Stanley Gibbons

STAMPS OF THE WORLD 1978

FORTY-THIRD EDITION

An illustrated and priced guide to the postage stamps of the whole world, excluding changes of paper, perforation, shade and watermark

Lists over 192,500 stamps over 40,500 illustrations

STANLEY GIBBONS PUBLICATIONS LTD
391 STRAND LONDON WC2R 0LX

Retail price £8·95 in U.K.

A—SC

By Appointment to H.M. the Queen
Stanley Gibbons Ltd, Philatelists

ISSN: 0081–4210
ISBN: 0 85259 940 4

Printed in Great Britain by Bemrose & Sons Ltd, London & Derby

Stanley Gibbons

STAMPS OF THE WORLD

This popular work is a straightforward listing, with prices, of the stamps of the whole world, omitting changes of paper, perforation, shade and watermark, and excluding such issues as locals, postal fiscals, etc. Published for thirty-six years as the 'Simplified Catalogue', it has an enviable world-wide reputation.

Features of this edition:

It is **the only guide** to the stamps of the whole world **in one volume.**

Its catalogue numbers are world-recognised **Stanley Gibbons numbers** throughout.

Based on the listings of the standard catalogue volumes: **British Commonwealth** (1978 edition), **Europe** Vol. 1 (3rd edition), **Europe** Volumes 2 and 3 (2nd editions), **Overseas** Volumes 1 and 2 (2nd editions), **Overseas** Volumes 3 and 4 (1st editions).

In addition Germany, Korea, Laos, Liberia, Liechtenstein, Luxembourg, Netherlands, Norway, Panama, Paraguay, Peru, Philippines, Russia, Saar, Spain, Surinam, Sweden, Switzerland, Thailand, Turkey, U.N., U.S.A., Uruguay, Vatican City, Venezuela, Yugoslavia specially **repriced for Stamps of the World.**

Over **6,000** new stamps and **1,900** illustrations added.

New **Index** for ease of reference.

New, helpful **Introduction** including table of **World Population Figures.**

Easy to understand!
Authoritative!

'Stamps of the World' is unquestionably the standard guide for the modern stamp collector, untroubled by variations of watermark and perforation.

STANLEY GIBBONS INTERNATIONAL

Stanley Gibbons Ltd.
391 Strand, London WC2R 0LX. Sales and buying departments for popular stamps, albums, catalogues and accessories; new issues and approvals.
Retail Shop: 391 Strand, London WC2R 0LX.
Specialist and Rare Stamp Departments: Romano House, 399 Strand, London WC2R 0LX. Classic and rare material, Specialist Register, investment advice, the Gibbons Gallery of changing exhibitions.

Stanley Gibbons Publications Ltd
Editorial Offices: Drury House, Russell Street, Drury Lane, London WC2B 5HD. The S.G. catalogues, books and albums. Mail order service (hotline 01–836 0974).
Wholesale and Trade: Stangib House, Sarehole Road, Hall Green, Birmingham B28 8EE.

Stanley Gibbons Auctions Ltd
Drury House, Russell Street, Drury Lane, London WC2B 5HD. Valuations and sales by auction and private treaty.

Stanley Gibbons Magazines Ltd.
Drury House, Russell Street, Drury Lane, London WC2B 5HD. Editorial offices for *Stamp Monthly* and *Flora.*

Stanley Gibbons Currency Ltd
395 Strand, London WC2R 0LX. Fine banknotes and coins of the world, publications and accessories.

Stanley Gibbons Products Ltd
Birmingham Envelope Co Ltd
Stangib House, Sarehole Road, Hall Green, Birmingham B28 8EE. Manilla and plastic folders, specialised envelopes, box and other files, binders, filing trays, cabinets and office equipment.

Stanley Gibbons Advertising Services Ltd
Drury House, Russell Street, Drury Lane, London WC2B 5HD. Advertising for the S.G. Group and the Crown Agents.

Mapsellers Ltd
37 Southampton Street, London WC2E 7HE. Antiquarian map specialists.

StanGib Ltd
601 Franklin Avenue, Garden City, New York, NY 11530, U.S.A. Stamp sales for the British Post Office and the Crown Agents, retail and wholesale publications.

Stanley Gibbons Merkur GmbH
D–6000 Frankfurt am Main, Zeil 83, West Germany. Rare stamps, covers, postal history material, expertising and auctions.

	Telephone numbers	*Telex numbers*
All London addresses	01–836 8444	28883
Birmingham offices	021–777 7255	—
New York office	(516) 746–4666 and 4667	96–7733
Frankfurt office	0611–287477 and 287454	4189148

Information for users

Aim

The aim of *Stamps of the World* is to provide a straightforward illustrated and priced guide to the postage stamps of the whole world to help you to enjoy the greatest hobby of the present day.

Arrangement

The catalogue lists countries in alphabetical order and there is a complete index at the end of the volume. For ease of reference country names are also printed at the head of each page.

Within each country, postage stamps are listed first. They are followed by separate sections for such other categories as postage due stamps, parcel post stamps, express stamps, official stamps, etc.

All catalogue lists are set out according to dates of issue of the stamps, starting from the earliest and working through to the most recent. New issues received too late for inclusion in the main lists will be found as "Addenda" at the end of the volume.

Scope of the Catalogue

Stamps of the World is a simplified catalogue of postage stamps only. Apart from the ordinary definitive, commemorative and airmail stamps of each country – which appear first in each list – there are sections for the following where appropriate:

- postage due stamps
- parcel post stamps
- official stamps
- express and special delivery stamps
- charity and compulsory tax stamps
- newspaper and journal stamps
- printed matter stamps
- registration stamps
- acknowledgement of receipt stamps
- late fee and too late stamps
- military post stamps
- recorded message stamps
- personal delivery stamps

We receive numerous enquiries from collectors about other items which do not fall within the categories set out above and which consequently do not appear in the catalogue lists. It may be helpful, therefore, to summarise the other kinds of stamp that exist but which we deliberately exclude from this postage stamp catalogue.

We do **not** list the following:

1. *Fiscal or revenue stamps:* stamps used solely in collecting taxes or fees for non-postal purposes. Examples would be stamps which pay a tax on a receipt, represent the stamp duty on a contract or frank a customs document. Common inscriptions found include: Documentary, Proprietary, Inter. Revenue, Contract Note.
2. *Local stamps:* postage stamps whose validity and use are limited in area, say to a single town or city, though in some cases they provided, with official sanction, services in parts of countries not covered by the respective government.
3. *Local carriage labels and Private local issues:* many labels exist ostensibly to cover the cost of ferrying mail from one of Great Britain's offshore islands to the nearest mainland post office. They are not recognised as valid for national or international mail. Examples: Calf of Man, Davaar, Herm, Lundy, Pabay, Stroma. Items from some other places have only the status of tourist souvenir labels.
4. *Telegraph stamps:* stamps intended solely for the prepayment of telegraphic communication.
5. *Bogus or "phantom" stamps:* labels from mythical places or non-existent administrations. Examples in the classical period were Sedang, Counani, Clipperton Island and in modern times Thomond and Monte Bello Islands. Numerous labels have also appeared since the War from dissident groups as propaganda for their claims and without authority from the home governments. Common examples are labels for "Free Albania", "Free Rumania" and "Free Croatia" and numerous issues for Nagaland, Indonesia and the South Moluccas ("Republik Maluku Selatan"). All these are classified as bogus stamps.
6. *Railway letter fee stamps:* special stamps issued by railway companies for the conveyance of letters by rail. Example: Talyllyn Railway. Similar services are now offered by some bus companies and the labels they issue likewise do not qualify for inclusion in the catalogue.
7. *Perfins* ("perforated initials"): numerous postage stamps may be found with

initial letters or designs punctured through them by tiny holes. These are applied by private and public concerns as a precaution against theft and do not qualify for separate mention.

8. *Labels:* innumerable items exist resembling stamps but – as they do not prepay postage – they are classified as labels. The commonest categories are:

   (*a*) propaganda and publicity labels: designed to further a cause or campaign;

   (*b*) exhibition labels: particularly souvenirs from philatelic events;

   (*c*) testing labels: stamp-size labels used in testing stamp-vending machines;

   (*d*) Post Office training school stamps: British stamps overprinted with two thick vertical bars or SCHOOL SPECIMEN are produced by the Post Office for training purposes;

   (*e*) seals and stickers: numerous charities produce stamp-like labels, particularly at Christmas and Easter, as a means of raising funds and these have no postal validity.

9. *Cut-outs:* items of postal stationery, such as envelopes, cards and wrappers, often have stamps impressed or imprinted on them. They may usually be cut out and affixed to envelopes, etc., for postal use if desired, but such items are not listed in this catalogue.

Collectors wanting further information about exact definitions are referred to *Philatelic Terms Illustrated,* published by Stanley Gibbons and containing many illustrations in colour.

There is also a priced listing of the postal fiscals of Great Britain in our *British Commonwealth* Catalogue and in Volume 1 of the *Great Britain Specialised* Catalogue (5th and later editions).

Although, as stated, none of the above qualify for inclusion in this postage stamp catalogue, this does not imply that they are of no interest to certain collectors. Indeed, in the 1950s, a group was formed in Great Britain called the "Cinderella Stamp Club", whose object is the study of all those stamps which Stanley Gibbons do *not* list in their catalogues.

Catalogue Numbers

Stanley Gibbons catalogue numbers are recognised universally and any individual stamp can be identified by quoting the catalogue number (the one at the left of the column) prefixed by the name of the country and the letters "S.G.". Do not confuse the catalogue number with the type numbers which refer to illustrations.

Prices

Prices in the left-hand column are for unused stamps and those in the right-hand column for used. Prices are given in pence and pounds: 100 pence (p) = 1 pound (£1).

Prices are shown as follows:
5 means 5p (5 pence);
1·75 means £1·75 (1 pound and 75 pence);
For £100 and above, prices are in whole pounds.

Our prices are for stamps in fine average condition, and in issues where condition varies we may ask more for the superb and less for the sub-standard. In the case of unused stamps, prices will be for stamps lightly hinged and used will be for postally used (or cancelled-to-order in some modern issues).

The minimum price quoted is 5p which represents a handling charge rather than a basis for valuing common stamps.

The prices quoted are generally for the cheapest variety of stamps but it is worth noting that differences of watermark, perforation, or other details, outside the scope of this catalogue, may often increase the value of the stamp.

Where prices are not given in either column it is either because the stamps are not known to exist in that particular condition, or, more usually, because there is no reliable information as to value.

All prices are subject to change without prior notice and we give no guarantee to supply all stamps priced. Prices quoted for albums, publications, etc. advertised in this catalogue are also subject to change without prior notice.

Value Added Tax

Stanley Gibbons Ltd. announce that stamp pricing in this and all other current S.G. catalogues is on a tax inclusive basis as at the date of going to press. They are able to absorb V.A.T. due to their vast exports and the fact that much of their business is in stamps over 100 years old. However, as in the past, price changes will reflect the international market and in addition, if there is any change in the rate of V.A.T. this may be reflected in an increase or decrease in the quoted prices.

Guarantee

All stamps supplied by us are guaranteed originals in the following terms:
If not as described, and returned by the purchaser within six years, we undertake to refund the price paid to us and our liability will thereby be discharged. If any stamp is certified as genuine by the Expert Committee of the Royal Philatelic Society, London, or of the British Philatelic Federation Limited, the purchaser shall not be entitled to make any claim against us for any error, omission or mistake in such certificate.

Country Notes

Following the heading, brief notes provide the geographical location of the country, together with details of its form of government and any subsequent changes during the period covered by its stamp issues.

World Population Figures

We feel that collectors need information on the populations of stamp-issuing territories and we now include these figures and update them annually. They can be helpful when considering the stamp output of certain countries. See page xii.

Currency

At the beginning of each country brief details give the currencies in which the values of the stamps are expressed. The dates, where given, are those of the earliest stamp issues in the particular currency. Where the currency is obvious, e.g. where the colony has the same currency as the mother country, no details are given.

Illustrations

Illustrations of stamps of British Commonwealth countries (indicated by "BC" in the country headings) and of any surcharges and overprints which are shown and not described are actual size; stamps of all foreign countries are reduced to ¾ linear, unless otherwise stated.

"Key-Types"

A number of standard designs occur so frequently in the stamps of the French, German, Portuguese and Spanish colonies that it would be a waste of space to repeat them each time. Instead these are all illustrated on page x together with the descriptive names and letters by which they are referred to in the lists.

Type Numbers

These are the bold figures found below each illustration. References to "Type **6**", for example, in the lists of a country should therefore be understood to refer to the illustration below which the number **"6"** appears. These type numbers are also given in the second column of figures alongside each list of stamps, thus indicating clearly the design of each stamp. In the case of Key-Types—see above—letters take the place of the type numbers.

Where an issue comprises stamps of similar design, represented in this catalogue by one illustration, the corresponding type numbers should be taken as indicating this general design.

Where there are blanks in the type number column it means that the type of the corresponding stamps is that shown by the last number above in the type column of the same issue.

A dash (–) in the type column means that no illustration of the stamp is shown.

Where type numbers refer to stamps of another country, e.g. where stamps of one country are overprinted for use in another, this is always made clear in the text.

Stamp Designs

Brief descriptions of the subjects of the stamp designs are given either below or beside the illustrations, at the foot of the list of the issue concerned, or in the actual lists. Where a particular subject, e.g. the portrait of a well-known monarch, recurs frequently the description is not repeated, nor are obvious designs described.

Generally, the unillustrated designs are in the same shape and size as the one illustrated, except where otherwise indicated.

Information for users (contd.)

Surcharges and Overprints

Surcharges and overprints are usually described in the headings to the issues concerned. Where the actual wording of a surcharge or overprint is given it is shown in bold type.

Some stamps are described as being "Surcharged in words", e.g. **TWO CENTS,** and others "Surcharged in figures and words", e.g. **20 CENTS,** although of course many surcharges are in foreign languages and combinations of words and figures are numerous. There are often bars, etc., obliterating old values or inscriptions but in general these are only mentioned where it is necessary to avoid confusion.

No attention is paid in this catalogue to colours of overprints and surcharges so that stamps with the same overprints in different colours are not listed separately.

Numbers in brackets after the descriptions of overprinted or surcharged stamps are the catalogue numbers of the unoverprinted stamps.

Note—the words "inscribed" or "inscription" always refer to wording incorporated in the design of a stamp and not surcharges or overprints.

Perforations

All stamps are perforated unless otherwise stated. No distinction is made between the various gauges of perforation but early stamp issues which exist both imperforate and perforated are usually listed separately.

Where a heading states "Imperf. or perf." or "Perf. or rouletted" this does not necessarily mean that all values of the issue are found in both conditions.

Watermarks

Stamps having different watermarks, but otherwise the same, are not listed separately. No reference is therefore made to watermarks in this volume.

Stamp Colours

Colour names are only required for the identification of stamps, therefore they have been made as simple as possible. Thus "scarlet", "vermilion", "carmine" are all usually called red. Qualifying colour names have been introduced only where necessary for the sake of clearness.

Where stamps are printed in two or more colours the central portion of the design is in the first colour given, unless otherwise stated.

Coloured Papers

Where stamps are printed on coloured paper the description is given as e.g. "4 c. black on blue"—a stamp printed in black on blue paper. No attention is paid in this catalogue to differences in the texture of paper, e.g. laid, wove.

Dates of Issue

The date given at the head of each issue is that of the appearance of the earliest stamp in the series. As stamps of the same design or issue are usually grouped together a list of King George VI stamps, for example, headed "1938" may include stamps issued from 1938 to the end of the reign.

Miniature Sheets

These are outside the scope of this catalogue but are listed in all other Stanley Gibbons catalogues.

"Appendix" Countries

We regret that, since 1968, it has been necessary to establish an Appendix (at the end of the volume) to which numerous stamps have had to be consigned. Several countries imagine that by issuing huge quantities of unnecessary stamps they will have a ready source of income from stamp collectors – and particularly from the less-experienced ones. Stanley Gibbons refuse to encourage this exploitation of the hobby and we do not deal in the stamps concerned.

Two kinds of stamp are therefore given the briefest of mentions in the Appendix, purely for the sake of record. Administrations issuing stamps greatly in excess of true postal needs have the offending issues placed there. Likewise it contains stamps which have not fulfilled all the normal conditions for full catalogue listing.

These conditions are that stamps (i) have been issued by a legitimate postal authority; (ii) they are valid for proper postal use in prepaying the fee for the class of service for which they were issued; (iii) they are available to the public in reasonable quantities at face value; and (iv) there are no artificial

Information for users (contd.)

restrictions imposed on their distribution.
Stamps in the Appendix are kept under review in the light of any newly acquired information about them. If we are satisfied that a stamp qualifies for proper listing in the body of the catalogue it is moved there.

The Appendix has well justified its existence and it will be continued until it becomes unnecessary.

Where to Look for More Detailed Listings

The present work deliberately omits details of paper, perforation, shade and watermark. But as you become more absorbed in stamp collecting and wish to get greater enjoyment from the hobby you may well want to study these matters.

All the information you require about any particular postage stamp will be found in the main Stanley Gibbons Catalogues. There is a separate volume for British Commonwealth countries; all other Foreign countries are split between those in Europe (three volumes) and the remainder (in four volumes) classed Overseas.

You can easily find which catalogue to consult by looking at the country headings in the present book.

To the right of each country name are code letters specifying which volume of our main catalogues contains that country's listing.

The code letters are as follows:

BC	British Commonwealth
E1	Europe 1
E2	Europe 2
E3	Europe 3
O1	Overseas 1
O2	Overseas 2
O3	Overseas 3
O4	Overseas 4

So, for example, if you want to know more about Chinese stamps than is contained in *Stamps of the World* the reference to

CHINA O1

guides you to the Gibbons *Overseas 1* Catalogue listing for the details you require.

The *British Commonwealth* Catalogue is published annually in the autumn; new editions of the other catalogues mentioned appear at longer intervals.

Correspondence

Whilst we welcome information and suggestions we must ask correspondents to include the cost of postage for the return of any stamps submitted plus registration where appropriate.

Where information is solicited purely for the benefit of the enquirer we regret we cannot undertake to reply unless stamps or reply coupons are sent to cover the postage.

We regret we do not give opinions as to the genuineness of stamps, nor do we identify stamps or number them by our Catalogue.

Building Your Collection

We would like to help you build your collection and Stanley Gibbons offers an unrivalled range of services which make this possible.

To see our world-famous stock we hope you can arrange a visit to our 391 Strand shop or our Specialist and Rare Stamp showrooms at Romano House, 399 Strand. The Specialist Register is available to record your special requirements if we cannot offer immediately.

If you would prefer to examine stamps in your own home the Approval Service can send you attractive selections of fine stamps in various price ranges, no matter where you live.

Our auctions frequently include material of interest and *Stamp Monthly* carries hundreds of offers every month. Brochures with full details of all these services are available on request.

We are proud that we are helping many thousands of people throughout the world build their collections and enjoy a lifetime's hobby. We would welcome hearing from you so that we may be of service.

Supplements

New issue Supplements to this Catalogue and to the Addenda, together with informative and helpful articles, news and many attractive stamp offers, are included in our magazine **Stamp Monthly** (from your newsagent or by postal subscription). The first supplement to this edition was included in the **July 1977** number.

Key-Types (see note on page vii)

French Group

A. " Blanc."

B. " Mouchon."

C. " Merson."

D. " Tablet."

E.

F.

G.

H.

" International Colonial Exhibition."

I. " Faidherbe."

J. " Palms."

K. " Balay."

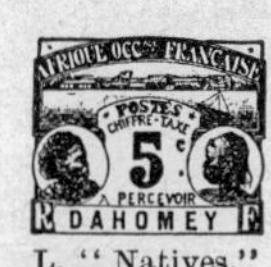

L. " Natives."

M. " Figure."

German Group

N. " Yacht."

O. " Yacht."

Spanish Group

X. " Alfonso XII."

Y. " Baby."

Z. "Curly Head."

Portuguese Group

P. " Crown."

Q. " Embossed."

R. " Figures."

S. " Carlos."

T. " Manoel."

U. " Ceres."

V. " Newspaper."

W. " Due."

Abbreviations

Anniv.	denotes	Anniversary
Assn.	,,	Association
Bis.	,,	Bistre
Bl.	,,	Blue
Bldg.	,,	Building
Blk.	,,	Black
Br.	,,	British *or* Bridge
Brn.	,,	Brown
B.W.I.	,,	British West Indies
C.A.R.I.F.T.A.	,,	Caribbean Free Trade Area
Cent.	,,	Centenary
Chest.	,,	Chestnut
Choc.	,,	Chocolate
Clar.	,,	Claret
Coll.	,,	College
Commem.	,,	Commemoration
Conf.	,,	Conference
Diag.	,,	Diagonally
E.C.A.F.E.	,,	Economic Commission for Asia and Far East
Emer.	,,	Emerald
E.P.T. Conference	,,	European Postal and Telecommunications Conference
Exn.	,,	Exhibition
F.A.O.	,,	Food and Agriculture Organization
Fig.	,,	Figure
G.A.T.T.	,,	General Agreement on Tariffs and Trade
G.B.	,,	Great Britain
Gen.	,,	General
Govt.	,,	Government
Grn.	,,	Green
Horiz.	,,	Horizontal
H.Q.	,,	Headquarters
Imperf.	,,	Imperforate
Inaug.	,,	Inauguration
Ind.	,,	Indigo
Inscr.	,,	Inscribed or inscription
Int.	,,	International
I.A.T.A.	,,	International Air Transport Association
I.C.A.O.	,,	International Civil Aviation Organization
I.C.Y.	,,	International Co-operation Year
I.G.Y.	,,	International Geophysical Year
I.L.O.	,,	International Labour Office (or later, Organization)
I.M.C.O.	,,	Inter-Governmental Maritime Consultative Organization
I.T.U.	denotes	International Telecommunication Union
Is.	,,	Island
Lav.	,,	Lavender
Mag.	,,	Magenta
Mar.	,,	Maroon
mm.	,,	Millimetres
Mult.	,,	Multicoloured
Mve.	,,	Mauve
Nat.	,,	National
N.A.T.O.	,,	North Atlantic Treaty Organization
O.D.E.C.A.	,	Organization of Central American States
Ol.	,,	Olive
Optd.	,,	Overprinted
Orge. *or* oran.	,,	Orange
P.A.T.A.	,,	Pacific Area Travel Association
Perf.	,,	Perforated
Post.	,,	Postage
Pres.	,,	President
P.U.	,,	Postal Union
Pur.	,,	Purple
R.	,,	River
R.S.A.	,,	Republic of South Africa
Roul.	,,	Rouletted
Sep.	,,	Sepia
S.E.A.T.O.	,,	South East Asia Treaty Organization
Surch.	,,	Surcharged
T.	,,	Type
T.U.C.	,,	Trade Unions Congress
Turq.	,,	Turquoise
Ultram.	,,	Ultramarine
U.N.E.S.C.O.	,,	United Nations Educational, Scientific and Cultural Organization
U.N.I.C.E.F.	,,	United Nations Children's Fund
U.N.O.	,,	United Nations Organization
U.N.R.W.A.	,,	United Nations Relief and Works Agency for Palestine Refugees in the Near East
U.N.T.E.A.	,,	United Nations Temporary Executive Authority
U.N.R.R.A.	,,	United Nations Relief and Rehabilitation Administration
U.P.U.	,,	Universal Postal Union
Verm.	,,	Vermilion
Vert.	,,	Vertical
Vio.	,,	Violet
W.F.T.U.	,,	World Federation of Trade Unions
W.H.O.	,,	World Health Organization
Yell.	,,	Yellow

Arabic Numerals

As in the case of European figures, the details of the Arabic numerals vary in different stamp designs, but they should be readily recognised with the aid of this illustration:

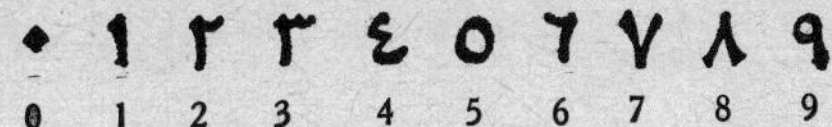

POPULATIONS OF TODAY'S STAMP-ISSUING TERRITORIES

These population figures, from the latest available census figures or estimates, are published by kind permission of the *Geographical Digest 1977*, George Philip & Son Ltd., London.

Afghanistan	19 280 000
Albania	2 482 000
Algeria	16 776 000
Andorra	27 000
Angola	6 761 000
Antigua	69 000
Argentine Republic	25 383 000
Ascension	500
Australia[a]	13 502 000
Austria	7 523 000
Bahamas	204 000
Bahrain	256 000
Bangladesh	76 815 000
Barbados	245 000
Barbuda	1 100
Belgium	9 796 000
Belize	140 000
Benin	3 112 000
Bermuda	56 000
Bhutan	1 173 000
Bolivia	5 634 000
Botswana	691 000
Brazil	107 145 000
Brunei	147 000
Bulgaria	8 722 000
Burma	31 240 000
Burundi	3 763 000
Cambodia	8 110 000
Cameroun	6 400 000
Canada	22 831 000
Canal Zone	44 000
Cape Verde Islands	294 000
Cayman Islands	11 000
Central African Republic	1 716 000
Chad	4 030 000
Chile	10 253 000
China, People's Republic	838 803 000
China, Taiwan	15 500 000
Christmas Island	3 000
Cocos (Keeling) Islands	1 000
Colombia	23 542 000
Comoro Islands	306 000
Congo Republic	1 345 000
Cook Islands[b]	25 000
Costa Rica	1 968 000
Cuba	9 162 000
Cyprus	639 000
Czechoslovakia	14 802 000
Denmark	5 059 000
Dominica	75 000
Dominican Republic	4 697 000
Ecuador	6 733 000
Egypt	37 233 000
El Salvador	4 007 000
Equatorial Guinea	310 000
Ethiopia	27 946 000
Falkland Islands[c]	2 000
Faroe Islands	41 000
Fiji	573 000
Finland	4 707 000
France[d]	54 191 000
French Polynesia	128 000
French Southern and Antarctic Territories	*no permanent population*
French Territory of the Afars and Issas	106 000
Gabon	526 000
Gambia	524 000
Germany, West Germany[e]	61 832 000
Germany, East Germany	16 850 000
Ghana	9 866 000
Gibraltar	27 000
Gilbert Islands	60 000
Great Britain[f]	56 149 000
Greece	9 046 000
Greenland	54 000
Grenada	96 000
Grenadines of Grenada	8 200
Grenadines of St. Vincent	6 500
Guatemala	5 540 000
Guinea	4 416 000
Guinea–Bissau	525 000
Guyana	791 000
Haiti	4 584 000
Honduras	3 037 000
Hong Kong	4 367 000
Hungary	10 540 000
Iceland	218 000
India	598 079 000
Indonesia[g]	131 269 000
Iran	33 019 000
Iraq	11 124 000
Ireland	3 127 000
Israel[h]	3 371 000
Italy	55 810 000
Ivory Coast	4 885 000
Jamaica	2 029 000
Japan	110 953 000
Jordan	2 702 000
Kenya	13 399 000
Korea, North Korea	15 852 000
Korea, South Korea	34 663 000
Kuwait	996 000
Laos	3 303 000
Lebanon	2 869 000
Lesotho	1 039 000
Liberia	1 708 000
Libya	2 444 000
Liechtenstein	24 000
Luxembourg	357 000
Macao	271 000
Malagasy Republic	6 750 000
Malawi	5 044 000
Malaysia	11 900 000
Maldive Islands	119 000
Mali Republic	5 697 000
Malta	300 000
Mauritania	1 318 000
Mauritius	899 000
Mexico	60 145 000
Monaco	25 000
Mongolia	1 444 000
Montserrat	13 000
Morocco	17 305 000
Mozambique	9 239 000
Nauru	8 000
Nepal	12 572 000
Netherlands	13 653 000
Netherlands Antilles	242 000
New Caledonia	125 000
New Hebrides	95 000
New Zealand[i]	3 087 000
Nicaragua	2 155 000
Niger Republic	4 600 000
Nigeria	62 925 000
Niue	5 000
Norfolk Island	2 000
Norway	4 007 000
Oman	766 000
Pakistan	70 260 000
Panama	1 668 000
Papua New Guinea	2 756 000
Paraguay	2 647 000
Peru	15 869 000
Philippine Islands	42 513 000
Pitcairn Islands	80
Poland	34 020 000
Portugal[j]	8 760 000
Qatar	92 000
Rhodesia	6 310 000
Rumania	21 245 000
Russia	254 382 000
Rwanda	4 198 000
St. Christopher – Nevis – Anguilla	66 000
St. Helena	6 000
St. Lucia	108 000
St. - Pierre et Miquelon	5 000
St. Thomas and Prince Islands	80 000
St. Vincent	94 000
Samoa (Western)	152 000
San Marino	20 000
Saudi Arabia	8 966 000
Senegal	4 136 000
Seychelles[k]	60 000
Sierra Leone	2 707 000
Singapore	2 250 000
Solomon Islands	190 000
Somalia	3 170 000
South Africa	25 471 000
South West Africa	883 000
Spain[l]	35 472 000
Spanish Sahara[m]	117 000
Sri Lanka	13 986 000
Sudan	17 757 000
Surinam	422 000
Swaziland	494 000
Sweden	8 195 000
Switzerland	6 403 000
Syria	7 355 000
Tanzania	15 155 000
Thailand	41 869 000
Togo	2 222 000
Tokelau Islands	2 000
Tonga	102 000
Trinidad and Tobago	1 070 000
Tristan da Cunha	200
Tunisia	5 772 000
Turkey	39 180 000
Turks and Caicos Islands	6 000
Tuvalu	5 800
Uganda	11 549 000
United Arab Emirates	222 000
United States[n]	217 048 000
Upper Volta	6 032 000
Uruguay	3 064 000
Vatican City	1 000
Venezuela	11 993 000
Vietnam	42 588 000
Virgin Islands (British)	11 000
Wallis and Futuna Islands	9 000
Yemen Arab Republic	6 668 000
Yemen People's Republic	1 690 000
Zaïre	24 902 000
Zambia	4 896 000

NOTES

a. includes Australian Antarctic Territory, which does not have a permanent population.

b. includes Aitutaki and Penrhyn (*pop.* 2800 and 600 respectively, from 1971 census, quoted in *The Statesman's Yearbook 1976–1977*).

c. includes British Antarctic Territory and South Georgia, which do not have permanent populations.

d. includes French Guiana (*pop.* 60 000), Guadeloupe (*pop.* 354 000), Martinique (*pop.* 363 000) and Réunion (*pop.* 501 000), all of which use the stamps of France.

e. includes West Berlin (*pop.* 2 024 000), a 1974 estimate quoted in *The Statesman's Yearbook 1976–1977*).

f. comprising: England (*pop.* 46 454 000), Wales (*pop.* 2 765 000), Scotland (*pop.* 5 206 000), Northern Ireland (*pop.* 1 537 000), Channel Islands (*pop.* 128 000) and Isle of Man (*pop.* 59 000).

g. includes Irian Jaya and former Portuguese Timor (*pop.* 918 000 and 590 000 respectively, from the *Geographical Digest 1971*).

h. includes all Israeli citizens in those parts of Egypt, Jordan and Syria occupied by Israel, and Arabs living in East Jerusalem, but no other Arabs living in the occupied territories (these are included in the figures for Egypt, Jordan and Syria and total about one million).

i. includes Ross Dependency, which does not have a permanent population.

j. includes Azores and Madeira (*pop.* 285 000 and 251 000 respectively, from the provisional 1970 census, quoted in *The Statesman's Yearbook 1976–1977*).

k. includes former British Indian Ocean Territory (*pop.* 2000).

l. includes Balearic and Canary Islands (*pop.* 558 300 and 1 138 800 respectively, from 1970 census, quoted in *The Statesman's Yearbook 1976–1977*), also the Spanish towns of Alhucemas, Ceuta, Chafarinas, Melilla and Peñón de Vélez de la Gomera on the coast of Morocco (*total pop.* 164 000, from the *Geographical Digest 1971*).

m. now divided between Morocco and Mauritania.

n. includes Eastern Samoa (*pop.* 29 000), Guam (*pop.* 104 000), Johnstone Island (*pop.* 1000), Midway Island (*pop.* 2000), Pacific Islands Trust Territory (*pop.* 120 000), Puerto Rico (*pop.* 3 087 000), U.S. Virgin Islands (*pop.* 92 000) and Wake Island (*pop.* 2000), all of which use the stamps of the United States.

SOURCES
U.N. Statistical Yearbook 1975.
U.N. Demographic Yearbook 1974.
U.N. Population and Vital Statistics Report, July 1976.

STANLEY GIBBONS
STAMPS OF THE WORLD CATALOGUE—43rd EDITION

ABU DHABI — BC; O1

The largest of the Trucial States in the Persian Gulf. Treaty relations with Great Britain expired on 31st December, 1966, when the Abu Dhabi Post Office took over the postal services. On 18th July, 1971, seven of the Gulf shaikhdoms, including Abu Dhabi, agreed to form the State of the United Arab Emirates. The federation came into being on 1 Aug., 1972.

100 naye paise = 1 rupee.
1966. 1,000 fils = 1 dinar.

1. Shaikh Shakhbut bin Sultan.

2. Ruler's Palace.

1964.

No.	Type	Description	Un.	Used
1.	1.	5 n.p. green	15	15
2.		15 n.p. brown	15	15
3.		20 n.p. blue	15	15
4.		30 n.p. orange	15	25
5.	–	40 n.p. violet	15	12
6.	–	50 n.p. bistre	20	25
7.	–	75 n.p. black	30	30
8.	2.	1 r. green	35	35
9.		2 r. black	95	1·10
10.	–	5 r. red	2·25	2·75
11.	–	10 r. blue	4·50	5·00

DESIGNS—As T **1**: 40 n.p. to 75 n.p. Arabian Gazelle. As T **2**: 5 r., 10 r. Oil rig and camels.

3. Falcon on Gloved Hand.

1965. Falconry.

No.	Type	Description	Un.	Used
12.	3.	20 n.p. brown & grey-blue	20	20
13.	–	40 n.p. brown and blue ..	30	30
14.	–	2 r. sepia and turquoise ..	1·00	1·00

DESIGNS: 40 n.p., 2 r. Other types of falcon on gloved hand.

1966. Nos. 1/11 surch. in new currency (" Fils " only on Nos. 5/7) and ruler's portrait obliterated with bars.

No.	Type	Description	Un.	Used
15.	1.	5 f. on 5 n.p. green ..	8	25
16.		15 f. on 15 n.p. brown ..	8	35
17.		20 f. on 20 n.p. blue ..	10	35
18.		30 f. on 30 n.p. orange ..	15	45
19.	–	40 f. violet	15	45
20	–	50 f. bistre	2·00	2·25
21.	–	75 f. black	2·00	2·25
22.	2.	100 f. on 1 r. green ..	2·00	2·25
23.		200 f. on 2 r. black ..	3·75	5·00
24.	–	500 f. on 5 r. red	7·00	9·00
25.	–	1 d. on 10 r. blue ..	12·00	14·00

4. Shaikh Zaid bin Sultan al Nahayyan. 5.

1967.

No.	Type	Description	Un.	Used
26.	–	5 f. red and green ..	5	5
27.	–	15 f. red and brown ..	5	5
28.	–	20 f. red and indigo ..	5	5
29.	–	35 f. red and violet ..	8	10
30.	4.	40 f. green	10	12
38.	5.	40 f. green	10	10
31.	4.	50 f. brown	12	12
39.	5.	50 f. brown	12	12
32.	4.	60 f. blue	15	15
40.	5.	60 f. blue	15	15
33.	4.	100 f. red	25	25
41.	5.	100 f. red	25	25
34.	–	125 f. brown and green ..	25	30
35.	–	200 f. brown and blue ..	40	45
36.	–	500 f. violet and orange ..	1·00	1·10
37.	–	1 d. blue and green ..	2·25	2·40

DESIGNS—As T **4/5**—VERT. 5 f. to 35. f. National flag. HORIZ. (47 × 27 mm.). 125 f. Antelope. 200 f. Falcon. 500 f., 1 d. Palace. Each with portrait of Ruler.

6. Human Rights Emblem and Shaikh Zaid.

1968. Human Rights Year.

No.	Type	Description	Un.	Used
42.	6.	35 f. multicoloured ..	8	8
43.		60 f. multicoloured ..	15	15
44.		150 f. multicoloured ..	30	30

7. Arms and Shaikh Zaid.

1968. Shaikh Zaid's Accession. Anniv.

No.	Type	Description	Un.	Used
45.	7.	5 f. blk., silv., red and grn.	5	5
46.		10 f. blk., silv., red & orge.	5	5
47.		100 f. blk., gold, red and mauve	25	25
48.		125 f. blk., gold, red and blue	30	35

8. New Construction.

1968. Shaikh's Accession. 2nd Anniv. "Progress in Abu Dhabi". Multicoloured.

No.	Description	Un.	Used
49.	5 f. Type **8**	5	5
50.	10 f. Airport buildings (46½ × 34 mm.)..	5	5
51.	35 f. Shaikh Zaid, bridge and falcon (59 × 34 mm.) ..	10	10

9. Petroleum Installations.

10. Shaikh Zaid.

1969. Shaikh's Accession. 3rd Anniv. Petroleum Industry. Multicoloured.

No.	Description	Un.	Used
52.	35 f. Type **9**	8	8
53.	60 f. Marine drilling platform	15	15
54.	125 f. Separator platform, Zakum field	30	35
55.	200 f. Tank farm	50	50

1970.

No.	Type	Description	Un.	Used
56.	–	5 f. multicoloured ..	5	5
57.	10.	10 f. multicoloured ..	5	5
58.	–	25 f. multicoloured ..	8	8
59.	10.	35 f. multicoloured ..	8	8
60.		50 f. multicoloured ..	12	12
61.	–	60 f. multicoloured ..	15	15
62.	10.	70 f. multicoloured ..	20	20
63.	–	90 f. multicoloured ..	25	25
64.	–	125 f. multicoloured ..	30	30
65.	–	150 f. multicoloured ..	35	35
66.	–	500 f. multicoloured ..	1·25	1·25
67.	–	1 d. multicoloured ..	2·75	2·75

DESIGNS: Nos. 56, 58, 61 and 63 as T **10**, but frames changed, and smaller country name. 125 f. Arab stallion. 150 f. Gazelle. 500 f. Fort Jahili. 1 d. Great Mosque.

No. 67 has face value in Arabic only.

11. Shaikh Zaid and "Mt. Fuji" (T. Hayashi).

1970. Expo 70. World Fair, Osaka, Japan.

No.	Type	Description	Un.	Used
68.	11.	25 f. multicoloured ..	5	5
69.		35 f. multicoloured ..	8	8
70.		60 f. multicoloured ..	15	15

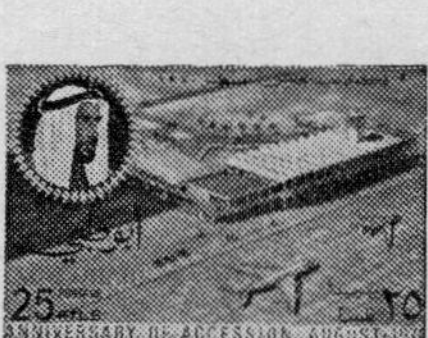

12. Abu Dhabi Airport.

13. Pres. G. A. Nasser.

1970. Shaikh's Accession. 4th Anniv. Multicoloured.

No.	Description	Un.	Used
71.	25 f. Type **12**	8	8
72.	60 f. Airport entrance ..	15	15
73.	150 f. Aerial view of Abu Dhabi (vert.)	40	40

1971. Gamal Nasser, President of Egypt. Commem.

No.	Type	Description	Un.	Used
74.	13.	25 f. black on pink ..	8	8
75.		35 f. black on lilac ..	8	8

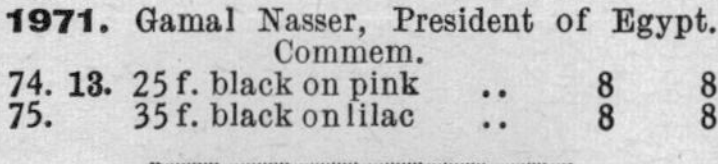

14. Motorised Patrol.

1971. Shaikh's Accession. 5th Anniv. Defence Force. Multicoloured.

No.	Description	Un.	Used
76.	35 f. Type **14**	8	8
77.	60 f. Patrol-boat ..	15	15
78.	125 f. Armoured car ..	30	30
79.	150 f. "Hunter" jet-fighters	40	40

1971. No. 60 surch.

No.	Type	Description	Un.	Used
80.	10.	5 f. on 50 f. multicoloured	1·25	1·25

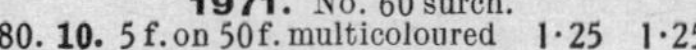

15. Dome of the Rock.

1972. Dome of the Rock, Jerusalem. Multicoloured.

No.	Description	Un.	Used
81.	35 f. Type **15**	8	8
82.	60 f. Mosque entrance ..	15	15
83.	125 f. Mosque dome ..	30	30

1972. Provisional Issue. Nos. 56/67 optd. **UAE** and arabic inscription.

No.	Type	Description	Un.	Used
84.	–	5 f. multicoloured ..	5	5
85.	10.	10 f. multicoloured ..	5	5
86.	–	25 f. multicoloured ..	8	8
87.	10.	35 f. multicoloured ..	10	10
88.		50 f. multicoloured ..	15	15
89.	–	60 f. multicoloured ..	15	15
90.	10.	70 f. multicoloured ..	20	20
91.	–	90 f. multicoloured ..	25	25
92.	–	125 f. multicoloured ..	35	35
93.	–	150 f. multicoloured ..	40	40
94.	–	500 f. multicoloured ..	1·40	1·40
95.	–	1 d. multicolcured	2·75	2·75

For later issues see **UNITED ARAB EMIRATES.**

ADEN — BC

Peninsula on S. coast of Arabia. Formerly part of the Indian Empire. A Crown Colony from April 1st, 1937 to January 18th, 1963, when Aden joined the South Arabian Federation, whose stamps it then used. Attained independence on 30th November, 1967, when the area was called Southern Yemen. It is now known as Yemen People's Democratic Republic. Aden stamps were also used in the Aden Protectorate.

1937. 16 annas = 1 rupee.
1951. 100 cents = 1 shilling.

1. Dhow.

1937.

No.	Type	Description	Un.	Used
1.	1.	½ a. green	30	30
2.		9 p. green	40	40
3.		1 a. brown	35	30
4.		2 a. red	60	65
5.		2½ a. blue	80	1·00
6.		3 a. red	1·00	1·50
7.		3½ a. blue	95	1·40
8.		8 a. purple	1·75	2·75
9.		1 r. brown..	3·25	3·25
10.		2 r. yellow	9·00	9·00
11.		5 r. purple	30·00	32·00
12.		10 r. olive	70·00	75·00

2. King George VI and Queen Elizabeth.

1937. Coronation.

No.	Type	Description	Un.	Used
13.	2.	1 a. brown	10	10
14.		2½ a. blue	15	20
15.		3½ a. grey-blue	30	30

3. Aidrus Mosque, Crater.

1939.

No.	Type	Description	Un.	Used
16.	3.	½ a. green	10	12
17.	–	¾ a. brown	10	20
18.	–	1 a. blue	15	12
19.	–	1½ a. red	30	25
20.	3.	2 a. brown	12	12
21.	–	2½ a. blue	20	15
22.	–	3 a. brown and red ..	35	25
23.	–	8 a. orange	35	15
23a.	–	14 a. brown and blue ..	85	70
24.	–	1 r. green	30	55
25.	–	2 r. blue and mauve ..	1·25	1·10
26.	–	5 r. brown and olive ..	3·25	3·25
27.	–	10 r. brown and violet ..	4·50	5·00

DESIGNS: ¾ a., 5 r. Camels. 1 s., 2 r. Harbour. 1½ a., 1 r. Adenese dhow. 3 a., 14 a., 10 r. Capture of Aden, 1839. 2½ a., 8 a. Mukalla.

4. Houses of Parliament, London.

1946. Victory.

No.	Type	Description	Un.	Used
28.	4.	1½ a. red	12	12
29.		2½ a. blue	20	20

5. King George VI and Queen Elizabeth. 6.

1949. Royal Silver Wedding.

30. 5. 1½ a. red 15 15
31. 6. 10 r. purple .. .. 7·50 8·50

1949. U.P.U. As T **14** to **17** of Antigua. surch. with new values.

32. 2½ a. on 20 c. blue .. 20 30
33. 3 a. on 30 c. red 40 40
34. 8 a. on 50 c. orange .. 75 85
35. 1 r. on 1s. blue .. .. 1·25 1·40

1951. Stamps of 1939 surch. in cents or shillings.

36. 5 c. on 1 a. blue 10 15
37. 10 c. on 2 a. brown .. 10 15
38. 15 c. on 2½ a. blue .. 25 35
39. 20 c. on 3 a. brown & red 15 20
40. 30 c. on 8 a. orange .. 30 35
41. 50 c. on 8 a. orange .. 30 25
42. 70 c. on 14 a. brown & blue 35 30
43. 1s. on 1 r. green 40 35
44. 2s. on 2 r. blue and mauve 1·25 1·10
45. 5s. on 5 r. brown & olive 2·50 2·25
46. 10s. on 10 r. brown & violet 5·00 5·50

7. Queen Elizabeth II. 8. Minaret.

9. Camel Transport.

1953. Coronation.

47. 7. 15 c. black and green .. 35 35

1953.

48. 8. 5 c. yellow-green .. 5 5
49. 5 c. blue-green .. 5 8
50. 9. 10 c. orange 5 5
51. 10 c. vermilion.. .. 5 10
52. – 15 c. blue-green .. 5 5
53. – 15 c. grey 15 15
54. – 25 c. red 5 5
56. – 35 c. ultramarine .. 10 12
58. – 50 c. pale blue .. 25 25
59a. – 50 c. deep blue.. .. 20 20
60. – 70 c. grey 25 30
61a. – 70 c. black 15 12
62. – 1s. sepia and violet .. 25 25
63. – 1s. black and violet .. 15 20
64. – 1s. 25 blue and black .. 35 35
65. – 2s. sepia and red .. 95 95
66. – 2s. black and red .. 40 35
67. – 5s. sepia and pale blue 3·00 3·00
68. – 5s. black and deep blue 95 95
69. – 10s. sepia and olive .. 6·00 8·00
70. – 10s. black and bronze .. 2·25 1·75
71. – 20s. chocolate and lilac 9·50 9·50
72. – 20s. black and lilac .. 4·50 4·50

DESIGNS—HORIZ. 15 c. Crater. 25 c. Mosque. 1s. Dhow. building 20s. (38 × 27 mm.). Aden in 1572. VERT. 35 c. Dhow. 50 c. Map of Arabia. 70 c. Salt works. 1s. 25, Colony's badge. 2s. Levy on camel. 5s. Crater Pass. 10s. Tribesman.

1954. Royal Visit. As No. 62 but inscr. "ROYAL VISIT 1954".

73. 1s. sepia and violet .. 30 35

1959. Revised Constitution. Optd. **REVISED CONSTITUTION 1959** (in Arabic on No. 74).

74. 15 c. grey-green (No. 53) .. 20 20
75. 1s. 25 blue and blk. (No. 64) 55 55

10. Protein Foods.

1963. Freedom from Hunger.

76. 10. 1s. 25 c. green 55 65

For later issues see **SOUTH ARABIAN FEDERATION, SOUTHERN YEMEN, YEMEN—PEOPLE'S DEMOCRATIC REPUBLIC.**

ADEN PROTECTORATE STATES

BC

The states of the Eastern Aden Protectorate commonly known as the Hadhramaut.

The National Liberation Front took control on 1st October, 1967, and full independence was granted by Great Britain on 30th November, 1967. Now part of Yemen People's Democratic Republic.

1937. 16 annas = 1 rupee.
1951. 100 cents = 1 shilling.
1966. 1,000 fils = 1 dinar.

SEIYUN

1. Sultan of Seiyun. 3. Tarim.

2. Seiyun.

1942.

1. 1. ½ a. green 10 20
2. ¾ a. brown 10 20
3. 1 a. blue 10 20
4. 2. 1½ a. red 10 25
5. 3. 2 a. sepia 10 30
6. – 2½ a. blue 12 35
7. – 3 a. sepia and red .. 15 30
8. – 8 a. red 20 35
9. – 1 r. green 35 40
10. – 2 r. blue and purple .. 75 1·50
11. – 5 r. brown and green .. 1·40 2·50

DESIGNS—VERT. 2½ a. Mosque at Seliyun. 1 r. South Gate, Tarim, HORIZ. 3 a. Fortress at Tarim. 8 a. Mosque at Seiyun. 2 r. A Kathiri House. 5 r. Mosque Entrance, Tarim.

1946. Victory. Optd. **VICTORY ISSUE 8th JUNE 1946.**

12. 2. 1½ a. red 5 5
13. – 2½ a. blue (No. 6) .. 8 8

1949. Silver Wedding. As T **5/6** of Aden.

14. 1½ a. red 8 8
15. 5 r. green .. .. .. 2·00 2·50

1949. U.P.U. As at T **14/17** of Antigua surch.

16. 2½ a. on 20 c. blue .. 12 30
17. 3 a on 30 c. red 12 35
18. 8 a. on 50 c. orange .. 45 1·10
19. 1 r. on 1s. blue .. .. 75 1·75

1951. 1942 stamps surch. in cents or shillings.

20. 1. 5 c. on 1 a. blue 10 20
21. 3. 10 c. on 2 a. sepia .. 10 20
22. – 15 c. on 2½ a. blue .. 10 30
23. – 20 c. on 3 a. sepia and red 10 30
24. – 50 c. on 8 a. red 12 35
25. – 1s. on 1 r. green 30 60
26. – 2s. on 2 r. blue and purple 60 1·40
27. – 5s. on 5 r. brown and green 1·40 2·25

1953. Coronation. As T 7 of Aden.

28. 15 c. black and green .. 25 25

4. Sultan Hussein.

DESIGNS—VERT. 35 c. Mosque at Seiyun. 70 c. Qarn Adh Dhabi. 2s. South Gate, Tarim. 10s. Mosque entrance, Tarim HORIZ. 50 c. Fortress at Tarim. 1s. Mosque at Seiyun. 1s. 25, Seiyun. 1s. 50, Gheil Omer. 5s. Kathiri house.

1954. As 1942 issue and new designs, but with portrait of Sultan Hussein as in T **4.**

29. 4. 5 c brown 12 12
30. 10 c. blue 12 12
31. 2. 15 c. green.. .. .. 12 15
32. 3. 25 c. red 12 15
33. – 35 c. blue 12 15
34. – 50 c. brown and red .. 15 20
39. – 70 c. black.. .. .. 12 25
35. – 1s. orange 25 30
40. – 1s. 25 green 20 35
41. – 1s. 50 violet 30 45
36. – 2s. green 60 70
37. – 5s. blue and violet .. 1·10 1·75
38. – 10s. brown and violet .. 2·25 2·00

1966. Nos. 29 etc. surch. **SOUTH ARABIA** in English and Arabic, with value and bar.

55. 4. 5 f. on 5 c. 5 5
56. – 5 f. on 10 c. 5 5
57. 2. 10 f. on 15 c. 5 5
58. 3. 15 f. on 25 c 5 5
59. – 20 f. on 35 c. 5 5
60. – 25 f. on 50 c. 5 5
61. – 35 f. on 70 c. 8 5
62. – 50 f. on 1s.. .. .. 10 10
63. – 65 f. on 1s. 25 .. .. 15 20
64. – 75 f. on 1s. 50 .. .. 20 25
65. – 100 f. on 2s. 25 35
66. – 250 f. on 5s. 60 90
67. – 500 f. on 10s. .. .. 1·25 2·00

Each value has two similar surcharges.

1966. Nos. 57, 59, 61/7 variously optd. as given below, together with Olympic "rings".

68. 10 f. on 15 c. **(LOS ANGELES 1932)** .. 5 5
69. 20 f. on 35 c. **(BERLIN 1936)** 5 5
70. 35 f. on 70 c. **(INTERNATIONAL COOPERATION, etc.)** .. 5 5
71. 50 f. on 1s. **(LONDON 1948)** 10 12
72. 65 f. on 1s. 25 **(HELSINKI 1952)** 12 15
73. 75 f. on 1s. 50 **(MELBOURNE 1956)** 15 20
74. 100 f. on 2s. **(ROME 1960)** 25 35
75. 250 f. on 5s. **(TOKYO 1964)** 50 75
76. 500 f. on 10s. **(MEXICO CITY 1968)** .. 1·00 1·75

1966. World Cup Football Championships. Nos. 57, 59, 61/2, 65/7 optd. **CHAMPIONS ENGLAND** (10 f., 50 f. and 250 f.) or **FOOTBALL 1966** (others). Both with football symbol.

77. 10 f. on 15 c. 5 5
78. 20 f. on 35 c. 5 5
79. 35 f. on 70 c. 8 10
80. 50 f. on 1s. 10 10
81. 100 f. on 2s 25 30
82. 250 f. on 5s. 50 60
83. 500 f. on 10s. .. .. 1·00 1·25

5. "Telstar".

1966. I.T.U. Cent. (1965).

84. 5. 5 f. green, black & violet 5 5
85. – 10 f. maroon, black & green 5 5
86. – 15 f. blue, black & orange 5 5
87. 5. 25 f. green, black and red 8 8
88. – 35 f. maroon, black & yell. 12 12
89. – 50 f. blue, black & brown 20 20
90. 5. 65 f. green, black & yellow 25 25

DESIGNS: 10 f., 35 f. "Relay". 15 f., 50 f. "Ranger".

6. Churchill at Easel.

1966. Sir Winston Churchill's Paintings. Multicoloured.

91. 5 f. Type **6** 5 5
92. 10 f. "Antibes" 5 5
93. 15 f. "Flowers" 8 8
94. 20 f. "Tapestries" .. 10 10
95. 25 f. "Village, Lake Lugano" 12 12
96. 35 f. "Church, Lake Como" 20 20
97. 50 f. "Flowers at Chartwell" 25 25
98. 65 f. Type **6** 30 30

The 15, 35 and 50 f. are vert.

1967. "World Peace". Nos. 57, 59, 61/7 optd. **WORLD PEACE** and names as given below.

99. 10 f. on 15 c. **(PANDIT NEHRU)** 5 5
100. 20 f. on 35 c. **(WINSTON CHURCHILL)** 5 5
101. 35 f. on 70 c. **(DAG HAMMARSKJOELD)** .. 8 5
102. 50 f. on 1s. **(JOHN F. KENNEDY)** 12 12
103. 65 f. on 1s. 25 **(LUDWIG ERHARD)** 15 15
104. 75 f. on 1s. 50 **(LYNDON JOHNSON)** 20 20
105. 100 f. on 2s. **(ELEANOR ROOSEVELT)** .. 25 25
106. 250 f. on 5s. **(WINSTON CHURCHILL)** 60 60
107. 500 f. on 10s. **(JOHN F. KENNEDY)** .. .. 1·25 1·25

7. "Master Crewe as Henry VIII" (Sir Joshua Reynolds).

1967. Paintings.

108. 7. 5 f. multicoloured .. 5 5
109. – 10 f. multicoloured .. 5 5
110. – 15 f. multicoloured .. 5 5
111. – 20 f. multicoloured .. 8 8
112. – 25 f. multicoloured .. 8 8
113. – 35 f. multicoloured .. 12 12
114. – 50 f. multicoloured .. 15 15
115. – 65 f. multicoloured .. 20 20
116. – 75 f. multicoloured .. 25 25

PAINTINGS: 10 f. "The Dancer" (Degas). 15 f. "The Fifer" (Manet). 20 f. "Stag at Sharkey's" (boxing-match, G. Burrows). 25 f. "Don Manuel Osorio" (Goya). 35 f. "St. Martin Distributing His Cloak" (A. van Dyck). 50 f. "The Blue Boy" (Gainsborough). 65 f. "The White Horse" (Gauguin). (45 × 60 mm.): 75 f. "Mona Lisa" (Da Vinci).

1967. American Astronauts. Nos. 57, 59, 61/2 and 65/6 optd. as below, all with space capsule.

117. 10 ft. on 15 c. **(ALAN SHEPARD, JR.)** .. 5 5
118. 20 f. on 35 c. **(VIRGIL GRISSOM)** 5 5
119. 35 f. on 70 c. **(JOHN GLENN JR.)** 8 8
120. 50 f. on 1s. **(SCOTT CARPENTER)** .. 15 15
121 100 f. on 2s. **(WALTER SCHIRRA JR.)** .. 30 30
122. 250 f. on 5s. **(GORDON COOPER JR.)** .. 75 75

8. Churchill Crown.

1967. Churchill Commem.
123. **8.** 75 f. multicoloured .. 20 20

HADHRAMAUT

On the resignation of the Shaikh, the National Liberation Front took control on 17th September, 1967, and full independence was granted by Great Britain on 30th November, 1967. Now part of Southern Yemen.

(a) Issues inscribed "SHIHR and MUKALLA"

1. Sultan of Shihr and Mukalla.

2. Mukalla Harbour.

DESIGNS—VERT. 2 a. Gateway of Shihr. 3 a. Outpost of Mukalla. 1 r. Du'an. 2 r. Mosque in Hureidha. HORIZ. 8 a. 'Einat. 5 r. Meshed.

3. Shibam.

1942.
1. **1.** ½ a. green 10 15
2. ¾ a. brown 10 15
3. 1 a. blue 10 15
4. **2.** 1½ a. red 10 25
5. – 2 a. sepia 10 35
6. **3.** 2½ a. blue 10 30
7. – 3 a. sepia and red .. 12 30
8. – 8 a. red 20 50
9. – 1 r. green 30 55
10. – 2 r. blue and purple .. 1·00 1·50
11. – 5 r. brown and green .. 1·40 2·50

1946. Victory. Optd. **VICTORY ISSUE 8th JUNE 1946.**
12. **2.** 1½ a. red 8 8
13. **3.** 2½ a. blue 8 8

1949. Silver Wedding. As **T 5/6** of Aden.
14. 1½ a. red 10 12
15. 5 r. green .. .. .. 1·75 2·50

1949. U.P.U. As **T 14/17** of Antigua surch.
16. 2½ a. on 20 c. blue .. 15 30
17. 3 a. on 30 c. red 45 50
18. 8 a. on 50 c. orange .. 75 1·00
19. 1 r. on 1s. blue .. .. 1·25 1·60

1951. Stamps of 1942 surch. in cents or shillings.
20. 5 c. on 1 a. blue 10 12
21. 10 c. on 2 a. sepia .. 10 12
22. 15 c. on 2½ a. blue .. 10 12
23. 20 c. on 3 a. sepia and red 10 15
24. 50 c. on 8 a. red 10 20
25. 1s. on 1 r. green 20 70
26. 2s. on 2 r. blue and purple 65 1·25
27. 5s. on 5 r. brown and green 1·25 1·90

1953. Coronation. As **T 7** of Aden.
28. 15 c. black and blue .. 20 35

(b) Issues inscribed "HADHRAMAUT".

4. Metal Work. 5.

1955. Occupations. Portrait as in **T 4.** Nos. 36/40 horiz. designs.
29. **4.** 5 c. blue 12 12
30. – 10 c. black (Mat-making) 12 12
31. – 15 c. green (Weaving) .. 12 12
32. – 25 c. red (Pottery) .. 12 12
33. – 35 c. blue (Building) .. 12 12
34. – 50 c. orange (Date cultivation) 20 15
35. – 90 c. brown (Agriculture) 20 25
36. – 1s. black & lilac (Fisheries) 20 25
37. – 1s. 25 c. black and orange (Lime-burning) 30 35
38. – 2s. black and blue (Dhow building) 55 70
39. – 5s. black and green (Agriculture) .. .. 1·50 1·75
40. – 10s. black & red (as No. 37) 2·50 3·25

1963. Occupations. As Nos. 29/40 but with inset portrait of Sultan Awadh bin Saleh el Qu'aiti, as in **T 5.**
41. **5.** 5 c. blue 5 5
42. – 10 c. black 5 5
43. – 15 c. green 5 5
44. – 25 c. red 5 5
45. – 35 c. blue 5 5
46. – 50 c. orange 5 8
47. – 70 c. brown (As No. 35) .. 8 12
48. – 1s. black and lilac .. 10 20
49. – 1s. 25 black and orange .. 20 30
50. – 2s. black and blue .. 40 50
51. – 5s. black and green .. 75 1·40
52. – 10s. black and red .. 1·40 2·25

1966. Nos. 41/52 surch. **SOUTH ARABIA** in English and Arabic, with value and bar.
53. **5.** 5 f. on 5 c. 5 5
54. – 5 f. on 10 c. 5 5
55. – 10 f. on 15 c. 5 5
56. – 15 f. on 25 c. 5 5
57. – 20 f. on 35 c. 5 5
58. – 25 f. on 50 c. 5 8
59. – 35 f. on 70 c. 8 10
60. – 50 f. on 1s. 10 15
61. – 65 f. on 1s. 25 .. .. 20 30
62. – 100 f. on 2s. 40 60
63. – 250 f. on 5s. .. .. 1·00 1·50
64. – 500 f. on 10s. .. .. 2·00 3·00

1966. Churchill Commem. Nos. 54/6 optd. **1874-1965 WINSTON CHURCHILL.**
65. 5 f. on 10 c. 10 15
66. 10 f. on 15 c. 20 30
67. 15 f. on 25 c. 30 45

1966. Pres. Kennedy Commem. Nos. 57/9 optd. **1917-63 JOHN F. KENNEDY.**
68. 20 f. on 35 c. 40 60
69. 25 f. on 50 c. 55 80
70. 35 f. on 70 c. .. .. 70 1·25

6. World Cup Emblem (reduced size illustration. Actual size 55 × 55 mm.).

1966. World Cup Football Championships.
71. **6.** 5 f. maroon and orange .. 5 5
72. – 10 f. violet and green .. 5 5
73. – 15 f. maroon and orange .. 5 5
74. – 20 f. violet and green .. 8 8
75. **6.** 25 f. green and red .. 8 8
76. – 35 f. blue and yellow .. 12 12
77. – 50 f. green and red .. 20 20
78. **6.** 65 f. blue and yellow .. 25 25

DESIGNS: 10 f., 35 f. Wembley Stadium. 15 f., 50 f. Footballers. 20 f. Jules Rimet Cup and football.

7. Mexican Hat and Blanket (reduced size illustration. Actual size 63 × 63 mm.).

1966. Pre-Olympic Games, Mexico (1968).
79. **7.** 75 f. sepia and green .. 30 30

8. Telecommunications Satellite.

1966. Int. Co-operation Year.
80. **8.** 5 f. maroon, purple & emer. 5 5
81. – 10 f. vio., orge., grn. & blue 5 5
82. – 15 f. maroon, blue and red 5 5
83. **8.** 20 f. blue, purple and red .. 8 8
84. – 25 f. violet, yellow, red & emerald 8 8
85. **8.** 35 f. maroon, red and blue 12 12
86. – 50 f. maroon, green and red 20 20
87. **8.** 65 f. choc., violet and red 25 25

DESIGNS: 10 f. Olympic runner (inscr. "ROME 1960"). 15 f. Fishes. 25 f. Olympic runner (inscr. "TOKIO 1964"). 50 f. Tobacco plant.

MAHRA SULTANATE OF QISHN AND SOCOTRA

The National Liberation Front took control on 1st October, 1967, and full independence was granted by Great Britain on 30th November, 1967. Now part of Southern Yemen.

1. Mahra Flag.

1967.
1. **1.** 5 f. multicoloured .. 5 5
2. 10 f. multicoloured .. 5 5
3. 15 f. multicoloured .. 5 5
4. 20 f. multicoloured .. 5 5
5. 25 f. multicoloured .. 5 5
6. 35 f. multicoloured .. 8 5
7. 50 f. multicoloured .. 8 8
8. 65 f. multicoloured .. 10 10
9. 100 f. multicoloured .. 15 15
10. 250 f. multicoloured .. 50 35
11. 500 f. multicoloured .. 1·00 75

For later issues see **SOUTH ARABIAN FEDERATION, SOUTHERN YEMEN, YEMEN-PEOPLE'S DEMOCRATIC REPUBLIC.**

AEGEAN ISLANDS E1

A group of islands off the coast of Asia Minor occupied by Italy in May, 1912 and ceded to her by Turkey in 1920. The islands concerned were Calino, Carchi, Caso, Coo, Lero, Lipso, Nisiro, Patmo, Piscopi, Rodi, Scarpanto, Simi and Stampalia. Castelrosso was added in 1921. The Aegean Islands were restored to Greece on 15th September, 1947.

1916. Optd. **Rodi.**
14. **22.** 20 c. orange 10 10
15. **26.** 85 c. brown 30 40
16. **23.** 1 l. brown & green .. 12

1. Rhodian Windmill. 2. Knight kneeling before the Holy City.

1929. King of Italy's Visit.
17. **1.** 5 c. claret 5 5
18. – 10 c. brown 5 5
19. – 20 c. red 5 5
20. – 25 c. green 5 5
21. **2.** 30 c. blue 5 5
22. – 50 c. brown 5 5
23. – 1 l. 25 blue 5 5
24. **2.** 5 l. claret 8 8
25. 10 l. olive 20 12

DESIGNS—As Type **1**: 10 c. Galley. 20 c. and 25 c. Knight defending Christianity. 50 c. and 1 l. 25 c. Knight's Tomb.

1930. Ferrucci issue (colours changed), optd. for each individual island, as 1912 issue but in capitals and Cos becomes **COO.**
26. **85.** 20 c. violet 8 10
27. – 25 c. green 8 10
28. – 50 c. black 8 10
29. – 1 l. 25 blue 8 10
30. – 5 l. + 2 l. red 45 50
Same prices for each of the 13 islands.

1930. Air. Ferrucci stamps (colours changed) optd. **ISOLE ITALIANE DELL'EGEO.**
31. **88.** 50 c. purple 15 20
32. 1 l. blue 20 20
33. 5 l. + 2 l. red .. .. 1·40 1·75

1930. 21st Hydrological Congress. Nos. 17/25 of Aegean Islands optd. **XXI Congresso Idrologico.**
34. 5 c. claret 15 35
35. 10 c. brown 15 35
36. 20 c. red 25 35
37. 25 c. green 30 45
38. 30 c. blue 20 35
39. 50 c. brown .. .. 90·00 20·00
40. 1 l. 25 blue .. .. 70·00 16·00
41. 5 l. claret .. .. 9·00 14·00
42. 10 l. olive .. .. 9·00 14·00

1930. Virgil stamps. Optd. **ISOLE ITALIANE DELL'EGEO.**
43. **89.** 15 c. violet (postage) .. 8 10
44. 20 c. brown 8 10
45. 25 c. green 8 10
46. 30 c. brown 8 10
47. 50 c. purple 8 10
48. 75 c. red 10 15
49. 1 l. 25 blue 15 20
50. 5 l + 1 l. 50 purple .. 90 1·75
51. 10 l. + 2 l. 50 brown .. 1·50 1·75
52. 50 c. green (air) .. 45 20
53. 1 l. red 20 20
54. 7 l. 70 + 1 l. 30 brown .. 55 1·10
55. 9 l. + 2 l. grey .. .. 70 1·25

1931. Italian Eucharistic Congress. Nos 17/25 of Aegean Islands optd. **1931 CONGRESSO EUCARISTICO ITALIANO**
56. 5 c. claret 10 15
57. 10 c. brown 10 15
58. 20 c. red 20 15
59. 25 c. green 20 20
60. 30 c. blue 20 25
61. 50 c. brown .. .. 8·50 5·00
62. 1 l. 25 blue .. .. 8·50 5·00

ITALIAN OCCUPATION

Stamps of Italy overprinted unless otherwise stated.

1912. Optd. **EGEO.**
1. **26.** 25 c. blue 35 15
2. 50 c. mauve 35 15

1912. Issues for individual islands optd. with islands name, or surch. also.
A. Calimno, B. Caso, C. Cos, D. Karki, E. Leros, F. Lipso, G. Nisiros, H. Patmos, I. Piscopi, J. Rodi, K. Scarpanto, L. Simi, M. Stampalia.

		Calimno A.		Caso B.		Cos C.		Karki D.		Leros E.		Lipso F.	
3. **21.**	2 c. brown	30	25	30	25	30	25	35	25	35	25	30	25
4. **24.**	5 c. green	10	10	10	10	1·75	1·25	8	10	8	10	8	12
5.	10 c. rose	10	10	10	10	8	10	8	10	8	10	8	12
6. **25.**	15 c. grey	2·00	1·40	2·00	1·40	1·50	1·25	1·75	1·10	1·50	1·10	1·50	1·00
12. **24.**	15 c. grey	45	90	50	90	50	90	45	90	45	90	45	90
10. **25.**	20 c. on 15 c. grey	70	90	10	20	70	90	10	20	55	70	10	20
13.	20 c. orange	45	90	35	90	50	90	50	90	7·00	8·00	30	90
7. **26.**	25 c. blue	10	15	10	15	1·00	90	10	15	1·75	1·10	10	12
8.	40 c. brown	10	15	10	15	10	15	10	15	10	15	10	12
9.	50 c. mauve	10	15	10	15	10	15	10	15	10	15	10	12

		Nisiros G.		Patmos H.		Piscopi I.		Rodi J.		Scarpanto K.		Simi L.		Stampalia M.	
3. **21.**	2 c.	35	30	35	30	35	30	8	10	35	30	35	30	35	30
4. **24.**	5 c.	8	12	8	12	8	12	8	10	8	10	60	35	8	12
5.	10 c.	8	12	8	12	8	12	8	10	8	10	8	10	8	12
6. **25.**	15 c.	1·50	1·10	1·50	1·10	1 50	1 10	2 00	95	1·75	1·25	1·50	1·10	1·50	1·10
12. **24.**	15 c.	45	90	35	90	2·10	2·50	2·10	2·00	1·60	1·75	9·00	10·00	1·60	1·75
10. **25.**	20 c. on 15 c.	10	25	40	50	10	20	9·00	10·00	10	20	45	50	10	20
13.	20 c.	3·75	4·50	7·50	8·00	2·00	2·25	20	20	1·60	1·75	1·50	1·50	1·60	1·75
7. **26.**	25 c.	10	15	10	15	10	15	10	10	30	25	25	20	12	15
8.	40 c.	10	15	10	15	10	15	10	10	20	12	10	15	12	15
9.	50 c.	10	15	10	15	10	15	10	10	25	15	10	15	12	15

1932. St. Anthony of Padua stamps. Optd. **ISOLE ITALIANE DELL'EGEO.**

No.	Type	Description	Unused	Used
63.	92.	20 c. purple	1·50	1·50
64.	–	25 c. green	1·50	1·50
65.	–	30 c. brown	1·50	1·50
66.	–	50 c. purple	1·50	1·50
67.	–	75 c. red	1·50	1·50
68.	–	1 l. 25 blue	1·50	1·50
69.	–	5 l.+2 l. 50 orange	1·50	1·50

1932. Dante Stamps. Optd. **ISOLE ITALIANE DELL'EGEO.**

No.	Type	Description	Unused	Used
70.	–	10 c. green (postage)	5	8
71.	–	15 c. violet	5	8
72.	–	20 c. brown	5	8
73.	–	25 c. green	5	8
74.	–	30 c. red	5	8
75.	–	50 c. purple	5	8
76.	–	75 c. red	8	10
77.	–	1 l. 25 blue	8	10
78.	–	1 l. 75 sepia	12	20
79.	–	2 l. 75 red	30	40
80.	–	5 l.+2 l. violet	40	50
81.	96.	10 l.+2 l. 50 brown	50	55
82.	97.	50 c. red (air)	20	15
83.	–	1 l. green	10	10
84.	–	3 l. purple	10	10
85.	–	5 l. red	10	10
86.	97.	7 l. 70+2 l. sepia	20	20
87.	–	10 l.+2 l. 50 blue	20	20
88.	98.	100 l. olive and blue	4·50	4·50

No. 88 is inscribed instead of optd.

1932. Garibaldi issue, (colours changed), optd. for each individual island, as in 1912 but in capital letters.

No.	Type	Description	Unused	Used
89.	–	10 c. sepia	40	40
90.	99.	20 c. brown	40	40
91.	–	25 c. green	40	40
92.	99.	30 c. black	40	40
93.	–	50 c. lilac	40	40
94.	–	75 c. red	40	40
95.	–	1 l. 25 blue	40	40
96.	–	1 l. 75+25 c. sepia	40	40
97.	–	2 l. 55+50 c. red	40	40
98.	–	5 l.+1 l. violet	40	40

Same price for each of the 13 islands.

1932. Air. Garibaldi stamps. Optd. **ISOLE ITALIANE DELL'EGEO.**

No.	Type	Description	Unused	Used
99.	100.	50 c. green (air)	2·75	3·00
100.	–	80 c. red	2·75	3·00
101.	–	1 l.+25 c. blue	2·75	3·00
102.	–	2 l.+50 c. brown	2·75	3·00
103.	–	5 l.+1 l. black	2·75	3·00

3.

1932. Italian Occupation of Aegean Is. 20th Anniv.

No.	Type	Description	Unused	Used
106.	3.	5 c. red, black and green	15	20
107.		10 c. red, black and blue	10	20
108.		20 c. red, black and yellow	15	20
109.		25 c. red, black and violet	10	20
110.		30 c. red, black and red	10	20
111.	–	50 c. red, black and blue	10	20
112.	–	1 l. 25 red, maroon & blue	10	20
113.	–	5 l. red and blue	1·40	2·00
114.	–	10 l. red, green and blue	5·00	7·00
115.	–	25 l. red, brown and blue	£160	£170

DESIGN—VERT. 50 c. to 25 l. Arms on Map of Rodi.

4.

5. Wing from Arms of Francesco Sans.

1933. "Graf Zeppelin" Air stamps.

No.	Type	Description	Unused	Used
116.	4.	3 l. brown	35·00	15·00
117.		5 l. purple	7·50	15·00
118.		10 l. green	7·50	15·00
119.		10 l. blue	7·50	15·00
120.		15 l. red	7·50	15·00
121.		20 l. black	7·50	15·00

1933. Air. Balbo Air stamps. Optd. **ISOLE ITALIANE DELL'EGEO.**

No.	Type	Description	Unused	Used
122.	109.	5 l. 25+19 l. 75 red, green and blue	14·00	18·00
123.	110.	5 l. 25+44 l. 75 red, green and blue	14·00	18·00

1934. Air.

No.	Type	Description	Unused	Used
124.	5.	50 c. black and yellow	5	5
125.		80 c. black and red	8	5
126.		1 l. black and green	8	5
127.		5 l. black and violet	30	30

1934. World Football Championship stamps. Optd. **ISOLE ITALIANE DELL'EGEO.**

No.	Type	Description	Unused	Used
128.	–	20 c. red (postage)	1·50	1·25
129.	117.	25 c. green	1·50	1·25
130.		50 c. violet	11·00	90
131.		1 l. 25 blue	1·90	2·00
132.	–	5 l. + 2 l. 50 blue	2·25	3·50
133.	–	50 c. brown (air)	35	55
134.	–	75 c. red	35	55
135.	–	5 l. + 2 l. 50 orange	1·90	2·50
136.	–	10 l. + 5 l. green	1·90	2·50

1934. Military Medal Cent. stamps. Optd. **ITALIANE ISOL DELL'EGEO.**

No.	Type	Description	Unused	Used
157.	120.	10 c. grey (postage)	5·00	5·50
158.	–	15 c. brown	5·00	5·50
159.	–	20 c. orange	5·00	5·50
160.	–	25 c. green	5·00	5·50
161.	–	30 c. claret	5·00	5·50
162.	–	50 c. olive-green	5·00	5·50
163.	–	75 c. red	5·00	5·50
164.	–	1 l. 25 blue	5·00	5·50
165.	–	1 l. 75 + 1 l. violet	3·00	5·50
166.	–	2 l. 55 + 2 l. red	3·00	5·50
167.	–	2 l. 75 + 2 l. brown	3·00	5·50
168.	–	25 c. green (air)	9·00	10·00
169.	–	50 c. grey	9·00	10·00
170.	–	75 c. red	9·00	10·00
171.	–	80 c. brown	9·00	10·00
172.	–	1 l. + 50 c. green	7·50	10·00
173.	–	2 l. + 1 l. blue	7·50	10·00
174.	–	3 l. + 2 l. violet	7·50	10·00
175.	–	2 l. + 1 l. 25 blue (air express)	7·50	10·00
176.	–	4 l. 50 + 2 l. green	7·50	10·00

6.

1935. Holy Year.

No.	Type	Description	Unused	Used
177.	6.	5 c. orange	35	55
178.		10 c. brown	35	55
179.		20 c. red	35	55
180.		25 c. green	35	55
181.		30 c. purple	35	55
182.		50 c. brown	35	55
183.		1 l. 25 blue	35	55

1938. Augustus the Great. Birth Bimillenary. Optd. **ITALIANE ISOL DELL'EGEO.**

No.	Type	Description	Unused	Used
186.	136.	10 c. brown (postage)	12	12
187.	–	15 c. violet	12	12
188.	–	20 c. brown	12	12
189.	–	25 c. green	12	12
190.	–	30 c. purple	12	12
191.	–	50 c. green	12	12
192.	–	75 c. red	20	20
193.	–	1 l. 25 blue	20	20
194.	–	1 l. 75+ 1 l. orange	1·40	1·40
195.	–	2 l. 55+2 l. brown	1·50	1·50
196.	–	25 c. violet (air)	30	30
197.	–	50 c. green	45	40
198.	–	80 c. blue	55	60
199.	–	1 l.+1 l. purple	1·90	1·90
200.	138.	5 l.+1 l. red	2·75	2·75

1938. Giotto. 600th Death Anniv. Optd. **ITALIANE ISOL DELL'EGEO.**

No.	Type	Description	Unused	Used
201.		1 l. 25 blue (No. 527)	40	40
202.		2 l. 75+2 l. brn. (530)	40	50

7. Crown and Maltese Cross.

8. Dante House, Rhodes.

1940. Colonial Exhibition. Inscr. as in T 7/8.

No.	Type	Description	Unused	Used
203.	–	5 c. brown (postage)	5	5
204.	7.	10 c. orange	5	5
205.	8.	25 c. green	25	25
206.	–	50 c. violet	25	25
207.	7.	75 c. red	25	25
208.	8.	1 l. 25 blue	25	25
209.	7.	2 l. + 75 c. red	25	25

DESIGN—VERT. 5 c., 50 c. Roman Wolf statue.

No.	Type	Description	Unused	Used
210.		50 c. brown (air)	50	50
211.		1 l. violet	50	50
212.		2 l. + 75 c. blue	70	70
213.		5 l. + 2 l. 50 brown	70	70

DESIGNS—HORIZ. 50 c., 2 l. 'Plane and stag statue. 1 l., 5 l. 'Plane and buildings.

1943. Charity. Nos. 17/25 of Aegean Islands surch. **PRO ASSISTENZA EGEO** and value.

No.	Type	Description	Unused	Used
214.	1.	5 c. + 5 c. claret	5	5
215.	–	10 c. + 10 c. brown	5	5
216.	–	20 c. + 20 c. red	5	5
217.	–	25 c. + 25 c. green	5	5
218.	2.	30 c. + 30 c. blue	5	5
219.	–	50 c. + 50 c. brown	10	10
220.	–	1 l. 25 + 1 l. 25 blue	15	15
221.	2.	5 l. + 5 l. claret	20·00	8·50

1944. War Victims Relief. Nos. 17/20 and 22/23 of Aegean Islands surch. **PRO SINISTRATI DI GUERRA** and value.

No.	Type	Description	Unused	Used
224.	1.	5 c. + 3 l. claret	5	5
225.	–	10 c. + 3 l. brown	5	5
226.	–	20 c. + 3 l. red	5	5
227.	–	25 c. + 3 l. green	5	5
228.	–	50 c. + 3 l. brown	8	8
229.	–	1 l. 25 + 5l. blue	2·00	2·00

1944. Air. War Victims Relief. Surch. **PRO SINISTRATI DI GUERRA** and value.

No.	Type	Description	Unused	Used
232.	5.	50 c.+2 l. blk. & yellow	10	10
233.		80 c.+2 l. blk. & red	15	15
234.		1 l.+2 l. black & green	15	15
235.		5 l.+2 l. black & mag.	6·00	6·00

1945. Red Cross Fund. Nos. 24/5 of Aegean Islands surch. **FEBBRAIO 1945** and value.

No.	Type	Description	Unused	Used
236.		+10 l. on 5 l. claret	1·25	1·25
237.		+10 l. on 10 l. olive	1·25	1·25

EXPRESS STAMPS

1931. Air. Garibaldi Air Express stamps. Optd. **ISOL ITALIANE DELL'EGEO.**

No.	Type	Description	Unused	Used
E 104.	E 3.	2 l. 25 + 1 l. red &bl.	2·75	3·75
E 105.		4 l. 50+1 l. 50 grey and yellow	2·75	3·75

E 1.

1935.

No.	Type	Description	Unused	Used
E 184.	E 1.	1 l. 25 green	8	8
E 185.		2 l. 50 orange	20	20

1943. Charity. Surch. **PRO ASSISTENZA EGEO** and value

No.	Type	Description	Unused	Used
E 222.	E 1.	1 l. 25+1 l. 25 green	2·25	1·90
E 223.		2 l. 50+2 l. 50 orge.	4·75	2·50

1944. Nos. 19/20 surch. **ESPRESS** and value.

No.	Type	Description	Unused	Used
E 230.		1 l. 25 on 25 c. green	8	10
E 231.		2 l. 50 on 20 c. red	8	10

PARCEL POST STAMPS

P 1.

1934.

No.	Type	Description	Unused	Used
P 137.	P 1.	5 c. orange	5	5
P 138.		10 c. red	5	5
P 139.		20 c. green	5	5
P 140.		25 c. violet	5	5
P 141.		50 c. blue	5	5
P 142.		60 c. black	5	5
P 143.	–	1 l. orange	5	5
P 144.	–	2 l. red	5	5
P 145.	–	3 l. green	8	5
P 146.	–	4 l. violet	15	5
P 147.	–	10 l. blue	25	5

DESIGN: 1 l. to 10 l. Left half. Stag as in Type E 1. Right half, Castle.

POSTAGE DUE STAMPS

D 1. Badge of the Knights of St. John.

D 2. Immortelle.

1934.

No.	Type	Description	Unused	Used
D 148.	D 1.	5 c. orange	5	5
D 149.		10 c. red	5	5
D 150.		20 c. green	5	5
D 151.		30 c. violet	5	5
D 152.		40 c. blue	5	5
D 153.	D 2.	50 c. orange	5	5
D 154.		60 c. red	5	5
D 155.		1 l. green	5	5
D 156.		2 l. violet	5	5

AFGHANISTAN O1

An independent Country in Asia, to N.W. of Pakistan. Now a republic, the country was formerly ruled by monarchs from 1747 to 1973.

1870. 12 shahi = 6 sanar = 3 abasi = 1 rupee.
1920. 60 paisa = 2 kran = 1 rupee.
1926. 100 poul (pul) = 1 afghani (rupee).

> The issues from 1860 to 1892 (Types 1 to 8) are difficult to classify because the values of each set are expressed in native script and are generally all printed in the same colour. As it is not possible to list these in an intelligible simplified form we would refer users to the detailed list in the Stanley Gibbons Foreign Overseas Catalogue, Volume 1.

1.

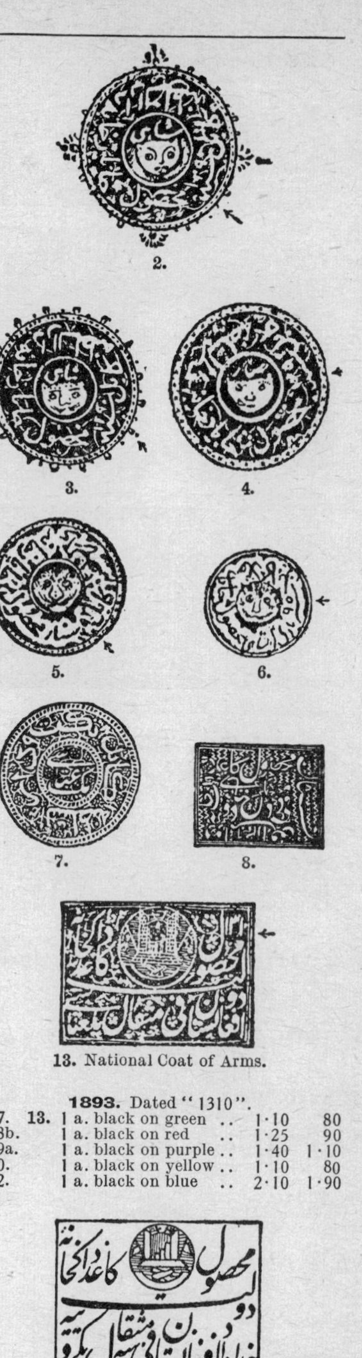

2. 3. 4. 5. 6. 7. 8.

13. National Coat of Arms.

1893. Dated "1310".

No.	Type	Description	Unused	Used
147.	13.	1 a. black on green	1·10	80
148b.		1 a. black on red	1·25	90
149a.		1 a. black on purple	1·40	1·10
150.		1 a. black on yellow	1·10	80
152.		1 a. black on blue	2·10	1·90

14.

1894. Undated.

No.	Type	Description	Unused	Used
153.	14.	2 abasi black on green	3·50	2·25
154.		1 rupee black on green	4·00	2·75

15.

18. National Coat of Arms.

19.

1907. Imperf., roul. or perf.

No.	Type	Description	Unused	Used
156a.	15.	1 a. green	1·50	1·40
157.	–	2 a. blue	70	45
158.	–	1 r. green	1·00	90

The 2 a. and 1 r. are in similar designs.

1909. Perf.

No.	Type	Description	Unused	Used
165.	18.	2 paisa brown	40	55
166.	19.	1 a. blue	20	15
167.		1 a. red	15	15
169.	–	2 a. green	30	30
170.	–	2 a. yellow-brown	45	45
171.	–	1 r. brown	50	50
172.	–	1 r. olive	50	50

The frames of the 2 a. and 1 r. differ from T 19.

22. Royal Star of Order of Independence. **23.** Crest of King Amanullah.

25a.

24. Crest of King Amanullah.

1920. New currency. End of War of Independence. 1st Anniv. Size 39 × 47 mm.

173. **22.** 10 paisa red .. .. 7·00 3·50
174. 20 paisa purple .. 17·00 10·00
175. 30 paisa green .. .. 28·00 20·00

1921. End of War of Independence. 2nd Anniv. Size 23 × 29 mm.

177. **22.** 10 paisa red 8 8
178. 20 paisa purple .. 15 15
180. 30 paisa green 30 25

1924. 6th Independence Day.

183. **23.** 10 paisa chocolate (24 × 32 mm.) .. 5 50 4·00

1924.

183b. **23a.** 5 kr. blue .. .. 3·75 3·75
183c. 5 r. purple .. .. 2·75 2·75

1925. 7th Independence Day.

184. **23.** 10 paisa red-brown (29 × 37 mm.) .. 4 50 3·25

1926. 7th Anniv. of Independence.

185. **23.** 10 paisa blue (26 × 33 mm. 60 60

1927. 8th Anniv. of Independence.

186. **24.** 10 p. purple .. .. 1·10 1·10

25.

26.

27.

Types 25/7, 29/34 show the National Seal.

1927. Perf. or imperf.

188. **25.** 15 pouls red 12 12
189. **26.** 30 pouls green 15 12
190. **27.** 60 pouls blue 35 35

28. Crest of King Amanullah.

1928. 9th Anniv. of Independence.

191. **28.** 15 pouls red 25 20

30.

31.

1928.

193. **30.** 10 pouls green 10 8
194. **31.** 25 pouls red 12 12
195. – 40 pouls blue 15 15
196. – 50 pouls red 20 20

The frames of the 40 and 50 p. differ from T 31.

34.

35. Independence Memorial.

1929. Nadir Shah Issue.

206. **30.** 10 pouls purple .. 50 50
207. 10 pouls brown .. 15 15
208. **25.** 15 pouls blue 25 20
209. **31.** 25 pouls blue 35 30
210. **34.** 30 pouls green .. 30 30
211. – 40 pouls red 35 35
212. – 50 pouls blue 50 50
213. **27.** 60 pouls black 60 50

1931. 13th Independence Day.

214. **35.** 20 pul. red 30 25

36. National Assembly Building.

37. Mosque at Balkh.

1932. National Council. Inaug.

215. – 40 p. brown (31 × 24 mm.) 20 12
216. – 60 p. violet (29 × 26 mm.) 45 30
217. **36.** 80 p. red 45 35
218. – 1 a. black (24 × 27 mm.) 2·75 1·50
219. – 2 a. blue (36 × 25 mm.) 2·00 1·25
220. – 3 a. green (36 × 24 mm.) 2·25 1·40

DESIGNS: Nos. 215/16, 218/19, Council Chamber. 3 a. National Assembly Building (different).

1932.

221. **37.** 10 p. brown 8 8
222. – 15 p. brown 12 8
223. – 20 p. red 20 15
224. – 25 p. green 15 10
225. – 30 p. red 20 15
226. – 40 p. orange 25 12
227. – 50 p. blue 45 20
228. – 60 p. blue 40 25
229. – 80 p. violet 75 70
230. – 1 a. blue .. .. 1·10 35
231. – 2 a. purple .. .. 1·50 1·10
232. – 3 a. red .. .. 1·75 1·40

DESIGNS: 15 p. Kabul Fortress. 20 p., 25 p. Parliament House, Darul Funun, Kabul. 30 p. Arch at Qualai Bust, Kandahar. 40 p. Memorial Pillar of Knowledge and Ignorance, Kabul. 50 p. Independence Memorial, Kabul. 60 p. Minaret at Herat. 80 p. Arch of Paghman. 1 a. Ruins at Balkh. 2 a. Minarets at Herat. 3 a. Great Buddha at Bamian.

See also Nos. 237/51.

38. Independence Memorial.

38a. National Liberation Monument, Kabul.

1932. 14th Independence Day.

233. **38.** 1 a. red 90 65
234. **38a.** 80 p. brown 45 35

39. Arch of Paghman.

1933. 15th Independence Day.

235. **39.** 50 p. blue 45 45

40. Independence Memorial.

1934. 16th Independence Day.

236. **40.** 50 p. green 45 45

1934. As 1932 issues but colours changed and new values.

237. **37.** 10 p. violet 5 5
238. – 15 p. green 8 8
239. – 20 p. mauve 10 5
240. – 25 p. red 15 10
241. – 30 p. orange 20 10
242. – 40 p. black 25 20
243. – 45 p. blue 40 35
244. – 45 p. red 12 10
245. – 50 p. red 15 8
246. – 60 p. violet 25 20
247. – 75 p. red 60 60
248. – 75 p. blue 30 25
249. – 1 a. mauve 55 40
250. – 2 a. grey .. .. 1·25 90
251. – 3 a. blue .. .. 1·75 1·60

DESIGNS: 15 p. Kabul Fortress. 20 p., 25 p. Parliament House, Darul Funun, Kabul. 30 p. Arch at Qualai Bust, Kandahar. 45 p. (2) Royal Palace, Kabul. 50 p. Independence Memorial, Kabul. 60 p. Minaret at Herat. 75 p. (2) Hunters Canyon Pass, Hindu Kush. 1 a. Ruins at Balkh. 2 a. Council Chamber. 3 a. National Assembly Building.

41. Independence Memorial.

42. Firework Display.

1935. 17th Independence Day.

252. **41.** 50 p. blue 55 55

1936. 18th Independence Day.

253. **42.** 50 p. purple 55 55

43. Independence Memorial and Mohamed Nadir Shah. **44.** Mohamed Nadir Shah.

1937. 19th Independence Day. Perf. or imperf.

254. **43.** 50 p. brown and violet 45 45

1938. 20th Independence Day. Perf. or imperf.

255. **44.** 50 p. brown and blue 35 35

45. Aliabad Hospital. **47.** Mohamed Nadir Shah.

1938. Int. Anti-Cancer Fund. Obligatory Tax.

256. **45.** 10 p. green .. .. 3·00 3·00
257. – 15 p. blue .. .. 3·00 3·00

DESIGN: 15 p. Pierre and Marie Curie (larger).

1939. 21st Independence Day.

258. **47.** 50 p. red 40 30

49. Darul Funun Parliament House, Kabul.

50. Independence Memorial.

51. Mohamed Zahir Shah.

52. Sugar Mill, Baghlan.

1939.

259. **49.** 10 p. purple 5 5
260. 15 p. green 5 5
261. 20 p. purple 8 5
262. – 25 p. red 12 8
263. – 25 p. green 8 5
264. – 30 p. orange 10 8
265. – 35 p. orange 20 20
266. – 40 p. grey 12 10
267. **50.** 45 p. red 12 10
268. 50 p. orange 15 10
269. 60 p. violet 15 12
270. – 70 p. violet 35 30
271. – 70 p. blue 40 35
272. – 75 p. blue 80 35
273. – 75 p. red 20 12
274. – 75 p. red 50 50
275. – 80 p. brown 25 15
276. **51.** 1 a. purple 45 30
277. – 1 a. purple 50 40
278. **52.** 1 a. 25 blue .. .. 1·00 1·00
279a. – 2 a. red 85 50
280. – 3 a. blue .. .. 1·25 55

DESIGNS: 25 p. (2), 30 p., 40 p. Royal Palace, Kabul. 35 p. Minarets at Herat. 80 p. (2) Ruins at Kandahar Fort. 75 p. (3), 80 p. Independence Memorial and Mohamed Nadir Shah. 1 a. (No. 277), 2 a. Mohamed Zahir Shah. 3 a. As T 51 but head turned more to left.

53. Aeroplane over Kabul.

1939. Air.

280a. **53.** 5 a. orange 85 85
280b. 10 a. blue .. .. 1·40 1·10
280c. 20 a. green .. .. 2·50 2·00

54. Mohamed Nadir Shah.

55. Arch of Paghman.

1940. 22nd Independence Day.

281. **54.** 50 p. green 35 35

1941. 23rd Independence Day.

282. – 15 p. green .. .. 1·75 65
283. **55.** 50 p. brown 35 35

DESIGN: (19 × 29½ mm.) 15 p. Independence Memorial.

56. Mohamed Nadir Shah and Arch of Paghman.

57. Independence Memorial and Mohamed Nadir Shah.

1942. 24th Independence Day.

284. – 35 p. green .. .. 1·40 1·10
285. **56.** 125 p. blue 85 85

DESIGN—VERT. 35 p. Independence Memorial in medallion.

1943. 25th Independence Day.

286. – 35 p. red .. .. 3·25 2·25
287. **57.** 1 a. 25 blue 85 85

DESIGN—HORIZ. 35 p. Independence Memorial seen through archway and Mohamed Nadir Shah in oval frame.

58. Arch of Paghman.

59. Independence Memorial and Mohamed Nadir Shah.

1944. 26th Independence Day.

288. **58.** 35 p. red 35 35
289. **59.** 1 a. 25 blue 80 80

60. Mohamed Nadir Shah and Independence Memorial.
61. Arch of Paghman and Mohamed Nadir Shah.

1945. 27th Independence Day.
290. **60.** 35 p. claret 40 40
291. **61.** 1 a. 25 blue .. .. 1·10 1·10

62. Independence Memorial.
63. M. Zahir Shah and Arch of Paghman.

1946. 28th Independence Day. Dated "1946".
292. – 15 p. green 20 20
293. **62.** 20 p. magenta 30 30
294. – 125 p. blue .. .. 1·10 1·10
DESIGNS—HORIZ. 15 p. Mohamed Zahir Shah. VERT. 125 p. Mohamed Nadir Shah.

1947. 29th Independence Day. Dated "1947".
295. – 15 p. green 12 12
296. **63.** 35 p. magenta 15 15
297. – 1 a. 25 blue 65 65
DESIGNS—HORIZ. 15 p. Mohamed Zahir Shah and ruins of Kandahar Fort. VERT. 1 a. 25, Independence Memorial and Mohamed Nadir Shah.

64. Hungry Boy.
65. Independence Memorial.

1948. Child Welfare Fund.
298. **64.** 35 p. green 55 40
299. – 1 a. 25 p. blue .. .. 1·10 80
DESIGN: 1 a. 25 p. Hungry boy in vert. frame (26×32½mm.).

1948. 30th Independence Day. Dated "1948".
300. – 15 p. green 15 12
301. **65.** 20 p. magenta 20 15
302. – 125 p. blue 50 45
DESIGNS—VERT. 15 p. Arch of Paghman. HORIZ. 125 p. Mohamed Nadir Shah.

66. U.N. Symbol.

1948. U.N.O. 3rd Anniv.
303. **66.** 1 a. 25 blue .. .. 5·50 3·50

67. Hungry Boy.
68. Victory Monument.

1949. Obligatory Tax. Child Welfare Fund.
307. – 35 p. orange 55 55
308. **67.** 125 p. blue .. .. 1·10 1·10
DESIGN—HORIZ. 35 p. as T **67** but 29×22½ mm.

1949. 31st Year of Independence. Dated "1949" (Nos. 310/11).
309. **68.** 25 p. green 20 15
310. – 35 p. magenta 25 20
311. – 1 a. 25 blue 50 50
DESIGNS—HORIZ. 35 p. Mohamed Zahir Shah and Ruins of Kandahar Fort. 1 a. 25, Independence Memorial and Mohamed Nadir Shah.

69. Arch of Paghman.

1949. U.N.O. 4th Anniv.
312. **69.** 125 p. green .. .. 8·00 8·00

70. Mohamed Zahir Shah and Map of Afghanistan.

1950. Return from Visit to Europe.
313. **70.** 125 p. green 55 55

71. Hungry Boy.
72. Mohamed Nadir Shah.

1950. Obligatory Tax. Child Welfare Fund.
314. **71.** 125 p. green .. .. 1·10 1·10

1950. 32nd Independence Day.
315. **72.** 35 p. brown 15 15
316. 125 p. blue 40 40

73.

1950. U.N.O. 5th Anniv.
317. **73.** 1 a. 25 blue .. .. 3·50 3·00

74.

1950. Medical Faculty. 19th Anniv. Inscr. "FACULTE DE MEDICINE".
318. **74.** 35 p. green (postage) .. 35 35
319. – 1 a. 25 blue .. .. 1·25 1·25
320. **74.** 35 p. carmine (obligatory tax) 15 15
321. – 1 a. 25 black 55 55
DESIGN: Nos. 319 and 321 Sanatorium. Nos. 318 and 320 measure 38½×25½ mm. and Nos. 318 and 321, 46×30 mm.

75. Minaret at Herat.
76. Mosque at Balkh.

77. Mohamed Zahir Shah.
78.

1951.
322. **75.** 10 p. brown and yellow 5 5
323. 15 p. brown and blue 5 5
324. – 20 p. black .. .. 1·25 1·00
325. **77.** 25 p. green 5 5
326. **76.** 30 p. red 8 5
327. **77.** 35 p. violet 5 5
328. – 40 p. brown 12 5
329. – 45 p. blue 10 5
330. – 50 p. black 25 12
331. – 60 p. black 12 5
332. – 70 p. black, red & green 15 5
333. – 75 p. red 35 12
334. – 80 p. black and red .. 35 15
335. – 1 a. violet and green .. 25 15
336. **78.** 1 a. 25 black & purple 25 15
337. – 2 a. blue 35 15
338. 3 a. blue and black .. 80 25
DESIGNS: 20 p. Buddha of Banian. 40 p. Ruins at Kandahar Fort. 45 p. Maiwand Victory Monument. 50 p. View of Kandahar. 60 p. Victory Towers, Ghazni. 70 p. Flag. 75 p. Mohamed Zahir Shah. 80 p., 1 a. Mohamed Zahir Shah.
See also Nos. 425/4251.

79. Aeroplane over Kabul.

81. Arch of Paghman.
80. Shepherdess.

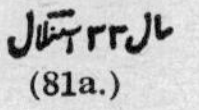

(81a.)  (81b.)

1951. Air.
339. **79.** 5 a. red 90 45
339a. 5 a. green 80 45
415a. 5 a. blue 55 40
340. 10 a. grey .. .. 2·25 55
415b. 10 a. violet .. .. 1·10 90
341. 20 a. blue .. .. 2·40 1·00

1951. Obligatory Tax. Child Welfare Fund.
342. **80.** 35 p. green 45 45
343. – 125 p. blue (Shepherd) 55 55

1951. 33rd Independence Day. Optd. with T **81a**.
344. **81.** 35 p. black and green .. 30 30
345. – 125 p. blue 70 70
DESIGN (34 × 18½ mm.): 125 p. Nadir Shah and Memorial.

For similar stamps but opt. T **81b** see Nos. 360/1, and see also Nos. 418/9.

IMPERF STAMPS. From 1951 many issues were made available imperf. from limited printings.

82. Flag of Pashtunistan.

1951. Obligatory Tax. Pashtunistan Day.
346. **82.** 35 p. brown 60 60
347. – 125 p. blue (Soldier) .. 1·40 1·40

83. Dove and Globe.
84. Avicenna (physician).

1951. Obligatory Tax. United Nations Day.
348. **83.** 35 p. purple 55 55
349. – 125 p. blue .. .. 2·00 2·00
DESIGN inscr. "U N O"—VERT. 125 p. Dove and globe.

1951. Obligatory Tax. Faculty of Medicine. 20th Anniversary.
350. **84.** 35 p. purple 30 30
351. 125 p. blue 85 85

85. Amir Sher Ali and First Stamp.
86. Children and Postman.

1951. Obligatory Tax. U.P.U. 76th Anniv. Dated "1951".
352. **85.** 35 p. brown 30 30
353. – 35 p. magenta 30 30
354. **85.** 125 p. blue 55 55
355. – 125 p. blue 55 55
DESIGN: Nos. 353 and 355, Mohamed Zahir Shah and first stamp.

1952. Obligatory Tax. Child Welfare Fund.
356. **86.** 35 p. brown 20 20
357. – 125 p. violet 50 50
DESIGN—HORIZ. 125 p. Girl dancing (33 × 23 mm.).

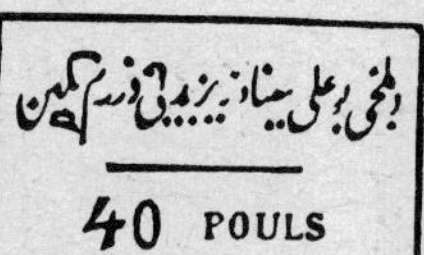

(87.)
88. Soldier and Flag of Pashtunistan.

1952. Millenary of Birth of Avicenna (poet). (a) Surch. with T **87**.
358. **76.** 40 p. on 30 p. red .. 60 60
(b) Surch. **MILLIEME ANNIVERSAIRE DE BOALI SINAI BALKI 125 POULS** in frame.
359. **76.** 125 p. on 30 p. red .. 1·10 1·10

1952. 34th Independence Day. As Nos. 344/5 but (a) optd. with T **81b**.
360. 35 p. black and green .. 30 30
361. 125 p. blue 70 70
(b) Without opt.
361a. 35 p. black and green .. 1·25 1·25
361b. 125 p. blue .. .. 1·25 1·25

1952. Obligatory Tax. Pashtunistan Day.
362. **88.** 35 p. red 15 15
363. 125 p. blue 40 40

89. Orderly and Wounded Soldier.
91. Staff of Aesculapius.

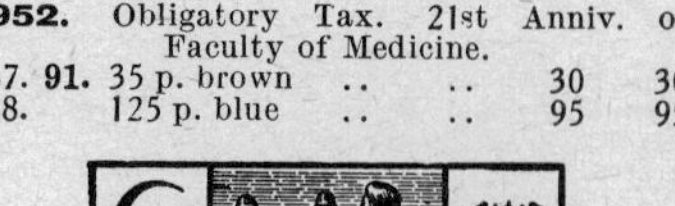

90.

1952. Obligatory Tax. Red Crescent Day.
364. **89.** 10 p. green 20 20

1952. Obligatory Tax. United Nations Day.
365. **90.** 35 p. red 40 40
366. 125 p. turquoise .. .. 1·00 1·00

1952. Obligatory Tax. 21st Anniv. of Faculty of Medicine.
367. **91.** 35 p. brown 30 30
368. 125 p. blue 95 95

92. Stretcher Bearers and Wounded.

1953. Obligatory Tax. Red Crescent Day.
369. **92.** 10 p. green and brown 25 20
370. – 10 p. choc. and orange 25 20
DESIGN: No. 370, Wounded soldier, orderly and eagle.

93. Prince Mohamed Nadir.
95. Flags of Afghanistan and Pashtunistan.

94. Mohamed Nadir Shah and Flag-bearer.

1953. Obligatory Tax. Children's Day.
371. 93. 35 p. orange 12 12
372. 125 p. blue 40 40

1953. 35th Year of Independence. Inscr "1953".
373. 94. 35 p. green 12 12
374. – 125 p. violet 45 40
DESIGN—VERT. 125 p. Independence Memorial and Mohamed Nadir Shah.

1953. Obligatory Tax. Pashtunistan Day. Inscr. "1953".
375. 95. 35 p. vermilion .. 12 12
376. – 125 p. blue 35 35
DESIGN—HORIZ. 125 p. Badge of Pashtunistan (26 × 20 mm.).

96. U.N. Emblem. 97. Mohamed Nadir Shah.

1953. Obligatory Tax. United Nations Day.
377. 96. 35 p. mauve 40 40
378. 125 p. blue .. .. 1·10 1·10

1953. Obligatory Tax. Faculty of Medicine. 22nd Anniversary.
379. 97. 35 p. orange 55 55
380. 125 p. blue .. .. 1·10 1·10

No. 379 was wrongly inscribed "23rd" in Arabic (the extreme right-hand figure in the second row of the inscription) and No. 380 was wrongly inscribed "XXIII" and had the words "ANNIVERSAIRE" and "MEDECINE" wrongly spelt "ANNIVERAIRE" and "MADECINE". These mistakes were subsequently corrected but the corrected stamps are much rarer than the original issue.

98. Children's Band and Map of Afghanistan. 99. Mohamed Nadir Shah and Cannon.

1954. Obligatory Tax. Child Welfare Fund.
381. 98. 35 p. violet 12 12
382. 125 p. blue 55 55

1954. 36th Independence Day.
383. 99. 35 p. red 15 15
384. 125 p. blue 50 50

100. Hoisting the Flag. 101.

1954. Obligatory Tax. Pashtunistan Day.
385. 100. 35 p. brown .. 15 15
386. 125 p. blue .. 50 50

1954. Red Crescent Day.
387. 101. 20 p. red and blue .. 20 20

102. U.N. Flag and Map. 103. Amir Sher Ali and Mohamed Zahir Shah.

1954. United Nations Day and 9th Anniv. of U.N.O.
388. 102. 35 p. red 55 55
389. 125 p. blue .. .. 1·75 1·75

1955. 85th Anniv. of Postal Service.
392. 103. 35 p. + 15 p. red .. 20 20
393. 125 p. + 25 p. blue .. 50 50

104. Children on Swing.

1955. Child Welfare Fund.
394. 104. 35 p. + 15 p. green .. 25 25
395. 125 p. + 25 p. violet .. 55 50

105. Globe and Clasped Hands. 106. U.N. Flag.

1955. 10th Anniv. of U.N.O.
(a) 1st issue. Inscr. and as T 105.
390. 105. 35 p. green 30 30
391. – 125 p. turquoise .. 85 85
DESIGN: 125 p. U.N. emblem and flags.

(b) 2nd issue.
403. 106. 35 p. brown 55 55
404. 125 p. blue .. .. 1·10 1·10

107. Mohamed Nadir Shah (centre) and brothers. 108.

1955. 37th Year of Independence.
396. 107. 35 p. blue 15 15
397. 35 p. magenta .. 15 15
398. – 125 p. violet 55 50
399. – 125 p. mauve 55 50
DESIGN: 125 p. Mohamed Zahir Shah and battle scene.

1955. Obligatory Tax. Pashtunistan Day.
400. 108. 35 p. brown 15 15
401. 125 p. green 50 50

109. Red Crescent. 110. Child on Slide.

1955. Obligatory Tax. Red Crescent Day.
402. 109. 20 p. red and grey .. 15 15

1956. Children's Day.
405. 110. 35 p. + 15 p. blue .. 20 20
406. 140 p. + 15 p. brown .. 45 45

111. Independence Memorial and Mohamed Nadir Shah. 112. Exhibition Building.

1956. 38th Year of Independence.
407. 111. 35 p. green 15 15
408. 140 p. blue 50 45

1956. International Exhibition, Kabul.
409. 112. 50 p. brown 20 15
410. 50 p. blue 20 15

113. Pashtan Square, Kabul. 114. Mohamed Zahir Shah and Crescent.

1956. Pashtunistan Day.
411. 113. 35 p. + 15 p. violet .. 15 15
412. 140 p. + 15 p. brown .. 45 45

1956. Obligatory Tax. Red Crescent Day.
413. 114. 20 p. green and red .. 15 15

115. Globe and Sun. 116. Children on See-saw.

1956. U.N. Day and 10th Anniv. of Admission of Afghanistan into U.N.O.
414. 115. 35 p. + 15 p. blue .. 75 75
415. 140 p. + 15 p. brown .. 1·25 1·25

1957. Child Welfare Fund.
416. 116. 35 p. + 15 p. red .. 25 25
417. 140 p. + 15 p. blue .. 60 60

1957. 39th Independence Day. As Nos. 344/5 but 35 p. has longer Arabic opt. (19 mm.) and 125 p. optd. 39 em Anv.
418. 81. 35 p. black and green .. 15 15
419. 125 p. blue 35 35

117. Pashtunistan Flag. 118. Red Crescent Headquarters, Kabul.

1957. Pashtunistan Day.
420. 117. 50 p. claret 25 25
421. 155 p. violet 55 55

No. 421 is inscr. "JOURNEE DU PASHTUNISTAN" beneath flag instead of Pushtu characters.

1957. Obligatory Tax. Red Crescent Day.
422. 118. 20 p. blue and red .. 15 15

119. U.N. Headquarters, New York. 121. Children Bathing.

120. Mounted Horsemen.

1957. U.N. Day.
423. 119. 35 p. + 15 p. brown .. 25 25
424. 140 p. + 15 p. blue .. 50 50

1957. As stamps of 1951 in new colours.
(a) With imprint "WATERLOW & SONS LIMITED LONDON".
425. 76. 30 p. brown 5 5
425a. – 40 p. red 8 5
425b. – 50 p. yellow 10 5
425c. – 60 p. blue 10 5
425d. – 75 p. violet 12 5
425e. – 80 p. brown & violet 15 5
425f. – 1 a. blue and red .. 20 8
425g. 120. 140 p. purple and green 45 30
425h. 78. 3 a. black and orange 55 40

(b) With imprint "THOMAS DE LA RUE & CO. LTD.".
425i – 75 p. violet 35 12
425j – 1 a. blue and red .. 45 15
425k. 78. 2 a. blue 60 25
425l. 3 a. black and red .. 1·60 35
DESIGNS: 40 p. Ruins at Kandahar Fort. 50 p. View of Kandahar. 60 p. Victory Towers, Ghazni. 75 p. (2), Mohamed Zahir Shah. 80 p., 1 a. (2), Mohamed Zahir Shah.

1958. Child Welfare Fund.
426. 121. 35 p. + 15 p. red .. 15 15
427. 140 p. + 15 p. brown 40 40

122. Mohamed Nadir Shah and Old Soldier. 123. Exhibition Building.

1958. 40th Independence Day.
428. 122. 35 p. green 8 8
429. 140 p. brown 30 30

1958. Int. Exn., Kabul.
430. 123. 35 p. green 8 8
431. 140 p. red 30 30

124. 125. President Bayar.

1958. Pashtunistan Day.
432. 124. 35 p. + 15 p. turquoise 12 12
433. 140 p. + 15 p. brown .. 30 30

1958. Visit of Turkish President.
434. 125. 50 p. blue 15 15
435. 100 p. brown 25 20

126. Red Crescent and Map of Afghanistan. 127.

1958. Red Crescent Day.
436. 126. 25 p. red and green .. 10 10

1958. "Atoms for Peace".
437. 127. 50 p. blue 30 30
438. 100 p. purple 55 55

128. Flags of U.N. and Afghanistan. 129. U.N.E.S.C.O. Headquarters, Paris.

1958. U.N. Day.
439. 128. 50 p. blue, red, green and black .. 45 45
440. 100 p. blue, red, black and green .. 90 90

1958. U.N.E.S.C.O. Headquarters Building. Inaug.
441. 129. 50 p. green 45 45
442. 100 p. brown 65 65

130. Globe and Torch. 131. Tug-of-War.

1958. Human Rights. 10th Anniv.
443. 130. 50 p. magenta .. 35 35
444. 100 p. lake 60 60

1959. Child Welfare Fund.
445. 131. 35 p. + 15 p. chocolate 15 15
446. 165 p. + 15 p. magenta 40 40

132. Mohamed Nadir Shah and Flags. 133. Tribal Dance.

1959. 41st Independence Day.
447. 132. 35 p. red 12 12
448. 165 p. violet 35 35

1959. Pashtunistan Day.
449. 133. 35 p. + 15 p. green .. 12 12
450. 165 p. + 15 p. yellow 40 40

134. Badge-sellers. 135. Horseman.

1959. Obligatory Tax. Red Crescent Day.
451. 134. 25 p. red and violet .. 8 5

1959. U.N. Day.

452. **135.** 35 p. + 15 p. yellow.. 12 12
453. 165 p. + 15 p. turquoise 35 35

136. "Uprooted Tree". **137.** Buzkashi Game.

138. Buzkashi Game.

1960. World Refugee Year.

454. **136.** 50 p. orange 8 8
455. 165 p. blue 25 25

1960.

456. **137.** 25 p. pink 12 12
457. 25 p. violet 10 8
458. 25 p. olive 10 8
459. 50 p. blue-green .. 30 25
460. 50 p. blue 12 12
460a. 50 p. orange 25 15
461. **138.** 100 p. olive 30 20
462. 150 p. orange 20 15
463. 175 p. brown 30 25
464. 2 a. green 65 30

139. Children receiving Ball.

1960. Child Welfare Fund.

465. **139.** 75 p.+25 p. blue .. 12 12
466. 175 p.+25 p. green .. 30 30

140. Aircraft over Mountains.

1960. Air.

467. **140.** 75 p. violet 12 10
468. 125 p. blue 20 15
469. 5 a. olive 45 40

141. Independence Monument, Kabul. **143.** Insecticide Sprayer.

142.

1960. 42nd Independence Day.

470. **141.** 50 p. blue 8 8
471. 175 p. magenta .. 25 20

1960. Pashtunistan Day.

472. **142.** 50 p.+50 p. red 15 15
473. 175 p.+50 p. blue 30 30

1960. Anti-Malaria Campaign Day.

474. **143.** 50 p.+50 p. orange .. 60 60
475. 175 p.+50 p. brown .. 1·40 1·25

144. Mohamed Zahir Shah.

1960. King's 46th Birthday.

476. **144.** 50 p. brown 12 12
477. 150 p. rose 35 35

145. Ambulance.

1960. Red Crescent Day.

478. **145.** 50 p.+50 p. violet & red 15 15
479. 175 p.+50 p. blue & red 40 40

146. Teacher with Globe and Children.

1960. Literacy Campaign.

480. **146.** 50 p. magenta .. 10 10
481. 100 p. green 30 30

147. Globe and Flags. **148.** Mir Wais Nika (patriot).

1960. U.N. Day.

482. **147.** 50 p. purple 15 15
483. 175 p. blue 45 40

1960. Olympic Games, Rome. Optd. **1960** in figures and in Arabic and Olympic Rings.

484. **138.** 175 p. brown .. .. 1·25 1·10

1960 World Refugee Year. Surch + **25 Ps.**

485. **136.** 50 p. + 25 p. orange.. 2·10 2·10
486. 165 p. + 25 p. blue .. 2·10 2·10

1960. Mir Wais Nika Commem.

487. **148.** 50 p. purple 12 12
488. 175 p. blue 30 30

The very numerous issues of Afghanistan which we do not list appeared between April 21st, 1961, and March 15th, 1964 (both dates inclusive), and were made available to the philatelic trade by an agency acting under the authority of a contract granted by the Afghanistan Government.

It later became evident that token supplies were only placed on sale in Kabul for a few hours and some of these sets contained stamps of very low denominations for which there was no possible postal use.

When the contract for the production of these stamps expired in 1963 it was not renewed and the Afghanistan Government set up a Philatelic Advisory Board to formulate stamp policy. The issues from No. 489 onwards were made in usable denominations and placed on sale without restriction in Afghanistan and distributed to the trade by the Philatelic Department of the G.P.O. in Kabul.

Issues not listed here will be found recorded in the Appendix at the end of this catalogue.

149. Band Amir Lake.

1961.

489. **149.** 3 a. blue 30 25
490. 10 a. purple 95 75

150. Independence Memorial.  **151.** Tribesmen.

1963. 45th Year of Independence.

491. **150.** 25 p. green 5 5
492. 50 p. orange 10 8
493. 150 p. magenta .. 25 20

1963. Pashtunistan Day.

494. **151.** 25 p. violet 5 5
495. 50 p. blue 10 10
496. 150 p. brown 30 25

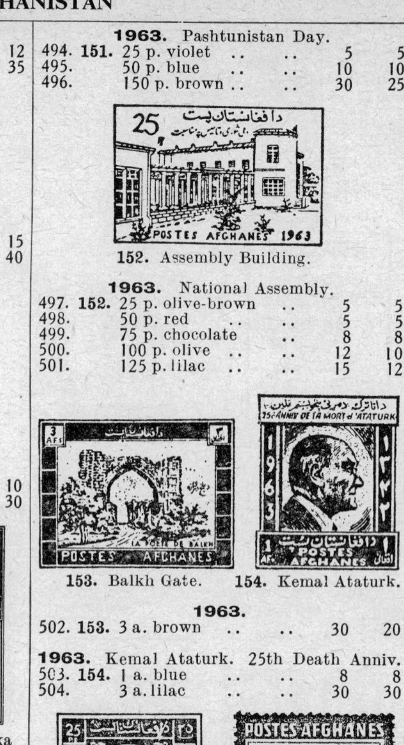

152. Assembly Building.

1963. National Assembly.

497. **152.** 25 p. olive-brown .. 5 5
498. 50 p. red 5 5
499. 75 p. chocolate .. 8 8
500. 100 p. olive 12 10
501. 125 p. lilac 15 12

153. Balkh Gate. **154.** Kemal Ataturk.

1963.

502. **153.** 3 a. brown 30 20

1963. Kemal Ataturk. 25th Death Anniv.

503. **154.** 1 a. blue 8 8
504. 3 a. lilac 30 30

155. Mohamed Zahir Shah. **156.** Afghan Stamp of 1878.

1963. King's 49th Birthday.

505. **155.** 25 p. green 5 5
506. 50 p. grey-drab .. 8 5
507. 75 p. red 10 8
508. 100 p. chocolate .. 15 10

1964. "Philately". Stamp Day.

509. **156.** 1 a. 25 blk., grn. & gold 10 10
510. 5 a. black, red and gold 25 25

157. Kabul International Airport.

1964. Air. Kabul Int. Airport. Inaug.

511. **157.** 10 a. green and purple 25 20
512. 20 a. purple and bronze 55 45
513. 50 a. turquoise and blue 1·40 1·10

158. Kandahar International Airport.

1964. Air. Kandahar Int. Airport. Inaug.

514. **158.** 7 a. 75 chocolate .. 25 20
515. 9 a. 25 blue .. 30 25
516. 10 a. 50 green .. 30 25
517. 13 a. 75 red 40 35

159. Unisphere and Flags. **160.** "Flame of Freedom".

1964. New York World's Fair.

518. **159.** 6 a. black, red & green 20 20

1964. 1st U.N. "Human Rights" Seminar Kabul.

519. **160.** 3 a. 75 multicoloured 15 15

161. Snow Leopard.

1964. Afghan Wild Life.

520. **161.** 25 p. blue and yellow.. 5 5
521. – 50 p. green and red .. 5 5
522. – 75 p. purple & turquoise 5 5
523. – 5 a. brown & blue-green 20 20

ANIMALS—VERT. 50 p. Ibex. HORIZ. 75 p. Marco Polo sheep. 5 a. Yak.

162. Herat. **163.** Hurdling.

1964. Tourist Publicity. Inscr. "1964".

524. **162.** 25 p. brown & violet-bl. 5 5
525. – 75 p. blue and ochre.. 5 5
526. – 3 a. black, red & green 10 10

DESIGNS—VERT. 75 p. Tomb of Gowhar Shad Herat. HORIZ. 3 a. Map and flag.

1964. Olympic Games, Tokyo.

527. **163.** 25 p. sepia, red & bistre 5 5
528. – 1 a. sepia, red & blue.. 5 5
529. – 3 a. 75 sepia, red & grn. 20 20
530. – 5 a. sepia, red & brown 25 25

DESIGNS—VERT. 1 a. Diving. HORIZ. 3 a. 75, Wrestling. 5 a. Football.

164. Afghan Flag. **165.** Pashtu Flag.

1964. 46th Independence Day.

531. **164.** 25 p. multicoloured .. 5 5
532. 75 p. multicoloured .. 5 5

On the above the Pashtu inscription "33rd Anniversary" is blocked out in gold.

1964. Pashtunistan Day.

533. **165.** 100 p. multicoloured.. 5 5

166. Mohamed Zahir Shah. **167.** "Blood Transfusion".

1964. King's 50th Birthday.

534. **166.** 1 a. 25 green and gold 5 5
535. 3 a. 75 red and gold.. 10 8
536. 50 a. black and gold.. 1·60 1·40

1964. Red Crescent Day.

537. **167.** 1 a.+50 p. red & black 8 5

168. Badges of Afghanistan and U.N.

1964. U.N. Day.

538. **168.** 5 a. blue, black & gold 15 12

169. Doves with Necklace. **170.** M. Jami (poet).

1964. Women's Day.
539. 169. 25 p. blue, green & pink 5 5
540. 75 p. blue, grn. & lt. bl. 5 5
541. 1 a. blue, green & silver 5 5

1964. Mowlana Jami. 550th Birth Anniv.
542. 170. 1 a. 50 cream, grn. & blk. 5 5

171. Lanceolated Jay. 172. "The Red City".

1965. Birds. Multicoloured.
543. 1 a. 25 Type 171 .. .. 8 8
544. 3 a. 75 White-capped "redstart" (vert.) 15 15
545. 5 a. Impeyan pheasant (vert.) 20 20

1965. Tourist Publicity. Inscr. "1965" Multicoloured.
547. 1 a. Type 172 .. .. 5 5
548. 3 a. 75 Bami Yan (valley and mountains) .. 15 12
549. 5 a. Band-E-Amir (lake and mountains) 20 15

173. I.T.U. Emblem and Symbols.

1965. I.T.U. Cent.
546. 173. 5 a. black, red and blue 15 15

174. I.C.Y. Emblem.

1965. Int. Co-operation Year.
550. 174. 5 a. multicoloured .. 20 15

DESIGNS: 5 a., 10 a. Airliner and emblem (different).

175. Airliner and Emblem.

1965. Afghan Airlines (ARIANA). 10th Anniv.
551. 175. 1 a. 25 black, grey & bl. 5 5
552. – 5 a. black, blue & pur. 20 15
553. – 10 a. multicoloured .. 40 40

176. Mohamed Nadir Shah. 177. Pashtu Flag.

1965. 47th Independence Day.
554. 176. 1 a. brown, blk. & green 5 5

1965. Pashtunistan Day.
555. 177. 1 a. multicoloured .. 5 5

178. Promulgation of New Constitution.

1965. New Constitution.
556. 178. 1 a. 50 black and green 8 8

179. Mohamed Zahir Shah. 180. First-Aid Post.

1965. King's 51st Birthday.
557. 179. 1 a. 25, brown, ultramarine and salmon 8 8
558. 6 a. indigo, pur. & blue 35 25

1965. Red Crescent Day.
559. 180. 1 a. 50+50 brown, green and red .. 8 8

181. U.N. and Afghan Flags.

1965. U.N. Day.
560. 181. 5 a. multicoloured .. 20 15

182. Lizard ("Eublepharis macularius").

1966. Reptiles. Multicoloured.
561. 3 a. Type 182 .. .. 10 10
562. 4 a. Lizard ("Agama caucasica") .. 15 15
563. 8 a. Tortoise 20 20

183. Cotton. 184. Footballer.

1966. Agriculture Day. Multicoloured.
564. 1 a. Type 183 .. .. 8 8
565. 5 a. Silkworm 15 15
566. 7 a. Oxen 20 20

1966. World Cup Football Championships.
567. 184. 2 a. black and red .. 8 8
568. 6 a. black and blue .. 20 20
569. 12 a. black and brown 55 55

185. Independence Memorial.

1966. Independence Day.
570. 185. 1 a. multicoloured .. 5 5
571. 3 a. multicoloured .. 15 15

186. Pashtu Flag.

1966. Pashtunistan Day.
572. 186. 1 a. blue 5 5

187. Founding Members.

1966. Red Crescent Day.
573. 187. 2 a.+1 a. green & red 10 10
574. 5 a.+1 a. brown & mag. 20 20

188. Map of Afghanistan.

1966. Tourism. Inscr. "1966". Multicoloured.
575. 2 a. Type 188 .. .. 8 8
576. 4 a. Bagh-i-Baba, former Palace of Abdur Rahman
577. 8 a Tomb of Abdur 12 12
Rahman Kabul .. 25 25

1966. King's 52nd Birthday. Portrait similar to T 179 but with position of inscr. changed. Dated "1966".
579. 1 a. green 5 5
580. 5 a. brown 20 20

189. Mohamed Zahir Shah and U.N. Emblem.

1966. U.N. Day. Inscr. "20TH ANNIVERSAIRE DES REFUGIES".
581. 189. 5 a. green, brn. & emer. 20 15
582. 10 a. red, emer. & lemon 35 30

190. Children Dancing.

1966. Child Welfare Day.
583. 190. 1 a.+1 a. red & green 8 8
584. 3 a.+2 a. brown & yell. 20 20
585. 7 a.+3 a. bronze & pur. 40 30

191. Construction of Power Station. 192. U.N.E.S.C.O. Emblem.

1967. Afghan Industrial Development. Multicoloured.
586. 2 a. Type 191 .. .. 8 8
587. 5 a. Handwoven carpet (vert.) 15 12
588. 8 a. Cement works .. 30 20

1967. U.N.E.S.C.O. 20th Anniv. (in 1966).
589. 192. 2 a. multicoloured .. 10 10
590. 6 a. multicoloured .. 20 20
591. 12 a. multicoloured .. 45 45

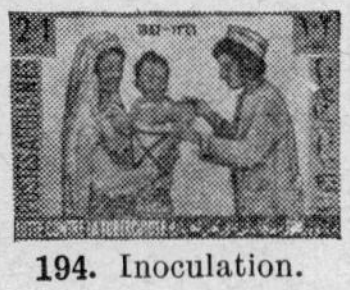

193. I.T.Y. Emblem. 194. Inoculation.

1967. Int. Tourist Year.
592. 193. 2 a. black, blue & yellow 8 8
593. – 6 a. black, blue & cinn. 20 20
DESIGN: 6 a. I.T.Y. emblem on map of Afghanistan.

1967. Anti-T.B. Campaign.
595. 194. 2 a.+1 a. black & yell. 8 8
596. 5 a.+2 a. brown & pink 20 20

195. Hydro-Electric Power Station, Dorunta. 196. Macaco.

1967. Development of Electricity for Agriculture.
597. 195. 1 a. lilac and green .. 5 5
598. – 6 a. turquoise & brown 20 15
599. – 8 a. blue and purple .. 30 20
DESIGNS—VERT. 6 a. Dam. HORIZ. 8 a. Reservoir, Jalalabad.

1967. Afghan Wildlife.
600. 196. 2 a. indigo and buff .. 8 5
601. – 6 a. sepia and green .. 25 20
602. – 12 a. brown and blue.. 45 30
ANIMALS—HORIZ. 6 a. Hyena. 12 a. Gazelles.

197. "Saving the Guns at Maiwand" (painting by Woodville). 198. Pashtu Dancers.

1967. Independence Day.
603. 197. 1 a. brown and red .. 5 5
604. 2 a. brown and magenta 8 5

1967. Pashtunistan Day.
605. 198. 2 a. violet and purple 8 5

1967. King's 53rd Birthday. Portrait similar to T 179 but with position of inscr. changed. Dated "1967".
606. 2 a. brown 10 5
607. 8 a. blue 20 15

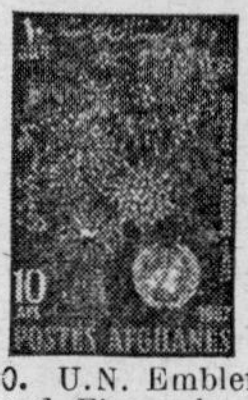

199. Red Crescent. 200. U.N. Emblem and Fireworks.

1967. Red Crescent Day.
608. 199. 3 a. + 1 a. red, black and olive 12 12
609. 5 a. + 1 a. red, black and blue 20 20

1967. U.N. Day.
610. 200. 10 a. multicoloured .. 30 25

201. Wrestling. 202. Said Jamaluddin Afghan.

1967. Olympic Games, Mexico City.
611. 201. 4 a. purple and green.. 15 12
612. – 6 a. brown and cerise.. 20 15
DESIGN: 6 a. Wrestling—a "throw".

1967. Said Afghan Commem.
614. 202. 1 a. purple 5 5
615. 5 a. brown 15 12

203 Bronze Vase. 204. W.H.O. Emblem.

1967. Archaeological Treasures. (1st Series). Ghasnavide era. (11th-12th Cent.) Inscr. "1967".
616. 203. 3 a. brown and green 10 8
617. – 7 a. green and yellow 20 20
DESIGN: 7 a. Bronze jar.
See also Nos. 645/6 and 661/3.

1968. World Health Organisation. 20th Anniv.
619. 204. 2 a. blue and bistre .. 5 5
620. 7 a. blue and claret .. 20 15

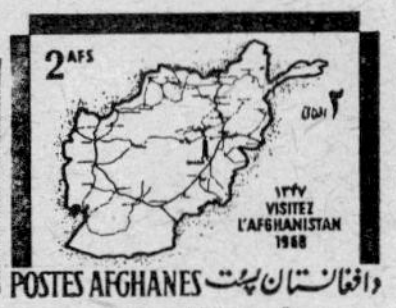

205. Karakul Sheep. 206. Map of Afghanistan.

1968. Agricultural Day.
621. 205. 1 a. black & yellow .. 5 5
622. 6 a. brown, blk. & blue 20 12
623. 12 a. brn., sep. & cobalt 30 15

1968. Tourist Publicity. Inscr. "1968". Multicoloured.
624. 2 a Type **206** 5 5
625. 3 a Tower (vert.) 8 8
626. 16 a. Mosque, Ghazni (vert.) 45 30
Nos. 625/6 are 21 × 31 mm.

207. Queen Humaira. **208.** Black Vulture.

1968. Mothers' Day.
627. **207.** 2 a.+2 a. brown .. 12 12
628. 7 a.+2 a. green .. 20 20

1968. Wild Birds. Multicoloured.
629. 1 a. Type **208** 8 8
630. 6 a. Eagle owl 20 15
631. 7 a. Greater flamingoes .. 25 20

209. "Peg-sticking". **210.** Flowers on Gun-carriage.

1968. Olympic Games, Mexico. Multicoloured.
632. 2 a Olympic flame and rings (vert.) 8 8
633. 8 a. Type **209** 20 15
634. 12 a. Buzkashi game .. 35 20
No. 632 is 21×31 mm.

1968. Independence Day.
635. **210.** 6 a. multicoloured .. 15 15

211. Pashtu Flag. **212.** Red Crescent.

1968. Pashtunistan Day.
636. **211.** 3 a. multicoloured .. 8 8

1968. King's 54th Birthday. Portrait similar to T **179** but differently arranged and in smaller size (21×31 mm.).
637. 2 a. ultramarine .. 5 5
638. 8 a. brown 25 20

1968. Red Crescent Day.
639. **212.** 4 a.+1 a. multicoloured 20 20

213. Human Rights Emblem. **214.** Maolala Djalalodine Balkhi.

1968. United Nations Day and Human Rights Year.
640. **213.** 1 a. brn., bistre & grn. 5 5
641. 2 a. blk., bistre & vio. 5 5
642. 6 a. vio., bistre & pur. 20 15

1968. Balkhi (historian) Commem.
644. **214.** 4 a. magenta and green 10 8

215. Temple Painting. **216.** I.L.O. Emblem.

1969. Archaeological Treasures (2nd Series). Bagram Era. Inscr. "1968".
645. **215.** 1 a. lake, yellow & grn. 5 5
646. – 3 a. purple and violet.. 10 8
DESIGN: 3 a. Carved vessel.

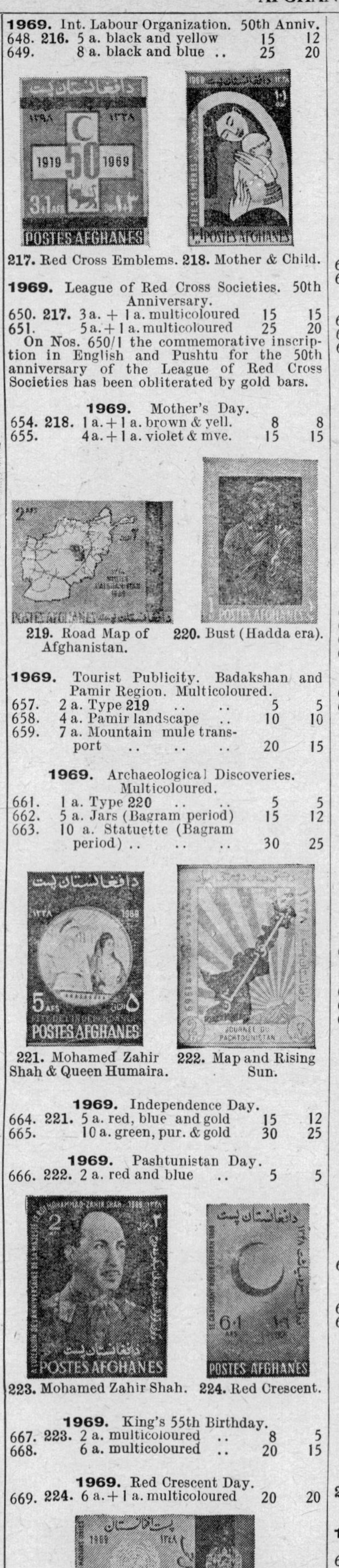

1969. Int. Labour Organization. 50th Anniv.
648. **216.** 5 a. black and yellow 15 12
649. 8 a. black and blue .. 25 20

217. Red Cross Emblems. **218.** Mother & Child.

1969. League of Red Cross Societies. 50th Anniversary.
650. **217.** 3 a. + 1 a. multicoloured 15 15
651. 5 a.+1 a. multicoloured 25 20
On Nos. 650/1 the commemorative inscription in English and Pushtu for the 50th anniversary of the League of Red Cross Societies has been obliterated by gold bars.

1969. Mother's Day.
654. **218.** 1 a.+1 a. brown & yell. 8 8
655. 4 a.+1 a. violet & mve. 15 15

219. Road Map of Afghanistan. **220.** Bust (Hadda era).

1969. Tourist Publicity. Badakshan and Pamir Region. Multicoloured.
657. 2 a. Type **219** 5 5
658. 4 a. Pamir landscape .. 10 10
659. 7 a. Mountain mule transport 20 15

1969. Archaeological Discoveries. Multicoloured.
661. 1 a. Type **220** 5 5
662. 5 a. Jars (Bagram period) 15 12
663. 10 a. Statuette (Bagram period) 30 25

221. Mohamed Zahir Shah & Queen Humaira. **222.** Map and Rising Sun.

1969. Independence Day.
664. **221.** 5 a. red, blue and gold 15 12
665. 10 a. green, pur. & gold 30 25

1969. Pashtunistan Day.
666. **222.** 2 a. red and blue .. 5 5

223. Mohamed Zahir Shah. **224.** Red Crescent.

1969. King's 55th Birthday.
667. **223.** 2 a. multicoloured .. 8 5
668. 6 a. multicoloured .. 20 15

1969. Red Crescent Day.
669. **224.** 6 a.+1 a. multicoloured 20 20

225. U.N. Emblem, Afghan Arms and Flag.

1969. United Nations Day.
670. **225.** 5 a. multicoloured .. 15 12

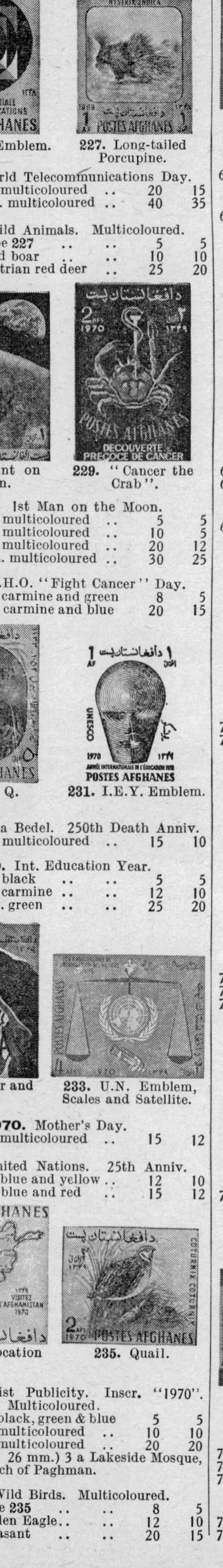

226. I.T.U. Emblem. **227.** Long-tailed Porcupine.

1969. World Telecommunications Day.
671. **226.** 6 a. multicoloured .. 20 15
672. 12 a. multicoloured .. 40 35

1969. Wild Animals. Multicoloured.
673. 1 a. Type **227** 5 5
674. 3 a. Wild boar 10 10
675. 8 a. Bactrian red deer .. 25 20

228. Footprint on the Moon. **229.** "Cancer the Crab".

1969. 1st Man on the Moon.
676. **228.** 1 a. multicoloured .. 5 5
677. 3 a. multicoloured .. 10 5
678. 6 a. multicoloured .. 20 12
679. 10 a. multicoloured .. 30 25

1970. W.H.O. "Fight Cancer" Day.
680. **229.** 2 a. carmine and green 8 5
681. 6 a. carmine and blue 20 15

230. M. A. Q. Bedel. **231.** I.E.Y. Emblem.

1970. Mirza Bedel. 250th Death Anniv.
682. **230.** 5 a. multicoloured .. 15 10

1970. Int. Education Year.
683. **231.** 1 a. black 5 5
684. 6 a. carmine 12 10
685. 12 a. green 25 20

232. Mother and Child. **233.** U.N. Emblem, Scales and Satellite.

1970. Mother's Day.
686. **232.** 6 a. multicoloured .. 15 12

1970. United Nations. 25th Anniv.
687. **233.** 4 a. blue and yellow .. 12 10
688. 6 a. blue and red .. 15 12

234. Tourist Location Map. **235.** Quail.

1970. Tourist Publicity. Inscr. "1970". Multicoloured.
689. **234.** 2 a. black, green & blue 5 5
690. – 3 a. multicoloured .. 10 10
691. – 7 a. multicoloured .. 20 20
DESIGNS (36 × 26 mm.) 3 a Lakeside Mosque, Kabul. 7 a. Arch of Paghman.

1970. Wild Birds. Multicoloured.
692. 2 a. Type **235** 8 5
693. 4 a. Golden Eagle.. .. 12 10
694. 6 a. Pheasant 20 15

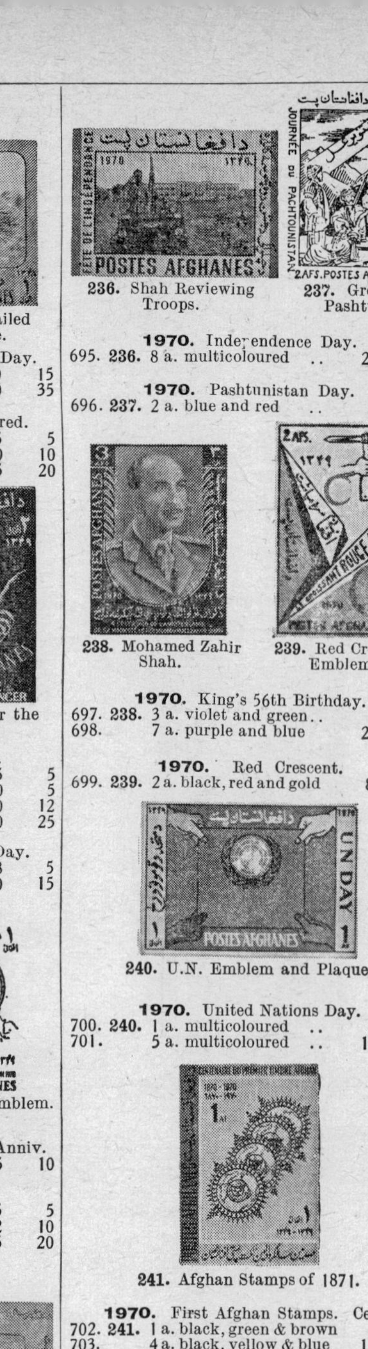

236. Shah Reviewing Troops. **237.** Group of Pashtus.

1970. Independence Day.
695. **236.** 8 a. multicoloured .. 25 20

1970. Pashtunistan Day.
696. **237.** 2 a. blue and red .. 8 5

238. Mohamed Zahir Shah. **239.** Red Crescent Emblems.

1970. King's 56th Birthday.
697. **238.** 3 a. violet and green.. 8 8
698. 7 a. purple and blue 20 15

1970. Red Crescent.
699. **239.** 2 a. black, red and gold 8 5

240. U.N. Emblem and Plaque.

1970. United Nations Day.
700. **240.** 1 a. multicoloured .. 5 5
701. 5 a. multicoloured .. 15 12

241. Afghan Stamps of 1871.

1970. First Afghan Stamps. Cent.
702. **241.** 1 a. black, green & brown 5 5
703. 4 a. black, yellow & blue 12 10
704. 12 a. black, blue & red 40 25

242. Global Emblem.

1971. World Telecommunications Day.
705. **242.** 12 a. multicoloured .. 45 30

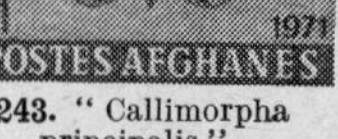

243. "Callimorpha principalis". **244.** Lower half of old Kushan Statue.

1971. Butterflies. Multicoloured.
706. 1 a. Type **243** 5 5
707. 3 a. "Epizygaenella sp." 10 8
708. 5 a. "Parnassius autocrator" 15 12

1971. U.N.E.S.C.O. Kushan Seminar.
709. **244.** 6 a. violet and yellow 15 12
710. 10 a. maroon and blue 30 20

245. Independence Memorial.

1971. Independence Day.

711. 245. 7 a. multicoloured .. 20 15
712. 9 a. multicoloured .. 25 20

246. Pashtunistan Square, Kabul.

1971. Pashtunistan Day.

713. 246. 5 a. purple 15 10

247. Mohamed Zahir Shah and Kabul Airport.

1971. Air. Multicoloured.

714. 50 a. Type 247 .. .. 1·40 1·10
715. 100 a. King, airline emblem and aircraft .. .. 3·00 2·25

248. Mohamed Zahir Shah. 249. Map, Nurse and Patients.

1971. King's 57th Birthday.

716. 248. 9 a. multicoloured .. 30 20
717. 17 a. multicoloured .. 55 40

1971. Red Crescent Day.

718. 249. 8 a. multicoloured .. 25 20

250. Emblem of Racial Equality Year. 251. Human Heart.

1971. United Nations Day.

719. 250. 24 a. blue 70 55

1972. World Health Day and World Heart Month.

720. 251. 9 a. multicoloured .. 25 20
721. 12 a. multicoloured .. 35 25

252. "Tulipa lanata". 253. Buddha of Hadda.

1972. Afghan Flora and Fauna. Mult.

722. 7 a. Type 252 .. .. 20 15
723 10 a. Chukar (rock partridge) (horiz.) 30 25
724. 12 a. Lynx (horiz.) 35 25
725. 18 a. "Allium stipitatum" 50 40

1972. Tourist Publicity.

726. 253. 3 a. blue and brown .. 8 5
727. – 7 a. green and red .. 20 12
728. – 9 a. purple and green .. 25 15

DESIGNS: 7 a. Greco-Bactrian seal, 250 B.C. 9 a. Greek temple, Ai-Khanum 3rd-2nd cent. B.C.

254. King with Queen Humaira at Independence Parade.

1972. Independence Day.

729. 254. 25 a. multicoloured .. 70 50

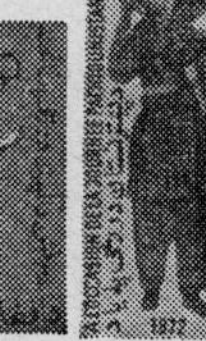

255. Wrestling. 256. Pathan and Mountain View.

1972. Olympic Games, Munich. Various Wrestling Holds.

730. 4 a. multicoloured .. 12 8
731. 8 a. multicoloured .. 25 15
732. 10 a. multicoloured .. 30 20
733. 19 a. multicoloured .. 55 35
734. 21 a. multicoloured .. 60 40

1972. Pashtunistan Day.

736. 256. 5 a. multicoloured .. 15 10

257. Mohamed Zahir Shah.

1972. King's 58th Birthday.

737. 257. 7 a. blue, black & gold 20 12
738. 14 a. brown, blk & gold. 40 25

258. Ruined Town and Refugees.

1972. Red Crescent Day.

739. 258. 7 a. black, red & blue.. 20 12

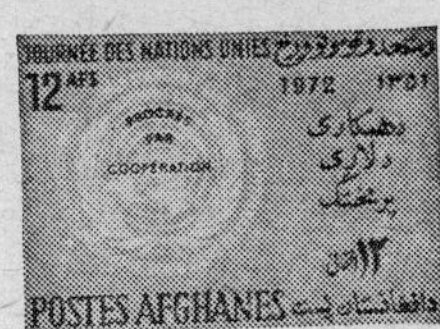

259. E.C.A.F.E Emblem.

1972. United Nations Day.

740. 259. 12 a. black and blue.. 30 20

260. Decorated boxes.

1973. Afghan Handicrafts. Multicoloured.

741. 7 a. Ceramics 20 12
742. 9 a. Embroidered coat (vert.) 25 15
743. 12 a. Coffee set (vert.) .. 35 20
744. 16 a. Type 260 .. .. 45 30

261. W.M.O. and Afghan Emblems.

1973. World Meteorological Organization. Cent.

746. 261. 7 a. green and mauve 15 12
747. 14 a. red and blue .. 30 25

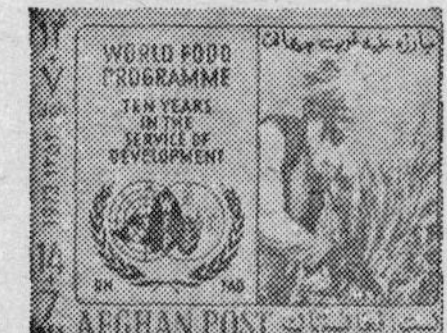

262. Emblems and Harvester.

1973. World Food Programme. 10th Anniv.

748. 262. 14 a + 7 a. pur. & blue 45 45

263. Al-Biruni. 264. Association Emblem.

1973. Abu-al Rayhan al-Biruni. 1000th Birth Anniv.

749. 263. 10 a. multicoloured.. 20 20

1973. Family Planning Week.

750. 264. 9 a. pur., orge. & red .. 20 15

265. Impeyan Pheasant.

1973. Birds of Afghanistan. Multicoloured.

751. 8 a. Type 265 .. .. 15 12
752. 9 a. Crested grebe 20 15
753. 12 a. Himalayan partridge 25 20

266. Buzkashi Game.

1973. Tourism.

754. 266. 8 a. black 15 12

267. Firework Display.

1973. Independence Day.

755. 267. 12 a. multicoloured .. 25 20

268. Landscape and Flag. 269. Red Crescent.

1973. Pashtunistan Day.

756. 268. 9 a. multicoloured .. 20 15

1973. Red Crescent.

757. 269. 10 a. multicoloured .. 25 20

270. Kemal Ataturk.

1973. Turkish Republic. 50th Anniv.

758. 270. 1 a. blue 5 5
759. 7 a. brown 20 15

271. Human Rights Flame.

1973. Declaration of Human Rights. 25th Anniv.

760. 271. 12 a. blue, blk. & silver 30 25

272. Asiatic Black Bears.

1974. Wild Animals. Multicoloured.

761. 5 a. Type 272 .. .. 10 5
762. 7 a. Afghan hound 15 10
763. 10 a. Persian goat 25 20
764. 12 a. Leopard 30 25

273. "Workers".

1974. Labour Day.

766. 273. 9 a. multicoloured .. 20 15

274. Paghman Arch and Independence Memorial.

1974. Independence Day.

767. 274. 4 a. multicoloured .. 8 5
768. 11 a. multicoloured .. 25 20

275. Arms of Afghanistan and Hands clasping Seedling.

1974. Republic. First Anniv. Multicoloured.

769. 4 a. Type 275 .. .. 8 5
770. 5 a. Republican flag (36×26 mm.) 10 5
771. 7 a. Gen. Mohammad Daoud (vert. 26×26 mm.) .. 15 10
772. 15 a. Soldiers and arms .. 30 25

276. Lesser Spotted Eagle.

1974. Afghan Birds. Multicoloured.
774. 1 a. Type **267** 5 5
775. 6 a. White-fronted goose, Ruddy shelduck and Grey lag goose 12 8
776. 11 a. Crane and coots .. 25 20

277. Flags of Pashtunistan and Afghanistan.

1974. Pashtunistan Day.
777. **277.** 5 a. multicoloured .. 12 8

278. Arms and Centenary Years.

1974. Universal Postal Union. Centenary.
778. **278.** 7 a. multicoloured .. 15 10

279. "UN" and U.N. Emblem.

1974. United Nations Day.
779. **279.** 5 a. blue and ultram. 12 8

280. Minaret, Jam.

1975. South Asia Tourist Year. Multicoloured.
780. 7 a. Type 280 .. .. 15 10
781. 14 a. "Griffon and Lady" (2nd cent. wood carving) 30 25
782. 15 a. Head of Buddha (4th-5th cent stone carving) .. 30 25

281. Afghan Flag.

1975. Independence Day.
784. **281.** 16 a. multicoloured .. 30 25

282. Celebrations and "2".

1975. Republic. 2nd Anniv.
785. **282.** 9 a. multicoloured .. 15 10
786. 12 a. multicoloured .. 25 12

283. I.W.Y. Emblem. **284.** Pashtunistan Flag and Rising Sun.

1975. International Women's Year.
787. **283.** 9a. black, blue & purple 15 10

1975. Pashtunistan Day.
788. **284.** 10 a. multicoloured .. 15 10

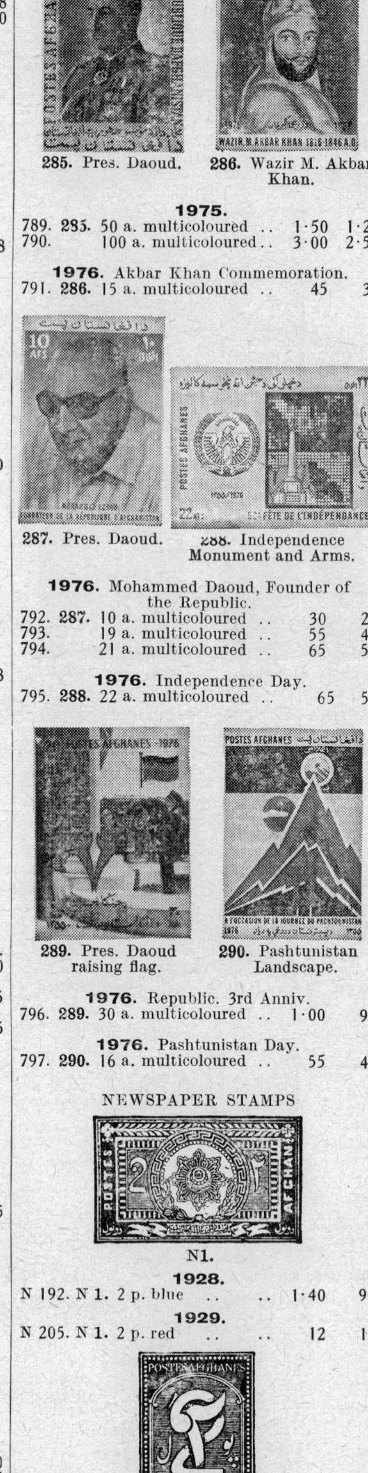

285. Pres. Daoud. **286.** Wazir M. Akbar Khan.

1975.
789. **285.** 50 a. multicoloured .. 1·50 1·25
790. 100 a. multicoloured .. 3·00 2·50

1976. Akbar Khan Commemoration.
791. **286.** 15 a. multicoloured .. 45 35

287. Pres. Daoud. **288.** Independence Monument and Arms.

1976. Mohammed Daoud, Founder of the Republic.
792. **287.** 10 a. multicoloured .. 30 20
793. 19 a. multicoloured .. 55 45
794. 21 a. multicoloured .. 65 55

1976. Independence Day.
795. **288.** 22 a. multicoloured .. 65 55

289. Pres. Daoud raising flag. **290.** Pashtunistan Landscape.

1976. Republic. 3rd Anniv.
796. **289.** 30 a. multicoloured .. 1·00 90

1976. Pashtunistan Day.
797. **290.** 16 a. multicoloured .. 55 45

NEWSPAPER STAMPS

N1.

1928.
N 192. N **1.** 2 p. blue .. .. 1·40 90

1929.
N 205. N **1.** 2 p. red 12 12

N 2.

1932.
N 215. N **2.** 2 p. red 5 5
N 216. 2 p. olive (to black) 5 5
N 219. 2 p. red 5 5

N 3. Coat of Arms.

1939.
N 259. N **3.** 2 p. green 5 5
N 260. 2 p. mauve 5 5

1969. As Type N 3, but inscr. differs.
N 652. 100 p. green 5 5
N 653. 150 p. brown 5 5

OFFICIAL STAMPS

O 1. O 2.

1909.
O 173. O **1.** red 40 50

1939. Design 22½ × 28 mm.
O 281. O **2.** 15 p. green .. 8 8
O 282. 30 p. brown .. 10 10
O 283. 45 p. red .. 12 12
O 284. 1 a. magenta .. 25 25

1954. Design 24½ × 31 mm.
O 285b. O2. 50 p. carmine .. 15 15

1965. Design 24 × 30½ mm.
O 286. O **2.** 50 p. cerise .. 35 35

PARCEL POST STAMPS

P 1.

1909.
P 173. P **1.** 3 sh. brown .. 20 35
P 174. 3 sh. green 30 30
P 175. 1 kr. brown .. 25 55
P 176. 1 kr. red 50 60
P 177. 1 rup. orange .. 1·00 1·00
P 179. 1 rup. brown .. 50 60
P 180. 2 rup. red .. .. 1·40 1·10
P 181. 2 rup. blue .. 1·25 1·25

P 2. Old Habibia College, Kabul.

1921.
P 182. P **2.** 10 p. brown .. 35 35
P 183. 15 p. brown .. 50 50
P 184. 30 p. purple .. 75 75
P 185. 1 r. blue .. .. 2·00 2·00

P 3. P 4.

1928.
P 192. P **3.** 2 a. orange .. 90 90
P 193. P **4.** 3 a. green .. 1·75 1·75

1930.
P 214. P **3.** 2 a. green .. 80 75
P 215. P **4.** 3 a. brown .. 1·75 1·75

REGISTRATION STAMP

R 1.

1894. Undated.
R 155. R **1.** 2 a. black on green. 3·25 3·25

AITUTAKI BC

Island in the S. Pacific.

A. NEW ZEALAND DEPENDENCY.

The British Govt., who had exercised a protectorate over the Cook Islands group since the 1880's handed the islands, including Aitutaki to New Zealand administration in 1901. Cook Is. stamps were used from 1932 to 1972.

Stamps of New Zealand overprinted **AITUTAKI** and value in native language.

1903. Pictorial stamps.
1. **21.** ½d. green .. .. .. 1·25 2·25
2. **35.** 1d. red .. .. .. 1·60 2·75
4. **24.** 2½d. blue .. .. .. 2·00 3·00
5. **25.** 3d. brown .. .. 1·00 4·50
6. **28.** 6d. red .. .. .. 3·75 9·00
8. **31.** 1s. red .. .. .. 20·00 24·00

1912. King Edward VII stamps.
9. **41.** ½d. green 30 80
10. **42.** 1d. red .. .. .. 45 1·25
11. **41.** 6d. red .. .. .. 11·00 21·00
12. 1s. red .. .. .. 21·00 26·00

1916. King George V stamps.
13. **43.** 6d. red .. .. .. 3·00 6·00
14. 1s. red .. .. .. 13·00 18·00

1917. King George V stamps optd. **AITUTAKI** only.
19. **43.** ½d. green 30 60
20. **42.** 1d. red 45 80
21. **43.** 1½d. grey .. .. 60 1·50
22. 1½d. brown .. .. 60 1·50
15. 2½d. blue .. .. 45 1·25
16. 3d. brown .. .. 75 2·25
17. 6d. red .. .. 1·25 2·25
18. 1s. red .. .. 2·25 4·50

1920. As 1920 pictorial stamps of Cook Is.
30. ½d. black and green .. 45 90
31. 1d. black and red .. 35 90
26. 1½d. black and brown .. 60 1·10
32. 2½d. black and blue .. 2·00 3·00
27. 3d. black and blue .. 75 1·50
28. 6d. brown and grey .. 1·50 3·25
29. 1s. black and purple .. 3·25 4·50

B. PART OF COOK ISLANDS.

On 9th August 1972, Aitutaki became a Port of Entry into the Cook Islands. Whilst remaining part of the Cook Islands, Aitutaki has a separate postal service.

1972. Nos. 227/8, 230, 233/4, 238, 240/1, 243 and 244 of Cook Islands optd. **Aitutaki.**
33. **33.** ½ c. multicoloured ..
34. – 1 c. multicoloured ..
35. – 2½ c. multicoloured ..
36. – 4 c. multicoloured ..
37. – 5 c. multicoloured ..
38. – 10 c. multicoloured ..
39. – 20 c. multicoloured ..
40. – 25 c. multicoloured ..
41. – 50 c. multicoloured ..
42. – $1 multicoloured ..
33/42. Set of 10 25·00 35·00

1972. Christmas. Nos. 406/8 of Cook Islands optd. **Aitutaki.**
43. **52.** 1 c. multicoloured .. 5 5
44. – 5 c. multicoloured .. 8 8
45. – 10 c. multicoloured .. 15 20

1972. Royal Silver Wedding. As Nos. 413 and 415 of Cook Islands, but inscr "COOK ISLANDS Aitutaki".
46. **53.** 5 c. black and silver .. 3·25 3·00
47. – 15 c. black and silver .. 1·50 1·50

1972. No. 245 of Cook Islands optd. **AITUTAKI.**
48. $2 multicoloured .. .. 2·50 3·00

1972. Nos. 227/8, 230, 233, 234, 238, 240, 241, 243 and 244 of Cook Islands optd. **AITUTAKI** within ornamental oval.
49. **33.** ½ c. multicoloured .. 5 5
50. – 1 c. multicoloured .. 5 5
51. – 2½ c. multicoloured .. 5 5
52. – 4 c. multicoloured .. 5 8
53. – 5 c. multicoloured .. 8 10
54. – 10 c. multicoloured .. 15 20
55. – 20 c. multicoloured .. 30 40
56. – 25 c. multicoloured .. 40 50
57. – 50 c. multicoloured .. 75 1·00
58. – $1 multicoloured .. 1·50 2·00

1. "Via Dolorosa" (Grunewald).

1973. Easter. Multicoloured.

59. 1 c. Type **1** 5 5
60. 1 c. "Veronica" (Van der Weyden) 5 5
61. 1 c. "Crucifixion" (Raphael) 5 5
62. 1 c. "Resurrection" (Piero della Francesca) 5 5
63. 5 c. "The Last Supper" (Master of Amiens) .. 10 12
64. 5 c. "Condemnation" (Holbein) 10 12
65. 5 c. "Crucifixion" (Rubens) 10 12
66. 5 c. "Resurrection" (El Greco) 10 12
67. 10 c. "Via Dolorosa" (El Greco) 20 25
68. 10 c. "Veronica" (Coneliz) 20 25
69. 10 c. "Crucifixion" (Rubens) 20 25
70. 10 c. "Resurrection" (Bouts) 20 25

1973. Silver Wedding Coinage. Nos. 417/23 of Cook Is. optd. **AITUTAKI.**

71. **54.** 1 c. black, red & gold .. 5 5
72. – 2 c. black, blue &gold .. 5 5
73. – 5 c. black, green & silver 10 12
74. – 10 c. black, blue & silver 20 25
75. – 20 c. black, green & silver 35 40
76. – 50 c. black, red & silver 75 85
77. – $1 black, blue & silver 1·75 2·00

1973. Treaty Banning Nuclear Testing. 10th Anniv. Nos. 236, 238, 240 and 243 of Cook Is. optd. **AITUTAKI** within ornamental oval and **TENTH ANNIVERSARY CESSION OF NUCLEAR TESTING TREATY.**

78. 8 c. multicoloured .. 12 15
79. 10 c. multicoloured .. 20 25
80. 20 c. multicoloured .. 35 40
81. 50 c. multicoloured .. 75 85

2. Red Hibiscus and Princess Anne.

1973. Royal Wedding. Multicoloured.

82. 25 c. Type **2** 40 45
83. 30 c. Capt. Mark Phillips and Blue Hibiscus .. 50 60

3. "Virgin and Child" (Montagna).

1973. Christmas. "Virgin and Child" paintings by artists listed below. Mult.

85. 1 c. Type **3** 5 5
86. 1 c. Crivelli 5 5
87. 1 c. Van Dyck 5 5
88. 1 c. Perugino 5 5
89. 5 c. Veronese 10 12
90. 5 c. Veronese 10 12
91. 5 c. Cima 10 12
92. 5 c. Memling 10 12
93. 10 c. Memling 20 25
94. 10 c. del Colle 20 25
95. 10 c. Raphael 20 25
96. 10 c. Garofalo 20 25

4. "Murex ramosus".

1974. Sea-shells. Multicoloured.

97. ½ c. Type **4** 5 5
98. 1 c. "Nautilus macromphallus" .. 5 5
99. 2 c. "Harpa major" .. 5 5
100. 3 c. "Phalium strigatum" 5 5
101. 4 c. "Cypraea talpa" .. 5 5
102. 5 c. "Mitra stictica" .. 5 5
103. 8 c. "Charonia tritonis" .. 8 8
104. 10 c. "Murex triremis" .. 10 10
105. 20 c. "Oliva sericea" .. 20 20
106. 25 c. "Tritonalia rubeta" 25 25
107. 60 c. "Strombus latissimus" 60 70
108. $1 "Biplex perca" .. 95 1·10
109. $2 Queen Elizabeth II and "Terebra maculata" .. 1·90 2·00
110. $5 Queen Elizabeth II and "Cypraea hesitat" .. 4·75 5·00

The $2 and $5 are larger, 53 × 25 mm.

5. Bligh and "Bounty".

1974. William Bligh's Discovery of Aitutaki. Multicoloured.

114. 1 c. Type **5** 5 5
115. 1 c. "Bounty" 5 5
116. 5 c. Bligh, and "Bounty" at Aitutaki 5 8
117. 5 c. Aitutaki chart of 1856 5 8
118. 8 c. Capt. Cook and "Resolution" 10 10
119. 8 c. Map of Aitutaki and inset location map 10 10

See also Nos. 123/8.

6. Aitutaki Surcharged ½d. and 1d. Stamps of 1903, and Map.

1974. Universal Postal Union. Cent. Multicoloured.

120. 25 c. Type **6** 30 35
121. 50 c. Surcharged 1903, and 1920, and map .. 60 65

1974. Air As Nos. 114/119 in larger size (46 × 26 mm.), additionally inscr. "AIR MAIL".

123. 10 c. Type **5** 12 15
124. 10 c. "Bounty" 12 15
125. 25 c. Bligh, and "Bounty" at Aitutaki 30 35
126. 25 c. Aitutaki chart of 1856 30 35
127. 30 c. Capt. Cook and "Resolution" 35 40
128. 30 c. Map of Aitutaki and inset location map .. 35 40

6. "Virgin and Child" (H. Van der Goes).

1974. Christmas. "Virgin and Child" paintings by artists named. Mult.

129. 1 c. Type **6** 5 5
130. 5 c. G. Bellini 5 5
131. 8 c. G. David 8 10
132. 10 c. A. da Messina .. 10 12
133. 25 c. J. Van Cleve .. 30 35
134. 30 c. Maitre Legende St. Catherine 35 40

7. Churchill as Schoolboy.

1974. Sir Winston Churchill. Birth Cent. Multicoloured.

136. 10 c. Type **7** 12 15
137. 25 c. Churchill as young man 30 35
138. 30 c. Churchill with troops 35 40
139. 50 c. Churchill painting .. 55 60
140. $1 Churchill giving "V"-sign .. .. .. 1·10 1·25

1974. Children's Christmas Fund. Nos. 129/34 surch.

142. **6.** 1 c. + 1 c. multicoloured 5 5
143. – 5 c. + 1 c. multicoloured 5 8
144. – 8 c. + 1 c. multicoloured 10 10
145. – 10 c. + 1 c. multicoloured 10 12
146. – 25 c. + 1 c. multicoloured 30 35
147. – 30 c. + 1 c. multicoloured 35 40

8. Soviet and U.S. Flags.

1975. "Apollo-Soyuz" Space Project. Multicoloured.

148. 25 c. Type **8** 25 30
149. 50 c. Daedalus with "Apollo" and "Soyuz" 50 55

9. "Madonna and Child" (Lorenzetti).

1975. Christmas. Multicoloured.

151. 6 c. } Type **9** 5 5
152. 6 c. } 5 5
153. 6 c. } 5 5
154. 7 c. } "Adoration of 8 8
155. 7 c. } the Magi" 8 8
156. 7 c. } (Van der Weyden) 8 8
157. 15 c. } "Madonna and .. 15 20
158. 15 c. } Child" .. 15 20
159. 15 c. } (Montagna) .. 15 20
160. 20 c. } "Adoration of .. 20 25
161. 20 c. } the Magi" .. 20 25
162. 20 c. } (Reni) .. 20 25

Type **9** shows the left-hand stamp of the 6 c. design.

1975. Children's Christmas Fund. Nos. 151/62 surch.

164. **9.** 6 c. + 1 c. multicoloured 8 8
165. – 6 c. + 1 c. multicoloured 8 8
166. – 6 c. + 1 c. multicoloured 8 8
167. – 7 c. + 1 c. multicoloured 8 10
168. – 7 c. + 1 c. multicoloured 8 10
169. – 7 c. + 1 c. multicoloured 8 10
170. – 15 c. + 1 c. multicoloured 15 20
171. – 15 c. + 1 c. multicoloured 15 20
172. – 15 c. + 1 c. multicoloured 15 20
173. – 20 c. + 1 c. multicoloured 20 25
174. – 20 c. + 1 c. multicoloured 20 25
175. – 20 c. + 1 c. multicoloured 20 25

10. "The Descent" (detail, Flemish School).

1976. Easter. Multicoloured.

176. 15 c. Type **10** 15 20
177. 30 c. "The Descent" (detail) 35 40
178. 35 c. "The Descent" (detail) 40 45

11. "The Declaration of Independence" (John Trumbull).

1976. American Revolution. Bicent. Multicoloured.

180. 30 c. } 35 40
181. 30 c. } Type **11** 35 40
182. 30 c. } 35 40
183. 35 c. } "Surrender of Lord 40 45
184. 35 c. } Cornwallis at York- 40 45
185. 35 c. } town" (John Trumbull) 40 45
186. 50 c. } "The Resignation of 55 60
187. 50 c. } General Washington" 55 60
188. 50 c. } (John Trumbull) .. 55 60

Type **11** shows the left-hand stamp of the 30 c. design.

12. Cycling.

1976. Olympic Games, Montreal. Multicoloured.

190. 15 c. Type **12** 15 20
191. 35 c. Sailing 40 45
192. 60 c. Hockey 70 80
193. 70 c. Sprinting 75 85

1976. Royal Visit to the U.S.A. Nos. 190/3 optd. **ROYAL VISIT JULY 1976.**

195. 15 c. multicoloured .. 15 20
196. 35 c. multicoloured .. 40 45
197. 60 c. multicoloured .. 70 80
198. 70 c. multicoloured .. 75 85

13. "The Visitation".

1976. Christmas. Multicoloured.

200. 6 c. } Type **13** 5 5
201. 6 c. } 5 5
202. 7 c. } "Angel and 8 8
203. 7 c. } Shepherds" .. 8 8
204. 15 c. } "The Holy Family" 15 20
205. 15 c. } 15 20
206. 20 c. } "The Magi" .. 20 25
207. 20 c. } .. 20 25

Type **13** shows the left-hand stamp of the 6 c. design.

1976. Children's Christmas Fund. Nos. 200/07 surch.

209. **13.** 6 c. + 2 c. multicoloured 8 10
210. – 6 c. + 2 c. multicoloured 8 10
211. – 7 c. + 2 c. multicoloured 10 10
212. – 7 c. + 2 c. multicoloured 10 10
213. – 15 c. + 2 c. multicoloured 20 20
214. – 15 c. + 2 c. multicoloured 20 20
215. – 20 c. + 2 c. multicoloured 20 25
216. – 20 c. + 2 c. multicoloured 20 25

INDEX

Countries can be quickly located by referring to the index at the end of this volume.

AJMAN O1

One of the Trucial States in the Persian Gulf. On 18th July, 1971, seven Gulf shaikhdoms, including Ajman, formed the State of the United Arab Emirates. The federation became effective on 1 Aug., 1972.

100 naye paise = 1 rupee.
1967. 100 dirhams = 1 riyal.

1. Shaikh Rashid bin Humaid al Naimi and Arab Stallion.

2. Kennedy in Football Kit.

1964. Multicoloured.

(a) Size 34½ × 23 mm.

1. 1 n.p. Type **1** 5 5
2. 2 n.p. Striped fish 5 5
3. 3 n.p. Camel 5 5
4. 4 n.p. Blue fish 5 5
5. 5 n.p. Tortoise 5 5
6. 10 n.p. Spotted fish 5 5
7. 15 n.p. Stork 5 5
8. 20 n.p. Gulls 5 5
9. 30 n.p. Hawk 12 8

(b) Size 42½ × 27 mm.

10. 40 n.p. Type **1** 15 12
11. 50 n.p. Striped fish.. .. 15 15
12. 70 n.p. Camel 20 15
13. 1 r. Blue fish 30 25
14. 1 r. 50 Tortoise 40 30
15. 2 r. Spotted fish 55 50

(c) Size 53 × 34 mm.

16. 3 r. Stork 85 75
17. 5 r. Gulls .. .. .. 1·60 1·50
18. 10 r. Hawk .. .. .. 3·00 2·75

1964. Pres. Kennedy Commem. Perf. or imperf.

19. **2.** 10 n.p. purple and green .. 5 5
20. – 15 n.p. violet & turquoise 5 5
21. – 50 n.p. blue and chestnut 15 10
22. – 1 r. blue-green and sepia .. 25 15
23. – 2 r. olive and purple .. 50 30
24. – 3 r. brown and green .. 80 50
25. – 5 r. brown and violet .. 1·60 80
26. – 10 r. brown and blue .. 3·00 1·50

DESIGNS—Various pictures of Kennedy: 15 n.p. Diving. 50 n.p. As naval officer. 1 r. Sailing with Mrs. Kennedy. 2 r. With Mrs. Eleanor Roosevelt. 3 r. With wife and child. 5 r. With colleagues. 10 r. Full-face portrait.

3. Start of Race.

1965. Olympic Games. Tokyo. Perf. or imperf.

27. **3.** 5 n.p. slate, brown & mve. 5 5
28. – 10 n.p. red, bronze & blue 5 5
29. **3.** 15 n.p. brn., violet & green 8 5
30. – 25 n.p. black, blue and red 10 8
31. – 50 n.p. slate, maroon & bl. 15 8
32. – 1 r. ultram., green & purple 25 12
33. – 1 r. 50 maroon, vio. & grn. 40 25
34. – 2 r. blue, vermilion & ochre 65 35
35. – 3 r. violet, choc. & blue .. 1·00 50
36. – 5 r. purple, green & yellow 1·60 80

DESIGNS: 10 n.p., 1 r. 50. Boxing. 25 n.p. 2 r. Judo. 50 n.p., 5 r. Gymnastics. 1 r., 3 r. Sailing.

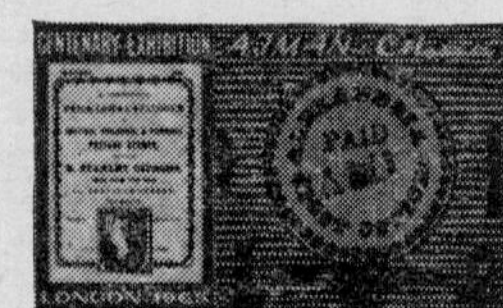

4. First Gibbons Catalogue and Alexandria (U.S.) 5 c. Postmaster's Stamp.

1965. Stanley Gibbons Catalogue Centenary Exhibition, London. Multicoloured.

37. 5 n.p. Type **4** 5 5
38. 10 n.p. Austria (6 k.) scarlet "Mercury" newspaper-tamp 5 5
39. 15 n.p. British Guiana "One Cent", 1856 .. .. 5 5
40. 25 n.p. Canada "Twelvepence Black", 1851 .. .. 8 5
41. 50 n.p. Hawaii "Missionary" 2 c., 1851 .. 15 8
42. 1 r. Mauritius "Post Office" 2d. blue, 1847 .. .. 25 12
43. 3 r. Switzerland "Double Geneva" 5 c.+5 c., 1843.. 1·00 50
44. 5 r. Tuscany 3 lire, 1860 .. 1·60 80

The 5, 15 and 50 n.p. and 3 r. also include the First Gibbons Catalogue and the others, the Gibbons "Elizabethan" Catalogue.

1965. Pan Arab Games, Cairo. Perf. or imperf. Nos. 29, 31 and 33/5 optd. (a) Optd. **PAN ARAB GAMES CAIRO 1965.**

45. **3.** 15 n.p. brown, violet & grn. 5 5
46. – 50 n.p. slate, maroon & blue 15 8
47. – 1 r. 50 maroon, vio. & grn. 65 30
48. – 2 r. blue, verm. & ochre .. 75 35
49. – 3 r. violet, chocolate & blue 1·40 75

(b) Optd. as Nos. 45/9 but equivalent in Arabic.

50. **3.** 15 n.p. brown, violet & grn. 5 5
51. – 50 n.p. slate, maroon & blue 15 8
52. – 1 r. 50 maroon, vio. & grn. 65 30
53. – 2 r. blue, verm. & ochre .. 75 35
54. – 3 r. violet, chocolate & blue 1·40 75

1965. Air. Designs similar to Nos. 1/9, but inscr. "AIR MAIL". Multicoloured.

(a) Size 42½ × 25½ mm.

55. 15 n.p. Type **1** 5 5
56. 25 n.p. Striped fish 5 5
57. 35 n.p. Camel 8 5
58. 50 n.p. Blue fish 12 5
59. 75 n.p. Tortoise 20 10
60. 1 r. Spotted fish 30 20

(b) Size 53 × 34 mm.

61. 2 r. Stork 55 40
62. 3 r. Gulls 85 70
63. 5 r. Hawk .. .. .. 1·60 1·40

1966. Stamp Cent. Exn., Cairo. Nos. 38/9 and 41/3 optd. **STAMP CENTENARY EXHIBITION CAIRO, JANUARY 1966,** and pyramid motif.

73. 10 n.p. multicoloured .. 5 5
74. 15 n.p. multicoloured .. 5 5
75. 50 n.p. multicoloured .. 15 8
76. 1 r. multicoloured .. 30 15
77. 3 r. multicoloured .. 90 45

5. Sir Winston Churchill and Tower Bridge.

1966. Churchill Commem. Each design includes portrait of Churchill. Multicoloured.

79. 25 n.p. Type **5** 5 5
80. 50 n.p. Buckingham Palace 15 8
81. 75 n.p. Blenheim Palace .. 20 10
82. 1 r. British Museum .. 30 20
83. 2 r. St. Paul's Cathedral in wartime 55 40
84. 3 r. National Gallery and St. Martin's in the Fields Church 80 60
85. 5 r. Westminster Abbey .. 1·50 1·00
86. 7 r. 50 Houses of Parliament at night .. .. .. 2·00 1·50

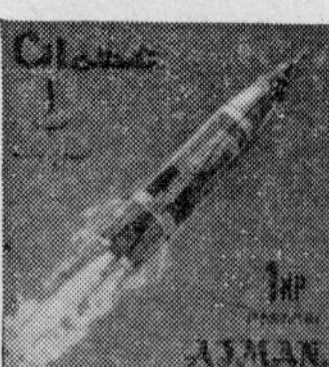

6. Rocket.

1966. Space Achievements. Multicoloured.

(a) Postage. Size As T **6**.

88. 1 n.p. Type **6** 5 5
89. 3 n.p. Capsule 5 5
90. 5 n.p. Astronaut entering capsule in space 5 5
91. 10 n.p. Astronaut outside capsule in space 5 5
92. 15 n.p. Astronauts & globe 5 5
93. 25 n.p. Astronaut in space.. 8 5

(b) Air. Size 38 × 38 mm.

95. 50 n.p. As Type **6** 12 8
96. 1 r. Astronauts and globe .. 25 12
97. 3 r. Astronaut outside capsule in space 80 40
98. 5 r. Capsule .. .. 1·40 70

1967. Various issues with currency names changed by overprinting in **Dh.** or **Riyals.**

(a) Postage. Nos. 1/18 (1964 Definitives).

99. 1 d. on 1 n.p. 5 5
100. 2 d. on 2 n.p. 5 5
101. 3 d. on 3 n.p. 5 5
102. 4 d. on 4 n.p. 5 5
103. 5 d. on 5 n.p. 5 5
104. 10 d. on 10 n.p. 5 5
105. 15 d. on 15 n.p. 5 5
106. 20 d. on 20 n.p. 5 5
107. 30 d. on 30 n.p. 8 5
108. 40 d. on 40 n.p. 10 5
109. 50 d. on 50 n.p. 12 8
110. 70 d. on 70 n.p. 20 10
111. 1 r. on 1 r. 25 15
112. 1 r. 50 on 1 r. 50 .. .. 35 20
113. 2 r. on 2 r. 50 25
114. 3 r. on 3 r. 75 35
115. 5 r. on 5 r. .. .. 1·25 65
116. 10 r. on 10 r. .. .. 2·50 1·25

(b) Air. Nos. 55/63 (Airmails).

117. 15 d. on 15 n.p. 5 5
118. 25 d. on 25 n.p. 5 5
119. 35 d. on 35 n.p. 8 5
120. 50 d. on 50 n.p. 12 8
121. 75 d. on 75 n.p. 20 10
122. 1 r. on 1 r. 25 15
123. 2 r. on 2 r. 50 25
124. 3 r. on 3 r. 75 35
125. 5 r. on 5 r. .. .. 1·25 65

NEW CURRENCY SURCHARGES. Nos. 19/44 and 79/98 are known surch. in new currency (dirhams and riyals), in limited quantities, but there is some doubt as to whether they were in use locally.

7. Motor-car.

1967. Transport.

135. **7.** 1 d. chest & black (post.) 5 5
136. – 2 d. blue and brown .. 5 5
137. – 3 d. magenta and black.. 5 5
138. – 4 d. ultram. and brown 5 5
139. – 5 d. emerald and black.. 5 5
140. – 15 d. blue and brown .. 5 5
141. – 30 d. brown and black .. 5 5
142. – 50 d. black and brown .. 12 8
143. – 70 d. violet and black .. 20 10
144. **7.** 1 r. green & brown (air) 25 15
145. – 2 r. magenta and black.. 50 25
146. – 3 r. black and brown .. 75 35
147. – 5 r. chestnut and black.. 1·25 65
148. – 10 r. blue and brown .. 2·50 1·25

DESIGNS: 2 d., 2 r. Motor-coach. 3 d., 3 r. Motor-cyclist. 4 d., 5 r. Jetliner. 5 d., 10 r. Ocean liner. 15 d. Sailing ship. 30 d. Cameleer. 50 d. Arab horse. 70 d. Helicopter.

OFFICIAL STAMPS

1965. Designs similar to Nos. 1/9, additionally inscr. "ON STATE'S SERVICE". Multicoloured.

(i) Postage. Size 43 × 26 mm.

O 64. 25 n.p. Type **1** 5 5
O 65. 40 n.p. Striped fish .. 12 12
O 66. 50 n.p. Camel 15 15
O 67. 75 n.p. Blue fish 20 20
O 68. 1 r. Tortoise 30 30

(ii) Air. (a) Size 43 × 26 mm.

O 69. 75 n.p. Spotted fish .. 20 10

(b) Size 53 × 34 mm.

O 70. 2 r. Stork 60 25
O 71. 3 r. Gulls 80 35
O 72. 5 r. Hawk .. .. .. 1·60 65

1967. Nos. O 64/72 with currency names changed by overprinting in **Dh.** or **Riyals.**

O 126. 25 d. on 25 n.p. 5 5
O 127. 40 d. on 40 n.p. 8 8
O 128. 50 d. on 50 n.p. 12 12
O 129. 75 d. on 75 n.p. (No. O 67) 20 20
O 130. 75 d. on 75 n.p. (No. O 69) 20 20
O 131. 1 r. on 1 r. 25 30
O 132. 2 r. on 2 r. 45 50
O 133. 3 r. on 3 r. 70 90
O 134. 5 r. on 5 r. .. .. 1·25 1·40

For later issues see **UNITED ARAB EMIRATES.**

ALAOUITES O4

A coastal district of Syria, placed under French mandate in 1920. Became the Republic of Latakia in 1930. Incorporated with Syria in 1937.

100 centiemes = 1 piastre.

1925. Stamps of France surch. **ALAOUITES** and value in English and Arabic.

1. **11.** 10 c. on 2 c. claret .. 30 30
2. **17.** 25 c. on 5 c. orange .. 20 20
3. **15.** 75 c. on 15 c. green .. 30 30
4. **17.** 1 pi. on 20 c. chocolate.. 30 20
5. 1 pi. 25 on 25 c. blue .. 50 35
6. 1 pi. 50 on 30 c. red .. 1·00 1·00
7. 2 pi. on 35 c. violet .. 25 15
8. **13.** 2 pi. on 40 c. red & blue 40 40
9. 2 pi. on 45 c. grn. & blue 1·10 1·10
10. 3 pi. on 60 c. vio. & blue 55 55
11. **15.** 3 pi. on 60 c. violet .. 1·00 1·00
12. 4 pi. on 85 c. red .. 10 10
13. **13.** 5 pi. on 1 f. red & yellow 65 65
14. 10 pi. on 2 f. orge. & green 75 75
15. 25 pi. on 5 f. blue & yell. 80 80

1925. "Pasteur" issue of France surch. **ALAOUITES** and value in English and Arabic.

16. **26.** 50 c. on 10 c. green .. 25 25
17. 75 c. on 15 c. green .. 25 25
18. 1 pi. 50 on 30 c. red .. 30 30
19. 2 pi. on 45 c. red.. .. 30 30
20. 2 pi. 50 on 50 c. blue .. 35 35
21. 4 pi. on 75 c. blue .. 30 30

1925. Air. Optd. **Avion** in English and Arabic.

22. **13.** 2 pi. on 40 c. (No. 8) .. 1·10 1·10
23. 3 pi. on 60 c. (No. 10) .. 1·10 1·10
24. 5 pi. on 1 f. (No. 13) .. 1·10 1·10
25. 10 pi. on 2 f. (No. 14) .. 1·10 1·10

Stamps of Syria overprinted **ALAOUITES** in English and Arabic.

1925. Pictorial stamps of 1925.

26. 10 c. violet 5 5
27. 25 c. black 15 15
28. 50 c. green 10 10
29. 75 c. red 12 12
30. 1 pi. claret 15 15
31. 1 pi. 25 green 15 15
32. 1 pi. 50 red 15 15
33. 2 pi. sepia 15 15
34. 2 pi. 50 blue 20 20
35. 3 pi. brown 10 10
36. 5 pi. violet 15 15
37. 10 pi. plum 20 20
38. 25 pi. blue 50 50

1925. Air. Air stamps of 1925 with **AVION** opt.

40. 2 pi. sepia 30 30
41. 3 pi. brown 30 30
42. 5 pi. violet 30 30
43. 10 pi. plum 30 30

1926. Air. Air stamps of 1926 with aeroplane optd.

44. 2 pi. sepia 35 35
45. 3 pi. brown 35 35
46. 5 pi. violet 35 35
47. 10 pi. plum 35 35

1926. Surcharged stamps of 1926 and 1928.

53. 5 c. on 10 c. violet .. 5 5
54. 2 pi. on 1 pi. 25 green .. 1·25 1·10
48. 3 pi. 50 on 75 c. red .. 20 15
49. 4 pi. on 25 c. black .. 20 20
56. 4 pi. 50 on 75 c. red .. 45 45
50. 6 pi. on 2 pi. 50 blue .. 20 20
57. 7 pi. 50 on 2 pi. 50 blue 25 25
51. 12 pi. on 1 pi. 25 green 20 20
58. 15 pi. on 2 pi. 50 blue .. 80 80
52. 20 pi. on 1 p. 25 green.. 25 25

1929. Air. Air stamps of 1929.

59. 50 c. green 20 20
60. 1 pi. claret 65 65
61. 2 pi. on 1 pi. 25 green 30 30
62. 15 pi. on 25 pi. blue .. 5·00 4·50
63. 25 pi. blue .. .. 3·75 3·75

POSTAGE DUE STAMPS

1925. Postage Due stamps of France surch. **ALAOUITES** and new value in English and Arabic.

D 26. **D 2.** 50 c. on 10 c. brown 50 50
D 27. 1 pi. on 20 c. olive .. 50 50
D 28. 2 pi. on 30 c. red .. 55 55
D 29. 3 pi. on 50 c. claret.. 55 55
D 30. 5 pi. on 1 f. claret on yellow 55 55

1925. Postage Due stamps of Syria optd. **ALAOUITES** in English and Arabic.

D 44. **D 1.** 50 c. brown on yellow 10 10
D 45. – 1 pi. black on red .. 10 10
D 46. – 2 pi. black on blue .. 12 12
D 47. – 3 pi. brown on orange 30 30
D 48. – 5 pi. black on green.. 35 35

For later issues see **LATAKIA.**

ALBANIA E1

Albania, formerly part of the Turkish Empire, was declared independent on 28th November, 1912, and this was recognised by Turkey in treaty of 30th May, 1913. After chaotic conditions during and after the First World War a republic was established in 1925. Three years later the country became a kingdom. From 7th April, 1939 until December, 1944, Albania was occupied, firstly by the Italians and then by the Germans. Following liberation a People's Republic was set up in 1946.

1913. 40 paras = 1 piastre or grosch.
1913. 100 qint = 1 franc.
1947. 100 qint = 1 lek.
1965. 10 old leks = 1 new lek.

1913. Various types of Turkey optd. with double-headed eagle and **SHQIPENIA.**

2. 11. 2 pa. olive (No. N 105) .. 27·00 25·00
3. 11. 5 pa. orange (No. 317) .. 22·00 19·00
12. 9. 10 pa. green (No. 265) .. 35·00 26·00
4. 11. 10 pa. green (No. 318) .. 16·00 13·00
11. 10 pa. on 20 pa. red .. 55·00 42·00
5. 20 pa. rose (No. 320) .. 14·00 10·00
6. 1 pi. blue (No. 323) .. 10·00 8·00
14. 1 pi. blk. on red (No. D 59) 80·00 65·00
7. 2 pi. black (No. 324) .. 25·00 16·00
8. 2½ pi. brown (No. 325) .. 40·00 30·00
9. 5 pi. purple (No. 326) .. 55·00 42·00
10. 10 pi. red (No. 327) .. £225 £170

1.

1913.

16. 1. 10 pa. violet .. .. 1·40 90
17. 20 pa. red and grey .. 1·40 90
18. 1 g. grey .. .. 1·40 90
19. 2 g. blue and violet .. 2·00 1·10
20. 5 g. violet and blue .. 2·25 1·75
21. 10 g. blue and violet .. 2·75 2·25

2. 3. Castriota Skanderbeg.

1913. Independence Anniversary.

22. 2. 10 pa. black and green .. 70 55
23. 20 pa. black and red .. 70 55
24. 30 pa. black and violet .. 70 55
25. 1 g. black and blue .. 75 65
26. 2 g. black .. .. 1·75 1·00

1913.

27. 3. 2 q. brown and yellow .. 25 25
28. 5 q. green and yellow .. 25 25
29. 10 q. red 20 20
30. 25 q. blue 30 30
31. 50 q. mauve and red .. 45 45
32. 1 f. brown .. .. 1·10 1·10

1914. Arrival of Prince William of Wied. Optd. **7 Mars 1461 RROFTE MBRETI 1914.**

33. 3. 2 q. brown and yellow .. 3·00 2·10
34. 5 q. green and yellow .. 3·00 2·10
35. 10 q. red .. .. 3·00 2·10
36. 25 q. blue .. .. 3·00 2·10
37. 50 q. mauve and red .. 3·00 2·10
38. 1 f. brown .. .. 3·00 2·10

1914. Surch.

40. 3. 5 pa. on 2 q. brown & yell. 12 12
41. 10 pa. on 5 q. green & yell. 12 12
42. 20 pa. on 10 q. red .. 20 20
43. 1 g. on 25 q. blue .. 25 25
44. 2 g. on 50 q. mauve & red 45 40
45. 5 g. on 1 f. brown .. 1·25 75

1914. Valona Provisional Issue. Optd. **POSTE D'ALBANIE** and Turkish inscr. in circle with star in centre.

45a. 3. 2 q. brown and yellow .. 55·00 55·00
45b. 5 q. green and yellow ..
45c. 10 q. red and rose .. 1·90 1·90
45d. 25 q. blue .. .. 2·00 2·00
45e. 50 q. mauve and red .. 1·90 1·90
45f. 1 f. brown .. £180
45g. 5 pa. on 2 q. br. & yell... 11·00 11·00
45h. 10 pa. on 5 q. grn. & yell. 20·00 20·00
45i. 20 pa. on 10 q. red & rose 3·50 3·50
45j. 1 gr. on 25 q. blue .. 1·90 1·90
45k. 2 gr. on 50 q. mve. & red 3·50 3·50
45l. 5 gr. on 1 f. brown .. 5·00 5·00

4. 5.

1917. Inscribed "SHQIPERIE KORCE VETQEVERITARE" or "REPUBLIKA KORCE SHQIPETARE" or "QARKU-POSTES-I-KORCES".

75. 4. 1 c. brown and green .. 45 35
76. 2 c. red and green .. 45 35
77. 3 c. grey and green .. 45 35
78. 5 c. green and black .. 45 35
79. 10 c. red and black .. 45 35
72. 25 c. blue and black .. 1·50 90
80. 50 c. violet and black .. 1·25 60
81. 1 f. brown and black .. 3·75 2·00

1919. Fiscal stamps used by the Austrians in Albania. Handstamped with control.

96. 5. (2) q. on 2 h. brown .. 1·75 1·75
97. 5 q. on 16 h. green .. 1·75 1·75
98. 10 q. on 8 h. red .. 1·75 1·75
86. 25 q. on 64 h. blue .. 1·25 1·00
93. 50 q. on 32 h. violet .. 1·75 1·40
101. 1 f. on 1.28 k. brn. on blue 1·75 1·75

Three sets may be made of this issue according to whether the handstamped control is a date, a curved comet or a comet with straight tail.

1919. No. 43 optd. **SHKODER 1919.**

103. 3. 1 g. on 25 q. blue .. 75 75

1919. Fiscal stamps surch. **POSTAT SHQIPTARE** and new value.

104. 5. 10 q. on 2 h. brown .. 1·10 1·10
111. 10 q. on 8 h. red .. 80 80
112. 15 q. on 8 h. red .. 80 80
113. 20 q. on 16 h. green .. 90 90
113a. 25 q. on 32 h. violet .. 90 90
107. 25 q. on 64 h. blue .. 1·10 1·10
108. 50 q. on 32 h. violet .. 1·25 1·25
113b. 50 q. on 64 h. blue .. 3·00 3·00
113c. 1 f. on 96 h. orange .. 1·00 1·00
113d. 2 f. on 160 h. violet .. 1·40 1·40

6. Prince William I. 7. Skanderbeg.

1920. Optd. with double-headed eagle and **SHKORDA** or surch. also.

114. 6. 1 q. grey .. .. 9·00 9·00
115. 2 q. on 10 q. red .. 1·75 1·75
116. 5 q. on 10 q. red .. 1·75 1·75
117. 10 q. red .. .. 1·10 1·10
118. 20 q. brown .. .. 5·00 5·00
119. 25 q. blue .. .. 65·00 65·00
120. 25 q. on 10 q. red .. 1·75 1·75
121. 50 q. violet .. .. 6·50 6·50
122. 50 q. on 10 q. red .. 1·75 1·75

1920. Optd with posthorn.

123. 7. 2 q. orange 30 25
124. 5 q. green .. .. 1·25 80
125. 10 q. red .. .. 1·40 90
126. 25 q. blue .. .. 3·25 2·00
127. 50 q. green 30 30
128. 1 f. mauve 35 35

Stamps as T 7 also exist optd. **BESA** meaning "Loyalty".

1922. No. 123 surch. with value in frame.

143. 7. 1 q. on 2 q. orange .. 12 10

8.

1922. Views.

144. 8. 2 q. orange (Gjinokaster) 20 15
145. 5 q. green (Kanina) .. 8 8
146. 10 q. red (Berat) .. 8 8
147. 25 q. blue (Veziri Bridge) 8 8
148. 50 q. blue-grn. (Rozafat) 8 8
149. 1 f. violet (Korce) .. 15 12
150. 2 f. olive (Durres) .. 35 25

1924. Opening of National Assembly. Optd. **TIRANE KALLNUER 1924** in frame with **Mbledhie Kushtetuese** above.

151. 8. 2 q. orange 35 35
152. 5 q. green 35 35
153. 10 q. red 35 35
154. 25 q. blue 35 35
155. 50 q. blue-green .. 35 35

1924. No. 143 surch. with value and bars.

156. 8. 1 on 2 q. orange .. 12 12

1924. Red Cross. (a) Surch. with small red cross and premium.

157. 8. 5 q.+5 q. green .. 75 75
158. 10 q.+5 q. red .. 75 75
159. 25 q.+5 q. blue .. 75 75
160. 50 q.+5 q. blue-green .. 75 75

(b) Nos. 157/60 with further surch. of large red cross and premium.

161. 8. 5 q.+5 q.+5 q. green .. 75 75
162. 10 q.+5 q.+5 q. red .. 75 75
163. 25 q.+5 q.+5 q. blue .. 75 75
164. 50 q.+5 q.+5 q. blue-grn. 75 75

1925. Return of Government to Capital. Optd. **Triumf' i legalitetit 24 Dhetuer 1924.**

164a. 8. 1 on 2 q. orange (No. 156) 30 30
165. 2 q. orange 30 30
166. 5 q. green 30 30
167. 10 q. red 30 30
168. 25 q. blue 30 30
169. 50 q. blue-green .. 30 30
170. 1 f. violet 30 30

1925. Proclamation of Republic. Optd. **Republika Shqiptare 21 Kallnduer 1925.**

171. 8. 1 on 2 q. orange (No. 156) 25 25
172. 2 q. orange 25 25
173. 5 q. green 25 25
174. 10 q. red 25 25
175. 25 q. blue 25 25
176. 50 q. blue-green .. 25 25
177. 1 f. violet 25 25

1925. Optd. **Republika Shqiptare.**

178. 8. 1 on 2 q. orange (No. 156) 15 15
179. 2 q. orange 15 15
180. 5 q. green 15 15
181. 10 q. red 15 15
182. 25 q. blue 15 15
183. 50 q. blue-green .. 15 15
184. 1 f. violet 15 15
185. 2 f. olive 25 25

9.

1925. Air.

186. 9. 5 q. green 20 20
187. 10 q. red 20 20
188. 25 q. blue 20 20
189. 50 q. green 25 25
190. 1 f. black and violet .. 70 70
191. 2 f. violet and olive .. 1·00 1·00
192. 3 f. green and brown .. 2·00 2·00

Ahmed Zogu, later King Zog I.
10. 11.

1925.

193. 10. 1 q. orange 5 5
194. 2 q. brown 5 5
195. 5 q. green 5 5
196. 10 q. red 5 5
197. 15 q. brown 45 40
198. 25 q. blue 5 5
199. 50 q. blue-green .. 15 15
200. 11. 1 f. blue and red .. 12 12
201. 2 f. orange and green .. 25 25
202. 3 f. purple and brown .. 35 30
203. 5 f. black and violet .. 1·25 1·00

1927. Air. Optd. **Rep. Shqiptare.**

204. 9. 5 q. green .. .. 1·50 1·50
205. 10 q. red .. .. 1·50 1·50
206. 25 q. blue 30 30
207. 50 q. green 30 30
208. 1 f. black and violet .. 35 35
209. 2 f. violet and olive .. 45 45
210. 3 f. green and brown .. 75 75

1927. Optd. **A.Z.** and wreath.

211. 10. 1 q. orange 5 5
212. 2 q. brown 5 5
213. 5 q. green 35 12
214. 10 q. red 5 5
215. 15 q. brown .. .. 1·90 1·40
216. 25 q. blue 5 5
217. 50 q. blue-green .. 5 5
218. 11. 1 f. blue and red .. 5 5
219. 2 f. orange and green .. 8 8
220. 3 f. purple and brown .. 20 12
221. 5 f. black and violet .. 35 35

1928. Air. Valona-Brindisi First Flight. Optd. **REP. SHQYPTARE Fluturim' i 1-ar Vlone-Brindisi 21.IV.1928.**

222. 9. 5 q. green 60 60
223. 10 q. red 60 60
224. 25 q. blue 60 60
225. 50 q. green 60 60
226. 1 f. black and violet .. 6·00 6·00
227. 2 f. violet and olive .. 6·50 6·50
228. 3 f. green and brown .. 6·50 6·50

1928. Surch in figures and bars.

229. 10. 1 on 10 q. red (No. 214) 8 8
230. 5 on 25 q. blue (No. 216) 8 8

12. King Zog I. 13. King Zog I.

1928. National Assembly. Optd. **Kujtim Mbledhjes Kushtetuese 25.8.28.**

231. 12. 1 q. brown 45 45
232. 2 q. grey 45 45
233. 5 q. green 65 65
234. 10 q. red 45 45
235. 15 q. brown .. .. 3·75 3·75
236. 25 q. blue 45 45
237. 50 q. lilac 50 45
238. 13. 1 f. black and blue .. 50 50

1928. Accession of King Zog I. Optd. **Mbretnia Shqiptar Zog I 1.IX.1928.**

239. 12. 1 q. brown .. .. 1·90 1·90
240. 2 q. grey .. .. 1·90 1·90
241. 5 q. green .. .. 1·60 1·60
242. 10 q. red .. .. 1·10 1·10
243. 15 q. brown .. .. 1·10 1·10
244. 25 q. blue .. .. 1·10 1·10
245. 50 q. lilac .. .. 1·10 1·10
246. 13. 1 f. black and blue .. 1·60 1·60
247. 2 f. black and green .. 2·00 2·00

1928. Optd. **Mbretnia-Shqiptare** only.

248. 12. 1 q. brown 5 5
249. 2 q. grey 5 5
250. 5 q. green 50 12
251. 10 q. red 5 5
252. 15 q. brown .. .. 2·25 1·60
253. 25 q. blue 5 5
254. 50 q. lilac 5 5
255. 13. 1 f. black and blue .. 5 5
256. 2 f. black and green .. 8 5
257. 3 f. olive and red .. 15 12
258. 5 f. black and violet .. 25 25

1929. Surch. **Mbr. Shqiptare** and new value.

259. 10. 1 on 50 q. blue-green .. 12 12
260. 5 on 25 q. blue .. 12 10
261. 15 on 10 q. red .. 25 12

1929. King Zog's 35th birthday. Optd. **RROFT-MBRETI 8.X.1929.**

262. 10. 1 q. orange .. .. 1·00 1·00
263. 2 q. brown .. .. 1·00 1·00
264. 5 q. green .. .. 1·00 1·00
265. 10 q. red .. .. 1·00 1·00
266. 25 q. blue .. .. 1·00 1·00
267. 50 q. green .. .. 1·50 1·50
268. 11. 1 f. blue and red .. 1·50 1·50
269. 2 f. orange and green .. 1·90 1·90

1929. Air. Optd. **Mbr. Shqiptare.**

270. 9. 5 q. green .. .. 1·90 1·90
271. 10 q. red .. .. 1·90 1·90
272. 25 q. blue .. .. 2·40 2·40
273. 50 q. green .. .. 12·00 12·00
274. 1 f. black and violet .. 48·00 48·00
275. 2 f. violet and olive .. 48·00 48·00
276. 3 f. green and brown .. 60·00 60·00

14. Lake of Butrinto. 15. King Zog I.

1930. Accession of King Zog I. 2nd Anniv. Various designs.

277. 14. 1 q. grey 5 5
278. 2 q. orange 5 5
279. 15. 5 q. green 5 5
280. 10 q. red 5 5
281. 15 q. brown 5 5
282. 25 q. blue 8 8
283. 14. 50 q. blue-green .. 10 10
284. – 1 f. violet 20 20
285. – 2 f. grey-blue 30 30
286. – 3 f. grey-green 45 45
287. – 5 f. brown 70 70

DESIGNS—VERT. 1 f., 2 f. Zog Bridge. HORIZ. 3 f., 5 f. Old Wall.

17.

1930. Air.

288. 17. 5 q. green 12 12
289. 15 q. red 15 15
290. 20 q. grey-blue .. 20 15
291. 50 q. olive 25 25
292. – 1 f. blue 50 45
293. – 2 f. brown .. .. 1·40 1·25
294. – 3 f. violet .. .. 2·00 1·90

1931. Air. Optd. **TIRANE-ROME 6 KORRIK 1931.**

295. 17. 5 q. green 90 90
296. 15 q. red 90 90
297. 20 q. grey-blue .. 90 90
298. 50 q. olive 90 90
299. – 1 f. blue .. .. 5·00 5·00
300. – 2 f. brown .. .. 5·00 5·00
301. – 3 f. violet .. .. 5·00 5·00

1934. 10th Anniv. of Revolution. Optd. **1924-24 Dhetuer-1934.**

302. 14. 1 q. grey 60 60
303. 2 q. orange 60 60
304. 15. 5 q. green 60 60
305. 10 q. red 60 60
306. 15 q. brown 60 60
307. 25 q. blue 60 60
308. 14. 50 q. blue-green .. 60 60
309. – 1 f. violet (No. 284) .. 1·90 1·90
310. – 2 f. grey-bl. (No. 285) .. 3·25 3·25
311. – 3 f. grey-grn. (No. 286) 5·50 5·50

18. Horse and Flag of Skanderbeg. 19. Albania (eagle) in chains.

1937. Independence. 25th Anniv.
312. **18.** 1 q. violet 8 8
313. **19.** 2 q. brown 10 10
314. – 5 q. green 12 12
315. **18.** 10 q. olive 12 12
316. **19.** 15 q. red 15 15
317. – 25 q. blue 30 30
318. **18.** 50 q. green 40 40
319. **19.** 1 f. violet .. .. 1·00 1·00
320. – 2 f. brown .. .. 1·75 1·75
DESIGNS: 5 q., 25 q., 2 f. As T **19**, but eagle with opened wings.

20. King Zog and Bride.

1938. Royal Wedding.
321. **20.** 1 q. purple 10 10
322. 2 q. brown 10 10
323. 5 q. green 10 10
324. 10 q. olive 12 12
325. 15 q. red 15 15
326. 25 q. blue 25 25
327. 50 q. green 60 60
328. 1 f. violet .. .. 1·50 1·50

21. National Emblems. **22.** King Zog.

1938. Accession. 10th Anniv.
329. – 1 q. violet 10 10
330. **21.** 2 q. red 12 12
331. – 5 q. green 15 15
332. **22.** 10 q. brown 15 15
333. – 15 q. red 30 30
334. **22.** 25 q. blue 40 40
335. **21.** 50 q. black 80 80
336. **22.** 1 f. green .. .. 1·60 1·60
DESIGN: 1 q., 5 q., 15 q. As T **22**, but Queen's portrait.

ITALIAN OCCUPATION

1939. Optd. **Mbledhja Kushtetuese 12—IV—1939 XVII.** (a) Postage.
337. **14.** 1 q. grey 5 5
338. 2 q. orange 8 8
339. **15.** 5 q. green 8 8
340. 10 q. red 8 8
341. 15 q. brown 8 8
342. 25 q. blue 10 10
343. **14.** 50 q. blue-green .. 15 15
344. – 1 f. violet (No. 284) .. 30 30
345. – 2 f. grey-blue (No. 285) .. 45 45
346. – 3 f. grey-green .. 85 85
347. – 5 f. brown .. .. 1·40 1·40

(b) Air. Optd. as Nos. 337/47 or surch. also.
348. **17.** 5 q. green 40 40
349. 15 q. red 25 25
350. 20 q. on 50 q. olive .. 60 40

23. Gheg. **25.** Broken Columns.

24. King Victor Emmanuel. **26.** King and Tirana-Rome Service Aeroplane.

1939.
351. **23.** 1 q. blue (postage) .. 5 5
352. – 2 q. olive 5 5
353. – 3 q. brown 5 5
354. – 5 q. green 5 5
355. **24.** 10 q. brown 8 5
356. 15 q. red 8 5
357. 25 q. blue 10 8
358. 30 q. violet 12 8
359. – 50 q. violet 15 10
360. – 65 q. brown 20 20
361. – 1 f. green 45 35
362. – 2 f. red 80 60
363. **25.** 3 f. black .. .. 1·60 1·25
364. – 5 f. purple .. .. 3·00 2·75
365. **26.** 20 q. brown (air) .. 2·50 85
DESIGNS—SMALL VERT. 2 q. Tosk man. 3 q. Gheg woman. 5 q., 65 q. Profile of King Victor Emmanuel. 50 q. Tosk woman. LARGE HORIZ. 1 f. Hillside landscape. 2 f. Veziri Bridge. 5 f. Amphitheatre Ruins, Berat.

27. Sheep Farming.

28. King Victor Emmanuel.

1940. Air.
366. **27.** 5 q. green 20 15
367. – 15 q. red 25 15
368. – 20 q. blue 25 15
369. – 50 q. brown 30 25
370. – 1 f. green 60 50
371. – 2 f. black .. .. 1·10 95
372. – 3 f. purple .. .. 3·00 2·75
DESIGNS—HORIZ. 20 q. King of Italy and harbour. 1 f. Bridge. VERT. 15 q. Aerial map. 50 q. Girl and valley. 2 f. Archway and wall. 3 f. Women waving to aeroplane.

1942. Italian Occupation. 3rd Anniv.
373. **28.** 2 q. green 5 5
374. 10 q. brown 5 5
375. 15 q. red 5 5
376. 25 q. blue 8 8
377. 65 q. brown 15 15
378. 1 f. olive 25 25
379. 2 f. purple 50 50

1942. No. 352 surch. **1 QIND.**
380. 1 q. on 2 q. olive .. 12 12

29.

1943. Anti-Tuberculosis Fund.
381. **29.** 5 q.+5 q. green .. 5 5
382. 10 q.+10 q. brown .. 8 8
383. 15 q.+10 q. red .. 8 8
384. 25 q.+15 q. blue .. 10 10
385. 30 q.+20 q. violet .. 12 12
386. 50 q.+25 q. orange .. 15 15
387. 65 q.+30 q. grey .. 15 15
388. 1 f.+40 q. brown .. 30 30

GERMAN OCCUPATION

1943. Postage stamps of 1939 optd. **14 Shtator 1943** or surch. also.
389. – 1 q. on 3 q. brn. (No. 353) 20 25
390. – 2 q. olive (No. 352) .. 20 25
391. – 3 q. brown (No. 353) .. 20 25
392. – 5 q. green (No. 354) .. 20 25
393. **24.** 10 q. brown 20 25
394. – 15 q. red (No. 356) .. 20 25
395. – 25 q. blue (No. 357) .. 20 25
396. – 30 q. violet (No. 358) .. 20 25
397. – 50 q. on 65 q. brown (No. 360) .. 30 35
398. – 65 q. brown (No. 360) .. 30 35
399. – 1 f. green (No. 361) .. 60 70
400. – 2 f. red (No. 362) .. 1·00 1·75
401. **25.** 3 f. black .. .. 2·50 2·75

30. War Refugees.

(30a.)

1944. War Refugees' Relief Fund.
402. **30.** 5 q. + 5 q. green .. 50 50
403. 10 q. + 5 q. brown .. 50 50
404. 15 q. + 5 q. lake .. 50 50
405. 25 q. + 10 q. blue .. 50 50
406. 1 f. + 50 q. olive .. 50 50
407. 2 f. + 1 f. violet .. 50 50
408. 3 f. + 1 f. 50 orange .. 50 50

INDEPENDENT STATE

1945. Nos. 353/8 and 360/2 surch. **QEVERIJA/DEMOKRAT./E SHQIPERISE/22-X-1944** and value.
409. 30 q. on 3 q. brown .. 30 30
410. 40 q. on 5 q. green .. 30 30
411. 50 q. on 10 q. brown .. 30 30
412. 60 q. on 15 q. red .. 30 30
413. 80 q. on 25 q. blue .. 30 30
414. 1 f. on 30 q. violet .. 40 40
415. 2 f. on 65 q. brown .. 40 40
416. 3 f. on 1 f. green .. 50 50
417. 5 f. on 2 f. red .. 85 85

1945. Albanian Army. 2nd Anniv. Surch. as T **30a.**
418. **14.** 30 q. on 1 q. grey .. 10 10
419. 60 q. on 1 q. grey .. 12 12
420. 80 q. on 1 q. grey .. 15 15
421. 1 f. on 1 q. grey .. 20 20
422. 2 f. on 2 q. orange .. 40 40
423. 3 f. on 50 q. green .. 60 60
424. – 5 f. on 2 f. blue (No. 285) 1·10 1·10

1945. Red Cross Fund. Surch. with Red Cross **JAVA EK.K. SHQIPTAR 4-11 MAJ 1945** and value.
425. **29.** 30 q.+15 q. on 5 q.+5 q. green 20 20
426. 50 q.+25 q. on 10 q.+10 q. brown .. 45 45
427. 1 f.+50 q. on 15 q.+10 q. red .. 70 70
428. 2 f.+1 f. on 25 q.+15 q. blue .. .. 1·40 1·40

31. Labinet.

32. Dove and Globe.

1945.
429. **31.** 20 q. green 5 5
430. – 30 q. orange 8 8
431. – 40 q. brown 8 8
432. – 60 q. claret 8 8
433. – 1 f. red 20 20
434. – 3 f. blue .. .. 1·00 1·00
DESIGNS: 40 q., 60 q. Bridge at Berat. 1 f., 3 f. Permet landscape.

1946. Constitutional Assembly. Optd. **ASAMBLEJA KUSHTETUESE 10 KALLNUER 1946.**
435. **31.** 20 q. green 5 5
436. 30 q. orange 10 10
437. – 40 q. brown (No. 431) 20 20
438. – 60 q. claret (No. 432) .. 35 35
439. – 1 f. red (No. 433) .. 55 55
440. – 3 f. blue (No. 434) .. 1·10 1·10

1946. Int. Women's Congress. Perf. or imperf.
441. **32.** 20 q. mauve and red 12 12
442. 40 q. lilac and red .. 15 15
443. 50 q. violet and red .. 25 25
444. 1 f. blue and red .. 30 30
445. 2 f. blue and red .. 50 50

PEOPLE'S REPUBLIC

1946. Proclamation of Albanian People's Republic. Optd. **REPUBLIKA POPULLORE E SHQIPERISE.**
446. **31.** 20 q. green 12 12
447. 30 q. orange 12 12
448. – 40 q. brown (No. 431) 20 20
449. – 60 q. claret (No. 432) .. 45 45
450. – 1 f. red (No. 433) .. 60 60
451. – 3 f. blue (No. 434) .. 1·75 1·75

1946. Albanian Red Cross Congress. Surch. **KONGRESI K.K.SH 24.25–11–46** and premium.
452. **31.** 20 q. + 10 q. green .. 1·50 1·25
453. 30 q. + 15 q. orange .. 1·50 1·25
454. – 40 q. + 20 q. brown .. 1·50 1·25
455. – 60 q. + 30 q. claret .. 1·50 1·25
456. – 1 f. + 50 q. red .. 1·50 1·25
457. – 3 f. + 1 f. 50 blue .. 1·50 1·25

33. Athletes.

34. Kemal Stafa.

1946. Balkan Games.
458. **33.** 1 q. black .. .. 1·40 1·00
459. 1 q. green .. .. 1·40 1·00
460. 5 q. brown .. .. 1·40 1·00
461. 10 q. red .. .. 1·40 1·00
462. 20 q. blue .. .. 2·10 1·75
463. 40 q. lilac .. .. 2·75 2·25
464. 1 f. orange .. .. 2·75 2·75

1947. Kemal Stafa (National hero). 5th Death Anniv.
465. **34.** 20 q. brown 35 20
466. 28 q. blue 45 30
467. 40 q. brown 55 45

35. Railway Construction.

1977. Durres-Elbasan Railway.
468. **35.** 1 q. black 20 15
469. 4 q. green 20 15
470. 10 q. brown 25 15
471. 15 q. red 30 25
472. 20 q. black 30 25
473. 28 q. blue 45 30
474. 40 q. purple 90 50
475. 68 q. brown .. .. 1·50 75

36. Partisans.

37. Enver Hoxha and Vasil Shanto.

1947. Albanian Army. 4th Anniv. Inscr. "1943–1947".
476. **36.** 16 q. brown 15 15
477. **37.** 20 q. brown 20 15
478. – 28 q. blue 35 35
479. – 40 q. brown and mauve 70 60
DESIGNS—HORIZ. 28 q. Infantry column. VERT. 40 q. Portrait of Vojo Kushi.

38. Ruined Conference Building.

1947. Peza Conf. 5th Anniv.
480. **38.** 2 l. purple 40 35
481. 2 l. 50 blue 40 35

39. War Invalids.

40. Peasants.

1947. 1st Congress of War Invalids.
482. **39.** 1 l. red 55 55

1947. Agrarian Reform. Inscr. "REFORMA AGRARE".
483. **40.** 1 l. 50 purple 40 40
484. – 2 l. brown 40 40
485. – 2 l. 50 blue 40 40
486. – 3 l. red 40 40
DESIGNS—HORIZ. 2 l. Banquet. 2 l. 50, Peasants rejoicing. VERT. 3 l. Soldier being chaired.

41. Burning Village.

1947. Liberation. 3rd Anniv. Inscr. "29–XI–1944–1947".
487. **41.** 1 l. 50 red 15 15
488. – 2 l. 50 maroon .. 20 20
489. – 5 l. blue 35 35
490. – 8 l. mauve 60 60
491. – 12 l. brown .. .. 1·25 1·25
DESIGNS: 2 l. 50 Riflemen. 5 l. Machine-gunners. 8 l. Mounted soldier. 12 l. Infantry column.

1948. Nos. 441/6 surch. in "lek".
492. **31.** 0 l. 50 on 30 q. orange .. 8 8
493. 1 l. on 20 q. green .. 10 10
494. – 2 l. 50 on 60 q. claret .. 15 15
495. – 3 l. on 1 f. red .. 20 20
496. – 5 l. on 3 f. blue .. 40 40
497. – 12 l. on 40 q. brown .. 1·00 1·00

42. Railway Construction.

1948. Durres-Tirana Railway.
498. **42.** 0 l. 50 claret 10 5
499. 1 l. green 10 8
500. 1 l. 50 red 15 12
501. 2 l. 50 brown 30 20
502. 5 l. blue 40 30
503. 8 l. orange 70 40
504. 12 l. purple 85 60
505. 20 l. black .. .. 2·00 1·10

43. Parade of Infantrymen. 44. Labourer, Globe and Flag.

1948. Albanian Army. 5th Anniv.
506. 43. 2 l. 50 brown 15 15
507. 5 l. blue 30 30
508. – 8 l. slate (Troops in action) 50 50

1949. Labour Day.
509. 44. 2 l. 50 brown 15 12
510. 5 l. blue 30 20
511. 8 l. purple 50 40

45. Soldier and Map. 46. Albanian and Kremlin Tower.

1949. Albanian Army. 6th Anniv.
512. 45. 2 l. 50 brown 15 12
513. 5 l. blue.. .. .. 25 25
514. 8 l. orange 45 40

1949. Albanian-Soviet Amity.
515. 46. 2 l. 50 brown 15 15
516. 5 l. blue.. .. .. 35 35

47. Gen. Enver Hoxha. 48. Soldier and Flag. 49. Joseph Stalin.

1949.
517. 47. 0 l. 50 purple 5 5
518. 1 l. green 8 5
519. 1 l. 50 rose 10 5
520. 2 l. 50 brown 15 5
521. 5 l. blue.. .. .. 30 15
522. 8 l. purple 35 20
523. 12 l. purple 65 35
524. 20 l. slate .. .. 1·25 70

1949. Liberation. 5th Anniv.
525. 48. 2 l. 50 brown 12 12
526. – 3 l. red 20 20
527. 48. 5 l. violet 25 25
528. – 8 l. black 45 45
DESIGN—HORIZ. 3 l., 8 l., Street fighting.

1949. Stalin's 70th Birthday.
529. 49. 2 l. 50 c. brown 15 15
530. 5 l. blue 30 30
531. 8 l. lake.. .. .. 45 45

50. 51. Sami Frasheri.

1950. 75th Anniv. of U.P.U.
532. 50. 5 l. blue 40 30
533. 8 l. purple 65 55
534. 12 l. black 90 80

1950. Literary Jubilee. Inscr. "1950—JUBILEU I SHKRIMTAREVE TE RILINDJES".
535. 51. 2 l. green 12 8
536. – 2 l. 50 brown 15 10
537. – 3 l. red 20 15
538. – 5 l. blue.. .. .. 25 20
PORTRAITS: 2 l. 40 A. Zako (Cajupi). 3 l. Naim Frasheri. 5 l. K. Kristoforidhi.

52. Vuno-Himare. 53. Stafa and Shanto.

1950. Air.
539. 52. 0 l. 50 black 5 5
540. – 1 l. purple 8 5
541. – 2 l. blue 12 8
542. 52. 5 l. green 25 15
543. – 10 l. blue 60 30
544. – 20 l. violet .. .. 1·10 75
DESIGNS: 1 l., 10 l. Rozafat Shkodor. 2 l., 20 l. Keshtjelle-Butrinto.

1950. Albanian Patriots.
545. – 2 l. green 12 12
546. – 2 l. 50 violet 15 15
547. – 3 l. red 20 20
548. – 5 l. blue 30 30
549. 53. 8 l. brown 45 45
DESIGNS: Nos. 545/8 each show five different portraits.

54. Arms and Flags. 55. Skanderberg.

1951. Republic. 5th Anniv.
550. 54. 2 l. 50 red 12 12
551. 5 l. blue 25 25
552. 8 l. black 40 40

1951. Skanderberg (patriot). 483rd Death Anniv.
553. 55. 2 l. 50 brown 12 12
554. 5 l. violet 25 25
555. 8 l. bistre 40 40

56. Gen. Enver Hoxha and Assembly. 57. Child and Globe.

1951. Permet Conf. 7th Anniv.
556. 56. 2 l. 50 brown 12 10
557. 3 l. lake.. .. .. 12 12
558. 5 l. blue.. .. .. 25 25
559. 8 l. mauve 40 40

1951. Int. Children's Day.
560. 57. 2 l. green 15 15
561. – 2 l. 50 brown 15 15
562. – 3 l. red 20 20
563. 57. 5 l. blue.. .. .. 40 40
DESIGN—HORIZ. 2 l. 50, 3 l. Nurse weighing baby.

58. Enver Hoxha and Meeting-house. 59. Young Partisans.

1951. Albanian Communists. 10th Anniv.
564. 58. 2 l. 50 brown 12 12
565. 3 l. lake.. .. .. 15 15
566. 5 l. blue 25 25
567. 8 l. black 40 35

1951. Albanian Young Communists. 10th Anniv. Inscr. "1941-1951".
568. 59. 2 l. 50 brown 12 12
569. – 5 l. blue 20 20
570. – 8 l. claret 35 35
DESIGNS: 5 l. Girl labourers. 8 l. Four portraits.

1952. Air. Surch. in figures.
571. – 0.50 l. on 2 l. blue (541) 13·00 6·50
572. 52. 0.50 l. on 5 l. green .. 1·75 1·10
573. 2 l. 50 on 5 l. green .. 18·00 12·00
574. – 2 l. 50 on 10 l. blue (543) 1·75 1·10

60. Factory. 61. Soldiers and Flags.

1953.
575. 60. 0 l. 50 brown 5 5
576. – 1 l. green 8 5
577. – 2 l. 50 sepia 12 8
578. – 3 l. red 15 8
579. – 5 l. blue 20 10
580. – 8 l. olive 30 10
581. – 12 l. purple 50 20
582. – 20 l. indigo 90 30
DESIGNS—HORIZ. 1 l. Canal. 2 l. 50, Girl and cotton mill. 3 l. Girl and sugar factory. 5 l. Film studio. 8 l. Girl and textile machinery. 20 l. Dam. VERT. 12 l. Pylon and hydro-electric station.

1954. Liberation. 10th Anniv.
583. 61. 0 l. 50 lilac 5 5
584. 1 l. green 5 5
585. 2 l. 50 brown 10 8
586. 3 l. red 12 8
587. 5 l. blue 20 12
588. 8 l. purple 45 35

62. First Albanian School. 63.

1956. Albanian Schools. 70th Anniv.
589. 62. 2 l. purple 5 5
590. – 2 l. 50 green 10 8
591. – 5 l. blue 20 10
592. 62. 10 l. turquoise 50 30
DESIGN: 2 l. 50, 5 l., Portraits of P. Sotiri, P. N. Luarasi and N. Naci.

1957. Albanian Worker's Party. 15th Anniv.
593. 63. 2 l. 50 brown 10 10
594. – 5 l. blue.. .. .. 20 12
595. – 8 l. purple 40 20
DESIGNS: 5 l. Party headquarters, Tirana. 8 l. Marx and Lenin.

64. Congress Emblem.

1957. 4th World Trade Unions Congress, Leipzig.
596. 64. 2 l. 50 slate-purple .. 12 8
597. 3 l. red 12 8
598. 5 l. blue 20 12
599. 8 l. green 35 25

65. Lenin and Cruiser "Aurora". 66. Raising the Flag.

1957. Russian Revolution. 40th Anniv.
600. 65. 2 l. 50 brown 12 8
601. 5 l. blue 20 12
602. 8 l. black 35 25

1957. Proclamation of Independence. 45th Anniv.
603. 66. 1 l. 50 purple 10 5
604. 2 l. 50 brown 10 8
605. 5 l. blue 15 12
606. 8 l. green 45 20

67. Naum Veqilharxhi. 68. Luigj Gurakuqi.

1958. Naum Veqilharxhi (patriot). 160th Birth Anniv.
607. 67. 2 l. 50 brown 12 8
608. 5 l. blue.. .. .. 20 15
609. 8 l. purple 35 20

1958. Removal of Ashes of L. Gurakuqi (patriot).
610. 68. 1 l. 50 green 8 5
611. 2 l. 50 brown 10 8
612. 5 l. blue.. .. .. 20 12
613. 8 l. sepia 40 30

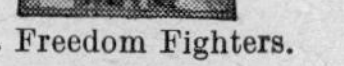

69. Freedom Fighters. 70. Soldiers in Action.

1958. Battle of Mashkullore. 50th Anniv.
614. 69. 2 l. 50 ochre 10 8
615. – 3 l. green 15 12
616. 69. 5 l. blue.. .. .. 20 15
617. 8 l. chestnut 35 25
DESIGN: 3 l., 8 l., Tree and buildings.

1958. Albanian People's Army. 15th Anniv.
618. 70. 1 l. 50 green 8 5
619. – 2 l. 50 chocolate 10 8
620. 70. 8 l. red 25 15
621. – 11 l. blue 40 25
DESIGN: 2 l. 50, 11 l. Tank-driver, sailor, infantryman and tanks.

71. Bust of Apollo and Butrinto Amphitheatre. 72. F. Joliot-Curie and Council Emblem.

1959. Cultural Monuments Week.
622. 71. 2 l. 50 chocolate 10 5
623. 6 l. 50 green 20 12
624. 11 l. blue 45 20

1959. World Peace Council. 10th Anniv.
625. 72. 1 l. 50 red 15 8
626. 2 l. 50 violet 25 12
627. 11 l. blue .. .. 1·10 45

73. Basketball. 74. Soldier.

1959. 1st National Spartacist Games.
628. 73. 1 l. 50 violet 10 8
629. – 2 l. 50 emerald 10 8
630. – 5 l. red 30 15
631. – 11 l. blue .. .. 1·00 50
DESIGNS: 2 l. 50, Football. 5 l. Running. 11 l. Runners with torches.

1959. Liberation. 15th Anniv.
632. 74. 1 l. 50 red 5 5
633. – 2 l. 50 brown 8 5
634. – 3 l. green 10 8
635. – 6 l. 50 red 35 15
DESIGNS: 2 l. 50, Security guard. 3 l. Harvester. 6 l. 50 Laboratory workers.

75. Mother and Child. 76.

1959. Human Rights. 10th Anniv.
636. 75. 5 l. blue.. .. .. 40 20

1960. Int. Women's Day. 50th Anniv.
637. 76. 2 l. 50 brown 12 5
638. 11 l. claret 50 25

77. Congress Building. 78. A. Moisiu (actor). 79. Lenin.

1960. Louchnia Congress. 40th Anniv.
639. 77. 2 l. 50 brown 12 5
640. 7 l. 50 blue 35 15

1960. Alexandre Moisiu. 80th Birth Anniv.
641. 78. 3 l. brown 10 5
642. 11 l. green 35 20

1960. Lenin 90th Birth Anniv.
643. 79. 4 l. turquoise 12 5
644. 11 l. crimson 35 20

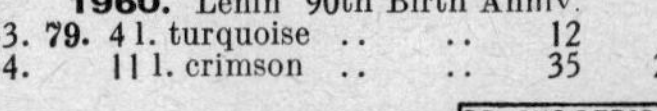

80. Pasha Vasa. 81. Frontier Guard. 82. Family with Policeman.

1960. Albanian Alphabet Study Assn. 80th Anniv.
645. 80. 1 l. olive 5 5
646. – 1 l. 50 brown 5 5
647. – 6 l. 50 blue 20 12
648. – 11 l. red. 40 20
DESIGNS: 1 l. 50 Jani Vreto. 6 l. 50, Sami Frasheri. 11 l. Association statutes.

1960. Frontier Force. 15th Anniv.
649. 81. 1 l. 50 cerise 5 5
650. 11 l. blue 35 20

1960. People's Police. 15th Anniv.
651. 82. 1 l. 50 green 5 5
652. 8 l. 50 brown 30 15

83. Normal School, Elbasan. 84. Soldier and Cannon.

1960. Normal School, Elbasan. 50th Anniv.
653. 83. 5 l. green 12 5
654. 6 l. 50 purple 20 12

1960. Battle of Vlore. 40th Anniv.
655. 84. 1 l. 50 sepia 5 5
656. 2 l. 50 lake 8 5
657. 5 l. blue 15 8

86. Tirana Clock Tower, Kremlin and TU-104 Airliner. 87. Federation Emblem.

1960. Tirana–Moscow Jet Air Service. 2nd Anniv.
658. 86. 1 l. brown 5 5
659. 7 l. 50 blue 30 20
660. 11 l. 50 grey 55 35

1960. World Democratic Youth Federation. 15th Anniv.
661. 87. 1 l. 50 blue 5 5
662. 8 l. 50 red 35 15

88. Ali Kelmendi (Communist). 89. Flags of Albania and Russia and Clasped Hands. 90. Marx and Lenin.

1960. Kelmendi. 60th Birth Anniv.
663. 88. 1 l. 50 olive 5 5
664. 11 l. maroon 35 15

1961. Albanian-Soviet Friendship Society. 15th Anniv.
665. 89. 2 l. violet 5 5
666. 8 l. claret 30 12

1961 4th Albanian Workers' Party Congress.
667. 90. 2 l. red 5 5
668. 8 l. blue 25 12

91. Malsi e Madhe (Shkoder) Costume. 92. Otter.

1961. Provincial Costumes
669. 91. 1 l. black 5 5
670. – 1 l. 50 brown-purple .. 8 5
671. – 6 l. 50 blue 25 15
672. – 11 l. red 55 35
COSTUMES: 1 l. 50, Malesia e Madhe (Shkoder) (female). 6 l. 50, Lume. 11 l. Mirdite.

1961. Albanian Fauna.
673. 92. 2 l. 50 blue 35 8
674. – 6 l. 50 green (Badger) .. 55 15
675. – 11 l. chocolate (Bear) .. 1·00 20

93. Pelicans. 94. Cyclamen.

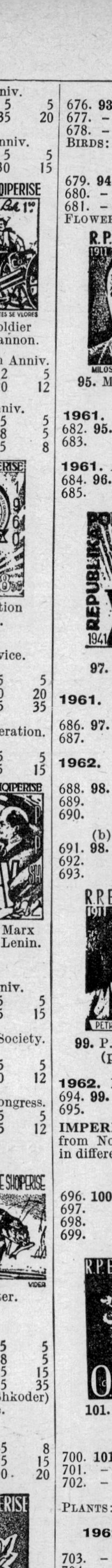
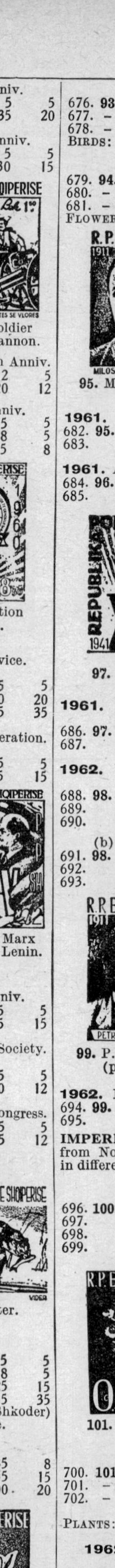

1961. Albanian Birds.
676. 93. 1 l. 50 red on pink .. 25 8
677. – 7 l. 50 violet on blue .. 65 12
678. – 11 l. brown on pink .. 2·25 35
BIRDS: 7 l. 50, Bittern. 11 l. Egret.

1961. Albanian Flowers.
679. 94. 1 l. 50 purple and blue .. 15 5
680. – 8 l. orange and purple .. 45 15
681. – 11 l. red and green .. 1·10 30
FLOWERS: 8 l. Forsythia. 11 l. Lily.

95. M. G. Nikolla. 96. Lenin and Marx on Flag.

1961. Nikolla (poet). 50th Birth Anniv.
682. 95. 0 l. 50 chocolate .. 8 5
683. 8 l. 50 slate-green .. 25 15

1961. Albanian Workers' Party. 20th Anniv.
684. 96. 2 l. 50 red 8 5
685. 7 l. 50 maroon 20 15

97. Workers. 98. Yuri Gagarin and "Vostok I".

1961. Albanian Young Communists Union. 20th Anniv.
686. 97. 2 l. 50 blue 8 5
687. 7 l. 50 purple 20 15

1962. World's First Manned Space Flight. (a) Postage.
688. 98. 0 l. 50 blue 10 8
689. 4 l. purple 20 15
690. 11 l. grey-green 75 40

(b) Air. Optd. **POSTA AJRORE.**
691. 98. 0 l. 50 blue on cream .. 3·50 2·75
692. 4 l. purple on cream .. 3·50 2·75
693. 11 l. grey-grn. on cream 3·50 2·75

99. P. N. Luarasi (patriot). 100. Campaign Emblem.

1962. Petro N. Luarasi. 50th Death Anniv.
694. 99. 0 l. 50 blue 5 5
695. 8 l. 50 brown 30 12

IMPERF. STAMPS. Many Albanian stamps from No. 696 onwards exist imperf. and/or in different colours from limited printings.

1962. Malaria Eradication.
696. 100. 1 l. 50 green 5 5
697. 2 l. 50 brown-red .. 8 5
698. 10 l. purple 30 15
699. 11 l. blue 45 20

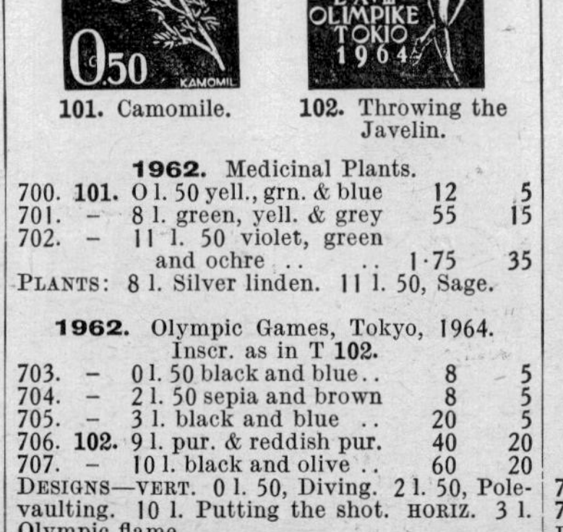

101. Camomile. 102. Throwing the Javelin.

1962. Medicinal Plants.
700. 101. 0 l. 50 yell., grn. & blue 12 5
701. – 8 l. green, yell. & grey 55 15
702. – 11 l. 50 violet, green and ochre .. .. 1·75 35
PLANTS: 8 l. Silver linden. 11 l. 50, Sage.

1962. Olympic Games, Tokyo, 1964. Inscr. as in T 102.
703. – 0 l. 50 black and blue .. 8 5
704. – 2 l. 50 sepia and brown 8 5
705. – 3 l. black and blue .. 20 5
706. 102. 9 l. pur. & reddish pur. 40 20
707. – 10 l. black and olive .. 60 20
DESIGNS—VERT. 0 l. 50, Diving. 2 l. 50, Pole-vaulting. 10 l. Putting the shot. HORIZ. 3 l. Olympic flame.

103. "Sputnik I" in Orbit.

104. Footballer and Ball in Net.

1962. Cosmic Flights.
708. 103. 0 l. 50 yellow and violet 5 5
709. – 1 l. sepia and green .. 12 5
710. – 1 l. 50 yellow and red .. 20 12
711. – 20 l. blue & reddish pur. 1·00 40
DESIGNS: 1 l. Dog "Laika" and "Sputnik II". 1 l. 50, Artificial satellite and Sun. 20 l. "Lunik III" photographing Moon.

1962. World Football Championships, Chile.
712. 104. 1 l. orange and purple 8 5
713. – 2 l. 50 emerald & turq. 12 5
714. 104. 6 l. 50 chestnut & mauve 30 12
715. – 15 l. turquoise & maroon 60 25
DESIGN: 2 l. 50, 15 l. As T 104 but Globe in place of ball in net.

105. "Europa" and Albanian Maps.

106. Dardhe Woman.

1962. Tourist Publicity.
716. 105. 0 l. 50 red, yell. & myrtle 5 5
717. – 1 l. red, violet and blue 5 5
718. – 2 l. 50 red, claret & blue 8 8
719. 105. 11 l. red, yellow & grey 70 20
DESIGN: 1 l., 2 l. 50, Statue and map.

1962. Costumes of Albania's Southern Region.
720. 106. 0 l. 50 red and blue .. 5 5
721. – 1 l. brown and buff .. 5 5
722. – 2 l. 50 violet and apple 8 8
723. – 14 l. brown and green 45 20
COSTUMES: 1 l. Devoll man. 2 l. 50 Lunxheri woman. 14 l. Gjirokaster man.

107. Chamois.

108. Eagle.

1962. Albanian Animals.
724. 107. 0 l. 50 pur. & grey-grn. 5 5
725. – 1 l. black and yellow .. 10 5
726. – 1 l. 50 black & brown 15 8
727. – 15 l. chest. & yell-grn. 65 35
ANIMALS—HORIZ. 1 l. Lynx. 1 l. 50, Wild boar. VERT. 15 l. Mountain deer.

1962. Independence. 50th Anniv. Inscr. "1912 1962".
728. 108. 1 l. chestnut and red .. 5 5
729. – 3 l. black & yellow-brown 8 5
730. – 16 l. black and red .. 45 20
DESIGNS: 3 l. I. Qemali. 16 l. "RPSH" and eagle.

109. Revolutionaries.

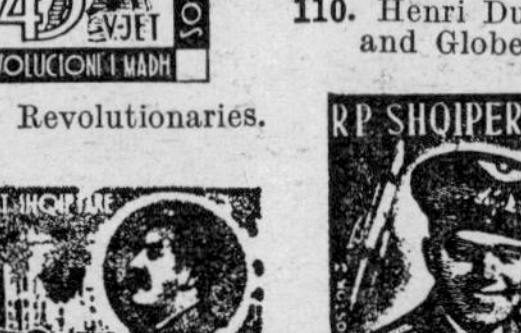

110. Henri Dunant and Globe.

111. Stalin and Battle.

112. A. Nikolaev and "Vostok 3".

1963. October Revolution. 45th Anniv.
731. 109. 5 l. slate-violet & yellow 12 8
732. – 10 l. black and red .. 30 20
DESIGN: 10 l. Statue of Lenin.

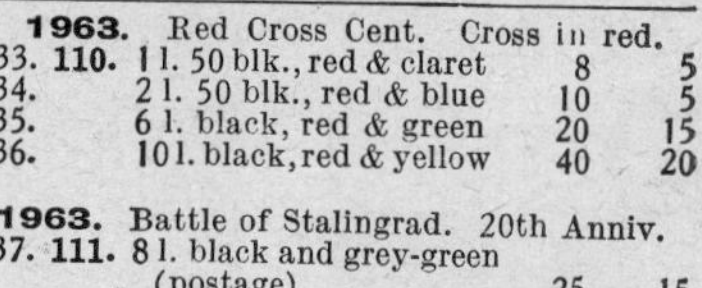

1963. Red Cross Cent. Cross in red.
733. 110. 1 l. 50 blk., red & claret 8 5
734. 2 l. 50 blk., red & blue 10 5
735. 6 l. black, red & green 20 15
736. 10 l. black, red & yellow 40 20

1963. Battle of Stalingrad. 20th Anniv.
737. 111. 8 l. black and grey-green (postage) 25 15
738. – 7 l. crimson & grn. (air) 35 15
DESIGN: 7 l. "Lenin" flag, map, tanks, etc.

1963. 1st "Team" Manned Space Flights.
739. 112. 2 l. 50 sepia and blue .. 10 5
740. – 7 l. 50 black & turquoise 30 20
741. – 20 l. sepia and violet .. 80 30
DESIGNS—HORIZ. 7 l. 50 Globe, "Vostok 3" and "Vostok 4". VERT. 20 l. P. Popovic and "Vostok 4".

113. "Polyphylla fullo".

114. Policeman and Allegorical Figure.

1963. Albanian Insects.
742. 113. 0 l. 50 brown & green .. 5 5
743. – 1 l. 50 brown and blue 12 5
744. – 8 l. violet and red .. 45 15
745. – 10 l. black and yellow 80 15
INSECTS: 1 l. 50, "Lucanus cervus". 8 l. "Procerus gigas". 10 l. "Cincindela albanica".

1963. Albanian Security Police. 20th Anniv.
746. 114. 2 l. 50 blk., pur. & red 10 5
747. 7 l. 50 blk., lake & verm. 20 12

115. Great Crested Grebe.

116. Official Insignia and Postmark of 1913.

1963. Birds. Multicoloured.
748. 0 l. 50 Type 115 .. .. 5 5
749. 3 l. Golden Eagle 15 8
750. 6 l. 50, Partridge 70 20
751. 11 l. Capercaillie .. .. 1·00 25

1963. First Albanian Stamps. 50th Anniv.
752. 116. 5 l. brown, black, blue and yellow 20 8
753. – 10 l. green, black and carmine 50 20
DESIGN: 10 l. Albanian stamps of 1913, 1937 and 1962.

117. Boxing.

118. Gen. Enver Hoxha and Labinoti Council Building.

1963. Olympic Games, Tokyo (1964).
754. 117. 2 l. slate, red & yellow 10 5
755. – 3 l. brn., bl. & orge.-buff 12 8
756. – 5 l. purple, brown and grey-blue 20 10
757. – 6 l. black, grey & green 35 15
758. – 9 l. blue and red-brown 60 20
SPORTS: 3 l. Basketball. 5 l. Athletes and umpire. 6 l. Cycling. 9 l. Gymnastics.

1963. Albanian People's Army. 20th Anniv.
759. 118. 1 l. 50 yell, blk. & red 5 5
760. – 2 l. 50 yellow-brown, chocolate and blue .. 8 5
761. – 5 l. blk., drab & bl.-grn. 15 8
762. – 6 l. blue, buff & brown 20 10
DESIGNS: 2 l. 50, Soldier with weapons. 5 l. Soldier attacking. 6 l. Peacetime soldier.

119. Gagarin.

120. Volleyball (Rumania).

1963. Soviet Cosmonauts. Portraits in yellow and brown.
763. 119. 3 l. reddish violet .. 12 5
764. – 5 l. deep blue .. 15 10
765. – 7 l. violet and grey .. 35 12
766. – 11 l. blue & reddish pur. 35 12
767. – 14 l. blue & blue-green 40 20
768. – 20 l. blue 70 25
COSMONAUTS: 5 l. Titov. 7 l. Nikolaev. 11 l. Popovich. 14 l. Bykovsky. 20 l. Valentina Tereshkova.

1963. European Sports Events, 1963.
769. 120. 2 l. red, black & olive 5 5
770. – 3 l. bistre, black & red 10 5
771. – 5 l. orange, black & grn. 12 10
772. – 7 l. green, black & pink 20 12
773. – 8 l. rose, black & blue 25 15
SPORTS: 3 l. Weightlifting (Sweden). 5 l. Football (European Cup). 7 l. Boxing (Russia). 8 l. Ladies' Canoeing (Russia).

121. Celadon Swallowtail.

1963. Butterflies and Moths. Multicoloured.
774. 1 l. Type 121 .. .. 15 5
775. 2 l. Jersey Tiger 15 5
776. 4 l. Brimstone 20 5
777. 5 l. Deaths Head Hawk Moth 40 8
778. 8 l. Orange Tip 60 12
779. 10 l. Peacock 90 15

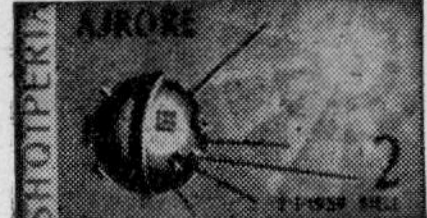

122. Lunik I.

DESIGNS: 3 l. Lunik II. 5 l. Lunik III. 8 l. Venus I. 12 l. Mars I.

1963. Air. Cosmic Flights.
780. 122. 2 l. olive, yell. & orge. 10 5
781. – 3 l. vermilion, yellow, mauve and green .. 15 8
782. – 5 l. olive, yell. & pur. 20 8
783. – 8 l. red, yell. & sl.-vio. 30 15
784. – 12 l. red, orange & blue 50 25

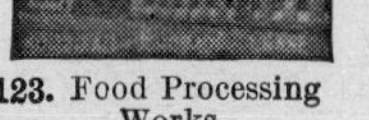

123. Food Processing Works. 124. Shield and Banner.

1963. Industrial Buildings.
785. 123. 2 l. 50 red on pink .. 5 5
786. – 20 l. green on green .. 50 25
787. – 30 l. purple on blue .. 80 40
788. – 50 l. yell-brn. on cream 1·25 60
DESIGNS—VERT. 20 l. Naphtha refinery. 30 l. Fruit-bottling plant. HORIZ. 50 l. Copper-processing works.

1963. First Army and Defence Aid Association, Congress.
789. 124. 2 l. deep blue, red, ochre and turquoise 8 5
790. 8 l. deep blue, red, ochre and light blue 25 15

125. Young Men of Three Races.

1963. Declaration of Human Rights. 15th Anniv.
791. 125. 3 l. black and ochre .. 12 8
792. 5 l. blue and ochre .. 15 10
793. 7 l. violet and ochre .. 25 15

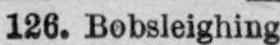

126. Bobsleighing.

127. Lenin.

1963. Winter Olympic Games, Innsbruck. Inscr. "1964".
794. 126. 0 l. 50 black and blue .. 5 5
795. – 2 l. 50 blk., red & grey 8 5
796. – 6 l. 50 blk., yell. & grey 25 8
797. – 12 l. 50 red, blk. & grn. 60 25
DESIGNS—VERT. 2 l. 50, Skiing. 12 l. 50, Figure-skating. HORIZ. 6 l. 50, Ice-hockey.

1964. Lenin. 40th Death Anniv.
798. 127. 5 l. olive and bistre .. 15 8
799. 10 l. olive and bistre .. 35 20

128. Hurdling. 129. Sturgeon.

1964. "GANEFO" Games. Jakarta (1963).
800. 128. 2 l. 50 ultram. and lilac 10 5
801. – 3 l. brown and green .. 10 5
802. – 6 l. 50 lake and blue .. 20 12
803. – 8 l. ochre and blue .. 30 15
SPORTS—HORIZ. 3 l. Running. 6 l. 50, Rifle-shooting. VERT. 8 l. Basketball.

1964. Albanian Fishes. Multicoloured.
804. 0 l. 50 Type 129 .. .. 5 5
805. 1 l. Gilthead 5 5
806. 1 l. 50 Striped mullet .. 8 5
807. 2 l. 50 Carp 12 5
808. 6 l. 50 Mackerel 30 8
809. 10 l. Salmon 65 20

130. Red Squirrel.

1964. Forest Animals. Multicoloured.
810. 1 l. Type 130 .. .. 8 5
811. 1 l. 50 Marten 10 5
812. 2 l. Fox 10 5
813. 2 l. 50 Hedgehog 10 5
814. 3 l. Hare 12 5
815. 5 l. Jackal 25 8
816. 7 l. Wild cat 45 10
817. 8 l. Wolf 80 15

131. Lighting Olympic Torch.

DESIGNS: 5 l. Torch and globes. 7 l. Olympic Flag and Mt. Fuji. 10 l. Olympic Stadium, Tokyo.

1964. Olympic Games, Tokyo. Inscr. "DREJT TOKIOS".
818. 131. 3 l. yell., buff & green 12 5
819. – 5 l. blue, violet and red 15 10
820. – 7 l. lt. blue, blue & yell. 20 10
821. – 10 l. bl., vio., orge. & blk. 30 20

132. Soldiers and hand clutching rifle, and Inscription.

1964. Permet Congress. 20th Anniv. Inscr. "24 MAJ 1944–1964".
822. 132. 2 l. sepia, red & orange 10 5
823. – 5 l. blk., red, yell. & grn. 12 10
824. – 8 l. sepia, red & red-brn. 20 12
DESIGNS (each with different inscription at right): 5 l. Albanian Arms. 8 l. Gen. Enver Hoxha.

133. Revolutionaries with Flag. 134. Full Moon.

1964. Revolution. 40th Anniv.
825. 133. 2 l. 50 black and red .. 10 5
826. 7 l. 50 black & magenta 20 12

1964. "Verso Tokyo" Stamp Exhibition, Rimini (Italy). Optd. **Rimini 25-VI-64.**
827. 10 l. blue, violet, orange and black (No. 821) .. 40 40

1964. Moon's Phases.
828. 134. 1 l. yellow and violet 8 5
829. – 5 l. yellow & ultramarine 15 10
830. – 8 l. yellow and blue .. 25 12
831. – 11 l. yellow and green 40 15
PHASES: 5 l. Waxing Moon. 8 l. Half-Moon. 11 l. Waning Moon.

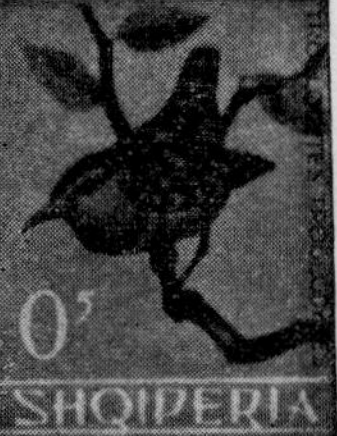

135. Wren. 136. Running and Gymnastics.

1964. Albanian Birds. Multicoloured.
832. 0 l. 50 Type 135 .. .. 5 5
833. 1 l. Penduline tit 5 5
834. 2 l. Green woodpecker .. 12 5
835. 3 l. Tree-creeper 15 5
836. 4 l. Nuthatch 20 5
837. 5 l. Great tit 25 8
838. 6 l. Goldfinch 40 15
839. 18 l. Golden oriole .. 90 20

1964. Air. Riccione "Space" Exn. Optd. **Riccione 23-8-1964.**
840. 122. 2 l. olive, yell. & orge. 90 90
841. – 8 l. red, yellow and slate-violet (No. 783) 1·50 1·50

1964. Olympic Games, Tokyo.
842. 136. 1 l. red, blue and green 5 5
843. – 2 l. brown, blue & violet 8 5
844. – 3 l. orge-brn., vio. & ol. 10 5
845. – 4 l. olive, turquoise & bl. 12 5
846. – 5 l. bl.-grn., pur. & red 12 5
847. – 6 l. ult., lt. blue & orge. 15 5
848. – 7 l. yell.-grn., orge. & bl. 20 8
849. – 8 l. grey, green & yellow 25 10
850. – 9 l. lt. bl., yell. & pur. 30 12
851. – 10 l. brn., grn. & bl.-grn. 60 20
SPORTS: 2 l. Weightlifting and judo. 3 l. Horse-jumping and cycling. 4 l. Football and water-polo. 5 l. Wrestling and boxing. 6 l. Various sports and hockey. 7 l. Swimming and yachting. 8 l. Basketball and netball. 9 l. Rowing and canoeing. 10 l. Fencing and pistol-shooting.

137. Chinese Republican Emblem. 138. Karl Marx.

1964. Chinese People's Republic. 15th Anniv. Inscr. "1 TETOR 1949 1964".
852. 137. 7 l. red, black & yellow 20 10
853. – 8 l. black, red & yellow 25 12
DESIGN—HORIZ. 8 l. Mao Tse-tung.

1964. "First International". Cent.
854. 138. 2 l. black, red & lavender 5 5
855. – 5 l. slate 12 10
856. – 8 l. black, red and buff 20 12
DESIGNS: 5 l. St. Martins Hall, London. 8 l. F. Engels.

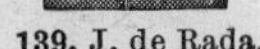

139. J. de Rada. 140. Arms and Flag.

1964. Jeronim de Rada (poet). 150th Birth. Anniv.
857. 139. 7 l. green 20 8
858. 8 l. violet 20 10

1964. Liberation. 20th Anniv.
859. 140. 1 l. black, orange, yellow and magenta .. 5 5
860. – 2 l. blue, red & yellow 5 5
861. – 3 l. brown, red & yellow 8 5
862. – 4 l. green, red & yellow 10 10
863. – 10 l. black, red and blue 40 12
DESIGNS—HORIZ. 2 l. Industrial scene. 3 l. Agricultural scene. 4 l. Laboratory worker. VERT. 10 l. Hands holding Constitution hammer and sickle.

141. Mercury. 142. Chestnut.

1964. Solar System Planets. Multicoloured.
864. 1 l. Type 141 .. .. 10 5
865. 2 l. Venus 12 5
866. 3 l. Earth 12 5
867. 4 l. Mars 15 8
868. 5 l. Jupiter 20 10
869. 6 l. Saturn 25 12
870. 7 l. Uranus 30 12
871. 8 l. Neptune 30 12
872. 9 l. Pluto 40 15

1965. Winter Fruits. Multicoloured.
873. 1 l. Type 142 .. .. 5 5
874. 2 l. Medlars 5 5
875. 3 l. Persimmon 10 5
876. 4 l. Pomegranate 15 5
877. 5 l. Quince 25 8
878. 10 l. Orange 40 12

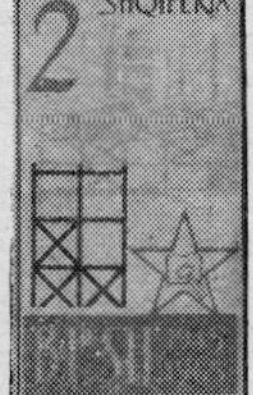

143. "Industry". 144. Cattle grazing.

1965. Albanian Professional Associations. 20th Anniv. Inscr. "B.P.S.H. 1945–1965".
879. 143. 2 l. red, pink & black 12 12
880. – 5 l. black, grey & ochre 25 20
881. – 8 l. blue, lt. blue & blk. 45 30
DESIGNS: 5 l. Set square, book and dividers ("Technocracy"). 8 l. Hotel, trees and sunshade ("Tourism").

1965. Albanian Cattle.
882. 144. 1 l. multicoloured .. 5 5
883. – 2 l. multicoloured .. 10 5
884. – 3 l. multicoloured .. 12 5
885. – 7 l. multicoloured .. 40 8
886. – 12 l. multicoloured .. 60 12
DESIGNS: 2 l. to 12 l. As Type 144 showing different views of cattle.

145. Coastal View.

1965. Albanian Scenery. Multicoloured.
887. 1 l. 50, Type 145 .. 5 5
888. 2 l. 50, Mountain forest .. 5 5
889. 3 l. Lugina Peak (vert.) .. 10 5
890. 4 l. White River, Thethi (vert.) 12 8
891. 5 l. Dry Mountain .. 12 8
892. 9 l. Lake of Flowers, Lure 25 12

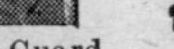

146. Frontier Guard 147. Rifleman.

1965. Frontier Army. 20th Anniv.
893. 146. 2 l. 50 multicoloured .. 12 5
894. 12 l. 50 multicoloured 45 30

1965. European Shooting Championships, Bucharest.
895. 147. 1 l. maroon, cerise & vio. 5 5
896. – 2 l. maroon, ultram. & bl. 5 5
897. – 3 l. red and pink .. 8 5
898. – 4 l. maroon, black, grey and ochre 12 8
899. – 15 l. maroon, black, brown and green .. 50 15
DESIGNS: 2 l., 15 l. Rifle-shooting (different). 3 l. "Target" map. 4 l. Pistol-shooting.

148. I.T.U. Emblem and Symbols.

149. Beliaiev.

1965. I.T.U. Cent.
900. 148. 2 l. 50 mag., blk. & grn. 12 5
901. 12 l. 50 blue, blk. & vio. 70 20

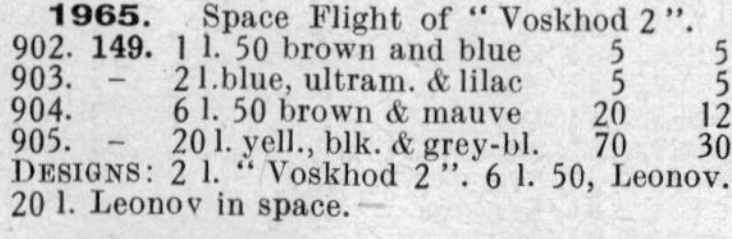

1965. Space Flight of "Voskhod 2".
902. 149. 1 l. 50 brown and blue 5 5
903. – 2 l. blue, ultram. & lilac 5 5
904. 6 l. 50 brown & mauve 20 12
905. – 20 l. yell., blk. & grey-bl. 70 30
DESIGNS: 2 l. "Voskhod 2". 6 l. 50, Leonov. 20 l. Leonov in space.

150. Marx and Lenin.

151. Mother and Child.

1965. Postal Ministers' Congress, Peking.
907. 150. 2 l. 50 sepia, red & yell. 10 5
908. " 7 l. 50 green, red & yell. 40 15

1965. Int. Children's Day. Multicoloured.
909. 1 l. Type 151 .. .. 5 5
910. 2 l. Children planting tree 5 5
911. 3 l. Children and construction toy (horiz.) .. 8 5
912. 4 l. Child on beach .. 12 8
913. 15 l. Child reading book .. 50 25

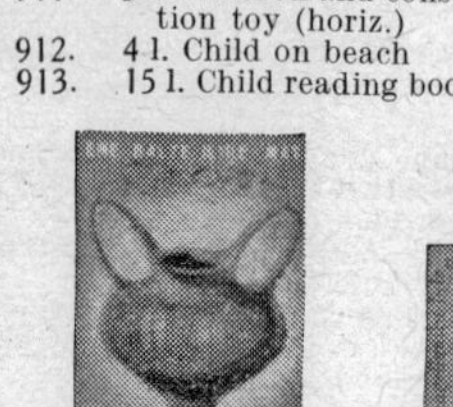
152. Wine Vessel.

153. Fuchsia.

1965. Albanian Antiquities. Multicoloured.
914. 1 l. Type 152 .. .. 5 5
915. 2 l. Helmet and shield .. 5 5
916. 3 l. Mosaic of animal (horiz.) 8 5
917. 4 l. Statuette of man .. 12 8
918. 15 l. Statuette of headless and limbless man .. 45 15

1965. Albanian Flowers. Multicoloured.
919. 1 l. Type 153 .. .. 5 5
920. 2 l. Cyclamen 5 5
921. 3 l. Lilies 8 5
922. 3 l. 40 Iris 8 5
923. 4 l. Dahlia 10 5
924. 4 l. 50 Hydrangea 20 8
925. 5 l. Rose 30 10
926. 7 l. Tulips 40 12
(Currency revaluation 10 (old) leks = 1 (new lek).

1965. Surch.
927. 5 q. on 30 l. (No. 794) .. 5 5
928. 15 p. on 30 l. (No. 794) .. 5 5
929. 25 q. on 50 l. (No. 795) .. 8 5
930. 80 q. on 50 l. (No. 795) .. 20 8
931. 1 l. 10 on 20 l. (No. 793) .. 40 12
932. 2 l. on 20 l. (No. 793) .. 65 20

154. White Stork.

155. "War Veterans" (after painting by B. Sejdini).

1965. Migratory Birds. Multicoloured.
933. 10 q. Type 154 .. .. 5 5
934. 20 q. Cuckoo 10 5
935. 30 q. Hoopoe 12 5
936. 40 q. Bee-eater 20 8
937. 50 q. Nightjar 25 10
938. 1 l. 50 Quail 65 20

1965. War Veterans Conf.
939. 155. 25 q. brown and black 10 5
940. 65 q. blue and black .. 20 10
941. 1 l. 10 black 40 15

156. Hunter stalking Game-bird.

157. "Nerium oleander".

1965. Hunting.
942. 156. 10 q. multicoloured .. 5 5
943. – 20 q. brown, sep. & grn. 5 5
944. – 30 q. multicoloured .. 8 5
945. – 40 q. purple and green 10 8
946. – 50 q. chest., blue & blk. 15 10
947. – 1 l. brown, bistre & grn. 35 15
DESIGNS: 20 q. Shooting deer. 30 q. Pheasant. 40 q. Shooting wild duck. 50 q. Dogs chasing wild boar. 1 l. Hunter.

1965. Mountain Flowers. Multicoloured.
948. 10 q. Type 157 .. .. 5 5
949. 20 q. "Myosotis alpestris" 10 5
950. 30 q. "Dianthus glacialis" 12 5
951. 40 q. "Nymphaea alba" .. 15 8
952. 50 q. "Lotus corniculatus" 25 10
953. 1 l. "Papaver rhoeas" .. 40 15

158. Tourist Hotel, Fier.

159. Freighter "Teuta".

1965. Public Buildings.
954. 158. 5 q. black and blue .. 5 5
955. – 10 q. black and buff .. 5 5
956. – 15 q. black and green 5 5
957. – 25 q. black and violet 8 5
958. – 65 q. black and brown 15 8
959. – 80 q. black and green 20 10
960. – 1 l. 10 black and purple 25 12
961. – 1 l. 60 black and blue 30 15
962. – 2 l. black and pink .. 50 25
963. – 3 l. black and grey .. 75 40
BUILDINGS: 10 q. Peshkopi Hotel. 15 q. Sanatorium, Tirana. 25 q. "House of Rest", Pegradec. 65 q. Partisans Sports Palace, Tirana. 80 q. "House of Rest", Dajti Mountain. 1 l. 10. Palace of Culture, Tirana. 1 l 60, Adriatic Hotel, Durres. 2 l. Migjeni Theatre, Shkoder. 3 l. "A. Moisiu" Cultural Palace, Durres.

1965. Evolution of Albanian Ships.
964. 159. 10 q. green 5 5
965. – 20 q. bistre and green 5 5
996. – 30 q. blue 8 5
967. – 40 q. violet 10 5
968. – 50 q. red and rose .. 15 10
969. – 1 l. brown and ochre .. 30 15
DESIGNS: 20 q. Punt. 30 q. 19th-century sailing ship. 40 q. 18th-century brig. 50 q. Freighter "Vlore". 1 l. Illyrian galliots.

160. Head of Brown Bear.

161. Championships Emblem.

1965. Bears. Different Bear designs, as T 160.
970. – 10 q. brown and buff .. 8 5
971. – 20 q. brown and buff .. 10 5
972. – 30 q. brown, red & buff 12 5
973. – 35 q. brown and buff .. 12 5
974. – 40 q. brown and buff .. 15 5
975. 160. 50 q. brown and buff .. 20 8
976. – 55 q. brown and buff .. 25 10
977. – 60 q. brown, red and buff 30 10
The 10 q. to 40 q. are vert.

1965. 7th Balkan Basketball Championships, Tirana. Multicoloured.
978. 10 q. Type 161 .. .. 5 5
979. 20 q. Competing players .. 8 5
980. 30 q. Clearing ball 10 5
981. 50 q. Attempted goal .. 12 10
982. 1 l. 40 Medal and ribbon .. 45 20

162. Arms on Book.

163. Cow.

1966. Albanian People's Republic. 20th Anniv.
983. 162. 10 q. gold, red & brown 5 5
984. – 20 q. gold, bl. & ultram. 5 5
985. – 30 q. gold, yell. & brn. 8 5
986. – 60 q. gold, apple & green 12 8
987. – 80 q. gold, red & brown 15 10
DESIGNS (Arms and): 20 q. Chimney stacks. 30 q. Ear of corn. 60 q. Hammer, sickle and open book. 80 q. Industrial plant.

1966. Domestic Animals. Animals in natural colours; inscr. in black: frame colours given.
988. 163. 10 q. turquoise .. 5 5
989. – 20 q. green 10 5
990. – 30 q. blue 12 5
991. – 35 q. lavender .. 12 5
992. – 40 q. pink 15 5
993. – 50 q. yellow 20 8
994. – 55 q. blue 20 8
995. – 60 q. yellow 25 10
ANIMALS—HORIZ. 20 q. Pig. 30 q. Sheep. 35 q. Goat. 40 q. Dog. VERT. 50 q. Cat. 55 q. Horse. 60 q. Ass.

164. Football.

165. A. Z. Cajupi.

1966. World Cup Football Championships (1st series).
996. 164. 5 q. orge., grey & buff 5 5
997. – 10 q. lilac, blue, ochre and buff .. 5 5
998. – 15 q. blue, yell. & buff 5 5
999. – 20 q. blue, ultramarine, orange and buff .. 8 5
1000. – 25 q. sepia, red and buff 10 5
1001. – 30 q. brn., green. & buff 12 5
1002. – 35 q. green, blue & buff 12 8
1003. – 40 q. brn., rose and buff 15 8
1004. – 50 q. red, purple, green and buff 15 8
1005. – 70 q. multicoloured .. 20 10
DESIGNS: 10 q. to 50 q. Different pictures of players with ball. Each design has a background map of a participating country. 70 q. World Cup and football.
See also Nos. 1035/42.

1966. Andon Cajupi (poet). Birth Cent.
1006. 165. 40 q. indigo and blue .. 12 5
1007. 1 l. 10 bronze and green 35 12

166. "Pyrameis cardui".

167. W.H.O. Building.

INDEX
Countries can be quickly located by referring to the index at the end of this volume.

1966. Butterflies and Dragonflies. Multicoloured.
1008. 10 q. Type 166 .. .. 8 5
1009. 20 q. "Calopteryx virgo" 10 5
1010. 30 q. "Colias hyale" .. 12 5
1011. 35 q. "Calopteryx splendens" 12 5
1012. 40 q. "Calopteryx splendens" (different) .. 12 8
1013. 50 q. "Papilio machaon" 15 8
1014. 55 q. "Colias myrmidone" 20 10
1015. 60 q. "Neptis lucilla" .. 20 10
The 20, 35 and 40 q. are dragonflies, remainder are butterflies.

1966. W.H.O. Headquarters, Geneva. Inaug.
1016. 167. 25 q. black and blue .. 5 5
1017. – 35 q. blue and orange 10 5
1018. – 60 q. red, blue & green 15 8
1019. – 80 q. blue, yell. & brn. 25 12
DESIGNS—VERT. 35 q. Ambulance and patient. 60 q. Nurse and mother weighing baby. HORIZ. 80 q. Medical equipment.

168. Leaf Star.

169. "Luna 10".

1966. "Starfish". Multicoloured.
1020. 15 q. Type 168 .. .. 8 5
1021. 25 q. Spiny Star .. 10 5
1022. 35 q. Brittle Star .. 12 5
1023. 45 q. Sea Star 12 5
1024. 50 q. Blood Star 15 8
1025. 60 q. Sea Cucumber .. 20 8
1026. 70 q. Sea Urchin .. 30 10

1966. "Luna 10". Launching.
1027. 169. 20 q. multicoloured .. 5 5
1028. – 30 q. multicoloured .. 8 5
1029. 169. 70 q. multicoloured .. 15 8
1030. – 80 q. multicoloured .. 30 10
DESIGN: 30 q., 80 q. Earth, Moon and trajectory of 'Luna 10".

170. Water-Level Map of Albania.

171. Footballers (Uruguay, 1930).

1966. Int. Hydrological Decade.
1031. 170. 20 q. black, orge. & red 5 5
1032. – 30 q. black, ochre, brown and green .. 10 5
1033. – 70 q. black and violet 20 10
1034. – 80 q. black, yellow, orange and blue .. 25 15
DESIGNS: 30 q. Water scale and fields. 70 q. Turbine and electricity pylon. 80 q. Hydrological decade emblem.

1966. World Cup Football Championships (2nd series). Inscriptions and values in black.
1035. 171. 10 q. purple and ochre 5 5
1036. – 20 q. olive and blue .. 5 5
1037. – 30 q. slate and red .. 8 5
1038. – 35 q. red and blue .. 8 5
1039. – 40 q. brown and green 10 5
1040. – 50 q. green and brown 12 8
1041. – 55 q. green and mauve 22 10
1042. – 60 q. ochre and claret 25 10
DESIGNS: (Various footballers representing World Cup winners): 20 q. Italy, 1934. 30 q. Italy, 1938. 35 q. Uruguay, 1950. 40 q. West Germany, 1954. 50 q. Brazil, 1958. 55 q. Brazil, 1962. 60 q. Football and names of 16 finalists in 1966 Championships.

172. Tortoise.

1966. Reptiles. Multicoloured.

1043. 10 q. Type **172** 5 5
1044. 15 q. Grass snake 8 5
1045. 25 q. Swamp tortoise .. 10 5
1046. 30 q. Lizard 10 5
1047. 35 q. Salamander .. 12 5
1048. 45 q. Green lizard .. 15 8
1049. 50 q. Slow-worm.. .. 20 10
1050. 90 q. Sand viper.. .. 30 12

173. Siamese Cat. **174.** P. Budi. (writer).

1966. Cats. Multicoloured.

1051. 10 q. Type **173** 5 5
1052. 15 q. Tabby 8 5
1053. 25 q. Kitten 10 5
1054. 45 q. Persian 15 5
1055. 60 q. Persian 20 8
1056. 65 q. Persian 25 10
1057. 80 q. Persian 40 12
Nos. 1053/7 are horiz.

1966. P. Budi. 400th Birth Anniv.

1058. **174.** 25 q. bronze and flesh 8 5
1059. 1 l. 75 maroon & green 40 20

175. U.N.E.S.C.O. Emblem.

1966. U.N.E.S.C.O. 20th Anniv. Multicoloured.

1060. 5 q. Type **175** 5 5
1061. 15 q. Tulip and open book 8 5
1062. 25 q. Albanian dancers.. 10 5
1063. 1 l. 55 Jug & base of column 50 20

176. Borzoi.

1966. Dogs. Multicoloured.

1064. 10 q. Type **176** 8 5
1065. 15 q. Kuvasz 10 5
1066. 25 q. Setter 12 5
1067. 45 q. Cocker Spaniel .. 15 5
1068. 60 q. Bulldog 20 8
1069. 65 q. St. Bernard .. 30 10
1070. 80 q. Dachshund .. 40 12

177. Hand holding Book. **178.** Ndre Mjeda (poet).

1966. 5th Workers Party Congress, Tirana. Multicoloured.

1071. 15 q. Type **177** .. 5 5
1072. 25 q. Emblems of agriculture and industry .. 8 5
1073. 65 q. Hammer and sickle, wheat and industrial skyline 15 8
1074. 95 q. Hands holding banner on bayonet & implements 30 10

1966. Ndre Mjeda Birth Cent.

1075. **178.** 25 q. brown and blue 8 5
1076. 1 l. 75 brown & green 50 20

179. Hammer and Sickle. **180.** Young Communists and Banner.

1966. Young Communists Union. 25th Anniv. Multicoloured.

1077. 15 q. Type **179** 5 5
1078. 25 q. Soldier leading attack 8 5
1079. 65 q. Industrial worker .. 15 8
1080. 95 q. Agricultural and industrial vista .. 30 10

1966. Young Communists Union. 25th Anniv. Multicoloured.

1081. 5 q. Manifesto (vert.) .. 5 5
1082. 10 q. Type **180** 5 5
1083. 1 l. 85 Partisans and banner (vert.) 45 20

181. Golden Eagle. **182.** Hake.

1966. Birds of Prey. Multicoloured.

1084. 10 q. Type **181** 5 5
1085. 15 q. White-tailed eagle.. 8 5
1086. 25 q. Griffon vulture .. 10 5
1087. 40 q. Sparrowhawk .. 15 5
1088. 50 q. Osprey 20 8
1089. 70 q. Egyptian vulture .. 35 10
1090. 90 q. Kestrel 55 12

1967. Fishes. Multicoloured.

1091. 10 q. Type **182** 5 5
1092. 15 q. Red Mullet 8 5
1093. 25 q. Opah 10 5
1094. 40 q. Wolf fish 12 5
1095. 65 q. Lumpsucker .. 20 8
1096. 80 q. Swordfish 30 10
1097. 1 l. 15 Father Lasher .. 50 12

183. Pelican.

1967. Pelicans. Multicoloured.

1098. 10 q. Type **183** 8 5
1099. 15 q. Three pelicans .. 8 5
1100. 25 q. Pelican and chicks at nest 12 5
1101. 50 q. Pelicans "taking off" and airborne 30 10
1102. 2 l. Pelican "yawning" .. 1·25 35

184. "Camellia williamsi". **185.** Congress Emblem.

1967. Flowers. Multicoloured.

1103. 5 q. Type **184** 5 5
1104. 10 q. "Chrysanthemum indicum" 8 5
1105. 15 q. "Althaea rosea" .. 10 5
1106. 25 q. "Abutilon striatum" 15 5
1107. 35 q. "Paeonia chinensis" 20 5
1108. 65 q. "Gladiolus gandavensis" 25 5
1109. 80 q. "Freesis hybrida" 30 10
1110. 1 l. 15 "Dianthus caryophyllus" .. .. 1·40 40

1967. 6th Trade Union Congress, Tirana.

1111. **185.** 25 q. red, sepia & lilac 10 5
1112. 1 l. 75 red, grn. & grey 45 25

186. Rose.

1967. Roses. As Type **186.**

1113. **186.** 5 q. multicoloured .. 5 5
1114. – 10 q. multicoloured.. 5 5
1115. – 15 q. multicoloured.. 10 5
1116. – 25 q. multicoloured.. 12 5
1117. – 35 q. multicoloured.. 15 5
1118. – 65 q. multicoloured.. 20 8
1119. – 80 q. multicoloured.. 30 10
1120. – 1 l. 65 multicoloured 50 15

187. Borsh Coast.

1967. Albanian Riviera. Multicoloured.

1121. 15 q. Butrinti (vert.) .. 5 5
1122. 20 q. Type **187** 8 5
1123. 25 q. Piqeras village .. 10 5
1124. 45 q. Coastal view .. 12 5
1125. 50 q. Himara coast .. 15 5
1126. 65 q. Saranda 20 8
1127. 80 q. Dhermi 30 10
1128. 1 l. Sunset at sea (vert.) .. 40 20

188. Fawn.

1967. Roe Deer. Multicoloured.

1129. 15 q. Type **188** 5 5
1130. 20 q. Head of buck (vert.) 8 5
1131. 25 q. Head of doe (vert.) 10 5
1132. 30 q. Doe and fawn .. 12 5
1133. 35 q. Doe and new-born fawn 15 5
1134. 40 q. Young buck (vert.) 20 5
1135. 65 q. Buck and doe (vert.) 25 10
1136. 70 q. Running deer .. 35 10

189. Costumes of Malesia e Madhe Region. **190.** Battle Scene and Newspaper.

1967. National Costumes. Multicoloured.

1137. 15 q. Type **189** 5 5
1138. 20 q. Zadrima 5 5
1139. 25 q. Kukesi 8 5
1140. 45 q. Dardhe 12 5
1141. 50 q. Myzeqe 12 5
1142. 65 q. Tirana 15 8
1143. 80 q. Dropulli 20 10
1144. 1 l. Laberise 25 12

1967. 25 Years of the Albanian Popular Press. Multicoloured.

1145. 25 q. Type **190** .. 8 5
1146. 75 q. Newspapers and printery.. .. .. 20 8
1147. 2 l. Workers with newspaper 50 20

191. University, Torch and Open Book. **192.** Soldiers and Flag.

1967. Tirana University. 10th Anniv.

1148. **191.** 25 q. multicoloured.. 8 5
1149. 1 l. 75 multicoloured 40 20

1967. Albanian Democratic Front. 25th Anniv. Multicoloured.

1150. 15 q. Type **192** .. 5 5
1151. 65 q. Pick, rifle and flag.. 12 8
1152. 1 l. 20 Torch and open book 30 12

193. Grey Rabbits.

1967. Rabbit-breeding. Similar designs showing rabbits.

1153. **193.** 15 q. multicoloured.. 5 5
1154. – 20 q. multicoloured.. 5 5
1155. – 25 q. multicoloured.. 10 5
1156. – 35 q. multicoloured.. 12 5
1157. – 40 q. multicoloured.. 15 5
1158. – 50 q. multicoloured.. 20 5
1159. – 65 q. multicoloured.. 30 8
1160. – 1 l. multicoloured .. 35 12
Nos. 1154 and 1158/9 are vert.

194. "The Marriage Ceremony" (detail, K. Idromeno).

1967. Albanian Paintings.

1161. **194.** 15 q. multicoloured.. 8 5
1162. – 20 q. multicoloured.. 10 5
1163. – 25 q. multicoloured.. 12 5
1164. – 45 q. multicoloured.. 15 5
1165. – 50 q. multicoloured.. 20 8
1166. – 65 q. multicoloured.. 20 8
1167. – 80 q. multicoloured.. 30 8
1168. – 1 l. multicoloured .. 35 10

DESIGNS—VERT. 20 q. "Head of the Prophet David" (detail, 16th-cent. fresco). 45 q. Ancient mosaic head (from Durres). 50 q. Detail, 16th-cent. icon. (30 × 51 mm.) 1 l. "Our Sister" (K. Idromeno). HORIZ.—(51 × 30 mm.): 25 q. "Commandos of the Hakmarrja Battalion" (S. Shijaku). 65 q. "Co-operative" (farm women, Z. Shoshi). 80 q. "Street in Korce" (V. Mio).

195. Lenin and Stalin.

1967. October Revolution. 50th Anniv. Multicoloured.

1169. 15 q. Type **195** .. 5 5
1170. 25 q. Lenin with soldiers 8 5
1171. 50 q. Lenin addressing meeting 15 8
1172. 1 l. 10 Revolutionaries 40 12
The 25 q. and 50 q. are vert.

196. Turkey. **197.** First Aid.

1967. Domestic Fowl. Multicoloured.

1173. 15 q. Type **196** .. 5 5
1174. 20 q. Goose 8 5
1175. 25 q. Hen 10 5
1176. 45 q. Cockerel 12 5
1177. 50 q. Guinea-fowl .. 15 5
1178. 65 q. Grey lag goose .. 20 8
1179. 80 q. Mallard 35 10
1180. 1 l. Chicks 40 12
Nos. 1178/80 are horiz.

1967. 6th Red Cross Congress, Tirana. Multicoloured.

1181. 15 q. + 5 q. Type **197** 15 10
1182. 25 q. + 5 q. Stretcher case 25 20
1183. 65 q. + 25 q. Heart patient 60 40
1184. 80 q. + 40 q. Nurse holding child 90 75

198. Arms of Skanderbeg.

SHQIPERIA
LOJNAT X OLIMPIKE DIMERORE
GRENOBLE 1968
15q 15q

199. Winter Olympic Emblem.

1967. Castriota Skanderbeg (patriot). 500th Death Anniv. (1st issue.) Multicoloured.
1185. 10 q. Type **198** .. 5 5
1186. 15 q. Skanderbeg .. 5 5
1187. 25 q. Helmet and sword 5 5
1188. 30 q. Kruja Castle .. 8 5
1189. 35 q. Petrela Castle .. 10 5
1190. 65 q. Berati Castle .. 15 8
1191. 80 q. Meeting of chiefs .. 20 10
1192. 90 q. Battle of Albulena 25 12
See also Nos. 1200/7.

1967. Winter Olympic Games, Grenoble. Multicoloured.
1193. 15 q. Type **199** .. 5 5
1194. 25 q. Ice-hockey .. 5 5
1195. 30 q. Figure-skating .. 8 5
1196. 50 q. Skiing (slalom) .. 15 8
1197. 80 q. Skiing (downhill) .. 20 10
1198. 1 l. Ski-jumping 30 12

200. Skanderbeg Memorial, Tirana. 201. Alpine Dianthus.

1968. Castrio Skanderbeg 500th Death Anniv. (2nd issue.) Multicoloured.
1200. 10 q. Type **200** .. 5 5
1201. 15 q. Skanderbeg portrait 5 5
1202. 25 q. Skanderbeg portrait (diff.) 5 5
1203. 30 q. Equestrian statue, Kruja 8 5
1204. 35 q. Skanderbeg and mountains 10 5
1205. 65 q. Bust of Skanderbeg 12 8
1206. 80 q. Title page of biography 15 12
1207. 90 q. "Skanderbeg battling with the Turks" (painting) 20 12
The 35 q. and 90 q. are horiz.

1968. Flowers. Multicoloured.
1208. 15 q. Type **201** .. 5 5
1209. 20 q. Chinese dianthus .. 8 5
1210. 25 q. Pink carnation .. 8 5
1211. 50 q. Red carnation & bud 10 8
1212. 80 q. Two red carnations 20 10
1213. 1 l. 10 Yellow carnations 40 12

202. Ear of Wheat and Electricity Pylon. 203. Long-horned Goat.

1968. 5th Agricultural Co-operative Congress. Multicoloured.
1214. 25 q. Type **202** 5 5
1215. 65 q. Tractor (horiz.) .. 15 8
1216. 1 l. 10 Cow 25 12

1968. Goats. Multicoloured.
1217 15 q. Zane female .. 5 5
1218. 20 q. Goatling 8 5
1219. 25 q. Long-haired Capore 10 5
1220. 30 q. Black goat at rest .. 12 5
1221. 40 q. Kids dancing .. 15 5
1222. 50 q. Red and piebald goats 20 8
1223. 80 q. Long-haired Ankara 30 10
1224. 1 l 40 Type **203**.. .. 50 15
The 15 q., 20 q. and 25 q. are vert.

SHQIPERIA 25

204. Zef Jubani (patriot). 205. Doctor using Stethoscope.

1968. Zef Jubani. 150th Birth Anniv.
1225. **204.** 25 q. chocolate & yell. 12 5
1226. 1 l. 75 ind., blk. & vio. 50 20

1968. World Health Organization. 20th Anniv.
1227 **205.** 25 q. claret & emerald 10 5
1228. – 65 q. blk , blue & yell. 20 8
1229. – 1 l. 10 brown & black 35 12
DESIGNS—HORIZ. 65 q. Hospital and microscope. VERT. 1 l. 10, Mother feeding child.

206. Servicewoman.

1968. Albanian Women's Union. 25th Anniv.
1230. **206.** 15 q. brn.-red & salmon 8 5
1231. – 25 q. bluish grn. & grn. 10 5
1232. – 60 q. brown and ochre 15 8
1233. – 1 l. bluish vio. & violet 35 12
DESIGNS: 25 q. Teacher. 60 q. Farm-girl. 1 l. Factory-worker.

207. Karl Marx. 208. Heliopsis.

1968. Karl Marx. 150th Birth Anniv. Multicoloured.
1234. 15 q. Type **207** .. 8 5
1235. 25 q. Marx addressing students 12 5
1236. 65 q. "Das Kapital", "Communist Manifesto" and marchers 30 10
1237. 95 q. Karl Marx 40 15

1968. Flowers. Multicoloured.
1238. 15 q. Type **208** .. 5 5
1239. 20 q. Red flax .. 8 5
1240. 25 q. Orchid .. 10 5
1241. 30 q. Gloxinia .. 15 5
1242. 40 q. Orange lily .. 30 8
1243. 80 q. Hippeastrum .. 40 8
1244. 1 l. 40 Purple magnolia 60 15

209. A. Frasheri and Torch. 210. "Shepherd" (A. Kushi).

1968. Prizren Defence League. 90th Anniv.
1245. **209.** 25 q. blk. & green .. 10 5
1246. – 40 q. multicoloured.. 12 8
1247. – 85 q. multicoloured.. 35 12
DESIGNS: 40 q. League headquarters. 85 q. Frasheri's manifesto and partisans.

1968. Paintings in Tirana Gallery. Multicoloured.
1248. 15 q. Type **210** .. 8 5
1249. 20 q. "Tirana" (V. Mio) (horiz.) 10 5
1250. 25 q. "Highlander" (G. Madhi) 12 5
1251. 40 q. "Refugees" (A. Buza) 15 8
1252. 80 q. "Partisans at Shahin Matrakut" (S. Zega) 25 10
1253. 1 l. 50 "Old Man" (S. Papadhimitri) .. 45 12
1254. 1 l. 70 "Shkoder Gate" (S. Rrota) 50 20

211. Soldiers and Armoured Vehicles.

1968. People's Army. 25th Anniv.
1256. **211.** 15 q. green, black, buff & cerise .. 8 5
1257. – 25 q. sepia, black, blue & yellow .. 12 5
1258. – 65 q. maroon, black, blue and ultram. .. 25 8
1259. – 95 q. orange, black, drab and green .. 40 10
DESIGNS—HORIZ. 25 q. Sailor and naval craft. 95 q. Soldier and patriots. VERT. 65 q. Pilot and aircraft.

212. Common Squid.

1968. Marine Fauna. Multicoloured.
1260. 15 q. Type **212** .. 5 5
1261. 20 q. Common Lobster .. 8 5
1262. 25 q. Whelk 10 5
1263. 50 q. Edible Crab .. 12 8
1264 70 q. Spiny Lobster .. 20 10
1265. 80 q. Common Green Crab 25 12
1266. 90 q. Norwegian Lobster (Scampi) 30 15

213. Relay-racing.

1968. Olympic Games, Mexico. Multicoloured.
1267 15 q. Type **213** .. 5 5
1268. 20 q. Running .. 5 5
1269. 25 q. Throwing the discus 5 5
1270. 30 q. Horse-jumping .. 8 5
1271. 40 q. High-jumping .. 10 5
1272. 50 q. Hurdling 12 8
1273. 80 q. Football 20 10
1274. 1 l. 40 High diving .. 35 12

214. Enver Hoxha (Party Secretary). 215. Alphabet Book.

1968. Enver Hoxha's 60th Birthday.
1276. **214.** 25 q. grey-blue .. 8 5
1277. 35 q. maroon .. 12 5
1278. 80 q. violet 20 12
1279. 1 l. 10 brown .. 45 15

1968. Monastir Language Congress. 60th Anniv.
1281. **215.** 15 q. lake and green 5 5
1282. 85 q. brown and green 40 12

216. Waxwing.

1968. Birds. Diamond-shaped designs as T **216.** Multicoloured.
1283. 15 q. Type **216** .. 8 5
1284. 20 q. Rose-coloured starling 10 5
1285. 25 q. Kingfishers .. 12 5
1286. 50 q. Long-tailed tits .. 20 8
1287. 80 q. Wall creeper .. 40 10
1288. 1 l. 10 Bearded tit .. 50 15

217. Mao Tse-tung.

1968. Mao Tse-tung's 75th Birthday.
1289. **217.** 25 q. blk., red & gold 20 12
1290. 1 l. 75 blk., red & gold 70 30

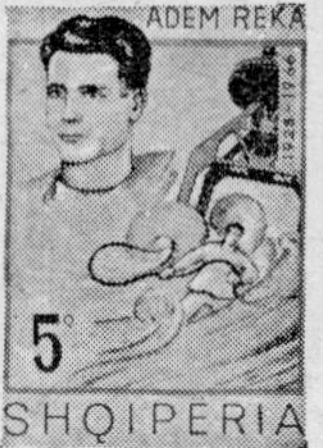

218. Adem Reka (dock foreman). 219. Meteorological Equipment.

1969. Contemporary Heroes. Multicoloured.
1291. 5 q. Type **218** 5 5
1292. 10 q. Pjeter Lleshi (telegraph linesman) .. 5 5
1293. 15 q. M. Shehu and M. Kepi (fire victims) .. 5 5
1294. 25 q. Shkurte Vata (railway worker) 5 5
1295. 65 q. Agron Elezi (earthquake victim) 15 8
1296. 80 q. Ismet Bruca (school teacher) 20 12
1297. 1 l. 30 Fuat Cela (blind Co-op leader) 35 25

1969. Albanian Hydro-Meteorology. 20th Anniv. Multicoloured.
1298. 15 q. Type **219** 5 5
1299. 25 q. "Arrow" indicator 10 8
1300. 1 l. 60 Met. balloon and isobar map 60 25

220. "Student Revolutionaries" (P. Mele).

1969. Albanian Paintings since 1944. Multicoloured.
1301. 5 q. Type **220** 5 5
1302. 25 q. "Partisans 1914" (F. Haxhiu) .. 8 5
1303. 65 q. "Steel Mill" (C. Ceka) 15 8
1304. 80 q. "Reconstruction" (V. Kilica) 20 8
1305. 1 l. 10 "Harvest" (N. Jonuzi) 35 15
1306. 1 l. 15 "Seaside Terraces" (S. Kaceli) 35 15
SIZES: The 25 q., 80 q., 1 l. 10, and 1 l. 15 are 50 × 30 mm.
Nos. 1302/6 are horiz.

221. "Self-portrait". 222. Congress Building.

1969. Leonardo da Vinci. 450th Death Anniv.
1308. 221. 25 q. agate, brn. & gold 8 5
1309. – 35 q. agate, brn. & gold 12 8
1310. – 40 q. agate, brn. & gold 20 8
1311. – 1 l. multicoloured .. 30 12
1312. – 2 l. agate, brn. & gold 65 20
DESIGNS–VERT. 35 q. "Lilies". 1 l. "Portrait of Beatrice". 2 l. "Portrait of a Lady". HORIZ: 40 q. Design for "Helicopter".

1969. Permet Congress. 25th Anniv. Multicoloured.
1314. 25 q. Type 222 .. 15 8
1315. 2 l. 25 Two partisans .. 85 35

223. "Viola albanica". 224. Plum.

1969. Flowers. Viola Family. Multicoloured.
1317. 5 q. Type 223 .. .. 5 5
1318. 10 q. "Viola hortensis" 8 5
1319. 15 q. "Viola heterophylla" 10 5
1320. 20 q. "Viola hortensis" (diff.) 12 5
1321. 25 q. "Viola odorata" .. 15 8
1322. 80 q. "Viola hortensis" (diff.) 30 10
1323. 1 l. 95 "Viola hortensis" (diff.) 50 20

1969. Fruit Trees (Blossom and Fruit). Multicoloured.
1324. 10 q. Type 224 .. 5 5
1325. 15 q. Lemon 5 5
1326. 25 q. Pomegranate .. 10 5
1327. 50 q. Cherry 20 5
1328. 80 q. Apricot 25 8
1329. 1 l. 20 Apple 50 20

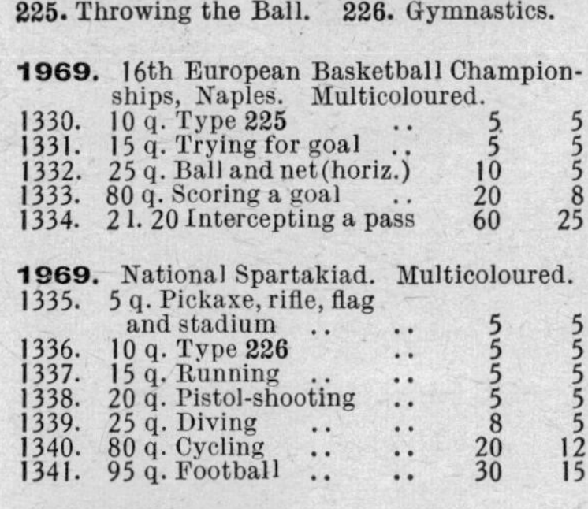

225. Throwing the Ball. 226. Gymnastics.

1969. 16th European Basketball Championships, Naples. Multicoloured.
1330. 10 q. Type 225 .. 5 5
1331. 15 q. Trying for goal .. 5 5
1332. 25 q. Ball and net (horiz.) 10 5
1333. 80 q. Scoring a goal .. 20 8
1334. 2 l. 20 Intercepting a pass 60 25

1969. National Spartakiad. Multicoloured.
1335. 5 q. Pickaxe, rifle, flag and stadium 5 5
1336. 10 q. Type 226 .. .. 5 5
1337. 15 q. Running 5 5
1338. 20 q. Pistol-shooting .. 5 5
1339. 25 q. Diving 8 5
1340. 80 q. Cycling 20 12
1341. 95 q. Football 30 15

227. Mao Tse-tung. 228. Enver Hoxha.

1969. Chinese People's Republic. 20th Anniv. Multicoloured.
1342. 25 q. Type 227 .. .. 15 5
1343. 85 q. Steel ladle and control room (horiz.) 25 8
1344. 1 l. 40 Rejoicing crowd .. 35 20

1969. 2nd. National Liberation Council Meeting, Berat. 25th Anniv. Multicoloured.
1345. 25 q. Type 228 .. .. 12 5
1346. 80 q. Star and Constitution 20 5
1347. 1 l. 45 Freedom-fighters 40 20

229. Entry of Provisional Government, Tirana.

1969. Liberation. 25th Anniv. Multicoloured.
1348. 25 q. Type 229 .. .. 8 5
1349. 30 q. Oil Refinery .. 10 5
1350. 35 q. Combine Harvester 10 5
1351. 45 q. Hydro-electric power station 12 8
1352. 55 q. Soldier & partisans 25 10
1353. 1 l. 10 People rejoicing .. 70 12

230. Stalin. 231. Head of Woman.

1969. Joseph Stalin. 90th Birth Anniv.
1354. 230. 15 q. lilac 5 5
1355. 25 q. blue 8 5
1356. 1 l. brown 25 8
1357. 1 l. 10 blue 30 12

1969. Mosaics. (1st Series.) Multicoloured.
1358. 15 q. Type 231 .. .. 5 5
1359. 25 q. Floor pattern .. 12 5
1360. 80 q. Bird and Tree .. 25 10
1361. 1 l. 10 Diamond floor pattern 40 12
1362. 1 l. 20 Corn in oval pattern 55 12
Nos. 1359/61 are horiz.
See also Nos. 1391/6, 1564/70 and 1657/62.

232. Manifesto and Congress Building. 234. "Lilium cernum".

233. "25" and Workers.

1970. Louchnia Congress. 50th Anniv.
1363. 232. 25 q. black, red & grey 8 5
1364. – 1 l. 25 blk., yell. & grn. 35 15
DESIGN: 1 l. 25, Louchnia postmark of 1920.

1970. Albanian Trade Union. 25th Anniv.
1365. 233. 25 q. black, red, brown and grey 10 5
1366. 1 l. 75 black, red, brn. and lilac 40 15

1970. Lilies. Multicoloured.
1367. 5 q. Type 234 .. .. 5 5
1368. 15 q. "Lilium candidum" 5 5
1369. 25 q. "Lilium regale" .. 12 5
1370. 80 q. "Lilium martagon" 25 10
1371. 1 l. 10 "Lilium tigrinum" 35 12
1372. 1 l. 15 "Lilium albanicum" 40 15
Nos. 1370/2 are horiz.

235. Lenin.

1970. Lenin. Birth Cent. All values black, silver and red.
1373. 5 q. Type 235 .. .. 5 5
1374. 15 q. Lenin making speech 5 5
1375. 25 q. As worker .. 8 5
1376. 95 q. As revolutionary .. 20 8
1377. 1 l. 10 Saluting 25 10
Nos. 1374/6 are all horiz.

236. Frontier Guard.

1970. Frontier Guards. 25th Anniv.
1378. 236. 25 q. multicoloured .. 10 5
1379. 1 l. 25 multicoloured 30 15

237. Jules Rimet Cup.

1970. World Cup Football Championships, Mexico. Multicoloured.
1380. 5 q. Type 237 .. .. 5 5
1381. 10 q. Aztec Stadium .. 5 5
1382. 15 q. Three footballers 5 5
1383. 25 q. Three footballers 8 5
1384. 65 q. Two footballers .. 15 8
1385. 80 q. Two footballers .. 20 8
1386. 2 l. Two footballers .. 50 20

238. New U.P.U. Headquarters Building.

1970. New U.P.U. Headquarters Building, Berne.
1388. 238. 25 q. blue, blk. & new bl. 8 5
1389. 1 l. 10 pink, blk. & orge. 25 8
1390. 1 l. 15 bl.-grn., blk. & grn. 30 12

239. Bird and Grapes.

1970. Mosaics (2nd Series). Multicoloured.
1391. 5 q. Type 239 .. .. 5 5
1392. 10 q. Waterfowl 5 5
1393. 20 q. Pheasant and tree-stump 5 5
1394. 25 q. Bird and leaves .. 8 5
1395. 65 q. Fish 12 8
1396. 2 l. 25 Peacock (vert.) .. 50 20

240. Harvesters and Dancers. 241. Partisans going into Battle.

1970. Agrarian Reform. 25th Anniv.
1397. 240. 15 q. lilac and black .. 5 5
1398. – 25 q. blue and black .. 8 5
1399. – 80 q. brown and black 20 8
1400. – 1 l. 30 brown & black 30 12
DESIGNS: 25 q. Ploughed fields and open-air conference. 80 q. Cattle and newspapers. 1 l. 30. Combine-harvester and official visit.

1970. Battle of Vlore. 50th Anniv.
1401. 241. 15 q. brn., orge. & blk. 5 5
1402. – 25 q. brn., yell. & blk. 8 5
1403. – 1 l. 60 myrtle, green and black 40 15
DESIGNS: 25 q. Victory parade. 1 l. 60, Partisans.

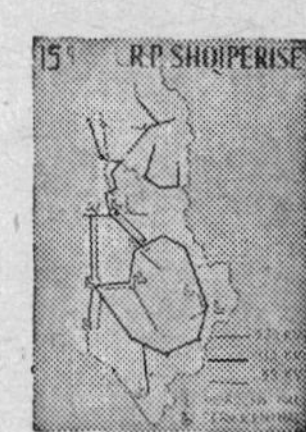

242. "The Harvesters" (I. Sulovari) 243. Electrification Map.

1970. Liberation. 25th Anniv. Prize winning Paintings. Multicoloured.
1404. 5 q. Type 242 .. .. 5 5
1405. 15 q. "Return of the Partisan" (D. Trebicka) 5 5
1406. 25 q. "The Miners" (N. Zajmi) 8 5
1407. 65 q. "Instructing the Partisans" (H. Nailbani) 15 5
1408. 95 q. "Making Plans" (V. Kilica) 25 10
1409. 2 l. "The Machinist" (Z. Shoshi) 50 20
The 15 q. and 2 l are vert.

1970. Rural Electrification Completion. Multicoloured.
1411. 15 q. Type 243 .. 5 5
1412. 25 q. Lamp and graph 8 5
1413. 80 q. Erecting power lines 20 8
1414. 1 l. 10 Uses of electricity 30 12

244. Engels. 245. Beethoven's Birthplace.

1970. Friedrich Engels. 150th Birth Anniv.
1415. 244. 25 q. blue and bistre 8 5
1416. – 1 l. 10 maroon & bistre 25 10
1417. – 1 l. 15 olive and bistre 30 12
DESIGNS: 1 l. 10, Engels as a young man. 1 l. 15, Engels making speech.

1970. Beethoven. Birth Bicent.
1418. 245. 5 q. violet and gold 5 5
1419. – 15 q. purple and silver 5 5
1420. – 25 q. green and gold 8 5
1421. – 65 q. purple and silver 20 8
1422. – 1 l. 10 blue and gold .. 35 12
1423. – 1 l. 80 black and silver 55 25
DESIGNS–VERT. Beethoven: 15 q. In silhouette. 25 q. As young man. 65 q. Full-face. 1 l. 10, Profile. HORIZ. 1 l. 80, Stage performance of "Fidelio".

246. Republican Emblem.

1971. Republic. 25th Anniv.
1424. 246. 15 q. multicoloured .. 5 5
1425. – 25 q. multicoloured .. 8 5
1426. – 80 q. blk., gold & grn. 25 8
1427. – 1 l. 30 blk., gold & grn. 30 12
DESIGNS: 25 q. Proclamation 80 q. Enver Hoxha. 1 l. 30 Patriots.

247. "Storming the Barricades".

1971. Paris Commune. Cent.
1428. – 25 q. blue & deep blue 8 5
1429. – 50 q. grn. & slate .. 12 5
1430. 247. 65 q. chest. & brn. .. 15 8
1431. – 1 l. 10 lilac & violet 25 12
DESIGNS—VERT. 25 q. "La Marseillaise". 50 q. Women Communards. HORIZ. 1 l. 10 Firing squad.

248. "Conflict of Race".

249. Tulip.

1971. Racial Equality Year.
1432. 248. 25 q. black & brown 5 5
1433. 1 l. 10 black & red .. 25 10
1434. 1 l. 15 black and red 30 15

1971. Hybrid Tulips. Designs as T 249.
1435. 249. 5 q. multicoloured .. 5 5
1436. – 10 q. multicoloured .. 5 5
1437. – 15 q. multicoloured .. 5 5
1438. – 20 q. multicoloured .. 5 5
1439. – 25 q. multicoloured .. 8 5
1440. – 80 q. multicoloured .. 20 8
1441. – 1 l. multicoloured .. 25 10
1442. – 1 l. 45 multicoloured 35 15

250. "Postrider".

251. Globe and Satellite.

1971. Albrecht Durer (painter and engraver). 500th Birth Anniv.
1443. 250. 10 q. black and green 5 5
1444. – 15 q. black and blue 5 5
1445. – 25 q. black and blue 5 5
1446. – 45 q. black and purple 10 5
1447. – 65 q. multicoloured . 20 8
1448. – 2 l. 40 multicoloured 60 20
DESIGNS.—VERT. 15 q. "Three Peasants" 25 q. "Peasant Dancers". 45 q. "The Bagpiper". HORIZ. 65 q. "View of Kalchreut". 2 l. 40 "View of Trient".

1971. Chinese Space Achievements. Multicoloured.
1450. 60 q. Type 251 .. 20 5
1451. 1 l. 05 Public Building, Tirana .. 35 12
1452. 1 l. 20 Globe and satellite 65 20
The date on No. 1451 refers to the passage of Chinese satellite over Tirana.

252. Mao Tse-tung applauding.

1971. Chinese Communist Party. 50th Anniv. Multicoloured.
1454. 25 q. Type 252 .. 8 5
1455. 1 l. 05 Party Birthplace (horiz.) 35 12
1456. 1 l. 20 Chinese celebrations (horiz.) 35 12

253. Crested Tit.

1971. Birds. Multicoloured.
1457. 5 q. Type 253 .. .. 5 5
1458. 10 q. Serin 5 5
1459. 15 q. Linnet 5 5
1460. 25 q. Goldcrest .. 8 5
1461. 45 q. Rock thrush .. 12 5
1462. 60 q. Blue tit 20 10
1463. 2 l. 40 Chaffinch .. 70 30

254. Running.

1971. Olympic Games (1972). Multicoloured.
1464. 5 q. Type 254 .. .. 5 5
1465. 10 q. Hurdling 5 5
1466. 15 q. Canoeing 5 5
1467. 25 q. Gymnastics .. 8 5
1468. 80 q. Fencing 20 10
1469. 1 l. 05 Football .. 25 12
1470. 3 l. 60 Diving 90 35

255. Workers with Banner.

1971. 6th Workers' Party Congress. Multicoloured.
1472. 25 q. Type 255 .. .. 8 5
1473. 1 l. 05 Congress hall .. 25 10
1474. 1 l. 20 "VI", flag, Congress Hall, star and rifle .. 30 15

1971. Albanian Workers' Party. 30th Anniv. Multicoloured.
1475. 15 q. Workers and industry (horiz.) 5 5
1476. 80 q. Type 255 .. .. 20 5
1477. 1 l. 55 Enver, Hoxha and flags (horiz.) 40 20

256. "Building Construction" (M. Fushekati).

1971. Albanian Paintings. Multicoloured.
1478. 5 q. "Young Man" (R. Kuci) (vert.) 5 5
1479. 15 q. Type 256 .. .. 5 5
1480. 25 q. "Partisan" (D. Jukniu) (vert.) .. 5 5
1481. 80 q. "Fighter Pilots" (S. Kristo) 20 8
1482. 1 l. 20 "Girl Messenger" (A. Sadikaj) 35 15
1483. 1 l. 55 "Medieval Warriors" (S. Kamberi) 45 15

257. Emblems and Flags.

1971. Albanian Young Communists' Union. 30th Anniv.
1485. 257. 15 q. multicoloured .. 8 5
1486. 1 l. 35 multicoloured 35 15

258. Village Girls.

1971. Albanian Ballet "Halili and Hajria". Multicoloured.
1487. 5 q. Type 258 .. .. 5 5
1488. 10 q. Parting of Halili and Hajria 5 5
1489. 15 q. Hajria before Sultan Suleiman 5 5
1490. 50 q. Hajria's marriage .. 15 8
1491. 80 q. Execution of Halili 25 12
1492. 1 l. 40 Hajria killing her husband .. 40 20

259. Rifle-shooting (Biathlon).

1972. Winter Olympic Games, Sapporo, Japan. Multicoloured.
1493. 5 q. Type 259 .. .. 5 5
1494. 10 q. Tobogganing .. 5 5
1495. 15 q. Ice-hockey 5 5
1496. 20 q. Bobsleighing .. 5 5
1497. 50 q. Speed-skating .. 12 5
1498. 1 l. Slalom skiing .. 30 12
1499. 2 l. Ski-jumping 60 25

260. Wild Strawberries.

1972. Wild Fruits. Multicoloured.
1501. 5 q. Type 260 .. .. 5 5
1502. 10 q. Blackberries .. 5 5
1503. 15 q. Hazelnuts 5 5
1504. 20 q. Walnuts 5 5
1505. 25 q. Strawberry-tree fruit 8 5
1506. 30 q. Dogwood berries 12 5
1507. 2 l. 40 Rowanberries .. 75 30

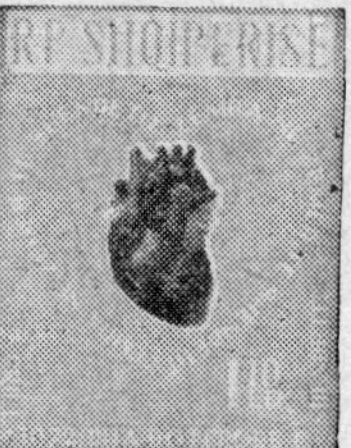
261. Human Heart.

262. Congress Delegates.

1972. World Health Day. Multicoloured.
1508. 1 l. 10 Type 261 .. .. 30 12
1509. 1 l. 20 Treatment of cardiac patient 30 12

1972. 7th Albanian Trade Unions Congress. Multicoloured.
1510. 25 q. Type 262 .. .. 8 5
1511. 2 l. 05 Congress Hall .. 55 25

263. Memorial Flame.

1972. Martyrs' Day. 30th Anniv. and Death of Kemal Stafa.
1512. 263. 15 q. multicoloured .. 5 5
1513. – 25 q. blk., orge. & grey 8 5
1514. – 1 l. 90 blk. & ochre .. 50 20
DESIGNS—VERT. 25 q. "Spirit of Defiance)" (statue). HORIZ. 1 l. 90 Kemal Stafa (martyr).

264. "Camellia japonica Kamelie".

1972. Camellias.
1515. 264. 5 q. multicoloured .. 5 5
1516. – 10 q. multicoloured .. 5 5
1517. – 15 q. multicoloured .. 5 5
1518. – 25 q. multicoloured .. 8 5
1519. – 45 q. multicoloured .. 12 5
1520. – 50 q. multicoloured .. 15 10
1521. – 2 l. 50 multicoloured 65 25
DESIGNS: 1516/21, Various Camellias as T 264.

265. High-jumping.

1972. Olympic Games, Munich. Mult.
1522. 5 q. Type 265 .. .. 5 5
1523. 10 q. Running 5 5
1524. 15 q. Putting the shot .. 5 5
1525. 20 q. Cycling 5 5
1526. 25 q. Pole-vaulting .. 8 5
1527. 50 q. Hurdling 15 8
1528. 75 q. Hockey 20 8
1529. 2 l. Swimming .. 50 25

266. Articulated bus.

1972. Modern Transport. Multicoloured.
1531. 15 q. Type 266 .. .. 5 5
1532. 25 q. Diesel railway locomotive 8 5
1533. 80 q. Freighter "Tirana" 20 8
1534. 1 l. 05 Motor-car .. 25 12
1535. 1 l. 20 Container lorry .. 30 15

267. "Trial of Strength".

1972. 1st Nat. Festival of Traditional Games. Multicoloured.
1536. 5 q. Type 267 .. .. 5 5
1537. 10 q. Pick-a-back ball game 5 5
1538. 15 q. Leaping game .. 5 5
1539. 25 q. Rope game .. 8 5
1540. 90 q. Leap-frog 25 10
1541. 2 l. Women's throwing game 60 25

268. Newspaper "Mastheads".

1972. Press Day. 30th Anniv.
1542. 268. 15 q. black and blue 5 5
1543. – 25 q. grn., red & blk. 8 5
1544. – 1 l. 90 blk. & mauve 55 25
DESIGNS: 25 q. Printing-press and partisan. 1 l. 90 Workers with newspaper.

269. Location Map and Commemorative Plaque.

1972. Peza Conf. 30th Anniv. Mult.
1545. 15 q. Type 269 .. .. 5 5
1546. 25 q. Partisans with flag .. 8 5
1547. 1 l. 90 Conference Memorial 45 20

270. "Partisans Conference" (S. Capo).

1972. Albanian Paintings. Multicoloured.
1548. 5 q. Type 270 .. .. 5 5
1549. 10 q. "Head of Woman" (I. Lulani) (vert.) .. 5 5
1550. 15 q. "Communists" (L. Shkreli) (vert.) .. 5 5
1551. 20 q. "Nendorit, 1941" (S. Shijaku) (vert.) .. 5 5

1252. 50 q. "Farm Woman" (Z. Shoshi) (vert.) .. 15 8
1553. 1 l. "Landscape" (D. Trebicka) 25 12
1554. 2 l. "Girls with Bicycles" (V. Kilica) 50 25

271. Congress Emblem. **272.** Hammer and Sickle.

1972. 6th Congress of Young Communists' Union.
1556. **271.** 25 q. gold, red & silver 8 5
1557. – 2 l. 05 multicoloured 45 20
DESIGN: 2 l. 05 Young worker and banner.

1972. Russian October Revolution. 55th Anniv. Multicoloured.
1558. **272.** 1 l. 10 multicoloured 25 10
1559. – 1 l. 20 red, blk. & pink 30 12
DESIGN: 1 l. 20 Lenin.

273. Albanian Soldiers.

1972. Independence. 60th Anniv.
1560. **273.** 15 q. blue, red & blk. 5 5
1561. – 25 q. multicoloured .. 8 8
1562. – 65 q. multicoloured .. 15 8
1563. – 1 l. 25 black and red 30 15
DESIGNS—VERT. 25 q. Ismail Qemali. 1 l. 25 Albanian double-eagle emblem. HORIZ. 65 q. "Proclamation of Independence".

274. Cockerel (mosaic).

1972. Ancient Mosaics from Apolloni and Butrint (3rd series). Multicoloured.
1564. 5 q. Type **274** 5 5
1565. 10 q. Bird (vert.) .. 5 5
1566. 15 q. Partridges (vert.) .. 5 5
1567. 25 q. Warrior's leg .. 5 5
1568. 45 q. Nude on dolphin (vert.) 12 5
1569. 50 q. Fish (vert.) .. 12 8
1570. 2 l. 50 Warrior's head .. 60 30

275. Nicolas Copernicus.

1973. Copernicus. 500th Birth Anniv. Multicoloured.
1571. 5 q. Type **275** 5 5
1572. 10 q. Copernicus and signatures .. 5 5
1573. 25 q. Engraved portrait .. 8 5
1574. 80 q. Copernicus at desk .. 20 10
1575. 1 l. 20 Copernicus and planets 30 15
1576. 1 l. 60 Planetary diagram 40 20

276. Policeman and Industrial Scene.

1973. State Security Police. 30th Anniv.
1577. **276.** 25 q. blk., bl. & light bl. 8 5
1578. – 1 l. 80 multicoloured 45 25
DESIGN: 1 l. 80 Prisoner under escort.

277/8. Cactus Flowers.

1973. Cacti. As **277/8**.
1579. **277.** 10 q. multicoloured .. 5 5
1580. **278.** 15 q. multicoloured .. 5 5
1581. – 20 q. multicoloured .. 5 5
1582. – 25 q. multicoloured .. 5 5
1583. – 30 q. multicoloured .. 8 5
1584. – 65 q. multicoloured .. 15 8
1585. – 80 q. multicoloured .. 25 12
1586. – 2 l. multicoloured .. 55 25
Nos. 1579/86 are arranged together se-tenant within the sheet and in alternate formats as Types **277/8**.

279. Common Tern.

1973. Sea Birds. Multicoloured.
1587. 5 q. Type **279** 5 5
1588. 15 q. White-winged black tern 5 5
1589. 25 q. Black-headed gull 8 5
1590. 45 q. Herring gull .. 12 8
1591. 80 q. Slender-billed tern 20 10
1592. 2 l. 40 Sandwich tern .. 65 35

280. Postmark of 1913, and Letters.

1973. First Albanian Stamps. 60th Anniv. Multicoloured.
1593. 25 q. Type **280** 8 5
1594. 1 l. 80 Postman and postmarks 45 20

281. Albanian Woman.

1973. 7th Albanian Women's Congress.
1595. **281.** 25 q. red and pink .. 8 5
1596. – 1 l. 80 black, orange & yellow 45 20
DESIGN: 1 l. 80 Albanian female workers.

282. "Creation of the General Staff" (G. Madhi).

1973. Albanian People's Army. 30th Anniv. Multicoloured.
1597. 25 q. Type **282** 8 5
1598. 40 q. "August 1949" (sculpture by Sh. Haderi) (vert.) 12 5
1599 60 q. "Generation after Generation" (Statue by H. Dule) (vert.) .. 15 8
1600. 80 q. "Defend Revolutionary Victories" (M. Fushekati) .. 20 10

283. "Electrification" (S. Hysa).

1973. Albanian Paintings. Multicoloured.
1601. 5 q. Type **283** 5 5
1602. 10 q. "Textile Worker" (E. Nallbani) (vert.) .. 5 5
1603. 15 q. "Gymnastics Class" (M. Fushekati) 5 5
1604. 50 q. "Aviator" (F. Stamo) (vert.) .. 12 5
1605. 80 q. "Downfall of Fascism" (A. Lakuriqi) 20 8
1606. 1 l. 20 "Koci Bako" (demonstrators—P. Mele) (vert.) 30 15
1607. 1 l. 30 "Peasant Girl" (Z. Shoshi) (vert.) .. 35 15

284. "Mary Magdalene". **286.** Weightlifting.

285. Goalkeeper with ball.

1973. Caravaggio. 400th Birth Anniv. Paintings. Multicoloured.
1609. 5 q. Type **284** 5 5
1610. 10 q. "The Guitar Player" (horiz.) .. 5 5
1611. 15 q. Self-portrait .. 5 5
1612. 50 q. "Boy carrying Fruit" 12 8
1613. 80 q. "Basket of Fruit" (horiz.) 20 10
1614. 1 l. 20 "Narcissus" .. 30 15
1615. 1 l. 30 "Boy peeling Apple" 35 15

1973. World Cup Football Championships, Munich (1974). Multicoloured.
1617. **285.** 5 q. multicoloured .. 5 5
1618. – 10 q. multicoloured .. 5 5
1619. – 15 q. multicoloured .. 5 5
1620. – 20 q. multicoloured .. 5 5
1621. – 25 q. multicoloured .. 8 5
1622. – 90 q. multicoloured .. 25 10
1623. – 1 l. 20 multicoloured 30 15
1624. – 1 l. 25 multicoloured 30 15
DESIGNS: Nos. 1618/24 are similar to T **285** showing goalkeepers saving goals.

1973. World Weightlifting Championships, Havana, Cuba.
1626. **286.** 5 q. multicoloured .. 5 5
1627. – 10 q. multicoloured 5 5
1628. – 25 q. multicoloured .. 5 5
1629. – 90 q. multicoloured .. 25 8
1630. – 1 l. 20 mult. (horiz.) 30 12
1631. – 1 l. 60 mult. (horiz.) 45 12
DESIGNS: Nos. 1627/31 are similar to T **286**, showing various lifts.

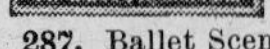

287. Ballet Scene. **288.** Mao Tse-tung.

1973. "Albanian Life and Work". Mult.
1632. 5 q. Cement Works, Kaveje 5 5
1633. 10 q. "Ali Kelmendi" Lorry factory .. 5 5
1634. 15 q. Type **287** .. 5 5
1635. 20 q. Combine-harvester 5 5
1636. 25 q. "Telecommunications" 8 5
1637. 35 q. Skier and hotel, Dajt 10 5
1638. 60 q. Llogora holiday village 15 5
1639. 80 q. Lake scene 20 10
1640. 1 l. Textile mill 30 15
1641. 1 l. 20 Furnaceman .. 35 20
1642. 2 l. 40 Welder & pipeline 80 40
1643. 3 l. Skanderbeg Statue, Tirana 90 40
1644. 5 l. Roman arches, Durres 1·60 70

1973. Mao Tse-tung. 80th Birth Anniv. Multicoloured.
1645. 85 q. Type **288** .. 40 20
1646. 1 l. 20 Mao saluting .. 50 25

289. "Male Model" (Gericault). **290.** "Lenin" (P. Mele).

1974. Jean-Louis Gericault (French painter). 150th Death Anniv.
1647. – 10 q. multicoloured .. 5 5
1648. **289.** 15 q. multicoloured .. 5 5
1649. – 20 q. black and gold .. 5 5
1650. – 25 q. blk., lav. & gold 8 5
1651. – 1 l. 20 multicoloured 30 12
1652. – 2 l. 20 multicoloured 60 25
DESIGNS—VERT. 10 q. "Horse's Head". 20 q. "Man and Dog". 25 q. "Head of a Negro". 1 l. 20 Self-portrait. HORIZ. 2 l. 20 "Battle of the Giants".

1974. Lenin. 50th Death Anniv. Mult.
1654. 25 q. Lenin with Crew of the "Aurora" (D. Trebicka) (horiz.) .. 8 5
1655. 60 q. Type **290** .. 15 8
1656. 1 l. 20 "Lenin" (seated) (V. Kilica) 30 15

291. Duck.

1974. Ancient Mosaics from Butrint, Pogradec and Apolloni (4th Series). Mult.
1657. 5 q. Duck (different) .. 5 5
1658. 10 q. Bird and flower 5 5
1659. 15 q. Ornamental basket and grapes 5 5
1660. 25 q. Type **291** .. 8 5
1661. 40 q. Donkey and cockerel 10 5
1662. 2 l. 50 Dragon .. 60 35

292. Shooting at Goal.

1974. World Cup Football Championships, West Germany.
1663. **292.** 10 q. multicoloured .. 5 5
1664. – 15 q. multicoloured .. 5 5
1665. – 20 q. multicoloured .. 5 5
1666. – 25 q. multicoloured .. 8 5
1667. – 40 q. multicoloured .. 12 8
1668. – 80 q. multicoloured .. 20 12
1669. – 1 l. multicoloured .. 30 15
1670. – 1 l. 20 multicoloured 35 20
DESIGNS: Nos. 1664/70, Players in action similar to Type **292**.

293. Memorial and Arms.

294. " Solanum dulcamara ".

1974. Permet Congress. 30th Anniv. Mult.
1672. 25 q. Type **293** 10 5
1673. 1 l. 80 Enver Hoxha and text 45 20

1974. " Useful Plants ". Multicoloured.
1674. 10 q. Type **294** 5 5
1675. 15 q. " Arbutus uva-ursi " (vert.) 5 5
1676. 20 q. " Convallaria majalis " (vert.) .. 5 5
1677. 25 q. "Colchicum autumnale " (vert.) .. 8 5
1678. 40 q. " Borago officinalis " 10 8
1679. 80 q. "Saponaria officinalis" 25 12
1680. 2 l. 20 " Gentiane lutea " 60 40

295. Revolutionaries.

1974. 1924 Revolution. 50th Anniv.
1681. **295.** 25 q. mve., blk. & red 10 5
1682. – 1 l. 80 multicoloured 45 20
DESIGN—VERT. 1 l. 80 Prominent revolutionaries.

296. Redwing.

1974. Song Birds. Multicoloured.
1683. 10 q. Type **296** 5 5
1684. 15 q. Robin 5 5
1685. 20 q. Greenfinch 5 5
1686. 25 q. Bullfinch (vert.) .. 8 5
1687. 40 q. Hawfinch (vert.) .. 10 8
1688. 80 q. Blackcap (vert.) .. 25 12
1689. 2 l. 50 Nightingale (vert.) 60 40

297. Globe and Post Office Emblem.

1974. Universal Postal Union. Cent. Multicoloured.
1690. **297.** 85 q. Multicoloured .. 25 12
1691. – 1 l. 20 green, lilac and violet 35 20
DESIGN: 1 l. 20 U.P.U. emblem.

298. "Widows" (Sali Shijaku).

1974. National Paintings. Multicoloured.
1693. 10 q. Type **298** 5 5
1694. 15 q. "Road Construction" (Danish Jukniu) .. 5 5
1695. 20 q. "Fulfilling the Plans" (Clirim Ceka) 5 5
1696. 25 q. "The Call to Action" (Spiro Kristo) 8 5
1697. 40 q. "The Winter Battle" (Sabaudin Xhaferi) .. 10 8
1698. 80 q. "Three Comrades" (Clirim Ceka) 20 10
1699. 1 l. "Step by Step, Aid the Partisans" (Guri Madhi) 30 15
1700. 1 l. 20 "At the War Memorial" (Kleo Nini) 35 20
Nos. 1694, 1696, and 1698 are vert. designs.

299. Chinese Festivities.

1974. Chinese People's Republic. 25th Anniv. Multicoloured.
1702. **299.** 85 q. multicoloured .. 35 15
1703. – 1 l. 20 blk., red & gold 50 30
DESIGN: 1 l. 20 Mao Tse-tung.

300. Volleyball. 301. Berat.

1974. National Spartakiade. Multicoloured.
1704. 10 q. Type **300** 5 5
1705. 15 q. Hurdling 5 5
1706. 20 q. Hoop exercises .. 5 5
1707. 25 q. Stadium parade .. 8 5
1708. 40 q. Weightlifting .. 10 8
1709. 80 q. Wrestling 20 10
1710. 1 l. Rifle shooting .. 30 15
1711. 1 l. 20 Football 35 20

1974. 2nd Berat Liberation Council Meeting. 30th Anniv.
1712. **301.** 25 q. red and black .. 8 5
1713. – 80 q. brn., yell. & blk. 20 10
1714. – 1 l. purple & black .. 30 15
DESIGNS—HORIZ. 80 q. "Liberation" frieze. VERT. 1 l. Council members walking to meeting.

302. Security Guards.

1974. Liberation. 30th Anniv. Multicoloured
1715. 25 q. Type **302** 8 5
1716. 35 q. Chemical industry 8 5
1717. 50 q. Agricultural produce 12 8
1718. 80 q. Cultural activities .. 20 10
1719. 1 l. Scientific technology 25 12
1720. 1 l. 20 Railway construction 35 20

303. Head of Artemis. 304. Clasped hands.

1974. Archaeological Discoveries. Mult.
1722. **303.** 10 q. blk., mau & silver 5 5
1723. – 15 q. blk., grn. & silver 5 5
1724. – 20 q. blk., buff & silver 5 5
1725. – 25 q. blk., mve. & silver 5 5
1726. – 40 q. multicoloured .. 10 8
1727. – 80 q. blk., blue & silver 20 10
1728. – 1 l. blk., grn. & silver 25 12
1729. – 1 l. 20 blk., sep. & silver 35 20
DESIGNS: 15 q. Statue of Zeus. 20 q. Statue of Poseidon. 25 q. Ulyrian helmet. 40 q. Greek amphora. 80 q. Bust of Agrippa 1 l. Bust of Remosthenes. 1 l. 20, Bust of Bilia

1945. Albanian Trade Unions. 30th Anniv. Multicoloured.
1731. 25 q. Type **304** 5 5
1732. 1 l. 80 Workers with arms raised 60 25

305. "Cichorium intybus". 306. "Head of Angel".

1975. Albanian Flowers. Multicoloured.
1733. 5 q. Type **305** 5 5
1734. 10 q. "Sempervivum montanum" 5 5
1735. 15 q. "Aquilegia alpina" 5 5
1736. 20 q. "Anemone hortensis" 5 5
1737. 25 q. "Hibiscus trionum" 5 5
1738. 30 q. "Gentiana kochiana" 8 5
1739. 35 q. "Lavatera arborea" 8 8
1740. 2 l. 70 "Iris graminea" .. 80 50

1975. Michelangelo. 500th Birth Anniv. Multicoloured.
1741. **306.** 5 q. multicoloured .. 5 5
1742. – 10 q. brn., grey & gold 5 5
1743. – 15 q. brn., grey & gold 5 5
1744. – 20 q. sepia, grey & gold 5 5
1745. – 25 q. multicoloured .. 5 5
1746. – 30 q. brn., grey & gold 8 5
1747. – 1 l. 20 brn., grey & gold 40 20
1748. – 3 l. 90 multicoloured 1·25 70
DESIGNS: 10 q. " The Slave ". 15 q. " Head of Dawn ". 20 q. " Awakening giant ". 25 q. " Cumaenian Sybil ". 30 q. " Lorenzo di Medici ". 1 l. 20 " David ". 3 l. 90 " Delphic Sybil ".

307. Horseman.

1975. " Albanian Transport of the Past ". Multicoloured.
1750. 5 q. Type **307** 5 5
1751. 10 q. Horse and cart .. 5 5
1752. 15 q. Punt 5 5
1753. 20 q. Schooner 5 5
1754. 25 q. Horse-drawn cab .. 5 5
1755. 3 l. 35 Early motor car .. 1·10 65

308. Frontier Guard.

1975. 30th Anniv. of Frontier Guards. Multicoloured.
1756. 25 q. Type **308** 5 5
1757. 1 l. 80 Guards patrolling industrial plant .. 65 35

309. Patriot affixing anti-fascist Placard.

1975. Victory over Fascism. 30th Anniv. Multicoloured.
1758. 25 q. Type **309** 5 5
1759. 60 q. Partisans in battle .. 20 10
1760. 1 l. 20 Patriot defeating Nazi soldier 35 20

310. " Anas penelope ".

1975. Albanian Wildfowl. Multicoloured.
1761. 5 q. Type **310** 5 5
1762. 10 q. " Netta rufina " .. 5 5
1763. 15 q. " Anser albifrons " 5 5
1764. 20 q. " Anas acuta " .. 5 5
1765. 25 q. " Mergus serrator " 5 5
1766. 30 q. " Pata somateria " 8 5
1767. 35 q. " Cignus cignus " .. 8 5
1768. 2 l. 70 " Spatula clypeata" 90 45

311. " Shyqyri Kanapari " (Musa Qarri).

1975. Albanian Paintings. People's Art Exhibition, Tirana. Multicoloured.
1769. 5 q. Type **311** 5 5
1770. 10 q. " Sea Rescue " (Agim Faja) 5 5
1771. 15 q. " 28 November 1912" (Petri Ceno) (horiz.) .. 5 5
1772. 20 q. " Workers' Meeting " (Sali Shijaka) 5 5
1773. 25 q. " Shota Galica " (Ismail Lulani) 5 5
1774. 30 q. " Victorious Fighters " (Nestor Jonuzi) .. 8 5
1775. 80 q. " Partisan Comrades " (Vilson Halimi) .. 25 12
1776. 2 l. 25 " Republic Day Celebration " (Fatmir Haxhiu) (horiz.) .. 80 45

312. Farmer with Declaration of Reform.

1975. Agrarian Reform. 30th Anniv. Mult
1778. 15 q. Type **312** 5 5
1779. 2 l. Agricultural scene .. 65 40

313. " Alcyonium palmatum ". 314. Cycling.

1975. Marine Corals. Multicoloured.
1780. 5 q. Type **313** 5 5
1781. 10 q. " Paramuricea chamaeleon " 5 5
1782. 20 q. " Coralium rubrum" 5 5
1783. 25 q. " Eunicella covalini " 5 5
1784. 3 l. 70 " Cladocora cespitosa " .. .. 1·25 65

1976. Olympic Games, Montreal (1976). Multicoloured.
1785. 5 q. Type **315** 5 5
1786. 10 q. Canoeing 5 5
1787. 15 q. Handball 5 5
1788. 20 q. Netball 5 5
1789. 25 q. Water-polo 5 5
1790. 30 q. Hockey 8 5
1791. 1 l. 20 Pole-vaulting .. 35 20
1792. 2 l. 05 Fencing 70 35

315. Power Lines leading to Village.

1975. Electrification of Albanian Countryside. Fifth Anniv. Multicoloured.
1794. **314.** 15 q. multicoloured .. 5 5
1795. – 25 q. vio., red-lilac & lilac 5 5
1796. – 80 q. blk., turq. & grn. 25 12
1797. – 85 q. buff, brn. & ochre 30 15
DESIGNS: 25 q. High power insulators. 80 q. Dam and power station. 85 q. T.V. plyons and emblems of agriculture and industry.

316. Berat.

1975. Air. Tourist Resorts. Mult.
1798. 20 q. Type **316** 5 5
1799. 40 q. Gjirokaster 10 5
1800. 60 q. Sarande 15 10
1801. 90 q. Durres 30 15
1802. 1 l. 20 Krujae 40 20
1803. 2 l. 40 Boga 80 40
1804. 4 l. 05 Tirana .. .. 1·40 1·75

317. Child, Rabbit and Bear planting Saplings.

1975. Children's Tales. Mult.
1805. 5 q. Type **317** 5 5
1806. 10 q. Mrs. Fox and cub .. 5 5
1807. 15 q. Ducks in school .. 5 5
1808. 20 q. Bears building .. 5 5
1809. 25 q. Animals watching television 5 5
1810. 30 q. Animals with log and electric light bulbs 5 5
1811. 35 q. Ants with spade and guitar 10 5
1812. 2 l. 70 Boy and girl with sheep and dog .. 1·00 50

318. Arms and Rejoicing Crowd.

1976. Albanian People's Republic. 30th Anniversary. Multicoloured.
1813. 25 q. Type **318** 5 5
1814. 1 c. 90 Folk-dancers .. 70 35

319. Ice-hockey.

1976. Winter Olympic Games, Innsbruck. Multicoloured.
1815. 5 q. Type **319** 5 5
1816. 10 q. Speed-skating .. 5 5
1817. 15 q. Rifle-shooting (biathlon) 5 5
1818. 50 q. Ski-jumping .. 15 5
1819. 1 l. 20 Skiing (slalom) .. 35 20
1820. 2 l. 30 Bobsleighing .. 70 40

320. "Colchicum autumnale".

1976. Medicinal Plants. Multicoloured.
1822. 5 q. Type **320** 5 5
1823. 10 q. "Atropa belladonna" 5 5
1824. 15 q. "Gentiana lutea" 5 5
1825. 20 q. "Aesculus hippocastanum" .. 5 5
1826. 70 q. "Polystichum filix" 25 12
1827. 80 q. "Althaea officinalis" 30 15
1828. 2 l. 30, "Datura stamonium" 80 40

321. Wooden Bowl and Spoon.

1976. Ethnographical Studies Conference, Tirina. Albanian Artifacts. Multicoloured.
1829. 10 q. Type **321** 5 5
1830. 15 q. Flask (vert.) .. 5 5
1831. 20 q. Ornamental handles (vert.) 5 5
1832. 25 q. Pistol and dagger .. 5 5
1833. 80 q. Hand-woven rug (vert.) 30 15
1834. 1 l. 20 Filigree buckle and earrings 35 20
1835. 1 l. 40 Jugs with handles (vert.) 40 25

322. "Founding the Co-operatives" (Zef Shoshi).

1976. Albanian Paintings. Multicoloured.
1836. 5 q. Type **322** 5 5
1837. 10 q. "Going to Work" (Agim Zajmi) (vert.) .. 5 5
1838. 25 q. "Listening to Broadcast" (Vilson Kilica) .. 5 5
1839. 40 q. "Female Welder" (Sabaudin Xhaferi) (vert.) 12 5
1840. 50 q. "Steel Workers" (Isuf Sulovari) (vert.) 15 5
1841. 1 l. 20 "1942 Revolt" (Lec Shkreli) (vert.) .. 35 20
1842. 1 l. 60 "Returning from Work" (Agron Dine) 50 25

EXPRESS LETTER STAMPS

ITALIAN OCCUPATION

E 1. King Victor Emmanuel.

1940.
E 373. **E 1.** 25 q. violet .. 30 30
E 374. 50 q. red 60 60
No. E 374 is inscr. "POSTAT EXPRES".

1943. Optd. **14 Shtator 1943.**
E 402. **E 1.** 25 q. violet .. 60 70

POSTAGE DUE STAMPS

1914. Optd. **TAKSE** through large letter **T.**
D 33. **3.** 2 q. brown and yellow 45 35
D 34. 5 q. green and yellow .. 45 35
D 35. 10 q. red 65 50
D 36. 25 q. blue 90 55
D 37. 50 q. mauve and red .. 90 50

1914. Nos. 28/31 optd. **TAKSE.**
D 46. **3.** 10 pa. on 5 q. grn. & yell. 60 45
D 47. 20 pa. on 10 q. red .. 60 45
D 48. 1 g. on 25 q. blue .. 60 45
D 49. 2 g. on 50 q. mve. & red 60 45

1919. Fiscal stamps optd. **TAXE.**
D 89. **5.** (4) q. on 4 h. pink .. 1·60 1·60
D 90. (10) q. on 10 k. red on grn. 1·60 1·60
D 91. 20 q. on 2 k. orange .. 1·60 1·60
D 92. 50 q. on 5 k. brown on yellow .. .. 1·60 1·60

D 1. Fortress of Scuta. **D 2.** **D 3.**

1920. Optd. with posthorn.
D 129. **D 1.** 4 q. olive 15 15
D 130. 10 q. red 12 15
D 131. 20 q. brown .. 20 20
D 132. 50 q. black 20 25

1922.
D 141. **D 2.** 4 q. black on red .. 20 30
D 142. 10 q. black on red .. 20 30
D 143. 20 q. black on red .. 20 30
D 144. 50 q. black on red .. 20 30

1922. Optd. **Republika Shiqiptare.**
D 186. **D 2.** 4 q. black on red .. 30 30
D 187. 10 q. black on red .. 30 30
D 188. 20 q. black on red .. 30 30
D 189. 50 q. black on red .. 30 30

1925.
D 204. **D 3.** 10 q. blue 8 8
D 205. 20 q. green .. 10 12
D 206. 30 q. brown .. 12 15
D 207. 50 q. dark brown .. 20 20

D 4. Arms of Albania. **D 5.**

1930.
D 288. **D 4.** 10 q. blue .. .. 1·40 1·40
D 299. 20 q. red 35 35
D 290. 30 q. violet 35 35
D 291. 50 q. green .. 55 55

1936. Optd. **Takse.**
D 312. **15.** 10 q. red .. .. 1·00 1·00

1940.
D 373. **D 5.** 4 q. red .. .. 3·25 3·25
D 374. 10 q. violet .. 50 50
D 375. 20 q. brown .. 55 55
D 376. 30 q. blue 75 75
D 377. 50 q. red .. .. 3·25 3·25

ALEXANDRIA O2

Issues of the French P.O. in this Egyptian port. The French Post Offices in Egypt closed on 31st March, 1931.
1899. 100 centimes = 1 franc.
1921. 1000 milliemes = £1 (Egyptian).

1899. Stamps of France optd. **ALEXANDRIE.**
1. **10.** 1 c. black on blue .. 15 15
2. 2 c. brown on yellow .. 30 30
3. 3 c. grey 25 20
4. 4 c. brown on grey .. 30 25
5. 5 c. green 50 30
7. 10 c. black on lilac .. 1·00 85
9. 15 c. blue .. .. 1·10 50
10. 20 c. red on green .. 1·75 1·10
11. 25 c. black on red .. 60 30
12. 30 c. brown .. .. 2·50 1·60
13. 40 c. red on yellow .. 2·25 1·90
15. 50 c. red .. .. 2·75 2·00
16. 1 f. olive .. .. 2·75 2·00
17. 2 f. brown on blue .. 15·00 12·00
18. 5 f. mauve on lilac .. 20·00 18·00

1902. "Blanc," "Mouchon" and "Merson" key-types, inscr. "ALEXANDRIE".
19. A. 1 c. grey 5 5
20. 2 c. claret 5 5
21. 3 c. orange 5 5
22. 4 c. brown 5 5
24. 5 c. green 8 5
25. B. 10 c. red 20 8
26. 15 c. red 10 8
28. 20 c. claret 20 12
29. 25 c. blue 5 5
30. 30 c. mauve 70 50
31. C. 40 c. red and blue .. 40 30
32. 50 c. brown & lavender 75 25
33. 1 f. red and green .. 80 30
34. 2 f. lilac and yellow .. 1·90 1·75
35. 5 f. blue and yellow .. 2·75 2·25

1915. Red Cross. Surch. **5 c.** and Red Cross.
36. B. 10 c. + 5 c. red .. 8 8

1921. Surch. thus, **15 Mill.** in one line.
37. A. 2 m. on 5 c. green .. 80 55
38. 3 m. on 3 c. orange .. 65 55
39. B. 4 m. on 10 c. red .. 45 45
40a. A. 5 m. on 1 c. grey .. 45 45
41. 5 m. on 4 c. brown .. 60 60
42. B. 6 m. on 15 c. orange 25 25
43. 8 m. on 20 c. claret .. 40 40
44. 10 m. on 25 c. blue .. 25 20
45. 12 m. on 30 c. mauve 1·60 1·60
46. A. 15 m. on 2 c. claret .. 55 55
47. C. 15 m. on 40 c. red&blue 1·60 1·60
48. 15 m. on 50 c. brown & lavender .. 65 65
49. 30 m. on 1 f. red & grn. 27·00 25·00
50. 60 m. on 2 f. lilac & yellow .. 38·00 38·00
51. 150 m. on 5 f. blue and yellow .. 50·00 50·00

1921. Surch. thus, **15 MILLIEMES** in two lines.
53. A. 1 m. on 1 c. grey .. 30 30
54. 2 m. on 5 c. green .. 20 20
55. B. 4 m. on 10 c. red .. 45 45
65. 4 m. on 10 c. green .. 25 20
56. A. 5 m. on 3 c. orange .. 65 45
57. B. 6 m. on 15 c. orange .. 20 20
58. 8 m. on 20 c. claret .. 12 12
59. 10 m. on 25 c. blue .. 8 8
60. 10 m. on 30 c. mauve 45 30
61. C. 15 m. on 50 c. brown and lavender .. 45 30
66. B. 15 m. on 50 c. blue .. 25 12
62. C. 30 m. on 1 f. red & grn. 20 20
63. 60 m. on 2 f. lilac and yellow .. £300 £300
67. 60 m. on 2 f. red & grn. 1·50 1·25
64. 150 m. on 5 f. bl. & yell. 1·00 90

1925. Surch. in milliemes with bars over old value.
68. A. 1 m. on 1 c. grey .. 10 10
69. 2 m on 5 c. orange .. 10 10
70. 2 m. on 5 c. green .. 15 15
71. B. 4 m. on 10 c. green .. 8 8
72. A. 5 m on 3 c. orange .. 10 10
73. B. 6 m. on 15 c. orange .. 10 10
74. 8 m. on 20 c. claret .. 10 10
75. 10 m. on 25 c. blue .. 5 5
76. 15 m. on 50 c. blue .. 15 12
77. C. 30 m. on 1 f. red & grn. 15 15
78. 60 m. on 2 f. red & grn. 50 40
79. 150 m. on 5 f. bl. & yell. 55 45

1927. Altered key-types, inscr. "Mm" below value.
80. A. 3 m. orange .. 25 25
81. B. 15 m. blue .. 20 15
82. 20 m. mauve 40 40
83. C. 50 m. red and green .. 1·25 1·25
84. 100 m. bl. and yellow 1·50 1·25
85. 250 m. green and red .. 2·50 2·25

1927. French "Sinking Fund" issue. Surch. + **5Mm Caisse d'Amortissement.**
86. B. 15 m. + 5 m. orange .. 30 30
87. 15 m. + 5 m. red .. 45 45
88. 15 m. + 5 m. brown .. 55 55
89. 15 m. + 5 m. lilac .. 80 80

POSTAGE DUE STAMPS

1922. Postage Due Stamps of France surch. in milliemes.

D 65. D 2. 2 m. on 5 c. brown .. 20 20
D 66. 4 m. on 10 c. brn. .. 20 20
D 67. 10 m. on 30 c. red .. 20 20
D 68. 15 m. on 50 c. pur... 20 20
D 69. 30 m. on 1 f. brn. .. 35 35

ILLUSTRATIONS British Commonwealth and all overprints and surcharges are FULL SIZE. Foreign Countries have been reduced to ¾-LINEAR.

D 1.

1928.

D 90. D 1. 1 m. grey 15 20
D 91. 2 m. blue .. 15 20
D 92. 4 m. pink .. 15 20
D 93. 5 m. olive .. 15 20
D 94. 10 m. red .. 15 20
D 95. 20 m. purple .. 20 20
D 96. 30 m. green .. 60 65
D 97. 40 m. lilac .. 45 50

This set was issued for use in both Alexandria and Port Said.

ALGERIA O1

French territory in N. Africa. Stamps of France were used in Algeria from July, 1958, until 3 July, 1962, when the country achieved independence following a referendum.

100 centimes = 1 franc.
1964. 100 centimes = 1 dinar.

1924. Stamps of France optd. **ALGERIE.**

1. 11. ½ c. on 1 c. grey .. 5 5
2. 1 c. grey .. 5 5
3. 2 c. claret .. 5 5
4. 3 c. red .. 5 5
5. 4 c. brown .. 5 5
6. 17. 5 c. orange .. 5 5
7. 11. 5 c. green .. 5 5
8. 26. 10 c. green .. 5 5
9. 17. 10 c. green .. 5 5
10. 15. 15 c. green .. 5 5
11. 26. 15 c. green .. 5 5
12. 17. 15 c. claret .. 5 5
13. 20 c. chocolate .. 5 5
14. 25 c. blue .. 5 5
15. 26. 30 c. red .. 5 5
16. 17. 30 c. blue .. 5 5
17. 30 c. red* .. 5 5
18. 35 c. violet .. 5 5
19. 13. 40 c. red and blue .. 5 5
20. 17. 40 c. olive .. 8 5
21. 13. 45 c. green and blue .. 5 5
22. 26. 45 c. red .. 5 5
23. 50 c. blue .. 5 5
24. 15. 60 c. violet .. 5 5
25. 65 c. red .. 5 5
26. 26. 75 c. blue .. 10 5
27. 15. 80 c. red .. 12 5
28. 85 c. red .. 10 5
29. 13. 1 f. red and green .. 25 5
30. 17. 1 f. 05 red .. 20 10
31. 13. 2 f. red and green .. 15 10
32. 3 f. violet and blue .. 50 15
33. 5 f. blue and yellow .. 2·50 2·00

* No. 17 was only issued pre-cancelled and the price in the unused column is for stamps with full gum.

1. Street in the Kasbah. 2. Mosque of Sidi Abderahman. 3. Grand Mosque.

4. Bay of Algiers.

1926. Surch. ½ **centime.**

71. 1. ½ c. on 1 c. olive .. 5 5

1926.

34. 1. 1 c. olive .. 5 5
35. 2 c. claret .. 5 5
36. 3 c. orange .. 5 5
37. 5 c. green .. 5 5
38. 10 c. mauve .. 5 5
39. 2. 15 c. brown .. 5 5
40. 20 c. green .. 5 5
41. 20 c. red .. 5 5
43. 25 c. green .. 5 5
45. 25 c. blue .. 5 5
46. 30 c. blue .. 8 5
47. 30 c. green .. 25 12
48. 35 c. violet .. 30 25
49. 40 c. olive .. 5 5
50. 3. 45 c. purple .. 8 5
51. 3. 50 c. blue .. 5 5
53. 50 c. red .. 5 5
54. 60 c. green .. 5 5
55. 65 c. brown .. 60 45
56. 1. 65 c. blue .. 5 5
57. 3. 75 c. red .. 12 8
58. 75 c. blue .. 80 5
59. 80 c. orange .. 10 10
60. 90 c. red .. 2·10 60
61. 4. 1 f. maroon and green .. 20 5
62. 3. 1 f. 05 brown .. 10 8
63. 1 f. 10 mauve .. 1·60 45
64. 4. 1 f. 25 blue .. 20 20
65. 1 f. 50 blue .. 55 5
66. 2 f. brown and green .. 70 5
67. 3 f. red and mauve .. 1·00 20
68. 5 f. mauve and red .. 1·75 55
69. 10 f. red and brown .. 14·00 9·00
70. 20 f. green and violet .. 50 40

1927. Wounded Soldiers of Moroccan War Charity Issue. Surch. with star and crescent and premium.

72. 1. 5 c.+5 c. green .. 10 10
73. 10 c.+10 c. mauve .. 10 10
74. 2. 15 c.+15c. brown .. 10 10
75. 20 c.+20 c. red .. 10 10
76. 25 c.+25 c. green .. 10 10
77. 30 c. +30 c. blue .. 10 10
78. 35 c.+35 c. violet .. 10 10
79. 40 c.+40 c. olive .. 10 10
80. 3. 50 c.+50 c. blue .. 10 10
81. 80 c.+80 c. orange .. 10 10
82. 4. 1 f.+1 f. maroon & green 10 10
83. 2 f. + 2 f. brown & green 4·00 4·00
84. 5 f.+5 f. mauve and red 4·00 4·00

1927. Surch. in figures.

85. 2. 10 on 35 c. violet .. 5 5
86. 25 c. on 30 c. blue .. 5 5
87. 30 on 25 c. green .. 5 5
88. 3. 65 on 60 c. green .. 30 20
89. 90 on 80 c. orange .. 10 8
90. 1 f. 10 on 1 f. 05 brown .. 10 5
91. 4. 1 f. 50 on 1 f. 25 blue .. 60 25

1927. Surch. **5 c.**

92. 11. 5 c. on 4 c. brown (No. 5) 5 5

5. Railway Terminus, Oran.

1930. Cent. of French Occupation.

93. 5. 5 c. orange .. 1·50 1·50
94. – 10 c. olive .. 1·50 1·50
95. – 15 c. brown .. 1·50 1·50
96. – 25 c. grey .. 1·50 1·50
97. – 30 c. red .. 1·50 1·50
98. – 40 c. green .. 1·50 1·50
99. – 50 c. blue .. 1·50 1·50
100. – 75 c. purple .. 1·50 1·50
101. – 1 f. orange .. 1·50 1·50
102. – 1 f. 50 blue .. 1·50 1·50
103. – 2 f. red .. 1·50 1·50
104. – 3 f. green .. 1·50 1·50
105. – 5 f. red and green .. 2·40 2·40

DESIGNS—HORIZ. 10 c. Constantine. 15 c. Admiralty, Algiers. 25 c. Algiers. 30 c. Ruins of Timgad. 40 c. Ruins of Djemila. VERT. 50 c. Ruins of Djemila. 75 c. Tlemcen. 1 f. Ghardaia. 1 f. 50, Tolga. 2 f. Touaregs. 3 f. Native Quarter, Algiers. 5 f. Mosque, Algiers.

7. Bay of Algiers.

1930. N. African Int. Philatelic Exn.

106. 7. 10 f. brown .. .. 4·00 4·00

10. Admiralty and Penon Lighthouse, Algiers.

DESIGNS—HORIZ. A. In the Sahara. B. Arc de Triomphe, Lambese. C. Ghardaia, Mzab. D. Marabouts, Touggourt. E. El Kebir Mosque Algiers. VERT. F. Colomb Bechar-Oued. G. Cemetery, Tlemcen.

1936.

107. A. 1 c. blue .. 5 5
108. F. 2 c. purple .. 5 5
109. B. 3 c. green .. 5 5
110. C. 5 c. mauve .. 5 5
111. 10. 10 c. green .. 5 5
112. D. 15 c. red .. 5 5
113. G. 20 c. green .. 5 5
114. E. 25 c. purple .. 15 5
115. C. 30 c. green .. 10 5
116. D. 40 c. maroon .. 5 5
117. G. 45 c. blue .. 20 15
118. 10. 50 c. red .. 20 5
119. A. 65 c. brown .. 75 70
120. 65 c. red .. 8 5
121. 70 c. brown .. 5 5
122. F. 75 c. slate .. 5 5
124. B. 90 c. red .. 5 5
125. E. 1 f. brown .. 5 5
126. 10. 1 f. 25 violet .. 15 8
127. 1 f. 25 red .. 5 5
128. F. 1 f. 50 blue .. 35 10
129. 1 f. 50 red .. 12 5
130. C. 1 f. 75 orange .. 5 5
131. B. 2 f. maroon .. 5 5
132. A. 2 f. 25 green .. 2·25 1·60
133. E. 2 f. 25 blue .. 5 5
134. C. 2 f. 50 blue .. 8 8
135. G. 3 f. mauve .. 5 5
136. E. 3 f. 50 blue .. 50 50
137. 10. 5 f. slate .. 5 5
138. F. 10 f. orange .. 5 5
139. D. 20 f. blue .. 20 20

11. Exhibition. Pavilion. 12. Constantine in 1837.

1937. Paris Int. Exn.

140. 11. 40 c. green .. 20 12
141. 50 c. red .. 5 5
142. 1 f. 50 blue .. 25 12
143. 1 f. 75 black .. 35 25

1937. Capture of Constantine. Cent.

144. 12. 65 c. red .. 15 5
145. 1 f. brown .. 1·25 15
146. 1 f. 75 blue .. 5 5
147. 2 f. 15 purple .. 5 5

13. Ruins of Roman Villa.

1938. Philippeville Cent.

148. 13. 30 c. green .. 20 15
149. 65 c. blue .. 5 5
150. 75 c. purple .. 20 20
151. 3 f. red .. 85 85
152. 5 f. brown .. 1·10 70

1938. Armistice Day. 20th Anniv. Surch. **1918–11 Nov.–1938** and value.

153. 65 c.+35 c. on 2 f. 25 green (No. 132) .. 15 15

1938. Surch. **0.25** between bars.

154. 10. 25 c. on 50 c. red .. 5 5

14. Caillie, Lavigerie and Duveyrier.

1939. Sahara Pioneers' Monument Fund.

155. 14. 30 c.+20 c. green .. 30 30
156. 90 c.+60 c. red .. 30 30
157. 2 f.+75 c. blue .. 2·50 2·50
158. 5 f.+5 f. black .. 5·50 5·50

15. Vessel in Algiers Harbour.

1939. New York World's Fair.

159. 15. 20 c. green .. 25 20
160. 40 c. purple .. 25 20
161. 90 c. brown .. 8 5
162. 1 f. 25 red .. 1·00 35
163. 2 f. 25 blue .. 25 25

1939. Surch. with new values and bars or cross.

173. 1. 50 c. on 65 c. blue .. 8 5
173c. B. 90 c.+60 c. red (No. 124) 5 5
164. 1. 1 f. on 90 c. red .. 5 5

16. Algerian Soldiers. 17. Algiers.

1940. Soldiers' Dependants' Relief Fund. Surch. + and premium.

166. 16. 1 f.+1 f. blue .. 20 20
167. 1 f.+2 f. red .. 20 20
168. 1 f.+4 f. green .. 20 20
169. 1 f.+9 f. brown .. 25 25

1941.

170. 17. 30 c. blue .. 5 5
171. 70 c. grey .. 5 5
172. 1 f. red .. 5 5

1941. Marshal Petain. As T 139 of France but inscr. "ALGERIE".

174. 1 f. blue .. 5 5

1941. National Relief Fund. As No. 154, but surch. +4 f. and colour changed.

175. 1 f.+4 f. black .. 5 5

1942. National Relief Fund. Surch. **SECOURS NATIONAL + 4 f.**

176. 1 f.+4 f. blue (No. 174) 5 5

1942. Various altered types.

(a) As T 17. but without "RF".

177. 17. 30 c. blue .. 5 5

(b) As T 3. but without "REPUBLIQUE FRANCAISE".

178. 3. 40 c. grey .. 5 5
179. 50 c. red .. 5 5

(c) As No. 129 but without "RF".

180. F. 1 f. 50 red .. 5 5

18. Arms of Oran. 19. Allegory of Victory. 20.

1942. Coats of arms.

190. A. 10 c. lilac .. 5 5
191. 18. 30 c. green .. 5 5
181. B. 40 c. purple .. 5 5
192. 40 c. lilac .. 5 5
182. 18. 60 c. red .. 5 5
194. B. 70 c. blue .. 5 5
195. A. 80 c. green .. 5 5
183. B. 1 f. 20 green .. 5 5
184. A. 1 f. 50 red .. 5 5
185. 18. 2 f. blue .. 5 5
186. B. 2 f. 40 red .. 5 5
187. A. 3 f. blue .. 5 5
188. B. 4 f. blue .. 5 5
201. 18. 4 f. 50 brown .. 5 5
189. 5 f. green .. 5 5

ARMS: A. Algiers. B. Constantine.

1943. As T 153 of France (Petain), but inscr. "POSTES ALGERIE"

202. 1 f. 50 red .. 5 5

1943.

203. 19. 1 f. 50 red .. 5 5
204. 20. 1 f. 50 blue .. 5 5

1943. Surch.

205. 18. 2 f. on 5 f. orange .. 5 5

21. Summer Palace. 22. Mother and Children.

1943.

206. 21. 15 f. grey .. 35 35
207. 20 f. green .. 20 12
208. 50 f. red .. 20 15
209. 100 f. blue .. 55 45
210. 200 f. brown .. 90 45

1943. Prisoners of War Relief Fund.

211. 22. 50 c.+4 f. 50 pink .. 15 15
212. 1 f. 50+8 f. 50 green .. 15 15
213. 3 f.+12 f. blue .. 15 15
214. 5 f.+15 f. brown .. 15 15

1944. As T 189 ("Marianne") of France, but inscr. "POSTES ALGERIE".

215. 10 c. grey .. 5 5
216. 30 c. lilac .. 5 5
217. 50 c. red .. 5 5
218. 80 c. green .. 5 5
219. 1 f. 20 lilac .. 5 5
220. 1 f. 50 blue .. 5 5
221. 2 f. 40 red .. 5 5
222. 3 f. violet .. 5 5
223. 4 f. 50 black .. 5 5

1944. As T 188 (Gallic cock) of France, but inscr. "POSTES ALGERIE".

224. 40 c. red .. 5 5
225. 1 f. green .. 5 5
226. 2 f. red .. 5 5
227. 2 f. brown .. 5 5
228. 4 f. blue .. 5 5
229. 10 f. black .. 15 8

1944. Surch. **O f. 30.**

230. 2. O f. 30 on 15 c. brown .. 5 5

No. 230 was only issued pre-cancelled and the price in the unused column is for stamp with full gum.

1945. Types of France optd. **ALGERIE.**

247. 217. 10 c. black and blue .. 5 5
231. 197. 40 c. magenta .. 5 5
232. 50 c. blue .. 5 5
248. – 50 c. brown, yellow and red (No. 973) .. 8 5

233. 198. 60 c. blue 5 5
236. 121. 80 c. green 5 5
237. 1 f. blue 5 5
234. 198. 1 f. red 5 5
238. 121. 1 f. 20 violet 5 5
235. 198. 1 f. 50 lilac 5 5
239. 121. 2 f. brown 5 5
242. 199. 2 f. green 5 5
240. 121. 2 f. 40 red 5 5
241. 3 f. orange 5 5
243. 199. 3 f. red 5 5
244. 4 f. 50 blue 15 5
245. 5 f. green 5 5
246. 10 f. blue 12 10

1945. Airmen and Dependants Fund. Type of France (aeroplanes), optd. **RF ALGERIE.**
249. 150. 1 f. 50 c. + 3 f. 50 c. bl. 5 5

1945. Postal Employees War Victims' Fund. Type of France overprinted **ALGERIE.**
250. 203. 4 f. + 6 f. brown 5 5

1945. Stamp Day. Type of France (Louis XI), overprinted **ALGERIE.**
251. 208. 2 f. + 3 f. brown 5 5

1946. Arms type surcharged **0 f. 50 RF.**
252. – 50 c. on 1 f. 50 c. red (No. 184) 5 5

1946. Type of France overprinted **ALGERIE** and surcharged **2 F.**
253. 121. 2 f. on 1 f. 50 c. brown 5 5

24. Aeroplane over Algiers.

1946. Air.
254. 24. 5 f. red 5 5
255. 10 f. blue 5 5
256. 15 f. green 10 5
257a. 20 f. brown 8 5
258. 25 f. violet 10 5
259. 40 f. black 15 5

1946. Stamp Day. Type of France (de la Varane), optd. **ALGERIE.**
260. 218. 3 f. + 2 f. red 15 15

25. Children at a Spring. 26. Arms of Constantine.

1946. Charity. Inscr. as in T 25.
261. 25. 3 f. + 17 f. green 35 35
262. – 4 f. + 21 f. red 35 35
263. – 8 f. + 27 f. purple 95 95
264. – 10 f. + 35 f. blue 35 35
DESIGNS—VERT. 4 f. Boy gazing skywards. 8 f. Laurel-crowned head. HORIZ. 10 f. Soldier looking at Algerian coast.

1947. Air Surch.—10%.
265. 24. "—10%" on 5 f. red 5 5

1947. Stamp Day. Type of France (Louvois), optd. **ALGERIE.**
266. 227. 4 ft. 50 + 5 f. 50 blue 12 12

1947. Various Arms.
267. 26. 10 c. green and red 5 5
268. A. 50 c. black and orange 5 5
269. B. 1 f. blue and yellow 5 5
364. C. 1 f. green and red 5 5
270. 26. 1 f. 30 black and blue 15 15
271. A. 1 f. 50 violet and yellow 5 5
272. B. 2 f. black and green 5 5
273. 26. 2 f. 50 black and red 10 8
274. A. 3 f. red and green 5 5
365. D. 3 f. blue and green 15 8
275. B. 3 f. 50 green and purple 5 5
276. 26. 4 f. brown and green 5 5
277. A. 4 f. 50 blue and red 5 5
278. 5 f. black and blue 5 5
366. E. 5 f. blue and yellow 5 5
279. B. 6 f. brown and red 5 5
367. A. 6 f. green and orange 15 10
280. B. 8 f. brown and blue 5 5
281. 26. 10 f. red and sepia 15 5
368. F. 12 gf. blue and red 15 15
282. A. 15 f. black and red 15 5
ARMS: A. Algiers. B. Oran. C. Bone. D. Mostagnem. E. Tlemcen. F. Orleansville.

1947. Air. 7th Anniv. of Gen. de Gaulle's Call to Arms. Surch with Lorraine Cross and **18 Juin 1940 + 10 Fr.**
283. 24. 10 f. + 10 f. blue 20 20

1947. Resistance Movement Type of France surch. **ALGERIE + 10 Fr.**
284. 235. 5 f. + 10 f. grey 12 12

1948. Stamp Day. Type of France (Arago) optd. **ALGERIE.**
285. 238. 6 f. + 4 f. green 20 20

1948. Air. 8th Anniv. of Gen. de Gaulle's Call to Arms. Surch. with Lorraine Cross and **18 JUIN 1940 + 10 Fr.**
286. 24. 5 f. + 10 f. red 20 20

1948. General Leclerc Memorial. T 241 of France surch. **ALGERIE + 4 Fr.**
287. 6 f. + 4 f. red 12 12

27. Battleship "Richelieu". 28. Storks over Minaret.

29a. Statue of Duke of Orleans. 29. French Colonials.

1949. Naval Welfare Fund.
288. 27. 10 f. + 15 f. blue 1·25 1·25
289. – 18 f. + 22 f. red 1·25 1·25
DESIGN: 18 f. Aircraft-carrier "Arromanches".

1949. Air.
290. 28. 50 f. green 90 5
291. – 100 f. brown 40 8
292. 28. 200 f. red 1·60 1·10
293. – 500 f. blue 5·00 3·50
DESIGN—HORIZ. 100 f., 500 f. Aeroplane over valley dwellings.

1949. Stamp Day. Type of France (Choiseul), optd. **ALGERIE.**
294. 248. 15 f. + 5 f. mauve 30 30

1949. 75th Anniv. of U.P.U.
295. 29. 5 f. green 30 30
296. 15 f. red 40 40
297. 25 f. blue 1·00 65

1949. Air. First Algerian Postage Stamp. 25th Anniv.
298. 29a. 15 f. + 20 f. brown 1·10 1·10

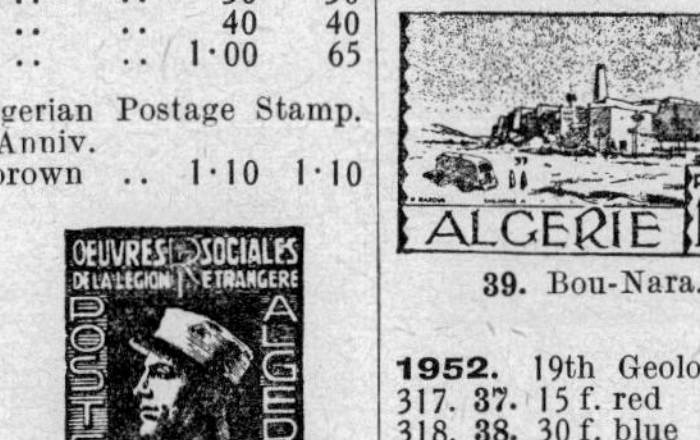

30. Grapes.

31. Legionary.

1950.
299. 30. 20 f. purple and green 30 8
300. – 25 f. orange and brown 40 12
301. – 40 f. brown and green 60 20
DESIGNS: 25 f. Dates. 40 f. Oranges and lemons.

1950. Stamp Day. Type of France (Postman), optd. **ALGERIE.**
302. 261. 12 f. + 3 f. brown 35 35

1950. Foreign Legion Welfare Fund.
303. 31. 15 f. + 5 f. green 35 35

32. R. P. de Foucauld and Gen. Laperrine.

1950. French in the Sahara. 50th Anniv. (25 f.) and Unveiling of Monument to Abd-el-Kader (40 f.).
304. 32. 25 f. + 5 f. blk. and olive 1·00 1·00
305. – 40 f. + 10 f. blk. and brn. 1·00 1·00
DESIGN: 40 f. Emir Abd-el-Kader and Marshal Bugeaud.

33. Col. C. d'Ornano.

1951. Col. d'Ornano Monument Fund.
306. 33. 15 f. + 5 f. purple, brown and black 20 20

1951. Stamp Day. Type of France (Sorting Van), optd. **ALGERIE.**
307. 268. 12 f. + 3 f. brown 25 25

34. Apollo of Cherchel. 35. Algerian War Memorial. 36. Military Medal.

1952.
308. 34. 10 f. sepia 8 5
309. – 12 f. brown 10 5
310. – 15 f. blue 8 5
311. – 18 f. red 12 8
312. – 20 f. green 10 5
313. 34. 30 f. blue 25 10
STATUES: 12 f., 18 f. Isis of Cherchel. 15 f., 20 f. Boy and eagle.

1952. Stamp Day. Type of France (Mail Coach), optd. **ALGERIE.**
314. 286. 12 f. + 3 f. blue 50 50

1952. African Army Commem.
315. 35. 12 f. green 15 10

1952. Military Medal Cent.
316. 36. 15 f. + 5 f. brown, yellow and green 45 45

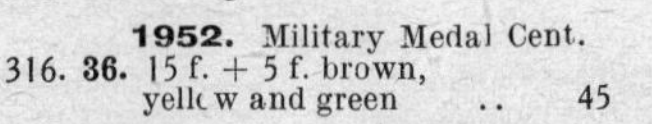

37. Fossil.

38. Phonolite Dyke, Hoggar.

39. Bou-Nara. 40. Members of Corps and Camel.

1952. 19th Geological Convention, Algiers.
317. 37. 15 f. red 15 8
318. 38. 30 f. blue 20 10

1952. Battle of Bir-Hakeim. 10th Anniv. Type of France surch. **ALGERIE + 5 F.**
319. 290. 30 f. + 5 f. blue 40 40

1952. Red Cross Fund.
320. – 8 f. + 2 f. red and blue 45 45
321. 39. 12 f. + 3 f. red 60 60
DESIGN: 8 f. El-Oued and map.

1952. Sahara Corps. 50th Anniv.
322. 40. 12 f. brown 20 15

1953. Stamp Day. Type of France (Count D'Argenson), optd. **ALGERIE.**
323. 297. 12 f. + 3 f. violet 20 20

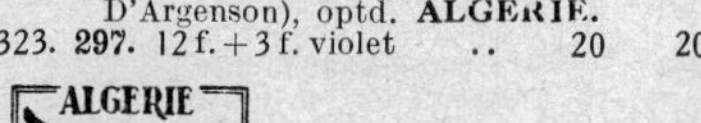

41. "Victory" of Cirta.

42. E. Millon.

1954. Army Welfare Fund.
324. 41. 15 f. + 5 f. brn. & sepia 20 20

1954. Military Health Service.
325. 42. 25 f. sepia and green 40 5
326. – 40 f. lake and chestnut 50 12
327. – 50 f. indigo and blue 50 5
DOCTORS—VERT. 40 f. F. Maillot. HORIZ. 50 f. A. Laveran.

1954. Stamp Day. Type of France (Lavalette), optd. **ALGERIE.**
328. 308. 12 f. + 3 f. red 20 20

43. French and Algerian Soldiers.

44. Foreign Legionary.

1954. Old Soldiers' Welfare Fund.
329. 43. 15 f. + 5 f. sepia 12 10

1954. Foreign Legion Welfare Fund.
330. 44. 15 f. + 5 f. green 25 25

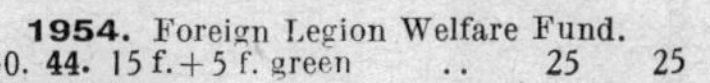

45.

46. Darguinah Hydro-electric Station.

47. Court-yard.

1954. 3rd Mediterranean Citrus Fruit Congress.
331. 45. 15 f. blue and indigo 15 15

1954. Liberation. 10th Anniv. Type of France ("D-Day"), optd. **ALGERIE.**
332. 310. 15 f. red 12 12

1954. Inaug. of River Agrioun Hydro-electric installations.
333. 46. 15 f. purple 15 12

1954.
334. 47. 10 f. brown 5 5
335. 12 f. orange & brn. (I) 8 5
336. 12 f. orge. & brn. (II) 5 5
337. 15 f. blue 8 5
338. 18 f. red 15 5
339. 20 f. green 10 8
340. 25 f. purple 12 5
12 f. "POSTES" and "ALGERIE" in orange (I), or in white (II).

1954. Presentation of First Legion of Honour. 15th Anniv. Type of France optd. **ALGERIE.**
341. 318. 12 f. green 20 15

48. Red Cross Nurses.

49. St. Augustine.

1954. Red Cross Fund. Cross in red.
342. 48. 12 f. + 3 f. indigo 50 50
343. 15 f. + 5 f. violet 50 50
DESIGN: 15 f. J.H. Dunant and Djemila ruins.

1954. St. Augustine. 1600th Birth Anniv.
344. 49. 15 f. chocolate 15 15

50. Earthquake Victims.

51. Statue of Aesculapius and El Kettar Hospital.

1954. Orleansville Earthquake Relief Fund. Inscr. as in T 50.
345. 50. 12 f. + 4 f. chocolate 55 55
346. 15 f. + 5 f. blue 55 55
347. 18 f. + 6 f. magenta 55 55
348. 20 f. + 7 f. violet 55 55
349. 25 f. + 8 f. lake 55 55
350. 30 f. + 10 f. turquoise 55 55
DESIGNS—HORIZ. 18 f., 20 f. Red Cross workers. 25 f., 30 f. Stretcher-bearers.

1955. Stamp Day. Type of France (Balloon Post), optd. **ALGERIE.**
351. 325. 12 f. + 3 f. blue 12 12

1955. 30th French Medical Congress.
352. 51. 15 f. red 12 10

52. Ruins of Tipasa.

53. Widows and Children.

55.

54. Grand Kabylie.

1955. Bimillenary of Tipasa.
353. **52.** 50 f. lake 20 5

1955. Rotary Int. 50th Anniv. Type of France, optd. **ALGERIE.**
354. **322.** 30 f. blue 20 15

1955. Type of France ("France") inscr. "ALGERIE".
355. **323.** 15 f. red 8 5
356. 20 f. blue 8 5

1955. War Victims Welfare Fund.
357. **53.** 15 f.+5 f. indigo & blue 15 15

1955.
369. – 30 f. purple (postage) 12 5
370. – 35 f. red 30 15
358. **54.** 100 f. indigo and blue.. 65 5
376. – 200 f. red (air) .. 1·75 30
DESIGNS: 30 f., 35 f. Oran. 200 f. Beni Bahde Barrage, Tlemcen.

1956. Anti-Cancer Fund.
359. **55.** 15 f.+5 f. brown .. 15 15

1956. Stamp Day. Type of France ("Francis of Taxis"), optd. **ALGERIE.**
360. **342.** 12 f.+3 f. red .. 15 15

56. Foreign Legion Retirement Home, Sidi Bel Abbes.

1956. Foreign Legion Welfare Fund.
361. **56.** 15 f.+5 f. green .. 20 15

57. Marshal Franchet d'Esperey (after J. Ebstein).

1956. Marshal Franchet d'Esperey. Birth Cent.
362. **57.** 15 f. indigo and blue .. 12 12

58. Marshal Leclerc and Memorial.

1956. Marshal Leclerc Commem.
363. **58.** 15 f. chestnut and sepia 12 12

1957. Stamp Day. Type of France. ("Felucca") optd. **ALGERIE.**
371. **360.** 12 f.+3 f. purple .. 25 25

59. Electric Train Crossing Viaduct.

1957. Electrification of Bone-Tebessa Railway Line.
372. **59.** 40 f. turquoise & green 15 5

60. Fennec.

61. "Horseman Crossing Ford" (after Delacroix).

1957. Red Cross Fund. Cross in red.
373. **60.** 12 f.+3 f. red-brown .. 1·00 1·00
374. – 15 f.+5 f. sepia (Storks) 1·00 1·00

1957. 17th Anniv. of Gen. de Gaulle's Call to Arms. Surch. **18 JUIN 1940+5 F.**
375. **58.** 15 f.+5 f. carmine & red 25 20

1957. Army Welfare Fund. Inscr. "Oeuvres Sociales De L'Armee".
377. **61.** 15 f.+5 f. red .. .. 1·00 1·00
378. – 20 f.+5 f. green .. 1·00 1·00
379. – 35 f.+10 f. blue .. 1·00 1·00
DESIGNS—HORIZ. 20 f. "Lakeside View" (after Fromentin). VERT. 35 f. "Arab Dancer" (after Chasseriau).

1958. Stamp Day. Type of France (rural service), optd. **ALGERIE.**
380. **376.** 15 f.+5 f. chestnut .. 15 15

1958. Arms. As T 26 but inscr. "REPUBLIQUE FRANCAISE" instead "RF" at foot.
381. 2 f. red and blue 15 12
382. 6 f. green and red.. .. 2·75 2·25
383. 10 f. maroon and green .. 20 15
ARMS: 2 f. Tizi-Ouzon. 6 f. Algiers. 10 f. Setif.

62. "Strelitzia Reginae".

63.

1958. Algerian Child Welfare Fund.
384. **62.** 20 f. + 5 f. orange, violet and green 70 70

1958. Marshal de Lattre Foundation.
385. **63.** 20 f.+5 f. red, grn. & bl. 35 35

INDEPENDENT STATE

1962. Stamps of France optd. **EA** (with serifs) and with bars obliterating "REPUBLIQUE FRANCAISE".
391. **306.** 10 c. green 12 8
392. **417.** 25 c. grey and claret .. 10 5
393. – 45 c. violet, purple and sepia (No. 1463) .. 1·10 95
394. – 50 c. maroon and bronze-green (No. 1464) .. 1·10 95
395. – 1 f. brown, blue and myrtle (No. 1549).. 65 40
The above also exist with similar overprints applied with handstamps.

1962. As pictorial types of France but inscr. "REPUBLIQUE ALGERIENNE".
396. – 5 c. blue-grn., grn. & brn. 5 5
397. **393.** 10 c. blue and sepia .. 5 5
398. – 25 c. red and grey-green 20 5
399. – 95 c. blue, buff & sepia 55 15
400. – 1 f. sepia and green .. 70 40
DESIGNS—VERT. 5 c. Kerrata Gorges. 25 c. Tlemcen Mosque. 95 c. Oil derrick and pipe-line at Hassi-Massaoud, Sahara. HORIZ. 1 f. Medea.

64. Flag, Rifle and Olive Branch.

65. Campaign Emblem and Globe.

1963. "Return of Peace". Flag in green and red. Inscription and background colours given.
401. **64.** 5 c. bistre 5 5
402. 10 c. blue 5 5
403. 25 c. red 45 5
404. 95 c. violet 30 25
405. – 1 f. green 25 8
406. – 2 f. brown 65 20
407. – 5 f. purple .. .. 1·25 50
408. – 10 f. black .. .. 3·75 3·00
DESIGN: 1 f. to 10 f. As T 64 but with dove and broken chain added.

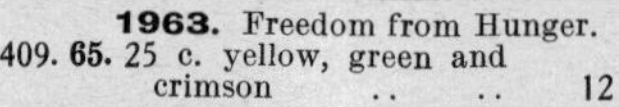

1963. Freedom from Hunger.
409. **65.** 25 c. yellow, green and crimson 12 5

66. Clasped Hands.

67. Map and Emblems.

1963. National Solidarity Fund.
410. **66.** 50 c.+20 c. red, green and black 30 25

1963. Independence. 1st Anniv.
411. **67.** 25 c. red, sepia, green and blue 15 10

68. "Arab Physicians" (13-cent. MS.).

69. Branch of Orange-tree.

1963. 2nd Arab Physicians Union Congress.
412. **68.** 25 c. brown, grn. & bistre 25 10

1963.
413. **69.** 8 c. orange and bronze* 5 5
414. 20 c. orange & grey-grn.* 8 8
415. 40 c. orange and turq.* 12 12
416. 55 c. orange and green* 20 15
* These stamps were only issued precancelled, the unused prices being for stamps with full gum.

70. "Constitution".

71. "Freedom Fighters".

1963. Promulgation of Constitution.
417. **70.** 25 c. red, green & sepia 12 8

1963. 9th Anniv. of Revolution.
418. **71.** 25 c. red, green & choc. 15 8

72. Centenary Emblem.

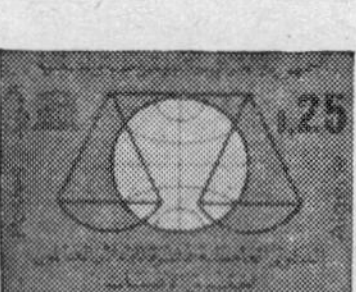
73. Globe and Scales of Justice.

1963. Red Cross Centenary.
419. **72.** 25 c. blue, crimson and yellow 15 8

1963. Declaration of Human Rights. 15th Anniv.
420. **73.** 25 c. black and blue .. 15 5

74. Labourers.

75. Map of Africa and Flags.

1964. Labour Day.
421. **74.** 50 c. blue, orange, maroon and red .. 25 10

1964. Africa Day, and African Unity Charter. 1st Anniv.
422. **75.** 45 c. red, orange & blue 25 10

76. Tractors.

77. Rameses II in War Chariot, Abu Simbel.

1964.
423. **76.** 5 c. purple 5 5
424. – 10 c. brown 5 5
425. – 12 c. green 5 5
426. – 15 c. ultramarine .. 5 5
427. – 20 c. yellow 8 5
428. **76.** 25 c. red 8 5
429. – 30 c. violet 10 5
430. – 45 c. lake 15 5
431. – 50 c. blue 15 5
432. – 65 c. orange 20 5
433. **76.** 85 c. green 25 5
434. – 95 c. red 30 5
DESIGNS: 10 c., 30 c., 65 c. Apprentices. 12 c. 15 c., 45 c. Research scientist. 20 c., 50 c. 95 c. Draughtsman and bricklayer.

1964. Nubian Monuments Preservation.
435. **77.** 20 c. maroon, red & blue 12 8
436. – 30 c. ochre, turq. & red 20 15
DESIGN: 30 c. Heads of Rameses II.

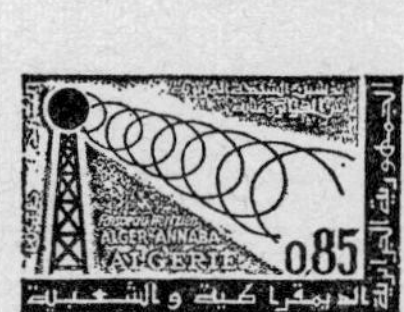
78. Hertzian-wave Radio Transmitting Pylon.

79. Fair Emblem.

1964. Algiers-Annaba Radio-Telephone Service. Inaug.
437. **78.** 85 c. black, blue & brn. 45 15

1964. Algiers Fair.
438. **79.** 30 c. blue, yell. & red .. 12 8

80. Gas Plant.

81. Planting Trees.

82. Children.

1964. Natural Gas Plant at Arzew. Inaug.
439. **80.** 25 c. blue, yellow & violet 15 10

1964. Reafforestation Campaign.
440. **81.** 25 c. green, red & yellow 10 5

1964. Children's Charter.
441. **82.** 15 c. blue, green & rose 10 5

83. Mehariste Saddle.

84. Books Aflame.

1965. Saharan Handicrafts.
442. **83.** 20 c. red, green, brown and black 8 5

1965. Reconstitution of Algiers University Library.
443. **84.** 20 c.+5 c. red, black and green 10 8

85. I.C.Y. Emblem.

1965. Int. Co-operation Year.
444. **85.** 30 c. black, green & red 15 8
445. 60 c. black, green & blue 30 10

86. I.T.U. Emblem and Symbols.

1965. I.T.U. Cent.

446. **86.** 60 c. violet, ochre & grn. 15 10
447. 95 c. choc., ochre & lake 25 15

87. Musicians playing Rebbah and Lute.

1965. Mohamed Racim's Miniatures. (1st series). Multicoloured.

448. 30 c. Type **87** 20 10
449. 60 c. Musicians Derbouka and Tarr 30 15
450. 5 d. Algerian princess .. 1·90 1·00

See also Nos. 471/3.

88. Cattle.

1966. Rock-paintings of Tassili-N-Ajjer (1st Series).

451. **88.** 1 d. brown, ochre & mar. 35 20
452. – 1 d. multicoloured .. 35 20
453. – 2 d. brn., buff & chocolate 70 30
454. – 3 d. brown, orange, black and cream .. .. 1·10 70

DESIGNS—VERT. No. 452. Peuhl shepherd. 454, Peuhl girls. HORIZ. 453 Ostriches.

See also Nos. 474/7.

89. Pottery. **90.** Meteorological instruments.

1966. Grand Kabylie Handicrafts.

455. **89.** 40 c. brown, sepia & blue 12 8
456. – 50 c. orge., green & red 20 8
457. – 70 c. black, red & ultram. 30 15

DESIGNS—HORIZ. 50 c. Weaving. VERT. 70 c. Jewellery.

1966. World Meteorological Day.

458. **90.** 1 d. maroon, green & blue 40 15

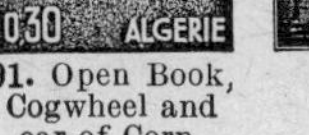

91. Open Book, Cogwheel and ear of Corn. **92.** W.H.O. Building.

1966. Literacy Campaign.

459. **91.** 30 c. black and ochre .. 12 5
460. – 60 c. red, black & grey 20 10

DESIGN: 60 c. Open primer, cogwheel and ear of corn.

1966. W.H.O. Headquarters, Geneva. Inaug.

461. **92.** 30 c. turq., green & brn. 8 5
462. 60 c. slate, blue & brown 10 10

93. Mohammedan Scout Emblem and Banner. **94.** Soldiers and Battle Casualty.

1966. Algerian Mohammedan Scouts, 30th Anniv., and 7th Arab Scout Jamboree, Jedaid (Tripoli). Multicoloured.

463. 30 c. Type **93** 10 5
464. 1 d. Jamboree emblem .. 35 15

1966. Freedom Fighters' Day.

465. **94.** 30 c.+10 c. mult. .. 20 20
466. 95 c.+10 c. mult. .. 50 50

95. Massacre Victims. **96.** Emir Abd-el-Kader.

1966. Deir Yasin Massacre (1948).

467. **95.** 30 c. black and red .. 12 5

1966. Return of Emir Abd-el-Kader Remains.

468. **96.** 30 c. multicoloured .. 10 8
469. 95 c. multicoloured .. 40 12

See also Nos. 496/502.

97. U.N.E.S.C.O. Emblems. **98.** Bardo Museum.

1966. U.N.E.S.C.O 20th Anniv.

470. **97.** 1 d. multicoloured .. 40 15

1966. Mohamed Racim's Miniatures (2nd series). As T **87**. Multicoloured.

471. 1 d. Horseman 40 15
472. 1 d. 50 Algerian bridge .. 55 20
473. 2 d. Barbarossa 75 25

1967. Rock-paintings of Tassili-N-Ajjer (2nd series). As T **88**.

474. 1 d. violet, buff & maroon 45 20
475. 2 d. chest., buff & maroon 90 45
476. 2 d. chest., maroon & buff 90 45
477. 3 d. chestnut, buff & black 1·40 80

DESIGNS: No. 474 Cow. 475, Antelope. 476, Archers. 477. Warrior.

1967. "Musulman Art". Multicoloured.

478. 35 c. Type **98** 40 15
479. 95 c. La Kalaa minaret (vert.) 15 5
480. 1 d. 30 Sedrata ruins .. 55 30

99. Aircraft over Ghardaia.

1967. Air.

481. **99.** 1 d. chest., green & pur. 40 20
482. – 2 d. chest., green & blue 80 40
483. – 5 d. chest., green & blue 1·75 1·00

DESIGN: 2 d. Aircraft over El Oued (Souf). 5 d. Aircraft over Tipasa.

100. View of Moretti.

1967. Int. Tourist Year. Multicoloured.

484. 40 c. Type **100** 20 8
485. 70 c. Tuareg, Tassili (vert.) 35 12

101. Boy and Girl, and Red Crescent. **102.** Ostrich.

1967. Algerian Red Cross Organization.

486. **101.** 30 c.+10 c. brown, red and green 20 10

1967. Sahara Fauna. Multicoloured.

487. 5 c. Lizard (horiz.) .. 5 5
488. 20 c. Type **102** 10 5
489. 40 c. Gazelle 20 10
490. 70 c. Fennecs (horiz. .. 35 20

103. Dancers with Tambourines. **104.** "Athletics".

1967. National Youth Festival.

491. **103.** 50 c. black, yellow & bl. 25 12

1967. 5th Mediterranean Games, Tunis.

492. **104.** 30 c. black, blue & red 10 5

105. Skiing. **106.** Scouts supporting Jamboree Emblem.

1967. Winter Olympic Games, Grenoble (1968).

493. **105.** 30 c. blue, grn. & ult. 15 10
494. – 95 c. grn., violet & chest. 40 25

DESIGN—(36 × 26 mm.)—HOR 95 c. Olympic rings and competitors.

1967.

498. **96.** 5 c. purple 5 5
499. 10 c. green 5 5
500. 25 c. orange 8 5
501. 30 c. black 10 5
502. 30 c. violet 10 5
496. 50 c. claret 25 12
497. 70 c. blue 30 15

The 10 c. value exists in two versions, differing in the figures of value and inscription at bottom right.

1967. World Scout Jamboree, Idaho.

503. **106.** 1 d. multicoloured .. 40 15

1967. No. 428 surch.

504. **76.** 30 c. on 25 c. red .. 12 5

107. Kouitra. **108.** Nememcha Carpet.

1968. Musical Instruments. Multicoloured.

505. 30 c. Type **107** 10 5
506. 40 c. Lute 15 10
507. 1 d. 30, Rebbah 60 30

1968. Algerian Carpets. Multicoloured.

509. 30 c. Type **108** 12 8
510. 70 c. Guergour 30 12
511. 95 c. Djebel-Amour .. 40 20
512. 1 d. 30 Kalaa 60 30

109. Human Rights Emblem and Globe.

1968. Human Rights Year.

513. **109.** 40 c. red, yellow & blue 15 8

110. W.H.O. Emblem. **111.** Emigrant.

1968. W.H.O. 20th Anniv.

514. **110.** 70 c. yellow, blk. & blue 25 12

1968. Emigration of Algerians to Europe.

515. **111.** 30 c. brn., slate & blue 12 8

112. Scouts holding Jamboree Emblem. **113.** Torch and Athletes.

1968. 8th Algerian Scout Jamboree.

516. **112.** 30 c. multicoloured .. 12 8

1968. Olympic Games, Mexico. Multicoloured.

517. 30 c. Type **113** 12 8
518. 50 c. Football 20 10
519. 1 d. Allegory of Games (horiz.) 45 20

114. Moufflons. **115.** "Neptune's Chariot", Timgad.

1968 Protected Animals. Multicoloured.

520. 40 c. Type **114** 15 10
521. 1 d. Red deer 45 20

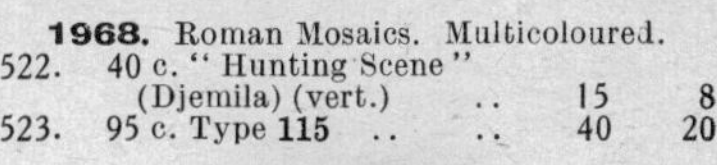

1968. Roman Mosaics. Multicoloured.

522. 40 c. "Hunting Scene" (Djemila) (vert.) .. 15 8
523. 95 c. Type **115** 40 20

116. Miner.

1968. "Industry, Energy and Mines".

524. **116.** 30 c. multicoloured .. 12 5
525. – 30 c. silver and red .. 12 5
526. – 95 c. red, blk. & silver 35 15

DESIGNS: No. 525, Coiled spring ("Industry"). 526, Symbol of radiation ("Energy").

117. Opuntia. **118.** Djorf Torba Dam, Oued Guir.

119. Desert Mail-coach of 1870.

120. The Capitol, Timgad.

1969. Algerian Flowers. Multicoloured.
527. 25 c. Type **117** 10 5
528. 40 c. Dianthus 15 10
529. 70 c. Rose 25 15
530. 95 c. Strelitzia 40 20
See also Nos. 621/4.

1969. Saharan Public Works. Multicoloured.
531. 30 c. Type **118** 10 5
532. 1 d. 50 Route Nationale No. 51 .. .. .. 55 30

1969. Stamp Day.
533. **119.** 1 d. sepia, brn. & blue 60 20

1969. Roman Ruins in Algeria. Multicoloured.
534. 30 c. Type **120** 12 5
535. 1 d. Septimius Temple, Djemila (horiz.) .. 40 12

121. I.L.O. Emblem.

122. Carved Bookcase.

1969. Int. Labour Organization. 50th Anniv.
536. **121.** 95 c. carmine, yellow and black 40 15

1969. No. 425 surch.
537. 20 c. on 12 c. green .. 8 5

1969. Handicrafts. Multicoloured.
538. 30 c. Type **122** 12 5
539. 60 c. Copper tray .. 20 8
540. 1 d. Arab saddle 35 12

123. "Africa" Head.

124. Astronauts on Moon.

1969. 1st Pan-African Cultural Festival, Algiers.
541. **123.** 30 c. multicoloured .. 12 5

1969. 1st Man on the Moon.
542. **124.** 50 c. multicoloured .. 15 12

125. Bank Emblem.

1969. African Development Bank. 5th Anniv.
543. **125.** 30 c. black, yellow & bl. 10 5

126. Flood Victims.

128. "Mother and Child".

127. "Algerian Women" (after Dinet).

1969. Aid for 1969 Flood Victims.
544. **126.** 30 c. + 10 c. black, flesh and blue 20 10
545. – 95 c. + 25 c. brown, blue and purple 50 25
DESIGN: 95 c. Helping hand for flood victims.

1969. Dinet's Paintings. Multicoloured.
546. 1 d. Type **127** 35 25
547. 1 d. 50 "The Look-outs" (Dinet) 60 30

1969. "Protection of Mother and Child".
548. **128.** 30 c. multicoloured .. 12 8

129. "Agriculture".

130. Postal Deliveries by Donkey and Mail Van.

131. Royal Prawn.

132. Oranges.

1970. Four Year Plan.
549. **129.** 25 c. multicoloured .. 10 5
550. – 30 c. multicoloured .. 10 5
551. – 50 c. black and purple 15 10
DESIGNS: (LARGER, 49 × 23 mm.): 30 c. "Industry and Transport". 50 c. "Industry" (abstract).

1970. Stamp Day.
552. **130.** 30 c. multicoloured .. 10 8

1970. Marine Life. Multicoloured.
553. 30 c. Type **131** 10 8
554. 40 c. Giant Pen 15 10
555. 75 c. Neptune's Basket .. 25 15
556. 1 d. Red coral 35 20

1970. "Expo 70". World Fair, Osaka, Japan. Multicoloured.
557. 30 c. Type **132** 10 5
558. 60 c. Algerian Pavilion .. 20 10
559. 70 c. Bunches of grapes .. 25 15

133. Olives and Bottle of Olive-oil.

1970. World Olive-oil Year.
560. **133.** 1 d. multicoloured .. 35 20

134. New U.P.U. H.Q. Building.

1970. New U.P.U. Headquarters Building. Inaug.
561. **134.** 75 c. multicoloured .. 25 15

135. Crossed Muskets.

1970. Algerian 18th-century Weapons. Multicoloured.
562. 40 c. Type **135** 15 8
563. 75 c. Sabre (vert.) 25 15
564. 1 d. Pistol 35 20

136. Arab League Flag. Arms and Map.

137. Lenin.

1970. Arab League. 25th Anniv.
565. **136.** 30 c. multicoloured .. 10 5

1970. Lenin. Birth Cent.
566. **137.** 30 c. bistre and ochre 10 5

138. Exhibition Palace.

1970. 7th International Algiers Fair.
567. **138.** 60 c. green 20 8

139. I.E.Y. and Education Emblems.

1970. Int. Education Year. Multicoloured.
568 30 c. Type **139** 10 5
569. 3 d. Illuminated Koran (vert.) .. .. .. 1·10 70

140. Great Mosque, Tlemcen.

1970. Mosques.
570 **140.** 30 c. multicoloured .. 10 8
571. – 40 c. brown & bistre .. 15 10
572. – 1 d. multicoloured .. 35 20
DESIGNS—VERT. 40 c. Ketchaoua Mosque, Algiers. 1 d. Sidi-Okba Mosque

141. "Fine Arts".

1970. Algerian Fine Arts.
573. **141.** 1 d. orange, green and apple-green 35 15

142. G.P.O., Algiers.

143. Hurdling.

144. "Racial Equality".

1971. Stamp Day.
574. **142.** 30 c. multicoloured .. 10 5

1971. 6th Mediterranean Games, Izmir (Turkey).
575. **143.** 20 c. grey and blue .. 8 5
576. – 40 c. grey and green .. 15 10
577. – 75 c. grey and brown 25 15
DESIGNS—VERT. 40 c. Gymnastics. 75 c. Basketball.

1971. Racial Equality Year.
578. **144.** 60 c. multicoloured .. 20 15

145. Symbols of Learning, and Students.

1971. Technological Institutes Inaug.
579. **145.** 70 c. multicoloured .. 25 10

146. Red Crescent Banner.

1971. Red Crescent Day.
580. **146.** 30 c. + 10 c. red & green 15 15

147. Casbah, Algiers.

1971. Air.
581. **147.** 2 d. multicoloured .. 65 40
582. – 3 d. violet and black .. 90 50
583. – 4 d. multicoloured .. 1·25 75
DESIGNS: 3 d. Port of Oran. 4 d. Rhumel Gorges.

148. Aures Costume.

149. U.N.I.C.E.F. Emblem, Tree and Animals.

1971. Regional Costumes (1st Series). Multicoloured.
584. 50 c. Type **148** 20 12
585. 70 c. Oran 25 15
586. 80 c. Algiers 30 20
587. 90 c. Djebel-Amour .. 35 25
See also Nos. 610/13, and 659/62.

1971. U.N.I.C.E.F. 25th Anniv.
588. **149.** 60 c. multicoloured .. 20 15

150. Lion of St. Mark's.

1971. U.N.E.S.C.O. "Save Venice" Campaign. Multicoloured.
589. 80 c. Type **150** 25 15
590. 1 d. 15 Bridge of Sighs .. 40 30

151. Cycling.

152. Book and Book-mark.

1972. Olympic Games, Munich. Multicoloured.
591. 25 c. Type **151** 10 8
592. 40 c. Throwing the javelin (vert.) 15 10
593. 60 c. Wrestling (vert.) .. 20 15
594. 1 d. Gymnastics (vert.) .. 30 25

1972. Int. Book Year.
595. **152.** 1d. 15 red, black & brn. 40 25

153. Algerian Postmen

154. Jasmine.

1972. Stamp Day.
596. **153.** 40 c. multicoloured .. 15 8

1972. Flowers. Multicoloured.
597. 50 c. Type **154** 15 10
598. 60 c. Violets 20 12
599. 1 d. 15 Polyanthus .. 40 20

155. Olympic Stadium.

156. Festival Emblem.

1972. Cheraga Olympic Stadium Inaug.
600. **155.** 50 c. grn., brn. & violet 15 10

1972. 1st Festival of Arab Youth.
601. **156.** 40 c. brn., yellow & grn. 15 8

157. Rejoicing Algerians.

158. Child posting Letter.

1972. Independence. 10th Anniv.
602. **157.** 1 d. multicoloured .. 35 20

1972. Regional Costumes (2nd Series). T. **148**. Multicoloured.
610. 50 c. Hoggar 15 10
611. 60 c. Kabylie 20 12
612. 70 c. Mzab 25 20
613. 90 c. Tlemcen 30 20

1973. Stamp Day.
614. **158.** 40 c. multicoloured .. 15 5

159. Ho-Chi-Minh and Map.

160. Annaba Embroidery.

1973. "Homage to the Vietnamese People".
615. **159.** 40 c. multicoloured .. 15 8

1973. Algerian Embroidery.
616. **160.** 40 c. multicoloured .. 12 8
617. – 60 c. multicoloured .. 20 12
618. – 80 c. black, gold & red 25 15
COSTUMES: 60 c. Algiers. 80 c. Constantine.

161. "Food Cultivation".

163. O.A.U. Emblem.

162. Serviceman and Flag.

1973. World Food Programme. 10th Anniv.
619. **161.** 1 d. 15 multicoloured 30 20

1973. National Service.
620. **162.** 40 c. multicoloured .. 15 8

1973. Algerian Flowers. As T **117**. Mult.
621. 30 c. Type **117** 8 5
622. 40 c. As No. 529 .. .. 10 8
623. 1 d. As No. 528 .. .. 25 12
624. 1 d. 15 As No. 530 .. 30 15

1973. O.A.U. 10th Anniv.
625. **163.** 40 c. multicoloured .. 10 5

164. Peasant Family.

1973. Agrarian Revolution.
626. **164.** 40 c. multicoloured .. 10 5

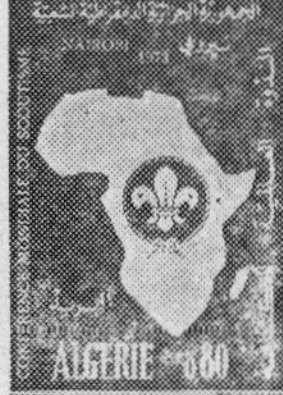

165. Scout Badge on Map.

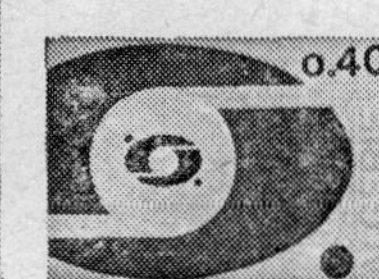

166. P.T.T. Symbol.

1973. 24th World Scouting Congress, Nairobi, Kenya.
627. **165.** 80 c. mauve 20 10

1973. New P.T.T. Symbol. Inaug.
628. **166.** 40 c. orange and blue 10 5

167. Conference Emblem.

168. "Skikda Harbour".

1973. Non-Aligned Countries. 4th Summit Conf., Algiers.
629. **167.** 40 c. multicoloured .. 10 5
630. 80 c. multicoloured .. 20 10

1973. Skikda Port. Opening.
631. **168.** 80 c. multicoloured .. 20 10

169. Young Workers.

170. Arms of Algiers.

1973. "Volontariat"—Students' Volunteer Service.
632. **169.** 40 c. multicoloured .. 10 5

1973. Millenary of Algiers.
633. **170.** 2 d. multicoloured .. 50 20

171. "Protected Infant".

1974. Anti-TB Campaign.
634. **171.** 80 c. multicoloured .. 20 10

172. Industrial Scene.

1974. Four Year Plan.
635. **172.** 80 c. multicoloured 20 10

173. Arabesque Motif.

1974. Al-Biruni (scientist). Millenary.
636. **173.** 1 d. 50 multicoloured 30 20

174. Map and Arrows.

175. Upraised Weapon and Fist.

1974. Meeting of Maghreb Committee for Co-ordination of Posts and Telecommunications, Tunis.
637. **174.** 40 c. multicoloured .. 10 5

1974. "Solidarity with South African People's Campaign".
638. **175.** 80 c. black and red .. 20 10

176. Algerian Family.

1974. Homage to Algerian Mothers.
639. **176.** 85 c. multicoloured .. 20 12

177. Urban Scene.

1974. Children's Drawings. Multicoloured.
640. 70 c. Type **177** 15 8
641. 80 c. Agricultural scene .. 20 10
642. 90 c. Tractor and sunrise 20 10
Nos. 641/2 are size, 49 × 33 mm.

1974. 'Floralies 1974'. Nos. 623/4 optd. **FLORALIES 1974.**
643. 1 d. multicoloured .. 25 12
644. 1 d. 15 multicoloured .. 30 15

178. Automatic Stamp-vending Machine.

179. U.P.U. Emblem on Globe.

1974. Stamp Day.
645. **178.** 80 c. multicoloured .. 20 10

1974. Universal Postal Union. Cent.
646. **179.** 80 c. multicoloured .. 20 10

180. Revolutionaries.

1974. Revolution. 20th Anniv. Mult.
647. 40 c. Type **180** 10 5
648. 70 c. Armed soldiers (vert.) 15 8
649. 95 c. Raising the flag (vert.) 20 10
650. 1 d. Algerians looking to independence 25 12

181. "Towards the Horizon".

182. Ewer.

1974. "Horizon 1980".
651. **181.** 95 c. red, brn. & blk.. 20 10

1974. Algerian 17th-century Brassware.
652. **182.** 50 c. grey, pink & red 12 5
653. – 60 c. brn. & yellow .. 15 8
654. – 95 c. brn., grn. & yell. 20 10
655. – 1 d. brn., bl. & ultram. 25 12
DESIGNS: 60 c. Coffee-pot. 95 c. Sugar-basin. 1 d. Bath vessel.

1975. No. 622 surch.
656. 50 c. on 40 c. multicoloured 12 5

183. Games Emblem.

1975. 7th Mediterranean Games (1st issue).
657. **183.** 50 c. vio., grn. & yell.. 12 5
658. 1 d. orge., vio. & blue.. 25 12

1975. Regional Costumes (3rd series). As Type **148**. Multicoloured.
659. 1 d. Algiers 25 12
660. 1 d. The Hogger 25 12
661. 1 d. Oran 25 12
662. 1 d. Teemcen 25 12

184. Labour Emblems.

1975. Arab Labour Organisations. 10th Anniv.
663. **184.** 50 c. brown 12 5

185. Transfusion.

1975. Blood Collection and Transfusion Service.
664. **185.** 50 c. multicoloured .. 12 5

186. El Kantara Post Office.

187. Policeman and Oil Rig on Map of Algeria.

1975. Stamp Day.
665. **186.** 50 c. multicoloured .. 12 5

1975. Police Day.
666. **187.** 50 c. multicoloured .. 12 5

188. Ground Receiving Aerial.

1975. Satellite Telecommunications. Multicoloured.
667. 50 c. Type **188** 12 5
668. 1 d. Map of receiving sites 25 12
669. 1 d. 20. Main and subsidiary ground stations 30 15

189. Revolutionary with Flag. 190. Swimming.

1975. "Skikda" Revolution. 20th Anniv.
670. **189.** 1 d. multicoloured .. 25 12

1975. 7th Mediterranean Games Algiers (2nd issue). Multicoloured.
671. 25 c. Type **190** 8 5
672. 50 c. Wrestling 12 5
673. 70 c. Football (vert.) .. 20 8
674. 1 d. Athletics (vert.) .. 25 12
675. 1 d. 20 Handball (vert.) .. 85 30

191. Commemorative Text. 192. Posthorn Emblem.

1975. Setif, Guelma and Kherrata Massacres 30th Anniv. (1st issue.)
677. **191.** 5 c. black and orange 5 5
678. 10 c. black and green 5 5
679. 25 c. black and blue .. 8 5
680. 30 c. black and brown 10 5
681. 50 c. black and green 12 5
682. 70 c. black and red .. 15 8
683. 1 d. black and red .. 25 12
See also No. 698.

1975. 10th Arab Postal Union Congress, Algiers.
684. **192.** 1 d. multicoloured .. 25 12

193. Mosaic Palace of the Bey, Constantine.

1975. Historic Buildings.
685. **193.** 1 d. multicoloured .. 25 12
686. – 2 d. multicoloured .. 50 25
687. – 2 d. 50 black and brown 65 30
DESIGNS—VERT. 2 d. Medersa Sidi-Boumediene Oratory, Tlemcen. HORIZ. 2 d. 50 Palace of the Bey, Algiers.

194. University Building.

195. "Lagonosticta senegals".

1975. Al-Azhar University, Cairo. Millenary.
688. **194.** 2 d. multicoloured .. 50 25

1976. Algerian Birds. Multicoloured.
689. 50 c. Type **195** 12 5
690. 1 d. 40 "Tchagra senegala cucullata" (horiz.) 30 15
691. 2 d. "Parus caeruleus ultramarinus" 50 25
692. 2 d. 50 "Pterocles orientalis" (horiz.) 65 30

196. Early and Modern Telephones.

197. Angolan Flag and Map.

1976. Telephone Cent.
693. **196.** 1 d. 40 multicoloured 30 15

1976. "Solidarity with Republic of Angola".
694. **197.** 50 c. multicoloured .. 12 5

198. Child on Map.

199. Postman making Deliveries.

1976. "Solidarity with Saharan People".
695. **198.** 50 c. multicoloured .. 12 5

1976. Stamp Day.
696. **199.** 1 d. 40 multicoloured 30 15

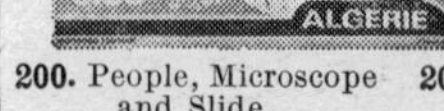

200. People, Microscope and Slide. 201. "Setif-Guelma-Kherrata".

1976. Campaign Against Tuberculosis.
697. **200.** 50 c. multicoloured .. 12 5

1976. Setif, Guelma and Kherrata Massacres. 30th Anniv. (2nd issue).
698. **201.** 50 c. grn., yell. & blue 12 5

MINIMUM PRICE

The minimum price quoted is 5p which represents a handling charge rather than a basis for valuing common stamps. For further notes about prices see introductory pages.

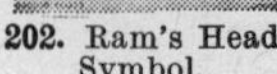

202. Ram's Head Symbol.

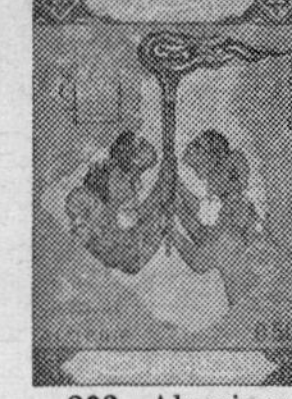

203. Algerians supporting Torch.

1976. Pastoral Agriculture.
699. **202.** 50 c. multicoloured .. 12 5

1976. National Charter.
700. **203.** 50 c. multicoloured .. 12 5

204. Flag and Map of Palestine.

1976. "Solidarity with the Palestinian People".
701. **204.** 50 c. multicoloured .. 12 5

205. Map of Africa.

206. Blind Craftsman.

1976. 2nd Pan-African Commercial Fair, Algiers.
702. **205.** 2 d. multicoloured .. 50 25

1976. Rehabilitation of the Blind. Multicoloured.
703. 1 d. 20 Type **206** .. 25 12
704. 1 d. 40 "The Blind Man" (E. Dinet) (horiz.) .. 30 15

POSTAGE DUE STAMPS

1926. As Postage Due stamps of France, but inscr. "ALGERIE".
D 34. D **2.** 5 c. blue 5 5
D 35. 10 c. brown 5 5
D 36. 20 c. olive 5 5
D 37. 25 c. red 15 15
D 38. 30 c. red 5 5
D 39. 45 c. green 15 15
D 40. 50 c. purple 5 5
D 41. 60 c. green 45 12
D 42. 1 f. claret on yellow 5 5
D 249. 1 f. 50 lilac 10 8
D 43. 2 f. mauve 8 8
D 250. 2 f. blue 10 8
D 44. 3 f. blue 5 5
D 251. 5 f. red 10 8
D 252. 5 f. green 45 30

1927. As last surch.
D 92. D **2.** 60 on 20 c. olive .. 25 8
D 93. 2 f. on 45 c. green .. 35 25
D 94. 3 f. on 25 c. red .. 10 8

1926. As Postage Due stamps of Feranc but inscr. "ALGERIE".
D 45. D **3.** 1 c. olive 5 5
D 46. 10 c. violet 10 8
D 47. 30 c. bistre 8 5
D 48. 60 c. red 8 5
D 49. 1 f. violet .. .. 2·75 70
D 50. 2 f. blue .. .. 2·50 15

1927. Nos. D 45/8 surch.
D 95. D **3.** 10 c. on 30 c. bistre 60 60
D 96. 1 f. on 1 c. olive .. 20 20
D 97. 1 f. on 60 c. red .. 3·50 5
D 98. 2 f. on 10 c. violet .. 1·75 1·75

1942. As 1926 issue, but without "RF".
D 181. D **2.** 30 c. red 5 5
D 182. 2 f. mauve 8 8

1944. Surch. **T O.50.**
D 231. **2.** 50 c. on 20 c. green .. 5 5

1947. Postage Due Stamps of France optd. **ALGERIE.**
D 283. – 10 c. brown (No. D 985) 5 5
D 284. – 30 c. purple (No. D 986) 5 5

D 1.

1947.
D 285. D **1.** 20 c. red 5 5
D 286. 60 c. blue 12 10
D 287. 1 f. brown 5 5
D 288. 1 f. 50 olive .. 20 15
D 289. 2 f. red 5 5
D 290. 3 f. violet 5 5
D 291. 5 f. blue 5 5
D 292. 6 f. black 5 5
D 293. 10 f. purple .. 5 5
D 294. 15 f. myrtle .. 20 20
D 295. 20 f. green .. 8 8
D 296. 30 f. red 15 15
D 297. 50 f. black 35 25
D 298. 100 f. blue .. .. 1·40 1·10

INDEPENDENT STATE

1962. Postage Due stamps of France optd. **EA** and with bar obliterating "REPUBLIQUE FRANCAISE".
D 391. D **6.** 5 c. magenta .. 45 45
D 392. 10 c. red 45 45
D 393. 20 c. brown .. 35 35
D 394. 50 c. slate-green .. 80 80
D 395. 1 f. green .. .. 1·50 1·50
The above also exist with larger overprint applied with handstamps.

D 2. Scales of Justice.

D 3. Ears of Corn.

1963.
D 411. D **2.** 5 c. red and olive .. 5 5
D 412. 10 c. olive and red 5 5
D 413. 20 c. blue and black 8 5
D 414. 50 c. brown and green 15 10
D 415. 1 f. violet and orange 40 25

1968. No. D 415 surch.
D 508. D **2.** 60 c. on 1 f. violet and orange .. 15 8

1972.
D 603. D **3.** 10 c. brown .. 5 5
D 604. 20 c. brown .. 5 5
D 605. 40 c. orange .. 8 5
D 606. 50 c. blue 12 5
D 607. 80 c. brown .. 20 8
D 608. 1 d. green 25 10
D 609. 2 d. blue 50 20

ALLENSTEIN E1

A district of E. Prussia retained by Germany as the result of a plebiscite in 1920. Stamps issued during the plebiscite period.

1920. Stamps of Germany inscr. "DEUTSCHES REICH" optd. **PLEBISCITE OLSZTYN ALLENSTEIN.**
1. **8.** 5 pf. green 8 8
2. 10 pf. red 8 8
3. **13.** 15 pf. violet 8 8
4. 15 pf. purple .. .. 1·60 1·50
5. **8.** 20 pf. blue 8 8
6. 30 pf. blk. & orge. on buff 8 8
7. 40 pf. black and red .. 12 12
8. 50 pf. blk. & pur. on buff 12 12
9. 75 pf. black and green .. 12 12
10. **9.** 1 m. red 45 45
11. 1 m. 25 green 25 25
12. 1 m 50 brown 25 25
13. **10.** 2 m. 50 claret .. .. 2·10 2·10
14. **11.** 3 m. black 70 80

1920. Stamps of Germany inscr. "DEUTSCHES REICH" optd. **TRAITE DE VERSAILLES** etc. in oval.
15 **8.** 5 pf. green 8 8
16. 10 pf. red 8 8
17. **13.** 15 pf. violet 8 8
18. 15 pf. purple .. .. 10·00 13·00
19. **8.** 20 pf. blue 8 8
20. 30 pf. blk. & orge. on buff 12 12
21. 40 pf black and red .. 12 12
22. 50 pf. blk. & pur. on buff 8 8
23. 75 pf. black and green .. 8 8
24. **9.** 1 m red 15 20
25. 1 m. 25 green 15 20
26. 1 m. 50 brown 15 20
27. **10.** 2 m. 50 claret 35 45
28. **11.** 3 m. black 35 45

ALSACE AND LORRAINE E2

Stamps used in parts of France occupied by the German army in the war of 1870–71, and afterwards temporarily in the annexed provinces of Alsace and Lorraine.

1.

1870.

1.	1.	1 c. green	32·00	65·00
3.		2 c. brown	60·00	80·00
6.		4 c. grey	55·00	38·00
8.		5 c. green	38·00	6·50
10.		10 c. brown	35·00	3·00
14.		20 c. blue	40·00	6·50
16.		25 c. brown	75·00	40·00

For 1940 issues see separate lists for Alsace and Lorraine under German Occupations.

ALWAR — BC

A state of Rajputana N. India. Now uses Indian stamps.

1. Native Dagger.

1877. Roul or perf.

1.	1.	¼ a. blue	40	20
5.		¼ a. green	1·50	75
2.		1 a. brown	45	35

ANDORRA — E1

An independent state in the Pyrenees under the joint suzerainty of France and Spain.

I. FRENCH POST OFFICES.

100 centimes = 1 franc.

1931. Stamps of France, optd. **ANDORRE.**

F 1.	11.	½ c. on 1 c. grey ..	12	12
F 2.		1 c. grey	12	12
F 3.		2 c. claret	15	15
F 4.		3 c. orange	15	15
F 5.		5 c. green	15	15
F 6.		10 c. lilac	15	15
F 7.	17.	15 c. claret	55	55
F 8.		20 c. mauve	75	75
F 9.		25 c. brown	75	75
F 10.		30 c. green	70	70
F 11.		40 c. blue	1·25	1·25
F 12.	15.	45 c. lilac	2·75	2·75
F 13.		50 c. red	1·40	1·40
F 14.		65 c. green	2·75	2·75
F 15.		75 c. mauve	3·75	3·75
F 16.	17.	90 c. red	4·25	4·25
F 17.	15.	1 f. blue	4·25	4·25
F 18.	17.	1 f. 50 blue	6·50	6·50
F 19.	13.	2 f. red and green ..	6·00	6·00
F 20.		3 f. mauve and red ..	14·00	14·00
F 21.		5 f. blue and orange ..	17·00	17·00
F 22.		10 f. green and red ..	60·00	60·00
F 23.		20 f. magenta & green	65·00	65·00

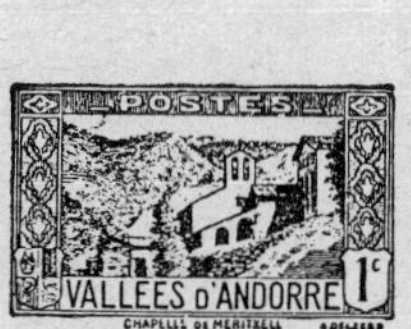

F 1. Notre Dame de Meritxell.

F 2. St. Miquel d'Engolasters.

1932.

F 24.	F 1.	1 c. slate	10	5
F 25.		2 c. violet	15	10
F 26.		3 c. brown	10	8
F 27.		5 c. blue-green ..	12	12
F 28.	A.	10 c. lilac	30	15
F 29.	F 1.	15 c. red	35	30
F 30.	A.	20 c. lake	2·25	1·40
F 31.	F 2.	25 c. brown ..	1·00	55
F 32.	A.	25 c. red	2·25	1·10
F 33.		30 c. green	35	25
F 34.		40 c. blue	2·00	1·25
F 35.		40 c. brown	25	25
F 36.		45 c. red	2·10	1·25
F 37.		45 c. green	1·10	70
F 38.	F 2.	50 c. claret	2·50	1·90
F 39.	A.	50 c. violet	1·10	65
F 40.		50 c. green	55	40
F 41.		55 c. violet	2·75	2·25
F 42.		60 c. brown ..	12	10
F 43.	F 2.	65 c. blue-green ..	8·50	6·50
F 44.	A.	65 c. blue	2·25	1·90
F 45.		70 c. red	30	20
F 46.	F 2.	75 c violet	1·10	50
F 47.	A.	75 c blue	1·10	65
F 48.		80 c. green	3·50	3·25
F 49.	B.	80 c. green	10	10
F 50.		90 c. red	1·10	80
F 51.		90 c. green	90	60
F 52.		1 f. blue-green ..	4·00	2·75
F 53.		1 f. red	3·50	3·25
F 54.		1 f. blue	12	10
F 55.		1 f. 20 violet ..	12	12
F 56.	F 1.	1 f. 25 claret ..	2·25	1·10
F 57.		1 f. 25 red	1·10	50
F 58.	B.	1 f. 30 brown ..	12	12
F 59.	C.	1 f. 50 blue	3·75	3·25
F 60.	B.	1 f. 50 red	10	12
F 61.		1 f. 75 violet ..	18·00	14·00
F 62.	B.	1 f. 75 blue	6·50	6·50
F 63.		2 f. purple	70	25
F 64.	F 1.	2 f. red	55	40
F 65.		2 f. green	12	12
F 66.		2 f. 15 violet ..	8·50	8·50
F 67.		2 f. 25 blue	1 60	1·10
F 68.		2 f. 40 red	12	12
F 69.		2 f. 50 black ..	1·60	90
F 70.		2 f. 50 blue	60	60
F 71.	B.	3 f. brown	55	55
F 72.	F 1.	3 f. brown	12	12
F 73.		4 f. blue	12	12
F 74.		4 f. 50 violet ..	20	12
F 75.	C.	5 f. brown	15	12
F 76.		10 f. violet	20	15
F 78.		15 f. blue	15	10
F 79.		20 f. red	20	15
F 81.	A.	50 f. blue	50	35

DESIGNS—HORIZ. A. St. Anthony's Bridge. C. Old Andorra. VERT. B. Gorge of St. Julia.

1935. Surch.

F 82.	4.	20 c. on 50 c. claret	12	5

F 3.

F 5. Old Andorra.

F 4. Arms of Andorra.

F 6. Councillor.

1937.

F 83.	F 3.	1 c. black	5	5
F 84.		2 c. blue	5	5
F 85.		3 c. brown	5	5
F 86.		5 c. mauve	5	5
F 87.		10 c. blue	5	5
F 88.		15 c. mauve	8	8
F 89.		20 c. green	5	5
F 90.		30 c. red	10	10
F 91.		30 c. black	5	5
F 92.		35 c. green	6·00	6·00
F 93.		40 c. brown ..	5	5
F 94.		50 c. green	5	5
F 95.		60 c. blue	5	5
F 96.		70 c. violet	5	5

1944.

F 97.	F 4.	10 c. violet ..	5	5
F 98		30 c. red	5	5
F 99.		40 c. blue	5	5
F 100.		50 c. orange ..	5	5
F 101.		60 c. black	5	5
F 102.		70 c. mauve ..	5	5
F 103.		80 c. green	5	5
F 104.	D	1 f. blue	12	10
F 105.	F 4.	1 f. purple	8	5
F 106.	D.	1 f. 20 blue ..	5	5
F 107.		1 f. 50 orange ..	8	5
F 108.		2 f. green	5	5
F 109.	E.	2 f. 40 red	8	5
F 110.		2 f. 50 red	10	5
F 111.		3 f. brown	5	5
F 112.	D.	3 f. red	1·10	80
F 113.	E.	4 f. blue	8	5
F 114.		4 f. green	30	25
F 115.	D.	4 f. sepia	60	45
F 116.	F 5.	4 f. 50 blue	35	20
F 117.	E.	4 f. 50 brown ..	5	5
F 118.	F 5.	5 f. blue	5	5
F 119.		5 f. green	10	8
F 120.	E.	5 f. emerald ..	55	35
F 121.		5 f. violet	45	30
F 122.	F 5.	6 f. red	8	5
F 123.		6 f. purple ..	15	15
F 124.	E.	6 f. emerald ..	45	30
F 125.	F 5.	8 f. indigo	45	30
F 126.	E.	8 f. brown	20	20
F 127.	F 5.	10 f. green ..	5	5
F 128.		10 f. blue	8	5
F 129.		12 f. red	12	12
F 130.		12 f. green ..	35	25
F 131.	F 6.	15 f. purple ..	8	8
F 132.	F 5.	15 f. red	20	20
F 133.		15 f. brown	30	20
F 134.	F 6.	18 f blue	30	25
F 135.	F 5.	18 f. red	1·60	1·60
F 136.	F 6.	20 f. blue	12	12
F 137.		20 f. violet	25	25
F 138.		25 f. red	20	20
F 139.		25 f. blue	40	40
F 140.		30 f. blue	1·75	80
F 141.		40 f. green ..	20	20
F 142.		50 f. brown	20	20

DESIGNS—HORIZ. D. Church of St. Jean de Caselles. E. "House of the Valleys".

F 7. Chamois and Pyrenees.

F 8. Les Escoldes.

F 10. East Valira River.

F 9. St. Coloma Belfry.

1950. Air.

F 143.	F 7.	100 f. blue ..	9·00	9·00

1955.

F 144.	F 8.	1 f. slate (postage)	5	5
F 145.		2 f. green ..	5	5
F 146.		3 f. red	5	5
F 147.		5 f. chocolate ..	5	5
F 148.	F 9.	6 f. green ..	10	10
F 149.		8 f. lake	12	12
F 150.		10 f. violet ..	15	15
F 151.		12 f. indigo ..	20	20
F 152.	–	15 f. vermilion ..	20	20
F 153.	–	18 f. turquoise ..	20	20
F 154.	–	20 f. violet ..	25	25
F 155.	–	25 f. sepia ..	25	25
F 156.	–	30 f. blue ..	4·50	3·75
F 157.	–	35 f. blue ..	1·10	1·10
F 158.	–	40 f. green ..	4·50	3·75
F 159.	–	50 f. red	55	55
F 160.	–	65 f. violet ..	1·10	1·00
F 161.	–	70 f. brown ..	1·10	1·10
F 162.	–	75 f. blue ..	7·50	6·50
F 163.	F 10.	100 f. green (air) ..	1·25	75
F 164.		200 f. red ..	2·50	2·00
F 165.		500 f. blue ..	11·00	8·00

DESIGNS—VERT. 15 f. to 25 f. Gothic Cross, Andorre la Vielle. HORIZ. 30 f. to 75 f. Les Bons village.

New currency. 100 (old) francs = 1 (new franc.)

F 11.

F 12. Gothic Cross, Meritxell.

1961.

F 166.	F 11.	1 c. grey, slate and blue (postage)	5	5
F 167.		2 c. orange & black	5	5
F 168.		5 c. green, emerald and black ..	5	5
F 169.		10 c. rose, red & blk.	5	5
F 170.		12 c. yell., grn. & mar.	5	5
F 171.		15 c. pale blue, blue and black ..	5	5
F 172.		18 c. pink, pur. & blk.	5	5
F 173.		20 c. red, yell. & brn.	5	5
F 174.	F 12.	25 c. blue, violet & and myrtle ..	10	10
F 175.		30 c. maroon, lake, green and olive	12	12
F 175a.		40 c. green & brown	20	20
F 176.		45 c. blue, indigo and green ..	1·25	1·00
F 176a.		45 c. bl., brn. & vio.	20	15
F 177.		50 c. sepia, pur., grn. and olive-brown	35	35
F 177a.	–	60 c. brown & chest.	20	20
F 178.	–	65 c. turquoise, olive and chocolate ..	1·40	1·10
F 179.	–	85 c. mauve, purple, violet & maroon	1·40	1·10
F 179a.	–	90 c. green, blue and brown ..	45	35
F 180.	–	1 f. turquoise, indigo and sepia	35	35
F 181.	–	2 f. red, sepia and maroon (air) ..	60	45
F 182.	–	3 f. blue, purple and myrtle	95	65
F 183.	–	5 f. mauve, orange and lake ..	1·40	1·10
F 184.	–	10 f. grn. & turq. ..	2·75	2·25

DESIGNS—As T F 12: 60 c. to 1 f. Engolasters Lake. 2 f. to 10 f. Incles Valley.

F 13. "Telstar" Satellite and part of Globe.

1962. 1st Trans-Atlantic TV Satellite Link.

F 185.	F 13.	50 c. violet & blue	55	55

INDEX

Countries can be quickly located by referring to the index at the end of this volume.

F 14. "La Sardane" (dance).

F 16. The Virgin of St. Coloma.

F 17. I.T.U. Emblem, "Syncom", Morse Key and Pleumeur- Bodou Centre.

F 15. St. Coloma Belfry and Grand Palais, Paris.

1963. Andorran History (1st issue).

F 186.	F 14.	20 c. purple, mag. and olive-green	50	35
F 187.	–	50 c. lake and slate-green	1·00	75
F 188.	–	1 f. blue-green, blue and brown ..	2·50	2·00

DESIGNS—LARGER (48½ × 27 mm.): 50 c. Charlemagne crossing Andorra. (48 × 27 mm.): 1 f. Foundation of Andorra by Louis le Debonnaire.

See also Nos. 190/1.

1964. "PHILATEC 1964" Int. Stamp Exhibition, Paris.

F 189.	F 15.	25 c. green, purple and sepia ..	35	15

1964. Andorran History (2nd issue). As Nos. F 187/8 inscr. "1964".

F 190.		60 c. bl., grn., chest. & brn.	1·00	85
F 191.		1 f. blue, sepia and orange-brown	1·10	85

DESIGNS (48½ × 27 mm.): 60 c. "Napoleon re-establishes the Andorran Statute, 1806". 1 f. "Confirmation of the Co-Government, 1288".

1964. Red Cross Fund.

F 192.	F 16.	25 c. + 10 c. red, green and blue	2·75	2·75

1965. I.T.U. Cent.

F 193.	F 17.	60 c. violet, blue and red	85	65

F 18. "Andorra House", Paris

F 19. Chair-lift.

1965. "Andorra House", Paris. Opening.

F 194.	F 18.	25 c. brown, olive and blue ..	20	12

1966. Winter Sports.

F 195.	F 19.	25 c. grn. brn. & bl.	15	15
F 196.	–	40 c. brn. blue & red	30	20

DESIGN—HORIZ. 40 c. Ski-lift.

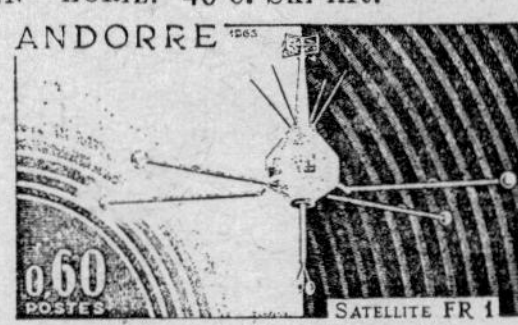

F 20. Satellite "FR 1".

1966. Launching of Satellite "FR 1".

F 197.	F 20.	60 c. blue, emerald and green ..	35	25

F 21. Europa "Ship".

F 22. Cogwheels.

1966. Europa.

F 198.	F 21.	60 c. brown ..	40	25

1967. Europa.

F 199.	F 22.	30 c. indigo & blue	15	12
F 200.		60 c. red and purple	35	30

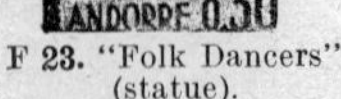

F 23. "Folk Dancers" (statue). F 24. Telephone and Dial.

1967. New Reform (1966). Cent.
F 201. F 23. 30 c. grn., ol. & slate 12 10

1967. Automatic Telephone Service. Inaug.
F 202. F 24. 60 c. blk., vio. & red 25 20

F 25. Andorran Family.

1967. Institution of Social Security.
F 203. F 25. 2 f. 30 brn. & mar. 90 65

F 26. "The Temptation". F 27. Downhill Skiing.

1967. 16th-Cent. Frescoes in the "House of the Valleys". (1st Series).
F 204. F 26. 25 c. red and black 15 15
F 205. – 30 c. purple & violet 20 20
F 206. – 60 c. blue & indigo 35 35
FRESCOES: 30 c. "The Kiss of Judas". 60 c. "The Descent from the Cross".
See also Nos. F 210/12.

1968. Winter Olympic Games, Grenoble.
F 207. F 27. 40 c. pur., orge. & red 20 15

F 28. Europa "Key".

1968. Europa.
F 208. F 28. 30 c. blue and slate 20 20
F 209. 60 c. violet & brown 35 30

1968. 16th-cent. Frescoes in the "House of the Valleys". (2nd Series). Designs as T F 26.
F 210. 25 c. bronze and green .. 12 12
F 211. 30 c. plum and chocolate 20 20
F 212. 60 c. chocolate and lake 35 35
FRESCOES: 25 c. "The Beating of Christ". 30 c. "Christ Helped by the Cyrenians". 60 c. "The Death of Christ".

F 29. High-jumping.

1968. Olympic Games, Mexico.
F 213. F 29. 40 c. brown & blue 20 15

F 30. Colonnade. F 31. Canoeing.

1969. Europa.
F 214. F 30. 40 c. slate, bl. & red 20 20
F 215. 70 c. red, ol. & blue 45 45

1969. World Kayak-canoeing Championships, Bourg-St. Maurice.
F 216. F 31. 70 c. blue and green 30 25

1969. European Water Charter. Similar to Type 590 of France.
F 217. 70 c. black, blue & ultram. 30 30

F 32. "The Apocalypse". F 33. Handball Player.

1969. Altar-screen, St. Jean-de-Caselles. (1st series.)
F 218. F 32. 30 c. red, vio. & brn. 15 15
F 219. – 40 c. brown & slate 20 20
F 220. – 70 c. pur., lake & red 30 30
Nos. F 219/20 show further sections of the screen.
See also Nos. F225/7 and F233/5.

1970. 7th World Handball Championships.
F 221. F 33. 80 c. blue, brown & ultramarine .. 30 25

F 34. "Flaming Sun". F 35. Putting the Shot.

1970. Europa.
F 222. F 34. 40 c. orange .. 20 12
F 223. 80 c. violet .. 30 20

1970. 1st European Junior Athletic Championships, Paris.
F 224. F 35. 80 c. maroon & blue 35 20

1970. Altar-screen, St. Jean-de-Caselles (2nd Series). Designs as T F 32.
F 225. 30 c. violet, brown & red 12 10
F 226. 40 c. green and violet .. 20 15
F 227. 80 c. red, indigo & green 35 30

F 36. Ice-skaters. F 37. Grouse.

1971. World Ice-skating Championships, Lyon.
F 228. F 36. 80 c. vio., pur. & red 30 20

1971. Nature Protection.
F 229. F 37. 80 c. multicoloured 35 20
F 230. – 80 c. brn., grn. & blue 35 20
DESIGN: No. F 230 Pyrenean bear.
See also Nos. F 238, F 251/2 and F 259/60.

F 38. Europa Chain.

1971. Europa.
F 231. F 38. 50 c. red .. 20 12
F 232. 80 c. green .. 35 30

1971. Altar-screen, St. Jean-de-Caselles (3rd series). As T F 32.
F 233. 30 c. grn., brn. & myrtle 12 10
F 234. 50 c. brn., orge. & lake 20 15
F 235. 90 c. blue, pur. & brn. 30 30
DESIGNS: 30 c. to 90 c. Further scenes from "The Revelation of St. John".

1972. Europa. As T 642 of France.
F 236. 50 c. multicoloured .. 20 12
F 237. 90 c. multicoloured .. 40 30

F 39. Golden Eagle.

1972. Nature Protection.
F 238. F 39. 60 c. grn., olive & pur. 25 15

F 40. Rifle-shooting. F 41. General De Gaulle.

1972. Olympic Games, Munich.
F 239. F 40. 1 f. plum 40 25

1972. Altar-screen, St. Jean-de-Caselles (4th Series). As T F 32.
F 240. 30 c. pur., grey & grn. 15 12
F 241. 50 c. grey and blue .. 25 20
F 242. 90 c. green and blue .. 30 30
DESIGNS: 30 c., 50 c., 90 c., Details from Altar-screen, St. Jean-de-Caselles.

1972. "Homage to General De Gaulle".
F 243. F 41. 50 c. blue .. 15 15
F 244. 90 c. brown .. 30 25

F 42. Europa "Posthorn".

1973. Europa.
F 245. F 42. 50 c. multicoloured 15 15
F 246. 90 c. multicoloured 35 35

F 43. "Virgin of Canolich" (wood carving). F 44. Lily.

1973. Andorra Art
F 247. F 43. 1 f. lilac, blue & drab 35 35

1973. Pyrenean Flowers (1st series). Mult.
F 248. 30 c. Type F 44 .. 8 8
F 249. 50 c. Columbine .. 12 12
F 250. 90 c. Wild pinks .. 25 25
See also Nos. F 253/5 and Nos. F 264/6.

F 45. Blue Tit. F 46. "The Virgin of Pal".

1973. Nature Protection (1st series). Multicoloured.
F 251. 90 c. Type F 45 .. 30 30
F 252. 1 f. Woodpecker .. 30 30
See also Nos. F 259/60.

1974. Pyrenean Wild Flowers (2nd series). As Type F 44. Multicoloured.
F 253. 45 c. Iris 12 12
F 254. 65 c. Tobacco Plant .. 20 15
F 255. 90 c. Narcissus 25 25

1974. Europa. Church Sculptures. Mult.
F 256. 50 c. Type F 46 .. 20 15
F 257. 90 c. "The Virgin of St. Coloma" 30 30

F 47. Arms of Andorra. F 48. Letters crossing Globe.

1974. Meeting of Co-Princes, Cahors.
F 258. F 47. 1 f. blue, violet and orange 30 30

1974. Nature Protection (2nd series). As Type F 45. Multicoloured.
F 259. 60 c. Citrail finch .. 15 15
F 260. 80 c. Bullfinch 25 25

1974. Universal Postal Union. Centenary.
F 261. F 48. 1 f. 20 red, grey & brn. 30 30

F 49. "Calvary"

1975. Europa. Multicoloured.
F 262. 80 c. Type F 49 .. 25 25
F 263. 1 f. 20 "Coronation of St. Marti" 30 30

1975. Pyrenean Flowers (3rd series). As Type F 44. Multicoloured.
F 264. 60 c. Gentian 12 12
F 265. 80 c. Anemone 20 20
F 266. 1 f. 20 Colchicum .. 25 25

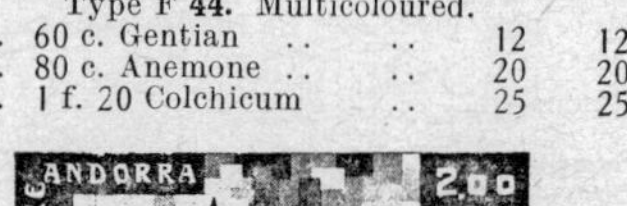

F 50. "Arphila" Motif.

1975. "Arphila 75" International Stamp Exhibition, Paris.
F 267. F 50. 2 f. red, grn. & blue 40 40

F 51. Pres. Pompidou (Co-Prince of Andorra). F 52. "La Pubilla" and Emblem.

1976. Pompidou Commem.
F 268. F 51. 80 c. blk. & vio. .. 20 20

1976. International Women's Year.
F 269. F 52. 1 f. 20 blk. pur. & bl. 25 25

F 53. Skier. F 54. Telephone and Satellite.

1976. Winter Olympic Games, Innsbruck.
F 270. F 53. 1 f. 30 bl. grn. & lt. bl. 25 25

1976. Telephone Centenary.
F 271. F 54. 1 f. grn., blk. & red 20 20

F 55. Catalan Forge. F 56. Thomas Jefferson.

1976. Europa.

F 272. F 55. 80 c. brn., bl. & grn. 20 20
F 273. – 1 f. 20 red, grn. and black .. 25 25

DESIGN: 1 f. 20, Andorran folk-weaving.

1976. American Revolution. Bicent.

F 274. F 56. 1 f. 20 slate, brown and green .. 25 25

F 57. Ball-trap (clay-pigeon) Shooting.

1976. Olympic Games, Montreal.

F 275. F 57. 2 f. brn., vio. & grn. 40 40

F 58. Rebuilt Chapel.

1976. Notre Dame Chapel, Meritxell. Reconstruction.

F 276. F 58. 1 f. grn., pur. & brn. 20 20

POSTAGE DUE STAMPS

1931. Postage Due stamps of France optd. **ANDORRE.**

FD 24. D 2. 5 c. blue 30 30
FD 25. 10 c. brown .. 25 25
FD 26. 30 c. red .. 12 12
FD 27. 50 c. purple .. 30 30
FD 28. 60 c. green .. 1·75 1·75
FD 29. 1 f. claret on yellow 25 25
FD 30. 2 f. mauve .. 1·60 1·60
FD 31. 3 f. red 35 35

1931. Postage Due stamps of France optd. **ANDORRE.**

FD 32. D 4. 1 c. olive 15 15
FD 33. 10 c. red 40 40
FD 34. 60 c. red .. .. 4·50 3·25
FD 35. 1 f. green .. .. 11·00 8·50
FD 36. 1 f. 20 on 2 f. blue 4·50 3·25
FD 37. 2 f. brown.. .. 13·00 9·50
FD 38. 5 f. on 1 f. violet .. 11·00 8·50

FD 1. FD 2. FD 3. Wheat Sheaves.

1935.

FD 82. FD 1. 1 c. olive-green .. 20 15

1937.

FD 97. FD 2. 5 c. blue .. .. 1·10 1·10
FD 98. 10 c. brown .. 1·00 1·00
FD 99. 2 f. violet .. 50 40
FD 100. 5 f. orange .. 25 25

1943.

FD 101. FD 3. 10 c. black .. 5 5
FD 102. 30 c. purple .. 10 10
FD 103. 50 c. green .. 15 15
FD 104. 1 f. blue .. 8 8
FD 105. 1 f. 50 red .. 30 30
FD 106. 2 f. blue .. 10 10
FD 107. 3 f. brown .. 15 15
FD 108. 4 f. violet .. 40 40
FD 109. 5 f. red 25 25
FD 110. 10 f. orange .. 50 50
FD 111. 20 f. brown .. 45 45

1946. As Type FD 3, but inscribed "TIMBRE-TAXE".

FD 143. 10 c. brown 15 15
FD 144. 1 f. blue 5 5
FD 145. 2 f. blue 5 5
FD 146. 3 f. brown 30 25
FD 147. 4 f. purple 30 25
FD 148. 5 f. red 12 12
FD 149. 10 f. orange 20 20
FD 150. 20 f. brown 25 25
FD 151. 50 f. green .. .. 2·25 2·00
FD 152 100 f. green .. .. 7·50 7·50

1961. As Type FD 3, but inscribed " Timbre-Taxe". With new values in currency.

FD 185. 5 c. crimson .. 15 15
FD 186. 10 c. orange .. 25 25
FD 187. 20 c. brown 50 50
FD 188. 50 c. myrtle .. 80 80

1964. Designs as Nos. D 1650/7 of France, but inscr. "ANDORRE".

FD 192. 5 c. red, grn. & pur. .. 5 5
FD 193. 10 c. blue, grn. & pur. 5 5
FD 194. 15 c. red, green & brn. 5 5
FD 195. 20 c. pur., grn. & turq. 5 5
FD 196. 30 c. blue, grn. & brn. 8 8
FD 197. 40 c. yell., red & grn. 10 10
FD 198. 50 c. red, grn. & blue 15 15

II. SPANISH POST OFFICES

100 centimos = 1 peseta.

1928. Stamps of Spain optd. **CORREOS ANDORRA.**

1. 35. 2 c. olive.. .. .. 10 12
2. 5 c. red 12 15
3. 10 c. green 15 15
5. 15 c. blue 50 45
6. 20 c. violet 50 45
7. 25 c. red 50 45
8. 30 c. brown .. .. 2·25 1·60
9. 40 c. blue .. .. 1·90 1·25
10. 50 c. orange .. .. 2·50 1·75
11. 36. 1 p. grey .. .. .. 5·00 2·25
12. 4 p. red .. .. .. 18·00 15·00
13. 10 p. brown .. .. 30·00 22·00

1. La Vall. **2.** General Council of Andorra.

1929.

14. 1. 2 c. olive 20 12
26. – 2 c. brown 12 10
15. – 5 c. claret 30 25
27. – 5 c. brown 12 10
16. – 10 c. green 30 25
17. – 15 c. grey-blue 50 35
29. – 15 c. green 40 20
18. – 20 c. violet 40 40
33. – 25 c. red 30 12
20. 1. 30 c. sepia.. .. .. 12·00 5·50
34. 30 c. red 30 12
21. – 40 c. blue 50 45
36. 1. 45 c. red 25 12
37. – 50 c. orange 90 30
38. 1. 60 c. blue 40 20
23. 2. 1 p. slate .. .. .. 1·25 1·10
39. 4 p. purple .. .. 4·00 1·50
40. 10 p. brown .. .. 5·00 1·75

DESIGNS: 5 c., 40 c. St. Juan de Caselles. 10 c., 20 c., 50 c. St. Julia de Loria. 15 c., 25 c. St. Coloma.

3. Councillor. **4.** Map.

1948.

41. F. 2 c. olive.. .. .. 15 10
42. 5 c. orange 15 10
43. 10 c. blue 15 10
44. 3. 20 c. purple 45 15
45. 25 c. yellow 35 10
46. G 30 c. green 60 15
47. H. 50 c. green 70 20
48. I. 75 c. blue .. .. 1·10 25
49. H. 90 c. claret 40 25
50. I. 1 p. red .. .. .. 1·00 20
51. G. 1 p. 35 blue 40 25
52. 4. 4 p. blue .. .. .. 1·00 35
53. 10 p. purple .. .. 1·25 90

DESIGNS—HORIZ. F. Edelweiss. VERT. G. Arms H. Market Place, Ordino. I. Shrine near Meritxell Chapel.

5. Shrine. **6.** St. Anthony's Bridge.

1951. Air.

54. 5. 1 p. purple .. .. 1·25 25

1963.

55. 6. 25 c. bistre & grey-black 5 5
56. – 70 c. sepia & blue-green .. 5 5
57. – 1 p. violet & grey-blue .. 5 5
58. – 2 p. reddish vio. & violet 10 5
59. – 2 p. 50 reddish purple .. 10 5
60. – 3 p. slate and black .. 20 5
61. – 5 p. dull purple & sepia .. 30 12
62. – 6 p. red and sepia .. 40 15

DESIGNS—VERT. 70 c. Aryos meadows. 1 p. Canillo. 2 p. St. Coloma belfry. 2 p. 50, Arms. 6 p. Madonna of Meritxell. HORIZ. 3 p. Andorra-la-vieja. 5 p. Ordino.

7. Narcissus ("N. pseudonarcissus"). **8.** "Communications".

1966. Pyrenean Flowers.

63. 7. 50 c. blue and slate .. 5 5
64. – 1 p. maroon and brown .. 5 5
65. – 5 p. slate and green .. 20 12
66. – 10 . slate-violet & violet 30 20

DESIGNS: 1 p. Carnation. 5 p. Narcissus ("N. poeticus"). 10 p. Anemone ("A pulsatilla") (wrongly inscr. "HELEBORUS CONI").

1972. Europa.

67. 8. 8 p. multicoloured .. 12·00 12·00

9. Encamp Valley. **10.** Volleyball.

1972. Multicoloured.

68. 1 p. Type 9 .. .. 8 5
69. 1 p. 50 La Massana .. 10 5
70. 2 p. Pas de la Casa (skis and snowscape) 12 10
71. 5 p. Pessons Lake (horiz.) 30 20

1972. Olympic Games, Munich. Multicoloured.

72. 2 p. Type 10 .. .. 20 12
73. 5 p. Swimming (horiz.) .. 40 30

11. St. Anthony Singers.

1972. Andorran Customs. Multicoloured.

74. 1 p. Type 11 .. .. 5 5
75. 1 p. 50 "Les Caramelles" (choir) 5 5
76. 2 p. "Nativity play" .. 8 8
77. 5 p. Giant Cigar (vert.) .. 12 10
78. 8 p. Carved shrine, Meritxell (vert.) .. 15 12
79. 15 p. "La Marratxa" (dance) 40 30

12. Peoples of Europe. **13.** "The Nativity".

1973. Europa.

80. 12. 2 p. black, red & blue .. 12 12
81. – 8 p. red, black & brown 40 40

DESIGN: 8 p. Europa "posthorn".

1973. Christmas. Multicoloured.

82. 2 p. Type 13 .. .. 5 5
83. 5 p. "The Adoration of the Kings" 10 10

14. "Virgin of Orchino". **15.** Oak Cupboard and Shelves.

1974. Europa. Sculptures. Multicoloured.

84. 2 p. Type 14 .. .. 5 5
85. 8 p. Cross 12 5

1974. Arts and Crafts. Multicoloured.

86. 10 p. Type 15 .. .. 25 20
87. 25 p. Crown of the Virgin of the Roses 60 50

16. U.P.U. Monument, Berne.

1974. Universal Postal Union. Centenary.

88. 16. 15 p. multicoloured .. 35 30

17. "The Nativity".

1974. Christmas. Carvings from Meritxell Chapel. Multicoloured.

89. 2 p. Type 17 .. .. 5 5
90. 5 p. "Adoration of the Kings" 10 8

18. 19th-century Postman. **19.** "Peasant with Knife".

1975. "Espana 75" International Stamp Exhibition, Madrid.

91. 18. 3 p. multicoloured 8 8

1975. Europa. 12th-century Romanesque Paintings from Ordino Church. Multicoloured.

92. 3 p. Type 19 .. .. 8 5
93. 12 p. "Christ" 30 25

20. Cathedral and Consecration Text.

1975. Consecration of Urgel Cathedral. 1100th Anniv.

94. 20. 7 p. multicoloured .. 12 10

21. "The Nativity". **22.** Copper Cauldron.

1975. Christmas Paintings from Ordino Church. Multicoloured.

95. 3 p. Type 21 .. .. 5 5
96. 7 p. "The Adoration of The Kings" 12 10

1976. Europa. Multicoloured.

97. 3 p. Type 22 .. .. 8 5
98. 12 p. Wooden chest .. 30 25

EXPRESS LETTER STAMPS

1928. Express Letter stamp of Spain optd. **CORREOS ANDORRA.**

E 14. E **1.**	20 c. red	3·00	2·00

E 1. Eagle over Pyrenees.

E 2. Squirrel (after Durer) and Coat of Arms

1929.

E 41. E **1.**	20 c. red	1·00	25

1949.

E 54. E **2.**	25 c. red	40	30

ANGOLA 01

Republic in Southern Africa. Independent of Portugal since 1975.

1870. 1000 reis = 1 milreis.
1913. 100 centavos = 1 escudo.
1932. 100 centavos = 1 angolar.
1954. 100 centavos = 1 escudo.

1870. "Crown" key-type inscribed "ANGOLA".

7. P.	5 r. black	1·00	60
8.	10 r. yellow	5·00	3·00
31.	10 r. green	1·10	70
9a.	20 r. olive	1·40	90
26.	20 r. red	1·75	1·40
10.	25 r. red	3·00	1·60
27.	25 r. lilac	50	40
19b.	40 r. blue	40·00	14·00
28.	40 r. yellow	2·00	1·10
12.	50 r. green	8·00	4·25
30.	50 r. blue	3·50	70
21a.	100 r. lilac	1·25	90
22b.	200 r. orange	1·50	90
23a.	300 r. brown	1·50	1·25

1886. "Embossed" key-type inscribed "PROVINCIA DE ANGOLA".

35. Q.	5 r. black	2·50	1·60
36.	10 r. green	2·75	1·60
47.	20 r. red	3·50	2·75
39.	25 r. mauve	3·25	80
40.	40 r. brown	3·50	1·50
41a.	50 r. blue	3·50	80
42.	100 r. brown	3·50	2·40
43.	200 r. violet	6·00	3·25
44.	300 r. orange	6·00	3·25

1894. "Figures" key-type inscribed "ANGOLA".

73. R.	5 r. orange	40	25
62.	10 r. mauve	90	40
53.	15 r. brown	1·00	80
54.	20 r. lavender	1·25	50
74.	25 r. green	60	50
66.	50 r. blue	90	40
67.	75 r. red	1·75	1·50
68.	80 r. green	2·50	1·90
69.	100 r. brown on buff	2·50	1·90
70.	150 r. red on rose	5·00	3·25
71.	200 r. blue on blue	5·00	3·25
72.	300 r. blue on brown	5·00	3·25

1894. No. N 3 with circular surch. **CORREIOS DE ANGOLA 25 REIS.**

79b. V.	25 r. on 2½ r. brown	11·00	9·00

1898. "King Carlos" key-type inscribed "ANGOLA".

80. S.	2½ r. grey	10	8
81.	5 r. orange	10	8
82.	10 r. green	12	8
83.	15 r. brown	45	30
142.	15 r. green	20	15
84.	20 r. lilac	20	15
85.	25 r. green	50	25
143.	25 r. red	15	10
86.	50 r. blue	40	25
144.	50 r. brown	1·50	80
145.	65 r. blue	2·50	2·40
87.	75 r. red	1·60	80
146.	75 r. purple	55	40
88.	80 r. mauve	1·60	80
89.	100 r. blue on blue	30	25
147.	115 r. brown on pink	1·75	1·60
148.	130 r. brown on yellow	1·75	1·60
90.	150 r. brown on buff	1·50	1·10
91.	200 r. purple on pink	80	30
92.	300 r. blue on pink	1·10	90
149.	400 r. blue on yellow	1·25	1·00
93.	500 r. black on blue	1·10	90
94.	700 r. mauve on yellow	5·00	4·00

1902. "Embossed," "Figures" and "Newspaper" key-types of Angola surch.

98. R.	65 r. on 5 r. orange	1·40	1·10
100.	65 r. on 10 r. mauve	1·40	1·10
102.	65 r. on 20 r. violet	1·40	1·00
104.	65 r. on 25 r. green	1·50	1·10
95. Q.	65 r. on 40 r. brown	1·50	1·10
96.	65 r. on 300 r. orange	1·75	1·40
106.	115 r. on 10 r. green	1·90	1·50
109. R.	115 r. on 80 r. green	2·40	1·75
111.	115 r. on 100 r. brn. on buff	2·50	2·25
113.	115 r. on 150 r. red on rose	2·50	2·10
108. Q.	115 r. on 200 r. violet	1·60	1·40
119. R.	130 r. on 15 r. brown	1·25	1·00
116. Q.	130 r. on 50 r. blue	2·75	2·00
122. R.	130 r. on 75 r. red	2·25	1·50
118. Q.	130 r. on 100 r. brown	1·75	1·40
126. R.	130 r. on 300 r. bl. on brn.	4·75	3·50
136. V.	400 r. on 2½ r. brown	30	25
127. Q.	400 r. on 5 r. black	4·00	3·50
128.	400 r. on 20 r. red	8·00	6·00
130.	400 r. on 25 r. mauve	2·50	2·75
131. R.	400 r. on 50 r. pale blue	75	60
133.	400 r. on 200 r. blue on blue	35	35

1902. "King Carlos" key-type of Angola optd. **PROVISORIO.**

138. S.	15 r. brown	60	30
139.	25 r. green	40	25
140.	50 r. blue	60	40
141.	75 r. red	1·25	1·00

1905. No. 145 surch. **50 REIS** and bar.

150. S.	50 r. on 65 r. blue	1·00	75

1911. "King Carlos" key-type optd. **REPUBLICA.**

151. S.	2½ r. grey	10	10
152.	5 r. orange	10	10
153.	10 r. green	12	10
154.	15 r. green	15	12
155.	20 r. lilac	15	12
156.	25 r. red	15	12
157.	50 r. brown	60	50
232.	50 r. blue (No. 140)	20	15
158.	75 r. purple	1·40	1·10
234.	75 r. red (No. 141)	80	70
159.	100 r. blue on blue	1·40	1·10
160.	115 r. brown on pink	50	40
161.	130 r. brown on yellow	50	40
162.	200 r. purple on pink	50	40
163.	400 r. blue on yellow	60	40
164.	500 r. black on blue	60	40
165.	700 r. mauve on yellow	75	45

1912. "King Manoel" key type inscr. "ANGOLA" optd. **REPUBLICA.**

166. T.	2½ r. lilac	12	10
167.	5 r. black	20	15
168.	10 r. green	20	15
169.	20 r. red	20	15
170.	25 r. brown	20	15
171.	50 r. blue	35	25
172.	75 r. brown	35	25
173.	100 r. brown on green	45	30
174.	200 r. green on pink	45	30
175.	300 r. black on blue	45	30

1912. "King Carlos" key-type of Angola, optd. **REPUBLICA** and surch.

176. S.	2½ on 15 r. green	1·00	75
177.	5 on 15 r. green	70	40
178.	10 on 15 r. green	70	40
179.	25 on 75 r. red	12·00	10·00
180.	25 on 75 r. purple	60	40

1913. Surch. **REPUBLICA ANGOLA** and value in figures on "Vasco da Gama" issues of

(a) **Portuguese Colonies.**

181.	¼ c. on 2½ r. green	35	30
182.	½ c. on 5 r. red	35	30
183.	1 c. on 10 r. purple	35	30
184.	2½ c. on 25 r. green	35	30
185.	5 c. on 50 r. blue	35	30
186.	7½ c. on 75 r. brown	1·40	1·40
187.	10 c. on 100 r. brown	50	45
188.	15 c. on 150 r. yell.-brn.	50	45

(b) **Macao.**

189.	¼ c. on ½ a. green	60	50
190.	½ c. on 1 a. red	60	50
191.	1 c. on 2 a. purple	60	50
192.	2½ c. on 4 a. green	50	40
193.	5 c. on 8 a. blue	50	40
194.	7½ c. on 12 a. brown	1·40	1·40
195.	10 c. on 16 a. brown	70	50
196.	15 c. on 24 a. yell.-brn.	70	50

(c) **Timor.**

197.	¼ c. on ½ a. green	60	50
198.	½ c. on 1 a. red	60	50
199.	1 c. on 2 a. purple	60	50
200.	2½ c. on 4 a. green	50	40
201.	5 c. on 8 a. blue	50	40
202.	7½ c. on 12 a. brown	1·40	1·40
203.	10 c. on 16 a. brown	70	50
204.	15 c. on 24 a. yell.-brn.	70	50

1914. "Ceres" key-type inscr. "ANGOLA".

296. U.	¼ c. olive	5	5
297.	½ c. black	5	5
298.	1 c. green	5	5
299.	1½ c. brown	5	5
300.	2 c. red	5	5
301.	2 c. grey	10	5
281.	2½ c. violet	5	5
303.	3 c. orange	5	5
304.	4 c. claret	5	5
305.	4½ c. grey	5	5
284.	5 c. blue	10	8
307.	6 c. mauve	5	5
308.	7 c. blue	5	5
287.	7½ c. brown	10	8
288.	8 c. grey	5	5
311.	10 c. brown	5	5
312.	12 c. brown	10	5
313.	12 c. green	15	5
291.	15 c. purple	5	5
314.	15 c. rose	5	5
315.	20 c. green	5	5
316.	24 c. blue	25	20
317.	25 c. brown	25	20
217.	30 c. brown on green	65	45
293.	30 c. green	12	10
218.	40 c. brown on pink	65	45
319.	40 c. blue	15	5
219.	50 c. orange on pink	2·00	1·25
320.	50 c. purple	20	10
321.	60 c. blue	12	5
322.	60 c. red	15·00	14·00
322a.	80 c. pink	20	10
220.	1 e. green on blue	1·40	1·00
323.	1 e. red	20	10
325.	1 e. blue	25	20
326.	2 e. purple	40	15
327.	5 e. brown	1·10	80
328.	10 e. pink	3·00	1·75
329.	20 e. green	9·50	7·00

1914. Provisional stamps of 1902 optd. **REPUBLICA.**

233. S.	50 r. on 65 r. blue	1·00	90
255. Q.	115 r. on 10 r. green	60	50
258. R.	115 r. on 80 r. green	35	25
261.	115 r. on 100 r. brown on buff	45	35
263.	115 r. on 150 r. red on rose	40	30
266. Q.	115 r. on 200 r. violet	45	30
267. R.	130 r. on 15 r. brown	40	30
246. Q.	130 r. on 50 r. blue	4·50	3·50
248. R.	130 r. on 75 r. red	40	30
273. Q.	130 r. on 100 r. brown	30	25
251. R.	130 r. on 300 r. bl. on brn.	1·60	1·25
254. V.	400 r. on 2½ r. brown	15	12

1919. Stamps of 1911, 1912 or 1914 surch.

332. S.	½ c. on 75 r. purple	25	20
331. T.	½ c. on 75 r. brown	25	20
336.	1 c. on 50 r. blue	25	20
334.	2½ c. on 100 r. blue on blue	25	20
335.	2½ c. on 100 r. brown on green	25	20
339. U.	4 c. on 15 c. purple	30	25
337. S.	4 c. on 130 r. brown on yellow	30	25
342. U.	5 c. on 7½ c. brown	30	25
341. T.	5 c. on 75 r. brown	30	25

1925. Nos. 136 and 133 surch. **Republica 40 c.**

345. V.	40 c. on 400 r. on 2½ r. brown	15	15
343. R.	40 c. on 400 r. on 200 r. blue on blue	20	15

1931. "Ceres" key-type of Angola surch.

347. U.	50 c. on 60 c. red	40	30
348.	70 c. on 80 c. pink	60	35
349.	70 c. on 1 e. blue	60	40
350.	1 e. 40 on 2 e. purple	60	40

2. Ceres.

ILLUSTRATIONS
British Commonwealth and all overprints and surcharges are FULL SIZE. Foreign Countries have been reduced to ¾-LINEAR.

1932.

351. **2.**	1 c. brown	5	5
352.	5 c. sepia	5	5
353.	10 c. mauve	5	5
354.	15 c. black	5	5
355.	20 c. grey	5	5
356.	30 c. green	5	5
357.	35 c. green	25	15
358.	40 c. red	5	5
359.	45 c. blue	12	10
360.	50 c. chocolate	5	5
361.	60 c. olive	5	5
362.	70 c. brown	5	5
363.	80 c. green	5	5
364.	85 c. red	60	40
365.	1 a. claret	12	5
366.	1 a. 40 blue	1·00	35
367.	1 a. 75 blue	60	15
368.	2 a. mauve	60	8
369.	5 a. green	1·00	20
370.	10 a. brown	2·50	25
371.	20 a. orange	5·00	50

1934. Surch.

380. **2.**	5 c. on 80 c. green (A)	10	12
419.	5 c. on 80 c. green (B)	15	12
372.	10 c. on 45 c. blue	25	20
381.	10 c. on 80 c. green	10	8
414.	15 c. on 45 c. blue	25	15
382.	15 c. on 80 c. green	35	25
415.	20 c. on 85 c. red	25	15
374.	30 c. on 1 a. 40 blue	25	20
416.	35 c. on 85 c. red	25	15
417.	50 c. on 1 a. 40 blue	25	15
418.	60 c. on 1 a. claret	1·00	90
375.	70 c. on 2 a. mauve	60	50
376.	80 c. on 5 a. green	70	40

(A) surch. **0.05 Cent.** in one line; (B) surch. **5 CENTAVOS** on two lines.

1935. "Due" key-type surch.

377. W.	5 c. on 6 c. brown	25	20
378.	30 c. on 50 c. grey	25	20
379.	40 c. on 50 c. grey	25	20

3. Vasco da Gama.

8. Aeroplane over Globe.

1938.

383. **3.**	1 c. olive (postage)	5	5
384.	5 c. brown	5	5
385.	10 c. red	5	5
386.	15 c. purple	8	5
387.	20 c. grey	10	5
388. –	30 c. purple	12	5
389. –	35 c. green	25	12
390. –	40 c. brown	12	5
391. –	50 c. mauve	12	5
392. –	60 c. black	12	5
393. –	70 c. violet	20	5
394. –	80 c. orange	20	5
395. –	1 a. red	20	5
396. –	1 a. 75 blue	30	10
397. –	2 a. red	40	10
398. –	5 a. olive	1·10	10
399. –	10 a. blue	2·50	35
400. –	20 a. brown	4·50	55
401. **8.**	10 c. red (air)	20	20
402.	20 c. violet	20	20
403.	50 c. orange	20	15
404.	1 a. blue	25	10
405.	2 a. red	30	12
406.	3 a. green	50	15
407.	5 a. brown	1·10	20
408.	9 a. red	2·25	60
409.	10 a. mauve	2·50	60

DESIGNS: 30 c. to 50 c. M. de Albuquerque. 60 c. to 1 a. "Fomento". 1 a. 75, 5 a. Prince Henry the Navigator. 10 a., 20 a. A. de Albuquerque.

9. Portuguese Colonial Column.

1938. President's Colonial Tour.

410. **9.**	80 c. green	1·00	90
411.	1 a. 75 blue	3·75	1·40
412.	20 a. brown	13·00	6·00

1945. Nos. 394/6 surch.

420.	5 c. on 80 c. orange	15	12
421.	50 c. on 1 a. red	15	12
422.	50 c. 1 a. 75 blue	15	12

11. S. Miguel Fortress, Luanda. **12.** Don John IV.

1948. Restoration of Angola. Tercent. Inscr. "Tricentenario da Restauracao de Angola 1648 1948".

424. **11.**	5 c. violet	5	5
425. –	10 c. brown	25	12
426. **12.**	30 c. green	12	8
427. –	50 c. purple	10	5
428. –	1 a. red	20	5
429. –	1 a. 75 blue	40	12
430. –	2 a. green	40	8
431. –	5 a. black	1·75	30
432. –	10 a. mauve	2·50	30
433. –	20 a. blue	6·00	85

DESIGNS—HORIZ. 10 c. Our Lady of Nazareth Hermitage, Luanda. 1 a. Surrender of Luanda. 5 a. Inscribed Rocks of Yelada. 20 a. Massangano Fortress. VERT. (portraits): 50 c. S. C. de Sa Benevides. 1 a. 75, Dioga Cao. 2 a. M. C. Pereira. 10 a. P. D. de Novals.

13. Our Lady of Fatima.

1948. Honouring Our Lady of Fatima.
434. **13.** 50 c. red 70 60
435. 3 a. blue .. .. 2·50 1·40
436. 6 a. orange .. .. 8·50 4·00
437. 9 a. claret .. .. 17·00 4·00

14. River Chiumbe. 15. Pedras Negras.

1949.
438. **14.** 20 c. blue 15 8
439. **15.** 40 c. brown 15 5
440. – 50 c. red 15 5
441. – 2 a. 50 blue 80 12
442. – 3 a. 50 grey 90 20
443. – 15 a. grn. (31×26 mm.) 4·50 90
444. – 50 a. green .. .. 30·00 2·00
DESIGNS—HORIZ. 50 c. Luanda 2 a. 50, Bandeira. 3 a. 50, Mocamedes. 15 a. River Cubal. 50 a. Braganza Falls..

16. Aeroplanes & Globe.

17. Sailing Vessel.

1949. Air.
445. **16.** 1 a. orange 20 5
446. 2 a. brown 40 8
447. 3 a. mauve 60 5
448. 6 a. green .. .. 1·50 40
449. 9 a. purple .. .. 2·50 90

1949. Founding of Mocamedes. Cent.
450. **17.** 1 a. purple 70 12
451. 4 a. green .. .. 1·25 25

18. Letter and Globe.

19. Reproduction of "Crown" key-type.

1949. U.P.U. 75th Anniv.
452. **18.** 4 a. green .. .. 2·25 40

1950. Philatelic Exn. and 80th Anniv. of first Angolan postage stamp.
453. **19.** 50 a. green 30 10
454. 1 a. red 30 12
455. 4 a. black 75 30

20. Bells and Dove.

21. Angels holding Candelabra.

1950. Holy Year.
456. **20.** 1 a. violet 50 8
457. **21.** 4 a. black .. .. 1·25 20

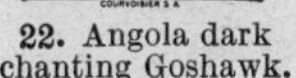

22. Angola dark chanting Goshawk.

23. Our Lady of Fatima.

1951. Birds. Multicoloured.
458. 5 c. Type **22** 10 8
459. 10 c. Racquet-tailed roller 10 8
460. 15 c. Bateleur eagle .. 15 12
461. 20 c. Bee-eater 25 20
462. 50 c. Giant kingfisher .. 20 8
463. 1 a. Yellow-fronted barbet 20 8
464. 1 a. 50 African openbill .. 35 10
465. 2 a. Ground hornbill .. 35 10
466. 2 a. 50 Scissor-billed tern or skimmer 35 10
467. 3 a. South African skikra 20 12
468. 3 a. 50 Barrow's bustard.. 20 12
469. 4 a. African golden oriole.. 30 12
470. 4 a. 50 Long-tailed shrike.. 35 25
471. 5 a. Red glossy starling .. 2·00 20
472. 6 a. Wedge-tailed glossy starling .. .. 2·75 70
473. 7 a. Red-shouldered widow bird .. .. 2·75 70
474. 10 a. Half-collared kingfisher .. .. 10·00 90
475. 12 a. 50 White-crowned shrike .. .. 3·50 2·00
476. 15 a. White-winged babbling starling .. .. 3·75 2·00
477. 20 a. Yellow-billed hornbill 35·00 4·50
478. 25 a. Violet-backed starling 9·00 3·50
479. 30 a. Sulphur-breasted bush shrike .. 10·00 5·00
480. 40 a. Secretary bird .. 15·00 5·50
481. 50 a. Rosy-faced lovebird 40·00 10·00
The 10, 15 and 20 c., 2 a. 50, 3 a., 4 a. 50, 12 a. 50 and 30 a. are horiz., the remainder are vert.

1951. Termination of Holy Year.
482. **23.** 4 a. orange 80 40

24. Laboratory.

25. The Sacred Face.

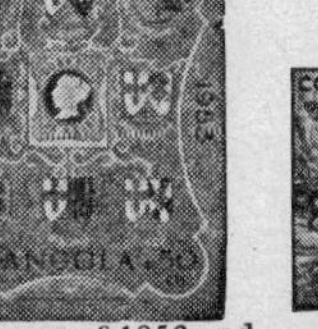

27. Stamp of 1853 and Colonial Arms.

26. Leopard.

1952. 1st Tropical Medicine Congress, Lisbon.
483. **24.** 1 a. grey and blue .. 20 8

1952. Missionary Art Exn.
484. **25.** 10 c. blue and salmon.. 5 5
485. 50 c. green and drab .. 5 5
486. 2 a. purple and salmon 50 8

1953. Animals as T **26** in natural colours. Inscr. in black.
487. 5 c. Leopard 5 5
488. 10 c. Sable antelope .. 5 5
489. 20 c. Elephant 5 5
490. 30 c. Eland 5 5
491. 40 c. Crocodile 5 5
492. 50 c. Impala 5 5
493. 1 a. Mountain zebra .. 15 5
494. 1 a. 50 Situtunga 8 5
495. 2 a. Black rhinoceros .. 15 5
496. 2 a. 30 Gemsbuck.. .. 15 5
497. 2 a. 50 Lion 25 5
498. 3 a. Buffalo 20 5
499. 3 a. 50 Gazelle 15 5
500. 4 a. Gnu .. .. .. 6·00 15
501. 5 a. Jungle cow 35 5
502. 7 a. Warthog 70 20
503. 10 a. Waterbuck .. .. 1·50 20
504. 12 a. 50 Hippopotamus .. 1·75 60
505. 15 a. Greater Kudu antelope 1·90 70
506. 20 a. Giraffe .. .. 4·00 50

1953. Portuguese Postage Stamp Centenary. Coat of arms mult.; insCr. in black.
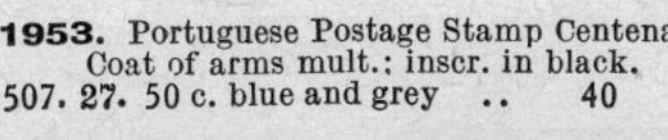
507. **27.** 50 c. blue and grey .. 40 30

28. Father M. da Nobrega and Sao Paulo.

29. Route of President's Tour.

1954. Sao Paulo. 4th Cent.
508. **28.** 1 e. black and buff .. 12 5

1954. Presidential Visit.
509. **29.** 35 c. red and green .. 5 5
510. 4 e. 50 violet, red, green, blue and black .. 40 15

30. Map of Angola.

31. Col. A. de Paiva.

1955. Map multicoloured. Angola territory in colour given.
511. **30.** 5 c. white 5 5
512. 20 c. salmon 5 5
513. 50 c. blue 5 5
514. 1 e. orange 8 5
515. 2 e. 30 yellow 20 5
516. 4 e. blue 50 5
517. 10 e. green 70 8
518. 20 e. white .. .. 1·50 15

1956. De Paiva's Birth Cent.
519. **31.** 1 e. black, blue & orge. 12 5

32. Quela Chief.

33. Father J. M. Antunes.

1957. Native types as T **32** in colourful costumes. Inscriptions in brown. Colours of backgrounds given.
520. **32.** 5 c. sepia and grey .. 5 5
521. – 10 c. red and buff .. 5 5
522. – 15 c. blue and turquoise 5 5
523. – 20 c. yell., brn. & claret 5 5
524. – 30 c. yellow, brn. & pink 5 5
525. – 40 c. brown and grey .. 5 5
526. – 50 c. yellow, brn. & olive 5 5
527. – 80 c. yell., brn. & lavender 10 8
528. – 1 e. 50 red, brown & buff 1·10 10
529. – 2 e. 50 blue and green.. 1·40 8
530. – 4 c. brown and salmon.. 25 5
531. – 10 e. brown and pink .. 70 20
DESIGNS: 10 c. Andulo flute player. 15 c. Dembos man and woman. 20 c. Quissama dancer (male). 30 c. Quibala family. 40 c. Bocoio dancer (female). 50 c. Quissama woman. 80 c. Cuanhama woman. 1 e. 50, Luanda widow. 2 e. 50, Bocoio dancer (male). 4 e. Muquixe man. 10 e. Cabinda chief.

1957. Father Antunes Birth Cent.
532. **33.** 1 e. brown, blk. & turq. 35 20

34. Exhibition Emblem, Globe and Arms.

1958. Brussels Int. Exn.
533. **34.** 1 e. 50 multicoloured .. 15 8

35. "Securidaca longipedunculata".

36. Native Doctor and Patient.

1958. 6th Int. Tropical Medicine Congress.
534. **35.** 2 e. 50 green, red, brown and buff 70 50

1958. Maria Pai Hospital, Luanda. 75th Anniv. Inscr. "1883 1958".
535. **36.** 1 e. brown, black & blue 8 5
536. – 1 e. 50 multicoloured .. 20 5
537. – 2 e. 50 multicoloured .. 40 8
DESIGNS: 1 e. 50, 17th-century doctor and patient. 2 e. 50, Present-day doctor, orderly and patients.

37. Welwitschia (plant).

38. Old Map of West Africa.

1959. Discovery of Welwitschia. Cent.
538. **37.** 1 e. 50 multicoloured .. 25 15
539. – 2 e. 50 multicoloured .. 40 20
540. – 5 e. multicoloured .. 75 20
541. – 10 e. multicoloured .. 2·25 70
DESIGNS: 2 e. 50, 5 e., 10 e. Various types of Welwitschia ("Welwitschia mirabilis").

1960. Prince Henry the Navigator. 500th Death Anniv.
542. **38.** 2 e. 50 multicoloured .. 10 8

39. "Agriculture" (distribution of seeds).

40.

1960. African Technical Co-operation Commission. 10th Anniv.
543. **39.** 2 e. 50 multicoloured .. 20 8

1961. Angolan Women. As T **40.** Portraits multicoloured: background colours given.
544. 10 c. yellow-green .. 5 5
545. 15 c. blue 5 5
546. 30 c. yellow 5 5
547. 40 c. grey.. .. .. 5 5
548. 60 c. chestnut 5 5
549. 1 e. 50 turquoise .. 8 5
550. 2 e. lilac 40 5
551. 2 e. 50 lemon 40 5
552. 3 e. pink .. .. 1·25 10
553. 4 e. olive 70 8
554. 5 e. blue 50 10
555. 7 e. 50 yellow 70 30
556. 10 e. buff 70 20
557. 15 e. brown 60 40
558. 25 e. rose .. .. 1·00 45
559. 50 e. grey .. .. 2·00 50

41. Weightlifting.

1962. Sports. Multicoloured.
560. 50 c. Flying 5 5
561. 1 e. Rowing 25 5
562. 1 e. 50 Water-polo .. 15 5
563. 2 e. 50 Putting the shot .. 10 5
564. 4 e. 50 High-jumping .. 20 12
565. 15 e. T **41** 60 30

42. "A. funestus" (mosquito).

43. Gen. Norton de Matos (statue).

1962. Malaria Eradication.
566. **42.** 2 e. 50 multicoloured .. 30 10

1962. Nova Lisboa. 50th Anniv.
567. **43.** 2 e. 50 multicoloured .. 12

44. Locusts.

47. Arms of Sanza-Pombo.

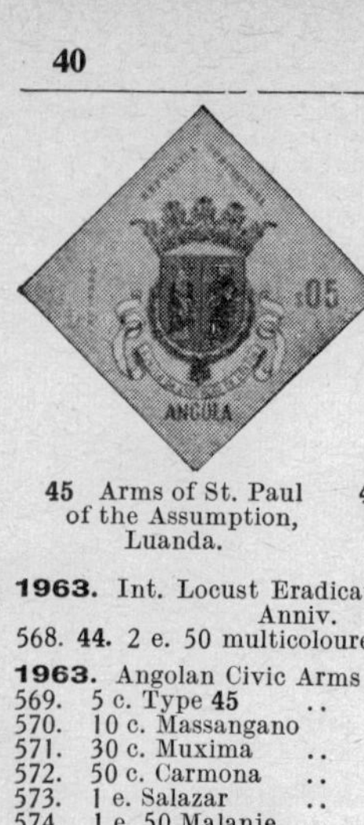

45 Arms of St. Paul of the Assumption, Luanda.

46. Rear-Admiral Tomas.

1963. Int. Locust Eradication Service. 15th Anniv.
568. 44. 2 e. 50 multicoloured .. 25 10

1963. Angolan Civic Arms (1st series). Mult.
569. 5 c. Type 45 .. .. 5 5
570. 10 c. Massangano .. 5 5
571. 30 c. Muxima 5 5
572. 50 c. Carmona 5 5
573. 1 e. Salazar 8 5
574. 1 e. 50 Malanje 20 5
575. 2 e. Henry of Carvalho .. 20 5
576. 2 e. 50 Mocamedes .. 60 5
577. 3 e. Novo Redondo .. 25 5
578. 3 e. 50 St. Salvador (Congo) 20 5
579. 5 e. Lusa 20 8
580. 7 e. 50 St. Philip (Benguela) 30 15
581. 10 e. Lobito 40 20
582. 12 e. 50 Gabela 50 35
583. 15 e. Sa da Bandeira .. 60 40
584. 17 e. 50 Silva Porto .. 1·10 50
585. 20 e. Nova Lisboa .. 75 45
586. 22 e. 50 Cabinda 90 50
587. 30 e. Serpa Pinto .. .. 1·25 60
See also Nos. 589/610.

1963. Presidential Visit.
588. 46. 2e. 50 multicoloured .. 20 10

1963. Angolan Civic Arms (2nd series). Mult.
589. 15 c. Type 47 .. .. 5 5
590. 20 c. St. Antonio do Zaire .. 5 5
591. 25 c. Ambriz 5 5
592. 40 c. Ambrizete 5 5
593. 50 c. Catete 5 5
594. 70 c. Quibaxe 5 5
595. 1 e. Maquela do Zombo .. 12 5
596. 1 e. 20 Bembe 8 5
597. 1 e. 50 Caxito 20 5
598. 1 e. 80 Dondo 12 5
599. 2 e. 50 Damba 70 5
600. 4 e. Cuimba 15 8
601. 6 e. 50 Negage 25 15
602. 7 e. Quitexe 25 15
603. 8 e. Mucaba 30 20
604. 9 e. 31 de Janeiro 30 25
605. 11 e. Novo Caipemba .. 40 30
606. 14 e. Songo 50 40
607. 17 e. Quimbele 65 50
608. 25 e. Noqui .. .. 1·00 60
609. 35 e. Santa Cruz .. .. 1·40 90
610. 50 e. General Freire .. 2·00 1·00

48. Map of Africa and Airliners.

49. Bandeira Cathedral.

1963. T.A.P. Airline. 10th Anniv.
611. 48. 1 e. multicoloured .. 15 8

1963. Angolan Churches. Mult.
612. 10 c. Type 49 .. .. 5 5
613. 20 c. Landana 5 5
614. 30 c. Luanda (Cathedral) 5 5
615. 40 c. Gabela 5 5
616. 50 c. St. Martin, Bay of Tigers (Chapel) 5 5
617. 1 e. Melange (Cathedral) .. 5 5
618. 1 e. 50 St. Peter, Chibia .. 8 5
619. 2 e. Benguela 8 5
620. 2 e. 50 Jesus, Luanda .. 10 5
621. 3 e. Camabatela 10 5
622. 3 e. 50 Cabinda Mission .. 12 5
623. 4 e. Folgares Villa .. 15 8
624. 4 e. 50 Arabida, Lobito .. 20 10
625. 5 e. Cabinda 20 10
626. 7 e. 50 Cacuso, Malange .. 30 20
627. 10 e. Lubanga Mission .. 40 20
628. 12 e. 50 Huila Mission .. 50 40
629. 15 e. Island Cape, Luanda 60 35
The 1 e., 2 e., 3 e., 4 e., 4e. 50, 7 e. 50 12 e. 50 and 15 e. are horiz., the rest vert.

50. Dr. A. T. de Sousa.

1964. National Overseas Bank Centenary.
630. 50. 2 e. 50 multicoloured .. 20 5

51. Arms and Palace of Commerce, Luanda.

52. I.T.U. Emblem and St. Gabriel.

53. Airliner over Petroleum Refinery.

54. Aircraft over Luanda Airport.

1964. Luanda Commercial Assn. Cent.
631. 51. 1 e. multicoloured .. 12 5

1965. I.T.U. Cent.
632. 52. 2 e. 50 multicoloured .. 30 12

1965. Air. Multicoloured.
633. 1 e. 50 Type 53 .. .. 60 5
634. 2 e. 50 Cambame Dam .. 70 5
635. 3 e. Salazar Dam .. .. 1·00 10
636. 4 e. Capt. T. Duarte Dam 45 12
637. 4 e. 50 Creveiro Lopes Dam 45 15
638. 5 e. Cuango Dam 50 12
639. 6 e. Quanza Bridge .. 60 20
640. 7 e. Capt. T. Duarte Bridge 80 20
641. 8 e. 50 Dr. Oliveira Salazar Bridge 90 30
642. 12 e. 50 Capt. S. Carvalho Bridge 90 50
Nos. 634/42 are horiz. and each design includes an airliner overhead.

1965. Direccao dos Transportes Aereos (Angolan airline). 25th Anniv.
643. 54. 2 e. 50 multicoloured .. 12 5

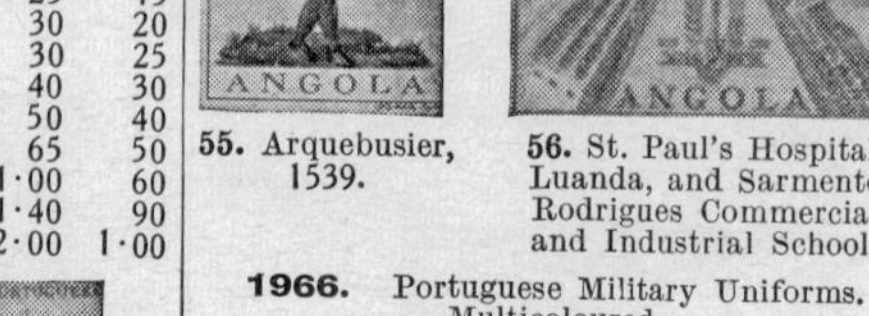

55. Arquebusier, 1539.

56. St. Paul's Hospital, Luanda, and Sarmento Rodrigues Commercial and Industrial School.

1966. Portuguese Military Uniforms. Multicoloured.
644. 50 c. Type 55 .. .. 5 5
645. 1 e. Arquebusier, 1640 .. 8 5
646. 1 e. 50 Infantry officer, 1777 .. .. .. 5 5
647. 2 e. Infantry standard-bearer, 1777 .. .. 10 5
648. 2 e. 50 Infantryman, 1777 10 5
649. 3 e. Cavalry officer, 1783 .. 12 5
650. 4 e. Trooper, 1783 .. 15 8
651. 4 e. 50, Infantry officer, 1807 .. .. .. 20 12
652. 5 e. Infantryman, 1807 .. 20 10
653. 6 e. Cavalry officer, 1807 25 20
654. 8 e. Trooper, 1807 .. 30 25
655. 9 e. Infantryman, 1873 .. 35 30

1966. National Revolution. 40th Anniv.
656. 56. 1 e. multicoloured .. 5 5

57. Emblem of Brotherhood.

58. M. Barata and Cruiser "Don Carlos I".

1966. Brotherhood of the Holy Spirit. Cent.
657. 57. 1 e. multicoloured .. 8 5

1967. Military Naval Assn. Cent. Multicoloured.
658. 1 e. Type 58 .. .. 10 5
659. 2 e. 50 A. de Castilho and corvette "Mindelo" .. 12 5

59. Basilica of Fatima.

60. 17th-Cent. Map and M. C. Pereira (founder).

1967. Fatima Apparitions. 50th Anniv.
660. 59. 50 c. multicoloured .. 5 5

1967. Benguela. 350th Anniv.
661. 60. 50 c. multicoloured .. 8 5

61. Town Hall. Uige-Carmona.

62. "The Three Orders".

1967. Uige-Carmona. 50th Anniv.
662. 61. 1 e. multicoloured .. 5 5

1967. Portuguese Civil and Military Orders. Multicoloured.
663. 50 c. Type 62 .. .. 5 5
664. 1 e. "Tower and Sword" 5 5
665. 1 e. 50 "Avis" 5 5
666. 2 e. "Christ" 8 5
667. 2 e. 50 "St. John of the Sword" 10 5
668. 3 e. "Empire" 12 5
669. 4 e "Prince Henry" .. 15 8
670. 5 e. "Benemerencia" .. 20 10
671. 10 e. "Public Instruction" 40 20
672. 20 e. "Agricultural and Industrial Merit" .. 80 40

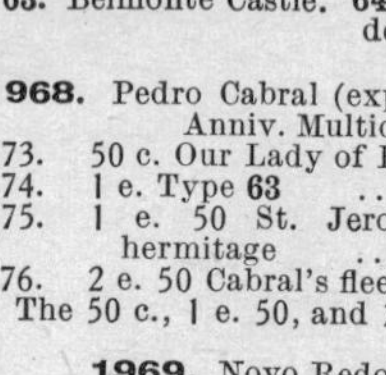

63. Belmonte Castle.

64. Francisco Inocencio de Souza Countinho.

1968. Pedro Cabral (explorer). 500th Birth Anniv. Multicoloured
673. 50 c. Our Lady of Hope .. 5 5
674. 1 e. Type 63 .. .. 12 5
675. 1 e. 50 St. Jeronimo's hermitage 20 5
676. 2 e. 50 Cabral's fleet .. 25 5
The 50 c., 1 e. 50, and 2 e. 50, are vert.

1969. Novo Redondo. Bicent.
677. 64. 2 e. multicoloured .. 8 5

65. Gunboat and Admiral Coutinho.

66. Compass.

1969. Admiral Gago Coutinho. Birth Cent.
678. 65. 2 e. 50 multicoloured .. 20 5

1969. Vasco da Gama (explorer). 500th Birth Anniv.
679. 66. 1 e. multicoloured .. 5 5

67. L. A. Rebello de Silva.

68. Gate of Jeronimos.

1969. Overseas Administrative Reforms. Cent.
680. 67. 1 e. 50 multicoloured .. 8 5

1969. Manoel I. 500th Birth Anniv.
681. 68. 3 e. multicoloured .. 12 5

69. "Angolasaurus bocagei".

70. Marshal Carmona.

1970. Fossils and Minerals. Multicoloured.
682. 50 c. Type 69 .. .. 5 5
683. 1 e. Ferro-meteorite .. 5 5
684. 1 e. 50 Dioptase 8 5
685. 2 e. "Gondwanidium validum" 8 5
686. 2 e. 50 Diamonds 10 5
687. 3 e. Estromatolitos .. 12 5
688. 3 e. 50 "Procarcharodon megalodon" 15 8
689. 4 e. "Microceratodus angolensis" 15 10
690. 4 e. 50 Muscovite (mica) .. 20 12
691. 5 e. Barytes 20 10
692. 6 e. Nostoceras (helicinum) 25 15
693. 10 e. "Rotula orbiculus angolensis" 40 15

1970. Marshal Carmona. Birth Cent.
694. 70. 2 e. 50 multicoloured .. 10 5

71. Cotton-picking.

1970. Malanje Municipality. Cent.
695. 71. 2 e. 50 multicoloured .. 10 5

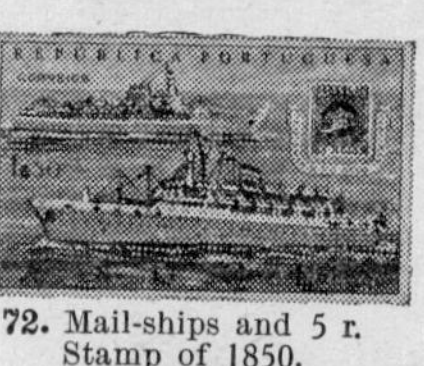

72. Mail-ships and 5 r. Stamp of 1850.

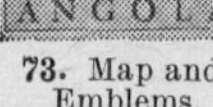

73. Map and Emblems.

1970. Stamp Centenary. Multicoloured.
696. 1 e. 50 Type 72 (postage) .. 12 5
697. 4 e. 50 Steam locomotive and 25 r. stamp of 1870 30 15
698. 2 e. 50 Mail-planes and 10 r. stamp of 1870 (air) 25 8

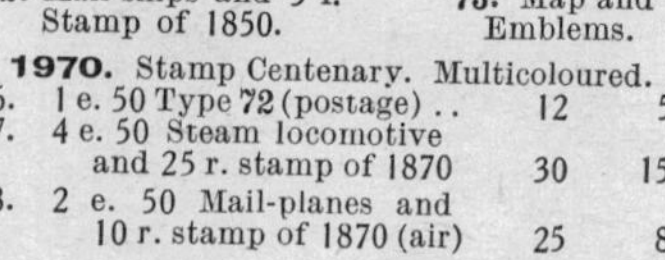

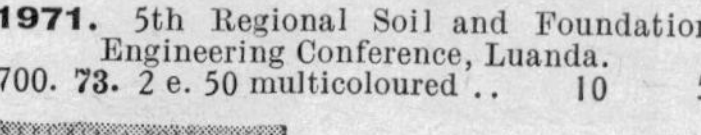

1971. 5th Regional Soil and Foundation Engineering Conference, Luanda.
700. 73. 2 e. 50 multicoloured .. 10 5

74. Galleon at Mouth of Congo.

75. Sailing.

1972. Camoen's "Lusiads" (epic poem) 400th Anniv.
704. 74. 1 e multicoloured .. 5 5

1972. Olympic Games, Munich.
705. 75. 50 c. multicicoloured .. 5 5

76. Seaplane "Santa Cruz" near Fernando de Noronha.

1972. 1st Flight Lisbon-Rio de Janeiro. 50th Anniv.
706. 76. 1 e. multicoloured .. 5 5

77. W. M. O. Emblem.

1974. W.M.O. Centenary.
707. 77. 1 e. multicoloured .. 5 5

78. Dish Aerials.

1974. Inauguration of Satellite Communications Station.
708. 78. 2 e multicoloured .. 8 5

79. "Harpa doris".

1974. Seashells. Multicoloured.
709. 25 c. Type 79 .. .. 5 5
710. 30 c. "Murex melanamathos" 5 5
711. 50 c. "Venus foliaceo lamellosa" 5 5
712. 70 c. "Lathyrus filosus" .. 5 5
713. 1 e. "Cymbium cisium" .. 5 5
714. 1 e. 50 "Cassis tesselata" 5 5
715. 2 e. "Cypraea stercoraria" 8 5
716. 2 e. 50 "Conus prometheus" 10 5
717. 3 e. "Strombus latus" .. 12 5
718. 3 e. 50 "Tympanotonus fuscatus" 15 8
719. 4 e. "Cardium costatum" 15 8
720. 5 e. "Natica fulminea" .. 20 10
721. 6 e. "Lyropecten nodosus" 25 12
722. 7 e. "Tonna galea" .. 30 15
723. 10 e. "Donax rogosus" .. 40 20
724. 25 e. "Cymatium trigonum" 1·00 50
725. 30 e. "Olivancilaria acuminata" .. .. 1·25 60
726. 35 e. "Semifusus morio" .. 1·40 70
727. 40 e. "Clavatula lineata" .. 1·60 80
728. 50 e. "Solarium granulatum" 2·00 1·00

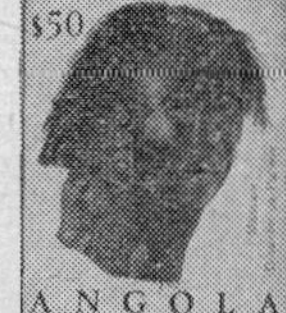

80. Arm with Rifle and Star. 81. Diquiche Mask.

1975. Independence.
730. 80. 1 e. 50 multicoloured .. 5 5

1975. Angolan Masks. Multicoloured.
731. 50 c. Type 81 .. .. 5 5
732. 3 e. Bui ou Congolo mask 12 12

82. "1st May" Emblem.

1976. Workers' Day.
733. 82. 1 e. multicoloured .. 8 8

1976. Stamp Day. Optd. **DIA DO SELO 15 Junho 1976 REP, POPULAR DE.**
734. 80. 10 c. multicoloured .. 80 80

CHARITY TAX STAMPS

The notes under this heading in Portugal also apply here.

1925. Marquis de Pombal Commem. stamps of Portugal but inscr. "ANGOLA".
C 343. C 4. 15 c. violet 12 10
C 344. – 15 c. violet 12 10
C 345. C 5. 15 c. violet 12 10

C 1. C 2. C 3. Old Man.

1929.
C 347. C 1. 50 c. blue 75 35

1939. No gum.
C 413. C 2. 50 c. green 50 5
C 414. 1 a. red .. .. 1·00 40

1955. Heads in brown.
C 519. C 3. 50 c. ochre 5 5
C 520. – 1 e. red (Boy) .. 8 5
C 521. – 1 e. 50 green (Girl) .. 12 8
C 522. – 2 e. 50 blue (Old woman) 25 12

1957. Surch.
C 535. C 3. 10 c. on 50 c. ochre .. 8 5
C 534. 30 c. on 50 c. ochre .. 15 8

C 4. Mother and Child. C 6. "Full Employment".

C 5. Yellow, White and Black Men.

1959.
C 538. C 4. 10 c. black & orange .. 5 5
C 539. – 30 c. black and slate .. 5 5
DESIGN: 30 c. Boy and girl.

1962. Provincial Settlement Committee.
C 568. C 5. 50 c. multicoloured 8 5
C 569. 1 e. multicoloured .. 12 5

1965. Provincial Settlement Committee.
C 643. C 6. 50 c. multicoloured .. 8 5
C 644. 1 e. multicoloured .. 10 5
C 645. 2 e. multicoloured .. 15 8

C 7. Planting Tree.

1972. Provincial Settlement Committee.
C 701. C 7. 50 c. red and brown 5 5
C 702. – 1 e. black and green 5 5
C 703. – 2 e. black and brown 8 5
DESIGNS: 1 e. Agricultural workers. 2 e. Corncobs and flowers.

NEWSPAPER STAMP

1893. "Newspaper" key-type inscribed "ANGOLA".
N 51. V. 2½ r. brown 50 30

POSTAGE DUE STAMPS

1904. "Due" key-type inscr. "ANGOLA".
D 150. W. 5 r. green 10 8
D 151. 10 r. grey 10 8
D 152. 20 r. brown 20 12
D 153. 30 r. orange 20 12
D 154. 50 r. brown 20 15
D 155. 60 r. brown .. 1·10 70
D 156. 100 r. mauve .. 75 45
D 157. 130 r. blue 75 50
D 158. 200 r. red .. .. 1·25 80
D 159. 500 r. lilac .. .. 1·25 80

1911. Nos. D150/9 optd. **REPUBLICA.**
D 166. W. 5 r. green 8 5
D 167. 10 r. grey 8 5
D 168. 20 r. brown 8 5
D 169. 30 r. orange 12 10
D 170. 50 r. brown 12 10
D 171. 60 r. brown 20 12
D 172. 100 r. mauve 20 12
D 173. 130 r. blue 20 12
D 174. 200 r. red 20 15
D 175. 500 r. lilac 30 20

1921. Values in new currency.
D 343. W. ½ c. green 5 5
D 344. 1 c. grey 5 5
D 345. 2 c. brown 5 5
D 346. 3 c. orange 5 5
D 347. 5 c. brown 5 5
D 348. 6 c. brown 5 5
D 349. 10 c. mauve 5 5
D 350. 13 c. blue 8 5
D 351. 20 c. red 8 5
D 352. 50 c. grey 10 8

1925. Marquis de Pombal stamps of Angola, as Nos. C343/5 optd. **MULTA.**
D 353. C 4. 30 c. violet .. 15 12
D 354. – 30 c. violet .. 15 12
D 355. C 5. 30 c. violet .. 15 12

1949. Surch. **PORTEADO** and value.
D 438. 2. 10 c. on 20 c. grey .. 10 10
D 439. 20 c. on 30 c. green .. 12 12
D 440. 30 c. on 50 c. brown .. 15 12
D 441. 40 c. on 1 a. claret .. 15 12
D 442. 50 c. on 2 a. mauve .. 20 15
D 443. 1 a. on 5 a. green .. 30 20

1952. As Type D1 of Macao. but inscr. "ANGOLA" Numerals in red, name in black.
D 483. 10 c. brown and olive .. 5 5
D 484. 30 c. green and blue .. 5 5
D 485. 50 c. brown & pale brown 5 5
D 486. 1 a. blue, green & orge. 5 5
D 487. 2 a. brown & vermilion 8 5
D 488. 5 a. brown and blue .. 20 10

ANGRA E1

A district of the Azores which used the stamps of the Azores from 1868.

1892. As T 9 of Portugal, inscr. "ANGRA"
3. 5 r. yellow 75 50
5. 10 r. mauve .. .. 1·00 70
6. 15 r. brown .. .. 1·25 1·00
7. 20 r. violet .. .. 1·25 1·00
2. 25 r. green 50 10
9. 50 r. blue .. .. 2·25 85
10. 75 r. red .. .. 3·00 1·40
11. 80 r. green .. .. 3·75 3·00
24. 100 r. brown on yellow .. 13·00 6·50
13. 150 r. red on rose .. 13·00 10·00
14. 200 r. blue on blue .. 13·00 10·00
15. 300 r. blue on brown .. 13·00 10·00

1897. "King Carlos" key-type inscr. "ANGRA".
28. S. 2½ r. grey 15 12
29. 5 r. red 15 12
30. 10 r. green 15 12
31. 15 r. brown .. .. 1·25 90
43. 15 r. green 35 25
32. 20 r. lilac 35 25
33. 25 r. green 70 20
44. 25 r. red 25 12
34. 50 r. blue 80 35
46. 65 r. blue 20 15
35. 75 r. red 60 40
47. 75 r. brown on yellow .. 2·00 1·90
36. 80 r. mauve 25 25
37. 100 r. blue on blue .. 45 30
48. 115 r. red on pink .. 35 30
49. 130 r. brown on cream 35 30
38. 150 r. brown on yellow 35 30
50. 180 r. grey on pink .. 45 40
39. 200 r. purple on pink .. 1·10 90
40. 300 r. blue on pink .. 1·40 1·25
41. 500 r. black on blue .. 3·25 2·40

ANGUILLA BC

St. Christopher, Nevis and Anguilla were granted Associated Statehood on 27th February, 1967, but following a referendum Anguilla declared her independence and the St. Christopher authorities withdrew. On 7th July, 1969, the Anguilla post office was officially recognised by the Government of St. Christopher, Nevis and Anguilla and normai postal communications via St. Christopher were resumed.

By the Anguilla Act of 28th July, 1971, the island was restored to direct British control.

100 cents = 1 West Indian dollar.

1967. Nos. 129/44 of St. Kitts-Nevis optd **Independent Anguilla** and bar.
1. – ½ c. sepia and blue .. 16·00 18·00
2. 12. 1 c. multicoloured .. 13·00 11·00
3. – 2 c. multicoloured .. 16·00 10·00
4. – 3 c. multicoloured .. 16·00 11·00
5. – 4 c. multicoloured .. 16·00 11·00
6. – 5 c. multicoloured .. 60·00 22·00
7. – 6 c. multicoloured .. 24·00 12·00
8. – 10 c. multicoloured .. 16·00 11·00
9. – 15 c. multicoloured .. 32·00 14·00
10. – 20 c. multicoloured .. 50·00 17·00
11. – 25 c. multicoloured .. 42·00 21·00
12. – 50 c. multicoloured .. — £350
13. – 60 c. multicoloured .. — £450
14. – $1 yellow and blue .. — £275
15. – $2. 50 multicoloured .. — £275
16. – $5 multicoloured .. — £275
Set of 16 .. £3000 £1600

The above stamps were issued by the governing Council and have been accepted for international mail. Owing to the limited stocks available for overprinting, the sale of the stamps was personally controlled by the Postmaster and no orders from the trade were accepted.

1. Mahogany Tree, The Quarter.

1967. Multicoloured.
17. 1 c. Type 1 .. .. 12 12
18. 2 c. Sombrero Lighthouse 12 12
19. 3 c. St. Mary's Church .. 12 12
20. 4 c. Valley Police Station 12 12
21. 5 c. Old Plantation House, Mt. Fortune 12 12
22. 6 c. Valley Post Office .. 12 12
23. 10 c. Methodist Church, West End 15 15
24. 15 c. Wall-Blake Airport .. 20 25
25. 20 c. Aircraft over Sandy Ground 25 30
26. 25 c. Island Harbour .. 25 30
27. 40 c. Map of Anguilla .. 50 50
28. 60 c. Hermit Crab & Starfish 65 75
29. $1 Hibiscus .. .. 95 1·25
30. $2.50 Local Scene .. 2·00 2·50
31. $5 Spiny Lobster .. 3·50 5·00

On 9th January, 1969, Anguilla reaffirmed her independence from St. Kitts and issued Nos. 17/31 optd. **INDEPENDENCE JANUARY, 1969.**

2. Yachts in Lagoon.

1968. Anguillan Ships. Multicoloured.
32. 10 c. Type 2 .. .. 15 15
33. 15 c. Boat on Beach .. 20 25
34. 25 c. Schooner "Warspite" 35 35
35. 40 c. "Atlantic Star" .. 55 55

3. Black-necked Stilt.

1968. Anguillan Birds. Multicoloured.
36. 10 c. Purple-throated Carib 10 12
37. 15 c. Bananaquit 15 20
38. 25 c. Type 3 .. .. 30 35
39. 40 c. Royal Tern 40 45

4. Guides Badge and Anniversary Years.

1968. Anguillan Girl Guides. 35th Anniv. Multicoloured.
40. 10 c. Type 4 .. .. 12 12
41. 15 c. Badge and Silhouettes of Guides (vert.) .. 15 25
42. 25 c. Guides Badge and Headquarters, Valley .. 25 35
43. 40 c. Association and Proficiency Badges (vert.) .. 40 45

5. The Three Kings.

1968. Christmas.
44. 5. 1 c. black and cerise .. 8 8
45. – 10 c. black and blue .. 12 12
46. – 15 c. black and chestnut 25 25
47. – 40 c. black and blue .. 40 40
48. – 50 c. black and green .. 60 60
DESIGNS—VERT. 10 c. The Wise Men. 15 c. Holy Family and Manger. HORIZ. 40 c. The Shepherds. 50 c. Holy Family and Donkey.

6. Bagging Salt.

1969. Anguillan Salt Industry. Multicoloured.
49. 10 c. Type **6** 12 12
50. 15 c. Packing salt 25 25
51. 40 c. Salt pond 35 35
52. 50 c. Loading salt .. 45 45

7. "The Crucifixion" (Studio of Massys).

1969. Easter Commem. Multicoloured.
53. 25 c. Type **7** 30 30
54. 40 c. "The Last Supper" (Ascr. to Roberti) .. 40 40

8. Amaryllis.

1969. Flowers of the Caribbean. Multicoloured.
55. 10 c. Type **8** 12 12
56. 15 c. Bougainvillea .. 20 20
57. 40 c. Hibiscus 35 35
58. 50 c. "Cattleya" Orchid .. 50 50

9. Turbans and Star Shells.

1969. Sea Shells. Multicoloured.
59. 10 c. Type **9** 12 12
60. 15 c. Spiny Oysters .. 20 20
61. 40 c. Scotch, Royal and Smooth Scotch Bonnets .. 45 45
62. 50 c. Triton Trumpet .. 60 60

1969. Christmas. Nos. 17, 25/8 optd. with different seasonal emblems.
63. 1 c. multicoloured 8 8
64. 20 c. multicoloured .. 35 30
65. 25 c. multicoloured .. 40 35
66. 40 c. multicoloured .. 65 55
67. 60 c. multicoloured .. 1·40 95

10. Red Goatfish.

1969. Fishes. Multicoloured.
68. 10 c. Type **10** 12 12
69. 15 c. Blue Striped Grunts .. 20 20
70. 40 c. Mutton Grouper .. 45 45
71. 50 c. Banded Butterfly Fish 50 50

11. "Morning Glory".

1970. Flowers. Multicoloured.
72. 10 c. Type **11** 12 12
73. 15 c. Blue Petrea 20 20
74. 40 c. Hibiscus 35 35
75. 50 c. "Flame Tree" .. 50 50

12. "Deposition" (Rosso Fiorentino).

1970. Easter. Multicoloured.
76. 10 c. "The Ascent to Calvary" (Tiepolo) 12 12
77. 20 c. "Crucifixion" (Masaccio) 25 25
78. 40 c. Type **12** 45 45
79. 60 c. "The Ascent to Calvary" (Murillo) .. 55 55
Nos. 76 and 79 are horiz.

13. Scout Badge and Map.

1970. Scouting in Anguilla. 40th Anniv. Multicoloured
80. 10 c. Type **13** 12 12
81. 15 c. Scout camp, and cubs practising First Aid .. 20 20
82. 40 c. Monkey bridge .. 35 35
83. 50 c. Scout H.Q. building and Lord Baden-Powell 50 50

14. Boatbuilding.

1970. Multicoloured
84. 1 c. Type **14** 5 5
85. 2 c. Road Construction .. 5 5
86. 3 c. Quay, Blowing Point .. 5 5
87. 4 c. Broadcaster, Radio Anguilla 8 8
88. 5 c. Cottage Hospital Extension 8 8
89. 6 c. Valley Secondary School 12 12
90. 10 c. Hotel Extension .. 12 15
91. 15 c. Sandy Ground .. 15 20
92. 20 c. Supermarket and Cinema 20 35
93. 25 c. Bananas and Mangoes 25 30
94. 40 c. Wall Blake Airport .. 35 40
95. 60 c. Sandy Ground Jetty .. 45 50
96. $1 Administration Buildings 80 85
97. $2·50 Livestock .. .. 2·00 2·25
98. $5 Sandy Hill Bay .. .. 3·50 3·75

15. "The Adoration of the Shepherds" (Reni).

1970. Christmas. Multicoloured.
99. 1 c. Type **15** 12 12
100. 20 c. "The Virgin and Child" (Gozzoli) .. 30 30
101. 25 c. "Manger Scene" (detail Botticelli) 30 30
102. 40 c. "The Santa Margherita Madonna" (detail, Mazzola) 35 35
103. 50 c. "L'Adorazione dei Magi" (detail, Tiepolo) .. 50 50

16. "Ecce Homo" (detail, Correggio).

1971. Easter. Paintings. Multicoloured.
104. 10 c. Type **16** 12 12
105. 15 c. "Christ appearing to St. Peter" (detail, Carracci) 20 20
106. 40 c. "Angels weeping over the Dead Christ" (detail, Guercino) 40 40
107. 50 c. "The Supper at Emmaus" (detail, Caravaggio) 50 50
The 40 c. and 50 c. designs are horiz.

17. "Hypolimnas missipus".

1971. Butterflies. Multicoloured.
108. 10 c. Type **17** 10 10
109. 15 c. "Junonia lavinia" .. 15 15
110. 40 c. "Agraulis vanillae" 30 30
111. 50 c. "Danaus plexippus" 40 40

18. "Magnanime" and "Amiable" in Battle.

1971. Sea-battles of the West Indies. Multicoloured.
112. 10 c. Type **18** 10 10
113. 15 c. H.M.S. "Duke", "Glorieux" and H.M.S. "Agamemnon" .. 15 15
114. 25 c. H.M.S. "Formidable" and H.M.S. "Namur" against "Ville de Paris" .. 25 25
115. 40 c. H.M.S. "Canada" .. 40 40
116. 50 c. H.M.S. "St. Albans" and wreck of "Hector" 50 55
Nos. 112/116 were issued in horizontal se-tenant strips within the sheet to form a composite design.

19. "The Ansidei Madonna" (detail, Raphael).

1971. Christmas. Multicoloured.
117. 20 c. Type **19** 20 20
118. 25 c. "Mystic Nativity" (detail, Botticelli) .. 25 25
119. 40 c. "Adoration of the Shepherds" (detail, ascr. to Murillo) .. 35 40
120. 50 c. "The Madonna of the Iris" (detail, ascr. to Durer) 45 45

20. Thomas Jefferys' Map, 1775.

1972. Caribbean Maps depicting Anguilla. Multicoloured.
121. 10 c. Type **20** 5 5
122. 15 c. Samuel Fahlberg's Map, 1814 .. .. .. 15 15
123. 40 c. Thomas Jefferys' Map, 1775 (horiz.) .. 30 30
124. 50 c. Capt. E. Barnett's Map, 1847 (horiz.) 35 40

21. "Jesus Buffeted".

1972. Easter Multicoloured.
125. 10 c. Type **21** 10 10
126. 15 c. "The Way of Sorrows" 15 15
127. 25 c. "The Crucifixion" .. 25 25
128. 40 c. "Descent from the Cross" 35 40
129. 50 c. "The Burial" .. 40 50

22. Loblolly Tree.

1972. Multicoloured.

130. 1 c. Spear fishing 5 5
131. 2 c. Type **22** 5 5
132. 3 c. Sandy ground .. 5 5
133. 4 c. Ferry at Blowing Point 5 5
134 5 c. Agriculture 5 5
135. 6 c. St. Mary's Church .. 8 10
136. 10 c. St. Gerrard's Church 10 10
137. 15 c. Cottage hospital extension 10 10
138. 20 c. Public library .. 12 15
139. 25 c. Sunset at Blowing Point 15 20
140. 40 c. Boat building .. 25 30
141. 60 c. Hibiscus 30 35
142. $1 Man-o'-War (bird) .. 45 50
143. $2·50 Frangipani .. 1·25 1·40
144. $5 Brown Pelican .. 2·25 2·50
144a. $10 Green-back turtle .. 4·00 4·25

1972. Royal Silver Wedding. As T **19**, of Ascension, but with Schooner and Dolphin in background.

145. 25 c. green .. .. .. 1·75 2·00
146. 40 c. brown .. .. 3·00 3·25

23. Flight into Egypt.

1972. Christmas. Multicoloured.

147. 1 c. Type **23** 5 5
148. 20 c. Star of Bethlehem 15 15
149. 25 c. Holy Family .. 20 20
150. 40 c. Arrival of the Magi 25 25
151. 50 c. Adoration of the Magi 35 35

24. " The Betrayal of Christ ".

1973. Easter. Multicoloured.

152. 1 c. Type **24** 5 5
153. 10 c. " The Man of Sorrows " 5 5
154. 20 c. " Christ bearing the Cross " 12 12
155. 25 c. " The Crucifixion " .. 15 15
156. 40 c. " The Descent from the Cross " 25 25
157. 50 c. " The Resurrection " 30 30

25. " Santa Maria ".

1973. Columbus Discovers the West Indies. Multicoloured.

159. 1 c. Type **25** 5 5
160. 20 c. Early map 15 15
161. 40 c. Map of voyages .. 30 30
162. 70 c. Sighting land .. 45 45
163. $1·20 Landing of Columbus 75 75

26. Princess Anne and Captain Mark Phillips.

1973. Royal Wedding. Multicoloured. Background colours given.

165. **26.** 60 c. green 40 40
166. $1·20 mauve 75 75

27. " The Adoration of the Shepherds " (Reni).

1973. Christmas. Multicoloured.

167. 1 c. Type **27** 5 5
168. 10 c. " The Virgin and Child " (Filippino Lippi) 8 8
169. 20 c. " The Nativity " (Meester Van de Brunswijkse Diptiek) .. 12 12
170. 25 c. " Madonna of the Meadow " (Bellini) .. 15 20
171. 40 c. " Virgin and Child " (Cima) 25 25
172. 50 c. " Adoration of the Magi " (Geertgen) .. 30 30

28. " The Crucifixion " (Raphael).

1974. Easter. Details of Raphael's " Crucifixion ".

174. **28.** 1 c. multicoloured .. 5 5
175. – 15 c. multicoloured .. 10 10
176. – 20 c. multicoloured .. 12 12
177. – 25 c. multicoloured .. 15 15
178. – 30 c. multicoloured .. 20 25
179. – $1 multicoloured .. 45 50

INDEX

Countries can be quickly located by referring to the index at the end of this volume.

29. Churchill Making " Victory " Sign.

1974. Sir Winston Churchill. Birth Cent. Multicoloured.

181. 1 c. Type **29** 5 5
182. 20 c. Churchill with Roosevelt 12 12
183. 25 c. Wartime broadcast .. 12 15
184. 40 c. Birthplace, Blenheim Palace 20 25
185. 60 c. Churchill's statue .. 25 30
186. $1·20 Country residence, Chartwell 50 60

30. U.P.U. Emblem.

1974. U.P.U. Centenary.

188. **30.** 1 c. black and blue .. 5 5
189. 20 c. black and orange .. 12 12
190. 25 c. black and yellow .. 12 15
191. 40 c. black and mauve .. 20 25
192. 60 c. black and green .. 25 30
193. $1. 20 black and blue .. 50 55

31. Anguillan pointing to Star.

1974. Christmas. Multicoloured.

195. 1 c. Type **31** 5 5
196. 20 c. Child in Manger .. 12 12
197. 25 c. King's offering .. 12 15
198. 40 c. Star over map of Anguilla 20 25
199. 60 c. Family looking at Star 25 30
200. $1.20 Angels of Peace .. 50 55

32. "Mary, John and Mary Magdalene" (Matthias Grunewald).

1975. Easter. Details from Isenheim Altarpiece, Colmar Museum. Multicoloured.

202. 1 c. Type **32** 5 5
203. 10 c. "The Crucifixion" .. 5 5
204. 15 c. "St. John the Baptist" 8 10
205. 20 c. "St. Sebastian and Angels" 10 12
206. $1 "The Entombment" (horiz.) 40 45
207. $1.50 "St. Anthony the Hermit" 60 70

33. Statue of Liberty.

1975. American Revolution. Bicent. Mult.

209. 1 c. Type **33** 5 5
210. 10 c. The Capitol 5 8
211. 15 c. Congress voting for independence 5 8
212. 20 c. Washington and map 8 10
213. $1 Boston Tea Party .. 40 45
214. $1.50 Bicentenary logo .. 60 70

34. " Madonna, Child and St. John " (Raphael).

1975. Christmas. " Madonna and Child " paintings by artists named. Mult.

216. 1 c. Type **34** 5 5
217. 10 c. Cima 5 8
218. 15 c. Dolci 5 8
219. 20 c. Durer 8 10
220. $1 Bellini 40 45
221. $1.50 Botticelli 60 70

1976. New Constitution. Nos. 130, etc. optd. **NEW CONSTITUTION 1976**, or surch. also.

223. 1 c. Spear fishing 5 5
224. 2 c. on 1 c. Spear fishing .. 5 5
225. 2 c. Type **22** 5 5
226. 3 c. on 40 c. Boat building 5 5
227. 4 c. Ferry at Blowing Point 5 5
228. 5 c. on 40 c. Boat building 5 5
229. 6 c. St. Mary's Church .. 5 5
230. 10 c. on 20 c. Public Library 5 5
231. 10 c. St. Gerard's Church 5 5
232. 15 c. Cottage Hospital extension 5 5
233. 20 c. Public Library .. 8 8
234. 25 c. Sunset at Blowing Point 10 10
235. 40 c. Boat Building .. 15 15
236. 60 c. Hibiscus 20 25
237. $1 Man-o'-War (bird) .. 35 40
238. $2.50 Frangipani .. .. 90 1·00
239. $5 Brown Pelican .. .. 1·75 2·00
240. $10 Green-back Turtle .. 3·50 4·00

35. Almond.

1976. Flowering Trees. Multicoloured.

241. 1 c. Type **35** 5 5
242. 10 c. Autograph 5 5
243. 15 c. Calabash 5 8
244. 20 c. Cordia 8 10
245. $1 Papaya 40 45
246. $1.50 Flamboyant .. 60 70

36. The Three Marys.

1976. Easter. Showing portions of the Altar Frontal Tapestry, Rheinau. Multicoloured.

248. 1 c. Type **36** 5 5
249. 10 c. The Crucifixion .. 5 5
250. 15 c. Two Soldiers .. 5 8
251. 20 c. The Annunciation .. 8 10
252. $1 The complete tapestry (horiz.) 40 45
253. $1.50 The Risen Christ .. 60 70

ANJOUAN O1

One of the Comoro Is. between Madagascar and the E. Coast of Africa. Used stamps of Madagascar from 1911 and became part of the Comoro Is. in 1950.

1892. "Tablet" key-type inscr. "SULTANAT D'ANJOUAN".

1. D. 1 c. black on blue .. 20 20
2. 2 c. brown on yellow .. 20 20
3. 4 c. claret on grey .. 35 20
4. 5 c. green 65 55
5. 10 c. black on lilac .. 75 65
14. 10 c. red .. .. 2·75 2·25
6. 15 c. blue 90 65
15. 15 c. grey .. .. 1·60 1·50
7. 20 c. red on green .. 1·40 1·10
8. 25 c. black on red .. 1·40 1·10
16. 25 c. blue .. .. 2·25 2·25
9. 30 c. brown .. .. 2·75 2·50
17. 35 c. black on yellow .. 1·10 65
10. 40 c. red on yellow .. 5·00 4·00
18. 45 c. black on green .. 19·00 15·00
11. 50 c. red on rose .. 4·00 3·25
19. 50 c. brown on blue .. 3·25 2·75
12. 75 c. brown on orange .. 3·00 2·75
13. 1 f. olive . .. 11·00 9·50

1912. Surch. in figures.

20. D. 05 on 2 c. brown .. 10 10
21. 05 on 4 c. claret .. 10 10
22. 05 on 15 c. blue .. 10 10
23. 05 on 20 c. red on green 10 10
24. 05 on 25 c. black on red 10 10
25. 05 on 30 c. brown .. 10 10
26. 10 on 40 c. red on yellow 10 10
27. 10 on 45 c. black on grn. 10 10
28. 10 on 50 c. red on rose .. 25 25
29. 10 on 75 c. brn. on orge. 15 15
30. 10 on 1 f. olive 15 15

ANNAM AND TONGKING O2

Later part of Indo-China and now included in Vietnam.

1888. Stamps of French Colonies, "Commerce" type, surch. **A & T** and value in figures.

1. 9. 1 on 2 c. brown on yellow .. 5·00 4·50
2. 1 on 4 c. lilac on grey .. 3·25 2·75
3. 5 on 10 c. black on lilac .. 3·75 3·25

ANTIGUA BC

One of the Leeward Is., Br. W. Indies. Used general issues for Leeward Is., concurrently with Antiguan stamps until 1st July, 1956. Ministerial Government introduced on 1st January, 1960. Achieved Associated Statehood on 3rd March, 1967.

1951. 100 cents = 1 West Indian dollar.

1.

2.

1862.

5. 1. 1d. mauve .. .. 35·00 16·00
25. 1d. red .. .. .. 1·20 5·00
29. 6d. green .. .. .. 20·00 27·00

1879.

21. 2. ½d. green .. .. 3·00 7·00
22. 2½d. brown .. .. 30·00 18·00
27. 2½d. blue .. .. 7·00 8·00
23. 4d. blue .. .. .. 80·00 17·00
28. 4d. brown .. .. 3·25 5·00
30. 1s. mauve .. .. £100 70·00

3. Seal of the Colony.

4.

5. St. John's Harbour.

1903.

31. 3. ½d. black and green .. 1·10 2·25
42. ½d. green .. .. .. 80 1·00
32. 1d. black and red .. 2·50 60
43. 1d. red .. .. .. 1·60 85
45. 2d. purple and brown .. 3·00 3·50
34. 2½d. black and blue .. 5·00 7·50
46. 2½d. blue .. .. .. 3·00 3·75
47. 3d. green and brown .. 5·00 7·00
48. 6d. purple and black .. 7·50 9·50
49. 1s. blue and purple .. 9·00 11·00
38. 2s. green and violet .. 21·00 26·00
39. 2s. 6d. black and purple .. 17·00 20·00
40. 4. 5s. green and violet .. 30·00 35·00

1913. Head of King George V.

51. 4. 5s. green and violet .. 25·00 28·00

1916. Optd. **WAR STAMP.**

52. 3. ½d. green 25 55
53. 1½d. orange 20 55

1921.

62. 5. ½d. green 25 35
64. 1d. red 35 30
66. 1d. mauve 80 80
67. 1½d. orange .. .. 2·75 4·50
68. 1½d. red 50 85
69. 1½d. brown .. .. 1·00 1·25
70. 2d. grey .. .. .. 80 1·00
72. 2½d. blue .. .. .. 2·75 2·75
73. 2½d. yellow .. .. 1·00 3·75
74. 3d. purple on yellow .. 2·00 3·50
56. 4d. black and red on yell. 2·50 4·00
75. 6d. purple .. .. .. 1·40 2·50
76. 1s. black on green .. 3·50 6·50
58. 2s. purple & blue on blue 5·50 8·50
59. 2s. 6d. blk. & red on blue 6·50 9·00
79. 3s. green and violet .. 10·00 13·00
80. 4s. black and red .. .. 12·00 15·00
60. 5s. green & red on yellow 11·00 15·00
61. £1 purple & black on red 80·00 95·00

6. Old Dockyard, English Harbour.

7. Sir Thomas Warner's Ship.

1932. Tercent. Designs with medallion portrait of King George V.

81. 6. ½d. green 55 70
82. 1d. red 70 85
83. 1½d. brown .. .. 1·40 1·50
84. 2d. grey .. .. .. 3·00 5·00
85. – 2½d. blue .. .. .. 3·25 5·00
86. – 3d. orange .. .. 5·50 8·00
87. – 6d. violet .. .. .. 11·00 12·00
88. – 1s. olive .. .. .. 12·00 14·00
89. – 2s. 6d. purple .. .. 23·00 25·00
90. 7. 5s black and brown .. 48·00 60·00

DESIGNS—HORIZ. 2d. to 3d. Government House, St. John's. 6d. to 2s. 6d. Nelson's "Victory".

11. Windsor Castle.

1935. Silver Jubilee.

91. 11. 1d. blue and red .. 90 90
92. 1½d. blue and grey .. 1·10 1·10
93. 2½d. brown and blue .. 2·75 4·00
94. 1s grey and purple .. 7·50 9·00

1937. Coronation. As T **2** of Aden.

95. 1d red 20 20
96. 1½d. brown 25 25
97. 2½d. blue 75 75

12. English Harbour.

13. Nelson's Dockyard.

1938.

98. 12. ½d. green 12 12
99. 13. 1d. red 35 35
100. 1½d. brown 50 55
101. 12. 2d. grey 12 12
102. 13. 2½d. blue 20 20
103. – 3d. orange 20 20
104. – 6d. violet 30 30
105. – 1s. black and brown .. 60 50
106. – 2s. 6d. purple .. .. 1·10 1·25
107. – 5s. olive .. .. 2·25 3·25
108. 13. 10s. magenta .. .. 7·00 8·00
109. – £1 green .. .. 12·00 13·00

DESIGNS: HORIZ. 3d., 2s. 6d., £1 Fort James. VERT. 6d., 1s., 5s. St. John's Harbour.

1946. Victory. As T **4** of Aden.

110. 1½d. brown 12 15
111. 3d. orange 12 15

1949. Silver Wedding. As T **5/6** of Aden.

112. 2½d. blue 10 12
113. 5s. green .. .. 3·00 5·00

14. Hermes, Globe and forms of Transport.

15. Hemispheres.

16. Hermes and Globe.

17. U.P.U. Monument.

1949. 75th Anniv. of U.P.U.

114. 14. 2½d. blue 20 30
115. 15. 3d. orange 80 60
116. 16. 6d. purple .. .. 1·40 1·40
117. 17. 1s. brown .. .. 1·40 1·75

18. Arms of University.

19. Princess Alice.

1951. B.W.I. University College. Inaug.

118. 18. 3 c. black and brown .. 15 35
119. 19. 12 c. black and violet .. 35 45

1953. Coronation. As T **7** of Aden.

120. 2 c. black and green .. 25 35

20. Martello Tower.

DESIGNS—HORIZ ½ c., 6 c., 60 c., $4.80, Fort James. VERT. 12 c., 24 c., $1.20, St. John's Harbour.

1953. Designs as 1938 issue but with portrait of Queen Elizabeth II as in T **20**.

120a. – ½ c. brown 5 5
150. 12. 1 c. grey 5 5
151. 13. 2 c. green 5 5
152. 3 c. black and yellow .. 8 8
153. 12. 4 c. red 10 10
154. 13. 5 c. black and lilac .. 12 12
155. – 6 c. yellow 12 12
156. 20. 8 c. blue 12 15
128. – 12 c. violet 25 15
129. – 24 c. black and brown 30 25
130. 20. 48 c. purple and blue .. 80 60
131. – 60 c. maroon .. .. 1·75 90
132. – $1.20 olive .. .. 2·75 3·25
133. 13. $2.40 purple .. .. 4·50 5·50
134. – $4.80 slate .. .. 8·00 9·50

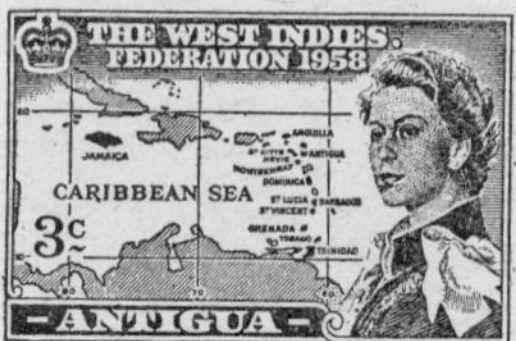

21. Federation Map.

1958. British Caribbean Federation.

135. 21. 3 c. green 10 10
136. 6 c. blue 30 30
137. 12 c. red 45 45

1960. New Constitution. Optd. **COMMEMORATION ANTIGUA CONSTITUTION.**

138. 13. 3 c. black and yellow .. 15 20
139. – 12 c. violet (No. 128) .. 30 25

22. Nelson's Dockyard and Admiral Nelson.

1961. Restoration of Nelson's Dockyard.

140. 22. 20 c. purple and brown 30 35
141. 30 c. green and blue .. 45 50

23. Stamp of 1862 and P.M.S.P. "Solent" at English Harbour.

1962. Stamp Cent.

142. 23. 3 c. purple and green .. 12 12
143. 10 c. blue and green .. 20 20
144. 12 c. sepia and green .. 25 25
145. 50 c. chestnut and green 65 70

1963. Freedom from Hunger. As T **10** of Aden.

146. 12 c. green 55 55

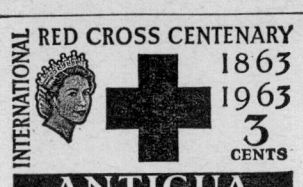

24. Red Cross Emblem.

1963. Red Cross Cent.

No.	Type	Description	Unused	Used
147.	**24.**	3 c. red and black ..	45	45
148.		12 c. red and blue ..	1·75	1·75

25. Shakespeare and Memorial Theatre, Stratford-upon-Avon.

1964. Shakespeare. 400th Birth Anniv.

No.	Type	Description	Unused	Used
164.	**25.**	12 c. brown	40	40

1965. No. 128 surch. **15c.** and bars.

No.	Type	Description	Unused	Used
165.	–	15 c. on 12 c. violet ..	30	30

26. I.T.U. Emblem.

1965. I.T.U. Cent.

No.	Type	Description	Unused	Used
166.	**26.**	2 c. blue and red ..	12	12
167.		50 c. yellow and ultram.	85	90

27. I.C.Y. Emblem.

1965. Int. Co-operation Year.

No.	Type	Description	Unused	Used
168.	**27.**	4 c. purple & turquoise	12	12
169.		15 c. green and lavender	40	35

28. Sir Winston Churchill, and St. Paul's Cathedral in Wartime.

1966. Churchill Commem. Designs in black, cerise and gold with background in colours given.

No.	Type	Description	Unused	Used
170.	**28.**	½ c. blue	5	5
171.		4 c. green	20	20
172.		25 c. brown	45	50
173.		35 c. violet	65	70

29. Queen Elizabeth II and Duke of Edinburgh.

1966. Royal Visit.

No.	Type	Description	Unused	Used
174.	**29.**	6 c. black and blue ..	30	30
175.		15 c. black and magenta	55	55

INDEX

Countries can be quickly located by referring to the index at the end of this volume.

30. Footballer's Legs, Ball and Jules Rimet Cup.

1966. World Cup Football Championships.

No.	Type	Description	Unused	Used
176.	**30.**	6 c. violet, green, lake and brown	15	15
177.		35 c. chocolate, turquoise lake and brown ..	50	50

31. W.H.O. Building.

1966. W.H.O. Headquarters, Geneva. Inaug.

No.	Type	Description	Unused	Used
178.	**31.**	2 c. black, green & blue	5	5
179.		15 c. black, pur. & ochre	35	40

32. Old Post Office, St. John's.

1966.

No.	Type	Description	Unused	Used
234.	–	½ c. green and turquoise	5	5
235a.	**32.**	1 c. purple and cerise ..	5	5
236a.	–	2 c. slate and orange ..	5	5
237.	–	3 c. red and black ..	5	5
238.	–	4 c. violet and brown ..	5	5
239a.	–	5 c. ultramarine & olive	8	8
240.	–	6 c. salmon and purple	10	12
241a.	–	10 c. emerald and red..	12	15
188.	–	15 c. brown and blue ..	15	20
189.	–	25 c. slate and sepia ..	30	35
190.	–	35 c. cerise and brown	45	50
191.	–	50 c. green and black ..	70	85
192.	–	75 c. blue & ultramarine	90	90
193.	–	$1 cerise and olive ..	1·40	1·60
194.	–	$2.50 black and cerise..	2·50	3·00
195.	–	$5 green and violet ..	5·00	5·50

DESIGNS: ½ c. Nelson's Dockyard. 2 c. Health Centre. 3 c. Teachers' Training College. 4 c. Martello Tower, Barbuda. 5 c. Ruins of Officers' Quarters, Shirley Heights. 6 c. Government House, Barbuda. 10 c. Princess Margaret School. 15 c. Air Terminal Building. 25 c. General Post Office. 35 c. Clarence House. 50 c. Government House, St. John's. 75 c. Administration Building. $1 Courthouse, St. John's. $2.50, Magistrates' Court. $5 St. John's Cathedral.

33. "Education".

34. "Science".

35. "Culture".

1966. U.N.E.S.C.O. 20th Anniv.

No.	Type	Description	Unused	Used
196.	**33.**	4 c. violet, yell. & orge.	5	5
197.	**34.**	25 c. yellow, violet & ol.	30	35
198.	**35.**	$1 black, purple & orge.	1·10	1·25

36. State Flag and Maps.

1967. Statehood. Multicoloured.

No.	Type	Description	Unused	Used
199.		4 c. Type **36**	5	5
200.		15 c. State Flag	20	25
201.		25 c. Premier's Office and State Flag	30	35
202.		35 c. State Flag	35	40

37. Gilbert Memorial Church.

1967. Attainment of Autonomy by the Methodist Church.

No.	Type	Description	Unused	Used
203.	**37.**	4 c. black and red ..	5	5
204.	–	25 c. black and green..	30	30
205.	–	35 c. black and blue ..	40	45

DESIGNS: 25 c. Nathaniel Gilbert's House. 35 c. Caribbean and Central American Map.

38. Coat of Arms.

1967. Treaty of Breda. 300th Anniv. and Grant of New Arms.

No.	Type	Description	Unused	Used
206.	**38.**	15 c. multicoloured ..	15	15
207.		35 c. multicoloured ..	30	35

39. Settlers' Ship.

1967. Barbuda Resettlement. 300th Anniv.

No.	Type	Description	Unused	Used
208.	**39.**	4 c. blue	5	5
209.	–	6 c. purple	12	12
210.	**39.**	25 c. green	30	30
211.	–	35 c. black	35	40

DESIGN: 6 c., 35 c. Blaeu's Map of 1665.

40. Tracking Station.

1968. N.A.S.A. Apollo Project. Dow Hill Tracking Station Inaug.

No.	Type	Description	Unused	Used
212.	**40.**	4 c. blue, yellow & black	5	5
213.	–	15 c. blue, yell. & black	20	25
214.	–	25 c. blue, yell. & black	30	30
215.	–	50 c. blue, yell. & black	35	55

DESIGNS: 15 c. Antenna and Spacecraft taking off. 25 c. Spacecraft approaching Moon. 50 c. Re-entry of Space Capsule.

41. Limbo Dancers.

1968. Tourism. Multicoloured.

No.	Type	Description	Unused	Used
216.		½ c. Type **41**	5	5
217.		15 c. Water-skier & Bathers	20	20
218.		25 c. Beach Scene ..	30	35
219.		35 c. Aqua-lung Diver ..	35	35
220.		50 c. Type **41**	45	45

42. Old Harbour in 1768.

1968. Opening of St. John's Deep Water Harbour.

No.	Type	Description	Unused	Used
221.	**42.**	2 c. blue and red ..	5	5
222.	–	15 c. green and sepia ..	20	20
223.	–	25 c. yellow and blue ..	25	25
224.	–	35 c. salmon and emer.	30	35
225.	**42.**	$1 black	65	70

DESIGNS: 15 c. Old Harbour in 1829. 25 c. Freighter and Chart of New Harbour. 35 c. New Harbour.

43. Parliament Building.

1968. Parliament. Tercent. Multicoloured.

No.	Type	Description	Unused	Used
226.		4 c. Type **43**	12	12
227.		15 c. Antigua Mace and Bearer	20	20
228.		25 c. House of Representatives Room ..	30	30
229.		50 c. Arms and Seal of Antigua..	50	50

44. Freight Transport.

1969. Caribbean Free Trade Area. 1st Anniv.

No.	Type	Description	Unused	Used
230.	**44.**	4 c. black and purple ..	5	5
231.		15 c. black and blue ..	20	20
232.	–	25 c. choc., black & ochre	25	25
233.	–	35 c. choc., black & brown	35	35

DESIGN—VERT. 25 c., 35 c. Crate of cargo.

45. Island of Redonda (Chart).

1969. Redonda Phosphate Industry. Cent. Multicoloured.

No.	Type	Description	Unused	Used
249.		15 c. Type **45**	25	25
250.		25 c. View of Redonda from the sea	35	40
251.		50 c. As Type **45** ..	55	60

46. "The Adoration of the Magi" (Marcillat).

1969. Christmas. Multicoloured.

252. 6 c. Type **46** 12 12
253. 10 c. "The Nativity" (unknown German, 15th Cent.) 20 20
254. 35 c. As Type **46** .. 35 35
255. 50 c. As 10 c. 45 50

1970. Surch. **20c.** and bars

256. 20 c. on 25 c. (No. 243) .. 30 30

47. Coat of Arms.

1970. Coil Stamps.

257. **47.** 5 c. blue 5 5
258. 10 c. emerald 5 5
259. 25 c. red 10 12

48. Sikorski "S-38".

1970. Antiguan Air Services. 40th Anniv. Multicoloured.

260. 5 c. Type **48** 15 15
261. 20 c. Dornier "DO-X" .. 35 35
262. 35 c. Hawker Siddeley "HS-748" 45 45
263. 50 c. Douglas "C-124C" (Globemaster II) .. 55 55
264. 75 c. Vickers "VC-10" .. 1·90 1·90

49. Dickens and Scene from "Nicholas Nickleby".

1970. Charles Dickens. Death Cent.

265. **49.** 5 c. bistre, sepia & blk. 12 12
266. – 20 c. turquoise-blue, sepia and black .. 30 30
267. – 35 c. vio.-bl., sep. & blk. 35 40
268. – $1 red, sepia & black .. 75 85

DESIGNS: All stamps show Dickens and scene from: 20 c. "Pickwick Papers". 35 c. "Oliver Twist". $1 "David Copperfield".

50. Carib Indian and War Canoe.

1970. Multicoloured.

269. ½ c. Type **50** 5 5
270. 1 c. Columbus and "Nina" 5 5
271. 2 c. Sir Thomas Warner's emblem and ship .. 5 5
272. 3 c. Viscount Hood and H.M.S. "Barfleur" .. 5 5
273. 4 c. Sir George Rodney and H.M.S. "Formidable" .. 8 8
274. 5 c. Nelson and H.M.S. "Boreas" 10 10
275. 6 c. William IV and H.M.S. "Pegasus" .. 10 12
276. 10 c. "Blackbeard" and pirate ketch 12 15
277. 15 c. Collingwood and H.M.S. "Pelican" .. 15 20
278. 20 c. Nelson and H.M.S. "Victory" 20 25
279. 25 c. R.M.S.P. "Solent" .. 25 25
280. 35 c. George V (when Prince George) and H.M.S. "Canada" 35 40
281. 50 c. H.M.S. "Renown" .. 40 50
282. 75 c. "Federal Maple" .. 65 75
283. $1 Yacht and class emblem 75 90
284. $2·50 H.M.S. "London" .. 2·25 2·50
285. $5 Tug "Pathfinder" .. 4·50 5·00

51. "The Small Passion" (detail) (Durer).

1970. Christmas.

286. **51.** 3 c. black and blue .. 12 12
287. – 10 c. purple and pink 15 15
288. **51.** 35 c. black and red .. 30 30
289. – 50 c. black and lilac .. 50 55

DESIGN: 10 c., 50 c. "Adoration of the Magi" (detail) (Durer).

52. 4th King's Own Regt., 1759.

1970. Military Uniforms (1st series). Multicoloured.

290. ½ c. Type **52** 20 20
291. 10 c. 4th West India Regt., 1804. .. .. .. 30 30
292. 20 c. 60th Regt., The Royal American, 1809 .. 45 45
293. 35 c. 93rd Regt., Sutherland Highlanders, 1826-34 .. 75 75
294. 75 c. 3rd West India Regt., 1851 .. .. .. 1·40 1·40

See also Nos. 303/7, 313/17, 353/7 and 380/4.

53. Market Woman casting Vote.

1971. Adult Suffrage. 20th Anniv.

296. **53.** 5 c. brown 5 5
297. – 20 c. olive 20 20
298. – 35 c. purple 25 30
299. – 50 c. blue 35 40

DESIGNS: People voting: 20 c. Executive. 35 c. Housewife. 50 c. Artisan.

54. "The Last Supper".

1971. Easter. Woodcuts by Durer.

300. **54.** 5 c. black, grey & red .. 10 10
301. – 35 c. black, grey & violet 30 30
302. – 75 c. black, grey & gold 45 45

DESIGNS: 35 c. "The Crucifixion". 75 c. "The Resurrection".

1971. Military Uniforms (2nd series). As T **52.** Multicoloured.

303. ½ c. Private, 12th Regt., The Suffolk (1704) .. 10 10
304. 10 c. Grenadier, 38th Regt., South Staffs. (1751) 20 20
305. 20 c. Light Company, 5th Regt., Royal Northumberland Fusiliers (1778) 35 35
306. 35 c. Private, 48th Regt., The Northamptonshire (1793) 65 65
307. 75 c. Private, 15th Regt., East Yorks (1805) .. 1·40 1·40

55. "Madonna and Child" (detail, Veronese).

1971. Christmas. Multicoloured.

309. 3 c. Type **55** 5 5
310. 5 c. "Adoration of the Shepherds" (detail, Veronese) 12 12
311. 35 c. Type **55** 40 40
312. 50 c. As 5 c. 45 45

1972. Military Uniforms (3rd Series). As T **52.** Multicoloured.

313. ½ c. Battalion Company Officer, 25th Foot, 1815 10 10
314. 10 c. Sergeant, 14th Foot, 1837 .. .. .. 15 15
315. 20 c. Private, 67th Foot, 1853 .. .. .. 35 35
316. 35 c. Officer, Royal Artillery, 1854 .. .. .. 65 65
317. 75 c. Private, 29th Foot, 1870 .. .. .. 1·40 1·40

56. Cowrie Helmet.

1972. Shells. Multicoloured.

319. 3 c. Type **56** 5 5
320. 5 c. Measeled Cowrie .. 10 10
321. 35 c. West Indian Fighting Conch 30 30
322. 50 c. Hawk Wing Conch .. 35 40

57. St. John's Cathedral, Side View.

1972. Christmas and St. John's Cathedral. 125th Anniv. Multicoloured.

335. 35 c. Type **57** 40 40
336. 50 c. Cathedral interior .. 55 55
337. 75 c. St. John's Cathedral 80 80

1972. Royal Silver Wedding. As T **19,** of Ascension, but with floral background.

339. 20 c. blue 20 25
340. 35 c. blue 30 40

58. Cricketer and Map.

1972. Rising Sun Cricket Club. 50th Anniv. Multicoloured.

341. 5 c. Type **58** 5 5
342. 35 c. Two cricketers .. 30 30
343. $1 Club badge 75 75

59. Yacht and Map.

1972. Antigua and Barbuda Tourist Office in New York. Inaug. Multicoloured.

345. 35 c. Type **59** 35 35
346. 50 c. Yachts 40 40
347. 75 c. Post Office 55 55
348. $1 Statue of Liberty, New York 80 80

60. Stained-glass window.

1973. Easter.

350. **60.** 5 c. multicoloured .. 5 5
351. – 35 c. multicoloured .. 30 30
352. – 75 c. multicoloured .. 40 45

Nos. 350/2 show different stained-glass windows from St. John's Cathedral.

1973. Military Uniforms (4th series). As T **52.** Multicoloured.

353. ½ c. Private, Zachariah Tiffin's Regt., of Foot, 1701 .. .. .. 5 5
354. 10 c. Private, 63rd Regt., of Foot, 1759 .. .. 12 12
355. 20 c. Light Company Officer, 35th Regt., of Foot, 1828 20 20
356. 35 c. Private, 2nd West India Regt., 1853 .. 30 30
357. 75 c. Sergeant, 49th Regt., 1858 .. .. .. 50 50

61. Butterfly Costumes.

1973. Carnival. Multicoloured.

359. 5 c. Type **61** 8 10
360. 20 c. Carnival street scene 20 20
361. 35 c. Carnival troupe 30 30
362. 75 c. Carnival Queen 45 50

62. " Virgin of the Milk Porridge " (Gerard David).

1973. Christmas. Multicoloured.

364. 3 c. Type **62** 5 5
365. 5 c. " Adoration of the Kings " (Stomer) 5 5
366. 20 c. " The Granduca Madonna " (Raphael) 20 20
367. 35 c. " Nativity with God the Father and Holy Ghost " (Battista) 30 30
368. $1 " Madonna and Child " (Murillo) 70 70

63. Princess Anne and Captain Mark Phillips.

1973. Royal Wedding.

370. **63.** 35 c. multicoloured 25 25
371. – $2 multicoloured 1·10 1·25

The $2 is as T **63** but has a different border.

1973. Nos. 370/1 optd. **HONEYMOON VISIT DECEMBER 16th 1973.**

373. **63.** 35 c. multicoloured 25 25
374. – $2 multicoloured 1·10 1·25

64. Coat of Arms of Antiqua and University.

1974. University of West Indies. 25th Anniv. Multicoloured.

376. 5 c. Type **64** 5 5
377. 20 c. Extra-mural art 20 20
378. 35 c. Antigua campus 30 30
379. 75 c. Antigua chancellor 45 50

1974. Military Uniforms (5th series). As T **52**. Multicoloured.

380. ½ c Officer, 59th Foot, 1797 5 5
381. 10 c. Gunner, Royal Artillery, 1800 5 5
382. 20 c. Private, 1st West India Regt., 1830 20 20
383. 35 c. Officer, 92nd Foot, 1843 30 30
384. 75 c. Private, 23rd Foot, 1846 45 50

65. English Postman, Mailcoach and Helicopter.

1974, U.P.U. Centenary. Multicoloured.

386. ½ c. Type **65** 5 5
387. 1 c. Bellman, mailboat " Orinoco " and satellite 5 5
388. 2 c. Train guard, post-bus and hydrofoil 5 5
389. 5 c. Swiss messenger, Wells Fargo coach and " Concorde " 5 5
390. 20 c. Postillion, Japanese postmen and carrier pigeon 20 20
391. 35 c. Antiguan postman, flying-boat and tracking station 30 30
392. $1 Medieval courier, American express train and Boeing " 747 " 50 55

66. Traditional Player.

1974. Antiguan Steel Bands.

394. **66.** 5 c. dull red, red & black 5 5
395. – 20 c. brn. light brn. & blk. 20 20
396. – 35 c. light grn. grn. & blk. 25 30
397. – 75 c. blue, dull bl. & blk. 45 45

DESIGNS—HORIZ. 20 c. Traditional band. 35 c. Modern band. VERT. 75 c. Modern player.

67. Footballers.

1974. World Cup Football Championships.

399. **67.** 5 c. multicoloured 5 5
400. – 35 c. multicoloured 20 25
401. – 75 c. multicoloured 40 40
402. – $1 multicoloured 50 50

Nos. 400/2 show various footballing designs similar to Type **67**.

1974. Earthquake Relief Fund. Nos. 400/2 and 397 optd. or surch. **EARTHQUAKE RELIEF.**

404. 35 c. multicoloured 25 25
405. 75 c. multicoloured 40 40
406. $1 multicoloured 50 50
407. $5 on 75 c. dull blue, blue and black 2·40 2·60

68. Churchill as Schoolboy and School College Building, Harrow.

1974. Sir Winston Churchill. Birth Cent. Multicoloured.

408. 5 c. Type **68** 5 5
409. 35 c. Churchill and St. Paul's Cathedral 25 25
410. 75 c. Coat of arms and catafalque 40 40
411. $1 Churchill, " reward " notice and South African escape route 50 50

69. "Madonna and Child" (Bellini).

1974. Christmas. "Madonna and Child" paintings by named artists. Multicoloured.

413. ½ c. Type **69** 5 5
414. 1 c. Raphael 5 5
415. 2 c. Van der Weyden 5 5
416. 3 c. Giorgione 5 5
417. 5 c. Mantegna 5 5
418. 20 c. Vivarini 15 15
419. 35 c. Montagna 20 20
420. 75 c. L. Costa 40 40

1975. Nos. 390/2 and 282 surch.

422. 50 c. on 20 c. multicoloured 25 30
423. $2.50 on 35 c. mult. 1·40 1·60
424. $5 on $1 multicoloured 2·50 2·75
425. $10 on 75 c. mult. 4·50 4·75

70. Carib War Canoe, English Harbour, 1300.

1975. Nelson's Dockyard. Multicoloured.

427. 5 c. Type **70** 5 5
428. 15 c. Ship of the line, English Harbour, 1770 8 8
429. 35 c. HMS " Boreas " at anchor, and Lord Nelson, 1787 20 20
430. 50 c. Yachts during " Sailing Week ", 1974 25 30
431. $1 Yacht Anchorage, Old Dockyard, 1970 45 50

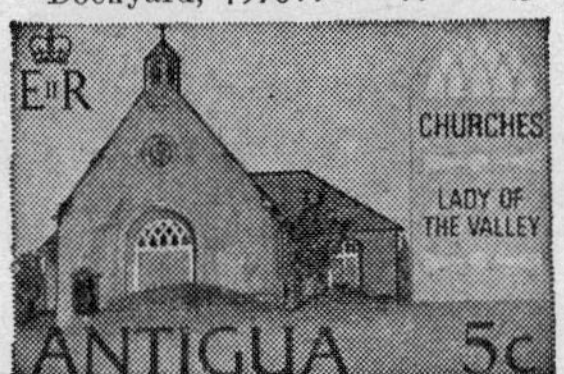

71. Lady of the Valley Church.

1975. Antiguan Churches. Multicoloured.

433. 5 c. Type **71** 5 5
434. 20 c. Gilbert Memorial 10 10
435. 35 c. Grace Hill Moravian 20 20
436. 50 c. St. Phillips 25 30
437. $1 Ebenezer Methodist 45 50

72. Map of 1721 and Sextant of 1640.

1975. Maps of Antigua. Multicoloured.

439. 5 c. Type **72** 5 5
440. 20 c. Map of 1775 and galleon 10 12
441. 35 c. Maps of 1775 and 1955 15 15
442. $1 1973 maps of Antigua and English Harbour 45 50

73. Scout Bugler.

1975. World Scout Jamboree, Norway. Multicoloured.

444. 15 c. Type **73** 5 8
445. 20 c. Scouts in camp 8 10
446. 35 c. Lord Baden-Powell 15 15
447. $2 Scout dancers from Dahomey 85 95

74. " Eurema elathea ".

1975. Butterflies. Multicoloured.

449. ½ c. Type **74** 5 5
450. 1 c. " Danaus plexippus " 5 5
451. 2 c. " Phoebis philea " 5 5
452. 5 c. " Marpoesia petreus thetys " 5 5
453. 20 c. " Eurema proterpia " 10 12
454. 35 c. " Papilio polydamus " 20 20
455. $2 " Vanessa cardui " 90 1·00

75. " Virgin and Child " (Correggio).

1975. Christmas. " Virgin and Child " paintings by artists named. Mult.

457. ½ c. Type **75** 5 5
458. 1 c. El Greco 5 5
459. 2 c. Durer 5 5
460. 3 c. Antonello 5 5
461. 5 c. Bellini 5 5
462. 10 c. Durer (different) 5 5
463. 35 c. Bellini (different) 15 15
464. $2 Durer (different again) 90 1·00

76. Vivian Richards.

1975. World Cricket Cup Winners. Mult.

466. 5 c. Type **76** 5 5
467. 35 c. Andy Roberts (horiz.) 15 15
468. $2 West Indies Team (horiz.) 90 1·00

77. Antillean Crested Hummingbird.

1976. Multicoloured.

469. ½ c. Type **77** 5 5
470. 1 c. Imperial Parrot 5 5
471. 2 c. Zenaida Dove 5 5
472. 3 c. Loggerhead Kingbird 5 5
473. 4 c. Red-necked Pigeon 5 5
474. 5 c. Rufous-throated Solitaire 5 5
475. 6 c. Orchid tree 5 5
476. 10 c. Bougainvillea 5 5
477. 15 c. Geiger tree 5 5
478. 20 c. Flamboyant 8 8
479. 25 c. Hibiscus 10 10
480. 35 c. Flame of the Wood 12 15
481. 50 c. Cannon at Fort James 20 20
482. 75 c. Premier's Office 25 30
483. $1 Potworks Dam 35 40
484. $2.50 Diamond irrigation scheme 90 1·00
485. $5 Government House 1·75 2·00
486. $10 Coolidge International Airport 3·50 4·00

Nos. 484/6 are larger, 44×28 mm.

78. Privates, Clark's Illinois. Regt.

1976. American Revolution. Bicent. Multicoloured.
487. ½ c. Type 78 .. .. 5 5
488. 1 c. Rifleman, Pennsylvania Militia 5 5
489. 2 c. Powder horn.. .. 5 5
490. 5 c. Water bottle.. .. 5 5
491. 35 c. American flags .. 20 20
492. $1 Privateer "Montgomery" 50 55
493. $5 Sloop "Ranger" .. 2·50 2·75

79. High Jump.

1976. Olympic Games, Montreal.
495. 79. ½ c. brown, yell. & blk. 5 5
496. – 1 c. violet and black .. 5 5
497. – 2 c. green and black .. 5 5
498. – 15 c. blue and black .. 8 10
499. – 30 c. brn., yell. and blk. 15 20
500. – $1 orange, red & black 50 55
501. – $2 red and black .. 90 1·00
DESIGNS: 1 c. Boxing. 2 c. Pole vault. 15 c. Swimming. 30 c. Running. $1 Cycling. $2 Shot put.

80. Water Skiing.

1976. Water Sports. Multicoloured.
503. ½ c. Type 80 .. .. 5 5
504. 1 c. Sailing 5 5
505. 2 c. Snorkeling 5 5
506. 20 c. Deep sea fishing .. 8 10
507. 50 c. Scuba diving .. 20 25
508. $2 Swimming 80 90

81. French Angelfish.

1976. Fish. Multicoloured.
510. 15 c. Type 81 .. .. 5 8
511. 30 c. Yellowfin Grouper.. 12 15
512. 50 c. Yellowtail Snappers 20 25
513. 90 c. Shy Hamlet .. 35 40

ANTIOQUIA O1

One of the states of the Granadine Confederation.

A department of Colombia from 1886, now uses Colombian stamps.

1. 2. 3.

1868. Various arms designs. Imperf.
1. 1. 2½ c. blue £200 £120
2. – 5 c. green .. .. .. £150 95·00
3. – 10 c. lilac £450 £180
4. – 1 p. red .. .. .. £120 75·00

1869. Various frames. Imperf.
5. 2. 2½ c. blue .. .. .. 1·10 70
6. 5 c. green .. .. .. 1·25 1·25
8. 10 c. mauve .. .. 1·75 1·00
9. 20 c. brown .. .. 1·90 1·10
10. 3. 1 p. red .. .. 2·75 2·75

4. 12.

1873. Arms designs inscr. "E.S." (or "Eo. So."or"Estado Soberono")"de Antioquia". Imperf.
11. 4. 1 c. green .. .. 1·40 1·10
12. – 5 c. green .. .. 1·60 1·25
13. – 10 c. mauve .. .. 7·00 5·00
14. – 20 c. brown .. .. 1·75 1·75
15. – 50 c. blue 55 55
16. – 1 p. red 80 80
17. – 2 p. black on yellow .. 1·50 1·50
18. – 5 p. black on red .. 10·00 8·00
The 5 p. is larger (25½ × 31½ mm).

1875. Imperf.
20. 12. 1 c. black on green .. 50 50
43. 1 c. mauve 65 65
21. 1 c. black 50 50
52. 1 c. green 70 70
22. – 2½ c. blue (Arms) .. 75 75
23. – 5 c. green ("Liberty") 5·50 4·50
25. – 10 c. mauve (J. Berrio) 7·00 4·50

16. Condor. 17. Liberty.

18. Liberty 19.

1879. Imperf.
30. 16. 2½ c. blue 80 80
38. 2½ c. green 70 65
45. 2½ c. black on buff .. 1·75 1·75
39. 17. 5 c. green 60 60
40. 5 c. violet .. .. 1·40 80
32. – 10 c. violet (Arms) .. £170 £140
36. 18. 10 c. violet .. .. 42·00 12·00
41. 10 c. red 65 65
42. 17. 20 c. brown 80 70

1883. Various frames. Head of Liberty to left. Imperf.
53. 19. 5 c. brown .. .. 1·25 90
47. 5 c. yellow .. .. 1·25 1·10
48. 5 c. green .. .. 35·00 21·00
49. 10 c. green .. .. 1·00 90
50. 10 c. mauve .. .. 2·00 2·00
55. 10 c. blue .. .. 1·40 1·25
51. 20 c. blue 90 90

20. 21.

1886. Imperf.
57. 20. 1 c. green on pink .. 25 25
65. 1 c. red on lilac 12 12
58. 2½ c. black on orange .. 20 20
66. 2½ c. mauve on pink .. 20 15
59. 5 c. blue on buff .. 65 35
67. 5 c. red on green .. 1·00 90
68. 5 c. lake on buff .. 40 35
60. 20. 10 c. red on buff .. 50 30
69. 10 c. brown on green .. 40 35
61. 20 c. purple on buff .. 60 35
62. 50 c. yellow on buff .. 80 80
63. 1 p. yellow on green .. 1·00 1·00
64. 2 p. green on lilac .. 1·00 1·00

1888. Various sizes and frames. Inscr. "MEDELLIN". Imperf.
70. 21. 2½ c. black on yellow .. 6·00 5·50
71. 2½ c. red on white .. 1·60 1·70
72. 5 c. black on yellow .. 1·25 1·25
73. 5 c. red on orange .. 1·00 1·00

22.  23. 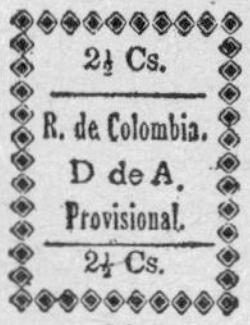 24.

1889. Arms in various frames.
74. 22. 1 c. black on red .. 5 5
75. 2½ c. black on blue .. 10 8
76. 5 c. black on yellow .. 15 12
77. 10 c. black on green .. 20 25
95. 10 c. brown 10 8
78. 20 c. blue 50 45
79. 50 c. brown .. .. 1·50 1·60
80. 50 c. green .. .. 1·00 1·00
81. 1 p. red 65 65
82. 23. 2 p. black on magenta.. 6·00 5·00
83. 5 p. black on red .. 7·00 6·00

1890. Perf.
84. 24. 2½ c. black on buff .. 30 30
85. 5 c. black on yellow .. 30 30
86. 10 c. black on buff .. 2·10 2·10
87. 10 c. black on red .. 1·75 1·75
88. 20 c. black on yellow .. 1·75 1·75

25. 26.

1892.
89. 25. 1 c. brown on buff .. 25 15
90. 1 c. blue 8 8
91. 2½ c. violet on lilac .. 15 12
92. 2½ c. green 15 12
93. 5 c. black 40 25
94. 5 c. red 8 5

1896.
96. 26. 2 c. grey 15 15
107. 2 c. claret 12 15
97. 2½ c. brown 15 15
108. 2½ c. blue 12 15
98. 3 c. red 20 20
109. 3 c. olive 12 15
99. 5 c. green 10 8
110. 5 c. yellow 10 12
100. 10 c. lilac 25 25
111. 10 c. brown 25 25
101. 20 c. brown 30 30
112. 20 c. blue 50 45
102. 50 c. sepia 45 45
113. 50 c. red 70 65
103. 1 p. black and blue .. 5·50 5·50
114. 1 p. black and red .. 5·50 5·50
104. 2 p. black and orange.. 20·00 20·00
115. 2 p. black and green .. 20·00 20·00
105. 5 p. black and mauve .. 23·00 23·00

27. Gen. Cordova. 28.

1899.
118. 27. ½ c. blue 5 5
119. 1 c. blue 5 5
120. 2 c. black 5 5
121. 3 c. red 5 10
122. 4 c. brown 5 5
123. 5 c. green 5 5
124. 10 c. red 5 5
125. 20 c. violet 5 5
126. 50 c. yellow 5 5
127. 1 p. grey-green 5 12
128. 2 p. green 5 20

1901. Various frames.
132. 28. 1 c. red 10 15
133. 1 c. brown 25 25
134. 1 c. blue 25 25
Nos. 132 and 134 also exist with "CENTAVO" inside the rectangle below figure "1".

29. 30. 31. Girardot.

1902.
138. 29. 1 c. red 5 5
139. 1 c. blue 5 5
140. 2 c. blue 5 5
141. 2 c. violet 5 5
142. 3 c. green 5 5
143. 4 c. purple 5 5
144. 30. 5 c. red 8 8
145. 10 c. mauve 8 8
147. 20 c. green 12 12
148. 30 c. red 12 10
149. 31. 40 c. blue 12 10
150. 50 c. brown on yellow.. 20 20
152. – 1 p. black and violet .. 40 45
153. – 2 p. black and red .. 40 45
154. – 5 p. black and blue .. 50 55
DESIGN: 1 p. to 5 p. Dr. J. Felix de Restrepo. No. 145 also exists with smaller head.

32. 33. 34. Zea.

1903.
159. 32. 4 c. brown 8 5
160. 5 c. blue 8 5
161. 33. 10 c. yellow 8 5
162. 20 c. lilac 8 10
163. 30 c. brown 30 30
164. 40 c. green 30 30
165. 50 c. red 10 12
166. 34. 1 p. grey-green .. 25 15
167. 2 p. mauve (Rovira) .. 25 15
168. 3 p. blue (La Pola) .. 30 30
169. 4 p. red (Restrepo) .. 50 30
170. 5 p. brown (Madrid) .. 50 30
171. 10 p. red (Corral) .. 2·25 2·25

ACKNOWLEDGMENT OF RECEIPT STAMPS

A 1.

1902.
AR157. A 1. 5 c. black on red.. 30 20
AR158. 5 c. grey-green .. 10 10

REGISTRATION STAMPS

R 1.

1896.
R 106. R 1. 2½ c. pink.. .. 40 40
R 117. 2½ c. blue.. .. 40 40

R 2. General Cordova. R 3.

1899.
R 130. R 2. 2½ c. blue 8 8
R 131. R 3. 10 c. claret.. .. 8 8

R 4.

1902.
R 156. R 4. 10 c. violet on green.. 10 10

TOO LATE STAMPS

T 1. Gen. Cordova. T 2.

1899.
L 129. T 1. 2½ c. green 5 8

1901. As T 28, but inscr. "RETARDO" at sides.
L 137a. – 2½ c. purple .. 30 30

1902.
L 155. T 2. 2½ c. lilac 8 8

ARBE E1

During the period of D'Annunzio's Italian Regency of Carnaro (Fiume), separate issues were made for Arbe (now Rab).

1920. No. 148, etc. of Fiume optd. **ARBE.**
1. 5 c. green 25 25
2. 10 c. red 85 40
3. 20 c. brown .. .. .. 1·00 60
4. 25 c. blue .. .. .. 3·25 1·90
5. 50 on 20 c. brown .. .. 1·40 85
6. 55 on 5 c. green .. .. 1·40 85

EXPRESS LETTER STAMPS.

1920. Nos. E163/4 of Fiume optd. **ARBE.**
E 7. 30 c. on 20 c. brown .. 21·00 7·00
E 8. 50 on 5 c. green .. .. 6·00 3·00

ARGENTINE REPUBLIC O1

A republic in the S.E. of S. America formerly part of the Spanish Empire.

100 centavos = 1 peso.
1970. 100 old pesos = 1 new peso.

1. Argentine Confederation. 2.

1858. Imperf.
1. 1. 5 c. red .. .. .. 20 3·00
2. 10 c. green .. .. .. 75 10·00
3. 15 c. blue .. .. .. 2·50 30·00

1862. Imperf.
10. 2. 5 c. red .. .. .. 5·00 3·50
8. 10 c. green .. .. .. 30·00 20·00
9. 15 c. blue .. .. .. 50·00 35·00

3. Rivadavia. 4.

1864. Imperf.
24. 3. 5 c. red .. .. .. 50·00 20·00
14. 4. 10 c. green £600 £350
15. 3. 15 c. blue £1200 £850

1864. Perf.
16. 3. 5 c. red .. .. .. 10·00 2·00
17. 4. 10 c. green .. .. .. 15·00 6·00
18. 3. 15 c. blue .. .. .. 20·00 12·00

5. B. Rivadavia. 6. Gen. Belgrano. 7. Gen. San Martin.

1867. Perf.
28. 5. 5 c. red 80 12
29. 6. 10 c. green .. .. .. 2·75 80
30a. 7. 15 c. blue .. .. .. 10·00 2·10

8. Balcarce. 13. Lopez. 14. Sarsfield.

1873. Portraits. Perf.
31. 8. 1 c. violet 80 35
32. – 4 c. brown (Moreno) .. 75 12
33. – 30 c. orange (Alvear) .. 14·00 2·00
34. – 60 c. black (Posadas) .. 12·00 80
35. – 90 c. blue (Saavedra) .. 2·25 35

1877. Surch. with large figure of value.
37. 5. 1 on 5 c. red .. .. 5·00 2·40
38. 2 on 5 c. red .. .. 16·00 7·00
39. 6. 8 on 10 c. green .. .. 9·50 2·25

1876. Roul.
36. 5. 5 c. red .. .. .. 21·00 9·00
40. 8 c. lake .. .. .. 2·40 10
41. 6. 16 c. green 65 15
42. 14. 20 c. blue 75 30
43. 7. 24 c. blue .. .. .. 3·50 40

1877. Perf.
46. 13. 2 c. green 55 15
44. 5. 8 c. lake 40 10
45. 7. 24 c. blue .. .. .. 2·25 20
47. – 25 c. lake (Alvear) .. 3·50 1·00

1882. Surch. **1/2 (PROVISORIO).**
51. 5. ½ on 5 c. red 15 15

15. 16.

1882.
52. 15. ½ c. brown 20 15
55. 1 c. red 45 25
54. 12 c. blue .. .. 7·00 1·25

1884. Surch. **1884** and value in figs. or words.
90. 5. ½ on 5 c. red 30 30
92. 7. ½ c. on 15 c. blue .. 35 35
94. 1 c. on 15 c. blue .. 90 70
100. 5. 4 c. on 5 c. red .. 1·00 30

1884.
101. 16. ½ c. brown 15 12
102. 1 c. red 45 10
103a. 12 c. blue .. .. 2·10 25

17. Urquiza. 28. Mitre.

1888. Portrait types, inscr. "CORREOS ARGENTINOS".
108. 17. ½ c. blue 10 8
110. – 2 c. green (Lopez) .. 1·60 1·25
111a. – 3 c. green (Celman) .. 25 12
113. – 5 c. red (Rivadavia) .. 65 12
114. – 6 c. red (Sarmiento) .. 2·25 1·75
115. – 10 c. brown (Avellaneda) 1·25 15
116. – 15 c. orge. (San Martin) 80 35
117a. – 20 c. green (Roca) .. 75 15
118. – 25 c. violet (Belgrano) 1·10 20
119. – 30 c. brown (Dorrego) 1·40 35
120a. – 40 c. slate (Moreno) .. 3·25 1·00
121. 28. 50 c. blue .. .. 8·00 1·10

29. Paz. 34. Rivadavia.

1888. Portrait types, inscr. "CORREOS Y TELEGRAFOS".
137. 29. ½ c. green 5 5
122. – ½ c. blue (Urquiza) .. 8 5
123. – 1 c. brown (Sarsfield) .. 10 8
125. – 2 c. violet (Derqui) .. 10 5
126. – 3 c. green (Celman) .. 15 12
127. 34. 5 c. red 30 8
129. – 6 c. blue (Sarmiento) .. 25 15
130. – 10 c. brown (Avellaneda) 30 8
131. – 12 c. blue (Alberti) .. 50 25
132. – 40 c. grey (Moreno) .. 65 12
133. – 50 c. orange (Mitre) .. 50 20
134. – 60 c. black (Posadas) .. 1·60 50

1890. No. 131 surch. **1/4** and bars.
135. – ¼ on 12 c. blue 10 8

41. Rivadavia. 43. La Madrid. 45. Rivadavia.

1890.
128a. 41. 5 c. red 10 5

1891. Portraits.
139. – 1 p. blue (San Martin) .. 4·25 1·10
140. 43. 5 p. blue .. .. 23·00 4·00
141. – 20 p. green (G. Brown) 28·00 18·00

1891.
138. 45. 8 c. red 15 12

46. Rivadavia. 47. Belgrano. 48. San Martin.

1892.
142. 46. ½ c. blue 5 5
143. 1 c. brown 8 5
144. 2 c. green 10 5
145. 3 c. orange 12 5
146. 46. 5 c. red 15 5
147. 47. 10 c. red 80 5
148. 12 c. blue 60 5
149. 16 c. slate .. .. 1·25 10
150. 24 c. sepia .. .. 1·00 12
257. 30 c. orange .. .. 2·00 8
151. 50 c. green .. .. 1·25 12
188. 80 c. lilac .. .. 1·40 20
152a. 48. 1 p. red .. .. 1·10 15
190. 1 p. 20 black .. .. 2·25 40
153. 2 p. green .. .. 3·50 70
154. 5 p. deep blue .. .. 5·50 70

49. Fleet of Columbus. 50. "Liberty" and Shield.

1892. Discovery of America. 4th Cent.
219. 49. 2 c. blue 60 40
220. 5 c. blue 70 50

1899.
221. 50. ½ c. brown 5 5
222. 1 c. green 5 5
223. 2 c. slate 5 5
224. 3 c. orange 10 5
225. 4 c. yellow 12 5
226. 5 c. red 5 5
227. 6 c. black 10 8
228. 10 c. green 15 5
229a. 12 c. blue 20 12
230a. 12 c. olive 12 5
231. 15 c. blue 12 5
232. 16 c. orange .. .. 1·40 1·25
233. 20 c. red 20 5
234a. 24 c. purple 30 12
235. 30 c. red 70 12
237. 50 c. blue 45 5
238. – 1 p. black and blue .. 1·25 8
239. – 5 p. black and orange .. 5·00 1·40
240. – 10 p. black and green .. 8·00 1·90
241. – 20 p. black and red .. 23·00 5·00

The peso values are larger (19 × 32 mm.).

52. Port Rosario. 53. Gen. San Martin.

1902. Completion of Port Rosario Dock.
290. 52. 5 c. blue 60 35

1908.
291. 53. ½ c. violet 5 5
292. 1 c. brown 5 5
293. 2 c. chocoolate 8 5
294. 3 c. green 8 5
295. 4 c. mauve 15 5
296. 5 c. red 5 5
297. 6 c. olive 10 8
298. 10 c. green 15 5
299. 12 c. brown 5 5
300. 12 c. blue 8 5
301. 15 c. green 8 5
302. 20 c. blue 10 5
303. 24 c. claret 25 15
304. 30 c. claret 40 15
305. 50 c. black 40 10
306. – 1 p. red and blue .. 1·00 25

The 1 p. is larger (21½ × 27 mm.) with portrait at upper left.

54. Pyramid of May. 57. Saavedra.

55. Azcuenaga and Alberti.

1910. Deposition of the Spanish Viceroy. Centenary.
366. 54. ½ c. blue and slate .. 8 5
367. – 1 c. black and green .. 15 10
368. – 2 c. black and olive .. 12 5
369. 55. 3 c. green 15 10
370. – 4 c. green and blue .. 15 10
371. 57. 5 c. red 15 5
372. – 10 c. black and brown .. 30 15
373. – 12 c. blue 30 12
374. – 20 c. black and sepia .. 30 15
375. – 24 c. blue and brown .. 35 25
376. – 30 c. black and lilac .. 35 15
377. – 50 c. black and red .. 80 25
378. – 1 p. blue .. .. 1·50 70
379. – 5 p. purple and orange 12·00 6·50
380. – 10 p. black and orange 24·00 13·00
381. – 20 p. black and blue .. 35·00 25·00

DESIGNS—VERT. 50 c. Crowds on 25 May, 1810. 10 p. Centenary Monument. 20 p. San Martin. HORIZ. 1 c. Pena and Vieytes. 2 c. Meeting at Pena's house. 4 c. Fort of the Viceroys, Buenos Aires. 10 c. Distribution of badges. 12 c. Congress Building. 20 c. Castelli and Matheu. 24 c. First National Council. 30 c. Belgrano and Larrea. 1 p. Moreno and Paso. 5 p. Oath of the Junta.

58. 59.

1911. President Sarmiento. Birth Cent.
382. 58. 5 c. black and brown .. 20 15

1911.
383. 59. 5 c. red 5 5
384. 12 c. blue 30 5

60. 61.

1911.
395. 60. ½ c. violet 5 5
396. 1 c. brown 5 5
397. 2 c. purple-brown .. 5 5
398. 3 c. green 8 5
399. 4 c. purple 8 5
400. 5 c. red 5 5
401. 10 c. green 12 5
402. 12 c. blue 10 5
403. 20 c. blue 50 10
404. 24 c. brown 60 25
405. 30 c. claret 45 15
406. 50 c. black .. .. 1·90 40
408. 61. 1 p. red and blue .. 1·10 20
409. 5 p. green and grey .. 3·75 1·25
410. 10 p. blue and violet 17·00 3·00
411. 20 p. claret and blue 38·00 16·00

62. Dr. F. N. Laprida. 63. Declaration of Independence.

64. San Martin. 65.

1916. Independence Cent. Inscr. "1816–1916".
417. 62. ½ c. violet 5 5
418. 1 c. orange-brown .. 8 5
419. 2 c. purple-brown .. 5 5
420. 3 c. green 8 5
421. 4 c. purple 10 5
422. 63. 5 c. red 5 5
423. 10 c. green 10 5
424. 64. 12 c. blue 8 5
425. 20 c. blue 15 8
426. 24 c. claret 25 15
427. 30 c. rose 25 15
428. 50 c. black 35 20
429. 1 p. red and blue .. 1·60 80
430. 5 p. green and grey .. 22·00 11·00
431. 10 p. blue and violet 27·00 21·00
432. 20 p. claret and slate 32·00 21·00

1917.
433. 65. ½ c. violet 5 5
434. 1 c. buff 5 5
435. 2 c. purple-brown .. 5 5
436. 3 c. green 10 5
454. 4 c. purple 10 5
455. 5 c. red 5 5
456. 10 c. green 8 5
457. – 12 c. blue 8 5
458. – 20 c. blue 10 5
459. – 24 c. claret 30 15
460. – 30 c. rose 20 8
461. – 50 c. black 50 10
445. – 1 p. red and blue .. 35 8
446. – 5 p. green and grey .. 2·40 60
447. – 10 p. blue and violet 7·00 1·90
448. – 20 p. claret and slate 10·00 4·75

The 12 c. to 20 p. values are larger (21 × 27 mm.).

66. Dr. Juan Pujol.

ILLUSTRATIONS
British Commonwealth and all overprints and surcharges are FULL SIZE. Foreign Countries have been reduced to ¾-LINEAR.

1918. Juan Pujol, 1st P.M.G. of Argentina. Birth Cent.
449. 66. 5 c. grey and bistre .. 15 10

67. Mausoleum of Belgrano. 68. Creation of Argentine Flag.

1920. Gen. Manuel Belgrano. Death Cent. Dated "1820-1920".
478. 67. 2 c. red 15 12
479. 68. 5 c. blue and red .. 20 12
480. – 12 c. blue and green .. 35 25
DESIGN—VERT. 12 c. Gen. Belgrano.

70. General Urquiza. 71. General Mitre. 72.

1920. Gen. Urquiza's Victory at Cepada.
488. 70. 5 c. blue 15 5

1921. Gen. Mitre. Birth Cent.
490. 71. 2 c. chocolate 12 8
491. 5 c. blue 12 8

1921. 1st Pan-American Postal Congress.
492. 72. 3 c. lilac 15 12
493. 5 c. blue 15 5
494. 10 c. brown 20 12
495. 12 c. red 20 15

1921. As T 72, but smaller. Inscr. "BUENOS AIRES AGOSTO DE 1921".
496. – 5 c. red 10 5

1921. As No. 488, but inscr. "REPUBLICA ARGENTINA" at foot
497. – 5 c. red.. .. 12 5

74. 75. B. Rivadavia.

1923. With or without stop below "c".
513. 74. ½ c. purple 5 5
530. 1 c. brown 5 5
515. 2 c. purple-brown .. 5 5
532. 3 c. green 5 5
533. 4 c. claret 5 5
518. 5 c. red 5 5
535. 10 c. green 5 5
520. 12 c. blue 8 5
537. 20 c. blue 10 5
538. 24 c. chocolate .. 20 8
539. 25 c. violet 12 5
540. 30 c. claret 20 5
541. 50 c. black 25 5
542. – 1 p. red and blue .. 40 5
543. – 5 p. green and lilac .. 2·25 25
544. – 10 p. blue and claret 5·00 80
545. – 20 p. lake and slate .. 8·50 2·75
The peso values are larger (21 × 27 mm.).

1926. Rivadavia Centenary.
546. 75. 5 c. red 10 5

76. Rivadavia. 77. San Martin.

78. G.P.O. 1926. 79. G.P.O. 1826.

1926. Postal Centenary.
547. 76. 3 c. green 5 5
548. 77. 5 c. red 5 5
549. 78. 12 c. blue 15 8
550. 79. 25 c. brown 20 5

80. 82.

1928. Air.
558. 80. 5 c. red 30 25
559. 10 c. blue 50 30
560. – 15 c. brown 50 30
561. 80. 18 c. violet .. .. 1·25 1·25
562. – 20 c. blue 70 40
563. – 24 c. blue 90 60
564. 82. 25 c. violet 90 45
565. 30 c. red 80 40
566. – 35 c. claret 55 40
567a. 80. 36 c. brown 60 60
568. – 50 c. black 80 30
569. – 54 c. purple-brown .. 90 80
570. – 72 c. green 85 65
571. 82. 90 c. purple .. .. 1·60 60
572. 1 p. red and blue .. 1·75 30
573. 1 p. 08 blue and claret 2·75 1·10
574. – 1 p. 26 green and violet 4·00 2·75
575. – 1 p. 80 claret and blue 3·75 3·00
576. – 3 p. 60 blue and grey .. 7·00 5·00
DESIGNS—VERT. 15 c., 20 c., 24 c., 54 c., 72 c. Eagle over sea. HORIZ. 35 c., 50 c., 1 p. 26, 1 p. 80, 3 p. 60. Eagle on mountain top.

84. Arms of Argentina and Brazil. 85. Torch illuminating New World.

86. Symbolical Figures, Spain and Argentina. 87. America offering Laurels to Columbus.

1928. Peace with Brazil. Cent.
577. 84. 5 c. red 20 12
578. 12 c. blue 30 15

1929. "Day of the Race" issue.
579. 85. 2 c. purple-brown .. 20 10
580. 86. 5 c. red 20 8
581. 87. 12 c. blue 25 15

'ZEPPELIN 1er VUELO 1930
(88.)

1930. Air. "Zeppelin" Europe-Pan-America Flight. Optd. with T 88.
587. – 20 c. blue (No. 562) .. 2·75 2·75
588. – 50 c. black (No. 568) .. 3·25 3·25
589. 82. 90 c. purple .. 3·25 3·25
584. 1 p. red and blue .. 4·75 4·75
585. – 1 p. 80 (No. 575) .. 10·00 10·00
586. – 3 p. 60 (No. 576) .. 27·00 27·00

89. Soldier and Civilian Insurgents. 90. The Victorious March, 6 Sept., '30.

1930. Revolution of 6 Sept., 1930.
592. 89. ½ c. violet 5 5
611. 90. ½ c. mauve 5 5
593. 89. 1 c. green 10 8
612. 90. 1 c. black 12 12
594. 2 c. lilac 8 5
595. 89. 3 c. green 12 8
613. 90. 3 c. green 10 8
596. 89. 4 c. violet 10 8
614. 90. 4 c. lake 12 8
597. 89. 5 c. red 5 5
615. 90. 5 c. red 8 5
598. 89. 10 c. black 30 15
616. 90. 10 c. green 25 12
599. 12 c. blue 15 8
600. 20 c. buff 12 8
601. 24 c. red-brown .. 45 35
602. 25 c. green 60 45
603. 30 c. violet 80 50
604. 50 c. black .. .. 1·40 70
605. 1 p. red and blue .. 2·25 2·00
606. 2 p. orange and black.. 3·75 2·10
607. 5 p. black and green .. 10·00 8·00
608. 10 p. blue and lake .. 14·00 6·00
609. 20 p. blue and green .. 45·00 23·00
610. 50 p. violet and green.. £140 95·00

1931. 1st Anniv. of 1930 Revolution. Optd. **6 Septiembre 1930-1931.**
617. 74. 3 c. green (postage) .. 5 5
618. 10 c. green 10 10
619. 30 c. claret 60 50
620. 50 c. black 70 55
621. 1 p. red and blue .. 80 70
623. 90. 2 p. orange and black.. 1·40 95
622. 74. 5 p. green and lilac .. 4·50 2·25
624. 80. 18 c. violet (air) .. 1·40 1·40
625. – 72 c. green (No. 570) .. 1·40 1·40
626. 82. 90 c. purple .. .. 1·40 1·40
627. – 1 p. 80 claret and blue (No. 575) .. .. 3·25 3·25
628. – 3 p. 60 blue and grey (No. 576) .. .. 7·00 7·00

1932. Zeppelin Air stamps. Optd. **GRAF ZEPPELIN 1932.**
629. 80. 5 c. red .. .. 1·90 1·75
630. 18 c. violet .. .. 2·25 2·25
631. 82. 90 c. purple .. .. 4·75 4·75

91. Refrigerating Plant. 92. Port La Plata.

1932. 6th Int. Refrigerating Congress.
632. 91. 3 c. green 15 8
633. 10 c. red 15 8
634. 12 c. blue 30 15

1933. La Plata City. 50th Anniv. Inscr. as in T 92.
635. 92. 3 c. chocolate and green 15 12
636. – 10 c. purple and orange 15 8
637. – 15 c. blue 80 50
638. – 20 c. brown and lilac .. 50 30
639. – 30 c. claret and green.. 2·10 1·50
DESIGNS: 10 c. President J. A. Roca. 15 c. Municipal buildings. 20 c. La Plata Cathedral. 30 c. Dr. D. Rocha.

94. Christ of the Andes. 95. "Liberty" with Arms of Brazil and Argentina.

1934. 32nd Int. Eucharistic Congress, Buenos Aires.
640. 94. 10 c. red 30 15
641. – 15 c. blue 30 15
DESIGN—HORIZ. 15 c. Buenos Aires Cathedral.

1935. Visit of President Vargas of Brazil. Inscr. "MAYO DE 1935".
642. 95. 10 c. red 12 8
643. – 15 c. blue 20 12
DESIGN: 15 c. Clasped hands and flags.

97. San Martin. 98. Prize Bull. 99. With Boundary Lines.

1935. Portraits.
644. ½ c. mauve (Belgrano) .. 5 5
645. 1 c. yellow (Sarmiento).. 5 5
646. 2 c. brown (Urquiza) .. 5 5
647. 3 c. green (T 97).. .. 5 5
648. 4 c. grey (G. Brown) .. 5 5
653b. 5 c. brown (Moreno) .. 5 5
650. 6 c. green (Alberdi) .. 5 5
653d 10 c. red (Rivadavia) .. 10 5
651. 12 c. maroon (Mitre) .. 5 5
754. 15 c. grey-blue (Martin Guemes) 10 5
652. 20 c. blue (Juan Martin Guemes) 12 5
653. 20 c. blue (Martin Guemes) 8 5
See also Nos. 671 etc.

1936. Production and Industry.
676. 98. 15 c. blue 5 5
677a. 20 c. blue (19½ × 26 mm.) 5 5
678c. 20 c. blue (22 × 33 mm.) 12 5
656. – 25 c. red and pink .. 8 5
657. – 30 c. brown and yellow 12 5
658. – 40 c. purple and mauve 12 5
659. – 50 c. red and salmon .. 12 5
660. 99. 1 p. blue and brown .. 1·00 15
660a. – 1 p. blue and brown .. 25 5
661. – 2 p. blue and chocolate 35 5
662. – 5 p. green and blue .. 60 5
763. – 10 p. black & chocolate 1·10 25
664. – 20 p. brown and blue .. 3·00 60
DESIGNS—VERT. 25 c. Ploughman. 50 c. Oil well. 1 p. (No. 660a) as T 99 but without country boundaries. 5 p. Iguazu Falls. 10 p. Grapes. 20 p. Cotton-plant. HORIZ. 30 c. Patagonian ram. 40 c. Sugar-cane and factory. 2 p. Fruit products.

101. 102. President Sarmiento.

1936. Pan-American Peace Conference.
665. 101. 10 c. red 12 10

1938. President's 50th Death Anniv.
666. 102. 3 c. green 8 5
667. 5 c. red 10 5
668. 15 c. blue 15 10
669. 50 c. orange .. 30 20

103. Frigate "Pres. Sarmiento". 104. Allegory of the Post.

1939. Last Voyage of Training-ship "President Sarmiento".
670. 103. 5 c. green 12 8

1939. Portraits as T 97.
671. – 2½ c. black 5 5
750. 97. 3 c. grey (San Martin) 5 5
751. – 3 c. grey (Moreno) .. 5 5
673. – 4 c. green 5 5
894. – 5 c. brn. (16½ × 22½ mm.) 5 5
674. – 8 c. orange 5 5
753. – 10 c. brown 10 5
675. – 12 c. red 5 5
895. – 20 c. lilac (21 × 27 mm.) 5 5
895b. – 20 c. lilac (19½ × 25½ mm.) 5 5
PORTRAITS: 2½ c. L. Braille. 4 c. G. Brown. 5 c. Jose Hernandez. 8 c. N. Avellaneda. 10c. B. Rivadavia. 12 c. B. Mitre. 20 c. G. Brown.

1939. 11th U.P.U. Congress, Buenos Aires.
679. 104. 5 c. red 12 5
680. – 15 c. slate 15 10
681. – 20 c. blue 12 10
682. – 25 c. green 30 20
683. – 50 c. brown 40 25
684. – 1 p. purple 60 35
685. – 2 p. magenta .. .. 3·25 1·50
686. – 5 p. violet .. .. 7·00 3·75
DESIGNS—VERT. 20 c. Seal of Argentina. 1 p. Symbols of postal communications. 2 p. Argentina, "Land of Promise" from a pioneer painting. HORIZ. 15 c. G.P.O. 25 c. Iguazu Falls. 50 c. Mt. Bonete. 5 p. Lake Frias.

105. Working-class Family and New Home. 106. North and South America.

1939. 1st Pan-American Housing Congress.
687. 105. 5 c. green 5 5

1940. Pan-American Union. 50th Anniv.
688. 106. 15 c. blue 12 8

107. Aeroplane and Envelope. 108. Gen. French, Col. Beruti and Rosette of the "Legion de Patricios".

1940. Air.
689. 107. 30 c. orange 45 5
690. – 50 c. brown 55 5
691. 107. 1 p. red 15 5
692. – 1 p. 25 green 20 5
693. 107. 2 p. 50 blue 35 12
DESIGNS—VERT. 50 c. "Mercury". 1 p. 25, Aeroplane in clouds.

1941. Rising against Spain. 131st Anniv.
694. 108. 5 c. blue 5 5

109. Marco M. de Avellaneda. **110.** Statue of Gen. J.A. Roca.

1941. Avellaneda. Death Cent.
695. **109.** 5 c. blue 5 5

1941. Dedication of Statue of Gen. Roca.
696. **110.** 5 c. olive 8 5

111. Pellegrini (founder) and National Bank.

112. Gen. Juan Lavalle.

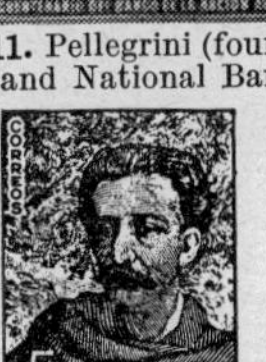

114. Jose Manuel Estrada. **113.** New P.O. Savings Bank.

1941. National Bank. 50th Anniv.
697. **111.** 5 c. lake 5 5

1941. Gen. Lavalle. Death Cent.
698. **112.** 5 c. blue 8 5

1942. P.O. Savings Bank Inaug.
699. **113.** 1 c. green 5 5

1942. Estrada (patriot). Birth Cent.
700. **114.** 5 c. purple 5 5

115. Proposed Columbus Lighthouse. **116.** G.P.O., Buenos Aires.

1942. Discovery of America. 450th Anniv.
721. **115.** 15 c. blue 10 5

1942. Postage and Express stamps.
717. **116.** 35 c. blue 12 5
746. 35 c. blue 10 5
No. 717 is inscribed "PALACIO CENTRAL DE CORREOS Y TELEGRAFOS" and No. 746. "PALACIO CENTRAL DE CORREOS Y TELECOMUNICACIONES".

117. Dr. Paz (founder of "La Prensa"). **118.** Books. **119.** Arms of Argentina.

1942. Dr. Jose C. Paz. Birth Cent.
722. **117.** 5 c. blue 5 5

1943. 1st National Book Fair.
723. **118.** 5 c. blue 5 5

1943. Revolution of 4th June, 1943.
724. **119.** 5 c. red 5 5
725. 15 c. green 10 5
726. 20 c. blue (larger) .. 10 8

120. National Independence House **121.** Head of Liberty, Money-box and Laurels.

1943. Tucuman Museum Inaug.
727. **120.** 5 c. green 5 5

1943. 1st Savings Bank Conf.
728. **121.** 5 c. brown .. 5 5

122. Buenos Aires in 1800.

1944. Export Day.
729. **122.** 5 c. black 5 5

123. Postal Union of the Americas and Spain. **124.** G. Bell. **125.** Ships.

1944. Postmen's Benefit Fund. Inscr. "PRO-CARTERO".
730. – 3 c.+2 c. black & violet 15 10
731. **123.** 5 c.+5 c. black & red 20 10
732. **124.** 10 c.+5 c. blk. & orge. 40 25
733. – 25 c.+15 c. blk. & brn. 50 40
734. – 1 p.+50 c. blk. & green 1·75 1·40
DESIGNS: 3 c. Samuel Morse. 25 c. Rowland Hill. 1 p. Columbus landing in America.

1944. Naval Week.
735. **125.** 5 c. blue 5 5

126. Argentina. **127.** Arms of Argentina.

1944. San Juan Earthquake Relief Fund.
736. **126.** 5 c.+10 c. blk. & olive 25 15
737. 5 c.+50 c. black & red 60 45
738. 5 c.+1 p. black & orge. 1·75 1·40
739. 5 c.+20 p. blk. & blue 3·50 3·00

1944. Revolutionary Govt. 1st Anniv.
740. **127.** 5 c. blue 5 5

128. Archangel Gabriel. **129.** Cross of Palermo. **130.** Allegory of Thrift.

1944. 4th National Eucharistic Congress.
741. **128.** 3 c. green 8 5
742. **129.** 5 c. red 8 5

1944. Universal Savings Day. 20th Anniv.
743. **130.** 5 c. black 5 5

131. Reservists.

1944. Reservists' Day.
744. **131.** 5 c. blue 5 5

132. Bernardino Rivadavia. **133.** Rivadavia's Mausoleum.

1945. Rivadavia's Death Cent.
770. **132.** 3 c. green 5 5
771. – 5 c. red 5 5
772. **133.** 20 c. blue 8 5
DESIGN—As T **132**: 5 c. Rivadavia and Scales of Justice.

134. San Martin. **135.** Memorial to Unknown Soldier.

1945.
773. **134.** 5 c. red 5 5

1946.
776. **135.** 5 c. purple 5 5

136. **137.** **138.**
Pres. Roosevelt. "Affirmation." Aeroplane over Iguazu falls.

1946. Pres. Franklin Roosevelt. 1st Death Anniv.
777. **136.** 5 c. grey 5 5

1946. Installation of President Juan Peron.
778. **137.** 5 c. blue 5 5

1946. Air.
779. **138.** 15 c. red .. 8 5
780. – 25 c. green .. 12 5
DESIGN: 25 c. Aeroplane over Andes.

DESIGN: 60 c. Hand upholding globe.

139. "Flight".

1946. Aviation Week.
781. **139.** 15 c. green on green .. 30 15
782. – 60 c. purple on buff .. 45 30

140. "Argentina and Populace".

1946. Peron's Defeat of Counter-Revolution. 1st Anniv.
783. **140.** 5 c. mauve 5 5
784. 10 c. green 8 5
785. 15 c. blue 10 5
786. 50 c. brown 15 12
787. 1 p. red 40 30

141. Money-box and Map. **142.** Industry.

1946. Annual Savings Day.
788. **141.** 30 c. red 12 8

1946. Industrial Exn.
789. **142.** 5 c. purple 5 5

143. International Bridge. **144.** South Pole, Arms of Argentina and Ship.

1947. Opening of International Bridge between Argentina and Brazil.
790. **143.** 5 c. green 5 5

1947. 1st Argentine Antarctic Mail. 43rd Anniv.
791. **144.** 5 c. violet 5 5
792. 20 c. red 15 5

145. "Justice". **146.** Icarus Falling.

1947. Col. Peron's Presidency. 1st Anniv.
793. **145.** 5 c. purple and buff .. 5 5

1947. Aviation Week.
794. **146.** 15 c. purple 8 5

147. Frigate "Pres. Sarmiento". **148.** Cervantes and "Don Quixote".

1947. Launching of Training Ship "Pres. Sarmiento". 50th Anniv.
795. **147.** 5 c. blue 8 5

1947. Cervantes. 400th Birth Anniv.
796. **148.** 5 c. olive 5 5

149. Gen. San Martin and Urn.

1947. Arrival from Spain of Ashes of Gen. San Martin's Parents.
797. **149.** 5 c. green 8 5

150. Young Crusaders. **151.** American Indian.

1947. Educational Crusade for Universal Peace.
798. **150.** 5 c. green 5 5
799. 20 c. brown 8 5

1948. American Indian Day.
801. **151.** 25 c. brown 10 5

152. Phrygian Cap and Sprig of Wheat. **153.** "Stop."

1948. Anti-Isolationist Revolution of 4th June. 5th Anniv.
802. **152.** 5 c. blue 5 5

1948. Safety First Campaign.
803. **153.** 5 c. yellow and brown 5 5

154. Posthorn. **155.** Peasant Family.

1948 Postal Service in Rio de la Plata. Bicent.
804. **154.** 5 c. mauve 5 5

1948. Agriculture Day.
805. **155.** 10 c. brown 5 5

156. "Liberty and plenty". **157.** Statue of Atlas.

158. Map, Globe and Compasses.

1948. Re-election of President Peron.

806. 156. 25 c. claret 8 5

1948. Air. 4th Meeting of Pan-American Cartographers.

807. 157. 45 c. brown 15 8

808. 158. 70 c. green 20 10

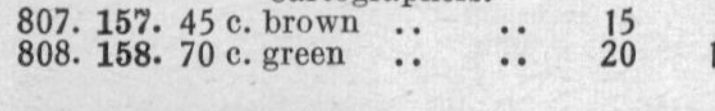

ILLUSTRATIONS
British Commonwealth and all overprints and surcharges are FULL SIZE. Foreign Countries have been reduced to ¾-LINEAR.

159. Winged Wheel.

1949. Nationalization of Argentine Railways. 1st Anniv.

809. 159. 10 c. blue 5 5

160. Head of Liberty.

1949. Constitution Day.

810. 160. 1 p. purple and red .. 15 5

161. Trophy and Target. 162. "Intercommunication."

1949. Air. Int. Shooting Championship.

811. 161. 75 c. brown 40 15

1949. U.P.U. 75th Anniv.

812. 162. 25 c. green and olive .. 10 5

163. San Martin.

DESIGNS—As T 163 10, 50, 75 c. Portraits of San Martin. 2 p. San Martin Mausoleum. As T 164: 1 p. House where San Martin died.

164. San Martin at Boulogne.

1950. San Martin's Death Cent. Dated "1850 1950".

813. – 10 c. purple and blue 5 5

814. 163. 20 c. brown and red .. 8 5

815. 164. 25 c. brown .. 8 5

816. – 50 c. blue and green .. 12 5

817. – 75 c. green and brown 20 8

818. – 1 p. green 30 10

819. – 2 p. purple 40 15

165. Stamp Designer. 166. S. America and Antarctic.

1950. Int. Philatelic Exn., Buenos Aires.

820. 165. 10 c.+10 c. vio. (post.) 8 8

821. – 45 c.+45 c. blue (air) 15 15

822. – 70 c.+70 c. brown .. 25 25

823. – 1 p.+1 p. red .. 50 50

824. – 2 p. 50+2 p. 50 olive 3·00 3·00

825. – 5 p.+5 p. green .. 3·75 3·25

DESIGNS: 45 c. Engraver. 70 c. Proofing. 1 p. Printer. 2 p. 50 Woman reading letter. 5 p. San Martin.

1951.

826. 166. 1 p. blue and brown .. 15 5

167. Aeroplane and Eagle.

1951. Air. State Airlines. 10th Anniv.

827. 167. 20 c. olive 8 5

168. Pegasus and Train.

DESIGNS—HORIZ. 25 c. Ship. VERT. 20 c. Aeroplane. 40 c. Telephone.

1951. Five-Year Plan.

828. 168. 5 c. brown (postage) .. 5 5

829. – 25 c. green 10 5

830. – 40 c. purple 12 8

831. – 20 c. blue (air) .. 8 5

169. Woman Voter. 170. "Piety".

1951. Women's Suffrage.

832. 169. 10 c. purple 5 5

1951. Air. Eva Peron Foundation Fund.

833. 170. 2 p. 45+7 p. 55 olive .. 6·50 4·50

171. Eva Peron. 172.

1952. (a) Size 20×26 mm.

834. 171. 1 c. brown 5 5

835. 5 c. grey 5 5

836. 10 c. claret 5 5

837. 20 c. red 5 5

838. 25 c. green 5 5

839. 40 c. purple 5 5

841. 45 c. blue 8 5

840. 50 c. bistre 5 5

(b) Size 22×33 mm. Without inscr. "EVA PERON".

842. 172. 1 p. brown 12 5

843. 1 p. 50 c. green .. 30 5

844. 2 p. red 20 5

845. 3 p. indigo 30 12

(c) Size 22×33 mm. Inscr. "EVA PERON".

846. 172. 1 p. brown 10 5

847. 1 p. 50 c. green .. 12 5

848. 2 p. crimson .. 25 5

849. 3 p. indigo .. 35 5

(d) Size 30½ × 40 mm. Inscr. "EVA PERON".

850. 172. 5 p. brown 35 12

851. 171. 10 p. red 80 30

852. 172. 20 p. green .. .. 1·90 80

853. 171. 50 p. blue .. .. 3·75 2·10

173. Indian Funeral Urn. 174. Rescue Ship "Uruguay".

1953. Santiago del Estero. 4th Cent.

854. 173. 50 c. green 8 5

1953. Rescue of the "Antarctic". 50th Anniv.

855. 174. 50 c. blue 15 5

175. Planting Flag in S. Orkneys. 176. "Telegraphs."

1954. Argentine P.O. in South Orkneys. 50th Anniv.

856. 175. 1 p. 45 blue 20 8

1954. Int. Telecommunications Conference. Symbolical designs inscr. as in T 176.

857. 176. 1 p. 50 slate-purple .. 15 8

858. – 3 p. blue 25 10

859. – 5 p. rose 45 20

DESIGNS—VERT. 3 p. "Radio". HORIZ. 5 p. "Television".

177. 178. Eva Peron.

1954. Argentine Stock Exchange. Cent.

860. 177. 1 p. green 15 5

1954. Eva Peron. 2nd Death Anniv.

861. 178. 3 p. red 30 12

179. San Martin. 180. Wheat.

181. Mt. Fitz Roy. 182. "Prosperity".

1954.

862. 179. 20 c. red 5 5

863. 40 c. red 5 5

868. – 50 c. blue (33×22 mm.) 5 5

869. – 50 c. blue (32×21 mm.) 8 5

870. 180. 80 c. brown 5 5

871. – 1 p. brown 8 5

872. – 1 p. 50 blue 8 5

873. – 2 p. lake 12 5

874. – 3 p. purple 10 5

875. – 5 p. green 15 5

876. – 10 p. yellow-green and grey-green 40 5

877. 181. 20 p. violet 60 8

1018. – 22 p. blue 20 5

878. – 50 p. indigo and blue (30½×40½ mm.) .. 90 40

1023. – 50 p. blue (29½×40 mm.) 25 8

1287. – 50 p. bl. (22½×32½ mm.) 15 8

DESIGNS—As T 180: HORIZ. 50 c. Port of Buenos Aires. 1 p. Cattle. 2 p. Eva Peron Foundation. 3 p. El Nihuil Dam. As T 181: VERT. 1 p. 50 c., 22 p. Industrial Plant. 5 p. Iguazu Falls. 50 p. San Martin. HORIZ. 10 p. Humahuaca Ravine.

For 43 p. in the design of the 1 p. 50 and 22 p. see No. 1021.

For 65 c in same design see No. 1313.

1954. Cent. of Argentine Corn Exchange.

867. 182. 1 p. 50 c. slate .. 15 5

183. Clasped Hands and Emblem. 184.

1955. Productivity and Social Welfare Congress.

879. 183. 3 p. brown 25 12

1955. Commercial Air Services. 25th Anniv.

880. 184. 1 p. 50 drab 12 5

185. "Liberation". 186. Forces Emblem.

1955. Anti-Peronist. Revolution of Sept. 16th, 1955.

881. 185. 1 p. 50 olive 12 5

1955. Armed Forces Commem.

882. 186. 3 p. blue 15 5

187. Gen. Urquiza (after J. M. Blanes). 188. Detail from "Antiope" (Coreggio).

1956. Battle of Caseros. 104th Anniv.

883. 187. 1 p. 50 green 15 5

1956. Infantile Paralysis Relief Fund.

884. 188. 20 c.+30 c. grey .. 12 5

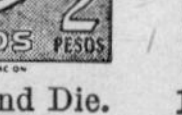

189. Coin and Die. 190. Stamp of 1856.

191. Dr. J. G. Pujol. 192. Cotton, Chaco.

1956. National Mint. 75th Anniv.
885. 189. 2 p. brown and sepia 12 8

1956. 1st Argentine Stamps. Cent.
886. 190. 40 c. blue and green .. 8 5
887. 2 p. 40 magenta & brn. 15 8
888. 191. 4 p. 40 blue 40 15
The 40 c. shows a 1 real stamp of 1856.

1956. New Provinces.
889. – 50 c. blue 5 5
890. 192. 1 p. lake 8 5
891. – 1 p. 50 green 15 5
DESIGNS—HORIZ. 50 c. Lumbering, La Pampa. VERT. 1 p. 50, Mate tea plant, Misiones.

193. Liberty. 194. Detail from "Virgin of the Rocks" (Leonardo)

1956. Revolution. 1st Anniv.
892. 193. 2 p. 40 magenta .. 15 10

1956. Air. Infantile Paralysis Victims, Gratitude for Help.
893. 194. 1 p. purple 15 10

196. Esteban Echeverria (poet). 197. F. Ameghino (anthropologist).

198. Roque Saenz Pena (statesman). 199. Franklin.

1956.
896. 196. 2 p. purple 10 5
897. 197. 2 p. 40 brown .. 15 10
898. 198. 4 p. 40 green 20 5

1956. Benjamin Franklin. 250th Birth Anniv.
899. 199. 40 c. blue 8 5

200. Frigate "Hercules". 201. Admiral G. Brown.

1957. Admiral Giullermo Brown. Death Cent.
900. 200. 40 c. blue (postage) .. 5 5
901. – 2 p. 40 olive 15 5
902. – 60 c. slate (air) .. 8 5
903. – 1 p. magenta 8 5
904. 201. 2 p. sepia 12 8
DESIGNS—HORIZ. 60 c. Battle of Montevideo. 1 p. L. Rosales and T. Espora. VERT. 2 p. 40, Admiral Brown in later years.

202. Church of Santo Domingo. 203. Map of the Americas and Badge of Buenos Aires.

1957. Defence of Buenos Aires. 150th Anniv.
905. 202. 40 c. green. 5 5

1957. Air. Inter-American Economic Conf.
906. 203. 2 p. purple 12 8

204. "La Porteña" (early Locomotive). 204a. Congress Symbol

1957. Argentine Railways. Cent.
907. 204. 40 c. sepia (postage) .. 5 5
908. – 60 c. grey (air) .. 8 5
DESIGN: 60 c. Diesel-electric locomotive.

1957. Air. Int. Tourist Congress Buenos Aires.
909. 204a. 1 p. brown 8 5
910. – 2 p. turquoise .. 20 5
DESIGN: 2 p. Symbolic key of tourism.

205. Head of Liberty. 206.

207. "Wealth in Oil". 208. La Plata Museum.

1957. Reform Convention.
911. 205. 40 c. red 5 5

1957. Air. Int. Correspondence Week.
912. 206. 1 p. blue 8 5

1957. Argentine Oil Industry. 50th Anniv.
913. 207. 40 c. blue 5 5

1958. Founding of La Plata. 75th Anniv.
914. 208. 40 c. black 5 5

209. Health Emblem and Flower.

1958. Air. Child Welfare.
915. 209. 1 p.+50 c. lake .. 12 12

210. Stamp of 1858 and River Ferry. 211. Stamp of 1858.

1958. Argentine Confederation Stamps Cent. and Philatelic Exhibition, Buenos Aires.
916. 210. 50 c.+20 c. purple and green (postage) .. 20 15
917. – 2 p. 40+1 p. 20 blue and black .. 30 25
918. – 4 p. 40+2 p. 20 maroon and blue .. 35 30
919. 211. 1 p.+50 c. blue and olive (air) .. 20 20
920. 2 p.+1 p. vio & crim. 25 25
921. 3 p.+1 p. 50 brown and green 35 35
922. 5 p.+2 p. 50 red and olive.. .. 50 50
923. 10 p.+5 p. sep. & olive 1·00 1·00

DESIGNS—HORIZ. 2 p. 40, Magnifier, stamp album and stamp of 1858. 4 p. 40, P.O. building of 1858.

212. Locomotive and Arms of Argentina and Bolivia. 213. Aeroplane and Map.

1958. Argentine-Bolivian Brotherhood.
(a) Inaug. of Yacuiba-Santa Cruz Railway.
924. 212. 40 c. red and slate .. 8 5
(b) Exchange of Presidential Visits.
925. 213. 1 p. brown 8 5

214. "Liberty and Flag". 215. Farman-type Biplane.

1958. Transfer of Presidential Mandate. Head of "Liberty" in grey; inscr. black; flag yellow and blue; background colours given.
926. 214. 40 c. buff 5 5
927. 1 p. salmon 8 5
928. 2 p. green 15 5

1958. Air. Argentine Aero Club. 50th Anniv.
929. 215. 2 p. brown 10 8

216. National Flag Monument, Rosario. 217. Map of Antarctica.

1958. National Flag Monument. Inaug. 1st Anniv.
930. 216. 40 c. grey and blue .. 5 5

1958. I.G.Y.
931. 217. 40 c. black and red .. 8 5

218. T 1 and "The Santa Fe Mail" (after J. L. Palliere). 219. Aerial view of Flooded Town.

1958. Argentine Confederation Stamps Cent.
932. – 40 c. grn. & blue (post.) 8 5
933. – 80 c. blue & yell. (air) 10 8
934. 218. 1 p. blue and orange.. 15 8
DESIGNS—HORIZ. 40 c. First local Cordoba 5 c. stamp of 1858 and mail-coach. 80 c. Buenos Aires T 1 of 1858 and "View of Buenos Aires" (after Deroy).

1958. Flood Disaster Relief Fund. Inscr. as in T 219.
935. 219. 40 c.+20 c. brn. (post.) 8 5
936. – 1 p.+50 c. plum (air) 12 10
937. – 5 p.+2 p. 50 c. slate-bl. 40 35
DESIGNS—HORIZ. 1 p. Different aerial view of flooded town. 5 p. Motor-truck in flood-water and garage.

220. 221. U.N. Emblem and "The Slave" (after Michelangelo).

1958. Leukaemia Relief Campaign.
938. 220. 1 p.+50 c. red and black 8 5

1959. Declaration of Human Rights. 10th Anniv.
939. 221. 40 c. grey and chocolate 5 5

222. "Comet" Jet Airliner.

1959. Air. Inaug. of "Comet" Jet Airliners by Argentine National Airlines.
940. 222. 5 p. black and olive .. 15 5

223. Orchids and Globe. 224. Pope Pius XII.

1959. 1st Int. Horticultural Exn., Buenos Aires.
941. 223. 1 p. maroon 8 5

1959. Pope Pius XII Commem.
942. 224. 1 p. black and yellow 8 5

PORTRAITS: 1 p. Claude Bernard. 1 p. 50 Ivan P. Pavlov.

225. William Harvey.

1959. 21st Int. Physiological Science Congress. Medical Scientists.
943. 225. 50 c. green 5 5
944. – 1 p. red 5 5
945. – 1 p. 50 brown .. 8 5

226. Creole Horse. 227. Tierra del Fuego.

1959.
946. – 10 c. green 5 5
947. – 20 c. maroon .. 5 5
948. – 50 c. ochre 5 5
950. 226. 1 p. red 5 5
1016. – 1 p. brown 5 5
1027. – 1 p. brown 5 5
1035. – 2 p. red 5 5
951. – 3 p. blue 5 5
1036. – 4 p. red 5 5
1283. 227. 5 p. brown 5 5
1037. – 8 p. red 8 5
1286. – 10 p. brown 5 5
1038. – 10 p. red 12 5
1028. – 12 p. purple 65 5
954. – 20 p. green 25 8
1039. – 20 p. red 8 5
1019. – 23 p. green 12 5
1020. – 25 p. lilac 12 5
1021. – 43 p. lake 20 5
1022. – 45 p. brown 15 5
1289. – 100 p. blue 35 12
1026. – 300 p. violet.. .. 25 5
1032. – 500 p. green.. .. 40 10
1033. – 1,000 p. blue .. 75 25
DESIGNS: As T 226—HORIZ. 10 c. Alligator. 20 c. Llama. 50 c. Puma. VERT. 2 p., 4 p., 8 p., 10 p. (No. 1038). 20 p. (No. 1039), San Martin. As T 227—HORIZ. 3 p. Zapata Hill, Catamarca. 300 p. Mar del Plata (40×29½ mm.). VERT. 1 p. (No. 1016) Sunflowers. 1 p. (No. 1027) Sunflower (22×32 mm.). 10 p. (No. 1286) Inca Bridge, Mendoza. 12 p. Quebracho Colorado (tree). 43 p., 45 p. Industrial plant (30×39½ mm.). 100 p. Ski-jumper. 500 p. Stag. 1,000 p. Leaping Salmon.
See also Nos. 1300/26 in revalued currency.

228. Athletes. 229.

1959. 3rd Pan-American Games, Chicago. Designs embody torch emblem. Centres and torch in black.
955. 228. 20 c.+10 c. grn. (post.) 5 5
956. – 50 c.+20 c. yellow .. 8 5
957. – 1 p.+50 c. maroon .. 10 8

958. – 2 p.+1 p. blue (air) .. 20 15
959. – 3 p.+1 p. 50 olive .. 25 20
DESIGNS—VERT. 50 c. Basketball. 1 p. Boxing. HORIZ. 2 p. Rowing. 3 p. High-diving.

1959. Red Cross Hygiene Campaign.
960. 229. 1 p. red, blue & black 5 5

230. Child with Toys.

231. Buenos Aires 1 p. stamp of 1859.

1959. Mothers' Day.
961. 230. 1 p. red and black .. 5 5

1959. Stamp Day.
962. 231. 1 p. blue and grey .. 8 5

232. B. Mitre and J. J. de Urquiza.

233. Andean Condor.

1959. Pact of San Jose de Flores. Cent.
963. 232. 1 p. plum 5 5

1960. Child Welfare. Birds.
964. 233. 20 c.+10 c. blue (post.) 5 5
965. – 50 c.+20 c. violet .. 5 5
966. – 1 p.+50 c. brown .. 8 5
967. – 2 p.+1 p. magenta (air) 15 8
968. – 3 p.+1 p. 50 grey-grn. 20 15
BIRDS: 50 c. Fork-tailed flycatcher. 1 p. Ivory-billed woodpecker. 2 p. Rufous tinamou. 3 p. Common rhea.

234. "Uprooted Tree".

235. Abraham Lincoln.

1960. World Refugee Year.
969. 234. 1 p. red and brown .. 5 5
970. 4 p. 20 pur. & yell.-grn. 10 8

1960. Abraham Lincoln. 150th Birth Anniv.
972. 235. 5 p. blue 12 8

236. Saavedra and Chapter Hall, Buenos Aires.

237. Dr. L. Drago.

1960. 150th Anniv. of May Revolution. Inscr. "25 DE MAYO 1810–1960".
973. 236. 1 p. purple (postage) .. 5 5
974. – 2 p. green .. 5 5
975. – 4 p. 20 grn. & grey-grn. 12 5
976. – 10 p. 70 blue and slate 25 12
977. – 1 p. 80 brown (air) .. 8 5
978. – 5 p. maroon & brown 15 8
DESIGNS—Chapter Hall and: 1 p. 80, Moreno, 2 p. Paso. 4 p. 20, Alberti and Azcuenaga. 5 p. Belgrano and Castelli. 10 p. 70, Larrea and Matheu.

1960. Drago. Birth Cent.
980. 237. 4 p. 20 brown .. 12 5

238. "Five Provinces".

239. "Market Place 1810" (Buenos Aires).

1960. Air. New Argentine Provinces.
981. 238. 1 p. 80 blue and red .. 8 5

1960. Air. Inter-American Philatelic Exn., Buenos Aires ("EFIMAYO") and 150th Anniv. of Revolution. Inscr. "EFIMAYO 1960".
982. 239. 2 p.+1 p. lake .. 8 5
983. – 6 p.+3 p. black .. 20 10
984 – 10 p. 70+5 p. 30 blue 35 25
985. – 20 p.+10 p. blue-green 60 50
DESIGNS: 6 p. "The Water Carrier". 10 p. 70, "The Landing Place", 20 p. "The Fort".

240. J. B. Alberdi.

241. Seibo (Argentine National Flower).

1960. J. B. Alberdi (statesman). 150th Birth Anniv.
986. 240. 1 p. green 5 5

1960. Air. Chilean Earthquake Relief Fund. Inscr. "AYUDA CHILE".
987. 241. 6 p.+3 p. carmine 15 12
988. – 10 p. 70+5 p. 30 red 25 20
DESIGN: 10 p. 70, Copihue (Chilean national flower).

242. Map of Argentina.

243. Galleon.

1960. National Census, 1960.
989. 242. 5 p. lilac 15 5

1960. 8th Spanish-American P.U. Congress.
990. 243. 1 p. green (postage) .. 5 5
991. 5 p. sepia .. 20 8
992. 1 p. 80 purple (air) .. 8 5
993. 10 p. 70 turquoise .. 20 15

1960. Air. U.N. Day. Nos. 990/3 optd. DIA DE LAS NACIONES UNIDAS 24 DE OCTUBRE.
994. 239. 2 p.+1 p. lake .. 12 8
995. – 6 p.+3 p. black .. 20 12
996. – 10 p. 70+5 p. 30 blue 30 20
997. – 20 p.+10 p. blue-grn. 60 45

244. Blessed Virgin of Lujan.

245. Jacaranda.

1960. 1st Inter-American Marian Congress.
998. 244. 1 p. blue 5 5

1960. Int. Thematic Stamp Exn. ("TEMEX"). Inscr. "TEMEX-61".
999. 245. 50 c.+50 c. blue .. 5 5
1000. – 1 p.+1 p. grey-green 5 5
1001. – 3 p.+3 p. chestnut.. 15 12
1002. – 5 p.+5 p. brown .. 25 20
FLOWERS: 1 p. Passion flowers ("Passiflora caerulea"). 3 p. Hibiscus ("Chorisia speciosa"). 5 p. Black lapacho ("Tabebuia ipe").

246. Argentine Scout Badge.

247. "Shipment of Cereals" (after B. Q. Martin).

1961. Int. Scout (Patrol) Camp.
1003. 246. 1 p. red and black .. 5 5

1961. Exports Campaign.
1004. 247. 1 p. brown 8 5

248. Emperor Penguin and Chick.

249. Battle Scene.

1961. Child Welfare. Inscr. "PRO-INFANCIA".
1005. – 4 p. 20+2 p. 10 brn. (postage) 15 15
1006. 248. 1 p. 80+90 c. blk. (air) 10 10
DESIGN: 4 p. 20, Blue-eyed shag.

1961. Battle of San Nicolas. 150th Anniv.
1007. 249. 2 p. black 5 5

250. Dr. M. Moreno.

251. Emperor Trajan.

1961. Dr. M. Moreno. 150th Death Anniv.
1008. 250. 2 p. blue 8 5

1961. Visit of President of Italy.
1009. 251. 2 p. green 8 5

1961. Americas Day. Nos. 999/1002 optd. 14 DE ABRIL DE LAS AMERICAS.
1010. 245. 50 c.+50 c. blue .. 5 5
1011. – 1 p.+1 p. grey-green 8 5
1012. – 3 p.+3 p. chestnut.. 15 12
1013. – 5 p.+5 p. brown .. 30 25

252. Tagore.

253. San Martin Monument, Madrid.

1961. Rabindranath Tagore (Indian Poet). Birth Cent.
1014. 252. 2 p. violet on green.. 8 5

1961. Spanish San Martin Monument. Inaug.
1015. 253. 1 p. black-olive .. 8 5

254. Gen. Belgrano (after monument by Rocha, Buenos Aires).

255. Antarctic Scene.

1961. Gen. Manuel Belgrano Commem.
1034. 254. 2 p. blue 8 5

1961. San Martin Antarctic Base. 10th Anniv.
1044. 255. 2 p. black 12 5

256. Conquistador and Sword.

257. Sarmiento Statue (Rodin).

1961. Jujuy City. 4th Cent.
1045. 256. 2 p. red and black .. 8 5

1961. Sarmiento. 150th Birth Anniv.
1046. 257. 2 p. violet 8 5

258. Cordoba Cathedral.

259. Argentine 10 c. Stamp of 1862.

261. "The Flight into Egypt" (after Ana Maria Moncalvo).

260.

1961. "Argentina 62" Int. Philatelic Exn.
1047. 258. 2 p.+2 p. purple (post.) 10 8
1048. 259. 3 p.+3 p. green .. 15 10
1049. – 10 p.+10 p. blue .. 35 30

1059. – 6 p. 50+6 p. 50 blue and turquoise (air) 30 25
DESIGNS—HORIZ. 10 p. Buenos Aires Cathedral. VERT. 6 p. 50. As T 259 but showing 15 c. value and different inscr.

1961. World Town-Planning Day.
1052. 260. 2 p. blue and yellow 8 5

1961. Child Welfare.
1053. 261. 2 p.+1 p. sepia & lilac 8 5
1054. 10 p.+5 p. mar. & mve. 25 20

262. Belgrano Statue.

263. Mounted Grenadier.

1962. National Flag. 150th Anniv.
1055. 262. 2 p. blue 8 5

1962. Gen. San Martin's Mounted Grenadiers. 150th Anniv.
1056. 263. 2 p. red 8 5

264. Mosquito and Emblem.

265. Lujan Basilica.

266. Juan Jufre (founder).

267. U.N.E.S.C.O. Emblem.

1962. Malaria Eradication.
1057. 264. 2 p. black and red .. 8 5

1962. Coronation of the Holy Virgin of Lujan. 75th Anniv.
1058. 265. 2 p. black and brown 8 5

1962. San Juan. 4th Cent.
1060. 266. 2 p. blue 8 5

1962. Air. U.N.E.S.C.O. 15th Anniv.
1061. 267. 13 p. brown and ochre 25 20

268. "Flight".

269. Juan Vucetich (finger-prints pioneer).

1962. Argentine Air Force. 50th Anniv.
1062. 268. 2 p. blue, black and brown-purple .. 8 5

1962. Vucetich Commem.
1063. 269. 2 p. green 8 5

270. 19th-century Mail-coach.

271. U.P.A.E. Emblem.

1962. Air. Postman's Day.
1064. 270. 5 p. 60 black and drab 12 8

1962. Air. Surch. AEREO and value.
1065. 227. 5 p. 60 on 5 p. brown 15 10
1066. 18 p. on 5 p. brn. on grn. 35 15

1962. Air. Postal Union of Latin America and Spain. 50th Anniv.
1067. 271. 5 p. 60 blue 10 8

272. Pres. Sarmiento. 272a. Jose Hernandez. 273. Mockingbird.

1962.

1068. 272. 2 p. green 5 5
1069. – 4 p. red 5 5
1070. – 6 p. red 5 5
1071. 272a. 6 p. brown 5 5
1288. – 90 p. bistre 30 10

PORTRAITS: 4 p., 6 p. Jose Hernandez. 90 p. G. Brown.

1962. Child Welfare.

1076. 273. 4 p.+2 p. sepia, turquoise and brown 15 12
1077. – 12 p.+6 p. brown, yellow and slate .. 45 35

DESIGN—VERT. 12 p. Rufous-collared sparrow.

See also Nos. 1101/2, 1124/5, 1165/6, 1191/2, 1214/15, 1264/5, 1293/4, 1394/5, 1415/6 and 1441/2.

274. "Skylark 3" Glider. 275. "20 de Febrero" Monument, Salta.

1963. Air. 9th World Gliding Championships, Junin.

1078. 274. 5 p. 60 black and blue 10 10
1079. – 11 p. black, red & blue 25 12

DESIGN: 11 p. "Super Albatross" glider.

1963. Battle of Salta. 150th Anniv.

1080. 275. 2 p. green 8 5

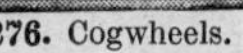

276. Cogwheels. 277. National College.

1963. Argentine Industrial Union. 75th Anniv.

1081. 276. 4 p. red and grey .. 8 5

1963. National College, Buenos Aires. Cent.

1082. 277. 4 p. black and buff .. 8 5

278. Child drinking Milk. 279. "Flight".

1963. Freedom from Hunger.

1083. 278. 4 p. ochre, black & red 8 5

1963. Air. (a) As T 279.

1084. 279. 5 p. 60 grn.,mag. & pur. 8 5
1085. 7 p. blk. & yellow (I) 12 5
1086. 7 p. blk. & yellow (II) 70 20
1087. 11 p. pur.,emer. & blk. 15 12
1088. 18 p. blue, red & mar. 25 10
1089. 21 p. grey, red & brn. 25 20

Two types of 7 p. I, "ARGENTINA" reads down, and II, "ARGENTINA" reads up as in T 279.

(b) As T 279 but inscr. "REPUBLICA ARGENTINA" reading down.

1147. 12 p. lake and brown .. 10 5
1148. 15 p. ultramarine and red 12 5
1149. 26 p. ochre. 8 5
1150. 27 p. 50 green and black 20 12
1151. 30 p. 50 brown and blue 20 15
1292. 40 p. lilac 12 8
1153. 68 p. green 20 15
1154. 78 p. ultramarine .. 25 15

See also Nos. 1374/80 in revalued currency.

280. Football. 281. Frigate "La Argentina" (after E. Biggeri).

1963. 4th Pan-American Games, Sao Paulo.

1090. 280. 4 p.+2 p. green, black and pink (postage) 12 5
1091. – 12 p.+6 p. maroon, black and salmon 25 20
1092. – 11 p.+5 p. red, black and green (air) .. 25 20

DESIGNS: 11 p. Cycling. 12 p. Show-jumping.

1963. Navy Day.

1093. 281. 4 p. blue 8 5

282. Assembly House and Seal. 284. Queen Nefertari (bas-relief).

283. Battle Scene.

1963. 1813 Assembly. 150th Anniv.

1094. 282. 4 p. black and blue 8 5

1963. Battle of San Lorenzo. 150th Anniv.

1095. 283. 4 p. blk. & grn. on grn. 10 5

1963. Preservation of Nubian Monuments. U.N.E.S.C.O. Campaign.

1096. 284. 4 p. black, turquoise and buff .. 8 5

285. Government House. 286. "Science".

1963. Presidential Installation.

1097. 285. 5 p. sepia and pink 8 5

1963. 10th Latin-American Neurosurgery Congress.

1098. 286. 4 p. blue, blk. & chest. 8 5

287. Blackboards. 288. F. de las Carreras (President of Supreme Court).

1963. "Alliance for Progress".

1099. 287. 5 p. red, black & blue 8 5

1963. Judicial Power Cent.

1100. 288. 5 p. green 8 5

1963. Child Welfare. Vert designs as T 352. Multicoloured.

1101. 4 p.+2 p. Vermilion flycatcher (postage) .. 12 10
1102. 11 p.+5 p. Great Kiskadee (air) 25 25

289. Kemal Ataturk. 290. "Payador" (after Castagnino).

1963. Kemal Ataturk. 25th Death Anniv.

1103. 289. 12 p. grey 12 8

1964. 4th Nat. Folklore Festival.

1104. 290. 4 p. blk., blue & ultram. 8 5

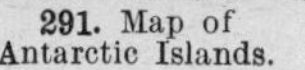

291. Map of Antarctic Islands. 292. Jorge Newbery in 'Plane.

1964. Antarctic Claims Issue.

1105. 291. 2 p. bl. & ochre (post.) 15 8
1106. – 4 p. bistre and blue .. 20 8
1107. – 18 p. bl. & bistre (air) 20 15

DESIGNS—VERT. (30×39½ mm.): 4 p. Map of Argentina and Antarctica. HORIZ. (as T 291): 518 p. Map of "Islas Malvinas" (Falkland Is.).

1964. Jorge Newbery (aviator). 50th Death Anniv.

1108. 292. 4 p. green 5

293. Pres. Kennedy. 294. Father Brochero.

1964. President Kennedy Memorial Issue.

1109. 293. 4 p. blue and magenta 10 5

1964. Father J. G. Brochero. 50th Death Anniv.

1110. 294. 4 p. brown 8 5

295. U.P.U. Monument, Berne. 296. Soldier of the Patricios Regiment.

1964. Air. 15th U.P.U. Congress, Vienna.

1111. 295. 18 p. purple and red .. 30 15

1964. Army Day.

1112. 296. 4 p. multicoloured . 8 5

See also Nos. 1170, 1201, 1223, 1246, 1343, 1363, 1406 and 1470.

297. Pope John XXIII. 298. Olympic Stadium.

1964. Pope John Commem.

1113. 297. 4 p. black and orange 8 5

1964. Olympic Games, Tokyo.

1114. 298. 4 p. + 2 p. brown, yellow and red (post.) 10 8
1115. – 12 p.+6 p. blk. & grn. 20 12
1116. – 11 p.+5 p. black and blue (air) .. 30 30

DESIGNS—VERT. 11 p. Sailing. 12 p. Fencing.

299. University Arms. 300. Olympic Flame and Crutch.

1964. Cordoba University. 350th Anniv.

1117. 299. 4 p. yellow, blue & blk. 8 5

1964. Air. Invalids Olympic Games, Tokyo.

1118. 300. 18 p.+9 p. mult. .. 30 30

301. "The Discovery of America" (Florentine woodcut). 302. Pigeons and U.N. Headquarters.

1964. Air. "Columbus Day" or ("Day of the Race").

1119. 301. 13 p. black and drab 15 12

1964. United Nations Day.

1120. 302. 4 p. ultramarine & blue 8 5

303. J. V. Gonzalez (medallion). 304. Gen. J. Roca.

1964. J. V. Gonzalez. Birth Cent.

1121. 303. 4 p. red 8 5

1964. General Julio Roca. 50th Death Anniv.

1122. 304. 4 p. blue 8 5

305. "Market-place, Montserrat Square" (after C. Morel). 306. Icebreaker "General San Martin".

1964. "Argentine Painters".

1123. 305. 4 p. sepia 12 5

1964. Child Welfare. Vert designs as T 273. Multicoloured.

1124. 4 p.+2 p. Cardinal (post.) 12 8
1125. 18 p.+9 p. Argentine swallow (air) 35 25

1965. "National Territory of Tierra del Fuego, Antarctic and South Atlantic Isles".

1126. – 2 p. maroon (postage) 8 5
1127. 306. 4 p. blue 10 5
1128. – 11 p. red (air) .. 15 10

DESIGNS: 2 p. General Belgrano Base (inscr. "BASE DE EJERCITO" erc.). 11 p. Teniente Matienzo Joint Antarctic Base (inscr. "BASE CONJUNTA" erc.).

1965. Air. First Rio Plata Philatelists' Day. Optd. **PRIMERAS JORNADAS FILATELICAS RIOPLATENSES.**

1129. 279. 7 p. black & yellow (II) 12 8

307. Young Saver. 308. I.T.U. Emblem.

1965. National Postal Savings Bank. 50th Anniv.

1130. 307. 4 p. black and red .. 5 5

1965. Air. I.T.U. Cent.

1131. 308. 18 p. multicoloured .. 20 12

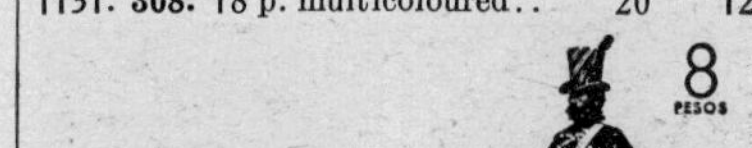

309. I.Q.S.Y. Emblem. 310. Soldier of the "Pueyrredon Hussars".

311. Ricardo Guiraldes. **312.** H. Yrigoyen (statesman).

1965. Int. Quiet Sun Year and Space Research.
1132. **309.** 4 p. black, orange and blue (postage) .. 8 5
1133. – 18 p. red (air) .. 20 12
1134. – 50 p. ultramarine .. 50 25
DESIGNS—VERT. 18 p. Rocket launching. HORIZ. 50 p. Earth, trajectories and space phenomena (both inscr. "INVESTIGACIONES ESPACIALES").

1965. Army Day (29th May).
1135. **310.** 8 p. multicoloured .. 10 5
See also Nos. 1170, 1201, 1223, 1246, 1343, 1363, 1399, 1450 and 1507.

1965. Argentine Writers. (1st Series). Each brown.
1136. 8 p. Type **311** 8 5
1137. 8 p. E. Larreta 8 5
1138. 8 p. L. Lugones 8 5
1139. 8 p. R J. Payro 8 5
1140. 8 p. R. Rojas 8 5
Nos. 1136/40 were arranged together in two horiz. rows of each design within the sheet.
See also Nos. 1174/8.

1965. Hipolito Yrigoyen Commem.
1141. **312.** 8 p. black and rose 8 5

313. "Children looking through a window".

1965. Int. Mental Health Seminar.
1142. **313.** 8 p. black and cinnamon 10 5

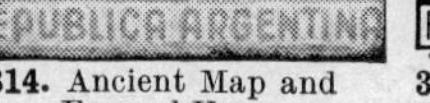

314. Ancient Map and Funeral Urn. **315.** Mgr. Dr. J. Cagliero.

1965. San Miguel de Tucuman. 400th Anniv.
1143. **314.** 8 p. red, yellow, brown and green .. 10 5

1965. Cagliero Commem.
1144. **315.** 8 p. violet 10 5

316. Dante (statue in Church of the Holy Cross, Florence). **317.** Clipper "Mimosa".

1965. Dante's 700th Birth Anniv.
1145. **316.** 8 p. blue 10 5

1965. Welsh Colonisation of Chubut and Foundation of Rawson. Cent.
1146. **317.** 8 p. black and red .. 10 5

318. Police Emblem. **319.** Schoolchildren.

1965. Federal Police Day.
1155. **318.** 8 p. red 8 5

1965. Law 1420 (Public Education). 81st Anniv.
1156. **319.** 8 p. black and green 10 5

320. St. Francis' Church, Catamarca. **321.** R. Dario (Nicaraguan poet).

1965. Brother Mamerto Esquiu Commem.
1157. **320.** 8 p. chestnut & yellow 8 5

1965. Ruben Dario. 50th Death Anniv.
1158. **321.** 15 p. violet on grey 10 5

322. "The Orange-seller" (detail).

1966. Prilidiano Pueyrredon's Paintings. Designs show details from the original works, each printed in green.
1159. 8 p. Type **322** 10 5
1160. 8 p. "A Halt at the Village Grocer's Shop" 10 5
1161. 8 p. "San Fernando Landscape" 10 5
1162. 8 p. "Bathing Horses on the Banks of the River Plate" 10 5

323. Rocket "Centaur" and Antarctic Map. **324.** Dr. Sun Yat-sen.

1966. Air. Rocket Launches in Antarctica.
1163. **323.** 27 p. 50 red, blk. & blue 25 12

1966. Dr. Sun Yat-sen. Birth Cent.
1164. **324.** 8 p. brown 8 5

1966. Child Welfare. Vert designs as T **273**, inscr. "R. ARGENTINA". Multicoloured.
1165. 8 p. + 4 p. Cayenne lapwing (postage) .. 12 10
1166. 27 p. 50 + 12 p. 50 Rufous oven-bird (air) .. 25 25

325. "Human Races".

1966. W.H.O. Headquarters, Geneva, Inaug.
1168. **325.** 8 p. black and brown 8 5

326. Seagull.

1966. Air. Naval Aviation School, Puerto Militar. 50th Anniv.
1169. **326.** 12 p. multicoloured .. 10 8

1966. Army Day (29th May). As T **310**.
1170. 8 p. multicoloured .. 8 5
DESIGN: 8 p. Militiaman of Guemes "Infernals".

327.

1966. Air. "Argentina '66" Philatelic Exn. Buenos Aires.
1171. **327.** 10 p. + 10 p. mult. 20 20

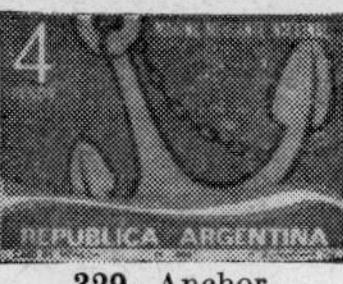

328. "Charity" Emblem. **329.** Anchor.

1966. Argentine Charities.
1173. **328.** 10 p. blue, black & grn. 8 5

1966. Argentine Writers (2nd Series). Portraits as T **311**. Each green.
1174. 10 p. H. Ascasubi .. 5 5
1175. 10 p. Estanislao del Campo 5 5
1176. 10 p. M. Cane .. 5 5
1177. 10 p. Lucio V. Lopez .. 5 5
1178. 10 p. R. Obligado .. 5 5

1966. Argentine Mercantile Marine. 25th Anniv.
1179. **329.** 4 p. multicoloured .. 5 5

330. L. Agote. **331.** Map and Flags of the American States.

1966. Argentine Scientists. Each violet.
1180. 10 p. Type **330** .. 5 5
1181. 10 p. J. B. Ambrosetti .. 5 5
1182. 10 p. M. I. Lillo 5 5
1183. 10 p. F. P. Moreno .. 5 5
1184. 10 p. F. J. Muniz .. 5 5

1966. 7th American Armies' Conf., Buenos Aires.
1185. **331.** 10 p. multicoloured 8 5

332. Bank Facade. **333.** La Salle Statue and College.

1966. Argentine National Bank. 75th Anniv.
1186. **332.** 10 p. green .. 8 5

1966. La Salle College, Buenos Aires. 75th Anniv.
1187. **333.** 10 p. black and brown 8 5

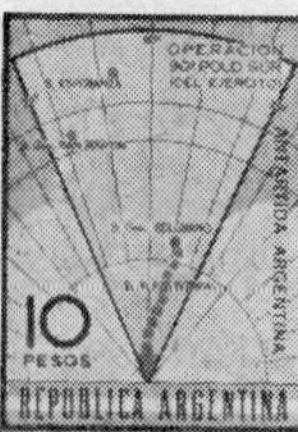

334. Antarctic Map. **335.** Gen. J. M. de Pueyrredon.

1966. Argentine South Pole Expedition, 1965-66.
1188. **334.** 10 p. multicoloured .. 10 5

1966. Gen. J. M. de Pueyrredon Commem.
1189. **335.** 10 p. lake 8 5

XX ANIVERSARIO UNESCO
10 PESOS
R. ARGENTINA

336. Gen. J. G. de Las Heras. **337.** Ancient Pot.

1966. Gen. Juan G. de Las Heras Commem.
1190. **336.** 10 p. black .. 8 5

1967. Child Welfare. Vert designs as T **273**, inscr. "R. ARGENTINA". Multicoloured.
1191. 10 p. + 5 p. Scarlet-headed marsh bird (horiz.) (post.) 12 10
1192. 15 p. + 7 p. Blue and yellow tanager (air) 20 15

1967. U.N.E.S.C.O. 20th Anniv.
1193. **337.** 10 p. multicoloured .. 8 5

338. "The Meal" (after F. Fader).

1967. Fernando Fader (painter).
1194. **338.** 10 p. brown 8 5

339. Juana Azurduy de Padilla. **340.** Schooner "Invincible".

1967. Famous Argentine Women. Each sepia.
1195. 6 p. Type **339** 5 5
1196. 6 p. J. M. Gorriti .. 5 5
1197. 6 p. C. Grierson .. 5 5
1198. 6 p. J. P. Manson .. 5 5
1199. 6 p. A. Storni 5 5

1967. Navy Day.
1200. **340.** 20p. multicoloured .. 12 5

1967. Army Day (29th May). As T **310.**
1201. 20 p. multicoloured .. 8 5
DESIGN: 20 p. Soldier of the Arribenos Regiment.

341. Suitcase and Dove. **342.** PADELAI Emblem and Sun.

1967. Int. Tourist Year.
1203. **341.** 20 p. multicoloured .. 8 5

1967. PADELAI (Argentine Children's Welfare Assn.). 75th Anniv.
1204. **342.** 20 p. multicoloured .. 8 5

343. Fels' Bleriot Aircraft. **344.** Ferreyra's Oxwagon and Skyscrapers.

1967. Air. 1st Argentine-Uruguay Airmail Flight. 50th Anniv.
1205. **343.** 26 p. brown, olive & bl. 15 8

1967. Villa Maria. Cent.
1206. **344.** 20 p. multicoloured .. 8 5

345. "General San Martin" (from statue by M. P. Nunez de Ibarra). **346.** Interior of Museum.

1967. Battle of Chacabuco. 150th Anniv.
1207. **345.** 20 p. brown & yellow 12 5
1208. – 40 p. indigo 15 10
DESIGN—(48 × 31 mm.)—HORIZ. 40 p. "Battle of Chacabuco" (from painting by P. Subercaseaux).

1967. Government House Museum. 10th Anniv.
1209. **346.** 20 p. blue 8 5

347. Pedro Zanni and Fokker Biplane.

1967. Aeronautics Week.
1210. **347.** 20 p. multicoloured.. 8 5

348. School Ship "General Brown" (from painting by E. Biggeri). **349.** Ovidio Lagos and Front Page of "La Capital" (newspaper).

1967. "Temex 67" Stamp Exn. and Naval Military School. 95th Anniv.
1211. **348.** 20 p. multicoloured.. 10 5

1967. "La Capital". Cent.
1212. **349.** 20 p. sepia 8 5

350. St. Barbara. **351.** "Sivori's Wife".

1967. Artillery Day (Dec. 4th).
1213. **350.** 20 p. red .. 10 5

1967. Child Welfare. Bird designs as T **273.** Multicoloured.
1214. 20 p.+10 p. Amazon kingfisher (postage) .. 12 10
1215. 26 p.+13 p. Toco toucan (air) 15 12

1968. Eduardo Sivori (painter). 50th Death Anniv.
1216. **351.** 20 p. green 12 5

352. "Almirante Brown" Scientific Station. **353.** Man in Wheel-chair.

1968. "Antarctic Territories".
1217. – 6 p. multicoloured .. 5 5
1218. **352.** 20 p. multicoloured.. 8 5
1219. – 40 p. multicoloured.. 15 8
DESIGNS—VERT. (22½×32 mm.). 6 p. Map of Antarctic radio-postal stations. HORIZ. (As T **352**). 40 p. Aircraft over South Pole ("Trans-Polar Round Flight").

1968. Rehabilitation Day for the Handicapped.
1220. **353.** 20 p. black and green 8 5

354. "St. Gabriel" (detail from "The Annunciation" by Leonardo da Vinci). **355.** Children and W.H.O. Emblem.

1968. St. Gabriel (patron saint of army communications).
1221. **354.** 20 p. magenta .. 8 5

1968. W.H.O. 20th Anniv.
1222. **355.** 20 p. blue & vermilion 8 5

1968. Army Day (29th May). As T **310.**
1223. 20 p. multicoloured .. 8 5
DESIGN: 20 p. Iriarte's artilleryman.

356. Frigate "Libertad" (E. Biggeri).

1968. Navy Day.
1224. **356.** 20 p. multicoloured.. 10 5

357. G. Rawson and Hospital.

1968. Guillermo Rawson Hospital. Cent.
1225. **357.** 6 p. bistre 5 5

358. Vito Dumas and "Legh II".

1968. Air. Vito Dumas' World Voyage in Yacht "Legh II".
1226. **358.** 68 p. multicoloured.. 20 15

359. Children crossing "Zebra".

1968. Road Safety.
1227. **359.** 20 p. multicoloured.. 8 5

360. "O'Higgins greeting San Martin" (P. Subercaseaux).

1968. Battle of the Maipu. 150th Anniv.
1228. **360.** 40 p. indigo 15 8

361. Dr. O. Magnasco (Lawyer). **362.** "The Sea" (E. Gomez).

363. "Grandmother's Birthday" (P. Lynch).

1968. Magnasco Commem.
1229. **361.** 20 p. brown 8 5

1968. Children's Stamp Design Competition.
1230. **362.** 20 p. multicoloured.. 8 5
1231. **363.** 20 p. multicoloured.. 8 5

364. Mar del Plata at Night. **365.** Mounted Gendarme.

1968. 4th Plenary Assembly of Int. Telegraph and Telephone Consultative Committee, Mar del Plata.
1232. **364.** 20 p. black, yellow & blue (postage) .. 8 5
1233. – 40 p. black, magenta and blue (air) .. 12 8
1234. – 68 p. blk., gold & bl. 20 15
DESIGNS: (As T **364**) 40 p. South America in Assembly hemisphere. (40×30 mm.). 68 p. Assembly emblem.

1968. National Gendarmerie.
1235. **365.** 20 p. black, yellow, green and brown .. 8 5

366. Coastguard Cutter. **367.** A. de Anchorens and "Pampero".

1968. National Maritime Prefecture (Coastguard).
1236. **366.** 20 p. blk., grey & bl. 8 5

1968. Aeronautics Week.
1237. **367.** 20 p. multicoloured.. 8 5

368. St. Martin of Tours (A. Guido). **369.** Bank Emblem.

1968. St. Martin of Tours (patron saint of Buenos Aires.)
1238. **368.** 20 p. brown and lilac 8 5

1968. Municipal Bank of Buenos Aires.
1239. **369.** 20 p. blk., grn., yell. 8 5

371. Anniversary and A.L.P.I. Emblems.

1968. "Fight Against Polio Assn."(A.L.P.I.) 25th Anniv.
1240. **371.** 20 p. green & cerise.. 8 5

372. "My Grandmother's Birthday. (Patricia Lynch).

1968. 1st "Solidarity" Philatelic Exn., Buenos Aires.
1241. **372.** 40 p.+20 p. mult. .. 20 15

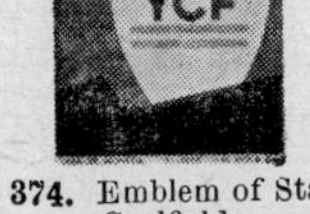

373. "The Potter Woman" (Ramon Gomez Cornet). **374.** Emblem of State Coalfields.

1968. Witcomb Gallery, Buenos Aires. Cent.
1242. **373.** 20 p. cerise 10 5

1968. Coal and Steel Industries.
1243. **374.** 20 p. multicoloured.. 8 5
1244. – 20 p. multicoloured.. 8 5
DESIGN: No 1244, Ladle and emblem of Military Steel-manufacturing Agency ("FM").

375. Illustration from Schmidl's book "Journey to the River Plate and Paraguay".

1969. Ulrich Schmidl Commem.
1245. **375.** 20 p. yellow, red & blk. 8 5

1969. Army Day (29th May). As T **310.**
1246. **376.** 20 p. Infantry Sapper 8 5

377. Frigate "Hercules".

1969. Navy Day.
1247. **377.** 20 p. multicoloured.. 8 5

378. "Freedom and Equality" (from poster by S. Zagorski). **379.** I.L.O. Emblem within Honeycomb.

1969. Human Rights Year.
1254. **378.** 20 p. black and yellow 8 5

1969. Int. Labour Organization. 50th Anniv.
1255. **379.** 20 p. multicoloured.. 5 5

380. P. N. Arata. (biologist). **381.** Dish Aerial and Satellite.

1969. Argentine Scientists.
1256. **380.** 6 p. brown on yellow.. 5 5
1257. – 6 p. brown on yellow.. 5 5
1258. – 6 p. brown on yellow.. 5 5
1259. – 6 p. brown on yellow.. 5 5
1260. – 6 p. brown on yellow.. 5 5
PORTRAITS: No. 1257, M. Fernandez (zoologist). 1307, A. P. Gallardo (biologist). 1259, C. M. Hicken (botanist). 1260, E. L. Holmberg (botanist).

1969. Satellite Communications.
1261. **381.** 20 p. blk. & yell. (post) 5 5
1262. – 40 p. blue (air) .. 12 8
DESIGN—HORIZ. 40 p. Earth station and dish aerial.

382. Nieuport "28" Fighter and Route-map.

1969. 1st Argentine Airmail Service. 50th Anniv.
1263. **382.** 20 p. multicoloured.. 8 5

1969. Child Welfare. Vert designs as T **273.** inscr. R. ARGENTINA. Multicoloured.
1264. 20 p. + 10 p. Widow duck (postage) 12 10
1265. 26 p. + 13 p. Red-headed striped woodpecker (air) 12 12

383. College Entrance. **384.** General Pacheco.

1969. Argentine Military College. Cent.
1266. **383.** 20 p. multicoloured .. 8 5

1969. General Angel Pacheco. Death Cent.
1267. **384.** 20 p. green 8 5

385. Bartolome Mitre and Logotypes of "La Nacion". **386.** J. Aguirre.

1969. Newspapers "La Nacion" and "La Prensa". Cent.
1268. **385.** 20 p. blk., emer. & grn. 8 5
1269. – 20 p. blk. orge. & yell. 8 5
DESIGN: No. 1269. "The Lantern" (mast-head) and logotypes of "La Prensa".

1969. Argentine Musicians.
1270. **386.** 6 p. green and blue 5 5
1271. – 6 p. green and blue 5 5
1272. – 6 p. green and blue 5 5
1273. – 6 p. green and blue 5 5
1274. – 6 p. green and blue 5 5
MUSICIANS: No. 1271, F. Boero. 1272,, C. Gaito. 1273, C. L. Buchardo. 1274, A. Williams.

387. Chocon-Cerros Colorados Hydro-electric Project.

1969. National Development Projects. Multicoloured.
1275. 6 p. Type **387** (postage) .. 5 5
1276. 20 p. Parana-Santa Fe river tunnel 8 5
1277. 26 p. Atomic Power Plant, Atucha (air) .. 12 5

388. Lieut. B. Matienzo and Nieuport Aircraft.

1969. Aeronautics Week.
1278. **388.** 20 p. multicoloured .. 8 5

389. Capital "L" and Lions' Emblem. **390.** "Madonna and Child" (after R. Soldi).

1969. Lions' International. 50th Anniv.
1279. **389.** 20 p. olive, orge. & grn. 8 5

1969. Christmas.
1280. **390.** 20 p. multicoloured .. 8 5

1970. Child Welfare. As T **273**, but differently arranged and inscr. "REPUBLICA ARGENTINA". Multicoloured.
1293. 20 c. + 10 c. Hummingbird (postage) 12 8
1294 40 c. + 20 c. Flamingo (air) 15 10
See also Nos. 1401/2, 1421/2 and 1461/2.

391. "General Belgrano" (from lithograph by Gericault). **392.** Early Fire Engine.

1970. General Manuel Belgrano. Birth Bicent.
1295. **391.** 20 c. brown 8 5
1296. – 50 c. blk., flesh & blue 15 10
DESIGN—HORIZ. (56 × 15 mm.): 50 c. "Monument to the Flag" (bas-relief by Jose Fioravanti).

1970. Air. Buenos Aires Fire Brigade. Cent.
1297. **392.** 40 c. multicoloured 12 8

393. Schooner "Juliet", 1814.

1970. Navy Day.
1298. **393.** 20 c. multicoloured .. 8 5

394. San Jose Palace.

1970. President Josto de Urquiza Commem.
1299. **394.** 20 c. multicoloured .. 8 5

395. Sunflower. **396.** General Belgrano.

1970. Revalued currency. Previous designs with values in centavos and pesos as T **395/6**. Inscr. "REPUBLICA ARGENTINA" or "ARGENTINA".
1300. **395.** 1 c. green (postage) .. 5 5
1301. – 3 c. red (No. 951) .. 5 5
1302. **227.** 5 c. blue 5 5
1303. **396.** 6 c. blue 5 5
1304. – 8 c. green 5 5
1305. – 10 c. brown (No. 953) 5 5
1306. – 10 c. red (No. 953) .. 5 5
1308. **396.** 10 c. brown 5 5
1307. – 10 c. brown 5 5
1309. – 25 c. brown 5 5
1310. **396.** 30 c. maroon .. 5
1311. – 50 c .red 8 5
1313. – 65 c. brown (No. 1024) 10 5
1314. – 70 c. blue 12 5
1315. – 90 c. green (No. 1024) 15 5
1316. – 1 p. brown (No. 1025) 15 5
1317. – 1 p. 15 blue (No. 1072) 15 8
1318. – 1 p. 20 orange(No.1024) 20 8
1319. – 1 p. 20 red (As No. 1288) 10 5
1320. – 1 p. 80 brn. (As No. 1288) 30 10
1321. **396.** 1 p. 80 blue 5 5
1322. – 2 p. brown 8 5
1323. – 2 p. 70 bl. (As No. 1287) 20 8
1392. – 4 p. 50 green (as No. 1288) (G. Brown) .. 10 8
1325. – 5 p. gr. (As No. 1032) 35 15
1326. – 6 p. red 15 8
1327. – 6 p. green 15 8
1328. – 7 p. 50 gr. (As No. 1287) 20 8
1329. – 10 p. bl. (As No. 1033) 70 25
1330. – 13 p. 50 red (As No. 1288) 30 12
1331. – 13 p. 50 red (As No. 1288 but larger, 16 × 24 mm.) .. 30 12
1332. – 22 p. 50 bl. (As No. 1287) (22 and 32½ mm) .. 50 20
1393. – 22 p. 50 blue (26 × 39 mm) (San Martin) .. 50 20
DESIGN—VERT. As T **396**. 25 c., 50 c., 70 c. 1 p. 20, 2 p., 6 p., General San Martin.

397. Wireless Set of 1920 and Radio "Waves".

1970. 1st Radio Outside Broadcast. 50th Anniv.
1341. **397.** 20 c. multicoloured 8

398. Emblem of Education Year. **399.** Military Courier 1879.

1970. Air. Int. Education Year.
1342. **398.** 68 c. black and blue 20 12

1970. Military Uniforms.
1343. **399.** 20 c. multicoloured .. 8 5

400. "Liberation Fleet leaving Valparaiso" (A. Abel).

1970. Air. Peruvian Liberation 150th Anniv.
1344. **400.** 26 c. multicoloured .. 10 5

401. "United Nations".

1970. United Nations. 25th Anniv.
1345. **401.** 20 c. multicoloured 8 5

402. Sumampa Chapel, Santiago del Estero.

1970. Tucuman Diocese. 400th Anniv.
1346. – 50 c. blk. & grey (post.) 15 8
1347. **402.** 40 c. multicoloured (air) 12 8
DESIGN—VERT. 50 c. Cordoba Cathedral.

403. Planetarium.

1970. Air. Buenos Aires Planetarium.
1348. **403.** 40 c. multicoloured .. 12 10

404. "Liberty" and Mint Building.

1970. State Mint Building, Buenos Aires. 25th Anniv.
1349. **404.** 20 c. blk., grn. & gold 8 5

405. "The Manger" (H. G. Gutierrez).
(Illustration reduced. Actual size 77 × 33 mm).

1970. Christmas.
1350. **405.** 20 c. multicoloured .. 8 5

406. Jorge Newbery and "Morane Saulnier" Aircraft.

1970. Air, Aeronautics Week.
1351. **406.** 26 c. multicoloured .. 10 5

407. St. John Bosco and Mission Building.

1970. Salesian Mission in Patagonia.
1352. **407.** 20 c. black and olive .. 8 5

408. "Planting the Flag".

1971. Argentine Expedition to the South Pole. 5th Anniv.
1353. **408.** 20 c. multicoloured .. 8 5

409. Dorado.
Illustration reduced. Actual size 75 × 15 mm.)

1971. Child Welfare. Fishes. Multicoloured.
1354. 20 c. + 10 c. Type **409** (postage) 12 10
1355. 40 c. + 20 c. Mackerel (air) 15 12

410. Einstein and Scanners. **411.** E. I. Allippi.

1971. Electronics in Postal Development.
1356. **410.** 25 c. multicoloured .. 10 5

1971. Argentine Actors and Actresses. Each black and sepia.
1357. 15 c. Type **411** .. 5 5
1358. 15 c. J. A. Casaberta .. 5 5
1359. 15 c. R. Casaux .. 5 5
1360. 15 c. Angelina Pagano 5 5
1361. 15 c. F. Perravicini .. 5 5

412. Federation Emblem.

1971. Inter-American Regional Meeting of Int. Roads Federation.
1362. **412.** 25 c. black and blue 8 5

1971. Army Day. Vert. designs as T **310.**
1363. 25 c. multicoloured .. 8 5
DESIGN: 25 c. Artilleryman of 1826.

1971. Navy Day. Horiz designs as T **393.**
1364. 25 c. multicoloured .. 8 5
DESIGN: Sloop "Carmen".

413. "Guemes" (L. Gigli).

1971. General M. de Guemes. 150th Death Anniv. Multicoloured.
1365. 25 c. Type **413** 8 5
1366. 25 c. "Death of Guemes" (A. Alice) 8 5
No. 1366 is larger, 84×29 mm.

414. Order of the Peruvian Sun.

1971. Peruvian Independence. 150th Anniv.
1367. **414.** 31 c. yell., blk. & red 10 5

415. Stylised Tulip.

416. Dr. A. Saenz (founder) (after Jose Gut).

1971. 3rd Int., and 8th National Horticultural Exhibition.
1368. **415.** 25 c. multicoloured .. 8 5

1971. Buenos Aires University. 150th Anniv.
1369. **416.** 25 c. multicoloured .. 8 5

417. Arsenal Emblem.

1971. Fabricaciones Militares (Arsenals) 30th Anniv.
1370. **417.** 25 c. multicoloured .. 8 5

418. Road Transport.

1971. Nationalised Industries (1st series).
1371. **418.** 25 c. mult. (postage) 8 5
1372. – 65 c. multicoloured .. 20 10
1373. – 31 c. yell., blk., & red (air) .. 12 5
DESIGNS: 31 c. Refinery and formula ("Petrochemicals"). 65 c. Tree and paper roll ("Paper and Cellulose").

1971. Air. Revalued currency. Face values in centavos.
1374. **279.** 45 c. brown 8 5
1375. 68 c. red 10 5
1376. 70 c. blue 10 5
1377. 90 c. green 15 15
1378. 1 p. 70 blue 25 10
1379. 1 p. 95 green 30 12
1380. 2 p. 65 purple .. 40 15

419. Constellation and Telescope.

1971. Cordoba Observatory. Cent.
1381. **419.** 25 c. multicoloured 10 5

420. Capt. D. L. Candelaria and Morane-Saulnier Aircraft.

1971. 25th Aeronautics and Space Week.
1382. **420.** 25 c. multicoloured 8 5

421. "Stamps". (Mariette Lydis).

422. "Christ in Majesty" (tapestry by Butler).

1971. 2nd Charity Stamp Exhibition.
1383. **421.** 1 p. + 50 c. mult. .. 35 30

1971. Christmas.
1384. **422.** 25 c. multicoloured .. 8 5

1972. Child Welfare. As T **273**, but differently arranged and inscribed "REPUBLIC ARGENTINA".
1394. 25 c. + 10 c. Saffron finch (vert.) 10 5
1395. 65 c. + 30 c. Chocolate tyrant (horiz.) 25 15

423. "Maternity" (J. Castagnino).

1972. U.N.I.C.E.F. 25th Anniv.
1396. **423.** 25 c. black & brown 5 5

424. Treaty Emblem and "Almirante Brown" Base.

1972. Antarctic Treaty, 10th Anniv.
1397. **424.** 25 c. multicoloured 10 5

425. Postman's Mail Pouch.

1972. 1st Buenos Aires Postman. Bicent.
1398. **425.** 25 c. multicoloured 5 5

1972. Army Day. As T **310.** Multicoloured.
1399. 25 c. Sergeant of Negro and Mulatto Battalion (1806-7) 10 5

1972. Navy Day. As T **393.** Multicoloured.
1400. 25 c. Brigantine "Santisima Trinidad" 10 5

426. Sonic Balloon. **427.** Oil Pump.

1972. National Meteorological Service.
1401. **426.** 25 c. multicoloured .. 10 5

1972. State Oilfields (YPF). 50th Anniv.
1402. **427.** 45 c. blk., blue & gold 15 8

428. Forest of Trees.

1972. 7th World Forestry Congress, Buenos Aires.
1403. **428.** 25 c. blk., bl. & light bl. 10 5

429. Arms and Frigate "Presidente Sarmiento".

1972. Naval School. Cent.
1404. **429.** 25 c. multicoloured .. 10 5

430. Baron A. de Marchi, Balloon and Aeroplane. **431.** Bartolome Mitre.

1972. Aeronautics Week.
1405. **430.** 25 c. multicoloured .. 10 5

1972. General Bartolome Mitre. 150th Birth Anniv.
1406. **431.** 25 c. blue 10 5

432. Heart and Flower.

433. "Martin Fierro" (J. C. Castignino).

1972. World Health Day.
1407. **432.** 90 c. black, violet-blue and blue 20 12

1972. Int. Book Year and Publication of "Martin Fierro" (poem by Jose Hernandez). Cent. Multicoloured.
1408. 50 c. Type **433** 12 8
1409. 90 c. "Spirit of the Gaucho" (V. Forte) 20 12

434. "Wise Man on Horseback" (18th-century wood-carving).

436. Cockerel Emblem.

435. Iguazu Falls.

1972. Christmas.
1411. **434.** 50 c. multicoloured .. 15 8

1972. American Tourist Year.
1410. **435.** 45 c. multicoloured .. 15 8

1973. Federal Police Force. 150th Anniv.
1412. **436.** 50 c. multicoloured .. 15 8

437. Bank Emblem and First Coin.

439. Presidential Chair.

438. Douglas "DC-3" Planes and Polar Map.

1973. Provincial Bank of Buenos Aires. 150th Anniv.
1413. **437.** 50 c. multicoloured .. 12 8

1973. 1st Argentine Flight to South Pole. 10th Anniversary.
1414. **438.** 50 c. multicoloured 10 5

1973. Child Welfare. As T **273**, but differently arranged and inscr. "R. ARGENTINA". Multicoloured.
1415. 50 c. + 25 c. Southern crested screamer (vert.) 15 10
1416. 90 c. + 45 c. Yellow-headed marshbird (horiz.) .. 25 15

1973. Presidential Inaug.
1417. **439.** 50 c. multicoloured .. 10 5

440. San Martin and Bolivar.

1973. San Martin's Farewell to People of Peru. Multicoloured.
1418. 50 c. Type **440** 8 5
1419. 50 c. "San Martin" (after Gil de Castro) (vert.) .. 8 5

441. "Eva Peron-Eternally with her People".

1973. Eva Peron Commemoration.
1420. **441.** 70 c. multicoloured .. 12 5

442. "House of Viceroy Sobremonte" (H. de Virgilio).

1973. Cordoba. 4th Centenary.
1421. **442.** 50 c. multicoloured .. 8 5

443. " Woman " (L. Spilimbergo).

1973. Philatelists' Day. Argentine Paintings. Multicoloured.

1422. 15 c.+15 c. " Nature Study " (A. Guttero) (horiz.) 5 5
1423. 70 c. Type **443** 10 5
1424. 90 c.+90 c. " Nude " (M. C. Victorica) (horiz.) 30 20

See also Nos. 1434/6 and 1440.

444. " La Argentina ". **445.** Early and Modern Telephones.

1973. Navy Day.

1425. **444.** 70 c. multicoloured .. 10 5

1973. National Telecommunications Enterprise (E.N.T.E.L.). 25th Anniv.

1426. **445.** 70 c. multicoloured .. 10 5

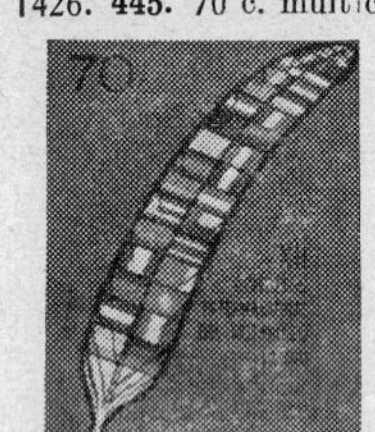

446. Quill Pen of Flags. **447.** Lujan Basilica.

1973. 12th International Latin Notaries Congress.

1427. **446.** 70 c. multicoloured .. 10 5

1973.

1428. **447.** 18 c. brown and orange 5 5
1429. 50 c. purple and black 8 5
1429a. 50 c. blue and brown 5 5
1430. 50 c. purple 5 5

1973. Transfer of Presidency to General Juan Peron. No. 1318 optd. **TRANSMISION DEL MANDO PRESIDENCIAL 12 OCTUBRE 1973.**

1431. 1 p. 20 orange .. 20 8

448. " Virgin and Child " (stained-glass window).

1973. Christmas. Multicoloured.

1432. 70 c. Type **448** 10 5
1433. 1 p. 20 " The Manger " (B. Venier) 20 8

449. " Houses " (E. Daneri).

1974. Argentine Paintings. Multicoloured.

1434. 50 c. Type **449** 8 5
1435. 70 c. " The Lama " (J. B. Planas) (vert.) .. 10 5
1436. 90 c. " Homage to the Blue Grotto " (E. Pettoruti) 12 5

450. View of Mar del Plata.

1974. Mar del Plata. Centenary.

1437. **450.** 70 c. multicoloured .. 10 5

451. " Fray Justo Santa Maria de Oro " (anon.). **452.** Weather Contrasts.

1974. Fray Justo Santa Maria de Oro. Birth Bicent.

1438. **451.** 70 c. multicoloured 10 5

1974. World Meteorological Organization. Cent.

1439. **452.** 1 p. 20 multicoloured 20 8

453. " The Lama " (J. B. Planas). **454.** B. Roldan.

1974. " Prenfil 74 " Philatelic Press Exn., Buenos Aires.

1440. **453.** 70 c.+30 c multicoloured 15 8

1974. Child Welfare. As T **273** but differently arranged and inscribed " REPUBLICA ARGENTINA ". Multicoloured.

1441. 70 c.+30 c. Seedeater (" Sphorophila caerulescens ") .. 15 8
1442. 1 p. 20 + 60 c. Black-headed siskin .. 30 15

No. 1461 is inscr. " Sphorophila caerulescems ".

1974. Belisario Roldan (writer). Birth Cent.

1443. **454.** 70 c. brown and blue 10 5

455. O.E.A. Member Countries.

1974. Organization of American States' Charter. 25th Anniv.

1444. **455.** 1 p. 38 multicoloured 25 12

456. Posthorn Emblem.

1974. Creation of State Posts & Telecommunications Enterprise (E.N.C.O.T.E.L.).

1445. **456.** 1 p. 20 bl., blk. & gold 20 8

457. Flags of Member Countries. **458.** El Chocon Hydro-electric Complex.

1974. Sixth Meeting of River Plate Countries' Foreign Ministers.

1446. **457.** 1 p. 38 multicoloured 25 12

1974. Nationalised Industries (2nd series). Multicoloured.

1447. 70 c. Type **458** 10 5
1448. 1 p. 20 Blast furnace, Somisa steel mills .. 15 8
1449. 4 p. 50 General Belgrano Bridge 65 30

No. 1449 is a horiz. design, size 61 × 25 mm.

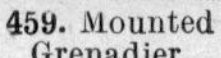

459. Mounted Grenadier. **460.** A. Mascias and "Bleriot" Aircraft.

1974. Army Day.

1450. **459.** 1 p. 20 multicoloured 15 8

See also No. 1507.

1974. Air Force Day.

1451. **460.** 1 p. 20 multicoloured 15 8

461. Brigantine "Belgrano".

1974. San Martin's Departure into Exile. 150th Anniv.

1452. **461.** 1 p. 20 multicoloured 15 8

462. San Francisco Convent, Santa Fe.

1974. Santa Fe. 400th Anniv.

1453. **462.** 1 p. 20 multicoloured 15 8

463. Symbolic Posthorn.

1974. Universal Postal Union. Centenary.

1454. **463.** 2 p. 65 multicoloured 30 15

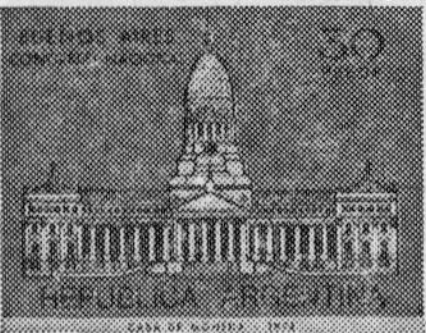

464. Congress Building, Buenos Aires.

1974.

1456. **464.** 30 p. mar. & yell. .. 3·25 1·50

465. Young Philatelist.

1974. International Year of Youth Philately.

1457. **465.** 1 p. 70 blk. & yell. .. 20 10

466. " Christmas in Peace ".

1974. Christmas. Multicoloured.

1458. 1 p. 20 Type **466** .. 12 8
1459. 2 p. 65 " St. Anne and the Virgin Mary " 15 0

467. " Space Monsters " (R. Forner).

1975. Contemporary Argentine Paintings. Multicoloured.

1460. 2 p. 70 Type **467** 25 15
1461. 4 p. 50 " Sleep " (E. Centurion) 40 20

468. Church and Weaver, Catamarca. (Illustration reduced. Actual size 83 × 29 mm.)

1975. Tourist Views. (1st series.) Multicoloured.

1462. 1 p. 20 Type **468** .. 8 5
1463. 1 p. 20 Street scene and carved pulpit, Jujuy .. 8 5
1464. 1 p. 20 Monastery and tree-felling, Salta .. 8 5
1465. 1 p. 20 Dam and gourd, Santiago del Estero .. 8 5
1466. 1 p. 20 Colonial mansion and farm-cart, Tucuman 8 5

See also Nos. 1491/3.

469. " We're Vaccinated Now ". (M. L. Alonso). **470.** " Don Quijote " (Zuloaga).

1975. Children's Vaccination Campaign.

1467. **469.** 2 p. multicoloured .. 8 5

1975. Air. " Espana 75 " International Stamp Exhibition, Madrid.

1468. **470.** 2 p. 75 black, yell. & red 10 5

471. Hugo S. Acuna and South Orcadas Base. (Illustration reduced. Actual size 83 × 29 mm).

1975. Antarctic Pioneers. Multicoloured.

1469. 2 p. Type **471** 8 5
1470. 2 p. Francisco P. Moreno and Quetrihue Peninsula 8 5
1471. 2 p. Capt. Carlos M. Moyano and Cerra Torre, Santa Cruz 8 5
1472. 2 p. Lt. Col. Luis Piedra Buena and Cutter " Luisito " 8 5
1473. 2 p. Ensign Jose M. Sobral and "Snow Hill" House 8 5

472. Valley of the Moon, San Juan Province. **473.** E. Bradley and Balloon.

1975.
1474. **472.** 50 p. multicoloured .. 1·50 90

1975. Air. Surch.
1475. **279.** 9 p. 20 on 5 p. 60 gr., blue and purple .. 40 20
1476. 19 p. 70 on 5 p. 60 gr., blue and purple .. 65 35
1477. 100 p. on 5 p. 60 gr., blue and purple .. 3·00 1·75

1975. Air Force Day.
1478. **473.** 6 p. multicoloured .. 15 8

474. Frigate " 25th of May ".

1975. Navy Day.
1479. **474.** 6 p. multicoloured .. 15 8

475. " Oath of the 33 Orientales on the Beach of La Agraciada " (J. Blanes).

1975. Uruguayan Independence. 150th Anniv.
1480. **475.** 6 p. multicoloured .. 15 8

1975. Air. Surch. **REVALORIZADO** and value.
1481. **279.** 9 p. 20 on 5 p. 60 gr., blue and purple .. 40 20
1482. 19 p. 70 on 5. 60 gr., blue and purple .. 65 35

476. Flame Emblem.

1975. Pres. Peron's Seizure of Power. 30th Anniv.
1483. **476.** 6 p. multicoloured .. 15 8

1975. Surch. **REVALORIZADO** and value.
1484. **447.** 5 p. on 18 c. br. & yell. 15 8

477. Bridge and Flags of Argentina and Uruguay.

1975. " International Bridge " between Colon (Argentina) and Paysandu (Uruguay).
1485. **477.** 6 p. multicoloured .. 15 8

INDEX

Countries can be quickly located by referring to the index at the end of this volume.

478. Posthorn Emblem. **479.** " The Nativity " (stained-glass window.)

1975. Introduction of Postal Codes.
1486. **478.** 10 p. on 20 c. yellow, black and green .. 20 10

1975. Nos. 951 and 1288 surch. **REVALORIZADO** and value.
1487. 6 c. on 3 p. blue 15 8
1488. 30 c. on 90 p. bistre .. 60 30

1975. Christmas.
1489. **479.** 6 p. multicoloured .. 15 8

480. Stylised Nurse and Child. **481.** " Numeral "

1975. Children's Hospital. Cent.
1490. **480.** 6 p. multicoloured .. 15 8

1975. Tourist Views (2nd series). As No. **468.** Multicoloured.
1491. 6 p. Mounted patrol and oil rig, Chubut .. 15 8
1492. 6 p. Glacier and sheep-shearing, Santa Cruz .. 15 8
1493. 6 p. Lake Lapataia, Tierra del Fuego, and Antarctic scene 15 8

1976.
1494. **481.** 12 c. grey and black 5 5
1495. 50 c. slate and black 5 5
1496. 1 p. red and black .. 5 5
1497. 4 p. blue and black .. 5 5
1498. 5 p. yellow and black 5 5
1499. 6 p. brown and black 5 5
1500. 10 p. grey and blue .. 8 5
1501. 27 p. green and black 20 10
1502. 45 p. yellow and black 35 20
1503. 50 p. green and black 40 20
1504. 100 p. green and red 75 40

482. Airliner in Flight.

1976. " Aerolineas Argentinas ". 25th Anniv.
1505. **482.** 30 p. multicoloured .. 25 12

483. Frigate " Heroina " and Map of Malvinas

1976. Argentine Claims to Falkland Islands (Malvinas).
1506. **483.** 6 p. multicoloured .. 5 5

1976. Army Day. As T **459.** Multicoloured.
1507. 12 p. Infantryman of Conde's 7th Regiment 10 5

484. Louis Braille. **485.** " Cyanocorax chrysops ".

1976. Louis Braille (inventor of characters for the Blind). Commemoration.
1508. **484.** 19 p. 70 blue .. 15 8

1976. Argentine Philately. Multicoloured.
1509. 7 p. + 3 p. 50 Type **485** .. 8 8
1510. 13 p. + 6 p. 50 " Ara auricolis " (parrot) .. 15 15
1511. 20 p. + 10 p. " Begonia micranthera " .. 25 25
1512. 40 p. + 20 p. " Echinopsis shaferi " (teasel) .. 50 50

486. Schooner " Rio de la Plata ".

1976. Navy Day.
1513. **486.** 12 p. multicoloured .. 10 5

487. Dr. Bernardo Houssay (Medicine).

1976. Argentine Nobel Prizewinners.
1514. **487.** 10 p. blk., orge. & grey 8 5
1515. – 15 p. blk., yell. & grey 12 5
1516. – 20 p. blk., ochre & grey 15 8
DESIGNS: 15 p. Dr. Luis Leloir (Chemistry). 20 p. Dr. Carlos Lamas (Peace).

488. Bridge and Ship.

1976. " International Bridge " between Unzue (Argentina) and Fray Bentos (Uruguay).
1517. **488.** 12 p. multicoloured .. 10 5

OFFICIAL STAMPS

1884. Optd. **OFICIAL.**
O 66. **16.** ½ c. brown .. .. 2·25 2·25
O 69. 1 c. red 15 15
O 70. **13.** 2 c. green 20 15
O 71. – 4 c. brown (No. 32) .. 12 15
O 72. **5.** 8 c. lake 12 12
O 73. **6.** 10 c. green .. .. 11·00 5·50
O 76. **16.** 12 c. blue 25 20
O 77. **6.** 16 c. green 30 25
O 78. **14.** 20 c. blue .. .. 1·00 80
O 80. **7.** 24 c. blue (roul.) .. 35 35
O 79. 24 c. blue (perf.) .. 35 30
O 81. – 25 c. lake (No. 47) .. 2·75 1·90
O 82. – 30 c. orange (No. 33) 5·00 3·75
O 83. – 60 c. black (No. 34) .. 2·75 1·90
O 84. – 90 c. blue (No. 35) .. 2·10 1·60

O 1.

1901.
O 275. O **1.** 1 c. grey 5 5
O 276. 2 c. brown 8 5
O 277. 5 c. red 8 5
O 278. 10 c. green 12 8
O 279. 30 c. blue 30 20
O 280. 50 c. orange .. 20 10

1938. Optd. **SERVICIO OFICIAL** in two lines.
O 668. – 1 c. yellow (No. 645) 5 5
O 669. – 2 c. brown (No. 646) 5 5
O 670. **97.** 3 c. green (No. 647) 5 5
O 679. 3 c. grey (No. 750) 5 5
O 771. – 3 c. grey (No.751) 20 8
O 671. – 5 c. brown (No. 653b) 5 5
O 782. **134.** 5 c. red (No. 773) .. 5 5
O 667. – 10 c. red (No. 653d) 5 5
O 773. – 10 c. brown (No. 753) 5 5
O 681. **98.** 15 c. blue (No. 676) 5 5
O 774. – 15 c. grey-blue (No. 754) 5 5
O 683. **98.** 20 c. blue (19½ × 26 mm.) 5 5
O 872. **179.** 20 c. red 5 5
O 813. – 25 c. (No. 656) .. 5 5
O 674. – 40 c. (No. 658) .. 10 5
O 675. – 50 c. (No. 659) .. 5 5
O 676. **99.** 1 p. (No. 660a) .. 5 5
O 828. **166.** 1 p. (No. 826) .. 50 5
O 778. – 2 p. (No. 661) .. 10 5
O 779. – 5 p. (No. 662) .. 12 5
O 780. – 10 p. (No. 763) .. 25 10
O 781. – 20 p. (No. 664) .. 40 20

(b) Optd. **SERVICIO OFICIAL** in one line.
O 897. – 20 c. lilac (No. 895) 5 5

1953. Eva Peron stamps optd. **SERVICIO OFICIAL.**
O 854. **171.** 5 c. grey 5 5
O 855. 10 c. claret 5 5
O 856. 20 c. red 5 5
O 857. 25 c. green 5 5
O 858. 40 c. purple 5 5
O 859. 45 c. blue 10 5
O 860. 50 c. bistre 5 5
O 862. **172.** 1 p. brown (No. 846) 5 5
O 863. 1 p. 50 green (No. 847) 12 5
O 864. 2 p. crimson (No. 848) 20 5
O 865. 3 p. indigo (No. 849) 25 10
O 866. 5 p. brown 40 12
O 867. **171.** 10 p. red .. .. 1·25 70
O 868. **172.** 20 p. green .. .. 3·00 2·10

1955. Stamps of 1954 optd. **SERVICIO OFICIAL** in one line.
O 869. **179.** 20 c. red 5 5
O 870. 40 c. red 5 5
O 880. – 1 p. brown (No. 871) 5 5
O 882. – 3 p. purple (No. 874) 5 5
O 883. – 5 p. green (No. 875) .. 8 5
O 884. – 10 p. yellow-green & grey-grn. (No. 876) 20 8
O 886. **181.** 20 p. violet 20 10

1955. Various stamps overprinted.
(a) Optd. **S. OFICIAL.**
O 896. – 5 c. brown (No. 894) 5 5
O 955. – 10 c. green (No. 946) 5 5
O 956. – 20 c. mar. (No. 947) .. 5 5
O 879. – 50 c. blue (No. 868) .. 5 5
O 957. – 50 c. ochre (No. 948) 5 5
O 1034. – 1 p. brn. (No. 1016) .. 5 5
O 899. **196.** 2 p. purple 10 5
O 1050. – 2 p. red (No. 1035) .. 8 5
O 959. – 3 p. blue (No. 951) .. 12 8
O 1051. – 4 p. red (No. 1036) .. 8 5
O 961. **227.** 5p. brown 8 5
O 1052. – 8 p. red (No .1037) 8 5
O 962. – 10 p. brown(No.1286) 20 10
O 1053. – 10 p. red (No. 1038) .. 10 5
O 1036. – 12 p. dull purple (No. 1028) 15 5
O 964. – 20 p. green (No. 954) 35 15
O 1055. – 20 p. red (No. 1039) . 10 5
O 1037. – 22 p. blue (No. 1018) 25 5
O 1038. – 23 p. green (No. 1019) 15 5
O 1039. – 25 p. lilac (No. 1020) 15 5
O 1040. – 43 p. lake (No. 1021) 40 5
O 1041. – 45 p. brn. (No. 1022) 40 5
O 1042. – 50 p. blue (No. 1023) 30 5
O 1043. – 50 p. blue (No. 1024) 20 5
O 1044. – 100 p. blue (No. 1025) 95 15
O 1045. – 100 p. blue (No. 1025) 60 15
O 1046. – 300 p. violet (No. 1026) 1·40 40

The overprint on No. O 1044 is horiz. and on No. O 1045 it reads vert. upwards.

(b) Optd. **SERVICIO OFICIAL.**
O 900. **197.** 2 p. 40 brown .. 12 5
O 958. – 3 p. blue (No. 951) 8 5
O 901. **198.** 4 p. 40 green .. 20 5
O 960. **227.** 5 p. brown 12 5
O 887. – 50 p. indigo and blue (No. 878) 65 30
O 1049. – 500 p. grn. (No. 1032) 1·75 80

For lists of stamps optd. **M.A., M.G., M.H., M.I., M.J.I., M.M., M.O.P.** or **M.R.C.** for use in ministerial offices see the Stanley Gibbons' Foreign Overseas Catalogue Vol. 1.

1963. Nos. 1068, etc., optd. **S. OFICIAL.**
O 1076. **272.** 2 p. green 5 5
O 1080. – 4 p. red (No. 1069) .. 5 5
O 1081. – 6 p. red (No. 1079) .. 12 5
O 1078. – 90 p. bistre (No. 1288) 40 15

RECORDED MESSAGE STAMPS.

ILLUSTRATIONS
British Commonwealth and all overprints and surcharges are FULL SIZE. Foreign Countries have been reduced to ¾-LINEAR.

RM **1.** Winged Messenger.

1939. Various symbolic designs inscribed " CORREOS FONOPOSTAL ".
RM 688. RM **1.** 1 p 18 blue .. 2·00 1·10
RM 689. – 1 p. 32 blue .. 2·00 1·10
RM 690. – 1 p. 50 brown .. 4·75 2·50
DESIGNS—VERT. 1 p. 32 Head of Liberty and National Arms. HORIZ. 1 p. 50. Record and winged letter.

ARMENIA E1

Formerly part of Transcaucasian Russia. Temporarily independent after the Russian revolution of 1917. From 12th March, 1922, Armenia, Azerbaijan and Georgia formed the Transcaucasian Federation. Issues for the federation were superseded by those of the Soviet Union in 1924.

NOTE. Only one price is given throughout and applies to unused or cancelled to order thus. Postally used copies are worth more.

All the overprints and surcharges were handstamped and consequently were applied upright or inverted indiscriminately, some occurring only inverted.

I. NATIONAL REPUBLIC.

28 May 1918 to 2 Dec. 1920 and 18 Feb. to 2 April 1921.

1919. Arms type of Russia and unissued Postal Savings Bank stamp (No. 6) surch. thus **k. 60. k** with or without stops. Imperf. or perf.

3. 11. 60 k. on 1 k. orange 8
6. – 60 k. on 1 k. red on buff .. 5·00

Surch. in figures only.

7. 11. 60 on 1 k. orange .. .. 18·00
8. 120 on 1 k. orange .. .. 18·00

(1.)

(2.)

1919. Stamps of Russia optd. as T 1 in various sizes, with or without frame. Imperf. or perf.

(a) Arms types.

53. 11. 1 k. orange .. .. .. 5·00
54B. 2 k. green 8
55B. 3 k. red 8
11B. 12. 4 k. red 12
39B. 11. 5 k. claret 8
40B. 12. 10 k. blue 30
41B. 11. 10 on 7 k. blue 8
42B. 4. 15 k. blue and purple .. 15
43B. 7. 20 k. red and blue 10
44B. 4. 25 k. mauve and green .. 25
45B. 35 k. green and purple .. 10
46B. 7. 50 k. green and purple .. 10
57B. 11. 60 k. on 1 k. orange (No. 3) 30
31B. 4. 70 k. orange and brown .. 12
59B. 8. 1 r. orange and brown .. 12
33B. 5. 3 r. 50 green and brown .. 20
23B. 13. 5 r. green and blue 55
62. 5. 7 r. yellow and black .. 8·00
24B. 7 r. pink and green 75
25B. 13. 10 r. grey, red and yellow .. 70

(b) Romanov type.

63B. 4 k. red (No. 129) 70

(c) Unissued Postal Savings Bank stamp.

64A. 1 k. red on buff 90

1920. Stamps of Russia surch. as T 2 in various types and sizes. Imperf. or perf.

(a) Arms types.

94B. 11. 1 r. on 60 k. on 1 k. orange (No. 3) 40
65B. 1 r. on 1 k. orange 10
66B. 3 r. on 3 k. red 5
67B. 3 r. on 4 k. red .. .. 2·75
97B. 5 r. on 2 k. green 12
69B. 12. 5 r. on 4 k. red 12
70B. 11. 5 r. on 5 k. claret 8
71B. 5 r. on 7 k. blue 15
72B. 12. 5 r. on 10 k. blue 8
73B. 11. 5 r. on 10 on 7 k blue .. 10
74B. 4. 5 r. on 14 k. red and blue .. 60
75B. 5 r. on 15 k. blue and purple 12
76B. 7. 5 r. on 20 k. red and blue .. 15
76aB. 4. 5 r. on 20 on 14 k. red & bl. 3·25
77B. 5 r. on 25 k. mauve & grn.. 1·40
111B. 11. 5 r. on 3 r. on 5 k. claret .. 2·50
78B. 4. 10 r. on 25 k. mauve & grn. 20
79B. 10 r. on 35 k. green & pur. 12
80B. 7. 10 r. on 50 k. green & purple 20
80aB. 3. 25 r. on 1 k. orange .. 7·00
80bB. 25 r. on 3 k. red .. .. 7·00
80cB. 25 r. on 5 k. pruple.. .. 7·00
80dB. 11. 25 r. on 10 on 7 k. blue .. 7·00
80eB. 4. 25 r. on 15 k. blue & purple 7·00
81B. 7. 25 r. on 20 k. red and blue 45
82B. 4. 25 r. on 25 k. mauve & green 45
83B. 25 r. on 35 k. green & purple 45
84B. 7. 25 r. on 50 k. green & purple 40
104B. 4. 25 r. on 70 k. orange & brn. 50
104aB. 3. 50 r. on 1 k. orange .. 7·00
104bB. 50 r. on 3 k. red .. .. 7·00
85bB. 7. 50 r. on 4 k. red .. .. 7·00
104cB. 3. 50 r. on 5 k. purple.. .. 7·00
85cB. 4. 50 r. on 15 k. blue & purple 7·00
85dB. 7. 50 r. on 20 k. red and blue 7·00
85eB. 4. 50 r. on 35 k. green & purple 7·00
85fB. 7. 50 r. on 50 k. green & purple 4·75
85gB. 4. 50 r. on 70 k. orange & brn. 1·75
106B. 8. 50 r. on 1 r orange & brown 40
107B. 100 r. on 1 r. orange & brn. 1·25
87B. 5. 100 r. on 3 r. 50 grn. & brn. 70
88B. 13. 100 r. on 5 r. green and blue 60
89B. 5. 100 r. on 7 r. yellow & black 4·25
90B. 100 r. on 7 r. pink and green 80
93B. 13. 100 r. on 10 r. grey, red and yellow 70

(b) Romanov issue of 1913.

112. 1 r. on 1 k. orange .. .. 1·25
113. 3 r. on 3 k. red .. .. 1·40
114. 5 r. on 4 k. red 70
115. 5 r. on 10 on 7 k. brown .. 40
116. 5 r. on 14 k. green .. .. 5·00
117. 5 r. on 20 on 14 k. green .. 1·00
118. 25 r. on 4 k. red 80
118a. 100 r. on 1 k. orange .. 13·00
119. 100 r. on 2 k. green .. 13·00
120. 100 r. on 3 r. violet .. 10·00

(c) War Charity issues of 1914 and 1915.

121. 20. 25 r. on 1 k. grn. & red on yell. 11·00
122. 25 r. on 3 k. grn & red on rose 9·00
123. 50 r. on 7 k. grn. & brn. on buff 7·00
124. 50 r. on 10 k. brown and blue 7·00
125. 100 r. on 1 k. grn. & red on yell. 7·00
126. 100 r. on 1 k. grey and brown 7·00
127. 100 r. on 3 k. grn. & red on rose 7·00
128. 100 r. on 7 k. grn. & brn. on buff 7·00
129. 100 r. on 10 k. brown & blue .. 7·00

1920. Arms types of Russia optd. as T 1 in various sizes, with or without frame and surch. as T 2 in various types and sizes. Imperf. or perf.

155A. 11. 1 r. on 60 k. on 1 k. orange (No. 3) 60
156A. 3 r. on 3 k. red 75
157A. 5 r. on 2 k. green 25
141A. 12. 5 r. on 4 k. red .. .. 1·00
158A. 11. 5 r. on 5 k. claret .. .. 1·50
142A. 12. 5 r. on 10 k. blue .. .. 1·00
143A. 11. 5 r. on 10 on 7 k. blue .. 75
144A. 4. 5 r on 15 k. blue and purple 40
145A. 7. 5 r. on 20 k. red and blue .. 40
132B. 4. 10 r. on 15 k. blue & purple 3·25
145aB. 7. 10 r. on 20 k. red and blue .. 3·75
146A. 4. 10 r. on 25 k. mauve & grn. 75
147A. 10 r. on 35 k. green and pur. 60
148A. 7. 10 r. on 50 k. green & purple 85
159A. 4. 10 r. on 70 k. orange & brn. 2·75
163A. 11. 10 r. on 5 r. on 5 k. claret .. 7·00
164A. 4. 10 r. on 5 r. on 25 k. mauve and green .. .. .. 7·50
165A. 10 r. on 5 r. on 35 k. green and purple .. .. .. 2·50
160. 25 r. on 70 k. orge. & brown 1·25
161B. 8. 50 r. on 1 r. orange & brown 60
135B. 5. 100 r. on 3 r. 50 green & brown 70
151. 13. 100 r. on 5 r. green and blue 1·75
136a. 5. 100 r. on 7 r. pink and green 14·00
154a. 13. 100 r. on 10 r. grey, red & yell. 3·00
166. 100 r. on 25 r. on 5 r. green and blue .. .. .. 8·00

1920. Stamps of Russia optd. as T 1 in various sizes, with or without frame and surch. **10.** Perf.

(a) Arms types.

168. 7. 10 on 20 k. red and blue .. 6·00
169. 4. 10 on 25 k. mauve and green 6·00
170. 10 on 35 k. green and purple 4·75
171. 7. 10 on 50 k. green and purple 5·50

(b) Romanov type.

172. 10 on 4 k. red (No. 129) .. 10·00

1920. Stamps of Russia optd. with monogram as in T 2 in various types and sizes and surch. **10.** Imperf. or perf.

(a) Arms types.

173. 12. 10 on 4 k. red .. .. 10·00
174. 11. 10 on 5 k. claret .. .. 10·00
175. 4. 10 on 15 k. blue and purple .. 10·00
176. 7. 10 on 20 k. red and blue .. 7·00
176a. 4. 10 on 20 on 14 k. red and blue 5·00
177. 10 on 25 k. mauve and green 5·00
178. 10 on 35 k. green and purple .. 5·00
179. 7. 10 on 50 k. green and purple.. 5·00

(b) Romanov type.

181. 10 on 4 k. red (No. 129) .. 11·00

3.

4. Mt. Ararat.

Stamps in T 3, 4 and a similar horizontal type showing a woman spinning were printed in Paris to the order of the Armenian National Government, but were not issued in Armenia as the Bolshevists had assumed control. (Price 5p. each.)

II. SOVIET REPUBLIC.

2 Dec. 1920 to 18 Feb. 1921 and 2 April 1921 to 12 Mar. 1922.

(5.)

ILLUSTRATIONS
British Commonwealth and all overprints and surcharges are FULL SIZE. Foreign Countries have been reduced to ¾-LINEAR.

1921. Arms types of Russia surch. with T 5. Perf.

182. 8. 5000 r. on 1 r. orange & brown 2·50
183. 5. 5000 r. on 3 r. 50 grn. & brn. 2·50
184. 13. 5000 r. on 5 r. green and blue 2·50
185. 5. 5000 r. on 7 r. pink and green 2·50
186. 13. 5000 r. on 10 r. grey, red & yell. 2·50

6. Crane.

7. Village Scene.

1922. Unissued stamps surch. in gold kopek Imperf.

187. 6. 1 on 250 r. rose 90
188. 1 on 250 r. slate .. .. 3·25
189. 7. 2 on 500 r. rose .. .. 1·25
190. 3 on 500 r. slate 70
191. – 4 on 1000 r. rose 70
192. – 4 on 1000 r. slate .. .. 3·75
193. – 5 on 2000 r. slate 65
194. – 10 on 2000 r. rose 65
195. – 15 on 5000 r. rose .. .. 6·50
196. – 20 on 5000 r. slate 70

DESIGNS (sizes in mm.): 1000 r. Woman at well (17 × 26). 2000 r. Erivan railway station (35 × 24½). 5000 r. Horseman and Mt. Ararat (39½ × 24½).

8. Soviet Emblems.

9. Wall sculpture at Ani.

10. Mt. Aragatz.

1922. Unissued stamps as T 8/10 surch. in gold kopeks in figures. Imperf. or perf.

210a. 8. 1 on 1 r. green .. .. 2·75
198. 9. 2 on 2 r. slate .. .. 2·00
199. – 3 on 3 r. red .. .. 7·00
213. – 4 on 25 r. green .. .. 1·75
214. – 5 on 50 r. red.. .. .. 1·50
202. – 10 on 100 r. orange .. 1·25
203. – 15 on 250 r. blue .. .. 1·00
204. 10. 20 on 500 r. purple .. .. 1·00
216. – 35 on 20,000 r. lake .. 18·00
206a. – 50 on 25,000 r. olive .. 15·00
209. – 50 on 25,000 r. blue .. .. 2·50

DESIGNS (sizes in mm: 3 r. (29 × 22) and 250 r. (21 × 35) Soviet emblems. 25 r. (30 × 22½). 100 r. (34½ × 23) and 20,000 r. (43 × 27) Mythological sculptures. Ani.50 r. (25½ × 37). Armenian soldier. 25,000 r. (45½ × 27½) Mt. Ararat.

The above and other values were not officially issued without the surcharges.

III. TRANSCAUCASIAN FEDERATION ISSUES FOR ARMENIA.

1923. As T 10, etc., surch. in gold kopeks in figures. Imperf. or perf.

219. – 1 on 250 r. blue .. .. 2·40
220. 10. 2 on 500 r. purple .. .. 2·75
218. – 3 on 20,000 r. lake .. .. 4·00

11. Mt. Ararat and Soviet Emblems.

12. Ploughing.

1923. Unissued stamps in various designs as T 11/12 surch. in Transcaucasian roubles in figures. Perf.

227. 11. 10,000 r. on 50 r. green & red 40
228. – 15,000 r. on 300 r. blue & buff 40
229. – 25,000 r. on 400 r. indigo & pink 40
230. – 30,000 r. on 500 r. violet & lilac 40
231. – 50,000 r. on 1000 r. blue .. 40
232. – 75,000 on 3000 r. blk. & grn.. 65
233. – 100,000 r. on 2000 r. blk. & grey 55
234. – 200,000 r. on 4000 r. blk. & brn. 50
235. – 300,000 r. on 5000 r. blk. & red 70
236. 12. 500,000 r. on 10,000 r. blk. & red 55

DESIGNS (Sizes in mm.): 300 r. (26 × 35) Star over Mt. Ararat. 400 r. (26 × 34½) Soviet emblems. 500 r. (26 × 34½) Crane (bird). 1000 r. (19 × 25) Peasant. 2000 r. (26 × 31) Human-headed bird from old bas-relief. 3000 r. (26½ × 36) Sower. 4000 r. (26 × 31½) Star and dragon. 5000 r. (26 × 32) Blacksmith.

ASCENSION BC

An island in S. Atlantic. A dependency of St. Helena.

1922. Stamps of St. Helena, optd. **ASCENSION.**

1. ½d. black and green .. .. 60 1·75
2. 1d. green .. .. .. 1·00 1·75
3. 1½d. red .. .. .. 2·25 6·00
4. 2d. black and slate .. .. 2·25 3·50
5. 3d. blue .. .. .. 2·50 5·50
6. 8d. black and purple .. 8·50 8·50
9. 1s. black on green .. .. 9·00 11·00
7. 2s. black and blue on blue.. 32·00 35·00
8. 3s. black and violet .. .. 45·00 55·00

1. Badge of St. Helena.

1924.

10. 1. ½d. black 45 75
11. 1d. black and green 65 90
12. 1½d. red .. .. .. 1·25 2·25
13. 2d. black and grey .. 1·25 1·00
14. 3d. blue .. .. .. 80 1·75
15. 4d. black on yellow .. 9·00 11·00
15a. 5d. purple and green .. 4·50 7·00
16. 6d. black and purple .. 18·00 23·00
17. 8d. black and violet .. 4·00 6·50
18. 1s. black and brown .. 7·00 8·50
19. 2s. black & blue on blue.. 17·00 18·00
20. 3s. black on blue .. .. 23·00 25·00

2. Georgetown.

3. Ascension Island.

DESIGNS—HORIZ. 1½d. The Pier. 3d. Long Beach. 5d. Three Sisters. 1s. Sooty Tern and Wideawake Fair. 5s. Green mountain.

1934. Medallion portrait of King George V. (except 1s.).

21. 2. ½d. black and violet .. 12 25
22. 3. 1d. black and green .. 45 45
23. – 1½d. black and red .. 45 50
24. 3. 2d. black and orange .. 45 45
25. – 3d. black and blue .. 60 85
26. – 5d. black and blue .. 1·10 1·75
27. 3. 8d. black and brown .. 2·75 3·25
28. – 1s. black and red.. .. 7·00 7·00
29. 3. 2s. 6d. black and purple.. 15·00 16·00
30. – 5s. black and brown .. 20·00 23·00

1935. Silver Jubilee. As T 11 of Antigua

31. 1½d. blue and red .. 1·75 1·40
32. 2d. blue and grey .. 2·00 3·00
33. 5d. green and blue .. 6·00 7·00
34. 1s. grey and purple .. 13·00 17·00

1937. Coronation. As T 2 of Aden.

35. 1d. green 15 25
36. 2d. orange 25 25
37. 3d. blue 80 80

9. Georgetown.

1938.

38. 9. ½d. black and violet .. 12 15
39. A. 1d. black and green .. 5·00 2·25
39b. 1d. black and orange .. 12 15
39d. B. 1d. black and green .. 12 20
40a. C. 1½d. black and red .. 25 45
40c. 1½d. black and pink .. 15 25
41. A. 2d. black and orange .. 15 25
41c. 2d. black and red .. 20 25

42. D. 3d. black and blue .. 11·00 6·00
42b. 3d. black 30 15
42c. A. 4d. black and blue .. 25 40
43. B. 6d. black and blue .. 40 45
44a. 9. 1s. black and brown .. 50 60
45. C. 2s. 6d. black and red .. 2·75 2·75
46. D. 5s. black and brown .. 4·00 2·50
47a. B. 10s. black and purple .. 5·50 7·00
DESIGNS: A, Green Mountain. B, Three Sisters. C, Pier. D, Long Beach.

1946. Victory. As T 4 of Aden.
48. 2d. orange 12 20
49. 4d. blue 12 20

1948. Silver Wedding. As T 5/6 of Aden.
50. 3d. black 12 20
51. 10s. mauve .. .. .. 6·50 11·00

1949. U.P.U. As T 14/17 of Antigua.
52. 3d. red 30 30
53. 4d. blue 60 60
54. 6d. olive .. .. 1·10 1·10
55. 1s. black .. .. 1·75 2·00

1953. Coronation. As Type 7 of Aden.
56. 3d. black and grey .. .. 1·10 1·90

10. Water Catchment.

1956.
57. 10. ½d. black and brown .. 12 12
58. – 1d. black and magenta .. 12 12
59. – 1½d. black and orange .. 12 12
60. – 2d. black and red .. 20 20
61. – 2½d. black and chestnut 25 30
62. – 3d. black and blue .. 30 30
63. – 4d. black and turquoise .. 35 40
64. – 6d. black and indigo .. 45 45
65. – 7d. black and olive .. 60 65
66. – 1s. black and vermilion 1·40 1·60
67. – 2s. 6d. black and maroon 4·00 4·50
68. – 5s. black and emerald .. 7·00 8·00
69. – 10s. black and purple .. 14·00 15·00
DESIGNS: 1d. Map of Ascension. 1½d. Georgetown. 2d. Map showing Atlantic cables. 2½d. Mountain road. 3d. Boatswain Bird. 4d. Long-finned tunny. 6d. Rollers on seashore. 7d. Turtles. 1s. Land crab. 2s. 6d. Wideawake (Sooty Tern). 5s. Perfect Crater. 10s. View of Ascension.

11. Brown Booby.

1963. Birds. Multicoloured.
70. 1d. T 11 .. .. .. 5 5
71. 1½d. Black Noddy 5 5
72. 2d. Fairy Tern 8 8
73. 3d. Red-billed Tropic Bird 10 12
74. 4½d. Brown Noddy .. 12 12
75. 6d. Wideawake Tern .. 15 15
76. 7d. Frigate-bird 20 25
77. 10d. White Booby 25 25
78. 1s. Yellow-billed Tropic Bird 25 35
79. 1s. 6d. Red-billed Tropic Bird 50 65
80. 2s. 6d. Madeiran Storm Petrel 90 1·10
81. 5s. Red-footed Booby (brown phase) .. 1·60 1·90
82. 10s. Frigate-birds .. .. 2·75 3·25
83. £1 Red-footed Booby (white phase) .. .. .. 5·50 6·50

1963. Freedom from Hunger. As T 10 of Aden.
84. 1s. 6d. red .. .. .. 2·75 2·25

1963. Red Cross Cent. As T 24 of Antigua.
85. 3d. red and black 80 80
86. 1s. 6d. red and blue .. 3·25 3·25

1965. I.T.U. Cent. As T 26 of Antigua.
87. 3d. magenta and violet .. 40 40
88. 6d. turquoise and chestnut 75 75

1965. I.C.Y. As T 27 of Antigua.
89. 1d. purple and turquoise .. 15 15
90. 6d. green and lavender .. 55 55

1966. Churchill Commem. As T 28 of Antigua.
91. 1d. blue 20 20
92. 3d. green 35 30
93. 6d. brown 65 55
94. 1s. 6d. violet .. .. 1·90 1·60

1966. World Cup Football Championships. As T 30 of Antigua.
95. 3d. vio., green, lake & brn. 30 25
96. 6d. choc., turq., lake & brn. 50 40

1966. W.H.O. Headquarters, Geneva. Inaug. As T 31 of Antigua.
97. 3d. black, green and blue .. 25 20
98. 1s. 6d. black, purple & ochre 85 85

12. Satellite Station.

1966. Opening of Apollo Communication Satellite Earth Station.
99. 12. 4d. black and violet .. 20 20
100. 8d. black and green .. 30 30
101. 1s. 3d. black and brown 50 50
102. 2s. 6d. black and blue .. 1·00 1·00

13. B.B.C. Emblem.

1966. Opening of B.B.C. Relay Station.
103. 13. 1d. gold & ultramarine 12 12
104. 3d. gold and green .. 15 15
105. 6d. gold and violet .. 30 25
106. 1s. 6d. gold and red .. 65 65

1966. U.N.E.S.C.O. 20th Anniv. As T 33/5 of Antigua.
107. 3d. vio., red, yellow & orge. 30 30
108. 6d. yellow, violet and olive 65 65
109. 1s. 6d. black, pur. & orge. 1·25 1·50

14. Human Rights Emblem and Chain Links.

1968. Human Rights Year.
110. 14. 6d. orge., red and blk... 30 30
111. 1s. 6d. blue, red & blk... 55 55
112. 2s. 6d. grn., red & blk... 85 85

15. Ascension Black-Fish.

1968. Fishes (1st series).
113. 15. 4d. black and blue .. 20 20
114. – 8d. multicoloured .. 30 30
115. – 1s. 9d. multicoloured .. 70 70
116. – 2s. 3d. multicoloured .. 80 80
DESIGNS: 8d. Leather-jacket. 1s. 9d. Tunny. 2s. 3d. Mako Shark.
See also Nos. 117/120 and 126/9.

1969. Fishes (2nd series). As T 15. Multicoloured.
117. 4d. Sailfish 12 12
118. 6d. Old Wife 20 20
119. 1s. 6d. Yellowtail .. 50 50
120. 2s. 11d. Jack 95 95

16. H.M.S. "Rattlesnake".

1969. Royal Naval Crests (1st series).
121. 16. 4d. multicoloured .. 15 15
122. – 9d. multicoloured .. 30 30
123. – 1s. 9d. blue and gold .. 65 65
124. – 2s. 3d. multicoloured .. 80 80
DESIGNS: 9d. H.M.S. "Weston". 1s. 9d. H.M.S. "Undaunted". 2s. 3d. H.M.S. "Eagle".
See also Nos. 130/3, 149/52, 154/7 and 166/9.

1970. Fishes (3rd series). As T 15. Multicoloured.
126. 4d. Wahoo 10 10
127. 9d. Coal-fish 20 25
128. 1s. 9d. Dolphin 45 45
129. 2s. 3d. Soldier fish .. 55 55

1970. Royal Naval Crests (2nd series). As T 16. Multicoloured.
130. 4d. H.M.S. "Penelope" 15 15
131. 9d. H.M.S. "Carlisle" .. 30 30
132. 1s. 6d. H.M.S. "Amphion" 55 55
133. 2s. 6d. H.M.S. "Magpie" 80 80

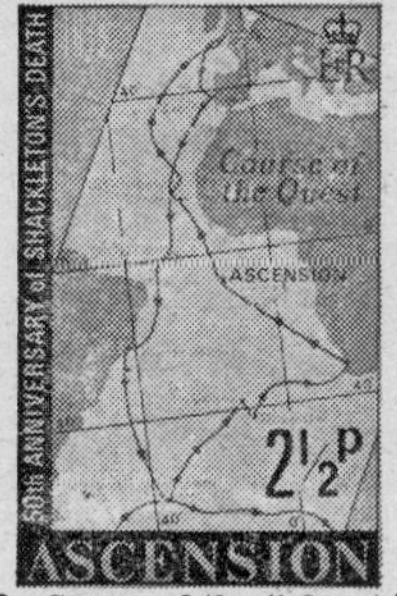

17. Early Chinese Rocket.

1971. Decimal Currency. Evolution of Space Travel. Multicoloured.
135. ½p. Type 17 .. .. 5 5
136. 1p. Medieval Arab astronomers 5 5
137. 1½p. Tycho Brahe's observatory, quadrant and supernova 5 5
138. 2p. Galileo, Moon and telescope 5 5
139. 2½p. Isaac Newton, instruments and apple .. 5 5
140. 3½p. Harrison's chronometer and ship .. 10 12
141. 4½p. Space rocket taking off 12 12
142. 5p. World's largest telescope, Palomar .. 12 15
143. 7½p. World's largest radio telescope, Jodrell Bank 20 20
144. 10p. "Mariner VII" and Mars 30 30
145. 12½p. "Sputnik II" and Space dog, Laika .. 30 35
146. 25p. Walking in Space .. 60 70
147. 50p. "Apollo XI" crew on Moon .. .. 1·25 1·40
148. £1 Future Space Research station .. .. .. 2·50 2·75
Nos. 137/40, 142/5 and 147/8 are horiz.

1971. Royal Naval Crests (3rd series). As T 16. Multicoloured.
149. 2p. H.M.S. "Phoenix" .. 15 15
150. 4p. H.M.S. "Milford" .. 30 30
151. 9p. H.M.S. "Pelican" .. 55 55
152. 15p. H.M.S. "Oberon" .. 85 85

1972. Royal Naval Crests (4th series). As T 16. Multicoloured.
154. 1½p. H.M.S. "Lowestoft" 8 8
155. 3p. H.M.S. "Auckland" 15 20
156. 6p. H.M.S. "Nigeria" .. 35 40
157. 17½p. H.M.S. "Bermuda" 70 75

18. Course of the "Quest".

1972. Shackleton's Death. 50th Anniv. Multicoloured.
159. 2½p. Type 18 .. .. 15 20
160. 4p. Shackleton and "Qeust" (horiz.) .. 30 35
161. 7½p. Shackleton's cabin and "Quest" (horiz.) .. 40 45
162. 11p. Shackleton's statue and memorial 60 70

19. Land Crab and Mako Shark.

1972. Royal Silver Wedding. Multicoloured.
164. 19. 2p. violet 10 12
165. 16p. red 70 80

1973. Royal Naval Crests (5th series). As T 16. Multicoloured.
166. 2p. H.M.S. "Birmingham" 12 12
167. 4p. H.M.S. "Cardiff" .. 25 25
168. 9p. H.M.S. "Penzance" 45 50
169. 13p. H.M.S. "Rochester" 60 65

20. Green Turtle.

1973. Turtles. Multicoloured.
171. 4 p. Type 20 .. .. 15 15
172. 9p. Loggerhead turtle .. 40 40
173. 12p. Hawksbill turtle .. 65 70

21. Sergeant, R.M. Light Infantry, 1900.

1973. Departure of Royal Marines from Ascension. 50th Anniv. Multicoloured.
174. 2p. Type 21 .. .. 8 12
175. 6p. R.M. Private, 1816 .. 20 25
176. 12p. R.M. Light Infantry Officer, 1880 .. .. 40 45
177. 20p. R.M. Artillery Colour Sergeant, 1910 .. .. 65 70

1973. Royal Wedding. As T 26 of Anguilla. Multicoloured. Background colours given.
178. 2p. brown 5 8
179. 18p. green 55 65

22. Letter and H.Q., Berne.

1974. Universal Postal Union. Cent. Mult.
180. 2p. Type **22** 8 8
181. 9p. Hermes and U.P.U. monument 35 40

23. Churchill as a Boy, and Birthplace, Blenheim Palace.

1974. Sir Winston Churchill. Birth Cent. Multicoloured.
182. 5p. Type **23** 15 20
183. 25p. Churchill as statesman, and U.N. Building 55 60

24. "Skylab 3" and Photograph of Ascension.

1975. Space Satellites. Multicoloured.
185. 2 p. Type **24** 5 5
186. 18p. "Skylab 4" Command module and photograph 45 50

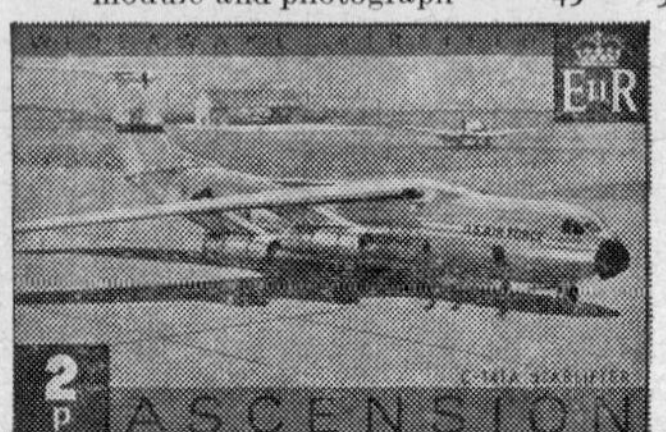

25. U.S.A.F. "Starlifter".

1975. Wideawake Airfield. Multicoloured.
187. 2p. Type **25** 5 5
188. 5p. R.A.F. "Hercules" .. 12 15
189. 9p. Vickers "VC-10" .. 25 25
190. 24p. U.S.A.F. "Galaxy" 55 60

1975. "Apollo-Soyuz" Space Link. Nos. 141 and 145/6 optd, **APOLLO-SOYUZ LINK 1975.**
192. 4½p. multicoloured .. 25 25
193. 12½p. multicoloured .. 55 65
194. 25p. multicoloured .. 1·25 1·40

26. Arrival of Royal Navy, 1815.

1975. Occupation. 160th Anniversary. Multicoloured.
195. 2p. Type **26** 5 5
196. 5p. Water supply, Dampiers Drip 12 15
197. 9p. First landing, 1815 .. 25 25
198. 15p. The garden on Green Mountain 35 40

27. Canary.

1976. Multicoloured.
199. 1p. Type **27** 5 5
200. 2p. Fairy Tern (vert.) .. 5 5
201. 3p. Waxbill 5 5
202. 4p. Black Noddy (vert.) .. 8 8
203. 5p. Brown Noddy 8 10
204. 6p. Common Mynah .. 8 10
205. 7p. Madeiran Storm Petrel (vert.) 10 12
206. 8p. Wideawake or Sooty Tern 15 15
207. 9p. White Booby (vert.) .. 15 15
208. 10p. Red-footed Booby .. 20 20
209. 15p. Red-throated Francolin (vert.) 20 25
210. 18p. Brown Booby (vert.) 30 35
211. 25p. Red-billed Bo'sun Bird 40 45
212. 50p. Yellow-billed Bo'sun Bird 85 1·00
213. £1 Ascension Frigatebird (vert.) .. .. 1·75 2·00
214. £2 Boatswain Bird Island Sanctuary .. .. 3·50 4·00
No. 214 is larger, 50×38 mm.

28. Penny Red with Ascension Postmark.

1976. Festival of Stamps, London.
215. **28.** 5p. red, black & brown 12 15
216. – 9p. green, black & brn. 25 25
217. – 25p. multicoloured .. 60 65
DESIGNS—VERT. 9p. ½d. stamp of 1922. HORIZ. 25p. Cargo vessel "Southampton Castle".

29. U.S. Base, Ascension.

1976. American Revolution. Bicent. Multicoloured.
219. 8p. Type **29** 20 25
220. 9p. NASA Station at Devils Ashpit 25 25
221. 25p. "Viking" landing on Mars 55 60

AUSTRALIA BC

An island continent to the S.E. of Asia. A Commonwealth consisting of the states of New S. Wales, Queensland, S. Australia, Tasmania, Victoria and W. Australia.

1966. 100 cents = 1 dollar.

ILLUSTRATIONS British Commonwealth and all overprints and surcharges are FULL SIZE. Foreign Countries have been reduced to ¾-LINEAR.

1. Kangaroo.

1913.
1. **1.** ½d. green .. .. .. 3·00 25
2. 1d. red .. .. .. 3·00 10
3. 2d. grey .. .. .. 7·00 1·00
36. 2½d. blue .. .. .. 7·00 1·50
37. 3d. olive .. .. .. 5·00 75
6. 4d. orange .. .. 35·00 20·00
8. 5d. brown .. .. 30·00 20·00
38. 6d. blue .. .. 12·00 75
73. 6d. brown .. .. 5·00 1·50
133. 9d. violet .. .. 5·50 60
40. 1s. green .. .. 11·00 75
41. 2s. brown .. .. 70·00 12·00
212. 2s. claret .. .. 1·25 25
42. 5s. grey and yellow .. £110 30·00
136. 10s. grey and red .. £200 50·00
44. £1 brown and blue .. £700 £300
137. £1 grey £225 £100
138. £2 black and red .. £1100 £160

2.

3. Kookaburra.

1913.
17. **2.** 1d. red .. .. 3·00 2·50
19. **3.** 6d. claret .. .. 50·00 28·00
For 3d. blue, T **3**, see No. 106.

4.

1914.
51. **4.** ½d. green 50 10
94. ½d. orange 30 5
30c. 1d. red .. .. .. 3·00 10
57. 1d. violet .. .. .. 1·50 50
95. 1d. green 30 5
58. 1½d. black-brown .. .. 1·00 20
55a. 1½d. brown .. .. 1·75 12
61. 1½d. green .. .. 1·75 10
97. 1½d. red 50 5
62. 2d. orange .. .. 3·00 10
127. **4.** 2d. red 40 10
78. 2d. brown .. .. 5·00 1·50
79. 3d. blue .. .. .. 6·00 40
32d. 4d. orange .. .. 28·00 1·50
64. 4d. blue .. .. .. 10·00 4·00
65. 4d. blue .. .. .. 22·00 3·50
129. 4d. olive .. .. .. 6·50 40
81. 4½d. violet .. .. 6·00 2·00
130. 5d. brown .. .. 3·00 35
131. 1s. 4d. blue .. .. 35·00 4·50

5. Parliament House, Canberra.

1927. Opening of Parliament House.
105. **5.** 1½d. red 20 10

1928. Melbourne Philatelic Exn.
106. **3.** 3d. blue .. .. .. 2·50 95

6.

1929. Air.
115. **6.** 3d. green.. .. .. 3·50 3·50

7. Black Swan.

1929. Western Australia Cent.
116. **7.** 1½d. red 30 20

8. Capt. Chas. Sturt. **12.** Lyre Bird.

9. The "Southern Cross" above Hemispheres.

1930. Sturt's Exploration of River Murray. Cent.
117. **8.** 1½d. red 25 10
118. 3d. blue .. .. .. 2·25 2·00

1930. Surch. in words.
119. **4.** 2d. on 1½d. red .. 50 10
120. 5d. on 4½d. violet .. 2·50 2·00

1931. Kingsford Smith's Flights.
121. **9.** 2d. red (postage) .. 25 10
122. 3d. blue .. .. 2·25 1·25
123. 6d. purple (air) .. 6·00 4·00

1931. Air. As T **9** but inscr. "AIR MAIL SERVICE".
139. – 6d. brown .. .. 11·00 9·00

1931. Air. No. 139, Opt. **O.S.**
139a. – 6d. brown .. .. 15·00 15·00

1932.
140. **12.** 1s. green .. .. 35·00 1·00

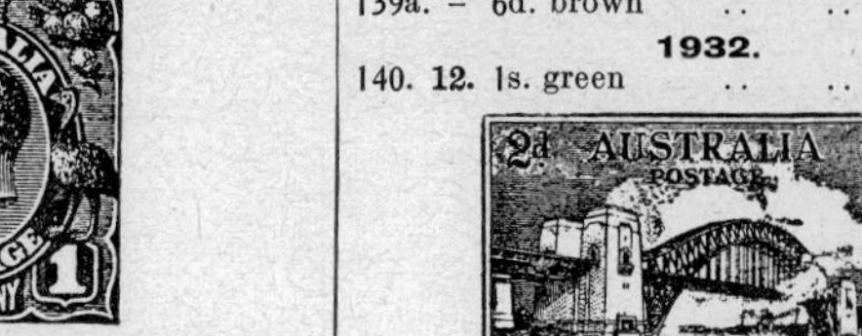

13. Sydney Harbour Bridge.

1932.
141. **13.** 2d. red 75 25
142. 3d. blue.. .. .. 2·50 2·00
143. 5s. green £400 £225

14. Kookaburra.

1932.
146. **14.** 6d. claret .. .. 6·00 30

15. Melbourne and R. Yarra.

1934. Victoria Cent.
147. **15.** 2d. red 45 25
148. 3d. blue.. .. 1·75 1·00
149. 1s. black .. .. 25·00 10·00

16. Merino Sheep.

1934. Capt. MacArthur Cent.
150. **16.** 2d. red 50 20
151. 3d. blue.. .. 3·50 3·00
152. 9d. purple .. .. 18·00 12·00

17. Hermes.

1934.
153b. **17.** 1s. 6d. purple.. .. 1·30 30

18. Cenotaph, Whitehall. **19.** King George V on "Anzac".

1935. Gallipoli Landing. 20th Anniv.
154. **18.** 2d. red 20 5
155. 1s. black .. .. 30·00 20·00

1935. Silver Jubilee.
156. **19.** 2d. red 25 10
157. 3d. blue.. .. 1·75 1·50
158. 2s. violet .. .. 25·00 15·00

20. Amphitrite and Telephone Cable.

1936. Opening of Submarine Telephone Cable to Tasmania.
159. **20.** 2d. red 20 5
160 3d. blue .. .. .. 1·50 1·25

21. Site of Adelaide, 1836. Old Gum Tree Glenelg; King William St., Adelaide.

1936. South Australia Cent.
161. **21.** 2d. red 20 5
162. 3d. blue .. .. 1·50 75
163. 1s. green .. .. 12·00 4·50

22. Kangaroo.  **23.** Queen Elizabeth.

24. King George VI. **25.**

26. King George VI.

28. Merino Ram.

33. Queen Elizabeth.

DESIGNS—As T **22**. 4d. Koala. 6d. Kookaburra. 1s. Lyre Bird. As T **28**: 9d. Duck-billed Platypus. As T **33**. 10s. K. George VI.

35. King George VI and Queen Elizabeth.

1937.
164. **22.** ½d. orange 8 5
165. **23.** 1d. green 5 5
180. – 1d. green 12 5
181. **22.** 1d. maroon 5 5
166. **24.** 1½d. maroon 75 15
183. 1½d. green 5 5
167. **25.** 2d. red 5 5
184. – 2d. red 12 5
185. **25.** 2d. purple 5 5
169. **26.** 3d. blue .. .. 6·00 15
187. 3d. brown 5 5
188. – 4d. green 10 5
171. **28.** 5d. purple 50 5
189a. – 6d. brown 50 5
190. – 9d. brown 20 5
191. – 1s. green 30 5
175a. **26.** 1s. 4d. mauve .. 90 20
176. **33.** 5s. claret .. .. 8·00 2·00
177. – 10s. purple .. .. 20·00 10·00
178. **35.** £1 slate .. .. 80·00 20·00
Nos. 180 and 184 are as Types **23** and **25** but with completely shaded background.

36. Governor Phillip at Sydney Cove.

1937. New South Wales. 150th Anniv.
193. **36.** 2d. red 20 5
194. 3d. blue .. .. .. 1·50 60
195. 9d. purple .. .. 12·00 6·00

37. A.I.F. and Nurse.

1940. Australian Imperial Forces.
196. **37.** 1s. green 25 5
197. 2d. red 25 5
198. 3d. blue .. .. .. 1·50 1·75
199. 6d. purple .. .. 7·50 5·00

1941. Surch. with figures and bars.
200. **25.** 2½d. on 2d. red .. 12 5
201. **26.** 3½d. on 3d. blue .. 20 20
202. **28.** 5½d. on 5d. purple .. 1·25 60

38. Queen Elizabeth.

39. King George VI.

40. King George VI.

41.

42. Emu.

43. Duke and Duchess of Gloucester.

1942.
203. **38.** 1d. purple 5 5
229. 1½d. green 8 8
230. **39.** 2d. purple 12 5
205. **40.** 2½d. red 5 5
206. **41.** 3½d. blue 10 5
207. **42.** 5½d. grey 8 5

1945. Royal Visit.
209. **43.** 2½d. red 5 5
210. 3½d. blue 12 12
211. 5½d. grey 15 12

44.

1946. Victory. Inscr. "PEACE 1945".
213. **44.** 2½d. red 5 5
214. – 3½d. blue 12 8
215. – 5½d. green 25 20
DESIGNS—HORIZ. 3½d. Flag and dove. VERT. 5½d. Angel.

47. Sir Thomas Mitchell and Queensland.

1946. Mitchell's Central Queensland Exploration. Cent.
216. **47.** 2½d. red 8 5
217. 3½d. blue 12 10
218. 1s. green 15 15

48. Lt. John Shortland, R.N.

49. Steel Foundry.

1947. City of Newcastle. 150th Anniv.
219. **48.** 2½d. lake 5 5
220. **49.** 3½d. blue 8 8
221. – 5½d. green 12 15
DESIGN—As T **49**, HORIZ. 5½d. Coal carrier cranes.

51. Queen Elizabeth II when Princess.

1947. Wedding of Princess Elizabeth.
222. **51.** 1d. purple 5 5

52. Hereford Bull.

53. Hermes and Globe.

54. Aboriginal Art.

55. Commonwealth Coat-of-Arms.

1948.
223. **52.** 1s. 3d. brown 90 25
223a. **53.** 1s. 6d. brown .. .. 1·00 8
224. **54.** 2s. brown .. .. 1·00 5
224a. **55.** 5s. claret .. .. 2·75 20
224b. 10s. purple .. .. 7·50 1·00
224c. £1 blue .. .. 25·00 3·75
224d. £2 green .. .. 75·00 13·00

56. William J. Farrer.

57. Ferdinand von Mueller.

1948. W. J. Farrer (wheat research).
225. **56.** 2½d. red 5 5

1948. Sir Ferdinand von Mueller (botanist).
226. **57.** 2½d. red 5 5

58. Boy Scout.

59. Henry Lawson.

1948. Pan-Pacific Scout Jamboree, Yarra Brae.
227. **58.** 2½d. lake 8 5
For 3½d. value dates "1952–53", see No. 254.

1949. Henry Lawson (poet). Birth Anniv.
231. **59.** 2½d. maroon 5 5

60. Mounted Postman and Aeroplane.

1949. U.P.U. 75th Anniv.
232. **60.** 3½d. blue 15 12

61. Lord Forrest of Bunbury.

ILLUSTRATIONS British Commonwealth and all overprints and surcharges are FULL SIZE. Foreign Countries have been reduced to ¾-LINEAR.

1949. Lord Forrest (explorer and politician).
233. **61.** 2½d. red 5 5

62. Queen Elizabeth.

63. King George VI.

64. King George VI. **65.**

66. Aborigine.

67. King George VI.

1950.
236. **62.** 1½d. green 5 5
237. 2d. olive 5 5
234. **63.** 2½d. red 5 5
235a. 2½d. brown 5 5
235. 3d. red 5 5
235b. 3d. myrtle 5 5
243. **64.** 3½d. maroon 8 8
249. 4½d. red 10 10
250. 6½d. brown 15 15
251. 6½d. green 10 8
247. **65.** 7½d. blue 20 15
238. **66.** 8½d. brown 25 15
252. **67.** 1s. 0½d. blue 25 8
253. **66.** 2s. 6d. brown (larger) 70 30

68.

69.

First Stamps of N.S.W. and Victoria.

1950. Australian Stamp Cent.
239. **68.** 2½d. maroon 5 5
240. **69.** 2½d. maroon 5 5

70. Sir Henry Parkes.

DESIGNS—As T **70**: No. 242 Sir Edmund Barton. As T **71**: 5½d. Opening first Federal Parliament.

71. Federal Parliament House, Canberra.

1951. Commonwealth. 50th Anniv. Inscr. as in T **70/71**.
241. **70.** 3d. lake 5 5
242. – 3d. lake 5 5
243. – 5½d. blue 20 35
244. **71.** 1s. 6d. brown 35 35

72. E. H. Hargraves. 73. C. J. Latrobe.

1951. Discovery of Gold in Australia. Cent.
245. 72. 3d. maroon 5 8

1951. Responsible Government in Victoria. Cent.
246. 73. 3d. maroon 5 8

1952. Pan-Pacific Scout Jamboree, Greystanes. As T 58 but dated "1952–53".
254. 58. 3½d. lake 8 5

74. Butter. 75. Queen Elizabeth II.

1953. Food Production. Inscr. "PRODUCE FOOD!"
255. 74. 3d. emerald 40 15
256. – 3d. emerald (Wheat) .. 40 15
257. – 3d. emerald (Beef) .. 40 15
258. 74. 3½d. red 40 15
259. – 3½d. red (Wheat) .. 40 15
260. – 3½d. red (Beef) 40 15

1953.
261. 75. 1d. purple 5 5
261a. 2½d. blue 12 5
262. 3d. green 12 5
262a. 3½d. red 10 5
262b. 6½d. orange 35 8

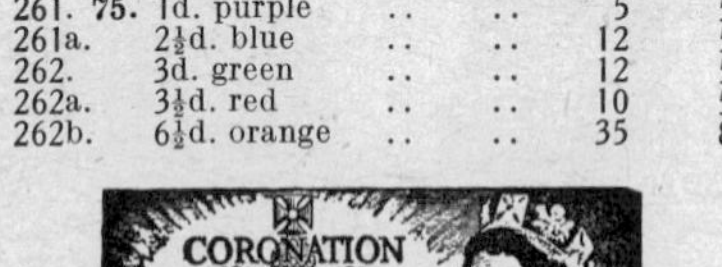

76. Queen Elizabeth II.

1953. Coronation.
264. 76. 3½d. red 8 5
265. 7½d. violet 40 40
266. 2s. blue-green .. .. 1·25 1·00

77. Young Farmers and Calf.

1953. Australian Young Farmers' Clubs. 25th Anniv.
267. 77. 3½d. brown and green .. 12 5

78. Lt.-Gov. D. Collins. 79. Lt.-Gov. W. Paterson.

80. Sullivan Cove, Hobart, 1804.

1953. Settlement in Tasmania. 150th Anniv.
268. 78. 3½d. maroon 15 10
269. 79. 3½d. maroon 15 10
270. 80. 2s. green .. .. 2·00 3·25

81. Stamp of 1853.

1953. Tasmania Postage Stamps. 1st Cent.
271. 81. 3d. red 12 8

82. Queen Elizabeth II and Duke of Edinburgh.

83. Queen Elizabeth II. 84. "Telegraphic Communications".

1954. Royal Visit.
272. 82. 3½d. red 10 5
273. 83. 7½d. purple 50 65
274. 82. 2s. green .. .. 1·25 1·25

1954. Telegraph Centenary.
275. 84. 3½d. brown 12 5

85. Red Cross and Globe.

1954. Australian Red Cross Society. 40th Anniv.
276. 85. 3½d. blue and red .. 12 5

86. Black Swan.

1954. Western Australian Stamp Cent.
277. 86. 3½d. black 15 5

87. Locomotives of 1854 and 1954.

1954. Australian Railways Cent.
278. 87. 3½d. maroon 12 5

88. Antarctic Map and Flora and Fauna. 89. Olympic Games Symbol.

1954. Australian Antarctic Research.
279. 88. 3½d. black 20 5

1954. Olympic Games Propaganda.
280. 89. 2s. blue 90 90
280a. 2s. green 90 90

90. Rotary Symbol, Globe and Flags. 91. American Memorial, Canberra.

1955. Rotary International 50th Anniv.
281. 90. 3½d. red 12 5

1955. Australian-American Freindship.
283. 91. 3½d. blue 12 5

92. Queen Elizabeth II. 93.

1955.
294. 92. 4d. lake 15 5
300. 7½d. violet 55 35
295. 10d. blue 25 15
282. 93. 1s. 0½d. blue 70 25
282a. 1s. 7d. brown .. .. 1·25 25
See also Nos. 308, etc.

94. Cobb & Co. Coach.

1955. Mail-coach Pioneers Commem.
284. 94. 3½d. sepia 15 5
285. 2s. brown .. .. 1·25 90

95. Y.M.C.A. Emblem and Map of the World.

1955. World Cent. of Y.M.C.A.
286. 95. 3½d. green and red .. 12 5

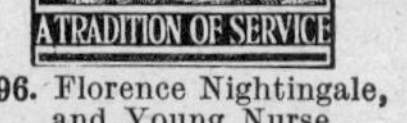

96. Florence Nightingale, and Young Nurse. 97. Queen Victoria.

1955. Nursing Profession Commemoration.
287. 96. 3½d lilac 12 5

1955. South Australian Postage Stamp Centenary.
288. 97. 3½d. green 12 5

98. Badges of N.S.W., Victoria and Tasmania.

1956. Centenary of Responsible Govt. in N.S.W., Victoria and Tasmania.
289. 98. 3½d. lake 12 5

99. Arms of Melbourne. 100. Olympic Torch and Symbol.

101. Collins Street, Melbourne.

1956. Olympic Games, Melbourne.
290. 99. 4d. red 12 5
291. 100. 7½d. blue 35 35
292. 101. 1s. multicoloured .. 50 30
293. – 2s. multicoloured .. 1·10 90
DESIGN As T 101: 2s. Melbourne across R. Yarra.

102. S. Australia Coat of Arms.

1957. Responsible Government in South Australia. Cent.
296. 102. 4d. brown 12 5

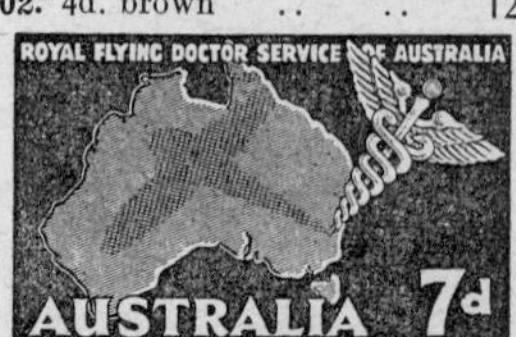

103. Map of Australia and Caduceus.

1957. Royal Flying Doctor Service of Australia.
297. 103. 7d. blue 30 12

104. "The Spirit of Christmas" (Child) after Sir Joshua Reynolds).

1957. Christmas.
298. 104. 3½d. red 12 5
299. 4d. purple 20 5

105. Super-Constellation Airliner.

1958. Inaug. of Australian "Round-the-World" Air Service.
301. 105. 2s. blue 90 65

106. Hall of Memory, Sailor and Airmen.

1958.
302. 106. 5½d. lake 50 35
303. – 5½d. lake 50 35
No. 303 shows a soldier and servicewoman instead of the sailor and airman.

107. Sir Charles Kingsford Smith and the "Southern Cross". 109. The Nativity.

108. Silver Mine, Broken Hill.

1958. 1st Air Crossing of the Tasman Sea. 30th Anniv.
304. **107.** 8d. blue 35 35

1958. Founding of Broken Hill. 75th Anniv.
305. **108.** 4d. brown 12 5

1958. Christmas Issue.
306. **109.** 3½d red 20 5
307. 4d. violet 20 5

109a. Queen Elizabeth II.

110. Queen Elizabeth II. 111.

112. Queen Elizabeth II. 113.

1959.
308 – 1d. slate-purple .. 5 5
309. **109a.** 2d. brown 5 5
311. **110.** 3d. turquoise 5 5
312. **111.** 3½d. green 10 5
313. **112.** 4d. red 25 5
314. **113.** 5d. blue 15 5

No. 308 shows a head and shoulders portrait as in T 112 and is vert.

118. Kangaroos. 119. Flannel Flower.

119a. Aboriginal Stockman.

1959.
316. – 6d. brown 25 5
317. – 8d. red-brown .. 25 5
318 **118.** 9d. sepia 35 12
319 – 11d. indigo 35 15
320. – 1s. green 90 12
321. – 1s. 2d. purple .. 45 20
322. – 1s. 6d. red on yellow .. 55 20
323. **119.** 2s. blue 45 8
324. – 2s. 3d. green on cream 65 20
324a. – 2s. 3d. green .. .. 1·75 80
325. – 2s. 5d. brown on cream 1·25 30
326. – 3s. red 90 20
327. **119a.** 5s. brown .. .. 8·00 85

DESIGNS—As T **118**—VERT. 6d. Banded Ant-eater. 8d. Tiger Cat. 11d. Rabbit Bandicoot. 1s. Platypus. HORIZ. 1s. 2d. Tasmanian Tiger. As T **119**. 1s. 6d. Christmas Bells (flower). 2s. 3d. Wattle. 2s. 5d. Banksia (plant). 3s. Waratah.

120. Postmaster Isaac Nichols boarding the Brig "Experiment".

1959. Australian P.O. 150th Anniv.
331. **120.** 4d. slate 12 5

121. Parliament House, Brisbane, and Arms of Queensland. 122. "The Approach of the Magi".

1959. Queensland Self-Government Cent.
332. **121.** 4d. lilac and green .. 15 5

1959. Christmas.
333. **122.** 5d. violet 15 5

123. Girl Guide and Lord Baden-Powell.

1960. Girl Guide Movement. Golden Jubilee.
334. **123.** 5d. ultramarine .. 15 5

124. "The Overlanders" (after Sir Daryl Lindsay).

1960. Northern Territory Exploration Cent.
335. **124.** 5d. magenta .. 12 5

125. "Archer" and Melbourne Cup. 126. Queen Victoria (after Chalon from first Queensland stamp).

1960. 100th Melbourne Cup Race Commem.
336. **125.** 5d. sepia 12 5

1960. Queensland Stamp Cent.
337. **126.** 5d. green 12 5

127. Open Bible and Candle.

ILLUSTRATIONS
British Commonwealth and all overprints and surcharges are FULL SIZE. Foreign Countries have been reduced to ¾-LINEAR.

129. Melba (after bust by Sir Bertram Mackennal). 128.

1960. Christmas Issue.
338. **127.** 5d. lake 15 5

1961. Colombo Plan.
339. **128.** 1s. brown 35 10

1961. Dame Nellie Melba (singer). Birth Cent.
340. **129.** 5d. blue 15 8

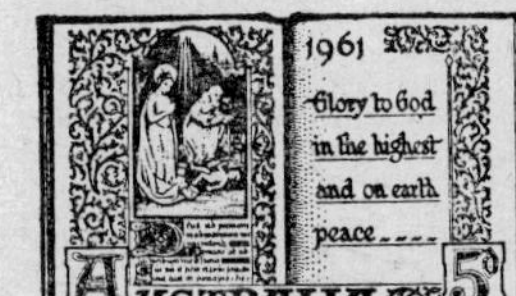

130. Open Prayer Book and Text.

1961. Christmas. issue.
341. **130.** 5d. brown 20 5

131. J. M. Stuart. 132. Flynn's Grave and Nursing Sister.

1962. Stuart's South to North Crossing of Australia. Cent.
342. **131.** 5d. red 15 5

1962. Australian Inland Mission. 50th Anniv.
343. **132.** 5d. multicoloured .. 15 5

133. "Woman". 134. "Madonna and Child".

1962. "Associated Country Women of the World" Conference, Melbourne.
344. **133.** 5d. green 15 5

1962. Christmas.
345. **134.** 5d. violet 20 5

135. Perth and Kangaroo Paw (plant).

1962. British Empire and Commonwealth Games, Perth.
346. **135.** 5d. multicoloured .. 20 10
347. – 2s. 3d. black, red, blue and green .. .. 6·00 3·50

DESIGN: 2s. 3d. Arms of Perth and running track.

136. Queen Elizabeth II. 138. Centenary Emblem.

137. Arms of Canberra and W. B. Griffin (architect).

1963. Royal Visit.
348. **136.** 5d. green 15 5
349. – 2s. 3d. lake .. .. 3·50 3·00

DESIGN: 2s. 3d. Queen Elizabeth II and Duke of Edinburgh.

1963. Canberra. 50th Anniv.
350. **137.** 5d. green 20 12

1963. Red Cross Cent.
351. **138.** 5d. red, grey-brn. & bl. 15 5

139. Explorers on Mt. York.

1962. First Crossing of Blue Mountains, 150th Anniv.
352. **139.** 5d. blue 15 5

140. "Export".

1963.
353. **140.** 5d. red 15 5

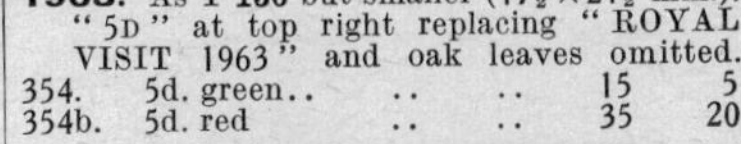

1963. As T **136** but smaller (17½ × 21½ mm.), "5D" at top right replacing "ROYAL VISIT 1963" and oak leaves omitted.
354. 5d. green 15 5
354b. 5d. red 35 20

141. Tasman and Ship.

1963. Navigators.
355. **141.** 4s. ultramarine .. 1·50 90
356. – 5s. chestnut .. .. 2·00 90
357. – 7s. 6d. olive .. .. 7·50 7·50
358a. – 10s. maroon .. .. 9·00 4·00
359a. – £1 violet .. .. 30·00 14·00
360. – £2 sepia .. .. 75·00 75·00

DESIGNS—HORIZ. (As T **141**): 7s. 6d. Captain Cook. 10s. Flinders and "Investigator". VERT. (20½ × 25½ mm.): Dampier and "Roebuck". £1 Bass and whaler. £2, Admiral King and "Mermaid".

142. "Peace on Earth . . .". 144. Black-backed Magpie.

143. "Commonwealth Cable".

1963. Christmas.
361. **142.** 5d. blue 25 5

1963. Opening of COMPAC (Trans-Pacific Telephone Cable).
362. **143.** 2s. 3d. red, blue, black and pale blue .. 3·50 3·00

1964.

363. – 6d. multicoloured .. 30 15
364. 144. 9d. black, grey & green 1·50 1·25
365. – 1s. 6d. pink, grey, pur. and black 70 65
366. – 2s. yellow, black & pink 80 30
367. – 2s. 5d. multicoloured .. 2·50 60
368. – 2s. 6d. black, red, grey and green .. .. 2·50 1·50
369. – 3s. blk., red, buff & grn. 1·60 60

BIRDS—HORIZ. 6d. Yellow-tailed Thornbill. 2s. 6d. Scarlet Robin. VERT. 1s. 6d. Galah (cockatoo). 2s. Golden Whistler (Thickhead). 2s. 5d. Blue Wren. 3s. Straw-necked Ibis.

145. " Bleriot " Aircraft (type flown by M. Guillaux, 1914).

1964. 1st Australian Airmail Flight. 50th Anniv.

370. 145. 5d. green 20 5
371. 2s. 3d. red .. .. 3·50 2·50

146. Child looking at Nativity Scene. **147.** " Simpson and his Donkey ".

1964. Christmas.

372. 146. 5d. red, blue, buff & blk. 20 5

1965. Gallipoli Landing. 50th Anniv.

373. 147. 5d. brown 15 10
374. 8d. blue 70 70
375. 2s. 3d. purple .. .. 2·50 2·50

148. " Telecommunications ". **149.** Sir Winston Churchill.

1965. I.T.U. Cent.

376. 148. 5d. black, brown & blue 20 5

1965. Churchill Commem.

377. 149. 5d. black, grey & blue 15 15

150. General Monash. **152.** I.C.Y. Emblem.

152. Hargrave and " Seaplane " (1902).

1965. General Sir John Monash (engineer and soldier). Birth Cent.

378. 150. 5d. multicoloured .. 15 5

1965. Lawrence Hargrave (aviation pioneer). 50th Death Anniv.

379. 151. 5d. brown, black, ochre and purple 20 5

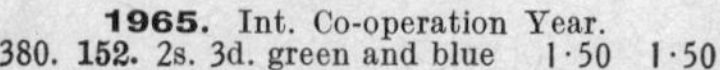

1965. Int. Co-operation Year.

380. 152. 2s. 3d. green and blue 1·50 1·50

153. " Nativity Scene ".

1965. Christmas.

381. 153. 5d. multicoloured .. 20 5

154. Queen Elizabeth II. **155.** Blue-faced Honeyeater.

1966. Decimal currency. As earlier issues but with values in cents and dollars as in T 154/5. Also some new designs.

382. 154. 1 c. brown 5 5
383. 2 c. green 8 5
384. 3 c. green 10 5
404. 3 c. blk., blue & green 25 20
385. 4 c. red 5 5
405. 4 c. blk., brn. & red .. 25 20
405a. 5 c. blk., brown & blue 70 25
386. 5 c. brn., yell., blk. & green (as 363) .. 40 10
386b.154. 5 c. blue .. 3·25 5
387. 155. 6 c. yell., blk., bl. & grey 70 25
387a. 6 c. orange 8 5
388. – 7 c. blk., grey, salmon and brown 30 5
388a.154. 7 c. purple 15 5
389. 8 c. red. yell., bl-green and green 90 15
390. · 9 c. red, mar., blk. & ol. 90 15
391. – 10 c. orange, brown, blue and chocolate 1·25 12
392. 13 c. red, black, grey and turquoise .. 1·40 35
393. – 15 c. red, black, grey and green (as 365) .. 1·40 40
394. – 20 c. yell., blk. & pink (as 366) .. .. 1·40 25
395. – 24 c. bl., yell., blk. & brn. 1·75 60
396. 25 c. blk., red, grey and green (as 368) .. 1·75 30
397. – 30 c. blk., red, buff and green (as 369) .. 10·00 30
398. 141. 40 c. blue .. .. 17·00 60
399. – 50 c. brown (as 356) .. 17·00 60
400. – 75 c. olive (as 357) .. 2·25 1·25
401. – $1 maroon (as 358a) .. 2·50 50
402. – $2 violet (as 359a) .. 5·00 2·00
403. – $4 brown (as 360) .. 9·50 5·50

DESIGNS—VERT. 7 c. Humbug fish. 8 c. Coral fish. 9 c. Hermit crab. 10 c. Anemone fish. 13 c. Red-necked avocet. HORIZ.—24 c. Azure kingfisher.

156. " Saving Life ".

1966. Royal Life Saving Society. 75th Anniv.

406. 156. 4 c. black and blue .. 20 10

157. " Adoration of the Shepherds ".

1966. Christmas.

407. 157. 4 c. black and olive .. 20 10

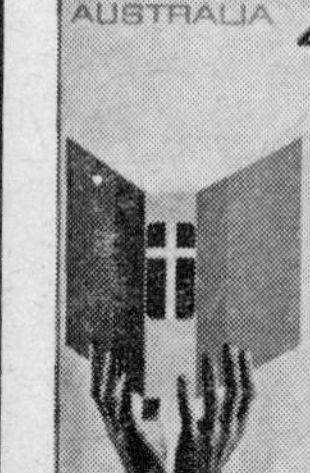

158. Dutch Ship. **159.** Open Bible.

1966. Dirk Hartog's Landing in Australia. 350th Anniv.

408. 158. 4 c. multicoloured .. 20 10

1967. British and Foreign Bible Society in Australia. 150th Anniv.

409. 159. 4 c. multicoloured .. 20 10

160. Ancient Keys and Modern Lock.

1967. Australian Banking. 150th Anniv.

410. 160. 4 c. black, blue & green 10 5

161. Lions Badge and 50 Stars.

1967. Lions Int. 50th Anniv.

411. 161. 4 c. black, gold & blue 25 10

162. Y.W.C.A. Emblem.

1967. World Y.W.C.A. Council Meeting, Monash University, Victoria.

412. 162. 4 c. multicoloured .. 20 10

163. Anatomical Figures.

1967. 5th World Gynaecology and Obstetrics Congress, Sydney.

413. 163. 4 c. black, blue & violet 20 10

1967. No. 385 surch.

414. 154. 5 c. on 4 c. red .. 25 5

164. Christmas Bells and Gothic Arches.

1967. Christmas. Multicoloured.

415. 5 c. Type 164 .. .. 15 5
416. 25 c. Religious symbols (vert.) .. .. 1·25 1·25

165. Satellite in Orbit.

1968. World Weather Watch. Multicoloured.

417. 5 c. Type 165 .. .. 20 10
418. 20 c. World Weather Map 2·25 1·25

166. Radar Antenna. **167.** Kangaroo Paw (Western Australia).

1968. World Telecommunications Intelsat II.

419. 166. 25 c. blue, black & grn. 2·25 1·50

1968. State Floral Emblems. Multicoloured.

420. 6 c. Type 167 .. .. 25 15
421. 13 c. Pink Heath (Victoria) 35 20
422. 15 c. Tasmanian Blue Gum (Tasmania) 45 15
423. 20 c. Sturt's Desert Pea (South Australia) .. 60 12
424. 25 c. Cooktown Orchid (Queensland) .. .. 1·00 25
425. 30 c. Waratah (New South Wales) .. .. .. 1·50 12

168. Soil Sample Analysis.

1968. Int. Soil Science Congress and World Medical Assn. Assembly.

426. 168. 5 c. chestnut, stone, blue and black .. 25 15
427. 5 c. blue, yellow, red and black 25 15

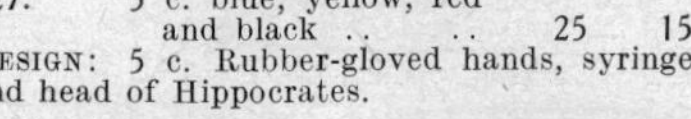

DESIGN: 5 c. Rubber-gloved hands, syringe and head of Hippocrates.

169. Athletic carrying Torch and Sunstone Symbol. **170.** Houses and Dollar Signs.

1968. Olympic Games, Mexico City. Multicoloured.

428. 5 c. Type 169 .. .. 20 10
429. 25 c. Sunstone Symbol and Mexican Flag .. .. 1·00 1·00

1968. Building and Savings Societies Congress.

430. 170. 5 c. multicoloured .. 20 10

171. Church Window and View of Bethlehem. **172.** Edgeworth David (geologist).

1968. Christmas.

431. 171. 5 c. multicoloured .. 25 5

1968. Famous Australians. (1st series).

432. 172. 5 c. green on myrtle .. 85 12
433. – 5 c. black on blue .. 85 12
434. 5 c. brown on buff .. 85 12
435. – 5 c. violet on lilac .. 85 12

DESIGNS: 433, A. B. Paterson (poet). 434, Albert Namatjira (artist). 435, Caroline Chrisholm (social worker).

Nos. 432/5 were only issued in booklets and exist with one or two sides imperf.

See also Nos. 446/9, 479/82, 505/8, 537/40, 590/5 and 602/7.

173. Macquarie Lighthouse.

1968. Macquarie Lighthouse. 150th Anniv.
436. 173. 5 c. black on yellow .. 20 12

174. Early Settlers and Modern Building, Darwin.

1969. Northern Territory Settlement. Cent.
437. 174. 5 c. brn. olive & ochre 20 12

175. Melbourne Harbour.

1969. Int. Ports and Harbours Conf.
438. 175. 5 c. multicoloured .. 20 12

176. Concentric Circles (Symbolising Management, Labour and Government).

1969. Int. Labour Organisation. 50th Anniv.
439. 176. 5 c. multicoloured .. 20 12

177. Sugar Cane. 178. " The Nativity " (stained glass window).

1969. Primary Industries. Multicoloured.
440. 7 c. Type 177 .. .. 65 50
441. 15 c. Timber .. .. 1·25 1·00
442. 20 c. Wheat 85 50
443. 25 c. Wool .. .. 1·25 75

1969. Christmas. Multicoloured.
444. 5 c. Type 178 .. .. 20 10
445. 25 c. " Tree of Life ", Christ in crib and Christmas Star (abstract) .. .. 1·50 1·25

1969. Famous Australians. (2nd series). As T 172. Prime Ministers.
446. 5 c. black on green .. 60 10
447. 5 c. black on green .. 60 10
448. 5 c. black on green .. 60 10
449. 5 c. black on green .. 60 10
DESIGNS: No. 446, Edmund Barton. 447, Alfred Deakin. 448, J. C. Watson. 449, G. H. Reid.
Nos. 446/9 were only issued in booklets and only exist with one or two adjacent sides imperf.

179. Capt. Ross Smith's Vickers " Vimy ", 1919.

1969. 1st England-Australia Flight. 50th Anniv.
450. 179. 5 c. multicoloured .. 25 12
451. – 5 c. red, black & green 25 12
452. – 5 c. multicoloured .. 25 12
DESIGNS: No. 451, Lt. H. Fysh and Lt. P. McGinness 1919 Survey with Ford car. 452, Capt. Wrigley and Sgt. Murphy in " BE 2E " take off to meet the Smiths.

180. Symbolic Track and Diesel Locomotive.

1970. Sydney-Perth Standard Gauge Railway Link.
453. 180. 5 c. multicoloured .. 15 10

181. Australian Pavilion, Osaka.

1970. World Fair, Osaka. Expo. 70.
454. 181. 5 c. multicoloured .. 12 12
455. – 20 c. red and black .. 70 60
DESIGN: 20 c. " Southern Cross " and " from the Country of the south with warm feelings " (message).

182. Australian Flag.

1970. Royal Visit.
456. – 5 c. black and ochre .. 15 12
457. 182. 30 c. multicoloured .. 90 75
DESIGN: 5 c. Queen Elizabeth II and Duke of Edinburgh.

183. Lucerne Plant, Bull and Sun.

1970. 11th Int. Grasslands Congress.
458. 183. 5 c. multicoloured .. 15 12

184. " Cook, giant among navigators, enters the Pacific." 185. Sturt's Desert Rose.

1970. Captain Cook's Discovery of Australia's East Coast. Bicent. Multicoloured.
459. 5 c. Type 184 .. .. 25 25
460. 5 c. " Fixes the position of the eastern part of Australia " 25 25
461. 5 c. " He finds new people and strange animals " ..
462. 5 c. " He and his scientists chart the shores and sketch the flora " .. 25 25 25 25
463. 5 c. " Sovereignty is proclaimed over the land discovered " 25 25
464. 30 c. Captain Cook, H.M.S. " Endeavour ", Quadrant, Aborigines and Kangaroo (84×30 mm.) .. .. 1·50 1·50
Nos. 459/63 were issued together se-tenant in horiz. strips of five, forming a composite design.

1970. Coil Stamps. Multicoloured.
465a. 2 c. Type 185 .. .. 20 5
466. 4 c. Type 185 .. .. 25 10
467. 5 c. Golden Wattle .. 5 5
468. 6 c. Type 185 .. .. 30 5
468b. 7 c. Sturt's Desert Pea .. 10 5
468d. 10 c. As 7 c. 12 5

186. Oil and Natural Gas.

1970. National Development (1st series). Multicoloured.
469. 7 c. Snowy Mountains scheme 65 30
470. 8 c. Ord River scheme .. 10 8
471. 9 c. Bauxite to Aluminium 10 5
472. 10 c. Type 186 .. .. 65 12

187. Rising Flames.

1970. 16th Commonwealth Parliamentary Association Conference, Canberra.
473. 187. 6 c. multicoloured .. 20 5

188. Milk Analysis and Dairy Herd.

1970. International Dairy Congress, Sydney.
474. 188. 6 c. multicoloured .. 20 5

189. " The Nativity ". 190. U.N. " Plant " and Dove of Peace.

1970. Christmas.
475. 189. 6 c. multicoloured .. 20 5

1970. United Nations. 25th Anniv.
476. 190. 6 c. multicoloured .. 20 5

191. Boeing " 707 " and Avro " 504 ".

1970. QANTAS Airline. 50th Anniv.
477. 191. 6 c. multicoloured .. 20 8
478. – 30 c. multicoloured .. 95 80
DESIGN: 30 c. Avro "504" and Boeing "707".

1970. Famous Australians (3rd series). As T 172.
479. 6 c. blue on pink 55 8
480. 6 c. black on flesh .. 55 8
481. 6 c. purple on pink .. 55 8
482. 6 c. lake on pink 55 8
DESIGNS: No. 479, The Duigan brothers (pioneer aviators). No. 480, Lachlan Macquarie (Governor of N.S.W.). No. 481, Adam Lindsay Gordon (poet). No. 482, E. J. Eyre (explorer).
These stamps were only issued in booklets and have one or two sides imperf.

192. " Theatre ".

1971. " Australia-Asia ". Multicoloured.
483. 7 c. Type 192 .. .. 25 12
484. 15 c. " Music " 45 40
485. 20 c. " Sea Craft " .. 60 55

193. The Southern Cross.

1971. Australian Natives' Assoc. Cent.
486. 193. 6 c. blk., verm. & blue 20 5

194. Market " Graph ".

1971. Sydney Stock Exchange Cent.
487. 194. 6 c. multicoloured .. 20 5

195. Rotary Emblem.

1971. Rotary International. 50th Anniv.
488. 195. 6 c. multicoloured .. 20 5

196. "Mirage" Jets and " D.H.9a " Biplane. 197. Draught-horse, Cat and Dog.

1971. R.A.A.F. 50th Anniv.
489. 196. 6 c. multicoloured .. 20 5

1971. Animals. Multicoloured.
490. 6 c. Type 197 .. .. 20 12
491. 12 c. Vet and lamb (" Animal Science ") .. 35 20
492. 8 c. Red Kangaroo (" Fauna Conservation ") 45 30
493. 24 c. Guide-dog (" Animals Aid to Man ") 65 40
The 6 c. commemorates the Centenary of the Australian R.S.P.C.A.

198. Bark Painting.

1971. Aboriginal Art. Multicoloured.

494. 20 c. Type **198** 45 20
495. 25 c. Body decoration .. 55 40
496. 30 c. Cave painting (vert) 65 40
497. 35 c. Grave posts (vert) .. 45 35

199. The Three Kings and the Star.

1971. Christmas. Colours of star and colour of " AUSTRALIA " given.

498. **199.** 7 c. blue, mve. & brn. 1·00 25
499. 7 c. brn., mve. & white 1·00 25
500. 7 c. mve., white & blk. 1·00 25
501. 7 c. blk., green & red 1·00 25
502. 7 c. lilac, grn. & red .. 1·00 25
503. 7 c. blk., brn. & white 1·00 25
504. 7 c. blue, mve. & green 1·00 25

1972. Famous Australians. (4th series). As T **172**. Prime Ministers.

505. 7 c. blue 35 5
506. 7 c. blue 35 5
507. 7 c. red 35 5
508. 7 c. red 35 5

DESIGNS: No. 505, Andrew Fisher. No. 506, W. M. Hughes. No. 507, Joseph Cook. 508, S. M. Bruce.

Nos. 505/8 were only issued in booklets and only exist with one or two adjacent sides imperf.

200. Cameo Brooch.

1972. Country Women's Assn. 50th Anniv.

509. **200.** 7 c. multicoloured .. 20 5

201. Fruit.

1972. Primary Industries. Multicoloured.

510. 20 c. Type **201** .. .. 1·75 1·00
511. 25 c. Rice .. .. .. 1·75 1·10
512. 30 c. Fish .. .. .. 1·90 1·40
513. 35 c. Beef .. .. .. 6·50 4·50

202. Worker in Wheelchair. 204. Athletics.

203. Telegraph Line.

1972. Rehabilitation of the Disabled.

514. **202.** 12 c. brown & green .. 15 10
515. – 18 c. green & orange .. 30 20
516. – 24 c. blue and brown 30 20

DESIGNS—HORIZ. 18 c. Patient and teacher. VERT. 24 c. Boy playing with ball.

1972. Overland Telegraph Line. Cent.

517 **203.** 7 c. multicoloured .. 20 5

1972. Olympic Games, Munich. Mult.

518. 7 c. Type **204** 20 12
519. 7 c. Rowing 20 12
520. 7 c. Swimming 20 12
521. 35 c. Equestrian .. .. 2·25 1·75

205. Numerals and Computer Circuit.

1972. 10th Int. Congress of Accountants, Sydney.

522. **205.** 7 c. multicoloured .. 20 5

206. Australian-built Harvester.

1972. Pioneer Life. Multicoloured.

523. 5 c. Pioneer Family (vert.) 5 5
524. 10 c. Water-pump (vert.) 12 8
525. 15 c. Type **206** 20 12
526. 40 c. House 50 30
527. 50 c. Stage Coach .. 60 40
528. 60 c. Morse key (vert.) .. 75 50
529. 80 c. Paddle-steamer .. 1·00 70

207. Jesus with Children.

1972. Christmas. Multicoloured.

530. 7 c. Type **207** 15 5
531. 35 c. Dove and spectrum motif .. .. .. 3·25 85

208. " Length ".

1973. Metric Conversion. Multicoloured.

532. 7 c. Type **208** 45 12
533. 7 c. " Volume " 45 12
534. 7 c. " Mass " 45 12
535. 7 c. " Temperature " (horiz.) 45 12

209. Caduceus and Laurel Wreath.

1973. World Health Organisation. 25th Anniv.

536. **209.** 7 c. multicoloured .. 15 5

1973. Famous Australians (5th series). As T **172**.

537. 7 c. brown and black .. 30 5
538. 7 c. lilac and black .. 30 5
539. 7 c. brown and black .. 30 5
540. 7 c. lilac and black .. 30 5

PORTRAITS: No. 537, William Wentworth statesman and explorer). No. 538, Isaac Isaacs (1st Australian-born Governor-General). No. 539, Mary Gilmore (writer). No. 540, Marcus Clarke (author).

210. Shipping. 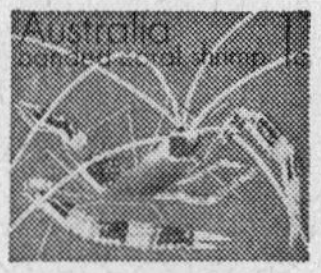 211. Banded Coral Shrimp.

1973. National Development (2nd series). Multicoloured.

541. 20 c. Type **210** 65 45
542. 25 c. Iron ore and steel .. 85 60
543. 30 c. Beef roads 80 60
544. 35 c. Mapping .. .. 1·60 1·40

1973. Marine Life and Gemstones. Mult.

545. 1 c. Type **211** 5 5
546. 2 c. Fiddler crab 5 5
547. 3 c. Coral crab 5 5
548. 4 c. Mauve stinger .. 5 5
549. 6 c. Chrysoprase 8 5
550. 7 c. Agate 10 5
551. 8 c. Opal 10 5
552. 9 c. Rhodonite 12 8
552a. 10 c. Star sapphire .. 12 8

212. Children at Play.

1973. Legacy (Welfare Organization). 50th Anniv.

553. **212.** 7 c. brown, red & green 15 8

213. John Baptising Jesus.

1973. Christmas. Multicoloured.

554. 7 c. Type **213** 20 10
555. 30 c. The Good Shepherd 1·00 80

214. Sydney Opera House.

1973. Architecture.

556. **214.** 7 c. blue and pale blue 20 12
557. – 10 c. ochre and brown 35 35
558. – 40 c. grey, brown & blk. 85 85
559. – 50 c. multicoloured .. 1·10 1·10

DESIGNS—HORIZ. 10 c. Buchanan's Hotel, Townsville. 40 c. Como House, Melbourne. VERT. 50 c. St. James' Church, Sydney.

215. Wireless Receiver and Speaker.

1973. Regular Radio Broadcasting. 50th Anniv.

560. **215.** 7 c. blue, red and black 15 12

216. Wombat.  217. " Sergeant of Light Horse" (G. Lambert).

1974. Animals. Multicoloured.

561. 20 c. Type **216** 25 15
562. 25 c. Spiny Ant-eater .. 35 15
563. 30 c. Brushtail Possum .. 35 20
564. 75 c. Feather-tailed Glider 90 60

1974. Australian Paintings. Multicoloured.

565. $1 Type **217** .. .. 1·25 25
566. $2 " Red Gums of the Far North " (H. Heysen) .. 2·40 80
567. $4 " Shearing the Rams " (Tom Roberts) .. 5·00 2·25

218. Supreme Court Judge.

1974. Australia's Third Charter of Justice. 150th Anniv.

568. **218.** 7 c. multicoloured .. 10 12

219. Rugby Football.

1974. Non-Olympic Sports. Multicoloured.

569. 7 c. Type **219** 20 12
570. 7 c. Bowls 20 12
571. 7 c. Australian football (vert.) 20 12
572. 7 c. Cricket (vert.) .. 20 12
573. 7 c. Golf (vert.) 20 12
574. 7 c. Surfing (vert.) .. 20 12
575. 7 c. Tennis (vert.) .. 20 12

220. " Transport of Mails ".

1974. U.P.U Centenary. Multicoloured.

576. 7 c. Type **220** 15 12
577. 30 c. Three-part version of Type **220** 65 65

221. Letter " A " and W. C. Wentworth (co-founder). 222. " The Adoration of the Magi ".

1974. First Independent Newspaper, " The Australian ", 150th Anniv.

578. **221.** 7 c. black and brown .. 8 5

1974. No. 551 surch.
579. 9 c. on 8 c. multicoloured 12 12

1974. Christmas. Woodcuts by Durer.
580. **222.** 10 c. black on cream .. 15 15
581. – 35 c. black on cream .. 60 60
DESIGN: 35 c. " The Flight into Egypt ".

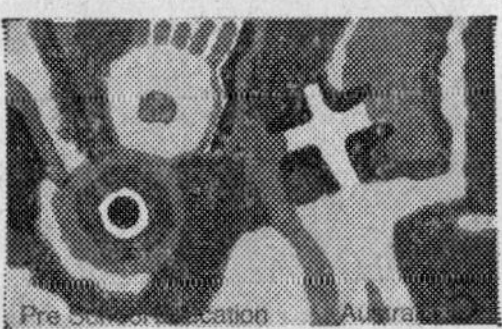

223. " Pre-School Education ".

1974. Education in Australia. Multicoloured.
582. 5 c. Type **223** 5 5
583. 11 c. " Correspondence Schools " 15 12
584. 15 c. " Science Education " 20 15
585. 60 c. " Advanced Education " (vert.) 75 60

224. " Road Safety ". **225.** Australian Women's Year Emblem.

1975. Environmental Dangers. Multicoloured.
586. 10 c. Type **224** 15 15
587. 10 c. " Pollution " (horiz.) 15 15
588. 10 c. " Bush Fires " (horiz.) 15 15

1975. International Women's Year.
589. **225.** 10 c. bl., grn. & vio... 15 15

226. J. H. Scullin.

1975. Famous Australians (6th series). Prime Ministers. Multicoloured.
590. 10 c. Type **226** 15 15
591. 10 c. J. A. Lyons 15 15
592. 10 c. Earle Page 15 15
593. 10 c. Arthur Fadden .. 15 15
594. 10 c. John Curtin 15 15
595. 10 c. J. B. Chifley 15 15

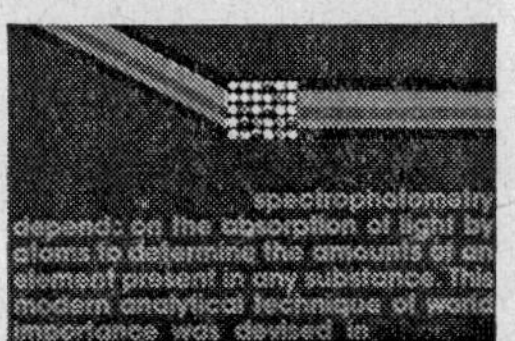

227. Atomic Absorption Spectrophotometry

1975. Scientific Development. Multicoloured.
596. 11 c. Type **227** 12 10
597. 24 c. Radio astronomy .. 30 25
598. 33 c. Immunology .. 40 35
599. 48 c. Oceanography .. 60 50

228. Logo of Australian Postal Commission.

1975. Australian Postal and Telecommunications Commissions. Inauguration.
600. **228.** 10 c. blk., red & grey 12 15
601. – 10 c. blk., orge. & grey 12 15
DESIGN: No. 601, Logo of Australian Telecommunications Commission.

229. Edith Cowan. **230.** " Helichrysum thomsonii ".

1975. Famous Australians (7th series). Australian Women. Multicoloured.
602. 10 c. Type **229** 12 15
603. 10 c. Louisa Lawson .. 12 15
604. 10 c. Henry Richardson (pen-name of Ethel Richardson) 12 15
605. 10 c. Catherine Spence 12 15
606. 10 c. Constance Stone .. 12 15
607. 10 c. Truganini 12 15

1975. Wild Flowers. Mult.
608. 18 c. Type **230** 20 15
609. 45 c. " Callistemon teretifolius " (horiz.) 55 45

231. "Tambaran" House and Sydney Opera House. **232.** Epiphany Scene.

1975. Papua New Guinea Independence. Mult.
610. 18 c. Type **231** 30 25
611. 25 c. " Freedom " (bird in flight) 40 40

1975. Christmas.
612. **232.** 15 c. multicoloured . 20 20
613. – 45 c. vio., bl. & silver 2·75 2·25
DESIGN: 45 c. " Shining Star ".

233. Australian Coat of Arms.

1975. Nationhood. 75th Anniversary.
614. **233.** 18 c. multicoloured .. 20 25

234. Telephone-user, 1878.

1976. Telephone Centenary.
615. **234.** 18 c. multicoloured .. 25 25

235. John Oxley.

1976. 19th Century Explorers. Multicoloured.
616. 18 c. Type **235** 25 25
617. 18 c. Hume and Hovell .. 25 25
618. 18 c. John Forest .. 25 25
619. 18 c. Ernest Giles .. 25 25
620. 18 c. William Gosse .. 25 25
621. 18 c. Peter Warburton .. 25 25

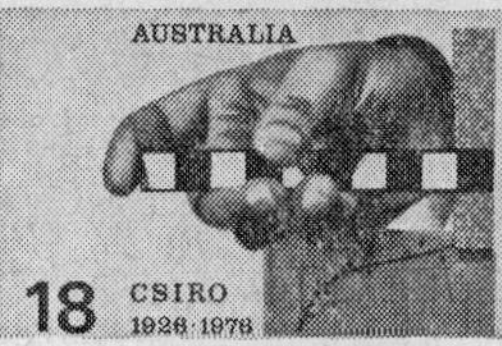

236. Measuring Stick, Graph and Computer Tape.

1976. Commonwealth Scientific and Industrial Research Organisation. 50th Anniv.
622. **236.** 18 c. multicoloured .. 25 25

237. Football.

1976. Olympic Games, Montreal. Multicoloured.
623. 18 c. Type **237** 25 30
624. 18 c. Gymnastics (vert.) .. 25 30
625. 25 c. Diving (vert.) .. 35 40
626. 40 c. Cycling 55 65

238. Richmond Bridge, Tasmania.

1976. Australian Scenes. Multicoloured
627. 5 c. Type **238** 5 8
628. 25 c. Broken Bay, N.S.W. 30 35
629. 35 c. Wittenoom Gorge, W.A. 45 50
630. 50 c. Mt. Buffalo, Victoria (vert.) 60 70
631. 70 c. Barrier Reef .. 85 95
632. 85 c. Ayers Rock, N.T... 1·00 1·10

239. Blamire Young (designer of first Australian stamp).

1976. National Stamp Week.
633. **239.** 18 c. multicoloured .. 25 30

OFFICIAL STAMPS

1931. Overprinted **O.S.**

(a) Kangaroo issue.
O 13. **1.** 6d. brown .. .. 10·00 10·00

(b) King George V issue.
O 7. **4.** ½d. orange .. .. 3·00 75
O 8. 1d. green .. .. 1·00 30
O 4. 2d. red .. .. 1·25 60
O 10. 3d. blue .. .. 6·00 4·50
O 5. 4d. olive .. .. 6·00 3·50
O 11. 5d. brown .. .. 22·00 15·00

(c) Various issues.
O 1. **9.** 2d. red .. .. 25·00 12·00
O 16. **13.** 2d. red .. .. 3·00 1·50
O 2. **9.** 3d. blue .. .. 90·00 30·00
O 17. **13.** 3d. blue .. .. 8·00 8·00
O 18. **12.** 1s. green .. .. 25·00 25·00

POSTAGE DUE STAMPS

D 1. D 2.

1902. White space below value at foot.
D 1. **D 1.** ½d. green .. .. 1·25 1·25
D 2. 1d green .. .. 2·25 1·00
D 3. 2d. green .. .. 2·25 1·00
D 4. 3d. green .. .. 3·75 1·50
D 5. 4d. green .. .. 3·75 1·50
D 6. 6d green .. .. 3·75 1·50
D 7. 8d green .. .. 18·00 12·00
D 8. 5s. green .. .. 42·00 14·00

1902. White space filled in.
D 45. **D 2.** ½d. green 75 30
D 23. 1d. green 60 15
D 47. 2d. green 60 20
D 25. 3d. green .. .. 1·25 30
D 49. 4d. green .. .. 3·00 90
D 17. 5d. green .. .. 3·00 65
D 28. 6d. green .. .. 3·50 80
D 29. 8d. green .. .. 10·00 1·50
D 18. 10d. green .. .. 4·50 1·00
D 19. 1s. green .. .. 4·50 1·00
D 20. 2s. green .. .. 9·00 1·50
D 33. 5s. green .. .. 22·00 2·00
D 43. 10s. green £325 £200
D 44. 20s. green £625 £400

1908. As Type D 2, but stroke after figure of value, thus "5/–".
D 58. **D 2.** 1s. green .. .. 10·00 3·00
D 60. 2s. green £150 £120
D 59. 5s. green .. .. 55·00 12·00
D 61. 10s. green £350 £225
D 62. 20s. green £750 £500

D 3. D 4.

1909.
D 91. **D 3.** ½d. red and green .. 30 30
D 120. 1d. red and green .. 15 5
D 93. 1½d. red and green 3·00 3·00
D 121. 2d. red and green .. 60 5
D 134. 3d. red and green .. 10 10
D 123. 4d. red and green .. 60 5
D 124. 5d. red and green .. 75 40
D 137. 6d. red and green .. 30 30
D 126. 7d. red and green .. 75 40
D 138. 8d. red and green .. 2·25 75
D 139. 10d. red and green 75 25
D 128. 1s. red and green .. 3·00 50
D 70. 2s. red and green .. 4·00 1·50
D 71. 5s. red and green .. 10·00 2·50
D 72. 10s. red and green.. 65·00 30·00
D 73. £1 red and green .. £110 55·00

1953.
D 140a. **D 4.** 1s. red and green.. 75 15
D 141. 2s. red and green.. 1·25 20
D 131a. 5s. red and green.. 6·00 1·25

AUSTRALIAN ANTARCTIC TERRITORY BC

By an Order in Council of 7th February, 1933, the territory S. of latitude 60°S. between 160th and 145th meridians of East longitude (excepting Adelie Land) was placed under Australian administration.

1966. 100 cents = 1 dollar.

1. 1954 Expedition at Vestfold Hills and Map.

1957.
1. **1.** 2s. blue 90 35

AUSTRALIAN
ANTARCTIC TERRITORY

2. Members of Shackleton Expedition at S. Magnetic Pole 1909.

DESIGNS—As T **3**—VERT. 1s. Map of Antarctica, dog-team and iceberg. 2s. 3d. Similar map and Emperor penguins.

3. Weazel and Team.

1959.

2.	2.	5d. on 4d. sepia and black	25	20
3.	3.	8d. on 7d. blue	40	40
4.	–	1s. myrtle	90	90
5.	–	2s. 3d. green	1·25	1·10

4. First Attainment of Magnetic Pole.

5. Sir Douglas Mawson (Expedition leader).

1961.

6.	4.	5d. blue	35	20

1961. 1911-14 Australasian Antarctic Expedition.

7.	5.	5d. myrtle	25	15

6. Aurora and Camera Dome.

1966. Multicoloured.

8.	1 c. Type 6	5	5
9.	2 c. Banding penguins ..	5	5
10.	4 c. Ship and iceberg ..	8	8
11.	5 c. Banding elephant seals	10	10
12.	7 c. Measuring snow strata..	12	20
13.	10 c. Wind gauges	25	25
14.	15 c. Weather balloon ..	35	55
15.	20 c. Helicopter (horiz.) ..	60	90
16.	25 c. Radio operator (horiz)	80	1·25
17.	50 c. Ice-compression tests (horiz.)	1·75	2·00
18.	$1 Parahelion ("mock sun") (horiz.)	3·50	4·50

7. Sastrugi (Snow Ridges).

1971. Antarctic Treaty. 10th Anniv.

19.	7.	6 c. blue and black ..	25	25
20.	–	30 c. multicoloured ..	80	80

DESIGN: 30 c. Pancake ice.

8. Capt. Cook, Sextant and Compass.

1972. Cook's Circumnavigation of Antarctica. Bicent. Multicoloured.

21.	7 c. Type 8	20	20
22.	35 c. Chart and the Resolution	90	90

9. Plankton.

1973. Multicoloured.

23.	1 c. Type 9	5	5
24.	5 c. Mawson's "Gipsy Moth", 1931	5	8
25.	7 c. Adelie penguin ..	8	10
26.	8 c. Rymill's "Fox Moth", 1934-7	10	10
27.	9 c. Leopard seal (horiz.) ..	10	12
28.	10 c. Killer whale (horiz.)..	12	12
29.	20 c. Albatross (horiz.) ..	25	25
30.	25 c. Wilkins' Lockheed "Vega", 1928 (horiz.) ..	30	35
31.	30 c. Ellsworth's Northrop "Gamma", 1935 ..	35	40
32.	35 c. Christensen's Avro "Avian", 1934 (horiz.)..	40	45
33.	50 c. Byrd's "Tri-Motor", 1929	60	65
34.	$1 Sperm whale	1·25	1·40

AUSTRIA E1

A state of Central Europe, part of the Austro-Hungarian Monarchy and Empire until 1918. At the end of the First World War the Empire was dismembered and German-speaking Austria became a Republic.

Austria was absorbed into the German Reich in 1938 and remained part of Germany until 1945. Following occupation by the four Allied Powers the Austrian Republic was re-established on the 14th May, 1945.

1850. 60 kreuzer = 1 gulden.
1858. 100 kreuzer = 1 gulden.
1899. 100 heller = 1 krone.
1925. 100 groschen = 1 schilling.
1938. 100 pfenning = 1 German reichsmark.
1945. 100 groschen = 1 schilling.

1. Arms of Austria.

2.

3.

1850. Imperf.

6a.	1.	1 k. yellow	£550	38·00
7.		2 k. black	£400	25·00
3d.		3 k. red	£180	1·50
9.		6 k. brown	£225	1·50
10.		9 k. blue	£300	85

For stamps in T 1 with values in "CENTES", see Lombardy and Venetia.

1858.

22.	3.	2 k. yellow	£350	15·00
23.	2.	3 k. black	£425	£110
24.		3 k. green	£400	55·00
25.	3.	5 k. red	£120	50
26.		10 k. brown	£275	1·25
27.		15 k. blue	£250	65

For stamps in T 2 and 3 with values in 'SOLDI'', see Lombardy and Venetia.

The portraits on Austrian stamps to 1906 are of the Emperor Francis Joseph I.

4.

5. Arms of Austria.

1860.

33.	4.	2 k. yellow	£180	11·00
34.		3 k. green	£170	9·00
35.		5 k. red	£100	30
36.		10 k. brown	£130	85
37.		15 k. blue	£130	50

1863.

45.	5.	2 k. yellow	65·00	4·25
46.		3 k. green	65·00	4·25
47.		5 k. red	25·00	12
48.		10 k. blue	60·00	1·10
49.		15 k. brown	60·00	55

6. 7. 8. Arms of Austria.

1867.

59.	6.	2 k. yellow	4·50	30
60.		3 k. green	13·00	20
62.		5 k. red	50	10
63.		10 k. blue	30·00	10
64.		15 k. brown	2·50	1·40
65.		25 k. lilac	1·25	18·00
66.	7.	50 k. brown	6·00	30·00

1883.

70.	8.	2 k. brown	2·50	8
71.		3 k. green	2·50	5
72.		5 k. red	5·00	5
73.		10 k. blue	2·50	5
74.		20 k. grey	22·00	70
75a.		50 k. lilac	£150	20·00

9.

10.

11.

1890. Figures in black on T 9.

79.	9.	1 k. slate..	1·25	5
80.		2 k. brown	20	5
81.		3 k. green	20	5
82.		5 k. red	20	5
83.		10 k. blue	35	5
84.		12 k. red	1·40	12
85.		15 k. mauve	75	12
86.		20 k. olive	20·00	80
87.		24 k. blue	1·50	40
88.		30 k. brown	80	10
89.		50 k. mauve	4·75	3·00
90.	10.	1 g. blue	65	80
105.		1 g. lilac	24·00	1·25
91.		2 g. red	2·25	3·75
106.		2 g. green	15·00	11·00

1891. Figures in black.

92.	11.	20 k. green	65	5
93.		24 k. blue	1·40	20
94.		30 k. brown	65	5
95.		50 k. mauve	1·00	12

12.

13.

14.

15.

1899. Corner numerals in black on heller values.

107.	12.	1 h. mauve	50	5
139.		2 h. grey	45	5
140.		3 h. brown	20	5
141.		5 h. green	8	5
142.		6 h. orange	8	5
143.	13.	10 h. red	12	5
113.		20 h. brown	50	5
145.		25 h. blue	45	5
146.		30 h. mauve	1·00	20
147.	14.	35 h. green	50	5
148.		40 h. green	85	1·00
149.		50 h. blue	1·75	1·50
150.		60 h. brown	1·00	15
119.	15.	1 k. red	3·25	5
120.		2 k. lavender	32·00	20
121.		4 k. green	3·25	2·75

16.

17.

1904. Types as before, but with corners containing figures altered as T 16 and 17. Figures in black on white on 10 h. to 30 h. only.

169.	16.	1 h. purple	8	5
170.		2 h. black	10	5
171.		3 h. brown	12	5
183.		5 h. green	15	5
173.	16.	6 h. orange	20	5
160.	13.	10 h. red	1·75	5
161.		20 h. brown	22·00	25
162.		25 h. blue	24·00	25
163.		30 h. mauve	28·00	55
178.	17.	35 h. green	1·10	10
179.		40 h. purple	1·10	35
180.		50 h. blue	1·25	1·40
181.		60 h. brown	1·25	20
168.		72 h. red	60	30

1906. Figures on plain white ground and stamps printed in one colour.

184.	13.	10 h. red	25	5
185.		12 h. violet	45	25
186.		20 h. brown	1·00	5
187.		25 h. blue	1·25	15
188.		30 h. claret	1·50	12

18. Charles VI.

19. Francis Joseph I.

21. Francis Joseph I.

20. Schonbrunn.

1908 60th year of Reign of Francis Joseph I.

189.	18.	1 h. black	12	10
190.	–	2 h. violet	15	10
191.	–	3 h. purple	5	5
192.	–	5 h. green	5	5
193.	–	6 h. brown	60	12
194.	–	10 h. red	5	5
195.	–	12 h. red	1·00	20
196.	–	20 h. brown	1·25	8
197.	–	25 h. blue	55	5
198.	–	30 h. olive	2·10	8
199.	–	35 h. slate	1·75	8
200.	19.	50 h. green	50	10
201.	–	60 h. red	25	5
202.	19.	72 h. brown	1·25	10
203.	–	1 k. violet	9·00	5
204.	20.	2 k. olive and red ..	14·00	15
205.	–	5 k. purple and brown..	26·00	2·25
206.	21.	10 k. brown and blue ..	£130	27·00

DESIGNS—As T 18: 2 h. Maria Theresa. 3 h. Joseph II. 5 h., 10 h., 25 h. Francis Joseph I. 6 h. Leopold II. 12 h. Francis I. 20 h. Ferdinand. 30 h. Francis Joseph I in 1848. 35 h. Same in 1878. As T 19: 60 h. Francis Joseph I on horseback. 1 k. Same in ceremonial robes. As T 20: 5 k. Hofburg.

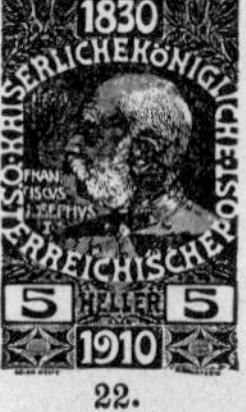

22.

23.

1910. 80th Birthday of Francis Joseph I. As T 18/21, but with dates added as T 22.

223.	1 h. black	4·00	2·50
224.	2 h. lilac	4·50	3·50
225.	3 h. purple	4·25	3·00
226.	5 h. green	10	8
227.	6 h. brown	1·50	1·25
228.	10 h. red	10	8
229.	12 h. red	1·50	1·25
230.	20 h. brown	3·25	2·50
231.	25 h. blue	35	30
232.	30 h. olive	2·40	2·10
233.	35 h. slate	2·50	2·10
234.	50 h. green	3·00	3·00
235.	60 h. red	3·00	3·00
236.	1 k. violet	3·25	3·25
237.	2 k. olive and red ..	£100	£100
238.	5 k. purple and brown	85·00	80·00
239.	10 k. brown and blue ..	£160	£160

1914. War Charity Funds.

240.	23.	5+2 h. green	10	8
241.		10+2 h. red	12	8

24. Cavalry.

DESIGNS: 3 h. Infantry. 10 h. Artillery. 20 h. Navy. 25 h. Biplane.

1915. War Charity Funds.
242. – 3+1 h. chocolate .. 10 10
243. 24. 5+2 h. green .. 5 5
244. – 10+2 h. red .. 5 5
245. – 20+3 h. blue-green .. 30 30
246. – 35+3 h. blue .. 2·40 1·25

26. Imperial Austrian Crown. 27. Francis Joseph I.

28. Arms of Austria. 29.

1916.
247. 26. 3 h. violet 5 5
248. 5 h. green 5 5
249. 6 h. orange 15 15
250. 10 h. claret 5 5
251. 12 h. blue 15 15
252. 27. 15 h. red 35 5
253. 20 h. brown .. .. 2·50 5
254. 25 h. blue .. .. 5·00 20
255. 30 h. slate .. .. 4·50 30
256. 28. 40 h. olive 8 5
257. 50 h. green 15 5
258. 60 h. blue 10 5
259. 80 h. red-brown .. 10 5
260. 90 h. purple 10 8
261. 1 k. red on yellow .. 20 8
262aa. 29. 2 k. blue 8 8
263aa. 3 k. red 15 10
264a. 4 k. green 60 40
265aa. 10 k. violet .. .. 4·00 4·50

ILLUSTRATIONS
British Commonwealth and all overprints and surcharges are FULL SIZE. Foreign Countries have been reduced to ¾-LINEAR.

30. Charles I.

1917.
290. 30. 15 h. red 5 5
291a. 20 h. green 5 5
292. 25 h. blue 12 5
293. 30 h. violet 10 5

1918. Air. Optd. **FLUGPOST** or surch. also.
296. 29. 1 k. 50 on 2 k. mauve .. 1·40 1·60
297. 2 k. 50 on 3 k. yellow .. 7·50 8·50
298. 4 k. grey .. .. 3·25 4·00

1918. Optd. **Deutschosterreich.**
299. 26. 3 h. violet 5 5
300. 5 h. green 5 5
301. 6 h. orange 8 20
302. 10 h. claret 5 5
303. 12 h. blue 10 20
304. 30. 15 h. red 8 10
305. 20 h. green 5 5
306. 25 h. blue 10 5
307. 30 h. violet 8 5
308. 28. 40 h. olive 10 5
309. 50 h. green 40 30
310. 60 h. blue 40 25
311. 80 h. red-brown .. 8 5
312. 90 h. claret 10 8
313. 1 k. red on yellow .. 12 8
314. 29. 2 k. blue 5 5
315. 3 k. red 15 12
316. 4 k. green 55 55
317. 10 k. violet .. .. 6·50 6·50

31. Posthorn. 32. Republican Arms. 33. "New Republic".

1919. Imperf. or perf.
336. 31. 3 h. grey 5 5
337. 32. 5 h. green 5 5
338. 5 h. grey 5 5
339. 31. 6 h. orange 5 5
340. 32. 10 h. red 5 5

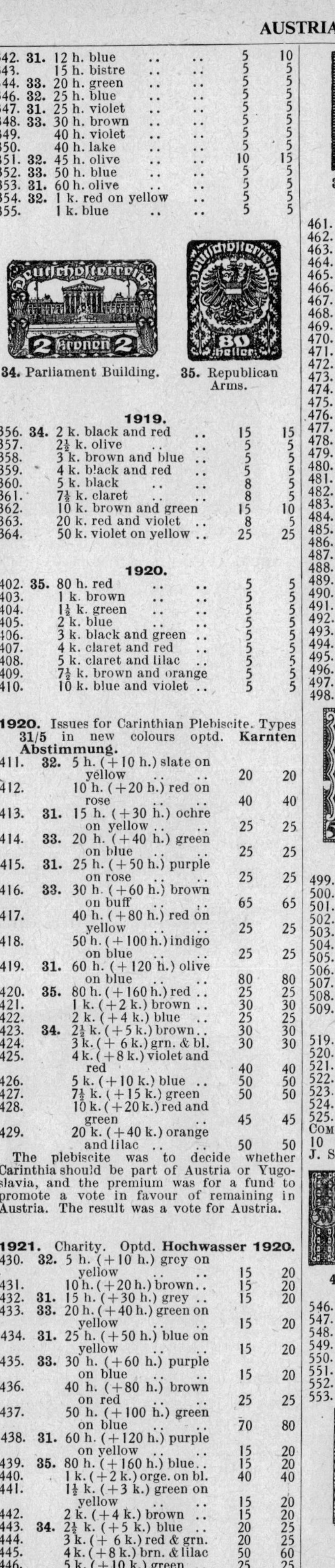

342. 31. 12 h. blue 5 10
343. 15 h. bistre 5 5
344. 33. 20 h. green 5 5
346. 32. 25 h. blue 5 5
347. 31. 25 h. violet 5 5
348. 33. 30 h. brown 5 5
349. 40 h. violet 5 5
350. 40 h. lake 5 5
351. 32. 45 h. olive 10 15
352. 33. 50 h. blue 5 5
353. 31. 60 h. olive 5 5
354. 32. 1 k. red on yellow .. 5 5
355. 1 k. blue 5 5

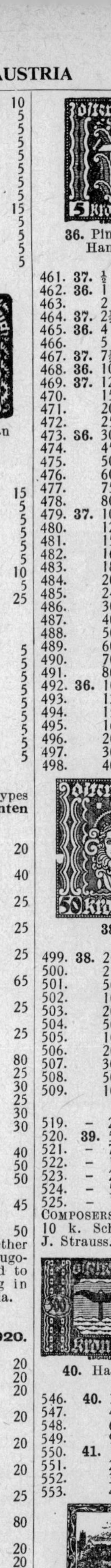

34. Parliament Building. 35. Republican Arms.

1919.
356. 34. 2 k. black and red .. 15 15
357. 2½ k. olive 5 5
358. 3 k. brown and blue .. 5 5
359. 4 k. black and red .. 5 5
360. 5 k. black 8 5
361. 7½ k. claret 8 5
362. 10 k. brown and green 15 10
363. 20 k. red and violet .. 8 5
364. 50 k. violet on yellow .. 25 25

1920.
402. 35. 80 h. red 5 5
403. 1 k. brown 5 5
404. 1½ k. green 5 5
405. 2 k. blue 5 5
406. 3 k. black and green .. 5 5
407. 4 k. claret and red .. 5 5
408. 5 k. claret and lilac .. 5 5
409. 7½ k. brown and orange .. 5 5
410. 10 k. blue and violet .. 5 5

1920. Issues for Carinthian Plebiscite. Types 31/5 in new colours optd. **Karnten Abstimmung.**
411. 32. 5 h. (+10 h.) slate on yellow 20 20
412. 10 h. (+20 h.) red on rose 40 40
413. 31. 15 h. (+30 h.) ochre on yellow 25 25
414. 33. 20 h. (+40 h.) green on blue 25 25
415. 31. 25 h. (+50 h.) purple on rose 25 25
416. 33. 30 h. (+60 h.) brown on buff 65 65
417. 40 h. (+80 h.) red on yellow 25 25
418. 50 h. (+100 h.) indigo on blue 25 25
419. 31. 60 h. (+120 h.) olive on blue 80 80
420. 35. 80 h. (+160 h.) red .. 25 25
421. 1 k. (+2 k.) brown .. 30 30
422. 2 k. (+4 k.) blue .. 25 25
423. 34. 2½ k. (+5 k.) brown .. 30 30
424. 3 k. (+6 k.) grn. & bl. 30 30
425. 4 k. (+8 k.) violet and red 40 40
426. 5 k. (+10 k.) blue .. 50 50
427. 7½ k. (+15 k.) green 50 50
428. 10 k. (+20 k.) red and green 45 45
429. 20 k. (+40 k.) orange and lilac 50 50

The plebiscite was to decide whether Carinthia should be part of Austria or Yugoslavia, and the premium was for a fund to promote a vote in favour of remaining in Austria. The result was a vote for Austria.

1921. Charity. Optd. **Hochwasser 1920.**
430. 32. 5 h. (+10 h.) grey on yellow 15 20
431. 10 h. (+20 h.) brown .. 15 20
432. 31. 15 h. (+30 h.) grey .. 15 20
433. 33. 20 h. (+40 h.) green on yellow 15 20
434. 31. 25 h. (+50 h.) blue on yellow 15 20
435. 33. 30 h. (+60 h.) purple on blue 15 20
436. 40 h. (+80 h.) brown on red 25 25
437. 50 h. (+100 h.) green on blue 70 80
438. 31. 60 h. (+120 h.) purple on yellow 15 20
439. 35. 80 h. (+160 h.) blue .. 15 20
440. 1 k. (+2 k.) orge. on bl. 40 40
441. 1½ k. (+3 k.) green on yellow 15 20
442. 2 k. (+4 k.) brown .. 15 20
443. 34. 2½ k. (+5 k.) blue .. 20 25
444. 3 k. (+6 k.) red & grn. 20 25
445. 4 k. (+8 k.) brn. & lilac 50 60
446. 5 k. (+10 k.) green .. 25 25
447. 7½ k. (+15 k.) red .. 25 25
448. 10 k. (+20 k.) grn. & bl. 25 25
449. 20 k. (+40 k.) purple and red 40 45

36. Pincers and Hammer. 37. Ear of Corn.

1922.
461. 37. ½ k. bistre 5 12
462. 36. 1 k. brown 5 5
463. 2 k. blue 5 5
464. 37. 2½ k. brown 5 5
465. 36. 4 k. purple 5 15
466. 5 k. green 5 5
467. 37. 7½ k. violet 5 5
468. 36. 10 k. claret 5 5
469. 37. 12½ k. green 5 5
470. 15 k. blue-green .. 5 5
471. 20 k. blue 5 5
472. 25 k. claret 5 5
473. 36. 30 k. grey 5 5
474. 45 k. red 5 5
475. 50 k. brown 5 5
476. 60 k. green 5 5
477. 75 k. blue 5 5
478. 80 k. yellow 5 5
479. 37. 100 k. grey 5 5
480. 120 k. brown 5 5
481. 150 k. orange 5 5
482. 160 k. green 5 5
483. 180 k. red 5 5
484. 200 k. pink 5 5
485. 240 k. violet 5 5
486. 300 k. blue 5 5
487. 400 k. green 25 5
488. 500 k. yellow 5 5
489. 600 k. slate 5 5
490. 700 k. brown 10 5
491. 800 k. violet 20 40
492. 36. 1000 k. mauve 12 5
493. 1200 k. red 8 5
494. 1500 k. orange 25 5
495. 1600 k. slate 30 20
496. 2000 k. blue .. .. 1·00 12
497. 3000 k. blue .. .. 2·75 25
498. 4000 k. blue on blue .. 1·25 30

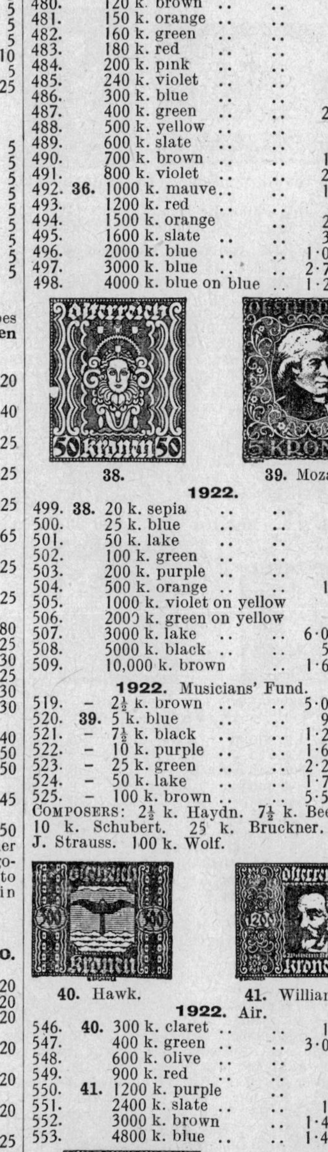

38. 39. Mozart.

1922.
499. 38. 20 k. sepia 5 5
500. 25 k. blue 5 5
501. 50 k. lake 5 5
502. 100 k. green 5 5
503. 200 k. purple 5 5
504. 500 k. orange 10 15
505. 1000 k. violet on yellow 5 5
506. 2000 k. green on yellow 8 5
507. 3000 k. lake .. .. 6·00 10
508. 5000 k. black 50 35
509. 10,000 k. brown .. 1·60 1·50

1922. Musicians' Fund.
519. – 2½ k. brown .. .. 5·00 4·25
520. 39. 5 k. blue 90 80
521. – 7½ k. black .. .. 1·25 95
522. – 10 k. purple .. .. 1·60 1·25
523. – 25 k. green .. .. 2·25 2·10
524. – 50 k. lake .. .. 1·75 1·50
525. – 100 k. brown .. .. 5·50 4·25
COMPOSERS: 2½ k. Haydn. 7½ k. Beethoven. 10 k. Schubert. 25 k. Bruckner. 50 k. J. Strauss. 100 k. Wolf.

40. Hawk. 41. William Kress.

1922. Air.
546. 40. 300 k. claret 12 15
547. 400 k. green .. .. 3·00 3·25
548. 600 k. olive 8 10
549. 900 k. red 8 10
550. 41. 1200 k. purple 8 12
551. 2400 k. slate 10 12
552. 3000 k. brown .. .. 1·40 1·50
553. 4800 k. blue .. .. 1·40 1·50

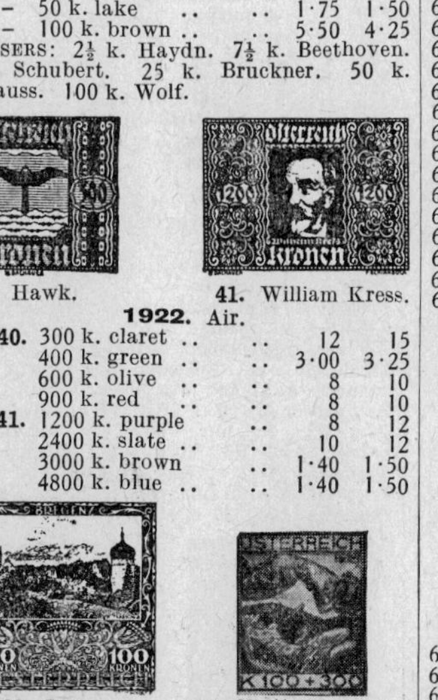

42. Bregenz. 43. "Art the Comforter".

1923. Artists' Charity Fund.
554. 42. 100 k. green .. .. 3·00 2·10
555. – 120 k. blue .. .. 2·50 2·00
556. – 160 k. purple .. .. 2·50 2·00
557. – 180 k. claret .. .. 2·50 2·00

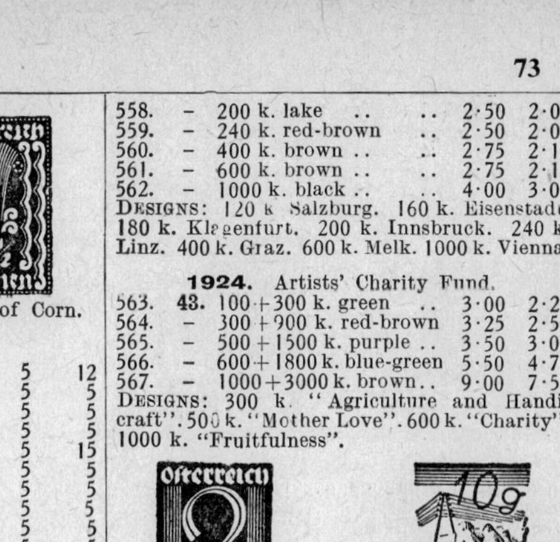

558. – 200 k. lake .. .. 2·50 2·00
559. – 240 k. red-brown .. 2·50 2·00
560. – 400 k. brown .. .. 2·75 2·10
561. – 600 k. brown .. .. 2·75 2·10
562. – 1000 k. black .. .. 4·00 3·00
DESIGNS: 120 k. Salzburg. 160 k. Eisenstadt. 180 k. Klagenfurt. 200 k. Innsbruck. 240 k. Linz. 400 k. Graz. 600 k. Melk. 1000 k. Vienna.

1924. Artists' Charity Fund.
563. 43. 100+300 k. green .. 3·00 2·25
564. – 300+900 k. red-brown 3·25 2·50
565. – 500+1500 k. purple .. 3·50 3·00
566. – 600+1800 k. blue-green 5·50 4·75
567. – 1000+3000 k. brown .. 9·00 7·50
DESIGNS: 300 k. "Agriculture and Handicraft". 500 k. "Mother Love". 600 k. "Charity". 1000 k. "Fruitfulness".

45.

46. Plains.

47. Eagle on Mountains.

48. Minorite Church, Vienna.

1925.
568. 45. 1 g. grey 30 5
569. 2 g. claret 45 5
570. 3 g. red 50 5
571. 4 g. blue 85 5
572. 5 g. orange .. .. 1·90 5
573. 6 g. blue .. .. 1·50 5
574. 7 g. brown .. .. 1·50 5
575. 8 g. green .. .. 6·50 5
576. 46. 10 g. orange 40 5
577. 15 g. claret 40 5
578. 16 g. blue 40 5
579. 18 g. olive 65 15
580. 47. 20 g. violet 50 5
581. 24 g. red 55 15
582. 30 g. brown 50 5
583. 40 g. blue 60 5
584. 45 g. brown 90 5
585. 50 g. grey .. .. 1·25 8
586. 80 g. blue .. .. 3·50 2·00
587. 48. 1 s. green .. .. 13·00 20·00
588. 2 s. claret .. .. 5·00 2·50

49. Airman.

50. De Havilland "D.H. 34" and Bird.

1925. Air.
616. 49. 2 g. brown 50 20
617. 5 g. red 20 10
618. 6 g. blue 95 60
619. 8 g. green 95 50
620. 50. 10 g. orange .. .. 1·40 65
621. 49. 10 g. orange .. .. 1·00 60
622. 50. 15 g. lake 45 25
623. 49. 15 g. claret 70 45
624. 20 g. brown .. .. 8·50 3·00
625. 25 g. violet .. .. 3·25 2·75
626. 50. 30 g. purple 85 55
627. 49. 30 g. bistre .. .. 7·00 3·75
628. 50. 50 g. slate 75 55
629. 49. 50 g. blue .. .. 16·00 7·00
630. 80 g. green .. .. 1·75 1·25
631. 50. 1 s. blue .. .. 2·00 1·60
632. 2 s. green .. .. 1·50 1·25
633. 3 s. red-brown .. .. 38·00 30·00
634. 5 s. blue .. .. 9·00 8·00
635. 10 s. brown on grey .. 7·50 6·50

51. Siegfried and Dragon. 52. Dr. Michael Hainisch.

1926. Child Welfare. Scenes from the Nibelung Legend.
636. 51. 3+2 g. sepia 60 45
637. – 8+2 g. indigo 10 12
638. – 15+5 g. lake 10 12
639. – 20+5 g. olive 20 20
640. – 24+6 g. violet 20 20
641. – 40+10 g. brown .. 6·00 2·75
DESIGNS: 8 g. Gunther's voyage. 15 g. Kriemhild and Brunhild. 20 g. Hagen and the Rhine-maidens. 24 g. Rudiger and the Nibelungs. 40 g. Dietrich's fight with Hagen.

1928. 10th Anniv. of Republic, and War Orphans and Invalid Children's Fund.
642. 52. 10 g. (+10 g.) sepia .. 5·00 4·00
643. 15 g. (+15 g.) brown 5·00 4·00
644. 30 g. (+30 g.) black .. 5·00 4·00
645. 40 g. (+40 g.) blue .. 5·00 4·00

53. Gussing. 54. National Library, Vienna.

1929. Views. 25½×21½ mm.
646. 53. 10 g. orange .. .. 1·25 5
647. 10 g. bistre .. .. 1·10 5
648. – 15 g. plum 75 30
649. – 16 g. grey 25 5
650. – 18 g. blue-green .. 55 15
651. – 20 g. grey 60 5
653. – 24 g. lake .. .. 6·50 15
654. – 30 g. violet .. .. 5·00 5
655. – 40 g. blue .. .. 9·00 8
656. – 50 g. violet .. .. 38·00 8
657. – 60 g. olive .. .. 29·00 15
658. 54. 1 s. sepia .. .. 8·00 15
659. – 2 s. green .. .. 11·00 3·25
VIEWS—HORIZ. 15 g. Hochosterwitz. 16 g. 20 g. Durnstein. 18 g. Traunsee. 24 g. Salzburg. 30 g. Seewiesen. 40 g. Innsbruck. 50 g. Worthersee. 60 g. Hohenems. VERT. 2 s. St. Stephen's Cathedral, Vienna.

CONVENTION WIEN 1931
56. Pres. Wilhelm, Miklas. (57.)

1930. Anti-tuberculosis Fund.
660. 56. 10 g. brown .. .. 8·50 7·50
661. 20 g. red .. .. 8·50 7·50
662. 30 g. purple .. .. 8·50 7·50
663. 40 g. (+40 g.) blue .. 8·50 7·50
664. 50 g. (+50 g.) green .. 8·50 7·50
665. 1 s. (+1 s.) sepia .. 8·50 7·50

1930. Rotarian Congress. Optd. with T 57.
666. 53. 10 g. (+10 g.) bistre .. 28·00 23·00
667. – 20 g. (+20 g.) grey (No. 651) .. .. 28·00 23·00
668. – 30 g. (+30 g.) violet (No. 654) .. .. 28·00 23·00
669. – 40 g. (+40 g.) blue (No. 655) .. .. 28·00 23·00
670. – 50 g. (+50 g.) violet (No. 656) .. .. 28·00 23·00
671. 54. 1 s. (+1 s.) sepia .. 28·00 23·00

58. Johann Nestroy. 59. Gussing.

1931. Austrian Writers and Youth Unemployment Fund.
672. – 10 g. (+10 g.) purple .. 12·00 10·00
673. – 20 g. (+20 g.) grey .. 12·00 10·00
674. 58. 30 g. (+30 g.) red .. 12·00 10·00
675. – 40 g. (+40 g.) blue .. 12·00 10·00
676. – 50 g. (+50 g.) green .. 12·00 10·00
677. – 1 s. (+1 s.) brown .. 12·00 10·00
DESIGNS: 10 g. F. Raimund. 20 g. E. Grillparzer. 40 g. A. Stifter. 50 g. L. Anzengruber. 1 s. P. Rosegger.

1932. Designs as No. 646, etc. but size reduced to 20½×16 mm. as T 59.
678. 59. 10 g. brown .. .. 1·10 5
679. – 12 g. blue-green .. 1·90 5
680. – 18 g. blue-green .. 1·75 45
681. – 20 g. grey .. .. 1·40 5
682. – 24 g. lake .. .. 6·00 5
683. – 24 g. violet .. .. 3·00 5
684. – 30 g. violet .. .. 19·00 5
685. – 30 g. red .. .. 4·00 5
686. – 40 g. blue .. .. 22·00 40
687. – 40 g. violet .. .. 6·00 12
688. – 50 g. violet .. .. 25·00 12
689. – 50 g. blue .. .. 6·00 12
690. – 60 g. olive .. .. 65·00 75
691. – 64 g. olive .. .. 5·00 8
DESIGNS (new values): 12 g. Traunsee. 64 g. Hohenems.

60. Ignaz Seipel. 61. Hans Makart.

1932. Death of Dr. Seipel (Chancellor), and Ex-Servicemen's Fund.
692. 60. 50 g. (+50 g.) blue .. 13·00 12·00

1932. Austrian Painters.
693. – 12 g. (+12 g.) green .. 15·00 14·00
694. – 24 g. (+24 g.) lilac .. 13·00 12·00
695. – 30 g. (+30 g.) red .. 13·00 12·00
696. 61. 40 g. (+40 g.) grey .. 15·00 14·00
697. – 64 g. (+64 g.) sepia .. 15·00 14·00
698. – 1 s. (+1 s.) claret .. 22·00 18·00
DESIGNS: 12 g. F. G. Waldmuller. 24 g. Von Schwind. 30 g. Alt. 64 g. Klimt. 1 s. A. Egger-Lienz.

62. The Climb.

1933. Int. Ski Championship Fund.
699. 62. 12 g. (+12 g.) green .. 6·50 5·00
700. – 24 g. (+24 g.) violet .. 85·00 60·00
701. – 30 g. (+30 g.) red .. 12·00 9·00
702. – 50 g. (+50 g.) blue .. 85·00 55·00
DESIGNS: 24 g. Start. 30 g. Race. 50 g. Ski-jump.

63. " The Honeymoon ". 64. John Sobieski.

1933. Int. Philatelic Exn. Vienna (WIPA).
703. 63. 50 g. (+50 g.) blue .. £140 £120

1933. 250th Anniv. of Relief of Vienna. Inscr. 1683 "1933".
706. – 12 g. (+12 g.) green .. 23·00 18·00
707. – 24 g. (+24 g.) violet .. 22·00 16·00
708. – 30 g. (+30 g.) scarlet .. 22·00 16·00
709. 64. 40 g. (+40 g.) grey-blk. 32·00 25·00
710. – 50 g. (+50 g.) ultram... 22·00 16·00
711. – 64 g. (+64 g.) brown .. 27·00 21·00
DESIGNS—VERT. 12 g. Vienna in 1683. 24 g. Marco d'Aviano. 30 g. Count von Starhemberg. 50 g. Charles of Lorraine. 64 g. Burgomaster Leibenberg.

1933. Winter Relief Fund. Surch. **Winterhilfe** or **WINTERHILFE** and premium.
712. 45. 5 g. +2 g. green .. 30 25
713. 59. 12 g. +3 g. blue .. 30 25
714. 24 g. +6 g. orange .. 30 25
715. 54. 1 s. +50 g. red .. 28·00 24·00

65. Burgenland. 66. Tyrol.

1934.
716. 65. 1 g. violet 5 5
717. – 3 g. red 5 5
718. – 4 g. olive-green .. 8 5
719. – 5 g. purple 8 5
721. – 6 g. blue 20 8
722. – 8 g. green 10 5
723. – 12 g. brown 10 5
724. – 20 g. yellow-brown .. 12 5
725. – 24 g. greenish blue .. 12 5
726. – 25 g. violet 20 8
727. – 30 g. claret 15 5
728. – 35 g. red 35 15
729. 66. 40 g. grey 40 5
730. – 45 g. chestnut 30 5
731. – 60 g. blue 65 10
732. – 64 g. brown 70 5
733. – 1 s. purple 70 15
735. – 2 s. green .. .. 2·25 2·00
736. – 3 s. orange .. .. 12·00 8·50
737. – 5 s. black .. .. 25·00 22·00
DESIGNS: Austrian costumes of the districts named—As T 65: 4 g., 5 g. Carinthia. 6 g., 8 g. Lower Austria. 12 g., 20 g. Upper Austria. 24 g., 25 g. Salzburg. 30 g., 35 g. Styria (Steiermark). As T 66: 60 g., 64 g. Vorarlberg. 1 s. Vienna. 2 s. Army officer and soldiers. LARGER: 3 s. Harvesters (30×30 mm.). 5 s. Builders (29×31 mm.).

67. Chancellor Dollfuss. 68. A. Pilgram.

1934. Dollfuss Mourning Stamps.
738. 67. 24 g. black 50 15
762. 24 g. blue 95 50

1934. Welfare Funds. Austrian Architects.
739. 68. 12 g. (+12 g.) black .. 9·50 8·00
740. – 24 g. (+24 g.) violet 9·50 8·00
741. – 30 g. (+30 g.) red .. 9·50 8·00
742. – 40 g. (+40 g.) brown 9·50 8·00
743. – 60 g. (+60 g.) blue .. 9·50 8·00
744. – 64 g. (+64 g.) green 9·50 8·00
DESIGNS: 24 g. Fischer von Erlach. 30 g. J. Prandtauer. 40 g. A. von Siccardsburg and E. Van der Null. 60 g. H. von Ferstel. 64 g. Otto Wagner.

69. " Mother and Child ".

1935. Mothers' Day.
745. 69. 24 g. blue 50 15

70. Maria Worth. 71. Zugspitze Aerial Railway.

1935. Air. Designs as T 70 and 71 (schilling values).
763. – 5 g. purple 15 8
764. 70. 10 g. orange 5 5
765. – 15 g. green .. .. 1·00 80
766. – 20 g. blue 12 12
767. – 25 g. purple 12 12
768. – 30 g. red 12 12
769. – 40 g. olive-green .. 15 15
770. – 50 g. blue 15 15
771. – 60 g. sepia 40 30
772. – 80 g. brown 35 25
773. – 1 s. red 45 25
774. – 2 s. olive-green .. 2·25 2·00
775. – 3 s. brown .. .. 11·00 9·00
776. 71. 5 s. green .. .. 3·75 3·50
777. – 10 s. blue .. .. 48·00 45·00
DESIGNS: Aeroplane and views. 5 g. Gussing Castle. 15 g. Durnstein. 20 g. Hallstatt. 25 g. Salzburg. 30 g. Dachstein Mts. 40 g. Wettersee. 50 g. Stuben am Arlberg. 60 g. St. Stephen's Cathedral, Vienna. 80 g. Minorite Church, Vienna. 1s. River Danube. 2 s. Tauern railway viaduct. 3 s. Grossglockner mountain roadway. 10 s. Glider and sailing boats on the Attersee.

1935. Winter Relief Fund. Designs as T 65/6 surch. **Winterhilfe** or **WINTERHILFE** and premium.
778. 65. 5 g. +2 g. green .. 30 25
779. 12 g. +3 g. blue .. 65 35
780. 24 g. +6 g. brown .. 40 25
781. 66. 1 s. +50 g. red .. 25·00 21·00

72. Prince Eugene of Savoy. 73. Slalom Course Skier.

1935. Welfare Funds. Austrian Heroes.
782. 72. 12 g. (+12 g.) brown .. 9·50 7·50
783. – 24 g. (+24 g.) green .. 9·50 7·50
784. – 30 g. (+30 g.) maroon 9·50 7·50
785. – 40 g. (+40 g.) blue .. 9·50 7·50
786. – 60 g. (+60 g.) blue .. 9·50 7·50
787. – 64 g. (+64 g.) violet .. 9·50 7·50
PORTRAITS: 24 g. Baron von Laudon. 30 g. Archduke Charles. 40 g. Field-Marshal Radetzky. 60 g. Vice-Admiral von Tegetthoff. 64 g. Field-Marshal Conrad von Hotzendorff.

1936. Int. Ski Championship Fund. Inscr. " WETTKAMPFE 1936 ".
788. 73. 12 g. (+12 g.) green .. 2·40 1·90
789. – 24 g. (+24 g.) violet .. 3·50 2·75
790. – 35 g. (+35 g.) red .. 27·00 22·00
791. – 60 g. (+60 g.) blue .. 27·00 22·00
DESIGNS: 24 g. Skier. 35 g. Woman Skier. 60 g. Maria-Theresienstrasse, Innsbruck.

74. Madonna and Child.

1936. Mothers' Day.
792. 74. 24 g. blue 30 15

75. Chancellor Dollfuss. 76. " St. Martin sharing cloak ".

1936.
793. 75. 10 s. blue £500 £400

1936. Winter Relief Fund. Inscr. " WINTERHILFE 1936/37 ".
794. 76. 5 g. +2 g. green .. 20 20
795. – 12 g. +3 g. violet .. 20 20
796. – 24 g. +6 g. blue .. 20 20
797. – 1 s. +1 s. red .. .. 7·50 7·00
DESIGNS: 12 g. " Healing the sick ". 24 g. " St. Elizabeth feeding the hungry ". 1 s. " Warming the poor ".

77. J. Ressel. 78. Mother and Child.

79. The " Maria Anna ". 80. " Child Welfare ".

1936. Welfare Funds. Austrian Inventors.
798. 77. 12 g. (+12 g.) brown .. 3·00 2·75
799. – 24 g. (+24 g.) violet .. 3·00 2·75
800. – 30 g. (+30 g.) red .. 3·00 2·75
801. – 40 g. (+40 g.) black .. 3·00 2·75
802. – 60 g. (+60 g.) blue .. 3·00 2·75
803. – 64 g. (+64 g.) green .. 3·00 2·75
PORTRAITS: 24 g. Karl Ritter v. Ghega. 30 g. Josef Werndl. 40 g. Carl Freih. Auer von Welsbach. 60 g. Robert v. Lieben. 64 g. Viktor Kaplan.

1937. Mothers' Day.
804. 78. 24 g. red 25 15

1937. Danube Steam Navigation Co. Cent.
805. 79. 12 g. red 85 25
806. – 24 g. blue 85 20
807. – 64 g. green 50 20
STEAMBOATS: 24 g. Passenger steamer " Helios ". 64 g. Freighter " Oesterreich ".

1937. Winter Relief Fund. Inscr. " WINTERHILFE 1937 1938 "
808. 80. 5 g. + 2 g. green .. 15 15
809. – 12 g. + 3 g. brown .. 20 20
810. – 24 g. + 6 g. blue .. 15 15
811. – 1 s. + 1 s. red .. 4·00 3·25
DESIGNS: 12 g. " Feeding the Children ". 24 g. " Protecting the Aged ". 1 s. " Nursing the Sick."

81. " Austria ". 82. Dr. G. Van Swieten.

1937. Railway Centenary.
812. 81. 12 g. brown 10 5
813. – 25 g. violet 40 20
814. – 35 g. red .. .. 1·25 95
DESIGNS: 25 g. Modern steam locomotion. 35 g. Electric locomotion.

1937. Welfare Funds. Austrian Doctors.
815. 82. 5 g. (+5 g.) brown .. 2·40 2·00
816. – 8 g. (+8 g.) red .. 2·40 2·00
817. – 12 g. (+12 g.) brown .. 2·40 2·00
818. – 20 g. (+20 g.) green .. 2·40 2·00
819. – 24 g. (+24 g.) violet .. 2·40 2·00
820. – 30 g. (+30 g.) red .. 2·40 2·00
821. – 40 g. (+40 g.) olive .. 2·40 2·00
822. – 60 g. (+60 g.) blue .. 2·40 2·00
823. – 64 g. (+64 g.) purple .. 2·40 2·00
DESIGNS: 8 g. L. A. von Auenbrugg. 12 g. K. von Rokitansky. 20 g. J. Skoda. 25 g. F. von Hebra. 30 g. F. von Arit. 40 g. J. Hyrtl. 60 g. T. Billroth. 64 g. T. Meynert.

83. Nosegay and Signs of the Zodiac.

(83a.)

1937. Christmas Greetings.
824. **83.** 12 g. green 10 5
825. 24 g. red 10 5

The following stamps (Nos. 826 to 840 and 841 to 863) were issued in Vienna and Graz respectively. They were later replaced by two separate issues: a joint issue for the British French and American Zones of occupation (Nos. 906/22), and a separate issue for the Russian Zone (Nos. 868/90). No. 923 and onwards were for use throughout Austria.

1945. Hitler portrait stamps of Germany optd.
(a) Optd. **Osterreich** only.
826. **128.** 5 pf. green 5 5
827. 8 pf. red 5 5

(b) Optd. **Osterreich** and bar.
828. **128.** 6 pf. violet 5 5
829. 12 pf. red 5 5

1945. Stamps of Germany surch. **OSTERREICH** new value and single bar
830. **141.** 5 pf. on 12+88 pf. .. 35 40
831. 6 pf. on 6+14 pf. (No. 811) .. 6·00 6·00
832. **174.** 8 pf. on 42+108 pf. .. 90 1·00
833. – 12 pf. on 3+7 pf. (No. 810) .. 25 35

1945. 1941 and 1944 Hitler stamps of Germany optd. as T **83a.**
835. **128.** 5 pf. green 12 20
836. 6 pf. violet 10 15
837. 8 pf. red 8 20
838. 12 pf. red 10 15
839. 30 pf. olive .. .. 2·10 2·50
840. **179.** 42 pf. green .. .. 18·00 19·00

(83b.)

ILLUSTRATIONS
British Commonwealth and all overprints and surcharges are FULL SIZE.
Foreign Countries have been reduced to ¾-LINEAR

1945. 1941 and 1944 Hitler stamps of Germany optd. as T **83b.**
841. **128.** 1 pf. grey .. .. 1·25 1·50
842. 3 pf. brown .. .. 1·40 1·60
843. 4 pf. slate .. .. 6·00 6·50
844. 5 pf. green .. .. 1·25 1·40
845. 6 pf. violet 20 20
846. 8 pf. red 35 45
847. 10 pf. brown .. .. 1·25 1·50
848. 12 pf. red 20 30
849. 15 pf. red 45 60
850. 16 pf. green .. .. 9·50 10·00
851. 20 pf. blue .. .. 1·10 1·25
852. 24 pf. brown .. .. 10·00 12·00
853. 25 pf. blue .. .. 1·10 1·25
854. 30 pf. green .. .. 1·10 1·25
855. 40 pf. mauve .. .. 1·25 1·50
856. **179.** 42 pf. green .. .. 2·50 3·00
857. **128.** 50 pf. green .. .. 1·75 2·25
858. 60 pf. brown .. .. 2·40 2·75
859. 80 pf. blue .. .. 2·00 2·75
860. **137.** 1 m. green .. .. 8·50 9·50
861. 2 m. violet .. .. 9·00 9·50
862. 3 m. red .. .. 18·00 20·00
863. 5 m. blue £160 £170

84. New National Arms. **85.**

1945.
868. **84.** 3 pf. brown 5 5
869. 4 pf. blue 5 5
870. 5 pf. green 5 5
871. 6 pf. violet 5 5
872. 8 pf. orange 5 5
873. 10 pf. brown 5 5
874. 12 pf. red 5 5
875. 15 pf. orange 5 5
876. 16 pf. blue 5 5
877. **84.** 20 pf. blue 5 5
878. 24 pf. orange 5 5
879. 25 pf. blue 5 5
880. 30 pf. green 5 5
881. 38 pf. blue 5 5
882. 40 pf. purple 5 5
883. 42 pf. grey 5 5
884. 50 pf. green 5 5
885. 60 pf. red 5 5
886. 80 pf. violet 5 5
887. **85.** 1 rm. green 5 12
888. 2 rm. violet 8 15
889. 3 rm. purple 8 20
890. 5 rm. brown 10 20
Nos. 877/890 are larger (24×28½ mm.).

86. Allegorical of the Home Land.

87. Posthorn.

1945. Charity.
905. **86.** 1 s.+10 s. green .. 60 65

1945.
906. **87.** 1 g. blue 5 5
907. 3 g. orange 5 5
908. 4 g. brown 5 5
909. 5 g. green 5 5
910. 6 g. purple 5 5
911. 8 g. red 5 5
912. 10 g. grey 5 5
913. 12 g. brown 5 5
914. 15 g. red 5 5
915. 20 g. brown 5 5
916. 25 g. blue 5 5
917. 30 g. mauve 5 5
918. 40 g. blue 5 5
919. 60 g. olive 5 5
920. 1 s. violet 5 8
921. 2 s. yellow 12 25
922. 5 s. blue 15 25

88. Salzburg.

89. Durnstein.

1945. Views as T **88/89.**
923. – 3 g. blue (Lermoos) .. 5 5
924. – 4 g. orange (Iron-ore mine) .. 5 5
925. – 5 g. red (Leopoldsberg) 5 5
926. **88.** 6 g. green 5 5
927. – 8 g. brown (Vienna) .. 5 5
928. – 8 g. purple (Park, Vienna) 5 5
929. – 8 g. green (Park, Vienna) 5 5
930. – 10 g. green (Hochosterwitz) .. 5 5
931. – 10 g. purple (Hochosterwitz) .. 5 5
932. – 12 g. brown (Schafberg) 5 5
933. – 15 g. blue (Forchtenstein) .. 5 5
934. – 16 g. brown (Gesauseeingang) .. 5 5
935. – 20 g. blue (Gebhartsberg) .. 5 5
936. – 24 g. green (Holdrichsmuhle) .. 5 5
937. – 25 g. grey (Otztal) .. 5 5
938. – 30 g. red (Neusiedler Lake) .. 5 5
939. – 30 g. grey-blue (Neusiedler Lake) .. 5 5
940. – 35 g. red (Belvedere Palace) .. 5 5
941. – 38 g. olive (Langbath Lake) .. 5 5
942. – 40 g. grey (Mariazell) .. 5 5
943. – 42 g. brown (Traunstein) 5 5
944. – 45 g. blue (Burg Hartenstein) 12 20
945. – 50 g. blue (Silvretta peaks, Vorarlberg) .. 5 5
946. – 50 g. purple (Silvretta peaks, Vorarlberg) .. 15 10
947. – 60 g. violet (Semmering) 5 5
948. – 60 g. purple (Semmering) 1·10 95
949. – 70 g. blue (Badgastein) 8 8
950. – 80 g. brown (Kaisergebirge) 12 12
951. – 90 g. green (Shrine near Tragoss) .. 50 60
952. **89.** 1 s. brown 30 25
953. – 2 s. green (St. Christof) 1·25 1·25
954. – 3 s. green (Heiligenblut) 35 35
955. – 5 s. red (Schonbrunn Palace) 65 65
Nos. 935/51 are larger (23½ × 29 mm.).
See also Nos. 1072/86a and 1244.

1946. United Nations. No. 938 surch. with value, globe and **26 JUNI 1945/6.**
971. 30 g.+20 g. red .. 65 70

90. Dr. Karl Renner.

1946. Renner Government. 1st Anniv.
972. **90.** 1 s.+1 s. green .. 1·75 1·90
973. 2 s.+2 s. violet .. 1·75 1·90
974. 3 s.+3 s. purple .. 1·75 1·99
975. 5 s.+5 s. brown .. 1·75 1·90

91. Dagger and Map of Austria.

(**92.**)

1946. Anti-Fascist Exn.
977. **91.** 5 g.+3 g. sepia .. 40 40
978. – 6 g.+4 g. green .. 25 30
979. – 8 g.+6 g. orange .. 25 30
980. – 12 g.+12 g. blue .. 25 30
981. – 30 g.+30 g. violet .. 25 30
982. – 42 g.+42 g. brown .. 25 30
983. – 1 s.+1 s. red .. 35 35
984. – 2 s.+2 s. red .. 40 45

DESIGNS: 6 g. Broom. 8 g. St. Stephen's Cathedral in flames. 12 g. Hand and barbed wire. 30 g. Hand strangling snake. 42 g. Hammer and broken column. 1 s. Hand and Austrian flag. 2 s. Eagle and smoking Nazi emblem.

1946. Austro-Soviet Relations Congress. No. 932 optd. with Type **92.**
985. 12 g. brown 10 12

93. Mare and foal.

94. Ruprecht's Church, Vienna.

1946. Austria Prize Race Fund. Inscr. as in T **93.**
986. **93.** 16+16 g. red .. 1·75 1·90
987. – 24+24 g. violet .. 1·25 1·40
988. – 60+60 g. green .. 1·25 1·40
989. – 1+1 s. blue .. 1·25 1·40
990. – 2+2 s. brown .. 2·25 2·40

DESIGNS: 24 g. Two horses' heads. 60 g. Racehorse over hurdle. 1 s. Three horses racing. 2 s. Three horses' heads.

1946. 950th Anniv. of first recorded use of name "Osterreich"
991. **94.** 30 g.+70 g. red .. 25 30

95. Statue of Duke Rudolf.

96. Franz Grillparzer (Poet).

1946. St. Stephen's Cathedral Reconstruction Fund.
992. **95.** 3 g.+12 g. brown .. 15 15
993. – 5 g.+20 g. purple .. 15 15
994. – 6 g.+24 g. blue .. 15 15
995. – 8 g.+32 g. green .. 15 15
996. – 10 g.+40 g. blue .. 20 25
997. – 12 g.+48 g. violet .. 25 30
998. – 30 g.+1 s. 20 red .. 90 1·10
999. – 50 g.+1 s. 80 blue .. 1·25 1·40
1000. – 1 s.+5 s. purple .. 1·75 1·90
1001. – 2 s.+10 s. brown .. 2·75 3·00

DESIGNS—VERT. 5 g. Tomb of Frederick III. 6 g. Pulpit. 8 g. Statue of St. Stephen. 10 g. Statue of Madonna and Child. 12 g. Altar. 30 g. Organ. 50 g. Antony Pilgram. 1 s. North-east Tower. 2 s. South-west Spire.

1947. Famous Austrians.
1002. – 12 g. green 5 5
1003. **96.** 18 g. purple 5 5
1004. – 20 g. green 12 8
1005. – 40 g. brown .. .. 1·90 1·40
1006. – 40 g. green .. .. 3·25 3·00
1007. – 60 g. lake 15 10

PORTRAITS: 12 g. Schubert (composer). 20 g. Carl Michael Zieher (composer). 40 g. (No. 1005), Adalbert Stifter (poet). 40 g. (No. 1006), Anton Bruckner (composer). 60 g. Friedrich von Amerling (painter).

97. Harvesting.

98. Aeroplane over Hinterstoder.

1947. Vienna Fair.
1009. **97.** 3 g.+2 g. brown .. 25 30
1010. – 8 g.+2 g. green .. 25 30
1011. – 10 g.+5 g. slate .. 25 30
1012. – 12 g.+8 g. violet .. 25 30
1013. – 18 g.+12 g. olive .. 25 30
1014. – 30 g.+10 g. purple 25 30
1015. – 35 g.+15 g. red .. 25 30
1016. – 60 g.+20 g. blue .. 25 30

DESIGNS: 8 g. Logging. 10 g. Factory. 12 g. Pithead. 18 g. Oil wells. 30 g. Textile machinery. 35 g. Foundry. 60 g. Electric cables.

1947. Air.
1017. – 50 g. brown.. .. 12 15
1018. – 1 s. purple 15 20
1019. – 2 s. brown .. 25 30
1020. **98.** 3 s. brown .. .. 1·50 1·60
1021. – 4 s. green 85 95
1022. – 5 s. blue 85 95
1023. – 10 s. blue 50 60

DESIGNS: 50 g. Aeroplane over windmill at St. Andra. 1 s. Heidentor. 2 s. Gmund. 4 s. Pragraten. 5 s. Torsaule. 10 s. St. Charles Church, Vienna.

99. Beaker (15th cent.).

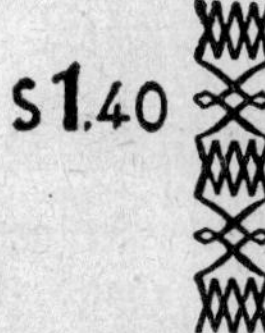

(**100.**)

1947. National Art Exn.
1024. **99.** 3 g.+2 g. brown .. 20 25
1025. – 8 g.+2 g. green .. 20 25
1026. – 10 g.+5 g. claret .. 20 25
1027. – 12 g.+8 g. violet .. 20 25
1028. – 18 g.+12 g. brown .. 20 25
1029. – 20 g.+10 g. violet .. 20 25
1030. – 30 g.+10 g. green .. 20 25
1031. – 35 g.+15 g. red .. 20 25
1032. – 48 g.+12 g. purple 20 25
1033. – 60 g.+20 g. blue .. 25 35

DESIGNS: 8 g. Statue of "Providence" (Donner). 10 g. Benedictine Monastery, Melk. 12 g. "Wife of Dr. Brante of Vienna". 18 g. "Children in a Window" (Waldmuller). 20 g. Belvedere Palace Gateway. 30 g. Figure of "Egeria" on fountain at Schonbrunn. 35 g. National Library, Vienna. 48 g. "Engraver at Work". 60 g. "Girl in Straw Hat" (Amerling).

1947. Nos. 934 and 941 such. as T **100.**
1069. **87.** 75 g. on 38 g. olive .. 12 15
1070. 1 s. 40 on 16 g. brown 5 5

101. Racehorse.

102. Prisoner-of-War.

1947. Vienna Prize Race.
1034. **101.** 60+20 g. blue 8 12

1947. Prisoners-of-War Relief Fund.
1063. **102.** 8 g.+2 g. green .. 8 10
1064. – 12 g.+8 g. brown .. 12 15
1065. – 18 g.+12 g. black .. 8 12
1066. – 35 g.+15 g. maroon 8 12
1067. – 60 g.+20 g. blue .. 8 12
1068. – 1 s.+40 g. brown .. 10 15

DESIGNS: 12 g. Letter from home. 18 g. Gruesome camp visitor. 35 g. Soldier and family reunited. 60 g. Industry beckons returned soldier. 1 s. Soldier sowing.

103. Globe and Tape Machine.

104. Sacred Olympic Flame.

1947. Telegraph Cent.
1071. 103. 40 g. violet 5 5

1947. Currency Revaluation. As T 88.
1072. 3 g. vermilion (Lermoos) 5 5
1073. 5 g. verm. (Leopoldsberg) 5 5
1074. 10 g. verm. (Hochosterwitz) 5 5
1075. 15 g. verm. (Forshtenstein) 65 50

As T 88 but larger (23½ × 29 mm.).
1076. 20 g. verm.(Gebhartsberg) 15 5
1077. 30 g. vermilion (Neusiedler Lake) 30 5
1078 40 g. verm. (Mariazell).. 30 5
1079. 50 g.verm.(Silvretta Peaks) 45 5
1080. 60 g. verm. (Semmering) 3·75 60
1081. 70 g. verm. (Badgastein) 1·60 5
1082. 80 g. verm. (Kaisergebirge) 1·90 5
1083. 90 g. vermilion (Wayside Shrine, Tragoss) .. 2·25 20

As T 89.
1084. 1 s. violet (Durnstein) .. 25 5
1085. 2 s. violet (St. Christof).. 40 5
1086. 3 s. violet (Heiligenblut) 4·50 55
1086a. 5 s. violet (Schonbrunn) 5·00 55
Nos. 1072/86a in new currency replaced previous issue at rate of 3 s. (old) = 1 s. (new).

1948. 5th Winter Olympic Games, St. Moritz. Entries Fund.
1087. 104. 1 s. + 50 g. blue .. 20 15

105. Bridge Reconstruction.

106. Violets.

1948. Reconstruction Fund.
1088. 105. 10 g. + 5 g. grey .. 15 12
1089. – 20 g. + 10 g. violet.. 15 12
1090. – 30 g. + 10 g. green.. 20 20
1091. – 40 g. + 20 g. olive .. 12 12
1092. – 45 g. + 20 g. blue .. 5 5
1093. – 60 g. + 30 g. lake .. 5 5
1094. – 75 g. + 35 g. purple 8 8
1095. – 80 g. + 40 g. purple 8 8
1096. – 1 s. + 50 g. blue .. 8 8
1097. – 1 s. 40 + 70 g. lake 20 20
DESIGNS (showing reconstruction): 20 g. Aqueduct. 30 g. Docks. 40 g. Quarry. 45 g. Railway. 60 g. Flats. 75 g. Factory. 80 g. Oil wells. 1 s. Mountain roadway. 1 s. 40, Parliament Building.

1948. Anti-T.B. Fund. Flowers in natural colours.
1098. 106. 10 g. + 5 g. violet .. 15 8
1099. – 20 g. + 10 g. green 5 5
1100. – 30 g. + 10 g. brown 2·25 1·50
1101. – 40 g. + 20 g. green 30 25
1102. – 45 g. + 20 g. purple 8 8
1103. – 60 g. + 30 g. lake .. 10 8
1104. – 75 g. + 35 g. green 10 8
1105. – 80 g. + 40 g. blue .. 20 20
1106. – 1 s. + 50 g. violet .. 15 15
1107. – 1 s. 40 + 70 g. olive.. 60 55
FLOWERS: 20 g. Anemone. 30 g. Crocus. 40 g. Primrose. 45 g. Cow-Bell. 60 g. Rhododendrom. 75 g. Wild rose. 80 g. Cyclamen 1 s. Gentian. 1 s. 40, "Edelweiss".

107. Voralberg Montafon.

1948. Provincial Costumes.
1108. – 3 g. grey 20 20
1109. – 5 g. green 5 5
1110. – 10 g. blue 5 5
1111. – 15 g. brown 25 5
1112. 107. 20 g. green 5 5
1113. – 25 g. brown 5 5
1114. – 30 g. claret .. .. 1·10 5
1115. – 30 g. violet 25 5
1116. – 40 g. violet .. .. 1·10 5
1117. – 40 g. green 10 5
1118. – 45 g. blue .. .. 1·10 12
1119. – 50 g. brown 35 5
1120. – 60 g. red 10 5
1121. – 70 g. green 10 5
1122. – 75 g. blue .. .. 1·75 12
1123. – 80 g. rose 20 5
1124. – 90 g. purple .. .. 12·00 5
1125. – 1 s. blue .. .. 2·50 5
1126. – 1 s. red .. .. 30·00 5
1127. – 1 s. green 10 5
1128. – 1 s. 20 violet .. 12 5
1129. – 1 s. 40 brown .. 1·25 8
1130. – 1 s. 45 red 55 5
1131. – 1 s. 50 blue 25 5
1132. – 1 s. 60 red 10 5
1133. – 1 s. 70 blue .. .. 1·00 15
1134. – 2 s. green 20 5
1135. – 2 s. 20 slate .. 2·50 5
1136. – 2 s. 40 blue 50 5
1137. – 2 s. 50 brown .. 80 20
1138. – 2 s. 70 brown.. .. 15 15
1139. – 3 s. lake 80 5
1140. – 3 s. 50 green .. 2·25 5
1141. – 4 s. 50 purple .. 25 25
1142. – 5 s. purple 50 8
1143. – 7 s. olive .. .. 2·50 70
1144. – 10 s. grey .. .. 20·00 2·50
DESIGNS: 3 g. "Tirol Inntal". 5 g. "Salzburg Pinzgau". 10 g., 75 g. "Steiermark Salzkammergut" (different designs). 15 g., "Burgenland Lutzmannsburg". 20 g. "Voralberg Montafon". 25 g., 1 s. 60, "Wien 1850" (two different designs). 30 g. (2) "Salzburg Pongau". 40 g. (2) "Wien 1840". 45 g. "Karnten Lesachtal". 50 g. "Vorarlberg Bregenzerwald". 60 g. "Karnten Lavanttal". 70 g. "Niederosterreich Wachau". 80 g. "Steiermark Ennstal". 90 g. "Steiermark Mittelsteier". 1 s. (3) "Tirol Pustertal". 1 s. 20, "Niederosterreich Wienerwald". 1 s. 40, "Oberosterreich Innviertel". 1 s. 45, "Wilten bei Innsbruck". 1 s. 50, "Wien 1853". 1 s. 70, "Ost Tirol Kals". 2 s. "Oberosterreich". 2 s. 20, "Ischl 1820". 2 s. 40, "Kitzbuhel". 2 s. 50 "Obersteiermark 1850". 2 s. 70. "Kleines Walsertal". 3 s. "Burgenland", 3 s. 50, "Niederosterreich 1850". 4 s. 50, "Gailtal". 5 s. "Zillertal". 7 s. "Steiermark Sulmtal". 10 s. (larger) "Wien, 1850".

108. "Kunstlerhaus".

109. Hans Makart.

1948. Creative Artists' Assn. 80th Anniv.
1145. 108. 20 g. + 10 g. green .. 3·00 2·50
1146. 109. 30 g. + 15 g. brown .. 1·10 1·00
1147. – 40 g. + 20 g. blue .. 1·10 1·00
1148. – 50 g. + 25 g. violet .. 3·00 2·50
1149. – 60 g. + 30 g. red .. 3·00 2·50
1150. – 1 s. + 50 g. blue .. 3·00 2·50
1151. – 1 s. 40 g. + 70 g. brown 7·50 7·00
PORTRAITS: 40 g. Kundmann. 50 g. Siccardsburg. 60 g. A. von Canon. 1 s. W. Unger. 1 s. 40 g. Friedr. Schmidt.

110. St. Rupert.

111. Pres. Renner.

1948. Salzburg Cathedral Reconstruction Fund.
1152. 110. 20 g. + 10 g. green .. 3·50 2·50
1153. – 30 g. + 15 g. brown .. 1·75 1·50
1154. – 40 g. + 20 g. green .. 1·75 1·50
1155. – 50 g. + 25 g. brown .. 30 25
1156. – 60 g. + 30 g. red .. 30 25
1157. – 80 g. + 40 g. purple .. 30 25
1158. – 1 s. + 50 g. blue .. 50 40
1159. – 1 s. 40 + 70 g. green 80 80
DESIGNS: 30, 40, 50, 80 g. Views of Salzburg Cathedral. 60 g. St. Peter's. 1 s. Cathedral and Fortress. 1s. 40, Madonna.

1948. 30th Anniv. of Republic.
1160. 111. 1 s. blue .. .. 1·60 90
See also No. 1333.

112. F. Gruber and J. Mohr.

113. Boy and Hare.

1948. Carol "Silent Night, Holy Night". 130th Anniv. of Composition.
1161. 112. 60 g. lake .. .. 3·75 3·00

1949. Child Welfare Fund.
1162. 113. 40 g. + 10 g. purple 7·50 7·00
1163. – 60 g. + 20 g. lake .. 7·50 7·00
1164. – 1 s. + 25 g. blue .. 7·50 7·00
1165. – 1 s. 40 + 35 g. green 8·00 7·50
DESIGNS: 60 g. Two girls and apples in boot. 1 s. Boy and birthday cake. 1 s. 40, Girl praying before candle.

114. Boy and Dove.

115. Johann Strauss.

1949. U.N. Int. Children's Emergency Fund.
1166. 114. 1 s. blue .. .. 2·10 80

1949. Johann Strauss, Junior (composer). 50th Death Anniv.
1167. 115. 1 s. blue .. .. 2·10 80

116. Esperanto Star.

117. St. Gebhard.

1949. Esperanto Congress, Vienna.
1168. 116. 20 g. green 80 40

1949. St. Gebhard (Bishop of Vorarlberg). Birth Millenary.
1169. 117. 30 g. violet .. .. 1·40 75

118. Seal of Duke Friedrich II, 1230.

119. Allegory of U.P.U.

1949. Prisoners-of-War Relief Fund. Arms.
1170. 118. 40 g. + 10 g. yellow and brown .. 4·25 3·25
1171. – 60 g. + 15 g. mauve and pink .. 3·50 3·25
1172. – 1 s. + 25 g. blue and red .. 3·50 3·25
1173. – 1 s. 60 + 40 g. pink and green .. 3·50 3·25
ARMS: 60 g. Princes of Austria, 1450. 1 s. Austria, 1600. 1 s. 60, Austria, 1945.

1949. Johann Strauss, the elder (composer). Death Cent. Portrait as T 115.
1174. 30 g. purple .. .. 1·60 1·50

1949. U.P.U. 75th Anniv. As T 119 inscr. "WELTPOSTVEREIN".
1175. 119. 40 g. green .. .. 1·75 1·10
1176. 60 g. lake .. .. 1·75 1·25
1177. 1 s. blue .. .. 4·50 3·75

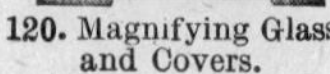

120. Magnifying Glass and Covers.

121. M. M. Daffinger.

1949. Stamp Day.
1206. 129. 60 g. + 15 g. lake .. 1·50 1·25

1949. Karl Millocker (composer). 50th Death Anniv. portrait as T 115 inscr. "1842-1899 KARL MILLOCKER".
1207. 1 s. blue .. .. 6·50 5·50

1950. Moritz Daffinger (painter). 160th Birth Anniv.
1208. 121. 60 g. lake .. .. 3·75 2·75

122. Andreas Hofer.

1950. Andreas Hofer (Tirolese patriot). 140th Death Anniv.
1209. 122. 60 g. violet .. .. 6·50 5·00

123. Reproduction of T 1.

124. Arms of Austria and Carinthia.

1950. Austrian Stamp Centenary.
1210. 123. 1 s. black on yellow .. 1·10 50

1950. J. Madersperger (sewing machine inventor). Death Cent. Portrait as T 121 inscr. "1768 1850".
1211. 60 g. violet .. .. 2·75 1·60

1950. Carinthian Plebiscite. 30th Anniv.
1212. 124. 60 g. + 15 g. grn. & brn. 16·00 12·00
1213. – 1 s. + 25 g. red .. 17·00 12·00
1214. – 1 s. 70 + 40 g. blue.. 18·00 14·00
DESIGNS: 1 s. Carinthian waving Austrian flag. 1 s. 70, Ballot box.

125. Rooks.

126. Philatelist.

1950. Air.
1215. 125. 60 g. violet 90 80
1216. – 1 s. violet (Swallows) 10·00 6·50
1217. – 2 s. blue (Gulls) .. 6·50 2·75
1218. – 3 s. blue-green (Cormorants) .. .. 65·00 40·00
1219. – 5 s. choc. (Buzzard) 60·00 40·00
1220. – 10 s. purple (Heron) 26·00 12·00
1221. – 20 s. sepia (Eagle) .. 5·50 1·50

1950. Stamp Day.
1222. 126. 60 g. + 15 g. green 5·00 4·00

1950. Alexander Girardi (actor). Birth Cent. Portrait as T 121 inscr. "1850 1918".
1223. 30 g. blue .. .. 1·10 45

127. Dr. Renner.

128. Miner.

1951. Death of President Karl Renner.
1224. 127. 1 s. black on lemon 1·25 15

1951. Reconstruction Fund. Inscr. "WIEDERAUFBAU".
1225. 128. 40 g. + 10 g. purple.. 7·00 6·50
1226. – 60 g. + 15 g. green .. 7·00 5·50
1227. – 1 s. + 25 g. brown .. 7·50 7·00
1228. – 1 s. 70 + 40 g. blue .. 7·50 7·00
DESIGNS: 60 g. Bricklayer. 1 s. Bridgebuilder. 1 s. 70, Telegraph engineer.

1951. Joseph Lanner (composer). 150th Birth Anniv. As T 115 but portrait of Lanner inscr. "1801 1843".
1229. 60 g. green .. 2·00 60

129. M. J. Schmidt.

130. Scout Badge.

1951. Schmidt (painter). 150th Death Anniv.
1230. **129.** 1 s. brown .. .. 3·00 1·60

1951. Boy Scout Jamboree.
1231. **130.** 1 s. red, yellow & green 2·75 1·60

131. W. Kienzl. **132.** Olympic Emblem.

1951. Kienzl (composer). 10th Death Anniv.
1232. **131.** 1 s. 50 blue .. .. 2·10 60
See also Nos. 1234, 1235, 1239, 1243 and 1253.

1952. 6th Winter Olympic Games, Oslo.
1233. **132.** 2 s. 40+60 g. green 10·00 9·00

1952. Karl Ritter von Ghega (engineer). 150th Birth Anniv. As T **131** but portrait of Von Ghega inscr. " 1802–1860 ".
1234. 1 s. green .. .. 3·00 85

1952. Schrammel (composer). Birth Cent. As T **131** but portrait of Schrammel inscr. " 1852–1895 ".
1235. 1 s. 50 g. blue .. 3·00 65

133. Cupid and Letter. **134.** Breakfast Pavilion.

1952. Stamp Day.
1236. **133.** 1 s. 50 g.+35 g. purple 11·00 10·00

1952. Schonbrunn Menagerie. Bicent.
1237. **134.** 1 s. 50 green .. .. 3·00 60

135. **136.**

1952. Int. Union of Socialist Youth Camp, Vienna.
1238. **135.** 1 s. 50 blue .. .. 3·25 50

1952. Lenau (writer). 150th Birth Anniv. As T **131** but portrait inscr. " NIKOLAUS LENAU 1802–1850 ".
1239. 1 s. green .. .. 3·25 75

1952. Int. Children's Correspondence.
1240. **136.** 2 s. 40 violet .. 6·00 1·75

137. " Christus Pantocrator" (sculpture). **138.** Hugo Wolf.

1952. Austrian Catholics' Day.
1241. **137.** 1 s.+25 g. olive .. 6·00 5·50

1953. Wolf (composer). 50th Death Anniv.
1242. **138.** 1 s. 50 blue .. .. 3·75 50

1953. President Korner's 80th Birthday. As T **131** but portrait of Korner.
1243. 1 s. 50 blue .. .. 3·50 45
For 1 s. 50 black, see No. 1288.

1953. Austrian Trade Union Movement. 60th Anniv. As No. 955 (colour changed) surch. **GEWERKSCHAFTS BEWEGUNG 60 JAHRE 1 s. + 25 g.**
1244. 1 s.+25 on 5 s. blue .. 2·00 1·90

139. Linz National Theatre. **140.** Meeting-house, Steyr.

1953. Linz National Theatre. 150th Anniv.
1245. **139.** 1 s. 50 slate .. .. 3·75 70

1953. Vienna Evangelical School Rebuilding Fund.
1246. **140.** 70 g.+15 g. purple .. 8 8
1247. – 1 s.+25 g. blue .. 12 10
1248. – 1 s. 50+40 g. choc. 20 20
1249. – 2 s. 40+60 g. green 1·90 1·90
1250. – 3 s.+75 g. lilac .. 4·00 3·75
DESIGNS: 1 s. J. Kepler (astronomer). 1 s. 50, Lutheran Bible, 1534. 2 s. 40, T. von Hansen (architect). 3 s. School after reconstruction.

141. Child and Christmas Tree. **142.**

1953. Christmas.
1251. **141.** 1 s. green .. .. 1·00 12
1266. 1 s. blue .. .. 2·00 25

1953. Stamp Day.
1252. **142.** 1 s.+25 g. chocolate 1·90 1·75

1954. M. von Schwind (painter). 150th Birth Anniv. As T **131** but portrait of Von Schwind.
1253. 1 s. 50 lilac .. .. 5·00 90

143. Baron K. von Rokitansky. **144.** St. Christof.

1954. Von Rokitansky (anatomist). 150th Birth Anniv.
1254. **143.** 1 s. 50 violet .. 5 50 1·10
See also No. 1264.

1954. Avalanche Fund.
1255. **144.** 1 s.+20 g. blue .. 15 5

145. Surgeon with Microscope. **146.** Esperanto Star.

1954. Health Service Fund.
1256. – 30 g.+10 g. violet .. 75 55
1257. **145.** 70 g.+15 g. brown .. 12 8
1258. – 1 s.+25 g. blue .. 15 12
1259. – 1 s. 45+35 g. green 20 15
1260. – 1 s. 50+35 g. red .. 2·50 2·50
1261. – 2 s. 40+60 g. maroon 3·25 3·25
DESIGNS: 30 g. Boy patient and sun-ray lamp. 1 s. Mother and children. 1 s. 45, Operating theatre. 1 s. 50, Baby on scales. 2 s. 40, Red Cross nurse and ambulance.

1954. Esperanto Movement in Austria. 50th Anniv.
1262. **146.** 1 s. green & olive-brn. 2·50 12

147. J. M. Rottmayr von Rosenbrunn. **148.** Organ, Church of St. Florian.

1954. Von Rosenbrunn (painter). Birth Tercent.
1263. **147.** 1 s. green .. .. 5·00 1·10

1954. Carl Auer-Welsbach (inventor). 25th Death Anniv. As T **143** but portrait of Welsbach.
1264. 1 s. 50 blue .. .. 10·00 90

1954. 2nd Int. Congress of Catholic Church Music, Vienna.
1265. **148.** 1 s. brown .. .. 1·90 15

149. " Ulmer Ordinari " (18th Century River-boat).

1954. Stamp Day.
1267. **149.** 1 s.+25 g. green .. 2·50 2·50

150. Arms of Austria and Newspapers.

1954. State Ptg. Wks. 150th Anniv. and "Wiener Zeitung" (newspaper). 250th Anniv.
1268. **150.** 1 s. black & vermilion 1·60 15

151. " Freedom ".

1955. 10th Anniv. of Re-establishment of Austrian Republic. Inscr. " 1945 1955 ".
1269. – 70 g. purple 60 10
1270. – 1 s. blue .. .. 3·75 8
1271. **151.** 1 s. 45 red .. .. 5·50 1·25
1272. – 1 s. 50 brown .. 10·00 10
1273. – 2 s. 40 green .. .. 4·50 2·40
DESIGNS—HORIZ. 70 g. Parliament Buildings. 1 s. Western Railway Terminus. 1 s. 50, Modern houses. 2 s. 40, Limberg Dam.

1955. Austrian State Treaty. As No. 920 (colour changed) optd. **STAATSVERTRAG 1955.**
1274. **86.** 2 s. slate .. .. 1·25 20

152. "Strength through Unity".

1955. 4th World Trades' Union Congress, Vienna.
1275. **152.** 1 s. blue .. .. 1·25 1·25

153. " Return to Work ".

1955. Returned Prisoners of War Relief Fund.
1276. **153.** 1 s.+25 g. brown .. 1·25 1·25

154. Burgtheater, Vienna.

1955. Re-opening of Burgtheater and State Opera House, Vienna.
1277. **154.** 1 s. 50 brown .. 2·10 8
1278. – 2 s. 40 blue (Opera House) .. .. 2·25 1·10

155. Globe and Flags. **156.** Stamp Collector.

1955. 10th Anniv. of U.N.
1279. **155.** 2 s. 40 green .. .. 4·50 1·25

1955. Stamp Day.
1280. **156.** 1 s.+25 g. brown .. 2·10 1·90

157. Mozart. **158.**

1956. Mozart's Birth Bicent.
1281. **157.** 2 s. 40 blue .. .. 2·00 45

1956. Admission of Austria into U.N.
1282. **158.** 2 s. 40 brown .. 4·25 1·00

159. **160.** Vienna and Five New Towns.

1956. 5th World Power Conference, Vienna.
1283. **159.** 2 s. 40 blue .. .. 5·50 1·75

1956. 23rd Int. Town Planning Congress.
1284. **160.** 1 s. 45 red, blk. & grn. 2·50 50

161. J. B. Fischer von Erlach. **162.** "Stamp Day".

1956. Fischer von Erlach (architect). Birth Tercent.
1285. **161.** 1 s. 50 brown .. 1·10 1·00

1956. Stamp Day.
1286. **162.** 1 s.+25 g. red .. 1·75 1·75

1956. Hungarian Relief Fund. As No. 1173, colours changed, surch. **1956 UNGARNHILFE** and value.
1287. 1 s. 50+50 g. on 1 s. 60 +40 g. red and grey 25 15

1957. Death of President Korner. As No. 1243 but colour changed.
1288. 1 s. 50 black .. .. 1·00 95

163. Dr. J. Wagner Jauregg. **164.** Anton Wildgans.

1957. Wagner Jauregg (psychiatrist) Birth Cent.
1289. **163.** 2 s. 40 chocolate .. 2·40 1·10

1957. Anton Wildgans (poet). 25th Death Anniv.
1290. **164.** 1 s. blue 45 12

165. Early and Modern Postal Coaches.

1957. Postal Coach Service. 50th Anniv.
1291. 165. 1 s. black on yellow .. 30 12

166. Mt. Gasherbrum II. 167. Mariazell Basilica.

1957. Austrian Himalaya-Karakorum Expedition, 1956.
1293. 166. 1 s. 50 blue 45 10

1957. Buildings.

1295.	–	20 g. purple	5	5
1296.	–	30 g. myrtle	5	5
1297.	–	40 g. red	5	5
1298.	–	50 g. slate	5	5
1324.	–	50 g. grey (smaller) ..	5	5
1299.	–	60 g. brown	5	5
1300.	–	70 g. blue	5	5
1301.	–	80 g. brown	5	5
1294.	167.	1 s. deep brown ..	70	5
1302.		1 s. light brown ..	25	5
1325.		1 s. brown (smaller)	5	5
1303.	–	1 s. sepia	5	5
1304.	–	1 s. 20 mauve ..	8	5
1305.	–	1 s. 30 brown ..	10	5
1306.	–	1 s. 40 turquoise ..	10	5
1307.	–	1 s. 50 claret ..	20	5
1326.	–	1 s. 50 claret (smaller)	12	10
1308.	–	1 s. 80 blue	12	5
1309.	–	2 s. blue	2·50	5
1310.	–	2 s. blue	20	5
1311.	–	2 s. 20 green.. ..	15	5
1312.	–	2 s. 50 violet ..	25	8
1313.	–	3 s. ultramarine ..	25	5
1314.	–	3 s. 40 green.. ..	25	20
1315.	–	3 s. 50 cerise.. ..	20	5
1316.	–	4 s. mauve	40	5
1317.	–	4 s. 50 green.. ..	35	20
1318.	–	5 s. 50 grey	35	12
1319.	–	6 s. violet	70	5
1320.	–	6 s. 40 blue	50	40
1321.	–	8 s. purple	55	15
1322.	–	10 s. green	1·10	15
1323.	–	20 s. purple	1·25	50

DESIGNS: 20 g. Old Courtyard, Morbisch. 30 g. Vienna Town Hall. 40 g. Porcia Castle, Spittal. 50 g. Heiligenstadt Flats. 60 g. Lederer Tower, Wels. 70 g. Archbishop's Palace, Salzburg. 80 g. Old farmhouse, Pinzgau. 1 s. (1303.) Millstatt. 1 s. 20, Corn Measurer's House, Bruck-on-the-Mur. 1 s. 30, Schattenburg Castle, 1 s. 40, Klagenfurt Town Hall. 1 s. 50 "Rabenhof" Flats, Erdberg, Vienna. 1 s. 80, Mint Tower, Hall-in-Tyrol. 2 s. (1309) Christkindl Church. 2 s. (1310) Dragon Fountain, Klagenfurt. 2 s. 20, Beethoven's House, Heiligenstadt, Vienna. 2 s. 50, Danube Bridge, Linz. 3 s. "Swiss Portal", Imperial Palace, Vienna, 3 s. 40, Stein Gate, Krems-on-Danube. 3 s. 50, Esterhazy Palace, Eisenstadt. 4 s. Vienna Gate Hainburg. 4 s. 50, Schwechat Airport. 5 s. 50, Chur Gate, Feldkirck. 6 s. Graz Town Hall. 6 s. 40, "Golden Roof", Innsbruck. 8 s. Steyr Town Hall. 10 s. (22×28½ mm.), Heidenreichstein Castle. 20 s. (28½×37½ mm.), Melk Abbey.

Nos. 1324, 1325 and 1326 are 17½×21 mm. and the others are as T 167, 20¼×24½mm.

168. Post Office, Linz. 169. Badgastein.

1957. Stamp Day.
1327. 168. 1 s.+25 g. green .. 2·10 2·10

1958. Int. Ski Championships, Badgastein.
1328. 169. 1 s. 50 blue 20 5

HAVE YOU READ THE NOTES AT THE BEGINNING OF THIS CATALOGUE?

These often provide answers to the enquiries we receive.

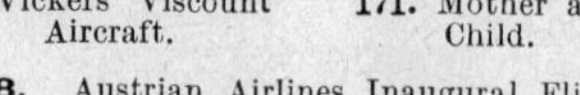

170. Vickers "Viscount" Aircraft. 171. Mother and Child.

1958. Austrian Airlines Inaugural Flight. Vienna-London.
1329. 170. 4 s. red 45 15

1958. Mothers Day.
1330. 171. 1 s. 50 blue 20 8

172. Walther von der Vogel (after 12th-century manuscript). 173. Dr. O. Redlich (historian).

1958. 3rd Austrian Choir Festival.
1331. 172. 1 s. 50 multicoloured 20 8

1958. Dr. Oswald Redlich. Birth Cent.
1332. 173. 2 s. 40 blue 40 15

1958. Republic. 40th Anniv. As T 111 but inscr. "40 JAHRE".
1333. 111. 1 s. 50 green.. .. 25 25

1958. Stamp Day. As T 168 but inscr. "1958".
1334. – 2 s. 40+60 g. blue .. 65 60
DESIGN: 2 s. 40, Post Office, Kitzbuhel.

174. "E" building on Map of Europe. 175. Monopoly Emblem and Cigars.

1959. Europa.
1335. 174. 2 s. 40 green.. .. 30 25

1959. Austrian Tobacco Monopoly. 175th Anniv.
1336. 175. 2 s. 40 brown .. 25 15

176. Archduke Johann. 177. Capercailzie.

1959. Archduke Johann. Death Cent.
1337. 176. 1 s. 50 green.. .. 25 8

1959. Int. Hunting Congress, Vienna.

1338.	177.	1 s. purple	25	5
1339.	–	1 s. 50 blue (Roebuck)	50	8
1340.	–	2 s. 40 grn. (Wild boar)	45	45
1341.	–	3 s. 50 brn. (Stag and family)	35	15

178. Haydn. 179. Tyrolean Eagle.

1959. Haydn. 150th Death Anniv.
1342. 178. 1 s. 50 brown .. 45 8

1959. Tyrolese Rising. 150th Anniv.
1343. 179. 1 s. 50 red 20 8

180. Microwave Transmitting Aerial Zugspitze. 181. Handball Player.

1959. Austrian Microwave Network. Inaug.
1344. 180. 2 s. 40 turquoise .. 25 15

1959. Sports.

1345.	–	1 s. violet (Runner) ..	15	10
1346.	181.	1 s. 50 turquoise ..	45	12
1347.	–	1 s. 80 red (Gymnast)	25	20
1348.	–	2 s. purple (Hurdling)	12	10
1349.	–	2 s. 20 (Hammer-thrower)	20	12

182. Orchestral Instruments. 183. Roman Coach.

184. Refugees. 185. Pres. Adolf Scharf.

1959. Vienna Philharmonic Orchestra's World Tour.
1350. 182. 2 s. 40 black & slate-bl. 25 15

1959. Stamp Day.
1351. 183. 2 s. 40+60 g. black and mauve .. 50 50

1960. World Refugee Year.
1352. 184. 3 s. blue-green .. 55 25

1960. President's 70th Birthday.
1353. 185. 1 s. 50 bronze-green.. 50 12

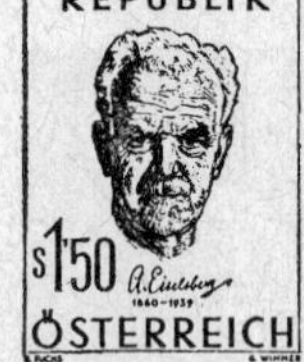

186. Youth Hostellers. 187. Dr. Anton Eiselsberg.

1960. Youth Hostels Movement.
1354. 186. 1 s. red 20 8

1960. Dr. Anton Eiselsberg (surgeon). Birth Cent.
1355. 187. 1 s. 50 sepia and cream 50 12

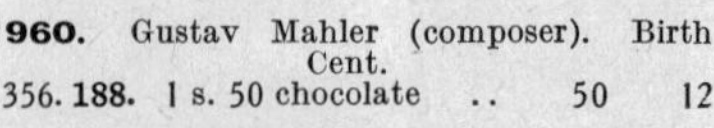

188. Gustav Mahler. 189. Jakob Prandtauer.

1960. Gustav Mahler (composer). Birth Cent.
1356. 188. 1 s. 50 chocolate .. 50 12

1960. Jakob Prandtauer (architect). Birth Tercent.
1357. 189. 1 s. 50 brown .. 50 12

190. Grossglockner Highway. 191. Ionic Capital.

1960. Grossglockner Alpine Highway. 25th Anniv.
1358. 190. 1 s. 80 blue 50 40

1960. United Europe.
1359. 191. 3 s. black .. .. 1·10 65

192. Griffen, Carinthia.

1960. Carinthian Plebiscite. 40th Anniv.
1360. 192. 1 s. 50 green 30 20

193. Examining Proof of Engraved Stamp. 194. "Freedom".

1960. Stamp Day.
1361. 193. 3 s.+70 g. chocolate 65 65

1961. Austrian Freedom Martyrs Commem.
1362. 194. 1 s. 50 red 25 8

195. "Hansa-Brandenburg C1 Albatross" Aircraft of 1918. 196. Transport.

1961. "LUPOSTA" Exn., Vienna, and 1st Austrian Airmail Service Commem.
1363 195. 5 s. blue 50 25

1961. European Transport Ministers' Meeting.
1364. 196. 3 s. olive and red .. 40 35

197. "Mower in the Alps" (detail, after A. Egger-Lienz). 198. Observatory on Sonnblick Mountain.

1961. Cent. of Kunstlerhaus, Vienna. Inscr. as in T 197.

1365.	197.	1 s. maroon & brown	12	8
1355.	–	1 s. 50 lilac & brown	15	10
1367.	–	3 s. bronze-grn. & brn.	65	65
1368.	–	5 s. violet & brown ..	40	85

PAINTINGS: 1 s. 50, "The Kiss" (after A. von Pettenkofen). 3 s. "Portrait of a Girl" (after A. Romako). 5 s. "The Triumph of Ariadne" (detail of Ariadne, after Hans Makart).

1961. Sonnblick Meteorological Observatory. 75th Anniv.
1369. 198. 1 s. 80 blue 25 25

199. Lavanttaler Colliery.

200. Mercury.

1961. Nationalised Industries. 15th Anniv. Inscr. "15 JAHRE VERSTAATLICHTE UNTERNEHMUNGEN".

1370. 199. 1 s. black 8 5
1371. – 1 s. 50 green 12 8
1372. – 1 s. 80 red 40 40
1373. – 3 s. mauve 50 50
1374. – 5 s. blue 50 45

DESIGNS: 1 s. 50, Turbine. 1 s. 80, Industrial plant. 3 s. Steelworks, Linz. 5 s. Oil refinery, Schwechat.

1961. World Bank Congress, Vienna.

1375. 200. 3 s. black 45 35

201. Arms of Burgenland.

202. Liszt.

1961. Burgenland. 40th Anniv.

1376. 201. 1 s. 50 red, yell. & sep. 25 8

1961. Franz Liszt (composer). 150th Birth Anniv.

1377. 202. 3 s. brown 45 30

203. Rust Post Office.

1961. Stamp Day.

1378. 203. 3 s.+70 g. deep blue-green 60 60

204. Court of Accounts.

1961. Court of Accounts Bicent.

1379. 204. 1 s. sepia 15 8

205. Glockner-Kaprun Power Station.

206. J. Nestroy and Theatrical Masks.

1962. Electric Power Nationalization. 15th Anniv. Inscr. as in T 205.

1380. 205. 1 s. blue 12 8
1381. – 1 s. 50 purple 15 10
1382. – 1 s. 80 green.. .. 40 35
1383. – 3 s. brown 30 30
1384. – 4 s. red 30 15
1385. – 6 s. 40 black.. .. 80 65

DESIGNS: 1 s. 50, Ybbs-Persenbeug (Danube). 1 s. 80, Luner See. 3 s. (Grossraming (Enns River). 4 s. Bisamberg Transformer Station. 6 s. 40, St. Andra Power Stations.

1962. J. Nestroy (playwright). Death Cent.

1386. 206. 1 s. violet 15 8

207. F. Gauermann (painter).

208. Scout Badge and Handclasp.

1962. Friedrich Gauermann. Death Cent.

1387. 207. 1 s. 50 blue 15 8

1962. Austrian Scout Movement. 50th Anniv.

1388. 208. 1 s. 50 green 20 8

209. Forest and Lake.

1962. "The Austrian Forest".

1389. 209. 1 s. grey 12 8
1390. – 1 s. 50 brown .. 20 15
1391. – 3 s. myrtle 60 60

DESIGNS: 1 s. 50, Deciduous forest. 3 s. Fir and larch forest.

210. Electric Locomotive and First Steam Loco. "Austria."

1962. Austrian Railways. 125th Anniv.

1392. 210. 3 s. black and buff .. 50 30

211. Engraving Die.

212. Postal Officials of 1863.

1962. Stamp Day.

1393. 211. 3 s.+70 g. violet .. 1·00 1·00

1963. Paris Postal Conference Cent.

1394. 212. 3 s. sepia and olive-yell. 50 30

213. Hermann Bahr.

214. St. Florian (statue).

1963. Hermann Bahr (writer). Birth Cent.

1395. 213. 1 s. 50 sepia and blue.. 20 8

1963. Austrian Voluntary Fire Brigade Cent.

1396. 214. 1 s. 50 black and pink 20 8

215. Flag and Emblem.

217. Prince Eugene of Savoy.

INDEX

Countries can be quickly located by referring to the index at the end of this volume.

218. Centenary Emblem.

216. Crests of Tyrol and Austria.

1963. 5th Austrian Trade Unions Federation Congress.

1397. 215. 1 s. 50 red, sepia & grey 20 8

1963. Tyrol as an Austrian province. 600th Anniv.

1398. 216. 1 s. 50 red, yellow, black and drab .. 20 8

1963. Prince Eugene of Savoy. Birth Tercent.

1399. 217. 1 s. 50 violet .. 20 8

1963. Red Cross Cent.

1400. 218. 3 s. silver, red & black 40 25

219. Skiing (slalom).

1963. Winter Olympic Games, Innsbruck, 1964. Centres black; inscr. gold; background colours given.

1401. 219. 1 s. grey 5 5
1402. – 1 s. 20 grey-blue .. 8 8
1403. – 1 s. 50 grey 10 8
1404. – 1 s. 80 purple.. .. 12 12
1405. – 2 s. 20 green 45 45
1406. – 3 s. slate 80 25
1407. – 4 s. cobalt 65 65

DESIGNS: 1 s. 20, Skiing (biathlon). 1 s. 50, Ski-jumping. 1 s. 80, Figure-skating. 2 s. 20, Ice-hockey. 3 s. Tobogganing. 4 s. Bob-sleighing.

220. Vienna "101" Post Office and Railway Shed.

221. "The Holy Family" (after Josef Stammel).

1963. Stamp Day.

1408. 220. 3 s.+70 g. black and drab 50 50

1963. Christmas.

1409. 221. 2 s. green 20 5

222. Nasturtium.

223. Gothic Statue and Stained-glass Window.

1964. Int. Horticultural Exn., Vienna. Multicoloured.

1410. 1 s. Type 222 .. .. 5 5
1411. 1 s. 50 Peony 10 5
1412. 1 s. 80 Clematis 20 20
1413. 2 s. 20 Dahlia 20 20
1414. 3 s. Convolvulus .. 30 30
1415. 4 s. Mallow 20 15

1964. Romanesque Art Exhibition, Vienna.

1416. 223. 1 s. 50 slate-bl. & black 15 12

224. Pallas Athene and Interior of Assembly Hall, Parliament Building.

225. "The Kiss" (after Gustav Klimt).

1964. 2nd Parliamentary and Scientific Conference. Vienna.

1417. 224. 1 s. 80 black & emerald 20 15

1964. Reopening of "Viennese Secession" Exhibition Hall.

1418. 225. 3 s. multicoloured .. 35 30

226. "Comforting the Sick".

227. "Bringing News of the Victory at Kunersdorf" (Bellotto).

1964. Order of Brothers of Mercy. 350th Anniv.

1419. 226. 1 s. 50 blue .. 15 8

1964. 15th U.P.U. Congress, Vienna. Paintings.

1420. 227. 1 s. reddish purple .. 5 5
1421. – 1 s. 20 sepia 10 10
1422. – 1 s. 50 blue 8 5
1423. – 1 s. 80 violet .. 20 20
1424. – 2 s. 20 black.. .. 12 12
1425. – 3 s. claret 20 20
1426. – 4 s. grey-green .. 20 15
1427. – 6 s. 40 maroon .. 65 65

PAINTINGS: 1 s. 20, "Changing horses" Hormann). 1 s. 50, "The Wedding Trip" (Schwind). 1 s. 80, "Postboys returning home" (Raffelt). 2 s. 20, "The Vienna Mail-coach" (Klein). 3 s. "Changing horses" (Gauermann). 4 s. "Postal tracked-vehicle in mountain village" (Pilch). 6 s. 40, "Saalbach Post Office and post-bus" (Pilch).

228. Vienna, from the Hochhaus (North).

229. "Workers".

1964. "WIPA" Stamp Exn., Vienna (1965) (1st issue). Multicoloured.

1428. 1 s. 50+30 g. Type 228 12 12
1429. 1 s. 50+30 g. North-east 12 12
1430. 1 s. 50+30 g. East .. 12 12
1431. 1 s. 50+30 g. South-east 12 12
1432. 1 s. 50+30 g. South .. 12 12
1433. 1 s. 50+30 g. South-west 12 12
1434. 1 s. 50+30 g. West .. 12 12
1435. 1 s. 50+30 g. North-west 12 12

DESIGNS: Each show a panoramic view of Vienna, looking to different points of compass (indicated on stamps). The inscription reads "Vienna welomes you to WIPA 1965".

See also Nos. 1447/52.

1964. Austrian Workers' Movement. Cent.

1436. 229. 1 s. black 8 8

230. Europa "Flower".

231. Radio Receiver Dial.

1964. Europa.

1437. 230. 3 s. blue 20 15

1964. Austrian Broadcasting Service. 40th Anniv.

1438. 321. 1 s. sepia and red .. 12 8

232. Old Printing Press.

233. Post-bus Station, St. Gilgen.

1964. 6th Int. Graphical Federation Congress, Vienna.
1439. **232.** 1 s. 50 black and drab 12 8

1964. Stamp Day.
1440. **233.** 3 s.+70 g. mult. .. 25 25

234. Dr. Adolf Scharf. **235.** "Reconstruction".

1965. President Scharf Commem.
1441. **234.** 1 s. 50 indigo & black 20 20

1965. "20 Years of Reconstruction".
1442. **235.** 1 s. 80 lake 12 8

236. University Seal. **237.** "St. George" (after engraving by Altdorfer).

1965. Vienna University. 600th Anniv.
1443. **236.** 3 s. red and gold .. 20 20

1965. Danubian Art.
1444. **237.** 1 s. 80 indigo .. 20 15

238. I.T.U. Emblem, Morse Key and T.V. Aerial. **239.** F. Raimund (actor and playwright).

1965. I.T.U. Cent.
1445. **238.** 3 s. violet 20 15

1965. Ferdinand Raimund. 175th Birth Anniv.
1446. **239.** 3 s. maroon 20 12

240. Writing on Clay Tablet. **241.** Gymnasts with Wands.

1965. "WIPA" Stamp Exhibition, Vienna (2nd issue). "Development of the Letter".
1447. **240.** 1 s. 50+40 g. blk. & pink 8 8
1448. – 1 s. 80+50 g. blk. & yell. 10 10
1449. – 2 s. 20+60 g. blk. & lilac 45 45
1450. – 3 s. +80 g. black & olive 15 15
1451. – 4 s.+1 s. black & blue 50 50
1452. – 5 s. +1s. 20 blk. & emer. 60 60
DESIGNS: 1 s. 80, Cuneiform writing. 2 s. 20, Latin. 3 s. Ancient letter and seal. 4 s. 19th-century letter. 5 s. Typewriter.

1965. 4th Gymnaestrada, Vienna.
1453. **241.** 1 s. 50 black and blue 10 8
1454. – 3 s. black and ochre 25 20
DESIGN: 3 s. Girls exercising with tambourines.

242. Dr. I. Semmelweis (physician) **243.** F. G. Waldmuller (self-portrait).

1965. Ignaz Semmelweis. Death Cent.
1455. **242.** 1 s. 50 violet .. 12 8

1965. F. G. Waldmuller (painter). Death Cent.
1456. **243.** 3 s. black 20 15

244. Red Cross and Gauze. **245.** Flag and Crowned Eagle.

1965. Red Cross Conf., Vienna.
1457. **244.** 3 s. red and black .. 20 15

1965. Austrian Towns Union. 50th Anniv.
1458. **245.** 1 s. 50 black, red, gold and grey 12 10

246. Austrian Flag, U.N. Emblem and Headquarters.

1965. Austria's Readmission to U.N.O. 10th Anniv.
1459. **246.** 3 s. sepia, red and blue 20 15

247. University Building. **248.** Bertha von Suttner.

1965. University of Technology, Vienna. 150th Anniv.
1460. **247.** 1 s. 50 violet .. 10 8

1965. Nobel Peace Prize Award to Bertha von Suttner. 60th Anniv.
1461. **248.** 1 s. 50 black.. .. 10 8

249. Postman delivering Mail.

1965. Stamp Day.
1462. **249.** 3 s.+70 g. green .. 25 25

250. Postal Code Map.

1966. Postal Code System Introduction.
1463. **250.** 1 s. 50 blk., red & yell. 10 5

251. P.T.T. Headquarters. **252.** M. Ebner-Eschenbach.

1966. Austrian Posts and Telegraphs Administration. Cent.
1464. **251.** 1 s. 50 black on cream 10 8

1966. Maria Ebner-Eschenbach (writer). 50th Death Anniv.
1465. **252.** 3 s. maroon 20 12

253. Big Wheel. **254.** Josef Hoffmann.

1966 Vienna Prater. 200th Anniv.
466. **253.** 1 s. 50 green.. .. 10 8

1966. Josef Hoffmann (architect). 10th Death Anniv.
1467. **254.** 3 s. brown 20 12

255. Bank Emblem. **256.** Arms of Wiener Neustadt.

1966. Austrian Nat. Bank. 150th Anniv.
1468. **255.** 3 s. brown, green & drab 20 12

1966. "Wiener Neustadt 1440-93" Art Exn.
1469. **256.** 1 s. 50 multicoloured 12 8

257. Puppy. **258.** Columbine.

1966. Vienna Animal Protection Society. 120th Anniv.
1470. **257.** 1 s. 80 black and yellow 12 8

1966. Alpine Flora. Multicoloured.
1471. 1 s. 50, Type **258** .. 10 5
1472. 1 s. 80 Turk's Cap .. 12 12
1473. 2 s. 20 Wulfenia .. 25 25
1474. 3 s. Globe Flower .. 25 25
1475. 4 s. Orange Lily.. .. 30 12
1476. 5 s. Alpine Anemone .. 35 30

259. Fair Building. **260.** Peter Anich.

261. "Suffering". **262.** Theatre Collection.

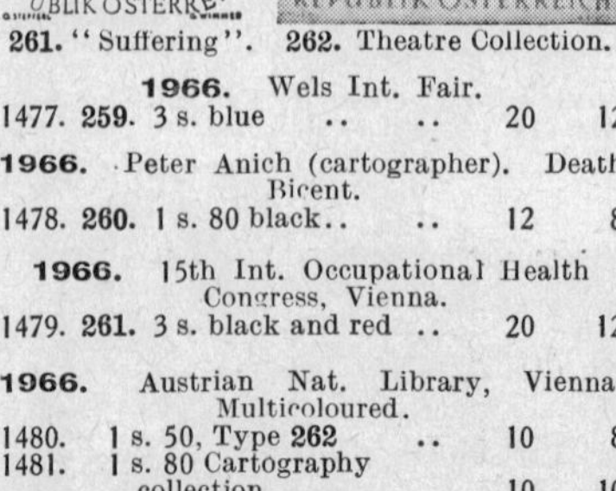

1966. Wels Int. Fair.
1477. **259.** 3 s. blue 20 12

1966. Peter Anich (cartographer). Death Bicent.
1478. **260.** 1 s. 80 black.. .. 12 8

1966. 15th Int. Occupational Health Congress, Vienna.
1479. **261.** 3 s. black and red .. 20 12

1966. Austrian Nat. Library, Vienna. Multicoloured.
1480. 1 s. 50, Type **262** .. 10 8
1481. 1 s. 80 Cartography collection 10 10
1482. 2 s. 20 Pictures and portraits collection .. 20 15
1483. 3 s. Manuscripts collection 20 20

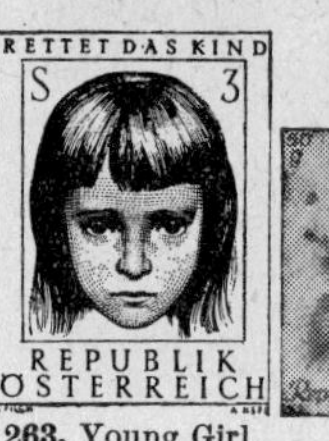

263. Young Girl. **264.** Strawberries. **265.** 16th-cent Postman.

1966. Austrian "Save the Children" Fund.
1484. **263.** 3 s. black and blue .. 20 12

1966. Fruits. Multicoloured.
1485. 50 g. Type **264** 12 12
1486. 1 s. Grapes 10 10
1487. 1 s. 50 Apple 10 10
1488. 1 s. 80 Blackberries .. 12 12
1489. 2 s. 20 Apricots 12 12
1490. 3 s. Cherries 20 15

1966. Stamp Day.
1491. **265.** 3 s. 70 g. multi-coloured 25 25

266. Arms of Linz University. **267.** Skater of 1867.

1966. Linz University. Inaug.
1492. **266.** 3 s. multicoloured .. 20 15

1967. Vienna Skating Assn. Cent.
1493. **267.** 3 s. indigo and blue 20 15

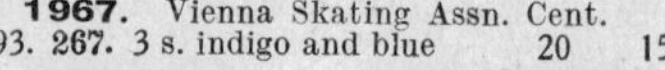

268. Dancer with Violin. **269.** Dr. Schonherr.

1967. "Blue Danube" Waltz. Cent.
1494. **268.** 3 s. maroon 25 20

1967. Dr. Karl Schonherr (poet). Birth Cent.
1495. **269.** 3 s. brown 20 12

270. Ice-hockey Goalkeeper. **271.** Violin and Organ.

1967. World Ice-hockey Championships, Vienna.
1496. **270.** 3 s. blue and green .. 20 12

1967. Vienna Philharmonic Orchestra. 125th Anniv.
1497. **271.** 3 s. 50 blue 20 15

272. "Mother and Children", after aquarelle by P. Fendi, 1841. **273.** "Madonna" (Gothic wood-carving).

1967. Mothers' Day.
1498. **272.** 2 s. multicoloured .. 15 12

1967. "Gothic Art in Austria" Exn., Krems.
1499. **237.** 3 s. green 20 12

274. Jewelled Cross. **275.** "The White Swan" (from Kokoschka's tapestry, "Cupid and Psyche").

1967. "Salzburg Treasures" Exn.
1500. **274.** 3 s. 50 multicoloured 20 15

1967. "Art of the Nibelungengau District" Exn., Pochlarn.
1501. **275.** 2 s. multicoloured .. 15 12

276. Vienna.

1967. 10th European Talks, Vienna.
1502. **276.** 3 s. black and red .. 20 15

277. Champion Bull.

1967. Ried Fair. Cent.
1503. **277.** 2 s. maroon 15 10

278. Colorado Beetle.

1967. 6th Int. Plant Protection Congress Vienna.
1504. **278.** 3 s. multicoloured .. 20 15

279. Locomotive of 1867. **280.** "Christ" (fresco detail).

1967. Brenner Railway. Cent.
1505. **279.** 3 s. 50 green and brown 25 20

1967. Lambach Frescoes.
1506. **280.** 2 s. multicoloured .. 15 12

281. Prater Hall, Vienna. **282.** Medallion and Chain.

1967. Int. Trade Fairs Congress, Vienna.
1507. **281.** 2 s. maroon and cream 15 12

1967. Fine Arts Academy, Vienna. 275th Anniv.
1508. **282.** 2 s. brown, yell. & ind. 15 12

283. Bible on Rock (from commemorative coin of 1717). **285.** Memorial, Vienna.

284. Forest Trees.

1967. Reformation. 450th Anniv.
1509. **283.** 3 s. 50 ultramarine .. 20 15

1967. 100 Years of Austrian University Forestry Studies.
1510. **284.** 3 s. 50 green.. .. 20 15

1967. Land Registry. 150th Anniv.
1511. **285.** 2 s. olive 15 12

286. "St. Leopold" (stained-glass window, Heiligenkreuz Monastery). **287.** "Music and Art".

1967. Margrave Leopold the Holy.
1512. **286.** 1 s. 80 multicoloured 12 10

1967. Academy of Music and Dramatic Art, Vienna. 150th Anniv.
1513. **287.** 3 s. 50 black and violet 20 15

288. St. Mary's Altar, Nonnberg Convent, Salzburg. **289.** "The Letter-carrier" (from playing card).

1967. Christmas.
1514. **288.** 2 s. green 15 12

1967. Stamp Day.
1515. **289.** 3 s. 50+80 g. mult. 30 30

290. Ski-jump, Stadium and Mountains.

1968. Winter University Games, Innsbruck.
1516. **299.** 2 s. blue 15 12

291. C. Sitte. **292.** Mother and Child.

1968. Camillo Sitte (architect). 125th Birth Anniv.
1517. **291.** 2 s. brown 15 12

1968. Mothers' Day.
1518. **292.** 2 s. olive 15 12

293. "Veterinary Medicine". **294.** Bride with Lace Veil.

1968. Vienna Veterinary College Bicent.
1519. **293.** 3 s. 50 gold, pur. & drab 25 20

1968. Voralberg Lace. Cent.
1520. **294.** 3 s. 50 indigo .. 25 20

295. Etrich "Dove" Aircraft. **297.** Dr. K. Landsteiner.

298. P. Rosegger. **296.** Horse-racing.

1968. "IFA Wien 1968" Airmail Stamp Exn., Vienna.
1521. **295.** 2 s. brown 20 20
1522. – 3 s. 50 green.. .. 35 35
1523. – 5 s. blue 50 50
DESIGNS: 3 s. 50, "Caravelle" jetliner. 5 s. Douglas "DC-8" jetliner.

1968. Freudenau Gallop Races. Cent.
1524. **296.** 3 s. 50 sepia 25 20

1968. Dr. Karl Landsteiner (physician and pathologist). Birth Cent.
1525. **297.** 3 s. 50 blue 25 20

1968. Peter Rosegger (writer) 50th Death Anniv.
1526. **298.** 2 s. green 15 10

299. A. Kauffmann (self-portrait). **300.** Statue of Young Man (Helenenberg site.)

1968. Exn. of Angelica Kauffmann's Paintings, Bregenz.
1527. **299.** 2 s. violet 15 10

1968. Magdalensberg Excavations, Carinthia
1528. **300.** 2 s. black and green 15 10

301. "The Bishop" (Romanesque carving). **302.** K. Moser

1968. Graz-Seckau Diocese. 750th Anniv.
1529. **301.** 2 s. grey 15 10

1968. Koloman Moser. 50th Death Anniv.
1530. **302.** 2 s. agate and verm. 15 10

303. Human Rights Emblem. **304.** Arms and Provincial Shields.

1968. Human Rights Year.
1531. **303.** 1 s. 50 red, grn. & grey 15 10

1968. Republic. 50th Anniv. Multicoloured.
1532. 2 s. Type **304** 25 20
1533. 2 s. President Renner .. 25 20
1534. 2 s. First Article of Constitution 25 20

305. Crib, Oberndorf, Salzburg. **306.** Mercury.

1968. "Silent Night, Holy Night" (carol). 150th Anniv.
1535. **305.** 2 s. green 15 8

1968. Stamp Day.
1536. **306.** 3 s. 50+80 g. blackish green 30 30

307. Fresco (Troger), Melk Monastery. **308.** "Madonna and Child".

1968. Baroque Frescoes. Showing frescoes in locations given. Multicoloured.
1537. 2 s. Type **307** 25 25
1538. 2 s. Altenburg Monastery 25 25
1539. 2 s. Rohrenbach-Greillenstein 25 25
1540. 2 s. Ebengurth Castle .. 25 25
1541. 2 s. Halbthurn Castle .. 25 25
1542. 2 s. Maria Treu Church, Vienna.. .. .. 25 25
Nos. 1537/9 are the work of Anton Troger and Nos. 1540/2 that of Franz Maulbertsch.

1969. Vienna Diocese. 500th Anniv.
1543. **308.** 2 s. blue 25 25
1544. – 2 s. slate 25 25
1545. – 2 s. green 25 25
1546. – 2 s. maroon 25 25
1547. – 2 s. black 25 25
1548. – 2 s. brown 25 25
DESIGNS: No. 1544, "St. Christopher". 1545, "St. George". 1546, "St. Paul". 1547, "St. Sebastian". 1548, "St. Stephen".

309. Parliament Building, Vienna.

1969. Inter-Parliamentary Union Meeting, Vienna.
1549. **309.** 2 s. blue-green .. 15 12

310. Colonnade.

1969. Europa
1550. **310.** 2 s. multicoloured .. 20 15

311. "Council Members". 312. Soldiers.

1969 Council of Europe. 20th Anniv.
1551. **311.** 3s. 50 multicoloured 30 25

1969. Austrian Armed Forces.
1552. **312.** 2 s. sepia and red .. 15 12

313. Maximilian's Armour. 314. Viennese "Privilege" Seal.

1969. Maximilian I Exn., Innsbruck.
1554. **313.** 2 s. black 15 10

1969. 19th Int. Union of Local Authorities Congress, Vienna.
1555. **314.** 2 s. red, brown & ochre 15 10

315. Young Girl. 316. Hands clasping Spanner.

1969. "SOS" Children's Villages Movement. 20th Anniv.
1556. **315.** 2 s. brown and green 15 10

1969. Int. Labour Organization. 50th Anniv.
1557. **316.** 2 s. green 15 10

317. Austrian "Flag" encircling Globe. 318. "El Cid killing a Bull" (Goya).

1969. "Austrians Living Abroad" Year.
1558. **317.** 3 s. 50 red and green 25 20

1969. Albertina Art Collection, Vienna. Bicent. Multicoloured.
1559. 2 s. Type **318** 20 20
1560. 2 s. "Young Hare" (Durer) 20 20
1561. 2 s. "Madonna with Pomegranate" (Raphael) .. 20 20
1562. 2 s. "The Painter and the Amateur" (Bruegel) .. 20 20
1563. 2 s. "Rubens' Son, Nicholas" (Rubens) .. 20 20
1564. 2 s. "Self-portrait" (Rembrandt) 20 20
1565. 2 s. "Madam Pompadour" (detail, Guerin) 20 20
1566. 2 s. "The Artist's Wife" (Schiele) 20 20

319. President Jonas. 320. Posthorn and Lightning over Globe.

1969. President Franz Jonas's 70th Birthday.
1567. **319.** 2 s. ultramarine & grey 15 10

1969. P.T.T. Employees Union. 50th Anniv.
1568. **320.** 2 s. multicoloured .. 15 10

321. Savings Bank (c. 1450). 322. "The Madonna" (Egger-Lienz).

1969. Austrian Savings Bank. 150th Anniv.
1569. **321.** 2 s. green and silver .. 15 10

1969. Christmas.
1570. **322.** 2 s. maroon and yellow 15 10

323. Unken, Salzburg, Post-house Sign (after F. Zeller). 324. J. Schoffel.

1969. Stamp Day.
1571. **323.** 3 s. 50+80 g. black, red and grey .. 30 30

1970. Josef Schoffel ("Saviour of the Vienna Woods"). 60th Death Anniv.
1572. **324.** 2 s. purple 15 12

325. St. Clement Hofbauer. 327. Krimml Waterfalls.

326. Chancellor Leopold Figl.

1970. St. Clement Hofbauer (theologian). 150th Death Anniv.
1573. **325.** 2 s. brown and green 15 12

1970. Austrian Republic. 25th Anniv.
1574. **326.** 2 s. olive 15 12
1575. – 2 s. chocolate .. 15 12
DESIGN: No. 1575, Belvedere Castle.

1970. Nature Conservation Year.
1576. **327.** 2 s. blackish green .. 15 12

328. Oldest University Seal. 330. Tower Clock, 1450–1550.

329. "Musikverein" Organ.

1970. Leopold Franz University, Innsbruck. 300th Anniv.
1577. **328.** 2 s. black and vermilion 15 12

1970. "Musikverein" Building. Cent.
1578. **329.** 2 s. purple and gold 15 12

1970. Antique Clocks.
1579. **330.** 1 s. 50 brown & cream 15 15
1580. – 1 s. 50 green.. .. 15 15
1581. – 2 s. blue and pale blue 20 15
1582. – 2 s. lake and claret .. 20 15
1583. – 3 s. 50 chocolate & buff 30 25
1584. – 3 s. 50 purple & lilac 30 25
DESIGNS: No. 1580, Empire "lyre" clock, 1790-1815. 1581, Pendant ball clock, 1600-50. 1582, Pocket-watch and signet, 1800-30. 1583, Bracket clock, 1720-60. 1584, "Biedermeier" pendulum clock and musical-box, 1820-50.

331. "The Beggar Student" (Millocker). 332. Scene from "The Gipsy Baron" (J. Strauss).

1970. Famous Operettas.
1585. **331.** 1 s. 50 blue-grn. & grn. 15 15
1586. – 1 s. 50 blue and yellow 15 15
1587. – 2 s. violet and pink.. 20 15
1588. – 2 s. brown and green 20 15
1589. – 3 s. 50 blue & pale blue 30 25
1590. – 3s. 50 blue and buff 30 25
OPERETTAS: No. 1586, "Die Fledermaus" (Johann Strauss the younger). 1587, "A Waltz Dream" (O. Strauss). 1588, "The Birdseller" (C. Zeller). 1589, "The Merry Widow" (F. Lehar). 1590, "Two Hearts in Waltz-time" (R. Stolz).

1970. Bregenz Festival. 25th Anniv.
1591. **332.** 3 s. 50 blue, buff & ult. 25 20

333. Festival Emblem. 334. T. Koschat.

1970. Salzburg Festival. 50th Anniv.
1592. **333.** 3 s. 50 multicoloured 25 20

1970. Thomas Koschat (composer and poet). 125th Birth Anniv.
1593. **324.** 2 s. brown 15 10

335. "Head of St. John", from sculpture "Mount of Olives", Ried Church (att. to T. Schwanthaler).

1970. 13th World Veterans Federation General Assembly.
1594. **335.** 3 s. 50 sepia 25 20

336. Climbers and Mountains. 337. A. Cossmann.

1970. "Walking and Mountaineering".
1595. **336.** 2 s. blue and mauve 15 10

1970. Alfred Cossmann (engraver). Birth Cent.
1596. **337.** 2 s. brown 15 10

338. Arms of Carinthia. 339. U.N. Emblem.

1970. Carinthian Plebiscite. 50th Anniv.
1597. **338.** 2 s. multicoloured .. 15 10

1970. United Nations. 25th Anniv.
1598. **339.** 3 s. 50 blue and black 25 20

340. "Adoration of the Shepherds". (Carving from Garsten Monastery).

1970. Christmas.
1599. **340.** 2 s. blue 15 10

341. Saddle, Harness and Posthorn. 342. Pres. K. Renner.

1970. Stamp Day.
1600. **341.** 3 s. 50+80 g. black, yellow and grey .. 30 25

1970. Pres. Renner. Birth Cent.
1601. **342.** 2 s. purple 15 10

343. Beethoven (after painting by Waldmuller). 344. E. Handel-Mazzetti.

1970. Beethoven. Birth Bicent.
1602. **343.** 3 s. 50 black and grey 25 20

1971. Enrica Handel-Mazzetti (novelist). Birth Cent.
1603. **344.** 2 s. brown 15 10

345. "Safety for Children".

1971. Road Safety.
1604. **345.** 2 s. multicoloured .. 20 12

346. Florentine Bowl, circa 1580.

1971. Austrian Art Treasures (1st series).
1605. **346.** 1 s. 50 green and grey 20 15
1606. – 2 s. maroon and grey 20 15
1607. – 3 s. 50 yell., brn. & grey 30 25
DESIGNS: 2 s. Ivory equestrian statuette of Joseph I (Matthias Steinle, circa 1693), 3 s. 50, Salt-cellar (Cellini, circa 1570).
See also Nos. 1609/11, 1632/4 and 1651/3.

347. Shield of Trade Association. 348. "Jacopo de Strada" (Titian).

1971. Int. Chamber of Commerce Congress, Vienna.
1608. **347.** 3 s. 50 multicoloured 25 20

1971. Austrian Art Treasures (2nd series).
1609. **348.** 1 s. 50 maroon .. 20 15
1610. – 2 s. black 20 15
1611. – 3 s. 50 brown .. 30 25
PAINTINGS: 2 s. "The Village Feast" (Brueghel). 3 s. 50 "Young Venetian Woman" (Durer).

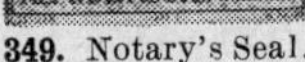

349. Notary's Seal. **350.** "St. Matthew" (altar sculpture).

1971. Austrian Notarial Statute Cent. Congress.
1612. **349.** 3 s. 50 purple & brown 25 20

1971. "Krems Millennium of Art" Exhib.
1613. **350.** 2 s. brown & purple 15 12

351. Dr. A. Neilreich. **352.** Singer with Lyre.

1971. Dr. August Neilreich (botanist). Death Cent.
1614. **351.** 2 s. brown 15 10

1971. Int. Choir Festival, Vienna.
1615. **352.** 4 s. bl., gold & pale bl. 30 25

353. Arms of Kitzbuhel.

1971. Kitzbuhel. 700th Anniv.
616. **353.** 2 s. 50 multicoloured 20 12

354. Stock Exchange Building.

1971. Vienna Stock Exchange. Bicent.
1617. **354.** 4 s. brown 25 20

355. Old and New Fair Halls. **356.** O.G.B. Emblem.

1971. 50 Years of Vienna Int. Fairs.
1618. **355.** 2 s. 50 purple .. 15 12

1971. "Osterreichischer Gewerkschaftsbund" (Austrian Trades Unions Federation). 25th Anniv.
1619. **356.** 2 s. multicoloured .. 12 10

357. Arms and Insignia. **358.** "Marcus" Veteran Car.

1971. Burgenland Province. 50th Anniv.
1620. **357.** 4 s. multicoloured .. 12 10

1971. Austrian Automobile, Motor-cycle and Touring Club. 75th Anniv.
1621. **358.** 4 s. black and green 25 20

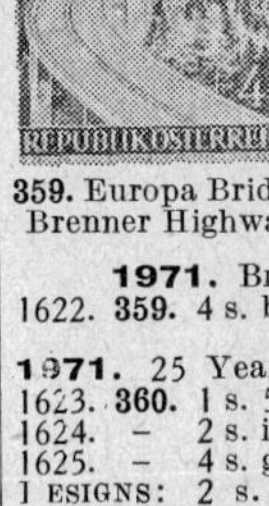

359. Europa Bridge, Brenner Highway. **360.** Iron-ore Workings, Erzberg.

1971. Brenner Highway. Inaug.
1622. **359.** 4 s. blue 25 20

1971. 25 Years of Nationalised Industries.
1623. **360.** 1 s. 50 brown .. 15 15
1624. – 2 s. indigo 15 15
1625. – 4 s. green 25 25
DESIGNS: 2 s. Nitrogen Works, Linz. 4 s. Iron and Steel works, Linz.

361. Electric Train on the Semmering Line. **362.** E. Tschermak-Seysenegg.

1971. Railway Anniversaries.
1626. **361.** 2 s. red 12 10

1971. Dr. E. Tshermak-Seysenegg (biologist). Birth Cent.
1627. **362.** 2 s. purple & grey .. 12 10

363. Angling. **364.** "The Infant Jesus as Saviour" (from miniature by Durer).

1971. Sports.
1628. **363.** 2 s. brown 12 10

1971. Christmas.
1629. **364.** 2 s. multicoloured .. 12 10

365. "50 Years".

1971. Austrian Philatelic Clubs. 50th Anniv.
1630. **365.** 4 s. + 1 s. 50 pur. & gold 35 35

366. "Franz Grillparzer" (Daffinger). **367.** "Roman Fountain" Friesach.

1972. Death Cent. of Grillparzer (dramatist).
1631. **366.** 2 s. brown and stone 15 10

1972. Austrian Art Treasures (3rd series). Fountains.
1632. **367.** 1 s. 50 purple .. 12 12
1633. – 2 s. brown 12 12
1634. – 2 s. 50 olive 10 15
DESIGNS—VERT. 2 s. "Lead Fountain", Heiligenkreuz Abbey. 2 s. 50, "Leopold Fountain", Innsbruck.

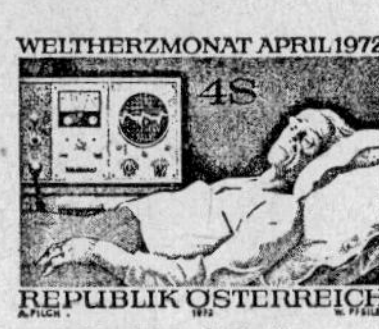

368. Hofburg Palace. **369.** Heart Patient.

1972. 4th European Postal Ministers' Conference, Vienna.
1635. **368.** 4 s. violet 30 25

1972. World Heart Month.
1636. **369.** 4 s. brown 25 20

370. "Woman's Head" (sculpture, Gurk Cathedral). **371.** Vienna Town Hall and Congress Emblem.

1972. Gurk Diocese. 900th Anniv.
1637. **370.** 2 s. purple and gold 15 10

1972. 9th Int. Public and Co-operative Economy Congress, Vienna.
1638. **371.** 4 s. blk., red and yellow 25 20

372. Lienz-Pelos Pylon Line.

1972. Electric Power Nationalisation. 25th Anniv.
1639. **372.** 70 g. violet and grey 8 5
1640. – 2 s. 50 brown and grey 20 15
1641. – 4 s. blue and grey .. 25 20
DESIGNS: 2 s. 50 Vienna-Simmering power station. 4 s. Zemm Dam and lake.

373. Runner with Torch. **374.** "Hermes" (C. Laib).

1972. Passage of the Olympic Torch through Austria.
1642. **373.** 2 s. brown and red .. 12 10

1972. "Late Gothic Art" Exhib. Salzburg.
1643. **374.** 2 s. maroon 12 10

375. Pears. **376.** University Arms.

1972. Amateur Gardeners' Congress, Vienna.
1644. **375.** 2 s. 50 multicoloured 15 12

1972. University of Agriculture, Vienna. Cent.
1646. **376.** 2 s. multicoloured .. 10 5

377. Old University Buildings (after F. Danreiter). **378.** C. M. Ziehrer.

1972. Paris Lodron University, Salzburg. 350th Anniv.
1647. **377.** 4 s. brown 25 20

1972. Carl M. Ziehrer (composer and conductor). 50th Death Anniv.
1648. **378.** 2 s. brown 12 10

379. "Virgin and Child", Inzersdorf Church.

1972. Christmas.
1649. **379.** 2 s. purple and green 12 10

380. 18th-century Viennese Postman. **381.** State Sledge of Maria Theresa.

1972. Stamp Day.
1650. **380.** 4 s. + 1 s. green .. 35 30

1972. Austrian Art Treasures (4th series). Carriages from the Imperial Coach House.
1651. **381.** 1 s. 50 brown and bistre 12 12
1652. – 2 s. green & bistre .. 12 12
1653. – 2 s. 50 purple & bistre 20 15
DESIGNS: 2 s. Coronation landau. 2 s. 50 Hapsburg State Coach.

382. Telephone Network. **384.** A. Petzold.

383. "Drug Addict".

1972. Completion of Austrian Telephone System Automation.
1654. **382.** 2 s. black and yellow 12 10

1973. Campaign against Drug Abuse.
1655. **383.** 2 s. multicoloured .. 1·00 40

1973. Alfons Petzold (writer). 50th Death Anniv.
1656. **384.** 2 s. violet 12 8

385. Pres. Theodor Korner. **386.** Douglas "DC-9" Jetliner.

1973. Pres. Korner. Birth Cent.
1657. **385.** 2 s. maroon and grey 12 8

1973. Austrian Aviation Annivs.
1658. **386.** 2 s. blue and red .. 12 8

387. Otto Loewi. **388.** "Succour"

1973. Otto Loewi (pharmacologist). Birth Cent.
1659. **387.** 4 s. violet 25 20

1973. Nat. Federation of Austrian Social Insurance Institutes. 25th Anniv.
1660. **388.** 2 s. blue 12 8

389. Telephone Dial within Posthorn.

391. Military Pentathlon.

390. Fair Emblem.

1973. Europa.
1661. **389.** 2 s. 50 blk., yell. & brn. 15 12

1973. 25th Dornbirn Fair.
1662. **390.** 2 s. multicoloured .. 12 8

1973. International Military Sports Council. 25th Anniv. and 23rd Military Pentathlon Championships, Wiener Neustadt.
1663. **391.** 4 s. brown 25 15

392. Leo Slezak.

393. Main Entrance, Hofburg Palace.

1973. Leo Slezak (operatic tenor). Birth Centenary.
1664. **392.** 4 s. maroon 25 15

1973. 39th Int. Statistical Institute's Congress, Vienna.
1665. **393.** 2 s. brn., red & grey 12 8

394. "The Admiral Tegetthof Icebound" (J. Player).

395. I.U.L.C.S. Arms.

1973. Discovery of Franz Josef Land. Cent.
1666. **394.** 2 s. 50 green.. .. 15 12

1973. 13th Int. Union of Leather Chemist's Societies Congress, Vienna.
1667. **395.** 4 s. multicoloured .. 25 15

396. "Academy of Sciences, Vienna" (B. Bellotto).

397. Max Reinhardt.

1973. Int. Meteorological Organisation.
1668. **396.** 2 s. 50 violet .. 15 12

1973. Max Reinhardt (theatrical director). Birth Cent.
1669. **397.** 2 s. violet 12 8

398. F. Hanusch.

399. Light Harness Racing.

1973. Ferdinand Hanusch (politician). 50th Death Anniv.
1670. **398.** 2 s. brown 12 8

1973. Vienna Trotting Assn. Cent.
1671. **399.** 2 s. green 12 8

400. Radio Operator.

1973. International Criminal Police Organization (Interpol). 50th Anniv.
1672. **400.** 4 s. violet 25 15

401. Petzval Camera Lens.

402. Aqueduct, Hollen Valley.

1973. "Europhot" (professional photographers) Congress, Vienna.
1673. **401.** 2 s. 50 multicoloured 15 12

1973. Vienna's First Mountain-spring Aqueduct. Cent.
1674. **402.** 2 s. brown, red & blue 12 8

403. Almsee.

404. "The Nativity" (stained-glass window, St. Erhard Church, Bretenau).

1973. Views.
1675. – 50 g. green and grey.. 5 5
1676. – 1 s. sepia & brown .. 5 5
1677. – 1 s. 50 pur., brn. & clar. 8 5
1678. – 2 s. blue & deep blue 12 5
1679. – 2 s. 50 blk. & violet.. 15 5
1680. – 3 s. ultram. and blue 20 5
1681. **403.** 4 s. violet and lilac.. 25 5
1683. – 5 s. violet and lilac.. 30 5
1684. – 6 s. rose and lilac .. 35 5
1685. – 7 s. grn. & dull grn... 40 8
1686. – 8 s. brown and pink 40 15
1687. – 10 s. myrtle and green 50 10
1689. – 50 s. slate and violet 2·50 1·00

DESIGNS: 50 g. Zillertal. 1 s. Kahlenbergerdorf, Vienna. 1 s. 50 Bludenz. 2 s. Old bridge, Alt Finstermunz. 2 s. 50 Steiermark, Murau. 3 s. Bischofsmutze and Alpine farm. 5 s. Ruins of Aggstein Castle. 6 s. Lindauer Hut, Ratchon Massif. 7 s. Falkenstein Castle. 8 s. Votive column, Reiteregg, Styria. 10 s. Neusiedlersee, (33×43 mm.). 50 s. Hofburg, Vienna.

1973. Christmas.
1691. **404.** 2 s. multicoloured .. 12 8

405. "Archangel Gabriel" (carving by Lorenz Luchsperger).

406. F. Pregl.

1973. Stamp Day.
1692. **405.** 4 s.+1 s. brown .. 35 30

1973. Award of Nobel Prize for Chemistry to Fritz Pregl. 50th Anniversary.
1693. **406.** 4 s. blue 25 15

407. Telex Machine and Globe.

408. H. von Hofmannsthal.

1974. Radio Austria. 50th Anniv.
1694. **407.** 2 s. 50 blue & ultram. 15 12

1974. Hugo von Hofmannsthal (writer). Birth Cent.
1695. **408.** 4 s. blue 25 15

409. Anton Bruckner (composer).

1974. Bruckner Memorial Centre, Linz. Inauguration.
1696. **409.** 4 s. brown 25 15

410. Vegetables.

1974. 2nd International Horticultural Show, Vienna. Multicoloured.
1697. 2 s. Type **410.** 15 12
1698. 2 s. 50 Fruit 20 15
1699. 4 s. Flowers 30 20

411. Head from Ancient Seal.

412. Karl Kraus.

1974. Judenburg. 750th Anniv.
1700. **411.** 2 s. multicoloured .. 15 10

1974. Karl Kraus (poet). Birth Centenary.
1701. **412.** 4 s. red 25 20

413. "St. Michael" (wood-carving, Thomas Schwanthaler).

414. "King Arthur" (statue, Innsbruck).

1974. "Sculptures by the Schwanthaler Family" Exhibition, Reichersberg.
1702. **413.** 2 s. 50 green.. .. 15 12

1974. Europa.
1703. **414.** 2 s. 50 blue & brown 15 12

415. Early Dion Bouton Motor-tricycle.

417. I.R.U. Emblem.

416. Mask of Satyr's Head.

1974. ARBO—Austrian Association of Motoring, Motor-cycling and Cycling. 75th Anniv.
1704. **415.** 2 s. purple and brown 12 10

1974. Renaissance Exhibition, Schallburg Castle.
1705. **416.** 2 s. blk., brn. & gold 12 10

1974. 14th International Road Haulage Union Congress, Innsbruck.
1706. **417.** 4 s. black and organge 25 15

418. F. A. Maulbertsch.

419. Gendarmes of 1849 and 1974.

1974. Franz Maulbertsch (painter). 250th Birth Anniv.
1707. **418.** 2 s. brown 12 10

1974. Austrian Gendarmerie. 125th Anniv.
1708. **419.** 2 s. multicoloured .. 12 10

420. Fencing.

421. Transport Emblems.

1974. Sports.
1709. **420.** 2 s. 50 blk. & orange 15 10

1974. European Transport Ministers' Conference, Vienna.
1710. **421.** 4 s. multicoloured .. 25 15

422. " St. Virgilius " (wood-carving).

423. Pres. F. Jonas.

1974. 1200 Years of Chrsitianity in Salzburg.
1711. **422.** 2 s. blue 12 10

1974. President Franz Jonas. Commemoration.
1712. **423.** 2 s. black 12 10

424. F. Stelzhamer.

425. Diving.

1974. Franz Stelzhamer (poet). Death Cent.
1713. **424.** 2 s. blue 12 10

1974. 13th European Swimming, Diving and Water-polo Championships.
1714. **425.** 4 s. brown and blue 25 15

426. F. R. von Hebra (founder of German scientific dermatology).

427. A. Schonberg.

1974. 30th Meeting of German-speaking Dermatologists Association.
1715. **426.** 4 s. brown .. 25 15

1974. Arnold Schonberg (composer). Birth Cent.
1716. **427.** 2 s. 50 purple .. 15 10

428. Broadcasting Studios, Salzburg.

429. E. Eysler.

1974. Austrian Broadcasting. 50th Anniv.
1717. 428. 2 s. multicoloured .. 12 10

1974. Edmund Eysler (composer). 25th Death Anniv.
1718. 429. 2 s. green 12 10

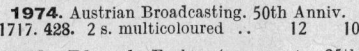

430. Postman and Mail Transport, 19th Cent.

1974. Universal Postal Union. Cent.
1719. 430. 2 s. brown & lilac .. 12 10
1720. – 4 s. blue and grey .. 25 20
DESIGN: 4 s. Modern postman and mail transport.

431. Sports Emblem.

1974. "Football Pools in Austria". 25th Anniv.
1721. 431. 70 g blk, grn. & red 5 5

432. Steel Gauntlet grasping Rose.

1974. Nature Protection.
1722. 432. 2 s. multicoloured .. 12 10

433. C. D. von Dittersdorf. 434. Mail-coach and Post Office, of 1905.

1974. Carl Ditters von Dittersdorf (composer). 175th Death Anniv.
1723. 433. 2 s. green 12 10

1974. Stamp Day.
1724. 434. 4 s.+2 s. blue .. 35 30

435. "Virgin Mary and Child" (wood-carving). 436. F. Schmidt.

1974. Christmas.
1725. 435. 2 s. brown and gold 12 8

1974. Franz Schmidt (composer). Birth Centenary.
1726. 436. 4 s. black and brown 25 15

MINIMUM PRICE

The minimum price quoted is 5p which represents a handling charge rather than a basis for valuing common stamps. For further notes about prices see introductory pages.

437. "St. Christopher and Child" (alterpiece).

439. Seat-belt around Skeletal Limbs.

438. Slalom-skiing.

1975. European Architectural Heritage Year and 125th Anniv. of Austrian Commission for Preservation of Monuments.
1727. 437. 2 s. 50 brn. & grey .. 15 10

1975. Winter Olympics, Innsbruck (1976). Multicoloured.
1728. 1 s.+50 g. Type 438 .. 12 12
1729. 1 s. 50+70 g. Ice-hockey 15 15
1730. 2 s.+90 g. Ski-jumping 20 20
1731. 4 s.+1 s. 90 Bobsleighing 35 35

1975. Car Safety-belts Campaign.
1732. 439. 70 g. multicoloured.. 5 8

440. "Stained-glass Window". 441. "The Buffer State".

1975. 11th European Communities' Day.
1733. 440. 2 s. 50 multicoloured 15 10

1975. Second Republic. 30th Anniv.
1734. 441. 2 s. black and buff .. 12 10

442. Forest Scene.

1975. Austrian Forests Administration. 50th Anniv.
1735. 442. 2 s. green 12 10

443. "The High Priest" (M. Pacher). 444. Gosaukamm Cable-way.

1975. Europa.
1736. 443. 2 s. 50 multicoloured 15 12

1975. 4th International Ropeways Congress, Vienna.
1737. 444. 2 s. grey and red .. 12 8

445. J. Misson.

1975. Josef Misson (poet). Death Cent.
1738. 445. 2 s. brown and red .. 12 8

446. "Setting Sun". 448. L. Fall.

447. F. Porsche.

1975. National Pensioners' Association Meeting, Vienna.
1739. 446. 1 s. 50 multicoloured 10 8

1975. Professor Ferdinand Porsche (motor engineer). Birth Cent.
1740. 447. 1 s. 50 pur. & blk. .. 10 8

1975. Leo Fall (composer). 50th Death Anniv.
1741. 448. 2 s. violet 12 8

449. Judo "Shoulder Throw". 450. T. Von Heinrich Angeli.

1975. World Judo Championships, Vienna.
1742. 449. 2 s. 50 purple .. 15 10

1975. Todestag von Heinrich Angeli (Court painter). 50th Death Anniv.
1743. 540. 2 s. purple 12 8

451. J. Strauss.

1975. Johann Strauss the Younger (composer). 150th Birth Anniv.
1744. 451. 4 s. brown and ochre 25 15

452. "The Cellist". 453. "One's Own House".

1975. Vienna Symphonic Orchestra. 75th Anniv.
1745. 452. 2 s. 50 blue & silver.. 15 10

1975. Austrian Building Societies. 50th Anniversary.
1746. 453. 2 s. multicoloured .. 12 8

1975. Winter Olympic Games, Innsbruck (1976) (2nd series). As T 438. Mult.
1747. 70 g.+30 g. Figure-skating (pairs) 8 8
1748. 2 s.+1 s. skiing 20 20
1749. 2 s. 50+1 s. Tobogganing 25 25
1750. 4 s.+2 s. Biathlon rifle-shooting 40 40

454. Scene on Folding Fan.

1975. Salzburg Land Theatre. Bicent.
1751. 454. 1 s. 50 multicoloured 8 8

455. Austrian Stamps of 1850, 1922 and 1945.

456. "Virgin and Child" (Schottenaltar, Vienna).

1975. Stamp Day and Austrian Postage Stamps. 125th Anniv.
1752. 455. 4 s.+2 s. multicoloured 35 35

1975. Christmas.
7153. 456. 2 s. lilac and gold .. 12 10

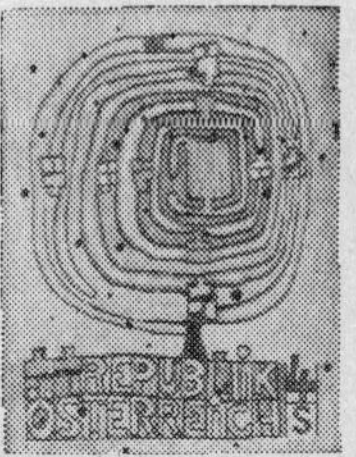

457. "Spiralbaum" (F. Hundertwasser). 458. Dr. R. Barany.

1975. Modern Austrian Art.
1754. 457. 4 s. multicoloured .. 25 15

1976. Dr. Robert Barany (Nobel prizewinner for Medicine). Birth Centenary.
1756. 458. 3 s. brown and blue.. 20 12

459. Ammonite Fossil. 460. 9th Century Coronation Throne.

1976. Centenary Exhibition, Vienna Natural History Museum.
1757. 459. 3 s. multicoloured .. 20 12

1976. Carinthia. Millenary.
1758. 460. 3 s. black and yellow 20 12

461. Stained-glass Window. Klosterneuburg. 462. "The Siege of Linz" (contemporary engraving).

1976. Babenberg Exhibition, Lilienfeld.
1759. 461. 3 s. multicoloured .. 20 12

1976. The Peasants' War in Upper Austria. 350th Anniv.
1760. 462. 4 s. black and green 25 15

463. Bowler delivering Ball.

1976. 11th World Skittles Championships, Vienna.
1761. 463. 4 s. black & orange.. 25 15

464. "St. Wolfgang" (altar painting by Michael Pacher). 465. Tassilo Cup, Kremsmunster.

1976. International Art Exhibition, St. Wolfgang.
1762. **464.** 6 s. purple .. 35 25

1976. Europa.
1763. **465.** 4 s. multicoloured .. 25 15

466. Fair Emblem. **467.** Constantin Economo.

1976. 25th Austrian Timber Fair, Klagenfurt.
1764. **466.** 3 s. multicoloured .. 20 12

1976. Constantin Economo (brain specialist). Birth Cent.
1765. **467.** 3 s. brown .. 20 12

JOURNAL STAMPS

J **1.** Arms. J **2.** Arms of Austria. J **3.**

1853. Imperf.
J 67. J **1.** 1 k. blue .. .. 7·00 40
J 15. 2 k. green .. .. £800 25·00
J 68. 2 k. brown .. .. 5·00 40
J 32. 4 k. brown £200 £425
For similar values in black and red, see Lombardy and Venetia Journal stamps, Nos. J 22/4.

1890. Imperf.
J 76. J **2.** 1 k. brown .. .. 6·00 40
J 77. 2 k. green .. .. 6·50 75

1890. Perf.
J 78. J **3.** 25 k. red .. .. 55·00 75·00

NEWSPAPER STAMPS

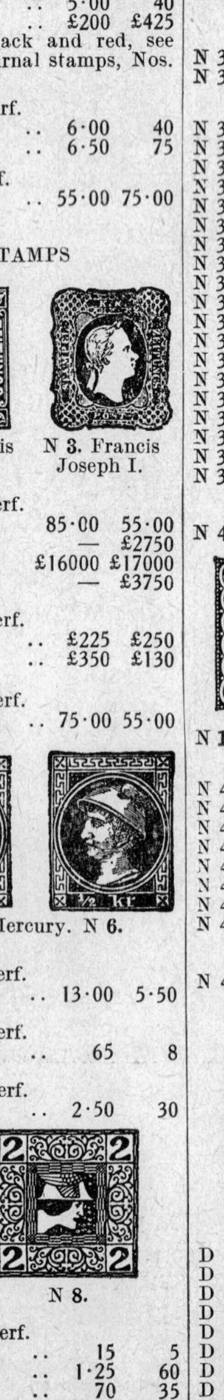

N **1.** Mercury. N **2.** Francis Joseph I. N **3.** Francis Joseph I.

1851. Imperf.
N 11b. N **1.** (0.6 k.) blue 85·00 55·00
N 12. (6 k.) yellow — £2750
N 13. (6 k.) red £16000 £17000
N 14. (30 k.) rose .. — £3750

1858. Imperf.
N 28. N **2.** (1 k.) blue £225 £250
N 29. (1 k.) lilac £350 £130

1861. Imperf.
N 38. N **3.** (1 k.) lilac .. .. 75·00 55·00

N **4.** Arms of Austria. N **5.** Mercury. N **6.**

1863. Imperf.
N 44. N **4.** (1 k. 05) lilac .. 13·00 5·50

1867. Imperf.
N 58b. N **5.** (1 k.) lilac 65 8

1880. Imperf.
N 69. N **6.** ½ k. green .. .. 2·50 30

N **7.** Mercury. N **8.**

1899. Imperf.
N 122. N **7.** 2 h. blue 15 5
N 123. 6 h. orange .. 1·25 60
N 124. 10 h. brown .. 70 35
N 125. 20 h. pink .. 75 55

1908. Imperf.
N 207. N **8.** 2 h. blue 20 5
N 208. 6 h. orange .. .. 1·10 10
N 209. 10 h. red .. .. 1·10 10
N 210. 20 h. brown .. 1·10 8

N **9.** Mercury. N **10.**

1916. Imperf.
N 266. N **9.** 2 h. brown 5 5
N 267. 4 h. green 15 25
N 268. 6 h. blue 12 20
N 269. 10 h. orange .. 20 25
N 270. 30 h. claret 20 25

1916. For Express. Perf.
N 271. N **10.** 2 h. red on yell. .. 25 20
N 272. 5 h. grn. on yell. .. 25 20

N **11.** Mercury. N **12.**

1917. For Express. Perf.
N 294. N **11.** 2 h. red on yell. .. 8 5
N 295. 5 h. grn. on yell. .. 8 5

1919. Optd. **Deutschosterreich.** Imperf.
N 318. N **9.** 2 h. brown 5 5
N 319. 4 h. green 10 12
N 320. 6 h. blue 10 15
N 321. 10 h. orange .. 20 25
N 322. 30 h. claret 12 15

1919. For Express. Optd. **Deutschosterreich.** Perf.
N 334. N **11.** 2 h. red on yell. .. 5 5
N 335. 5 h. grn. on yell. .. 5 5

1920. Imperf.
N 365. N **12.** 2 h. violet 5 5
N 366. 4 h. brown 5 5
N 367. 5 h. slate 5 5
N 368. 6 h. blue 5 5
N 369. 8 h. green 5 5
N 370. 9 h. bistre 5 5
N 371. 10 h. red 5 5
N 372. 12 h. blue 5 5
N 373. 15 h. mauve 5 5
N 374. 18 h. blue-green .. 5 5
N 375. 20 h. orange 5 5
N 376. 30 h. brown 5 5
N 377. 45 h. green 5 5
N 378. 60 h. claret 5 5
N 379. 72 h. brown 5 5
N 380. 90 h. violet 5 5
N 381. 1 k. 20 red 5 10
N 382. 2 k. 40 green .. 5 10
N 383. 3 k. grey 5 10

1921. For Express. No. N 334 surch.
N 450. N **11.** 50 on 2 h. red on yell. 5 5

N **13.** Mercury. N **14.** Posthorn and Arrow.

1921. Imperf.
N 452. N **13.** 45 h. grey 5 5
N 453. 75 h. red-brown .. 5 8
N 454. 1 k. 50 bistre .. 5 8
N 455. 1 k. 80 blue .. 5 8
N 456. 2 k. 25 brown .. 5 8
N 457. 3 k. green 5 8
N 458. 6 k. claret 5 8
N 459. 7 k. 50 yellow .. 5 8

1921. For Express. Perf.
N 460. N **14.** 50 h. lilac on yellow 5 10

POSTAGE DUE STAMPS

D **1.** D **2.**

1894. Perf.
D 96. D **1.** 1 k. brown .. .. 1·00 25
D 97. 2 k. brown .. .. 1·40 25
D 98. 3 k. brown .. .. 1·40 12
D 99. 5 k. brown .. .. 1·25 12
D 100. 6 k. brown .. .. 1·10 1·00
D 101. 7 k. brown 25 45
D 102. 10 k. brown .. .. 1·90 12
D 103. 20 k. brown 25 50
D 104. 50 k. brown .. 13·00 11·00

1899. As Type D **1**, but value in heller. Perf. or imperf.
D 126. D **1.** 1 h. brown 10 8
D 127. 2 h. brown 10 8
D 128. 3 h. brown 8 5
D 129. 4 h. brown 15 5
D 130. 5 h. brown 12 5
D 131. 6 h. brown 12 5
D 132. 10 h. brown .. 10 5
D 133. 12 h. brown .. 20 12
D 134. 15 h. brown .. 20 12
D 135. 20 h. brown .. 25 10
D 136. 40 h. brown .. 35 12
D 137. 100 h. brown .. 1·90 75

1908. Perf.
D 210. D **2.** 1 h. red 60 30
D 211. 2 h. red 12 5
D 212. 4 h. red 12 5
D 213. 6 h. red 12 5
D 214. 10 h. red 25 5
D 215. 14 h. red .. .. 2·25 35
D 216. 20 h. red .. .. 2·50 5
D 217. 25 h. red .. .. 5·50 90
D 218. 30 h. red .. .. 3·50 5
D 219. 50 h. red .. .. 5·00 5
D 220. 100 h. red .. .. 8·00 8
D 221. 5 k. violet .. .. 26·00 4·25
D 222. 10 k. violet .. .. £140 1·60

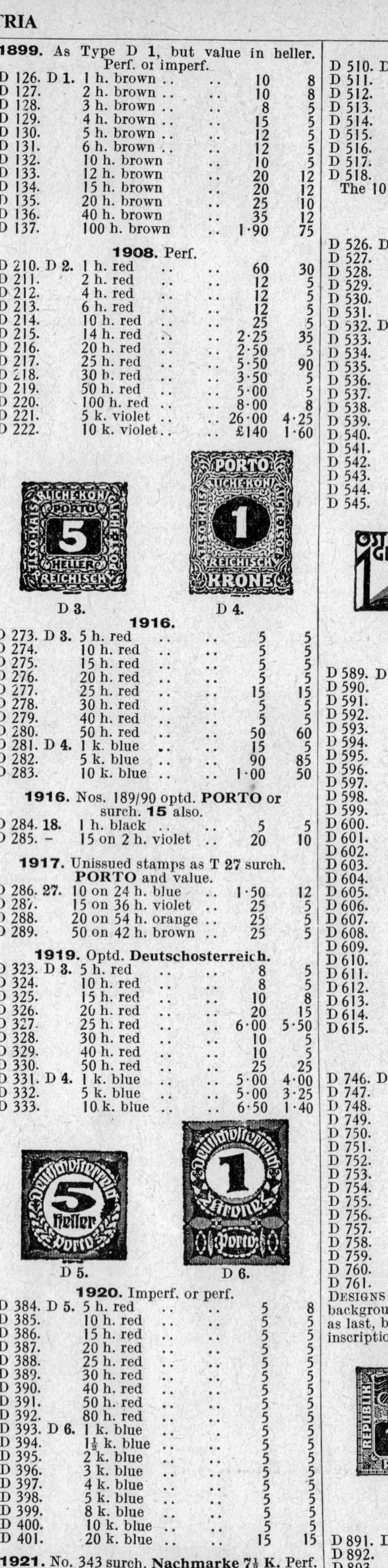

D **3.** D **4.**

1916.
D 273. D **3.** 5 h. red 5 5
D 274. 10 h. red 5 5
D 275. 15 h. red 5 5
D 276. 20 h. red 5 5
D 277. 25 h. red 15 15
D 278. 30 h. red 5 5
D 279. 40 h. red 5 5
D 280. 50 h. red 50 60
D 281. D **4.** 1 k. blue 15 5
D 282. 5 k. blue 90 85
D 283. 10 k. blue .. .. 1·00 50

1916. Nos. 189/90 optd. **PORTO** or surch. **15** also.
D 284. **18.** 1 h. black 5 5
D 285. – 15 on 2 h. violet 20 10

1917. Unissued stamps as T **27** surch. **PORTO** and value.
D 286. **27.** 10 on 24 h. blue .. 1·50 12
D 287. 15 on 36 h. violet .. 25 5
D 288. 20 on 54 h. orange .. 25 5
D 289. 50 on 42 h. brown .. 25 5

1919. Optd. **Deutschosterreich.**
D 323. D **3.** 5 h. red 8 5
D 324. 10 h. red 8 5
D 325. 15 h. red 10 8
D 326. 20 h. red 20 15
D 327. 25 h. red .. .. 6·00 5·50
D 328. 30 h. red 10 5
D 329. 40 h. red 10 5
D 330. 50 h. red 25 25
D 331. D **4.** 1 k. blue .. .. 5·00 4·00
D 332. 5 k. blue .. .. 5·00 3·25
D 333. 10 k. blue .. .. 6·50 1·40

D **5.** D **6.**

1920. Imperf. or perf.
D 384. D **5.** 5 h. red 5 8
D 385. 10 h. red 5 5
D 386. 15 h. red 5 5
D 387. 20 h. red 5 5
D 388. 25 h. red 5 5
D 389. 30 h. red 5 5
D 390. 40 h. red 5 5
D 391. 50 h. red 5 5
D 392. 80 h. red 5 5
D 393. D **6.** 1 k. blue 5 5
D 394. 1½ k. blue 5 5
D 395. 2 k. blue 5 5
D 396. 3 k. blue 5 5
D 397. 4 k. blue 5 5
D 398. 5 k. blue 5 5
D 399. 8 k. blue 5 5
D 400. 10 k. blue 5 5
D 401. 20 k. blue 15 15

1921. No. 343 surch. **Nachmarke 7½ K.** Perf.
D 451. **31.** 7½ k. on 15 h. bistre 5 5

D **7.** D **8.**

1921.
D 510. D **7.** 1 k. brown 5 5
D 511. 2 k. brown 5 5
D 512. 4 k. brown 5 5
D 513. 5 k. brown 5 5
D 514. 7½ k. brown 5 5
D 515. – 10 k. blue 5 5
D 516. – 15 k. blue 5 5
D 517. – 20 k. blue 5 5
D 518. – 50 k. blue 5 5
The 10 k. to 50 k. are larger (22×30 mm.).

1922.
D 526. D **7.** 10 k. blue-green .. 5 5
D 527. 15 k. blue-green .. 5 5
D 528. 20 k. blue-green .. 5 5
D 529. 25 k. blue-green .. 5 5
D 530. 40 k. blue-green .. 5 5
D 531. 50 k. blue-green .. 5 5
D 532. D **8.** 100 k. purple .. 5 5
D 533. 150 k. purple .. 5 5
D 534. 200 k. purple .. 5 5
D 535. 400 k. purple .. 5 5
D 536. 600 k. purple .. 5 5
D 537. 800 k. purple .. 5 5
D 538. 1000 k. purple .. 5 5
D 539. 1200 k. purple .. 20 20
D 540. 1500 k. purple .. 5 5
D 541. 1800 k. purple .. 90 1·00
D 542. 2000 k. purple .. 12 12
D 543. 3000 k. purple .. 2·10 2·40
D 544. 4000 k. purple .. 1·75 2·25
D 545. 6000 k. purple .. 1·75 2·25

D **9.** D **10.**

1925.
D 589. D **9.** 1 g. red 5 5
D 590. 2 g. red 5 5
D 591. 3 g. red 5 5
D 592. 4 g. red 5 5
D 593. 5 g. red 5 5
D 594. 6 g. red 15 12
D 595. 8 g. red 12 5
D 596. 10 g. blue 5 5
D 597. 12 g. blue 5 5
D 598. 14 g. blue 12 5
D 599. 15 g. blue 8 5
D 600. 16 g. blue 20 5
D 601. 18 g. blue 70 60
D 602. 20 g. blue 8 5
D 603. 23 g. blue 60 5
D 604. 24 g. blue 80 5
D 605. 28 g. blue 25 5
D 606. 30 g. blue 15 5
D 607. 31 g. blue 50 5
D 608. 35 g. blue 40 5
D 609. 39 g. blue .. .. 1·10 5
D 610. 40 g. blue 60 50
D 611. 60 g. blue 50 30
D 612. 1 s. green .. .. 3·25 25
D 613. 2 s. green .. .. 25·00 1·25
D 614. 5 s. green .. .. 80·00 11·00
D 615. 10 s. green .. .. 38·00 1·60

1935.
D 746. D **10.** 1 g. red 5 5
D 747. 2 g. red 5 5
D 748. 3 g. red 5 5
D 749. 5 g. red 5 5
D 750. – 10 g. blue 5 5
D 751. – 12 g. blue 5 5
D 752. – 15 g. blue 10 20
D 753. – 20 g. blue 5 5
D 754. – 24 g. blue 8 5
D 755. – 30 g. blue 10 5
D 756. – 39 g. blue 12 5
D 757. – 60 g. blue 25 25
D 758. – 1 s. green 45 10
D 759. – 2 s. green 80 20
D 760. – 5 s. green .. .. 1·50 45
D 761. – 10 s. green .. .. 2·25 25
DESIGNS: Nos. D 750/7, as Type D **10**, but with background of horizontal lines. Nos. D 758/61, as last, but with positions of figures, arms and inscriptions reversed.

D **11.** D **12.**

1945.
D 891. D **11.** 1 pf. red 5 5
D 892. 2 pf. red 5 5
D 893. 3 pf. red 5 5
D 894. 5 pf. red 5 5
D 895. 10 pf. red 5 5
D 896. 12 pf. red 5 5
D 897. 20 pf. red 5 5
D 898. 24 pf. red 5 5
D 899. 30 pf. red 5 5
D 900. 60 pf. red 5 5
D 901. 1 rm. violet 5 5
D 902. 2 rm. violet 5 5
D 903. 5 rm. violet 5 8
D 904. 10 rm. violet 5 8

1946. Optd. **PORTO.**

D 956. **87.** 3 g. orange 5 5
D 957. 5 g. green 5 5
D 958. 6 g. purple 5 5
D 959. 8 g. red 5 5
D 960. 10 g. grey 5 5
D 961. 12 g. brown 5 5
D 962. 15 g. red 5 5
D 963. 20 g. brown 5 5
D 964. 25 g. blue 5 5
D 965. 30 g. mauve .. 5 5
D 966. 40 g. blue 5 5
D 967. 60 g. olive 5 5
D 968. 1 s. violet 5 5
D 969. 2 s. yellow 15 15
D 970. 5 s. blue 15 15

1947.

D 1035. **D 12.** 1 g. brown .. 5 5
D 1036. 2 g. brown .. 5 5
D 1037. 3 g. brown .. 5 5
D 1038. 5 g. brown .. 5 5
D 1039. 8 g. brown .. 5 5
D 1040. 10 g. brown .. 5 5
D 1041. 12 g. brown .. 5 5
D 1042. 15 g. brown .. 5 5
D 1043. 16 g. brown .. 10 12
D 1044. 17 g. brown .. 10 12
D 1045. 18 g. brown .. 10 12
D 1046. 20 g. brown .. 20 5
D 1047. 24 g. brown .. 12 12
D 1048. 30 g. brown .. 8 8
D 1049. 36 g. brown .. 25 25
D 1050. 40 g. brown .. 5 5
D 1051. 42 g. brown .. 20 20
D 1052. 48 g. brown .. 20 20
D 1053. 50 g. brown .. 25 5
D 1054. 60 g. brown .. 5 5
D 1055. 70 g. brown .. 5 5
D 1056. 80 g. brown .. 1·90 1·90
D 1057. 1 s. blue 5 5
D 1058. 1 s. 15 blue .. 1·10 10
D 1059. 1 s. 20 blue .. 1·25 30
D 1060. 2 s. blue 10 8
D 1061. 5 s. blue 12 8
D 1062. 10 s. blue 15 8

D 13.

1949.

D 1178. **D 13.** 1 g. red 5 5
D 1179. 2 g. red 5 5
D 1180. 4 g. red 20 5
D 1181. 5 g. red 60 15
D 1182. 8 g. red 60 50
D 1183. 10 g. red 40 5
D 1184. 20 g. red 45 5
D 1185. 30 g. red 60 5
D 1186. 40 g. red 5 5
D 1187. 50 g. red 95 5
D 1188. 60 g. red .. .. 4·50 5
D 1189. 63 g. red 60 50
D 1190. 70 g. red 60 5
D 1191. 80 g. red 5 5
D 1192. 90 g. red 8 8
D 1193. 1 s. violet .. .. 1·25 5
D 1194. 1 s. 20 violet .. 8 5
D 1195. 1 s. 35 violet .. 8 5
D 1196. 1 s. 40 violet .. 60 30
D 1197. 1 s. 50 violet .. 2·50 5
D 1198. 1 s. 65 violet .. 12 12
D 1199. 1 s. 70 violet .. 12 12
D 1200. 2 s. violet 50 5
D 1201. 2 s. 50 violet .. 3·25 5
D 1202. 3 s. violet .. .. 4·25 5
D 1203. 4 s. violet 25 15
D 1204. 5 s. violet .. .. 3·00 10
D 1205. 10 s. violet .. .. 3·00 10

AUSTRIAN POST OFFICES IN CRETE E1

100 centimes = 1 franc.

For use in Austrian post offices at Canea, Candia and Rethymnon in Crete, and in other Austrian Levant post offices which used French currency. The post offices in Crete were closed in December 1914.

1903. Stamps of Austria surcharged **CENTIMES or FRANC.**

1. **12.** 5 c. green .. .. 80 1·25
2. **13.** 10 c. red (No. 143) .. 55 1·40
3. 25 c. blue (No. 145) .. 17·00 11·00
4. **14.** 50 c. blue .. .. 3·00 35·00
5. **15.** 1 f. red .. .. 1·10 28·00
6. 2 f. lavender .. .. 6·00 75·00
7. 4 f. green .. .. 6·50 £160

1904. Stamps of Austria surch. **CENTIMES.**

8. **16.** 5 c. green .. .. 2·10 2·50
9. **13.** 10 c. red (No. 160) .. 10·00 9·00
10. 25 c. blue (No. 162) .. 30 26·00
11. **17.** 50 c. blue 75 £140

1906. Type of Austria surch. **CENTIMES.**

15. **13.** 10 c. red (No. 184) .. 55 9·00
16. 15 c. violet (As No. 185) 70 8·00

The 15 c. has figures of value in black.

1.

2.

1908. Francis Joseph I. 60th year of Reign.

17. **1.** 5 c. green on yellow .. 20 20
18. 10 c. red on pink .. 25 30
19. 15 c. brown on buff .. 30 70
20. 25 c. blue on blue .. 5·50 2·00
21. **2.** 50 c. red on yellow .. 1·10 8·00
22. 1 f. brown on grey .. 1·60 12·00

AUSTRIAN POST OFFICES IN TURKEY E3

Various Austrian P.Os in the Turkish Empire. Such offices closed in 1914.

1867. 100 soldi = 1 guiden.
1886. 40 paras = 1 piastre.

1. 2.

3.

1867.

1. **1.** 2 s. yellow .. .. 60 5·50
9. 3 s. green .. .. 45 4·75
10. 5 s. red .. .. 12 4·25
11. 10 s. blue .. .. 21·00 35
5. 15 s. brown .. .. 4·00 1·60
6. 25 s. lilac .. .. 3·00 9·50
7a. **2.** 50 s. brown .. .. 30 9·50

1883.

14. **3.** 2 s. brown .. .. 5 12·00
15. 3 s. green .. .. 40 3·50
16. 5 s. red .. .. 5 2·10
17. 10 s. blue 35 15
18. 20 s. grey .. .. 2·10 1·25
19. 50 s. mauve .. .. 55 3·75

1886. Surch. **10 PARA 10.**

21. **3.** 10 p. on 3 s. green .. 12 1 25

1888. Stamps of Austria of 1883 surch.

22. **8.** 10 pa. on 3 k. green .. 1·10 1·50
23. 20 pa. on 5 k. red .. 20 1·25
24. 1 pi. on 10 k. blue .. 18·00 30
25. 2 pi. on 20 k. grey .. 60 65
26. 5 pi. on 50 k. lilac .. 70 3·25

1890. Stamps of Austria of 1890, the kreuzer values with lower figures of value removed, surch. at foot.

27. **9.** 8 pa. on 2 k. brown .. 8 8
28. 10 pa. on 3 k. green .. 25 8
29. 20 pa. on 5 k. red .. 5 5
30. 1 pi. on 10 k. blue .. 15 5
31. 2 pi. on 20 k. olive .. 3·25 8·00
32. 5 pi. on 50 k. mauve .. 5·00 19·00
33. **10.** 10 pi. on 1 g. blue .. 4·00 4·75
37. 10 pi. on 1 g. lilac .. 4·50 4·00
34. 20 pi. on 2 g. red .. 4·75 7·50
38. 20 pi. on 2 g. green .. 17·00 10·00

1890. Stamps of Austria of 1891, with lower figures of value removed, surch. at foot.

35. **11.** 2 pi. on 20 k. green .. 1·25 20
36. 5 pi. on 50 k. mauve .. 1·10 60

1900. Stamps of Austria of 1899, the heller values with lower figures of value removed, surch. at foot.

46. **12.** 10 pa. on 5 h. green .. 75 60
40. **13.** 20 pa. on 10 h. red .. 2·00 25
48. 1 pi. on 25 h. blue .. 40 15
49. **14.** 2 pi. on 50 h. blue .. 1·00 60
43. **15.** 5 pi. on 1 k. red .. 35 5
44. 10 pi. on 2 k. lavender .. 1·00 70
45. 20 pi. on 4 k. green .. 75 1·75

1903. Stamps of Austria of 1899, with all figures of value removed, surch. at top and at foot.

55. **12.** 10 pa. green 15 35
56. **13.** 20 pa. red 35 15
57. 30 pa. mauve 25 75
58. 1 pi. blue 15 5
59. **14.** 2 pi. blue 40 20

1908. Emperor's Accession. 60th Anniv. T 1/2 of Austrian P.Os in Crete, but value in paras or piastres.

60. 10 pa. green on yellow .. 5 5
61. 20 pa. red on pink .. 8 5
62. 30 pa. brown on buff .. 10 12
70. 1 pi. blue on blue .. 25 12
63. 60 pa. purple on blue .. 12 70
65. 2 pi. red on yellow .. 10 5
66. 5 pi. brown on grey .. 12 12
67. 10 pi. green on yellow .. 25 30
68. 20 pi. blue on grey .. 95 60

POSTAGE DUE STAMPS

1902. Postage Due stamps as Type D 1 of Austria, but with value in heller, surch. with new value.

D 50. **D 1.** 10 pa. on 5 h. green 40 55
D 51. 20 pa. on 10 h. green 40 55
D 52. 1 pi. on 20 h. green .. 75 80
D 53. 2 pi. on 40 h. green .. 80 80
D 54. 5 pi. on 100 h. green 80 55

D 1.

1908.

D 71. **D 1.** ¼ pi. green .. .. 1·40 85
D 72. ½ pi. green .. .. 75 1·00
D 73. 1 pi. green .. .. 1·00 1·00
D 74. 1½ pi. green .. .. 30 2·75
D 75. 2 pi. green .. .. 1·00 3·00
D 76. 5 pi. green .. .. 1·00 1·90
D 77. 10 pi. green .. .. 6·50 27·00
D 78. 20 pi. green .. .. 5·50 32·00
D 79. 30 pi. green .. .. 7·50 3·50

AUSTRO-HUNGARIAN MILITARY POST E1

A. GENERAL ISSUES

100 heller = 1 krone.

1915. Stamps of Bosnia optd. **K.U.K. FELDPOST.**

1. **10.** 1 h. olive 12 8
2. 2 h. blue 12 8
3. 3 h. lake 12 8
4. 5 h. green 8 8
5. 6 h. black 12 8
6. 10 h. red 8 8
7. 12 h. olive 15 12
8. 20 h. brown 20 15
9. 25 h. blue 20 15
10. 30 h. red .. .. 2·25 1·90
11. **11.** 35 h. green .. .. 1·90 1·60
12. 40 h. violet .. .. 1·90 1·60
13. 45 h. brown .. .. 2·00 1·75
14. 50 h. blue .. .. 1·90 1·60
15. 60 h. purple-brown .. 25 20
16. 72 h. blue .. .. 1·60 1·25
17. **10.** 1 k. brown on cream .. 1·90 1·75
18. 2 k. indigo on blue .. 1·75 1·60
19. **11.** 3 k. red on green .. 17·00 16·00
20. 5 k. lilac on grey .. 17·00 14·00
21. 10 k. blue on grey .. £110 £100

1. Francis Joseph.

1915.

22. **1.** 1 h. olive 8 5
23. 2 h. blue 10 8
24. 3 h. lake 8 5
25. 5 h. green 8 5
26. 6 h. black 8 5
27. 10 h. red 10 5
28. 10 h. blue 10 8
29. 12 h. olive 10 8
30. 15 h. red 5 5
31. 20 h. brown 20 10
32. 20 h. olive 20 10
33. 25 h. blue 10 8
34. 30 h. red 10 8
35. 35 h. green 20 20
36. 40 h. violet 20 20
37. 45 h. brown 20 20
38. 50 h. deep green 20 10
39. 60 h. purple 20 15
40. 72 h. blue 20 15
41. 80 h. brown 10 8
42. 90 h. lake 60 45
43. – 1 kr. purple on cream .. 1·40 70
44. – 2 kr. grey on blue .. 80 30
45. – 3 kr. red on green .. 60 55
46. – 4 kr. violet on grey .. 60 55
47. – 5 kr. violet on grey .. 15·00 14·00
48. – 10 kr. blue on grey .. 2·00 2·25

The kronen values are larger, with profile portrait.

1917. As 1917 issue of Bosnia, but inscr. "K. u. K. FELDPOST".

49. 1 h. blue 5 5
50. 2 h. orange 5 5
51. 3 h. grey 5 5
52. 5 h. green 5 5
53. 6 h. violet 8 5
54. 10 h. brown 5 5
55. 12 h. blue 5 5
56. 15 h. red 5 5
57. 20 h. brown 5 5
58. 25 h. blue 25 10
59. 30 h. grey-blue 5 5
60. 40 h. bistre 5 5
61. 50 h. green 5 5
62. 60 h. red 5 5
63. 80 h. blue 5 5
64. 90 h. purple 25 15
65. 2 k. red on buff 8 5
66. 3 k. green on blue 60 50
67. 4 k. red on green .. .. 10·00 8·00
68. 10 k. violet on grey .. 1·50 1·60

The kronen values are larger and the border is different.

1918. Emperor's Welfare Fund. As 1918 issue of Bosnia, but inscr. "K. UND K. FELDPOST".

69. **20.** 10 h. (+10 h.) green .. 25 12
70. – 20 h. (+10 h.) claret .. 25 12
71. **20.** 45 h. (+10 h.) blue .. 25 12

NEWSPAPER STAMPS

N 1. Mercury.

1916.

N 49. **N 1.** 2 h. blue 5 5
N 50. 6 h. orange 60 25
N 51. 10 h. red 70 25
N 52. 20 h. brown 40 20

B. ISSUES FOR ITALY

100 centesimi = 1 lira.

1918. General Issue stamps of 1917 surch. in figs. and word

1. 2 c. on 1 h. blue 5 5
2. 3 c. on 2 h. orange .. 5 5
3. 4 c. on 3 h. grey 5 5
4. 6 c. on 5 h. green .. 8 8
5. 7 c. on 6 h. violet .. 8 8
6. 11 c. on 10 h. brown .. 5 5
7. 13 c. on 12 h. blue .. 5 5
8. 16 c. on 15 h. red 5 5
9. 22 c. on 20 h. brown .. 5 5
10. 27 c. on 25 h. blue .. 20 15
11. 32 c. on 30 h. grey-blue .. 10 8
12. 43 c. on 40 h. bistre .. 8 8
13. 53 c. on 50 h. green .. 5 5
14. 64 c. on 60 h. red 8 8
15. 85 c. on 80 h. blue .. 5 5
16. 95 c. on 90 h. purple .. 8 8
17. 2 l. 11 on 2 k. red on buff .. 12 12
18. 3 l. 16 on 3 k. green on blue 35 30
19. 4 l. 22 on 4 k. red on green .. 50 50

NEWSPAPER STAMPS

1918. Newspaper stamps of General Issue surch. in figs. and words.

N 20. **N 1.** 3 c. on 2 h. blue 5 5
N 21. 7 c. on 6 h. orange .. 20 20
N 22. 11 c. on 10 h. red .. 20 20
N 23. 22 c. on 20 h. brown 12 10

1918. For Express. Newspaper stamps of Bosnia surch. in figs. and words.

N 24. **N 2.** 3 c. on 2 h. red .. 3·25 3·25
N 25. 6 c. on 5 h. green 3·25 3·25

POSTAGE DUE STAMPS

1918. Postage Due stamps of Bosnia surch. in figs. and words.

D 20. **D 2.** 6 c. on 5 h. red .. 1·25 1·25
D 21. 11 c. on 10 h. red .. 1·90 1·75
D 22. 16 c. on 15 h. red .. 40 40
D 23. 27 c. on 25 h. red .. 40 40
D 24. 32 c. on 30 h. red .. 40 40
D 25. 43 c. on 40 h. red .. 40 40
D 26. 53 c. on 50 h. red .. 40 40

C. ISSUES FOR MONTENEGRO

100 heller = 1 krone.

1917. General Issue stamps optd. **K.U.K. MILIT. VERWALTUNG MONTENEGRO.**

1. **1.** 10 h. blue .. .. 4·50 2·50
2. 15 h. red .. .. 4·50 2·50

D. ISSUES FOR RUMANIA

100 bani = 1 leu.

1917. General Issue stamps of 1917, optd. **BANI** or **LEI.**

1. 3 b. grey 70 60
2. 5 b. green 60 40
3. 6 b. violet 60 40
4. 10 b. brown 12 5
5. 12 b. blue 65 50
6. 15 b. red 55 40
7. 20 b. brown 10 5
8. 25 b. blue 12 8
9. 30 b. grey-blue 20 15
10. 40 b. bistre 20 12
11. 50 b. green 20 12
12. 60 b. red 20 12
13. 80 b. blue 10 5
14. 90 b. purple 25 12
15. 2 l. red on buff 30 20
16. 3 l. green on blue .. 40 25
17. 4 l. red on green .. 40 25

1. Charles I.

1918.

18. **1.** 3 b. grey 12 10
19. 5 b. green 12 10
20. 6 b. violet 15 15
21. 10 b. brown 15 15
22. 12 b. blue 12 12
23. 15 b. red 10 10
24. 20 b. brown 12 12
25. 25 b. blue 12 12
26. 30 b. grey-blue 12 12
27. 40 b. bistre 12 12

28. 1.	50 b. green	15	15
29.	60 b. red	15	15
30.	80 b. blue	10	10
31.	90 b. purple	12	15
32.	2 l. red on buff	15	15
33.	3 l. green on blue	20	20
34.	4 l. red on green	20	20

E. ISSUES FOR SERBIA

100 heller = 1 krone.

1916. Stamps of Bosnia optd. **SERBIEN**

22. 10.	1 h. olive	1·50	1·25
23.	2 h. blue	1·50	1·25
24.	3 h. lake	1·40	1·90
25.	5 h. green	25	25
26.	6 h. black	75	65
27.	10 h. red	25	25
28.	12 h. olive	75	65
29.	20 h. brown	40	40
30.	25 h. blue	35	35
31.	30 h. red	35	35
32. 11.	35 h. green	35	35
33.	40 h. violet	35	35
34.	45 h. brown	35	35
35.	50 h. blue	35	35
36.	60 h. purple-brown	35	35
37.	72 h. blue	35	35
38. 10.	1 k. brown on cream	45	45
39.	2 k. indigo on blue	40	40
40. 11.	3 k. red on green	40	40
41.	5 k. lilac on grey	40	40
42.	10 k. blue on grey	8·00	8·00

AZERBAIJAN E1

Formerly part of the Russian Empire. Became independent on 27 May 1918, following the Russian Revolution. Soviet troops invaded the country on 27 April 1920, and a Soviet Republic followed. From 1 Oct. 1923 stamps of the Transcaucasian Federation were used but these were superseded by those of the Soviet Union in 1924.

1. Standard-bearer.

4. Famine Supplies.

2. "Labour". 3. Petroleum Well.

1919. Imperf. Various designs.

1. 1.	10 k. grn., blue, blk. & red	15	30
2. –	20 k. blue, grn., blk. & red	12	25
3. –	40 k. olive, black & yellow	5	10
4. –	60 k. orange, blk. & yellow	5	10
5. –	1 r. blue, black and yellow	5	10
6. –	2 r. red, black and yellow	5	10
7. –	5 r. blue, black and yellow	5	12
8. –	10 r. olive, black & yellow	25	35
9. –	25 r. blue, black and red	25	30
10. –	50 r. olive, black and red	25	45

DESIGNS—HORIZ. 40 k. to 1 r. Reaper. 2 r. to 10 r. Citadel. Baku. 25 r., 50 r. Temple of Eternal Fires.

1921. Imperf.

11. 2.	1 r. green	5	15
12. 3.	2 r. sepia	5	10
13. –	5 r. brown	5	10
14. –	10 r. slate	10	15
15. –	25 r. orange-brown	5	15
16. –	50 r. violet	5	25
17. –	100 r. orange-brown	8	25
18. –	150 r. blue	8	15
19. –	200 r. violet and buff	8	15
20. –	400 r. blue	8	12
21. –	500 r. black and lilac	8	25
22. –	1000 r. red and blue	8	15
23. –	2000 r. black and blue	8	15
24. –	3000 r. brown and blue	8	15
25. –	5000 r. green on olive	10	20

DESIGNS—HORIZ. 5 r., 3000 r. Bibi Eibatt Oilfield. 100 r., 5000 r. Goukasoff House. 400 r., 1000 r. Hall of Judgment, Khan's Palace. VERT. 10 r., 2000 r. Khan's Palace, Baku. 25 r., 250 r. Globe and Workers. 50 r. Maiden's Tower, Baku. 150 r., 500 r. Blacksmiths.

1921. Famine Relief. Imperf.

26. 4.	500 r. blue	15	25
27. –	1000 r. brown	20	40

DESIGN—VERT. 1000 r. Starving family.

For stamps of the above issues surcharged with new values, see Stanley Gibbons' "Europe" Catalogue, Volume I.

AZORES E1

A group of islands in the Atlantic Ocean. Now uses the stamps of Portugal.

NOTE. Except where otherwise stated the following are all stamps of Portugal overprinted **AZORES.**

1868. Curved value labels. Imperf.

1. 4.	5 r. black	£700	£500
2.	10 r. yellow	£1800	£1200
3.	20 r. olive	65·00	42·00
4.	50 r. green	85·00	55·00
5.	80 r. orange	£100	45·00
6.	100 r. purple	75·00	48·00

1868. Curved value labels. Perf.

7. 4.	5 r. black	10·00	6·00
9.	10 r. yellow	28·00	16·00
10.	20 r. olive	22·00	14·00
11.	25 r. red	14·00	1·50
12.	50 r. green	40·00	30·00
13.	80 r. orange	55·00	32·00
14.	100 r. lilac	42·00	30·00
16.	120 r. blue	35·00	16·00
17.	240 r. mauve	£130	60·00

1871. Straight value labels.

38. 5.	5 r. black	3·25	1·75
28.	10 r. yellow	4·25	3·25
73.	10 r. green	9·00	4·50
96.	15 r. brown	3·25	2·25
31.	20 r. olive	4·25	3·25
109.	20 r. red	10·00	7·00
21.	25 r. red	2·75	40
33.	50 r. green	8·00	3·50
54.	50 r. blue	14·00	7·00
111.	80 r. orange	7·50	2·75
103.	100 r. mauve	3·00	1·40
25.	120 r. blue	30·00	15·00
37.	150 r. blue	38·00	17·00
82.	150 r. yellow	5·00	2·25
26.	240 r. lilac	£180	90·00
105.	300 r. mauve	11·00	6·00
84.	1000 r. black	13·00	12·00

1880.

51. 6.	5 r. black	3·00	1·90
61.	25 r. grey	2·75	1·60
61a.	25 r. grey	2·75	1·60
65. 7.	25 r. grey	10·00	4·25
62. 6.	50 r. blue	13·00	8·00

1882.

124. 8.	5 r. grey	1·10	50
125.	10 r. green	1·75	1·10
139.	20 r. red	2·50	1·75
126.	25 r. brown	1·60	60
141.	25 r. mauve	1·60	20
119.	50 r. blue	1·75	1·00
128.	500 r. black	40·00	20·00
129.	500 r. mauve	22·00	15·00

1894. Prince Henry the Navigator.

143. 10.	5 r. orange	70	55
144.	10 r. red	1·00	60
145.	15 r. brown	1·60	70
146.	20 r. lilac	1·60	80
147.	25 r. green	1·60	80
148.	50 r. blue	2·00	1·10
149.	75 r. red	3·25	2·75
150.	80 r. green	3·50	3·00
151.	100 r. brown on buff	3·00	1·75
152.	150 r. red	5·50	4·75
153.	300 r. blue on buff	6·00	4·75
154.	500 r. purple	7·50	5·50
155.	100 r. black on buff	12·00	7·50

1895. St. Anthony of Padua.

156. 13.	2½ r. black	1·00	90
157. –	5 r. orange	1·50	1·25
158. –	10 r. mauve	2·10	1·60
159. –	15 r. brown	3·00	2·50
160. –	20 r. grey	3·00	2·50
161. –	25 r. purple and green	2·00	1·50
162. 15.	50 r. brown and blue	6·50	6·00
163. –	75 r. brown and red	10·00	8·50
164. –	80 r. brown and green	14·00	12·00
165. –	100 r. black and brown	13·00	9·50
166. –	150 r. red and brown	26·00	17·00
167. –	200 r. blue and brown	30·00	19·00
168. –	300 r. black and brown	42·00	30·00
169. –	500 r. brown & green	55·00	38·00
170. –	1000 r. lilac and green	£110	75·00

1898. Vasco da Gama stamps as Nos. 378/385 of Portugal but inscr. "ACORES".

171.	2½ r. green	35	30
172.	5 r. red	50	45
173.	10 r. purple	1·25	75
174.	25 r. green	60	45
175.	50 r. blue	1·50	1·25
176.	75 r. brown	2·75	2·50
177.	100 r. brown	2·75	2·00
178.	150 r. yellow-brown	4·25	3·25

1906. "King Carlos" key-type inscr. "ACORES" and optd. with letters "**A**", "**H**" and "**PD**" in three of the corners.

179. S.	2½ r. grey	15	12
180.	5 r. orange	15	12
181.	10 r. green	15	12
182.	20 r. lilac	25	20
183.	25 r. red	12	12
184.	50 r. blue	1·25	80
185.	75 r. brown on yellow	35	30
186.	100 r. blue on blue	45	40
187.	200 r. purple on pink	50	40
188.	300 r. blue on pink	55	50
189.	500 r. black on blue	80	60

1.

1910.

190. 1.	2½ r. lilac	20	15
191.	5 r. black	20	20
192.	10 r. green	25	25
193.	15 r. brown	45	30
194.	20 r. red	45	30
195.	25 r. brown	20	12
196.	50 r. blue	70	55
197.	75 r. brown	85	65
198.	80 r. grey	85	65
199.	100 r. brown on green	1·40	1·25
200.	200 r. green on pink	1·25	90
201.	300 r. black on blue	1·75	1·40
202.	500 r. brown and olive	2·25	1·75
203.	1000 r. black and blue	4·50	3·50

1910. Optd. **REPUBLICA.**

204. 1.	2½ r. lilac	12	10
205.	5 r. black	15	12
206.	10 r. green	20	15
207.	15 r. brown	30	25
208.	20 r. red	55	50
209.	25 r. brown	12	10
210.	50 r. blue	40	30
211.	75 r. brown	20	12
212.	80 r. grey	35	25
213.	100 r. brown on green	25	20
214.	200 r. green on pink	25	20
215.	300 r. black on blue	45	30
216.	500 r. brown and olive	65	55
217.	1000 r. black and blue	1·10	90

1911. Vasco da Gama stamps of Azores optd. **REPUBLICA**, some surch. also.

218.	2½ r. green	25	20
219.	15 r. on 5 r. red	20	20
220.	25 r. green	20	20
221.	50 r. blue	40	35
222.	75 r. brown	30	30
223.	80 r. on 150 r. brown	30	30
224.	100 r. brown	30	30
225.	1000 r. on 10 r. purple	2·75	2·40

1911. Postage Due stamps optd. **REPUBLICA ACORES**, some surch. also.

226 D 1.	5 r. black	30	25
227.	10 r. mauve	50	40
228.	20 r. orange	1·00	70
229.	200 r. brown	2·50	2·40
230.	300 r. on 50 r. grey	2·50	2·40
231.	500 r. on 100 r. red	2·50	2·40

1912. "Ceres" type.

250. 28.	¼ c. olive	8	5
251.	½ c. black	10	5
252.	1 c. green	30	15
274.	1 c. brown	10	5
254.	1½ c. brown	40	30
275.	1½ c. green	15	15
256.	2 c. red	25	20
257.	2 c. yellow	15	10
258.	2½ c. lilac	25	12
259.	3 c. red	15	10
278.	3 c. blue	15	12
260.	3½ c. green	15	10
279.	4 c. green	12	8
401.	4 c. orange	15	12
262.	5 c. blue	25	15
263.	5 c. brown	20	15
264.	6 c. claret	15	10
282.	6 c. brown	20	15
265.	7½ c. brown	1·10	70
266.	7½ c. blue	40	30
267.	8 c. grey	25	20
283.	8 c. green	20	20
284.	8 c. orange	30	25
268.	10 c. brown	1·00	35
285.	10 c. red	15	10
286.	12 c. grey-blue	35	35
287.	12 c. green	30	25
288.	13½ c. blue	35	25
249.	14 c. blue on yellow	45	40
269.	15 c. maroon	25	20
289.	15 c. black	15	10
290.	16 c. blue	15	10
243.	20 c. brown on green	2·75	1·60
291.	20 c. chocolate	20	15
292.	20 c. green	20	15
293.	20 c. drab	25	20
294.	24 c. turquoise	20	15
295.	25 c. pink	15	10
244.	30 c. brown on rose	16·00	11·00
245.	30 c. brown on yellow	45	35
296.	30 c. brown	35	30
406.	32 c. green	50	45
298.	36 c. red	20	15
299.	40 c. blue	20	15
300.	40 c. sepia	15	12
407.	40 c. green	35	20
301.	48 c. pink	65	55
246.	50 c. orange on salmon	1·10	70
302.	50 c. yellow	35	30
409.	50 c. brown	1·00	55
271.	60 c. blue	35	30
304.	64 c. blue	70	60
411.	64 c. lake	70	55
305.	75 c. pink	70	60
412.	75 c. red	70	55
306.	80 c. claret	50	40
307.	80 c. violet	50	40
413. 28.	80 c. green	65	60
308.	90 c. blue	50	40
309.	96 c. red	1·25	1·00
248.	1 e. green on blue	1·60	1·25
310.	1 e. lilac	50	40
314.	1 e. slate-purple	55	35
414.	1 e. red	9·00	7·50
311.	1 e. 10 brown	50	40
312.	1 e. 20 green	50	40
315.	1 e. 20 ochre	1·25	1·00
415.	1 e. 25 blue	35	30
316.	1 e. 50 slate-purple	90	65
317.	1 e. 50 lilac	90	65
318.	1 e. 60 blue	90	80
313.	2 e. green	1·25	1·00
319.	2 e. 40 green	8·50	7·50
320.	3 e. pink	8·00	7·50
321.	3 e. 20 bronze	1·60	1·50
322.	5 e. turquoise-green	2·25	1·75
323.	10 e. rose	4·50	4·00
324.	20 e. blue	22·00	15·00

1925. Branco Centenary.

325. 37.	2 c. orange	12	12
326.	3 c. green	12	12
327.	4 c. blue	12	12
328.	5 c. red	12	12
329. –	10 c. blue	12	12
330. –	16 c. orange	15	15
331. 39.	25 c. red	15	15
332. –	32 c. green	25	25
333. 39.	40 c. black and green	20	20
334.	48 c. maroon	35	35
335. –	50 c. green	35	35
336. –	64 c. brown	35	35
337. –	75 c. grey	50	50
338. 39.	80 c. brown	50	50
339. –	96 c. red	50	50
340. –	1 e. 50 blue on blue	50	50
341. 39.	1 e. 60 blue	50	50
342. –	2 e. green on green	75	75
343. –	2 e. 40 red on orange	1·00	1·00
344. –	3 e. 20 black on green	1·00	1·00

1926. First Independence Issue.

345. 47.	2 c. black and orange	20	20
346. –	3 c. black and blue	20	20
347. 47.	4 c. black and green	20	20
348. –	5 c. black and brown	20	20
349. 47.	6 c. black and orange	20	20
350. –	15 c. black and green	25	25
351. 48.	20 c. black and violet	25	25
352. –	25 c. black and red	30	30
353. 48.	32 c. black and green	30	30
354. –	40 c. black and brown	30	30
355. –	50 c. black and olive	65	65
356. –	75 c. black and red	65	65
357. –	1 e. black and violet	90	90
358. –	4 e. 50 black and green	2·10	2·10

1927. Second Independence Issue.

359. 49.	2 c. black and brown	20	20
360. –	3 c. black and blue	20	20
361. 49.	4 c. black and orange	20	20
362. –	5 c. black and brown	20	20
363. 50.	6 c. black and brown	20	20
364. –	15 c. black and brown	20	20
365. 49.	25 c. black and grey	35	35
366. 50.	32 c. black and green	35	35
367. –	40 c. black and green	35	35
368. –	96 c. black and red	1·10	1·10
369. –	1 e. 60 black and blue	1·10	1·10
370. –	4 e. 50 black and yellow	2·00	2·00

1928. Third Independence Issue.

371. –	2 c. black and blue	20	20
372. –	3 c. black and green	20	20
373. –	4 c. black and red	20	20
374. –	5 c. black and olive	20	20
375. –	6 c. black and brown	20	20
376. 52.	15 c. black and grey	25	25
377. –	16 c. black and purple	30	30
378. –	25 c. black and blue	30	30
379. –	32 c. black and green	30	30
380. 53.	40 c. black and brown	30	30
381. –	50 c. black and red	60	60
382. 52.	80 c. black and grey	60	60
383. –	96 c. black and red	90	90
384. 53.	1 e. black and mauve	90	90
385. –	1 e. 60 black and blue	90	90
386. –	4 e. 50 black and yellow	2·00	2·00

1929. "Ceres" type surch. **ACORES** and new value.

387. 28.	4 c. on 25 c. pink	20	20
388.	4 c. on 60 c. blue	20	20
389.	10 c. on 25 c. pink	45	40
390.	12 c. on 25 c. pink	35	35
391.	15 c. on 25 c. pink	35	35
392.	20 c. on 25 c. pink	35	35
393.	40 c. on 1 e. 10 brown	1·10	1·10

CHARITY TAX STAMPS

The notes under this heading in Portugal also apply here.

1911. No. 206 optd. **ASSISTENCIA.**

C 218. 1.	10 r. green	35	30

1913. No. 252 optd. **ASSISTENCIA.**

C 250. 28.	1 c. green	70	60

1915. For the Poor. Charity stamp optd. **ACORES.**

C 251. C 2.	1 c. red	12	10

1925. No. C 251 surch. **15 ctvs.**

C 325. C 2.	15 c. on 1 c. red	20	20

1925. Portuguese Army in Flanders.
C 345. C **3.** 10 c. red 35 35
C 346. 10 c. green 35 35
C 347. 10 c. blue 35 35
C 348. 10 c. brown 35 35

1925. As Marquis de Pombal.
C 349. C **4.** 20 c. green 30 25
C 350. – 20 c. green 30 25
C 351. C **5.** 20 c. green 30 25

NEWSPAPER STAMPS

1876.
N 146. N **1.** 2 r. black 40 30
N 149. N **2.** 2½ r. olive 50 20
N 151. 2½ r. yellow-brown 50 30

PARCEL POST STAMPS

1921.
P 325. P **1.** 1 c. brown 15 15
P 326. 2 c. orange 15 15
P 327. 5 c. brown 15 15
P 328. 10 c. brown 20 15
P 329. 20 c. blue 20 15
P 330. 40 c. red 20 15
P 331. 50 c. black 25 20
P 332. 60 c. blue 25 20
P 333. 70 c. brown 50 50
P 334. 80 c. blue 50 50
P 335. 90 c. violet 50 50
P 336. 1 e. green 50 50
P 337. 2 e. lilac 80 70
P 338. 3 e. olive 1·25 1·00
P 339. 4 e. blue 1·60 1·50
P 340. 5 e. lilac 1·75 1·60
P 341. 10 e. brown 4·25 3·50

POSTAGE DUE STAMPS

1904.
D 179. D **2.** 5 r. brown 30 25
D 180. 10 r. orange 30 25
D 181. 20 r. mauve 45 40
D 182. 30 r. green 45 40
D 183. 40 r. lilac 65 60
D 184. 50 r. red 1·00 90
D 185. 100 r. blue 1·10 1·00

1911. As last optd. **REPUBLICA.**
D 218. D **2.** 5 r. brown 15 12
D 219. 10 r. orange 15 12
D 220. 20 r. mauve 15 15
D 221. 30 r. green 20 15
D 222. 40 r. lilac 20 15
D 223. 50 r. red 1·00 80
D 224. 100 r. blue 50 45

1918. Value in centavos.
D 325. D **2.** ½ c. brown 15 15
D 326. 1 c. orange 15 15
D 327. 2 c. claret 15 15
D 328. 3 c. green 15 15
D 329. 4 c. lilac 15 15
D 330. 5 c. red 15 15
D 331. 10 c. blue 20 20

1922.
D 332. D **2.** ½ c. green 12 12
D 333. 1 c. green 12 12
D 334. 2 c. green 12 12
D 335. 3 c. green 20 20
D 336. 8 c. green 15 15
D 337. 10 c. green 20 20
D 338. 12 c. green 20 15
D 339. 16 c. green 20 20
D 340. 20 c. green 20 20
D 341. 24 c. green 15 15
D 342. 32 c. green 15 15
D 343. 36 c. green 15 15
D 344. 40 c. green 20 20
D 345. 48 c. green 20 20
D 346. 50 c. green 25 20
D 347. 60 c. green 25 20
D 348. 72 c. green 15 15
D 349. 80 c. green 40 35
D 350. 1 e. 20 green 55 45

1925. Portuguese Army in Flanders.
D 351. D **3.** 20 c. brown 25 25

1925. De Pombal stamps optd. **MULTA.** New colour. As Nos. C 349/51
D 352. C **4.** 40 c. green 25 25
D 353. – 40 c. green 25 25
D 354. C **5.** 40 c. green 25 25

BADEN E2

In S.W. Germany. Formerly a Grand Duchy now part of West Germany.

60 kreuzer = 1 Gulden.

1. 2.

1851. Imperf.
1. **1.** 1 k. black on buff £400 £275
8. 1 k. black on white 75·00 8·50
3. 3 k. black on yellow 80·00 5·00
9. 3 k. black on green 85·00 1·75
10. 3 k. black on blue £170 8·50
5. 6 k. black on green £225 18·00
11. 6 k. black on orange £150 6·00
6. 9 k. black on rose 38·00 6·50

1860. Shaded background behind Arms. Perf.
21. **2.** 1 k. black 20·00 30·00
16. 3 k. blue 45·00 6·50
17. 6 k. orange 70·00 22 00
22. 6 k. blue 60·00 20·00
19. 9 k. red £150 50·00
25. 9 k. brown 50·00 30·00

1892. Uncoloured background behind Arms.
27. 1 k. black 25·00 5·00
28. 3 k. red 20·00 35
30. 6 k. blue 5·00 6 00
34. 9 k. brown 5·00 7·00
36. 18 k. green £170 £170
38. 30 k. orange 16·00 £350

1868. "K.R." instead of "KREUZER".
39. 1 k. green 2·00 1·75
41. 3 k. red 1·25 50
44. 7 k. blue 10·00 12·00

For issues of 1947 to 1949 see Germany (French Zone).

RURAL POSTAGE DUE STAMPS

D 1.

1862
D 39. D **1.** 1 k. black on yellow 2·00 £100
D 40. 3 k. black on yellow 2·00 38·00
D 41. 12 k. black on yellow 19·00 £7500

BAGHDAD BC

A city in Iraq. Special stamps issued during Br. occupation in the War of 1914/18.

1917. Various issues of Turkey surch. **BAGHDAD IN BRITISH OCCUPATION** and new value in annas.

A. Pictorial issues of 1913.
1. **14.** ½ a. on 2 pa. claret 30·00 30·00
2. **16.** ½ a. on 5 pa. purple 25·00 25·00
3. – ½ a. on 10 pa. grn. (516) £140 £120
4. **13.** ½ a. on 10 pa. green £300 £325
5. – 1 a. on 20 pa. red (504) £140 £120
6. – 2 a. on 1 pi. blue (No. 518) 45·00 45·00

B. As last but optd. with small star.
7. – 1 a. on 20 pa. red £110 £110
8. – 2 a. on 1 pi. blue £1400 £2400

C. Postal Jubilee issue.
9. **36.** ½ a. on 10 pa. red £110 £110
10. 1 a. on 20 pa. blue £250 £250
11. 2 a. on 1 pi. blk. & violet 25·00 25·00

D. Optd. with Turkish letter "B".
12. **12.** 2 a. on 1 pi. blue £100 £100

E. Optd. with star and Arabic date within crescent.
13. **12.** ½ a. on 10 pa. green 25·00 25·00
14. 1 a. on 20 pa. red £110 £110
15. **7.** 1 a. on 20 pa. rose £120 £120
16. **5.** 1 a. on 20 pa. red (No. N 185) £1500 £1600
17. **12.** 2 a. on 1 pi. blue 30·00 30·00
18. **5.** 2 a. on 1 pi. blue 60·00 60·00

F. Optd. as last but with date between star and crescent.
19. **7.** ½ a. on 10 pa. green 30·00 30·00
20. **36.** ½ a. on 10 pa. red 55·00 55·00
21. **12.** 1 a. on 20 pa. red 28·00 28·00
22. **11.** 1 a. on 20 pa. rose 60·00 60·00
23. **4.** 1 a. on 10 pa. on 20 pa. red 70·00 70·00
24. **12.** 2 a. on 1 pi. blue 60·00 60·00
25. **11.** 2 a. on 1 pi. blue £350 £350

BAHAMAS BC

A group of islands in the Br. W. Indies, S.E. of Florida. Self-Government introduced on 7th January, 1964. The islands became an independent member of the British Commonwealth on 10th July, 1973.

1966. 100 cents = 1 dollar.

ILLUSTRATIONS
British Commonwealth and all overprints and surcharges are FULL SIZE. Foreign Countries have been reduced to ¾-LINEAR.

1.

1859. Imperf.
2. **1.** 1d. rose 18·00 £250

2. 3.

1860. Perf.
40. **1.** 1d. red 16·00 12·00
26. **2.** 4d. rose 95·00 32·00
30. 6d. violet 40·00 24·00
39. **3.** 1s. green 3·50 4·50

1883. Surch. **FOURPENCE.**
45. **2.** 4d. on 6d. violet £200 90·00

4. **5.** Queen's Staircase, Nassau.

1884.
48. **4.** 1d. red 3·00 1·60
52. 2½d. blue 3·00 2·50
53. 4d. yellow 3·75 2·75
54. 6d. mauve 4·00 4·25
56. 5s. green 25·00 25·00
57. £1 red £130 85·00

1901.
122. **5.** 1d. black and red 1·10 2·00
96. 3d. purple on yellow 1·50 3·00
110. 3d. black and brown 90 3·00
69. 5d. black and orange 10·00 13·00
97. 5d. black and mauve 1·50 4·50
70. 2s. black and blue 10·00 15·00
71. 3s. black and green 14·00 17·00

6. 7.

1902.
72. **6.** ½d. green 2·25 65
73. 1d. red 2·50 50
61. 2½d. blue 5·00 3·25
62. 4d. yellow 7·50 9·50
64. 6d. brown 7·00 9·00
65. 1s. black and red 8·00 11·00
67. 5s. purple and blue 32·00 32·00
68. £1 green and black £180 £250

1912.
76. **7.** ½d. green 45 50
125. 1d. red 25 25
139. 1½d. brown 50 60
125a. 2d. grey 45 1·00
126. 2½d. blue 50 1·00
140. 3d. purple on yellow 3·00 5·00
127. 4d. yellow 75 2·25
128. 6d. brown 60 2·25
129. 1s. black and red 1·75 4·50
130. 5s. purple and blue 15·00 19·00
91. £1 green and black 75·00 85·00

1917. Optd. **1.1.17** and Red Cross.
100. **5.** 1d. black and red 25 60

WAR TAX
(8.)

1918. Optd. with T 8.
101. **7.** ½d. green 2·00 2·50
102. 1d. red 60 90
105. **5.** 1d. black and red 1·60 2·50
103. 3d. purple on yellow 2·25 2·75
104. **7.** 1s. black and red 25·00 32·00

WAR TAX (9.) WAR TAX (10.)

1918. Optd. with T 9 or 10 (3d.).
106. **7.** ½d. green 20 50
107. 1d. red 20 60
108. **5.** 3d. purple on yellow 45 1·25
111. 3d. black and brown 50 2·50
109. **7.** 1s. black and red 65 1·50

1919. Optd. **WAR CHARITY 3.6.18.**
112. **5.** 1d. black and red 30 1·10

1919. Optd. **WAR TAX** in two lines.
113. **7.** ½d. green 20 75
114. 1d. red 20 75
116. **5.** 3d. black and brown 60 2·25
115. **7.** 1s. black and red 2·00 3·75

11.

1920. Peace Commem.
117. **11.** ½d. green 25 75
118. 1d. red 1·00 1·10
119. 2d. grey 2·00 3·00
120. 3d. brown 1·90 4·50
121. 1s. green 11·00 15·00

12. Seal of the Colony.

1930. Tercentenary of the Colony.
132. **12.** 1d. black and red 1·25 1·90
133. 3d. black and brown 2·50 3·50
134. 5d. black and violet 5·00 7·00
135. 2s. black and blue 13·00 18·00
136. 3s. black and green 17·00 23·00

1931. As T 12, but without dates at top.
137. 2s. black and blue 60 45
138. 3s. black and green 70 75

1935. Silver Jubilee. As T 11 of Antigua.
141. 1½d. blue and red 35 35
142. 2½d. brown and blue 1·10 1·10
143. 6d. blue and olive 2·50 3·25
144. 1s. grey and purple 4·00 5·00

13. Flamingoes.

1935.
145. **13.** 8d. blue and red 4·50 3·00

1937. Coronation. As T 2 of Aden.
146. ½d. green 15 15
147. 1½d. brown 30 30
148. 2½d. blue 75 45

14. King George VI.

DESIGNS—As T **15** HORIZ. 6d. Fort Charlotte. 8d. Flamingoes.

15. Sea Garden, Nassau.

1938.
149. **14.** ½d. green 12 12
149a. ½d. purple 12 30
150. 1d. red 1·00 1·10
150a. 1d. grey 10 10
151a. 1½d. brown 15 20
152. 2d. grey 5·50 4·00
152a. 2d. red 10 20
152b. 2d. green 30 50
153. 2½d. blue 80 1·00
153a. 2½d. violet 10 15
154. 3d. violet 70 2·75
154a. 3d. blue 10 30
154b. 3d. red 40 60
158. **15.** 4d. blue and orange 25 30
159. – 6d. green and blue 15 20
160. – 8d. blue and red 25 45
154c. **14.** 10d. orange 25 25
155. 1s. black and red 45 45
156a. 5s. purple and blue 4·50 4·00
157. £1 green and black 8·00 11·00

1940. Surch.
161. **14.** 3d. on 2½d. blue 10 40

1942. Landing of Columbus. 450th Anniv. Optd. **1492 LANDFALL OF COLUMBUS 1942.**
162. **14.** ½d. green 10 15
163. 1d. grey 10 15
164. 1½d. brown 12 20
165. 2d. red 12 20
166. 2½d. blue 12 20
167. 3d. blue 12 20

168. 15. 4d. blue and orange .. 25 35
169. – 6d. grn. & blue (No. 159) 30 40
170. – 8d. blue & red (No. 160) 30 35
171. 14. 1s. black and red .. 30 50
172. 12. 2s. black and blue .. 2·00 2·50
173a. 3s. black and green .. 1·50 2·50
174. 14. 5s. purple and blue .. 1·75 2·50
175. £1 green and black .. 10·00 11·00

1946. Victory. As T 4 of Aden.
176. 1½d. brown 5 10
177. 3d. blue.. .. .. .. 10 12

16. Infant Welfare Clinic.

1948. Tercentenary of Settlement of Island of Eleuthera. Inscr. as in T 16.
178. 16. ½d. orange 10 20
179. – 1d. olive 10 20
180. – 1½d. yellow 12 25
181. – 2d. red 15 25
182. – 2½d. brown 15 35
183. – 3d. blue.. .. .. 25 35
184. – 4d. black 25 50
185. – 6d. green 30 50
186. – 8d. violet 30 55
187. – 10d. red 25 30
188. – 1s. brown 40 50
189. – 2s. purple .. .. 4·00 4·50
190. – 3s. blue .. .. 3·50 4·00
191. – 5s. mauve .. .. 2·50 3·50
192. – 10s. grey .. .. 3·00 5·50
193. – £1 red .. .. .. 6·00 8·50
DESIGNS: 1d. Agriculture. 1½d. Sisal. 2d. Straw work. 2½d. Dairy. 3d. Fishing fleet. 4d. Island settlement. 6d. Tuna fishing. 8d. Paradise Beach. 10d. Modern hotels. 1s. Yacht racing. 2s. Water sports — skiing. 3s. Shipbuilding. 5s. Transportation. 10s. Salt production. £1 Parliament Buildings.

1948. Silver Wedding. As T 5/6 of Aden.
194. 1½d. brown 8 12
195. £1 grey .. .. .. 14·00 17·00

1949. U.P.U. As T 14/17 of Antigua.
196. 2½d. violet 15 20
197. 3d. blue 30 30
198. 6d. blue 70 70
199. 1s. red .. .. .. 1·00 1·00

1953. Coronation. As T 7 of Aden.
200. 6d. black and blue .. 40 55

17. Infant Welfare Clinic.

1954. Designs as Nos. 178/93 but with portrait of Queen Elizabeth II and without commemorative inscr. as in T 17.
201. 17. ½d. black and vermilion 10 10
202. – 1d. olive and brown .. 10 10
203. – 1½d. blue and black .. 10 10
204. – 2d. chestnut and green 12 12
205. – 3d. black and red .. 15 15
206. – 4d. turquoise and purple 15 15
207. – 5d. brown and blue .. 25 25
208. – 6d. blue and black .. 25 20
209. – 8d. black and lilac .. 30 20
210. – 10d. black and blue .. 30 30
211. – 1s. blue and brown .. 40 45
212. – 2s. orange and black .. 1·10 1·40
213. – 2s. 6d. black and blue 1·60 1·90
214. – 5s. emerald and orange 2·50 3·00
215. – 10s. black and slate .. 5·00 6·00
216. – £1 black and violet .. 9·50 11·00
DESIGNS: 1½d. Island settlement. 4d. Water sports—Skiing. 5d. Dairy. 6d. Transportation. 2s. Sisal. 2s. 6d. Shipbuilding. 5s. Tuna fishing. Other values the same as for the corresponding values in Nos. 178/93.

18. Queen Elizabeth II.

1959. Bahamas Stamp Cent.
217. 18. 1d. black and red .. 10 12
218. 2d. black and green .. 15 25
219. 6d. black and blue .. 30 40
220. 10d. black and brown.. 50 50

19. Christ Church Cathedral.

1962. Nassau Centenary.
221. 19. 8d. green 40 45
222. – 10d. violet 40 45
DESIGN: 10d. Nassau Public Library.

1963. Freedom from Hunger. As T 10 of Aden.
223. 8d. sepia 75 75

1963. Bahamas Talks. Nos. 209/10 optd. **BAHAMAS TALKS 1962.**
224. 8d. black and lilac .. 90 1·00
225. 10d. black and blue .. 1·60 1·60

1963. Red Cross Cent. As T 24 of Antigua.
226. 1d red and black .. 15 20
227. 10d. red and blue .. 75 1·10

1964. New Constitution. Nos. 201/16 optd. **NEW CONSTITUTION 1964.**
228. 17. ½d. black and vermilion 8 10
229. – 1d. olive and brown .. 8 10
230. – 1½d. blue and black .. 10 10
231. – 2d. chestnut and green 10 10
232. – 3d. black and red .. 12 12
233. – 4d. turquoise and purple 15 20
234. – 5d. brown and blue .. 20 25
235. – 6d. blue and black .. 25 25
236. – 8d. black and lilac .. 30 30
237. – 10d. black and blue .. 35 35
238. – 1s blue and brown .. 50 55
239. – 2s. orange and black .. 1·40 1·60
240. – 2s. 6d. black and blue 1·60 1·90
241. – 5s. emerald and orange 2·75 3·00
242. – 10s. black and slate .. 4·75 5·50
243. – £1 black and violet .. 9·50 11·00

1964. Shakespeare. 400th Birth Anniv. As T 25 of Antigua.
244. 6d. turquoise 45 45

1964. Olympic Games, Tokyo. No. 211 surch. with Olympic "rings" symbol and value.
245. 8d. on 1s. blue and brown 40 45

20. Colony's Badge.

1965.
247. 20. ½d. multicoloured .. 5 5
248. – 1d. slate, blue & orange 5 5
249. – 1½d. red, green & brown 5 5
250. – 2d. slate, green & blue 8 8
251. – 3d. red, blue and purple 10 8
252. – 4d. green, blue & chest. 12 20
253. – 6d. green, blue and red 20 15
254. – 8d. purple, blue & bronze 30 30
255. – 10d. brown, green & vio. 25 20
256a. – 1s. multicoloured .. 40 35
257. – 2s. brown, blue & green 85 95
258. – 2s. 6d. olive, blue & red 1·00 1·40
259. – 5s. chestnut, ult. & grn. 1·90 2·25
260. – 10s. red, blue & choc. 3·00 3·75
261. – £1 chestnut, blue & red 5·50 6·00
DESIGNS: 1d. Out Island Regatta. 1½d. Hospital. 2d. High School. 3d. Flamingo. 4d. R.M.S. "Queen Elizabeth". 6d. "Development". 8d. Yachting. 10d. Public Square. 1s. Sea Garden. 2s. Old Cannons at Fort Charlotte. 2s. 6d. Sikorsky "S-38" Seaplane (1929) and Boeing "707" Airliner. 5s. Williamson Film Project (1914) and Undersea Post Office (1939). 10s. Conch Shell. £1 Columbus's Flagship.

1965. I.T.U. Cent. As T 26 of Antigua.
262. 1d. green and orange .. 12 12
263. 2s. purple and olive .. 90 90

1965. No. 254 surch.
264. – 9d. on 8d. purple, blue and bronze 40 40

1965. I.C.Y. As T 27 of Antigua.
265. ½d. purple and turquoise 12 12
266. 1s. green and lavender .. 55 55

1966. Churchill Commem. As T 28 of Antigua.
267. ½d. blue 5 5
268. 2d. green 15 15
269. 10d. brown 65 75
270. 1s. violet 75 90

1966. Royal Visit. As T 29 of Antigua but "to the Caribbean" omitted.
271. 6d. black and blue .. 30 30
272. 1s. black and magenta .. 40 40

1966. Decimal currency. Nos. 247/61 surch.
273. 20. 1 c. on ½d. multicoloured 5 5
274. – 2 c. on 1d. slate, blue and orange 5 5
275. – 3 c. on 2d. slate, green and blue 5 5
276. – 4 c. on 3d. red, bl. & pur. 8 10
277. – 5 c. on 4d. green, blue and chestnut .. 10 12
278. – 8 c. on 6d. grn., bl. & red 15 15
279. – 10 c. on 8d. purple, blue and bronze .. 20 25
280. – 11 c. on 1½d. red, green and brown 20 25
281. – 12 c. on 10d. brown, green and violet .. 25 25
282. – 15 c. on 1s. multicoloured 30 35
283. – 22 c. on 2s. brown, blue and green 55 65
284. – 50 c. on 2s. 6d. olive, blue and red .. 95 1·10
285. – $1 on 5s. chestnut, ultramarine and green .. 1·90 2·25
286. – $2 on 10s. red, bl. & choc. 3·25 3·75
287. – $3 on £1 chest., bl. & red 6·50 7·50

1966. World Cup Football Championships. As T 30 of Antigua.
288. 8 c. violet, grn., lake & brn. 25 25
289. 15 c. choc., turq. lake & brn. 35 35

1966. W.H.O. Headquarters, Geneva. Inaug. As T 31 of Antigua.
290. 11 c. black, green and blue 35 35
291. 15 c. black, purple & ochre 40 45

1966. U.N.E.S.C.O. 20th Anniv. As T 33/5 of Antigua.
292. 3 c. violet, red, yell. & orge. 5 5
293. 15 c. yellow, violet & olive 50 60
294. $1 black, purple & orange 1·90 1·90

1967. As Nos. 247/61 but values in decimal currency, and new designs for 5 c. and $2.
295. 20. 1 c. multicoloured .. 5 5
296. – 2 c. slate, blue & orange 8 10
297. – 3 c. slate, green & blue 10 10
298. – 4 c. red, blue and purple 10 12
299. – 5 c. green, blue & chest. 12 12
300. – 8 c. green, blue and red 12 15
301. – 10 c. pur., blue & bronze 15 12
302. – 11 c. red, green & brown 25 20
303. – 12 c. brown, grn. & olive 30 20
304. – 15 c. multicoloured .. 40 30
305. – 22 c. brown, blue & grn. 45 45
306. – 50 c. olive, blue and red 85 75
307. – $1 chest., ultram. & grn. 1·75 2·00
308. – $2 red, blue & chocolate 3·25 3·75
309. – $3 chestnut, blue & red 6·00 6·50
NEW DESIGNS: 5 c. "Oceanic". $2 Conch Shell (different).

21. Bahamas Crest.

1967. World Scouting. Diamond Jubilee. Multicoloured.
310. 3 c. Type 21 .. .. 5 5
311. 15 c. Scout badge.. .. 25 25

22. Globe and Emblem.

1968. Human Rights Year. Multicoloured.
312. 3 c. Type 22 .. .. 10 10
313. 12 c. Scales of Justice and Emblem 55 55
314. $1 Bahamas Crest & Emblem 1·40 1·75

23. Golf.

1968. Tourism. Multicoloured.
315. 5 c. Type 23 .. .. 10 10
316. 11 c. Yachting 20 30
317. 15 c. Horse-racing .. 25 30
318. 50 c. Water-skiing .. 60 70

24. Racing Yacht and Olympic Monument.

1968. Olympic Games, Mexico City.
319. 24. 5 c. brown yell. & grn. 10 10
320. – 11 c. multicoloured .. 20 25
321. – 50 c. multicoloured .. 90 1·00
322. 24. $1 grey blue & violet 1·75 2·00
DESIGNS: 11 c. Long jumping and Olympic Monument. 50 c. Running and Olympic Monument.

25. Legislative Building.

1968. 14th Commonwealth Parliamentary Conf. Multicoloured.
323. 3 c. Type 25 .. .. 5 5
324 10 c. Bahamas Mace and Westminster Clock Tower 25 25
325. 12 c. Local Straw Market 25 30
326. 15 c. Horse drawn Surrey 35 35
Nos. 324/5 are vert.

26. Obverse and reverse of $100 Gold Coin.

1968. Gold Coins Commemorating the first General Election under the New Constitution.
327. 26. 3 c. red on gold .. 10 10
328. – 12 c. gold on green .. 25 25
329. – 15 c. purple on gold .. 35 35
330. – $1 black on gold .. 1·60 1·60
OBVERSE AND REVERSE OF: 12 c. $50 Gold Coin. 15 c. $20 Gold Coin. $1, $10 Gold Coin.

27. First Flight Postcard of 1919.

1969. Bahamas Airmail Services. 50th Anniv.
331. 27. 12 c. multicoloured .. 40 50
332. – 15 c. multicoloured .. 50 55
DESIGN: 15 c. Sikorsky "S-38" Seaplane of 1929.

28. Game-Fishing Boats.

1969. Tourism. One Millionth Visitor to Bahamas. Multicoloured.

No.	Description	Unused	Used
333.	3 c. Type **28**	5	5
334.	11 c. Paradise Beach ..	20	20
335.	12 c. Sunfish Sailing boats	25	25
336.	15 c. Rawson Square and parade	30	30

29. "The Adoration of the Shepherds" (Louis le Nain).

1969. Christmas. Multicoloured.

No.	Description	Unused	Used
338.	3 c. Type **29**	8	8
339.	11 c. "The Adoration of the Shepherds" (Poussin) ..	30	30
340.	12 c. "The Adoration of the Kings" (Gerard David)	30	30
341.	15 c. "The Adoration of the Kings" (Vincenzo Foppa)	40	40

30. Flags, Guides and Globe.

1970. Girl Guides' Association Diamond Jubilee.

No.	Description	Unused	Used
342. **30.**	3 c. yell., verm. & blue	10	10
343. –	12 c. yellow, brn. & grn.	25	25
344. –	15 c. yellow, grn. & blue	30	30

DESIGNS: 12 c. Sprite and Yellow Elder. 15 c. Globe inside Guides' emblem.

31. New U.P.U. Headquarters and emblem.

1970. New U.P.U. Headquarters Building.

No.	Description	Unused	Used
345. **31.**	3 c. multicoloured ..	12	12
346.	15 c. multicoloured ..	50	55

32. Coach and Globe.

1970. "Goodwill Caravan". Multicoloured.

No.	Description	Unused	Used
347.	3 c. Type **32**	5	5
348.	11 c. Train and globe ..	30	30
349.	12 c. Liner, yacht & globe	35	35
350.	15 c. Airliner and globe ..	40	40

33. Nurse, Patients and Flamingo.

1970. British Red Cross. Cent. Multicoloured.

No.	Description	Unused	Used
352.	3 c. Type **33**	5	5
353.	15 c. Hospital and dolphin	35	40

34. "The Nativity" (detail, Pittoni).

1970. Christmas. Multicoloured.

No.	Description	Unused	Used
354.	3 c. Type **34**	10	10
355.	11 c. "The Holy Family" (detail, Anton Raphael Mengs)	20	20
356.	12 c. "Adorazione dei Pastori" (detail, Giorgione)	25	30
357.	15 c. "The Adoration of the Shepherds" (detail, School of Seville) ..	30	35

35. "VC-10" at Airport Terminal.

1971. Multicoloured.

No.	Description	Unused	Used
359.	1 c. Type **35**	5	5
360.	2 c. Breadfruit	8	8
361.	3 c. Straw Market ..	5	5
362.	4 c. Hawksbill turtle ..	10	10
363.	5 c. Grouper	10	10
364.	6 c. As 4 c.	5	5
365.	7 c. Hibiscus	8	8
399.	8 c. Yellow Elder ..	12	12
367.	10 c. Bahamian sponge boat	12	15
368.	11 c. Flamingoes ..	8	10
369.	12 c. As 7 c.	25	20
370.	15 c. Bonefish	15	15
371.	18 c. Royal Poinciana ..	15	20
372.	22 c. As 18 c.	30	35
373.	50 c. Nassau Post Office	60	70
374.	$1 Pineapple (vert) ..	1·25	1·40
408.	$2 Crawfish (vert) ..	1·90	2·00
376.	$3 Junkanoo (vert) ..	3·00	3·25

36. Snowflake.

1971. Christmas.

No.	Description	Unused	Used
377. **36.**	3 c. pur., orge. & gold	8	8
378. –	11 c. blue and gold ..	25	25
379. –	15 c. multicoloured ..	30	30
380. –	18 c. green, blue & gold	40	40

DESIGNS: 11 c. "Peace on Earth" (doves) 15 c. Arms of Bahamas and holly. 18 c. Starlit lagoon.

MINIMUM PRICE

The minimum price quoted is 5p which represents a handling charge rather than a basis for valuing common stamps. For further notes about prices see introductory pages.

37. High jumping.

1972. Olympic Games, Munich. Multicoloured.

No.	Description	Unused	Used
382.	10 c. Type **37**	20	20
383.	11 c. Cycling	20	20
384.	15 c. Running	25	25
385.	18 c. Sailing	40	40

38. Shepherd.

1972. Christmas. Multicoloured.

No.	Description	Unused	Used
387.	3 c. Type **38**	8	8
388.	6 c. Bells	12	12
389.	15 c. Holly and Cross ..	30	35
390.	20 c. Poinsettia	40	45

1972. Royal Silver Wedding. As T **19**, of Ascension but with Mace and Galleon in background.

No.	Description	Unused	Used
393.	11 c. pink	20	25
394.	18 c. violet	30	35

39. Weather Satellite.

1973. I.M.O./W.M.O. Cent. Multicoloured.

No.	Description	Unused	Used
410.	15 c. Type **39**	25	25
411.	18 c. Weather radar	30	30

40. C. A. Bain (national hero).

1973. Independence. Multicoloured.

No.	Description	Unused	Used
412.	3 c. Type **40**	5	5
413.	11 c. Coat of arms ..	15	15
414.	15 c. Bahamas flag ..	25	25
415.	$1 Governor-General, M. B. Butler	1·10	1·25

41 "Madonna in Prayer" (Sassoferrato).

1973. Christmas. Multicoloured.

No.	Description	Unused	Used
417.	3 c. Type **41**	5	5
418.	11 c. "Virgin and Child with St. John" (Filippino Lippi) ..	15	15
419.	15 c. "A Choir of Angels" (Simon Marmion) ..	25	25
420.	18 c. "The Two Trinities" (Murillo) ..	30	30

42. "Agriculture and Sciences".

1974. University of West Indies. 25th Anniv. Multicoloured.

No.	Description	Unused	Used
422.	15 c. Type **42**	25	25
423.	18 c. "Arts, Engineering and General Studies" ..	30	30

43. U.P.U. Monument, Berne.

1974. U.P.U. Centenary.

No.	Description	Unused	Used
424. **43.**	3 c. multicoloured ..	5	5
425. –	13 c. multicoloured (vert.)	20	20
426. –	14 c. multicoloured ..	25	25
427. –	18 c. multicoloured (vert.)	30	30

DESIGNS: As Type **43** but showing different arrangements of the U.P.U. Monument.

44. Roseate Spoonbills.

1974. Bahamas National Trust. 15th Anniv. Multicoloured.

No.	Description	Unused	Used
429.	13 c. Type **44**	15	20
430.	14 c. White-crowned Pigeon	20	20
431.	21 c. White-tailed Tropic Birds	25	25
432.	36 c. Bahamian Parrot ..	40	40

45. "The Holy Family" (Jacques de Stella).

1974. Christmas. Multicoloured.

No.	Description	Unused	Used
434.	8 c. Type **45**	10	10
435.	10 c. "Madonna and Child" (Romanino)	12	12
436.	12 c. "Virgin and Child with St. John the Baptist and St. Catherine" (Previtali)	15	15
437.	21 c. "Virgin and Child with Angels" (Previtali) ..	30	30

46. "Anteos maerula".

1975. Butterflies. Multicoloured.

No.	Description	Unused	Used
439.	3 c. Type **46**	5	5
440.	14 c. "Eurema nicippe"	20	20
441.	18 c. "Papilio andraemon bonhotei"	25	30
442.	21 c. "Euptoieta hegesia"	25	25

47. Sheep Husbandry.

1975. Economic Diversification. Mult.
444. 3 c. Type **47** 5 5
445. 14 c. Electric-reel fishing 15 20
446. 18 c. Farming 20 20
447. 21 c. Oil Refinery .. 20 25

48. Rowena Rand (evangelist).

1975. International Women's Year.
449. **48.** 14 c. brn., light bl. & bl. 20 20
450. – 18 c. yell., grn. & brn.. 25 30
DESIGN: 18 c. I.W.Y. symbol and Harvest symbol.

49. " Adoration of the Shepherds " (Perugino).

1975. Christmas. Multicoloured.
451. 3 c. Type **49** 5 5
452. 8 c. " Adoration of the Magi " (Ghirlandaio) 10 10
453. 18 c. As 8 c. 20 20
454. 21 c. Type **49** 25 25

50. Telephones, 1876 and 1976.

1976. Telephone Centenary. Multicoloured.
456. 3 c. Type **50** 5 5
457. 16 c. Radio-telephone link, Deleporte .. 20 25
458. 21 c. Alexander Graham Bell 25 30
459. 25 c. Satellite 35 40

51. Map of North America.

1976. American Revolution. Bicent. Multicoloured.
475. 16 c. Type **51** 15 20
476. $1 John Murray, Earl of Dunmore .. .. 1·10 1·25

52. Cycling.

1976. Olympic Games, Montreal.
478. **52.** 8 c. purple, blue and light blue .. 8 10
479. – 16 c. orange, brown and light blue .. 15 20
480. – 25 c. blue, purple and light blue .. 30 35
481. – 40 c. brown, orange and light blue .. 45 50
DESIGNS: 16 c. Jumping. 25 c. Sailing. 40 c. Boxing.

53. " Virgin and Child " (detail, Lippi).

1976. Christmas. Multicoloured.
482. 3 c. Type **53** 5 5
483. 21 c. " Adoration of the Shepherds " (School of Seville) 20 25
484. 25 c. " Adoration of the Kings " (detail, Foppa) 30 35
485. 40 c. " Virgin and Child " (detail, Vivarini) .. 45 50

SPECIAL DELIVERY STAMPS

1916. Optd. **SPECIAL DELIVERY** (letters with serifs).
S 1. **5.** 5d. black and orange .. 5·00 5·50

1917. Optd. **SPECIAL DELIVERY** (letters without serifs).
S 2. **5.** 5d. black and orange .. 75 1·50
S 3. 5d. black and mauve .. 40 1·00

BAHAWALPUR BC

A former state of Pakistan, now merged in West Pakistan.

1. Amir Muhammad Bahawal Khan I Abbasi

1948. Bicentenary Commem.
1. **1.** ½ a. black and red .. 10

2. H.H. the Ameer of Bahawalpur.

3. The Tombs of the Ameers.

1948.
2. **2.** 3 p. black and blue .. 5
3. ½ a. black and claret .. 5
4. 9 p. black and green .. 5
5. 1 a. black and red .. 5
6. 1½ a. black and violet .. 5
7. **3.** 2 a. green and red .. 5
8. – 4 a. orange and brown .. 5
9. – 6 a. violet and blue .. 5
10. – 8 a. red and violet .. 8
11. – 12 a. green and red .. 10
12. – 1 r. violet and brown .. 12
18. – 1 r. green and orange .. 8
13. – 2 r. green and claret .. 25
19. – 2 r. black and red .. 15
14. – 5 r. black and violet .. 60
20. – 5 r. chocolate and blue .. 30
15. – 10 r. red and black .. 1·00
21. – 10 r. brown and green .. 50
DESIGNS—HORIZ. as T **3**: 6 a. Fort Derawar. 8 a. Nur-Mahal Palace. 12 a Sadiq-Garh Palace. Larger (46 × 32 mm.): 10 r. Three generations of Rulers. VERT. as T **3**: 4 a. Mosque in Sadiq-Garh. 1 r., 2 r., 5 r. H.H. the Ameer of Bahawalpur.

6. Soldiers of 1848 and 1948.

1948. Multan Campaign Cent.
17. **6.** 1½ a. black and red .. 10

7. H.H. the Ameer of Bahawalpur and Mr. Jinnah.

1948. Union with Pakistan. 1st Anniv.
16. **7.** 1½ a. red and green .. 5

8. Irrigation.

1949. Silver Jubilee of Accession of H.H. the Ameer of Bahawalpur.
22. **8.** 3 p. black and blue .. 5
23. – ½ a. black and orange .. 5
24. – 9 p. black and green .. 5
25. – 1 a. black and red .. 5
DESIGNS: ½ a. Wheat. 9 p. Cotton. 1 a. Sahiwal bull.

9. U.P.U. Monument, Berne.

26. **9.** 9 p. black and green .. 5
27. 1 a. black and magenta .. 5
28. 1½ a. black and orange .. 5
29. 2½ a. black and blue .. 5

OFFICIAL STAMPS

O 1. Pelicans.

1945. As Type O **1** with Arabic opt.
O 1. – ½ a. black and green .. 8 15
O 2. – 1 a. black and red .. 15 25
O 7. – 1 a. black and brown.. 10·00 10·00
O 3. – 2 a. black and violet .. 15
O 4. O **1.** 4 a. black and olive .. 20
O 5. – 8 a. black and brown.. 20
O 6. – 1 r. black and orange.. 25
DESIGNS: ½ a. Panjnad Weir. 1 a. (No. O 2), Camel and calf. 1 a. (No. O 3), Baggage camels. 2 a. Blackbuck Antelopes. 8 a. Juma Masjid Palace, Fort Derawar. 1 r. Temple at Pattan Munara.

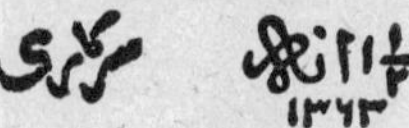
(O **2**.)

1945. Types as Nos. O 1, etc., in new colours and without Arabic opt. (a) Surch. as Type O **2**.
O 11. ½ a. on 8 a. black and purple (as No. O 5) .. 60 45
O 12. 1½ a. on 1 r. black and orange (as No. O 6) .. 1·25 1·00
O 13. 1½ a. on 2 r. black and blue (as No. O 1) .. 2·00 1·75
(b) Optd. **SERVICE** and Arabic inscription.
O 14. ½ a. black and red (as No. O 1) 10 10
O 15. 1 a. black and red (as No. O 2) 15 20
O 16. 2 a. black and orange (as No. O 3) 20 25

1946. As T **2** but inscr. " SERVICE " at left.
O 17. 3 p. black and blue .. 5 5
O 18. 1½ a. black and violet .. 5 5

O 3. Allied Banners.

1946. Victory.
O 19. O **3.** 1½ a. green and grey 15 20

1948. Stamps of 1948 with Arabic opt. as in Type O **1**.
O 20. **2.** 3 p. black and blue .. 5
O 21. 1 a. black and red .. 5
O 22. **3.** 2 a. green and red .. 5
O 23. – 4 a. orange and brown.. 5
O 24. – 1 r. green and orange .. 8
O 25. – 2 r. black and red .. 12
O 26. – 5 r. chocolate and blue 25
O 27. – 10 r. brown and green.. 50

1949. U.P.U. 75th Anniv. Optd. as in Type O **1**.
O 28. **9.** 9 p. black and green .. 5
O 29. 1 a. black and magenta 5
O 30. 1½ a. black and orange 5
O 31. 2½ a. black and blue .. 5

BAHRAIN BC; O1

An archipelago in the Persian Gulf on the Arabian coast. An independent shaikhdom with Indian and, later, British postal administration. The latter was closed on 1st January 1966, when the Bahrain Post Office took over.

Stamps of India overprinted **BAHRAIN.**
1966. 1000 fils = dinar.

1933. King George V.
1. **40.** 3 p. grey 30 30
2. **41.** ½ a. green 75 60
15. **62.** ½ a. green 30 8
3. 9 p. green 65 40
4. **42.** 1 a. chocolate 40 40
16. **64.** 1 a. chocolate 75 12
5. **63.** 1 a. 3 p. mauve .. 50 30
6. **45.** 2 a. orange-red.. .. 80 70
17a. **44.** 2 a. orange-red .. 4·00 40
7. **48.** 3 a. blue .. .. 3·50 3·00
18. 3 a. red .. .. .. 1·50 15

8.	**66.**	3 a. 6 p. blue	45	35
9.	**50.**	4 a. green	3·50	2·00
19.	**49.**	4 a. olive	1·00	20
10.	**52.**	8 a. mauve	50	30
11.	**53.**	12 a. claret	75	40
12.	**54.**	1 r. brown and green ..	3·50	1·00
13.		2 r. red and orange ..	7·50	3·50
14.		5 r. blue and violet ..	18·00	14·00

1938. King George VI.

20.	**74.**	3 p. slate..	40	30
21.		½ a. brown	5	5
22.		9 p. green	15	12
23.		1 a. red	8	5
24.	**76.**	2 a. red	40	15
26.	–	3 a. green (No. 253) ..	1·50	50
27.	–	3½ a. blue (No. 254) ..	50	75
28.	–	4 a. brown (No. 255) ..	7·50	8·50
30.	–	8 a. violet (No. 257) ..	14·00	12·00
31.	–	12 a. red (No. 258) ..	13·00	13·00
32.	**77.**	1 r. slate and brown ..	50	40
33.		2 r. purple and brown ..	3·25	90
34.		5 r. green and blue ..	6·00	4·00
35.		10 r. purple and red ..	10·00	6·00
36.		15 r. brown and green ..	8·00	9·00
37.		25 r. slate and purple ..	18·00	14·00

1942. King George VI.

38.	**78.**	3 p. slate..	5	8
39.		½ a. mauve	5	8
40.		9 p. green	5	20
41.		1 a. red	5	5
42.	**79.**	1 a 3 p. bistre	15	45
43.		1½ a. violet	20	8
44.		2 a. red	20	8
45.		3 a. violet	30	40
46.		3½ a. blue	75	60
47.	**80.**	4 a. brown	40	15
48.		6 a. green	1·50	90
49.		8 a. violet	20	30
50.		12 a. purple	50	40

Stamps of Great Britain surcharged **BAHRAIN** and new value in Indian currency.

1948. King George VI.

51.	**103.**	½ a. on ½d. pale green..	5	8
71.		½ a. on ½d. orange ..	5	10
52.		1 a. on 1d. pale red ..	5	8
72.		1 a. on 1d. blue ..	5	10
53.		1½ a. on 1½d. pale brown	5	15
73.		1½ a. on 1½d. green ..	5	20
54.		2 a. on 2d. pale orange	5	5
74.		2 a. on 2d. brown ..	5	5
55.		2½ a. on 2½d. light blue	15	20
75.		2½ a. on 2½d. red ..	5	30
56.		3 a. on 3d. pale violet..	5	5
76.	**104.**	4 a. on 4d. blue ..	12	20
57.		6 a. on 6d. purple ..	5	8
58.	**105.**	1 r. on 1s. brown ..	25	25
59.	**106.**	2 r. on 2s. 6d. green ..	65	1·10
60.		5 r. on 5s. red ..	2·00	3·00
60a.	–	10 r. on 10s. bright blue (No. 478a)	11·00	9·00

1948. Silver Wedding.

61.	**110.**	2½ a. on 2½d. blue ..	5	5
62.	**111.**	15 r. on £1 blue ..	6·00	7·00

1948. Olympic Games.

63.	**112.**	2½ a. on 2½d. blue ..	5	8
64.	**113.**	3 a. on 3d. violet ..	12	15
65.	–	6 a. on 6d. purple ..	15	20
66.	–	1 r. on 1s. brown ..	35	45

1949. U.P.U.

67.	**114.**	2½ a. on 2½d. blue ..	10	12
68.	**115.**	3 a. on 3d. violet ..	12	20
69.	–	6 a. on 6d. purple ..	25	35
70.	–	1 r. on 1s. brown ..	40	45

1951. Pictorial stamps (Nos. 509/11).

77.	**116.**	2 r. on 2s. 6d. green ..	1·25	75
78.	–	5 r. on 5s. red	1·00	1·00
79.	–	10 r. on 10 s. blue ..	3·00	2·50

1952. Queen Elizabeth II.

80.	**118.**	½ a. on ½d. orange ..	5	5
81.		1 a. on 1d. blue ..	5	5
82.		1½ a. on 1½d. green ..	5	5
83.		2 a. on 2d. brown ..	5	5
84.	**119.**	2½ a. on 2½d. red ..	5	8
85.		3 a. on 3d. lilac ..	8	10
86.		4 a. on 4d. blue ..	12	12
87.	**120.**	6 a. on 6d. purple ..	12	15
88.	**122.**	12 a. on 1s. 3d. green ..	20	20
89.		1 r. on 1s. 6d. indigo ..	25	20

1953. Coronation.

90.	**123.**	2½ a. on 2½d. red ..	15	25
91.	–	4 a. on 4d. ultramarine	25	35
92.	**124.**	12 a. on 1s. 3d. green ..	70	70
93.	–	1 r. on 1s. 6d. blue ..	75	80

1955. Pictorial stamps (Nos. 595a/598a).

94.	**125.**	2 r. on 2s. 6d. brown ..	50	65
95.	–	5 r. on 5s. red	2·00	2·00
96.		10 r. on 10s. blue ..	2·50	2·25

1957. Queen Elizabeth II.

102.	**120.**	1 n.p. on 5d. brown ..	5	5
103.	**118.**	3 n.p. on ½d. orange ..	5	8
104.		6 n.p. on 1d. blue ..	8	8
105.		9 n.p. on 1½d. green ..	8	8
106.		12 n.p. on 2d. pale brn.	8	8
107.	**119.**	15 n.p. on 2½d. red ..	10	10
108.		20 n.p. on 3d. lilac ..	8	8
109.		25 n.p. on 4d. blue ..	12	15
110.	**120.**	40 n.p. on 6d. purple	12	15
111.		50 n.p. on 9d. olive ..	25	25
112.		75 n.p. on 1s. 3d. green	25	30

1957. World Scout Jubilee Jamboree.

113.	**126.**	15 n.p. on 2½d. red ..	12	15
114.	**127.**	25 n.p. on 4d. blue ..	15	20
115.	–	75 n.p. on 1s. 3d. green	30	35

1. Shaikh Sulman bin Hamed al-Khalifa.

2. Shaikh Isa bin Sulman al-Khalifa.

3. Air Terminal Muharraq.

1960.

117.	**1.**	5 n.p. blue	5	5
118.		15 n.p. orange	5	5
119.		20 n.p. violet	5	5
120.		30 n.p. bistre-brown ..	5	8
121.		40 n.p. grey	8	10
122.		50 n.p. green	10	12
123.		75 n.p. red-brown ..	12	10
124.	–	1 r. grey	15	20
125.	–	2 r. red	30	25
126.	–	5 r. blue	85	65
127.	–	10 r. green	1·50	1·00

The rupee values are larger (27 × 32½ mm.).

1964.

128.	**2.**	5 n.p. blue	5	5
129.		15 n.p. orange	5	5
130.		20 n.p. violet	5	5
131.		30 n.p. bistre-brown ..	5	8
132.		40 n.p. slate	8	8
133.		50 n.p. green	8	8
134.		75 n.p. brown	12	10
135.	**3.**	1 r. black	15	10
136.		2 r. red	30	20
137.	–	5 r. blue	75	65
138.	–	10 r. myrtle	1·50	1·10

DESIGNS—As T **3**: 5 r., 10 r. Deep water harbour.

4. Shaikh Isa bin Sulman al-Khalifa.

5. Ruler and Bahrain Airport.

1966.

139.	**4.**	5 f. green	5	5
140.		10 f. red	5	5
141.		15 f. blue	5	5
142.		20 f. purple	5	5
143.	**5.**	30 f. black and green ..	8	5
144.		40 f. black and blue ..	10	8
145.	–	50 f. black and magenta	10	10
146.	–	75 f. black and violet ..	20	20
147.	–	100 f. blue and yellow ..	35	45
148.	–	200 f. green and orange..	80	55
149.	–	500 f. brown and yellow	1·60	1·10
150.	–	1 d. multicoloured ..	3·25	2·40

DESIGNS—As T **5**: 50 f., 75 f. Ruler and Mina Sulman deep-water harbour. VERT. (26½ × 42½ mm.): 100 f. Pearl-diving. 200 f. Falconry and horse-racing. 500 f. Serving coffee, and Ruler's Palace. LARGER (37 × 52½ mm.): 1 d. Ruler, crest, date-palm, horse, dhow, pearl necklace, mosque, coffee-pot and Bab-al-Bahrain (gateway).

6. Produce.

7. W.H.O. Emblem and Map of Bahrain.

1966. Trade Fair and Agricultural Show.

151.	**6.**	10 f. turquoise and red..	5	5
152.		20 f. lilac and green ..	5	5
153.		40 f. blue and brown ..	15	15
154.		200 f. rose and indigo ..	65	65

1968. World Health Organization. 20th Anniv.

155.	**7.**	20 f. black and grey ..	5	5
156.		40 f. black & turq.-green	10	10
157.		150 f. black and red ..	40	30

8. View of Isa Town.

1968. Isa New Town. Inaug. Multicoloured.

158.		50 f. Type **8**	12	12
159.		80 f. Shopping centre ..	20	20
160.		120 f. Stadium	35	35
161.		150 f. Mosque	45	45

9. Symbol of Learning.

1969. School Education in Bahrain. 50th Anniv.

162.	**9.**	40 f. multicoloured ..	10	10
163.		60 f. multicoloured ..	15	15
164.		150 f. multicoloured ..	40	40

10. Dish Aerial and Map.

1969. Opening of Satellite Earth Station, Ras Abu Jarjour. Multicoloured.

165.		20 f. Type **10**	5	5
166.		40 f. Dish Aerial and palms (vert.)	10	10
167.		100 f. Type **10**	25	25
168.		150 f. As 40 f.	40	40

11. Arms, Map and Manama Municipality Building.

1970. 2nd Arab Cities Organization Conf., Manama.

169.	**11.**	30 f. multicoloured ..	8	8
170.		150 f. multicoloured	40	40

12. Copper Bull's Head, Barbar.

1970. 3rd Int. Asian Archaeology Conf., Bahrain. Multicoloured.

171.		60 f. Type **12**	15	15
172.		80 f. Palace of Dilmun excavations	20	20
173.		120 f. Desert gravemounds	30	30
174.		150 f. Dilmun seal ..	40	40

13. "VC-10", Globe, Big Ben, London, and Bahrain Minaret.

1970. 1st "Gulf Aviation" "VC-10" Flight Doha–London.

175.	**13.**	30 f. multicoloured ..	8	8
176.		60 f. multicoloured ..	15	15
177.		120 f. multicoloured ..	35	35

14. I.E.Y. Emblem and Open Book.

1970. Int. Education Year. Multicoloured.

178.		60 f. Type **14**	15	12
179.		120 f. Emblem and Bahraini children	30	25

15. Allegory of Independence.

17. Human Heart.

16. Arab Dhow.

1971. Independence Day and Ruler's Accession. 10th Anniv. Multicoloured.

180.		30 f. Type **15**	8	8
181.		60 f. Government House	15	12
182.		120 f. Arms of Bahrain ..	30	25
183.		150 f. Arms of Bahrain (gold background) ..	40	35

1972. Bahrain's Membership of Arab League and United Nations. Multicoloured.

184.		30 f. Type **16**	8	8
185.		60 f. Type **16**	15	12
186.		120 f. Dhow Sails (vert.) ..	30	25
187.		150 f. As 120 f.	40	35

1972. World Health Day.

188.	**17.**	30 f. multicoloured ..	8	8
189.		60 f. multicoloured ..	15	12

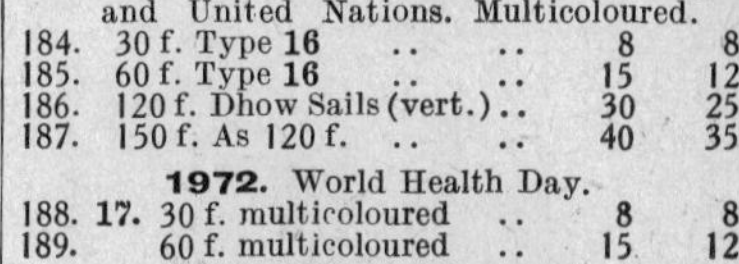

18. F.A.O. and U.N. Emblems.

1973. World Food Programme. 10th Anniv.

190.	**18.**	30 f. brn., red & green..	8	8
191.		60 f. brn., grn. & light brn.	15	12

19. " Races of the World ".

1973. Declaration of Human Rights. 25th Anniv.

192.	**19.**	30 f. blue, brn. & black	8	8
193.		60 f. red, brown and blk.	15	12

20. Flour Mill.

1973. National Day. " Progress in Bahrain ". Multicoloured.

194.		30 f. Type **20**	8	8
195.		60 f. International Airport	15	12
196.		120 f. Sulmaniya Medical Centre	30	25
197.		150 f. Aluminium Smelter	45	40

21. U.P.U. Emblem within Letters.

1974. Admission of Bahrain to U.P.U Multicoloured.

199.		30 f. Type **21**	8	8
200.		60 f. U.P.U. emblem on letters	15	15
201.		120 f. Ruler and emblem on dove with letter in beak	30	30
202.		150 f. As 120 f.	45	45

Nos. 201/2 are larger, size 37 × 28 mm.

22. Traffic Lights and Directing Hands.

1974. International Traffic Day.

203. **22.** 30 f. multicoloured .. 10 10
204. 60 f. multicoloured .. 20 20

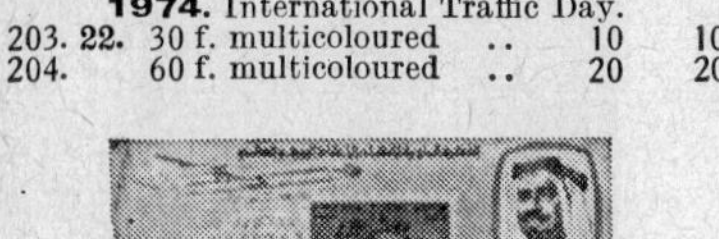

23. U.P.U. "Stamp" and Mail Transport.

1974. Universal Postal Union. Cent.

205. **23.** 30 f. multicoloured .. 10 10
206. 60 f. multicoloured .. 20 20
207. 120 f. multicoloured .. 35 35
208. 150 f. multicoloured .. 45 45

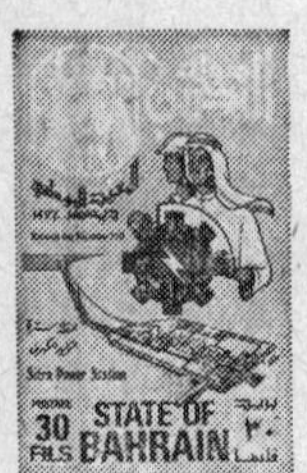

24. Emblem and Sitra Power Station. **25.** Costume and Headdress.

1974. National Day. Multicoloured.

209. 30 f. Type **24** 10 10
210. 60 f. Type **24** 20 20
211. 120 f. Emblem and Bahrain Dry Dock 35 35
212. 150 f. As 120 f. 45 45

1975. Bahrain Women's Costumes.

213. **25.** 30 f. multicoloured .. 10 10
214. – 60 f. multicoloured .. 20 20
215. – 120 f. multicoloured .. 35 35
216. – 150 f. multicoloured .. 45 45

DESIGNS: Nos. 214/16, Costumes similar to Type **25**.

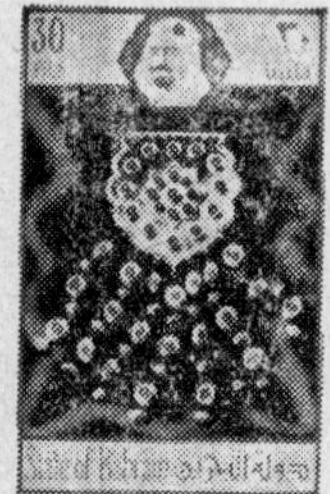

26. Jewelled Pendant. **27.** Woman planting "Flower".

1975. Costume Jewellery. Multicoloured.

217. 30 f. Type **26** 10 10
218. 60 f. Gold crown 20 20
219. 120 f. Jewelled necklace .. 35 35
220. 150 f. Gold necklace .. 45 45

1975. International Women's Year. Mult.

221. 30 f. Type **27** 10 10
222. 60 f. Woman holding I.W.Y. emblem 20 20

28. National Flag. **29.** Map of Bahrain within Cog and Laurel Branch.

1976.

224. **28.** 5 f. multicoloured .. 5 5
225. 10 f. multicoloured .. 5 5
226. 15 f. multicoloured .. 8 5
227. 20 f. multicoloured .. 8 5
228. **29.** 40 f. black and blue .. 10 10
229. 80 f. black and mauve 25 25
230. 150 f. black and yellow 45 45
231. 200 f. black and yellow 60 60

30. Concorde Taking-off.

1976. Concorde's Inaugural Commercial Flight, Bahrain-London. Mult.

232. 80 f. Type **30** 25 25
233. 80 f. Concorde landing .. 25 25
234. 80 f. Concorde en route .. 25 25
235. 80 f. Concorde on tarmac 25 25

31. Soldier, Crest and Flag.

1976. Defence Force Cadets' Day.

237. **31.** 40 f. multicoloured .. 10 10
238. 80 f. multicoloured .. 25 25

32. King Khaled and Shaikh Isa.

1976. Visit of King Khaled of Saudi Arabia.

239. **32.** 40 f. multicoloured .. 10 10
240. 80 f. multicoloured .. 25 25

BAMRA BC

A state in India. Now uses Indian stamps.

1. **2.**

1888. Imperf.

1. **1.** ½ a. black on yellow .. 15·00
2. ½ a. black on rose .. 14·00
3. 1 a. black on blue .. 14·00
4. 2 a. black on green .. 12·00
5. 4 a. black on yellow .. 12·00
6. 8 a. black on rose .. 12·00

1890. Imperf.

8. **2.** ¼ a. black on rose .. 15 20
11. ½ a. black on green .. 30 30
30. 1 a. black on yellow .. 45 60
32. 2 a. black on rose .. 40 60
34. 4 a. black on rose .. 75 1·00
37. 8 a. black on rose .. 1·50 1·50
25. 1 r. black on rose .. 10·00 10·00

BANGKOK BC

Capital of Thailand. Stamps of Straits Settlements, specially overprinted, were used for a time.

1882. Stamps of Straits Settlements optd. **B.** On issue of 1867.

1. **5.** 32 c. on 2 a. orange .. £1300 £1500

On issues of 1867-83.

14. **1.** 2 c. brown .. .. 12·00 12·00
12. **3.** 2 c. on 32 c. oran. (No. 60) 90·00 £120
15. **1.** 2 c. rose .. .. .. 4·00 3·75
16. 4 c. rose .. .. .. 20·00 16·00
17. 4 c. brown .. .. .. 7·00 7·00
4. **4.** 5 c. brown .. .. .. 12·00 12·00
18. 5 c. blue .. .. .. 18·00 12·00
19. **1.** 6 c. lilac .. .. .. 11·00 10·00
20. 8 c. orange .. .. .. 7·00 6·00
21. **5.** 10 c. grey .. .. .. 11·00 9·00
8. **1.** 12 c. blue .. .. .. 45·00 28·00
22. 12 c. purple .. .. 16·00 12·00
9. 24 c. green .. .. .. 28·00 11·00
10. **2.** 30 c. claret £750 £500
11. **3.** 96 c. grey £150 £160

BANGLADESH BC

Formerly the Eastern wing of Pakistan. Following a landslide victory at the Pakistan General Election in December 1970, for the local party favouring autonomy, the constitution was suspended and military rule imposed from West Pakistan. Unrest continued, culminating in guerilla warfare and the intervention of India on the side of the East Bengalis. The new state became effective after the surrender of the Pakistan army in December 1971.

1971. 100 paisa = 1 rupee.
1972. 100 paisa = 1 taka.

1. Map of Bangladesh **2.** "Martyrdom".

1971.

1. **1.** 10 p. indigo, orange & blue 5 5
2. – 20 p. multicoloured .. 5 5
3. – 50 p. multicoloured .. 8 8
4. – 1 r. multicoloured .. 12 15
5. – 2 r. greenish bl., blk. & red 25 30
6. – 3 r. apple-green, grn. & blue 35 40
7. – 5 r. multicoloured .. 60 65
8. – 10 r. gold, red & blue .. 1·25 1·40

DESIGNS: 20 p. "Dacca University Massacre". 50 p. "75 Million People". 1 r. Flag of Independence. 2 r. Ballot box. 3 r. Broken chain. 5 r. Shaikh Mujibur Rahman. 10 r. "Support Bangla Desh" and map.

1971. Liberation. Nos. 1 and 7/8 optd. **BANGLA DESH LIBERATED.**

9. 10 p. bl., orge. & pale blue 10 10
10. 5 r. multicoloured .. 75 75
11. 10 r. gold, red and blue .. 1·40 1·40

The remaining values of the original issue were also overprinted and placed on sale in Great Britain but were not issued in Bangladesh.

On the 1st February 1972 the Agency placed on sale a further issue in the flag, map and Sheikh Mujib designs in new colours and new currency (100 paisa = 1 taka). This issue proved to be unacceptable to the Bangla Desh authorities and was never put on sale there and so has no postal validity. The values comprise 1, 2, 3, 5, 7, 10, 15, 20, 25, 40, 50, 75 p., 1, 2 and 5 t.

1972. In Memory of the Martyrs.

12. **2.** 20p. green and red .. 5 5

3. Flames of Independence.

1972. Independence. 1st Anniv.

13. **3.** 20p. lake and red .. 5 5
14. 60p. blue and red .. 8 10
15. 75p. violet and red .. 10 10

4. Doves of Peace.

1972. Victory Day Anniv.

16. **4.** 20 p. multicoloured .. 5 5
17. 60 p. multicoloured .. 8 10
18. 75 p. multicoloured .. 10 10

5. 'Homage to Martyrs". **6.** Embroidered Quilt.

7. Court of Justice.

1973. In Memory of the Martyrs.

19. **5.** 20 p. multicoloured .. 5 5
20. 60 p. multicoloured .. 8 10
21. 1 t. 35 multicoloured .. 20 20

1973.

22. **6.** 2 p. black 5 5
23. – 3 p. green 5 5
24. – 5 p. brown 5 5
25. – 10 p. black 5 5
26. – 20 p. green 5 5
27. – 25 p. mauve 5 5
28. – 50 p. purple 5 5
29. – 60 p. grey 5 5
30. – 75 p. orange 8 10
31. – 90 p. brown 8 10
32. **7.** 1 t. violet 10 12
33. – 2 t. green 20 25
34. – 5 t. blue 50 55
35. – 10 t. pink .. .. .. 1·00 1·10

DESIGNS—VERT. As T **6**. 3 p. Jute field. 5 p. Jack fruit. 10 p. Bullocks ploughing. 20 p. Rakta jaba (flower). 25 p. Bengal tiger. 60 p. Bamboo grove. 75 p. Plucking tea. 90 p. Handicrafts. As T **7**. 2 t. Date tree. HORIZ. (28 × 22 mm.). 50 p. Hilsa (fish). As T **7**. 5 t. Fishing boat. 10 t. Sixty dome-mosque, Bagerhat.

See also Nos. 49/50 and 63 etc.

8. Flame Emblem.

1973. Declaration of Human Rights. 25th Anniv.

36. **8.** 10 p. multicoloured .. 5 5
37. 1 t. 25 multicoloured .. 12 15

9. Family, Map and Graph.

1974. First Population Census.

38. **9.** 20 p. multicoloured .. 5 5
39. 25 p. multicoloured .. 5 5
40. 75 p. multicoloured .. 10 12

10. Copernicus and Heliocentric System.

1974. Copernicus. 500th Birth Anniv.

41. 10. 25 p. orge., vio. & blk. .. 5 5
42. 75 p. orge., grn. & blk. .. 8 8

11. U.N. H.Q. and Bangladesh Flag.

1974. Bangladesh's Admission to the U.N.

43. 11. 25 p. multicoloured .. 5 5
44. 1 t. multicoloured .. 10 10

12. U.P.U. Emblem.

1974. Universal Postal Union. Centenary. Multicoloured.

45. 25 p. Type 12 .. .. 5 5
46. 1 t. 25 Mail runner .. 12 15
47. 1 t. 75 Type 12 .. .. 15 20
48. 5 t. As 1 t. 25 .. .. 50 55

13. Courts of Justice.

1974. As Nos. 32/3 with revised inscriptions.

49. 13. 1 t. violet 10 12
50. – 2 t. olive (As No. 33) .. 20 25

14. Royal Bengal Tiger. 15. Symbolic Family.

1974. Wildlife Preservation. Multicoloured.

51. 25 p. Type 14 .. .. 5 5
52. 50 p. Tiger whelp 5 8
53. 2 r. Tiger in stream .. 20 25

1974. World Population Year. "Family Planning for All". Multicoloured.

54. 25p. Type 15 .. .. 5 5
55. 70 p. Village family 10 12
56. 1 t. 25 Heads of family (horiz.) 12 15

16. Radar Antenna.

1975. Betbunia Satellite Earth Station. Inaug.

57. 16. 25 p. black, silver and red 5 5
58. – 1 t. black, silver and blue 10 12

17. Woman's Head.

1975. International Women's Year.

59. 17. 50 p. multicoloured .. 5 5
60. 2 t. multicoloured .. 20 20

1976. As Nos. 22, etc., but redrawn in a smaller size.

63. – 5 p. green 5 5
64. – 10 p. black 5 5
65. – 20 p. green 5 5
67. – 50 p. purple 5 5
71. 13. 1 t. blue 10 12
72. – 2 t. green 20 25

Nos. 63/5 and 67 are 23×18 mm. and Nos 71/2 are 31×20 mm.

18. Telephones of 1876 and 1976.

1976. Telephone Centenary.

75. 18. 2 t. multicoloured .. 25 30
76. – 5 t. red, green and black 55 65

DESIGN: 5 t. Alexander Graham Bell.

19. Eye and Nutriments.

1976. Prevention of Blindness.

77. 19. 30p. multicoloured .. 5 5
78. 2t. 25 multicoloured .. 25 30

20. Liberty Bell.

1976. American Revolution. Bicent. Multicoloured.

79. 30 p. Type 20 .. .. 5 5
80. 2 t. 25 Statue of Liberty .. 25 30
81. 5 t. "Mayflower" .. 55 65
82. 10 t. Mount Rushmore .. 1·10 1·25

21. Industry, Science, Agriculture and Education.

1976. Colombo Plan. 25th Anniversary.

84. 21. 30 p. multicoloured .. 5 5
85. 2 t. 25 multicoloured .. 25 30

BARBADOS BC

An island in the Br. W. Indies, E. of the Windward Is., attained self-government on 16th October, 1961 and achieved independence within the Commonwealth on 30th November, 1966.

1950. 100 cents = 1 West Indian dollar.

1. Britannia. 2.

1852. Imperf.

8. 1. (½d.) green .. .. 42·00 80·00
9. (1d.) blue .. .. 22·00 22·00
4a. (2d) slate £120
5. (4d.) red .. .. 13·00 £160
11. 2. 6d. red .. .. £225 50·00
12a. 1s. black .. .. 45·00 25·00

1860. Perf.

21. 1. (½d.) green .. .. 3·00 3·00
24. (1d.) blue .. .. 7·00 2·25
25. (4d.) red .. .. 18·00 9·00
29. 2. 6d. red .. .. 55·00 6·00
32. 6d. orange .. .. 14·00 5·00
35. 1s. black .. .. 7·50 6·00

1873. Perf.

72. 2. ½d. green .. .. 2·50 1·40
73. 1d. blue .. .. 6·00 60
63. 3d. brown-purple .. £150 40·00
75. 3d. mauve .. .. 28·00 5·50
77. 4d. red .. .. 50·00 2·75
79. 6d. yellow .. .. 42·00 2·75
81. 1s. purple .. .. 42·00 6·50

3. 4.

1873.

64. 3. 5s. rose £300 £180

1878. Half of No. 64 surch. **1 D.**

86. 3. 1d. on half 5s. rose .. £800 £200

1882.

89. 4. ½d. green .. .. 2·00 70
92. 1d. red .. .. 1·75 45
94. 2½d. blue .. .. 12·00 90
96. 3d. purple .. .. 2·75 3·25
97. 4d. grey .. .. 55·00 2·25
99. 4d. brown .. .. 2·00 1·25
100. 6d. olive-brown .. 14·00 7·00
102. 1s. red-brown .. 9·00 9·00
103. 5s. pale olive .. 95·00 £100

1892. Surch. **HALF-PENNY.**

104. 4. ½d. on 4d. brown .. 20 55

5. Seal of Colony.  6.

1892.

105. 5. ¼d. grey and red .. 20 30
163. ¼d. brown 20 25
106. ½d. green 10 30
107. 1d. red 20 20
108. 2d. black and orange .. 2·50 1·50
166. 2d. grey .. .. 4·00 5·00
109. 2½d. blue .. .. 2·25 60
110. 5d. olive .. .. 3·50 2·50
111. 6d. mauve and red .. 3·50 2·75
168. 6d. purple .. .. 7·00 7·00
112. 8d. orange and blue .. 1·75 4·00
113. 10d. green and red .. 5·00 6·00
169. 1s. black on green .. 12·00 13·00
114. 2s. 6d. black and orange 14·00 15·00
144. 2s. 6d. violet and green 21·00 23·00

1897. Diamond Jubilee.

116. 6. ¼d. grey and red .. 30 35
117. ½d. green 70 35
118. 1d. red .. .. 1·25 50
119. 2½d. blue .. .. 3·50 75
120. 5d. brown .. .. 6·50 7·50
121. 6d. mauve and carmine 8·00 7·00
122. 8d. orange and blue 7·00 6·50
123. 10d. green and red .. 12·00 13·00
124. 2s. 6d. black and orange 12·00 13·00

7. Monument to Nelson.

1906. Nelson Cent.

145. 7. ¼d. black and grey .. 45 50
146. ½d. black and green .. 1·60 55
147. 1d. black and red .. 1·60 35
148. 2d. black and yellow .. 3·50 5·00
149 2½d. black and blue .. 4·00 4·50
150. 6d. black and mauve .. 11·00 12·00
151. 1s. black and rose .. 12·00 12·00

8. The "Olive Blossom". 9.

1906. Annexation of Barbados. Tercent.

152. 8. 1d. black, blue and green 6·00 1·75

1907. Surch. **Kingston/Relief/Fund/1d.**

153. 5. 1d. on 2d. black & orange 1·40 1·75

1912.

170. 9. ¼d. brown 8 12
171. ½d. green 8 8
172. 1d. red 55 25
173. 2d. grey .. .. 1·25 3·50
174. 2½d. blue 90 70
175. 3d. purple on yellow .. 1·00 2·25
176. 4d. red & black on yellow 1·00 3·25
177. 6d. purple .. .. 2·25 3·00

Larger type, with portrait at top centre.

178. 1s. black on green .. 3·50 5·00
179. 2s. blue and pur. on blue 22·00 20·00
180. 3s. violet and green .. 22·00 22·00

11. Badge of Colony.

1916.

181.	11.	¼d. brown	15	20
185.		½d. green	30	30
188.		1d. red	1·25	50
189.		2d. grey	2·00	3·00
190.		2½d. blue	50	75
191.		3d. purple on yellow	1·00	1·10
192.		4d. red on yellow	85	3·25
199.		4d. black and red	45	1·90
193.		6d. purple	1·00	1·50
194.		1s. black on green	2·50	2·25
195.		2s. purple on blue	11·00	11·00
196.		3s. violet	21·00	23·00
200.		3s. green and violet	10·00	11·00

1917. Optd. WAR TAX.

197.	9.	1d. red	15	20

12. Victory.

1920. Victory. Inscr. "VICTORY 1919".

201.	12.	¼d. black and brown	15	35
202.		½d. black and green	15	35
203.		1d. black and red	20	30
204.		2d. black and grey	80	2·50
205.		2½d. indigo and blue	1·50	2·50
206.		3d. black and purple	85	1·50
207.		4d. black and green	85	2·25
208.		6d. black and orange	1·00	2·25
209.	–	1s. black and green	3·25	5·50
210.	–	2s. black and brown	6·50	9·50
211.	–	3s. black and orange	14·00	17·00

The 1s. to 3s. show Victory full-face.

14. 15.

1921.

217.	14.	¼d. brown	15	5
219.		½d. green	15	25
220.		1d. red	25	25
221.		2d. grey	90	25
222.		2½d. blue	55	1·10
213.		3d. purple on yellow	40	1·25
214.		4d. red on yellow	70	1·25
225.		6d. purple	95	2·25
215.		1s. black on green	3·00	5·50
227.		2s. purple on blue	12·00	14·00
228.		3s. violet	15·00	18·00

1925. Inscr. "POSTAGE & REVENUE".

229.	15.	¼d. brown	5	5
230.		½d. green	5	5
231.		1d. red	5	5
231a.		1½d. orange	35	15
232.		2d. grey	20	65
233a.		2½d. blue	1·50	8
234.		3d. purple on yellow	25	20
235.		4d. red on yellow	50	50
236.		6d. purple	75	75
237.		1s. black on green	1·50	2·50
238.		2s. purple on blue	3·00	4·00
238a.		2s. 6d. red on blue	12·00	16·00
239.		3s. violet	7·00	9·00

16. Kings Charles I and George V.

1927. Settlement of Barbados. Tercent.

240.	16.	1d. red	45	45

1935. Silver Jubilee. As T 11 of Antigua.

241.	1d. blue and red	8	12
242.	1½d. blue and grey	20	30
243.	2½d. brown and blue	85	85
244.	1s. grey and purple	3·50	4·00

1937. Coronation. As T 2 of Aden.

245.	1d. red	20	20
246.	1½d. brown	25	20
247.	2½d. blue	70	70

17. Badge of the Colony.

1938. "POSTAGE & REVENUE" omitted.

248.	17.	½d. green	15	12
248b.		½d. yellow	10	15
249a.		1d. red	85	12
249c.		1d. green	8	8
250.		1½d. orange	15	8
250b.		2d. claret	35	35
250c.		2d. red	10	8
251.		2½d. blue	20	25
252a.		3d. brown	20	20
252b.		3d. blue	12	12
253.		4d. slate	20	8
254.		6d. violet	12	8
254a.		8d. mauve	45	40
255a.		1s. olive	60	35
256.		2s. 6d. purple	1·75	75
256a.		5s. blue	2·00	1·25

18. Kings Charles I, George VI, Assembly Chamber and Mace.

1939. General Assembly. Tercent.

257.	18.	½d. green	25	15
258.		1d. red	25	15
259.		1½d. orange	85	55
260.		2½d. blue	1·10	1·25
261.		3d. brown	1·10	2·00

1946. Victory. As T 4 of Aden.

262.	1½d. orange	5	5
263.	3d. brown	5	5

1947. Surch. ONE PENNY.

264.	17.	1d. on 2d. red	30	60

1948. Silver Wedding. As T 5/6 of Aden.

265.	1½d. orange	8	5
266.	5s. blue	2·50	5·00

1949. U.P.U. As T 14/17 of Antigua.

267.	1½d. orange	10	12
268.	3d. blue	25	20
269.	4d. grey	45	45
270.	1s. olive	55	55

19. Dover Fort.

20. Seal of Barbados.

1950.

271.	19.	1 c. indigo	12	20
272.	–	2 c. green	10	12
273.	–	3 c. brown and grey	12	20
274.	–	4 c. red	12	15
275.	–	6 c. blue	10	15
276.	–	8 c. blue and purple	20	20
277.	–	12 c. blue and olive	50	35
278.	–	24 c. red and black	40	40
279.	–	48 c. violet	1·25	1·25
280.	–	60 c. green and lake	1·25	1·10
281.	–	$1.20 c. red and olive	2·00	1·25
282.	20.	$2.40 c. black	4·00	5·00

DESIGNS—As T 19: HORIZ. 2 c. Sugar cane breeding. 3 c. Public building. 6 c. Casting net. 8 c. Inter-Colonial schooner. 12 c. Flying fish. 24 c. Old Main Guard Garrison. 60 c. Careenage. VERT. 4 c. Nelson's Monument. 48 c. The Cathedral. $1.20 c. Map and wireless mast.

1951. B.W.I. University College. Inaug. As T 18/19 of Antigua.

283.	3 c. brown and blue	5	10
284.	12 c. blue and olive	35	40

21. King George VI and Stamp of 1852.

1952. Barbados Stamp Cent.

285.	21.	3 c. green and slate	12	15
286.		4 c. blue and red	12	20
287.		12 c. slate and emerald	20	20
288.		24 c. brown and sepia	35	45

1953. Coronation. As T 7 of Aden.

289.	4 c. black and orange	12	12

22. Harbour Police.

1953. As 1950 issue but with portrait or cypher (No. 319) of Queen Elizabeth II as in T 22.

290.	19.	1 c. indigo	12	15
291.	–	2 c. orange & turquoise	12	12
292.	–	3 c. black and green	12	12
293.	–	4 c. black and orange	12	15
294.	22.	5 c. blue and red	12	12
295.	–	6 c. brown	12	12
296.	–	8 c. black and blue	15	15
297.	–	12 c. blue and olive	25	25
298.	–	24 c. red and black	25	35
299.	–	48 c. violet	80	65
318.	–	60 c. green and lake	1·10	1·40
301.	–	$1.20 red and olive	2·75	2·00
302.	20.	$2.40 black	3·75	2·75

1958. British Caribbean Federation. As T 21 of Antigua.

303.	3 c. green	12	12
304.	6 c. blue	25	30
305.	12 c. red	30	30

23. Deep Water Harbour, Bridgetown.

1961. Opening of Deep Water Harbour.

306.	23.	4 c. black and orange	12	12
307.		8 c. black and blue	20	20
308.		24 c. red and black	40	40

24. Scout Badge and Map of Barbados.

1962. Barbados Boy Scout Association. Golden Jubilee.

309.	24.	4 c. black and orange	12	12
310.		12 c. blue & olive-brown	30	30
311.		$1.20 red & olive-green	1·10	1·40

1965. I.T.U. Cent. As T 26 of Antigua.

320.	2 c. lilac and red	8	10
321.	48 c. yellow and drab	65	65

25. Deep Sea Coral.

1965.

342.	25.	1 c. black, pink and blue	5	5
343.	–	2 c. brown, yell. & mag.	5	5
324.	–	3 c. brown and orange	8	8
344.	–	3 c. brown and orange	5	5
345.	–	4 c. blue and green	5	5
346.	–	5 c. sepia, rose and lilac	5	5
347.	–	6 c. multicoloured	5	8
348.	–	8 c. multicoloured	8	8
349.	–	12 c. multicoloured	10	10
350.	–	15 c. black, yellow & red	10	12
351.	–	25 c. blue and ochre	15	15
352.	–	35 c. red and green	30	30
353.	–	50 c. blue and green	40	40
354.	–	$1 multicoloured	1·00	1·00
355.	–	$2.50 multicoloured	1·75	1·75
355a.	–	$5 multicoloured	4·00	4·00

DESIGNS: 2 c. Lobster (wrongly inscr. "Panulirus" for "Palinurus"). 324. Sea Horse (wrongly inscr. "Hippocanpus"). 344. (correctly inscr. "Hippocampus"). 4 c. Sea Urchin. 5 c. Staghorn Coral. 6 c. Butterfly Fish. 8 c. File Shell. 12 c. Balloon Fish. 15 c. Angel Fish. 25 c. Brain Coral. 35 c. Brittle Star. 50 c. Flying Fish. $1, Queen Conch Shell. $2·50. Fiddler Crab. VERT. $5, Dolphin.

1966. Churchill Commem. As T 28 of Antigua.

336.	1 c. blue	5	5
337.	4 c. green	8	5
338.	25 c. brown	35	45
339.	35 c. violet	55	65

1966. Royal Visit. As T 29 of Antigua.

340.	3 c. black and blue	12	12
341.	35 c. black and magenta	50	50

26. Arms of Barbados.

1966. Independence. Multicoloured.

356.	4 c. Type 26	12	12
357.	25 c. Hilton Hotel	30	30
358.	35 c. G. Sobers (Test cricketer)	40	40
359.	50 c. Pine Hill Dairy	50	55

1967. U.N.E.S.C.O. 20th Anniv. As T 33/5 of Antigua.

360.	4 c. vio., red, yell. & orge.	12	12
361.	12 c. yellow, violet & olive	35	35
362.	25 c. black, purple & orange	55	55

27. Policeman and Anchor.

1967. Harbour Police. Cent. Multicoloured.

363.	4 c. Type 27	8	10
364.	25 c. Policeman with telescope	25	25
365.	35 c. Police launch	35	35
366.	50 c. Policeman outside H.Q.	55	55

The 25 c. and 50 c. are horiz.

28. Governor-General Sir Winston Scott, G.C.M.G.

1967. Independence. 1st Anniv. Multicoloured.

367. 4 c. Type **28** 8 8
368. 25 c. Independent Arch .. 25 25
369. 35 c. Treasury Building .. 35 35
370. 50 c. Parliament Building 55 55

Nos. 368/70 are horiz.

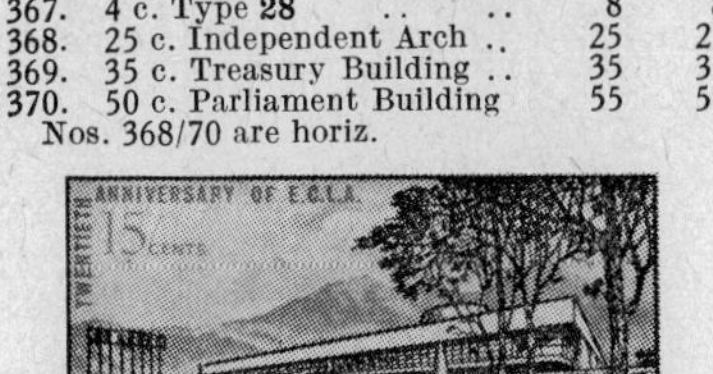

29. U.N. Building, Santiago de Chile.

1968. Economic Commission for Latin America. 20th Anniv.

371. **29.** 15 c. multicoloured .. 20 20

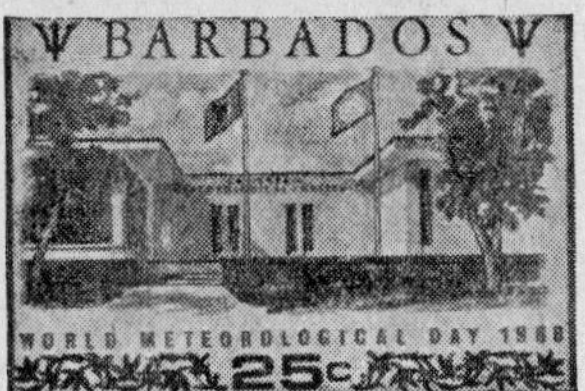

30. Meteorological Institute.

1968. World Meteorological Day. Multicoloured.

372. 3 c. Radar Antenna .. 10 10
373. 25 c. Type **30** 25 25
374. 50 c. Harp Gun and Coat of Arms .. 40 40

Nos. 372 and 374 are vert.

31. Lady Baden-Powell and Guide at Camp Fire.

1968. Girl Guiding in Barbados. Golden Jubilee.

375. **31.** 3 c. ultram., blk. & gold 10 10
376. – 25 c. blue, blk. & gold 30 30
377. – 35 c. yell., blk. & gold 45 45

DESIGNS: 25 c. Lady Baden-Powell and Pax Hill. 35 c. Lady Baden-Powell and Guides' Badge.

32. Hands breaking Chain, and Human Rights Emblem.

1968. Human Rights Year.

378. **32.** 4 c. violet, brown & grn. 10 10
379. – 25 c. blk., blue & yellow 25 25
380. – 35 c. multicoloured .. 40 40

DESIGNS: 25 c. Human Rights Emblem and family enchained. 35 c. Shadows of refugees beyond opening fence.

33. Racehorses in the Paddock.

1969. Horse-Racing. Multicoloured.

381. 4 c. Type **33** 10 10
382. 25 c. Starting-Gate .. 25 25
383. 35 c. On the flat 40 40
384. 50 c. The Winning-post .. 1·10 1·10

INDEX

Countries can be quickly located by referring to the index at the end of this volume.

34. Map showing " CARIFTA " Countries.

1969. " CARIFTA " 1st Anniv. Multicoloured.

386. 5 c. Type **34** 10 10
387. 12 c. " Strength in Unity " 15 20
388. 25 c. Type **34** 25 30
389. 50 c. As 12 c. 40 40

35. I.L.O. Emblem and " 1919-1969 ".

1969. I.L.O. 50th Anniv.

390. **35.** 4 c. multicoloured .. 10 10
391. 25 c. multicoloured .. 35 35

1969. No. 363 Surch.

392. **27.** 1 c. on 4 c. mult. .. 15 15

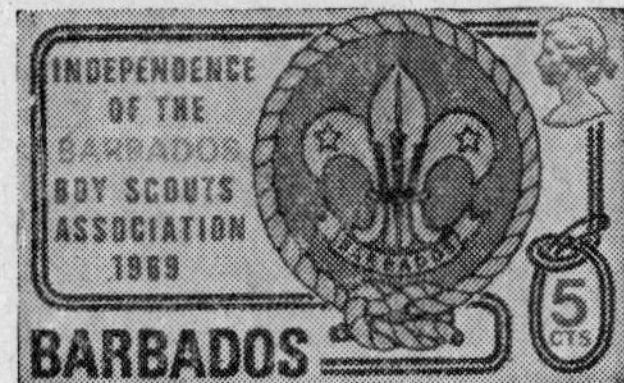

36. National Scout Badge.

1969. Independence of Barbados Boy Scouts Assn., and 50th Anniv. of Barbados Sea Scouts. Multicoloured.

393. 5 c. Type **36** 8 8
394. 25 c. Sea Scouts rowing .. 30 30
395. 35 c. Scouts around camp-fire 35 35
396. 50 c. Scouts and National Scout H.Q. 40 45

1970. No. 346 surch.

398. 4 c. on 5 c. sepia, red & lilac 8 8

37. Lion at Gun Hill.

1970. Multicoloured.

399. 1 c. Type **37** 5 5
400. 2 c. Trafalgar Fountain .. 5 5
401. 3 c. Montefiore Drinking Fountain 5 5
402. 4 c. St. James' Monument 5 5
403. 5 c. St. Ann's Fort .. 5 5
457. 6 c. Old Sugar Mill, Morgan Lewis 5 5
405. 8 c. The Cenotaph .. 5 8
406. 10 c. South Point Lighthouse 8 8
407. 12 c. Barbados Museum .. 8 10
408. 15 c. Sharon Moravian Church 10 12
462. 25 c. George Washington House 20 20
463. 35 c. Nicholas Abbey .. 20 25
464. 50 c. Bowmanston Pumping Station 30 35
465. $1 Queen Elizabeth Hospital 55 60
466. $2.50 Sugar Factory .. 1·40 1·60
467. $5 Seawell Int. Airport .. 2·75 3·00

Nos. 407/8 and 462/7 are horiz.

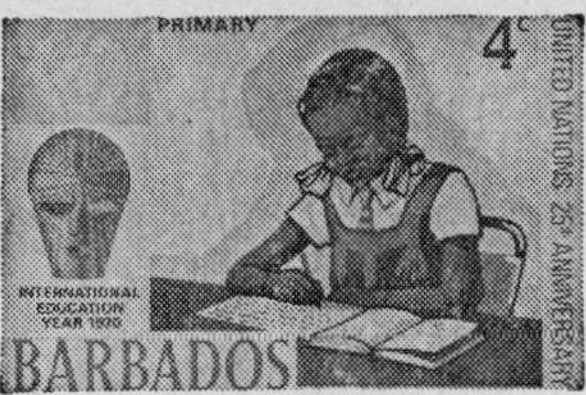

38. Primary Schoolgirl.

1970. U.N. 25th Anniv. Multicoloured.

415. 4 c. Type **38** 5 5
416. 5 c. Secondary Schoolboy 5 5
417. 25 c. Technical Student .. 20 20
418. 50 c. University Building 40 40

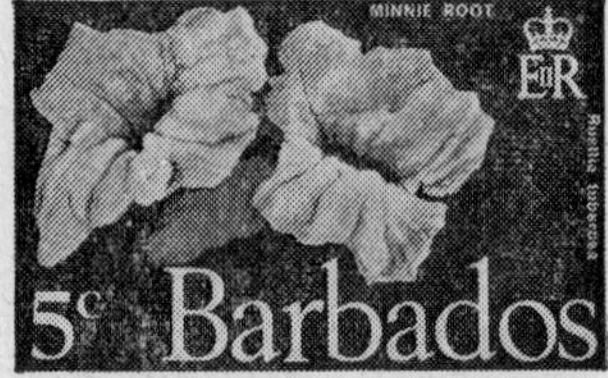

39. Minnie Root.

1970. Flowers of Barbados. Multicoloured.

419. 1 c. Barbados Easter Lily 5 5
420. 5 c. Type **39** 5 5
421. 10 c. Eyelash Orchid .. 5 5
422. 25 c. Pride of Barbados .. 20 20
423. 35 c. Christmas Hope 30 35

The 1 c. and 25 c. are vert.

40. Window, St. Margaret's Church, St. John.

1971. Easter. Multicoloured.

425. 4 c. Type **40** 8 8
426. 10 c. "The Resurrection" (Benjamin West) .. 12 12
427. 35 c. Type **40** 35 35
428. 50 c. As 10 c. 45 45

41. Sail-fish Craft.

1971. Tourism. Multicoloured.

429. 1 c. Type **41** 8 8
430. 5 c. Tennis 10 10
431. 12 c. Horse-riding .. 15 15
432. 25 c. Water-skiing .. 25 25
433. 50 c. Scuba-diving .. 45 45

42. S. J. Prescod.

1971. Samuel Jackman Prescod (politician). Death Cent.

434. **42.** 3 c. multicoloured .. 8 8
435. 35 c. multicoloured .. 30 30

43. Arms of Barbados.

1971. Independence. Fifth Anniv. Multicoloured.

436. 4 c. Type **43** 8 8
437. 15 c. National flag and map 15 15
438. 25 c. Type **43** 30 35
439. 50 c. As 15 c. 50 55

44. Transmitting " Then and Now ".

1972. Cable Link Cent. Multicoloured.

440. 4 c. Type **44** 8 8
441. 10 c. Cable Ship " Stanley Angwin " 12 12
442. 35 c. Barbados Earth Station and " Intelsat 4 " .. 35 35
443. 50 c. Mt. Misery and Tropospheric Scatter Station .. 50 50

45. Map and Badge.

1972. Scouts. Diamond Jubilee. Mult.

444. 5 c. Type **45** 8 8
445. 15 c. Pioneers of Scouting 15 10
446. 25 c. Scouts 30 35
447. 50 c. Flags 45 50

46. Mobile Library.

1972. Int. Book Year. Multicoloured.

448. 4 c. Type **46** 8 8
449. 15 c. Visual-aids van .. 12 12
450. 25 c. Public Library .. 30 30
451. $1 Codrington College .. 1·00 1·25

47. Potter's Wheel.

1973. Pottery in Barbados. Mult.

468. 5 c. Type **47** 8 8
469. 15 c. Kilns 12 12
470. 25 c. Finished products .. 20 25
471. $1 Market scene 50 60

48. First Flight, 1911.

1973. Aviation.

472. 48.	5 c. multicoloured		5	5
473. –	15 c. multicoloured	..	12	12
474. –	25 c. blue, blk. & cobalt		20	20
475. –	50 c. multicoloured	..	35	35

DESIGNS: 15 c. First flight to Barbados, 1928. 25 c. Passenger aircraft, 1939. 50 c. Jet airliner, 1973.

49. University Chancellor.

1973. University of West Indies. 25th Anniv. Multicoloured.

476.	5 c. Type 49	5	5
477.	25 c. Sherlock Hall ..	15	15
478.	35 c. Cave Hill Campus ..	25	25

1974. No. 462 surch.

479.	4 c. on 25 c. multicoloured	8	8

50. Old Sail Boat.

1974. Fishing Boats of Barbados. Multicoloured.

480.	15 c. Type 50	12	12
481.	35 c. Rowing-boat ..	25	25
482.	50 c. Motor fishing-boat ..	30	30
483.	$1 U.N.D.P. vessel, "Calamar"	50	60

51. "Cattleya Gaskelliana Alba".

1974. Orchids. Multicoloured.

485.	1 c. Type 51	5	5
486.	2 c. "Renanthera storiei"	5	5
487.	3 c. "Dendrobium" "Rose Marie"	5	8
513.	4 c. "Epidendrum ibaguense"	5	5
489.	5 c. "Schomburgkia humboldtii"	5	5
490.	8 c. "Oncidium ampliatum"	5	5
491.	10 c. "Arachnis maggie oei"	8	8
492.	12 c. "Dendrobium aggregatum"	5	5
493.	15 c. "Paphiopedilum puddle"	12	12
494.	25 c. "Epidendrum ciliare" (Eyelash)	12	15
495.	35 c. "Bletia patula" ..	20	25
496.	50 c. "Phalaenopsis schilleriana" "Sunset Glow"	25	30
497.	$1 "Ascocenda" "Red Gem"	55	60
498.	$2.50 "Brassolaeliocattleya" "Nugget"	1·40	1·50
499.	$5 "Caularthron bicornatum" ..	2·75	3·00
500.	$10 "Vanda" "Josephine Black"	5·50	6·00

Nos. 485, 494 and 498/9 are horiz. designs, and the remainder are vert.

52. 4d. Stamp of 1882, and U.P.U. Emblem.

1974. Universal Postal Union. Cent.

501. 52.	8 c. mve., oran. & grn. ..	8	5
502. –	35 c. red, oran. & orn. ..	25	25
503. –	50 c. ultram., bl. & silver	30	30
504. –	$1 bl., brn. & black ..	50	50

DESIGNS: 35 c. Letters encircling the globe. 50 c. U.P.U. emblem and arms of Barbados. $1 Map of Barbados, sailing ship and aeroplane.

53. R. Y. "Britannia".

1975. Royal Visit. Multicoloured.

506.	8 c. Type 53	5	5
507.	25 c. Type 53	15	20
508.	35 c. Sunset and palms ..	25	25
509.	$1 As 35 c.	50	60

54. St. Michael's Cathedral.

1975. Anglican Diocese. 150th Anniv. Mult.

526.	5 c. Type 54	5	5
527.	15 c. Bishop Coleridge ..	8	8
528.	50 c. All Saints' Church ..	20	25
529.	$1 Stained-glass window, St. Michael's Cathedral	45	50

55. Pony Float.

1975. Crop-over Festival. Multicoloured.

531.	8 c. Type 55	5	5
532.	25 c. Man on stilts ..	12	15
533.	35 c. Maypole dancing ..	20	20
534.	50 c. Cuban dancers ..	20	25

56. Barbados Coat of Arms. 57. 17th-Century Sailing Ship.

1975. Coil Stamps.

536. 56.	5 c. blue	5	5
537.	25 c. violet	12	15

1975. First Settlement. 350th Anniv. Mult.

538.	4 c. Type 57	5	5
539.	10 c. Bearded fig tree and fruit	5	5
540.	25 c. Ogilvy's 17-century map	12	15
541.	$1 Captain John Powell ..	45	50

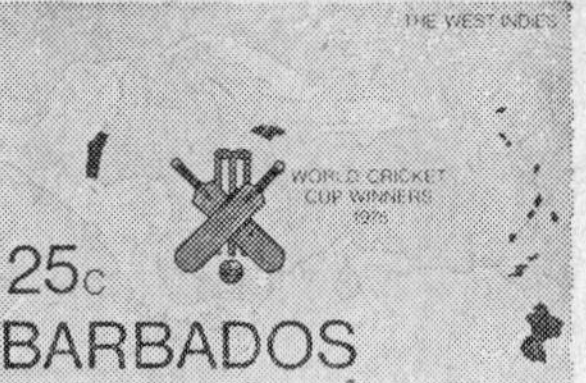

58. Map of the Caribbean.

1976. West Indian Victory in World Cricket Cup.

559. 58.	25 c. multicoloured ..	15	15
560. –	45 c. black and purple ..	25	30

DESIGN—VERT 45 c. The Prudential Cup.

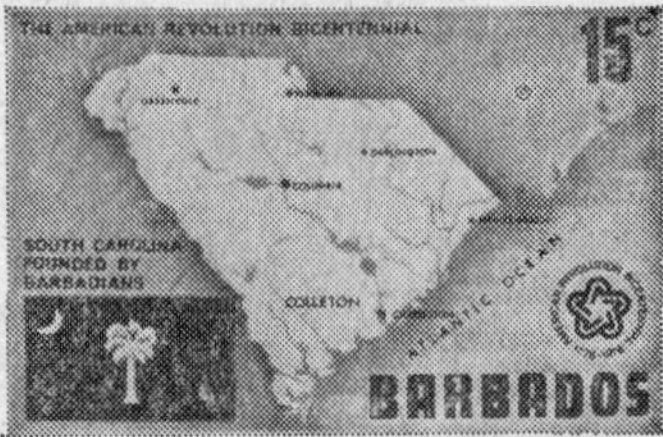

59. Flag and Map of South Carolina.

1976. American Revolution. Bicent. Multicoloured.

561.	15 c. Type 59	8	10
562.	25 c. George Washington and map of Bridgetown	15	15
563.	50 c. Independence Declaration	30	35
564.	$1 Prince Hall	55	65

60. Early Postman.

1976. Post Office Act. 125th Anniv. Multicoloured.

565.	8 c. Type 60	5	5
566.	35 c. Modern postman ..	20	20
567.	50 c. Early letter	30	35
568.	$1 Delivery van	55	65

POSTAGE DUE STAMPS

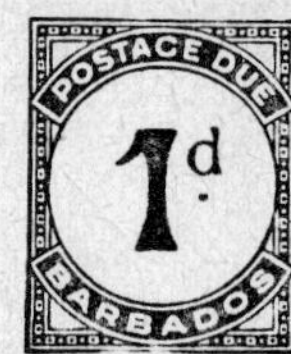

D 1. D 2.

1934.

D 1. D 1.	½d. green	12	10
D 2.	1d. black	40	25
D 3.	3d. red	3·50	90

1950. Values in cents.

D 7. D 1.	1 c. green	8	8
D 8.	2 c. black	8	8
D 9.	6 c. red	8	8

1976.

D 14. D 2.	1 c. mauve and pink	5	5
D 15. –	2 c. blue and lt. blue	5	5
D 16. –	5 c. brown and yellow	5	5
D 17. –	10 c. blue and lilac ..	5	5
D 18. –	25 c. dark grn. & grn.	12	15
D 19. –	$1 red and dark red ..	50	60

DESIGNS: Nos. 15/19 show different floral backgrounds.

BARBUDA BC

One of the Leeward Is., Br. W. Indies. Dependency of Antigua. Used stamps of Antigua and Leeward Is. concurrently. The issues from 1968 are also valid for use in Antigua. From 1971 to 1973 the stamps of Antigua were again used.

1922. Stamps of Leeward Islands optd. BARBUDA.

1. 4.	½d. green	90	2·25
2.	1d. red	90	2·25
3.	2d. grey	1·10	2·75
4.	2½d. blue	1·10	2·25
9.	3d. purple on yellow ..	1·00	2·25
5.	6d. purple	2·50	5·50
10.	1s. black on green ..	2·50	4·00
6.	2s. purple and blue on blue	7·50	11·00
7.	3s. green and violet ..	17·00	20·00
8.	4s. black and red	20·00	26·00
11.	5s. green & red on yellow	45·00	65·00

1. Map of Barbuda.

1968.

12. 1.	½ c. brown, black and pink	5	5
13.	1 c. orange, black & flesh	5	5
14.	2 c. brown, red and rose	5	5
15.	3 c. brown, yell. & lemon	5	5
16.	4 c. black, green & apple	5	5
17.	5 c. blue-green and black	5	5
18.	6 c. black, purple and lilac	8	8
19.	10 c. blk., ultram. & cobalt	10	12
20.	15 c. black, green & turq.	12	15

2. Longspine Squirrelfish.

1968. Fishes. Multicoloured.

20a.	20 c. Great Barracuda ..	15	20
21.	25 c. Great Amberjack ..	20	25
22.	35 c. French Angelfish ..	25	30
23.	50 c. Porkfish	35	45
24.	73 c. Striped Parrotfish ..	50	60
25.	$1 Type 2	90	1·40
26.	$2·50 Catalufa	2·25	2·50
27.	$5 Blue Chromis	4·00	4·50

3. Sprinting and Aztec Sun-stone.

1968. Olympic Games, Mexico. Multicoloured.

28.	25 c. Type 3	30	30
29.	35 c. High-jumping and Aztec Statue ..	40	40
30.	75 c. Yachting and Aztec Lion Mask	65	70

4. "The Ascension" (Orcagna).

1969. Easter Commem.

32. 4.	25 c. black and blue ..	25	25
33.	35 c. black and red ..	30	35
34.	75 c. black and lilac ..	55	55

5. Scout Enrolment Ceremony.

1969. 3rd Caribbean Scout Jamboree. Multicoloured.

35.	25 c. Type **5**	20	25
36.	35 c. Scouts around camp fire	30	35
37.	75 c. Sea Scouts rowing boat	50	60

5. " Sistine Madonna " (Raphael).

1969. Christmas.

38. **6.**	½ c. multicoloured ..	10	10
39.	25 c. multicoloured ..	25	30
40.	35 c. multicoloured ..	35	35
41.	75 c. multicoloured ..	65	80

7. William I (1066–87).

1970. English Monarchs. Multicoloured.

42.	35 c. Type **7**	35	40
43.	35 c. William II (1087-1100)	35	40
44.	35 c. Henry I (1100-35) ..	35	40
45.	35 c. Stephen (1135-54) ..	35	40
46.	35 c. Henry II. (1154-89) ..	35	40
47.	35 c. Richard I (1189-99) ..	35	40
48.	35 c. John (1199-1216) ..	35	40
49.	35 c. Henry III (1216-72) ..	35	40
50.	35 c. Edward I (1272-1307)	35	40
51.	35 c. Edward II (1307-27) .	35	40
52.	35 c. Edward III (1327-77)	35	40
53.	35 c. Richard II (1377-99) .	35	40
54.	35 c. Henry IV (1399-1413)	35	40
55.	35 c. Henry V (1413-22) ..	35	40
56.	35 c. Henry VI (1422-61) ..	35	40
57.	35 c. Edward IV (1462-83) ..	35	40
58.	35 c. Edward V (April-June 1483)	35	40
59.	35 c. Richard III (1483-85)	35	40
60.	35 c. Henry VII (1485-1509)	35	40
61.	35 c. Henry VIII (1509-47)	35	40
62.	35 c. Edward VI (1547-53) .	35	40
63.	35 c. Lady Jane Grey (1553)	35	40
64.	35 c. Mary I (1553-8) ..	35	40
65.	35 c. Elizabeth I (1558-1603)	35	40
66.	35 c. James I (1603-25) ..	35	40
67.	35 c. Charles I (1625-49) ..	35	40
68.	35 c. Charles II (1649-1685)	35	40
69.	35 c. James II (1685-1688) .	35	40
70.	35 c. William III (1689-1702)	35	40
71.	35 c. Mary II (1689-1694) ..	35	40
72.	35 c. Anne (1702-1714) ..	35	40
73.	35 c. George I (1714-1727) ..	35	40
74.	35 c. George II (1727-1760)	35	40
75.	35 c. George III (1760-1820)	35	40
76.	35 c. George IV (1820-1830)	35	40
77.	35 c. William IV (1830-1837)	35	40
78.	35 c. Victoria (1837-1901) ..	35	40

1970. No. 12 surch.

79. **1.**	20 c. on ½ c. brn., blk. & pink	30	45

8. " The Way to Calvary " (Ugolino).

1970. Easter. Multicoloured.

80.	25 c. Type **8**	25	30
81.	35 c. " The Deposition from the Cross " (Ugolino) ..	30	35
82.	75 c. Crucifix (The Master of S. Francesco)	55	65

9. Oliver is introduced to Fagin (" Oliver Twist ").

1970. Charles Dickens. Death Cent. Multicoloured.

83.	20 c. Type **9**	25	30
84.	75 c. Dickens and scene from "The Old Curiosity Shop"	55	55

10. " Madonna of the Meadows " (G. Bellini).

1970. Christmas. Multicoloured.

85.	20 c. Type **10**	25	25
86.	50 c. " Madonna, Child and Angels " (from Wilton diptych)	35	50
87.	75 c. " The Nativity " (della Francesca)	55	70

11. Nurse with Patient in Wheelchair.

1970. British Red Cross. Cent. Multicoloured.

88.	20 c. Type **11**	25	25
89.	35 c. Nurse giving Patient Magazines (horiz.) ..	35	50
90.	75 c. Nurse and Mother weighing Baby (horiz.) ..	55	70

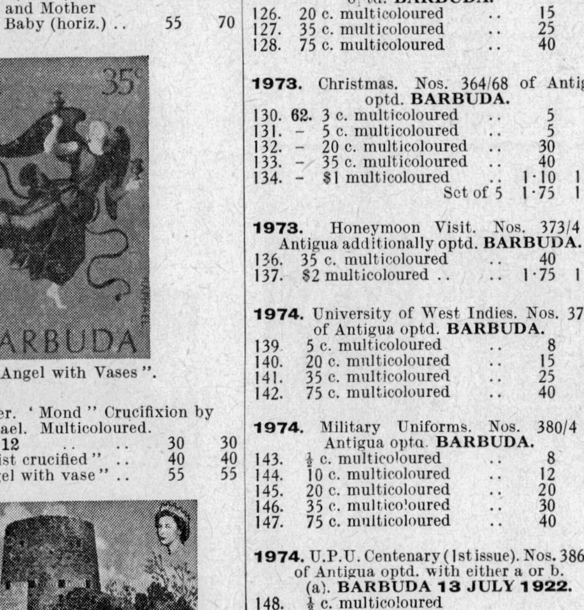

12. " Angel with Vases ".

1971. Easter. ' Mond " Crucifixion by Raphael. Multicoloured.

91.	35 c. Type **12**	30	30
92.	50 c. " Christ crucified " ..	40	40
93.	75 c. " Angel with vase " ..	55	55

13. Martello Tower.

1971. Tourism. Multicoloured.

94.	20 c. Type **13**	25	25
95.	25 c. Sailing boats	30	30
96.	50 c. Hotel bungalows ..	45	45
97.	75 c. Government House and Mystery Stone	65	65

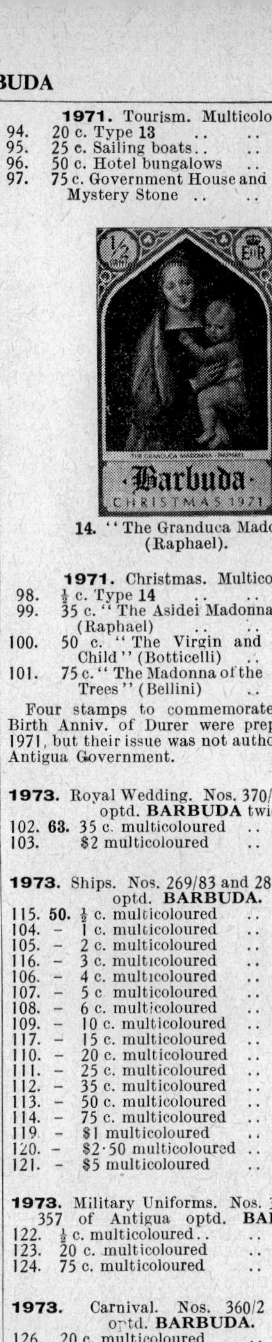

14. " The Granduca Madonna " (Raphael).

1971. Christmas. Multicoloured.

98.	½ c. Type **14**	10	10
99.	35 c. " The Asidei Madonna " (Raphael)	30	35
100.	50 c. " The Virgin and Child " (Botticelli) ..	40	45
101.	75 c. " The Madonna of the Trees " (Bellini) ..	55	60

Four stamps to commemorate the 500th Birth Anniv. of Durer were prepared in late 1971, but their issue was not authorised by the Antigua Government.

1973. Royal Wedding. Nos. 370/1 of Antigua optd. **BARBUDA** twice.

102. **63.**	35 c. multicoloured ..	5·00	5·50
103.	$2 multicoloured ..	2·50	3·00

1973. Ships. Nos. 269/83 and 285 of Antigua optd. **BARBUDA.**

115. **50.**	½ c. multicoloured ..	5	5
104. –	1 c. multicoloured ..	5	5
105. –	2 c. multicoloured ..	5	5
116. –	3 c. multicoloured ..	5	5
106. –	4 c. multicoloured ..	5	5
107. –	5 c. multicoloured ..	5	8
108. –	6 c. multicoloured ..	8	10
109. –	10 c. multicoloured ..	10	12
117. –	15 c. multicoloured ..	8	10
110. –	20 c. multicoloured ..	12	12
111. –	25 c. multicoloured ..	20	20
112. –	35 c. multicoloured ..	25	30
113. –	50 c. multicoloured ..	30	40
114. –	75 c. multicoloured ..	40	45
119. –	$1 multicoloured ..	55	60
120. –	$2·50 multicoloured ..	6·50	6·50
121. –	$5 multicoloured ..	2·50	2·75

1973. Military Uniforms. Nos. 353, 355 and 357 of Antigua optd. **BARBUDA.**

122.	½ c. multicoloured ..	8	8
123.	20 c. multicoloured ..	20	20
124.	75 c. multicoloured ..	45	55

1973. Carnival. Nos. 360/2 of Antigua optd. **BARBUDA.**

126.	20 c. multicoloured ..	15	15
127.	35 c. multicoloured ..	25	25
128.	75 c. multicoloured ..	40	45

1973. Christmas. Nos. 364/68 of Antigua optd. **BARBUDA.**

130. **62.**	3 c. multicoloured ..	5	5
131. –	5 c. multicoloured ..	5	5
132. –	20 c. multicoloured ..	30	30
133. –	35 c. multicoloured ..	40	40
134. –	$1 multicoloured ..	1·10	1·25
	Set of 5	1·75	1·75

1973. Honeymoon Visit. Nos. 373/4 of Antigua additionally optd. **BARBUDA.**

136.	35 c. multicoloured ..	40	40
137.	$2 multicoloured	1·75	1·75

1974. University of West Indies. Nos. 376/9 of Antigua optd. **BARBUDA.**

139.	5 c. multicoloured ..	8	8
140.	20 c. multicoloured ..	15	15
141.	35 c. multicoloured ..	25	25
142.	75 c. multicoloured ..	40	40

1974. Military Uniforms. Nos. 380/4 of Antigua optd. **BARBUDA.**

143.	½ c. multicoloured ..	8	8
144.	10 c. multicoloured ..	12	12
145.	20 c. multicoloured ..	20	20
146.	35 c. multicoloured ..	30	30
147.	75 c. multicoloured ..	40	45

1974. U.P.U. Centenary (1st issue). Nos. 386/92 of Antigua optd. with either a or b.

(a). **BARBUDA 13 JULY 1922.**

148. ½ c. multicoloured
150. 1 c. multicoloured
152. 2 c. multicoloured
154. 5 c. multicoloured
156. 20 c. multicoloured
158. 35 c. multicoloured
160. $1 multicoloured

(b). **BARBUDA 15 SEPT. 1874 G.P.U.** ("General Postal Union").

149.	½ c. multicoloured		
151.	1 c. multicoloured		
153.	2 c. multicoloured		
155.	5 c. multicoloured		
157.	20 c. multicoloured		
159.	35 c. multicoloured		
161.	$1 multicoloured		
148/161.	Set of 14	8·00	9·00

1974. Antiguan Steel Bands. Nos. 394/97 of Antigua optd. **BARBUDA.**

163.	5 c. dull red, red & blk. ..	5	5
164.	20 c. brn., light brn. & blk.	15	15
165.	35 c. light grn., grn. & blk.	20	25
166.	75 c. dull blue, blue & blk.	40	40

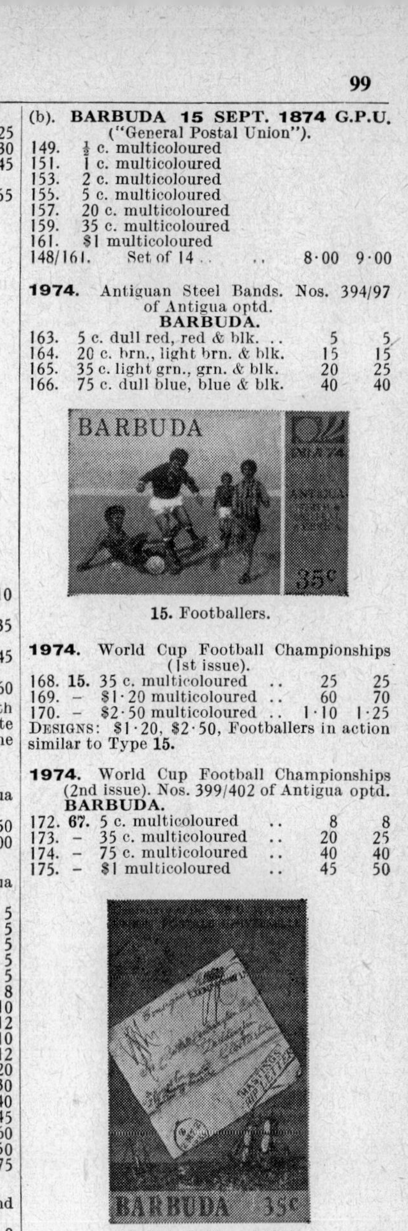

15. Footballers.

1974. World Cup Football Championships (1st issue).

168. **15.**	35 c. multicoloured ..	25	25
169. –	$1·20 multicoloured ..	60	70
170. –	$2·50 multicoloured ..	1·10	1·25

DESIGNS: $1·20, $2·50, Footballers in action similar to Type **15.**

1974. World Cup Football Championships (2nd issue). Nos. 399/402 of Antigua optd. **BARBUDA.**

172. **67.**	5 c. multicoloured ..	8	8
173. –	35 c. multicoloured ..	20	25
174. –	75 c. multicoloured ..	40	40
175. –	$1 multicoloured ..	45	50

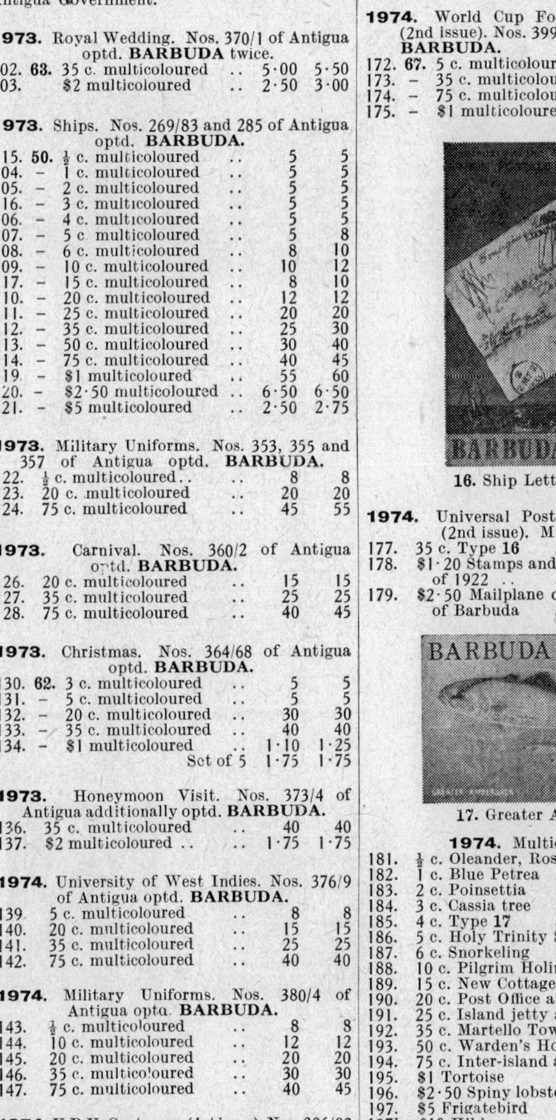

16. Ship Letter of 1833.

1974. Universal Postal Union. Centenary (2nd issue). Multicoloured.

177.	35 c. Type **16**	20	20
178.	$1·20 Stamps and postmark of 1922	55	60
179.	$2·50 Mailplane over map of Barbuda	1·10	1·40

17. Greater Amberjack.

1974. Multicoloured.

181.	½ c. Oleander, Rose Bay ..	5	5
182.	1 c. Blue Petrea	5	5
183.	2 c. Poinsettia	5	5
184.	3 c. Cassia tree	5	5
185.	4 c. Type **17**	5	5
186.	5 c. Holy Trinity School ..	5	5
187.	6 c. Snorkeling	5	5
188.	10 c. Pilgrim Holiness Church	5	5
189.	15 c. New Cottage Hospital	5	5
190.	20 c. Post Office and Treasury	8	10
191.	25 c. Island jetty and boats	10	12
192.	35 c. Martello Tower ..	12	15
193.	50 c. Warden's House ..	20	25
194.	75 c. Inter-island aircraft	25	30
195.	$1 Tortoise	35	40
196.	$2·50 Spiny lobster ..	90	1·00
197.	$5 Frigatebird	1·75	2·00
197b.	$10 Hibiscus	3·50	4·00

The $10 is vert., 34 × 48 mm.

1974. Sir Winston Churchill. Birth Cent. (1st issue). Nos. 408/11 of Antigua optd. **BARBUDA.**

198. **68.**	5 c. multicoloured ..	10	10
199. –	35 c. multicoloured ..	40	40
200. –	75 c. multicoloured ..	85	90
201. –	$1 multicoloured ..	1·40	1·40

18. Churchill making Broadcast.

1974. Sir Winston Churchill. Birth Cent. (2nd issue). Multicoloured.

203.		5 c. Type **18**	5	5
204.		35 c. Churchill and Chartwell	20	20
205.		75 c. Churchill painting ..	35	40
206.		$1 Churchill making "V"-sign	45	50

1974. Christmas. Nos. 413/20 of Antigua optd. **BARBUDA.**

208.	**69.**	½ c. multicoloured ..	5	5
209.	–	1 c. multicoloured ..	5	5
210.	–	2 c. multicoloured ..	5	5
211.	–	3 c. multicoloured ..	5	5
212.	–	5 c. multicoloured ..	5	5
213.	–	20 c. multicoloured ..	12	12
214.	–	35 c. multicoloured ..	15	15
215.	–	75 c. multicoloured ..	35	35

1975. Nelson's Dockyard. Nos. 427/31 of Antigua optd. **BARBUDA.**

217.	**70.**	5 c. multicoloured ..	5	5
218.	–	15 c. multicoloured ..	10	10
219.	–	35 c. multicoloured ..	20	20
220.	–	50 c. multicoloured ..	25	30
221.	–	$1 multicoloured ..	45	50

19. Ships of the Line.

1975. Sea Battles. Battle of the Saints, 1782. Multicoloured.

223.		35 c. Type **19**	20	20
224.		50 c. English three-masters	25	30
225.		75 c. Ships firing broadsides	35	40
226.		95 c. Sailors fleeing burning ship	45	50

1975. "Apollo-Soyuz" Space Project. No. 197 optd. **U.S.A.-U.S.S.R. SPACE CO-OPERATION 1975** with **APOLLO** (No. 227) and **SOYUZ** (No. 228).

227.		$5 multicoloured	2·50	2·75
228.		$5 multicoloured	2·50	2·75

20. Officer, 65th Foot, 1763.

1975. Military Uniforms. Multicoloured.

229.		35 c. Type **20**	20	20
230.		50 c. Grenadier, 27th Foot 1701-10	25	30
231.		75 c. Officer, 21st Foot, 1793-6	35	40
232.		95 c. Officer, Royal Regt. of Artillary, 1800 ..	40	45

1975. United Nations. 25th Anniv. Nos. 203/6 optd. **30TH ANNIVERSARY UNITED NATIONS 1945 - 1975.**

233.	**18.**	5 c. multicoloured ..	5	5
234.	–	35 c. multicoloured ..	20	20
235.	–	75 c. multicoloured ..	30	35
236.	–	$1 multicoloured ..	45	50

1975. Christmas. Nos. 457/64 of Antigua optd. **BARBUDA.**

237.	**121.**	½ c. multicoloured ..	5	5
238.	–	1 c. multicoloured ..	5	5
239.	–	2 c. multicoloured ..	5	5
240.	–	3 c. multicoloured ..	5	5
241.	–	5 c. multicoloured ..	5	5
242.	–	10 c. multicoloured ..	8	8
243.	–	35 c. multicoloured ..	20	20
244.	–	$2 multicoloured ..	85	95

1975. World Cup Cricket Winners. Nos. 466/8 of Antigua optd. **BARBUDA.**

246.	**122.**	5 c. multicoloured ..	5	5
247.	–	35 c. multicoloured ..	20	20
248.	–	$2 multicoloured ..	85	95

21. Surrender of Cornwallis.

1976. American Revolution. Bicent. Mult.

249.	15 c.	Type **21**	5	5
250.	15 c.	Type **21**	5	5
251.	15 c.	Type **21**	5	5
252.	35 c.	The Battle of Princetown ..	12	15
253.	35 c.	The Battle of Princetown ..	12	15
254.	35 c.	The Battle of Princetown ..	12	15
255.	$1	Surrender of General Burgoyne at Saratoga ..	35	40
256.	$1	Surrender of General Burgoyne at Saratoga ..	35	40
257.	$1	Surrender of General Burgoyne at Saratoga ..	35	40
258.	$2	Jefferson presenting Declaration of Independence ..	70	80
259.	$2	Jefferson presenting Declaration of Independence ..	70	80
260.	$2	Jefferson presenting Declaration of Independence ..	70	80

Type **21** shows the left-hand stamp of the 15 c. design.

22. Bananaquits.

1976. Birds. Multicoloured.

262.		35 c. Type **22**	15	15
263.		50 c. Blue-headed Euphonia	20	25
264.		75 c. Royal Tern ..	30	35
265.		95 c. Killdeer ..	35	40
266.		$1·25 Glossy Cowbird ..	50	60
267.		$2 Purple Gallinule ..	80	90

1976. Royal Visit to the U.S.A. Nos. 249/60 additionally inscr. "H.M. QUEEN ELIZABETH ROYAL VISIT 6th JULY. H.R.H. DUKE OF EDINBURGH".

268.		15 c. multicoloured ..	5	8
269.		15 c. multicoloured ..	5	8
270.		15 c. multicoloured ..	5	8
271.		35 c. multicoloured ..	15	15
272.		35 c. multicoloured ..	15	15
273.		35 c. multicoloured ..	15	15
274.		$1 multicoloured ..	40	45
275.		$1 multicoloured ..	40	45
276.		$1 multicoloured ..	40	45
277.		$1 multicoloured ..	80	90
278.		$2 multicoloured ..	80	90
279.		$2 multicoloured ..	80	90

BARWANI BC

A state of Central India. Now uses Indian stamps.

1. Rana Ranjitsingh. **2.**

1921.

8.	**1.**	¼ a. green	3·25	
29.		¼ a. blue	40	45
31.		¼ a. black	40	80
18.		¼ a. pink	50	45
4.		½ a. blue	6·50	6·50
30.		½ a. green	40	45
10.	**2.**	1 a. red	65	2·00
38.		1 a. brown	1·00	1·25
12.		2 a. purple	80	
40.		2 a. red	5·50	
23.		4 a. brown	8·00	
41a.	–	4 a. green	2·10	3·00

DESIGN: 4 a. Another portrait of Rana Ranjitsingh.

3. Rana Devi Singh. **4.**

1932.

31.	**3.**	¼ a. slate	40	80
32.		½ a. green	45	65
33.		1 a. brown	80	1·25
34.		2 a. purple	1·25	
35.		4 a. olive	2·75	4·00

1938.

42.	**4.**	1 a. brown	4·00	

BASUTOLAND BC

An African territory under Br. protection, N.E. of Cape Province. Self-Government introduced on 1st April, 1965. Attained independence on 4th October, 1966, when the country was renamed Lesotho.

1961. 100 cents = 1 rand.

1. King George V, Crocodile and Mountains.

1933.

1.	**1.**	½d. green	25	30
2.		1d. red	15	30
3.		2d. purple	30	40
4.		3d. blue	40	1·10
5.		4d. grey	90	1·75
6.		6d. yellow	1·10	2·25
7.		1s. orange	2·50	4·00
8.		2s. 6d. brown	6·00	10·00
9.		5s. violet	16·00	18·00
10.		10s. olive	35·00	40·00

1935. Silver Jubilee. As T **11** of Antigua.

11.		1d. blue and red	15	20
12.		2d. blue and grey ..	30	65
13.		3d. brown and blue ..	1·10	1·40
14.		6d grey and purple ..	1·75	2·25

1937. Coronation. As T **2** of Aden.

15.		1d. red	10	12
16.		2d. purple	12	20
17.		3d. blue	20	30

1938. As T **1**, but portrait of King George VI.

18.		½d. green	10	12
19.		1d. red	12	12
20.		1½d. blue	10	10
21.		2d. purple	10	10
22.		3d. blue	10	20
23.		4d. grey	40	40
24.		6d. yellow	30	35
25.		1s. orange	40	50
26.		2s. 6d. brown	1·10	1·25
27.		5s. violet	2·25	2·75
28.		10s. olive	4·50	5·00

1945. Victory. Stamps of South Africa optd. **Basutoland.** Alternate stamps inscr. in English or Afrikaans.

29.	**49.**	1d. brown and red ..	10	10
30.		2d. blue and violet ..	10	15
31.		3d. blue	12	30

Prices are for bi-lingual pairs.

2. King George VI and Queen Elizabeth.

1947. Royal Visit.

32.	–	1d. red	5	8
33.	**2.**	2d. green	5	8
34.	–	3d. blue	12	12
35.	–	1s. mauve	20	20

DESIGNS—VERT. 1d. King George VI. HORIZ. 3d. Queen Elizabeth II as Princess and Princess Margaret. 1s. The Royal Family.

1948. Silver Wedding. As T **5/6** of Aden.

36.		1½d. blue	5	5
37.		10s. green	2·50	3·50

1949. U.P.U. As T **14/17** of Antigua.

38.		1½d. blue	12	15
39.		3d. blue	25	30
40.		6d. orange	30	35
41.		1s brown	40	45

1953. Coronation. As T **7** of Aden.

42.		2d. black and purple ..	15	20

3. Qiloane.

4. Mohair (Shearing Goats).

DESIGNS — HORIZ. 1d. Orange River. 2d. Mosuto horseman. 3d. Basuto household. 4½d. Maletsunyane Falls. 6d. Herd-boy with lesiba. 1s. Pastoral scene. 1s. 3d. 'Plane over Lancers' Gap. 2s. 6d. Old Fort, Leribe. 5s. Mission cave house.

1954.

43.	**3.**	½d. black and sepia ..	8	10
44.	–	1d. black and green ..	8	10
45.	–	2d. blue and orange ..	10	12
46.	–	3d. sage and red ..	15	15
47.	–	4½d. indigo and blue ..	25	35
48.	–	6d. chestnut and green ..	30	25
49.	–	1s. bronze and purple ..	35	35
50.	–	1s. 3d. brown & turquoise	60	70
51.	–	2s. 6d. blue and crimson ..	1·40	1·60
52.	–	5s. black and red	1·60	1·90
53.	**4.**	10s. black and maroon	3·25	3·50

1959. Surch. ½d. and bar.

54.		½d. on 2d. blue and orange (No. 45)	10	12

5. Paramount Chief Moshesh.

DESIGNS: 1s. Council House. 1s. 3d. Mosuto horseman.

1959. National Council Inaug.

55.	**5.**	3d. black and olive ..	12	15
56.	–	1s. red and green	30	30
57.	–	1s. 3d. blue & orange ..	40	45

1961. Nos. 43/53 surch.

58.	**3.**	½ c. on ½d. black & sepia ..	5	5
59.	–	1 c. on 1d. black & green ..	5	5
60.	–	2 c. on 2d. blue & orange	8	8
61a.	–	2½ c. on 3d. sage and red ..	12	15
62.	–	3½ c. on 4½d. indigo & blue	20	25
63.	–	5 c. on 6d. chestnut & grn.	12	20
64.	–	10 c. on 1s. bronze & pur.	30	30
65a.	–	12½ c. on 1s. 3d. brown and turquoise	40	55
66.	–	25 c. on 2s. 6d. bl. & crim.	75	1·00
67a.	–	50 c. on 5s. black and red	1·75	2·00
68b.	**4.**	1 r. on 10s. blk. & maroon	3·00	4·00

6. Basuto Household.

1961. As 1954 but value in new currency as in T **6.**

69.	**3.**	½ c. black and sepia ..	5	5
70.	–	1 c. black & green (as 1d.)	5	5
71.	–	2 c. blue & orange (as 2d.)	5	8
86.	**6.**	2½ c. sage and red ..	5	5
73.	–	3½ c. ind. & blue (as 4½d.)	8	10
74.	–	5 c. chest. & green (as 6d.)	12	12
75.	–	10 c. bronze & pur. (as 1s.)	25	25
76.	–	12½ c. brown and turquoise (as 1s. 3d.)	35	40
77.	–	25 c. blue and crimson (as 2s. 6d.)	1·10	1·25
92.	–	50 c. black & red (as 5s.)	1·25	1·60
79.	–	1 r. black & mar. (as 10s.)	3·75	4·25

1963. Freedom from Hunger. As T **10** of Aden.
80. 12½ c. violet 35 35

1963. Red Cross Cent. As T **24** of Antigua.
81. 2½ c. red and black .. 12 12
82. 12½ c. red and blue .. 40 45

7. Mosotho Woman and Child.

1965. New Constitution. Inscr. "SELF GOVERNMENT 1965". Multicoloured.
94. 2½ c. Type 7 .. .. 5 5
95. 3½ c. Maseru Border Post 12 15
96. 5 c. Mountain Scene .. 15 15
97. 12½ c. Legislative Buildings 30 35

1965. I.T.U. Cent. As T **26** of Antigua.
98. 1 c. red and purple .. 5 5
99. 20 c. blue and brown .. 45 55

1965. I.C.Y. As T **27** of Antigua.
100. ½ c. purple and turquoise 8 8
101. 12½ c. green and lavender 35 45

1966. Churchill Commem. As T **28** of Antigua.
102. 1 c. blue 5 5
103. 2½ c. green 8 5
104. 10 c. brown 30 35
105. 22½ c. violet 55 60

POSTAGE DUE STAMPS

1933. As Type D **1** of Barbados.
D 1b. 1d. red 15 25
D 2a. 2d. violet 12 25

D 1.

1956.
D 3. D **1.** 1d. red 15 25
D 4. 2d. violet 20 30

1961. Surch.
D 5. D **1.** 1 c. on 1d. red .. 5 8
D 6. 1 c. on 2d. violet .. 5 8
D 7. 5 c. on 2d. violet .. 12 12
D 8. – 5 c. on 2d. vio. (No. D2a) 2·00 2·50

1964. As Type D **1**, but values in decimal currency.
D 9. 1 c. red 5 5
D 10. 5 c. violet 10 15

For later issues see **LESOTHO.**

BATUM BC

City of Georgia on Black Sea. Stamps issued during Br. occupation after War of 1914/18.

1. (2.)

1919.
1. 1. 5 k. green 12 20
2. 10 k. blue 12 20
3. 50 k. yellow 15 25
4. 1 r. brown 15 25
5. 3 r. violet 45 55
6. 5 r. brown 60 70

1919. Arms types of Russia surch. as T **2.**
7. 10 r. on 1 k. orange .. 4·00 4·00
8. 10 r. on 3 k. red .. .. 2·00 2·25
9. 10 r. on 5 k. purple .. 20·00 20·00
10. 10 r. on 10 on 7 k. blue .. 17·00 17·00

1919. Arms type of Russia surch. with Russian inscription, **BRITISH OCCUPATION** and new value.
11. 10 r. on 3 k. red .. .. 2·00 2·25
12. 15 r. on 1 k. orange .. 4·00 4·00
22. 25 r. on 5 k. purple .. 2·25 2·50
24. 25 r. on 10 on 7 k. blue .. 3·00 3·00
25. 25 r. on 20 on 14 k. red and blue .. .. .. 4·00 4·00
27. 25 r. on 25 k. pur. & grn. .. 4·00 4·00
29. 25 r. on 50 k. grn. & purple 2·00 2·00
31. 50 r. on 2 k. green .. 4·50 4·50
32. 50 r. on 3 k. red .. .. 4·50 4·50
33. 50 r. on 4 k. red .. .. 4·50 4·50
34. 50 r. on 5 k. purple .. 4·00 4·00

1919. T **1** optd. **BRITISH OCCUPATION.**
13. **1.** 5 k. green 35 35
14. 10 k. blue 35 35
15. 25 k. yellow 35 35
16. 1 r. blue 15 25
17. 2 r. pink 15 20
18. 3 r. violet 15 25
19. 5 r. brown 25 40
20. 7 r. red 40 50

1920. Nos. 13, 15 and 3 surch. with new value and Russian words (50 r. with **BRITISH OCCUPATION** also).
46. **1.** 25 r. on 5 k. green .. 2·50 2·50
48. 25 r. on 25 k. yellow .. 2·00 2·25
50. 50 r. on 50 k. yellow .. 2·00 2·00

1920. T **1** optd. **BRITISH OCCUPATION.**
52. **1.** 1 r. brown 5 5
53. 2 r. blue 5 5
54. 3 r. pink 5 5
55. 5 r. black 5 5
56. 7 r. yellow 5 5
57. 10 r. green 8 10
58. 15 r. violet 15 20
59. 25 r. red 25 30
60. 50 r. blue 30 40

BAVARIA E2

In S. Germany. A kingdom till 1918; then a republic. Now part of West Germany.

1849. 60 kreuzer = 1 gulden.
1874. 100 pfennige = 1 mark.

1. 2. (Circle cut.)

1849. Imperf.
2. **1.** 1 k. black £300 £550

1849. Imperf. Circle cut by labels.
3. **2.** 3 k. blue .. .. .. 22·00 1·60
24. 3 k. red .. .. .. 22·00 75
7. 6 k. brown .. .. .. £2000 60·00

1850. Imperf. As T **2**, but circle not cut.
8a. **2.** 1 k. red .. .. .. 25·00 10·00
21. 1 k. yellow .. .. .. 35·00 10·00
11. 6 k. brown .. .. .. 22·00 1·00
25. 6 k. blue .. .. .. 32·00 3·75
16. 9 k. green .. .. .. 35·00 6·00
28. 9 k. brown .. .. .. 45·00 7·50
18. 12 k. red .. .. .. 65·00 80·00
31. 12 k. green .. .. .. 80·00 30·00
19. 18 k. yellow .. .. .. 75·00 85·00
32. 18 k. red .. .. .. 75·00 £100

3. 4. 5.

1867. Imperf.
34. **3.** 1 k. green .. .. .. 32·00 2·00
37. 3 k. red .. .. .. 25·00 25
39. 6 k. blue .. .. .. 17·00 7·50
41. 6 k. brown .. .. .. 35·00 25·00
43. 7 k. blue .. .. .. £170 6·00
46. 9 k. brown .. .. .. 25·00 18·00
48. 12 k. mauve .. .. .. £160 38·00
50. 18 k. red .. .. .. 55·00 70·00
65. **4.** 1 m. mauve .. .. .. £200 38·00

1870. Perf.
51. **3.** 1 k. green 70 35
69. 3 k. red .. .. .. 20 1·50
55. 6 k. brown .. .. .. 20·00 17·00
57. 7 k. blue .. .. .. 1·00 1·00
59. 9 k. brown .. .. .. 1·25 1·25
60. 10 k. yellow .. .. .. 2·50 6·00
61. 12 k. mauve £170 £350
63. 18 k. red .. .. .. 5·00 6·00

1876. Perf.
102. **5.** 2 pf. grey 50 5
103. 3 pf. green .. .. .. 2·00 10
121. 3 pf. brown 5 5
122. 5 pf. green 5 5
107. 5 pf. mauve .. .. .. 1·40 40
123. 10 pf. red 5 5
124. 20 pf. blue 5 5
114. 25 pf. brown .. .. .. 10·00 70
125. 25 pf. orange 10 8
126. 30 pf. olive 10 10
127. 40 pf. yellow 10 12
86. 50 pf. red .. .. .. 15·00 1·10
117. 50 pf. brown .. .. .. 13·00 40
128. 50 pf. purple-brown .. 10 10
129. 80 pf. mauve 50 75
100. **4.** 1 m. mauve .. .. .. 1·25 20
101. 2 m. orange .. .. .. 3·75 75
136. 3 m. brown .. .. .. 5·50 7·50
137. 5 m. green .. .. .. 7·00 10·00

6. Prince Luitpold. 7.

1911. Prince Regent Luitpold's 90th Birthday.
138. **6.** 3 pf. brown on drab .. 12 5
139. 5 pf. green on green .. 12 5
140. 10 pf. red on buff .. 12 5
141. 20 pf. blue on blue .. 1·00 5
142. 25 pf. deep brown on buff 1·40 20
143. – 30 pf. orange on buff .. 75 12
144. – 40 pf. olive on buff .. 1·10 15
145. – 50 pf. claret on drab .. 1·40 20
146. – 60 pf. green on buff .. 1·50 25
147. – 80 pf. violet on drab .. 2·50 60
148. **7.** 1 m. brown on drab .. 1·25 50
149. 2 m. green on green .. 1·25 85
150. 3 m. red on buff .. 7·50 7·50
151. 5 m. blue on buff .. 6·00 10·00
152. 10 m. orange on yellow 11·00 21·00
153. 20 m. brown on yellow .. 12·00 12·00

The 30 pf. to 80 pf. values are similar to T **9**, but larger.

8.

1911. Jubilee of the Prince Regent.
169. **8.** 5 pf. yellow, green & black 50 40
170. 10 pf. yellow, red & black 50 65

9. King Ludwig III. 10.

1914. Imperf. or perf.
171. **9.** 2 pf. slate 5 12
172. 2½ on 2 pf. slate .. 5 12
173. 3 pf. brown 5 5
175. 5 pf. green 5 5
176. 7½ pf. green 5 5
177. 10 pf. red 5 5
179. 15 pf. red 5 5
181. 20 pf. blue 5 10
183. 25 pf. grey 5 12
184. 30 pf. orange 5 12
185. 40 pf. olive 5 12
186. 50 pf. brown 5 12
187. 60 pf. green 12 20
188. 80 pf. violet 10 35
189. **10.** 1 m. brown 20 25
190. 2 m. violet 30 80
191. 3 m. red .. .. 50 1·25
192. – 5 m. blue .. .. 75 2·50
193. – 10 m. green .. .. 1·25 4·50
194. – 20 m. brown .. .. 2·50 9·00

The 5, 10 and 20 m. are larger.

1919. Peoples' State Issue. Overprinted **Volksstaat Bayern.** Imperf. or perf.
195. **9.** 3 pf. brown 5 20
196. 5 pf. green 5 12
197. 7½ pf. green 5 20
198. 10 pf. lake 5 12
199. 15 pf. red 5 12
200. 20 pf. blue 5 20
201. 25 pf. grey 5 20
202. 30 pf. orange 5 20
203. 35 pf. orange 5 35
204. 40 pf. olive 5 20
205. 50 pf. brown 5 20
206. 60 pf. blue-green .. 5 25
207. 75 pf. brown 10 35
208. 80 pf. violet 15 25
209. **10.** 1 m. brown 20 30
210. 2 m. violet 25 50
211. 3 m. red .. .. 35 1·25
212. – 5 m. blue (No. 192) .. 65 2·50
213. – 10 m. green (No. 193) .. 75 6·00
214. – 20 m. brown (No. 194) 1·75 8·50

1919. 1st Free State Issue. Stamps of Germany optd. **Freistaat Bayern.**
215. **13.** 2½ pf. grey 5 10
216. **8.** 3 pf. brown 5 10
217. 5 pf. green 5 10
218. **13.** 7½ pf. orange 5 10
219. **8.** 10 pf. red 5 10
220. **13.** 15 pf. violet 5 10
221. **8.** 20 pf. blue 5 10
222. 25 pf. blk. & red on yell. 12 20
223. **13.** 35 pf. brown 12 20
224. **8.** 40 pf. black and red .. 25 25
225. 75 pf. black and green .. 35 35
226. 80 pf. blk. & red on rose 35 75
227. **9.** 1 m. red .. .. 1·00 1·00
228. **10.** 2 m. blue .. .. 1·10 1·50
229. **11.** 3 m. black .. .. 1·25 2·00
230. **12.** 5 m. red and black .. 1·60 2·10

1919. 2nd Free State Issue. Stamps of Bavaria overprinted **Freistaat Bayern.** Imperf. or perf.
231. **9.** 3 pf. brown 5 20
232. 5 pf. green 5 12
233. 7½ pf. green 5 75
234. 10 pf. lake 5 10
235. 15 pf. red 5 10
236. 20 pf. blue 5 15
237. 25 pf. grey 12 25
238. 30 pf. orange 12 25
239. 40 pf. olive 25 75
240. 50 pf. brown 10 20
241. 60 pf. blue-green .. 45 75
242. 75 pf. brown .. .. 35 1·10
243. 80 pf. violet 15 75
244. **10.** 1 m. brown 20 25
245. 2 m. violet 20 90
246. 3 m. red .. .. 35 1·25
247. – 5 m. blue (No. 192) .. 55 3·75
248. – 10 m. green (No. 193) .. 1·10 6·00
249. – 20 m. brown (No. 194) 1·40 7·50

1919. War Wounded. Surch. **5 Pf. fur Kreigs-beschadigte Freistaat Bayern.** Perf.
250. **9.** 10 pf. + 5 pf. lake .. 25 30
251. 15 pf. + 5 pf. red .. 25 30
252. 20 pf. + 5 pf. blue .. 25 30

1920. Surch. **Freistaat Bayern** and value. Imperf. or perf.
253. **10.** 1 m. 25 pf. on 1 m. grn. 10 50
254. 1 m. 50 pf. on 1 m. oran. 10 75
255. 2 m. 50 pf. on 1 m. slate 15 1·10

1920. No. 121 surch. on four corners.
256. **5.** 20 on 3 pf. brown .. 5 15

12. 13. 14.

15. 16.

1920.
257. **12.** 5 pf. green 5 5
258. 10 pf. orange 5 5
259. 15 pf. red 5 5
260. **13.** 20 pf. violet 5 5
261. 30 pf. blue 5 15
262. 40 pf. brown 5 20
263. **14.** 50 pf. red 10 35
264. 60 pf. blue-green .. 10 50
265. 75 pf. claret 10 85
266. **15.** 1 m. red and grey .. 25 50
267. 1¼ m. blue and brown 15 60
268. 1½ m green and grey .. 15 60
269. 2½ m. black and grey .. 15 75
270. **16.** 3 m. blue .. .. 25 3·50
271. 5 m. orange .. .. 45 3·75
272. 10 m. green .. .. 90 5·00
273. 20 m. black .. .. 1·10 7·00

OFFICIAL STAMPS

O 1.

1916.
O 195. O **1.** 3 pf. brown 5 5
O 196. 5 pf. green 5 5
O 197. 7½ pf. green on green 5 5
O 198. 7½ pf. green 5 5
O 199. 10 pf. red 5 5
O 200. 15 pf. red on buff .. 5 5
O 201. 15 pf. red 5 5
O 202. 20 pf. blue on blue 35 12
O 203. 20 pf. blue 5 5
O 204. 25 pf. grey 5 5
O 205. 30 pf. orange 5 5
O 206. 60 pf. blue-green .. 5 10
O 207. 1 m. purple on buff .. 50 50
O 208. 1 m. purple .. .. 2·40 16·00

1919. Optd. **Volksstaat Bayern.**
O 215. O **1.** 3 pf. brown 5 50
O 216. 5 pf. green 5 5
O 217. 7½ pf. green 5 10
O 218. 10 pf. red 5 5
O 219. 15 pf. red 5 5
O 220. 20 pf. blue 5 5
O 221. 25 pf. grey 5 5
O 222. 30 pf. orange 5 5
O 223. 35 pf. orange 5 5
O 224. 50 pf. olive 5 5
O 225. 60 pf. blue-green .. 5 50
O 226. 75 pf. brown 12 30
O 227. 1 m. purple on buff 40 60
O 228. 1 m. purple .. .. 2·00 17·00

O 2.

O 3.

O 4.

1920.

O 274. O 2. 5 pf. green 5 25
O 275. 10 pf. orange 5 25
O 276. 15 pf. red 5 25
O 277. 20 pf. violet 5 25
O 278. 30 pf. blue 5 30
O 279. 40 pf. brown 5 30
O 280. O 3. 50 pf. red 5 50
O 281. 60 pf. green 5 50
O 282. 70 pf. lilac 5 60
O 283. 75 pf. claret 5 60
O 284. 80 pf. blue 5 60
O 285. 90 pf. olive 5 75
O 286. O 4. 1 m. brown.. .. 5 60
O 287. 1¼ m. green 5 60
O 288. 1½ m. red .. .. 5 1·00
O 289. 2½ m. blue .. .. 5 1·25
O 290. 3 m. lake .. .. 12 2·50
O 291. 5 m. deep olive .. 75 6·50

POSTAGE DUE STAMPS

D 1.

1862. Inscr. "Bayer. Posttaxe" at top. Imperf.
D 34. D 1. 3 k. black .. .. 60·00 £140

1870. As Type D 1, but inscr. "Bayr. Posttaxe" at top. Perf.
D 65. D 1. 1 k. black .. .. 6·00 £225
D 66. 3 k. black .. .. 6·00 £160

1876. Optd. **Vom Empfanger zahibar.**
D 130. 5. 2 pf. grey 35 35
D 131. 3 pf. grey 25 60
D 132. 5 pf. grey 50 50
D 133. 10 pf. grey 35 25

RAILWY OFFICIALS' STAMPS

1908. Stamps of 1876 optd. **E.**
R 133. 5. 3 pf. brown .. .. 75 2·00
R 134. 5 pf. green 5 5
R 135. 10 pf. red 5 5
R 136. 20 pf. blue 15 15
R 137. 50 pf. purple-brown .. 2·50 3·00

BECHUANALAND BC

A colony and protectorate in Central S. Africa. British Bechuanaland (colony) was annexed to Cape of Good Hope in 1895. Internal Self-Government in the protectorate introduced on 1st March, 1965. Attained independence on 30th September, 1966, when the country was renamed Botswana.

1961. 100 cents = 1 rand.

A. BRITISH BECHUANALAND

British

Bechuanaland
(1.)

BRITISH

BECHUANALAND
(2.)

1885. Stamps of Cape of Good Hope ("Hope" seated) optd. with T 1.
4. 4. ½d. black .. .. .. 2·50 2·50
5. 1d. red .. .. .. 2·50 2·50
6. 2d. brown .. .. .. 8·00 6·50
2. 3d. claret .. .. .. 7·00 9·00
3. 4d. blue .. .. .. 15·00 18·00
7. 6d. purple .. .. .. 10·00 12·00
8. 1s. green .. .. .. 75·00 50·00

1887. Stamps of Gt. Britain (Queen Victoria) optd. with T 2.
9. 54. ½d. red 45 35

3.

4.

1887.
10. 3. 1d. lilac and black .. 6·00 1·60
11. 2d. lilac and black .. 6·50 1·60
12. 3d. lilac and black .. 1·60 1·60
13. 4d. lilac and black .. 12·00 3·25
14. 3. 6d. lilac and black .. 11·00 8·50
15. 4. 1s. green and black .. 11·00 4·00
16. 2s. green and black .. 13·00 6·50
17. 2s. 6d. green and black .. 14·00 10·00
18. 5s. green and black .. 32·00 26·00
19. 10s. green and black .. 55·00 55·00
20. – £1 lilac and black .. £275 £300
21. – £5 lilac and black .. £700 £300
Nos. 20/1 are as T 4 but larger, 23×39½ mm.

1888. Surch.
22. 3. "1d." on 1d. lilac & black 2·75 1·60
23. "2d." on 2d. lilac & black 3·25 2·10
25. "4d." on 4d. lilac & black 26·00 22·00
26. "6d." on 6d. lilac & black 20·00 10·00
28. 4. "1s." on 1s. green & black 26·00 18·00

1888. Surch. **ONE HALF-PENNY** and bars.
29. 3. ½d. on 3d. lilac and black 17·00 17·00

British

Bechuanaland.
(5.)

British Bechuanaland
(6.)

1889. Stamp of Cape of Good Hope ("Hope" seated) optd. with T 5.
30. 4. ½d. black .. .. 2·75 4·00

1891. Stamps of Cape of Good Hope ("Hope" seated) optd. with T 6, reading up or down.
38. 4. 1d. red 60 60
39. 2d. brown .. .. .. 1·10 60

1891. Stamps of Gt. Britain (Queen Victoria) optd. **BRITISH BECHUANALAND.**
33. 40. 1d. lilac 65 25
34. 56. 2d. green and red .. 1·10 75
35. 59. 4d. green and brown .. 1·40 80
36. 62. 6d. purple on red .. 1·60 1·10
37. 65. 1s. green .. .. 3·50 5·50

B. BECHUANALAND PROTECTORATE.

1888. No. 9 to 19 optd. **Protectorate** or surch. also.
40. 54. ½d. red .. .. 1·25 2·25
41. 3. 1d. on 1d. lilac and black 1·40 2·25
42. 2d. on 2d. lilac and black 4·50 4·50
43. 3d. on 3d. lilac and black 20·00 21·00
51. 4d. on 4d. lilac and black 16·00 11·00
45. 6d. on 6d. lilac and black 12·00 11·00
46. 4. 1s. green and black .. 18·00 12·00
47. 2s. green and black .. 65·00 65·00
48. 2s. 6d. green and black.. £120 £110
49. 5s. green and black .. £250 £270
50. 10 s. green and black .. £650 £650

1889. Stamp of Cape of Good Hope ("Hope" seated) optd. **Bechuanaland Protectorate.**
52. 4. ½d. black .. .. 1·25 2·10

1889. No. 9 surch. **Protectorate Fourpence.**
53. 54. 4d. on ½d. red .. 2·25 2·25

1897. Stamp of Cape of Good Hope ("Hope" seated) optd. as T 2.
56. 4. ½d. green .. .. .. 70 1·25

Stamps of Gt. Britain overprinted **BECHUANALAND PROTECTORATE.**

1897. Queen Victoria.
59. 54. ½d. red 30 60
60. ½d. green.. .. .. 30 60
61. 40. 1d. lilac 30 40
62. 56. 2d. green and red .. 1·50 1·75
63. 58. 3d. purple on yellow .. 2·50 2·50
64. 59. 4d. green and brown .. 3·25 3·50
65. 62. 6d. purple on red .. 8·00 8·50

1904. King Edward VII.
66. 66. ½d. blue-green .. .. 1·40 1·25
67. ½d. yellow-green .. .. 1·60 1·60
68. 1d. red .. .. .. 1·60 90
69. 2½d. blue.. .. .. 3·25 3·25
70. – 1s. green & red (No. 314) 6·50 9·00

1912. King George V.
73. 85. ½d. green.. .. .. 45 40
72. 83. 1d. red .. .. .. 1·10 1·00
74. 84. 1d. red 50 40
75. 85. 1½d. brown 60 85
76. 86. 2d. orange .. .. 80 1·00
78. 84. 2½d. blue.. .. .. 1·00 1·10
94. 86. 3d. violet .. .. 1·60 2·00
95. 4d. grey-green .. .. 1·60 2·40
81. 87. 6d. purple .. .. 2·00 2·50
82. 88. 1s. brown .. .. 3·25 3·50
88. 89. 2s. 6d. brown .. .. 23·00 29·00
89. 5s. red .. .. .. 25·00 32·00

7. King George V, Baobab Tree and Cattle.

1932.
99. 7. ½d. green.. .. .. 15 30
100. 1d. red 25 40
101. 2d. brown 70 60
102. 3d. blue 80 80
103. 4d. orange 65 80
104. 6d. purple .. .. .. 80 1·00
105. 1s. black and olive .. 2·00 2·50
106. 2s. black and orange .. 7·00 8·00
107. 2s. 6d. black and red .. 9·00 11·00
108. 3s. black and purple .. 12·00 14·00
109. 5s. black and blue .. 15·00 18·00
110. 10s. black and brown .. 27·00 30·00

1935. Silver Jubilee. As T 11 of Antigua.
111. 1d. blue and red .. 10 20
112. 2d. blue and black .. 25 40
113. 3d. brown and blue .. 30 60
114. 6d. grey and purple .. 60 85

1937. Coronation. As T 2 of Aden.
115. 1d. red 12 12
116. 2d. brown 12 15
117. 3d. blue 15 25

1938. As T 7, but portrait of King George VI.
118. ½d. green.. .. .. 50 50
119. 1d. red 10 12
120a. 1½d. blue.. .. .. 15 12
121. 2d. brown 10 15
122. 3d. blue 10 15
123. 4d. orange 15 25
124a. 6d. purple 90 80
125. 1s. black and olive .. 30 50
126. 2s. 6d. black and red .. 1·25 1·50
127. 5s. black and blue .. 2·00 2·25
128. 10s. black and brown .. 6·50 7·00

1945. Victory. Stamps of South Africa optd. **Bechuanaland.** Alternate stamps inscr. in English or Afrikaans.
129. 49. 1d. brown and red .. 10 12
130. 2d. blue & vio. (No. 109) 12 20
131. 3d. blue (No. 110) .. 20 25
Prices for bi-lingual pairs.

1947. Royal Visit. As Nos. 32/5 of Basutoland.
132. 1d. red 5 5
133. 2d. green 5 5
134. 3d. blue.. .. .. 5 5
135. 1s. mauve 25 25

1948. Silver Wedding. As T 5/6 of Aden.
136. 1½d. blue 10 10
137. 10s. grey .. .. 2·75 4·00

1949. U.P.U. As T 14/17 of Antigua.
138. 1½d. blue 12 12
139. 3d. blue.. .. .. 12 15
140. 6d. magenta 30 30
141. 1s. olive.. .. .. 55 55

1953. Coronation. As T 7 of Aden.
142. 2d. black and brown .. 15 20

1955. As T 7 but portrait of Queen Elizabeth II, facing right.
143. ½d. green.. .. .. 5 5
144. 1d. red 5 5
145. 2d. brown 8 8
146. 3d. blue 10 10
146a. 4d. orange 20 25
147. 4½d. indigo 25 25
148. 6d. purple 20 20
149. 1s. black and olive .. 30 30
150. 1s. 3d. black and lilac .. 50 65
151. 2s. 6d. black and red .. 1·10 1·40
152. 5s. black and blue .. 1·90 2·25
153. 10s. black and brown .. 3·75 4·25

8. Queen Victoria. Queen Elizabeth II and Landscape.

1960 75th Anniv. of Protectorate.
154. 8. 1d. sepia and black .. 5 5
155. 3d. magenta and black.. 12 12
156. 6d. blue and black .. 25 25

1961. Stamps of 1955 surch.
157. 1 c. on 1d. red 10 10
158. 2c. o n 2d. brown .. 10 10
159. 2½ c. on 2d. brown .. 12 15
160. 2½ c. on 3d. blue 70 70
161d. 3½ c. on 4d. orange .. 12 15
162a. 5 c. on 6d. purple .. 25 25
163. 10 c. on 1s. black and olive 30 35
164. 12½ c. on 1s. 3d. blk. & lilac 40 50
165. 25 c. on 2s. 6d. black & red 85 1·10
166. 50 c. on 5s. black and blue 1·75 2·00
167b. 1 r. on 10s. black & brown 3·50 4·00

9. Golden Oriole.

1961.
168. 1 c. yellow, red, black and lilac (Type 9) .. 5 5
169. 2 c. orange, black & olive 5 5
170. 2½ c. red, grn., blk., & bistre 5 8
171. 3½ c. yell., blk., sepia & pink 8 10
172. 5 c. yell., blue, black & buff 10 12
173. 7½ c. brn., red, blk. & apple 15 20
174. 10 c. red, yell., sepia & turq. 25 25
175. 12½ c. buff, blue, red & grey 30 30
176. 20 c. brown and drab .. 35 40
177. 25 c. sepia and lemon .. 45 55
178. 35 c. blue and orange .. 65 80
179. 50 c. sepia and olive .. 95 1·40
180. 1 r. black and brown .. 1·90 2·25
181. 2 r. brown and turquoise.. 3·75 4·25
DESIGNS—VERT. 2 c. African Hoopoe. 2½ c. Scarlet-chested Sunbird. 3½ c. Cape Widow-bird. 5 c. Swallow-tailed Bee-eater. 7½ c. Grey Hornbill. 10 c. Red-headed Weaver. 12½ c. Brown-hooded Kingfisher. 20 c. Woman musician. 35 c. Woman grinding maize. 1 r. LION. 2 r. Police Camel Patrol. HORIZ. 25 c. Baobab tree. 50 c. Bechuana Ox.

1963. Freedom from Hunger. As T 10 of Aden.
182. 12½ c. green 35 40

1963. Red Cross Cent. As T 24 of Antigua.
183. 2½ c. red and black .. 12 20
184. 12½ c. red and blue .. 35 45

1964. Shakespeare. 400th Birth Anniv. As T 25 of Antigua.
185. 12½ c. brown 25 30

C. BECHUANALAND

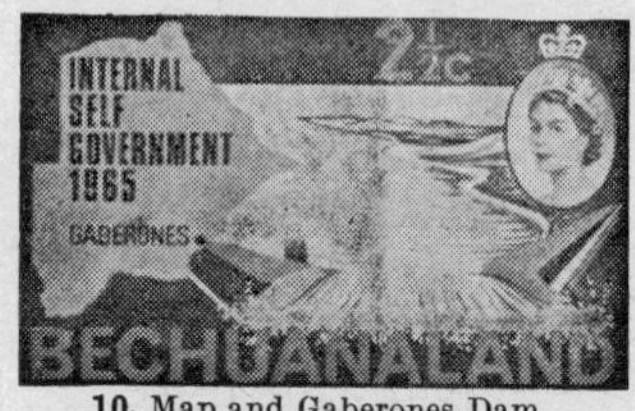

10. Map and Gaberones Dam.

1965. New Constitution.
186. 10. 2½ c. red and gold .. 5 5
187. 5 c. ultramarine & gold 8 8
188. 12½ c. brown and gold.. 25 30
189. 25 c. green and gold .. 35 40

1965. I.T.U. Cent. As T 26 of Antigua.
190. 2½ c. red and yellow .. 8 10
191. 12½ c. mauve and brown.. 35 35

1965. I.C.Y. As T 27 of Antigua.
192. 1 c. purple and turquoise 5 5
193. 12½ c. green and lavender 35 35

1966. Churchill Commem. As T 28 of Antigua.
194. 1 c. blue 5 5
195. 2½ c. green 8 8
196. 12½ c. brown 30 30
197. 20 c. violet 55 60

11. Haslar Smoke Generator.

1966. Bechuanaland Royal Pioneer Corps.
198. 11. 2½ c. blue, red & emerald 5 5
199. – 5 c. brown and blue .. 10 12
200. – 15 c. blue, red & emerald 30 30
201. – 35 c. buff, brown, red and green 60 65
DESIGNS: 5 c. Bugler. 15 c. Gun-site. 35 c. Regimental Cap Badge.

POSTAGE DUE STAMPS

1926. Postage Due stamps of Gt. Britain optd. **BECHUANALAND PROTECTORATE.**
D 1. D 1. ½d. green 20 25
D 2. 1d. red.. .. .. 25 30
D 3. 2d. black 40 50

D 1.

1932.
D 4. D 1. ½d. green 70 80
D 5a. 1d. red.. .. .. 12 15
D 6a. 2d. violet 15 30

1961. Surch.
D 7a. D 1. 1 c. on 1d. red .. 8 10
D 8. 2 c. on 2d. violet .. 12 20
D 9. 5 c. on ½d. green .. 20 30

1961. As Type D 1 but values in decimal currency.

D 10.	1 c. red	8	10
D 11.	2 c. violet	8	10
D 12.	5 c. green	12	25

For later issues see **BOTSWANA**.

BELGIAN CONGO

A Belgian colony in Central Africa. Became independent in July, 1960. For later issues see Congo, Zaire and Katanga.

A. INDEPENDENT STATE OF THE CONGO

The Independent State of the Congo was established on 2 May 1885, with King Leopold II of the Belgians as ruler.

1. Leopold II.

2. Leopold II.

1886. Various frames.

1.	1.	5 c. green	3·25	3·00
2.		10 c. red	1·25	1·25
3.		25 c. blue	13·00	10·00
4.		50 c. green	1·50	1·25
5.		5 f. lilac	£100	70·00

1887. Surch. **COLIS-POSTAUX Fr. 3.50.**

6.	1.	3 f. 50 on 5 f. lilac	£120	£110

1887.

7.	2.	5 c. green	15	15
8.		10 c. red	30	30
9.		25 c. blue	25	25
10.		50 c. brown	15·00	6·00
11.		50 c. grey	80	1·60
12.		5 f. lilac	£150	80·00
13.		5 f. grey	30·00	20·00
14.		10 f. orange	80·00	50·00

1887. Surch. **COLIS-POSTAUX Fr. 3.50.**

15.	2.	3 f. 50 on 5 f. violet	£130	£110

1889. Surch. **COLIS-POSTAUX Fr. 3.50.** in frame.

16.	2.	3 f. 50 on 5 f. violet	£100	80·00
17.		3 f. 50 on 5 f. grey	£120	£110

3. Port of Matadi.

4. Stanley Falls.

5. Coconut Trees.

6. Inkissi Falls (horiz.).
8. Railway Bridge over the M'pozo (horiz.).
9. Elephant hunt (horiz.).
10. Congo village (horiz.).
11. Bangala chief Morangi and wife (vert).
12. Stern-wheel steamer (horiz.).

7. Native Canoe.

1894. Inscr. "ETAT INDEPENDANT DU CONGO".

18.	3.	5 c. black and blue	2·75	3·00
24.		5 c. black and red-brown	1·10	45
30.		5 c. black and green	55	15
19.	4.	10 c. black and brown	2·75	3·00
25.		10 c. black & blue-green	35	30
31.		10 c. black and red	55	15
26.	5.	15 c. black and yellow	1·10	15
20.	6.	25 c. black and orange	1·00	50
32.		25 c. black and blue	1·00	50
27.	7.	40 c. black and green	1·25	90
21.	8.	50 c. black and green	50	35
33.		50 c. black and ochre	1·00	20
22.	9.	1 f. black and mauve	7·50	3·50
35.		1 f. black and red	38·00	75
28.	10.	3 f. 50 black and red	30·00	12·00
23.	11.	5 f. black and lake	12·00	4·25
29.	12.	10 f. black and green	25·00	4·00

B. BELGIAN CONGO

The Congo was annexed to Belgium by Act of the Belgian Parliament on 18 Oct. 1908, and was renamed the Belgian Congo.

1909. Optd. **CONGO BELGE.**

36.	3.	5 c. black and green	60	50
37.	4.	10 c. black and red	60	50
38.	5.	15 c. black and yellow	1·50	80
39.	6.	25 c. black and blue	1·60	1·10
50.	7.	40 c. black and green	55	55
41.	8.	50 c. black and ochre	1·10	75
42.	9.	1 f. black and red	6·00	70
53.	10.	3 f. 50 black and red	5·00	3·75
54.	11.	5 f. black and lake	11·00	5·00
55.	12.	10 f. black and green	42·00	22·00

1909. As 1894 but inscr. "CONGO BELGE".

56.	3.	5 c. black and green	35	30
57.	4.	10 c. black and red	15	12
58.	5.	15 c. black and yellow	4·00	2·75
59.	8.	50 c. black and bistre	1·25	70

1910. As 1894 but inscr. "CONGO BELGE"—"BELGISCH-CONGO" with values in French and Flemish.

60.	3.	5 c. black and green	40	10
61.	4.	10 c. black and red	20	8
62.	5.	15 c. black and yellow	25	8
63a.	6.	25 c. black and blue	50	12
64.	7.	40 c. black and green	55	50
65.	8.	50 c. black and olive	70	55
66.	8.	1 f. black and red	1·10	75
68.	10.	3 f. black and red	4·25	3·50
67.	11.	5 f. black and lake	5·50	5·00
69.	12.	10 f. black and green	5·00	4·50

13. Port of Matadi.

14. Stanley Falls.

15. Inkissi Falls.

1915. New types as 13 to 15 (with value in words at top) and other types as 1910 all inscr. "CONGO BELGE" and "BELGISCH-CONGO".

70.	13.	5 c. black and green	8	5
71.	14.	10 c. black and red	10	5
72b.	5.	15 c. black and green	8	5
73.	15.	25 c. black and blue	50	12
74.	7.	40 c. black and lake	1·25	60
75.	8.	50 c. black and lake	1·60	50
76.	9.	1 f. black and olive	55	25
77.	11.	5 f. black and orange	45	25

1918. Types as before surch. with red cross and premium.

78.	13.	5 c.+10 c. blue & green	8	8
79.	14.	10 c.+15 c. blue and red	8	8
80.	5.	15 c.+20 c. blue & green	8	8
81.	15.	25 c.+25 c. blue	12	8
82.	7.	40 c.+40 c. blue & lake	12	8
83.	8.	50 c.+50 c. blue & lake	12	10
84.	9.	1 f.+1 f. blue and olive	75	75
85.	11.	5 f.+5 f. blue & orange	1·90	1·90
86.	12.	10 f.+10 f. blue & green	22·00	22·00

16. Wharf on the Congo.

1920. Air.

87.	16.	50 c. black and orange	10	5
88.	–	1 f. black and violet	12	5
89.	–	2 f. black and blue	25	12
90.	–	5 f. black and green	45	20

DESIGNS—HORIZ. 1 f. District stores. 2 f. Congo landscape. VERT. 5 f. Provincial prison.

1921. Stamps of 1910 surch.

91.	7.	5 c. on 40 c. black & green	10	10
92.	8.	10 c. on 5 c. black & green	10	10
93.	8.	15 c. on 50 c. blk. & olive	10	10
94.	5.	25 c. on 15 c. blk. & yell.	60	45
95.	4.	30 c. on 10 c. blk. & red	8	8
96.	6.	50 c. on 25 c. blk. & blue	45	35

1921. Stamps of 1910 optd. **1921.**

97.	9.	1 f. black and red	35	30
98.	10.	3 f. black and red	1·00	80
99.	11.	5 f. black and lake	1·25	1·25
100.	12.	10 f. black and green	1·50	1·00

1922. Stamps of previous issues variously surch. without bars.

101.	8.	5 c. on 50 c. black and lake (No. 75)	15	12
102.	13.	10 c. on 5 c. black and green (No. 70)	15	12
114.	4.	0.25 on 30 c. on 10 c. black & red (No. 95)	2·00	2·00
115.	14.	0.25 on 30 c. on 10 c. blk. & red (No. 104)	2·00	2·00
103.	7.	25 c. on 40 c. lake (No. 74)	45	12
104.	14.	30 c. on 10 c. black and red (No. 71)	8	8
105.	15.	50 c. on 25 c. black and blue (No. 73)	15	20

1922. Stamps of 1915 surch. with new value and two bars through old values.

106.	13.	10 c. on 5 c. black & green	20	15
110.	9.	10 c. on 1 f. black & olive	15	15
112.	7.	25 c. on 40 c. black & lake	20	12
113.	1.	25 c. on 5 f. blk. & orange	65	65

20. Wood Carver.

21. Native Cattle.

1923.

117.	A.	5 c. yellow	8	5
118.	B.	10 c. green	8	5
119.	C.	15 c. brown	8	5
120.	D.	20 c. olive	5	5
121.	E.	20 c. green	8	8
122.	F.	25 c. brown	10	5
123.	20.	30 c. red	8	8
124.		30 c. olive	8	8
125.		35 c. green	15	15
126.	D.	40 c. purple	8	8
142.	21.	45 c. purple	15	12
127.	G.	50 c. blue	8	5
128.		50 c. orange	15	5
143.	21.	60 c. lake	15	8
129.	E.	75 c. orange	15	12
130.		75 c. blue	15	10
131.	20.	75 c. red	12	8
132.	H.	1 f. brown	20	8
133.		1 f. blue	15	8
134.		1 f. red	15	8
135.	D.	1 f. 25 blue	35	8
136.		1 f. 50 blue	15	10
137.		1 f. 75 blue	1·25	85
138.	I.	3 f. brown	1·00	35
139.	J.	5 f. slate	2·25	1·00
140.	K.	10 f. black	4·75	1·50

DESIGNS: A. Ubangi woman. B. Baluba woman. C. Babuende woman. D. Ubangi man. E. Weaver. F. Basketmaker. G. Archer. H. Potter. I. Rubber worker. J. Palm oil. K. Elephant.

23.

24. H. M. Stanley.

25. Nurse weighing Native Children.

26. Doctor and Tent Surgery.

1925. Colonial campaigns, 1914/18. Inscr. in French or in Flemish.

141.	23.	25 c.+ 25 c. black & red	10	10

1927. No. 137 surch. **1.75.**

144.		1.75 on 1 f. 50 blue	15	15

1928. Stanley's Exploration of the Congo. 50th Anniv.

145.	24.	5 c. olive	5	5
146.		10 c. violet	5	5
147.		20 c. red	8	8
148.		35 c. green	30	20
149.		40 c. brown	8	8
150.		60 c. sepia	8	8
151.		1 f. red	8	5
152.		1 f. 60 slate	1·00	75
153.		1 f. 75 blue	35	25
154.		2 f. brown	30	10
155.		2 f. 75 purple	1·00	12
156.		3 f. 50 lake	35	20
157.		5 f. blue-green	30	8
158.		10 f. violet-blue	45	15
159.		20 f. claret	1·10	70

1930. Congo Natives Protection Fund.

160.	25.	10 c.+5 c. red	15	15
161.	–	20 c.+10 c. brown	20	20
162.	26.	35 c.+15 c. green	30	30
163.	–	60 c.+30 c. purple	35	35
164.	–	1 f.+50 c. red	55	55
165.	–	1 f. 75+75 c. blue	75	75
166	–	3 f. 50+1 f. 50 lake	1·75	1·75
167.	–	5 f.+2 f. 50 brown	1·40	1·40
168.	–	10 f.+5 f. black	1·50	1·50

DESIGNS—VERT. 20 c. Missionary and child. 1 f. Dispenser attending patients. HORIZ. 60 c. Local hospital. 1 f. 75 Nurses and native patients. 3 f. 50, Nurse bathing native baby. 5 f. Operating theatre. 10 f. Native children in school.

DESIGN: 30 f. Native porters.

27. Native Kraal.

1930. Air.

169.	27.	15 f. black and sepia	1·00	45
170.	–	30 f. black and purple	1·25	45

1931. Surch.

171.	40 c. on 35 c. grn. (No. 148)	20	15
177.	40 c. on 35 c. green (125)	1·50	1·40
178.	50 c. on 45 c. purple (142)	1·00	30
172.	1 f. 25 on 1 f. red (151)	15	5
173.	2 f. on 1 f. 60 slate (152)	25	10
174.	2 f. on 1 f. 75 blue (153)	25	10
179.	2 f. on 1 f. 75 blue (137)	2·25	2·10
175.	3 f. 25 on 2 f. 75 purple (155)	70	50
180.	3 f. 25 on 3 f. sepia (138)	90	65
176.	3 f. 25 on 3 f. 50 lake (156)	1·00	60

29. Sankur River.

30. Flute Players.

1931.

181.	29.	10 c. brown	5	5
182.	–	15 c. grey	5	5
183.	–	20 c. magenta	5	5
184.	–	25 c. blue	5	5
185.	30.	40 c. green	5	5
186.	–	50 c. violet	5	5
187.	–	60 c. purple	5	5
188.	–	75 c. lake	5	5
189.	–	1 f. red	10	5
190.	–	1 f. 25 brown	5	5
190a.	–	1 f. 50 black	8	5
191.	–	2 f. blue	8	5
191a.	–	2 f. 50 blue	15	12
192.	–	3 f. 25 grey	30	15
193.	–	4 f. lilac	10	8
194.	–	5 f. purple	30	12
195.	–	10 f. orange-red	25	20
196.	–	20 f. sepia	75	50

DESIGNS—HORIZ. 15 c. Native kraal. 20 c. Waterfall. 25 c. Native kraal. 50 c. Native musicians. 1 f. 50, 2 f., 4 f. Riverside scenes (different views). 2 f. 50, 3 f. 25, Okapi. VERT. 60 c. Drummers. 75 c. Mangbethu woman. 1 f. Elephant transport. 1 f. 25, Native chief. 5 f. Pressing tapioca. 10 f. Witch doctor. 20 f. Woman carrying latex.

31. Aeroplane over Congo.

32. King Albert I.

1934. Air.

197.	31.	50 c. black	5	5
198.		1 f. red	10	5
199.		1 f. 50 green	5	5
200.		3 f. lake	10	5
201.		4 f. 50 blue	15	5
202.		5 f. red	12	5
203.		15 f. purple	25	15
204.		30 f. red	50	45
205.		50 f. violet	1·25	70

1934. Death of King Albert.

206.	32.	1 f. 50 black	35	10

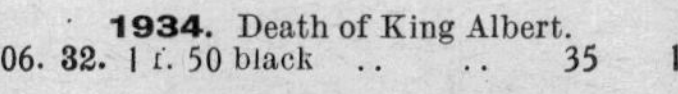

33. Four Belgian Kings.

1935. Independent State of the Congo. 50th Anniv.

207.	33.	50 c. green	25	20
208.		1 f. 25 red	25	8
209.		1 f. 50 purple	25	5
210.		2 f. 40 orange	75	70
211.		2 f. 50 blue	60	30
212.		4 f. violet	80	40
213.		5 f. brown	80	35

1936. Air. Surch. **3.50 F** and bars.

214.	31.	3 f. 50 on 3 f. lake	12	8

1936. King Albert Memorial Fund. Surch. **+50 c.**

215. 33. 1 f. 50+50 c. purple .. 60 60
216. 2 f. 50+50 c. blue .. 50 50

34. Queen Astrid and Congo Children.
35. R. Molindi.

1936. Charity. Congo Children's Fund.

217. 34. 1 f. 25+5 c. brown .. 25 20
218. 1 f. 50+10 c. red .. 25 20
219. 2 f. 50+25 c. blue .. 30 25

1938. Promotion of National Parks.

220. 35. 5 c. black and violet .. 5 5
221. – 90 c. brown and red .. 25 20
222. – 1 f. 50 black & choc. .. 5 5
223. – 2 f. 40 brown & slate .. 8 8
224. – 2 f. 50 black and blue .. 12 8
225. – 4 f. 50 brown & green .. 15 8

DESIGNS—VERT. 90 c. Bamboo-canes 1 f. 50 R. Suza. 2 f. 40, R. Rutshuru. HORIZ. 2 f. 50, Mt. Karisimbi. 4 f. 50, Mitumba Forest.

36. Vultures and Marabou-storks.

DESIGNS: 1 f. 25, Kob antelope. 1 f. 50, Chimpanzees. 4 f. 50, Crocodiles. 5 f. Lioness.

1939. Leopoldville Zoological Gardens.

226. 36. 1 f.+1 f. maroon .. 1·50 1·50
227. – 1 f. 25+1 f. 25 red .. 1·50 1·50
228. – 1 f. 50+1 f. 50 violet .. 2·50 2·50
229. – 4 f. 50+4 f. 50 green .. 1·50 1·50
230. – 5 f.+5 f. brown .. 1·75 1·50

37. King Albert Memorial, Leopoldville.
38. "Belgium shall rise again".

1941.

231. 37. 10 c. grey 8 5
232. 15 c. brown 8 5
233. 25 c. blue 8 5
234. 50 c. lilac 8 5
235. 75 c. pink 35 10
236. 1 f. 25 brown 10 8
237. 1 f. 75 orange 25 20
238. 2 f. 50 red 30 5
239. 2 f. 75 blue 35 30
240. 5 f. olive 50 45
241. 10 f. red 85 80

1941. Surch.

242. – 5 c. on 1 f. 50 (No. 222) (postage) 5 5
243. 37. 75 c. on 1 f. 75 orange .. 20 20
244. – 2 f. 50 on 2 f. 40 brown and slate (No. 223) .. 30 20
245. 31. 50 c. on 1 f. 50 green (air) 15 15

1942. War Relief Fund.

246. 38. 10 f.+40 f. blue .. 60 60
247. 10 f.+40 f. green .. 60 60

39. Oil Palms.
40. Leopard.

1942. Inscr. "BELGISCH CONGO BELGE".

248. 39. 5 c. red 5 5
249. – 50 f. black and blue .. 1·00 20
250. – 100 f. black and red .. 2·00 35

Inscr. "CONGO BELGE BELGISCH CONGO", or vice versa.

251. 39. 10 c. olive 5 5
252. 15 c. brown 5 5
253. 20 c. blue 5 5
254. 25 c. purple 5 5
255. 30 c. blue 5 5
256. 50 c. green 5 5
257. 60 c. brown 5 5
258. – 75 c. black and violet .. 5 5
259. – 1 f. black and brown .. 8 5
260. – 1 f. 25 black and red 8 5
261. 40. 1 f. 75 brown 25 25
262. 2 f. yellow 25 5
263. 2 f. 50 red 25 5
264. – 3 f. 50 olive 12 5
265. – 5 f. orange 25 8
266. – 6 f. blue 20 5
267. – 7 f. black 20 5
268. – 10 f. brown 25 5
269. – 20 f. black and claret .. 1·10 30

DESIGNS—As T 39: 75 c. to 1 f. 25, Head of a native woman. 3 f. 50 to 10 f. Askari sentry. As T 40: 20 f. Okapi. LARGER (28×33 mm.): 50 f. Negress head. 100 f. Askari sentry.

1944. Red Cross Fund. Surch.

269a. 39. 50 c.+50 f. green (No. 256) .. .. 1·00 1·10
269b. – 1 f. 25+100 f. black & red (No. 260) .. 1·00 1·25
269c. 40. 1 f. 75+100 f. brown (No. 261) .. .. 1·00 1·25
269d. – 3 f. 50+100 f. green (No. 264) .. .. 1·00 1·25

PORTRAITS — As T 42: 1 f. 50, Lavigerie. 3 f. Dhanis. 3 f. 50, Lambermont.

41. Driving Slaves to Market.
42. Leopold II.

1947. Abolition of Slavery in Belgian Congo. 50th Anniv.

270. 41. 1 f. 25 brown .. 10 5
270a. – 1 f. 50 violet .. 50 10
270b. – 3 f. brown .. 50 5
271. – 3 f. 50 blue .. 12 5
272. 42. 10 f. orange .. 30 8

43. Seated Figure.
44. Railway Train and Map.

45. Globe and Ship.
46. Allegorical Figure and Map.

1947. Native masks and carvings as T 43.

273. 10 c. orange 5 5
274. 15 c. blue 5 5
275. 20 c. blue 5 5
276. 25 c. red 12 5
277. 40 c. violet 5 5
278. 50 c. sepia 5 5
279. 70 c. green 5 5
280. 75 c. mauve 5 5
281. 1 f. purple and yellow .. 30 5
281a. 1 f. 20 brown and grey .. 8 8
282. 1 f. 25 mauve and blue 12 8
282a. 1 f. 50 mauve and olive .. 1·50 35
282b. 1 f. 60 blue and grey .. 10 8
283. 2 f. claret and red .. 8 5
283a. 2 f. 40 green and blue .. 12 10
284. 2 f. 50 green and brown .. 8 5
284a. 3 f. black and blue .. 85 5
285. 3 f. 50 black and blue .. 75 8
286. 5 f. claret and olive .. 15 5
287. 6 f. myrtle & brown-orge. 15 5
287a. 6 f. 50 brown and orange 45 5
287b. 8 f. green and blue .. 20 5
288. 10 f. brown and violet .. 50 5
289. 20 f. purple and red .. 35 5
290. 50 f. black and brown .. 1·00 12
291. 100 f. black and red .. 1·50 25

1948. Matadi-Leopoldville Railway. 50th Anniv.

292. 44. 2 f. 50 green and blue .. 20 8

1949. U.P.U. 75th Anniv.

293. 45. 4 f. blue 25 10

1950. Katanga Province. 50th Anniv.

294. 46. 3 f. slate and blue .. 50 8
295. 6 f. 50 sepia and red .. 60 10

47. "Littonia".
48. St. Francis Xavier.

1952. Flowers. Multicoloured.

296. 10 c. "Dissotis" 5 5
297. 15 c. "Protea" 5 5
298. 20 c. "Vellozia" 5 5
299. 25 c. Type 47 .. .. 5 5
300. 40 c. "Ipomoea" 5 5
301. 50 c. "Angraecum" .. 5 5
302. 60 c. "Euphorbia" .. 5 5
303. 75 c. "Ochna" 5 5
304. 1 f. "Hibiscus" 5 5
305. 1 f. 25 "Pretea" 30 25
306. 1 f. 50 "Schizoglossum" .. 5 5
307. 2 f. "Ansellia" 12 5
308. 3 f. "Costus" 10 5
309. 4 f. "Nymphaea" 12 5
310. 5 f. "Thunbergia" 15 5
311. 6 f. 50 "Thonningia" .. 25 5
312. 7 f. "Gerbera" 25 5
313. 8 f. "Gloriosa" 30 8
314. 10 f. "Silene" 60 5
315. 20 f. "Aristolochia" .. 50 5
316. 50 f. "Eulophia" .. .. 2·25 25
317. 100 f. "Cryptosepalum" .. 3·25 55

SIZES: Nos. 296/315, 21×25½ mm. Nos. 316/7, 22½×32½ mm.

1953. St. Francis Xavier. 400th Death Anniv.

318. 48. 1 f. 50 c. black & blue 30 25

49. Lake Kivu.
50. Medallion.

1953. Kivu Festival.

319. 49. 3 f. black and red .. 50 12
320. 7 f. brown and blue .. 60 15

1954. 25th Anniv. of Belgian Royal Colonial Institute. No. 322 has different frame.

321. 50. 4 f. 50 grey and blue .. 50 12
322. 6 f. 50 brown and green 60 15

51. King Baudouin and Mountains.
52. Badge and Map.

1955. Inscr. "CONGO BELGE. BELGISCH CONGO" or vice versa.

323. 51. 1 f. 50 c. black and red 12 10
324. – 3 f. black and green .. 10 5
325. – 4 f. 50 c. black and blue 12 5
326. – 6 f. 50 c. black & maroon 20 5

DESIGNS—HORIZ. 3 f. Forest. 4 f. 50 c. River. 6 f. 50 c. Grassland.

1955. 5th Int. Congress of African Tourism. Inscr. in Flemish or French.

327. 52. 6 f. 50 blue 90 15

1956. Mozart Birth Bicent. As T 226/7 of Belgium.

328. 226. 4 f. 50+1 f. 50 violet 50 55
329. 227. 6 f. 50+2 f. 50 blue .. 75 80

DESIGNS—HORIZ. 4 f. 50 c. Doctor inoculating patient. 6 f. 50 c. Nurse in tropical kit bandaging patient.

53. Nurse with Children.

1957. Red Cross Fund. Cross in red.

330. 53. 3 f.+50 c. indigo .. 35 35
331. – 4 f. 50 c.+50 c. brown 40 40
332. – 6 f. 50 c.+50 c. brown 50 50

54. Belgian Monarchs.
55. Roan Antelope.

1958. Belgian Annexation of the Congo 50th Anniv.

333. 54. 1 f. claret 8 5
334. 1 f. 50 blue 10 5
335. 3 f. red 10 5
336. 5 f. green 30 25
337. 6 f. 50 brown 20 5
338. 10 f. slate-violet .. 25 5

1959. Wild Animals.

339. 55. 10 c. brn., sepia & blue 5 5
340. – 20 c. grey-blue & verm. 5 5
341. – 40 c. brown and blue .. 5 5
342. – 50 c. red, ol., blk. & bl. 5 5
343. – 1 f. black, green & brn. 5 5
344. – 1 f. 50 black and yellow 5 5
345. – 2 f. black, brown & red 5 5
346. – 3 f. black, pur. & slate 10 5
347. – 5 f. brown, green & sepia 15 8
348. – 6 f. 50 brn., yell. & blue 20 5
349. – 8 f. bistre, violet & chest. 25 15
350. – 10 f. brown, black, orange and yellow .. 25 8

DESIGNS—HORIZ. 20 c. White rhinoceros. 50 c. Galago. 1 f. 50 Black buffaloes. 3 f. Elephants. 6 f. 50 Impala. 10 f. Eland and zebras. VERT. 40 c. Giraffe. 1 f. Gorilla. 2 f. Colobus monkey. 5 f. Okapis. 8 f. Giant pangolin.

56. Madonna and Child.
57. "African Resources".

1959. Christmas.

351. 56. 50 c. brn., ochre & chest. 5 5
352. 1 f. brown, violet & blue 5 5
353. 2 f. brown, blue & slate 8 5

1960. African Technical Co-operation Commission. 10th Anniv. Inscr. in French or Flemish.

354. 57. 3 f. salmon and slate .. 12 8

DESIGNS: 1 f. 50, Hurdling. 2 f. Football. 3 f. Throwing the javelin. 6 f. 60, Throwing the discus.

58. High-jumping.

1960. Child Welfare Fund.

355. 58. 50 c.+25 c. blue and red 5 5
356. – 1 f. 50+50 c. red & grn. 10 10
357. – 2 f.+1 f. green and red 12 12
358. – 3 f.+1 f. 25 pur. & blue 45 45
359. – 6 f. 60+3 f. 50 brown and red 50 50

POSTAGE DUE STAMPS

D 1.
D 2.

1923.

D 141. D 1. 5 c. sepia 5 5
D 142. 10 c. red 8 5
D 143. 15 c. violet 8 8
D 144. 30 c. green 15 15
D 145. 50 c. blue 20 20
D 146. 1 f. slate 20 20

1943.

D 270. D 2. 10 c. olive 5 5
D 271. 20 c. blue 5 5
D 272. 50 c. green 5 5
D 273. 1 f. brown 5 5
D 274. 2 f. orange 8 8

D 3.

1957.

D 330. D 3. 10 c. brown .. 5 5
D 331. 20 c. maroon .. 5 5
D 332. 50 c. green .. 5 5
D 333. 1 f. blue .. 12 12
D 334. 2 f. red .. 20 15
D 335. 4 f. violet .. 25 20
D 336. 6 f. blue .. 30 25

For later issues see **CONGO (KINSHASA)** and **ZAIRE REPUBLIC.**

BELGIAN OCCUPATION OF GERMANY E2

Stamps used in German territory occupied by Belgian Forces at the end of the War of 1914/18, and including the districts of Eupen and Malmedy, now incorporated in Belgium.

1919. Stamps of Belgium optd. **ALLEMAGNE DUITSCHLAND.**

No.	Type	Description	Unused	Used
1.	37.	1 c. orange	5	5
2.		2 c. brown	5	5
3.		3 c. grey	5	5
4.		5 c. green	10	10
5.		10 c. red	35	30
6.		15 c. violet	10	8
7.		20 c. purple	12	10
8.		25 c. blue	50	35
9.	38.	25 c. blue	1·00	90
10.	39.	35 c. black and brown	20	15
11.	40.	40 c. black and green	35	25
12.	41.	50 c. black and red	2·00	1·60
13.	42.	65 c. black and claret	65	55
14.	43.	1 f. violet	6·00	3·50
15.	44.	2 f. grey	13·00	11·00
16.	45.	5 f. bl. (FRANK, No. 151)	2·10	2·00
17.	46.	10 f. sepia	18·00	18·00

1920. Stamps of Belgium surch. **EUPEN & MALMEDY** and value.

No.	Type	Description	Unused	Used
18.	37.	5 pf. on 5 c. green	15	15
19.		10 pf. on 10 c. red	12	12
20.		15 pf. on 15 c. violet	12	12
21.		20 pf. on 30 c. purple	12	12
22.		30 pf. on 25 c. blue	15	15
23.	41.	75 pf. on 50 c. blk. & red	6·50	5·50
24.	43.	1 m. 25 on 1 f. violet	6·50	5·50

1920. Stamps of Belgium optd. **Eupen.**

No.	Type	Description	Unused	Used
25.	37.	1 c. orange	5	5
26.		2 c. brown	5	5
27.		3 c. grey	5	5
28.		5 c. green	15	10
29.		10 c. red	50	20
30.		15 c. violet	35	20
31.		20 c. purple	35	20
32.		25 c. blue	55	25
33.	38.	25 c. blue	1·00	55
34.	39.	35 c. black and brown	35	35
35.	40.	40 c. black and green	1·00	85
36.	41.	50 c. black and red	2·25	1·75
37.	42.	65 c. black and claret	55	55
38.	43.	1 f. violet	6·00	4·00
39.	44.	2 f. grey	10·00	7·50
40.	45.	5 f. bl. (FRANK, No. 151)	2·40	2·25
41.	46.	10 f. sepia	18·00	18·00

1920. Stamps of Belgium optd. **Malmedy.**

No.	Type	Description	Unused	Used
42.	37.	1 c. orange	5	5
43.		2 c. brown	5	5
44.		3 c. grey	5	5
45.		5 c. green	12	10
46.		10 c. red	35	25
47.		15 c. violet	35	25
48.		20 c. purple	35	25
49.		25 c. blue	55	35
50.	38.	25 c. blue	1·00	85
51.	39.	35 c. black and brown	35	35
52.	40.	40 c. black and green	65	55
53.	41.	50 c. black and red	2·25	1·75
54.	42.	65 c. black and claret	55	55
55.	43.	1 f. violet	6·00	4·00
56.	44.	2 f. grey	11·00	8·50
57.	45.	5 f. bl. (FRANK, No. 151)	2·50	2·50
58.	46.	10 f. sepia	18·00	18·00

POSTAGE DUE STAMPS

1920. Postage Due stamps of Belgium, 1919.

(a) Optd. **Eupen.**

No.	Description	Unused	Used
D 1.	5 c. green	20	20
D 2.	10 c. red	25	25
D 3.	20 c. green	85	80
D 4.	30 c. blue	85	80
D 5.	50 c. grey	4·25	3·75

(b) Optd. **Malmedy.**

No.	Description	Unused	Used
D 6.	5 c. green	20	20
D 7.	10 c. red	25	25
D 8.	20 c. green	4·00	3·50
D 9.	30 c. blue	85	80
D 10.	50 c. grey	3·25	3·00

BELGIUM E1

An independent Kingdom of N.W. Europe.
100 centimes = 1 franc.

1. Leopold I. 2. Leopold I.

1849. Imperf.

No.	Type	Description	Unused	Used
1a.	1.	10 c. brown	£800	32·00
2a.		20 c. blue	£1100	20·00

1849. Imperf.

No.	Type	Description	Unused	Used
12.	2.	1 c. green	95·00	70·00
13.		10 c. brown	£160	2·25
14.		20 c. blue	£160	2·75
8.		40 c. red	£950	32·00

1863. Perf.

No.	Type	Description	Unused	Used
24.	2.	1 c. green	17·00	10·00
21.		10 c. brown	28·00	30
22.		20 c. blue	28·00	20
23.		40 c. red	£160	7·50

3. Leopold I. 4. 5.

1865.

No.	Type	Description	Unused	Used
34.	3.	10 c. grey	40·00	30
35.		20 c. blue	45·00	30
36.		30 c. brown	90·00	2·00
37.	4.	40 c. red	£120	5·00
38.	3.	1 f. lilac	2·75	35·00

1866.

No.	Type	Description	Unused	Used
43.	5.	1 c. grey	13·00	6·00
41.		2 c. blue	50·00	27·00
42.		5 c. brown	50·00	27·00

6. 7. 8.

9. 10.

T 7 to 10 and all later portraits to T 27 are of Leopold II.

1869.

No.	Type	Description	Unused	Used
46.	6.	1 c. green	3·00	8
47b.		2 c. blue	2·50	12
48a.		5 c. buff	20·00	15
49.		8 c. lilac	30·00	20·00
50a.	7.	10 c. green	11·00	8
51b.	8.	20 c. blue	35·00	15
52a.	9.	25 c. bistre	24·00	30
53a.	7.	30 c. buff	30·00	1·25
54.		40 c. red	45·00	1·50
55a.	9.	50 c. grey	60·00	2·00
56.	7.	1 f. mauve	70·00	6·50
57a.	10.	5 f. brown	£700	£250

11. 15.

1883. Various frames. Perf. or imperf.

No.	Type	Description	Unused	Used
63.	11.	10 c. red	12·00	25
64.	–	20 c. grey	50·00	1·00
65.	–	25 c. blue	85·00	11·00
66.	–	50 c. violet	70·00	8·50

1884. Various frames to portrait stamps.

No.	Type	Description	Unused	Used
67.	6.	1 c. olive	3·50	25
68.		1 c. grey	1·75	5
69.		2 c. brown	4·00	10
70.		5 c. green	5·00	5
71.	15.	10 c. red	2·50	5
72.	–	20 c. olive	45·00	15
73.	–	25 c. blue on red	4·25	12
74.	–	35 c. brown	7·00	1·00
75.	–	50 c. bistre	4·75	55
76.	–	1 f. brown on green	£200	2·75
77.	–	2 f. lilac	55·00	7·00

21. 22. 23. Arms of Antwerp.

1893.

No.	Type	Description	Unused	Used
78a.	21.	1 c. grey	35	5
79.		2 c. yellow	50	50
80.		2 c. brown	1·00	8
81.		5 c. green	1·40	8
82.	22.	10 c. brown	1·75	8
83.		10 c. red	1·75	8
84.		20 c. olive	12·00	15
85.		25 c. blue	10·00	15
86a.		35 c. brown	18·00	35
87.		50 c. brown	24·00	3·00
88.		50 c. grey	30·00	70
89.		1 f. red on green	32·00	5·50
90.		1 f. orange	55·00	1·75
92.		2 f. mauve	75·00	5·50

The prices for the above and all following issues with the tablet are for stamps with the tablet attached. Without tablet, the prices will be about half those quoted.

1894. Antwerp Exn.

No.	Type	Description	Unused	Used
93a.	23.	5 c. green on red	2·75	85
94.		10 c. red on blue	2·50	35
95.		25 c. blue on red	15	20

24. St. Michael encountering Satan. 25.

1896. Brussels Exn. of 1897

No.	Type	Description	Unused	Used
96.	24.	5 c. violet	35	20
97.	25.	10 c. red	5·00	1·00
98.		10 c. brown	20	15

26. 27. 29. St. Martin and the Beggar.

1905. Various frames.

No.	Type	Description	Unused	Used
99.	26.	10 c. red	1·40	5
100.		20 c. olive	10·00	25
101.		25 c. blue	8·00	20
102.		35 c. maroon	14·00	50
103.	27.	50 c. grey	38·00	55
104.		1 f. orange	50·00	1·75
105.		2 f. mauve	45·00	5·50

1907. As T 21 but no scroll pattern between stamps and labels.

No.	Description	Unused	Used
106.	1 c. grey	90	8
107.	2 c. claret	2·75	60
108a.	5 c. green	3·25	8

1910. Brussels Exhibition. A. Unshaded background. B. Shaded background.

A.

No.	Type	Description	Unused	Used
109.	29.	1 c. (+1 c.) grey	60	35
110.		2 c. (+2 c.) maroon	5·50	4·25
111.		5 c. (+5 c.) green	1·40	1·10
112.		10 c. (+5 c.) red	1·40	1·10

B.

No.	Type	Description	Unused	Used
113.	29.	1 c. (+1 c.) green	1·50	80
112.		2 c. (+2 c.) maroon	4·25	2·75
115.		5 c. (+5 c.) green	1·40	1·10
116.		10 c. (+5 c.) red	1·40	1·10

1911. Nos. 109/16 optd. **1911.**

A.

No.	Type	Description	Unused	Used
117.	29.	1 c. (+1 c.) grey	7·00	5·50
118.		2 c. (+2 c.) maroon	19·00	15·00
119.		5 c. (+5 c.) green	2·25	1·75
120.		10 c. (+5 c.) red	2·25	1·75

B.

No.	Type	Description	Unused	Used
121.	29.	1 c. (+1 c.) green	14·00	11·00
122.		2 c. (+2 c.) maroon	13·00	10·00
123.		5 c. (+5 c.) green	2·25	1·75
124.		10 c. (+5 c.) red	2·25	1·75

1911. Charleroi Exhibition. Nos. 109/16 optd **CHARLEROI—1911.**

A.

No.	Type	Description	Unused	Used
125.	29.	1 c. (+1 c.) grey	1·40	70
126.		2 c. (+2 c.) maroon	6·50	5·50
127.		5 c. (+5 c.) grey	3·25	2·75
128.		10 c. (+5 c.) red	2·10	1·75

B.

No.	Type	Description	Unused	Used
129.	29.	1 c. (+1 c.) green	2·10	1·10
130.		2 c. (+2 c.) maroon	5·00	4·25
131.		5 c (+5 c.) green	2·40	1·90
132.		10 c. (+5 c.) red	2·10	1·90

30. 31. 32.

33. Albert I. 34.

1912.

No.	Type	Description	Unused	Used
133.	30.	1 c. orange	5	5
134.	31.	2 c. brown	8	5
135.	32.	5 c. green	5	5
136.	33.	10 c. red	50	12
137.		20 c. olive	7·50	35
138.		35 c. brown	65	25
139.		40 c. green	9·00	5·50
140.		50 c. grey	60	25
141.		1 f. orange	3·75	1·25
142.		2 f. violet	11·00	6·50
143.	–	5 f. purple	65·00	13·00

The 5 f. is as T 33 but larger (23 × 35 mm.).

1912. Large head.

No.	Type	Description	Unused	Used
144.	34.	10 c. red	10	5
145.		20 c. olive	15	10
150.		25 c. blue	15	10
147.		40 c. green	20	15

35. Merode Monument. 36. Albert I.

1914. Red Cross.

No.	Type	Description	Unused	Used
151.	35.	5 c. (+5 c.) red & green	1·40	1·10
152.		10 c. (+10 c.) red & pink	1·40	1·10
153.		20 c. (+20 c.) red & vio.	20·00	16·00

1914. Red Cross.

No.	Type	Description	Unused	Used
154.	36.	5 c. (+5 c.) red & green	40	25
155.		10 c. (+10 c.) red	15	15
156.		20 c. (+20 c.) red & vio.	6·00	5·50

37. Albert I.

1915. Red Cross.

No.	Type	Description	Unused	Used
157.	37.	5 c. (+5 c.) red & green	3·50	1·10
158.		10 c. (+10 c.) red & pink	5·50	1·50
159.		20 c. (+20 c.) red & vio.	18·00	4·25

38. Albert I. 39. "Perron" at Liege.

40. Cloth Hall, Ypres.

41. Dinant (28×22½ mm.).

42. Louvain (28×22½ mm.).

43. Hotel de Ville, Termonde (28×22½ mm.).

44. Freeing of the Scheldt.

45. Annexation of the Congo (33×24 mm.).

46. King Albert at Furnes (33×24 mm.).

47. The Kings of Belgium (33×25 mm.).

1915.

No.	Type	Description	Unused	Used
170.	38.	1 c. orange	12	5
178.		2 c. brown	10	5
179.		3 c. grey	8	5
180.		5 c. green	30	5
173.		10 c. red	50	5
174.		15 c. violet	50	5
175.		20 c. purple	40	5
176.		25 c. blue	40	12
236.	39.	25 c. blue	£150	£130
188.	40.	35 c. black and brown	35	8
189.	41.	40 c. black and green	55	8
190.	42.	50 c. black and red	2·10	8
308.	43.	65 c. black and claret	60	10
191.	44.	1 f. violet	10·00	15
192.	45.	2 f. grey	16·00	55
193.	46.	5 f. blue (FRANKEN)	£120	35·00
194.		5 f. blue (FRANK)	£175	70
195.	47.	10 f. sepia	20·00	14·00

1918. Red Cross. Surch. with new value and cross.
222. **38.** 1 c.+1 c. orange .. 20 20
223. 2 c.+2 c. brown .. 20 20
224. 5 c.+5 c. green .. 85 60
225. 10 c.+10 c. red .. 1·25 1·10
226. 15 c.+15 c. violet .. 2·10 1·60
227. 20 c.+20 c. purple .. 4·25 3·50
228. 25 c.+25 c. blue .. 4·75 3·50
229. **40.** 35 c.+35 c. blk. & vio. 6·00 5·50
230. **41.** 40 c.+40 c. blk. & brn. 6·00 5·50
231. **42.** 50 c.+50 c. blk. & bl. 7·00 6·00
232. **44.** 1 f.+1 f. slate .. .. 21·00 17·00
233. **45.** 2 f.+2 f. green.. .. 65·00 60·00
234. **46.** 5 f.+5 f. brown (FRANKEN) £150 £120
235. **47.** 10 f.+10 f. blue .. £275 £250

48. Albert I.

1919.
237. **48.** 1 c. brown 5 5
238. 2 c. olive 5 5
239. 5 c. green 20 12
240. 10 c. red 8 5
241. 15 c. violet 8 5
242. 20 c. sepia 55 50
243. 25 c. blue 65 60
244. 35 c. brown 85 75
245. 40 c. red .. .. 1·50 1·25
246. 50 c. brown .. .. 3·00 3·00
247. 1 f. orange .. .. 21·00 15·00
248. 2 f. purple £225 £170
249. 5 f. lake .. .. 65·00 55·00
250. 10 f. claret .. .. 70·00 60·00
Sizes: 1 c., 2 c., 18½×21½ mm., 5 c. to 2 f., 22½×26½ mm., 5 f., 10 f., 28×33 mm.

49. Discus thrower. **50.** Charioteer.

1920. Antwerp Olympic Games.
256. **49.** 5 c. (+5 c.) green .. 2·25 1·50
257. **50.** 10 c. (+5 c.) red .. 2·10 1·40
258. – 15 c. (+5 c.) brown .. 4·25 80
DESIGN—VERT. 15 c. Runner.

1921. Surch. **20 c.** and cross and bar.
309. **49.** 20 c. on 5 c. green .. 75 15
310. **50.** 20 c. on 10 c. red .. 55 15
311. – 20 c. on 15 c. (No. 258) 60 15

51. Albert I. **52.** **53.** Albert I.

1921.
313. **51.** 50 c. blue 20 5
314. 75 c. red 12 5
315. 75 c. blue 30 5
316. 1 f. sepia 60 5
317. 1 f. blue 40 5
318. 2 f. green 55 10
319. 5 f. purple .. .. 7·00 6·50
320. 5 f. brown .. .. 7·50 7·50
321. 10 f. claret .. .. 7·50 1·10

1921. Surch. **55 c.** and bars.
322. **42.** 55 c. on 65 c. blk. & clar. 70 15

1922. Charity.
348. **52.** 20 c.+20 c. brown .. 90 55

1922.
349. **53.** 1 c. orange 5 5
350. 2 c. olive 5 5
351. 3 c. red-brown 5 5
352. 5 c. slate 5 5
353. 10 c. green 10 5
354. 15 c. plum 15 5
355. 20 c. brown 30 5
356. 25 c. purple 20 5
357. 25 c. violet 45 5
358. 30 c. red 45 5
359. 30 c. mauve 45 5
360. 35 c. brown 20 5
361. 35 c. green .. .. 1·25 5
362. 40 c. red 50 5
363. 50 c. bistre 45 5
364. 60 c. olive .. .. 1·50 5
365. 75 c. violet 50 20
366. 1 f. yellow 45 8
367. 1 f. red .. .. 1·10 5
368. 1 f. 25 blue 40 25
369. 1 f. 50 blue .. .. 1·60 8
370. 1 f. 75 blue .. .. 1·75 5
371. 2 f. blue .. .. 2·40 5
372. 5 f. green .. .. 15·00 20
373. 10 f. brown .. .. 29·00 65

54. Wounded Soldier.

ILLUSTRATIONS
British Commonwealth and all overprints and surcharges are FULL SIZE. Foreign Countries have been reduced to ¾-LINEAR.

1923. Charity.
374. **54.** 20 c.+20 c. slate .. 1·90 1·00

55. Leopold I and Albert I.

1925. 1st Belgian Stamps. 75th Anniv.
410. **55.** 10 c. green .. .. 5·00 4·50
411. 15 c. violet .. .. 3·50 3·25
412. 20 c. brown .. .. 3·50 3·25
413. 25 c. slate .. .. 3·50 3·25
414. 30 c. red .. .. 3·50 3·25
415. 35 c. blue .. .. 3·50 3·25
416. 40 c. sepia .. .. 3·50 3·25
417. 50 c. brown .. .. 3·50 3·25
418. 75 c. blue .. .. 3·50 3·25
419. 1 f. purple .. .. 5·00 4·50
420. 2 f. blue .. .. 3·50 3·25
421. 5 f. black .. .. 3·75 3·50
422. 10 f. red .. .. 5·50 4·75

56.

57.

1925. Anti-T.B. Fund.
423. **56** 15 c.+5 c. red & mauve 20 20
424. 30 c.+5 c. red and grey 15 8
425. 1 f.+10 c. red and blue 80 70

1926. Flood Relief. Type of 1922 surch. **Inondations 30 c. Watersnood.**
426. **53.** 30 c.+30 c. blue-green 50 40

1926. Charity. A. Shaded background. B. Solid background.
A.
427. **57.** 1 f.+1 f. blue .. .. 5·50 5·00
B.
428. **57.** 1 f.+1 f. blue .. .. 1·00 85

58.

59. Queen Elisabeth and King Albert.

1926. Anti-T.B. Fund.
429. **58.** 5 c.+5 c. brown .. 8 8
430. 20 c.+5 c. red-brown .. 35 30
431. 50 c.+5 c. violet .. 20 5
432. **59.** 1 f. 50+25 c. blue .. 55 55
433. 5 f.+1 f. red .. .. 5·00 4·75

1927. Stamps of 1922 surch.
434. **53.** 3 c. on 2 c. olive .. 5 5
435. 10 c. on 15 c. plum .. 10 5
436. 35 c. on 40 c. red .. 30 5
437. 1 f. 75 on 1 f. 50 blue .. 1·10 30

60.

1927. Anti-T.B. Fund.
438. **60.** 25 c.+10 c. brown .. 55 40
439. 35 c.+10 c. green .. 55 40
440. 60 c.+10 c. violet .. 40 15
441. 1 f. 75+25 c. blue .. 1·25 1·10
442. 5 f.+1 f. purple .. 4·25 3·50

61. Ogives.

62. Ruins of Orval Abbey.

1928. Orval Abbey Restoration Fund Inscr. "ORVAL 1928" or "ORVAL".
461. **61.** 5 c.+5 c. red and gold 15 15
462. – 25 c.+5 c. violet & gold 30 30
463. – 35 c.+10 c. green .. 1·10 75
464. – 60 c.+15 c. brown .. 1·50 15
465. – 1 f. 75+25 c. blue .. 3·75 1·75
466. – 2 f.+40 c. purple .. 11·00 7·50
467. – 3 f.+1 f. red .. .. 14·00 10·00
468. **62.** 5 f.+5 f. lake .. .. 15·00 14·00
469. – 10 f.+10 f. sepia .. 15·00 14·00
DESIGNS—VERT. 35 c., 2 f. Cistercian monk stone-carving. 60 c., 1 f. 75, 3 f. Duchess Matilda retrieving her ring.

65. Mons Cathedral.

66. Malines Cathedral.

1928. Anti-T.B. Fund.
472. **65.** 5 c.+5 c. red 12 8
473. – 25 c.+15 c. sepia .. 25 20
474. **66.** 35 c.+10 c. green .. 85 55
475. – 60 c.+15 c. brown .. 30 8
476. – 1 f. 75+25 c. violet .. 7·00 5·50
477. – 5 f.+5 f. purple .. 13·00 11·00
DESIGNS—As T **65**: 25 c. Tournai Cathedral. As T **66**: 60 c. Ghent Cathedral. 1 f. 75, St. Gudule Cathedral, Brussels. 5 f. Louvain Library.

1929. Surch. **BRUXELLES 1929. BRUSSEL 5 c.** in frame.
478. **52.** 5 c. on 30 c. mauve .. 5 5
479. 5 c. on 75 c. violet .. 15 8
480. 5 c. on 1 f. 25 c. blue .. 8 8
The above cancellation, whilst altering the original face value of the stamps, also constitutes a pre-cancel, although stamps also come with additional ordinary postmark. The unused prices are for stamps with full gum and the used prices for stamps without gum, with or without postmarks.

67. The Belgian Lion.

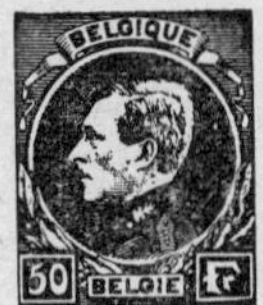

68. Albert I.

1929.
487. **67.** 1 c. orange 5 5
488. 2 c. green 15 15
489. 3 c. brown 5 5
490. 5 c. slate 8 5
491. 10 c. olive 8 5
492. 20 c. violet 65 5
493. 25 c. red 45 5
494. 35 c. green 55 5
495. 40 c. mauve 55 5
496. 50 c. blue 45 5
497. 60 c. magenta .. .. 1·75 5
498. 70 c. chestnut .. .. 1·25 5
499. 75 c. violet .. .. 2·00 5
500. 75 c. brown .. .. 6·50 5
501. **68.** 10 f. sepia .. .. 13·00 2·75
502. 20 f. green .. .. 70·00 3·25
503a. 50 f. purple .. .. 2·50 2·10
564a. 100 f. lake .. .. 6·50 6·00

1929. Laying of first Stone towards Restoration of Orval Abbey. Nos. 461/9 optd. with crown over ornamental letter "L" and **19-8-29.**
543. 5 c.+5 c. red and gold ..
544. 25 c.+5 c. violet & gold ..
545. 35 c.+10 c. green.. ..
546. 60 c.+15 c. brown
547. 1 f. 75 c.+25 c. blue
548. 2 f.+40 c. purple
549. 3 f.+1 f. red
550. 5 f.+5 f. lake
551. 10 f.+10 f. sepia
Set of 9 .. .. £425 £400

DESIGNS—HORIZ. 5 c. Waterfall at Coo. 60 c. Promenade d'Orleans, Spa. 1 f. 75, Antwerp Harbour. VERT. 25 c. Bayard Rock, Dinant. 5 f. Canal and Belfry, Bruges.
69. Menin Gate, Ypres.

1929. Anti-T.B. Fund.
552. – 5 c.+5 c. brown .. 12 12
553. – 25 c.+15 c. grey .. 45 35
554. **69.** 35 c.+10 c. green .. 70 55
555. – 60 c.+15 c. lake .. 30 8
556. – 1 f. 75+25 c. blue .. 3·00 2·50
557. – 5 f.+5 f. purple .. 20·00 15·00

71. Paul Rubens.

72. Zenobe Gramme.

1930. Antwerp and Liege Exns.
558. **71.** 35 c. green 55 12
559. **72.** 35 c. green 55 12

73. Ostend.

74. Leopold II by Jef Lempoels.

1930. Air.
560. **73.** 50 c. blue 30 10
561. – 1 f. 50 brn. (St. Hubert) 1·60 1·00
562. – 2 f. green (Namur) .. 1·50 25
563. – 5 f. claret (Brussels) .. 2·00 40
564. – 5 f. violet (Brussels) .. 20·00 17·00

1930. Independence Cent.
565. – 60 c. purple 12 5
566. **74.** 1 f. red .. .. 2·00 90
567. – 1 f. 75 blue .. .. 4·25 65
PORTRAITS: 60 c. "Leopold I" by Lievin de Winne. 1 f. 75 King Albert I.

1930. "B.I.T." Congress. Nos. 565/7 optd. **B.I.T. OCT. 1930.**
569. 60 c. purple .. .. 1·10 1·00
570. 1 f. red .. .. 5·50 3·50
571. 1 f. 75 blue .. .. 11·00 8·50

76. Wynendaele.

77. Gaesbeek.

1930. Anti-T.B. Fund.
572. – 10 c.+5 c. mauve .. 10 8
573. **76.** 25 c.+15 c. sepia .. 30 20
574. – 40 c.+10 c. purple .. 35 30
575. – 70 c.+15 c. slate .. 20 10
576. – 1 f.+25 c. red .. .. 2·00 1·75
577. – 1 f. 75+25 c. blue .. 2·00 1·40
578. **77.** 5 f.+5 f. green.. .. 19·00 15·00
DESIGNS: 10 c. Bornhem. 40 c. Beloeil. 70 c. Oydonck. 1 f. Ghent. 1 f. 75, Bouillon.

1931. Surch.
579. **67.** 2 c. on 3 c. brown .. 8 5

1931. Surch. **BELGIQUE 1931 BELGIE 10c.**
580. **67.** 10 c. on 60 c. magenta 40 5
See note below No. 480.

78.

Albert I.

79.

1931.
582. **78.** 75 c. brn. (18×22 mm.) 40 5
583. 1 f. lake (21×23½ mm.) 50 5
584. **79.** 1 f. 25 black 55 10
585. 1 f. 50 purple 95 8
586. 1 f. 75 blue 70 5
587. 2 f. brown .. .. 1·10 5
588. 2 f. 45 violet .. .. 1·50 10
589. 2 f. 50 sepia .. .. 14·00 10
590. 5 f. green .. .. 11·00 20
591. 10 f. claret .. .. 30·00 2·75

81. Queen Elisabeth. 82. Reaper. 83. Mercury.

1931. Anti-T.B. Fund.
593. 81. 10 c.+5 c. brown 15 15
594. 25 c.+15 c. violet 75 65
595. 50 c.+10 c. green 70 45
596. 75 c.+15 c. sepia 40 8
597. 1 f.+25 c. lake 4·25 3·75
598. 1 f. 75+25 c. blue 3·75 1·75
599. 5 f.+5 f. purple 35·00 32·00

1932. Surch. **BELGIQUE 1932. BELGIE 10 c.**
600. 67. 10 c. on 40 c. mauve 2·40 15
601. 10 c. on 70 c. chestnut 1 90 15
See Note below No. 480.

1932.
602. 82. 2 c. green 20 20
603. 83. 5 c. red 10 5
604. 82. 10 c. green 25 5
605. 83. 20 c. lilac 70 5
606. 82. 25 c. red 55 5
607. 83. 35 c. green 4·00 5

84. Cardinal Mercier. 85.

1932. Cardinal Mercier Monument Fund.
609. 84. 10 c.+10 c. purple 20 20
610. 50 c.+30 c. mauve 1·50 70
611. 75 c.+25 c. brown 1·25 35
612. 1 f.+2 f. red 4·50 4·00
613. – 1 f. 75+75 c. blue 45·00 43·00
614. – 2 f. 50+2 f. 50 brown 45·00 40·00
615. – 3 f.+4 f. 50 green 45·00 40·00
616. – 5 f.+20 f. purple 50·00 45·00
617. – 10 f.+40 f. claret £110 £100
DESIGNS: 1 f. 75, 3 f. Mercier protecting refugees at Malines. 2 f. 50, 5 f. Mercier with busts of Aristotle and Thomas Aquinas. 10 f. Mercier when Professor at Louvain University.

1932. Infantry Memorial.
618. 85. 75 c.+3 f. 25 red-brn. 30·00 27·00
619. 1 f. 75+4 f. 25 blue 30·00 27·00

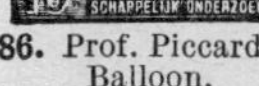

86. Prof. Piccard's Balloon. 88. Hulpe-Waterloo Sanatorium.

1932. Scientific Research Fund.
621. 86. 75 c. brown 4·50 8
622. 1 f. 75 blue 8·50 65
623. 2 f. 50 violet 8·50 3·00

1932. Anti-T.B. Fund.
624. 88. 10 c.+5 c. purple 15 15
625. 25 c.+15 c. claret 70 55
626. 50 c.+10 c. red-brown 70 40
627. 75 c.+15 c. brown 70 10
628. 1 f.+25 c. lake 7·50 6·50
629. 1 f. 75+25 c. blue 6·00 5·00
630. 5 f.+5 f. green 65·00 55·00

1933. Lion type surch. **BELGIQUE 1933 BELGIE 10 c.**
631. 67. 10 c. on 40 c. mauve 9·00 1·40
632. 10 c. on 70 c. chestnut 5·00 35
See note below No. 480.

90. The Transept. 93. Anti-T.B. Symbol.

1933. Orval Abbey Restoration Fund. Inscr. "ORVAL".
633. – 5 c.+5 c. yellow-green 34·00 29·00
634. – 10 c.+15 c. dp. green 27·00 23·00
635. – 25 c.+15 c. brown 27·00 23·00
636. 90. 50 c.+25 c. lake 27·00 23·00
637. – 75 c.+50 c. dp. green 27·00 23·00
638. – 1 f.+1 f. 25 lake 27·00 23·00
639. – 1 f. 25+1 f. 75 sepia 27·00 23·00
640. – 1 f. 75+2 f. 75 blue 34·00 32·00
641. – 2 f.+3 f. mauve 29·00 26·00
642. – 2 f. 50+5 f. chocolate 29·00 26·00
643. – 5 f.+20 f. purple 29·00 26·00
644. – 10 f.+40 f. blue £145 £135
DESIGNS—VERT. 10 c. Abbey Ruins. 75 c. Belfry, new abbey. 1 f. Fountain, new abbey. HORIZ. 5 c. The old abbey. 25 c. Guests' Courtyard, new abbey. 1 f. 25 Cloister, new abbey. 1 f. 75 Foundation of Orval Abbey in 1131. 2 f. Restoration of the abbey, XVI and XVII centuries. 2 f. 50 Orval Abbey, XVIII century. 5 f. Prince Leopold laying foundation stone of new abbey. 10 f. The Virgin Mary (30×45 mm.).

1933. Anti-tuberculosis Fund.
646. 93. 10 c.+5 c. grey 30 30
647. 25 c.+15 c. mauve 1·50 1·10
648. 50 c.+10 c. chestnut 1·25 70
649. 75 c.+15 c. sepia 6·50 12
650. 1 f.+25 c. claret 7·00 6·00
651. 1 f. 75+25 c. blue 5·50 4·75
652. 5 f.+5 f. purple 90·00 75·00

1934. Lion type surch. **BELGIQUE 1934 BELGIE 10 c.**
653. 67. 10 c. on 40 c. mauve 4·50 20
See note below No. 480.

1934. King Albert's Mourning stamp.
654. 78. 75 c. black 35 5

94. Peter Benoit. 95. Brussels Palace.

1934. Benoit Centenary Memorial Fund.
658. 94. 75 c.+25 c. brown 5·50 3·75

1934. International Exhibition, Brussels.
659. – 35 c. green 1·10 5
660. 95. 1 f. red 1·50 8
661. – 1 f. 50 brown 2·50 60
662. – 1 f. 75 blue 6·00 8
DESIGNS: 35 c. Congo Palace. 1 f. 50, Old Brussels. 1 f. 75, Grand Palace of the Belgian section.

96. King Leopold III. 97. King Leopold III.

1934. War Invalids' Fund. (a) Size 18×22 mm. (b) Size 21 × 24 mm.
(i) Exhibition Issue.
663. 96. 75 c.+25 c. green (a) 15·00 11·00
664. 1 f.+25 c. purple (b) 13·00 9·00
(ii) Ordinary postage stamps.
665. 96. 75 c.+25 c. purple (a) 85 70
666. 1 f.+25 c. red (b) 6·50 5·00

1934.
667. 96. 70 c. olive-green 25 5
668. 75 c. brown 80 5
669. 97. 1 f. red 5·00 12

ILLUSTRATIONS
British Commonwealth and all overprints and surcharges are FULL SIZE. Foreign Countries have been reduced to ¾-LINEAR.

98. Health Crusader.

1934. Anti-tuberculosis Fund. Cross in red.
670. 98. 10 c.+5 c. black 15 15
671. 20 c.+15 c. brown 85 75
672. 50 c.+10 c. green 85 65
673. 75 c.+15 c. dull purple 50 10
674. 1 f.+25 c. red 5·50 4·50
675. 1 f. 75+25 c. blue 5·00 4·00
676. 5 f.+5 f. purple 80·00 70·00

99. The Royal Children.

1935. Queen Astrid's Appeal.
680. 99. 35 c.+15 c. green 50 30
681. 70 c.+30 c. red 50 30
682. 1 f. 75+50 c. blue 3·00 2·50

100. "Mail-diligence." 102. Queen Astrid.

1935. Brussels Int. Exn.
683. 100. 10 c.+10 c. olive 70 55
684. 25 c.+25 c. brown 2·00 1·60
685. 35 c.+25 c. green 2·25 1·90

1935. Air. Surch. thus **1 Fr. 1 Fr.** × ×
686. 73. 1 f. on 1 f. 50 brown 25 20
687. 4 f. on 5 f. claret 6·00 1·75

1935. Death of Queen Astrid. Mourning stamps.
713. 102. 70 c.+5 c. black 8 5

1935. Anti-Tuberculosis Fund. Black borders.
714. 102. 10 c.+5 c. olive 5 5
715. 25 c.+15 c. brown 15 12
716. 35 c.+5 c. green 15 12
717. 50 c.+10 c. magenta 35 20
718. 1 f.+25 c. red 95 70
719. 1 f. 75+25 c. blue 3·00 1·60
720. 2 f. 45+55 c. violet 3·25 2·40

103. State arms. 104. 105. King Leopold III.

1936.
727. 103. 2 c. green 5 5
728. 5 c. orange 5 5
729. 10 c. olive 5 5
730. 15 c. blue 5 5
731. 20 c. violet 5 5
732. 25 c. red 5 5
733. 25 c. yellow 5 5
734. 30 c. brown 10 5
735. 35 c. green 5 5
736. 40 c. lilac 25 5
737. 50 c. blue 20 5
738. 60 c. grey 15 5
739. 65 c. mauve 35 5
740. 70 c. green 15 5
741. 75 c. mauve 50 5
742. 80 c. green 4·25 20
743. 90 c. violet 20 5
744. 1 f. brown 30 5

1936. Various frames.
(a) Size 17½ × 22 mm.
745. 104. 70 c. brown 35 5
746. 75 c. olive 30 5
747. 1 f. red 5 5
(b) Size 21 × 24 mm.
748. 104. 1 f. red 40 5
749. 1 f. 20 brown 70 5
750. 1 f. 50 lilac 35 5
751. 1 f. 75 blue 10 8
752. 1 f. 75 red 35 5
753. 2 f. violet 40 12
754. 2 f. 25 myrtle 20 5
755. 2 f. 50 vermilion 5·00 5
756. 3 f. 25 brown 20 5
757. 5 f. green 1·50 12

1936.
760. 105. 1 f. 50 mauve 30 5
761. 1 f. 75 blue 15 5
762. 2 f. violet 40 5
763. 2 f. 25 violet 25 5
764. 2 f. 45 black 27·00 10
765. 2 f. 50 black 2·25 5
770. 3 f. brown 1·10 5
766. 3 f. 25 brown 25 5
771. 4 f. blue 2·25 8
767. 5 f. green 1·40 10
772. 6 f. red 5·00 5
768. 10 f. purple 85 5
769. 20 f. red 1·40 5

108. Prince Baudouin. 109. Queen Astrid and Prince Baudouin.

1936. Anti-Tuberculosis Fund.
777. 108. 10 c.+5 c. brown 5 5
778. 25 c.+5 c. violet 15 10
779. 35 c.+5 c. green 15 10
780. 50 c.+5 c. chocolate 20 12
781. 70 c.+5 c. olive 8 5
782. 1 f.+25 c. red 70 35
783. 1 f. 75+25 c. blue 90 40
784. 2 f. 45+2 f. 55 purple 4·00 3·25

1937. Stamp of 1929 surcharged **BELGIQUE 1937 BELGIE 10 c.**
785. 67. 10 c. on 40 c. mauve 25 10
See note below No. 480.

1937. International Stamp Day.
786. 108. 2 f. 45 c.+2 f. 55 c. slate 1·25 1·00

1937. Queen Astrid Public Utility Fund.
787. 109. 10 c.+5 c. purple 5 5
788. 25 c.+5 c. olive 12 10
789. 35 c.+5 c. green 12 10
790. 50 c.+5 c. violet 30 20
791. 70 c.+5 c. black 15 8
792. 1 f.+25 c. red 70 40
793. 1 f. 75 c.+25 c. blue 1·25 60
794. 2 f. 45 c.+1 f. 55 c. brown 3·50 1·90

119 Queen Elisabeth. 111. Princess Josephine Charlotte.

1937. Eugene Ysaye Memorial Fund.
795. 110. 70 c.+5 c. black 25 8
796. 1 f. 75+25 c. blue 50 35

1937. Anti-Tuberculosis Fund.
798. 111. 10 c.+5 c. green 5 5
799. 25 c.+5 c. brown 15 10
800. 35 c.+5 c. green 15 10
801. 50 c.+5 c. olive 20 15
802. 70 c.+5 c. maroon 20 5
803. 1 f. +25 c. red 60 35
804. 1 f. 75+25 c. blue 80 40
805. 2 f. 45+2 f. 55 purple 4·25 3·00

112. King Leopold.

1938. Aeronautical Propaganda.
810. 112. 10 c.+5 c. maroon 8 8
811. 35 c.+5 c. green 20 15
812. 70 c.+5 c. black 55 15
813. 1 f. 75+25 c. blue 1·60 1·10
814. 2 f. 45+2 f. 55 violet 3·25 2·75

113. Basilica of the Sacred Heart, Koekelberg.

DESIGNS — HORIZ. 35 c., 1 f. and 2 f. 45c. Front of Basilica. VERT. 5 f. Nave of Basilica.

1938. Building (Completion) Fund.
815. 113. 10 c.+5 c. brown 5 5
816. – 35 c.+5 c. green 10 8
817. 113. 70 c.+5 c. grey 20 5
818. – 1 f.+25 c. red 65 40
819. 113. 1 f. 75+25 c. blue 70 50
820. – 2 f. 45+2 f. 55 claret 2·75 2·40
821. – 5 f.+5 f. green 14·00 10·00

1938. Surch. in figures and bars.
823. 105. 2 f. 50 on 2 f. 45 black 15·00 10

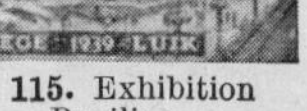

115. Exhibition Pavilion. 116. Prince Albert of Liege.

1938. Int. Exhibition, Liege (1939). Inscr. "LIEGE 1939 LUIK".
824. – 35 c. green 12 5
825. 115. 1 f. red 75 8
826. – 1 f. 50 brown 1·60 20
827. – 1 f. 75 blue 1·75 5
DESIGNS—VERT. 35 c. view of Liege. HORIZ. 1 f. 50, R. Meuse at Liege. 1 f. 75, Albert Canal and King Albert.

1938. Koekelberg Basilica Fund. Surch.
828. – 40 c. on 35 c.+5 c. grn. (No. 816) 20 15
829. 113. 75 c. on 70 c.+5 c. grey 25 12

830. – 2 f. 50+2 f. 50 on 2 f. 45+2 f. 55, claret (No. 820) .. .. 5·50 5·00

1938. Anti-Tuberculosis Fund.
831. 116. 10 c.+5 c. brown .. 5 5
832. 30 c.+5 c. purple .. 12 10
833. 40 c.+5 c. olive .. 20 15
834. 75 c.+5 c. grey .. 15 8
835. 1 f.+25 c. red .. 70 40
836. 1 f. 75+25 c. blue .. 70 40
837. 2 f. 50+2 f. 50 green 4·25 3·25
838. 5 f.+5 f. maroon .. 12·00 7·00

117. King Leopold and Royal Children.

1939. Int. Red Cross Society. 75th Anniv.
839. – 10 c.+5 c. brown .. 5 5
840. – 30 c.+5 c. claret .. 20 15
841. – 40 c.+5 c. olive .. 12 10
842. 117. 75 c.+5 c. black .. 50 8
843. – 1 f.+25 c. red .. 2·10 85
844. 117. 1 f. 75+25 c. blue .. 90 65
845. – 2 f. 50+2 f. 50 violet 1·50 1·25
846. – 5 f.+5 f. green .. 5·50 3·75
DESIGNS—VERT. 10 c. H. Dunant. 30 c. Florence Nightingale. 40 c. and 1 f. Queen Elisabeth and Royal children. 2 f. 50 Queen Astrid. HORIZ. 5 f. Queen Elisabeth and wounded soldier (larger).

120. Rubens' House after engraving by Harrewijn. 122. Portrait by Memling.

1939. Rubens' House Restoration Fund. Reproductions of Rubens' works, etc.
847. 120. 10 c.+5 c. brown .. 8 5
848. – 40 c.+5 c. maroon .. 20 15
849. – 75 c.+5 c. olive .. 75 20
850. – 1 f.+25 c. red .. 2·10 1·10
851. – 1 f. 50+25 c. brown .. 2·25 1·25
852. – 1 f. 75+25 c. blue .. 2·50 1·50
853. – 2 f. 50+2 f. 50 purple 12·00 8·00
854. – 5 f.+5 f. grey .. 15·00 10·00
DESIGNS—As T 120, VERT. 40 c. Rubens' sons. 1 f. Rubens' second wife and children. 1 f. 50, Rubens and his first wife. 1 f. 75, Rubens after engraving by Pontius. 2 f. 50, "Chapeau de paille". (35×45 mm.). "Descent from the Cross". HORIZ. 75 c. Arcade of Rubens' house.

1939. Exn. of Memling's Paintings, Bruges.
855. 122. 75 c.+75 c. olive .. 2·25 1·50

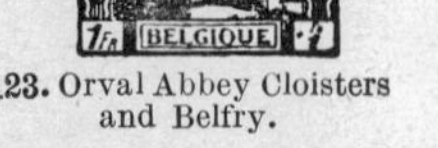

123. Orval Abbey Cloisters and Belfry. 125. Thuin.

1939. Orval Abbey Restoration Fund. Inscr. "ORVAL".
861. – 75 c.+75 c. olive .. 2·10 2·00
862. 123. 1 f.+1 f. red .. 1·40 1·25
863. – 1 f. 50+1 f. 50 brown 1·40 1·25
864. – 1 f. 75+1 f. 75 blue .. 1·40 1·25
865. – 2 f. 50+2 f. 50 mauve 7·50 5·00
866. – 5 f.+5 f. maroon .. 7·50 5·00
DESIGNS—VERT. 75 c. Monks in laboratory. HORIZ. 1 f. 50, Monks harvesting. 1 f. 75, Aerial view of Orval Abbey. 2 f. 50, Cardinal Van Roey, Statue of the Madonna and Abbot of Orval. 5 f. Kings Albert and Leopold III and shrine (35×45 mm.).

1939. Anti-Tuberculosis Fund. Belfries.
868. – 10 c.+5 c. olive .. 5 5
869. 125. 30 c.+5 c. brown .. 12 12
870. – 40 c.+5 c. purple .. 15 15
871. – 75 c.+5 c. grey .. 15 5
872. – 1 f.+25 c. red .. 55 45
873. – 1 f. 75+25 c. blue .. 70 55
874. – 2 f. 50+2 f. 50 brown 6·00 5·00
875. – 5 f.+5 f. violet .. 8·00 6·50
DESIGNS—As T 125: 10 c. Bruges. 40 c. Lier. 75 c. Mons. LARGER (21½×34 mm.); 1 f. Furnes. 1 f. 74, Namur. 2 f. 50, Alost. 5 f. Tournai.

126. Arms of Mons. 127. Painting.

128. Monks studying Plans of Orval Abbey.

1940. Winter Relief Fund.
901. 126. 10 c.+5 c. black, red and green 5 5
902. – 30 c.+5 c. green, black, red and yellow .. 12 5
903. – 40 c.+10 c. brn., red, blue and black .. 8 5
904. – 50 c.+10 c. lilac, blue, red and yellow .. 10 5
905. – 75 c.+15 c. violet, blk., red and yellow .. 8 5
906. – 1 f.+25 c. red, orange, green and black .. 30 20
907. – 1 f. 75 c.+50 c. blue, red, yellow & black 35 25
908. – 2 f. 50 c.+2 f. 50 c. olive, red & black .. 1·10 1·00
909. – 5 f.+5 f. purple, red, yellow and black .. 1·40 1·25
DESIGNS: 30 c. to 5 f. Arms of Ghent, Arlon, Bruges, Namur, Hasselt, Brussels, Antwerp, and Liege, respectively.

1941. Orval Abbey Restoration Fund.
935. 127. 10 c.+15 c. brown .. 40 30
936. – 30 c.+30 c. grey .. 40 30
937. – 40 c.+60 c. brown .. 40 30
938. – 50 c.+65 c. violet .. 40 30
939. – 75 c.+1 f. mauve .. 40 30
940. – 1 f.+1 f. 50 c. red .. 40 30
941. 127. 1 f. 25 c.+1 f. 75 c. grn. 40 30
942. – 1 f. 75 c.+2 f. 50 c. bl. 40 30
943. – 2 f.+3 f. 50 c. mauve .. 40 30
944. – 2 f. 50 c.+4 f. 50 c. brn. 40 30
945. – 3 f.+5 f. olive .. 40 30
946. 128. 5 f.+10 f. black .. 5·00 3·75
DESIGNS: 30 c., 1 f., 2 f. 50 c. Sculpture. 40 c., 2 f. Goldsmiths (Monks carrying candlesticks and cross). 50 c., 1 f. 75 c. Stained glass (Monks at prayer). 75 c., 3 f. Sacred music.

1941. Surch.
955. 103. 10 c. on 30 c. brown .. 5 5
956. 10 c. on 40 c. lilac .. 5 5
957. 104. 10 c. on 70 c. brown .. 5 5
958. 50 c. on 75 c. olive .. 30 5
959. 105. 2 f. 25 on 2 f. 50 black 50 15

129. Maria Theresa. 130. St. Martin, Dinant.

1941. Soldiers' Families Relief Fund.
960. 129. 10 c.+5 c. black .. 5 5
961. – 35 c.+5 c. green .. 5 5
962. – 50 c.+10 c. brown .. 5 5
963. – 60 c.+10 c. violet .. 5 5
964. – 1 f.+15 c. red .. 5 5
965. – 1 f. 50+1 f. mauve .. 25 20
966. – 1 f. 75+1 f. 75 blue .. 25 20
967. – 2 f. 25+2 f. 25 brown 30 25
968. – 3 f. 25+3 f. 25 brown 35 35
969. – 5 f.+5 f. green .. 35 35
PORTRAITS: 35 c. to 5 f. Charles of Lorraine, Margaret of Parma, Charles V, Johanna of Castile, Philip the Good, Margaret of Austria, Charles the Bold, Archduke Albert and Archduchess Isabella respectively.

1941. Winter Relief Fund. Statues.
970. 130. 10 c.+5 c. brown .. 5 5
971. – 35 c.+5 c. green .. 8 8
972. – 50 c.+10 c. violet .. 8 8
973. – 60 c.+10 c. brown .. 8 8
974. – 1 f.+15 c. red .. 8 8
975. – 1 f. 50+25 c. green .. 25 20
976. – 1 f. 75+50 c. blue .. 30 20
977. – 2 f. 25+2 f. 25 mauve 30 25
978. – 3 f. 25+3 f. 25 brown 30 30
979. – 5 f.+5 f. grn. (larger) 35 35
DESIGNS: (Statues of St. Martin in churches at)—Dinant (10 c., 1 f. 50): Lennick, St. Quentin (35 c., 1 f.); Beck, Limburg (50 c., 3 f. 25); Dave on the Meuse (60 c., 2 f. 25); Hal, Brabant (1 f. 75); St. Trond (5 f.) (35×33 mm.).

132. Mercator. 133. Prisoner writing Letter.

1942. Anti-Tuberculosis Fund. Portraits.
986. – 10 c.+5 c. brown .. 5 5
987. – 35 c.+5 c. green .. 5 5
988. – 50 c.+10 c. brown .. 5 5
989. – 60 c.+10 c. green .. 5 5
990. – 1 f.+15 c. red .. 5 5
991. 132. 1 f. 75+50 c. blue .. 20 20
992. – 3 f. 25+3 f. 25 claret 15 15
993. – 5 f.+5 f. violet .. 20 20
994. – 10 f.+30 f. brown .. 1·10 1·10
DESIGNS: (Portraits of scientists)—Bolland (10 c.), Versale (35 c.), S. Stevin (50 c.), van Helmont (60 c.), Dodoens (1 f.), Oertell (3 f. 25), Juste Lipse (5 f.) and Plantin (10 f.). The 10 f. is larger (24½×28½ mm.).

1942. Prisoners of War Relief Fund.
1000. 133. 5 f.+45 f. grey .. 4·00 4·00

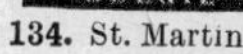

134. St. Martin. 135. St. Martin sharing his cloak,

1942. Winter Relief Fund.
1001. 134. 10 c.+5 c. orange .. 5 5
1002. – 35 c.+5 c. green .. 5 5
1003. – 50 c.+10 c. brown .. 8 8
1004. – 60 c.+10 c. black .. 8 8
1005. – 1 f.+15 c. red .. 8 5
1006. – 1 f. 50+25 c. green .. 25 20
1007. – 1 f. 75+50 c. blue .. 30 25
1008. – 2 f. 25+2 f. 25 brn. 30 25
1009. – 3 f. 25+3 f. 25 purple 30 30
1010. 135. 5 f.+10 f. brown .. 35 35
1011. 10 f.+20 f. brown and violet 75 75
1012. 10 f.+20 f. red & vio. 75 75
DESIGNS: 60 c., 2 f. 25, 3 f. 25, horiz.; others vert.

136. Soldiers and Vision of Home.

1943. Prisoners of War Relief Fund.
1013. 136. 1 f.+30 f. red .. 2·00 2·00
1014. – 1 f.+30 f. brown .. 2·00 2·00
DESIGN: No. 1014, Soldiers emptying parcel of books and vision of home.

137. Tiler.

DESIGNS: 35 c. Blacksmith. 50 c. Coppersmith. 60 c. Gunsmith. 1 f. Armourer. 1 f. 75 c. Goldsmith. 3 f. 25 c. Fishmonger. 5 f. Clockmaker.

1943. Anti-Tuberculosis Fund. Trades.
1015. 137. 10 c.+5 c. brown .. 5 5
1016. – 35 c.+5 c. green .. 5 5
1017. – 50 c.+10 c. brown .. 8 5
1018. – 60 c.+10 c. green .. 8 8
1019. – 1 f.+15 c. red .. 15 10
1020. – 1 f. 75+75 c. blue .. 35 30
1021. – 3 f. 25+3 f. 25 purple 45 45
1022. – 5 f.+25 f. violet .. 1·60 1·40

138. Ornamental Letter.

139. Ornamental Letters.

1943. Orval Abbey Restoration Fund. Designs showing single letters forming "ORVAL".
1023. 138. 50 c.+1 f. black .. 50 40
1024. – 60 c.+1 f. 90 violet 20 20
1025. – 1 f.+3 f. red .. 20 20
1026. – 1 f. 75+5 f. 25 blue 20 20
1027. – 3 f. 25+16 f. 75 green 30 25
1028. 139. 5 f.+30 f. brown .. 60 50

140. St. Leonard's Church, Leon, and St. Martin.

141. Church of Notre Dame, Hal, and St. Martin.

142. St. Martin and River Scheldt.

DESIGNS: (Various churches and statues of St. Martin sharing his cloak). As T. 140: HORIZ. 35 c. Dionle-Val. 50 c. Alost. 60 c. Liege. 3 f. 25, Lopnem. VERT. 1 f. Courtrai. 1 f. 75, Angre. As T 142: 10 f. brown Meuse landscape.

1943. Winter Relief Fund.
1029. 140. 10 c.+5 c. brown .. 5 5
1030. – 35 c.+5 c. green .. 8 5
1031. – 50 c.+15 c. green .. 8 5
1032. – 60 c.+20 c. purple .. 10 8
1033. – 1 f.+1 f. red .. 15 8
1034. – 1 f. 75+4 f. 25 blue 90 80
1035. – 3 f. 25+11 f. 75 mve. 90 80
1036. 141. 5 f.+25 f. blue .. 1·25 1·10
1037. 142. 10 f.+30 f. green .. 90 90
1038. – 10 f.+30 f. brown .. 90 90

143. "Daedalus and Icarus". 144. Jan van Eyck.

1944. Red Cross. Paintings of Van Dyck.
1039. 143. 35 c.+1 f. 65 green .. 30 25
1040. – 50 c.+2 f. 50 grey .. 30 25
1041. – 60 c.+3 f. 40 brown 30 25
1042. – 1 f.+5 f. red .. 30 25
1043. – 1 f. 75+8 f. 25 blue 35 30
1044. – 5 f.+30 f. brown .. 35 35
DESIGNS: 50 c. "The Good Samaritan". 60 c. from "Christ healing the Paralytic". 1 f. "Madonna and Child". 1 f. 75 Self-portrait of Van Dyck. 5 f. "St. Sebastian".

1944. Prisoners of War Relief Fund.
1045. 144. 10 c.+15 c. violet .. 25 20
1046. – 35 c.+15 c. green .. 25 20
1047. – 50 c.+25 c. brown .. 25 20
1048. – 60 c.+40 c. olive .. 25 20
1049. – 1 f.+50 c. red .. 25 20
1050. – 1 f. 75+4 f. 25 blue 25 20
1051. – 2 f. 25+8 f. 25 slate 45 45
1052. – 3 f. 25+11 f. 25 brn. 25 20
1053. – 5 f.+35 f. grey .. 50 40
PORTRAITS: 35 c. "Godefroid de Bouillon". 50 c. "Jacob van Maerlant". 60 c. "Jean Joses de Dinant". 1 f. "Jacob van Artevelde". 1 f. 75, "Charles Joseph de Ligne". 2 f. 25, "Andre Gretry". 3 f. 25, "Jan Morteus-Plantin". 5 f. "Ruusbroeck".

145. "Bayard and Four Sons of Aymon", Namur.

146. Lion Rampant.

1944. Anti-Tuberculosis Fund. Provincial legendary types.

1054.	145.	10 c.+5 c. brown	5	5
1055.	–	35 c.+5 c. green	5	5
1056.	–	50 c.+10 c. violet	5	5
1057.	–	60 c.+10 c. brown	5	5
1058.	–	1 f.+15 c. red	5	5
1059.	–	1 f. 75+2 f. 25 blue	25	20
1060.	–	3 f. 25+11 f. 75 grn.	25	20
1061.	–	5 f.+25 f. blue	30	25

DESIGNS—VERT. 35 c. "Brabo severing the giant's hand" Antwerp. 60 c. "Thyl Ulenspiegel" and "Nele", Flanders. 1 f. "St. George and the Dragon," Hainaut. 1 f. 75, "Genevieve of Brabant, with the Child and the Hind," Brabant. HORIZ. 50 c. "St. Hubert encounters the Hind with the Cross," Luxemburg. 3 f. 25, "Tchantches wrestling with the Saracen," Liege. 5 f. "St. Gertrude rescuing the Knight with the cards," Limbourg.

1944. Inscr. "BELGIQUE-BELGIE" or "BELGIE-BELGIQUE".

1062.	146.	5 c. brown	5	5
1063.		10 c. green	5	5
1064.		25 c. blue	5	5
1065.		35 c. brown	5	5
1066.		50 c. green	5	5
1067.		75 c. violet	5	5
1068.		1 f. red	5	5
1069.		1 f. 25 brown	10	8
1070.		1 f. 50 orange	20	10
1071.		1 f. 75 blue	8	5
1072.		2 f. blue	60	20
1073.		2 f. 75 mauve	10	5
1074.		3 f. claret	25	25
1075.		3 f. 50 grey	25	25
1076.		5 f. olive	2·40	1·60
1077.		10 f. black	60	35

1944. Overprinted with large **V.**

1078.	103.	2 c. green	5	5
1079.		15 c. blue	5	5
1080.		20 c. violet	5	5
1081.		60 c. grey	10	5

147. King Leopold III and "V".

148. War Victims.

149. Rebuilding Homes.

1944.

1082.	147.	1 f. red	12	5
1083.		1 f. 50 mauve	12	5
1084.		1 f. 75 blue	12	5
1085.		2 f. violet	70	5
1086.		2 f. 25 green	25	10
1087.		3 f. 25 brown	30	5
1088.		5 f. green	1·40	5

1945. War Victims' Relief Fund.

1114.	148.	1 f.+30 f. red	75	75
1115.	149.	1¾ f.+30 f. blue	75	75

Nos. 1114/5 measure 50×35 mm.

1945. Post Office Employers' Relief Fund.

1119.	148.	1 f.+9 f. red	15	15
1120.	149.	1 f.+9 f. red	15	15

150. Resister.

151. Group of Resisters.

1945. Prisoners of War Relief Fund.

1121.	150.	10 c.+15 c. orange	5	5
1122.	–	20 c.+20 c. violet	5	5
1123.	–	60 c.+25 c. brown	8	8
1124.	–	70 c.+30 c. green	8	8
1125.	150.	75 c.+50 c. brown	10	10
1126.	–	1 f.+75 c. green	12	12
1127.	–	1 f. 50+1 f. red	12	12
1128.	–	3 f. 50+3 f. 50 blue	70	65
1129.	151.	5 f.+40 f. brown	70	65

DESIGNS—VERT. 20 c., 1 f. Father and child. 60 c., 1 f. 50, Victim tied to stake. HORIZ. 70 c., 3 f. 50, Rifleman.

152. West Flanders.

153. Douglas "Skymaster".

1945. Anti-Tuberculosis Fund.

1130.	152.	10 c.+15 c. green	5	5
1131.	–	20 c.+20 c. red	8	8
1132.	–	60 c.+25 c. brown	8	8
1133.	–	70 c.+30 c. green	8	8
1134.	–	75 c.+50 c. brown	8	8
1135.	–	1 f.+75 c. violet	8	8
1136.	–	1 f. 50+1 f. red	8	8
1137.	–	3 f. 50+1 f. 50 blue	12	12
1138.	–	5 f.+45 f. mauve	1·10	1·10

ARMS DESIGNS—VERT. 20 c. to 5 f. Arms of Luxembourg, East Flanders, Namur, Limburg, Hainut, Antwerp, Liege and Brabant respectively.

1946. Air.

1165.	153.	6 f. blue	25	5
1166.		8 f. 50 claret	40	20
1167.		50 f. green	3·00	25
1168.		100 f. grey	5·50	35

1946. Surch. — 10% reducing the original value by 10%.

1171.	147.	"—10%" on 1 f. 50 mve.	30	5
1172.		"—10%" on 2 f. violet	1·00	20
1173.		"—10%" on 5 f. green	1·00	5

154. Paddle Steamer "Marie Henriette".

DESIGNS: 1 f. 35, M.V. "Prince Baudouin" (21½×18½ mm. or 21×17 mm.). 3 f. 15, Paddle Steamer "Diamant", formerly "Le Chemin de Fer".

1946. Ostend-Dover Mail-boat Service Cent.

1174.	–	1 f. 35 blue	15	5
1175.	154.	2 f. 25 green	30	5
1176.	–	3 f. 15 grey	30	8

155. Paratrooper.

1946. Air. Bastogne Monument Fund.

1177.	155.	17 f. 50+62 f. 50 grn.	80	75
1178.		17 f. 50+62 f. 50 pur.	80	75

156. Father Damien.

157. E. Vandervelde.

158. Francois Bovesse.

1946. Belgian Patriots.

(a) Father Damien.

1179.	156.	65 c.+75 c. blue	50	50
1180.	–	1 f. 35+2 f. brown	50	50
1181.	–	1 f. 75+18 f. lake	50	50

DESIGNS—HORIZ. 1 f. 35, Molokai Leper Colony. VERT. 1 f. 75, Damien's statue.

(b) Emile Vandervelde.

1182.	157.	65 c.+75 c. green	65	65
1183.	–	1 f. 35+2 f. blue	65	65
1184.	–	1 f. 75+18 f. red	75	75

DESIGNS—HORIZ. 1 f. 35, Vandervelde, miner, mother and child. VERT. 1 f. 75, Sower.

(c) Francois Bovesse.

1185.	–	65 c.+75 c. violet	50	50
1186.	158.	1 f. 35+2 f. brown	50	50
1187.	–	1 f. 75+18 f. red	60	60

DESIGNS—VERT. 65 c. Symbols of Patriotism and Learning. 1 f. 75, Draped memorial figures holding wreath and torch.

159. Pepin d'Herstal.

160. "Flight".

1946. War Relief Fund.

1188.	159.	75 c.+25 c. green	20	15
1189.	–	1 f.+50 c. violet	40	30
1190.	–	1 f. 50+1 f. purple	40	30
1191.	–	3 f. 50+1 f. 50 blue	50	40
1192.	–	5 f.+45 f. mauve	7·00	7·00
1194.	–	5 f.+45 f. orange	6·00	6·00

DESIGNS: 1 f. Charlemagne; 1 f. 50, Godfrey of Bouillon; 3 f. 50, Robert of Jerusalem; 5 f. Baudouin of Constantinople.

1946. Air.

1193.	160.	2 f.+8 f. violet	40	40

161. Malines.

162. Joseph Platcau.

1946. Anti-Tuberculosis Fund. No date.

1195.	161.	65 c.+35 c. red	20	15
1196.	–	90 c.+60 c. olive	20	15
1197.	–	1 f. 35+1 f. 15 green	20	15
1198.	–	3 f. 15+1 f. 85 blue	35	45
1199.	–	4 f. 50+45 f. 50 brn.	8·50	8·50

DESIGNS—(Arms and Industries): 90 c. Dinant. 1 f. 35, Ostend. 3 f. 15, Verviers. 4 f. 50, Louvain.

1947. Int. Film and Belgian Fine Arts Festival.

1200.	162.	3 f. 15 blue	30	5

163. Adrien de Gerlache.

164. Explorers landing from "Belgica".

1947. Belgian Antarctic Expedition. 50th Anniv.

1201.	163.	1 f. 35 red	20	5
1202.	164.	2 f. 25 grey	70	40

1947. War Relief Fund. Mediaeval Princes as T **159**.

1207.		65 c.+35 c. blue	25	25
1208.		90 c.+60 c. green	45	45
1209.		1 f. 35+1 f. 15 red	60	60
1210.		3 f. 15+1 f. 85 blue	75	75
1211.		20 f.+20 f. purple	19·00	17·00

DESIGNS: 65 c. John II, Duke of Brabant. 90 c. Philippe of Alsace. 1 f. 35, William the Good. 3 f. 15, Notger, Bishop of Liege. 20 f. Philip the Noble.

1947. Anti-Tuberculosis Fund. Arms designs as T **161**, but dated "1947".

1212.		65 c.+35 c. orange	25	20
1213.		90 c.+60 c. purple	25	20
1214.		1 f. 35+1 f. 15 brown	25	20
1215.		3 f. 15+1 f. 85 blue	50	45
1216.		20 f.+20 f. green	11·00	11·00

DESIGNS (Arms and Industries): 65 c. Nivelles. 90 c. St. Truiden. 1 f. 35, Charleroi. 3 f. 15, St. Nicholas. 20 f. Bouillon.

166. Chemical Industry.

168. Textile Machinery.

167. Antwerp Docks.

DESIGNS—As T **166**. 1 f. 35, 1 f. 75 green, Woman making lace. 1 f. 75 red, 2 f. 50, Agricultural produce. As T **167**: 6 f., 6 f. 30, Steel works.

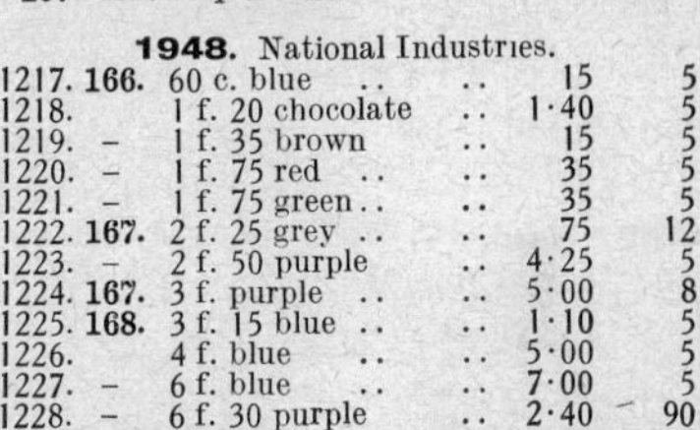

1948. National Industries.

1217.	166.	60 c. blue	15	5
1218.		1 f. 20 chocolate	1·40	5
1219.	–	1 f. 35 brown	15	5
1220.	–	1 f. 75 red	35	5
1221.	–	1 f. 75 green	35	5
1222.	167.	2 f. 25 grey	75	12
1223.	–	2 f. 50 purple	4·25	5
1224.	167.	3 f. purple	5·00	8
1225.	168.	3 f. 15 blue	1·10	5
1226.		4 f. blue	5·00	5
1227.	–	6 f. blue	7·00	5
1228.	–	6 f. 30 purple	2·40	90

169. St. Benedict and King Totila.

170. St. Bega and Chevremont Castle.

1948. Achel Abbey Fund. Inscr. "ACHEL".

1232.	169.	65 c.+65 c. brown	45	30
1233.	–	1 f. 35+1 f. 35 green	60	45
1234.	–	3 f. 15+2 f. 85 blue	2·00	1·50
1235.	–	10 f.+10 f. purple	10·00	9·00

DESIGNS—HORIZ. 1 f. 35, Achel Abbey. VERT. 3 f. 15, St. Benedict as Law-Giver. 10 f. Death of St. Benedict.

1948. Chevremont Abbey Fund. Inscr. "CHEVREMONT".

1236.	170.	65 c.+65 c. blue	45	30
1237.	–	1 f. 35+1 f. 35 red	60	40
1238.	–	3 f. 15+2 f. 85 blue	1·60	1·25
1239.	–	10 f.+10 f. brown	9·00	7·50

DESIGNS—HORIZ. 1 f. 35, Chevremont Basilica and Convent. VERT. 3 f. 15, Madonna of Chevremont and Chapel. 10 f. Monk and Madonna of Mt. Carmel.

171. Statue of Anseele.

172. Ghent and E. Anseele.

1948. Unveiling of E. Anseele Statue (Socialist).

1245.	171.	65 c.+35 c. red	90	60
1246.	172.	90 c.+60 c. grey	2·00	1·40
1247.	–	1 f. 35+1 f. 15 brn.	1·10	75
1248.	–	3 f. 15+1 f. 85 blue	3·75	3·50

DESIGNS: 1 f. 35, Statue and Ed. Anseele. 3 f. 15, Reverse side of statue.

173. " Liberty ". 174. " Resistance ".

1948. Antwerp and Liege Monuments Funds.
1253. **173.** 10 f.+10 f. green .. 12·00 11·00
1254. **174.** 10 f.+10 f. brown .. 7·00 7·00

175. Cross of Lorraine.

1948. Anti-Tuberculosis Fund.
1255. **175.** 20 c.+5 c. green .. 10 10
1256. 1 f. 20+30 c. purple 50 40
1257. 1 f. 75+25 c. red .. 60 50
1258. – 4 f.+3 f. 25 blue .. 3·25 3·25
1259. – 20 f.+20 f. green .. 16·00 16·00
DESIGNS—As T **159**: 4 f. Isabel of Austria. 20 f. Albert, Archduke of Austria.

1949. Surch. **1-1-49** at top, **31-XII-49** and value at bottom with posthorn in between. (a) Arms type.
1262. **103.** 5 c. on 15 c. blue .. 8 5
1263. 5 c. on 30 c. brown .. 8 5
1264. 5 c. on 40 c. lilac .. 8 5
1265. 20 c. on 70 c. green .. 10 10
1266. 20 c. on 75 c. mauve 5 5

(b) Anseele Statue.
1267. **171.** 10 c. on 65 c.+35 c. red .. .. .. 2·25 2·10
1268. **172.** 40 c. on 90 c.+60 c. grey .. 65 50
1269. – 80 c. on 1 f. 35+1 f. 15 brown .. 30 25
1270. – 1 f. 20 on 3 f. 15+1 f. 85 blue .. .. 1·25 1·10

177. King Leopold I. **178.** Forms of Postal Transport.

1949. Belgian Stamp Cent.
1271. **177.** 90 c. green (postage) 30 20
1272. 1 f. 75 brown .. 20
1273. 3 f. red .. 1·50 1·25
1274. 4 f. blue .. 3·00 35
1275. **178.** 50 f. brown (air) .. 9·50 4·25

179. St. Madeleine from " The Baptism of Christ ". **180.** Hemispheres and Allegorical Figure.

1949. Exhibition of Paintings by Gerard David, Bruges.
1276. **179.** 1 f. 75 brown .. 50 10

1949. U.P.U. 75th Anniv
1296. **180.** 4 f. blue .. .. 1·75 85

181. Guido Gezelle. **182.** Arnica.

1949. Gezelle (poet). 50th Death Anniv.
1297. **181.** 1 f. 75+75 c. green .. 1·25 1·10

1949. Anti-Tuberculosis and other Funds (a) Flowers.
1298. **182.** 20 c.+5 c. black, yellow and green .. 15 10
1299. – 65 c.+10 c. black, green and buff .. 60 50
1300. – 90 c.+10 c. black, blue and red .. 75 60
1301. – 1 f. 20+30 c. black, green, red and blue 90 75
FLOWERS: 65 c. Thistle. 90 c. Periwinkle 1 f. 20, Poppy.

(b) Portraits as T **159**.
1302. 1 f. 75+25 c. orange .. 45 10
1303. 3 f.+1 f. 50 claret .. 3·25 3·00
1304. 4 f.+2 f. blue .. 3·50 3·25
1305. 6 f.+3 f. brown .. 6·00 5·50
1306. 8 f.+4 f. green .. 6·00 6·00
PORTRAITS: 1 f. 75, Philip the Good. 3 f. Charles V. 4 f. Maria Christina. 6 f. Charles of Lorraine. 8 f. Maria Theresa.

183. Anglo-Belgian Monument, Hertain. **184.** Allegory of Saving.

1950. Liberation. 6th Anniv. Anglo-Belgian Union.
1307. – 80 c.+20 c. green .. 70 65
1308. – 2 f. 50+50 c. red .. 2·10 1·90
1309. **183.** 4 f.+2 f. blue .. 3·25 2·75
DESIGNS—HORIZ. 80 c. Arms of Great Britain and Belgium. 2 f. 50, British tanks at Tournai.

1950. National Savings Bank Cent.
1310. **184.** 1 f. 75 sepia 35 8

185. Hurdling. **186.** Helicopter leaving Melsbroeck.

1950. European Athletic Championships. Inscr. "HEYSEL 1950".
1311. **185.** 20 c.+5 c. emerald .. 15 12
1312. – 90 c.+10 c. purple .. 1·25 1·10
1313. – 1 f. 75+25 c. red .. 1·50 1·40
1314. – 4 f.+2 f. blue .. 12·00 11·00
1315. – 8 f.+4 f. green .. 14·00 13·00
DESIGNS—HORIZ. 1 f. 75, Relay racing. VERT. 90 c. Javelin throwing. 4 f. Pole vaulting. 8 f. Sprinting.

1950. Air. Inaug. of Helicopter Airmail Services and Aeronautical Fund.
1317. **186.** 7 f.+3 f. blue .. 1·60 1·60

187. Gentian. **188.** Sijsele Sanatorium.

1950. Anti-Tuberculosis and other Funds. Cross in red.
1326. **187.** 20 c.+5 c. blue, green and claret 12 12
1327. – 65 c.+10 c. green and brown 50 45
1328. – 90 c.+10 c. claret, yellow and green .. 60 60
1329. – 1 f. 20+30 c. blue and green 70 70
1330. **188.** 1 f. 75+25 c. red .. 50 35
1331. – 4 f.+2 f. blue .. 6·00 5·00
1332. – 8 f.+4 f. green .. 8·00 7·00
DESIGNS—Flowers as T **187**: 65 c. Rushes. 90 c. Foxglove. 1 f. 20, Sea Lavender. Sanatoria as T **188**: 4 f. Jauche (horiz.). 8 f. Tombeek (vert.).

189. The Belgian Lion. **190.** " Science ".

1951. (a) 17½×20½ mm.
1334. **189.** 2 c. brown 5 5
1335. 3 c. violet 5 5
1336. 5 c. lilac 5 5
1336a. 5 c. pink 5 5
1337. 10 c. orange 5 5
1338. 15 c. mauve 5 5
1333. 20 c. blue 15 5
1339. 20 c. lake 5 5
1340. 25 c. green 85 5
1341. 25 c. turquoise .. 5 5
1342. 30 c. grey 5 5
1343. 40 c. olive 15 5
1344. 50 c. blue 5 5
1345. 60 c. magenta .. 5 5
1346. 65. c maroon .. 7·00 5
1347. 75 c. lavender .. 15 5
1348. 80 c. emerald .. 50 5
1349. 90 c. blue 55 5
1359. 1 f. red (17½×22 mm.) 1·00 45
1350. 1 f. red 5 5
1351. 1 f. 50 olive-grey .. 5 5
1352. 2 f. emerald 20 5
1360. 2 f. green (17½×22 mm.) 10 5
1354. 2 f. 50 brown .. 8 5
1355. 3 f. magenta 8 5
1355a. 4 f. purple 12 5
1355b. 4 f. 50 blue 12 5
1355c. 5 f. purple 15 5

(b) 20½×24½ mm.
1356. **189.** 50 c. blue 30 5
1358. 60 c. purple .. 2·00 50
1357. 1 f. red 5 5

1951. U.N.E.S.C.O. Fund. Inscr. "UNESCO".
1365. **190.** 80 c.+20 c. green .. 70 55
1366. – 2 f. 50+50 c. choc. .. 5·50 5·00
1367. – 4 f.+2 f. blue .. 5·50 4·50
DESIGNS—HORIZ. 2 f. 50, "Education". VERT. 4 f. "Peace".

191. "Tipsy" Monoplane.

1951. Air. National Aero Club. 50th Anniv.
1368. – 6 f.+37 f. blue } 17·00 17·00
1369. **191.** 7 f. red }
DESIGN: 6 f.+37 f. Glider.

1951. Air.
1370. – 6 f. brown (glider) .. 2·00 5
1371. **191.** 7 f. green .. .. 2·40 30

192. Monument. **193.** Queen Elisabeth.

1951. Political Prisoners' National Monument Fund.
1372. **192.** 1 f. 75+25 c. brown 90 60
1373. – 4 f.+2 f. blue .. 9·00 8·00
1374. – 8 f.+4 f. green .. 10·00 8·00
DESIGNS—HORIZ. 4 f. Breendonk Fort. VERT. 8 f. Side view of monument.

1951. Queen Elisabeth Medical Foundation Fund.
1376. **193.** 90 c.+10 c. grey .. 55 40
1377. 1 f. 75+25 c. claret 1·25 45
1378. 3 f.+1 f. green .. 7·50 7·50
1379. 4 f.+2 f. blue .. 10·00 8·50
1380. 8 f.+4 f. sepia .. 11·00 10·00

194. Lorraine Cross and Dragon. **195.** Beersel Castle.

1951. Anti-Tuberculosis and other Funds.
1381. **194.** 20 c.+5 c. vermilion 8 8
1382. 65 c.+10 c. blue 20 15
1383. 90 c.+10 c. brown .. 30 20
1384. 1 f. 20+30 c. violet 50 80
1385. **195.** 1 f. 75+75 c. brown 50 8
1386. – 3 f.+1 f. green .. 4·75 4·25
1387. – 4 f.+2 f. blue .. 5·00 4·75
1388. – 8 f.+4 f. black .. 7·00 6·00
CASTLES—As T **195**—VERT. 3 f. Horst Castle. 8 f. Veves Castle. HORIZ. 4 f. Lavaux St. Anne Castle.

For stamps as T **194** but dated " 1952 " see Nos. 1516/23, and for those dated " 1953 " see Nos. 1507/14.

196. Consecration of the Basilica.

1952. Koekelberg Basilica Fund.
1389. – 1 f. 75+25 c. brown 50 20
1390. – 4 f.+2 f. blue .. 6·00 5·50
1391. **196.** 8 f.+4 f. purple .. 9·00 8·00
DESIGNS—VERT. 1 f. 75, Altar. 4 f. Exterior of Koekelberg Basilica.

197. King Baudouin. **198.** King Baudouin.

1952.
1393. **197.** 1 f. 50 grey 25 5
1394. 2 f. red 30 5
1395. 4 f. blue .. 2·25 8
1396. **198.** 50 f. purple .. .. 1·10 15
1397. 100 f. red .. .. 2·25 15

199. Francis of Taxis. **200.** A. Vermeylen.

1952. 13th U.P.U. Congress, Brussels. Portraits of Members of the House of Thurn and Taxis.
1398. **199.** 80 c. green 15 15
1399. – 1 f. 75 orange .. 12 5
1400. – 2 f. purple 35 8
1401. – 2 f. 50 red 50 25
1402. – 3 f. olive 50 10
1403. – 4 f. blue 50 8
1404. – 5 f. brown 80 30
1405. – 5 f. 75 violet .. 2·10 45
1406. – 8 f. black .. 5·00 45
1407. – 10 f. purple .. 5·00 45
1408. – 20 f. grey .. .. 13·00 6·00
1409. – 40 f.+10 f. blue-green 70·00 70·00
DESIGNS—VERT. 1 f. 75, John Baptist. 2 f. Leonard. 2 f. 50, Lamoral. 3 f. Leonard Francis. 4 f. Lamoral Claud. 5 f. Eugene Alexander. 5 f. 75, Anselm Francis. 8 f. Alexander Ferdinand. 10 f. Charles Anselm. 20 f. Charles Alexander. 40 f. Beaulieu Chateau.

1952. Culture Fund. Writers.
1410. **200.** 65 c.+30 c. lilac .. 95 75
1411. – 80 c.+40 c. green .. 95 75
1412. – 90 c.+45 c. olive .. 95 75
1413. – 1 f. 75+75 c. lake .. 1·25 75
1414. – 4 f.+2 f. blue .. 12·00 11·00
1415. – 8 f.+4 f. sepia .. 13·00 12·00
PORTRAITS: 80 c. K. van de Woestijne. 90 c. C. de Coster. 1 f. 75, M. Maeterlinck. 4 f. E. Verhaeren. 8 f. H. Conscience.

A 4 f. blue as No. 1414 and an 8 f. lake as No 1415 each se-tenant with a label showing a laurel wreath and bearing a premium " +9 fr." were put on sale by subscription only.

201. Arms, Malmedy. **202.** Dewe and Monument at Liege.

1952. Anti-Tuberculosis and other Funds. As T **194** but dated "1952" and designs as T **201**.
1416. **194.** 20 c.+5 c. brown .. 8 5
1417. 80 c.+20 c. green .. 20 15
1418. 1 f. 20+30 c. purple 45 25
1419. 1 f. 50+50 c. olive .. 40 25

1420. 201. 2 f. + 75 c. red .. 90 60
1421. – 3 f. + 1 f. 50 brown .. 7·00 6·50
1422. – 4 f. + 2 f. blue .. 6·00 5·50
1423. – 8 f. + 4 f. maroon .. 7·00 6·50
DESIGNS—HORIZ. 3 f. Ruins, Burgreuland VERT. 4 f. Dam, Eupen. 8 f. Saint and lion, St. Vith.

1953. Walthere Dewe Memorial Fund.
1435. 202. 2 f. + 1 f. lake .. 1·00 75

203. Princess Josephine Charlotte. 204. Fishing Vessels.

1953. Red Cross National Disaster Fund. Cross in red.
1436. 203. 80 c. + 20 c. green .. 55 40
1437. 1 f. 20 + 30 c. brown .. 55 40
1438. 2 f. + 50 c. lake .. 55 30
1439. 2 f. 50 + 50 c. red .. 6·00 5·50
1440. 4 f. + 1 f. blue .. 3·75 3·25
1441. 5 f. + 2 f. black .. 4·50 3·50

1953. Tourist Propaganda and Cultural Funds.
1442. 204. 80 c. + 20 c. green .. 45 30
1443. – 1 f. 20 + 30 c. brown .. 65 45
1444. – 2 f. + 50 c. sepia .. 65 45
1445. – 2 f. 50 + 50 c. magenta 5·00 4·00
1446. – 4 f. + 2 f. blue .. 8·00 7·00
1447. – 8 f. + 4 f. grey-green 9·50 8·00
DESIGNS—HORIZ. 1 f. 20, Bridge Bouillon. 2 f. Antwerp. VERT. 2 f. 50, Namur. 4 f. Ghent. 8 f. Freyr Rocks and River Meuse.

205. King Baudouin. 206.

1953.
(a) 22 × 24 mm.
1453. 205. 1 f. 50 black 10 5
1454. 2 f. red .. .. 9·50 5
1455. 2 f. green 10 5
1456. 2 f. 50 chestnut .. 20 5
1457. 3 f. purple 15 5
1458. 3 f. 50 green 15 5
1459. 4 f. blue 30 5
1460. 4 f. 50 brown .. 20 5
1461. 4 f. 50 red 40 5
1462. 5 f. violet .. .. 1·10 5
1463. 6 f. magenta 30 5
1464. 6 f. 50 grey .. .. 42·00 4·25
1465. 7 f. blue 25 5
1466. 7 f. 50 brown .. 35·00 5·50
1467. 8 f. grey-blue .. 40 5
1468. 8 f. 50 maroon .. 13·00 15
1469. 9 f. olive .. .. 35·00 35
1470. 12 f. turquoise .. 45 5
1471. 30 f. orange .. .. 1·25 8
(b) $17\frac{1}{2}$ × 22 mm.
1472. 205. 1 f. 50 black 10 5
1473. 2 f. 50 brown .. 3·00 2·25
1474. 3 f. mauve 25 5
1475. 3 f. 50 green 20 5
1476. 4 f. 50 brown .. 45 20
Nos. 1472/6 come from booklets and have one or two adjacent sides imperf.

1953. European Child Welfare Fund.
1482. 206. 80 c. + 20 c. green .. 1·50 1·25
1483. 2 f. 50 + 1 f. red .. 13·00 11·00
1484. 4 f. + 1 f. 50 blue .. 15·00 13·00

207. E. Malvoz.

208. King Albert Statue.

1953. Anti-Tuberculosis and other Funds. As T 194 but dated "1953" and portrait as T 207.
1507. 194. 20 c. + 5 c. blue .. 5 5
1508. 80 c. + 20 c. purple .. 20 15
1509. 1 f. 20 + 30 c. brown 30 25
1510. 1 f. 50 + 50 c. slate .. 35 30
1511. 207. 2 f. + 75 c. green .. 55 45
1512. – 3 f. + 1 f. 50 red .. 5·00 4·25
1513. – 4 f. + 2 f. blue .. 5·00 4·50
1514. – 8 f. + 4 f. brown .. 6·50 5·50
PORTRAITS—VERT. 3 f. C. Forlanini. 4 f. A. Calmette. HORIZ. 8 f. R. Koch.

1954. Surch. **20 c.** and **1-1-54** at top **31-XII-54** at bottom and bars in between.
1515. 189. 20 c. on 65 c. maroon 1·00 15
1516. 20 c. on 90 c. blue .. 1·00 15
See note below No. 480.

1954. King Albert Memorial Fund.
1520. 208. 2 f. + 50 c. chestnut .. 1·25 60
1521. – 4 f. + 2 f. blue .. 7·00 5·50
1522. – 9 f. + 4 f. 50 black .. 8·00 6·50
DESIGNS—HORIZ. 4 f. King Albert Memorial. VERT. 9 f. Marche-les-Dames Rocks and medallion portrait.

209. Monument. 210. Breendonk Camp and Fort.

1954. Political Prisoners' National Monument Fund.
1531. 209. 2 f. + 1 f. red .. 4·50 3·75
1532. 210. 4 f. + 2 f. brown .. 10·00 9·00
1533. – 9 f. + 4 f. 50 green .. 11·00 9·50
DESIGN—VERT. 9 f. As T 209 but viewed from different angle.

211. Entrance to Beguinal House.

DESIGNS—HORIZ. 2 f. River scene VERT. 4 f. Convent Buildings. 7 f. Cloisters. 8 f. Doorway. 9 f. Statue of our Lady of the Vineyard (larger 35 × 53 mm.).

1954. Beguinage of Bruges Restoration Fund.
1534. 211. 80 c. + 20 c. green .. 60 45
1535. – 2 f. + 1 f. red .. 5·00 2·40
1536. – 4 f. + 2 f. violet .. 8·00 6·50
1537. – 7 f. + 3 f. 50 purple .. 18·00 6·50
1538. 8 f. + 4 f. brown .. 17·00 40·00
1539. 9 f. + 4 f. 50 blue .. 21·00 19·00

212. Map of Europe and Rotary Symbol.

DESIGNS: Mermaid, "Mercury" and Rotary symbol. (80 c.) Rotary symbol and hemispheres (4 f.).

1954. 50th Anniv. of Rotary Int. and 5th Regional Conference, Ostend.
1540. 212. 20 c. red 8 5
1541. – 80 c. green 30 12
1542. – 4 f. blue .. .. 1·10 25

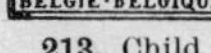

213. Child. 214. "The Blind Man and the Paralytic" (after Anto-Carte).

1954. Anti-T.B. and other Funds.
1543. 213. 20 c. + 5 c. green .. 10 8
1544. 80 c. + 20 c. black .. 25 20
1545. 1 f. 20 + 30 c. brown 30 25
1546. 1 f. 50 + 50 c. violet 35 30
1547. 214. 2 f. + 75 c. red .. 3·25 2·50
1548. 4 f. + 1 f. blue .. 9·00 7·50

215. Begonia and the Rabot.

DESIGNS—VERT. 2 f. 50, Azaleas and Chateau des Comtes. 4 f. Orchid and the "Three Towers".

1955. Ghent Flower Show.
1549. 215. 80 c. red 25 8
1550. – 2 f. 50 sepia .. 2·75 1·40
1551. – 4 f. lake .. 2·25 35

216. "Homage to Charles V" (A. De Vriendt). 217. "Charles V" (Titian).

1955. Emperor Charles V. Exn., Ghent.
1552. 216. 20 c. red 5 5
1553. 217. 2 f. green .. .. 1·00 5
1554. – 4 f. blue .. .. 2·75 60
DESIGN—As T 216. 4 f. "Abdication of Charles V" (L. Gallait).

218. Emile Verhaeren (after C. Montald). 219. "Textile Industry".

1955. Verhaeren (poet). Birth Cent.
1555. 218. 20 c. black 5 5

1955. 2nd Int. Textile Exn., Brussels.
1556. 219. 2 f. maroon 75 5

220. "The Foolish Virgin" (R. Wouters). 221. "The Departure of the Liege Volunteers in 1830" (Soubre).

1955. 3rd Biennial Sculpture Exn., Antwerp.
1557. 220. 1 f. 20 green 65 40
1558. 2 f. violet .. .. 1·10 5

1955. Liege Exn. 1830 Revolution. 125th Anniv.
1559. 221. 20 c. green 8 5
1560. 2 f. brown 65 5

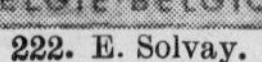

222. E. Solvay. 223. "The Joys of Spring".

224. E. Holboll. 225. Blood Donors' Emblem.

1955. Cultural Fund. Scientists.
1561. 222. 20 c. + 5 c. brown .. 8 5
1562. – 80 c. + 20 c. violet .. 35 30
1563. – 1 f. 20 + 30 c. indigo 50 45
1564. – 2 f. + 50 c. red .. 2·10 1·50
1565. – 3 f. + 1 f. green .. 5·00 4·75
1566. – 4 f. + 2 f. brown .. 5·00 4·75
PORTRAITS—VERT. 80 c. J. J. Dony. 2 f. L. H. Baekeland. 3 f. J. E. Lenoir. HORIZ. 1 f. 20 E. Walschaerts. 4 f. E. Fourcault and E. Gobbe.

1955. Anti-T.B. and other Funds.
1567. 223. 20 c. + 5 c. mauve .. 8 5
1568. 80 c. + 20 c. green .. 30 25
1569. 1 f. 20 + 30 c. brown 35 30
1570. 1 f. 50 + 50 c. violet 50 45
1571. 224. 2 f. + 50 c. red .. 3·00 2·25
1572. – 4 f. + 2 f. blue .. 6·00 5·00
1573. – 8 f. + 4 f. sepia .. 8·00 7·50
PORTRAITS—As T 244: 4 f. J. D. Rockefeller (philanthropist). 8 f. Sir R. W. Philip (physician).

1956. Blood Donors.
1574. 225. 2 f. red 35 5

226. Mozart when a Child.

DESIGN—VERT. As T 226.: 80 c. Palace of Charles de Lorraine, Brussels.

227. Queen Elisabeth and Mozart Sonata.

1956. Mozart. 200th Birth Anniv. Inscr. as in T 226.
1575. – 80 c. + 20 c. green .. 25 20
1576. 226. 2 f. + 1 f. purple .. 2·25 1·90
1577. 227. 4 f. + 2 f. lilac .. 4·00 3·50

228. 229. Queen Elisabeth Medallion (Courtens).

1956. "Scaldis" Exn. in Tournai, Ghent and Antwerp.
1578. 228. 2 f. blue 30 5

1956. Queen Elisabeth. 80th Birthday and Foundation Fund.
1579. 229. 80 c. + 20 c. green .. 35 30
1580. 2 f. + 1 f. lake .. 1·50 1·00
1581. 4 f. + 2 f. sepia .. 2·50 2·25

230. 231.

1956. Europa.
1582. 230. 2 f. green .. .. 1·40 5
1583. 4 f. violet .. .. 1·75 35

1956. Electrification of Brussels-Luxembourg Railway Line.
1584. 231. 2 f. blue 35 8

232. E. Anseele.

1956. Anseele (statesman) Birth Cent.
1588. 232. 20 c. purple 5 5

233. Ship. 234. Weighing a Baby.

1956. Anti-Tuberculosis and other Funds.
1589. 233. 20 c. + 5 c. brown .. 8 5
1590. 80 c. + 20 c. green .. 35 20
1591. 1 f. 20 + 30 c. purple 35 25
1592. 1 f. 50 + 50 c. slate .. 35 30
1593. 234. 2 f. + 50 c. green .. 1·00 60
1594. – 4 f. + 2 f. maroon .. 5·00 4·75
1595. – 8 f. + 4 f. red .. 5·00 4·75
DESIGNS—As T 234: HORIZ. 4 f. X-ray examination. VERT. 8 f. Convalescence and rehabilitation.

235. "Atomium" and Exhibition Emblem.

236. Emperor Maximilian I. with Messenger.

1957. Brussels Int. Exhibition, 1958.

1596. **235.**	2 f. red	.. ..	15	5
1597.	2 f. 50 green..	..	30	5
1598.	4 f violet	.. ..	30	8
1599.	5 f. maroon ..	..	70	40

1957. Stamp Day.

1603. **236.**	2 f. claret	.. ..	35	5

237. C. Plisnier and A. Rodenbach.

PORTRAITS: 80 c. E. Vliebergh and M. Wilmotte. 1 f. 20 P. Pastur and J. Hoste. 2 f. L. de Raet and J. Destree. 3 f. C. Meunier and C. Permeke. 4 f. L. Gevaert and E. Empain.

1957. Cultural Fund. Belgian Celebrities.

1604. **237.**	20 c.+5 c. violet	..	8	5
1605. –	80 c.+20 c. chestnut		20	15
1606. –	1 f. 20+30 c. sepia..		30	25
1607. –	2 f.+50 c. claret	..	75	60
1608. –	3 f.+1 f. green	..	1·75	1·60
1609. –	4 f.+2 f. blue	..	2·25	2·10

238. Sikorsky S58 Helicopter.

1957. Celebrating 100,000th Passenger carried by Belgian Helicopter Service.

1610. **238.**	4 f. blue, green & grey	60	35

239. Zeebrugge Harbour.

1957. Completion of Zeebrugge Harbour. 50th Anniv.

1611. **239.**	2 f. blue	.. ..	30	5

240. King Leopold I entering Brussels (after Simonau).

241. Scout and Guide Badges.

1957. Arrival of King Leopold I in Belgium. 126th Anniv.

1612. **240.**	20 c. grey-green	..	5	5
1613. –	2 f. mauve	..	50	10

DESIGN—HORIZ. 2 f. King Leopold I arriving at the frontier (after Wappers).

1957. Boy Scout Movement, 50th Anniv. and Lord Baden-Powell, Birth Cent.

1614. **241.**	80 c. brown ..	..	15	8
1615. –	4 f. green	.. ..	1·00	35

DESIGN—VERT. 4 f. Lord Baden-Powell.

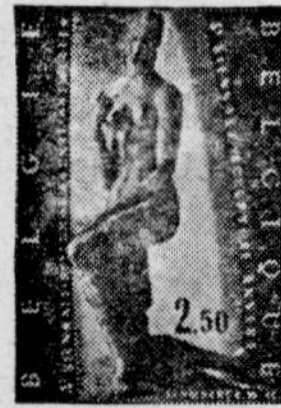

242. "Kneeling Woman" (after Lehmbruck).

243. "Agriculture and Industry".

1957. 4th Biennial Sculpture Exn., Antwerp.

1616. **242.**	2 f. 50 green..	..	95	60

1957. Europa.

1617. **243.**	2 f. purple	.. ..	40	8
1618.	4 f. blue	.. ..	55	30

244. Sledge-dog Team.

1957. Belgian Antarctic Expedition, 1957-58.

1619. **244.**	5 f.+2 f. 50 orange, brown and grey ..	1·60	1·60

245. General Patton's grave at Hamm.

246. Adolphe Max.

1957. General Patton Memorial Issue.

1621. **245.**	1 f.+50 c. black	..	50	45
1622. –	2 f. 50+50 c. green..		60	55
1623. –	3 f.+1 f. chestnut	..	1·50	1·25
1624. –	5 f.+2 f. 50 slate	..	3·50	3·00
1625. –	6 f.+3 f. red	..	5·00	4·75

DESIGNS—HORIZ. 2 f. 50, Patton Memorial project at Bastogne. 3 f. Gen. Patton decorating Brig.-General A. MacAuliffe. 6 f. (51 × 35½ mm.) Tanks in action. VERT. 5 f. General Patton.

1957. Burgomaster Adolphe Max (patriot). 18th Death Anniv.

1626. **246.**	2 f. 50+1 f. blue	..	1·10	1·00

247. Queen Elisabeth with Doctors Depage and Debaisieux at a surgical operation.

1957. "Edith Cavell-Marie Depage" and "St. Camille" Nursing Schools. 50th Anniv.

1627. **247.**	30 c. claret ..	..	20	5

248. "Carnival Kings of Fosses" (Namur).

249. "Infanta Isabella with Crossbow" (Brussels).

1957. Anti-Tuberculosis and other Funds. Provincial Legends.

1628. **248.**	30 c.+20 c. pur. & yell.	5	5
1629. –	1 f.+50 c. sepia & blue	20	15
1630. –	1 f. 50+50 c. grey & red	25	20
1631. –	2 f.+1 f. black & grn.	35	25
1632. **249.**	2 f. 50+1 f. green and mauve	60	45
1633. –	5 f.+2 f. black & blue	2·25	2·00
1634. –	6 f.+2 f. 50 lake & red	2·50	2·40

DESIGNS: As T **248**—HORIZ. 1 f. 50, "St. Remacle and the Wolf" (Liege). VERT. 1 f. "Op Signoorken" (Antwerp). 2 f. "The Long Man and the Pea Soup" (Limburg). As T **249**—HORIZ. 6 f. "Carnival Kings of Binche" (Hainaut). VERT. 5 f. "The Virgin with the Inkwell" (West Flanders).

250. Posthorn and Postillion's Badges.

1958. Postal Museum Day.

1635. **250.**	2 f. 50 grey ..	..	20	5

251. Benelux Gate.

DESIGNS — HORIZ. 1 f. Civil Engineering Pavilion. 1 f. 50, Belgian Congo and Ruanda – Urundi Pavilion. 2 f. 50, "Belgium, 1900". 3 f. Atomium. 5 f. (49 × 33½ mm.) Telexpo Pavilion.

1958. Inaug. of Brussels Int. Exhibition. Inscr. as in T **251**.

1636. **251.**	30 c.+20 c. sepia, chestnut and violet		8	5
1637. –	1 f.+50 c. pur., slate and emerald	..	12	10
1638. –	1 f. 50+50 c. red-vio. turquoise and grn.		15	15
1639. –	2 f. 50+1 f. red, blue and vermilion		25	25
1640. –	3 f.+1 f. 50 blue, blk. and red	.. ..	1·00	80
1641. –	5 f.+3 f. mve., black and blue	.. ..	1·40	1·00

252. Emblems of F.A.O.

1958. United Nations Commem.

1642. –	50 c. grey (postage)..		60	55
1643. **252.**	1 f. claret	.. ..	8	8
1644. –	1 f. 50 blue	.. ..	8	8
1645. –	2 f. slate-purple	..	45	45
1646. –	2 f. 50 green..	..	15	15
1647. –	3 f. turquoise	..	50	50
1648. –	5 f. mauve	..	20	20
1649. –	8 f. brown	..	60	60
1650. –	11 f. slate-lilac	..	90	85
1651. –	20 f. rose	..	1·10	1·00
1652. –	5 f. blue (air)	..	15	15
1653. –	6 f. green	..	50	50
1654. –	7 f. 50 violet	..	25	25
1655. –	8 f. sepia	..	25	25
1656. –	9 f. red	..	30	30
1657. –	10 f. brown ..	..	80	80

DESIGNS (Emblems and symbols)—HORIZ. 50 c. I.L.O. 2 f. 50, U.N.E.S.C.O. 3 f. U.N. Pavilion, Brussels Int. Exn. 6 f. World Meteorological Organization. 8 f. (No. 1649), Int. Monetary Fund. 8 f. (No. 1655), General Agreement on Tariffs and Trade. 10 f. Atomic Energy Agency. 11 f. W.H.O. 20 f. U.P.U. VERT. 1 f. 50, U.N.O. 2 f. World Bank. 5 f. (No. 1648), I.T.U. 5 f. (No. 1652), I.C.A.O. 7 f. 50, Protection of Refugees. 9 f. UNICEF.

253. Eugene Ysaye.

254. "Europa".

1958. Ysaye (violinist). Birth Cent.

1658. **253.**	30 c. blue and claret	5	5

1958. Europa.

1659. **254.**	2 f. 50, blue & red ..	15	5
1660.	5 f. red and blue	25	15

255. "Marguerite Van Eyck" (after Jan Van Eyck).

1958. Cultural Relief Funds. Paintings as T **255**. Frames in brown and yellow.

1661. **255.**	30 c.+20 c. myrtle..	12	10
1662. –	1 f.+50 c. lake ..	40	30
1663. –	1 f. 50+50 c. ultram.	60	45
1664. –	2 f. 50+1 f. sepia ..	1·75	1·50
1665. –	3 f.+1 f. 50 red ..	2·75	2·40
1666. –	5 f.+3 f. blue ..	4·75	4·25

PAINTINGS—HORIZ. 1 f. "Le portement de la Croix" (Bosch). 3 f. "The Rower" (Ensor). VERT. 1 f. 50, "St. Donatien" (Gossart). 2 f. 50, Self-portrait (Lombard). 5 f. "Henriette au grand chapeau" (Evenepoel).

256. "Hoogstraten".

257. Pax—"Creche Vivante".

1958. Anti-Tuberculosis and other Funds Provincial Legends.

1667. **256.**	40 c.+10 c. bl. & grn.	8	5
1668. –	1 f.+50 c. sepia and yellow	25	15
1669. –	1 f. 50+50 c. purple and green	35	25
1670. –	2 f.+1 f. brown & red	45	35
1671. **257.**	2 f. 50+1 f. claret and green	1·25	1·00
1672. –	5 f.+2 f. purple & blue	1·75	1·60
1673. –	6 f.+2 f. 50 blue and red	2·25	2·25

DESIGNS: As T **257**—VERT. 1 f. "Jean de Nivelles". 1 f. 50, "Jeu de Saint Evermare a Russon". HORIZ. 2 f. 'Les penitents de Furnes". As T **258**—HORIZ. "Marches de l'Entre Sambre et Meuse". VERT. 6 f. "Pax—Vierge".

258. "Human Rights".

259. "Europe of the Heart".

1958. Human Rights Declaration. 10th Anniv.

1674. **258.**	2 f. 50 slate ..	..	30	5

1959. "Heart of Europe". Fund for Displaced Persons.

1675. **259.**	1 f.+50 c. purple ..	35	30
1676.	2 f. 50+1 f. green ..	90	75
1677.	5 f.+2 f. 50 brown ..	1·60	1·50

260. J. B. de Taxis taking the oath at the hands of Charles V (after J.-E. Van den Bussche).

261. N.A.T.O. Emblem.

1959. Stamp Day.

1680. **260.**	2 f. 50 green.. ..	40	5

1959. N.A.T.O. 10th Anniv.

1681. **261.**	2 f. 50 blue and red ..	45	5
1682.	5 f. blue and green ..	1·00	50

On the 5 f. value the French and Flemish inscriptions are transposed.

For similar design but inscr. "1969", see No. 2112

262. "Blood Transfusion".

DESIGN—As T **262**—HORIZ. 2 f. 50, 3 f. Red Cross and broken sword ("Aid for the wounded").

263. J. H. Dunant and battle scene at Solferino, 1859.

1959. Red Cross Commem. Inscr. "1859 1959".

1683. **262.**	40 c.+10 c. red & grey	15	15
1684.	1 f.+50 c. red & sepia	35	30
1685.	1 f. 50+50 c. red and lilac	65	60
1686. –	2 f. 50+1 f. red and myrtle	1·10	95
1687. –	3 f.+1 f. 50, red and ultramarine ..	2·10	2·00
1688. **263.**	5 f.+3 f. red & sepia	2·75	2·50

264. Philip the Good.

265. Arms of Philip the Good.

1959. Royal Library of Belgium Fund. Nos. 1689/94 have background in deep blue and yellow-brown and bottom panel in deep olive.

1689. 264. 40 c.+10 c. brown-red 10 10
1690. – 1 f.+50 c. brown-red 25 25
1691. – 1 f. 50+50 c. brown-red 70 60
1692. – 2 f. 50+1 f. red .. 1·00 90
1693. – 3 f.+1 f. 50 red .. 2·10 2·00
1694. 265. 5 f.+3 f. red, blue, ochre and brown .. 2·50 2·50

DESIGNS—As T 264 (Holders of Order of the Golden Fleece): 1 f. Charles the Bold. 1 f. 50, Maximilian of Austria. 2 f. 50, Philip the Fair. 3 f. Charles V.

266. Town Hall, Oudenarde.

267. Pope Adrian VI.

1959. Oudenarde Town Hall Commem.

1699. 266. 2 f. 50 maroon .. 25 5

1959. Pope Adrian VI. Birth Quincent.

1700. 267. 2 f. 50 red 20 5
1701. 5 f. blue 50 25

268. "Europa".

269. Boeing "707" Inter-continental Jet Airliner.

1959. Europa.

1702. 268. 2 f. 50 red 12 5
1703. 5 f. turquoise 30 20

1959. Boeing "707" Airliners by SABENA. Inaug.

1704. 269. 6 f. blue, grey & red .. 1·25 60

270. Antwerp fish (float).

271. Stavelot "Blancs Moussis" (carnival figures).

1959. Anti-Tuberculosis and other Funds. Carnival scenes.

1705. 270. 40 c.+10 c. green, red and bistre 8 8
1706. – 1 f.+50 c. green, vio. and olive 20 15
1707. – 2 f.+50 c. yellow, maroon & brown .. 30 25
1708. 271. 2 f. 50+1 f. blue vio. and grey 40 35
1709. – 3 f.+1 f. maroon, yell. and grey .. .. 1·00 75
1710. – 6 f.+2 f. blue, red and olive .. .. 1·50 1·40
1711. – 7 f.+3 f. black, yell., and blue .. .. 2·40 2·40

DESIGNS—As T 270—HORIZ. 1 f. Mons dragon (float). 2 f. Eupen and Malmedy clowns in chariot. As T 271—VERT. 3 f. Ypres jester. HORIZ. 6 f. Holy Family. 7 f. Madonna and child.

272. Countess Alexandrine of Taxis (tapestry).

273. Indian Azalea.

1960. Stamp Day.

1712. 272. 3 f. blue 70 8

1960. Ghent Flower Show. Inscr. as in T 273.

1713. 273. 40 c. red and violet .. 8 5
1714. – 3 f. yell, red. & green 60 5
1715. – 6 f. red, green & blue 80 60

FLOWERS: 3 f. Begonia. 6 f. Anthurium and bromelia.

274. Refugee.

275. "Labour" (after Meunier).

1960. World Refugee Year. Inscr. as in T 274.

1716. – 40 c.+10 c. purple .. 10 5
1717. 274. 3 f.+1 f. 50 sepia .. 90 85
1718. – 6 f.+3 f. blue .. 1·00 90

DESIGNS: 40 c. Child refugee. 6 f. Woman refugee.

1960. Belgian Socialist Party. 75th Anniv. Inscr. as in T 275.

1720. 275. 40 c. purple and red .. 8 5
1721. – 3 f. chocolate and red 60 15

DESIGN—HORIZ. 3 f. "Workers" (after Meunier).

276. Parachutist on ground.

DESIGNS — HORIZ. 40 c., 1 f.. Parachutists dropping from Douglas DC-4 aircraft. VERT. 2 f., 2 f. 50, Parachutists descending.

1960. Parachuting. Designs bearing emblem of National Parachuting Club.

1726. – 40 c.+10 c. blk. & bl. 10 8
1727. – 1 f.+50 c. blk. & bl. 50 45
1728. – 2 f.+50 c. black, turquoise and green .. 75 65
1729. – 2 f. 50+1 f. black, turquoise & olive .. 1·25 90
1730. 276. 3 f.+1 f. blue and bronze-green .. 1·75 1·60
1731. 6 f.+2 f. black, blue and green .. .. 2·00 2·00

277. Ship's Officer and Helmsman.

1960. Congo Independence.

1732. 277. 10 c. red 5 5
1733. – 40 c. lake 8 5
1734. – 1 f. purple 60 20
1735. – 2 f. green 50 30
1736. – 2 f. 50 blue 50 25
1737. – 3 f. indigo 65 5
1738. – 6 f. blue-violet .. 75 60
1739. – 8 f. brown .. .. 4·00 3·25

DESIGNS—As T 277: 40 c. Doctor and nurses with patient. 1 f. Tree-planting. 2 f. Sculptors. 2 f. 50, Sport (putting the shot). 3 f. Broadcasting from studio. (52×35½ mm.): 6 f. Children with doll. 8 f. Child with globe.

278. Refugee Airlift.

DESIGNS—As T 278. 3 f. Mother and child: (35×51½ mm.): 6 f. SABENA Boeing 707 airliner spanning map of airlift route.

1960. Congo Refugees Relief Fund.

1740. 278. 40 c.+10 c. turquoise 5 5
1741. – 3 f.+1 f. 50 red .. 95 90
1742. – 6 f.+3 f. violet .. 1·40 1·25

1960. Surch.

1743. 189. 15 c. on 30 c. green .. 20 5
1744. 15 c. on 50 c. blue .. 5 5
1745. 20 c. on 30 c. green .. 20 5

See note below No. 480.

279. Conference Emblem.

280. Young Stamp Collectors.

1960. E.P.T. Conf. 1st Anniv.

1746. 279. 3 f. lake 20 5
1747. 6 f. grey-green .. 40 25

1960. "Philately for the Young" Propaganda.

1748. 280. 40 c. black and bistre 5 5

No. 1748 was issued in sheets se-tenant with labels depicting posthorn.

281. Pouring Milk for Child.

282. Frere Orban (founder).

1960. UNICEF Commem. and Belgian Fund.

1749. 281. 40 c.+10 c. yellow, green and brown .. 8 5
1750. – 1 f.+50 c. crimson, blue and drab .. 60 50
1751. – 2 f.+50 c. bistre, green and violet .. 75 60
1752. – 2 f. 50+1 f. sepia, blue and red .. 90 80
1753. – 3 f.+1 f. violet, oran. and turquoise .. 1·00 90
1754. – 6 f.+2 f. brown, green and blue .. .. 1·50 1·50

DESIGNS: 1 f. Nurse embracing children. 2 f. Child carrying clothes, and ambulance. 2 f. 50, Nurse weighing baby. 3 f. Children with linked arms. 6 f. Refugee worker and child.

1960. Credit Communal (Co-operative Bank) Cent.

1755. 282. 10 c. brown and yellow 5 5
1756. 40 c. brown and green 8 5
1757. 1 f. 50 brown & violet 50 45
1758. 3 f. brown and red .. 90 5

283. Tapestry.

DESIGNS—VERT. 1 f. Crystalware. 2 f. Lace. HORIZ. 2 f. 50, Brassware. 3 f. Diamond-cutting. 6 f. Ceramics.

1960. Anti-T.B. and other Funds. Arts and Crafts.

1759. 283. 40 c.+10 c. ochre, chocolate and blue 8 8
1760. – 1 f.+50 c. blue, brn. and indigo .. 60 50
1761. – 2 f.+50 c. olive, blk. and brown .. 80 75
1762. – 2 f. 50+1 f. yellow and chocolate .. 1·25 1·10
1763. – 3 f.+1 f. black, chestnut and blue .. 1·50 1·50
1764. – 6 f.+2 f. lemon and black .. .. 2·10 1·90

284. King Baudouin and Queen Fabiola.

285. Nicolaus Rockox (after Van Dyck).

1960. Royal Wedding.

1765. 284. 40 c. sepia and green 5 5
1766. 3 f. sepia and purple .. 40 5
1767. 6 f. sepia and blue .. 70 30

1961. Surch. in figs. and **1961.** at top, **1962** at bottom and bars in between.

1768. 189. 15 c on 30 c. green .. 50 5
1769. 20 c. on 30 c. green .. 50 15

See note below No. 480.

1961. Nicolaus Rockox (Burgomaster of Antwerp) 400th Birth Anniv.

1770. 285. 3 f. black, bis. & brn. 30 5

286. Seal of Jan Bode.

287. K. Kats (playwright) and Father N. Pietkin (poet).

1961. Stamp Day.

1771. 286. 3 f. sepia and brown .. 30 5

1961. Cultural Funds. Portrait in maroon.

1772. 40 c.+10 c. lake and pink 8 8
1773. 1 f.+50 c. lake & brown .. 60 55
1774. 2 f.+50 c. red & yellow .. 1·00 90
1775. 2 f. 50+1 f. myrtle & sage 1·25 1·10
1776. 3 f.+1 f. blue & lt. blue .. 1·90 1·60
1777. 6 f.+2 f. blue & lavender 1·90 1·75

PORTRAITS: 40 c. T 287. 1 f. A. Mockel and J. F. Willems (writers). 2 f. J. van Rijswijck and X. Neujean (politicians). 2 f. 50, J. Demarteau (journalist) and A. van der Perre (politician). 3 f. J. David (literateur) and A. Du Bois (writer). 6 f. H. Vieuxtemps (violinist) and W. de Mol (composer).

288. White Rhinoceros.

289. Cardinal A.P. de Granville (first Archbishop).

1961. Philanthropic Funds. Animals of Antwerp Zoo.

1778. 40 c.+10 c. choc. & brn. 8 8
1779. 1 f.+50 c. brn. & grey-grn. 60 60
1780. 2 f.+50 c. sepia, red and black 95 90
1781. 2 f. 50+1 f. brn. & verm. 80 80
1782. 3 f.+1 f. brown & orange 90 75
1783. 6 f.+2 f. ochre and blue .. 1·10 1·00

ANIMALS—VERT. 40 c. T 288. 1 f. Przewalski horse and foal. HORIZ. 2 f. 50 Giraffe. 3 f. Panda. 6 f. Elk.

1961. Archbishopric of Malines. 400th Anniv.

1784. 289. 40 c.+10 c. brown, crimson & purple .. 8 8
1785. – 3 f.+1 f. 50 crimson, orge., blk. & violet 60 50
1786. – 6 f.+3 f. bistre, violet and purple .. 1·10 1·00

DESIGNS: 3 f. Cardinal's Arms. 6 f. Symbols of Archbishopric and Malines.

290. "Interparliamentary Union".

1961. 50th Interparliamentary Union Conf., Brussels.

1791. 290. 3 f. brown & turq. .. 25 5
1792. 6 f. maroon and red .. 50 40

291. Doves.

1961. Europa.

1793. 291. 3 f. black and olive .. 12 5
1794. 6 f. black & chestnut 25 15

292. Reactor BR 2, Mol.

293. "The Mother and Child" (after Paulus).

1961. Euratom Commem.
1795. **292.** 40 c. green 5 5
1796. – 3 f. mauve 30 5
1797. – 6 f. blue 35 35
DESIGNS—VERT. 3 f. Heart of reactor BR 3, Mol. HORIZ. 6 f. View of reactor BR 3, Mol.

1961. Anti-T.B. and other Funds. Belgian paintings of mothers and children. Frames in gold.
1798. **293.** 40 c.+10 c. sepia .. 8 8
1799. – 1 f.+50 c. blue .. 30 30
1800. – 2 f.+50 c. red .. 50 40
1801. – 2 f. 50+1 f. lake .. 75 65
1802. – 3 f.+1 f. violet .. 1·00 90
1803. – 6 f.+2 f. myrtle .. 1·10 1·00
PAINTINGS: 1 f. "Maternal Love" (Navez). 2 f. "Maternity" (Permeke). 2 f. 50, "The Virgin and the Child" (Van der Weyden). 3 f. "The Virgin with the Apple" (Memling). 6 f. "The Myosotis Virgin" (Rubens).

294. Horta Museum.

295. Male Castle.

1962. Victor Horta (architect). Birth Cent.
1804. **294.** 3 f. brown 20 5

1962. Cultural and Patriotic Funds. Buildings.
1805. **295.** 40 c.+10 c. green .. 5 5
1806. – 90 c.+10 c. mauve .. 15 12
1807. – 1 f.+50 c. lilac .. 25 20
1808. – 2 f.+50 c. violet .. 50 45
1809. – 2 f. 50+1 f. brown .. 65 60
1810. – 3 f.+1 f. turquoise .. 75 70
1811. – 6 f.+2 f. red .. 1·25 1·10
BUILDINGS—HORIZ. 90 c. Royal Library, Brussels. 2 f. Collegiate Church, Soignies. 6 f. Ypres Halls. VERT. 1 f. Notre-Dame Basilica, Tongres. 2 f. 50, Notre-Dame Church, Hanswijk. 3 f. St. Denis-en-Broqueroie Abbey.

296. 16th-Century Postilion.

297. G. Mercator (after F. Hogenberg).

1962. Stamp Day.
1812. **296.** 3 f. brown and green 30 5

1962. Mercator (geographer). 450th Birth Anniv.
1813. **297.** 3 f. sepia 30 5

298. Brother A. M. Gochet (scholar).

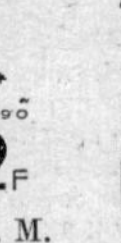
299. Cock of the Rock.

1962. Gochet and Triest Commem.
1814. **298.** 2 f. blue 20 5
1815. – 3 f. brown 25 5
PORTRAIT: 3 f. Canon P.-J. Triest (benefactor of the aged).

1962. Philanthropic Funds. Birds of Antwerp Zoo. Birds, etc., in natural colours. Colours of name panel and inscription given.
1816. **299.** 40 c.+10 c. blue .. 8 8
1817. – 1 f.+50 c. blue & red 20 20
1818. – 2 f.+50 c. mag. & blk. 50 40
1819. – 2 f. 50+1 f. turq. & red 60 50
1820. – 3 f.+1 f. brn. & grn. 80 75
1821. – 6 f.+2 f. ult. & red .. 1·00 90
BIRDS: 1 f. Red lory. 2 f. Senegalese touraco. 2 f. 50, Short-beaked toucan. 3 f. Great bird of paradise. 6 f. Congolese peacock.

300. Europa "Tree".

301. "Captive Hands" (after sculpture by Lanchelivici).

1962. Europa.
1822. **300.** 3 f. black, yell. & red 15 5
1823. 6 f. black, yell. & olive 30 12

1962. Concentration Camp Victims.
1824. **301.** 40 c. blue and black .. 5 5

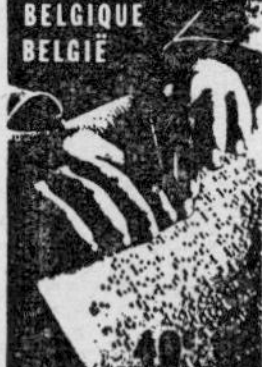
302. Reading Braille.

303. "Adam" (After Michelangelo).

1962. Handicapped Children Relief Funds.
1825. **302.** 40 c.+10 c. brown .. 5 5
1826. – 1 f.+50 c. red .. 20 15
1827. – 2 f.+50 c. mauve .. 45 35
1828. – 2 f. 50+1 f. green .. 60 50
1829. – 3 f.+1 f. blue .. 65 60
1830. – 6 f.+2 f. sepia .. 1·10 1·00
DESIGNS—VERT. 1 f. Girl solving puzzle. 2 f. 50, Crippled child with ball. 3 f. Girl walking with crutches. HORIZ. 2 f. Child with ear-phones. 6 f. Crippled boys with football.

1962. "The Rights of Man".
1831. **303.** 3 f. sepia & grey-green 20 5
1832. 6 f. sepia and chestnut 25 15

304. Queen Louise-Marie.

305. Menin Gate, Ypres.

1962. Anti-tuberculosis and other Funds. Belgian Queens in grey-green and gold.
1833. 40 c.+10 c. T **304** .. 5 5
1834. 40 c.+10 c. As T **304** but inscr. "ML" .. 5 5
1835. 1 f.+50 c. Marie-Henriette 35 30
1836. 2 f.+1 f. Elisabeth .. 60 50
1837. 3 f.+1 f. 50 Astrid .. 75 70
1838. 8 f.+2 f. 50 Fabiola 1·25 1·10

1962. Ypres Millenary.
1839. **305.** 1 f.+50 c. brown, grn., blue and black .. 20 20

306. H. Pirenne.

307. "Peace Bell".

1963. Henri Pirenne (historian). Birth Cent.
1841. **306.** 3 f. blue 30 5

1963. Cultural Funds and Installation of "Peace Bell" in Koekelberg Basilica. Bell in yellow; "PAX" in black.
1842. **307.** 3 f.+1 f. 50 grn. & blue 80 80
1843. 6 f.+3 f. chestnut and brown .. 80 80

HAVE YOU READ THE NOTES AT THE BEGINNING OF THIS CATALOGUE?
These often provide answers to the enquiries we receive.

308. "The Sower" (after Brueghel).

309. 17th-century Duel.

1963. Freedom from Hunger.
1845. **308.** 2 f.+1 f. sepia, green and orange .. 20 20
1846. – 3 f.+1 f. black, orange and mauve .. 45 40
1847. – 6 f.+2 f. apple, olive and brown .. 65 60
PAINTINGS—HORIZ. 3 f. "The Harvest" Breughel). VERT. 6 f. "The Loaf" (Anto Carte).

1963. Royal Guild and Knights of St. Michael. 350th Anniv.
1848. **309.** 1 f. brown-red & blue 8 8
1849. – 3 f. violet and lemon 20 5
1850. – 6 f. multicoloured .. 30 20
DESIGNS—HORIZ. 3 f. Modern fencing. VERT. 6 f. Arms of the Guild.

310. 19-century Mail-coach.

1963. Stamp Day.
1851. **310.** 3 f. black and ochre .. 25 5

311. Hotel des Postes, Paris, and Belgian 1 c. Stamp of 1863.

312. Child in Wheatfield.

1963. Paris Postal Conference Cent.
1852. **311.** 6 f. sep., mar. & grn. 45 30

1963. "8th May" Peace Movement.
1853. **312.** 3 f. yellow-green, brn., yellow and black .. 20 5
1854. 6 f. yellow, orange, brown and black .. 30 12

313. "Transport".

313a. Town Seal.

1963. European Transport Ministers' Conf., Brussels.
1855. **313.** 6 f. black and blue .. 35 15

1963. Int. Union of Towns Congress, Brussels.
1856. **313a.** 6 f. multicoloured .. 35 15

314. Racing Cyclists.

315. "Caravelle" Airliner

1963. Belgian Cycling Team's Participation in Olympic Games, Tokyo (1964).
1857. **314.** 1 f.+50 c. red, orge-brn., blk. & sepia .. 15 15
1858. – 2 f.+1 f. red, turq.-blue, blk. & olive .. 25 25
1859. – 3 f.+1 f. 50 red, blk., green and blue .. 35 35
1860. – 6 f.+3 f. blue, red, black and green .. 60 60
DESIGNS—HORIZ. 2 f. Group of cyclists. 3 f. Cyclists rounding bend. VERT. 6 f. Cyclists being paced by motor-cyclists.

1963. SABENA Airline. 40th Anniv.
1861. **315.** 3 f. black & bl.-green 20 5

316. "Co-operation".

137. Princess Paola with Princess Astrid.

1963. Europa.
1862. **316.** 3 f. blk., brn. & claret 20 5
1863. 6 f. blk., brn. & blue .. 35 15
No. 1863 is inscr. with "6 F" on the left. "BELGIE" at foot and "BELGIQUE" on right.

1963. Red Cross Cent. and Belgian Red Cross Fund. Cross in red.
1864. – 40 c.+10 c. crimson and yellow .. 5 5
1865. **317.** 1 f.+50 c. grey & yell. 25 20
1866. – 2 f.+50 c. mag. & yell. 30 25
1867. – 2 f. 50+1 f. bl. & yell. 45 35
1868. – 3 f.+1 f. sep. & yell. 45 35
1869. – 3 f.+1 f. bronze & yell. 1·50 1·50
1870. – 6 f.+2 f. black-green and yellow .. 70 65
DESIGNS—VERT. 40 c. Prince Phillippe. 2 f. Princess Astrid. 2 f. 50, Princess Paola. 6 f. Prince Albert. HORIZ. (46×35 mm.), 3 f. (2). Prince Albert and family.
No. 1869 was issued in a special sheet of 8 stamps in booklets.

318. J. Destree (writer).

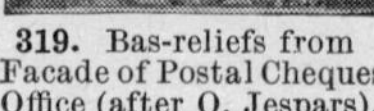
319. Bas-reliefs from Facade of Postal Cheques Office (after O. Jespars).

320. Balthasar Gerbier's Daughter.

1963. Jules Destree and H. Van de Vedle Commems.
1871. **318.** 1 f. reddish purple .. 8 8
1872. – 1 f. green 8 8
DESIGN: No. 1872, H. Van de Vedle (architect).

1963. Belgian Postal Cheques Office. 50th Anniv.
1873. **319.** 50 c. blk., blue & red 5 5

1963. T.B. Relief and Other Funds. Rubens' Drawings. Background buff; inscr. in black; designs colour given.
1874. **320.** 50 c.+10 c. grey-blue 8 8
1875. – 1 f.+40 c. brown-red 12 12
1876. – 2 f.+50 c. reddish vio. 20 20
1877. – 2 f. 50+1 f. green .. 40 40
1878. – 3 f.+1 f. orange-brn. 45 40
1879. – 6 f.+2 f. black .. 65 60
DRAWINGS—VERT. Rubens' children—1 f. Nicolas (aged 2). 2 f. Franz (aged 4). 2 f. 50, Nicolas (aged 6). 3 f. Albert (aged 3). HORIZ. (46½×35½ mm.), 6 f. Infant Jesus, St. John and two angels.

321. Dr. G. Hansen and Laboratory.

1964. Leprosy Relief Campaign.
1880. **321.** 1 f. black & chestnut 5 5
1881. – 2 f. chestnut & black 20 5
1882. – 5 f. black & chestnut 45 15
DESIGNS: 2 f. Leprosy hospital. 5 f. Father Damien.

322. A. Vesale (anatomist) with Model of Human Arm.

323. Postilion.

1964. Belgian Celebrities.
1884. **322.** 50 c. blk. & yell.-grn. 5 5
1885. – 1 f. blk. & yell.-grn... 10 5
1886. – 2 f. blk. & yell.-grn... 15 8
DESIGNS—HORIZ. 1 f. J. Boulvin (engineer) and internal combustion engine. 2 f. H. Jaspar (statesman) and medallion.

1964. Stamp Day.
1887. **323.** 3 f. grey 12 5

324. Admiral Lord Gambier and U.S. Ambassador J. Q. Adams after signing treaty (from painting by Sir A. Forestier).

1964. Treaty of Ghent. 150th Anniv.
1888. **324.** 6 f.+3 f. grey-blue .. 1·25 1·25

325. Arms of Ostend. **326.** Ida of Bure (Calvin's wife).

1964. Millenary of Ostend.
1889. **325.** 3 f. blk., gold, red & bl. 15 5

1964. "Protestantism in Belgium".
1890. – 1 f.+50 c. grey-blue 15 15
1891. **326.** 3 f.+1 f. 50 red 35 30
1892. – 6 f.+3 f. brown .. 60 55
PORTRAITS: 1 f. P. Marnix of St. Aldegonde (Burgomaster of Antwerp). 6 f. J. Jordaens (painter).

327. Globe, Hammer and Flame. **328.** Infantryman of 1918.

1964. Socialist International. Cent.
1893. **327.** 50 c. red and deep blue 5 5
1894. – 1 f. red and deep blue 10 5
1895. – 2 f. red and deep blue 15 5
DESIGNS: 1 f. "SI" on Globe. 2 f. Flames.

1964. German Invasion of Belgium. 50th Anniv. Multicoloured.
1896. 1 f.+50 c. Type 328 .. 12 12
1897. 2 f.+1 f. Colour-sergeant of the Guides Regt., 1914 20 20
1898. 3 f.+1 f. 50 Trumpeter of the Grenadiers & Drummers of the Infantry and Carabineers, 1914 .. 25 25

329. Soldier at Bastogne. **330.** Europa "Flower".

1964. "Liberation-Resistance". Multicoloured.
1899. 3 f.+1 f. Type 329 .. 20 20
1900. 6 f.+3 f. Soldier at estuary of the Scheldt 35 35

1964. Europa.
1901. **330.** 3 f. grey, lake & green 12 5
1902. 6 f. blue, green & lake 25 15

DESIGN: 3 f. Waterside view of Abbey.

331. Pand Abbey, Ghent.

1964. Pand Abbey Restoration Fund.
1905. **331.** 2 f.+1 f. blue, turq. and black 25 20
1906. – 3 f.+1 f. brown, blue and purple .. 30 30

Stamps of 1 f., 2 f. and 3 f. in vert. format showing respectively Philippe le Bon, Portrait of a Lady and Man with an arrow and an 8 f. value in horiz. format showing The Descent from the Cross, all paintings of Rogier Van der Weyden, come from two miniature sheets issued to commemorate the fifth centenary of his death on 19th Sept., 1964.

332. King Baudouin, Queen Juliana and Grand Duchess Charlotte.

1964. "BENELUX". 20th Anniv.
1907. **332.** 3 f. brown-purple, blue and olive 15 5

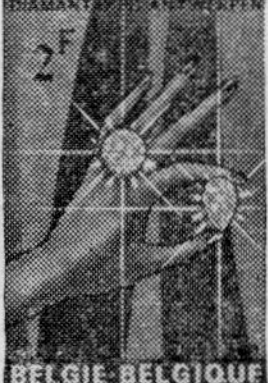

333. "One of Charles I's Children" (Van Dyck). **334.** "Diamonds".

1964. T.B. Relief and Other Funds. Paintings of Royalty.
1908. **333.** 50 c.+10 c. purple .. 5 5
1909. – 1 f.+40 c. rose .. 10 10
1910. – 2 f.+1 f. maroon .. 20 15
1911. – 3 f.+1 f. grey .. 25 20
1912. – 4 f.+2 f. violet .. 30 25
1913. – 6 f.+3 f. reddish violet 45 40
DESIGNS—VERT. 1 f. "William of Orange and his fiancee, Marie" (Van Dyck). 2 f. "Portrait of a little boy" (E. Quellin and Jan Fyt). 3 f. "Alexander Farnese at the age of 12 years" (A. Moro). 4 f. "William II, Prince of Orange" (Van Dyck). HORIZ—LARGER (46×35 mm.): 6 f. "Two children of Cornelis De Vos" (C. de Vos).

1965. "Diamantexpo" (Diamonds Exn.), Antwerp.
1914. **334.** 2 f. red, purple, blue and black 20 5

335. "Textiles". **336.** Vriesia.

1965. "Textirama" (Textile Exn.), Ghent.
1915. **335.** 1 f. black, red and blue 8 8

1965. Ghent Flower Show. Inscr. "FLORALIES GANTOISES", etc. Multicoloured.
1916. 1 f. Type **336** 8 5
1917. 2 f. Echinocactus .. 20 15
1918. 3 f. Stapelia 10 5

337. Paul Hymans. **338.** Rubens.

1965. Paul Hymans (statesman). Birth Cent.
1919. **337.** 1 f. violet 5 5

1965 General Savings and Pensions Funds. Cent. Painters.
1920. **338.** 1 f. sepia and magenta 5 5
1921. – 2 f. sepia and turquoise 10 10
1922. – 3 f. sepia and purple.. 15 5
1923. – 6 f. sepia and red .. 25 8
1924. – 8 f. sepia and blue .. 35 30
PAINTERS: 2 f. Snyders. 3 f. Van Noort. 6 f. Van Dyck. 8 f. Jordaens.

339. "Sir Rowland Hill with young collectors" (detail from mural by J. Van den Bussche). **340.** 19th-century Postmaster.

1965. "Philately for the Young".
1925. **339.** 50 c. green 5 5

1965. Stamp Day.
1926. **340.** 3 f. green 20 5

341. Globe and Telephone.

1965. I.T.U. Cent.
1928. **341.** 2 f. black and purple 12 8

342. Handclasp. **343.** Abbey Staircase

1965. Liberation of Prison Camps. 20th Anniv.
1929. **342.** 50 c.+50 c. flesh, blk., and bistre.. .. 5 5
1930. – 1 f.+50 c. flesh, black, yellow and grey .. 10 8
1931. – 3 f.+1 f. 50 black, maroon & turquoise 20 20
1932. – 8 f.+5 f. mult. .. 45 45
DESIGNS—VERT. 1 f. Hand reaching for barbed wire. HORIZ. 3 f. Tank entering prison camp. 8 f. Rose within broken wall.

1965. Affligem Abbey.
1933. **343.** 1 f. slate-blue .. 8 5

344. St. Jean Berchmans, Birthplace and Residence. **345.** Toc H Lamp and Arms of Poperinge.

1965. St. Jean Berchmans.
1934. **344.** 2 f. brown & maroon 12 5

1965. Founding of Toc H Movement at Talbot House, Poperinge. 50th Anniv.
1935. **345.** 3 f. multicoloured .. 10 5

346. Maison Stoclet, Brussels. **347.** Tractor ploughing.

1965. Josef Hoffman (architect) Commem.
1936. **346.** 3 f.+1 f. grey & drab 15 15
1937. – 6 f.+3 f. brown .. 30 30
1938. – 8 f.+4 f. pur. & drab 45 40
DESIGNS—Maison Stoclet: VERT. 6 f. Entrance hall. HORIZ. 8 f. Rear of building.

1965. Boerenbond (Belgian Farmers' Assn.). 75th Anniv.
1939. **347.** 50 c. black, olive, brown and blue 5 5
1940. – 3 f. black, olive, green and blue 10 5
DESIGN: 3 f. Horse-drawn plough.

348. Europa "Sprig".

1965. Europa.
1941. **348.** 1 f. black and pink .. 5 5
1942. 3 f. black and green.. 10 5

349. Jackson's Chameleon.

1965. Philanthropic Funds. Reptiles of Antwerp Zoo. Multicoloured.
1943. 1 f.+50 c. Type **349** .. 5 5
1944. 2 f.+1 f. Iguana.. .. 10 8
1945. 3 f.+1 f. 50 Nile lizard.. 15 15
1946. 6 f.+3 f. Komodo lizard 30 30

350. J. Lebeau (after A. Schollaert). **351.** Leopold I (after 30 c. and 1 f. Stamps of 1865).

1965. Joseph Lebeau (statesman). Death Cent.
1948. **350.** 1 f. multicoloured .. 10 5

1965. King Leopold I. Death Cent.
1949. **351.** 3 f. sepia 12 5
1950. – 6 f. violet 25 25
DESIGN: 6 f. As 3 f. but with different portrait frame.

352. Huy. **353.** Guildhouse.

1965. Tourist Publicity. Multicoloured.
1951. 50 c. Type **352** 8 5
1952. 50 c. Hoeilaart (vert.) .. 8 5
See also Nos. 1995/6, 2025/6, 2083/4, 2102/3, 2123/4, 2159/60, 2240/1, 2250/1, 2275/6, 2321, 2328/9 2368/70 and 2394/5.

1965. T.B. Relief and Other Funds. Public Buildings, Brussels.
1953. **353.** 50 c.+10 c. blue .. 5 5
1954. – 1 f.+40 c. turquoise 8 5
1955. – 2 f.+1 f. purple .. 10 10
1956. – 3 f.+1 f. 50 violet .. 20 20
1957. – 10 f.+4 f. 50 sepia & grey 50 45
BUILDINGS—HORIZ. 1 f. Brewers' House 2 f. Builders' House 3 f. House of the Dukes of Brabant. VERT. (24½×44½ mm.): 10 f. Tower of Town Hall.

354. Queen Elisabeth (from medallion by A. Courtens). **355.** "Peace on Earth".

1965. Queen Elisabeth Commem.
1958. **354.** 3 f. black 15 5

1966. "Rerum Novarum" (papal encyclical). 75th Anniv. Multicoloured.

1959. 50 c. Type **355** 5 5
1960. 1 f. "Building for To-morrow" (family and new building) 5 5
1961. 3 f. Arms of Pope Leo XIII (vert. $24\frac{1}{2} \times 45$ mm.) .. 12 5

356. Rural Postman.

357. High Diving.

1966. Stamp Day.

1964. **356.** 3 f. blk., lilac & buff .. 15 5

1966. Swimming.

1965. **357.** 60 c.+40 c. brown, green and blue .. 8 5
1966. – 10 f.+4 f. brown, purple and green .. 45 40

DESIGN: 10 f. Diving from block.

358. Iguanodon Fossil (Royal Institute of Natural Sciences).

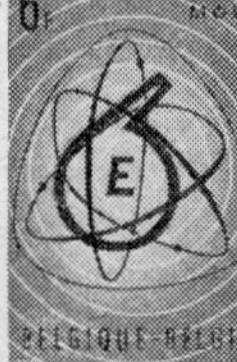

359. Eurochemic Symbol.

1966. National Scientific Institutions.

1967. **358.** 1 f. black and green 5 5
1968. – 2 f. blk., orge. & cream 5 5
1969. – 2 f. black, yellow, ultramarine & blue .. 8 5
1970. – 3 f. multicoloured .. 10 5
1971. – 3 f. gold, blk., & red .. 12 5
1972. – 6 f. yellow, black, blue and ultramarine .. 20 10
1973. – 8 f. multicoloured .. 35 30

DESIGNS—HORIZ. No. 1968, Kasai head (Royal Central African Museum). 1969, Snow crystals (Royal Meteorological Institute). VERT. 1970, "Scholar" (Royal Library). 1971, Seal (General Archives). 1972, Arend-Roland comet and telescope (Royal Observatory). 1973, Satellite and rocket (Space Aeronomy Inst.).

1966. European Chemical Plant, Mol.

1974. **359.** 6 f. blk., red and drab 30 15

360. A. Kekule.

361. Rik Wouters (self-portrait).

1966. Professor August Kekule's Benzine Formula, Cent.

1975. **360.** 3 f. brown, blk. & bl. 10 5

1966. 19th World I.P.T.T. Congress, Brussels. Optd. **XIXe CONGRES IPTT** and emblem.

1976. **356.** 3 f. black, lilac & buff 15 5

1966. Rik Wouters (painter). 50th Death Anniv.

1977. **361.** 60 c. multicoloured .. 8 5

362. Minorites Convent, Liege.

1966. Cultural Series.

1978. **362.** 60 c.+40 c. maroon, blue and brown .. 5 5
1979. – 1 f.+50 c. blue, purple and turquoise-blue 8 5
1980. – 2 f.+1 f. maroon, cerise and brown .. 10 8
1981. – 10 f.+4 f. 50 maroon, turquoise and green 40 35

DESIGNS: 1 f. Val-Dieu Abbey, Aubel. 2 f. Huy and town seal. 10 f. Statue of Ambiorix and castle Tongres.

363. Europa "Ship".

364. Surveying.

1966. Europa.

1989. **363.** 3 f. green 15 5
1990. 6 f. purple 30 15

1966. Antarctic Expeditions.

1991. **364.** 1 f.+50 c. green .. 8 8
1992. – 3 f.+1 f. 50 violet .. 15 15
1993. – 6 f.+3 f. lake .. 30 30

DESIGNS: 3 f. Commander A. de Gerlache and ships. 6 f. "Magga Dan" and meteorological operations.

1966. Tourist Publicity. As T **352**. Multicoloured.

1995. 2 f. Bouillon 10 5
1996. 2 f. Lier (vert.) .. 10 5

1966. Royal Federation of Belgian Philatelic Circles. 75th Anniv. Stamps similar to Nos. 1812 and 1851 but optd. **1890 1966** and F.I.P. emblem.

1997. **296.** 60 c. maroon & green 5 5
1998. **310.** 3 f. maroon & ochre .. 10 5

365. Children with Hoops.

366. Lions Emblem

1966. "Solidarity" (Child Welfare).

1999. – 1 f.+1 f. blk. & pink 5 5
2000. – 2 f.+1 f. blk. & green 12 10
2001. – 3 f.+1 f. 50 blk. & lav. 15 15
2002. **365.** 6 f.+3 f. brn. & flesh 25 25
2003. – 8 f.+3 f. 50 brn. & grn. 35 35

DESIGNS—VERT. 1 f. Boy with ball and dog. 2 f. Girl with skipping-rope. 3 f. Boy and girl blowing bubbles. HORIZ. 8 f. Children and cat playing "Follow My Leader".

1967. Lions Int.

2004. **366.** 3 f. sepia, blue & olive 10 5
2005. 6 f. sepia, violet & grn. 20 10

367. Part of Cleuter Pistol.

1967. Arms Museum, Liege.

2006. **367.** 2 f. black, yell. & red 8 5

368. I.T.Y. Emblem.

1967. Int. Tourist Year.

2007. **368.** 6 f. blue, red and blk. 15 8

369. Woodland and Trientalis (flowers), Hautes Fagnes.

1967. Nature Conservation. Multicoloured.

2009. 1 f. Type **369** 5 5
2010. 1 f. Dunes and eryngium (flowers), Westhoek .. 5 5

370. Paul-Emile Janson.

371. 19th-cent. Postman.

1967. Janson (statesman) Commem.

2011. **370.** 10 f. blue 40 20

1967. Stamp Day.

2012. **371.** 3 f. purple and red .. 12 5

372. Cogwheels.

373 Flax Plant and Shuttle.

1967. Europa.

2013. **372.** 3 f. black, red & blue 12 5
2014. 6 f. black, yell. & grn. 20 10

1967. Belgian Linen Industry.

2015. **373.** 6 f. multicoloured .. 15 5

374. Kursaal in 19th Century.

1967. Ostend's Rank as Town. 700th Anniv.

2016. **374.** 2 f. sepia, buff & blue 12 5

375. With F.I.T.C.E. Emblem.

376. Robert Schuman (statesman).

1967. European Telecommunications Day. "Stamp Day" design of 1967 incorporating F.I.T.C.E. emblem of T **375** in green.

2021. **375.** 10 f. sepia and blue .. 40 20

"F.I.T.C.E." "Federation des Ingenieurs des Tele-communications de la Communaute Europeenne."

1967. Charity.

2022. **376.** 2 f.+1 f. green .. 25 20
2023. – 5 f.+2 f. brown, yellow and black .. 25 25
2024. – 10 f.+5 f. yellow, red, black and blue .. 45 40

DESIGNS—HORIZ. 5 f. Kongolo Memorial, Gentinnes (Congo Martyrs). VERT. 10 f. "Colonial Brotherhood" emblem (Colonial Troops Memorial).

1967. Tourist Publicity. As T **352**. Multicoloured.

2025. 1 f. Ypres 8 5
2026. 1 f. Spontin 8 5

377. "Caesar Crossing the Rubicon" (Tournai Tapestry).

378. "Jester in Pulpit" (from Erasmus' Praise of Folly).

1967. Charles Plisnier and Lodewijk de Raet Foundations.

2028. **377.** 1 f. multicoloured .. 5 5
2029. – 1 f. multicoloured .. 5 5

DESIGN No. 2029. "Maximilian hunting boar" (Brussels tapestry).

1967. Cultural Series. "Erasmus and His Time".

2030. 1 f.+50 c. black, red, blue and cream 8 8
2031. 2 f.+1 f. black, red and cream 12 12
2032. 3 f.+1 f. 50 multicoloured 15 15
2033. 5 f.+2 f. blk., red & crm. 20 20
2034. 6 f.+3 f. multicoloured .. 25 25

DESIGNS—VERT. 1 f. Type **378**. 2 f. "Jester declaiming" (from Erasmus' Praise of Folly). 3 f. Erasmus. 6 f. Pierre Gilles "Aegidius"; from painting by Metzijs). HORIZ. 5 f. "Sir Thomas More's Family" (Holbein)

379. "Princess Margaret of York" (from miniature).

380. Arms of Ghent University.

1967. "British Week".

2035. **379.** 6 f. multicoloured .. 20 12

1967. Universities of Ghent and Liege. Multicoloured.

2036. 3 f. Type **380** 12 5
2037. 3 f. Liege 12 5

381. Our Lady of Virga Jesse, Hasselt.

1967. Christmas.

2039. **381.** 1 f. blue 5 5

382. "Children's Games" (section of Brueghel's painting).

1967. "Solidarity".

2040. **382.** 1 f.+50 c. mult. .. 12 10
2041. – 2 f.+50 c. mult. .. 15 15
2042. – 3 f.+1 f. mult. .. 20 20
2043. – 6 f.+3 f. mult. .. 30 30
2044. – 10 f.+4 f. mult. .. 35 35
2045. – 13 f.+6 f. mult. .. 60 60

Nos. 2040/45 together form the complete painting.

383. Worker in Protective Hand.

384. Army Postman (1916).

1968. Industrial Safety Campaign.

2046. **383.** 3 f. blk., red, bl. & grn. 12 5

1968. Stamp Day.

2068. **384.** 3 f. pur.-brn., brn. & bl. 12 5

385. Belgian 1 c. "Small Lion" Stamp of 1866.

386. Grammont and Seal of Baudouin VI.

1968. State Printing Works, Malines. Cent.

2069. **385.** 1 f. olive 5 5

1968. "Historical Series". Multicoloured.

2070. 2 f. Type **386** 12 8
2071. 3 f. Theux-Franchimont Castle & battle emblems 15 5
2072. 6 f. Archaeological discoveries, Spiennes .. 20 10
2073. 10 f. Roman oil lamp and town crest Wervik .. 35 25

387. Europa "Key". **388.** Queen Elisabeth and Dr. Depage.

1968. Europa.

2074. **387.** 3 f. gold, blk. & green 10 5
2075. 6 f. silver, black & red 20 10

1968. Belgian Red Cross Fund. Cross in red.

2076. **388.** 6 f.+3 f. sepia, black and green 35 30
2077. – 10 f.+5 f. sepia, black and green 45 40

DESIGN: 10 f. Queen Fabiola and baby.

389. Gymnastics. **390.** "Explosion".

1968. Olympic Games, Mexico. Multicoloured.

2078. 1 f.+50 c. Type **389** .. 5 5
2079. 2 f.+1 f. Weightlifting .. 12 12
2080. 3 f.+1 f. 50 Hurdling .. 15 15
2081. 6 f.+2 f. Cycling .. 30 30
2082. 13 f.+5 f. Yachting (vert. 24½×45 mm.) .. 65 65

Each design includes the Olympic "rings" and a Mexican cultural motif.

1968. Tourist Publicity. As Type **352**.

2083. 2 f. black, yellow, green and blue 12 5
2084. 2 f. blk., blue & emerald .. 12 5

DESIGNS: No. 2083, Farm-house and windmill Bokrijk. 2084, Bath-house and fountain, Spa.

1968. Belgian Disasters. Victims Fund. Multicoloured.

2085. 10 f.+5 f. Type **390** .. 50 50
2086. 12 f.+5 f. "Fire" .. 65 65
2087. 13 f.+5 f. "Typhoon" .. 75 75

391. St. Laurent Abbey, Liege.

1968. "National Interest".

2088. **391.** 2 f. black, bistre and ultramarine .. 20 10
2089. – 3 f. green, grey & brn. 25 5
2090. – 6 f. black, blue, and slate 30 8
2091. – 10 f. black, blue, green and bistre.. 40 25

DESIGNS: 3 f. Church, Lissewege. 6 f. Canal-lock, Zandvliet. 10 f. Canal-"lift", Ronquieres.

392. Undulate Triggerfish.

1968. "Solidarity" and 125th Anniv. of Antwerp Zoo. Designs showing fish. Multicoloured.

2092. 1 f.+50 c. Type **392** .. 12 12
2093. 3 f.+1 f. 50 Angel fish .. 15 15
2094. 6 f. +3 f. Scorpion fish .. 40 40
2095. 10 f.+5 f. Red Striped Butterfly 50 50

393. King Albert in Bruges (October, 1918). **394.** Lighted Candle.

1968. Patriotic Funds.

2096. **393.** 1 f.+50 c. mult. .. 8 8
2097. – 3 f.+1 f. 50 mult. .. 20 20
2098. – 6 f.+3 f. mult. .. 30 30
2099. 10 f.+5 f. blk., orge., brown and yellow .. 50 50

DESIGNS—HORIZ. 3 f. King Albert entering Brussels (November, 1918)). 6 f. King Albert in Liege (November, 1918. LARGER (46×35 mm.) 10 f. Tomb of the Unknown Soldier, Brussels.

1968. Christmas.

2100. **394.** 1 f. multicoloured .. 5 5

395. Ship in Ghent Canal.

1968. Ghent Maritime Canal.

2101. **395.** 6 f. black, brn., & blue 20 8

1969. Tourist Publicity. As T **352**.

2102. 1 f. blk., bl. & pur. (vert.) 8 5
2103. 1 f. black, olive and blue .. 10 5

DESIGN: No. 2102, Town Hall, Louvain. No. 2103, Valley of the Ourthe.

396. "Albert Magnis" (detail of wood carving by Quellin, Confessional, St. Paul's Church, Antwerp).

1969. St. Paul's Church, Antwerp, and Aulne Abbey Commem.

2104. **396.** 2 f. sepia 10 5
2105. – 3 f. black and mauve 10 5

DESIGN: 3 f. Aulne Abbey.

397. "The Travellers" (sculpture, Archaeological Museum, Arlon). **398.** Broodjes Chapel, Antwerp.

1969. Arlon. 2,000th Anniv.

2106. **397.** 2 f. purple 8 5

1969. "150 Years of Public Education in Antwerp."

2107. **398.** 3 f. black & olive-grey 10 5

399. Mail Train. **400.** Colonnade.

1969. Stamp Day.

2108. **399.** 3 f. multicoloured .. 15 5

1969. Europa.

2109. **400.** 3 f. multicoloured .. 15 5
2110. 6 f. multicoloured .. 30 12

401. NATO Emblem. **402.** "The Builders" (F. Leger).

1969. NATO. 20th Anniv.

2112. **401.** 6 f. blue and chestnut 30 15

1969. Int. Labour Organization. 50th Anniv.

2113. **402.** 3 f. multicoloured .. 15 5

403. "Houses" (I. Dimitrova). **404.** Racing Cyclist.

1969. UNICEF "Philanthropy" Funds. Multicoloured.

2114. 1 f.+50 c. Type **403** .. 12 12
2115. 3 f.+1 f. 50 "My Art" (C. Patric) 20 15
2116. 6 f.+3 f. "In the Sun" (H. Rejchlova) .. 40 40
2117. 10 f.+5 f. "Out for a Walk" (P. Sporn) .. 50 45

No. 2117 is horiz.

1969. World Championship Cycle Races, Zolder.

2118. **404.** 6 f. multicoloured .. 30 15

405. Mgr. V. Scheppers. **406.** National Colours.

1969. Monseigneur Victor Scheppers. Commem.

2119. **405.** 6 f.+3 f. purple .. 60 60

1969. "Benelux". 25th Anniv.

2120. **406.** 3 f. red., bl., yell. & blk. 15 5

407. Pascali Rose and Annevoie Gardens.

1969. Flowers and Gardens. Multicoloured

2121. 2 f. Type **407** 15 5
2122. 2 f. Begonia and Lochristi Gardens 15 5

1969. Tourist Publicity. As T **3520**.

2123. 2 f. brown, red and blue .. 10 5
2124. 2 f. black, green and blue 12 5

DESIGNS: No. 2123, Veurne Furnes. No. 2124 Vielsalm.

408. "Feats of Arms" from "History of Alexander the Great" (Tournai, 15th century). **410.** Wounded Soldier (design of 1923 charity stamp).

409. Astronauts and Location of Moon Landing.

1969. "Cultural Works" Tapestries. Multicoloured.

2125. 1 f.+50 c. Type **408** .. 10 8
2126. 3 f.+1 f. 50 "The Violinist" from "Festival" (David Teniers II, Oudenarde, circa 1700) 20 20
2127. 10 f.+4 f. "The Paralytic", from "The Acts of the Apostles" (Brussels, circa 1517) .. 60 60

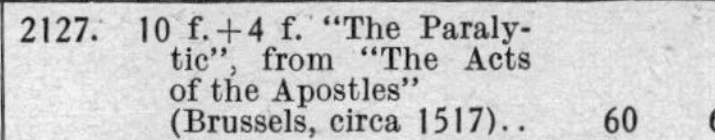

1969. 1st Man on the Moon.

2128. **409.** 6 f. blackish brown .. 30 15

1969. National War Invalids Works (O.N.I.G.).

2130. **410.** 1 f. green 5 5

411. "The Postman". **413.** Count H. Carton de Wiart.

412. John F. Kennedy Motorway Tunnel, Antwerp.

1969. "Philately for the Young".

2131. **411.** 1 f. multicoloured .. 5 5

1969. Completion of Belgian Road-works. Multicoloured.

2132. 3 f. Type **412** 25 5
2133. 6 f. Loncin flyover, Wallonie motorway 25 12

1969. Count Henry Carton de Wiart (statesman). Birth Cent.

2134. **413.** 6 f. sepia 25 8

414. "Barbu d' Anvers" (Cockerel).

1969. "The Poultry-yard" (poultry-breeding).

2135. **414.** 10 f.+5 f. mult. .. 90 90

415. "Le Denombrement de Bethleem" (detail, Bruegel).

1969. Christmas.

2136. **415.** 1 f. 50 multicoloured 12 5

416. Emblem, "Coin" and Machinery. **417.** Window, St. Waudru Church, Mons.

1969. National Credit Society (S.N.C.I.). 50th Anniv.

2137. **416.** 3 f. 50 brown and blue 12 5

1969. "Solidarity". Musicians in Stained-glass Windows. Multicoloured.

2138. 1 f. 50+50 c. Type **417** .. 15 15
2139. 3 f. 50+1 f. 50 Window, 's-Herenelderen Church 25 25
2140. 7 f.+3 f. Window, St. Jacques Church, Liege 40 40
2141. 9 f.+4 f. Window, Royal Museum of Art and History, Brussels .. 50 50

No. 2141 is larger, 36×52 mm.

418. Camellias.

419. Beech Tree in National Botanical Gardens.

1970. Ghent Flower Show. Multicoloured.
2142. 1 f. 50 Type **418** 10 5
2143. 2 f. 50 Water-lily 20 10
2144. 3 f. 50 Azaleas 20 5

1970. Nature Conservation Year. Multi-coloured.
2146. 3 f. 50 Type **419** 25 5
2147. 7 f. Birch 30 12

420. Young "Postman".

1970. "Philately for the Young".
2148. **420.** 1 f. 50 multicoloured 5 5

421. New U.P.U. Headquarters Building.

1970. New U.P.U. Headquarters Building.
2149. **421.** 3 f. 50 emerald .. 30 5

422. "Flaming Sun".

1970. Europa.
2150. **422.** 3 f. 50 cream, blk. & lake 15 5
2151. 7 f. flesh, black & blue 25 12

423. Relay Post-house, Courcelles.

424. Clock-tower, Virton.

1970. Cultural Works. Multicoloured.
2152. 1 f. 50+50 c. Open-air Museum, Bokrijk .. 20 15
2153. 3 f. 50+1 f. 50 Type **423** .. 30 30
2154. 7 f.+3 f. "The Reaper of Trevires" (bas-relief, Virton) 40 40
2155. 9 f.+4 f. Open-air Museum, Middleheim (Antwerp) 60 60

1970. Virton and Zelzate.
2156. **424.** 2 f. 50 violet & ochre 15 8
2157. – 2 f. 50 black and blue 15 8
DESIGN—HORIZ. No. 2157, Canal bridge, Zelzate.

425. Co-operative Alliance Emblem.

1970. Int. Co-operative Alliance. 75th Anniv.
2158. **425.** 7 f. black and orange 20 5

INDEX

Countries can be quickly located by referring to the index at the end of this volume.

1970. Tourist Publicity. As T **352**.
2159. 1 f. 50 green, blue & black 12 8
2160. 1 f. 50 buff and blue .. 12 8
DESIGNS—HORIZ. No. 2159, Kasterlee. VERT. 2160, Nivelles.

426. Allegory of Resistance Movements.

427. King Baudouin.

1970. Prisoner of War and Concentration Camps Liberation. 25th Anniv.
2161. **426.** 3 f. 50+1 f. 50 black, cerise and green .. 20 20
2162. – 7 f.+3 f. black, cerise and mauve .. 40 40
DESIGN: 7 f. Similar to T **426**, but inscr. "LIBERATION DES CAMPS", etc.

1970. King Baudouin's 40th Birthday.
2163. **427.** 3 f. 50 brown .. 30 5
See also Nos. 2207/23 and 2335/9.

428. Fair Emblem.

429. U.N. Headquarters, New York.

1970. 25th Int. Ghent Fair.
2164. **428.** 1 f. 50 multicoloured 5 5

1970. United Nations, 25th Anniv.
2165. **429.** 7 f. blue and black .. 25 10

430. Queen Fabiola.

431. Angler's Rod and Reel.

1970. Queen Fabiola Foundation.
2166. **430.** 3 f. 50 black and blue 15 5

1970. Sports. Multicoloured.
2167. 3 f. 50+1 f. 50, Type **431** 30 30
2168. 9 f.+4 f. Hockey stick and ball 70 70

432. "The Mason" (sculpture by G. Minne).

434. "Madonna and child" (J. Gossart).

433. Man, Woman and Hillside Town.

1970. National Housing Society. 50th Anniv.
2170. **432.** 3 f. 50 brown & yellow 10 5

1970. Belgian Social Security. 25th Anniv.
2171. **433.** 2 f. 50 multicoloured 12 5

1970. Christmas.
2172. **434.** 1 f. 50 brown .. 8 5

435. C. Huysmans (statesman).

436. Arms of Eupen, Malmedy and St. Vith.

1970. Cultural Works. Famous Belgians.
2173. **435.** 1 f. 50+50 c. brown and red 15 12
2174. – 3 f. 50+1 f. 50 brown and purple .. 25 20
2175. – 7 f.+3 f. brn. & green 35 35
2176. – 9 f.+4 f. brn. & blue 55 55
PORTRAITS: 3 f. 50 Cardinal J. Cardijn. 7 f Maria Baers (Catholic social worker). 9 f. P Pastur (social reformer).

1970. Annexation of Eupen, Malmedy and St. Vith. 50th Anniv.
2177. **436.** 7 f. brown and sepia .. 30 8

437. "The Uneasy Town" (detail, Paul Delvaux).

438. Telephone.

1970. "Solidarity". Paintings. Multi-coloured.
2178. 3 f. 50+1 f. 50 Type **437** .. 25 25
2179. 7 f.+3 f. "The Memory" (Rene Magritte) .. 45 45

1971. Automatic Telephone Service Inaug.
2183. **438.** 1 f. 50 multicoloured 10 5

439. "Auto" Car.

440. Touring Club Badge.

1971. 50th Brussels Motor Show.
2184. **439.** 2 f. 50 black and red 15 8

1971. Royal Touring Club of Belgium. 75th Anniv.
2185. **440.** 3 f. 50 gold, red & blue 12 5

441. Tournai Cathedral.

442. "The Letter-box" (T. Lobrichon).

1971. Tournai Cathedral. 800th Anniv.
2186. **441.** 7 f. blue 35 15

1971. "Philately for the Young".
2187. **442.** 1 f. 50 brown .. 8 5

443. Notre-Dame Abbey, Marche-les-Dames.

1971. Cultural Works.
2190. **443.** 3 f. 50+1 f. 50 blk., grn. & brn. .. 25 25
2191. – 7 f.+3 f. black, red and yellow .. 45 45
DESIGN: 7 f. Convent, Turnhout.

444. King Albert I, Jules Destree and Academy.

1971. Royal Academy of French Language and Literature. 50th Anniv.
2201. **444.** 7 f. black and grey .. 30 12

445. Postman of 1855.

446. Europa Chain.

1971. Stamp Day.
2202. **445.** 3 f. 50 multicoloured 12 5

1971. Europa.
2203. **446.** 3 f. 50 brown & black 20 5
2204. 7 f. green and black .. 25 12

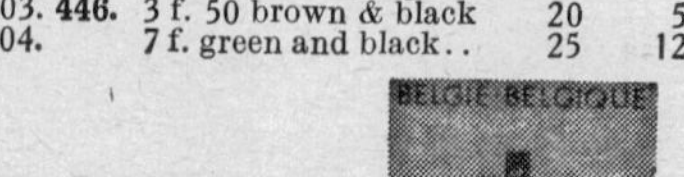

447. Satellite Earth Station.

448. Red Cross.

1971. World Telecommunications Day.
2205. **447.** 7 f. multicoloured .. 30 10

1971. Belgian Red Cross.
2206. **448.** 10 f.+5 f. red & blk. 75 70

1971. As Type **427**, but without dates.
2207. 1 f. 75 green 35 5
2208. 2 f. 25 green 35 5
2208a. 2 f. 50 green 12 5
2209. 3 f. green 12 5
2209a. 3 f. 25 plum 8 5
2210. 3 f. 50 brown 30 5
2211. 4 f. blue 15 5
2212. 4 f. 50 maroon .. 20 5
2212a. 4 f. 50 blue 12 5
2213. 5 f. violet 12 5
2214. 6 f. red 15 5
2214a. 6 f. 50 violet .. 20 5
2215. 7 f. red 20 5
2215a. 7 f. 50 mauve .. 20 5
2216. 8 f. black 20 5
2217. 9 f. brown 40 5
2218. 10 f. red 25 5
2219. 12 f. blue 30 5
2219a. 13 f. blue 35 5
2220. 15 f. violet 35 8
2220a. 17 f. purple 40 8
2221. 18 f. blue 45 8
2222. 20 f. blue 50 10
2222a. 22 f. black 55 12
2222b. 25 f. purple 65 8
2223. 30 f. orange 65 10
See also Nos. 2335/9.

449. Scientists, Penguins and "Erika Dan".

1971. Antarctic Treaty. Tenth Anniv.
2230. **449.** 10 f. multicoloured .. 50 25

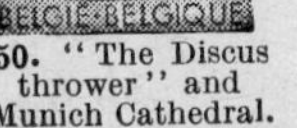

450. "The Discus thrower" and Munich Cathedral.

451. G. Hubin (statesman).

1971. Olympic Games, Munich (1972).
2231. **450.** 7 f. + 3 f. blk. and blue 90 90

1971. Georges Hubin Commemoration.
2232. **451.** 1 f. 50 violet & black 8 5

452. Notre-Dame Abbey, Orval.

453. Processional Giants, Ath.

1971. Notre-Dame Abbey, Orval. 900th Anniv.
2233. **452.** 2 f. 50 brown .. 10 5

1971. Historic Towns.
2234. **453.** 2 f. 50 multicoloured 10 5
2235. – 2 f. 50 brown .. 10 5
DESIGN—HORIZ. (46×35 mm.) No. 2235, View of Ghent.

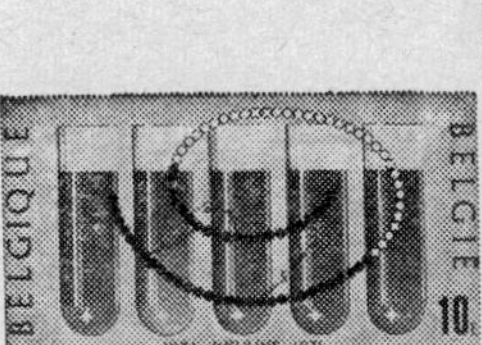

454. Test-tubes and Diagram.

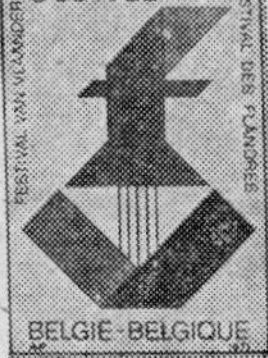

455. Flemish Festival Emblem.

1971. Discovery of Insulin. 50th Anniv.
2236. **454.** 10 f. multicoloured .. 40 15

1971. Cultural Works. Festivals. Multicoloured.
2237. 3 f. 50 + 1 f. 50 Type **455** .. 25 25
2238. 7 f. + 3 f. Walloon Festival emblem 45 45

456. Belgian Family and "50".

457. Dr. Jules Bordet (medical scientist) (10th Death Anniv.)

1971. League of Large Families. 50th Anniv.
2239. **456.** 1 f. 50 multicoloured 8 5

1971. Tourist Publicity. Designs similar to Type **352.**
2240. 2 f. 50 blk., brn. & blue 12 5
2241. 2 f. 50 blk., brn. & blue 12 5
DESIGNS: No. 2240, St. Martin's Church, Alost. No. 2241, Town Hall and belfry, Mons.

1971. Belgian Celebrities.
2242. **457.** 3 f. 50 green 15 5
2243. – 3 f. 50 brown .. 15 5
DESIGN: No. 2243, "Stijn Streuvels" (Frank Lateur, writer) (Birth Cent.).

458. Achaemenid Tomb, Buzpar.

459. Elewijt Chateau.

1971. Persian Empire. 2500th Anniv.
2244. **458.** 7 f. multicoloured .. 30 10

1971. "Belgica 72" Stamp Exhibition, Brussels. (2nd issue).
2245. – 3 f. + 1 f. 50 green .. 45 45
2246. **459.** 7 f. + 3 f. brown .. 60 60
2247. – 10 f. + 5 f. blue .. 90 90
DESIGNS—HORIZ. (52×35½ mm.): 3 f. Attre Chateau. 10 f. Royal Palace, Brussels.

460. F.I.B./V.B.N. Emblem.

461. "The Flight into Egypt" (15th century Dutch School.

1971. Federation of Belgian Industries. 25th Anniv.
2248. **460.** 3 f. 50 gold, blk. & bl. 12 5

1971. Christmas.
2249. **461.** 1 f. 50 multicoloured 8 5

1971. Tourist Publicity. Designs similar to Type **352.**
2250. 1 f. 50 indigo and buff .. 15 5
2251. 2 f. 50 blue and buff .. 12 5
DESIGNS—HORIZ. 1 f. 50 Town Hall, Malines. VERT. 2 f. 50 Basilica, St. Hubert.

462. Head of "Polistes gallicus".

1971. 'Solidarity". Heads of Insects in Antwerp Zoo. Multicoloured.
2252. 1 f. 50 + 50 c. "Actias luna" 12 12
2253. 3 f. 50 + 1 f. 50 "Tabanus bromius" 20 20
2254. 7 f. + 3 f. Type **462** .. 40 40
2255. 9 f. + 4 f. "Cicindela campestris" .. .. 1·10 1·10
The 1 f. 50 and 9 f. are vert. designs.

463. Road Signs and Traffic Signals.

464. Book Year Emblem.

1972. "Via Secura" Road Safety. Organisation. 20th Anniv.
2263. **463.** 3 f. 50 multicoloured 12 5

1972. International Book Year.
2264. **464.** 7 f. blue, brn. & black 20 8

465. Coins of Belgium and Luxembourg.

466. "Auguste Vermeylen" (I. Opsomer).

1972. Belgo-Luxembourgeoise Economic Union. 50th Anniv.
2265. **465.** 1 f. 50 sil., blk. & orge. 10 5

1972. Auguste Vermeylen (writer) Birth Cent.
2267. **466.** 2 f. 50 multicoloured 12 8

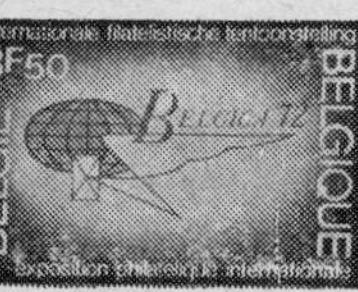

467. "Belgica 72" Emblem.

469. Astronaut cancelling Letter on Moon.

468. Heart Emblem.

1972. "Belgica 72" Stamp Exn., Brussels (3rd Issue).
2268. **467.** 3 f. 50 purple, bl. & brn. 12 5

1972. World Heart Month.
2269. **468.** 7 f. multicoloured .. 25 8

470. "Communications".

1972. Stamp Day.
2270. **469.** 3 f. 50 multicoloured 15 5

1972. Europa.
2271. **470.** 3 f. 50 multicoloured 15 5
2272. 7 f. multicoloured .. 25 12

471. Quill Pen and Newspaper.

472. "UIC" on Coupled Wagons.

1972. "Liberty of the Press", Belga News Agency. 50th Anniv. and 25th Congress of International Federation of Newspaper Editors (F.I.E.J.).
2273. **471.** 2 f. 50 multicoloured 12 5

1972. Int. Railways Union (U.I.C.). 50th Anniv.
2274. **472.** 7 f. multicoloured .. 25 8
See also No. P 2266.

1972. Tourist Publicity. Designs similar to T **352.**
2275. 2 f. 50 pur., blue & green 8 5
2276. 2 f. 50 brown and blue .. 8 5
DESIGNS—HORIZ. (30×22 mm.) No. 2275, Couvin. VERT. (22×30 mm.) No. 2276, Aldeneik Church, Maaseik.

473. Leopold I 10c. "Epaulettes" Stamp of 1849.

474. "Beatrice" (after G. De Smet).

1972. "Belgica 72" Stamp Exhib., Brussels (4th issue).
2277. **473.** 1 f. 50 + 50 c. brown black and gold .. 15 15
2278. – 2 f. + 1 f. brown-red, brown and gold .. 20 20
2279. – 2 f. 50 + 1 f. red, brown and gold 35 35
2280. – 3 f. 50 + 1 f. 50 lilac, black and gold .. 45 45
2281. – 6 f. + 3 f. violet, black and gold 90 90
2282. – 7 f. + 3 f. red, black and gold .. .. 1·25 1·25
2283. – 10 f. + 5 f. blue, black and gold .. .. 1·75 1·75
2284. – 15 f. + 7 f. 50 green, blue-green & gold .. 2·25 2·25
2285. – 20 f. + 10 f. chestnut, brown and gold .. 2·10 2·10
DESIGNS: 2 f. Leopold I 40 c. "Medallion" of 1849. 2 f. 50 Leopold II 10 c. of 1883. 3 f. 50 Leopold II 50 c. of 1883. 6 f. Albert I 2 f. "Tin Hat" of 1919. 7 f. Albert I 50 f. of 1929. 10 f. Albert I 1 f. 75 of 1931. 15 f. Leopold III 5 f. of 1936. 20 f. Baudouin 3 f. 50 of 1970.

1972. "Philately for the Young".
2287. **474.** 3 f. multicoloured .. 8 5

475. Emblem of William Lennox Centre.

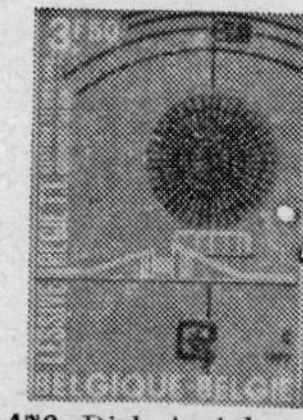

476. Dish Aerial and "Intelstat 4" Satellite.

1972. William Lennox Epileptic Centre, Ottignies. Inaug.
2288. **475.** 10 f. + 5 f. mult. .. 60 50

1972. Satellite Earth Station, Lessive. Inaug.
2289. **476.** 3 f. 50 blk., silver & bl. 15 5

477. Frans Masereel (wood-carver and painter).

478. "The Adoration of the Magi" (F. Timmermans).

1972. Masereel Commem.
2290. **477.** 4 f. 50 black and green 15 5

1972. Christmas.
2291. **478.** 3 f. 50 multicoloured 8 5

479. "Empress Maria Theresa" (unknown artist).

1972. Belgian Royal Academy of Sciences, Letters and Fine Arts. Bicent.
2292. **479.** 2 f. multicoloured .. 15 8

480. Falcon.

481. "Fire".

1972. "Solidarity". Birds from Zwin Nature Reserve. Multicoloured.
2293. 2 f. + 1 f. Grey lag goose (vert.) 15 12
2294. 4 f. 50 + 2 f. Lapwing (vert.) 30 25
2295. 8 f. + 4 f. White stork (vert.) 45 45
2296. 9 f. + 4 f. 50 Type **480** .. 55 55

1973. Industrial Buildings Fire Protection Campaign.
2297. **481.** 2 f. multicoloured .. 20 8

482. W.M.O. Emblem and Meteorological Equipment.

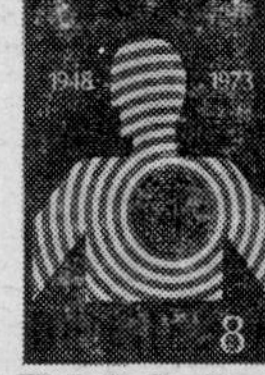

484. W.H.O. Emblem as Man's "Heart".

483. Bijoke Abbey and Museum, Ghent.

1973. World Meteorological Organisation. Centenary.
2298. **482.** 9 f. multicoloured .. 30 10

1973. Cultural Works. Religious Buildings.
2299. **483.** 2 f. + 1 f. green .. 20 20
2300. – 4 f. 50 + 2 f. brown .. 35 35
2301. – 8 f. + 4 f. red .. 55 55
2302. – 9 f. + 4 f. 50 blue .. 65 65

DESIGNS: 4 f. 50 Collegiate Church of St. Ursmer, Lobbes. 8 f. Park Abbey, Heverlee, 9 f. Floreffe Abbey.

1973. W.H.O. 25th Anniv.
2303. **484.** 8 f. black, red & yell. 30 15

485. Ball in Hands.

1973. 1st World Basketball Championships for the Handicapped, Bruges.
2304. **485.** 10 f.+5 f. mult. .. 75 70

486. Europa "Posthorn". **487.** Thurn and Taxis Courier (17th-cent.).

1973. Europa.
2305. **486.** 4 f. 50 bl., yell. & brn. 15 5
2306. 8 f. bl., yell. and grn. 30 15

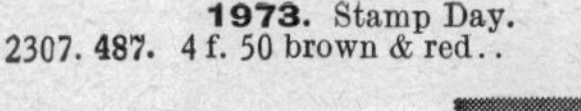

1973. Stamp Day.
2307. **487.** 4 f. 50 brown & red.. 15 5

488. Fair Emblem. **489.** Arrows encircling Globe.

1973. 25th International Fair, Liege.
2308. **488.** 4 f. 50 multicoloured 15 5

1973. 5th World Telecommunications Day.
2309. **489.** 3 f. 50 multicoloured 12 5

490. "Sport" (poster for Ghent Exhibition, 1913).

1973. Workers' Int., Sports Organization. 60th Anniv.
2310. **490.** 4 f. 50 multicoloured 20 5

491. SABENA "DC-10".

1973. SABENA. 50th Anniv.
2311. **491.** 8 f. blk., bl. & grey-bl. 30 15

492. "Tips" Biplane of 1908.

1973. "Les Vieilles Tiges de Belgique" (pioneer aviators' association). 35th Anniv. (1972).
2312. **492.** 10 f. blk., bl., & grn... 60 20

493. 15th-Century Printing-press.

494. "Woman Bathing" (fresco by Lemaire).

1973. Historical Events and Anniversaries.
2313. **493.** 2 f.+1 f. blk., brn. & red 35 25
2314. – 3 f. 50+1 f. 50 mult. 55 45
2315. – 4 f. 50+2 f. mult. .. 70 65
2316. – 8 f.+4 f. multicoloured 1·10 1·00
2317. – 9 f.+4 f. 50 mult. .. 1·25 1·25
2318. – 10 f.+5 f. mult. .. 1·60 1·60

DESIGNS—VERT. (As Type **493**.). 2 f. (500th anniv., of first Belgian printed book, produced by Dirk Martens). 3 f. 50 Head of Amon (Queen Elisabeth Egyptological Foundation. 50th anniv.). 4 f. 50 "Portrait of a Young Girl" (Petrus Christus, 500th death anniv.). HORIZ. (36×25 mm.). 8 f. Gold coins of Hadrian and Marcus Aurelius (Discovery of Roman treasure at Luttre-Liberchies). (52×35 mm.). 9 f. "Members of the Great Council" (Coessaert) (Great Council of Malines. 500th anniv.). 10 f. 18th-century sailing-ship (Ostend Merchant Company. 250th anniv.).

1973. Thermal Treatment Year.
2319. **494.** 4 f. 50 multicoloured 15 5

495. Adolphe Sax and Tenor Saxophone.

496. St. Nicholas Church, Eupen.

1973. Belgian Musical Instrument Industry.
2320. **495.** 9 f. multicoloured .. 30 5

1973. Tourist Publicity.
2321. **496.** 2 f. multicoloured .. 5 5
See also Nos. 2328/9, 2368/70 and 2394/5.

497. "Little Charles" (Evenepoel).

498. J. B. Moens (philatelist) and Perforations.

1973. "Philately for the Young".
2322. **497.** 3 f. multicoloured .. 8 5

1973. Belgian Stamp Dealers Association. 50th Anniv.
2323. **498.** 10 f. multicoloured .. 35 5

499. "Adoration of the Shepherds" (H. van der Goes)

500. Motorway and Emblem.

1973. Christmas.
2324. **499.** 4 f. blue 12 5

1973. "Vlaamse Automobilistenbond" (VAB) (motoring organization). 50th Anniv.
2325. **500.** 5 f. multicoloured .. 15 5

501. L. Pierard (after sculpture by Lanchelevici).

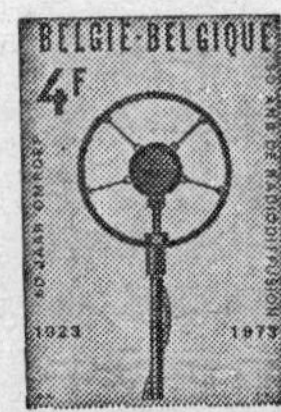

502. Early Microphone.

1973. Louis Pierard (politician and writer). 21st Death Anniv.
2326. **501.** 4 f. red and cream .. 12 5

1973. Belgium Radio. 50th Anniv.
2327. **502.** 4 f. black and blue .. 12 5

503. Town Hall, Lean.

1973. Tourist Publicity.
2328. **503.** 3 f. grey, brn. & blue 15 5
2329. – 4 f. grey and green .. 15 5
DESIGN: 4 f. Chimay Castle.

504. F. Rops (self-portrait). **505.** Jack of Diamonds.

1973. Felicien Rops (artist and engraver). 75th Death Anniv.
2330. **504.** 7 f. black and brown 25 8

1973. "Solidarity". Old Playing Cards. Mult.
2331. 5 f.+2 f. 50 Type **505** .. 60 60
2332. 5 f.+2 f. 50 Jack of Spades 60 60
2333. 5 f.+2 f. 50 Queen of Hearts 60 60
2334. 5 f.+2 f. 50 King of Clubs 60 60

1973. As Nos. 2207/23 but smaller, size 22×17 mm.
2335. **427.** 3 f. green 70 30
2336. 4 f. blue 30 5
2336a. 4 f. 50 green 60 60
2337. 4 f. 50 blue 20 5
2338. 5 f. mauve 12 8
2338a. 6 f. 50 black 30 5
2339. 6 f. 50 violet 50 40

506. King Albert (Baron Opsomer).

507. Blood donation.

1974. King Albert I. 40th Death Anniv.
2340. **506.** 4 f. blue and black .. 15 5

1974. Belgian Red Cross. Multicoloured.
2341. 4 f.+2 f. Type **507** .. 30 25
2342. 10 f.+5 f. "Traffic Lights" (Road Safety) 60 60

508. "Protection of the Environment".

509. "Armand Jamar" (Self-portrait).

1974. Robert Schuman Association for the Protection of the Environment.
2343. **508.** 3 f. multicoloured .. 15 5

1974. Belgian Cultural Celebrities. Multi-coloured.
2344. 4 f.+2 f. Type **509** .. 30 30
2345. 5 f.+2 f. 50 Tony Bergmann (author) and view of Lier 30 30
2346. 7 f.+3 f. 50 Henri Vieuxtemps (violinist) and view of Verviers .. 45 45
2347. 10 f.+5 f. "James Ensor" (self-portrait with masks) (35×52 mm.) 70 70

510. N.A.T.O. Emblem.

511. Hubert Krains (Belgian postal administrator).

1974. North Atlantic Treaty Organization. 25th Anniv.
2348. **510.** 10 f. blue and lt. blue 30 8

1974. Stamp Day.
2349. **511.** 5 f. black and grey .. 15 5

512. "Destroyed Gown" (O. Zadkine).

513. Heads of Boy and Girl.

1974. Europa. Sculptures.
2350. **512.** 5 f. black and red .. 15 5
2351. – 10 f. black & blue .. 35 12
DESIGN: 10 f. "Solidarity" (G. Minne).

1974. Lay Youth Festival.
2352. **513.** 4 f. multicoloured .. 15 5

514. Pillory, Braine-le-Chateau.

1974. "Historical Series".
2354. – 3 f. brown & blue .. 12 5
2355. **514.** 4 f. brown & red .. 15 5
2356. – 5 f. brown & reen .. 20 8
2357. – 7 f. brown & yellow.. 25 8
2358. – 10 f. brown, orge. & bl. 30 12
DESIGNS—HORIZ. 3 f. New Planetarium, Brussels. 5 f. Rains of Soleilmont Abbey. 7 f. "procession" (fountain sculpture, Ghent). VERT. 10 f. Belfry, Bruges.

515. "BENELUX".

1974. Benelux. 30th Anniv.
2359. **515.** 5 f. turquoise & green 15 5

516. "Jan Vekemans at the Age of Five". **517.** Self-portrait and Van Gogh House, Cuesmes.

1974. "Philately for the Young".
2360. **516.** 3 f. multicoloured .. 12 5

1974. Opening of Vincent Van Gogh Memorial Museum, Cuesmes.
2361. **517.** 10 f.+5 f. multicoloured 70 70

518. Corporal Tresignies and Brule Bridge.

1974. Corporal Leon Tresignies (war hero). 60th Death Anniv.
2362. **518.** 4 f. green & brown .. 12 5

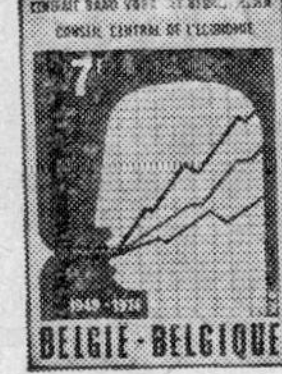

519. Montgomery Blair and U.P.U. Emblem. **520.** Graph within Head.

1974. Universal Postal Union. Cent.
2363. **519.** 5 f. black & green .. 20 8
2364. – 10 f. black and red .. 35 10
DESIGN: 10 f. H. von Stephan and U.P.U. emblem.

1974. Central Economic Council. 25th Anniv.
2365. **520.** 7 f. multicoloured .. 25 8

521. Rotary Emblem on Belgian Flag. **522.** Wild Boar.

1974. Rotary International in Belgium.
2366. **521.** 10 f. multicoloured .. 30 12

1974. Granting of Colours to Ardennes Regiment of Chasseurs. 40th Anniv.
2367. **522.** 3 f. multicoloured .. 12 5

1974. Tourist Publicity. As Type **496.**
2368. 3 f. black, yell. & brn. .. 10 5
2369. 4 f. black, green & blue .. 12 5
2370. 4 f. black, green & blue .. 15 5
DESIGNS—VERT. 3 f. Aarschot. HORIZ. 4 f. (No. 2369), Nassogne. 4 f. (No. 2320), Gemmenich.

523. "The Mystic Lamb" (angel-detail, Van Eyck brothers). **524.** Gentian.

1974. Christmas.
2371. **523.** 4 f. purple 10 5

1974. "Solidarity". Flora and Fauna. Mult.
2372. 4 f.+2 f. Type **524** .. 20 20
2373. 5 f.+2 f. 50 Badger (horiz.) 30 30
2374. 7 f.+3 f. 50 Golden Beetle (horiz.) 50 50
2375. 10 f.+5 f. Spotted Cat's-ear ("Hypochoeris maculata") 60 60

525. Adolphe Quetelet. (after J. Odevaere). **526.** Exhibition Emblem.

1974. Adolphe Quetelet (scientist). Death Centenary.
2376. **525.** 10 f. black & brown.. 30 10

1975. "Themabelga" Stamp Exhibition, Brussels.
2377. **526.** 6 f. 50 orge., blk. & grn. 20 5

527. "Neoregelia carolinae". **528.** Student and Young Boy.

1975. Ghent Flower Show. Multicoloured.
2378. 4 f. 50 Type **527** 15 5
2379. 5 f. "Tussilago petasites" 15 5
2380. 6 f. 50 "Azalea japonica" 20 5

1975. Charles Buls Normal School. Cent.
2381. **528.** 4 f. 50 multicoloured 15 5

529. Foundation Emblem. **530.** King Albert I

1975. Davids Foundation. Cent.
2382. **529.** 5 f. multicoloured .. 15 5

1975. King Albert I. Birth Cent.
2383. **530.** 10 f. black and purple 30 8

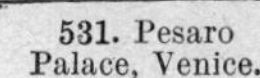

531. Pesaro Palace, Venice. **532.** "Postman of 1840" (J. Thiriar).

1975. Cultural Works.
2384. **531.** 6 f. 50+2 f. 50 brown 30 30
2385. – 10 f.+4 f. 50 maroon 55 55
2386. – 15 f.+6 f. 50 blue .. 70 70
DESIGNS—HORIZ. 10 f. Sculpture Museum, St. Bavon Abbey, Ghent. VERT. 15 f. "Virgin and Child". (Michelangelo, 500th Birth Anniv.)

1975. Stamp Day.
2387. **532.** 6 f. 50 maroon .. 20 5

533. "An Apostle" (detail, "The Last Supper" Dirk Bouts). **534.** Prisoners' Identification Emblems.

1975. Europa. Paintings.
2388. **533.** 6 f. 50 black, bl. & grn. 20 5
2389. – 10 f. blk., red & orge. 30 10
DESIGN: 10 f. "The Suppliant's Widow" (detail, "The Justice of Otho", Dirk Bouts).

1975. Concentration Camps' Liberation. 30th Anniv.
2390. **534.** 4 f. 50 multicoloured 15 5

535. St. John's Hospice, Bruges.

1975. European Architectural Heritage Year.
2391. **535.** 4 f. 50 purple .. 15 5
2392. – 5 f. green 20 5
2393. – 10 f. blue 30 10
DESIGNS—VERT. 5 f. St. Loup's Church, Namur. 10 f. Martyrs Square, Brussels.

1975. Toursit Publicity. As T **496.**
2394. 4 f. 50 brown, buff and red 15 5
2395. 5 f. multicoloured .. 15 5
DESIGN—VERT. 4 f. 50, Church, Dottignies. HORIZ. 5 f. Market Square, Saint Truiden.

536. G. Ryckmans and L. Cerfaux (founders), and Louvian University Library. **537.** "Metamorphosis" (P. Mara).

1975. Louvain Colloquium Biblicum (Biblical Scholarship Association). 25th Anniv.
2396. **536.** 10 f. sepia and blue.. 30 8

1975. Queen Fabiola Foundation. For the Mentally Ill.
2397. **537.** 7 f. multicoloured .. 20 8

538. Marie Popelin (women's rights pioneer) and Palace of Justice. **539.** "Assia" (Charles Despiau).

1975. International Women's Year.
2398. **538.** 6 f. 50 purple & green 15 5

1975. Middelheim Open-air Museum. Antwerp. 25th Anniv.
2399. **539.** 5 f. black and green.. 15 5

540. Dr. Hemerijckx and Leprosy Hospital, Zaire.

1975. Dr. Frans Hemerijckx, treatment of leprosy pioneer. Commemoration.
2400. **540.** 20 f.+10 f. mult. .. 95 95

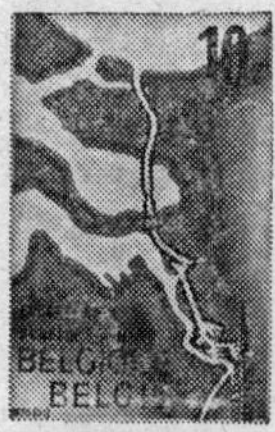

541. Canal Map. **542.** "Cornelia Vakemans at the Age of Seven" (Cornelia de Vos).

1975. Opening of Rhine-Scheldt Canal.
2401. **541.** 10 f. multicoloured .. 30 10

1975. "Philately for the Young".
2402. **542.** 4 f. 50 mult coloured 15 5

543. National Bank and F. Orban (founder).

1975. Belgian National Bank. 125th Anniv.
2403. **543.** 5 f. multicoloured .. 65 15

544. Edmond Thieffry (pilot) and Handley-Page aircraft, "Princess Marie-Jose". **545.** University Seal.

1975. First Flight, Brussels–Kinshasa. 50th Anniv.
2404. **544.** 7 f. purple and black 20 10

1975. Louvain University. 550th Anniv.
2405. **545.** 6 f. 50 blk., grn. & blue 20 5

546. "Angels" (detail, "The Nativity" R. de le Pasture). **547.** Emile Moyson (Flemish Leader).

1975. Christmas.
2406. **546.** 5 f. multicoloured .. 15 5

1975. "Solidarity".
2407. **547.** 4 f. 50+2 f. purple.. 30 30
2408. – 6 f. 50+3 f. green .. 35 35
2409. – 10 f.+5 f. vio., blk. & bl. 60 60
2410. – 13 f.+6 f. multicoloured 70 70
DESIGNS—VERT. 6 f. 50 Dr. Augustus Snellaert (Flemish literature scholar). 13 f. Detail of retable, St. Dymphne Church, Geel. HORIZ. 10 f. Eye within hand, and Braille characters (150th anniv. of introduction of Braille).

548. Cheese Seller. **549.** "African" Collector.

1975. "Themabelga" International Thematic Stamp Exhibition, Brussels. Traditional Belgian Trades. Multicoloured.
2411. 4 f. 50+1 f. 50 Type **548** 25 25
2412. 6 f. 50+3 f. Potato seller 35 35
2413. 6 f. 50+3 f. Basket-carrier 35 35
2414. 10 f.+5 f. Prawn fisher-man and pony (horiz.) 45 45
2415. 10 f.+5 f. Knife-grinder and cart (horiz.) .. 45 45
2416. 30 f.+15 f. Milk-woman with dog-cart (horiz.) 1·50 1·50

1976. "Conservatoire Africain" (Charity organization). Centenary.
2417. **549.** 10 f.+5 f. multicoloured 60 60

550. Owl Emblem and Flemish Buildings. **551.** Bicentennial Symbol.

1976. Willems Foundation (Flemish cultural organization). 125th Anniv.
2418. **550.** 5 f. multicoloured .. 15 5

1976. American Revolution. Bicent.
2419. **551.** 14 f. multicoloured .. 45 12

552. Caridnal Mercier.

553. " Vlaams Ekonomisch Verbond."

1976. Cardinal Mercier. 50th Death Anniv.

2420.	**552.**	4 f. 50 purple	15	5

1976. Flemish Economic Federation. 50th Anniv.

2421.	**553.**	6 f. 50 multicoloured	20	5

554. Swimming.

555. Money Centre Building, Brussels.

1976. Olympic Games, Montreal. Multicoloured.

2422.	4 f. 50+1 f. 50 Type **554**	20	15
2423.	5 f.+2 f. Running (vert.)	20	15
2424.	6 f. 50+2 f. 50 Horse-jumping	30	25

1976. Stamp Day.

2425.	**555.**	6 f. 50 brown	20	5

556. Queen Elizabeth playing Violin.

557. Basket-making.

1976. Queen Elizabeth International Music Competitions. 25th Anniv.

2426.	**556.**	14 f.+6 f. red & blk.	60	60

1976. Europa. Traditional Crafts. Multicoloured.

2427.	6 f. 50 Type **557**	20	5
2428.	14 f. Pottery (horiz.)	40	8

558. Lorry on Motorway.

559. Queen Elizabeth.

1976. 14th Congress of International Road Haulage Union, Brussels.

2429.	**558.**	14 f. blk., red & yell.	40	8

1976. Queen Elizabeth. Birth Cent.

2430.	**559.**	14 f. myrtle-green	40	8

560. Ardennes Horses.

1976. Ardennes Draught Horses Society. 50th Anniv.

2436.	**560.**	5 f. multicoloured	15	5

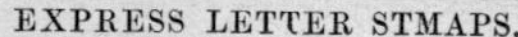

EXPRESS LETTER STAMPS.

E 1. Ghent.

DESIGNS: 1 f. 75, Town Hall, Brussels. 2 f. 45, Eupen. 3 f. 50, Bishop's Palace, Liege. 5f. 25 Antwerp Cathedral.

1929.

E 530.	–	1 f. 75 blue	55	8
E 531.	**E 1.**	2 f. 35 red	1·60	10
E 581.	–	2 f. 45 green	9·00	50
E 532.	–	3 f. 50 purple	3·00	2·10
E 533.	–	5 f. 25 olive	3·00	2·10

1932. No. E 581 surch. **2 Fr 50** and cross.

E 608.	2 f. 50 on 2 f. 45 grn.	7·00	40

MILITARY STAMPS

1967. As T **205.** (Baudouin) but with letter " M " within oval at foot.

M 2027.	1 f. 50 green	35	5

1971. As No. 2207/8a and 2209a but with letter " M " within oval at foot.

M 2224.	1 f. 75 green	60	12
M 2225.	2 f. 25 green	80	12
M 2226.	2 f. 50 green	30	10
M 2227	3 f. 25 plum	10	8

NEWSPAPER STAMPS

1928. Railway Parcels stamps of 1923 optd. **JOURNAUX DAGBLADEN 1928.**

N 443.	**P 10.**	10 c. red	12	8
N 444.		20 c. green	12	8
N 445.		40 c. olive	10	5
N 446.		60 c. orange	25	8
N 447.		70 c. brown	12	5
N 448.		80 c. violet	25	5
N 449.		90 c. slate	1·00	35
N 450.		1 f. blue	45	5
N 451.		2 f. olive	80	12
N 452.		3 f. red	85	15
N 453.		4 f. red	85	15
N 454.		5 f. violet	85	12
N 455.		6 f. brown	1·00	35
N 456.		7 f. orange	1·75	35
N 457.		8 f. brown	1·60	35
N 458.		9 f. purple	2·50	55
N 459.		10 f. green	1·60	35
N 460.		20 f. pink	4·00	1·00

1929. Railway Parcels stamps of 1923 optd. **JOURNAUX DAGBLADEN** only.

N 505.	**P 10.**	10 c. red	10	5
N 506.		20 c. green	10	5
N 507.		40 c. olive	10	8
N 508.		60 c. orange	25	10
N 509.		70 c. brown	10	5
N 510.		80 c. violet	30	8
N 511.		90 c. slate	1·00	35
N 512.		1 f. blue	35	5
N 513.		1 f. 10 brown	2·50	45
N 514.		1 f. 50 blue	2·50	55
N 515.		2 f. olive	80	10
N 516.		2 f. 10 slate	11·00	3·50
N 517.		3 f. red	95	15
N 518.		4 f. red	95	15
N 519.		5 f. violet	95	15
N 520.		6 f. brown	1·25	35
N 521.		7 f. orange	1·75	35
N 522.		8 f. brown	1·60	35
N 523.		9 f. purple	2·25	60
N 524.		10 f. green	1·40	35
N 525.		20 f. pink	4·75	1·00

PARCEL POST STAMPS

Stamps issued at Belgian Post Offices only.

1928. Optd. **COLIS POSTAL POSTCOLLO.**

B 470.	**53.**	4 f. brown	1·60	15
B 471.		5 f. bistre	1·60	25

B 1. G.P.O., Brussels.

1929.

B 526.	**B 1.**	3 f. sepia	75	8
B 527.		4 f. slate	75	5
B 528.		5 f. red	75	5
B 529.		6 f. purple	11·00	7·00

1933. Surch. **X4 4X**

B 645.	**B 1.**	4 f. on 6 f. purple	12·00	8

RAILWAY PARCELS STAMPS

In Belgium the parcels service is largely operated by the Belgian Railways (a private company) for which the following stamps were issued.

Certain stamps under this heading were also on sale at post offices in connection with a "small parcels" service. These show a posthorn in the design except for Nos. P 1116/18.

P 1.

1879.

P 63.	**P 1.**	10 c. brown	11·00	70
P 64.		20 c. blue	40·00	4·00
P 65.		25 c. green	50·00	1·90
P 66.		50 c. red	£300	1·75
P 67.		80 c. yellow	£325	10·00
P 68.		1 f. grey	38·00	3·75

P 2.

1882.

P 69.	**P 2.**	10 c. brown	4·25	20
P 73.		15 c. slate	2·50	2·50
P 75.		20 c. blue	13·00	80
P 77.		25 c. green	14·00	1·10
P 78.		50 c. red	14·00	10
P 83.		80 c. yellow	17·00	50
P 84.		80 c. brown	13·00	15
P 85.		1 f. grey	85·00	70
P 86.		1 f. purple	70·00	70
P 88.		2 f. buff	60·00	13·00

P 3.

1895. Numerals in black except 1 and 2.).

P 96.	**P 3.**	10 c. brown	2·25	12
P 97.		15 c. slate	1·75	1·25
P 98.		20 c. blue	4·50	20
P 99.		25 c. green	4·50	30
P 100.		30 c. orange	6·00	45
P 101.		40 c. green	6·50	45
P 102.		50 c. red	5·50	10
P 103.		60 c. lilac	10·00	12
P 104.		70 c. blue	8·00	12
P 105.		80 c. yellow	8·00	12
P 106.		90 c. red	13·00	15
P 107.		1 f. purple	32·00	25
P 108.		2 f. buff	35·00	85

P 4.

1902.

P 109a.	**P 3.**	10 c. slate & brown	5	5
P 110.		15 c. pur. & slate	5	5
P 111.		20 c. brn. & blue	5	5
P 112.		25 c. red & green	10	5
P 113.		30 c. green & orge.	5	5
P 114.		35 c. green & brn.	5	5
P 115.		40 c. mauve & grn.	10	5
P 116.		50 c. mauve & pink	5	5
P 117.		55 c. blue & purple	5	5
P 118.		60 c. red and lilac	5	5
P 119.		70 c. red and blue	5	5
P 120.		80 c. purple & yell.	5	5
P 121.		90 c. green and red	5	5
P 122.	**P 4.**	1 f. orange & purple	5	5
P 123.		1 f. 10 black & red	5	5
P 124.		2 f. green & bistre	5	5
P 125.		3 f. blue and black	5	5
P 126.		4 f. red & green	40	25
P 127.		5 f. green & orange	25	20
P 128.		10 f. purple & yell.	20	20

P 5.

P 6.

1916.

P 201.	**P 5.**	10 c. blue	30	5
P 202.		15 c. olive	35	15
P 203.		20 c. red	50	15
P 204.		25 c. brown	50	15
P 205.		30 c. mauve	50	5
P 206.		35 c. grey	35	5
P 207.		40 c. orange	70	25
P 208.		50 c. bistre	55	10
P 209.		55 c. brown	60	40
P 210.		60 c. lilac	55	5
P 211.		70 c. green	40	5
P 212.		80 c. brown	50	5
P 213.		90 c. blue	50	10
P 214.	**P 6.**	1 f. grey	45	5
P 215.		1 f. 10 bl. (FRANKEN)	4·00	3·50
P 216.		1 f. 10 bl. (FRANK)	60	5
P 217.		2 f. red	5·00	10
P 218.		3 f. violet	5·00	5
P 219.		4 f. green	7·00	25
P 220.		5 f. brown	8·00	30
P 221.		10 f. orange	8·00	20

P 7.

P 8.

1920.

P 259.	**P 7.**	10 c. blue	40	10
P 280.		10 c. red	12	5
P 260.		15 c. olive	60	25
P 281.		15 c. green	8	5
P 261.		20 c. red	50	12
P 282a.		20 c. green	20	5
P 262.		25 c. brown	70	15
P 283.		25 c. blue	25	5
P 263.		30 c. mauve	3·25	3·50
P 284.		30 c. brown	30	5
P 285.		35 c. brown	35	15
P 286.		40 c. orange	35	15
P 265.		50 c. bistre	1·75	15
P 287.		50 c. red	30	5
P 266.		55 c. brown	1·25	75
P 288.		55 c. yellow	80	50
P 267.		60 c. purple	2·40	15
P 289		60 c. red	35	5
P 290.		70 c. green	1·10	8
P 269.		80 c. brown	10·00	20
P 291.		80 c. violet	85	5
P 270.		90 c. blue	2·50	15
P 292.	**P 7.**	90 c. yellow	4·00	3·00
P 293.		90 c. claret	1·75	12
P 271.	**P 8.**	1 f. grey	18·00	35
P 295.		1 f. brown	1·75	8
P 296.		1 f. 10 blue	65	10
P 273.		1 f. 20 green	4·25	35
P 297.		1 f. 20 orange	85	5
P 274.		1 f. 40 brown	1·75	10
P 298.		1 f. 40 yellow	3·50	25
P 299.		1 f. 60 green	6·00	15
P 300.		2 f. red	7·00	10
P 276.		3 f. mauve	21·00	12
P 301.		3 f. red	7·00	10
P 302.		4 f. green	7·00	10
P 278.		5 f. brown	24·00	15
P 303.		5 f. violet	5·50	10
P 279.		10 f. orange	20·00	12
P 304.		10 f. yellow	32·00	75
P 305.		10 f. brown	6·00	8
P 306.		15 f. red	6·00	8
P 307.		20 f. blue	65·00	40

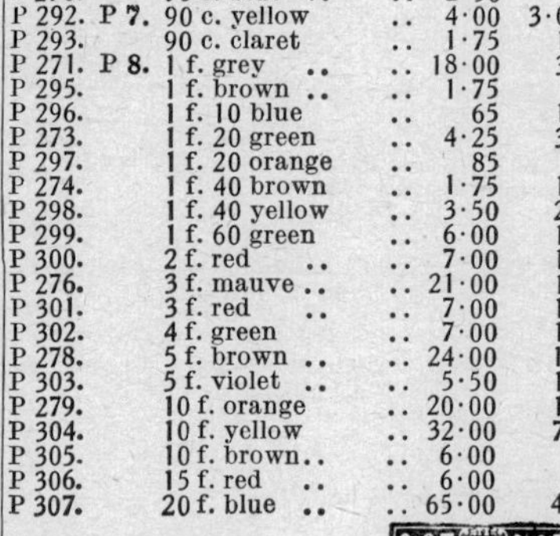

P 9.

P 10.

1922.

P 341.	**P 9.**	2 f. black	1·25	8
P 342.		3 f. brown	16·00	8
P 343.		4 f. green	3·50	8
P 344.		5 f. claret	3·50	8
P 345.		10 f. brown	3·50	8
P 346.		15 f. red	3·75	8
P 347.		20 f. blue	20·00	8

1923.

P 375.	**P 10.**	5 c. brown	10	8
P 376.		10 c. red	5	5
P 377.		15 c. blue	10	10
P 378.		20 c. green	5	5
P 379.		30 c. purple	5	5
P 380.		40 c. olive	5	5
P 381.		50 c. red	5	5
P 382.		60 c. orange	10	5
P 383.		70 c. brown	5	5
P 384.		80 c. violet	8	5
P 385.		90 c. slate	70	8

Similar type, but horiz.

P 387.		1 f. blue	15	5
P 388.		1 f. 10 orange	1·60	5
P 389.		1 f. 50 green	1·60	5
P 390.		1 f. 70 brown	30	5
P 391.		1 f. 80 claret	2·00	8
P 392.		2 f. olive	15	5
P 393.		2 f. 10 green	4·25	10
P 394.		2 f. 40 violet	2·10	20
P 395.		2 f. 70 grey	7·00	5
P 396.		3 f. red	25	5
P 397.		3 f. 30 brown	8·00	10
P 398.		4 f. red	25	5
P 399.		5 f. violet	40	5
P 400.		6 f. brown	25	5
P 401.		7 f. orange	50	5
P 402.		8 f. brown	40	5
P 403.		9 f. purple	1·40	5
P 404.		10 f. green	55	5
P 405.		20 f. pink	80	5
P 406.		30 f. green	2·50	5
P 407.		40 f. slate	17·00	10
P 408.		50 f. bistre	4·25	8

See Nos. P911/34.

1924. No. P 394 surch. **2 F 30** and bars.
P 409. 2 f. 30 on 2 f. 40 violet .. 1·25 15

P 13. "Goliath". **P 14.** Diesel Locomotive.

1934.
P 655. **P 13.** 3 f. green .. .. 2·00 65
P 656. 4 f. mauve .. 1·00 5
P 657. 5 f. red .. 1·60 5

1935. Belgian Railway Cent.
P 689. **P 14.** 10 c. red 12 5
P 690. 20 c. violet .. 15 5
P 691. 30 c. brown .. 20 5
P 692. 40 c. blue .. 25 5
P 693. 50 c. orange .. 25 5
P 694. 60 c. green .. 35 5
P 695. 70 c. blue 40 5
P 696. 80 c. black .. 35 5
P 697. 90 c. claret .. 40 10
Horiz. type. Early engine, "Le Belge".
P 698. 1 f. purple .. 40 5
P 699. 2 f. black .. 85 5
P 700. 3 f. orange .. 1·00 5
P 701. 4 f. purple .. 1·10 5
P 702. 5 f. purple .. 1·25 5
P 703. 6 f. green .. .. 1·50 5
P 704. 7 f. violet .. .. 1·75 5
P 705. 8 f. black .. .. 2·25 5
P 706. 9 f. blue .. .. 2·50 5
P 707. 10 f. red .. .. 2·50 5
P 708. 20 f. green .. 8·50 5
P 709. 30 f. violet .. 35·00 25
P 710. 40 f. brown .. 35·00 60
P 711. 50 f. red .. .. 35·00 35
P 712. 100 f. blue.. .. 65·00 7·50

P 16. Winged Wheel and Posthorn.

1938.
P 806. **P 16.** 5 f. on 3 f. 50 green 3·75 10
P 807. 5 f. on 4 f. 50 pur. 10 5
P 808. 6 f. on 5 f. 50 red.. 15 5
P 1162. 8 f. on 5 f. 50 brn. 20 5
P 1163. 10 f. on 5 f. 50 blue 20 5
P 1164. 12 f. on 5 f. 50 vio. 25 5

1939. Surch. **M. 3 Fr.**
P 867. **P 16.** 3 f. on 5 f. 50 red.. 12 5

P 17. Seal of the Congress.

1939. Int. Railway Congress, Brussels.
P 856. **P 17.** 20 c. brown .. 1·50 1·50
P 857. 50 c. blue .. .. 1·50 1·50
P 858. 2 f. red .. .. 1·50 1·50
P 859. 9 f. green .. 1·50 1·50
P 860. 10 f. purple .. 1·50 1·50

1940. As Nos. P 399 and P 404 but colours changed.
P 876. **P 10.** 5 f. brown.. 15 15
P 877. 10 f. black .. 85 85

1940. Optd. **B** in oval and two vert. bars.
P 878. **P 10.** 10 c. red 5 5
P 879. 20 c. green .. 5 5
P 880. 30 c. purple .. 5 5
P 881. 40 c. olive .. 5 5
P 882. 50 c. red .. 5 5
P 883. 60 c. orange .. 8 5
P 884. 70 c. brown .. 5 5
P 885. 80 c. violet .. 5 5
P 886. 90 c. slate.. .. 5 5
P 887. 1 f. blue .. 5 5
P 888. 2 f. olive .. 15 8
P 889. 3 f. red .. 15 8
P 890. 4 f. red .. 15 8
P 891. 5 f. violet .. 15 8
P 892. 6 f. brown.. .. 30 8
P 893. 7 f. orange .. 35 8
P 894. 8 f. brown.. .. 35 8
P 895. 9 f. purple.. .. 35 8
P 896. 10 f. green .. 35 5
P 897. 20 f. pink 75 8
P 898. 30 f. green .. 1·00 25
P 899. 40 f. slate .. 1·25 60
P 900. 50 f. bistre .. 1·40 20

1940. As Type P 10 but colours changed.
P 911. **P 10.** 10 c. olive .. 5 5
P 912. 20 c. violet .. 5 5
P 913. 30 c. red .. 5 5
P 914. 40 c. blue .. 5 5
P 915. 50 c. green .. 5 5
P 916. 60 c. grey .. 5 5
P 917. 70 c. green .. 5 5
P 918. 80 c. orange .. 8 5
P 919. 90 c. lilac .. 10 5

Similar design, but horizontal.
P 920. 1 f. green 10 5
P 921. 2 f. brown 12 5
P 922. 3 f. grey 15 5
P 923. 4 f. olive 20 5
P 924. 5 f. lilac 25 5
P 925. 5 f. black 35 5
P 926. 6 f. red 35 5
P 927. 7 f. violet 35 5
P 928. 8 f. green 35 5
P 929. 9 f. blue 40 5
P 930. 10 f. mauve .. 40 5
P 931. 20 f. blue .. .. 1·00 5
P 932. 30 f. yellow .. 1·90 5
P 933. 40 f. red .. .. 2·40 5
P 934. 50 f. red .. .. 3·00 5

P 18. Engine Driver. **P 19.** Mercury.

1942. Various designs.
P 1090. **P 18.** 10 c. grey .. 5 5
P 1091. 20 c. violet .. 5 5
P 1092. 30 c. red 8 5
P 1093. 40 c. blue .. 5 5
P 1094. 50 c. turquoise .. 5 5
P 1095. 60 c. black .. 5 5
P 1096. 70 c. green .. 5 5
P 1097. 80 c. orange .. 5 5
P 1078. 90 c. chocolate .. 5 5
P 1099. – 1 f. green .. 5 5
P 1100. – 2 f. brown .. 5 5
P 1101. – 3 f. black .. 50 5
P 1102. – 4 f. blue 5 5
P 1103. – 5 f. brown .. 10 5
P 1104. – 6 f. green .. 50 5
P 1105. – 7 f. violet .. 15 5
P 1106. – 8 f. orange .. 15 5
P 1107. – 9 f. blue 30 5
P 996. – 9 f. 20 c. orange.. 25 25
P 1108. – 10 f. red .. .. 1·00 5
P 1109. – 10 f. sepia .. 55 5
P 997. **P 18.** 12 f. 30 c. green.. 30 30
P 998. – 14 f. 30 c. red .. 30 30
P 1110. – 20 f. green .. 35 5
P 1111. – 30 f. violet .. 50 5
P 1112. – 40 f. red 35 5
P 1113. – 50 f. blue .. 4·00 5
P 999. – 100 f. blue .. 6·50 6·50
Designs: 1 f. to 9 f. 20 c. Platelayer. 10 f. and 14 f. 30 c. to 50 f. Railway Porter. 100 f. Electric train (24½ × 34½ mm.).

1945. Inscribed "BELGIQUE-BELGIE" or vice-versa.
P 1116. **P 19.** 3 f. green .. 12 5
P 1117. 5 f. blue 5 5
P 1118. 6 f. red 5 5

P 20. Level Crossing.

1947.
P 1203. **P 20.** 100 f. green .. 4·00 8

P 21. Archer.

1946. As Type **P 21**, but without surch.
P 1204. 8 f. sepia 50 8
P 1205. 10 f. blue and black .. 50 8
P 1206. 12 f. violet 60 8

1948. Surch. as in Type **P 21.**
P 1229. 9 f. on 8 f. sepia .. 50 5
P 1230. 11 f. on 10 f. bl. & blk. 55 5
P 1231. 13 f. 50 on 12 f. vio... 60 5

P 22. "Parcel Post".

1948.
P 1250. **P 22.** 9 f. brown .. 1·75 5
P 1251. 11 f. red .. .. 1·75 5
P 1252. 13 f. 50 black .. 2·10 5

P 23. Locomotive, 1862.

1949. Locomotives from 1835 to 1951. Year given in brackets.
P 1277. ½ f. brown (1835) .. 12 5
P 1278. 1 f. red (Type P 23) .. 15 5
P 1279. 2 f. blue (1875) .. 25 5
P 1280. 3 f. claret (1884) .. 45 5
P 1281. 4 f. green (1901) .. 50 5
P 1282. 5 f. red (1902) .. 50 5
P 1283. 6 f. purple (1904) .. 60 5
P 1284. 7 f. green (1905) .. 80 5
P 1285. 8 f. blue (1906) .. 85 5
P 1286. 9 f. brown (1909) .. 1·25 5
P 1287. 10 f. olive (1910) .. 1·25 5
P 1295. 10 f. black & red (1905) 1·40 25
P 1288. 20 f. orange (1920) .. 1·75 5
P 1289. 30 f. blue (1928) .. 3·50 5
P 1290. 40 f. red (1930) .. 4·25 5
P 1291. 50 f. mauve (1935) .. 5·50 5
P 1292. 60 f. brown (1949) .. 5·50 8
P 1293. 100 f. red (1939) .. 10·00 5
P 1294. 300 f. violet (1951) .. 21·00 25
The 300 f. is larger (37½ × 25 mm.).

Designs—horiz. 11 f., 12 f., 17 f. Dispatch counter. 13 f., 15 f. Sorting compartment.

P 24. Loading Parcels.

1950.
P 1318. 11 f. orange .. 1·50 10
P 1319. – 12 f. purple .. 3·50 40
P 1320. – 13 f. green .. 1·50 8
P 1321. – 15 f. blue .. 3·25 15
P 1322. **P 24.** 16 f. grey .. 1·50 8
P 1323. – 17 f. brown .. 2·00 8
P 1324. **P 24.** 18 f. red .. 3·25 20
P 1325. 20 f. orange .. 2·00 10

P 25. Mercury.

1951. National Belgian Railway Society. 25th Anniv.
P 1375. **P 25.** 25 f. blue .. 2·50 2·25

1953. Nos. P 1318, P 1321 and P 1324 surch.
P 1448. – 13 f. on 15 f. blue 11·00 15
P 1449. – 17 f. on 11 f. orge. 7·50 12
P 1450. **P 24.** 20 f. on 18 f. red 5·00 35

P 26. Electric Train and Brussels Skyline.

1953. Inaug. of Nord-Midi Junction.
P 1451. **P 26.** 200 f. green .. 45·00 50
P 1452. 200 f. olive-green and chocolate .. 50·00 1·75

P 27. "Nord" Station. **P 28.** Central Station.

1953. Brussels Railway Stations.
P 1485. **P 27.** 1 f. ochre .. 10 5
P 1486. 2 f. black .. 15 5
P 1487. 3 f. green .. 20 5
P 1488. 4 f. orange .. 35 5
P 1489. 5 f. red-brown .. 35 5
P 1490. – 5 f. chocolate .. 1·50 5
P 1491. **P 27.** 6 f. purple .. 45 5
P 1492. 7 f. green .. 45 5
P 1493. 8 f. red 50 5
P 1494. 9 f. blue 50 5
P 1495. – 10 f. green .. 65 5
P 1496. – 10 f. black .. 25 5
P 1497. – 15 f. red .. .. 2·00 5
P 1498. – 20 f. blue .. 1·00 5
P 1498a. – 20 f. green .. 45 5
P 1499. – 30 f. purple .. 1·60 5

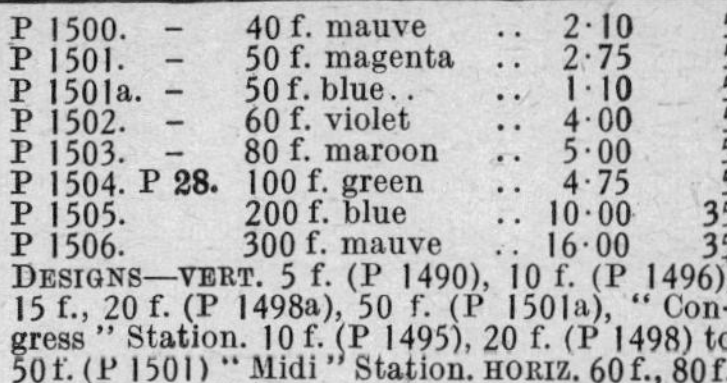
P 1500. – 40 f. mauve .. 2·10 5
P 1501. – 50 f. magenta .. 2·75 5
P 1501a. – 50 f. blue.. .. 1·10 5
P 1502. – 60 f. violet .. 4·00 5
P 1503. – 80 f. maroon .. 5·00 5
P 1504. **P 28.** 100 f. green .. 4·75 5
P 1505. 200 f. blue .. 10·00 35
P 1506. 300 f. mauve .. 16·00 35
Designs—vert. 5 f. (P 1490), 10 f. (P 1496), 15 f., 20 f. (P 1498a), 50 f. (P 1501a), "Congress" Station. 10 f. (P 1495), 20 f. (P 1498) to 50 f. (P 1501) "Midi" Station. horiz. 60 f., 80 f. "Chapelle" Station.

P 29. Electric Train and "Nord" Station, Brussels. **P 30.** Mercury and Winged Wheel.

1953.
P 1517. **P 29.** 13 f. brown .. 3·50 5
P 1518. 18 f. blue .. 3·50 5
P 1519. 21 f. mauve .. 3·50 15

1956. Surch. in figures.
P 1585. **P 29.** 14 f. on 13 f. brown 3·25 5
P 1586. 19 f. on 18 f. blue 3·25 5
P 1587. 22 f. on 21 f. mauve 3·25 10

1957.
P 1600. **P 30.** 14 f. green .. 2·75 8
P 1601. 19 f. sepia .. 2·75 8
P 1602. 22 f. red .. .. 2·75 8

1959. Surch. **20 F.**
P 1678. **P 30.** 20 f. on 19 f. sepia 11·00 15
P 1679. 20 f. on 22 f. red.. 11·00 30

Designs—vert. 24 f. Brussels "Midi" station, 1869-1949. **horiz.** 26 f. Antwerp Central station, 1905. 28 f. Ghent St. Pieter's station.

P 31. Brussels "Nord" Station, 1861–1954.

1959.
P 1695. **P 31.** 20 f. olive .. 5·50 5
P 1696. – 24 f. red .. 2·25 10
P 1697. – 26 f. blue .. 2·25 20
P 1698. – 28 f. purple .. 2·25 20

P 32. Congress Seal, Diesel and Electric Locomotives.

1960. Int. Railway Congress Assn. 75th Anniv.
P 1722. **P 32.** 20 f. red .. .. 20·00 15·00
P 1723. 50 f. blue .. 20·00 15·00
P 1724. 60 f. purple .. 20·00 15·00
P 1725. 70 f. green .. 20·00 15·00

1961. Nos. P 1695/8 surch.
P 1787. **P 31.** 24 f. on 20 f. olive 17·00 8
P 1788. – 26 f. on 24 f. red 2·50 5
P 1789. – 28 f. on 26 f. blue 2·50 5
P 1790. – 35 f. on 28 f. purple 2·50 5

P 33. Arlon Station.

1967.
P 2017. **P 33.** 25 f. ochre .. 4·00 5
P 2018. 30 f. green .. 1·50 5
P 2019. 35 f. blue .. 1·60 20
P 2020. 40 f. red .. 5·00 5

P 34. Electric Train ("Type 122").

1968.
P 2047. P 34. 1 f. bistre .. 5 5
P 2048. 2 f. green .. 5 5
P 2049. 3 f. green .. 8 5
P 2050. 4 f. orange .. 10 5
P 2051. 5 f. brown .. 12 5
P 2052. 6 f. plum .. 15 5
P 2053. 7 f. green .. 20 5
P 2054. 8 f. red .. 20 5
P 2055. 9 f. blue .. 25 5
P 2056. – 10 f. green .. 25 5
P 2057. – 20 f. blue .. 45 5
P 2058. – 30 f. lilac .. 70 5
P 2059. – 40 f. violet .. 90 5
P 2060. – 50 f. purple .. 1·10 5
P 2061. – 60 f. violet .. 1·40 5
P 2062. – 70 f. brown .. 1·50 5
P 2063. – 80 f. purple .. 1·75 8
P 2063a. – 90 f. green .. 2·00 5
P 2064. – 100 f. green .. 2·10 5
P 2065. – 200 f. violet .. 4·25 30
P 2066. – 300 f. magenta .. 6·50 1·00
P 2067. – 500 f. yellow .. 10·00 50
DESIGNS: 10 f. to 40 f. Electric train ("Type 126"). 50 f., 60 f., 70 f., 80 f., 90 f. Electric train ("Type 160"). 100 f., 200 f., 300 f. Diesel-electric train ("Type 205"). 500 f. Diesel-electric train ("Type 210").

1970. Surch.
P 2180. P 33. 37 f. on 25 f. ochre 15·00
P 2181. 48 f. on 35 f. blue 5·00
P 2182. 53 f. on 40 f. red 5·00

P 35. Ostend Station.

1971.
P 2192. P 35. 32 f. ochre .. 90
P 2193. 37 f. grey .. 1·10
P 2194. 42 f. blue .. 1·25
P 2195. 44 f. magenta .. 1·25
P 2196. 46 f. violet .. 1·25
P 2197. 50 f. red .. 1·40
P 2198. 52 f. brown .. 1·40
P 2199. 54 f. green .. 1·50
P 2200. 61 f. blue .. 1·60

1972. Nos. P 2192/5 and P 2198/200. Surch. in figures.
P 2256. P 35. 34 f. on 32 f. ochre 60
P 2257. 40 f. on 37 f. grey 75
P 2258. 47 f. on 44 f. mag. 85
P 2259. 53 f. on 42 f. blue 1·00
P 2260. 56 f. on 52 f. brown 1·10
P 2261. 59 f. on 54 f. green 1·10
P 2262. 66 f. on 61 f. blue 1·25

P 36. Emblems within Bogie Wheels.

1972. Int. Railways Union (UIC). 50th Anniv.
P 2266. P 36. 100 f. blk., red & grn 6·00 1·25
See also No. 2274.

P 37. Global Emblem.

1974. 4th International Symposium of Railway Cybernetics, Washington.
P 2353. P 37. 100 f. black, red and yellow .. 3·25 55

RAILWAY OFFICIAL STAMPS

For use on the official mail of the Railway Company.

Optd. with winged wheel.

1929. Stamps of 1922.
O 481. 53. 5 c. slate 8 8
O 482. 10 c. green 12 12
O 483. 35 c. green 15 5
O 484. 60 c. olive 10 5
O 485. 1 f. 50 blue .. .. 2·25 80
O 486. 1 f. 75 blue 50 50

1929. Stamps of 1929.
O 534. 67. 5 c. slate 8 8
O 535. 10 c. olive 15 10
O 536. 25 c. red 40 15
O 537. 35 c. green 50 15
O 538. 40 c. mauve 35 8
O 539. 50 c. blue 25 5
O 540. 60 c. magenta .. 1·40 40
O 541. 70 c. red-brown .. 1·40 25
O 542. 75 c. violet .. 1·10 20

1932. Stamps of 1931-34.
O 620. 82. 10 c. green 20 12
O 677. 83. 35 c. green .. .. 3·75 10
O 678. 96. 70 c. olive (No. 667) 1·00 8
O 679. 78. 75 c. brown (No. 668) 55 8

1936. Stamps of 1936.
O 721. 103. 10 c. olive 8 8
O 722. 35 c. green 10 5
O 723. 40 c. lilac 15 5
O 724. 50 c. blue 30 5
O 725. 104. 70 c. brown .. 65 10
O 726. 75 c. olive 35 5

1941. Optd. B in oval frame.
O 948. 103. 10 c. olive 5 5
O 949. 40 c. lilac 15 10
O 950. 50 c. blue 5 5
O 951. – 1 f. red (No. 747) .. 12 5
O 952. – 1 f. red (No. 748) .. 12 5
O 953. 104. 2 f. 25 myrtle .. 15 15
O 954. 105. 2 f. 25 violet .. 15 15

1942. Nos. O 722, O 725 and O 726 surch.
O 983. 103. 10 c. on 35 c. green 8 5
O 984. 104. 50 c. on 70 c. brown 5 5
O 985. 50 c. on 75 c. olive 5 5

O 1.

O 2.

1946. Designs incorporating letter "B".
O 1156. O 1. 10 c. olive 5 5
O 1157. 20 c. violet .. 65 5
O 1158. 50 c. blue 5 5
O 1159. 65 c. purple .. 90 12
O 1160. 75 c. mauve .. 5 5
O 1161. 90 c. violet .. 1·25 8
O 1240. – 1 f. 35 brn. (as 1219) 85 10
O 1241. – 1 f. 75 grn. (as 1221) 85 8
O 1242. 167. 3 f. purple .. 3·75 1·25
O 1243. 168. 3 f. 15 blue .. 2·10 1·60
O 1244. 4 f. blue .. 4·00 3·25

1952.
O 1424. O 2. 10 c. orange .. 8 5
O 1425. 20 c. lake .. 8 5
O 1426. 30 c. green .. 35 20
O 1427. 40 c. olive .. 15 8
O 1428. 50 c. blue .. 30 10
O 1429. 60 c. mauve .. 40 30
O 1430. 65 c. purple .. 6·50 6·00
O 1431. 80 c. emerald .. 50 10
O 1432. 90 c. blue .. 1·40 15
O 1433. 1 f. red .. 10 5
O 1433a. 1 f. 50 grey .. 5 5
O 1434. 2 f. 50 brown .. 10 5

1954. As T 205 (King Baudouin) but with letter "B" incorporated in design.
O 1523. 1 f. 50 black .. 12 5
O 1524. 2 f. red .. 15·00 5
O 1525. 2 f. green .. 12 5
O 1526. 2 f. 50 brown .. 10·00 10
O 1527. 3 f. mauve .. 60 5
O 1528. 3 f. 50 green .. 15 5
O 1529. 4 f. blue .. 35 10
O 1530. 6 f. cerise .. 1·75 15

1971. As Nos. 2209/20, but with letter "B" incorporated in design.
O 2224. 3 f. green .. 35 35
O 2225. 3 f. 50 brown .. 30 12
O 2226. 4 f. blue .. 12 10
O 2227. 4 f. 50 maroon .. 15 12
O 2228. 4 f. 50 blue .. 15 12
O 2229. 5 f. violet .. 15 12
O 2231. 7 f. red .. 1·50 70
O 2232. 10 f. red .. 30 20
O 2233. 15 f. violet .. 60 20

POSTAGE DUE STAMPS

D 1.

D 2.

1870.
D 63. D 1. 10 c. green .. 1·75 55
D 64. 20 c. blue .. 8·00 1·00

1895.
D 96a. D 2. 5 c. green .. 8 8
D 97. 10 c. brown .. 2·25 40
D 101. 10 c. red .. 8 5
D 98a. 20 c. green .. 8 8
D 102. 30 c. blue .. 15 10
D 99. 50 c. brown .. 4·25 1·75
D 103. 50 c. grey .. 30 20
D 100. 1 f. red .. 12·00 7·50
D 104. 1 f. yellow .. 2·50 2·25

1919. As Type D 2, but value in colour on white background.
D 251. D 2. 5 c. green .. 15 8
D 323. 5 c. grey .. 5 5
D 252. 10 c. red .. 40 10
D 324. 10 c. green .. 5 5
D 253. 20 c. green .. 2·50 12
D 325. 20 c. brown .. 8 5
D 254. 30 c. blue .. 80 10
D 326a. 30 c. red .. 15 5
D 327. 35 c. green .. 20 15
D 328. 40 c. brown .. 15 5
D 330. 50 c. grey .. 15 5
D 329. 50 c. blue .. 70 5
D 331. 60 c. red .. 20 10
D 1146. 65 c. green .. 2·25 1·75
D 332. 70 c. red-brown .. 20 8
D 333. 80 c. grey .. 20 8
D 334. D 2. 1 f. violet .. 25 5
D 335. 1 f. purple .. 25 5
D 336. 1 f. 20 olive .. 35 12
D 337. 1 f. 40 green .. 35 10
D 338. 1 f. 50 olive .. 35 12
D 1147. 1 f. 60 magenta .. 2·75 1·60
D 1148. 1 f. 80 red .. 4·25 1·60
D 339. 2 f. mauve .. 45 8
D 1149. 2 f. 40 lavender .. 2·40 70
D 1150. 3 f. red .. 40 10
D 340. 3 f. 50 blue .. 50 8
D 1151. 4 f. blue .. 3·00 12
D 1152. 5 f. brown .. 1·00 12
D 1153. 7 f. violet .. 1·00 90
D 1154. 8 f. purple .. 2·10 1·75
D 1155. 10 f. violet .. 2·25 1·50

D 3.

D 4.

1945. Inscr. "A PAYER" at top and "TE BETALEN" at bottom, or vice versa.
D 1139. D 3. 10 c. olive .. 5 5
D 1140. 20 c. blue .. 5 5
D 1141. 30 c. red .. 5 5
D 1142. 40 c. blue .. 5 5
D 1143. 50 c. green .. 5 5
D 1144. 1 f. brown .. 5 5
D 1145. 2 f. orange .. 5 5

1966.
D 1982. D 4. 1 f. magenta .. 5 5
D 1983. 2 f. green .. 5 5
D 1984. 3 f. blue .. 5 5
D 1985. 5 f. violet .. 12 8
D 1986. 6 f. brown .. 15 10
D 1987. 7 f. vermilion .. 15 12
D 1988. 20 f. olive .. 45 30

BELIZE BC

100 cents = 1 dollar.

British Honduras was renamed Belize on the 1st June 1973.

1973. Nos. 256/66 and 277/8 of British Honduras optd. **BELIZE** and two stars.
347. – ½ c. mult. and yellow .. 5 5
348. 19. 1 c. black, brn. & yell. 5 5
349. – 2 c. black, green & yell. 5 5
350. – 3 c. black, brown & lilac 5 8
351. – 4 c. multicoloured .. 8 8
352. – 5 c. black and red .. 8 10
353. – 10 c. multicoloured .. 10 12
354. – 15 c. multicoloured .. 20 20
355. – 25 c. multicoloured .. 25 30
356. – 50 c. multicoloured .. 40 50
357. – $1 multicoloured .. 95 1·10
358. – $2 multicoloured .. 1·90 2·25
359. – $5 multicoloured .. 3·75 4·25

1973. Royal Wedding. As T 16 of Anguilla. Background colours given. Multicoloured.
360. 26 c. blue .. 20 25
361. 50 c. brown .. 35 40

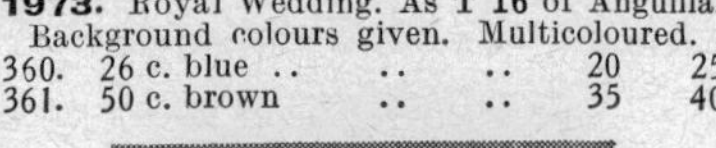

33. Crana.

1974. As Nos. 256/66 and 276/78 of British Honduras. Multicoloured.
362. ½ c. Type 33 .. 5 5
363. 1 c. Jew Fish .. 5 5
364. 2 c. Waree .. 5 5
365. 3 c. Grouper .. 5 5
366. 4 c. Ant Bear .. 5 5
367. 5 c. Bone Fish .. 5 5
368. 10 c. Gibnut .. 8 8
369. 15 c. Dolphin .. 10 10
370. 25 c. Night Walker .. 15 20
371. 50 c. Mutton Snapper .. 30 35
372. $1 Bush Dog .. 55 60
373. $2 Great Barracuda .. 1·10 1·25
374. $5 Mountain Lion .. 2·75 3·00

34. Deer.

1974. Mayan Artefacts. Pottery Motifs. Multicoloured.
375. 3 c. Type 34 .. 5 8
376. 6 c. Jaguar deity .. 8 10
377. 16 c. Sea monster .. 12 15
378. 26 c. Cormorant .. 20 20
379. 50 c. Scarlet macaw .. 40 45

35. "Parides arcas".

1974. Butterflies of Belize. Multicoloured.
380. ½ c. Type 35 .. 8 5
381. 1 c. "Thecla regalis" .. 5 5
382. 2 c. "Colombura dirce" .. 5 5
383. 3 c. "Catonephele numilia" 5 5
384. 4 c. "Battus belus" .. 5 5
385. 5 c. "Callicore patelina" .. 5 5
386. 10 c. "Callicore astala" .. 5 5
387. 15 c. "Nessaea aglaura" .. 10 12
388. 16 c. "Prepona pseudojoiceyi" 8 8
389. 25 c. "Papilio thoas" .. 12 15
390. 26 c. "Hamadryas arethusa" 20 25
391. 50 c. "Thecla bathildis" .. 25 30
392. $1 "Caligo uranus" .. 50 55
393. $2 "Heliconius sapho" .. 1·00 1·10
433. $5 "Eurytides philolaus" 2·25 2·50
395. $10 "Philaethria dido" .. 5·00 5·25

36. Churchill when Prime Minister, and Coronation Scene.

1974. Sir Winston Churchill. Birth Cent. Multicoloured.
396. 50 c. Type 36 .. 25 30
397. $1 Churchill in stetson, and Williamsburg Liberty Bell 50 55

37. The Actun Balam Vase.

1975. Mayan Artefacts. Multicoloured.
398. 3 c. Type 37 .. 5 5
399. 6 c. Seated figure .. 5 5
400. 16 c. Costumed priest .. 10 10
401. 26 c. Head and headdress .. 12 15
402. 50 c. Layman and priest .. 25 30

38. Musicians.

1975 Christmas. Multicoloured.
435. 6 c. Type 38 .. 5 5
436. 26 c. Children and "crib" 12 15
437. 50 c. Dancer and drummers (vert.) .. 25 30
438. $1 Family and map (vert.) 50 55

39. William Wrigley Jr. and Chicle Tapping.

1976. American Revolution. Bicent. Mult.
439. 10 c. Type 39 .. 5 8
440. 35 c. Charles Lindbergh .. 20 25
441. $1 J. L. Stephens (archaeologist) .. 25 30

40. Cycling.

1976. Olympic Games Montreal. Multicoloured.
442. 35 c. Type **40** .. ..
443. 45 c. Running .. ..
444. $1 Shooting .. ..

1976. No. 390 surch.
445. 20 c.on 26 c. multicoloured 10 12

1976. West Indian Victory in World Cricket Cup. As Nos. 559/60 of Barbados.
446. 35 c. multicoloured .. 20 20
447. $1 black and purple .. 55 65

POSTAGE DUE STAMPS

D 2.

1972.
D 6. D 2. 1 c. red and green .. 5 5
D 7. – 2 c. purple and violet 5 5
D 8. – 5 c. green and brown 5 5
D 9. – 15 c. green and red.. 8 8
D 10. – 25 c. orange & green 12 15
DESIGNS: Nos. D 7/10 as Type D 2 but with different frames.

BENIN O2

A French possession on the W. coast of Africa incorporated, in 1899, into the colony of Dahomey.

A. FRENCH COLONY

1892. Stamps of French Colonies. "Commerce" type, optd. **BENIN**
1. 9. 1 c. black on blue .. 25·00 22·00
2. 2 c. brown on yellow .. 23·00 21·00
3. 4 c. lilac on grey .. 8·00 8·00
4. 5 c. green on pale green 3·25 2·75
5. 10 c. black on lilac .. 14·00 11·00
6. 15 c. blue on pale blue .. 5·00 2·00
7. 20 c. red on green .. 40·00 35·00
8. 25 c. black on red .. 14·00 8·50
9. 30 c. brown on drab .. 25·00 22·00
10. 35 c. black on orange .. 27·00 27·00
11. 40 c. red on yellow .. 25·00 25·00
12. 75 c. red on pink .. 60·00 55·00
13. 1 f. olive .. .. 60·00 55·00

1892. Surch. in figures
14. 9. 01 on 5 c. green .. .. 42·00 32·00
15. 40 on 15 c. blue .. .. 32·00 10·00
16. 75 on 15 c. blue .. .. £120 8·00

1893. "Tablet" key-type inscr. "GOLFE DE BENIN".
17. D. 1 c. black on blue .. 55 55
18. 2 c. brown on yellow .. 65 65
19. 4 c. lilac on grey .. 45 45
20. 5 c. green 90 65
21. 10 c. black on lilac .. 1·00 75
22. 15 c. blue .. .. 4·50 3·25
23. 20 c. red on green .. 2·75 1·60
24. 25 c. black on red .. 6·50 3·25
25. 30 c. brown .. .. 2·40 2·10
26. 40 c. red on yellow .. 55 30
27. 50 c. red.. .. .. 45 45
28. 75 c. brown on orange.. 1·25 1·10
29. 1 f. olive .. .. 8·00 6·50

1894. "Tablet" key-type inscr. "BENIN".
33. D. 1 c. black on blue .. 45 45
34. 2 c. brown on yellow .. 45 45
35. 4 c. claret on grey .. 45 45
36. 5 c. green 40 30
37. 10 c. black on lilac .. 1·00 75
38. 15 c. blue.. .. .. 1·10 55
39. 20 c. red on green .. 1·25 1·10
40. 25 c. black on red .. 1·00 75
41. 30 c. brown 75 75
42. 40 c. red on yellow .. 2·40 1·50
43. 50 c. red .. .. 2·75 2·25
44. 75 c. brown on orange .. 2·25 1·10
45. 1 f. olive 45 45

POSTAGE DUE STAMPS

1894. Postage Due stamps of French Colonies optd. **BENIN.** Imperf.
D 46. D 1. 5 c. black .. .. 25·00 14·00
D 47. 10 c. black .. .. 25·00 14·00
D 48. 20 c. black .. .. 24·00 13·00
D 49. 30 c. black .. .. 25·00 14·00

B. PEOPLE'S REPUBLIC

The Republic of Dahomey was renamed the People's Republic of Benin on 30th November 1975.

157. Celebrations.

1976. Republic of Benin Proclamation. Multicoloured.
603. 50 f. Type **157** 20 12
604. 60 f. President Kerekou making Proclamation .. 25 15
605. 100 f. Benin arms and flag 50 30

158. Skiing.

1976. Air. Winter Olympic Games, Innsbruck. Multicoloured.
606. 60 f. Type **158** 25 15
607. 150 f. Bobsleighing (vert.) 70 40
608. 300 f. Figure-skating .. 1·50 80

159. Alexander Graham Bell, Early Telephone and Satellite.

1976. Telephone Centenary.
609. 159. 200 f. red, violet & brn. 1·00 60

160. Long-jumping.

1976. Air. Olympic Games, Montreal. Multicoloured.
610. 60 f. Type **160** 25 15
611. 150 f. Basketball (vert.).. 70 40
612. 200 f. Hurdling .. .. 1·00 60

161. Scouts and Camp-fire.

1976. African Scout Jamboree, Jos, Nigeria.
618. 161. 50 f. purple, brn. & blk. 20 12
619. – 70 f. brn., olive & blk. 30 20
DESIGN: 70 f. "Comradeship".

162. Konrad Adenauer.

1976. Air. Konrad Adenauer (German statesman). Birth Cent.
620. 162. 90 f. slate, blue & red 45 25
621. – 250 f. blue, red & lt. bl. 1·25 75
DESIGN—HORIZ. 250 f. Adenauer and Cologne Cathedral.

163. Dahomey 60 f. Stamp of 1965, and Children's Silhouettes.

1976. Air. "Juvarouen 76" Youth Stamp Exhibition, Rouen.
622. 163. 60 f. blue & turquoise 25 15
623. – 210 f. red, brn. & olive 1·10 65
DESIGN—VERT. 210 f. Benin 1 c. stamp of 1893 and lion cub.

BERGEDORF E2

A German city on the Elbe, governed by Hamburg and Lubeck till 1867 when it was purchased by the former. Now part of West Germany.

16 schillinge = 1 Hamburg mark.

1.

1861. Various sizes. Imperf.
1. 1. ½ s. black on lilac £250
2. ½ s. black on blue .. .. 13·00 £350
4. 1 s. black on white .. 13·00 £180
5. 1½ s. black on yellow .. 6·00 £500
6. 3 s. black on red .. £350
7. 3 s. blue on red .. .. 7·50 9·00
8. 4 s. black on brown .. 7·50 £1100

BERMUDA BC

A group of islands in the W. Atlantic, E. of N. Carolina. Usually regarded by collectors as part of the Br. W. Indies group, though this is not strictly correct.

1970. 100 cents. = 1 dollar (U.S.)

1. Queen Victoria.

5. Dock.

1865. Portrait. Various frames.
19. 1. ½d. brown .. .. 90 1·10
21a. ½d. green 80 60
24a. 1d. red 70 20
25. 2d. blue .. .. .. 6·00 1·25
26a. 2d. purple .. .. 1·25 2·25
27a. 2½d. blue .. .. .. 2·50 45
10. 3d. yellow .. .. 45·00 14·00
28. 3d. grey .. .. .. 4·00 1·25
20. 4d. orange.. .. .. 2·25 1·40
10a. 6d. mauve .. .. 5·50 6·00
11. 1s. green .. .. .. 6·00 7·50
29a. 1s brown .. .. .. 7·00 6·00

1874. Surch. in words
15. 1. 1d. on 2d. blue .. .. £190 95·00
16. 1d. on 3d. yellow.. .. £135 £135
17. 1d. on 1s. green .. .. 75·00 75·00
12. 3d. on 1d. red £1600
13. 3d. on 1s. green £325 £250

1901. Surch. **ONE FARTHING** and bar.
30a. 1. ¼d. on 1s. grey 20 25

1902.
34a. 5. ¼d. brown and violet .. 75 1·10
35. ½d. black and green .. 2·75 1·60
41. ½d. green.. .. .. 1·75 1·25
32. 1d. brown and red .. 3·00 15
42. 1d. red .. .. .. 1·75 30
37. 2d. grey and orange .. 2·50 3·50
38. 2½d. brown and blue .. 4·00 7·00
43. 2½d. blue.. .. .. 7·50 6·00
33. 3d. magenta and green.. 1·25 1·75
39. 4d. blue and chocolate .. 2·25 3·50

INDEX

Countries can be quickly located by referring to the index at the end of this volume.

6. Badge of the Colony.

7.

1910.
76a. 6. ¼d. brown 30 40
77. ½d. green.. .. .. 15 10
79. 1d. red 25 20
79b. 1½d. brown .. .. 1·75 55
80. 2d. grey 55 75
82a. 2½d. blue.. .. .. 1·10 40
81a. 2½d. green .. .. 1·40 1·60
84. 3d. purple on yellow .. 60 65
83. 3d. blue .. .. .. 7·00 9·50
85. 4d. red on yellow .. 65 1·00
86. 6d. purple .. .. 1·10 1·25
51a. 1s. black on green .. 4·00 5·00
51b. 7. 2s. purple & blue on blue 4·00 8·50
52. 2s. 6d. black & red on bl. 8·50 12·00
52a. 4s. black and carmine .. 16·00 18·00
53. 5s. green & red on yell. 16·00 18·00
54. 10s. green & red on green 32·00 38·00
93. 12s. 6d. black & orange 70·00 80·00
55. £1 purple & black on red 80·00 £120

1918. Optd. **WAR TAX.**
56a. 6. 1d. red 12 20

8.
Tercent. of Representative Institutions.

(a) **1920.** 1st Issue.
59. 8. ¼d. brown.. .. .. 35 60
60. ½d. green .. .. .. 60 1·60
65. 1d. red 55 65
61. 2d. grey .. .. .. 3·25 4·50
66. 2½d. blue .. .. .. 2·75 4·00
62. 3d. purple on yellow .. 4·00 7·00
63. 4d. black & red on yellow 7·00 8·50
67. 6d. purple .. .. 9·50 10·00
64. 1s. black on green .. 10·00 11·00

9.

(b) **1921.** 2nd Issue.
74. 9. ¼d. brown 40 65
75. ½d. green .. .. 1·25 1·40
76. 1d. red 75 50
68. 2d. grey .. .. .. 4·00 5·00
69. 2½d. blue .. .. .. 3·50 2·50
70. 3d. purple on yellow .. 3·50 3·25
71. 4d. red on yellow .. 5·00 4·50
72. 6d. purple .. .. 5·00 7·00
73. 1s. black on green .. 10·00 11·00

1935. Silver Jubilee. As T 11 of Antigua.
94. 1d. blue and red 15 20
95. 1½d. blue and grey .. 30 35
96. 2½d. brown and blue .. 75 1·40
97. 1s. grey and purple .. 4·00 5·00

10. Hamilton Harbour.

12. The "Lucie".

1936.

No.	Type	Description	Mint	Used
98.	10.	½d. green	10	12
99.	–	1d. black and red	15	12
100.	–	1½d. black and brown	30	25
101.	12.	2d. black and blue	2·25	2·75
102.	–	2½d. blue	50	60
103.	–	3d. black and red	1·40	1·60
104.	–	6d. red and violet	30	20
105.	–	1s. green	4·00	4·50
106.	10.	1s. 6d. brown	25	30

DESIGNS—HORIZ. 1d., 1½d. South Shore, nr. Spanish Rock. 3d. Point House, Warwick Parish. VERT. 2½d., 1s. Grape Bay, Paget Parish. 6d. House at Par-la-Ville, Hamilton.

The 1d., 1½d., 2½d. and 1s. values include a portrait of King George V.

1937. Coronation. As T 2 of Aden.

No.	Description	Mint	Used
107.	1d. red	12	15
108.	1½d. brown	20	10
109.	2½d. blue	50	50

16. Ships in Hamilton Harbour.

DESIGNS—VERT. 3d. St. David's Lighthouse. The 2½d. and 1s. are as 1936, but with King George VI portrait.

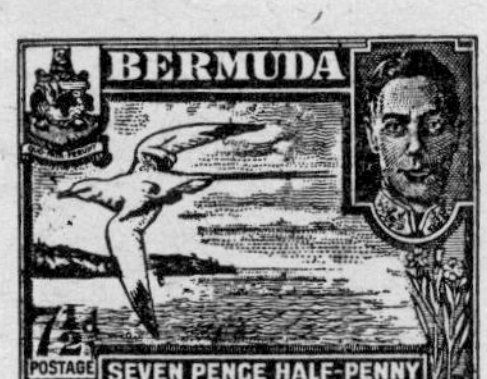

17. Longtail, Arms and Flower.

1938.

No.	Type	Description	Mint	Used
110a.	16.	1d. black and red	15	15
111.		1½d. blue and brown	30	30
112.	12.	2d. blue and black	7·00	4·00
112a.		2d. blue and red	90	1·00
113.	–	2½d. blue	1·40	55
113a.	–	2½d. blue and sepia	35	30
114.	–	3d. black and red	1·40	90
114a.	–	3d. black and blue	20	15
114b.	17.	7½d. blk., blue & green	40	50
115.	–	1s. green	40	40

As T 7, but King George VI portrait.

No.	Description	Mint	Used
116b.	2s. purple & blue on blue	1·10	1·00
117a.	2s. 6d. blk. & red on blue	1·25	2·00
118b.	5s. green and red on yell.	2·50	3·25
119ba.	10s. green & red on grn.	3·25	5·00
120c.	12s. 6d. grey and orange	7·00	7·50
121b.	£1 purple & black on red	7·00	7·50

1940. Surch. **HALFPENNY XX.**

No.	Type	Description	Mint	Used
122.	16.	½d. on 1d. black and red	25	35

1946. Victory. As T 4 of Aden.

No.	Description	Mint	Used
123.	1½d. brown	12	12
124.	3d. blue	20	15

1948. Silver Wedding. As T 5 and 6 of Aden.

No.	Description	Mint	Used
125.	1½d. brown	15	15
126.	£1 red	14·00	15·00

18. Postmaster Perot's Stamp.

1949. Postmaster Perot's Stamp Cent.

No.	Type	Description	Mint	Used
127.	18.	2½d. blue and brown	25	20
128.		3d. black and blue	25	30
129.		6d. violet and green	30	40

1949. U.P.U. As T 14 to 17 of Antigua.

No.	Description	Mint	Used
130.	2½d. black	12	15
131.	3d. blue	20	30
132.	6d purple	25	35
133.	1s. green	45	45

1953. Coronation. As T 7 of Aden.

No.	Description	Mint	Used
134.	1½d. black and blue	30	30

19. Easter Lily.

20. Hog Coin.

1953.

No.	Type	Description	Mint	Used
135.	–	½d. olive	5	5
136.	–	1d. black and red	5	5
137.	19.	1½d. green	8	8
138.	–	2d. blue and red	10	10
139.	–	2½d. red	12	12
140a.	–	3d. purple	10	10
141.	–	4d. black and blue	12	15
142.	–	4½d. green	35	35
143.	–	6d. black and turquoise	25	25
156.	–	6d. black and mauve	20	25
143a.	–	8d. black and red	25	30
143b.	–	9d. violet	35	35
144.	–	1s. orange	30	25
145b.	–	1s. 3d. blue	40	35
146.	–	2s. brown	70	60
147.	–	2s. 6d. red	80	75
148.	20.	5s. red	2·25	2·00
149.	–	10s. blue	3·75	4·25
150.	–	£1 brown, blue, red, green and olive	8·00	9·50

DESIGNS—HORIZ. ½d. Easter lilies. 1d., 4d. Postmaster Perot's stamp. 2d. Bermuda racing dinghy. 2½d. Sir George Somers and "Sea Venture". 3d., 1s. 3d. Map of Bermuda, 4½d., 9d "Sea Venture", inter-island boat, coin and Perot stamp. 6d. (No. 143), 8d. Longtail, or Boatswain Bird. 6d. (No. 156), Perot's Post Office. 1s. Early Bermuda coins. 2s. Arms of St. George's. 10s. Obverse and reverse of hog coin. £1 Arms of Bermuda. VERT. 2s. 6d. Warwick Fort. No. 156 commemorates the restoration and re-opening of Perot's Post Office.

1953. Royal Visit. As No. 143 but inscr. "ROYAL VISIT 1953".

No.	Description	Mint	Used
151.	6d. black and turquoise	25	25

1953. Three Power Talks. Nos. 140a and 145b optd. **Three Power Talks December, 1953.**

No.	Description	Mint	Used
152.	3d. purple	20	20
153.	1s. 3d. blue	40	45

1956. 50th Anniv. United States-Bermuda Yacht Race. Nos. 143a and 145b optd. **50TH ANNIVERSARY US-BERMUDA OCEAN RACE 1956.**

No.	Description	Mint	Used
154.	8d. black and red	30	30
155.	1s. 3d. blue	40	40

21. Arms of King James I. and Queen Elizabeth II.

1959. Settlement. 350th Anniv. Arms in red, yellow and blue. Frame colours given.

No.	Type	Description	Mint	Used
157.	21.	1½d. blue	12	15
158.		3d. grey	20	20
159.		4d. purple	30	30
160.		8d. violet	70	85
161.		9d. olive	70	85
162.		1s 3d. brown	1·25	1·50

22. The Old Rectory, St. George's, c. 1730.

1962.

No.	Type	Description	Mint	Used
163.	22.	1d. purple, black & orge.	5	8
195.	–	2d. lilac, ind., yell. & grn.	8	8
165.	–	3d. brown and blue	8	10
166.	–	4d. brown and magenta	10	10
167.	–	5d. grey and rose	20	20
168.	–	6d. grey, green and blue	12	10
196.	–	8d. blue, green & orange	30	25
170.	–	9d. blue and brown	20	15
197.	–	10d. violet and ochre	30	35
198.	–	1s. blk., bl., grn. & orge.	30	30
172.	–	1s. 3d. lake, grey & bis.	30	25
173.	–	1s. 6d. violet and ochre	1·25	1·50
199.	–	1s. 6d. blue and red	35	40
200.	–	2s. brown and orange	50	35
175.	–	2s. 3d. sepia & yell-grn.	1·25	1·40
176.	–	2s. 6d. sepia, green and yellow	65	50
177.	–	5s. maroon and green	1·25	1·40
178.	–	10s. magenta, green and buff	2·25	2·50
179.	–	£1 black, olive & orange	5·00	5·50

DESIGNS: 2d. Church of St. Peter, St. George's. 3d. Government House, 1892. 4d. The Cathedral, Hamilton, 1894. 5d., 1s. 6d. (No. 199) H.M. Dockyard, 1811. 6d. Perot's Post Office, 1848. 8d. G.P.O., Hamilton, 1869. 9d. Library, Par-la-Ville. 10d., 1s. 6d. (No. 173) Bermuda Cottage, c. 1705. 1s. Christ Church, Warwick, 1719. 1s. 3d. City Hall, Hamilton, 1960. 2s. Town of St. George. 2s. 3d. Bermuda House, c. 1710. 2s. 6d. Bermuda House, early 18th century. 5s. Colonial Secretariat, 1833. 10s. Old Post Office, Somerset, 1890. £1, The House of Assembly, 1815.

1963. Freedom from Hunger. As T 10 of Aden.

No.	Description	Mint	Used
180.	1s. 3d. sepia	1·75	1·50

1963. Red Cross Cent. As T 24 of Antigua.

No.	Description	Mint	Used
181.	3d. red and black	30	30
182.	1s. 3d. red and blue	1·75	1·75

23. Finn Boat.

1964. Olympic Games, Tokyo.

No.	Type	Description	Mint	Used
183.	23.	3d. red, violet and blue	20	25

1965. I.T.U. Cent. As T 26 of Antigua.

No.	Description	Mint	Used
184.	3d. blue and green	25	25
185.	2s. yellow & ultramarine	1·50	1·50

24. Scout Badge and St. Edward's Crown.

1965. Bermuda Boy Scouts Assn. 50th Anniv.

No.	Type	Description	Mint	Used
186.	24.	2s. multicoloured	60	70

1965. I.C.Y. As T 27 of Antigua.

No.	Description	Mint	Used
187.	4d. purple and turquoise	20	15
188.	2s. 6d. green and lavender	1·00	1·00

1966. Churchill Commem. As T 28 of Antigua.

No.	Description	Mint	Used
189.	3d. blue	15	15
190.	6d. green	30	35
191.	10d. brown	50	55
192.	1s. 3d. violet	80	85

1966. World Cup Football Championships. As T 30 of Antigua.

No.	Description	Mint	Used
193.	10d. violet, grn., lake & brn.	30	30
194.	2s. 6d. chocolate, turquoise, lake and brown	70	75

1966. U.N.E.S.C.O. 20th Anniv. As T 33/5 of Antigua.

No.	Description	Mint	Used
201.	4d. violet, red, yell. & orge.	12	12
202.	1s. 3d. yellow, violet & olive	50	55
203.	2s. black, purple & orange	1·00	1·00

25. G.P.O. Building.

1967. Opening of New General Post Office.

No.	Type	Description	Mint	Used
204.	25.	3d. multicoloured	10	10
205.		1s. multicoloured	25	25
206.		1s. 6d. multicoloured	35	35
207.		2s. 6d. multicoloured	50	50

26. Cable Ship and Chain Links.

1967. Bermuda-Tortola Telephone Service. Inaug. Multicoloured.

No.	Description	Mint	Used
208.	3d. Type **26**	8	8
209.	1s. Map, Telephone and Microphone	30	30
210.	1s. 6d. Telecommunications Media	35	40
211.	2s. 6d. Cable Ship and Marine Fauna	60	65

27. Human Rights Emblem and Doves.

1968. Human Rights Year.

No.	Type	Description	Mint	Used
212.	27.	3d. indigo, blue & green	8	8
213.		1s. brown, blue & lt. bl.	30	30
214.		1s. 6d. black, blue & rose	40	40
215.		2s. 6d. grn., bl. & yellow	55	55

28. Mace and Queen's Profile.

1968. New Constitution.

No.	Type	Description	Mint	Used
216.	28.	3d. multicoloured	8	8
217.		1s. multicoloured	30	30
218.	–	1s. 6d. yell., blk. & bl.	40	40
219.	–	2s. 6d. lilac, black and yellow	55	55

DESIGN: 1s. 6d., 2s. 6d., Houses of Parliament, and House of Assembly, Bermuda.

29. Football, Athletics and Yachting.

1968. Olympic Games, Mexico.

No.	Type	Description	Mint	Used
220.	29.	3d. multicoloured	10	10
221.		1s. multicoloured	30	30
222.		1s. 6d. multicoloured	40	40
223.		2s. 6d. multicoloured	70	70

30. Brownie and Guide.

1969. Girl Guides. 50th Anniv. Multicoloured.

No.	Description	Mint	Used
224.	3d. Type **30**	8	8
225.	1s. Type **30**	30	30
226.	1s. 6d. Guides and Badge	45	45
227.	2s 6d. As 1s. 6d.	70	70

31. Emerald-studded Gold Cross and Seaweed.

1969. Underwater Treasure. Multicoloured.
228. 4d. Type **31** 10 10
229. 1s. 3d. Emerald-studded gold cross and sea-bed .. 30 30
230. 2s. As Type **31** 40 40
231. 2s. 6d. As 1s. 3d. .. 60 60

1970. Decimal Currency. Nos. 163/79 surch.
232. 1 c. on 1d. pur., blk. & orge. 5 5
233. 2 c. on 2d. lilac, indigo, yellow and green .. 5 5
234. 3 c. on 3d. brown and blue 5 5
235. 4 c. on 4d. brown & magenta 5 5
236. 5 c. on 8d. blue, grn. & orge. 8 8
237. 6 c. on 6d. grey, grn. & blue 8 10
238. 9 c. on 9d. blue and brown 12 12
239. 10 c. on 10d. violet & ochre 15 15
240. 12 c. on 1s. black, blue, green and orange .. 20 20
241. 15 c. on 1s. 3d. lake, grey and bistre .. 40 55
242. 18 c. on 1s. 6d. blue & red 25 25
243. 24 c. on 2s. brown & orange 35 45
244. 30 c. on 2s. 6d. sepia, green and yellow 40 50
245. 36 c. on 2s. 3d. sepia & grn. 50 55
246. 60 c. on 5s. maroon & green 1·10 1·50
247. $1.20 on 10s. magenta, green and buff.. .. 2·50 3·00
248. $2.40 on £1 black, olive and orange .. .. 4·50 5·50

32. Spathiphyllum.

1970. Flowers. Multicoloured.
249. 1 c. Type **32** 5 5
250. 2 c. Bottlebrush 5 5
251. 3 c. Oleander (vert.) .. 5 5
252. 4 c. Bermudiana 5 5
253. 5 c. Poinsettia 5 8
254. 6 c. Hibiscus 8 8
255. 9 c. Cereus 10 8
256. 10 c. Bougainvillea (vert.) 10 8
257. 12 c. Jacaranda 25 25
258. 15 c. Passion Flower .. 15 20
258a. 17 c. As 15 c. 15 20
259. 18 c. Coralita 20 20
259a. 20 c. As 18 c. 20 20
260. 24 c. Morning Glory .. 30 35
260a. 25 c. As 24 c. 25 30
261. 30 c. Tecoma 35 40
262. 36 c. Angel's Trumpet .. 35 40
262a. 40 c. as 36 c. 40 45
263. 60 c. Plumbago 75 85
263a. $1 As 60 c. .. .. 95 1·10
264. $1.20 Bird of Paradise Flower .. .. .. 1·50 1·75
264a. $2 As $1.20 .. .. 1·90 2·10
265. $2.40 Chalice Cup .. 2·75 3·00
265a. $3 As $2.40 .. .. 3·00 3·25

33. The State House, St. George's.

1970. Bermuda Parliament. 350th Anniv. Multicoloured.
266. 4 c. Type **33** 8 8
267. 15 c. The Sessions House, Hamilton 25 25
268. 18 c. St. Peter's Church, St. George's 30 30
269. 24 c. Town Hall, Hamilton 40 40

34. Street Scene, St. George's.

1971. "Keep Bermuda Beautiful". Multicoloured.
271. 4 c. Type **34** 8 8
272. 15 c. Horseshoe Bay .. 30 30
273. 18 c. Gibbs Hill Lighthouse 35 35
274. 24 c. Hamilton Harbour .. 45 45

35. Building of the "Deliverance".

1971. Voyage of the "Deliverance". Multicoloured.
275. 4 c. Type **35** 12 12
276. 15 c. "Deliverance" and "Patience" at Jamestown (vert.) 35 35
277. 18 c. Wreck of the "Sea Venture" (vert.) 35 35
278. 24 c. "Deliverance" and "Patience" on high seas 45 45

36. Green overlooking Ocean View.

1971. Golfing in Bermuda. Multicoloured.
279. 4 c. Type **36** 10 10
280. 15 c. Golfers at Port Royal 30 30
281. 18 c. Castle Harbour .. 35 35
282. 24 c. Belmont 50 50

1971. Anglo-American Talks. Nos. 252 and 258/60 optd. **HEATH-NIXON DECEMBER 1971.**
283. 4 c. Bermudiana 10 10
284. 15 c. Passion Flower .. 25 30
285. 18 c. Coralita 35 35
286. 24 c. Morning Glory .. 45 45

37. Bonefish.

1972. World Fishing Records. Multicoloured.
287. 4 c. Type **37** 8 8
288. 15 c. Wahoo 25 25
289. 18 c. Yellowfin Tuna .. 30 30
290. 24 c. Greater Amberjack 45 45

1972. Royal Silver Wedding. As T **19** of Ascension, but with "Admiralty Oar" and Mace in background.
291. 4 c. violet.. .. .. 8 10
292. 15 c. red 35 40

38. Palmetto.

1973. Tree Planting Year. Multicoloured.
293. 4 c. Type **38** 5 5
294. 15 c. Olivewood Bark .. 30 30
295. 18 c. Bermuda Cedar .. 35 35
296. 24 c. Mahogany 40 40

1973. Royal Wedding. As Type **26** of Anguilla. Background colour given. Mult.
297. 15 c. mauve 25 25
298. 18 c. blue 30 35

39. Bernard Park, Pembroke, 1973.

1973. Lawn Tennis Centenary. Multicoloured.
299. 4 c. Type **39** 8 8
300. 15 c. Clermont Court, 1873 25 25
301. 18 c. Leamington Spa Court, 1872 .. .. 35 35
302. 24 c. Staten Island Courts, 1874 .. .. .. 40 35

40. Weather Vane, City Hall.

1974. Rotary in Bermuda. 50th Anniv. Multicoloured.
320. 5 c. Type **40** 10 10
321. 17 c. St. Peter's Church St. George's 25 25
322. 20 c. Somerset Bridge .. 30 30
323. 25 c. Map of Bermuda, 1626 30 35

41. Jack of Clubs and "good bridge hand".

1975. World Bridge Championships, Bermuda. Multicoloured.
324. 5 c. Type **41** 10 10
325. 17 c. Queen of Diamonds and Bermuda Bowl .. 25 25
326. 20 c. King of Hearts and Bermuda Bowl 30 30
327. 25 c. Ace of Spades and Bermuda Bowl 30 35

42. Queen Elizabeth II and the Duke of Edinburgh.

1975. Royal Visit.
328. **42.** 17 c. multicoloured .. 25 25
329. 20 c. multicoloured .. 30 30

43. "Cavalier" Flying-boat, 1937.

1975. Air-mail Service 50th Anniv. Mult.
330. 5 c. Type **43** 5 5
331. 17 c. Airship "Los Angeles", 1925 .. .. .. 25 25
332. 20 c. Lockheed "Constellation", 1946 .. .. 25 30
333. 25 c. Boeing "747", 1970 30 35

44. Supporters of American Army raiding Royal Magazine.

1976. Gunpowder Plot, St. George's. Bicent. Multicoloured.
335. 5 c. Type **44** 8 8
336. 17 c. Settin off for raid .. 20 20
337. 20 c. Loading gunpowder aboard American ship . 20 25
338. 25 c. Gunpowder on beach 25 30

45. Launching Bathysphere.

1976. Bermuda Biological Station. 50th Anniversary. Multicoloured.
357. 5 c. Type **45** 5 8
358. 17 c. View from the sea (horiz.) 20 20
359. 20 c. H.M.S. "Challenger". 1873 (horiz.) 20 25
360. 2 c. Beebe's Bathysphere descent, 1934 .. .. 25 30

46. "Christian Radich".

1976. Tall Ships Race, 1976. Multicoloured.
361. 5 c. Type **46** 5 8
362. 12 c. "Juan Sebastian de Elcano" 12 15
363. 17 c. U.S.C.G. "Eagle" 20 20
364. 20 c. "Winston S. Churchill" 20 25
365. 40 c. "Kruzenshtern".. 45 50
366. $1 "Cutty Sark" trophy 1·10 1·25

47. Silver Trohpy and Club Flags.

1976. St. George's v. Somerset Cricket Cup Match. 75th Anniversary. Multicoloured.
367. 5 c. Type **47** 5 5
368. 17 c. Badge and Pavilion, St. George's Club .. 20 20
369. 20 c. Badge and Pavilion, Somerset Club 20 25
370. 25 c. Somerset playing field 30 35

BHOPAL BC

A state of C. India. Now uses Indian stamps.

1.

2.

1876. Imperf.
5. **1.** ½ a. black 20 25
4. ½ a. red .. .. .. 1·10 1·10

1878. Imperf. or perf.
6. 2. ¼ a. green .. .. .. 2·75 3·25
12. ¼ a. blue 65
15. ½ a. red 50 55
8. ½ a. red .. .. .. 1·00 1·00
9. ½ a. brown .. .. 8·00

1881. As T 1, but larger. Imperf. or perf.
29. ¼ a. black 25 40
38. ¼ a. red 45 45
46. ½ a. black 40 40
30. 1 a. brown 40 50
31. 2 a. blue 25 45
32. 4 a. yellow 40 80

4. 5.

1884. Perf.
49. 4. ¼ a. green 65 80
76. ¼ a. black 30 30

1884. Imperf. or perf.
63. 5. ¼ a. green 8 8
65. ¼ a. black 10 10
52. ½ a. black 20 20
59. ½ a. red 20 30

6.

1890. Imperf. or perf.
67. 6. 8 a. greenish black .. 6·50 6·50

7. 8. State arms.

1902. Imperf.
89. 7. ¼ a. red 12 12
91. ½ a. black 12 20
82. 1 a. brown .. .. 1·00 90
94. 2 a. blue 80 80
96. 4 a. yellow .. .. 11·00 11·00
97. 8 a. lilac .. .. 12·00 12·00
98. 1 r. rose .. .. 18·00 18·00

1908. Perf.
100. 8. 1 a. green 65 10

OFFICIAL STAMPS

1908. As T 8, but inscr. "H.H. BEGUM'S SERVICE" optd. **SERVICE.**
305. ½ a. green 60 5
302. 1 a. red 65 8
307. 2 a. blue .. .. 2·00 10
304. 4 a. brown .. .. 5·50 5

O 1.

1930. Type O 1 optd. **SERVICE.**
309. O 1. ½ a. green 30 8
310. 1 a. red 40 5
311. 2 a. blue 45 5
312. 4 a. brown 65 10

1932. As T 8, but inscr. "POSTAGE" at left and "BHOPAL STATE" at right, optd. **SERVICE.**
313. – ¼ a. orange 65 5

1932. As T 8, but inscr. "POSTAGE" at left and "BHOPAL GOVT" at right, optd. **SERVICE.**
314. – ½ a. green 8 5
315. – 1 a. red 10 5
316. – 2 a. blue 35 30
317. – 4 a. brown 50 45

1935. Nos. 314, etc., surch.
318. – ¼ a. on ½ a. green .. 2·75 1·50
320. – ¼ a. on 2 a. blue .. 2·75 80
323. – ¼ a. on 4 a. brown .. 6·50 5·00
319. – 3 p. on ½ a. green .. 12 5
321. – 3 p. on 2 a. blue .. 30 30
325. – 3 p. on 4 a. brown .. 1·00 65
326. – 1 a. on ½ a. green .. 20 20
327. – 1 a. on 2 a. blue .. 20 12
329. – 1 a. on 4 a. brown .. 25 10

O 2.

1935.
330. O 2. 1 a. 3 p. blue & claret 10 8
331. 1 a. 6 p. blue & claret 10 10
332. 1 a. 6 p. claret .. 10 10
Nos. 331/2 are similar to Type O 2, but inscr. "BHOPAL STATE POSTAGE".

O 3.

1936. Type O 3 optd. **SERVICE.**
334. O 3. ½ a. yellow 5 5
335. 1 a. red 5 5

O 4. The Moti Mahal.

1936. As Type O 4 optd. **SERVICE.**
336. O 4. ½ a. purple and green 8 5
337. – 2 a. brown and blue .. 8 8
338. – 2 a. green and violet .. 30 5
339. – 4 a. blue and brown .. 35 35
340. – 8 a. purple and blue .. 50 40
341. – 1 r. blue and purple .. 80 40
DESIGNS: 2 a. The Moti Masjid. 4 a. Taj Mahal and Be-Nazir Palaces. 8 a. Ahmadabad Palace. 1 r. Rait Ghat.
No. 336 is inscribed "BHOPAL GOVT" below the arms, other values have "BHOPAL STATE".

1940. Animal designs, as Type O 4, but inscr. "SERVICE" in bottom panel.
344. – ¼ a. blue (Tiger) .. 45 10
345. – 1 a. purple (Chital) .. 1·25 20

1941. As Type O 2 but "SERVICE" inscr. instead of optd.
346. O 2. 1 a. 3 p. green .. 10 5

1944. Palaces as Type O 4 but smaller.
347. ½ a. green (Moti Mahal) .. 20 20
348. 2 a. violet (Moti Masjid) .. 30 30
348c. 2 a. purple (Moti Masjid) 30 30
349. 4 a. brown (Be Nazir) .. 40 30
The 2 a. and 4 a. are inscribed "BHOPAL STATE", and the other "BHOPAL GOVT"

O 6. Arms of Bhopal.

1945.
350. O 6. 3 p. blue 5 5
351. 9 p. brown .. .. 1·00 50
352. 1 a. purple 10 5
352b. 1 a. violet .. .. 1·00 25
353. 1½ a claret 25 25
354. 3 a. yellow 12 20
354d. 3 a. brown .. .. 6·50
355. 6 a. red .. .. 2·75 2·75

1949. Surch. **2 As.** and bars.
356. O 6. 2 a. on 1½ a. claret .. 20 35

1949. Surch. **2 As.** and ornaments.
357. O 6. 2 a. on 1½ a. claret .. 80·00 55·00

BHOR BC

A state of W. India, Bombay district. Now uses Indian stamps.

1. 2. Pant Sachiv Shankarro Chimnaji.

1879. Imperf.
1. 1. ½ a. red 80 90
Similar to T 1, but rectangular
2. 1 a red 80 90

1901. Imperf.
3. 2. ½ a. red .. .. .. 2·00 11·00

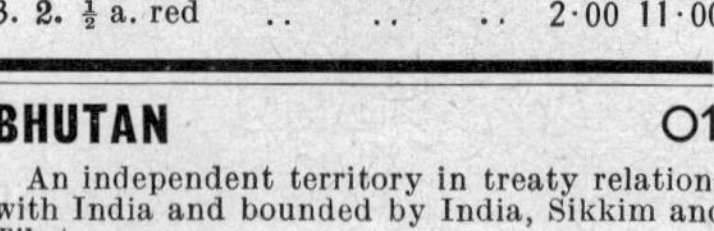

BHUTAN O1

An independent territory in treaty relations with India and bounded by India, Sikkim and Tibet.

100 chetrum = 1 ngultrum or rupee.

1. Postal Runner. 2. "Uprooted Tree" Emblem and Crest of Bhutan.

1962.
1. 1. 2 ch. red and grey .. 5 5
2. – 3 ch. red & violet-blue .. 5 5
3. – 5 ch. sepia and green .. 25 25
4. – 15 ch. yellow, black & red 5 5
5. 1. 33 ch. turquoise & mauve 12 12
6. – 70 ch. ultramarine & blue 30 30
7. – 1 n. 30 black and blue .. 55 55
DESIGNS—HORIZ. 3 ch., 70 ch. Archer. 5 ch., 1 n. 30, Wild yak. 15 ch. Map of Bhutan, Maharaja, fortress and monastery.

1962. World Refugee Year.
8. 2. 1 n. red and blue .. 40 40
9. 2 n. mauve and apple .. 85 85

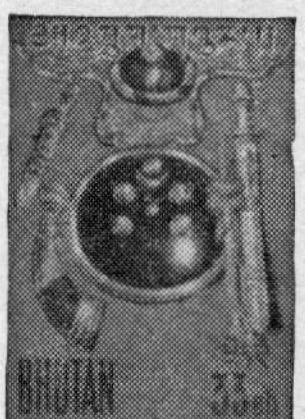

3. Accoutrements of Ancient Warrior. 4. "Boy filling box" (with grain).

1962. Membership of Colombo Plan.
10. 3. 33 ch. multicoloured .. 12 12
11. 70 ch. multicoloured .. 20 20
12. 1 n. 30 multicoloured .. 45 45

1963. Freedom from Hunger.
13. 4. 20 ch. brown, blue & yell. 12 12
14. 1 n. 50 pur., brn. & turq. 50 50

1964. Winter Olympic Games, Innsbruck, and Bhutanese Winter Sports Committee Fund. Surch. with Olympic Rings, Games Emblem and **INNSBRUCK 1964 + 50 ch.**
15. 3. 33 ch. + 50 ch. mult. .. 2·00 2·00
16. 70 ch. + 50 ch. mult. .. 2·00 2·00
17. 1 n. 30 + 50 ch. mult. .. 2·00 2·00

5. Dancer with upraised Hands.

1964. Bhutanese Dancers. Multicoloured.
18. 2 ch. Standing on one leg 5 5
19. 3 ch. Type 5 .. .. 5 5
20. 5 ch. With "tambourine" 5 5
21. 20 ch. Standing on one leg 8 8
22. 33 ch. Type 5 .. .. 10 10
23. 70 ch. With sword .. 15 15
24. 1 n. With tasselled hat .. 25 25
25. 1 n. 30 With "tambourine" 30 30
26. 2 n. With sword 50 50
The 2 ch., 5 ch., 20 ch., 1 n. and 1 n. 30 are vert.

6. Bhutanese Athlete. 8. Primula.

7. Flags at Half-mast.

1964. Olympic Games, Tokyo. Multicoloured.
27. 2 ch. Type 6 .. .. 5 5
28. 5 ch. Boxing 5 5
29. 15 ch. Type 6 .. .. 5 5
30. 33 ch. Boxing 10 10
31. 1 n. Archery 30 30
32. 2 n. Football 60 60
33. 3 n. Archery 90 90

1964. Pres. Kennedy. Commem.
34. 7. 33 ch. multicoloured .. 15 15
35. 1 n. multicoloured .. 30 30
36. 3 n. multicoloured .. 75 75

1965. Flowers. Multicoloured.
37. 2 ch. Type 8 .. .. 5 5
38. 5 ch. Gentian 5 5
39. 15 ch. Type 8 .. .. 5 5
40. 33 ch. Gentian 8 8
41. 50 ch. Rhododendron .. 12 12
42. 75 ch. Peony 20 20
43. 1 n. Rhododendron .. 25 25
44. 2 n. Peony 55 55

1965. Churchill Commem. Optd. **WINSTON CHURCHILL 1874-1965.**
45. 1. 33 ch. turquoise & mauve 15 15
46. 7. 1 n. multicoloured .. 40 40
47. – 1 n. multicoloured (No. 43) 40 40
48. – 2 n. multicoloured (No. 44) 75 75
49. 7. 3 n. multicoloured .. 1·10 1·10

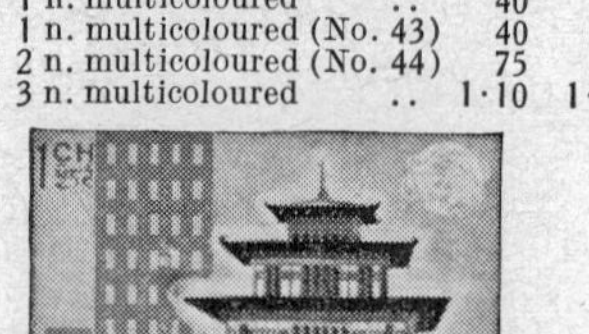

9. Pavilion and Skyscrapers.

1965. New York World's Fair. Multi-coloured.
50. 1 ch. Type 9 .. .. 5 5
51. 10 ch. Buddha and Michelangelo's "Pieta" .. 5 5
52. 20 ch. Bhutan houses and New York skyline .. 5 5
53. 33 ch. Bhutan and New York bridges 10 10
54. 1 n. 50, Type 9 .. .. 40 40
55. 2 n. As 10 ch 55 55

1965. Surch.
56. 2. 5 ch. on 1 n. (No. 8) .. 10·00 10·00
57. – 5 ch. on 2 n. (No. 9) .. 10·00 10·00
58. – 10 ch. on 70 ch. (No. 23) 7·00 7·00
59. – 10 ch. on 2 n. (No. 26) .. 3·50 3·50
60. – 15 ch. on 70 ch. (No. 6) .. 1·75 1·75
61. – 15 ch. on 1 n. 30 (No. 7) 1·50 1·50
62. – 20 ch. on 1 n. (No. 24) .. 3·50 3·50
63. – 20 ch. on 1 n. 30 (No. 25) .. 3·50 3·50

10. "Telstar" and Portable Transmitter.

1966. I.T.U. Cent. Multicoloured.
64. 35 ch. Type 10 .. .. 10 10
65. 2 n. "Telstar" & morse key 55 55
66. 3 n. "Relay" and ear-phones 80 80

INDEX

Countries can be quickly located by referring to the index at the end of this volume.

11. Bear.

1966. Animals. Multicoloured.
68. 1 ch. Type **11** 5 5
69. 2 ch. Leopard 5 5
70. 4 ch. Wild boar 5 5
71. 8 ch. Tiger 5 5
72. 10 ch. Wild dog 5 5
73. 75 ch. Tiger 20 15
74. 1 n. Buffalo 30 30
75. 1 n. 50 Wild dog 40 30
76. 2 n. Wild boar 60 40
77. 3 n. Leopard 70 50
78. 4 n. Type **11** .. .. 1·00 80
79. 5 n. Buffalo .. .. 1·25 90

12. Simtoke Dzong (fortress).

1966.
80. – 5 ch. chestnut 5 5
81. **12.** 15 ch. brown 5 5
82. 20 ch. green 8 8
DESIGN: 5 ch. Rinpung Dzong (fortress).

13. King Jigme Darji Wangchuk (obverse of 50 n.p. coin).

1966. King Jigme Wangchuk's Accession (father of King Jigme Dorji Wangchuk). 40th Anniv. Circular designs, embossed on gold foil, backed with multicoloured patterned paper. Imperf.
Sizes: (*a*) Diameter 1½ in.
(*b*) Diameter 1 in.
(*c*) Diameter 2½ in.
(i) 50 n.p. Coin.
83. **13.** 10 ch. green (*a*) 5 5
(ii) 1 r. Coin.
84. **13.** 25 ch. green (*b*) 8 8
(iii) 3 r. Coin.
85. **13.** 50 ch. green (*c*) 15 15
(iv) 1 sertum Coin.
86. **13.** 1 n. red (*a*) 20 20
87. – 1 n. 30 red (*a*) 30 30
(v) 2 sertum Coin.
88. **13.** 2 n. red (*b*) 60 60
89. – 3 n. red (*b*) 75 75
(vi) 5 sertum Coin.
90. **13.** 4 n. red (*c*) .. .. 1·00 1·00
91. – 5 n. red (*c*) .. .. 1·40 1·40
Nos. 87, 89 and 91 show the reverse side of the coins (Symbol).

14. "Abominable Snowman".

1966. "Abominable Snowman". Various triangular designs.
92. **14.** 1 ch. multicoloured .. 5 5
93. – 2 ch. multicoloured .. 5 5
94. – 3 ch. multicoloured .. 5 5
95. – 4 ch. multicoloured .. 5 5
96. – 5 ch. multicoloured .. 5 5
97. – 15 ch. multicoloured .. 5 5
98. – 30 ch. multicoloured .. 8 8
99. – 40 ch. multicoloured .. 8 8
100. – 50 ch. multicoloured .. 10 10
101. – 1 n. 25 multicoloured .. 30 30
102. – 2 n. 50 multicoloured .. 50 50
103. – 3 n. multicoloured .. 60 60
104. – 5 n. multicoloured .. 75 75
105. – 6 n. multicoloured .. 1·00 1·00
106. – 7 n. multicoloured .. 1·25 1·25

1967. Air. Optd. **AIR MAIL** and helicopter motif.
107. **5.** 33 ch. multicoloured .. 5 5
108. – 50 ch. mult. (No. 41) .. 8 8
109. – 70 ch. mult. (No. 23) .. 10 10
110. – 75 ch. mult. (No. 42) .. 15 15
111. – 1 n. mult. (No. 24) .. 20 20
112. – 1 n. 50 mult. (No. 75) .. 25 25
113. – 2 n. mult. (No. 76) .. 30 30
114. – 3 n. mult. (No. 77) .. 55 55
115. **11.** 4 n. multicoloured .. 70 70
116. – 5 n. mult. (No. 79) .. 80 80
These stamps come with two types of opt. **AIR MAIL** curved and **AIR MAIL** in one line.

15. "Lilium sherriffiae".

1967. Bhutan Flowers. Multicoloured.
117. 3 ch. Type **15** 5 5
118. 5 ch. "Meconopsis" .. 5 5
119. 7 ch. "Rhododendron dhwoju" 5 5
120. 10 ch. "Pleione hookeriana" 5 5
121. 50 ch. Type **15** 8 8
122. 1 n. "Meconopsis" .. 25 25
123. 2 n. 50 "Rhododendron dhwoju" 45 45
124. 4 n. "Pleione hookeriana" 80 80
125. 5 n. "Rhododendron giganteum" 90 90

16. Scouts Tree Planting.

1967. Bhutanese Boy Scouts. Multicoloured.
126. 5 ch. Type **16** 5 5
127. 10 ch. Scouts preparing meal 5 5
128. 15 ch. Scout mountaineering 8 8
129. 50 ch. Type **16** 10 10
130. 1 n. 25. As 10 ch. .. 25 25
131. 4 n. As 15 ch. 60 60

1967. World Fair, Montreal. Nos. 53/5 optd. **expo 67** and emblem.
133. – 33 ch. multicoloured .. 12 12
134. **9.** 1 n. 50 multicoloured .. 30 30
135. – 2 n. multicoloured .. 40 40

17. "Lancaster" Bomber.

1967. Churchill and Battle of Britain Commem. Multicoloured.
137. 45 ch. Type **17** 12 12
138. 2 n. "Spitfire" fighter .. 30 30
139. 4 n. "Hurricane" fighter 60 60

1967. World Scout Jamboree, Idaho. Nos. 126/31 optd. **WORLD JAMBOREE IDAHO, U.S.A. AUG. 1–9/67.**
141. **16.** 5 ch. multicoloured .. 5 5
142. – 10 ch. multicoloured .. 5 5
143. – 15 ch. multicoloured .. 5 5
144. – 50 ch. multicoloured .. 10 10
145. – 1 n. 25 multicoloured .. 20 20
146. – 4 n. multicoloured .. 60 60

18. Painting.

1967. Bhutan Girl Scouts. Multicoloured.
148. 5 ch. Type **18** 5 5
149. 10 ch. Playing musical instrument 5 5
150. 15 ch. Picking fruit .. 5 5
151. 1 n. 50 Type **18** 20 20
152. 2 n. 50 As 10 ch. .. 45 45
153. 5 n. As 15 ch. 85 85

19. Astronaut in Space.

1967. Space Achievements. With laminated prismatic-ribbed plastic surface. Multicoloured.
155. 3 ch. Type **19** (postage) .. 12 12
156. 5 ch. Space vehicle and astronaut 12 12
157. 7 ch. Astronaut and landing vehicle 12 12
158. 10 ch. Three astronauts in space 20 20
159. 15 ch. Type **19** 20 20
160. 30 ch. As 5 ch. 20 20
161. 50 ch. As 7 ch. 25 25
162. 1 n. 25 As 10 ch. .. 50 50
163. 2 n. 50 Type **19** (air) .. 45 45
164. 4 n. As 5 ch. 70 70
165. 5 n. As 7 ch. 80 80
166. 9 n. As 10 ch. .. .. 1·75 1·75
The laminated plastic surface gives the stamps a three-dimensional effect.

20. Tashichho Dzong.

1968.
168. **20.** 10 ch. purple and green 5 5

21. Tongsa Dzong.

22. Daga Dzong.

24. Wangdiphodrang Dzong and Bridge.

23. Mahatma Gandhi.

1968.
169. **21.** 50 ch. green 10 10
170. **22.** 75 ch. brown & ultram. 15 15
171. – 1 n. ultram. and violet 20 20
DESIGN: 1 n. Lhuntsi Dzong.

1969. Mahatma Gandhi. Birth Cent.
172. **23.** 20 ch. brown and blue 10 10
173. 2 n. brown and yellow 60 60

1970. Various stamps surch **20 CH.**
(a) Animals.
174. – 20 ch. on 3 n. (No. 77) .. 35 35
175. **11.** 20 ch. on 4 n. 35 35
176. – 20 ch. on 5 n. (No. 79) 35 35
(b) Abominable Snowmen.
177. 20 ch. on 3 n. (No. 103) .. 50 50
178. 20 ch. on 5 n. (No. 104) .. 50 50
179. 20 ch. on 6 n. (No. 105) .. 50 50
180. 20 ch. on 7 n. (No. 106) .. 50 50
(c) Flowers.
181. 20 ch. on 4 n. (No. 124) .. 50 50
182. 20 ch. on 5 n. (No. 125) .. 50 50
(d) Scouts.
183. 20 ch. on 4 n. (No. 131) .. 30 30
(e) Pheasants (Appendix).
184. 20 ch. on 4 n. multicoloured 50 50
(f) Mythological Creatures (Appendix).
185. 20 ch. on 2 n. multicoloured (postage) 50 50
186. 20 ch. on 5 n. multicoloured (air) 50 50
187. 20 ch. on 10 n. multicoloured 50 50
(g) Rare Birds (Appendix).
188. 20 ch. on 2 n. multicoloured (postage) 25 25
189. 20 ch. on 2 n. 50 multicoloured (air) 50 50
190. 20 ch. on 4 n. multicoloured 50 50
191. 20 ch. on 5 n. multicoloured 40 40
192. 20 ch. on 10 n. multicoloured 40 40

1972. Various stamps surch. similar to Nos. 174/92.
(a) Freedom from Hunger.
193. **4.** 20 ch. on 1 n. 50 .. 1·00 1·00
(b) Animals.
194. – 20 ch. on 1 n. 50 (No. 75) 1·00 1·00
195. – 20 ch. on 2 n. (No. 76).. 1·00 1·00
(c) Abominable Snowmen.
196. – 20 ch. on 1 n. 25 (No. 101) 1·25 1·25
197. – 20 ch. on 2 n. 50 (No. 102) 1·00 1·00
(d) Boy Scouts.
198. – 20 ch. on 1 n. 25 (No. 130) 1·00 1·00
(e) Churchill.
199. – 20 ch. on 2 n. (No. 138).. 1·25 1·25
200. – 20 ch. on 4 n. (No. 139).. 1·25 1·25
(f) Pheasants (Appendix).
201. – 20 ch. on 2 n. mult. .. 1·00 1·00
202. – 20 ch. on 7 n. mult. .. 1·00 1·00
(g) Mythological Creatures (Appendix).
203. – 5 ch. on 30 ch. mult. (post.) 15 15
204. – 5 ch. on 50 ch. mult. .. 15 15
205. – 5 ch. on 1 n. 25 mult. .. 15 15
206. – 5 ch. on 2 n. mult. .. 15 15
207. – 5 ch. on 1 n. 50 mult. (air) 25 25
208. – 5 ch. on 2 n. 50 mult. .. 25 25
(h) Rare Birds (Appendix).
209. – 20 ch. on 30 ch. mult. (post.) 1·00 1·00
210. – 20 ch. on 50 ch. mult. .. 1·00 1·00
211. – 20 ch. on 1 n. 25 mult. .. 1·00 1·00
212. – 20 ch. on 1 n. 50 mult. (air) 1·25 1·25
(i) U.P.U. (Appendix).
213. – 20 ch. on 1 n. 05 mult. .. 1·25 1·25
214. – 20 ch. on 1 n. 40 mult. .. 1·25 1·25
215. – 20 ch. on 4 n. mult. .. 1·25 1·25

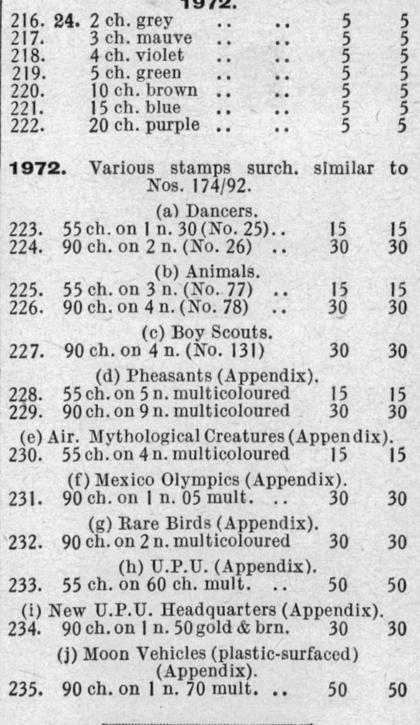

1972.
216. **24.** 2 ch. grey 5 5
217. 3 ch. mauve 5 5
218. 4 ch. violet 5 5
219. 5 ch. green 5 5
220. 10 ch. brown 5 5
221. 15 ch. blue 5 5
222. 20 ch. purple 5 5

1972. Various stamps surch. similar to Nos. 174/92.
(a) Dancers.
223. 55 ch. on 1 n. 30 (No. 25).. 15 15
224. 90 ch. on 2 n. (No. 26) .. 30 30
(b) Animals.
225. 55 ch. on 3 n. (No. 77) .. 15 15
226. 90 ch. on 4 n. (No. 78) .. 30 30
(c) Boy Scouts.
227. 90 ch. on 4 n. (No. 131) 30 30
(d) Pheasants (Appendix).
228. 55 ch. on 5 n. multicoloured 15 15
229. 90 ch. on 9 n. multicoloured 30 30
(e) Air. Mythological Creatures (Appendix).
230. 55 ch. on 4 n. multicoloured 15 15
(f) Mexico Olympics (Appendix).
231. 90 ch. on 1 n. 05 mult. .. 30 30
(g) Rare Birds (Appendix).
232. 90 ch. on 2 n. multicoloured 30 30
(h) U.P.U. (Appendix).
233. 55 ch. on 60 ch. mult. .. 50 50
(i) New U.P.U. Headquarters (Appendix).
234. 90 ch. on 1 n. 50 gold & brn. 30 30
(j) Moon Vehicles (plastic-surfaced) (Appendix).
235. 90 ch. on 1 n. 70 mult. .. 50 50

25. Book Year Emblem.

1972. Int. Book Year.
236. **25.** 2 ch. green, turq.-green and turq.-blue 5 5
237. 3 ch. pur., yell. & brn. 5 5
238. 5 ch. brn., pink & orge. 5 5
239. 20 ch. multicoloured .. 5 5

26. King and Good Luck Signs.

1974. Coronation of King Jigme Singe Wangchuk. Multicoloured.

240.	10 ch. King and Crest ..	5	5
241.	25 ch. Bhutan Flag ..	5	5
242.	1 n. 25 Type **26**	20	20
243.	2 n. Punakha Dzong ..	35	35
244.	3 n. Royal Crown	50	50

27. Mail Delivery by Horse.

1974. Universal Postal Union. Cent. Mult.

246.	1 ch. Type **27** (postage) ..	5	5
247.	2 ch. Early and modern locomotives	5	5
248.	3 ch. Early and modern ships	5	5
249.	4 ch. Early & modern aircraft	5	5
250.	25 ch. Mail runner and jeep	5	5
251.	1 n. As 25 ch. (air) ..	15	15
252.	1 n. 40 As 2 ch.	20	20
253.	2 n. As 4 ch.	30	30

28. Family and W.P.Y. Emblem.

1974. World Population Year.

255.	**28.**	25 ch. multicoloured ..	5	5
256.		50 ch. multicoloured ..	8	8
257.		90 ch. multicoloured ..	15	15
258.		2 n. 50 multicoloured ..	35	35

29. " Sephisa chandra ".

1975. Butterflies. Multicoloured.

260.	1 ch. Type **29**	5	5
261.	2 ch. " Lethe kansa " ..	5	5
262.	3 ch. " Neope bhandra " ..	5	5
263.	4 ch. " Euthalia duda " ..	5	5
264.	5 ch. " Vindula erota " ..	5	5
265.	10 ch. " Bhutanitis lidderdalei "	5	5
266.	3 n. " Limenitis zayla " ..	50	50
267.	5 n. " Delias thysbe " ..	70	70

30. " Apollo ".

1976. " Apollo–Soyuz " Space Link. Multicoloured.

269.	10 n. Type **30**	1·50	1·50
270.	10 n. " Soyuz "	1·50	1·50

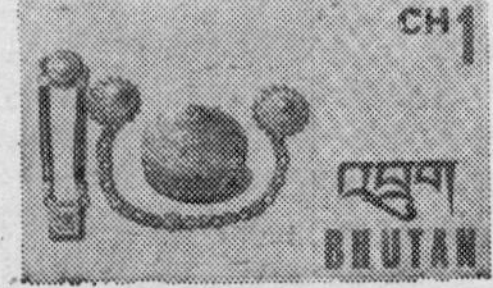

31. Jewellery.

1976. Handicrafts and Craftsmen. Multicoloured.

272.	1 ch. Type **31**	5	5
273.	2 ch. Coffee-pot, bell and sugar dish	5	5
274.	3 ch. Vessel and drinking-horn	5	5
275.	4 ch. Pendants and inlaid box	5	5
276.	5 ch. Painter	5	5
277.	15 ch. Silversmith ..	5	5
278.	20 ch. Wood-carver with tools	5	5
279.	1 n. 50 Mat-maker ..	20	20
280.	10 n. Printer	1·50	1·50

32. King Jigme Singye Wangchuk.

1976. King Jigme's 20th Birthday. Circular designs embossed on gold foil. Imperf.

		(a) Diameter 1½ in.		
282.	**32.**	15 ch. green	5	5
283.		1 n. red	15	15
284.	–	1 n. 30 red	20	20
		(b) Diameter 2 in.		
285.	**32.**	25 ch. green	5	5
286.		2 n. red	30	30
287.		3 n. red	45	45
		(c) Diameter 2½ in.		
288.	**32.**	90 ch. green	12	12
289.		4 n. red	60	60
290.	–	5 n. red	75	75

DESIGN: Nos. 284, 287, 290 National Symbol.

33. " Rhododendron Cinnabarinum ".

1976. Rhododendrons. Multicoloured.

291.	1 ch. Type **33**	5	5
292.	2 ch. " R. campanulatum "	5	5
293.	3 ch. " R. fortunei " ..	5	5
294.	4 ch. " R. arboreum " ..	5	5
295.	5 ch. " R. arboreum " (different)	5	5
296.	1 n. " R. falconeri " ..	15	15
297.	3 n. " R. hodgsonii " ..	45	45
298.	5 n. " R. keysii "	75	75

34. Slalom-skiing.

1976. Winter Olympic Games, Innsbruck. Multicoloured.

300.	1 ch. Type **34**	5	5
301.	2 ch. Bobsleighing ..	5	5
302.	3 ch. Ice-hockey	5	5
303.	4 ch. Cross-country skiing	5	5
304.	5 ch. Women's figure-skating	5	5
305.	2 n. Downhill skiing ..	30	30
306.	4 n. Speed skating ..	60	60
307.	10 n. Figure-skating (pairs)	1·50	1·50

BIAFRA BC

The following stamps were issued by Biafra (the Eastern Region of Nigeria) during the civil war with the Federal Government, 1967-70.

They were in regular use within Biafra from the time when supplies of Nigerian stamps were exhausted, and towards the end of the conflict they began to be used on external mail carried by air via Libreville.

Biafra was overrun by Federal troops on 10 January, 1970, and surrender took place on 15 January.

1. Map of Republic. 2. Weapon Maintenance

1968. Independence. Multicoloured.

1.	2d. Type **1**	5	10
2.	4d. Arms, Flag and Date of Independence	10	15
3.	1s. Mother and Child (17×22 mm.	20	40

1968. Stamps of Nigeria optd. with Arms and **SOVEREIGN BIAFRA.**

4.	½d. mult. (No. 172) ..	30	25
5.	1d. mult. (No. 173) ..	40	30
6.	1½d. mult. (No. 174) ..	50	40
7.	2d. mult. (No. 175) ..	2·00	2·00
8.	4d. mult. (No. 177) ..	2·00	2·00
9.	6d. mult. (No. 178) ..	55	70
10.	9d. blue & red (No. 179) ..	60	85
11.	1s. mult. (No. 180) ..	25·00	25·00
12.	1s. 3d. mult. (No. 181) ..	18·00	20·00
13.	2s. 6d. mult. (No. 182) ..	1·00	1·25
14.	5s. mult. (No. 183) ..	1·25	2·50
15.	10s. mult. (No. 184) ..	5·00	6·00
16.	£1 mult. (No. 185) ..	6·00	6·50

1968. Nos. 172/3 of Nigeria surch. **BIAFRA-FRANCE FRIENDSHIP 1968 SOVEREIGN BIAFRA** and value.

16b.	–	½ d. + 5 s. multicoloured	70	
16c.	**45.**	1 d. + £1 multicoloured	1·75	

1968. Independence. 1st Anniv. Multicoloured.

17.	4d. Type **2**	8	8
18.	1s. Victim of Atrocity ..	12	20
19.	2s. 6d. Nurse and Refugees	25	50
20.	5s. Biafran Arms and Banknote	45	80
21.	10s. Orphaned Child ..	85	1·75

1968. Nos. 17/21 surch. **HELP BIAFRAN CHILDREN** and value.

22.	**2.**	4d. + 2d. multicoloured ..	8	10
23.	–	1s. + 6d. multicoloured ..	20	25
24.	–	2s. 6d. + 1s. multicoloured	35	50
25.	–	5s. + 2s. 6d. multicoloured	75	1·25
26.	–	10s. + 2s. 6d. multicoloured	1·25	2·00

3. " Papilio dardanus " (butterfly) and " Lankesteria barteri " (plant).

1969. Butterflies and Plants. Multicoloured.

27.	4d. Type **3**	8	8
28.	1s. 6d. " Papilio antimachus " and " Ipomoea involucrata "	20	25
29.	2s. 6d. " Papilio zalmoxis " and " Haemanthus cinnabarinus "	35	45
30.	5s. " Papilio hesperus " and " Clerodendrum splendens "	65	85

1968. Olympic Games, Mexico. Nos. 27/30 optd. **MEXICO OLYMPICS 1968** and Olympic Rings.

31.	**3.**	4d. multicoloured ..	8	8
32.	–	1s. 6d. multicoloured ..	20	25
33.	–	2s. 6d. multicoloured ..	35	45
34.	–	5s. multicoloured	65	85

4. Child in chains, and Globe.

1969. Independence. 2nd Anniv. Multicoloured; frame colours given.

35.	**4.**	2d. orange	5	5
36.		4d. red	8	10
37.		1s. blue	12	20
38.		2s. 6d. emerald	35	60

5. Pope Paul VI, Africa, and Papal Arms.

1969. Visit of Pope Paul to Africa. Multicoloured; background colours given.

39.	**5.**	4d. orange	8	8
40.	–	6d. blue	8	12
41.	–	9d. green	12	20
42.	–	3s. magenta	45	65

DESIGNS: Pope Paul VI, map of Africa and—6d. Arms of Vatican. 9d. St. Peter's Basilica. 3s. Statue of St. Peter.

On December 17, the French Agency released a Christmas issue consisting of Nos. 39/42 overprinted **" CHRISTMAS 1969 PEACE ON EARTH AND GOODWILL TO ALL MEN ".** Later Nos. 35/38 were released overprinted **" SAVE BIAFRA 9TH JAN 1970 "** with a premium of 8d., 1s. 4d., 8s. and 10s. respectively. We have no evidence that these issues were put on sale in Biafra before the collapse.

BIJAWAR BC

A state of Central India. Now uses Indian stamps.

1. Maharaja Sir Sarwant Singh Bahadur. 2.

1935.

1.	**1.**	3 p. brown	20	25
2.		6 p. red	20	25
3.		9 p. violet	20	35
4.		1 a. blue	25	40
5.		2 a. green	40	50

1937.

11.	**2.**	4 a. orange	65	1·10
12.		6 a. lemon	1·00	1·25
13.		8 a. green	1·25	1·40
14.		12 a. blue	1·50	2·00
15.		1 r. violet	5·50	6·50

BOHEMIA AND MORAVIA E1

Following the proclamation of Slovak Independence on 14 March, 1939, the Czech provinces of Bohemia and Moravia became a German Protectorate. The area was liberated in 1945 and returned to Czechoslovakia.

100 haleru = 1 koruna.

1939. Stamps of Czechoslovakia optd. **BOHMEN U. MAHREN** and **CECHY a MORAVA.**

1.	**22.**	5 h. blue	5	5
2.		10 h. brown	5	5
3.		20 h. red	5	5
4.		25 h. green	5	5
5.		30 h. purple	5	5
6.	**50.**	40 h. blue	55	75
7.	**63.**	50 h. green	5	5
8.	**65.**	60 h. violet	25	45
10.	**46.**	1 k. red	15	20
11.	–	1 k. 20 purple (No. 354)	1·75	2·00
12.	**51.**	1 k. 50 red	1·40	1·75
13.	–	1 k. 60 olive (No. 355a)	1·40	1·75
14.	–	2 k. green (No. 356) ..	30	45
15.	–	2 k. 50 blue (No. 357) ..	1·40	1·75
16.	–	3 k. chocolate (No. 358)	1·75	2·00
17.	**52.**	4 k. violet	1·75	2·00
18.	–	5 k. green (No. 361)	2·00	2·50
19.	–	10 k. blue (No. 362)	2·50	3·00

1. Linden Leaves and Buds. 3. Zlin.

2. Karluv Tyn Castle.

DESIGNS—As T 2: 40 h. Svikov Castle. 60 h. St. Barbara's Church, Kutna Hora. 1 k. St. Vitus's Cathedral, Prague. As T 3—VERT. 1 k. 20, 1 k. 50 Brno Cathedral. 2 k., 2 k. 50, Olomouc. HORIZ. 4 k. Ironworks, Moravska-Ostrava. 5 k., 10 k., 20 k. Karlsburg, Prague.

1939.

20.	1.	5 h. blue	5	5
21.		10 h. brown	5	5
22.		20 h. red	5	5
23.		25 h. green	8	5
24.		30 h. purple	5	5
25.	–	40 h. blue	5	5
26.	2.	50 h. green	5	5
27.	–	60 h. violet	5	5
28.	–	1 k. red	5	5
29.	–	1 k. 20 purple	20	20
30.	–	1 k. 50 red	5	5
31.	–	2 k. green	5	5
32.	–	2 k. 50 blue	5	5
33.	3.	3 k. mauve	8	5
34.	–	4 k. slate	10	5
35.	–	5 k. green	30	15
36.	–	10 k. blue	25	25
37.	–	20 k. bistre	40	55

1940. As 1939 issue, but colours changed and new values.

38.	1.	30 h. brown	5	5
39.		40 h. orange	5	5
40.		50 h. slate	5	5
44.	–	50 h. green	8	10
41.	1.	60 h. violet	5	5
42.		80 h. orange	5	5
45.	–	80 h. blue	8	10
43.	1.	1 k. brown	5	5
46.	–	1 k. 20 brown	25	12
47.	–	1 k. 20 red	5	5
48.	–	1 k. 50 lilac	5	5
49.	–	2 k. green	8	8
50.	–	2 k. blue	5	5
51.	–	2 k. 50 blue	5	5
52.	–	3 k. olive	8	8
53.	–	5 k. green	10	8
54.	–	6 k. purple	12	10
55.	–	8 k. green	15	20
56.	–	10 k. blue	25	20
57.	–	20 k. brown	60	65

DESIGNS—As T 2: 50 h. (No. 44), Neuhaus Castle. 80 h. (No. 45), 3 k. Pernstyn Castle. 1 k. 20 (No. 46). 2 k. 50, Brno Cathedral. 1 k. 20 (No. 47), St. Vitus's Cathedral, Prague. 1 k. 50, St. Barbara's Church, Kutna Hora. 2 k. Pardubitz Castle. As T 3—HORIZ. 5 k. Bridge at Beching. 6 k. Sampson Fountain, Budweis. 8 k. Kremsier. 10 k. Wallenstein Palace, Prague. 20 k. Karlsburg, Prague.

4. Red Cross Nurse and Patients. 5.

1940. Red Cross Relief Fund.

58.	4.	60 h.+40 h. blue	25	25
59.		1 k. 20+80 h. plum	30	40

1941. Red Cross Relief Fund.

60.	5.	60 h.+40 h. blue	10	15
61.		1 k. 20+80 h. plum	10	15

6. Anton Dvorak (composer).

1941. Dvorak. Birth Cent.

62.	6.	60 k. violet	5	8
63.		1 k. 20 brown	10	12

7. Harvesting. 8. Blast-furnace, Pilsen

1941. Prague Fair.

64.	7.	30 h. brown	5	5
65.		60 h. green	5	5
66.	8.	1 k. 20 plum	5	8
67.		2 k. 50 blue	8	12

9. "Standetheater", Prague. 10. Mozart. (11.

1941. Mozart. 150th Death Anniv.

68.	9.	30 h.+30 h. brown	5	5
69.		60 h.+60 h. green	5	8
70.	10.	1 k. 20+1 k. 20 red	8	12
71.		2 k. 50+2 k. 50 blue	12	15

1942. German Occupation. 3rd Anniv. Optd. with T 11.

72.		1 k. 20 red (No. 47)	12	15
73.		2 k. 50 blue (No. 51)	12	15

12. Adolf Hitler. 13.

1942. Hitler's 53rd Birthday.

74.	12.	30 h.+20 h. brown	5	5
75.		60 h.+40 h. green	5	5
76.		1 k. 20+80 h. maroon	5	5
77.		2 k. 50+1 k. 50 blue	5	8

1942. Various sizes.

78.	13.	10 h. black	5	5
79.		30 h. brown	5	5
80.		40 h. blue	5	5
81.		50 h. green	5	5
82.		60 h. violet	5	5
83.		80 h. orange	5	5
84.		1 k. brown	5	5
85.		1 k. 20 red	5	5
86.		1 k. 50 claret	5	5
87.		1 k. 60 green	5	8
88.		2 k. blue	5	5
89.		2 k. 40 brown	5	10
90.		2 k. 50 blue	5	5
91.		3 k. olive	5	5
92.		4 k. purple	5	5
93.		5 k. green	5	5
94.		6 k. brown	5	5
95.		8 k. blue	5	5
96.		10 k. green	8	8
97.		20 k. violet	12	12
98.		30 k. red	30	35
99.		50 k. blue	40	60

SIZES—17½ × 21½ mm. 10 h. to 80.; 1 h8½ × 21 mm. 1 k. to 2 k. 40 h.; 19 × 24 mm. 2 k. 50 h. to 8 k.; 24 × 30 mm. 10 k. to 50 k.

14. Nurse and Patient. 15. Mounted Postman.

1942. Red Cross Relief Fund.

100.	14.	60 h.+40 h. blue	5	5
101.		1 k. 20+80 h. claret	5	5

1943. Stamp Day.

102.	15.	60 h. purple	5	5

16. Peter Parler. 17. Adolf Hitler.

1943. Winter Relief Fund.

103.	–	60 h.+40 h. violet	5	5
104.	16.	1 k. 20+80 h. red	5	5
105.	–	2 k. 50+1 k. 50 blue	5	5

DESIGNS: 60 h. Charles IV. 2 k. 50, King John of Luxembourg.

1943. Hitler's 54th Birthday.

106.	17.	60 h.+1 k. 40 violet	5	5
107.		1 k. 20+3 k. 80 red	5	5

18. Scene from "The Mastersingers of Nuremberg". 19. Richard Wagner.

1943. Wagner's 130th Birth Anniv.

108.	18.	60 h. violet	5	5
109.	19.	1 k. 20 red	5	5
110.	–	2 k. 50 blue	5	5

DESIGN: 2 k. 50, Blacksmith scene from "Siegfried".

20. Reinhard Heydrich. 21. Arms of Bohemia and Moravia and Red Cross.

1943. Heydrich. 1st Death Anniv.

111.	20.	60 h.+4 k. 40 black	12	15

1943. Red Cross Relief Fund.

112.	21.	1 k. 20 + 8 k. 80 black and red	5	5

22. National Costumes. 23. Arms of Bohemia and Moravia.

1944. German Occupation. 5th Anniv.

113.	22.	1 k. 20+3 k. 80 red	5	5
114.	23.	4 k. 20+18 k. 80 brown	5	5
115.	22.	10 k. + 20 k. blue	8	10

24. Adolf Hitler. 25. Friedrich Smetana.

1944. Hitler's 55th Birthday.

116.	24.	60 h.+1 k. 40 brown	5	5
117.		1 k. 20 + 3 k. 80 green	5	5

1944. Smetana (composer). 60th Death Anniv.

118.	25.	60 h.+1 k. 40 green	5	5
119.		1 k. 20+3 k. 80 claret	5	5

26. St. Vitus's Cathedral, Prague. 27. Adolf Hitler.

1944.

120.	26.	1 k. 50 purple	5	5
121.		2 k. 50 violet	5	8

1944.

122.	27.	4 k. 20 green	8	10

NEWSPAPER STAMPS

N 1. Dove. N 2.

1939. Imperf.

N 38.	N 1.	2 h. brown	5	5
N 39.		5 h. blue	5	5
N 40.		7 h. orange	5	5
N 41.		9 h. green	5	5
N 42.		10 h. lake	5	5
N 43.		12 h. blue	5	5
N 44.		20 h. green	5	8
N 45.		50 h. brown	5	8
N 46.		1 k. grey	5	10

1940. No. N 42 optd. GD-OT.

N 60.	N 1.	10 h. lake	10	12

1943. Imperf.

N 106.	N 2.	2 h. brown	5	5
N 107.		5 h. blue	5	5
N 108.		7 h. orange	5	5
N 109.		9 h. green	5	5
N 110.		10 h. lake	5	5
N 111.		12 h. blue	5	5
N 112.		20 h. green	5	5
N 113.		50 h. brown	5	5
N 114.		1 k. grey	5	5

OFFICIAL STAMPS

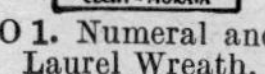

O 1. Numeral and Laurel Wreath. O 2. Eagle and Numeral.

1941.

O 60.	O 1.	30 h. brown	5	5
O 61.		40 h. blue	5	5
O 62.		50 h. green	5	5
O 63.		60 h. green	5	5
O 64.		80 h. red	5	5
O 65.		1 k. brown	5	5
O 66.		1 k. 20 red	5	5
O 67.		1 k. 50 maroon	5	5
O 68.		2 k. blue	5	5
O 69.		3 k. olive	5	5
O 70.		4 k. purple	8	8
O 71.		5 k. yellow	15	15

1943.

O 106.	O 2.	30 h. brown	5	5
O 107.		40 h. blue	5	5
O 108.		50 h. green	5	5
O 109.		60 h. violet	5	5
O 110.		80 h. red	5	5
O 111.		1 k. brown	5	5
O 112.		1 k. 20 red	5	5
O 113.		1 k. 50 brown	5	5
O 114.		2 k. blue	5	5
O 115.		3 k. olive	5	5
O 116.		4 k. purple	5	8
O 117.		5 k. green	5	5

PERSONAL DELIVERY STAMPS

P 1.

1939.

P 38.	P 1.	50 h. blue	30	45
P 39.		50 h. red	30	50

POSTAGE DUE STAMPS

D 1.

1939.

D 38.	D 1.	5 h. red	5	5
D 39.		10 h. red	5	5
D 40.		20 h. red	5	5
D 41.		30 h. red	5	5
D 42.		40 h. red	5	5
D 43.		50 h. red	5	5
D 44.		60 h. red	5	5
D 45.		80 h. red	5	5
D 46.		1 k. blue	10	10
D 47.		1 k. 20 blue	8	8
D 48.		2 k. blue	12	15
D 49.		5 k. blue	15	15
D 50.		10 k. blue	35	40
D 51.		20 k. blue	55	65

BOLIVAR O1

One of states of the Granadine Confederation. A department of Colombia from 1806, now uses Colombian stamps.

1. 2. 3.

1863. Imperf.

1.	1.	10 c. green	£250	£175
2.		10 c. red	10·00	10·00
3.		1 p. red	4·00	4·00

1872. Various frames. Imperf.

4.	2.	5 c. blue	1·00	1·50
5.	3.	10 c. mauve	1·50	1·50
6.	–	20 c. green	7·50	7·50
7.	–	80 c. red	20·00	18·00

4. 5. 6.

1874. Imperf.

8.	4.	5 c. blue	7·00	2·00
9.	5.	5 c. blue	3·50	1·75
10.	6.	10 c. mauve	50	50

7. Bolivar 8. Bolivar.

1879. Various frames. Dated "1879". White or blue paper. Perf.
14. 7. 5 c. blue .. 15 15
12. 10 c. mauve 15 15
13. 20 c. red 20 15

1880. Various frames. Dated "1880". White or blue paper.
19. 7. 5 c. blue 12 12
20. 10 c. mauve 20 20
21. 20 c. red 20 20
22. 80 c. green .. .. 1·00 1·00
23. 1 p. orange .. .. 1·50 1·50

1882.
30. 8. 5 p. red and blue 75 75
31. 10 p. blue and maroon .. 75 75

9. Bolivar. 10. Bolivar.

1882. Various frames. Dated "1882".
32. 9. 5 c. blue 12 15
33. 10 c. mauve 12 12
34. 20 c. red 20 25
35. 80 c. green 50 40
36. 1 p. orange 50 55

1883. Various frames. Dated "1883".
37. 9. 5 c. blue 12 12
38. 10 c. mauve 12 15
39. 20 c. red 12 15
40. 80 c. green 35 40
41. 1 p. orange 40 60

1884. Various frames. Dated "1884".
42. 9. 5 c. blue 30 30
43. 10 c. mauve 10 10
44. 20 c. red 10 10
45. 80 c. green 15 20
46. 1 p. orange 35 40

1885. Various frames. Dated "1885".
47. 9. 5 c. blue 8 5
48. 10 c. mauve 8 5
49. 20 c. red 8 5
50. 80 c. green 15 20
51. 1 p. orange 20 25

1891.
56. 10. 1 c. black 12 15
57. 5 c. orange 25 20
58. 10 c. red 40 40
59. 20 c. blue 50 50
60. 50 c. green 70 70
61. 1 p. violet 70 70

11. Bolivar. 12. J. M. del Castillo. 31.

1903. Various sizes and portraits. Imperf. or perf. On paper of various colours.
63. 11. 50 c. green 45 45
64. 50 c. blue 30 30
65. 50 c. violet 80 80
67. – 1 p. red 50 50
68. – 1 p. green 70 70
69. – 5 p. red 35 40
70b. – 10 p. blue 40 45
71. – 10 p. violet .. .. 2·50 2·50
PORTRAITS: 1 p. Fernandez Madrid. 5 p. Rodriguez Torices. 10 p. Garcia de Toledo.

1904. Various portraits. Imperf. or perf.
77. 12. 5 c. black 12 12
78. – 10 c. brn. (M. Anguiano) 12 12
79. – 20 c. red (P. G. Ribon) .. 20 20

1904. Figures in various frames. Imperf.
81. 13. ½ c. black 30 25
82. 1 c. blue (horiz.) .. 50 50
83. 2 c. violet 75 70

ACKNOWLEDGMENT OF RECEIPT STAMPS

A 1. A 2.

1903. Imperf. On paper of various colours.
AR 75. A 1. 20 c. orange .. 60 60
AR 76. 20 c. blue .. 45 45

1904. Imperf.
AR 85. A 2. 2 c. red 40 40

REGISTRATION STAMPS

1879. As T 7 but additionally inscr. "CERTIFICADA".
R17. 7. 40 c. brown 40 40

1880. As previous issue dated "1880".
R 28. 7. 40 c. brown 25 30

1882. As T 9, but additionally inscr. "CERTIFICADA" Dated as shown.
R52. 9. 40 c. brown ("1882") 20 30
R53. 40 c. brown ("1883") 30 30
R54. 40 c. brown ("1884") 12 12
R55. 40 c. brown ("1885") 25 30

R 1.

1903. Imperf. On paper of various colours.
R 72. R 1. 20 c. orange 50 50

R 2.

1904. Imperf.
R 84. R 2. 5 c. black .. .. 2·00 2·00

LATE FEE STAMPS.

L 1.

1903. Imperf. On paper of various colours.
L 73. L 1. 20 c. red 30 30
L 74. 20 c. violet 30 30

BOLIVIA

A republic of Central S. America.

1866. 100 centavos = 1 boliviano.
1963. 100 cents = 1 peso boliviano (equivalent to 1000 old bolivianos.

1. Condor. 2.

1867. Imperf.
4a. 1. 5 c. green .. .. .. 40 1·00
10. 5 c. mauve .. .. 30·00 30·00
7. 10 c. brown .. .. 35·00 40·00
8. 50 c. yellow .. .. 3·00 7·00
11. 50 c. blue .. .. 75·00 75·00
9. 100 c. blue .. .. 10·00 20·00
12. 100 c. green .. .. 25·00 30·00

1868. Nine stars below Arms. Perf.
32. 2. 5 c green .. .. 2·00 45
33. 10 c. red .. .. 3·50 50
34 50 c. blue .. .. 4·00 2·00
35. 100 c. orange .. .. 4·00 3·50
36. 500 c. black £150 £150

1871. Eleven stars below Arms. Perf.
37. 2. 5 c. green .. .. 1·50 40
38. 10 c. red .. .. 2·00 50
39. 50 c. blue .. .. 3·50 2·00
40. 100 c. orange .. .. 3·50 1·50
41. 500 c. black £250 £250

3. 4.

1878. Perf.
42. 3. 5 c. blue .. .. 1·90 85
43. 10 c. orange .. .. 1·60 40
44. 20 c. green .. .. 4·50 80
45. 50 c. red .. .. 27·00 3·00

1887. Eleven stars below Arms. Roul.
46. 2. 1 c. red 30 20
47. 2 c. violet 30 20
48. 5 c. blue .. .. 1·75 35
49. 10 c. orange .. .. 1·75 35

1890. Nine stars below Arms. Perf.
50. 2. 1 c. red 35 30
58. 2 c. violet 35 30
52. 5 c. blue 45 25
53. 10 c. orange .. .. 1·25 35
54. 20 c. green .. .. 3·00 50
55. 50 c. red 95 50
56. 100 c. yellow .. .. 2·25 1·25

1893. Eleven stars below Arms. Perf.
59. 2. 5 c. blue 30 30

1894.
63. 4. 1 c. bistre 20 30
64. 2 c. red 20 30
65. 5 c. green 20 30
66. 10 c. brown 20 30
67. 20 c. blue .. .. 90 2·00
68. 50 c. claret .. .. 2·25 4·00
69. 100 c. red .. .. 5·50 10·00

5. Frias. 7.

1897.
77. 5. 1 c. green 35 25
78. – 2 c. red (Linares) .. 70 45
79. – 5 c. green (Murillo) .. 30 20
80. – 10 c. pur. (Monteagudo) .. 60 20
81. – 20 c. black and red (J. Ballivian) .. 1·10 35
82. – 50 c. orange (Sucre) .. 1·25 70
83. – 1 b. blue (Bolivar) .. 1·40 1·40
84. 7. 2 b. blk., red, yell. & grn. 9·00 13·00

8. Sucre. 9. A. Ballivian. 14.

1899.
92. 8. 1 c. blue 20 20
93. 2 c. red 15 12
94. 5 c. green 60 20
95. 5 c. red 40 25
96. 10 c. orrange 30 15
97. 20 c. red 40 15
98. 50 c. brown 80 30
99. 1 b. lilac 30 30

1901.
100. 9. 1 c. claret 12 8
101. – 2 c. green (Camacho) .. 12 8
102. – 5 c. red (Campero) .. 12 8
103. – 10 c. blue (J. Ballivian) 30 8
104. – 20 c. black and purple (Santa Cruz) .. 15 8
105. 14. 2 b. brown .. .. 1·00 80

15. 16. Murillo.

1909. Issued in La Paz. Cent. of Revolution of July, 1809. Centres in black.
110. 15. 5 c. blue .. .. 2·00 1·50
111. 16. 10 c. green .. .. 2·00 1·50
112. – 20 c. orange (Lanza) .. 2·00 1·75
113. – 2 b. red (Montes) .. 3·50 2·25

17. P. D. Murillo. 18. Figure of Justice.

1909. Beginning of War of Independence, 1809-25. Cent.
115. – 1 c. black and brown .. 20 12
116. – 2 c. black and green .. 20 15
117. 17. 5 c. black and red .. 20 8
118. – 10 c. black and blue .. 20 8
119. – 20 c. black and violet .. 25 15
120. – 50 c. black and bistre .. 25 25
121. – 1 b. black and brown .. 35 30
122. – 2 b. black and brown .. 45 40
PORTRAITS: 1 c. M. Betanzos. 2 c. I. Warnes. 10 c. B. Monteagudo. 20 c. E. Arze. 50 c. A. J. Sucre. 1 b. S. Bolivar. 2 b. M. Belgrano.

1910. Liberation of Santa Cruz, Potosi and Cochabamba. Cent. Portraits as T 17.
123. 5 c. black and green .. 8 5
124. 10 c. black and red .. 8 5
125. 20 c. black and blue .. 20 15
PORTRAITS: 5 c. I. Warnes. 10 c. M. Betanzos. 20 c. E. Arze.

1911. Nos. 101 and 104 surch. **5 Centavos 1911.**
127. 5 c. on 2 c. green .. 20 15
128. 5 c. on 20 c. blk. & pur. .. 4·75 4·75

1912. Stamps similar to T 18 optd. **CORREOS 1912** or surch. also.
130. 18. 2 c. green 12 12
131. 5 c. orange 12 12
132. 10 c. red 30 15
129. 10 c. on 1 c. blue .. 12 12

1913. Portraits as 1901 and new types.
133. 9. 1 c. pink 10 8
134. – 2 c. red 8 5
135. – 5 c. green 10 5
136. – 8 c. yellow (Frias) .. 20 15
137. – 10 c. grey 20 8
139. – 50 c. purple (Sucre) .. 35 15
140. – 1 b. blue (Bolivar) .. 50 30
141. 14. 2 b. black .. .. 1·00 75

23. Monolith. 24. Potosi.

1916. Various sizes.
142. 23. ½ c. brown 8 8
143. 24. 1 c. green 5 5
144. – 2 c. black and red .. 5 5
145. – 5 c. blue 12 8
147. – 10 c. blue and orange .. 20 5
DESIGNS—HORIZ. 2 c. Lake Titicaca. 5 c. Mt. Illimani. 10 c. Parliament Building, La Paz.

28. 29.

1919.
158a. 28. 1 c. lake 5 5
158b. 2 c. violet 10 5
151. 5 c. green 10 5
152. 10 c. red 10 5
179. 15 c. blue 20 5
180. 20 c. blue 15 5
154 22 c. blue 15 15
155. 24 c. violet 20 12
156. 50 c. orange .. .. 1·00 15
163. 1 b. brown 30 12
164. 2 b. brown 20 12
See also Nos. 194/206.

1923. Surch **Habilitada** and value.
165. 28. 5 c. on 1 c. lake .. 15 10
169. 15 c. on 10 c. red .. 25 10
168. 15 c. on 22 c. blue .. 25 8

1924. Air. Establishment of National Aviation School.
170. 29. 10 c. black and red .. 10 10
171. 15 c. black and lake .. 75 60
172. 25 c. black and blue .. 30 30
173. 50 c. black and orange 75 55
174. – 1 b. black and brown 1·00 90
175. – 2 b. black and brown 1·60 1·60
176. – 5 b. black and violet .. 1·90 1·90
Nos. 174/6 have a different view.

32. Hermes.

1925. Independence. Cent.
184. – 5 c. red on green .. 30 15
185. – 10 c. red on yellow .. 1·00 40
186. – 15 c. red 20 10
187. – 25 c. blue 80 25
183. – 50 c. purple 20 12
189. – 1 b. red 30 30
190. 32. 2 b. orange 45 40
191. 5 b. sepia 55 50
DESIGNS—HORIZ. 25 c. Condor. VERT. 5 c. Torch of Freedom. 10 c. Immortelle blooms. 15 c. Pres. Saavedra. 50 c. Head of Liberty. 1 b. Mounted archer. 5 b. Marshal Sucre.

1927. Surch. **1927** and value.
192. 28. 5 c. on 1 c. lake .. 50 45
193. 10 c. on 24 c. violet .. 50 45

1928.
194. 28. 2 c. yellow 10 8
195. 3 c. pink 12 10
196. 4 c. claret 10 8
197. 20 c. olive 15 8
198. 25 c. blue 12 8
199. 30 c. violet 15 10
200. 40 c. orange 30 12
201. 50 c. brown 30 12
202. 1 b. red 40 12
203. 2 b. purple 60 15
204. 3 b. green 60 50
205. 4 b. lake .. .. 1·00 65
206. 5 b. brown .. .. 1·25 50

1928. Optd. **Octubre 1927** and star.
207. 28. 5 c. green 8 8
208. 10 c. grey 12 10
209. 15 c. red 12 8

1928. Surch. **15 cts. 1928.**
211. **28.** 15 c. on 20 c. blue .. 3·50 3·50
213. 15 c. on 24 c. violet .. 55 20
216. 15 c. on 50 c. orange .. 40 20

33.  **34.** Condor.

1928. Air.
217. **33.** 15 c. green 35 35
218. 20 c. blue 10 10
219. 35 c. red 25 25

1928.
221. **34.** 5 c. green 50 10
222. – 10 c. blue 8 5
223. – 15 c. red 25 5
DESIGNS: 10 c. Pres. Siles. 15 c. Map of Bolivia.

1930. Stamps of 1913 and 1916 surch. **R.S. 21—4 1930** and value.
224. – 0.01 c. on 2 c. (No. 134) 30 30
225. – 0.03 c. on 2 c. (No. 144) 35 35
226. **23.** 25 c. on ½ c. brown .. 25 25
227. – 25 c. on 2 c. (No. 144) 30 25

1930. Air. Optd. **CORREO AEREO R.S. 6-V-1930** or surch. **5 Cts.** also
228. **29.** 5 c. on 10 c. blk. & red .. 2·75 2·75
229. 10 c. black and red .. 2·75 2·75
231. 15 c. black and lake .. 2·75 2·75
232. 25 c. black and blue .. 2·75 2·75
233. 50 c. black and orange 2·75 2·75
235. 1 b. black and brown .. 45·00 45·00

1930. "Graf Zeppelin" Air stamps. Stamps of 1928 surch. **Z 1930** and value.
241. **33.** 1 b. 50 on 15 c. green .. 8·00 8·00
242. 3 b. on 20 c. blue .. 8·00 8·00
243. 6 b. on 35 c. red .. 12·00 16·00

37. Aircraft over Bullock Cart.  **39.** Pres. Siles.

40. Map of Bolivia.  **41.** Field-Marshal Sucre

1930. Air.
244. **37.** 5 c. violet 20 12
245. – 15 c. red 20 12
246. – 20 c. yellow 20 12
247. **37.** 35 c. green 15 12
248. – 40 c. blue 15 12
249. **37.** 1 b. brown 20 12
250. – 2 b. red 20 20
251. **37.** 3 b. grey .. .. 2·00 1·25
DESIGN: Others, 'Plane over River Boat.

1930.
252. **39.** 1 c. brown 5 5
253. – 2 c. green (Potosi) .. 10 8
254. – 5 c. blue (Illimani) .. 8 5
255. – 10 c. red (E. Abaroa) .. 10 5
256. **40.** 15 c. violet 15 5
257. 35 c. red 30 20
258. 45 c. orange 30 25
259. **41.** 50 c. slate 15 12
260. – 1 b. brown (Bolivar) .. 50 50

42.

1931. Revolution. 1st Anniv.
263. **42.** 15 c. red 40 20
264. 50 c. lilac 30 30

43.

1932. Air.
265. **43.** 5 c. blue 30 25
266. 10 c. grey 12 10
267. 15 c. red 35 30
268. 25 c. orange 40 30
269. 30 c. green 20 20
270. 50 c. purple 25 25
271. 1 b. brown 40 30

1933. Surch. **Habilitada D.S. 13-7-1933** and value.
273. **28.** 5 c. on 1 b. red .. 15 8
274. **40.** 15 c. on 35 c. red .. 8 8
275. 15 c. on 45 c. orange .. 8 8
276. **28.** 15 c. on 50 c. brown .. 15 8
277. 25 c. on 40 c. orange .. 15 8

44.  **44a.** M. Baptista.

1933.
278. **44.** 2 c. green 8 5
279. 5 c. blue 5 5
280. 10 c. red 15 10
281. 15 c. violet 8 5
282. 25 c. blue 20 15

1935. Air.
283. **44a.** 15 c. violet 12 8

45. Map of Bolivia.  **46.** 'Plane and Map.

1935.
284. **45.** 2 c. blue 5 5
285. 3 c. yellow 5 5
286. 5 c. green 5 5
287. 5 c. red 5 5
288. 10 c. brown 5 5
289. 15 c. blue 5 5
290. 15 c. red 5 5
291. 20 c. green 8 5
292. 25 c. blue 8 5
293. 30 c. red 20 10
294. 40 c. orange 20 8
295. 50 c. violet 20 5
296. 1 b. yellow 25 15
297. 2 b. brown 35 25

1935. Air.
298. **46.** 5 c. brown 5 5
299. 10 c. green 5 5
300. 20 c. violet 5 5
301. 30 c. blue 5 5
302. 50 c. orange 8 8
303. 1 b. brown 10 8
304. 1½ b. yellow 25 5
305. 2 b. red 25 8
306. 5 b. green 65 20
307. 10 b. brown .. .. 1·10 40

1937. Surch. **Comunicaciones D.S. 25-2-37** and value in figures.
308. **44.** 5 c. on 2 c. green .. 8 8
310. 15 c. 25 c. blue .. 8 8
311. 30 c. on 25 c. blue .. 10 10
312. **28.** 45 c. on 1 b. brown .. 12 12
313. 1 b. on 2 b. purple .. 20 20
314. **44.** 2 b. on 25 c. blue .. 20 35
315. **42.** 3 b. on 50 c. lilac .. 40 40
316. 5 b. on 50 c lilac .. 70 70

1937. Air. Surch. **Correo Aereo D.S. 25-2-37** and value in figures.
321. **37.** 5 c. on 35 c. green .. 12 10
322. **33.** 20 c. on 35 c. red .. 15 10
323. 50 c. on 35 c. red .. 20 15
324. 1 b. on 35 c. red .. 30 20
325. **29.** 2 b. on 50 c. blk. & orge. 50 30
317. – 3 b. on 50 c. purple (No. 188) 65 50
318. – 4 b. on 1 b. red (No. 189) 75 65
319. **32.** 5 b. on 2 b. orange .. 90 80
320. – 10 b. on 5 b. sepia (No. 191) .. .. 1·75 1·50
326. **29.** 12 b. on 10 c. blk. & red 1·90 1·50
327. 15 b. on 10 c. blk. & red 1·90 1·50

48. Native School.  **49.** Oil Wells.

52. Aeroplane over Cornfield.

1938.
328. **48.** 2 c. red (postage) .. 12 8
329. **49.** 10 c. orange 12 8
330. – 15 c. green 15 8
331. – 30 c. yellow 20 8
332. – 45 c. red 40 12
333. 60 c. violet 30 8
334. – 75 c. blue 40 10
335. – 1 b. brown 40 10
336. – 2 b. buff 50 15
DESIGNS—VERT. 15 c. Industrial buildings. 30 c. Pincers and torch. 75 c. Indian and eagle. HORIZ. 45 c. Sucre-Camiri railway map. 60 c. Natives and book. 1 b. Machinery. 2 b. Agriculture.

337. – 20 c. red (air) 10 8
338. – 30 c. grey 10 8
339. – 40 c. yellow 15 8
340. **52.** 50 c. green 15 8
341. – 60 c. blue 15 8
342. – 1 b. red 20 8
343. – 2 b. buff 45 10
344. – 3 b. brown 60 10
345. – 5 b. violet .. .. 1·00 5
DESIGNS—VERT. 20 c. Mint, Potosi. 30 c. Miner. 40 c. Symbolical of women's suffrage. 1 b. Pincers, torch and slogan. 3 b. New Government emblem. 5 b. Aeroplanes over map of Bolivia. HORIZ. 60 c. Aeroplane and monument. 2 b. Aeroplane over river.

53. Llamas.  **54.** Arms.

1939.
346. **53.** 2 c. green 50 15
347. 4 c. cinnamon 50 15
348. 5 c. mauve 50 15
349. – 10 c. black 50 15
350. – 15 c. green 50 15
351. – 20 c. green 50 15
352. **54.** 25 c. yellow 20 12
353. 30 c. blue 20 12
354. – 40 c. red 35 20
355. – 45 c. black 35 20
356. – 60 c. red .. .. 1·00 25
357. – 75 c. slate .. .. 1·00 25
358. – 90 c. orange .. .. 2·25 40
359. – 1 b. blue .. .. 2·25 40
360. – 2 b. claret .. .. 2·50 40
361. – 3 b. violet .. .. 3·50 50
362. – 4 b. brown .. .. 3·50 50
363. – 5 b. purple .. .. 5·00 70
DESIGNS—HORIZ. 10 c., 15 c., 20 c. Vicuna. 60 c., 75 c. Chinchilla. 90 c., 1 b. Toucan. 2 b., 3 b. Condor. 4 b., 5 b. Jaguar. VERT. 40 c., 45 c. Herons.

56. Virgin of Copacabana.  **57.** Workman.

1939. Air. 2nd National Eucharistic Congress. Inscr. "II° CONGRESO EUCARISTICO NACIONAL".
364. – 5 c. violet 15 8
365. **56.** 30 c. green 15 5
366. – 45 c. blue 15 5
367. – 60 c. red 20 8
368. – 75 c. red 20 20
369. – 90 c. blue 25 10
370. – 2 b. brown 40 8
371. – 4 b. mauve 65 20
372. **56.** 5 b. blue .. .. 1·40 10
373. – 10 b. yellow .. .. 3·75 15
DESIGNS—TRIANGULAR: 5 c., 10 b. Allegory of the Light of Religion. VERT. 45 c., 4 b. The "Sacred Heart of Jesus". 75 c., 90 c. S. Anthony of Padua. HORIZ. 60 c., 2 b. Facade of St. Francis's Church, La Paz.

1939. Obligatory Tax. Workers' Home Building Fund.
374. **57.** 5 c. violet 8 5

58. Flags of 21 American Republics.

1940. Pan-American Union. 50th Anniv.
375. **58.** 9 b. red, blue and yellow 1·25 70

59. Murillo dreaming in Prison.  **60.** Shadow of Aeroplane on Lake Titicaca.

1941. P. D. Murillo (patriot). 130th Death Anniv. Dated "1810 1940".
376. – 10 c. purple 5 5
377. – 15 c. green 8 5
378. **59.** 45 c. red 8 5
379. – 1 b. 05 blue 10 5
DESIGNS—VERT. 10 c. Murillo statue. 1 b. 05 Murillo portrait. HORIZ. 15 c. Coffins of Murillo and Sagarnaga.

1941. Air.
380. **60.** 10 b. green .. .. 1·50 12
381. 20 b. blue .. .. 2·10 30
382. 50 b. mauve .. .. 4·50 60
383. – 100 b. brown .. .. 11·00 2·25
DESIGN: 50, 100 b. Condor over Mt. Illimani.

61. 1866 and 1941 Issues.  **62.** "Union is Strength".

1942. First Students' Philatelic Exn., La Paz.
384. **61.** 5 c. mauve 20 12
385. 10 c. orange 20 12
386. 20 c. green 40 20
387. 40 c. red 50 35
388. 90 c. blue .. .. 1·25 45
389. 1 b. violet .. .. 2·25 1·00
390. 10 b. brown .. .. 8·00 3·50

1942. Air. Chancellors' Meeting, Rio de Janeiro.
391. **62.** 40 c. claret 12 5
392. 50 c. blue 12 5
393. 1 b. brown 25 10
394. 5 b. mauve 85 12
395. 10 b. purple .. .. 2·00 1·10

63. Mt. Potosi.  **64.** Chaquiri Dam.

1943. Mining Industry.
396. **63.** 15 c. brown 10 8
397. – 45 c. blue 10 8
398. – 1 b. 25 purple 15 12
399. – 1 b. 50 green 15 12
400. – 2 b. brown 20 15
401. **64.** 2 b. 10 blue 20 15
402. – 3 b. orange 35 30
DESIGNS—VERT. 45 c. Quechisia (at foot of Mt. Choroloque), 1 b. 25, Miner Drilling. HORIZ. 1 b. 50, Dam. 2 b. Truck Convoy. 3 b. Entrance to Pulacavo Mine.

65. Gen. Ballivian leading Cavalry Charge.

1943. Battle of Ingavi. Cent.
403. **65.** 2 c. green 5 5
404. 3 c. orange 5 5
405. 25 c. maroon 5 5
406. 45 c. blue 10 5
407. 3 b. red 25 15
408. 4 b. purple 30 25
409. 5 b. sepia 40 30

66. Gen. Ballivian and Trinidad Cathedral.

1943. Founding of El Beni. Cent. Centres in brown.
410. 66. 5 c. green (postage) .. 5 5
411. 10 c. purple 8 5
412. 30 c. red 10 8
413. 45 c. blue 15 10
414. 2 b. 10 orange 30 25

415. – 10 c. violet (air) .. 5 5
416. – 20 c. green 8 5
417. – 30 c. red 10 8
418. – 3 b. blue 15 12
419. – 5 b. black 30 20
DESIGN: Nos. 415/9 Gen. Ballivian and mule convoy crossing bridge below aeroplane.

67. " Honour-Work-Law/All for the country ".
68. Allegory of " Flight ".

1944. Revolution of 20th December, 1943.
420. 67. 20 c. orange (postage) 5 5
421. 20 c. green 5 5
422. 90 c. blue 5 5
423. 90 c. red 5 5
424. – 1 b. purple 8 5
425. – 2 b. 40 brown 15 12
DESIGN—VERT. 1 b., 2 b. 40, Clasped hands and flag.

426. 68. 40 c. mauve (air) .. 5 5
427. – 1 b. violet 5 5
428. – 1 b. 50 green 8 5
429. – 2 b. 50 blue 12 10
DESIGN—HORIZ. 1 b. 50, 2 b. 50, Aeroplane and sun.

69. Posthorn and Envelope.
70. National Airways Route Map.

1944. Obligatory Tax.
430. 69. 10 c. red 8 5
432. 10 c. blue 8 5
Smaller Posthorn and Envelope.
469. 10 c. red 5 5
470. 10 c. yellow 5 5
471. 10 c. green 5 5
472. 10 c. brown 5 5

1945. Air. Panagra Airways. 10th Anniv. of First La Paz-Tacna Flight.
433. 70. 10 c. red 5 5
434. 50 c. orange 5 5
435. 90 c. green 5 5
436. 5 b. blue 12 8
437. 20 b. brown 65 25

71. Lloyd-Aereo Boliviano Air Routes.
72. Composers of National Anthem.

1945. Air. First National Air Service. 20th Anniv.
438. 71. 20 c. blue, orge. & violet 5 5
439. 30 c. blue, orge. & brown 5 5
440. 50 c. blue, orge. & green 5 5
441. 90 c. blue, orge. & purple 5 5
442. 2 b. blue, orge. and blue 8 5
443. 3 b. blue, orge. & claret 10 8
444. 4 b. blue, orge. & olive 12 8

1946. National Anthem. Cent.
445. 72. 5 c. black and mauve .. 5 5
446. 10 c. black and blue .. 5 5
447. 15 c. black and green .. 5 5
448. 30 c. brown and red .. 8 5
449. 90 c. brown and blue .. 8 5
450. 2 b. brown and black .. 15 8

1947. Surch. **1947 Habilitada Bs. 1.40.**
451. 1 b. 40 on 75 c. blue (No. 334) (postage) .. 10 8
452. 1 b. 40 on 75 c. slate (No. 357) 10 8
455. 1 b. 40 on 75 c. red (No. 368) (air) 10 8

73. Seizure of Government Palace.
74. Mt. Illimani.

1947. Popular Revolution of July 21, 1946.
456. 73. 20 c. green (postage) .. 5 5
457. 50 c. purple 5 5
458. 1 b. 40 blue 8 5
459. 3 b. 70 orange 12 8
460. 4 b. violet 15 10
461. 10 b. olive 40 25

462. 74. 1 b. red (air) 5 5
463. 1 b. 40 green 5 5
464. 2 b. 50 blue 8 5
465. 3 b. orange 10 8
466. 4 b. mauve 12 8

75. Arms of Bolivia and Argentina.
76. Cross and Child.

1947. Meeting of Presidents of Bolivia and Argentina.
467. 75. 1 b. 40 orange (postage) 5 5
468. 2 b. 90 blue (air) .. 15 12

1948. 3rd Inter-American Catholic Education Congress.
473. – 1 b. 40 bl. & yell. (post.) 8 5
474. 76. 2 b. green and orange .. 12 8
475. – 3 b. green and blue .. 25 10
476. – 5 b. violet and orange .. 40 25
477. – 5 b. brown and green 40 25

478. – 2 b. 50 orge. & yell. (air) 20 10
479. 76. 3 b. 70 red and buff .. 30 12
480. – 4 b. mauve and blue .. 35 15
481. – 4 b. blue and orange .. 35 12
482. – 13 b. 60 blue and green 55 20
DESIGNS: 1 b. 40, 2 b. 50, Christ the Redeemer, Monument. 3 b., 4 b. (No. 480), Don Bosco. 5 b. (No. 476), 4 b. (No. 481), Virgin of Copacabana. 5 b. (No. 477), 13 b. 60, Pope Pius XII.

77. Map of S. America and Badge.
78. Posthorn, Globe and Pres. G. Pacheco.

1948. Pan-American Motor Race.
483. 77. 5 b. blue & pink (post.) 1·60 25
484. 10 b. grn. & cream (air) 1·50 35

1950. U.P.U. 75th Anniv.
485. 78. 1 b. 40 blue (postage) .. 5 5
486. 4 b. 20 red 8 5
487. 1 b. 40 brown (air) .. 8 8
488. 2 b. 50 orange 5 5
489. 3 b. 30 purple 8 8

1950. Air. Surch. **XV ANIVERSARIO PANAGRA 1935-1950** and value.
490. 70. 4 b. on 10 c. red .. 8 8
491. 10 b. on 20 b. brown .. 20 12

1950. No. 379 surch. **Bs 2.—Habilitada D.S. 6.VII.50.**
492. 2 b. on 1 b. 05 blue .. 10 8

79. Apparition at Potosi.
80. Aeroplane.

1950. Apparition at Potosi. 400th Anniv.
493. 79. 20 c. violet 5 5
494. 30 c. orange 5 5
495. 50 c. purple 5 5
496. 1 b. red 8 5
497. 2 b. blue 10 5
498. 6 b. brown 12 8

1950. Air. Lloyd-Aereo Boliviano. 25th Anniv.
499. 80. 20 c. orange 5 5
500. 30 c. violet 5 5
501. 50 c. green 5 5
502. 1 b. yellow 5 5
503. 3 b. blue 5 5
504. 15 b. red 20 5
505. 50 b. brown 55 20

1950. Air. Surch. **Triunfo de la Democracia 24 de Sept. 49 Bs. 1.40.**
506. 74. 1 b. 40 on 3 b. orange .. 8 5

81. U.N. Emblem and Globe.
83. St. Francis Gate.
82. Sun Gate.

1950. U.N.O. 5th Anniv.
507. 81. 60 c. blue (postage) .. 75 10
508. 2 b. green .. .. 1·10 15
509. 3 b. 60 red (air) .. 35 12
510. 4 b. 70 brown 70 20

1951. La Paz. 4th Cent. Centres in black.
511. 82. 20 c. green (postage) .. 10 5
512. 83. 30 c. orange 5 5
513. A. 40 c. brown 5 5
514. B. 50 c. red 5 5
515. C. 1 b. slate-purple .. 5 5
516. D. 1 b. 40 violet .. 5 5
517. E. 2 b. slate-purple .. 5 5
518. F. 3 b. magenta 8 5
519. G. 5 b. red 12 8
520. H. 10 b. sepia 20 12
521. 82. 20 c. red (air) 5 5
522. 83. 30 c. violet 5 5
523. A. 40 c. slate 5 5
524. B. 50 c. green 5 5
525. C. 1 b. red 8 5
526. D. 2 b. orange 12 8
527. E. 3 b. blue 15 10
528. F. 4 b. red 12 12
529. G. 5 b. green 15 12
530. H. 10 b. brown 30 25
DESIGNS—HORIZ. AS T 82: A. Camacho Avenue. B. Consistorial Palace. C. Legislative Palace. D. Palace of Communications. E. Arms. F. Pedro de la Casca authorizes plans of City. G. Founding the City. H. City Arms and Captain A. de Mendoza.

84. Tennis.
85. Condor and Flag.

1951. Sports. Centres in black.
531. – 20 c. blue (postage) .. 8 5
532. 84. 50 c. red 10 5
533. – 1 b. purple 12 8
534. – 1 b. 40 yellow 12 8
535. – 2 b. red 20 10
536. – 3 b. brown 40 30
537. – 4 b. blue 55 40
538. – 20 c. violet (air) .. 10 5
539. – 30 c. purple 20 5
540. – 50 c. orange 30 8
541. – 1 b. brown 30 8
542. – 2 b. 50 orange 50 25
543. – 3 b. sepia 70 40
544. – 5 b. red .. .. 1·10 75
DESIGNS—HORIZ. As T 84—POSTAGE: 20 c. Boxing. 1 b. Diving. 1 b. 40 c. Football. 2 b. Ski-ing. 3 b. Pelota. 4 b. Cycling. AIR: 20 c. Horse-jumping. 30 c. Basket-ball. 50 c. Fencing. 1 b. Hurdling. 2 b. 50 c. Javelin. 3 b. Relay race. 5 b. La Paz Stadium.

1951. 100th National Flag Anniv. Flag in red, yellow and green.
545. 85. 2 b. green 5 5
546. 3 b. 50 c. blue 5 5
547. 5 b. violet 5 5
548. 7 b. 50 c. grey 8 8
549. 15 b. claret 20 10
550. 30 b. brown 50 30

86. Posthorn and Envelope.
87. E. Abaroa.

1951. Obligatory Tax.
551. – 20 c. blue 8 5
551a. – 20 c. green 8 5
552. – 20 c. orange 8 5
553. 86. 50 c. green 8 5
553a. 50 c. red 5 5
553b. 3 b. green 5 5
553c. 3 b. bistre 50 50
553d. 5 b. violet 8 5
DESIGN: 20 c. Condor over posthorn and envelope.

1952. Abaroa (patriot). 73rd Death Anniv.
554. 87. 80 c. claret (postage) .. 5 5
555. 1 b. orange 5 5
556. 2 b. green 5 5
557. 5 b. ultramarine .. 8 5
558. 10 b. magenta 20 10
559. 20 b. chocolate 35 20

560. 50 c. red (air) 5 5
561. 2 b. yellow 5 5
562. 3 b. green 5 5
563. 5 b. blue 5 5
564. 50 b. purple 45 25
565. 100 b. black .. .. 1·10 80

88. Isabella the Catholic.
89. Columbus Lighthouse.

1952. Isabella the Catholic. 500th Birth Anniv.
566. 88. 2 b. blue (postage) .. 8 5
567. 6 b. 30 red 10 5

568. 50 b. green (air) .. 25 12
569. 100 b. brown 50 25

1952. Columbus Memorial Lighthouse. On tinted papers.
570. 89. 2 b. blue (postage) .. 8 5
571. 5 b. red 12 10
572. 9 b. emerald 20 15

573. 2 b. purple (air) .. 8 5
574. 3 b. 70 blue-green .. 8 8
575. 4 b. 40 orange 10 5
576. 20 b. brown 30 10

90. Miner.
92. Revolutionaries.

91. Villarroel, Paz Estenssoro and Siles Zuazo.

1953. Nationalization of Mining Industry.
577. 90. 2 b. 50 c. red 5 5
578. 8 b. violet 8 5

1953. Revolution of April 9th, 1952. 1st Anniv.
579. 91. 50 c. mauve (postage) .. 5 5
580. 1 b. red 5 5
581. 2 b. blue 5 5
582. 3 b. green 5 5
583. 4 b. yellow 5 5
584. 5 b. violet 5 5

585. 3 b. 70 choc. (air) .. 5 5
590. 92. 6 b. mauve 5 5
586. 91. 9 b. claret 5 5
587. 10 b. turquoise 5 5
588. 16 b. orange 8 5
591. 92. 22 b. 50 brown 8 8
589. 91. 40 b. grey 12 5

1953. Obligatory Tax. No. 551a. and similar stamp surch. **50 cts.**
592. 50 c. on 20 c. mauve .. 8 5
593. 50 c. on 20 c. green .. 8 5

93.
94. Ear of Wheat and Map.

1954. Obligatory Tax.
594. 93. 1 b. lake 8 5
595. 1 b. brown 8 5

1954. 1st National Agronomical Congress.
596. 94. 25 b. blue 8 5
597. 85 b. brown 20 15

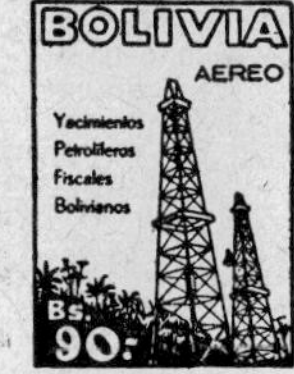
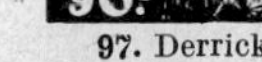

95. Pres. Paz embracing Indian. 97. Derricks.

96. Refinery.

1954. Air. 3rd Inter-American Indigenous Congress.
598. 95. 20 b. chestnut 5 5
599. 100 b. turquoise .. 25 10

1954. Agrarian Reform. 1st Anniv. As T 94, but designs inscr. "REFORMA AGRARIA".
600. 5 b. red (postage) .. 5 5
601. 17 b. turquoise 5 5
602. 27 b. magenta (air) .. 5 5
603. 30 b. orange 8 5
604. 45 b. purple 10 5
605. 300 b. green 60 20
DESIGNS—5 b., 17 b. Cow's head and map. 27 b. to 300 b. Indian peasant woman and map.

1955. Obligatory Tax. Surch. **BS 5.—/ D.S./21-IV-55.**
606. 86. 5 b. on 3 b. green .. 8 5
607. 5 b. on 3 b. bistre .. 8 5

1955. Development of Petroleum Industry.
608. 96. 10 b. blue (postage) .. 5 5
609. 35 b. red 5 5
610. 40 b. green 5 5
611. 50 b. purple 8 5
612. 80 b. brown 10 8
613. 97. 55 b. blue (air) 10 5
614. 70 b. black 10 5
615. 90 b. green 10 5
616. 500 b. mauve 40 30
617. 1000 b. brown 80 65

98. Control Tower. 99. Aeroplanes.

1957. Obligatory Tax. Airport Building Fund.
(a) As T 98.
618. 98. 5 b. blue 8 5
620. – 5 b. red 8 5
(b) As T 99.
619. 99. 10 b. green 8 5
620a. – 20 b. brown 8 5
DESIGNS: 5 b. (No. 620). Aeroplane and runway. 20 b. Aeroplane in flight.

1957. Currency revaluation. Founding of La Paz stamps of 1951 surch. Centres in black.
621. F. 50 b. on 3 b. mag. (post.) 5 5
622. E. 100 b. on 2 b. slate-pur. 5 5
623. C. 200 b. on 1 b. slate-pur. 5 5
624. D. 300 b. on 1 b. 40 violet 8 5
625. 82. 350 b. on 20 c. green .. 10 5
626. A. 400 b. on 40 c. brown .. 10 5
627. 83. 600 b. on 30 c. orange 12 8
628. B. 800 b. on 50 c. red .. 15 8
629. H. 1000 b. on 10 b. sepia .. 20 12
630. G. 2000 b. on 5 b. red .. 40 30
631. E. 100 b. on 3 b. blue (air) 5 5
632. D. 200 b. on 2 b. orange .. 5 5
633. F. 500 b. on 4 b. red .. 8 5
634. C. 600 b. on 1 b. red .. 10 8
635. 82. 700 b. on 20 c. red .. 10 8
636. A. 800 b. on 40 c. slate .. 15 10
637. 83. 900 b. on 30 c. violet .. 20 8
638. B. 1800 b. on 50 c. green 35 20
639. G. 3000 b. on 5 b. green .. 55 45
640. H. 5000 b. on 10 b. brown 1·40 1·00

100. Congress Building. 101. "Latin America" on Globe.

1957. 7th Latin-America Economic Congress, La Paz.
641. 100. 150 b. bl. & grey (post.) 5 5
642. 350 b. grey and brown 8 5
643. 550 b. sepia and blue 10 8
644. 750 b. green and red .. 15 10
645. 900 b. brown and green 25 15
646. 101. 700 b. vio. & lilac (air) 20 12
647. 1200 b. brown .. 25 20
648. 1350 b. claret & mag. 40 30
649. 2700 b. olive & turq. 70 35
650. 4000 v. bio. & ultram. 1·10 50

102. Train and Presidents of Bolivia and Argentina.

1957. Yacuiba-Santa Cruz Railway Inaug.
651. 102. 50 b. orange (postage) 5 5
652. 350 b. blue 8 5
653. 1000 b. brown & cinna. 20 8
654. 102. 600 b. pur. & pink (air) 12 5
655. 700 b. violet and blue 15 8
656. 900 b. green 20 8

103. Presidents and Flags of Bolivia and Mexico.

1960. Visit of Mexican President.
657. 103. 350 b. olive (postage) .. 8 5
658. 600 b. chestnut .. 10 8
659. 1,500 b. sepia 25 15
660. 103. 400 b. claret (air) .. 15 8
661. 800 b. slate-blue .. 15 12
662. 2,000 b. slate-green .. 40 30
The President's visit to Bolivia did not take place.

104. Indians and Mt. Illimani. 105. "Gate of the Sun", Tiahuanacu.

1960. Tourist Publicity.
663. 104. 500 b. bistre (postage) 8 5
664. 1000 b. blue 15 8
665. 2000 b. sepia 30 20
666. 4000 b. green 65 30
667. 105. 3000 b. grey (air) .. 40 30
668. 5000 b. orange .. 70 55
669. 10,000 b. purple .. 1·25 1·10
670. 15,000 b. violet .. 2·25 2·00

106. Refugees. 107. "Uprooted Tree".

1960. World Refugee Year.
671. 106. 50 b. brown (postage) 5 5
672. 350 b. maroon .. 8 5
673. 400 b. slate-blue .. 10 8
674. 1000 b. sepia 35 20
675. 3000 b. bronze-green .. 1·00 60
676. 107. 600 b. blue (air) .. 12 10
677. 700 b. chestnut .. 15 12
678. 900 b. blue-green .. 20 20
679. 1800 b. violet 40 30
680. 2000 b. black 50 40

108. Jaime Laredo (violinist). 109.

1960. Jaime Laredo Commem.
681. 108. 100 b. ol-grn. (post) .. 8 5
682. 350 b. lake 8 5
683. 500 b. slate-blue .. 10 5
684. 1000 b. brown .. 15 10
685. 1500 b. violet 30 15
686. 500 b. black 85 55
687. 109. 600 b. plum (air) .. 10 8
688. 700 b. olive 12 10
689. 800 b. chocolate .. 15 10
690. 900 b. blue 20 12
691. 1800 b. blue-green .. 40 25
692. 4000 b. violet-grey .. 60 55

110. Rotary Emblem and Nurse with Children. 111.

1960. Founding of Children's Hospital by La Paz Rotary Club. Wheel in blue and yellow, foreground in yellow; background given.
693. 110. 350 b. green (postage) 5 5
694. 500 b. sepia 10 5
695. 600 b. violet 10 8
696. 1000 b. grey 15 12
697. 110. 600 b. chestnut (air) .. 15 12
698. 1000 b. olive 20 15
699. 1800 b. purple .. 30 25
700. 5000 b. black .. 90 70

1960. Air. Unissued stamp, surch. as in T **111.**
701. 111. 1200 b. on 10 b. orange 25 20

112. 113. Flags of Argentina and Bolivia.

1960. Unissued Tiahuanacu Excavations stamps surch. as in T **112.** Gold backgrounds.
702. 50 b. on ½ c. red .. 12 12
703. 100 b. on 1 c. red .. 5 5
704. 200 b. on 2 c. black .. 15 12
705. 300 b. on 5 c. green .. 10 8
706. 350 b. on 10 c. green .. 12 12
707. 400 b. on 15 c. indigo .. 12 10
708. 500 b. on 20 c. red .. 15 12
709. 500 b. on 50 c. red .. 15 12
710. 600 b. on 22½ c. green .. 20 15
711. 600 b. on 60 c. violet .. 20 15
712. 700 b. on 25 c. violet .. 25 25
713. 700 b. on 1 b. green .. 25 25
714. 800 b. on 30 c. red .. 25 25
715. 900 b. on 40 c. green .. 30 25
716. 1000 b. on 2 b. blue .. 35 30
717. 1800 b. on 3 b. grey .. 1·40 1·10
718. 4000 b. on 4 b. grey .. 12·00 11·00
719. 5000 b. on 5 b. grey .. 1·90 1·90
DESIGNS: Various gods, motifs and ornaments.
SIZES: Nos. 702/6, As T 112. Nos. 707/17, As T 112 but horiz. No. 718, 49 × 23 mm. No. 719, 50 × 52½ mm.

1961. Air. Visit of Pres. Frondizi of Argentina.
720. 113. 4000 b. multicoloured 55 45
721. – 6000 b. sepia and green 75 60
DESIGN: 6000 b. Presidents of Argentina and Bolivia.

114. Miguel de Cervantes (First Mayor of La Paz). 115. "United in Christ".

1961. M. de Cervantes Commem. and 4th Cent. of Santa Cruz de la Sierra (1500 b.).
722. 114. 600 b. violet and ochre (postage) 12 8
723. – 1500 b. blue & salmon 25 15
724. – 1400 b. olive-brown & green (air) .. 25 20
DESIGNS: 1400 b. Portrait as T 114 (diamond shape, 30½ × 30½ mm.). 1500 b. Nuflo de Chaves (vert. as T 114).
See also Nos. 755/6.

1962. 4th National Eucharistic Congress, Santa Cruz.
725. 115. 1000 b. yellow, red and myrtle (postage) .. 20 15
726. – 1400 b. yellow, pink & sepia (air) 25 20
DESIGN: 1400 b. Virgin of Cotoca.

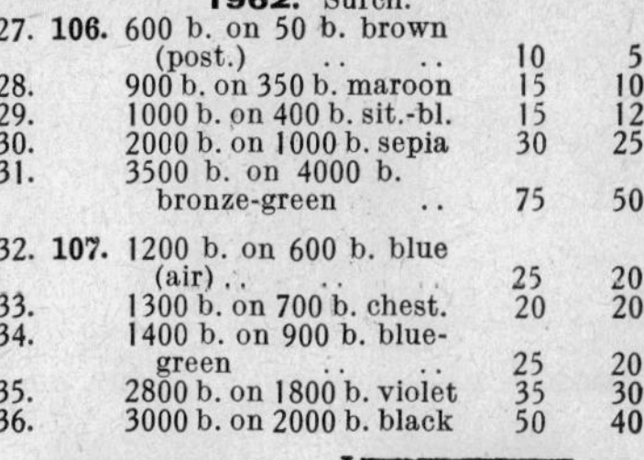

1962. Surch.
727. 106. 600 b. on 50 b. brown (post.) 10 5
728. 900 b. on 350 b. maroon 15 10
729. 1000 b. on 400 b. sit.-bl. 15 12
730. 2000 b. on 1000 b. sepia 30 25
731. 3500 b. on 4000 b. bronze-green .. 75 50
732. 107. 1200 b. on 600 b. blue (air) 25 20
733. 1300 b. on 700 b. chest. 20 20
734. 1400 b. on 900 b. blue-green 25 20
735. 2800 b. on 1800 b. violet 35 30
736. 3000 b. on 2000 b. black 50 40

116. Hibiscus. 117. Infantry.

1962. Flowers in actual colours; background colours given.
737. 200 b. slate-green (postage) 5 5
738. 400 b. brown 10 5
739. 600 b. deep blue 15 10
740. 1000 b. violet 25 12
741. 100 b. blue (air) 5 5
742. 800 b. bronze-green .. 15 10
743. 1800 b. violet 60 25
744. 10,000 b. deep blue .. 1·75 1·50
FLOWERS: Nos. 738, 740 Orchids. No. 739, St. Janos' lily. Nos. 741/4, Types of Kantuta (national flower).

1962. Armed Forces Commem.
745. 117. 400 b. mult. (postage) 5 5
746. – 500 b. multicoloured .. 8 5
747. – 600 b. multicoloured .. 10 5
748. – 2000 b. multicoloured 25 20
749. – 600 b. mult. (air) .. 8 5
750. – 1200 b. multicoloured 15 12
751. – 2000 b. multicoloured 25 15
752. – 5000 b. multicoloured 60 45
DESIGNS: No. 746, Cavalry. 747, Artillery. 748, Engineers. 749, Parachutists and 'planes. 750, 752, "Overseas Flights" ('plane over oxen-cart). 751, "Aerial Survey" ('plane photographing ground).

118. Campaign Emblem. 119. Goal-keeper Diving to save goal.

1962. Malaria Eradication.
753. 118. 600 b. yellow, violet and lilac (postage) .. 15 15
754. – 2000 b. yellow, green and indigo (air) .. 30 25
DESIGN: 2000 b. As No. 753 but with laurel wreath and inscription encircling emblem.

1962. Spanish Discoverers. As T **114** but inscribed "1548–1962".
755. 600 b. magenta on blue (post.) 10 5
756. 1200 b. brown on yellow (air) 15 12
PORTRAITS: 600 b. A. de Mendoza. 1200 b. P. de la Gasca.

1963. 21st S. American Football Championships, La Paz. Multicoloured.
757. 60 c. T **119** (postage) .. 10 5
758. 1 p. Goal-keeper saving ball 15 12
759. 1 p. 40 Eagle on football (air) 25 20
760. 1 p. 80 Football in corner of net 30 25
Nos. 758/60 are vert.

120. Globe and Emblem. 121. Alliance Emblem.

1963. Freedom from Hunger.
761. 120. 60 c. yellow, blue and indigo (postage) .. 8 5
762. – 1 p. 20 yellow, blue and myrtle (air) 20 15
DESIGN: 1 p. 20, Ear of wheat across Globe.

1963. Air. "Alliance for Progress".
763. 121. 1 p. 20 grn., bl. & bistre 25 20

122. Oil Derrick.

1963. Revolution (1962). 10th Anniv. Inscr. "1952–1962".
764. 122. 10 c. grn. & brn. (post.) 5 5
765. – 60 c. sepia & orge.-brn. 10 5
766. – 1 p. yellow, violet & grn. 12 8
767. – 1 p. 20 pink, brown and grey (air) 12 10
768. – 1 p. 40 green & ochre 20 12
769. – 2 p. 80 buff and slate 30 25
DESIGNS: 60 c. Map of Bolivia. 1 p. Students. 1 p. 20, Ballot box and voters. 1 p. 40, Peasant breaking chain. 2 p. 80, Miners.

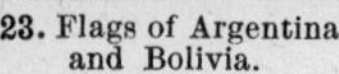

123. Flags of Argentina and Bolivia. 124. Marshal Santa Cruz.

1966. Marshal Santa Cruz. Death Cent.
770. 123. 10 c. mult. (postage) 5 5
771. 60 c. multicoloured .. 8 5
772. 1 p. multicoloured .. 10 8
773. 2 p. multicoloured .. 20 12
774. 124. 20 c. blue (air) .. 5 5
775. 60 c. green 8 5
776. 1 p. 20 brown .. 12 8
777. 2 p. 80 black 30 25

125. Generals Barrientos and Ovando, Bolivian Map and Flag. 126. Needy Children.

1966. Co-Presidents Commem.
778. 125. 60 c. mult. (postage).. 8 8
779. 1 p. multicoloured .. 12 10
780. 125. 2 p. 80 mult. (air) .. 70 50
781. 10 p. multicoloured .. 1·10 90

1966. Aid for Poor Children.
783. 126. 30 c. brown, sepia and ochre (postage) .. 5 5
784. – 1 p. 40 blk. & blue (air) 30 25
DESIGN: 1 p. 40, Mother and needy children.

1966. Commem. Issues. Various stamps surch. with inscr. (as given below) and value.

(i) Red Cross Cent. Surch. **Centenario de la Cruz Roja Internacional.** (a) Postage.
785. 20 c. on 150 b. (No. 641) 5 5

(b) Air.
786. 4 p. on 4000 b. (No. 650).. 45 30

(ii) General Azurduy de Padilla. Surch. **Homenaje a la Generala J. Azurduy de Padilla.**
787. 30 c. on 550 b. (No. 643) .. 5 5
788. 2 p. 80 on 750 b. (No. 644) 30 25

(iii) Air. Tupiza Cent. Surch. **Centenario de Tupiza.**
789. 60 c. on 1350 b. (No. 648) 5 5

(iv) Air. Bolivian Motor Club. 25th Anniv. Surch. **XXV Aniversario Automovil Club Boliviano.**
790. 2 p. 80 on 2700 b. (No. 649) 75 55

(v) Air. Cochabamba Philatelic Society Anniv. Surch. **Anniversario Centro Filatelico Cochabamba.**
791. 1 p. 20 on 800 b. (No. 742) 12 10
792. 1 p. 20 on 1800 b. (No. 743) 12 10

(vi) Rotary Help for Children's Hospital. Surch. with value only. (a) Postage.
793. 1 p. 60 on 350 b. (No. 693) 20 15
794. 2 p. 40 on 500 b. (No. 694) 25 15

(b) Air.
795. 1 p. 40 on 1000 b. (No. 698) 15 12
796. 1 p. 40 on 1800 b. (No. 699) 15 12

(vii) Coronilla Heroines. 150th Anniv. Surch. **CL Aniversario Heroinas Coronilla.** (a) Postage.
797. 60 c. on 350 b. (No. 682).. 8 5

(b) Air.
798. 1 p. 20 on 800 b. (No. 689) 12 10

(viii) Air. Hymn La Paz. Cent. Surch. **Centenario Himno Paceno.**
799. 1 p. 40 on 4000 b. (No. 692) 15 12

(ix) Air. Agrarian Reform. 12th Anniv. Surch. **XII Aniversario Reforma Agraria.**
800. 10 c. on 27 b. (No. 602) .. 5 5

(x) Air. Chaco Peace Settlement. 25th Anniv Surch. **XXV Aniversario Paz del Chaco.**
801. 10 c. on 55 b. (No. 613) .. 5 5

All the following are surch. on Revenue stamps. The design shows a beach scene with palms, size 27 × 21½ mm.

(xi) Rurrenabaque. Cent. Surch. **Centenario de Rurrenabaque.**
802. 1 p. on 10 b. brown .. 12 10

(xii) Busch Government. 25th Anniv. Surch. **XXV Aniversario Gobierno Busch.**
803. 20 c. on 5 b. red 5 5

(xiii) Villarroel Government. 20th Anniv. Surch. **XX Aniversario Gob. Villarroel.**
804. 60 c. on 2 b. green .. 10 10

xiv) Pando Department. 25th Anniv. Surch. **XXV Aniversario Dpto. Pando** (a) Postage.
805. 1 p. 60 on 50 c. violet .. 20 15

(b) Air. Surch. **Aereo** also.
806. 1 p. 20 on 1 b. blue .. 12 10

127. Sower. 128. "Macheteros".

1967. Lions Int. 50th Anniv. Multicoloured.
807. 70 c. Type 127 postage) .. 10 8
808. 2 p. Lions emblem and Inca obelisks (air) 20 15

1968. 9th Congress of the U.P.A.E (Postal Union of the Americas and Spain). Bolivian Folklore. Designs showing costumed figures. Multicoloured.
810. 30 c. Type 128 (postage) 5 5
811. 60 c. "Chunchos" .. 8 5
812. 1 p. "Wiphala" .. 10 8
813. 2 p. "Diablada" .. 20 15
814. 1 p. 20 "Pujllay" (air) .. 12 10
815. 1 p. 40 "Ujusiris" .. 15 12
816. 2 p. "Morenada" .. 20 15
817. 3 p. "Auki-aukis" .. 30 25

129. Arms of Tarija. 130. President G. Villarroel.

1968. Battle of the Tablada (1817). 150th Anniv.
819. 129. 20 c. mult. (postage).. 5 5
820. 30 c. multicoloured .. 5 5
821. 40 c. multicoloured .. 5 5
822. 60 c. multicoloured .. 8 5
823. 1 p. multicoloured (air) 10 8
824. – 1 p. 20 multicoloured 12 10
825. – 2 p. multicoloured .. 25 20
826. – 4 p. multicoloured .. 40 30
DESIGNS: Nos. 823/6, Moto Mendez.

1968. Cochabamba. 400th Anniv.
827. 130. 20 c. brn. & orge. (post.) 5 5
828. 30 c. brn. & turq.-grn. 5 5
829. 40 c. brown & maroon 5 5
830. 50 c. brown and green 5 5
831. 1 p. brown and bistre 10 8
832. – 1 p. 40 blk. & red (air) 15 12
833. – 3 p. black and blue .. 30 20
834. – 4 p. black and red .. 40 30
835. – 5 p. black and green .. 50 40
836. – 10 p. black and violet 1·10 80
DESIGN—HORIZ. 1 p. 40 to 10 p. Similar portrait of President.

131. I.T.U. Emblem. 132. Copper Urn.

1968. I.T.U. Cent. (1965).
837. 131. 10 c. black grey and yellow (postage) .. 5 5
838. 60 c. black, orange and bistre 8 5
839. 131. 1 p. 20 black, grey and yellow (air).. .. 12 10
840. 1 p. 40 blk., blue & brn. 15 12

1968. U.N.E.S.C.O. (1966). 20th Anniv.
841. 132. 20 c. mult. (postage).. 5 5
842. 60 c. multicoloured .. 5 5
843. – 1 p. 20 blk. & blue (air) 12 10
844. – 2 p. 80 black & green.. 30 25
DESIGNS: Nos. 843/4, U.N.E.S.C.O. emblem.

133. President J. F. Kennedy. 134. Tennis Player.

1968. Kennedy Commem.
845. 133. 10 c. blk. & grn. (post.) 5 5
846. 4 p. black and violet.. 40 30
847. 133. 1 p. black & green (air) 10 8
848. 10 p. black and red .. 1·00 85

1968. South American Tennis Championships, La Paz.
850. 134. 10 c. black, brown and grey (postage) .. 5 5
851. 20 c. black, brn. & yell. 5 5
852. 30 c. black, brown & bl. 5 5
853. 134. 1 p. 40 black, brown & orange (air).. .. 15 12
854. 2 p. 80 blk., brn. & blue 30 20

135. Unofficial 1 r. Stamp of 1867. 136. Running.

1968. Stamp Cent.
856. 135. 10 c. brown, black and green (postage) .. 5 5
857. 30 c. brn., blk. & blue 5 5
858. 2 p. brown, black & drab 20 15
859. – 1 p. 40 green, black and yellow (air) .. 15 12
860. – 2 p. 80 grn., blk. & pink 30 25
861. – 3 p. grn. blk. & lilac.. 35 30
DESIGNS: Nos. 859/61 First Bolivian stamp.

1969. Olympic Games, Mexico (1968).
863. – 40 c. black, red & orge. (postage) 5 5
864. – 50 c. black, red and green 8 5
865. – 60 c. black, blue & green 8 8
866. 136. 1 p. 20 black, green and ochre (air) .. 25 15
867. – 2 p. 80 blk., red & yell. 50 30
868. – 5 p. multicoloured .. 80 60
DESIGNS—HORIZ. 40 c. Rifle-shooting. 50 c. Horse-jumping. 60 c. Canoeing. 5 p. Hurdling. VERT. 2 p. 80 Throwing the discus.

137. F. D. Roosevelt. 138. "Temensis laothoe violetta".

1969. Air. Roosevelt Commem.
870. 137. 5 p. black, orge. & brn. 65 50

1970. Butterflies. Multicoloured.
871. 5 c. Type 138 (postage) .. 5 5
872. 10 c. "Papilio crassus" .. 5 5
873. 20 c. "Catagramma cynosura" 8 5
874. 30 c. "Eunica eurota flora" 10 8
875. 80 c. "Ituna phenarete" 20 15
876. 1 p. "Metamorpha dido wernichei" (air) .. 20 8
877. 1 p. 80 "Heliconius felix" 30 15
878. 2 p. 80 "Morpho casica" 50 20
879. 3 p. "Papilio yuracares" 50 25
880. 4 p. "Heliconsus melitus" 80 40

139. Scout mountaineering. 140. President Ovando and Revolutionaries.

1970. Bolivian Scout Movement. Mult.
882. 5 c. Type 139 (postage) .. 5 5
883. 10 c. Girl-scout planting shrub 5 5
884. 50 c. Scout laying bricks (air) 8 5
885. 1 p. 20 Bolivian scout badge 20 12

1970. Obligatory Tax. Revolution and National Day.
886. 140. 20 c. blk. & red (post.) 5 5
887. – 30 c. blk. & green (air) 5 5
DESIGN: 30 c. Pres. Ovando, oil derricks and laurel sprig.

1970. "Exfilca 70" Stamp Exhib., Caracas. No. 706 further surch. **EXFILCA 70** and new value.
888. 30 c. on 350 b. on 10 c. .. 5 5

1970. Provisionals. Various stamps surch.
889. 106. 60 c. on 900 b. on 350 b. (postage) 8 5
890. – 1 p. 20 on 1500 b. (No. 723).. .. .. 15 8
891. 113. 1 p. 20 on 4000 b. (air) 15 10

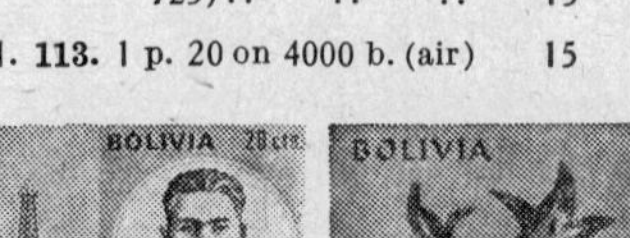

141. Pres. Busch and Oil Derrick. 142. "Amaryllis escobar uriae".

1971. President G. Busch. 32nd Death Anniv. and Pres. Villarroel. 25th Death Anniv.
892. 141. 20 c. blk. & lilac (post.) 5 5
893. – 30 c. black & blue (air) 5 5
DESIGN: 30 c. Pres. Villarroel and oil refinery.

1971. Bolivian Flora. Multicoloured.
894. 30 c. Type 142 (postage) 5 5
895. 40 c. "Amaryllis evansae" 5 5
896. 50 c. "Amaryllis yungacensis" (vert.).. .. 5 5
897. 2 p. "Gymnocalycium chiquitanum" (vert.) 25 12
898. 1 p. 20 "Amaryllis pseudopardina" (air) .. 12 8
899. 1 p 40 "Rebutia kruegeri" (vert.) 15 10
900. 2 p. 80 "Lobivia pentlandii" 35 15
901. 4 p. "Rebutia tunariensis" (vert.) 45 25

143. Sica Sica Cathedral. 144. Pres. Banzer.

1971. "Exfilima" Stamp Exhibition, Lima, Peru.
903. 143. 20 c. multicoloured .. 5 5

1972. "Bolivia's Development".
904. 144. 1 p. 20 multicoloured.. 15 8

145. Chiriwano de Achocalla Dance. 146. "Virgin and Child" (B. Bitti).

1972. Folk Dances. Multicoloured.

905. 20 c. Type 145 (postage) .. 5 5
906. 40 c. Rueda Chapaca .. 5 5
907. 60 c. Kena-Kena 8 5
908. 1 p. Waca Thokori .. 12 8
909. 1 p. 20 Kusillo (air) .. 15 10
910. 1 p. 40 Taquirari 20 12

1972. Bolivian Paintings. Multicoloured.

911. 10 c. "The Washerwoman" (M. P. Holguin) (post.) 5 5
912. 50 c. "Coronation of the Virgin" (G. M. Berrio) 5 5
913. 70 c. "Arquebusier" (anon.) 8 5
914. 80 c. "St. Peter of Alcantara" (M. P. Holguin) 8 5
915. 1 p. Type 146 .. .. 12 10
916. 1 p. 40 "Chola Pacena" (G. de Rojas) (air) .. 15 10
917. 1 p. 50 "Adoration of the Kings" (G. Gamarra) .. 15 10
918. 1 p. 60 "Pachamama Vision" (A. Borda) .. 15 10
919. 2 p. "Idol's Kiss" (G. de Rojas) 20 12

147. Tarija Cathedral.

1972. "EXFILIBRA 72" Stamp Exhib., Rio de Janeiro.

920. 147. 30 c. multicoloured .. 5 5

148. National Arms.

1972. Air.

921. 148. 4 p. multicoloured .. 40 25

149. Santos Dumont and Aircraft.

1973. Air. Santos Dumont. Birth Cent.

922. 149. 1 p. 40 black & yellow 12 8

150. "Echinocactus notocactus". 151. Power Station, Santa Isabel.

1973. Cacti. Multicoloured.

923. 20 c. Type 150 (postage).. 5 5
924. 40 c. "Echinocactus lenninghaussii" .. 5 5
925. 50 c. "Mammillaria bocasana" 5 5
926. 70 c. "Echinocactus lenninghaussii" (different) 5 5
927. 1 p. 20 "Mammillaria bocasana" (different) (air) 8 5
928. 1 p. 90 "Opuntia cristata" 12 8
929. 2 p. "Echinocactus rebutia" 15 12

1973. Bolivian Development. Multicoloured.

930. 10 c. Type 151 (postage).. 5 5
931. 20 c. Tin foundry 5 5
932. 90 c. Bismuth plant .. 5 5
933. 1 p. Gas plant 8 5
934. 1 p. 40 Bridge, Highway 1Y4 (air) 12 8
935. 2 p. Railcar crossing bridge, Al Beni 15 12

INDEX

Countries can be quickly located by referring to the index at the end of this volume.

152. "Cattleya nobilior". 153. Early Aircraft and Emblem.

1974. Bolivian Orchids. Multicoloured.

936. 20 c. Type 152 (postage) 5 5
937. 50 c. "Zygopetalum bolivianum" .. 5 5
938. 1 p. "Huntleya melagris" 8 8
939. 2 p. 50 "Cattleya luteola" (horiz.) (air) 20 12
940. 3 p. 80 "Stanhopaea" .. 30 20
941. 4 p. "Catasetum" (horiz.) 30 20
942. 5 p. "Maxillaria".. .. 35 25

1974. Air. Bolivian Air Force. 50th Anniv. Multicoloured.

944. 3 p. Type 153 .. .. 20 12
945. 3 p. 80 Aircraft crossing Andes 25 15
946. 4 p. 50 Early and modern training aircraft .. 25 15
947. 8 p. Col. Rafael Pabon and fighter aircraft .. 50 30
948. 15 p. Aircraft on "50" .. 1·00 60

154. General Sucre.

1974. Battle of Ayacucho. 150th Anniv.

949. 154. 5 p. multicoloured .. 30 20

155. U.P.U. and Exhibition Emblems.

1974. Cent. of U.P.U. and Expo U.P.U. (Montevideo) and Prenfil U.P.U. (Buenos Aires) Exhibitions.

950. 155. 3 p. 50 grn., blk. & bl. 20 12

156. Lions Emblem and Steles.

1975. Lions International in Bolivia. 50th Anniv.

951. 156. 30 c. multicoloured .. 5 5

157. Exhibition Emblem.

1975. "Espana 75" International Stamp Exhibition, Madrid.

952. 157. 4 p. 50 multicoloured 25 15

158. Emblem of Meeting. 159. Arms of Pando.

1975. Cartagena Agreement. First Meeting of Postal Ministers, Quito, Ecuador.

953. 158. 2 p. 50 silver, vio. & blk. 20 12

1975. Republic. 150th Anniv. (1st issue). Provincial Arms. Multicoloured.

955. 20 c. Type 159 (postage).. 5 5
956. 2 p. Chuzuisaca 15 10
957. 3 p. Cochabamba.. .. 20 12
958. 20 c. Beni (air) 5 5
959. 30 c. Tarija 5 5
960. 50 c. Potosi 5 5
961. 1 p. Oruro.. .. .. 8 5
962. 2 p. 50 Santa Cruz .. 20 12
963. 3 p. La Paz 20 12

See also Nos. 965/80.

160. Presidents Perez and Banzer. 161. Simon Bolivar.

1975. Air. Visit of Pres. Perez of Venezuela.

964. 160. 3 p. multicoloured .. 25 15

1975. Republic. 150th Anniv. (2nd issue).

965. 30 c. Victor Paz Estenssoro (post) 5 5
966. 60 c. Pres. Thomas Frias.. 5 5
967. 1 p. Ismael Montes .. 8 5
968. 2 p. 50 Aniceto Arce .. 20 10
969. 7 p. Bautista Saavedra .. 50 25
970. 10 p. Jose Manuel Pando.. 75 40
971. 15 p. Jose Maria Linares.. 1·10 75
972. 50 p. Type 161 .. .. 3·75 2·25
973. 50 c. Rene Barrientos Ortuno (air) 5 5
974. 2 p. Francisco B. O'Connor 15 10
975. 3 p. 80 Gualberto Villaroel 20 12
976. 4 p. 20 German Busch .. 25 15
977. 4 p. 50 Pres. Hugo Banzer Suarez 35 15
978. 20 p. Jose Ballivian .. 1·50 90
979. 30 p. Pres. Andres de Santa Cruz .. .. .. 2·25 1·25
980. 40 p. Pres. Antonic Jose de Sucre .. .. .. 3·00 1·75

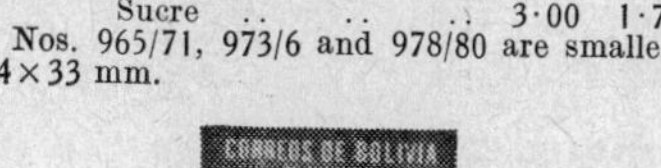

Nos. 965/71, 973/6 and 978/80 are smaller, 24×33 mm.

162. Airline Emblem.

1975. Air. Lloyd-Aereo Boliviano. 50th Anniversary. Multicoloured.

981. 1 p. Type 162 .. .. 10 8
982. 1 p. 50 L. A. B. route map 12 10
983. 2 p. Guillermo Kyllmann (founder) 15 10

1975. Obligatory Tax. As No. 893 but inscr. "XXV ANIVERSARIO DE SU GOBIERNO".

984. 30 c. black and blue .. 5 5

163. "EXFIVIA".

1975. "Exfivia 75". Stamp Exhibition.

985. 163. 3 p. multicoloured .. 20 12

164. U.P.U. Emblem.

1975. Universal Postal Union. Cent. (1974).

986. 164. 25 p. multicoloured .. 1·90 1·10

165. Chiang Kai-shek. 166. Naval Insignia.

1976. President Chiang Kai-shek of Taiwan. 1st Death Anniv.

987. 165. 2 p. 50 multicoloured 20 10

1976. Navy Day.

988. 166. 50 c. multicoloured .. 5 5

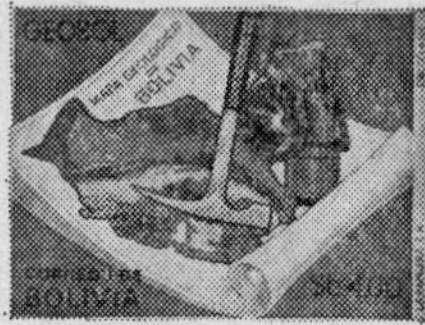

167. Axe, Lamp and Map.

1976. Bolivian Geological Institute.

989. 167. 4 p. multicoloured .. 30 20

168. Airliner and Divided Roundel.

1976. Lufthansa Airline. 50th. Anniv.

990. 168. 3 p. multicoloured .. 20 12

169. Bolivian Boy Scout (vert.).

1976. Boy Scout Movement. 60th Anniv.

991. 169. 1 p. multicoloured .. 8 5

170. Battle Scene.

1976. American Revolution. Bicent.

992. 170. 4 p. 50 multicoloured 35 25

POSTAGE DUE STAMPS

D 1. D 2.

1931.

D 265. D 1. 5 c. blue 20 20
D 266. 10 c. red 20 20
D 267. 15 c. yellow 20 20
D 268. 30 c. green 30 30
D 269. 40 c. violet 35 35
D 270. 50 c. sepia 35 35

1938. Triangular designs.

D 346. D 2. 5 c. red 20 15
D 347. – 10 c. green 20 15
D 348. – 30 c. blue 20 15

DESIGNS: 10 c. Torch of Knowledge. 30 c. Date and Symbol of 17 May, 1936, Revolution.

BOSNIA AND HERZEGOVINA E1

AUSTRO-HUNGARIAN MILITARY POST

Turkish provinces administered by Austria from 1878 and annexed by her in 1908. Now part of Yugoslavia.

1879. 100 kreuzer (or novics) = 1 gulden.
1900. 100 heller = 1 krone.

1.

2.

1879.

119. 1. ½ k. black .. .. 4·75 7·50
120. 1 k. grey .. .. 1·75 30
136. 2 k. yellow 90 15
137. 3 k. green .. .. 1·50 80
146a. 5 k. red .. .. .. 1·10 15
139. 10 k. blue .. .. 1·60 15
140. 15 k. brown .. .. 1·50 75
141. 20 k. green .. .. 2·25 1·50
142. 25 k. purple .. .. 3·00 2·50

1900.

148. 2. 1 h. black 15 5
149. 2 h. grey 15 5
151. 3 h. yellow 20 5
152. 5 h. green 20 5
154. 6 h. brown 30 5
155. 10 h. red 15 5
156. 20 h. pink .. .. 48·00 2·50
158. 25 h. blue 45 12
159. 30 h. brown .. .. 55·00 3·00
160. 40 h. orange .. .. 90·00 4·50
161. 50 h. purple 55 20

Larger stamps with value in each corner.

162. 1 k. red 65 30
163. 2 k. blue 90 75
164. 5 k. green .. .. 2·00 2·00

1901. Black figures of value.

177. 2. 20 h. pink and black .. 65 15
178. 30 h. brown and black 65 15
179. 35 h. blue and black .. 5·00 45
181. 40 h. orange and black .. 75 20
182. 45 h. blue-green and black 65 20

4. View of Doboj.

DESIGNS—As T 4: 2 h. Mostar. 3 h. The old castle, Jajce. 5 h. Naretva pass and Prenz Planina. 6 h. Valley of the Rama. 10 h. Valley of the Vrbas. 12 h. Jajce. 20 h. Old Bridge, Mostar. 25 h. The Begova Djamia (Bey's Mosque), Sarajevo. 30 h. Post by beast of burden. 35 h. Village and lake, Jezero. 40 h. Mail wagon. 45 h. Bazaar at Sarajevo. 50 h. Postal motor-car. 60 h. Konjica. 72 h. Vishegrad. As T 5: 2 k. St. Luke's Campanile at Jajce. 5 k. Francis Joseph I.

5. In the Carshija, Sarajevo.

1906.

186. 4. 1 h. black 10 5
187. – 2 h. violet 12 5
188. – 3 h. olive.. .. 12 5
189. – 5 h. green 15 5
190. – 6 h. brown 15 8
191. – 10 h. red.. .. .. 20 5
359. – 12 h. blue .. .. 2·40 1·00
192. – 20 h. sepia 55 10
193. – 25 h. blue .. .. 1·50 50
194. – 30 h. green .. .. 1·60 20
195. – 35 h. green .. .. 1·60 20
196. – 40 h. orange .. .. 1·60 20
197. – 45 h. red.. .. .. 1·60 75
198. – 50 h. purple .. .. 1·90 50
360. – 60 h. blue .. .. 4·00 1·25
361. – 72 h. red .. .. 5·00 4·00
199. 5. 1 k. lake .. .. 4·00 1·25
200. – 2 k. green .. .. 6·50 5·50
201. – 5 k. blue .. .. 4·00 3·75

1910. 80th Birthday of Francis Joseph I. As stamps of 1906 with date-label at foot.

343. 1 h. black 30 10
344. 2 h. violet 30 10
345. 3 h. olive 35 12
346. 5 h. green 40 8
347. 6 h. brown 40 12
348. 10 h. red 40 8
349. 20 h. sepia .. .. 1·00 80
350. 25 h. blue .. .. 2·00 1·50
351. 30 h. green .. .. 1·50 1·25
352. 35 h. green .. .. 1·75 1·25
353. 40 h. orange .. .. 2·00 1·50
354. 45 h. red .. .. 3·25 3·00
355. 50 h. purple .. .. 3·75 3·00
356. 1 k. lake .. .. 3·75 3·00
357. 2 k. green .. .. 14·00 10·00
358. 5 k. blue .. .. 1·60 1·75

10. Francis Joseph I. 11.

1912. Nos. 378/82 are larger (27×25 mm.)

362. 10. 1 h. olive 40 5
363. 2 h. blue 40 5
364. 3 h. lake 40 5
365. 5 h. green 40 5
366. 6 h. black 40 5
367. 10 h. red 40 5
368. 12 h. green .. .. 1·00 10
369. 20 h. brown .. .. 4·75 5
370. 25 h. blue .. .. 1·75 5
371. 30 h. red .. .. 1·75 5
372. 11. 35 h. green .. .. 1·90 5
373. 40 h. brown .. .. 6·00 5
374. 45 h. brown .. .. 2·25 10
375. 50 h. blue .. .. 2·25 5
376. 60 h. purple-brown .. 2·25 5
377. 72 h. blue .. .. 2·50 1·60
378. 10. 1 k. brown on cream .. 11·00 20
379. 2 k. blue on blue .. 4·50 12
380. 11. 3 k. red on green .. 7·50 4·00
381. 5 k. lilac on grey .. 18·00 12·00
382. 10 k. blue on grey .. 75·00 48·00

1914. Surch. **1915** and value.

383. 7 h. on 5 h. grn (No. 189).. 25 25
384. 12 h. on 10 h. red (No. 191) 25 25

1915. Surch **1915** and value.

385. 7 h. on 5 h. grn. (No. 189) 6·50 6·00
386. 12 h. on 10 h. red (No. 191) 20 20

1915. Surch. **1915** and value.

387. 10. 7 h. on 5 h. green .. 45 40
388. 12 h. on 10 h. red .. 1·25 1·10

1916. Surch. **1916** and value.

389. 10. 7 h. on 5 h green .. 30 20
390. 12 h. on 10 h. red .. 30 20

12.

DESIGN: 10 h. Blind soldier and girl.

1916. Charity. War Invalids Fund.

391. 12. 5 h. (+2 h.) green .. 65 35
392. – 10 h. (+2 h.) claret .. 95 50

See also Nos. 434/5.

14. Francis Joseph I. 15.

1916.

393. 14. 3 h. black 15 12
394. 5 h. olive 25 20
395. 6 h. violet 25 25
396. 10 h. bistre .. .. 1·25 95
397. 12 h. blue-grey .. 30 30
398. 15 h. red 8 5
399. 20 h. brown 30 25
400. 25 h. blue 20 15
401. 30 h. green 20 15
402. 40 h. red 20 15
403. 50 h. green 20 15
404. 60 h. lake 20 20
405. 80 h. brown 50 8
406. 90 h. purple 55 30
407. 15. 2 k. claret on yellow .. 35 30
408. 3 k. green on blue .. 1·10 1·10
409. 4 k. red on green .. 4·75 4·00
410. 10 k. violet on grey .. 12·00 11·00

1917. Charity. Optd. **WITWEN. UND WAISENWOCHE 1917.**

411. 14. 10 h. (+2 h.) bistre .. 5 5
412. 15 h. (+2 h.) red .. 5 5

18. Design for Memorial Church, Sarajevo. 19. Charles I.

1917. Assassination of Archduke Ferdinand.

413. 18. 10 h. (+2 h.) violet .. 12 12
414. – 15 h. (+2 h.) lake .. 12 12
415. – 40 h. (+2 h.) blue .. 12 12

PORTRAITS—HORIZ. 40 h. Archduke and Archduchess. VERT. 15 h. Archduke Ferdinand.

1917.

416. 19. 3 h. grey 12 8
417. 5 h. olive 8 5
418. 6 h. violet 30 30
419. 10 h. brown 12 5
420. 12 h. blue 35 40
421. 15 h. red 8 5
422. 20 h. brown 8 5
423. 25 h. blue 55 25
424. 30 h. green 15 10
425. 40 h. bistre 15 8
426. 50 h. green 65 25
427. 60 h. red 55 25
428. 80 h. blue 20 12
429. 90 h. lilac 70 60
430. – 2 k. red on yellow .. 40 15
431. – 3 k. green on blue .. 11·00 10·00
432. – 4 k. red on green .. 4·00 3·75
433. – 10 k. violet on grey .. 2·50 2·50

The kronen values are larger (25×25 mm).

1918. Charity.

434. – 10 h. (+2 h.) blue (as No. 392) 35 30
435. 12. 15 h. (+2 h.) brown .. 35 30

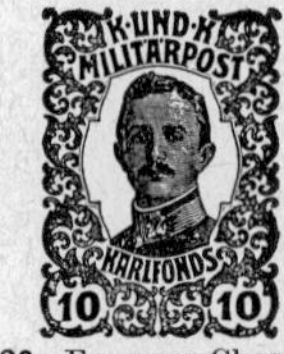
20. Emperor Charles.

ILLUSTRATIONS British Commonwealth and all overprints and surcharges are FULL SIZE. Foreign Countries have been reduced to ¾-LINEAR.

1918.

436. 20. 10 h. (+10 h.) green .. 25 25
437. – 15 h. (+10 h.) brown.. 25 25
438. 20. 40 h. (+10 h.) purple.. 25 25

DESIGN—15 h. Empress Zita.

1918. Optd. **1918.**

439 – 2 h. violet (No. 344) .. 40 50
440. 10. 2 h. blue 40 50

NEWSPAPER STAMPS

N 1. Girl in Bosnian Costume.

N 2. Mercury.

1913. Imperf.

N 383. N 1. 2 h. blue 45 40
N 384. 6 h. mauve .. 1·25 75
N 385. 10 h. red .. .. 1·25 75
N 386. 20 h. green .. 1·75 90

For these stamps perforated see Yugoslavia, Nos. 25 to 28.

1916. For Express.

N 411. N 2. 2 h. red 15 15
N 412. 5 h. green 35 35

POSTAGE DUE STAMPS

D 1. D 2.

1904. Imperf or perf.

D 183. D 1. 1 h. black, red & yell. 35 5
D 184. 2 h. black, red & yell. 35 5
D 185. 3 h. black, red & yell. 35 5
D 186. 4 h. black, red & yell. 35 5
D 187. 5 h. black, red & yell. 35 5
D 188. 6 h. black, red & yell. 30 5
D 189. 7 h. black, red & yell. 2·25 1·10
D 190. 8 h. black, red & yell. 2·25 45
D 191. 10 h. blk., red & yell. 65 5
D 192. 15 h. blk., red & yell. 55 8
D 193. 20 h. blk., red & yell. 2·75 10
D 194. 50 h. blk., red & yell. 1·90 10
D 195. 200 h. blk., red & grn. 9·00 55

1916.

D 411. D 2. 2 h. red 30 30
D 412. 4 h. red 25 25
D 413. 5 h. red 30 20
D 414. 6 h. red 15 15
D 415. 10 h. red 25 20
D 416. 15 h. red .. .. 2·40 2·10
D 417. 20 h. red 25 25
D 418. 25 h. red 75 75
D 419. 30 h. red 65 65
D 420. 40 h. red .. .. 6·00 5·50
D 421. 50 h. red .. .. 20·00 18·00
D 422. 1 k. blue .. .. 2·50 2·50
D 423. 3 k. blue .. .. 11·00 11·00

BOTSWANA BC

Formerly Bechuanaland Protectorate, attained independence on 30th September 1966, and changed its name to Botswana.
1976. 100 thebe = 1 pula.

1. National Assembly Building.

1966. Independence. Multicoloured.

202. 2½ c. Type 1 .. .. 5 5
203. 5 c. Abattoir, Lobatsi .. 12 12
204. 15 c. National Airways "Dakota" 35 35
205. 35 c. State House, Gaberones 55 55

1966. Nos. 168/81 of Bechuanaland optd. **REPUBLIC OF BOTSWANA.**

206. 9. 1 c. yell., red, black & lilac 5 5
207. – 2 c. orange, black & olive 8 8
208. – 2½ c. red grn. blk. & bis. 10 10
209. – 3½ c. yell., blk., sep. & pink 12 12
210. – 5 c. yell., bl., blk. & buff 15 15
211. – 7½ c. brn., red, blk. & apple 20 25
212. – 10 c. red, yell., sep. & turq. 25 25
213. – 12½ c. buff, bl., red & grey 30 30
214. – 20 c. brown and drab .. 40 40
215. – 25 c. sepia and lemon .. 45 50
216. – 35 c. blue and orange .. 65 75
217. – 50 c. sepia and olive .. 1·25 1·60
218. – 1 r. black and brown .. 2·25 2·75
219. 2 r. brown and turquoise 4·00 5·50

2. Golden Oriole.

1967. Multicoloured.

220. 1 c. Type 2 .. .. 5 5
221. 2 c. African Hoopoe .. 5 5
222. 3 c. Ground-scraper Thrush 5 8
223. 4 c. Blue Waxbill.. .. 8 10
224. 5 c. Secretary Bird .. 10 12
225. 7 c. Yellow-billed Hornbill 12 15
226. 10 c. Crimson-breasted Shrike 15 20
227. 15 c. Malachite Kingfisher 30 55
228. 20 c. Fish Eagle 35 45
229. 25 c. Grey Lory 45 55
230. 35 c. Scimitar-bill.. .. 55 65
231. 50 c. Knob-billed duck .. 1·40 1·60
232. 1 r. Crested Barbet .. 2·00 2·50
233. 2 r. Diederick Cuckoo .. 3·75 4·75

3. Students and University.

1967 1st Conferment of University Degrees.

234. 3. 3 c. sepia, blue & orange 5 5
235. 7 c. sepia, blue & turquoise 15 15
236. 15 c. sepia, blue and red 30 30
237. 35 c. sepia, blue & violet 50 50

4. Chobe Bush-buck.

1967. Chobe Game Reserve. Multicoloured.

238. 3 c. Type 4 .. .. 5 5
239. 7 c. Sable Antelope .. 12 15
240. 35 c. Fishing on the Chobe River 55 60

5. Arms of Botswana and Human Rights Emblem.

1968. Human Rights Year.

241. **5.** 3 c. multicoloured .. 8 8
242. – 15 c. multicoloured .. 30 35
243. – 25 c. multicoloured .. 45 45

The designs of Nos. 242/3 are similar, but are arranged differently.

6. Rock Paintings, Tsodilo Hills.

1968. Opening of National Museum and Art Gallery. Multicoloured.

244. 3 c. Type **6** 5 5
245. 7 c. Girl wearing ceremonial beads .. 12 15
246. 10 c. " Baobab Trees " (Thomas Baines) .. 20 25
247. 15 c. National Museum and art gallery (72 × 19 mm) 30 35

No. 245 is vert. and the size is 31 × 48 mm.

7. African Family, and Star over Village.

1968. Christmas.

249. **7.** 1 c. multicoloured .. 5 5
250. 2 c. multicoloured .. 8 8
251. 5 c. multicoloured .. 12 15
252. 25 c. multicoloured .. 55 60

8. Scout, Lion and Badge in frame.

1969. 22nd World Scout Conf., Helsinki. Multicoloured.

253. 3 c. Type **8** 8 10
254. 15 c. Scouts cooking over open fire 30 45
255. 25 c. Scouts around camp fire 45 55

The 15 c. is vert.

9. Woman, Child and Christmas Star.

1969. Christmas.

256. **9.** 1 c. blue and chocolate .. 5 5
257. 2 c. olive and chocolate .. 8 8
258. 4 c. yellow and chocolate 10 12
259. 35 c. chocolate and violet 50 55

10. Diamond Treatment Plant, Orapa.

1970. Developing Botswana. Multicoloured.

261. 3 c. Type **10** 5 5
262. 7 c. Copper-Nickel mining 15 15
263. 10 c. Copper-Nickel mine, Selebi Pickwe 20 20
264. 35 c. Orapa Diamond mine and diamonds .. 55 65

11. Mr. Micawber (" David Copperfield ").

1970. Charles Dickens. Death Cent. Multicoloured.

265. 3 c. Type **11** 12 12
266. 7 c. Scrooge (" A Christmas Carol ") 15 15
267. 15 c. Fagin (" Oliver Twist ") 30 30
268. 25 c. Bill Sykes (" Oliver Twist ") 45 50

12. U.N. Building and Emblem. (Illustration reduced. Actual size 59 × 21 mm.)

1970. United Nations. 25th Anniv.

270. **12.** 15 c. blue, brown & silver 35 35

13. Crocodile.

1970. Christmas. Multicoloured.

271. 1 c. Type **13** 5 5
272. 2 c. Giraffe 8 8
273. 7 c. Elephant 15 15
274. 25 c. Rhinoceros 55 60

14. Sorghum.

1971. Important Crops. Multicoloured.

276. 3 c. Type **14** 5 5
277. 7 c. Millet 15 15
278. 10 c. Maize 25 25
279. 35 c. Groundnuts 55 60

15. Map and Head of Cow.

1971. Independence. Fifth Anniv.

280. **15.** 3 c. black, brown & grn. 8 8
281. – 4 c. black, new bl. & bl. 10 10
282. – 7 c. black & orange .. 20 20
283. – 10 c. multicoloured .. 25 25
284. – 20 c. multicoloured .. 80 85

DESIGNS: 4 c. Map and cogs. 7 c. Map and zebra. 10 c. Map and sorghum stalk crossed by tusk. 20 c. Arms and map of Botswana.

16. King bringing Gift of Gold.

1971. Christmas. Multicoloured.

285. 2 c. Type **16** 8 8
286. 3 c. King bringing frankincense 10 10
287. 7 c. King bringing myrrh 20 25
288. 20 c. Three Kings behold the star 40 45

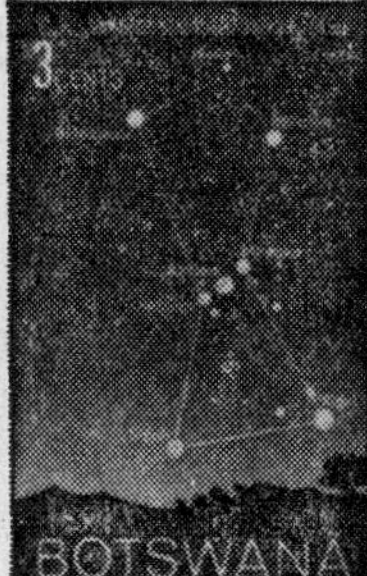

17. Orion.

1972. " Night Sky ".

290. **17.** 3c. blue, blk. and red .. 5 5
291. – 7c. blue, black and yell. 15 15
292. – 10c. grn., blk. and orge. 20 25
293. – 20c. blue, blk. and green 35 45

CONSTELLATIONS: 7c. The Scorpion. 10c. The Centaur. 20c. The Cross.

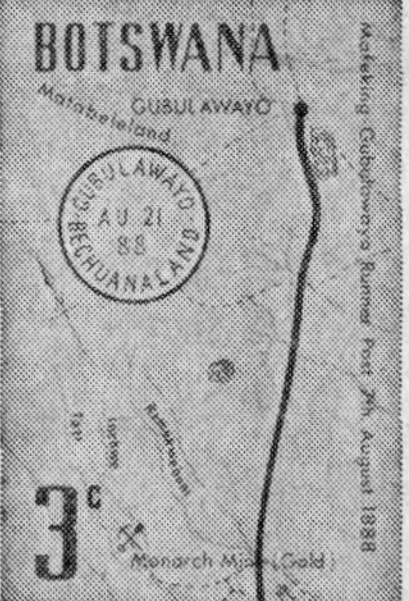

18. Postmark and Map.

1972. Mafeking-Gubulawayo Runner Post. Multicoloured.

294. 3 c. Type **18** 8 8
295. 4 c. Bechuanaland stamp and map 10 10
296. 7 c. Runners and map .. 20 25
297. 20 c. Mafeking postmark and map 55 60

19. Cross, Map and Bells.

1972. Christmas. Each with Cross and Map. Multicoloured.

299. 2 c. Type **19** 5 5
300. 3 c. Candle 8 8
301. 7 c. Christmas tree .. 15 20
302. 20 c. Star and holly .. 50 55

20. Thor.

1973. I.M.O./W.M.O. Centenary. Norse myths. Multicoloured.

304. 3 c. Type **20** 5 5
305. 4 c. Sun God's chariot (horiz.) 8 8
306. 7 c. Ymir, the frost giant .. 15 15
307. 20 c. Odin and Sleipnir (horiz.) 35 40

21. Livingstone and River Scene.

1973. Dr. Livingstone. Death Centenary. Multicoloured.

308. 3 c. Type **21** 8 8
309. 20 c. Livingstone meeting Stanley 50 55

22. Donkey and Foal at Village Trough.

1973. Christmas. Multicoloured.

310. 3 c. Type **22** 5 5
311. 4 c. Shepherd and flock (horiz.) 8 8
312. 7 c. Mother and child .. 15 15
313. 20 c. Kgotla meeting (horiz.) 35 40

23. Gaberone Campus.

1974. University of Botswana, Lesotho and Swaziland. 10th Anniv. Multicoloured.

314. 3 c Type **23** 5 5
315. 7 c. Kwaluseni Campus .. 10 12
316. 20 c. Roma Campus .. 35 35
317. 35 c. Map and flags of the three countries 55 60

24. Methods of Mail Transport.

1974. U.P.U. Centenary. Multicoloured.

318. 2 c. Type **24** 5 5
319. 3 c. Post Office, Palapye, circa 1889 .. .. 8 8
320. 7 c. Bechuanaland Police Camel Post, circa 1900 12 15
321. 20 c. Mail-planes of 1920 and 1974 .. .. 40 45

25. Amethyst.

1974. Botswana Minerals. Multicoloured.

322.	1 c. Type **25**	5	5
323.	2 c. Agate—"Botswana Pink"	5	5
324.	3 c. Quartz	5	5
325.	4 c. Copper nickel ..	8	8
326.	5 c. Moss agate	8	8
327.	7 c. Agate	10	12
328.	10 c. Stilbite	12	15
329.	15 c. Moshaneng Banded Marble	20	20
330.	20 c. Gem diamonds ..	25	30
331.	25 c. Chrysotile	30	35
332.	35 c. Jasper	45	50
333.	50 c. Moss quartz ..	60	70
334.	1 r. Citrine	1·25	1·40
335.	2 r. Chalcopyrite	2·50	2·75

26. "Stapelia variegata".

1974. Christmas. Multicoloured.

336.	2 c. Type **26**	5	5
337.	7 c. "Hibiscus lunarifolius"	10	12
338.	15 c. "Ceratotheca triloba"	25	25
339.	20 c. "Nerine laticoma" ..	30	35

27. President Sir Seretse Khama.

1975. Self-Government. Tenth Anniv.

341. 27.	4 c. multicoloured ..	8	8
342.	10 c. multicoloured ..	15	20
343.	20 c. multicoloured ..	35	30
344.	35 c. multicoloured ..	45	50

28. Ostrich.

1975. Rock Paintings, Tsodilo Hills. Mult.

346.	4 c. Type **28**	8	8
347.	10 c. Rhinoceros	15	20
348.	25 c. Hyena	35	40
349.	35 c. Scorpion	45	55

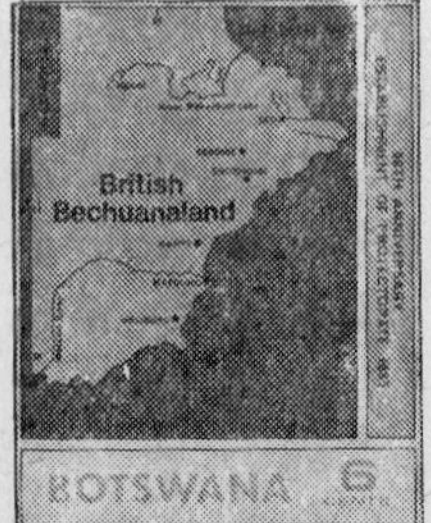

29. Map of British Bechuanaland, 1885.

1975. Anniversaries. Multicoloured.

351.	6 c. Type **29**	8	10
352.	10 c. Chief Khama, 1875 ..	15	20
353.	25 c. Chiefs Sebele, Bathoen and Khama, 1895 (horiz.)	35	35

EVENTS: 6 c. 90th Anniv. of Protectorate. 10 c. Centenary of Khama's Accession. 25 c. 80th Anniv. of Chiefs' visit to London.

30. " Aloe marlothii ".

1975. Christmas. Aloes. Multicoloured.

354.	3 c. Type **30**	5	5
355.	10 c. " Aloe lutescens " ..	12	15
356.	15 c. " Aloe zebrina " ..	15	20
357.	25 c. " Aloe littoralis " ..	30	35

31. Drum.

1976. Traditional Musical Instruments. Mult.

358.	4 c. Type **31**	5	5
359.	10 c. Hand piano	10	12
360.	15 c. Segankuru (violin) ..	15	15
361.	25 c. Kudu signal horn ..	25	30

32. One Pula Note.

1976. First National Currency. Multicoloured.

362.	4 c. Type **32**	5	5
363.	10 c. Two pula note ..	12	15
364.	15 c. Five pula note ..	20	20
365.	25 c. Ten pula note ..	30	35

1976. Nos. 322/35 surch. in new currency.

367.	1 t. on 1 c. multicoloured ..	5	5
368.	2 t. on 2 c. multicoloured ..	5	5
369.	3 t. on 3 c. multicoloured ..	5	5
370.	4 t. on 4 c. multicoloured ..	5	5
371.	5 t. on 5 c. multicoloured ..	5	5
372.	7 t. on 7 c. multicoloured ..	8	8
373.	10 t. on 10 c. multicoloured	12	12
374.	15 t. on 15 c. multicoloured	15	20
375.	20 t. on 20 c. multicoloured	20	25
376.	25 t. on 25 c. multicoloured	30	30
377.	35 t. on 35 c. multicoloured	40	45
378.	50 t. on 50 c. multicoloured	55	60
379.	1 p. on 1 r. multicoloured	1·10	1·25
380.	2 p. on 2 r. multicoloured	2·25	2·50

33. Botswanan Cattle.

1976. Independence. 10th Anniv. Multicoloured.

381.	4 t. Type **33**	5	5
382.	10 t. Deer, Okavango Delta (vert.)	12	15
383.	15 t. School and pupils ..	20	20
384.	25 t. Rural weaving (vert.)	30	35
385.	35 t. Miner (vert.) ..	45	50

34. " Colophospermum mopane ".

1976. Christmas. Trees. Multicoloured.

386.	3 t. Type **34**	5	5
387.	4 t. " Baikiaea plurijuga "	5	5
388.	10 t. " Sterculia rogersii "	12	15
389.	25 t. " Acacia nilotica " ..	30	35
390.	40 t. " Kigelia africana "	50	55

POSTAGE DUE STAMPS

1967 Nos. D 10/2 of Bechuanaland optd. **REPUBLIC OF BOTSWANA.**

D 13. D 1.	1 c. red	5	8
D 14.	2 c. violet	8	10
D 15.	5 c. green	10	12

D 1. Elephant.

1971.

D 16. D 1.	1 c. red	5	5
D 17.	2 c. violet	5	5
D 18.	6 c. brown	5	8
D 19.	14 c. green	15	20

BOYACA O1

One of the states of the Granadine Confederation.

A Department of Colombia from 1806, now uses Colombian stamps.

1. Mendoza Perez.

1899. Imperf. or perf.

1. 1.	5 c. green	40	40

2.

3. Battle of Boyaca Monument.

1903. Imperf. or perf.

3. 2.	10 c. grey	12	12
4.	10 c. blue	60	60
12. –	10 c. orange	15	12
5. 2.	20 c. brown	20	20
5a.	20 c. lake	25	25
6. –	50 c. blue-green	15	15
8. –	1 p. red	20	15
9. –	1 p. claret	1·40	1·40
10. 3.	5 p. black on red ..	50	35
11. –	10 p. black on buff ..	50	40

DESIGNS—As T 2: 10 c. orange, Building. 50 c. Gen. Pinzon. 1 p. Figure of value. As T 3: 10 p. Pres. Marroquin.

BRAZIL O1

A country in the N.E. of S. America. Portuguese settlement, 1500. Kingdom, 1815. Empire, 1822. Republic from 1889.

1843.	1000 reis = 1 milreis.
1942.	100 centavos = 1 cruzeiro.
1967.	Revaluation: 100 (old) cruzeiros = 1 (new) cruzeiro.

1.

1843. Imperf.

4. 1.	30 r. black	£100	50·00
5.	60 r. black	70·00	35·00
6.	90 r. black	£250	£150

2. 3. 4.

1844. Imperf.

10. 2.	10 r. black	6·00	2·00
11.	30 r. black	10·00	3·50
12.	60 r. black	6·00	1·50
13.	90 r. black	50·00	30·00
14.	180 r. black	£350	£250
15.	300 r. black	£500	£300
16.	600 r. black	£500	£300

1850. Imperf.

17. 3.	10 r. black	3·00	1·00
18.	20 r. black	10·00	10·00
19.	30 r. black	75	35
20.	60 r. black	75	35
21.	90 r. black	5·00	2·00
22.	180 r. black	12·00	8·00
23.	300 r. black	35·00	15·00
24.	600 r. black	40·00	25·00

1854. Imperf.

25. 3.	10 r. blue	2·00	1·00
26.	30 r. blue	5·00	5·00
27. 4.	280 r. red	30·00	20·00
28.	430 r. yellow	40·00	30·00

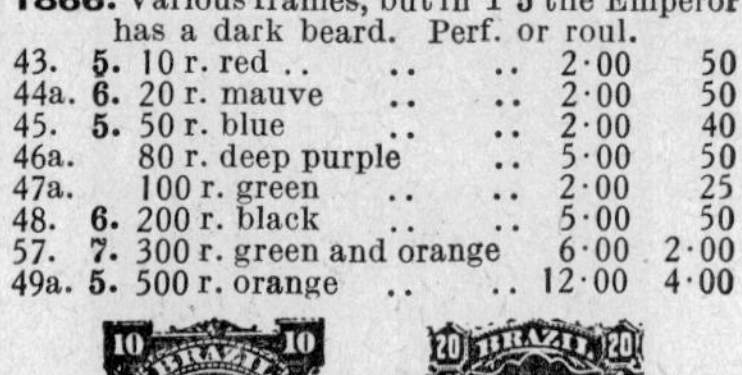

5. 6. 7. Emperor Dom Pedro II.

1866. Various frames, but in T 5 the Emperor has a dark beard. Perf. or roul.

43. 5.	10 r. red	2·00	50
44a. 6.	20 r. mauve	2·00	50
45. 5.	50 r. blue	2·00	40
46a.	80 r. deep purple ..	5·00	50
47a.	100 r. green	2·00	25
48. 6.	200 r. black	5·00	50
57. 7.	300 r. green and orange	6·00	2·00
49a. 5.	500 r. orange	12·00	4·00

8.

9.

1878. Various frames, but in T 8 the Emperor's beard is white. Roul.

58. 8.	10 r. red	75	40
59. 9.	20 r. mauve	75	20
60. 8.	50 r. blue	90	25
61.	80 r. lake	3·00	90
62.	100 r. green	2·00	10
63.	200 r. black	15·00	2·00
64.	260 r. sepia	10·00	2·50
65.	300 r. bistre	5·00	75
66.	700 r. brown	25·00	15·00
67.	1000 r. slate	25·00	4·00

10.

13.

1881. Various frames. Perf.

71. 10.	10 r. black	60	50
72.	10 r. orange	30	30
73.	50 r. blue	2·50	40
74.	100 r. olive	3·25	45
77.	100 r. lilac	7·50	45
75a.	200 r. rose	8·00	40

No. 77 is inscr. " CORREIO ".

1884.

81. 13.	100 r. lilac	15·00	70

14. 15.

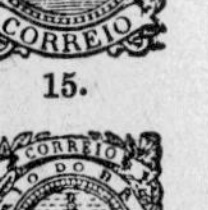

16.

17. Southern Cross. 18.

19.

20. Entrance to Bay of Rio de Janeiro. 21. Southern Cross.

1884.

No.	Type	Description	Unused	Used
78.	14.	20 r. green	55	20
80.	15.	50 r. blue	2·25	30
83.	16.	100 r. lilac	5·00	40
84.	17.	300 r. blue	11·00	1·00
85a.	18.	500 r. olive	10·00	90
86.	19.	700 r. lilac	2·75	2·50
87.	20.	1000 r. blue	30·00	6·00

1890.

No.	Type	Description	Unused	Used
97a.	21.	20 r. green	60	40
89.		50 r. green	70	35
110a.		100 r. purple	10·00	20
91.		200 r. violet	2·00	30
100.		300 r. slate	6·00	1·25
92.		300 r. blue	3·75	1·00
93.		500 r. buff	4·00	1·25
94.		500 r. grey	4·50	1·60
95.		700 r. brown	4·00	4·25
96.		1000 r. yellow	5·00	45

22. Head of Liberty. 23. Head of Liberty.

1891.

No.	Type	Description	Unused	Used
111d.	22.	100 r. red and blue	3·75	20

1893.

No.	Type	Description	Unused	Used
114.	23.	100 r. rose	4·00	20

24. Sugar-loaf Mountain. 25. Head of Liberty. 26. Head of Mercury.

1894.

No.	Type	Description	Unused	Used
124.	24.	10 r. blue and red	8	5
125.		20 r. blue and orange	12	5
126.		50 r. blue	12	8
232.		50 r. green	20	5
127.	25.	100 r. black and red	60	5
239.		100 r. red	70	5
128.		200 r. black and orange	20	5
234.		200 r. blue	1·00	5
129.		300 r. black and green	60	5
153.		500 r. black and blue	20	5
131a.		700 r. black and mauve	1·10	10
132.	26.	1000 r. mauve and green	4·50	12
133.		2000 r. purple and grey	20·00	4·75

1897. As T 24, but "REIS REIS" instead of "DEZ REIS".

No.	Type	Description	Unused	Used
165a.		10 r. blue and red	8	5

1898. Newspaper stamps of 1889 surch. **1898** between value twice in figures.

No.	Type	Description	Unused	Used
168.	N 1.	100 r. on 50 r. orange	60	40
169.		200 r. on 100 r. mauve	30	30
170.		300 r. in 200 r. black	40	30
171.		500 r. on 300 r. red	55	30
173.		700 r. on 500 r. green	1·10	45
172.		700 r. on 500 r. orange	2·00	1·50
174.		1000 r. on 700 r. orange	3·00	2·40
175.		1000 r. on 700 r. blue	3·25	2·75
176.		2000 r. on 1000 r. orge.	2·75	1·90
177.		2000 r. on 1000 r. brn.	2·50	1·75

1898. Newspaper stamp of 1890 surch. **200** over **1898**.

No.	Type	Description	Unused	Used
180.	N 2.	200 r. on 100 r. mauve	3·00	1·90

1898. Newspaper stamps of 1890 surch. **1898** over new value.

No.	Type	Description	Unused	Used
182.	N 3.	20 r. on 10 r. blue	70	50
183.		50 r. on 20 r. green	60	30
184.		100 r. on 50 r. green	1·60	1·75

1899. Postage stamps of 1890 surch. **1899** over new value.

No.	Type	Description	Unused	Used
194.	21.	50 r. on 20 r. green	30	25
195.		100 r. on 50 r. green	20	20
196.		300 r. on 200 r. violet	1·25	1·00
190b.		500 r. on 300 r. slate	40	40
190.		500 r. on 300 r. blue	2·00	1·40
191.		700 r. on 500 r. buff	1·40	90
192a.		1,000 r. on 700 r. brown	1·25	1·00
193.		2,000 r. on 1,000 r. yell.	3·25	60

28. Discovery of Brazil. 30. Emancipation of Slaves.

1900. Discovery of Brazil. 400th Anniv.

No.	Type	Description	Unused	Used
226.	28.	100 r. red	1·00	1·00
227.	–	200 r. green and yellow	1·00	1·00
228.	30.	500 r. blue	1·00	1·00
229.	–	700 r. green	1·00	1·00

DESIGNS—HORIZ. 200 r. Declaration of Independence. VERT. 700 r. Allegory of Republic.

32. Pan-American Congress.

1906.

No.	Type	Description	Unused	Used
259a.	32.	100 r. red	9·00	3·50
259b.		200 r. blue	11·00	4·50

33. Aristides Lobo. 42. Liberty.

1906.

No.	Type	Description	Unused	Used
260.	33.	10 r. grey	5	5
261.	–	20 r. violet	5	5
262.	–	50 r. green	5	5
264.	–	100 r. red	20	5
265.	–	200 r. blue	15	5
267.	–	300 r. sepia	75	5
268.	–	400 r. olive	70	8
269.	–	500 r. violet	75	8
271.	–	600 r. olive	30	5
273.	–	700 r. brown	45	20
274.	42.	1000 r. red	4·75	25
275.	–	1000 r. green	40	15
276.	–	1000 r. slate	1·25	12
277a.	42.	2000 r. green	1·50	12
278.		2000 r. blue	2·50	15
279.		5000 r. lake	2·00	40
280.	–	5000 r. brown	5·50	1·75
281.	–	10,000 r. brown	75	20

PORTRAITS: 20 r. B. Constant. 50 r. A. Cabral. 100 r. Wandenkolk. 200 r. D. da Fonseca. 300 r. F. Peixoto. 400 r., 600 r. P. de Moraes. 500 r. C. Salles. 700 r., 5000 r. (No. 280) R. Alves. 1000 r. (Nos. 275/6) B. do Rio Branco. 10,000 r. N. Pecanha.

47. King Carlos and Affonso Penna and Emblems of Portuguese-Brazilian Amity. 48. Emblems of Peace, Commerce and Industry.

1908. Opening of Brazilian Ports to Foreign Commerce. Cent.

No.	Type	Description	Unused	Used
282.	47.	100 r. red	1·50	25

1908. National Exn., Rio de Janeiro.

No.	Type	Description	Unused	Used
283.	48.	100 r. red	3·50	35

49. Bonifacio, San Martin, Hidalgo, Washington, O'Higgins, Bolivar. 50. Cape Frio.

1909. Pan-American Congress, Rio de Janeiro.

No.	Type	Description	Unused	Used
284.	49.	200 r. blue	1·10	20

1915. Discovery of Cape Frio. Tercent.

No.	Type	Description	Unused	Used
285.	50.	100 r. blue-green on yell.	80	40

51.

1916. City of Belem. Tercent.

No.	Type	Description	Unused	Used
286.	51.	100 r. red	90	45

52. Revolutionary Flag.

1917. Pernambuco Revolution. Cent.

No.	Type	Description	Unused	Used
287.	52.	100 r. blue	5·00	1·75

53. Liberty 54. 55. Inscr. "BRAZIL".

1918. Various frames.

No.	Type	Description	Unused	Used
288.	53.	10 r. brown	5	5
289.		20 r. violet	5	5
290.		25 r. grey	8	5
291.		50 r. green	20	5
292.	54.	100 r. red	15	5
293.		200 r. blue	40	8
294.		300 r. orange	1·25	8
295.		500 r. purple	1·60	12
296.		600 r. orange	50	30
297.	55.	1000 r. blue	55	10
298.		2000 r. brown	3·00	45
299.		5000 r. lilac	1·10	55
301.		10,000 r. claret	90	8

56. Locomotive. 57. "Industry". 58. "Agriculture".

59. "Aviation". 60. Mercury. 61. "Shipping".

1920. T 55 inscr. "BRASIL".

No.	Type	Description	Unused	Used
302.	56.	10 r. purple	5	5
387.	59.	10 r. brown	5	5
318.	56.	20 r. grey	5	5
388.	59.	20 r. violet	5	5
389.	57.	25 r. purple	5	5
321.	58.	40 r. brown	10	8
306.	57.	50 r. green	5	5
323.		50 r. brown	8	5
390.	59.	50 r. claret	5	5
391.		50 r. blue-green	5	5
308.	58.	80 r. blue-green	10	8
309.	59.	100 r. red	20	5
392.		100 r. orange	5	5
327.		100 r. blue-green	5	5
311.		150 r. violet	15	5
312.		200 r. blue	30	8
330a.		200 r. red	10	5
383.		200 r. grey	25	8
394.	60.	300 r. grey	5	5
333.		300 r. red	8	5
395.		400 r. blue	5	5
335.		400 r. orange	10	5
396.		500 r. brown	8	5
337.		500 r. blue	20	5
361.	61.	600 r. chestnut	30	10
397.	60.	600 r. orange	8	5
398.		700 r. violet	12	5
342.	61.	1000 r. purple	40	5
423.	60.	1000 r. blue	30	5
411.	55.	2000 r. violet	30	5
344.		5000 r. brown	1·40	20
364.		10,000 r. claret	1·25	15

62. King Albert of Belgium and Pres. Pessoa.

1920. Visit of King of the Belgians.

No.	Type	Description	Unused	Used
431.	62.	100 r. red	35	20

63. Declaration of Ypiranga. 66. Brazilian Army entering Bahia.

1922. Independence Cent.

No.	Type	Description	Unused	Used
432.	63.	100 r. blue	60	15
433.	–	200 r. red	60	15
434.	–	300 r. green	1·10	25

DESIGNS: 200 r. Dom Pedro I and J. Bonifacio. 300 r. National Exn. and Pres. Pessoa.

1923. Capture of Bahia from the Portuguese. Cent.

No.	Type	Description	Unused	Used
435.	66.	200 r. red	2·50	90

67. Arms of 1824. 68. Ruy Barbosa.

1924. Confederation of the Equator. Cent.

No.	Type	Description	Unused	Used
436.	67.	200 r. blue, red, yellow and black	90	40

1925.

No.	Type	Description	Unused	Used
438a.	68.	1000 r. claret	40	8

69. "Justice". DESIGN: 200 r. Map and Balances.

1927. Law Courses. Cent.

No.	Type	Description	Unused	Used
439.	69.	100 r. blue	40	20
440.	–	200 r. red	35	15

1928. Air. Official stamps of 1913, Type O 2, surch. **SERVICO AEREO** and new value. Centres in black.

No.	Type	Description	Unused	Used
441.		50 r. on 10 r. grey	8	8
442.		200 r. on 1000 r. brown	25	20
443.		200 r. on 2000 r. brown	60	40
444.		200 r. on 5000 r. bistre	20	20
445.		300 r. on 500 r. yellow	25	20
446.		300 r. on 600 r. purple	20	20
447.		500 r. on 50 r. grey	25	20
448.		1000 r. on 20 r. olive	20	8
449.		2000 r. on 100 r. red	40	30
450.		2000 r. on 200 r. blue	65	40
451.		2000 r. on 10,000 r. black	40	30
452.		5000 r. on 20,000 r. blue	90	65
453.		5000 r. on 50,000 r. green	1·25	70
454.		5000 r. on 100,000 r. red	9·00	7·50
455.		10,000 r. on 500,000 r. brn.	6·50	5·00
456.		10,000 r. on 100,0,000 r. sepia	6·50	5·00

71. Liberty holding Coffee Leaves. 72. Ruy Barbosa.

1928. Introduction of the Coffee Plant. Bicent.

No.	Type	Description	Unused	Used
457.	71.	100 r. green	40	25
458.		200 r. red	35	25
459.		300 r. black	1·90	35

1928. Official stamps of 1919 surch.

No.	Type	Description	Unused	Used
460.	O 3.	700 r. on 500 r. orange	50	30
461.		1000 r. on 100 r. red	35	12
462.		2000 r. on 200 r. blue	40	12
463.		5000 r. on 50 r. green	55	20
464.		10,000 r. on 10 r. brown	2·50	60

1929.

No.	Type	Description	Unused	Used
468b.	72.	5000 r. blue	30	5

73. Santos Dumont's Airship. 74. Santos Dumont.

1929. Air.

No.	Type	Description	Unused	Used
469.	–	50 r. green	8	5
470.	73.	200 r. red	12	5
471.	–	300 r. blue	15	5
472.	–	500 r. purple	10	5
473.	–	1000 r. brown	70	10
479.	–	2000 r. green	65	8
480.	–	5000 r. red	1·10	10
481.	74.	10,000 r. grey	2·50	20

DESIGNS: 50 r. De Gusmao's monument. 300 r. A. Severo's airship "Pax". 500 r. S. Dumont's biplane "14 bis". 1000 r. R. de Barro's seaplane "Jahu", 2000 r. De Gusmao. 5000 r. A. Severo.

75. 76.

1930. Air.

No.	Type	Description	Unused	Used
486.	75.	3000 r. violet	60	12

1930. 4th Pan-American Architectural Congress.

No.	Type	Description	Unused	Used
487.	–	100 r. blue-green	60	30
488.	76.	200 r. grey	70	30
489.	–	300 r. red	1·40	40

DESIGNS: 100 r. Sun rays inscr. "ARCHITECTOS". 300 r. Architrave and Southern Cross.

77. G. Vargas and J. Pessoa. 78. O. Aranha.

1931. Charity. Revolution of 3rd Oct., 1930.
490. **77.** 10 r.+10 r. blue .. 5 5
491. 20 r.+20 r. brown .. 5 5
492. **78.** 50 r.+50 r. green, red and yellow 5 5
493. **77.** 100 r.+50 r. orange .. 8 8
494. 200 r.+100 r. green .. 10 8
495. – 300 r.+150 r. black green, yellow and red 12 8
496. **77.** 400 r.+200 r. red .. 15 12
497. 500 r.+250 r. blue .. 20 12
498. 600 r.+300 r. purple .. 25 20
499. – 700 r.+350 r. black, green, yellow and red 25 15
500. – 1 $+500 r. green, red and yellow 50 12
501. – 2 $+1 $ grey and red .. 2·10 25
502. – 5 $+2$500 r. blk. & red 6·50 2·25
503. – 10 $+5 $ green and yell. 8·00 4·00
DESIGNS: 300 r., 700 r. as T 77, but portraits in circles and frames altered. Milreis values as T 78 with different portraits and frames.

1931. No. 333 surch. **1931 200 Reis.**
507. **69.** 200 r. on 300 r. red .. 20 5

1931. Zeppelin Air Stamps. Surch. **ZEPPELIN** and value.
508. **73.** 2$500 on 200 r red (No. 470) .. .. 3·50 2·50
511. **72.** 3$500 on 5000 r. blue (No. 468b) .. .. 3·00 2·50
509. – 5$000 on 300 r. blue (No. 471) .. .. 3·50 2·50
512. **55.** 7$000 on 10,000 r. claret (No. 364) .. .. 3·00 2·50

1931. Air. No. 486 surch **2.500 REIS**.
510. **75.** 2500 r. on 3000 r. violet 3·00 3·00

79. Brazil.

1932. Colonization of Sao Vicente. 4th Cent.
513. **79.** 20 r. purple 10 8
514. – 100 r. black 20 12
515. – 200 r. violet 40 8
516. – 600 r. brown 80 25
517. – 700 r. blue 90 40
DESIGNS: 100 r. Natives. 200 r. M. Afonso de Souza. 600 r. King John III of Portugal. 700 r. Founding of Sao Vicente.

80. Soldier and Flag. **81.** "Justice".

1932. Sao Paulo Revolutionary Government issue.
518. – 100 r. chestnut 40 40
519. **80.** 200 r. red 40 30
520. – 300 r. green 50 50
521. – 400 r. blue 50 50
522. – 500 r. sepia 60 70
523. – 600 r. red 70 90
524. **80.** 700 r. violet 70 90
525. – 1000 r. orange 70 90
526. – 2000 r. brown .. .. 8·00 9·00
527. – 5000 r. green .. .. 10·00 11·00
528. **81.** 10,000 r. purple .. .. 12·00 12·00
DESIGNS—As T **80**: 100 r., 500 r. Map of Brazil. 300 r., 600 r. Symbolical of freedom, etc., 400 r., 1000 r. Soldier in tin helmet. As T **81**; 2000 r. "LEX" and sword. 5000 r. "Justice" and soldiers with bayonets.

82. Campo Bello Square and road memorial. Vassouras.

1933. Vassouras. Cent.
529. **82.** 200 r. red 30 15

83. Flag and Aeroplane.

1933. Air.
530. **83.** 3 $500 blue, grn. & yell. 75 25

1933. Surch. **200 REIS.**
536. **80.** 200 r. on 300 r. red .. 15 5

84. Flag of the Race.

1933. "Day of the Race".
537. **84.** 200 r. red 30 20

85. **86.** From Santos Dumont Statue, St. Cloud. **87.** Faith and Energy.

1933. 1st Eucharistic Congress.
538. **85.** 200 r. red 30 20

1933. Obligatory Tax for Airport Fund.
539. **86.** 100 r. maroon 12 5

1933.
540. **87.** 200 r. red 10 5
543. 200 r. violet 5 5

88. "Republic" and Flags. **89.** Santos Dumont Statue, St. Cloud.

1933. Visit of Pres. Justo of Argentina.
545. **88.** 200 r. blue 25 15
546. 400 r. green 40 30
547. 600 r. red .. .. 1·25 1·00
548 1000 r. violet .. .. 1·75 1·25

1934. 1st National Aviation Congress, Sao Paulo.
549. **89.** 200 r. blue 35 15

90. Exhibition Building. **91.**

1934. 7th Int. Exn., Rio de Janeiro.
550. **90.** 200 r. brown 35 20
551. 400 r. red 90 45
552. 700 r. blue 90 45
553. 1000 r. orange .. .. 1·75 70

1934. National Philatelic Exn. Imperf.
555. **91.** 200 r.+100 r. purple 25 25
556. 300 r.+100 r. red .. 25 25
557. 700 r.+100 r. blue .. 2·75 3·00
558. 1000 r.+100 r. black .. 2·75 3·00

92. Christ of Mt. Corcovado. **93.** Jose de Anchieta.

1934. Visit of Cardinal Pacelli.
559. **92.** 300 r. red .. .. 2·50 1·40
560. 700 r. blue .. .. 3·00 1·60

1934. Founding of Sao Paulo by Anchieta. 4th Cent.
561. **93.** 200 r. brown 60 20
562. 300 r. violet 40 20
563. 700 r. blue .. .. 1·10 70
564. 1000 r. green .. .. 1·25 80

94. **96.** Primitive Settlement.

1935. Visit of President Terra of Uruguay.
565. – 200 r. orange 40 20
566. **94.** 300 r. yellow 60 25
567. 700 r. blue .. .. 1·40 90
568. – 1000 r. violet .. .. 2·50 1·25
DESIGN—HORIZ. 200 r., 1000 r. Female figures as in T **94** and bridge.

1935. Pernambuco. 4th Cent.
569. **96.** 200 r. brown and claret 70 30
570. 300 r. olive and violet .. 70 30

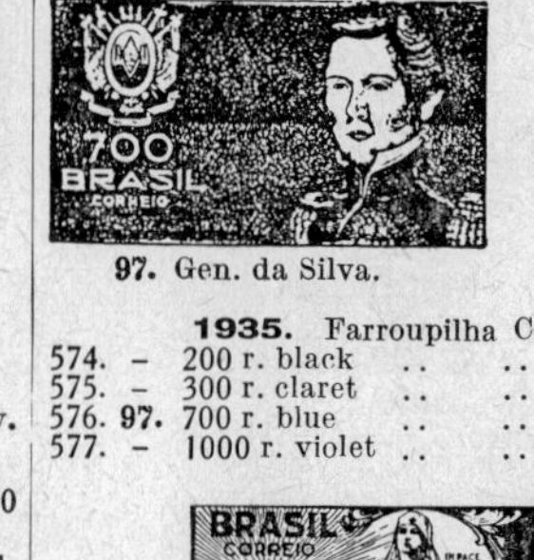

97. Gen. da Silva.

DESIGNS: 200 r., 300 r. Mounted Gaucho. 1000 r. Marshal Caxias.

1935. Farroupilha Cent.
574. – 200 r. black 40 30
575. – 300 r. claret 40 30
576. **97.** 700 r. blue .. .. 1·90 1·00
577. – 1000 r. violet .. .. 1·90 1·00

98. Nurse and Patient.

1935. 3rd Pan-American Red Cross Conference.
571. **98.** 200 r.+100 r. violet .. 70 45
572. 300 r.+100 r. brown .. 70 45
573. 700 r.+100 r. blue .. 4·00 2·50

99. Gavea.

1935. Children's Day.
578. **99.** 300 r. violet and brown 80 40
579. 300 r. turquoise & black 80 40
580. 300 r. blue and green 80 40
581. 300 r. black and red .. 80 40

100. Coutinho's Ship.

1935. Colonization of Espirito Santo. 400th Anniv.
583. **100.** 300 r. claret 45 25
584. – 700 r. blue 85 70
DESIGN—VERT. 700 r. Arms of Coutinho.

101. Federal District Coat-of-Arms.

1935. 8th Int. Fair.
582. **101.** 200 r. blue .. .. 1·00 40

101a. Viscount Cairu. **102.** Cameta.

1936. Cairu. Death Cent.
585. **101a.** 1200 r. violet .. 3·25 1·60

1936. Tercent. of Cameta.
586. **102.** 200 r. buff 55 35
587. 500 r. green 55 35

103. Coin Press. **104.** "Justice".

1936. Numismatic Congress, S. Paulo.
588. **103.** 300 r. brown 35 20

1936. First National Juridical Congress.
589. **104.** 300 r. red 30 20

105. C. Gomes.

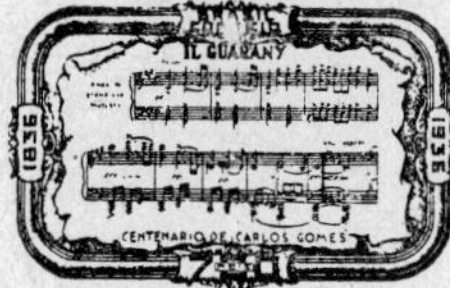

106. "Il Guarany".

1936. C. Gomes. Birth Cent.
590. **105.** 300 r. red 40 30
591. 300 r. brown 40 30
592. **106.** 700 r. blue .. .. 1·50 75
593. 700 r. buff .. .. 1·75 1·10

1936. 9th Int. Fair, Rio de Janeiro. As T **101** with inscription and date altered.
594. **101.** 200 r. red 35 25

107. Congress Seal. **108.** Botafogo Bay.

1936. 2nd Eucharistic Congress.
595. **107.** 300 r. blue, yellow, green and black .. 30 20

1937. Dr. Francisco Pereira Passos. Birth Cent.
596. **108.** 700 r. blue 40 20
597. 700 r. black 40 20

109. Esperanto Star and National Flags.

1937. 9th Brazilian Esperanto Congress.
598. **109.** 300 r. green 40 20

110. Bay of Rio de Janeiro. **111.**

1937. 2nd S. American Radio Conference.
599. **110.** 300 r. black and orange 25 15
600. 700 r. brown and blue 35 25

1937. Golden Jubilee of Esperanto.
601. **111.** 300 r. green 25 15

113. Iguazu Falls.

DESIGNS—HORIZ. 200 r., 2000 r. Monroe Palace, Rio. VERT. 300 r. 10,000 r. Botanical Gardens, Rio.

1937. Tourist Propaganda.
602. – 200 r. blue and brown 15 12
603. – 300 r. green & orange 25 12
604. **113.** 1000 r. brown & sepia 65 25
605. – 2000 r. red and green 1·50 80
606. **113.** 5000 r. green & black 8·00 2·10
607. – 10,000 r. blue and red 13·00 5·50

115. J. Da Silva Paes. **116.** Eagle and Shield.

1937. Rio Grande do Sul. Bicent.
608. **115.** 300 r. blue 20 15

1937. U.S. Constitution. 150th Anniv.
609. **116.** 400 r. blue 30 15

117. Coffee. **118.** "Grito" Memorial.

1938. Coffee Propaganda.
610. **117.** 1200 r. multicoloured 75 45

1938. Commem. of Abortive Proclamation of Republic.
611. **118.** 400 r. brown 50 20

119. Arms of Olinda.

1938. Olinda. 4th Cent.
612. **119.** 400 r. violet 25 12

120. Couto de Magalhaes. **121.** National Archives.

1938. De Megalhaes. Birth Cent.
613. **120.** 400 r. green 25 15

1938. National Archives Cent.
614. **121.** 400 r. brown 20 10

122. Rio de Janeiro. **123.** Santos.

1939.
615. **122.** 1200 r. purple .. 40 10

1939. Santos City. Cent.
616. **122.** 400 r. blue 25 15

124. Chalice-vine and Cup-of-gold Blossoms. **125.**

1939. 1st S. American Botanical Congress, Rio.
617. **124.** 400 r. green 45 20

1939. 3rd National Eucharistic Congress, Reafe.
618. **125.** 400 r. red 20 12

126. Duke of Caxias. **127.** Washington.

1939. Soldiers' Day.
619. **126.** 400 r. blue 20 12

1939. New York World's Fair. Inscr. "FEIRA MUNDIAL DE NOVA YORK".
620. **127.** 400 r. orange 30 12
621. – 800 r. green 20 8
633. – 1 m. violet 90 40
622. – 1200 r. red 30 10
623. – 1600 r. blue 35 15
634. – 5 m. red .. .. 1·00 60
635. – 10 m. slate .. .. 1·10 40
DESIGNS—HORIZ. 1200 r. Grover Cleveland. VERT. 800 r. Dom Pedro II. 1 m. Water lily. 1600 r. Statue of Liberty, Rio de Janeiro. 5 m. Bust of Pres. Vargas. 10 m. Relief map of Brazil.

128. Benjamin Constant. **131.** Roosevelt, Vargas and American Continents.

1939. Constitution. 50th Anniv.
624. **128.** 400 r. green 15 8
625. – 800 r. black 25 15
626. – 1200 r. brown .. 35 20
DESIGNS—VERT: 800 r. Marshal da Fonseca. HORIZ. 1200 r. Marshal and Pres Vargas.

1940. Pan-American Union. 50th Anniv.
631. **131.** 400 r. blue 60 30

132. Child and Southern Cross. **133.** Map of Brazil.

1940 Child Welfare.
627. – 100 r.+100 r. violet .. 30 25
628. – 200 r.+100 r. blue .. 50 35
629. **132.** 400 r.+200 r. olive .. 50 20
630. – 1,200 r.+400 r. red .. 2·10 75
DESIGNS: 100 r. Three Wise Men. 200 r. Angel and Child. 1,200 r. Mother and Child.

1940. 9th National Geographical Congress, Florianopolis.
632. **133.** 400 r. red 25 15

134. Two Workers. **136.** Brazilian Flags and Head of Liberty.

135. Acclaiming King John IV.

1940. Machado de Assis (writer). Birth Cent. As T 120, but portrait of de Assis, dated "1839–1939".
636. 400 r. black 20 12

1940. Colonization of Porto Alegre. Bicent.
637. **134.** 400 r. green 20 12

1940. Centenaries of Portugal (1140–1640–1940).
638. **135.** 1200 r. grey 35 15
See also Nos. 642/5.

1940. 10th Anniv. of Govt. of President Vargas.
639. **136.** 400 r. purple .. 20 12

137. Date of Fifth Census. **138.** Globe showing Spotlight on Brazil.

1941. 5th General Census.
640. **137.** 400 r. blue & red (post.) 20 10
641. **138.** 1200 r. brown (air) .. 75 15

139. Father Antonio Vieira.

1941. Centenaries of Portugal (2nd issue).
642. – 200 r. pink 15 10
643. **139.** 400 r. blue 15 8
644. – 800 r. violet 20 10
645. – 5400 r. green 50 25
DESIGNS-VERT. 200 r. Alfonso Henriques. 800 r. Governor-Gen. Benevides. HORIZ. 5400 r. Carmona and Vargas.

140. Father Jose Anchieta. **141.** Oil Wells. **142.** Count of Porto Alegre.

1941. Jesuits. 400th Anniv.
646. **140.** 1 m. violet 40 25

1941. Value in reis.
647. **141.** 10 r. orange 5 5
648. 20 r. olive 5 5
649. 50 r. brown 5 5
650. 100 r. turquoise .. 5 5
651. – 200 r. chestnut .. 5 5
652. – 300 r. claret .. 5 5
653. – 400 r. blue .. 5 5
654. – 500 r. red .. 8 5
655. – 600 r. violet .. 10 5
656. – 700 r. red .. 10 5
657. – 1000 r. grey .. 10 5
658. – 1200 r. blue .. 10 5
659. – 2000 r. purple .. 12 5
660. – 5000 r. blue .. 30 5
661. **142.** 10,000 r. red .. 65 5
662. – 20,000 r. brown .. 90 12
663. – 50 m. red .. 2·00 30
664. – 100 m. blue .. 30 25
DESIGNS: 200 r. to 500 r. Wheat harvesting machinery. 600 r. to 1200 r. Smelting works. 2000 r. "Commerce". 5000 r. Marshal F. Peixoto. 20,000 r. Admiral Maurity. 50 m. "Armed Forces". 100 m. Pres. Vargas.
For stamps with values in centavos and cruzeiros see Nos. 751, etc.

143. Amador Bueno. **144.** Brazilian Air Force Emblem.

1941. Amador Bueno as King of S. Paulo. 300th Anniv.
665. **143.** 400 r. black 25 10

1941. Aviation Week.
666. **144.** 5400 r. green 80 40

1941. Air. Pres. Vargas' New Constitution. 4th Anniv. Optd. **AERO "10 Nov." 937–941.**
667. 5400 r. green (No. 642) 70 30

145. Bernardino de Campos. **146.** Indo-Brazilian Cattle.

1942. B. de Campos and P. de Morais (lawyers and statesmen). 100th Birth Anniv.
670. **145.** 1000 r. red 75 25
671. – 1200 r. blue 95 25
PORTRAIT: 1200 r. Prudente de Morais.

1942. 2nd Agriculture and Cattle Show, Uberaba.
668a. **146.** 200 r. blue 15 10
669a. 400 r. brown 20 12

147. Torch of Learning. **148.** Map of Brazil showing Goiania.

1942. 8th National Education Congress.
672. **147.** 400 r. brown 15 10

1942. Founding of Goiania City.
673. **148.** 400 r. violet 20 10

149. Congressional Seal. **150.** Tributaries of R. Amazon.

1942. 4th National Eucharistic Congress, Sao Paulo.
674. **149.** 400 r. brown 25 12

1942. Air. Pres. Vargas' New Constitution. 5th Anniv. No. 645 surch. **AEREO "10 Nov." 937–942** and value.
675. 5 cr. 40 on 5,400 r. green 70 25

1943. Discovery of River Amazon. 400th Anniv.
676. **150.** 40 c. brown 20 10

151. Early Brazilian Stamp. **152.** Memorial Tablet.

1943. Petropolis Cent.
677. **151.** 40 c. violet 30 12

1943. Air. Visit of Pres. Morinigo of Paraguay.
678. **152.** 1 cr. 20 blue 35 15

153. Do Amaral. **154.** Indo-Brazilian Cattle.

1943. Ubaldino do Amaral. Birth Cent.
687. **153.** 40 c. grey 15 12

1943. 9th Cattle Show, Bahia.
688. **154.** 40 c. brown .. 25 15

155. Map of S. America showing Brazil. **156.** Book of the Law.

1943. Air. Visit of President Penaranda of Bolivia.
679. **155.** 1 cr. 20 black, green red and yellow .. 35 20

1943. Air. Inter-American Advocates Conference.
686. **156.** 1 cr. 20 red and brown 20 10

157. "Bull's-eye".

158.

1943. Brazilian Stamp Cent.

(a) Postage, Imperf.

680. **157.** 30 c. black 30 20
681. 60 c. black 30 20
682. 90 c. black 30 25

(b) Air. Perf.

683. **158.** 1 cr. black and yellow 1·60 1·10
684. 2 cr. black and green .. 2·10 1·10
685. 5 cr. black and red .. 2·50 1·10

159. Justice and Seal. **160.** Santa Casa de Misericordia Hospital.

1943. Institute of Brazilian Lawyers. Cent.

689. **159.** 2 cr. red 35 20

1943. Santa Casa de Misericordia Hospital, Santos. 400th Anniv.

690. **160.** 1 cr. blue 20 12

161. Barbosa Rodrigues. **162.** Pedro Americo.

1943. B. Rodrigues (botanist). Birth Cent.

691. **161.** 40 c. green 20 12

1943. Americo (artist and author). Birth Cent.

692. **162.** 40 c. brown 12 8

1944. Air. No. 629 surch. **AEREO** and value.

693. **132.** 20 c. on 400 r. + 200 r. 25 10
694. 40 c. on 400 r. + 200 r. 30 10
695. 60 c. on 400 r. + 200 r. 40 25
696. 1 cr. on 400 r. + 200 r. 60 30
697. 1 cr. 20 on 400 r. + 200 r. 70 30

163. Gen. Carneiro and Defenders of Lapa. **164.** Baron do Rio Branco.

1944. Siege of Lapa. 50th Anniv.

698. **163.** 1 cr. 20 c. red 20 15

1944. Monument to Baron do Rio Branco. Inaug.

699. **164.** 1 cr. blue 20 15

165. Duke of Caxias. **166.** Emblems of Y.M.C.A.

1944. Pacification of Revolutionary Uprising of 1842. Cent.

700. **165.** 1 cr. 20 green & yellow 25 15

1944. Y.M.C.A. Cent.

701. **166.** 40 c. blue, red & yell. 15 10

167. Rio Grande Chamber of Commerce. **168.** "Bartolomeo de Gusmao and the Aerostat".

1944.

702. **167.** 40 c. brown 20 12

1944. Air Week.

703. **168.** 1 cr. 20 red 30 15

169. Martim F. R. de Andrada. **170.** Meeting between Caxias and Canabarro.

1945. M. de Andrada (statesman). Death Cent.

704. **169.** 40 c. blue 20 15

1945. Pacification of Rio Grande do Sul. Cent.

705. **170.** 40 c. blue 20 12

171. Dr. L. L. Zamenhof. **172.** Baron do Rio Branco (statesman).

1945. 10th Brazilian Esperanto Congress Rio de Janeiro.

706. – 40 c. green (postage) .. 20 12
707. **171.** 1 cr. 20 brown (air) .. 25 10

DESIGN: 40 c. Woman and map.

1945. Baron do Rio Branco. Birth Cent.

708. – 40 c. blue (postage) .. 20 12
709. – 1 cr. 20 purple (air) .. 20 12
710. **172.** 5 cr. purple 40 20

DESIGNS—HORIZ. 40 c. Bookplate view of Rio de Janeiro Harbour. VERT. 1 cr. 20, Map of S. America.

173. "Glory". **174.** "Co-operation".

1945. Victory of United Nations. Roul.

711. – 20 c. violet 12 5
712. **173.** 40 c. red 15 5
713. – 1 cr. orange 20 10
714. – 2 cr. blue 25 15
715. **174.** 5 cr. green 60 30

SYMBOLICAL DESIGNS—VERT. 20 c. (inscr. "SAUDADE"), "Salute to the Dead". HORIZ. 1 cr. (inscr. "VITORIA"), Flags of the U.N. 2 cr. (inscr. "PAZ"), Head of Liberty.

175. F. M. da Silva. **176.** Bahia Institute.

1945. Francisco Manoel da Silva (composer of Brazilian National Anthem). 150th Birth Anniv.

716. **175.** 40 c. red 15 10

1945. Institute of Geography and History, Bahia. 50th Anniv.

717. **176.** 40 c. blue 15 10

ILLUSTRATIONS
British Commonwealth and all overprints and surcharges are FULL SIZE. Foreign Countries have been reduced to ¾-LINEAR.

177. Wireless Mast and map.

1945. 3rd Inter-American Radio Communication Conf.

723. **177.** 1 cr. 20 black 30 12

177a. 5th Army Shoulder Flash. **178.** "V" Sign and Shoulder Flashes.

1945. Return of Brazilian Expeditionary Force.

718. **177a.** 20 c. blue, red & grn. 8 5
719. – 40 c. green, yell., blue and red 10 5
720. – 1 cr. blue, red, green and yellow .. 30 15
721. – 2 cr. blue, yellow, green and red .. 40 20
722. **178.** 5 cr. blue, red, green and yellow .. 75 35

DESIGNS (embodying shoulder flashes)—As T 177a: 40 c. B.E.F. flash. As T 178. HORIZ. 1 cr. U.S.A. flag. 2 cr. Brazilian flag.

179. Saldanha da Gama. **180.** "Liberty".

1946. Admiral S. da Gama. Birth Cent.

724. **179.** 40 c. grey 10 10

1946. New Constitution.

734. **180.** 40 c. grey 8 5

181. Princess Isabel d'Orleans-Braganza. **182.** P.O., Rio de Janeiro.

184. Aeroplane over Bay of Rio de Janeiro.

1946. Princess Isabel d'Orleans-Braganza. Birth Cent.

725. **181.** 40 c. black 12 10

1946. 5th P.U. Congress of the Americas and Spain.

726. – 40 c. orange and black 15 8
727. **184.** 1 cr. 30 orge. & green 15 10
728. 1 cr. 70 orange and red 20 12
729. **183.** 2 cr. blue and slate .. 20 10
730. **184.** 2 cr. 20 orange & blue 25 12
731. **183.** 5 cr. blue and brown .. 60 40
732. 10 cr. blue and violet .. 90 50

DESIGN—(25×37 mm.): 40 c. Post-horn, V and envelope.

185. Proposed Columbus Lighthouse. **186.** Orchid.

1946. Construction of Columbus Lighthouse, Dominican Republic.

733. **185.** 5 cr. blue .. .. 1·00 55

1946. 4th National Exn. of Orchids, Rio de Janeiro.

735. **186.** 40 c. blue, red & yellow 25 15

187. Gen. A. E. Gomes Carneiro. **188.** Academy of Arts.

1946. Gen. Carneiro. Birth Cent.

736. **187.** 40 c. green 8 5

1946. Academy of Arts. 50th Anniv.

737. **188.** 40 c. blue 10 5

189. Antonio de Castro Alves. **190.** Pres. Gonzalez.

1947. Alves (poet). Birth Cent.

738. **189.** 40 c. blue-green .. 8 5

1947. Visit of Chilean President.

739. **190.** 40 c. brown 8 5

191. Pres. Truman, Map of S. America and Statue of Liberty.

1947. Visit of U.S. President.

742. **191.** 40 c. blue 12 8

192. "Peace and Security." **193.** "Dove of Peace".

1947. Inter-American Defence Conference, Petropolis.

740. **192.** 1 cr. 20 blue (postage) 10 8
741. **193.** 2 cr. 20 green (air) .. 25 15

194. Pres. Enrico Gaspar Dutra. **195.** Woman and Child.

1947. Commemorating Pres. Dutra.

743. **194.** 20 c. green 8 5
744. 40 c. red 10 5
745. 1 cr. 20 blue 15 10

1947. Children's Week. 1st Brazilian Infant Welfare Convention.

747. **195.** 40 c. blue 12 5

196. Icarus.

1947. Obligatory Tax. "Week of the Wing" Aviation Fund.

748. **196.** 40 c. + 10 c. orange .. 12 5

197. Santos Dumont Monument, St. Cloud, France.

198. Arms of Belo Horizonte.

1947. Air. Homage to Santos Dumon
749. 197. 1 cr. 20 c. chest. & grn. 15 10

1947. City of Belo Horizonte. (50th Anniv.)
750. 198. 1 cr. 20 c. red.. 12 8

1947. As postage stamps of 1941, but values in centavos or cruzeiros.

751.	141.	2 c. olive	5	5
752.		5 c. brown	5	5
753.		10 c. turquoise ..	5	5
754.	–	20 c. chestnut (No. 651)	5	5
755.	–	30 c. claret (No. 652)..	5	5
756.	–	40 c. blue (No. 653) ..	5	5
757.	–	50 c. red (No. 654) ..	5	5
758.	–	60 c. violet (No. 655)..	5	5
759.	–	70 c. red (No. 656) ..	5	5
760.	–	1 cr. grey (No. 657) ..	5	5
761.	–	1 cr. 20 blue (No. 658)	5	5
762.	–	2 cr. purple (No. 659)..	10	5
763.	–	5 cr. blue (No. 660) ..	45	5
764.	142.	10 cr. red	50	5
765.	–	20 cr. brown (No. 662)	60	5
766.	–	50 cr. red (No. 663) ..	3·25	15

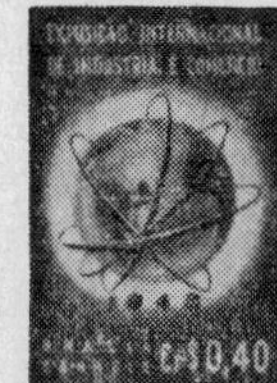

199. Bay of Rio de Janeiro and Rotary Symbol. 200. Globe.

261. Quitandinha Hotel.

1948. Air. Rotary Congress.
769. 199. 1 cr. 20 claret.. .. 20 15
770. 3 cr. 80 violet.. .. 50 25

1948. Int. Industrial and Commercial Exn., Petropolis.
771. 200. 40 c. grn. & mve. (post) 8 5
772. 201. 1 cr. 20 brown (air) .. 15 12
773. 3 cr. 80 violet .. 30 15

202. President Berres.

1948. Air. Visit of Uruguayan President.
777. 202. 1 cr. 70 blue 15 10

203. Three Muses.

204. Girl Reading.

1948. Air. National School of Music. Cent.
776. 203. 1 cr. 20 blue 15 10

1948. National Children's Campaign.
775. 204. 40 c. green 15 8

205. Arms of Paranagua.

206. Eucharistic Congress Seal.

1948. Founding of Paranagua. Tercent.
774. 205. 5 cr. brown 90 30

1948. Air. 5th National Eucharistic Congress, Porto Alegre.
779. 206. 1 cr. 20 purple .. 20 12

207. Ram.

208. " Tiradentes ".

1948. Air. Int. Cattle Show, Bage.
778. 207. 1 cr. 20 orange .. 25 12

1948. J. J. da Silva Xavier (patriot). Birth Bicent.
780. 208. 40 c. orange 8 5

209. Crab and Globe.

210. Adult Student.

1948. Anti-Cancer Campaign.
781. 209. 40 c. purple 10 5

1949. Campaign for Adult Education.
782. 210. 60 c. purple 10 5

211. Battle of Guararapes.

1949. 2nd Battle of Guararapes. Tercent.
783. 211. 60 c. blue (postage) .. 30 15
784. – 1 cr. 20, pink (air) .. 70 20
DESIGN: 1 cr. 20, View of Guararapes.

212. St. Francis of Paula Church.

213. Father Nobrega.

214. De Souza meeting Indians.

215. Franklin D. Roosevelt.

1949. Founding of Ouro Fino. Bicent.
785. 212. 60 c. brown 12 8

1949. Founding of Bahia. 4th Cent.
(a) Postage. Imperf.
786. 213. 60 c. violet 8 5
(b) Air. Perf.
787. 214. 1 cr. 20 c. blue .. 15 10

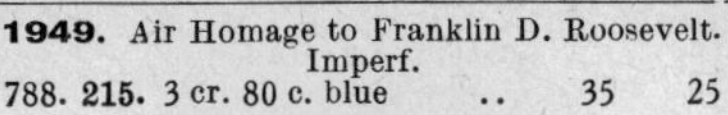

1949. Air Homage to Franklin D. Roosevelt. Imperf.
788. 215. 3 cr. 80 c. blue .. 35 25

216. Aeroplane and Air Force Badge.

1949. Homage to Brazilian Air Force. Imperf.
789. 216. 60 c. violet 8 5

217. Joaquim Nabuco.

218. " Revelation ".

1949. Air. J. Nabuco (lawyer and author). Birth Cent.
790. 217. 3 cr. 80 c. purple .. 30 20

1949. 1st Sacerdotal Vocational Congress, Bahia.
791. 218. 60 c. magenta .. 8 5

219. Globe.

1949. U.P.U. 75th Anniv.
792. 219. 1 cr. 50 blue 20 8

220. Ruy Barbosa.

221. Cardinal Arcoverde.

222. " Agriculture and Industry ".

223. Virgin of the Globe.

1949. Barbosa (statesman). Birth Cent.
793. 220. 1 cr. 20 red 20 8

1950. Arcoverde's Birth Cent.
794. 221. 60 c. pink 8 5

1950. Italian Immigration into Rio Grande do Sul. 75th Anniv.
795. 222. 60 c. claret 10 5

1950. Establishment of Daughters of Charity of St. Vincent de Paul. Cent.
796. 223. 60 c. blue and black .. 12 5

224. Globe and Footballers. 225. Stadium.

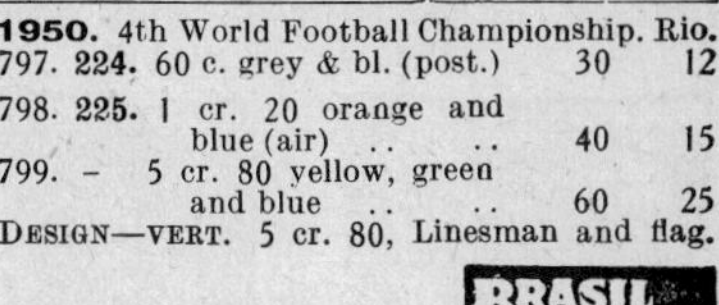

1950. 4th World Football Championship. Rio.
797. 224. 60 c. grey & bl. (post.) 30 12
798. 225. 1 cr. 20 orange and blue (air) 40 15
799. – 5 cr. 80 yellow, green and blue 60 25
DESIGN—VERT. 5 cr. 80, Linesman and flag.

226. Map and Graph. 227. Map.

1950. National Survey, 1950.
800. 226. 60 c. claret (postage) 8 5
801. 227. 1 cr. 20 brown (air) .. 12 8

228. O. Cruz.

229. Blumenau and Itajai River.

1950. 5th Int. Microbiological Congress.
802. 228. 60 c. brown 8 5

1950. Blumenau. Cent.
803. 229. 60 c. pink 8 5

230. Government Offices.

231. Arms.

1950. Amazon Province. Cent.
804. 230. 60 c. red 8 5

1950. Juiz de Fora City. Cent.
805. 231. 60 c. red 8 5

232. P.O. Building, Recife.

1951. Head Post Office, Pernambuco Province. Inaug.
806. 232. 60 c. red 8 5
807. 1 cr. 20 red 12 8

233. Arms of Joinville.

234. Heart and Flowers.

1951. Joinville. Cent.
808. 233. 60 c. brown 8 5

1951. Mothers' Day.
811. 234. 60 c. purple 10 8

235. De La Salle.

236. S. Romero.

1951. Jean-Baptiste de la Salle (educator). Birth Tercent.
810. 235. 60 c. blue 10 8

1951. Sylvio Romero (poet). Birth Cent.
809. **236.** 60 c. brown 8 5

237. J. Caetano and Stage.

238. O. A. Derby.

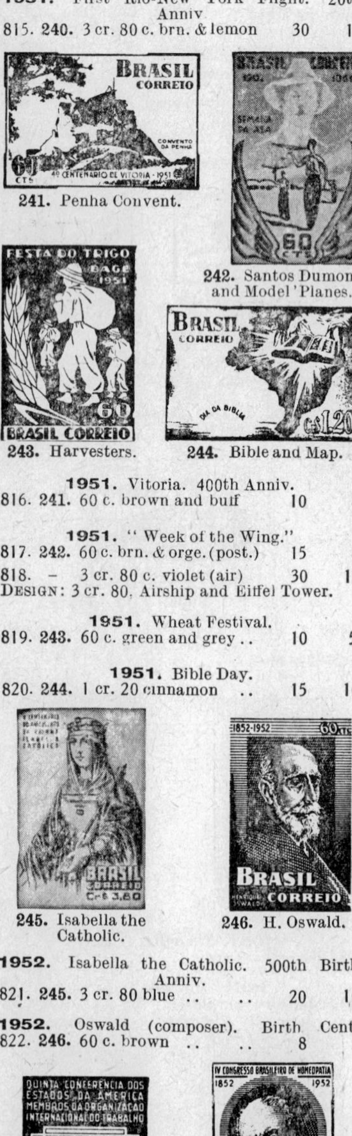

239. Cross and Congregation.

240. Pilot and Map.

1951. 1st Brazilian Theatrical Congress.
812. **237.** 60 c. blue 8 5

1951. Derby (geologist). Birth Cent.
813. **238.** 2 cr. slate 12 8

1951. 4th Inter-American Catholic Education Congress
814. **239.** 60 c. brown and buff 8 5

1951. First Rio-New York Flight. 20th Anniv.
815. **240.** 3 cr. 80 c. brn. & lemon 30 15

241. Penha Convent.

242. Santos Dumont and Model 'Planes.

243. Harvesters.

244. Bible and Map.

1951. Vitoria. 400th Anniv.
816. **241.** 60 c. brown and buff 10 8

1951. "Week of the Wing."
817. **242.** 60 c. brn. & orge. (post.) 15 8
818. – 3 cr. 80 c. violet (air) 30 12
DESIGN: 3 cr. 80, Airship and Eiffel Tower.

1951. Wheat Festival.
819. **243.** 60 c. green and grey .. 10 5

1951. Bible Day.
820. **244.** 1 cr. 20 cinnamon .. 15 10

245. Isabella the Catholic.

246. H. Oswald.

1952. Isabella the Catholic. 500th Birth Anniv.
821. **245.** 3 cr. 80 blue 20 10

1952. Oswald (composer). Birth Cent.
822. **246.** 60 c. brown 8 5

247. Map and Symbol of Labour.

248. Dr. L. Cardoso.

1952. 5th Conf. of American Members of Int. Labour Organization.
823. **247.** 1 cr. 50 c. claret .. 12 8

1952. Cardoso (scientist) Birth Cent. and 4th Brazilian Homoeopathic Congress, Porto Alegre.
824. **248.** 60 c. blue 8 5

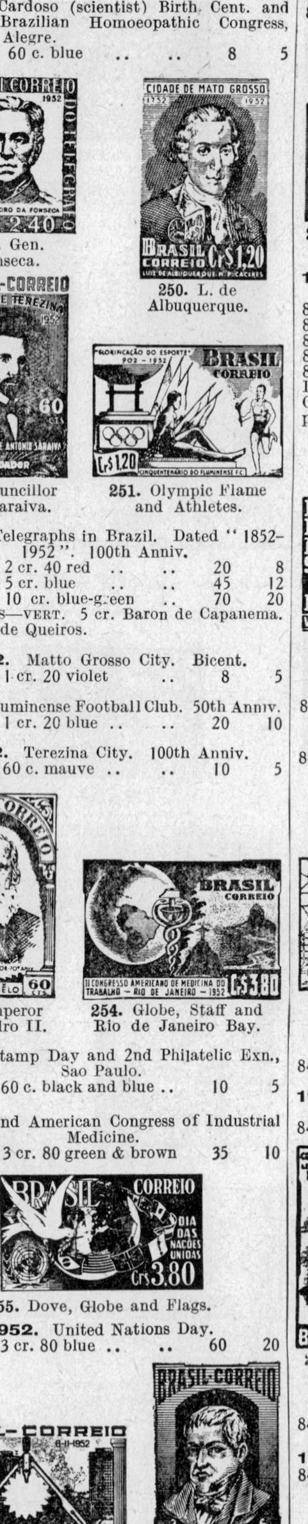

249. Gen. Fonseca.

250. L. de Albuquerque.

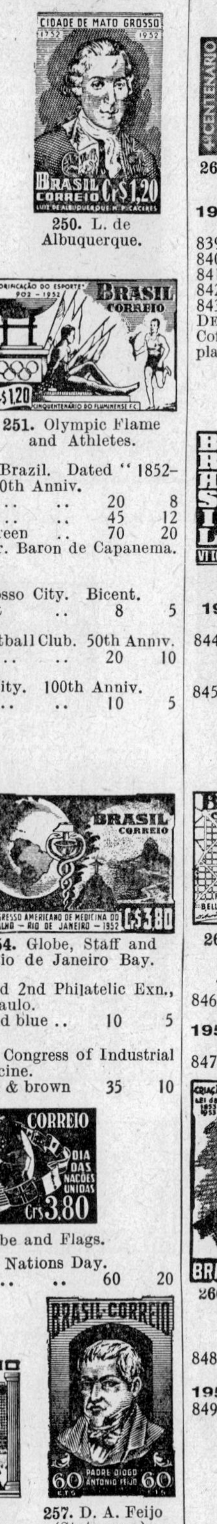

252. Councillor J. A. Saraiva.

251. Olympic Flame and Athletes.

1952. Telegraphs in Brazil. Dated "1852–1952". 100th Anniv.
825. **249.** 2 cr. 40 red 20 8
826. – 5 cr. blue 45 12
827. – 10 cr. blue-green .. 70 20
PORTRAITS—VERT. 5 cr. Baron de Capanema. 10 cr. E. de Queiros.

1952. Matto Grosso City. Bicent.
828. **250.** 1 cr. 20 violet .. 8 5

1952. Fluminense Football Club. 50th Anniv.
829. **251.** 1 cr. 20 blue 20 10

1952. Terezina City. 100th Anniv.
830. **252.** 60 c. mauve 10 5

253. Emperor Dom Pedro II.

254. Globe, Staff and Rio de Janeiro Bay.

1952. Stamp Day and 2nd Philatelic Exn., Sao Paulo.
831. **253.** 60 c. black and blue .. 10 5

1952. 2nd American Congress of Industrial Medicine.
832. **254.** 3 cr. 80 green & brown 35 10

255. Dove, Globe and Flags.

1952. United Nations Day.
833. **255.** 3 cr. 80 blue 60 20

256. Compasses and Modern Buildings.

257. D. A. Feijo (Statesman).

1952. City Planning Day.
834. **256.** 60 c. yell., grn. & blue 10 5

1952. Homage to D. A. Feijo.
835. **257.** 60 c. brown 8 5

258. Father Damien.

259. R. Bernardelli.

1952. Obligatory Tax. Leprosy Research Fund.
836. **258.** 10 c. brown 8 5
837. 10 c. green 5 5

1952. Bernardelli (Sculptor). Birth Cent.
838. **259.** 60 c. blue 5 5

260. Arms of Sao Paulo and Settler.

261. "Expansion".

1953. Founding of Sao Paulo. 400th Anniv. (1st issue).
839. **260.** 1 cr. 20 black & brown 12 5
840. – 2 cr. green and yellow 80 20
841. – 2 cr. 80 brown & orange 20 8
842. **261.** 3 cr. 80 brown & green 20 10
843. 5 cr. 80 blue and green 30 12
DESIGNS—VERT. (Inscr. as T 261): 2 cr. Coffee blossom and berries. 2 cr. 80, Monk planting tree.

262.

263. J. Ramalho.

1953. 6th Brazilian Accountancy Congress, Port Alegre.
844. **262.** 1 cr. 20 brown .. 10 5

1953. Santo Andre City. 4th Cent.
845. **263.** 60 c. blue 8 5

264. A. Reis and Plan of Belo Horizonte.

265. The "Admiral Saldanha".

1953. A. Reis (engineer). Birth Cent.
846. **264.** 1 cr. 20 brown .. 8 5

1953. 4th Voyage of Circumnavigation by Training Ship "Admiral Saldanha".
847. **265.** 1 cr. 50 blue 12 5

266. Viscount de Itaborahy.

267. Lamp and Rio-Petropolis Highway.

1953. Bank of Brazil Cent.
848. **266.** 1 cr. 20 violet .. 10 5

1953. 10 Int. Nursing Congress, Petropolis.
849. **267.** 1 cr. 20 grey .. 10 5

268. Bay of Rio de Janeiro.

1953. 4th World Conf. of Young Baptists.
850. **268.** 3 cr. 80 c. blue-green 15 8

INDEX

Countries can be quickly located by referring to the index at the end of this volume.

269. Arms and Map.

270. Ministry of Health and Education.

1953. Jau City. Cent.
852. **269.** 1 cr. 20 violet .. 8 5

1953. Stamp Day and 1st National Philatelic Exn. of Education.
851. **270.** 1 cr. 20 blue-green .. 8 5

271. Maria Quiteria de Jesus.

272. Pres. Odria.

1953. Maria Quiteria de Jesus Death Cent.
853. **271.** 60 c. blue 8 5

1953. Visit of President of Peru.
854. **272.** 1 cr. 40 maroon .. 8 5

273. Caxias leading Troops.

274. Quill-pen and Map.

1953. Duke of Caxias. 150th Birth Anniv. Inscr. "1803–1953".
855. **273.** 60 c. blue-green .. 12 5
856. – 1 cr. 20 purple .. 12 5
857. – 1 cr. 70 blue 12 5
858. – 3 cr. 80 brown .. 20 10
859. – 5 cr. 80 violet .. 30 10
DESIGNS: 1 cr. 20, Tomb. 1 cr. 70, 5 cr. 80, Portrait. 3 cr. 80, Arms.

1953. 5th National Congress of Journalists, Curitiba.
860. **274.** 60 c. blue 10 5

275. H. Hora.

276. President Somoza.

1953. H. Hora (painter). Birth Cent.
861. **275.** 60 c. purple and orange 10 5

1953. Visit of President of Nicaragua.
862. **276.** 1 cr. 40 maroon .. 10 5

277. A. de Saint-Hilaire.

278. J. do Patrocinio and "Spirit of Emancipation".

1953. A de Saint-Hilaire (explorer and botanist). Death Cent.
863. **277.** 1 cr. 20 lake 10 5

1953. J. do Patrocinio (slavery abolitionist).
864. **278.** 60 c. slate 8 5

279. Clock Tower, Crato.

280. C. de Abreu.

1953. Crato City. Cent.
865. 279. 60 c. green 8 5

1953. Abreu (historian). Birth Cent.
866. 280. 60 c. blue 8 5
867. 5 cr. violet 20 8

281. "Justice".

282. Harvesting.

1953. Treaty of Petropolis. 50th Anniv.
868. 281. 60 c. indigo 8 5
869. 1 cr. 20 purple 12 8

1953. 3rd National Wheat Festival, Erechim.
870. 282. 60 c. blue-green .. 8 5

283. Teacher and Pupils.

284. Porters with Trays of Coffee Beans.

1953. 1st National Congress of Elementary School-teachers.
871. 283. 60 c. red 8 5

1953. Cent. of Political Emancipation of Parana. Inscr. "CENTENARIO DO PARANA".
872a. – 2 cr. brown and black 30 20
873. 284. 5 cr. orange and black 35 10
DESIGN: 2 cr. Portrait of Z. de Gois e Vasconcellos.

285. A. de Gusmao.

286. Growth of Sao Paulo.

287. Sao Paulo and Arms.

1954. De Gusmao (statesman). Death Bicent.
874. 285. 1 cr. 20 purple .. 8 5

1954. 400th Anniv of Founding of Sao Paulo (2nd issue). Inscr. "1554–1954".
875. 286. 1 cr. 20 chocolate .. 20 8
876. – 2 cr. magenta.. .. 35 10
877. – 2 cr. 80 slate 25 10
878. 287. 3 cr. 80 green .. 30 12
879. 5 cr. 80 red 30 15
DESIGNS—VERT. 2 cr. Priest, settler and Indian. 2 cr. 80, J. de Anchieta.

288. J. F. Vieira, A. V. de Negreiros, A. F. Camarao and H. Dias.

1954. Recovery from the Dutch of Pernambuco. 3rd Cent.
880. 288. 1 cr. 20 blue 12 8

289. Sao Paulo and Allegorical Figure.

1954. 10th Int. Congress of Scientific Organization, Sao Paulo.
881. 289. 1 cr. 50 purple .. 10 5

290. Grapes and Winejar.

291. Immigrants' Monument.

1954. Grape Festival, Rio Grande do Sul.
882. 290. 40 c. lake 8 5

1954. Immigrants' Monument, Rio Caxias do Sul.
883. 291. 60 c. violet 8 5

292. First Loco used in Brazil.

293. Pres. Chamoun.

1954. Brazilian Railways Cent.
884. 292. 40 c. red 20 8

1954. Visit of President of Lebanon.
885. 293. 1 cr. 50 lake .. 10 5

294. Sao Jose College, Rio de Janeiro.

295. Vel Marcelino Champagnat.

296. Apolonia Pinto.

297. Admiral Tamandare.

1954. Marists in Brazil. 50th Anniv.
886. 294. 60 c. violet 8 5
887. 295. 1 cr. 20 blue 15 8

1954. Apolonia Pinto (actress). Birth Cent.
888. 296. 1 cr. 20 emerald .. 8 5

1954. Portraits.
889. 297. 2 c. blue 8 5
890. 5 c. vermilion.. .. 5 5
891. 10 c. green 5 5
892. – 20 c. claret 5 5
893. – 30 c. slate 5 5
894. – 40 c. red 5 5
895. – 50 c. lilac 8 5
896. – 60 c. blue-green .. 5 5
897. – 90 c. salmon 25 8
898. – 1 cr. brown 12 5
899. – 1 cr. 50 blue 5 5
900. – 2 cr. green 15 5
901. – 5 cr. purple 12 5
902. – 10 cr. green 12 5
903. – 20 cr. red 20 5
904. – 50 cr. blue 35 5
PORTRAITS—20 c., 30 c., 40 c. O. Cruz. 50 c. to 90 c. J. Murtinho. 1 cr., 1 cr. 50 c., 2 cr. Duke of Caxias. 5 cr., 10 cr. R. Barbosa. 20 cr., 50 cr. J. Bonifacio.

298. Boy Scout.

299. B. Fernandes.

300. Cardinal Piazza.

1954. Int. Scout (Patrol) Camp, Sao Paulo.
905. 298. 1 cr. 20 blue 20 10

1954. Sorocaba City Tercent.
906. 299. 60 c. red 8 5

1954. Visit of Cardinal Piazza.
907. 300. 4 cr. 20 red 15 8

301. Virgin and Map.

302. Benjamin Constant and Braille Book.

1954. Marian Year. Inscr. "ANO MARIANO".
908. 301. 60 c. lake 30 12
909. – 1 cr. 20 blue 40 12
DESIGN: 1 cr. 20, Virgin and globe.
No. 909 also commemorates the Centenary of the Proclamation of the Dogma of the Immaculate Conception.

1954. Education for the Blind in Brazil. Cent.
910. 302. 60 c. myrtle .. 8 5

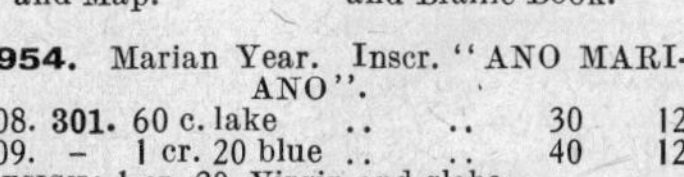

303. Battle Scene. 304. Admiral Barroso.

1954. Barroso. 150th Birth Anniv.
911. 303. 40 c. claret 10 5
912. 304. 60 c. violet 12 5

305. S. Hahnemann (physician).

306. Nisia Floresta (suffragist).

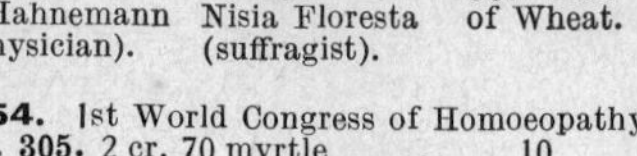
307. Ears of Wheat.

1954. 1st World Congress of Homoeopathy.
913. 305. 2 cr. 70 myrtle .. 10 5

1954. Removal of Ashes of Floresta from France to Brazil.
914. 306. 60 c. magenta .. 5 5

1954. 4th Wheat Festival, Carazinho.
915. 307. 60 c. olive 8 5

308. Globe and Basketball Player.

309. Girl, Torch and Spring Flowers.

310. Father Bento.

1954. 2nd World Basketball Championship.
916. 308. 1 cr. 40 vermilion .. 12 8

1954. 6th Spring Games.
917. 309. 60 c. chocolate .. 10 5

1954. Leprosy Research Fund.
918. 310. 10 c. blue 5 5
919. 10 c. magenta 5 5
919a. 10 c. salmon 5 5
919b. 10 c. green 5 5
919c. 10 c. lilac 5 5
919d. 10 c. brown 5 5
919e. 10 c. slate 5 5
919f. 2 cr. lake 5 5
919g. 2 cr. lilac 5 5
919h. 2 cr. orange 5 5
See also Nos. 1239/40.

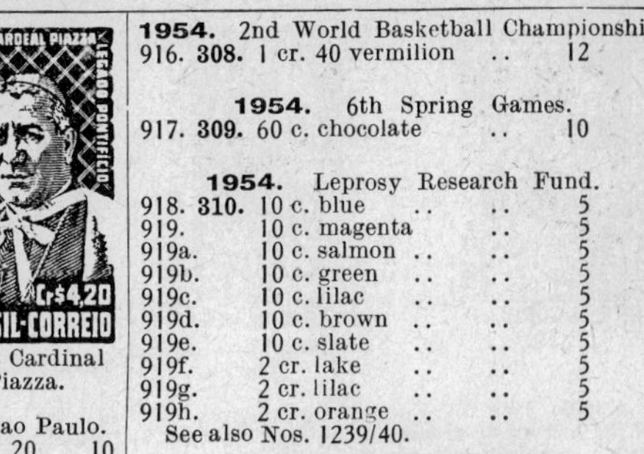

311. S. Francisco Power Station.

1955. S. Francisco Power Station Inaug.
920. 311. 60 c. orange 5 5

312. Itutinga Power Plant.

1955. Itutinga Hydro-Electric Station. Inaug.
921. 312. 40 c. blue 5 5

313. Rotary Symbol and Rio Bay.

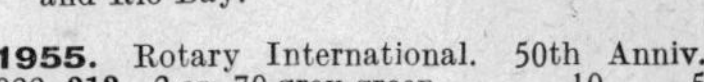
314. Aviation Symbols.

1955. Rotary International. 50th Anniv.
922. 313. 2 cr. 70 grey-green .. 10 5

1955. 3rd Aeronautical Congress, Sao Paulo.
923. 314. 60 c. blue-green .. 5 5

315. Fausto Cardoso Palace.

1955. Aracaiu. Cent.
924. 315. 40 c. chestnut .. 5 5

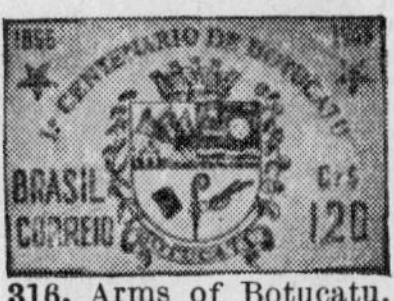
316. Arms of Botucatu.

1955. Botucatu. Cent.
925. 316. 60 c. chestnut .. 5 5
926. 1 cr. 20 green 8 5

317. Young Athletes.

318. Marshal Da Fonseca.

1955. 5th Children's Games, Rio de Janeiro.
927. 317. 60 c. chestnut .. 12 5

1955. Marshal Da Fonseca. Birth Cent.
928. 318. 60 c. violet 5 5

319. **319a.** Cardinal Masella.

1955. 36th Int. Eucharistic Congress.
929. **319.** 1 cr. 40 green 5 5
930. – 2 cr. 70 lake (St. Pascoal) 10 5

1955. Visit of Cardinal Masella (Papal Legate) to Eucharistic Congress.
931. **319a.** 4 cr. 20 blue 15 5

320. Gymnasts.

1955. 7th Spring Games.
932. **320.** 60 c. mauve 12 5

321. Monteiro Lobato. **322.** Lt.-Col. T. C. Vilagran Cabrita.

1955. Honouring M. Lobato (author).
933. **321.** 40 c. green 5 5

1955. Cent. of 1st Battalion of Engineers.
935. **322.** 60 c. blue 5 5

323. A. Lutz. **324.** Salto Grande Dam.

1955. Lutz (public health pioneer). Birth Cent.
934. **323.** 60 c. green 5 5

1956. Salto Grande Dam.
936. **324.** 60 c. red 5 5

325. **326.** Arms of Mococa.

1956. 18th Int. Geographic Congress, Rio.
937. **325.** 1 cr. 20 blue 8 5

1956. Mococa, Sao Paulo. Cent.
938. **326.** 60 c. red 5 5

327. Girls Running. **328.** Aeroplane and Map.

1956. Children's Games.
939. **327.** 2 cr. 50 blue 12 5

1956. 25th Anniv. of National Air Mail.
940. **328.** 3 cr. 30 blue 8 5

329. Rescue Work.

1956. Firemen's Corps, Rio de Janeiro Cent.
941. **329.** 2 cr. 50 red 8 5

330. Franca Cathedral. **331.** Open book with Inscription and Map.

1956. City of Franca. Cent.
942. **330.** 2 cr. 50 blue 8 5

1956. 50th Anniv. of Arrival of Marist Brothers in N. Brazil. Inscr. as on book in T **331.**
943. **331** 2 cr. 50 blue (postage) 8 5
944. – 3 cr. 30 purple (air) . . 12 5
DESIGN—VERT. 3 cr. 30, J. B. Marcelino Champagra.

332. Hurdler.

333.

335. Commemorative Stamp from Panama. **334.** Baron da Bocaina and Express Letter.

1956. 8th Spring Games.
945. **332.** 2 cr. 50 red 15 8

1956. Afforestation Campaign.
946. **333.** 2 cr. 50 green 8 5

1956. Baron da Bocaina. Birth Cent.
947. **334.** 2 cr. 50 brown 8 5

1956. Pan-American Congress. Panama.
948. **335.** 3 cr. 30 black & green 12 5

336. Dumont's Aeroplane.

1956. Air. Santos Dumont Commemoration.
949. **336.** 3 cr. green 30 15
950. 3 cr. 30 blue 12 5
951. 4 cr. lake 15 5
952. 6 cr. 50 brown 20 5
953. 11 cr. 50 chestnut 45 30

337. Volta Redonda Steel Mill, and Molten Steel. **338.** J. E. Gomes da Silva (civil engineer).

1957. National Steel Company's Expansion Campaign.
955. **337.** 2 cr. 50 brown 8 5

1957. J. E. Gomes da Silva. Birth Cent.
956. **338.** 2 cr. 50 green 8 5

339. Allan Kardec, Code and Globe.

1957. Spiritualism Code. Cent.
957. **339.** 2 cr. 50 chocolate . . 8 5

340. Young Gymnast. **341.** Gen. Craveiro Lopes.

1957. Children's Games.
958. **340.** 2 cr. 50 lake 10 5

1957. Visit of President of Portugal.
959. **341.** 6 cr. 50 blue 12 5

342. Stamp of 1932. **343.** Lord Baden-Powell.

1957. Sao Paulo Revolutionary Government. 25th Anniv.
960. **342.** 2 cr. 50 red 8 5

1957. Air. Lord Baden-Powell. Birth Cent.
961. **343.** 3 cr. 30 lake 12 5

344. Convent of San Antonio.

1957. Emancipation of San Antonio Province. Tercent.
962. **344.** 2 cr. 50 purple 8 5

345. Volleyball. **346.** Basketball.

1957. 9th Spring Games.
963. **345.** 2 cr. 50 chestnut . . 20 5

1957. 2nd Women's World Basketball Championships.
964. **346.** 3 cr. 30 green & chestnut 20 5

347. U.N. Emblem, Map of Suez Canal and Soldier.

1957. Air. United Nations Day.
965. **347.** 3 cr. 30 blue 15 5

348. C. do Pinhal (founder), Arms and Locomotive. **349.** Auguste Comte (philosopher).

1957. City of San Carlos. Cent.
966. **348.** 2 cr. 50 red 8 5

1957. Comte. Death Cent.
967. **349.** 2 cr. 50 brown 8 5

350. Sarapui Radio Station.

1957. Sarapui Radio Station. Inaug.
968. **350.** 2 cr. 50 myrtle 8 5

351. Admiral Tamandare and Cruiser. **352.** Coffee beans and Emblem.

1957. Brazilian Navy. 150th Anniv.
969. **351.** 2 cr. 50 blue 10 5
970. – 3 cr. 30 green 10 5
DESIGN: 3 cr. 30 Aircraft-carrier.

1957. City of Ribeirao Preto. Cent.
971. **352.** 2 cr. 50 claret 8 5

353. King John VI of Portugal and Sailing Ship.

1958. Opening of Ports to Foreign Trade 150th Anniv.
972. **353.** 2 cr. 50 purple 8 5

354. Bugler. **355.** Early Locomotive and Skyscraper.

1958. Corps of Brazilian Marines. 150th Anniv.
973. **354.** 2 cr. 50 red 8 5

1958. Central Brazil Railway Cent.
974. **355.** 2 cr. 50 brown 5 5

356. High Court Building. **357.** Brazilian Pavilion.

1958. Military High Courts. 150th Anniv.
975. **356.** 2 cr. 50 green 5 5

1958. Brussels Int. Exn.
976. **357.** 2 cr. 50 blue 5 5

358. Marshal da Silva Rondon. **359.** Jumping.

1958. Marshal Rondon Commem. and "Day of the Indian".
977. **358.** 2 cr. 50 purple 5 5

1958. Children's Games, Rio de Janeiro.
978. **359.** 2 cr. 50 red 10 5

360.

1958. Salto Grande Hydro-Electric Station. Inaug.
979. **360.** 2 cr. 50 purple .. 5 5

361. National Printing Works.

362 Marshal Osorio.

1958. National Printing Works, Rio de Janeiro. 150th Anniv.
980. **361.** 2 cr. 50 brown .. 5 5

1958. Marshal Osorio. 150th Birth Anniv.
981. **362.** 2 cr. 50 violet.. .. 5 5

363. Pres. Morales of Honduras.

364. Botanical Gardens, Rio de Janeiro.

1958. Visit of President of Honduras.
982. **363.** 6 cr. 50 green .. 25 10

1958. Botanical Gardens, Rio de Janeiro. 150th Anniv.
983. **364.** 2 cr. 50 green .. 8 5

365. Hoe, Rice and Cotton.

366. Prophet Joel.

1958. Japanese Immigration in Brazil. 50th Anniv.
984. **365.** 2 cr. 50 claret .. 5 5

1958. Basilica of the Good Jesu . Matosinhos. 200th Anniv.
985. **366.** 2 cr. 50 blue 5 5

367. Brazil on Globe.

1958. Int. Investments Conf., Belo Horizonte.
986. **367.** 2 cr. 50 brown .. 5 5

368. Tiradentes Palace, Rio de Janeiro.

369. J. B. Brandao (statesman).

1958. 47th Inter-Parliamentary Union Conf.
987. **368.** 2 cr. 50 brown .. 5 5

1958. Brandao. Cent.
988. **369.** 2 cr. 50 chestnut .. 8 5

370. Dawn Palace, Brasilia.

1958. Construction of Presidential Palace.
989. **370.** 2 cr. 50 blue 5 5

371. Merchant Ships.

1958. Govt. Aid for Brazilian Merchant Navy.
990. **371.** 2 cr. 50 blue 5 5

372. J. C. da Silva.

373. Pres. Gronchi.

1958. Da Silva. Birth Cent.
991. **372.** 2 cr. 50 brown .. 5 5

1958. Visit of President of Italy.
992. **373.** 7 cr. blue 10 5

374. Archers.

375. Old People within Hour-glass.

1958. 10th Spring Games, Rio de Janeiro.
993. **374.** 2 cr. 50 orange .. 10 5

1958. Old People's Day.
994. **375.** 2 cr. 50 lake 5 5

376. Machado de Assis (writer).

377. Pres. Vargas with oily Hand.

1958. Machado de Assis. 50th Death Anniv.
995. **376.** 2 cr. 50 brown .. 5 5

1958. State Petroleum Law. 5th Anniv.
996. **377.** 2 cr. 50 blue 5 5

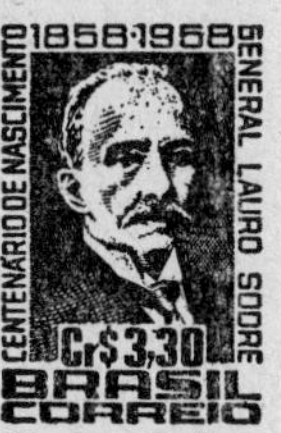

378. Globe showing Brazil and the Americas.

379. Gen. L. Sodre.

1958. 7th Inter-American Municipalities Congress, Rio de Janeiro.
997. **378.** 2 cr. 50 blue 5 5

1958. Gen. Sodre. Birth Cent.
998. **379.** 3 cr. 30 green .. 5 5

380. U.N. Emblem.

381. Footballer.

1958. Human Rights Declaration. 10th Anniv.
999. **380.** 2 cr. 50 blue 5 5

1959. World Football Cup Victory, 1958.
1000. **381.** 3 cr. 30 chest. & green 15 5

382. Map and Railway Line.

383. Pres. Sukarno.

1959. Patos-Campina Grande Railway Cent.
1001. **382.** 2 cr. 50 chestnut .. 8 5

1959. Visit of President of Indonesia.
1002. **383.** 2 cr. 50 blue .. 5 5

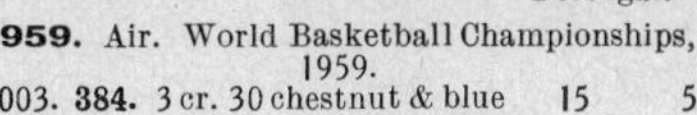

384. Basketball Player.

385. Polo Players.

386. King John VI of Portugal.

1959. Air. World Basketball Championships, 1959.
1003. **384.** 3 cr. 30 chestnut & blue 15 5

1959. Children's Games.
1005. **385.** 2 cr. 50 chestnut .. 10 5

1959.
1004. **386.** 2 cr. 50 red 5 5

387. Dockside Scene.

388. Church Organ, Diamantina.

1959. Rehabilitation of National Ports Law.
1006. **387.** 2 cr. 50 slate-green .. 8 5

1959. Carmelite Order in Brazil. Bicent.
1007. **388.** 3 cr. 30 lake 5 5

389. Dom J. S. de Souza (First Archbishop).

390.

1959. Archbishop of Diamantina. Birth Cent.
1008. **389.** 2 cr. 50 brown .. 5 5

1959. 11th Int. Roads Congress.
1009. **390.** 3 cr. 30 blue and green 5 5

391. Londrina and Parana.

392.

394. Globe and "Snipe" Class Yachts.

393. Daedalus.

1959. Londrina. 25th Anniv.
1010. **391.** 2 cr. 50 slate-green .. 5 5

1959. Spring Games.
1011. **392.** 2 cr. 50 magenta .. 12 5

1959. Air. Aviation Week.
1012. **393.** 3 cr. 30 blue .. 8 5

1959. World Sailing Championships, Porto Alegre.
1013. **394.** 6 cr. 50 slate-green .. 12 5

395.

396. Gunpowder Factory.

1959. 4th Int. Brazilian-Portuguese Study Conference, Bahia University.
1014. **395** 6 cr. 50 blue 8 5

1959. President Vargas Gunpowder Factory. 50th Anniv.
1015. **396.** 3 cr. 30 chestnut .. 5 5

397.

398. "Caravelle" Airliner.

1959. Thanksgiving Day.
1016. **397.** 2 cr. 50 blue .. 8 5

1959. Air. Inaug. of "Caravelle" Jet Airliners by Brazilian National Airlines.
1017. **398.** 6 cr. 50 blue.. .. 10 5

399. P. da Silva.

1959. Discovery and Identification of "Schistosoma Mansoni" (Fluke). 50th Anniv.
1019. **399.** 2 cr. 50 purple .. 5 5

400. Burning Bush.

1959. Presbyterian Work in Brazil. Cent.
1018. **400.** 3 cr. 30 green .. 5 5

401. L. de Matos and Church.

402. Pres. Lopez Mateos of Mexico.

1960. Luiz de Matos (Christian evangelist). Birth Cent.
1020. **401.** 3 cr. 30 brown .. 5 5

1960. Air. Visit of Mexican President.
1021. **402.** 6 cr. 50 brown .. 10 5

403. Pres. Eisenhower.

404. Dr. L. Zamenhof.

1960. Air. Visit of President Eisenhower.
1022. **403.** 6 cr. 50 chestnut .. 10 5

1960. Dr. L. Zamenhof (inventor of Esperanto). Birth Cent.
1023. **404.** 6 cr. 50 green .. 8 5

405. Adel (engineer).

406. Hands protecting Refugee.

1960. Adel. Birth Cent.
1024. **405.** 11 cr. 50 red.. .. 12 5

1960. Air. World Refugee Year.
1025. **406.** 6 cr. 50 blue.. .. 10 5

407. Plan of Brasilia.

1960. Brasilia Capital. Inaug.
1026. – 2 cr. 50 green (postage) 5 5
1027. – 3 cr. 30 violet (air) .. 5 5
1028. – 4 cr. blue .. 10 5
1029. – 6 cr. 50 magenta .. 8 5
1030. **407.** 11 cr. 50 brown .. 12 8
DESIGNS—Outlines representing: HORIZ. 2 cr. 50, President's Palace of the Plateau. 3 cr. 30, Parliament Buildings. 4 cr. Cathedral. VERT. 6 cr. 50, Tower. HORIZ. (105×47 mm.)

408.

1960. Air. 7th National Eucharistic Congress. Curitiba.
1032. **408.** 3 cr. 30 magenta .. 5 5

409.

410. Boy Scout.

1960. Air. 10th Baptist World Alliance Congress, Rio de Janeiro.
1033. **409.** 6 cr. 50 blue.. .. 8 5

1960. Air. Scouting in Brazil. 50th Anniv.
1034. **410.** 3 cr. 30 orange .. 5 5

411. "Agriculture". 412. Caravel. 413. P. de Frontin.

1960. Brazilian Ministry of Agriculture. Cent.
1035. **411.** 2 cr. 50 brown .. 5 5

1960. Air. Prince Henry the Navigator. 5th Death Cent.
1036. **412.** 6 cr. 50 black .. 10 5

1960. Paulo de Frontin (engineer). Birth Cent.
1037. **413.** 2 cr. 50 orange .. 5 5

414. Locomotive Piston Gear.

415. Athlete.

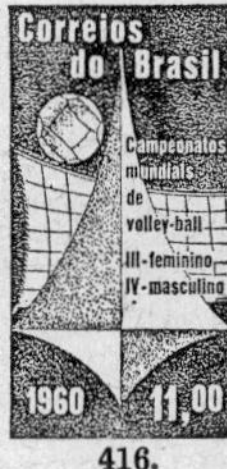

416.

1960. 10th Pan-American Railways Congress.
1038. **414.** 2 cr. 50 blue.. .. 10 5

1960. 12th Spring Games.
1039. **415.** 2 cr. 50 blue-green .. 8 5

1960. World Volleyball Championships.
1040. **416.** 11 cr. blue 15 5

417. Maria Bueno in play.

1960. Air. Maria Bueno's Wimbledon Tennis Victories, 1959–60.
1041. **417.** 6 cr. brown 12 5

418. Exhibition Emblem.

1960. Int. Industrial and Commercial Exn., Rio de Janeiro.
1042. **410.** 2 cr. 50 choc. & yell. 5 5

419. War Memorial, Rio de Janeiro.

420. Pylon and Map.

1960. Air. Return of Ashes of World War II Heroes from Italy.
1043. **419.** 3 cr. 30 lake 5 5

1961. Air. Tres Marias Hydro-Electric Station Inaug.
1044. **420.** 3 cr. 30 magenta .. 5 5

421. Emperor Haile Selassie.

422. Book with Seal of College.

1961. Visit of Emperor of Ethiopia.
1045. **421.** 2 cr. 50 chocolate .. 5 5

1961. "Sacre-Coeur de Marie" College. 50th Anniv.
1046. **422.** 2 cr. 50 blue.. .. 5 5

423. Map of Guanabara State.

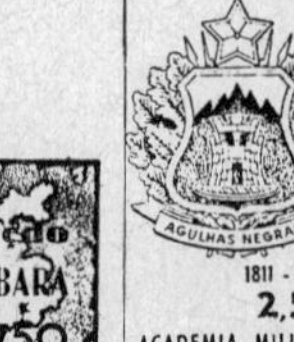

424. Arms of Academy.

1961. Promulgation of Guanabara Constitution.
1047. **423.** 7 cr. 50 chestnut .. 8 5

1961. Agulhas Negras Military Academy. 150th Anniv.
1048. **424.** 2 cr. 50 green .. 5 5
1049. – 3 cr. 30 red 5 5
DESIGN: 3 cr. 30, Military cap and sabre.

425. "Spanning the Atlantic Ocean".

426. View of Ouro Preto.

1961. Visit of Foreign Minister to Senegal.
1050. **425.** 27 cr. blue 10 5

1961. 250th Anniv. of Ouro Preto.
1051. **426.** 1 cr. orange 5 5

427. Arsenal. Rio de Janeiro.

428. Coffee Plant.

429. Tagore.

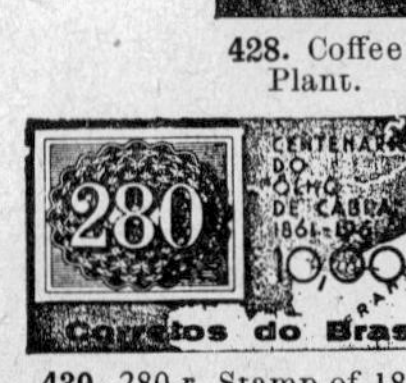

430. 280 r. Stamp of 1861 and Map of France.

1961. Rio de Janeiro Arsenal. 150th Anniv.
1052. **427.** 5 cr. brown 5 5

1961. Int. Coffee Convention, Rio de Janeiro.
1053. **428.** 20 cr. brown.. .. 15 8

1961. Rabindranath Tagore. Birth Cent.
1054. **429.** 10 cr. magenta .. 8 5

1961. "Goat's Eyes" Stamp Centenary.
1055. **430.** 10 cr. red 30 5
1056. – 20 cr. orange .. 50 10
DESIGN: 20 cr. 430 r. stamp of 1861 and map of the Netherlands.

431. Cloudburst.

432. Pinnacle, Rope and Haversack.

1962. World Meteorological Day.
1057. **431.** 10 cr. brown.. .. 10 5

1962. 1st Ascent of "Finger of God" Mountain. 50th Anniv.
1058. **432.** 8 cr. green 8 5

433. Dr. G. Vianna and parasites.

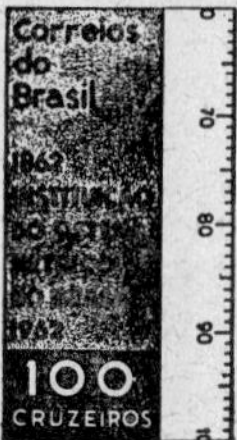

436. Metric Measure.

434. Campaign Emblem.

435. H. Dias (patriot).

1962. Dr. Gaspar Vianna's Cure for Leishman's Disease. 50th Anniv.
1059. **433.** 8 cr. blue 8 5

1962. Air. Malaria Eradication.
1060. **434.** 21 cr. blue 5 5

1962. Dias. 300th Death Anniv.
1061. **435.** 10 cr. maroon .. 5 5

1962. Brazil's Adoption of Metric System. Cent.
1062. **436.** 100 cr. red 45 20

437. "Snipe" Sailing-boats.

438. J. Mesquita and Newspaper.

439. Empress Leopoldina.

440. Brasilia.

1962. 13th "Snipe" Class Sailing Championships, Rio de Janeiro.
1063. **437.** 8 cr. turquoise .. 8 5

1962. Mesquita (journalist and founder of "O Estado de Sao Paulo"). Birth Cent.
1064. **438.** 8 cr. bistre 5 5

1962. Independence. 140th Anniv.
1065. **439.** 8 cr. magenta .. 5 5

1962. 51st Interparliamentary Conference, Brasilia.
1066. **440.** 10 cr. orange .. 5 5

441. Foundry Ladle.

442. U.P.A.E. Emblem.

1962. Inaug. of "Usiminas" (national iron and steel foundry).
1067. **441.** 8 cr. orange 5 5

1962. Postal Union of the Americas and Spain. 50th Anniv.
1068. **442.** 8 cr. magenta .. 5 5

443. Emblems of Industry. **444.** Q. Bocaiura. **445.** Footballer.

1962. National Bank. 10th Anniv.
1069. **443.** 10 cr. turquoise .. 5 5

1962. Bocaiura. 50th Death Anniv.
1070. **444.** 8 cr. brown 5 5

1962. Brazil's Victory in World Football Championships, 1962.
1071. **445.** 10 cr. turquoise .. 5 5

446. Carrier Pigeon. **447.** Dr. S. Neiva (first Brazilian P.M.G.).

1962. Brazilian Posts Tercent.
1072. **446.** 8 cr. blue, red, green and yellow 5 5

1963.
1073. **447.** 8 cr. violet 5 5
1073a. – 30 cr. turquoise (Euclides da Cunha) 30 10
1073b. – 50 cr. brown (Prof. A. Moreira da Costa Lima) 25 5
1073c. – 100 cr. blue (G. Dias) 15 5
1073d. – 200 cr. orange-red (Tiradentes) .. 30 8
1073e. – 500 cr. brown (Dom Pedro I) 80 25
1073f. – 1000 cr. indigo (Dom Pedro II) .. .. 1·25 30

448. Rockets and "Dish" Aerial. **449.** Cross.

1963. Int. Aeronautics and Space Exn. Sao Paulo.
1074. **448.** 21 cr. blue 8 5

1963. Ecumenical Council, Vatican City.
1075. **449.** 8 cr. purple 5 5

459. "abc" Symbol. **451.** Basketball. **452.** Torch Emblem.

1963. National Education Week.
1076. **450.** 8 cr. blue 5 5

1963. 4th World Basketball Championships.
1077. **451.** 8 cr. magenta .. 5 5

1963. 4th Pan-American Games Sao Paulo.
1078. **452.** 10 cr. red 5 5

453. "OEA" and Map. **454.** J. B. de A. e Silva.

1963. O.E.A. (Organization of American States) Charter. 15th Anniv.
1079. **453.** 10 cr. orange .. 5 5

1963. Jose B. de Andrade e Silva ("Father of Independence"). Birth Bicent.
1080. **454.** 8 cr. bistre .. 5 5

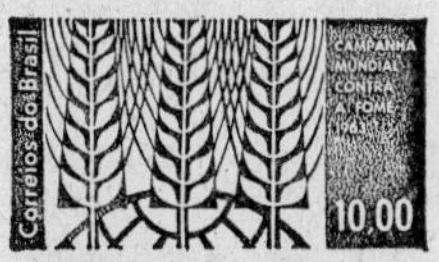

455. Campaign Emblem.

1963. Freedom from Hunger.
1081. **455.** 10 cr. blue 5 5

456. Centenary Emblem. **457.** J. Caetano. **458.** "Atomic" Development.

1963. Red Cross Cent.
1082. **456.** 8 cr. red and yellow .. 5 5

1963. John Caetano (actor). Death Cent.
1083. **457.** 8 cr. black 5 5

1963. Nat. Nuclear Energy Commission. 1st Anniv.
1084. **458.** 10 cr. magenta .. 5 5

459. Throwing the Hammer. **460.** Marshal Tito. **461.** Cross and Map.

1963. Int. Students' Games, Porto Alegre.
1085. **459.** 10 cr. black and grey 5 5

1963. Visit of President Tito of Yugoslavia.
1086. **460.** 80 cr. drab .. 20 8

1963. 8th Int. Leprology Congress, Rio de Janeiro.
1087. **461.** 8 cr. turquoise .. 5 5

462. Petroleum Installations.

463. "Jogos da Primavera". **464.** A. Borges de Medeiros.

1963. Nat. Petroleum Industry. 10th Anniv.
1088. **462.** 8 cr. grey-green .. 5 5

1963. Spring Games.
1089. **463.** 8 cr. yellow .. 5 5

1963. A. Borges de Medeiros (politician). Birth Cent.
1090. **464.** 8 cr. brown 5 5

465. Bridge of Sao Joao del Rey.

466. Dr. A. Alvim. **467.** Viscount de Maua.

1963. Sao Joao del Rey. 250th Anniv.
1091. **465.** 8 cr. blue 5 5

1963. Dr. Alvaro Alvim (scientist). Birth Cent.
1092. **466.** 8 cr. slate 5 5

1963. Viscount de Maua (founder of Brazilian Railway). Birth Cent.
1093. **467.** 8 cr. magenta .. 5 5

468. Cactus. **469.** C. Netto.

1964. North-East Bank. 10th Anniv.
1094. **468.** 8 cr. grey-green .. 5 5

1964. Coelho Netto (author). Birth Cent.
1095. **469.** 8 cr. violet 5 5

470. L. Muller. **471.** Child with Spoon.

1964. Lauro Muller. Birth Cent.
1096. **470.** 8 cr. red 5 5

1964. Schoolchildren's Nourishment Week.
1097. **471.** 8 cr. yellow and brown 5 5

472. "Chalice" (carved rock), Vila Velha, Parana. **473.** A. Kardec (author).

1964. Tourism.
1098. **472.** 80 cr. red 15 5

1964. Spiritual Code, "O Evangelho" Cent.
1099. **473.** 30 cr. grey-green .. 8 5

474. Pres. Lubke. **475.** Pope John XXIII.

1964. Visit of President Lubke of West Germany.
1100. **474.** 100 cr. chestnut .. 20 8

1964. Pope John Commem.
1101. **475.** 20 cr. lake 10 5

476. Pres. Senghor. **477.** "Visit Rio de Janeiro".

1964. Visit of Pres. Senghor of Senegal.
1102. **476.** 20 cr. sepia 8 5

1964. Rio de Janeiro. 400th Anniv. (1965). Inscr. "IV CENTENARIO" or "IV Centenario", etc.
1103. **477.** 15 cr. blue and orange 12 5
1104. – 30 cr. red and blue .. 5 5
1105. – 30 cr. black and blue 5 5
1106. – 35 cr. black and orange 5 5
1107. – 100 cr. brown and green on yellow .. 20 8
1108. – 200 cr. red and green 30 12

DESIGNS: As T **477**—HORIZ. 30 cr. (No. 1105), Tramway viaduct. 200 cr. Copacabana Beach. VERT. 35 cr. Estacio de Sa's statue. 100 cr. Church of Our Lady of the Rock. SMALLER. (24½ × 37 mm.): 30 cr. (No. 1104), Statue of St. Sebastian.

478. Pres. De Gaulle. **479.** Pres. Kennedy. **480.** Nahum (statue).

1964. Visit of Pres. De Gaulle of France.
1110. **478.** 100 cr. brown .. 15 5

1964. Pres. Kennedy Commem.
1111. **479.** 100 cr. black .. 15 5

1964. A. F. Lisboa (sculptor). 150th Death Anniv.
1112. **480.** 10 cr. black .. 5 5

481. Cross and Sword. **482.** V. Brazil (scientist).

1965. Democratic Revolution. 1st Anniv.
1113. **481.** 120 cr. grey 15 8

1965. Vital Brazil. Birth Cent.
1114. **482.** 120 cr. orange .. 15 8

483. Shah of Iran. **484.** Marshal Rondon and Map.

1965. Visit of Shah of Iran.
1115. **483.** 120 cr. red 15 8

1965. Marshal C. M. da S. Rondon. Birth Cent.
1116. **484.** 30 cr. maroon .. 5 5

485. Lions Emblem.

486. I.T.U. Emblem and Symbols.

1965. Brazilian Lions Clubs National Convention, Rio de Janeiro.
1117. **485.** 35 cr. black and lilac 5 5

1965. I.T.U. Cent.
1118. **486.** 120 cr. green & yellow 10 5

487. E. Pessoa. 488. Barroso's Statue.

1965. Epitacio Pessoa. Birth Cent.
1119. **487.** 35 cr. slate 5 5

1965. Naval Battle of Riachuelo. Cent.
1120. **488.** 30 cr. blue 5 5

489. Author and Heroine. 490. Sir Winston Churchill.

1965. Publication of Jose de Alencar's "Iracema". Cent.
1121. **489.** 30 cr. maroon .. 5 5

1965. Churchill Commem.
1122. **490.** 200 cr. slate 25 15

491. Scout Badge and Emblem of Rio's 400th Anniv.

492. I.C.Y. Emblem.

1965. 1st Pan-American Scout Jamboree, Rio de Janeiro.
1123. **401.** 30 cr. green 5 5

1965. Int. Co-operation Year.
1124. **492.** 120 cr. black & blue.. 15 5

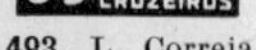

493. L. Correia.

494. Exhibition Emblem.

1965. Leoncia Correia poet). Birth Cent.
1125. **493.** 35 cr. green .. 5 5

1965. Sao Paulo Biennale (Art Exn.).
1126. **494.** 30 cr. red 5 5

495. President Saragat. 496. Grand Duke and Duchess of Luxembourg.

1965. Visit of President of Italy.
1127. **495.** 100 cr. green on pink 10 5

1965. Visit of Grand Duke and Duchess of Luxembourg.
1128. **496.** 100 cr. brown .. 12 8

497. Biplane on Map.

498. O.E.A. Emblem.

1965. Aviation Week and 3rd Philatelic Exn.
1129. **497.** 35 cr. blue 5 5

1965. Inter-American Conf., Rio de Janeiro.
1130. **498.** 100 cr. black and blue 12 8

499. King Baudouin and Queen Fabiola. 500. Coffee Beans.

1965. Visit of King and Queen of the Belgians.
1131. **499.** 100 cr. slate 12 8

1965. Brazilian Coffee.
1132. **500.** 30 cr. brown on cream 5 5

501. F. A. Varnhagen.

503. Sister and Globe.

502. Emblem and Map.

1965. Air. Francisco Varnhagen (historian). 150th Birth Anniv.
1133. **501.** 45 cr. brown.. .. 5 5

1966. Air. Alliance for Progress. 5th Anniv.
1134. **502.** 120 cr. blue & turquoise 12 8

1966. Air. Dorothean Sisters Educational Work in Brazil. Cent.
1135. **503.** 35 cr. violet 5 5

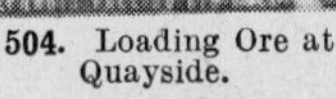

504. Loading Ore at Quayside.

505. "Steel".

1966. Rio Doce Iron-ore Terminal Tubarao, Espirito Santo. Inaug.
1136. **504.** 110 cr. black and bistre 10 5

1966. National Steel Company. Silver Jubilee.
1137. **505.** 30 cr. black on orange 5 5

506. Prof. Rocha Lima.

507. Battle Scene.

1966. Professor Lima's Discovery of the Characteristics of "Rickettsia prowazeki" (cause of typhus fever). 50th Anniv.
1138. **506.** 30 cr. turquoise .. 5 5

1966. Battle of Tuiuti. Cent.
1139. **507.** 30 cr. green 5 5

508. "The Sacred Face".

509. M. e Barros.

1966. Air. "Concilio Vaticano II".
1140. **508.** 45 cr. brown.. .. 5 5

1966. Air. Commander Mariz e Barros. Death Cent.
1141. **509.** 35 cr. chestnut .. 5 5

510. Decade Symbol. 511. Pres. Shazar.

1966. Int. Hydrological Decade.
1142. **510.** 100 cr. blue & brown 10 5

1966. Visit of President Shazar of Israel.
1143. **511.** 100 cr. ultramarine .. 10 5

512. "Youth". 513. Imperial Academy of Fine Arts.

514. Military Service Emblem. 515. R. Dario.

1966. Air. Eliseu Visconti (painter). Birth Cent.
1144. **512.** 120 cr. chestnut .. 12 5

1966. French Art Mission's arrival in Brazil. 150th Anniv.
1145. **513.** 100 cr. chestnut .. 10 5

1966. New Military Service Law.
1146. **514.** 30 cr. blue & yellow.. 5 5

1966. Ruben Dario (Nicaraguan poet). 50th Death Anniv.
1148. **515.** 100 cr. purple .. 10 5

516. Santarem Candlestick.

517. Arms of Santa Cruz.

1966. Goeldi Museum. Cent.
1149. **516.** 30 cr. brown on salmon 5 5

1966. 1st National Tobacco Exn., Santa Cruz.
1150. **517.** 30 cr. green 5 5

518. U.N.E.S.C.O. Emblem. 519. Capt. A. C. Pinto and Map.

1966. U.N.E.S.C.O. 20th Anniv.
1151. **518.** 120 cr. black .. 12 5

1966. Arrival of Captain A. C. Pinto. Bicent.
1153. **519.** 30 cr. red 10 5

520. Maltese Cross and Southern Cross.

521. Madonna and Child.

1966. "Lubrapex 1966". Stamp Exn. Rio de Janeiro.
1154. **520.** 100 cr. green .. 12 5

1966. Christmas.
1155. **521.** 30 cr. green 10 5
1156. – 35 cr. blue & salmon 10 5
1157. – 150 cr. pink and blue 50 40

DESIGN—DIAMOND—(34 × 34 mm.). 35 cr. Madonna and child (different). VERT. (46 × 103 mm.). 150 cr. As 35 cr. inscr. "Pax Haminibus" but not "Brazil Correio".

522. Arms of Laguna.

1967. Laguna Postal and Telegraphic Agency. Cent.
1158. **522.** 60 cr. sepia 8 5

523. Railway Bridge.

1967. Santos-Jundiai Railway. Cent.
1159. **523.** 50 cr. orange .. 8 5

524. Polish Cross and "Black Madonna".

1967. Polish Millennium.
1160. **524.** 50 cr. red, bl. & yell... 15 5

525. Research Rocket. **526.** Anita Garibaldi.

1967. World Meteorological Day.
1161. **525.** 50 cr. black & blue . . 15 5

1967.
1162. – 1 c. ultramarine . . 5 5
1163. – 2 c. vermilion . . 5 5
1164. – 3 c. green 5 5
1165. **526.** 5 c. black 5 5
1166. – 6 c. brown 5 5
1167. – 10 c. green 5 5
PORTRAITS: 1 c. Mother Angelica. 2 c. Marilia de Dirceu. 3 c. Dr. R. Lobato. 6 c. Ana Neri. 10 c. Darci Vargas.

527. "VARIG 40 Years". **528.** Lions Emblem and Globes.

1967. Varig Airlines. 40th Anniv.
1171. **527.** 6 c. black and blue 5 5

1967. Lions Int. 50th Anniv.
1172. **528.** 6 c. green 5 5

529. "Madonna and Child". **530.** Prince Akihito and Princess Michiko.

1967. Mother's Day.
1174. **529.** 5 c. violet 5 5

1967. Visit of Crown Prince and Princess of Japan.
1176. **530.** 10 c. black and red 10 5

531. Radar Aerial and Pigeon. **532.** Brother Vicente do Salvador.

1967. Communications Ministry Brasilia. Inaug.
1177. **531.** 10 c. black & magenta 10 5

1967. Brother Vicente do Salvador (founder of Franciscan Brotherhood, Rio de Janeiro). 400th Birth Anniv.
1178. **532.** 5 c. brown 5 5

533. Emblem and Members. **534.** Mobius Symbol.

1967. National 4-S ("4-H") Clubs Day.
1179. **533.** 5 c. green and black . . 5 5

1967. 6th Brazilian Mathematical Congress. Rio de Janeiro.
1180. **534.** 5 c. black and blue . . 5 5

535. Fish and "Waves".

1967. Piracicaba. Bicent.
1181. **535.** 5 c. black and blue 5 5

536. Papal Arms and "Golden Rose". **537.** General A. de Sampaio.

1967. Pope Paul's "Golden Rose" Offering to Our Lady of Fatima.
1182. **536.** 20 c. magenta & yell. 15 5

1967. Gen. Sampaio Commem.
1183. **537.** 5 c. blue 5 5

538. King Olav of Norway. **539.** Sun and Rio de Janeiro.

1967. Visit of King Olav.
1184. **538.** 10 c. chestnut . . 10 5

1967. Meeting of Int. Monetary Fund, Rio de Janeiro.
1185. **539.** 10 c. black and red . . 10 5

540. N. Pecanha (statesman). **541.** Our Lady of the Apparition and Basilica.

1967. Nilo Pecanha. Birth Cent.
1186. **540.** 5 c. purple 5 5

1967. Discovery of Statue of Our Lady of the Apparition. 250th Anniv.
1187. **541.** 5 c. blue and ochre 8 5

542. "Song Bird". **543.** Balloon, Rocket and Aircraft.

1967. Int. Song Festival.
1189. **542.** 20 c. multicoloured . . 15 5

1967. Aviation Week.
1190. **543.** 10 c. blue 10 5

543a. Pres. Wenceslau Braz. **544.** Rio Carnival.

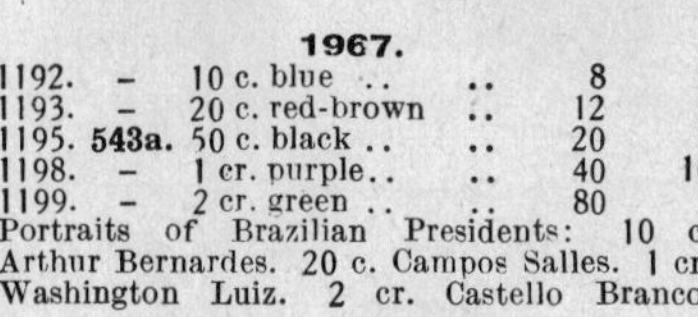

1967.
1192. – 10 c. blue 8 5
1193. – 20 c. red-brown . . 12 5
1195. **543a.** 50 c. black 20 5
1198. – 1 cr. purple 40 10
1199. – 2 cr. green 80 5
Portraits of Brazilian Presidents: 10 c. Arthur Bernardes. 20 c. Campos Salles. 1 cr. Washington Luiz. 2 cr. Castello Branco.

1967. Int. Tourist Year.
1200. **544.** 10 c. multicoloured . . 5 5

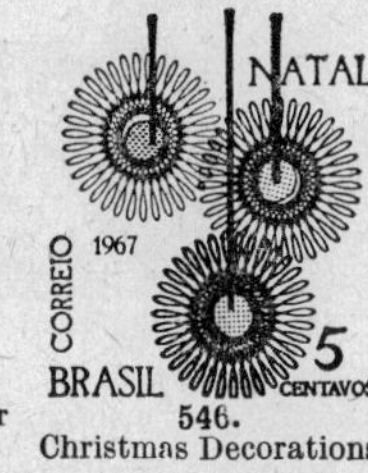

545. Sailor, Anchor and Ships. **546.** Christmas Decorations.

1967. Navy Week.
1202. **545.** 10 c. blue 10 5

1967. Christmas.
1203. **546.** 5 c. multicoloured . . 10 5

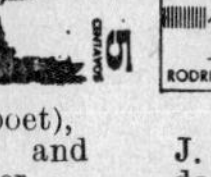

547. O. Bilac (poet), Aircraft, Tank and Aircraft-carrier. **548.** J. Rodrigues de Carvalho.

1967. Reservists Day.
1204. **547.** 5 c. blue and yellow . . 8 5

1967. Jose Rodriques de Carvalho (jurist and writer). Birth Cent.
1205. **548.** 10 c. green 8 5

549. O. Rangel.

1968. Orlando Rangel (pioneer pharmacologist). Birth Cent.
1206. **549.** 5 c. black and blue . . 8 5

550. Madonna and Diver. **551.** Map of Free Zone.

1968. Paranagua Underwater Exploration. 250th Anniv.
1207. **550.** 10 c. yellow-green and slate-green . . 8 5

1968. Manaus Free Zone.
1208. **551.** 10 c. red, grn. & yellow 10 5

552. Human Rights Emblem. **553.** Paul Harris.

1968. Declaration of Human Rights. 20th Anniv.
1209. **552.** 10 c. red and blue . . 10 5

GUM. All the following issues to No. 1415 are without gum, except where otherwise stated.

1968. Paul Harris Birth Cent.
1210. **553.** 20 c. chestnut & grn. 15 5

554. College Arms.

1968. St. Luiz College. Cent. With gum
1211. **554.** 10 c. gold, blue & red 10 5

555. Cabral and Ships.

1968. Pedro Cabral (discoverer of Brazil). 500th Birth Anniv.
1212. **555.** 10 c. multicoloured . . 8 5
1213. – 20 c. multicoloured . . 15 5
DESIGN: 20 c. "The First Mass"

556. "Maternity" (after H. Bernardeli). **557.** Harpy Eagle.

1968. Mother's Day.
1214. **556.** 5 c. multicoloured . . 10 5

1968. National Museum. 150th Anniv. With gum.
1215. **557.** 20 c. black and blue 25 5

558. Women of Brazil and Japan.

1968. "VARIG" Brazil—Japan Air Service. Inaug.
1216. **558.** 10 c. multicoloured 10 5

559. Horse-racing.

560. Cardinal.

1968. Brazilian Jockey Club. Cent.
1217. **559.** 10 c. multicoloured .. 10 5

1968. Birds.
1218. **560.** 10 c. multicoloured .. 8 5
1219. – 20 c. chestnut, green and blue .. 15 5
1220. – 50 c. sepia, red, green and blue 30 12
DESIGNS—HORIZ. 20 c. Wren. VERT. 50 c. Swainson's Royal Flycatcher.

561. Ancient Post-box.

562. Marshal E. Luiz Mallet.

1968. Stamp Day. With gum.
1221. **561.** 5 c. black green and yellow 5 5

1968. Mallet Commem. With gum.
1222. **562.** 10 c. lilac 8 5

563. Map of South America.

564. Lyceum Badge.

1968. Visit of Chilean President. With gum.
1223. **563.** 10 c. orange 8 5

1968. Portuguese Literacy Lyceum (High School). Cent. With gum.
1224. **564.** 5 c. green and pink 8 5

565. Map and Telex Tape.

1968. Telex Service for 25th City (Curitiba). With gum.
1225. **565.** 20 c. green and yell. 12 5

566. Soldiers on Medallion.

567. "Cock" shaped as Treble Clef.

1968. 8th American Armed Forces Conf.
1226. **566.** 5 c. black and blue .. 8 5

1968. 3rd. Int. Song Festival, Rio de Janeiro.
1227. **567.** 6 c. multicoloured .. 8 5

568. "Petrobas" Refinery.

569. Boy walking towards Rising Sun.

1968. National Petroleum Industry. 15th Anniv.
1228. **568.** 6 c. multicoloured .. 8 5

1968. U.N.I.C.E.F.
1229. **569.** 5 c. black and blue .. 10 5
1230. – 10 c. blk. red & blue 10 5
1231. – 20 c. black, grey, red, pink and olive .. 15 8
DESIGNS—HORIZ. 10 c. Hand protecting child. VERT. 20 c. Young girl in plaits.

570. Children with Books.

1968. Book Week.
1232. **570.** 5 c. multicoloured .. 5 5

571. W.H.O. Emblem and Flags.

1968. World Health Organisation. 20th Anniv.
1233. **571.** 20 c. multicoloured .. 12 5

572. J. B. Debret (painter).

1968. Jean Baptiste Debret. Birth Bicent.
1234. **572.** 10 c. black and yellow 10 5

573. Queen Elizabeth II.

1968. State Visit of Queen Elizabeth II.
1235. **573.** 70 c. multicoloured .. 50 30

574. Brazilian Flag.

575. F. Braga and part of "Hymn of National Flag".

1968. Brazilian Flag Day.
1236. **576.** 10 c. blue, yell., green and black 10 5

1968. Francisco Braga (composer). Birth Cent. With gum.
1237. **575.** 5 c. maroon 8 5

576. Clasped Hands.

1968. Blood Donors' Day.
1238. **576.** 5 c. red, black & blue 8 5

1968. Obligatory Tax. Leprosy Research Fund. Revalued currency. With gum.
1239. **310.** 5 c. green 5 5
1240. 5 c. red 5 5

577. Steam Locomotive of 1868.

1968. Sao Paulo Railway. Cent.
1241. **577.** 5 c. multicoloured .. 20 10

578. Angelus Bell.

579. F.A.V. Caldas Jr.

1968. Christmas. Multicoloured.
1242. 5 c. Type 578 .. .. 5 5
1243. 6 c. Father Christmas giving present 8 5

1968. Francisco Caldas, Junior (founder of "Correio do Povo" newspaper). Birth Cent.
1244. **579.** 10 c. blk., pink & red 8 5

580. Reservists' Emblem and Memorial.

1968. Reservists' Day. With gum.
1245. **580.** 5 c. green and brown 8 5

581. Dish Aerial.

582. Viscount do Rio Branco.

1969. Satellite Communications System. Inaug.
1246. **581.** 30 c. black and blue .. 15 5

1969. Viscount do Rio Branco. 150th Birth Anniv.
1247. **582.** 5 c. sepia and drab .. 8 5

583. St. Gabriel.

584. Shoemaker's Last and Globe.

585. Kardec and Monument.

1969. St. Gabriel's Day (Patron Saint of Telecommunications).
1248. **583.** 5 c. multicoloured .. 8 5

1969. 4th Int. Shoe Fair, Novo Hamburgo.
1249. **584.** 5 c. multicoloured .. 8 5

1969. "Allan Kardec" (Professor H. Rivail) (French educationalist and spiritualist). Death Cent.
1250. **585.** 5 c. chestnut and green 8 5

586. Men of Three Races and Arms of Cuiaba.

1969. Cuiaba (capital of Mato Grosso state). 250th Anniv.
1251. **586.** 5 c. multicoloured .. 8 5

587. Mint and Banknote Pattern.

1969. Opening of New State Mint Printing Works.
1252. **587.** 5 c. bistre and orange 10 5

588. Society Emblem and Stamps.

1969. Sao Paulo Philatelic Society. 50th Anniv.
1253. **588.** 5 c. multicoloured .. 10 5

589. "Our Lady of Santana" (statue).

1969. Mothers' Day.
1254. **589.** 5 c. multicoloured .. 10 5

590. ILO Emblem.

1969. Int. Labour Organisation. 50th Anniv. With gum.
1255. **590.** 5 c. gold and red .. 10 5

591. Diving Platform and Swimming Pool.

592. "Mother and Child at Window" (after Di Cavalcanti).

1969. Cearense Water Sports Club, Fortaleza. 40th Anniv.
1256. **591.** 20 c. blk., grn. and brn. 12 5

1969. 10th Biennale Art Exhib. Sao Paulo. Multicoloured.

1257. 10 c. Type **592** 15 8
1258. 20 c. "Sclupture" (F. Leirner) 15 8
1259. 50 c. "Sunset in Brasilia" (D. di Prete) 25 12
1260. 1 cr. "Angelfish" (A. Martins) 60 20

No. 1258 is square, size 33 × 33 mm. and Nos. 1259/60 vert., size 55 × 35 mm.

593. Angelfish. **594.** L. O. Teles de Manezes (founder).

1969. A.C.A.R.P.I. Fish Preservation and Development.

1261. **593.** 20 c. multicoloured .. 12 5

1969. Spiritualist Press. Cent.

1263. **594.** 50 c. green and orange 35 12

595. Postman delivering Letter. **597.** General Fragoso.

1969. Stamp Day.

1264. **595.** 30 c. blue 20 12

1969. General Tasso Fragoso. Birth Cent.

1265. **597.** 20 c. green 12 8

598. Map of Army Bases. **599.** Jupia Dam.

1969. Army Week. Multicoloured.

1266. 10 c. Type **598** 5 5
1267. 20 c. Monument and railway bridge (39 × 22 mm) 12 8

1969. Jupia Dam. Inaug.

1268. **599.** 20 c. multicoloured .. 12 8

600. Mahatma Gandhi and Spinning-wheel.

1969. Mahatma Gandhi. Birth Cent.

1269. **600.** 20 c. black and yellow 12 8

601. Santos-Dumont, Eiffel Tower and Moon Landing.

1969. 1st Man on the Moon and Santos-Dumont's Flight. Commem.

1270. **601.** 50 c. multicoloured .. 35 10

602. Smelting Plant.

1969. Expansion of USIMINAS Steel Consortium.

1271. **602.** 20c. multicoloured .. 12 5

603. Steel Furnace. **605.** Exhibition Emblem.

604. "The Water Cart" (after Debret).

1969. ACESITA Steel Works. 25th Anniv.

1272. **603.** 10 c. multicoloured .. 8 5

1969. J. B. Debret (painter). Birth Bicent. (2nd issue). Multicoloured. No. 1274 dated "1970".

1273. **604.** 20 c. Type **604** .. 15 5
1274. 30 c. "Street Scene" 20 8

1969. "Abuexpo 69" Stamp Exn.

1275. **605.** 10 c. multicoloured .. 8 5

606. Air Force "Bandeirante" Aircraft.

1969. Brazilian Aeronautical Industry. Expansion Year.

1276. **606.** 50 c. multicoloured .. 25 8

607. Pele scoring Goal. **608.** "Madonna and Child".

1969. Footballer Pele's 1,000th Goal.

1277. **607.** 10 c. multicoloured .. 20 8

1969. Christmas.

1279. **608.** 10 c. multicoloured .. 10 5

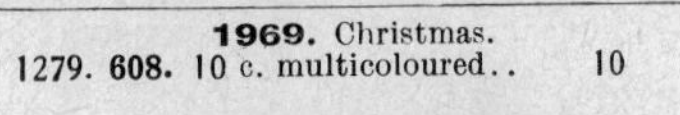

609. Destroyer and Submarine.

1969. Navy Day.

1281. **609.** 5 c. blue 8 5

610. Dr. H. Blumenau.

1969. Dr. Hermann Blumenau (German immigrant leader). 150th Birth Anniv.

1282. **610.** 20 c. green 12 5

611. Carnival Dancers.

1969. Carioca Carnival, Rio de Janeiro. Multicoloured.

1283. 5 c. Type **611** 8 5
1284. 10 c. Samba dancers .. 10 8
1285. 20 c. Clowns 20 10
1286. 30 c. Confetti and mask.. 25 12
1287. 50 c. Tambourine-player 30 15

Nos. 1284 and 1285 are horiz.

612. Carlos Gomes conducting.

1970. Opera "Il Guarani" by A. Carlos Gomes. Cent.

1288. **612.** 20 c. multicoloured .. 12 5

613. Monastery.

1970. Penha Monastery, Vilha Velha. 400th Anniv.

1289. **613.** 20 c. multicoloured 15 10

614. National Assembly Building.

1970. Brasilia. 10th Anniv. Multicoloured.

1290. 20 c. Type **614** 12 8
1291. 50 c. Reflecting Pool .. 25 12
1292. 1 cr. Presidential Palace 50 25

615. Emblem on Map.

1970. Rondon Project (students' practical training scheme).

1293. **615.** 50 c. multicoloured 25 12

616. Marshal Osorio and Arms.

1970. Marshal Osorio Historical Park. Opening.

1294. **616.** 20 c. multicoloured .. 15 5

617. "Madonna and Child" (San Antonio Monastery). **618.** Brasilia Cathedral (stylised).

1970. Mothers' Day

1295. **617.** 20 c. multicoloured .. 15 8

1970. 8th National Eucharistic Congress, Brasilia.

1296. **618.** 20 c. green 15 5

619. Census Symbol. **620.** Jules Rimet Cup and Map.

1970. 8th National Census.

1297. **619.** 20 c. yellow and green 12 5

1970. World Cup Football Championships, Mexico.

1298. **620.** 50 c. blk., gold & blue 25 12

621. Christ's Statue.

1970. Marist Students. 6th World Congress.

1299. **621.** 50 c. multicoloured .. 25 12

622. Bellini and Swedish Flag (1958).

1970. Brazil's Third Victory in World Cup Football Championships. Multicoloured.
1300. 1 cr. Type **622** 60 20
1301. 2 cr. Garrincha and Chilean flag (1962) .. 1·00 35
1302. 3 cr. Pele and Mexican flag (1970) .. .. 1·60 60

623. Pandia Calogeras.

624. Brazilian Forces Badges and Map.

1970. Calogeras (author and politician) Birth Cent.
1303. **623.** 20 c. green 15 5

1970. World War II. Victory. 25th Anniv.
1304. **624.** 20 c. multicoloured .. 15 5

625. "The Annunciation" (Cassio M'Boy)

1970. St. Gabriel's Day (Patron Saint of Telecommunications).
1305. **625.** 20 c. multicoloured 15 8

626. Boy in Library.

627. U.N. Emblem.

1970. Book Week.
1306. **626.** 20 c. multicoloured .. 15 10

1970. United Nations. 25th Anniv.
1307. **627.** 50 c. blue, silver and ultram. 25 12

628. "Rio de Janeiro, circa 1820".

1970. 3rd Brasilian-Portuguese Stamp Exhib. "Lubrapex 70". Rio de Janeiro.
1308. **628.** 20 c. multicoloured 15 5
1309. – 50 c. brown and black 30 10
1310. – 1 cr. multicoloured .. 60 20
DESIGNS: 50 c. Exhibition emblem. 1 cr. Rio de Janeiro (modern view).

629. "The Holy Family" (C. Portinari).

630. Warship.

1970. Christmas.
1312. **629.** 50 c. multicoloured .. 30 12

1970. Navy Day.
1314. **630.** 20 c. multicoloured 15 5

631. Congress Emblem.

632. Links and Globe.

1971. 3rd Inter-American Housing Congress, Rio de Janeiro.
1315. **631.** 50 c. red and black .. 25 10

1971. Racial Equality Year.
1316. **632** 20 c. multicoloured .. 15 8

633. "Morpho melacheilus".

1971. Butterflies. Multicoloured.
1317. 20 c. Type **633** 15 8
1318. 1 cr. "Papilio thoas brasiliensis" 60 20

634. Madonna and Child.

635. Hands reaching for Ball.

1971. Mothers' Day.
1319. **634.** 20 c. multicoloured .. 15 5

1971. 6th Women's Basketball World Championships.
1320. **635.** 70 c. multicoloured .. 40 10

636. Eastern Part of Highway Map.

1971. Trans-Amazon Highway Project. Multicoloured.
1321. 40 c. Type **636** 25 10
1322. 1 cr. Western part of Highway Map 60 20
Nos. 1321/2 were issued together se-tenant with stamp size label.

637. "Head of Man" (V. M. Lima).

1971. Stamp Day. Multicoloured.
1323. 40 c. Type **637** 25 10
1324. 1 cr. "Arab Violinist" (Pedro Americo) .. 60 20

638. General Caxias and Map.

639. Anita Garibaldi.

1971. Army Week.
1325. **638.** 20 c. red and green .. 12 5

1971. Anita Garibaldi. 150th Birth Anniv.
1326. **639.** 20 c. multicoloured .. 15 5

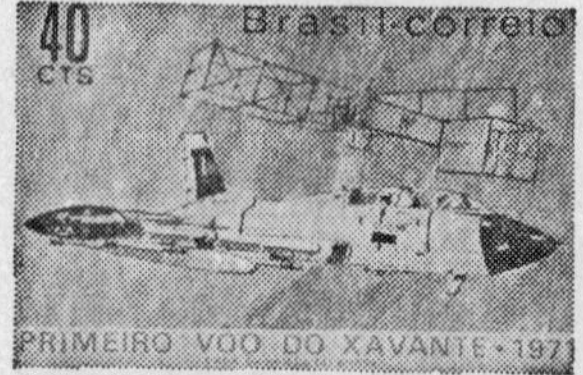

640. "Xavante" Jet Fighter and Early Aircraft.

1971. First Flight of "Xavante" Jet Fighter.
1327. **640.** 40 c. multicoloured .. 25 10

641. Flags of Central American Republics.

642. Exhibition Emblem.

1971. Central American Republics' Independence. 150th Anniv.
1328. **641.** 40 c. multicoloured .. 25 10

1971. "Franca 71" Industrial, Technical and Scientific Exhibition, Sao Paulo.
1329. **642.** 1 cr. 30 multicoloured 70 20

643. "The Black Mother" (L. de Albuquerque).

644. Archangel Gabriel.

1971. Slaves Emancipation Law. Cent.
1330. **643.** 40 c. multicoloured .. 25 10

1971. St. Gabriel's Day (Patron Saint of Communications).
1331. **644.** 40 c. multicoloured .. 25 10

645. "Couple on Bridge" (Marisa da Silva Chaves).

1971. Children's Day. Multicoloured.
1332. 35 c. Type **645** 20 5
1333. 45 c. "Couple on Riverbank" (Mary Rosa e Silva) 20 8
1334. 60 c. "Girl in Hat" (Teresa A. Prata Ferreira) 30 10

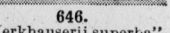

646. "Werkhauserii superba".

647. Eunice Weaver.

1971. Brazilian Orchids.
1335. **646.** 40 c. multicoloured .. 25 10

1971. Obligatory Tax. Leprosy Research Fund.
1336. **647.** 10 c. green 8 5
1337. 10 c. purple 8 5

648. "25 Senac".

1971. SENAC (apprenticeship service) and SESC (commerical social service). 25th Anniv.
1338. **648.** 20 c. new blue & blk. 10 5
1339. – 40 c. orange & black 15 5
DESIGN: 40 c. As Type **648** but inscr. "sesc". Nos. 1338/9 were issued together in horiz. se-tenant pairs.

649. Patrolboat.

650. Cruciform Symbol.

1971. Navy Day.
1340. **649.** 20 c. multicoloured .. 10 5

1971. Christmas.
1341. **650.** 20 c. lilac, red and blue 10 5
1342. 75 c. black on silver .. 25 8
1343. 1 cr. 30 multicoloured 50 15

651. Washing Bomfim Church.

1972. Tourism. Multicoloured.
1344. 20 c. Type **651** 10 5
1345. 40 c. Cogwheel and Grapes (Grape Festival, Rio Grande do Sul) 15 5
1346. 75 c. Nazareth Festival procession, Belem .. 25 12
1347. 1 cr. 30 Street scene (Winter Festival of Ouro Preto) 50 20

652. Pres. Lanusse.

1972. Visit of President Lanusse of Argentina
1348. **652.** 40 c. multicoloured .. 15 5

653. Presidents Castello Branco, Costa le Silva and Medici.

654. Post Office Symbol.

1972. 1964 Revolution. 8th Anniv.
1349. **653.** 20 c. multicoloured .. 10 5

1972.
1350. **654.** 20 c. brown 8 5

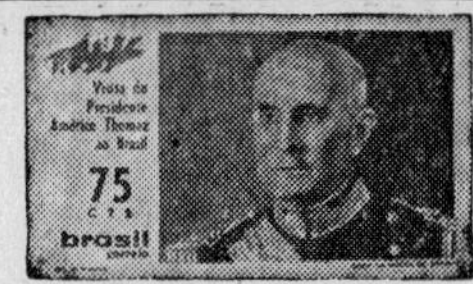
655. Pres. Tomas.

1972. Visit of Pres. Tomas of Portugal.
1351. **655.** 75 c. multicoloured 25 10

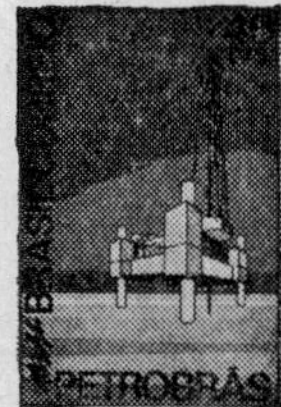

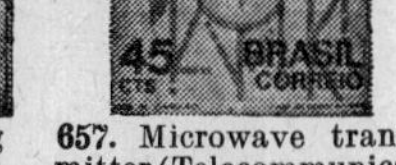
656. Drilling Rig (PETROBRÁS).
657. Microwave transmitter (Telecommunications).

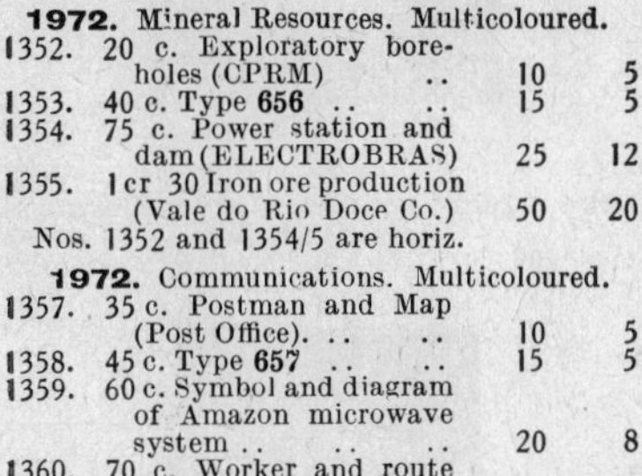

1972. Mineral Resources. Multicoloured.
1352. 20 c. Exploratory boreholes (CPRM) .. 10 5
1353. 40 c. Type **656** 15 5
1354. 75 c. Power station and dam (ELECTROBRAS) 25 12
1355. 1 cr 30 Iron ore production (Vale do Rio Doce Co.) 50 20
Nos. 1352 and 1354/5 are horiz.

1972. Communications. Multicoloured.
1357. 35 c. Postman and Map (Post Office). 10 5
1358. 45 c. Type **657** 15 5
1359. 60 c. Symbol and diagram of Amazon microwave system 20 8
1360. 70 c. Worker and route map (Amazon Basin development) .. 25 10
Nos. 1359/60 are horiz.

658. Three Hulls. (Shipbuilding).
659. Footballer (Independence Cup Championships).

1972. Major Industries.
1361. – 35 c. orge., red & blk. 10 5
1362. **658.** 45 c. multicoloured .. 15 5
1363. – 70 c. multicoloured .. 25 10
Designs–vert. 35 c. Motor cars. horiz. 70 c. Metal blocks (Iron and Steel Industry).

1972. " Sports and Pastimes ".
1364. **659.** 20 c. black and brown 8 5
1365. – 75 c. black and red .. 25 10
1366. – 1 cr. 30 black and blue 50 20
Designs: 75 c. Treble clef in open mouth (" Popular Music "). 1 cr. 30 Hand grasping plastic (" Plastic Arts ").

660. Diego Homem's Map of Brazil, 1568.

1972. "EXFILBRA 72" 4th Int. Stamp Exhib., Rio de Janeiro. Multicoloured.
1367. 70 c. Type **660** 25 8
1368. 1 cr. Nicolau Visscher's Map of Americas, c 1652 40 12
1369. 2 cr. Lopo Homem's World Map, 1519 .. 70 25

661. Figurehead, Sao Francisco River.

662. " Institution of Brazilian Flag.

1972. Brazilian Folklore. Multicoloured.
1371. 45 c. Type **661** 12 5
1372. 60 c. Frandango, Rio Grande do Sul.. .. 15 8
1373. 75 c. Capoeira (game), Bahia 25 10
1374. 1 cr. 15 Karaja statuette 35 15
1375. 1 cr. 30 "Bumba-Meu-Boi" (folk play) .. 50 20

1972. Independence. 150th Anniv.
1376. **662.** 30 c. green & yellow 10 5
1377. – 70 c. mauve & pink 20 8
1378. – 1 cr. red and brown 40 15
1379. – 2 cr. black & brown 75 30
1380. – 3 cr. 50 black & grey 1·25 40
Designs–horiz. 70 c. " Proclamation of Emperor Pedro I " (lithograph after Debret). 2 cr. Commemorative gold coin of Pedro I. 3 cr. 50 Declaration of Ypiranga monument. vert. 1 cr. " Emperor Pedro I " (H. J. da Silva).

663. Numeral and P.T.T. Symbol.

665. Writing Hand and People (" Mobral " Literacy Campaign).

664. Scroll.

1972.
1383. **663.** 5 c. orange 5 5
1384. 10 c. brown 5 5
1394. 15 c. blue 5 5
1385. 20 c. blue 5 5
1396. 25 c. brown 5 5
1386. 30 c. red 5 5
1387. 40 c. green 8 5
1388. 50 c. green 8 5
1398. 70 c. purple 10 5
1389. **664.** 1 cr. purple 20 12
1390. 2 cr. blue 40 25
1391. 4 cr. orange and lilac 70 15
1392. 5 cr. brn., cinnamon and red 90 60
1393. 10 cr. grn., brn., & blk. 1·80 1·20
Nos. 1392/3 have a background of multiple postal emblems.

1972. Social Development. Multicoloured.
1412. 10 c. Type **665** 5 5
1413. 20 c. Graph and people (National Census Cent.) 8 5
1414. 1 cr. House in hand (Pension Fund system) 35 15
1415. 2 cr. Workers and factory (Gross National Product) 70 20

666. Legislative Building, Brasilia.

667. Pottery Crib.

1972. National Congress Building, Brasilia.
1416. **666.** 1 cr. blk., orge. & blue 30 10

1972. Christmas.
1417. **667.** 20 c. black and brown 8 5

668. Children and Traffic Lights (Transport System development).

1972. Government Services.
1418. – 10 c. blk., orge. & bl. 5 5
1419. **668.** 10 c. multicoloured.. 5 5
1420. – 70 c. blk., brown & red 20 10
1421. – 2 cr. multicoloured.. 75 25
Designs—vert. 10 c. (No. 1418) Farmworker and pension book (Rural Security Scheme). 70 c. Dr. Oswald Cruz, public health pioneer (birth cent.). horiz. 2 cr. Bull, fish and produce (Agricultural exports).

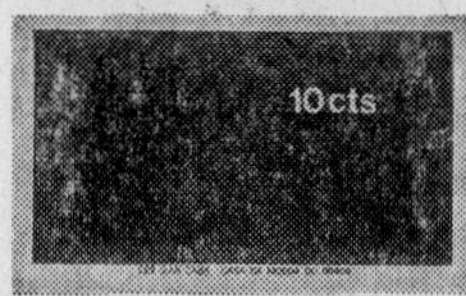
669. " Expeditionary Force " (Monument).

1972. Armed Forces' Day.
1422. **669.** 10 c. brown, purple and orange-brown 5 5
1423. – 30 c. multicoloured.. 10 5
1424. – 30 c. multicoloured.. 10 5
1425. – 30 c. black, brown and lilac 10 5
Designs: No. 1423, Sailing-ship (Navy). No. 1424. Trooper (Army). No. 1425, " Mirage III " jet-fighter (Air Force).

670. Emblem and Cogwheels.

1973. Rotary in Brazil. 50th Anniv.
1426. **670.** 1 cr. blue, light blue and yellow 25 10

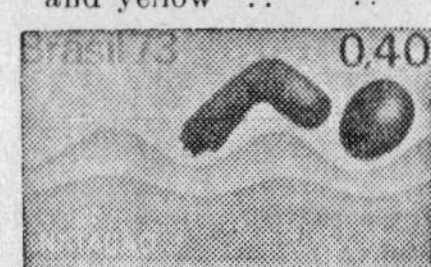
671. Swimming.

1973. Sports Events.
1427. **671.** 40 c. brown and blue 10 5
1428. – 40 c. brown & green.. 10 5
1429. – 40 c. brown & purple 10 5
Designs and event – horiz. No. 1427, (" Latin Cup " Swimming Championships). No. 1428, Gymnast (Olympic Festival of Gymnastics, Rio de Janeiro). vert. No. 1429, Volleyball player (International Volleyball Championships, Rio de Janeiro).

672. Paraguayan Flag.

1973. Visit of Pres. Stroessner of Paraguay.
1430. **672.** 70 c. multicoloured.. 15 8

673. " Communications ".

1973. Ministry of Communications Building, Brasilia, Inaug.
1431. **673.** 70 c. multicoloured.. 20 8

674. Neptune and Map.

1973. " Bracan 1 " Submarine Cable Inaug.
1432. **674.** 1 cr. multicoloured .. 30 10

675. " World Commerce ".

676. Manakin and " Acacia decurrens ".

1973. 24th Int. Chamber of Commerce Congress.
1433. **675.** 1 cr. purple and orge. 25 10

1973. Tropical Birds and Plants. Mult.
1434. 20 c. Type **676** 8 5
1435. 20 c. Oriole and " Cereus peruvianos " 8 5
1436. 20 c. Ruby hummingbird and " Tecoma umbellata" 8 5

677. " Tourism ".
678. " Cabolco " Festival Cart.

1973. National Tourism Year.
1437. **677.** 70 c. multicoloured.. 20 8

1973. Anniversaries. Multicoloured.
1438. 20 c. Type **678** 8 5
1439. 20 c. Arariboia (Indian chief) 8 5
1440. 20 c. Convention delegates 8 5
1441. 20 c. " The Graciosa Road " 8 5
Events: No. 1438, Liberation Day. 150th anniv. No. 1439, Niteroi. 400th anniv. No. 1440, Itu Convention, Cent. No. 1441, Nhundiaquara highway, Cent.

679. " Institute of Space Research ".

1973. Scientific Research Institute. Mult.
1442. 20 c. Type **679** 8 5
1443. 70 c. " Federal Engineering School ", Itajuba (Opening Ceremony) .. 20 8
1444. 1 cr. " Institute for Pure and Applied Mechanics " 25 10

680. Santos Dumont and " 14-Bis ".

1973. Alberto Santos Dumont. Birth Cent.
1445. **680.** 20 c. brown, green and pale green .. 8 5
1446. – 70 c. brown. red & yell. 20 8
1447. – 2 cr. brn., ultram. & bl. 55 15
Designs: 70 c. Airship No. 6. 2 cr. " Demoiselle " aircraft.

681. Map of the World.

1973. Stamp Day.

1448. **681.** 40 c. black and red .. 12 5
1449. – 40 c. black and red .. 12 5

The design of No. 1449 differs from T 681 in that the red portion is to the top and right, instead of to the top and left.

682. G. Dias. **683.** Festival Banner.

1973. Goncalves Dias (poet). 150th Birth Anniv.

1450. **682.** 40 c. black and violet 12 5

1973. National Folklore Festival.

1452. **683.** 40 c. multicoloured .. 12 5

684. Masonic Emblems.

1973. Brazilian Freemasonry.

1553. **684.** 1 cr. blue 25 10

685. Fire Protection. **686.** St. Theresa.

1973. National Protection Campaign. Mult.

1454. 40 c. Type **685** 12 5
1455. 40 c. Cross and Cornice (Cultural Protection) .. 12 5
1456. 40 c. Winged emblem (Protection in Flight) .. 12 5
1457. 40 c. Leaf (Protection of Nature) .. 12 5

1973. St. Theresa of Lisieux. Birth Cent.

1459. **686.** 2 cr. brn. & orange .. 20 8

687. M. Lobato and " Emilia ".

1973. Monteiro Lobato's Children's Stories. Multicoloured.

1460. 40 c. Type **687** 12 5
1461. 40 c. Aunt Nastasia .. 12 5
1462. 40 c. Nazarinho, Pedrinho and Quindim the Rhinoceros 12 5
1463. 40 c. Visconde de Sabugosa 12 5
1464. 40 c. Dona Benta .. 12 5

688. Father J. M. Nunes Garcia.

1973. " The Baroque Age ". Mult.

1465. 40 c. Wood carving, Church of St. Francia Bahia .. 12 5
1466. 40 c. " Prophet Isaiah " (detail, sculpture by Aleijadinho) 12 5
1467. 70 c. Type **688** 20 8
1468. 1 cr. Portal, Church of Conceicao da Praia .. 25 12
1469. 2 cr. " Glorification of Holy Virgin", ceiling, St. Francis Assisi Church, Ouro Preto 55 25

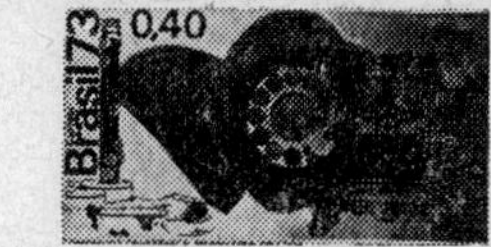

689. Early Telephone, and Dial.

1973. Brazilian Telephone Company. 50th Anniv.

1470. **689.** 40 c. multicoloured .. 12 5

690. " Angel ".

1973. Christmas.

1471. **690.** 40 c. multicoloured .. 12 5

691. " Gailoa " (river steamboat).

1973. Brazilian Boats. Multicoloured.

1472. 40 c. Type **691** 12 5
1473. 70 c. " Regatao " (Amazon trading boat) 20 8
1474. 1 cr. " Jangada " (coastal raft) 25 10
1475. 2 cr. " Saveiro " transport boat) 50 15

692. Scales of Justice. **693.** P. de Castro.

1973. " Homage to Judiciary Power ".

1476. **692.** 40 c. violet and mauve 12 5

1973. Placido de Castro, " Liberator of Acre ". Birth Cent.

1477. **693.** 40 c. black and red .. 12 5

694. Scarlet Ibis and Victoria Regia Lilies. **695.** Saci Perere (hoblin).

1973. Brazilian Flora and Fauna Mult.

1478. 40 c. Type 694 .. .. 12 5
1479. 70 c. Jaguar and Indian tulip 20 8
1480. 1 cr. Red macaw and palm 25 10
1481. 2 cr. Rhea and " mulungu " plant 50 15

1974. Brazilian Folk Tales. Multicoloured.

1482. 40 c. Type **695** 10 5
1483. 80 c. Zumbi (warrior) .. 20 8
1484. 1 cr. Chico Rei (African king) 25 10
1485. 1 cr. 30 Little black boy of the pasture 30 12
1486. 2 cr. 50 Iara, queen of the waters 45 15

696. President Costa e Silva Bridge.

1974. Inauguration of President Costa e Silva Bridge.

1487. **696.** 40 c. multicoloured .. 8 5

697. "Imprensa".

1974. Brazilian Communications Pioneers.

1488. **697.** 40 c. red, blue & brn. 8 5
1489. – 40 c. brn., bl. & bistre 8 5
1490. – 40 c. blue, pink & brn. 8 5

Designs and events: No. 1488, (Hipolito da Costa. Birth bicent. (founder of newspaper " Correiro Braziliense ", 1808)). No. 1489, Radio waves (Edgar R. Pinto, founder of Radio Sociedade do Rio de Janeiro, 1923). No. 1490, Television screen (F. de Assis Chateaubriand, founder of first T.V. station, Sao Paulo, 1950).

698. "Construction".

1974. "Ten Years of Brazilian Construction".

1491. **698.** 40 c. multicoloured .. 8 5

699. "Christ of the Andes".

1974. G. Marconi (radio pioneer). Birth Cent.

1492. **699.** 2 cr. 50 multicoloured 45 15

700. Artwork and Stamp-printing Press.

1974. State Mint Commemoration.

1493. **700.** 80 c. multicoloured .. 15 5

701. Heads of White, Indian and Negro Peoples.

1974. Ethnical Origins and Immigration. Multicoloured.

1494. 40 c. Type **701** 8 5
1495. 40 c. Heads of many races 8 5
1496. 2 cr. 50 German immigration 45 15
1497. 2 cr. 50 Italian immigration 45 15
1498. 2 cr. 50 Japanese immigration 45 15

702. Rock Formation, Sete Cidades National Park.

1974. Tourism. Multicoloured.

1499. 40 c. Type **702** 8 5
1500. 80 c. Ruins of church of St. Michael of the Missions 15 8

703. Caraca College.

1974. Caraca College. Bicent.

1502. **703.** 40 c. multicoloured .. 8 5

704. Wave Pattern.

1974. Third Brazilian Telecommunications Congress, Brasilica.

1503. **704.** 40 c. black and blue .. 8 5

705. F. Dias Paes and Rifle.

1974. Fernao Dias Paes' Expedition. 300th Anniv.

1504. **705.** 20 c. multicoloured .. 5 5

706. Mexican Flag.

1974. Visit of President Alvarez of Mexico

1505. **706.** 80 c. multicoloured .. 15 8

707. Flags and Map. **708.** "Raul Pederneiras". (caricature by J. Carlos).

1974. World Cup Football Championships.

1506. **707.** 40 c. multicoloured .. 8 5

1974. Raul Pederneiras (lawyer, author and artist). Birth Centenary.

1508. **708.** 40 c. blk. & yell. on brn. 8 5

709. Emblem and Seascape.

1974. 13th Int., Union of Building Societies and Savings Associations' Congress, Rio de Janeiro.

1509. **709.** 1 cr. 30 multicoloured 20 12

710. "UPU" on World Map.

1974. Universal Postal Union. Cent.
1511. **710.** 2 cr. 50 black & blue 45 25

711. "The Hammock" (Aruak culture).

1974. "Popular Culture".
1512. **711.** 50 c. purple 10 5
1513. – 50 c. light blue & blue 10 5
1514. – 50 c. brn., red & yell. 10 5
1515. – 50 c. brn. & yellow .. 10 5
DESIGNS—SQUARE No. 1513, Bilro Lace. VERT. (24×37 mm.), No. 1514 Guitar player (folk literature). No. 1515, Horseman (statuette by Vitalino).

712. Coffee Beans.

1974. City of Campinas. 200th Anniv.
1516. **712.** 50 c. multicoloured .. 10 5

713. Hornless Tabapua.

1974. Domestic Animals. Multicoloured.
1517. 80 c. Type **713** 15 5
1518. 1 cr. 30 Creole horse .. 20 10
1519. 2 cr. 50 Brazilian mastiff 45 15

714. Ilha Solteira Dam. 715. Herald Angel.

1974. Ilha Solteira Hydro-electric Power Project.
1520. **714.** 50 c. brn., grey & yell. 10 5

1974. Christmas.
1521. **715.** 50 c. multicoloured .. 10 5

716. "The Girls". 718. Athlete.

717. "Justice for Juveniles".

1974. "Lubrapex 74" Stamp Exhibition, Sao Paulo.
1522. **716.** 1 cr. 30 multicoloured 20 12

1974. Brazilian Juvenile Court. 50th Anniv.
1523. **717.** 90 c. multicoloured.. 15 5

1974. Sao Silvestre Long-distance Race. 50th Anniv.
1524. **718.** 3 cr. 30 multicoloured 60 20

719. Mounted Newsvendor and Newspaper Masthead.

1975. Newspaper "O Estado de S. Paulo". Centenary.
1525. **719.** 50 c. multicoloured .. 10 5

720. Industrial Complex, Sao Paulo.

1975. Economic Resources.
1526. **720.** 50 c. yellow and blue 10 5
1527. – 1 cr. 40 yell. & brn... 25 10
1528. – 4 cr. 50 yell. & blk... 75 30
DESIGNS: 1 cr. 40 Rubber industry, Acre. 4 cr. 50 Manganese industry, Amapa.

721. Santa Cruz Fortress, Rio de Janeiro.

1975. Colonial Forts.
1529. **721.** 50 c. brown on yellow 10 5
1530. – 50 c. brown on yellow 10 5
1531. – 50 c. brown on yellow 10 5
1532. – 90 c. brown on yellow 15 8
DESIGNS: No. 1530, Dos Reis Magos Fort, Rio Grande do Norte. No. 1531, Mont Serrat Fort, Bahia. No. 1532, Nossa Senhora dos Remedios Fort, Fernando de Noronha.

722. Modern Architecture, Brazilia.

1975. Brazilian Architecture. Multicoloured.
1533. 50 c. Type **722** (yellow line at right) 8 5
1534. 50 c. Type **722** (yellow line at left) 8 5
1535. 1 cr. "Palafita" House, Amazonas 15 8
1536. 1 cr. 40 Indian hut, Rondonia (yellow line at left) .. 20 10
1537. 1 cr. 40 As No. 1536 but yellow line at right .. 20 10
1538. 3 cr. 30 "Enxaimel" house, Santa Catarina (yellow line at right) 50 20
1539. 3 cr. 30 As No. 1538 but yellow line at left .. 50 20

723. "Astronotus Ocellatus

1975. Freshwater Fishes. Multicoloured.
1540. 50 c. Type **723** 8 5
1541. 50 c. "Colomesus psitacus" 8 5
1542. 50 c. "Phallocerus caudimaculatus" 8 5
1543. 50 c. "Symphysodon discus" 8 5

724. Flags forming Serviceman's Head. 725. Brazilian Pines.

1975. Honouring Ex-Servicemen of Second World War.
1544. **724.** 50 c. multicoloured .. 8 5

1975. Fauna and Flora Preservation. Mult.
1545. 70 c. Type **725** 8 5
1546. 1 cr. Ariranha (otter) (vert) 12 5
1547. 3 cr. 30 Marsh cayman .. 50 20

726. Inga Carved Stone, Paraiba State. 727. Statue of the Virgin Mary.

1975. Archaeology. Multicoloured.
1548. 70 c. Type **726** 8 5
1549. 1 cr. Marajoara pot from Para 12 5
1550. 1 cr. Fossilized fish from Ceara (horiz.) 12 5

1975. Holy Year. Franciscan Province of Our Lady of the Immaculate Conception. 300th Anniv.
1551. **727.** 3 cr. 30 multicoloured 50 20

728. Ministry of Communications Building, Rio de Janeiro. 729. "Congada" Sword Dance, Minas Gerais.

1975. Stamp Day.
1552. **728.** 70 c. red 8 5

1975. Folk Dances. Multicoloured.
1553. 70 c. Type **729** 8 5
1554. 70 c. "Frevo" umbrella dance, Pernamouco .. 8 5
1555. 70 c. "Warrior" dance, Alagoas.. .. .. 8 5

730. Stylised Trees.

1975. Tree Festival.
1556. **730.** 70 c. multicoloured .. 8 5

731. Dish Aerial and Globe. 732. Woman holding Globe.

1975. Tangua Satellite Telecommunications Station. Inauguration.
1557. **731.** 3 cr. 30 multicoloured 50 20

1975. International Women's Year.
1558. **732.** 3 cr. 30 multicoloured 50 20

733. Tile, Balcony Rail and Memorial Column, Alcantara.

1975. Historic Towns. Multicoloured.
1559. 70 c. Type **733** 8 5
1560. 70 c. Belfry, weather vane and jug, Goias (26×38 mm.) 8 5
1561. 70 c. Sao Francisco Convent, Sao Cristovao (40×22 mm.) 8 5

734. Children greeting "Book Man".

1975. National Book Day.
1562. **734.** 70 c. multicoloured .. 8 5

735. Congress Emblem.

1975. 24th American Society of Travel Agents Congress, Rio de Janeiro.
1563. **735.** 70 c. multicoloured .. 8 5

736. "Angels". 737. Map of the Americas.

1975. Christmas.
1564. **736.** 70 c. brown and red 8 5

1975. 2nd Inter-American Telecommunications Conference (C.I.T.E.L.), Rio de Janeiro.
1565. **737.** 5 cr. 20 multicoloured 80 30

738. Firar Nicodemus. 739. "Thanksgiving" (figures with upraised arms).

1975. Obligatory Tax. Leprosy Research Fund.
1566. **738.** 10 c. brown 8 5

1975. Thanksgiving Day.
1567. **739.** 70 c. turquoise & blue 8 5

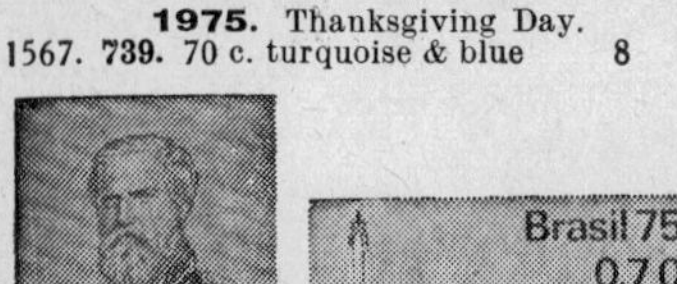

740. Emperor Pedro II. **741.** Salt Stone Beach, Piaui.

1975. Emperor Pedro II. 150th Birth Anniv.
1568. **740.** 70 c. brown 8 5

1975. Tourism. Multicoloured.
1569. 70 c. Type **741** 8 5
1570. 70 c. Guarapari Beach (Espirito Santo) 8 5
1571. 70 c. Torres Cliffs (Rio Grande do Sol) .. 8 5

742. Triple Jump.

1975. 7th Pan-American Games, Santo Domingo, Dominican Republic.
1572. **742.** 1 cr. 60 turquoise & black 25 10

743. U.N. Emblem and H.Q., New York.

1975. United Nations. 30th Anniv.
1573. **743.** 1 cr. 30 violet on blue 25 10

744. Electric-light Bulbs and House.

1976. "Preservation of Fuel Resources". Multicoloured.
1574. 70 c. Type **744** 8 5
1575. 70 c. Drops of petrol and car 8 5

745. "Concorde" in Flight.

1976. "Concorde's First Commercial Flight, Paris–Rio de Janeiro.
1576. **745.** 5 cr. 20 black & grey 90 40

746. Early and Modern Telephone Equipment.

1976. Telephone Centenary.
1578. **746.** 5 cr. 20 black & orange 60 25

747. "Eye"-part of Exclamation Mark. **748.** Kaiapo Body-painting.

1976. World Health Day.
1579. **747.** 1 cr. lake, brn. & violet 12 5

1976. Brazil's Indigenous Culture. Multicoloured.
1580. 1 cr. Type **748** 12 5
1581. 1 cr. Bakairi ceremonial mask 12 5
1582. 1 cr. Karaja feather head-dress 12 5

749. Itamaraty Palace, Brasilia.

1976. Diplomats' Day.
1583. **749.** 1 cr. multicoloured .. 12 5

750. "The Sprinkler" (J. Tarcisio). **751.** Basketball.

1976. Modern Brazilian Art. Multicoloured.
1584. 1 cr. Type **750** 12 5
1585. 1 cr. "Beribboned Fingers" (P. Checcacci) (horiz.) 12 5

1976. Olympic Games, Montreal.
1586. **751.** 1 cr. black and green 12 5
1587. – 1 cr. 40 black & blue 15 5
1588. – 5 cr. 20 black & orge. 60 25
DESIGNS: 1 cr. 40 Sailings. 5 cr. 20 Judo.

752. Golden-faced Lion-monkey. **753.** Cine Camera on Screen.

1976. Nature Protection. Multicoloured.
1589. 1 cr. Type **752** 12 5
1590. 1 cr. Orchid ("Acacallis cyanea") 12 5

1976. Brazilian Cinematograph Industry.
1591. **753.** 1 cr. multicoloured .. 12 5

754. Bahia Woman.

1976.
1592. **754.** 15 c. brown 5 5
1593. – 20 c. blue 5 5
1594. – 30 c. mauve 5 5
1595. – 50 c. brown 5 5
1596. – 80 c. green 10 5
1597. – 1 cr. black 12 5
1598. – 7 cr. lilac 85 40
1599. – 20 cr. blue .. .. 2·40 1·10
DESIGNS—HORIZ. 20 c. Raft Fisherman. VERT. 30 c. Rubber Tapper. 50 c. Gaucho. 80 c. Gold Prospector. 1 cr. Banana Picker. 7 cr. Salt Raker. 20 cr. Lace-maker.

755. "Hyhessobrycon innesi".

1976. Brazilian Freshwater Fishes. Mult.
1600. 1 cr. Type **755** 12 5
1601. 1 cr. "Copeina arnoldi" .. 12 5
1602. 1 cr. "Prochilodus insignis" 12 5
1603. 1 cr. "Crenicichla lepidota" 12 5
1604. 1 cr. "Agenieosus sp." .. 12 5
1605. 1 cr. "Corydoras reticlatus" 12 5

756. Santa Marta Lighthouse.

1976. Laguna 300th Anniv.
1606. **756.** 1 cr. blue 12 5

757. "Magic Carpet".

1976. Stamp Day.
1607. **757.** 1 cr. multicoloured .. 12 5

758. Oil Lamp and Profile.

1976. Brazilian Nursing Association. 50th Anniv.
1608. **758.** 1 cr. multicoloured .. 12 5

759. Puppet Soldier. **760.** Winner's Medal.

1976. Mamulengo Puppet Theatre. Mult.
1609. 1 cr. Type **759** .. 12 5
1610. 1 cr. 30 Puppet girl .. 15 5
1611. 1 cr. 60 Finger puppets .. (horiz.) 20 8

1976. 27th International Military Athletics Championships, Rio de Janeiro.
1612. **760.** 5 cr. 20 multicoloured 60 35

761. Family within "House". **762.** Rotten Tree.

1976. SESC and SENAC National Organisations.
1613. **761.** 1 cr. blue 12 5

1976. Conservation of Environment.
1614. **762.** 1 cr. multicoloured .. 12 5

763. "Atomic Energy".

1976. 20th International Atomic Energy Conference, Rio de Janeiro.
1615. **763.** 5 cr. 20 multicoloured 60 35

764. Tube Train. **766.** School Building.

765. St. Francis of Assisi.

1976. Sao Paulo Underground Railway. Inauguration.
1616. **764.** 1 cr. 60 multicoloured 20 8

1976. St. Francis of Assisi. 750th Death Anniv.
1617. **765.** 5 cr. 20 multicoloured 60 35

1976. Ouro Preto Mining School. Cent.
1618. **766.** 1 cr. violet 12 5

EXPRESS STAMP

1930. Surch. **1000 REIS EXPRESSO** and bars.
E 490. **49.** 1000 r. on 200 r. blue 75 35

NEWSPAPER STAMPS

N 1. N 2.

1889. Roul.
N 88. N 1. 10 r. orange 70 40
N 89. 20 r. orange .. .. 1·75 90
N 90. 50 r. orange .. .. 2·25 1·75
N 91. 100 r. orange .. 1·40 90
N 92. 200 f. orange .. 70 50
N 93. 300 r. orange .. 70 50
N 94. 500 r. orange .. 5·00 3·25
N 95. 700 r. orange .. 85 75
N 96. 1000 r. orange .. 1·75 1·00

1889. Roul.
N 97. N 1. 10 r. grey-green .. 12 10
N 98. 20 r. green .. 12 12
N 99. 50 r. buff .. 20 12
N 100a. 100 r. mauve .. 20 12
N 101. 200 r. black .. 35 30
N 102. 300 r. red .. 95 80
N 103. 500 r. green .. 7·00 6·50
N 104. 700 r. blue .. 7·50 7·00
N 105. 100 r. brown .. 2·25 2·10

1890. Perf.
N 111. N 2. 10 r. blue .. .. 1·25 95
N 112a. 20 r. green .. 3·50 1·40
N 118. 100 r. mauve .. 1·50 1·40

N 3. Southern Cross and Sugar Loaf Mountain.

1890. Perf.

N 119. N 3. 10 r. blue 12 10
N 123a. 20 r. green 30 15
N 127. 50 r. green .. .. 1·00 1·00

OFFICIAL STAMPS

O 1. Pres. Affonso Penna. O 2. Pres. Hermes de Fonseca. O 3. Pres. Wenceslao Braz.

1906. Various frames.

O 282. O 1. 10 r. green and orange 5 5
O 283. 20 r. green and orange 5 5
O 284. 50 r. green and orange 8 5
O 285. 100 r. green & orange 8 5
O 286. 200 r. green & orange 8 5
O 287. 300 r. green & orange 12 5
O 288. 400 r. green & orange 35 12
O 289. 500 r. green & orange 30 10
O 290. 700 r. green & orange 40 20
O 291. 1000 r. green & orange 30 10
O 292. 2000 r. green & orange 35 20
O 293. 5000 r. green & orange 1·10 45
O 294. 10,000 r. green & orge. 40 20

1913. Various frames.

O 295. O 2. 10 r. black and grey .. 10 8
O 296. 20 r. black and olive 10 8
O 297. 50 r. black and grey .. 10 8
O 298. 100 r. black and red .. 8 5
O 299. 200 r. black and blue 10 8
O 300. 500 r. black & yellow 15 12
O 301. 600 r. black & purple 25 12
O 302. 1000 r. black & brown 35 12
O 303. 2000 r. black & brown 45 20
O 304. 5000 r. black & bistre 60 30
O 305. 10,000 r. black .. 80 40
O 306. 20,000 r. black & blue 2·75 1·75
O 307. 50,000 r. black & grn. 7·50 5·00
O 308. 100,000 r. black & red 28·00 21·00
O 309. 500,000 r. black & brn. 48·00 42·00
O 310. 1,000,000 r. blk. & brn. 60·00 48·00

1919.

O 311. O 3. 10 r. brown .. 12 12
O 312. 50 r. green .. 12 12
O 313. 100 r. red .. 15 12
O 314. 200 r. blue .. 30 15
O 315. 500 r. orange .. 1·25 1·10

POSTAGE DUE STAMPS

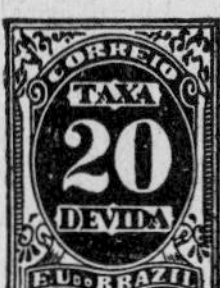

D 1. D 2. D 3.

1889. Roul.

D 88. D 1. 10 r. red 20 15
D 89. 20 r. red 25 15
D 90. 50 r. red 40 25
D 91. 100 r. red 15 12
D 92. 200 r. red .. .. 5·00 2·75
D 93. 300 r. red .. .. 1·00 60
D 94. 500 r. red 45 40
D 95. 700 r. red 65 50
D 96. 1000 r. red .. .. 1·40 1·00

1890. Roul.

D 97. D 1. 10 r. orange .. 10 8
D 98. 20 r. blue 10 8
D 99. 50 r. olive 10 8
D 100. 200 r. claret .. 40 15
D 101. 300 r. green .. 40 20
D 102. 500 r. grey .. 45 30
D 103. 700 r. violet .. 65 50
D 104. 1000 r. purple .. 1·00 75

1895. Perf.

D 172. D 2. 10 r. blue 30 20
D 173. 20 r. green 40 25
D 174. 50 r. green 65 30
D 175. 100 r. red 30 8
D 176b. 200 r. lilac 40 10
D 177a. 300 r. blue .. .. 1·00 35
D 178. 2000 r. brown .. 5·50 3·75

1906.

D 282. D 3. 10 r. slate 5 5
D 283. 20 r. violet 5 5
D 284. 50 r. green 8 5
D 285. 100 r. red 10 5
D 286. 200 r. blue 10 5
D 287. 300 r. grey 12 8
D 288. 400 r. deep olive .. 25 12
D 289. 500 r. lilac .. .. 10·00 8·00
D 290. D 3. 600 r. purple .. 35 20
D 291. 700 r. brown .. 8·00 6·00
D 292. 1000 r. red 35 30
D 293. 2000 r. green .. 80 35
D 294. 5000 r. brown .. 90 35

D 4.

1919.

D 345. D 4. 5 r. brown 5 5
D 403. 10 r. mauve 5 5
D 365. 20 r. olive 5 5
D 404. 20 r. black 5 5
D 405. 50 r. green 5 5
D 375. 100 r. red 5 5
D 407. 200 r. blue 5 5
D 408. 400 r. brown .. 12 5
D 401. 600 r. violet .. 10 5
D 350. 600 r. orange .. 15 8
D 409. 1000 r. blue-green .. 15 8
D 439. 2000 r. brown .. 50 20
D 411. 5000 r. blue 75 40

BREMEN E2

A free city of the Hanseatic League, situated on the R. Weser in N. Germany. Now part of West Germany.

22 grote = 10 silbergroschen.
72 grote = 1 thaler.

1. 2. 3.

1855. Imperf.

1. 1. 3 g. black and blue .. £110 £160

1856. Imperf.

3. 2. 5 g. black on rose £110 £140
4. 7 g. black on yellow .. £120 £350
5. 3. 5 sg. green .. .. .. 75·00 £110

4. 5.

1861. Zigzag roulette or perf.

17. 4. 2 g. orange .. .. 42·00 £170
19. 1. 3 g. black on blue .. 42·00 £160
12. 2. 5 g. black on rose .. 75·00 90·00
21. 7 g. black on yellow .. 70·00 £1400
22. 5. 10 g. black £110 £550
24. 3. 5 sg. green .. .. 90·00 90·00

BRITISH ANTARCTIC TERRITORY BC

Constituted in 1962 comprising territories south of latitude 60° S., from the former Falkland Is. Dependencies.

1. M.V. "Kista Dan".

1963.

1. 1. ½d. blue 5 5
2. – 1d. brown 5 5
3. – 1½d. red and maroon .. 8 8
4. – 2d. purple 10 12
5. – 2½d. myrtle 12 12
6. – 3d. turquoise 15 15
7. – 4d. sepia 20 20
8. – 6d. olive and ultramarine 20 20
9. – 9d. olive-green 30 35
10. – 1s. turquoise-blue .. 40 45
11. – 2s. violet and bistre .. 1·25 1·75
12. – 2s. 6d. blue .. .. 1·40 1·90
13. – 5s. orange and red .. 2·50 3·00
14. – 10s. ultram. and emerald 5·50 7·00
15. – £1 black and blue .. 11·00 14·00
15a.– £1 red and black .. 15·00 17·00

DESIGNS: 1d. Manhauling. 1½d. Muskeg (tractor). 2d. Skiing. 2½d. Beaver (aircraft). 3d. R.R.S. "John Biscoe". 4d. Camp scene. 6d. H.M.S. "Protector". 9d. Sledging. 1s. Otter (aircraft). 2s. Huskies. 2s. 6d. Helicopter. 5s. Snocat (tractor). 10s. R.R.S. "Shackleton". £1 (No. 15), Antarctic map. £1 (No. 15a.), H.M.S. "Endurance".

1966. Churchill Commem. As T **28** of Antigua.

16. ½d. blue .. .. .. 12 12·00
17. 1d. green .. .. .. 30 30·00
18. 1s. brown .. .. .. 3·50 4·50
19. 2s. violet .. .. .. 4·50 5·50

2. Lemaire Channel and Icebergs.

1969. Continuous Scientific Work. 25th Anniv.

20. **2.** 3½ blk., bl. & ultram. .. 20 25
21. – 6d. multicoloured .. 35 45
22. – 1s. black, blue & verm. .. 55 65
23. – 2s. blk. orange & turq. .. 1·10 1·40

DESIGNS: 6d. Radio Sonde Balloon. 1s. Muskeg pulling Tent Equipment. 2s. Surveyors with Theodolite.

1971. Decimal Currency. Nos. 1/14 surch.

24. ½p. on ½d. blue 5 5
25. 1p. on 1d. brown 5 8
26. 1½p. on 1½d. red and purple 8 8
27. 2p. on 2d. purple 8 10
28. 2½p. on 2½d. green 10 12
29. 3p. on 3d. blue 15 20
30. 4p. on 4d. brown 20 25
31. 5p. on 6d. green and blue 25 30
32. 6p. on 9d. green 30 30
33. 7½p. on 1s. blue 30 45
34. 10p. on 2s. violet & brown 45 65
35. 15p. on 2s. 6d. blue .. 90 1·10
36. 25p. on 5s. orange & red .. 1·60 1·90
37. 50p. on 10s. blue & green 3·25 3·75

3. Setting up Camp.

1971. Antarctic Treaty. 10th Anniv. Multicoloured.

38. 1½p. Type **3** 8 8
39. 4p. Snow petrels 35 40
40. 5p. Weddell seals 35 40
41. 10p. Adelie penguins .. 75 85

Nos. 38/41 each include Antarctic Map and Queen Elizabeth in their design.

1972. Royal Silver Wedding. As T **19** of Ascension, but with Seals and Emperor Penguins in background.

42. 5p. brown .. .. .. 50 1·00
43. 10p. green .. .. .. 1·00 2·25

4. James Cook and "Resolution".

1973. Multicoloured.

64. ½p. Type **4** 8 8
45. 1p. Thaddeus Von Bellinghausen and "Vostok" .. 5 5
46. 1½p. James Weddell and "Jane" 5 5
47. 2p. John Biscoe and "Tula" 5 5
48. 2½p. J.S.C. Dumont d'Urville and "Astrolabe" .. 8 8
49. 3p. James Clark Ross and "Erebus" 5 8
50. 4p. C. A. Larsen and "Jason" 8 8
51. 5p. Adrien de Gerlache and "Belgica" 8 10
52. 6p. Otto Nordenskjold and "Antarctic" 10 12
53. 7½p. W. S. Bruce and "Scotia" 12 15
54. 10p. Jean-Baptiste Charcot and "Pourquoi Pas?" .. 20 20
55. 15p. Ernest Shackleton and "Endurance" 25 30

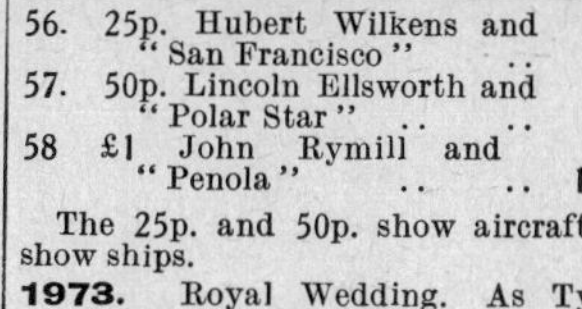

56. 25p. Hubert Wilkens and "San Francisco" 45 50
57. 50p. Lincoln Ellsworth and "Polar Star" 85 95
58 £1 John Rymill and "Penola" .. .. 1·75 2·00

The 25p. and 50p. show aircraft; the rest show ships.

1973. Royal Wedding. As Type **26** of Anguilla. Background colour given. Mult.

59. 5p. brown 15 20
60. 15p. blue 35 40

5. Churchill and Churchill Peninsular, B.A.T.

1974. Sir Winston Churchill. Birth Cent. Multicoloured.

61. 5p. Type **5** 25 30
62. 15p. Churchill and "Trespassey" 50 55

BRITISH COLUMBIA AND VANCOUVER ISLAND BC

Former British colonies, now a Western province of the Dominion of Canada, whose stamps are used.

1.

1860. Imperf. or perf.

2. 1. 2½d. pink .. .. .. £120 90·00

VANCOUVER ISLAND

2.

1865. Imperf. or perf. Various frames.

13. 2. 5 c. rose .. .. .. 75·00 65·00
14. – 10 c. blue .. .. .. 75·00 65·00

BRITISH COLUMBIA

4. Emblems of United Kingdom.

1865.

21. 4. 3d. blue .. .. .. 24·00 20·00

1868. Surch. in words or figures and words.

28. 4. 2 c. brown .. .. 25·00 22·00
29. 5 c. red .. .. 32·00 30·00
24. 10 c. lake £180 £150
31. 25 c. yellow .. .. 42·00 38·00
26. 50 c. mauve £160 £150
27. 1 dol. green £375 £300

BRITISH EAST AFRICA BC

Now incorporated in Kenya and Uganda.

1890. Stamps of Gt. Britain (1881) surch. **BRITISH EAST AFRICA COMPANY** and value in annas.

1. 40. ½ a. on 1d. lilac .. .. £150 85·00
2. 56. 1 a. on 2d. green & red .. £150 85·00
3. 61. 4 a. on 5d. purple & blue £140 70·00

1. Arms of the Company. **2.**

1890. Nos. 16/19 are larger (24 × 25 mm.).
4c. 1. ½ a. brown 30 30
5b. 1 a. green 30 1·10
6. 2 a. red 1·10 1·25
7b. 2½ a. black on yellow 1·75 1·00
8a. 3 a. black on red 60 70
9. 4 a. brown 1·10 1·75
11a. 4½ a. purple 1·10 3·75
29. 5 a. black on blue 70 3·50
30. 7½ a. black 70 3·50
12. 8 a. blue 1·75 2·25
13. 8 a. grey 65·00 70·00
14. 1 r. red 2·10 3·00
15. 1 r. grey 50·00 60·00
16. – 2 r. red 4·25 4·75
17. – 3 r. purple 3·00 4·75
18. – 4 r. blue 4·50 5·50
19. – 5 r. green 12·00 9·50

1891. With handstamped or pen surcharges Initialled in black.
20. 1. ½ a. on 2 a. red £280 £130
31. ½ a. on 3 a. black on red 42·00 17·00
32. 1 a. on 3 a. black on red £450 £325
26. 1 a. on 4 a. brown £325 £160

1894. Surch. in words and figures.
27. 1. 5 a. on 8 a. blue 13·00 28·00
28. 7½ a. on 1 r. red 14·00 28·00

1895. Optd. **BRITISH EAST AFRICA.**
33. 1. ½ a. brown 10·00 6·50
34. 1 a. green 14·00 15·00
35. 2 a. red 26·00 26·00
36. 2½ a. black on yellow 23·00 15·00
37. 3 a. black on red 12·00 12·00
38. 4 a. brown 12·00 12·00
39. 4½ a. purple 28·00 26·00
40. 5 a. black on blue 40·00 30·00
41. 7½ a. black 20·00 20·00
42. 8 a. blue 23·00 23·00
43. 1 r. red 13·00 14·00
44. – 2 r. red 30·00 35·00
45. – 3 r. purple 26·00 30·00
46. – 4 r. blue 35·00 30·00
47. – 5 r. green 65·00 80·00

1895. Surch. with large **2½**.
48. 1. 2½ a. on 4½ a. purple 20·00 17·00

1895. Stamps of India (Queen Victoria) optd. **British East Africa.**
49. 14. ½ a. blue-green 80 80
50. – 1 a. purple 1·10 1·40
51. – 1½ a. brown 1·75 1·75
52. – 2 a. blue 80 1·10
53. – 2½ a. green 3·00 1·75
54. – 3 a. orange 3·00 3·00
55. – 4 a. green (No. 96) 4·50 4·50
56. – 6 a. brown (No. 80) 8·00 7·00
57. – 8 a. mauve 13·00 14·00
58. – 12 a. purple on red 6·50 8·00
59. – 1 r. grey (No. 101) 13·00 16·00
60. 26. 1 r. green and red 7·00 9·00
61. 27. 2 r. red and orange 15·00 20·00
62. 3 r. brown and green 20·00 22·00
63. 5 r. blue and violet 22·00 23·00

1895. No. 51 surch. with small **2½**.
64. "2½" on 1½ a. brown 12·00 12·00

1896.
65. 2. ½ a. green 15 15
66. 1 a. red 35 12
67. 2 a. chocolate 85 65
68. 2½ a. blue 1·25 70
69. 3 a. grey 90 1·40
70. 4 a. green 1·75 70
71. 4½ a. yellow 1·25 2·00
72. 5 a. brown 3·00 2·00
73. 7½ a. mauve 3·00 3·50
74. 8 a. grey 1·25 2·10
75. 1 r. blue 7·00 6·00
76. 2 r. orange 11·00 7·00
77. 3 r. violet 11·00 7·00
78. 4 r. red 11·00 9·00
79. 5 r. brown 11·00 9·00

1897. Stamps of Zanzibar. 1896, optd. **British East Africa.**
80. 1. ½ a green and red 14·00 10·00
81. 1 a. blue and red 26·00 26·00
82. 2 a. brown and red 14·00 10·00
83. 4½ a. orange and red 15·00 10·00
84. 5 a. brown and red 15·00 11·00
85. 7½ a. mauve and red 22·00 17·00

1897. As last, surch. **2½**.
86. 1. "2½" on 1 a. blue and red 20·00 16·00
89. "2½" on 3 a. grey and red 17·00 16·00

1897. As T 2, but larger.
92. 1 r. blue 8·50 8·00
93. 2 r. orange 20·00 20·00
94. 3 r. violet 22·00 25·00
95. 4 r. red 35·00 42·00
96. 5 r. brown 42·00 60·00
97. 10 r. brown 80·00 85·00
98. 20 r. green £225 £225
99. 50 r. mauve £550 £600

MORE DETAILED LISTS

are given in the Stanley Gibbons Catalogues referred to in the country headings:

BC British Commonwealth
E1, E2, E3 Europe 1, 2, 3
O1, O2, O3, O4 Overseas 1, 2, 3, 4

BRITISH GUIANA BC

Situated on the N.E. coast of S. America. A British colony granted full internal self-Government in August, 1951. Attained independence on 26th May, 1966, when the country was renamed Guyana.

100 cents = 1 dollar.

1.

1850. Imperf.
1. 1. 2 c. black on red — £38000
2. 4 c. black on orange £7500 £1500
4. 8 c. black on green £5000 £1200
5. 12 c. black on blue £2500 £1100

Prices are for used stamps cut round. Stamps cut square are worth much more.

2.

3. Seal of the Colony.

1852. Imperf.
9. 2. 1 c. black on magenta £4000 £2500
10. 4 c. black on blue £5000 £2500

1853. Imperf.
11. 3. 1 c. red £1200 £300
20. 4 c. blue £300 £150

4.

1856. Imperf.
23. 4. 1 c. black and magenta — £300000
24. 4 c. black on magenta — £2700
26. 4 c. black on blue — £13000

5.

6.

1860. Perf.
29. 5. 1 c. red £225 55·00
40. 1 c. brown 60·00 23·00
85. 1 c. black 3·00 1·50
88. 2 c. orange 5·50 1·50
90. 4 c. blue 12·00 2·75
71. 6. 6 c. blue 18·00 9·00
73. 5. 8 c. rose 21·00 4·50
47. 12 c. lilac 18·00 6·00
99. 12 c. grey 23·00 5·50
64. 24 c. green 30·00 14·00
78. 6. 24 c. green 21·00 3·75
82. 48 c. red 24·00 11·00

The prices quoted for Nos. 29/82 are for fine copies with four margins. Medium specimens can be supplied at much lower rates.

7.

8.

1862. Various borders. Roul.
116. 7. 1 c. black on red £375 75·00
117. 2 c. black on yellow £375 60·00
122. 4 c. black on blue £375 60·00

The above prices are for stamps signed in the centre by the Postmaster. Unsigned stamps are worth considerably less.

1876.
126. 8. 1 c. grey 1·50 35
171. 2 c. orange 3·75 55
172. 4 c. blue 12·00 5·50
173. 6 c. brown 3·00 3·00
174. 8 c. rose 17·00 90
131. 12 c. violet 14·00 2·75
132. 24 c. green 14·00 4·50
133. 48 c. brown 17·00 6·00
134. 96 c. olive 90·00 75·00

1878. Optd. with thick horiz. or horiz. and vert. bars. (a) On postage stamps.
137. 8. 1 c. on 6 c. brown 11·00 12·00
141. 6. 1 c. on 6 c. blue 24·00 9·00

(b) On official stamps of 1875 and 1877.
138. 5. 1 c. black 20·00 11·00
139. 8. 1 c. grey 20·00 7·50
140. 2 c. orange 21·00 11·00
144. 4 c. blue 20·00 11·00
145. 6 c. brown 23·00 11·00
146. 5. 8 c. rose 23·00 12·00
148. 8. 8 c. rose 24·00 14·00

1881. Surch. with figure. Old value barred out in ink. (a) On postage stamps.
152. 6. "1" on 48 c. red 5·00 2·10
149. 8. "1" on 96 c. olive 1·90 1·90
150. "2" on 96 c. olive 1·90 3·50

(b) On stamps optd. **OFFICIAL.**
154. 5. "1" on 12 c. lilac 12·00 9·00
153. 8. "1" on 48 c. brown 20·00 14·00
155. "2" on 12 c. violet 9·00 6·50
157. "2" on 24 c. green 12·00 6·50

9.

10.

1882.
162. 9. 1 c. black on rose 9·00 7·00
163. 2 c. black on yellow 11·00 7·00

Each stamp is perforated with the word "SPECIMEN".

1888. T 8 without value in bottom tablet, surch. **INLAND REVENUE** and value.
175. 8. 1 c. purple 40 40
176. 2 c. purple 40 40
177. 3 c. purple 40 40
178. 4 c. purple 70 55
179. 6 c. purple 1·40 70
180. 8 c. purple 55 55
181. 10 c. purple 1·75 1·50
182. 20 c. purple 3·50 3·00
183. 40 c. purple 5·50 4·25
184. 72 c. purple 5·50 5·00
185. $1 green 85·00 60·00
186. $2 green 45·00 35·00
187. $3 green 27·00 23·00
188. $4 green 75·00 60·00
189. $5 green 42·00 38·00

1889. No. 176 surch. with additional **2.**
192. 8. "2" on 2 c. purple 40 40

1889.
193. 10. 1 c. purple and grey 55 45
213. 1 c. green 15 15
194. 2 c. purple and orange 45 25
234. 2 c. purple and red 1·40 25
235. 2 c. purple & black on red 45 12
253a. 2 c. red 85 25
195. 4 c. purple and blue 1·40 1·40
254. 4 c. brown and purple 1·60 90
255. 5 c. blue 85 35
243. 5 c. pur. and blue on blue 2·25 1·60
198. 6 c. purple and brown 3·50 1·90
236. 6 c. black and blue 3·50 4·00
256. 6 c. grey and black 5·00 2·50
199. 8 c. purple and rose 2·25 90
215. 8 c. purple and black 1·75 2·25
200. 12 c. purple and mauve 3·50 75
257. 12 c. orange and purple 2·50 1·60
201. 24 c. purple and green 3·50 1·25
202. 48 c. purple and red 7·00 3·00
247. 48 c. grey and brown 8·00 8·50
248. 60 c. green and rose 8·00 9·00
203. 72 c. purple and brown 7·50 4·50
205. 96 c. purple and red 20·00 18·00
250. 96 c. blk. & red on yell. 17·00 17·00

1890. Nos. 185/8 surch. **ONE CENT.**
207. 8. 1 cent on $1 green 75 55
208. 1 cent on $2 green 40 75
209. 1 cent on $3 green 70 60
210. 1 cent on $4 green 1·50 2·25

11. Mount Roraima.

12. Kaieteur Falls.

13.

1898. Jubilee.
216. 11. 1 c. black and carmine 1·60 45
217. 12. 2 c. brown and blue 1·75 55
219. 11. 5 c. green and brown 6·00 2·75
220. 12. 10 c. black and red 8·00 5·00
221. 11. 15 c. brown and blue 8·00 5·50

1899. Nos. 219/21 surch. **TWO CENTS.**
222. 11. 2 c. on 5 c. grn. & brn. 70 80
223. 12. 2 c. on 10 c. blk. & red 45 60
224. 11. 2 c. on 15 c. brn. & blue 1·00 1·00

1905. T 10, but inscr. "REVENUE", optd. **POSTAGE AND REVENUE.**
251. 10. $2.40 green and violet 90·00 £100

1913.
272. 13. 1 c. green 15 12
260. 2 c. red 30 12
274. 2 c. violet 15 10
275. 4 c. brown and purple 60 20
262. 5 c. blue 50 50
263. 6 c. grey and black 55 55
276. 6 c. blue 60 35
277. 12 c. orange and violet 85 75
278. 24 c. purple and green 1·40 1·40
279. 48 c. grey and purple 3·25 3·50
280. 60 c. green and rose 6·50 6·50
281. 72 c. purple and brown 7·00 7·00
269a. 96 c. black & red on yell. 9·50 9·50

1918. Optd. **WAR TAX** in two lines.
271. 13. 2 c. red 15 15

14. Ploughing Rice Field.

15. Indian shooting Fish.

16. Kaieteur Falls.

17. Public Buildings, Georgetown.

1931. County Union. Cent.
283. 14. 1 c. green 35 35
284. 15. 2 c. brown 55 35
285. 16. 4 c. red 1·50 1·00
286. 17. 6 c. blue 3·00 3·25
287. 16. $1 violet 15·00 17·00

18. Ploughing Rice Field.

19. Gold mining. 20. South America.

1934.

288. 18. 1 c. green 5 5
289. 15. 2 c. brown 10 5
290. 19. 3 c. red 5 5
291. 16. 4 c. violet 35 20
292. – 6 c. blue 80 80
293. – 12 c. orange 5 15
294. – 24 c. purple .. .. 2·25 2·25
295. – 48 c. black .. .. 5·50 6·00
296. 16. 50 c. green .. .. 7·00 7·50
297. – 60 c. brown .. .. 16·00 15·00
298. – 72 c. purple .. .. 1·10 1·10
299. – 96 c. black .. .. 15·00 16·00
300. – $1 violet .. .. 15·00 16·00

DESIGNS—HORIZ. 6 c. Shooting logs over falls. 12 c. Stabroek Market. 24 c. Sugar canes in punts. 48 c. Forest road. 60 c. Victoria Regia lilies. 72 c. Mt. Roraima. $1 Botanical Gardens. VERT. 96 c. Sir Walter Raleigh and his son.

The 2 c., 4 c. and 50 c. are without the dates shown in T 15/16 and the 12 c., 48 c., 72 c. and 96 c. have no portrait.

1935. Silver Jubilee. As T 11 of Antigua.

301. 2 c. blue and grey .. 5 5
302. 6 c. brown and blue .. 60 50
303. 12 c. green and blue .. 80 90
304. 24 c. grey and purple .. 1·75 1·75

1937. Coronation. As T 2 of Aden.

305. 2 c. brown 5 5
306. 4 c. grey 12 15
307. 6 c. blue 20 25

1938. Designs as for same values of 1934 issue (except where indicated) but with portrait of King George VI (as in T 20) where portrait of King George V previously appeared.

308aa.18. 1 c. green 5 5
309. – 2 c. violet (As 4 c.) .. 5 5
310. 20. 4 c. red and black .. 5 5
311a. – 6 c. blue (As 2 c.) .. 8 8
312a. – 24 c. green .. .. 1·25 20
313. – 36 c. violet (As 4 c.) .. 25 25
314. – 48 c. orange 35 20
315. – 60 c. brown (As 6 c.) .. 40 40
316a. – 96 c. purple .. .. 1·10 1·10
317. – $1 violet .. .. 1·10 90
318a. – $2 purple (As 72 c.) .. 1·75 3·00
319b. – $3 brown .. .. 4·00 4·00

DESIGN—HORIZ. $3 Victoria Regia lilies.

1946. Victory. As T 4 of Aden.

320. 3 c. red 8 5
321. 6 c. blue 8 5

1948. Silver Wedding. As T 5 and 6 of Aden.

322. 3 c. red 8 8
323. $3 brown .. .. .. 4·00 5·00

1949. U.P.U. As T 14 to 17 of Antigua.

324. 4 c. red 20 15
325. 6 c. blue 35 30
326. 12 c. orange 45 40
327. 24 c. green 65 65

1951. Inaug. of B.W.I. University College. As T 18 and 19 of Antigua.

328. 3 c. black and red .. 15 12
329. 6 c. black and blue .. 25 20

1953. Coronation. As T 7 of Aden.

330. 4 c. black and red .. 12 8

21. G.P.O., Georgetown.

1954.

331. 21. 1 c. black 5 5
332. – 2 c. myrtle 5 5
333. – 3 c. olive and brown .. 5 5
334. – 4 c. violet 5 5
356. – 5 c. red and black .. 5 8
336. – 6 c. green 8 8
337. – 8 c. blue 8 10
359. – 12 c. black and brown 12 5
339. – 24 c. black and orange 35 30
361. – 36 c. red and black .. 30 5
362. – 48 c. blue and brown .. 35 35
342. – 72 c. red and green .. 70 75
343. – $1 pink, yell., grn. & blk. 75 50
344. – $2 mauve .. .. 1·50 90
345. – $5 blue and black .. 3·75 4·00

DESIGNS—HORIZ. 2 c. Botanical Garden 3 c. s. Victoria Regia lilies. 5 c. Map. 6 c. Rice combine-harvester. 8 c. Sugar cane entering factory. 24 c. Bauxite mining. 36 c. Mt. Roraima. $1 Toucan. $2 Dredging gold. VERT. 4 c. Shooting fish. 12 c. Felling Greenheart. 48c. Kaieteur Falls. 72 c. Arapaima (fish). $5 Arms.

22.

1961. History and Culture Week.

346. 22. 5 c. sepia and red .. 10 12
347. 6 c. sepia and green .. 12 12
348. 30 c. sepia and orange 30 40

1963. Freedom from Hunger. As T 10 of Aden.

349. 20 c. violet 30 30

1963. Red Cross Cent. As T 24 of Antigua.

350. 5 c. red and black .. 12 12
351. 20 c. red and blue .. 45 50

23. Weightlifting.

1964. Olympic Games, Tokyo.

367. 23. 5 c. orange 10 10
368. 8 c. blue 12 12
369. 25 c. magenta 30 30

1965. I.T.U. Cent. As T 26 of Antigua.

370. 5 c. green and olive .. 8 8
371. 25 c. blue and magenta .. 25 25

1965. I.C.Y. As T 27 of Antigua.

372. 5 c. purple and turquoise 8 8
373. 25 c. green and lavender 25 25

24. St. George's Cathedral, Georgetown.

1966. Churchill Commem.

374. 24. 5 c. black, red and gold 10 10
375. 25 c. black, blue & gold 30 30

1966. Royal Visit. As T 29 of Antigua.

376. 3 c. black and blue .. 8 8
377. 25 c. black and magenta .. 25 25

OFFICIAL STAMPS

1875. Optd. **OFFICIAL.**

O 1. 5. 1 c. black .. .. 4·25 4·25
O 2. 2 c. orange .. .. 21·00 4·25
O 3. 8 c. rose .. .. 50·00 22·00
O 4. 12 c. lilac .. .. £130 70·00
O 5. 6. 24 c. green .. .. 85·00 35·00

1877. Optd. **OFFICIAL.**

O 6. 8. 1 c. grey .. .. 38·00 18·00
O 7. 2 c. orange .. .. 11·00 4·25
O 8. 4 c. blue .. .. 17·00 8·50
O 9. 6 c. brown £325 £100
O 10. 8 c. rose .. .. £300 85·00

POSTAGE DUE STAMPS

1940. As Type D 1 of Barbados, but inscr. " BRITISH GUIANA ".

D 1a. 1 c. green 10 10
D 2aa. 2 c. black 10 10
D 3. 4 c. blue 10 10
D 4a. 12 c. red 10 10

For later issues see **GUYANA.**

BRITISH HONDURAS BC

A Br. colony on the E. coast of Central America. Self-government was granted on 1 Jan. 1964. The country was renamed Belize from 1 June 1973.

1866. Sterling.
1888. 100 cents = 1 dollar.

1.

2 CENTS (2.) 2 CENTS (3.)

1866.

12. 1. 1d. blue .. .. .. 12·00 4·50
18. 1d. red .. .. .. 6·50 5·50
13. 3d. brown .. .. 32·00 6·50
20. 4d. mauve .. .. 26·00 2·75
9. 6d rose .. .. .. 55·00 9·50
21. 6d. yellow .. .. 90·00 6·00
16. 1s. green .. .. 60·00 6·50
22. 1s. grey .. .. 90·00 55·00

1888. Surch. as T 2.

27. 1. 2 c. on 1d. red .. .. 3·25 6·00
25. 2 c. on 6d. rose .. 25·00 25·00
26. 3 c. on 3d. brown .. 24·00 24·00
28. 10 c. on 4d. mauve .. 12·00 5·50
29. 20 c. on 6d. yellow .. 12·00 8·00
30. 50 c. on 1s. grey .. 85·00 95·00

No. 30 surch. **TWO.**

35. 1. " TWO " on 50 c. on 1s. grey .. .. .. 16·00 20·00

1888. Surch. as T 3.

36. 1. 1 c. on 1d. green .. 25 25
37. 2 c. on 1d. red .. 25 55
38. 3 c. on 3d. brown .. 35 70
39. 6 c. on 3d. blue .. 80 2·00
40. 10 c. on 4d. mauve .. 80 80
41. 20 c. on 6d. yellow .. 2·75 5·50
42. 50 c. on 1s. grey .. 6·50 12·00

1891. No. 39 surch. **6** and bar.

43. 1. " 6 " on 10 c. on 4d. mauve 45 1·60

Nos. 38 and 47 surch.

49. 1. " FIVE " on 3 c. on 3d. brown .. .. .. 75 1·60
50. " 15 " on 6 c. on 3d. blue 3·75 5·00

4.

NOTE: 10 c. (A) inscr. "POSTAGE POSTAGE "; (B) inscr. "POSTAGE & REVENUE ".

1891.

51. 4. 1 c. green 25 35
52. 2 c. red 25 30
53. 3 c. brown .. .. 40 1·10
54. 5 c. blue .. .. 5·00 55
55. 5 c. black & blue on blue .. 85 65
56. 6 c. blue 90 45
57. 10 c. mauve and green (A) 3·25 3·00
58. 10 c. purple and green (B) 1·60 3·00
59. 12 c. mauve and green .. 12·00 2·25
60. 24 c. yellow and blue .. 1·60 3·25
61. 25 c. brown and green .. 8·00 10·00
62. 50 c. green and red .. 6·50 8·50
63. $1 green and red .. 11·00 12·00
64. $2 green and blue .. 26·00 30·00
65. $5 green and black .. £130 £160

1899. Optd. **REVENUE.**

66. 4. 5 c. blue .. .. .. 1·25 1·25
67. 10 c. mauve and green .. 2·00 2·25
68. 25 c. brown and green .. 1·60 2·25
69. 1. 50 c. on 1s. grey .. .. 38·00 30·00

5.

6.

1902.

84. 5. 1 c. green 30 40
85. 2 c. purple & black on red 30 15
96. 2 c. red 30 25
86. 5 c. black & blue on blue 75 50
97. 5 c. blue .. .. .. 1·10 55
87. 10 c. purple and green .. 2·25 3·00
83. 20 c. purple .. .. 5·00 5·00
89. 25 c. purple and orange 4·00 6·50
100. 25 c. black on green .. 8·50 9·50
90. 50 c. green and red .. 13·00 14·00
91. $1 green and red .. 13·00 14·00
92. $2 green and blue .. 38·00 42·00
93. $5 green and black .. £120 £130

1913.

101. 6. 1 c. green 12 12
102. 2 c. red 25 30
103. 3 c. orange 5 20
104. 5 c. blue 70 75
105. 10 c. purple and green .. 1·60 1·75
106. 25 c. black on green .. 1·60 1·90
107. 50 c. purple & blue on blue 1·60 3·50
108. $1 black and red .. 3·25 3·50
109. $2 purple and green .. 26·00 28·00
110. $5 purple & black on red £110 £120

1915. Optd. with pattern of wavy lines.

111a. 6. 1 c. green .. .. 50 1·60
112. 2 c. red 30 40
113. 5 c. blue .. .. 35 1·60

1916. Optd. **WAR** in small letters.

114. 6. 1 c. green (No. 111a) .. 12 12
116. 1 c. green (No. 101) .. 15 35
118. 3 c. orange 30 40

1918. Optd. **WAR** in large letters 3 mm. high.

119. 6. 1 c. green 20 35
120. 3 c. orange 20 50

7. 8.

1921. Peace.

121. 7. 2 c. red .. .. .. 1·25 1·00

As last, but without word " PEACE ".

122. 4 c. grey .. .. .. 2·50 90

1922.

126. 8. 1 c. green 15 30
127. 2 c. brown 12 12
128. 2 c. red 12 12
129. 3 c. orange 75 60
130. 4 c. grey 65 35
131. 5 c. blue 60 35
132. 10 c. purple and olive .. 60 1·10
133. 25 c. black on green .. 90 1·00
134. 50 c. purple & blue on blue 2·75 4·00
136. $1 black and red .. 7·00 9·00
137. $2 green and purple .. 15·00 18·00
125. $5 purple and black on red 70·00 80·00

1932. Optd. **BELIZE RELIEF FUND PLUS** and value.

138. 8. 1 c.+1 c. green .. .. 45 1·60
139. 2 c.+2 c. red .. .. 65 1·60
140. 3 c.+3 c. orange .. 85 2·25
141. 4 c.+4 c. grey .. 1·25 2·75
142. 5 c.+5 c. blue .. 2·75 5·50

1935. Silver Jubilee. As T 11 of Antigua.

143. 3 c. blue and black .. 20 25
144. 4 c. green and blue .. 30 35
145. 5 c. brown and blue .. 85 95
146. 25 c. grey and purple .. 1·60 1·90

1937. Coronation. As T 2 of Aden.

147. 3 c. orange 8 10
148. 4 c. grey 10 12
149. 5 c. blue 10 15

9. Maya figures.

1938.

150. 9. 1 c. purple and green .. 10 12
151. – 2 c. black and red .. 10 12
152. – 3 c. purple and brown .. 12 15
153. – 4 c. black and green .. 12 15
154. – 5 c. purple and blue .. 12 15
155. – 10 c. green and brown .. 20 15
156. – 15 c. brown and blue .. 30 25
157. – 25 c. blue and green .. 50 35
158. – 50 c. black and purple .. 80 80
159. – $1 red and olive .. 1·40 1·40
160. – $2 blue and purple .. 3·25 2·50
161. – $5 red and brown .. 9·00 6·50

DESIGNS—VERT. 2 c. Chicle tapping. 3 c. Cohune palm. $1 Court House, Belize. $2 Mahogany felling. $5 Arms. HORIZ. 4 c. Local products. 5 c. Grape fruit. 10 c. Mahogany logs in river. 15 c. Sergeant's Cay. 25 c. Dorey. 50 c. Chicle industry.

1946. Victory. As T 4 of Aden.

162. 3 c. brown 8 5
163. 5 c. blue 8 5

1948. Silver Wedding. As T 5 and 6 of Aden.

164. 4 c. green 8 5
165. $5 brown .. .. .. 8·00 10·00

10. St. George's Cay.

1949. Battle of St. George's Cay. 150th Anniv.

166. 10. 1 c. blue and green .. 12 12
167. 3 c. blue and brown .. 12 15
168. 4 c. olive and violet .. 15 20
169. – 5 c. brown and blue .. 25 25
170. – 10 c. green and brown 35 35
171. – 15 c. green and blue .. 45 50

DESIGNS: 5, 10 and 15 c. H.M. Sloop " Merlin ".

1949. U.P.U. As T 14/17 of Antigua.

172. 4 c. green 20 20
173. 5 c. blue 30 40
174. 10 c. brown 55 60
175. 25 c. blue .. .. 1·00 1·25

1951. Inaug. of B.W.I. University Coll. As T 18/19 of Antigua.

176. 3 c. violet and brown .. 15 15
177. 10 c. green and brown 30 30

1953. Coronation As T 7 of Aden.

178. 4 c. black and green .. 30 35

11. Mountain Cow.

12. Mountain Orchid.

DESIGNS—HORIZ. 1 c. Arms. 3 c. Mace and Council Chamber. 4 c. Pine industry. 5 c. Spiny lobster. 10 c. Stanley Field Airport. 15 c. Maya Frieze. 25 c. Blue Butterfly. $1 Armadillo. $2 Hawkesworth Bridge. VERT. 50 c. Maya Indian.

1953.

179. – 1 c. green and black .. 5 5
180. 11. 2 c. brown and black .. 8 10
181. – 3 c. lilac and magenta .. 5 5
182. – 4 c. brown and green .. 5 10
183a. – 5 c. olive and red .. 15 15
184. – 10 c. slate and blue .. 10 12
185. – 15 c. green and violet .. 30 30
186. – 25 c. blue and brown .. 35 30
187. – 50 c. brown and purple 90 1·10
188. – $1 slate and brown .. 1·90 2·75
189. – $2 red and grey .. 3·75 4·75
190. 12. $5 purple and slate .. 8·50 9·50

13. Belize from Fort George, 1842.

1960. Cent. of Br. Honduras P.O.

191. 13. 2 c. green 10 10
192. – 10 c. red 20 20
193. – 15 c. blue 35 35

DESIGNS: 10 c. Public Seals, 1860 and 1960. 15 c. Tamarind tree, Newtown Barracks.

1961. New Constitution. Stamps of 1953 optd. **NEW CONSTITUTION 1960.**

194. 11. 2 c. brown and black .. 5 8
195. – 3 c. lilac and magenta .. 12 15
196. – 10 c. slate and blue .. 35 35
197. – 15 c. green and violet .. 45 50

1962. Hurricane Hattie Relief Fund. Stamps of 1953 optd. **HURRICANE HATTIE.**

198. 1 c. green and black .. 5 8
199. 10 c. slate and blue .. 12 20
200. 25 c. blue and brown .. 25 30
201. 50 c. brown and purple .. 50 55

14. Great Curassow.

1962. Birds in natural colours; portrait and inscr. in black; background colours given.

239. 14. 1 c. greenish yellow .. 5 8
240. – 2 c. grey 5 5
204. – 3 c. olive-green .. 5 5
241. – 4 c. pale grey 8 10
242. – 5 c. buff 12 15
243. – 10 c. stone 20 25
244. – 15 c. stone 30 35
209. – 25 c. slate 15 20
245. – 50 c. greenish grey .. 80 90
211. – $1 blue .. .. 1·25 1·50
212. – $2 stone .. .. 2·50 3·00
213. – $5 blue-grey .. .. 4·50 5·50

BIRDS: 2 c. Red Legged Honeycreeper. 3 c. American Jacana. 4 c. Great Kiskadee. 5 c. Scarlet-rumped Tanager. 10 c. Scarlet Macaw. 15 c. Massena Trogon. 25 c. Red-footed Booby. 50 c. Keel-billed Toucan. $1, Magnificent Frigate Bird. $2, Rufous-tailed Jacamar. $5, Montezuma Oropendola.

1963. Freedom from Hunger. As T 10 of Aden.

214. 22 c. green 40 45

1963. Red Cross Cent. As T 24 of Antigua.

215. 4 c. red and black .. 5 8
216. 22 c. red and blue .. 50 50

1964. New Constitution. Nos. 239, 204, 241, 243 and 209 optd. **SELF GOVERNMENT 1964.**

217. 14. 1 c. greenish yellow .. 5 5
218. 3 c. olive-green .. 5 5
219. – 4 c. pale grey 5 5
220. – 10 c. stone 15 15
221. – 25 c. slate 25 30

1965. I.T.U. Cent. As T 26 of Antigua.

222. 2 c. red and green .. 5 5
223. 50 c. yellow and purple .. 40 45

1965. I.C.Y. As T 27 Antigua.

224. 1 c. purple and turquoise .. 5 5
225. 22 c. green and lavender .. 25 30

1966. Churchill Commem. As T 28 of Antigua.

226. 1 c. blue 5 5
227. 4 c. green 5 5
228. 22 c. brown 30 30
229. 25 c. violet 40 50

1966. Dedication of new Capital Site. Nos. 239, 204, 241, 243 and 209 optd. **DEDICATION OF SITE NEW CAPITAL 9th OCTOBER 1965.**

230. 14. 1 c. greenish yellow .. 5 5
231. – 3 c. olive-green .. 5 5
232. – 4 c. pale grey .. 5 5
233. – 10 c. stone 15 15
234. – 25 c. slate 30 30

15. Citrus Grove.

1966. Stamp Cent. Multicoloured.

235. 5 c. Type 15 .. .. 5 5
236. 10 c. Half Moon Cay .. 15 15
237. 22 c. Hidden Valley Falls 30 30
238. 25 c. Maya Ruins, Xunantunich 45 45

16. Sailfish.

1967. Int. Tourist Year.

246. 16. 5 c. blue, black & yellow 5 5
247. – 10 c. brown, black & red 5 8
248. – 22 c. orge., blk. and grn. 25 25
249. – 25 c. blue, black & yell. 30 35

DESIGNS: 10 c. Deer. 22 c. Jaguar. 25 c. Tarpon.

17. "Schomburgkia tibiscinus".

18. Monument to Belizean Patriots.

1968. Economic Commission for Latin America. 20th Anniv. Multicoloured.

250. 5 c. Type 17 .. .. 5 5
251. 10 c. "Maxillaria tenuifolia" 5 8
252. 22 c. "Bletia purpurea" .. 20 25
253. 25 c. "Sobralia macrantha" 25 30

1968. Human Rights Year. Multicoloured.

254. 22 c. Type 18 .. .. 20 20
255. 50 c. Monument at Site of New Capital .. 30 35

19. Jew Fish.

1968.

276. – ½ c. mult. and blue .. 10 10
277. – ½ c. mult. and yellow .. 5 5
256. 19. 1 c. blk., brn. & yell. .. 5 5
257. – 2 c. blk., grn. & yell. .. 5 5
258. – 3 c. black, brn. & lilac 5 5
259. – 4 c. multicoloured .. 5 5
260. – 5 c. black and red .. 8 8
261. – 10 c. multicoloured .. 10 12
262. – 15 c. multicoloured .. 15 15
263. – 25 c. multicoloured .. 35 35
264. – 50 c. multicoloured .. 45 55
265. – $1 multicoloured .. 90 1·10
266. – $2 multicoloured .. 1·75 2·00
267. – $5 multicoloured .. 3·25 3·75

DESIGNS: ½ c. (276 and 277) Crana Fish. 2 c. Warree. 3 c. Grouper. 4 c. Ant Bear. 5 c. Bonefish. 10 c. Gibnut. 15 c. Dolphin. 25 c. Night Walker. 50 c. Mutton Snapper. £1 Bush Dog. $2 Great Barracuda. $5 Mountain Lion.

20. "Rhycholaelia digbyana".

1969. "Orchids of Belize" (1st Series). Multicoloured.

268. 5 c. Type 20 .. .. 8 8
269. 10 c. "Cattleya boweringiana" 15 15
270. 22 c. "Lycaste cochleatum" 30 35
271. 25 c. "Coryanthes speciocum" 35 40

See also Nos. 287/90.

21. Ziricote Tree.

1969. Indigenous Hardwoods (1st Series). Multicoloured.

272. 5 c. Type 21 .. .. 8 8
273. 10 c. Rosewood 12 12
274. 22 c. Mayflower 25 25
275. 25 c. Mahogany 30 30

See also Nos. 291/4 and 315/8.

22. "The Virgin and Child" (Bellini).

23. Santa Maria.

1969. Christmas. Multicoloured.

279. 5 c. Type 22 .. .. 5 5
280. 15 c. As Type 22 .. 15 15
281. 22 c. "The Adoration of the Magi" (Veronese) .. 25 25
282. 25 c. As No. 281 .. 30 30

1970. Population Census. Nos. 260/3 optd. **POPULATION CENSUS 1970.**

283. 5 c. multicoloured .. 5 5
284. 10 c. multicoloured .. 12 12
285. 15 c. multicoloured .. 20 20
286. 25 c. multicoloured .. 25 30

1970. "Orchids of Belize" (2nd Series). As T 20. Multicoloured.

287. 5 c. Black Orchid .. 8 8
288. 15 c. White Butterfly Orchid 15 15
289. 22 c. Swan Orchid .. 20 20
290. 25 c. Butterfly Orchid .. 25 25

1970. Indigenous Hardwoods (2nd Series). Multicoloured.

291. 5 c. Type 23 .. .. 15 12
292. 15 c. Nargusta 20 15
293. 22 c. Cedar 25 20
294. 25 c. Sapodilla 30 25

24. "The Nativity" (A. Hughes).

1970. Christmas. Multicoloured.

295. ½ c. Type 24 .. .. 5 5
296. 5 c. "The Mystic Nativity" (Botticelli) 10 10
297. 10 c. Type 24 .. .. 12 12
298. 15 c. As 5 c. 15 15
299. 22 c. Type 24 .. .. 30 30
300. 50 c. As 5 c. 45 45

25. Legislative Assembly House.

1971. Establishment of New Capital. Multicoloured.

301. 5 c. Old Capital, Belize .. 5 5
302. 10 c. Government Plaza .. 10 10
303. 15 c. Type 25 .. .. 12 12
304. 22 c. Magistrates' Court .. 25 25
305. 25 c. Police H.Q. .. 25 25
306. 50 c. New G.P.O. .. 40 40

The 5 c. and 10 c. are larger, 60 × 22 mm.

26. "Tabebuia chrysantha".

1971. Easter. Flowers. Multicoloured.

307. ½ c. Type 26 .. .. 5 5
308. 5 c. "Hymenocallis littoralis" 8 8
309. 10 c. "Hippeastrum equestre" 10 10
310. 15 c. Type 26 .. .. 12 12
311. 22 c. As 5 c. 20 20
312. 25 c. As 10 c. 25 25

1971. Racial Equality Year. Nos. 261 and 264 optd. **RACIAL EQUALITY YEAR-1971.**

313. 10 c. multicoloured .. 10 10
314. 50 c. multicoloured .. 35 40

27. Tubroos.

1971. Indigenous Hardwoods (3rd Series). Multicoloured.

315. 5 c. Type 27 .. .. 12 12
316. 15 c. Yemeri 15 15
317. 26 c. Billywebb 30 30
318. 50 c. Logwood 45 50

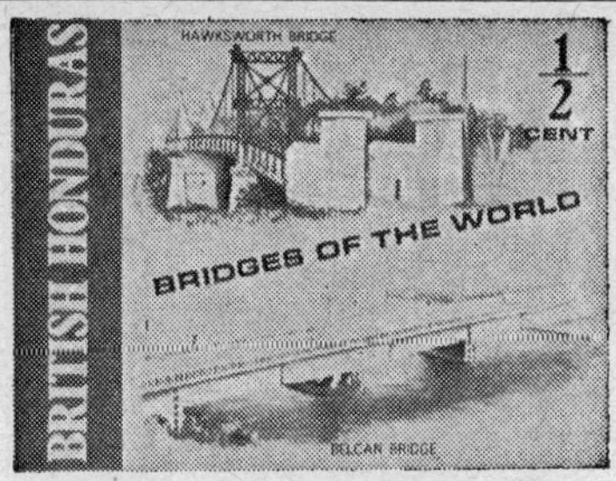

28. Hawksworth and Belcan Bridges.

1971. Bridges of the World. Multicoloured.

320. ½ c. Type **28** 5 25
321. 5 c. Narrows Bridge, N.Y. and Quebec Bridge .. 8 8
322. 26 c. London Bridge (1871) and reconstructed, Arizona (1971) .. 25 25
323. 50 c. Belize Mexican Bridge and Swing Bridge .. 50 50

29. " Petrae volubis ". 30. Pendant.

1972. Easter. Wild Flowers. Multicoloured.

324. 6 c. Type **29** 10 10
325. 15 c. Yemeri 20 20
326. 26 c. Mayflower 25 25
327. 50 c. Tiger's Claw .. 40 45

1972. Mayan Artefacts. Multicoloured.

328. 3c. Type **30** 10 10
329. 6c. Priest in "dancing" pose 10 10
330. 16 c. Sun God's Head (horiz.) 25 25
331. 26c. Priest and Sun God .. 30 30
332. 50c. Full-front figure .. 45 50

Nos. 328/32 are inscribed on the reverse with information about the artefacts depicted.

31. Banak.

1972. Indigenous Hardwoods (4th Series). Multicoloured.

333. 3 c. Type **31** 8 8
334. 5 c. Quamwood 10 10
335. 16 c. Waika Chewstick .. 15 15
336. 26 c. Mamee-Apple .. 30 30
337. 50 c. My Lady 40 45

1972. Royal Silver Wedding. As T **19** of Ascension, but with Orchids of Belize in background.

341. 26 c. blue 45 25
342. 50 c. violet 40 40

32. Baron Bliss Day.

1973. Festivals of Belize. Multicoloured.

343. 3 c. Type **32** 5 5
344. 10 c. Labour Day .. 10 10
345. 26 c. Carib Settlement .. 15 15
346. 50 c. Pan-American Day .. 35 35

POSTAGE DUE STAMPS

D 1.

1923.

D 1a. D **1.** 1 c. black 5 8
D 2a. 2 c. black 5 8
D 3a. 4 c. black 5 8

For later issues see **BELIZE.**

BRITISH INDIAN OCEAN TERRITORY BC

This Crown Colony, created on 8th November, 1965, comprised the Chagos Archipelago, previously administered by Mauritius, Aldabra, Farquhar and Desroches, previously administered by Seychelles. In 1976 all the islands, except Aldabra, were transferred to Seychelles.

100 cents = 1 rupee.

1968. Nos. 233, 197/200, 202/4 and 206/12 of Seychelles optd. **B.I.O.T.**

1. **9.** 5 c. multicoloured .. 8 8
2. – 10 c. multicoloured .. 8 10
3. – 15 c. multicoloured .. 10 10
4. – 20 c. multicoloured .. 12 12
5. – 25 c. multicoloured .. 12 15
6. – 40 c. multicoloured .. 20 25
7. – 45 c. multicoloured .. 25 25
8. – 50 c. multicoloured .. 25 35
9. – 75 c. multicoloured .. 40 60
10. – 1 r. multicoloured .. 90 1·10
11. – 1 r. 50 multicoloured .. 1·40 1·75
12. – 2 r. 25 multicoloured .. 2·25 3·00
13. – 3 r. 50 multicoloured .. 3·50 4·50
14. – 5 r. multicoloured .. 4·00 5·00
15. – 10 r. multicoloured .. 9·00 11·00

1. Lascar.

1968. Fish. Multicoloured.

16. 5 c. Type **1** 15 15
17. 10 c Hammerhead Shark (vert.) 12 10
18. 15 c. Tiger Shark 12 10
19. 20 c. Bat Ray 12 10
20. 25 c. Butterfly Fish (vert.) 12 10
20a. 30 c. Robber Crab 12 10
21. 40 c. Caranx 12 10
22. 45 c. Garfish (vert.) .. 30 35
23. 50 c. Barracuda 20 15
23a. 60 c. Spotted Pebble Crab 25 20
24. 75 c. Parrot Fish 60 60
24a. 85 c. Dorade ("Elegatis bipinnulatus") 30 30
25. 1 r. Giant Hermit Crab .. 50 60
26. 1 r. 50 Humphead .. .. 1·00 1·25
27. 2 r. 25 Rock Cod .. .. 2·75 3·50
28. 3 r. 50 Black Marlin .. 2·25 2·75
29. 5 r. black, green and blue (Whale Shark) (vert.) .. 2·25 2·75
30. 10 r. Lion Fish .. .. 4·50 6·00

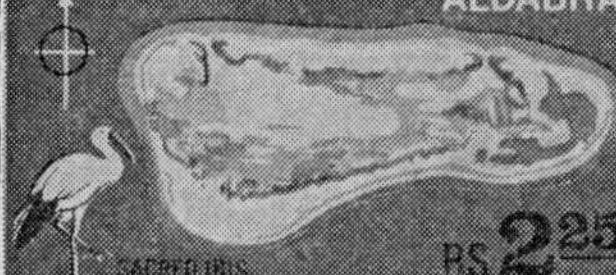

2. Sacred Ibis and Aldabra Coral Atoll.

1969. Coral Atolls.

31. **2.** 2 r. 25 multicoloured .. 70 75

3. Out-Rigger.

1969. Ships of the Islands. Multicoloured.

32. 45 c. Type **3** 30 30
33. 75 c. Pirogue 45 45
34. 1 r. M.V. " Nordvaer " .. 55 55
35. 1 r. 50 " Isle of Farquhar " 75 80

4. Giant Land Tortoise.

1971. Aldabra Nature Reserve. Multicoloured.

36. 45 c. Type **4** 25 25
37. 75 c. Aldabra lily .. 40 40
38. 1 r. Aldabra snail 50 50
39. 1 r. 50 Dimorphic egrets .. 75 75

5. Arms of Royal Society and Flightless Rail.

1971. Opening of Royal Society Research Station, Aldabra.

40. **5.** 3 r. 50 multicoloured .. 2·00 2·00

6. Staghorn Coral.

1972. Coral. Multicoloured.

41. 40 c. Type **6** 20 20
42. 60 c. Brain coral 30 30
43. 1 r. Mushroom coral .. 50 50
44. 1 r. 75 Organ Pipe coral .. 75 80

1972. Royal Silver Wedding. As T **19** of Ascension, but with Flightless Rail and Sacred Ibis in background.

45. 95 c. green .. .. .. 70 1·10
46. 1 r. 50 violet .. .. 1·00 1·60

7. " Christ on Cross ".

1973. Easter. Multicoloured.

47. 45 c. Type **7** 15 15
48. 75 c. " Joseph and Nicodemus Burying Jesus " 25 25
49. 1 r. Type **7** 40 40
50. 1 r. 50 As 75 c. 50 55

8. Upsidedown Jellyfish.

1973. Wildlife. (1st series). Multicoloured.

53. 50 c. Type **8** 20 25
54. 1 r. Butterflies 40 45
55. 1 r. 50 Spider 50 50

See also Nos. 75/8.

9. M.V. "Nordvaer".

1974. "Nordvaer" Travelling Post Office. 5th Anniv. Multicoloured.

56. 85 c. Type **9** 30 30
57. 2 r. 50 "Nordvaer" off shore 65 75

10. Auger Shells.

1974. Wildlife (2nd series). Shells. Mult.

58. 45 c. Type **10** 12 12
59. 75 c. Green Turban .. 20 20
60. 1 r. Drupe Snail 25 25
61. 1 r. 50 Helmet Shell .. 40 40

11. Aldabra Drongo.

1975. Birds. Multicoloured.

62. 5 c. Type **11** 5 5
63. 10 c. Malagasy Coucal .. 5 5
64. 20 c. Red-headed Forest Fody 5 5
65. 25 c. Fairy Tern 5 5
66. 30 c. Crested Tern 5 5
67. 40 c. Brown Booby .. 5 5
68. 50 c. Noddy Tern (horiz.) .. 8 8
69. 60 c. Grey Heron 8 10
70. 65 c. Blue-faced Booby (horiz.) 8 10
71. 95 c. Malagasy White-eye (horiz.) 12 12
72. 1 r. Green-backed Heron (horiz.) 12 15
73. 1 r. 75 Lesser Frigatebird (horiz.) 25 30
74. 3 r. 50 White-tailed Tropic Bird 45 50
75. 5 r. Souimanga Sunbird (horiz.) 65 75
76. 10 r. Malagasy Turtle Dove (horiz.) .. .. .. 1·25 1·50

12. " Grewia salicifola ".

1975. Wildlife (3rd series). Seashore Plants. Multicoloured.

77. 50 c. Type **12** 10 12
78. 65 c. " Cassia aldabrensis " 15 20
79. 1 r. " Hypoestes aldabrensis " 20 25
80. 1 r. 60 " Euphorbia pyrifolia " 30 35

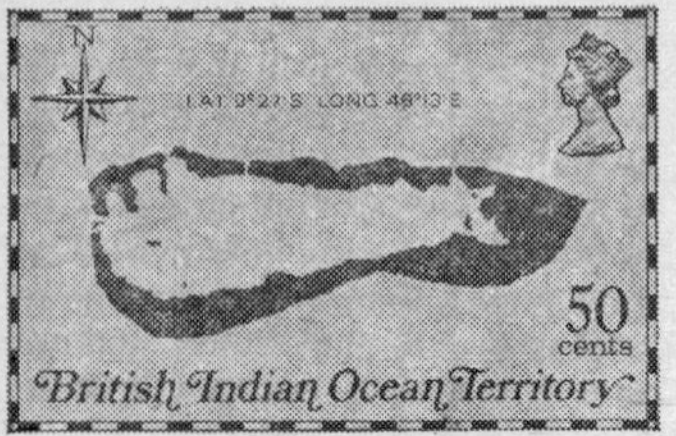

13. Map of Aldabra.

1975. Maps. Multicoloured.

81. 50 c. Type **13** 10 12
82. 1 r. Desroches 20 25
83. 1 r. 50 Farquhar 30 35
84. 2 r. Diego Garcia 35 45

14. Crimson Speckled Moth.

1976. Wildlife (4th series). Mult.

86. 65 c. Type **14** 10 12
87. 1 r. 20 " Dysdercus fasiatus " 20 25
88. 1 r. 50 " Sphex torridus " 25 30
89. 2 r. " Oryctes rhinoceros " 30 35

BRITISH LEVANT BC

Stamps used at Br. post offices in the Turkish Empire. These offices closed in 1914. The stamps were again in use after 1918, during the British Occupation of Turkey.

40 paras = 1 piastre.

Stamps of Great Britain surcharged or overprinted.

80 PARAS
(1.)

Queen Victoria.

1885. Surch as T **1**.

1. **46.** 40 par. on 2½d. purple 5·50 1·40
2. **45.** 80 par. on 5d. green 48·00 3·00
3a. **41.** 12 pi. on 2s. 6d. lilac 11·00 5·00

1887. Surch as T **1**.

4. **57.** 40 par. on 2½d. pur. on bl. 55 20
5. **61.** 80 par. on 5d. pur. & blue 1·40 35
6. **64.** 4 pi. on 10d. pur. & red 4·50 3·00

1893. Handstamped surcharge.

7. **54.** 40 par. on ½d. red 80·00 42·00

King Edward VII.

1902. Surch. as T **1**.

26. – 30 par. on 1½d. pur. & grn. 40 50
8. **66.** 40 par. on 2½d. blue 60 20
9. – 80 par. on 5d. pur. & blue 90 80
23. **66.** 1 pi. on 2½d. blue 90 15
40. – 2 pi. on 5d. purple & blue 90 85
10. – 4 pi. on 10d. purple & red 2·75 1·10
42. – 5 pi. on 1s. green and red 3·00 3·25
43a. – 12 pi. on 2s. 6d. purple 11·00 12·00
44. – 24 pi. on 5s red 19·00 21·00

1905. Optd. **LEVANT.**

13. **66.** ½d. yellow-green 35 20
14. 1d. red 35 20
15. – 1½d. purple and green 1·90 1·40
16a. – 2d. green and red 1·40 1·60
17. **66.** 2½d. blue 3·50 3·50
18. – 3d. purple on yellow 2·50 2·75
19. – 4d. green and brown 2·40 2·75
20. – 5d. purple and blue 5·50 6·00
21. **66.** 6d. purple 4·50 5·50
22. – 1s green and red 7·50 7·50

1906. Surch. **1 Piastre.**

25. – 1 pi. on 2d. green and red £500 £200

1 PIASTRE
10 PARAS
(2.)

1909. Surch. as T **2**.

27. – 1 pi. 10 par. on 3d. purple on yellow 2·75 3·50
28. – 1 pi. 30 par. on 4d. green and brown 2·75 3·25
29. – 1 pi. 30 par. on 4d. orge. 3·00 3·25
30. **66.** 2 pi. 20 par. on 6d. purple 5·50 6·00

1910. Surch. in two lines.

32. – 1¼ pi. on 3d. pur. on yell. 35 75
33. – 1¾ pi. on 4d. orange 40 60
34. **66.** 2½ pi. on 6d. purple 90 90

King George V.

1911. Optd. **LEVANT.**

46. **80.** ½d. green 65 80
48. – ½d. green 20 10
47. **81.** 1d. red 65 80
49. **83.** 1d. red 20 10

1913. Optd. **LEVANT.**

50. **85.** ½d. green 15 15
51. **84.** 1d. red 25 50
68. **86.** 2d. orange 60 1·10
69. 3d. violet 1·40 80
70. 4d. grey-green 1·10 1·25
71. **87.** 5d. brown 2·25 2·50
72. 6d. purple 2·25 2·75
73. **88.** 1s. brown 1·60 1·40
74. **89.** 2s. 6d. brown 15·00 19·00

1913. Surch. in one or two lines.

58. **85.** 30 par. on ½d. green 10 35
52. 30 par. on 1½d. brown 95 1·25
53. **84.** 1 pi. on 2½d. blue 20 12
54. **86.** 1½ pi. on 3d. violet 55 1·25
59. **84.** 1¾ pi. on 1d. red 10 15
55. **86.** 1¾ pi. on 4d. grey-green 75 1·60
60. **84.** 3¾ pi on 2½d. blue 20 30
56. **88.** 4 pi. on 10d. blue 3·50 3·50
61. **86.** 4½ pi. on 3d. violet 35 70
57. **88.** 5 pi. on 1s. brown 6·00 8·00
62. **87.** 7½ pi. on 5d. brown 15 15
63. **88.** 15 pi. on 10d. blue 30 20
64. 18¾ pi. on 1s. brown 1·60 1·10
65. **89.** 45 pi. on 2s 6d. brown 7·50 10·00
66. 90 pi. on 5s. red 16·00 8·50
67. 180 pi. on 10s. blue 38·00 20·00

BRITISH FIELD OFFICE IN SALONICA

Levant
(3.)

1916. King George V stamps of Great Britain optd. with T **3**.

S 1. **85.** ½d. green 6·00 11·00
S 2. **84.** 1d. red 6·00 11·00
S 3. **86.** 2d. orange 22·00 35·00
S 4. 3d. violet 17·00 28·00
S 5. 4d. grey-green 23·00 35·00
S 6. **87.** 6d. purple 17·00 28·00
S 7. **88.** 9d. black 55·00 75·00
S 8. 1s. brown 55·00 75·00

The above stamps were overprinted at Salonica during the war of 1914–18.

BRITISH OCCUPATION OF JAPAN BC

Stamps used by British Commonwealth Occupation Forces, 1946–49.

1945. Stamps of Australia optd. **B.C.O.F. JAPAN 1946.**

B 1. **22.** ½d. orange 1·00 1·25
B 2. **38.** 1d. purple 1·00 1·25
B 3. **26.** 3d. brown 1·20 1·50
B 4. – 6d. brown (No. 189a) 4·00 5·00
B 5. – 1s. green (No. 191) 5·00 6·00
B 6. **1.** 2s. claret 18·00 22·00
B 7. **33.** 5s. claret 75·00 85·00

BRITISH POSTAL AGENCIES IN EASTERN ARABIA BC

British stamps were surcharged for use in the area of the Persian Gulf.

The stamps were used in Muscat from 1st April 1948 to 29th April 1966; in Dubai from 1st April 1948 to 6th January 1961; in Qatar: Doha from August 1950, Umm Said from February 1956 to 31st March 1957; and in Abu Dhabi from 30th March 1963 (Das Island from December 1960) to 29th March 1964.

Certain of them were placed on sale in Kuwait Post Offices in 1951 and in 1953 due to shortages of stamps with "KUWAIT" overprint; and they can all be found commercially used from that state and from Bahrain.

Stamps of Great Britain surcharged in Indian currency.

1948. King George VI.

16. **103.** ½ a. on ½d. pale green 5 5
35. ½ a. on ½d. orange 8 10
17. 1 a. on 1d. pale red 8 8
36. 1 a. on 1d. blue 8 10
18. 1½a. on 1½d pale brown 8 8
37. 1½ a. on 1½d. green 20 25
19. 2 a. on 2d. pale orange 10 15
38. 2 a. on 2d. brown 8 15
20. 2½ a. on 2½d. light blue 8 20
39. **103.** 2½ a. on 2½d. red 20 20
21. 3 a. on 3d. pale violet 8 8
40. **104.** 4 a. on 4d. blue 15 25
22. 6 a. on 6d. purple 10 10
23. **105.** 1 r. on 1s. brown 35 40
24. **106.** 2 r. on 2s. 6d. green 2·50 3·50

1948. Royal Silver Wedding.

25. **110.** 2½ a. on 2½d. blue 8 10
26. **111.** 15 r. on £1 blue 4·50 6·50

1948. Olympic Games.

27. **112.** 2½ a. on 2½d. blue 10 15
28. **113.** 3 a. on 3d. violet 12 25
29. – 6 a. on 6d. purple 12 30
30. – 1 r. on 1s. brown 35 50

1949. U.P.U.

31. **114.** 2½ a. on 2½d. blue 15 15
32. **115.** 3 a. on 3d. violet 20 25
33. – 6 a. on 6d. purple 25 30
34. – 1 r. on 1s. brown 45 45

1951. Pictorial.

41. **116.** 2 r. on 2s. 6d. green 1·50 1·75

1952. Queen Elizabeth.

42. **118.** ½ a. on ½d. orange 5 5
43. 1 a. on 1d. blue 5 5
44. 1½ a. on 1½d. green 5 5
45. 2 a. on 2d. brown 5 5
46. **119.** 2½ a. on 2½d. red 12 12
47. 3 a. on 3d. lilac 5 8
48. 4 a. on 4d. blue 12 12
49. **120.** 6 a. on 6d. purple 15 15
50. **122.** 12 a. on 1s. 3d. green 30 40
51. 1 r. on 1s. 6d. indigo 35 50

1953. Coronation.

52. **123.** 2½ a. on 2½d. red 25 30
53. – 4 a. on 4d. ultramarine 30 35
54. **124.** 12 a. on 1s. 3d. green 80 90
55. – 1 r. on 1s. 6d. blue 75 1·10

1955. Pictorials.

92. **125.** 2 r. on 2s. 6d. brown 60 75
93. – 5 r. on 5s. red 1·50 1·75

1957. Value in naye paise. Queen Elizabeth II stamps surch. **NP** twice and value.

65. **120.** 1 n.p. on 5d. brown 5 5
66. **118.** 3 n.p. on ½d. orange 5 5
81. 5 n.p. on 1d. blue 5 5
67. 6 n.p. on 1d. blue 5 5
68. 9 n.p. on 1½d. green 5 5
83. 10 n.p. on 1½d. green 10 10
69. 12 n.p. on 2d. pale brown 10 20
85. **119.** 15 n.p. on 2½d. red 10 10
71. 20 n.p. on 3d. lilac 5 5
72. 25 n.p. on 4d. blue 10 8
87. 30 n.p. on 4½d. chestnut 15 15
73. **120.** 40 n.p. on 6d. purple 12 10
74. **121.** 50 n.p. on 9d. olive 15 15
75. **122.** 75 n.p. on 1s. 3d. green 25 25

1957. World Scout Jubilee Jamboree.

76. **126.** 2½d. red 20 20
77. **127.** 4d. blue 30 30
78. – 1s. 3d. green 30 35

BRITISH POST OFFICES IN CHINA BC

Stamps for use in Weihaiwei, and the neighbouring islands, leased to Great Britain from 1898 to October 1st, 1930, when they were returned to China.

1917. Stamps of Hong Kong (King George V) optd. **CHINA.**

1. **6.** 1 c. brown 10 15
2. 2 c. green 20 20
3. 4 c. red 10 10
4. 6 c. orange 20 15
5. 8 c. grey 40 20
6. 10 c. blue 30 10
7. 12 c. purple on yellow 60 45
24. 20 c. purple and olive 35 30
25. 25 c. purple 45 1·25
11. 30 c. purple and orange 1·75 55
12b. 50 c. black on green 1·50 80
13a. $1 purple and blue on blue 5·50 80
28. $2 red and black 7·00 9·00
15. $3 green and purple 16·00 12·00
16. $5 green and red on green 14·00 14·00
17. $10 purple & black on red 30·00 35·00

BRITISH POST OFFICES IN CRETE BC

1.

2.

1898.

1. **1.** 20 parades, violet 85·00 80·00

1898.

2. **2.** 10 par. blue 2·25 3·50
3. 10 par. brown 2·25 3·50
4. 20 par. green 2·50 4·50
5. 20 par. red 4·50 5·00

BRUNEI BC

A Sultanate on the N. Coast of Borneo.

100 cents = 1 dollar (Straits or Malayan).

1906. Stamps of Labuan optd. **BRUNEI,** or surch. also.

1. **4.** 1 c. black and purple 4·50 6·50
2. 2 c. on 3 c. black & brown 1·25 1·60
3. 2 c. on 8 c. black & orange 6·50 6·50
4. 3 c. black and brown 6·50 6·50
5. 4 c. on 12 c. black & yellow 80 1·60
6. 5 c. on 16 c. green & brown 6·50 5·00
7. 8 c. black and orange 2·00 2·75
8. 10 c. on 16 c. green & brn. 1·60 2·25
9. 25 c. on 16 c. green & brn. 27·00 32·00
10. 30 c. on 16 c. green & brn. 22·00 28·00
11. 50 c. on 16 c. green & brn. 22·00 28·00
12. $1 on 8 c. black & orange 22·00 28·00

1. On the Brunei River.

1907.

14. **1.** 1 c. black and green 40 65
15. 2 c black and red 50 1·00
16. 3 c. black and brown 2·75 2·75
17. 4 c. black and mauve 2·50 2·75
18. 5 c. black and blue 9·00 10·00
19. 8 c. black and orange 2·00 4·50
20. 10 c. black and green 4·50 5·00
21. 25 c. blue and brown 6·00 7·00
22. 30 c. violet and black 6·00 7·00
23. 50 c. green and brown 6·00 7·00
24. $1 red and grey 20·00 27·00

1908.

26. **1.** 1 c. green 15 20
51. 1 c black 12 15
66. 1 c. brown 12 12
27. 2 c. black and brown 35 30
52. 2 c. brown 30 35
52a. 2 c. green 15 15
67ab. 2 c. grey 12 35
28. 3 c. red 60 60
53. 3 c. green 55 1·00
30. 4 c. claret 25 25
55. 4 c. orange 55 30
31. 5 c. black and orange 1·60 1·60
69. 5 c. orange 25 35
57. 5 c. grey 1·75 1·40
57b. 5 c. brown 20 25
32. 8 c. blue and indigo 1·60 1·60
60. 8 c. blue 1·10 1·00
60a. 8 c. black 90 55
70. 8 c. red 15 12
33a. 10 c. purple on yellow 45 60
71. 10 c. violet 5 5
72. 15 c. blue 20 8
73. 25 c. lilac 8 15
35. 30 c. purple and orange 1·75 1·75
74. 30 c. black and orange 15 25
36a. 50 c. black on green 3·50 5·00
75. 50 c. black 15 50
37. $1 black and red on blue 6·00 8·00
76. $1 black and red 45 45
38. $5 red on green 27·00 32·00
77. $5 green and red 4·00 5·00
78. $10 black and purple 8·00 11·00
39. $25 black on red 85·00 £125

1922. Optd. **MALAYA-BORNEO EXHIBITION 1922.**

42. **1.** 1 c. green 90 3·25
43. 2 c. black and brown 1·90 2·25
44. 3 c. red 2·25 6·00
45. 4 c. claret 2·00 8·50
46. 5 c. orange 3·00 11·00
47. 10 c. purple on yellow 4·00 15·00
48. 25 c. lilac 8·00 20·00
49. 50 c. black on green 20·00 42·00
50. $1 black and red on blue 24·00 42·00

2. Native houses, Brunei Town.

1924.

68. **2.** 3 c. green 20 35
69d. 6 c. black 12 30
59. 6 c. red 1·40 2·50
61. 12 c. blue 2·00 2·25

For Japanese issues see " Japanese Occupation of Brunei ".

3. Sultan Ahmed Tajudin and Brunei Town.

1949. Silver Jubilee of H.H. the Sultan.

79.	3.	8 c. black and red ..	35	65
80.		25 c. purple and orange ..	35	25
81.		50 c. black and blue ..	50	75

1949. U.P.U. As T 14/17 of Antigua.

82.		8 c. red	12	25
83.		15 c. blue	30	30
84.		25 c. magenta	35	35
85.		50 c. black	50	60

4. Sultan Omar Ali Saifuddin.

1952. Dollar values as T, 3 but with arms instead of portrait inset.

104.	4.	1 c. black	5	5
105.		2 c. black and orange ..	5	5
106.		3 c. black and brown ..	5	5
107.		4 c. black and green ..	5	5
108.		6 c. black and grey ..	5	5
109a.		8 c. black and red ..	5	5
110.		10 c. black and sepia ..	8	8
111.		12 c. black and violet ..	12	10
112.		15 c. black and blue ..	12	12
113.		25 c. black and purple ..	15	12
114.		50 c. black and blue ..	25	30
115a.	3.	$1 black and green ..	45	45
116.		$2 black and red ..	90	80
117.		$5 black and purple ..	2·25	2·00

5. Brunei Mosque and Sultan Omar.

1958. Opening of the Brunei Mosque.

100.	5.	8 c. black and green ..	12	12
101.		15 c. black and red ..	15	15
102.		35 c. black and lilac ..	30	30

6. "Protein Foods".

1963. Freedom from Hunger.

103.	6.	12 c. sepia	40	40

7. I.T.U. Emblem.

1965. I.T.U. Cent.

118.	7.	4 c. mauve and chestnut	8	8
119.		75 c. yellow and green ..	40	40

8. I.C.Y. Emblem.

1965. Int. Co-operation Year.

120.	8.	4 c. purple and turquoise	8	8
121.		15 c. green and lavender	25	25

9. Sir Winston Churchill and St. Paul's Cathedral in Wartime.

1966. Churchill Commem. Designs in black, cerise and gold and with background in colours given.

122.	9.	3 c. blue	5	5
123.		10 c. green	10	10
124.		15 c. brown	12	12
125.		75 c. violet	45	45

10. Footballer's Legs, Ball and Jules Rimet Cup.

1966. World Cup Football Championships.

126.	10.	4 c. vio., grn., lake & brn.	8	8
127.		75 c. chocolate, turquoise, lake and brown ..	40	40

11. W.H.O. Building.

1966. W.H.O. Headquarters, Geneva. Inaug.

128.	11.	12 c. black, grn. & blue	8	8
129.		25 c. blk., pur. & ochre	15	15

12. "Education".

1966. U.N.E.S.C.O. 20th Anniv.

130.	12.	4 c. vio., red, yell. & orge.	8	8
131.	–	15 c. yellow, violet & ol.	12	12
132.	–	75 c. black, pur. & orge.	40	40

DESIGNS: 15 c. "Science". 75 c. "Culture".

13. Banguan Pejabat Pejabat Hal Ehwal Ugama (Religious Headquarters building).

1967. Al-Quran's Descent to Universe. 1400th Year.

133.	13.	4 c. multicoloured ..	5	5
134.		10 c. multicoloured ..	8	8
135.	–	25 c. multicoloured ..	15	15
136.	–	50 c. multicoloured ..	30	30

Nos. 135/6 have sprigs of laurel flanking the main design (which has a smaller circle) in place of flagpoles.

INDEX

Countries can be quickly located by referring to the index at the end of this volume.

14. Sultan of Brunei, Mosque and Flags.

1968. Installation of Y.T.M. Seri Paduka Duli Pengiran Temenggong. Multicoloured.

137.		4 c. Type 14	5	5
138.		12 c. Sultan of Brunei, Mosque and Flags (different)	8	8
139.		25 c. Type 14	20	20

No. 138 is horiz.

15. Sultan of Brunei.

1968. Sultan's Birthday.

140.	15.	4 c. multicoloured ..	5	5
141.		12 c. multicoloured ..	8	8
142.		25 c. multicoloured ..	20	20

16. Sultan of Brunei.

1968. Coronation of Sultan of Brunei.

143.	16.	4 c. multicoloured ..	5	5
144.		12 c. multicoloured ..	8	8
145.		25 c. multicoloured ..	20	20

17. New Building and Sultan's Portrait.

1968. Opening of Hall of Language and Culture. Multicoloured.

146.		10 c. Type 17	5	5
147.		15 c. New Building and Sultan's portrait ($48\frac{1}{2} \times 22$ mm.) ..	10	10
148.		30 c. As 15 c.	15	15

MORE DETAILED LISTS

are given in the Stanley Gibbons Catalogues referred to in the country headings:

BC	British Commonwealth
E1, E2, E3	Europe 1, 2, 3
O1, O2, O3, O4	Overseas 1, 2, 3, 4

18. Human Rights Emblem and struggling Man.

1968. Human Rights Year.

149.	18.	12 c. blk., yell. & grn...	5	5
150.		25 c. blk., yell. & bl. ..	12	12
151.		75 c. blk., yell. & pur...	40	40

19. Sultan of Brunei and W.H.O. Emblem.

1968. World Health Organization. 20th Anniv.

152.	19.	4 c. yell., blk. & cobalt	5	5
153.		15 c. yell., blk. & vio...	10	10
154.		25 c. yell., blk. & olive	20	20

20. Deep Sea Oil-Rig, Sultan of Brunei and inset portrait of Di-Gadong Sahibol Mal.

1969. Installation (9th May, 1968) of Pengiran Shar-bandar as Y.T.M. Seri Paduka Duli Pengiran Di-Gadong Sahibol Mal.

155.	20.	12 c. multicoloured ..	5	5
156.		40 c. multicoloured ..	20	20
157.		50 c. multicoloured ..	25	25

21. Aerial View of Royal Assembly Hall.

1969. Opening of Dewan Majlis and Lapau Di-Raja.

158.	21.	12 c. multicoloured ..	5	5
159.		25 c. multicoloured ..	12	12
160.	–	50 c. red and violet ..	25	25

DESIGN: 50 c. Side view of Royal Assembly Hall.

22. Youth Centre and Sultan's Portrait.

1969. Opening of New Youth Centre.

161.	22.	6 c. multicoloured ..	5	5
162.		10 c. multicoloured ..	10	10
163.		30 c. multicoloured ..	30	30

23. Soldier, Sultan and Arms.

1971. Royal Brunei Malay Regiment. 10th Anniv. Multicoloured.
164. 10 c. Type **23** 5 5
165. 15 c. Helicopter, Sultan and Arms (horiz.) 8 8
166. 75 c. Patrolboat, Sultan and Arms (horiz.) .. 35 35

24. Badge, and Officer in Full-dress Uniform.

1971. Royal Brunei Police Force. 50th Anniv. Multicoloured.
167. 10 c. Type **24** 5 5
168. 15 c. Badge and Patrol Constable 8 8
169. 50 c. Badge and Traffic Constable 25 25

25. Perdana Wazir, Sultan of Brunei and View of Brunei Town.

1971. Installation of the Yang Teramat Malia as the Perdana Wazir.
170. **25.** 15 c. multicoloured .. 8 8
171. – 25 c. multicoloured .. 15 15
172. – 50 c. multicoloured .. 30 30
Nos. 170/2 show various views of Brunei Town.

26. Pottery.

1972. Opening of Brunei Museum. Multicoloured.
173. 10 c. Type **26** 5 5
174. 12 c. Straw-work 5 5
175. 15 c. Leather-work .. 8 8
176. 25 c. Gold-work 12 12
177. 50 c. Museum Building (58×21 mm.) 30 30

27. Modern Building, Queen Elizabeth and Sultan of Brunei.

1972. Royal Visit. Each design with portrait of Queen and Sultan. Multicoloured.
178. 10 c. Type **27** 5 5
179. 15 c. Native houses .. 10 10
180. 25 c. Mosque 15 20
181. 50 c. Royal Assembly Hall 30 35

28. Bangunan Secretariat.

1972. Renaming of Brunei Town as Bandar Seri Begawan.
182. **28.** 10 c. multicoloured .. 5 5
183. – 15 c. green, yell. & blk. 8 8
184. – 25 c. blue, yell. & black 12 12
185. – 50 c. red, blue and black 25 30
VIEWS: 15 c. Istana Darul Hana. 25 c. Bandar Brunei Lama. 50 c. Bandar Dan Kampong Ayer.

29. Blackburn "Beverley" parachuting supplies.

1972. Opening of R.A.F. Museum, Hendon. Multicoloured.
186. 25 c. Type **29** 12 12
187. 75 c. Blackburn "Beverley" landing 35 35

1972. Royal Silver Wedding. As T **19** of Ascension, but with Girl with Traditional Flower-pot, and Boy with Bowl and Pipe in background.
196. 12 c. red 8 8
197. 75 c. green 40 40

30. Interpol H.Q., Paris.

1973. Interpol. 50th Anniv.
198. **30.** 25 c. grn., pur. & black 12 12
199. – 50 c. blue, ultramarine and red 25 25
DESIGN: 50 c. Different view of the H.Q.

31. Sultan, Princess Anne and Capt. Phillips.

1973. Royal Wedding.
200. **31.** 25 c. multicoloured .. 12 12
201. 50 c. multicoloured .. 25 25

32. Churchill Painting. 33. Sultan Sir Muda Hassanal Balkiah Muizzaddin Waddaulah.

1973. Churchill Memorial Exhibition. Mult.
202. 12 c. Type **32** 5 5
203. 50 c. Churchill making "V" sign 15 20

1974. Multicoloured. Background colours given.
204. **33.** 4 c. green 5 5
205. 5 c. blue 5 5
206. 6 c. brown 5 5
207. 10 c. lilac 5 5
208. 15 c. brown 5 5
209. 20 c. grey 5 8
210. 25 c. green 8 10
211. 30 c. blue 10 12
212. 35 c. grey 12 15
213. 40 c. purple 12 15
214. 50 c. brown 15 20
215. 75 c. green 25 30
216. $1 buff 35 40
217. $2 yellow 70 80
218. $5 silver .. .. 1·75 2·00
219. $10 gold .. .. 3·25 3·50

34. Aerial View of Airport.

1974. Brunei Int. Airport. Inaug. Mult.
220. 50 c. Type **34.** 25 25
221. 75 c. Sultan in Air Force uniform, and airport .. 35 35

35. U.P.U. Emblem and Sultan.

1974. Universal Postal Union. Cent.
222. **35.** 12 c. multicoloured .. 8 8
223. 50 c. multicoloured .. 20 20
224. 75 c. multicoloured .. 25 30

36. Sir Winston Churchill.

1974. Sir Winston Churchill. Birth Cent.
225. **36.** 12 c. blk., blue and gold 8 8
226. – 75 c. blk., grn. & gold.. 30 30
DESIGN: 75 c. Churchill smoking cigar (profile)

37. Boeing '737' and Tail-fin bearing RBA Crest.

1975. Royal Brunei Airlines Inaug. Mult.
227. 12 c. Type **37** 5 5
228. 35 c. '737' over Bander Seri Begawan Mosque .. 12 15
229. 75 c. '737' in flight .. 25 30

1976. Surch.
246. **33.** 10 c. on 6 c. brown .. 5 5

BRUNSWICK E2

Formerly a Duchy of N. Germany. Joined North German Confederation in 1868. Now part of West Germany.

30 silbergroschen = 1 thaler.

1.

1852. Imperf.
1. **1.** 1 sg. red £1300 £150
2. 2 sg. blue £800 £110
3. 3 sg. vermilion £800 £110

1853. Imperf. or roul.
4. **1.** $\frac{1}{4}$ g. black on brown .. £150 95·00
5. $\frac{1}{3}$ g. black .. .. .. 75·00 £170
15. $\frac{1}{2}$ sg. black on green .. 10·00 85·00
7. 1 sg. black on buff .. 80·00 28·00
25. 1 sg. yellow .. .. 75·00 38·00
9. 2 sg. black on blue .. 50·00 17·00
10. 3 sg. black on rose .. £140 25·00
18. 3 sg. rose .. .. .. £130 60·00

2. 3.

1857. Imperf.
12. **2.** 4/4 g. black on brown .. 14·00 42·00

1865. Roul.
28. **3.** $\frac{1}{3}$ g. black .. .. .. 11·00 £190
31. 1 g. red .. .. .. 75 14·00
33. 2 g. blue .. .. .. 5·00 55·00
34. 3 g. brown .. 3·75 70·00

BUENOS AIRES O1

A province of the Argentine Republic. Issued its own stamps from 1858–1862.

8 reales = 1 peso.

1. 2.

1858. Imperf.
P 13. **1.** 4 r. brown.. .. 35·00 25·00
P 17. 1 (IN) p. brown .. 40·00 25·00
P 20. 1 (IN) p. blue .. .. 25·00 15·00
P 25. 1 (TO) p. blue .. .. 50·00 25·00
P 1. 2 p. blue .. .. .. 35·00 20·00
P 4. 3 p. green £200 £100
P 7. 4 p. red £900 £600
P 10. 5 p. yellow £950 £500

1859. Imperf.
P 37. **2.** 4 r. green on blue .. 25·00 15·00
P 38. 1 p. blue .. .. 4·00 3·00
P 45. 1 p red .. .. 10·00 6·00
P 43. 2 p. red .. .. 30·00 20·00
P 48. 2 p. blue .. .. 20·00 12·00

BULGARIA E1

Formerly a Turkish province; a principality under Turkish suzerainty from 1878 to 1908, when an independent kingdom was proclaimed. A People's Republic since 1946.

1879. 100 centimes = 1 franc.
1881. 100 stotinki = 1 leva.

1. Large Lion 2.

1879. Value in centimes and franc.
1. **1.** 5 c. black and yellow .. 32·00 11·00
3. 10 c. black and green .. £160 30·00
5. 25 c. black and purple .. 75·00 8·50
7. 50 c. black and blue .. £150 27·00
8. 1 f. black and red .. 22·00 11·00

1881. Value in stotinki.
10. **2.** 3 s. red and grey .. 7·50 1·75
11. 5 s. black and yellow .. 8·00 1·75
14. 10 s. black and green .. 29·00 3·50
15. 15 s. red and green .. 32·00 3·50
18. 25 s. black and purple .. £150 15·00
19. 30 s. blue and brown .. 11·00 3·50
See also Nos. 275/9.

A.

B.

C.

D.

1882.

46. **2.** 1 s. violet (Type A) .. 6·50 2·25
48. 1 s violet (Type B) .. 40 10
47. 2 s. green (Type C) .. 6·00 1·25
49. 2 s. green (Type D) .. 40 10
24. 3 s. orange and yellow .. 4·50 40
23. 5 s. green .. .. 4·50 40
26. 10 s. red .. .. 4·75 25
28. 15 s. purple and mauve .. 2·50 25
31. 25 s. blue .. .. 3·00 40
33. 30 s. lilac and green .. 3·50 40
34. 50 s. blue and red .. 3·50 45
50. 1 l. black and red .. 11·00 1·40

1884. Surch. with large figure of value.

38. **2.** 3 on 10 s. red .. .. 23·00 23·00
43. 5 on 30 s. blue and brown 24·00 24·00
45. 15 on 25 s. blue .. .. 26·00 26·00
40. 50 on 1 f. black and red .. £140 £100

3.

4. Arms of Bulgaria.

5. Cherry wood Cannon used against the Turks.

1889.

51. **3.** 1 s. mauve 12 5
52. 2 s. grey 30 5
53. 3 s. brown 20 5
54. 5 s. green .. .. 2·25 5
55. 10 s. red .. .. 2·75 5
56. 15 s. orange .. .. 3·00 5
57. 25 s. blue .. .. 2·40 5
58. 30 s. brown .. .. 2·40 5
59. 50 s. green 35 5
60. 1 l. red 25 12
83. 2 l. rose and pink .. 1·25 70
84. 3 l. black and buff .. 2·00 1·25

1892. Surch. **15.**

61. **3.** 15 on 30 s. brown .. 2·75 35

1895. Surch. **01.**

74. **2.** 01 on 2 s. green (No. 49) 20 10

1896. Baptism of Prince Boris.

78. **4.** 1 s. green 12 5
79. 5 s. blue 12 5
81. 15 s. violet 20 8
82. 25 s. red .. .. 1·60 25

1901. Surch. in figures.

102. **3.** 5 on 3 s. brown 60 60
103. 10 on 50 s. green .. 70 70

1901. Uprising against Turkey. 25th Anniv.

104. **5.** 5 s. red 55 55
105. 15 s. green 55 55

6. Prince Ferdinand.

7. Fighting at Shipka Pass.

1901.

106. **6.** 1 s. black and purple .. 5 5
107. 2 s. blue and green .. 5 5
108. 3 s. black and orange .. 12 5
109. 5 s. brown and green .. 1·25 5
110. 10 s. brown and red .. 60 5
113. 15 s. black and lake .. 50 5
114. 25 s. black and blue .. 50 5
116. 30 s. black and brown .. 8·00 15
117. 50 s. brown and blue .. 65 8
118. 1 l. green and red .. 1·25 5
120. 2 l. black and red .. 3·25 60
123. 3 l. claret and grey .. 4·50 1·75

1902. Battle of Shipka Pass. 25th Anniv.

124. **7.** 5 s. red 75 25
125. 10 s. green 85 30
126. 15 s. blue .. .. 2·25 1·25

1903. Surch.

140. **6.** 5 on 15 s. black and lake 70 35
127. 10 on 15 s. blk. and lake 4·50 20
143. 25 on 30 s. blk. & brown 4·00 40

8. Ferdinand I in 1887 and 1907.

1907. King's Accession. 20th Anniv.

132. **8.** 5 s. green .. .. 3·25 60
134. 10 s. red-brown .. .. 7·50 70
137. 25 s. blue .. .. 10·00 1·60

1909. Optd. **1909.**

146. **3.** 1 s. mauve 45 15
149. 5 s. green 30 20

1909. Surch. **1909** and new value.

151. **3.** 5 on 30 s. brown .. 60 20
154. 10 on 15 s. orange .. 75 15
156. 10 on 50 s. green .. 70 20

1910. Surch. **1910** and new value.

157. **6.** 1 on 3 s. black and orange 1·65 55
158. 5 on 15 s. black and lake 75 40

9. King Asen Tower.

10. Tsar in Generals Uniform.

11. Tirnovo City

Designs—vert. 5 s. 10 s., 25 s., 1 l. Portraits of Tsar Ferdinand. horiz. 15 s. R. Isker. 30 s. Rila Monastery. 50 s. Tsars and Princes. 2 l. Monastery of the Holy Trinity. 3 l. Varna.

1911.

159. **9.** 1 s. green 5 5
182a. 1 s. slate 5 5
160. **10.** 2 s. black and red .. 5 5
161. **11.** 3 s. black and lake .. 10 5
162. – 5 s. black and green .. 35 5
181. – 5 s. purple and green .. 40 5
163. – 10 s. black and red .. 65 5
181a. – 10 s. sepia and brown .. 5 5
164. – 15 s. bistre 75 5
183. – 15 s. olive 12 5
165. – 25 s. black and blue .. 25 5
166. – 30 s. black and blue .. 1·90 5
182. – 30 s. brown and olive .. 8 5
167. – 50 s. black and yellow .. 6·50 8
168. – 1 l. brown .. .. 3·25 8
169. – 2 l. black and purple .. 90 30
170. – 3 l. black and violet .. 4·25 1·40

See also Nos. 234/5 and 241/2.

21. King Ferdinand.

1912. 25th Year of the Reign.

171. **21.** 5 s. grey .. .. 1·60 75
172. 10 s. lake .. .. 2·00 1·25
173. 25 s. blue .. .. 2·50 1·40

ОСВОБ. ВОЙНА
1912-1913
(22.)

3
СТОТИНКИ
(23.)

1913. Victory over Turks. Stamps of 1911 optd. as T **22.**

174. **9.** 1 s. green 12 5
175. **10.** 2 s. black and red .. 12 8
176. **11.** 3 s. black and lake .. 15 8
177. – 5 s. black and green .. 12 8
178. – 10 s. black and red .. 20 5
179. – 15 s. bistre 45 25
180. – 25 s. black and blue .. 1·40 15

1915. No. 165 surch. **10 CT.** and bar.

180a. – 10 s. on 25 s. blk. & blue 25 8

1916. Red Cross Fund. Surch. with T **23.**

185. **8.** 3 s. on 1 s. mauve .. 2·75 2·50

Nos. 186/9 formerly listed here will now be found under Bulgarian Occupation of Rumania.

25. Veles.

26. Bulgarian Ploughman.

27.

28. Bulgarian peasant.

1917. Liberation of Macedonia.

193. **25.** 1 s. grey 5 5
194. **26.** 1 s. green 5 5
195. – 5 s. green 5 5
186. **27.** 5 s. green 15 5
187. **28.** 15 s. grey 5 5
188. – 25 s. blue 5 5
189. – 30 s. orange 5 5
190. – 50 s. violet 20 5
191. – 2 l. brown 20 5
192. – 3 l. claret 30 8

Designs—As T **25**: 5 s. Monastery of St. John, Ochrid. As T **27**: 25 s. Soldier and Mt. Sonichka. 50 s. Ochrid and Lake. As T **28**: 30 s. Nish. 2 l. Demir kapija. 3 l. Gevgeli.

34.

1918. Tsar's Accession. 30th Anniv.

196. **34.** 1 s. slate 5 5
197. 2 s. brown 5 5
198. 3 s. blue 12 5
199. 10 s. red 12 8

36. Parliament Building.
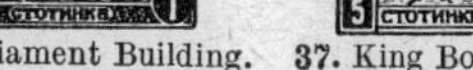
37. King Boris III.

1919.

201. **36.** 1 s. black 5 5
202. 2 s. olive 5 5

1919. Enthronement of King Boris III. 1st Anniv.

203. **37.** 3 s. chestnut 5 5
204. 5 s. green 5 5
205. 10 s. red 5 5
206. 15 s. violet 5 5
207. 25 s. blue 5 5
208. 30 s. chocolate 5 5
209. 50 s. brown 5 5

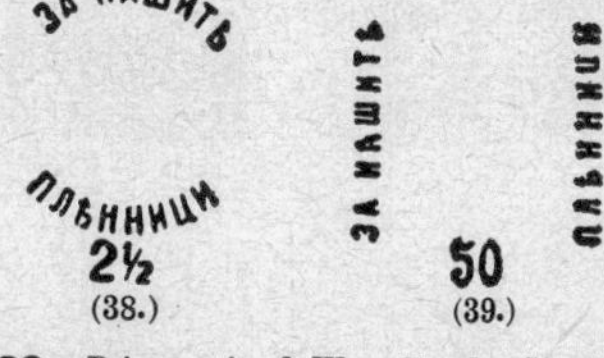

(38.) (39.)

1920. Prisoners' of War Fund. Surch. as T 38/39.

210. **36.** 1 on 2 s. olive .. 5 5
211. **37.** 2½ on 5 s. green .. 5 5
212. 5 on 10 s. red 5 5
213. 7½ on 15 s. violet .. 5 5
214. 12½ on 25 s. blue .. 5 5
215. 15 on 30 s. chocolate .. 5 5
216. 25 on 50 s. brown .. 5 5
217. – 50 on 1 l. brn. (No. 168) 10 10
218. – 1 on 2 l. brn. (No. 191) 12 12
219. – 1½ on 3 l. clar. (No. 192) 25 25

40. Vazov's Birthplace at Sopot and Chreeywood Cannon.

41. "The Bear-fighter", character from "Under the Yoke"

1920. Ivan Vazov (writer). 70th Birth Anniv.

220. **40.** 30 s. red 5 5
221. **41.** 50 s. green 8 5
222. – 1 l. sepia 12 5
223. – 2 l. brown 45 20
224. – 3 l. violet 45 20
225. – 5 l. blue 65 25

Designs—horiz. 1 l. Ivan Vazov in 1870 and 1920. 3 l. Vazov's Houses in Plovdiv and Sofia. vert. 2 l. Vazov. 5 l. Monk Paissi quoted by Vazov.

46.

48. Mt. Shar.

1921.

226. **46.** 10 s. claret 5 5
227. – 10 s. claret 5 5
228. **48.** 10 s. claret 5 5
229. – 10 s. mauve 5 5
230. – 20 s. blue 15 10

Designs—vert. No. 227, King and Lion. horiz. 229, Bridge over Vardar at Skopje. 230, Lake Ochrid.

51. Sofia.

54. King Boris III.

1921.

231. **51.** 10 s. violet 5 5
232. – 20 s. green 5 5
233. **54.** 25 s. blue 5 5
234. **11.** 50 s. orange 5 5
235. 50 s. blue .. .. 1·25 95
236. – 75 s. purple 8 5
237. – 75 s. blue 8 5
238. **54.** 1 l. red 12 5
239. 1 l. blue 12 5
240. – 2 l. brown 20 5
241. – 3 l. purple 25 5
242. – 5 l. blue .. .. 1·25 15
243. **54.** 10 l. claret .. .. 3·25 25

Designs—horiz. 20 s. Alexander II "The Liberator" Monument Sofia. 75 s. Shipka Pass Monastery. 5 l. Rila Monastery. vert. 2 l. Girl with wheatsheaf. 3 l. King Asen Tower.

58. Bourchier in Bulgarian Costume.

59. J. D. Bourchier.

60. Rila Monastery, Bourchier's Resting-place.

1921. J. D. Bouchier ("Times" Correspondent) commem.

244. **58.** 10 s. red 5 5
245. 20 s. orange 5 5
246. **59.** 30 s. slate 5 5
247. 50 s. lilac 5 5
248. 1 l. purple 15 5
249. **60.** 1½ l. olive 8 5
250. 2 l. green 10 5
251. 3 l. blue 30 12
252. 5 l. claret 70 30

1924. Surch.

253. **36.** 10 s. on 1 s. black .. 5 5
254. **D 4.** 10 s. on 20 s. orange .. 5 5
255. 20 s. on 5 s. green .. 5 5
256. 20 s. on 10 s. violet .. 5 5
257. 20 s. on 30 s. orange .. 5 5
258. **37.** 1 l. on 5 s. green .. 8 5
259. **11.** 3 l. on 50 s. blue .. 12 8
260. **54.** 6 l. on 1 l. red .. 25 15

61.

62.

63. King Boris III. **64.** Nevski Church, Sofia.

65. **66.** Proposed Rest-home.

1925.

261.	**61.**	10 s. blue & red on rose	5	5
262.		15 s. brn. & lake on blue	5	5
263.		30 s. buff and black ..	5	5
264.	**62.**	50 s. brown on green ..	5	5
265.	**63.**	1 l. olive	8	5
266.		1 l. green	25	5
267.	**64.**	2 l. green and buff ..	20	5
267a.	**63.**	2 l. grey-brown ..	55	5
268.	**65.**	4 l. lake and yellow ..	25	5

1925. Sunday Delivery Stamps.

268a.	**66.**	1 l. black on green ..	1·00	5
268b.		1 l. brown	70	5
268c.		1 l. orange	1·25	8
268d.		1 l. pink	1·25	5
268e.		1 l. violet on rose ..	1·90	8
268f.	–	2 l. green	15	8
268g.	–	2 l. violet	15	5
268h.	–	5 l. blue	1·75	25
268j.	–	5 l. red	1·75	25

DESIGN: 2 l., 5 l. Proposed Sanatorium.

68. Sveta Nedelya Cathedral, Sofia after Bomb Outrage. **69.** C. Botev (poet).

1926.

269.	**68.**	50 s. black	5	5

1926. Botev Commem.

270.	**69.**	1 l. green	20	10
271.		2 l. lilac	35	10
272.		4 l. claret	35	20

70. **71.** King Boris III. **72.** Saint Clement of Ochrid.

1926.

273.	**70.**	6 l. olive and blue ..	1·00	15
274.		10 l. orange and sepia ..	3·25	50

1927. Air. Various stamps optd. with aeroplane and 6 l. surch. also.

281.	**70.**	1 l. on 6 l. olive and blue	50	50
282.	**63.**	2 l. grey-brown ..	60	55
283.	**65.**	4 l. lake and yellow ..	75	70
284.	**70.**	10 l. orange and sepia ..	10·00	7·00

1927. As T 2 in new colours.

275.		10 s. red and green ..	5	5
276.		15 s. black and yellow ..	5	5
277.		30 s. slate and buff ..	5	5
278.		30 s. blue and buff ..	5	5
279.		50 s. black and red ..	5	5

1928.

285.	**71.**	1 l. green	8	5
286.		2 l. brown	10	5

1929. 50th Anniv. of Liberation of Bulgaria and Millenary of Tsar Simeon. Various sizes.

287.	**72.**	10 s. violet	12	5
288.	–	15 s. purple	12	5
289.	–	30 s. red	12	5
290.	–	50 s. olive	20	5
291.	–	1 l. red-brown	40	5
292.	–	2 l. blue	40	5
293.	–	3 l. green	1·10	20
294.	–	4 l. brown	1·60	8
295.	–	5 l. brown	1·40	20
296.	–	6 l. blue-green	1·40	30

DESIGNS: 15 s. K. Miladinov. 30 s. George S. Rakovski. 50 s. Drenovo Monastery. 1 l. Father Paissi. 2 l. Tsar Simeon. 3 l. Liuben Karavelov. 4 l. Vasil Levski. 5 l. George Benkovski. 6 l. Tsar Alexander II of Russia.

82. Convalescent Home, Varna.

1930. Sunday Delivery stamps.

297.	**82.**	1 l. green and purple ..	2·25	8
298.		1 l. yellow and green	25	8
299.		1 l. brown and claret ..	25	8

83. **85.** King Boris III.

1930. Marriage of King Boris and Princess Giovanna.

300.	**83.**	1 l. green	15	12
301.	–	2 l. purple	25	12
302.	**83.**	4 l. red	25	15
303.	–	6 l. blue	35	15

DESIGN: 2 l., 6 l. Portraits in separate ovals.

1931. The 20 l. is $24\frac{1}{2} \times 33\frac{1}{2}$ mm.

304.	**85.**	1 l. green (A) ..	10	5
305.		2 l. red (A)	20	5
306.		4 l. orange (A) ..	15	5
308a.		4 l. orange (B) ..	55	5
307.		6 l. blue (A)	15	5
308b.		6 l. blue (B)	55	5
308c.		7 l. blue (B)	15	5
308d.		10 l. slate (B)	4·75	20
308.		12 l. brown (A) ..	25	5
308e.		14 l. brown (B) ..	25	12
308f.	–	20 l. brown & purple (B)	50	20

(A) Without coloured frame-lines at top and bottom: (B) with frame-lines.

86.

DESIGNS—VERT. (23 × 28 mm.): 2 l. Footballer. 4 l. Horse-riding. As T 86—HORIZ. 6 l. Fencing. 10 l. Cycling. VERT. 12 l. Diving. 50 l. Spirit of Victory.

1931. Balkan Olympic Games.

309.	**86.**	1 l. green	85	50
326.		1 l. blue-green	1·10	65
310.	–	2 l. lake	1·00	50
327.	–	2 l. blue	1·60	75
311.	–	4 l. red	2·25	70
328.	–	4 l. purple	2·75	90
312.	–	6 l. blue-green	4·25	90
329.	–	6 l. red	5·50	1·60
313.	–	10 l. orange	10·00	8·25
330.	–	10 l. brown	15·00	7·00
314.	–	12 l. blue	20·00	6·50
331.	–	12 l. orange	38·00	20·00
315.	–	50 l. brown	22·00	20·00
332.	–	50 l. claret	90·00	75·00

89. **90.** Rila Monastery.

1931. Air.

316.	**89.**	1 l. green	15	5
316a.		1 l. maroon	15	8
317.		2 l. claret	15	5
317a.		2 l. green	15	8
318.		6 l. blue	20	8
318a.		6 l. red	40	15
319.		12 l. red	40	12
319a.		12 l. blue	55	20
320.		20 l. violet	55	25
321.		30 l. orange	75	45
322.		50 l. brown	1·75	60

1932. Air.

323.	**90.**	18 l. green	18·00	11·00
324.		24 l. red	18·00	11·00
325.		28 l. blue	9·00	8·50

1934. Surch. **2.**

333.	**85.**	2 on 3 l. olive	2·00	12

91. Defending the pass. **93.** Convalescent Home, Troyan.

1934. Shipka Pass Memorial Unveiling.

334.	**91.**	1 l. green	15	15
340.		1 l. yellow-green ..	20	15
335.	–	2 l. red	12	8
341.	–	2 l. orange	12	8
336.	–	3 l. brown	35	40
342.	–	3 l. yellow	60	40
337.	–	4 l. carmine	80	25
343.	–	4 l. rose	80	25
338.	–	7 l. blue	1·25	90
344.	–	7 l. light blue	1·50	90
339.	–	14 l. purple	3·75	3·00
345.	–	14 l. bistre	3·50	3·25

DESIGNS—VERT. (dated " 1934 "): 2 l. Shipka Memorial. 3 l., 7 l. Veteran standard-bearer. 14 l. Widow showing orphans memorial. HORIZ. 4 l. Bulgarian Veteran.

1935. Sunday Delivery stamps.

346.	**93.**	1 l. red and brown ..	15	10
347.		1 l. blue and green ..	15	10
348.	–	5 l. blue and red ..	1·00	25

DESIGN: 5 l. Convalescent Home, Banya.

96. Capt. Mamarchef. **98.** Cathedral.

1935. Tirnovo Insurrection Cent.

349.	–	1 l. blue	70	15
350.	**96.**	2 l. claret	70	20

DESIGN: 1 l. Velcho A. Djamdjyata.

1935. 5th Balkan Football Tournament.

351.	–	1 l. green	1·10	80
352.	**98.**	2 l. grey	2·25	1·40
353.	–	4 l. red	5·00	2·10
354.	–	7 l. blue	7·50	2·75
355.	–	14 l. orange	6·50	3·25
356.	–	50 l. brown	60·00	48·00

DESIGNS—HORIZ. 1 l. Match in progress. 4 l. Footballers. VERT. 7 l. Herald and map. 14 l. Footballer and trophy. 50 l. Football trophy.

102. Girl Gymnast. **103.** Janos Hunyadi.

1935. 8th Bulgarian Gymnastic Tournament. Dated " 12-14. VII. 1935 ".

357.	–	1 l. green	80	80
358.	–	2 l. blue	1·60	1·25
359.	**102.**	4 l. red	4·50	2·25
360.	–	7 l. blue	4·75	2·50
361.	–	14 l. brown	4·00	2·50
362.	–	50 l. orange	45·00	40·00

DESIGNS—VERT. 1 l. Parallel bars. 2 l. Male gymnast in uniform. 7 l. Pole jump. 50 l. Athlete and lion. HORIZ. 14 l. Stadium Sofia.

1935. Unveiling of Monument to Ladislas III of Poland at Varna. Inscr. " WARNENCZYK(A) ", etc.

363.	**103.**	1 l. orange	80	20
364.	–	2 l. claret	1·10	20
365.	–	4 l. red	4·00	60
366.	–	7 l. blue	1·40	70
367.	–	14 l. green	1·40	65

DESIGNS—VERT. 2 l. King Ladislas of Hungary enthroned (22 × 32 mm.). 7 l. King Ladislas in armour (20 × 31 mm.). HORIZ. 4 l. Varna Memorial (33 × 24 mm.). 14 l. Battle scene (30 × 25 mm.).

104. H. Dimitr. **104a.** **105.**

1935. Hadji Dimitr. 67th Death Anniv.

368.	–	1 l. green	75	40
369.	**104.**	2 l. brown	1·25	90
370.	–	4 l. red	2·75	2·00
371.	–	7 l. blue	4·25	3·00
372.	–	14 l. orange	5·00	3·25

DESIGNS—VERT. 1 l. H. Dimitr's monument at Sliven. 7 l. Revolutionary group (dated 1868). HORIZ. 4 l. H. Dimitr and S. Karaja. 14 l. Dimitr's birthplace at Silven.

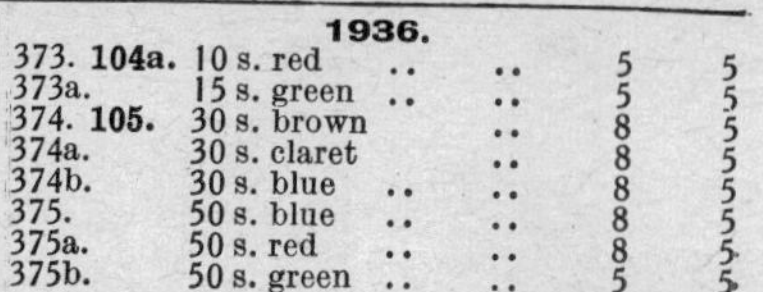

1936.

373.	**104a.**	10 s. red	5	5
373a.		15 s. green	5	5
374.	**105.**	30 s. brown ..	8	5
374a.		30 s. claret ..	8	5
374b.		30 s. blue	8	5
375.		50 s. blue	8	5
375a.		50 s. red	8	5
375b.		50 s. green	5	5

106. Nesebur. **107.** St. Cyril and St. Methodius.

1936. Slav Geographical and Ethnographical Congress, Sofia. Inscr. as in T **106.**

376.	–	1 l. violet	1·25	50
377.	–	2 l. blue	80	35
378.	**106.**	7 l. blue	2·00	1·10

DESIGNS—VERT. 1 l. Meteorological Bureau, Mt. Mousala. 2 l. Peasant Girl.

1937. Millenary of Cyrillic Alphabet and Slavonic Liturgy.

379.	**107.**	1 l. green	5	5
380.		2 l. purple	5	5
381.	–	4 l. red	15	5
382.	**107.**	7 l. blue	1·00	60
383.	–	14 l. red	90	70

DESIGN: 4 l., 14 l. The Saints Preaching.

109. Princess Marie Louise. **110.** King Boris III.

1937.

384.	**109.**	1 l. green	15	5
385.		2 l. red	15	8
386.		4 l. red	30	12

1937. 19th Anniv. of Accession.

387.	**110.**	2 l. red	15	10

111. Harvesting. **114.** Prince Simeon.

1938. Trade Propaganda.

388.	**111.**	10 s. orange	5	5
389.		10 s. vermilion ..	5	5
390.	–	15 s. red	15	5
391.	–	15 s. purple	15	5
392.	–	30 s. brown	5	5
393.	–	30 s. red-brown ..	5	5
394.	–	50 s. slate-blue ..	20	5
395.	–	50 s. black	20	5
396.	–	1 l. green	35	5
397.	–	1 l. yellow-green ..	50	5
398.	–	2 l. red	25	5
399.	–	2 l. brown	25	5
400.	–	3 l. purple	1·00	30
401.	–	3 l. maroon	1·00	30
402.	–	4 l. brown	35	10
403.	–	4 l. purple	60	10
404.	–	7 l. violet	70	45
405.	–	7 l. blue	70	45
406.	–	14 l. red-brown ..	1·00	55
407.	–	14 l. chocolate ..	1·10	55

DESIGNS—VERT. 15 s. Sunflower. 30 s. Wheat. 50 s. Chickens and eggs. 1 l. Grapes. 3 l. Strawberries. 4 l. Girl carrying grapes. 7 l. Roses. 14 l. Tobacco leaves. HORIZ. 2 l. " Attar of Roses ".

1938. Heir Apparent's First Birthday.

408.	**114.**	1 l. green	5	5
409.		2 l. red	8	5
410.	–	4 l. orange	12	8
411.	**114.**	7 l. blue	40	20
412.	–	14 l. brown	40	20

DESIGN: 4 l., 14 l. Another portrait.

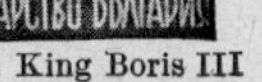

116. King Boris III **117.** Primitive Railway-engine.

1938. 20th Anniv of King's Accession Portraits of King in various uniforms.
413. **116.** 1 l. green 8 5
414. – 2 l. red 45 5
415. – 4 l. brown 8 5
416. – 7 l. blue 20 10
417. – 14 l. mauve 20 15

1939. Bulgarian Railways' Jubilee, Locomotive types dated "1888–1938".
418. **117.** 1 l. green 10 5
419. – 2 l. brown 12 8
420. – 4 l. orange 40 20
421. – 7 l. blue .. .. 1·00 75
DESIGNS: 2 l. Modern express train. 4 l. Train crossing viaduct. 7 l. King Boris as engine-driver.

118. P.O. Emblem. **120.** Gymnast.

1939. Bulgarian P.O. 60th Anniv. Inscr. "1879 1939".
422. **118.** 1 l. green 8 5
423. – 2 l. red (G.P.O., Sofia) 10 5

1939. Yunak Gymnastic Society's Rally.
424. **120.** 1 l. green 20 10
425. – 2 l. red 20 12
426. – 4 l. brown 35 12
427. – 7 l. blue 70 45
428. – 14 l. mauve .. .. 3·00 1·60
DESIGNS: 2 l. Yunak badge. 4 l. Throwing discus. 7 l. Rhythmic dancer. 14 l. Weight-lifting.

1939. Sevlievo and Tirnovo Floods' Relief Fund. Surch **Наводнението** (=Inundation) **1939** and value.
429. **28.** 1 l.+1 l. on 15 s. grey .. 8 8
430. **60.** 2 l.+1 l. on 1½ l. olive 8 8
431. 4 l.+2 l. on 2 l. green .. 10 10
432. 7 l.+4 l. on 3 l. blue .. 25 25
433. 14 l.+7 l. on 5 l. claret 35 35

121. King Boris III. **122.** Mail 'Plane.

1940.
433a. **121.** 1 l. green 5 5
434. 2 l. red 8 5

1940. Air.
435. **122.** 1 l. green 5 5
436. – 2 l. red 40 5
437. – 4 l. orange 5 5
438. – 6 l. blue 10 5
439. – 10 l. brown 15 5
440. – 12 l. brown 20 8
441. – 16 l. violet 25 12
442. – 19 l. blue 25 15
443. – 30 l. mauve 45 25
444. – 45 l. violet .. .. 1·10 60
445. – 70 l. red 95 50
446. – 100 l. blue .. .. 3·25 2·00
DESIGNS—VERT. Aeroplanes over King Asen's Tower (2 l.). Bachovo Monastery (4 l.), Nevski Church, Sofia (45 l.) and Shipka Pass Memorial (70 l.). 10 l. Aeroplane mail train and express motor-cycle. 30 l. Aeroplane and swallow. 100 l. Aeroplane and Royal cypher. HORIZ. 6 l. Loading mails at aerodrome. Aeroplanes over Sofia Palace (12 l.), Mt. El Tepe (16 l.), Rila Lakes and mountains (19 l.).

123. First Bulgarian Postage Stamp.

ILLUSTRATIONS
British Commonwealth and all overprints and surcharges are FULL SIZE. Foreign Countries have been reduced to ¾-LINEAR.

1940. 1st Adhesive Postage Stamp Cent.
447. **123.** 10 l. olive 80 70
448. – 20 l. blue 90 70
DESIGN: 20 l. has scroll dated "1840–1940".

124. Peasant Couple and King.

125. King Boris and Map of Dobrudja.

1940. Recovery of the Dobrudja from Rumania. Designs incorporating miniature portrait of King Boris.
449. **124.** 1 l. green 8 5
450. – 2 l. red 8 5
451. **125.** 4 l. brown 10 5
452. 7 l. blue 30 15
DESIGN—VERT. 2 l. Bulgarian flags and wheat-field.

126. Grapes.

127. Ploughing.

1940.
453. **126.** 10 s. orange 5 5
454. – 15 s. blue 5 5
455. **127.** 30 s. brown 5 5
456. – 50 s. violet 5 5
456a. – 50 s. green 5 5
DESIGNS—As T **126**: 15 s. Beehive. As T **127**: 50 s. Shepherd and flock.

128. King Boris III.

129. Bee-keeping.

1940.
457. **128.** 1 l. green 5 5
458. 2 l. red 5 5
459. 4 l. orange 5 5
460. 6 l. violet 12 5
461. 7 f. blue 5 5
462. 10 l. green 8 5

1941. Agricultural Propaganda.
468. – 10 s. purple 5 5
469. – 10 s. blue 5 5
470. – 15 s. green 5 5
471. – 15 s. olive 5 5
472. **129.** 30 s. orange 5 5
473. 30 s. green 5 5
474. – 50 s. violet 5 5
475. – 50 s. purple 5 5
476. – 3 l. brown 12 5
477. – 3 l. black 70 20
478. – 5 l. brown 50 15
479. – 5 l. blue 70 25
DESIGNS: 10 s. Threshing. 15 s. Ploughing with oxen. 50 s. Picking apples. 3 l. Shepherd. 5 l. Cattle.

130. P. R. Slaveykov.

131. St. Ivan Rilski.

1940. National Relief. Patriots.
480. **130.** 1 l. green 5 5
481. – 2 l. red 5 5
482. **131.** 3 l. brown 8 5
483. – 4 l. orange 8 5
484. – 7 l. blue 80 55
485. – 10 l. brown 90 65
DESIGNS: 2 l. Bishop Sofroni of Vratsa. 4 l. M. S. Drinov. 7 l. Chernorisev the Brave. 10 l. K. Ficheto.

132. J. Gutenberg.

132a. N. Karastoyanov.

1940. Printing 500th Anniv. and Bulgarian printer, Karastoyanov. Cent.
486. **132.** 1 l. green 8 5
487. **132a.** 2 l. brown 8 5

133. C. Botev.

134. Arrival in Kosiodul.

1941. 65th Anniv. of Botev's Death.
488. **133.** 1 l. green 5 5
489. **134.** 2 l. red 8 5
490. – 3 l. brown 30 25
DESIGN—VERT. 3 l. Botev Memorial Cross.

135. Palace of Justice.

DESIGNS: 20 l. Workers' Hospital. 50 l. National Bank, Sofia.

1941.
491. **135.** 14 l. brown 12 8
492. – 20 l. green 20 8
493. – 50 l. blue .. .. 1·10 70

136. Thasos Island.

137. Ochrid.

1941. Reacquisition of Macedonia.
494. – 1 l. green 5 5
495. **136.** 2 l. orange 5 8
496. – 2 l. red 5 5
497. – 4 l. brown 8 5
498. **137.** 7 l. blue 25 15
DESIGNS—VERT. 1 l. Macedonian Girl. HORIZ. 2 l. (No. 496) King Boris and map (dated "1941"). 4 l. Cloister of Poganowski.

137a. Children on Beach.

1942. Sunday Delivery. Inscr. as in T **142a**.
499. – 1 l. olive 5 5
500. **137a.** 2 l. orange 5 5
501. – 5 l. blue 12 8
DESIGNS: 1 l. Sanatorium. 5 l. Sun-bathing.

138.

139.

1942. "Work and Joy". Inscr. as at foot of T **139**.
502. – 1 l. green 5 5
503. – 2 l. red 5 5
504. – 4 l. black 8 5
505. **138.** 7 l. blue 8 8
506. **139.** 14 l. brown 20 12
DESIGNS—VERT. 1 l. Girl with guitar. 2 l. Camp orchestra. 4 l. Hoisting the flag.

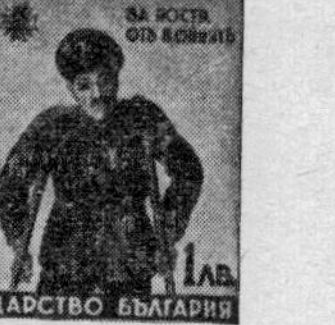
140. Wounded Soldier.

141. Queen visiting Wounded.

1942. War Invalids. Inscr. as T **140/1**.
507. **140.** 1 l. green 5 5
508. – 2 l. red 5 5
509. – 4 l. orange 5 5
510. – 7 l. blue 5 5
511. – 14 l. brown 8 5
512. **141.** 20 l. black 15 10
DESIGNS—HORIZ. 2 l. Soldier and family. 4 l. First aid on battlefield. 7 l. Widow and orphans at grave. 14 l. Unknown Soldiers Memorial.

142. Legend of Kubrat.

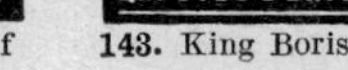
143. King Boris III.

1942. Historical series.
513. **142.** 10 s. black 5 5
514. – 15 s. blue 5 5
515. – 30 s. mauve 5 5
516. – 50 s. blue 5 5
517. – 1 l. green 5 5
518. – 2 l. red 5 5
519. – 3 l. brown 5 5
520. – 4 l. orange 5 5
521. – 5 l. green 5 5
522. – 7 l. blue 5 5
523. – 10 l. black 8 5
524. – 14 l. olive 12 5
525. – 20 l. brown 25 12
526. – 30 l. black 35 20
DESIGNS: 15 s. Cavalry charge. 30 s. Equestrian statue. 50 s. Baptism of King Boris I. 1 l. St. Naum's School. 2 l. Coronation of Tsar Simeon. 3 l. Golden Era of Bulgarian literature. 4 l. Trial of Bogomil Vasili. 5 l. Proclamation of Second Bulgarian Empire. 7 l. Ivan Asen II at Trebizond. 10 l. Expulsion of Patriarch Ertimi. 14 l. Wandering minstrels. 20 l. Father Paissi. 30 l. Shipka Pass Memorial.

1944. King Boris Mourning Issue. Portraits dated "1894–1943". Perf. or imperf.
527. **143.** 1 l. olive 5 5
528. – 2 l. brown 5 5
529. – 4 l. brown 8 8
530. – 5 l. violet 20 20
531. – 7 l. blue 20 20

144. King Simeon II.

145.

1944.
532. **144.** 3 l. orange 5 5

1945. "All for the Front". Parcels Post stamps optd. **ВСИЧКО ЗА ФРОНТА** or surch. also.
533. **P 3.** 1 l. red 5 5
534. 4 l. on 1 l. red .. 5 5
535. 7 l. mauve 5 5
536. 20 l. brown 8 5
537. 30 l. purple 10 5
538. 50 l. orange 20 8
539. 100 l. blue 40 15

1945. Air. Optd. with aeroplane or surch. also.
540. **128.** 1 l. green 5 5
541. 4 l. orange 5 5
542. **P 3.** 10 l. on 100 l. yellow 10 5
543. 45 l. on 100 l. yellow 12 10
544. 75 l. on 100 l. yellow 20 15
545. 100 l. yellow 30 25
Nos. 567/8 are perf.; the rest imperf.

1945. Slav Congress. Perf. or imperf.
546. **145.** 4 l. red 5 5
547. 10 l. blue 5 5
548. 50 l. claret 12 12

СЪБИРАЙТЕ
ВСЪКАКВИ
ПАРЦАЛИ
(**146.**) "Collect All Rags".

СЪБИРАЙТЕ
СТАРО
ЖЕЛЪЗО
(**147.**) "Collect Old Iron".

СЪБИРАЙТЕ
ХАРТИЕНИ
ОТПАДЪЦИ
(**148.**) "Collect Wastepaper".

1945. Salvage Campaign. Nos. 457/9 optd. with T **146/8**.
549. **128.** 1 l. green 5 5
550. 2 l. red 5 5
551. 4 l. orange 5 5
Prices are the same for these stamps with any one of the overprints illustrated.

149. Lion Rampant. 150.

1945. Lion Rampant, in various frames.
552. – 30 s. green 5 5
553. – 50 s. green 5 5
554. 149. 1 l. green 5 5
555. – 2 l. brown 5 5
556. – 4 l. blue 5 5
557. – 5 l. violet 5 5
558. 150. 9 l. grey 5 5
559. – 10 l. blue 5 5
560. – 15 l. brown 5 5
561. – 20 l. black 10 5
562. – 20 l. red 10 5

151. Chain-breaker. 152. "VE Day".

1945 Liberty Loan. Imperf.
563. 151. 50 l. orange 5 5
564. 50 l. lake 5 5
565. – 100 l. blue 10 8
566. – 100 l. brown 10 8
567. – 150 l. red 20 15
568. – 150 l. green 20 15
569. – 200 l. olive 45 30
570. – 200 l. blue 45 30
DESIGNS: 100 l. Hand holding coin. 150 l. Water-mill. 200 l. Coin and symbols of industry and agriculture.

1945. VE Day.
571. 152. 10 l. green and brown 5 5
572. 50 l. green and red .. 15 8

153. 154.

1945. "Fatherland Front". 1st Anniv.
573. 153. 1 l. olive 5 5
574. 4 l. blue 5 5
575. 5 l. mauve 5 5
576. 154. 10 l. blue 5 5
577. 20 l. red 12 8
578. 153. 50 l. green 30 20
579. 100 l. brown 40 25

155. Refugee Children. 156. Red Cross Train.

1946. Red Cross.
580. 155. 2 l. olive 5 5
645d. 2 l. brown 5 5
581. – 4 l. violet 5 5
645e. – 4 l. black 5 5
582. 155. 10 l. purple 5 5
645f. 10 l. green 8 8
583. – 20 l. dark blue 5 5
645g. – 20 l. light blue .. 12 12
584. – 30 l. brown 10 5
645h. – 30 l. green 15 15
585. 156. 35 l. black 12 12
645i. 35 l. green 20 20
586. – 50 l. maroon 20 15
645j. – 50 l. lake 30 30
587. 156. 100 l. brown 50 40
645k. 100 l. blue 50 50
DESIGNS—HORIZ. 4 l. 20 l. Soldier on stretcher. VERT. 30 l., 50 l. Nurse and wounded soldier.

157. Postal Savings Emblem. 157. Savings Bank-Note.

1946. Savings Bank. 50th Anniv.
588. 157. 4 l. red 5 5
589. 158. 10 l. olive 15 5
590. – 20 l. blue 8 5
591. – 50 l. black 40 35
DESIGNS—VERT. 20 l. Child filling money-box. 50 l. Postal Savings Bank.

159. Arms of Russia and Bulgaria and Oak Spray. 160. Lion Rampant.

1946. Bulgo-Russian Congress.
592. 159. 4 l. claret .. .. 1·75 1·40
593. 4 l. orange 8 5
594. 20 l. blue .. .. 3·25 2·50
595. 20 l. green 12 8

1946. Stamp Day. Imperf.
596. 160. 20 l. blue 20 8

161. 162.

1946. Air. Inscr. "PAR AVION".
597. 161. 1 l. lilac 5 5
598. 2 l. grey 5 5
599. – 4 l. black 5 5
600. – 6 l. blue 5 5
601. – 10 l. green 5 5
602. – 12 l. brown 5 5
603. – 16 l. purple 5 5
604. – 19 l. red 5 5
605. – 30 l. orange 8 5
606. – 45 l. green 15 8
607. – 75 l. brown 20 10
608. 162. 100 l. red 50 25
609. – 100 l. slate 50 25
DESIGNS—HORIZ. 4 l. Bird and envelope. 100 l. (No. 609), Aeroplane. VERT. 6 l. Aeroplane and envelope. 10 l., 12 l. and 19 l. Wings and posthorn. 16 l. Wings and envelope. 30 l. Aeroplane. 45 l., 75 l. Dove and posthorn.

163. A. Stamboliiski. 164. Balkan Flag.

1946. A. Stamboliiski (Agrarian Leader). 23rd Death Anniv.
610. 163. 100 l. orange .. 2·00 2·00

1946. Balkan Games.
611. 164. 100 l. brown 50 45

166. Aeroplanes. 167. Artillery.

1946. Military and Air Services.
612. – 2 l. claret 5 5
613. – 4 l. grey 5 5
614. 167. 5 l. red 5 5
615. 166. 6 l. brown 5 5
616. – 9 l. mauve 5 5
617. – 10 l. violet 5 5
618. – 20 l. blue 10 5
619. – 30 l. orange 10 5
620. – 40 l. olive 20 10
621. – 50 l. green 20 12
622. – 60 l. brown 30 20
DESIGNS—HORIZ. 2 l., 20 l. Grenade thrower and machine-gunner. 9 l. Pontoon-bridge builders. 10 l., 30 l. Cavalry charge. 40 l. Supply column. 50 l. Motor convoy. 60 l. Tanks. VERT. 4 l. Grenade thrower.

167a. St. Ivan Rilsky. 168. "New Republic".

1946. Millenary of St. Ivan Rilsky.
623. 167a. 1 l. brown 5 5
624. – 4 l. sepia 5 5
625. – 10 l. green 5 5
626. – 20 l. blue 15 5
627. – 50 l. red 55 40
DESIGNS—HORIZ. 4 l., 10 l., 50 l. Views of Rila Monastery. VERT. 20 l. Cathedral.

1946. Referendum.
628. 168. 4 l. claret 5 5
629. 20 l. blue 5 5
630. 50 l. olive 15 12

169. Assault.

170. Ambuscade. 171. Nurse and Children

1946. Partisan Activities.
631. 169. 1 l. purple 5 5
632. 170. 4 l. green 5 5
633. 5 l. brown 8 8
634. 170. 10 l. red 8 8
635. 169. 20 l. blue 8 8
636. – 30 l. brown 10 8
637. – 50 l. black 20 15
DESIGNS—VERT. 5 l., 50 l. Partisan riflemen. 30 l. Partisan leader.

1947. Winter Relief.
638. 171. 1 l. violet 5 5
639. – 4 l. red 5 5
640. – 9 l. olive 5 5
641. 171. 10 l. grey 5 5
642. – 20 l. blue 8 5
643. – 30 l. brown 10 8
644. – 40 l. claret 15 12
645. 171. 50 l. green 30 20
DESIGNS: 4 l., 9 l. Child carrying gifts. 20 l., 40 l. Hungary child. 30 l. Destitute mother and child.

171a. Partisans. 172. Olive Branch. 173. Dove of Peace.

1947. Anti-fascists of 1923, 1941 and 1944 Commem.
645a. – 10 l. brown and orange-brown .. 12 12
645b. 171a. 20 l. deep blue and pale blue .. 15 15
645c. – 70 l. purple-brown and claret .. 6·50 6·50
DESIGNS—HORIZ. 10 l. Group of fighters. 70 l. Soldier addressing crowd.

1947. Peace
646. 172. 4 l. olive 5 5
647. 173. 10 l brown 5 5
648. 20 l. blue 12 12
"BULGARIA" is in Roman characters on the 20 l.

174. "U.S.A." and "Bulgaria". 175. Esperanto Emblem and Map of Bulgaria.

1947. Air. Stamp Day and New York Int. Philatelic Exn.
649. 174. 70 l.+30 l. brown .. 75 60

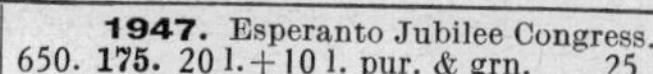

1947. Esperanto Jubilee Congress.
650. 175. 20 l.+10 l. pur. & grn. 25 25

176. Parliament Building. 177. National Theatre, Sofia.

178. G.P.O., Sofia. 179. Presidency. 180. G.P.O., Sofia.

1947. Government Buildings.
(a) T 176.
651. 1 l. green 5 5
(b) T 177.
652. 50 s. green 5 5
653. 2 l. red 5 5
654. 4 l. blue 5 5
655. 9 l. red 8 5
(c) T 178.
656. 50 s. green 5 5
657. 2 l. blue 5 5
658. 4 l. blue 5 5
659. 20 l. blue 20 12
(d) T 179.
660. 1 l. green 5 5
(e) T 180.
661. 1 l. green 5 5
662. 2 l. blue 5 5
663. 4 l. blue 5 5

181. Hydro-Electric Power Station and Dam. 182. Emblem of Industry.

1947. Reconstruction.
664. 181. 4 l. green 5 5
665. – 9 l. brown (Miner) .. 8 5
666. 182. 20 l. blue 12 10
667. – 40 l. ol. (Motor plough 30 25

183. Exhibition Building. 184. Former Residence of the French Poet Lamartine.

185. Rose and Grapes. 186. Aeroplane over City.

1947. Plovdiv Fair. (a) Postage.
668. 183. 4 l. red 5 5
669. 184. 9 l. claret 5 5
670. 185. 20 l. blue 20 8
(b) Air. Imperf.
671. 186. 40 l. green 40 40

187. Cycle Racing.

DESIGNS—VERT. 9 l. Chess. 20 l. Football. 60 l. Balkan flags.

188. Basketball. 189. V. E. Aprilov.

1947. Balkan Games.

672. **187.** 2 l. lilac 15 8
673. **188.** 4 l. green 15 8
674. – 9 l. brown 30 8
675. – 20 l. blue 40 12
676. – 60 l. claret .. .. 1·10 60

1947. V. E. Aprilov (patriot and writer). Death Cent.

678. – 4 l. claret 8 5
677. **189.** 40 l. blue 25 15

DESIGN: 4 l. Another portrait of Aprilov.

190. Postman.

191.

1947. Postal Employees' Relief Fund.

679. **190.** 4 l.+2 l. olive .. 5 5
680. – 10 l.+5 l. red 8 5
681. – 20 l.+10 l. blue .. 10 10
682. – 40 l.+20 l. brown .. 40 40

DESIGNS: 10 l. Linesman. 20 l. Telephonists. 40 l. Wireless masts.

1947. Theatrical Artists' Benevolent Fund.

683. **191.** 50 s. brown 5 5
684. – 1 l. green 5 5
685. – 2 l. green 5 5
686. – 3 l. blue 5 5
687. – 4 l. red 5 5
688. – 5 l. maroon 5 5
689. – 9 l.+5 l. green .. 5 5
690. – 10 l.+6 l. claret .. 5 5
691. – 15 l.+7 l. violet .. 8 8
692. – 20 l.+15 l. blue .. 12 12
693. – 30 l.+20 l. purple .. 40 40

PORTRAITS: 50 st. Kirov. 1 l. Nedeva. 2 l. Popov. 3 l. Kirchev. 4 l. Snezhina. 5 l. Buchvarov. 9 l. Ganchev. 10 l. Budevska. 15 l. Kirkov. 20 l. Ognianov. 30 l. Sarafov.

192. S.S. "Rodina".

1947. National Shipping Revival.

694. **192.** 50 l. blue 25 15

193. Worker and Flag.

194. Worker and Globe.

1948. 2nd National Trades Union Congress.

695. **193.** 4 l. blue (postage) .. 8 5
696. **194.** 60 l. brown (air) .. 25 20

195.

1948. Leisure and Culture.

697. **195.** 4 l. red 8 5
698. **196.** 20 l. blue 12 8
699. – 40 l. green 20 10
700. – 60 l. brown 30 20

DESIGNS—VERT. 40 l. Workers' musical interlude. 60 l. Sports Girl.

197. Vaptsarov.

198. Aeroplane over Fortress.

1948. Poets and Writers.

701. **197.** 4 l. red 5 5
702. – 9 l. brown 8 5
703. – 15 l. purple 8 8
704. – 20 l. blue 12 10
705. – 45 l. green 25 20

PORTRAITS: 9 l. Yavorov. 15 l. Smirnensky. 20 l. Vazov. 45 l. Slaveykov.

1948. Air. Stamp Day.

706. **198.** 50 l. brown 60 45

199. Soldier.

200. Peasants and Soldiers.

1948. Soviet Army Monument.

707. **199.** 4 l. red 5 5
708. **200.** 10 l. green 5 5
709. – 20 l. blue 10 8
710. – 60 l. olive 35 30

DESIGNS—HORIZ. 20 l. Soldiers of 1878 and 1944. VERT. 60 l. Stalin and Spasski Tower, Kremlin.

200a. D. Blagoev.

200b. Youths marching.

1948. 1923 Insurrection. 25th Anniv.

711. **200a.** 4 l. brown 5 5
712. – 9 l. orange 5 5
713. – 20 l. blue 8 8
714. **200b.** 60 l. brown 45 30

DESIGNS—VERT. 9 l. Genov. HORIZ. 20 l. Bishop Andrey Monument.

201. Christo Smirnensky.

202. Bath, Gorna Banya.

1948. Smirnensky (poet and revolutionary). 50th Birth Anniv.

715. **201.** 4 l. blue 5 5
716. 16 l. brown 8 5

1948. Bulgarian Health Resorts.

717. **202.** 2 l. claret 5 5
718. – 3 l. orange 5 5
719. – 4 l. blue 5 5
723. – 5 l. brown 5 5
720. – 10 l. purple 5 5
724. – 15 l. olive 12 8
721. **202.** 20 l. blue 20 10
722. – 20 l. blue 25 15

DESIGNS: 3 l., 10 l. Bath, Bankya. 4 l., 20 l. (No. 724), Mineral bath, Sofia. 5 l., 15 l. Malyovitsa Peak.

202a. Lion Emblem.

202b. Miner.

203. Battle of Grivitza.

1948.

725. **202a.** 50 s. orange .. 5 5
725a. 50 s. brown .. 5 5
726. 1 l. green 5 5
727. 9 l. black 8 5

1948.

728. **202b.** 4 l. blue 8 5

1948. Treaty of Friendship with Rumania.

729. **203.** 20 l. blue (postage) .. 10 5
730. – 40 l. black (air) .. 15 12
731. – 100 l. mauve 40 30

DESIGNS: 40 l. Parliament Buildings in Sofia and Bucharest. 100 l. Projected Danube Bridge.

204. Botev's House, Kalofer.

205. Christo Botev (poet).

1948. Botev Birth Cent. Inscr. "1848–1948".

732. **204.** 1 l. green 5 5
733. **205.** 4 l. chocolate 5 5
734. 4 l. purple 5 5
735. – 9 l. violet 5 5
736. – 15 l. brown 5 5
737. – 20 l. blue 8 5
738. – 40 l. brown 20 10
739. – 50 l. black 30 20

DESIGNS—HORIZ. 9 l. River-steamer "Radetski". 15 l. Village of Kalofer. 40 l. Botev's mother and verse of poem. VERT. 20 l. Botev in uniform. 50 l. Quill, pistol and laurel wreath.

206. V. I. Lenin.

207. Road Construction.

1949. Lenin. 25th Death Anniv. Inscr. "1924-1949".

740. **206.** 4 l. brown 5 5
741. – 20 l. claret 15 10

DESIGN—(27×37 mm.): 20 l. Lenin as an orator.

1949. Workers' Cultural Organization.

742. **207.** 4 l. red 5 5
743. – 5 l. brown 8 5
744. – 9 l. green 10 8
745. – 10 l. violet 20 10
746. – 20 l. blue 30 25
747. – 40 l. brown .. .. 1·25 90

DESIGNS—HORIZ. 5 l. Tunnel construction. 9 l. Locomotive. 10 l. Textile workers. 20 l. Girl driving tractor. 40 l. Workers in lorry.

208. Pleven Mausoleum.

1949. Air. 7th Philatelic Congress, Pleven.

748. **208.** 50 l. bistre .. .. 1·00 1·00

209. G. Dimitrov. **210.**

1949. Death of G. Dimitrov (statesmen).

749. **209.** 4 l. claret 8 5
750. **210.** 20 l. blue 25 12

211. Hydro-electric Power Station.

212. Symbols of Agriculture and Industry.

1949. 5 Year Industrial and Agricultural Plan.

751. **211.** 4 l. olive (postage) .. 5 5
752. – 9 l. red 10 8
753. – 15 l. violet 12 8
754. – 20 l. blue 40 20
755. **212.** 50 l. brown (air) .. 1·10 55

DESIGNS—VERT. 9 l. Cement works. 15 l. Tractors in garage. HORIZ. 20 l. Tractors in field.

213. Javelin and Grenade Throwing.

214. Motor-cyclist and Tractor.

1949. Physical Culture Campaign.

756. **213.** 4 l. red 20 12
757. – 9 l. olive 35 25
758. **214.** 20 l. blue 75 45
759. – 50 l. claret .. .. 1·50 1·00

DESIGNS—HORIZ. 9 l. Hurdling and leaping barbed-wire. VERT. 50 l. Two athletes marching.

215. Globe.

ILLUSTRATIONS British Commonwealth and all overprints and surcharges are FULL SIZE. Foreign Countries have been reduced to ¾-LINEAR.

1949. Air. U.P.U. 75th Anniv.

760. **215.** 50 l. blue .. .. 1·00 50

216. Guardsman and Peasant.

217. Guardsman with Dog.

1949. Frontier Guardsmen.

761. **216.** 4 l. brown (postage) .. 5 5
762. – 20 l. blue 30 20
763. **217.** 60 l. olive (air) .. 70 70

DESIGNS—VERT. 20 l. Coast-guard.

218. G. Dimitrov. **219.** "Unanimity". **220** Joseph Stalin.

1949. Fatherland Front.

764. **218.** 4 l. brown 8 5
765. **219.** 9 l. violet 10 5
766. – 20 l. blue 20 12
767. – 50 l. red 40 35

DESIGNS: 20 l. Man and woman with wheelbarrow and spade. 50 l. Young people marching with banners.

1949. Stalin's 70th Birthday.

768. **220.** 4 l. orange 5 5
769. – 40 l. claret 40 30

DESIGN—VERT. (25×37 mm.): 40 l. Stalin as an orator.

221. Haralampi Stoyanov.

222. Strikers and Train.

224. Locomotive.

223. Miner.

1950. Railway Strike. 30th Anniv.

770. **221.** 4 l. brown 8 5
771. **222.** 20 l. blue 12 8
772. – 60 l. olive 50 35

DESIGN—VERT. 60 l. Two workers and flag.

1950.

773. 223. 1 l. olive 5 5
773a. 1 l. violet 5 5
774. 224. 2 l. black 8 5
774a. 2 l. brown 8 5
775. – 3 l. blue 10 5
776a. – 4 l. green 20 5
777. – 5 l. red 30 8
778. – 9 l. grey 10 5
779. – 10 l. purple 10 5
780. – 15 l. red 20 5
781. – 20 l. blue 25 8

DESIGNS—VERT. 3 l. Ship under construction. 10 l. Power station. 15 l., 20 l. Woman in factory. HORIZ. 4 l. Tractor. 5 l., 9 l. Agricultural machinery.

225. Vasil Kolarov.

DESIGN: (27×40 mm.): 20 l. Portrait as T 225, but different frame.

1950. Kolarov (statesman). Death Cent. Inscr. "1877-1950".

782. 225. 4 l. brown 5 5
783. – 20 l. blue 30 25

226. Dospevski (self-portrait).

226a. Peasant (Stanchev).

227. Vazov and Birthplace.

228. G. Dimitrov (statesman).

1950. Painters and paintings.

784. 226. 1 l. green 10 5
785. – 4 l. orange 25 8
786. – 9 l. chocolate 40 8
787. 226a. 15 l. brown 40 12
788. 20 l. blue 60 30
789. – 40 l. brown 90 50
790. – 60 l. orange .. .. 1·40 80

DESIGNS—VERT. 4 l. King Kaloyan and Desislava. 9 l. Pavlovich. 40 l. Debelianov Statue. 60 l. Peasant (Dimitrov).

1950. Vazov (poet). Birth Cent.

791. 227. 4 l. olive 8 5

1950. G. Dimitrov. 1st Death Anniv.

792. – 50 s. brown (postage) 5 5
793. – 50 s. green 5 5
794. 228. 1 l. brown 8 5
795. – 2 l. slate 8 8
796. – 4 l. purple 10 8
797. – 9 l. red 20 15
798. – 10 l. red 40 25
799. – 15 l. grey 45 35
800. – 20 l. blue 75 45
801. – 40 l. brown (air) .. 1·60 80

DESIGNS—HORIZ. 50 s. green, Dimitrov and birthplace. 2 l. Dimitrov's house, Sofia. 15 l. Dimitrov signing new constitution. 20 l. Dimitrov. 40 l. Mausoleum. VERT. 50 s. brown, 4 l., 9 l., 10 l. Dimitrov in various poses.

229. Runners.

230. Workers and Tractor.

1950.

802. 229. 4 l. green 25 12
803. – 9 l. brown (Cycling) .. 30 20
804. – 20 l. blue (Putting the shot) .. 50 35
805. – 40 l. purple (Volley-ball) 1·00 70

1950. 2nd National Peace Congress.

806. 230. 4 l. red 5 5
807. – 20 l. blue 12 8

DESIGN—VERT. 20 l. Stalin on flag and three heads.

230a.

231. Children on Beach.

1950. Arms designs.

807a. – 2 l. brown 5 5
807b. – 3 l. red 5 5
807c. 230a. 5 l. claret 5 5
807d. – 9 l. blue 8 5

Although inscribed "OFFICIAL MAIL", the above were issued as regular postage stamps.

1950. Sunday Delivery.

808. – 1 l. green (Sanatorium) 5 5
809. 231. 2 l. red 5 5
810. – 5 l. orange (Sun bathing) 8 5
811. 231. 10 l. blue 25 12

232. Molotov, Kolarov, Stalin and Dimitrov.

233. Russian and Bulgarian Girls.

1950. Soviet-Bulgarian Treaty of Friendship. 2nd Anniv.

812. 232. 4 l. brown 5 5
813. – 9 l. claret 8 5
814. 233. 20 l. blue 15 12
815. – 50 l. green 55 35

DESIGNS—VERT. 9 l. Spasski Tower and flags. 50 l. Ship and tractor.

234. Marshal Tolbukhin.

235. A. S. Popov.

236. Kirkov.

1950. Marshal Tolbukhin.

816. 234. 4 l. magenta 12 8
817. – 20 l. blue 35 20

DESIGN—HORIZ. 20 l. Bulgarians greeting Tolbukhin.

1951. A. S. Popov (inventor).

818. 235. 4 l. brown 20 12
819. 20 l. blue 30 25

1951. Anti-Fascist Heroes.

823. – 1 l. magenta 10 5
824. – 2 l. plum 10 5
825. 236. 4 l. red 12 10
826. – 9 l. brown 25 15
827. – 15 l. olive 40 25
828. – 20 l. blue 80 40
829. – 50 l. grey .. .. 1·40 80

PORTRAITS: 1 l. Chankova, Antonov-Malchika, Sasho Dimitrov and Lilyana Dimitrova. 2 l. Stanke Dimitrov. 9 l. Ivanov. 15 l. Mihailov. 20 l. Dimitrov at Leipzig. 50 l. Ivanov and Stoyanov.

238. Truck.

239. Embroidery.

1951. National Occupations.

(a) As T 238.

820. – 1 l. violet (Tractor) .. 5 5
821. – 2 l. grn. (Steam-roller) 5 5
822. 238. 4 l. brown 5 5

(b) As T 239.

830. – 1 l. brown (Tractor) .. 8 5
831. – 2 l. vio. (Steam-roller) 10 8
832. – 4 l. brown (Truck) .. 12 8
833. 239. 9 l. violet 15 10
834. – 15 l. purple (Carpets) .. 30 20
835. – 20 l. blue (Roses and Tobacco) .. 35 25
836. – 40 l. green (Fruit) .. 1·10 60

The 9 l. and 20 l. are vert., the remainder horiz.

240. Turkish Attack.

DESIGNS—HORIZ. 4 l. Proclamation of Uprising. 9 l. Cannon and cavalry. 20 l. Patriots in 1876 and 1944. 40 l. G. Benkovsky and G. Dimitrov.

1951. April Insurrection. 75th Anniv.

837. 240. 1 l. brown 10 8
838. – 4 l. green 12 8
839. – 9 l. purple 35 20
840. – 20 l. blue 40 30
841. – 40 l. lake 70 55

241. Blagoev as Orator.

1951. First Bulgarian Communist Congress 60th Anniv.

842. 241. 1 l. violet 10 5
843. 4 l. green 20 10
844. 9 l. purple 45 25

242. Babies in Creche.

DESIGNS: 4 l. Children building models. 9 l. Girl and children's playground. 20 l. Boy bugler and children marching.

1951. Children's Day.

845. 242. 1 l. brown 8 5
846. – 4 l. purple 15 8
847. – 9 l. green 30 20
848. – 20 l. blue 70 55

243. Workers.

244. Obverse.

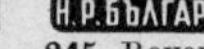

245. Reverse.

1951. 3rd National Workers' Union Congress.

849. 243. 1 l. black 5 5
850. – 4 l. brown 5 5

DESIGN inscr. "16 XII 1951": 4 l. Dimitrov and Chervenkov.

1952. Order of Labour.

851. 244. 1 l. red 5 5
852. 245. 1 l. brown 5 5
853. 244. 4 l. green 5 5
854. 245. 4 l. green 5 5
855. 244. 9 l. violet 20 8
856. 245. 9 l. blue 20 8

246. Kolarov Dam.

249. N. Vaptsarov (revolutionary).

247. G. Dimitrov and Chemical Works.

248. Republican Power Station.

1952.

857. 246. 4 s. green 5 5
858. 12 s. violet 5 5
859. 16 s. brown 5 5
860. 44 s. claret 20 8
861. 80 s. blue 45 12

1952. Dimitrov (statesman). 70th Birth Anniv. Dated "1882–1952".

862. 247. 16 s. brown 15 5
863. – 44 s. chocolate 25 10
864. – 80 s. blue 50 30

DESIGNS—HORIZ. 44 s. Dimitrov and Chervenkov. VERT. 80 s. Dimitrov full-face.

1952.

866. 248. 16 s. sepia 12 5
867. 44 s. purple 25 8

1952. Vaptsarov. 10th Death Anniv. Portraits dated "1942 1952".

869. 249. 16 s. lake 12 10
870. – 44 s. brown 25 15
871. – 80 s. sepia 75 40

PORTRAITS: 44 s. Facing bayonets. 80 s. Full-face.

250. Congress Delegates.

1952. 1st Bulgarian Socialist Youth Congress. 40th Anniv.

872. 250. 2 s. lake 5 5
873. – 16 s. violet 8 5
874. – 44 s. green 30 15
875. – 80 s. sepia 50 40

DESIGNS: 16 s. Young partisans attacking. 44 s. Factory and guards. 80 s. Dimitrov addressing young workers.

251. Attack on Winter Palace, St. Petersburg.

DESIGNS: 8 s Volga - Don canal. 16 s. Dove and globe. 44 s. Lenin and Stalin. 80 s. Lenin, Stalin and Himlay hydro-electric station.

1952. Russian Revolution. 35th Anniv. Dated "1917 1952".

876. 251. 4 s. lake 5 5
877. – 8 s. green 5 5
878. – 16 s. blue 5 5
879. – 44 s. sepia 20 10
880. – 80 s. olive 40 25

252.

253. Vintagers and Grapes.

1952. Wood Carvings depicting National Products.

881. – 2 s. sepia 5 5
882. – 8 s. green 5 5
883. – 12 s. brown 8 5
884. – 16 s. green 8 5
885. 252. 28 s. green 10 5
886. – 44 s. sepia 20 5
887. 253. 80 s. blue 50 8
888. 1 l. violet 80 12
889. 4 l. lake .. .. 2·10 60

DESIGNS—VERT. 2 s. Numeral in carved frame. HORIZ. 8 s. Gift-offering to idol. 12 s. Birds and grapes. 16 s. Rose-gathering. 44 s. "Attar of Roses."

254. V. Levski.

DESIGN: 44 s. Levsky addressing crowd.

1953. Execution of V. Levski (revolutionary). 80th Anniv.

890. 254. 16 s. brown on cream .. 8 5
891. – 44 s. brown on cream .. 20 8

255. Russian Army Crossing R. Danube.

256. Mother and Children.

1953. Bulgarian Independence. 75th Anniv.

892. 255. 8 s. blue 5 5
893. – 16 s. brown 12 5
894. – 44 s. green 30 10
895. – 80 s. lake 50 20
896. – 1 l. black 70 25

DESIGNS—VERT. 16 s. Battle of Shipka Pass. HORIZ. 44 s. Peasants welcoming Russian soldiers. 80 s. Bulgarians and Russians embracing. 1 l. Shipka Pass memorial and Dimitrovgrad.

1953. Int. Women's Day.

897. 256. 16 s. blue 5 5
898. 16 s. green 5 5

257. Karl Marx. **258.** May Day Parade.

1953. Karl Marx. 70th Death Anniv.
899. **257.** 16 s. blue 8 5
900. – 44 s. brown 20 12
DESIGN—VERT. 44 s. Book " Das Kapital ".

1953. Labour Day.
901. **258.** 16 s. red 8 5

259. Stalin. **260.** G. Dlechev.

1953. Death of Stalin.
902. **259.** 16 s. brown 8 5
903. 16 s. black 12 8

1953. Macedonian Insurrections. 50th Anniv.
904. **260.** 16 s. brown 5 5
905. – 44 s. violet 20 12
906. – 1 l. maroon 40 20
DESIGNS: 44 s. Insurgents and flag. HORIZ. 1 l. Insurgents and flag.

261. Soldier and Insurgents. **262.** G. Dimitrov and V. Kolarov.

1953. Army Day.
907. **261.** 16 s. red 5 5
908. – 44 s. blue 15 10
DESIGN: 44 s. Soldier, factories and combine-harvester.

1953. September Insurrection. 30th Anniv.
911. **262.** 8 s. black 8 5
912. – 16 s. brown 8 5
913. – 44 s. red 25 15
DESIGNS: 16 s. Insurgent and flag. 44 s. Crowd of Insurgents.

263. D. Blagoev. **264.** Railway Viaduct.

1953. Bulgarian Socialist-Democratic Party. 50th Anniv.
909. **263.** 16 s. brown 10 5
910. – 44 s. chestnut 20 10
DESIGN: 44 s. Dimitrov and Blagoev.

1953. Bulgarian-Russian Friendship.
914. **264.** 8 s. blue 5 5
915. – 16 s. slate 5 5
916. – 44 s. chestnut .. 20 12
917. – 80 s. orange 35 25
DESIGNS—HORIZ. 16 s. Welder and industrial plant. 80 s. Combine-harvester. VERT. 44 s. Iron foundry.

265. Kolarov Library. **266.** Wild Rose.

1953. Kolarov Library, Sofia. 75th Anniv.
932. **265.** 44 s. brown 15 10

1953. Medicinal Flowers.
918. – 2 s. blue 8 5
919. – 4 s. orange 8 5
920. – 8 s. turquoise 8 5
921. **266.** 12 s. green 8 5
922. – 12 s. vermilion 8 5
923. – 16 s. blue 10 5
924. – 16 s. maroon 10 5
925. – 20 s. red 15 8
926. – 28 s. grey-green 25 8
927. – 40 s. blue 30 15
928. – 44 s. brown 30 15
929. – 80 s. brown 60 30
930. – 1 l. chestnut .. .. 1·10 40
931. – 2 l. purple .. .. 1·60 75
FLOWERS: 2 s. Deadly Nightshade. 4 s. Thorn-apple. 8 s. Sage. 16 s. Gentian. 20 s. Opium Poppy. 28 s. Peppermint. 40 s. Bear berry. 44 s. Coltsfoot. 30 s. Cowslip. 1 l. Dandelion. 2 l. Foxglove.

267. Singer and Musician. **268.** Aeroplane over Mountains.

1953. Amateur Theatricals.
933. **267.** 16 s. brown 5 5
934. – 44 s. green 15 10
DESIGN: 44 s. Folk-Dancers.

1954. Air.
935. **268.** 8 s. grey-green .. 5 5
936. – 12 s. lake .. 5 5
937. – 16 s. brown .. 5 5
938. – 20 s. salmon .. 5 5
939. – 28 s. blue .. 5 5
940. – 44 s. maroon .. 12 5
941. – 60 s. brown .. 20 5
942. – 80 s. green .. 25 5
943. – 1 l. green .. 35 10
944. – 4 l. blue .. 1·50 40
DESIGNS—VERT. 12 s. Exhibition buildings. 80 s. Hillside town. 4 l. Statue. HORIZ. 16 s. Seaside promenade. 20 s. Combine-harvester in cornfield. 20 s. Monastery. 44 s Hydro-electric barrage. 60 s. Industrial plant. 1 l. Building and equestrian statue.

269. Lenin and Stalin. **270.** D. Blagoev and Crowd.

1954. Lenin. 30th Death Anniv.
945. **269.** 16 s. brown 5 5
946. – 44 s. lake 12 5
947. – 80 s. blue 20 10
948. – 1 l. green 25 12
DESIGNS—VERT. 44 s. Lenin statue. 80 s. Lenin–Stalin Mausoleum and Kremlin. 1 l. Lenin.

1954. Blagoev. 30th Death Anniv.
949. **270.** 16 s. brown 10 5
950. – 44 s. sepia 20 10
DESIGN: 44 s. Blagoev writing at desk.

271. Dimitrov Speaking. **272** Locomotive.

1954. Dimitrov. 5th Death Anniv.
951. **271.** 44 s. lake 12 8
952. – 80 s. brown 25 12
DESIGN—HORIZ. 80 s. Dimitrov and blast-furnace.

1954. Railway Workers' Day.
953. **272.** 44 s. turquoise 20 8
954. 44 s. black 20 8

273. Miner Operating Machinery. **274.** Marching Soldiers.

1954. Miners' Day.
955. **273.** 44 s. green 15 5

1954. 10th Anniv. of Liberation.
956. **274.** 12 s. lake 5 5
957. – 16 s. red 5 5
958. – 28 s. slate 8 5
959. – 44 s. brown 12 5
960. – 80 s. blue 40 8
961. – 1 l. green 45 12
DESIGNS—VERT. 16 s. Soldier and parents. 80 s. Girl and boy pioneers. 1 l. Dimitrov. HORIZ. 28 s. Industrial plant. 44 s. Dimitrov and workers.

275. Academy Building. **276.** Gymnast.

1954. Academy of Sciences. 85th Anniv.
962. **275.** 80 s. black 45 15

1954. Sports. Cream paper.
963. **276.** 16 s. green 40 12
964. – 44 s. red 45 20
965. – 80 s. brown .. .. 1·00 50
966. – 2 l. blue .. .. 2·40 1·25
DESIGNS—VERT. 44 s. Wrestlers. 2 l. Ski-jumper. HORIZ. 80 s. Horse-jumper.

277. Velingrad Rest Home.

DESIGNS—VERT. 44 s. Foundryman. HORIZ. 80 s. Dimitrov, Blagoev and Kirkov.

1954. Trade Union Movement. 50th Anniv.
967. **277.** 16 s. green 5 5
968. – 44 s. chestnut .. 15 5
969. – 80 s. blue 30 15

278. Geese. **279.** Communist Party Building.

1955.
970. **278.** 2 s. green 8 5
971. – 4 s. olive 8 5
972. – 12 s. brown 15 5
973. – 16 s. chestnut .. 20 5
974. – 28 s. blue 12 5
975. **279.** 44 s. red .. .. 1·75 12
976. – 80 s. chocolate .. 30 8
977. – 1 l. green 65 15
DESIGNS: 4 s. Rooster and hens. 12 s. Sow and piglets. 16 s. Ewe and lambs. 28 s. Telephone exchange. 80 s. Flats. 1 l. Cellulose factory.

280. Mill Girl. **281.** Rejoicing Crowds.

1955. Int. Women's Day.
978. **280.** 12 s. brown 5 5
979. – 16 s. green 8 5
980. – 44 s. blue 20 8
981. – 44 s. red 20 8
DESIGNS—HORIZ. 16 s. Girl feeding cattle. VERT. 44 s. Mother and baby.

1955. As Nos. 820 and 822 surch. **16 CT.**
981a. – 16 s. on 1 l. violet .. 10 5
982. **238.** 16 s. on 4 l. chocolate .. 30 5

1955. Labour Day.
983. **281.** 16 s. red 5 5
984. – 44 s. blue 15 5
DESIGN: 44 s. Three workers and globe.

282. St. Cyril and St. Methodius. **283.** S. Rumyantsev.

1955. 1st Bulgarian Literature. 1100th Anniv. On cream paper.
985. **282.** 4 s. blue 5 5
986. – 8 s. olive 5 5
987. – 16 s. black 5 5
988. – 28 s. red 8 5
989. – 44 s. brown 12 5
990. – 80 s. red 25 15
991. – 2 l. black 90 35
DESIGNS: 8 s. Monk writing. 16 s. Early printing press. 28 s. Christo Botev. 44 s. Ivan Vazov. 80 s. D. Blagoev and Books. 2 l. Building.

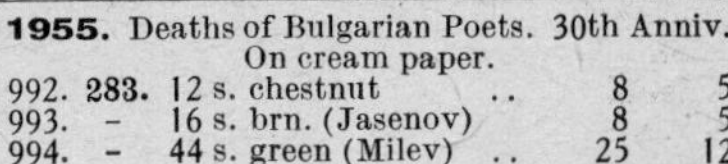

1955. Deaths of Bulgarian Poets. 30th Anniv. On cream paper.
992. **283.** 12 s. chestnut .. 8 5
993. – 16 s. brn. (Jasenov) 8 5
994. – 44 s. green (Milev) .. 25 12

284. F. Engels and Book. **285.** Mother and Children.

1955. Engels. 60th Death Anniv.
995. **284.** 44 s. brown on cream .. 20

1955. World Mothers' Congress, Lausanne.
996. **285.** 44 s. lake on cream .. 20 8

286. " Youth of the World." **287.** Main Entrance in 1892.

1955. 5th World Youth Festival, Warsaw.
997. **286.** 44 s. blue on cream .. 15 8

1955. 16th Int. Fair, Plovdiv. On cream paper.
998. **287.** 4 s. brown 5 5
999. – 16 s. red 5 5
1000. – 44 s. olive 12 8
1001. – 80 s. blue 35 10
DESIGNS—VERT. 16 s. Sculptured group. 80 s. Fair poster. HORIZ. 44 s. Fruit.

288. Schiller. **289.** Industrial Plant.

1955. Cultural Annivs. Writers. On cream paper.
1002. **288.** 16 s. brown .. 8 5
1003. – 44 s. red 20 8
1004. – 60 s. blue 25 10
1005. – 80 s. black 35 12
1006. – 1 l. purple 70 20
1007. – 2 l. olive .. .. 1·10 30
PORTRAITS: 44 s. Mickiewicz. 60 s. Hans Anderson. 80 s. Montesquieu. 1 l. Cervantes. 2 l. Walt Whitman.

1955. Bulgarian-Russian Friendship. On cream paper.
1008. **289.** 2 s. slate 5 5
1009. – 4 s. blue 5 5
1010. – 16 s. green 8 5
1011. – 44 s. brown 12 5
1012. – 80 s. green 25 8
1013. – 1 l. black 55 15
DESIGNS—HORIZ. 4 s. Dam. 16 s. Danube Bridge. VERT. 44 s. Monument. 80 s. Michurin. 1 l. V. Mayakovsky.

290. Emblem. **291.** Quinces.

1956. Library Reading Rooms. Cent. On cream paper.
1014. **290.** 12 s. red 5 5
1015. – 16 s. brown 5 5
1016. – 44 s. myrtle 15 10
DESIGNS: 16 s. K. Pshourka reading. 44 s. B. Kiro writing.

1956. Fruits.
1017. **291.** 4 s. red 65 8
1017a. 4 s. yellow-green .. 5 5
1018. – 8 s. green (Pears) .. 20 5
1018a. – 8 s. chestnut (Pears) 5 5
1019. – 16 s. crimson (Apples) 55 5
1019a. – 16 s. carmine (Apples) 8 5
1020. – 44 s. violet (Grapes) 55 15
1020a. – 44 s. ochre (Grapes) 45 8

292. Artillerymen.

293. Blagoev and Birthplace.

1956. April Rising. 80th Anniv.
1021. **292.** 16 s. chocolate .. 8 5
1022. – 44 s. green (Cavalry charge) 12 8

1956. Blagoev (writer). Birth Cent.
1023. **293.** 44 s. turquoise .. 20 8

294. Cherries.

295. Football.

1956. Fruits.
1024. **294.** 2 s. lake 5 5
1025. – 12 s. blue (Plums) .. 8 5
1026. – 28 s. buff (Greengages) 12 8
1027. – 80 s. red (Strawberries) 40 15

1956. Olympic Games.
1028. – 4 s. blue 12 8
1029. – 12 s. red 12 8
1030. – 16 s. chestnut .. 20 8
1031. **295.** 44 s. green 25 15
1032. – 80 s. brown 60 40
1033. – 1 l. lake 75 50
DESIGNS—VERT. 4 s. Gymnastics. 12 s. Throwing the discus. 80 s. Basket-ball. HORIZ. 16 s. Pole-vaulting. 1 l. Boxing.

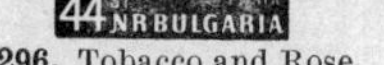

296. Tobacco and Rose.

297.

1956. 17th Int. Fair, Plovdiv.
1034. **296.** 44 s. red 25 10
1035. 44 s. green 25 10

1956. Air. 30th Anniv. of Gliding Club.
1036. – 44 s. blue 15 8
1037. – 60 s. violet 20 10
1038. **297.** 80 s. green 30 12
DESIGNS: 44 s. Launching glider. 60 s. Glider over hangar.

298. National Theatre.

299. Mozart.

1956. National Theatre. Cent.
1039. **298.** 16 s. brown 8 5
1040. – 44 s. turquoise .. 15 8
DESIGN: 44 s. D. Voinikov and S. Dobroplodni.

1956. Cultural Anniversaries.
1041. – 16 s. olive 10 5
1042. – 20 s. brown 5 5
1043. **299.** 40 s. red 15 5
1044. – 44 s. chocolate .. 20 5
1045. – 60 s. slate 20 5
1046. – 80 s. brown 30 8
1047. – 1 l. green 50 12
1048. – 2 l. slate-green .. 1·00 40
PORTRAITS: 16 s. Franklin. 20 s. Rembrandt. 44 s. Heine. 60 s. Shaw. 80 s. Dostoievsky. 1 l Ibsen. 2 l Curie.

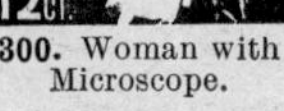

300. Woman with Microscope.

301. The "New Times".

1957. Int. Women's Day. Inscr. as in T **301.**
1049. **300.** 12 s. blue 5 5
1050. – 16 s. chestnut .. 5 5
1051. – 44 s. green 20 12
DESIGNS: 16 s. Woman and children. 44 s. Woman feeding poultry.

1957. "New Times" (book). 60th Anniv.
1052. **301.** 16 s. red 10 5

302. Cyclists.

303. Bulgarian Airliner.

1957. Tour of Egypt Cycle Race.
1053. **302.** 80 s. chestnut .. 45 15
1054. 80 s. turquoise .. 45 15

1957. Air. Bulgarian Airways. 10th Anniv.
1055. **303.** 80 s. blue 40 20

304. St. Cyril and St. Methodius.

305. Basketball.

1957. Canonization of Saints Cyril and Methodius (founders of Cyrillic alphabet). Cent.
1056. **304.** 44 s. olive and buff 30 15

1957. 10th European Basketball Championships.
1057. **305.** 44 s. green 70 20

306. Girl in National Costume.

307. G. Dimitrov.

1957. 6th World Youth Festival, Moscow.
1058. **306.** 44 s. blue 20 10

1957. G. Dimitrov (statesman). 75th Birth Anniv.
1059. **307.** 44 s. red 20 8

308. V. Levski.

309. View of Tirnovo and Dr. Zamenhof.

1957. Levski (revolutionary). 120th Birth Anniv.
1060. **308.** 44 s. green 20 8

1957. Esperanto. 70th Anniv. and Bulgarian Esperanto Assn. 50th Anniv.
1060. **309.** 44 s. green 45 12

310. Soldiers in Battle.

311. Woman Planting Tree.

1957. Bulgarian Independence. 80th Anniv. Inscr. "1878-1958".
1062. – 16 s. green 8 5
1063. **310.** 44 s. brown 20 8
DESIGN: 16 s. Old and young soldiers.

1957. Reafforestation Campaign.
1064. **311.** 2 s. green 5 5
1065. – 12 s. brown 5 5
1066. – 16 s. blue 5 5
1067. – 44 s. blue-green .. 15 8
1068. – 80 s. green 30 12
DESIGNS—HORIZ. 12 s. Deer in forest. 16 s. Dam and trees. 44 s. Aeroplane over forest. 80 s. Trees and cornfield.

312. Two Hemispheres.

313. Lenin.

1957. 4th World T.U.C., Leipzig.
1069. **312** 44 s. blue 15 8

1957. Russian Revolution. 40th Anniv. Inscr. "1917–1957".
1070. **313.** 12 s. brown 5 5
1071. – 16 s. turquoise .. 8 5
1072. – 44 s. blue 15 8
1073. – 60 s. red 25 10
1074. – 80 s. green 40 20
DESIGNS: 16 s. Cruiser "Aurora". 44 s. Dove of Peace over Europe. 60 s. Revolutionaries. 80 s. Oil refinery.

314. Youth and Girl.

315. Partisans.

1957. National Youth Movement. 10th Anniv.
1075. **314.** 16 s. red 12 5

1957. "Fatherland Front". 15th Anniv.
1076. **315.** 16 s. chocolate .. 12 5

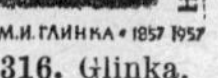

316. Glinka.

317. Kolarov.

1957. Cultural Celebrities.
1077. **316.** 12 s. brown 8 5
1078. – 16 s. green (Comenius) 12 5
1079. – 40 s. blue (Linnaeus) 30 5
1080. – 44 s. brown (Blake).. 35 5
1081. – 60 s. chestnut (Goldoni) 45 10
1082. – 80 s. purple (Comte) 75 20

1958. Holiday Resorts.
1083. – 4 s. blue 5 5
1084. – 8 s. brown 5 5
1085. – 12 s. green 5 5
1086. **317.** 16 s. green 8 5
1087. – 44 s. turquoise .. 10 8
1088. – 60 s. blue 15 8
1089. – 80 s. chestnut .. 25 12
1090. – 1 l. chocolate .. 40 15
DESIGNS—HORIZ. 4 s. Skis and Pirin Mts. 8 s. Old house in Koprivshtita. 12 s. Hostel at Velingrad. 44 s. Hotel at Momin-Prohod. 60 s. Seaside hotel and peninsula, Nesebur. 80 s. Beach scene, Varna. 1 l. Modern hotels, Varna.

318. Hare.

319. Marx and Lenin.

320. Wrestlers.

1958. Forest Animals.
1091. **318.** 2 s. bronze-green and yellow-green .. 5 5
1092. – 12 s. chestnut and bronze-green .. 8 5
1093. – 16 s. brown & green 10 5
1094. – 44 s. brown and blue 12 5
1095. – 80 s. brown and bistre 50 15
1096. – 1 l. sepia and blue 70 25
DESIGNS—VERT. 12 s. Doe. HORIZ. 16 s. Stag. 44 s. Mountain goat. 80 s. Bear. 1 l. Wild boar.

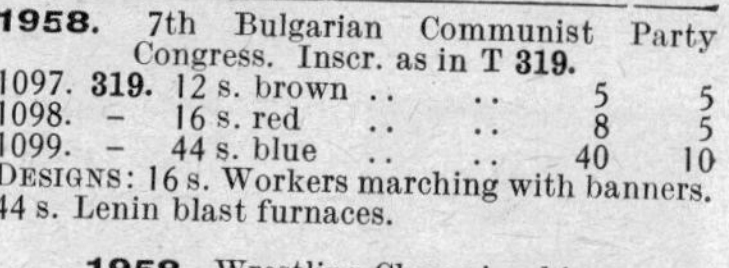

1958. 7th Bulgarian Communist Party Congress. Inscr. as in T **319.**
1097. **319.** 12 s. brown 5 5
1098. – 16 s. red 8 5
1099. – 44 s. blue 40 10
DESIGNS: 16 s. Workers marching with banners. 44 s. Lenin blast furnaces.

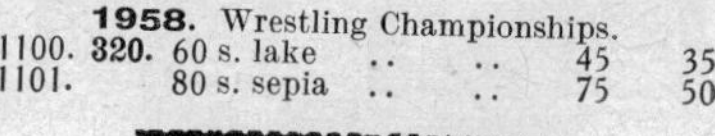

1958. Wrestling Championships.
1100. **320.** 60 s. lake 45 35
1101. 80 s. sepia 75 50

321. Chessmen and "Oval Chessboard".

1958. 5th Students' World Chess Championships, Sofia.
1102. **321.** 80 s. green .. .. 1·00 35

322. Russian Pavilion.

1958. 18th Int. Fair, Plovdiv.
1103. **322** 44 s. red 30 12

323. Swimmer.

1958. Bulgarian Students' Games.
1104. **323.** 16 s. blue 12 8
1105. – 28 s. brown .. 15 10
1106. – 44 s. green 25 12
DESIGNS. 28 s. Dancer. 44 s. Volley ball players at net.

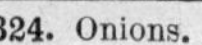

324. Onions.

325. Insurgent with Rifle.

1958. "Agricultural Propaganda".
1107. **324.** 2 s. brown 5 5
1108. – 12 s. lake (Garlic) .. 5 5
1109. – 16 s. myrtle (Peppers) 5 5
1110. – 44 s. red (Tomatoes) 12 5
1111. – 80 s. green (Cucumbers) 30 10
1112. – 1 l. violet (Aubergines) 45 15

1958. September Insurrection. 35th Anniv. Inscr. as in T **325.**
1113. **325.** 16 s. orange 8 5
1114. – 44 s. lake 20 8
DESIGN—HORIZ.: 44 s. Insurgent helping wounded comrade.

326. Conference Emblem.

1958. 1st. World T.U. Young Workers' Conf., Prague.
1115. **326.** 44 s. blue 20 12

327. Exhibition Emblem.

1958. Brussels Int. Exn.
1116. **327.** 1 l. blue and black .. 2·25 2·25

328. Sputnik over Globe. **329.** Running.

1958. Air. I.G.Y.
1117. **328.** 80 s. turquoise .. 2·00 80

1958. Balkan Games. Inscr. "1958".
1118. **329.** 16 s. brown .. 25 12
1119. – 44 s. olive 30 20
1120. – 60 s. blue 40 25
1121. – 80 s. green 60 25
1122. – 4 l. lake .. .. 3·25 1·10
DESIGNS—HORIZ. 44 s. Throwing the javelin. 60 s. High-jumping. 80 s. Hurdling. VERT. 4 l. Putting the shot.

330. Young Gardeners. **331.** Christo Smirnenski.

1958. 4th Dimitrov Youth Movement Congress. Inscr. as in T **330**.
1123. **330.** 8 s. myrtle 5 5
1124. – 12 s. brown 5 5
1125. – 16 s. brown-purple .. 8 5
1126. – 40 s. blue 12 5
1127. – 44 s. red 40 10
DESIGNS—HORIZ. 12 s. Farm girl with cattle. 40 s. Youth with wheel-barrow. VERT. 16 s. Youth with pickaxe and girl with spade. 44 s. Communist Party Building.

1958. Smirnenski (poet and revolutionary). 60th Birth Anniv.
1128. **331.** 16 s. red 10 5

332. First Cosmic Rockets. **333.** Footballers.

1959. Air. Launching of First Cosmic Rocket.
1129. **332.** 2 l. brown and blue .. 2·75 2·00

1959. Youth Football Games, Sofia.
1130. **333.** 2 l brown on cream 1·10 60

334. U.N.E.S.C.O. Headquarters, Paris. **335.** Skier.

1959. U.N.E.S.C.O. Headquarters Building. Inaug.
1131. **334.** 2 l. purple on cream 1·40 75

1959. 40 Years of Skiing in Bulgaria.
1132. **335.** 1 l. blue on cream .. 65 25

1959. No. 1110 surch. **45 CT.**
1133. – 45 s. on 44 s. red .. 25 8

336. Military Telegraph Linesman.

1959. 1st Bulgarian Postage Stamps. 80th Anniv. Insce. "1879–1959".
1134. **336.** 12 s. yellow and green 5 5
1135. – 16 s. mauve & purple 8 5
1136. – 60 s. yellow & ol.-brn. 15 8
1137. – 80 s. salmon and red 25 10
1138. – 1 l. blue 30 12
1139. – 2 l. chocolate .. 80 40
DESIGNS—HORIZ. 16 s. 19th-cent. mail-coach. 80 s. Early postal car. 2 l. Riot scene. VERT. 60 s. Bulgarian 1879 stamp. 1 l. Radio tower.

337. Tits. **338.** Cotton-picking.

1959. Birds.
1140. **337.** 2 s. slate & yellow-ol. 5 5
1141. – 8 s. bronze-green and chestnut 5 5
1142. – 16 s. sepia and brown 10 8
1143. – 45 s. myrtle & brown 15 10
1144. – 60 s. grey and blue .. 20 15
1145. – 80 s. drab & turquoise 50 20
DESIGNS—HORIZ. 8 s. Hoopoe. 60 s. Red-legged partridge. 80 s. Cuckoo. VERT. 16 s. Woodpecker. 45 s. Partridge.

1959. Five Year Plan.
1146. – 2 s. chestnut 5 5
1147. – 4 s. yellow-brown .. 5 5
1148. **338.** 5 s. green 5 5
1149. – 10 s. brown 5 5
1150. – 12 s. brown 5 5
1151. – 15 s. mauve 5 5
1152. – 16 s. violet 5 5
1153. – 20 s. orange 5 5
1154. – 25 s. blue 5 5
1155. – 28 s. green 8 5
1156. – 40 s. blue 12 8
1157. – 45 s. brown 12 8
1158. – 60 s. red 15 8
1159. – 80 s. olive 20 12
1160. – 1 l. lake 25 15
1161. – 1 l. 25 blue 50 15
1162. – 2 l. red 70 20
DESIGNS—HORIZ. 2 s. Children at play. 10 s. Dairymaid milking cow. 16 s. Industrial plant. 20 s. Combine-harvester. 40 s. Hydro-electric barrage. 60 s. Furnaceman. 1 l. 25, Machinist. VERT. 4 s. Woman doctor examining child. 12 s. Tobacco harvesting. 15 s. Machinist. 25 s. Power linesman. 28 s. Tending sunflowers. 45 s. Miner. 80 s. Fruit-picker. 1 l. Workers with symbols of agriculture and industry. 2 l. Worker with banner.

339. Patriots. **340.** Piper.

1959. Batak Tercent.
1163. **339.** 16 s. chocolate .. 10 5

1959. Spartacist Games. Insce. "1958–1959".
1164. **340.** 4 s. olive on cream .. 5 5
1165. – 12 s. red on yellow .. 5 5
1166. – 16 s. lake on salmon 5 5
1167. – 20 s. blue on blue .. 5 5
1168. – 80 s. green on green 35 10
1169. – 1 l. brown on orange 50 20
DESIGNS—VERT. 12 s. Gymnastics. 1 l. Urn. HORIZ. 16 s. Girls exercising with hoops. 20 s. Dancers leaping. 80 s. Ballet dancers.

341. Soldiers in Lorry.

1959. Liberation. 15th Anniv. Inscr. "1944-1959".
1170. **341.** 12 s. slate-blue and red 5 5
1171. – 16 s. black-pur. & red 5 5
1172. – 45 s. blue and red .. 12 5
1173. – 60 s. green and red 15 8
1174. – 80 s. yell.-brn. & red 25 10
1175. – 1 l. 25, brown and red 50 15
DESIGNS—HORIZ. 16 s. Partisans meeting Red Army soldiers. 45 s. Blast furnaces. 60 s. Tanks. 80 s. Combine-harvester in cornfield. VERT. 1 l. 25, "Pioneers" with banner.

342. Footballer.

1959. Football in Bulgaria. 50th Anniv.
1176. **342.** 1 l. 25 green on yellow 2·75 1·60

343. Airliner and Statue of Liberty. **344.** Globe and Letter.

1959. Air. Visit of Russian Prime Minister to U.S.A.
1177. **343.** 1 l. pink and blue .. 1·10 60

1959. Int. Correspondence Week.
1178. **344.** 45 s. black and green 20 8
1179. – 1 l. 25 red, blk. & blue 35 20
DESIGN: 1 l. 25, Pigeon and letter.

345. Parachutist. **346.** N. Vaptsarov.

1960. 3rd Voluntary Defence Congress.
1180. **345.** 1 l. 25, cream & bl.-grn. 1·00 40

1960. Vaptsarov (poet). 50th Birth Anniv.
1181. **346.** 80 st. brown and green 30 12

347. Dr. L. Zamenhof. **348.**

1960. Birth Cent. of Zamenhof (inventor of Esperanto).
1182. **347.** 1 l. 25 green & apple 50 25

1960. State Opera. 50th Anniv.
1183. **348.** 80 s. black and green 30 12
1184. – 1 l. 25 black and red 45 15
DESIGN: 1 l. 25, Lyre.

349. Track of Lunik 3 around the Moon.

1960. Flight of Lunik 3.
1185. **349.** 1 l. 25 grn., yell. & bl. 2·75 1·25

350. Skier.

1960. Winter Olympic Games.
1186. **350.** 2 l. brn., blue & black 90 30

351. Vela Blagoeva. **352.** Lenin.

1960. Int. Women's Day. 50th Anniv. Inscr. "1910-1960".
1187. **351.** 16 s. chestnut & pink 5 5
1188. – 28 s. yellow-olive and olive-yellow .. 5 5
1189. – 45 s. green & ol.-grn. 10 5
1190. – 60 s. blue & pale blue 15 8
1191. – 80 s. brn. & vermilion 25 10
1192. – 1 l. 25 olive and ochre 30 20
PORTRAITS: 28 s. Anna Maimunkowa. 45 s. Vela Piskova. 60 s. Rosa Luxemburg. 80 s. Clara Zetkin. 1 l. 25, N. K. Krupskaya.

1960. Lenin. 90th Birth Anniv. Inscr. "1870–1960".
1193. **352.** 16 s. flesh & chestnut 15 10
1194. – 45 s. black and pink 25 12
DESIGN: 45 s. "Lenin at Smolny" (writing in chair).

354. Basketball Players. **355.** Moon Rocket.

1960. 7th European Women's Basketball Championships.
1195. **354.** 1 l. 25 black and yell. 65 25

1960. Air. Landing of Russian Rocket on Moon.
1196. **355.** 1 l. 25 blk., yell. & blue 2·75 1·60

356. Parachutist. **357.** "Gentiana lutea".

1960. World Parachuting Championships, 1960.
1197. **356.** 16 s. blue and lilac .. 40 15
1198. – 1 l. 25 claret & blue 1·00 30
DESIGN: 1 l. 25, Parachutes descending.

1960. Flowers.
1199. **357.** 2 s. orge., grn. & drab 8 5
1200. – 5 s. red, green and yellow-green .. 8 5
1201. – 25 s. orange, green & salmon 12 5
1202. – 45 s. magenta, green and lilac 20 8
1203. – 60 s. vermilion, green and buff 35 12
1204. – 80 s. blue, grn. & drab 50 20
FLOWERS: 5 s. "Tulipa rhodopea". 25 s. "Lilium jankae". 45 s. "Rhododendron ponticum". 60 s. "Cypripedium calceolus". 80 s. "Haberlea rhodopensis".

358. Football.

1960. Olympic Games.
1205. **358.** 8 s. pink and brown 5 5
1206. – 12 s. pink and violet 5 5
1207. – 16 s. pink & turq. .. 5 5
1208. – 45 s. pink and purple 15 8
1209. – 80 s. pink and blue .. 25 12
1210. – 2 l. pink and green .. 80 25
DESIGNS: 12 s. Wrestling. 16 s. Weightlifting. 45 s. Gymnastics. 80 s. Canoeing. 2 l. Running.

359. Racing Cyclists.

1960. Tour of Bulgaria Cycle Race.
1211. **359.** 1 l. blk., yell. & red 60 40

360. Globes.

1960. W.F.T.U. 15th Anniv.
1212. **360.** 1 l. 25 cobalt and blue 50 15

361. Popov. 362. Y. Veshin.

1960. Popov (Russian inventor). Birth Cent.
1213. **361.** 90 s. black and blue 60 15

1960. Veshin (painter). Birth Cent.
1214. **362.** 1 l. olive & olive-yell. 1·25 60

363. U.N. Headquarters, New York 364. Boyana Church.

1961. U.N.O. 15th Anniv.
1215. **363.** 1 l. cream and brown 90 65

1961. Boyana Murals (1959). 700th Anniv.
1216. **364.** 60 s. black, emerald and green 25 10
1217. – 80 s. green, cream and orange .. 30 12
1218. – 1 l. 25 crimson, cream and green 60 20
DESIGNS (Frescoes of): 80 s. Theodor Tiron. 1 l. 25, Desislava.

365. Cosmic Rocket.

1961. Russian Cosmic Rocket Flight of August, 1960.
1219. **365.** 1 l. 25 blue and red 3·75 2·25

366. Pleven Costume. 367. Clock Tower, Vratsa.

1961. Provincial Costumes.
1220. – 12 s. yell., grn. & sal. 8 5
1221. **366.** 16 s. chocolate, buff and lilac 8 5
1222. – 28 s. rose, blk. & grn. 8 5
1223. – 45 s. blue and red .. 20 5
1224. – 60 s. yell., blue & turq. 25 8
1225. – 80 s. rose, grn. & yell. 30 15
COSTUMES: 12 s. Kyustendil. 28 s. Sliven. 45 s. Sofia. 60 s. Rhodope. 80 s. Karnobat.

1961. Museums and Monuments. Values and star in red.
1226. **367.** 8 s. green 5 5
1227. – 12 s. violet 5 5
1228. – 16 s. brown 5 5
1229. – 20 s. blue 5 5
1230. – 28 s. turquoise .. 5 5
1231. – 40 s. brown 8 5
1232. – 45 s. olive 10 8
1233. – 60 s. slate 15 8
1234. – 80 s. olive brown .. 25 10
1235. – 1 l. blue-green .. 40 12
DESIGNS—As T **368**—VERT. 12 s. Clock Tower, Bansko. 20 s. "Agushev" building, Mogilitsa (Smolensk). HORIZ. 28 s. Oslekoff House, Koprivshtitsa. 40 s. Pasha's House, Melnik. SQUARE (27×27) mm.): 16 s. Wine jug. 45 s. Lion (bas-relief). 60 s. "Horseman of Madara". 80 s. Fresco, Bachkovo Monastery. 1 l. Coin of Tsar Konstantin-Asen (13th century).

369. Pelican. 370. "Communications and Transport".

1961. Birds.
1236. 2 s. turq., black and red 5 5
1237. 4 s. orge., black & apple 5 5
1238. 16 s. orge., choc. & green 5 5
1239. 80 s. yell., brn. & turq. 20 8
1240. 1 l. yellow, sepia & blue 30 10
1241. 2 l. yell., brn. & grey-blue 75 20
BIRDS: 2 s. Capercailzie. 4 st. T **369.** 16 s. Pheasant. 80 s. Great Bustard. 1 l. Vulture. 2 l. Grouse.

1961. Transport Workers' Union. 50th Anniv.
1242. **370.** 80 s. green and black 25 10

371. Gagarin and Rocket.

1961. World's First Manned Space Flight.
1243. **371.** 4 l. turq., blk & red 2·75 1·00

372. Shevchenko (poet).

1961. Shevchenko Commem.
1244. **372.** 1 l. sepia and olive .. 1·25 50

373. Tennis.

1961. World Students' Games. Values and inscr. in black.
1245. – 4 s. blue 5 5
1246. **373.** 5 s. vermilion 5 5
1247. – 16 s. olive 8 5
1248. – 45 s. slate-blue .. 12 8
1249. – 1 l. 25 brown .. 40 15
1250. – 2 l. mauve 55 25
DESIGNS—VERT. 4 s. Water polo. 2 l. Basketball. HORIZ. 16 s. Fencing. 45 s. Throwing the discus. 1 l. 25, Sports Palace, Sofia.

374. Sea-horse. 375. "Space" Dogs.

1961. Black Sea Fauna.
1251. – 2 s. sepia and green.. 5 5
1252. – 12 s. pink and blue.. 5 5
1253. – 16 s. vio.-bl. & cobalt 5 5
1254. **374.** 45 s. brown and blue 12 5
1255. – 1 l. slate-blue & green 25 12
1256. – 1 l. 25 brn. & vio.-bl. 40 15
DESIGNS—HORIZ. 2 s. Seals. 12 s. Jellyfish. 16 s. Dolphins. 1 l. Sturgeons. 1 l. 25, Thornback Ray.

1961. Air. Space Exploration.
1257. **375.** 2 l. slate & brn.-pur. 1·50 75
1258. – 2 l. bl., yell. & orge. 2·75 1·40
DESIGN: No. 1258, "Venus" rocket in flight (24×41½ mm.).

376. Blagoev as Orator.

1961. 1st Bulgarian Communist Congress. 70th Anniv.
1259. **376.** 45 s. red and cream 12 8
1260. 80 s. blue and pink.. 20 10
1261. 2 l. sepia and green.. 50 25

377. Hotel. 378. "The Golden Girl".

1961. Tourist issue. Inscr. in black; designs green. Background colours given.
1262. **377.** 4 s. green 5 5
1263. – 12 s. blue (Hikers) .. 5 5
1264. – 16 s. green (Tents) .. 5 5
1265. – 1 l. 25 bistre (Climber) 40 10
Nos. 1263/5 are vert.

1961. Bulgarian Fables
1266. 2 s. blk., yell., grey & bl. 8 5
1267. 8 s. grey, black & purple 10 5
1268. 12 s. pink, black & green 12 5
1269. 16 s. grey, blk., bl. & red 12 8
1270. 45 s. pink, blk., grey & ol. 40 12
1271. 80 s. red, black, grey and brown 75 25
DESIGNS: 2 s. T **378.** 8 s. Man and woman ("The Living Water"). 12 s. Archer and dragon ("The Golden Apple"). 16 s. Horseman ("Krali Marko"; national hero). 45 s. Female archer on stag ("Samovila-Vila", fairy). 80 s. "Tom Thumb" and cockerel.

379. Major Titov in Space-suit. 380. "Amanita caesarea".

1961. Air. 2nd Russian Manned Space Flight.
1272. **379.** 75 s. flesh, blue & ol. 1·60 75
1273. – 1 l. 25 pink, blue and violet-blue .. 2·00 1·10
DESIGN: 1 l. 25, "Vostok-2" in flight.

1961. Mushrooms.
1274. 2 s. red, bistre and black (T **380**).. .. .. 5 5
1275. 4 s. brown, green & black 5 5
1276. 12 s. brown, bistre & blk. 5 5
1277. 16 s. brn., mauve & blk. 5 5
1278. 45 s. red, yell., orge. & blk. 10 5
1279. 80 s. orange, sepia & blk. 15 8
1280. 1 l. 25 lav., choc. & black 25 8
1281. 2 l. brn., yell.-brn. & blk. 60 25
MUSHROOMS: 4 s. "Psalliota silvatica". 12 s. "Boletus elegans". 16 s. "Boletus edulis". 45 s. "Lactarius deliciosus". 80 s. "Lepiota procera". 1 l. 25, "Pleurotus ostreatus". 2 l. "Armillariella mellea".

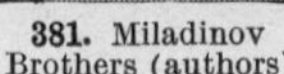

381. Miladinov Brothers (authors). 382. Isker River.

1961. Publication Cent. of "Collected Folk-songs".
1282. **381.** 1 l. 25 black and olive 40 12

(Currency revaluation.)

1962. Surch.
1283. 1 s. on 10 s. brown (1149) 5 5
1284. 1 s. on 12 s. brown (1150) 5 5
1285. 2 s. on 15 s. mauve (1151) 5 5
1286. 2 s. on 16 s. violet (1152) 5 5
1287. 2 s. on 20 s. orge. (1153)(A) 5 5
1288. 2 s. on 20 s. orge. (1153)(B) 5 5
1289. 3 s. on 25 s. blue (1154).. 5 5
1290. 3 s. on 28 s. green (1155) 5 5
1291. 5 s. on 44 s. turq. (1087) 8 5
1292. 5 s. on 44 s. red (1110) .. 8 5
1293. 5 s. on 45 s. brown (1157) 8 5
1294. 10 s. on 1 l. lake (1160).. 20 8
1295. 20 s. on 2 l. red (1162) .. 40 15
1296. 40 s. on 4 l. lake (889) .. 85 30
(A) Surch. in one line; (B) in two lines.

1962. Air.
1297. **382.** 1 s. slate-blue and slate-violet .. 5 5
1298. – 2 s. blue and pink.. 5 5
1299. – 3 s brown & chestnut 5 5
1300. – 10 s. black & bistre.. 15 5
1301. – 40 s. black & emerald 80 30
DESIGNS: 2 s. Sailing boat at Varna. 3 s. Melnik. 10 s. Tirnovo. 40 s. Pirin Mts.

383. Freighter "Varna". 384. Rila Mountains.

1962. Bulgarian Merchant Navy.
1302. **383.** 1 s. green and blue .. 5 5
1303. – 5 s. pale blue & green 12 5
1304. – 20 s. vio.-blue & blue 40 12
SHIPS: 5 s. Tanker "Komsomol". 20 s. Liner "G. Dimitrov".

1963. Views.
1305. **384.** 1 s. blue-green .. 5 5
1306. 2 s. blue 5 5
1307. 6 s. turquoise .. 10 5
1308. 8 s. purple 12 8
1309. 13 s. green 20 10
1310. 1 l. deep green .. 1·40 40
VIEWS: 2 s. Pirin Mts. 6 s. Fishing boats, Nesebur. 8 s. Danube shipping. 13 s. Viden Castle. 1 l. Rhodope Mts.

385. Dimitrov as Printer. 386. Pink Roses.

1962. State Printing Office. 80th Anniv.
1311. **385.** 2 s. red, black & yell. 5 5
1312. – 13 s. blk., orge. & yell. 25 10
DESIGN: 13 s. Emblem of Printing Office.

1962. Bulgarian Roses. T **368** and similar designs.
1313. 1 s. pink, green and violet 5 5
1314. 2 s. red, green and buff .. 5 5
1315. 3 s. red, green and blue.. 8 5
1316. 4 s. yell., blue-grn. & grn. 10 5
1317. 5 s. pink, green and blue 15 8
1318. 6 s. red, green & turquoise 20 8
1319. 8 s. red, green & yell.-grn. 50 12
1320. 13 s. yellow, green & blue 1·00 35

387. "The World United against Malaria".

1962. Malaria Eradication.
1321. **387.** 5 s. yell., blk. & chest. 25 8
1322. – 20 s. yell., grn. & blk. 60 20
DESIGN: 20 s. Campaign emblem.

388. Lenin and Front Page of "Pravda". 389. Text-book and Blackboard.

1962. "Pravda" Newspaper. 50th Anniv.
1323. **388.** 5 s. indigo, red & black 25 12

1962. Bulgarian Teachers' Congress.
1324. **389.** 5 s. black, yell. & blue 12 5

390. Footballer. 391. Dimitrov.

1962. World Football Championships, Chile.
1325. **390.** 13 s. chest., grn. & blk. 75 25

1962. Dimitrov. 80th Birth Anniv.
1326. **391.** 2 s. olive-green .. 5 5
1327. 5 s. grey-blue .. 12 5

392. Bishop. **393.** Festival Emblem.

1962. 15th Chess Olympiad, Varna. Inscr. "1962". Inscr. in black.
1328. **392.** 1 s. green and grey .. 5 5
1329. – 2 s. bistre and grey .. 5 5
1330. – 3 s. purple and grey 8 5
1331. – 13 s. orange and grey 30 15
1332. – 20 s. blue and grey .. 55 25
CHESS PIECES: 2 s. Rook. 3 s. Queen. 14 s. Knight. 20 s. Pawn.

1962. 35th Esperanto Congress, Burgas. Surch. **XXXV КОНГРЕС 1962 13** and bars.
1333. **309.** 13 s. on 44 s. green .. 1·40 75

1962. World Youth Festival, Helsinki. Inscr. "1962".
1334. **393.** 5 s. blue, pink & green 10 5
1335. – 13 s. blue, pur. & grey 25 8
DESIGN: 13 s. Girl and emblem.

394. Tu-114 Airliner.

1962 Air. TABSO Airline. 15th Anniv.
1336. **394.** 13 s. bl., ultram. & blk. 70 8

395. "Parnassius apollo" (butterfly).

1962. Butterflies and Moths. Insects in natural colours; Inscr. and frame colours given.
1337. **395.** 1 s. grey and olive .. 5 5
1338. – 2 s. sepia and rose .. 5 5
1339. – 3 s. brown and stone 5 5
1340. – 4 s. sepia & slate-vio. 8 5
1341. – 5 s. sepia & pale grey 10 5
1342. – 6 s. sepia and grey .. 12 8
1343. – 10 s. olive-brn. & sage 50 15
1344. – 13 s. chestnut & buff 70 30
DESIGNS: 2 s. "Thair cerisyi". 3 s. "Lycaena meleager". 4 s. "Vanessa antiopa". 5 s. "Catocala dilecta". 6 s. "Arctia hebe". 10 s. "Colias balcanica". 13 s. "Argynnis pandora".

396. K. E. Tsiolkovsky (scientist).

1962. Air. 13th Int. Astronautics Congress. Inscr. "1962".
1345. **396.** 5 s. drab and green .. 1·40 60
1346. – 13 s. blue and yellow 70 25
DESIGN: 13 s. Moon rocket

397. Combine Harvester. **398.** Cover of "History of Bulgaria"

1962. 8th Bulgarian Communist Party Congress.
1347. **397.** 1 s. olive & blue-green 5 5
1348. – 2 s. blue-green & blue 8 5
1349. – 3 s. brown and red .. 8 5
1350. – 13 s. sepia, red & pur. 30 12
DESIGNS: 2 s. Electric train. 3 s. Steel furnace. 13 s. Blagoev and Dimitrov.

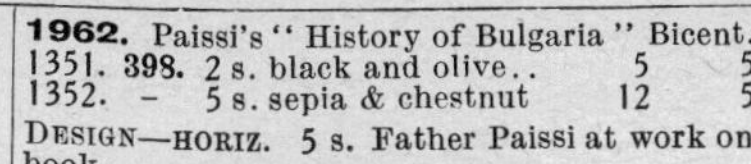

1962. Paissi's "History of Bulgaria" Bicent.
1351. **398.** 2 s. black and olive .. 5 5
1352. – 5 s. sepia & chestnut 12 5
DESIGN—HORIZ. 5 s. Father Paissi at work on book.

399. Nikolaev and "Vostok 3". **400.** Parachutist.

1962. Air. 1st "Team" Manned Space Flight.
1353. **399.** 1 s. olive, blue & black 10 8
1354. – 2 s. olive, green & blk. 25 8
1355. – 40 s. pink, turq. & blk. 1·50 60
DESIGNS: 2 s. Popovich and "Vostok 4". 40 s. "Vostoks 3 and 4" in flight.

1963.
1356. – 1 s. lake 5 5
1357. – 1 s. brown 5 5
1358. – 1 s. blue-green 5 5
1359. – 1 s. green 5 5
1360. **400.** 1 s. blue 5 5
DESIGNS—VERT. No. 1356, State crest. HORIZ. 1357, Sofia University. 1358, "Vasil Levski" Stadium, Sofia. 1359, "The Camels" (archway), Hisar.

No. 1361 was printed with "se-tenant" label in brown, showing Bai Ganyu, hero of one of the author's novels.

401. Aleko Konstantinov.

1963. Konstantinov (author). Birth Cent.
1361. **401.** 5 s. green and red .. 12 5

402. Mars and Space Station.

1963. Air. Launching of Soviet Space Station, "Mars 1"
1362. **402.** 5 s. violet, blue-green, rose and black .. 40 12
1363. – 13 s. turq., rose & blk. 85 25
DESIGN: 13 s. Release of station from rocket.

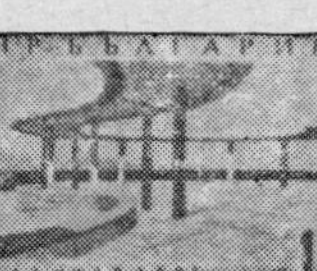

403. Terrace, "Orpheus" Restaurant. **404.** V. Levski.

1963. Black Sea Coast Resorts.
1364. **403.** 1 s. blue 5 5
1365. – 2 s. vermilion .. 5 5
1365a. – 2 s. carmine 5 5
1366. – 3 s. yellow-brown .. 5 5
1367. – 5 s. purple 8 5
1368. – 13 s. turquoise .. 25 5
1369. – 20 s. green 50 12
VIEWS ("Sunny Beach"): 5 s. The Dunes Restaurant. 20 s. Hotel, "Golden Sands". 2 s., 3 s., 13 s. Various hotels.

1963. Execution of Vasil Levski (revolutionary). 90th Anniv.
1370 **404.** 13 s. blue and yellow .. 40 12

405. Dimitrov, Boy and Girl. **406.** Squirrel.

1963. 10th Dimitrov Communist Youth Union Congress, Sofia.
1371. **405.** 2 s. brown, red & blk. 5 5
1372. – 13 s. brn., turq. & blk. 25 10
DESIGN: 13 s. Girl and youth holding book and hammer aloft.

1963. Woodland Animals.
1373. **406.** 1 s. brown, red & green on blue-green .. 5 5
1374. – 2 s. black, red & green on yellow 5 5
1375. – 3 s. sepia, red & olive on olive-drab .. 5 5
1376. – 5 s. brown, red & blue on violet-blue .. 8 5
1377. – 13 s. blk., red & brown on pink 30 12
1378. – 20 s. sepia, red & blue on blue .. 60 15
ANIMALS—HORIZ. 2 s. Hedgehog. 3 s. Polecat. 5 s. Marten. 13 s. Badger. VERT. 20 s. Otter.

DESIGN—HORIZ. 20 s. As T **407** but different hold.

407. Wrestling.

1963. 15th Int. Open Wrestling Championships, Sofia.
1379. **407.** 5 s. bistre and black .. 10 5
1380. – 20 s. chestnut & black 40 15

408. Congress Emblem and Allegory. **409.** Esperanto Star and Sofia Arms.

410. Rocket, Globe and Moon. **411.** Bykovsky in Space-suit.

1963. World Women's Congress, Moscow.
1381. **408.** 20 s. blue and black .. 40 15

1963. 48th World Esperanto Congress, Sofia.
1382. **409.** 13 s. green, grey, brown and buff .. 30 10

1963. Launching of Soviet Moon Rocket "Luna 4". Inscr. "2.IV.1963".
1383. **410.** 1 s. ultramarine .. 5 5
1384. – 2 s. purple 5 5
1385. – 3 s. turquoise-blue .. 8 5
DESIGNS: 2 s. Tracking equipment. 3 s. Sputniks.

1963. Air. Second "Team" Manned Space Flights. Inscr. "14.VI.1963".
1386. **411.** 1 s. turq.-blue & lilac 8 5
1387. – 2 s. brown and yellow 8 5
1388. – 5 s. red and light red 12 5
1389. – 20 s. + 10 s. olive-grn. and light blue .. 70 30
DESIGNS: 2 s. Tereshkova in space-suit. 5 s. Globe. 20 s. Bykovsky and Tereshkova.

1963. Europa Fair, Riccione. Nos. 1314/5 and 1318 (Roses) optd. **MOSTRA EUROPEISTICA. 1963 RICCIONE** and sailing boat motif or additionally surch.
1390. 2 s. red, grn. & buff .. 15 8
1391. 5 s. on 3 s. red, green and blue .. 25 10
1392. 13 s. on 6 s. red, green and turquoise .. 60 25

412. Relay-racing.

1963. Balkan Games. Flags in red, yellow, blue, green and black.
1393. **412.** 1 s. green 5 5
1394. – 2 s. violet 8 5
1395. – 3 s. turquoise-blue 8 5
1396. – 5 s. brown-red .. 30 15
1397. – 13 s. brown .. .. 1·10 65
DESIGNS: 2 s. Throwing the hammer. 3 s. Long-jumping. 5 s. Pole-vaulting. 13 s. Throwing the discus. Each design includes the flags of the competing countries.

413. Slavonic Scroll. **414.** Insurgents.

1963. 5th Int. Slav Congress, Sofia.
1398. **413.** 5 s. red, yellow and deep green .. 12 5

1963. September Insurrection. 40th Anniv.
1399. **414.** 2 s. black and red .. 5 5

415. Aquilegia. **416.** Christo Smirnensky.

1963. Nature Protection. Flowers in natural colours; background colours given.
1400. **415.** 1 s. greenish blue .. 5 5
1401. – 2 s. grey-olive .. 5 5
1402. – 3 s. yellow 5 5
1403. – 5 s. blue 8 5
1404. – 6 s. purple 10 5
1405. – 8 s. light grey .. 15 5
1406. – 10 s. mauve 25 8
1407. – 13 s. yellow-olive .. 65 20
FLOWERS: 2 s. Edelweiss. 3 s. Primula. 5 s. Water-lily. 6 s. Tulip. 8 s. Viola. 10 s. Clematis. 13 s. Anemone.

1963. Smirnensky (poet and revolutionary). 65th Birth Anniv.
1408. **416.** 13 s. black and lilac . 25 8

417. Chariot Horses (wall-painting). **418.** Hemispheres and Centenary Emblem.

1963. Thracian Tombs, Kazanlik.
1409. **417.** 1 s. red, yell. & grey 5 5
1410. – 2 s. violet, yell. & grey 5 5
1411. – 3 s. greenish blue, yellow and grey .. 5 5
1412. – 5 s. brown, yell. & grn. 8 5
1413. – 13 s. blk., yell. & grn. 30 8
1414. – 20 s. clar., yell. & grn. 45 15
DESIGNS (wall paintings on tombs): 2 s. Chariot race. 3 s. Flautists. 5 s. Tray-bearer. 13 s. Funeral feast. 20 s. Seated woman.

1964. Red Cross Centenary.
1415. **418.** 1 s. olive-yellow, red and black 5 5
1416. – 2 s. blue, red & black 5 5
1417. – 3 s. slate, red, black and grey 8 5
1418. – 5 s. turq., red & black 12 8
1419. – 13 s. blk., red & orge. 40 10
DESIGNS: 2 s. Blood transfusion. 3 s. Bandaging wrist. 5 s. Nurse. 13 s. Henri Dunant.

DESIGNS: 2 s. Figure-skating. 3 s. Cross-country skiing. 5 s. Ski-jumping. Ice-hockey: — 10 s. Goalkeeper. 13 s. Players.

419. Speed-skating.

1964. Winter Olympic Games, Innsbruck.
1420. **419.** 1 s. ind., chest. & blue 5 5
1421. – 2 s. olive, mauve & blk. 5 5
1422. – 3 s. grn., chest. & blk. 5 5
1423. – 5 s. multicoloured .. 10 5
1424. – 10 c. orge., blk. & grey 20 10
1425. – 13 s. magenta, violet and black .. 35 15

420. Head (2nd-cent.). **421.** "The Unborn Maid".

1964. 2500 years of Bulgarian Art. Borders in grey.
1426. **420.** 1 s. blue-green & red 5 5
1427. – 2 s. olive-black & red 5 5
1428. – 3 s. bistre and red .. 5 5
1429. – 5 s. blue and red .. 8 5
1430. – 6 s. chestnut and red 10 5
1431. – 8 s. brown-red and red 15 5
1432. – 10 s. yellow-olive & red 20 8
1433 – 13 s. olive and red .. 30 12
DESIGNS: 2 s. Horseman (1st to 4th cent.). 3 s. Jug (19th cent.). 5 s. Buckle (19th cent.). 6 s. Pot (19th cent.). 8 s. Angel (17th cent.). 10 s. Animals (8th to 10th cent.). 13 s. Peasant woman (20th cent.).

1964. Folk Tales. Multicoloured.
1434. 1 s. Type **421** 5 5
1435. 2 s. "Grandfather's Glove" 5 5
1436. 3 s. "The Big Turnip" .. 5 5
1437. 5 s. "The Wolf and the Seven Kids" 8 5
1438. 8 s. "Cunning Peter" .. 15 8
1439. 13 s. "The Loaf of Corn" 35 12

422. "Ascalaphus otomanus".

1964. Insects.
1440. 1 s. black, yellow & chest. 5 5
1441. 2 s. black. ochre & bl.-grn. 5 5
1442. 3 s. green, black & drab 5 5
1443. 5 s. violet, black and olive 8 5
1444. 13 s. brown, black & violet 30 12
1445. 20 s. yell. black & slate-bl. 50 20
DESIGNS—HORIZ. 1 s. T **422**. 3 s. "Saga natalia". 20 s. "Scolia flavitrons". VERT. 2 s. "Nemoptera coa". 5 s. "Rosalia alpina". 13 s. "Anisoplia austriaca".

423. Football.

1964. Levski Physical Culture Association. 50th Anniv. Multicoloured.
1446. 2 s. Type **423** 8 5
1447. 13 s. Handball 30 15

424. Title Page and P. Beron (author).

1964. First Bulgarian Primer. 140th Anniv.
1448. **424.** 20 s. black & chestnut 70 50

425. Stephenson's "Rocket".

1964. Railway Transport. Multicoloured.
1449. 1 s. Type **425** 5 5
1450. 2 s. Steam loco. 5 5
1451. 3 s. Diesel loco. 5 5
1452. 5 s. Electric loco. .. 10 5
1453. 8 s. Steam train on bridge 15 8
1454. 13 s. Diesel train emerging from tunnel 45 10

МЕЖДУНАРОДНА КОСМИЧЕСКА ИЗЛОЖБА РИЧИОНЕ · 1964 ST 10

426. Alsatian. (**427.**)

1964. Dogs. Multicoloured.
1455. 1 s. Type **426** 5 5
1456. 2 s. Setter 5 5
1457. 3 s. Poodle 5 5
1458. 4 s. Pomeranian 8 5
1459. 5 s. St. Bernard 10 5
1460. 6 s. Fox terrier 15 5
1461. 10 s. Pointer 65 15
1462. 13 s. Dachshund .. 1·10 40

1964. Air. Int. Cosmic Exn., Riccione. No. 1386 surch. with T **427** and No. 1387 surch. as T **427**, but in Italian.
1463. **411.** 10 s. on 1 s. turquoise-blue and lilac .. 30 12
1464. – 20 s. on 2 s. brn. & yell. 50 20

428. Partisans and Flag.

1964. Liberation. 20th Anniv. Flag in red.
1465. **428.** 1 s. blue and light blue 5 5
1466. – 2 s. olive and bistre 5 5
1467. – 3 s. lake and mauve .. 5 5
1468. – 4 s. violet and lavender 5 5
1469. – 5 s. brown & orange 10 5
1470. – 6 s. blue & light blue 12 5
1471. – 8 s. green & light green 15 5
1472. – 13 s. brown & salmon 30 10
DESIGNS: 2 s. Greeting Soviet troops. 3 s. Soviet aid—arrival of goods. 4 s. Industrial plant, Kremikovtsi. 5 s. Combine-harvester. 6 s. "Peace" campaigners. 8 s. Soldier of National Guard. 13 s. Blagoev and Dimitrov. All with flag as T **428**.

М М панаир ПЛОВДИВ - 1964 ST 20

(**429.**) **430.** Transport.

1964. 21st Int. Fair, Plovdiv. Surch. with T **429**.
1473. 20 s. on 44 s. ochre (No. 1020a) 45 20

1964. 1st National Stamp Exn., Sofia.
1474. **430.** 20 s. blue 65 30
No. 1474 was issued in sheets containing 12 stamps with "se-tenant" labels and one blank centrepiece.

431. Gymnastics. **432.** Vratcata.

1964. Olympic Games, Tokyo. Rings and values in red.
1475. **431.** 1 s. green & light green 5 5
1476. – 2 s. blue and lavender 5 5
1477. – 3 s. blue & turq.-blue 5 5
1478. – 5 s. violet and rose .. 8 5
1479. – 13 s. blue & light blue 30 10
1480. – 20 s. green & yell-buff 45 12
DESIGNS: 2 s. Long-jumping. 3 s. Diving. 5 s. Football. 13 s. Netball. 20 s. Wrestling.

1964. Landscapes.
1481. **432.** 1 s. slate-green .. 5 5
1482. – 2 s. brown .. 5 5
1483. – 3 s. blue .. 5 5
1484. – 4 s. red-brown .. 8 5
1485. – 5 s. green .. 10 5
1486. – 6 s. violet .. 12 5
DESIGNS: 2 s. The Ritli. 3 s. Maliovitsa. 4 s. Broken Rocks. 5 s. Erkyupria. 6 s. Rhodope mountain pass.

433. Paper and Cellulose Factory, Bukovitza.

1964. Air. Industrial Buildings.
1487. **433.** 8 s. turquoise .. 15 5
1488. – 10 s. purple .. 20 5
1489. – 13 s. violet .. 25 8
1490. – 20 s. blue 40 10
1491. – 40 s. green 75 20
DESIGNS: 10 s. Metal works, Plovdiv. 13 s. Metallurgical works, Kremikovtzi. 20 s. Petrol refinery, Burgas. 40 s. Fertiliser factory, Stara-Zagora.

434. Rila Monastery.

1964. Philatelic Exn. for Franco-Bulgarian Amity.
1492. **434.** 5 s. black and drab .. 12 8
1493. – 13 s. black and blue .. 35 12
DESIGN: 13 s. Notre-Dame, Paris (inscr. in French).

435. 500-year-old Walnut. **436.**

1964. Ancient Trees. Values and inscr. in black.
1494. **435.** 1 s. brown 5 5
1495. – 2 s. maroon 5 5
1496. – 3 s. sepia 5 5
1497. – 4 s. blue 5 5
1498. – 10 s. green 20 8
1499. – 13 s. olive 40 10
TREES: 2 s. Plane (1000 yrs.). 3 s. Plane (600 yrs.). 4 s. Poplar (800 yrs.). 10 s. Oak (800 yrs.). 13 s. Fir (1200 yrs.).

1964. 8th Congress of Int. Union of Students, Sofia.
1500. **436.** 13 s. black and blue 30 8

437. Bulgarian Veteran and Soviet Soldier. (Sculpture by T. Zlatarev). **438.** "Gold Medal".

1965. Bulgarian-Soviet Society. Cent.
1501. **437.** 2 s. red and black .. 10 5

1965. Olympic Games, Tokyo (1964).
1502. **438.** 20 s. blk., gold & chest. 40 15

439. Komarov.

1965. Flight of "Voskhod 1". Multicoloured.
1503. 1 s. Type **439** 5 5
1504. 2 s. Feoktistov 5 5
1505. 5 s. Egorov 10 5
1506. 13 s. The three astronauts 25 8
1507. 20 s. "Voskhod 1" .. 50 12

440. Corn-cob. **441.** "Victory against Fascism".

1965. Agricultural Products.
1508. **440.** 1 s. yellow 5 5
1509. – 2 s. green 5 5
1510. – 3 s. orange 5 5
1511. – 4 s. olive 5 5
1512. – 5 s. cerise 10 5
1513. – 10 s. blue 20 8
1514. – 13 s. bistre 30 10
DESIGNS: 2 s. Ears of Wheat. 3 s. Sunflowers. 4 s. Sugar beet. 5 s. Clover. 10 s. Cotton. 13 s. Tobacco.

1965. "Victory of 9 May, 1945". 20th Anniv.
1515. **441.** 5 s. black, bistre & grey 10 5
1516. – 13 s. blue, black & grey 25 8
DESIGN: 13 s. Globes on dove ("Peace").

442. Bullfinch. **443.** Transport, Globe and Whale.

1965. Song Birds. Multicoloured.
1517. 1 s. Type **442** 5 5
1518. 2 s. Golden oriole .. 5 5
1519. 3 s. Rock thrush 5 5
1520. 5 s. Swallows .. 8 5
1521. 8 s. Roller .. 15 8
1522. 10 s. Goldfinch 60 10
1523. 13 s. Rosy pastor .. 75 20
1524. 20 s. Nightingale .. 1·00 40

1965. 4th Int. Transport Conf., Sofia.
1525. **443.** 13 s. silver, blue, magenta and yellow 25 8

444. I.C.Y. Emblem. **445.** I.T.U. Emblem and Symbols.

1965. Int. Co-operation Year.
1526. **444.** 20 s. orge., olive & blk. 40 15

1965. I.T.U. Cent.
1527. **445.** 20 s. yell., green & blue 40 15

446. Beliaiev and Leonov.

1965. "Voskhod 2" Space Flight.
1528. **446.** 2 s. pur., grn. & drab 10 5
1529. – 20 s. violet, black, olive and grey .. 1·00 40
DESIGN: 20 s. Leonov in space.

447. Sting-ray. **448.** Marx and Lenin.

1965. Fishes. Borders in grey.
1530. **447.** 1 s. gold, black & orge. 5 5
1531. – 2 s. silver, indigo & bl. 5 5
1532. – 3 s. gold, black & grn. 5 5
1533. – 5 s. gold, black & red 8 5
1534. – 10 s. silver, indigo and turquoise 25 12
1535. – 13 s. gold, blk. & brn. 75 25
FISHES: 2 s. Belted bonito. 3 s. Scorpion-fish. 5 s. Gurnard. 10 s. Horse mackerel. 13 s. Turbot.

1965. Postal Ministers' Congress, Peking.
1536. **448.** 13 s. brown and red .. 25 10

449. Film and Screen.

450. Quinces.

1965. Balkan Film Festival, Varna.
1537. **449.** 13 s. black, silver & bl. 20 10

1965. Fruits.
1538. **450.** 1 s. orange 5 5
1539. – 2 s. olive (Grapes) .. 5 5
1540. – 3 s. bistre (Pears) .. 5 5
1541. – 4 s. orange (Plums) .. 5 5
1542. – 5 s. red (Strawberries) 12 5
1543. – 6 s. brown (Walnuts) 20 8

451. Ballerina.

452. Dove, Emblem and Map.

1965. Ballet Competitions, Varna.
1544. **451.** 5 s. black and magenta 15 5

1965. "Balkanphila" Stamp Exn., Varna.
1545. **452.** 1 s. silver, ult. & yell. 5 5
1546. – 2 s. silver, violet & yell. 5 5
1547. – 3 s. gold, green & yell. 8 5
1548. – 13 s. gold, red & yell. 40 35
1549. – 20 s. brn., bl. & silver 50 40
DESIGNS: 2 s. Yacht emblem. 3 s. Stylised fish and flowers. 13 s. Stylised Sun, planet and rocket. LARGER (45 × 25½ mm.): 20 s. Cosmonauts Beliaiev and Leonov.

453. Escapes in Boat.

455. Gymnast.

2 Ст

ПЪРВИ НАЦИОНАЛЕН
СЪБОР НА НАРОДНО
ТО ТВОРЧЕСТВО
12–15–VIII
1965

=

(454.)

1965. Political Prisoners' Escape from "Bolshevik Island". 40th Anniv.
1551. **453.** 2 s. black and slate 12 10

1965. National Folklore Competition. No. 1084 surch. with T **454.**
1552. – 2 s. on 8 s. brown .. 30 20

1965. Balkan Games.
1553. **455.** 1 s. black and red .. 5 5
1554. – 2 s. purple and black 5 5
1555. – 3 s. pur., blk. & cerise 5 5
1556. – 5 s. brown, black & red 5 5
1557. – 10 s. purple, blk. & mag. 25 8
1558. – 13 s. purple and black 45 15
DESIGNS: 2 s. Gymnastics on bars 3 s. Weight-lifting. 5 s. Rally car and building. 10 s. Basketball. 13 s. Rally car and map.

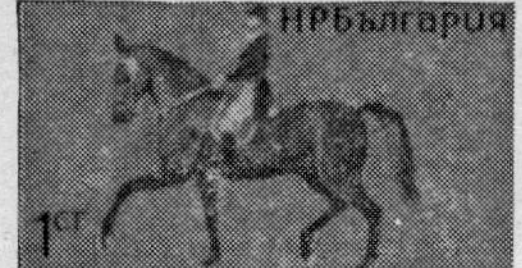

456. Dressage.

1965. Horsemanship.
1559. **456.** 1 s. plum, blk. & blue 5 5
1560. – 2 s. brn., blk. & ochre 5 5
1561. – 3 s. crimson, black and slate-purple .. 5 5
1562. – 5 s. brown and green 5 5
1563. – 10 s. brown, blk. & grey 20 8
1564. – 13 s. brown, green and cinnamon 60 25
DESIGNS: 5 s. Horse-racing. Others, Horse-jumping (various).

456. Young Pioneers.

1965. Dimitrov Young Pioneers Movement.
1566. **457.** 1 s. green & turquoise 5 5
1567. – 2 s. mauve and violet 5 5
1568. – 3 s. bistre and olive .. 5 5
1569. – 5 s. ochre and blue .. 8 5
1570. – 8 s. orange and brown 25 12
1571. – 13 s. violet and red .. 50 15
DESIGNS: 2 s. Admitting recruit. 3 s. Camp bugler. 5 s. Flying model aircraft. 8 s. Girls singing. 13 s. Young athlete.

458. "Ju-52" Aircraft over Tirnovo.

459. Women of N. and S. Bulgaria.

1965. Bulgarian Civil Aviation. Multi-coloured.
1572. 1 s. Type **458** 5 5
1573. 2 s. "Il-14" over Plovdiv 5 5
1574. 3 s. "Mi-4" helicopter over Dimitrovgrad 5 5
1575. 5 s. "Tu-104" over Ruse 8 5
1576. 13 s. "Il-18" over Varna 30 10
1577. 20 s. "Tu-114" over Sofia 55 25

1965. North and South Bulgarian Union. 80th Anniv.
1578. **459.** 13 s. black and green 30 12

460. I.Q.S.Y. Emblem and Earth's Radiation Zones.

461. "Spring Greetings".

1965. Int. Quiet Sun Year.
1579. **460.** 1 s. yell., green & blue 5 5
1580. – 2 s. yell., brn., red & pur. 5 5
1581. – 13 s. yell., grn., blk. & bl. 30 12
DESIGNS (I.Q.S.Y. emblem and): 2 s. Sun and solar flares. 13 s. Total eclipse of the Sun.

1966. "Spring". National Folklore.
1582. **461.** 1 s. mauve, ultram. and drab 5 5
1583. – 2 s. red, black & drab 5 5
1584. – 3 s. violet, red & grey 5 5
1585. – 5 s. red, violet & black 5 5
1586. – 8 s. pur., brn. & mve. 15 8
1587. – 13 s. mauve, blk. & bl. 30 10
DESIGNS: 2 s. Drummer. 3 s. "Birds" (stylised). 5 s. Folk dancer. 8 s. Vase of flowers. 13 s. Bagpiper.

462. Biela Bridge.

DESIGNS: 1589, Svilengrad Bridge. 1590, Fountain, Samokov. 1591, Ruins of Matochnitza Castle. 1592, Cherven Castle. 1593, Cafe, Bozhentsi.

1966. Ancient Monuments.
1588. **462.** 1 s. turquoise 5 5
1589. – 1 s. emerald 5 5
1590. – 2 s. green 5 5
1591. – 2 s. maroon 5 5
1592. – 8 s. brown 15 5
1593. – 13 s. blue 25 10

463. "Christ" (from fresco Boyana Church).

1966. "2,500 Years of Culture". Mult.
1594. 1 s. Type **463** 25 25
1595. 2 s. "Destruction of the Idols" (from fresco, Boyana Church) (horiz.) 20 12
1596. 3 s. Bachkovo Monastery 20 15
1597. 4 s. Zemen Monastery (horiz.) 20 20
1598. 5 s. John the Baptist Church, Nesebur .. 25 20
1599. 13 s. "Nativity" (icon, Monumental Church of Alexander Nevski, Sofia) 30 25
1600. 20 s. "Virgin and Child" (icon, Archaeological Museum, Sofia) .. 70 60

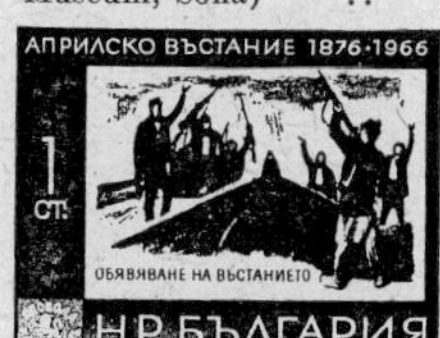

464. "The First Gunshot" at Koprivshtitsa.

1966. April Uprising. 90th Anniv.
1601. **464.** 1 s. black, brn. & gold 5 5
1602. – 2 s. black, red & gold 5 5
1603. – 3 s. black, green & gold 5 5
1604. – 5 s. black, blue & gold 5 5
1605. – 10 s. black, pur. & gold 15 8
1606. – 13 s. black, vio. & gold 25 12
DESIGNS: 2 s. G. Benkovski and T. Kableskov. 3 s. "Showing the Flag" at Panagyurishte. 5 s. V. Petleshkov and Z. Dyustabanov. 10 s. Landing of Botev's detachment at Kozlodui. 13 st. P. Volov and I. Dragostinov.

465. W.H.O. Building.

1966. W.H.O. Headquarters, Geneva. Inaug.
1608. **465.** 13 s. blue and silver .. 40 15

466. Worker.

1966. 6th Trades Union Congress, Sofia.
1609. **466.** 20 s. black and pink 40 20

467. Elephant.

468. Boy and Girl holding Banners.

1966. Sofia Zoo Animals. Multicoloured.
1610. 1 s. Type **467** 5 5
1611. 2 s. Tiger 5 5
1612. 3 s. Chimpanzee .. 5 5
1613. 4 s. Mountain goat .. 5 5
1614. 5 s. Polar bear .. 5 5
1615. 8 s. Lion 12 10
1616. 13 s. Bison 25 12
1617. 20 s. Kangaroo .. 70 25

1966. 3rd Congress of Bulgarian Sports Federation.
1618. **468.** 13 s. bl., orge. & cobalt 25 12

469. Paddle-steamer "Radetzky" and Pioneer.

470. Standard-bearer B.N. Simov-Kuruto.

1966. Botev's Seizure of Paddle-steamer "Radetzky". 90th Anniv.
1619. **469.** 2 s. black, red, blue and ultramarine .. 8 5

1966. Simov-Kuruto (hero of the Uprising against Turkey). 90th Anniv.
1620. **470.** 5 s. multicoloured .. 12 8

471. Federation Emblem.

1966. 7th Int. Youth Federation Assembly, Sofia.
1621. **471.** 13 s. blue and black .. 25 12

472. U.N.E.S.C.O. Emblem.

1966. U.N.E.S.C.O. 20th Anniv.
1622. **472.** 20 s. ochre, red & blk. 40 25

473. Footballer with Ball.

1966. World Cup Football Championships. Showing players in action. Borders in grey.
1623. **473.** 1 s. black and brown 5 5
1624. – 2 s. black and red .. 5 5
1625. – 5 s. black and bistre 8 5
1626. – 13 s. black and blue .. 20 10
1627. – 20 s. black and blue .. 35 15

474. Wrestling.

1966. 3rd Int. Wrestling Championships, Sofia.
1629. **474.** 13 s. sepia, grn & brn. 25 12

475. Throwing the Javelin.

1966. 3rd Youth Spartakiade.
1630. **475.** 2 s. green, red & yellow 5 5
1631. – 13 s. green, red & yell. 20 8
DESIGN: 13 s. Running.

476. Map of Balkans, Globe and U.N.E.S.C.O. Emblem.

1966. Int. Balkan Studies Congress, Sofia.
1632. 476. 13 s. green, pink & blue 20 10

477. Children with Construction Toy.

DESIGNS: 2 s. Rabbit and Teddy Bear. 3 s. Children as astronauts. 13 s. Children with gardening equipment.

1966. Children's Day.
1633. 477. 1 s. blk., yellow & red 5 5
1634. – 2 s. black, brn. & grn. 5 5
1635. – 3 s. blk., yell. & ult. 8 5
1636. – 13 s. blk., mve. & blue 25 10

478. Gagarin and "Vostok 1".

1966. Russian Space Exploration.
1637. 478. 1 s. slate and grey .. 5 5
1638. – 2 s. purple and grey .. 5 5
1639. – 3 s. brown and grey .. 5 5
1640. – 5 s. lake and grey .. 5 5
1641. – 8 s. blue and grey .. 10 8
1642. – 13 s. turquoise & grey 20 10
1643. – 20 s. + 10 s. violet & grey 70 30
DESIGNS: 2 s. Titov and "Vostok 2". 3 s. Nikolaev, Popovich and "Vostoks 3" and "4". 5 s. Tereshkova, Bykovsky and "Vostoks 5" and "6". 8 s. Komorov, Yegorov, Feoktistov and "Voskhod 1". 13 s. Beliaiev, Leonov and "Voskhod 2". 20 s. Gagarin, Leonov and Tereshkova.

479. St. Clement (14th-cent. wood-carving).

480. M. Shatorov.

1966. St. Clement of Ochrid. 1050th Birth Anniv.
1645. 479. 5 s. brown, red & drab 12 5

1966. Anti-Fascist Fighters. Frames in gold; value in black.
1646. 480. 2 s. violet and red .. 5 5
1647. – 3 s. brown & magenta 5 5
1648. – 5 s. blue and red .. 5 5
1649. – 10 s. brown & orange 15 8
1650. – 13 s. brown & verm. 25 10
PORTRAITS: 3 s. V. Trichkov. 5 s. V. Ivanov. 10 s. R. Daskalov. 13 s. Gen. V. Zaimov.

481. G. Dimitrov (statesman).
482. Deer's head Vessel.

1966. 9th Bulgarian Communist Party Congress, Sofia.
1651. 481. 2 s. black and crimson 5 5
1652. – 20 s. black, red & grey 35 15
DESIGN: 20 s. Furnaceman and steelworks.

1966. The Gold Treasures of Panagyurishte. Multicoloured.
1653. 1 s. Type 482 .. .. 5 5
1654. 2 s. Amazon 5 5
1655. 3 s. Ram 5 5
1656. 5 s. Plate 5 5
1657. 6 s. Venus 8 5
1658. 8 s. Roe-buck 25 10
1659. 10 s. Amazon (different) 30 10
1660. 13 s. Amphora 35 12
1661. 20 s. Goat 50 20
Except for the 5 s. and 13 s. the designs show vessels with animal heads.

483. Bansko Hotel.
484. Christmas Tree.

1966. Tourist Resorts.
1662. 483. 1 s. blue 5 5
1663. – 2 s. grn. (Belogradchik) 5 5
1664. – 2 s. lake (Triavna) .. 5 5
1665. – 20 s. purple (Maliovitsa, Rila) .. 25 12

1966. New Year. Multicoloured.
1666. 2 s. Type 484 .. .. 5 5
1667. 13 s. Money-box .. 25 10

485. P. Slaveikov (writer).
486. Dahlias.

1966. Cultural Celebrities.
1668. 485. 1 s. bistre, blue & orge. 5 5
1669. – 2 s. brown, orge. & grey 5 5
1670. – 3 s. blue, bistre & orge. 5 5
1671. – 5 s. mar., drab & orge. 8 5
1672. – 8 s. grey, purple & blue 15 5
1673. – 13 s. violet, blue & pur. 25 10
CELEBRITIES, Writers (with pen emblem): 2 s. D. Debelianov. 3 s. P. Todorov. Painters (with brush emblem): 5 s. D. Dobrovich. 8 s. I. Markvichka. 13 s. I. Bechkov.

1966. Flowers. Multicoloured.
1674. 1 s. Type 486 .. .. 5 5
1675. 1 s. Clematis 5 5
1676. 2 s. Narcissi 5 5
1677. 2 s. Foxgloves 5 5
1678. 3 s. Snowdrops 5 5
1679. 5 s. Petunias 10 5
1680. 13 s. Tiger lilies .. 25 8
1681. 20 s. Campanulas .. 50 20

487. Pheasant.

1967. Hunting. Multicoloured.
1682. 1 s. Type 487 .. .. 5 5
1683. 2 s. Partridge 5 5
1684. 3 s. Hen partridge .. 5 5
1685. 5 s. Hare 8 5
1686. 8 s. Deer 25 10
1687. 13 s. Stag 45 15

488. "Philately".
489. 6th-cent. B.C. Coin of Thrace.

1967. 10th Congress of Bulgarian Philatelists Union, Sofia.
1688. 488. 10 s. yell., black & green 50 25

1967. Ancient Bulgarian Coins. Coins in silver on black background except 13 s. (gold on black). Frame colours given.
1689. 489. 1 s. brown 5 5
1690. – 2 s. purple 5 5
1691. – 3 s. green 8 5
1692. – 5 s. chestnut .. 10 8
1693. – 13 s. turquoise .. 50 15
1694. – 20 s. violet 75 50
COINS—SQUARE. 2 s. 2nd-cent. B.C. Macedonian tetradrachm. 3 s. 2nd-cent. B.C. Odessos (Varna) tetradrachm. 5 s. 4th-cent. B.C. Macedonian coin of Philip II. HORIZ. (38×25 mm.): 13 s. Obverse and reverse of 4th-cent. B.C. coin of King Sevt (Thrace). 20 s. Obverse and reverse of 5th-cent. B.C. coin of Apollonia (Sozopol).

490. Partisans listening to radio.

1967. "Patriotic Front" Union. 25th Anniv. Multicoloured.
1695. 1 s. Type 490 .. .. 5 5
1696. 20 s. Dimitrov speaking at rally 35 15

491. Nikola Kofardjiev.
492. "Cultural Development".

1967. Anti-Fascist Fighters.
1697. 491. 1 s. lake, black & blue 5 5
1698. – 2 s. green, black & blue 5 5
1699. – 5 s. ochre, black & blue 5 5
1700. – 10 s. blue, blk. & lilac 15 8
1701. – 13 s. pur., black & grey 30 10
PORTRAITS: 2 s. P. Napetov. 5 s. P. D. Petkov. 10 s. E. Markov. 13 s. T. Kostov.

1967. 1st Cultural Conf., Sofia.
1702. 492. 13 s. yell., green & gold 25 8

493. Angora Kitten.
494. "Golden Sands" Resort.

1967. Cats. Multicoloured.
1703. 1 s. Type 493 .. .. 5 5
1704. 2 s. Siamese (horiz.) .. 5 5
1705. 3 s. Abyssinian 5 5
1706. 5 s. European black and white 5 5
1707. 13 s. Persian (horiz.) .. 30 12
1708. 20 s. European tabby .. 45 15

1967. Int. Tourist Year.
1709. 494. 13 s. green, yellow, black and blue .. 20 8
1710. – 20 s. green, buff, black and turquoise .. 25 10
1711. – 40 s. green, buff, black and blue-green .. 70 25
DESIGNS: 20 s. Pamporovo. 40 s. Old church, Nesebur.

495. Scene from Iliev's Opera, "The Master of Boyana".

1967. 3rd Int. Young Opera singers' Competition, Sofia.
1712. 495. 5 s. cerise, bl. & grey 8 5
1713. – 13 s. red, blue & grey 20 8
DESIGN—VERT. 13 s. "Vocal Art" (song-bird on piano-keys).

496. G. Kirkov (patriot).

1967. Georgi Kirkov. Birth Cent.
1714. 496. 2 s. bistre and red .. 8 5

497. Roses and Distillery.

1967. Economic Achievements. Multicoloured.
1715. 1 s. Type 497 .. .. 5 5
1716. 1 s. Chick and incubator 5 5
1717. 2 s. Cucumber and glass-houses 5 5
1718. 2 s. Lamb and farm building 5 5
1719. 3 s. Sunflower and oil-extraction plant .. 5 5
1720. 4 s. pigs and piggery .. 5 5
1721. 5 s. Hops and vines .. 5 5
1722. 6 s. Grain and irrigation canals 5 5
1723. 8 s. Grapes and "Bulgar" tractor 10 5
1724. 10 s. Apples and tree .. 12 8
1725. 13 s. Bees and honey .. 20 10
1726. 20 s. Bee on flower, and hives 40 15

498. D.K.M.S. Emblem.
499. Map and Spasski Tower, Kremlin.

1967. Bulgarian Youth Organisation (D.K.M.S.). 11th Anniv.
1727. 498. 13 s. black, red & blue 25 10

1967. October Revolution. 50th Anniv.
1728. 499. 1 s. multicoloured .. 5 5
1729. – 2 s. olive and purple .. 5 5
1730. – 3 s. violet and purple 5 5
1731. – 5 s. red and purple .. 5 5
1732. – 13 s. ultramarine and purple 20 8
1733. – 20 s. blue and purple 30 12
DESIGNS: 2 s. Lenin directing revolutionaries. 3 s. Bulgarian revolutionaries. 5 s. Marx, Engels and Lenin. 13 s. Soviet oil refinery. 20 s. "Molyna" satellite and Moon (Soviet space research).

500. Scenic "Fish" and Rod.
502. Bogdan Peak, Sredna Mts.

501. Ski-walking.

1967. 7th World Angling Championships, Varna.
1734. 500. 10 s. multicoloured .. 20 10

1967. Winter Olympic Games, Grenoble (1968).
1735. 501. 1 s. black, red & turq. 5 5
1736. – 2 s. black, bistre & bl. 5 5
1737. – 3 s. black, blue & mar. 5 5
1738. – 5 s. black, yell. & grn. 8 5
1739. – 13 s. blk., buff. & ult. 20 10
1740. – 20 s. + 10 s. black, red, drab and blue .. 45 25
DESIGNS: 2 s. Ski-jumping. 3 s. Biathlon. 5 s. Ice-hockey. 13 s. Pair dancing. 20 s. Men's slalom.

1967. Tourism. Mountain Peaks.
1742. 502. 1 s. green and yellow 5 5
1743. – 2 s. sepia and blue .. 5 5
1744. – 3 s. indigo and blue .. 5 5
1745. – 5 s. green and blue .. 5 5
1746. – 10 s. brown and blue 15 5
1747. – 13 s. black and blue 20 8
1748. – 20 s. blue and purple 40 12
DESIGNS—HORIZ. 2 s. Cherni Vruh, Vitosha. 5 s. Persenk, Rhodopes. 10 s. Botev, Stara-Planina. 20 s. Vihren, Pirin. VERT. 3 s. Ruen, Osogovska Planina. 13 s. Musala, Rila.

503. G. Rakovski (revolutionary).

1967. G. Rakovski. Death Cent.
1794. 503. 13 s. black and green 25 12

504. Gagarin, Tereshkova and Leonov.

1967. Space Exploration. Multicoloured.
1750. 1 s. Type 504 .. .. 5 5
1751. 2 s. Glenn and White .. 5 5
1752. 5 s. "Molyna 1" .. 5 5
1753. 10 s. "Gemini 6 and 7" .. 15 8
1754. 13 s. "Luna 13" .. 20 8
1755. 20 s. "Gemini 10" .. 40 20

505. View of Town.

1967. Views of Tirnovo (Ancient Capital).
1756. 505. 1 s. black, drab & blue 5 5
1757. – 2 s. multicoloured .. 5 5
1758. – 3 s. multicoloured .. 5 5
1759. – 5 s. black, slate & red 8 5
1760. – 13 s. multicoloured .. 20 10
1761. – 20 s. blk., orge. & lav. 35 15
DESIGNS: 2 s. Hadji Nikola's Inn. 3 s. Houses on hillside. 5 s. Town and river. 13 s. "House of the Monkeys". 20 s. Gurko street.

506. "The Ruchenitsa" (folk dance, from painting by Markvitchka).

1967. Belgian-Bulgarian "Painting and Philately" Exn., Brussels.
1762. 506. 20 s. green and gold 75 50
No. 1762 was issued in sheets of 8 (4 × 2) with se-tenant commem. labels in the upper and lower margins inscr. in Bulgarian, Flemish and French.

507. "The Shepherd" (Z. Boiadjiev).

1967. Paintings in the National Gallery Sofia. Multicoloured.
1763. 1 s. Type 507 .. .. 5 5
1764. 2 s. "The Wedding" (V Dimitrov) 8 5
1765. 3 s. "The Partisans" (I. Petrov) 10 8
1766. 5 s. "Anastasia Pentchovich" (N. Pavlovich) .. 20 12
1767. 13 s. "Self-Portrait" (Z. Zograf) 60 20
1768. 20 s. "Old Town of Plovdiv" (T. Lavrenov) 70 30
The 3 s. design is 55 × 35 mm. and those of the 2, 5 and 13 s. are vert.

508. Linked Satellites "Cosmos 186 and 188". 509. "Crossing the Danube" (Orenburgski).

1968. "Cosmic Activities". Multicoloured.
1770. 20 s. Type 508 .. .. 35 15
1771. 40 s. "Venus 4" and orbital diagram (horiz.) 75 30

1968. Liberation from Turkey. 90th Anniv. Paintings. Inscr. and frames in black and gold; centre colours below.
1772. 509. 1 s. green 5 5
1773. – 2 s. indigo 5 5
1774. – 3 s. brown 5 5
1775. – 13 s. blue 25 12
1776. – 20 s. turquoise .. 45 20
DESIGNS—VERT. 2 s. "Flag of Samara" (Veschin). 13 s. "Battle of Orlovo Gnezdo" (Popov). HORIZ. 3 s. "Battle of Pleven" (Orenburgski). 20 s. "Greeting Russian Soldiers" (Goudienov).

510. Karl Marx. 511. Maxim Gorky.

1968. Karl Marx. 150th Birth Anniv.
1777. 510. 13 s. grey, verm. & blk. 25 8

1968. Maxim Gorky (writer). Birth Cent.
1778. 511. 13 s. grn., orge. & blk. 25 8

512. Dancers.

1968. 9th Youth Congress, Sofia. Multicoloured.
1779. 2 s. Type 512 .. .. 5 5
1780. 5 s. Running 5 5
1781. 13 s. "Doves" 15 8
1782. 20 s. "Youth" (symbolic design) 30 15
1783. 40 s. Bulgarian 5 c. stamp of 1879 under magnifier and Globe 70 30

513. "Campanula alpina". 514. "The Unknown Hero" (Ran Bosilek).

1968. Wild Flowers. Multicoloured.
1784. 1 s. Type 513 .. .. 5 5
1785. 2 s. "Gentiana acaulis" 5 5
1786. 3 s. "Crocus veluchensis" 5 5
1787. 5 s. "Iris sibirica" .. 5 5
1788. 10 s. "Erythronium dens-canis" 12 5
1789. 13 s. "Sempervivum eucanthum" 20 8
1790. 20 s. "Dictamnus albus" 40 12

1968. Bulgarian—Danish Stamp Exn. Fairy Tales. Multicoloured.
1791. 13 s. Type 514 .. 25 10
1792. 20 s. "The Witch and the Young Men" (Hans Andersen) 35 20

515. Memorial Temple, Shipka. 516. Copper Rolling-mill, Medet.

1968. Bulgarian—West Berlin Stamp Exn.
1793. 515. 13 s. multicoloured 30 15
No. 1793 was issued in sheets with se-tenant label inscr. in Bulgarian and German.

1968. Air
1794. 516. 1 l. red .. .. 1·10 30

517. Lake Smolian. 518. Gymnastics.

1968.
1795. 517. 1 s. green 5 5
1796. – 2 s. myrtle 5 5
1797. – 3 s. sepia 5 5
1798. – 8 s. olive-green .. 10 5
1799. – 10 s. brown 12 5
1800. – 13 s. olive 15 5
1801. – 40 s. blue 55 20
1802. – 2 l. brown .. .. 2·50 80
DESIGNS: 2 s. Ropotamo River. 3 s. Lomnitza Gorge, Erma River. 8 s. Isker River. 10 s. Hotel-ship "Die Fregatte". 13 s. Cape Kaliakra. 40 s. Sosopol. 2 l. Mountain road, Kamchia River.

1968. Olympic Games, Mexico.
1803. 518. 1 s. black and red .. 5 5
1804. – 2 s. black, brn. & grey 5 5
1805. – 3 s. black & magenta 5 5
1806. – 10 s. blk., yell. & turq. 10 5
1807. – 13 s. blk., pink & ultramarine .. 20 10
1808. – 20 s. +10 s. grey, pink & blue .. 50 25
DESIGNS: 2 s. Horse-jumping. 3 s. Fencing. 10 s. Boxing. 13 s. Throwing the discus. 20 s. Rowing.

519. Dimitr on Mt. Bouzloudja. 520. Human Rights Emblem.

1968. Exploits of Hadji Dimitr and Stephan Kharadja. (partisan leaders). Cent.
1810. 519. 2 s. chestnut & drab 5 5
1811. – 13 s. green and gold 20 12
DESIGN: 13 s. Hadji Dimitr and Stephan Kharadja.

1968. Human Rights Year.
1812. 520. 20 s. gold and blue .. 30 12

521. Vulture. 522. Battle Scene.

1968. Sofia Zoo. 80th Anniv.
1813. 521. 1 s. black, cinnamon and blue 5 5
1814. – 2 s. blk., yell. & chest. 5 5
1815. – 3 s. black and green 5 5
1816. – 5 s. blk., yell. & lake 15 5
1817. – 13 s. black, bistre & green 40 12
1818. – 20 s. blk., grn. & blue 50 15
DESIGNS: 2 s. Crowned crane. 3 s. Zebra. 5 s. Panther. 13 s. Python. 20 s. Crocodile.

1968. Tchiprovtzi Rising. 280th Anniv.
1819. 522. 13 s. olive, yellow, green and grey 25 8

523. "Calosoma sycophanta". 524. Flying Swans.

1968. Insects.
1820. 523. 1 s. green 5 5
1821. – 1 s. brown 5 5
1822. – 1 s. blue 5 5
1823. – 1 s. chestnut 5 5
1824. – 1 s. purple 15 10
DESIGNS—VERT. No. 1821, "Lucanus cervus". 1822, "Procerus scabrosus". HORIZ. 1823, "Oryctes nasicornis". 1824, "Perisomena caecigena".

1968. "Co-operation with Scandinavia".
1825. – 2 s. ochre and green 50 40
1826. 524. 5 s. bl., grey & blk. .. 50 40
1827. – 13 s. purple & maroon 60 50
1828. – 20 s. grey & violet .. 60 50
DESIGNS: 2 s. Wooden flask. 13 s. Rose. 20 s. "Viking ships".
Nos. 1825. 1828 and 1826, 1827 were issued in panes of 20 with intervening se-tenant label (size 45×25 mm.) showing a stylised "bridge of flags".

525. Congress Building and Emblem.

1968. Int. Dental Congress, Varna.
1829. 525. 20 s. gold, grn. & red 30 15

526. C. Smirnensky (poet) and part of poem "Red Squadrons".

1968. Christo Smirnensky's 70th Birth Anniv.
1830. 526. 13 s. blk., orge. & gold 25 12

527. Dove with Letter.

1968. National Stamp Exn., Sofia and 75th Anniv. of "National Philately".
1831. 527. 20 s. emerald .. 30 15
No. 1831 was issued in small sheets containing 4 stamps and 5 se-tenant stamp size labels in two designs, (a) "Arms", in gold and red; (b) "Magnifier and tweezers", in bright scarlet.

528. Dalmatian Pelican.

1968. Srebirna Wildlife Reservation. Birds. Multicoloured.
1832. 1 s. Type 528 .. .. 5 5
1833. 2 s. Little Egret .. 5 5
1834. 3 s. Great Crested Grebe 5 5
1835. 5 s. Common Tern .. 8 5
1836. 13 s. Spoonbill .. 15 8
1837. 20 s. Glossy Ibis .. 40 12

529. Silistra Costume.

1968. Provincial Costumes. Multicoloured.
1838. 1 s. Type 529 .. .. 5 5
1839. 2 s. Lovetch 5 5
1840. 3 s. Yambol 5 5
1841. 13 s. Tchirpan .. 15 5
1842. 20 s. Razgrad .. 30 10
1843. 40 s. Ixhtiman .. 70 20

530. "St. Arsenius" (icon).

1968. Rila Monastery Icons and murals. Multicoloured.

1844. 1 s. Type **530** 5 5
1845. 2 s. "Carrying St. Ivan Rila's Relics" (horiz.) 5 5
1846. 3 s. "St. Michael torments the Rich Man's Soul" 10 5
1847. 13 s. "St. Ivan Rila" .. 30 8
1848. 20 s. "Prophet Iona" .. 55 12
1849. 40 s. "St. George" .. 1·00 30

531. "Matricaria chamomilla".

1968. Medicinal Plants. Multicoloured.

1851. 1 s. Type **531** 5 5
1852. 1 s. "Mespilus oxyacantha" .. 5 5
1853. 2 s. "Convallaria majalis" 5 5
1854. 3 s. "Atropa belladonna" 5 5
1855. 5 s. "Malva silvestris" 5 5
1856. 10 s. "Adonis vernalis" 12 5
1857. 13 s. "Papaver rhoeas" 20 8
1858. 20 s. "Thymus serpyllum" 35 15

532. Silkworms and Spindles.

1969. Silk Industry. Multicoloured.

1859. 1 s. Type **532** 5 5
1860. 2 s. Worm, cocoons and pattern 5 5
1861. 3 s. Cocoons and spinning wheel 5 5
1862. 5 s. Cocoons and pattern 5 5
1863. 13 s. Moth, cocoon and spindles 20 8
1864. 20 s. Moth, eggs and shuttle 35 12

533. "Death of Ivan Assen". **534.** "Saints Cyril and Methodius" (mural, Troian Monastery).

1969. Manasses Chronicle (1st Series). Multicoloured.

1865. 1 s. Type **533** 5 5
1866. 2 s. "Emperor Nicephorus invading Bulgaria" .. 5 5
1867. 3 s. "Khan Krum's Feast" 5 5
1868. 13 s. "Prince Sviatoslav invading Bulgaria" .. 15 8
1869. 20 s. "The Russian invasion" 25 12
1870. 40 s. "Jesus Christ, Tsar Ivan Alexander and Constantine Manasses" 80 35

See also Nos. 1911/16.

1969. Saints Cyril and Methodius Commem.
1871. **534.** 28 s. multicoloured .. 55 25

535. Galleon. **536.** Posthorn Emblem.

1969. Air. "SOFIA 1969" Int. Stamp Exn. "Transport". Multicoloured.

1872. 1 s. Type **535** 5 5
1873. 2 s. Mail-coach 5 5
1874. 3 s. Steam locomotive .. 5 5
1875. 5 s. Early motor-car .. 5 5
1876. 10 s. Montgolfier's balloon 12 8
1877. 13 s. Early flying-machines 15 8
1878. 20 s. Modern aircraft .. 25 12
1879. 40 s. Rocket and planets 55 25

1969. Bulgarian Postal Services. 90th Anniv.
1881. **536.** 2 s. yellow and green 5 5
1882. – 13 s. multicoloured .. 25 8
1883. – 20 s. blue 40 12

DESIGNS: 13 s. Bulgarian Stamps of 1879 and 1946. 20 s. Post Office workers' strike, 1919.

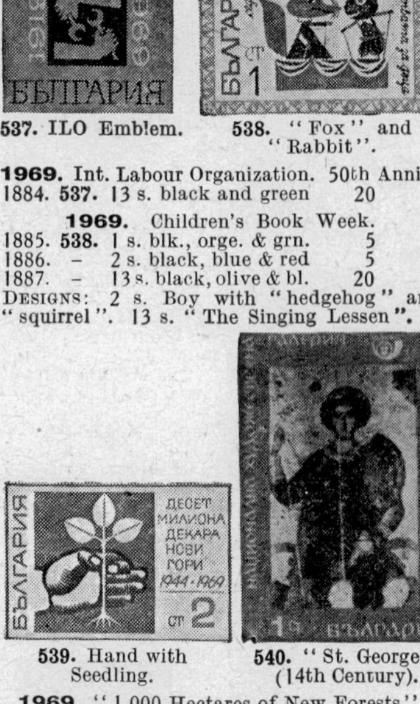

537. ILO Emblem. **538.** "Fox" and "Rabbit".

1969. Int. Labour Organization. 50th Anniv.
1884. **537.** 13 s. black and green 20 8

1969. Children's Book Week.
1885. **538.** 1 s. blk., orge. & grn. 5 5
1886. – 2 s. black, blue & red 5 5
1887. – 13 s. black, olive & bl. 20 10

DESIGNS: 2 s. Boy with "hedgehog" and "squirrel". 13 s. "The Singing Lesson".

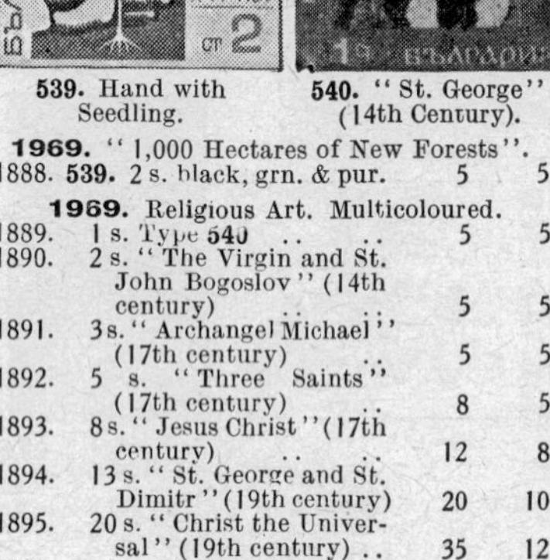

539. Hand with Seedling. **540.** "St. George" (14th Century).

1969. "1,000 Hectares of New Forests".
1888. **539.** 2 s. black, grn. & pur. 5 5

1969. Religious Art. Multicoloured.

1889. 1 s. Type **540** 5 5
1890. 2 s. "The Virgin and St. John Bogoslov" (14th century) 5 5
1891. 3 s. "Archangel Michael" (17th century) .. 5 5
1892. 5 s. "Three Saints" (17th century) .. 8 5
1893. 8 s. "Jesus Christ" (17th century) 12 8
1894. 13 s. "St. George and St. Dimitr" (19th century) 20 10
1895. 20 s. "Christ the Universal" (19th century) .. 35 12
1896. 60 s. "The Forty Martyrs" (19th century) .. .. 1·00 45
1897. 80 s. "The Transfiguration" (19th century).. 1·25 55

541. Roman Coin.

542. St. George and the Dragon.

1969. "SOFIA 1969" Int. Stamp Exhibition. "Sofia Through the Ages".

1899. **541.** 1 s. silver, blue & gold 5 5
1900. – 2 s. silver, grn. & gold 5 5
1901. – 3 s. silver, lake & gold 5 5
1902. – 4 s. silver, vio. & gold 5 5
1903. – 5 s. silver, pur. & gold 5 5
1904. – 13 s. silver, grn. & gold 12 8
1905. – 20 s. silver, bl. & gold 35 12
1906. – 40 s. silver, red & gold 65 25

DESIGNS: 2 s. Roman Coin showing Temple of Aesculapius. 3 s. Church of St. Sophia. 4 s. Boyana Church. 5 s. Parliament Building. 13 s. National Theatre. 20 s. Alexander Nevsky Church. 40 s. Sofia University.

1969. F.I.P. Congress, Sofia.
1908. **542.** 40 s. blk., orge. & silver 60 25

543. St. Cyril.

1969. St. Cyril. 1,000th Birth Anniv.
1909. **543.** 2 s. grn. & red on silver 8 5
1910. – 28 s. bl. & red on silver 45 20

DESIGN: 28 s. St. Cyril and procession.

Nos. 1909/10 were issued in sheets vertically se-tenant with half stamp-size labels.

1969. Manasses Chronicle (Second Series). Designs at T **533**, but all horiz. Multicoloured.

1911. 1 s. "Nebuchadnezzar II and Balthasar of Babylon, Cyrus and Darius of Persia" 5 5
1912. 2 s. "Cambyses, Gyges and Darius of Persia" 5 5
1913. 5 s. "Prophet David and Tsar Ivan Alexander" 10 5
1914. 13 s. "Rout of the Byzantine Army, 811" 20 8
1915. 20 s. "Christening of Khan Boris" .. 35 12
1916. 60 s. "Tsar Simeon's attack on Constantinople" 90 45

544. Partisans.

1969. People's Republic. 25th Anniv.
1917. **544.** 1 s. lilac, red & black 5 5
1918. – 2 s. brn., red & black 5 5
1919. – 3 s. green, red & black 5 5
1920. – 5 s. brn., red & black 5 5
1921. – 13 s. blue, red & blk. 15 5
1922. – 20 s. brown, green, red and black .. 30 10

DESIGNS: 2 s. Combine-harvester. 3 s. Dam. 5 s. Folk singers. 13 s. Petroleum Refinery. 20 s. Lenin, Dimitrov and flags.

545. Gymnastics.

1969. Third National Spartakiad. Multicoloured.
1923. 2 s. Type **545** 5 5
1924. 20 s. Wrestling .. 25 12

546. "Construction" and soldier.

547. T. Tcherkovski.

1969. Army Engineers. 25th Anniv.
1925. **546.** 6 s. black and blue .. 8 5

1969. Tzanke Tcherkovski (poet). Birth Cent.
1926. **547.** 13 s. multicoloured .. 15 5

548. "Wolf" (bronze).

1969. Silistra. 1,800th Anniv.
1927. – 2 s. grey, blue & silver 5 5
1928. **548.** 13 s. brn., grn. & silver 25 8

DESIGN: 2 s. "Woman" (Roman statue).

549. Skipping-rope Exercise.

1969. World Gymnastics Competition, Varna.
1929. **549.** 1 s. grey, blue & grn. 5 5
1930. – 2 s. grey and blue .. 5 5
1931. – 3 s. grey, grn. & emer. 5 5
1932. – 5 s. grey, pur. & red 8 5
1933. – 13 s. + 5 s. grey, blue and red 20 10
1934. – 20 s. + 10 s. grey, green and yellow 40 15

DESIGNS: 2 s. Hoop exercise (pair). 3 s. Hoop exercise (solo). 5 s. Ball exercise (pair). 13 s. Ball exercise (solo). 20 s. Solo gymnast.

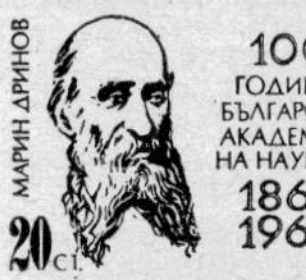

550. Marin Drinov (founder).

1969. Bulgarian Academy of Sciences. Cent.
1935. **550.** 20 s. black and red .. 30 10

551. "Workers' Family" (Balkanski).

1969. Paintings in National Gallery, Sofia. Multicoloured.

1936. 1 s. "Neophit Rilski" (Z. Zogrov) (vert.) .. 5 5
1937. 2 s. "Village Girl" (V. Stoianov (vert.) .. 5 5
1938. 3 s. Type **551** 5 5
1939. 4 s. "Woman Dressing" (I. Nenov) (vert.) .. 5 5
1940. 5 s. "Portrait of a Woman" (N. Pavlovich) (vert.) 8 5
1941. 13 s. "Sarafov as Falstaff" (D. Uzunov) (vert.) 25 10
1942. 20 s. "Artist's Wife" (N. Michailov) .. 40 15
1943. 20 s. "Worker's Lunch" (S. Sotirov) 70 30
1944. 40 s. "Self portrait" (T. Todorov) .. 1·75 85

552. Pavel Bania.

1969. Sanatoria.
1945. **552.** 2 s. blue 5 5
1946. – 5 s. blue 5 5
1947. – 6 s. green 8 5
1948. – 20 s. green 25 12

SANATORIA: 5 s. Chisar. 6 s. Kotel. 20 s. Marachen Polyclinic.

553. Deep-sea Trawler.

1969. Ocean Fisheries.
1949. **553.** 1 s. grey and blue .. 5 5
1950. – 1 s. green and black 5 5
1951. – 2 s. violet and black 5 5
1952. – 3 s. blue and black .. 5 5
1953. – 5 s. mauve and black 5 5
1954. – 10 s. grey and black 12 8
1955. – 13 s. flesh, orge. & blk. 15 10
1956. – 20 s. brn., ochre & blk. 30 12

DESIGNS: 1 s. (No. 1950), Cape hake. 2 s. Scad. 3 s. Pilchard. 5 s. Sea bream. 10 s. Chub-mackerel. 13 s. Salmon-bass. 20 s. Leer-fish.

554. Trapeze Act.

555. Cosmonauts and "Soyuz 6".

1969. Circus. Multicoloured.

1957. 1 s. Type **554** 5 5
1958. 2 s. Acrobats 5 5
1959. 3 s. Balancing act with hoops 5 5
1960. 5 s. Juggler, and bear on cycle 5 5
1961. 13 s. Equestrian act .. 20 8
1962. 20 s. Clowns 40 12

1970. Space Flights of "Soyuz 6, 7 and 8".

1963. **555.** 1 s. multicoloured .. 5 5
1964. – 2 s. multicoloured .. 5 5
1965. – 3 s. multicoloured .. 5 5
1966. – 28 s. pink and blue .. 40 15

DESIGNS: 2 s. Cosmonauts and "Soyuz 7". 3 s. Cosmonauts and "Soyuz 8". 28 s. Three "Soyuz" spacecraft in orbit.

556. Khan Asparerch and "Old-Bulgars" crossing the Danube, 679.

1970. History of Bulgaria. Multicoloured.

1967. 1 s. Type **556** 5 5
1968. 2 s. Khan Krum and defeat of Emperor Nicephorus, 811 .. 5 5
1969. 3 s. Conversion of Khan Boris I to Christianity, 865 .. .. .. 5 5
1970. 5 s. Tsar Simeon and Battle of Akhelo, 917 5 5
1971. 8 s. Tsar Samuel and defeat of Byzantines, 976 .. .. .. 10 5
1972. 10 s. Tsar Kaloyan and victory over Emperor Baldwin, 1205 .. 12 5
1973. 13 s. Tsar Ivan Assen II and defeat of Komnine of Epirus, 1230 .. 20 8
1974. 20 s. Coronation of Tsar Ivailo, 1277 .. .. 40 10

557. Bulgarian Pavilion.

1970. "Expo 70" World's Fair, Osaka, Japan (First Issue).

1975. **557.** 20 s. silver, yell. & brn. 40 25

558. Footballers.

1970. World Football Cup, Mexico.

1976. **558.** 1 s. multicoloured .. 5 5
1977. – 2 s. multicoloured .. 5 5
1978. – 3 s. multicoloured .. 5 5
1979. – 5 s. multicoloured .. 8 5
1980. – 20 s. multicoloured 25 10
1981. – 40 s. multicoloured 70 20

DESIGNS: 2 s. to 40 s. various football scenes.

559. Lenin. **560.** " Tephrocactus Alexanderi v. bruchi ".

1970. Lenin. Birth Cent. Multicoloured.

1983. 2 s. Type **559** 5 5
1984. 13 s. Full-face portrait .. 25 8
1985. 20 s. Lenin writing .. 30 12

1970. Flowing Cacti. Multicoloured.

1986. 1 s. Type **560** 5 5
1987. 2 s. "Opuntia drummondii" 5 5
1988. 3 s. "Hatiora cilindrica" 5 5
1989. 5 s. " Gymnocalycium vatteri " 8 5
1990. 8 s. " Heliantho cereus grandiflorus " 10 5
1991. 10 s. " Neochilenia andreaeana " 25 12
1992. 13 s. " Peireskia vargasii v. longispina " .. 40 15
1993. 20 s. "Neobesseya rosiflora" 65 25

561. Union Badge. **562.** Rose.

1970. Agricultural Union. 70th Anniv.

1994. **561.** 20 s. blk., gold & red 20 8

1970. Bulgarian Roses.

1995. **562.** 1 s. multicoloured .. 5 5
1996. – 2 s. multicoloured .. 5 5
1997. – 3 s. multicoloured .. 5 5
1998. – 4 s. multicoloured .. 5 5
1999. – 5 s. multicoloured .. 8 5
2000. – 13 s. multicoloured 15 8
2001. – 20 s. multicoloured .. 35 12
2002. – 28 s. multicoloured .. 50 20

DESIGNS: 2 s. to 28 s. various roses.

563. Gold Bowl.

1970. Gold Treasures of Thrace.

2003. **563.** 1 s. blk., blue & gold 5 5
2004. – 2 s. blk., lilac & gold 5 5
2005. – 3 s. blk., red & gold .. 5 5
2006. – 5 s. blk., green & gold 5 5
2007. – 13 s. blk., orge. & gold 25 8
2008. – 20 s. blk., violet & gold 35 12

DESIGNS: 2 s. Three small bowls. 3 s. Plain lid. 5 s. Pear shaped ornaments. 13 s. Large lid with pattern. 20 s. Vase.

564. Rose and Woman with Baskets of Produce.

1970. " Expo 70 " World's Fair, Osaka, Japan (Second issue) Multicoloured.

2009. 1 s. Type **564** 5 5
2010. 2 s. Three Dancers .. 5 5
2011. 3 s. Girl in National costume 5 5
2012. 28 s. Dancing couples .. 50 20

565. U.N. Emblem.

1970. United Nations. 25th Anniv.

2014. **565.** 20 s. gold and blue .. 30 12

566. I. Vasov.

1970. Ivan Vasov (poet). 120th Birth Anniv.

2015. **566.** 13 s. blue 25 8

567. Golden Retriever.

1970. Dogs. Multicoloured.

2016. 1 s. Type **567** 5 5
2017. 2 s. Retriever (vert.) .. 5 5
2018. 3 s. Great Dane (vert.) 5 5
2019. 4 s. Boxer (vert.) 5 5
2020. 5 s. Cocker spaniel (vert.) 5 5
2021. 13 s. Dobermann pinscher (vert.) 30 12
2022. 20 s. Scottish terrier (vert.) 45 15
2023. 28 s. Collie 50 20

568. Fireman with Hose. **569.** Congress Emblem.

1970. Fire Protection.

2024. **568.** 1 s. grey, yell. & blk. 5 5
2025. – 3 s. red, grey & blk. 5 5

DESIGN. 3 s. Fire-engine.

1970. 7th World Sociological Congress, Varna.

2026. **569.** 13 s. multicoloured .. 25 8

570. Two Male Players. **571.** Cyclists.

1970. World Volleyball Championships.

2027. **570.** 2 s. black and brown 5 5
2028. – 2 s. orge., blk. & blue 5 5
2029. – 20 s. yell., blk. & green 40 12
2030. – 20 s. green, yellow, black and blue .. 40 12

DESIGNS (No. 2028). Two female players. 20 s. (No. 2029), Male player. (No. 2030), Female player.

1970. 20th Round-Bulgaria Cycle Race.

2031. **571.** 20 s. mauve, yell. & grn. 30 12

572. Caruso and Scene from " Il Pagliacci ".

1970. Opera Singers. Multicoloured.

2032. **572.** 1 s. Type **571** .. 5 5
2033. 2 s. C. Morfova and " The Bartered Bride " 5 5
2034. 3 s. P. Raichev and " Tosca " 5 5
2035. 10 s. S. Tabakova and " The Flying Dutchman " 12 5
2036. 13 s. K. Popova and " The Masters of Nuremberg " .. 15 5
2037. 20 s. Chaliapin and " Boris Godunov " 50 12

575. Beethoven.

1970. Beethoven Birth Bicent.

2038. **573.** 28 s. blue and purple 25 8

574. Ivan Assen II Coin.

1970. Bulgarian Coins of the 14th century. Multicoloured.

2039. **574.** 1s s. Type **574** .. 5 5
2040. 2 s. Theodor Svetoslav 5 5
2041. 3 s. Mikhail Chichman 5 5
2042. 13 s. Ivan Alexander and Mikhail Assen 12 5
2043. 20 s. Ivan Stratsimir 20 8
2044. 28 s. Ivan Chichman (initials) 25 10

575. Engels. **576.** Snow Crystal.

1970. Friedrich Engels. 150th Birth Anniv.

2046. **575.** 13 s. brown and red .. 12 5

1970. New Year.

2047. **576.** 2 s. multicoloured .. 5 5

577. " Girl's Head " (Z. Spiridonov). **578.** Edelweiss Sanatorium, Borovets.

1971. Modern Bulgarian Sculpture.

2049. **577.** 1 s. violet and gold .. 5 5
2050. – 2 s. green and gold .. 5 5
2051. – 3 s. brown and gold .. 5 5
2052. – 13 s. green and gold .. 15 5
2053. – 20 s. red and gold .. 30 12
2054. – 28 s. brown and gold 40 15

SCULPTURES: 2 s. " Third Class Carriage " (I. Funev). 3 s. " Elin Pelin " (M. Markov). 13 s. " Nina " (A. Nikolov). 20 s. " Kneeling Woman " (Yavorov monument, I. Lazarov). 28 s. " Engineer " (I. Funev).

1971. Health Resorts.

2056. **578.** 1 s. green 5 5
2057. – 2 s. olive 5 5
2058. – 4 s. blue 5 5
2059. – 8 s. blue 8 5
2060. – 10 s. blue 15 5

DESIGNS: 2 s. Panorama Hotel, Pamporovo. 4 s. Yachts, Albena. 8 s. Harbour scene, Rousalka. 10 s. Shtastlivetsa Hotel, Mt. Vitosa.

579. Birds and Flowers.

1971. Spring.

2061. **579.** 1 s. multicoloured .. 5 5
2062. – 2 s. multicoloured .. 5 5
2063. – 3 s. multicoloured .. 5 5
2064. – 5 s. multicoloured .. 5 5
2065. – 13 s. multicoloured .. 15 5
2066. – 20 s. multicoloured .. 35 15

DESIGNS: 2 s. to 20 s. Various designs of birds and flowers similar to T **579**.

580. " Khan Asparuch Crossing Danube " (B. Angelushev).

1971. Bulgarian History. Paintings. Multicoloured.

2067. 2 s. Type **580** 5 5
2068. 3 s. " Ivajlo Meeting Tirnovo " (I. Petrov) .. 5 5
2069. 5 s. " Cavalry Charge, Benkovski " (P. Morosov) 10 5
2070. 8 s. ' Gen. Gurko entering Sofia, 1878 " (D. Gudjenko) 15 8
2071. 28 s. " Greeting Red Army " (S. Venov) .. 75 35

581. Running.

1971. 2nd European Indoor Track and Field Championships. Multicoloured.
2073. 2 s. Type **581** 5 5
2074. 20 s. Putting the shot .. 45 15

582. School Building.

1971. Foundation of First Bulgarian Secondary School, Bolgrad.
2075. **582.** 2 s. grn., brn. & silver 5 5
2076. – 20 s. vio., brn. & silver 35 12
DESIGN: 20 s. Prince Bogoridi, Dimitr Mutev and Sada Radulov (founders).

583. Communards.

1971. Paris Commune. Cent.
2077. **583.** 20 s. black and red .. 30 12

584. Dimitrov challenging Goering. 585. G. Rakovski.

1971. "Federation Internationale des Resistants". 20th Anniv.
2078. **584.** 2 s. multicoloured .. 5 5
2079. 13 s. multicoloured .. 30 12

1971. Georgi Rakovski (polititian and Revolutionary). 150th Birth Anniv.
2081. **585.** 13 s. brn., cream & grn. 20 8

586. Symbols of "Technical Progress".

1971. 10th Bulgarian Communist Party Congress. Multicoloured.
2082. 1 s. Worker and Banner ("People's Progress") 5 5
2083. 2 s. Type **586** 5 5
2084. 12 s. Men clasping hands ("Bulgarian-Soviet Friendship") 20 10

587. Pipkov and Music.

1971. Panayot Pipkov. Birth Cent.
2085. 587. 13 s. blk., grn. & silver 20 10

588. "Three Races". 589. Mammoth.

1971. Racial Equality Year.
2086. **588.** 13 s. multicoloured .. 20 10

1971. Prehistoric Animals. Multicoloured.
2087. 1 s. Type **589** 5 5
2088. 2 s. Bear (vert.) .. 5 5
2089. 3 s. Hipparion .. 5 5
2090. 13 s. Mastodon .. 15 8
2091. 20 s. Deinodon (vert.) 25 10
2092. 28 s. Sabre-toothed tiger 35 15

590. Facade of Ancient Building. 591. Tweezers, Magnifying Glass and "Stamp".

1971. Ancient Buildings of Koprivshtitsa.
2093. **590.** 1 s. grn., brn. & grn. 5 5
2094. – 2 s. brn., grn. & buff 5 5
2095. – 6 s. violet, brn. & blue 8 5
2096. – 13 s. red, blue & orge. 35 10
DESIGNS: 1 s. to 13 s. Different facades.

1971. 9th Congress of Bulgarian Philatelic Federation.
2097. **591.** 20 s.+10 s. brown, black and red 60 25

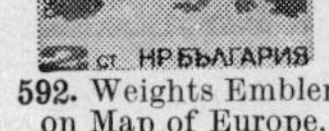

592. Weights Emblem on Map of Europe. 593. Frontier Guard and Dog.

1971. 30th European Weightlifting Championships. Sofia. Multicoloured.
2098. 2 s. Type **592** 5 5
2099. 13 s. Figures supporting weights 30 12

1971. Frontier Guards. 25th Anniv.
2100. **593.** 2 s. olive, grn. & bl.-grn. 5 5

594. Congress Meeting (sculpture).

1971. Buzlodja Congress. 80th Anniv.
2101. **594.** 2 s. grn., cream & red 8 5

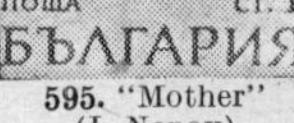

595. "Mother" (I. Nenov) 596. Factory, Polyprovadnitsi.

1971. Paintings from the National Art Gallery (1st series). Multicoloured.
2102. 1 s. Type **595** 5 5
2103. 2 s. "Lagorova" (S. Ivanov) 5 5
2104. 3 s. "Portrait of U. H." (C. Zonev) 5 5
2105. 13 s. "Portrait of a Lady" (D. Uzonov) .. 15 8
2106. 30 s. "Young Woman from Kalotina" (V. Dimitrov) 30 10
2107. 40 s. "Gorjanin" (S. Venev) 60 15

See also Nos. 2145/50.

1971. Industrial Buildings.
2108. **596.** 1 s. violet 5 5
2109. – 2 s. red 5 5
2110. – 10 s. violet 12 5
2111. – 13 s. red 15 8
2112. – 40 s. brown .. 50 15
DESIGNS—VERT. 2 s. Petro-chemical plant, Tsliben. HORIZ. 10 s. Chemical works, Vratna. 13 s. "Marine-Istok" plant, Dimitrovgrad. 40 s. Zavod electronics factory, Sofia.

597. Free Style Wrestling. 598. Posthorn Emblem

1971. European Wrestling Championships, Sofia.
2113. **597.** 2 s. grn., blk. & blue 5 5
2114. – 13 s. blk., red & blue 25 8
DESIGN: 13 s. Greco-Roman wrestling.

1971. 8th Congress of Socialist Postal Administrations.
2115. **598.** 20 s. gold and green.. 30 10

599. Entwined Ribbons.

1971. 7th European Biochemical Congress, Varna.
2116. **599.** 13 s. brown and black 25 8

600. "New Republic" Statue. 601. Cross-country Skiing.

1971. People's Republic. 25th Anniv.
2117. **600.** 2 s. red, yell. & gold 5 5
2118. – 13 s. grn., red & gold 25 10
DESIGN: 13 s. Bulgarian flag.

1971. Winter Olympic Games, Sapporo, Japan. Multicoloured.
2119. 1 s. Type **601** 5 5
2120. 2 s. Downhill skiing .. 5 5
2121. 3 s. Ski-jumping .. 5 5
2122. 4 s. Figure-skating .. 5 5
2123. 13 s. Ice-hockey .. 15 8
2124. 28 s. Slalom skiing .. 40 15

602. Brigade Members. 603. U.N.E.S.C.O. Emblem and Wreath.

1971. Youth Brigades. 25th Anniv.
2126. **602.** 2 s. blue 5 5

1971. U.N.E.S.C.O. 25th Anniv.
2127. **603.** 20 s. multicoloured 30 10

604. "The Footballer" (C. Zonev).

1971. Paintings by Cyril Zonev. Multicoloured.
2128. 1 s. Type **604** 5 5
2129. 2 s. "Landscape" (horiz.) 5 5
2130. 3 s. Self-portrait .. 5 5
2131. 13 s. "Lilies 15 8
2132. 20 s. "Woodland Scene" (horiz.) 25 10
2133. 40 s. "Portrait of a Young Woman" 60 20

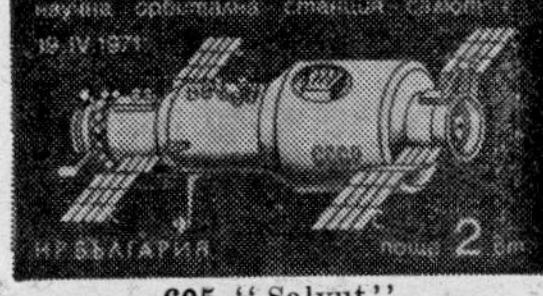

605. "Salyut".

1971. Space Flights of "Salyut" and "Soyuz 11". Multicoloured.
2134. 2 s. Type **605** 5 5
2135. 13 s. "Soyuz 11" .. 20 10
2136. 40 s. "Salyut" and "Soyuz 11" joined together .. 70 20

606. Tanker "Vihren".

1972. "One Million Tons of Bulgarian Shipping".
2138. **606.** 18 s. lilac, red & blk. 30 12

607. G. Delchev.

1972. Bulgarian Patriots' Birth Cents. Centenary year in brackets.
2139. **607.** 2 s. black and red .. 5 5
2140. – 5 s. black and green 5 5
2141. – 13 s. black and yell. 20 8
PATRIOTS: 5 s. J. Sandanski (1972). 13 s. D. Gruev (1971).

608. Gymnast with Ball.

1972. World Gymnastics Championships, Havana (Cuba). Multicoloured.
2142. 13 s. Type **608** 25 8
2143. 18 s. Gymnast with hoop 35 12

1972. Paintings in Bulgarian National Gallery (2nd series. As Type **595**. Multicoloured.
2145. 1 s. "Melnik" (Mladenov) (vert.) 5 5
2146. 2 s. "Ploughman" (Georgiev) (vert.) 5 5
2147. 3 s. "By the Death-bed" (Djendov) (horiz.) .. 5 5
2148. 13 s. "Family" (Dimitrov) (horiz.) .. 12 8
2149. 20 s. "Family" (Balkasnki) (vert.) 25 12
2150. 40 s. "Paisi" (Denchev) (vert.) 50 20
SIZES—VERT. 32 × 47 mm. HORIZ. 47 × 32 mm.

609. Worker. 610. "Singing Harvesters" (V. Dimitrov).

1972. 7th Bulgarian Trade Unions' Congress.
2151. **609.** 13 s. multicoloured .. 20 8

1972. Vladimir Dimitrov (painter). 90th Birth Anniv. Multicoloured.

2152. 1 s. Type 610 .. 5 5
2153. 2 s. "Farm Worker" .. 5 5
2154. 3 s. "Women Cultivators" (horiz.) .. 5 5
2155. 13 s. "Peasant Girl" (horiz.) 15 8
2156. 20 s. "My Mother" .. 25 10
2157. 40 s. Self-portrait .. 60 20

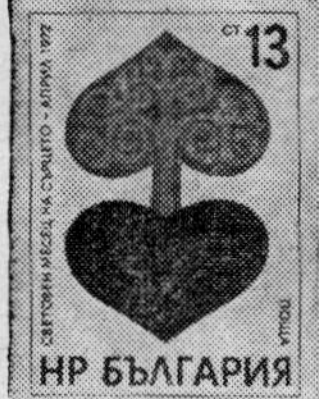

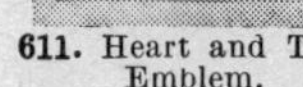

611. Heart and Tree Emblem. **612.** St. Mark's Cathedral.

1972. World Heart Month.

2158. **611.** 13 s. multicoloured .. 25 10

1972. U.N.E.S.C.O. "Save Venice" Campaign.

2159. **612.** 2 s. grn., bl.-grn. & bl. 5 5
2160. – 13 s. brn., violet & grn. 25 10

DESIGN: 13 s. Doge's Palace.

613. Dimitrov and Printing-press.

1972. Georgi Dimitrov (statesman). 90th Birth Anniv. Multicoloured.

2161. 1 s. Type 613 .. .. 5 5
2162. 2 s. Dimitrov leading uprising of 1923 .. .. 5 5
2163. 3 s. Dimitrov at Leipzig Trial 5 5
2164. 5 s. Dimitrov addressing workers 5 5
2165. 13 s. Dimitrov with Bulgarian crowd .. 15 8
2166. 18 s. Addressing young people 25 8
2167. 28 s. Dimitrov with children 35 15
2168. 40 s. Dimitrov's mausoleum 75 20
2169. 80 s. Portrait head (green and gold) .. .. 1·75 45
2173. 80 s. As No. 2169 .. 3·25 1·00

No. 2173 has the centre in red and gold, and is imperforate.

614. "Lamp of Learning" and Quotation.

1972. Father Paissi (monastic historian). 250th Birth Anniv.

2171. **614.** 2 s. brn., grn. & gold 5 5
2172. – 13 s. brn., grn. & gold 25 12

DESIGN: 13 s. Paissi writing.

615. Canoeing.

1972. Olympic Games, Munich. Mult.

2174. 1 s. Type 615 .. .. 5 5
2175. 2 s. Gymnastics 5 5
2176. 3 s. Swimming 5 5
2177. 13 s. Volleyball 15 8
2178. 18 s. Hurdling 20 12
2179. 40 s. Wrestling 60 20

616. A. Kanchev.

1972. Angel Kanchev (patriot). Death Cent.

2181. **616.** 2 s. mar., gold & pur. 5 5

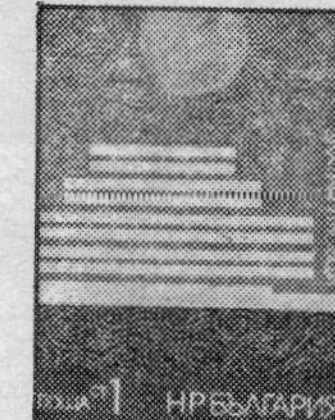

617. Zlatni Piasatzi.

1972. Black Sea Resorts. Hotels. Multicoloured.

2182. – 1 s. Type 617 .. 5 5
2183. – 2 s. Drujba 5 5
2184. – 3 s. Slanchev Briag .. 5 5
2185. – 13 s. Primorsko .. 15 8
2186. – 28 s. Rusalka .. 40 15
2187. – 40 s. Albena 60 20

618. Canoeing (Bronze Medal).

1972. Olympic Games, Munich (2nd series). Medals and Sports. Multicoloured.

2188. – 1 s. Type 618 .. 5 5
2189. – 2 s. Long jumping (Silver Medal) .. 5 5
2190. – 3 s. Boxing (Gold Medal) 5 5
2191. – 18 s. Wrestling (Gold Medal) 20 12
2192. – 40 s. Weightlifting (Gold Medal) .. 55 25

619. S. Dimitrov.

621. "Lilium rhodopaeum".

620. Commemorative Text.

1972. Freedom Fighters. Multicoloured.

2193. 1 s. Type 619 .. .. 5 5
2194. 2 s. T. Radoinov 5 5
2195. 3 s. J. Lutibrodsky .. 5 5
2196. 5 s. M. Ganev 8 8
2197. 13 s. N. Nikolov .. 20 8

1972. U.S.S.R. 50th Anniv.

2198. **620.** 13 s. red, yellow & gold 15 8

1972. Protected Flowers. Multicoloured.

2199. 1 s. Type 621 .. .. 5 5
2200. 2 s. "Gentiana pneumonanthe" .. 5 5
2201. 3 s. "Pancratium maritimum" 5 5
2202. 4 s. "Trollius europaeus" 5 5
2203. 18 s. "Primula frondosa" 15 10
2204. 23 s. "Pulsatilla vernalis" .. 25 15
2205. 40 s. "Fritillaria stribrnyi" .. 50 25

(**622.**) **623.** Forehead Ornament. (19th-century).

1972. "Olympic Glory", Munich. No. 2192 optd. with T **622**.

2206. 40 s. brn., green and gold 60 25

1972. Antique Ornaments.

2208. **623.** 1 s. black and brown 5 5
2209. – 2 s. black and green 5 5
2210. – 3 s. black and blue .. 5 5
2211. – 8 s. black and red .. 10 8
2212. – 23 s. black and brown 30 15
2213. – 40 s. black and violet 70 30

DESIGNS: 2 s. Belt-buckle (19th-century). 3 s. Amulet (18th-century). 8 s. Pendant (18th-century). 23 s. Earrings (14th-century). 40 s. Necklace (18th-century).

624. Divers with Cameras.

1973. Underwater Research in the Black Sea.

2214. **624.** 1 s. blk., yellow & blue 5 5
2215. – 2 s. blk., yellow & blue 5 5
2216. – 18 s. blk., yell. & blue 25 15
2217. – 40 s. blk., yell. & blue 80 25

DESIGNS—HORIZ. 2 s. Divers with underwater laboratory, "Shelf 1". VERT. 18 s. Divers and "NIV 100" underwater camera. 40 s. Lifting balloon.

625. Vasil Levski (G. Danchev).

626. Elhovo Mask.

1973. Vasil Levski (patriot). Death Cent.

2219. – 2 s. green and red .. 5 5
2220. **625.** 20 s. brn., cream & grn. 55 15

DESIGN: 2 s. "The Hanging of Vasil Levski" (B. Angelushev).

1973. Koukeris' Festival Masks. Mult.

2221. 1 a. Type 626 .. .. 5 5
2222. 2 s. Breznik 5 5
2223. 3 s. Hisar 5 5
2224. 13 s. Radomir 20 10
2225. 20 s. Karnobat 25 15
2226. 40 s. Pernik .. .. 1·60 1·10

627. Copernicus.

628. Vietnamese "Working-girl".

1973. Copernicus. 500th Birth Anniv.

2227. **627.** 28 s. pur., blk. & brn. 45 20

1973. "Peace in Vietnam".

2229. **628.** 18 s. multicoloured .. 25 12

629. Poppy.

630. C. Botev (T. Todorov).

1973. Wild Flowers. Multicoloured.

2231. 1 s. Type 629 .. .. 5 5
2232. 2 s. Marguerite 5 5
2233. 3 s. Peony 5 5
2234. 13 s. Centaury .. 15 10
2235. 18 s. Corn-cockle .. 80 60
2236. 28 s. Ranunculas .. 60 25

1973. Christo Botov. 150th Birth Anniv.

2237. **630.** 2 s. yellow, brown and green 15 5
2238. 18 s. green, pale green and brown 30 20

631. Asen Halachev and insurgents.

1973. June Uprising. 50th Anniv.

2239. **631.** 1 s. blk., red and gold 5 5
2240. – 2 s. blk., orge. & gold 5 5

DESIGNS: 2 s. Crawling Worker, ("September", B. Angelushev).

632. A. Stamboliisky (from sculpture by A. Nikolov).

1973. Alexander Stamboliisky. 50th Death Anniv.

2241. **632.** 18 s. light-brown, brown and orange 40 25
2242. 18 s. bright orange .. 40 25

633. Musk-rat.

1973. Bulgarian Fauna. Multicoloured.

2243. 1 s. Type 633 .. .. 5 5
2244. 2 s. Raccoon-dog .. 5 5
2245. 3 s. Moufflon (vert.) .. 5 5
2246. 12 s. Fallow deer (vert.) 15 10
2247. 18 s. European Bison .. 25 15
2248. 40 s. Elk .. .. .. 1·25 90

634. Tirnova.

636. Congress Emblem.

635. Insurgents on the March (B. Angelushev).

1973. Air. Tourism. Views of Bulgarian Towns and Cities. Multicoloured.

2249. 2 s. Type 634 .. .. 5 5
2250. 13 s. Rusalka 15 8
2251. 20 s. Plovdiv 65 40
2252. 28 s. Sofia 40 25

1973. September Uprising. 50th Anniv.

2253. **635.** 2 s. multicoloured .. 5 5
2254. 5 s. violet, pink & lake 8 5
2255. 13 s. multicoloured .. 15 12
2256. 18 s. olive, cream & lake 50 30

1973. 8th World Trade Union Congress, Varna.

2257. **636.** 2 s. multicoloured. .. 8 5

DESIGNS—HORIZ. 5 s. "Armed Train" (B. Angelushev). VERT. 13 s. Patriotic poster by N. Mirtchev. HORIZ. 18 s. Georgi Dimitrov and Vasil Kolarov.

637. " Sun " Emblem and Olympic Rings.

638. "Prince Kalojan"

1973. Olympic Congress, Varna. Mult.

2258. 13 s. Type **637** 40 25
2259. 28 s. Lion Emblem of Bulgarian Olympic Committee (vert.) 55 35

1973. Fresco Portraits, Bonjano Church. Multicoloured.

2261. 1 s. Type **638** 5 5
2262. 2 s. " Desislava " .. 5 5
2263. 3 s. " Saint " 5 5
2264. 5 s. " St. Eustratius " .. 5 5
2265. 10 s. " Tsar Constantine-Assen " 12 5
2266. 13 s. " Deacon Laurentius " 15 8
2267. 18 s. " Virgin Mary " .. 20 12
2268. 20 s. " St. Ephraim " .. 25 15
2269. 28 s. " Jesus Christ " .. 50 20

639. Smirnenski and Cavalry Charge.

1973. Christo Smirnenski (poet and revolutionary). 75th Birth Anniv.

2271. **639.** 1 s. blue, red and gold 5 5
2272. 2 s. blue, red and gold 5 5

640. Human Rights Emblem.

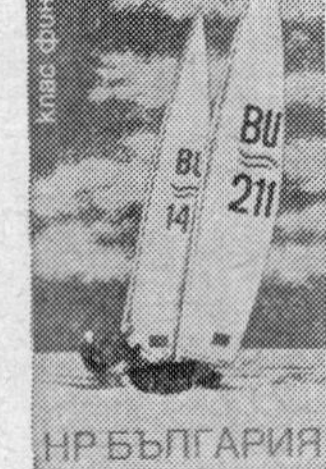

642. " Finn " Class Yacht.

641. Tsar Todor Svetoslav meeting the Byzantine Embassy, 1307.

1973. Declaration of Human Rights. 25th Anniv.

2273. **640.** 13 s. gold, red and blue 20 12

1973. Bulgarian History. Multicoloured.

2274. – 1 s. Type **641** .. 5 5
2275. – 2 s. Tsar Mihail Shishman in battle against Byzantines, 1328 .. 5 5
2276. – 3 s. Battle of Rosokastro, 1332, and Tsar, Ivan Alexander .. 5 5
2277. – 4 s. Defence of Tirnovo, 1393 and Patriarch Evtimi 5 5
2278. – 5 s. Tsar Ivan Shishaman's attack on the Turks 5 5
2279. – 13 s. Momchil attacks Turkish ships at Umur, 1344 .. .. 15 8
2280. – 18 s. Meeting of Tsar Ivan Strabzimir and Crussaders, 1396 .. 20 10
2281. – 28 s. Embassy of Empress Anne of Savoy meets Boyar Balik .. 35 20

HAVE YOU READ THE NOTES AT THE BEGINNING OF THIS CATALOGUE?

These often provide answers to the enquiries we receive.

1973. Sailing. Various Yachts. Multicoloured.

2282. 1 s. Type **642** 5 5
2283. 2 s. " Flying Dutchman " class 5 5
2284. 3 s. " Soling " class .. 5 5
2285. 13 s. " Tempest " class 15 8
2286. 20 s. " 470 " class .. 25 12
2287. 40 s. " Tornado " class .. 1·10 75

643. " Balchik " (B. Obreshkov).

1973. National Art Gallery, Sofia. 25th Anniv. and Stanislav Dospevski (painter). 150th Birth Anniv. Multicoloured.

2288. 1 s. Type **643** 5 5
2289. 2 s. " Mother and Child " (S. Venev) 5 5
2290. 3 s. " Rest " (T. Boyadjiev) 5 5
2291. 13 s. " Vase with Flowers " (S. Skitnik) (vert.) .. 15 8
2292. 18 s. " Mery Kaneva " (I. Petrov) (vert.) 20 12
2293. 40 s. " Winter in Plovdiv " (Z. Boyadjiev) (vert) .. 50 25

644. Old Testament Scene (Wood-carving). 646. Social Economic Integration Emblem.

645. " Lenin " (N. Mirtchev).

1974. Wood-Carvings from Rogen Monastery.

2296. – 1 s. dark brn., cream and brown .. 5 5
2297. **644.** 2 s. dark brown, cream and brown .. 5 5
2298. – 3 s. dark brown, cream and brown .. 5 5
2299. – 5 s. olive, cream & grn. 10 8
2300. – 8 s. olive, cream & grn. 15 12
2301. – 13 s. brn., cream and chestnut 25 20
2302. – 28 s. brn., cream and chestnut 65 40

DESIGNS: No. 2296/8, " Passover Table ". No. 2299/2300, " Abraham and the Angel ". No. 2301/2. " The Expulsion from Eden ". Nos. 2296/8, 2299/300 and 2301/2 form three composite designs.

1974. Lenin. 50th Death Anniv. Mult.

2303. 2 s. Type **645** 5 5
2304. 18 s. " Lenin with Workers " (W. A. Serov) 45 15

1974. D. Blagoev (founder of Bulgarian Communist Party). 50th Death Anniv. As Type **645**. Multicoloured.

2305. 2 s. "Blagoev addressing Meeting" (G. Kovachev) 5 5

1974. Council for Mutual Economic Aid. 25th Anniv.

2306. **646.** 13 s. multicoloured .. 15 10

647. Sheep.

1974. Domestic Animals.

2307. **647.** 1 s. brn., buff & grn. .. 5 5
2308. – 2 s. pur., vio. & red .. 5 5
2309. – 3 s. brn., pink & grn. 5 5
2310. – 5 s. brn., buff & blue 5 5
2311. – 13 s. blk., bl. & brn. .. 15 10
2312. – 20 s. brn., pink & blue 45 20

DESIGNS: 2. s. Goat. 3 s. Pig. 5 s. Cow. 13 s. Buffalo. 20 s. Horse.

648. Footballers.

1974. World Cup Football Championships.

2313. **648.** 1 s. multicoloured .. 5 5
2314. – 2 s. multicoloured .. 5 5
2315. – 3 s. multicoloured .. 5 5
2316. – 13 s. multicoloured .. 15 10
2317. – 28 s. multicoloured .. 35 20
2318. – 40 s. multicoloured .. 95 45

DESIGNS: Nos. 2314/18, various designs similar to T **648**.

649. Folk-singers.

650. "Cosmic Research".

1974. Amateur Arts and Sports Festival. Multicoloured.

2320. 1 s. Type **649** 5 5
2321. 2 s. Folk-dancers .. 5 5
2322. 3 s. Piper and drummer 5 5
2323. 5 s. Wrestling 5 5
2324. 13 s. Athletics 40 25
2325. 18 s. Gymnastics .. 25 12

1974. Youth Stamp Exhibition. Multicoloured.

2326. 1 s. Type **650** 5 5
2327. 2 s. " Salt Production " (M. Bliznakaa) .. 5 5
2328. 3 s. " Fire-dancer " (D. Lalova) 5 5
2329. 28 s. " Friendship " (V. Bojanova) 50 35

651. Motor-cars.

1974. World Automobile Federation's Spring Congress, Sofia.

2331. **651.** 13 s. multicoloured .. 15 10

652. Period Architecture.

1974. U.N.E.S.C.O. Executive Council's 94th Session, Varna.

2332. **652.** 18 s. multicoloured .. 20 12

653. Chinese Aster.

1974. Bulgarian Flowers. Multicoloured.

2333. 1 s. Type **653** 5 5
2334. 2 s. Mallow 5 5
2335. 3 s. Columbine 5 5
2336. 18 s. Tulip 20 12
2337. 20 s. Marigold 25 12
2338. 28 s. Pansy 65 12

654. Postilion.

1974. Universal Postal Union. Cent.

2340. **654.** 2 s. vio. & blk. on orge. 5 5
2341. – 18 s. grn. & blk. on orge. 35 20

DESIGN: 18 s. First Bulgarian mail-coach.

655. Young Pioneer and Komsomol Girl.

656. Communist soldiers with Flag.

1974. Dimitrov's "Septemvriiche" Pioneer Organization. 30th Anniv. Multicoloured.

2343. 1 s. Type **655** 5 5
2344. 2 s. Pioneer with doves 5 5

1974. Bulgarian People's Republic. 30th Anniv. Multicoloured.

2346. 1 s. Type **656** 5 5
2347. 2 s. "Soviet Liberators" 5 5
2348. 5 s. "Industrialisation" 5 5
2349. 13 s. "Modern Agriculture" 15 10
2350. 18 s. "Science and Technology" 30 12

657. Gymnast on Beam.

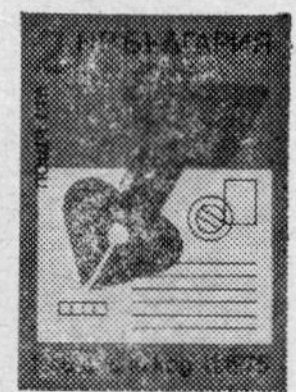

658. Envelope with arrow pointing to Postal Code.

1974. World Gymnastic Championships, Varna. Multicoloured.

2352. 2 s. Type **657** 5 5
2353. 13 s. Gymnast on horse .. 20 12

1974. Introduction of Postal Coding System (1 January, 1975).

2355. **658.** 2 s. green, orge. & blk. 5 5

659. " Sourovachka " (twig decorated with coloured ribbons).

1974. New Year.

2356. **659.** 2 s. multicoloured .. 5 5

660. Ikon of St. Theodore. 661. Apricot.

1974. Bulgarian History.

2357. **660.** 1 s. multicoloured .. 5 5
2358. 2 s. grey, mve. & blk. 5 5
2359. 3 s. grey, blue & blk. 5 5
2360. 5 s. grey, lilac & blk. 5 5
2361. 8 s. black, buff & brn. 5 8
2362. 13 s. grey, grn. & blk. 12 8
2363. 18 s. blk., gold & red 20 12
2364. 28 s. grey, blue & blk. 35 25

DESIGNS: 2 s. Bronze medallion. 3 s. Carved capital. 5 s. Silver bowl of Sivin Jupan. 8 s. Clay goblet. 13 s. Lioness (torso). 18 s. Gold tray. 28 s. Double-headed eagle.

1975. Fruit-tree Blossoms. Multicoloured.

2365. 1 s. Type **661** 5 5
2366. 2 s. Apple 5 5
2367. 3 s. Cherry 5 5
2368. 19 s. Pear 20 12
2369. 28 s. Peach 35 25

662. Star and Arrow.

663. " Weights and Measures ".

1975. May 9th Victory. 30th Anniv.
2372. **662.** 2 s. red, blk. & brn... 5 5
2373. – 13 s. blk., brn. & blue 20 10
DESIGNS: 13 s. Peace dove and broken sword.

1975. Metre Convention. Cent.
2374. **663.** 13 s. vio., blk. & silver 20 10

664. Tree and Open Book.

1975. Forestry School. 50th Anniv.
2375. **664.** 2 s. multicolour d .. 5 5

665. Michelangelo.

666. Festival Emblem.

1975. Michelangelo. 500th Birth Anniv.
2376. **665.** 2 s. purple and blue 5 5
2377. – 13 s. vio. & purple .. 15 8
2378. – 18 s. brown & green 20 10
DESIGNS—HORIZ. 13 s., 18 s. Roof sculptures.

1975. Festival of Humour and Satire, Gabrovo.
2380. **666.** 2 s. multicoloured .. 5 5

667. Woman's Head.

1975. International Women's Year.
2381. **667.** 13 s. multicoloured .. 15 8

668. Nikolov and Sava Kokarechkov.

1975. " Young Martyrs to Fascism ".
2382. **668.** 1 s. black, green & gold .. 5 5
2383. 2 s. black, mauve & gold 5 5
2384. 5 s. black, red and gold 5 5
2385. 13 s. black, blue and gold 15 8
DESIGNS—HORIZ: 2 s. Mitko Palaouzov and Ivan Vassilev. 5 s. Nicolas Nakev and Stevtcho Kraychev. 13 c. Ivanka Pachkolouva and Detelina Mintcheva.

INDEX

Countries can be quickly located by referring to the index at the end of this volume.

669. " Mother feeding Child."
670. Gabrovo Costume.

1975. World Graphics Exhibition, Sofia Celebrated Drawings and Engravings. Mult.
2386. 1 s. Type **669** 5 5
2387. 2 s. " Mourning a Dead Daughter " (Goya) .. 5 5
2388. 3 s. " The Reunion " (Bemkov) 5 5
2389. 13 s. " Seated Nude " (Renoir) 20 10
2390. 20 s. " Man in a Fur Hat " (Rembrandt) 30 10
2391. 40 s. " The Dream " (Daumier) (horiz.) 45 15

1975. Women's Regional Costumes. Mult.
2393. 2 s Type **670** 5 5
2394. 3 s. Trin Costume .. 5 5
2395. 5 s. Vidin Costume .. 5 5
2396. 13 s. Gotze Deltchev Costume 15 8
2397. 18 s. Rousse Costume .. 20 10

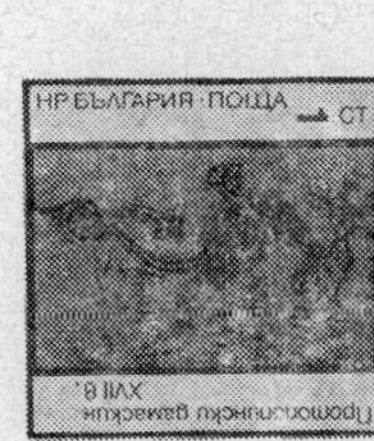

671. " Bird " (manuscript illumination).
672. Ivan Vasov.

1975. Original Bulgarian Manuscripts. Multicoloured.
2398. 1 s. Type **671** 5 5
2399. 2 2. " Head " 5 5
2400. 3 s. Abstract design .. 5 5
2401. 8 s. " Pointing finger " .. 8 5
2402. 13 s. " Imaginary creature " 15 8
2403. 18 s. Abstract design .. 20 12

1975. Ivan Vasov (writer). 125th Birth Anniv. Multicoloured.
2404. 2 s. Type **672** 5 5
2405. 13 s. Vasov seated .. 15 10

673. " Soyuz " and Leonov.

1975. " Apollo-Soyuz " Space Link. Multicoloured.
2406. 13 s. Type **673** 15 10
2407. 18 s. " Apollo " and Stafford 20 12
2408. 28 s. Linking manoeuvre 35 15

674. Boat, Map and Emblems.

1975. International Exposition, Okinawa.
241·. ·74. 13 s. multicoloured .. 15 8

675. St. Cyril and St. Methodius.
676. Footballer.

1975. " Balkanphila V " Stamp Exhibition, Sofia.
2411. **675.** 2 s. brn., lt. brn. & red 5 5
2412. – 13 s. brn., lt. brn. & grn. 15 8
DESIGN: 13 s. St. Constantine and St. Helene.

1975. 8th Inter-Toto (Football Pools) Congress, Varna.
2414. **676.** 2 s. multicoloured .. 5 5

677. " Acherontia atropos ".

1975. Moths. Multicoloured.
2415. 1 s. Type **677** 5 5
2416. 2 s. " Daphnis neri " .. 5 5
2417. 3 s. " Smerinthus ocellata " 5 5
2418. 10 s. " Deilaphila nicea " 12 5
2419. 13 s. " Choerocampa elpenor " 15 8
2420. 18 s. " Macroglossum fuciformis " .. 20 10

678. U. N. Emblem.
679. D. Hristov.

1975. United Nations Organization. 30th Anniv.
2421. **678.** 13 s. red, brn. & blk. 15 8

1975. Dobri Hristov (composer). Birth Cent.
2422. **679.** 5 s. brn., yell. & grn. 5 5

680. Constantine's Rebellion against the Turks.

1975. Bulgarian History. Multicoloured.
2423. 1 s. Type **680** 5 5
2424. 2 s. Vladislav III's campaign 5 5
2425. 3 s. Battle of Turnova .. 5 5
2426. 10 s. Battle of Liprovsko 10 5
2427. 13 s. 17th-Century Partisans 15 8
2428. 18 s. Return of banished peasants 20 10

681. European Map on Peace Dove.

1975. European Security and Co-operation Conference, Helsinki.
2429. **681.** 18 s. lilac, blue & yell. 20 15

682. " First Aid ".

1975. Bulgarian Red Cross. 90th Anniv.
2430. **682.** 2 s. brn., blk. and red 5 5
2131. – 13 s. grn., blk. & red 15 8
DESIGN: 13 s. " Peace and international Co-operation ".

683. Egyptian Galley.

1975. Ancient Ships. Multicoloured.
2432. 1 s. Type **683** 5 5
2433. 2 s. Phoenician galley .. 5 5
2434. 3 s. Greek trireme .. 5 5
2435. 5 s. Roman galley .. 5 5
2436. 13 s. Viking long-ship .. 15 8
2437. 18 s. Venetian galley .. 20 10

684. Ethnographical Museum, Plovidiv.

1975. European Architectural Heritage Year.
2438. **684.** 80 s. brn., yell. & grn. 90 90

685. Christmas Lanterns.

1975. Christmas and New Year. Multicoloured.
2439. 2 s. Type **685** 5 5
2440. 13 s. Stylised peace dove 15 8

686. Modern Articulated Tram-car.

1976. Sofia Tramways. 75th Anniv. Mult.
2441. 2 s. Type **686** 5 5
2442. 13 s. Early 20th-Century tram-car 12 5

687. Skiing.

1976. Winter Olympic Games, Innsbruck. Multicoloured.
2443. 1 s. Type **687** 5 5
2444. 2 s. Cross-country skiing (vert.) 5 5
2445. 2 s. Ski-jumping .. 5 5
2446. 13 s. Ski-trekking (vert.) 15 5
2447. 18 s. Ice-hockey (vert.) .. 20 8
2448. 18 s. Speed-skating (vert.) 25 15

688. Stylised Bird.

1976. 11th Bulgarian Communists Party Congress. Multicoloured.
2450. 2 s. Type **688** 5 5
2451. 5 s. " 1956-1976, Fulfilment of the Five Year Plans " 5 5
2452. 13 s. Hammer and Sickle 15 5

689. Swan.

1976. Waterfowl. Multicoloured.
2454. 1 s. Type **689** 5 5
2455. 2 s. Ruddy Shelduck .. 5 5
2456. 3 s. Shelduck 5 5
2457. 5 s. Garganey 5 5
2458. 13 s. Mallard 15 5
2459. 18 s. Red-crested Pochard 20 8

690. Alexander Graham Bell and early Telephone. **692.** New Industrial Building Complex.

691. Guerillas' Briefing.

1976. Telephone Centenary.
2460. **690.** 18 s. light brown, brown and purple .. 20 8

1976. 1876 Uprising. Cent. Multicoloured.
2461. 1 s. Type **691** 5 5
2462. 2 s. Peasants briefing .. 5 5
2463. 5 s. Krishina, horse and guard 5 5
2464. 13 s. Rebels with cannon 15 5

1976. Modern Industrial Installations.
2465. **692.** 5 s. green 5 5
2466. – 8 s. red 8 5
2467. – 10 s. green 10 5
2468. – 13 s. violet 15 8
2469. – 20 s. green 20 10
DESIGNS: 8 s. Factory. 10 s. Office block. 13 s. Chemical works. 20 s. Saw-mill.

693. Guard with Patrol-dog.

1976. Border Guards. 30th Anniv. Multicoloured.
2470. 2 s. Type **693** 5 5
2471. 13 s. Mounted guards .. 15 8

694. Worker with Spade. **695.** Christo Botev.

1976. Young Workers.
2472. **694.** 2 s. multicoloured .. 5 5

1976. Christo Botev (poet). Death Cent.
2473. **695.** 13 s. green and brown 15 8

MORE DETAILED LISTS

are given in the Stanley Gibbons Catalogues referred to in the country headings:

BC British Commonwealth
E1, E2, E3 Europe 1, 2, 3
O1, O2, O3, O4 Overseas 1, 2, 3, 4

696. " Martyrs of First Congress ". (relief) **697.** Dimitar Blagoev.

1976. 1st Congress of the Bulgarian Social-Democratic Party. 85th Anniv. Multicoloured.
2474. 2 s. Type **696** 5 5
2475. 5 s. Modern memorial, Busladya Peak .. 5 5

1976. Dimitar Blagoev (socialist). 120th Birth Anniv.
2476. **697.** 13 s. black, red & gold 15 8

698. Children Playing.

1976. Child Welfare.
2478. 1 s. multicoloured .. 5 5
2479. 2 s. multicoloured .. 5 5
2480. 5 s. multicoloured .. 5 5
2481. 23 s. multicoloured .. 25 12

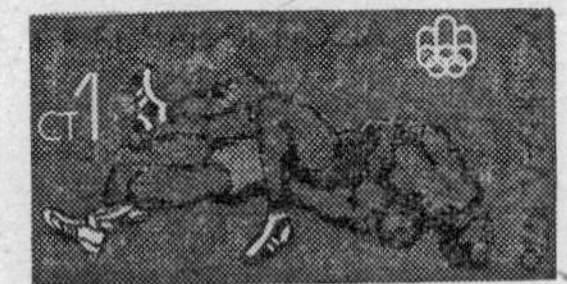

699. Wrestling.

1976. Olympic Games, Montreal. Multicoloured.
2482. 1 s. Type **699** 5 5
2483. 2 s. Boxing 5 5
2484. 3 s. Weight-lifting .. 5 5
2485. 13 s. Canoeing 15 8
2486. 18 s. Gymnastics .. 15 8
2487. 28 s. Diving 30 15
2488. 40 s. Athletics 40 20
Nos. 2483/8 are vert.

700. Belt Buckle, Virin.

1976. Thracian Art (8th-4th-Century BC). Multicoloured.
2490. 1 s. Type **700** 5 5
2491. 2 s. Brooch, Darjanitza 5 5
2492. 3 s. Mirror handle, Tchukarka 5 5
2493. 5 s. Helmet cheek guard, Garlo 5 5
2494. 13 s. Gold decoration, Orizovo 15 8
2495. 18 s. Decorated horse-harness 15 8
2496. 20 s. Greave, Mogilanska Mogila 20 10
2497. 28 s. Pendant, Bukyovitzi 30 15

701. " Partisans at Night " (Petrov).

1976. Paintings by Irya Petrov and Stanko Davrelov from the National Gallery. Multicoloured.
2498. 2 s. Type **701** 5 5
2499. 5 s. " Townscape " (Davrelov) 5 5
2500. 13 s. " Seated Woman " (Petrov) 15 8
2501. 18 s. " Boy seated in chair " (Petrov) .. 15 8
2502. 28 s. " The Visit " (Davrelov) 30 15
The 18 s. and 28 s. are vert.

EXPRESS STAMPS

E 1. Express Delivery Van.

DESIGNS—VERT. 5 l. 20 l. Bicycle messenger. 7 l. Motorcyclist and sidecar.

1939.
E 429. – 5 l. blue 40 12
E 430. E 1. 6 l. brown 15 12
E 431. – 7 l. brown 30 12
E 432. E 1. 8 l. red 35 15
E 433. – 20 l. red 70 40

OFFICIAL STAMPS

O 1. O 2.

1942.
O 507. O 1. 10 s. green 5 5
O 508. 30 s. orange .. 5 5
O 509. 50 s. brown .. 5 5
O 510. – 1 l. blue 5 5
O 511. – 2 l. green 5 5
O 534. – 2 l orange 5 5
O 512. – 3 l. mauve 5 5
O 513. – 4 l. pink 5 5
O 514. – 5 l. red 5 5
The 1 l. to 5 l. are larger (19×23 mm.)

1945. Arms designs. Imperf. or perf.
O 580. – 1 l. mauve 5 5
O 581. O 2. 2 l. green 5 5
O 582. – 3 l. brown 5 5
O 583. – 4 l. blue 5 5
O 584. – 5 l. claret 5 5

PARCEL POST STAMPS

P 1. Weighing Machine. P 2. Loading Motor Lorry.

1941.
P 494. P 1. 1 l. green 5 5
P 495. A. 2 l. red 5 5
P 496 P 2. 3 l. brown 5 5
P 497. B. 4 l. orange 5 5
P 498. P 1. 5 l. blue 5 5
P 506. 5 l. green 5 5
P 499. B. 6 l. purple 5 5
P 507. 6 l. brown 5 5
P 500. P 1. 7 l. blue 5 5
P 508. 7 l. sepia 5 5
P 501. P 2. 8 l. blue-green .. 5 5
P 509. 8 l. grey-green .. 5 5
P 502. A. 9 l. olive 5 5
P 503. B. 10 l. orange 8 5
P 504. P 2. 20 l. violet 12 5
P 513. A. 30 l. black 25 5
DESIGNS—HORIZ. A. Loading mail coach. B. Motor-cycle combination.

P 3.

ILLUSTRATIONS
British Commonwealth and all overprints and surcharges are FULL SIZE. Foreign Countries have been reduced to ¾-LINEAR.

1944. Imperf.
P 532. P 3. 1 l. red 5 5
P 533. 3 l. green 5 5
P 534. 5 l. green 5 5
P 535. 7 l. mauve 5 5
P 536. 10 l. blue 5 5
P 537. 20 l. brown 8 5
P 538. 30 l. purple.. .. 10 5
P 539. 50 l. orange .. 20 12
P 540. 100 l. blue .. 45 15

POSTAGE DUE STAMPS

D 1. D 2. D 3.

1884. Perf.
D 53. D 1. 5 s. orange .. .. 4·25 60
D 54. 25 s. lake .. .. 2·50 1·10
D 55. 50 s. blue .. .. 1·50 1·10

1886. Imperf.
D 50. D 1. 5 s. orange .. .. 55·00 2·10
D 51. 25 s. lake .. .. 65·00 2·10
D 52a. 50 s. blue .. .. 2·50 1·75

1893. Surch. with bar and **30.**
D 78. D 1. 30 s. on 50 s. bl. (perf.) 4·00 1·75
D 79. 30 s. on 50 s. blue (imperf.) .. .. 3·75 1·75

1896. Perf.
D 83. D 2. 5 s. orange .. .. 1·25 25
D 84. 10 s. violet .. .. 1·25 30
D 85. 30 s. green .. .. 1·75 25

1901.
D 124. D 3. 5 s. red 10 8
D 125. 10 s. green 30 8
D 126. 20 s. blue .. .. 2·00 10
D 127. 30 s. claret 25 15
D 128. 50 s orange .. .. 3·75 2·75

D 4. D 5.

1915.
D 181. D 4. 5 s green 10 8
D 201. 10 s. violet 8 5
D 202. 20 s. red 8 5
D 222. 20 s. orange 10 5
D 203. 30 s. orange 80 80
D 204. 50 s. blue 8 5
D 224. 1 l. green 10 5
D 225. 2 l. red 10 5
D 226. 3 l. brown 12 5

1932.
D 326. D 5. 1 l. bistre 30 25
D 327. 2 l. red 30 25
D 328. 6 l. purple 95 35

D 6. D 7. D 8.

1933.
D 333. D 6. 20 s. sepia 5 5
D 334. 40 s. blue 5 5
D 335. 80 s. red 5 5
D 336. D 7. 1 l. brown 5 5
D 337. 2 l. olive 5 5
D 338. 6 l. violet 10 8
D 339. 14 l. blue 15 10

1947. As Type D 7, but larger (18×24 mm.).
D 646. D 7. 1 l. brown 5 5
D 647. 2 l. claret 5 5
D 648. 8 l. orange 8 5
D 649. 20 l. blue 10 8

1951.
D 849. D 8. 1 l. chocolate .. 5 5
D 850. 2 l. maroon.. .. 5 5
D 851. 8 l. orange 10 8
D 852 20 l. blue 30 20

HAVE YOU READ THE NOTES AT THE BEGINNING OF THIS CATALOGUE?

These often provide answers to the enquiries we receive.

BULGARIAN OCCUPATION OF RUMANIA E3

(DOBRUDJA DISTRICT)

Поща въ Ромъния 1916—1917

(1.)

1916. Bulgarian stamps of 1911 optd. with T **1.**

No.	Type	Description	Unused	Used
1.	9.	1 s. slate	5	5
2.	–	5 s. purple and green	40	20
3.	–	10 s. sepia and brown	60	20
4.	–	25 s. black and blue	5	5

BUNDI BC

A state of Rajasthan, India. Now uses Indian stamps.

1. Native Dagger.

2. Maharao Raja Sir Raghubir Singh.

1894. Imperf.

No.	Type	Description	Unused	Used
12.	1.	½ a. grey	30	20
13.		1 a. red	50	20
14.		2 a. green	1·00	80
8.		4 a. green	6·50	5·00
15.		8 a. red	1·90	1·90
16.		1 r. yellow on blue	3·25	3·25

1898. As T 1, but dagger point to left.

No.	Type	Description	Unused	Used
17.	1.	4 a. green	2·00	2·50

1914. Roul. or perf.

No.	Type	Description	Unused	Used
26.	2.	¼ a. blue	35	35
38.		½ a. black	25	35
28a.		1 a. red	45	50
20a.		2 a. green	50	80
30.		2½ a. yellow	80	1·00
51.		3 a. brown	4·50	4·50
32.		4 a. green	1·25	1·60
33.		6 a. blue	3·25	
42.		8 a. orange	3·00	3·00
43.		10 a. olive	3·00	4·00
44.		12 a. green	3·00	4·00
45.		1 r. lilac	5·50	6·50
46.		2 r. brown and black	14·00	
47.		3 r. blue and brown	26·00	28·00
71.		4 r. green and red	45·00	
72.		5 r. red and green	50·00	

3.

4. Maharao Rajah Bahadur Singh.

1941. Perf.

No.	Type	Description	Unused	Used
79.	3.	3 p. blue	8	20
80.		6 p. blue	20	30
81.		1 a. red	30	40
82.		2 a. brown	2·00	2·00
83.		4 a. green	3·00	3·00
84.		8 a. green	5·00	5·50
85.		1 r. blue	5·00	

1947.

No.	Type	Description	Unused	Used
86.	4.	¼ a. green	10	1·00
87.		½ a. violet	10	1·75
88.		1 a. green	30	2·25
89.	–	2 a. red	50	
90.	–	4 a. orange	65	
91.	–	8 a. blue	1·25	
92.	–	1 r. brown	3·25	

DESIGNS: 2 a., 4 a. Rajah in Indian dress. 8 a., 1 r. View of Bundi.

OFFICIAL STAMPS

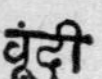

सरविस

(S 1.)

A. Type S **1.**

B/C. Optd. **BUNDI SERVICE.**

1918. Optd.

No.	Type	Description	A. Unused	A. Used	B/C. Unused	B/C. Used
O 6a.	2.	¼ a. blue	40	40	3·25	4·50
O 16a.		½ a. black	40		8·00	8·00
O 8a.		1 a. red	50		1·25	
O 1a.		2 a. green	2·25		4·00	
O 2.		2½ a. yell.	1·00	1·50	2·25	3·25
O 3.		3 a. brown	1·60	2·25	3·25	
O 10.		4 a. green	3·25		6·00	
O 11a.		6 a. blue	3·25		4·50	
O 12.		8 a. orge.	7·00		13·00	
O 13.		10 a. olive	7·00		13·00	
O 22.		12 a. green	7·00	7·00	8·00	
O 5.		1 r. lilac	8·00		9·00	
O 24a.		2 r. brn & black	40·00	40·00	40·00	
O 25.		3 r. blue & brown	55·00		55·00	
O 26.		4 r. green & red	£110		£125	
O 27.		5 r. red & green	£110		£125	

1941. Optd. **SERVICE.**

No.	Type	Description	Unused	Used
O 53.	3.	3 p. blue	40	45
O 54.		6 p. blue	65	80
O 55.		1 a. red	1·50	1·50
O 56.		2 a. brown	2·25	3·00
O 57.		4 a. green	7·00	6·00
O 58.		8 a. green	9·00	11·00
O 59.		1 r. blue	12·00	13·00

For later issues see **RAJASTHAN.**

BURMA BC; O1

A territory in the east of India. Formerly part of the Indian Empire, but separated from it on April 1st, 1937. Japanese forces were in occupation from 1942 to 1945 and Independence was established in 1948.

1937. 12 pies = 1 anna. 16 annas = 1 rupee.
1953. 100 pyas = 1 kyat (rupee).

1937. Stamps of India (King George V.) optd. **BURMA.**

No.	Type	Description	Unused	Used
1.	40.	3 p. grey	12	5
2.	62.	½ a. green	12	5
3.	63.	9 p. green	15	5
4.	64.	1 a. chocolate	15	12
5.	44.	2 a. orange-red	15	12
6.	47.	2½ a. orange	25	15
7.	48.	3 a. red	45	35
8.	66.	3½ a. blue	45	30
9.	49.	4 a. olive	40	12
10.	51.	6 a. yellow-brown	40	25
11.	52.	8 a. mauve	50	30
12.	53.	12 a. claret	65	60
13.	54.	1 r. brown and green	70	30
14.		2 r. red and orange	1·75	55
15.		5 r. blue and violet	3·75	3·00
16.		10 r. green and red	7·50	4·00
17.		15 r. blue and olive	30·00	18·00
18.		25 r. orange and blue	50·00	35·00

1. King George VI and "Chinthes".

2. King George VI and "Nagas".

3. Royal Barge.

7. King George VI and Peacock.

1938. King George VI.

No.	Type	Description	Unused	Used
18a.	1.	1 p. orange	8	25
19.		3 p. violet	8	25
20.		6 p. blue	5	5
21.		9 p. green	10	20
22.	2.	1 a. brown	5	5
23.		1½ a. green	10	12
24.		2 a. red	15	12
25.	3.	2 a. 6 p. claret	30	30
26.	–	3 a. mauve	50	40
27.	–	3 a. 6 p. blue	1·00	1·40
28.	2.	4 a. blue	20	20
29.	–	8 a. green	40	40
30.	7.	1 r. purple and blue	85	45
31.		2 r. brown and purple	2·00	15
32.	–	5 r. violet and red	6·50	3·50
33.	–	10 r. brown and green	14·00	14·00

DESIGNS—HORIZ. As T **3**: 3 a. Burma teak. 3 a., 6 p. Burma Rice. 8 a. Irrawaddy. VERT. As T **7**: 5 r., 10 r. King George VI and "Nats".

1940. Cent. of First Adhesive Postage Stamp. Surch. **COMMEMORATION POSTAGE STAMP 6TH MAY, 1840,** and value in figures and letters.

No.	Type	Description	Unused	Used
34.	3.	1 a. on 2 a. 6 p. claret	75	80

For Japanese issues see "Japanese Occupation of Burma".

1945. British Military Administration Stamps of 1938 optd. **MILY ADMN.**

No.	Type	Description	Unused	Used
35.	1.	1 p. orange	5	5
36.		3 p. violet	5	10
37.		6 p. blue	5	10
38.		9 p. green	5	10
39.	2.	1 a. brown	5	10
40.		1½ a. green	5	10
41.		2 a. red	5	10
42.	3.	2 a. 6 p. claret	5	8
43.	–	3 a. mauve	5	8
44.	–	3 a. 6 p. blue	5	8
45.	2.	4 a. blue	5	10
46.	–	8 a. green	5	10
47.	7.	1 r. purple and blue	12	20
48.		2 r. brown and purple	25	30
49.	–	5 r. violet and red	55	65
50.	–	10 r. brown and green	1·40	1·40

1946. British Civil Administration. As 1938, but colours changed.

No.	Type	Description	Unused	Used
51.	1.	3 p. brown	5	8
52.		6 p. violet	5	5
53.		9 p. green	8	8
54.	2.	1 a. blue	8	8
55.		1½ a. orange	5	5
56.		2 a. claret	8	10
57.	3.	2 a. 6 p. blue	5	5
57a.	–	3 a. blue	10	8
57b.	–	3 a. 6 p. black and blue	5	10
58.	2.	4 a. purple	5	8
59.	–	8 a. mauve	8	12
60.	7.	1 r. violet and mauve	15	12
61.		2 r. brown and orange	30	30
62.	–	5 r. green and brown	80	80
63.	–	10 r. claret and violet	1·75	2·00

8. Elephant.

ကြားဖြတ်
အစိုးရ။

(9. Trans. "Interim Government").

1946. Victory.

No.	Type	Description	Unused	Used
64.	–	9 p. green (Burman)	5	5
65.	–	1½ a. vio. (Burmese woman)	5	5
66.	–	2 a. red (Chinthe)	5	5
67.	8.	3 a. 6 p. blue	5	8

1947. Stamps of 1946 optd. with T **9** or with larger opt. on large stamps.

No.	Type	Description	Unused	Used
68.	1.	3 p. brown	8	10
69.		6 p. violet	5	10
70.		9 p. green	5	10
71.	2.	1 a. blue	5	10
72.		1½ a. orange	12	10
73.		2 a. claret	5	10
74.	3.	2 a. 6 p. blue	10	10
75.	–	3 a. blue	5	10
76.	–	3 a. 6 p. black and blue	5	10
77.	2.	4 a. purple	10	10
78.	–	8 a. mauve	10	12
79.	7.	1 r. violet and mauve	25	20
80.		2 r. brown and orange	45	35
81.	–	5 r. green and brown	80	85
82.	–	10 r. claret and violet	1·40	1·60

10. Gen. Aung San, Chinthe and Map of Burma.

11. Martyrs' Memorial.

1948. Independence Day.

No.	Type	Description	Unused	Used
83.	10.	½ a. green	5	5
84.		1 a. pink	5	5
85.		2 a. red	5	5
86.		3½ a. blue	10	8
87.		8 a. brown	15	15

1948. Murder of Aung San and his Ministers. 1st Anniv.

No.	Type	Description	Unused	Used
88.	11.	3 p. blue	5	5
89.		6 p. green	5	5
90.		9 p. red	5	5
91.		1 a. violet	5	5
92.		2 a. mauve	5	5
93.		3½ a. green	5	5
94.		4 a. brown	5	5
95.		8 a. red	10	5
96.		12 a. purple	15	8
97.		1 r. green	15	10
98.		2 r. blue	30	20
99.		5 r. brown	85	55

12. Boys Playing.

13. Bell.

14. Planting Rice.

15. Royal Throne.

1949. Independence. First Anniv.

No.	Type	Description	Unused	Used
100.	12.	3 p. blue	40	15
120.		3 p. vermilion	20	10
101.	–	6 p. green	5	5
121.	–	6 p. purple	5	5
102.	–	9 p. red	5	5
122.	–	9 p. blue	5	5
103.	13.	1 a. salmon	5	5
123.		1 a. blue	5	5
104.	–	2 a. orange	12	5
124.	–	2 a. green	12	5
105.	14.	2 a. 6 p. magenta	5	5
125.		2 a. 6 p. green	5	5
106.	–	3 a. violet	5	5
126.	–	3 a. vermilion	8	8
107.	–	3 a. 6 p. green	8	5
127.	–	3 a. 6 p. salmon	8	8
108.	–	4 a. brown	8	5
128.	–	4 a. vermilion	8	8
109.	–	8 a. red	10	8
129.	–	8 a. blue	12	10
110.	15.	1 r. green	30	12
130.		1 r. lilac	25	25
111.		2 r. blue	50	25
131.		2 r. green	45	45
112.		5 r. brown	1·00	80
132.		5 r. blue	1·25	1·25
113.		10 r. orange	2·00	1·10
133.		10 r. blue	2·25	2·25

DESIGNS—As T **12**: 6 p. Dancer. 9 p. Girl musician. 2 a. Legendary bird. As T **13**: 4 a. Elephant hauling log. As T **14**: 3 a. Girl weaving. 3 a. 6 p. Royal Palace. 8 a. Ploughing.

16. U.P.U. Monument, Berne.

17. Monument and Map.

1949. U.P.U. 75th Anniv.

No.	Type	Description	Unused	Used
114.	16.	2 a. orange	5	5
115.		3½ a. green	8	8
116.		6 a. violet	12	12
117.		8 a. red	15	12
118.		12½ a. blue	30	20
119.		1 r. green	45	35

1953. Independence. 5th Anniv.

No.	Type	Description	Unused	Used
134.	17.	14 p. grn. (22 × 18 mm.)	8	5
135.		20 p. red (36½ × 26½ mm.)	10	5
136.		25 p. blue (36½ × 26½ mm.)	15	8

1954. New Currency. As 1949 but values in pyas and kyats.

No.	Type	Description	Unused	Used
137.	12.	1 p. vermilion	15	5
138.	–	2 p. purple (as 6 p.)	5	5
139.	–	3 p. blue (as 9 p.)	5	5
140.	13.	5 p. blue	5	5
141.	14.	10 p. green	5	5
142.	–	15 p. green (as 2 a.)	8	5
143.	–	20 p. vermilion (as 3 a.)	5	5
144.	–	25 p. salmon (as 3 a. 6 p.)	5	5
145.	–	30 p. vermilion (as 4 a.)	8	5
146.	–	50 p. blue (as 8 a.)	10	5
147.	15.	1 k. violet	20	10
148.		2 k. green	60	15
149.		5 k. blue	1·50	30
150.		10 k. blue	2·50	50

18. "Kaba-Aye", Rock Cave and Monuments.

DESIGNS—HORIZ. 10 p. Sangha of Cambodia. 15 p. Buddhist priests and temples. 50 p. Sangha of Thailand. 1 k. Sangha of Ceylon. 2 k. Sangha of Laos.

1954. 6th Buddhist Council, Rangoon.
151. – 10 p. blue 5 5
152. – 15 p. maroon 5 5
153. 18. 35 p. brown 12 10
154. – 50 p. green 15 12
155. – 1 k. red 30 20
156. – 2 k. violet 60 45

19. Fifth Buddhist Council Monuments.

DESIGNS: 40 p. Pagoda. 60 p. Shwedagon Pagoda. 1 k.25 Site of 6th Buddhist Council.

1956. Buddha Jayanti. Inscr. "2500TH BUDDHIST ERA".
157. 19. 20 p. myrtle and blue .. 8 5
158. – 40 p. green and blue .. 12 10
159. – 60 p. yellow and green 15 12
160. – 1 k. 25 slate-blue and yellow 40 35

မြန္တလာ-နှစ်တရာ
၁၂၂၁-၁၃၂၁
15 P ၁၅ပြား
(20.)
"Mandalay Town 100 Years/1221-1321").

1959. Mandalay Cent. No. 144 surch. with T 20 and Nos. 147/8 with two-line opt. only.
161. – 15 p. on 25 p. salmon 8 5
162. 15. 1 k. violet 35 25
163. 2 k. green 50 40

1961. Surch. as right-hand characters in T 20.
164. 17. 15 p. on 14 p. green .. 10 8

21. Torch-bearer in Rangoon.  22. Children at Play.

1961. 2nd S.E.A.P. Games.
165. 21. 15 p. blue and red .. 8 5
166. – 25 p. chestnut & green 10 8
167. – 50 p. cerise and blue .. 15 10
168. – 1 k. yellow and green .. 40 25
DESIGNS—VERT. 25 p. Contestants. 50 p. Women sprinting in Aung San Stadium, Rangoon. HORIZ. 1 k. Contestants.

1961. U.N.I.C.E.F. 15th Anniv.
169. 22. 15 p. crimson and pink 8 5

အလုပ်သမားနေ့
၁၉၆၃

23. Flag and Map. (24.)

1963. Military Coup by General Ne Win. 1st Anniv.
170. 23. 15 p. red 10 5

1963. Freedom from Hunger. Nos. 141 and 146 optd. **FREEDOM FROM HUNGER.**
171. 14. 10 p. green 20 15
172. – 50 p. blue 35 25

1963. Labour Day. No. 143 optd. with T 24.
173. 20 p. vermilion 10 5

25. Fantailed Flycatcher.  26. I.T.U. Emblem and Symbols.

1964. Burmese Birds. (1st Series).
174. 25. 1 p. black 5 5
175. 2 p. red 5 5
176. 3 p. turquoise 5 5
177. – 5 p. violet 5 5
178. – 10 p. chestnut 8 5
179. – 15 p. olive 8 5
180. – 20 p. brown and red .. 10 5
181. – 25 p. brown and yellow 10 5
182. – 50 p. slate, black & red 25 8
183. – 1 k. indigo, yell. & grey 35 20
184. – 2 k. indigo, red & olive 85 30
185. – 5 k. multicoloured .. 1·75 70

BIRDS—VERT. (22×26 mm.). 5 p. to 15 p. Roller. (27×37 mm.). 25 p. Crested serpent-eagle. 50 p. Sarus crane. 1 k. Pied hornbill. 5 k. Peafowl. HORIZ. (35½×25 mm.): 20 p. Red-whiskered bulbul (37×27 mm.): 2 k. Silver pheasant.

See also Nos. 195/206.

1965. I.T.U. Cent.
186. 26. 20 p. magenta 8 8
187. 50 p. grn. (34×24½ mm.) 15 15

27. I.C.Y. Emblem.  28. Harvesting.

1965. Int. Co-operation Year.
188. 27. 5 p. blue 5 5
189. 10 p. brown 5 5
190. 15 p. olive 8 5

1966. Peasants' Day.
191. 28. 15 p. multicoloured .. 8 5

29. Cogwheel and Hammer. 30. Bogyoke Aung San and Agricultural Cultivation.

1967. May Day.
192. 29. 15 p. yell., black & blue 8 5

1968. Independence. 20th Anniv.
193. 30. 15 p. multicoloured .. 8 5

31. Burma Pearls. 32. Spike of Paddy.

1968. Burmese Gems, Jades and Pearls Emporium, Rangoon.
194. 31. 15 p. ultram., blue & yell. 5 5

1968. Burmese Birds (2nd series). Designs and colours as Nos. 174/85 but formats and sizes changed.
195. 25. 1 p. black 5 5
196. 2 p. red 5 5
197. 3 p. turquoise 5 5
198. – 5 p. violet 5 5
199. – 10 p. chestnut 5 5
200. – 15 p. olive 5 5
201. – 20 p. brown and red .. 8 5
202. – 25 p. brown and yellow 10 5
203. 50 p. slate, black & red 15 8
204. – 1 k. indigo, yell. & grey 25 8
205. – 2 k. indigo, red & olive 55 20
206. – 5 k. multicoloured .. 1·40 50
NEW SIZES—HORIZ. (21×17 mm.). 1, 2, 3 p. (39×21 mm.). 20 p., 2 k. VERT. (23×28 mm.). 5, 10, 15 p. (21×39 mm.). 25, 50 p., 1 k., 5 k.

1969. Peasants' Day.
218. 32. 15 p. yellow, blue & grn. 8 5

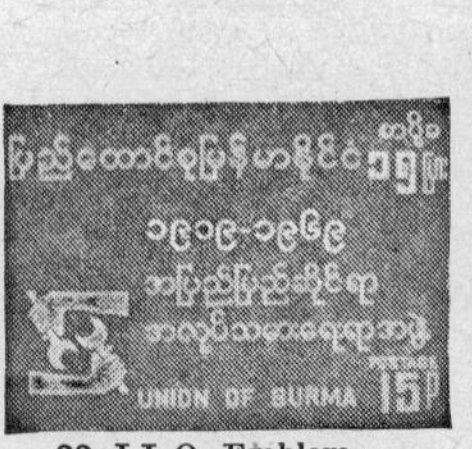

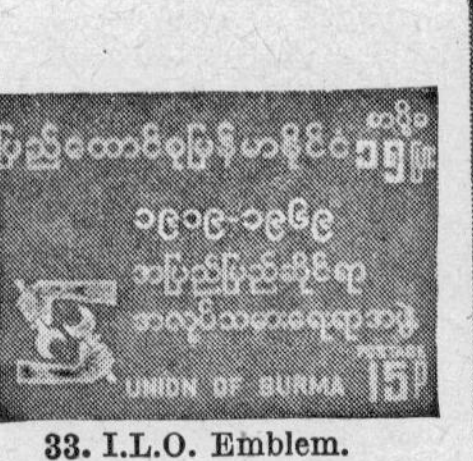

33. I.L.O. Emblem. 34. Football.

1969. Int. Labour Organisation. 50th Anniv.
219. 33. 15 p. gold and green 5 5
220. 50 p. gold and carmine 12 10

1969. 5th South East Asian Peninsular Games, Rangoon.
221. 34. 15 p. multicoloured .. 5 5
222. – 25 p. multicoloured .. 8 5
223. – 50 p. multicoloured .. 12 10
224. – 1 k. blk., grn. & blue .. 25 15
DESIGNS—HORIZ. 25 p. Running. VERT. 50 p. Weightlifting. 1 k. Volleyball.

35. Marchers with Independence, Resistance and Union Flags.

1970. Burmese Armed Forces. 25th Anniv.
225. 35. 15 p. multicoloured .. 8 5

36. "Peace and Progress".

1970. United Nations. 25th Anniv.
226. 36. 15 p. multicoloured .. 10 5

37. Boycott Declaration and Marchers.

1970. Burmese National Day. 50th Anniv. of University Boycott Multicoloured
227. 15 p. Type 37 .. .. 5 5
228. 25 p. Students on boycott march 8 5
229. 50 p. Banner and demonstrators 15 10

38. Burmese Workers.

1971. First Burmese Socialist Programme Party Congress. Multicoloured.
230. 5 p. Type 38 .. .. 5 5
231. 15p. Burmese races and flags 8 5
232. 25 p. Hands holding scroll 10 5
233. 50 p. Party Flag 20 10

39. Child drinking Milk.

1971. U.N.I.C.E.F. 25th Anniv. Multicoloured.
235. 15 p. Type 39 .. .. 5 5
236. 50 p. Marionettes .. 12 8

40. Aung San and Independence Monument, Panglong.

1972. Independence. 25th Anniv. Mult.
237. 15 p. Type 40 .. .. 5 5
238. 50 p. Aung San and Burmese in national costumes .. 12 8
239. 1 k. Flag and map (vert.) 25 10

41. Burmese and Stars.

1972. Revolutionary Council. 10th Anniv.
240. 41. 15 p. multicoloured .. 5 5

42. Human Heart.  44. Casting Vote.

43. Burmese Races.

1972. World Health Day.
241. 42. 15 p. red, blk. & yellow 5 5

1973. National Census.
242. 43. 15 p. multicoloured .. 5 5

1973. National Referendum.
243. 44. 5 p. red and black .. 5 5
244. – 10 p. multicoloured .. 5 5
245. – 15 p. multicoloured .. 5 5
DESIGNS—HORIZ. 10p. Voter supporting map. VERT. 15 p. Burmese with ballot papers.

45. Open-air Meeting.

1974. Opening of 1st Pyithu Hluttaw. Mult.
246. 15 p. Flags of 8 nations .. 5 5
247. 50 p. Type 45 .. .. 12 8
248. 1 k. Burmese badge .. 25 12
No. 246 is larger, size 80×26 mm.

46. U.P.U. Emblem and Carrier Pigeon.

1974. Universal Postal Union. Cent. Multicoloured.
249. 15 p. Type 46 .. .. 5 5
250. 20 p. Woman reading letter (vert.) 5 5
251. 50 p. U.P.U. emblem on "stamps" (vert.) .. 12 8
252. 1 k. Stylised doll (vert.) .. 25 12
253. 2 k. Postman delivering letter to family .. 50 30

47. Dancers. 48. Burmese Couple.

1974. Burmese Costumes.
254. 47. 1 p. pur., & pale pur. .. 5 5
255. 3 p. brown and pink .. 5 5
256. 5 p. violet and lilac .. 5 5
257. 15 p. green & pale green 5 5
258. 48. 20 p. brown, blue & black 5 5
259. – 50 p. pur., brn. & ochre 12 8
260. – 1 k. mve, pink & black 25 12
261. – 5 k. multicoloured .. 1·25 60
DESIGNS—As T 47: 3 p. Girl. 5 p. Man and woman. 15 p. Man and woman (different). As T 48: 50 p. Girl with fan. 1 k. Girl sitting. 5 k. Musician.

49. Burmese Woman.

1976. International Women's Year.
262. 49. 50 p. black and green .. 5 5
263. – 2 k. black and blue .. 50 25
DESIGN—VERT. 2 k. Globe within lotus.

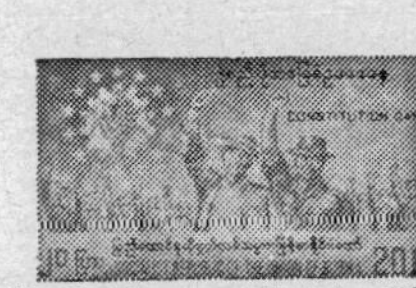

50. Emblem and Rejoicing People. **51.** Learning to Read.

1976. Constitution Day.

264. **50.** 20 p. black and blue .. 5 5
265. – 50 p. brown and blue .. 5 5
266. – 1 k. multicoloured 25 12

DESIGNS—As Type **50**: 50 p. Emblem and procession. 57×21 mm. 1 k. Emblem and procession.

1976. International Literacy Year. Multicoloured.

267. 10 p. Type **51** 5 5
268. 15 p. Abacus (horiz.) .. 5 5
269. 50 p. Emblem (horiz.) .. 5 5
270. 1 k. Emblem, open book and globe 25 12

OFFICIAL STAMPS

1937. Stamps of India (King George V) optd. **BURMA SERVICE.**

O 1. **40.** 3 p. grey 5 10
O 2. **62.** ½ a. green 25 12
O 3. **63.** 9 p. green 20 12
O 4. **64.** 1 a. chocolate 20 12
O 5. **44.** 2 a. orange-red .. 20 12
O 6. **47.** 2½ a. orange 25 20
O 7. **49.** 4 a. olive 25 15
O 8. **51.** 6 a. yellow-brown .. 60 45
O 9. **52.** 8 a. mauve 35 25
O 10. **53.** 12 a. claret 55 45
O 11. **54.** 1 r. brown and green 60 50
O 12. 2 r. red and orange .. 1·60 1·40
O 13. 5 r. blue and violet .. 4·50 4·00
O 14. 10 r. green and red .. 11·00 8·50

1939. Stamps of 1938 optd. **SERVICE.**

O 15. **1.** 3 p. violet 5 10
O 16. 6 p. blue 5 10
O 17. 9 p. green 8 10
O 18. **2.** 1 a. brown 5 10
O 19. 1½ a. green 30 10
O 20. 2 a. red 12 15
O 21. **3.** 2 a. 6 p. claret 35 35
O 22. **2.** 4 a. blue 55 20
O 23. – 8 a. green (No. 29) .. 60 45
O 24. **7.** 1 r. purple and blue .. 85 65
O 25. 2 r. brown and purple 1·40 65
O 26. – 5 r. violet & red (No. 32) 4·00 2·25
O 27. – 10 r. brn. & grn. (No. 33) 6·00 3·50

1946. Stamps of 1946 optd. **SERVICE.**

O 28. **1.** 3 p. brown 5 10
O 29. 6 p. violet 10 10
O 30. 9 p. green 5 10
O 31. **2.** 1 a. blue 5 10
O 32. 1½ a. orange 8 10
O 33. 2 a. claret 5 10
O 34. **3.** 2 a. 6 p. blue 5 10
O 35. **2.** 4 a. purple 5 10
O 36. – 8 a. mauve (No. 59) .. 5 12
O 37. **7.** 1 r. violet and mauve .. 10 12
O 38. 2 r. brown and orange 40 45
O 39. – 5 r. green & brn. (No. 62) 80 1·45
O 40. – 10 r. claret and violet (No. 63) .. .. 1·25 2·25

1947. Interim Govt. Nos. O 28, etc., optd. with T **9** or with large opt. on larger stamps.

O 41. **1.** 3 p. brown 5 5
O 42. 6 p. violet 5 5
O 43. 9 p. green 5 5
O 44. **2.** 1 a. blue 12 8
O 45. 1½ a. orange 15 8
O 46. 2 a. claret 15 8
O 47. **3.** 2 a. 6 p. blue 15 10
O 48. **2.** 4 a. purple 15 8
O 49. – 8 a mauve 15 10
O 50. **7.** 1 r. violet and mauve .. 35 30
O 51. 2 r. brown and orange .. 60 45
O 52. – 5 r. green and brown .. 1·00 1·40
O 53. – 10 r. claret and violet .. 2·00 2·40

အစိုးရကိစ္စ အစိုးရကိစ္စ

(O **1.**) (13 mm. long). (O **2.**) (11½ mm. long).

1949. 1st Anniv. of Independence. Stamps of 1949 optd. as Type O **1.**

O 114. **12.** 3 p. blue 20 5
O 115. – 6 p. green 5 5
O 116. – 9 p. red 5 5
O 117. **13.** 1 a. red 5 5
O 118. – 2 a. orange 5 5
O 119. – 3 a. 6 p. green 5 5
O 120. – 4 a. brown 8 8
O 121. – 8 a. red 8 8
O 122. **15.** 1 r. green 20 15
O 123. 2 r. blue 40 30
O 124. 5 r. brown .. 1·00 90
O 125. 10 r. orange .. .. 2·75 2·00

1954. Nos. 137, etc., optd. as Type O **1.**

O 151. **12.** 1 p. vermilion .. 20 5
O 152. – 2 p. purple 5 5
O 153. – 3 p. blue 5 5
O 154. **13.** 5 p. blue 5 5
O 155. – 15 p. green 5 5
O 156. – 20 p. vermilion .. 5 5
O 157. – 25 p. salmon 5 5
O 158. – 30 p. vermilion .. 10 5
O 159. – 50 p. blue 12 8
O 160. **15.** 1 k. violet 25 12
O 161. 2 k. green 40 25
O 162. 5 k. blue .. .. 1·10 60
O 163. 10 k. blue .. .. 2·00 1·25

1964. No. 139 optd. **Service** in English.

O 174. – 3 p. blue .. .. 2·50 1·60

1964. Nos. 137, 139/40 and 142 optd. with Type O **2.**

O 175. **12.** 1 p. vermilion .. 5 5
O 176. – 3 p. blue 5 5
O 177. **13.** 5 p. blue 5 5
O 178. – 15 p. green 5 5

1965. Nos. 175/7, 179 and 181 optd. with Type O **2.**

O 186. **25.** 2 p. red 5 5
O 187. 3 p. turquoise .. 5 5
O 188. – 5 p. violet 5 5
O 189. – 15 p. olive 8 8
O 190. – 25 p. brown & yellow 10 10

အစိုးရကိစ္စ အစိုးရကိစ္စ အစိုးရကိစ္စ

(O **3.**) (O **4.**) (O **5.**)
(15 mm. long). (12 mm. long). (14½ mm. long).

1966. Nos. 174/6 optd. with Type O **3,** and No. 179 optd. with Type O **4.**

O 192. **25.** 1 p. black 5 5
O 193. 2 p. red 5 5
O 194. 3 p. turquoise .. 5 5
O 195. – 15 p. olive 5 5

1966. Nos. 174/7 and 179/85 optd. with Type O **5.**

O 196. **25.** 1 p. black 5 5
O 197. 2 p. red 5 5
O 198. 3 p. turquoise .. 5 5
O 199. – 5 p. violet 5 5
O 200. – 15 p. olive 5 5
O 201. – 20 p. brown and red .. 5 5
O 202. – 25 p. brown & yellow 5 5
O 203. – 50 p. slate, blk. & red 12 12
O 204. – 1 k. indigo, yell. & grey 25 20
O 205. – 2 k. indigo, red & olive 60 35
O 206. – 5 k. multicoloured .. 1·75 1·00

1968. Nos. 195/8 and 200/6 optd. as Type O **9**, but 13 mm. long (1, 2 p.), 15 mm. long (5 p. 15 p.), or 14 mm. long (others).

O 207. 1 p. black 5 5
O 208. 2 p. red 5 5
O 209. 3 p. turquoise 5 5
O 210. 5 p. violet 5 5
O 211. 15 p. Olive 5 5
O 212. 20 p. brown and red .. 8 8
O 213. 25 p. brown and yellow 8 8
O 214. 50 p. blue, black and red 12 10
O 215. 1 k. blue, yellow & grey 25 14
O 216. 2 k. blue, red and olive 50 40
O 217. 5 k. multicoloured .. 1·40 1·00

BURUNDI O1

Once part of the Belgian territory, Ruanda-Urundi. Independent on 1st July, 1962, when a monarchy was established. After a revolution in 1967 Burundi became a republic.

Currency: Belgian.

1962. Stamps of Ruanda-Urundi optd. **Royaume du Burundi** and bar or surch. also.

(a) Flowers. (Nos. 167, etc.)

1. 25 c. orange and green .. 8 8
2. 40 c. salmon and green .. 8 8
3. 60 c. purple and green .. 12 12
4. 1 f. 25 blue and green .. 6·50 6·50
5. 1 f. 50 green and violet .. 25 25
6. 5 f. green and purple .. 30 30
7. 7 f. brown and green .. 65 65
8. 10 f. olive and purple .. 1·10 1·10

(b) Animals (Nos. 192, etc.)

9. 10 c. black, red and brown 5 5
10. 20 c. black and green .. 5 5
11. 40 c. black, ol.-blk. & mag. 5 5
12. 50 c. brown, yellow & green 5 5
13. 1 f. black, blue and brown 5 5
14. 1 f. 50 black and orange .. 5 5
15. 2 f. black, brown and turq. 5 5
16. 3 f. black, red and brown .. 10 5
17. 3 f. 50 on 3 f. blk., red & brn. 12 10
18a. 4 f. on 10 f. brown, black, magenta and yellow .. 12 12
19. 5 f. brn., blk., grn. & yell. 12 12
20. 6 f. 50 brown, yellow & red 20 15
21. 8 f. black, magenta & blue 25 25
23. 10 f. brn., blk., mag. & yell. 25 25

(c) Animals (Nos. 211/12).

24. 20 f. yellow, red, black and blue-green 45 40
25. 50 f. bis., blk., bl. & verm. 85 85

1. King Mwambutsa IV and Royal Drummers.

1962. Independence. Inscr. "1.7.1962".

26. **1.** 50 c. sepia and lake .. 5 5
27. A. 1 f. green, red & deep grn. 5 5
28. B. 2 f. sepia and olive .. 5 5
29. **1.** 3 f. sepia and red .. 8 5
30. A. 4 f. green, red and blue .. 10 5
31. B. 8 f. sepia and violet .. 20 8
32. **1.** 10 f. sepia and green .. 25 10
33. A. 20 f. green, red and sepia 50 12
34. B. 50 f. sepia and magenta .. 1·25 30

DESIGNS—VERT. A, Burundi flag and arms. HORIZ. B, King and outline map of Burundi.

1962. Dag Hammarskjoeld Commem. No. 204 of Ruanda-Urundi surch. **HOMMAGE A DAG HAMMARSKJOLD ROYAUME DU BURUNDI** and new value. U.N. emblem and wavy pattern at foot. Inscr. in French or Flemish.

35. 3 f. 50 on 3 f. salmon & bl. 12 12
36. 6 f. 50 on 3 f. salmon & bl. 20 20
37. 10 f. on 3 f. salmon & blue 25 25

1962. Malaria Eradication. As Nos. 31 and 34 but colours changed and with campaign emblem superimposed on map.

38. B. 8 f. sepia, turq. & bistre 25 15
39. 50 f. sepia turq. & olive 1·40 40

2. Prince Louis Rwagasore.

3. "Sowing".

1963. Prince Rwagasore Memorial and Stadium Fund.

40. **2.** 50 c.+25 c. violet .. 5 5
41. – 1 f.+50 c. blue and orange 5 5
42. 1 f. 50+75 c. vio. & bistre 5 5
43. **2.** 3 f. 50+1 f. 50 magenta .. 8 5
44. – 5 f.+2 f. blue and pink .. 12 8
45. – 6 f. 50+3 f. violet & olive 20 8

DESIGNS—HORIZ. 1 f., 5 f. Prince and stadium. 1 f. 50, 6 f. 50 Prince and memorial.

1963. Freedom from Hunger.

46. **3.** 4 f. purple and olive .. 10 5
47. 8 f. purple and olive .. 20 15
48. 15 f. purple and green .. 30 15

1963. "Peaceful Uses of Outer Space" Nos. 28 and 34 optd. **UTILISATIONS PACIFIQUES DE L'ESPACE** around globe encircled by rocket.

49. B. 2 f. sepia and olive .. 1·25 1·10
50. 50 f. sepia and magenta .. 1·50 1·40

1963. Independence. 1st Anniv. Nos. 30/3 but with colours changed and optd. **Premier Anniversaire.**

51. A. 4 f. green, red and olive .. 8 5
52. B. 8 f. sepia and orange .. 15 8
53. **1.** 10 f. sepia and mauve .. 25 10
54. A. 20 f. green, red and grey 55 20

1963. Nos. 27 and 33 surch.

55. A. 6 f. 50 on 1 f. green, red and deep green .. 25 8
56. 15 f. on 20 f. green, red and sepia 50 25

4. Globe and Red Cross Flag.

5. "1962" and U.N.E.S.C.O. Emblem.

1963. Red Cross Centenary.

57. **4.** 4 f. green, red and grey .. 10 5
58. 8 f. brown, red and grey .. 20 8
59. 10 f. blue, red and grey .. 30 15
60. 20 f. violet, red and grey .. 65 30

IMPERF. STAMPS. Many Burundi stamps from No. 61 onwards exist imperf. from limited printings and/or miniature sheets.

1963. Admission to U.N.O. 1st Anniv. Emblems and values in black.

61. **5.** 4 f. olive and yellow .. 10 5
62. 8 f. blue and lilac 15 8
63. 10 f. violet and blue .. 20 10
64. 20 f. green & yellow-green 45 15
65. 50 f. red-brown and ochre 1·10 35

EMBLEMS: 8 f. I.T.U.; 10 f. W.M.O.; 20 f. U.P.U.; 50 f. F.A.O.

6. U.N.E.S.C.O. Emblem and Scales of Justice

1963. Declaration of Human Rights. 15th Anniv.

66. **6.** 50 c. blk., blue and pink .. 5 5
67. 1 f. 50 black, blue & orge. 5 5
68. – 3 f. 50 black, green & chest. 8 5
69. 6 f. 50 black, green & lilac 15 8
70. 10 f. black, bistre & blue 20 10
71. – 20 f. blk., bistre, bl. & brn. 45 20

DESIGNS: 3 f. 50, 6 f. 50, Scroll. 10 f., 20 f. Lincoln.

7. Ice-hockey.

9. Burundi Dancer.

8. Hippopotamus.

1964. Winter Olympic Games, Innsbruck.

72. **7.** 50 c. black, gold & olive .. 5 5
73. – 3 f. 50 black, gold & cinn. 10 5
74. – 6 f. 50 black, gold and greenish grey 20 10
75. – 10 f. black, gold and grey 30 12
76. – 20 f. blk., gold. & yell.-bis. 65 30

DESIGNS: 3 f. 50, Figure-skating. 6 f. 50, Olympic flame. 10 f. Speed-skating. 20 f. Skiing (slalom).

1964. Burundi Animals. Multicoloured.

(i) Postage. (a) Size as T **8.**

77. 50 c. Impala 5 5
78. 1 f. T **8** 5 5
79. 1 f. 50 Giraffe 5 5
80. 2 f. Buffalo 8 5
81. 3 f. Zebra 8 5
82. 3 f. 50 Defassa waterbuck .. 10 5

(b) Size 16×42½ mm. or 42½×26 mm.

83. 4 f. Impala 10 5
84. 5 f. Hippopotamus .. 10 5
85. 6 f. 50 Zebra 12 5
86. 8 f. Buffalo 15 8
87. 10 f. Giraffe 20 8
88. 15 f. Defassa waterbuck .. 30 12

(c) Size 53½×33½ mm.

89. 20 f. Spotted leopard .. 40 15
90. 50 f. Elephant .. .. 1·10 30
91. 100 f. Lion .. .. 2·25 50

(ii) Air. Inscr. "POSTE AERIENNE" and optd. with gold border.

(a) Size 26×42½ mm. or 42½×26 mm.

92. 6 f. Zebra 12 5
93. 8 f. Buffalo 20 5
94. 10 f. Impala 20 5
95. 14 f. Hippopotamus .. 30 8
96. 15 f. Defassa waterbuck .. 35 10

(b) Size 53½×33½ mm.

97. 20 f. Spotted leopard .. 50 20
98. 50 f. Elephant .. .. 1·40 50

The impala, giraffe and waterbuck stamp are all vert. designs, and the remainder are horiz.

1964. World's Fair, New York (1st series). Gold backgrounds.
99. 9. 50 c. multicoloured .. 5 5
100. – 1 f. multicoloured .. 5 5
101. – 4 f. multicoloured .. 10 5
102. – 6 f. 50 multicoloured .. 15 8
103. – 10 f. multicoloured .. 30 12
104. – 15 f. multicoloured .. 45 15
105. – 20 f. multicoloured .. 55 25
DESIGNS: 1 f. to 20 f. Various dancers and drummers as T 9.
See also Nos. 175/81.

10. Pope Paul and King Mwambutsa IV.

1964. Canonisation of 22 African Martyrs. Inscriptions in gold.
106. 10. 50 c. lake and blue .. 5 5
107. – 1 f. indigo and purple .. 5 5
108. – 4 f. sepia and mauve .. 8 5
109. – 8 f. brown and red .. 20 8
110. – 14 f. brown & turquoise 35 12
111. 10. 20 f. green and red .. 50 25
DESIGNS—VERT. 1 f., 8 f. Group of martyrs. HORIZ. 4 f., 14 f. Pope John XXIII and King Mwambutsa IV.

11. Putting the Shot.

1964. Olympic Games Tokyo. Inscr. "TOKYO 1964". Multicoloured.
112. 50 c. Type 11 .. .. 5 5
113. 1 f. Throwing the discus .. 5 5
114. 3 f. Swimming 5 5
115. 4 f. Relay-racing .. 8 5
116. 6 f. 50 Throwing the javelin 10 8
117. 8 f. Hurdling 20 10
118. 10 f. Long-jumping .. 20 12
119. 14 f. High-diving 30 15
120. 18 f. High-jumping .. 40 20
121. 20 f. Gymnastics .. 50 30
The 3, 8, 10, 18, and 20 f. are horiz. designs.

12. Scientist, Map and Emblem.

1965. Anti-T.B. Campaign. Country name values and Lorraine Cross in red.
122. 12. 2 f.+50 c. sepia & drab 5 5
123. 4 f.+1 f. 50 grn. & pink 12 8
124. 5 f.+2 f. 50 vio. & buff 15 10
125. 8 f.+3 f. ultram. & grey 20 10
126. 10 f.+5 f. red & grey-grn. 30 15

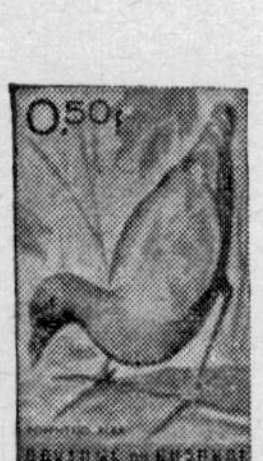

13. African Gallinule. **14.** "Relay" Satellite and Telegraph Key.

1965. Birds. Multicoloured.
(i) Postage. (a) Size as T 13.
127. 50 c. Type 13 .. .. 5 5
128. 1 f. Little bee-eater .. 5 5
129. 1 f. 50 Secretary bird .. 5 5
130. 2 f. Wood ibis 5 5
131. 3 f. Congolese peacock .. 5 5
132. 3 f. 50 African darter .. 5 5
(b) Size 26 × 42½ mm.
133. 4 f. Type 13 .. .. 5 5
134. 5 f. Little bee-eater .. 8 5
135. 6 f. 50 Secretary bird .. 10 8
136. 8 f. Wood ibis .. 10 8
137. 10 f. Congolese peacock .. 15 10
138. 15 f. African darter .. 20 12
(c) Size 33½ × 53 mm.
139. 20 f. Saddle-billed stork or jabiru 25 15
140. 50 f. Abyssinian ground hornbill 60 40
141. 100 f. Crowned crane .. 1·25 65
ii) Air. Inscr. "POSTE AERIENNE" optd. with gold border.
(a) Size 26 × 42½ mm.
142. 6 f. Secretary bird .. 10 5
143. 8 f. African darter .. 12 8
144. 10 f. Congolese peacock .. 15 8
145. 14 f. Little bee-eater .. 20 10
146. 15 f. Wood ibis .. 20 10
(b) Size 33½ × 53 mm.
147. 20 f. Saddle-billed stork, or jabiru 30 20
148. 50 f. Abyssinian ground hornbill 70 50
149. 75 f. Martial eagle .. .. 1·10 70
150. 130 f. Lesser flamingo .. 1·75 1·10

1965. I.T.U. Cent. Multicoloured.
151. 1 f. Type 14 .. .. 5 5
152. 3 f. "Telstar 1" and hand telephone .. 8 5
153. 4 f. "Lunik 3" and wall telephone 8 5
154. 6 f. 50 Weather satellite and tracking station .. 10 8
155. 8 f. "Telstar 2" and head-phones 12 10
156. 10 f. "Sputnik" and radar scanner 20 10
157. 14 f. "Syncom" and aerial 25 15
158. 20 f. "Pioneer 5" space probe and radio aerial .. 30 20

15. Arms (reverse of 10 f. coin).

1965. 1st Independence Anniv. Gold Coinage Commem. Circular designs on gold foil, backed with multicoloured patterned paper. Imperf.
(i) Postage. (a) 10 f. coin. Diameter 1½ in.
159. 15. 2 f.+50 c. red & yellow 5 5
160. – 4 f.+50 c. blue & verm. 8 8
(b) 25 f. coin. Diameter 1¾ in.
161. 15. 6 f.+50 c. orange & grey 12 12
162. – 8 f.+50 c. blue & maroon 15 15
(c) 50 f. coin. Diameter 2½ in.
163. 15. 12 f.+50 c. green & pur. 20 20
164. – 15 f.+50 c. emer. & lilac 25 25
(d) 100 f. coin. Diameter 2⅝ in.
165. 15. 25 f.+50 c. blue & flesh 40 40
166. – 40 f.+50 c. mauve & brn. 60 60
(ii) Air. (a) 10 f. coin. Diameter 1½ in.
167. 15. 3 f.+1 f. violet & lav. 8 8
168. – 5 f.+1 f. verm. & turq. 10 10
(b) 25 f. coin. Diameter 1¾ in.
169. 15. 11 f.+1 f. pur. & yellow 20 20
170. – 14 f.+1 f. emerald & red 20 20
(c) 50 f. coin. Diameter 2½ in.
171. 15. 20 f.+1 f. black & blue 30 30
172. – 30 f.+1 f. lake & orange 40 40
(d) 100 f. coin. Diameter 2⅝ in.
173. 15. 50 f.+1 f. violet & blue 75 75
174. – 100 f.+1 f. maroon and magenta .. .. 1·40 1·40
DESIGNS: The 4, 5, 8, 14, 15, 30, 40 and 100 f. each show the obverse side of the coins (King Mwambutsa IV).

1965. Worlds Fair, New York (2nd series). As Nos. 99/105, but with silver backgrounds.
175. 9. 50 c. multicoloured .. 5 5
176. – 1 f. multicoloured .. 5 5
177. – 4 f. multicoloured .. 8 5
178. – 6 f. 50 multicoloured .. 12 10
179. – 10 f. multicoloured .. 15 12
180. – 15 f. multicoloured .. 25 20
181. – 20 f. multicoloured .. 30 25

16. Globe and I.C.Y. Emblem.

1965. Int. Co-operation Year. Multicoloured.
182. 1 f. Type 16 .. .. 5 5
183. 4 f. Map of Africa and cog-wheel emblem of U.N. Science and Technology Conference 8 5
184. 8 f. Map of South-East Asia and Colombo Plan emblem 10 5
185. 10 f. Globe & U.N. emblem 12 8
186. 18 f. Map of Americas and "Alliance for Progress" emblem 25 12
187. 25 f. Map of Europe and C.E.P.T. emblems .. 35 20
188. 40 f. Space map and satellite (U.N.—"Peaceful Uses of Outer Space") 60 40

17. Prince Rwagasore and Memorial.

1966. Prince Rwagasore and Pres. Kennedy Commem.
189. 17. 4 f.+1 f. brown & blue 8 5
190. – 10 f.+1 f. blue, brown and green 12 8
191. – 20 f.+2 f. green & lilac 30 20
192. – 40 f.+2 f. brown & grn. 55 35
DESIGNS—HORIZ. 10 f. Prince Rwagasore and Pres. Kennedy. 20 f. Pres. Kennedy and memorial library. VERT. 40 f. King Mwambutsa at Pres. Kennedy's grave.

18. Protea.

1966. Flowers. Multicoloured.
(i) Postage. (a) Size as T 18.
194. 50 c. Type 18 .. .. 5 5
195. 1 f. Crossandra 5 5
196. 1 f. 50 Ansellia 5 5
197. 2 f. Thunbergia 5 5
198. 3 f. Schizoglossum .. 5 5
199. 3 f. 50 Dissotis 5 5
(b) Size 41 × 41 mm.
200. 4 f. Type 18 .. .. 5 5
201. 5 f. Crossandra 8 5
202. 6 f. 50 Ansellia 10 5
203. 8 f. Thunbergia 12 8
204. 10 f. Schizoglossum .. 12 8
205. 15 f. Dissotis 20 10
(c) Size 50 × 50 mm.
206. 20 f. Type 18 .. .. 25 10
207. 50 f. Gazania 65 40
208. 100 f. Hibiscus .. 1·25 80
209. 150 f. Markhamia .. 1·75 1·10
(ii) Air. (a) Size 41 × 41 mm.
210. 6 f. Dissotis 8 5
211. 8 f. Crossandra 12 5
212. 10 f. Ansellia 12 5
213. 14 f. Thunbergia 15 5
214. 15 f. Schizoglossum .. 15 5
(b) Size 50 × 50 mm.
215. 20 f. Gazania 30 10
216. 50 f. Type 18 .. .. 70 25
217. 75 f. Hibiscus 90 35
218. 130 f. Markhamia .. 1·75 70

1967. Various stamps optd.
(i) Nos. 127, etc. (Birds) optd. REPUBLIQUE DU BURUNDI and bar. (a) Postage.
221. 50 c. multicoloured .. 5 5
222. 1 f. 50 multicoloured .. 5 5
223. 3 f. 50 multicoloured .. 8 8
224. 5 f. multicoloured .. 10 10
225. 6 f. 50 multicoloured .. 12 10
226. 8 f. multicoloured .. 15 12
227. 10 f. multicoloured .. 20 25
228. 15 f. multicoloured .. 30 30
229. 20 f. multicoloured .. 50 50
230. 50 f. multicoloured .. 1·10 1·10
231. 100 f. multicoloured .. 2·50 2·50
(b) Air.
232. 6 f. multicoloured .. 12 8
233. 8 f. multicoloured .. 15 10
234. 10 f. multicoloured .. 20 12
235. 14 f. multicoloured .. 30 20
236. 15 f. multicoloured .. 30 20
237. 20 f. multicoloured .. 50 25
238. 50 f. multicoloured .. 1·40 70
239. 75 f. multicoloured .. 2·00 95
240. 130 f. multicoloured .. 3·25 1·60
(ii) Nos. 193, etc. (Flowers) optd. as Nos. 221, etc., but with two bars. (a) Postage.
241. 50 c. multicoloured .. 5 5
242. 1 f. multicoloured .. 5 5
243. 1 f. 50 multicoloured .. 5 5
244. 2 f. multicoloured .. 5 5
245. 3 f. multicoloured .. 8 5
246. 3 f. 50 multicoloured .. 10 5
247. 4 f. multicoloured .. 12 8
248. 5 f. multicoloured .. 15 8
249. 6 f. 50 multicoloured .. 15 10
250. 8 f. multicoloured .. 20 12
251. 10 f. multicoloured .. 20 12
252. 15 f. multicoloured .. 30 20
253. 50 f. multicoloured .. 1·10 35
254. 100 f. multicoloured .. 2·25 70
255. 150 f. multicoloured .. 3·25 1·25
(b) Air.
256. 6 f. multicoloured .. 10 8
257. 8 f. multicoloured .. 12 8
258. 10 f. multicoloured .. 15 8
259. 14 f. multicoloured .. 20 10
260. 15 f. multicoloured .. 25 15
261. 20 f. multicoloured .. 30 20
262. 50 f. multicoloured .. 70 30
263. 75 f. multicoloured .. 1·10 45
264. 130 f. multicoloured .. 2·25 70

19. Sir Winston Churchill and St. Paul's Cathedral.

1967. Churchill Commem.
265. 19. 4 f.+1 f. multicoloured 8 5
266. – 15 f.+2 f. multicoloured 25 20
267. – 20 f.+3 f. multicoloured 30 25
DESIGNS (Churchill and): 15 f. Tower of London. 20 f. Big Ben and Boadicea statue, Westminster.

20. Egyptian Mouthbreeder.

1967. Fishes. Multicoloured.
(a) Postage. (i) Size as T 20.
269. 50 c. Type 20 .. .. 5 5
270. 1 f. Spotted Climbing Perch 5 5
271. 1 f. 50 Six Banded Panchax 5 5
272. 2 f. Congo Tetra 5 5
273. 3 f. Red Jewel Fish .. 5 5
274. 3 f. 50 White Spotted Cichlid 5 5
(ii) Size 53½ × 27 mm.
275. 4 f. As 50 c. 5 5
276. 5 f. As 1 f. 5 5
277. 6 f. 50. As 1 f. 50 .. 8 8
278. 8 f. As 2 f. 10 10
279. 10 f. As 3 f. 15 15
280. 15 f. As 3 f. 50 .. .. 20 15
(iii) Size 63½ × 31½ mm.
281. 20 f. As 50 c. 25 15
282. 50 f. Snakehead 65 40
283. 100 f. Tooth Carp .. 1·40 50
284. 150 f. African Tetra .. 1·90 70
(b) Air. (i) Size 50 × 23 mm.
285. 6 f. Type 20 .. .. 8 5
286. 8 f. As 1 f. 10 5
287. 10 f. As 1 f. 50 .. .. 12 8
288. 14 f. As 2 f. 15 8
289. 15 f. As 3 f. 20 10
(ii) Size 59 × 27 mm.
290. 20 f. As 3 f. 50 .. .. 25 10
291. 50 f. As 50 f. (postage) .. 60 25
292. 75 f. As 100 f. 90 40
293. 130 f. As 150 f. .. .. 1·50 60

21. Baule Ancestral Figures.

1967. "African Art". Multicoloured.
294. 50 c. Type **21** (postage) .. 5 5
295. 1 f. "Master of Buli's" carved seat .. 5 5
296. 1 f. 50, Karumba antelope's head 5 5
297. 2 f. Bobo buffalo's head .. 5 5
298. 4 f. Guma-Goffa funeral figures 8 5
299. 10 f. Bakoutou "spirit" (carving) (air) .. 15 8
300. 14 f. Bamum sultan's throne 20 10
301. 17 f. Bebin bronze head .. 25 12
302. 24 f. Statue of 109th Bakouba king 35 15
303. 26 f. Burundi basketwork and lances 55 20

1967. Lions Int. 50th Anniv. Nos. 265/7 optd. **1917 1967** and emblem.
304. 4 f.+1 f. multicoloured .. 8 8
305. 15 f.+2 f. multicoloured .. 25 15
306. 20 f.+3 f. multicoloured .. 35 20

22. Lord Baden-Powell (founder).

1967. Scout Movement. 60th Anniv. and World Scout Jamboree, Idaho.
308. 50 c. Scouts climbing (post.) 5 5
309. 1 f. Scouts preparing meal 5 5
310. 1 f. 50, Type **22** 5 5
311. 2 f. Two scouts 5 5
312. 4 f. Giving first aid .. 8 5
313. 10 f. As 50 c. (air) .. 15 10
314. 14 f. As 1 f. 20 12
315. 17 f. Type **22** 20 12
316. 24 f. As 2 f. 35 15
317. 26 f. As 4 f. 65 20

23. "The Gleaners" (Millet).

1967. World Fair, Montreal. Multicoloured.
318. 4 f. Type **23** 8 8
319. 8 f. "The Water-carrier of Seville" (Velasquez) .. 12 8
320. 14 f. "The Triumph of Neptune and Amphitrite" (Poussin) 25 12
321. 18 f. "Acrobat with a ball" (Picasso) 30 15
322. 25 f. "Margaret van Eyck" (Van Eyck) 40 20
323. 40 f. "St. Peter denying Christ" (Rembrandt) .. 70 35

24. Boeing "707".

1967. Air. Opening of Bujumbura Airport. Aircraft and inscr. in black and silver.
325. **24.** 10 f. green 15 5
326. – 14 f. yellow 20 10
327. – 17 f. blue 25 12
328. – 26 f. purple 35 15

AIRCRAFT: 14 f. Boeing "727" over lakes. 17 f. "VC-10" over lake. 26 f. Boeing "727" over Bujumbura Airport.

25. Pres. Micombero and Flag.

1967. Republic. 1st Anniv. Multicoloured.
329. 5 f. Type **25** 10 5
330. 14 f. Memorial and Arms .. 20 10
331. 20 f. View of Bujumbura and Arms 25 15
332. 30 f. "Place de la Revolution" and President Micombero 40 20

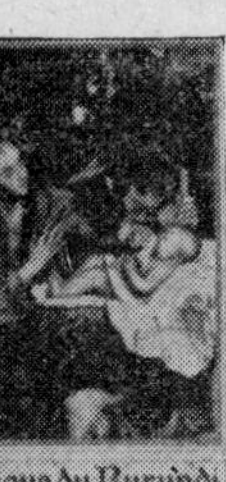

26. "The Adoration of the Shepherds" (J. B. Mayno). **27.** Downhill Skiing.

1967. Christmas. Religious Paintings. Multicoloured.
333. 1 f. Type **26** 5 5
334. 4 f. "The Holy Family" (A. van Dyck) 8 5
335. 14 f. "The Nativity" (Maitre de Moulins) .. 20 15
336. 26 f. "Madonna and Child" (C. Crivelli) 40 20

1968. Winter Olympic Games, Grenoble. Multicoloured.
339. 5 f. Type **27** 8 5
340. 10 f. Ice-hockey 10 8
341. 14 f. Figure-skating .. 20 10
342. 17 f. Bobsleighing .. 25 12
343. 26 f. Ski-jumping .. 35 20
344. 40 f. Speed-skating .. 45 30
345. 60 f. Olympic torch .. 70 40

28. "Portrait of a Young Man" (Botticelli).

1968. Famous Paintings. Multicoloured.
347. 1 f. 50 Type **28** (postage) 5 5
348. 2 f. "La Maja Vestida" (Goya) (horiz.) .. 5 5
349. 4 f. "The Lacemaker" (Vermeer) 8 5
350. 17 f. "Woman and Cat" (Renoir) (air) 25 8
351. 24 f. "The Jewish Bride" (Rembrandt) (horiz.) .. 30 15
352. 26 f. "Pope Innocent X" (Velasquez) 35 15

29. Module landing on Moon.

1968. Space Exploration. Multicoloured.
353. 4 f. Type **29** (postage) .. 8 5
354. 6 f. Russian cosmonaut in Space 10 5
355. 8 f. Weather satellite .. 12 8
356. 10 f. American astronaut in Space 20 10
357. 14 f. Type **29** (air) .. 20 10
358. 18 f. As 6 f. 25 10
359. 25 f. As 8 f. 30 15
360. 40 f. As 10 f. 50 20

30. "Salamis aethiops".

1968. Butterflies. Multicoloured.

(a) Postage. (i) Size as T **27**.
362. 50 c. Type **30** 5 5
363. 1 f. "Graphium ridleyanus" 5 5
364. 1 f. 50 "Cymothoe" .. 5 5
365. 2 f. "Charaxes eupale" .. 5 5
366. 3 f. "Papilio bromius" .. 5 5
367. 3 f. 50 "Teracolus annae" 5 5

(ii) Size 34 × 38 mm.
386. 4 f. Type **30** 5 5
369. 5 f. As 1 f. 8 5
370. 6 f. 50 As 1 f. 50 .. 10 8
371. 8 f. As 2 f. 10 8
372. 10 f. As 3 f. 12 10
373. 15 f. As 3 f. 50 .. .. 20 12

(iii) Size 41 × 46 mm.
374. 20 f. Type **30** 30 15
375. 50 f. "Papilio zenobia" .. 70 25
376. 100 f. "Danais chrysippus" .. .. 1·40 50
377. 150 f. "Salamis temora" 2·00 90

(b) Air. With gold frames.

(i) Size 33 × 37 mm.
378. 6 f. As 3 f. 50 .. .. 8 5
379. 8 f. As 1 f. 10 5
380. 10 f. As 1 f. 50 .. .. 12 5
381. 14 f. As 2 f. 20 8
382. 15 f. As 3 f. 20 8

(ii) Size 39 × 44 mm.
383. 20 f. As 50 f. (postage) .. 30 10
384. 50 f. Type **30** 70 20
385. 75 f. As 100 f. .. .. 1·00 30
386. 130 f. As 150 f. .. .. 1·50 50

31. "Woman by the Manzanares" (Goya).

1968. Int. Letter-writing Week. Mult.
387. 4 f. Type **31** (postage) .. 8 5
388. 7 f. "Reading a Letter" (De Hooch) 10 5
389. 11 f. "Woman reading a Letter" (Terborch) .. 12 8
390. 14 f. "Man writing a Letter" (Metsu) .. 20 10
391. 17 f. "The Letter" (Fragonard) (air) 25 10
392. 26 f. "Young Woman reading Letter" (Vermeer) .. 30 15
393. 40 f. "Folding a Letter" (Vigee-Lebrun) .. 45 20
394. 50 f. "Mademoiselle Lavergne" (Liotard) .. 55 25

32. Football.

1968. Olympic Games, Mexico. Mult.
396. 4 f. Type **32** (postage) .. 8 5
397. 7 f. Basketball 12 8
398. 13 f. High jumping .. 15 10
399. 24 f. Relay racing 30 15
400. 40 f. Throwing the javelin 55 30
401. 10 f. Putting the shot (air) 10 5
402. 17 f. Running 20 8
403. 26 f. Throwing the hammer 30 10
404. 50 f. Hurdling 65 20
405. 75 f. Long jumping .. 85 30

33. "Virgin and Child" (Lippi). **35.** Hand holding Flame.

34. W.H.O. Emblem and Map.

1968. Christmas. Paintings. Multicoloured.
407. 3 f. Type **33** (postage) .. 5 5
408. 5 f. "The Magnificat" (Botticelli) 8 5
409. 6 f. "Virgin and Child" (Durer) 10 8
410. 11 f. "Virgin and Child" (Correggio) 15 10
411. 10 f. "Madonna" (Raphael) (air) 10 10
412. 14 f. "The Nativity" (Baroccio) 20 15
413. 17 f. "The Holy Family" (El Greco) 20 15
414. 26 f. "Adoration of the Magi (Maino) 35 20

1969. World Health Organisation Operations in Africa. 20th Anniv.
416. **34.** 5 f. multicoloured .. 8 5
417. 6 f. multicoloured .. 10 5
418. 11 f. multicoloured .. 15 10

1969. Air. Human Rights Year.
419. **35.** 10 f. multicoloured .. 12 8
420. 14 f. multicoloured .. 15 10
421. 26 f. multicoloured .. 30 15

1969. Space Flight of "Apollo 8". Nos. 407/14 optd. ***VOL DE NOEL APOLLO 8*** and space module.
422. 3 f. multicoloured (postage) 5 5
423. 5 f. multicoloured 5 5
424. 6 f. multicoloured 10 8
425. 11 f. multicoloured .. 15 10
426. 10 f. multicoloured (air) .. 10 8
427. 14 f. multicoloured .. 15 12
428. 17 f. multicoloured .. 20 15
429. 26 f. multicoloured .. 30 25

36. Map showing African Members. **37.** "Resurrection" (Isenmann).

1969. Yaounde Agreement between Common Market Countries and African-Malagasy Economic Community. 5th Anniv. Mult.

430.	5 f. Type **36**	8	5
431.	14 f. Ploughing with tractor	20	12
432.	17 f. Teacher and pupil	25	15
433.	26 f. Maps of Africa and Europe (horiz.)	35	25

1969. Easter. Multicoloured.

434.	11 f. Type **37**	15	10
435.	14 f. "Resurrection" (Caron)	20	15
436.	17 f. "Noli me Tangere" (Schongauer)	25	20
437.	26 f. "Resurrection" (El Greco)	35	25

38. Potter.

1969. Int. Labour Organization. 50th Anniv. Multicoloured.

439.	3 f. Type **38**	5	5
440.	5 f. Farm workers	8	5
441.	7 f. Foundry worker	10	5
442.	10 f. Harvester	12	8

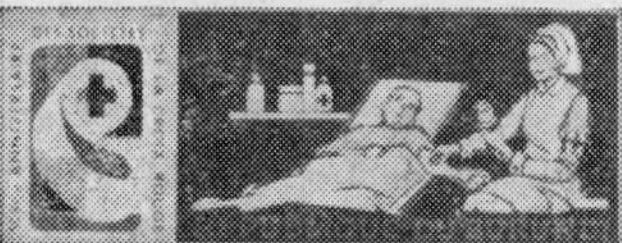

39. Nurse and Patient.

1969. League of Red Cross Societies. 50th Anniv. Multicoloured.

443.	4 f.+1 f. Type **39** (postage)	8	8
444.	7 f.+1 f. Stretcher bearers	12	8
445.	11 f.+1 f. Operating theatre	15	12
446.	17 f.+1 f. Blood bank	20	15
447.	26 f.+3 f. Laboratory (air)	40	15
448.	40 f.+3 f. Red Cross truck in African village	50	20
499.	50 f.+3 f. Nurse and woman patient	60	25

40. Steel Works.

1969. African Development Bank. 5th Anniv. Multicoloured.

451.	10 f. Type **40**	10	5
452.	17 f. Broadcaster	20	10
453.	30 f. Language laboratory	35	15
454.	50 f. Tractor and harrow	50	25

41. Pope Paul VI.

42. "Girl reading Letter" (Vermeer).

1969. 1st Papal Visit to Africa. Mult.

456.	3 f.+2 f. Type **41**	5	5
457.	5 f.+2 f. Pope Paul and map of Africa	10	8
458.	10 f.+2 f. Pope Paul and African flags	15	10
459.	14 f.+2 f. Pope Paul and the Vatican	20	15
460.	17 f.+2 f. Type **41**	20	15
461.	40 f.+2 f. Pope Paul and Uganda Martyrs	55	30
462.	50 f.+2 f. Pope Paul enthroned	60	40

Nos. 457/59 and 461/62 are horiz.

1969. Int. Letter-writing Week. Mult.

464.	4 f. Type **42**	5	5
465.	7 f. "Graziella" (Renoir)	8	8
466.	14 f. "Woman writing a Letter" (Terborch)	20	12
467.	26 f. "Galileo" (unknown painter)	30	15
468.	40 f. "Beethoven" (unknown painter)	45	25

43. Blast-off.

44. "Adoration of the Magi" (detail, Rubens).

1969. 1st Man on the Moon. Multicoloured.

470.	4 f. Type **43** (postage)	8	5
471.	6 f. 50 Rocket in Space	10	5
472.	7 f. Separation of lunar module	10	5
473.	14 f. Module landing on Moon	15	10
474.	17 f. Command module in orbit	25	15
475.	26 f. Astronaut descending ladder (air)	30	15
476.	40 f. Astronaut on Moon's surface	45	20
477.	50 f. Module in sea	55	25

1969. Christmas. Multicoloured.

479.	5 f. Type **44** (postage)	5	5
480.	6 f. "Virgin and Child with St. John" (Romano)	8	5
481.	10 f. "Madonna of the Magnificat" (Botticelli)	12	8
482.	17 f. "Virgin and Child" (Garofalo) (air)	20	10
483.	26 f. "Madonna and Child" (Negretti)	35	15
484.	50 f. "Virgin and Child" (Barbarelli)	50	30

Nos. 482/4 are horiz.

45. "Chelorrhina polyphemus".

1970. Beetles. Multicoloured.

(a) Postage. (i) Size 39×28 mm.

486.	50 c. "Sternotomis bohemani"	5	5
487.	1 f. "Tetralobus flabellicornis"	5	5
488.	1 f. 50 Type **45**	5	5
489.	2 f. "Brachytritus hieroglyphicus"	5	5
490.	3 f. "Goliathus goliathus"	5	5
491.	3 f. 50 "Homoderus mellyi"	5	5

(ii) Size 46×32 mm.

492.	4 f. As 50 c.	8	5
493.	5 f. As 1 f.	8	5
494.	6 f. 50 Type **45**	8	8
495.	8 f. As 2 f.	10	8
496.	10 f. As 3 f.	12	8
497.	15 f. As 3 f. 50	15	10

(iii) Size 62×36 mm.

498.	20 f. As 50 c.	25	12
499.	50 f. "Stephanorrhina guttata"	75	25
500.	100 f. "Phyllocnema viridocostata"	1·50	40
501.	150 f. "Mecynorrhina oberthueri"	2·25	60

(b) Air. (i) Size 46×32 mm.

502.	6 f. As 3 f. 50	8	5
503.	8 f. As 1 f.	10	8
504.	10 f. Type **45**	12	8
505.	14 f. As 2 f.	15	10
506.	15 f. As 3 f.	20	10

(ii) Size 52×36 mm.

507.	20 f. As 50 f. (No. 499)	25	12
508.	50 f. As 50 c.	60	15
509.	75 f. As 100 f.	90	20
510.	130 f. As 150 f.	1·10	30

46. "Jesus Condemned to Death".

1970. Easter. "The Stations of the Cross" (Carredano). Multicoloured.

511.	1 f. Type **46** (postage)	5	5
512.	1 f. 50 "Carrying the Cross"	5	5
513.	2 f. "Jesus falls for the First Time"	5	5
514.	3 f. "Jesus meets His Mother"	5	5
515.	3 f. 50 "Simon of Cyrene takes the Cross"	5	5
516.	4 f. "Veronica wipes the face of Christ"	5	5
517.	5 f. "Jesus falls for the Second Time"	8	8
518.	8 f. "The Women of Jerusalem" (air)	10	8
519.	10 f. "Jesus falls for the Third Time"	12	10
520.	14 f. "Christ stripped"	15	12
521.	15 f. "Jesus nailed to the Cross"	20	15
522.	18 f. "The Crucifixion"	25	20
523.	20 f. "Descent from the Cross"	30	25
524.	50 f. "Christ laid in the Tomb"	70	30

47. Japanese Parade.

1970. World Fair, Osaka, Japan (EXPO '70). Multicoloured.

526.	4 f. Type **47**	8	5
527.	6 f. 50 Exhibition site from the air	8	5
528.	7 f. African pavilions	10	5
529.	14 f. Pagoda (vert.)	20	12
530.	26 f. Recording pavilion and pool	35	20
531.	40 f. Town of the Sun (vert.)	60	30
532.	50 f. National flags (vert.)	70	40

48. Burundi Cow.

1970. Sources of the Nile. Multicoloured.

534.	7 f. Any design (postage)	10	5
535.	14 f. Any design (air)	20	8

Nos. 534 and 535 were each issued in se-tenant sheets of 18 stamps as T **48**, showing map sections, animals and birds, forming a map of the Nile from Cairo to Burundi.

49. European Redstart.

1970. Birds. Multicoloured.

(a) Postage. Size 44×33 or 33×44 mm.

536.	2 f. Northern shrike (vert.)	5	5
537.	2 f. European starling (vert.)	5	5
538.	2 f. Yellow wagtail (vert.)	5	5
539.	2 f. Bank swallow (vert.)	5	5
540.	3 f. Wren	5	5
541.	3 f. Firecrest	5	5
542.	3 f. Skylark	5	5
543.	3 f. Crested lark	5	5
544.	3 f. 50 Wood shrike (vert.)	5	5
545.	3 f. 50 Rock thrush (vert.)	5	5
546.	3 f. 50 Black redstarts (vert.)	5	5
547.	3 f. 50 Ring ouzel (vert.)	5	5
548.	4 f. Type **49**	5	5
549.	4 f. Hedge sparrow	5	5
550.	4 f. Grey wagtail	5	5
551.	4 f. Meadow pipit	5	5
552.	5 f. Eurasian hoopoe (vert.)	8	5
553.	5 f. Flycatcher (vert.)	8	5
554.	5 f. Great reed warbler (vert.)	8	5
555.	5 f. Kingfisher (vert.)	8	5
556.	6 f. 50 House martin	10	5
557.	6 f. 50 Sedge warbler	10	5
558.	6 f. 50 Fieldfare	10	5
559.	6 f. 50 Golden oriole	10	5

(b) Air. Size 52×44 mm. or 44×52 mm.

560.	8 f. As No. 536	10	8
561.	8 f. As No. 537	10	8
562.	8 f. As No. 538	10	8
563.	8 f. As No. 539	10	8
564.	10 f. As No. 540	12	10
565.	10 f. As No. 541	12	10
566.	10 f. As No. 542	12	10
567.	10 f. As No. 543	12	10
568.	14 f. As No. 544	20	12
569.	14 f. As No. 545	20	12
570.	14 f. As No. 546	20	12
571.	14 f. As No. 547	20	12
572.	20 f. Type **49**	25	15
573.	20 f. As No 549	25	15
574.	20 f. As No. 550	25	15
575.	20 f. As No. 551	25	15
576.	30 f. As No. 552	40	20
577.	30 f. As No. 553	40	20
578.	30 f. As No. 554	40	20
579.	30 f. As No. 555	40	20
580.	50 f. As No. 556	70	30
581.	50 f. As No. 557	70	30
582.	50 f. As No. 558	70	30
583.	50 f. As No. 559	70	30

50. Library.

1970. Int. Educational Year. Multicoloured.

584.	3 f. Type **50**	5	5
585.	5 f. Examination	8	5
586.	7 f. Experiments in the laboratory	8	8
587.	10 f. Students with electron microscope	12	10

51. United Nations Building, New York.

1970. Air. United Nations. 25th Anniv Multicoloured.

588.	7 f. Type **51**	8	5
589.	11 f. Security Council in session	15	8
590.	26 f. Paul VI and U Thant	40	20
591.	40 f. U.N. and National flags	50	30

52. Pres. Micombero and Wife.

1970. Republic. 4th Anniv.

593.	4 f. Type **52**	5	5
594.	7 f. Pres. Micombero and flag	8	5
595.	11 f. Revolution Memorial	15	10

INDEX

Countries can be quickly located by referring to the index at the end of this volume.

53. King Baudouin and Queen Fabiola.

1970. Air. Visit of King and Queen of the Belgians. Each brown, purple and gold.

597.	6 f. Type **53**	8	5
598.	20 f. Pres. Micombero and King Baudouin	25	15
599.	40 f. Pres. Micombero in evening dress	50	25

54. " Adoration of the Magi " (Durer).

1970. Christmas. Multicoloured.

601.	6 f. 50+1 f. Type **54** (post.)	12	8
602.	11 f.+1 f. " The Virgin of the Eucharist " (Botticelli)	15	10
603.	20 f.+1 f. " The Holy Family " (El Greco)	25	15
604.	14 f.+3 f. " The Adoration of the Magi " (Velasquez) (air)	20	12
605.	26 f.+3 f. " The Holy Family " (Van Cleve)	35	20
606.	40 f.+3 f. " Virgin and Child " (Van der Weyden)	60	30

55. Lenin in Discussion. 57. " The Resurrection " (Il Sodoma).

56. Lion.

1970. Lenin. Birth Cent. Each brown and gold.

608.	3 f. 50 Type **55**	5	5
609.	5 f. Lenin addressing Soviet	8	5
610.	6 f. 50 Lenin with soldier and sailor	8	8
611.	15 f. Lenin speaking to crowd	20	15
612.	50 f. Lenin	75	40

1971. African Animals. Multicoloured.

(a) Postage. Size 38×38 mm.

613.	1 f. Type **56**	5	5
614.	1 f. Water buffalo	5	5
615.	1 f. Hippopotamus	5	5
616.	1 f. Giraffe	5	5
617.	2 f. Damas gazelles	5	5
613.	2 f. Rhinoceros	5	5
619.	2 f. Zebra	5	5
620.	2 f. Leopard	5	5
621.	3 f. Grant's gazelle	5	5
622.	3 f. Cheetah	5	5
623.	3 f. Vultures	5	5
624.	3 f. Okapi	5	5
625.	5 f. Chimpanzee	8	5
626.	5 f. Elephant	8	5
627.	5 f. Spotted hyena	8	5
628.	5 f. Oryx	8	5
629.	6 f. Gorilla	8	5
630.	6 f. Gnu	8	5
631.	6 f. Warthog	8	5
632.	6 f. Wild dog	8	5
633.	11 f. Sable antelope	20	8
634.	11 f. Caracal lynx	20	8
635.	11 f. Ostriches	20	8
636.	11 f. Bongo	20	8

(b) Air. Size 44×44 mm.

637.	10 f. Type **56**	15	8
638.	10 f. As No. 614	15	8
639.	10 f. As No. 615	15	8
640.	10 f. As No. 616	15	8
641.	14 f. As No. 617	20	12
642.	14 f. As No. 618	20	12
543.	14 f. As No. 619	20	12
644.	14 f. As No. 620	20	12
645.	17 f. As No. 621	20	12
646.	17 f. As No. 522	20	12
647.	17 f. As No. 623	20	12
648.	17 f. As No. 624	20	12
649.	24 f. As No. 625	35	20
650.	24 f. As No. 626	35	20
651.	24 f. As No. 627	35	20
652.	24 f. As No. 628	35	20
653.	26 f. As No. 629	35	20
654.	26 f. As No. 630	35	20
655.	26 f. As No. 631	35	20
656.	26 f. As No. 632	35	20
657.	31 f. As No. 633	40	25
658.	31 f. As No. 634	40	25
659.	31 f. As No. 635	40	25
660.	31 f. As No. 636	40	25

1971. Easter. Multicoloured.

661.	3 f. Type **57** (postage)	5	5
662.	6 f. " The Resurrection " (Del Castagno)	8	5
663.	11 f. " Noli Me Tangere " (Correggio)	15	10
664.	14 f. " The Resurrection " (Borrassi) (air)	20	10
665.	17 f. " The Resurrection " (Della Francesca)	25	10
666.	26 f. " The Resurrection " (Pleydenwyurff)	30	15

1971. Air. United Nations Campaigns. Nos. 637/48 optd. or surch.

(a) Optd. **LUTTE CONTRE LE RACISME ET LA DISCRIMINATION RACIALE** and Racial Equality Year emblem.

668.	10 f. multicoloured	15	8
669.	10 f. multicoloured	15	8
670.	10 f. multicoloured	15	8
671.	10 f. multicoloured	15	8

(b) Surch. **LUTTE CONTRE L'ANALPHABETISME,** U.N.E.S.C.O. emblem and premium (Campaign against Illiteracy).

672.	14 f.+2 f. multicoloured	20	12
673.	14 f.+2 f. multicoloured	20	12
674.	14 f.+2 f. multicoloured	20	12
675.	14 f.+2 f. multicoloured	20	12

(c) Surch. **AIDE INTERNATIONALE AUX REFUGIES,** emblem and premium (Int. Help for Refugees).

676.	17 f.+1 f. multicoloured	20	12
677.	17 f.+1 f. multicoloured	20	12
678.	17 f.+1 f. multicoloured	20	12
679.	17 f.+1 f. multicoloured	20	12

1971. Air. Olympic Commems. Nos. 653/60 surch.

(a) Surch. **75eme ANNIVERSAIRE DES JEUX OLYMPIQUES MODERNES (1896-1971),** Olympic rings and premium.

680.	26 f.+1 f. multicoloured	65	30
681.	26 f.+1 f. multicoloured	65	30
682.	26 f.+1 f. multicoloured	65	30
683.	26 f.+1 f. multicoloured	65	30

(b) Surch. **JEUX PRE-OLYMPIQUES MUNICH 1972,** rings and premium (Olympic Games, Munich (1972)).

684.	31 f.+1 f. multicoloured	70	40
685.	31 f.+1 f. multicoloured	70	40
686.	31 f.+1 f. multicoloured	70	40
687.	31 f.+1 f. multicoloured	70	40

58. " Venetian Girl ". 59. " The Virgin and Child " (Il Perugino).

1971. Int. Letter-writing Week. Paintings by Durer. Multicoloured.

688.	6 f. Type **58**	8	5
689.	11 f. " Jerome Holzschuhers "	15	8
690.	14 f. " Emperor Maximilian "	20	12
691.	17 f. Altar painting, Paumgartner	20	12
692.	26 f. " The Halle Madonna "	35	20
693.	31 f. Self portrait	45	25

1971. 6th Congress of Int. Institute of French Law, Bujumbura. Nos. 668/693 optd. **VIeme CONGRES DE L'INSTITUT INTERNATIONAL DE DROIT D'EXPRESSION FRANCAISE.**

695.	6 f. multicoloured	8	5
696.	11 f. multicoloured	15	8
697.	14 f. multicoloured	20	10
698.	17 f. multicoloured	20	10
699.	26 f. multicoloured	35	15
700.	31 f. multicoloured	45	20

1971. Christmas. Paintings of " Virgin and Child " by following artists. Mult.

702.	3 f. Type **59** (postage)	5	5
703.	5 f. Del Sarte	8	5
704.	6 f. Morales	8	8
705.	14 f. Da Conegliano (air)	20	12
706.	17 f. Lippi	20	12
707.	31 f. Leonardo da Vinci	45	20

1971. U.N.I.C.E.F. 25th Anniv. Nos. 702/707 surch. **UNICEF XXVe ANNIVERSAIRE 1946-1971,** emblem and premium.

709.	3 f.+1 f. mult. (postage)	8	8
710.	5 f.+1 f. multicoloured	10	10
711.	6 f.+1 f. multicoloured	20	20
712.	14 f.+1 f. mult. (air)	25	12
713.	17 f.+1 f. multicoloured	25	12
714.	31 f.+1 f. multicoloured	50	25

60. " Archangel Michael " (icon, St. Mark's).

1971. U.N.E.S.C.O. " Save Venice " Campaign. Multicoloured.

716.	3 f.+1 f. Type **60** (postage)	5	5
717.	5 f.+1 f. " La Polenta " (Longhi)	8	5
718.	6 f.+1 f. " Gossip " (Longhi)	12	8
719.	11 f.+1 f. " Diana's Bath " (Pittoni)	20	10
720.	10 f.+1 f. Casa d'Oro (air)	15	10
721.	17 f.+1 f. Doge's Palace	20	12
722.	24 f.+1 f. St. John and St. Paul Church	30	20
723.	31 f.+1 f. " Doge's Palace and Piazzetta " (Canaletto)	45	25

61. " Lunar Orbiter ". 63. " Ecce Homo " (Metzys).

62. Slalom skiing.

1972. Conquest of Space. Multicoloured.

725.	6 f. Type **61**	8	5
726.	11 f. " Vostok " spaceship	15	8
727.	14 f. " Luna 1 "	20	12
728.	17 f. First Man on Moon	25	15
729.	26 f. " Soyuz 11 " space flight	30	20
730.	40 f. " Lunar Rover "	50	30

1972. Winter Olympic Games, Sapporo, Japan. Multicoloured.

732.	5 f. Type **62**	5	5
733.	6 f. Pair skating	8	5
734.	11 f. Figure-skating	15	8
735.	14 f. Ski-jumping	20	12
736.	17 f. Ice-hockey	25	12
737.	24 f. Speed skating	30	20
738.	26 f. Snow scooting	30	20
739.	31 f. Downhill skiing	40	20
740.	50 f. Bobsleighing	60	30

1972. Easter. Paintings. Multicoloured.

742.	3 f. 50 Type **63**	5	5
743.	6 f. 50 " The Crucifixion " (Rubens)	8	5
744.	10 f. " The Descent from the Cross " (Portormo)	15	8
745.	18 f. " Pieta " (Gallegos)	25	10
746.	27 f. " The Trinity " (El Greco)	30	20

64. Gymnastics

1972. Olympic Games, Munich. Mult.

748.	5 f. Type **64** (postage)	8	5
749.	6 f. Throwing the javelin	8	5
750.	11 f. Fencing	15	8
751.	14 f. Cycling	20	10
752.	17 f. Pole-vaulting	25	12
753.	24 f. Weightlifting (air)	30	15
754.	26 f. Hurdling	35	20
755.	31 f. Throwing the discus	40	25
756.	40 f. Football	50	30

65. Prince Rwagasore, Pres. Micombero and Drummers.

1972. Independence. 10th Anniv. Mult.

758.	5 f. Type **65** (postage)	8	5
759.	7 f. Rwangasore, Micombero and map	8	8
760.	13 f. Pres. Micombero and Burundi flag.	20	10
761.	15 f. Type **65** (air)	20	12
762.	18 f. As 7 f.	25	15
763.	27 f. As 13 f.	35	25

66. " Madonna and Child " (A. Solario).

1972. Christmas. " Madonna and Child " paintings by artists given below. Mult.

765.	5 f. Type **66** (postage)	8	5
766.	10 f. Raphael	15	8
767.	15 f. Botticelli	20	12
768.	18 f. S. Mainardi (air)	25	15
769.	27 f. H. Memling	30	20
770.	40 f. Lotto	50	25

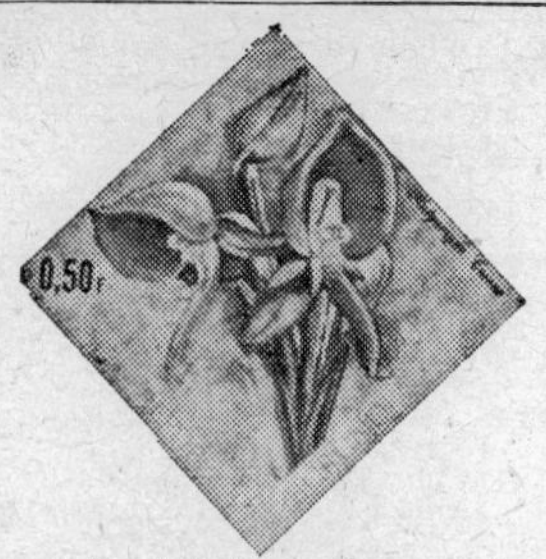

67. "Platycoryne croces"

1972. Orchids. Multicoloured.

772. 50 c. Type **67** (postage) .. 5 5
773. 1 f. "Cattleya trianaei" .. 5 5
774. 2 f. "Eulophia cucullata" 5 5
775. 3 f. "Cymbidium hamsey" 5 5
776. 4 f. "Thelymitra pauciflora" 5 5
777. 5 f. "Miltassia" 8 5
778. 6 f. "Miltonia" 8 5
779. 7 f. Type **67** 10 8
780. 8 f. As 1 f... .. .. 10 8
781. 9 f. As 2 f... .. .. 12 10
782. 10 f. As 3 f... .. .. 15 10

783. 13 f. As 4 f. (air) 20 12
784. 14 f. As 5 f... .. .. 20 12
785. 15 f. As 6 f... .. .. 20 12
786. 18 f. Type **67** 25 15
787. 20 f. As 1 f... .. .. 30 15
788. 27 f. As 2 f... .. .. 35 15
789. 36 f. As 3 f... .. .. 45 25

Nos. 779/89 are size, 54 × 54 mm.

1972. Christmas Charity. Nos. 765/770 surch.

790. 5 f. + 1 f. mult. (postage).. 8 5
791. 10 f. + 1 f. multicoloured.. 15 8
792. 15 f. + 1 f. multicoloured.. 20 15

793. 18 f. + 1 f. mult. (air) .. 30 20
794. 27 f. + 1 f. multicoloured.. 40 25
795. 40 f. + 1 f. multicoloured.. 60 30

68. H. M. Stanley.

1973. Stanley/Livingstone African Exploration. Cent. Multicoloured.

797. 5 f. Type **68** (postage) .. 5 5
798. 7 f. Expedition bearers .. 8 5
799. 13 f. Stanley directing foray 15 12

800. 15 f. Dr. Livingstone (air) 20 12
801. 18 f. Stanley meets Livingstone 25 15
802. 27 f. Stanley conferring with Livingstone .. 35 20

69. "The Scourging" (Caravaggio).

1973. Easter. Multicoloured.

804. 5 f. Type **69** (postage) .. 5 5
805. 7 f. "Crucifixion" (Van der Weiden) 8 5
806. 13 f. "The Deposition" (Raphael) 15 12

807. 15 f. "Christ bound to the Pillar" (Guido Reni) (air) 20 12
808. 18 f. "Crucifixion" (M. Grunewald) 25 15
809. 27 f. "The Descent from the Cross" (Caravaggio) 35 20

70. Interpol Emblem.

1973. Interpol. 50th Anniv. Multicoloured.

811. 5 f. Type **70** (postage) .. 5 5
812. 10 f. Burundi flag.. .. 12 8
813. 18 f. Interpol H.Q., Paris 20 15

814. 27 f. As 5 f. (air) .. 35 20
815. 40 f. As 10 f. 50 35

71/74. Signs of the Zodiac.

1973. Copernicus. 500th Birth Anniv.

816. **71.** 3 f. gold, red & blk. (post.) 5 5
817. **72.** 3 f. gold, red and black 5 5
818. **73.** 3 f. gold, red and black 5 5
819. **74.** 3 f. gold, red and black 5 5
820. – 5 f. multicoloured .. 8 5
821. – 5 f. multicoloured .. 8 5
822. – 5 f. multicoloured .. 8 5
823. – 5 f. multicoloured .. 8 5
824. – 7 f. multicoloured .. 10 8
825. – 7 f. multicoloured .. 10 8
826. – 7 f. multicoloured .. 10 8
827. – 7 f. multicoloured .. 10 8
828. – 13 f. multicoloured .. 20 15
829. – 13 f. multicoloured .. 20 15
830. – 13 f. multicoloured .. 20 15
831. – 13 f. multicoloured .. 20 15

832. – 15 f. multicoloured (air) 20 15
833. – 15 f. multicoloured .. 20 15
834. – 15 f. multicoloured .. 20 15
835. – 15 f. multicoloured .. 20 15
836. – 18 f. multicoloured .. 25 20
837. – 18 f. multicoloured .. 25 20
838. – 18 f. multicoloured .. 25 20
839. – 18 f. multicoloured .. 25 20
840. – 27 f. multicoloured .. 35 25
841. – 27 f. multicoloured .. 35 25
842. – 27 f. multicoloured .. 35 25
843. – 27 f. multicoloured .. 35 25
844. – 36 f. multicoloured .. 45 35
845. – 36 f. multicoloured .. 45 35
846. – 36 f. multicoloured .. 45 35
847. – 36 f. multicoloured .. 45 35

DESIGNS: Nos. 820/23, Greek and Roman Gods. Nos. 824/7, Ptolemy and Ptolemaic System. Nos. 828/31, Copernicus and Solar System. Nos. 832/5, Copernicus, Earth, Pluto and Jupiter. Nos. 836/39, Copernicus, Venus, Saturn and Mars. Nos. 840/43, Copernicus, Uranus, Neptune and Mercury. Nos. 844/7, Earth and spacecraft.

The four designs of each value were issued se-tenant in blocks of four within the sheet, forming composite designs.

75. "Protea cynaroides".

76. "Virgin and Child" (Van Eyck).

1973. Flora and Butterflies. Multicoloured.

849. 1 f. Type **75** (postage) .. 5 5
850. 1 f. "Precis octavia" .. 5 5
851. 1 f. "Epiphora bauhiniae" 5 5
852. 1 f. "Gazania longiscapa" 5 5
853. 2 f. "Kniphofia" – "Royal Standard" 5 5
854. 2 f. "Cymothoe coccinata hew" 5 5
855. 2 f. "Nudaurelia zambesina" 5 5
856. 2 f. "Freesia refracta" .. 5 5
857. 3 f. "Calotis eupompe" .. 5 5
858. 3 f. Narcissus 5 5
859. 3 f. "Cineraria hybrida" 5 5
860. 3 f. "Cyrestis camillus".. 5 5
861. 5 f. "Iris tingitana" .. 8 5
862. 5 f. "Papilio demodocus" 8 5
863. 5 f. "Catopsilia avelaneda" 8 5
864. 5 f. "Narine sarniensis" 8 5
865. 6 f. "Hypolimnas dexithea" 8 5
866. 6 f. "Zantedeschia tropicalis" 8 5
867. 6 f. "Sandersonia aurantiaca" 8 5
868. 6 f. "Drurya antimachus" 8 5
869. 11 f. "Nymphaea capensis" 15 10
870. 11 f. "Pandoriana pandora" 15 10
871. 11 f. "Precis orythia" .. 15 10
872. 11 f. "Pelargonium domesticum" – "Aztec" 15 10

873. 10 f. Type **75** (air) .. 12 10
874. 10 f. As No. 850 .. .. 12 10
875. 10 f. As No. 851 .. .. 12 10
876. 10 f. As No. 852 .. .. 12 10
877. 14 f. As No. 853 .. .. 15 12
878. 14 f. As No. 854 .. .. 15 12
879. 14 f. As No. 855 .. .. 15 12
880. 14 f. As No. 856 .. .. 15 12
881. 17 f. As No. 857 .. .. 20 15
882. 17 f. As No. 858 .. .. 20 15
883. 17 f. As No. 859 .. .. 20 15
884. 17 f. As No. 860 .. .. 20 15
885. 25 f. As No. 861 .. .. 25 20
886. 25 f. As No. 862 .. .. 25 20
887. 25 f. As No. 863 .. .. 25 20
888. 25 f. As No. 864 .. .. 25 20
889. 26 f. As No. 865 .. .. 30 25
890. 26 f. As No. 866 .. .. 30 25
891. 26 f. As No. 867 .. .. 30 25
892. 26 f. As No. 868 .. .. 30 25
893. 31 f. As No. 869 .. .. 35 30
894. 31 f. As No. 870 .. .. 35 30
895. 31 f. As No. 871 .. .. 35 30
896. 31 f. As No. 872 .. .. 35 30

Nos. 849, 852/3, 856, 858/9, 861, 864, 866/7, 869, 872, 876/7, 880, 882/3, 885, 888, 890/1, 893 and 896 depict flora and the remainder butterflies.

The four designs of each value were issued se-tenant in blocks of four within the sheet, forming composite designs.

1973. Christmas. Various paintings of "The Virgin and Child" by artists listed below. Multicoloured.

897. 5 f. Type **76** (postage) .. 8 5
898. 10 f. G. Bellini 15 10
899. 15 f. P. Perugino 20 15

900. 18 f. G. A. Boltraffio (air) 20 15
901. 27 f. Titian 35 30
902. 40 f. Raphael 55 40

1973. Nos. 897/902 surch.

904. **76.** 5 f. + 1 f. mult. (postage) 8 5
905. 10 f. + 1 f. multicoloured 15 10
906. – 15 f. + 1 f. multicoloured 20 15

907. – 18 f. + 1 f. multicoloured (air) 25 20
908. – 27 f. + 1 f. multicoloured 40 30
909. – 40 f. + 1 f. multicoloured 60 40

77. "The Pieta" (Veronese).

1974. Easter. Religious Paintings. Multicoloured.

911. 5 f. Type **77** 8 5
912. 10 f. "The Virgin and St. John" (Van der Weiden) 15 10
913. 18 f. "The Crucifixion" (Van der Weiden) .. 25 20
914. 27 f. "The Entombment" (Titian) 40 30
915. 40 f. "The Pieta" (El Greco) 50 40

78. "Haplochromis multicolor".

1974. Fishes. Multicoloured.

917. 1 f. Type **78** 5 5
918. 1 f. "Tropheus duboisi" .. 5 5
919. 1 f. "Pantodon buchholzi" 5 5
920. 1 f. "Distichodus sexfasciatus" 5 5
921. 2 f. "Pelmatochromis kribensis" 5 5
922. 2 f. "Polycentropsis abbreviata" 5 5
923. 2 f. "Nannaethiops tritaeniatus" 5 5
924. 2 f. "Hemichromis bimaculatus" 5 5
925. 3 f. "Ctenopoma acutirostre" 5 5
926. 3 f. "Tilapia melanopleura" 5 5
927. 3 f. "Synodontis angelicus" 5 5
928. 3 f. "Aphyosemion bivittatum" 5 5
929. 5 f. "Monodactylus argenteus" 8 5
930. 5 f. "Pygoplites diacanthus" 8 5
931. 5 f. "Zanclus canescens" .. 8 5
932. 5 f. "Cephalopholis argus" 8 5
933. 6 f. "Priacanthus arenatus" 10 8
934. 6 f. "Scarus guacamaia" .. 10 8
935. 6 f. "Pomacanthus arcuatus" 10 8
936. 6 f. "Zeus faber" 10 8
937. 11 f. "Lactophrys quadricornis" 20 15
938. 11 f. "Acanthurus bahianus" 20 15
939. 11 f. "Balistes vetula" .. 20 15
940. 11 f. "Holocanthus ciliaris" 20 15

941. 10 f. Type **78** (air) .. 15 12
942. 10 f. As No. 918 .. .. 15 12
943. 10 f. As No. 919 .. .. 15 12
944. 10 f. As No. 920 .. .. 15 12
945. 14 f. As No. 921 .. .. 20 15
946. 14 f. As No. 922 .. .. 20 15
947. 14 f. As No. 923 .. .. 20 15
948. 14 f. As No. 924 .. .. 20 15
949. 17 f. As No. 925 .. .. 25 20
950. 17 f. As No. 926 .. .. 25 20
951. 17 f. As No. 927 .. .. 25 20
952. 17 f. As No. 928 .. .. 25 20
953. 24 f. As No. 929 .. .. 35 30
954. 24 f. As No. 930 .. .. 35 30
955. 24 f. As No. 931 .. .. 35 30
956. 24 f. As No. 932 .. .. 35 30
957. 26 f. As No. 933 .. .. 40 35
958. 26 f. As No. 934 .. .. 40 35
959. 26 f. As No. 935 .. .. 40 35
960. 26 f. As No. 936 .. .. 40 35
961. 31 f. As No. 937 .. .. 45 40
962. 31 f. As No. 938 .. .. 45 40
963. 31 f. As No. 939 .. .. 45 40
964. 31 f. As No. 940 .. .. 45 40

The four designs of each value are arranged together in se-tenant blocks of four within the sheet, forming composite designs.

79. Footballers and World Cup.

1974. World Cup Football Championships.

965. **79.** 5 f. multicoloured (postage) 8 5
966. – 6 f. multicoloured .. 10 8
967. – 11 f. multicoloured .. 20 15
968. – 14 f. multicoloured .. 25 20
969. – 17 f. multicoloured .. 25 20

970. – 20 f. multicoloured (air) 30 25
971. – 26 f. multicoloured .. 40 35
972. – 40 f. multicoloured .. 55 45

DESIGNS: Nos. 966/72, Football scenes as Type **79**.

80. Burundi Flag.

1974. Universal Postal Union. Cent. Mult.

974. 6 f. Type **80** (postage) .. 10 8
975. 6 f. Burundi P.T.T. Building 10 8
976. 11 f. Postmen carrying .. 20 15
977. 11 f. letters 20 15
978. 14 f. U.P.U. Monument .. 20 15
979. 14 f. Mail transport .. 20 15
980. 17 f. Burundi on map .. 25 20
981. 17 f. Dove and letter .. 25 20

982. 24 f. Type **80** (air) .. 35 30
983. 24 f. As No. 975 .. .. 35 30
984. 26 f. As No. 976 .. .. 40 35
985. 26 f. As No. 977 .. .. 40 35
986. 31 f. As No. 978 .. .. 45 40
987. 31 f. As No. 979 .. .. 45 40
988. 40 f. As No. 980 .. .. 55 45
989. 40 f. As No. 981 .. .. 55 45

The two designs in each denomination were arranged together in se-tenant pairs within the sheet, each pair forming a composite design.

81. "St. Ildefonso writing a letter". (El Greco).

1974. International Letter-writing Week. Multicoloured.

991.	6 f. Type **81**	10	8
992.	11 f. " Lady sealing a letter " (Chardin)	20	15
993.	14 f. " Titus at desk " (Rembrandt)	20	15
994.	17 f. " The Love-letter " (Vermeer)	25	20
995.	26 f. " The Merchant G. Gisze " (Holbein)	40	35
996.	31 f. " A. Lenoir " (David)	45	40

82. " Virgin and Child ". (Van Orley).

1974. Christmas. Showing " Virgin and Child " paintings by artists named. Mult.

998.	5 f. Type **82** (postage)	8	5
999.	10 f. Hans Memling	15	12
1000.	15 f. Botticelli	20	15
1001.	18 f. Hans Memling (different) (air)	25	20
1002.	27 f. F. Lippi	40	35
1003.	40 f. L. di Gredi	55	45

1974. Christmas Charity. Nos. 998/1003 surch.

1005.	**82.**	5 f.+1 f. mult. (post.)	10	8
1006.	–	10 f.+1 f. multicoloured	20	15
1007.	–	15 f.+1 f. multicoloured	20	15
1008.	–	18 f.+1 f. mult. (air)	25	20
1009.	–	27 f.+1 f. multicoloured	40	35
1010.	–	40 f.+1 f. multicoloured	55	45

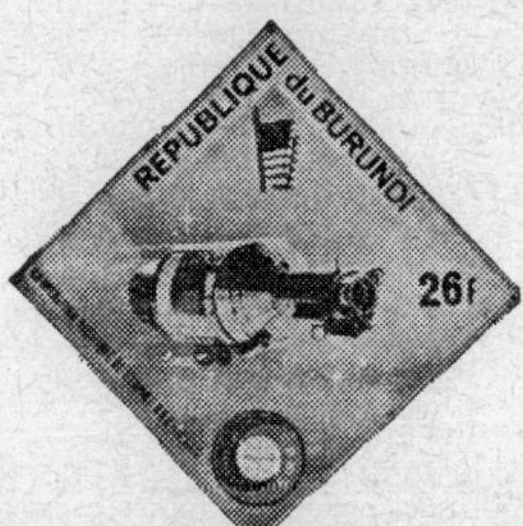

83. " Apollo " Spacecraft.

1975. " Apollo-Soyuz " Space Project.

1012.	26 f. Type **83** (postage)	15	12
1013.	26 f. Leonov and Kubasov	15	12
1014.	26 f. " Soyuz " Spacecraft	15	12
1015.	26 f. Slayton, Brand and Stafford	15	12
1016.	31 f. " Soyuz " launch	45	30
1017.	31 f. " Apollo " and " Soyuz " spacecraft	45	30
1018.	31 f. " Apollo " third stage separation	45	30
1019.	31 f. Slayton, Brand, Stafford, Leonov and Kubasov	45	30
1020.	27 f. Type **83** (air)	40	35
1021.	27 f. As No. 1012	40	35
1022.	27 f. As No. 1013	40	35
1023.	27 f. As No. 1014	40	35
1024.	40 f. As No. 1015	55	45
1025.	40 f. As No. 1016	55	45
1026.	40 f. As No. 1017	55	45
1027.	40 f. As No. 1018	55	45

The four designs in each value were issued together in se-tenant blocks of four within the sheet.

84. Addax.

1975. Animals. Multicoloured.

1028.	1 f. Type **84** (postage)	5	5
1029.	1 f. Roan antelope	5	5
1030.	1 f. Nyala	5	5
1031.	1 f. White rhinoceros	5	5
1032.	2 f. Mandrill	5	5
1033.	2 f. Oryx	5	5
1034.	2 f. Dik-dik	5	5
1035.	2 f. Thomson's gazelles	5	5
1036.	3 f. Small-clawed civet	5	5
1037.	3 f. Reed buck	5	5
1038.	3 f. Indian civet	5	5
1039.	3 f. Cape buffalo	5	5
1040.	5 f. White-tailed gnu	8	5
1041.	5 f. Donkeys	8	5
1042.	5 f. Colobus monkey	8	5
1043.	5 f. Gerenuk	8	5
1044.	6 f. Dama gazelle	10	10
1045.	6 f. Wild dog	10	10
1046.	6 f. Sitatungas	10	10
1047.	6 f. Striped duiker	10	10
1048.	11 f. Fennec	20	15
1049.	11 f. Lesser kudus	20	15
1050.	11 f. Blesbok	20	15
1051.	11 f. Serval	20	15
1052.	10 f. Type **84** (air)	15	12
1053.	10 f. As No. 1029	15	12
1054.	10 f. As No. 1030	15	12
1055.	10 f. As No. 1031	15	12
1056.	14 f. As No. 1032	20	15
1057.	14 f. As No. 1033	20	15
1058.	14 f. As No. 1034	20	15
1059.	14 f. As No. 1035	20	15
1060.	17 f. As No. 1036	25	20
1061.	17 f. As No. 1037	25	20
1062.	17 f. As No. 1038	25	20
1063.	17 f. As No. 1039	25	20
1064.	24 f. As No. 1040	35	30
1065.	24 f. As No. 1041	35	30
1066.	24 f. As No. 1042	35	30
1067.	24 f. As No. 1043	35	30
1068.	26 f. As No. 1044	40	35
1069.	26 f. As No. 1045	40	35
1070.	26 f. As No. 1046	40	35
1071.	26 f. As No. 1047	40	35
1072.	31 f. As No. 1048	45	40
1073.	31 f. As No. 1049	45	40
1074.	31 f. As No. 1050	45	40
1075.	31 f. As No. 1051	45	40

The four designs in each value were issued together in horiz. se-tenant strips within the sheet, forming composite designs.

1975. Air. International Women's Year. Nos. 1052/9. optd. with **ANNEE INTERNATIONALE DE LA FEMME.**

1076.	**84.**	10 f. multicoloured	15	12
1077.	–	10 f. multicoloured	15	12
1078.	–	10 f. multicoloured	15	12
1079.	–	10 f. multicoloured	15	12
1080.	–	14 f. multicoloured	20	15
1081.	–	14 f. multicoloured	20	15
1082.	–	14 f. multicoloured	20	15
1083.	–	14 f. multicoloured	20	15

1975. Air. United Nations. 30th Anniv. Nos. 1068/75. optd. with **30eme ANNIVERSAIRE DES NATIONS UNIES.**

1084.	26 f. multicoloured	40	35
1085.	26 f. multicoloured	40	35
1086.	26 f. multicoloured	40	35
1087.	26 f. multicoloured	40	35
1088.	31 f. multicoloured	45	40
1089.	31 f. multicoloured	45	40
1090.	31 f. multicoloured	45	40
1091.	31 f. multicoloured	45	40

85. " Jonah ".

1975. Christmas. Michelangelo. 500th Birth Anniversary. Multicoloured.

1092.	5 f. Type **85** (postage)	8	5
1093.	5 f. " Cumaean Sybil "	8	5
1094.	13 f. " Isaiah "	20	15
1095.	13 f. " Delphic Sybil "	20	15
1096.	27 f. " Daniel "	40	35
1097.	27 f. " Cumaean Sybil " (different)	40	35
1098.	18 f. " Zachariah " (air)	25	20
1099.	18 f. " Joel "	25	20
1100.	31 f. " Erythrian Sybil "	45	40
1101.	31 f. " Ezekiel "	45	40
1102.	40 f. " Persian Sybil "	55	45
1103.	40 f. " Jeremiah "	55	45

1975. Christmas Charity. Nos. 1092/1103. surch. with premium.

1105.	**85.**	5 f.+1 f. mult. (postage)	8	5
1106.	–	5 f.+1 f. multicoloured	8	5
1107.	–	13 f.+1 f. multicoloured	20	15
1108.	–	13 f.+1 f. multicoloured	20	15
1109.	–	27 f.+1 f. multicoloured	40	35
1110.	–	27 f.+1 f. multicoloured	40	35
1111.	–	18 f.+1 f. mult. (air)	25	20
1112.	–	18 f.+1 f. multicoloured	25	20
1113.	–	31 f.+1 f. multicoloured	45	40
1114.	–	31 f.+1 f. multicoloured	45	40
1115.	–	40 f.+1 f. multicoloured	55	45
1116.	–	40 f.+1 f. multicoloured	55	45

86. Speed Skating. **87.** Basketball.

1976. Winter Olympic Games, Innsbruck. Multicoloured.

1118.	17 f. Type **86** (postage)	25	20
1119.	24 f. Figure-skating	35	30
1120.	26 f. Two-man bobsleigh	40	35
1121.	31 f. Cross-country skiing	45	40
1122.	18 f. Ski-jumping (air)	25	20
1123.	36 f. Skiing (slalom)	45	40
1124.	50 f. Ice-hockey	80	70

1976. Olympic Games, Montreal. Multicoloured.

1126.	14 f. Type **87** (postage)	20	15
1127.	14 f. Pole-vaulting	20	15
1128.	17 f. Running	25	20
1129.	17 f. Football	25	20
1130.	28 f. As No. 1127	45	40
1131.	28 f. Ar No. 1128	45	40
1132.	40 f. As No. 1129	65	55
1133.	40 f. Type **87**	65	55
1134.	27 f. Hurdling (air)	40	35
1135.	27 f. High-jumping (horiz.)	40	35
1136.	31 f. Gymnastics (horiz.)	45	40
1137.	31 f. As No. 1134 (horiz.)	45	40
1138.	50 f. As No. 1135 (horiz.)	80	20
1139.	50 f. As No. 1136 (horiz.)	80	20

BUSHIRE BC

A Persian seaport. Stamps issued during the Br. occupation in the 1914-18 War.

1915. Portrait stamps of Persia (1911) optd. **BUSHIRE Under British Occupation.**

1.	**29.**	1 ch. orange and green	5·00	6·00
2.		2 ch. brown and red	5·00	6·00
3.		3 ch. green and grey	5·00	6·00
4.		5 ch. red and brown	55·00	65·00
5.		6 ch. lake and green	5·00	6·00
6.		9 ch. lilac and brown	7·00	9·00
7.		10 ch. brown and red	7·00	9·00
8.		12 ch. blue and green	10·00	12·00
9.		24 ch. green & purple	9·00	11·00
10.		1 kr. red and blue	9·00	9·00
11.		2 kr. claret and green	22·00	24·00
12.		3 kr. black and lilac	55·00	60·00
13.		5 kr. blue and red	20·00	24·00
14.		10 kr. rose and brown	19·00	20·00

1915. Coronation issue of Persia optd. **BUSHIRE Under British Occupation.**

15.	**31.**	1 ch. blue and red	£110
16.		2 ch. red and blue	£1100
17.		3 ch. green	£130
18.		5 ch. red	£1000
19.		6 ch. red and green	£950
20.		9 ch. violet and brown	£190
21.		10 ch. brown and green	£325
22.		12 ch. blue	£350
23.		24 ch. black and brown	£130
24.	**32.**	1 kr. black, brn. & silver	£120
25.		2 kr. red, blue and silver	£110
26.		3 kr. black, lilac & silver	£130
27.		5 kr. slate, black & silver	£130
28.	–	1 t. black, violet and gold	£120
29.	–	3 t. red and gold	£400

1915. No. 552 of Persia optd. **BUSHIRE Under British Occupation.**

30.	**29.**	1 ch. on 5 ch. red & brown	£650

MORE DETAILED LISTS

are given in the Stanley Gibbons Catalogues referred to in the country headings:

BC	British Commonwealth
E1, E2, E3	Europe 1, 2, 3
O1, O2, O3, O4	Overseas 1, 2, 3, 4

BUSSAHIR (BASHAHR) BC

A state in the Punjab, India. Now uses Indian stamps.

1.

1895. Various frames. Imperf., perf. or roul.

9.	**1.**	¼ a. pink	8·50	9·50
2.		½ a. grey	4·00	
3.		1 a. red	4·00	
4.		2 a. yellow	4·00	38·00
13.		4 a. violet	8·00	30·00
6.		8 a. brown	5·50	6·00
15.		12 a. green	13·00	
16.		1 r. blue	13·00	

1896. Similar types, but inscriptions on white ground and inscr. " POSTAGE " instead of " STAMP ".

27.	**1.**	¼ a. violet	1·50	4·00
31.		¼ a. red	65	
25.		½ a. blue	1·00	7·00
26.		1 a. olive	4·50	7·00
38.		1 a. red	65	1·50
41.		2 a. yellow	2·75	3·50
36.		4 a. claret	6·00	20·00

CAMBODIA O1

Once part of Indo-China but from 1946 an associated state within the French Union. Became an independent sovereign state on 29th Dec., 1954, and left the French Union on 25th Sept., 1955. Following the introduction of a republican constitution in 1971 the name of the country was changed to Khmer Republic, but it reverted to Cambodia in 1975.

1951. 100 cents = 1 piastre.
1955. 100 cents = 1 riel.

1. " Apsara" or Dancing Nymph.

2. Throne Room, Phnom-Penh.

4. " Kinnari ". **3.** King Norodom Sihanouk.

1951.

1.	**1.**	10 c. green & blue-green	25	25
2.		20 c. brown and lake	15	15
3.		30 c. indigo and violet	15	15
4.		40 c. green and blue	15	15
5.	**2.**	50 c. green & blue-green	15	15
6.	**3.**	80 c. green and indigo	35	35
7.	**2.**	1 p. violet and indigo	50	50
8.	**3.**	1 p. 10 red and lake	50	50
9.	**1.**	1 p. 50 rose and lake	60	50
10.	**2.**	1 p. 50 blue and indigo	60	50
11.	**3.**	1 p. 50 purple & chocolate	60	65
12.		1 p. 90 blue and indigo	90	1·00
13.	**2.**	2 p. chestnut and lake	70	35
14.	**3.**	3 p. chestnut and lake	1·00	1·00
15.	**1.**	5 p. violet and indigo	3·25	2·00
16.	**2.**	10 p. indigo and violet	6·50	3·25
17.	**3.**	15 p. violet	8·50	4·50

1952. Students Aid Fund. Surch. **AIDE A L'ETUDIANT** and value.

18.	**3.**	1 p. 10+40 c. red and lake	1·75	1·75
19.		1 p. 90+60 c. blue & indigo	1·75	1·75
20.		3 p.+1 p. chestnut & lake	1·75	1·75
21.	**1.**	5 p.+2 p. violet & indigo	1·75	1·75

1953. Air.
22. 4. 50 c. green 25 25
23. 3 p. brown 30 25
24. 3 p. 30 violet 45 30
25. 4 p. blue and brown 55 35
26. 5 p. 10 yell., red & brown 70 45
27. 6 p. 50 purple and brown 80 65
28. 9 p. green and magenta 1·25 1·10
29. 11 p. 50 orange, red, magenta, green and black 2·00 1·75
30. 30 p. yellow, brn. & turq. 3·50 1·75

5. Arms of Cambodia. 6. "Postal Transport".

1954.
31. – 10 c. red 5 5
32. – 20 c. green 5 5
33. – 30 c. indigo 5 5
34. – 40 c. violet 5 5
35. – 50 c. brown-purple 5 5
36. – 70 c. chocolate 8 8
37. – 1 p. violet 10 10
38. – 1 p. 50 red 12 12
39. 5. 2 p. red 20 15
40. 2 p. 50 green 30 30
41. 6. 2 p. 50 green 50 35
42. 5. 3 p. blue 60 45
43. 6. 4 p. sepia 60 60
44. 5. 4 p. 50 violet 70 60
45. 6. 5 p. red 70 60
46. 5. 6 p. chocolate 85 70
47. 6. 10 p. violet 85 80
48. 15 p. blue 1·00 90
49. – 20 p. blue 1·75 1·10
50. – 30 p. green 2·50 2·00
DESIGNS—VERT. 10 c. to 50 c. View of Phnom-Daun Penh. HORIZ. 70 c., 1 p., 1 p. 50, 20 p., 30 p. East Gate, Temple of Angkor.

7. King Norodom Suramarit. 8. King and Queen of Cambodia.

1955.
51. – 50 c. indigo 5 5
52. 7. 50 c. violet 5 5
53. 1 r. red 10 10
54. 2 r. blue 15 15
55. – 2 r. 50 chocolate 25 25
56. – 4 r. green 25 25
57. – 6 r. lake 45 40
58. 7. 7 r. brown 55 50
59. – 15 r. lilac 1·00 70
60. 7. 20 r. green 1·50 1·10
PORTRAIT: Nos. 51, 55/7 and 59, Queen Kossumak.
For stamps as Nos. 58 and 60, but with black border, see Nos. 101/2.

1955. Coronation (1st issue).
61. 8. 1 r. 50 brown and sepia 25 25
62. 2 r. black and blue 25 25
63. 3 r. red and orange 25 25
64. 5 r. black and green 30 30
65. 10 r. lake and violet 50 50

9. King Norodom Suramarit. 10. Prince Sihanouk, Flags and Globe.

1956. Coronation. 2nd issue. Inscr. "COURONNEMENT".
66. 9. 2 r. red 50 50
67. – 3 r. blue 75 75
68. – 5 r. green 75 75
69. 9. 10 r. myrtle 2·50 2·50
70. 30 r. violet 5·50 5·50
71. – 50 r. magenta 10·00 10·00
PORTRAIT—VERT. 3 r., 5 r., 50 r. Queen of Cambodia.

1957. Admission of Cambodia to U.N.O. 1st Anniv.
72. 10. 2 r. red, blue and green 50 50
73. 4 r. 50 blue 50 50
74. 8 r. 50 red 50 50

11. 12. Mythological Bird.

1957. Buddhism. 2,500th Anniv. Temple in bistre (a) With premiums.
75. 11. 1 r. 50+50 c. red & indigo 60 60
76. 6 r. 50+1 r. 50 red and purple 90 90
77. 8 r.+2 r. red and blue 1·50 1·50
(b) Colours changed and premiums omitted.
78. 11. 1 r. 50 red 40 40
79. 6 r. 50 violet 50 50
80. 8 r. green 50 50

1957. Air.
81. 12. 50 c. lake 5 5
82. 1 r. green 10 10
83. 4 r. blue 40 30
84. 50 r. red 2·50 2·00
85. 100 r. red, green and blue 4·25 3·00

13. King Ang Duong. 14. King Norodom I.

1958. King Ang Duong Commem.
86. 13. 1 r. 50 brown and violet 12 12
87. 5 r. bistre and black 20 20
88. 10 r. sepia and purple 40 25

1958. King Norodom I Commem.
89. 14. 2 r. olive and blue 12 12
90. 6 r. green and orange 20 20
91. 15 r. olive and green 40 25

15. Children.

1959. Children's World Friendship.
92. 15. 20 c. purple 8 8
93. 50 c. blue 12 12
94. 80 c. red 20 20

1959. Red Cross Fund. Surch. with red cross and premium in red.
95. 15. 20 c.+20 c. purple 10 8
96. 50 c.+30 c. blue 15 12
97. 80 c.+50 c. red 20 15

16. Prince Sihanouk, Plan of Port and Ship. 17. Sacred Plough in Procession.

1960. Sihanoukville Port. Inaug.
98. 16. 2 r. sepia and red 15 15
99. 5 r. chocolate and blue 20 20
100. 20 r. blue and violet 75 50

1960. King Norodom Suramarit Mourning issue. Nos. 58 and 60 reissued with black border.
101. 7. 7 r. brown and black 90 90
102. 20 r. green and black 90 90

1960. Festival of the Sacred Furrow.
103. 17. 1 r. purple 15 15
104. 2 r. brown 15 15
105. 3 r. turquoise 20 15

18. Child and Book ("Education").

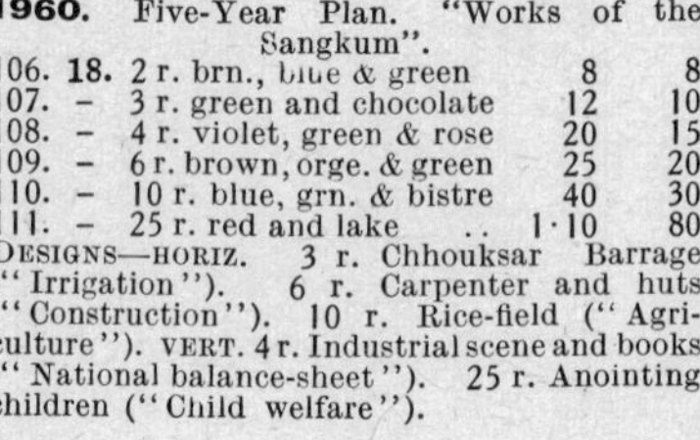
19. Flag and Dove of Peace. 20. Jasmine. 21. "Rama" (from temple door, Baphoun).

1960. Five-Year Plan. "Works of the Sangkum".
106. 18. 2 r. brn., blue & green 8 8
107. – 3 r. green and chocolate 12 10
108. – 4 r. violet, green & rose 20 15
109. – 6 r. brown, orge. & green 25 20
110. – 10 r. blue, grn. & bistre 40 30
111. – 25 r. red and lake 1·10 80
DESIGNS—HORIZ. 3 r. Chhouksar Barrage ("Irrigation"). 6 r. Carpenter and huts ("Construction"). 10 r. Rice-field ("Agriculture"). VERT. 4 r. Industrial scene and books ("National balance-sheet"). 25 r. Anointing children ("Child welfare").

1961. Peace. Flag in red and blue.
112. 19. 1 r. 50 green and choc. 15 15
113. 5 r. red 25 20
114. 7 r. blue and green 30 25

1961. Cambodian Flowers.
115. 20. 2 r. yell., green & mag. 12 12
116. – 5 r. mag., green & blue 25 25
117. – 10 r. red, green & violet 50 50
FLOWERS: 5 r. Lavender. 10 r. Rose lily.

1961. Cambodian Soldiers Commem.
118. 21. 1 r. violet 5 5
118a. 2 r. blue 70 60
119. 3 r. green 12 10
120. 6 r. orange 30 15

22. Prince Norodom Sihanouk and Independence Monument.

1961. Independence Monument.
121. 22. 2 r. green (postage) 15 15
122. 4 r. sepia 20 20
123. 7 r. chestnut, purple, green and sepia (air) 30 25
124. 30 r. red, blue and grn. 1·00 80
125. 50 r. violet, blue-green yellow-green and brn. 1·60 1·25

1961. 6th World Buddhist Conf. Optd. **VIe CONFERENCE MONDIALE BOUDDHIQUE 12-11-1961.**
126. 6. 2 p. 50 (2 r. 50) green 15 15
127. 4 p. 50 (4 r. 50) violet 20 20

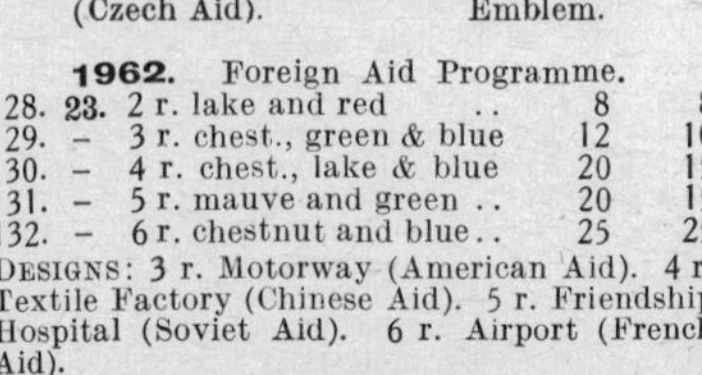
23. Power Station (Czech Aid). 24. Campaign Emblem.

1962. Foreign Aid Programme.
128. 23. 2 r. lake and red 8 8
129. – 3 r. chest., green & blue 12 10
130. – 4 r. chest., lake & blue 20 15
131. – 5 r. mauve and green 20 15
132. – 6 r. chestnut and blue 25 25
DESIGNS: 3 r. Motorway (American Aid). 4 r. Textile Factory (Chinese Aid). 5 r. Friendship Hospital (Soviet Aid). 6 r. Airport (French Aid).

1962. Malaria Eradication.
133. 24. 2 r. purple and brown 8 8
134. 4 r. green and chocolate 12 10
135. 6 r. violet and bistre 15 12

25. Curcumas.

1962. Cambodian Fruits (1st issue).
136. 25. 2 r. yell.-orge. & olive 15 15
137. – 4 r. dark olive and turq. 20 20
138. – 6 r. lake, green and blue 30 30
FRUITS: 4 r. Lichees. 6 r. Mangosteens.

1962. Cambodian Fruits (2nd issue).
139. 2 r. brown & blue-green 12 12
140. 5 r. green and brown 25 20
141. 9 r. brown & blue-green 35 25
DESIGNS—VERT. 2 r. Pineapples. 5 r. Sugar-cane. 9 r. "Bread" trees.

1962. Surch.
142. 15. 50 c. on 80 c. red 5 5
150. – 3 r. on 2 r. 50 chocolate (No. 55) 12 12

1962. Independence Monument Inaug. Optd. **INAUGURATION DU MONUMENT** and surch. also.
143. 22. 3 r. on 2 r. green (post.) 10 8
144. 12 r. on 7 r. chest., pur., green and sepia (air) 60 50

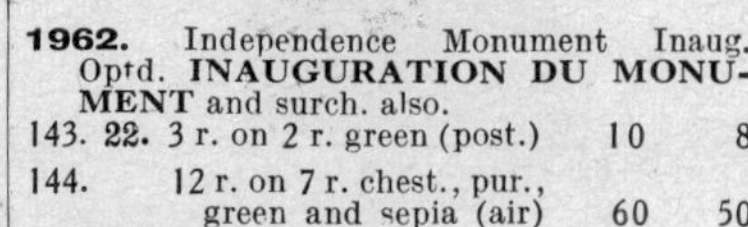
26. Campaign Emblem, Corn and Maize.

28. Kep sur Mer. 27. Temple Preah Vihear

1963. Freedom from Hunger.
145. 26. 3 r. chestnut, yellow-brown and blue 15 15
146. 6 r. chestnut, yellow-brown & ultramarine 25 25

1963. Reunification of Preah Vihear Temple with Cambodia.
147. 27. 3 r. brn., purple & green 12 10
148. 6 r. bronze, orge. & turq. 25 20
149. 15 r. choc., blue & green 50 45

1963. Cambodian Resorts. Multicoloured.
151. 3 r. Koh Tonsay 12 10
152. 7 r. Popokvil (waterfall) 30 20
153. 20 r. Type 28 70 45
The 3 r. and 7 r. are vert.

1963. Red Cross Centenary. Surch. **1863 1963 CENTENAIRE DE LA CROIX-ROUGE** and premium.
154. 24. 4 r.+40 c. grn. & choc. 25 25
155. 6 r.+60 c. violet & bis. 35 35

29. Scales of Justice.

1963. Declaration of Human Rights. 15th Anniv.
156. 29. 1 r. green, red and blue 5 5
157. 3 r. red, blue and green 10 10
158. 12 r. blue, green & red 40 40

30. Water-buffalo.

31. Magpie.

32. "Hanuman". 33. Airline Emblem.

1964. Wild Animal Protection.
159. **30.** 50 c. brn., grn. & chest. 5 5
160. 3 r. brn., chest. & grn. 15 12
161. 6 r. brown, blue & green 25 15

1964. Birds
162. **31.** 3 r. blue, green & indigo 12 10
163. – 6 r. orge., mar. & slate-bl. 25 25
164. – 12 r. turquoise & maroon 40 30
BIRDS: 6 r. Kingfisher. 12 r. Heron.

1964. Air.
165. **32.** 5 r. multicoloured .. 15 10
166. 10 r. multicoloured .. 25 15
167. 20 c. multicoloured .. 60 35
168. 40 r. multicoloured .. 1·40 70
169. 80 r. multicoloured .. 2·50 1·50

1964. Air Olympic Games, Tokyo. Surch. **JEUX OLYMPIQUES TOKYO–1964,** Olympic rings and value.
170. **32.** 3 r. on 5 mult... .. 15 15
171. 6 r. on 10 r. mult. .. 25 25
172. 9 r. on 20 r. mult. .. 35 30
173. 12 r. on 40 r. mult. .. 50 40

1964. Royal Air Cambodia. 8th Anniv.
174. **33.** 1 r. 50 red and violet .. 8 8
175. 3 r. vermilion and blue 12 12
176. 7 r. 50 red and ultram. 30 20

34. Prince Norodom Sihanouk. **35.** Weaving.

1964. Foundation of Sangkum. 10th Anniv.
177. **34.** 2 r. violet 5 5
178. 3 r. brown 12 10
179. 10 r. blue 30 20

1965. Native Handicrafts.
180. **35.** 1 r. vio., brn. & bistre 8 8
181. – 3 r. brown, green & pur. 12 12
182. – 5 r. red, maroon & green 25 15
DESIGNS: 3 r. Engraving. 5 r. Basket-making.

1965. Indo-Chinese People's Conf. Nos. 178/9 Optd. **CONFERENCE DES PEUPLES INDOCHINOIS.**
183. **34.** 3 r. brown 15 15
184. 10 r. blue 30 15

36. I.T.U. Emblem and Symbols. **37.** Cotton.

1965. I.T.U. Cent.
185. **36.** 3 r. bistre and green .. 10 8
186. 4 r. blue and red .. 15 12
187. 10 r. purple and violet .. 30 25

1965. Industrial Plants. Multicoloured.
188. 1 r. 50 Type **37** .. 8 5
189. 3 r. Groundnuts .. 12 10
190. 7 r. 50 Coconut palms .. 30 25

38. Preah Ko.

1966. Cambodian Temples.
191. **38.** 3 r. bronze, green and chestnut 12 10
192. – 5 r. brn., grn. & purple 20 15
193. – 7 r. brn., green & ochre 25 20
194. – 9 r. plum, green & blue 30 25
195. – 12 r. red, green & orge. 40 30
TEMPLES: 5 r. Baksei Chamkrong. 7 r. Banteay Srei. 9 r. Angkor Vat. 12 r. Bayon.

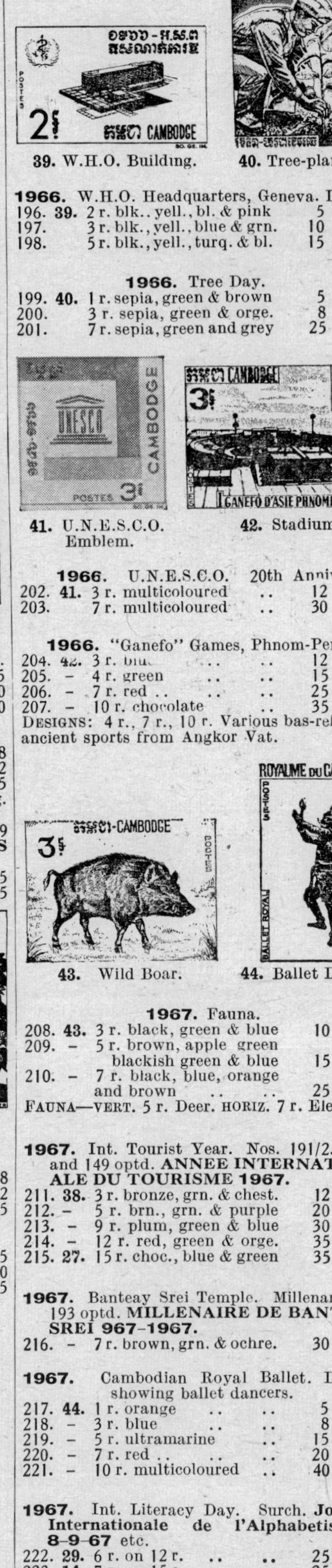

39. W.H.O. Building. **40.** Tree-planting.

1966. W.H.O. Headquarters, Geneva. Inaug.
196. **39.** 2 r. blk., yell., bl. & pink 5 5
197. 3 r. blk., yell., blue & grn. 10 8
198. 5 r. blk., yell., turq. & bl. 15 15

1966. Tree Day.
199. **40.** 1 r. sepia, green & brown 5 5
200. 3 r. sepia, green & orge. 8 8
201. 7 r. sepia, green and grey 25 15

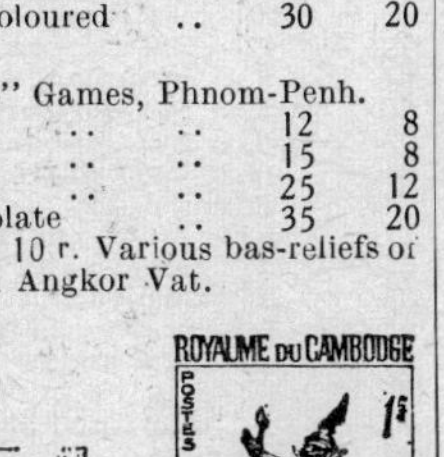

41. U.N.E.S.C.O. Emblem. **42.** Stadium.

1966. U.N.E.S.C.O. 20th Anniv.
202. **41.** 3 r. multicoloured .. 12 10
203. 7 r. multicoloured .. 30 20

1966. "Ganefo" Games, Phnom-Penh.
204. **42.** 3 r. blue 12 8
205. – 4 r. green 15 8
206. – 7 r. red 25 12
207. – 10 r. chocolate .. 35 20
DESIGNS: 4 r., 7 r., 10 r. Various bas-reliefs of ancient sports from Angkor Vat.

43. Wild Boar. **44.** Ballet Dancer.

1967. Fauna.
208. **43.** 3 r. black, green & blue 10 10
209. – 5 r. brown, apple green blackish green & blue 15 12
210. – 7 r. black, blue, orange and brown 25 20
FAUNA—VERT. 5 r. Deer. HORIZ. 7 r. Elephant.

1967. Int. Tourist Year. Nos. 191/2. 194/5 and 149 optd. **ANNEE INTERNATIONALE DU TOURISME 1967.**
211. **38.** 3 r. bronze, grn. & chest. 12 10
212. – 5 r. brn., grn. & purple 20 15
213. – 9 r. plum, green & blue 30 20
214. – 12 r. red, green & orge. 35 30
215. **27.** 15 r. choc., blue & green 35 30

1967. Banteay Srei Temple. Millenary. No. 193 optd. **MILLENAIRE DE BANTEAY SREI 967–1967.**
216. – 7 r. brown, grn. & ochre. 30 15

1967. Cambodian Royal Ballet. Designs showing ballet dancers.
217. **44.** 1 r. orange 5 5
218. – 3 r. blue 8 8
219. – 5 r. ultramarine .. 15 12
220. – 7 r. red 20 20
221. – 10 r. multicoloured .. 40 25

1967. Int. Literacy Day. Surch. **Journee Internationale de l'Alphabetisation 8–9–67** etc.
222. **29.** 6 r. on 12 r. 25 15
223. **14.** 7 r. on 15 r. 25 15

45. Decade Emblem. **46.** Royal University of Kompong-Cham.

1967. Int. Hydrological Decade.
224. **45.** 1 r. orge., blue & black 5 5
225. 6 r. orge, blue & violet 20 12
226. 10 r. orge. & blue-green 35 20

1968. Cambodian Universities and Institutes.
227. **46.** 4 r. purple, blue & brown 15 12
228. – 6 r. brown, green & blue 25 15
229. – 9 r. brown, green & blue 30 20
DESIGNS: 6 r. "Khmero-Soviet Friendship" Higher Technical Institute. 9 r. Sangkum Reaster Niyum University Centre.

47. Doctor tending child.

1968. World Health Organisation. 20th Anniv.
230. **47.** 3 r. blue 5 5
231. – 7 r. blue 15 12
DESIGN: 7 r. Man using insecticide.

48. Stadium.

1968. Olympic Games, Mexico.
232. **48.** 1 r. brown, green & red 5 5
233. – 2 r. brown, red & blue .. 5 5
234. – 3 r. brn., bl. & purple .. 10 10
235. – 5 r. violet .. 12 10
236. – 7 r. 50, brown, grn. & red 20 15
DESIGNS—HORIZ. 2 r. Wrestling. 3 r. Cycling. VERT. 5 r. Boxing. 7 r. 50 Runner with torch.

49. Stretcher-party.

1968. Cambodian Red Cross Fortnight.
237. **49.** 3 r. red, green & blue .. 8 5

50. Prince Norodom Sihanouk.

1968. Independence. 15th Anniv.
238. **50.** 7 r. vio., grn. & ultrm. 15 12
239. – 8 r. brown, green & blue 20 12
DESIGN: 8 r. Soldiers wading through stream.

51. Human Rights Emblem and Prince Norodom Sihanouk.

1968. Human Rights Year.
240. **51.** 3 r. blue 8 5
241. 5 r. purple 12 8
242. 7 r. black, orge. & grn. 15 12

52. I.L.O. Emblem.

1969. Int. Labour Organization. 50th Anniv.
243. **52.** 3 r. ultramarine .. 5 5
244. 6 r. red 12 8
245. 9 r. green 20 10

53. Red Cross Emblems around Globe.

1969. League of Red Cross Societies. 50th Anniv.
246. **53.** 1 r. multicoloured .. 5 5
247. 3 r. multicoloured .. 8 5
248. 10 r. multicoloured .. 20 12

54. "Papilio oeacus".

1969. Butterflies.
249. **54.** 3 r. black, yellow & violet 12 10
250. – 4 r. black, green & verm. 15 12
251. – 8 r. black, orge. & green 25 20
DESIGNS: 4 r. "Papilio agamenon". 8 r. "Danaus plexippus"

55. Diesel Train and Route Map.

1969. Opening of Phnom Penh-Sihanoukville Railway.
252. **55.** 3 r. multicoloured .. 8 8
253. – 6 r. brn., blackish brn. & grn. 20 12
254. – 8 r. black .. 25 20
255. – 9 r. blue, greenish bl. & grn. 30 20
DESIGN: 6 r. Phnom-Penh Station. 8 r. Diesel locomotive and rural station. 9 r. Steam locomotive at Sihanoukville Station.

56. Triple Tail.

1970. Fishes. Multicoloured.
256. 3 r. Type **56** 8 5
257. 7 r. Marbled Goby .. 15 10
258. 9 r. Striped Snakehead .. 20 15

57. Vat Tepthidaram. **58.** Dish Aerial and Open Book.

1970. Buddhist Monasteries in Cambodia. Multicoloured.
259. 2 r. Type **57** 5 5
260. 3 r. Vat Maniratanaram (horiz.) 8 5
261. 6 r. Vat Patumavati (horiz.) 15 10
262. 8 r. Vat Ummalom (horiz.) 20 12

1970. World Telecommunications Day.
263. **58.** 3 r. multicoloured .. 5 5
264. 4 r. multicoloured .. 10 5
265. 9 r. multicoloured .. 20 10

59. New Headquarters Building.

1970. Opening of New U.P.U. Headquarters Building, Berne.
266. **59.** 1 r. multicoloured .. 5 5
267. 3 r. multicoloured .. 5 5
268. 4 r. multicoloured .. 10 5
269. 10 r. multicoloured .. 20 12

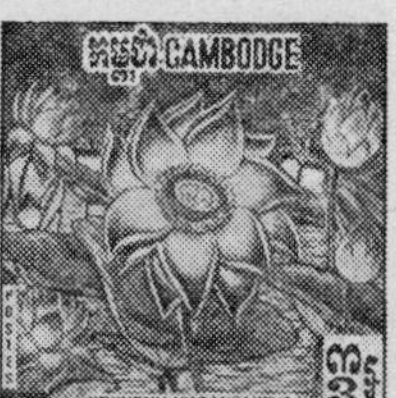

60. "Nelumbium speciosum".

1970. Aquatic Plants. Multicoloured.
270. 3 r. Type **60** 5 5
271. 4 r. "Eichhornia crassipes solms" 12 5
272. 13 r. "Nymphea lotus" 35 15

61. "Banteay-srei" (bas-relief).

1970. World Meteorological Day.
273. **61.** 3 r. red and green .. 5 5
274. 4 r. red, green and blue 10 5
275. 7 r. green, blue and black 15 10

62. Rocket, Dove and Globe.

1970. United Nations. 25th Anniv.
276. **62.** 3 r. multicoloured .. 8 5
277. 5 r. multicoloured .. 12 5
278. 10 r. multicoloured .. 20 12

63. I.E.Y. Emblem.

1970. International Education Year.
279. **63.** 1 r. blue 5 5
280. 3 r. purple 8 5
281. 8 r. green 20 12

64. Samdech Nath (founder of national language).

1971. Samdech Chuon-Nath (Cambodian language scholar). 2nd Death Anniv.
282. **64.** 3 r. multicoloured .. 5 5
283. 8 r. multicoloured .. 15 10
284. 9 r. multicoloured .. 20 12

POSTAGE DUE STAMPS

D 1.

1957.
D 81. D **1.** 10 c. red, blue & black 5 5
D 82. 50 c. red, blue & black 8 8
D 83. 1 r. red, blue & black 12 12
D 84. 3 r. red, blue & black 20 20
D 85. 5 r. red, blue & black 30 30

For later issues see **KHMER REPUBLIC.**

CAMEROUN O1; BC

A. GERMAN COLONY OF KAMERUN.

A German possession prior to the War of 1914-18.

100 pfennig = 1 mark.

1897. Stamps of Germany optd. **Kamerun.**
K 1a. **6.** 3 pf. brown .. .. 2·50 3·00
K 2. 5 pf. green .. .. 1·75 1·00
K 3. **7.** 10 pf. red .. .. 90 1·00
K 4. 20 pf. blue .. .. 1·40 2·00
K 5. 25 pf. orange .. .. 5·50 9·50
K 6. 50 pf. brown .. .. 4·50 8·00

1900. "Yacht" key-types inscr. "KAMERUN".
K 7. A. 3 pf. brown 30 30
K 8. 5 pf. green .. .. 5·50 30
K 9. 10 pf. red .. .. 15·00 55
K 10. 20 pf. blue .. .. 8·00 90
K 11. 25 pf. blk. & red on yell. 35 2·50
K 12. 30 pf. blk. & orge. on buff 55 1·75
K 13. 40 pf. black and red .. 55 2·10
K 14. A. 50 pf. blk. & pur. on buff 70 2·50
K 15. 80 pf. blk. & red on rose 90 3·25
K 16. B. 1 m. red .. .. 22·00 18·00
K 17. 2 m. blue .. .. 2·75 18·00
K 18. 3 m. black .. .. 2·75 35·00
K 19. 5 m. red and black .. 55·00 £140

B. BRITISH OCCUPATION OF CAMEROONS.

The German colony was occupied by British and French troops during 1914-16. The country was divided between them and the two areas were administered under the United Nations mandate from 1922. The British section was administered as part of Nigeria until 1960. (See Southern Cameroons).

1915. "Yacht" key-types of German Kamerun surch. **C.E.F.** and value in English currency.
1. N. ½d. on 3 pf. brown .. 1·25 1·25
2. ½d. on 5 pf. green .. 50 75
3. 1d. on 10 pf. red .. 50 65
4. 2d. on 20 pf. blue .. 50 85
5. 2½d. on 25 pf. black and red on yellow .. 90 1·25
6. 3d. on 30 pf. black and orange on buff .. 90 1·40
7. 4d. on 40 pf. black & red 90 1·40
8. 6d. on 50 pf. black and purple on buff .. 90 1·25
9. 8d. on 80 pf. black and red on rose .. .. 90 1·25
10. O. 1s. on 1 m. red .. 18·00 22·00
11. 2s. on 2 m. blue .. 18·00 22·00
12. 3s. on 3 m. black .. 18·00 22·00
13. 5s. on 5 m. red & black 38·00 45·00

C. FRENCH ADMINISTRATION OF CAMEROUN.

Area occupied by French troops during 1914-16 and administered under the League of Nations mandate from 1922. Created an autonomous state within the French community in 1958.

1915. Stamps of Gabon with inscription "AFRIQUE EQUATORIALE-GABON" optd. **Corps Expeditionnaire Franco-Anglais CAMEROUN.**
1. **2.** 1 c. brown and orange .. 13·00 5·00
2. 2 c. black and brown .. 28·00 25·00
3. 4 c. violet and blue .. 30·00 25·00
4. 5 c. olive and green .. 3·25 1·50
5. 10 c. red and lake (on No. 37 of Gaboon) .. 3·25 1·25
6. 20 c. brown and violet 30·00 25·00
7. **3.** 25 c. brown and blue .. 8·00 2·25
8. 30 c. red and grey .. 22·00 18·
9. 35 c. green and violet .. 5·00 2·25
10. 40 c. blue and brown .. 27·00 25·00
11. 45 c. violet and red .. 30·00 25·00
12. 50 c. grey and green .. 28·00 22·00
13. 75 c. brown and orange .. 38·00 23·00
14. **4.** 1 f. yellow and brown .. 32·00 25·00
15. 2 f. brown and red .. 35·00 25·00

1916. Stamps of French Congo and Middle Congo (1 c. to 5 c., 35 c., 45 c.) optd. **Occupation Francaise du Cameroun.**
16. **1.** 1 c. olive and brown .. 12·00 12·00
17. 2 c. violet and brown .. 12·00 12·00
18. 4 c. blue and brown .. 12·00 12·00
19. 5 c. green and blue .. 4·25 3·25
22. 15 c. violet and green .. 6·50 6·50
23. **2.** 20 c. green and orange .. 27·00 13·00
24. 30 c. red and yellow .. 12·00 8·50
20. 35 c. brown and blue .. 16·00 12·00
25. 40 c. brown and green .. 10·00 8·00
21. 45 c. violet and red .. 10·00 8·00
26. 50 c. violet and lilac .. 12·00 8·50
27. 75 c. purple and yellow .. 12·00 8·50
28. – 1 f. grey and green .. 17·00 11·00
29. – 2 f. red and brown .. 17·00 11·00

1916. Stamps of Middle Congo optd. **CAMEROUN Occupation Francaise.**
30. **1.** 1 c. olive and brown .. 5 5
31. 2 c. violet and brown .. 5 5
32. 4 c. blue and brown .. 5 5
33. 5 c. green and blue .. 5 5
34. 10 c. red and blue .. 12 8
34a. 15 c. purple and red .. 12 5
35. 20 c. brown and blue .. 5 5
36. **2.** 25 c. blue and green .. 8 5
37. 30 c. red and green .. 8 5
38. 35 c. brown and blue .. 5 5
39. 40 c. green and brown .. 12 5
40. 45 c. violet and red .. 12 8
41. 50 c. green and red .. 12 8
42. 75 c. brown and blue .. 15 10
43. **3.** 1 f. green and violet .. 15 10
44. 2 f. violet and green .. 1·25 75
45. 5 f. blue and red .. 1·40 1·10

1921. Stamps of Middle Congo optd. **CAMEROUN.**
46. **1.** 1 c. orange and olive .. 5 5
47. 2 c. red and brown .. 5 5
48. 4 c. green and grey .. 5 5
49. 5 c. orange and red .. 5 5
50. 10 c. green 5 5
51. 15 c. orange and blue .. 5 5
52. 20 c. grey and purple .. 5 5
53. **2.** 25 c. orange and black .. 5 5
54. 30 c. red 5 5
55. 35 c. blue and grey .. 8 8
56. **2.** 40 c. orange and olive .. 5 5
57. 45 c. red and brown .. 5 5
58. 50 c. blue 5 5
59. 75 c. green and claret .. 8 8
60. **3.** 1 f. orange and black .. 15 15
61. 2 f. red and olive .. 75 60
62. 5 f. grey and red .. 1·10 80

1924. Stamps of Middle Congo optd. **CAMEROUN** and surch. also.
63. **1.** 25 c. on 15 c. orge. & bl. 10 10
64. **3.** 25 c. on 2 f. red & olive 10 10
65. 25 c. on 5 f. grey and red 10 10
66. **2.** "65" on 45 c. red & brown 25 25
67. "85" on 75 c. grn. & clar. 25 25

1. Cattle at Ford.

2. Tapping for rubber (vertical).

3. Liana suspension bridge.

1925.
68. **1.** 1 c. mauve and olive .. 5 5
69. 2 c. green & red on grn. 5 5
70. 4 c. black and blue .. 5 5
71. 5 c. mauve and yellow 5 5
72. 10 c. orge. & pur. on yell. 5 5
73. 15 c. green 5 5
88. 15 c. red and lilac .. 15 15
74. **2.** 20 c. brown and olive 5 5
89. 20 c. green 5 5
90. 20 c. brown and red 5 5
75. 25 c. black and green .. 5 5
76. 30 c. red and green .. 5 5
91. 30 c. green and olive .. 5 5
77. 35 c. black and brown 5 5
91a. 35 c. green 15 8
78. 40 c. violet and orange 12 5
79. 45 c. red 5 5
92. 45 c. brown and mauve 40 30
80. 50 c. red and green .. 5 5
93. 55 c. red and blue .. 12 12
81. 60 c. black and mauve 5 5
94. 60 c. red 5 5
82. 65 c. brown and blue 5 5
83. 75 c. blue 5 5
95. 75 c. mauve and brown 8 5
95a. 80 c. brown and red 20 15
84. 85 c. blue and red .. 5 5
96. 90 c. red 30 20
85. **3.** 1 f. brown and blue .. 8 5
97. 1 f. blue 5 5
98. 1 f. mauve and brown 8 5
99. 1 f. brown and green 15 12
100. 1 f. 10 brown and red .. 60 50
100a. 1 f. 25 blue and brown 50 40
101. 1 f. 50 blue 10 5
101a. 1 f. 75 red and brown .. 15 8
101b. 1 f. 75 blue 15 8
86. 2 f. orange and olive .. 30 8
102. 3 f. mauve and brown 1·00 20
87. 5 f. blk. & brn. on blue 40 20
103. 10 f. mauve and orange 1·60 1·00
104. 20 f. green and red .. 3·25 1·60

1926. Surch. with new value.
105. **3.** 1 f. 25 on 1 f. blue .. 5 5

1931. "Colonial Exhibition" key-types inscribed "CAMEROUN".
106. E. 40 c. green 40 40
107. F. 50 c. mauve 70 70
108. G. 90 c. orange 60 60
109. H. 1 f. 50 blue 75 75

5. Sailing Ships.

1937. Paris International Exn. Inscr. "EXPOSITION INTERNATIONALE PARIS 1937".
110. 20 c. violet 15 10
111. 30 c. green 15 10
112. 40 c. red 15 12
113. 50 c. brown 8 8
114. 90 c. red 15 15
115. 1 f. 50 blue 15 15

DESIGNS—VERT. 20 c. Allegory of Commerce. 50 c. Allegory of Agriculture. HORIZ. 40 c. Berber, Negress and Annamite. 90 c. France with torch of Civilization. 1 f. 50, Diane de Poitiers.

10. Pierre and Marie Curie.

1938. International Anti-Cancer Fund.
116. **10.** 1 f. 75+50 c. blue .. 1·25 1·10

11.

1939. New York World's Fair.
117. **11.** 1 f. 25 red 8 8
118. 2 f. 25 blue 8 8

12. Lamido Woman.

13. Banyo Waterfall. (Vert.)

14. Elephants. (Horiz.)

15. Native Boatman. (Vert.)

1939.
119. **12.** 2 c. black 5 5
120. 3 c. magenta 5 5
121. 4 c. blue 5 5
122. 5 c. brown 5 5
123. 10 c. green 5 5
124. 15 c. red 5 5
125. 20 c. purple 5 5
126. **13.** 25 c. black 8 8
127. 30 c. orange 5 5
128. 40 c. blue 8 8
129. 45 c. green 20 20
130. 50 c. brown 5 5
131. 60 c. blue 5 5
132. 70 c. purple 25 25
133. **14.** 80 c. blue 20 20
134. 90 c. blue 5 5
135. 1 f. red 15 12
135a. 1 f. brown 5 5
136. 1 f. 25 red 25 25
137. 1 f. 40 orange 12 12
138. 1 f. 50 brown 8 8
139. 1 f. 60 brown 25 25
140. 1 f. 75 blue 5 5
141. 2 f. green 5 5
142. 2 f. 25 blue 10 10
143. 2 f. 50 purple 12 12
144. 3 f. violet 5 5
145. **15.** 5 f. brown 8 8
146. 10 f. purple 12 12
147. 20 f. green 20 20

16. Storming the Bastille.

1939. Revolution. 150th Anniv.
148. **16.** 45 c.+25 c. green .. 1·40 1·40
149. 70 c.+30 c. brown .. 1·40 1·40
150. 90 c.+35 c. orange .. 1·40 1·40
151. 1 f. 25+1 f. red .. 1·40 1·40
152. 2 f. 25+2 f. blue .. 1·40 1·40

1940. Adherence to General de Gaulle. Optd. **CAMEROUN FRANCAIS 27.8.40.**
153. **12.** 2 c. black 5 5
154. 3 c. magenta 5 5
155. 4 c. blue 5 5
156. 5 c. brown 20 20
157. 10 c. green 5 5
158. 15 c. red 8 8
159. 20 c. purple .. .. 1·10 90
160. **13.** 25 c. black 8 5
161. 30 c. orange 90 70
162. 40 c. blue 20 20
163. 45 c. green 10 10
164. **2.** 50 c. red and green .. 8 5
165. **13.** 60 c. blue 40 35
166. 70 c. purple 10 10
167. **14.** 80 c. blue 45 45
168. 90 c. blue 10 8
169. **11.** 1 f. 25 red 45 45
170. **14.** 1 f. 25 red 8 8
171. 1 f. 40 orange 30 30
172. 1 f. 50 brown 10 10
173. 1 f. 60 brown 12 12
174. 1 f. 75 blue 15 15
175. **11.** 2 f. 25 blue 45 45
176. **14.** 2 f. 25 blue 8 8
177. 2 f. 50 purple 8 8
178. **3.** 5 f. blk. & brn. on blue .. 2·00 1·50
179. **15.** 5 f. brown .. .. 2·10 1·50
180. **3.** 10 f. mauve and orange 3·25 2·75
181. **15.** 10 f. purple .. .. 5·00 3·75
182. **3.** 20 f. green and red .. 6·00 5·50
183. **15.** 20 f. green .. .. 30·00 22·00

1940. War Relief Fund Surch. **OEUVRES DE GUERRE** and premium.
184. **3.** 1 f. 25+2 f. blue & brn. 2·00 2·00
185. 1 f. 75+3 f. red & brn. 2·00 2·00
186. 2 f.+5 f. orange & olive 2·00 2·00

1940. Spitfire Fund Surch. **+5 Frs. SPITFIRE**
187. **13.** 25 c.+5 f. brown .. 14·00 11·00
188. 45 c.+5 f. green .. 14·00 11·00
189. 60 c.+5 f. blue .. 16·00 13·00
190. 70 c.+5 f. purple .. 16·00 13·00

1941. Spitfire Fund. Surch. **SPITFIRE 10 fr. General de GAULLE.**

190a.	**1.**	1 f. 25+10 f. red ..	11·00	8·00
190b.		2 f. 25+10 f. blue ..	11·00	8·00

16a. 'Plane over Map. **16b.** Flying Boat.

1941. Air.

190c.	**16a.**	25 c. brown-red	5	5
190d.		50 c. green	5	5
190e.		1 f. purple	5	5
190f.	**16b.**	2 f. olive	5	5
190g.		3 f. brown	5	5
190h.		4 f. blue	5	5
190i.		6 f. myrtle	5	5
190j.		7 f. purple	5	5
190k.		12 f. orange	60	60
190l.		20 f. red	15	15
190m.	–	50 f. ultramarine ..	25	25

DESIGN: 50 f. 'Plane over harbour.

17. Cross of Lorraine, Sword and Shield. **18.** Modern Aeroplane.

1941. Laquintinie Hospital Fund. Surch. **+10 Frs. AMBULANCE LAQUINTINIE.**

191.	**11.**	1 f. 25+10 f. red ..	2·50	1·60
192.		2 f. 25+10 f. blue ..	2·50	1·60

1942. Free French Issue.

193.	**17.**	5 c. brown (postage) ..	5	5
194.		10 c. blue	5	5
195.		25 c. green	5	5
196.		30 c. red	5	5
197.		40 c. green	5	5
198.		80 c. maroon	5	5
199.		1 f. mauve	5	5
200.		1 f. 50 red	5	5
201.		2 f. black	5	5
202.		2 f. 50 blue	5	5
203.		4 f. violet	8	8
204.		5 f. yellow	12	10
205.		10 f. brown	12	8
206.		20 f. green	20	10
207.	**18.**	1 f. orange (air) ..	5	5
208.		1 f. 50 red	5	5
209.		5 f. maroon	5	5
210.		10 f. black	8	8
211.		25 f. blue	12	12
212.		50 f. green	20	15
213.		100 f. claret	25	20

19. **20.** Felix Eboue.

1944. Mutual Aid and Red Cross Funds.

214.	**19.**	5 f.+20 f. red ..	25	25

1945. Surch.

215.	**17.**	50 c. on 5 c. brown ..	5	5
216.		60 c. on 5 c. brown ..	5	5
217.		70 c. on 5 c. brown ..	5	5
218.		1 f. 20 on 5 c. brown ..	5	5
219.		2 f. 40 on 25 c. green ..	5	5
220.		3 f. on 25 c. green ..	8	8
221.		4 f. 50 on 25 c. green ..	12	12
222.		15 f. on 2 f. 50 blue ..	15	15

1945.

223.	**20.**	2 f. black	5	5
224.		25 f. green	10	10

21. "Victory".

1946. Air. Victory.

225.	**21.**	8 f. purple	8	8

22. Chad.

1946. Air. From Chad to the Rhine. Inscr. "DU TCHAD AU RHIN".

226.	**22.**	5 f. blue	8	8
227.	–	10 f. purple	12	12
228.	–	15 f. red	12	12
229.	–	20 f. blue	15	15
230.	–	25 f. brown	20	20
231.	–	50 f. black	25	25

DESIGNS: 10 f. Koufra. 15 f. Mareth. 20 f. Normandy. 25 f. Paris. 50 f. Strasbourg.

23. Zebu and Herdsman. **24.** Aeroplane, African and Mask.

1946.

232.	**23.**	10 c. green (postage) ..	5	5
233.		30 c. orange	5	5
234.		40 c. blue	5	5
235.	–	50 c. sepia	5	5
236.	–	60 c. purple	5	5
237.	–	80 c. brown	5	5
238.	–	1 f. orange	5	5
239.	–	1 f. 20 green	5	2
240.	–	1 f. 50 red	20	15
241.	–	2 f. black	5	5
242.	–	3 f. red	5	5
243.	–	3 f. 60 claret	8	8
244.	–	4 f. blue	5	5
245.	–	5 f. red	8	5
256.	–	6 f. blue	5	5
247.	–	10 f. green	8	5
248.	–	15 f. blue	20	5
249.	–	20 f. green	20	5
250.	–	25 f. black	30	5

DESIGNS—VERT. 50 c. to 80 c. Tikar women. 1 f. to 1 f. 50, Banana porters. 2 f. to 4 f. Bowman. 5 f. to 10 f. Lamido horsemen. 15 f. to 25 f. Native head.

251.	–	50 f. green (air) ..	35	20
252.	–	100 f. brown	65	8
253.	**24.**	200 f. olive	1·25	30
253a.	–	500 f. indigo, bl. & lilac	3·25	65

DESIGNS—HORIZ. 50 f. Birds over mountains. 100 f. Horseman and aeroplane. VERT. 500 f. Aeroplane over Piton d'Humsiki.

25. Africans, Globe and Aeroplane.

1949. Air. U.P.U. 75th Anniv.

254.	**25.**	25 f. red, purple, green and blue ..	85	85

26. Doctor and Patient. **27.** Military Medal.

1950. Colonial Welfare Fund.

255.	**26.**	10 f.+2 f. green ..	50	50

1952. Military Medal Centenary.

256.	**27.**	15 f. red, yellow & green	60	45

28. Edea Barrage.

1953. Air. Opening of Edea Barrage.

257.	**28.**	15 f. blue, lake & brown	50	25

29. "D-Day".

1954. Air. Liberation. 10th Anniv.

258.	**29.**	15 f. green and turquoise	65	65

30. Dr. Jamot and Students.

1954. Air, Dr. Jamot (physician). 75th Birthday.

259.	**30.**	15 f. brn., blue & green	70	70

31. Porters Carrying Bananas.

DESIGNS—VERT. As T **31**: 40 f. Woman gathering coffee. HORIZ. As T **32**: 100 f. Aeroplane over giraffes. 200 f. Douala Port.

32. Transporting Logs.

1954.

260.	**31.**	8 f. violet, orange and purple (postage) ..	8	5
261.		15 f. choc., yellow & red	25	5
262.	–	40 f. brown, pink & choc.	25	5
263.	**32.**	50 f. ol., brn. & sep. (air)	40	5
264.	–	100 f. sepia, brn. & turq.	80	10
265.	–	200 f. choc., blue & grn.	1·25	20

33. Native Cattle.

DESIGNS: 15 f. R. Wouri bridge. 20 f. Technical education. 25 f. Mobile medical unit.

1956. Economic and Social Development Fund. Inscr. "F.I.D.E.S.".

266.	**33.**	5 f. chestnut and sepia	10	8
267.	–	15 f. turq., indigo & blk.	15	5
268.	–	20 f. turquoise & indigo	20	10
269.	–	25 f. indigo	25	12

1956. Coffee. As T **15** of New Caledonia.

270.		15 f. vermilion and red ..	10	5

34. Woman, Child and Flag. **35.** "Human Rights".

1958. 1st Anniv. of First Cameroun Govt.

271.	**34.**	20 f. brown, green, red, yellow and blue ..	20	5

1958. Declaration of Human Rights. 10th Anniv.

272.	**35.**	20 f. chocolate and red	25	20

1959. Tropical Flora. As T **21** of French Equatorial Africa.

273.		20 f. brn., pur., grn. & yell.	15	8

DESIGN—VERT. "Randia malleifera".

36. Loading Bananas on Ship. **37.** Prime Minister A. Ahidjo.

1959.

274.	**36.**	20 f. orange, brown, blue and myrtle	15	5
275.	–	25 f. grn., brown & purple	20	8

DESIGN—VERT. 25 f. Bunch of bananas and native bearers in jungle path.

D. FEDERAL REPUBLIC OF CAMEROUN.

Independence was granted in 1960. In 1961 the southern part of the former British mandate united with Cameroun to form a Federal Republic.

1960. Proclamation of Independence. Inscr. "1 ER JANVIER 1960".

276.	–	20 f. red, yellow, green and chocolate ..	20	5
277.	**37.**	25 f. grn., bistre & black	25	5

DESIGN: 20 f. Cameroun flag and map.

38. "Uprooted Tree". **39.** C.C.T.A. Emblem.

1960. World Refugee Year.

278.	**38.**	30 f. green, blue & brown	25	25

1960. African Technical Co-operation Commission. 10th Anniv.

279.	**39.**	50 f. black and maroon	40	30

40. Map and Flag. **41.** U.N. Headquarters, Emblem and Cameroun Flag.

1961. Red Cross Fund. Flag in green, red and yellow; cross in red; background colours given.

280.	**40.**	20 f.+5 f. green & red ..	25	25
281.		25 f.+10 f. red & green	30	30
282.		30 f.+15 f. red & green	40	40

1961. Admission to U.N.O. Flag in green, red and yellow; emblem in blue; buildings and inscr. in colours given.

283.	**41.**	15 f. chocolate & green	20	15
284.		25 f. green and blue ..	20	20
285.		85 f. purple, blue & red	60	50

1961. Surch. **REPUBLIQUE FEDERALE** and value in sterling currency.

286.	–	½d. on 1 f. orge. (238) (postage)	12	8
287.	–	1d. on 2 f. black (241)	12	8
288.	**33.**	1½d. on 5 f. chest. & sep.	15	10
289.	–	2d. on 10 f. green (247)	15	10
290.	–	3d. on 15 f. turq., ind. & black (267) ..	20	12
291.	–	4d. on 15 f. vermilion and red (270) ..	30	20
292.	–	6d. on 20 f. brn., pur., green & yellow (273)	30	20
293.	**37.**	1s. on 25 f. grn., bistre and black ..	60	50
294.	**38.**	2s. 6d. on 30 f. green, blue and brown ..	1·10	1·00

295. – 5s. on 100 r. sepia. brn. & turq. (264) (air) .. 2·25 2·25
296. – 10s. on 200 f. choc., blue and green (265) .. 4·25 4·25
297. – £1 on 500 f. ind., blue and lilac (253a) .. 8·00 8·00

The above were for use in the former Southern Cameroons pending the introduction of the Cameroun franc.

42. Pres. Ahidjo and Prime Minister Foncha.

1962. Reunification. (a) T 42.

298. 20 f. chocolate & violet
299. 25 f. choc. & bronze-green
300. 60 f. green and red ..
Set of 3 .. .. 14·00 12·00

(b) T 42 surch. in sterling currency.

301. 3d. on 20 f. choc. & violet
302. 6d. on 25 f. chocolate and bronze-green ..
303. 2s. 6d. on 60 f. grn. & red
Set of 3 .. .. 95·00 90·00

43. Lions International Badge. Doctor and Leper.

1962. World Leprosy Day. Lions International Relief Fund.

304. 43. 20 f. + 5 f. mar. & brn. 20 20
305. 25 f. + 10 f. mar. & blue 30 30
306. 50 f. + 15 f. mar. & grn. 70 70

44. European, African and Airliners.

1962. Air. Foundation of "Air Afrique" Airline.

307. 44. 25 f. purple, vio. & grn. 25 25

45. Campaign Emblem.

46. Giraffes and Waza Camp.

1962. Malaria Eradication.

308. 45. 25 f. + 5 f. mauve .. 25 20

1962. (a) Postage. Animals.

309. A. 50 c. sep., bl. & bl.-grn. 5 5
310. B. 1 f. black, turq. & orge. 5 5
311. C. 1 f. 50 brn., sage. & ol.-blk. 5 5
312. D. 2 f. black, blue & green 5 5
313. C. 3 f. brown, orange & pur. 5 5
314. B. 4 f. sepia, green & turq. 5 5
315. D. 5 f. slate-pur., grn. & cin. 8 5
316. A. 6 f. sepia, blue & lemon 8 5
317. E. 8 f. blue, red and green 10 5
318. F. 10 f. black, orange & blue 10 5
319. A. 15 f. brown, blue & turq. 15 5
320. 46. 20 f. chocolate and grey 20 8
321. F. 25 f. brown, yell. & grn. 25 12
322. E. 30 f. black, blue & chest. 25 12
323. 46. 40 f. lake and apple .. 30 15

(b) Air.

324. – 50 f. brown, myrtle & bl. 40 20
325. – 100 f. red, brn., ol. & bl. 80 25
326. – 200 f. black, chestnut and blue-green .. 1·75 40
327. – 500 f. buff, maroon & bl. 4·00 1·10

DESIGNS—HORIZ. as T 46: A, Moustac monkey. B, Elephant and Ntem Falls. C, Buffon's cob, Dschang. D, Hippopotamus, Hippo Camp. E, Manatee, Lake Ossa. F, Buffalo, Batoun Region (48 × 27 mm.): 50 f. Cocotiers Hotel, Douala. 100 f. "Cymothoe sangaris" (butterfly). 200 f. Ostriches. 500 f. Kapsikis, Mokalo (landscape).

47. Union Flag.

1962. Union of African and Malagasy States. 1st Anniv. Flag in green, red and gold.

328. 47. 30 f. chocolate 30 25

48. Map and View. 49. "The School Under the Tree."

1962. Reunification. 1st Anniv.

329. 48. 9 f. bistre, vio. & choc... 10 8
330. 14 f. red, green & blue.. 20 12
331. – 20 f. bistre, ind. & pur. 20 12
332. – 25 f. orge., sepia & blue 20 15
333. – 50 f. blue, sepia & red.. 50 35

DESIGNS: 20 f., 25 f. Sunrise over Cameroun 50 f. Commemorative scroll.

1962. Literacy and Popular Education Plan.

334. 49. 20 f. red, yellow & green 15 8

50. Globe and "Telstar".

1963. 1st Trans-Atlantic Television Satellite Link.

335. 50. 1 f. ol., vio. & blue (post) 5 5
336. 2 f. lake, green and blue 5 5
337. 3 f. olive, maroon & green 5 5
338. 25 f. maroon, blue & grn. 40 30
339. 100 f. chestnut and bronze-green (air) (48 × 27 mm.) 85 55

51. Globe and Emblem. 52. VHF Station, Mt. Bankolo, Yaounde.

1963. Freedom from Hunger.

340. 51. 18 f. + 5 f. blue, brown and green 20 15
341. 25 f. + 5 f. grn. & brown 25 20

1963. Duoala-Yaounde VHF Radio Service Inaug.

342. 52. 15 f. multicoloured (post) 12 10
343. – 20 f. multicoloured 15 12
344. – 100 f. multicoloured (air) 85 55

DESIGNS: 20 f. Aerials and control panel. 100 f. Edea relay station (26 × 44 mm.).

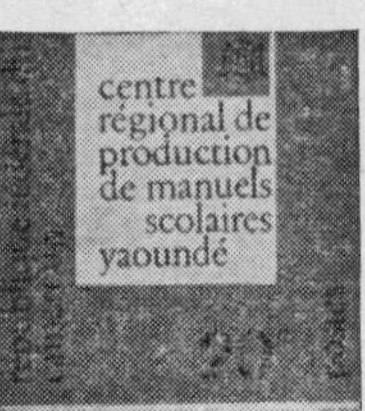

53. "Centre regional . . ." 54. Pres. Ahidjo.

1963. U.N.E.S.C.O. Regional Schoolbooks Production Centre. Yaounde. Inaug.

345. 53. 20 f. red, black & green 15 10
346. 25 f. red, black & orange 20 12
347. 100 f. red, black & gold 85 45

1963. Air. African and Malagasian Posts and Telecommunications Union. As T 10 of Central African Republic.

348. 85 f. red, buff, blue and ultramarine 75 65

1963. Reunification. 2nd Anniv. Mult.

349. 9 f. Type 54 .. .. 8 8
350. 18 f. Map and flag .. 15 10
351. 20 f. Type 54 .. .. 15 15

1963. Air. "Air Afrique" 1st Anniv. and "DC-8" Service Inaug. As T 10 of Congo Republic.

352. 50 f. black, green, drab and pink 40 30

55. Globe and Scales of Justice.

1963. Declaration of Human Rights. 15th Anniv.

353. 55. 9 f. chest., black & blue 10 8
354. 18 f. red, black & green 15 12
355. 25 f. green, black & red 20 12
356. 75 f. blue, black & yell. 65 40

56. Lion.

1964. Waza National Park.

357. 56. 10 f. bistre green & brown 10 5
358. 25 f. bistre and green .. 25 12

DESIGNS: 18 f. Sports Equipment. 30 f. Stadium Entrance. Yaounde.

57. Football Stadium, Yaounde.

1964. Tropics Cup. Inscr. as in T 57.

359. 57. 10 f. chest., turq. & grn. 8 5
360. – 18 f. green, red & violet 15 8
361. – 30 f. blue, brown & black 30 12

58. Palace of Justice, Yaounde.

1964. European-African Economic Convention. 1st Anniv.

362. 58. 15 f. brown, grey, red and green 20 15
363. – 40 f. red, green, black and slate 45 30

DESIGN—VERT. 40 f. Sun, Moon and various emblems of agriculture, industry and science.

59. Olympic Flame and Hurdling.

1964. Olympic Games, Tokyo.

364. 59. 9 f. red, blk. & grn. (post) 25 20
365. – 10 f. brown-olive, violet and red 25 20
366. – 300 f. blue-green, chocolate and red (air) .. 2·50 1·75

DESIGNS—VERT. 10 f. Running. HORIZ. 300 f. Wrestling.

DESIGNS—As T 60. VERT. 9 f. Bamileke dance costume. 18 f. Bamenda dance mask. HORIZ. 25 f. Fulani horseman. LARGER (48 × 27½ mm.): 50 f. View of Kribi and Longji. 250 f. Rhinoceros.

60. Ntem Falls.

1964. Folklore and Tourism.

367. – 9 f. red, bl. & grn. (post) 8 5
368. – 18 f. blue, brown & red 15 8
369. 60. 20 f. drab, green & red 15 10
370. – 25 f. red, choc. & orange 20 12
371. – 50 f. brn., grn. & bl. (air) 40 25
372. – 250 f. sep., grn. & chest. 2·25 85

1964. French, African and Malagasy Co-operation. As T 500 of France.

373. 18 f. choc., grn. & blue 15 12
374. 30 f. choc., turq. & brown 30 15

61. Pres. Kennedy.

1964. Air. Pres. Kennedy Commem.

375. 61. 100 f. sepia, grn. & apple 75 75

62. Inscription recording laying of First Rail.

1965. Opening of Mbanga-Kumba Railway.

376. 62. 12 f. indigo, grn. & blue 10 8
377. – 20 f. yellow, grn. & red 15 10

DESIGN—HORIZ. (36 × 22 mm.): 20 f. Diesel locomotive.

63. Abraham Lincoln.

1965. Air. Abraham Lincoln Death Cent.

378. 63. 100 f. multicoloured .. 90 65

DESIGN — VERT. 50 f. Nurse and child.

64. Ambulance and First Aid Post.

1965. Cameroun Red Cross

379. 64. 25 f. yellow, green & red 20 12
380. – 50 f. brown, red and grey 40 25

65. "Syncom" and I.T.U. Emblem.

1965. Air. I.T.U. Cent.

381. 65. 70 f. black, blue and red 60 45

66. Churchill giving "V" Sign. 67. "Map" Savings Bank.

1965. Air. Churchill Commem. Multi-coloured.

382. 12 f. Type 66 .. .. 55 45
383. 18 f. Churchill, oak spray and battleship 55 45

Nos. 382/3 were issued together in sheets with a se-tenant stamp-size label inscr. "SIR WINSTON CHURCHILL 1874-1965".

1965. Federal Postal Savings Bank.

384. 67. 9 f. yellow, red & green 8 8
385. – 15 f. choc., emer. & blue 12 10
386. – 20 f. brn., chest. & turq. 15 12

DESIGNS—HORIZ. (48 × 27 mm.): 15 f. Savings Bank building. VERT. (27 × 48 mm.): 20 f. "Cocoa-bean" savings bank.

68. Africa Cup and Players.

1965. Winning of Africa Cup by Oryx Football Club.
387. 68. 9 f. choc., yellow & red 8 8
388. 20 f. blue, yellow and red 15 12

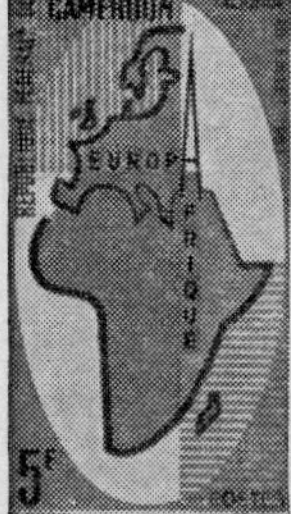

69. Map of Europe and Africa. 70. U.P.U. Monument Berne, and Doves.

1965. "Europafrique".
389. 69. 5 f. red, lilac and black 5 5
390. – 40 f. multicoloured .. 35 25
DESIGN: 40 f. Yaounde Conference.

1965. Admission to U.P.U. 5th Anniv.
391. 70. 30 f. purple and red .. 25 20

71. I.C.Y. Emblem.

1965. Int. Co-operation Year.
392. 71. 10 f. red & blue (postage) 10 10
393. 100 f. blue and red (air) 90 60

72. Pres. Ahidjo and Government House.

1965. Re-election of Pres. Ahidjo. Multicoloured.
394. 9f. Pres. Ahidjo wearing hat, and Government House (vert.) 8 5
395. 18 f. Type 72 .. .. 15 10
396. 20 f. As 9 f. 20 12
397. 25 f. Type 72 .. .. 25 12

73. Musgum Huts, Pouss.

1965. Folklore and Tourism.
398. 73. 9 f. green, brown and red (postage) .. 8 5
399. – 18 f. brown, green & blue 15 10
400. – 20 f. brown and blue .. 20 12
401. – 25 f. grey, lake & emer. 20 12
402. – 50 f. brown, indigo and green (48×27 mm.) (air) 45 25
DESIGNS—HORIZ. 18 f. Great Calao's dance (N. Cameroons). 25 f. National Tourist office, Yaounde. 50 f. Racing pirogue on Sanaga River, Edea. VERT. 20 f. Sultan's palace gate, Foumban.

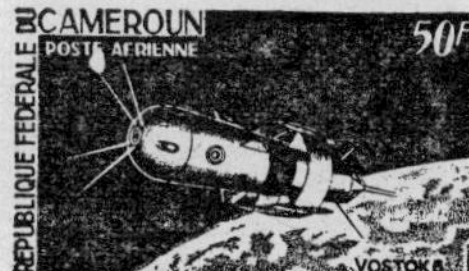

74. "Vostock 6".

1966. Air. Spacecraft.
403. 74. 50 f. green and lake .. 45 25
404. – 100 f. ultram. & purple 90 55
405. – 200 f. violet and ultram. 1·75 1·10
406. – 500 f. blue and indigo .. 4·25 2·50
DESIGNS: 100 f. "Gemini 4", and White in space. 200 f. "Gemini 5". 500 f. "Gemini 6" and "Gemini 7" making rendezvous.

75. Mountain's Hotel, Buea.

1966. Cameroun Hotels.
407. 75. 9 f. bistre, green & red (postage) 5 5
408. – 20 f. black, green & blue 15 10
409. – 35 f. red, choc. & green 30 15
410. 75. 18 f. blk., grn. & bl. (air) 12 10
411. – 25 f. indigo, red & blue 20 12
412. – 50 f. choc., orge. & green 40 25
413. – 60 f. choc., green & blue 60 30
414. – 85 f. blue, red and green 85 40
415. – 100 f. pur., indigo & grn. 90 45
416. – 150 f. orge., brn. & blue 1·10 55
HOTELS—HORIZ. 20 f. Deputies, Yaounde. 25 f. Akwa Palace, Douala. 35 f. Dschang. 50 f. Terminus, Yaounde. 60 f. Imperial, Yaounde. 85 f. Independence, Yaounde. 150 f. Huts, Waza Camp. VERT. 100 f. Hunting Lodge, Mora.

76. Foumban Bas-relief.

1966. World Festival of Negro Arts, Dakar.
417. 76. 9 f. black and red .. 8 5
418. – 18 f. mar., chest & green 15 8
419. – 20 f. brown, blue & violet 20 10
420. – 25 f. chocolate and plum 25 12
DESIGNS—VERT. 18 f. Ekoi mask. 20 f. Bamileke statue. HORIZ. 25 f. Bamoun stool.

77. W.H.O. Headquarters, Geneva. 78. "Phaeomeria magnifica".

1966. U.N. Agency Buildings.
421. 77. 50 f. lake, blue & yellow 45 25
422. – 50 f. yellow, blue & grn. 45 25
DESIGN: No. 422, I.T.U. Headquarters, Geneva.

1966. Flowers. Multicoloured.
(a) Postage. Size as T 78.
423. 9 f. Type 78 .. .. 8 5
424. 15 f. "Strelitzia reginae" 12 5
425. 18 f. "Hibiscus schizopetalus X, rosa sinensis" .. 15 5
426. 20 f. "Antigonon leptopus" 20 5
(b) Air. Size 26×45½ mm.
427. 25 f. "Hibiscus mutabilis" ("Caprice des dames") 20 8
428. 50 f. "Delonix regia" .. 40 10
429. 100 f. "Bougainvillea glabra" 85 20
430. 200 f. "Thevetia peruviana" 1·60 70
431. 250 f. "Hippeastrum equestre" .. .. 2·25 95
For stamps at T 78 but showing fruits, see Nos. 463/71.

79. Mobile Gendarmerie.

1966. Air. Cameroun Armed Forces.
432. 79. 20 f. ultram., chest. & plum 15 10
433. – 25 f. green, violet & brn. 20 12
434. – 60 f. indigo, green & blue 55 20
435. – 100 f. blue, red & mar. 85 45
DESIGNS: 25 f. Paratrooper. 60 f. Gunboat "Vigilant". 100 f. Transport aircraft.

80. Wembley Stadium.

1966. Air. World Cup Football Championships.
436. 80. 50 f. green, indigo & red 40 25
437. – 200 f. red, blue & green 1·75 1·00
DESIGN: 200 f. Footballers.

81. Aircraft and "Air Afrique" Emblem.

1966. Air. "DC-8" Air Services. Inaug.
438. 81. 25 f. grey, black & pur. 20 10

82. U.N. General Assembly.

1966. Admission to U.N. 6th Anniv.
439. 82. 50 f. pur., green & blue 40 8
440. – 100 f. blue, brown & grn. 85 40
DESIGN—VERT. 100 f. Africans encircling U.N. emblem within figure "6".

83. 1st Minister's Residency, Buea (side view).

1966. Cameroun's Reunification. 5th Anniv. Designs show Ministerial Residencies. Multicoloured.
441. 9 f. Type 83 .. .. 8 5
442. 18 f. Prime Minister's Residency, Yaounde (front view) 12 5
443. 20 f. As 18 f. but side view 15 5
444. 25 f. As Type 83 but front view 20 8

84. Learning to Write.

1966. U.N.E.S.C.O. and U.N.I.C.E.F. 20th Anniv.
445. 84. 50 f. brown, pur. & blue 45 25
446. – 50 f. black, blue & pur. 45 25
DESIGN: No. 446, Cameroun children.

85. Buea Cathedral.

1966. Air. Religious Buildings.
447. 85. 18 f. maroon, blue & grn. 15 10
448. – 25 f. violet, brown & grn. 20 12
449. – 30 f. lake, green & purple 25 15
450. – 60 f. green, lake & turq. 50 25
BUILDINGS: 25 f. Yaounde Cathedral. 30 f. Orthodox Church, Yaounde. 60 f. Garoua Mosque.

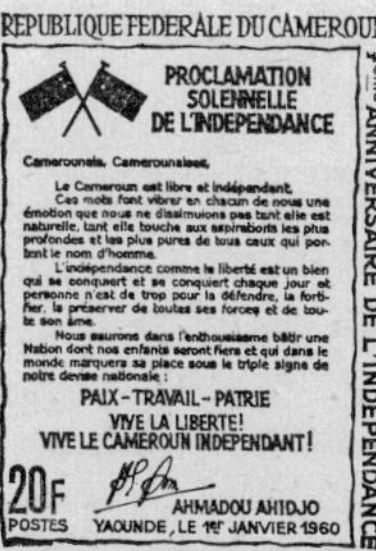

86. Proclamation.

1967. Independence. 7th Anniv.
451. 86. 20 f. red, green & yellow 20 12

87. Map of Africa, Railway Lines and Signals. 89. Aircraft and I.C.A.O. Emblem.

88. Lions Emblem and Jungle.

1967. 5th African and Malagasy Railway Technicians Conf., Yaounde. Multicoloured.
452. 20 f. Type 87 .. .. 20 10
453. 20 f. Map of Africa and diesel train 25 12

1967. Lions Int. 50th Anniv. Multicoloured.
454. 50 f. Type 88 .. .. 45 25
455. 100 f. Lions emblem and palms 85 50

1967. Int. Civil Aviation Organisation.
456. 89. 50 f. multicoloured .. 40 20

90. Dove and I.A.E.A. Emblem.

1967. Int. Atomic Energy Agency.
457. 90. 50 f. blue and green .. 40 25

91. Rotary Banner and Emblem.

1967. Cameroun Branch, Rotary Int. 10th Anniv.
458. 91. 25 f. red, gold & blue .. 20 12

92. "Pioneer A".

1967. Air. "Conquest of the Moon".
459. 92. 25 f. green, brown & blue 20 12
460. – 50 f. violet, pur. & grn. 45 25
461. – 100 f. purple, brn. & bl. 85 45
462. – 250 f. mar., grey & brn. 2·25 1·25
DESIGNS: 50 f. "Ranger 6". 100 f. "Luna 9". 250 f. "Luna 10".

93. Grapefruit. 94. Sanaga Waterfalls.

1967. Fruits. Multicoloured.

463. 1 f. Type **93** 5 5
464. 2 f. Papaw 5 5
465. 3 f. Custard-apple .. 5 5
466. 4 f. Breadfruit 5 5
467. 5 f. Coconut 5 5
468. 6 f. Mango 5 5
469. 8 f. Avocado pear 8 5
470. 10 f. Pineapple 10 5
471. 30 f. Bananas 25 12

1967. Int. Tourist Year.

472. **94.** 30 f. grn., bl., brn. & blk. 25 10

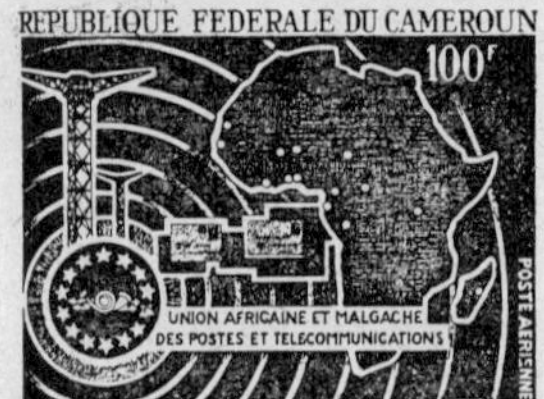

95. Map, Letters and Pylons.

1967. Air. African and Malagasy Posts and Telecommunications Union (U.A.M.P.T.). 5th Anniv.

473. **95.** 100 f. purple, lake and turquoise 90 50

96. Harvesting Coconuts (carved box). **97.** Crossed Skis.

1967. Cameroun Art.

474. **96.** 10 f. brown, red & blue 8 5
475. – 20 f. brown, green & yell. 15 8
476. – 30 f. brown, red & green 25 10
477. – 100 f. brown, verm. & grn. 80 35

DESIGNS (Carved boxes): 20 f. Lion-hunting. 30 f. Harvesting coconuts (different). 100 f. Carved chest.

1967. Air. Winter Olympic Games, Grenoble.

478. **97.** 30 f. chocolate and blue 30 15

98. Cameroun Exhibit.

1967. Air. World Fair, Montreal.

479. **98.** 50 f. brown, chest. & pur. 40 20
480. – 100 f. choc., mar. & grn. 80 30
481. – 200 f. grn., pur. & brn. 1·60 60

DESIGNS: 100 f. Totem poles. 200 f. African pavilion.

For No. 481 optd., **PREMIER HOMME SUR LA LUNE 20 JUILLET 1969/FIRST MAN LANDING ON MOON 20 JULY 1969** see note below Nos. 512/17.

99. Chancellor Adenauer and Cologne Cathedral. **100.** Arms of the Republic.

1967. Air. Adenauer Commem. Mult.

482. 30 f. Type **99** 30 15
483. 70 f. Adenauer and Chancellor's residence, Bonn .. 65 30

Nos. 482/3 were issued together with an intervening se-tenant label showing the C.E.P.T. emblem.

1968. Independence. 8th Anniv.

484. **100.** 30 f. multicoloured 25 10

101. Pres. Ahidjo and King Faisal of Saudi Arabia.

1968. Air. Pres. Ahidjo's Pilgrimage to Mecca and Visit to the Vatican. Multicoloured.

485. 30 f. Type **101** 20 12
486. 60 f. Pope Paul VI greeting Pres. Ahidjo 45 25

102. "Explorer VI" (televised picture of Earth).

1968. Air. Telecommunications Satellites.

487. **102.** 20 f. grey, red and blue 20 8
488. – 30 f. blue, indigo & red 25 12
489. – 40 f. green, red & plum 30 15

DESIGNS: 30 f. "Molnya". 40 f. "Molnya" (televised picture of Earth).

103. Douala Port.

1968. Air. Five-Year Development Plan.

490. – 20 f. blue, red & green 15 8
491. – 30 f. blue, green & brn. 25 12
492. – 30 f. blue, chocolate & green 25 12
493. – 40 f. brn., grn. & turq. 30 15
494. **103.** 60 f. maroon, indigo & blue 40 20

DESIGNS—VERT. 20 f. Steel forge. 30 f. (No. 491), "Transcamerounais" express train leaving tunnel. 30 f. (No. 492), Tea-harvesting. 40 f. Rubber-tapping.

104. Spiny Lobster.

1968. Fishes and Crustaceans.

495. **104.** 5 f. grn., brn. & violet 5 5
496. – 10 f. slate, brn. & blue 5 5
497. – 15 f. brn., chest. & pur. 8 5
498. – 20 f. brown and blue 8 5
499. – 25 f. blue, brn. & grn. 10 5
500. – 30 f. choc., ultram. & red 12 8
501. – 40 f. blue, brown & orge. 20 10
502. – 50 f. cerise, slate & grn. 30 15
503. – 55 f. mar.. chest. & bl. 40 20
504. – 60 f. blue, mar. & grn 50 25

FISHES AND CRUSTACEANS—HORIZ. 10 f. Fresh water crayfish. 15 f. Nile mouthbreeder. 20 f. Sole. 25 f. Pike. 30 f. Swimming crab. 55 f. Snakehead. 60 f. Threadfin. VERT. 40 f. Sickle fish. 50 f. Prawn.

105. Refinery and Tanker.

1968. Petroleum Refinery, Port Gentil, Gabon. Inaug.

505. **105.** 30 f. multicoloured .. 20 8

106. Boxing. **107.** Human Rights.

1968. Air. Olympic Games, Mexico.

506. **106.** 30 f. choc., grn. & emer. 20 12
507. – 50 f. choc., red & emer. 35 20
508. – 60 f. choc., bl. & emer. 40 25

DESIGNS: 50 f. Long-jumping. 60 f. Gymnastics.

1968. Human Rights Year

510. **107.** 15 f. bl. & salmon (post.) 12 8
511. **107.** 30 f. grn. & pur. (air) .. 20 12

108. Mahatma Gandhi and Map of India. **109.** "The Letter" (A. Cambon).

1968. Air. "Apostles of Peace".

512. **108.** 30 f. blk., yell. & blue 25 12
513. – 30 f. black and blue .. 25 12
514. – 40 f. black and pink 30 15
515. – 60 f. black and lilac .. 45 25
516. – 70 f. blk., bl. & buff .. 50 30
517. – 70 f. black and green 50 30

PORTRAITS: No. 513, Martin Luther King. 514, J. F. Kennedy. 515, R. F. Kennedy. 516, Gandhi (full-face). 517, Martin Luther King (half-length).

Nos. 512 and 516, 513 and 517, and 514/5 were respectively issued together in sheets se-tenant with stamp-size labels bearing commemorative inscr.

During 1969, Nos. 481 and 512/17 were issued optd. **PREMIER HOMME SUR LA LUNE 20 JUILLET 1969/FIRST MAN LANDING ON MOON 20 JULY 1969** in very limited quantities.

1968. Air. "Philexafrique" Stamp Exn., Abidjan (in 1969). (1st Issue.)

519. **109.** 100 f. multicoloured 80 80

No. 519 was issued in sheets with a se-tenant stamp-size label inscr. "PHILEXAFRIQUE ABIDJAN 14-23 FEVRIER 1969" and showing the U.A.M.P.T. posthorn emblem.

110. Wouri Bridge and 1 f. stamp of 1925.

1969. Air. "Philexafrique" Stamp Exn., Abidjan, Ivory Coast (2nd Issue).

520. **110.** 50 f. blue, olive and grn. 40 35

111. President Ahidjo.

1969. Independence. 9th Anniv.

521. **111.** 30 f. multicoloured 20 10

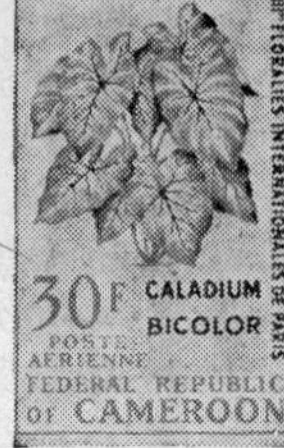

112. Vat of Chocolate. **113.** "Caladium bicolor".

1969. Chocolate Industry Development.

522. **112.** 15 f. indigo, choc. & red 10 5
523. – 30 f. brn., choc. & grn. 20 8
524. – 50 f. red, grn. & bistre 25 15

DESIGNS—HORIZ. 30 f. Chocolate factory. VERT. 50 f. Making confectionery.

1969. Air. 3rd Int. Flower Show, Paris. Multicoloured.

525. 30 f. Type **113** 20 12
526. 50 f. "Aristolochia elegans" 40 25
527. 100 f. "Gloriosa simplex" 80 45

114. Reproduction Symbol.

1969. Abbia Arts and Folklore.

528. **114.** 5 f. purple, turquoise-blue and blue .. 5 5
529. – 10 f. orge., olive & blue 8 5
530. – 15 f. indigo, red & blue 10 5
531. – 30 f. green, brown & bl. 20 8
532. – 70 f. red, green and blue 50 25

DESIGNS—HORIZ. 10 f. "Two Toucans". 30 f. "Vulture attacking Monkey". VERT. 15 f. Forest Symbol. 70 f. Olifant-player.

115. G.P.O., Douala.

1969. Air. New Post Office Buildings.

533. **115.** 30 f. brn., blue & green 20 10
534. – 50 f. red, slate and blue-green 40 20
535. – 100 f. brn. & blue-green 80 40

DESIGNS: 50 f. G.P.O., Buea. 100 f. G.P.O., Bafoussam.

116. "Coronation of Napoleon" (J. L. David).

1969. Air. Napoleon Bonaparte. Birth Bicent.

536. **116.** 30 f. multicoloured .. 25 15
537. – 1,000 f. gold .. .. 13·00

DESIGN: 1,000 f. "Napoleon crossing the Alps".

No. 537 is embossed on gold foil.

117. Kumba Station. **118.** Bank Emblem.

1969. Opening of Mbanga-Kumba Railway. Multicoloured.

538. 30 f. Type **117** 20 8
539. 50 f. Diesel train on bridge (vert.) 40 15

1969. African Development Bank. 5th Anniv.

540. **118.** 30 f. brn., grn. & violet 25 10

1969. Air. Negro Writers. Portrait designs as T **108**.

541. 15 f. brown and blue .. 10 5
542. 30 f. brown and brn.-purple 20 8
543. 30 f. brown and yellow .. 20 8
544. 50 f. brown and emerald 35 20
545. 50 f. brown and agate .. 35 20
546. 100 f. brown and yellow .. 70 45

DESIGNS—VERT. No. 541, Dr. P. Mars (Haiti). No. 542, W. Dubois (U.S.A.). No. 543, A. Cessaire (Martinique). No. 544, M. Garvey (Jamaica). No. 545, L. Hughes (U.S.A.). No. 546, R. Maran (Martinique).

119. I.L.O. Emblem.

1969. Air. Int. Labour Organization. 50th Anniv.

548. **119.** 30 f. black and turquoise 20 10
549. 50 f. black and magenta 35 20

120. Astronauts and "Apollo 11".

1969. Air. 1st Man on the Moon. Mult.

550. 200 f. Type **120** .. .. 1·40 80
551. 500 f. Astronaut and module on Moon.. .. .. 3·50 2·25

121. Aircraft, Map and Airport.

1969. Aerial Navigation Security Agency for Africa and Madagascar. (Agence pour la Securite de la Navigation Aerienne=ASECNA.) 10th Anniv.

552. **121.** 100 f. green 60 50

122. President Ahidjo, Arms and Map.

1970. Air. Independence. 10th Anniv.

553. **122.** 1,000 f. gold and mult. 7·00

No. 553 is embossed on gold foil.

123. Mont Febe Hotel, Yaounde.

1970. Air. Tourism.

554. **123.** 30 f. grey, grn. & brn. 20 8

124. Lenin. **125.** "Lantana camara".

1970. Air. Lenin. Birth Cent.

555. **124.** 50 f. brown and yellow 30 20

1970. African Climbing Plants. Multicoloured.

556. 15 f. Type **125** (postage).. 10 5
557. 30 f. "Passiflora quadrangularis" 20 8
558. 50 f. "Cleome speciosa" (air) 30 25
559. 100 f. "Mussaenda erythrophylla" 60 35

126. Lions' Emblem and Map of Africa.

1970. Air. 13th Congress of Lions Int. District 403, Yaounde.

560. **126.** 100 f. multicoloured .. 65 40

127. New U.P.U. H.Q. Building.

1970. New U.P.U. Headquarters Building, Berne.

561. **127.** 30 f. green, violet & bl. 20 8
562. 50 f. blue, red & grey.. 35 10

128. U.N. Emblem and Stylised Doves.

1970. Air. United Nations. 25th Anniv.

563. **128.** 30 f. brown and orange 20 12
564. – 50 f. indigo and blue.. 35 15

DESIGN—VERT. 50 f. U.N. emblem and stylised dove.

129. Fermenting Vats. **130.** Expo Emblem and Map of Japan.

1970. Brewing Industry.

565. **129.** 15 f. brn., grn. & slate 10 5
566. – 30 f. red, choc. & blue 20 8

DESIGN: 30 f. Storage tanks.

1970. Air. Expo 70.

567. – 50 f. blue, red and green 35 15
568. **130.** 100 f. red, blue and grn. 65 25
569. – 150 f. brn., slate and bl. 1·00 45

DESIGNS—HORIZ. 50 f. Japanese Pavilion. 150 f. Australian Pavilion.

131. Gen. De Gaulle in Tropical Kit. **133.** Dancers.

132. Aztec Stadium, Mexico City.

1970. Air. "Homage to General De Gaulle".

570. **131.** 100 f. brown, ultramarine and green .. 70 40
571. – 200 f. ultramarine, green and brown .. 1·25 70

DESIGN: 200 f. Gen. De Gaulle in military uniform.

Nos. 576/7 were issued together as a triptych, separated by a stamp-size label showing Maps of France and Cameroun.

1970. Air. World Cup Football Championships, Mexico. Multicoloured.

572. 50 f. Type **132** 30 15
573. 100 f. Mexican team .. 65 30
574. 200 f. Pele and Brazilian team with World Cup (vert.) .. .. .. 1·25 70

1970. Ozilia Dancers.

575. **133.** 30 f. red, orge. & grn. 20 8
576. 50 f. red, brn. and scarlet 30 12

134. Doll in National Costume. **135.** Beethoven (after Stieler).

1970. Cameroun Dolls.

577. **134.** 10 f. grn., black and red 5 5
578. 15 f. red, grn. and yell. 8 5
579. 30 f. brn., grn. and blk. 15 8

1970. Air. Beethoven. Birth Bicentenary.

580. **135.** 250 f. multicoloured.. 1·75 1·00

1970. Air. Rembrandt Paintings. Horiz. designs similar to T **116**. Multicoloured.

581. 70 f. "Christ at Emmaus" 45 20
582. 150 f. "The Anatomy Lesson" 90 50

136. "Industry and Agriculture". **137.** Bust of Dickens.

1970. "Europafrique" Economic Community.

583. **136.** 30 f. multicoloured .. 20 8

1970. Charles Dickens. Death Cent.

584. **137.** 40 f. brown and red .. 30 12
585. – 50 f. multicoloured .. 35 15
586. – 100 f. multicoloured.. 70 30

DESIGNS: 50 f. Characters from David Copperfield. 100 f. Dickens writing.

Nos. 590/2 were issued together as a triptych within the sheet.

1971. Air. De Gaulle Memorial Issue. Nos. 570/1 optd. **IN MEMORIAM 1890-1970.**

587. **131.** 100 f. brn., ultram. & grn. 60 30
588. – 200 f. ultram., grn. & brn. 1·25 65

138. University Buildings.

1971. Federal University, Yaounde.

589. **138.** 50 f. grn., blue & brn. 25 12

139. Presidents Ahidjo and Pompidou.

1971. Visit of Pres. Pompidou of France.

590. **139.** 30 f. multicoloured .. 25 15

140. "Cameroun Youth".

1971. 5th National Youth Festival.

591. **140.** 30 f. multicoloured .. 20 5

141. Timber Yard, Douala.

1971. Air. Industrial Expansion.

592. **141.** 40 f. brn., grn. & red .. 25 10
593. – 70 f. brn., grn. & blue 45 20
594. – 100 f. red, blue & grn. 55 30

DESIGNS—VERT. 70 f. "Alucam" aluminium plant, Edea. HORIZ. 100 f. Mbakaou Dam.

142. "Gerbera hybrida". **143.** "World Races".

1971. Flowers. Multicoloured.

595. 20 f. Type **142** .. 12 5
596. 40 f. "Opuntia polyantha" 25 10
597. 50 f. "Hemerocallis hybrida" 30 15

For similar designs inscr. "United Republic of Cameroon" etc., see Nos. 648/52.

1971. Racial Equality Year. Multicoloured.

598. 20 f. Type **143** .. 12 5
599. 30 f. Hands of four races clasping globe 20 8

144. Flamingoes, Camp de Waza.

1971. Landscapes.

600. **144.** 10 f. blue, red & green 8 5
601. – 20 f. red, brn. & grn. .. 12 5
602. – 30 f. grn., blue & brn. 20 8

DESIGNS: 20 f. African pirogue. 30 f. Sanaga River.

145. Relay-racing.

1971. Air. Modern Olympic Games. 75th Anniv.

603. **145.** 30 f. blue, red & brn. 20 10
604. – 50 f. purple and blue .. 30 20
605. – 100 f. blk., grn. & red 60 30

DESIGNS—VERT. 50 f. Olympic runner with torch. HORIZ. 100 f. Throwing the discus.

146. Deep-sea Trawler.

1971. Air. Fishing Industry.
606. **146.** 30 f. brn., grn. & blue 20 10
607. – 40 f. maroon, bl. & grn. 25 15
608. – 70 f. brown, red & blue 45 20
609. – 150 f. brown, yellow, blue and green 1·00 50

DESIGNS: 40 f. Traditional fishing method, Northern Cameroun. 70 f. Fish quay, Douala. 150 f. Shrimp-boats, Douala.

147. Peace Palace, The Hague.

1971. Int. Court of Justice, The Hague. 25th Anniv.
610. **147.** 50 f. brn., bl. & green 30 12

148. 1916 French Occupation 20 c. and 1914–18 War Memorial, Yaounde.

1971. Air. "Philatecam 71" Stamp Exhibition, Yaounde (1st issue).
611. **148.** 20 f. brn., ochre & grn. 15 5
612. – 25 f. brn., grn. & blue 20 8
613. – 40 f. grn., grey & brn. 25 15
614. – 50 f. black, red, sepia and brown 30 20
615. – 100 f. grn., brn. & orge. 65 35

DESIGNS: 25 f. 1954 15 f. Jamot stamp and memorial. 40 f. 1965 25 f. Tourist Office stamp and public buildings, Yaounde. 50 f. German stamp and Imperial German postal emblem. 100 f. 1915 Expeditionary Force optd., error, and Expeditionary Force memorial. See also No. 620.

149. Rope Bridge. **150.** Bamoun Horseman (carving).

1971. "Rural Life". Multicoloured.
616. 40 f. Type **149** 25 10
617. 45 f. Local market (horiz.) 30 10

1971. Cameroun Carving.
618. **150.** 10 f. brown and yellow 8 5
619. – 15 f. brown and yellow 10 5

DESIGN: 15 f. Fetish statuette.

151. Pres. Ahidjo, Flag and "Reunification" Road.

1971. Air. "Philatecam 72" Stamp Exhib., Yaounde (2nd issue).
620. **151.** 250 f. multicoloured.. 2·00

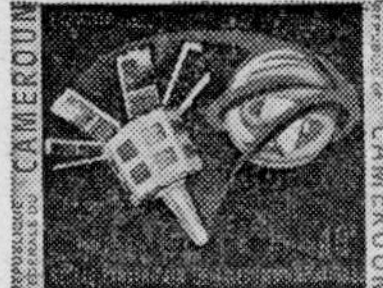

152. Satellite and Globe.

1971. Pan-African Telecommunications Network.
621. **152.** 40 f. multicoloured. .. 25 10

153. U.A.M.P.T. Headquarters, Brazzaville and Carved Stool.

1971. Air. African and Malagasy Posts and Telecommunications Union. 10th Anniv.
622. **153.** 100 f. multicoloured .. 65 30

154. Ear of Wheat and Emblem. **155.** "The Holy Family with the Lamb" (detail, Raphael).

1971. U.N.I.C.E.F. 25th Anniv.
623. – 40 f. pur., blue & slate 30 12
624. **154.** 50 f. red, green & blue 40 20

DESIGN—HORIZ. 40 f. Children acclaiming emblem.

1971. Air. Christmas. Paintings. Multicoloured.
625. 40 f. "The Annunciation" (Fra Angelico) 20 10
626. 45 f. "Virgin and Child" (Del Sarto) 20 12
627. 150 f. Type **155** .. .. 1·00 45

The 40 f. and 45 f. are horiz.

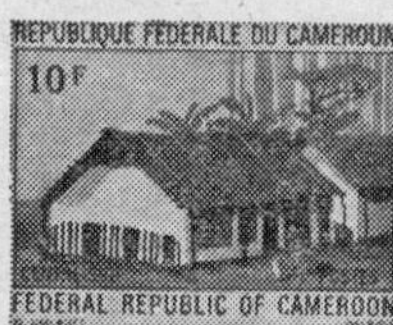

156. Cabin, South-Central Region.

1972. Traditional Cameroun Houses. Multicoloured.
628. 10 f. Type **156** 5 5
629. 15 f. Adamaoua round house 8 5

157. Airline Emblem.

1972. Air. Cameroun Airlines' Inaugural Flight.
630. **157.** 50 f. multicoloured .. 30 15

158. Giraffe and Palm Tree. **160.** "St. Mark's Square and Doge's Palace" (detail-Caffi).

159. Players with ball.

1972. Festival of Youth. Multicoloured.
631. 2 f. Type **158** 5 5
632. 5 f. Domestic scene 5 5
633. 10 f. Blacksmith (horiz.) .. 5 5
634. 15 f. Women 8 5

1972. African Football Cup Championships. Multicoloured.
635. 20 f. Africa Cup (vert.) .. 10 8
636. 40 f. Type **159** 20 12
637. 45 f. Team captains (vert.) 25 15

1972. Air. U.N.E.S.C.O. "Save Venice" Campaign. Multicoloured.
638. 40 f. Type **160** 25 10
639. 100 f. "La Regata Grand Canal" (detail - Canaletto) 55 25
640. 200 f. "La Regata Grand Canal" (detail - Canaletto) (different) .. 1·10 50

161. Assembly Building, Yaounde.

1972. Inter-Parliamentary Council, Yaounde. 110th Session.
641. **161.** 40 f. multicoloured .. 20 10

162. Horseman, North Cameroun.

1972. "Countryside and Folklore". Multicoloured.
642. 15 f. Type **162** 8 5
643. 20 f. Bororo woman (vert.) 10 5
644. 40 f. River Wouri and Mt. Cameroun 20 12

163. Pataiev, Dobrovolsky and Volkov.

1972. Air. "Soyuz 11" Cosmonauts Memorial Issue.
645. **163.** 50 f. multicoloured .. 25 12

E. UNITED REPUBLIC OF CAMEROUN.

164. U.N. Building, New York, Gate of Heavenly Peace, Peking and Chinese Flag.

1972. Air. Admission of Chinese People's Republic to U.N.
646. **164.** 50 f. multicoloured .. 25 12

165. Chemistry Laboratory, Federal University.

1972. Pres. Ahidjo Prize.
647. **165.** 40 f. red, green & purple 20 10

1972. Flowers. As T **142**, but inscr. "UNITED REPUBLIC OF CAMEROON", etc. Multicoloured.
648. 40 f. "Solanum macranthum" 20 10
649. 40 f. "Kaempferia aethiopica" 20 10
650. 45 f. "Hoya carnosa" .. 25 12
651. 45 f. "Cassia alata" .. 25 12
652. 50 f. "Crinum sanderianum" 30 15

166. Swimming.

1972. Air. Olympic Games, Munich.
653. **166.** 50 f. grn., brn. & lake 30 12
654. – 50 f. brn., blue and blackish-brown .. 30 12
655. – 200 f. lake, grey & pur. 1·10 55

DESIGNS—HORIZ. No. 655, Horse-jumping. VERT. No. 654, Boxing.

167. "Charaxes ameliae". **168.** Giant (Great Blue) Turacos.

1972. Butterflies. Multicoloured.
657. 40 f. Type **167** 20 10
658. 45 f. "Papiliotynderaeus" 20 12

1972. No. 471 surch.
659. 40 f. on 30 f. multicoloured 20 10

1972. Air. Olympic Gold Medal Winners. Nos. 653/5 optd. as listed below.
660. 50 f. green, brown & lake 30 15
661. 50 f. brown, blue and blackish-brown .. 30 15
662. 200 f. lake, grey and purple 1·10 55

OVERPRINTS: No. 660, **NATATION MARK SPITZ 7 MEDAILLES D'OR.** No. 661, **SUPER-WELTER KOTTYSCH MEDAILLE D'OR.** No. 662, **CONCOURS COMPLET MEADE MEDAILLE D'OR.**

1972. Birds. Multicoloured.
663. 10 f. Type **168** 5 5
664. 45 f. Red-headed lovebirds (horiz.) 20 10

169. "The Virgin with Angels" (Cimabue). **170.** St. Theresa.

1972. Air. Christmas. Multicoloured.
665. 45 f. Type **169** 20 10
666. 140 f. "The Madonna of the Rose Arbour" (S. Lochner) 60 30

1973. Air. St. Theresa of Lisieux. Birth Cent.
667. **170.** 45 f. blue, brn. & violet 20 12
668. – 100 f. mauve, brn. & bl. 60 30

DESIGN: 100 f. Lisieux Basilica.

171. Emperor Haile Selassie and "Africa Hall", Addis Ababa.

1973. Air. Emperor Haile Selassie of Ethiopia. 80th Birthday.
669. **171.** 45 f. multicoloured .. 20 12

172. Cotton Cultivation, North Cameroun. **174.** Human Hearts.

173. " Food for All ".

1973. 3rd Five Year Plan. Multicoloured.

670. 5 f. Type **172** 5 5
671. 10 f. Cacao pods, South-central region 5 5
672. 15 f. Forestry, South-eastern area 8 5
673. 20 f. Coffee plant, West Cameroun 10 8
674. 45 f. Tea-picking, West Cameroun 25 10

1973. World Food Programme. 10th Anniv.

675. **173.** 45 f. multicoloured .. 20 12

1973. W. H. O. 25th Anniv.

676. **174.** 50 f. red and blue .. 20 12

175. Pres. Ahidjo, Map, Flag and Cameroun Stamp.

1973. United Republic. 1st Anniv. Mult.

677. 10 f. Type **175** (postage).. 5 5
678. 20 f. Pres. Ahidjo, proclamation and stamp .. 10 8
679. 45 f. Pres. Ahidjo, route-map and stamp (air) .. 20 12
680. 70 f. Significant dates .. 35 20

176. Bamoun Mask. 177. Dr. G. A Hansen.

1973. Masks.

681. **176.** 5 f. blk., brn. & green 5 5
682. – 10 f. brn., blk. & purple 5 5
683. – 45 f. brn., black & red 20 12
684. – 100 f. brn., blk. & blue 45 25

DESIGNS: 10 f., 45 f., 100 f., as T **176**, but different masks.

1973. Hansen's Discovery of Leprosy Bacillus. Cent.

685. **177.** 45 f. bl., light bl. & brn. 20 12

178. Scout Emblem and Flags. 179. Folk-dancers.

1973. Air. Admission of Cameroun to World Scout Conference.

686. **178.** 40 f. multicoloured .. 20 12
687. 45 f. multicoloured .. 25 15
688. 100 f. multicoloured.. 45 35

1973. African Solidarity " Drought Relief ". No. 670 surch. **SECHERESSE SOLIDARITE AFRICAINE** and value.

689. **172.** 100 f. on 5 f. mult. .. 45 35

1973. Folklore Dances of South-west Cameroun. Multicoloured.

690. 10 f. Type **179** 5 5
691. 25 f. Dancer in plumed hat 12 8
692. 45 f. Dancers with "totem" 20 12

180. W.M.O. Emblem.

1973. I.M.O./W.M.O. Cent.

693. **180.** 45 f. blue and green .. 20 12

181. Garoua Party H.Q. Building.

1973. Cameroun National Union. 7th Anniv.

694. **181.** 40 f. multicoloured .. 20 12

182. U.A.M.P.T. Emblem and Crane.

1973. U.A.M.P.T.

695. **182.** 100 f. bl., light bl. & grn. 45 35

183. African Mask and Old Town Hall, Brussels. 184. Avocado.

1973. Air. African Fortnight, Brussels.

696. **183.** 40 f. brown and maroon 20 12

1973. Cameroun Fruits. Multicoloured.

697. 10 f. Type **184** 5 5
698. 20 f. Mango 10 5
699. 45 f. Plum 10 12
700. 50 f. Custard-apple .. 25 15

185. Map of Africa.

1973. Air. Aid for Handicapped Children.

701. **185.** 40 f. red, brn. & grn... 20 12

186. Kirdi Village.

1973. Cameroun Villages.

702. **186.** 15 f. blk., grn. & brn. 5 5
703. – 45 f. brn., red & orge. 20 12
704. – 50 f. blk., grn. & orge. 25 15

DESIGNS: 45 f. Mabas. 50 f. Fishing village.

187. Earth Station.

1973. Satellite Earth Station, Zamengoe. Inauguration.

705. **187.** 100 f. brn., blue & grn. 45 35

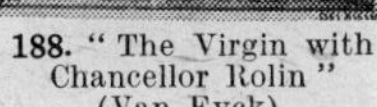

188. " The Virgin with Chancellor Rolin " (Van Eyck). 189. Handclasp on Map of Africa.

1973. Christmas. Multicoloured.

706. 45 f. Type **188** 20 12
707. 140 f. " The Nativity " (Federico Fiori–Il Barocci) 65 45

1974. Organization of African Unity. 10th Anniv.

708. **189.** 40 f. blue, red & green 20 10
709. 45 f. green, blue & red 25 12

190. Mill-worker.

1974. C.I.C.A.M. Industrial Complex.

710. **190.** 45 f. brown, green & red 25 12

191. Carved Panel of Bilinga (detail).

1974. Cameroun Art.

711. **191.** 10 f. brown and green 5 5
712. – 40 f. brown and red .. 20 10
713. – 45 f. red and blue .. 25 12

DESIGN: 40 f. Tubinga carving (detail). 45 f. Acajou Ngollon carved panel (detail).

1974. No. 469 surch.

714. 40 f. on 8 f. multicoloured 20 10

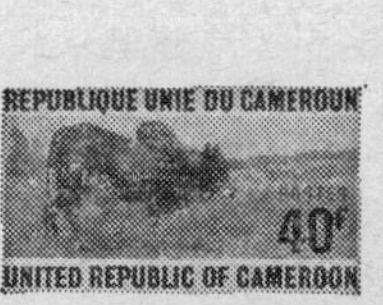

192. Cameroun Cow. 193. Route-map and Track.

1974. Cattle-raising in North Cameroun. Multicoloured.

715. 40 f. Type **192** (postage).. 20 12
716. 45 f. Cattle in pen (air) .. 25 15

1974. Trans-Cameroun Railway. Inauguration of Yaounde–Ngaoundere Line.

717. **193.** 5 f. brown, blue & green 5 5
718. – 20 f. brn., bl. & violet 8 5
719. – 40 f. red, blue & green 20 12
720. – 100 f. green, bl. & brn. 45 35

DESIGNS—HORIZ. 20 f. Laying track. 100 f. Railway bridge over Djerem River. VERT. 40 f. Welding rails.

194. Sir Winston Churchill.

1974. Air. Sir Winston Churchill. Birth Cent.

721. **194.** 100 f. black, red & blue 45 35

195. Footballer and City Crests.

1974. Air. World Cup Football Championships.

722. **195.** 45 f. orange, slate & grey 25 12
723. – 100 f. orge., slate & grey 45 30
724. – 200 f. bl., orge. & blk. 90 60

DESIGNS: 100 f. Goalkeeper and city crests. 200 f. World Cup.

Nos. 722/4 were issued together in se-tenant strips of three within the sheet.

196. U.P.U. Emblem and Hands with Letters.

1974. Universal Postal Union. Cent.

725. **196.** 40 f. red, bl. & grn. (post.) 20 12
726. – 100 f. grn., vio. & bl. (air) 45 30
727. – 200 f. green, red & blue 90 60

DESIGNS: 100 f. Cameroun U.P.U. headquarters stamps of 1970. 200 f. Cameroun U.P.U. 75th anniv. stamps of 1949.

1974. Air. West Germany's Victory in World Cup Football Championships. Nos. 722/4 optd. **7th JULY 1974 R.F.A. 2 HOLLANDE 1 7 JUILLET 1974.**

728. **195.** 45 f. orge., slate & grey 25 15
729. – 100 f. orge., slate & grey 45 35
730. – 200 f. bl., orge. & blk. 90 70

197. Copernicus and Solar System.

1974. Air. Copernicus. 500th Birth Anniv. (1973).

731. **197.** 250 f. blue, red & brown 1·00 70

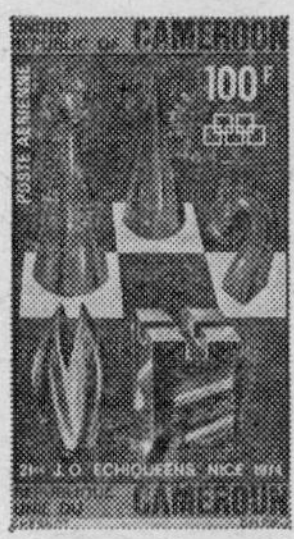

198. Modern Chess Pieces.

1974. Air. Chess Olympics, Nice.

732. **198.** 100 f. multicoloured .. 45 35

199. African Mask and " Arphila " Emblem.

1974. Air. " Arphila 75 " Stamp Exhibition, Paris.

733. **199.** 50 f. brown and red .. 25 15

200. African Leaders, U.D.E.A.C. H.Q. and Flags.

1974. Central African Customs and Economics Union. 10th Anniv.
734. **200.** 40 f. multicoloured (post.) 20 12
735. – 100 f. multicoloured (air) 45 30
DESIGN: 100 f. Similar to Type **200.**

1974. No. 717 surch. **10 DECEMBRE 1974** and value.
736. **193.** 100 f. on 5 f. brown, blue and green .. 45 35

201. "Apollo" Emblem, Astronaut, Module and Astronaut's Boots.

1974. Air. First Landing on Moon. 5th Anniv.
737. **201.** 200 f. brown, red & blue 80 55

202. "Virgin of Autun" (15th-century sculpture).

1974. Christmas. Multicoloured.
738. 40 f. Type **202** 20 12
739. 45 f. "Virgin and Child" (Luis de Morales) .. 25 15

203. De Gaulle and Eboue.

1975. Air. Felix Eboue. 30th Death Anniv.
740. **203.** 45 f. multicoloured .. 25 15
741. 200 f. multicoloured .. 80 55

204. "Celosia cristara". **206.** Afo Akom Statue.

205. Fish and Fishing-boat.

1975. Flowers of North Cameroun. Mult.
742. 5 f. Type **204** 5 5
743. 40 f. "Costus spectabilis" 20 12
744. 45 f. "Mussaenda erythrophylla" .. 25 15

1975. Offshore Fishing.
745. **205.** 40 f. brn., blue & choc. 20 12
746. – 45 f. brn., bistre & blue 25 15
DESIGN: 45 f. Fishing-boat and fish in net.

1975.
747. **206.** 40 f. multicoloured .. 20 12
748. 45 f. multicoloured .. 25 15
749. 200 f. multicoloured .. 80 55

207. "Polypore" (fungus). **209.** Presbyterian Church, Elat.

208. View of Building.

1975. Natural History. Multicoloured.
750. 15 f. Type **207** 8 5
751. 40 f. Nymphalis crysalis .. 20 12

1975. New Ministry of Posts Building. Inaug.
752. **208.** 40 f. blue, grn. & brn. 20 12
753. 45 f. brn., grn. & blue 25 15

1975. Church and Mosques.
754. **209.** 40 f. brn., blue & blk. 20 12
755. – 40 f. brn., blue & slate 65 45
756. – 45 f. brn., grn. & blk. 25 15
DESIGNS: No. 755, Foumban Mosque. No. 576, Catholic Church, Ngaoundere.

210. Lafayette and Ship. **211.** Harvesting Maize.

1975. Air. American Revolution. Bicent. (1976).
757. **210.** 100 f. bl., turq. & brn. 45 30
758. – 140 f. bl., brn. & grn... 65 45
759. – 500 f. green, brn. & bl. 2·25 2·00
DESIGNS: 140 f. George Washington and soldiers. 500 f. Benjamin Franklin.

1975. "Green Revolution". Multicoloured.
760. 40 f. Type **211** 20 12
761. 40 f. Ploughing with oxen (horiz.) 20 12

212. "The Burning Bush" (N. Froment).

1975. Air. Christmas. Multicoloured.
762. 50 f. Type **212** 25 15
763. 500 f. "Adoration of the Magi" (Gentile da Fabriano) (horiz.) .. 2·25 1·75

213. Tracking Aerial.

1976. Satellite Monitoring Station, Zamengoe. Inauguration. Multicoloured.
764. 40 f. Type **213** 20 12
765. 100 f. Close-up of tracking aerial (vert.) 55 45

214. Porcelain Rose.

1976. Cameroun Flowers. Multicoloured.
766. 40 f. Type **214** 20 12
767. 50 f. Flower of North Cameroun 30 20

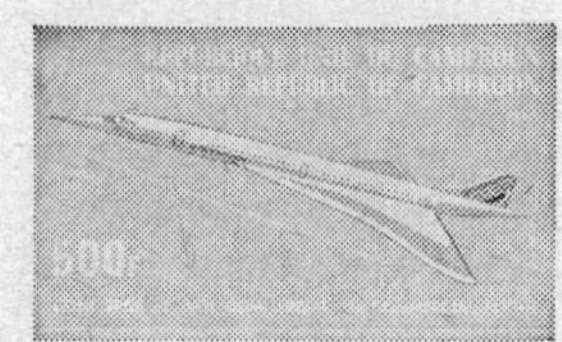

215. "Concorde".

1976. "Concorde's" First Commercial Flight. Paris to Rio de Janeiro.
768. **215.** 500 f. multicoloured .. 2·75 2·25

POSTAGE DUE STAMPS

D 1. Felling Mahogany Tree.

D 2. Native Idols.

1925.
D 88. **D 1.** 2 c. black and blue .. 5 5
D 89. 4 c. purple and olive 5 5
D 90. 5 c. black and lilac .. 8 8
D 91. 10 c. black and red .. 8 8
D 92. 15 c. black and grey 10 10
D 93. 20 c. black and olive 10 10
D 94. 25 c. black & yellow 12 12
D 95. 30 c. orange & blue 20 20
D 96. 50 c. black & brown 20 20
D 97. 60 c. red and green 25 25
D 98. 1 f. grn. & red on grn. 30 30
D 99. 2 f. mauve and red 50 50
D 100. 3 f. blue and brown 60 60

1939.
D 148. **D 2.** 5 c. purple 5 5
D 149. 10 c. blue 10 10
D 150. 15 c. red 5 5
D 151. 20 c. brown 5 5
D 152. 30 c. blue 5 5
D 153. 50 c. green 5 5
D 154. 60 c. purple .. 5 5
D 155. 1 f. violet 8 8
D 156. 2 f. orange 15 15
D 157. 3 f. blue 20 20

D 3.

1947.
D 254. **D 3.** 10 c. red 5 5
D 255. 30 c. orange .. 5 5
D 256. 50 c. black 5 5
D 257. 1 f. red 5 5
D 258. 2 f. green 5 5
D 259. 3 f. mauve 5 5
D 260. 4 f. blue 5 5
D 261. 5 f. brown 8 8
D 262. 10 f. blue 10 10
D 263. 20 f. sepia 20 20

D **4.** "Hibiscus rosa sinensis".

1963. Flowers. Multicoloured.
D 342. 50 c. Type D 4 .. 5 5
D 343. 50 c. "Erythrine" .. 5 5
D 344. 1 f. "Plumeria lutea" .. 5 5
D 345. 1 f. "Ipomoca sp." .. 5 5
D 346. 1 f. 50 "Grinum sp." .. 5 5
D 347. 1 f. 50 "Hoodia gordonii" 5 5
D 348. 2 f. "Ochna" 5 5
D 349. 2 f. "Gloriosa" 5 5
D 350. 5 f. "Costus spectabilis" 5 5
D 351. 5 f. "Bougainvillea spectabilis" 5 5
D 352. 10 f. "Delonix regia" .. 5 5
D 353. 10 f. "Haemanthus" .. 5 5
D 354. 20 f. "Titanopsis" .. 8 8
D 355. 20 f. "Ophthalmophyllum" 8 8
D 356. 40 f. "Zingiberacee" .. 12 12
D 357. 40 f. "Amorphophalus" 12 15

The two designs in each value are arranged se-tenant in "tete-beche" pairs throughout the sheet.

MILITARY FRANK STAMP

M 1.

1963. No value indicated.
M 1. M **1.** (–) lake 25 25

CANADA BC

A British dominion consisting of the former province of Canada with Br. Columbia, New Brunswick, Newfoundland, Nova Scotia, and Prince Edward Is.

1851. 12 pence = 1 shilling. (Canadian) = 1s. 3d. sterling.

1859. 100 cents = 1 dollar.

1. **2.** Beaver.

3. Prince Albert. **4.**

5. Jacques Cartier. **6.**

1851. Imperf.
23. **1.** ½d. rose £230 £110
10. **2.** 3d. red .. .. £350 65·00
2. **3.** 6d. purple £3000 £500
22a. **4.** 7½d. green £3500 £700
20. **5.** 10d. blue £3500 £475
4. **6.** 12d. black £25000 £23000

1858. Perf.
25. **1.** ½d. rose .. .. £400 1·50
26. **2.** 3d. red .. .. £550 1·50
27. **3.** 6d. purple £2000 £850

1859. Values in cents. Perf.
29. **1.** 1 c. red .. .. .. 30·00 6·50
44. 2 c. red .. .. .. 95·00 50·00
31. **2.** 5 c. red .. .. .. 45·00 6·00
37. **3.** 10 c. violet .. .. £110 16·00
36. 10 c. brown .. .. £140 16·00
40. **4.** 12½ c. green .. .. 75·00 14·00
42. **5.** 17 c. blue .. .. .. £130 20·00

DOMINION OF CANADA

13.  14.

1868.

54. **13.** ½ c. black .. .. 14·00 14·00
55. **14.** 1 c. brown .. .. 85·00 13·00
76. 1 c. yellow .. .. £200 20·00
56. 2 c. green .. .. £120 9·00
58. 3 c. red .. .. .. £160 5·00
70. 5 c. olive .. .. £350 35·00
59. 6 c. brown .. .. £150 9·00
61. 12½ c. blue .. .. 85·00 9·00
113. 15 c. purple .. .. 25·00 9·00
67. 15 c. blue .. .. 80·00 11·00

16.  17.

1870.

101. **16.** ½ c. black .. .. 1·25 1·25
80. **17.** 1 c. yellow .. .. 5·50 5
82. 2 c. green .. .. 9·00 5
106. 3 c. red .. .. 4·00 5
107. 5 c. grey .. .. 10·00 5
88. 6 c. brown .. .. 17·00 2·75
118. – 8 c. grey .. .. 20·00 1·40
112. **17.** 10 c. magenta .. .. 32·00 3·00

On 8 c. head is to left.

19.

1893.

115. **19.** 20 c. red .. .. 60·00 15·00
116. 50 c. blue .. .. 80·00 10·00

20. 21.

1897. Jubilee.

121. **20.** ½ c. black .. .. 30·00 32·00
123. 1 c. orange .. .. 2·25 1·50
124. 2 c. green .. .. 4·00 3·00
126. 3 c. red .. .. .. 2·75 70
128. 5 c. blue .. .. 15·00 9·00
129. 6 c. brown .. .. 60·00 55·00
130. 8 c. violet .. .. 12·00 12·00
131. 10 c. purple .. .. 20·00 20·00
132. 15 c. slate .. .. 45·00 45·00
133. 20 c. red .. .. 50·00 50·00
134. 50 c. blue .. .. 55·00 55·00
136. $1 red £250 £180
137. $2 violet £425 £200
138. $3 yellow-brown .. £575 £325
139. $4 violet £550 £300
140. $5 green £550 £300

1897. Maple-leaves in four corners.

142. **21.** ½ c. black .. .. 3·00 3·00
143. 1 c. green .. .. 4·00 12
144. 2 c. violet .. .. 6·00 12
145. 3 c. red .. .. 6·00 10
146. 5 c. blue .. .. 15·00 2·25
147. 6 c. brown .. .. 15·00 11·00
148. 8 c. orange .. .. 25·00 5·00
149. 10 c. purple .. .. 55·00 35·00

1898. As T 21 but figures in lower corners.

150. ½ c. black 55 55
151. 1 c. green .. .. 5·00 8
154. 2 c. purple .. .. 3·75 8
155. 2 c. red .. .. 5·00 8
156. 3 c. red .. .. 10·00 8
157. 5 c. blue .. .. 25·00 15
159. 6 c. brown .. .. 30·00 14·00
160. 7 c. yellow .. .. 14·00 5·00
161. 8 c. orange .. .. 32·00 7·00
163. 10 c. purple .. .. 60·00 6·00
165. 20 c. olive .. .. £110 30·00

23.

24.

1898. Imperial Penny Postage.

166. **23.** 2 c. black, red and blue 7·00 2·00

1899. Surch. **2 CENTS.**

171. 2 c. on 3 c. red (No. 145).. 2·25 1·50
172. 2 c. on 3 c. red (No. 156).. 2·25 1·50

1903.

175. **24.** 1 c. green .. .. 4·00 8
177. 2 c. red .. .. 4·50 8
178. 5 c. blue .. .. 20·00 90
180. 7 c. olive .. .. 18·00 1·10
182. 10 c. purple .. .. 50·00 2·50
186. 20 c. olive .. .. £110 12·00
187. 50 c. mauve .. .. £180 30·00

25. King George V and Queen Mary, when Prince and Princess of Wales.

1908. Quebec Tercent. Dated "1608 1908".

188. **25.** ½ c. brown .. .. 2·25 2·25
189. – 1 c. green .. .. 3·00 2·50
190. – 2 c. red .. .. 6·00 55
191. – 5 c. blue .. .. 18·00 12·00
192. – 7 c. olive .. .. 25·00 14·00
193. – 10 c. violet .. .. 40·00 38·00
194. – 15 c. orange .. .. 55·00 50·00
195. – 20 c. brown .. .. 70·00 60·00

DESIGNS: 1 c. Cartier and Champlain. 2 c. King Edward VII and Queen Alexandra. 5 c. Champlain's House in Quebec. 7 c. Gen. Montcalm and Wolfe. 10 c. Quebec in 1700. 15 c. Champlain's departure for the West. 20 c. Cartier's arrival before Quebec.

ILLUSTRATIONS
British Commonwealth and all overprints and surcharges are FULL SIZE. Foreign Countries have been reduced to ¾-LINEAR.

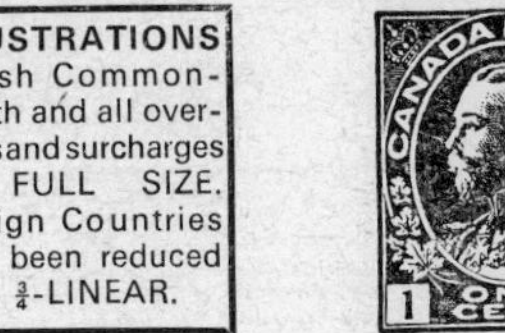

33.

1912.

196. **33.** 1 c. green .. .. 2·00 5
200. 2 c. red .. .. 2·00 5
205. 3 c. brown .. .. 2·50 8
205b. 5 c. blue .. .. 20·00 12
209. 7 c. yellow .. .. 6·00 45
210. 10 c. purple .. .. 32·00 30
212. 20 c. olive .. .. 14·00 25
214. 50 c. deep brown .. 14·00 70

1915. Optd. **WAR TAX** diagonally.

225. **33.** 5 c. blue .. .. 90·00 90·00
226. 20 c. olive .. .. 20·00 20·00
227. 50 c. deep brown .. 30·00 30·00

34.  35.

1915.

228. **34.** 1 c. green 80 8
229. 2 c. red 80 12

1916.

231. **35.** 2 c.+1 c. red .. .. 3·00 50
239. 2 c.+1 c. brown .. 1·25 8

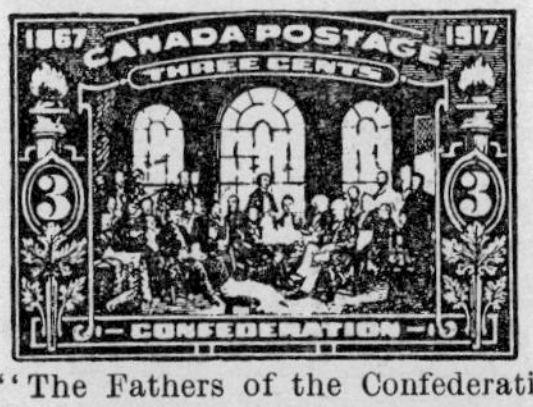

36. "The Fathers of the Confederation".

1917. Confederation. 50th Anniv.

244. **36.** 3 c. brown .. .. 7·50 25

1922.

246. **33.** 1 c. yellow .. .. 1·75 8
247. 2 c. green .. .. 1·50 5
248. 3 c. red .. .. 1·25 5
249a. 4 c. yellow .. .. 7·00 60
250. 5 c. violet .. .. 3·50 25
251. 7 c. brown .. .. 6·50 1·50
252. 8 c. blue .. .. 9·00 1·50
253. 10 c. blue .. .. 9·00 25
254. 10 c. brown .. .. 9·00 25
255. $1 orange .. .. 35·00 1·50

1926. Surch. **2 CENTS** in one line.

264. **33.** 2 c. on 3 c. red .. 24·00 24·00

1926. Surch. **2 CENTS** in two lines.

265. **33.** 2 c. on 3 c. red .. 9·00 9·00

37.
Sir J. A. Macdonald.

DESIGNS — HORIZ. A T 38: 3 c. Parliament Buildings, Ottawa. 12 c. Map of Canada, 1867/1927. VERT. As T 37: 5 c. Sir W. Laurier.

38. "The Fathers of the Confederation".

1927. Confederation. 60th Anniv. I. Commemoration Issue. Dated "1867 1927".

266. **37.** 1 c. orange .. .. 1·00 30
267. **38.** 2 c. green 50 8
268. – 3 c. red .. .. 3·50 2·25
269. – 5 c. violet .. .. 1·50 1·00
270. – 12 c. blue .. .. 3·00 1·75

42. Darcy McGee.

DESIGNS — HORIZ. As T 44: 20 c. R. Baldwin and L. H. Lafontaine. VERT. As T 42: 10 c. Sir G. E. Cartier.

44. Sir W. Laurier and Sir J. A. Macdonald.

II. Historical Issue.

271. **42.** 5 c. violet .. .. 1·50 90
312. – 10 c. olive .. .. 4·00 8
272. **44.** 12 c. green .. .. 3·00 2·00
273. – 20 c. red .. .. 5·00 2·00

46.

1928. Air.

274. **46.** 5 c. brown .. .. 2·00 1·00

47. King George V.

DESIGNS—HORIZ. 12 c. Quebec Bridge. 20 c. Harvesting with horses. 50 c. Fishing smack "Bluenose". $1 Parliament Buildings, Ottawa.

48. Mt. Hurd and Indian Totem Poles.

1928.

275. **47.** 1 c. orange 50 12
276. 2 c. green 20 8
277. 3 c. red .. .. 5·00 3·00
278. 4 c. yellow .. .. 4·00 1·50
279. 5 c. violet .. .. 2·00 70
280. 8 c. blue .. .. 3·00 1·50
281. **48.** 10 c. green .. .. 2·25 25
282. 12 c. black .. .. 4·00 2·50
283. – 20 c. red .. .. 5·00 3·00
284. – 50 c. blue .. .. £100 20·00
285. – $1 olive .. .. £125 30·00

53.

54. Parliamentary Library, Ottawa.

55. The Old Citadel, Quebec.

1930.

288. **53.** 1 c. orange 20 10
300. 1 c. green 30 5
289. 2 c. green 25 8
301. 2 c. red 40 5
302b. 2 c. brown 25 10
303. 3 c. red 40 5
290. 4 c. yellow .. .. 3·00 2·00
291. 5 c. violet 90 90
304. 5 c. blue 55 5
292. 8 c. blue .. .. 4·50 3·75
305. 8 c. red .. .. 1·25 1·25
293. **54.** 10 c. olive .. .. 3·00 60
294. **55.** 12 c. black .. .. 4·00 2·00
325. 13 c. violet .. .. 6·50 1·00
295. – 20 c. red .. .. 5·00 15
296. – 50 c. blue .. .. 65·00 5·00
297. – $1 olive.. .. .. 60·00 8·00

DESIGNS—HORIZ. 20 c. Harvesting with tractor. 50 c. Acadian Memorial Church, Grand Pre, Nova Scotia. $1 Mt. Edith Cavell.

59. Mercury and Western Hemisphere.

1930. Air.

310. **59.** 5 c. brown .. .. 14·00 9·00

1932. Air. Surch. **6** and bars.

313. **46.** 6 c. on 5 c. brown .. 2·25 1·10

1932. Surch. **3** between bars.

314a. **53.** 3 c. on 2 c. red .. 25 5

60. King George V.  **61.** Duke of Windsor when Prince of Wales.

62. Allegory of British Empire.

1932. Ottawa Conf. (a) Postage.
315. **60.** 3 c. red 25 8
316. **61.** 5 c. blue .. .. 1·75 80
317. **62.** 13 c. green .. .. 2·25 1·75

(b) Air. Surch. **6 OTTAWA CONFERENCE 6 1932** between bars.
318. **59.** 6 c. on 5 c. brown .. 5·50 4·50

63. King George V.

ILLUSTRATIONS British Commonwealth and all overprints and surcharges are FULL SIZE. Foreign Countries have been reduced to ¾-LINEAR.

1932.
319. **63.** 1 c. green 25 8
320. 2 c. brown 35 8
321b. 3 c. red 40 8
322. 4 c. brown .. .. 10·00 1·50
323. 5 c. blue .. .. 1·25 8
324. 8 c. orange .. .. 2·00 1·25

64. Parliament Buildings, Ottawa.

1933. U.P.U. Congress. (Preliminary Meeting).
329. **64.** 5 c. blue .. .. 3·25 1·25

1933. Optd. **WORLD'S GRAIN EXHIBITION & CONFERENCE REGINA 1933.**
330. – 20 c. red (No. 295) .. 14·00 5·00

65. S.S. "Royal William".

1933. 1st Transatlantic Steamboat Crossing. Cent.
331. **65.** 5 c. blue .. .. 3·25 1·25

66. Jacques Cartier approaching Land.

1934. Discovery of Canada. 4th Cent.
332. **66.** 3 c. blue .. .. 1·75 65

67. U.E.L. Statue, Hamilton.

1934. Arrival of United Empire Loyalists. 150th Anniv.
333. **67.** 10 c. olive .. .. 8·00 3·25

MINIMUM PRICE

The minimum price quoted is 5p which represents a handling charge rather than a basis for valuing common stamps. For further notes about prices see introductory pages.

68. Seal of New Brunswick.

1934. New Brunswick. 150th Anniv.
334. **68.** 2 c. brown 80 60

69. Queen Elizabeth II when Princess. **70.** King George VI when Duke of York.

71. King George V and Queen Mary.

1935. Silver Jubilee. Dated "1910–1935".
335. **69.** 1 c. green 20 8
336. **70.** 2 c. brown 35 8
337. **71.** 3 c. red 80 8
338. – 5 c. blue .. .. 2·25 1·25
339. – 10 c. green .. .. 2·50 1·25
340. – 13 c. blue .. .. 3·25 2·50

DESIGNS—VERT. 5 c. Duke of Windsor when Prince of Wales. HORIZ. 10 c. Windsor Castle. 13 c. Royal Yacht "Britannia".

75. King George V.

DESIGNS—HORIZ. 13 c. Confederation, Charlottetown, 1864. 20 c. Niagara Falls. 50 c. Parliament Buildings, Victoria, B.C. $1 Champlain Monument, Quebec.

76. Royal Canadian Mounted Policeman.

1935.
341. **75.** 1 c. green 12 8
342. 2 c. brown 15 8
343. 3 c. red 30 8
344. 4 c. yellow .. .. 1·25 20
345. 5 c. blue .. .. 1·25 8
346. 8 c. orange .. .. 1·25 40
347. **76.** 10 c. red .. .. 3·25 8
348. – 13 c. violet .. .. 3·25 20
349. – 20 c. olive-green .. 10·00 25
350. – 50 c. violet .. .. 12·00 2·00
351. – $1 blue .. .. 30·00 4·00

81. Daedalus.

1935. Air.
355. **81.** 6 c. brown 80 60

82. King George VI and Queen Elizabeth.

1937. Coronation.
356. **82.** 3 c. red 15 5

83. King George VI. **84.** Memorial Chamber, Parliament Buildings, Ottawa.

85. Fort Garry Gate, Winnipeg.

1937.
357. **83.** 1 c. green 12 5
358. 2 c. brown 15 5
359. 3 c. red 25 5
360. 4 c. yellow .. .. 1·25 15
361. 5 c. blue 70 12
362. 8 c. orange .. .. 1·25 12
363. **84.** 10 c. red .. .. 5·00 12
364. – 13 c. blue .. .. 6·00 20
365. **85.** 20 c. brown .. .. 12·00 25
366. – 50 c. green .. .. 17·00 2·50
367. – $1 violet .. .. 35·00 3·25

DESIGNS—HORIZ. 13 c. Halifax Harbour. 50 c. Vancouver Harbour. $1 Chateau de Ramezay, Montreal.

86. Seaplane over S.S. "Discoverer" on Mackenzie River.

1938. Air.
371. **86.** 6 c. blue 80 12

87. Queen Elizabeth II when Princess and Princess Margaret.

1939. Royal Visit.
372. **87.** 1 c. black and green .. 15 5
373. – 2 c. black and brown .. 10 5
374. – 3 c. black and red .. 10 5

DESIGNS—HORIZ. 3 c. King George VI and Queen Elizabeth. VERT. 2 c. War Memorial, Ottawa.

88. King George VI in naval uniform. **89.** King George VI in military uniform.

90. Grain Elevator. **91.** Farm Scene.

92. Air Training Camp.

1942. War Effort.
375 **88.** 1 c. green (postage) .. 12 5
376. **89.** 2 c. brown 20 5
377. – 3 c. red 25 5
378. – 3 c. purple 25 5
379. **90.** 4 c. grey 80 20
380. **89.** 4 c. red 20 5
381. **88.** 5 c. blue 50 5
382. **91.** 8 c. sepia .. .. 1·00 20
383. – 10 c. brown .. .. 1·75 5
384. – 13 c. green .. .. 2·50 1·75
385. – 14 c. green .. .. 3·00 20
386. – 20 c. brown .. .. 2·50 10
387. – 50 c. violet .. .. 11·00 1·00
388. – $1 blue .. .. 35·00 3·50
399. **92.** 6 c. blue (air) .. .. 1·40 35
400. 7 c. blue 35 10

DESIGNS—As T 89: 3 c. King George VI. As T 92. VERT. 10 c. Parliament Buildings. HORIZ. 13 c., 14 c. Ram tank. 20 c. Corvette. 50 c. Munitions factory. $1, Destroyer.

93. Ontario Farm Scene.

1946. Re-conversion to Peace-time.
401. **93.** 8 c brown (postage) .. 50 20
402. – 10 c. green 85 5
403. – 14 c. brown .. .. 1·40 8
404. – 20 c. grey .. .. 1·75 8
405. – 50 c. green .. .. 12·00 70
406. – $1 purple .. .. 25·00 1·25
407. – 7 c. blue (air) 35 5

DESIGNS: 10 c. Great Bear Lake. 14 c. St. Maurice River Power-station. 20 c. Combine harvester. 50 c. Lumbering in Br. Columbia. $1 Train ferry. 7 c. Canada geese in flight.

94. Alexander Graham Bell and "Fame". **95.**

1947. Graham Bell (inventor of the telephone). Birth Cent.
408. **94.** 4 c. blue 10 8

1947. Advent of Canadian Citizenship and 80th Anniv. of Confederation.
409. **95.** 4 c. blue 10 8

96. Queen Elizabeth II when Princess. **96a.** King George VI.

1948. Princess Elizabeth's Wedding.
410. **96.** 4 c. blue 10 5

97. Queen Victoria, Parliament Building, Ottawa, and King George VI.

1948. Responsible Government. Cent.
411. **97.** 4 c. grey 10 5

98. Cabot's Ship "Matthew".

1949. Entry of Newfoundland into Canadian Confederation.

412. **98.** 4 c. green 10 5

99. "Founding of Halifax, 1749" (after C. W. Jeffries).

1949. Halifax Bicent.

413. **99.** 4 c. violet 10 5

1949. Portraits of King George VI.

414. **96a.** 1 c. green 8 5
415. – 2 c. brown 10 5
415a. – 2 c. olive 10 5
416. – 3 c. purple 10 5
417. – 4 c. lake 15 5
417a. – 4 c. vermilion .. 15 5
418. – 5 c. blue 35 8

1950. As Nos. 414/8 but without "POSTES POSTAGE".

424. 1 c. green 8 5
425. 2 c. brown 15 10
426. 3 c. purple 12 5
427. 4 c. red 15 5
428. 5 c. blue 40 35

100. Canada Goose.

101. Drying Furs.

102. Oil Wells in Alberta.

1950.

443. **100.** 7 c. blue 20 8
432. **101.** 10 c. purple 50 5
441. – 20 c. grey 70 8
431. **102.** 50 c. green .. .. 5·00 50
433. – $1 blue .. .. 40·00 4·50

DESIGNS: 20 c. Forestry products. $1. Fisherman.

103. Mackenzie King.

1951. Canadian Prime Ministers.

434. – 3 c. green (Borden) .. 12 5
444. – 3 c. purple (Abbott) .. 12 8
435. **103.** 4 c. red 12 5
445. – 4 c. red (A. Mackenzie) 15 8
475. – 4 c. violet (Thompson) 20 5
483. – 4 c. violet (Bennett) .. 15 5
476. – 5 c. blue (Bowell) .. 20 5
484. – 5 c. blue (Tupper) .. 15 5

104. Mail Trains, 1851 and 1951.

105. Reproduction of 3d., 1851

DESIGNS—As T **104:** 5 c. S.S. "City of Toronto" and S.S. "Prince George". 7 c. Mail coach and aeroplane.

1951. Centenary of First Canadian Postage Stamp. Dated "1851 1951".

436. **104.** 4 c. black 25 8
437. – 5 c. violet .. .. 1·00 70
438. – 7 c. blue 50 12
439. **105.** 15 c. red 50 12

106. Queen Elizabeth II when Princess and Duke of Edinburgh.

1951. Royal Visit.

440. **106.** 4 c. violet 12 5

107. Red Cross Emblem.

1952. 18th Int. Red Cross Conf., Toronto.

442. **107.** 4 c. red and blue .. 12 5

108. Eskimo Hunter.

110. Textile Industry.

109. Gannet.

111. Pacific Coast Indian House and Totem Pole.

1953.

477. **108.** 10 c. chocolate .. 25 8
474. **109.** 15 c. black 50 10
488. – 20 c. green 70 5
489. – 25 c. red 90 5
462. **110.** 50 c. green .. .. 2·50 15
446. **111.** $1 black .. .. 11·00 50

DESIGNS—As T **110**—HORIZ. 20 c. Pulp and paper industry. VERT. 25 c. Chemical industry.

112. Polar Bear.

113. Queen Elizabeth II

1953. National Wild Life Week.

447. **112.** 2 c. blue 10 5
448. – 3 c. sepia (Moose) .. 12 5
449. – 4 c. slate (Sheep) .. 20 5

1953.

450. **113.** 1 c. brown 5 5
451. 2 c. green 8 5
452. 3 c. red 12 5
453. 4 c. violet 12 5
454. 5 c. blue 15 5

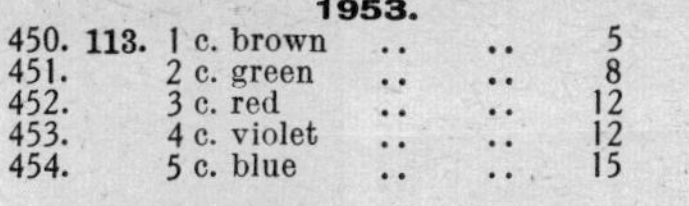

114. Queen Elizabeth II. **115.**

1953. Coronation.

461. **114.** 4 c. violet 12 5

1954.

463. **115.** 1 c. brown 5 5
464. 2 c. green 5 5
465. 3 c. red 10 5
466. 4 c. violet 12 5
467. 5 c. blue 15 5
468. 6 c. orange 25 15

1954. National Wild Life Week. As T **112.**

472. 4 c. slate (Walrus) .. 20 5
473. 5 c. blue (Beaver) .. 20 5

116. Musk-ox.

118. Dove and Torch.

117. Whooping Cranes.

1955. National Wild Life Week.

478. **116.** 4 c. violet 20 8
479. **117.** 5 c. blue 20 8

1955. I.C.A.O. 10th Anniv.

480. **118.** 5 c. blue 25 5

119. Pioneer Settlers.

1955. Alberta and Saskatchewan Provinces. 50th Anniv.

481. **119.** 5 c. blue 25 5

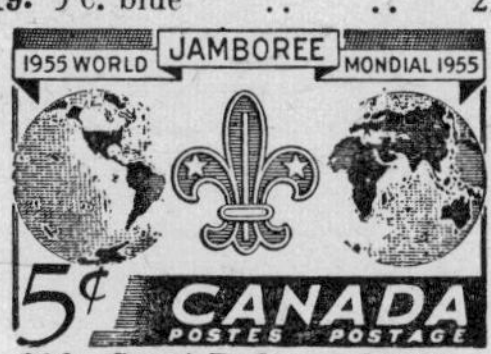

120. Scout Badge and Globe.

1955. 8th World Scout Jamboree.

482. **120.** 5 c. brown and green .. 25 8

121. Ice-Hockey Players.

1956. Ice-hockey Commem.

485. **121.** 5 c. blue 20 5

1956. National Wild Life Week. As T **112.**

486. 4 c. violet (Caribou) .. 20 5
487. 5 c. blue (Mountain goat) 20 5

122.

124. Common Loon.

123. Hunting.

1956. Fire Prevention Week.

490. **122.** 5 c. red and black .. 15 5

1957. Outdoor Recreation.

491. – 5 c. blue (Fishing) .. 15 5
492. – 5 c. blue (Swimming) 15 5
493. **123.** 5 c. blue 15 5
494. – 5 c. blue (Skiing) .. 15 5

Nos. 491/4 were printed together in the sheet and are obtainable in various combinations according to position.

1957. National Wild Life Week.

495. **124.** 5 c. black 20 5

125. Thompson with Sextant, and North American Map.

1957. David Thompson (explorer). Death Cent.

496. **125.** 5 c blue 20 5

126. Parliament Buildings, Ottawa.

127. Miner.

1957. 14th U.P.C. Congress, Ottawa.

497. **126.** 5 c. slate 20 5
498. – 15 c. slate .. .. 1·10 85

DESIGN—HORIZ. (33½×22 mm.): 15 c. Globe within posthorn.

1957. Mining Industry.

499. **127.** 5 c. black 15 5

128. Queen Elizabeth and Duke of Edinburgh.

130. Microscope.

129. "A Free Press".

1957. Royal Visit.

500. **128.** 5 c. black 12 5

1958. The Canadian Press.

501. **129.** 5 c. black 15 5

1958. Int. Geophysical Year.

502. **130.** 5 c blue 20 5

131. Miner Panning for Gold.

1958. Br. Columbia. Cent.
503. 131. 5 c turquoise .. 15 5

132. La Verendrye Statue.

1958. La Verendrye (explorer) Commem.
504. 132. 5 c. blue 15 5

133. Champlain and Heights of Quebec.

1958. Founding of Quebec by Samuel de Champlain. 350th Anniv.
505. 133. 5 c. brown and green 15 5

134. Nurse.

1958. National Health.
506. 134. 5 c. purple 15 5

135. "Petroleum 1858-1958".

1958. Canadian Oil Industry Cent.
507. 135. 5 c. red and olive .. 15 5

136. Speaker's Chair and Mace.

1958. First Elected Assembly. Bicent.
508. 136. 5 c. slate 15 5

137. The "Silver Dart".

1959. First Flight of the "Silver Dart" in Canada. 50th Anniv.
509. 137. 5 c. black and blue .. 15 5

138. Globe showing N.A.T.O. Countries.

1959. N.A.T.O. 10th Anniv.
510. 138. 5 c. blue 15 5

139.

140.

1959. "Associated Country Women of the World" Commem.
511. 139. 5 c. black & yell.-olive 15 5

1959. Royal Visit.
512. 140. 5 c. red 15 5

141. Maple Leaf linked with American Eagle.

1959. Opening of St. Lawrence Seaway.
513. 141. 5 c. blue and red .. 15 5

142. Maple Leaves.

1959. Battle of Quebec Bicent.
514. 142. 5 c. green and red .. 15 5

143. Girl Guides Badge.

144. Dollard des Ormeaux.

1960. Golden Jubilee of Canadian Girl Guides Movement.
515. 143. 5 c. blue and chestnut 15 5

1960. Battle of Long Sualt. Tercent.
516. 144. 5 c. blue and brown . 15 5

145. Surveyor, Bulldozer and Compass Rose.

146. E. Pauline Johnson.

1961. Northern Development.
517. 145. 5 c. green and red .. 15 5

1961. E. Pauline Johnson (Mohawk poetess) Birth Cent.
518. 146. 5 c green and red .. 15 5

147. Arthur Meighen (statesman).

1961. Arthur Meighen Commem.
519. 147. 5 c. blue 15 5

148. Dam and Technicians.

1961. Colombo Plan.
520. 148. 5 c. brown and blue .. 15 5

149. "Resources for Tomorrow".

150. "Education".

1961. Natural Resources.
521. 149. 5 c. green and brown.. 15 5

1962. Education Year.
522. 150. 5 c. black and brown 15 5

151. Lord Selkirk and Farmer.

1962. Red River Settlement. 150th Anniv.
523. 151. 5 c. chocolate & green 15 5

152. Talon bestowing Gifts on Married Couple.

153. British Columbia and Vancouver Is. 2½d. stamp of 1860, and Parliament Bldgs., B.C.

1962. Jean Talon Commem.
524. 152. 5 c. blue 15 5

1962. Victoria, B.C. Cent.
525. 153. 5 c. red and black .. 15 5

154. Highway (map version) and Provincial Arms.

1962. Opening of Trans-Canada Highway.
526. 154. 5 c. black and brown 15

155. Queen Elizabeth II.

156. Sir Casimir Gzowski.

1962. Different symbols in top left corner.
527. 155. 1 c. chocolate.. .. 5 5
528. 2 c. green 5 5
529. 3 c. violet 10 5
530. 4 c. red 10 5
531. 5 c. blue 15 10

SYMBOLS: 1 c. Crystals (Mining). 2 c. Tree (Forestry). 3 c. Fish (Fisheries). 4 c. Electricity pylon (Industrial power). 5 c. Wheat (Agriculture).

1963. Gzowski (engineer). 150th Birth Anniv.
535. 156. 5 c. purple 15 5

157. "Export Trade".

1963.
536: 157. $1 red .. .. .. 18·00 1·50

158. Frobisher and barque "Gabriel".

1963. Sir Martin Frobisher Commem.
537. 158. 5 c. blue 20 5

159. Horseman and Map.

1963. Quebec—Trois-Rivieres—Montreal Postal Service. Bicent.
538. 159. 5 c. brown and green 15 5

160. Jet Airliner (composite) and Uplands Airport, Ottawa.

161. Canada Geese.

1963.
540. 160. 7 c. blue 20 20
540a. 8 c. blue 20 20
539. 161. 15 c. blue .. .. 1·40 15

162. "Peace on Earth".

1964. "Peace".
541. 162. 5 c. ochre, blue & turq. 15 5

163. Maple Leaves.

1964. "Canadian Unity".
542. 163. 5 c. lake and blue .. 15 8

164. White Trillium and Arms of Ontario.

1964. Provincial Badges.
543. 164. 5 c. green, brown & orge. 20 8
544. – 5 c. green, brown & yell. 20 8
545. – 5 c. red, green & violet 20 8
546. – 5 c. blue, red & green.. 20 8
547. – 5 c. purple, green & brn. 20 8
548. – 5 c. brown, green & mve. 20 8
549. – 5 c. lilac, green & pur. 20 8
550. – 5 c. green, yellow & red 20 8

551. – 5 c. sepia, orange & grn. 20 8
552. – 5 c. black, red & green 20 8
553. – 5 c. drab, green & yell. 20 8
554. – 5 c. blue, green and red 20 8
555. – 5 c. red and blue .. 20 8

FLOWERS AND ARMS OF: No. 544, Madonna Lily, Quebec. 545, Purple Violet, New Brunswick. 546, Mayflower, Nova Scotia. 547, Dogwood, British Columbia. 548, Prairie Crocus, Manitoba. 549, Lady's Slipper, Prince Edward Island. 550, Wild Rose, Alberta. 551, Prairie Lily, Saskatchewan. 552 Pitcher Plant, Newfoundland. 553, Mountain Avens, Northwest Territories. 554, Fireweed, Yukon Territory. 555, Maple Leaf, Canada.

1964. Surch.
556. **160.** 8 c. on 7 c. blue .. 25 20

165. Fathers of the Confederation Memorial, Charlottetown.

1964. Cent. of Charlottetown Conf.
557. **165.** 5 c. black 15 5

166. Maple Leaf and Hand with Quill Pen.

1964. Cent. of Quebec Conf.
558. **166.** 5 c. red and chocolate 15 5

167. Queen Elizabeth II. **168.** "Canadian Family".

1964. Royal Visit.
559. **167.** 5 c. purple 15 5

1964. Christmas.
560. **168.** 3 c. red 12 5
561. 5 c. blue 15 8

169. Co-operation.

1965. Int. Co-operation Year.
562. **169.** 5 c. green 15 8

170. Sir W. Grenfell.

1965. Sir Wilfred Grenfell (missionary). Birth Cent.
563. **170.** 5 c. green .. 15 5

171. National Flag.

1965. National Flag Inauguration.
564. **171.** 5 c. red and blue .. 15 5

172. Sir Winston Churchill. **173.** Peace Tower, Parliament Bldgs., Ottawa.

1965. Churchill Commem.
565. **172.** 5 c. brown 15 8

1965. Inter-Parliamentary Union Conf., Ottawa.
566. **173.** 5 c. green 15 8

174. Parliament Buildings, Ottawa, 1865.

1965. Proclamation of Ottawa as Capital. Cent.
567. **174.** 5 c. brown 15 5

175. "Gold, Frankincense and Myrrh". **176.** "Alouette 2" over Canada.

1965. Christmas.
568. **175.** 3 c. green 10 5
569. 5 c. blue 15 5

1966. Launching of Canadian Satellite, "Alouette 2".
570. **176.** 5 c. blue 15 5

177. La Salle. **178.** Road Signs.

1966. La Salle's Arrival in Canada. 300th Anniv.
571. **177.** 5 c. green 15 5

1966. Highway Safety.
572. **178.** 5 c. yellow, blue & blk. 15 5

179. Canadian Delegation and Houses of Parliament.

1966. London Conf., Cent.
573. **179.** 5 c. brown 15 5

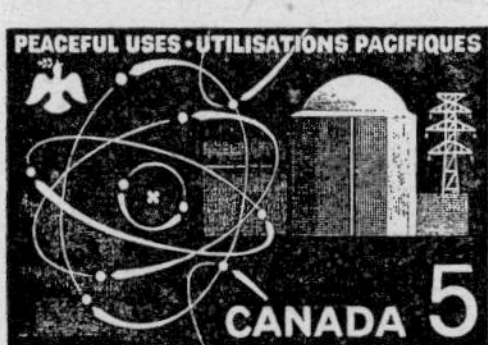

180. Douglas Point Nuclear Power Station.

1966. Peaceful Uses of Atomic Energy.
574. **180.** 5 c. ultramarine .. 15 5

181. Parliamentary Library, Ottawa. **182.** "Hands in Prayer", after Dürer.

1966. Commonwealth Parliamentary Assn. Conf., Ottawa.
575. **181.** 5 c. purple 15 5

1966. Christmas.
576. **182.** 3 c. red 8 5
577. 5 c. orange 15 5

183. Flag, and Canada on Globe. **184.** Queen Elizabeth, Northern Lights and Dog-team.

185. "Alaska Highway" (A. Y. Jackson).

1967. Canadian Centennial.
578. **183.** 5 c. red and blue .. 15 8

1967.
579. **184.** 1 c. brown 5 5
580. – 2 c. green 5 5
581. – 3 c. purple 10 10
582. – 4 c. red 10 5
583. – 5 c. blue 8 5
606. – 6 c. orange-red .. 15 5
607. – 6 c. black 15 5
609. – 7 c. green 12 5
584. **185.** 8 c. maroon 15 5
610. – 8 c. black 12 5
585. – 10 c. olive 15 5
586. – 15 c. purple 25 8
587. – 20 c. blue 35 10
588. – 25 c. green 50 10
589. – 50 c. cinnamon .. 1·00 20
590. – $1 red .. .. 3·50 50

DESIGNS—As T **184**—Queen Elizabeth and: 2 c. Totem Pole. 3 c. Combine-harvester and Oil Derrick. 4 c. Ship in Lock. 5 c. (No. 583), Harbour Scene. 6 c. (Nos. 606/7), 7 c. "Transport". 8 c. (No. 609a), Library of Parliament. As T **185**. 10 c. "The Jack Pine" (T. Thomson). 15 c. "Bylot Island" (L. Harris). 20 c. "Quebec Ferry" (J. W. Morrice). 25 c. "The Solemn Land" (J. E. H. MacDonald). 50 c. "Summer's Stores" (Grain elevators, J. Ensor). $1, "Oilfield" (near Edmonton, H. G. Glyde).

186. Canadian Pavilion.

1967. World Fair, Montreal.
611. **186.** 5 c. blue and red .. 12 5

187. Allegory of "Womanhood" on Ballot-box. **188.** Queen Elizabeth. II and Centennial Emblem.

1967. Women's Franchise. 50th Anniv.
612. **187.** 5 c. purple and black .. 12 5

1967. Royal Visit.
613. **188.** 5 c. plum and chestnut 12 5

189. Athletic.

1967. Pan-American Games, Winnipeg.
614. **189.** 5 c. red 12 5

190. "World News".

1967. Canadian Press. 50th Anniv.
615. **190.** 5 c. blue 12 5

191. Governor-General Vanier.

1967. Vanier Commem.
616. **191.** 5 c. black 12 5

192. People of 1867, and Toronto, 1967.

1967. Cent. of Toronto as Capital City of Ontario.
617. **192.** 5 c. green & vermilion 12 5

193. Carol Singers. **194.** Grey Jays.

1967. Christmas.
618. **193.** 3 c. red 10 5
619. 5 c. green 12 5

1968. Wild Life.
620. **194.** 5 c. multicoloured .. 20 10
See also Nos. 638/40.

195. Weather Map and Instruments.

1968. First Meteorological Readings. 20th Anniv.
621. **195.** 5 c. multicoloured .. 12 5

196. Narwhal.

1968. Wild Life.
622. **196.** 5 c. multicoloured .. 12 5

197. Globe, Maple Leaf and Rain Gauge.

1968. Int. Hydrological Decade.
623. **197.** 5 c. multicoloured .. 12 5

198. The " Nonsuch ".

1968. Voyage of the " Nonsuch ". 300th Anniv.
624. **198.** 5 c. multicoloured .. 12 5

No. 624 and some latter commemorative issues may be found with either one, or two adjacent sides imperforate.

199. Lacrosse Players.

1968. Lacrosse.
625. **199.** 5 c. multicoloured .. 12 5
The footnote after No. 624 applies here also.

200. Front page of " The Globe ", George Brown and Legislative Building.

1968. George Brown (politician and journalist). 150th Birth Anniv.
626. **200.** 5 c. multicoloured .. 12 5
The footnote after No. 624 applies here also.

201. H. Bourassa (politician and journalist).

203. Armistice Monument, Vimy.

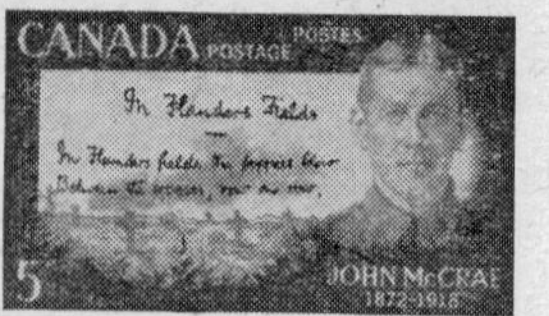
202. John Macrae. Battlefield and First Lines of " In Flanders Fields ".

1968. Henri Bourassa. Birth Cent.
627. **201.** 5 c. black, red & cream 12 5

1968. John Macrae (soldier and poet). 50th Death Anniv.
628. **202.** 5 c. multicoloured .. 12 5

1968. 1918 Armistice. 50th Anniv.
629. **203.** 15 c. black 40 35

204. Eskimo Family (carving).

1968. Christmas.
630. **204.** 5 c. black and blue .. 10 5
631. – 6 c. black and ochre .. 15 5
DESIGN: 6 c. " Mother and Child " (carving).

205. Curling.

1969. Curling.
632. **205.** 6 c. black, blue and red 15 5

206. Vincent Massey.

208. Globe and Tools.

207. " Return from the Harvest Field " (Suzor-Cote).

1969. Vincent Massey, First Canadian-born Governor-General.
633. **206.** 6 c. sepia and ochre .. 10 5

1969. Aurele de Foy Suzor-Cote (painter). Birth Cent.
634. **207.** 50 c. multicoloured .. 90 70

1969. Int. Labour Organisation. 50th Anniv.
635. **208.** 6 c. green 10 5

209. Vickers Vimy Aircraft over Atlantic Ocean.

1969. 1st Non-stop Transatlantic Flight. 50th Anniv.
636. **209.** 15 c. choc., grn. & blue 40 35

210. Sir William Osler.

211. White-throated Sparrow.

1969. Sir William Osler (physician). 50th Death Anniv.
637. **210.** 6 c. blue and chestnut 10 5

1969. Birds. Multicoloured.
638. 6 c. Type **211** 12 8
639. 10 c. Ipswich sparrow .. 30 20
640. 25 c. Hermit thrush .. 55 50
The 10 c. and 25 c. are horiz.

212. Flags of Winter and Summer Games.

214. Sir Isaac Brock and Memorial Column.

213. Outline of Prince Edward Island showing Charlottetown.

1969. Canadian Games.
641. **212.** 6 c. emerald, red & blue 10 5

1969. Bicent. of Charlottetown as Capital of Prince Edward Is.
642. **213.** 6 c. brown, blk. & blue 10 5

1969. Sir Isaac Brock. Birth Bicent.
643. **214.** 6 c. orge., bistre & brn. 10 5

215. Children of the World in Prayer.

1969. Christmas.
644. **215.** 5 c. multicoloured .. 10 5
645. 6 c. multicoloured .. 10 5

216. Stephen Butler Leacock, Mask and " Mariposa ".

1969. Stephen Butler Leacock (humorist). Birth Cent.
646. **216.** 6 c. multicoloured .. 10 5

217. Symbolic Cross-roads.

1970. Manitoba Cent.
647. **217.** 6 c. ultramarine, lemon and vermilion .. 10 8

218. " Enchanted Owl " (Kenojuak).

1970. Northwest Territories. Cent.
648. **218.** 6 c. red and black .. 10 5

219. Microscopic View of Inside of Leaf.

1970. Int. Biological Programme.
649. **219.** 6 c. emer., yell. & ultram. 10 5

220. Dogwood and Stylised Cherry Blossom.

1970. World Fair, Osaka. Expo 70. Multicoloured.
650. 25 c. Expo '67 Emblem (red) 85 70
651. 25 c. Type **220** (violet) .. 85 70
652. 25 c. White Trillium (green) 85 70
653. 25 c. White Garden Lily (bl.) 85 70

NOTE: Each stamp shows a stylized Cherry Blossom, in a different colour, given above in brackets.

Nos. 650/3 were issued together in se-tenant blocks of four, within the sheet.

221. Henry Kelsey.

1970. Henry Kelsey (explorer). 300th Birth Anniv.
654. **221.** 6 c. multicoloured .. 10 5

222. " Towards Unification ".

1970. U.N. 25th Anniv.
655. **222.** 10 c. blue 30 25
656. 15 c. magenta and lilac 50 40

223. Louis Riel (Metis leader).

224. Mackenzie's Inscription, Dean Channel.

1970. Louis Riel Commem.
657. **223.** 6 c. blue and vermilion 10 5

1970. Sir Alexander Mackenzie (explorer).
658. **224.** 6 c. brown 10 5

225. Sir Oliver Mowat (statesman).

1970. Sir Oliver Mowat Commen.
659. **225.** 6 c. vermilion and black 10 5

226. " Isles of Spruce " (A. Lismer).

1970. " Group of Seven " (artists). 50th Anniv.
660. **226.** 6 c. multicoloured .. 10 5

227. " Horse-drawn Sleigh". 228. Sir Donald A. Smith.

1970. Christmas. Multicoloured.

661.	5 c. Type **227**	12	5
662.	5 c. " Stable and Star of Bethlehem "	12	5
663.	5 c. " Snowmen "	12	5
664.	5 c. " Skiing "	12	5
665.	5 c. " Santa Claus "	12	5
666.	6 c. " Santa Claus " (different)	12	5
667.	6 c. " Christ in Manger "	15	5
668.	6 c. " Toy Shop "	15	5
669.	6 c. " Christmas Tree "	15	5
670.	6 c. " Church "	15	5
671.	10 c. " Christ in Manger " (37 × 20 mm.)	20	20
672.	15 c. " Trees and Sledge " (37 × 20 mm.)	30	30

The 5 c. and the 6 c. values were each issued in se-tenant strips of the five designs.

1970. Sir Donald Alexander Smith. 150th Birth. Anniv.

673. **228.** 6 c. yell., brn and grn. 10 5

229. "Big Raven". (E. Carr). 230. Laboratory Equipment.

1971. Emily Carr (painter). Birth Cent.

674. **229.** 6 c. multicoloured .. 10 5

1971. Discovery of Insulin. 50th Anniv.

675. **230.** 6 c. multicoloured .. 10 5

231. "The Atom".

1971. Sir Ernest Rutherford (scientist). Birth Cent.

676. **231.** 6 c. yellow, red & brn. 10 5

232. Maple " Keys". 233. Louis Papineau.

1971. "The Maple Leaf in Four Seasons". Multicoloured.

677.	6 c. Type **232** (Spring)	15	5
678.	6 c. Green leaves (summer)	15	5
679.	7 c. Autumn leaves	15	5
680.	7 c. Withered leaves and snow (winter)	15	5

1971. Louis-Joseph Papineau (politician). Death Cent.

681. **233.** 6 c. multicoloured .. 10 5

234. Chart of Coppermine River.

1971. Samuel Hearne's Expedition to the Coppermine. Bicent.

682. **234.** 6 c. red, brown & buff 10 5

235. " People " and Computer Tapes.

1971. Census. Cent.

683. **235.** 6 c. blue, red & black 10 5

236. Maple Leaves.

1971. Radio Canada International.

684. **236.** 15 c. red, yell. & blk. 45 35

237. " B. C."

1971. British Columbia's Entry into the Confederation. Cent.

685. **237.** 7 c. multicoloured .. 10 8

238. " Indian Encampment on Lake Huron " (Kane).

1971. Paul Kane (painter). Death Cent.

686. **238.** 7 c. multicoloured .. 15 10

239. " Snowflake". 240. Pierre Laporte (Quebec Cabinet Minister).

1971. Christmas.

687.	**239.**	6 c. blue	10	5
688.		7 c. green	10	5
689.	–	10 c. silver and red	15	12
690.	–	15 c. silver, pur. & lav.	25	20

DESIGN: 10 c., 15 c. "Snowflake" design similar to T **239** but square (26 × 26 mm.).

1971. Assassination of Pierre Laporte. 1st Anniv.

691. **240.** 7 c. black on buff .. 10 8

241. Skaters.

1972. World Figure Skating Championships, Calgary.

692. **243.** 8 c. purple 10 5

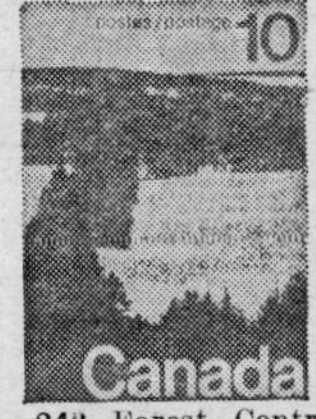

242. J. A. MacDonald. 243. Forest, Central Canada.

244. Vancouver.

1972.

693.	**242.**	1 c. orange	5	5
694.	–	2 c. green	5	5
695.	–	3 c. brown	5	5
696.	–	4 c. black	8	5
697.	–	5 c. mauve	8	5
698.	–	6 c. red	5	5
699.	–	7 c. brown	5	5
700.	–	8 c. blue	5	8
701.	–	10 c. brown	10	12
702.	**243.**	10 c. green, blue-green and orange	20	12
703.	–	15 c. blue and brown	20	8
704.	–	20 c. orge., vio. & blue	30	10
705.	–	25 c. ultram. & blue	35	10
706.	–	50 c. grn., blue & brn.	80	12
709.	**244.**	$1 multicoloured	2·50	1·10
710.	–	$2 multicoloured	2·10	1·25

DESIGNS: As T **242** (1 to 7 c. show Canadian Prime Ministers). 2 c. W. Laurier. 3 c. R. Borden. 4 c. W. L. Mackenzie King. 5 c. R. B. Bennett. 6 c. L. B. Pearson. 7 c. Louis St. Laurent. 8 and 10 c. Queen Elizabeth II. As T **243**. 15 c. Mountain sheep. 20 c. Prairie landscape from the air. 25 c. Polar Bears. 50 c. Seashore. As T **244**. $2 Quebec.

245. Heart.

1972. World Health Day.

719. **245.** 8 c. red 10 5

246. Frontenac and Fort Saint-Louis, Quebec.

1972. Governor Frontenac's Appointment to New France. 300th Anniv.

720. **246.** 8 c. brown-red, orange-brown & blue .. 10 8

247. Plains Indian's Artefacts.

248. Dancer in Ceremonial Costume.

1972. Canadian Indians.

721.	**247.**	8 c. multicoloured	10	8
722.	–	8 c. multicoloured	10	8
723.	–	8 c. multicoloured	10	8
724.	–	8 c. multicoloured	10	8
725.	–	10 c. multicoloured	12	15
726.	–	10 c. brn., blk. & grn.	12	15
727.	–	8 c. orge., red & black	10	8
728.	**248.**	8 c. multicoloured	10	8
729.	–	8 c. red, violet & black	10	8
730.	–	8 c. multicoloured	10	8
731.	–	8 c. red and black	10	8
732.	–	8 c. multicoloured	10	8
733.	–	8 c. multicoloured	10	8
734.	–	8 c. multicoloured	10	8
735.		8 c. multicoloured	5	8
736.		8 c. multicoloured	5	8
737.		8 c. multicoloured	5	8
738.		8 c. brown and black	5	8
739.	–	10 c. multicoloured	12	15
740.	–	10 c. grn., red & black	12	15

DESIGN—As T **247**: No. 722, " Buffalo Chase ". No. 723, Pacific Coast Indians' artefacts. No. 724, " The Inside of a House in Nootka Sound ". No. 725, Iroquoian artefacts. No. 726, Iroquoian encampment. No. 733, Algonkian artefacts. No. 734, " Micmac Indians ". No. 735, Sub-arctic Indians artefacts. No. 736, " The Dance of Kutcha-Kutchin ". As T **248**: No. 727, Plains Indians' Thunderbird. and decorative pattern. No. 729, Algonkians' Thunderbird and decorative pattern. No. 730, Algonkian Indians. No. 731, Pacific Coast Indians' Thunderbird and decorative pattern. No. 732, Gitksan Tsimshian chief. No. 737, Ceremonial costume, Kutchin tribe. No. 738, Ojibwa Thunderbird and Nuskapi pattern. No. 739, Iroquoian costume. No. 740, Iroquoian thunderbird.

249. Photogrammetric Surveying. 250. Candles.

1972. Earth Sciences.

741.	**249.**	15 c. multicoloured	50	45
742.	–	15 c. grey, blue & blk.	50	45
743.	–	15 c. multicoloured	50	45
744.	–	15 c. green, orge. & blk.	50	45

DESIGNS AND EVENTS: No. 741 (12th Congress of Int. Society of Photogrammetry). No. 742, " Siegfried " lines (6th Conf. of Int. Cartographic Assn.). No. 743, Earth's crust (24th Int. Geological Congress). No. 744, Diagram of village at road-intersection (22nd Int. Geographical Congress).

1972. Christmas. Multicoloured.

745.	6 c. Type **250**	10	8
746.	8 c. Type **250**	10	8
747.	10 c. Candles with fruits and pine boughs (horiz.)	12	10
748.	15 c. Candles with prayer-book, caskets and vase (horiz.)	20	15

Nos. 747/8 are size 36 × 20 mm.

251. "The Blacksmith's Shop". (Krieghoff).

1972. Cornelius Krieghoff (painter). Death Cent.

749. **251.** 8 c. multicoloured .. 12 8

252. F. de Montmorency-Laval.

1973. Monsignor de Laval (1st Bishop of Quebec). 350th Birth Anniv.

750. **252.** 8 c. blue, gold & silver 10 8

253. Commissioner French and Route of the March West.

1973. Royal Canadian Mounted Police. Cent.

751. **253.** 8 c. brown, orge. & red .. 12 8
752. – 10 c. multicoloured .. 15 12
753. – 15 c. multicoloured .. 20 20

DESIGNS: 10 c. Spectrograph. 15 c. Mounted policemen.

254. Jeanne Mance.

1973. Jeanne Mance (nurse). 300th Death Anniv.

754. **254.** 8 c. multicoloured .. 10 8

255. Joseph Howe. **256.** "Mist Fantasy" (MacDonald).

1973. Joseph Howe (Nova Scotian politician). Death Cent.

755. **255.** 8 c. gold and black .. 10 8

1973. J. E. H. MacDonald (artist). Birth Cent.

756. **256.** 15 c. multicoloured .. 20 20

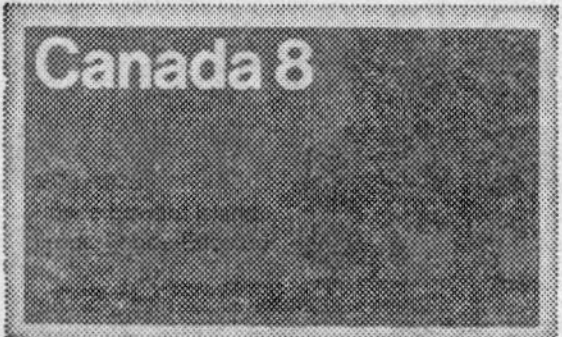

257. Oaks and Harbour.

1973. Prince Edward Island's Entry into the Confederation. Cent.

757. **257.** 8 c. orange and red .. 10 8

258. Scottish Settlers.

1973. Arrival of Scottish Settlers at Pictou, Nova Scotia. Bicentenary.

758. **258.** 8 c. multicoloured .. 10 8

259. Queen Elizabeth II.

1973. Royal Visit and Commonwealth Heads of Government Meeting, Ottawa.

759. **259.** 8 c. multicoloured .. 10 8
760. 15 c. multicoloured .. 20 15

260. Nellie McClung. **261.** 1976 Olympics Emblem.

1973. Nellie McClung (feminist). Birth Cent.

761. **260.** 8 c. multicoloured .. 10 8

1973. 1976 Olympic Games, Montreal. (1st issue).

762. **261.** 8 c. multicoloured .. 12 15
763. 15 c. multicoloured .. 20 25

See also Nos. 768/71, 772/4, 786/9, 798/802, 809/11, 814/16, 829/31 and 833/7.

262. Ice-skate.

1973. Christmas. Multicoloured.

764. 6 c. Type **262** 5 5
765. 8 c. Bird decoration .. 10 8
766. 10 c. Santa Claus (20×36 mm.) 12 10
767. 15 c. Shepherd (20×36 mm.) 20 15

263. Diving.

1974. 1976 Olympic Games, Montreal. (2nd issue). "Summer Activities". Each blue.

768. 8 c. Type **263** 10 10
769. 8 c. "Jogging" 10 10
770. 8 c. Cycling 10 10
771. 8 c. Hiking 10 10

1974. 1976 Olympic Games, Montreal. (3rd issue). As Type **261** but smaller (20×36½ mm.).

772. **261.** 8 c.+2 c. multicoloured 12 10
773. 10 c.+5 c. multicoloured 20 15
774. 15 c.+5 c. multicoloured 25 20

264. Winnipeg Signpost, 1872.

1974. Winnipeg Centennial.

775. **264.** 8 c. multicoloured .. 10 8

265. Postmaster and Customer.

1974. Canadian Letter Carrier Delivery Service. Cent. Multicoloured.

776. 8 c. Type **265** 10 8
777. 8 c. Postman collecting mail 10 8
778. 8 c. Mail handler 10 8
779. 8 c. Mail sorters 10 8
780. 8 c. Postman making delivery 10 8
781. 8 c. Rural delivery by car 10 8

266. "Canada's Contribution to Agriculture".

1974. "Agricultural Education". Ontario Agricultural College. Cent.

782. **266.** 8 c. multicoloured .. 10 5

267. Telephone Development.

1974. Invention of Telephone by Alexander Graham Bell. Cent.

783. **267.** 8 c. multicoloured .. 10 8

268. Bicycle Wheel.

1974. World Cycling Championships, Montreal.

784. **268.** 8 c. black, red & silver 10 8

269. Mennonite Settlers.

1974. Arrival of Mennonites in Manitoba. Cent.

785. **269.** 8 c. multicoloured .. 10 8

1974. 1976 Olympic Games, Montreal (4th issue). "Winter Activities". As Type **263**. Each red.

786. 8 c. Snow-shoeing .. 10 8
787. 8 c. Skiing 10 8
788. 8 c. Skating 10 8
789. 8 c. Curling 10 8

270. Mercury, Winged Horses and U.P.U. Emblem.

1974. U.P.U. Centenary.

790. **270.** 8 c. violet, red & blue 10 8
791. 15 c. red, violet & blue 20 15

271. "The Nativity" (J. P. Lemieux).

1974. Christmas. Multicoloured.

792. 6 c. Type **271** 8 5
793. 8 c. "Skaters in Hull" (H. Masson) 10 8
794. 10 c. "The Ice Cone, Montmorency Falls" (R. C. Todd) 12 10
795. 15 c. "Village in the Laurentian Mountains" (C. A. Gagnon) 20 15

No. 793 is smaller 34×31 mm.

272. Marconi and St. John's Harbour, Newfoundland.

1974. Guglielmo Marconi (radio pioneer). Birth Centenary.

796. **272.** 8 c. multicoloured .. 10 8

273. Merritt and Welland Canal.

1974. Commencement of Welland Canal Construction. 150th Anniv.

797. **273.** 8 c. multicoloured .. 10 8

274. Swimming.

1975. 1976 Olympic Games, Montreal (5th issue). Multicoloured.

798. 8 c.+2 c. Type **274** .. 12 10
799. 10 c.+5 c. Rowing .. 20 15
800. 15 c.+5 c. Sailing 25 20

275. "The Sprinter".

1975. 1976 Olympic Games, Montreal (6th issue). Multicoloured.

801. $1 Type **275** .. .. 1·40 1·10
802. $2 "The Diver" .. .. 2·75 2·25

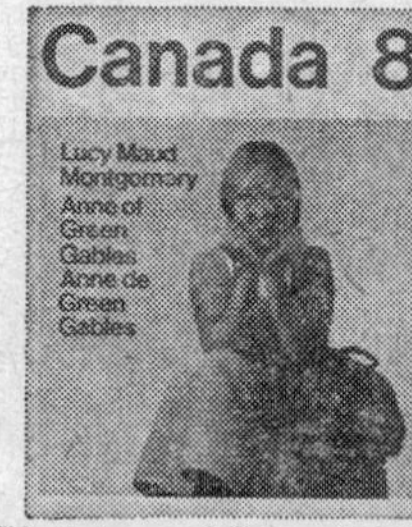

276. "Anne of Green Gables". (Lucy Maud Montgomery).

1975. Canadian Writers. (1st series). Multicoloured.

803. 8 c. Type **276** 10 8
804. 8 c. "Maria Chapdelaine" (Louis Hemon). .. 10 8

See also Nos. 846/7.

277. Marguerite Bourgeoys. (founder of the Order of Notre Dame).

278. S. D. Chown.
(founder of United Church of Canada).

1975. Canadian Celebrities.

805. **277.** 8 c. multicoloured .. 10 8
806. – 8 c. multicoloured .. 10 8
807. **278.** 8 c. multicoloured .. 10 8
808. – 8 c. multicoloured .. 10 8

DESIGNS—As T 277. No. 806, Alphouse Desjardins (leader of Credit Union movement). As T 278 No. 808, Dr. J. Cook (first moderator of Presbyterian Church in Canada).

279. Pole-vaulting.

1975. 1976 Olympics (7th issue). Mult.

809. 20 c. Type **279** 25 25
810. 25 c. Marathon-running .. 30 30
811. 50 c. Hurdling 70 60

280. " Untamed ".

1975. Calgary Centenary.

812. **280.** 8 c. multicoloured .. 10 8

281. I.W.Y. Symbol. **282.** Fencing.

1975. International Women's Year.

813. **281.** 8 c. grey, brn. and blk. 10 8

1975. 1976 Olympics Funds. (8th issue). Multicoloured.

814. 8 c.+2 c. Type **282** .. 12 12
815. 10 c.+5 c. Boxing.. .. 20 20
816. 15 c.+5 c. Judo 25 25

283. " Justice-Justitia ".

1975. Canadian Supreme Court. Centenary.

817. **283.** 8 c. multicoloured .. 10 8

284. " The William D. Lawrence ".

1975. Coastal Ships.

818. **284.** 8 c. yell., brn. & black 10 8
819. – 8 c. yell., grn. & black 10 8
820. – 8 c. blue, grn. & black 10 8
821. – 8 c. yell., brn. & black 10 8

DESIGNS: No. 819, " Beaver ". No. 820 " Neptune ". No. 821, " Quadra ".

285. " Santa Claus " (G. Kelly).

1975. Christmas. Multicoloured.

822. 6 c. Type **285** 8 5
823. 6 c. " Skater " (B. Cawsey) 8 5
824. 8 c. " Child " (D. Hebert) 10 5
825. 8 c. " Family " (L. Caldwell) 10 5
826. 10 c. " Gift " (D. Lovely) 12 10
827. 15 c. " Trees " (R. Kowalski) (horiz.) 20 15

286. Text, Badge and Bugle.

1975. Royal Canadian Legion. 50th Anniv.

828. **286.** 8 c. multicoloured .. 10 5

287. Basketball. **288.** Games Symbol and Snow Crystal.

1976. Olympics. (9th issue). Multicoloured.

829. 8 c.+2 c. Type **287** .. 12 10
830. 10 c.+5 c. Gymnastics .. 20 15
831. 20 c.+5 c. Soccer .. 30 25

1976. 12th Winter Olympic Games, Innsbruck.

832. **288.** 20 c. multicoloured .. 25 20

289. " Communications Arts ".

1976. Olympics. (10th issue). Multicoloured.

833. 20 c. Type **289** 25 20
834. 25 c. " Performing Arts " 30 25
835. 50 c. " Handicrafts " .. 70 55

290. Place Ville Marie and Notre-Dame Church.
(Illustration reduced. Actual size 58×22 mm.)

1976. Olympics. (11th issue). Multicoloured.

836. $1 Type **290** .. .. 1·25 1·00
837. $2 Olympic stadium and flags .. .. .. 2·50 2·00

291. Flower and Urban Sprawl.

1976. HABITAT. U.N. Conf. on Human Settlements, Vancouver.

838. **291.** 20 c. multicoloured .. 25 25

292. Benjamin Franklin and Map.

1976. American Revolution. Bicent.

839. **292.** 10 c. multicoloured .. 10 12

293. Wing Parade before Mackenzie Building.

1976. Royal Military College. Centenary. Multicoloured.

840. 8 c. Type **293** 10 10
841. 8 c. Colour party and Memorial Arch .. 10 10

294. Transfer of Olympic Flame by Satellite.

1976. Olympics (12th issue). Multicoloured.

842. 8 c. Type **294** 10 10
843. 20 c. Carrying the Olympic flag 25 25
844. 25 c. Athletes with medals 35 30

295. Archer.

1976. Disabled Olympics.

845. **295.** 20 c. multicoloured .. 25 25

296. " Sam McGee " (Robert W. Service).

1976. Canadian Writers (2nd series). Mult.

846. 8 c. Type **296** 10 10
847. 8 c. " Le Survenant " (Germaine Guevremont) 10 10

297. " Nativity " (F. Mayer).

1976. Christmas. Stained-glass Windows. Multicoloured.

848. 8 c. Type **297** 10 10
849. 10 c. " Nativity " (G. Maile & Son) 12 12
850. 20 c. " Nativity " (Yvonne Williams) 25 25

OFFICIAL STAMPS

1949. Optd. **O.H.M.S.**

O 1. **88.** 1 c. green (postage) .. 70 70
O 2. **89.** 2 c. brown .. .. 5·00 5·00
O 3. 3 c. purple (No. 378).. 50 35
O 4. **89.** 4 c. red 70 20
O 5. – 10 c. green (No. 402) 1·40 20
O 6. – 14 c. brown (No. 403) 1·75 50
O 7. – 20 c. grey (No. 404) .. 4·50 90
O 8. – 50 c. green (No. 405) 70·00 65·00
O 9. – $1 purple (No. 406) .. 20·00 17·00
O 10. – 7 c. blue (No. 407) (air) 2·75 1·75

1949. Optd. **O.H.M.S.**

O 11. **100.** 1 c. green 15 10
O 12. – 2 c. brown (No. 415) 30 15
O 13. – 3 c. purple (No. 416) 35 20
O 14. – 4 c. red (No. 417) .. 50 15
O 15. – 5 c. blue (No. 418) .. 70 35
O 16. **102.** 50 c. green .. .. 12·00 10·00

1950. Optd. **G.**

O 17. **100.** 1 c. green (postage).. 5 5
O 18. – 2 c. brown (No. 415) 25 15
O 19. – 2 c. olive (No. 415a) 15 5
O 20. – 3 c. purple (No. 416) 25 12
O 21. – 4 c. red (No. 417) .. 35 5
O 22. – 4 c. verm. (No. 417a) 35 5
O 23. – 5 c. blue (No. 418) .. 50 35
O 32. **100.** 7 c. blue .. .. 1·25 30
O 24. – 10 c. green (No. 402) 1·00 15
O 30. **101.** 10 c. purple 70 10
O 25. – 14 c. brown (No. 403) 3·50 90
O 26. – 20 c. grey (No. 404) 5·50 40
O 33. – 20 c. grey (No. 441) 1·00 15
O 27. **102.** 50 c. green .. .. 4·50 3·00
O 28. – $1 purple (No. 406) 38·00 35·00
O 31. – $1 blue (No. 433) .. 38·00 35·00
O 29. – 7 c. blue (No. 407)(air) 3·00 2·50

1953. 1st Queen Elizabeth II stamps optd. **G.**

O 35. **113.** 1 c. brown 10 5
O 36. 2 c. green 12 5
O 37. 3 c. red 12 5
O 38. 4 c. violet 20 5
O 39. 5 c. blue 20 8

1953. Pictorial stamps optd. **G.**

O 45. **108.** 10 c. chocolate .. 30 5
O 46. – 20 c. green (No. 488) 80 12
O 40. **110.** 50 c. green .. .. 2·50 40
O 34. **111.** $1 black .. .. 5·00 3·00

1955. 2nd Queen Elizabeth II stamps optd. **G.**

O 41. **115.** 1 c. brown 10 5
O 42. 2 c. green 10 5
O 43. 4 c. violet 30 8
O 44. 5 c. blue 15 5

1963. 3rd Queen Elizabeth II stamps optd. **G.**

O 47. **155.** 1 c. chocolate .. 40 40
O 48. 2 c. green 40 40
O 49. 4 c. red 40 40
O 50. 5 c. blue 25 25

OFFICIAL SPECIAL DELIVERY STAMPS

1950. Optd. **O.H.M.S.**

OS 1. – 10 c. green (No. S 15).. 6·00 6·00

1950. Optd. **G.**

OS 2. – 10 c. green (No. S 15).. 10·00 10·00

POSTAGE DUE STAMPS

D 1.

D 2.

1906.

D 2. D **1.** 1 c. violet .. .. 2·00 1·00
D 3. 2 c. violet .. .. 3·00 35
D 5. 4 c. violet .. .. 11·00 6·00
D 7. 5 c. violet .. .. 3·00 35
D 8. 10 c. violet .. .. 9·00 3·00

1930.

D 9. D **2.** 1 c. violet .. .. 2·00 2·00
D 10. 2 c. violet .. .. 1·00 30
D 11. 4 c. violet .. .. 2·00 1·50
D 12. 5 c. violet .. .. 2·00 1·50
D 13. 10 c. violet .. .. 25·00 3·50

D 3.

D 4.

1933.

D 14. D **3.** 1 c. violet .. .. 2·50 2·00
D 15. 2 c. violet .. .. 1·00 40
D 16. 4 c. violet .. .. 2·50 1·75
D 17. 10 c. violet .. .. 3·50 2·00

1935.

D 18. D **4.** 1 c. violet 5 5
D 19. 2 c. violet 5 5
D 20. 3 c. violet 70 65
D 21. 4 c. violet 12 5
D 22. 5 c. violet 15 5
D 23. 6 c. violet 50 45
D 24. 10 c. violet 15 5

D 5.

1967.

(a) Size 21 × 17 mm.

D 25. D **5.** 1 c. red 12 8
D 26. 2 c. red 10 8
D 27. 3 c. red 10 10
D 28. 4 c. red 35 15
D 29. 5 c. red .. .. 1·25 1·10
D 30. 6 c. red 20 15
D 31. 10 c. red 30 25

(b) Size 20 × 15½ mm.

D 32. D **5.** 1 c. red 5 5
D 34. 3 c. red 5 5
D 35. 4 c. red 5 5
D 36. 5 c. red .. .. 10·00 10·00
D 37. 6 c. red 5 5
D 38. 8 c. red 8 5
D 39. 10 c. red 10 5
D 40. 12 c. red 12 5
D 41 16 c. red 15 12

REGISTRATION STAMPS

R 1.

1875.

R 1. R **1.** 2 c. orange .. .. 12·00 1·50
R 6. 5 c. green .. .. 15·00 1·00
R 8. 8 c. blue .. .. 90·00 65·00

SPECIAL DELIVERY STAMPS

S 1.

1898.

S 2. S **1.** 10 c. green .. .. 12·00 2·50

S 2.

1922.

S 4. S **2.** 20 c. red .. .. 14·00 2·50

S 3. Mail-carrying, 1867 and 1927.

1927. Confederation. 60th Anniv.

S 5. S. **3.** 20 c. orange .. .. 3·00 3·00

S 4.

1930.

S 6. S **4.** 20 c. red .. .. 14·00 4·50

1932. As Type S **4**, but inscr. "CENTS" instead of "TWENTY CENTS".

S 7. – 20 c. red .. .. 10·00 5·00

S 5. Allegory of Progress.

1935.

S 8. S **5.** 20 c. red .. .. 2·00 1·75

S **6.** Canadian Coat of Arms.

1938.

S 9. S **6.** 10 c. green .. .. 2·00 90
S 10. 20 c. red .. .. 9·00 6·00

1939. Surch. **10 10** and bars.

S 11. S **6.** 10 c. on 20 c. red .. 1·50 1·50

S **7.** Coat of Arms and Flags.

S **8.** Two-engined Air Liner.

1942.

S 12. S **7.** 10 c. green (postage) .. 1·00 50
S 13. S **8.** 16 c. blue (air) .. 90 70
S 14. 17 c. blue .. 1·00 1·00

1946.

S 15. 10 c. green (postage) .. 90 40
S 17. 17 c. blue (air) .. .. 2·00 2·00

DESIGNS: 10 c. as Type S **7**, but with wreath of leaves. 17 c. as Type S **8**, but with four-engined transatlantic 'plane.

CANAL ZONE

O1

Territory adjacent to the Panama Canal leased by the U S.A. from the Republic of Panama.

100 cents = 1 balboa.

1904. Stamps of Panama (with **PANAMA** optd. twice) optd. **CANAL ZONE** horiz. in one line.

1. **3.** 2 c. red (No. 54) .. .. 65·00 65·00
2. 5 c. blue (No. 55) .. 35·00 27·00
3. 10 c. orange (No. 56) .. 50·00 45·00

1904. Stamps of the United States of 1902 optd. **CANAL ZONE PANAMA.**

4. **53.** 1 c. green .. .. .. 3·50 3·25
5. **54.** 2 c. red .. .. .. 4·00 4·00
6. **57.** 5 c. blue .. .. .. 10·00 10·00
7. **59.** 8 c. violet .. .. 18·00 18·00
8. **60.** 10 c. brown .. .. 19·00 19·00

Stamps of Panama overprinted.

1904. 1905 stamps optd. **CANAL ZONE** in two lines.

9. **4.** 1 c. green 45 30
10. 2 c. red 60 50

1904. Stamps with **PANAMA** optd. twice, optd. **CANAL ZONE** in two lines or surch. also.

11. **3.** 2 c. red (No. 54) .. 1·10 90
12. 5 c. blue (No. 55) .. 1·00 60
14. 8 c. on 50 c. brn. (No. 65) 2·75 2·25
13. 10 c. orange (No. 56) .. 2·75 1·90

1906. 1892 stamps surch. **PANAMA** on both sides and **CANAL ZONE** and new value in centre between bars.

19. **3.** 1 c. on 20 c. violet (No. 64) 25 25
22. 2 c. on 1 p. lake (No. 66) .. 40 40

1906. 1906 stamps optd. **CANAL ZONE** vert.

26. **5.** 1 c. black and green .. 40 35
27. **7.** 2 c. black and red .. 45 35
28A. **9.** 5 c. black and blue .. 1·00 40
29. **10.** 8 c. black and purple .. 2·25 90
30. **11.** 10 c. black and violet .. 2·25 90

1909. 1909 stamps optd. **CANAL ZONE** vert.

35. **14.** 1 c. black and green .. 45 35
36. **15.** 2 c. black and red .. 65 35
37. **17.** 5 c. black and blue .. 1·40 45
38. **18.** 8 c. black and purple .. 1·40 90
39. **19.** 10 c. black and purple .. 6·50 3·00

1911. Surch. **CANAL ZONE 10 cts.**

53. **4.** 10 c. on 13 c. grey .. 75 35

1914. Optd. **CANAL ZONE** vert.

54. **4.** 10 c. grey .. .. 4·50 1·25

1915. 1915 and 1918 stamps optd. **CANAL ZONE** vert.

55. 1 c. black and green (No. 162) 1·40 95
56. 2 c. black and red (No. 163) 1·25 90
57. 5 c. black and blue (No. 166) 1·40 90
58. 10 c. blk. & orange (No. 167) 2·75 2·25
59. 12 c. blk. and violet (No. 178) 1·60 80
60. 15 c. blk. and blue (No. 179) 4·50 2·50
61. 24 c. blk. & brown (No. 180) 3·50 1·40
62. 50 c. blk. & orange (No. 181) 50·00 32·00
63. 1 b. blk. and violet (No. 182) 25·00 9·50

1921. 1921 stamps optd. **CANAL ZONE** vert.

64. **24.** 1 c. green 50 25
65. – 2 c. red (No. 186) .. 50 20
66. **26.** 5 c. blue .. .. 1·25 60
67. – 10 c. violet (No. 191) .. 2·10 1·10
68. – 15 c. blue (No. 192) .. 3·75 1·75
69. – 24 c. sepia (No. 194) .. 7·00 3·25
70. – 50 c. black (No. 195) .. 19·00 11·00

1924. 1924 stamps optd. **CANAL ZONE** vert.

72. **29.** 1 c. green .. .. 1·40 80
73. 2 c. red .. .. 1·10 50

1924. Stamps of the United States of 1922 optd. **CANAL ZONE** horiz.

74. ½ c. sepia (No. 559) .. 10 10
75. 1 c. green (No. 602) .. 15 12
76. 1½ c. brown (No. 603) .. 15 15
103. 2 c. red (No. 604) .. 15 10
87. 3 c. violet (No. 638a) .. 50 35
88. 5 c. blue (No. 640) .. 50 35
106. 10 c. yellow (No. 645) .. 1·90 1·25
90. 12 c. purple (No. 693) .. 2·00 1·75
141. 14 c. blue (No. 695) .. 40 30
92. 15 c. grey (No. 696) .. 60 50
93. 17 c. black (No. 697) .. 45 40
94. 20 c. red (No. 698) .. 60 40
95. 30 c. sepia (No. 700) .. 70 50
84. 50 c. mauve (No. 701) .. 5·00 4·00
97. $1 brown (No. 579) .. 11·00 5·50

1926. Liberty Bell stamp of U.S.A. optd. **CANAL ZONE.**

101. **110.** 2 c. red .. .. 1·00 70

1. Gen. Gorgas.

3. Panama Canal under Construction.

1928. Portraits.

107. **1.** 1 c. green 5 5
108. – 2 c. red (Goethals) .. 8 5
109. **3.** 5 c. blue 25 10
111. – 12 c. purple (Gaillard) .. 20 15
116. – 50 c. mauve (Blackburn) 45 12

1929. Air. Stamps of 1928 surch. **AIR MAIL** and value.

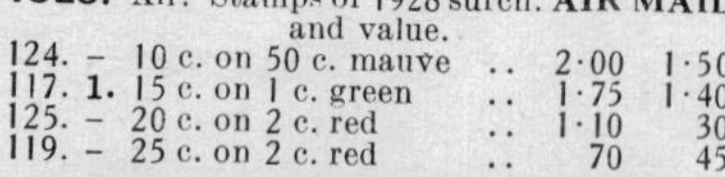

124. – 10 c. on 50 c. mauve .. 2·00 1·50
117. **1.** 15 c. on 1 c. green .. 1·75 1·40
125. – 20 c. on 2 c. red .. 1·10 30
119. – 25 c. on 2 c. red .. 70 45

6. Panama Canal.

7. H. F. Hodges.

1931. Air.

126. **6.** 4 c. purple 12 10
127. 5 c. green 8 8
128. 6 c. brown 15 8
129. 10 c. orange 20 8
130. 15 c. blue 20 5
131. 20 c. violet 35 8
132. 30 c. red 40 20
133. 40 c. yellow 60 25
134. $1 black .. .. 1·75 50

1931.

110. **7.** 10 c. orange 10 5
112. – 14 c. blue 25 20
113. – 15 c. grey 15 8
114. – 20 c. sepia 20 8
115. – 30 c. black 30 20

PORTRAITS: 14 c. Gen. Sibert. 15 c. Jackson Smith. 20 c. Admiral Rousseau. 30 c. Col. S. B. Williamson.

1933. No. 720 of United States optd. **CANAL ZONE.**

140. 3 c. violet 40 8

11. Gen. Goethals.

12. Balboa (before construction).

1934.

142. **11.** 3 c. violet 5 5

1939. Stamps of United States (1938) optd. **CANAL ZONE.**

165. **192.** ½ c. orange 5 5
166. – 1½ c. brown (No 801) 5 5

1939. Opening of Panama Canal, 25th Anniv. and Canal Zone Airmail Service, 10th Anniv. (a) Postage. As T **12** Inscr. "25TH ANNIVERSARY 1939 OPENING PANAMA CANAL 1914".

143. **12.** 1 c. green 10 10
144. – 2 c. red 12 10
145. – 3 c. violet 10 5
146. – 5 c. blue 25 20
147. – 6 c. orange 40 40
148. – 7 c. black 40 40
149. – 8 c. green 70 60
150. – 10 c. blue 70 60
151. – 11 c. green .. .. 1·25 1·25
152. – 12 c. maroon .. .. 1·25 1·10
153. – 14 c. violet .. .. 1·40 1·40
154. – 15 c. olive .. .. 1·75 75
155. – 18 c. red .. .. 1·40 1·40
156. – 20 c. brown .. .. 1·75 90
157. – 25 c. orange .. .. 3·25 2·50
158. – 50 c. purple .. .. 4·00 70

DESIGNS: 2 c. Balboa (after construction). 3 c., 5 c. Gaillard Cut. 6 c., 7 c. Bas Obispo. 8 c., 10 c. Gatun Locks. 11 c., 12 c. Canal Channel. 14 c., 15 c. Gamboa. 18 c., 20 c. Pedro Miguel Locks. 25 c., 50 c. Gatun Spillway.

(b) Air. Inscr. "TENTH ANNIVERSARY AIR MAIL" and "25TH ANNIVERSARY OPENING PANAMA CANAL".

159. 5 c. black 60 60
160. 10 c. violet 75 60
161. 15 c. brown 75 25
162. 25 c. blue .. .. 2·75 2·10
163. 30 c. red .. .. 2·10 1·50
164. $1 green .. .. 7·00 5·50

DESIGNS.—HORIZ.: As T **12**.—5 c. Seaplane over Sosa Hill. 10 c. Seaplane and map of C. America. 15 c. Seaplane and Fort Amador. 25 c. Seaplane at Cristobal Harbour, Manzanillo Is. 30 c. Seaplane over Culebra Cut. $1 Seaplane and palm trees.

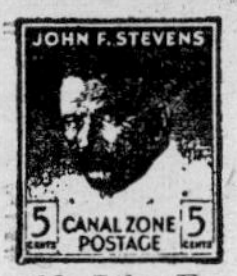

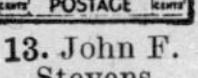

13. John F. Stevens. 14. Coati-mundi and Barro Colorado Island.

1946. Portraits.
188. – ½ c. orange (Davis) .. 5 5
189. – 1½ c. brown (Magoon) .. 5 5
190. – 2 c. red (Theodore Roosevelt) .. 5 5
191. **13.** 5 c. blue (Stevens) .. 5 5
192. – 25 c. green (Wallace) .. 25 15

1948. Canal Zone Biological Area. 25th Anniv.
194. **14.** 10 c. black 75 25

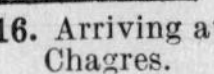

16. Arriving at Chagres. 17. Western Hemisphere.

1949. Gold Rush Cent. Inscr. "1849 GOLD RUSH CENTENNIAL 1949".
195. **16.** 3 c. blue 15 10
196. – 6 c. violet 15 12
197. – 12 c. green 30 25
198. – 18 c. magenta 40 35
DESIGNS: 6 c. "Up the Chagres River to Las Cruces". 12 c. "Las Cruces Trail to Panama". 18 c. "Leaving Panama for San Francisco".

1951. Air.
199. **17.** 4 c. purple 12 8
200. 5 c. green 15 10
201. 6 c. brown 12 8
202. 7 c. olive 15 8
210. 8 c. red 15 8
203. 10 c. orange 25 10
204. 15 c. maroon 70 40
205. 21 c. blue .. .. 1·00 60
206. 25 c. yellow .. .. 1·00 30
207. 31 c. claret .. .. 1·25 50
208. 35 c. blue .. .. 1·25 45
209. 80 c. black .. .. 1·50 45

18. Labourers in Gaillard Cut. 19. Early Train.

1951. West Indian Panama Canal Labourers.
211. **18.** 10 c. red 45 40

1955. Panama Railway Cent.
212. **19.** 3 c. violet 15 12

20. Gorgas Hospital.

1957. Gorgas Hospital, 75th Anniv.
213. **20.** 3 c. black on green .. 10 8

21. S.S. "Ancon".

22. Roosevelt Medal and Map of Canal Zone. 23. "First Class" Scout Badge.

1958.
214. **21.** 4 c. turquoise 10 8

1958. Theodore Roosevelt Birth Cent.
215. **22.** 4 c. brown 12 10

1960. American Boy Scout Movement. 50th Anniv.
216. **23.** 4 c. ochre, red and blue 20 15

24. Administration Building, Balboa. 25. U.S. Army Caribbean School Crest

1960.
217. **24.** 4 c. purple 8 5

1961. Air.
221. **25.** 15 c. blue and red .. 35 25

26. Girl Scouts Emblem and Camp.

1962. U.S. Girl Scouts Movement. 50th Anniv.
222. **26.** 4 c. ochre, green & blue 12 10

27. Campaign Emblem and Mosquito.

1962. Air. Malaria Eradication.
223. **27.** 7 c. black on yellow .. 15 12

28. Thatcher Ferry Bridge.

1962. Thatcher Ferry Bridge Opening.
224. **28.** 4 c. black and silver .. 10 8

29. Torch of Progress.

1963. Air. "Alliance for Progress".
225. **29.** 15 c. blue, green & black 40 25

30. Cristobal.

1964. Air. Panama Canal. 50th Anniv.
226. **30.** 6 c. black and green .. 10 8
227. – 8 c. black and red .. 15 10
228. – 15 c. black and blue .. 30 20
229. – 20 c. black and purple .. 40 25
230. – 30 c. black and brown .. 60 40
231. – 80 c. black and bistre .. 1·25 85
DESIGNS: 8 c. Gatun Lock. 15 c. Madden Dam. 20 c. Gaillard Cut. 30 c. Miraflores Locks. 80 c. Balboa.

31. Seal and Jetliner.

1965. Air.
232. **31.** 6 c. black and green .. 8 5
233. 8 c. black and red .. 10 5
234. 10 c. black and orange 10 5
235. 11 c. black and green .. 12 8
236. 13 c. black and green .. 12 8
237. 15 c. black and blue .. 15 8
238. 20 c. black and violet .. 20 10
238a. 22 c. black and violet .. 30 12
239. 25 c. black and green .. 25 10
240. 30 c. black and brown .. 30 12
240a. 35 c. black and red .. 50 25
241. 80 c. black and ochre .. 75 30

32. Goethal's Memorial, Balboa. 33. Dredge "Cascadas".

1968.
242. **32.** 6 c. blue and green .. 5 5
243. – 8 c. multicoloured .. 8 5
DESIGN: 8 c. Fort San Lorenzo.

1976.
247. **33.** 13 c. blk., grn. and blue 20 10

OFFICIAL STAMPS

1941. Optd. **OFFICIAL PANAMA CANAL.**
O 180. **1.** 1 c. green 12 8
O 181. **11.** 3 c. violet 25 12
O 182. **3.** 5 c. blue .. .. — 5·50
O 183. **7.** 10 c. orange 60 35
O 184. – 15 c. grey (No. 113) 90 40
O 185. – 20 c. sepia (No. 114) 1·10 45
O 186. – 50 c. mauve (No. 116) 2·75 1·10

1941. Air. Optd. **OFFICIAL PANAMA CANAL.**
O 167. **6.** 5 c. green 80 30
O 168. 6 c. brown .. .. 1·50 80
O 169. 10 c. orange .. .. 1·10 40
O 170. 15 c. blue .. .. 1·25 40
O 171. 20 c. violet .. .. 1·60 1·25
O 172. 30 c. red .. .. 2·00 1·10
O 173. 40 c. yellow .. .. 2·50 1·25
O 174. $1 black .. .. 3·25 1·60

1947. No. 192 optd. **OFFICIAL PANAMA CANAL.**
O 193. **13.** 5 c. blue 85 50

POSTAGE DUE STAMPS

1914. Postage Due stamps of United States of 1894 optd. **CANAL ZONE** diag.
D 55. D **2.** 1 c. red .. .. 4·75 1·60
D 56. 2 c. red .. .. 12·00 3·50
D 57. 10 c. red .. .. 45·00 5·00

1915. Postage Due stamps of Panama of 1915 optd. **CANAL ZONE** vert.
D 59. D **1.** 1 c. brown .. .. 1·40 50
D 60. D **2.** 2 c. brown .. .. 9·50 2·75
D 61. – 10 c. brown (No. D 172) 4·50 1·75

1915. Postage Due stamps of Panama of 1915 surch. **CANAL ZONE** vert. and value in figures.
D 62. D **1.** 1 c. on 1 c. brown .. 9·00 1·50
D 63. D **2.** 2 c. on 2 c. brown .. 3·00 85
D 66. – 4 c. on 4 c. (No. D 171) 4·50 2·10
D 64. – 10 c. on 10 c. brown (No. D 172) .. 2·75 85

1924. Postage Due stamps of United States of 1894 optd. **CANAL ZONE** horiz. in two lines.
D 92. D **2.** 1 c. red 60 40
D 93. 2 c. red .. .. 2·10 55
D 94. 10 c. red .. .. 13·00 1·40

1925. Stamps of Canal Zone of 1924 optd. **POSTAGE DUE.**
D 89. 1 c. green (No. 75) .. 8·50 1·75
D 90. 2 c. red (No. 103) .. 2·10 70
D 91. 10 c. yellow (No. 106) 4·75 1·40

1929. No. 109 surch. **POSTAGE DUE** and value and bars.
D 120. **3.** 1 c. on 5 c. blue .. 20 20
D 121. 2 c. on 5 c. blue .. 60 30
D 122. 5 c. on 5 c. blue .. 50 40
D 123. 10 c. on 5 c. blue .. 60 40

D 1. Canal Zone Seal.

1932.
D 135. D **1.** 1 c. claret 5 5
D 136. 2 c. claret 5 5
D 137. 5 c. claret 8 8
D 138. 10 c. claret 25 25
D 139. 15 c. claret 20 20

CANTON O1

A treaty port in S. China. Stamps issued at the French Indo-Chinese P.O. which was closed in 1922.

1901. 100 centimes = 1 franc.
1919. 100 cents = 1 piastre.

Stamps of Indo-China overprinted or surcharged.

CANTON
州廣
(1.)

1901. "Tablet" key-type, optd. with T **1.** The Chinese characters represent "Canton" and are therefore the same on every value.
1. D. 1 c. black on blue .. 15 15
2. 2 c. brown on yellow .. 15 15
3. 4 c. claret on grey .. 25 25
4. 5 c. green 25 25
6. 10 c. black on lilac .. 70 60
7. 15 c. blue 35 35
8. 15 c. grey 35 35
9. 20 c. red on green .. 1·40 1·40
10. 25 c. black on red .. 1·25 1·25
11. 30 c. brown .. .. 3·25 3·00
12. 40 c. red on yellow .. 3·25 3·00
13. 50 c. red on rose .. 5·50 5·00
14. 75 c. brown on orange .. 6·50 6·50
15. 1 f. olive .. .. 3·75 3·75
16. 5 f. mauve on lilac .. 40·00 40·00

1903. "Tablet" key-type, surch. as T **1.** The Chinese characters indicate the value and therefore differ for each value.
17. D. 1 c. black on blue .. 30 30
18. 2 c. brown on yellow .. 35 35
19. D. 4 c. claret on grey .. 35 35
20. 5 c. green 25 25
21. 10 c. red 25 25
22. 15 c. grey 30 25
23. 20 c. red on green .. 1·75 1·25
24. 25 c. blue 65 45
25. 25 c. black on red .. 90 65
26. 30 c. brown .. .. 2·75 2·25
27. 40 c. red on yellow .. 8·50 2·00
28. 50 c. red on rose .. 50·00 42·00
29. 50 c. brown on blue .. 13·00 13·00
30. 75 c. brown on orange .. 13·00 13·00
31. 1 f. olive .. .. 13·00 13·00
32. 5 f. mauve on lilac .. 12·00 12·00

1906. Surch. **CANTON** (letters without serifs) and value in Chinese.
33. **1.** 1 c. olive 15 12
34. 2 c. claret on yellow .. 15 12
35. 4 c. purple on grey .. 15 15
36. 5 c. green 20 15
37. 10 c. red 30 20
38. 15 c. brown on blue .. 40 40
39. 20 c. red on green .. 20 15
40. 25 c. blue 25 25
41. 30 c. brown on cream .. 45 45
42. 35 c. black on yellow .. 20 15
43. 40 c. black on grey .. 50 50
44. 50 c. olive on cream .. 65 50
45. D. 75 c. olive on orange .. 8·00 8·00
46. **1.** 1 f. green .. .. 2·10 2·00
47. 2 f. brown on yellow .. 5·00 4·00
48. D. 5 f. mauve on lilac .. 12·00 10·00
49. **1.** 10 f. red on green .. 12·00 12·00

1908. 1907 stamps surch. **CANTON** and value in Chinese.
50. **2.** 1 c. black and olive .. 12 10
51. 2 c. black and brown .. 12 10
52. 4 c. black and blue .. 20 12
53. 5 c. black and green .. 20 12
54. 10 c. black and red .. 25 15
55. 15 c. black and violet .. 30 25
56. **3.** 20 c. black and violet .. 30 30
57. 25 c. black and blue .. 55 40
58. 30 c. black and purple .. 1·10 90
59. 35 c. black and green .. 1·10 90
60. 40 c. black and brown .. 1·10 90
61. 50 c. black and red .. 1·00 80
62. **4.** 75 c. black and orange .. 1·25 1·00
63. – 1 f. black and red .. 2·25 2·25
64. – 2 f. black and green .. 6·00 5·50
65. – 5 f. black and blue .. 7·00 6·50
66. – 10 f. black and violet .. 12·00 12·00

1919. As last but additionally surch.
67. **2.** ⅖ c. on 1 c. blk. & olive .. 12 12
68. ⅘ c. on 2 c. black & brown 5 5
69. 1⅗ c. on 4 c. black & blue .. 15 15
70. 2 c. on 5 c. blk. & grn. .. 15 12
71. 4 c. on 10 c. black and red 12 12
72. 6 c. on 15 c. black & violet 20 10
73. **3.** 8 c. on 20 c. black & violet 25 15
74. 10 c. on 25 c. black & blue 30 12
75. 12 c. on 30 c. black & pur. 30 15
76. 14 c. on 35 c. black & grn. 20 10
77. 16 c. on 40 c. black & brn. 20 12
78. 20 c. on 50 c. black & red 20 12
79. **4.** 30 c. on 75 c. blk. & orge. 20 12
80. – 40 c. on 1 f. black and red 1·40 60
81. – 80 c. on 2 f. black & green 1·40 1·10
82. – 2 p. on 5 f. black and blue 1·60 1·60
83. – 4 p. on 10 f. black & violet 1·60 1·60

CAPE JUBY O4

Former Spanish possession on the N.W. coast of Africa, ceded to Morocco in 1958.

1916. Stamps of Rio de Oro surch. **CABO JUBI** and value.
1. **4.** 5 c. on 4 p. red .. .. 6·50 3·50
2. 10 c. on 10 p. violet .. 6·50 3·50
3. 15 c. on 50 c. brown .. 6·50 3·50
4. 40 c. on 1 p. lilac .. .. 10·00 7·00

1919. Stamps of Spain optd. **CABO JUBY.**
5. **17.** ¼ c. green 5 5
18. **33.** 1 c. green (imperf.) .. 3·50 2·25
6. **32.** 2 c. brown 5 5
7. 5 c. green 8 5
8. 10 c. red 12 8
9. 15 c. yellow 40 15
10. 20 c. green .. .. 1·60 70
19. 20 c. violet .. .. 22·00 11·00
11. 25 c. blue 40 12
12. 30 c. green 40 20
13. 40 c. pink 40 20
14. 50 c. blue 60 20
15. 1 p. red .. .. 1·10 70
16. 4 p. purple .. .. 6·00 3·00
17. 10 p. orange .. .. 7·00 3·00

1925. Stamps of Spain optd. **CABO JUBY.**
19a. **35.** 2 c. green .. .. 4·75 4·50
20. 5 c. purple 55 35
21. 10 c. green 70 35
22. 20 c. violet .. .. 1·75 1·10

1926. As Red Cross stamps of Spain of 1926 optd. **CABO-JUBY.**
23. **37.** 1 c. orange 70 45
24. – 2 c. red 70 45
25. – 5 c. grey 25 20
26. – 10 c. green 20 20
27. **37.** 15 c. violet 15 10
28. – 20 c. purple 15 10
29. **38.** 25 c. red 15 10
30. **37.** 30 c. olive 15 10
31. – 40 c. blue 5 5
32. – 50 c. brown 5 5
33. – 1 p. red 5 5
34. – 4 p. brown 8 8
35. **38.** 10 p. lilac 15 15

1929. Seville and Barcelona Exhibition stamps of Spain (Nos. 504/14) optd. **CABO JUBY.**

36. – 5 c. red	8	8
37. – 10 c. green	8	8
38. 42. 15 c. blue	8	8
39. 43. 20 c. violet	8	8
40. 42. 25 c. red	8	8
41. – 30 c. brown	10	10
42. – 40 c. blue	10	10
43. 43. 50 c. orange	20	20
44. – 1 p. grey	1·40	1·10
45. – 4 p. red	2·50	2·25
46. – 10 p. brown	2·25	1·75

1934. Stamps of Spanish Morocco of 1928 optd. **Cabo Juby.**

47. 1. 1 c. red	35	20
48. 2 c. violet	30	15
49. 5 c. blue	40	15
50. 10 c. green	45	25
51. 15 c. brown	1·40	70
52. – 25 c. red	55	35
53. 2. 1 p. green	3·50	1·75
54. – 2 p. 50 purple	9·00	4·25
55. – 4 p. blue	11·00	6·00

1934. Stamps of Spanish Morocco of 1933 optd. **Cabo Juby.**

56. 3. 1 c. red	8	8
57. – 10 c. green	35	30
58. 3. 20 c. green	70	55
59. – 30 c. lake	70	55
60. 4. 40 c. blue	3·25	1·40
61. 50 c. red	5·50	2·75

1935. Stamps of Spanish Morocco of 1933 optd. **CABO JUBY.**

62. 3. 1 c. red	8	5
63. – 2 c. green	10	5
64. – 5 c. magenta	20	10
65. – 10 c. green	1·40	55
66. – 15 c. yellow	55	35
67. 3. 20 c. green	70	55
68. – 25 c. red	7·00	4·25
73. – 25 c. violet	55	35
74. – 30 c. red	55	30
75. – 40 c. red	70	35
76. – 50 c. blue	1·10	35
77. – 60 c. green	1·60	55
69. – 1 p. grey	1·25	90
78. – 2 p. lake	7·00	4·25
70. – 2 p. 50 brown	5·00	3·50
71. – 4 p. green	5·50	3·50
72. – 5 p. black	6·50	4·25

1937. Civil War. 1st Anniv. Nos. 184/99 of Spanish Morocco optd. **CABO JUBY.**

79. 1 c. blue	5	5
80. 2 c. brown	5	5
81. 5 c. mauve	5	5
82. 10 c. green	5	5
83. 15 c. blue	8	8
84. 20 c. maroon	8	8
85. 25 c. mauve	8	8
86. 30 c. red	8	8
87. 40 c. orange	20	20
88. 50 c. blue	20	20
89. 60 c. green	20	20
90. 1 p. violet	20	20
91. 2 p. blue	3·25	3·25
92. 2 p. 50 black	3·25	3·25
93. 4 p. brown	3·25	3·25
94. 10 p. black	3·25	3·25

1938. Air. Nos. 203/12 of Spanish Morocco optd. **CABO-JUBY.**

95. 5 c. brown	8	5
96. 10 c. green	8	5
97. 25 c. red	5	5
98. 40 c. blue	70	35
99. 50 c. mauve	8	5
100. 75 c. blue	8	8
101. 1 p. brown	10	10
102. 1 p. 50 violet	35	20
103. 2 p. red	55	35
104. 3 p. black	2·40	1·40

1939. Nos. 213/6 of Spanish Morocco optd. **CABO-JUBY.**

105. 5 c. orange	10	8
106. 10 c. green	10	8
107. 15 c. brown	15	10
108. 20 c. blue	15	10

1940. Nos. 217/32 of Spanish Morocco optd. **CABO JUBY.**

109. 1 c. brown	5	5
110. 2 c. olive	5	5
111. 5 c. blue	5	5
112. 10 c. lilac	8	5
113. 15 c. green	8	5
114. 20 c. purple	8	5
115. 25 c. sepia	8	8
116. 30 c. green	8	8
117. 40 c. green	20	10
118. 45 c. orange	20	10
119. 50 c. brown	20	10
120. 75 c. blue	30	15
121. 1 p. brown and blue	35	15
122. 2 p. 50 green and brown	1·10	70
123. 5 p. sepia and pink	90	55
124. 10 p. brown and olive	3·50	2·50

1942. Air. Nos. 258/62 of Spanish Morocco, but without "Z" opt. and inscr. "CABO JUBY".

125. 5 c. blue	5	5
126. 10 c. brown	5	5
127. 15 c. green	5	5
128. 90 c. red	8	8
129. 5 p. black	55	55

1944. Nos. 269/82 (agricultural scenes) Spanish Morocco optd. **CABO JUBY.**

130. – 1 c. blue and brown	5	5
131. – 2 c. green	5	5
132. 11. 5 c. black and brown	5	5
133. – 10 c. orange and blue	5	5
134. – 15 c. green	5	5
135. – 20 c. black and claret	5	5
136. – 25 c. brown and blue	5	5
137. – 30 c. blue and green	5	5
138. – 40 c. purple and brown	5	5
139. 11. 50 c. brown and blue	5	5
140. – 75 c. blue and green	8	8
141. – 1 p brown and blue	8	8
142. – 2 p. 50 blue and black	50	50
143. – 10 p. black and orange	2·40	2·40

1946. Nos. 285/94 (craftsmen) of Spanish Morocco optd. **CABO JUBY.**

144. – 1 c. brown and purple	5	5
145. 12. 2 c. violet and green	5	5
146. – 10 c. blue and orange	5	5
147. 12. 15 c. green and blue	5	5
148. – 25 c. blue and green	5	5
149. – 40 c. brown and blue	5	5
150. 12. 45 c. red and black	8	8
151. – 1 p. blue and green	12	12
152. – 2 p. 50 green and orange	45	45
153. – 10 p. grey and blue	1·40	1·40

1948. Nos. 307/17 (transport and commerce of Spanish Morocco optd. **CABO JUBY.**

154. 15. 2 c. brown and violet	5	5
155. – 5 c. violet and claret	5	5
156. – 15 c. green and blue	5	5
157. – 25 c. green and black	5	5
158. – 35 c. black and blue	5	5
159. – 50 c. violet and orange	5	5
160. – 70 c. blue and green	5	5
161. – 90 c. green and red	5	5
162. – 1 p. violet and blue	10	10
163. 15. 2 p. 50 green & maroon	20	20
164. 10 p. blue and black	45	45

EXPRESS LETTER STAMPS

1919. Express letter stamp of Spain optd. **CABO JUBY.**

E 18. E 1. 20 c. red	20	20

1926. Red Cross stamp. As Express letter stamp of Spain optd. **CABO-JUBY.**

E 36. E 2. 20 c. black and blue	25	15

1934. Stamp of Spanish Morocco optd. **Cabo Juby.**

E 62. E 1. 20 c. black	1·00	55

1935. Stamp of Spanish Morocco optd. **CABO JUBY.**

E 79. E 2. 20 c. red	55	25

1937. No. E 200 of Spanish Morocco optd. **CABO JUBY.**

E 95. E 3. 20 c. red	15	15

1940. No. E 233 Spanish Morocco optd. **CABO JUBY.**

E 125. E 4. 25 c. red	12	8

CAPE OF GOOD HOPE BC

Formerly a Br. Colony, later the southernmost province of the Union of S. Africa.

1. "Hope".

1853. Imperf.

18. 1. 1d. red	80·00	£120
19. 4d. blue	60·00	28·00
20. 6d. lilac	£120	£180
8a. 1s. green	£140	£300

2.

1861. Imperf.

13. 2. 1d. red	£8000	£1200
14. 4d. blue	£3250	£1100

3. "Hope" seated 4.

1864. With outer frame line. Perf.

23. 3. 1d. red	12·00	3·25
24. 4d. blue	14·00	80
52a. 6d. violet	5·50	1·00
53a. 1s. green	10·00	1·00

1871. No outer frame line.

48. 4. ½d. black	10	8
49a. 1d. red	15	8
36. 3d. rose	20·00	2·50
40. 3d. claret	1·20	55
51. 4d. blue	40	10
66. 5s. orange	6·00	90

1868. Surch.

32. 3. 1d. on 6d. violet	45·00	7·00
33. 1d. on 1s. green	5·00	5·00
34. 4. 3d. on 4d. blue	13·00	1·80
27. 3. 4d. on 6d. violet	18·00	4·50

1880. Surch. **THREEPENCE.**

35. 4. 3d. on 4d. rose	6·50	85

1880. Surch. **3.**

37. 4. "3" on 3d. rose	5·00	50

1882. Surch. **One Half-penny** and bar.

42. 4. ½d. on 3d. claret	1·40	1·00

1882.

59. 4. ½d. green	10	8
60. 2d. brown	20	8
56. 2½d. olive	55	10
61a. 2½d. blue	30	8
62. 3d. magenta	50	18
63. 4d. olive	70	18
64. 1s. green	3·50	35
65. 1s. yellow	1·20	25

On the 2½d. stamps the value is in a white square at upper right-hand corner as well as at foot.

1891. Surch. **2½d.**

55a. 4. 2½d. on 3d. magenta	1·20	50

1893. Surch. **ONE PENNY** and bar.

57a. 4. 1d. on 2d. brown	25	8

ILLUSTRATIONS
British Commonwealth and all overprints and surcharges are FULL SIZE. Foreign Countries have been reduced to ¾-LINEAR.

5. "Hope" and Table Mountain.

1893.

67. 5. ½d. green	10	8
58a. 1d. red	10	8
68. 3d. mauve	85	40

6. Table Mountain and Bay and Arms. 7.

1900.

69. 6. 1d. red	10	8

1902. Various frames.

70. 7. ½d. green	12	8
71. 1d. red	10	8
72. 2d. brown	45	20
73. 2½d. blue	95	1·80
74. 3d. purple	55	8
75. 4d. green	95	20
76. 6d. mauve	95	20
77. 1s. olive-yellow	1·50	25
78. 5s. orange	7·50	2·25

CAPE VERDE ISLANDS O1

Islands in the Atlantic; formerly Portuguese which became independent in 1975.

1877. "Crown" key-type inscr. "CABO VERDE".

1. P. 5 r. black	1·25	90
2a. 10 r. yellow	4·50	3·75
18. 10 r. green	1·10	90
3. 20 r. olive	90	70
19. 20 r. red	1·60	1·10
4. 25 r. red	90	50
20. 25 r. lilac	1·25	1·10
5. 40 r. blue	22·00	15·00
21. 40 r. yellow	90	75
6. 50 r. green	22·00	12·00
22. 50 r. blue	2·40	1·75
7. 100 r. lilac	2·75	1·25
8a. 200 r. orange	2·00	1·60
9b. 300 r. brown	2·50	2·10

1886. "Embossed" key-type inscr. "PROVINCIA DE CABO VERDE".

33. Q. 5 r. black	1·25	90
34. 10 r. green	1·25	90
25. 20 r. red	1·75	1·40
26a. 25 r. mauve	1·60	1·25
27. 40 r. brown	1·75	1·40
28. 50 r. blue	1·75	1·40
29. 100 r. brown	2·00	1·25
30. 200 r. lilac	3·50	3·25
32. 300 r. orange	5·00	3·50

1894. "Figures" key-type inscr. "CABO VERDE".

37. R. 5 r. orange	50	40
38. 10 r. mauve	60	50
39. 15 r. brown	1·25	1·00
40. 20 r. lilac	1·25	1·00
41. 25 r. green	1·10	1·00
42. 50 r. blue	1·10	1·00
51. 75 r. red	3·00	2·50
43. 80 r. green	3·50	3·00
44. 100 r. brown on buff	2·40	1·25
58. 150 r. red on rose	6·00	5·00
59. 200 r. blue on blue	5·00	4·00
46. 300 r. blue on buff	6·00	3·75

1898. "King Carlos" key-type inscr. "CABO VERDE".

60. S. 2½ r. grey	15	12
61. 5 r. orange	15	12
62. 10 r. green	15	12
63. 15 r. brown	1·10	70
111. 15 r. green	50	35
64. 20 r. lilac	40	30
65. 25 r. green	90	50
112. 25 r. red	35	12
66. 50 r. blue	1·00	60
113. 50 r. brown	1·10	90
114. 65 r. blue	3·50	3·00
67. 75 r. red	2·10	80
115. 75 r. purple	90	80
68. 80 r. mauve	2·10	1·25
69. 100 r. blue on blue	80	55
116. 115 r. brown on pink	2·10	2·00
117. 130 r. brown on yellow	2·10	2·00
70. 150 r. brown on yellow	2·10	1·50
71. 200 r. purple on pink	1·10	80
72. 300 r. blue on pink	2·00	1·50
118. 400 r. blue on yellow	2·10	2·00
73. 500 r. black on blue	2·00	1·50
74. 700 r. mauve on yellow	5·50	4·25

1902. Key-types of Cape Verde Is. surch.

119. S. 50 r. on 65 r. blue	1·10	90
75. Q. 65 r. on 5 r. black	1·60	1·50
78. R. 65 r. on 10 r. mauve	1·75	1·40
79. 65 r. on 20 r. lilac	1·75	1·40
80. 65 r. on 100 r. brn. on buff	2·75	1·75
76. Q. 65 r. on 200 r. lilac	1·60	1·50
77. 65 r. on 300 r. orange	1·60	1·50
85. R. 115 r. on 5 r. orange	1·40	1·25
82. Q. 115 r. on 10 r. green	1·50	1·40
83. 115 r. on 20 r. red	1·50	1·40
87. R. 115 r. on 25 r. green	1·25	1·00
88. 115 r. on 150 r. red on rose	2·75	2·40
90. Q. 130 r. on 50 r. blue	1·50	1·40
93. R. 130 r. on 75 r. red	1·25	1·10
95. 130 r. on 80 r. green	1·40	1·10
92. Q. 130 r. on 100 r. brown	1·50	1·40
97. R. 130 r. on 200 r. bl. on blue	1·40	1·25
104. V. 400 r. on 2½ r. brown	60	55
98. Q. 400 r. on 25 r. mauve	1·10	1·00
99. 400 r. on 40 r. brown	1·50	1·25
101. R. 400 r. on 50 r. blue	1·75	1·40
103. 400 r. on 300 r. blue on buff	70	60

1902. "King Carlos" key-type of Cape Verde Is. optd. **PROVISORIO.**

107. S. 15 r. brown	60	55
108. 25 r. green	60	55
109. 50 r. blue	60	55
110. 75 r. red	1·00	80

1911. "King Carlos" key-type of Cape Verde Is. optd. **REPUBLICA.**

120. S. 2½ r. grey	15	15
121. 5 r. orange	15	15
122. 10 r. green	40	30
123. 15 r. green	25	20
124. 20 r. lilac	40	30
125. 25 r. red	40	30
126. 50 r. brown	1·75	1·50
127. 75 r. purple	45	30
128. 100 r. blue on blue	45	30
129. 115 r. brown on pink	35	30
130. 130 r. brown on yellow	35	30
131. 200 r. purple on pink	1·50	1·10
132. 400 r. blue on yellow	60	30
133. 500 r. black on blue	60	30
134. 700 r. mauve on yellow	60	40

1912. "King Manoel" key-type inscr. "CABO VERDE" and optd. **REPUBLICA.**

135. T. 2½ r. lilac	15	12
136. 5 r. black	15	12
137. 10 r. green	20	15
138. 20 r. red	80	70
139. 25 r. brown	30	15
140. 50 r. blue	1·25	1·10
141. 75 r. brown	40	35
142. 100 r. brown on green	40	35
143. 200 r. green on pink	50	30
144. 300 r. black on blue	50	30
145. 400 r. blue and black	80	70
146. 500 r. brown and olive	80	70

1913. Surch. **REPUBLICA CABO VERDE** and new value on "Vasco da Gama" issues of

(a) Portuguese Colonies.

147.	¼ c. on 2½ r. green	50	40
148.	½ c. on 5 r. red	50	40
149.	1 c. on 10 r. purple	50	40
150.	2½ c. on 25 r. green	50	40
151.	5 c. on 50 r. blue	75	65
152.	7½ c. on 75 r. brown	1·10	1·00
153.	10 c. on 100 r. brown	80	70
154.	15 c. on 150 r. yell.-brn.	1·00	90

(b) Macao.

155.	¼ c. on ½ a. green	65	55
156.	½ c. on 1 a. red	65	55
157.	1 c. on 2 a. purple	65	55
158.	2½ c. on 4 a. green	65	55
159.	5 c. on 8 a. blue	1·90	1·90
160.	7½ c. on 12 a. brown	1·60	1·10
161.	10 c. on 16 a. brown	90	80
162.	15 c. on 24 a. yell.-brown	1·50	1·50

(c) Timor.

163.	¼ c. on ½ a. green	65	55
164.	½ c. on 1 a. red	65	55
165.	1 c. on 2 a. purple	65	55
166.	2½ c. on 4 a. green	65	55
167.	5 c. on 8 a. blue	1·60	1·50
168.	7½ c. on 12 a. brown	1·60	1·50
169.	10 c. on 16 a. brown	90	80
170.	15 c. on 24 a. yell.-brown	1·10	90

1914. Stamps of 1902 optd. **REPUBLICA.**

171. S.	75 r. red (No. 110)	1·10	1·00
192. R.	115 r. on 5 r. (No. 85)	40	35
193. Q.	115 r. on 10 r. (No. 82)	90	75
195.	115 r. on 20 r. (No. 83)	1·00	90
198. R.	115 r. on 25 r. (No. 87)	60	50
200.	115 r. on 150 r. (No. 88)	25	20
201. Q.	130 r. on 50 r. (No. 90)	90	70
203. R.	130 r. on 75 r. (No. 93)	65	60
204.	130 r. on 80 r. (No. 95)	60	50
206. Q.	130 r. on 100 r. (No. 92)	60	50
208. R.	130 r. on 200 r. (No. 97)	60	50

1914. "Ceres" key-type inscr. "CABO VERDE".

219. U.	¼ c. olive	5	5
220.	½ c. black	5	5
221.	1 c. green	5	5
222.	1½ c. brown	5	5
223.	2 c. red	5	5
224.	2 c. grey	10	10
214.	2½ c. violet	8	5
215.	3 c. orange	8	8
216.	4 c. red	8	8
228.	4½ c. grey	12	12
229.	5 c. blue	12	12
230.	6 c. mauve	12	12
231.	7 c. blue	12	12
232.	7½ c. brown	12	10
233.	8 c. grey	12	10
234.	10 c. brown	12	10
235.	12 c. green	15	15
236.	15 c. claret	12	12
237.	20 c. green	12	10
238.	24 c. blue	35	30
239.	25 c. brown	35	30
188.	30 c. brown on green	1·40	1·25
240.	30 c. green	15	15
189.	40 c. brown on rose	1·10	80
241.	40 c. blue	15	12
190.	50 c. orange on pink	1·00	90
242.	50 c. mauve	25	20
243.	60 c. blue	35	25
244.	60 c. red	35	30
245.	80 c. red	1·40	45
191.	1 e. green on blue	1·00	90
246.	1 e. red	1·10	70
247.	1 e. blue	90	50
248.	2 e. purple	1·00	70
249.	5 e. brown	1·75	1·60
250.	10 e. pink	3·75	3·00
251.	20 e. green	9·00	6·50

1921. Vasco da Gama stamps surch. with new values and bars.

252.	2 c. on 15 c. on 150 r. yellow-brown (No. 154)	60	50
253.	4 c. on 10 c. on 100 r. brown (No. 153)	70	70

1921. No. 69 surch. **REPUBLICA 6 c.**

254. S.	6 c. on 100 r. bl. on blue	50	45

1921. Vasco da Gama stamp of Port Colonies optd. **CABO VERDE CORREIOS** or surch. also.

255.	¼ c. on 1 c. green	12	10
256.	½ c. on 1 c. green	15	12
257.	1 c. green	15	12

1922. Provisionals of 1914 surch. **$04.**

260. R.	4 c. on 130 r. on 75 r. red (No. 203)	40	35
262.	4 c. on 130 r. on 80 r. green (No. 204)	45	40
265.	4 c. on 130 r. on 200 r. blue (No. 208)	30	30

1925. Provisional stamps of 1902 surch. **Republica 40 c.**

267. V.	40 c. on 400 r. on 2½ r. brown (No. 104)	20	20
268. R.	40 c. on 400 r. on 300 r. blue on buff (No. 103)	30	25

1931. No. 245 surch. **70 c.** and bars.

269. U.	70 c. on 80 c. red	60	50

1934. As T **2** of Angola (new "Ceres" type).

270. 2.	1 c. brown	5	5
271.	5 c. sepia	5	5
272.	10 c. mauve	5	5
273.	15 c. black	5	5
274.	20 c. grey	5	5
275.	30 c. green	8	5
276.	40 c. red	8	5
277.	45 c. blue	25	25
278.	50 c. chocolate	25	15
279.	60 c. olive	25	20
280.	70 c. brown	25	20
281.	80 c. green	25	20
282.	85 c. red	65	60
283.	1 e. claret	50	15
284.	1 e. 40 blue	60	50
285.	2 e. mauve	60	55
286.	5 e. green	1·75	1·25
287.	10 e. brown	3·00	2·10
288.	20 e. orange	6·50	5·00

1938. As Nos. 383/409 of Angola.

289.	1 c. olive (postage)	5	5
290.	5 c. brown	8	8
291.	10 c. red	8	8
292.	15 c. purple	40	25
293.	20 c. slate	20	15
294.	30 c. purple	20	15
295.	35 c. green	20	15
296.	40 c. brown	20	15
297.	50 c. mauve	20	15
298.	60 c. black	20	15
299.	70 c. violet	25	20
300.	80 c. orange	25	20
301.	1 e. red	25	20
302.	1 e. 75 blue	60	35
303.	2 e. green	70	40
304.	5 e. olive	1·50	70
305.	10 e. blue	2·40	1·00
306.	20 e. brown	5·50	1·50
307.	10 c. red (air)	30	25
308.	20 c. violet	30	25
309.	50 c. orange	35	30
310.	1 e. blue	35	30
311.	2 e. red	60	40
312.	3 e. green	90	55
313.	5 e. brown	1·40	70
314.	9 e. red	2·40	1·40
315.	10 e. mauve	2·75	1·50

1. Route of President's African Tour.

ILLUSTRATIONS
British Commonwealth and all overprints and surcharges are FULL SIZE. Foreign Countries have been reduced to ¾-LINEAR.

1939. Pres. Carmona's 2nd Colonial Tour.

316. 1.	80 c. violet	2·40	1·60
317.	1 e. 75 blue	5·50	3·00
318.	20 e. brown	21·00	11·00

1948. Nos. 276 and 294 surch.

319.	10 c. on 30 c. purple	35	30
320.	25 c. on 40 c. red	35	30

2. St. Vincent.

3. St. Nicholas.

1948.

321. 2.	5 c. purple	25	15
322. –	10 c. green	25	15
323. 3.	50 c purple	45	25
324. –	1 e. violet	1·50	80
325. –	1 e. 75 blue and green	1·50	1·00
326. –	2 e. violet and buff	2·75	1·25
327. –	5 e. green and yellow	6·50	4·00
328. –	10 e. red and orange	11·00	7·50
329. –	20 e. violet and flesh	20·00	11·00

DESIGNS—VERT. 10 c. Ribeira Grande. HORIZ. 1 e. Porto Grande, St. Vincent. 1 e. 75, 5 e. Mindelo. 2 e. Joao de Evora beach, St. Vincent. 10 e. Volcano. 20 e. Paul.

1938. Honouring the Statue of Our Lady of Fatima. As T **13** of Angola.

330.	50 c. blue	5·50	4·25

1949. U.P.U. 75th Anniv. As T **18** of Angola.

331.	1 e. magenta	4·25	2·50

1950. Holy Year. As T **20/1** of Angola.

332.	1 e. brown	35	25
333.	2 e. blue	1·60	1·00

1951. Holy Year. As T **23** of Angola.

340.	2 e. violet	50	40

1951. Surch. with figures and bars over old value.

334.	10 c. on 35 c. (No. 295)	20	20
335.	20 c. on 70 c. (No. 299)	40	35
336.	40 c. on 70 c. (No. 299)	40	35
337.	50 c. on 80 c. (No. 300)	40	35
338.	1 e. on 1 e. 75 (No. 302)	40	35
339.	2 e. on 10 e. (No. 305)	1·50	90

1952. No. 302 surch. with figures and cross over old values.

341.	10 c. on 1 e. 75 blue	65	60
342.	20 c. on 1 e. 75 blue	65	60
343.	50 c. on 1 e. 75 blue	2·10	2·10
344.	1 e. on 1 e. 75 blue	12	10
345.	1 e. 50 on 1 e. 75 blue	12	10

4. Map, about 1371.

5. V. Dias and G. de Cintra.

1952. Portuguese Navigators as T **5**. Multicoloured.

346.	5 c. T **4**	8	8
347.	10 c. T **5**	8	8
348.	30 c. D. Afonso and A. Fernandes	8	8
349.	50 c. Lancarote and S da Costa	10	8
350.	1 e. D. Gomes & A. da Nola	15	10
351.	2 e. Princes Fernando and Henry the Navigator	60	12
352.	3 e. A. Goncalves and D. Dias	2·10	25
353.	5 e. A. Goncalves Baidaia and J. Fernandes	1·25	35
354.	10 e. D. Eanes da Gra and A. de Freitas	3·00	1·00
355.	20 c. Map. 1502	4·75	1·10

6. Doctor giving Injection.

7. Facade of Monastery.

1952. 1st Tropical Medicine Congress, Lisbon.

356. 6.	20 c. black and green	20	15

1953. Missionary Art Exhibition.

357. 7.	10 c. brown and olive	5	5
358.	50 c. violet and salmon	8	8
359.	1 e. green and orange	15	12

1953. Portuguese Stamp Centenary. As T **27** of Angola.

360.	50 c. blue, grey & purple	55	35

1954. 4th Cent. of Sao Paulo. As T **28** of Angola.

361.	1 e. black, green and buff	12	10

8. Arms of Cape Verde Is. and Port Guinea.

9. Arms of Praia.

10. Prince Henry the Navigator.

1955. Presidential Visit.

362. 8.	1 e. multicoloured	12	10
363.	1 e. 60 c. multicoloured	20	12

1958. City of Praia Cent. Multicoloured.

364. 9.	1 e. on yellow	12	10
365.	2 e. 50 on salmon	20	12

1958. Brussels Int. Exn. As T **34** of Angola.

366.	2 e. multicoloured	20	12

1958. 6th Int. Congress of Tropical Medicine. As T **35** of Angola.

367.	3 c. yellow, green, red, brown and lilac	1·75	90

DESIGN—VERT. DIAMOND: 3 e. "Aloe vera" (plant).

1960. Prince Henry the Navigator. 500th Death Anniv.

368. 10.	2 e. multicoloured	10	5

11. Antonio da Nola.

12. "Education".

1960. Colonization of Cape Verde Is. 5th Cent. Inscr. "v centenario de cabo verde".

369. 11.	1 e. multicoloured	15	12
370. –	2 e. 50 multicoloured	25	20

DESIGNS: 2 e. 50, Diogo Gomes.

1960. African Technical Co-operation Commission. 10th Anniv.

371. 12.	2 e. 50 multicoloured	30	15

13. Arms of Praia.

14. Militia Regiment Drummer, 1806.

1961. Urban Arms. As T **13.** Arms multicoloured; inscriptions in red and green; background colours given.

372.	5 c. buff	5	5
373.	15 c. blue	5	5
374.	20 c. yellow	5	5
375.	30 c. lilac	5	5
376.	1 e green	30	8
377.	2 e. lemon	30	8
378.	2 e. 50 pink	35	12
379.	3 e. brown	60	20
380.	5 e. cobalt	40	15
381.	7 e. 50 olive	30	20
382.	15 e. mauve	60	40
383.	30 e. yellow	1·25	80

ARMS: 15 c. Nova Sintra. 20 c. Ribeira Brava. 30 c. Assomada. 1 e. Maio. 2 e. Mindelo. 2 e. 50 Santa Maria. 3 e. Pombas. 5 e. Sal-Rei. 7 e 50, Tarrafal. 15 e. Maria Pia. 30 e. San Felipe.

1962. Sports. As T **41** of Angola. Multicoloured.

384.	50 c. Throwing the javelin	5	5
385.	1 e. Discus-thrower	15	10
386.	1 e. 50 Batsman (cricket)	5	5
387.	2 e. 50 Boxing	10	8
388.	4 e. 50 Hurdler	15	15
389.	12 e. 50 Golfers	50	50

1962. Malaria Eradication. Mosquito design as T **42** of Angola. Multicoloured.

390.	2 e. 50 "A. pretoriensis"	35	20

1963. T.A.P. Airline. 10th Anniv. As T **48** of Angola.

391.	2 e. 50 multicoloured	25	15

1964. National Overseas Bank Cent. As Angola T **50** but portrait of J. da S. M. Leal.

392.	1 e. 50 multicoloured	20	12

1965. I.T.U. Cent. As T **52** of Angola.

393.	2 e. 50 multicoloured	60	40

1965. Portuguese Military Uniforms. Multicoloured.

394.	50 c. Type **14**	8	8
395.	1 e. Militiaman, 1806	15	12
396.	1 e. 50 Infantry Grenadiers officer, 1833	30	12
397.	2 e. 50 Infantry grenadier, 1833	40	20
398.	3 e. Cavalry officer, 1834	40	20
399.	4 e. Infantry grenadier, 1835	55	25
400.	5 e. Artillery officer, 1848	60	35
401.	10 e. Infantry drum-major, 1856	1·10	80

1966. National Revolution. 40th Anniv. As T **56** of Angola, but showing different building. Multicoloured.

402.	1 e. Dr. A. Moreira's Academy and Public Assistance Building	5	5

1967. Military Naval Assn. Cent. As T **58** of Angola. Multicoloured.

403.	1 e. F. da Costa and gunboat "Mandovy"	15	10
404.	1 e. 50 C. Araujo and minesweeper "Augusto Castilho"	20	15

1967. Fatima Apparitions. 50th Anniv. As T **59** of Angola. Multicoloured.

405.	1 e. Image of Virgin Mary	5	5

15. President Tomas.

16. Port of Sao Vicente.

1968. Visit of President Tomas of Portugal.

406. 15.	1 e. multicoloured	5	5

1968. Pedro Cabral (explorer). 500th Birth Anniv. As T **63** of Angola. Multicoloured.

407.	1 e. Cantino's map, 1502	15	8
408.	1 e. 50 Pedro Alvares Cabral (vert.)	20	10

1968. "Produce of Cape Verde Islands". Multicoloured.

409. 50 c. Type **16** 5 5
410. 1 e. "Purgueira" (Tatrophus curcus) 5 5
411. 1 e. 50 Groundnuts 5 5
412. 2 e. 50 Castor-oil Plant 10 5
413. 3 e. 50 "Inhame" (Dioscorea alata) 15 8
414. 4 e. Date Palm 20 8
415. 4 e. 50 "Goiabeira" (Psidium guajava) 20 10
416. 5 e. Tamarind 20 10
417. 10 e. Manioc 40 20
418. 30 e. Girl of Cape Verde 1·25 70

The 1 e. to 30 e. values are vert.

1969. Admiral Gago Coutinho. Birth Cent. As T **65** of Angola but different design.

419. 30 c. Seaplane and map of Lisbon–Rio flight 5 5

1969. Vasco da Gama (explorer). 500th Birth Anniv. Multicoloured. As T **66** of Angola.

420. 1 e. 50 Vasco da Gama (vert.) 5 5

1969. Overseas Administrative Reforms. Cent. As T **67** of Angola.

421. 2 e. multicoloured 8 5

1969. Manoel I. 500th Birth Anniv. Multicoloured. As T **68** of Angola.

422. 3 e. Manoel I 12 5

1970. Marshal Carmona. Birth Cent. Multicoloured. As T **70** of Angola.

423. 2 e. 50 Half-length portrait 10 5

17. Desalination Installation.

1971. Desalination Works, Mindelo. Inaug.

424. **17.** 4 e. multicoloured 15 12

1972. Camoens' "Lusiad" (epic poem). 400th Anniv. As T **74** of Angola. Mult.

425. 5 e. Galleons at Cape Verde 20 12

1972. Olympic Games, Munich. As T **75** of Angola. Multicoloured.

426. 4 e. Basketball and boxing 15 10

1972. 1st Flight Lisbon-Rio de Janeiro. 50th Anniv. As T **76** of Angola. Multicoloured.

427. 3 e. 50 Seaplane "Lusitania" near Sao Vicente 15 5

1973. I.M.O./W.M.O. Centenary. As Type **77** of Angola.

428. 2 e. 50 multicoloured 10 5

1976. Independence. No. 407 optd. **INDEPENDENCIA 5 JULHO 1975.**

429. 1 e. multicoloured 20 10

18. Cabral, Flag and People.

1976. Amilcar Cabral's Assassination. Third Anniv.

430. **18.** 5 e. multicoloured 40 20

CHARITY TAX STAMPS

The notes under this heading in Portugal also apply here.

1925. Marquis de Pombal Commem. Stamps of Portugal but inscr. "CABO VERDE".

C 266. C **4.** 15 c. violet 20 15
C 267. – 15 c. violet 20 15
C 268. C **5.** 15 c. violet 20 15

C 1. St. Isabel. C 2. C 3.

1948.

C 321. C **1.** 50 c. green 80 70
C 322. 1 e. chestnut 1·00 90

1959. Surch.

C 368. C **1.** 50 e. on 1 e. chestnut 60 45

1959. Colours changed.

C 369. C **1.** 50 e. cerise 35 30
C 370. 1 e. blue 35 30

1967.

C 406. C **2.** 30 c. multicoloured 8 8
C 407. 50 c. (purple panel) 20 20
C 408. 50 c. mult. (brown panel) 5 5
C 409. 1 e. mult. (brown panel) 35 35
C 410. 1 e. mult. (pur. panel) 10 10

1968. Pharmaceutical Tax stamps surch. as in Type C **3.**

C 411b. C **3.** 50 c. on 1 c. black, orange and green 8 8
C 412c. 50 c. on 2 c. black, orange and green 8 8
C 413. 50 c. on 3 c. black, orange and green 10 10
C 414. 50 c. on 5 c. black, orange and green 10 10
C 415. 50 c. on 10 c. black, orange and green 10 10
C 416. 1 e. on 1 c. black, orange and green 55 55
C 417a. 1 e. on 2 c. black, orange and green 10 10

NEWSPAPER STAMP

1893. "Newspaper" key-type inscr. "CABO VERDE".

N. 37. V. 2½ r. brown 40 35

POSTAGE DUE STAMPS

1904. "Due" key-type inscr. "CABO VERDE".

D 119. W. 5 r. green 12 12
D 120. 10 r. grey 12 12
D 121. 20 r. brown 20 15
D 122. 30 r. orange 35 15
D 123. 50 r. brown 25 15
D 124. 60 r. brown 65 60
D 125. 100 r. mauve 40 30
D 126. 130 r. blue 40 30
D 127. 200 r. red 40 30
D 128. 500 r. lilac 90 80

1911. "Due" key-type inscr. "CABO VERDE" and optd. **REPUBLICA.**

D 135. W. 5 r. green 10 10
D 136. 10 r. grey 10 10
D 137. 20 r. brown 10 8
D 138. 30 r. orange 15 12
D 139. 50 r. brown 15 12
D 140. 60 r. brown 15 12
D 141. 100 r. mauve 15 12
D 142. 130 r. blue 15 12
D 143. 200 r. red 15 12
D 144. 500 r. lilac 30 20

1921. "Due" key-type inscr "CABO VERDE" with currency in centavos.

D 252. W. ½ c. green 5 5
D 253. 1 c. slate 5 5
D 254. 2 c. brown 5 5
D 255. 3 c. orange 5 5
D 256. 5 c. brown 5 5
D 257. 6 c. brown 5 5
D 258. 10 c. mauve 5 5
D 259. 13 c. blue 10 8
D 260. 20 c. red 12 10
D 261. 50 c. grey 15 12

1925. As Nos. C266/8 optd. **MULTA.**

D 266. C **4.** 30 c. violet 20 15
D 267. – 30 c. violet 20 15
D 268. C **5.** 30 c. violet 20 15

1952. As Type D **1** of Macao, but inscr. "CABO VERDE". Numerals in red; name in black.

D 356. 10 c. brown and olive 5 5
D 357. 30 c. black, blue & mauve 5 5
D 358. 50 c. slate, green & yellow 5 5
D 359. 1 e. indigo and blue 5 5
D 360. 2 e. brown and orange 8 8
D 361. 5 e. green and olive 20 20

CAROLINE ISLANDS O1

A group of islands in the Pacific Ocean, formerly a German protectorate; under Japanese mandate after 1918. Now under United States trusteeship.

100 pfennig = 1 mark.

1899. Stamps of Germany optd. **Karolinen.**

7. **6.** 3 pf. brown 2·75 3·00
8. 5 pf. green 4·00 3·50
9. **7.** 10 pf. red 6·00 6·00
10. 20 pf. blue 6·00 9·00
11. 25 pf. orange 18·00 20·00
12. 50 pf. brown 19·00 22·00

1901. "Yacht" key-types inscr. "KAROLINEN".

13. N. 3 pf. brown 15 40
14. 5 pf. green 20 70
15. 10 pf. red 15 2·10
16. 20 pf. blue 35 3·50
17. 25 pf. black & red on yell. 55 6·00
18. 30 pf. blk. & orge. on buff 55 6·00
19. 40 pf. black and red 55 7·00
20. 50 pf. blk. & pur. on buff 60 9·00
21. 80 pf. blk. & red on rose 90 11·00
22. O. 1 m. red 1·25 22·00
23. 2 m. black 2·10 27·00
24. 3 m. black 3·00 50·00
29b. 5 m. red and black 9·00

CASTELROSSO E1

One of the Aegean Is. Occupied by the French Navy on 27 December 1915. The French withdrew in August 1921 and, after a period of Italian Naval administration, the island was included in the Dodecanese territory.

(a) FRENCH OCCUPATION.

1920. Stamps of 1902-20 of French Levant optd. **B. N. F. CASTELLORIZO.**

1. A. 1 c. grey 5·50 5·50
2. 2 c. claret 5·50 5·50
3. 3 c. red 5·50 5·50
4. 5 c. green 5·50 5·50
5. B. 10 c. red 7·00 7·00
6. 15 c. orange 10·00 10·00
7. 20 c. brown 11·00 11·00
8. 1 pi. on 20 c. blue 11·00 11·00
9. 30 c. lilac 11·00 11·00
10. C. 40 c. red and blue 26·00 26·00
11. 2 pi. on 50 c. brn. & blue 22·00 22·00
12. 4 pi. on 1 f. brn. & green 26·00 26·00
13. 20 pi. on 5 f. bl. & brown 80·00 80·00

1920. Stamps of 1902-20 of French Levant optd. **O. N. F. Castellorizo.**

14. A. 1 c. grey 3·00 3·00
15. 2 c. claret 3·00 3·00
16. 3 c. red 3·25 3·25
17. 5 c. green 3·25 3·25
18. B. 10 c. red 3·25 3·25
19. 15 c. claret 4·25 4·25
20. 20 c. brown 10·00 10·00
21. 1 pi. on 25 c. blue 7·00 7·00
22. 30 c. lilac 7·00 7·00
23. C. 40 c. red and blue 7·00 7·00
24. 2 pi. on 50 c. brn. & blue 7·00 7·00
25. 4 pi. on 1 f. brn. and green 10·00 10·00
26. 20 pi. on 5 f. blue & brn. 45·00 45·00

1920. Nos. 334 and 339 of France optd. **O. N. F. Castellorizo.**

27. **17.** 10 c. red 2·00 2·50
28. 25 c. blue 2·00 2·50

1920. Stamps of France optd. **O. F. CASTELLORISO.**

29. **17.** 5 c. green (332) 17·00 13·00
30. 10 c. red (334) 17·00 13·00
31. 20 c. chocolate (337) 17·00 13·00
32. 25 c. blue (339) 17·00 13·00
33. **13.** 50 c. brown & lav. (305) £160 £140
34. 1 f. brown & green (306) £160 £140

(b) ITALIAN OCCUPATION.

1922. Stamps of Italy optd. **CASTELROSSO.**

1. **24.** 5 c. green 15 20
2. 10 c. red 15 20
3. 15 c. grey 15 20
4. **25.** 20 c. orange 15 20
5. **26.** 25 c. blue 15 20
20. 40 c. brown 20 45
21. 50 c. mauve 20 45
22. 60 c. red 30 70
23. 85 c. brown 30 1·00
24. **23.** 1 l. brown and green 40 1·25

1.

1923.

10. **1.** 5 c. green 25 40
11. 10 c. red 25 40
12. 25 c. blue 25 40
13. 50 c. purple 25 40
14. 1 l. brown 25 40

1930. As Ferrucci stamps of Italy optd. **CASTELROSSO.**

25. **85.** 20 c. violet 20 25
26. – 25 c. green (No. 283) 20 25
27. – 50 c. black (as No. 284) 20 25
28. – 1 l. 25 blue (No. 285) 20 25
29. – 5 l. + 2 l. red (as No. 286) 70 90

1932. As Garibaldi stamps of Italy optd. **CASTELROSSO.**

30. – 10 c. sepia 75 75
31. **99.** 20 c. brown 75 75
32. – 25 c. green 75 75
33. **99.** 30 c. black 75 75
34. – 50 c. lilac 75 75
35. – 75 c. red 75 75
36. – 1 l. 25 blue 75 75
37. – 1 l. 75 + 25 c. sepia 75 75
38. – 2 l. 55 + 50 c. red 75 75
39. – 5 l. + 1 l. violet 75 75

CAUCA O1

A State of Colombia, reduced to a Department in 1886, now uses Colombian stamps.

1.

1902. Imperf.

2. **1.** 10 c. black on red 65 70
3. 20 c. black on orange 50 60

CAVALLA (KAVALLA) E3

French P.O. in a former Turkish port, now closed.

100 centimes = 1 franc.
40 paras = 1 piastre.

1893. Stamps of France optd. **Cavalle** or surch. also in figures and words.

42. **10.** 5 c. green 2·75 2·25
43. 10 c. black on lilac 2·25 1·60
45a. 15 c. blue 2·75 2·25
46. 1 pi. on 25 c. blk. on red 3·50 2·75
47. 2 pi. on 50 c. red 11·00 9·50
48a. 4 pi. on 1 f. olive 11·00 8·00
49. 8 pi. on 2 f. brn. on blue 17·00 16·00

1902. "Blanc", "Mouchon" and "Merson" key-types inscr. "CAVALLE". The four higher values surch. also.

50. A. 5 c. green 15 12
51. B. 10 c. red 15 12
53. 15 c. orange 15 15
54. 1 pi. on 25 c. blue 35 35
55. C. 2 pi. on 50 c. brown & lav. 65 55
56. 4 pi. on 1 f. red and green 1·40 1·10
57. 8 pi. on 2 f. lilac & yellow 2·25 2·10

CAYMAN ISLANDS BC

A group of islands in the Br. W. Indies. A dependency of Jamaica until August, 1962, when it became a Crown Colony.

1969. 100 cents = 1 Jamaica Dollar.

1. 2.

1900.

1a. **1.** ½d. green 45 1·00
2. 1d. red 1·75 80

1901.

8. **2.** ½d. green 35 90
4. 1d. red 3·00 2·75
10. 2½d. blue 2·00 3·50
13. 4d. brown and blue 15·00 17·00
6. 6d. brown 12·00 11·00
14. 6d. olive and red 15·00 17·00
7. 1s. orange 25·00 27·00
15. 1s. violet and green 28·00 32·00
16. 5s. red and green £100 £130

1907. Surch. **One Halfpenny.**

17. **2.** ½d. on 1d. red 25·00 32·00

1907. Surch.

18. **2.** "½d." on 5s. red & green £100 £130
19. "1d." on 5s. red & green £100 £130
24. "2½d." on 4d. brn. & blue £900 £1000

3. 4.

1907.

38. **3.** ¼d. brown 12 25
25. **4.** ½d. green 60 65
26. 1d. red 60 60
27. 2½d. blue 3·50 4·50
28. 3d. purple on yellow 2·50 4·00
29. 4d. black & red on yellow 30·00 32·00
30a. 6d. purple 3·50 7·50
31. 1s. black on green 4·00 7·50
32. 5s. green & red on yellow 28·00 32·00
34. 10 s. green & red on green £110 £130

5. 6.

1912.

40. **5.** ¼d. brown 15 30
41. ½d. green 30 70
42. 1d. red 60 90
43. 2d. grey 60 1·00
44a. 2½d. blue 2·25 3·50
45a. 3d. purple on yellow 3·50 3·75
46. 4d. black & red on yellow 85 1·60
47. 6d. purple 1·40 2·20
48. 1s. black on green 3·00 3·50
49. 2s. pur. and blue on blue 7·50 10·00
50. 3s. green and violet 10·00 12·00
51. 5s. green & red on yellow 25·00 35·00
52b. 10s. green & red on green 50·00 65·00

1917. Surch. 1½d. with WAR STAMP in two lines.

54. 5. 1½d. on 2½d blue .. .. 45 1·25

1917. Optd. or surch. as last, but with WAR STAMP in one line.

57. 5. ½d. green 25 25
58. 1½d. on 2d. grey .. 60 1·10
56. 1½d. on 2½d. blue .. 12 15
59. 1½d. on 2½d. orange .. 60 85

1921.

69. 6. ¼d. brown 20 30
70. ½d. green 30 40
71. 1d. red 35 50
72. 1½d. brown .. 40 60
73. 2d. grey 60 90
74. 2½d. blue 70 90
75. 3d. purple on yellow .. 70 1·00
62. 4d. red on yellow .. 75 2·50
76. 4½d. green.. .. 1·10 2·50
77. 6d. claret .. .. 2·50 4·00
63. 1s. black on green .. 2·25 4·50
80. 2s. violet on blue.. .. 5·50 10·00
81. 3s. violet .. .. 12·00 16·00
82. 5s. green on yellow .. 16·00 18·00
83. 10s. red on green .. 35·00 48·00

7. Kings William IV and George V.

1932. "Assembly of Justices and Vestry" Cent.

84. 7. ¼d. brown 35 55
85. ½d. green 50 80
86. 1d. red 50 75
87. 1½d. orange 70 80
88. 2d. grey .. .. .. 90 1·10
89. 2½d. blue .. .. .. 90 1·10
90. 3d. green .. .. .. 1·75 3·50
91. 6d. purple .. .. .. 6·00 9·00
92. 1s. black and brown .. 11·00 14·00
93. 2s. black and blue .. 22·00 25·00
94. 5s. black and green .. 55·00 65·00
95. 10s. black and red .. £140 £180

1935. Silver Jubilee. As T 11 of Antigua.

96. ½d. black and green .. 12 25
97. 2½d. brown and blue .. 90 1·40
98. 6d. blue and olive .. 1·50 2·25
99. 1s. grey and purple .. 2·25 3·00

8. Cayman Islands.

1935.

100. 8. ¼d. black and brown .. 8 8
101. – ½d. blue and green .. 15 20
102. – 1d. blue and red .. 1·50 45
103. – 1½d. black and orange .. 70 45
104. – 2d. blue and purple .. 70 35
105. – 2½d. blue and black .. 3·00 70
106. 8. 3d. black and olive-green 90 75
107. – 6d. purple and black .. 3·25 3·25
108. – 1s. blue and orange .. 3·00 3·00
109. – 2s. blue and black .. 18·00 20·00
110. – 5s. green and black .. 22·00 25·00
111. – 10s. black and red .. 32·00 38·00

DESIGNS—HORIZ. ½d., 2d., 1s. Cat boat. 1d., 2s. Booby birds. 2½d., 6d., 5s. Hawksbill turtles. VERT. 1½d., 10s. Conch shells and coco-nut palms.

1937. Coronation. As T 2 of Aden.

112. ½d. green.. .. .. 30 12
113. 1d. red 30 20
114. 2½d. blue.. .. .. 60 65

13. Beach View.

17. Hawksbill Turtles.

DESIGNS—HORIZ. ¼d., 1s. Caribbean Dolphin. 1d., 3d. Map of Islands. 2½d., 5s. Cayman Schooner.

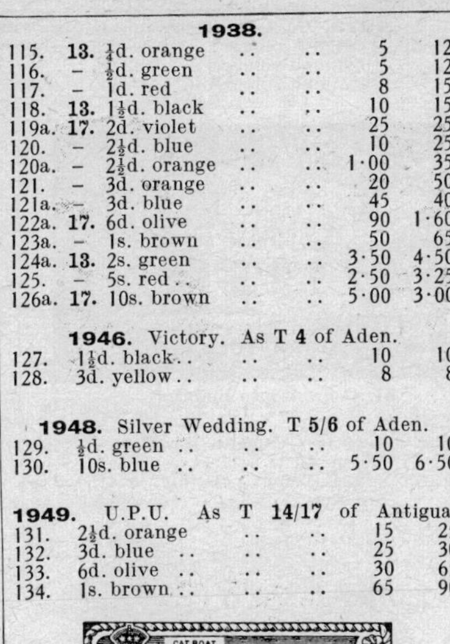

1938.

115. 13. ¼d. orange 5 12
116. – ½d. green 5 12
117. – 1d. red 8 15
118. 13. 1½d. black 10 15
119a. 17. 2d. violet 25 25
120. – 2½d. blue 10 25
120a. – 2½d. orange .. .. 1·00 35
121. – 3d. orange 20 50
121a. – 3d. blue 45 40
122a. 17. 6d. olive .. .. 90 1·60
123a. – 1s. brown 50 65
124a. 13. 2s. green .. .. 3·50 4·50
125. – 5s. red .. .. 2·50 3·25
126a. 17. 10s. brown .. .. 5·00 3·00

1946. Victory. As T 4 of Aden.

127. 1½d. black.. .. .. 10 10
128. 3d. yellow.. .. .. 8 8

1948. Silver Wedding. T 5/6 of Aden.

129. ½d. green 10 10
130. 10s. blue .. .. .. 5·50 6·50

1949. U.P.U. As T 14/17 of Antigua.

131. 2½d. orange 15 25
132. 3d. blue 25 30
133. 6d. olive 30 65
134. 1s. brown 65 90

31. Cat Boat.

1950.

135. 31. ¼d. blue and red .. 15 25
136. – ½d. violet and green .. 15 25
137. – 1d. olive and blue .. 30 40
138. – 1½d. green and brown.. 20 25
139. – 2d. violet and red .. 30 40
140. – 2½d. blue and black .. 40 20
141. – 3d. green and blue .. 80 70
142. – 6d. brown and blue .. 80 80
143. – 9d. red and green .. 1·50 1·40
144. – 1s. brown and orange .. 1·40 1·75
145. – 2s. violet and purple .. 2·50 3·25
146. – 5s. olive and violet .. 3·50 4·00
147. – 10s. black and red .. 5·50 8·00

DESIGNS: ½d. Coconut grove, Cayman Brac. 1d. Green turtle. 1½d. Making thatch rope. 2d. Cayman seamen. 2½d. Map. 3d. Parrot fish. 6d. Bluff, Cayman Brac. 9d. Georgetown Harbour. 1 s. Turtle in "crawl". 2 s. Cayman schooner. 5s. Boat-building. 10s. Government offices, Grand Cayman.

Portrait faces right on ¼d., 2d., 2½d., 4d., 1s. and 10s. values and left on others. The £1 shows a larger portrait of the Queen (vert.).

32. Lighthouse, South Sound, Grand Cayman.

1953. As 1950 issue but with portrait of Queen Elizabeth II as in T 32.

148. ¼d. blue and red .. 8 10
149. ½d. violet and green .. 8 10
150. 1d. olive and blue .. 8 10
151. 1½d. green and brown .. 8 10
152. 2d. violet and red .. 10 12
153. 2½d. blue and black .. 12 15
154. 3d. green and blue .. 20 25
155. 4d. black and blue .. 30 35
156. 6d. brown and blue .. 25 35
157. 9d. red and green .. 30 35
158. 1s. brown and orange .. 35 40
159. 2s. violet and purple .. 1·50 1·75
160. 5s. olive and violet .. 3·00 3·75
161. 10s. black and red .. 6·00 7·50
161a. £1 blue .. .. .. 12·00 14·00

1953. Coronation. As T 7 of Aden.

162. 1d. black and green .. 20 30

33. Arms of the Cayman Is.

1959. New Constitution.

163. 33. 2½d. black and blue .. 35 40
164. 1s. black and orange .. 45 45

34. Cat Boat.

1962. Portrait as in T 34.

165. – ¼d. emerald and red .. 5 8
166. 34. 1d. black and olive .. 5 8
167. – 1½d. yellow and purple 5 8
168. – 2d. blue and brown .. 5 8
169. – 2½d. violet & blue-green 5 8
170. – 3d. blue and red .. 8 10
171. – 4d. green and purple .. 12 12
172. – 6d. blue-green & sepia 15 15
173. – 9d. ultram. and purple 20 20
174. – 1s. sepia and red .. 25 30
175. – 1s. 3d. blue-green and orange-brown .. 75 95
176. – 1s. 9d. turquoise & violet 85 1·10
177. – 5s. plum and green .. 1·75 2·25
178. – 10s. olive and blue .. 2·75 2·25
179. – £1 carmine and black.. 5·50 6·50

DESIGNS—VERT. ¼d. Cayman Parrot. 9d. Angler with Kingfish. 10s. Arms. £1 Q. Elizabeth II. HORIZ. 1½d. "Schomburgkia thomsoniana" (orchid). 2d. Cayman Is. map. 2½d. Fisherman casting net. 3d. West Bay Beach. 4d. Green Turtle. 6d. Cayman Schooner. 1s. Iguana. 1s 3d. Swimming pool, Cayman Brac. 1s. 9d. Water Sports. 5s. Fort George.

1963. Freedom from Hunger. As T 10 of Aden.

180. 1s. 9d. red.. .. .. 1·25 1·25

1963. Red Cross Cent. As T 24 of Antigua.

181. 1d. red and black .. 5 5
182. 1s. 9d. red and blue .. 1·50 1·50

1964. Shakespeare. 400th Birth Anniv. As T 25 of Antigua.

183. 6d. magenta 15 20

1965. I.T.U. Cent. As T 26 of Antigua.

184. 1d. blue and purple .. 5 5
185. 1s. 3d. purple and green.. 45 50

1965. I.C.Y. As T 27 of Antigua.

186. 1d. purple and turquoise 5 5
187. 1s. green and lavender .. 40 45

1966. Churchill Commem. As T 28 of Antigua.

188. ¼d. blue 5 5
189. 1d. green 5 5
190. 1s. brown 35 40
191. 1s. 9d. violet 55 60

1966. Royal Visit. As T 29 of Antigua.

192. 1d. black and blue .. 5 5
193. 1s. 9d. black and magenta 40 45

1966. World Cup Football Championships. As T 30 of Antigua.

194. 1½d. vio., grn., lake & brn. 5 5
195. 1s. 9d. chocolate, turquoise, lake and brown .. 35 40

1966. W.H.O. Headquarters, Geneva. Inaug. T 31 of Antigua.

196. 1½d. black, green and blue 8 8
197. 1s. 3d. black, purple & ochre 45 45

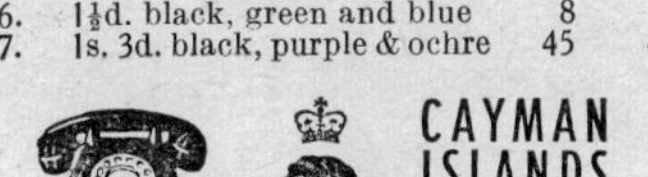

35. Telephone and Map.

1966. Int. Telephone Links.

198. 35. 4d. red, blk., bl. & grn. 15 15
199. 9d. blue, blk., red & grn. 30 30

1966. U.N.E.S.C.O. 20th Anniv. As T 33/5 of Antigua.

200. 1d. violet, red, yell. & orge. 5 5
201. 1s. 9d. yellow, violet & olive 40 45
202. 5s. black, purple & orange 1·00 1·10

36. BAC-11 Airliner over Cayman Schooner.

1966. Opening of Cayman Jet Service.

203. 36. 1s. black, blue and green 20 25
204. 1s. 9d. maroon, bl. & grn. 30 35

37. Water-skiing.

1967. Int. Tourist Year. Multicoloured.

205. 4d. Type 37 .. .. 5 5
206. 6d. Skin diving 10 10
207. 1s. Sport fishing 20 20
208. 1s. 9d. Sailing 30 30

38. Former Slaves and Emblem.

1968. Human Rights Year.

209. 38. 3d. green, black & gold 8 8
210. 9d. brown, gold & green 20 20
211. 5s. ultram., gold & green 70 75

39. Long-Jumping.

1968. Olympic Games, Mexico. Multicoloured.

212. 1s. Type 39 .. .. 25 25
213. 1s. 3d. High-jumping .. 30 30
214. 2s. Pole-vaulting 45 45

40. "The Adoration of the Shepherds" (Fabritius).

1968. Christmas. Multicoloured.

215. ¼d. Type 40 .. .. 5 5
221. ¼d. Type 40 .. .. 5 5
216. 1d. "The Adoration of the Shepherds" (Rembrandt).. .. 5 5
217. 6d. Type 40 .. .. 12 12
218. 8d. As 216 .. .. 20 20
219. 1s. 3d. Type 40 .. .. 25 25
220. 2s. As 216.. .. .. 45 45

No. 215 has brown background and No. 221 a bright purple one.

41. Cayman Thrush.

1969. Multicoloured.

222. ¼d. Type 41 .. .. 5 5
223. 1d. Brahmin Cattle .. 5 5
224. 2d. Blowholes on the coast 5 5
225. 2½d. Map of Grand Cayman 8 8
226. 3d. Georgetown scene .. 10 10
227. 4d. Royal "Poinciana" .. 12 15
228. 6d. Cayman Brac and Little Cayman on Chart .. 15 20
229. 8d. Motor vessels at berth 20 25
230. 1s. Basket making .. 25 30
231. 1s. 3d. Beach scene .. 40 50
232. 1s. 6d. Straw rope making 50 60
233. 2s. Barracuda 60 75
234. 4s. Government House .. 1·00 1·10
235. 10s. Arms of the Cayman Islands .. .. 2·25 2·50
236. £1 black, ochre and red (Queen Elizabeth II) .. 4·25 4·75

Nos. 235/6 are vert.

1969. Decimal Currency. Nos. 222/36 surch. Multicoloured.

238. 41. ¼ c. on ¼d. 5 5
239. – 1 c. on 1d. 5 5
240. – 2 c. on 2d. 5 5
241. – 3 c. on 4d. 5 5
242. – 4 c. on 2½d. 5 8

243.	–	5 c. on 6d.	8	10
244.	–	7 c. on 8d.	10	12
245.	–	8 c. on 3d.	12	15
246.	–	10 c. on 1s.	15	20
247.	–	12 c. on 1s. 3d.	30	40
248.	–	15 c. on 1s. 6d.	40	50
249.	–	20 c. on 2s.	50	60
250.	–	40 c. on 4s.	75	85
251.	–	$1 on 10s.	2·25	2·50
252.	–	$2 on £1	4·50	5·50

42. " Madonna and Child " (Vivarinin).

1969. Christmas. Multicoloured. Background colours given.

253.	42.	¼ c. orange-red	5	5
254.		¼ c. magenta	5	5
255.		¼ c. emerald	5	5
256.		¼ c. blue	5	5
257.	–	1 c. ultramarine	5	5
258.	42.	5 c. orange-red	8	10
259.	–	7 c. green	15	20
260.	42.	12 c. emerald	25	30
261.	–	20 c. purple	40	45

DESIGNS: 1 c., 7 c., 20 c. " The Adoration of the Kings " (Gossaert).

43. " Noli me tangere " (Titian).

1970. Easter. Multicoloured; frame colours given.

262.	43.	¼ c. carmine	5	5
263.		¼ c. green	5	5
264.		¼ c. brown	5	5
265.		¼ c. violet	5	5
266.		10 c. blue	15	20
267.		12 c. chestnut	25	25
268.		40 c. plum	55	55

44. Barnaby ("Barnaby Rudge").

1970. Charles Dickens. Death Cent.

269.	44.	1 c. blk., grn. & yellow	8	8
270.	–	12 c. black, brown & red	25	25
271.	–	20 c. black, brn. & gold	35	40
272.	–	40 c. black, ultram. & blue	60	65

DESIGNS: 12 c. Sairey Gamp ("Martin Chuzzlewit"). 20 c. Mr. Micawber and David ("David Copperfield"). 40 c. The "Marchioness" ("The Old Curiosity Shop").

45. Cayman Thrush.

1970. Decimal Currency. Designs as Nos. 222/36, but with values inscr. in decimal currency as in T **45**.

273.		¼ c. multicoloured (Type **45**)	5	5
274.		1 c. multicoloured	5	5
275.		2 c. multicoloured	5	5
276.		3 c. multicoloured	5	5
277.		4 c. multicoloured	5	5
278.		5 c. multicoloured	8	8
279.		7 c. multicoloured	10	10
280.		8 c. multicoloured	10	12
281.		10 c. multicoloured	12	15
282.		12 c. multicoloured	20	25
283.		15 c. multicoloured	25	30
284.		20 c. multicoloured	35	35
285.		40 c. multicoloured	70	80
286.		$1 multicoloured	2·00	2·25
287.		$2 black, ochre and red	4·00	4·50

46. The Three Wise Men.

1970. Christmas.

288.	46.	¼ c. green, grey and emer.	5	5
289.	–	1 c. black, yell. and grn.	5	5
290.	46.	5 c. grey, orange and red	8	8
291.	–	10 c. black, yell. and red	15	15
292.	46.	12 c. grey, green and blue	20	25
293.	–	20 c. black, yell. and grn.	30	35

DESIGN: 1 c., 12 c., 20 c. Nativity Scene and Globe.

47. Grand Cayman Terrapin.

1971. Turtles. Multicoloured.

294.		5 c. Type **47**	12	15
295.		7 c. Green turtle	20	25
296.		12 c. Hawksbill turtle	15	40
297.		20 c. Turtle farm	50	60

48. " Dendrophylax fawcetti ".

49. " Adoration of the Magi ". (Flemish, 15th cent.).

1971. Orchids. Multicoloured.

298.		¼ c. Type **48**	5	5
299.		2 c. " Schomburgkia thomsoniana "	8	8
300.		10 c. " Vanilla claviculata "	25	30
301.		40 c. "Oncidium variegatum"	65	70

1971. Christmas. Multicoloured.

302.		¼ c. Type **49**	8	8
303.		1 c. " The Nativity " (Parision, 14th cent.)	8	8
304.		5 c. " Adoration of the Magi " (Burgundian, 15th cent.)	10	10
305.		12 c. Type **49**	25	30
306.		15 c. As 1 c.	30	35
307.		20 c. As 5 c.	40	45

50. Turtle and Telephone Cable.

1972. Co-Axial Telephone Cable.

309.	50.	2 c. multicoloured	8	8
310.		10 c. multicoloured	25	30
311.		40 c. multicoloured	90	95

51. Court House Building.

1972. New Government Buildings. Mult.

312.		5 c. Type **51**	8	8
313.		15 c. Legislative Assembly Building	30	30
314.		25 c. Type **51**	45	45
315.		40 c. As 15 c.	65	65

1972. Royal Silver Wedding. As T **19** of Ascension but with Hawksbill Turtle and Conch Shell in background.

317.		12 c. violet	20	20
318.		30 c. green	45	50

52. $1 Coin and Note.

1972. 1st Issue of Currency. Multicoloured.

319.		3 c. Type **52**	5	5
320.		6 c. $5 Coin and note	12	12
321.		15 c. $10 Coins and note	25	30
322.		25 c. $25 Coin and note	35	40

53. " The Way of Sorrow ".

1973. Easter. Stained-Glass Windows. Multicoloured.

324.		10 c. Type **53**	15	15
325.		12 c. " Christ Resurrected "	20	20
326.		20 c. " The Last Supper " (horiz.)	30	30
327.		30 c. " Christ on the Cross " (horiz.)	40	40

54. " The Nativity " (Storza Book of Hours).

1973. Christmas.

329.	54.	3 c. multicoloured	5	5
330.	–	5 c. multicoloured	8	8
331.	54.	9 c. multicoloured	12	12
332.	–	12 c. multicoloured	20	20
333.	54.	15 c. multicoloured	25	25
334.	–	25 c. multicoloured	35	35

DESIGN: 5, 12, 25 c. " The Adoration of the Magi " (Breviary of Queen Isabella).

1973. Royal Wedding. As Type **26** of Anguilla. Background colour given. Mult.

335.		10 c. green	20	25
336.		30 c. mauve	45	50

55. White-winged Dove.

1974. Birds (1st series). Multicoloured.

337.		3 c. Type **55**	5	5
338.		10 c. Vitelline Warbler	12	12
339.		12 c. Greater Antillean Grackle	15	15
340.		20 c. West Indian Red-bellied Woodpecker	25	30
341.		30 c. Stripe-headed Tanager	35	40
342.		50 c. Yucatan Vireo	55	60

See also Nos. 383/8.

56. Old School Building.

1974. University of West Indies. 25th Anniv. Multicoloured.

343.		12 c. Type **56**	20	20
344.		20 c. New Comprehensive School	25	30
345.		30 c. Creative Arts Centre, Mona	35	40

57. Hermit Crab and Staghorn Coral.

1974. Multicoloured.

346.		1 c. Type **57**	5	5
347.		3 c. Treasure-chest and lion's paw	5	5
348.		4 c. Treasure and spotted scorpion-fish	5	5
349.		5 c. Flintlock pistol and brain coral	5	8
350.		6 c. Blackbeard and green turtle	8	8
369.		8 c. As 9 c.	12	15
351.		9 c. Jewelled pomander and pork-fish	10	12
352.		10 c. Spiny lobster & treasure	15	20
353.		12 c. Jewelled sword and dagger and sea-fan	15	15
354		15 c. Cabrit's murex and treasure	20	20
355.		20 c. Queen Conch & treasure	30	35
356.		25 c. Hogfish and treasure	30	35
357.		40 c. Gold chalice and sea-whip	50	55
358.		$1 Coat of arms	1·25	1·40
359.		$2 Queen Elizabeth II	2·40	2·60

58. Sea Captain and Ship (Shipbuilding)

1974. Local Industries. Multicoloured.

360.		8 c. Type **58**	12	12
361.		12 c. Thatcher and cottage	20	20
362.		20 c. Farmer and plantation	30	30

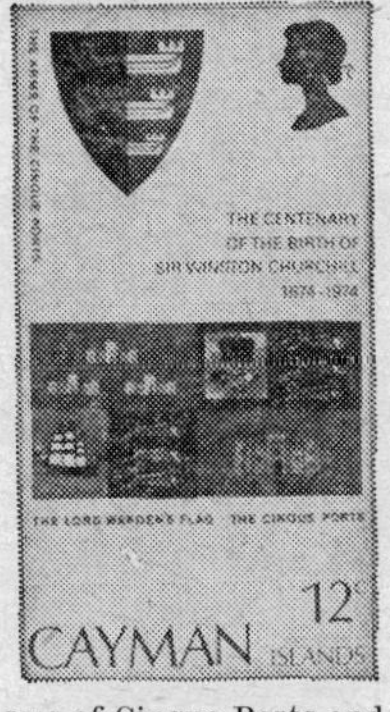

59. Arms of Cinque Ports and Lord Warden's Flag.

1974. Sir Winston Churchill. Birth Cent. Multicoloured.
380. 12 c. Type **59** 20 20
381. 50 c. Churchill's coat of arms 60 70

1975. Birds (2nd series). As Type **55**. Mult.
383. 3 c. Yellow-shafted Flicker 5 5
384. 10 c. West Indian Tree Duck 10 12
385. 12 c. Yellow Warbler .. 15 20
386. 20 c. White-bellied Dove 25 30
387. 30 c. Magnificent Frigate-bird 35 40
388. 50 c. Cayman Amazona .. 60 70

60. " The Crucifixion ".

1975. Easter. French Pastoral Staffs.
389. **60.** 15 c. multicoloured .. 20 25
390. – 35 c. multicoloured .. 35 40
DESIGN: 35 c. Pastoral staff similar to Type **60**.

61. Israel Hands.

1975. Pirates. Multicoloured.
392. 10 c. Type **61** 12 15
393. 12 c. John Fenn 20 25
394. 20 c. Thomas Anstis .. 25 30
395. 30 c. Edward Low .. 35 40

1975. Christmas. " Virgin and Child with Angels ". As T **60**.
396. 12 c. multicoloured .. 20 25
397. 50 c. multicoloured .. 60 70

62. Registered Cover Government House and Sub-Post Office.

1975. First Cayman Islands Postage Stamp. 75th Anniv. Multicoloured.
399. 10 c. Type **62** 10 12
400. 20 c. ½d. stamp and 1890–94 postmark 20 25
401. 30 c. 1d. stamp and 1908 surcharge 30 35
402. 50 c. ½d. and 1d. stamps .. 50 60

63. Seals of Georgia, Delaware and New Hampshire.

1976. American Revolution. Bicent. Mult.
404. 10 c. Type **63** 12 15
405. 15 c. S.Carolina, New Jersey and Maryland seals .. 20 25
406. 20 c. Virginia, Rhode Is. and Massachusetts seals 25 30
407. 25 c. New York, Connecticut and N. Carolina seals 30 35
408. 30 c. Pennsylvania seal, Liberty Bell and U.S. Great Seal 35 40

64. Racing Dinghies.

1976. Olympic Games, Montreal. Mult.
410. 20 c. Type **64** 25 30
411. 50 c. Racing dinghy .. 65 75

CENTRAL AFRICAN REPUBLIC O1

Formerly Ubangui Chari. An independent republic within the French Community.

1. President Boganda.

2. " Dactyloceras widenmanni ".

1959. Republic. 1st Anniv. Centres multicoloured. Frame colours given.
1. **1.** 15 f. blue 12 10
2. – 25 f. red 20 10
DESIGN—HORIZ. 25 f. As T **1** but flag behind portrait.

1960. African Technical Co-operation Commission. 10th Anniv. As T **39** of Cameroun.
3. 50 f. blue and green .. 60 45

3. Abyssinian Roller.

1960.
4. – 50 c. brown, red and turquoise (postage) .. 5 5
5. – 1 f. myrt., chest. & violet 5 5
6. – 2 f. myrt., brn. & slate-grn. 5 5
7. – 3 f. brown, red and olive 5 5
8. **2.** 5 f. brown and green .. 5 5
9. – 10 f. blue, black & green 10 5
10. – 20 f. crimson, blk. & green 15 8
11. – 85 f. crimson, black & grn. 65 40
12. – 50 f. turquoise, red and myrtle (air) 40 20
13. **3.** 100 f. vio., chest. & green 75 30
14. – 200 f. grn., vio., red & turq. 1·50 65
15. – 250 f. red, grn., bl. & mar. 1·90 1·10
16. – 500 f. brn., indigo & grn. 3·75 1·50
BUTTERFLIES—As T **2**: 50 c., 3 f. " Cymothoe sangaris ". 1 f., 2 f., " Charaxe mobilis ". 10 f. " Charaxes ameliae ". 20 f. " Charaxes zingha ". 85 f. " Drurya antimachus ". BIRDS—As T **3**: 50 f. Giant touraco. 200 f. Persian turaco. 250 f. Red headed love-birds. 500 f. Fish Eagle.
See also Nos. 42/5.

1960. Air. Olympic Games. No. 276 of French Equatorial Africa optd. with Olympic rings, **XVIIe OLYMPIADE 1960 REPUBLIQUE CENTRAFRICAINE** and surch. **250 F** and bars.
17. 250 f. on 500 f. blue, black and green .. .. 3·25 3·25

1960. National Festival. No. 2 optd. **FETE NATIONALE 1-12-1960.**
18. 25 f. multicoloured .. 55 55

4. Pasteur Institute, Bangui.

1961. Opening of Pasteur Institute, Bangui.
19. **4.** 20 f. crimson, blue-green, brown & yellow-green .. 35 30

5. U.N. Emblem, Map and Flag.

1960. Admission into U.N.O.
20. **5.** 15 f. multicoloured .. 15 12
21. 25 f. multicoloured .. 20 15
22. 85 f. multicoloured .. 75 55

1961. National Festival. Optd. with star and **FETE NATIONALE 1-12-61.**
23. **5.** 25 f. multicoloured .. 75 75

1962. Air. " Air Afrique " Airline. As T **44** of Cameroun.
24. 50 f. violet, brown & green 40 40

1962. Union of African States and Madagascar Conference, Bangui. Surch. **U.A.M. CONFERENCE DE BANGUI 25-27 MARS 1962 50 F.**
25. **5.** 50 f. on 85 f. multicoloured 60 60

1962. Malaria Eradication. As T **45** of Cameroun.
26. 25 f. + 5 f. slate 30 30

6. Hurdling. **7.** Pres. Dacko.

1962. Sports.
27 **6.** 20 f sepia, yellow & green (postage) 15 12
28. – 50 f. sepia, yellow & green 40 25
29. – 100 f. sepia, yellow and green (air) 75 55
DESIGNS—As T **6**: 50 f. Cycling. VERT. (26 × 47 mm.): 100 f. Pole-vaulting.

1962.
30. **7.** 20 f. sepia, yellow, brown and green 15 5
31. 25 f. sepia, grn., red & yell. 20 8

1962. Union of African and Malagasy States. 1st Anniv. As T **47** of Cameroun.
32. 30 f. yellow-green .. 25 20

8. Athlete.

10. " Posts and Telecommunications ".

9. " National Army ".

11. " Telecommunications ".

1962. Air. " Coupe des Tropiques " Games, Bangui.
33. **8.** 100 f. choc., blue-grn. & red 70 50

1963. Freedom from Hunger. As T **51** of Cameroun.
34. 25 f. + 5 f. blue-green, brown and bistre .. 30 30

1963. Proclamation of Republic. 3rd Anniv.
35. **9.** 20 f. multicoloured .. 12 8

1963. Air. African and Malagasy Posts and Telecommunications Union.
36. **10.** 85 f. red, buff, blue-green and green 65 45

1963. Space Telecommunications.
37. **11.** 25 f. green and purple .. 20 20
38. – 100 f. green, orge. & blue 90 90
DESIGN: 100 f. Radio waves and globe.

12. " Young Pioneers ". **13.** Boali Falls.

1963. Young Pioneers.
39. **12.** 50 f. brown, blue and turquoise-blue 30 25

1963.
40. **13.** 30 f. maroon, grn. & blue 20 12

14. Map of Africa and Sun.

1963. Air. " African Unity ".
41. **14.** 25 f. ultram., yell & blue 20 15

15. Colotis evippe.

16. " Europafrique ".

17. Diesel Train.

18. U.N.E.S.C.O. Emblem, Scales of Justice and Tree.

1963. Butterflies. Mult.
42. 1 f. Type **15** 8 8
43. 3 f. " Papilio dardanus " .. 10 10
44. 4 f. " Papilio lormieri " .. 10 10
45. 60 f. " Papilio zalmoxis " .. 50 50

1963. Air. European–African Economic Convention.
46. **16.** 50 f. brown, yellow, ochre and blue 55 40

1963. Air. Bangui-Douala Railway Project.
47. – 20 f. myrtle, mar. & brn. 15 10
48. **17.** 25 f. choc., blue & brown 20 15
49. – 50 f. violet, pur. & brown 40 25
50. – 100 f. maroon, blue-green and brown 75 50
DESIGNS: (Diesel rolling stock)—HORIZ. 20 f. Rail-car. 100 f. Locomotive. VERT. 50 f. Shunter.

1963. Declaration of Human Rights. 15th Anniv.

51. **18.** 25 f. bistre, grn. and brn. 20 15

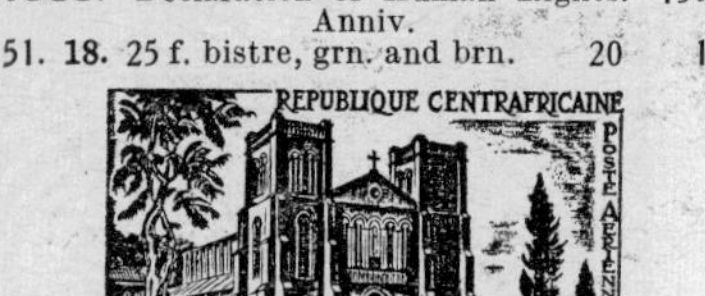

19. Bangui Cathedral.

1964. Air.

52. **19.** 100 f. chest., green & blue 70 50

20. Cleopatra, Temple of Kalabsha. **22.** " Tree " and Sun Emblem.

21. Radar Scanner.

1964. Air. Nubian Monuments Preservation.

53. **20.** 25 f.+10 f. magenta, blue and bronze-green .. 35 35

54. 50 f.+10 f. brown, olive and blue-green .. 65 65

55. 100 f. + 10 f. maroon, violet and bronze-green 1·00 1·00

1964. Air World Meteorological Day.

56. **21.** 50 f. violet, chest. & blue 40 35

1964. International Quiet Sun Years.

57. **22.** 25 f. orge., ochre & bl.-grn. 45 35

23. Map and African Heads of State. **25.** Pres. Kennedy.

24. Throwing the Javelin.

1964. Air. Equatorial African Heads of State Conf. 5th Anniv.

58. **23.** 100 f. multicoloured .. 70 50

1964. Air. Olympic Games, Tokyo.

59. **24.** 25 f. brown, green & blue 20 12

60. – 50 f. red, black and green 35 20

61. – 100 f. brown, blue & green 75 45

62. – 250 f. black, green & red 1·90 1·25

DESIGNS: 50 f. Basketball. 100 f. Running. 250 f. Diving and swimming.

1964. Air. Pres. Kennedy Memorial Issue.

63. **25.** 100 f. brown, black and reddish violet 75 65

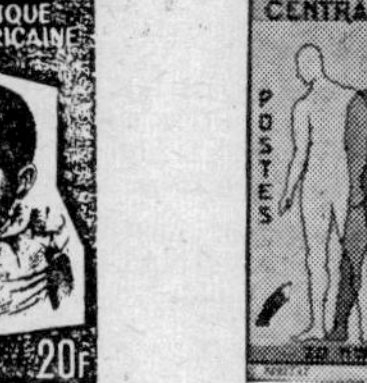

26. African Child. **27.** Silhouettes of European and African.

1964. Child Welfare. Different portraits of children. As T **26.**

64. **26.** 20 f. brown, green & pur. 15 12

65. – 25 f. brown, blue and red 20 12

66. – 40 f. brown, pur. & grn. 25 20

67. – 50 f. brown, grn. & claret 40 25

1964. French, African and Malagasy Co-operation. As T **500** of France.

68. 25 f. chocolate, red & green 20 12

1964. National Unity.

69. **27.** 25 f. multicoloured .. 20 12

28. " Economic Co-operation ".

1964. Air. " Europafrique ".

70. **28.** 50 f. green, red & yellow 40 35

29. Handclasp.

1965. Air. Int. Co-operation Year.

71. **29.** 100 f. brown, flesh, blue and yellow 75 50

30. Weather Satellite.

1965. Air. World Meteorological Day.

72. **30.** 100 f. blue and brown .. 75 50

31. Abraham Lincoln.

1965. Air. Abraham Lincoln Death Cent.

73. **31.** 100 f. flesh, indigo & green 75 50

32. Team of Oxen.

1965. Harnessed Animals in Agriculture.

74. **32.** 25 f. red, brown & green 20 12

75. – 50 f. maroon, green & blue 40 25

76. – 85 f. brown, green & blue 65 40

77. – 100 f. multicoloured .. 75 50

DESIGNS: 50 f. Ploughing with bullock. 85 f. Ploughing with oxen. 100 f. Oxen with hay cart.

33. Pouget-Maisonneuve Telegraph Instrument.

1965. I.T.U. Cent.

78. **33.** 25 f. bl., red & grn. (post) 20 12

79. – 30 f. lake and green .. 25 15

80. – 50 f. red and violet .. 35 25

81. – 85 f. indigo and purple .. 65 40

82. – 100 f. brown, blue & green (48½ × 27 mm.) (air) 75 50

DESIGNS—VERT. 30 f. Chappe's telegraph instrument. 50 f. Doignon regulator for Hughes telegraph. HORIZ. 85 f. Pouillet's telegraph apparatus. 100 f. " Relay " satellite and I.T.U. emblem.

34. Women and Loom (" To Clothe "). **35.** Coffee Plant, Hammer Grubs and Moth.

1965. " M.E.S.A.N." Welfare Campaign. Designs depicting " Five Aims ".

83. **34.** 25 f. green, chocolate and blue (postage) .. 20 12

84. – 50 f. choc., blue & green 35 20

85. – 60 f. choc., blue & green 40 30

86. – 85 f. multicoloured 65 40

87. – 100 f. blue, choc. & green (48 × 27 mm.) (air) .. 75 50

DESIGNS: 50 f. Doctor examining child, and hospital (" To care for "). 60 f. Student and school (" To instruct "). 85 f. Women and child, and harvesting scene (" To nourish "). 100 f. Village houses (" To house "). " M.E.S. A.N.—Mouvement Evolution Social Afrique Noire ".

1965. Plant Protection.

88. **35.** 2 f. purple, red & green 5 5

89. – 3 f. carm., green & black 5 5

90. – 30 f. purple, green & red 25 15

DESIGNS—HORIZ. 3 f. Coffee plant, caterpillar and hawk-moth. VERT. 30 f. Cotton plant, caterpillar and rose-moth.

1965. Surch.

91. – 2 f. on 3 f. (No. 43) .. 1·00

92. **1.** 5 f. on 15 f. .. .. 1·00

93. – 5 f. on 85 f. (No. 76) .. 12 12

94. **7.** 10 f. on 20 f. .. .. 1·00

95. – 10 f. on 100 f. (No. 77) .. 20 20

36. Camp Fire.

37. U.N. and Campaign Emblems. **38.** " Industry and Agriculture ".

1965. Scouting.

96. **36.** 25 f. red, purple and blue 20 12

97. – 50 f. brown and blue (Boy Scout) 40 25

1965. Freedom from Hunger.

98. **37.** 50 f. brown, blue & green 40 30

1965. Air. " Europafrique ".

99. **38.** 50 f. multicoloured .. 40 25

39. Mercury (statue after Coysevox). **40.** Father and Child.

1965. Air. Admission to U.P.U. 5th Anniv.

100. **39.** 100 f. black, blue & red 75 50

1965. Air. Red Cross.

101. **40.** 50 f. black, blue & red 40 25

102. – 100 f. brown, green & red (Mother and Child) .. 75 55

41. Grading Diamonds. **42.** Mbaka Porter.

1966. National Diamond Industry.

103. **41.** 25 f. brown, violet & red 20 10

1966. World Festival of Negro Arts, Dakar.

104. **42.** 25 f. multicoloured .. 20 10

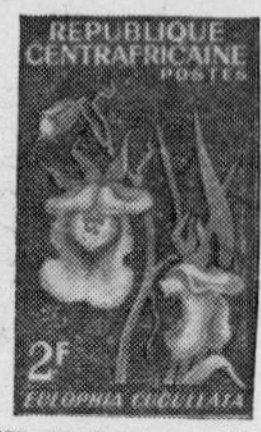

43. W.H.O. Building. **44.** "Eulophia cucullata".

1966. W.H.O. Headquarters, Geneva. Inaug.

105. **43.** 25 f. violet, blue & yell. 20 10

1966. Flowers. Multicoloured.

106. 2 f. Type **44** 5 5

107. 5 f. "Lissochilus horsfalii" 5 5

108. 10 f. "Tridactyle bicaudata" 8 5

109. 15 f. "Polystachya" .. 10 8

110. 20 f. " Eulophia alta " .. 15 10

111. 25 f. " Microcelia macrorrhynchium " 20 10

45. Aircraft and " Air Afrique " Emblem.

1966. Air. " DC–8 " Air Services. Inaug.

112. **45.** 25 f. yell., grn., blk. & bl. 20 8

46. " Deomys ferrugineus ".

1966. Rodents. Multicoloured.

113. 5 f. Type **46** 5 5

114. 10 f. "Hybomis univittatus" 8 5

115. 20 f. " Prionomys batesi " (vert.) 15 10

47. " Luna 9 ".

1966. Air. " Conquest of the Moon ". Multicoloured.

116. 130 f. Type **47** .. .. 1·00 65

117. 130 f. " Surveyor " .. 1·00 65

118. 200 f. " From the Earth to the Moon " (Jules Verne) 1·50 90

48. Cernan. **49.** U.N.E.S.C.O. Emblem.

1966. Air. Astronauts. Multicoloured.

120. 50 f. Type **48** 40 20

121. 50 f. Popovich 40 20

1966. Air. Launching of Satellite " D 1 ". As T **521** of France.

122. 100 f. purple and brown .. 75 40

1966. U.N.E.S.C.O. 20th Anniv.

123. **49.** 30 f. multicoloured .. 20 12

50. Symbols of Industry and Agriculture. **51.** Pres. Bokassa.

1966. Air. Europafrique.
124. **50.** 50 f. multicoloured .. 40 20

1967.
125. **51.** 30 f. black, ochre & grn. 25 12

1967. Provisional Stamps. (a) Postage. No. 111 surch. **XX** and value.
126. 10 f. on 25 f. multicoloured 8 5

(b) Air. No. 112 with face value altered by obliteration of figure " 2 " in " 25 ".
127. **45.** 5 f. yellow, green, black and blue 5 5

52. Bangui M'Poko Airport.

1967. Air.
128. **52.** 100 f. indigo, grn. & choc. 75 40

53. Aerial View of Fair.

1967. Air. World Fair, Montreal.
129. **53.** 100 f. choc., ult. & blue 75 40

54. Central Market, Bangui.

1967. Multicoloured.
130. 30 f. Type **54** 25 10
131. 30 f. Safari Hotel, Bangui 25 10

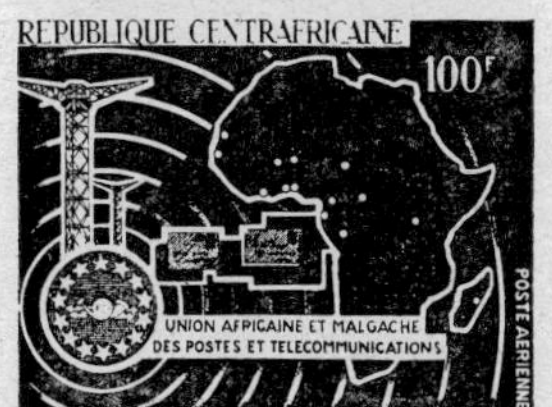

55. Map, Letters and Pylons.

1967. Air. African and Malagasy Posts and Telecommunications Union (U.A.M.P.T.). 5th Anniv.
132. **55.** 100 f. purple, grn. & red 75 40

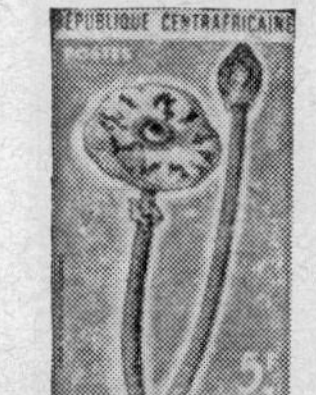

56. " Leucocoprinus africanus ". **57.** Projector, Africans and Map.

1967. Mushrooms. Multicoloured.
133. 5 f. Type **56** 5 5
134. 10 f. " Synpodia arborescens " 8 5
135. 15 f. "Phlebopus sudanicus" 10 5
136. 30 f. "Termitomyces schimperi" 25 10
137. 50 f. "Psalliota sebedulis" 40 20

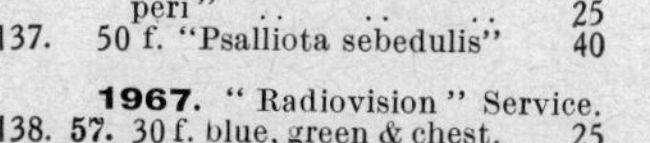

1967. " Radiovision " Service.
138. **57.** 30 f. blue, green & chest. 25 10

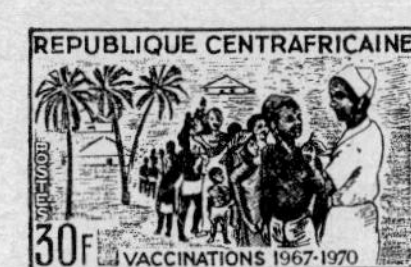

58. Coiffure. **59.** Inoculation Session.

1967. Female Coiffures. Showing different hairstyles.
139. **58.** 5 f. brown, choc. & blue 5 5
140. – 10 f. brown, choc. & red 8 5
141. – 15 f. brown, choc. & grn. 10 8
142. – 20 f. brown, choc. & orge. 15 8
143. – 30 f. brown, choc. & pur. 25 10

1967. Vaccination Programme, 1967-70.
144. **59.** 30 f. brown, green & lake 25 10

60. Douglas " DC-3 ".

1967. Aircraft.
145. **60.** 1 f. slate, green & brown (post.) 5 5
146. – 2 f. black, blue & purple 5 5
147. – 5 f. black, green & blue 5 5
148. – 100 f. brn., grn. & bl. (air) 75 40
149. – 200 f. ult., choc. & green 1·50 70
150. – 500 f. slate, red & blue 3·75 2·10

DESIGNS: 2 f. Beechcraft " Baron ". 5 f. Douglas " DC-4 ". (48 × 27 mm.): 100 f. Potez " 25-TOE ". 200 f. Junkers " 52 ". 500 f. Caravelle " 11-R ".

61. Presidents Boganda and Bokassa.

1967. Air. Republic. 9th Anniv.
151. **61.** 13 f. multicoloured .. 1·00 60

62. Primitive Shelter, Toulou.

1967. 6th Pan-African Prehistory Congress, Dakar.
152. **62.** 30 f. indigo, mar. & red 25 12
153. – 50 f. bistre, ochre & grn. 35 20
154. – 100 f. mar, brown & blue 75 30
155. – 130 f. red, green & brown 1·00 45

DESIGNS—VERT. 50 f. Kwe perforated stone. 100 f. Megaliths, Bouar. HORIZ. 130 f. Rock drawings, Toulou.

63. Pres. Bokassa.

1968. Air.
156. **63.** 30 f. multicoloured .. 20 12

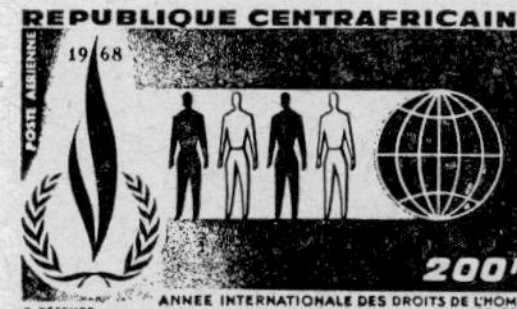

64. Human Rights Emblem, Human Figures and Globe.

1968. Air. Human Rights Year.
157. **64.** 200 f. verm., grn. & violet 1·50 80

65. Human Figure and W.H.O. Emblem.

1968. Air. W.H.O. 20th Anniv.
158. **65.** 200 f. red, blue & brown 1·50 80

66. Downhill Skiing. **67.** Parachute-landing on Venus.

1968. Air. Olympic Games, Grenoble and Mexico.
159. **66.** 200 f. brown, blue & red 1·60 80
160. – 200 f. brown, blue & red 1·60 80

DESIGN: No. 160, Throwing the javelin.

1968. Air. " Venus 4." Exploration of planet Venus.
161. **67.** 100 f. blue, turq.-green and green 75 30

68. Marie Curie and impaled Crab (of Cancer).

1968. Air. Marie Curie Commem.
162. **68.** 100 f. brown, violet & bl. 75 30

69. Refinery and Tanker.

1968. Petroleum Refinery, Port Gentil, Gabon. Inaug.
163. **69.** 30 f. blue, red, green and chestnut 15 8

1968. Air. Surch. Nos. 165/6 are obliterated with digit.
164. **47.** 5 f. on 130 f. (No. 116) .. 5 5
165. – 10 f. (100 f. No. 148) .. 8 5
166. – 20 f. (200 f. No. 149) .. 12 8
167. – 50 f. on 130 f. (No. 117) 40 25

70. "CD-8" Bulldozer.

1968. Bokassa Project.
168. **70.** 5 f. brn., blk. & grn. .. 5 5
169. – 10 f. black, brn. & grn. .. 8 5
170. – 20 f. grn., yell. & brn. .. 12 8
171. – 30 f. bl., drab & brn. .. 20 8
172. – 30 f. red, bl. & grn. .. 20 8

DESIGNS: 10 f. Baoule cattle; 20 f. Spinning-machine; 30 f. (No. 171), Automatic looms; 30 f. (No. 172), "D4-C" bulldozer.

71. Bangui Mosque.

1968. Bangui Mosque. 2nd. Anniv.
173. **71.** 30 f. flesh, green & bl. 20 8

72. Za Throwing-knife.

1968. Hunting Weapons.
174. **72.** 10 f. blue and bistre .. 10 5
175. – 20 f. green, brown & bl. 12 5
176. – 30 f. green, orge. & blue 20 8

DESIGNS: 20 f. Kpinga-Gbengue Throwing-knife; 30 f. Mbano Cross-bow.

73. " Ville de Bangui " (1958).

1968. River Craft.
177. **73.** 10 f. blue, grn. & pur. (postage) 8 5
178. – 30 f. brown, bl. & grn... 20 8
179. – 50 f. black, brn. & grn. 35 20
180. – 100 f. brn., grn. & bl. (air) 75 30
181. – 130 f. blue, grn. & pur. 1·00 45

DESIGNS: 30 f. " J.B. Gouandjia " (1968); 50 f. " Lamblin " (1944). LARGER (48 × 27 mm.): 100 f. " Pie X " (Bangui, 1894); 130 f. " Ballay " (Bangui, 1891).

74. " Madame de Savigne " (French School, 17th century).

1968. Air. " Philexafrique " Stamp Exn., Abidjan (1969).
182. **74.** 100 f. multicoloured .. 75 75

No. 182 was issued in sheets with se-tenant stamp-size label inscr. " PHILEXAFRIQUE ".

75. President Bokassa, Cotton Plantation, and Ubangui Chari stamp of 1930.

1969. Air "Philexafrique" Stamp Exn. Abidjan, Ivory Coast (2nd Issue).
183. **75.** 50 f. blk., grn. & brown 40 40

76. " Holocerina anguatal ".

1969. Air. Butterflies. Multicoloured.
184. 10 f. Type **76** 5 5
185. 20 f. " Nudaurelia dione " 12 5
186. 30 f. " Eustera troglophylla " (vert.) 20 8
187. 50 f. " Aurivillius aratus " 30 12
188. 100 f. " Epiphora albida " 65 25

77. Throwing the Javelin. **78.** Miner and Emblems.

1969. Sports. Multicoloured.
189. 5 f. Type **77** (postage) .. 5 5
190. 10 f. Start of race 8 5
191. 15 f. Football 10 5
192. 50 f. Boxing (air) 30 15
193. 100 f. Basketball .. 65 30
Nos. 192/3 are 48 × 28 mm.

1969. Int. Labour Organization. 50th Anniv.
194. **78.** 30 f. multicoloured .. 20 10
195. 50 f. multicoloured .. 30 15

79. "Apollo 8" Moon's Surface.

1969. Air. Flight of "Apollo 8" Around Moon.
196. **79.** 200 f. multicoloured 1·25 60

80. Nuremberg Spire and Toys.

1969. Air. Int Toy Fair, Nuremberg.
197. **80.** 100 f. blk., pur. & emer. 60 50

1969. Air. Napoleon Bonaparte. Birth Bicent. As T **116** of Cameroun. Multicoloured.
198. 100 f. "Napoleon as First Consul" (Girodet-Trioson) (vert.) .. 75 45
199. 130 f. "Meeting of Napoleon and Francis II of Austria" (Gros) .. 1·00 65
200. 200 f. "Marriage of Napoleon and Marie-Louise" (Rouget) .. .. 1·60 1·25

81. President Bokassa in Military Uniform.

82. Pres. Bokassa, Flag and Map.

1969.
201. **81.** 30 f. multicoloured .. 20 8

1969. A.S.E.C.N.A. 10th Anniv. As T **121** of Cameroun.
202. 100 f. blue 65 30

1970. Air. Die-stamped on gold foil.
203. **82.** 2000 f. gold .. .. 13·00

83. Ngombi.

84. F. D. Roosevelt.

83a. Flour Storage Depot.

1970. Musical Instruments.
204. – 10 f. brown, sepia & grn. 5 5
205. **83.** 15 f. brown and green .. 10 5
206. – 30 f. brown, lake & yellow 20 8
207. – 50 f. indigo and red .. 25 12
208. – 130 f. brown, olive & blue 95 35
DESIGNS—VERT. 10 f. Garayah. 130 f. Gatta and Babylon. HORIZ. 30 f. Xylophone. 50 f. Ndala.

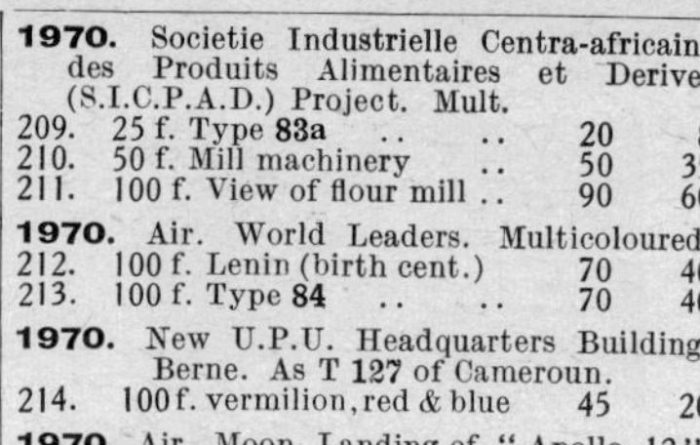

1970. Societie Industrielle Centra-africaine des Produits Alimentaires et Derives (S.I.C.P.A.D.) Project. Mult.
209. 25 f. Type **83a** 20 8
210. 50 f. Mill machinery .. 50 35
211. 100 f. View of flour mill .. 90 60

1970. Air. World Leaders. Multicoloured.
212. 100 f. Lenin (birth cent.) 70 40
213. 100 f. Type **84** 70 40

1970. New U.P.U. Headquarters Building, Berne. As T **127** of Cameroun.
214. 100 f. vermilion, red & blue 45 20

1970. Air. Moon Landing of "Apollo 12". No. 196 optd. **ATTERRISSAGE d'APOLLO 12 19 novembre 1969.**
215. **79.** 200 f. multicoloured .. 4·25 3·50

85. Pres. Bokassa.

87. Silkworm.

86. Sarki Project.

1970.
216. **85.** 30 f. multicoloured .. 90 65
217. 40 f. multicoloured .. 1·60 90

1972. "Operation Bokassa" Development Projects. Multicoloured.
218. 5 f. Type **86** (postage) .. 10 5
219. 10 f. M'Bali Ranch .. 2·00 1·50
220. 20 f. Zebu bull and herdsman (vert.) 30 15
221. 40 f. Type **87** 50 30
222. 140 f. Type **87** (air) .. 90 55

88. African Dancer.

1970. Air. "Knokphila 70" Stamp Exhib., Knokke, Belgium. Multicoloured.
223. 100 f. Type **88** 65 25
224. 100 f. African produce .. 65 25
Nos. 223/4 were issued with an intervening se-tenant label.

89. Footballer.

1970. Air. World Cup Football Championships, Mexico.
225. **89.** 200 f. multicoloured .. 1·25 70

90. Central African Republic's Pavilion, Expo 70.

1970. Air. "EXPO 70", Osaka, Japan.
226. **90.** 200 f. multicoloured .. 1·25 65

91. Dove and Cogwheel.

1970. Air. United Nations. 25th Anniv.
227. **91.** 200 f. black, yell. & blue 1·25 65

92. Presidents Mobutu, Bokassa and Tombalbaye.

1970. Air. Reconciliation with Chad and Zaire.
228. **92.** 140 f. multicoloured .. 90 40

93. Guineafowl and Partridge.

1971. Wildlife. Multicoloured.
229. 5 f. + 5 f. Type **93** .. 35 25
230. 10 f. + 5 f. Duiker and snails 50 40
231. 20 f. + 5 f. Hippopotamus, elephant and tortoise in tug-of-war 90 60
232. 30 f. + 10 f. Tortoise and cuckoo .. .. .. 1·25 80
233. 50 f. + 20 f. Monkey and leopard .. .. .. 2·50 2·00

94. Lengue Dancer.

1971. Traditional Dances. Multicoloured.
234. 20 f. + 3 f. Type **94** .. 12 8
235. 40 f. + 10 f. Lengue (diff.) 30 15
236. 100 f. + 40 f. Teke 75 40
237. 140 f. + 40 f. Englabolo .. 1·00 55

95. "Gnathonemus monteiri".

1971. Fishes. Multicoloured.
244. 10 f. Type **95** 5 5
245. 20 f. "Mornyrus proboscirostris" 12 8
246. 30 f. "Marcusenius wilverthi" 15 10
247. 40 f. "Gnathonemus elephas" 25 12
248. 50 f. "Gnathonemus curvirostris" 30 20

96. Satellite and Globe.

1971. Air. World Telecommunications Day.
249. **96.** 100 f. multicoloured 60 30

97. Berberati Cathedral.

98. Gen. De Gaulle.

1971. Consecration of Roman Catholic Cathedral, Berberati.
250. **97.** 5 f. multicoloured .. 5 5

1971. De Gaulle. 1st Death Anniv.
251. **98.** 100 f. multicoloured .. 60 30

99. Calabar Potto.

1971. Animals: Primates. Multicoloured.
252. 30 f. Grey galago (vert.) 20 15
253. 40 f. Elegant galago (vert.) 30 15
254. 100 f. Type **99** 65 35
255. 150 f. Bosman's potto .. 1·00 50
256. 200 f. Oustalet's colobus monkey .. .. .. 1·50 70

1971. Air. African and Malagasy Posts and Telecommunications Union. 10th Anniv. Similar to T **153** of Cameroun. Mult.
257. 100 f. Headquarters and carved head 60 30

100. Shepard in Capsule.

1971. Space Achievements. Multicoloured.
258. 40 f. Type **100** 20 10
259. 40 f. Gagarin in helmet .. 20 10
260. 100 f. Aldrin in Space .. 50 30
261. 100 f. Leonov in Space .. 50 30
262. 200 f. Armstrong on Moon 1·10 50
263. 200 f. "Lunokhod 1" on Moon .. .. .. 1·10 50

101. Crab Emblem.

102. "Operation Bokassa".

1971. Air. Anti-Cancer Campaign.
264. **101.** 100 f. multicoloured .. 50 50

1971. 12th Year of Independence.
265. **102.** 40 f. multicoloured .. 20 10

103. Racial Equality Year Emblem.

1971. Racial Equality Year.
266. **103.** 50 f. multicoloured .. 25 12

104. Int. I.E.Y. Emblem and Child with Toy Bricks.

1971. Air. U.N.E.S.C.O. 25th Anniv.
267. **104.** 140 f. multicoloured .. 80 40

105. African Children.

1971. Air. U.N.I.C.E.F. 25th Anniv.
268. **105.** 140 f. + 50 f. multicoloured. .. .. 1·00 70

106. Arms and Parade. **107.** Pres. G. Nasser.

1972. Bokassa Military School.
269. **106.** 30 f. multicoloured .. 15 8

1972. Air. Nasser Commem.
270. **107.** 100 f. ochre, brn. & red 50 30

108. Book Year Emblem. **109.** Heart Emblem.

1972. Int. Book Year.
271. **108.** 100 f. gold, yell. & brn. 50 30

1972. World Heart Month.
272. **109.** 100 f. red, blk. & yellow 50 30

110. First-Aid Post. **111.** Global Emblem.

1972. Red Cross Day.
273. **110.** 150 f. multicoloured .. 80 45

1972. World Telecommunications Day.
274. **111.** 50 f. blk., yellow & red 25 12

112. Boxing.

1972. Air. Olympic Games, Munich.
275. **112.** 100 f. bistre & brown 50 30
276. – 100 f. violet and green 50 30
DESIGN—VERT. No. 276, Long-jumping.

113. Pres. Bokassa and Family.

1972. Mothers' Day.
278. **113.** 30 f. multicoloured .. 15 8

114. Pres. Bokassa planting Cotton Bush. **115.** Savings Bank Building.

1972. "Operation Bokassa" Cotton Development.
279. **114.** 40 f. multicoloured .. 20 12

1972. Opening of New Postal Cheques and Savings Bank Building.
280. **115.** 30 f. multicoloured .. 15 8

116. "La Pacifique" Hotel.

1972. "Operation Bokassa" Completion of "La Pacifique" Hotel.
281. **116.** 30 f. blue, red & green 15 8

117. Hunting Scene. **118.** Postal Runner.

119. Tiling's Postal Rocket, 1931.

1972. Clock-faces from Central African HORCEN Factory. Multicoloured.
282. 5 f. Type **117** 5 5
283. 10 f. Camp fire and Native warriors 5 5
284. 20 f. Fishermen 12 5
285. 30 f. Giraffe and monkeys 15 8
286. 40 f. Warriors fighting .. 20 12

1972. "CENTRAPHILEX" Stamp Exhibition, Bangui.
287. **118.** 10 f. mult. (postage) .. 5 5
288. – 20 f. multicoloured .. 12 5
289. **119.** 40 f. orange, blue and slate-blue (air) .. 20 10
290. – 50 f. bl., slate-bl. & orge. 25 10
291. – 150 f. grey, orge. & brn. 80 40
292. – 200 f. blue, orge. & brn. 1·10 55
DESIGNS—As T **118**. HORIZ. Protestant Youth Centre. As T **119**. VERT. 50 f. "DC-3" aircraft and camel postman. 150 f. "Sirio" satellite and rocket. HORIZ. 200 f. "Intelstat 4" satellite and rocket.

120. University Buildings.

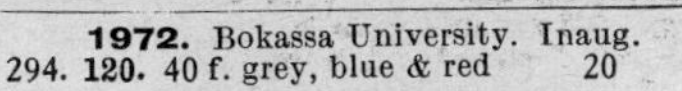

1972. Bokassa University. Inaug.
294. **120.** 40 f. grey, blue & red 20 12

121. Mail Van.

1972. World U.P.U. Day.
295. **121.** 100 f. multicoloured .. 50 30

122. Paddy Field.

1972. Bokassa Plan. State Farms. Mult.
296. 5 f. Type **122** 5 5
297. 25 f. Rice cultivation .. 12 8

123. Four Linked Arrows. **124.** Hotel Swimming Pool.

1972. Air. "Europafrique".
298. **123.** 100 f. multicoloured .. 55 30

1972. Air. Munich Olympic Gold Medal Winners. Nos. 275/6 optd. as listed below.
299. **112.** 100 f. bistre and brown 50 25
300. – 100 f. violet and green 50 25
OVERPRINTS: No. 299, **POIDS MOYEN-LEMECHEV-MEDAILLE D'OR.** No. 300. **LONGUEUR - WILLIAMS - MEDAILLE D'OR.**

1972. Opening of Hotel St. Sylvestre.
302. **124.** 30 f. brn., blue-grn. & grn. 15 8
303. – 40 f. pur., grn. & blue 20 12
DESIGN: 40 f. Facade of Hotel.

125. Landing Module and Lunar Rover on Moon.

1972. Air. Moon Flight of "Apollo 16".
304. **125.** 100 f. green, blue & grey 50 30

126. "Virgin and Child" (F. Pesellino).

1972. Air. Christmas. Multicoloured.
305. 100 f. Type **126** 50 25
306. 150 f. "Adoration of the Child" (F. Lippi) .. 85 45

127. Learning to Write.

1972. "Central African Mothers". Mult.
307. 5 f. Type **127** 5 5
308. 10 f. Baby-care 5 5
309. 15 f. Dressing hair .. 8 5
310. 20 f. Learning to read .. 10 5
311. 180 f. Suckling baby .. 1·00 40
312. 190 f. Learning to walk .. 1·10 45

128. Louys (marathon), Athens, 1896.

1972. Air. Revival of Olympic Games. 75th Anniv.
313. **128.** 30 f. pur., brn. & green 15 5
314. – 40 f. green, blue & brn. 20 10
315. – 50 f. violet, blue & red 25 10
316. – 100 f. pur., brn. & grey 55 25
317. – 150 f. blk., blue & pur. 85 40
DESIGNS: 40 f. Barrelet (sculling), Paris, 1900. 50 f. Prinstein (triple-jump), St. Louis, U.S.A., 1904. 100 f. Taylor (400 m. freestyle swimming), London, 1908. 150 f. Johansson (Graeco-Roman wrestling), Stockholm, 1912.

129. W.H.O. Emblem, Doctor and Nurse.

1973. Air. World Health Organization. 25th Anniversary.
318. **129.** 100 f. multicoloured .. 45 30

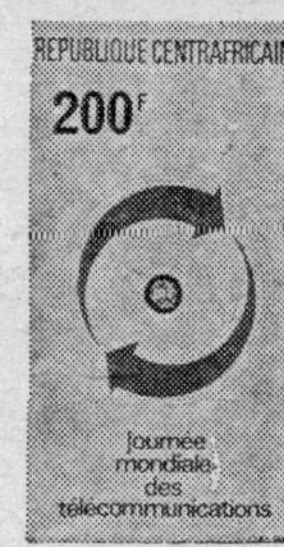

130. "Telecommunications".

1973. World Telecommunications Day.
319. **130.** 200 f. orge., blue & blk. 90 60

131. Harvesting.

1973. World Food Programme. 10th Anniv.
320. **131.** 50 f. multicoloured .. 25 12

132. "Garcinia punctata".

1973. "Flora". Multicoloured.
321. 10 f. Type **132** 5 5
322. 20 f. "Bertiera racemosa" 10 5
323. 30 f. "Carynanthe pachyceras" 12 8
324. 40 f. "Combretodendron africanum" 20 12
325. 50 f. "Xylopia villosa" .. 25 15

133. Pygmy Chameleon.

1973.
326. **133.** 15 f. multicoloured .. 8 5

134. "Mboyo Ndili".

1973. Caterpillars. Multicoloured.
327. 3 f. Type **134** 5 5
328. 5 f. "Piwili" 5 5
329. 25 f. "Loulia Konga" .. 12 8

1973. African Solidarity "Drought Relief". No. 321 surch. **SECHERESSE SOLIDARITE AFRICAINE** and value.
330. **132.** 100 f. on 10 f. mult. .. 45 35

1973. U.A.M.P.T. As Type **182** of Cameroun.
331. 100 f. red, brn. & olive-brn. 45 35

1973. Air. African Fortnight, Brussels. As Type **183** of Cameroun.
332. 100 f. brn., violet & yell.-brn. 45 35

135. African and Symbolic Map.

1973. Air. Europafrique.
333. **135.** 100 f. red, grn. & brn. 45 35

136. Bird with Letter.

1973. Air. World U.P.U. Day.
334. **136.** 200 f. multicoloured .. 90 70

137. Weather Map.

1973. Air. I.M.O./W.M.O. Cent.
335. **137.** 150 f. multicoloured .. 65 35

138. Copernicus.

1973. Air. Copernicus. 500th Birth Anniv.
336. **138.** 100 f. multicoloured .. 45 35

139. Pres. Bokassa. 140. Blast-off.

1973.
337. **139.** 1 f. multicoloured (post.) 5 5
338. 2 f. multicoloured .. 5 5
339. 3 f. multicoloured .. 5 5
340. 5 f. multicoloured .. 5 5
341. 10 f. multicoloured .. 5 5
342. 15 f. multicoloured .. 8 5
343. 20 f. multicoloured .. 10 5
344. 30 f. multicoloured .. 15 8
345. 40 f. multicoloured .. 20 15
346. – 50 f. multicoloured (air) 25 15
347. – 100 f. multicoloured 45 35
DESIGNS-SQUARE (35×35 mm.). 50 f. Pres. Bokassa facing left. VERT. (26×47 mm.). 100 f. Pres. Bokassa in military uniform.

1973. Air. Moon Flight of "Apollo 17".
348. **140.** 50 f. red, grn. & brn. 25 15
349. – 65 f. grn., red & purple 30 20
350. – 100 f. blue, brn. & red 45 35
351. – 150 f. grn., brn. & red-brn. 65 50
352. – 200 f. grn., red and blue 90 70

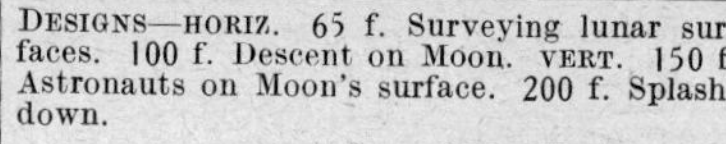
DESIGNS—HORIZ. 65 f. Surveying lunar surfaces. 100 f. Descent on Moon. VERT. 150 f. Astronauts on Moon's surface. 200 f. Splashdown.

141. Interpol Emblem within "Eye". 142. St. Theresa.

1973. Interpol. 50th Anniv.
353. **141.** 50 f. multicoloured .. 25 15

1973. Air. St. Theresa of Lisieux. Birth Cent.
354. **142.** 500 f. blue & light blue 2·25 1·40

143. Main Entrance.

1974. Opening of "Catherine Bokassa" Mother-and-Child Centre.
355 **143.** 30 f. brn., red & blue 15 8
356. – 40 f. brn., blue & red 20 12
DESIGN: 40 f. General view of Centre.

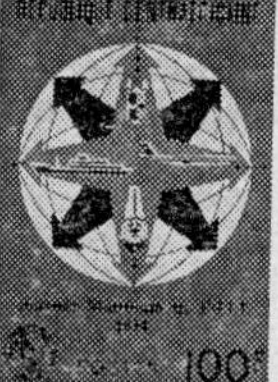

144. Cigarette-packing Machine. 145. "Telecommunications".

1974. "Centra" Cigarette Factory.
357. **144.** 5 f. pur., green & red .. 5 5
358. – 10 f. blue, green & brn. 5 5
359. – 30 f. blue, green & red 15 8
DESIGNS: 10 f. Administration block and factory building. 30 f. Tobacco warehouse.

1974. World Telecommunications Day.
360. **145.** 100 f. multicoloured .. 40 30

146. "Peoples of the World". 147. Mother and Baby.

1974. World Population Year.
361. **146.** 100 f. green, red & brown 40 30

1974. World Health Organization. 26th Anniv.
362. **147.** 100 f. brn., bl. & grn... 40 30

148. Letter and U.P.U. Emblem. 150. Modern Building.

149. Battle Scene.

1974. Universal Postal Union. Centenary.
363. **148.** 500 f. red, grn. & brn. 2·00 1·50

1974. "Activities of Forces' Veterans". Multicoloured.
364. 10 f. Type **149** 5 5
365. 15 f. "Today" (Peace-time activities) 5 5
366. 20 f. Planting rice .. 8 5
367. 25 f. Cattle-shed 10 8
368. 30 f. Workers hoeing .. 12 8
369. 40 f. Veterans' houses .. 15 10

1974. Central African Customs and Economics Union. 10th Anniv. As Nos. 734/5 of Cameroun.
370. 40 f. multicoloured (post.) 20 10
371. 100 f. multicoloured (air) 45 30

1975. "OCAM City" Project.
372. **150.** 30 f. multicoloured .. 15 8
373. – 40 f. multicoloured .. 20 10
374. – 50 f. multicoloured .. 25 15
375. – 100 f. multicoloured .. 45 25
DESIGNS: Nos. 373/5, Various views similar to Type **150**.

1975. "J. B. Bokassa Pilot Village Project". As Type **150**, but inscr. "VILLAGE PILOTE J. B. BOKASSA".
376. 25 f. multicoloured .. 10 5
377. 30 f. multicoloured .. 15 8
378. 40 f. multicoloured .. 20 10
DESIGNS: Nos. 376/8, Various views similar to Type **150**.

151. President Bokassa's Sword.

1975. "Homage to President Bokassa". Multicoloured.
379. 30 f. Type **151** (postage) .. 15 8
380. 40 f. President Bokassa's baton 20 12
381. 50 f. Bokassa in Pres. uniform (air) 25 15
382. 100 f. Pres. Bokassa in cap and cape 45 30
Nos. 381 and 382 are vertical, 36×49 mm.

152. Foreign Minister and Ministry.

1975. Government Buildings. Mult.
383. 40 f. Type **152** 20 12
384. 40 f. Television Centre .. (36×23 mm.) 20 12

152. "No Entry".

1975. Road Signs.
385. 5 f. red and blue 5 5
386. 10 f. red and blue 5 5
387. 20 f. red and blue 10 5
388. 30 f. multicoloured .. 15 8
389. 40 f. multicoloured .. 20 10
SIGNS: 10 f. "Stop". 20 f. "No stopping". 30 f. "School". 40 f. "Crossroads".

154. Buffon's Gazelle. 155. Carved Wooden Mask.

1975. Wild Animals. Multicoloured.
390. 10 f. Type **154** 5 5
391. 15 f. Warthog 8 5
392. 20 f. Defassa buck .. 10 5
393. 30 f. Lion 15 8

1975. AIR. "Arphila" International Stamp Exhibition. Paris.
394. **155.** 100 f. red, rose & blue 40 30

156. Dr. Schweitzer and Canoe. 157. Forest Scene.

1975. Air. Dr. Albert Schweitzer. Birth Cent.
395. **156.** 200 f. blk., bl. & brn... 80 60

1975. Central African Woods.
396. **157.** 10 f. brn., grn. & lake 5 5
397. – 15 f. brn., grn. & bl... 8 5
398. – 50 f. bl., brn. & grn... 20 15
399. – 100 f. brn., bl. & grn... 40 30
400. – 150 f. bl., brn. & grn... 60 45
401. – 200 f. brn., red & grn. 80 60
DESIGNS—VERT. 15 f. Cutting sapeles. HORIZ. 50 f. Mobile crane. 100 f. Log stack. 150 f. Floating logs. 200 f. Timber-sorting yard.

158. African Women.

1975. International Women's Year.
402. **158.** 40 f. multicoloured .. 20 10
403. 100 f. multicoloured .. 40 30

159. River-boat "Jean Bedel Bokassa".

1976. Air. Multicoloured.
404. 30 f. Type **159** 15 8
405. 40 f. Frontal view of "Jean Bedel Bokassa" .. 20 10

160. Co-operation Monument.

1976. Air. Central African-French Co-operation and Visit of President Giscard d' Estaing. Multicoloured.
406. 100 f. Type **160** 45 25
407. 200 f. Presidents Giscard d' Estaing, Bokassa and flags 90 50

161. Alexander Graham Bell.

1976. Telephone Centenary.
408. **161.** 100 f. black and yellow 45 25

162. Telecommunications Satellite and Emblems.

1976. World Telecommunications Day.
409. 162. 100 f. pur., blue & grn. 45 25

163. Rocket on Launch-pad.

1976. Apollo-Soyuz Space Link. Multicoloured.
410. 40 f. Type **163** (postage) .. 20 10
411. 50 f. Blast-off .. 25 12
412. 100 f. "Soyuz" in flight (air) 45 25
413. 200 f. "Apollo" in flight 90 50
414. 300 f. Crew meeting in space 1·40 70

1976. Air. American Revolution Bicent. Multicoloured.
416. 100 f. Type **164** .. 45 25
417. 125 f. Black Watch soldier 60 30
418. 150 f. German Dragoons' officer 70 35
419. 200 f. British Grenadiers' officer 90 50
420. 250 f. American Ranger .. 1·10 55

MILITARY FRANK STAMPS

1963. Optd. **FM.** No. M1 also has the value obliterated with two bars. Centre multicoloured; frame colour given.
M 35. 1. (–) on 15 f. blue .. 2·25
M 36. 15 f. blue .. .. 2·75

OFFICIAL STAMPS

O 1. Arms. O 2. Arms.

1965.
O 78. O 1. 1 f. multicoloured .. 5 5
O 79. 2 f. multicoloured .. 5 5
O 80. 5 f. multicoloured .. 5 5
O 81. 10 f. multicoloured .. 8 5
O 82. 20 f. multicoloured .. 12 10
O 83. 30 f. multicoloured .. 25 20
O 84. 50 f. multicoloured .. 40 20
O 85. 100 f. multicoloured 75 30
O 86. 130 f. multicoloured 1·25 60
O 87. 200 f. multicoloured 1·50 1·00

1971.
O 238. O 2. 5 f. multicoloured .. 5 5
O 239. 30 f. multicoloured 15 10
O 240. 40 f. multicoloured 20 12
O 241. 100 f. multicoloured 50 25
O 242. 140 f. multicoloured 90 25
O 243. 200 f. multicoloured 1·10 55

POSTAGE DUE STAMPS

D 1. "Sternotomis gama" (Beetle).

1962. Beetles.
D 33. 50 c. brown and blue-green 5 5
D 34. 50 c. blue-green and brown 5 5
D 35. 1 f. brown and green .. 5 5
D 36. 1 f. green and brown .. 5 5
D 37. 2 f. pink and black .. 5 5
D 38. 2 f. green, black & pink 5 5
D 39. 5 f. green and chestnut .. 5 5
D 40. 5 f. green and chestnut .. 5 5
D 41. 10 f. green, black & drab 8 8
D 42. 10 f. drab, black & green 8 8
D 43. 25 f. brown, blk. & emerald 15 15
D 44. 25 f. brown, emerald & blk. 15 15

DESIGNS: Nos. D 33, Type D 1. D 34, "Sternotomis virescens". D 35, "Augosoma centaurus". D 36, "Phosphorus virescens" and "Ceroplesis carabarica". D 37, "Ceroplesis S.P.". D 38, "Cetoine scaraboidae". D 39, "Cetoine scaraboidae". D 40, "Macrorhina S.P.". D 41, "Taurina longiceps". D 42, "Phryneta leprosa". D 43, "Monohamus griseoplagiatus". D 44, "Jambonus trifasciatus".

The two designs in each value are arranged in "tete-beche" pairs throughout the sheet.

CENTRAL LITHUANIA E2

Became temporarily independent in 1918 and was subsequently absorbed by Poland.
100 fenigow = mark.

1.

2.

1920. Imperf. or perf.
1. 1. 25 f. red 5 5
20. 25 f. green 5 5
2. 1 m. blue 5 5
21. 1 m. brown 5 5
3. 2 m. violet 5 5
22. 2 m. yellow 5 5

1920. Stamps of Lithuania of 1919 surch. **SRODKOWA LITWA POCZTA,** new value and Arms of Poland and Lithuania. Perf.
4. 2. 2 m. on 15 s. violet .. 1·10 1·10
5. 4 m. on 10 s red 80 80
6. 4 m. on 20 s. blue .. 1·10 1·10
7. 4 m. on 30 s. orange .. 80 80
8. 3. 6 m. on 50 s. green .. 1·60 1·60
9. 6 m. on 60 s. red and violet 1·60 1·60
10. 6 m. on 75 s. red & yellow 1·60 1·60
11. 4. 10 m. on 1 a. red & grey 5·00 5·00
12. 10 m. on 3 a. red & brown 32·00 32·00
13. 10 m. on 5 a. red and green 30·00 30·00

1920. Imperf. or perf. Inscr. "LITWA SRODKOWA".
14. 2. 25 f. grey 5 5
15. – 1 m orange 5 5
16. – 2 m. claret 5 5
17. – 4 m. olive and yellow .. 5 5
18. – 6 m. grey and red .. 10 10
19. – 10 m. yellow and brown 12 12

DESIGNS: 1 m. Warrior. 2 m. Ostrabrama Sanctuary, Vilna. 4 m. Cathedral, Vilna. 6 m. Royal Regalia. 10 m. Gen. Zeligowski.

1921. Surch. **NA SLASK** and new value. Imperf. or perf.
23. 1. 25 f. + 2 m. red 10 10
24. 25 f. + 2 m. green .. 10 10
25. 1 m. + 2 m. blue .. 15 15
26. 1 m. + 2 m. brown .. 15 15
27. 2 m. + 2 m. violet .. 15 15
28. 2 m. + 2 m. yellow .. 15 15

1921. Red Cross. Nos. 16/17 surch. with cross and value. Imperf. or perf.
29. 2 m. + 1 m. claret .. 15 15
30. 4 m. + 1 m. olive & yellow 20 20

1921. White Cross. As Nos. 16, 17 and 19, but with cross and value in white added. Imperf. or perf.
31. 2 m. + 1 m. claret .. 8 8
32. 4 m. + 1 m. olive & yellow 8 8
33. 10 m. + 2 m. yellow & brn. 8 8

8. St. Nicholas Cathedral.

9. St. Stanislaus Cathedral.

1921. Imperf. or perf.
34. 8. 1 m. yellow and slate .. 5 5
35. 9. 2 m. green and red .. 5 5
36. – 3 m. green 5 5
37. – 4 m. brown 5 5
38. – 5 m. brown 5 5
39. – 6 m. buff and green .. 5 5
40. – 10 m. buff and purple .. 8 8
41. – 20 m. buff and brown .. 12 12

DESIGNS—HORIZ. 4 m. Queen Jadwiga and King Wladislaw Jagiello. 6 m. Tyschkewitsch Castle. 10 m. Union of Lithuania and Poland, 1569. 20 m. Kosciuszko and Micklewicz. VERT. 3 m. Arms (Eagle). 5 m. Arms (Shield).

16. Entry into Vilna.

17. General Zeligowski.

1921. Entry of Gen. Zeligowski into Vilna Anniv. Imperf. or perf.
42. 16. 100 m. blue and bistre .. 45 45
43. 17. 150 m. green and brown 65 65

19. Arms.

DESIGNS—HORIZ. 50 m. National Assembly. Vilna. VERT. 10 m. Girl Sower. 75 m. Industry.

1922. Opening of National Parliament. Inscr. "SEJM—WILNIE". Imperf. or perf.
44. – 10 m. brown 30 45
45. 19. 25 m. red and buff .. 30 45
46. – 50 m. blue 45 55
47. – 75 m. lilac 55 75

POSTAGE DUE STAMPS

D 1. Government Offices.

DESIGNS—HORIZ. 2 m. Island. VERT. 1 m. Castle Hill, Vilna. 3 m. City Gate, Vilna. 5 m. St. Stanislaus Cathedral. 20 m. St. Nicholas Cathedral.

1921. Inscr. "DOPLATA". Imperf. or perf.
D 23. D 1. 50 f. red 5 5
D 24. – 1 m. green 5 5
D 25. – 2 m. purple .. 5 5
D 26. – 3 m. purple .. 5 5
D 27. – 5 m. purple .. 5 5
D 28. – 20 m. red 10 10

CEPHALONIA AND ITHACA E2

(ITALIAN OCCUPATION)

Two of the Greek Ionian Islands off the W. coast of Greece, under Italian occupation in 1941.

1941. Stamps of Greece optd. **ITALIA Occupazione Militare Italiana isole Cefalonia e Itaca** across a pair of stamps.

PRICES. Prices are for unsevered pairs. Single stamps from severed pairs are worth ½ unused and ½ used prices.

(a) On postage stamps of 1937.
1. 69. 5 l. blue and brown .. 8 8
2. – 10 l. brown and blue .. 8 8
3. – 20 l. green and black .. 12 12
4. – 40 l. black and green .. 12 12
5. – 50 l. black and brown .. 8 8
6. – 80 l. brown and violet .. 15 15
7. 72. 1 d. green .. .. 4·50 3·00
8. 72a. 1 d. 50 green .. 6·00 3·25
9. – 2 d. blue 8 8
10. – 5 d. red 65 40
11. – 6 d. olive 70 40
12. – 7 d. brown 85 45
13. 72. 8 d. blue .. .. 9·00 6·00
14. – 10 d. brown .. .. 3·25 2·10
15. – 15 d. green .. .. 6·00 3·25
16. – 25 d. blue .. .. 14·00 10·00
17. 72a. 30 d. red .. .. 21·00 12·00

(b) On air stamps of 1938 and 1935.
18. D 2. 50 l. brown (No. 521) .. 29·00 21·00
19. 66. 1 d. red .. .. 1·90 1·50
20. – 2 d. blue 30 25
21. – 5 d. mauve 65 40
22. – 7 d. blue .. .. 1·50 85
23. – 25 d. red .. .. 18·00 15·00
24. – 30 d. green .. .. 17·00 10·00
25. – 50 d. mauve .. .. £150 90·00
26. – 100 d. brown .. .. 85·00 38·00

(c) On Charity Tax stamps.
27. D 2. 10 l. red (No. C 498) .. 2·10 1·75
28. C 14. 10 l. red .. .. 1·75 1·25
29. 50 l. green (No. C 525) 40 40
30. 50 l. green (No. C 554) .. 40 40
31. 1 d. blue (No. C526) .. 3·50 2·25

CEYLON BC

An island to the S. of India formerly under British administration, then a self-governing Dominion. The island became a Republic within the Commonwealth on 22 May 1972 and was renamed Sri Lanka (q.v.).
1872. 100 cents = 1 rupee.

1.

2.

3.

4.

1857. Imperf.
4. 1. ½d. lilac .. .. .. 50·00 35·00
5. 3. 1d. blue .. .. .. £120 11·00
8. 2d. green .. .. .. £125 35·00
9. 2. 4d. red £25000 £1900
10. 3. 5d. brown .. .. £350 50·00
11. 6d. brown .. .. £600 90·00
13. 2. 8d. brown £3000 £750
14. 9d. brown £5500 £550
15. 3. 10d. orange .. .. £350 90·00
16. 1s. violet £2000 £130
17. 2. 1s. 9d. green £250 £200
19. 2s. blue £1750 £550

The prices of these imperf. stamps vary greatly according to condition. The above prices are for fine copies with four margins. Poor to medium specimens are worth much less.

1861. Perf.
71. 1. ½d. lilac .. .. .. 5·50 3·50
74. 3. 1d. blue .. .. .. 8·50 2·15
78. 2d. green .. .. .. 17·00 4·25
98. 2d. yellow .. .. .. 7·50 2·75
100. 2. 4d. red .. .. .. 7·00 3·50
27. 3. 5d. brown .. .. 30·00 7·50
103. 5d. green .. .. .. 7·50 7·00
106. 6d. brown .. .. .. 8·00 2·75
108. 2. 8d. brown .. .. 8·00 5·50
110. 9d. brown .. .. .. 7·00 4·25
53a. 3. 10d. red .. .. .. 50·00 8·00
111a. 10d. orange .. .. 11·00 3·50
114. 1s. violet .. .. .. 17·00 4·00
116. 2. 2s. blue .. .. .. 17·00 4·50

1866. The 3d. has portrait in circle.
119. 4. 1d. blue .. .. .. 4·50 2·75
120. – 3d. red .. .. .. 13·00 7·00

6.

7.

16.

1872. Various frames.
121. 6. 2 c. brown .. .. 1·10 30
147. 2 c. green 30 10
256. 2 c. orange-brown .. 35 15
122. 7. 4 c. grey .. .. 3·50 30
148. 4 c. purple 35 10
149. 4 c. red .. .. 1·10 2·40
258. 4 c. yellow 35 45
150a. – 8 c. yellow .. .. 1·60 2·40
126. – 16 c. violet .. .. 8·50 1·75
127. – 24 c. green .. .. 7·00 1·75
128. – 32 c. grey .. .. 12·00 4·00
129. – 36 c. blue .. .. 12·00 4·00
130. – 48 c. red .. .. 12·00 4·00
131. – 64 c. brown .. .. 24·00 10·00
132. – 96 c. grey .. .. 18·00 7·00
201. 16. 1 r. 12 red .. .. 4·50 4·50
138. 2 r. 50 red .. .. 75·00 32·00
249. 2 r. 50 purple on red .. 8·00 8·50

1882. Nos. 127 and 131 surch. in words and figures.
142. – 16 c. on 24 c. green .. 7·00 4·00
143. – 20 c. on 64 c. brown .. 4·50 1·75

1885. As Nos. 148/132 surch. **Postage & Revenue** and value in words.
177. 5 c. on 4 c. purple .. 50·00 42·00
178. 5 c. on 4 c. red.. .. 2·10 30
179. 5 c. on 8 c. yellow .. 4·25 1·40
180. 5 c. on 16 c. violet .. 6·00 3·50
154. 5 c. on 24 c. green .. £180 14·00
182. 5 c. on 24 c. purple .. 50·00 28·00
155b. 5 c. on 32 c. grey .. 6·00 4·00
156. 5 c. on 36 c. blue .. 8·50 1·75
157. 5 c. on 48 c. red .. 28·00 6·00
158. 5 c. on 64 c. brown .. 5·50 1·75
159. 5 c. on 96 c. grey .. 24·00 8·50

1885. As Nos. 126/249 surch. with new value in words.
161. 10 c. on 16 c. violet .. £140 £100
162. 10 c. on 24 c. green .. 70·00 20·00
185. 10 c. on 24 c. purple .. 4·00 2·75
163. 10 c. on 36 c. blue .. 35·00 25·00
174. 10 c. on 64 c. brown .. 10·00 10·00
186. 15 c. on 16 c. violet .. 4·00 3·25
165. 20 c. on 24 c. green .. 10·00 5·50
166a. 20 c. on 32 c. grey .. 6·00 5·50
167a. 25 c. on 32 c. grey .. 4·00 2·10
168. 28 c. on 48 c. red .. 6·00 2·75
169. 30 c. on 36 c. blue .. 4·25 4·25
170. 56 c. on 96 c. grey .. 6·00 4·50
176. 1 r. 12 on 2 r. 50 red .. 9·00 8·50

1885. Surch. **REVENUE AND POSTAGE 5 CENTS.**
187. – 5 c. on 8 c. lilac (as No. 150a) .. 2·00 30

1885. As Nos. 126/32 surch. in words and figures.
188. 10 c. on 24 c. purple .. 4·00 2·10
189. 15 c. on 16 c. yellow .. 5·00 2·75
190. 28 c. on 32 c. grey .. 4·00 1·20
191. 30 c. on 36 c. olive .. 5·50 4·50
192. 56 c. on 96 c. grey .. 5·50 4·00

1885. Surch. **1 R. 12 C.**
193. 16. 1 r. 12 on 2 r. 50 red .. 10·00 11·00

17. 18.

19.

1886.
245. 17. 3 c. brown and green .. 40 30
257. 3 c. green 35 15
195. 18. 5 c. purple 30 8
259. 17. 6 c. red and black .. 35 15
260. 12 c. olive and red .. 95 1·00
197. 15 c. olive 50 20
261. 15 c. blue 95 60
198. 25 c. brown 60 70
199. 28 c. grey .. .. 1·25 65
247. 30 c. mauve and brown 1·00 70
262. 75 c. black and brown.. 1·75 1·10
263. 19. 1 r. 50 red .. .. 8·50 8·50
264. 2 r. 25 blue .. .. 11·00 11·00

1887. Nos. 148/9 surch.
A. Surch. **TWO CENTS.**
202. 7. 2 c. on 4 c. purple .. 20 15
203. 2 c. on 4 c. red.. .. 20 20
B. Surch. **TWO.**
204. 7. 2 c. on 4 c. purple .. 42 15
205. 2 c. on 4 c. red.. .. 35 15
C. Surch. **2 Cents** and bar.
206. 7. 2 c. on 4 c. purple .. 7·00 6·00
207. 2 c. on 4 c. red.. .. 50 60
D. Surch. **Two Cents** and bar.
208. 7. 2 c. on 4 c. purple .. 6·50 8·00
209. 2 c. on 4 c. red.. .. 50 35
E. Surch. **2 Cents** without bar.
210. 7. 2 c. on 4 c. purple .. 6·00 6·00
211. 2 c. on 4 c. red.. .. 85 35

1890. Surch. **POSTAGE Five Cents REVENUE.**
233. 17. 5 c. on 15 c. olive .. 35 45

1891. Surch. **FIFTEEN CENTS.**
239. 17. 15 c. on 25 c. brown .. 2·75 2·75
240. 15 c. on 28 c. grey .. 2·75 2·75

1892. Surch. **3 Cents** and bar.
241. 7. 3 c. on 4 c. purple .. 30 30
242. 3 c. on 4 c. red.. .. 48 85
243. 17. 3 c. on 28 c. grey .. 30 45

1899. Surch. **Six Cents.**
250. 17. 6 c. on 15 c. olive .. 25 25

1899. Surch. with value and bar.
254. 16. 1 r. 50 on 2 r. 50 grey.. 7·50 8·50
255. 2 r. 25 on 2 r. 50 yellow 10·00 11·00

20. 21.

1903. Various frames.
277. 20. 2 c. brown 30 15
278. 21. 3 c. green (A) 30 15
293. 3 c. green (B) 40 15
279. 4 c. orange and blue .. 20 35
268. – 5 c. purple } see footnote .. 40 8
289. – 5 c. purple } 40 12
281. – 6 c. red } 30 15
291. – 6 c. red } .. 40 15
294. 21. 10 c. olive and claret .. 65 35
282. 12 c. olive and red .. 70 35
283. 15 c. blue 35 20
284. 25 c. brown .. .. 2·50 1·25
295. 25 c. grey .. .. 1·25 50
285. 30 c. violet and green.. 1·10 35
296. 50 c. brown .. .. 2·25 1·75
286. 75 c. blue and orange .. 1·90 2·50
297. 1 r. purple on yellow .. 3·00 3·00
287. 1 r. 50 grey .. .. 3·25 4·50
298. 2 r. red on yellow .. 4·00 4·50
288. 2 r. 25 brown and green 6·50 5·50
299. 5 r. black on green .. 20·00 20·00
300. 10 r. black on red .. 45·00 42·00
(A) has value in shaded tablet; (B) in white tablet as in T 21.

Nos. 268 and 281 have the value in words; Nos. 289 and 291 in figures.

26. 29.

1912.
301. 26. 1 c. brown 8 12
302. 2 c. orange 20 15
306. 3 c. green 20 15
355. 3 c. grey 5 10
308. 5 c. purple 10 12
310. 6 c. red 65 15
356. 6 c. violet 8 15
357. 9 c. red on yellow .. 15 20
360a. 10 c. olive 35 20
360b. 12 c. red .. .. 90 1·10
315. 15 c. blue 80 35
360c. 15 c. green on yellow .. 60 60
360d. 20 c. blue 30 35
317. 25 c. yellow and blue .. 80 35
319. 30 c. green and violet 70 45
321. 50 c. black and red .. 55 60
322. 1 r. purple on yellow 75 1·10
323. 2 r. black & red on yell. 1·60 2·50
324. 5 r black on green .. 4·00 4·50
325. 10 r. pur. & blk. on red 17·00 14·00
326. 20 r. blk. & red on blue 32·00 26·00
Large type, as Bermuda T 7.
327. 50 r. purple £200
328. 100 r. black £850
360. 100 r. purple and blue.. £750

1918. Optd. **WAR STAMP** or surch. **ONE CENT** and bar also.
335. 26. 1 c. on 5 c. purple .. 8 12
330. 2 c. orange 10 15
331. 3 c. green 12 20
333. 5 c. purple 5 12

1918. Surch. **ONE CENT** and bar.
337. 26. 1 c. on 5 c. purple .. 10 15

1926. Surch. with new value and bar.
361. 26. 2 c. on 3 c. grey .. 35 25
372. 5 c. on 6 c violet .. 35 30

1927.
363. 29. 1 r. purple .. .. 1·60 90
364. 2 r. green and red .. 3·25 2·00
365. 5 r. green and purple .. 10·00 6·50
366. 10 r. green and orange.. 13·00 14·00
367. 20 r. purple and blue .. 26·00 21·00

1935. Silver Jubilee. As T 11 of Antigua.
368. 6 c. blue and grey .. 5 8
369. 9 c. green and blue .. 20 20
370. 20 c. brown and blue .. 35 35
371. 50 c. grey and purple.. 1·10 85

31. Adam's Peak.

1935. King George V.
372. – 2 c. black and red .. 5 8
373. 31. 3 c. black and green .. 12 12
374. – 6 c. black and blue .. 25 15
375. – 9 c. green and red .. 20 15
376. – 10 c. black and purple.. 20 15
377. – 15 c. brown and green.. 70 35
378. – 20 c. black and blue .. 50 30
379. – 25 c. blue and brown .. 55 30
380. – 30 c. red and green .. 55 50
381. – 50 c. black and violet.. 2·25 50
382. – 1 r. violet and brown.. 2·50 2·25
DESIGNS—VERT. 2 c. Tapping rubber. 6 c. Colombo Harbour. 9 c. Plucking tea. 20 c. Coconut plams. HORIZ. 10 c. Hill paddy (rice). 15 c. River scene. 25 c. Temple of the Tooth, Kandy. 30 c. Ancient irrigation tank. 50 c. Wild elephants. 1 r. Trincomalee.

1937. Coronation. As T 2 of Aden.
383. 6 c. red 5 5
384. 9 c. green 12 15
385. 20 c. blue 25 25

41. Sigiriya (Lion Rock).

1938. As 1935 issue but with portrait of King George VI and "POSTAGE & REVENUE" omitted.
386b. – 2 c. black and red .. 5 8
387d. 31. 3 c. black and green .. 5 8
387g. – 5 c. green and orange.. 10 10
388. – 6 c. black and blue .. 5 8
389a. 41. 10 c. black and blue .. 8 8
390. – 15 c. green and brown 5 8
391. – 20 c. black and blue.. 10 8
392a. – 25 c. blue and brown.. 10 8
393a. – 30 c. red and green .. 70 50
394d. – 50 c. black and violet.. 25 8
395a. – 1 r. blue and brown .. 85 35
396. – 2 r. black and red .. 80 50
396a. – 2 r. black and violet.. 70 35
DESIGNS—VERT. 5 c. Coconut palms. 20 c. Plucking tea. 2 r. Ancient Guard-stone, Anuradhapura. Others, same as for corresponding values of 1935 issue.

1938. As T 29, but head of King George VI to right.
397a. 5 r. green and purple.. 2·00 55

1940. Surch. with new value and bars.
398. – 3 c. on 6 c. black & blue (No. 388) .. 12 5
399. – 3 c. on 20 c. black & blue (No. 391) .. 12 20

1946. Victory. As T 4 of Aden.
400. 6 c. blue 5 8
401. 15 c. brown 5 10

42. Parliament Building.

1947. New Constitution.
402. 42. 6 c. black and blue .. 5 10
403. – 10 c. black, orge. & red 5 12
404. – 15 c. green and purple.. 8 12
405. – 25 c. yellow and green.. 15 15
DESIGNS—VERT. 10 c. Adam's Peak. 25 c. Anuradhapura. HORIZ. 15 c. Temple of the Tooth.

43. Lion Flag of Dominion. 44. D. S. Senanayake.

1949. Independence. 1st Anniv.
406. 43. 4 c. red, yellow & brown 5 10
407. 44. 5 c. brown and green .. 10 12
408. 43. 15 c. red, yellow & orge. 10 12
409. 44. 25 c. brown and blue .. 15 15
No. 408 is larger (28 × 22 mm.).

INDEX

Countries can be quickly located by referring to the index at the end of this volume.

45. Globe and Forms of Transport.

1949. U.P.U. 75th Anniv. Inscr. as in T 45. Designs show globe.
410. 45. 5 c. brown and green .. 8 8
411. – 15 c. blk. & red (horiz.) 30 12
412. – 25 c. blk. & blue (vert.) 35 12

46. Kandyan Dancer. 47. Sigiriya (Lion Rock).

48. Ruins of Madirgiriya.

1950.
413. 46. 4 c. purple and red .. 5 8
414. 5 c. green 8 8
415. – 15 c. green and violet.. 12 8
416. 47. 30 c. red and yellow .. 12 8
417. – 75 c. blue and orange .. 25 8
418. 48. 1 r. blue and brown .. 30 45
DESIGNS—VERT. As T 46/7: 5 c. Kiri Vehera, Polonnaruwa. 15 c. Vesak orchid. As T 48: 75 c. Octagon Library, Temple of the Tooth.

49. Coconut Trees. 50. Tea Plantation.

1951.
419. – 2 c. brown & blue-green 5 5
420. – 3 c. black and violet .. 5 5
421. – 6 c. sepia and green .. 5 5
422. 49. 10 c. green and grey .. 5 5
423. – 25 c. orange and blue.. 8 5
424a. – 35 c. red and green .. 20 5
425. – 40 c. brown 12 5
426. – 50 c. slate 12 5
427. 50. 85 c. black & blue-green 25 10
428. – 2 r. blue and brown .. 50 20
429. – 5 r. brown and orange.. 1·25 40
430. – 10 r. brown and buff .. 4·00 1·25
DESIGNS—As T 49. VERT. 2 c. Ruhuna National Park. 3 c. Ancient Guard-stone, Anuradhapura. 6 c. Harvesting rice. 25 c. Sigiriya fresco. 35 c. Star orchid. HORIZ. 40 c. Rubber plantation. 50 c. Outrigger canoe. As T 50. HORIZ 2 r. River Gal Dam. VERT. 5 r. Bas-relief, Anuradhapura. 10 r. Harvesting rice.

51. Mace and Symbols of Progress.

1952. Colombo Plan Exn.
431. 51. 5 c. green 8 8
432. 15 c. blue 12 15

1952. As No. 397a but inscr. "REVENUE" at sides.
F 1. 10 r. green and orange .. 4·50 2·00

This fiscal stamp was on sale for postal use from Dec., 1952, to March, 1954. Our used price is for postally used copies.

52. Queen Elizabeth II. 54. King Coconuts.

53. Ceremonial Procession.

1953. Coronation.
433. 52. 5 c. green 8 8

1954. Royal Visit.
434. 53. 10 c. blue 5 5

1954.
435. 54. 10 c. orge., brn. & buff 5 5

55. Farm Produce.

1955. Royal Agricultural and Food Exn.
436. 55. 10 c. brown and orange 5 5

56. Sir J. Kotelawala and House of Representatives.

1956. Prime Minister's 25 years of Public Service.
437. 6. 10 c. green 5 5

57. Arrival of Vijaya.

58. Lampstand and the Dharmachakra.

DESIGNS—VERT. 10 c. Hand of Peace and Dharmachakra. HORIZ. 15 c. Dharmachakra encircling world.

1956. Buddha Jayanti. Inscr. "2500".
438. 57. 3 c. blue and grey .. 5 5
439. 58. 4 c.+2 c. yellow & blue 5 5
440. – 10 c.+5 c. red, yellow and grey 10 10
441. – 15 c. blue 10 5

59. Mail Transport. 60. Reproduction of T 1.

1957. Stamp Centenary.
442. 59. 4 c. red and turquoise 5 5
443. 10 c. red and blue .. 5 5
444. 60. 35 c. choc., yell. & blue 10 5
445. 85 c. choc., yell. & grn. 20 15

1958. Nos. 439/40 with premium obliterated with bars.
446. 58. 4 c. yellow and blue .. 5 5
447. – 10 c. red, yellow & grey 5 5

61. Kandyan Dancer.

1958. As Nos. 413 and 419, etc., and 435, but with inscriptions changed as in T 61.
448. 2 c. brown and blue-green 5 5
449. 3 c. black and violet .. 5 5
450. 4 c. purple and red .. 5 5
451. 5 c. green 5 5
452. 6 c. sepia and green .. 5 5
453. 10 c. orange, brown & buff 5 5
454. 15 c. green and violet .. 5 5
455. 25 c. orange and blue .. 5 5
456. 30 c. red and yellow .. 5 5
457. 35 c. red and green .. 5 5
459. 50 c. slate 8 5
460. 75 c. blue and orange .. 12 5
461. 85 c. black and blue-green 15 10
462. 1 r. blue and brown .. 20 8
463. 2 r. blue and brown .. 35 10
464. 5 r. brown and orange .. 1·00 20
465. 10 r. brown and buff .. 2·25 1·00

62. "Human Rights".

1958. Declaration of Human Rights. 10th Anniv.
466. 62. 10 c. red, brn. and pur. 5 5
467. 85 c. red, turq. and grn... 20 20

63. Portraits of Founders and University Buildings.

1959. Institution of Pirivona Universities.
468. 63. 10 c. orange and blue .. 5 5

64. "Uprooted Tree". 65. S.W.R.D. Bandaranaike.

1960. World Refugee Year.
469. 64. 4 c. brown and gold .. 5 5
470. 25 c. blksh. violet & gold 5 5

1961. Prime Minister Bandaranaike Commem.
471. 65. 10 c. blue & greenish bl. 5 5
See also Nos. 475 and 481.

66. Ceylon Scout Badge. 67. Campaign Emblem.

1962. Ceylon Boy Scouts Association. Golden Jubilee.
472. 66. 35 c. buff and blue .. 8 5

1962. Malaria Eradication.
473. 67. 25 c. red and drab .. 5 5

68. Moth and Comet Aircraft.

1963. Airmail Services. 25th Anniv.
474. 68. 50 c. black and blue .. 12 12

69. "Produce" and Campaign Emblem.

1963. Freedom from Hunger.
475. 69. 5 c. red and blue .. 5 5
476. 25 c. brown and olive.. 5 5

ශත
2
சதம்
■ ■

(70.)

1963. No. 450 surch. with T 70.
477. 2 c. on 4 c. purple and red 5 5

71. "Rural Life".

1963. Golden Jubilee of Ceylon Co-operative Movement.
478. 71. 60 c. red and black .. 12 12

1963. Design similar to T 65, but smaller (21 × 26 mm.) and with inscription rearranged at top.
479. 10 c. blue 5 5
481. 10 c. violet and grey .. 5 5
No. 481 has a decorative pattern at foot instead of the inscription.

72. Terrain, Elephant and Tree.

1963. National Conservation Week.
480. 72. 5 c. sepia and blue .. 5 5

73. Anagarika Dharmapala (Buddhist missionary).

1964. A. Dharmapala (founder of Maha Bodhi Society). Birth Cent.
482. 73. 25 c. sepia and yellow 5 5

73a. D. S. Senanayake.  75. Jungle Fowl.

74. Ruins of Madirigiriya.

1964.
485. – 5 c. multicoloured .. 5 5
486. 73a. 10 c. green 5 5
488. – 15 c. multicoloured .. 5 5
489. 74. 20 c. maroon and buff 5 5
494. 75. 60 c. multicoloured .. 8 5
495. – 75 c. multicoloured .. 8 5
497. – 1 r. brown and green.. 12 5
499. – 5 r. multicoloured .. 55 25
500. – 10 r. multicoloured .. 1·10 50

DESIGNS: As T 75—HORIZ. 5 c. Grackle. 15 c. Peacock. 75 c. Oriole. 5 r. Girls transplanting Rice (23 × 36 mm.). VERT. 1 r. Tea Plantation (as T 50, but larger, 21 × 35 mm.). 10 r. Map of Ceylon on Scroll (23 × 36 mm.).

76. Exhibition Buildings and Cogwheels.

1964. Industrial Exn.
501. – 5 c. multicoloured .. 5 5
502. 76. 5 c. multicoloured .. 5 5
No. 501 is inscribed "INDUSTRIAL EXHIBITION" in Sinhala and Tamil, No. 502 in Sinhala and English. The stamps were issued together se-tenant in alternate vert. rows, producing horiz. pairs.

77. Trains of 1864 and 1964.

1964. Ceylon Railways. Cent.
503. – 60 c. blue, purple & grn. 12 15
504. 77. 60 c. blue, purple & grn. 12 15
No. 503 is inscribed "RAILWAY CENTENARY" in Sinhala and Tamil, No. 504 in Sinhala and English. The stamps were issued together se-tenant in alternate horiz. rows, producing vert. pairs.

78. I.T.U. Emblem and Symbols.

1965. I.T.U. Cent.

505.	78.	2 c. blue and red ..	5	5
506.		30 c. brown and red ..	8	10

79. I.C.Y. Emblem.

1965. Int. Co-operation Year.

507.	79.	3 c. blue and red ..	8	5
508.		50 c. black, red & gold	10	8

80. Town Hall, Colombo.

1965. Colombo Municipal Council Cent.

509.	80.	25 c. green and sepia ..	8	5

1965. No. 481 surch.

510.		5 c. on 10 c. violet and grey	8	5

82. Kandy and Council Crest.

1966. Kandy Municipal Council Cent.

512.	82.	25 c. multicoloured ..	5	5

83. W.H.O. Building.

1966. W.H.O. Headquarters, Geneva. Inaug.

513.	83.	4 c. multicoloured ..	5	5
514.		1 r. multicoloured ..	15	12

84. Rice Paddy and Map of Ceylon.

1966. Int. Rice Year. Multicoloured.

515.		6 c. Type **84**	5	5
516.		30 c. Rice Paddy and Globe..	8	8

85. U.N.E.S.C.O. Emblem.

1966. U.N.E.S.C.O. 20th Anniv.

517.	85.	3 c. multicoloured ..	5	5
518.		50 c. multicoloured ..	10	8

86. Water-resources Map.

1966. Int. Hydrological Decade.

519.	86.	2 c. brown, yellow & blue	5	5
520.		2 r. brn., yell., bl. & grn.	30	25

87. Devotees at Buddhist Temple.

1967. Poya Holiday System. Multicoloured.

521.		5 c. Type **87**	5	5
522.		20 c. Mihintale	5	5
523.		35 c. Sacred Bo-tree, Anuradhapura	5	8
524.		60 c. Adam's Peak ..	12	10

88. Galle Fort and Clock Tower.

1967. Galle Municipal Council. Cent.

525.	88.	25 c. multicoloured ..	5	5

89. Field Research.

1967. Ceylon Tea Industry. Cent. Multicoloured.

526.		4 c. Type **89**	5	5
527.		40 c. Tea-tasting equipment	8	8
528.		50 c. Leaves and bud ..	8	8
529.		1 r. Shipping tea ..	15	12

90. Elephant Ride.

1967. Int. Tourist Year.

530.	90.	45 c. multicoloured ..	8	8

91. Ranger, Jubilee Emblem and Flag.

1967. Ceylon Girl Guides' Assn. Golden Jubilee.

532.	91.	3 c. multicoloured ..	5	5
533.		25 c. multicoloured ..	8	8

92. Col. Olcott (theosophist) and Buddhist Flag.

1967. Colonel Olcott. 60th Death Anniv.

534.	92.	15 c. multicoloured ..	5	5

93. Independence Hall.

1968. Independence. 20th Anniv. Multicoloured.

535.		5 c. Type **93**	5	5
536.		1 r. Lion Flag and Sceptre	15	12

94. Sir D. B. Jayatilleke.

1968. Sir Baron Jayatilleke (scholar and statesman). Birth Cent.

537.	94.	25 c. brown	5	5

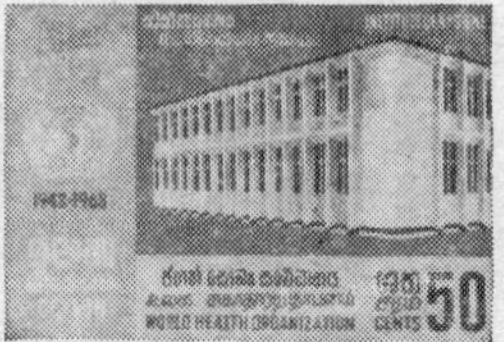

95. Institute of Hygiene.

1968. World Health Organization. 20th Anniv.

538.	95.	50 c. multicoloured ..	8	8

96. Aircraft over Terminal Building.

1968. Colombo Airport. Opening.

539.	96.	60 c. blue, chestnut, red and yellow	10	10

97. Open Quran and "1400".

1968. Holy Quran. 1400th Anniv.

541.	97.	25 c. multicoloured ..	5	5

98. Human Rights Emblem.

1968. Human Rights Year.

542.	98.	2 c. multicoloured ..	5	5
543.		20 c. multicoloured ..	5	5
544.		40 c. multicoloured ..	8	8
545.		2 r. multicoloured ..	25	25

99. All Ceylon Buddhist Congress Headquarters,

1968. All Ceylon Buddhist Congress. Golden Jubilee.

546.	99.	5 c. multicoloured ..	8	5

100. E. W. Perera (patriot).

101. Symbols of Strength in Savings.

1969. Perera Commem.

547.	100.	60 c. brown	12	10

1969. National Savings Movement. Silver Jubilee.

548.	101.	3 c. multicoloured ..	5	5

102. Seat of Enlightenment under Sacred Bodhi Tree.

103. A. E. Goonesingha.

1969. Vesak Day. Inscr. "Wesak".

549.	102.	4 c. multicoloured ..	5	5
550.	–	6 c. multicoloured ..	5	5
551.	102.	35 c. multicoloured ..	5	8

DESIGN: 6 c. Buduresmala (Six-fold Buddha-Rays).

1969. Goonesingha Commem.

552.	103.	15 c. multicoloured ..	5	5

104. I.L.O. Emblem.

1969. Int. Labour Organisation. 50th Anniv.

553.	104.	5 c. black and blue ..	5	5
554.		25 c. black and red ..	5	5

105. Convocation Hall, University of Ceylon.

1969. Educational Cent. Multicoloured.

555.		4 c. Type **105**	5	5
556.		35 c. Lamp of learning, globe and flags ..	5	5
557.		50 c. Uranium atom ..	8	10
558.		60 c. Symbols of scientific education	10	10

106. Ath Pana (Elephant Lamp).

1969. Archaeological Cent. Multicoloured.
559. 6 c. Type **106** 5 5
560. 1 r. Rock fortress of Sigiriya 15 12

107. Leopard.

1970. Wild Life Conservation. Multicoloured.
561. 5 c. Wild Buffalo 5 5
562. 15 c. Slender Loris .. 5 5
563. 50 c. Spotted Deer .. 8 8
564. 1 r. Type **107** 15 12

108. Emblem and Symbols.

1970. Asian Productivity Year.
565. **108.** 60 c. multicoloured .. 10 10

109. New U.P.U. Headquarters Building.

1970. New U.P.U. Headquarters Building.
566. **109.** 50 c. orge., blk. and blue 10 8
567. 1 r. 10, vermilion, black and blue 20 15

110. Oil Lamp and Caduceus.

1970. Colombo Medical School. Cent.
568. **110.** 5 c. multicoloured .. 5 5
569. 45 c. multicoloured .. 15 20

111. Victory March and S.W.R.D. Bandaranaike.

1970. Establishment of United Front Government.
570. **111.** 10 c. multicoloured .. 5 5

112. U.N. Emblem and Dove of Peace.

1970. United Nations. 25th Anniv.
571. **112.** 2 r. multicoloured .. 25 25

113. Keppetipola Dissawa.

1970. Keppetipola Dissawa (Kandyan patriot) 152nd Death Anniv.
572. **113.** 25 c. multicoloured .. 10 10

114. Ola Leaf Manuscript.

1970. Int. Education Year.
573. **114.** 15 c. multicoloured .. 8 15

115. C. H. De Soysa. **116.** D. E. H. Pedris (patriot).

1971. C. H. De Soysa (philanthropist). 135th Birth Anniv.
574. **115.** 20 c. multicoloured .. 8 8

1971. D. E. H. Pedris. Commemoration.
575. **116.** 25 c. multicoloured .. 8 8

117. Lenin. **118.** Ananda Rajakaruna.

1971. Lenin Commemoration.
576. **117.** 40 c. multicoloured .. 8 8

1971. Poets and Philosophers.
577. **118.** 5 c. blue 5 5
578. – 5 c. brown 5 5
579. – 5 c. orange 5 5
580. – 5 c. blue 5 5
581. – 5 c. brown 5 5
PORTRAITS: No. 578. Arumuga Navalar. No. 579, Rev. S. Mahinda. No. 580, Ananda Coomaraswamy. No. 581, Cumaratunga Munidasa.

1972. Surch. in figures.
582. **102.** 5 c. on 4 c. multicoloured 8 10
583. **105.** 5 c. on 4 c. multicoloured 8 10
584. **111.** 15 c. on 10 c. multicoloured .. 5 5
585. – 25 c. on 6 c. multicoloured (No. 550) 10 12
586. **106.** 25 c. on 6 c. multicoloured 10 12

119. Colombo Plan Emblem and Ceylon.

1971. Colombo Plan. 20th Anniv.
587. **119.** 20 c. multicoloured .. 8 8

120. Globe and C.A.R.E. Package.

1971. Co-operative for American Relief Everywhere. 20th Anniv.
588. **120.** 50 c. blue, violet & lilac 8 8

121. W.H.O. Emblem and Heart.

1972. World Health Day.
589. **121.** 25 c. multicoloured .. 8 8

122. Map of Asia and U.N. Emblem.

1972. E.C.A.F.E. 25th Anniv.
590. **122.** 85 c. multicoloured .. 12 12

OFFICIAL STAMPS.

1895. Stamps of Queen Victoria optd. **On Service.**
O 1. **6.** 2 c. green 95 12
O 8. 2 c. brown 30 10
O 2. **17.** 3 c. brown and green 85 50
O 9. 3 c. green 55 25
O 3. **18.** 5 c. purple 35 10
O 4. **17.** 15 c. olive 95 20
O 10. 15 c. blue 50 25
O 5. 25 c. brown 75 25
O 6. 30 c. mauve and brown 60 15
O 11. 75 c. black and brown 65 60
O 7. **16.** 1 r. 12 red .. .. 4·50 3·50

1903. Stamps of King Edward VII optd. **On Service.**
O 12. **20.** 2 c. brown 85 60
O 13. **21.** 3 c. green 60 60
O 14. – 5 c. purple (No. 268) 80 30
O 15. **21.** 15 c. blue .. .. 1·40 75
O 16. 25 c. brown .. .. 4·00 4·00
O 17. 30 c. violet and green 1·60 65

For later issues see **SRI LANKA.**

CHAD O1

Formerly a dependency of Ubangui-Chari. Became one of the separate colonies of Fr. Equatorial Africa in 1937. In 1958 became a republic within the French Community.

1922. Stamps of Middle Congo, colours changed, optd. **TCHAD.**
1. **1.** 1 c. red and violet .. 5 5
2. 2 c. brown and red .. 5 5
3. 4 c. blue and violet .. 5 5
4. 5 c. brown and green .. 10 10
5. 10 c. green 15 15
6. 15 c. violet and red .. 20 20
7. 20 c. green and violet .. 50 50
8. **2.** 25 c. brown .. .. 1·10 1·10
9. 30 c. red 12 12
10. 35 c. blue and red .. 30 30
11. 40 c. brown and green .. 30 30
12. 45 c. violet and green .. 30 30
13. 50 c. blue 30 30
14. 60 on 75 c. violet on red .. 40 40
15. 75 c. red and violet .. 20 20
16. **3.** 1 f. blue and red .. 1·40 1·40
17. 2 f. blue and violet .. 2·25 2·25
18. 5 f. blue and brown .. 1·50 1·50

1924. Stamps of Middle Congo optd. **TCHAD** and further optd. **AFRIQUE EQUATORIALE FRANCAISE.**
19. **1.** 1 c. red and violet .. 5 5
20. 2 c. brown and red .. 5 5
21. 4 c. blue and violet .. 5 5
22. 5 c. brown and green .. 5 5
23. 10 c. green 5 5
24. 10 c. red and grey .. 5 5
25. 15 c. violet and red .. 8 8
26. 20 c. green and violet .. 8 8
27. **2.** 25 c. brown 5 5
28. 30 c. red 5 5
29. 30 c. grey and blue .. 5 5
30. 30 c. green 10 10
31. 35 c. blue and red .. 5 5
32. 40 c. brown and green .. 12 12
33. 45 c. violet and green .. 8 8
34. 50 c. blue 8 8
35. 50 c. green and violet .. 12 12
36. 60 on 75 c. violet on red 5 5
37. 65 c. brown and blue .. 20 20
38. 75 c. red and violet .. 5 5
39. 75 c. blue 5 5
40. 75 c. claret and brown .. 25 25
41. 90 c. red .. .. 1·10 1·10
42. **3.** 1 f. blue and red .. 12 12
43. 1 f. 10 blue and green .. 20 20
44. 1 f. 25 blue and red .. 1·10 1·10
45. 1 f. 50 blue .. .. 1·10 1·10
46. 1 f. 75 mauve and brown 7·50 7·50
47. 2 f. blue and violet .. 20 20
48. 3 f. magenta on red .. 1·10 1·10
49. 5 f. blue and brown .. 25 25

1925. Stamps of Middle Congo optd. **TCHAD** and **AFRIQUE EQUATORIALE FRANCAISE** and surch. also.
50. **3.** 65 on 1 f. brown & green .. 12 12
51. 85 on 1 f. brown & green .. 12 12
52. **2.** 90 on 75 c. red and pink .. 10 10
53. **3.** 1 f. 25 on 1 f. blue & ultram. 5 5
54. 1 f. 50 on 1 f. blue & ultram 25 25
55. 3 f. on 5 f. brown and red 50 50
56. 10 f. on 5 f. green and red 1·75 1·75
57. 20 f. on 5 f. violet & orge. 2·00 2·00

1931. "Colonial Exhibition" key-types inscr. "TCHAD".
58. E. 40 c. green 60 60
59. F. 50 c. mauve 60 60
60. G. 90 c. red 60 60
61. H. 1 f. 50 blue 60 60

1. "Birth of the Republic". **2.** Flag, Map and U.N. Emblem.

1959. Republic. 1st Anniv.
62. **1.** 15 f. lake, green, yellow and blue 12 8
63. – 25 f. lake and myrtle .. 20 8
DESIGN: 25 f. Map and Birds.

1960. African Technical Co-operation Commission. 10th Anniv. As **T39** of Cameroun.
64. 50 f. violet and purple .. 45 45

1960. Air. Olympic Games. No. 276 of French Equatorial Africa optd. with Olympic rings, **XVIIe OLYMPIADE 1960 REPUBLIQUE DU TCHAD** and surch. **250F** and bars.
65. 250 f. on 500 f. blue, black and green .. .. 3·25 3·25

1961. Admission into U.N.
66. **2.** 15 f. multicoloured .. 20 10
67. 25 f. multicoloured .. 25 15
68. 85 f. multicoloured .. 75 55

3. Shari Bridge and Hippopotamus. **4.** "Euplectes oryx".

1961.
69. – 50 c. yellow-green & black 5 5
70. – 1 f. green and black .. 5 5
71. – 2 f. brown and black .. 5 5
72. – 3 f. orange and green .. 5 5
73. – 4 f. red and black .. 5 5
74. **3.** 5 f. lemon and black .. 5 5
75. – 10 f. pink and black .. 8 5
76. – 15 f. violet and black .. 10 5
77. – 20 f. red and black .. 15 8
78. – 25 f. blue and black .. 20 8
79. – 30 f. ultramarine and black 20 12
80. – 60 f. yellow and black .. 45 12
81. – 85 f. orange and black .. 55 25

DESIGNS (with animal silhouettes)—VERT. 50 c. Biltine and Dorcas gazelle. 1 f. Logone and elephant. 2 f. Batha and lion. 3 f. Salamat and buffalo. 4 f. Ouaddai and greater kudu. 10 f. Abtouyour and bullock. 15 f. Bessada and Derby's eland. 20 f. Tibesti and moufflon. 25 f. Tikem Rocks and hartebeest. 30 f. Kanem and cheetah. 60 f. Borkou and oryx. 85 f. Guelta D'Archei and addax.

1961. Air.

82. **4.** 50 f. black, crimson & grn. .. 45 15
83. – 100 f. indigo, red, green and maroon 75 40
84. – 200 f. red, bl., vio. & mar. 1·50 60
85. – 250 f. blue, orange & green 1·75 85
86. – 500 f. red, grn., brn. & bl. 3·50 1·90

BIRDS: 100 f. "Chalcomitra senegalensis". 200 f. "Tchitrea viridis". 250 f. "Corythornis cristada". 500 f. "Merops nubicus".

1962. Air. "Air Afrique" Airline. As T **44** of Cameroun.

87. 25 f. blue, chestnut & black 20 15

1962. Malaria Eradication. As T **45** of Cameroun.

88. 25 f. + 5 f. orange 30 30

1962. Sports. As T **6** of Central African Republic.

89. 20 f. brown, red-brown, green and black (postage) .. 15 10
90. 50 f. brn., red-brn., grn. & blk. 40 25
91. 100 f. brown, red-brown, green and black (air) .. 75 50

DESIGNS—HORIZ. 20 f. Relay-racing. 50 f. High-jumping. VERT. (26 × 47 mm.): 100 f. Throwing the discus.

1962. Union of African and Malagasy States. 1st Anniv. As No. 328 of Cameroun.

92. **47.** 30 f. deep blue .. 25 20

1963. Freedom from Hunger. As T **51** of Cameroun.

93. 25 f. + 5 f. indigo, brown and myrtle. 25 25

5. Pres. Tombalbaye. **6.** Carved Thread-weight.

1963.

94. **5.** 20 f. multicoloured .. 15 5
95. 85 f. multicoloured .. 55 25

1963. Air. African and Malagasy Posts and Telecommunications Union. As T **10** of Central African Republic.

96. 85 f. red, buff, light bl. & bl. 60 40

1963. Space Telecommunications. As Nos. 37/8 of Central African Republic.

97. 25 f. violet, emerald & green 20 15
98. 100 f. blue and pink .. 75 65

1963. Air. "Air Afrique" 1st Anniv. and "DC-8" Service Inaug. As T **10** of Congo Republic.

99. 50 f. blk., grn., drab & chest. 55 40

1963. Air. European-African Economic Convention. As T **16** of Central African Republic.

100. 50 f. brn., yell., ochre & grn. 40 30

1963. Sao Art.

101. **6.** 5 f. orge.-red & bl.-green 5 5
102. – 15 f. maroon, slate & red 10 8
103. – 25 f. brown and blue .. 20 10
104. – 60 f. bronze and brown 40 20
105. – 80 f. bronze and chestnut 60 25

DESIGNS: 15 f. Ancestral mask. 25 f. Ancestral statuette. 60 f. Gazelle's-head pendant. 80 f. Pectoral.

1963. Declaration of Human Rights. 15th Anniv. As Central African Republic T **18**.

106. 25 f. maroon and green .. 20 15

7. Broussard Monoplane.

1963. Air.

107. **7.** 100 f. blue, green & chest. 70 45

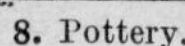

8. Pottery.

DESIGNS: 30 f. Canoe-building. 50 f. Carpet-weaving. 85 f. Blacksmith working iron.

1964. Sao Handicrafts.

108. **8.** 10 f. black, orge. & blue 5 5
109. – 30 f. red, black & yellow 20 8
110. – 50 f. black, red & green 30 15
111. – 85 f. black, yellow & pur. 60 25

9. Rameses II in War Chariot, Abu Simbel

1964. Air. Nubian Monuments Preservation Fund.

112. **9.** 10 f. + 5 f. vio., grn. & red 15 15
113. 25 f. + 5 f. mar., grn. & red 25 25
114. 50 f. + 5 f. blue-green, green and red .. 50 50

1964. World Meteorological Day. As T **13** of Congo Republic.

115. 50 f. violet, blue and purple 40 25

10. Cotton.

1964.

116. **10.** 20 f. bl., yell., red & blk. 15 10
117. – 25 f. red, brn., grn. & bl. 15 10

DESIGN: 25 f. Flamboyant tree.

1964. Air. Equatorial African Heads of State Conf. 5th Anniv. As T **23** of Central African Republic.

118. 100 f. multicoloured .. 70 45

11. Globe, Chimneys and Ears of Wheat.

1964. Air. Europafrique.

119. **11.** 50 f. orge., pur. & brn. 30 25

12. Football.

1964. Air. Olympic Games, Tokyo.

120. **12.** 25 f. green, apple & brn. 20 12
121. – 50 f. brn., indigo & blue 35 25
122. – 100 f. blk., green & red 70 55
123. – 200 f. blk., bistre & red 1·50 90

DESIGNS—VERT. 50 f. Throwing the javelin. 100 f. High-jumping. HORIZ. 200 f. Running.

1964. Air. Pan-African and Malagasy Posts and Telecommunications Congress, Cairo. As T **22** of Congo Republic.

124. 25 f. sepia, brn-red & mve. 20 10

1964. French, African and Malagasy Co-operation. As T **500** of France.

125. 25 f. chocolate, blue and red 20 15

13. Pres. Kennedy. **14.** National Guard.

1964. Air. Pres. Kennedy Commem.

126. **13.** 100 f. sepia, purple, blk. and blue 75 60

1964. Chad Army. Multicoloured.

127. 20 f. Type **14** 15 10
128. 25 f. Standard-bearer and troops of Land Forces .. 20 12

15. Mouflon.

1964. Fauna. Protection. Multicoloured.

129. 5 f. Type **15** 5 5
130. 10 f. Addax 8 5
131. 20 f. Oryx 12 8
132. 25 f. Derby's Eland .. 20 10
133. 30 f. Giraffe, buffalo and lion (Zakouma Park) .. 20 10
134. 85 f. Great Kudu .. 55 35

Nos. 132/4 are vert.

16. Perforator of Olsen's Telegraph Apparatus.

1965. I.T.U. Cent.

135. **16.** 30 f. choc., red & green 20 12
136. – 60 f. green, red & choc. 40 30
137. – 100 f. green, choc. & red 70 50

DESIGNS—VERT. 60 f. Milde's telephone. HORIZ. 100 f. Distributor of Baudot's telegraph apparatus.

17. Badge and Mobile Gendarmes.

1965. National Gendarmerie.

138. **17.** 25 f. multicoloured .. 20 12

18. I.C.Y. Emblem.

1965. Air. Int. Co-operation Year.

139. **18.** 100 f. multicoloured .. 75 45

19. Abraham Lincoln.

1965. Air. Abraham Lincoln Death Cent.

140. **19.** 100 f. multicoloured 75 45

20. Guitar. **21.** Sir Winston Churchill

1965. Native Musical Instruments.

141. – 1 f. choc. & green (post.) 5 5
142. **20.** 2 f. brown, purple and red 5 5
143. – 3 f. lake, black and brown 5 5
144. – 15 f. green, orge. & red 10 8
145. – 60 f. green and lake .. 45 20
146. – 100 f. ultramarine, chestnut & blue (48½ × 27 mm.) (air) 70 45

DESIGNS—VERT. 1 f. Drum and seat. 3 f. Shoulder drum. 60 f. Harp. HORIZ. 15 f. Viol. 100 f. Xylophone.

1965. Air. Churchill Commem.

147. **21.** 50 f. black and green .. 40 25

22. Dr. Albert Schweitzer (philosopher and missionary) and "Appealing Hands".

1966. Air. Schweitzer Commem.

148. **22.** 100 f. multicoloured .. 70 45

23. Mask in Mortar.

1966. World Festival of Negro Arts, Dakar.

149. **23.** 15 f. mar., bistre & blue 10 8
150. – 20 f. brown, red & green 12 8
151. – 60 f. maroon, blue & verm. 40 25
152. – 80 f. grn., brn. & violet 60 30

DESIGNS—Sao Art: 20 f. Mask. 60 f. Mask (different). (All from J. Courtin's excavations at Bouta Kebira). 80 f. Armband (from I.N.T.S.H. excavations, Gawi).

1966. No. 94 surch.

153. **5.** 25 f. on 20 f. mult. .. 20 10

24. W.H.O. Building. **25.** Caduceus and Map of Africa.

1966. W.H.O. Headquarters, Geneva. Inaug.

154. **24.** 25 f. blue, yellow & red 20 12
155. 32 f. blue, yellow & grn. 20 15

1966. Central African Customs and Economic Union.

156. **25.** 30 f. multicoloured .. 15 10

26. Footballer. **27.** Youths, Flag and Arms.

1966. World Cup Football Championships

157. **26.** 30 f. claret, green and emerald 20 10
158. – 60 f. red, black and blue 45 20

DESIGN—VERT. 60 f. Footballer (different).

1966. Youth Movement.

159. **27.** 25 f. multicoloured .. 20 10

28. Columns. **29.** Skull of Lake Chad Man ("Tchadanthropus uxoris").

1966. U.N.E.S.C.O. 20th Anniv.

160. **28.** 32 f. blue, violet and red 20 10

1966. Air. "DC-8" Air Services. Inaug. As T **45** of Central African Republic.

161. 30 f. grey, black and green 20 10

1966. Archaeological Excavation.

162. **29.** 30 f. slate, yellow & red 20 10

30. White-throated Bee-eater.

1966. Air. Birds. Multicoloured.

163. 50 f. Hartlaub's glossy starling 25 12
164. 100 f. Type **30** 55 25
165. 200 f. Pigmy kingfisher .. 1·10 50
166. 250 f. Red-throated bee-eater .. .. 1·40 65
167. 500 f. Little green bee-eater 2·75 1·40

31. Battle-axe. **33.** Sportsmen and Dais on Map.

32. Congress Palace.

1966. Prehistoric Implements.

168. **31.** 25 f. brown, blue & red 15 8
169. – 30 f. black, brown & blue 20 8
170. – 85 f. brown, red and blue 55 25
171. – 100 f. brn., turq. & sepia 65 25

DESIGNS: 30 f. Arrowhead. 85 f. Harpoon. 100 f. Sandstone grindstone and pounder. From Tchad National Museum.

1967. Air.

173. **32.** 25f. multicoloured .. 20 10

1967. Sports Day.

174. **33.** 25 f. multicoloured .. 15 8

34. "Colotis protomedia klug".

37. H.Q. Building **35.** Lions Emblem.

36. Dagnaux's Breguet "19" Aircraft.

1967. Butterflies. Multicoloured.

175. 5 f. Type **34** 5 5
176. 10 f. "Charaxes jasius epijasius L" 8 5
177. 20 f. "Junonia cebrene trim" 12 8
178. 130 f. "Danaida petiverana H.D.". 75 50

1967. Air. Lions Int. 50th Anniv.

179. **35.** 50 f. + 10 f. mulitcoloured 40 25

1967. Air. Air Chad Airline. 1st Anniv.

180. **36.** 25 f. green, blue & brown 20 10
181. – 30 f. indigo, emer. & blue 20 15
182. – 50 f. brown, green & blue 35 20
183. – 100 f. red, blue & green 75 40

DESIGNS: 20 f. Latecoere "631" flying-boat. 50 f. Douglas "DC-3". 100 f. Piper Cherokee "6".

1967. Air. U.A.M.P.T. 5th Anniv. As T **55** of Central African Republic.

184. 100 f. chest., bistre & mag. 75 40

1967. Opening of W.H.O. Regional Headquarters, Brazzaville.

185. **37.** 30 f. multicoloured .. 20 8

38. Scouts and Jamboree Emblem.

1967. World Scout Jamboree, Idaho. Multicoloured.

186. 25 f. Type **38** 15 5
187. 32 f. Scout and Jamboree emblem 20 10

39. Flour Mills.

1967. Economic Development.

188. **39.** 25 f. slate, brown & blue 15 8
189. – 30 f. blue, brown & green 20 12

DESIGN: 30 f. Land reclamation, Lake Bol.

40. Woman and Harpist. **41.** Emblem of Rotary International.

1967. Bailloud Mission in the Ennedi. Rock paintings.

190. – 2 f. chocolate, brn. & red (postage) 5 5
191. – 10 f. red, brn. and violet 5 5
192. **40.** 15 f. lake, chest. & blue 10 5
193. – 20 f. red, brn., & green .. 12 8
194. – 25 f. red, brown and bl. 15 10
195. – 30 f. lake, chest. & blue 20 12
196. – 50 f. lake, chest. & green 30 15
197. – 100 f. lake, chestnut and green (air) 70 30
198. – 125 f. lake, chest. & blue 90 25

DESIGNS: 2 f. Archers. 10 f. Male and female costumes. 20 f. Funeral vigil. 25 f. "Dispute". 30 f. Giraffes. 50 f. Cameleer pursuing ostrich. (48×27 mm.) 100 f. Masked dancers. 125 f. Hunters and hare.

1968. Rotary Club, Fort Lamy. 10th Anniv.

199. **41.** 50 f. multicoloured .. 30 20

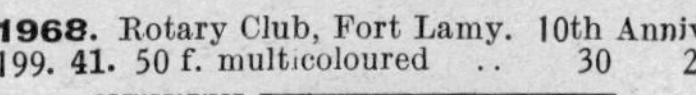

42. Downhill Skiing.

1968. Air. Winter Olympic Games, Grenoble.

200. **42.** 30 f. brn., grn. & purple 20 12
201. – 100 f. blue, green and greenish blue .. 75 50

DESIGN—VERT. 100 f. Ski-jumping.

43. Chancellor Adenauer.

1968. Air. Adenauer Commem.

202. **43.** 52 f. brown, lilac & green 35 20

44. "Health Services". **45.** Allegory of Irrigation.

1968. W.H.O. 20th Anniv.

204. **44.** 25 f. multicoloured .. 15 10
205. 32 f. multicoloured .. 20 12

1968. Int. Hydrological Decade.

206. **45.** 50 f. blue, brown & grn. 30 15

46. "The Snake-charmer".

1968. Air. Paintings by Henri Rousseau. Multicoloured.

207. 100 f. Type **46** 65 40
208. 130 f. "The War" (horiz.—49×35 mm.) 80 50

47. College Building, Student and Emblem.

1968. National College of Administration.

209. **47.** 25 f. purple, indigo & red 15 8

48. Child writing and Blackboard.

49. Harvesting Cotton. **50.** "Utetheisa pulchella".

1968. Literacy Day.

210. **48.** 60 f. black, blue & choc. 40 15

1968. Cotton Industry.

211. **49.** 25 f. maroon, grn. & blue 15 5
212. – 30 f. brn., blue & green 20 8

DESIGN—VERT. 30 f. Loom, Fort Archambault Mill.

1968. Butterflies and Moths. Multicoloured.

213. 25 f. Type **50** 12 5
214. 30 f. "Ophideres materna" 15 8
215. 50 f. "Gynanisa maja" .. 30 15
216. 100 f. "Epiphora bauhiniae" 55 20

51. Hurdling.

1968. Air. Olympic Games, Mexico.

217. **51.** 32 f. chocolate, green and brown 20 15
218. – 80 f. mar., blue & cerise 45 30

DESIGN: 80 f. Relay-racing.

52. Human Rights Emblem within Man.

1968. Human Rights Year.

219. **52.** 32 f. verm., grn. & blue 20 12

1969. Air. "Philexafrique" Stamp Exn., Abidjan, Ivory Coast (1st Issue). Mult.

(a) As T **109** of Cameroun.

220. 100 f. "The actor Wolf, called Bernard" (J. L. David) 70 70

(b) As T **110** of Cameroun.

221. 50 f. Moundangs dancers and Chad postage due stamp of 1930 .. .. 35 35

No. 220 was issued in sheets with se-tenant "PHILEXAFRIQUE" stamp-size label.

53. G. Nachtigal and Tibesti landscape, 1879.

1969. Air. Chad Explorers.

222. **53.** 100 f. violet, green & blue 65 40
223. – 100 f. mar., ult. & ches . 65 40

DESIGN: No. 223. H. Barth (portrait) and aboard canoe, Lake Region, 1851.

54. "Apollo 8" circling Moon.

1969. Air. Flight of "Apollo 8" around the Moon.

224. **54.** 100f. black, blue & orge. 65 40

54a. St. Bartholomew.

1972. Catholic Church. Jubilee. Mult.

225. 50 c. St. Paul .. ..
226. 1 f. St. Peter .. ..
227. 2 f. St. Thomas .. ..
228. 5 f. St. John the Evangelist
229. 10 f. Type **54a** .. ..
230. 20 f. St. Matthew .. ..
231. 25 f. St. James the Less ..
232. 30 f. St. Andrew .. ..
233. 40 f. St. Jude .. ..
234. 50 f. St. James the Greater
235. 85 f. St. Philip .. ..
236. 100 f. St. Simon .. ..
Set of 12 2·00 2·00

Nos. 225/36 were issued printed together in small sheets without inscription.

55. Mahatma Gandhi. **56.** Motor Vehicles and I.L.O. Emblem.

1969. Air. "Apostles of Peace".
237. 55. 50 f. brown and green .. 30 20
238. – 50 f. blackish brn. & agate 30 20
239. – 50 f. brown and pink .. 30 20
240. – 50 f. brown and blue .. 30 20
DESIGNS: No. 238 President Kennedy. No. 239 Martin Luther King. No. 240 Robert F. Kennedy.

1969. Int. Labour Organization. 50th Anniv.
242. 56. 32 f. blue, purple & green 15 10

56a. Cipolla, Baran and Sambo (pair with cox). 56b. "African Woman" (Bezombes).

1969. "World Solidarity". Multicoloured.

(a) Gold Medal Winners, Mexico Olympics.
243. 1 f. Type 56a 15 15
244. 1 f. D. Beamon (long-jump) 15 15
245. 1 f. I. Becker (women's pentathlon) 15 15
246. 1 f. C. Besson (women's 400 metres) 15 15
247. 1 f. W. Davenport (110 metres hurdles) .. 15 15
248. 1 f. K. Dibiasi (diving) .. 15 15
249. 1 f. R. Fosbury (high-jumping) 15 15
250. 1 f. M. Gamoudi (5000 metres) 15 15
251. 1 f. Great Britain (sailing) 15 15
252. 1 f. J. Guyon (cross-country riding) .. 15 15
253. 1 f. D. Hemery (200 metres hurdles) 15 15
254. 1 f. S. Kato (gymnastics) .. 15 15
255. 1 f. B. Klinger (small bore rifle-shooting) 15 15
256. 1 f. R. Matson (shot put) .. 15 15
257. 1 f. R. Matthes (100 metres backstroke) 15 15
258. 1 f. D. Meyer (women's 200 metres freestyle) .. 15 15
259. 1 f. Morelon and Trentin (tandem cycle) 15 15
260. 1 f. D. Rebillard (4000 m. cycle pursuit) 15 15
261. 1 f. T. Smith (200 metres) 15 15
262. 1 f. P. Trentin (1000 metres cycle) 15 15
263. 1 f. F. Vianelli (196 kilo-metre cycle race) .. 15 15
264. 1 f. West Germany (dressage) 15 15
265. 1 f. M. Wolke (welterweight boxing) 15 15
266. 1 f. Zimmermann and Esser (women's kayak pair) .. 15 15

(b) Paintings.
267. 1 f. Type 56b 15 15
268. 1 f. "Mother and Child" (Gauguin) 15 15
269. 1 f. "Holy Family" (Murillo) (horiz.) .. 15 15
270. 1 f. "Adoration of the Kings" (Rubens) .. 15 15
271. 1 f. "Three Negroes" (Rubens) 15 15
272. 1 f. "Woman with Flowers" (Veneto) 15 15

57. Presidents Tombalbaye and Mobutu.

1969. Air. Central African States Union. 1st Anniv.
273. 57. 1,000 f. gold, red & blue 7·00
This stamp is embossed in gold foil; colours of flags enamelled.

58. "Cochlospermum tinctorium".

1969. Flowers. Multicoloured.
274. 1 f. Type 58 .. .. 5 5
275. 4 f. "Parkia biglobosa" .. 5 5
276. 10 f. "Pancratium trianthum" 5 5
277. 15 f. "Ipomoea aquatica" 8 5

1969. Air. Napoleon Bonaparte. Birth Bicent. Multicoloured. As T 80 of Congo Republic.
278. 30 f. "Napoleon visiting the Hotel des Invalides" (Veron-Bellecourt) .. 25 20
279. 85 f. "The Battle of Wagram" (H. Vernet) .. 70 50
280. 130 f. "The Battle of Austerlitz" (Gerard) .. 1·10 1·00

59. Frozen Carcases.

1969. Frozen Meat Industry.
281. 59. 25 f. red, green & orange 12 8
282. – 30 f. brown, slate & green 15 8
DESIGN: 30 f. Cattle and refrigerated abattoir, Farcha.

1969. African Development Bank. 5th Anniv. As T 118 of Cameroun.
283. 30 f. brown, emerald & red 15 10

60. Astronaut and Lunar Module.

1969. Air. 1st Man on the Moon. Embossed on gold foil.
289. 60. 1,000 f. gold .. .. 7·00

61. Nile Mouth Breeder. 62. President Tombalbaye.

1969. Fishes.
290. 61. 2 f. maroon, slate & green 5 5
291 – 3 f. slate, red and blue .. 5 5
292. – 5 f. indigo, lemon & ochre 5 5
293. – 20 f. indigo, green and red 10 5
FISHES. 3 f. Moonfish. 5 f. Puffer fish. 20 f. Tiger fish.

1969. A.S.E.C.N.A. 10th Anniv. As T 121 of Cameroun.
294. 30 f. orange 12 5

1970. President Tombalbaye.
295. 62. 25 f. multicoloured .. 15 10

63. "Village Life" (G. Narcisse).

1970. Air. African Paintings. Multicoloured.
296. 100 f. Type 63 .. .. 50 35
297. 250 f. "Market Woman" (I. N'Diaye) .. .. 1·10 70
298. 250 f. "Flower-seller" (I. N'Diaye) (vert.) .. 1·10 70

64. Lenin. 66. Osaka Print.

65. Class and Torchbearers.

1970. Lenin. Birth Cent.
299. 64. 150 f. blk., cream & gold 80 45

1970. New U.P.U. Headquarters Building, Berne.
As T 127 of Cameroun.
300. 30 f. brn., violet & carmine 15 8

1970. Int. Education Year.
301. 65. 100 f. multicoloured .. 55 30

1970. Air. World Fair "EXPO 70", Osaka, Japan.
302. 66. 50 f. green, blue & red 25 20
303. – 100 f. blue, green & red 55 30
304. – 125 f. slate, brn. & carmine 65 45
DESIGNS: 100 f. Tower of the Sun. 125 f. Osaka print (different).

1970. Air. "Apollo" Moon Flights. Nos. 164/6 surch. with new value, and optd. with various inscriptions and diagrams concerning space flights.
305. 30. 50 f. on 100 f. ("Apollo 11") 25 15
306. – 100 f. on 200 f. ("Apollo 12") 55 30
307. – 125 f. on 250 f. ("Apollo 13") 65 45

67. Meteorological Equipment and "Agriculture".

1970. World Meteorological Day.
308. 67. 50 f. grey, grn. & orge. 25 12

68. "DC 8-63" over Airport.

1970. Air. "Air Afrique" DC-8 "Fort Lamy".
309. 68. 30 f. multicoloured .. 15 10

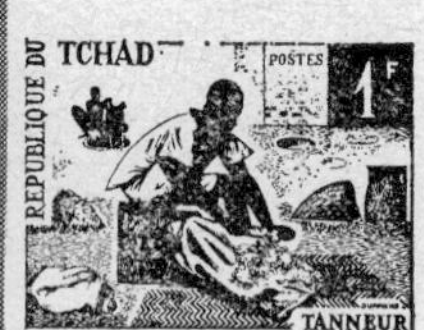

70. Ahmed Mangue (Minister of Education). 71. Tanning.

1970. Ahmed Mangue (air crash victim). Commem.
310. 70. 100 f. black, red and gold 50 25

1970. Trades and Handicrafts.
311. 71. 1 f. bistre, brn. & blue 5 5
312. – 2 f. brn., blue & green 5 5
313. – 3 f. violet, brn & mag. 5 5
314. – 4 f. brn., bistre & green 5 5
315. – 5 f. brn., green and red 5 5
DESIGNS—VERT. 2 f. Dyeing. 4 f. Water-carrying. HORIZ. 3 f. Milling palm-nuts for oil. 5 f. Copper-founding.

72. U.N. Emblem and Dove. 73. "The Visitation" (Venetian School 15th cent.).

1970. United Nations. 25th Anniv.
316. 72. 32 f. multicoloured .. 15 8

1970. Air. Christmas. Multicoloured.
317. 20 f. Type 73 .. .. 10 8
318. 25 f. "The Nativity" (Venetian School, 15th cent.) 12 8
319. 30 f. "Virgin and Child" (Veneziano) 15 10

74. Map and O.C.A.M. Building.

1971. O.C.A.M. (Organisation Commune Africane et Malgache) Conference, Fort Lamy.
320. 74. 30 f. multicoloured .. 15 8

75. Maritius "Post Office" 2d. of 1847.

1971. Air. "PHILEXOCAM" Stamp Exhib., Fort-Lamy.
321. 75. 10 f. slate, brn. & turq. 8 5
322. – 20 f. brn., black & turq. 10 8
323. – 30 f. brn., black & red 15 12
324. – 60 f. black, brn. & pur. 30 20
325. – 80 f. slate, brn. and blue 40 35
326. – 100 f. brn., slate & blue 55 40
DESIGNS—20 f. Tuscany 3 lire of 1860. 30 f. France 1 f. of 1849. 30 f., 60 f. U.S.A. 10 c. of 1847. 80 f. Japan 5 sen of 1872. 100 f. Saxony 3 pf. of 1850.

76. Pres. Nasser. 77. "Racial Harmony" Tree.

1971. Air. Gamal Abdel Nasser (Egypt). 1st Death Anniv.
328. 76. 75 f. multicoloured .. 40 20

1971. Racial Equality Year.
329. 77. 40 f. red, grn. and blue 20 10

78. Presidents Mobutu, Bokassa and Tombalbaye.

1971. Air. Reconciliation with Central African Republic and Zaire.
330. 78. 100 f. multicoloured .. 50 25

79. Map and Dish Aerial.

1971. World Telecommunications Day.
331. **79.** 5 f. orange, red & blue (postage) 5 5
332. – 40 f. grn., brn. & purple 20 5
333. – 50 f. black, brown & red 25 15
334. – 125 f. red, green & blue (air) 65 40

DESIGNS: 40 f. Map and communications tower. 50 f. Map and satellite. (49 × 27 mm.) 125 f. Map and telecommunications symbols. No. 288 commemorates Pan-African Telecommunications.

80. Scouts by Camp-fire.

1971. Air. World Scout Jamboree, Asagiri, Japan.
335. **80.** 250 f. multicoloured .. 1·40 75

81. Great White Heron.

1971. Air.
336. **81.** 1,000 f. multicoloured .. 5·50 3·75

82. Ancient Marathon Race.

1971. Air. Modern Olympic Games. 75th Anniv. Multicoloured.
337. 40 f. Type **82** 20 8
338. 45 f. Ancient stadium, Olympia 25 15
339. 75 f. Ancient wrestling .. 35 20
340. 130 f. Athens Stadium, Games 1896 .. .. 60 35

83. Sidney Bechet. **84.** Gen. de Gaulle.

1971. Air. Famous American Black Musicians. Multicoloured.
341. 50 f. Type **83** 25 15
342. 75 f. Duke Ellington .. 40 20
343. 100 f. Louis Armstrong .. 55 30

1971. Air. De Gaulle. 1st Death Anniv.
344. – 200 f. gold, bl. & light bl. 1·50
345. **84.** 200 f. gold, grn. & yell. 1·50

DESIGN: No. 298, Governor-General Felix Eboue.

1971. Air. African and Malagasy Posts and Telecommunications Union. 10th Anniv. As T **153** of Cameroun. Multicoloured.
347. 100 f. U.A.M.P.T. H.Q. and Sao carved animal head.. .. .. 50 30

85. Children's Heads.

1971. U.N.I.C.E.F. 25th Anniv.
348. **85.** 50 f. blue, grn. & purple 25 15

On the above stamp, "24e" has been obliterated and "25e" inserted in the commemorative inscription.

86. Gorane Nangara Dancers.

1971. Chad Dancers Multicoloured.
349. 10 f. Type **86** 8 5
350. 15 f. Yondo initiates .. 12 5
351. 30 f. M'Boum (vert.) .. 25 8
352. 40 f. Sara Kaba (vert.) .. 35 10

88. Presidents Pompidou and Tombalbaye.

1972. Visit of French President.
354. **88.** 40 f. multicoloured .. 20 12

89. Bob-sleighing.

1972. Air. Winter Olympic Games, Sapporo, Japan.
355. **89.** 50 f. red and blue .. 25 15
356. – 100 f. green and purple 55 30

DESIGN: 100 f. Downhill skiing.

90. Human Heart.

1972. World Heart Month.
357. **90.** 100 f. red, blue & violet 50 25

91. "Gorrizia dubiosa". **92.** Hurdling.

1972. Insects (1st series). Multicoloured.
358. 1 f. Type **91** 5 5
359. 2 f. "Argiope sector" .. 5 5
360. 3 f. "Nephila senegalense" 5 5
361. 4 f. "Oryctes boas" .. 5 5
362. 5 f. "Hemistigma albipunctata" .. 5 5
363. 25 f. "Dinothrombium tinctorium" 10 5
364. 30 f. "Bupreste sternocera H." 12 5
365. 40 f. "Hyperechia bomboides" 15 8
366. 50 f. "Chrysis" (Hymenoptere) 20 10
367. 100 f. "Tithoes confinis" (Longicome) 40 20
368. 130 f. "Galeodes araba" (Solifuge) 50 30

1972. Air. U.N.E.S.C.O. "Save Venice" Campaign. As T **160** of Cameroun. Mult.
369. 40 f. "Harbour Panorama" (detail Caffi) 20 10
370. 45 f. "Venice Panorama" (detail Caffi) (horiz.) .. 25 15
371. 140 f. "Grand Canal" (detail, Caffi) 70 45

1972. Olympic Games, Munich. Mult.
372. 50 f. Type **92** 25 12
373. 130 f. Gymnastics.. .. 60 35
374. 150 f. Swimming 75 45

93. Alphonse Daudet and "Tartarin de Tarascon".

1972. Air. Int. Book Year.
376. **93.** 100 f. brn., red & purple 55 25

94. Dromedary.

1972. Domestic Animals.
377. **94.** 25 f. brown and violet 12 5
378. – 30 f. blue and mauve.. 15 8
379. – 40 f. brown and green.. 20 10
380. – 45 f. brown and blue .. 25 12

DESIGNS: 30 f. Horse. 40 f. Saluki hound. 45 f. Goat.

95. "Luna 16" and Moon Probe. **96.** Tobacco Production.

1972. Air. Russian Moon Exploration.
381. **95.** 100 f. violet, brn. & blue 50 30
382. – 150 f. brn., blue and pur. 75 45

DESIGN—HORIZ. 150 f. "Lunokhod 1" Moon vehicle.

1972. Economic Development.
383. **96.** 40 f. grn., red & brown 20 10
384. – 50 f. brown, green & blue 25 12

DESIGN: 50 f. Ploughing with oxen.

97. Microscope, Cattle and Laboratory.

1972. Air. Farcha Veterinary Laboratory. 20th Anniv.
385. **97.** 75 f. multicoloured .. 35 15

98. Massa Warrior.

1972. Chad Warriors. Multicoloured.
386. 15 f. Type **98** 12 8
387. 20 f. Moudang archer .. 12 5

99. King Faisal and Pres. Tombalbaye.

1972. Visit of King Faisal of Saudi Arabia. Multicoloured.
388. 100 f. Type **99** (postage).. 50 30
389. 75 f. King Faisal and Kaaba, Mecca (air) 35 20

100. Gen. Gowon, Pres. Tombalbaye and Map.

1972. Visit of Gen. Gowon, Nigerian Head-of-State.
390. **100.** 70 f. multicoloured .. 35 15

101. "Madonna and Child" (G. Bellini).

1972. Air. Christmas. Paintings. Mult.
391. 40 f. Type **101** 20 12
392. 75 f. "Virgin and Child" (bas-relief, Da Santivo, Dall' Occhio) 40 25
393. 80 f. "Nativity" (B. Angelico) (horiz.) .. 40 25
394. 90 f. "Adoration of the Magi" (P. Perugino) .. 55 40

102. Commemorative Scroll.

1972. U.S.S.R. 50th Anniv.
395. **102.** 150 f. multicoloured .. 70 30

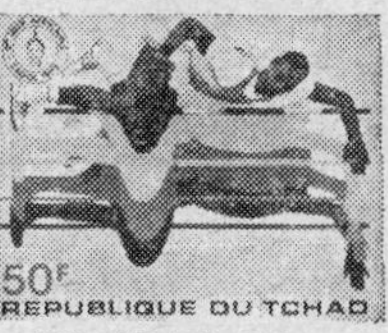

103. High-jumping.

1973. 2nd African Games, Lagos. Mult.
396. 50 f. Type **103** 20 10
397. 125 f. Running 55 25
398. 200 f. Putting the shot .. 90 40

104. Copernicus and Planetary System Diagram.

1973. Air. Nicholas Copernicus. 500th Birth Anniv.
400. **104.** 250 f. grey, brn. & mve. 1·10 65

1973. African Solidarity "Drought Relief" No. 377 surch. **SECHERESSE SOLIDARITE AFRICAINE** and value.
401. **94.** 100 f. on 25 f. brn. & vio. 45 30

1973. U.A.M.P.T. As Type **182** of Cameroun.
402. 100 f. green, red & brown 45 30

105. "Skylab" over Globe.

1974. Air. "Skylab" Exploits.
403. 105. 100 f. brn., red & blue 45 25
404. – 150 f. turq., blue & brn. 70 40
DESIGN: 150 f. Close-up of "Skylab".

106. Chad Mother and Children.

1974. Chad Red Cross. First Anniv.
405. 106. 30 f.+10 f. multicoloured 15 12

107. Football Players.

1974. Air. World Cup Football Championships, West Germany.
406. 107. 50 f. brown and red .. 20 12
407. – 125 f. green and red .. 55 30
408. – 150 f. red and green .. 70 40
DESIGNS: Nos. 407/8, Footballers in action similar to Type 107.
No. 407 is vert.

108. Chad Family. 110. Rotary Emblem.

109. U.P.U. Emblem and Mail Canoe.

1974. Air. World Population Year.
409. 108. 250 f. brn., grn. & blue 1·00 70

1974. Air. Universal Postal Union. Cent.
410. 109. 30 f. brn., red and grn. 12 8
411. – 40 f. black and blue .. 15 8
412. – 100 f. blue, brn. & blk. 45 25
413. – 150 f. violet, green and turquoise-green .. 70 40
DESIGNS—U.P.U. Emblem and: 40 f. Electric train. 100 f. Jetliner. 150 f. Space satellite.

1975. Rotary International. 70th Anniv.
414. 110. 50 f. multicoloured .. 20 12

111. Heads of Women of Four Races.

1975. Air. International Women's Year.
415. 111. 250 f. multicoloured .. 1·10 70

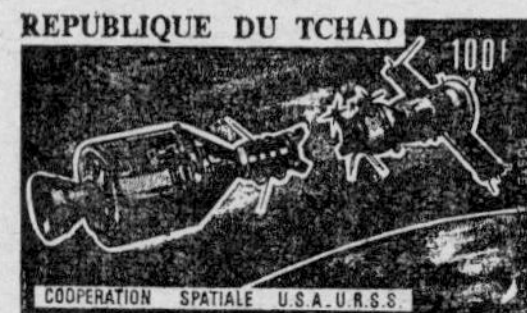

112. "Apollo" and "Soyuz" Spacecraft about to dock.

1975. Air. "Apollo-Soyuz" Test Project.
416. 112. 100 f. brn., blue & emer. 40 25
417. – 130 f. brn., blue & emer. 60 40
DESIGN: 130 f. "Apollo" and "Soyuz" spacecraft docked.

113. "Craterostigma plantagineum".

1975. Flowers. Multicoloured.
418. 5 f. Type 113 .. .. 5 5
419. 10 f. "Tapinanthus globiferus" 5 5
420. 15 f. "Commelina forskalaei" (vert.) 5 5
421. 20 f. "Adenium obasum" 8 5
422. 25 f. "Hibiscus esulentus" 10 5
423. 30 f. "Hibiscus sabdariffa" 12 5
424. 40 f. "Kigelia africana" .. 15 8

114. Football.

1975. Air. Olympic Games, Montreal (1976).
425. 120. 75 f. green and red .. 35 20
426. – 100 f. choc., blue & red 40 30
427. – 125 f. blue and brown 45 35
DESIGNS: 100 f. Throwing the discus. 152 f. Running.

1975. Air. Successful Rendezvous of "Apollo-Soyuz" Mission. Optd. **JONCTION 17 JUILLET 1975.**
428. 112. 100 f. brn., bl. & grn... 40 25
429. – 130 f. brn., bl. & grn... 60 40

115. Figures "200" and Flags.

1975. Air. American Revolution. Bicent.
430. 115. 150 f. bl., red & brn... 60 45

116. "Adoration of the Shepherds" (Murillo).

1975. Air. Christmas. Religious Paintings. Multicoloured.
431. 40 f. Type 116 .. .. 15 8
432. 75 f. "Adoration of the Shepherds" (G. de la Tour) 30 25
433. 80 f. "Virgin of the Bible" (R. van der Weyden) (vert.) 30 25
434. 100 f. "Holy Family with the Lamb" (attrib. Raphael) (vert.) .. 40 30

117. A. Graham Bell.

1976. Telephone Centenary.
435. 117. 100 f. multicoloured .. 70 60
436. 125 f. multicoloured .. 90 80

118. Ice Hockey.

1976. Winter Olympics. Medal-winners, Innsbruck. Multicoloured.
437. 60 f. Type 118 (postage) . 45 35
438. 90 f. Ski-jumping (K. Schnabl, Austria) .. 65 55
439. 250 f. Bobsleighing (West Germany) (air).. .. 1·75 1·50
440. 300 f. Speed-skating (J. E. Storholt, Norway) .. 2·10 1·75
These stamps were not issued without overprints.

119. Paul Revere's Night Ride.

1976. Air. American Revolution. Bicent.
442. 100 f. Type 119 .. .. 70 60
443. 125 f. Washington crossing the Delaware 90 80
444. 150 f. Lafayette offering his services to America 1·10 95
445. 200 f. Rochambeau and Washington at Yorktown .. .. .. 1·40 1·10
446. 250 f. Franklin presenting the Declaration of Independence .. .. 1·75 1·50

120. Hurdling.

1976. Olympic Games, Montreal. Mult.
448. 45 f. Type 120 (postage).. 30 20
449. 100 f. Boxing (air) .. 70 60
450. 200 f. Pole vaulting .. 1·40 1·10
451. 300 f. Shot-putting .. 2·10 1·75

121. Launch of "Viking".

1976. "Viking" landing on Mars. Mult.
453. 45 f. Type 121 (postage).. 30 20
454. 90 f. Trajectory of flight.. 65 55
455. 100 f. Descent to Mars (air) 70 60
456. 200 f. "Viking" in flight 1·40 1·10
457. 250 f. "Viking" on landing approach .. .. 1·75 1·50

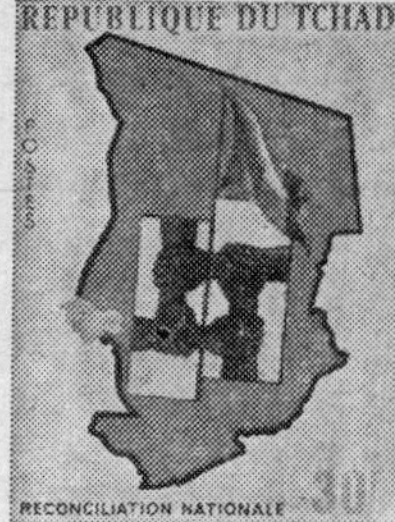

122. Handclasp and Flag on Map.

1976. National Reconciliation. Mult.
459. 30 f. Type 122 .. .. 20 10
460. 60 f. Type 122 .. .. 40 20
461. 120 f. People joining hands on map 90 80

123. Release of Political Prisoners.

1976. April 13th Revolution. First Anniv. Multicoloured.
462. 30 f. Type 123 .. .. 20 10
463. 60 f. Officer-cadets on parade 40 20
464. 120 f. Type 123 .. .. 90 80

OFFICIAL STAMPS

O 1. Flag and Map.

1966. Flag in blue, yellow and red.
O 148. O 1. 1 f. blue 5 5
O 149. 2 f. grey 5 5
O 150. 5 f. black 5 5
O 151. 10 f. ultramarine .. 8 8
O 152. 25 f. orange .. 15 15
O 153. 30 f. turquoise .. 20 20
O 154. 40 f. red 25 25
O 155. 50 f. purple .. 30 30
O 156. 85 f. green 50 50
O 157. 100 f. brown .. 60 60
O 158. 200 f. red .. .. 1·40 1·40

POSTAGE DUE STAMPS

1928. Postage Due type of France optd. **TCHAD A.E.F.**
D 58. D 2. 5 c. blue 5 5
D 59. 10 c. brown 5 5
D 60. 20 c. olive 5 5
D 61. 25 c. red 5 5
D 62. 30 c. red 8 8
D 63. 45 c. green 10 10
D 64. 50 c. purple 10 10
D 65. 60 c. brown on cream 25 25
D 66. 1 f. claret on cream .. 25 25
D 67. 2 f. red 60 60
D 68. 3 f. violet 30 30

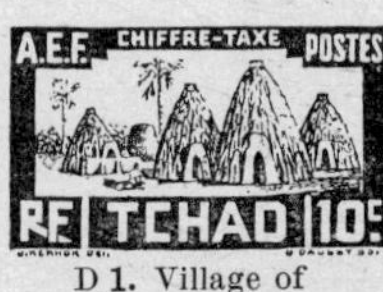

D 1. Village of Straw Huts. D 2. Pirogue on Lake Chad.

1930.
D 69. D 1. 5 c. olive and blue .. 5 5
D 70. 10 c. brown and red.. 8 8
D 71. 20 c. brown and green 15 15
D 72. 25 c. brown and blue 15 15
D 73. 30 c. green and brown 15 15
D 74. 45 c. olive and green 15 15
D 75. 50 c. brn. and mauve 15 15
D 76. 60 c. black and lilac.. 20 20

D 77. D 2. 1 f. black and brown 30 30
D 78. 2 f. brown and mauve 50 50
D 79. 3 f. brown and red .. 4·25 4·25

D 3. Gonoa Hippopotamus.

1962.
D 89. 50 c. yellow-bistre .. 5 5
D 90. 50 c. red-brown .. 5 5
D 91. 1 f. blue 5 5
D 92. 1 f. green 5 5
D 93. 2 f. vermilion 5 5
D 94. 2 f. claret 5 5
D 95. 5 f. myrtle 5 5
D 96. 5 f. blue-violet 5 5
D 97. 10 f. chocolate 10 10
D 98. 10 f. chestnut 10 10
D 99. 25 f. purple 20 20
D 100. 25 f. violet 20 20

DESIGNS (rock-paintings): No. D 89, Type D 3. D 90, Gonoa kudu. D 91, Two Gonoa antelopes. D 92, Three Gonoa antelopes. D 93, Gonoa antelope. D 94, Tibestiram. D 95, Tibestiox. D 96, Oudingueur boar. D 97, Gonoa elephant. D 98, Gira-Gira rhinoceros. D 99, Bardai warrior. D 100, Gonoa masked archer. The two designs in each value are arranged in tetebeche pairs throughout the sheet.

D 4. Kanem Puppet.

1969. Native Puppets.
D 284. D 4. 1 f. brn., verm. & emer. 5 5
D 285. – 2 f. brn., grn. & verm. 5 5
D 286. – 5 f. green and brown 5 5
D 287. – 10 f. brn., pur. & emer. 8 5
D 288. – 25 f. brn., pur. & emer. 15 10

DESIGNS: 2 f. Kotoko doll. 5 f. Copper doll. 10 f. Kotoko (diff.). 25 f. Guera doll.

MILITARY FRANK STAMPS

1965. No. 77 optd. **F.M.**
M 148. 20 f. red and black ..

M 1. Soldier with Standard.

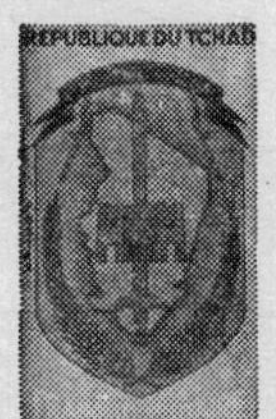

M 2. Shoulder Flash of 1st Chad Regiment.

1966. No value indicated.
M 149. M 1. (—) multicoloured 20 12

1972. No value indicated.
M 353. M 2. (—) multicoloured 20 15

CHAMBA BC

An Indian "convention" state of the Punjab. Stamps of India optd. **CHAMBA STATE.**

1886. Queen Victoria.
1. 14. ½ a. blue-green 5 5
2. – 1 a. purple 5 5
4. – 1½ a. brown 25 45
5. – 2 a. blue 12 12
7. – 2½ a. green .. .. 2·25 2·00
9. – 3 a. orange 20 20
11. – 4 a. green (No. 96) .. 30 25
12. – 6 a. brown (No. 80) .. 40 55
15. – 8 a. mauve 30 60
16. – 12 a. purple on red .. 50 65
17. – 1 r. grey (No. 101) .. 3·50 6·00
18. 26. 1 r. green and red .. 50 70
19. 27. 2 r. red and orange .. 8·00
20. 3 r. brown and green .. 10·00
21. 5 r. blue and violet .. 11·00

1900. Queen Victoria.
22. 25. 3 p. red 5 5
23. 3 p. grey 8 5
24. 14. ½ a. green 5 5
26. – 1 a. red 5 5
27. – 2 a. lilac .. .. 1·25 1·50

1903. King Edward VII.
29. 23. 3 p. grey 5 5
30. – ½ a. green (No. 122) .. 5 5
31. – 1 a. red (No. 123) .. 5 5
33. – 2 a. lilac 10 10
34. – 3 a. orange 30 25
35. – 4 a. olive 40 35
36. – 6 a. yellow-brown .. 50 65
37. – 8 a. mauve 50 55
39. – 12 a. purple on red .. 60 65
40. – 1 r. green and red .. 80 90

1907. King Edward VII.
41. – ½ a. green (No. 149) .. 5 5
42. – 1 a. red (No. 150) .. 10 12

1913. King George V. Optd. in two lines.
43. 40. 3 p. grey 5 5
44. 41. ½ a. green 5 5
45. 42. 1 a. red 5 5
55. 1 a. chocolate 5 5
56. 43. 1½ a. brown (No. 163) .. 4·50 5·00
57. 1½ a. brown (No. 165) .. 10 12
58. 1½ a. red 30 35
47. 44. 2 a. lilac 5 8
59. 47. 2½ a. blue 30 35
60. 2½ a. orange 30 35
48. 48. 3 a. orange 12 25
61. 3 a. blue 50 65
49. 49. 4 a. olive 25 25
50. 51. 6 a. yellow-brown .. 25 25
51. 52. 8 a. mauve 30 40
52. 53. 12 a. claret 60 80
53. 54. 1 r. brown and green .. 90 1·30

1921. No. 192 of India optd. **CHAMBA.**
54. 42. 9 p. on 1 a. red 40 50

1927. Stamps of India (King George V) optd. **CHAMBA STATE** in one line.
62. 40. 3 p. grey 5 5
63. 41. ½ a. green 5 5
76. 62. ½ a. green 5 5
64. 63. 9 p. green 5 5
65. 42. 1 a. chocolate 5 5
77. 64. 1 a. chocolate 5 5
66. 65. 1¼ a. mauve 5 5
67. 43. 1½ a. red 5 5
68. 45. 2 a. lilac 12 12
78. 44. 2 a. orange-red .. 8 8
69. 47. 2½ a. orange 25 25
70. 48. 3 a. blue 30 30
80. 3 a. red 30 30
71. 50. 4 a. green 25 30
81. 49. 4 a. olive 35 35
72. 51. 6 a. yellow-brown .. 21·00
73. 52. 8 a. mauve 35 40
74. 53. 12 a. claret 50 90
75. 54. 1 r. brown and green .. 80 90

1938. Stamps of India (King George V Nos. 247/64) optd. **CHAMBA STATE.**
82. 74. 3 p. slate 8 10
83. ½ a. brown 12 30
84. 9 p. green 30 30
85. 1 a. red 8 12
86. 76. 2 a. red 25 35
87. – 2½ a. violet 30 35
88. – 3 a. green .. .. 1·10 1·30
89. – 3½ a. blue 30 50
90. – 4 a. brown 30 50
91. – 6 a. green .. .. 2·50 4·00
92. – 8 a. violet .. .. 50 1·30
93. – 12 a. red .. .. 1·10 1·75
94. 77. 1 r. slate and brown .. 2·50 3·00
95. 2 r. purple and brown .. 3·75 5·25
96. 5 r. green and blue .. 7·00 8·00
97. 10 r. purple and red .. 17·00 20·00
98. 15 r. brown and green .. 25·00 30·00
99. 25 r. slate and purple .. 40·00 50·00

1948. Stamps of India (King George VI) optd. **CHAMBA.**

(a) On issue of 1938.
100. 74. ½ a. brown 50 45
101. 1 a. red 60 50
102. 77. 1 r. slate and brown .. 4·00 4·50
103. 2 r. purple and brown .. 4·00 5·00
104. 5 r. green and blue .. 16·00 17·00
105. 10 r. purple and red .. 25·00 26·00
106. 15 r. brown and green .. 26·00 29·00
107. 25 r. slate and purple .. 40·00 45·00

(b) On issue of 1940.
108. 78. 3 p. slate 8 8
109. ½ a. mauve 8 8
110. 9 p. green 8 8
111. 1 a. red 8 8
112. 79. 1½ a. violet 8 8
113. 2 a. red 8 25
114. 3 a. violet 10 25
115. 3½ a. blue 10 30
116. 80. 4 a. brown 10 30
117. 6 a. green 30 65
118. 8 a. violet .. .. 30 1·20
119. 12 a. purple .. .. 65 1·30
120. – 14 a. purple (No. 277) .. 2·25 4·00

OFFICIAL STAMPS

Stamps of India optd. **SERVICE CHAMBA STATE.**

1886. Queen Victoria.
O 1. 14. ½ a. blue-green .. 5 5
O 3. – 1 a. purple 5 5
O 5. – 2 a. blue 5 8
O 7. – 3 a. orange 45 50
O 8. – 4 a. green (No. 96) .. 8 8
O 10. – 6 a. brown (No. 80) .. 30 35
O 12. – 8 a. mauve 30 40
O 14. – 12 a. purple on red .. 1·75 3·75
O 15. – 1 r. grey (No. 101) .. 3·50 3·50
O 16. 26. 1 r. green and red .. 1·10 1·30

1902. Queen Victoria.
O 17. 25. 3 p. grey 5 5
O 19. 14. ½ a. yellow-green .. 5 5
O 20. – 1 a. red 8 5
O 21. – 2 a. lilac 50 80

1903. King Edward VII.
O 23. 28. 3 p. grey 5 5
O 24. ½ a. green (No. 122) .. 5 5
O 25. 1 a. red (No. 123) .. 5 5
O 27. – 2 a. lilac 5 5
O 28. – 4 a. olive 25 25
O 29. – 8 a. mauve 40 45
O 31. – 1 r. green and red .. 40 45

1907. King Edward VII.
O 32. – ½ a. green (No. 149) .. 8 5
O 33. – 1 a. red (No. 150) .. 30 25

1913. King George V Official stamps optd. **CHAMBA STATE.**
O 34. 40. 3 p. grey 5 5
O 37. 41. ½ a. green 5 5
O 38. 42. 1 a. red 5 5
O 47. 1 a. chocolate 5 5
O 40. 44. 2 a. lilac (No. O 83) .. 8 12
O 41. 49. 4 a. olive (No. O 86) .. 25 30
O 42. 52. 8 a. mauve 40 45
O 43. 54. 1 r. brown and green .. 50 55

1914. King George V Official stamps optd. **SERVICE CHAMBA STATE.**
O 44. 44. 2 a. lilac (No. 166) .. 2·00 3·00
O 45. 49. 4 a. olive (No. 210) .. 4·50 5·50

1921. No. O 97 of India optd. **CHAMBA.**
O 46. 42. 9 p. on 1 a. red .. 8 25

1927. King George V Postage stamps optd. **CHAMBA STATE SERVICE.**
O 48. 40. 3 p. grey 5 5
O 49. 41. ½ a. green 5 5
O 61. 62. ½ a. green 5 5
O 50. 63. 9 p. green 5 5
O 51. 42. 1 a. chocolate 5 5
O 62. 64. 1 a. chocolate 5 5
O 52. 65. 1¼ a. mauve 5 5
O 53. 45. 2 a. lilac 8 10
O 63. 44. 2 a. orange-red .. 5 5
O 54. 50. 4 a. olive 5 5
O 65. 49. 4 a. green 5 5
O 55. 52. 8 a. mauve 10 30
O 56. 53. 12 a. claret 40 45
O 57. 54. 1 r. brown and green .. 50 55
O 58. 2 r. red and orange .. 4·00
O 59. 5 r. blue and violet .. 6·00
O 60. 10 r. green and red .. 7·00

1938. King George VI Postage stamps of India optd. **CHAMBA STATE SERVICE.**
O 66. 74. 9 p. green 25 30
O 67. 1 a. red 12 25
O 68. 77. 1 r. slate and brown .. £110 £110
O 69. 2 r. purple and brown 2·50 3·00
O 70. 5 r. green and blue .. 4·50 5·00
O 71. 10 r. purple and red .. 9·00 10·00

1941. Official stamps of India optd. **CHAMBA.**
O 72. O 1. 3 p. slate 8 5
O 73. ½ a. brown 30 12
O 74. ½ a. purple 25 8
O 75. 9 p. green 8 5
O 76. 1 a. red 8 8
O 77. 1 a. 3 p. bistre .. 2·50 1·30
O 78. 1½ a. violet 10 25
O 79 2 a. orange 12 25
O 80. 2½ a. violet 35 35
O 81. 4 a. brown 40 60
O 82. 8 a. violet 80 90

1942. King George VI Postage stamps of India optd. **CHAMBA SERVICE.**
O 83. 77. 1 r. slate and brown .. 2·00 3·00
O 84. 2 r. purple and brown 2·25 3·00
O 85. 5 r. green and blue .. 4·50 7·00
O 86. 10 r. purple and red .. 8·00 9·00

CHARKHARI BC

A state of Central India. Now uses Indian stamps.

1.

2.

1894. Imperf.
5a. 1. ½ a. purple 65 65
6. ½ a. purple .. .. 80 1·25
7. 1 a. green .. .. 1·50 1·50
8. 2 a. green .. .. 3·00 3·00
9. 4 a. green .. .. 3·00 4·00

INDEX

Countries can be quickly located by referring to the index at the end of this volume.

1909. Perf. or imperf.
23. 2. 1 p. brown .. .. 85 4·00
16. 1 p. blue 15 25
33. 1 p. violet .. .. 2·75
32. 1 p. green .. .. 6·00 7·00
37. ½ a. red .. .. 4·00 6·00
35. ½ a. brown .. .. 25 2·00
34. ½ a. olive 12
36. ½ a. black .. .. 11·00 8·00
39. 1 a. green .. .. 25 1·50
40. 1 a. chocolate .. .. 20 1·50
41. 1 a. red .. .. 16·00 24·00
42. 2 a. blue .. .. 35 2·00
43. 2 a. grey .. .. 11·00 18·00
20. 4 a. green .. .. 1·25
44. 4 a. red .. .. 3·00 6·00
21. 8 a. red .. .. 1·25
22. 1 r. brown .. .. 3·00

3.

1918. Imperf.
28. 8. 1 p. violet .. .. 3·25 3·25

4. (Actual size 63 × 25 mm.)

1925. Imperf.
29. 4. 1 a. violet .. .. 8·00 8·00

5. The Lake.

DESIGNS—HORIZ. 1 a. Imlia Palace. 2 a. Industrial school. 4 a. Bird's-eye view of city. 8 a. Fort. 1 r. Guest House. 2 r. Palace Gate. 3 r. Temples at Rainpur. 5 r. Goverdhan Temple.

1931. Perf.
45. 5. ½ a. green 5 5
46. – 1 a. sepia 5 5
47. – 2 a. violet 5 5
48. – 4 a. olive 5 5
49. – 8 a. mauve 5 5
50. – 1 r. green and red .. 12 10
51. – 2 r. red and brown .. 30 10
52. – 3 r. brown and green .. 45 10
53. – 5 r. blue and lilac .. 65 25

1940. Nos. 21/2 surch.
54. 2. ½ a. on 8 a. red .. 5·00 6·00
55. 1 a. on 1 r. brown .. 10·00 12·00
56. "1 ANNA" on 1 r. brown £100

CHILE O1

A republic on the W. coast of S. America.

100 centavos = 1 peso.
1960. 10 milesimos = 1 centesimo.
100 centesimos = 1 escudo.

ILLUSTRATIONS
British Commonwealth and all overprints and surcharges are FULL SIZE. Foreign Countries have been reduced to ¾-LINEAR.

1. Columbus.

1853. Imperf.
29. 1. 1 c. yellow .. .. 6·00 10·00
17. 5 c. brown .. .. 55·00 3·00
37. 5 c. red .. .. 4·50 1·25
31. 10 c. blue .. .. 15·00 1·75
33. 20 c. green .. .. 18·00 14·00

2.

3.

1867. Perf.
41 2. 1 c. orange .. .. 2·00 75
43. 2 c. black .. .. 3·50 1·00
45. 5 c. red .. .. 2·50 12
46. 10 c. blue .. .. 2·50 20
48. 20 c. green .. .. 3·00 60

1877. Roul.

No.	Type	Description		
49.	3.	1 c. slate	30	10
50.		2 c. orange	2·00	40
51.		5 c. lake	2·00	8
52.		10 c. blue	2·50	10
53.		20 c. green	2·50	45

4. 5.

1878. Roul.

No.	Type	Description		
55.	4.	1 c. green	20	5
57.		2 c. red	30	5
58.		5 c. red	1·40	15
59a.		5 c. blue	30	5
60a.		10 c. orange	45	8
61.		15 c. slate-green	20	12
62.		20 c. grey	50	5
63.		25 c. brown	35	12
64.		30 c. red	70	30
65a.		50 c. violet	20	15
66.	5.	1 p. black and brown	1·75	15

6. 7.

1900. Roul.

No.	Type	Description		
82.	6.	1 c. green	8	5
83.		2 c. lake	8	5
84a.		5 c. blue	45	10
78.		10 c. lilac	90	10
79.		20 c. grey	50	15
80.		30 c. chestnut	60	20
81.		50 c. brown	60	20

1900. Surch. **5.**

No.	Type	Description		
86.	4.	5 c. on 30 c. red	12	8

1901. Perf.

No.	Type	Description		
87.	7.	1 c. green	8	5
88.		2 c. red	12	5
89.		5 c. blue	12	5
90.		10 c. black and red	25	12
91.		30 c. black and violet	80	15
92.		50 c. black and red	95	25

1903. Surch. **Diez CENTVAOS.**

No.	Type	Description		
93.	6.	10 c. on 30 c. chestnut	15	10

8. Huemal. 9. Pedro Valdivia.

1904. Animal supporting shield at left without mane and tail. Optd. **CORREOS** in frame.

No.	Type	Description		
94.	8.	2 c. brown	10	5
95.		5 c. red	12	5
96.		10 c. olive	30	12

1904. As T 8, but animal with mane and tail. Optd. **CORREOS** in frame and the 1 p. also surch. **CENTAVOS 3 3.**

No.	Type	Description		
97.	8.	2 c. brown	1·00	1·00
98.		3 c. on 1 p. brown	8	8
99.		5 c. red	2·25	2·25
100.		10 c. olive	2·75	2·75

1904. Surch. **CORREOS** in frame and new value.

No.	Type	Description		
101.	9.	1 c. on 20 c. blue	5	5
102.		3 c. on 5 c. red	10·00	10·00
103.		12 c. on 5 c. red	20	10

10. 11. 12.
Christopher Columbus.

1905.

No.	Type	Description		
104.	10.	1 c. green	5	5
105.		2 c. red	5	5
106.		3 c. brown	10	8
107.		5 c. blue	10	5
108.	11.	10 c. black and grey	15	5
109.		12 c. black and lake	40	40
110.		15 c. black and lilac	20	8
111.		20 c. black and brown	30	10
112.		30 c. black and green	35	15
113.		50 c. black and blue	35	12
114.	12.	1 p. grey and green	2·00	2·00

1910. Optd. **ISLAS DE JUAN FERNANDEZ** or surch. also.

No.	Type	Description		
115.	11.	5 c. on 12 c. blk. & lake	8	8
116.	12.	10 c. on 1 p. grey & grn.	15	15
117.		20 c. on 1 p. grey & grn.	20	20
118.		1 p. grey and green	90	85

13. Battle of Chacabuco. 14. San Martin Monument.

1910. Independence Cent. Dated "1810–1910". Centres in black.

No.	Type	Description		
119.	–	1 c. green	8	5
120.	13.	2 c. lake	5	5
121.	–	3 c. chestnut	10	10
122.	–	5 c. blue	8	5
123.	–	10 c. brown	20	15
124.	–	12 c. red	40	30
125.	–	15 c. slate	25	20
126.	–	20 c. orange	30	25
127.	–	25 c. blue	65	45
128.	–	30 c. mauve	50	30
129.	–	50 c. olive	70	40
130.	14.	1 p. yellow	2·50	1·75
131.	–	2 p. red	1·75	90
132.	–	5 p. green	9·00	8·00
133.	–	10 p. purple	26·00	21·00

DESIGNS—HORIZ. 1 c. Oath of Independence. 3 c. Battle of Roble. 5 c. Battle of the Maipu. 10 c. Fight between frigates "Lautaro" and "Esmeralda". 12 c. Capture of the "Maria Isabella". 15 c. First sortie of the liberating forces. 20 c. Abdication of O'Higgins. 25 c. First Chilean Congress. VERT. 30 c. O'Higgins Monument. 50 c. Carrera Monument. 2 p. General Blanco. 5 p. General Zenteno. 10 p. Admiral Cochrane.

16. Columbus. 17. Valdivia. 18. O'Higgins.

19. Admiral Cochrane. 20. Freire. 21. Prieto.

22. M. Rengifo. 23. A. Pinto.

1911. Inscr. "CHILE CORREOS".

No.	Type	Description		
135.	16.	1 c. green	5	5
136.	17.	2 c. red	5	5
150.	16.	2 c. red	5	5
137.	–	3 c. sepia	5	5
151.	–	4 c. sepia	5	5
138.	18.	5 c. blue	5	5
161.	19.	5 c. blue	5	5
152.	–	8 c. grey	5	5
139.	20.	10 c. black and grey	8	5
153.	18.	10 c. black and blue	12	5
140.	–	12 c. black and red	8	5
154.	–	14 c. black and red	8	5
141.	21.	15 c. black and purple	8	5
142.	–	20 c. black and orange	15	5
167.	–	25 c. black and blue	10	5
168.	–	30 c. black and brown	15	5
155.	21.	40 c. black and purple	30	10
169.	22.	40 c. black and violet	10	5
170.	–	50 c. black and green	25	5
156.	–	60 c. black and blue	50	30
171.	–	80 c. black and sepia	30	25
188.	23.	1 p. black and green	20	5
189.	–	2 p. black and red	60	10
174.	–	5 p. black and olive	1·25	15
190a.	–	10 p. black and orange	1·25	40

PORTRAITS: 3 c., 4 c. Toro Z. 8 c. Freire. 12 c., 14 c. F. A. Pinto. 20 c. Bulnes. 25 c., 60 c. Montt. 30 c. Perez. 50 c. Errazuriz Z. 80 c. Admiral Latorre. 2 p. Santa Maria. 5 p. Balmaceda. 10 p. Errazuriz E.

24. Columbus. 25. P. de Valdivia. 25a. Columbus.

1915. Larger Stars.

No.	Type	Description		
157a.	24.	1 c. green	5	5
158.	25.	2 c. red	5	5
160.	24.	4 c. brown (small head)	5	5
159.	25a.	4 c. brown (large head)	12	5

26. Chilean Congress Building. 26a. O'Higgins.

1923. Pan-American Conf.

No.	Type	Description		
176.	26.	2 c. red	8	8
177.		4 c. brown	8	8
178.		10 c. black and blue	10	8
179.		20 c. black and orange	10	8
180.		40 c. black and mauve	20	10
181.		1 p. black and green	30	12
182.		2 p. black and red	85	20
183.		5 p. black and green	2·40	1·00

1927. Air. Unissued stamp surch. **Correo Aereo** and value.

No.	Type	Description		
184.	26.	40 c. on 10 c. bl. & brn.	£100	22·00
184a.		80 c. on 10 c. bl. & brn.	£130	24·00
184b.		1.20 p. on 10 c. blue and brown	£130	24·00
184c.		1.60 p. on 10 c. blue and brown	£130	24·00
184d.		2 p. on 10 c. bl. & brn.	£130	24·00

1928. Air. Optd. **CORREO AEREO** and bird or surch. also.

No.	Type	Description		
191.	–	20 c. blk. & orge. (No. 142)	25	25
199.	22.	40 c. black and violet	15	10
200.	23.	1 p. black and green	20	10
194.	–	2 p. blk. & red (No. 189)	60	25
201.	19.	3 p. on 5 c. blue	14·00	14·00
195.	–	5 p. blk. & ol. (No. 174)	2·00	40
196.	18.	6 p. on 10 c. black & bl.	14·00	14·00
198.	–	10 p. black and orange (No. 190a)	2·50	1·10

1928. As Types of 1911, but inscr. "CORREOS DE CHILE".

No.	Type	Description		
205.	19.	5 c. blue	5	5
206.		5 c. green	8	5
204.	18.	10 c. black and blue	10	5
208.	21.	15 c. black and purple	15	5
209.	–	20 c. black and orange (As No. 142)	1·00	8
210.	–	25 c. black and blue (As No. 167)	15	5
211.	–	30 c. black and brown (As No. 168)	12	5
212.	–	50 c. black and green (As No. 170)	15	5

1929. Air. Nos. 209/12 optd. **CORREO AEREO** and bird.

No.	Type	Description		
213a.		20 c. black and orange	12	5
214.		25 c. black and blue	8	5
215.		30 c. black and brown	10	8
216.		50 c. black and green	10	5

27. Winged Wheel. 28. Sower.

1930. Nitrate Industry Cent.

No.	Type	Description		
217.	27.	5 c. green	10	5
218.		10 c. brown	10	5
219.		15 c. violet	15	5
220.	–	25 c. slate (Girl harvester)	40	25
221.	28.	70 c. blue	70	30
222.		1 p. green (24½ × 30 mm.)	70	15

29. 31. Los Cerrillos Airport.

1931. Air. Inscr. "LINEA AEREA NACIONAL".

No.	Type	Description		
223.	29.	5 c. green	5	5
224.		10 c. brown	5	5
225.		20 c. red	8	5
226a.	–	50 c. sepia	12	5
227.	31.	50 c. blue	40	30
228.	–	1 p. violet	25	8
229.	–	2 p. slate	40	12
230.	31.	5 p. red	60	20

DESIGN: 50 c. sepia. 1 p., 2 p. Aeroplane over mountain and river.

32. O'Higgins. 35. M. Egana.

1931.

No.	Type	Description		
231.	32.	10 c. blue	8	5
232.	–	20 c. brown (Bulnes)	8	5
233.	–	30 c. magenta (Perez)	10	5

1934. Constitution of 1833. Cent.

No.	Type	Description		
234.	35.	30 c. magenta	8	5
235.	–	1 p. 20 blue	15	10

PORTRAIT: 1 p. 20, Joaquin Tocornal (24½ × 29 mm).

36. Aeroplanes above Globe. 37. Diego de Almagro.

1934. Air. As T 36.

No.	Type	Description		
236.		10 c. green	5	5
237.		15 c. green	5	5
238.		20 c. blue	5	5
239.		30 c. black	5	5
239a.		40 c. blue	5	5
240.		50 c. brown	5	5
241.		60 c. black	5	5
356.		70 c. blue	5	5
243.		80 c. black	5	5
244.		1 p. grey	5	5
245.		2 p. blue	8	5
246.		3 p. brown	8	5
247.		4 p. brown	8	5
248.		5 p. red	8	5
249.		6 p. brown	12	5
250.		8 p. green	15	5
251.		10 p. maroon	20	5
252.		20 p. olive	35	5
366b.		30 p. grey	30	15
366c.		40 p. violet	40	20
366e.		50 p. purple	40	12

DESIGNS—VERT. (21 × 25 mm.): 10 c. 15 c., 20 c. Aeroplane over Santiago. 30 c., 40 c., 50 c. Aeroplane over landscape. 60 c. Condor in flight. 70 c. Aeroplane and star. 80 c. Condor and statue of Caupolican. (25 × 29 mm.): 1 p., 2 p. T 36. 3 p., 4 p., 5 p. Seaplane in flight. 6 p., 8 p., 10 p. Aeroplane and rainbow. 20 p., 30 p. Flying boat and compass. 40 p., 50 p. Aeroplane riding a storm.

1936. Discovery of Chile. 4th Cent. Inscr. "1536–1936" (except 2 p.).

No.	Type	Description		
256.	–	5 c. red	5	5
257.	–	10 c. violet	5	5
258.	–	20 c. magenta	5	5
259.	–	25 c. blue	15	15
260.	–	30 c. green	8	5
261.	–	40 c. black	25	25
262.	–	50 c. blue	12	10
263.	–	1 p. green	35	12
264.	–	1 p. 20 blue	35	12
265.	37.	2 p. brown	60	35
266.	–	5 p. red	2·75	2·00
267.	–	10 p. purple	5·00	3·50

DESIGNS: 5 c. Atacama desert. 10 c. Fishing boats. 20 c. Coquito palms. 25 c. Sheep. 30 c. Coal mines. 40 c. Lonquimay forests. 50 c. Lota coal port. 1 p. Ships at Valparaiso. 1 p. 20, Mt. Puntiaguda. 5 p. Cattle. 10 p. Shovelling nitrate.

39. Laja Waterfall. 40. Fishing Smack.

1938.

268. 39. 5 c. purple 5 5
269. – 10 c. red 5 5
269a. – 15 c. red 5 5
270. – 20 c. blue 5 5
271. – 30 c. red 5 5
272. – 40 c. green 5 5
273. – 50 c. violet 5 5
274. 40. 1 p. orange 15 5
275. – 1 p. 80 blue 20 8
338h. – 2 p. red 10 5
338i. – 5 p. green 10 5
338j. – 10 p. purple 25 5

DESIGNS—As T 39: 10 c. Rural landscape. 15 c. Boldo tree. 20 c. Nitrate works. 30 c. Mineral spas. 40 c. Copper mine. 50 c. Petroleum tanks. As T 40: 1 p. 80. Osorno Volcano. 2 p. Merchant ship at Valparaiso. 5 p. Lake Villarrica. 10 p. Railway train.

41. "Abtao" and Policarpo Toro.

42. Map of Western Hemisphere.

1940. Occupation of Easter Island and Local Hospital Fund. 50th Anniv. Inscr. "OCUPACION DE PASCUA 1888–1938".

279. 41. 80 c. + 2 p. 20 red & grn. 30 25
280. – 3 p. 60 + 6 p. 40 green and red 30 25

DESIGN: 3 p. 60, "Abtao" and E. Eyraud.

1940. Pan-American Union. 50th Anniv.

281. 42. 40 c. green 20 10

1940. Air. Surch. with winged device above new values.

282. 29. 80 c. on 20 c. red .. 12 5
283. 31. 1 p. 60 on 5 p. red .. 40 25
284. – 5 p. 10 on 2 p. slate (No. 229) 65 60

43. Fray Camilo Henriquez.

44. Founding of Santiago.

1941. Santiago. 4th Cent.

285. 43. 10 c. red 15 12
286. – 40 c. green 12 5
287. – 1 p. 10 red 15 12
288. 44. 1 p. 80 blue 20 15
289. – 3 p. 60 blue 55 40

PORTRAITS—As T 43: 40 c. P. Valdivia. 1 p. 10, B. V. MacKenna. 3 p. 60, D. B. Arana.

45. Aeroplane and Globe.

46. Flying boat and Galleon.

1941. Air. No. 304 is dated "1541 1941" and commemorates the 4th Cent. of Santiago.

290. – 10 c. olive 5 5
292. 45. 20 c. red 5 5
295. – 30 c. violet 5 5
296. – 40 c. brown 5 5
325. – 50 c. orange 5 5
299a. – 60 c. green 5 5
328. – 70 c. red 8 5
301. – 80 c. blue 70 35
303a. – 90 c. brown 5 5
331. 46. 1 p. blue 8 5
307. – 2 p. lake 25 15
309. – 3 p. green 35 30
311. – 4 p. violet and brown .. 40 40
336a. – 5 p. chestnut 15 5
314. – 10 p. green and blue .. 1·40 1·10

DESIGNS (each incorporating a different type of aeroplane): 10 c. Steeple. 30 c. Flag. 40 c. Stars. 50 c. Mountains. 60 c. Tree. 70 c. Estuary. 80 c. Wake of ship. 90 c. Sun rays. 2 p. Compass. 3 p. Telegraph pole. 4 p. Rainbow. 5 p. Factory. 10 p. Snow-peaked mountain landscape.

INDEX

Countries can be quickly located by referring to the index at the end of this volume.

1942. Air. Various designs as T 45 and 46. I. Imprint at foot "ESPECIES VALORADAS-CHILE".

(a) Colours changed.

316. – 10 c. blue 5 5
317. – 10 c. mauve 5 5
319. 45. 20 c. brown 5 5
318. – 20 c. green 5 5
295a. – 30 c. olive 5 5
297. – 40 c. blue 5 5
324. – 50 c. red 5 5
326. – 60 c. orange 8 5
302. – 80 c. olive 5 5
304a. 46. 1 p. green and blue .. 5 5
308. – 2 p. brown 10 5
334. – 3 p. violet and orange 8 5
310a. – 3 p. violet and yellow 20 5
335. – 4 p. green 12 5
336a. – 5 p. red 15 5
337. – 10 p. blue 30 20

DESIGNS: The same as in the preceding issue.

(b) New values and new designs.

395. 20 c. brown 5 5
396. 40 c. violet 5 5
397. 60 c. blue 5 5
398. 1 p. green 5 5
305. 1 p. 60 violet 5 5
306. 1 p. 80 violet 5 5
399. 2 p. brown 5 5
404f. 3 p. blue 5 5
404g. 4 p. orange 5 5
404h. 5 p. violet 8 5
403. 10 p. green 15 5
404j. 20 p. chocolate 25 10

DESIGNS (each including an aeroplane): 20 c. Mountains. 40 c. Coastline. 60 c. Fishing vessel. 1 p. Araucanian pine tree. 1 p. 60, 1 p. 80, Wireless mast. 2 p. Chilean flag. 3 p. Dock crane. 4 p. River. 5 p. Industrial plant. 10 p. Landscape. 20 p. Aerial railway.

II. Imprint at foot "CASA DE MONEDA DE CHILE".

478. 1 p. green (as 398) .. 80 25
479. 10 p. green (as 403) .. 8 5
480. 20 p. chocolate (as 404) .. 8 5
481. 50 p. green 15 8
482. 100 p. red 25 15
483. 200 p. blue 50 20

DESIGNS (each including an aeroplane): 50 p. Mountainous coastline. 100 p. Antarctic map. 200 p. Rock "bridge" in sea.

48. V. Letelier.

49. National University.

50. Coat of arms and Aeroplane.

1942. Santiago de Chile University Cent.

339. 48. 30 c. red (postage) .. 5 5
340. – 40 c. green 8 5
341. – 90 c. violet 15 10
342. 49. 1 p. brown 20 10
343. – 1 p. 80 blue 35 30
344. 50. 100 p. red (air) .. 20·00 16·00

DESIGNS—As T 48: 40 c. A. Bello. 90 c. M. Bulnes. 1 p. 80, M. Montt.

51. Manuel Bulnes.

52. Straits of Magellan.

1944. Occupation of Magellan Straits. Cent.

345. 51. 15 c. black 5 5
346. – 30 c. red 5 5
347. – 40 c. green 8 5
348. – 1 p. brown 10 8
349. 52. 1 p. 80 blue 30 15

PORTRAITS: 30 c. J. W. Wilson. 40 c. D. D. Almeida. 1 p. Jose de los Santos Mardones.

53. "Lamp of Life".

DESIGN: 1 p. 80, Serpent and chalice symbol of Hygiene.

1944. International Red Cross.

350. 53. 40 c. black, red & green 12 8
351. – 1 p. 80 red and blue .. 25 10

54. O'Higgins.

55. Battle of Rancagua.

1944. Bernardo O'Higgins. Death Cent. Inscr. as in T 55.

367. 54. 15 c. black and red .. 5 5
368. – 30 c. black and brown 5 5
369. – 40 c. black and green .. 8 5
370. 55. 1 p. 80 black and blue .. 20 15

DESIGNS—As T 55: 30 c. Battle of the Maipo. 40 c. Abdication of O'Higgins.

56. Columbus Lighthouse.

57. Andres Bello.

1945. Discovery of America. 450th Anniv.

371. 56. 40 c. green 8 5

1946. Andres Bello (educationist). 80th Death Anniv.

372. 57. 40 c. green 8 5
373. 1 p. 80 blue 8 5

58. Antarctic Territory.

60. Miguel de Cervantes.

59. Eusebio Lillo and Ramon Carnicer.

1947.

374. 58. 40 c. red 15 8
375. 2 p. 50 blue 40 10

1947. National Anthem. Cent.

376. 59. 40 c. green 12 8

1947. Cervantes. 400th Birth Anniv.

377. 60. 40 c. red 8 5

61. Arturo Prat.

1948. Arturo Prat. Birth Cent.

378. 61. 40 c. blue 8 5

62. O'Higgins.

63. Chiasognathus Grantil.

1948.

379. 62. 60 c. black 5 5

1948. No. 272 surch. **VEINTE CTS.** and bar.

380. 20 c. on 40 c. green .. 5 5

1948. Cent. of Publication on Chilean Flora and Fauna. Botanical and zoological designs, as T 63. inscr. "CENTENARIO DEL LIBRO DE GAY 1844–1944".

381. 60 c. blue (postage) .. 25 10
382. 2 p. 60 green 40 15
383. 3 p. red (air) 40 40

Each value in 25 different designs.

64. Airline Badge.

65. B. V. Mackenna.

1979. Air. National Airline. 20th Anniv.

384. 64. 2 p. blue 10 5

1949. Vicuna Mackenna Museum.

385. 65. 60 c. blue (postage) .. 5 5
386. 3 p. red (air) 12 12

66. Wheel and Lamp.

DESIGNS: 2 p. 60, Shield and book. 5 p. Shield, book and factory. 10 p. Wheel and column.

1949. School of Arts and Crafts, Santiago. Cent. Inscr. as in T 66.

387. 66. 60 c. magenta (postage) 5 5
388. – 2 p. 60 blue 12 8
389. – 5 p. green (air) 15 12
390. – 10 p. brown 25 15

67. H. von Stephan.

68. Plane and Globe.

1950. U.P.U. 75th Anniv.

391. 67. 60 c. red (postage) .. 5 5
392. 2 p. 50 blue 15 10
393. 68. 5 p. green (air) 15 8
394. 10 p. brown 25 15

69. Crossing the Andes.

70. Isabella the Catholic.

1951. Gen. San Martin. Death Cent.

405. – 60 c. blue (postage) .. 5 5
406. 69. 5 p. purple (air) .. 15 10

PORTRAIT (25×29 mm.): 60 c. San Martin.

1951. Air. No. 303a surch. **UN PESO.**

407. 1 p. on 90 c. brown .. 5 5

1952. Isabella the Catholic. 500th Birth Anniv.

408. 70. 60 c. blue (postage) .. 5 5
409. 10 p. red (air) 25 15

1952. Surch. **40 Ctvs.**

410. 62. 40 c. on 60 c. black .. 5 5

1952. Air. No. 302 surch. **40 Centavos.**

411. 40 c. on 80 c. olive .. 5 5

ILLUSTRATIONS
British Commonwealth and all overprints and surcharges are FULL SIZE. Foreign Countries have been reduced to ¾-LINEAR.

71. M. de Toroy Zambrano.

1952.

379a. **71.** 80 c. green 5 5
379b. – 1 p. blue-grn. (O'Higgins) 5 5
446. – 2 p. lilac (Carrera) .. 5 5
447. – 3 p. blue (R. Freire) .. 5 5
448. – 5 p. sepia (M. Bulnes) 5 5
449. – 10 p. violet (F. A. Pinto) 5 5
450. – 50 p. red (M. Montt) .. 15 5

72. Arms of Valdivia. **73.** Old Spanish Watch-tower.

1953. Valdivia. 4th Cent. Inscr.
414. **72.** 1 p. blue (postage) .. 5 5
415. – 2 p. violet 5 5
416. – 3 p. green 8 5
417. – 5 p. brown 12 5
418. **73.** 10 p. red (air) .. 20 20
DESIGNS—As T **73**: 2 p. Ancient cannons, Corral Fort. 3 p. Valdivia from the river. 5 p. Street scene (after old engraving).

74. J. Toribio Medina. **75.** Stamp of 1853.

1953. Toribio Medina. Birth Cent.
419. **74.** 1 p. brown 5 5
420. 2 p. 50 blue 8 5

1953. First Chilean Postage Stamp. Cent.
421. **75.** 1 p. brown (postate) .. 12 5
422. 100 p. turquoise (air) .. 2·50 1·40

76. Map and Graph. **77.** Aeroplanes of 1929 and 1954.

1953. 12th National Census.
423. **76.** 1 p. green 5 5
424. 2 p. 50 blue 5 5
425. 3 p. brown 5 5
426. 4 p. red 8 5

1954. Air. National Air Line. 25th Anniv.
427. **77.** 3 p. blue 5 5

78. Arms of Angol. **79.** I. Domeyko.

1954. Angol City. 4th Cent.
428. **78.** 2 p. red 5 5

1954. Domeyko (educationist and mineralogist). 150th Birth Anniv.
429. **79.** 1 p. blue (postage) .. 5 5
430. 5 p. brown (air) .. 5 5

80. Early Locomotive. **81.** Arturo Prat.

1954. Chilean Railways Cent.
431. **80.** 1 p. red (postage) .. 10 5
432. 10 p. purple (air) .. 25 12

1954. Naval Battle of Iquique. 75th Anniv.
433. **81.** 2 p. violet 5 5

82. Arms of Vina del Mar. **83.** Dr. A. del Rio

1955. Int. Philatelic Exn., Vina del Mar.
434. **82.** 1 p. blue 5 5
435. – 2 p. red 5 5
DESIGN: 2 p. Arms of Valparaiso.

1955. 14th Pan-American Sanitary Conf.
436. **83.** 2 p. blue 5 5

84. Christ of the Andes. **85.** "Comet" Airliner.

1955. Exchange of Visits between Argentine and Chilean Presidents.
437. **84.** 1 p. blue (postage) .. 8 5
438. 100 p. red (air) .. 1·25 1·25

1955. Air.
441a. **85.** 100 p. green 20 5
441b. – 200 p. blue 50 8
441c. – 500 p. red .. .. 1·00 20
DESIGNS: 200 p. "Beechcraft" monoplane. 600 p. Four-engined airliner.
See also Nos. 516/18.

86. M. Rengifo. **87.** Helicopter and Bridge.

1955. President Prieto. Death Cent.
442. **86.** 3 p. blue 5 5
443. – 5 p. red (Egana) .. 5 5
444. – 50 p. purple (Portales) 15 5
For 15p in similar design see under Compulsory Tax Stamps.

1956. Air.
451. – 1 p. claret 5 5
452. **87.** 2 p. sepia 5 5
455. – 5 p. violet 5 5
456. – 10 p. green 5 5
456a. – 20 p. blue 5 5
456b. – 50 p. red 12 5
DESIGNS: 1 p. Jet 'plane. 5 p. Train and 'plane. 10 p. Oil derricks and 'plane. 20 p. Jet 'plane and monolith. 50 p. 'Plane and control tower.
See also Nos. 512/5.

88. F. Santa Maria. **89.** Atomic Symbol and Cogwheels.

1956. Santa Maria Technical University, Valparaiso. 25th Anniv. Inscr. as in T **89**.
457. **88.** 5 p. brown (postage) .. 5 5
458. **89.** 20 p. green (air) .. 15 5
459. – 100 p. violet 35 20
DESIGN—As T **89**: 100 p. Aerial view of University.

90. Gabriela Mistral. **91.** Arms of Osorno.

1958. Gabriela Mistral (poet).
460. **90.** 10 p. brown (postage) .. 5 5
461. 100 p. green (air) .. 20 10

1958. Osorno. 4th Cent. Inscr. as in T **91**.
462. **91.** 10 p. red (postage) .. 5 5
463. – 50 p. green 12 8
464. – 100 p. blue (air) .. 25 12
PORTRAITS: 50 p. G. H. de Mendoza. 100 p. O'Higgins.

92. "La Araucana" (poem) and Antarctic Map. **93.** Arms of Santiago de Chile.

1958. Antarctic issue.
465. **92.** 10 p. blue (postage) .. 8 5
466. – 200 p. purple 40 35
467. **92.** 20 p. violet (air) .. 12 5
468. – 500 p. blue .. .. 1·50 50
DESIGN: 200 p., 500 p. Chilean map of 1588.

1958. National Philatelic Exn., Santiago.
469. **93.** 10 p. purple (postage) 5 5
470. 50 p. green (air) .. 15 8

94. **95.** Antarctic Territory.

1958. Chilean Civil Servants' Savings Bank Cent.
471. **94.** 10 p. blue (postage) .. 5 5
472. 50 p. brown (air) .. 12 5

1958. I.G.Y.
473. **95.** 40 p. red (postage) .. 25 8
474. 50 p. green (air) .. 15 8

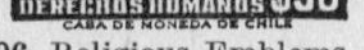

96. Religious Emblems. **97.** Bridge, Valdivia.

1959. Air. Human Rights Day.
475. **96.** 50 p. red 25 15

1959. German School, Valdivia. Cent. and Philatelic Exn.
476. **97.** 40 p. green (postage) .. 10 5
477. – 20 p. red (air) 8 5
DESIGN—VERT. 20 p. A. C. Anwandter. (founder).

98. Expedition Map. **99.** D. Barros-Arana.

1959. Juan Ladrillero's Expedition of 1557 400th Anniv.
484. **98.** 10 p. violet (postage) .. 8 5
485. 50 p. green (air) .. 15 5

1959. D. Barros-Arana (historian). 50th Death Anniv.
486. **99.** 40 p. blue (postage) .. 10 5
487. 100 p. lilac (air) .. 20 15

ILLUSTRATIONS
British Commonwealth and all overprints and surcharges are FULL SIZE. Foreign Countries have been reduced to ¾-LINEAR.

100. J. H. Dunant.

1959. Red Cross Commem.
488. **100.** 20 p. lake & red (post) 10 5
489. 50 p. black & red (air) 12 8

101. F. A. Pinto. **101a.** Choshuenco Volcano.

1960. (a) Portraits as T **101**.
490. – 5 m. turquoise .. 5 5
491. **101.** 1 c. red 5 5
493. – 5 c. blue 5 5

(b) Views as T **101a**.
492. **101a.** 2 c. blue 5 5
492a. 2 c. blue (23½ × 18 mm.) 5 5
494. – 10 c. green 10 5
495. – 20 c. blue 20 5
496. – 1 E. turquoise .. 25 10
DESIGNS—As T **101**: 5 m. M. Bulnes. 5 c. M. Montt. As T **101a**: 10 c. R. Manle Valley. 20 c., 1 E. Inca Lake.

102. 'Plane and Dock Crane. **130.** Refugee Family.

1960. Air (Inland).
497. – 1 m. orange 5 5
498. – 2 m. yellow-green .. 5 5
499. **102.** 3 m. violet 5 5
500. – 4 m. olive 5 5
501. – 5 m. turquoise .. 5 5
502. – 1 c. blue 5 5
503. – 2 c. brown 5 5
504. – 5 c. green 5 5
505. – 10 c. red 15 8
506. – 20 c. blue 25 15
DESIGNS: 'Plane over— 1 m. Araucanian pine. 2 m. Chilean flag. 4 m. River; 5 m. Industrial plant. 1 c. Landscape. 2 c. Aerial railway. 5 c. Mountainous coastline. 10 c. Antarctic map. 20 c. Rock "bridge" in sea.

1960. World Refugee Year.
507. **103.** 1 c. green (postage) .. 10 5
508. 10 c. violet (air) .. 15 10

104. Arms of Chile. **105.** Rotary Emblem and Map.

1960. 1st National Government. 150th Anniv. (1st issue)
509. **104.** 1 c. brn. & lake (post.) 5 5
510. 10 c. chest. & brn. (air) 12 5
See also Nos. 519/30.

1960. Air. Rotary International S. American Regional Conference, Santiago.
511. **105.** 10 c. blue 15 8

1960. Air (Foreign). As T **87** or **86** (10 c. and 50 c.), but values in new currency.
512. 5 m. brown 5 5
513. 1 c. blue 5 5
514. 2 c. ultramarine 5 5
515. 5 c. red 5 5
516. 10 c. ultramarine 5 5
517. 20 c. lake 15 10
518. 50 c. turquoise 15 10
DESIGNS: 'Plane over—5 m. Locomotive. 1 c. Oil derricks. 2 c. Monolith. 5 c. Control tower. 10 c. Comet airliner. 20 c. "Beechcraft" monoplane. 50 c. Four-engined airliner.

106. J. M. Carrera.

107. "Population".

1960. 1st National Government. 150th Anniv. (2nd issue). Inscr. as in T **106**.

(a) Postage.
519. – 1 c. purple and brown 5 5
520. – 5 c. turquoise & green 5 5
521. – 10 c. maroon and brown 5 5
522. – 20 c. green and indigo 8 5
523. – 50 c. lake and brown .. 25 5
524. **106.** 1 E. brn. & bronze-grn. 1·00 60
DESIGNS—HORIZ. 1 c. Palace of Justice. 10 c. M. de Toro y Zambrano and M. de Rozas. 20 c. M. de Salas and Juan Egana. 50 c. M. Rodriguez and J. Mackenna. VERT. 5 c. Temple of the National Vow.

(b) Air.
525. – 2 c. violet and lake .. 5 5
526. – 5 c. purple and blue .. 5 5
527. – 10 c. bistre & chocolate 10 5
528. – 20 c. violet and blue .. 12 15
529. – 50 c. blue and green .. 25 30
530. – 1 E. brown and lake .. 40 55
DESIGNS—HORIZ. 2 c. Palace of Justice. 10 c. J. G. Marin and J. G. Argomedo. 20 c. J. A. Eyzaguirre and J. M. Infante. 50 c. Bishop J. I. Clenfuegos and Fray C. Henriquez. VERT. 5 c. Temple of the National Vow. 1 E. O'Higgins.

1960. National Census. 13th Population Census (5 c.); 2nd Housing Census (10 c.).
531. **107.** 5 c. green 10 5
532. – 10 c. violet (buildings) 12 5

108. Pedro de Valdivia.

109. Congress Building.

1961. Earthquake Relief Fund. Inscr. "ESPANA A CHILE".
533. 5 c.+5 c. myrtle & flesh (postage) 25 8
534. 10 c.+10 c. violet and buff 15 10
535. 10 c.+10 c. brn. & sal. (air) 20 15
536. 20 c.+20 c. lake and blue 40 35
PORTRAITS: No. 533, T **108**. 534, J. T. Medina. 535, A. de Ercilla. 536, Gabriela Mistral.

1961. 1st National Congress. 150th Anniv.
537. **109.** 2 c. brown (postage) 5 5
538. 10 c. green (air) .. 12 10

110. Footballers and Globe.

111. Mother and Child.

1962. World Football Championships, Chile.
539. **110.** 2 c. blue (postage) .. 5 5
540. – 5 c. green 5 5
541. – 5 c. purple (air) .. 12 5
542. **110.** 10 c. lake 15 10
DESIGN: Nos. 540/1, Goalkeeper and stadium.

1963. Freedom from Hunger.
543. **111.** 3 c. maroon (postage) 5 5
544. – 20 c. green (air) .. 20 15
DESIGN—HORIZ. 20 c. Mother holding out food bowl.

112. Centenary Emblem.

113. Fire Brigade Monument.

1963. Red Cross Cent.
545. **112.** 3 c. red & slate (post.) 5 5
546. – 20 c. red and grey (air) 15 12
DESIGN—HORIZ. 20 c. Centenary emblem and silhouette of aircraft.

1963. Santiago Fire Brigade Centenary.
547. **113.** 3 c. violet (postage) .. 5 5
548. – 30 c. red (air) .. 30 20
DESIGN—HORIZ. (39×30 mm.): 30 c. Fire engine of 1863.

114. Band encircling Globe.

115. Enrique Molina.

1964. Air. "Alliance for Progress" and Pres. Kennedy Commem.
549. **114.** 4 c. blue 5 5

1964. Molina Commem. (founder of Concepcion University).
550. **115.** 4 c. bistre (postage) .. 5 5
551. 60 c. violet (air) .. 20 15

1965. Casanueva Commem. As T **115** but portrait of Mons. Carlos Casanueva, Rector of Catholic University.
552. 4 c. purple (postage) .. 5 5
553. 60 c. green (air) .. 20 15

116. Battle Scene.

1965. Air. Battle of Rancagua. 150th Anniv.
554. **116.** 5 c. brown and green 5 5

117. Monolith.

118. I.T.U. Emblem and Symbols.

1965. Easter Island Discoveries.
555. **117.** 6 c. purple 5 5
556. 10 c. magenta 5 5

1965. Air I.T.U. Cent.
557. **118.** 40 c. maroon and red .. 15 10

119. Crusoe on Juan Fernandez.

120. Skier descending slope.

1965. Robinson Crusoe Commem.
558. **119.** 30 c. claret 10 5

1965. World Skiing Championships.
559. **120.** 4 c. green (postage) .. 5 5
560. – 20 c. blue (air) .. 10 8
DESIGN—HORIZ. 20 c. Skier crossing slope.

121. Angelmo Harbour.

122. Aviators Monument.

1965. Air.
561. **121.** 40 c. brown 12 5
562. **122.** 1 E. red 20 15

123. Copihue (National Flower).

124. A. Bello.

1965.
563. **123.** 15 c. red and green .. 5 5
563a. 20 c. red and green .. 5 5

1965. Air. Andres Bello (poet). Death Cent.
564. **124.** 10 c. red 5 5

125. Dr. L. Sazie.

126. Skiers.

1966. Dr. L. Sazie. Death Cent.
565. **125.** 1 E. green 30 15

1966. Air. World Skiing Championships.
566. – 75 c. claret and lilac .. 20 12
567. – 3 E. ultramarine & blue 75 40
568. **126.** 4 E. brown and blue .. 75 65
DESIGN—HORIZ. (38×25 mm.): 75 c. and 3 E. Skier in Slalom Race.

127. Ball and Basket.

128. J. Montt.

1966. Air. World Basketball Championships
569. **127.** 13 c. red 5 5

1966.
570. **128.** 30 c. violet 10 5
571. – 50 c. brown (G. Riesco) 15 5

129. W. Wheelwright and Paddle-steamer "Chile". **130.** "Learning".

1966. Arrival of Paddle-steamers "Chile" and "Peru". 125th Anniv. (in 1965).
572. **129.** 10 c. ultram. & bl. (post.) 5 5
573. 70 c. blue and green (air) 12 8

1966. Education Campaign.
574. **130.** 10 c. maroon 5 5

131. I.C.Y. Emblem.

132. Chilean Flag and Ships.

1966. Int. Co-operation Year (1965).
575. **131.** 1 E. brn. & green (post) 30 20
576. 3 E. red and blue (air) 1·00 1·00

1966. Air. Antofagasta Cent.
577. **132.** 13 c. maroon 5 5

133. Capt. Pardo and Rescue Vessel.

134. Chilean Family.

1967. Pardo's Rescue of Shackleton Expedition. 50th Anniv.
578. **133.** 20 c. turquoise (post) .. 8 5
579. – 40 c. ultramarine (air) 15 12
DESIGN: 40 c. Capt. Pardo and Antarctic sectoral map.

1967. 8th Int. Family Planning Conf.
580. **134.** 10 c. black and purple (postage) 5 5
581. 80 c. black & blue (air) 20 12

135. R. Dario (poet). **136.** Pine Forest.

1967. Air. Ruben Dario. Birth Cent.
582. **135.** 10 c. ultramarine .. 5 5

1967. National Afforestation Campaign.
583. **136.** 10 c. green & bl. (post) 5 5
584. **136.** 75 c. green & chest. (air) 15 12

137. Lions Emblem. **138.** Chilean Flag.

1967. Lions Int. 50th Anniv.
585. **137.** 20 c. turq. & yell. (post.) 8 5
586. **137.** 1 E. violet & yell. (air) 20 15
587. 5 E. ultram. & yellow 1·00 75

1967. National Flag. 150th Anniv.
588. **138.** 80 c. red & blue (post.) 15 12
589. **138.** 50 c. red and blue (air) 12 10

139. I.T.Y. Emblem.

140. Cardinal Caro.

1967. Air. Int. Tourist Year.
590. **139.** 30 c. black and blue .. 10 8

1967. Cardinal Caro. Birth Cent.
591. **140.** 20 c. lake (postage) .. 5 5
592. 40 c. violet (air) .. 12 8

141. San Martin and O'Higgins. **142.** Farmer and Wife.

1968. Battles of Chacabuco and Maipu. 150th Anniv.
593. **141.** 3 E. blue (postage) .. 60 30
594. 2 E. violet (air) .. 40 30

1968. Agrarian Reform.
595. **142.** 20 c. black, green and orange (postage) .. 5 5
596. 50 c. black, green and orange (air) 10 5

143. Juan I. Molina (scientist) and "Lamp of Learning". **144.** Hand supporting Cogwheel.

1968. Molina Commem.
597. **143.** 2 E. purple (postage) .. 30 15
598. – 1 E. green (air) .. 15 12
DESIGN: 1 E. Molina and books.

1968. 4th Manufacturing Census.
599. **144.** 30 c. red 8 5

145. Map, Galleon and Ferry-boat.

1968. "Five Towns" Cent.
600. **145.** 30 c. ultram. (postage) 8 5
601. – 1 E. purple (air) .. 10 8
DESIGN—VERT. 1 E. Map of Chiloe Province.

146. Club Emblem.

1968. Chilean Automobile Club. 40th Anniv.
602. **146.** 1 E. red (postage) .. 12 8
603. 5 E. blue (air) .. 60 45

147. Chilean Arms.

1968. Air. State Visit of Queen Elizabeth II.
604. **147.** 50 c. brown & green .. 8 5
605. – 3 E. brown and blue .. 30 20
606. – 5 E. purple and plum 60 35
DESIGN—HORIZ. 3 E. Royal arms of Great Britain. VERT. 5 E. St. Edward's Crown on map of South America.

148. Don Francisco Garcia Huidobro (founder).

1968. Chilean Mint. 225th Anniv.
608. **148.** 2 E. blue & red (post.) 25 15
609. – 5 E. brown and green 60 35
610. – 50 c. mar. & yell. (air) 8 5
611. – 1 E. red and blue .. 15 12
DESIGNS: 50 c. First Chilean coin and press. 1 E. First Chilean stamp printed by the mint (1915). 5 E. Philip V. of Spain.

149. Satellite and Dish Aerial.

1969. Inaug. of "Entel-Chile" Satellite Communications Ground Station, Longovilo (1st issue).
613. **149.** 30 c. blue (postage) .. 5 5
614. 2 E. purple (air) .. 25 12

150. Red Cross Symbols.

1969. League of Red Cross Societies. 50th Anniv.
615. **150.** 2 E. red & violet (post.) 25 15
616. 5 E. red and black (air) 55 40

151. Rapel Dam.

1969. Rapel Hydro-Electric Project.
617. **151.** 40 c. green (postage) .. 5 5
618. 3 E. blue (air) .. 40 20

152. Rodriguez Memorial.

1969. Col. Manuel Rodriguez. 150th Death Anniv.
619. **152.** 2 E. red (postage) .. 20 15
620. 30 c. brown (air) .. 5 5

153. Open Bible.

1969. Spanish Translation of Bible. 400th Anniv.
621. **153.** 40 c. brown (postage) 5 5
622. 1 E. emerald (air) .. 12 8

154. Hemispheres and I.L.O. Emblem.

1969. Int. Labour Organization. 50th Anniv.
623. **154.** 1 E. grn. & blk. (post.) 12 8
624. 2 E. purple & blk. (air) 30 15

155. Human Rights Emblem. **156.** "Expo" Emblem.

1969. Human Rights Year (1968).
625. **155.** 4 E. red and blue (post.) 50 35
626. 4 E. red & chocolate (air) 50 35

1969. Expo 70.
628. **156.** 3 E. blue (postage .. 40 25
629. 5 E. vermilion (air) .. 60 45

157. Mint, Valparaiso (18th cent.)

1970. Spanish Colonization of Chile.
630. **157.** 2 E. maroon 15 10
631. – 3 E. red 20 15
632. – 4 E. blue 30 20
633. – 5 E. brown 40 30
634. – 10 E. green 80 60
DESIGNS—HORIZ. 5 E. Cal y Canto Bridge. VERT. 3 E. Pedro de Valdivia. 4 E. Santo Domingo Church, Santiago. 10 E. Ambrosio O'Higgins.

158. P. Toro and Map.

1969. Seizure of Easter Island. 80th Anniv.
636. **158.** 5 E. violet (postage) .. 65 50
637. 50 c. turquoise (air) .. 5 5

159. Chilean Schooner and Arms. **160.** Paul Harris.

1970. Capture of Valdivia by Lord Cochrane. 150th Anniv.
640. **159.** 40 c. lake (postage) .. 5 5
641. 2 E. ultramarine (air) 20 15

1970. Paul Harris (founder of Rotary Int.). Birth Cent.
642. **160.** 10 E. ultramarine (post.) 1·00 80
643. 1 E. red (air) 10 5

161. Mahatma Gandhi. **162.** Education Year Emblem.

1970. Gandhi. Birth Cent.
644. **161.** 40 c. green (postage) .. 5 5
645. 1 E. brown (air) .. 10 5

1970. Int. Education Year.
648. **162.** 2 E. red (postage) .. 15 12
649. 4 E. brown (air) .. 45 30

163. "Virgin and Child". **164.** Snake and Torch Emblem.

1970. O'Higgins National Shrine. Maipo.
650. **163.** 40 c. green (postage) .. 5 5
651. 1 E. blue (air) .. 10 5

1970. 10th Int. Cancer Congress, Houston, U.S.A.
652. **164.** 40 c. purple and blue (postage) 5 5
653. 2 E. brn. and olive (air) 15 10

165. Chilean Arms and Copper Symbol. **166.** Globe, Peace Dove and Cogwheel.

1970. Copper Mines Nationalisation.
654. **165.** 40 c. red & brn. (postage) 5 5
655. 3 E. green & brown (air) 30 20

1970. United Nations. 25th Anniv.
656. **166.** 3 E. violet and claret (postage) 30 20
657. 5 E. green & lake (air) 50 25

1970. Nos. 613/4 surch.
658. **149.** 52 c. on 30 c. blue (postage) 5 5
659. **149.** 52 c. on 2 E. purple (air) 5 5

167. Bow of Freighter and Ship's Wheel. **169.** Scout Badge.

168. O'Higgins and Fleet.

1971. State Maritime Corporation.
660. **167.** 52 c. claret (postage) 5 5
661. 5 E. brown (air) .. 40 25

1971. Peruvian Liberation Expedition. 150th Anniv.
662. **168.** 5 E. grn. & blue (postage) 35 25
663. 1 E. pur. & blue (air) .. 10 5

1971. Chilean Scouting Association. 60th Anniv.
664. **169.** 1 E. brn. & grn. (postage) 10 5
665. 5 c. grn. & lake (air) .. 5 5

170. Young People and U.N. Emblem.

1971. 1st Latin-American Meeting of U.N.I.C.E.F. Executive Council, Santiago (1969).
666. 170. 52 c. brn. & blue (postage) 5 5
667. 2 E. grn. & blue (air) 15 12

1971. Longovilo Satellite Communications Ground Station (2nd issue). As T 149, but with "LONGOVILO" added to centre inscr. and wording at foot of design changed to "PRIMERA ASTACION LATINOAMERICANA".
668. 40 c. green (postage) .. 5 5
669. 2 E. brown (air) .. 20 12

171. Diver with Harpoon-gun.

1971. 10th World Underwater Fishing Championships, Iquique.
670. 171. 1 E. 15 myrtle and grn. 8 5
671. 2 E. 35 ultram. & blue 15 10

172. Magellan and Caravel.

1971. Discovery of Magellan Straits. 450th Anniv.
676. 172. 35 c. plum and blue .. 5 5

173. D. Godoy and Plane across Andes.

1971. 1st Trans-Andes Flight (1918). Commem.
677. 173. 1 E. 15 green and blue 8 5

174. U.P.A.E. Emblem.

1971. Spanish-American Postal Union Congress, Santiago.
678. – 1 E. 15 blue 8 5
679. 174. 2 E. 35 blue and red.. 15 12
680. – 4 E. 35 red 30 20
681. – 9 E. 35 lilac 65 50
682. – 18 E. 35 mauve .. 1·50 1·00
DESIGNS—VERT. 1 E. 15 Statue of the Virgin, San Cristobal. 4 E. 35 St. Francis' Church, Santiago. HORIZ. 9 E. 35 Central Post Office, Santiago. 18 E. 35 Corregidor Inn.

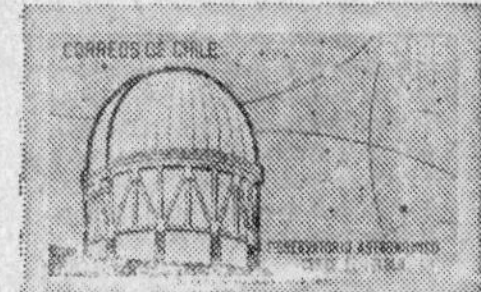

175. Cerro el Tololo Observatory.

1972. Astronomical Observatory, Cerro el Tololo. Inaug.
683. 175. 1 E. 95 bl. and new bl. 8 5

176. Boeing "707" over Easter Island.

1972. 1st Air Service Santiago-Easter Island-Tahiti.
684. 176. 2 E. 35 purple & ochre 15 10

177. Alonso de Ercilla y Zuniga.

179. Human Heart.

178. Antarctic Map and Dog-sledge.

1972. "La Araucana" (epic poem by de Ercilla y Zungia) (1969). 400th Anniv.
685. 177. 1 E. brown (postage).. 8 5
686. 177. 2 E. blue (air).. .. 12 10

1972. Antarctic Treaty. 10th Anniv.
687. 178. 1 E. 15 black & blue.. 8 5
688. 3 E. 50 blue & green.. 25 15

1972. World Heart Month.
689. 179. 1 E. 15 red and black.. 8 5

180. Conference Hall, Santiago de Chile.

1972. 3rd United Nations Conf., on Trade and Development, Santiago.
690. – 35 c. green & brown .. 5 5
691. 180. 1 E. 15 violet and blue 8 5
692. – 4 E. violet and pink .. 30 20
693. 180. 6 E. blue and orange.. 50 35
DESIGNS: 35 c. 4 E. Text of speech by Pres. Allende.

Nos. 690 and 692 were issued in sheets with se-tenant stamp-size labels showing Chilean workers and inscr. "CORREOS DE CHILE". These two values were only valid for postage with the se-tenant label attached.

181. Soldier and Crest.

1972. O'Higgins Military Academy, 150th Anniv.
694. 181. 1 E. 15 yellow and blue 8 5

182. Copper Miner.

183. Training Ship "Esmerelda".

1972. Copper Mines Nationalization Law (1971).
695. 182. 1 E. 15 blue and red.. 8 5
696. 5 E. black, blue & red 45 25

1972. Arturo Prat Naval College. 150th Anniv.
697. 183. 1 E. 15 maroon .. 5 5

184. Observatory and Telescope.

185. Dove with Letter.

1972. Cerro Calan Observatory. Inaug.
698. 184. 50 c. blue 5 5

1972. Int. Correspondence Week.
699. 185. 1 E. 15 violet and mve. 8 5

186. Gen. Schneider and Flag.

1972. General Rene Schneider. 2nd Death Anniv.
700. 186. 2 E. 30 multicoloured 15 12

187. Book and Students.

1972. International Book Year.
701. 187. 50 c. black and red .. 5 5

188. Folklore and Handicrafts.

1972. Tourist Year of the Americas.
702. 188. 1 E. 15 black and red 8 5
703. – 2 E. 65 purple & blue 20 12
704. – 3 E. 50 brown & red.. 25 15
DESIGNS—HORIZ. 2 E. 65 Natural produce. VERT. 3 E. 50 Stove and rug.

189. Carrera in Prison.

190. Antarctic Map.

1973. General J. M. Carrera. 150th Death Anniv.
705. 189. 2 E. 30 blue 5 5

1973. General Bernardo O'Higgins Antarctic Base. 25th Anniv.
706. 190. 10 E. red and blue .. 12 8

191. Destroyer and Emblem.

192. Astronomical Telescope.

1973. "50 Years of Chilean Naval Aviation".
707. 191. 20 E. blue and brown.. 10 5

1973. La Silla Astronomical Observatory. Inaug.
708. 192. 2 E. 30 black and blue 8 5

193. Interpol Emblem.

194. Bunch of Grapes.

1973. Interpol. 50th Anniv.
709. 193. 30 E. bl., brn. & blk... 12 5
710. – 50 E. black and red .. 20 10
DESIGN: 50 E. Fingerprint on globe.

1973. Chilean Wine Exports.
711. 194. 20 E. pur., red & orge. 8 5
712. – 100 E. blue and red .. 40 25
DESIGN: 100 E. Inscribed globe.

1974. World Meteorological Organization. Cent. No. 668 surch. "**Centenario de la Organizacion Meteorologica Mundial IMO-W-MO 1973**" and value.
713. 27 E. + 3 E. on 40 c. green 8 5

195. New U.P.U. H.Q. Building, Berne.

1974. U.P.U. Cent. Unissued stamp surch
714. 195. 500 E. on 45 c. green.. 1·25 60

196. Bernardo O'Higgins and Emblems.

1974. Chilean Armed Forces.
715. 196. 30 E. yellow and red 5 5
716. – 30 E. lake and red 5 5
717. – 30 E. blue and light blue 5 5
718. – 30 E. blue and lilac .. 5 5
719. – 30 E. emerald and grn. 5 5
DESIGNS: No. 716, Soldiers with mortar. No. 717, Naval gunners. No. 718, Air-force pilot. No. 719, Mounted policeman.

1974. Copernicus. 500th Birth Anniv. (1973). No. 683 surch. "**V Centenario del Nacimiento de Copernico 1473-1973**" and value.
720. 175. 27 E. + 3 E. on 1 E. 95 blue & new blue .. 8 5

1974. Vina del Mar. Cent. No. 496 surch. "**Centenario de la ciudad de Vina del Mar 1874-1974**" and value.
721. 27 E. + 3 E. on 1 E. turquoise 8 5

197. Football and Globe.

198. Gloved Hand and Police Staff.

1974. World Cup Football Championships, West Germany.

722. **197.** 500 E. orange & red .. 1·00 50
723. – 1000 E. bl. & deep bl. 1·90 1·00
DESIGN—HORIZ. 1000 E. Football on disk.

1974. Various stamps surch.

724. **151.** 47 E.+3 E. on 40 c. grn. 10 8
725. **165.** 67 E.+3 E. on 40 c. red and brown .. 15 10
726. **153.** 97 E.+3 E. on 40 c. brn. 20 15
727. **161.** 100 E. on 40 c. green .. 20 15
728. – 300 E. on 50 c. brown (No. 571) 60 25

1974. Campaign for Prevention of Traffic Accidents.

729. **198.** 30 E. brown & green .. 5 5

199. Manutara and Part of Globe.

200. Core of Globe.

1974. Inaugural LAN Flight to Tahiti, Fiji and Australia. Each green and brown.

730. 200 E. Type **199** 25 12
731. 200 E. Tahitian dancer and part of Globe 25 12
732. 200 E. Map of Fiji and part of Globe 25 12
733. 200 E. Kangaroo and part of Globe 25 12

1974. Int. Symposium of Volcanology, Santiago de Chile.

734. **200.** 500 E. orge. & brown 60 40

1974. Votive Temple. Inauguration. No. 650 surch. **24 OCTUBRE 1974 INAUGURACION TEMPLO VOTIVO** and value.

735. **163.** 100 e. on 40 c. green .. 12 8

201. Map of Robinson Crusoe Island.

203. F. Vidal Gormaz and Seal.

202. O'Higgins and Bolivar.

1974. Discovery of Juan Fernandez Archipelago. 400th Anniv. Each brown and blue.

736. 200 E. Type **201** 25 12
737. 200 E. Chontas (hardwood palm-trees) 25 12
738. 200 E. Mountain goat .. 25 12
739. 200 E. Spiny lobster .. 25 12

1974. Battles of Junin and Ayacucho. 150th Anniv.

740. **202.** 100 E. brown and buff 12 8

1975. Naval Hydrographic Institute. Cent.

741. **203.** 100 E. blue and mauve 12 8

1975. Surch **Revalorizada 1975** and value.

742. **165.** 70 c. on 40 c. red and brown 5 5

204. Dr. Schweitzer.

205. Lighthouse.

1975. Dr. Albert Schweitzer (missionary). Birth Cent.

743. **204.** 500 E. brown & yellow 25 12

1975. Valparaiso Lifeboat Service. 50th Anniv. Each blue and green.

744. 150 E. Type **205** 10 5
745. 150 E. Wreck of ship .. 10 5
746. 150 E. Lifeboat 10 5
747. 150 E. Survivor in water .. 10 5

206. Corvette " Barquedano ".

1975. 30th Anniv. of Shipwreck of Frigate " Lautaro ".

749. **206.** 500 E. black and emer. 20 10
750. – 500 E. black and emer. 20 10
751. – 500 E. black and emer. 20 10
752. – 500 E. black and emer. 20 10
753. **206.** 800 E. black and brown 30 15
754. – 800 E. black and brown 30 15
755. – 800 E. black and brown 30 15
756. – 800 E. black and brown 30 15
757. **206.** 1000 E. black and blue 35 20
758. – 1000 E. black and blue 35 20
759. – 1000 E. black and blue 35 20
760. – 1000 E. black and blue 35 20
DESIGNS: Nos. 750, 754, 758: Frigate "Lautaro". Nos. 751, 755, 759: Cruiser " Chacabuco ". Nos. 752, 756, 760: Brigantine " Goleta Esmeralda ".

207. " The Happy Mother " (A. Valenzuela).

208. Diego Portales.

1975. International Women's Year. Chilean Paintings. Multicoloured.

761. 50 c. Type **207** 8 5
762. 50 c. " Girl " (F. J. Mandiola) 8 5
763. 50 c. " Lucia Guzman " (P. L. Rencoret) .. 8 5
764. 50 c. " Unknown Woman " (Magdalena M. Mena) .. 8 5

1975.

765. **208.** 10 c. green 5 5
766. 50 c. brown 8 8
767. 1 p. blue 15 8
768. 5 p. mauve 75 40

209. Lord Cochrane and Fleet, 1820.

1975. Lord Thomas Cochrane. Birth Bicent. Multicoloured.

769. 1 p. Type **209** 15 8
770. 1 p. Cochrane's conquest of Valdivia, 1820 .. .. 15 8
771. 1 p. Capture of " La Esmeralda ", 1820 .. 15 8
772. 1 p. Cruiser " Cochrane ", 1874 .. .. .. 15 8
773. 1 p. Destroyer " Cochrane ", 1962 .. .. .. 15 8

210. Flags of Chile and Bolivia.

1976. Bolivia's Independence. 150th Anniv.

774. **210.** 1 p. 50 multicoloured 20 12

211. Lake of the Inca.

1976. 6th General Assembly of Organization of American States.

775. **211.** 1 p. 50 multicoloured 20 12

212. George Washington.

213. Minerva and Academy Emblem.

1976. American Revolution. Bicent.

776. **212.** 5 p. multicoloured .. 70 60

1976. Polytechnic Military Academy. 50th Anniv.

777. **213.** 2 p. 50 multicoloured 35 25

ACKNOWLEDGMENT OF RECEIPT STAMP

1894. Portrait of Columbus. Inscr. "A.R." Perf. or Imperf.

AR 77. 5 c. brown 45 45

OFFICIAL STAMPS

1928. Stamps of 1911 inscr. " CHILE CORREOS " optd. **Servicio del ESTADO.**

O 190. **18.** 10 c. black and blue 3·00 30
O 191. – 20 c. (No. 142) .. 3·00 30
O 192. – 25 c. (No. 167) .. 3·25 40
O 193. – 50 c. (No. 170) .. 3·25 40
O 194. **23.** 1 p. black and green 4·00 40

1930. Stamps inscr. " CORREOS DE CHILE " optd. **Servicio del ESTADO.**

O 217. **18.** 10 c. (No. 204) .. 45 30
O 234. **32.** 10 c. blue 15 5
O 219. – 20 c. (No. 209) .. 25 15
O 235. – 20 c. brown (No. 232) 15 8
O 220. – 25 c. (No. 167) .. 30 10
O 221. – 50 c. (No. 168) .. 40 15

1934. Stamps inscr. " CORREOS DE CHILE " optd. **OFICIAL.**

O 236. **19.** 5 c. green (No. 206) 15 12
O 237. **32.** 10 c. blue 15 12
O 238. – 20 c. brown (No. 232) 4·50 15

1939. Optd. **Servicio del ESTADO.**

O 279. – 50 c. violet (No. 273) 1·10 1·00
O 280. **40.** 1 p. orange .. .. 1·60 70

1941. Nos. 269/77 optd. **OFICIAL.**

O 281. – 10 c. red 80 60
O 282. – 15 c. red 25 8
O 283. – 20 c. blue 30 5
O 284. – 30 c. red 30 5
O 285. – 40 c. green 30 5
O 286. – 50 c. violet .. .. 1·00 75
O 339. **40.** 1 p. orange .. .. 1·40 50
O 288. – 1 p. 80 blue .. .. 4·00 3·50
O 289. – 2 p. red .. .. 2·10 45
O 383. – 5 p. green .. .. 5·50 80

1953. No. 379b optd. **OFICIAL.**

O 386. 1 p. blue-green .. .. 1·25 50

1955. Nos. 276 and 278 optd. **OFICIAL.**

O 442. 2 p. red .. .. .. 2·50 1·00
O 443. 10 p. purple .. .. 4·00 1·50

1956. Nos. 446/450 opd. **OFICIAL.**

O 451. 2 p. lilac .. .. .. 1·50 1·10
O 452. 3 p. blue .. .. 6·00 6·00
O 453. 5 p. sepia .. .. 1·50 1·10
O 454a. 10 p. violet .. .. 3·00 65
O 455. 50 p. red .. .. 14·00 3·50

1958. Optd. **OFICIAL.**

O 469. **92.** 10 p. blue .. .. £110 10·00

1960. No. 493 optd. **OFICIAL.**

O 507. 5 c. blue .. .. 3·75 1·25

COMPULSORY TAX STAMPS

T 1. Arms of Talca.

T 2. Chilean Arms.

1942. Talca Bicent.

T 338. **T 1.** 10 c. blue 5 5

1955. Pres. Prieto, Death Cent. As T **86.**

T 455. 15 p. green 8 5
PORTRAIT: 15 p. Pres. Prieto.

1970. Postal Tax. No. 492 and 555 surch. **E° O, 10 Art. 77 LEY 17272.**

T 638. **101a.** 10 c. on 2 c. blue .. 5 5
T 639. **117.** 10 c. on 6 c. purple 5 5

1971. Postal Modernization.

T 646. **T 2.** 10 c. blue 5 5
T 647. 15 c. red 5 5

1971. Postal Modernization. Nos. T 646/7 surch.

T 672. **T 2.** 15 c. on 10 c. blue .. 5 5
T 674. 20 c. on 15 c. red .. 5 5
T 675. 50 c. on 15 c. red .. 5 5

POSTAGE DUE STAMPS

D 1.

D 2.

D 3.

1895.

D 98. **D 1.** 1 c. red on yellow .. 20 15
D 99. 2 c. red on yellow .. 20 15
D 100. 4 c. red on yellow .. 20 15
D 101. 6 c. red on yellow .. 20 15
D 102. 8 c. red on yellow .. 20 15
D 103. 10 c. red on yellow .. 20 15
D 104. 20 c. red on yellow .. 20 15
D 93. 40 c. red on yellow .. 25 25
D 94. 50 c. red on yellow .. 40 40
D 95. 60 c. red on yellow .. 95 95
D 96. 80 c. red on yellow .. 1·60 1·60
D 109. 100 c. red on yellow 10·00 7·00
D 97. 1 p. red on yellow .. 1·75 1·75

1898.

D 110. **D 2.** 1 c. red 5 5
D 111. 2 c. red 20 20
D 112. 4 c. red 5 5
D 113. 10 c. red 5 5
D 114. 20 c. red 5 5

1924.

D 184. **D 3.** 2 c. red and blue .. 15 15
D 185. 4 c. red and blue .. 15 15
D 186. 8 c. red and blue .. 15 15
D 187. 10 c. red and blue 8 8
D 188. 20 c. red and blue .. 8 8
D 189. 40 c. red and blue .. 8 8
D 190. 60 c. red and blue .. 15 15
D 191. 80 c. red and blue .. 20 20
D 192. 1 p. red and blue .. 35 35
D 193. 2 p. red and blue .. 1·50 1·50
D 194. 5 p. red and blue .. 2·00 2·00

CHINA

O1

A republic in the E. of Asia.

1878. 100 candarins = 1 tael.
1897. 100 cents = 1 dollar (Chinese).
1948. 100 cents = 1 Gold Yuan.
1949. 100 cents = 1 Silver Yuan.
1955. 100 fen = 1 yuan.

CHINESE CHARACTERS

Simple	Formal	
半	半	= ½
一	壹	= 1
二	貳	= 2
三	叁	= 3
四	肆	= 4
五	伍	= 5
六	陸	= 6
七	柒	= 7
八	捌	= 8
九	玖	= 9
十	拾	= 10
百	佰	= 100
千	仟	= 1,000
萬	萬	= 10,000
	分	= cent
	圓	= dollar

Examples:

十五	= 15
五十	= 50
叁佰圓	= 300 dollars
伍仟圓	= 5,000 dollars

1. Dragon. 2.

1878.

1.	1.	1 c. green	10·00	5·00
2.		3 c. red	5·00	2·50
3.		5 c. orange	6·00	2·50

1885.

13.	2.	1 c. green	75	50
14.		3 c. mauve	1·00	25
15.		5 c. yellow	1·00	35

3. 6.

1894. Dowager Empress's 60th Birthday.

16.	3.	1 c. orange	1·00	1·00
17.	–	2 c. green	1·00	1·00
18.	–	3 c. yellow	75	50
19.	–	4 c. pink	3·00	3·00
20.	–	5 c. orange	4·00	3·00
21.	–	6 c. brown	1·50	1·00
22.	6.	9 c. green	2·50	1·50
23.		12 c. orange	5·00	2·50
24.	–	24 c. red	6·00	3·50

DESIGNS—VERT. (as T 3): 2 c. to 6 c. Dragon. HORIZ. (as T 6): 24 c. Junks.

1897. Surch. in English and Chinese characters.

37.	–	½ c. on 3 c. yellow (No. 18)	25	25
34.	2.	1 c. on 1 c. green	1·00	75
79.	3.	1 c. on 1 c. orange	40	40
59.	–	2 c. on 2 c. green (No. 17)	35	35
35.	2.	2 c. on 3 c. mauve	2·00	1·00
40.	–	4 c. on 4 c. pink (No. 19)	40	40
36.	2.	5 c. on 5 c. yellow	1·00	1·00
41.	–	5 c. on 5 c. orange (No. 20)	40	40
42.	–	8 c. on 6 c. brown (No. 21)	1·00	60
43.	–	10c. on 6 c. brown (No. 21)	2·00	2·50
44.	6.	10 c. on 9 c. green	3·00	3·00
64.		10 c. on 12 c. orange	4·00	3·50
65.	–	30 c. on 24 c. red (No. 24)	6·50	5·00

9. 10.   11. 12.

1897. Surch. in English and Chinese characters.

88.	9.	1 c. on 3 c. red	1·00	50
89.		2 c. on 3 c. red	2·00	1·00
90.		4 c. on 3 c. red	5·00	4·00
91.		$1 on 3 c. red	35·00	20·00
92.		$5 on 3 c. red	£275	£250

1897. Inscr. "IMPERIAL CHINESE POST".

96.	10.	½ c. purple	20	15
97.		1 c. yellow	20	12
98.		2 c. orange	10	8
99.		4 c. brown	30	15
100.		5 c. red	50	20
101.		10 c. green	75	20
102.	11.	20 c. lake	2·00	1·00
103.		30 c. red	2·00	2·00
104.		50 c. green	3·00	3·00
105.	12.	$1 red	10·00	6·00
106.		$2 orange and yellow	50·00	60·00
107.		$5 green and red	20·00	25·00

13. 14. 15.

1898. Inscr. "CHINESE IMPERIAL POST".

108.	13.	½ c. brown	5	5
122.		1 c. buff	5	5
110a.		2 c. red	8	5
151.		2 c. green	10	5
152.		3 c. green	12	5
124.		4 c. brown	15	5
153.		4 c. red	15	5
112.		5 c. pink	75	15
126.		5 c. orange	1·00	25
154.		5 c. mauve	25	5
155.		7 c. lake	60	25
127.		10 c. green	35	5
156.		10 c. blue	70	5
157.	14.	16 c. olive	2·00	45
128.		20 c. claret	75	12
115.		30 c. red	85	40
130.		50 c. green	1·40	15
131.	15.	$1 red and salmon	3·50	40
132.		$2 claret and yellow	8·00	1·25
133.		$5 green and salmon	12·00	5·50

16. Temple of Heaven.  17. Dr. Sun Yat-sen.

1909. 1st Year of Reign of Emperor "Hsuan T'ung".

165.	16.	2 c. green and orange	15	15
166.		3 c. blue and orange	20	20
167.		7 c. purple and orange	50	50

1912. Optd. vert. with four Chinese characters signifying "Republic of China".

192.	13.	½ c. brown	8	5
193.		1 c. buff	8	5
194.		2 c. green	8	5
195a.		3 c. green	8	5
196.		4 c. red	15	5
197.		5 c. mauve	15	5
198.		7 c. lake	30	10
199.		10 c. blue	25	5
200.	14.	16 c. olive	40	25
201		20 c. claret	60	8
202.		30 c. red	1·10	20
203.		50 c. green	1·10	12
230.	15.	$1 red and salmon	3·75	30
205.		$2 claret and yellow	5·00	1·25
206.		$5 green and salmon	16·00	16·00

1912. Revolution Commem.

242.	17.	1 c. orange	15	15
243.		2 c. green	20	20
244.		3 c. blue	20	20
245.		5 c. mauve	20	20
246.		8 c. sepia	30	25
247.		10 c. blue	20	20
248.		16 c. olive	60	45
249.		20 c. lake	70	45
250.		50 c. green	2·75	2·25
251.		$1 red	5·50	3·50
252.		$2 brown	30·00	28·00
253.		$5 slate	10·00	10·00

1912. As T 17 but portrait of Pres. Yuan Shih-kai, inscr. "Commemoration of the Republic".

254.		1 c. orange	15	15
255.		2 c. green	15	15
256.		3 c. blue	15	15
257.		5 c. mauve	15	15
258.		8 c. sepia	45	30
259.		10 c. blue	25	20
260.		16 c. olive	40	30
261.		20 c. lake	60	35
262.		50 c. green	3·25	2·00
263.		$1 red	5·00	3·00
264.		$2 brown	6·00	4·00
265.		$5 slate	16·00	15·00

19. Junk.  20. Reaper.  21. Imperial Academy Gateway, Peking.

1913.

309.	19.	½ c. sepia	5	5
310.		1 c. orange	5	5
311.		1½ c. purple	60	12
312.		2 c. green	5	5
313.		3 c. green	8	5
272.		4 c. red	25	5
314.		4 c. grey	40	5
315.		4 c. olive	10	5
316.		5 c. mauve	8	5
294.		6 c. grey	15	5
317.		6 c. red	10	5
318.		6 c. brown	1·60	35
319.		7 c. violet	15	5
320.		8 c. orange	10	5
321.		10 c. blue	12	5
298.	20.	13 c. brown	15	5
299.		15 c. brown	1·25	20
323.		15 c. blue	25	5
300.		16 c. olive	25	8
301.		20 c. lake	40	5
302.		30 c. purple	30	5
327.		50 c. green	40	5
304.	21.	$1 black and yellow	1·75	8
328.		$1 sepia and brown	2·25	15
305.		$2 black and blue	3·50	25
329.		$2 brown and blue	3·75	20
306.		$5 black and red	6·50	2·00
330.		$5 green and red	8·00	60
307.		$10 black and green	25·00	12·00
331.		$10 mauve and green	15·00	3·25
308.		$20 black and orange	£160	£150
332.		$20 blue and purple	60·00	11·00

1920. Surch. with new value in English and Chinese characters.

349.	19.	1 c. on 2 c. green	90	40
361.		2 c. on 3 c. green	35	12
350.		3 c. on 4 c. red	1·10	75
351.		5 c. on 6 c. grey	1·60	1·10

22. Aeroplane over Great Wall of China.

I  II

1921. Air. Tail fin of aeroplane as Type I.

352.	22.	15 c. black and green	4·25	3·00
353.		30 c. black and red	2·75	2·00
354.		45 c. black and purple	2·75	2·00
355.		60 c. black and blue	3·75	2·25
356.		90 c. black and olive	4·25	3·00

For similar stamps in this type but with tail fin as Type II, see Nos. 384a/8.

23. Yen Kung-cho, Pres. Hsu Shih-chang and Chin Yung-peng.  24. Temple of Heaven.

1921. Chinese National Postal Service. 25th Anniv.

357.	23.	1 c. orange	40	25
358.		3 c. blue-green	40	25
359.		6 c. grey	90	70
360.		10 c. blue	90	70

1923. Adoption of the Constitution.

362.	24.	1 c. orange	30	15
363.		3 c. blue-green	40	20
364.		4 c. red	60	20
365.		10 c. blue	1·10	60

1925. Surch. in English and Chinese characters.

366.	19.	1 c. on 2 c. green	10	5
367.		1 c. on 3 c. green	8	5
369.		1 c. on 4 c. olive	12	5
370.		3 c. on 4 c. grey	20	5

The figures in this surcharge are at the top and are smaller than for the 1920 provisionals.

25. Marshal Chang Tso-lin.  26. General Chiang Kai-shek.

1928. Assumption of Naval and Military Commands.

372.	25.	1 c. orange	15	12
373.		4 c. olive	20	15
374.		10 c. blue	60	30
375.		$1 red	6·00	3·75

1929. Unification of China.

376.	26.	1 c. orange	30	12
377.		4 c. olive	50	12
378.		10 c. blue	1·50	25
379.		$1 red	8·00	4·75

27. Mausoleum at Nanking.  28. Dr. Sun Yat-sen.

1929. State Burial of Dr. Sun Yat-sen.

380.	27.	1 c. orange	15	10
381.		4 c. olive	25	15
382.		10 c. blue	75	30
383.		$1 red	8·00	4·00

1929. Air. As T 22, but tail fin of aeroplane as Type II.

384a.	22.	15 c. black and green	50	10
385.		30 c. black and red	1·50	65
386.		45 c. black and purple	1·50	75
387.		60 c. black and blue	1·75	75
388.		90 c. black and olive	2·00	1·50

1931.

389.	28.	1 c. orange	5	5
390.		2 c. olive	5	5
391.		4 c. green	5	5
398.		5 c. green	5	5
399.		15 c. green	25	5
400.		15 c. red	10	5
392.		20 c. blue	10	5
402.		25 c. blue	5	5
403a.		$1 sepia and brown	30	5
735.		$1 violet	5	5
404a.		$2 brown and blue	70	8
736.		$2 olive	5	5
405a.		$5 black and red	1·10	8
737.		$20 green	5	5
738.		$30 brown	5	5
739.		$50 orange	5	5

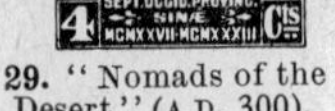

29. "Nomads of the Desert" (A.D. 300).

30. General Teng Keng.

1932. North-West China Scientific Expedition.

No.	Type	Description		
406.	29.	1 c. orange	2·40	3·00
407.		4 c. olive	2·40	3·00
408.		5 c. claret	2·40	3·00
409.		10 c. blue	2·40	3·00

1932. Martyrs of the Revolution.

No.	Type	Description		
410.	30.	½ c. sepia	5	5
411.	–	1 c. orange	5	5
509.	–	2 c. blue	5	5
412.	30.	2½ c. red	5	5
413.	–	3 c. brown	5	5
512.	30.	4 c. lilac	5	5
513.	–	5 c. orange	5	5
514.	–	8 c. orange	5	5
515.	–	10 c. purple	5	5
416.	–	13 c. green	5	5
517.	–	15 c. maroon	5	5
518.	–	17 c. green	5	5
418.	–	20 c. lake	8	5
519.	–	20 c. blue	5	5
520.	–	21 c. sepia	5	5
521.	–	25 c. purple	5	5
522.	–	28 c. olive	5	5
542.	–	30 c. maroon	5	5
524.	–	40 c. orange	5	5
525.	–	50 c. green	5	5

DESIGNS: 1 c., 25 c., 50 c. Chen Ying Shih. 2 c., 10 c., 17 c., 28 c. Chung Chiao-Jen. 3 c., 5 c., 15 c., 30 c. Liao Chung Kai. 8 c., 13 c., 21 c. Chu-chih Hsing. 20 c., 40 c. Huang Hsing.

31. Aeroplane over Great Wall.

1932. Air.

No.	Type	Description		
555.	31.	15 c. green	5	5
556.		25 c. orange	5	5
557.		30 c. red	5	5
558.		45 c. purple	5	5
559.		50 c. chocolate	5	5
560.		60 c. blue	5	5
561.		90 c. olive	5	5
562.		$1 green	5	5
563.		$2 brown	8	8
564.		$5 red	8	8

32. Tan Yen-kai.

33.

1933. Tan Yen-kai Memorial.

No.	Type	Description		
440.	32.	2 c. olive	20	20
441.		5 c. green	30	20
442.		25 c. blue	1·00	30
443.		$1 red	7·00	5·00

1936. New Life Movement. Symbolic designs as T 33.

No.	Type	Description		
444.	33.	2 c. olive	20	12
445.		5 c. green	25	12
446.	–	20 c. blue (various emblems)	1·00	20
447.	–	$1 red (Lighthouse)	4·00	1·10

34. "Postal Communications."

35. Dr. Sun Yat-sen.

1936. Chinese National Postal Service. 40th Anniv.

No.	Type	Description		
448.	35.	2 c. orange	12	10
449.	–	5 c. green	15	10
450.	–	25 c. blue	90	15
451.	–	100 c. red	3·00	1·00

DESIGNS: 5 c. The Bund, Shanghai. 25 c. G.P.O., Shanghai. 100 c. Ministry of Communications, Nanking.

1936. Surch. in figures and Chinese characters.

No.	Type	Description		
452.	20.	5 c. on 15 c. blue	15	5
453.		5 c. on 16 c. olive	15	5

1937. Surch. in figures and Chinese characters.

No.	Type	Description		
454.	28.	1 on 4 c. green	8	5
455.	–	8 on 40 c. orange (No. 420)	12	5
456.	28.	10 on 25 c. blue	12	5

1938.

No.	Type	Description		
462.	35.	2 c. olive	5	5
464.		3 c. lake	5	5
465.		5 c. green	5	5
466.		5 c. olive	5	5
467.		8 c. olive	5	5
469.		10 c. green	5	5
470.		15 c. red	5	5
471.		16 c. olive	25	10
472.		25 c. blue	5	5
494.		30 c. red	5	5
495.		50 c. blue	5	5
496.		$1 brown and red	12	5
479.		$2 brown and blue	20	5
498.		$5 green and red	20	5
499.		$10 violet and green	25	10
500.		$20 blue and claret	50	20

For stamps as T 35 but emblem at top redrawn with solid background, see Nos. 666 etc.

For 15 c. brown see Japanese Occupation of China, IV Shanghai and Nanking No. 12.

36. Chinese and U.S. Flags and Map of China.

1939. U.S. Constitution. 150th Anniv. Flags in red and blue.

No.	Type	Description		
501.	36.	5 c. green	20	15
502.		25 c. blue	40	35
503.		50 c. brown	50	40
504.		$1 red	1·00	90

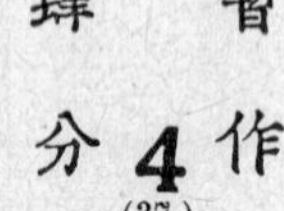

暫作
肆分 4

(37.)

1940. Surch. as T 37.

No.	Type	Description		
580b.	35.	3 c. on 5 c. green	8	5
579b.		3 c. on 5 c. olive	5	5
582.		4 c. on 5 c. green	5	5
619.		7 c. on 8 c. olive	8	8

38. Dr. Sun Yat-sen.

39. Industry

1941.

No.	Type	Description		
583.	38.	½ c. sepia	5	5
584.		1 c. orange	5	5
585.		2 c. blue	5	5
586.		5 c. green	5	5
587.		8 c. orange	5	5
588.		8 c. green	5	5
589.		10 c. green	5	5
590		17 c. olive	15	12
591.		25 c. claret	5	5
592.		30 c. red	5	5
593		50 c. blue	5	5
594.		$1 black and brown	5	5
595.		$2 black and blue	5	5
596.		$5 black and red	12	12
597.		$10 black and green	30	25
598.		$20 black and claret	35	25

1941. Thrift Movement.

No.	Type	Description		
599.	39.	8 c. green	5	5
600.		21 c. brown	5	5
601.		28 c. olive	8	8
602.		33 c. red	15	15
603.		50 c. blue	20	25
604.		$1 purple	30	30

中華民國創立
三十週年紀念
日十月十年十三

(40.)

改作
伍角 50

(41.)

42. Dr. Sun Yat-sen.

1941. Republic. 30th Anniv. Optd. with T 40.

No.	Type	Description		
606.	–	1 c. orange (No. 411)	5	5
607.	35.	2 c. olive	5	5
608.	30.	4 c. lilac	5	5
609.	35.	8 c. olive	5	5
610.		10 c. green	5	5
611.		16 c. olive	5	5
612.	–	21 c. sepia (No. 520)	5	5
613.	–	28 c. olive (No. 522)	5	5
614.	35.	30 c. red	10	10
615.		$1 brown and red	15	15

1942. Provincial surcharges. Surch. as T 41.

No.	Type	Description		
622.	30.	1 c. on ½ c. sepia	8	5
624.	38.	1 c. on ½ c. sepia	8	5
692b.	30.	20 c. on 13 c. green	5	5
691b.	35.	20 c. no 16 c. olive	5	5
693c.	30.	20 c. on 17 c. olive	5	5
697a.	38.	20 c. on 17 c. olive	5	5
694b.	30.	20 c. on 21 c. sepia	5	5
695b.		20 c. on 28 c. olive	5	5
625.	35.	40 c. on 50 c. blue	10	5
627.	38.	40 c. on 50 c. blue	5	5
626.	30.	40 c. on 50 c. green	8	8
701g.	42.	50 c. on 16 c. olive	12	8

1942.

No.	Type	Description		
628.	42.	10 c. green	5	5
629.		16 c. olive	1·50	1·50
630.		20 c. olive	5	5
631.		25 c. purple	5	5
632.		30 c. red	5	8
642.		30 c. brown	5	8
633.		40 c. brown	5	5
634.		50 c. green	5	5
635.		$1 red	8	5
636.		$1 olive	5	5
637.		$1·50 blue	5	5
638.		$2 green	5	5
645.		$2 blue	5	5
646.		$2 purple	5	5
639.		$3 yellow	5	5
648.		$4 brown	5	5
649.		$5 red	5	5
650.		$6 violet	5	5
651.		$10 brown	5	5
652.		$20 blue	5	5
653.		$50 green	5	5
654.		$70 violet	5	5
655.		$100 brown	5	5

1942. As T 35 but emblem at top redrawn with solid background. Perf., Imperf. or roul.

No.	Type	Description		
666.	35.	$4 blue	5	5
667.		$5 grey	5	5
656.		$10 brown	5	5
657.		$20 green	5	5
658.		$20 red	55	15
671.		$30 purple	5	5
660.		$40 red	5	5
673.		$50 blue	10	5
662.		$100 brown	30	12

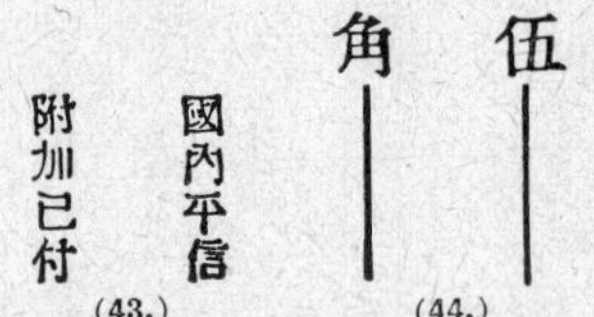

國內平信
附加已付

(43.)

伍角

(44.)

(T 43. Trans. "Surcharge for Domestic Postage. Paid".)

1942. Surch. as T 43.

No.	Type	Description		
688e.	42.	16 c. olive	30	40

1943. No. 688e. surch. as T 44.

No.	Type	Description		
689a.	42.	50 c. on 16 c. olive	5	5

45. Dr. Sun Yat-sen.

47. Savings Bank and Money Box.

46. War Refugees.

1944.

No.	Type	Description		
702.	45.	40 c. red	5	5
703.		$2 brown	5	5
704.		$3 red	5	5
705.		$3 brown	5	5
706.		$6 grey	5	5
707.		$10 red	5	5
708.		$20 pink	5	5
709.		$50 brown	5	5
710.		$70 violet	5	5

1944. War Refugees' Relief Fund. Various frames.

No.	Type	Description		
724.	46.	$2+$2 on 50 c.+50 c. blue	15	20
725.		$4+$4 on 8 c.+8 c. grn.	15	20
726.		$5+$5 on 21 c.+21 c. brown	30	30
727.		$6+$6 on 28 c.+28 c. olive	40	40
728.		$10+$10 on 33 c.+33 c. red	75	75
729.		$20+$20 on $1+$1 vio.	1·25	1·50

1944.

No.	Type	Description		
731.	47.	$40 slate	5	5
732.		$50 green	5	5
733.		$100 brown	5	5
734.		$200 green	5	5

48. Dr. Sun Yat-sen.

49.

1944. Kuomintang. 50th Anniv.

No.	Type	Description		
740.	48.	$2 green	5	25
741.		$5 brown	8	25
742.		$6 purple	10	30
743.		$10 blue	20	40
744.		$20 red	30	80

1945. Dr. Sun Yat-sen. 20th Death Anniv.

No.	Type	Description		
746.	49	$2 green	5	12
747.		$5 brown	5	12
748.		$6 blue	8	12
749.		$10 blue	12	15
750.		$20 red	15	20
751.		$30 buff	25	25

50. Dr. Sun Yat-sen.

52. Pres. Lin Sen.

51. Gen. Chiang Kai-shek.

1945.

No.	Type	Description		
758.	50.	$2 green	5	5
759.		$5 green	5	5
760.		$10 blue	5	5
761.		$20 red	5	5

1945. Equal Treaties with Great Britain and U.S.A., abolishing Foreign Concessions. Flags in National colours.

No.	Type	Description		
762.	51.	$1 blue	5	5
763.		$2 green	5	5
764.		$5 olive	8	8
765.		$6 brown	15	20
766.		$10 claret	25	30
767.		$20 red	35	50

1945. In Memory of President Lin Sen.

No.	Type	Description		
768.	52.	$1 black and blue	5	5
769.		$2 black and green	5	5
770.		$5 black and red	5	5
771.		$6 black and violet	10	15
772.		$10 black and brown	12	20
773.		$20 black and olive	25	35

暫售
貳佰圓 200.00

(53.)

國幣
壹圓

(54.)

國幣
貳拾圓

(55.)

1945. Chinese National Currency (C.N.C.). Various issues surch. as T 53 (for Japanese controlled Government at Shanghai and Nanking) and further surch. as T 54.

No.	Type	Description		
774.	35.	10 c. on $20 on 3 c. lake	5	5
775.	30.	15 c. on $30 on 2 c. blue	5	5
776.	38.	25 c. on $50 on 1 c. orge.	5	5
777.	35.	$1 on $100 on 3 c. lake	5	5
778.	30.	$1 on $200 on 1 c. orge.	5	5
779.	35.	$2 on $400 on 3 c. lake	5	5
780.	38.	$5 on $1000 on 1 c. orge.	5	5

1945. Kaifeng provisionals. C.N.C. surcharges. Stamps of Japanese Occupation of North China surch. as T 55.

No.	Type	Description		
781.	30.	$10 on 20 c. lake (No. 166)	20	35
782.		$20 on 40 c. orge. (No. 168)	30	35
783.		$50 on 30 c. clar. (No. 167)	35	35

56. Pres. Chiang Kai-Shek. 57.

1945. Inaug. of Pres. Chiang Kai-shek. Flag in blue and red.
784. 56. $2 green 10 30
785. $4 blue 10 30
786. $5 olive 10 30
787. $6 brown 20 50
788. $10 grey 30 70
789. $20 red 45 90

1945. Victory. Flag in red.
790. 57. $20 green and blue .. 5 5
791. $50 brown and blue .. 10 10
792. $100 blue 8 8
793. $300 red and blue .. 8 8

58. Dr. Sun Yat-sen. 59.)

1945.
794. 58. $20 red 5 5
795. $30 blue 5 5
796. $40 orange 5 10
797. $50 green 5 5
798. $100 brown 5 5
799. $200 chocolate 5 5

1945. C.N.C. surcharges. Surch. as T 59 (value tablet at top).
800. 30. $3 on 2½ c. red 15 20
801. $10 on 15 c. maroon .. 5 5
802. $20 on 8 c. orange .. 5 5
803. $20 on 20 c. blue .. 5 5
804. $30 on ½ c. sepia .. 5 5
805. $50 on 21 c. sepia .. 5 5
807. $70 on 13 c. green .. 5 5
808. $100 on 28 c. olive .. 5 5

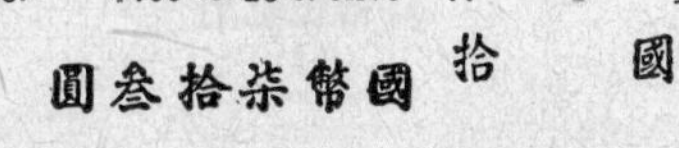

(60.) (61.)

1946. Air. C.N.C. surcharges. Surch. as T 60.
820. 31. $23 on 30 c. red .. 5 5
821. $53 on 15 c. green .. 5 5
822. $73 on 25 c. orange .. 5 5
823. $100 on $2 brown .. 5 5
824. $200 on $5 red .. 5 5

1946. C.N.C. surcharges. Surch. as T 61 (octagonal value tablet at bottom).
898. 30. $10 on 1 c. orange .. 5 5
903. 41. $10 on 1 c. orange .. 5 5
896. 38. $20 on 2 c. olive .. 5 5
904. 41. $20 on 2 c. blue .. 5 5
899. 30. $20 on 3 c. brown .. 5 5
897. 38. $20 on 3 c. lake .. 5 5
879. 30. $20 on 8 c. orange .. 5 5
869. 38. $20 on 8 c. olive .. 5 5
882. 41. $20 on 8 c. orange .. 5 5
883. $20 on 8 c. green .. 5 5
900. 30. $30 on 4 c. lilac .. 5 5
880. $50 on 5 c. orange .. 5 5
875. 38. $50 on 5 c. green .. 8 5
872. $50 on 5 c. olive .. 5 5
884. 41. $50 on 5 c. green .. 8 5

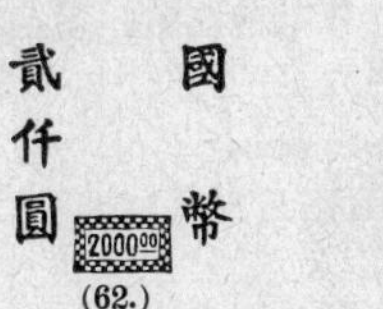

(62.) 63. Dr. Sun Yat-sen.

1946. C.N.C. surcharges. Surch. as T 62 (rectangular value tablet at bottom).

(a) Box with chequered pattern.
831. 35. $20 on 3 c. lake .. 5 5
846. 30. $20 on 8 c. orange .. 5 5
832. 35. $50 on 3 c. lake .. 5 5
844. $50 on 5 c. green .. 5 5
833. $50 on 5 c. olive .. 5 5
847. 30. $50 on 5 c. orange .. 5 5
851. 38. $50 on 5 c. green .. 5 5
854. 42. $50 on $1 olive .. 5 5
848. 30. $100 on 1 c. orange .. 5 5
834. 35. $100 on 3 c. lake .. 5 5
836. $100 on 8 c. olive .. 5 5
852. 38. $100 on 8 c. green .. 5 5
860. 28. $100 on $1 purple .. 5 5
868. 63. $100 on $20 red .. 5 5
837. 35. $200 on 10 c. green .. 5 5
861. 28. $200 on $4 blue .. 5 5
855. 42. $250 on $1·50 blue .. 5 5
862. 28. $250 on $2 olive .. 5 5
863. $250 on $5 red .. 5 5
838. 35. $300 on 10 c. green .. 5 5
853. 38. $300 on 10 c. green .. 5 5
839. 35. $500 on 3 c. lake .. 5 5
864. 28. $500 on $20 green .. 5 5
865. $800 on $30 brown .. 5 5
830. $1000 on 2 c. olive .. 5 5
856. 42. $1000 on $2 green .. 8 5
857. $1000 on $2 blue .. 12 5
858. $1000 on $2 purple .. 8 5
866. 50. $1000 on $2 green .. 20 12
859. 42. $2000 on $5 red .. 15 10
867. 50. $2000 on $5 green .. 12 8

(b) Box with diamond pattern.
978. 23. $500 on $20 green .. 5 5
979. 63. $1250 on $70 orange 5 5
980. 72. $1800 on $350 buff .. 5 5
974. 42. $2000 on $3 yellow .. 5 5
976. 45. $2000 on $3 red .. 5 5
975. 42. $3000 on $3 yellow .. 5 5
977. 45. $3000 on $3 brown .. 8 8

1946.
885. 63. $20 red 5 5
886. $30 blue 5 5
887. $50 violet 5 5
888. $70 orange 8 5
889. $100 claret 5 5
890. $200 green 5 5
891. $500 green 5 5
892. $700 brown 8 5
893. $1000 purple 5 5
894. $3000 blue 20 10
895. $5000 red and green .. 30 12

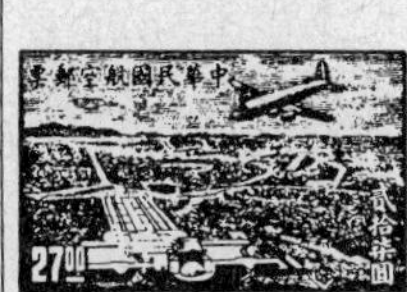

64. Aeroplane over Mausoleum of Dr. Sun Yat-sen. 65. Pres. Chiang Kai-shek.

1946. Air.
905. 64. $27 blue 8 5

1946. President's 60th Birthday.
906. 65. $20 red 5 5
907. $30 green 5 5
908. $50 orange 8 8
909. $100 green 8 8
910. $200 yellow 8 8
911. $300 claret 15 15

For stamps of this type, but additionally inscribed with four characters around head, see Taiwan Nos. 30/5, or North Eastern Provinces, Nos. 48/53.

66. National Assembly House, Nanking. 67. Entrance to Sun Yat-sen Mausoleum.

1946. Opening of National Assembly, Nanking.
912. 66. $20 green 5 5
913. $30 blue 8 8
914. $50 brown 10 10
915. $100 red 10 10

1947. 1st Anniv. of Return of Government to Nanking.
942. 67. $100 green 5 5
943. $200 blue 5 5
944. $250 red 8 8
945. $350 brown 8 8
946. $400 purple 8 8

For stamps of this type but additionally inscribed with four characters above numeral of value, see Taiwan, Nos. 36/40, or North Eastern Provinces, Nos. 64/68.

68. Dr. Sun Yat-sen. 69. Confucius. 70. Confucius' Lecture School.

71. Tomb of Confucius. 72. Dr. Sun Yat-sen.

1947.
947. 68. $500 olive 5 5
948. $1,000 red and green .. 5 5
949. $2,000 lake and blue .. 8 8
950. $5,000 black and orange 12 12

1947. Confucius Commem.
951. 69. $500 red 5 5
952. 70. $800 brown 5 5
953. 71. $1,250 green 5 5
954. – $1,800 blue 5 5
DESIGN—HORIZ. $1,800 Confucian Temple.

1947. (a) With noughts for cents.
955. 72. $150 blue 5 5
956. $250 violet 5 5
957. $500 green 5 5
958. $1,000 red 5 5
959. $2,000 orange 5 5
960. $3,000 blue 5 5
961. $4,000 grey 5 5
962. $5,000 brown 5 5
963. $6,000 purple 5 5
964. $7,000 brown 5 5
965. $10,000 red and blue .. 12 8
966. $20,000 green and red 8 8
967. $50,000 blue and green 10 8
968. $100,000 green & orange 12 8
969. $200,000 blue & purple 15 8
970. $300,000 orange & brown 30 15
971. $500,000 brown & green 50 40

(b) Without noughts for cents.
1032. 72. $20,000 red 5 5
1033. $30,000 brown 5 5
1034. $40,000 green 5 5
1035. $50,000 blue 5 5
1036. $100,000 olive 5 5
1037. $200,000 purple 5 5
1038. $300,000 green 5 5
1039. $500,000 mauve 10 8
1040. $1,000,000 claret 10 8
1041. $2,000,000 orange .. 12 8
1042. $3,000,000 bistre .. 10 8
1043. $5,000,000 blue .. 55 30

73. Taiwan and Chinese Flag. 74. Postal Kiosk.

1947. Restoration of Taiwan (Formosa). (1st issue).
972. 73. $500 red 5 5
973. $1,250 green 5 5
See also Nos. 1003/4.

1947. Progress of the Postal Service.
981. – $500 red 5 5
982. 74. $1,000 violet 5 5
983. $1,250 green 5 5
984. – $1,800 blue 8 8
DESIGN: $500, $1,800 Mobile Post Office.

75. Air, Sea and Rail Transport. 76. Postboy and Motor Van.

1947. Directorate General of Posts. 50th Anniv.
985. 75. $100 violet 5 5
986. 76. $200 green 5 5
987. $300 lake 5 5
988. – $400 red 5 5
989. – $500 blue 5 5
DESIGN—HORIZ. $400, $500 Junk and aeroplane (as in T 75).

77. Book of the Constitution and National Assembly Building.

1947. Adoption of the Constitution.
990. 77. $2,000 red 5 5
991. $3,000 blue 5 5
992. $5,000 green 5 5

78. Reproductions of 1947 and 1912 Stamps.

1948. Perf. or Imp.(a) Nanking Philatelic Exn.
1001. 78. $5,000 claret 8 8

(b) Shanghai Philatelic Exhibition.
1002. 78. $5,000 green .. 8 8

79. Sun Yat-sen Memorial Hall.

1948. Restoration of Taiwan (Formosa). (2nd issue).
1003. 79. $5,000 lilac 5 5
1004. $10,000 red 5 5

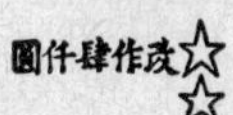

(80.) (81.)

(82.)

1948. "Re-valuation" surcharges.

(a) Surch. as T 80.
1012. 72. $4,000 on $100 red .. 10 8
1013. $5,000 on $100 red .. 10 8
1014. $8,000 on $800 brown 10 8

(b) Surch. as T 81.
1005. 43. $5,000 on $1 olive .. 5 5
1007. $5,000 on $2 green .. 8 8
1008. 58. $10,000 on $20 red .. 8 8
1018. 43. $15,000 on 10 c. green 10 8
1015. $15,000 on 50 c. green 8 8
1019. $15,000 on $4 purple 10 8
1020. $15,000 on $6 blue .. 10 8
1009. $20,000 on 10 c. green 8 8
1010. $20,000 on 50 c. green 8 8
1011. $30,000 on 30 c. red 8 8
1016. $40,000 on 20 c. olive 8 8
1017. $60,000 on $4 brown 15 10

(c) Air. Surch. as T 82.
1022. 31. $10,000 on 30 c. red 5 5
1028. 64. $10,000 on $27 blue 5 5
1023. 31. $20,000 on 25 c. orange 5 5
1024. $30,000 on 90 c. olive 5 5
1025. $50,000 on 60 c. blue 5 5
1026. $50,000 on $1 green 5 5

In No. 1028 the Chinese characters read vertically.

83. Great Wall of China. 84. S.S. "Hai Tien" and Steamship of 1872.

85. S.S. "Kiang Ya".

伍 國
千
圓5000幣
(85a).

1948. Tuberculosis Relief Fund. Cross in red. Perf. or Imperf.
1029. 83. $5,000 + $2,000 violet 5 50
1030. $10,000 + $2,000 brown 5 50
1031. $15,000 + $2,000 grey 5 50

1948. China Merchants' Steam Navigation Company 75th Anniv.
1044. 84. $20,000 blue .. 5 5
1045. $30 000 mauve .. 5 5
1046. 85. $40,000 brown .. 5 5
1047. $60,000 red 8 5

1948 C.N.C. surcharge. Surch. with T **85a.**
1048. **61.** $5,000 on $100 claret 45 60

金 圓 壹 金

1/2分 (86.) 3 分 (87.) 金圓 角 10 圓 (88.)

1948. Gold Yuan surcharges.
(a) Surch. as T **86** or **87.**
1049. **42.** ½ c. on 30 c. brown .. 5 5
1050. **72.** ½ c. on $500 green .. 5 5
1051. **61.** 1 c. on $20 red .. 5 5
1052. **42.** 2 c. on $1 50 c. blue .. 5 5
1053. 3 c. on $5 red .. 5 5
1054. 4 c. on $1 red .. 5 5
1055. 5 c. on 50 c. green .. 5 5
(b) Surch. as T **88.**
1056. **45.** 5 c. on $20 pink .. 5 5
1057. **58.** 5 c. on $30 blue .. 5 5
1058. **35.** 10 c. on 2 c. olive .. 5 5
1059. **30.** 10 c. on 2½ c. mauve .. 5 5
1061. **42.** 10 c. on 25 c. purple .. 5 5
1062. **45.** 10 c. on 40 c. red .. 5 5
1063. **42.** 10 c. on $1 olive .. 5 5
1064. **45.** 10 c. on $2 brown .. 5 5
1065. **42.** 10 c. on $20 blue .. 5 5
1067. **45.** 10 c. on $20 pink .. 7·50 7·50
1068. **50.** 10 c. on $20 red .. 5 5
1069. **61.** 10 c. on $20 red .. 12 12
1070. **58.** 10 c. on $30 blue .. 5 5
1071. **45.** 10 c. on $70 violet .. 5 5
1072. **72.** 10 c. on $7,000 brown .. 5 5
1073. 10 c. on $20,000 red .. 5 5
1074. **45.** 20 c. on $6 grey .. 5 5
1075. **29.** 20 c. on $30 yrown .. 5 5
1076. **61.** 20 c. $30 blue .. 5 5
1077. 20 c. on $100 claret .. 5 5
1079. **30.** 50 c. on ½ c. sepia .. 5 5
1081. **42.** 50 c. on 20 c. olive .. 5 5
1082. 50 c. on 30 c. red .. 5 5
1083. 50 c. on 40 c. brown .. 5 5
1084. **48.** 50 c. on 40 c. red .. 5 5
1085. **42.** 50 c. on $4 brown .. 5 5
1086. 50 c. on $20 blue .. 5 5
1087. **50.** 50 c. on $20 red .. 5 5
1088. **61.** 50 c. on $20 red .. 5 5
1089. **42.** 50 c. on $70 violet .. 5 5
1090. **72.** 50 c. on $6,000 purple .. 5 5
1091. **42.** $1 on 30 c. brown .. 5 5
1092. $1 on 40 c. brown .. 5 5
1093. $1 on $1 red .. 5 5
1094. $1 on $5 red .. 5 5
1095. **45.** $2 on $2 brown .. 5 5
1096. **59.** $2 on $20 red .. 5 5
1097. **61.** $2 on $100 claret .. 5 5
1098. **30.** $5 on 17 c. olive .. 5 5
1099. **45.** $5 on $2 brown .. 5 5
1100. **72.** $5 on $3,000 blue .. 5 5
1101. **30.** $8 on 20 c. blue .. 5 5
1102. **72.** $8 on $30,000 brown .. 5 5
1103. **30.** $10 on 40 c. orange .. 5 5
1104. **45.** $10 on $2 brown .. 5 5
1105. $20 on $2 brown .. 5 5
1106. **61.** $20 on $20 red .. 10 10
1107. **42.** $50 on 30 c. red .. 5 5
1108. **45.** $50 on $2 brown .. 8 5
1109. **61.** $80 on $20 red .. 5 5
1110. **42.** $100 on $1 olive .. 5 5
1111. **45.** $100 on $2 brown .. 5 5
1112. **72.** $20,000 on $40,000 green 40 40
1113. $50,000 on $20,000 red 25 25
1114. $50,000 on $30,000 brn. 40 40
1115. $100,000 on $20,000 red 25 25
1116. $100,000 on $30,000 brn. 10 10
1117. $200,000 on $40,000 grn. 60 70
1118. $200,000 on $50,000 blue 60 70

金圓貳佰圓 2000̲0̲ (89.) 改作郵票

90. Ship, Train and Aeroplane.

中華民國郵政 1.00 金圓壹圓 (91.)

92. Dr. Sun Yat-sen.

1949. Gold Yuan surcharges. Parcels Post stamps surch. as T **89.**
1119. **P 2.** $200 on $3,000 orange 5 5
1120. $500 on $5,000 blue 5 8
1121. $1,000 on $10,000 vio. 8 10

1949. Gold Yuan surcharges. Revenue stamps surch. (a) As T **91.**
1122. **90.** 50 c. on $20 brown .. 5 5
1137. $1 on $15 orange .. 5 5
1123. $2 on $50 blue .. 5 5
1128. $3 on $50 blue .. 5 5
1138. $5 on $50 chocolate .. 5 5
1129. $10 on $30 mauve .. 5 5
1140. $15 on $20 brown .. 5 5
1141. **90.** $25 on $20 brown .. 5 5
1145. $50 on $50 blue .. 5 5
1147. $50 on $300 green .. 5 5
1130. $80 on $50 blue .. 5 5
1131. $100 on $50 blue .. 5 5
1124. $200 on $50 blue .. 5 5
1145. $200 on $500 chocolate 5 5
1125. $300 on $50 blue .. 5 5
1143. $500 on $14 orange .. 5 5
1134. $500 on $30 mauve .. 5 8
1135. $1,000 on $50 blue .. 20 12
1150. $1,000 on $100 olive 40 30
1126. $1,500 on $50 blue .. 5 5
1151. $2,000 on $300 green 12 12

(b) As T **91** but with key pattern inverted at top and bottom.
1183. **90.** $50 on $10 green 25 20
1184. $100 on $10 green 90 65
1185. $500 on $10 green 90 60
1186. $1,000 on $10 green 35 12
1187. $5,000 on $20 brown 60 20
1188. $10,000 on $20 brown 50 25
1189. $50,000 on $20 brown 50 25
1190. $100,000 on $20 brown 60 40
1191. $500,000 on $20 brown 12·00 8·00
1192. $2,000,000 on $20 brn. 40·00 20·00
1193. $5,000,000 on $20 brn. 60·00 40·00

1949.
1152. **92.** $1 orange .. 5 5
1153. $10 green .. 5 5
1154. $20 purple .. 5 5
1155. $50 green .. 5 5
1156. $100 brown .. 5 5
1157. $200 red .. 5 5
1158. $500 mauve .. 5 5
1159. $800 red .. 5 5
1160. $1,000 blue .. 5 5
1168. $2,000 violet .. 5 5
1169. $5,000 blue .. 5 5
1177. $5,000 red .. 8 5
1170. $10,000 brown .. 5 5
1171. $20,000 green .. 5 5
1179. $20,000 orange .. 8 8
1172. $50,000 pink .. 5 5
1180. $50,000 blue .. 8 8
1173. $80,000 brown .. 12 20
1174. $100,000 green .. 5 5
1181. $200,000 blue .. 10 8
1182. $500,000 purple .. 15 8
For stamps of T **92** in Silver Yuan currency see Nos. 1348/56.

93. "Surface Transport." **94.** "Air Transport."

95. Postman on Motor-cycle. **96.** Mountains.

1949 No value indicated. Perf. or roul.
1211. **93.** Orange (Ord. postage) 15 8
1212. **94.** Green (Air Mail) .. 50 30
1213. **95.** Mauve (Express) .. 25 30
1214. **96.** Red (Registration) .. 25 10
Owing to the collapse of the Gold Yuan the above were sold at the rate for the day for the service indicated.

中華民國郵政 國內信函費 (97.)

中華郵政 國內掛號 分四 4 (98.)

1949. Gold Yuan currency. Revenue stamps optd. as T **97.**
1232. **90.** $10 green (B) .. .. 80 1·00
1233. $30 mauve (A) .. 1·50 1·25
1234. $50 blue (C) 70 80
1235. $100 olive (D) .. 2·00 2·00
1236. $200 purple (A) .. 70 25
1237. $500 green (A) .. 75 45
Opt. translation: (A) Domestic Letter Fee. (B) Express Letter Fee. (C) Registered Letter Fee. (D) Air Mail Fee.

1949. Silver Yuan surcharges. Revenue stamps surch. as T **98.**
1312. **90.** 1 c. on $20 brown 1·50 1·75
1284. 1 c. on $5,000 brown .. 12 12
1285. 4 c. on $100 olive .. 8 8
1286. 4 c. on $3,000 orange .. 8 8
1313. 10 c. on $20 brown .. 1·50 1·75
1287. 10 c. on $50 blue .. 8 8
1288. 10 c. on $1,000 red .. 10 8
1289. 20 c. on $1,000 red .. 10 10
1290. 50 c. on $30 mauve .. 20 12
1291. 50 c. on $50 blue .. 20 20
1292. $1 on $50 blue .. 30 30
In Nos. 1292 and 1313 the key pattern is inverted at top and bottom. See also Nos. 1183/93.

99. Flying Geese over Globe. **100.** Globe and Doves.

1949.
1344. **99.** $1 orange 40 35
1345. $2 blue .. .. 1·10 60
1346. $5 red .. .. 1·60 1·25
1347. $10 green .. .. 3·25 2·25

1949. Silver Yuan currency.
1348. **92.** 1 c. green 8 8
1349. 2 c. orange 8 8
1350. 4 c. green 5 5
1351. 10 c. lilac 5 5
1352. 16 c. red 25 25
1353. 20 c. blue 10 40
1354. 50 c. brown .. .. 40 1·00
1355. 100 c. blue .. .. 18·00 22·00
1356. 500 c. red .. .. 25·00 25·00

1949. U.P.U. 75th Anniv. Value optd. in black. Imperf.
1357. **100.** $1 orange 80 95

101. Buddha's Tower, Peking. **102.** Bronze Bull.

1949. Value optd. Roul.
1358. **101.** 15 c. green and brown 8 8
1359. **102.** 40 c. red and green .. 12 12

5 伍分 (103.) 15 壹角伍分 (104.)

1949. Silver Yuan surcharges.
(a) Chungking issue. Surch. as T **103.**
1360. **91.** 2½ c. on $50 green .. 8 8
1361. 2½ c. on $50,000 blue 8 8
1362. 5 c. on $1,000 blue .. 15 12
1363. 5 c. on $20,000 orange 15 12
1364. 5 c. on $200,000 blue 20 15
1365. 5 c. on $500,000 purple 20 15
1366. 10 c. on $5,000 red .. 25 20
1367. 10 c. on $10,000 brown 25 20
1368. 15 c. on $200 red .. 40 35
1369. 25 c. on $100 brown 50 1·00
(b) Canton issue. Surch. as T **104.**
1370. **91.** 1 c. on $100 brown .. 30 30
1372. 2½ c. on $500 mauve 50 50
1374. 15 c. on $10 green 1·25 1·25
1375. 15 c. on $20 purple 1·60 1·60
General issues for the People's Republic of China (Nos. 1401 onwards), follow the Regional issues after Nos. SW64.

EXPRESS DELIVERY STAMP

已付 國內快遞 函信 起重二十公分 郵資

E 1.

1941. Perf.
E616. **E 1.** (No value) red & yell. 35 35
This stamp was sold at $2 which included ordinary postage.

REGISTRATION STAMP

1941. Roul.
R 617. **E 1.** (No value) green & buff 35 35
This stamp was sold at $1·50 which included ordinary postage.

MILITARY POST STAMPS

郵 軍

M 2. M 2. Entrenched Soldiers.

1942. Optd. variously as Type M 1.
M 675. **33.** 8 c. olive 25 25
M 684. **41.** 8 c. green 30 25
M 676. 8 c. orange .. .. 5·00
M 683. **38.** 16 c. olive 60 50
M 677. **43.** 16 c. olive 30 30
M 678. 50 c. green 20 20
M 679. $1 red 20 20
M 680. $1 olive 30 20
M 681. $2 green 50 50
M 687. $2 purple .. .. 1·25 1·25

1945.
M 745. **M 2.** (No value) red .. 12 20

PARCELS POST STAMPS

P 1. P 2. P 3.

1944.
P 711. **P 1.** $500 green .. — 10
P 712. $1,000 blue .. — 10
P 713. $3,000 red .. — 10
P 714. $5,000 brown .. — 70
P 715. $10,000 purple .. — 1·25
P 716. $20,000 orange .. — 18·00

1946.
P 814. **P 2.** $3,000 orange .. — 5
P 815. $5,000 blue .. — 5
P 816. $10,000 violet .. — 5
P 817. $20,000 red .. — 15

1947. Type P 3 and similar design.
P 925. $1,000 yellow .. — 5
P 926. $3,000 green .. — 5
P 827. $5,000 red .. — 5
P 928. $7,000 blue .. — 5
P 929. $10,000 red .. — 5
P 930. $30,000 olive .. — 8
P 931. $50,000 black .. — 8
P 932. $70,000 brown .. — 8
P 933. $100,000 purple .. — 8
P 934. $200,000 green .. — 8
P 935. $300,000 pink .. — 8
P 936. $500,000 plum .. — 10
P 937. $3,000,000 blue .. — 15
P 938. $5,000,000 lilac .. — 15
P 939. $6,000,000 grey .. — 20
P 940. $8,000,000 red .. — 25
P 941. $10,000,000 olive .. — 30

圓拾伍圓金 50 圓拾伍圓金 (P 4).

1949. Gold Yuan surcharges. 1947 issue surch. as Type **P 4.**
P 1194. $10 on $3,000 green .. — 5
P 1195. $20 on $5,000 red .. — 5
P 1196. $50 on $10,000 red .. — 5
P 1197. $100 on $3,000,000 blue — 5
P 1198. $200 on $5,000,000 lilac — 5
P 1199. $500 on $1,000 yellow — 8
P 1200. $1,000 on $7,000 blue — 10
Parcels post stamps were not on sale in unused condition and those now on the market were probably stocks seized by the Communists.

POSTAGE DUE STAMPS

1904. Stamps of 1898 optd. **POSTAGE DUE** in English and Chinese characters.
D 137. **13.** ½ c. brown 55 20
D 138. 1 c. buff 55 20
D 139a. 2 c. red 55 25
D 140. 4 c. brown 70 30
D 141. 5 c. red 90 40
D 142. 10 c. green .. .. 1·10 40

D 1. 中華民國 (D 2.) D 3. D 4.

1904.
D 143. **D 1.** ½ c. blue 20 8
D 144. 1 c. blue 35 8
D 168. 1 c. brown 50 30
D 145. 2 c. blue 12 8
D 169. 2 c. brown 80 40
D 146. 4 c. blue 40 10
D 147. 5 c. blue 50 12
D 148. 10 c. blue 60 20
D 149. 20 c. blue .. .. 1·25 70
D 150. 30 c. blue .. .. 1·60 80

1912. Optd. with vertical row of Chinese characters.
D 207. **D 1.** ½ c. blue 5 5
D 208. 1 c. brown 8 8
D 209. 2 c. brown 8 8
D 210. 4 c. blue 20 10
D 211. 5 c. blue .. .. 10·00 10·00
D 212. 5 c. brown 25 12
D 213. 10 c. blue 35 20
D 214. 20 c. blue 70 35
D 215. 30 c. blue .. .. 1·40 80

1912. Optd. with Type D 2.

D 233.	D 1.	½ c. blue	70	35
D 234.		½ c. brown	8	8
D 235.		1 c. brown	8	8
D 236.		2 c. brown	20	15
D 237.		4 c. blue	40	20
D 238.		5 c. brown ..	50	25
D 239.		10 c. blue	1·25	50
D 240.		20 c. brown ..	2·50	1·40
D 241.		30 c. blue	3·00	1·60

1913.

D 333.	D 3.	½ c. blue	5	5
D 342.		1 c. blue	8	5
D 343.		2 c. blue	8	5
D 344.		4 c. blue	10	5
D 345.		5 c. blue	12	5
D 346.		10 c. blue	20	8
D 347.		20 c. blue	40	8
D 348.		30 c. blue	1·50	20

1932.

D 432.	D 4.	½ c. orange	5	5
D 433.		1 c. orange	5	5
D 434.		2 c. orange	5	5
D 435.		4 c. orange	8	5
D 436.		5 c. orange ..	8	5
D 437.		10 c. orange ..	12	10
D 438.		20 c. orange ..	12	10
D 439.		30 c. orange ..	12	10
D 573.		50 c. orange ..	5	5
D 574.		$1 orange	5	5
D 575.		$2 orange	5	5

暫作欠資

D 5. ("Temporary-use Postage Due.")

1940. Optd. with Type D 5.

D 505.	35.	$1 brown and red ..	15	12
D 506.		$2 brown and blue ..	25	20

D 6.  D 7.  D 8.

1944.

D 717.	D 6.	10 c. green	5	5
D 718.		20 c. blue	5	5
D 719.		40 c. red	5	5
D 720.		50 c. green	5	5
D 721.		60 c. blue	5	5
D 722.		$1 red	5	5
D 723.		$2 purple	5	5

1945.

D 752.	D 7.	$2 red	5	5
D 753.		$6 red	5	5
D 754.		$8 red	5	5
D 755.		$10 red	5	5
D 756.		$20 red	5	5
D 757.		$30 red	5	5

1947.

D 916.	D 8.	$50 purple	5	5
D 917.		$80 purple	5	5
D 918.		$100 purple ..	5	5
D 919.		$160 purple ..	5	5
D 920.		$200 purple ..	5	5
D 921.		$400 purple ..	5	5
D 922.		$500 purple ..	5	5
D 923.		$800 purple ..	5	5
D 924.		$2,000 purple ..	5	5

圓仟壹作改
1000 00
(D 9.)

資欠作改
金圓壹分
1
(D 10.)

1948. Surch. as Type D 9.

D 993.	D 7.	$1,000 on $20 pur.	5	5
D 994.		$2,000 on $30 pur.	5	5
D 995.		$3,000 on $50 pur.	5	5
D 996.		$4,000 on $100 pur.	5	5
D 997.		$5,000 on $200 pur.	5	5
D 998.		$10,000 on $300 pur.	5	5
D 999.		$20,000 on $500 pur.	5	5
D 1000.		$30,000 on $1,000 pur.	8	8

1949. Gold Yuan surcharges. Surch. as Type D 10.

D 1201.	58.	1 c. on $40 orange..	5	5
D 1202.		2 c. on $40 orange..	5	5
D 1203.		5 c. on $40 orange..	5	5
D 1204.		10 c. on $40 orange	5	5
D 1205.		20 c. on $40 orange	5	5
D 1206.		50 c. on $40 orange	5	5
D 1207.		$1 on $40 orange ..	5	5
D 1208.		$2 on $40 orange ..	5	5
D 1209.		$5 on $40 orange ..	5	5
D 1210.		$10 on $40 orange..	10	10

CHINA—MANCHURIA

A. KIRIN AND HEILUNGKIANG

用貼黑吉限 (1.)

吉黑貼用 (2.)

Stamps of China optd.

1927. Stamps of 1913 optd. with T 1.

1.	19.	½ c. sepia	5	5
2.		1 c. orange	5	5
3.		1½ c. purple	5	5
4.		2 c. green	10	5
5.		3 c. green	8	5
6.		4 c. olive	10	5
7.		5 c. mauve	10	5
8.		6 c. red	10	5
9.		7 c. violet	10	8
10.		8 c. orange	12	5
11.		10 c. blue	12	5
12.	20.	13 c. brown	30	12
13.		15 c. blue	15	10
14.		16 c. olive	15	10
15.		20 c. lake	25	10
16.		30 c. purple	25	10
17.		50 c. green	60	30
18.	21.	$1 sepia and brown	1·00	50
19.		$2 brown and blue	2·25	1·60
20.		$5 green and red ..	10·00	8·00

1928. Chang Tso-lin stamps optd. with T 2.

21.	25.	1 c. orange	12	10
22.		4 c. olive	15	12
23.		10 c. blue	40	35
24.		$1 red	3·50	3·25

1929. Unification stamps optd. as T 2.

25.	28.	1 c. orange	12	10
26.		4c. olive	25	15
27.		10 c. blue	70	40
28.		$1 red	4·25	4·00

1929. Sun Yat-sen Memorial stamps optd. as T 2.

29.	27.	1 c. orange	12	8
30.		4 c. olive.. ..	25	12
31.		10 c. blue	65	35
32.		$1 red	6·00	3·50

B. MANCHUKUO

Issues for the Japanese puppet Government set up in 1932 under President (later Emperor) Pu Yi.

100 fen = 1 yuan

1. White Pagoda, Liaoyang.  2. Pu Yi, later Emperor Kang-teh.

1932.

(a) With five characters in top panel as T 1 and 2.

1.	1.	½ f. sepia	8	5
2.		1 f. lake	8	5
25.		1½ f. mauve	30	12
26.		2 f. slate	30	5
27.		3 f. brown..	30	5
6.		4 f. olive	20	5
7.		5 f. green	20	5
8.		6 f. red	90	15
9.		7 f. grey	25	10
10.		8 f. yellow..	1·25	40
29.		10 f. orange	50	5
12.	2.	13 f. brown	75	30
13.		15 f. red	1·25	15
14.		16 f. blue	1·25	35
15.		20 f. sepia..	60	8
16.		30 f. orange	70	15
17.		50 f. green	1·90	35
31.		1 y. violet..	3·50	90

(b) With six characters in top panel.

40.	1.	½ f. sepia	5	5
41.		1 f. lake	8	5
42.		1½ f. mauve	10	5
43.		3 f. brown..	8	5
44.		5 f. blue	75	8
45.		5 f. slate	25	20
46.		6 f. red	25	8
47.		7 f. grey	30	10
48.		9 f. orange	15	8
55.		10 f. blue	35	8
56.	2.	13 f. brown	35	25
49.		15 f. red	15	8
50.		18 f. green	2·75	35
51.		20 f. sepia..	30	15
52.		30 f. brown	40	8
53.		50 f. olive	80	15
54.		1 y. violet..	1·60	35

3. Map and Flag.  5. Emperor's Palace.

1933. Republic. 1st Anniv.

19.	3.	1 f. orange	1·10	80
20.	–	2 f. green	1·50	1·00
21.	3.	4 f. red	1·10	80
22.	–	10 f. blue	2·75	1·60

DESIGN: 2 f., 10 f. Council Hall, Hsinking.

1934. Enthronement.

32.	5.	1½ f. brown	50	20
33.	–	3 f. red	1·25	30
34.	5.	6 f. green	1·40	75
35.	–	10 f. blue	2·10	75

DESIGN: 3 f., 10 f. Phoenixes.

1934. Stamps of 1932 surch. with four Japanese characters.

36.	1.	1 f. on 4 f. olive (No. 6)..	20	15
38.		3 f. on 4 f. olive (No. 6)..	25	15
39.	2.	3 f. on 16 f. blue (No. 14)..	2·25	1·10

In No. 38 the left hand upper character of the surcharge consists of three horizontal lines.

7. Orchid Crest of Manchukuo.  8. Changpai Mountain and Sacred Lake.

1935. China Mail.

64.	7.	2 f. green	12	8
65.		2½ f. violet	15	8
66.	8.	4 f. olive-green ..	20	5
67.		5 f. black	5	5
68.	7.	8 f. yellow	8	5
63.	8.	12 f. chestnut ..	75	50
70.		13 f. brown	10	5

9. Mt. Fuji.  10. Phœnixes.

1935. Visit of Emperor Kang-teh to Japan.

71.	9.	1½ f green	25	12
72.	10.	3 f. orange	25	12
73.	9.	6 f. red	35	20
74.	10.	10 f. blue	60	30

11. Symbolic of Accord.  13. State Council Building, Hsinking.  14. Chengte Palace, Johol.

1936. Japan-Manchukuo Postal Agreement.

75.	11.	1½ f. sepia	20	12
76.	–	3 f. mauve	20	12
77.	11.	6 f. red	75	30
78.	–	10 f. blue	80	60

DESIGN—HORIZ. 3 f., 10 f. Department of Communications.

1936.

79.	13.	½ f. brown	5	5
80.		1 f. lake	5	5
81.		1½ f. violet	30	12
82.	A.	2 f. green	5	5
83.	13.	3 f. chocolate ..	5	5
84.	B.	4 f. olive	5	5
85.	13.	5 f. grey	1·00	30
86.	A.	6 f. red	8	5
87.	B.	7 f. black	8	5
88.		9 f. orange	12	8
89.	14.	10 f. blue	8	5
90.	B.	12 f. orange	8	5
91.		13 f. chocolate ..	1·75	75
92.		15 f. red	15	10
93.	C.	18 f. green	80	50
94.		19 f. green	50	25
152.	A.	20 f. brown	25	12
153.	14.	30 f. brown	25	15
97.	D.	38 f. blue	80	40
98.		39 f. blue	50	12
99.	A.	50 f. orange	25	25
154.	14.	1 y. violet	1·00	70

DESIGNS: A. Carting soya-beans. B. Pelling Mausoleum. C Aeroplane and grazing sheep (domestic and China air mail). D. Aeroplane over R. Sungari bridge (air mail to Japan).

15. Sun rising over Fields.  16. Shadowgraph of old and new Hsinking.

1937. Founding of State. 5th Anniv.

101.	15.	1½ f. red	35	25
102.	16.	3 f. green	30	25

1937. China Mail. Surch in Chinese characters.

108.	7.	2½ f. on 2 f. green ..	25	15
110.	8.	5 f. on 4 f. olive-green ..	30	20
107.		13 f. on 12 f. chestnut ..	1·10	80

17. Pouter Pigeon and Hsinking.

DESIGN: 4 f., 20 f. Flag over Imperial Palace.

1937. Completion of Five Year Reconstruction Plan for Hsinking.

112.	17.	2 f. mauve	12	8
113.	–	4 f. red	12	8
114.	17.	10 f. green	50	30
115.	–	20 f. blue	60	50

19. Manchukuo.  20. Japanese Residents Assn. Bldg.

1937. Japan's Relinquishment of Extra-territorial Rights.

116.	19.	2 f. red	8	5
117.	20.	4 f. green	12	10
118.		8 f. orange	30	25
119.	–	10 f. blue	40	35
120.	–	12 f. violet	45	35
121.	–	20 f. lake	50	40

DESIGNS—As T 20—HORIZ. 10 f., 20 f. Dept. of Communications Bldg. VERT. 12 f. Ministry of Justice.

23. "Twofold Happiness".  24. Red Cross on Map and Globe.

1937. New Year's Greetings.

122.	23.	2 f. red and blue ..	30	15

1938. Manchukuo Red Cross Society Inaug.

123.	24.	2 f. red	20	15
124.		4 f. green	20	15

25. Map of Railway Lines.  26. "Asia" Express.

1939. Completion of 10,000 Kilometres of Manchurian Railways.

125.	25.	2 f. blue and orange ..	8	5
126.	26.	4 f. blue	15	12

27. Cranes over Shipmast.  28. Census Official.  29. Census Slogans in Chinese, and Mongolian.

1940. 2nd Visit of Emperor to Japan.

127.	27.	2 f. mauve	8	5
128.		4 f. green	15	12

1940. National Census.

129.	28.	2 f. brown and orange..	8	5
130.	29.	4 f. green and black ..	10	8

30. Message of Congratulation.  31. Dragon Dance.

1940. Japan. 2600th Anniv.

131.	30.	2 f. red	8	8
132.	31.	4 f. blue	10	10

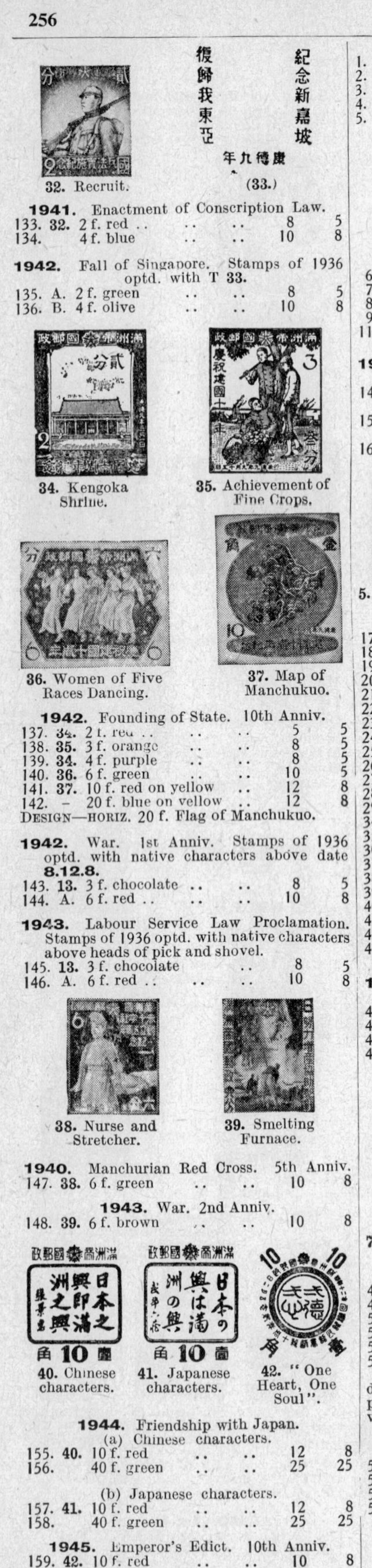

32. Recruit. (33.)

1941. Enactment of Conscription Law.
133. 32. 2 f. red 8 5
134. 4 f. blue 10 8

1942. Fall of Singapore. Stamps of 1936 optd. with T 33.
135. A. 2 f. green 8 5
136. B. 4 f. olive 10 8

34. Kengoka Shrine. 35. Achievement of Fine Crops.

36. Women of Five Races Dancing. 37. Map of Manchukuo.

1942. Founding of State. 10th Anniv.
137. 34. 2 f. red 5 5
138. 35. 3 f. orange 8 5
139. 34. 4 f. purple 8 5
140. 36. 6 f. green 10 5
141. 37. 10 f. red on yellow .. 12 8
142. – 20 f. blue on yellow .. 12 8
DESIGN—HORIZ. 20 f. Flag of Manchukuo.

1942. War. 1st Anniv. Stamps of 1936 optd. with native characters above date **8.12.8.**
143. 13. 3 f. chocolate 8 5
144. A. 6 f. red 10 8

1943. Labour Service Law Proclamation. Stamps of 1936 optd. with native characters above heads of pick and shovel.
145. 13. 3 f. chocolate 8 5
146. A. 6 f. red 10 8

38. Nurse and Stretcher. 39. Smelting Furnace.

1940. Manchurian Red Cross. 5th Anniv.
147. 38. 6 f. green 10 8

1943. War. 2nd Anniv.
148. 39. 6 f. brown 10 8

40. Chinese characters. 41. Japanese characters. 42. "One Heart, One Soul".

1944. Friendship with Japan.
(a) Chinese characters.
155. 40. 10 f. red 12 8
156. 40 f. green 25 25

(b) Japanese characters.
157. 41. 10 f. red 12 8
158. 40 f. green 25 25

1945. Emperor's Edict. 10th Anniv.
159. 42. 10 f. red 10 8

C. NORTH EASTERN PROVINCES

Issues made by the Chinese Nationalist Government of Chiang Kai-shek.

1. Dr. Sun Yat-sen. (2.)

1946. Surch. as T 2.
1. 1. 50 c. on $5 red 5 5
2. 50 c. on $10 green 5 5
3. $1 on $10 green 5 5
4. $2 on $20 purple 5 5
5. $4 on $50 brown 5 5

(3.) (4.)

1946. Stamps of China optd. with T 3.
6. 30. 1 c. orange 5 5
7. 3 c. brown 5 5
8. 5 c. orange 5 5
9. 38. 10 c. green 5 5
11. 20 c. blue 5 5

1946. Stamps of China surch. as T 4 but larger.
14. 30. $5 on $50 on 21 c. sepia (No. 805) .. .. 2·25 2·75
15. $10 on $100 on 28 c. olive (No. 808) .. .. 2·25 2·75
16. 47. $20 on $200 green .. 2·25 2·75

5. Dr. Sun Yat-sen. (6.)

1946.
17. 5. 5 c. lake 5 5
18. 10 c. orange 5 5
19. 20 c. green 5 5
20. 25 c. brown 5 5
21. 50 c. orange 5 5
22. $1 blue 5 5
23. $2 purple 5 5
24. $2·50 blue 5 5
25. $3 brown 5 5
26. $4 brown 5 5
27. $5 green 5 5
28. $10 red 5 5
29. $20 olive 5 5
34. $22 black .. .. 2·00 3·00
35. $44 red 20 20
30. $50 violet 5 5
37. $65 green .. .. 2·25 3·25
38. $100 green 5 5
39. $109 green .. .. 4·00 4·50
40. $200 brown 5 5
41. $300 green 5 5
42. $500 red 5 5
43. $1,000 orange 5 5

1946. Nanking National Assembly stamps of China surch. as T 6.
44. 66. $2 on $20 green 5 5
45. $3 on $30 blue 5 5
46. $5 on $50 brown 5 5
47. $10 on $100 red 5 5

7. Pres. Chiang Kai-shek. (8.)

1947. President's 60th Birthday.
48. 7. $2 red 5 5
49. $3 green 5 5
50. $5 red 5 5
51. $10 green 5 5
52. $20 orange 5 5
53. $30 claret 5 5

For other stamps as T 7 and 9 but with different 3rd and 4th Chinese characters in positions shown by arrows, see Chinese Provinces, etc. (Taiwan) T 4 and 5.

1947. Stamps of China surch. as T 8.
54. 61. $100 on $1,000 purple .. 5 5
55. $300 on $3,000 blue .. 5 5
56. 28. $500 on $30 brown .. 5 5
57. 61. $500 on $5,000 red & grn. 5 5

9. Entrance to Dr. Sun Yat-sen Mausoleum. (10.)

1947. Return of Govt. to Nanking. 1st Anniv.
64. 9. $2 green 5 5
65. $4 blue 5 5
66. $6 red 5 5
67. $10 brown 5 5
68. $20 purple 5 5

1948. Surch. as T 10.
70. 5. $1,500 on 20 c. green .. 8 20
71. $3,000 on $1 blue .. 8 8
72. $4,000 on 25 c. brown .. 8 8
73. $8,000 on 50 c. orange .. 8 8
74. $10 000 on 10 c. orange .. 8 8
75. $50,000 on $109 green .. 10 12
76. $100,000 on $65 green .. 10 12
77. $500,000 on $22 black .. 12 15

MILITARY POST STAMPS

1946. Military Post stamp of China optd. as T 3 but larger.
M 13. M 2. (No value) red .. 12 40

(M 1.)

1947. Surch. with Type M 1.
M 69. 5. $44 on 50 c. orange .. 25 60

PARCELS POST STAMPS

P 1. (P 2.)

1948.
P 78. P 1. $500 red .. .. — 75
P 79. $1,000 red .. .. — 75
P 80. $3,000 olive .. .. — 75
P 81. $5,000 blue .. .. — 1·25
P 82. $10,000 green .. .. — 1·25
P 83. $20,000 blue .. .. — 2·00

1948. Parcels Post stamp of China surch. wtih Type P 2.
P 84. $500,000 on $5,000,000 lilac (No. P 938) .. .. — 7·50
Parcels Post stamps were not on sale unused.

POSTAGE DUE STAMPS

D 1. (D 2.)

1947.
D 48. D 1. 10 c. blue 5 5
D 49. 20 c. blue 5 5
D 50. 50 c. blue 5 5
D 51. $1 blue 5 5
D 52. $2 blue 5 5
D 53. $5 blue 5 5

1948. Surch. as Type D 2.
D 85. D 1. $10 on 10 c. blue .. 5 5
D 86. $20 on 20 c. blue .. 5 5
D 87. $50 on 50 c. blue .. 5 5

D. NORTH EAST CHINA

Issues made in areas under Communist control; from November 1948, these comprised all Manchuria.

(See note at beginning of CHINESE PEOPLE'S REPUBLIC.)

In 1951 stamps of the Chinese People's Republic came into use.

1. Mao Tse-tung. 2. (3.)

1946. Perf. or imperf.
NE 1. 1. $1 violet 30 40
NE 2. 2. $2 red 15 20
NE 3. $5 orange 15 20
NE 4. $10 blue 15 25

1946. Chinese Revolution. 35th Anniv. Nos. 1, 3, 4 and 5 of N.E. Provinces optd. with T 3.
NE 26. 50 c. on $5 red .. 20 30
NE 27. $1 on $10 green .. 25 30
NE 28. $2 on $20 purple .. 40 50
NE 29. $4 on $50 brown .. 50 70

4. Map of China, Communist Lion, Japanese Wolf, and Chiang Kai-shek. 5. Railwaymen.

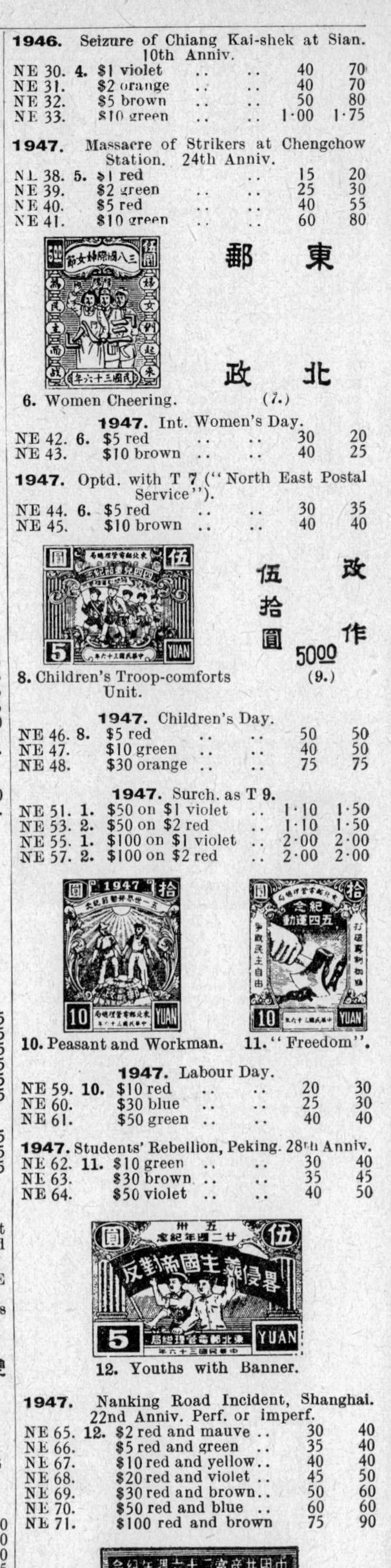

1946. Seizure of Chiang Kai-shek at Sian. 10th Anniv.
NE 30. 4. $1 violet 40 70
NE 31. $2 orange 40 70
NE 32. $5 brown 50 80
NE 33. $10 green .. .. 1·00 1·75

1947. Massacre of Strikers at Chengchow Station. 24th Anniv.
NE 38. 5. $1 red 15 20
NE 39. $2 green 25 30
NE 40. $5 red 40 55
NE 41. $10 green 60 80

6. Women Cheering. (7.)

1947. Int. Women's Day.
NE 42. 6. $5 red 30 20
NE 43. $10 brown 40 25

1947. Optd. with T 7 ("North East Postal Service").
NE 44. 6. $5 red 30 35
NE 45. $10 brown 40 40

8. Children's Troop-comforts Unit. (9.)

1947. Children's Day.
NE 46. 8. $5 red 50 50
NE 47. $10 green 40 50
NE 48. $30 orange 75 75

1947. Surch. as T 9.
NE 51. 1. $50 on $1 violet .. 1·10 1·50
NE 53. 2. $50 on $2 red .. 1·10 1·50
NE 55. 1. $100 on $1 violet .. 2·00 2·00
NE 57. 2. $100 on $2 red .. 2·00 2·00

10. Peasant and Workman. 11. "Freedom".

1947. Labour Day.
NE 59. 10. $10 red 20 30
NE 60. $30 blue 25 30
NE 61. $50 green 40 40

1947. Students' Rebellion, Peking. 28th Anniv.
NE 62. 11. $10 green 30 40
NE 63. $30 brown 35 45
NE 64. $50 violet 40 50

12. Youths with Banner.

1947. Nanking Road Incident, Shanghai. 22nd Anniv. Perf. or imperf.
NE 65. 12. $2 red and mauve .. 30 40
NE 66. $5 red and green .. 35 40
NE 67. $10 red and yellow .. 40 40
NE 68. $20 red and violet .. 45 50
NE 69. $30 red and brown .. 50 60
NE 70. $50 red and blue .. 60 60
NE 71. $100 red and brown 75 90

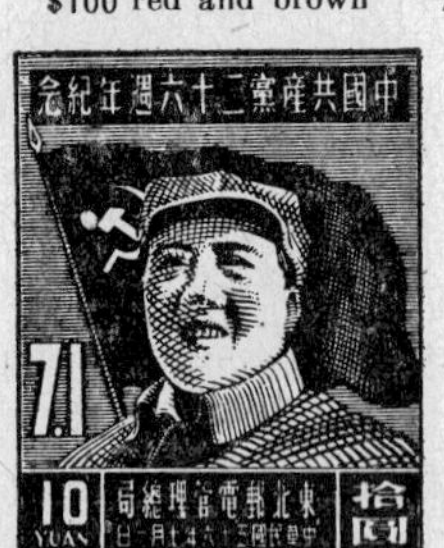

13. Mao Tse-tung.

1947. Chinese Communist Party. 26th Anniv.
NE 75. 13. $10 red .. .. 1·00 1·00
NE 76. $30 mauve .. .. 1·00 1·00
NE 77. $50 purple .. .. 1·00 1·00
NE 78. $100 red .. .. 1·50 1·50

14. Hand grasping rifle.

15. Mountains and River.

1947. War with Japan. 10th Anniv.

NE 79. **14.** $10 orange 40 40
NE 80. $30 green 50 60
NE 81. $50 blue 70 70
NE 82. $100 brown .. .. 1·00 1·25

1947. Japanese Surrender 2nd Anniv.

NE 84. **15.** $10 brown 30 30
NE 85. $30 olive 30 35
NE 86. $50 green 50 65
NE 87. $100 brown .. .. 1·00 1·40

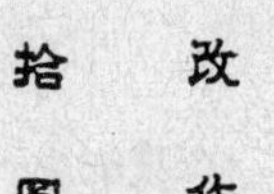

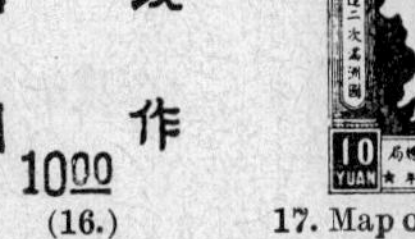

(16.)

17. Map of Manchuria.

1947. Surch. as T **16**.

NE 88. **1.** $5 on $1 violet .. 75 90
NE 91. **2.** $10 on $2 red .. 1·50 1·50

1947. Japanese Attack on Manchuria. 16th Anniv.

NE 102. **17.** $10 green 70 90
NE 103. $20 mauve .. 75 90
NE 104. $30 brown .. 1·00 1·40
NE 105. $50 red .. .. 1·50 1·60

18. Offices of N.E. Political Council.

19. Mao Tse-tung.

1947. Chinese Republic. 35th Anniv.

NE 106. **18.** $10 yellow .. 1·50 2·00
NE 107. $20 red .. 2·50 2·50
NE 108. $100 brown .. 8·00 10·00

1947.

NE 109. **19.** $1 purple 15 15
NE 110. $5 green 20 20
NE 111. $10 green 20 20
NE 112. $15 violet 25 30
NE 113. $20 red 25 30
NE 114. $30 green 30 30
NE 115. $50 sepia 15 20
NE 119. $50 green 30 30
NE 116. $90 blue 40 50
NE 117. $100 red 25 30
NE 120. $150 red 20 25
NE 121. $250 lilac 40 50
NE 123. $300 green .. 2·50 2·50
NE 118. $500 orange .. 70 80
NE 124. $1,000 yellow .. 40 55

For stamps as T **19** but with "YUAN" top right tablet, see Nos. NE 168/72.

20.

21. Tomb of Gen. Li Chao-lin.

1947. Seizure of Chiang Kai-shek at Sian. 11th Anniv.

NE 125. **20.** $30 red .. 50 50
NE 126. $90 blue .. 75 1·00
NE 127. $150 green .. 1·25 2·00

1948. Gen. Li Chao-lin. 2nd Death Anniv.

NE 128. **21.** $30 green 80 80
NE 129. $150 lilac .. .. 1·50 1·50

22. Flag and Globe.

ILLUSTRATIONS British Commonwealth and all overprints and surcharges are FULL SIZE. Foreign Countries have been reduced to ¾-LINEAR.

1948. Labour Day.

NE 143. **22.** $50 red .. .. 2·50 4·00
NE 144. $150 green .. 3·50 6·00
NE 145. $250 violet .. 6·00 12·00

23. Youth with Torch.

24. Crane Operator.

1948. Youth Day.

NE 146. **23.** $50 green .. 1·25 1·25
NE 147. $150 purple .. 1·25 1·25
NE 148. $250 lake .. .. 2·00 2·25

1948. All-China Labour Conf.

NE 149. **24.** $100 red and pink 40 60
NE 150. $300 brown and yell. 60 70
NE 151. $500 blue and green 75 80

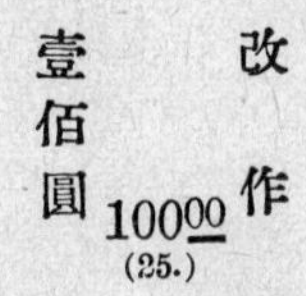

(25.)

26. Workman, Soldier and Peasant.

1948. Surch. as T **25**.

NE 153. **19.** $100 on $1 purple .. 2·00 2·50
NE 154. $100 on $15 violet .. 2·00 2·50
NE 156. $300 on $5 green .. 2·00 2·50
NE 157. $300 on $30 green .. 2·00 2·50
NE 158. $300 on $90 blue .. 2·00 2·50
NE 162. **2.** $500 on $2 red .. 40 50
NE 159. **19.** $500 on $50 green .. 50 80
NE 163. **2.** $1,500 on $5 orange 45 60
NE 160. **19.** $1,500 on $150 red 80 1·00
NE 164. **2.** $2,500 on $10 blue 60 75
NE 161. **19.** $2,500 on $300 grn. 1·25 1·60

1948. Liberation of the North East.

NE 165. **26.** $500 red 50 60
NE 166. $1,500 green .. 60 75
NE 167. $2,500 brown .. 75 90

1949. As T **19**, but "YUAN" at top right.

NE 168. $300 olive 10 12
NE 169. $500 orange .. 10 12
NE 170. $1,500 green .. 10 12
NE 171. $4,500 brown .. 20 25
NE 172. $6,500 blue 30 35

27. Workers and Banners.

28. "Production in Field and Industry".

1949. Labour Day.

NE 173. **27.** $1,000 red and blue 12 20
NE 174. $1,500 red and blue 15 20
NE 175. $4,500 red and brn. 20 30
NE 176. $6,500 brown & grn. 25 35
NE 177. $10,000 mar. & blue 30 40

1949.

NE 178. **28.** $5,000 blue .. 70 50
NE 179. $10,000 orange .. 25 50
NE 180. $50,000 green .. 1·00 1·25
NE 181. $100,000 violet .. 1·50 2·50

29. Workers' Procession.

30. N. E. Heroes Monument.

1949. Chinese Communist Party. 28th Anniv.

NE 182. **20.** $1,500 red, violet and blue .. 15 20
NE 183. $4,500 red, brown and blue .. 20 25
NE 184. $6,500 red, pink and blue .. 25 30

1949. Japanese Surrender. 4th Anniv.

NE 185. **30.** $1,500 red .. 15 20
NE 186. $4,500 green .. 20 25
NE 187. $6,500 blue .. 25 30

REPRINTS. The note above No. 1401 of China also refers here to Nos. NE 188/91, 200/206, 218/231 and 244/46.

1949. First Chinese People's Political Conf. As T **105** of China.

NE 188. $1,000 blue .. 30 40
NE 189. $1,500 red .. 50 60
NE 190. $3,000 green .. 75 1·00
NE 191. $4,500 purple .. 1·00 1·50

31. Factory.

貳 改
仟
圓 作
2000

(32.)

東北貼用

(33.)

1949.

NE 192. **31.** $1,500 red 15 20

1949. Surch. as T **32**.

NE 193. **19.** $2,000 on $300 olive 15 25
NE 194. $2,000 on $4,500 brn. 1·50 1·00
NE 195. $2,500 on $1,500 grn. 1·50 1·00
NE 196. $2,500 on $6,500 bl. 1·00 1·00
NE 197. **31.** $5,000 on $1,500 red 40 40
NE 198. **19.** $20,000 on $4,500 brown .. 40 50
NE 199. $35,000 on $300 ol. 40 50

The following issues are as Types of China, but with four extra characters, as in T **33**.

1949. World Federation of Trade Unions, Asiatic and Australasian Conf., Peking.

NE 200. **106.** $5,000 red .. 5·00 5·00
NE 201. $20,000 green .. 7·00 7·00
NE 202. $35,000 blue .. 10·00 10·00

1950. Chinese People's Political Conf.

NE 203. **107.** $1,000 red .. 50 50
NE 204. $1,500 blue .. 60 60
NE 205. **108.** $5,000 purple .. 75 75
NE 206. $20,000 green .. 1·50 1·50

1950.

NE 235. **109.** $250 brown .. 5 5
NE 207. $500 olive .. 5 5
NE 208. $1,000 orange .. 5 5
NE 209. $1,000 magenta .. 5 5
NE 210. $2,000 green .. 5 5
NE 211. $2,500 yellow .. 5 5
NE 212. $5,000 orange .. 10 10
NE 213. $10,000 brown .. 10 10
NE 242. $12,500 purple .. 20 20
NE 215. $20,000 maroon .. 20 20
NE 233. $30,000 red .. 75 75
NE 216. $35,000 blue .. 30 30
NE 217. $50,000 green .. 35 35
NE 234. $100,000 violet .. 1·10 75

1950. Foundation of People's Republic.

NE 218. **112.** $5,000 red, yellow and green .. 60 75
NE 219. $10,000 red, yellow and brown .. 60 75
NE 220. $20,000 red, yellow and purple .. 1·00 1·25
NE 221. $30,000 red, yellow and blue .. .. 1·50 2·00

1950. Peace Campaign. Additional characters below olive branch.

NE 222. **115.** $2,500 brown .. 40 30
NE 223. $5,000 green .. 60 50
NE 224. $20,000 blue .. 1·40 1·00

1950. 1st Anniv. of People's Republic. Flag in red, yellow and brown.

NE 225. **116.** $1,000 violet .. 30 25
NE 226. $2,500 brown .. 60 50
NE 227. $5,000 grn. (larger) 70 60
NE 228. $10,000 olive .. 1·10 1·00
NE 229. $20,000 blue .. 1·90 1·50

1950. 1st All-China Postal Conference.

NE 230. **117.** $2,500 brn. & grn. 25 25
NE 231. $5,000 green & red 40 40

1950. Sino-Soviet Treaty.

NE 244. **118.** $2,500 red .. 30 30
NE 245. $5,000 green .. 40 40
NE 246. $20,000 blue .. 80 80

PARCELS POST STAMPS

P 1.

1951. Nos. NEP 247/9 imperf.

NEP 247. P **1.** $100,000 violet .. 8·00
NEP 248. $300,000 claret .. 15·00
NEP 249. $500,000 turquoise 20·00
NEP 250. $1,000,000 red .. 50·00

E. PORT ARTHUR AND DAIREN

Stamps issued by the Chinese under a Sino-Soviet Treaty arrangement. Now uses stamps of the Chinese People's Republic.

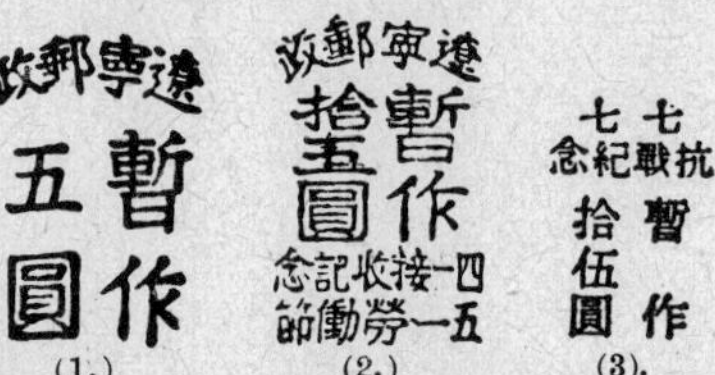

(1.) (2.) (3).

1946. Stamps of Manchuria and Japan handstamped "LIAONING POSTS" and new value at T **1**.

(a) On stamps of Manchuria.

1. **14.** 20 c. on 30 f. brown .. 50 50
2. – $1 on 12 f. orge. (No. 90) 50 50

(b) On stamps of Japan.

3. 20 c. on 3 s. green (No. 319) 40 50
4. $1 on 17 s. violet (No. 402) 60 70
5. $5 on 6 s. red (No. 242) .. 1·00 1·40
7. $5 on 6 s. orange (No. 322) 90 1·00
8. $15 on 40 s. purple (No. 406) .. .. .. 4·50 6·00

1946. Transfer of Administration and Labour Day. Stamps of Manchuria handstamped as T **2**.

9. **13.** $1 on 1 f. lake .. .. 1·25 1·60
10. – $5 on 4 f. olive (No. 84) 1·75 2·00
11. **14.** $15 on 30 f. brown .. 5·00 5·50

1946. Nos. 319 and 322 of Japan surch. as T **1** but with two horiz. bars instead of top line of characters.

12. $1 on 3 s. green .. 10·00 10·00
13. $5 on 6 s. orange .. 4·50 4·50

1946. War with Japan. 9th Anniv. Stamps of Manchuria surch. as T **3**.

14. $1 on 6 f. red (No. 86) .. 75 75
15. $5 on 2 f. green (No. 82) 1·25 1·25
16. $15 on 12 f. orange (No. 90) 5·00 5·00

復光國民華中
念紀年週一
壹 暫
圓 作
五 一•八
(4.)

國民華中
念紀節十雙
壹 暫
圓 作
(5.)

1946. Japanese Surrender. 1st Anniv. Stamps of Manchuria surch. as T **4**.

17. – $1 on 12 f. orge (No. 90) 1·00 1·25
18. **13.** $5 on 1 f. lake .. 3·50 5·00
19. **8.** $15 on 5 f. black .. 6·00 7·50

1946. Chinese Revolution. 35th Anniv. Stamps of Manchuria surch. as T **5**.

20. $1 on 6 f. red (No. 86) .. 2·00 2·00
21. $5 on 12 f. orge. (No. 90) 4·00 4·00
22. $15 on 2 f. green (No. 82) 8·00 8·00

國民華中
世逝迅魯
念紀年週十
五 暫
、圓 作
(6.)

建聯蘇祝慶
十二第節軍
念紀年週九
五 暫
圓 作
(7.)

1946. Lu Hsun (author). 10th Death Anniv. Stamps of Manchuria surch. as T **6**.

23. **13.** $1 on 1 f. lake .. 3·50 5·00
24. – $5 on 6 f. red (No. 86) .. 5·00 7·00
25. – $15 on 12 f. orge. (90) 8·00 10·00

1947. Red Army. 29th Anniv. Stamps of Manchuria surch. as T **7**.

26. – $1 on 2 f. green (No. 82) 3·00 5·00
27. – $5 on 6 f. red (No. 86) 8·00 10·00
28. **8.** $15 on 13 f. brown .. 15·00 18·00

國 中
政郵東關
五暫
念 紀
圓作
節動勞一五
(8.)

政郵東關國中
貳 暫
拾
圓 作
(9.)

1947. Labour Day. Stamps of Manchuria surch. as T **8**.

29. – $1 on 2 f. green (No. 82) 2·00 2·00
30. – $5 on 6 f. red (No. 86) .. 4·50 4·50
31. **14.** $15 on 30 f. brown .. 7·00 7·00

1947. Stamps of Manchuria surch. "KWANTUNG POSTAL SERVICE. CHINA" and new value as T **9**.

32. – $5 on 2 f. green (No. 82) 3·50 4·00
33. – $15 on 4 f. olive (No. 84) 6·00 6·50
34. **14.** $20 on 30 f. brown .. 8·00 9·00

(10.)

1948. Red Army. 30th Anniv. Surch. as T. **10**

(a) On stamps of Manchuria.

36. $10 on 2 f. green (No. 82) .. 12·00 12·00
37. $20 on 6 f. red (No. 86) .. 16·00 16·00

(b) On label commemorating 2,600th Anniv. of Japanese Empire.

38. $100 on (no value) bl. & brn. 60·00 60·00

中華郵政 暫作 五拾圓 關東郵電
(11.)

關東郵政 紀念一卅週年 暫作 壹佰圓 十月革命節
(12.)

1948. Stamps of Manchuria surch. "KWANTUNG POSTAL ADMINISTRATION" and new value as T 11.
39. $20 on 2 f. green (No. 82) 16·00 18·00
40. $50 on 4 f. olive (No. 84) 20·00 22·00
41. $100 on 20 f. brown (No. 152) 24·00 26·00

1948. Russian October Revolution. 31st Anniv. Stamps of Manchuria surch. as T 12.
42. 13. $10 on 1 f. lake 30·00 40·00
43. – $50 on 2 f. green (No. 82) 40·00 45·00
44. – $100 on 4 f. olive (No. 84) 90·00 £100

(13.) (14.)

1948. Kwantung Agricultural and Industrial Exn. Stamps of Manchuria surch. as T 13.
45. $10 on 2 f. green (No. 82) 20·00 28·00
46. $50 on 20 f. brown (No. 152) £120 £150

1948. Surch. "CHINESE POSTAL ADMINISTRATION: KWANTUNG POSTS AND TELEGRAPHS" and new value as T 14. (a) On No. 319 of Japan.
47. $5 on 3 s. green 3·50 3·50

(b) On stamps of Manchuria.
48. 13. $10 on 1 f. lake 22·00 25·00
51. – $10 on 2 f. green (No. 82) 16·00 18·00
52. 13. $50 on 1 f. lake 20·00 22·00
49. – $50 on 2 f. green (No. 82) 30·00 35·00
50. – $100 on 4 f. ol. (No. 84) 42·00 45·00

15. Peasant and Artisan. 16. Dock.

1949.
53. 15. $5 green 1·40 1·75
54. – $10 orange 2·00 2·50
55. 16. $50 red 3·00 3·50
DESIGN—VERT. $10, "Transport".

(17.) (18.) (19.)

1949. Nos. 54/5 surch. as T 17/9.
56. 17. $7 on $5 green 1·50 1·50
58. 18. $50 on $5 green 5·00 5·00
59. $100 on $10 orange 9·00 9·00
60. 19. $500 on $5 green £100
61. $500 on $10 orange 50·00 35·00

20. "Labour". 21. Mao Tse-tung.

1949. Labour Day.
62. 20. $10 red 1·00 1·25

1949. Chinese Communist Party. 28th Anniv.
64. 21. $50 red 3·00 3·00

22. Heroes' Monument, Dairen. 23. Acclamation of Mao Tse-tung

1949. 4th Anniv. of Victory over Japan and Opening of Dairen Industrial Fair.
66. 22. $10 red, blue and turq. 3·00 3·50
67. $10 red, blue and green 1·50 2·00

1949. Founding of Chinese People's Republic.
68. 23. $35 red, yellow and blue 1·50 2·00

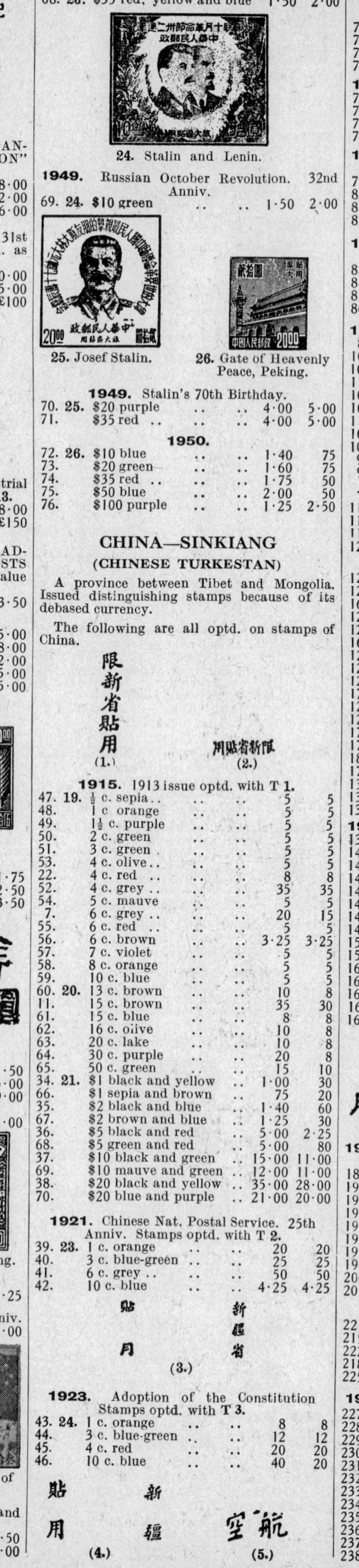

24. Stalin and Lenin.

1949. Russian October Revolution. 32nd Anniv.
69. 24. $10 green 1·50 2·00

25. Josef Stalin. 26. Gate of Heavenly Peace, Peking.

1949. Stalin's 70th Birthday.
70. 25. $20 purple 4·00 5·00
71. $35 red 4·00 5·00

1950.
72. 26. $10 blue 1·40 75
73. $20 green 1·60 75
74. $35 red 1·75 50
75. $50 blue 2·00 50
76. $100 purple 1·25 2·50

CHINA—SINKIANG
(CHINESE TURKESTAN)

A province between Tibet and Mongolia. Issued distinguishing stamps because of its debased currency.

The following are all optd. on stamps of China.

限新省貼用
(1.)

限新省貼用
(2.)

1915. 1913 issue optd. with T 1.
47. 19. ½ c. sepia 5 5
48. 1 c. orange 5 5
49. 1½ c. purple 5 5
50. 2 c. green 5 5
51. 3 c. green 5 5
53. 4 c. olive 5 5
22. 4 c. red 8 8
52. 4 c. grey 35 35
54. 5 c. mauve 5 5
7. 6 c. grey 20 15
55. 6 c. red 5 5
56. 6 c. brown 3·25 3·25
57. 7 c. violet 5 5
58. 8 c. orange 5 5
59. 10 c. blue 5 5
60. 20. 13 c. brown 10 8
11. 15 c. brown 35 30
61. 15 c. blue 8 8
62. 16 c. olive 10 8
63. 20 c. lake 10 8
64. 30 c. purple 20 8
65. 50 c. green 15 10
34. 21. $1 black and yellow 1·00 30
66. $1 sepia and brown 75 20
35. $2 black and blue 1·40 60
67. $2 brown and blue 1·25 30
36. $5 black and red 5·00 2·25
68. $5 green and red 5·00 80
37. $10 black and green 15·00 11·00
69. $10 mauve and green 12·00 11·00
38. $20 black and yellow 35·00 28·00
70. $20 blue and purple 21·00 20·00

1921. Chinese Nat. Postal Service. 25th Anniv. Stamps optd. with T 2.
39. 23. 1 c. orange 20 20
40. 3 c. blue-green 25 25
41. 6 c. grey 50 50
42. 10 c. blue 4·25 4·25

新疆省貼用
(3.)

1923. Adoption of the Constitution Stamps optd. with T 3.
43. 24. 1 c. orange 8 8
44. 3 c. blue-green 12 12
45. 4 c. red 20 20
46. 10 c. blue 40 20

新疆貼用
(4.)

航空
(5.)

1928. Assumption of Title of Marshal of the Army and Navy by Chang Tso-lin. Optd. with T 4.
71. 25. 1 c. orange 10 10
72. 4 c. blue-green 15 15
73. 10 c. blue 30 30
74. $1 red 2·40 2·40

1929. Unification of China. Optd. as T 4.
75. 26. 1 c. orange 15 15
76. 4 c. olive 20 20
77. 10 c. blue 40 40
78. $1 red 4·50 4·50

1929. Sun Yat-sen State Burial. Optd. as T 4.
79. 27. 1 c. orange 10 10
80. 4 c. olive 20 20
81. 10 c. blue 30 30
82. $1 red 2·50 2·50

1932. Air. Handstamped on Sinkiang issues as T 5 ("By Air Mail").
83. 19. 5 c. mauve (No. 54) 35·00 23·00
84. 10 c. blue (No. 59) 35·00 20·00
85. 20. 15 c. blue (No. 61) £300 85·00
86. 30 c. purple (No. 64) £425 £180

1932. Dr. Sun Yat-sen stamps optd with T 2.
87. 28. 1 c. orange 10 12
102. 2 c. olive 5 5
103. 4 c. green 5 5
113. 5 c. green 5 5
105. 15 c. green 10 5
106. 15 c. red 8 8
115. 20 c. blue 5 5
107. 25 c. blue 5 5
108. $1 sepia and brown 40 50
92. $2 brown and blue 1·00 1·10
93. $5 black and red 2·25 2·40

1933. Tan Yen-kai Memorial. Optd. as T 4.
117. 32. 2 c. olive 10 10
118. 5 c. green 15 15
119. 25 c. blue 30 30
120. $1 red 2·40 2·40

1933. Martyrs' issue optd. as T 2.
121. 30. ½ c. sepia 5 5
122. 1 c. orange 5 5
167. 2 c. blue 5 5
123. 2½ c. mauve 5 5
124. 3 c. brown 5 5
169. 4 c. lilac 5 5
125. 8 c. orange 5 5
126. 10 c. purple 5 5
127. 13 c. green 5 5
172. 15 c. maroon 5 5
128. 17 c. olive 8 8
129. 20 c. lake 8 8
174. 20 c. blue 5 5
175. 21 c. sepia 5 5
185. 25 c. purple 5 5
176. 28 c. olive 5 5
130. 30 c. claret 5 5
131. 40 c. orange 10 10
132. 50 c. green 12 12

1940. Dr. Sun Yat-sen stamps opt. as T 2.
139. 38. 2 c. olive 5 5
140. 3 c. red 5 5
141. 5 c. green 5 5
143. 8 c. olive 5 5
144. 10 c. green 5 5
145. 15 c. red 5 5
146. 16 c. olive 5 5
147. 25 c. blue 5 5
156. 30 c. red 5 5
158. 50 c. blue 5 5
160. $1 brown and red 5 5
161. $2 brown and blue 5 5
162. $5 green and red 12 12
163. $10 violet and green 20 20
164. $20 blue and claret 40 40

限新省貼用
(6.)

改作壹角貳分
(7.)

1942. Air. Air stamps optd. with T 6 or larger.
187. 31. 15 c. green 35 35
197. 25 c. orange 20 20
198. 30 c. red 30 30
190. 45 c. purple 30 30
199. 50 c. chocolate 30 30
192. 60 c. blue 30 25
193. 90 c. olive 3·00 3·00
194. $1 green 30 30
200. $2 brown 1·90 1·90
201. $5 red 1·90 1·90

1942. Thrift stamps optd. as T 6.
221. 42. 8 c. green 15 15
215. 21 c. brown 15 15
222. 33 c. red 15 15
218. 50 c. blue 35 35
225. $1 purple 30 30

1943. Dr. Sun Yat-sen stamps optd. as T 2.
227. 43. 10 c. green 5 5
228. 20 c. olive 5 5
229. 25 c. purple 5 5
230. 30 c. red 5 5
231. 40 c. brown 5 5
232. 50 c. green 5 5
233. $1 red 5 5
234. $1 olive 5 5
235. $1.50 blue 5 5
236. $2 green 5 5
237. $3 yellow 5 5
238. $5 red 5 5

限新省貼用
(8.)

1943. Stamps optd. with T 8.
239. 38. 10 c. green 30 35
240. 30. 20 c. blue 30 35
241. 38. 50 c. blue 30 35

1944. Dr. Sun Yat-sen stamps optd. as T 2.
248. 38. $4 blue 5 5
249. $5 grey 5 5
250. $10 brown 5 5
251. $20 green 15 15
243. $20 red 8 8
244. $30 purple 12 12
245. $40 red 15 15
255. $50 blue 30 30
247. $100 brown 20 20

1944. Nos. 227 and 229 of Sinkiang surch as T 7.
257 43. 12 c. on 10 c. green 5 10
258. 24 c. on 25 c. purple 5 10

1945. Stamps optd. as T 2.
259. 46. 40 c. red 5 5
260. $3 red 5 5

改作壹 限新疆貼用
(9.)

人民郵政 (新) 叁圓
(10.)

1949. Silver Yuan surcharges. Sun Yat-sen issues of China surch. as T 9.
261. 61. 1 c. on $100 claret (No. 889) 70 70
262. 3 c. on $200 green (No. 890) 50 50
263. 5 c. on $500 green (No. 891) 70 70
264. 72. 10 c. on $20,000 red (No. 1032) 1·00 1·00
265. 50 c. on $4,000 grey (No. 961) 6·00 6·00
266. $1 on $6,000 purple (No. 963) 7·50 7·50

After the Communists took over Sinkiang, they handstamped the above issue, and also China Nos. 1357/9, in October 1949, with characters meaning "People's Postal Service". Owing to the difficulty of distinguishing genuine handstamps, we do not list these stamps.

1949. Stamps of China optd. "People's Postal Service, Sinkiang" and surch. with new value as T 10.
267. 72. 10 c. on $50,000 blue (No. 1035) 50 50
268. 93. $1 on (–) orge. (No. 1211) 3·00 3·00
269. 72. $1.50 on $100,000 olive (No. 1036) 1·00 1·00
270. 96. $3 on (–) red (No. 1214) 3·00 3·00

CHINA—SZECHWAN PROVINCE

A province of China. Issued distinguishing stamps because of its debased currency.

限四川貼用
(1.)

Stamps of China optd. with T 1.

1933. Issue of 1913.
1. 19. 1 c. orange 15 5
2. 5 c. mauve 15 5
3. 20. 50 c. green 60 15

1933. Dr. Sun Yat Sen issue.
4. 28. 2 c. olive 5 5
5. 5 c. green 5 5
6. 15 c. green 20 8
7. 15 c. red 20 15
8. 25 c. blue 25 5
9. $1 sepia and brown 1·00 12
10. $2 brown and blue 2·10 30
11. $5 black and red 6·00 1·10

1933. Martyrs issue.
12. 30. ½ c. sepia 5 5
13. 1 c. orange 5 5
14. 2½ c. mauve 12 8
15. 3 c. brown 10 5
16. 8 c. orange 12 5
17. 10 c. purple 25 5
18. 13 c. green 25 5
19. 17 c. olive 30 15
20. 20 c. lake 30 5
21. 30 c. claret 35 5
22. 40 c. orange 1·25 5
23. 50 c. green 1·60 10

MORE DETAILED LISTS
are given in the Stanley Gibbons Catalogues referred to in the country headings:
BC British Commonwealth
E1, E2, E3 Europe 1, 2, 3
O1, O2, O3, O4 Overseas 1, 2, 3, 4

CHINA—YUNNAN PROVINCE

A province of China which issued distinguishing stamps because of its debased currency.

貼 滇

用貼省滇限 (1.) 用 省 (2.) 用貼省滇限 (3.)

Stamps of China optd.

1926. Issue of 1913, optd. with T **1.**

1. **19.** ½ c. sepia 5 5
2. 1 c. orange 5 5
3. 1½ c. purple 8 5
4. 2 c. green 8 5
5. 3 c. green 5 5
6. 4 c. olive 5 5
7. 5 c. mauve 8 5
8. 6 c. red 10 5
9. 7 c. violet 10 10
10. 8 c. orange 12 10
11. 10 c. blue 12 5
12. **90.** 13 c. brown 15 10
13. 15 c. blue 12 10
14. 16 c. olive 15 10
15. 20 c. lake 20 5
16. 30 c. purple 35 12
17. 50 c. green 50 15
18. **21.** $1 sepia and brown .. 1·10 30
19. $2 brown and blue .. 1·75 75
20. $5 green and red .. 8·00 7·00

1929. Unification of China. Optd. with T **2.**

21. **26.** 1 c. orange 12 10
22. 4 c. olive 12 10
23. 10 c. blue 40 30
24. $1 red .. .. 3·50 3·00

1929. Sun Yat-sen State Burial. Optd. as T **2.**

25. **27.** 1 c. orange 10 10
26. 4 c. olive 10 10
27. 10 c. blue 30 30
28. $1 red .. .. 2·75 2·75

1932. Dr. Sun Yat-sen stamps optd. with T **3.**

29. **28.** 1 c. orange 12 12
30. 2 c. olive 15 15
44. 4 c. green 20 20
45. 5 c. green 15 15
46. 15 c. green 70 60
47. 15 c. red 45 45
32. 20 c. blue 30 30
48. 25 c. blue 50 50
33. $1 sepia and brown .. 3·75 3·25
34. $2 brown and blue .. 6·50 5·50
51. $5 black and red .. 15·00 15·00

1933. Tan Yen-kai Memorial. Optd. with T **2.**

52. **32.** 2 c. olive 15 15
53. 5 c. green 15 15
54. 25 c. blue 45 45
55. $1 red .. .. 4·00 3·50

1933. Martyrs' issue optd. as T **3.**

40. **30.** ½ c. sepia 8 5
41. 1 c. orange 8 5
42. 2½ c. mauve 15 8
43. 3 c. brown 20 12
44. 8 c. orange 30 20
45. 10 c. purple 25 12
46. 13 c. green 30 10
47. 17 c. olive 50 20
48. 20 c. lake 30 15
49. 30 c. claret 40 25
50. 40 c. orange .. .. 3·25 2·50
51. 50 c. green .. .. 3·50 2·25

CHINESE P.O's IN TIBET

Post Offices at Yatung, Phari Jong, Guantse, Shigatse and Lhasa in Tibet. These offices were closed after a short time.

分貳
One Anna
ཨྣང་གཅིག།
(1.)

ILLUSTRATIONS
British Commonwealth and all overprints and surcharges are FULL SIZE.
Foreign Countries have been reduced to ¾-LINEAR.

1911. Stamps of China of 1898 surch. as T **1.**

C 1. **13.** 3 p. on 1 c. buff .. 75 1·25
C 2. ½ a on 2 c. green .. 1·00 1·50
C 3. 1 a. on 4 c. red .. 1·00 1·50
C 4. 2 a. on 7 c. lake .. 1·00 1·50
C 5. 2½ a. on 10 c. blue .. 1·00 1·50
C 6. **14.** 3 a. on 16 c. olive .. 1·50 2·00
C 7. 4 a. on 20 c. claret .. 2·00 3·00
C 8. 6 a. on 30 c. red .. 2·50 3·50
C 9. 12 a. on 50 c. green .. 4·50 6·00
C 10. **15.** 1 r. on $1 red & salmon 16·00 22·00
C 11. 2 r. on $2 claret & yell. 65·00 80·00

CHINESE PEOPLE'S REPUBLIC

I. REGIONAL ISSUES.

Many stamps were issued by Communist administrations in the years 1929 to 1949, during their warfare against the Nationalist government from 1929 to 1936 and 1945 to 1949 and against the Japanese from 1937 to 1945. They were much used for postal purposes, but with one exception, the areas in which they were used were of a shifting character; we consider the stamps to be outside the scope of this publication, but many are included in the first volume of the "Overseas" catalogue. The exception is the large Shensi-Kansu-Ninghsia Area in N.W. China, which was the Communist headquarters and was in continuous occupation by them from October 1935 onwards. We list such stamps of this area as are known to have been issued; earlier stamps have been reported, but no examples seem to be known to collectors.

The other issues listed below were issued by the postal administrations of the Liberation Areas of Central China, E. China, N. China, N.W. China, S. China and S.W. China, which were established in 1949 as regional administrative units each consisting of a group of provinces. These regional issues were in general use and were current anywhere in China. The regional issues were discontinued in 1950 and replaced by general issues for all China (see No. 1401 onwards).

North East China (Manchuria) where the currency had a lower value had independent issues of stamps until May, 1951, after the introduction of a unified currency (see separate list under CHINESE PROVINCES—MANCHURIA).

SHENSI-KANSU-NINGHSIA AREA

NW 1. Yenan Pagoda.

1946. Yenan Pagoda (1st issue). Imperf. or Roul.

NW 1. **1.** $1 green 50 50
NW 2. $5 blue .. .. 8·00 8·00
NW 3. $10 red 50 50
NW 4. $50 purple .. .. 1·00 1·00
NW 5. $100 chestnut .. .. 1·60 1·60

三十圓 暫作 (NW 2.) 三十元 暫作 (NW 3.)

三十元 暫作 (NW 4.) (NW 5.)

1946. Nos. NW 1/2 surch. as Types NW 2/5.

NW 6. $30 on $1 green (T NW 2) 75 75
NW 7. $30 on $1 green (T NW 3) 15 15
NW 8. $30 on $1 green (T NW 4) 20 20
NW 9. $60 on $1 green (T NW 2 with square bottom left character) .. 50·00 50·00
NW 10. $90 on $5 blue (T NW 5) 30 30

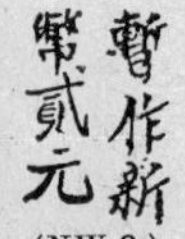

NW 6. Yenan Pagoda. NW 7. (NW 8.)

1948. Yenan Pagoda (2nd issue). Imperf.

NW 11. NW **6.** $100 buff .. 20·00 20·00
NW 12 $300 red .. 2·00 2·00
NW 13. $500 pink .. 60 60
NW 14 $1,000 blue .. 40 40
NW 15. $2,000 green .. 2·00 2·00
NW 16. $5,000 maroon .. 2·00 2·00

1948. Yenan Pagoda (3rd issue). Values in People's Currency. Imperf.

NW 17. NW **7.** 10 c. ochre .. 10 15
NW 18. 20 c. yellow .. 10 15
NW 19. $1 blue 10 15
NW 20. $2 red 30 40
NW 21. $5 green 50 60
NW 22. $10 violet .. 1·50 1·60

1949. Nos. NW 2 and NW 13 surch. in People's Currency as Type NW **8.**

NW 23. $1 on $5 blue .. 2·00 2·00
NW 24. $2 on $500 red .. 2·00 2·00

NW 9. Yenan Pagoda.

1949. Yenan Pagoda (4th issue). Values in People's Currency. Imperf.

NW 25. NW **9.** 50 c. yellow .. 10 15
NW 26. $1 indigo 10 15
NW 27. $3 yellow 10 15
NW 28. $5 green 10 15
NW 29. $10 violet 20 25
NW 30. $20 red 30 40

No. NW 25 is inscr. "5" in the bottom corners (=5 ten cent. pieces).

CENTRAL CHINA

政郵中華
用暫
100 圓壹
(1.)

1949. Stamps of China surch. as T **1.**

CC 44. **91.** $1 on $200 red .. 5 5
CC 52. $3 on $5,000 blue .. 5 5
CC 45. $6 on $10,000 brown 5 5
CC 53. $10 on $500 mauve .. 5 5
CC 46. $15 on $1 orange .. 5 5
CC 47. $30 on $100 brown .. 5 5
CC 49. $50 on $20 purple .. 5 5
CC 58. $80 on $1,000 blue .. 90 90
CC 59. $100 on $50 green .. 12 12

2. Peasant, Soldier and Workman. 3. 4. Star enclosing Map of Hankow Area.

1949.

CC 91. **2.** $1 orange 5 5
CC 92. $3 brown 5 5
CC 93. $6 green 5 5
CC 94. **3.** $7 brown 20 20
CC 95. **2.** $10 green 5 5
CC 96. **3.** $14 brown 50 50
CC 97. **2.** $15 blue 5 5
CC 98. $30 green 5 8
CC 99. **3.** $35 grey 50 50
CC 100. **2.** $50 purple 25 25
CC 101. **3.** $70 green 10 10
CC 102. **2.** $80 red 30 25
CC 103. **3.** $100 green 10 10
CC 104. $220 red 15 12

1949.

CC 106. **4.** $110 brown 5 8
CC 107. $130 violet 8 5
CC 108. $200 orange 5 5
CC 109. $290 brown 10 5
CC 110. $370 blue 15 12
CC 112. $500 blue 25 5
CC 114. $1,000 lake .. 1·50 70
CC 115. $5,000 sepia .. 60 50
CC 116. $10,000 pink .. 1·25 1·00

5. Communist Troops entering Hankow. 6. River Wall, Wuchang.

1949. Liberation of Hankow, Wuchang, and Hanyang. Perf. or imperf.

CC 127. **5.** $70 green 20 25
CC 128. $220 red 20 25
CC 129. – $290 brown 20 25
CC 130. – $370 blue 20 25
CC 131. **6.** $500 purple 25 30
CC 132. $1,000 red 40 40

DESIGN—HORIZ. $290, $370 River scene, Hanyang.

柒拾圓 人民幣 省南河 (7.)

人民幣 (8.)

河南省 人民幣 河南省 (9.)

1949. Issue for Honan. Nos. CC 93, CC 97 and CC 98 surch. as T **7.**

CC 133. **2.** $7 on $6 green .. 5 10
CC 134. $14 on $15 blue .. 5 8
CC 135. $70 on $30 green .. 15 15

This and the next three issues were made because the currency in Honan Province had a different value from that in the other provinces of Central China.

1949. Issues for Honan. Nos. CC 92/116 optd. as T **8.**

CC 136. **2.** $3 brown 5 8
CC 137. **3.** $7 brown 5 8
CC 138. **2.** $10 green 5 8
CC 139. **3.** $14 brown 8 10
CC 140. **2.** $30 green 8 10
CC 141. **3.** $35 grey 15 15
CC 142. **2.** $50 purple 15 15
CC 143. **3.** $70 green 25 25
CC 144. **4.** $110 brown 8 10
CC 145. **3.** $220 red 40 40
CC 146. **4.** $290 brown 8 10
CC 147. $370 blue 30 30
CC 148. $500 blue 40 40
CC 149. $1,000 lake .. 1·00 1·00
CC 150. $5,000 sepia .. 4·00 4·00
CC 151. $10,000 pink .. 10·00 10·00

1949. Issues for Honan. Nos. CC 127/32. optd. as T **9.** Perf. or Imperf.

CC 152. **5.** $70 green 20 25
CC 153. $220 red 20 25
CC 154. – $290 brown 20 25
CC 155. – $370 blue 25 30
CC 156. **6.** $500 purple 30 40
CC 157. $1,000 red 70 70

(10.) ($370)

作 改
圓 佰 貳
200^{00}
(11.)

1949. Issue for Honan. Central Plain Area issue of Jan. 1949 surch. as T **10.**

CC 158. $290 on $30 green .. 40 40
CC 159. $370 on $30 green (T **10**) 60 60

1950. Surch. as T **11.**

CC 164. **2.** $200 on $1 orange .. 5 12
CC 165. $200 on $3 brown .. 5 15
CC 166. $200 on $6 green .. 10 15
CC 167. **3.** $200 on $7 brown .. 10 15
CC 168. $200 on $14 brown .. 10 12
CC 169. $200 on $35 grey .. 10 15
CC 170. $200 on $70 green .. 10 10
CC 171. **2.** $200 on $80 red .. 8 10
CC 172. **3.** $200 on $220 red .. 10 15
CC 173. **4.** $200 on $370 blue .. 15 30
CC 174. **3.** $300 on $70 green .. 12 15
CC 175. **2.** $300 on $80 red .. 12 15
CC 176. **3.** $300 on $220 red .. 12 15
CC 177. **2.** $1,200 on $3 brown .. 40 40
CC 178. **3.** $1,200 on $7 brown .. 25 25
CC 179. $1,500 on $14 brown 25 35
CC 180. **2.** $2,100 on $1 orange 1·60 1·60
CC 181. $2,100 on $6 green .. 1·60 1·60
CC 182. **3.** $2,100 on $35 grey .. 50 25
CC 183. **4.** $5,000 on $370 blue .. 40 35

PARCEL POST STAMPS

P 1.

1949.

CCP 160. P **1.** $5,000 brown .. 75 90
CCP 161. $10,000 red .. 1·25 1·50
CCP 162. $20,000 green .. 2·75 3·00
CCP 163. $50,000 vermilion 5·00 6·00

EAST CHINA

1. Methods of Transport.

政郵東華
京
圓壹作暫
(2.)

1949. Shantung Communist Postal Admin. 7th Anniv. Perf. or imperf.

EC 307. **1.** $1 green 5 5
EC 308. $2 green 5 5
EC 309. $3 red 5 5
EC 310. $5 brown 5 5
EC 311. $10 blue 5 5
EC 312. $13 violet 5 5
EC 313. $18 blue 5 5
EC 314. $21 red 5 5
EC 315. $30 grey 5 5
EC 316. $50 red 8 8
EC 317. $100 olive .. 1·00 1·00

The $5 has an overprinted character obliterating a Japanese flag on the tower.

1949. Sun Yat-sen issue of China, Nos. 1153/4 surch. as T **2.**

EC 318. **92.** $1 on $10 green .. 10 15
EC 319. $3 on $20 purple .. 10 15

3. Train and Postal Runner. 4. Troops and Map of Battle.

1949. Dated "1949.2.7". Perf. or imperf.

EC 320. **3.** $1 green 5 5
EC 321. $2 green 5 5
EC 322. $3 red 5 5
EC 323. $5 brown 5 5
EC 324. $10 blue 5 5
EC 325. $13 violet 5 5
EC 326. $18 blue 5 5
EC 327. $21 red 5 5
EC 328. $30 grey 5 5
EC 329. $50 red 5 5
EC 330. $100 olive 10 10

For stamps as T **3**, but dated "1949", see Nos. EC 370/7.

1949. Victory of Hwai-Hai. Perf. or imperf.

EC 331.	**4.**	$1 green	5	5
EC 332.		$2 green	5	5
EC 333.		$3 red	5	5
EC 334.		$5 sepia	5	5
EC 335.		$10 blue	5	5
EC 336.		$13 violet	5	5
EC 337.		$18 blue	5	5
EC 338.		$21 red	5	5
EC 339.		$30 grey	5	5
EC 340.		$50 red	5	5
EC 341.		$100 olive	25	25

政郵東華 杭 圓壹作暫 (5.)

★200★ 郵政 華東 圓百貳作暫 (6.)

1949. Sun Yat-sen issue of China, surch. as T 5.

EC 342.	**91.**	$1 on $1 orange	5	5
EC 343.		$3 on $20 purple	5	5
EC 344.		$5 on $100 brown	5	5
EC 345.		$10 on $50 green	8	8
EC 346.		$13 on $10 green	10	10

1949. Sun Yat-sen issue of China, surch. as T 6.

EC 348.	**91.**	$50 on £1,000 blue	9·00	12·00
EC 349.		$100 on $5,000 blue	15·00	18·00
EC 350.		$200 on $20 purple	18·00	22·00

念圓 券民人 改作 (7.)

伍拾圓 人民券 東華 (8.) ($50)

1949. Stamps of Nationalist China surch.

(a) Revenue stamps with Gold Yuan surcharges surch. as T 7.

EC 351.	**89.**	$5 on 50 c. on $20 brn.	10	10
EC 352.		$10 on 50 c. on $20 brn.	10	10
EC 353.		$20 on 50 c. on $20 brn.	12	12
EC 354.		$20 on 50 c. on $20 brn.	15	15

(b) Sun Yat-sen issue of China, surch. as T 8.

EC 355.	**91.**	$30 on $1,000 blue	10	10
EC 357.		$50 on $200 red (T 8)	10	10
EC 358.		$100 on $5,000 blue	30	30
EC 359.		$300 on $10,000 brn.	1·00	1·00
EC 360.		$500 on $200 red	1·25	1·25

9. Maps of Shanghai and Nanking.

1949. Liberation of Nanking and Shanghai.

EC 361.	**9.**	$1 red	5	5
EC 362.		$2 green	5	5
EC 363.		$3 violet	5	5
EC 364.		$5 brown	5	5
EC 365.		$10 blue	5	5
EC 366.		$30 grey	5	5
EC 367.		$50 red	5	5
EC 368.		$100 olive	5	5
EC 369.		$500 orange	40	40

1949. As T 3, but dated "1949".

EC 370.		$10 blue	5	5
EC 371.		$15 red	8	8
EC 372.		$30 black	5	5
EC 373.		$50 red	5	5
EC 374.		$60 green	8	8
EC 375.		$100 olive	25	8
EC 376.		$1,600 blue	30	50
EC 377.		$2,000 purple	60	50

10. General Chu Teh, Mao Tse-Tung and Troops.

11. Mao Tse-tung.

1949. Chinese People's Liberation Army. 22nd Anniv.

EC 378.	**10.**	$70 orange	5	5
EC 379.		$270 red	5	5
EC 380.		$370 green	8	8
EC 381.		$470 purple	20	20
EC 382.		$570 blue	10	10

For other values in this design with only three characters in bottom panel, see South West China, Nos. SW 6/16.

1949.

EC 389.	**11.**	$10 blue	20	30
EC 390.		$15 red	20	30
EC 391.		$70 brown	5	5
EC 392.		$100 lilac	5	5
EC 393.		$150 orange	5	5
EC 394.		$200 grey	5	5
EC 395.		$500 grey	5	5
EC 396.		$1,000 red	5	8
EC 397.		$2,000 green	5	10

政郵民人華中 肆佰圓 華東區 ★★★★★ (12.)

("Chinese People's Postal Service East China Region".)

1949. Stamps of Nationalist China surch. as T 12.

EC 398.	**91.**	$400 on $200 red	50	8
EC 399.		$1,000 on $50 green	50	8
EC 400.		$1,200 on $100 brown	15	50
EC 401.		$1,600 on $20,000 grn.	5	40
EC 402.		$2,000 on $1,000 blue	10	10

PARCELS POST STAMPS

Stamps of Nationalist China surch.

紙印裹包 圓萬壹 政郵東華 (P 1.)

$200 $500 $1,000 $2,000 $5,000 $10,000

1949. No. 1056 surch. as Type P 1.

ECP 383.	**99.**	$200 on $10 green	1·50	70
ECP 384.		$500 on $10 green	1·50	70
ECP 385.		$1,000 on $10 green	1·50	1·00
ECP 386.		$2,000 on $10 green	3·00	1·25
ECP 387.		$5,000 on $10 green	8·00	2·50
ECP 388.		$10,000 on $10 grn	10·00	5·00

華東郵政 紙印裹包 圓萬壹 圓萬壹 紙印裹包 ★★★★★ (P 2.)

紙印裹包 圓萬貳 政郵東華 圓萬貳 (P 3.)

1950. Nos. 1353/5 and unissued 10 c. surch. as Type P 2.

ECP 403.	**99.**	$5,000 on 10 c. blue	3·00	2·00
ECP 404.		$10,000 on $1 orge.	5·00	4·00
ECP 405.		$20,000 on $2 blue	10·00	7·00
ECP 406.		$50,000 on $5 red	25·00	15·00

1950. Nos. P 711/2 and P 926/7 surch as Type P 3.

ECP 407.	**P 1.**	$5,000 on $500 grn.	1·00	2·00
ECP 408.		$10,000 on $1,000 blue	8·00	3·00
ECP 409.	**P 3.**	$20,000 on $3,000 green	15·00	7·00
ECP 410.		$50,000 on $5,000 red	4·00	10·00

NORTH CHINA

1. Infantry. **2.** Industry.

1949. Imperf.

NC 283.	**1.**	50 c. purple	15	20
NC 284.		$1 blue	30	40
NC 285.		$2 green	15	20
NC 286.		$3 violet	15	20
NC 287.		$5 brown	15	20
NC 288.	**2.**	$6 claret	15	20
NC 289.	**1.**	$10 green	15	20
NC 290.		$12 red	15	10

The 50 c. and $6 have value in Chinese characters only.

3. Pagoda.

暫作郵票 伍角 華北郵電 **4.** (50 c.)

壹 ($1) 叁 ($3)

("North China Postal Service Provisional Postage Stamps").

1949. Money Order stamps of China surch. as T 4. (top central character differs as shown).

NC 291.	**3.**	50 c. on $50 brown	10	20
NC 292.		$1 on $50 brown	20	35
NC 293.		$3 on $50 brown	20	35
NC 294.		$6 on $20 purple	8	12

壹百元 人民郵政 改作 北 (5.)

二元 人民郵政 暫作 華 (6.)

("People's Postal Service North China.")

1949. Surch. as T 5.

(a) On stamp of China.

NC 295.	**61.**	$100* on $100 claret	70	25

(b) On stamps of North Eastern Provinces.

NC 296.	**5.**	50 c. on 5 c. lake	5	5
NC 297.		$1 on 10 c. orange	5	5
NC 298.		$2 on 20 c. green	5	5
NC 299.		$3 on 50 c. orange	5	5
NC 300.		$4 on $5 green	5	5
NC 301.		$6 on $10 red	8	8
NC 302.		$10 on $300 green	10	10
NC 303.		$12 on $1 blue	10	10
NC 304.		$18 on $3 brown	10	10
NC 305.		$20* on 50 c. orange	10	10
NC 306.		$20 on $20 olive	5	5
NC 308.		$30 on $2.50 blue	25	20
NC 309.		$40 on 25 c. brown	25	25
NC 310.		$50 on $109 green	30	30
NC 311.		$80* on $1 blue	30	30
NC 312.		$100 on $65 green	40	40

1949. Surch as T 6.

(a) On stamps of China.

NC 313.	**61.**	$100* on $100 claret	30	20
NC 314.		$300* on $700 brn.	30	20
NC 315.	**72.**	$500* on $500 green	15	15
NC 316.		$3,000* on $3,000 bl.	1·00	70

(b) On stamps of North Eastern Provinces.

NC 317.		$1* on 25 c. brown	5	5
NC 318.		$2 on 20 c. green	8	8
NC 319.		$3 on 50 c. orange	10	10
NC 320.		$4 on $5 green	10	10
NC 321.		$6 on $10 red	10	10
NC 323.		$10* on $300 green	5	5
NC 324.		$12 on $1 blue	8	8
NC 325.		$20* on 50 c. orange	80	80
NC 326.		$20* on $20 olive	8	8
NC 327.		$40* on 25 c. brown	15	15
NC 328.		$50* on $109 green	40	40
NC 329.		$80* on $1 blue	12	12

* On these stamps the bottom character in the left-hand column of the overprints is square in shape.

7.

ILLUSTRATIONS British Commonwealth and all overprints and surcharges are FULL SIZE. Foreign Countries have been reduced to ¾-LINEAR.

1949. Labour Day. Perf. or imperf.

NC 330.	**7.**	$20 red	20	20
NC 331.		$40 blue	20	20
NC 332.		$60 brown	20	20
NC 333.		$80 green	25	25
NC 334.		$100 violet	30	30

8. Mao Tse-tung. **9.**

1949. Chinese Communist Party. 28th Anniv. Perf. or imperf.

NC 359.	**8.**	$10 red	10	10
NC 360.	**9.**	$20 blue	10	10
NC 361.	**8.**	$50 orange	10	10
NC 362.	**9.**	$80 green	15	15
NC 363.	**8.**	$100 violet	20	20
NC 364.	**9.**	$120 olive	25	25
NC 365.	**8.**	$140 maroon	30	30

政郵民人 暫用 拾圓 華北 (10.)

("People's Postal Service North China").

1949. Surch. as T 10.

(a) On stamp of China.

NC 366.	**72.**	$10 on $7,000 brn.	35	25

(b) On stamps of North Eastern Provinces.

NC 368.	**5.**	$10 on $10 red	20	12
NC 369.		$30 on 20 c. green	25	12
NC 370.		$50 on $44 red	20	8
NC 371.		$100 on $3 brown	35	12
NC 373.		$200 on $4 brown	1·50	1·50

11. Gate of Heavenly Peace, Peking. **12.** Field Workers and Factory.

1949.

NC 381.	**11.**	$50 orange	10	15
NC 382.		$100 red	8	10
NC 383.		$200 green	8	10
NC 384.		$300 purple	8	10
NC 385.		$400 blue	25	15
NC 386.		$500 brown	40	15
NC 387.		$700 violet	25	30

1949.

NC 388.	**12.**	$1,000 orange	40	15
NC 389.		$3,000 blue	15	15
NC 390.		$5,000 red	15	20
NC 391.		$10,000 brown	25	1·00

PARCELS POST STAMPS

Stamps of China surch.

政郵民人 元百捌 北華 (P 1.)

作圓佰伍暫 電郵北華 作暫 500 (P 2.)

1949. Surch. as Type P 1.

NCP 335.	**P 3.**	$300 on $6,000,000 grey	—	1·50
NCP 336.		$400 on $8,000,000 red	—	1·50
NCP 337.		$500 on $10,000,000 olive	—	2·00
NCP 338.		$800 on $5,000,000 lilac	—	3·00
NCP 339.		$1,000 on $3,000,000 blue	—	4·00

1949. Surch. as Type P 2.

NCP 340.	**P 3.**	$500 on $3,000,000 blue	—	2·00
NCP 341.		$1,000 on $5,000,000 lilac	—	4·00
NCP 342.		$3,000 on $8,000,000 red	—	10·00
NCP 343.		$5,000 on $10,000,000 olive	—	20·00

政郵民人 紙印裹包 元 六 北華 (P 3.)

北華 圓拾貳 紙印裹包 圓拾貳 北華 (P 4.)

圓拾貳 紙印裹包 圓拾貳 (P 5.)

1949. Money Order stamps as North China T 6 surch. as Type P 3.

NCP 344.	$6 on $5 red	25	25
NCP 345.	$6 on $50 grey	40	30
NCP 346.	$50 on $20 purple	70	40
NCP 347.	$100 on $10 olive	1·40	50

1949. Money Order stamps as North China T 6 surch. as Type P 4 or P 5 (No. NCP 349).

NCP 348.	$20 on $1 orange	40	20
NCP 349.	$20 on $1 orange	1·00	40
NCP 350.	$30 on $2 green	40	20
NCP 352.	$30 on $10 green	6·00	20
NCP 357.	$50 on $5 red	50	20
NCP 354.	$100 on $10 green	40	20

P 6.

1949.

NCP 374.	**P 6.**	$500 red	—	1·00
NCP 375.		$1,000 blue	—	1·50
NCP 376.		$2,000 green	—	2·00
NCP 377.		$5,000 olive	—	4·00
NCP 378.		$10,000 orange	—	8·00
NCP 379.		$20,000 red	—	20·00
NCP 380.		$50,000 purple	—	45·00

NORTH WEST CHINA

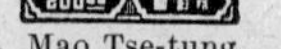

1. Mao Tse-tung.

2. Great Wall of China.

1949. Imperf.
NW 76. 1. $50 pink 10 10
NW 77. 2. $100 blue 8 8
NW 78. 1. $200 orange 25 25
NW 79. 2. $400 sepia 15 15

SOUTH CHINA

300
圓佰叁作改

1. Ho Nam Bridge, Canton. (2).

1949. Liberation of Canton. Imperf.
SC 1. 1. $10 green 5 5
SC 2. $20 brown 5 5
SC 3. $30 violet 5 5
SC 4. $50 red 5 5
SC 5. $100 blue 5 5

1949. Surch. as T 2.
SC 22. 1. $300 on $30 violet .. 10 5
SC 23. $500 on $20 brown .. 10 5
SC 24. $800 on $30 violet .. 20 10
SC 25. $1,000 on $10 green .. 30 15
SC 26. $1,000 on $20 brown 35 15

SOUTH WEST CHINA

1. Gen. Chu Teh, Mao Tse-tung and Troops.

1949.
SW 6. 1. $10 blue 5 8
SW 7. $20 purple 5 8
SW 8. $30 orange 5 8
SW 9. $50 green 5 5
SW 10. $100 red 5 5
SW 11. $200 blue 5 10
SW 12. $300 violet .. 10 12
SW 13. $500 grey 20 20
SW 14. $1,000 purple .. 40 50
SW 15. $2,000 green .. .. 1·50 1·75
SW 16. $5,000 orange .. 4·00 4·50
For other values in this design see East China, Nos. EC 378/82.

圓百叁 作改 (2.) （川東） (3.)

1949. Surch. as T 2 (number of characters and length as indicated).
SW 17. 1. $300 on $100 red (T 2) 15 15
SW 18. $500 on $100 red (5 characs., 17 mm.) 15 15
SW 19. $1,200 on $100 red (7 characters) .. 50 50
SW 20. $1,500 on $200 blue (7 characters) .. 50 50
SW 21. $2,000 on $200 blue (5 characters) .. 70 70

1950. East Szechwan issue. Nos. SW 10/11 optd. "East Szechwan" in Chinese characters as T 3.
SW 22. 1. $100 red 40 40
SW 23. $200 blue 40 40

壹仟伍百 (4.) 改作 川西 (5.)

1950. Surch. as T 4.
SW 24. 1. $1,200 on $200 red .. 1·25 1·25
SW 25. $1,500 on $200 blue 1·25 1·25

1950. West Szechwan issue. Nos. SW 10/12 optd. "West Szechwan" in Chinese characters as T 5.
SW 26. 1. $100 red 30 30
SW 27. $200 blue 60 60
SW 28. $300 violet .. 1·25 1·40

(6.) ($800) (7.) ($200) (8.) ($1,000)

1950. West Szechwan issue. Nos. SW 9/12 surch. as T 6.
SW 29. 1. $500 on $100 red 30 30
SW 30. $800 on $100 red (T 6) 25 25
SW 31. $1,000 on $50 green 50 35
SW 32. $2,000 on $200 blue 1·00 75
SW 33. $3,000 on $300 violet 2·50 2·00

1950. West Szechwan issue. Sun Yat-sen issue of China, surch. as T 7/8.
SW 34. 91. $100 on 4 c. green .. 30 30
SW 35. $200 on 4 c. grn. (T 7) 60 60
SW 36. $800 on 16 c. red .. 3·00 3·50
SW 37. $1,000 on 16 c. red (T 8) .. .. 5·00 5·00

9. Map of China with Flag in S.W. (10.)

1950. Liberation of the South West.
SW 39. 9. $20 blue 10 15
SW 40. $30 green 10 15
SW 41. $50 red 10 15
SW 42. $100 brown .. 10 15

1950. Nos. 1211 and 1213/14 of China optd. Perf. or rouletted.
SW 44. 93. (–) brown-orange 20·00 20·00
SW 45. 95. (–) magenta .. 20·00 20·00
SW 46. 96. (–) carmine .. 20·00 20·00

(11.) ($3,000)

($5,000) ($10,000) ($20,000) ($50,000)

1950. Surch. as T 11 (characters in left-hand column of surcharge differ as indicated in illustrations and footnote).
SW 50. 9. $60 on $30 green .. 40 40
SW 51. $150 on $30 green .. 40 25
SW 52. $300 on $20 blue .. 40 25
SW 53. $300 on $100 brown 50 30
SW 54. $1,500 on $100 brown 1·25 1·25
SW 55. $3,000 on $50 red .. 2·50 2·00
SW 56. $5,000 on $50 red .. 5·50 3·50
SW 57. $10,000 on $50 red .. 5·50 3·50
SW 58. $20,000 on $50 red .. 1·50 5·00
SW 59. $50,000 on $50 red .. 2·00 8·00
Nos. 50 and 52/3 have three characters in left-hand column. Nos. 51 and 54 have five.

(12.)

1950. Surch. as T 12.
SW 60. 9. $800 on $30 orange .. 2·50 3·00
SW 61. $1,000 on $50 red .. 50 30
SW 62. $2,000 on $100 brown 60 60
SW 63. $4,000 on $20 blue .. 2·00 2·00
SW 64. $5,000 on $30 green .. 2·75 2·75

II. General Issues for China.

GUM or NO GUM. Nos. 1401/1891 were issued without gum (except Nos. 1843/5 and 1850/7). From No. 1892 onwards all postage stamps were issued with gum, unless otherwise stated. From 1965 some issues seem to have no gum, though in fact they bear an adhesive substance.

SERIAL MARKINGS. Issues other than definitive issues are divided into two categories: "commemorative" and "special". Figures below the design of each stamp of such issues indicate: (a) serial number of the issue; (b) number of stamps in the issue; (c) number of stamps within the issue; and (d) year of issue (from No. 1557 on). Neither chronological order of issue nor sequence of value is always strictly followed. From No. 2343 these serial markings were omitted until No. 2433.

REPRINTS were later made in replacement of exhausted stocks by the Chinese Postal Administration for sale to stamp collectors and were not available for postal purposes. Nos. 1401/11, 1432/5, 1456/8, 1464/73, 1507/9, 1524/37, and 1543/52.

Our prices are for originals. For notes describing the distinguishing features of the reprints, see Stanley Gibbons' Overseas Stamp Catalogue, Volume 1.

For other values in the following types see North East China.

105. Gate of Heavenly Peace, Peking. 106.

1949. Chinese People's Political Conf. First Session Celebration.
1401. 105. $30 blue 15 15
1402. $50 red 20 20
1403. $100 green 30 25
1404. $200 purple 60 45

1949. World Federation of Trade Unions. Asiatic and Australasian Congress, Peking.
1405. 106. $100 red 25 25
1406. $300 green 35 35
1407. $500 blue 60 60

107. Conference Hall. 108. Mao Tse-tung.

1950. Chinese People's Political Conf.
1408. 107. $50 red 20 15
1409. $100 blue 30 20
1410. 108. $300 purple 55 40
1411. $500 green .. .. 1·00 60

109. Gate of Heavenly Peace, Peking.

1950.
1412. 109. $200 green 5 5
1413. $300 lake 5 5
1414. $500 red 5 5
1415. $800 orange .. 60 5
1420a. $1,000 lilac 5 5
1417. $2,000 olive 40 5
1420b. $3,000 brown 5 5
1418. $5,000 pink 8 8
1419. $8,000 blue 8 50
1420c. $10,000 brown .. 5 10
See also Nos. 1481a/7 and 1493/8.

中國人民郵政 壹佰圓 ★★ 100 (110.) 中國人民郵政 20000 貳萬圓 (111.)

1950. Surch. as T 110. Perf. or roul.
1427. 95. $100 on (–) mauve .. 5 8
1428. 96. $200 on (–) red .. 5 8
1429. 94. $300 on (–) green .. 10 12
1424. 93. $500 on (–) orange .. 8 8
1430. $800 on (–) orange .. 5 5
1426a. $1,000 on (–) orange .. 8 8

1950. Unissued stamp of East China surch. with T 111.
1431. $20,000 on $10,000 red 40·00 1·75
Design (21 × 18 mm.): Harvesters and ox.

中國人民郵政 伍拾圓 ☆ 50 (113.)

中國人民郵政 壹佰圓 ★★ 100 (114.)

112. Mao Tse-tung and Parade.

1950. Foundation of People's Republic in 1949.
1432. 112. $800 red, yellow & grn. 70 40
1433. $1,000 red, yell. & brn. 70 50
1434. $2,000 red, yell. & pur. 1·50 90
1435. $3,000 red, yell. & blue 1·75 1·25

1950. Stamps of North Eastern Provinces surch. as T 113.
1436. 5. $50 on 20 c. green .. 60 60
1437. $50 on 25 c. brown .. 10 45
1438. $50 on 50 c. orange .. 10 10
1439. $100 on $2.50 blue .. 10 10
1440. $100 on $3 brown .. 10 10
1441. $100 on $4 brown .. 10 50
1442. $100 on $5 green .. 10 10
1443. $100 on $10 red .. 45 50
1444. $400 on $20 olive .. 50 50
1445. $400 on $44 red .. 50 15
1446. $400 on $65 green .. 40 40
1447. $400 on $100 green .. 40 20
1448. $400 on $200 brown .. 40 20
1449. $400 on $300 green .. 40 20

1950. Surch. as T 114.
1450. 99. $50 on 10 c. blue .. 8 5
1451. $100 on 16 c. olive .. 8 5
1452. $100 on 50 c. green .. 10 8
1453. $200 on $1 orange .. 10 8
1453a. $200 on $2 blue .. 10 8
1454. $400 on $5 red .. 10 10
1455. $400 on $10 green .. 10 10
1455a. $400 on $20 purple .. 90 60
Nos. 1451/2 are imperf.

115. "Peace". 115a. Gate of Heavenly Peace, Peking.

1950. Peace Campaign (1st issue).
1456. 115. $400 brown 20 25
1457. $800 green 60 20
1458. $2,000 blue .. .. 1·00 40
See also Nos. 1510/12 and 1590/2.

1950. Clouds redrawn.
1481a. 115a. $100 blue 8 5
1482. $200 green 8 5
1460. $300 lake 5 8
1460a. $400 grey-green .. 15 8
1461. $500 red 5 5
1462. $800 orange 5 5
1485a. $1,000 violet 8 5
1463. $2,000 olive 12 15
1486a. $3,000 brown .. 15 30
1487. $5,000 pink .. 20 50

116. Flag. 117 "Communications".

1950. People's Republic. 1st Anniv. Flag in red, yellow and brown.
1464. 116. $100 violet 25 15
1465. $400 brown 25 15
1466. $800 green (44 × 53 mm) 60 25
1467. $1,000 olive 70 45
1468. $2,000 blue .. .. 1·00 75

1950. 1st All-China Postal Conf.
1469. 117. $400 brown and green 40 15
1470. $800 green and red 60 25

118. Stalin greets Mao Tse-tung.

1950. Sino-Soviet Treaty.
1471. 118. $400 red 40 50
1472. $800 green 60 50
1473. $2,000 blue .. .. 1·25 70

中國人民郵政 壹佰圓 ★★ 100 (119.) 肆佰圓 中國人民郵政 400 (120.)

1950. Nos. EC 370, etc., of East China surch. as T 119.
1474. $50 on $10 blue .. 5 5
1475. $100 on $15 red .. 5 5
1476. $300 on $50 red .. 5 5
1477. $400 on $1,600 purple .. 10 12
1478. $400 on $2,000 lilac .. 8 5

1950. Stamps of East China surch. as T 120.
1479. 11. $50 on $10 blue .. 8 5
1480. $400 on $15 red .. 8 5
1481. $400 on $2,000 green 8 5

121. Temple of Heaven and Aeroplane.

1951. Air.
1488. 121. $1,000 red 8 8
1489. $3,000 green .. 8 8
1490. $5,000 orange .. 12 15
1491. $10,000 green and pur. 25 30
1492. $30,000 brn. and blue 50 60

1951. Pink network background.
1493. 109. $10,000 brown .. 70 40
1494. $20,000 olive .. 70 25
1495. $30,000 green .. 1·25 70
1496. $50,000 violet .. 2·50 50
1497. $100,000 red .. 18·00 5·00
1498. $200,000 blue .. 35·00 7·00

中國人民郵政 貳拾伍圓 25 (122.)
伍拾圓 ★ 50 ★ 中國人民郵政 (123.)

1951. Surch. as T 122. Perf. or roul.
1499. 95. $5 on (–) mauve .. 8 8
1500. 94. $10 on (–) green .. 8 8
1501. 96. $15 on (–) red .. 8 8
1502. 93. $25 on (–) orange .. 8 8

124. Mao Tse-tung. 126. National Emblem.

125. Dove.

1951. Chinese Communist Party. 30th Anniv.
1507. 124. $400 brown 20 20
1508. $500 green 30 30
1509. $800 red 45 30

1951. Peace Campaign (2nd issue).
1510. 125. $400 brown 50 50
1511. $800 green 75 65
1512. $1,000 violet .. 1·00 80

1951. National Emblem Issue. Yellow network background.
1513. 126. $100 blue 12 8
1514. $200 brown 15 8
1515. $400 orange 30 10
1516. $500 green 45 20
1517. $800 red 60 25

1951. Money Order stamps as North China, T 6, but surch. with T 123.
1518. $50 on $2 green (perf.) .. 12 12
1519. $50 on $2 blue (roul.) .. 25 25
1520. $50 on $5 orange (roul.) 8 8
1521. $50 on $50 grey (roul.) 8 8
1523. $50 on $50 black (perf.) 8 5

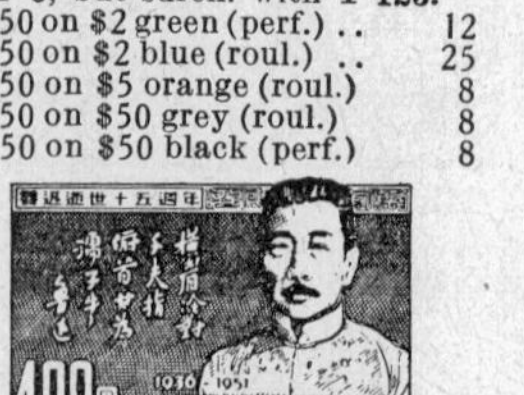
127. Lu Hsun (author).

1951. Lu Hsun. 15th Death Anniv.
1524. 127. $400 violet 30 25
1525. $800 green 50 25

128. Rebels at Chintien.

1951. Taiping Rebellion Cent. Inscr. "1851 1951".
1526. 128. $400 green 30 20
1527. $800 red 50 25
1528. – $800 orange 50 25
1529. – $1,000 blue 70 35
DESIGN: Nos. 1528/9 Coin and documents.

129. Peasants and Tractor.

1952. Agrarian Reform.
1530. 129. $100 red 25 25
1531. $200 blue 25 25
1532. $400 chocolate .. 40 30
1533. $800 green 60 50

130. The Potala, Lhasa. 131. "Child Protection".

1952. Liberation of Tibet.
1534. 130. $400 red 40 30
1535. – $800 green 50 40
1536. 130. $800 claret 50 40
1537. – $1,000 violet .. 75 60
DESIGN: Nos. 1535, 1537 Tibetan ploughing with yaks.

1952. Int. Child Protection Conf., Vienna.
1538. 131. $400 green 8 8
1539. $800 blue 8 8

132. Hammer and Sickle. 133. Gymnast.

1952. Labour Day. Dated "1952".
1540. 132. $800 red 12 8
1541. – $800 green 12 8
1542. – $800 brown 12 8
DESIGNS: No. 1541, Hand and dove. No. 1542, Hammer, dove and ear of corn.

1952. Gymnastics by Radio. As T 133.
1543. $400 scarlet (14–17) .. 12 8
1544. $400 deep blue (18–21) .. 12 8
1545. $400 brown-pur. (22–25) 12 8
1546. $400 green (26–29) .. 12 8
1547. $400 vermilion (30–33) .. 12 8
1548. $400 blue (34–37) .. 12 8
1549. $400 orange (38–41) .. 12 8
1550. $400 violet (42–45) .. 12 8
1551. $400 yellow-brn. (46–49) 12 8
1552. $400 pale blue (50–53) .. 12 8
DESIGNS: Various gymnastic exercises, the stamps in each colour being arranged in blocks of four throughout the sheet, each block showing four stages of the exercise depicted. Where two stages are the same, the stamps differ only in the serial number in brackets, in the right-hand corner of the bottom margin of the stamp. The serial numbers are shown above after the colours of the stamps.

Prices are for single stamps.

134. "A Winter Hunt" (A.D. 386–580).

1952. "Glorious Mother Country" 1st issue). Tun Huang Mural Paintings.
1553. 134. $800 brown-black .. 12 8
1554. – $800 red-brown .. 12 8
1555. – $800 slate-black .. 12 8
1556. – $800 slate-purple .. 12 8
PAINTINGS: No. 1554, "Benefactor" (A.D. 581–617). No. 1555, "Celestial Flight" (A.D. 618–906). No. 1556, "Dragon" (A.D. 618–906).

See also Nos. 1569/72, 1593/96, 1601/4 and 1628/31.

135. Marco Polo Bridge, Lukouchiao.

1952. War with Japan. 15th Anniv.
1557. 135. $800 blue 12 8
1558. – $800 green 12 8
1559. – $800 plum 12 8
1560. – $800 red 12 8
DESIGNS (dated "1937–1952"): Nos. 1558, Victory at Pinghsinkwan. 1559, Departure of New Fourth Army from C. China. 1560, Mao Tse-tung and Chu Teh.

136. Airman, Sailor and Soldier. 137. Dove over Pacific.

1952. People's Liberation Army. 25th Anniv.
1561. 136. $800 red 12 8
1562. – $800 green 12 8
1563. – $800 violet 12 8
1564. – $800 brown 12 8
DESIGNS (dated "1927–1952"): HORIZ. No. 1562, Soldier, tanks and guns. 1563, Sailor and warships. 1564, Pilot and aeroplanes.

1952. Asia and Pacific Ocean Peace Conf.
1565. 137. $400 claret 12 8
1566. – $800 orange 12 8
1567. 137. $800 red 12 8
1568. – $2500 green 25 15
DESIGN—HORIZ. Nos. 1566 and 1568, Doves and globe.

138. Huai River Barrage.

1952. "Glorious Mother Country". (2nd issue).
1569. 138. $800 violet 12 8
1570. – $800 red 12 8
1571. – $800 maroon 12 8
1572. – $800 green 12 8
DESIGNS: No. 1570, Chengtu railway viaduct. 1571, Oil refinery. 1572, Tractor, disc harrows and combine drill.

139. Peasants collecting food for the Front.

DESIGNS—(dated "1950 – 1952"): HORIZ. No. 1573, Marching troops. 1575, Infantry attack. 1576, Meeting of Chinese and North Korean soldiers.

1952. Chinese Volunteer Force in Korea. 2nd Anniv.
1573. – $800 blue 12 8
1574. 139. $800 vermilion .. 12 8
1575. – $800 violet 12 8
1576. – $800 lake 12 8

141. Textile Worker.

DESIGN: No. 1579, Woman harvesting grain.

1953. Int. Women's Day.
1578. 141. $800 red 12 8
1579. – $800 emerald 12 8

142. Shepherdess. 143. Karl Marx. 144. Workers and Flags.

1953.
1580. – $50 purple 8 8
1581. 142. $200 emerald .. 8 8
1582. – $250 blue 8 8
1583. – $800 blue-green .. 10 8
1584. – $1,600 grey 12 10
1585. – $2,000 orange .. 15 12
DESIGNS: $50 Mill girl. $250 Carved lion. $800 Lathe-operator. $1,600 Miners. $2,000 Old Palace, Peking.

1953. Karl Marx. 135th Birth Anniv.
1586. 143. $400 brown 8 8
1587. $800 green 12 10

1953. 7th National Labour Union Conf.
1588. 144. $400 blue 8 8
1589. $800 red 12 10

145. Dove of Peace.

1953. Peace Campaign (3rd issue).
1590. 145. $250 green 8 5
1591. $400 brown 10 8
1592. $800 violet 10 8

146. Horseman and Steed (A.D. 386–580).

PAINTINGS: No. 1594, Court players (A.D 386–580). No. 1595, Battle scene (A.D. 581–617). No. 1596, Ox-drawn palanquin (A.D. 618–906).

1953. "Glorious Mother Country" (3rd issue).
1593. 146. $800 green .. 15 10
1594. – $800 orange .. 15 10
1595. – $800 blue 15 10
1596. – $800 red 15 10

147. Mao Tse-tung and Stalin at Kremlin.

1953. Russian Revolution. 35th Anniv.
1597. 147. $800 green 15 10
1598. – $800 red 15 10
1599. – $800 blue 15 10
1600. – $800 brown 15 10
DESIGNS—HORIZ. No. 1598, Lenin addressing revolutionaries. VERT. 1599, Statue of Stalin. 1600, Stalin making speech.

148. Compass (300 B.C.). 149. Rabelais (writer).

1953. "Glorious Mother Country" (4th issue). Scientific instruments.
1601. 148. $800 black 15 10
1602. – $800 green 15 10
1603 – $800 slate 15 10
1604. – $800 chocolate .. 15 10
DESIGNS: No. 1602, Seismograph (A.D. 132). 1603, Drum cart for measuring distances (A.D. 300). 1604, Armillary sphere (A.D. 1437).

1953. Famous Men.
1605. 149. $250 green 8 5
1606. – $400 purple 12 8
1607. – $800 indigo 15 10
1608. – $2,200 chocolate .. 25 15
PORTRAITS: $400, J. Marti (revolutionary). $800, Chu Yuan (poet). $2,200 Copernicus (astronomer.)

150. Flax Mill, Harbin.

DESIGNS: $200, Tangku New Harbour. $250, Tienshui - Lanchow Rly. $400, Heavy machine works. No. 1613, Blast-furnace. No. 1614, Fuhsin open-cast mines. $2,000 Electric power station. $3,200 Geological survey team.

1954. Industrial Development.

1609.	150.	$100 olive-brown ..	8	8
1610.	–	$200 green ..	8	8
1611.	–	$250 violet ..	8	8
1612.	–	$400 sepia ..	10	8
1613.	–	$800 purple ..	12	8
1614.	–	$800 indigo ..	12	8
1615.	–	$2,000 red ..	25	12
1616.	–	$3,200 brown ..	25	12

151. Gate of Heavenly Peace, Peking.

152. Statue of Lenin and Stalin at Gorki.

153. Lenin Speaking.

154. Painted Pottery (c. 2000 B.C.).

1954.

1617.	151.	$50 claret	5	5
1618.		$100 blue	5	5
1619.		$200 green	5	5
1620.	151.	$250 ultramarine ..	5	5
1621.		$400 grey-green ..	5	5
1622.		$800 orange	8	8
1623.		$1,600 grey	25	15
1624.		$2,000 olive ..	35	25

1954. Lenin. 30th Death Anniv. Inscr. "1870–1924".

1625.	152.	$400 turquoise ..	12	8
1626.	–	$800 brown	15	10
1627.	153.	$2,000 lake	30	20

DESIGN—As T 153: $800, Full-face portrait.

1954. "Glorious Mother Country" (5th issue).

1628.	154.	$800 chocolate ..	10	8
1629.	–	$800 black ..	10	8
1630.	–	$800 turquoise ..	10	8
1631.	–	$800 lake	10	8

DESIGNS—As T 154: No. 1629, Musical stone (1200 B.C.). 1630, Bronze basin (816 B.C.). 1631, Lacquered wine cup and cosmetic tray (403-221 B.C.).

155. Heavy Rolling Mill.

156. Statue of Stalin.

1954. Anshan Steel Works.

1632.	–	$400 turquoise ..	8	8
1633.	155.	$800 maroon ..	12	8

DESIGN: $400, Seamless steel-tubing mill.

1954. Stalin. 1st Death Anniv. Inscr. "1953 1954".

1634.	156.	$400 black ..	8	8
1635.	–	$800 sepia	20	10
1636.	–	$2,000 red	25	15

DESIGNS—VERT. $800, Full-face portrait of Stalin (26×37 mm.). HORIZ. $2,000 Stalin and hydro-electric station (42½×25 mm.).

157. Exhibition Building.

1954. Russian Economic and Cultural Exn., Peking.

1637.	157.	$800 brown on yellow	1·25	50

158. The Universal Fixture.

159. Woman Worker.

160. Rejoicing Crowds.

1954. Workers' Inventions.

1638.	158.	$400 green	8	8
1639.	–	$800 red	15	12

DESIGN: $800, The reverse repeater.

1954. 1st Session of National Congress.

1640.	159.	$400 purple	8	8
1641.	160.	$800 red	20	12

161. "New Constitution".

1954. Constitution Commem.

1642.	161.	$400 brown on buff	8	8
1643.		$800 red on yellow ..	15	10

162. Pylons.

163. Nurse and Red Cross Worker.

1955. Overhead Transmission of Electricity.

1644.	162.	$800 blue	20	12

1955. Chinese Red Cross. 50th Anniv.

1645.	163.	8 f. red and green ..	50	20

164. Miner.

165. Gate of Heavenly Peace, Peking.

1955.

1646.	164.	½ f. brown	35	5
1647.	–	1 f. purple	35	5
1648.	–	2 f. green	35	5
1648a.	–	2½ f. blue	35	5
1649.	–	4 f. olive	35	8
1650.	–	8 f. red	1·50	8
1650b.	–	10 f. crimson ..	1·75	10
1651.	–	20 f. blue	3·25	15
1652.	–	50 f. grey	6·50	20
1653.	165.	$1 lake	2·00	30
1654.		$2 brown	4·00	45
1655.		$5 slate	8·00	80
1656.		$10 red	12·00	2·25
1657.		$20 violet	24·00	5·00

DESIGNS—As T 164: 1 f. Lathe operator. 2 f. Airman. 2½ f. Nurse. 4 f. Soldier. 8 f. Foundry worker. 10 f. Chemist. 20 f. Farm girl. 50 f. Sailor.

166. Workmen and Industrial Plant.

167. Chang-Heng (A.D. 78–139, astronomer).

1955. Sino-Russian Treaty. 5th Anniv.

1658.	–	8 f. brown	50	20
1659.	166.	20 f. olive	1·00	30

DESIGN—HORIZ. (37×32 mm.): 8 f. Stalin and Mao Tse-tung.

1955. Scientists of Ancient China.

1660.	167.	8 f. sepia on buff ..	20	10
1661.	–	8 f. blue on buff ..	20	10
1662.	–	8 f. black on buff ..	20	10
1663.	–	8 f. purple on buff ..	20	10

PORTRAITS: No. 1661, Tsu Chung-chi (429-500, mathematician). 1662, Chang-Sui (683-727 astronomer). 1663, Li-Shih-chen (1518-1593 pharmacologist).

168. Foundry.

169. Lenin.

1955. Five Year Plan. Frames in black.

1664.	168.	8 f. red and orange ..	20	8
1665.	–	8 f. brown and yellow	20	8
1666.	–	8 f. olive and black ..	20	8
1667.	–	8 f. mauve and blue	20	8
1668.	–	8 f. yellow and brown	20	8
1669.	–	8 f. yellow and red ..	20	8
1670.	–	8 f. grey and indigo	20	8
1671.	–	8 f. orange and brown	20	8
1672.	–	8 f. yellow and sepia	20	8
1673.	–	8 f. red, brown & yell.	20	8
1674.	–	8 f. yellow and green	20	8
1675.	–	8 f. red and yellow ..	20	8
1676.	–	8 f. yellow and brown	20	8
1677.	–	8 f. yellow and olive	20	8
1678.	–	8 f. yellow and blue	20	8
1679.	–	8 f. blue and ochre ..	20	8
1680.	–	8 f. yellow and sepia	20	8
1681.	–	8 f. red and brown ..	20	8

DESIGNS—No. 1665, Electricity pylons. 1666, Mining machinery. 1667, Oil tankers and derricks. 1668, Heavy machinery workshop. 1669, Factory guard and industrial plant. 1670, Textile machinery. 1671, Factory workers. 1672, Combine-harvester. 1673, Dairy herd farm girl. 1674, Dam. 1675, Artists decorating pottery. 1676, Workers' rest home. 1677, Lorry. 1678, Ship and wharf. 1679, Surveyors. 1680, Students. 1681, Man, woman and child.

1955. Lenin. 85th Birth Anniv.

1682.	169.	8 f. blue	40	15
1683.		20 f. lake	90	40

170. Engels.

171. Capture of Lu Ting Bridge.

1955. Engels. 60th Death Anniv.

1684.	170.	8 f. red	40	15
1685.		20 f. sepia	90	40

1955. Long March by Communist Army. 20th Anniv. Inscr. "1934.10 1935.10".

1686.	171.	8 f. red	60	15
1687.	–	8 f. blue	60	15

DESIGN—VERT. (28×46 mm.): No. 1687, Crossing the Ta Hsueh Mountains.

172. Convoy of Lorries.

DESIGNS—VERT. (21 × 42 mm.); No. 1689, Suspension bridge: Tatu River. HORIZ. As T 172: No. 1690, Opening ceremony, Lhasa.

1956. Opening of Sikang-Tibet and Tsinghai-Tibet Highways.

1688.	172.	4 f. blue	20	10
1689.	–	8 f. brown	30	15
1690.	–	8 f. red	30	15

173. Summer Palace.

VIEWS: Nos. 1692, Peihai Park. 1693, Gate of Heavenly Peace. 1694, Temple of Heaven. 1695, Tai Ho Palace.

1956. Views of Peking.

1691.	173.	4 f. red	15	5
1692.	–	4 f. green	15	5
1693.	–	8 f. red	30	12
1694.	–	8 f. blue	30	12
1695.	–	8 f. brown	30	12

174. Salt Production.

DESIGNS—HORIZ. (Brick carvings of Tung Han Dynasty, A.D. 25-200): No. 1697, Residence. 1698, Hunting and farming. 1699, Carriage crossing bridge.

1956. Archaeological Discoveries at Chengtu.

1696.	174.	4 f. green	15	5
1697.	–	4 f. black	15	5
1698.	–	8 f. brown-black ..	30	12
1699.	–	8 f. sepia	30	12

175.

1956. National Savings.

1700.	175.	4 f. buff	50	12
1701.		8 f. red	70	20

176. Gate of Heavenly Peace, Peking.

177. Dr. Sun Yat-sen.

1956. 8th National Communist Party Congress.

1702.	176.	4 f. green	40	8
1703.		8 f. vermilion ..	40	15
1704.		16 f. red	1·25	30

1956. Dr. Sun Yat-sen. 90th Birth Anniv.

1705.	177.	4 f. brown	5	5
1706.		8 f. blue	15	8

178. Putting the Shot.

1957. 1st Chinese Workers' Athletic Meeting, 1955. Inscr. "1955". Flower in red and green; inscr. in brown.

1707.	178.	4 f. lake	12	8
1708.	–	4 f. purple (Weight-lifting)	12	8
1709.	–	8 f. grn. (Sprinting)	25	12
1710.	–	8 f. blue (Football) ..	25	12
1711.	–	8 f. brown (Cycling)	25	12

179. Assembly Line.

1957. Lorry Production.

1712.	–	4 f. brown	12	8
1713.	179.	8 f. blue	25	12

DESIGN: 4 f. Changchun motor plant.

180. Nanchang Revolutionaries.

1957. People's Liberation Army. 30th Anniv.

1714.	180.	4 f. violet	50	20
1715.	–	4 f. green	50	20
1716.	–	8 f. brown	1·00	30
1717.	–	8 f. blue	1·00	30

DESIGNS: No. 1715, Meeting of Red Armies at Tsinkangchan. 1716, Liberation Army crossing the Yellow River. 1717, Liberation of Nanking.

181. Congress Emblem. **182.** Yangtse River Bridge.

1957. 4th W.F.T.U. Congress, Leipzig.
1718. **181.** 8 f. brown 30 8
1719. 22 f. blue 70 20

1957. Opening of Yangtse River Bridge.
1720. **182.** 8 f. red 20 8
1721. – 20 f. grey-blue .. 40 15
DESIGN: 20 f. Aerial view of bridge.

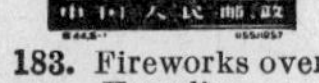

183. Fireworks over Kremlin. **184.** Airport Scene.

1957. Russian Revolution. 40th Anniv. Dated "1917–1957".
1722. **183.** 4 f. red 50 12
1723. – 8 f. sepia 70 25
1724. – 20 f. green 90 35
1725. – 22 f. brown .. .. 1·25 50
1726. – 32 f. blue .. .. 1·60 50
DESIGNS: 8 f. Soviet emblem, globe and broken chains. 20 f. Dove of Peace and plant. 22 f. Hands supporting book bearing portraits of Marx and Lenin. 32 f. Electricity power pylon.

1957. Air.
1727. **184.** 16 f. indigo .. .. 1·60 15
1728. – 28 f. olive .. .. 1·60 15
1729. – 35 f. black .. .. 2·50 30
1730. – 52 f. blue .. .. 4·50 50
DESIGNS ('Plane over): 28 f. Mountain highway. 35 f. Railway trucks. 52 f. Coaling station.

185. Yellow River Dam and Power Station. **186.** Ploughing.

1957. Harnessing of the Yellow River.
1731. – 4 f. orange 40 12
1732. **185.** 4 f. blue 40 12
1733. – 8 f. lake 60 20
1734. – 8 f. green 60 20
DESIGNS: No. 1731, Map of Yellow River. 1733, Motor-ship. 1734, Aerial view of irrigation on Yellow River.

1957. Co-operative Agriculture. Mult.
1735. 8 f. Farmer enrolling for farm 20 10
1736. 8 f. Type **186** 20 10
1737. 8 f. Tree-planting 20 10
1738. 8 f. Harvesting 20 10

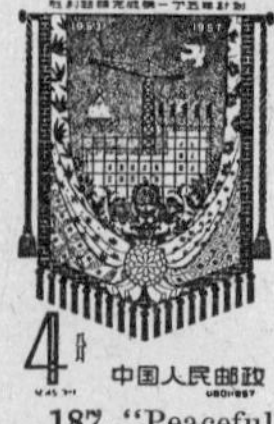

187. "Peaceful Construction". **188.** High Peak Pagoda, Tenfeng.

1958. Completion of First Five Year Plan.
1739. **187.** 4 f. green 20 12
1740. – 8 f. red 35 12
1741. – 16 f. blue 50 20
DESIGNS: 8 f. "Industry and Agriculture" (grapple and wheat-sheaves). 16 f. "Communications and Transport" (train on viaduct and ship).

1958. Ancient Chinese Pagodas.
1742. **188.** 8 f. olive-brown .. 30 8
1743. – 8 f. blue 30 8
1744. – 8 f. purple-brown .. 30 8
1745. – 8 f. green 30 8
DESIGNS: No. 1743, One Thousand League Pagoda, Tali. 1744, Buddha Pagoda, Yinghsien. 1745, Flying Rainbow Pagoda, Hungchao.

189. Trilobite of Hao Li Shan. **190.**

1958. Chinese Fossils.
1746. **189.** 4 f. indigo 15 10
1747. – 8 f. sepia 30 15
1748. – 16 f. slate-green .. 60 20
DESIGNS: 8 f. Dinosaur of Lufeng. 16 f. "Srnomegaceros pachyospeus" (deer).

1958. People's Heroes Monument, Peking. Unveiling.
1749. **190.** 8 f. red 50 15

191. Karl Marx (after Zhukov). **192.** Cogwheels of Industry.

1958. Karl Marx. 140th Birth Anniv.
1750. **191.** 8 f. chocolate .. 35 10
1751. – 22 f. myrtle .. .. 1·25 25
DESIGN: 22 f. Marx addressing German Workers' Educational Association, London.

1958. 8th All-China Trade Union Congress, Peking.
1752. **192.** 4 f. blue 20 12
1753. 8 f. purple 60 20

193. Federation Emblem. **194.** Mother and Child.

1958. 4th Int. Democratic Women's Federation Congress, Vienna.
1754. **193.** 8 f. blue 50 12
1755. 20 f. green 75 25

1958. Chinese Children. Centre multi-coloured. Inscriptions and values in green.
1756. 8 f. Type **194** .. .. 1·00 20
1757. 8 f. Watering sunflowers 1·00 20
1758. 8 f. "Hide and seek" .. 1·00 20
1759. 8 f. Children sailing boat 1·00 20

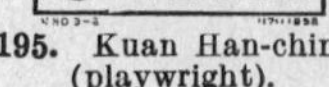

195. Kuan Han-ching (playwright). **196.** Peking Planetarium.

1958. Works of Kuan Han-ching. 700th Anniv.
1760. – 4 f. black-grn. on crm. 45 12
1761. **195.** 8 f. maroon on cream 70 20
1762. – 20 f. black on cream 1·25 25
DESIGNS: Scenes from Han-ching's comedies: 4 f. "The Butterfly Dream". 20 f. "The Riverside Pavilion".

1953. Peking Planetarium.
1763. **196.** 8 f. green 60 15
1764. – 20 f. indigo .. .. 1·25 30
DESIGN: 20 f. Planetarium in operation.

197. Marx and Engels. **198.** Wild Goose and Radio Pylon.

1958. "Communist Manifesto". 110th Anniv. Inscr. "1848–1958".
1765. **197.** 4 f. purple .. 60 15
1766. – 8 f. blue .. .. 1·10 25
DESIGN: 8 f. Front cover of first German "Communist Manifesto".

1958. Communist Postal Conf., Moscow.
1767. **198.** 4 f. blue 40 15
1768. 8 f. green .. .. 1·10 45

199. Peony and Doves. **200.** Chang Heng's Weather-cock.

1958. Int. Disarmament Conf., Stockholm.
1769. **199.** 4 f. red .. .. 1·25 70
1770. – 8 f. green .. .. 1·25 70
1771. – 22 f. brown .. .. 6·00 1·25
DESIGNS: 8 f. Olive branch. 22 f. Atomic symbol and factory plant.

1958. Chinese Meteorology
1772. **200.** 8 f. black on yellow .. 40 12
1773. – 8 f. black on blue .. 40 12
1774. – 8 f. black on green .. 40 12
DESIGNS No. 1773, Meteorological balloon. No 1774, Typhoon signal-tower

201. Union Emblem within figure "5". **202.** Chrysanthemum.

203. Telegraph Building, Peking.

1958. 5th Int. Students' Union Congress, Peking.
1775. **201.** 8 f. purple 40 12
1776. 22 f. green .. .. 1·25 20

1958. Flowers.
1777. – 1½ f. magenta (Peony) 1·50 10
1778. – 3 f. green (Hibiscus) .. 1·50 10
1779. **202.** 5 f. orange .. .. 1·50 8

1958. Peking Telegraph Building. Opening.
1780. **203.** 4 f. olive 12 8
1781. 8 f. red 30 12

204. Exhibition Emblem and Symbols.

1958. National Exn. of Industry and Communications.
1782. **204.** 8 f. green 60 12
1783. – 8 f. red 60 12
1784. – 8 f. brown 60 12
DESIGNS No. 1783, Chinese dragon riding the waves. 1784, Horses in the sky.

205. Labourer on Reservoir Site. **206.** "Sputnik" and ancient Theodolite.

1958. Ming Tombs Reservoir Inaug.
1885. **205.** 4 f. brown 12 8
1886. – 8 f. blue 25 12
DESIGN: 8 f. Ming Tombs Reservoir.

1954. Russian Space Satellite Commem.
1887. **206.** 4 f. red 60 15
1888. – 8 f. violet .. .. 1·25 20
1889. – 10 f. green .. .. 1·75 25
DESIGNS: 8 f. Third Russian "sputnik" encircling globe. 10 f. Three Russian "sputniks" encircling globe.

207. Chinese and Korean Soldiers. **208.** Forest Landscape.

1958. Return of Chinese People's Volunteers from Korea.
1790. **207.** 8 f. purple 25 10
1791. – 8 f. chestnut 25 10
1792. – 8 f. red 25 10
DESIGNS: No. 1791, Chinese soldier embracing Korean woman. 1792, Girl presenting bouquet to Chinese soldier.

1958. Afforestation Campaign.
1793. **208.** 8 f. green 25 10
1794. – 8 f. slate 25 10
1795. – 8 f. violet 25 10
1796. – 8 f. blue 25 10
DESIGNS—VERT. No. 1794, Forest patrol. HORIZ. 1795, Tree-felling by power-saw. 1796, Tree planting.

209. Atomic Reactor.

1958. China's First Atomic Reactor. Inaug.
1797. **209.** 8 f. blue 45 15
1798. – 20 f. brown 90 30
DESIGN: 20 f. Cyclotron in action.

210. Children with Model Aircraft. **211.** Rooster.

1958. Aviation Sports.
1799. **210.** 4 f. red 15 8
1800. – 8 f. myrtle 20 8
1801. – 10 f. sepia 25 12
1802. – 20 f. slate 45 12
DESIGNS: 8 f. Gliders in flight. 10 f. Parachutists. 20 f. Light planes in flight.

1959. Chinese Folk Paper-cuts.
1803. – 8 f. black on violet .. 50 8
1804. – 8 f. black on green .. 50 8
1805. **211.** 8 f. black on red .. 50 8
1806. – 8 f. black on blue .. 50 8
DESIGNS: No. 1803, Camel. 1804, Pomegranate. 1806, Acress on stage.

212. Mao Tse-tung and Steel Workers. **213.** Chinese Women.

1959. Steel Production Progress. Inscr. "1958".
1807. **212.** 4 f. red 25 8
1808. – 8 f. purple 40 8
1809. – 10 f. red 60 20
DESIGNS: 8 f. Battery of steel furnaces. 10 f. Steel "blowers" and workers.

1958. Int. Women's Day.
1810. **213.** 8 f. green on cream .. 25 8
1811. – 22 f. magenta on cream 50 15
DESIGN. 22 f. Russian and Chinese women.

214. Natural History Museum, Peking. **215.** Barley.

1959. Opening of Natural History Museum. Peking.
1812. **214.** 4 f. turquoise .. 10 8
1813. 8 f. sepia 25 8

1959. Successful Harvest, 1958.
1814. **215.** 8 f. red (Barley) .. 30 10
1815. – 8 f. red (Rice) .. 30 10
1816. – 8 f. red (Soya beans) 30 10
1817. – 8 f. red (Groundnuts and rape) 30 10

216. Workers with Marx-Lenin Banner. **217.** Airport Building.

1959. Labour Day. Inscr. "1889–1959".
1818. **216.** 4 f. blue 25 12
1819. – 8 f. red 50 12
1820. – 22 f. green 80 20
DESIGNS: 8 f. Hands clasping Red Flag. 22 f. Figures "5.1" (May 1st) and workers.

1959. Peking Airport Inaug.
1821. **217.** 8 f. black on lilac .. 25 8
1822. – 10 f. blk. on grey-grn. 45 15
DESIGN: 10 f. Chinese airliner at airport.

218. Students with Banners **219.** F. Joliot-Curie (first President).

1959. "May 4th" Students' Rising. 40th Anniv. Inscr. "1919–1959".
1823. **218.** 4 f. red, choc. & olive 45 12
1824. – 8 f. red, choc. & bis. 70 12
DESIGN: 8 f. Workers with banners.

1959. World Peace Council. 10th Anniv. Inscr. "1949–1959".
1825. **219.** 8 f. purple 50 12
1826. – 22 f. violet .. .. 1·10 25
DESIGN: 22 f. Silhouettes of European, Chinese and Negro.

220. Stamp Printing Works, Peking. **221.**

1959. Sino-Czech Co-operation in Postage Stamp Production.
1827. **220.** 8 f. myrtle 45 12

1959. World Table-Tennis Championships, Dortmund.
1828. **221.** 4 f. blue and black .. 30 15
1829. 8 f. red and black .. 50 15

222. Moon Rocket. **223.** "Prologue".

1959. Launching of First Lunar Rocket.
1830. **222.** 8 f. red, blue & black 4·00 80

1959. People's Communes. 1st Anniv.
1831. **223.** 8 f. rose-red 20 8
1832. – 8 f. dull purple .. 20 8
1833. – 8 f. orange 20 8
1834. – 8 f. bronze-green .. 20 8
1835. 8 f. blue 20 8
1836. – 8 f. olive 20 8
1837. – 8 f. indigo 20 8
1838. 8 f. magenta.. .. 20 8
1839. 8 f. black 20 8
1840. 8 f. emerald 20 8
1841. 8 f. violet 20 8
1842. 8 f. red 20 8
DESIGNS: No. 1832, Steel worker ("Rural Industries"). 1833, Farm girl ("Agriculture"). 1834, Salesgirl ("Trade"). 1835, Peasant ("Study"). 1836, Militiaman ("Militia"). 1837, Cook with tray of food ("Community Meals"). 1838, Child watering flowers ("Nursery"). 1839, Old man with pipe ("Old People's Homes"). 1840, Health worker ("Public Health"). 1841, Young flautist ("Recreation and Entertainment"). 1842, Star-shaped flower ("Epilogue").

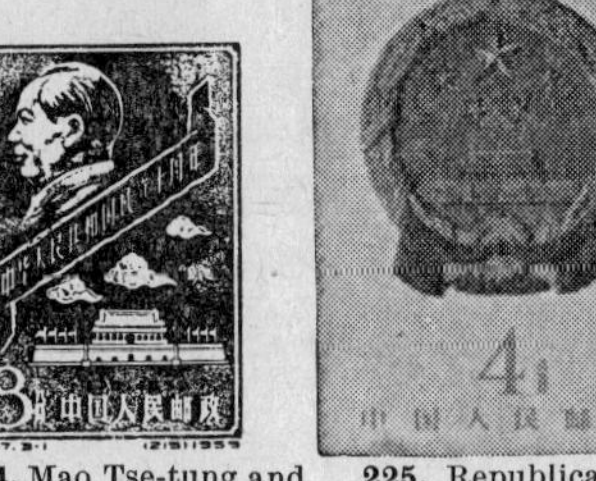

224. Mao Tse-tung and Gate of Heavenly Peace, Peking. **225.** Republican Emblem.

1959. People's Republic. 10th Anniv.

(a) 1st issue. Inscr. "1949–1959". With gum.
1843. **224.** 8 f. red and brown .. 50 25
1844. – 8 f. red and blue .. 50 25
1845. – 22 f. red and green .. 1·25 50
DESIGNS: No. 1844, Marx, Lenin and Kremlin. 1845, Dove of peace and globe.

(b) 2nd issue. Emblem in red and yellow; inscriptions in yellow; background colours given.
1846. **225.** 4 f. turquoise .. 20 10
1847. 8 f. lilac 20 10
1848. 10 f. blue 60 20
1849. 20 f. buff .. .. 1·00 30

226. Steel Plant.

DESIGNS: No. 1851, Coal-mine. 1852, Steel-mill. 1853, Double-decked bridge. 1854, Combine-harvester. 1855, Dam construction. 1856, Textile mill. 1857, Chemical works.

(c) 3rd issue. Inscr. "1949–1959". Frames in maroon; centre colours given. With gum.
1850. **226.** 8 f. rose-red 30 12
1851. – 8 f. grey-drab .. 30 12
1852. – 8 f. yellow-brown .. 30 12
1853. – 8 f. grey-blue .. 30 12
1854. – 8 f. salmon 30 12
1855. – 8 f. olive-green .. 30 12
1856. – 8 f. blue-green .. 30 12
1857. – 8 f. lilac 30 12

227. Rejoicing Populace.

DESIGNS—VERT. People rejoicing with background of industrial plant (10 f.) or banners and tree (20 f.).

(d) 4th Issue. Inscr. "1949–1959".
1858. **227.** 8 f. mult. on cream .. 30 12
1859. – 10 f. mult. on cream 40 20
1860. – 20 f. mult. on cream 60 30

228. Mao Tse-tung proclaiming Republic.

(e) 5th issue.
1861. **228.** 20 f. lake .. .. 3·00 1·75

229. Boy Bugler ("Summer Camps"). **230.** Exhibition Emblem and Symbols of Communication.

1959. Chinese Youth Pioneers. 10th Anniv.
1862. – 4 f. yell., verm. & blk. 15 8
1863. **229.** 4 f. red and blue .. 20 8
1864. – 8 f. red and brown .. 35 10
1865. – 8 f. red and blue .. 35 10
1866. – 8 f. red and green .. 35 10
1867. – 8 f. red and purple .. 35 10
DESIGNS: No. 1862, Pioneers' emblem. 1864, Schoolgirl with flowers and satchel ("Study"). 1865, Girl with rain gauge ("Science"). 1866, Boy with sapling ("Forestry"). 1867 Girl skater ("Athletic Sports").

1959. National Exn. of Industry and Communications, Peking. Inscr. "1949–1959".
1868. **230.** 4 f. blue 15 8
1869. – 8 f. red 30 10
DESIGN: 8 f. Exn. emblem and symbols of industry.

231. "Cultural Palace of the Nationalities". **232.** "Statue of Sport".

1959. Cultural Palace of the Nationalities, Peking. Inaug.
1870. **231.** 4 f. black and red .. 15 8
1871. 8 f. black and green 30 10

1959. 1st National Sports Meeting, Peking. Multicoloured.
1872. 8 f. Type **232** 15 8
1873. 8 f. Parachuting 15 8
1874. 8 f. Pistol-shooting .. 15 8
1875. 8 f. Diving 15 8
1876. 8 f. Table-tennis .. 15 8
1877. 8 f. Weight-lifting .. 15 8
1878. 8 f. High-jumping .. 15 8
1879. 8 f. Rowing 15 8
1880. 8 f. Running 15 8
1881. 8 f. Basketball 15 8
1882. 8 f. Fencing 15 8
1883. 8 f. Motor-cycling .. 15 8
1884. 8 f. Gymnastics 15 8
1885. 8 f. Cycling 15 8
1886. 8 f. Horse-racing .. 15 8
1887. 8 f. Football 15 8

233. Wheat (Main Pavilion).

DESIGNS: Meteorological symbols (Meteorological Pavilion). 10 f. Cattle (Animal Husbandry Pavilion). 20 f. Fishes (Aquatic Products Pavilion).

1960. Opening of National Agricultural Exn. Hall, Peking.
1888. **233.** 4 f. black, red & orge. 12 8
1889. – 8 f. black and blue .. 20 8
1890. – 10 f. black and brown 20 8
1891. – 20 f. black and turq. 45 15

234. Crossing the Chinsha River. **235.** Clara Zetkin (founder).

1960. Conference during the Long March, Tsunyi, Kweichow. 25th Anniv. Inscr. "1935–1960".
1892. – 4 f. blue 35 15
1893. – 8 f. sepia, turquoise, yellow and red .. 70 40
1894. **234.** 10 f. green 90 50
DESIGNS: 4 f. Conference Hall, Tsunyi. 8 f. Mao Tse-tung and flags.

1960. Int. Women's Day. 50th Anniv. Frame and inscriptions black. Centre colours given.
1895. **235.** 4 f. blue, black & flesh 15 10
1896. – 8 f. multicoloured .. 20 10
1897. – 10 f. multicoloured .. 30 15
1898. – 22 f. multicoloured .. 60 25
DESIGNS: 8 f. Mother, child and dove. 10 f. Woman tractor-driver. 22 f. Women of three races.

236. Chinese and Soviet Workers.

DESIGNS: 8 f. Flowers and Sino-Soviet emblems. 10 f. Chinese and Soviet soldiers.

1960. Sino-Soviet Treaty. 10th Anniv. Inscr. "1950–1960".
1899. **236.** 4 f. brown 40 25
1900. – 8 f. black, yell. & red 50 30
1901. – 10 f. blue .. .. 1·00 45

237. Flags of Hungary and China. **238.** Lenin speaking.

1960. Hungarian Liberation. 15th Anniv. Inscr. "1945–1960".
1902. **237.** 8 f. red, green, black and yellow .. 60 30
1903. – 8 f. red, black & blue 60 30
DESIGN: No. 1903, Parliament Building, Budapest.

1960. Lenin. 90th Birth Anniv. Inscr. "1870–1960".
1904. **238.** 4 f. lilac 25 10
1905. – 8 f. black & vermilion 30 12
1906. – 20 f. chocolate .. 70 20
DESIGNS: 8 f. Lenin (portrait). 20 f. Lenin talking with Red Guards (after Vasilyev).

239. Lunik II. **240.** Prague.

1960. Lunar Rocket Flights.
1907. **239.** 8 f. red 50 20
1908. – 10 f. green (Lunik 3) 75 30

1960. Liberation of Czechoslovakia. 15th Anniv. Inscr. "1945–1960".
1909. – 8 f. multicoloured .. 60 30
1910. **240.** 8 f. green 60 30
DESIGN—VERT. No. 1909, Child pioneers and flags of China and Czechoslovakia.

SERIAL NUMBERS. In this and many later multicoloured sets containing several stamps of the same denomination, the serial number is quoted in brackets to assist identification. This is the last figure in the bottom left corner of the stamp.

241. "Out-folded Operculum and Nostril Bouquet".

1960. Chinese Goldfish. Multicoloured.
1911. 4 f. (1) T **241** .. .. 1·00 20
1912. 4 f. (2) "Black-back Dragon-eye" .. .. 1·00 20
1913. 4 f. (3) "Bubble-eye" .. 1·00 20
1914. 4 f. (4) "Red Tigerhead" 1·00 20
1915. 8 f. (5) "Pearl-scale" .. 1·00 20
1916. 8 f. (6) "Blue Dragon-eye" 1·00 20
1917. 8 f. (7) "Skyward-eye" .. 1·00 20
1918. 8 f. (8) "Red-cap" .. 1·00 20
1919. 8 f. (9) "Purple-cap" .. 1·00 20
1920. 8 f. (10) "Red-head" .. 1·00 20
1921. 8 f. (11) "Red and White Dragon-eye" .. .. 1·00 20
1922. 8 f. (12) "Red Dragon-eye" 1·00 20

INDEX

Countries can be quickly located by referring to the index at the end of this volume.

242. Sow with Litter.

1960. Pig-breeding.

1923. 242. 8 f. black and red .. 50 12
1924. – 8 f. black and green 50 12
1925. – 8 f. black & magenta 50 12
1926. – 8 f. black and olive .. 50 12
1927. – 8 f. black and orange 50 12

DESIGNS: No. 1924, Pig being inoculated. 1925, Group of pigs. 1926, Pig and feeding pens. 1927, Pig and crop-bales.

243. "Serving the Workers".

244. N. Korean and Chinese Flags, and Flowers.

1960. 3rd National Literary and Art Workers' Congress, Peking. Inscr. "1960".

1928. 243. 4 f. red, sepia & green 20 12
1929. – 8 f. red, bistre & turq. 50 12

DESIGN: 8 f. Inscribed stone seal.

1960. Liberation of Korea. 15th Anniv. Inscr. "1945–1960".

1930. 244. 8 f. red, yellow & green 1·00 25
1931. – 8 f. red, indigo & blue 1·00 25

DESIGN: No. 1931, "Flying Horse" of Korea.

245. Peking Railway Station.

1960. Opening of New Peking Railway Station.

1932. 245. 8 f. brown, cream, black and blue .. 40 20
1933. – 10 f. indigo, cream and turquoise 70 30

DESIGN: 10 f. Train arriving in station.

246. Chinese and N. Vietnamese Flags, and Children.

247. Worker and Spray Fan.

1960. N. Vietnam Republic. 15th Anniv. Inscr. "1945-1960".

1934. 248. 8 f. red, yell. & black 40 20
1935. – 8 f. red, grey-green, green and black .. 40 20

DESIGN—VERT. No. 1935, "Lake of the Returning Sword", Hanoi.

1960. Public Health Campaign.

1936. 247. 8 f. black and orange 25 8
1937. – 8 f. grey-green and grey-blue 25 8
1938. – 8 f. brown and blue .. 25 8
1939. – 8 f. lake and chestnut 25 8
1940. – 8 f. blue and turquoise 25 8

DESIGNS: No. 1937, Spraying insecticide. 1938, Cleaning windows. 1939, Medical examination of child. 1940, "Tai Chi Chuan" (Chinese physical drill).

248. Façade of Great Hall.

1960. Completion of "Great Hall of the People". Multicoloured.

1941. 8 f. Type 248 .. 40 30
1942. 10 f. Interior of Great Hall 60 50

249. Dr. N. Bethune operating on Wounded Soldier.

250. Friedrich Engels.

1960. Dr. Norman Bethune (Canadian surgeon with 8th Route Army). Commem.

1943. 249. 8 f. sepia 20 8
1944. – 8 f. grey, black & red 30 10

PORTRAIT: No. 1944, Dr. N. Bethune.

1960. Engels. 140th Birth Anniv.

1945. – 8 f. chocolate .. 60 12
1946. 250. 10 f. orange and blue 90 25

DESIGN: 8 f. Engels addressing Congress at The Hague.

251. Big "Ju-I".

252. Freighter.

1960. Chrysanthemums. Background colours given. Multicoloured.

1947. – 4 f. blue 20 8
1948. – 4 f. pink 20 8
1949. – 8 f. grey 40 10
1950. 251. 8 f. blue 40 10
1951. – 8 f. green 40 10
1952. – 8 f. violet 40 10
1953. – 8 f. olive 40 10
1954. – 8 f. greenish-blue .. 40 10
1955. – 10 f. grey 45 15
1956. – 10 f. brown 45 15
1957. – 20 f. blue 70 20
1958. – 20 f. red 70 20
1959. – 22 f. brown 70 20
1960. – 22 f. red 70 20
1961. – 30 f. green .. 1·00 25
1962. – 30 f. mauve .. 1·00 25
1963. – 35 f. green .. 1·25 25
1964. – 52 f. purple .. 1·40 35

CHRYSANTHEMUMS: No. 1947, "Hwang Shih Pa". No. 1948, "Green Peony". No. 1949, "Er Chiao". No. 1951, "Ju-I" with Golden Hooks. No. 1952, "Golden Peony". No. 1953, "Generalissimo's Banner". No. 1954, "Willow Thread". No. 1955, "Cassia on Salver of Hibiscus". No. 1956, "Pearls on Jade Salver". No. 1957, "Red Gold Lion". No. 1958, "Milky White Jade". No. 1959, "Purple Jade with Fragrant Beads". No. 1960, "Cassia on Ice Salver". No. 1961, "Inky Black Lotus". No. 1962, "Jade Bamboo Shoot of Superior Class". No. 1963, "Smiling Face". No. 1964, "Swan Ballet".

1960. 1st Chinese-built Freighter. Launching. No gum.

1965. 252. 8 f. blue 40 12

253. Pantheon, Paris.

255. Chan Tien-yu.

254. Table-Tennis Match.

1961. Paris Commune. 90th Anniv.

1966. 253. 8 f. black and red .. 35 12
1967. – 8 f. sepia and red .. 35 12

DESIGN: No. 1967, Proclamation of Commune

1961. 26th World Table-Tennis Championships, Peking. Multicoloured.

1968. 8 f. Championship emblem and jasmine 30 10
1969. 10 f. Table-tennis bat and ball, and Temple of Heaven 40 10
1970. 20 f. T 254 .. .. 50 25
1971. 22 f. Peking Workers' Gymnasium 60 30

1961. Chan Tien-yu (railway construction engineer). Birth Cent. Inscr. "1861-1961".

1972. 255. 8 f. black and sage .. 25 10
1973. – 10 f. chestnut & sepia 40 10

DESIGN: 10 f. Train on Peking-Changchow-Railway.

256. Congress Building, Shanghai.

1961. Chinese Communist Party. 40th Anniv. Inscr. "1921-1961". Flags, red; frames, gold.

1974. 256. 4 f. purple 25 8
1975. – 8 f. green 35 10
1976. – 10 f. brown 60 12
1977. – 20 f. blue 80 15
1978. – 30 f. red .. .. 1·40 20

DESIGNS: 8 f. "August 1" Building, Nanchang. 10 f. Provisional Central Govt. Building, Juichin. 20 f. Pagoda Hill, Yenan. 30 f. Gate of Heavenly Peace, Peking.

257. "August 1" Building, Nanchang.

258. Flags of China and Mongolia.

1961. Size 24 × 16½ mm. No gum.

1979. 257. 1 f. blue 5 5
1980. 1½ f. lake 5 5
1981. 2 f. slate-blue .. 5 5
1982. A. 3 f. violet 5 5
1983. 4 f. green 5 5
1984. 5 f. grey-green .. 8 5
1985. B. 8 f. sepia 8 5
1986. 10 f. purple 20 5
1987. 20 f. deep blue .. 25 5
1988. C. 22 f. chocolate .. 30 5
1989. 30 f. blue 40 10
1990. 50 f. red 50 15

DESIGNS: A, Tree and Sha Chow Pa Building, Juichin. B, Yenan Pagoda. C, Gate of Heavenly Peace, Peking.

See also Nos. 2010/21.

1961. Mongolian People's Revolution. 40th Anniv. Inscr. "1921-1961".

1991. 258. 8 f. red, blue & yellow 15 10
1992. – 10 f. orge., yell. & olive 20 15

DESIGN: 10 f. Mongolian Government Building.

259. Military Museum.

1961. People's Revolutionary Military Museum.

1993. 259. 8 f. brown, grn. & bl. 40 10
1994. 10 f. blk., grn. & brn. 50 12

DESIGN—VERT. 10 f. Dr. Sun Yat-sen.

260. Uprising at Wuhan.

1961. Revolution of 1911. 50th Anniv. Inscr. "1911-1961".

1995. 260. 8 f. black and grey .. 40 10
1996. – 10 f. black and brown 50 12

261. Donkey.

262. Tibetans Rejoicing.

1961. Tang Dynasty Pottery (618-907 A.D.). Centres multicoloured. Background colours given.

1997. 261. 4 f. grey-blue .. 10 5
1998. – 8 f. grey-green .. 20 8
1999. – 8 f. purple 20 8
2000. – 10 f. slate-blue .. 20 8
2001. – 20 f. olive 30 15
2002. – 22 f. blue-green .. 30 15
2003. – 30 f. red 45 20
2004. – 50 f. slate 75 40

DESIGNS: No. 1998, Donkey. Nos. 1999/2002, Various horses. Nos. 2003/4, Various camels.

1961. "Rebirth of the Tibetan People".

2005. 262. 4 f. chocolate & buff 10 5
2006. – 8 f. chocolate & turq. 20 5
2007. – 10 f. chocolate & yell. 40 8
2008. – 20 f. chocolate & pink 1·10 12
2009. – 30 f. choc. & slate-blue 1·75 20

DESIGNS: 8 f. Sower. 10 f. Tibetan celebrating "bumper crop". 20 f. "Responsible Citizens". 30 f. Tibetan children.

1962. As T 257 but smaller (20½ × 16½ mm.). No gum.

2010. 257. 1 f. blue 5 5
2011. 2 f. green 5 5
2013. A. 3 f. violet 5 5
2014. 257. 3 f. brown 5 5
2015. A. 4 f. green 5 5
2016. C. 4 f. pink 5 5
2017. B. 8 f. brown 12 5
2018a. 10 f. purple 12 5
2019a. 20 f. blue 20 5
2020. C. 30 f. blue 40 12
2021. 52 f. red 60 40

263. Lu Hsun (after Hsieh Chia-seng).

ILLUSTRATIONS
British Commonwealth and all overprints and surcharges are FULL SIZE. Foreign Countries have been reduced to ¾-LINEAR.

1962. Lu Hsun (writer). 80th Birth Anniv.

2022. 263. 8 f. black and crimson 25 8

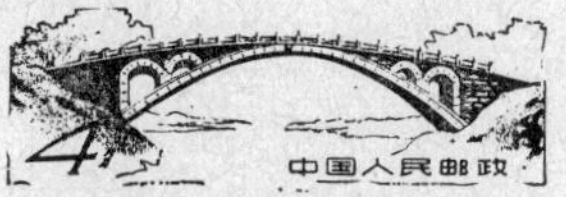

264. Anchi Bridge, Chaohsien.

1962. Ancient Chinese Bridge.

2023. 264. 4 f. violet and lavender 12 5
2024. – 8 f. slate-grn. & green 25 10
2025. – 10 f. sepia and bistre 40 15
2026. – 20 f. blue & turquoise 70 20

BRIDGES 8 f. Paotai, Soochow. 10 f. Chupu, Kuanhsien. 20 f. Chenvang, Sankiang.

265. Tu Fu.

266. Two Cranes and Trees.

1962. Tu Fu (poet). 1250th Birth Anniv.

2027. – 4 f. black and bistre .. 30 5
2028. 265. 8 f. black & turquoise 50 10

DESIGN: 4 f. Tu Fu's Memorial, Chengtu.

1962. "The Sacred Crane".

2029. 8 f. black, red, turq. & drab 25 8
2030. 10 f. blk., red, buff & blue 25 10
2031. 20 f. blk., red, blue & buff 50 15

DESIGNS: 8 f. T 266. 10 f. Two cranes in flight. 20 f. Crane on rock. All from paintings by Chen Chi-fo.

267. Cuban Soldier.

268. Torch and Map.

1962. "Support for Cuba".

2032. 267. 8 f. black and lake .. 50 15
2033. – 10 f. black and green 70 20
2034. – 22 f. black and blue 1·50 25

DESIGNS: 10 f. Sugar-cane planter. 22 f. Militia man and woman.

1962. "Support for Algeria".

2035. 268. 8 f. orange and brown 20 10
2036. – 22 f. chocolate & ochre 40 15

DESIGN: 22 f. Algerian patriots.

269. Mei Lan-fang (actor).

270. Han "Flower Drum" Dance.

1962. "Stage Art of Mei Lan-fang". Multicoloured. Each showing Lan-fang in stage costume with items given below.

2037. 4 f. T **269** 50 20
2038. 8 f. Drum 70 20
2039. 8 f. Fan 70 20
2040. 10 f. Swords .. .. .. 1·00 25
2041. 20 f. Bag .. .. .. 1·40 35
2042. 22 f. Ribbons .. .. .. 1·75 35
2043. 30 f. Loom .. .. .. 2·25 50
2044. 50 f. Long sleeves .. .. 3·00 1·00
Nos. 2042/4 are horiz.

1962. Chinese Folk Dances (1st issue). Multicoloured. No gum.

2045. 4 f. T **270** 8 5
2046. 8 f. Mongolian "Ordos" .. 12 5
2047. 10 f. Chuang "Catching shrimp" 15 8
2048. 20 f. Tibetan "Fiddle" .. 30 8
2049. 30 f. Yi "Friend" 40 15
2050. 50 f. Uighur "Tambourine" 65 30
See also Nos. 2104/15.

271. Soldiers storming the Winter Palace, Petrograd.

1962. Russian Revolution. 45th Anniv.

2051. – 8 f. brown and red .. 1·00 12
2052. **271.** 20 f. bronze and red .. 2·75 15
DESIGN—VERT. 8 f. Lenin leading soldiers.

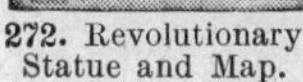

272. Revolutionary Statue and Map.

273. Tsai Lun (A.D. ?–121, inventor of paper making process).

1962. Albanian Independence. 50th Anniv.

2053. **272.** 8 f. sepia and blue .. 20 10
2054. – 10 f. multicoloured .. 30 15
DESIGN: 10 f. Albanian flag and pioneer.

1962. Scientists of Ancient China. Multicoloured.

2055. 4 f. Type **273** 10 8
2056. 4 f. Paper-making .. 10 8
2057. 8 f. Sun Szu-miao (581–682, physician) 15 10
2058. 8 f. Preparing medical treatise 15 10
2059. 10 f. Shen Ko (1031–1095, geologist) 25 12
2060. 10 f. Making field notes .. 25 12
2061. 20 f. Ku Shou-chin (1231–1316, astronomer) .. 60 20
2062. 20 f. Astronomical equipment 60 20

274. Tank Monument, Havana.

DESIGNS—As T **274**: No. 2064, Cuban revolutionaries. 2067 Cuban soldier. 2068, Castro and Cuban flag. LARGER (48½ × 27 mm.) 2065, Crowd in Havana (value on left). 2066, Crowd in Peking (value on right).

1963. Cuban Revolution. 4th Anniv.

2063. **274.** 4 f. sepia and red .. 30 12
2064. – 4 f. black and green 30 12
2065. – 8 f. lake and brown 60 20
2066. – 8 f. lake and brown .. 60 20
2067. – 10 f. black and buff .. 1·00 25
2068. – 10 f. sepia, red & blue 1·00 25

275. Tibetan Clouded Yellow.

276. Marx and Engels.

1963. Butterflies. Multicoloured. No gum.

2069. 4 f. (1) T **275** 8 5
2070. 4 f. (2) Tritailed Glory .. 8 5
2071. 4 f. (3) Neumogeni Jungle Queen 8 5
2072. 4 f. (4) Washan Swordtail 8 5
2073. 4 f. (5) Striped Ringlet .. 8 5
2074. 8 f. (6) Green Dragontail 15 5
2075. 8 f. (7) Dilunuleted Peacock 15 5
2076. 8 f. (8) Yamfly 15 5
2077. 8 f. (9) Golden Kaisar-i-Hind 15 5
2078. 8 f. (10) Mushaell Hairstreak 20 8
2079. 10 f. (11) Yellow Orange-tip 20 8
2080. 10 f. (12) Great Jay .. 20 8
2081. 10 f. (13) Striped Punch .. 20 8
2082. 10 f. (14) Hainan Violet-beak 20 8
2083. 10 f. (15) Omei Skipper .. 20 8
2084. 20 f. (16) Philippines Birdwing 30 12
2085. 20 f. (17) Richthofeni Red Apollo 30 12
2086. 22 f. (18) Blue-banded King Crow 30 15
2087. 30 f. (19) Solskyi Copper .. 50 20
2088. 50 f. (20) Yunnan Clipper 70 30

1963. Karl Marx. 145th Birth Anniv. Inscr. "1818-1963". No gum.

2089. – 8 f. black, flesh & gold 35 12
2090. – 8 f. red and gold .. 35 12
2091. **276.** 8 f. chocolate & gold 35 12
DESIGNS: No. 2089, Marx. 2090, Slogan "Workers of the World Unite!" over cover of 1st edition of "Communist Manifesto".

277. Child with Top.

278. Giant Panda eating Apples.

1963. Children. Designs multicoloured. Inscr. in black and red. Background colours given. No gum.

2092. **277.** 4 f. turquoise-blue .. 8 5
2093. – 4 f. cinnamon .. 8 5
2094. – 8 f. grey 15 5
2095. – 8 f. blue 15 5
2096. – 8 f. beige 15 5
2097. – 8 f. slate 15 5
2098. – 8 f. sage-green .. 15 5
2099. – 8 f. silver-grey .. 15 5
2100. – 10 f. grey-green .. 20 8
2101. – 10 f. violet 20 8
2102. – 20 f. yellow-drab .. 50 12
2103. – 20 f. green 50 12
DESIGNS (each shows a child): No. 2093, Eating candied hawberries. 2094, As "traffic policemen". 2095, With toy windmill. 2096, Listening to caged cricket. 2097, With toy sword. 2098, Embroidering. 2099, With umbrella. 2100, Playing with sand. 2101, Playing table-tennis. 2102, Doing sums. 2103, Flying kite.

1963. Chinese Folk Dances (2nd issue). As T **270** but inscr. "(261) 1962" to "(266) 1962" in bottom right corner. Multicoloured. No gum.

2104. 4 f. Puyi "Weaving Cloth" 10 5
2105. 8 f. Kazakh 15 8
2106. 10 f. Olunchun 15 8
2107. 20 f. Kaochan "Labour" 30 12
2108. 30 f. Miao "Reed-pipe" 40 20
2109. 50 f. Korean "Fan" .. 70 30

1963. Chinese Folk Dances (3rd issue). As T **270** but inscr. "(279) 1963" to "(284) 1963" in bottom right corner. Multicoloured. No gum.

2110. 4 f. Yu "Wedding Ceremony" 10 5
2111. 8 f. Pai "Encircling Mountain Forest" 15 8
2112. 10 f. Yao "Long Drum" .. 15 8
2113. 20 f. Li "Third Day of Third Month" 30 12
2114. 30 f. Kava "Knife" .. 40 20
2115. 50 f. Tai "Peacock" .. 70 30

1963. Giant Panda. Perf. or imperf.

2116. **278.** 8 f. black and blue .. 30 15
2117. – 8 f. black and green 30 15
2118. – 10 f. black and drab 40 15
DESIGNS: As T **278**: No. 2117, Giant panda eating bamboo shoots. HORIZ. (52×31 mm.): 10 f. Two giant pandas.

279. Table-Tennis Player.

280. Golden-haired Monkey.

1963. 27th World Table-Tennis Championships.

2119. **279.** 8 f. grey 30 12
2120. – 8 f. brown 30 12
DESIGN: No. 2120 Trophies won by Chinese team.

1963. Golden-haired Monkeys. Multicoloured.

2121. 8 f. Type **280** 20 10
2122. 10 f. Two monkeys .. 25 12
2123. 22 f. Two monkeys on branch of tree 45 20

281. Old Pines of Hwangshan.

1963. Hwangshan Landscapes. Multicoloured.

2124. 4 f. (1) Mount of Jade Screen 10 8
2125. 4 f. (2) "The Guest welcoming Pines" .. 10 8
2126. 4 f. (3) Pines and Rocks behind the Lake .. 10 8
2127. 4 f. (4) Terrace of Keeping Cool 10 8
2128. 8 f. (5) Mount of the Heavenly Capital .. 20 8
2129. 8 f. (6) Mount of Scissors 20 8
2130. 8 f. (7) Forest of Ten Thousand Pines .. 20 8
2131. 8 f. (8) "The Flowering Bush in a Dream" .. 20 8
2132. 10 f. (9) Mount of the Lotus Flower 25 10
2133. 10 f. (10) Cumulus Flood Waves of the Eastern Lake 25 10
2134. 10 f. (11) T **281** 25 10
2135. 10 f. (12) Cumulus on the Eastern Lake 25 10
2136. 20 f. (13) The Stalagmite Mountain Range .. 30 15
2137. 22 f. (14) "The Apes of Stone" watch the lake below 30 15
2138. 30 f. (15) The Forest of Lions 50 25
2139. 50 f. (16) The Fairy Isles of Peng Lai .. .. 1·00 30
The 4 f. and 8 f. values are vert.

282. Football.

283. Clay Rooster and Goat.

1963. "GANEFO" Athletic Games, Jakarta.

2140. **282.** 8 f. red & blk. on lav. 30 10
2141. – 8 f. blue & blk. on buff 30 10
2142. – 8 f. brn., & blk. on blue 30 10
2143. – 8 f. pur. & blk. on mve. 30 10
2144. – 10 f. multicoloured .. 50 15
DESIGNS—As T **282**: No. 2141, Throwing the discus. 2142, Diving. 2143, Gymnastics. HORIZ. (48½×27½ mm.): 10 f. Athletes on parade.

1963. Chinese Folk Toys. Multicoloured. No gum.

2145. 4 f. (1) T **283** 8 5
2146. 4 f. (4) Cloth camel .. 8 5
2147. 4 f. (7) Cloth tigers .. 8 5
2148. 8 f. (2) Clay ox and rider 15 8
2149. 8 f. (5) Cloth rabbit, wooden figure and clay cock .. 15 8
2150. 8 f. (8) Straw cock .. 15 8
2151. 10 f. (3) Cloth donkey and clay bird 20 10
2152. 10 f. (6) Clay lion .. 20 10
2153. 10 f. (9) Clay-paper tumbler and cloth tiger .. 20 10

284. Vietnamese Family.

285. Cuban and Chinese Flags.

1963. "Liberation of South Vietnam". Multicoloured.

2154. 8 f. T **284** 25 10
2155. 8 f. Vietnamese with flag 25 10

1964. Liberation of Cuba. 5th Anniv. Multicoloured.

2156. 8 f. T **285** .. 70 25
2157. 8 f. Boy waving flag .. 1·00 25

286. Woman driving Tractor.

287. "Sino-African Friendship".

1964. "Women of the People's Commune". Multicoloured.

2158. 8 f. (1) T **286** 15 10
2159. 8 f. (2) Harvesting .. 15 10
2160. 8 f. (3) Picking cotton .. 15 10
2161. 8 f. (4) Picking fruit .. 15 10
2162. 8 f. (5) Reading book .. 15 10
2163. 8 f. (6) Holding rifle .. 15 10

1964. African Freedom Day.

2164. **287.** 8 f. multicoloured .. 20 10
2165. – 8 f. chocolate & black 20 10
DESIGN: No. 2165, African beating drum.

DESIGN: No. 2167, Workers and banners.

288. Marx, Engels, Lenin and Stalin.

1964. Labour Day.

2166. **288.** 8 f. black, red & gold 40 15
2167. – 8 f. black, red & gold 40 15

289. Date Orchard, Yenan.

290. Map of Viet-Nam and Flag.

1964. "Yenan—Shrine of the Chinese Revolution". Multicoloured.

2168. 8 f. (1) Type **289** .. 30 10
2169. 8 f. (2) Central Auditorium, Yang Chia Ling .. 20 8
2170. 8 f. (3) Mao Tse-tung's Office and Residence at Date Orchard, Yenan .. 20 8

2171. 8 f. (4) Auditorium, Wang Chia Ping 20 8
2172. 8 f. (5) Border Region Assembly Hall .. 30 10
2173. 52 f. (6) Pagoda Hill .. 1·10 30

1964. South Vietnam Victory Campaign.
2174. **290.** 8 f. grey, blue, red and yellow .. 50 15

291. "The Alchemist's Glowing Crucible". (peony).

292. "Chueh" (wine cup).

1964. Chinese Peonies. Multicoloured.
2175. 4 f. (1) Type **291** .. 15 8
2176. 4 f. (2) Night-shining Jade 15 8
2177. 8 f. (3) Purple Kuo's Cap 20 10
2178. 8 f. (4) Chao Pinks .. 20 10
2179. 8 f. (5) Yao Yellows .. 20 10
2180. 8 f. (6) Twin Beauties .. 20 10
2181. 8 f. (7) Ice-veiled Rubies 20 10
2182. 10 f. (8) Gold-sprinkled Chinese Ink 25 10
2183. 10 f. (9) Cinnabar Jar .. 25 10
2184. 10 f. (10) Lantien Jade .. 25 10
2185. 10 f. (11) Imperial Robe Yellow.. .. 25 10
2186. 10 f. (12) Hu Reds .. 25 10
2187. 20 f. (13) Pea Green .. 50 15
2188. 43 f. (14) Wei Purples .. 90 25
2189. 52 f. (15) Intoxicated Celestial Peach .. 1·00 25

1964. Bronze Vessels of the Yin Dynasty (before 1050 B.C.). Centres in various shades of green, olive or blue; values, inscr. and frames in black.
2190. 4 f. (1) Type **292** .. 8 5
2191. 4 f. (2) "Ku" (beaker) .. 8 5
2192. 8 f. (3) "Kuang" (wine urn) 12 5
2193. 8 f. (4) "Chia" (wine cup) 12 5
2194. 10 f. (5) "Tsun" (wine vessel) 20 10
2195. 10 f. (6) "Yu" (wine urn) 20 10
2196. 20 f. (7) "Tsun" (wine vessel) 35 15
2197. 20 f. (8) "Ting" (ceremonial cauldron) .. 35 15

293. "Harvesting".

294. Marx, Engels and Trafalgar Square, London (vicinity of old St. Martin's Hall).

1964. Agricultural Students. Multicoloured.
2198. 8 f. (1) Type **293** .. 30 10
2199. 8 f. (2) "Sapling planting" 30 10
2200. 8 f. (3) "Study" .. 30 10
2201. 8 f. (4) "Scientific experiment" 30 10

1964. "First International". Cent.
2202. **294.** 8 f. red, brown & gold 5·00 3·00

295. Rejoicing People.

296. Oil Derrick.

1964. People's Republic. 15th Anniv. Multicoloured.
2203. 8 f. (1) Type **295** .. 70 15
2204. 8 f. (2) Chinese flag .. 70 15
2205. 8 f. (3) As T **295** in reverse 70 15
Nos. 2203/5 were issued in the form of a triptych, in sheets.

1964. Petroleum Industry. Multicoloured.
2206. 4 f. Geological surveyors and van 50 10
2207. 8 f. Type **286** 50 10
2208. 8 f. Oil-extraction equipment 50 10
2209. 10 f. Refinery 50 10
2210. 20 f. Railway petroleum trucks .. .. 1·75 30
The 4 f. and 20 f. are horiz. designs.

297. Albanian and Chinese Flags and Plants. **298.** Dam under Construction.

1964. Liberation of Albania. 20th Anniv.
2211. **297.** 8 f. red, black, green and yellow 35 12
2212. – 10 f. black, red & yell. 60 20
DESIGN: 10 f. Enver Hoxha and Albanian arms.

1964. Hsinankiang Hydro-Electric Power Station. Multicoloured.
2213. 4 f. Type **298** .. 40 12
2214. 8 f. Installation of turbo-generator rotor .. 40 12
2215. 8 f. Main dam 40 12
2216. 20 f. Pylon .. .. 2·25 30

299. Fertilisers.

1964. Chemical Industry. Main design and inscr. in black; background colours given.
2217. 8 f. (1) red 20 12
2218. 8 f. (2) green 20 12
2219. 8 f. (3) brown 20 12
2220. 8 f. (4) magenta 20 12
2221. 8 f. (5) blue 20 12
2222. 8 f. (6) orange 20 12
2223. 8 f. (7) violet 20 12
2224. 8 f. (8) blue-green .. 20 12
DESIGNS: (1) T **299**. (2) Plastics. (3) Medicinal drugs. (4) Rubber. (5) Insecticides. (6) Acids. (7) Alkalis. (8) Synthetic fibres.

300. Mao Tse-tung standing in Room.

1965. Tsunyi Conf. 30th Anniv. Multicoloured.
2225. 8 f. (1) Type **300** .. 2·00 1·60
2226. 8 f. (2) Mao Tse-tung .. 2·00 1·60
2227. 8 f. (3) "Victory at Loushan Pass" .. 2·00 1·60
No. 2226 is vert. (26½ × 36 mm.).

301. Conference Hall.

302. Lenin.

1965. Bandung Conf. 10th Anniv. Multicoloured.
2228. 8 f. Type **301** 25 8
2229. 8 f. Rejoicing Africans and Asians 25 8

1965. Lenin. 95th Birth Anniv.
2230. **302.** 8 f. multicoloured 45 20

303. Table-tennis Player.

304. Government Building.

1965. World Table-tennis Championships, Peking. Each red, gold, black and green.
2231. **303.** 8 f. (1) 20 10
2232. – 8 f. (2) 20 10
2233. – 8 f. (3) 20 10
2234. – 8 f. (4) 20 10
DESIGNS: Nos. 2232/4 each show different views of table-tennis players.

1965. No gum.
2235. **304.** 1 f. brown 5 5
2236. A. 1½ f. purple 5 5
2237. B. 2 f. grey-green .. 5 5
2238. C. 3 f. turquoise .. 5 5
2239. **304.** 4 f. blue 5 5
2239a. A. 5 f. plum 8 5
2240. B. 8 f. red 5 5
2241. C. 10 f. drab 8 5
2242. **304.** 20 f. violet 15 5
2243. A. 22 f. orange 20 5
2244. B. 30 f. green 30 5
2244a. C. 50 f. ultramarine .. 50 10
DESIGNS: A, Gate of Heavenly Peace. B, People's Hall. C, Military Museum.

305. All China T.U. Federation Team scaling Mt. Minya Konka.

306. Marx and Lenin.

1965. Chinese Mountaineering Achievements. Each black, yellow and blue.
2245. 8 f. (1) Type **305** .. 25 12
2246. 8 f. (2) Men and women's mixed team on slopes of Muztagh Ata 25 12
2247. 8 f. (3) Climbers on Mt. Jolmo Lungma .. 25 12
2248. 8 f. (4) Women's team camping on Kongur Tiuble Tagh 25 12
2249. 8 f. (5) Climbers on Shisha Pangma 25 12

1965. Postal Ministers' Congress, Peking.
2250. **306.** 8 f. multicoloured .. 60 20

307. Tseping.

1965. "Chingkang Mountains—Cradle of the Chinese Revolution". Multicoloured.
2251. 4 f. (1) Type **307** .. 8 5
2252. 8 f. (2) Sanwantsun .. 15 10
2253. 8 f. (3) Octagonal Building, Maoping 15 10
2254. 8 f. (4) River and bridge at Lungshih .. 15 10
2255. 8 f. (5) Tachingtsun .. 15 10
2256. 10 f. (6) Bridge at Lungyuankou 20 15
2257. 10 f. (7) Hwangyangchieh 20 15
2258. 52 f. (8) Chingkang peaks 90 50

308. Soldiers with Texts.

1965. People's Liberation Army. Multicoloured.
2259. 8 f. (1) Type **308** .. 40 20
2260. 8 f. (2) Soldiers reading book 40 20
2261. 8 f. (3) Soldier with grenade-thrower 40 20
2262. 8 f. (4) Giving tuition in firing rifle 40 20
2263. 8 f. (5) Soldiers at rest .. 40 20
2264. 8 f. (6) Bayonet charge .. 40 20
2265. 8 f. (7) Soldier with banners 40 20
2266. 8 f. (8) Military band .. 40 20
Nos. 2263/6 are vert.

309. "Welcome to Peking".

310. Soldier firing Weapon.

1965. Chinese—Japanese Youth Meeting, Peking. Multicoloured.
2267. 4 f. (1) Type **309** .. 10 8
2268. 8 f. (2) Chinese and Japanese youths with linked arms 15 8
2269. 8 f. (3) Chinese and Japanese girls 15 8
2270. 10 f. (4) Musical entertainment 25 12
2271. 22 f. (5) Emblem of Meeting 45 20

1965. "Viet-Namese People's Struggle".
2272. **310.** 8 f. (1) chestnut & red 30 12
2273. – 8 f. (2) olive and red 30 12
2274. – 8 f. (3) maroon & red 30 12
2275. – 8 f. (4) black & verm. 30 12
DESIGNS—VERT. (2) Soldier with captured weapons. (3) Soldier giving victory salute. HORIZ. (48½ × 26 mm.): (4) "Peoples of the world".

311. "Victory".

312. Football.

1965. Victory over Japanese. 20th Anniv.
2276. – 8 f. (1) multicoloured 60 25
2277. – 8 f. (2) green and red 60 25
2278. **311.** 8 f. (3) sepia and red 60 25
2279. – 8 f. (4) green and red 60 25
DESIGNS—HORIZ. (50½ × 36 mm.): (1) Mao Tse-tung writing. As T **311**—HORIZ. (2) Soldiers crossing Yellow River. (4) Recruits in cart.

1965. National Games. Multicoloured.
2280. 4 f. (1) Type **312** .. 20 5
2281. 4 f. (2) Archery 20 5
2282. 8 f. (3) Throwing the javelin 25 5
2283. 8 f. (4) Gymnastics .. 25 5
2284. 8 f. (5) Volleyball .. 25 5
2285. 10 f. (6) Opening ceremony 30 8
2286. 10 f. (7) Cycling 30 8
2287. 20 f. (8) Diving 50 12
2288. 22 f. (9) Hurdling .. 60 15
2289. 30 f. (10) Weightlifting .. 1·10 25
2290. 43 f. (11) Basketball .. 1·60 40
The 10 f. (6) is larger, 56 × 35½ mm.

313. Textile Workers.

1965. Women in Industry. Multicoloured.
2291. 8 f. (1) Type **313** 45 10
2292. 8 f. (2) Machine building 45 10
2293. 8 f. (3) Building construction 45 10
2294. 8 f. (4) Studying 45 10
2295. 8 f. (5) Militia guard .. 45 10

314. Children playing with ball.

1966. Children's Games. Multicoloured.
2296. 4 f. (1) Type **314** 10 5
2297. 4 f. (2) Racing 10 5
2298. 8 f. (3) Tobogganing .. 20 8
2299. 8 f. (4) Exercising .. 20 8
2300. 8 f. (5) Swimming .. 20 8
2301. 8 f. (6) Shooting 20 8
2302. 10 f. (7) Jumping with rope 25 10
2303. 52 f. (8) Playing table-tennis 90 40

315. Mobile Transformer.

1966. New Industrial Machines.
2304. **315.** 4 f. (1) black & yellow 10 5
2305. – 8 f. (2) black and blue 15 5
2306. – 8 f. (3) black and pink 15 5
2307. – 8 f. (4) black & olive 15 5
2308. – 8 f. (5) black & purple 15 5
2309. – 10 f. (6) black and grey 50 8
2310. – 10 f. (7) black & turq. 50 8
2311. – 22 f. (8) black & lilac 1·60 20
DESIGNS—VERT. (2), Electron microscope. (4), Vertical boring and turning machine. (6), Hydraulic press. (8), Electron accelerator. HORIZ. (3) Lathe. (5) Gear-grinding machine. (7), Milling machine.

316. Women of Military and Other Services.

1966. Women in Public Service. Mult.
2312. 8 f. (1) Type **316** 20 8
2313. 8 f. (2) Train conductress 20 8
2314. 8 f. (3) Red Cross worker 20 8
2315. 8 f. (4) Kindergarten teacher 20 8
2316. 8 f. (5) Roadsweeper .. 20 8
2317. 8 f. (6) Hairdresser .. 20 8
2318. 8 f. (7) Bus conductress .. 20 8
2319. 8 f. (8) Travelling saleswoman 20 8
2320. 8 f. (9) Canteen worker .. 20 8
2321. 8 f. (10) Rural postwoman 20 8

317. "Thunderstorm" (sculpture).

318. Dr. Sun Yat-sen.

1966. Afro-Asian Writers' Meeting.
2322. **317.** 8 f. black and red .. 20 12
2323. – 22 f. gold, yellow & red 40 15
DESIGN: 22 f. Meeting emblem.

1966. Dr. Sun Yat-sen. Birth Cent.
2324. **318.** 8 f. sepia and buff .. 80 40

319. Athletes with Mao Tse-tung's Portrait.

1966. "Cultural Revolution" Games. Multicoloured.
2325. 8 f. (1) Type **319** 40 20
2326. 8 f. (2) Athletes with linked arms hold Mao texts .. 40 20
2327. 8 f. (3) Two women athletes with Mao texts .. 40 20
2328. 8 f. (4) Athletes reading Mao texts 40 20
SIZES: No. 2326, As T **319**, but vert. Nos. 2327/8, 36½ × 25 mm.

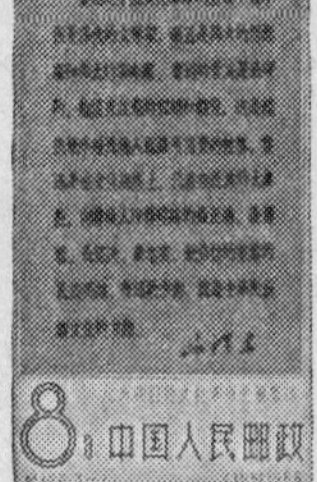

320. Mao's Appreciation of Lu Hsun (patriot and writer).

321. "Be Resolute . . ." (Mao Tse-tung).

1966. Lu Hsun Commem.
2329. **320.** 8 f. (1) black & orge. 40 30
2330. – 8 f. (2) blk., flesh & red 40 30
2331. – 8 f. (3) black & orge. 40 30
DESIGNS: (2) Lu Hsun. (3) Lu Hsun's manuscript.

1967. Heroic Oilwell Firefighters.
2332. **321.** 8 f. (1) gold, red & blk. 80 40
2333. – 8 f. (2) black & verm. 50 25
2334. – 8 f. (3) black & verm. 50 25
DESIGNS—HORIZ. (48 × 27 mm.): (2) Drilling Team No. 32111 fighting flames. VERT. (3) Smothering flames with tarpaulins.

322. Liu Ying-chun (military hero).

1967. Liu Ying-chun Commem. Multicoloured.
2335. 8 f. (1) Type **322** .. .. 1·00 30
2336. 8 f. (2) Liu Ying-chun holding book of Mao texts .. .. .. 1·00 30
2337. 8 f. (3) Liu Ying-chun holding horse's bridle .. 1·00 30
2338. 8 f. (4) Liu Ying-chun looking at film slide .. 1·00 30
2339. 8 f. (5) Liu Ying-chun lecturing .. .. 1·00 30
2340. 8 f. (6) Liu Ying-chun making fatal attempt to stop bolting horse .. 1·00 30

323. Soldier, Nurse, Workers and Banners.

1967. 3rd Five-Year Plan. Multicoloured.
2341. 8 f. (1) Type **323** 75 25
2342. 8 f. (2) Armed woman, peasants and banners 75 25

324. Mao Tse-tung.

325. Mao Text (39 characters).

1967. "Thoughts of Mao Tse-tung" (1st issue). Similar designs showing Mao texts each gold and red. To assist identification of Nos. 2344/53 the total number of Chinese characters within the frames are given.

(a) Type **324.**
2343. 8 f. multicoloured .. 2·75 60

(b) As Type **325.** Red outer frames.
2344. 8 f. Type **325** .. .. 2·75 60
2345. 8 f. (50 characters) .. 2·75 60
2346. 8 f. (39—in six lines) .. 2·75 60
2347. 8 f. (53) .. .. .. 2·75 60
2348. 8 f. (46) .. .. .. 2·75 60

(c) As Type **325.** Gold outer frames.
2349. 8 f. (41) .. .. .. 2·75 60
2350. 8 f. (49) .. .. .. 2·75 60
2351. 8 f. (35) .. .. .. 2·75 60
2352. 8 f. (22) .. .. .. 2·75 60
2353. 8 f. (29) .. .. .. 2·75 60
Nos. 2344/8 and 2349/53 were respectively issued together se-tenant in strips of five within the sheet.
See also No. 2405.

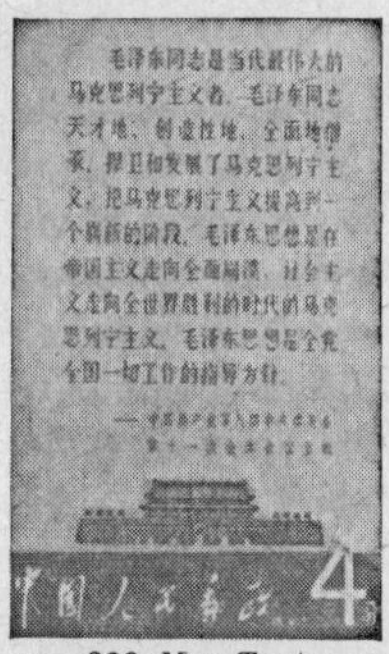
326. Mao Text.

1967. Labour Day.
2354. **326.** 4 f. multicoloured .. 5·00 1·25
2355. – 8 f. multicoloured .. 5·00 1·25
2356. – 8 f. multicoloured .. 5·00 1·25
2357. – 8 f. multicoloured .. 5·00 1·25
2358. – 8 f. multicoloured .. 5·00 1·25
DESIGNS (Mao Tse-tung and): No. 2355, Poem. 2356, Multi-racial crowd with texts. 2357, Red Guards. (36 × 50½ mm.): Mao with hand raised in greeting.
For stamps similar to No. 2358, see Nos. 2367/9.

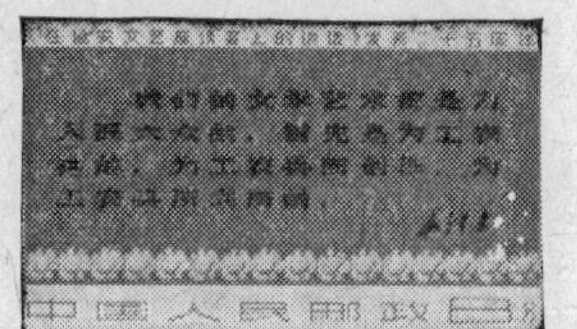

327. Mao Text.

1967. Mao Tse-tung's "Talks on Literature and Art". 25th Anniv.
2359. **327.** 8 f. black, red & yellow 4·00 1·25
2360. – 8 f. black, red & yellow 4·00 1·25
2361. – 8 f. multicoloured .. 4·00 1·25
DESIGNS: No. 2360, As Type **327** but different text. (50 × 36½ mm.): 2361, Mao supporters in procession.

328. Mao Tse-tung.

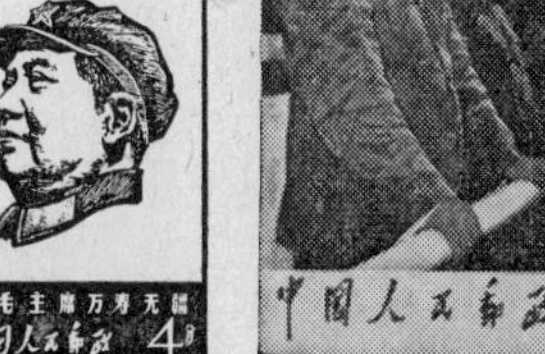

329. Mao Tse-tung and Lin Piao.

1967. Chinese Communist Party. 46th Anniv.
2362. **328.** 4 f. red 35 15
2363. 8 f. red 60 30
2364. 35 f. maroon .. 70 35
2365. 43 f. vermilion .. 80 50
2366. 52 f. cerise .. 1·25 70

1967. "Our Great Teacher". Multicoloured.
2367. 8 f. Type **329** .. 20·00 10·00
2368. 8 f. Mao Tse-tung (horiz.) 10·00 4·00
2369. 10 f. Mao Tse-tung conferring with Lin Piao (horiz.) .. .. 20·00 10·00
For 8 f. stamp showing Mao with hand raised in greeting, see No. 2358.

330. Mao Tse-tung as "Sun".

1967. People's Republic. 18th Anniv. Multicoloured.
2370. 8 f. Type **330** .. 5·50 1·25
2371. 8 f. Mao Tse-tung with representatives of Communist countries .. 5·50 1·25

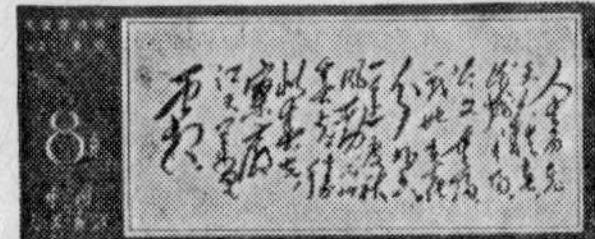
331. (Reduced size illustration. Actual size 62 × 26 mm.).

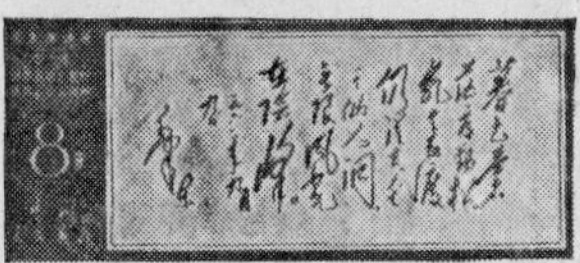
332. (Reduced size illustration. Actual size 62 × 26 mm.).

333. Mao Writing Poems at Desk.

1967. "Poems of Mao Tse-tung". (1st Series).
2372. **331.** 8 f. blk., yell. & red 3·00 45
2373. **332.** 8 f. blk., yell. & red 3·00 45
2374. **333.** 10 f. multicoloured 3·00 45
See also Nos. 2385/7 and 2389/96.

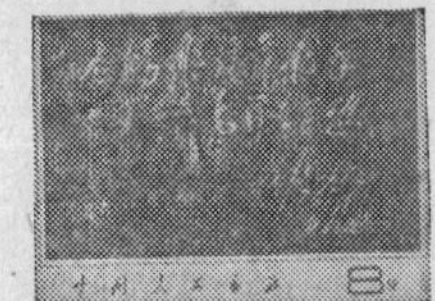
334. Epigram on Chairman Mao by Lin Piao.

1967. Fleet Expansionists' Congress.
2375. **334.** 8 f. gold and red .. 25·00 2·00

335. Mao Tse-tung and Procession.

1968. "Revolutionary Literature and Art" (1st issue). Multicoloured designs showing scenes from People's Operas.
2376. 8 f. Type **335** .. .. 2·00 50
2377. 8 f. "Raid on the White Tiger Regiment" .. 2·00 50
2378. 8 f. "Taking Tiger Mountain" .. .. .. 2·00 50
2379. 8 f. "On the Docks" .. 2·00 50
2380. 8 f. "Shachiapang" .. 2·00 50
2381. 8 f. "The Red Lantern" 2·00 50
No. 2381 is vert.

336. "Red Detachment of Women" (ballet).

1968. "Revolutionary Literature and Art". (2nd Series).

2382. **336.** 8 f. multicoloured .. 2·00 50
2383. – 8 f. multicoloured .. 2·00 50
2384. – 8 f. multicoloured .. 2·00 50

DESIGNS—As T **336**: No. 2383. "The White-haired Girl" (ballet). LARGER (50×36 mm): 2384, Mao Tse-tung, Symphony Orchestra and Chorus (scene from "Shachiapang" opera).

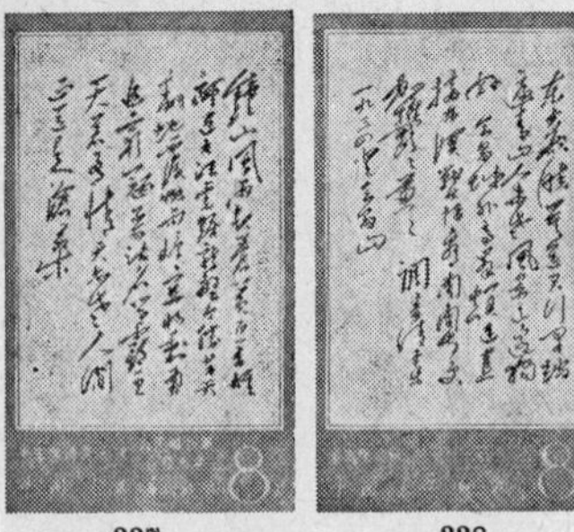

337. **338.**

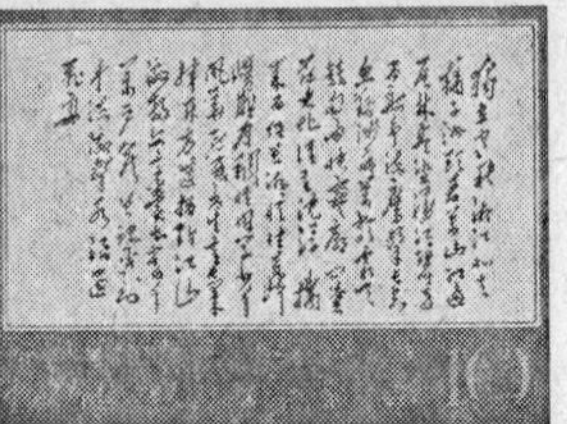

339.

1968. "Poems of Mao Tse-tung" (2nd Series).

2385. **337.** 8 f. blk., yell. & red 2·75 60
2386. **338.** 8 f. blk., yell. & red 2·75 60
2387. **339.** 10 f. blk., yell. & red 2·75 60

340. Mao Tse-tung ("Unite still more closely . . .").

1968. Mao's Anti-American Declaration.

2388. **340.** 8 f. brown, gold & red 10·00 3·00

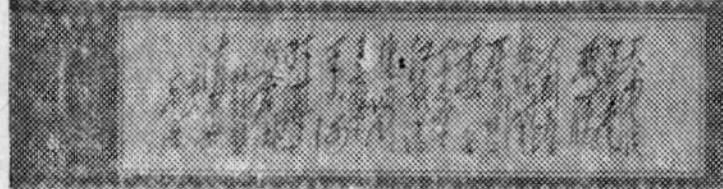

341. (Reduced size illustration. Actual size 81×20 mm.).

342. (Actual size 81×20 mm.).

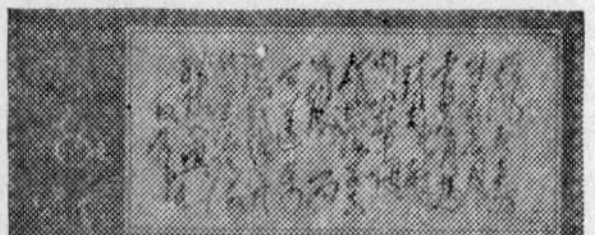

343. (Actual size 62×26 mm.).

344. (Actual size 62×26 mm.).

345. (Actual size 54×40 mm.).

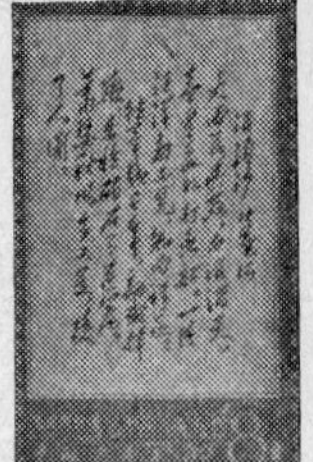

346. (Actual size 31×52 mm.). **347.** (Actual size 31×52 mm.).

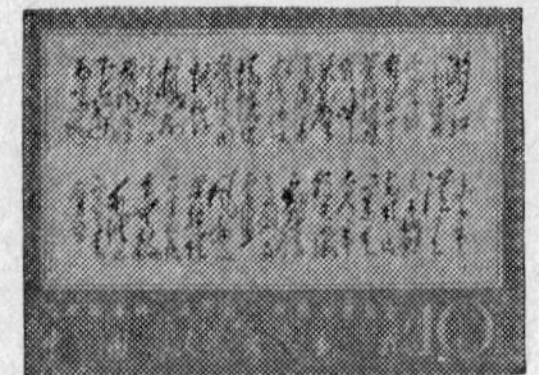

348. (Actual size 54×40 mm.).

1968. "Poems of Mao Tse-tung" (3rd Series).

2389. **341.** 4 f. blk., yell. & red 2·50 50
2390. **342.** 4 f. blk., yell. & red 2·50 50
2391. **343.** 8 f. blk., yell. & red 2·50 50
2392. **344.** 8 f. blk., yell. & red 2·50 50
2393. **345.** 8 f. blk., yell. & red 2·50 50
2394. **346.** 8 f. blk., yell. & red 2·50 50
2395. **347.** 8 f. blk., yell. & red 2·50 50
2396. **348.** 10 f. blk., yell. & red 2·50 50

349. **350.**

351. **352.**

353.

1968. "Directives of Mao Tse-tung".

2397. **349.** 8 f. brown, red & yell. 4·00 1·00
2398. **350.** 8 f. brown, red & yell. 4·00 1·00
2399. **351.** 8 f. brown, red & yell. 4·00 1·00
2400. **352.** 8 f. brown, red & yell. 4·00 1·00
2401. **353.** 8 f. brown, red & yell. 4·00 1·00

Nos. 2397/2401 were issued together se-tenant in strips of 5 within the sheet.

354. Inscription by Lin Piao. 26 July, 1965.

1968. People's Liberation Army. 41st Anniv.

2402. **354.** 8 f. black, gold & red 12·00 1·50

355. "Chairman Mao goes to Anyuan" (Chiang Ching).

1968. Mao's Youth.

2403. **355.** 8 f. multicoloured .. 15·00 4·00

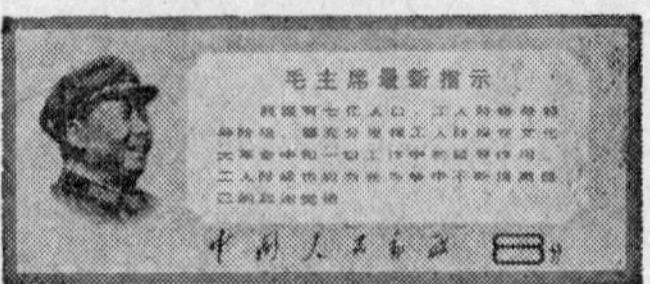

356. Mao Tse-tung and Text.

1968. "Thoughts of Mao Tse-tung" (2nd issue).

2405. **356.** 8 f. brown and red .. 10·00 1·50

357. Displaying "The Words of Mao Tse-tung".

1968. "The Words of Mao Tse-tung". No gum.

2406. **357.** 8 f. multicoloured .. 80 40

358. Yangtse Bridge.

1968. Completion of Yangtse Bridge Nanking. Multicoloured. No gum.

2407. 4 f. Type **358** 70 45
2408. 8 f. Buses on bridge .. 70 55
2409. 8 f. View of end portals .. 70 20
2410. 10 f. Aerial view .. 70 20

Nos. 2408/9 are larger, size 49×27 mm.

359. Li Yu-ho singing "I am filled with Courage and Strength".

1969. Songs from "The Red Lantern" Opera. Multicoloured. No gum.

2411. 8 f. Type **359** 80 20
2412. 8 f. Li Li-mei singing "Hatred in my Heart" .. 80 20

360. Pagoda Hill, Yenan. **361.** Conference Hall, Tsungi.

1969. Multicoloured. No gum.

2413. – 1½ f. red, brn. and lilac 15 5
2414. **360.** 8 f. brn., grn. & cream 15 5
2415. – 8 f. red and purple .. 15 5
2416. – 8 f. brown and blue .. 20 8
2417a. **361.** 20 f. blue, pur. and red 50 25
2418. – 50 f. brown and green 60 35

DESIGNS: As Type **360**. No. 2413, Communist Party Building, Shanghai. No. 2415, Gate of Heavenly Peace, Peking. No. 2418, Mao Tse-tung's house, Yenan. As Type **361**. No. 2416, Heroes' Monument, Peking.

See also Nos. 2455/65.

362. Rice Harvesters.

1969. Agricultural Workers. Multicoloured. No gum.

2419. 4 f. Type **362** 70 50
2420. 8 f. Grain harvest .. 70 30
2421. 8 f. Study Group with "Thoughts of Mao" .. 70 30
2422. 10 f. Red Cross worker with mother and child .. 70 30

363. Snow Patrol. **364.** Farmworker.

1969. Defence of Chen Pao Tao in the Ussuri River. Multicoloured. No gum.

2423. 8 f. Type **363** 20 10
2424. 8 f. Guards by river .. 20 10
2425. 8 f. Servicemen and Militia 20 10
2426. 35 f. As No. 2424 .. 60 25
2427. 43 f. Type **363** 70 30

1969. "The Chinese People" (woodcuts). No gum.

2428. **362.** 4 f. maroon and orge. 20 20
2429. – 8 f. purple and orange 20 20
2430. – 10 f. green and orange 20 20

DESIGNS: 8 f. Foundryman. 10 f. Soldier.

365. Chin Hsun-hua in Water. **366.** Cavalry Patrol.

1970. Heroic Death of Chin Hsun-hua in Kirin Border Floods. No gum.

2431. **365.** 8 f. black & vermilion 75 75

1970. People's Liberation Army. 43rd Anniv. No gum.

2432. **366.** 8 f. multicoloured .. 75 75

367. "Yang Tse-jung, Army Scout". **368.** Tractor Driver.

1970. "Taking Tiger Mountain" (Revolutionary opera). Multicoloured. No gum.

2433. 8 f. (1) Type **367** .. 30 30
2434. 8 f. (2) "The patrol sets out" (horiz.) 30 30
2435. 8 f. (3) "Leaping through the forest" 30 30
2436. 8 f. (4) "Li Yung-chi's farewell" 30 30
2437. 8 f. (5) "Yang Tse-jung in disguise" 30 30
2438. 8 f. (6) "Congratulating Yang Tse-jung" (horiz.) 30 30

Nos. 2436/7 are larger, 27×48 mm.

1970. No gum.

2439. **368.** 5 f. black, red & pink 12 10
2440. – 1 y. black and red .. 1·00 50

DESIGN-HORIZ. 1 y. Foundryman.

369. Soldiers in Snow.

1970. Defence of Chen Pao Tao. 2nd Anniv. No gum.

2441. **369.** 4 f. multicoloured .. 12 12

370. Communard Standard. **372.** Workers and People's Hall, Peking.

371. Communist Party Building, Shanghai.

1971. Paris Commune. Cent. Multicoloured. No gum.

2442. **370.** 4 f. multicoloured .. 12 12
2443. – 8 f. brn., pink and red 20 20
2444. – 10 f. red, brn. and pink 20 20
2445. – 22 f. brn., red and pink 35 35

DESIGNS—HORIZ. 8 f. Fighting in Paris, March 1871. 22 f. Communards in Place Vendome. VERT. 10 f. Commune proclaimed at the Hotel de Ville.

1971. Chinese Communist Party. 50th Anniv. Multicoloured. No gum.

2446. 4 f. (12) Type **371** .. 8 8
2447. 4 f. (13) National Peasant Movement Inst., Canton 8 8
2448. 8 f. (14) Chingkang Mountains 15 15
2449. 8 f. (15) Conference Building, Tsunyi 15 15
2450. 8 f. (16) Pagoda Hill Yenan 15 15
2452. 8 f. (18) Workers and Industry 15 15
2453. 8 f. (19) Type **372** 15 15
2454. 8 f. (20) Workers and Agriculture 15 15
2451. 22 f. (17) Gate of Heavenly Peace, Peking .. 35 35

SIZES: As Type **371**. Nos. 2447/2450 and 2451. As Type **372**. Nos. 2452/4.

373. National Peasant Movement Institute, Canton. **374.** Welcoming Bouquets.

1971. Revolutionary Sites. Multicoloured. No gum.

2455. 1 f. Communist Party Building, Shanghai (vert.) 5 5
2456. 2 f. Type **373** 5 5
2457. 3 f. Site of 1929 Congress, Kutien 5 5
2458. 4 f. Mao Tse-tung's house, Yenan 8 5
2459. 8 f. Gate of Heavenly Peace, Peking 12 8
2460. 10 f. Monument, Chingkang Mountains .. 15 8
2461. 20 f. River bridge, Yenan 25 12
2462. 22 f. Mao's birthplace, Shaoshan 25 12
2463. 35 f. Conference Building, Tsunyi 35 20
2464. 43 f. Start of the Long March, Chingkang Mountains 40 25
2465. 52 f. People's Palace, Peking 50 35

1971. "Afro-Asian Friendship" Table-tennis Tournament, Peking. Multicoloured. No gum.

2466. 8 f. (22) Type **455** .. 12 12
2467. 8 f. (23) Group of players 12 12
2468. 8 f. (24) Asian and African players 12 12
2469. 8 f. (21) Tournament badge 70 70

375. Enver Hoxha making speech. **376.** Soldier and Workers' Militia.

1971. Albanian Worker's Party. 30th Anniv. Multicoloured. No gum.

2470. 8 f. (25) Type **375** .. 12 12
2471. 8 f. (26) Party Headquarters 12 12
2472. 8 f. (27) Albanian flag, rifle and pick 12 12
2473. 52 f. (28) Type **376** .. 85 85

378. Conference Hall, Yenan.

1972. Publication of "Yenan Forum's Discussions on Literature and Art". 30th Anniv. Multicoloured. No gum.

2474. 8 f. (33) Type **373** .. 12 12
2475. 8 f. (34) Military choir .. 12 12
2476. 8 f. (35) "Brother and Sister" 12 12
2477. 8 f. (36) "Open-air Theatre" 12 12
2478. 8 f. (37) "The Red Lantern" (opera) 12 12
2479. 8 f. (38) Dancer of "The Red Company of Women" 12 12

379. Ball Games.

1972. Mao Tse-tung's Edict on Physical Culture. 10th Anniv. Multicoloured. No gum.

2480. 8 f. (39) Type **379** .. 12 12
2481. 8 f. (40) Physical exercises 12 12
2482. 8 f. (41) Tug-of-War .. 12 12
2483. 8 f. (42) Rock-climbing .. 12 12
2484. 8 f. (43) High-diving .. 12 12

Nos. 2481/4 are size 26 × 36 mm.

380. Freighter "Fenglei".

1972. Chinese Merchant Shipping. Multicoloured. No gum.

2485. 8 f. (29) Type **380** .. 12 12
2486. 8 f. (30) Tanker "Tacking No. 30" 12 12
2487. 8 f. (31) Ocean liner "Chang-seng" 12 12
2488. 8 f. (32) Dredger "Hsien-feng" 12 12

INDEX

Countries can be quickly located by referring to the index at the end of this volume.

381. Badge of Championships. **382.** Wang Chinphsi, the "Iron Man".

1972. 1st Asian Table-tennis Championships. Multicoloured. No gum.

2489. 8 f. (45) Type **381** .. 12 12
2490. 8 f. (46) Welcoming crowd (horiz.) 12 12
2491. 8 f. (47) Game in progress (horiz.) 12 12
2492. 22 f. (48) Players from three countries .. 30 30

1972. Wang Chin-hsi (workers' hero). Commem. No gum.

2493. **382.** 8 f. multicoloured .. 12 8

383. Road Construction. **384.** Panda eating Bamboo Shoots.

1972. Construction of Red Flag Canal. Multicoloured.

2494. 8 f. (49) Type **383** .. 12 8
2495. 8 f. (50) "Youth tunnel" 12 8
2496. 8 f. (51) Taoguan bridge .. 12 8
2497. 8 f. (52) Canal skirting cliff-edge 12 8

1973. China's Giant Pandas. Various designs as T **384**.

2498. **384.** 4 f. (61) multicoloured .. 8 5
2499. – 8 f. (59) mult. (horiz.) 8 5
2500. – 8 f. (60) mult. (horiz.) 8 5
2501. – 10 f. (58) multicoloured 10 5
2502. – 20 f. (57) multicoloured 20 8
2503. – 43 f. (62) multicoloured 30 15

385. "New Power in the Mines" (Yang Shi-guang). **386.** Girl Dancer.

1973. Int. Working Women's Day. Mult.

2504. 8 f. (63) Type **385** .. 8 5
2505. 8 f. (64) "Woman Committee Member" (Tang Hsiao-ming) 8 5
2506. 8 f. (65) "I am a Sea-gull" (Army telegraph line-woman) (Pan Jia-jun) 8 5

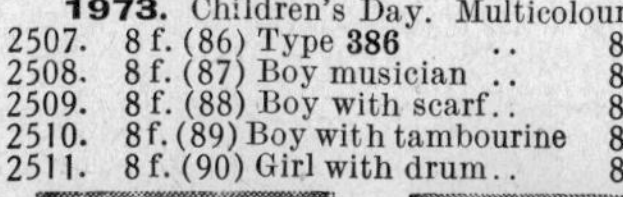

1973. Children's Day. Multicoloured.

2507. 8 f. (86) Type **386** .. 8 5
2508. 8 f. (87) Boy musician .. 8 5
2509. 8 f. (88) Boy with scarf .. 8 5
2510. 8 f. (89) Boy with tambourine 8 5
2511. 8 f. (90) Girl with drum .. 8 5

387. Badge of Championships. **388.** "Hsi-erh".

1973. Asian, African and Latin-American Table-tennis Invitation Championships. Multicoloured.

2512. 8 f. (91) Type **387** .. 8 5
2513. 8 f. (92) Visitors 8 5
2514. 8 f. (93) Player 8 5
2515. 22 f. (94) Guest players .. 15 8

1973. Revolutionary Ballet "The White-haired Girl". Multicoloured.

2516. 8 f. (53) Type **388** .. 8 5
2517. 8 f. (54) Hsi-erh escapes from Huang (horiz.) .. 8 5
2518. 8 f. (55) Hsi-erh meets Ta-chun (horiz.) 8 5
2519. 8 f. (56) Hsi-erh becomes a soldier 8 5

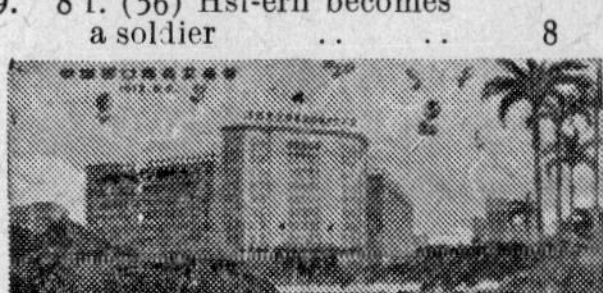

389. Fair Building.

1973. Chinese Exports Fair, Canton.

2520. **389.** 8 f. multicoloured .. 8 5

390. Mao's Birthplace, Shaoshan.

391. Steam and Diesel Trains.

1973. No gum.

2521. **390.** 1 f. grn. and pale grn. 5 5
2522. – 1½ f. red and yellow .. 5 5
2523. – 2 f. blue and yellow .. 5 5
2524. – 3 f. green and yellow 5 5
2525. – 4 f. red and yellow .. 5 5
2526. – 5 f. brown and yellow 5 5
2527. – 8 f. purple and mauve 5 5
2528. – 10 f. blue and mauve 5 5
2529. – 20 f. red and yellow .. 15 8
2530. – 22 f. violet and yellow 15 8
2531. – 35 f. red and yellow .. 20 20
2532. – 43 f. brown and buff .. 25 15
2534. – 52 f. brown and yellow 35 25
2535. **391.** 1 y. multicoloured .. 40 40
2536. – 2 y. multicoloured .. 60 60

DESIGNS. As T **390**: 1½ f. National Peasant Movement Institute, Shanghai. 2 f. National Institute, Kwangchow. 3 f. Headquarters Building, Nanching uprising. 4 f. People's Hall, Peking. 5 f. Wen Chia Shih. 8 f. Gate of Heavenly Peace, Peking. 10 f. Chingkang Mountains. 20 f. Kutien Congress Building. 22 f. Tsunyi Congress Building. 35 f. Bridge, Yenan. 43 f. Hsi Pai Po. 53 f. "Fairy Cave", Lushan. As T **391**. 2 y. Lorries.

392. "Phoenix" Pot. **393.** Dance Routine.

1973. Archaeological Treasures. Mult.

2537. 4 f. (66) Type **392** .. 5 5
2538. 4 f. (67) Silver pot .. 5 5
2539. 8 f. (68) Porcelain horse and groom 5 5
2540. 8 f. (69) Figure of woman 5 5
2541. 8 f. (70) Carved pedestals 5 5
2542. 8 f. (71) Bronze horse .. 5 5
2543. 8 f. (72) Gilded "frog" .. 5 5
2544. 8 f. (73) Lamp-holder figurine 5 5
2545. 10 f. (74) Tripod jar .. 8 5
2546. 10 f. (75) Bronze vessel .. 8 5
2547. 20 f. (76) Bronze wine vessel 15 8
2548. 52 f. (77) Tray with tripod 35 25

1974. Popular Gymnastics. Multicoloured.

2549. 8 f. (1) Type **393** 5 5
2550. 8 f. (2) Rings exercise .. 5 5
2551. 8 f. (3) Dancing on beam 5 5
2552. 8 f. (4) Handstand on parallel bars 5 5
2553. 8 f. (5) Trapeze exercise .. 5 5
2554. 8 f. (6) Vaulting over horse 5 5

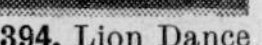

394. Lion Dance **395.** Man reading Book.

1974. Acrobatics. Multicoloured.
2555. 8 f. (1) Type **394** 5 5
2556. 8 f. (2) Handstand on chairs 5 5
2557. 8 f. (3) Diabolo team (horiz.) 5 5
2558. 8 f. (4) Revolving jar (horiz.) 5 5
2559. 8 f. (5) Spinning plates .. 5 5
2560. 8 f. (6) Foot-juggling with parasol 5 5

1974. Husein Paintings. Multicoloured.
2561. 8 f. (1) Type **395** 5 5
2562. 8 f. (2) Mineshaft (23×57 mm) 5 5
2563. 8 f. (3) Workers hoeing field (horiz.) 5 5
2564. 8 f. (4) Workers having meal (horiz.) 5 5
2565. 8 f. (5) Wheatfield landscape (horiz. 56×24 mm) 5 5
2566. 8 f. (6) Harvesting scene (horiz.) 5 5

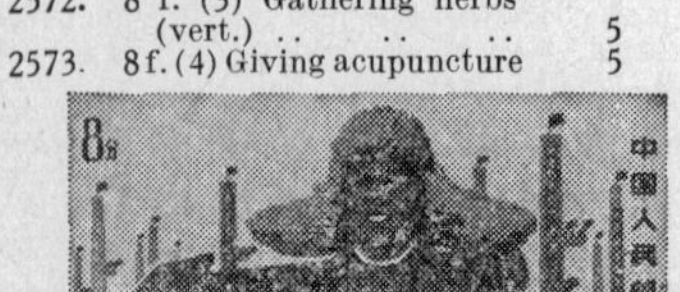

396. Postman.

1974. U.P.U. Cent. Multicoloured.
2567. 8 f. (1) Type **396** 5 5
2568. 8 f. (2) People of five races 5 5
2569. 8 f. (3) Great Wall of China 5 5

397. Innoculating Children.

1974. Country Doctors. Multicoloured.
2570. 8 f. (1) Type **397** 5 5
2571. 8 f. (2) On country visit (vert.) 5 5
2572. 8 f. (3) Gathering herbs (vert.) 5 5
2573. 8 f. (4) Giving acupuncture 5 5

398. Wang Chin-hsi, "The Iron Man".

1974. Chairman Mao's Directives on Industrial and Agricultural Teaching. Multicoloured.

(a) "Learning Industry from Taching".
2574. 8 f. (1) Type **398** 5 5
2575. 8 f. (2) Pupils studying Mao's works 5 5
2576. 8 f. (3) Oil-workers sinking well 5 5
2577. 8 f. (4) Consultation with management 5 5
2578. 8 f. (5) Taching oilfield as development site .. 5 5

(b) "Learning Agriculture from Tachai".
2579. 8 f. (1) Tachai workers looking to future .. 5 5
2580. 8 f. (2) Construction workers 5 5
2581. 8 f. (3) Agricultural workers making field tests .. 5 5
2582. 8 f. (4) Trucks delivering grain to State granaries 5 5
2583. 8 f. (5) Workers going to fields 5 5

399. National Day Celebrations.

400. Steel Worker, Taching.

1974. Chinese People's Republic. 25th Anniv. Multicoloured.

(a) National Day.
2584. 8 f. Type **399** 5 5

(b) Chairman Mao's Directives.
2585. 8 f. (1) Type **400** 5 5
2586. 8 f. (2) Agricultural worker, Tachai 5 5
2587. 8 f. (3) Coastal guard .. 5 5

401. Fair Building.

1974. Chinese Exports Fair, Canton.
2588. **401.** 8 f. multicoloured .. 5 5

402. Revolutionary Monument, Permet. **403.** Capital Stadium.

1974. Albania's Liberation. 30th Anniv. Multicoloured.
2589. 8 f. Type **402** 5 5
2590. 8 f. Albanian patriots .. 5 5

1974. Peking Buildings. No gum.
2591. **403.** 4 f. black and green 5 5
2592. – 8 f. black and blue .. 5 5
DESIGN: 8 f. Hotel Peking.

404. Water-cooled Turbine Generator.

1974. Industrial Production. Multicoloured.
2593. 8 f. (78) Type **404** .. 5 5
2594. 8 f. (79) Mechanical rice-sprouts transplanter .. 5 5
2595. 8 f. (80) Universal cylindrical grinding machine .. 5 5
2596. 8 f. (81) Mobile rock-drill (vert.) 5 5

405. Congress Delegates.

1975. Fourth National People's Congress, Peking, Multicoloured.
2597. 8 f. (1) Type **405** 5 5
2598. 8 f. (2) Flower-decked rostrum 5 5
2599. 8 f. (3) Farmer, worker and soldier 5 5

406. Teacher Studying.

1975. Country Women Teachers. Mult.
2600. 8 f. (1) Type **406** 5 5
2601. 8 f. (2) Teacher on rounds 5 5
2602. 8 f. (3) Open-air class .. 5 5
2603. 8 f. (4) Primary class aboard boat 5 5

407. "Broadsword".

1975. "Wushu" (popular sport). Mult.
2604. 8 f. (1) Type **407** 5 5
2605. 8 f. (2) Sword exercises .. 5 5
2606. 8 f. (3) "Boxing" 5 5
2607. 8 f. (4) Leaping with spear 5 5
2608. 8 f. (5) Cudgel exercise .. 5 5
2609. 43 f. (6) Cudgel versus spears (60×30 mm.) .. 25 15

408. "Mass Revolutionary Criticism". **409.** Parade of Athletes.

1975. Criticism of Confucius and Lin Piao. Multicoloured.
2610. 8 f. (1) Type **408** 5 5
2611. 8 f. (2) "Leaders of the production brigade" .. 5 5
2612. 8 f. (3) "The battle continues" (horiz.) .. 5 5
2613. 8 f. (4) "Liberated slave-pioneer critic" (horiz.) 5 5

1975. Third National Sports Meeting, Peking. Multicoloured.
2614. 8 f. (1) Type **409** 5 5
2615. 8 f. (2) Athletes studying (horiz.) 5 5
2616. 8 f. (3) Volleyball players (horiz.) 5
2617. 8 f. (4) Athlete, soldier, farmer and worker .. 5 5
2618. 8 f. (5) Various sports (horiz.) 5 5
2619. 8 f. (6) Ethnic types and horse racing (horiz.) .. 5 5
2620. 8 f. (7) Children and divers 20 12

410. Members of Expedition. **412.** Boy and Girl.

411. Workers and Book.

1975. Chinese Ascent of Mount Everest. Multicoloured.
2621. 8 f. (2) Type **410** 5 5
2622. 8 f. (3) Mountaineers with flag (horiz.) 5 5
2623. 8 f. (4) View of Mount Everest (horiz.) .. 25 15

1975. National Conference, "Learning Agriculture from Tachai". Mult.
2624. 8 f. Type **411** 5 5
2625. 8 f. Workers carrying load 5 5
2626. 8 f. Woman driving combine-harvester .. 5 5

1975. Children's Progress. Multicoloured.
2627. 8 f. Type **412** 5 5
2628. 8 f. Sticking-up posters .. 5 5
2629. 8 f. Studying 5 5
2630. 8 f. Harvesting 5 5
2631. 52 f. Tug-of-war 35 25

413. Mechanical Ploughing.

1975. Mechanised Farming. Multicoloured.
2632. 8 f. Type **413** 5 5
2633. 8 f. Mechanical rice-planting 5 5
2634. 8 f. Drainage and irrigation 5 5
2635. 8 f. Spraying insecticide 5 5
2636. 8 f. Combine harvester .. 5 5

414. Harvest Scene.

1976. 4th 5-Year Plan. Completion (1st series). Multicoloured.
2637. 8 f. Type **414** 8 5
2638. 8 f. Bridge over canal .. 8 5
2639. 8 f. Fertilizer plant .. 8 5
2640. 8 f. Textile factory .. 8 5
2641. 8 f. Iron foundry .. 8 5
See also Nos. 2637/41 and 2654/9.

1976. 4th 5-Year Plan. Completion (2nd series). As T **414**. Multicoloured.
2642. 8 f. Coal train 8 5
2643. 8 f. Hydro-electric power station 8 5
2644. 8 f. Shipbuilding .. 8 5
2645. 8 f. Oil industry .. 8 5
2646. 8 f. Pipe-line and harbour 8 5

415. Heart Surgery.

1976. Medical Services' Achievements. Multicoloured.
2647. 8 f. Type **415** 8 5
2648. 8 f. Restoration of tractor-driver's severed arm .. 8 5
2649. 8 f. Exercise of fractured arm 8 5
2650. 8 f. Cataract operation-patient threading needle 8 5

416. Students studying at "May 7" School.

1976. Mao's "May 7 Directive". 10th Anniversary. Multicoloured.
2651. 8 f. Type **416** 8 5
2652. 8 f. Students in agriculture 8 5
2653. 8 f. Students in production team 8 5

1976. 4th 5-Year Plan. Completion (3rd series). As T **414**. Multicoloured.
2654. 8 f. Train on viaduct .. 8 5
2655. 8 f. Crystal formation (scientific research) .. 8 5
2656. 8 f. Classroom (rural education) 8 5
2657. 8 f. Workers' health centre 8 5
2658. 8 f. Workers' tenements 8 5
2659. 8 f. Department store .. 8 5

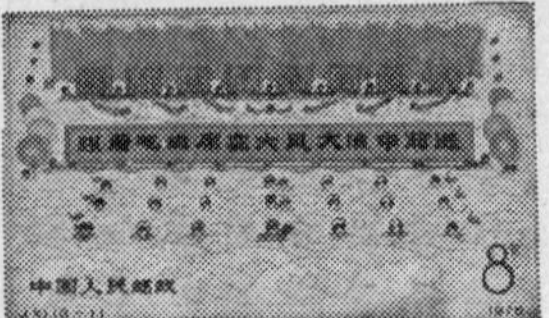

417. Formation of Swimmers.

1976. Chairman Mao's Swim in Yangtse River. 10th Anniv. Multicoloured.
2660. 8 f. Type **417** 8 5
2661. 8 f. Swimmers crossing Yangtse 8 5
2662. 8 f. Swimmers in surf .. 8 5
Nos. 2661/2 are larger, 35×28 mm.

418. Students with Rosettes.

1976. "Going to College". Multicoloured.
2663. 8 f. Type **418** 8 5
2664. 8 f. Study group .. 8 5
2665. 8 f. On-site instructions .. 8 5
2666. 8 f. Students operating computer 8 5
2667. 8 f. Return of graduates from college 8 5

419. Electricity Lineswoman.

1976. Maintenance of Electric Power Lines. Multicoloured.
2668. 8 f. Type **419** 8 5
2669. 8 f. Linesman replacing insulator 8 5
2670. 8 f. Linesman using hydraulic lift 8 5
2671. 8 f. Technician inspecting transformer 8 5

MILITARY POST STAMPS

M 3.

1953.
M 1593. **M 3.** $800 yell. & red .. 2·00 3·00
M 1594. $800 red, orge. & purple .. .. 10·00
M 1595. $800 red, yell. & bl. £325
Nos. M 1593/5 were issued for the use of the Army, Air Force and Navy respectively.

POSTAGE DUE STAMPS

D 11.

D 12.

1950.
D 1459. **D 11.** $100 blue .. 5 5
D 1460. $200 blue .. 5 5
D 1461. $500 blue .. 5 5
D 1462. $800 blue .. 40 5
D 1463. $1,000 blue .. 12 8
D 1464. $2,000 blue .. 20 12
D 1465. $5,000 blue .. 40 35
D 1466. $8,000 blue .. 55 45
D 1467. $10,000 blue .. 1·50 70

1954.
D 1628. **D 12.** $100 red 5 5
D 1629. $200 red 5 5
D 1630. $500 red 5 5
D 1631. $800 red 8 8
D 1632. $1,600 red .. 15 10

CHINA—TAIWAN (FORMOSA)

A. CHINESE PROVINCE.

The island of Taiwan was ceded by China to Japan in 1895 and was returned to China in 1945 after the defeat of Japan. From 1949 Taiwan was controlled by the remnants of the Nationalist Government under Chiang Kai-shek.

1946 100 sen = 1 dollar.

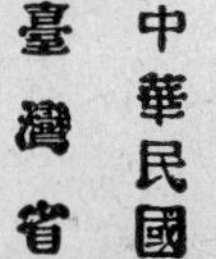

1. "Taiwan Province, Chinese Republic"

1945. Optd. as Type **1**.
(a) On stamps as Nos. J 1/3 of Japanese Formosa.
1. **1.** 3 s. red 8 5
2. 5 s. green 10 5
3. 10 s. blue 12 5
4. 30 s. blue 20 12
5. 40 s. purple 12 8
6. 50 s. brown 12 8
7. 1 y. green 15 12

(b) On stamps of Japan. Imperf.
8. **69.** 5 y. olive (No. 424) .. 50 30
9. **70.** 10 y. purple (No. 334) .. 60 40

限臺灣省貼用 3⁰⁰ 圓叁
(2.)

用貼灣臺限 錢 伍
(3.)

1946. Opening of National Assembly, Nanking. Issue of China. surch as T **2**.
10. **66.** 70 s. on $20 green .. 8 5
11. 1 y. on $30 blue .. 8 5
12. 2 y. on $50 brown .. 10 8
13. 3 y. on $100 red .. 10 8

1946. Stamps of China surch. as T **3** with two to four characters in lower line denoting value.
14. **30.** 2 s. on 2 c. blue .. 5 5
15. 5 s. on 5 c. orange .. 5 5
16. 10 s. on 4 c. lilac .. 5 5
17. 30 s. on 15 c. maroon .. 5 5
23. **61.** 50 s. on $20 red .. 5 5
20. **28.** 65 s. on $20 green .. 5 5
19. **30.** $1 on 20 c. blue .. 5 5
21. **28.** $1 on $30 brown .. 5 5
65. **30.** $2 on 2½ c. red .. 5 5
22. **28.** $2 on $50 orange .. 5 5
24. **61.** $3 on $100 red .. 5 5
77. **58.** $5 on $40 orange .. 5 5
78. **61.** $5 on $50 violet .. 5 5
79. $5 on $70 orange .. 5 5
80. $5 on $100 claret .. 5 5
25. $5 on $200 green .. 5 5
67. **43.** $10 on $3 yellow .. 5 5
82. **72.** $10 on $150 blue .. 5 8
26. **61.** $10 on $500 green .. 5 5
66. **38.** $20 on 2 c. olive .. 5 5
71. **46.** $20 on $3 red .. 12 5
83. **72.** $20 on $250 violet .. 5 5
27. **61.** $20 on $700 brown .. 8 8
68. **43.** $50 on 50 c. green .. 8 5
28. **61.** $50 on $1,000 red .. 25 25
72. **46.** $100 on $20 pink .. 5 5
73. **52.** $100 on $20 red .. 14·00 16·00
29. **61.** $100 on $3,000 blue .. 30 30
74. **52.** $200 on $10 blue .. 10 5
70. **38.** $500 on $30 purple .. 5 5
81. **61.** $600 on $100 claret .. 80 30
69. **43.** $800 on $4 brown .. 30 10
85. **72.** $1,000 on $20,000 red .. 40 15
75. **52.** $5,000 on $10 blue .. 30 5
76. $10,000 on $20 red .. 60 50
84. **72.** $200,000 on $3,000 blue 11·00 7·50

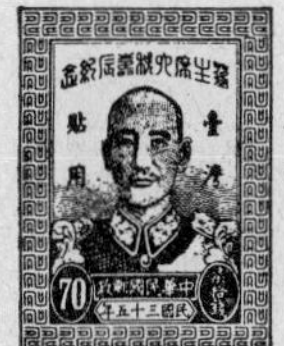

4. President Chiang Kai-shek.

5. Entrance to Dr. Sun Yat-sen Mausoleum.

1947. President's 60th Birthday.
30. **4.** 70 s. red 8 8
31. $1 green 8 8
32. $2 red 8 8
33. $3 green 8 8
34. $7 orange 10 10
35. $10 claret 12 12

1947. Chinese Nat. Currency. Return of Govt. to Nanking. 1st Anniv.
36. **5.** 50 s. green 8 8
37. $4 blue 8 8
38. $7.50 red 8 8
39. $10 brown 8 8
40. $20 purple 8 8
For other stamps as T **4** and **5**, but with different 3rd and 4th Chinese characters in positions shown by arrows, see N.E. Provinces T **7** and **9**.

6. Sun Yat-sen and Palms.

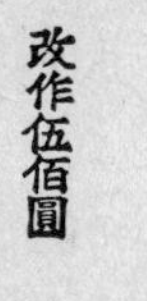

500⁰⁰
(7.)

1947.
41. **6.** $1 brown 5 5
42. $2 brown 5 5
43. $3 green 5 5
44. $5 orange 5 5
45. **6.** $9 blue 5 5
46. $10 red 5 5
47. $20 green 5 5
59. $25 green 5 5
48. $50 purple 8 5
49. $100 blue 5 5
50. $200 brown 10 10
60. $5,000 orange 12 8
61. $10,000 green 12 8
62. $20,000 brown 12 8
63. $30,000 blue 15 8
64. $40,000 purple 20 8

1948. "Re-valuation" surcharges. Surch. as T **7**.
51. **6.** $25 on $100 blue .. 15 8
52. $300 on $3 green .. 10 10
53. $500 on $7.50 orange .. 20 15
54. $1,000 on 30 c. grey .. 60 40
55. $1,000 on $3 green .. 20 8
56. $2,000 on $3 green .. 15 8
57. $3,000 on $3 green .. 40 15
58. $3,000 on $7.50 orange .. 2·00 50

1949. No value indicated. Stamps of China optd. with five Chinese characters, similar to T **3**.
86. **93.** (-) Orange (Ord. postage) 12 5
87. **94.** (-) Green (Air Mail) .. 15 15
88. **95.** (-) Mauve (Express) .. 12 15
89. **96.** (-) Red (Registration) .. 12 15

PARCELS POST STAMPS

1948. As Type P **3** of China with six Chinese characters in the sky above the lorry.
P 65. $100 green .. .. — 5
P 66. $300 red .. .. .. — 5
P 67. $500 olive .. .. — 5
P 68. $1,000 black .. .. — 5
P 69. $3,000 purple .. .. — 5
Parcels Post stamps were not on sale in unused condition.

POSTAGE DUE STAMPS

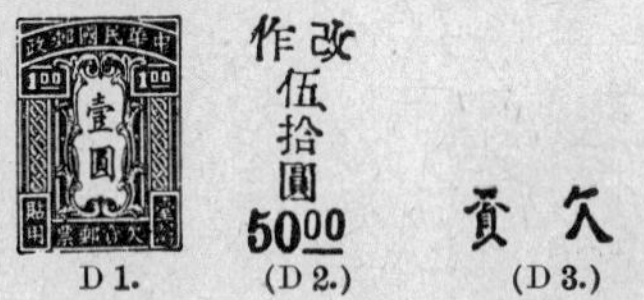

D 1. (D 2.) (D 3.)

1948.
D 51. **D 1.** $1 blue 5 5
D 52. $3 blue 5 5
D 53. $5 blue 5 5
D 54. $10 blue 5 5
D 55. $20 blue 5 5

1949. "Re-valuation" surcharges, Surch as Type D **2**.
D 65. **D 1.** $50 on $1 blue .. 40 40
D 66. $100 on $3 blue .. 40 40
D 67. $300 on $5 blue .. 40 40
D 68. $500 on $10 blue .. 90 90

1949. Handstamped with Type D **3**.
D 86. **6.** $1,000 on $3 green (No. 55) .. .. 1·10 85
D 87. $3,000 on $3 green (No. 57) .. .. 1·00 1·10
D 88. $5,000 orange (No. 60) 1·00 1·00

B. CHINESE NATIONALIST REPUBLIC

1949. 100 cents = 1 silver yuan (or New Taiwan Yuan).
Silver Yuan Surcharges.

臺幣壹角 10
(8.)

臺幣壹角 10
(9.)

1949. Stamps of Taiwan Province surch.
(a) With T **8**.
90. **6.** 10 c. on $50 purple .. 1·00 70

(b) As T **9** (figures at right).
91. **6.** 2 c. on $30,000 blue .. 80 75
92. 10 c. on $40,000 purple .. 90 75

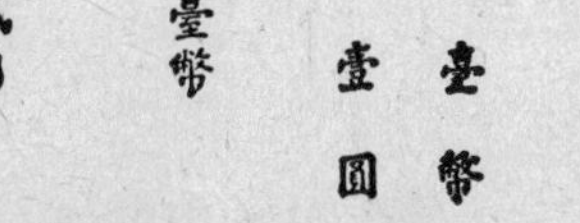

(10.) (11.)

1949. Stamps of North Eastern Provinces (Manchuria), surch. as T **10**.
93. **5.** 2 c. on $44 red 50 30
95. 5 c. on $44 red 40 40
96. 10 c. on $44 red 80 30
97. 20 c. on $44 red .. .. 2·00 80
98. 30 c. on $44 red .. .. 2·25 1·00
99. 50 c. on $44 red .. .. 4·25 1·75

1950. Surch. as T **11** on stamp of China but with no indication of value.
100. **99.** $1 on (-) green .. .. 3·00 40
101. $2 on (-) green .. .. 3·25 1·10
102. $5 on (-) green .. .. 55·00 4·50
103. $10 on (-) green .. 60·00 15·00
104. $20 on (-) green .. £120 50·00

1950. Stamps of China surch.
(a) As T **8** (figure "5" at left).
105. **72.** 5 c. on $200,000 purple 60 35
(b) As T **9** (figures at left).
106. **72.** 3 c. on $30,000 brown .. 40 25
107. 3 c. on $40,000 green .. 40 25
108. 3 c. on $50,000 blue .. 60 25
108a. 10 c. on $4,000 grey .. 1·10 50
109. 10 c. on $6,000 purple .. 1·00 40
110. 10 c. on $20,000 red .. 1·75 60
110a. 10 c. on $2,000,000 orge. 2·00 75
110b. 20 c. on $500,000 mauve 2·10 75
110c. 20 c. on $1,000,000 clar. 2·25 1·10
110d. 30 c. on $3,000,000 bistre 3·00 1·50
110e. 50 c. on $5,000,000 blue 4·75 2·25

12. Koxinga.

GUM.
All the following stamps to No. 616 were issued without gum except where otherwise stated.

1950. Rouletted. (a) Postage.
111. **12.** 3 c. grey 40 30
112. 10 c. brown 15 5
113. 15 c. yellow .. .. 1·75 70
114. 20 c. green 15 5
115. 30 c. claret .. .. 4·50 2·50
116. 40 c. orange 12 5
117. 50 c. chocolate .. 20 12
118. 80 c. red 90 25
119. $1 violet 60 5
120. $1.50 green .. .. 2·00 30
121. $1.60 blue .. .. 2·50 12
122. $2 magenta .. .. 3·50 20
123. $5 turquoise .. .. 10·00 2·25

(b) Air. With character at each side of head.
124. **12.** 60 c. blue .. .. 1·90 1·25

13. Peasant and Ballot Box. (14.) **15.** Peasant and Scroll.

1951. Division of Country into Self-governing Districts. Perf. or imperf.
125. **13.** 40 c. red 55 12
126. $1 blue .. .. 2·10 60
127. $1·60 purple .. .. 3·50 45
128. $2 brown .. .. 3·00 1·00

1951. Silver Yuan surcharges. As T **99** of China but without value, surch. as T **14**.
129. $5 on (-) green .. 6·00 1·50
130. $10 on (-) green .. 30·00 2·25
131. $20 on (-) green .. 40·00 5·50
132. $50 on (-) green .. 70·00 6·00

1952. Land Tax Reduction. Perf. or imperf.
133. **15.** 20 c. orange 70 20
134. 40 c. green 50 20
135. $1 brown .. .. 2·25 85
136. $1·40 blue .. .. 1·90 50
137. $2 grey .. .. 4·00 2·75
138. $5 red .. .. 5·00 4·00

16. President and Rejoicing crowds.

(17.)

1952. Re-election of Pres. Chiang Kai-shek. 2nd Anniv. Flag in red and blue. Eight characters in scroll. Perf. or imperf.

139. **16.** 40 c. red 30 5
140. $1 green .. .. 2·00 70
141. $1·60 orange .. .. 5·00 50
142. $2 blue .. .. .. 4·50 2·50
143. $5 purple .. .. 6·50 75

1952. Stamps of China surch. with T **17.**

144. **91.** 3 c. on 4 c. grn. (No. 1044) 30 15
145. 3 c. on 10 c. lilac (No. 1347) 30 15
146. 3 c. on 20 c. blue (No. 1349) 30 15
147. 3 c. on 50 c brown (No. 1350) 30 15

(18.) (19.)

1953. T **99** of China, but without value, surch. as T **18.**

148. $10 on (–) green .. 7·00 2·25
149. $20 on (–) green .. 25·00 3·50
150. $50 on (–) green .. 80·00 80·00

1953. 3rd Anniv. of Re-election of Pres. Chiang Kai-shek. As T **16** but eleven characters in scroll. Flag in red and blue. Perf. or imperf.

151. 10 c. orange 50 20
152. 20 c. green 50 20
153. 40 c. red 30 8
154. $1.40 blue .. .. 1·60 25
155. $2 sepia .. .. 2·25 40
156. $5 purple .. .. 7·50 3·25

1953. Surch. as T **19.**

157. **12.** 3 c. on $1 violet .. 20 8
158. 10 c. on 15 c. yellow .. 1·75 12
159. 10 c. on 30 c. claret .. 25 8
160. 20 c. on $1.60 blue .. 25 8

20. Doctor, Nurses and Patients.

21. Pres. Chiang Kai-shek.

1953. Establishment of Anti-tuberculosis Assn. Cross of Lorraine in red. On paper with coloured network.

161. **20.** 40 c. brown on stone .. 90 5
162. $1.60 blue on turquoise 4·00 8
163. $2 green on yellow .. 1·60 12
164. $5 red on flesh .. .. 9·00 60

1953.

165. **21.** 10 c. sepia 10 5
166. 20 c. purple 10 5
167. 40 c. green 10 5
168. 50 c. mauve 15 5
169. 80 c. brown 60 20
170. $1 olive 15 5
171. $1.40 blue 20 5
172. $1.60 red .. .. 3·50 5
173. $1.70 emerald 25 20
174. $2 brown 25 5
175. $3 blue .. .. .. 12·00 50
176. $4 turquoise 70 12
177. $5 red 75 12
178. $10 green .. .. 3·00 5·00
179. $20 lake .. .. 5·00 1·00

22. Silo Bridge over R. Cho-Shui-Chi.

23. Sapling, Tree and Plantation.

1954. Completion of Silo Bridge. Various frames.

180. **22.** 40 c. red 60 10
181. – $1.60 blue .. .. 5·00 20
182. **22.** $3.60 black .. .. 1·50 30
183. – $5 magenta .. .. 8·50 1·25

DESIGN: $1.60, $5 Silo Bridge.

1954. Afforestation Day.

184. **23.** 40 c. blue .. .. 2·00 15
185. – $10 purple .. .. 6·50 90
186. – $20 red .. .. .. 3·00 45
187. – $50 blue .. .. 6·50 1·75

DESIGNS: $10 Tree plantation and houses. $20 Planting seedling. $50 Map of Taiwan and tree.

24. Runner.

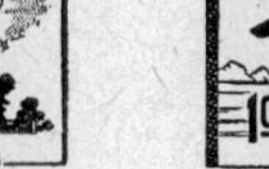

25. 'Plane over Taipeh City Gate.

1954. Youth Day.

188. **24.** 40 c. blue .. .. 3·75 60
189. $5 red .. .. .. 9·00 2·00

1954. Air. Air Force Day. 15th Anniv.

190. **25.** $1 brown 80 12
191. – $1·60 black 70 8
192. – $5 blue .. .. .. 1·25 15

DESIGNS: $1.60, Three jet fighters over Chung Shang Bridge, Taipeh. $5, Doves over Chi Kan Lee (Fort Zeelandia) in Tainan City.

26. Refugees crossing Pontoon Bridge.

27. Junk and Bridge.

1954. Relief Fund for Chinese Refugees from North Vietnam.

193. **26.** 40 c. + 10 c. blue .. 2·50 30
194. $1·60 + 40 c. purple .. 5·00 75
195. $5 + $1 red .. .. 12·00 7·00

1954. Overseas Chinese League. 2nd Anniv.

196. **27.** 40 c. red .. .. 2·50 10
197. $5 blue .. .. .. 1·60 40

28. "Chainbreaker"

(29.)

1955. Freedom Day.

198. **28.** 40 c. green 30 8
199. – $1 olive .. .. .. 2·50 60
200. – $1.60 red .. .. 2·50 45

DESIGNS: $1 Soldier with torch and flag. $1.60 Torch and figures "1·23".

1955. Surch. as T **29.**

201. **12.** 3 c. on $1 violet .. 30 10
202. 20 c. on 40 c. orange .. 30 10

31. Pres. Chiang Kai-shek and Sun Yat-sen Memorial Building.

1955. President Chiang Kai-shek's Second Re-election. 1st Anniv.

203. **31.** 20 c. olive 25 5
204. 40 c. green 40 5
205. $2 red 80 12
206. $7 blue .. .. 1·25 40

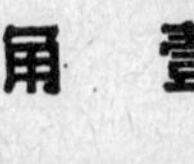

(32.)

33. Air Force Badge.

1955. Nos. 116/8, 120 and 124 surch. as T **32.** Nos. 212/4 have additional floral ornament below two characters at top.

207. **12.** 10 c. on 80 c. red .. 30 10
208. 10 c. on $1.50 green .. 30 10
212. 20 c. on 40 c. orange .. 40 10
213. 20 c. on 50 c. chocolate 40 10
214. 20 c. on 60 c. blue .. 50 10

1955. Armed Forces Day.

209. **33.** 40 c. blue 25 5
210. $2 red .. .. .. 2·10 15
211. $7 green .. .. 2·10 15

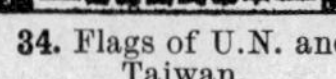

34. Flags of U.N. and Taiwan.

35. Pres. Chiang Kai-shek.

1955. U.N.O. 10th Anniv.

215. **34.** 40 c. blue 40 5
216. $2 red .. .. .. 1·50 20
217. $7 green .. .. 1·50 40

1955. President's 69th Birthday. With gum.

218. **35.** 40 c brown, blue & red 20 5
219. $2 blue, green and red 75 20
220. $7 green, brown & red 1·10 40

36. Sun Yat-sen's Birthplace.

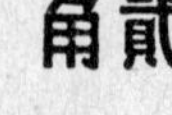

(37.)

1955. Dr. Sun Yat-sen. 90th Birth Anniv. (1956.)

221. **36.** 40 c. blue 20 5
222. $2 brown .. .. 1·25 20
223. $7 red .. .. .. 1·60 40

1956. Nos. 1025 and 1023 of China. surch. as T **37.**

232. **95.** 3 c. on (–) mauve .. 20 8
224. **93.** 20 c. on (–) orange I .. 8 5
304. 20 c. on (–) orange II .. 8 5

In No. 232 the characters are smaller and there are leaves on either side of the "3".

(I) Surch. with T **37.** (II) The characters are below the figures.

38. Old and Modern Postal Transport.

39. Children at Play.

1956. Postal Service. 60th Anniv.

225. **38.** 40 c. red 12 5
226. $1 blue 25 15
227. $1.60 brown 35 8
228. $2 green 50 12

1956. Children's Day.

229. **39.** 40 c. green 15 5
230. $1.60 blue 40 5
231. $2 red 50 12

40. Earliest and Latest Locomotives.

41. Pres. Chiang Kai-shek.

1956. Chinese Railways. 75th Anniv.

233. **40.** 40 c. red 20 5
234. $2 blue 30 5
235. $8 green 90 35

1956. President's 70th Birthday. Various portraits of President. With gum.

236. **41.** 20 c. orange 10 5
237. – 40 c. red 10 5
238. – $1 blue 15 5
239. – $1.60 purple 30 5
240. – $2 brown 70 8
241. – $8 turquoise .. .. 2·00 30

SIZES—$21\frac{1}{2} \times 30$ mm.: 20 c., 40 c.; $26\frac{1}{2} \times 26\frac{1}{2}$ mm.: $1, $1.60; $30 \times 21\frac{1}{2}$ mm.: $2, $8.

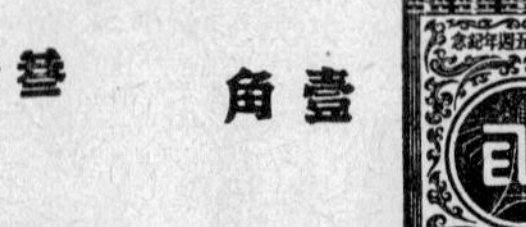

(42.) (43.)

41. Telecommunications Symbols.

1956. No. 1024 of China surch. with T **42.**

242. **94.** 3 c. on (–) green .. 20 8

1956. No. 1026 of China surch. with T **43.**

243. **96.** 10 c. on (–) red .. 20 8

1956. Chinese Telegraph Service. 75th Anniv.

244. **44.** 40 c. blue 5 5
245. $1.40 red 8 5
246. $1.60 green 20 5
247. $2 brown .. .. 1·00 12

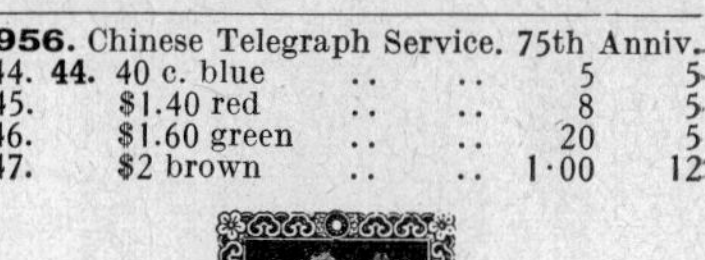

45. Map of China.

1957. (a) Printed in one colour.

248. **45.** 3 c. blue 8 5
249. 10 c. violet 8 5
250. 20 c. orange 8 5
251. 40 c. red 8 5
252. $1 brown 15 5
253. $1 60 green 20 5

(b) With frames in grey-blue.

268. **45.** 3 c. blue 8 5
269. 10 c. violet 8 5
270. 20 c. orange 8 5
271. 40 c. red 12 5
272. $1 brown 15 5
273. $1.60 green 30 5

46. Mencius with his Mother.

47. Chinese Scout Badges and Jubilee Jamboree Emblem.

1957. Mothers' Teaching.

254. **46.** 40 c. green 15 5
255. – $3 brown 40 12

DESIGN: $3, Marshal Yueh Fei with his mother.

1957. Boy Scout Movement. 50th Anniv. Jubilee Jamboree and Lord Baden-Powell. Birth Cent.

256. **47.** 40 c. violet 8 5
257. $1 green 15 5
258. $1.60 blue 25 8

48. Globe, Radio Mast and Microphone.

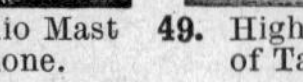

49. Highway Map of Taiwan.

1957. Chinese Broadcasting Service. 30th Anniv.

259. **48.** 40 c. salmon 8 5
260. 50 c. mauve 15 5
261. $3.50 blue 35 15

1957. Taiwan Cross-Island Highway Project. 1st Anniv.

262. **49.** 40 c. green 10 5
263. $1.40 blue 25 5
264. $2 sepia 30 15

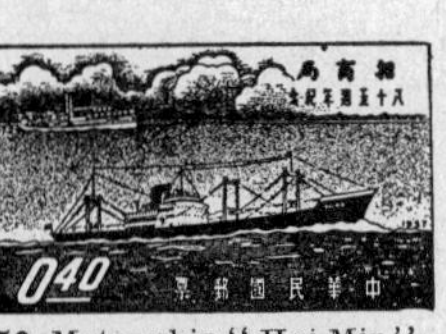

50. Motor-ship "Hai Min" and River-vessel "Kiang Foo".

51. "Batocera lineolata" (beetle).

1957. China Merchants' Steam Navigation Co. 80th Anniv.

265. **50.** 40 c. blue 5 5
266. 80 c. claret 15 5
267. $2.80 salmon 40 20

1958. Formosan Insects. Insects in natural colours; backgrounds in colours given. With gum.

274. **51.** 10 c. green 8 5
275. – 40 c. greenish yellow .. 8 5
276. – $1 apple-green .. 10 5
277. – $1.40 yellow 15 8
278. – $1.60 drab 20 8
279. – $2 lemon 25 10

DESIGNS: 40 c. "Agehana maraho" (butterfly). $1, "Attacus atlas" (moth). $1.40, "Erasmia pulchella chinensis" (moth). $1.60, "Propomacrus macleayi" (beetle). $2, "Papilio memnon agenor" (butterfly).

ORCHIDS—VERT. 40 c. "Laelia-cattleya" $1.40, "Cycnoches chlorochilon klotzsch". HORIZ. $3, "Dendrobium phalaenopsis".

52. "Phalaenopsis amabilis".

1958. Formosan Orchids. Orchids in natural colours; backgrounds in colours given. With gum.

280. 52. 20 c. brown 10 5
281. – 40 c. violet 12 5
282. – $1.40 maroon 20 10
283. – $3 indigo 30 20

53. W.H.O. Emblem.

54. Presidential Mansion, Taipeh.

1958. W.H.O. 10th Anniv.

284. 53. 40 c. blue 5 5
285. $1.60 red 12 5
286. $2 purple 20 12

1958.

286a. 54. $5 grey-green 75 5
286b. $5.60 violet .. .. 1·00 5
286c. $6 orange .. .. 1·10 5
287. $10 green .. .. 1·25 5
288. $20 red .. .. 1·90 5
289. $60 brown .. .. 6·50 60
290. $100 blue .. .. 10·00 1·25

55. Ploughman.

1958. Joint Commission on Chinese Rural Reconstruction. 10th Anniv.

291. 55. 20 c. green 5 5
292. 40 c. black 5 5
293. $1.40 purple 15 5
294. $3 blue 35 15

56. President Chiang Kai-shek Reviewing Troops.

1958. President's 72nd Birthday and National Day Review. With gum.

295. 56. 40 c. multicoloured .. 15 8

57. U.N.E.S.C.O. Headquarters Building, Paris.

58. Flame of Freedom encircling Globe.

1958. U.N.E.S.C.O. Headquarters. Inaug.

296. 57. 20 c. blue 5 5
297. 40 c. green 5 5
298. $1.40 red 12 5
299. $3 purple 25 15

1958. Declaration of Human Rights. 10th Anniv.

300. 58. 40 c. green 5 5
301. 60 c. sepia 5 5
302. $1 red 12 8
303. $3 blue 30 15

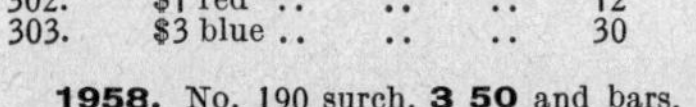

1958. No. 190 surch. **3 50** and bars.

305. – $3.50 on $5 blue .. 35 10

59. The Constitution.

60. Chu Kwang Tower, Quemoy.

1958. Constitution. 10th Anniv.

306. 59. 40 c. green 5 5
307. 50 c. purple 8 5
308. $1.40 red 20 8
309. $3.50 blue 35 15

1959.

310. 60. 3 c. orange 5 5
311. 5 c. olive 5 5
312. 10 c. lilac 5 5
313. 20 c. blue 5 5
314. 40 c. brown 5 5
315. 50 c. blue-green .. 8 5
316. $1 red 12 5
317. $1.40 yellow-green .. 20 5
318. $2 myrtle 20 5
319. $2.80 magenta .. 40 5
320. $3 slate 40 5

See also Nos. 367/82g.

61. Seagull.

62. I.L.O. Emblem and Headquarters, Geneva.

1959. Air. With gum.

321. 61. $8 black, blue and green 45 10

1959. I.L.O. 40th Anniv.

322. 62. 40 c. blue 5 5
323. $1.60 brown 10 5
324. $3 green 20 8
325. $5 red 50 15

64. Inscribed Rock on Mt. Tai-wu, Quemoy.

63. Scout Bugler.

65.

1959. 10th World Scout Jamboree, Manila.

326. 63. 40 c. red 5 5
327. 50 c. blue 20 8
328. $5 green 45 20

1959. Defence of Quemoy (Kinmen) and Matsu Islands, 1958.

329. 64. 40 c. brown 8 5
330. – $1.40 blue 15 8
331. – $2 green 30 12
332. 64. $3 blue 40 15

DESIGN—(41 × 23½ mm.): $1.40, $2. Map of Taiwan, Quemoy and Matsu Is.

1959. Int. Correspondence Week.

333. 65. 40 c. blue 5 5
334. $1 crimson 8 5
335. $2 sepia 15 5
336. $3.50 vermilion .. 40 15

66. National Science Hall.

67. Confederation Emblem.

1959. Taiwan National Science Hall Inaug. With gum.

337. 66. 40 c. multicoloured .. 15 8
338. – $3 multicoloured (different view) .. 50 20

1959. Int. Confed. of Free Trade Unions. 10th Anniv.

339. 67. 40 c. green 8 5
340. $1.60 purple 15 5
341. $3 orange 30 12

68. Sun Yat-sen and Abraham Lincoln.

69. "Bomb Burst" by "Thunder Tiger" Aerobatic Squadron.

1959. Lincoln. 150th Birth Anniv. With gum.

342. 68. 40 c. multicoloured .. 8 5
343. $3 multicoloured .. 45 10

1960. Air. Chinese Air Force Commem. With gum.

344. 69. $1 black, red and blue 40 15
345. – $2 multicoloured .. 50 10
346. – $5 multicoloured .. 90 20

DESIGNS—HORIZ. (Aerobatics): $2, "Loop". $5 Diamond formation flying over jet fighter.

70. Night Delivery.

71. "Uprooted Tree".

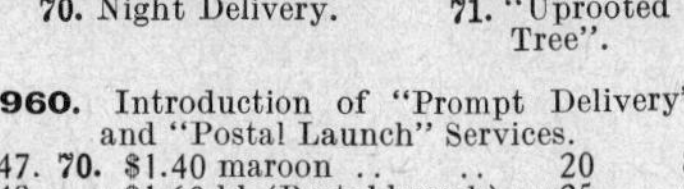

1960. Introduction of "Prompt Delivery" and "Postal Launch" Services.

347. 70. $1.40 maroon 20 8
348. $1.60 bl. (Postal launch) 25 8

1960. World Refugee Year. With gum.

349. 71. 40 c. green, brown & blk. 8 5
350. $3 green, orange & blk. 25 12

72. Cross-Island Highway.

73. Winged Tape-reel.

1960. Inaug. of Taiwan Cross-Island Highway.

351. 72. 40 c. green 8 5
352. – $1 blue 35 15
353. – $2 maroon 12 8
354. 72. $3 brown 40 10

DESIGN—VERT. $1, $2 Tunnels on the Highway.

1960. Visit of Pres. Eisenhower. Nos. 331/2 optd. **WELCOME U.S. PRESIDENT DWIGHT D. EISENHOWER 1960** in English and Chinese.

355. – $2 green 15 8
356. 64. $3 blue 35 15

1960. Phonopost (tape-recordings) Service.

357. 73. $2 salmon 25 8

74. "Flowers and Birds" (after Hsiao Yung).

75. Youth Corps Flag and Summer Activities.

1960. Ancient Chinese Paintings from Palace Museum Collection. (1st series). With gum.

358. – $1 multicoloured .. 30 12
359. – $1.40 multicoloured .. 40 12
360. 74. $1.60 multicoloured .. 50 15
361. – $2 multicoloured .. 80 30

PAINTINGS—HORIZ. $1, "Two Riders" (after Wei Yen). $1.40, "Two Horses and Groom" (after Han Kan). $2, "A Pair of Mandarin Ducks in a Rivulet" (after Monk Hui Ch'ung).

See also Nos. 451/4, 577/80 and 716/19.

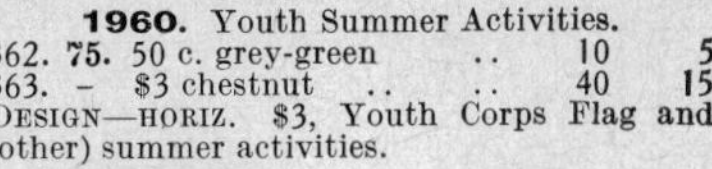

1960. Youth Summer Activities.

362. 75. 50 c. grey-green .. 10 5
363. – $3 chestnut .. 40 15

DESIGN—HORIZ. $3, Youth Corps Flag and (other) summer activities.

76. "Forest Cultivation".

77. Chu Kwang Tower, Quemoy.

1960. 5th World Forestry Congress, Seattle. With gum.

364. 76. $1 multicoloured .. 15 5
365. – $2 multicoloured .. 40 12
366. – $3 multicoloured .. 40 12

DESIGNS: $2, "Forest Protection" (trees). $3 "Lumber Production" (cable railway).

1960. As T 60 but redrawn.

367. 77. 3 c. brown 8 5
382. 10 c. emerald 25 5
368. 40 c. violet 8 5
369. 50 c. orange 8 5
370. 60 c. purple 8 5
371. 80 c. green 8 5
372. $1 green 35 5
373. $1.20 olive 15 5
374. $1.50 blue 15 5
375. $2 red 45 5
376. $2.50 blue 45 5
377. $3 blue-green 30 5
378. $3.20 chocolate .. 75 5
379. $3.60 blue 60 8
382f. $4 turquoise .. .. 1·50 5
382g. $4.50 red 85 10

78. Diving.

79. Bronze Wine Vase (Shang Dynasty).

1960. Sports. With gum.

383. 78. 50 c. chest., yell. & blue 10 5
384. – 80 c. violet, yellow & pur. 10 5
385. – $2 blk., grn., red & yell. 15 10
386. – $2.50 black and orange 30 12
387. – $3 black, red, brown and buff 30 20
388. – $3.20 black, orange, yellow and red .. 40 25

DESIGNS: 80 c. Discus-throwing. $2, Basket-ball. $2.50, Football. $3. Hurdling. $3.20, Sprinting.

1961. Ancient Chinese Art Treasures (1st issue). With gum.

389. 79. 80 c. purple, indigo, black and olive 12 5
390. – $1 indigo, blue & salmon 15 8
391. – $1.20 blue, black, sepia and yellow 30 15
392. – $1.50 sepia, blue & mauve 35 20
393. – $2 brown, violet & olive 40 15
394. – $2.50 blk., lilac & turq. 45 15

DESIGNS: $1, Bronze cauldron (Chou). $1.20, Porcelain vase (Sung). $1.50, Jade perforated tube (Chou). $2, Porcelain jug (Ming). $2.50, Jade flower vase (Ming).

See also Nos. 408/13 and 429/34.

80. Farmer and Mechanical Plough.

81. Mme Chiang Kai-shek.

1961. Agricultural Census.

395. 80. 80 c. purple 8 5
396. $2 green 30 15
397. $3.20 red 30 8

1961. Chinese Women's Anti-Aggression League. 10th Anniv.

398. 81. 80 c. blk., red & bl.-grn. 8 5
399. $1 blk., red & yel.-grn. 20 10
400. $2 black, red & brown 20 10
401. $3.20 blk., red & purple 60 20

82. Taiwan Lobster.

83. Jeme Tien-yao and Locomotive.

84. Pres. Chiang Kai-shek.

85. Convair 880-M Jet-liner ("The Mandarin Jet"), Biplane and Flag.

1961. Mail Order Service.
402. **82.** $3 myrtle 40 8

1961. Jeme Tien-yao (railway engineer). Birth Cent.
403. – 80 c. violet 10 5
404. **83.** $2 black 40 15
DESIGN: 80 c. As T **83** but locomotive heading right.

1961. Anniv. of President's Third Term Inauguration. With gum.
405. – 80 c. multicoloured .. 20 5
406. **84.** $2 multicoloured .. 80 25
DESIGN—HORIZ. 80 c. Map of China inscr. (in Chinese) "Recovery of the Mainland".

1961. Chinese Civil Air Service. 40th Anniv. With gum.
407. **85.** $10 multicoloured .. 1·00 15

1961. Ancient Chinese Art Treasures (2nd issue). As T **79**. With gum.
408. 80 c. bl., yell., blk. & red 12 5
409. $1 indigo, brn. & bistre 30 8
410. $1.50 indigo and salmon 40 20
411. $2 red, black and blue 40 15
412. $4 blue, sepia and red 1·40 15
413. $4.50 chest., sepia & bl. 1·25 40
DESIGNS—VERT. 80 c. Palace perfumer (Ching). $1, Corn vase (Warring States). $2, Jade tankard (Sung). HORIZ. $1.50, Bronze bowl (Chou). $4, Porcelain bowl (Southern Sung). $4.50, Jade chimera (Han).

86. Dr. Sun Yat-sen and Chiang Kai-shek.

87. Lotus Lake.

1961. 50th National Day. With gum.
414. **86.** 80 c. brn., blue & grey 15 5
415. – $5 bl., red brn. & grey 85 30
DESIGN—HORIZ. $5, Map and flag.

1961. Taiwan Scenery. Multicoloured. With gum.
416. 80 c. Pitan (Green Lake) 15 5
417. $1 Type **87** 50 12
418. $2 Sun-Moon Lake .. 50 12
419. $3.20 Wulai Waterfall 1·00 30
The 80 c. and $3.20 are vertical.

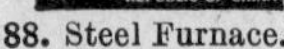

88. Steel Furnace.

89. Atomic Reactor, National Tsing Hwa University.

1961. Taiwan Industries. Multicoloured. With gum.
420. 80 c. Oil refinery .. 15 5
421. $1.50 Type **88** .. 50 30
422. $2.50 Aluminium manufacture 50 30
423. $3.20 Fertiliser plant 80 15
The $3.20 is horiz.

1961. First Taiwan Atomic Reactor Inaug. Multicoloured. With gum.
424. 80 c. Type **89** 30 5
425. $2 Interior of reactor .. 75 35
426. $3.20 Reactor building (horiz.) .. .. .. 1·10 30

90. Telegraph Wires and Micro-wave Reflector Pylons.

91. Postal Segregating, Facing and Cancelling Machine.

1961. Chinese Telecommunications. 80th Anniv. Inscr. "1881-1961". Multicoloured. With gum.
427. 80 c. Type **90** 15 5
428. $3.20 Micro-wave parabolic antenna (horiz.) .. 85 35

1962. Ancient Chinese Art Treasures (3rd issue). As T **79**. With gum.
429. 80 c. brown, violet and red 5 5
430. $1 pur., black, brown & bl. 10 5
431. $2.40 blue, sepia, and red 15 8
432. $3 grn., pink, black & blue 35 15
433. $3.20 rose, green and blue 45 5
434. $3.60 brn., blue, sep. & yell. 50 10
DESIGNS—VERT. 80 c. Jade topaz twin wine vessel (Chiang). $1, Bronze pouring vase (Warring States). $2.40, Porcelain vase (Ming). $3, Tsun bronze wine vase (Shang). $3.20, Porcelain jar (Ching). $3.60, Jade perforated disc (Han).

1962.
435. **91.** 80 c. maroon 15 5

92. Mt. Yu Weather Station.

93. Feeding Children.

1962. World Meteorological Day.
436. **92.** 80 c. brown 8 5
437. – $1 blue 70 15
438. – $2 green 75 30
DESIGNS—HORIZ. $1, Route-map of Typhoon Pamela. VERT. $2, Weather balloon passing globe.

1962. U.N.I.C.E.F. 15th Anniv.
439. **93.** 80 c. red 10 5
440. $3.20 green 65 30

94. Campaign Emblem.

95. Yu Yu-jen (journalist).

1962. Malaria Eradication. With gum.
441. **94.** 80 c. grn., red & indigo 15 5
442. $3.60 turquoise & sepia 40 30

1962. "Elder Reporter" Yü Yu-jen Commem. With gum.
443. **95.** 80 c. sepia and pink .. 15 5

96. Koxinga.

97. Co-operative Emblem.

1962. Koxinga's Recovery of Taiwan. Tercent. With gum.
444. **96.** 80 c. maroon 15 5
445. $2 slate-green .. 40 12

1962. 40th Int. Co-operative Day.
446. **97.** 80 c. brown 15 5
447. – $2 lilac 60 20
DESIGN: $2, Global handclasp.

98. U.N.E.S.C.O. Symbols.

99. Emperor T'ai Tsu (Ming Dynasty).

1962. U.N.E.S.C.O. Activities Commem.
448. **98.** 80 c. magenta 10 8
449. – $2 lake 35 25
450. – $3.20 green 40 15
DESIGNS—HORIZ. $2, U.N.E.S.C.O. emblem on open book. $3.20, Emblem linking hemispheres.

1962. Ancient Chinese Paintings from Palace Museum Collection. (2nd series.) Emperors. Multicoloured. With gum.
451. 80 c. T'ai Tsung (Tang) .. 35 10
452. $2 T'ai Tsu (Sung) .. 1·60 40
453. $3.20 Genghis Khan (Yuan) 2·00 40
454. $4 Type **99** .. .. 1·75 60

100. "Lions" Emblem and Activities.

101. Pole-vaulting.

1962. "Lions International". 45th Anniv. With gum.
455. **100.** 80 c. multicoloured .. 20 5
456. $3.60 multicoloured .. 90 30

1962. Sports. With gum.
457. **101.** 80 c. brn., blue & black 20 5
458. – $3.20 indigo, orange, blue-green & green.. 45 15
DESIGN—HORIZ. $3.20, Rifle-shooting.

102. Young Farmers.

103. Liner.

1962. Chinese 4-H Clubs. 10th Anniv.
459. **102.** 80 c. red 12 5
460. – $3.20 green 35 20
DESIGN: $3.20, 4-H Clubs emblem.

1962. China Merchants' Steam Navigation Co. 90th Anniv. With gum.
461. **103.** 80 c. multicoloured .. 20 5
462. – $3.60 multicoloured .. 90 35
DESIGN—HORIZ. $3.60, Freighter and Pacific route-map.

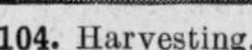
104. Harvesting.

105. Youth, Girl, Torch and Martyrs Monument, Huang Hua Kang.

1963. Freedom from Hunger. With gum.
463. **104.** $10 multicoloured .. 1·40 35

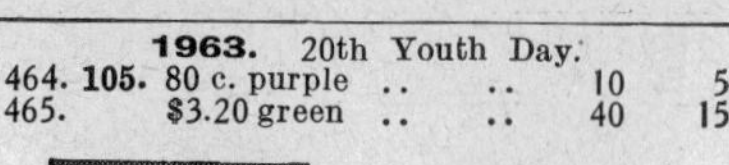

1963. 20th Youth Day.
464. **105.** 80 c. purple 10 5
465. $3.20 green 40 15

106. Swallows and Pagoda.

107. Refugee in Tears.

1963. Asian-Oceanic P.U. 1st Anniv. Inscr. "AOPU". With gum.
466. **106.** 80 c. red, black, grey and ochre 50 8
467. – $2 yellow, black, slate-blue and blue .. 50 8
468. – $6 red, blk. & brn.-red 1·60 70
DESIGNS—HORIZ. $2, Sea gulls. VERT. $6, Crane and pine tree.

1963. Refugees' Flight from Mainland.
469. **107.** 80 c. black 25 8
470. – $3.20 purple 60 10
DESIGN—HORIZ. $3.20, Refugees on march.

108. Jetliner over Tropic of Cancer Monument, Kiai.

109. Red Cross Nurse and Emblem.

1963. Air. Multicoloured. With gum.
471. $2.50 Suspension Bridge, Pitan 25 5
472. $6 Type **108** 50 8
473. $10 Lion-head Mountain, Sinchu .. .. 1·25 50
The $2.50 is horiz.

1963. Red Cross Centenary. With gum.
474. **109.** 80 c. red and black .. 35 8
475. – $10 red, grey-green and grey-blue .. .. 1·60 80
DESIGN: $10, Globe and scroll.

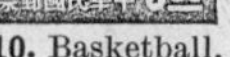
110. Basketball.

111. Freedom Torch.

1963. 2nd Asian Basketball Championships, Taipeh.
476. **110.** 80 c. magenta.. .. 10 5
477. – $2 violet 40 25
DESIGN: $2, Hands reaching for inscribed ball.

1963. Declaration of Human Rights. 15th Anniv.
478. **111.** 80 c. green 8 5
479. – $3.20 lake 25 8
DESIGN—HORIZ. $3.20, Human figures and scales of justice.

112. Country Scene.

113. Dr. Sun Yat-sen and his Book "Three Principles of the People".

1963. "Good-People, Good-Deeds" Campaign. Multicoloured. With gum.
480. 40 c. Type **112** 20 5
481. $4.50 Lighting candle .. 1·00 25

1963. Land-to-Tillers Programme. 10th Anniv With gum.
482. **113.** $5 multicoloured .. 80 12

114. Torch of Liberty. **115.** Broadleaf Cactus.

1964. Liberty Day. 10th Anniv.

483.	114.	80 c. orange	8	5
484.	–	$3.20 indigo	30	8

DESIGN—VERT. $3.20, Hands with broken manacles.

1964. Taiwan Cacti. Mult. With gum.

485.	80 c. T **115**	10	5
486.	$1 Crab cactus	35	12
487.	$3.20 Nopalxochia	50	5
488.	$5 Grizzly-Bear cactus	70	15

116. Wu Chih-hwei (politician). **117.** Chu Kwang Tower, Quemoy.

1964. 99th Birth Anniv. of Wu Chih-hwei.

489.	116.	80 c. sepia	20	5

1964.

490.	117.	3 c. purple	5	5
491.		5 c. green	5	5
492.		10 c. olive	5	5
493.		20 c. blue-green	5	5
494.		40 c. red	5	5
495.		50 c. claret	5	5
496.		80 c. orange	5	5
497.		$1 violet	8	5
498.		$1.50 purple	8	5
499.		$2 mauve	8	5
500.		$2.50 blue	10	5
501.		$3 grey	10	5
502.		$3.20 blue	12	5
504.		$4 green	15	5

118. Nurse and Florence Nightingale. **119.** Weir.

1964. Nurse Day.

506.	–	80 c. violet	12	5
507.	118.	$4 red	50	10

DESIGN—HORIZ. 80 c. Nurses holding candle-light ceremony.

1964. Shinmen Reservoir Inaug. With gum. Multicoloured.

508.	80 c. Type **119**	15	5
509.	$1 Irrigation channel	15	5
510.	$3.20 Dam and powerhouse	35	5
511.	$5 Main spillway	80	25

120. Ancient Treasure Ship and Modern Freighter. **121.** Bananas.

122. Aircraft, Warships and Artillery. **123.** Globe and Flags of Formosa and U.S.A.

1964. Navigation Day.

512.	120.	$2 orange	15	5
513.		$3.60 green	30	8

1964. Taiwan Fruits. Multicoloured. With gum.

514.	80 c. Type **121**	12	5
515.	$1 Oranges	35	15
516.	$3.20 Pineapples	40	10
517.	$4 Water-melons	70	25

1964. Armed Forces Day.

518.	122.	80 c. blue	8	5
519.		$6 brown-purple	60	15

1964. New York World's Fair (1st issue). With gum.

520.	123.	80 c. multicoloured	10	5
521.	–	$5 multicoloured	60	15

DESIGN—HORIZ. $5, Taiwan Pavilion at Fair.
See also Nos. 550/1.

124. Cowman holding calf. **125.** Cycling.

1964. Animal Protection.

522.	124.	$2 maroon	20	5
523.		$4 blue	50	15

1964. Olympic Games, Tokyo.

524.	125.	80 c. blue	8	5
525.	–	$1 red	15	5
526.	–	$3.20 green	40	5
527.	–	$10 violet	1·25	60

DESIGNS: $1, Runner breasting tape. $3.20, Gymnastics. $10, High-jumping.

126. Hsu Kuang-chi (statesman). **127.** Factory-bench ("Pharmaceutics").

1964. Famous Chinese.

528.	126.	80 c. indigo	25	5

See also Nos. 558/9, 586/7, 599, 606/9, 610, 738/40, 960 and 1072/7.

1964. Taiwan Industries. Multicoloured. With gum.

529.	40 c. Type **127**	8	5
530.	$1.50 Loom ("Textiles")	35	15
531.	$2 Refinery ("Chemicals")	45	8
532.	$3.60 Cement-mixer ("Cement")	75	12

The $1.50 and $3.60 are horiz. designs.

128. Dr. Sun Yat-sen (founder). **129.** Mrs. Eleanor Roosevelt and "Human Rights" Emblem.

1964. Kuomintang. 70th Anniv.

533.	128.	80 c. green	20	5
534.		$3.60 purple	35	10

1964. Declaration of Human Rights. 16th Anniv. With gum.

535.	129.	$10 brown and violet	50	15

130. Law Code and Scales of Justice. **131.** Rotary Emblem and Mainspring.

1965. 20th Judicial Day.

536.	130.	80 c. red	8	5
537.		$3.20 green	30	8

1965. Rotary Int. 60th Anniv.

538.	131.	$1.50 red	10	5
539.		$2 green	25	8
540.		$2.50 blue	35	10

132. "Double Carp". **133.** Mme. Chiang Kai-shek.

1965.

541.	132.	$5 violet	90	5
542.		$5.60 blue	45	12
543.		$6 brown	30	8
544.		$10 magenta	1·00	8
545.		$20 red	1·25	15
546.		$50 green	2·10	40
547.		$100 vermilion	5·50	90

1965. Chinese Women's Anti-Aggression League. 15th Anniv. With gum.

548.	133.	$2 multicoloured	30	5
549.		$6 multicoloured	1·00	35

134. Unisphere and Taiwan Pavilion, N.Y. Fair.

1965. New York World's Fair (2nd issue). Multicoloured. With gum.

550.	$2 Type **134**	30	5
551.	$10 Peacock and various birds ("100 birds paying tribute to Queen Phoenix")	1·40	30

135. I.T.U. Emblem and Symbols.

1965. I.T.U. Cent. Multicoloured. With gum.

552.	80 c. Type **135**	10	5
553.	$5 I.T.U. emblem and symbols (vert.)	70	20

136. Red Bream. **137.** I.C.Y. Emblem.

1965. Taiwan Fishes. Multicoloured. With gum.

554.	40 c. Type **136**	8	5
555.	80 c. White pomfret	20	5
556.	$2 Skipjack (vert.)	30	5
557.	$4 Moonfish	60	12

1965. Famous Chinese. Portraits as T **126**.

558.	$1 red (Confucius)	15	5
559.	$3.60 blue (Mencius)	45	8

1965. Int. Co-operation Year. Multicoloured. With gum.

560.	$2 Type **137**	20	5
561.	$6 I.C.Y. emblem (horiz.)	80	35

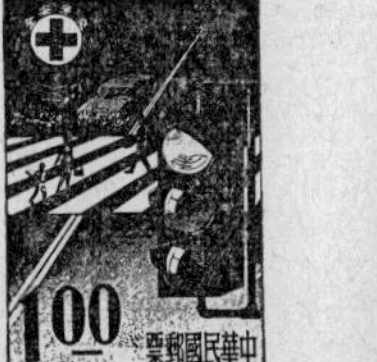

138. Road Crossing. **139.** Dr. Sun Yat-sen.

1965. Road Safety.

562.	138.	$1 maroon	20	5
563.		$4 red	45	10

1965. Dr. Sun Yat-sen's Birth Cent. Multicoloured. With gum.

564.	$1 Type **139**	15	5
565.	$4 As T **139** but with portrait, etc., on right	35	10
566.	$5 Dr. Sun Yat Sen and flags (horiz.)	1·00	45

140. Children with Firework. **141.** Lien Po, "Marshal and Prime Minister Reconciled".

1965. Chinese Folklore. (1st Series). Multicoloured. With gum.

567.	$1 Type **140**	40	5
568.	$4.50 Dragon dance	40	30

See also Nos. 581/3 and 617.

1966. Painted Faces of Chinese Opera. With gum.

569.	141.	$1 multicoloured	80	12
570.	–	$3 multicoloured	80	10
571.	–	$4 multicoloured	80	12
572.	–	$6 multicoloured	1·25	75

FACES (role and opera): $3, Kuan Yu, "Reunion at Ku City". $4, Chang Fei, "Long Board Slope". $6, Buddha, "The Flower-scattering Angel".

142. Pigeon holding Postal Emblem. **143.** "Fishing on a Snowy Day" (after artist of the "Five Dynasties").

1966. Chinese Postal Services. 70th Anniv. Multicoloured. With gum.

573.	$1 Type **142**	20	5
574.	$2 Postman by Chu memorial stone (horiz.)	20	5
575.	$3 Postal Museum (horiz.)	30	8
576.	$4 "Postman climbing"	60	20

1966. Ancient Chinese Paintings from Palace Museum Collection (3rd series). With gum. Multicoloured.

577.	$2.50 Type **143**	40	5
578.	$3.50 "Calves on the Plain"	25	5
579.	$4.50 "Snowscape"	25	15
580.	$5 "Magpies" (after Lin Ch'un)	80	20

Nos. 578/9 (both after Sung artists).

1966. Chinese Folklore (2nd Series). Designs as T **140**. With gum. Multicoloured.

581.	$2.50 Dragon-boat racing	60	5
582.	$4 "Lady Chang O Flying to the Moon"	50	5
583.	$6 Lion Dance	25	8

The $2.50 and $4 are horiz.

144. Flags of Argentine and Chinese Republics. **145.** Lin Sen.

1966. Argentine Republic's Independence. 150th Anniv. With gum.

584.	144.	$10 multicoloured	50	10

1966. Lin Sen (statesman). Birth cent.

585.	145.	$1 sepia	15	5

1966. Famous Chinese. Portraits as T **126**.

586.	$2.50 sepia	15	5
587.	$3.50 red	30	5

PORTRAITS: $2.50 General Yueh Fei. $3.50 Wen Tien-hsiang (statesman).

146. Flying Geese. **147.** Pres. Chiang Kai-shek.

1966.

588. **146.** $3.50 brown 10 5
589. $4 red 15 5
590. $4.50 emerald 15 5
591. $5 purple 15 5
592. $5.50 green 20 5
593. $6 blue 30 15
594. $6.50 violet 40 5
595. $7 black 40 5
596. $8 cerise 25 5

1966. President Chiang Kai-shek's re-election for 4th Term. With gum. Multicoloured.
597. $1 Type **147** 15 5
598. $5 President in Uniform .. 80 20

1966. Famous Chinese. Portrait as T **126.**
599. $1 ultramarine (Tsai Yuan-Pei (scholar)) .. 20 5

148. Various means of Transport. **149.** Boeing "727" over Chilin Pavilion, Grand Hotel, Taipei.

1967. Development of Taiwan Communications. Multicoloured. With gum.
600. $1 Mobile postman and micro-wave station (vert.) 15 5
601. $5 Type **148** 40 8

1967. Air. Multicoloured. With gum.
602. $5 Type **149** 30 5
603. $8 Boeing "727" over Palace Museum, Taipei .. 35 15

150. Pres. Chiang Kai-shek. **151.** "God of Happiness" (wood carving).

1967. Chiang Kai-shek's 4th Presidential Term. With gum.
604. **150.** $1 multicoloured .. 15 5
605. $4 multicoloured .. 50 8

1967. Famous Chinese. Poets. Portraits As T **126.**
606. $1 black (Chu Yuan) .. 12 5
607. $2 brown (Li Po) .. 20 5
608. $2.50 (Tu Fu) 30 8
609. $3 olive (Po Chu-i) .. 30 8

1967. Famous Chinese. Portrait as T **126.**
610. $1 black (Chiu Ching, female revolutionary) .. 15 5

1967. Chinese Handicrafts. Multicoloured. With gum.
611. $1 Type **151** 8 5
612. $2.50 Vase and dish .. 15 5
613. $3 Chinese dolls 20 5
614. $5 Palace lanterns .. 35 20

152. "WACL" on World Map. **153.** Formosan Barbet.

1967. 1st World Anti-Communist League Conf., Taipei.
615. **152.** $1 vermilion 5 5
616. $5 blue 20 10

GUM. From No. 617 all stamps were issued with gum unless otherwise stated.

1967. Chinese Folklore (3rd Series). Stilts Pastime. As T **140.**
617. $4.50 multicoloured .. 20 10
DESIGN: "The Fisherman and the Woodcutter" (Chinese play on stilts).

1967. Taiwan Birds. Multicoloured.
618. $1 Type **153** 8 5
619. $2 Maroon oriole (horiz.) .. 15 5
620. $2.50 Formosan green pigeon (horiz.) 15 8
621. $3 Blue magpie (horiz.) .. 20 8
622. $5 Crested serpent-eagle .. 40 12
623. $8 Mikado long-tailed pheasant (horiz.) .. 50 30

154. Chung Hsing Pagoda. **155.** Flags and China Park, Manila.

1967. Int. Tourist Year. Multicoloured.
624. $1 Type **154** 10 5
625. $2.50 Yeh Liu National Park (coastal scene) (horiz.) .. 25 12
626. $4 Statue of Buddha (horiz.) 30 8
627. $5 National Palace Museum, Taipei (horiz.) .. 40 20

1967. China-Philippines Friendship.
628. **155.** $1 multicoloured .. 10 5
629. $5 multicoloured .. 30 10

156. Sun Yat-sen Building, Yangmingshan. **157.** Taroko Gorge.

1968.

630. **156.** 5 c. brown 5 5
631. 10 c. green 5 5
632. 50 c. purple 5 5
633. $1 red 8 5
634. $1.50 green 10 5
635. $2 purple 12 5
636. $2.50 blue 12 5
637. $3 blue 15 5
For redrawn design see Nos. 791/8.

1968. 17th Pacific Area Travel Assn. Conf., Taipei. Multicoloured.
638. $5 Type **157** 30 10
639. $8 Sun Yat-sen Building, Yangmingshan 35 12

158. Harvesting Sugar-cane. **159.** Vice-Pres. Cheng.

1968. Sugar-cane Technologists Congress, Taiwan.
640. **158.** $1 multicoloured .. 15 5
641. $4 multicoloured .. 20 10

1968. Vice-Pres. Chen Cheng. 3rd Death Anniv.
642. **159.** $1 multicoloured .. 15 5

160. Flying Geese. **161.** Jade Cabbage. (Ching Dynasty).

1968. Chinese Postage Stamps. 90th Anniv.
643. **160.** $1 red 10 5

1968. Chinese Art Treasures, National Palace Museum. Multicoloured.
645. $1 Type **161** 8 5
646. $1.50 Jade battle-axe (Warring States period) 15 10
647. $2 Lung-ch'uan porcelain flower bowl (Sung dynasty) 15 8
648. $2.50 Yung Cheng enamelled vase (Ching dynasty) .. 20 10
649. $4 Agate "fingered" flower-holder (Ching dynasty) .. 20 10
650. $5 Sacrificial vessel (Western Chou) 30 15
The $2 and $4 are horiz.
See also Nos. 682/7 and 632/7.

162. W.H.O. Emblem on "20". **163.** Sun, Planets and "Rainfall".

1968. W.H.O. 20th Anniv.
651. **162.** $1 green 10 5
652. $5 red 20 12

1968. Int. Hydrological Decade.
653. **163.** $1 green and orange .. 10 5
654. $4 blue and orange .. 20 5

164. "A City of Cathay" (section of hand-scroll painting).

1968. "A City of Cathay" (Palace Museum).
655. **164.** $1 (1) multicoloured .. 10 5
656. – $1 (2) multicoloured .. 10 5
657. – $1 (3) multicoloured .. 10 5
658. – $1 (4) multicoloured .. 10 5
659. – $1 (5) multicoloured .. 10 5
660. – $5 multicoloured .. 50 25
661. – $8 multicoloured .. 70 35
DESIGNS—As T **164**: Nos. 660/4 together show panorama of the city ending with the palace. LARGER (61 × 32 mm.). $5, City wall and gate. $8, Great bridge.
The five $1 stamps were issued together se-tenant in horiz. strips, representing the last 11 feet of the 37 foot scroll, which is viewed from right to left as it is unrolled.
The stamps may be identified by the numbers given in brackets which correspond to the numbers in the bottom right-hand corners of the stamps.
See also Nos. 699/703 and 752/758.

165. Map and Radio "Waves". **166.** Human Rights Emblem.

1968. Chinese Broadcasting Service. 40th Anniv.
662. **165.** $1 grey, ultram. & blue 8 5
663. – $4 red & ultramarine .. 20 5
DESIGNS—VERT. $4, Stereo broadcast 'waves'.

1968. Human Rights Year.
664. **166.** $1 multicoloured .. 10 5
665. $5 multicoloured .. 20 8

167. Harvesting Rice. **168.** Throwing the Javelin.

1968. Rural Reconstruction.
666. **167.** $1 brown, ochre & yell. 10 5
667. $5 bronze, grn. & lemon. 25 20

1968. Olympic Games, Mexico. Multicoloured.
668. $1 Type **168** 5 5
669. $2.50 Weightlifting .. 12 5
670. $5 Pole-vaulting (horiz.) .. 15 5
671. $8 Hurdling (horiz) .. 30 12

169. President Chiang Kai-shek and Main Gate, Whampoa Military Academy.

1968. "President Chiang Kai-shek's Meritorious Services". Multicoloured.
672. $1 Type **169** 10 5
673. $2 Reviewing Northern Expedition Forces .. 15 8
674. $2.50 Suppression of bandits 15 8
675. $3.50 Marco Polo Bridge, and Victory Parade, Nanking, 1945 .. 20 10
676. $4 Chinese Constitution .. 25 15
677. $5 National flag 35 15
Each stamp bears the portrait of President Chiang Kai-shek as in T **169.**

170. Cockerel. **171.** National Flag.

1968. New Year Greetings. "Year of the Cock".
678. **170.** $1 multicoloured .. 85 8
679. $4.50 multicoloured .. 85 60

1968. Chinese Constitution. 20th Anniv.
680. **171.** $1 multicoloured .. 8 5
681. $5 multicoloured .. 25 10

1969. Chinese Art Treasures, National Palace Museum (2nd series). Multicoloured as T **161.**
682. $1 Jade buckle (Ching dynasty) (horiz.) .. 8 5
683. $1.50 Jade vase (Sung dynasty) .. 10 5
684. $2 Cloisonne enamel teapot (Ching dynasty) (horiz.) 10 5
685. $2.50 Bronze sacrificial vessel (Kuei) (horiz.) .. 15 8
686. $4 Hsuan-te "heavenly ball" vase (Ming dynasty.) 20 8
687. $5 "Gourd" vase (Ching dynasty) 25 15

172. Servicemen and Savings Emblem. **173.** Ti (flute).

1969. Forces' Savings Services. 10th Anniv.
688. **172.** $1 maroon 8 5
689. $4 blue 20 5

1969. Chinese Musical Instruments. Multicoloured.
690. $1 Type **173** 5 5
691. $2.50 Sheng (pipes) .. 8 5
692. $4 P'i-p'a (lute) .. 25 12
693. $5 Cheng (zither) .. 25 10

174. Chung Shan Building, Mt. Yangmin. **175.** "Double Carp".

1969. 10th Kuomintang Congress.
694. **174.** $1 multicoloured .. 8 5

1969.

695a. **175.** $10 blue 35 5
696a. $20 chocolate 35 5
697a. $50 green .. .. 1·25 15
698a. $100 vermilion .. 2·50 50
T **175** is a redrawn version of T **132.**

1969. "A City of Cathay" (scroll). (2nd series). As T **164**. Multicoloured.

699. $1 "Musicians" 10 5
700. $1 "Bridal chair" 10 5
701. $2.50 Emigrants with ox-cart 20 12
702. $5 "Scroll gallery" .. 25 15
703. $8 "Roadside cafe" .. 40 30

176. I.L.O. Emblem. **177.** "Food and Clothing".

1969. Int. Labour Organization. 50th Anniv.

704. **176.** $1 blue 8 5
705. $8 red 25 12

1969. "Model Citizen's Life" Movement.

706. **177.** $1 vermilion 5 5
707. – $2.50 blue 20 10
708. – $4 green 20 5

DESIGNS: $2.50 "Housekeeping and Road Safety". $4 "Schooling and Recreation".

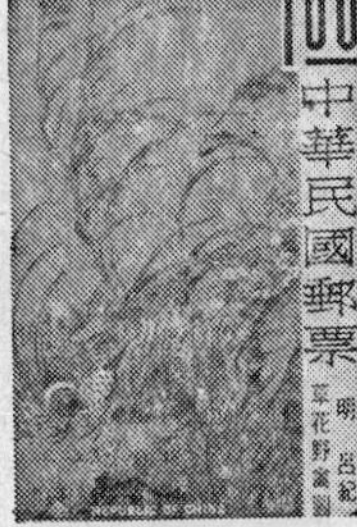

178. Wild Geese over Mountains. **179.** Children and Symbols of Learning.

1969. Air. Multicoloured.

709. $2·50 Type **178** 8 5
710. $5 Geese over sea 12 8
711. $8 Geese over land .. 20 10

No. 711 is horiz.

1969. Nine-Year Free Education System. 1st. Anniv.

712. **179.** $1 red 8 5
713. – $2.50 green 12 5
714. – $4 blue 15 8
715. **179.** $5 chocolate 20 10

DESIGNS—VERT. $2.50 and $4, Children and school.

180. "Flowers and Pheasants", Ming dynasty (Lu Chih). **181.** "Charles Mollerin" Rose.

1969. Ancient Chinese Paintings from Palace Museum Collection (4th Series). Birds and Flowers. Multicoloured.

716. $1 Type **180** 8 5
717. $2.50 "Bamboos and Birds", Sung dynasty (artist unknown) 12 8
718. $5 "Flowers and Birds", Sung dynasty (artist unknown) 25 10
719. $8 "Two Cranes and Flowers" Ching dynasty (C. Castiglione) 40 12

1969. Roses. Multicoloured.

720. $1 Type **181** 8 5
721. $2.50 "Golden Sceptre" .. 15 8
722. $5 "Peace" 30 20
723. $8 "Josephine Bruce" .. 30 15

182. Launching Missile. **183.** A.P.U. Emblem.

1969. Air. Defence Day.

724. **182.** $1 claret 8 5

1969. 5th Asian Parliamentarians' Union General Assembly, Taipei.

725. **183.** $1 claret 8 5
726. $5 green 20 8

184. Pekinese Dogs. **185.** Satellite and Earth Station.

1969. New Year Greetings.

727. **184.** 50 c. multicoloured .. 5 5
728. $4.50 multicoloured .. 80 25

1969. Communications Satellite Earth Station. Inaug.

729. **185.** $1 multicoloured .. 8 5
730. $5 multicoloured .. 25 15
731. $8 multicoloured .. 30 20

1970. Chinese Art Treasures, National Palace Museum (3rd Series). Multicoloured as T **161**.

732. $1 Lacquer vase (Ching dynasty) 8 5
733. $1.50 Agate grinding-stone (Ching dynasty) .. 10 5
734. $2 Jade carving (Ching dynasty) 10 5
735. $2.50 Jade "Shepherd and Ram" (Han dynasty) .. 12 8
736. $4 Porcelain jar (Ching dynasty) 20 8
737. $5 Porcelain urn (Northern Sung dynasty) .. 25 12

Nos. 733/5 are horiz.

1970. Famous Chinese. Portraits as T **126**.

738. $1 red 10 5
739. $2·50 green 15 8
740. $4 blue 20 8

PORTRAITS: $1 Hsuan Chuang (traveller). $2·50 Hua To (physician). $4 Chu Hsi (philosopher).

186. Taiwan Pavilion and EXPO Emblem. **187.** Sun Yat-sen Building, Yangmingshan.

1970. World Fair "EXPO 70", Osaka, Japan. Multicoloured.

741. $5 Type **186** 15 8
742. $8 Pavilion encircled by national flags 30 15

1970.

743. **187.** $1 red 8 5

For redrawn design see No. 1039.

188. Rain-cloud, Palm and Recording apparatus. **189.** Martyrs' Shrine.

1970. World Meteorological Day. Multicoloured.

744. $1 Type **188** 10 5
745. $8 "Nimbus 3" satellite (horiz.) 30 15

1970. Revolutionary Martyrs' Shrine. Mult.

746. $1 Type **189** 8 5
747. $8 Shrine gateway 25 15

190. General Yueh Fei ("Loyalty").

1970. Chinese Opera. "The Virtues". Multicoloured.

748. $1 Type **190** 10 5
749. $2·50 Emperor Shun tortured by stepmother ("Filial Piety") .. 15 10
750. $5 Chin Liang-yu "The Lady General" ("Chastity") 25 12
751. $8 Kuan Yu and groom ("Fidelity") 30 15

191. Three Horses at Play.

1970. "One Hundred Horses" (handscroll by Lang Shi-ning (G. Castiglione)). Multicoloured.

752. $1 (1) Horses on plain .. 8 5
753. $1 (2) Horses on plain (different) 8 5
754. $1 (3) Horses playing .. 8 5
755. $1 (4) Horses on river bank 8 5
756. $1 (5) Horses crossing river 8 5
757. $5 Type **191** 35 20
758. $8 Groom roping horses .. 45 25

SERIAL NUMBERS are indicated to aid identification of the above and certain other sets. For key to Chinese numerals see table at the beginning of CHINA.

192. Old Lai-tsu dropping buckets. **193.** Chiang Kai-shek's Moon Message.

1970. Chinese Folk-tales. (1st series). Mult.

759. 10 c. Type **192** 5 5
760. 10 c. Yien-tsu disguised as a deer 5 5
761. 10 c. Hwang Hsiang with fan 5 5
762. 10 c. Wang Shiang fishing 5 5
763. 10 c. Chu Hsiu-chang reunited with mother .. 5 5
764. 50 c. Emperor Wen tasting mother's medicine .. 5 5
765. $1 Lu Chi dropping oranges 8 5
766. $1 Yang Hsiang fighting tiger 8 5

See also Nos. 817/24, 1000/7 and 1064/7.

1970. 1st Man on the Moon. Multicoloured.

767. $1 Type **193** 10 5
768. $5 "Apollo 11" astronauts (horiz.) 20 10
769. $8 "First step on the Moon" 30 20

194. Productivity Symbol. **195.** Flags of Taiwan and U.N.

1970. Asian Productivity Year.

770. **194.** $1 multicoloured .. 5 5
771. $5 multicoloured .. 20 10

1970. United Nations. 25th Anniv.

772. **195.** $5 multicoloured .. 25 8

196. Postal Zone Map. **197.** "Cultural Activities" (10th month).

1970. Postal Zone Numbers Campaign. Multicoloured.

773. $1 Type **196** 8 5
774. $2.50 Postal Zone emblem (horiz.) 25 10

1970. "Occupations of the Twelve Months" Hanging Scrolls. Multicoloured.

(a) "Winter".

775. $1 Type **197** 8 5
776. $2·50 "School Buildings" (11th month) 20 12
777. $5 "Games in the Snow" (12th month) 30 15

(b) "Spring".

778. $1 "Lantern Festival" (1st month) 5 5
779. $2·50 "Apricots in Blossom" (2nd month) .. 12 8
780. $5 "Purification Ceremony" (3rd month) .. 25 15

(c) "Summer".

781. $1 "Summer Shower" (4th month) 5 5
782. $2·50 "Dragon-boat Festival" (5th month) .. 12 8
783. $5 "Lotus Pond" (6th month) 25 15

(d) "Autumn".

784. $1 "Weaver Festival" (7th month) 5 5
785. $2·50 "Moon Festival" (8th month) 12 8
786. $5 "Chrysanthemum Blossom" (9th month) 25 15

The month numbers are given by the Chinese characters in brackets, which follow the face value on the stamps.

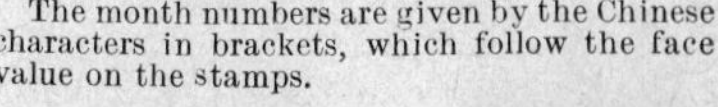

198. "Planned Family". **199.** Toy Pig.

1970. Family Planning. Multicoloured.

787. $1 Type **198** 8 5
788. $4 "Family excursion" (vert.) 25 8

1970. New Year Greetings.

789. **199.** 50 c. multicoloured .. 5 5
790. $4.50 multicoloured 40 15

200. Sun Yat-sen Building, Yangmingshan. **201.** "Tibia fusus".

1971.

791. **200.** 5 c. brown 5 5
792. 10 c. green 5 5
793. 50 c. red 5 5
794. $1 vermilion 5 5
795. $1·50 blue 5 5
796. $2 purple 8 5
797. $2·50 green 10 5
798. $3 blue 12 5

T **200** is a redrawn version of T **156**.

1971. Taiwan Shells. Multicoloured.

799. $1 Type **201** 8 5
800. $2·50 "Harpecla kuroda" 10 8
801. $5 "Conus stupa kuroda" .. 25 10
802. $8 "Entemnotrochus rumphii" 40 20

202. Savings Book and Certificate. **203.** Chinese greeting African Farmer.

1971. National Savings Campaign. Multicoloured.

803. $1 Type **202** 5 5
804. $4 Hand dropping coin in savings bank 20 8

1971. Sino-African Technical Co-operation Committee. 10th Anniv. Multicoloured.

805. $1 Type **203** 5 5
806. $8 Rice-growing (horiz.) .. 35 15

204. White-faced Flying Squirrel.

205. Pitcher delivering ball.

1971. Taiwan Animals. Multicoloured.
807. $1 Taiwan rock-monkey (vert.) 8 5
808. $2 Type **204** 10 8
809. $3 Chinese pangolin .. 15 8
810. $4 Taiwan sika deer .. 20 12

1971. World Little League Baseball Championships, Taiwan. Multicoloured.
811. $1 Type **205** 5 5
812. $2·50 Players at base (horiz.) 12 5
813. $4 Striker and catcher .. 20 8

(206.)

207. Yu Hsun and Elephant.

1971. Taiwan Giant's Victory in World Little League Baseball Championships. Optd. with T **206**.
814. **156.** $1 red 5 5
815. $2·50 blue 20 10
816. $3 blue 15 10

1971. Chinese Folk-tales (2nd series). Mult.
817. 10 c. Type **207** 5 5
818. 10 c. Tsai Hsun with mulberries 5 5
819. 10 c. Tseng Sun with fire-wood 5 5
820. 10 c. Kiang Keh and bandits 5 5
821. 10 c. Tsu Lu with sack of rice 5 5
822. 50 c. Meng Chung gathering bamboo shoots 5 5
823. $1 Tung Yung and wife .. 5 5
824. $1 Tzu Chien shivering with cold 5 5

208. Emblem and Flag.

1971. 60th National Day. Multicoloured.
825. $1 Type **208** 5 5
826. $2.50 National anthem, map and flag 12 5
827. $5 Pres. Chiang Kai-shek, constitution and flag .. 25 15
828. $8 Dr. Sun Yat-sen, " Three principles " and flag .. 35 12

209. A.O.P.U. Emblem. 210. " White Frost Hawk ".

1971. Asian-Oceanic Postal Union Executive Committee Session, Taipei.
829. **209.** $2.50 multicoloured .. 20 8
830. $5 multicoloured .. 20 8

1971. " Ten Prized Dogs " (paintings on silk by Lang Shih-ning (G. Castiglione)). Multicoloured.
831. $1 Type **210** 5 5
832. $1 " Black Dog with Snow-white Claws " 5 5
833. $2 " Star-glancing Wolf " 8 5
834. $2 " Yellow Leopard " .. 8 5
835. $2·50 " Golden-winged Face " 10 8
836. $2·50 " Flying Magpie " .. 10 8
837. $5 " Young Black Dragon " 20 10
838. $5 " Heavenly Lion " .. 20 10
839. $8 " Young Grey Dragon " .. 35 25
840. $8 " Mottle-coated Tiger " 35 25

211/214. Squirrels.

1971. New Year Greetings.
841. **211.** 50 c. multicoloured .. 5 5
842. **212.** 50 c. multicoloured .. 5 5
843. **213.** 50 c. multicoloured .. 5 5
844. **214.** 50 c. multicoloured .. 5 5
845. **211.** $4.50 multicoloured .. 15 12
846. **212.** $4.50 multicoloured .. 15 12
847. **213.** $4.50 multicoloured .. 15 12
848. **214.** $4.50 multicoloured .. 15 12

215. Flags of Taiwan and Jordan.

1971. Hashemite Kingdom of Jordan. 50th Anniv.
849. **215.** $5 multicoloured .. 25 5

216. Freighter " Hai King ".

1971. China Merchants Steam Navigation Company. Cent. Multicoloured.
850. **216.** $4 blue, red & green .. 15 8
851. – $7 multicoloured .. 25 8
DESIGN—VERT. $7 Liner on Pacific.

217. Downhill Skiing.

1972. Winter Olympic Games, Sapporo, Japan.
852. **217.** $1 blk., yell. and blue 5 5
853. – $5 black, orge. & grn. 15 5
854. – $8 blk., red & grey .. 25 20
DESIGNS: $5 Cross-country skiing. $8 Giant slalom.

218. Yung Cheng Vase.

219. Doves.

1972. Chinese Porcelain. (1st series). Ch'ing Dynasty. Multicoloured.
855. $1 Type **218** 5 5
856. $2 Kang Hsi jar .. 10 5
857. $2.50 Yung Cheng jug .. 12 5
858. $5 Chien Lung vase .. 20 10
859. $8 Chien Lung jar .. 30 20
See also Nos. 914/18, 927/31 and 977/81.

1972. Asian-Oceanic Postal Union. 10th Anniv.
860. **219.** $1 black and blue .. 5 5
861. $5 black and violet 20 10

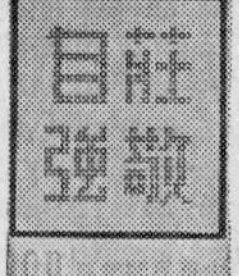
220. " Dignity with Self-Reliance " (Pres. Chiang Kai-shek).

222. Magnifying-glass, Perforation gauge and tweezers.

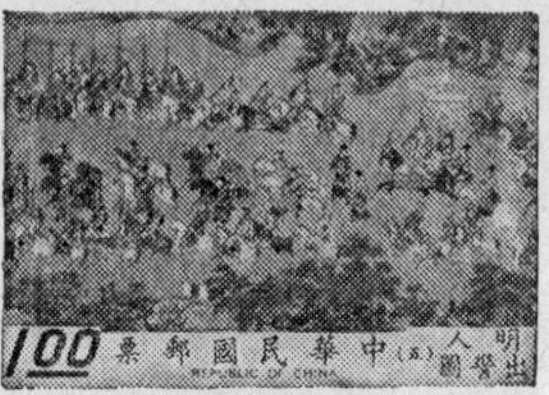
221. Horsemen and Emperor.

1972.
862. **220.** 5 c. brown & yellow .. 5 5
863. 10 c. blue & orange .. 5 5
864. 50 c. mauve & purple 5 5
865. $1 red and blue .. 5 5
866. $1·50 yellow and blue 5 5
867. $2 violet, pur. & orge. 5 5
868. $2·50 green and red .. 5 5
869. $3 red and green .. 8 5

1972. " The Emperor's Procession " (Ming dynasty handscrolls). Multicoloured.
(a) First issue.
870. $1 (1) Pagoda and crowds 5 5
871. $1 (2) Seven carriages .. 5 5
872. $1 (3) Emperor's coach .. 5 5
873. $1 (4) Horsemen with flags 5 5
874. $1 (5) Type **221** 5 5
875. $2·50 Mounted messengers 10 5
876. $5 Guards 20 8
877. $8 Imperial sedan chair .. 30 15
(b) Second issue.
878. $1 (1) Three barges .. 5 5
879. $1 (2) Sedan chairs .. 5 5
880. $1 (3) Two barges.. .. 5 5
881. $1 (4) Horsemen and mounted orchestra .. 5 5
882. $1 (5) Two carriages .. 5 5
883. $2·50 City gate 10 5
884. $5 Mounted orchestra .. 20 8
885. $8 Barges 30 15

1972. Philately Day.
886. – $1 blue 5 5
887. – $2·50 green 10 5
888. **222.** $8 red 25 20
DESIGNS—VERT. $1 First day covers. $2·50 Magnifying glass and stamps.

(223.)

224. Emperor Yao.

1972. Taiwan's Victories in Senior and Little World Baseball Leagues. Nos. 862/5 optd. with T **223**.
889. **220.** $1 red and blue .. 5 5
890. $1·50 yellow & blue.. 12 8
891. $2 violet, pur. & orge. 12 5
892. $3 red and green .. 12 5

1972. Chinese Cultural Heroes.
893. **224.** $3·50 blue 10 5
894. – $4 red 12 5
895. – $4·50 violet 12 5
896. – $5 green 15 8
897. – $5·50 purple 15 8
898. – $6 orange 15 10
899. – $7 brown 20 10
900. – $8 blue 20 15
DESIGNS: $4 Emperor Shun. $4.50 Yu the Great. $5 King T'ang. $5·50 King Weng. $6 King Wu. $7 Chou Kung. $8 Confucius.

225. Mountaineering.

226. Microwave Systems and Electronic Sorting machine.

1972. China Youth Corps. 20th Anniv. Multicoloured.
902. $1 Type **225** 5 5
903. $2·50 Winter exercises .. 10 5
904. $4 High-diving 15 8
905. $8 Parachuting 30 15

1972. Improvement of Communication.
906. **226.** $1 red 5 5
907. – $2·50 blue 12 8
908. – $5 purple 20 12
DESIGNS—HORIZ. $2·50 Container-ship and aircraft. $5 Road traffic and train (bridge).

227. " Eyes " and J.C.I. Emblem.

228. Cow and Calf.

1972. 27th Junior Chamber Int., World Congress, Taipei.
909. **227.** $1 multicoloured .. 5 5
910. $5 multicoloured .. 15 8
911. $8 multicoloured .. 25 20

1972. New Year Greetings.
912. **228.** 50 c. black and brown 5 5
913. $4·50 brn., red & yell. 20 12

1973. Chinese Porcelain (2nd Series). Ming Dynasty. As T **218**. Multicoloured.
914. $1 Fu vase 5 5
915. $2 Floral vase 5 5
916. $2·50 Ku vase 10 5
917. $5 Hu flask 15 10
918. $8 Garlic-head vase .. 25 20

229. " Kicking the Shuttlecock ".

230. Bamboo Sampan.

1973. Chinese Folklore. Multicoloured.
919. $1 Type **229** 5 5
920. $4 " The fisherman and the oyster fairy " (horiz.) 12 8
921. $5 " Lady in a boat " (horiz.) 15 10
922. $8 " The Old Man and the Lady " 25 15
See also Nos. 982/3 and 1037/8.

1973. Taiwan Handicrafts (1st series). Mult.
923. $1 Type **230** 5 5
924. $2·50 Marble vase (vert.) 10 5
925. $5 Glass plate 15 8
926. $8 Aborigine Doll (vert.).. 25 15
See also Nos. 988/91.

1973. Chinese Porcelain (3rd series). Ming Dynasty. Horiz. designs as T **218**. Mult.
927. $1 Dragon stem-bowl .. 5 5
928. $2 Dragon pot .. 8 5
929. $2·50 Covered jar with lotus decor 10 5
930. $5 Covered jar showing horses 15 8
931. $8 " Immortals " bowl .. 25 15

231. Contractors' Equipment.

232. Pres. Chiang Kai-shek and Flag.

1973. Int. Federation of Asian and Western Pacific Contractors' Association. 12th Convention.
932. **231.** $1 multicoloured .. 5 5
933. – $5 blue and black .. 15 8
DESIGN—HORIZ. $5 Bulldozer.

1973. Pres. Chiang Kai-shek's 5th Term of Office. Inaug.
934. **232.** $1 multicoloured .. 5 5
935. $4 multicoloured .. 15 8

233. Lin Tse-hsu (statesman).

1973. Lin Tse-hsu Commemoration.
936. 233. $1 maroon 5 5

234. Palace Gate.

1973. "Spring Morning in the Han Palace" (Ming dynasty handscroll). Multicoloured.
(a) First issue.
937. $1 (1) Type **234** 5 5
938. $1 (2) Feeding peacocks .. 5 5
939. $1 (3) Emperor's wife .. 5 5
940. $1 (4) Ladies and pear tree 5 5
941. $1 (5) Music pavilion .. 5 5
942. $5 Giant rock (vert.) .. 15 8
943. $8 Lady musicians (vert.) 20 12
(b) Second issue.
944. $1 (6) Game with flowers .. 5 5
945. $1 (7) Leisure room .. 5 5
946. $1 (8) Ladies with teapots 5 5
947. $1 (9) Artist at work .. 5 5
948. $1 (10) Palace wall and guards 5 5
949. $5 Playing game at table (vert.) 15 8
950. $8 Swatting insect (vert.) 20 12

235. "Bamboo" (Hsiang Te-hsin).

1973. Ancient Chinese Fan Paintings. (1st series). Multicoloured.
951. $1 Type **235** 5 5
952. $2·50 "Flowers" (Sun K'O-Hung) 10 5
953. $5 "Landscape" (Ch'iu Ying) 20 8
954. $8 "Seated Figure and Tree" (Shen Chou) .. 30 12
See also Nos. 1052/5.

236. Emblem of World Series. 237. Interpol Emblem.

1973. Little League World Baseball Series. Taiwan Victory in Twin Championships.
955. 236. $1 blue, red and yellow 5 5
956. $4 blue, green & yell. 12 8

1973. International Criminal Police Organization (Interpol). 50th Anniv.
957. 237. $1 blue and orange .. 5 5
958. $5 green and orange .. 15 8
959. $8 purple and orange 20 12

1973. Famous Chinese. Portrait as T **126**.
960. $1 violet (Ch'iu Feng-chia (poet)) 5 5

238. Part of Map of Reservoir.

1973. Opening of Tsengwen Reservoir. Multicoloured.
961. $1 Type **238** 5 5
962. $1 } Rest of Map .. 5 5
963. $1 } .. 5 5
964. $5 Dam and power station (30 × 22mm) 15 8
965. $8 Spillway (30 × 22mm) .. 20 12

239. "Snow-dotted Eagle".

1973. Paintings of Horses. Multicoloured.
966. 50 c. Type **239** 5 5
967. $1 "Comfortable Ride" .. 5 5
968. $1 "Red Flower Eagle" .. 5 5
969. $1 "Cloud-running Steed" 5 5
970. $1 "Sky-running Steed" 5 5
971. $2·50 "Red Jade Steed" 5 5
972. $5 "Thunder-clap Steed" 12 8
973. $8 "Arabian Champion" 20 12

240. Tiger. 241. Balancing pot.

1973. New Year Greetings. "Year of the Tiger".
975. 240. 50 c. multicoloured .. 5 5
976. $4. 50 multicoloured .. 10 5

1974. Chinese Porcelain (4th series). Sung Dynasty. As Type **218**. Multicoloured.
977. $1 Ko vase 5 5
978. $2 Kuan vase (horiz.) .. 5 5
979. $2·50 Ju bowl (horiz.) .. 5 5
980. $5 Kuan incense burner (horiz.) 12 8
981. $8 Chun incense burner .. (horiz.) 20 12

1974. Chinese Folklore (2nd series). Mult.
982. $1 Type **241** 5 5
983. $8 Magicians (horiz.) .. 20 12

242. Road Tunnel, Taroko Gorge. 243. "Fighting Cocks" (brass).

1974. Taiwan Scenery (1st series). Mult.
984. $1 Type **242** 5 5
985. $2·50 Luce Chapel, Tunghi University .. 5 5
986. $5 Tzu En Pagoda, Sun Moon Lake 12 8
987. $8 Goddess of Mercy Statue, Keelung .. 20 12
See also Nos. 992/5.

1974. Taiwan Handicrafts (2nd series). Mult.
988. $1 Type **243** 5 5
989. $2·50 "Fruits" (jade) .. 5 5
990. $5 "Fisherman" (wood-carving) (vert.) .. 12 8
991. $8 "Bouquet of Flowers" (plastic) (vert.) .. 20 12

1974. Taiwan Scenery (2nd series). As Type **242** but all horiz. Multicoloured.
992. $1 Dr. Sun Yat-Sen Memorial Hall, Taipei .. 5 5
993. $2·50 Reaching-Moon Tower, Cheng Ching Lake .. 5 5
994. $5 Seashore, Lanyu .. 12 8
995. $8 Inter-island bridge, Penghu 20 12

244. Pres. Chiang Kai-shek. 245. Long-distance Runner.

1974. Chinese Military Academy. 50th Anniv.
996. 244. $1 red 5 5
997. – $14 blue 35 25
DESIGN—VERT. $14 Cadets on parade.

1974. Int., Olympic Committee. 80th Anniv.
998. 245. $1 blue, black & red .. 5 5
999. – $8 multicoloured .. 20 12
DESIGN: $8 Female relay runner.

246. Wen Yen-po retrieving Ball. 247. "Crape Myrtle" (Wei Sheng).

1974. Chinese Folk tales (3rd series). Mult.
1000. 50 c. Type **246** 5 5
1001. 50 c. T'i Ying pleading for mercy 5 5
1002. 50 c. Wang Ch'i in battle 5 5
1003. 50 c. Wang Hua returning gold 5 5
1004. $1 Tung Yu at study .. 5 5
1005. $1 Szu Ma Kuang saving playmate from water-jar 5 5
1006. $1 Pu Shih offering sheep to the emperor .. 5 5
1007. $1 K'ung Yung selecting the smallest pear .. 5 5

1974. Ancient Chinese Moon-shaped Fan-paintings (1st series). Multicoloured.
1008. $1 Type **247** 5 5
1009. $2·50 "White Cabbage and Insects" (Hsu Ti) 5 5
1010. $5 "Hibiscus and Rock" (Li Ti) 12 8
1011. $8 "Pomegranates" (Wu Ping) 20 12
See also Nos. 1068/71 and 1115/16.

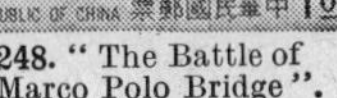

248. "The Battle of Marco Polo Bridge". 249. Chrysanthemum.

1974. Armed Forces' Day.
1012. 248. $1 multicoloured .. 5 5

1974. Chrysanthemums.
1014. 249. $1 multicoloured .. 5 5
1015. – $2·50 multicoloured 5 5
1016. – $5 multicoloured .. 12 8
1017. – $8 multicoloured .. 20 12
DESIGNS: Nos. 1015/17, various chrysanthemums.

250. Chinese Pavilion. 251. Steel Mill, Kaohsiung.

1974. "Expo 74" World Fair, Spokane, Washington. Multicoloured.
1018. $1 Type **250** 5 5
1019. $8 Fairground map .. 20 12

1974. Major Construction Projects. Mult.
1020. 50 c. Type **251** 5 5
1021. $1 Taiwan North link railway (green figures) 5 5
1021a. $1 As No. 1021 (red figures) 5 5
1022. $2 Petrochemical works, Kaohsiung 5 5
1022a. $2 As No. 1023 .. .. 5 5
1023. $2·50 TRA trunk line electrification 5 5
1024. $3 Taiching harbour (blue figures) (horiz.) .. 8 5
1024a. $3 As No. 1024 (violet figures) 8 5
1025. $3·50 Taoyuan international airport (horiz.) 10 5
1026. $4 Taiwan North–south motorway (yellow figures) (horiz.) .. 10 5
1026a. $4 As No. 1026 (red figures) 10 5
1027. $4·50 Giant shipyard, Kaohsiung (horiz.) .. 12 8
1028. $5 Su-ao port (horiz.) .. 12 8
1028a. $9 As No. 1028 .. .. 20 12

252. "Agaricus bisporus". 253. Baseball Strikers.

1974. Edible Fungi. Multicoloured.
1029. $1 Type **252** 5 5
1030. $2·50 "Pleurotus ostreatus" 5 5
1031. $5 "Dictyophora indusiata" 12 5
1032. $8 "Flammulina velutipes" 20 15

1974. Chinese Triple Championship Victories in World Little League Baseball Series, U.S.A. Multicoloured.
1033. $1 Type **253** 5 5
1034. $8 Player and banners .. 20 15

254. Hare. 255. Acrobat.

1974. New Year Greetings. "Year of the Hare".
1035. 254. 50 c. multicoloured .. 5 5
1036. $4·50 multicoloured .. 10 8

1975. Chinese Folklore (3rd series). Mult.
1037. $4 Type **255** 10 8
1038. $8 Jugglers with diabolo 20 12

256. Sun Yat-Sen Building, Yangmingshan. 258. Sun Yat-Sen Memorial Hall, Taipeh.

257. Puppet Show.

1975.
1039. 256. $1 red 5 5
T **256** is a redrawn version of T **187**.

1975. "New Year Festivals" (handscroll by Ting Kuan-p'eng). Multicoloured.
1040. $1 (1) Greetings 5 5
1041. $1 (2) Entertainer .. 5 5
1042. $1 (3) Crowd and musicians 5 5
1043. $1 (4) Picnic 5 5
1044. $1 (5) Type **257** 5 5
1045. $2·50 New Year greetings 5 5
1046. $5 Children buying fireworks 12 8
1047. $8 Entertainer with monkey and dog .. 20 12

1975. Dr. Sun Yat-Sen. 50th Death Anniv.
1048. $1 Type **258** 5 5
1049. $4 Sun Yat-Sen's handwriting 10 5
1050. $5 Bronze statue of Sun Yat-Sen (vert.) .. 12 8
1051. $8 Sun Yat-Sen Memorial Hall, St. John's University, USA 20 12

1975. Ancient Chinese Fan Paintings (2nd series). As T **235**. Multicoloured.
1052. $1 "Landscape" (Li Liu-fang) 5 5
1053. $2·50 "Landscape" (Wen Cheng-ming) 5 5
1054. $5 "Landscape" (Chou Ch'en) 12 8
1055. $8 "Landscape" (T'ang Yin) 20 12

259. "Yuan-chin" Coin (Chou dynasty).

260. "Lohan, the Cloth-bag Monk" (Chang Hung).

1975. Ancient Chinese Coins. (1st series). Multicoloured.

1056. $1 Type **259** 5 5
1057. $4 "Pan-liang" coin (Chin dynasty) .. 12 8
1058. $5 "Five chu" coin (Han dynasty) .. 12 8
1059. $8 "Five chu" coin (Liang dynasty) .. 20 12
See also Nos. 1111/14.

1975. Ancient Chinese Figure Paintings. Multicoloured.

1060. $1 Type **260** 5 5
1061. $4 "Lao-tzu on buffalo" (Chao Pu-chih) .. 12 8
1062. $5 "Shih-te" (Wang-wen) 12 8
1063. $8 "Splashed-ink Immortal" (Liang K'ai) .. 20 12

261. Chu-Yin reading by Light of Fireflies.

1975. Chinese Folk-tales (4th series). Mult.

1064. $1 Type **261** 5 5
1065. $2 Hua Mu-lan going to battle disguised as a man 8 5
1066. $2 Ling Kou Chien living a humble life .. 8 5
1067. $5 Chou Ch'u defeating the tiger 15 10

1975. Ancient Chinese Moon-shaped Fan Paintings. As T **247**. Multicoloured.

1068. $1 "Cherry-apple blossoms" (Lin Ch'un) 5 5
1069. $2 "Spring blossoms and a colourful butterfly" (Ma K'uei) 8 5
1070. $5 "Monkeys and deer" (I Yuan-chi) 20 12
1071. $8 "Tree sparrows among bamboo" (anon.) .. 30 20

1975. Famous Chinese. Martyrs of War against Japan. Portraits as T **216**.

1072. $2 red (Gen. Chang Tzu-chung) 10 5
1073. $2 brown (Maj.-Gen. Kao Chih-hong) 10 5
1074. $2 green (Capt. Sha Shih-Chiun) 10 5
1075. $5 purple (Maj.-Gen. Hsieh Lo-yuan) 20 12
1076. $5 blue (Lt. Yen Hai-wen) 20 12
1077. $5 indigo (Lt.-Gen. Tai An-lan) 20 12

262. "Lotus Pond with Willows".

1975. Madame Chiang Kai-Shek's Landscape Paintings. Multicoloured.

1078. $2 Type **262** 10 5
1079. $5 "Sun breaks through Mountain Clouds" .. 20 12
1080. $8 "A Pair of Pine Trees" 30 20
1081. $10 "Fishing and Farming" 40 25

263. Rectangular Cauldron.

264. Dragon, Nine-Dragon Wall, Peihai.

1975. Ancient Bronzes (1st series). Mult.

1082. $2 Type **263** 10 5
1083. $5 Cauldron with "Phoenix" handles (horiz.) .. 20 12
1084. $8 Flat jar (horiz.) .. 30 20
1085. $10 Wine vessel 40 25
See also Nos. 1119/22.

1975. New Year's Greetings. Year of the Dragon.

1086. **264.** $1 multicoloured .. 5 5
1087. $5 multicoloured .. 20 12

265. Techi Dam.

266. Biathlon.

1975. Techi Reservoir. Completion. Mult.

1088. $2 Type **265** 8 5
1089. $10 Dam and reservoir .. 35 25

1976. Winter Olympic Games, Innsbruck. Multicoloured.

1090. $2 Type **266** 8 5
1091. $5 Tobogganing 20 12
1092. $8 Skiing 30 20

267. "Chin".

1976. Chinese Musical Instruments. Mult.

1093. $2 Type **267** 8 5
1094. $5 "Se" 20 12
1095. $8 "Standing kong-ho" 30 20
1096. $10 "Sleeping kong-ho" 35 25

268. Postman collecting Mail.

1976. Chinese Postal Service. 80th Anniversary. Multicoloured.

1097. $2 Type **268** 8 5
1098. $5 Mail-sorting systems (vert.) 20 12
1099. $8 Mail transport (vert.) 30 20
1100. $10 Traditional and modern mail deliveries 35 25

269. Pres. Chiang Kai-shek.

1976. President Chiang Kai-shek. 1st Death Anniversary. Multicoloured.

1102. $2 Type **269** 8 5
1103. $2 People paying homage (horiz.) 8 5
1104. $2 Lying-in-state (horiz.) 8 5
1105. $2 Start of funeral procession (horiz.) .. 8 5
1106. $5 Roadside obeisance (horiz.) 20 12
1107. $8 Altar, Tzuhu Guest-house (horiz.) .. 30 20
1108. $10 Tzuhu Guest-house (horiz.) 35 25

270. Chinese and U.S. Flags.

271. "Kung Shou Pi" Coin (Shang/Chou Dynasties).

1976. American Revolution. Bicent.

1109. $2 multicoloured .. 8 5
1110. $10 multicoloured .. 35 25

1976. Ancient Chinese Coins (2nd series). Multicoloured.

1111. $2 Type **271** 8 5
1112. $5 "Chien Tsu Pu" coin (Chao Kingdom) .. 20 12
1113. $8 "Yuan Tsu Pu" coin (Tsin Kingdom) .. 30 20
1114. $10 "Fang Tsu Pu" coin (Chin/Han Dynasties) 35 25

1976. Ancient Chinese Moon-shaped Fan-paintings (3rd series). As T **247**. Mult.

1115. $2 "Hibiscus" (Li Tung) 8 5
1116. $5 "Lilies" (Lin Chun) 20 12
1117. $8 "Two Deer, Mushrooms and Pine" (Mou Chung-fu) 30 20
1118. $10 "Wild Flowers and Quail" (Li An-chung) 35 25

1976. Ancient Bronzes (2nd series). As T **263**. Multicoloured.

1119. $2 Square cauldron .. 8 5
1120. $5 Round cauldron .. 20 12
1121. $8 Wine vessel 30 20
1122. $10 Wine vessel with legs 35 25

No. 1119 is similar to Type **263**, but has four characters at left only.

272. Chiang Kai-shek and Mother.

1976. President Chiang Kai-shek's 90th Birth Anniv. Multicoloured.

1023. $2 Type **272** 8 5
1024. $5 Chiang Kai-shek .. 20 12
1025. $10 Chiang Kai-shek and Dr. Sun Yat-sen in railway carriage .. 35 25

273. Chinese and K.M.T. Flags.

1976. 11th Kuomintang National Congress. Multicoloured.

1026. $2 Type **273** 8 5
1027. $10 President Chiang Kai-shek and Dr. Sun Yat-sen 35 25

POSTAGE DUE STAMPS

(D 3.) (D 4.)

1950. Surch. as Type D **3**.

D 105. **6.** 4 c. on $100 blue .. 40 35
D 106. 10 c. on $100 blue .. 60 50
D 107. 20 c. on $100 blue .. 80 75
D 108. 40 c. on $100 blue .. 2·25 1·75
D 109. $1 on $100 blue .. 3·75 2·25

1951. No. 524 of China surch as Type D **4**.

D 133. 40 c. on 40 c. orange .. 85 60
D 134. 80 c. on 40 c. orange .. 1·00 60

(D 5.) D 6. (D 7.)

1953. Revenue stamps as T **89** of China surch. as Type D **5**.

D 151. 10 c. on $50 blue .. 70 25
D 152. 20 c. on $100 olive .. 70 25
D 153. 40 c. on $20 brown .. 90 10
D 154. 80 c. on $500 green .. 1·60 20
D 155. 100 c. on $30 mauve .. 1·50 70

1956.

D 236. D **6.** 20 c. red and blue 8 5
D 237. 40 c. green and buff 8 5
D 238. 80 c. brown and grey 15 5
D 239. $1 blue and mauve 15 5

1961. Surch. with Type D **7**.

D 429. **54.** $5 on $20 red .. 40 15

1964. Surch. as Type D **7**.

D 490. **77.** 10 c. on 80 c. green .. 5 5
D 491. 20 c. on $3.60 blue .. 5 5
D 492. 40 c. on $4.50 red .. 5 5

ILLUSTRATIONS
British Commonwealth and all overprints and surcharges are FULL SIZE. Foreign Countries have been reduced to ¾-LINEAR

D 9.

1966.

D 588. D **9.** 10 c. brown and lilac 5 5
D 589. 20 c. blue and yellow 5 5
D 590. 50 c. ultram. & blue 5 5
D 591. $1 violet and flesh .. 5 5
D 592. $2 green and blue .. 5 5
D 593. $5 red and buff .. 10 5

CHINA EXPEDITIONARY FORCE BC

Stamps used by Indian military forces in China.

Stamps of India optd. **C.E.F.**

1900. Queen Victoria.

C 1. **25.** 3 p. red 5 5
C 2. **14.** ½ a. green 5 5
C 3. – 1 a. purple 12 15
C 11. – 1 a. red .. .. 1·75 1·25
C 4. – 2 a. blue 30 50
C 5. – 2½ a. green 35 50
C 6. – 3 a. orange .. .. 1·00 1·75
C 7. – 4 a. green (No. 96) .. 50 70
C 8. – 8 a. mauve 50 75
C 9. – 12 a. purple on red .. 75 90
C 10. **26.** 1 r. green and red .. 1·25 1·25

1904. King Edward VII.

C 12. **28.** 3 p. grey 20 30
C 13. – 1 a. red (No. 123) .. 45 50
C 14. – 2 a. lilac 60 40
C 15. – 2½ a. blue 50 85
C 16. – 3 a. orange 55 85
C 17. – 4 a. olive .. .. 1·00 1·25
C 18. – 8 a. mauve .. .. 1·00 1·25
C 19. – 12 a. purple on red .. 1·50 2·50
C 20. – 1 r. green and red .. 1·25 2·00

1909. King Edward VII.

C 21. ½ a. green (No. 149) .. 40 40
C 22. 1 a. red (No. 150) .. 25 20

1913. King George V.

C 23. **40.** 3 p. grey 15 30
C 24. **41.** ½ a. green 20 30
C 25. **42.** 1 a. red 30 60
C 26. **43.** 1½ a. brown (No. 163) 65 1·50
C 27. **44.** 2 a. lilac .. .. 75 1·75
C 28. **47.** 2½ a. blue .. .. 1·00 1·75
C 29. **48.** 3 a. orange .. .. 1·50 2·25
C 30. **49.** 4 a. olive .. .. 2·00 3·50
C 32. **52.** 8 a. mauve .. .. 2·00 3·50
C 33. **53.** 12 a. claret .. .. 2·00 3·50
C 34. **54.** 1 r. brown and green 7·00 9·00

CHRISTMAS ISLAND BC

Situated in the Indian Ocean about 600 miles S. of Singapore. Formerly part of the Crown Colony of Singapore, it was transferred to Australian administration on 15 October, 1948.

100 cents = 1 dollar (Malayan).
1968. 100 cents = 1 dollar (Australian).

1. Queen Elizabeth II.

2. Map.

1958. Type of Australia with opt. and value in black.

No.	Type	Description	Unused	Used
1.	**1.**	2 c. orange	8	10
2.		4 c. brown	10	12
3.		5 c. mauve	12	12
4.		6 c. blue	15	20
5.		8 c. sepia	25	25
6.		10 c. violet	35	45
7.		12 c. red	60	70
8.		20 c. blue	1·25	1·50
9.		50 c. yellow-green	3·25	3·75
10.		$1 blue-green	7·00	8·00

1963.

No.	Type	Description	Unused	Used
11.	**2.**	2 c. orange	5	5
12.	–	4 c. brown	5	5
13.	–	5 c. purple	8	8
14.	–	6 c. indigo	10	10
15.	–	8 c. black	12	12
16.	–	10 c. violet	15	15
17.	–	12 c. red	25	25
18.	–	20 c. blue	45	55
19.	–	50 c. green	90	1·10
20.	–	$1 yellow	1·75	2·25

DESIGNS—VERT. 4c Moonflower. 5 c. Robber Crab. 8 c. Phosphate train. 10 c. Raising phosphate. HORIZ. 6 c. Island scene. 12 c. Flying Fish cove. 20 c. Loading cantilever. 50 c. Frigate bird. LARGER. (35 × 21 mm.): $1, Golden Bo'sun bird.

1965. Gallipoli Landing. 50th Anniv. As T 147 of Australia, but slightly larger (22 × 34½ mm.).

No.	Type	Description	Unused	Used
21.		10 c. brown, black and green	20	20

3. Golden Striped Grouper.

1968. Fishes. Multicoloured.

No.	Type	Description	Unused	Used
22.		1 c. Type 3	5	5
23.		2 c. Moorish Idol	5	5
24.		3 c. Forceps Fish	8	8
25.		4 c. Queen Triggerfish	10	10
26.		5 c. Regal Angelfish	12	12
27.		9 c. Surgeon Fish	15	20
28.		10 c. Scorpion Fish	20	25
28a.		15 c. Saddleback Butterfly	35	40
29.		20 c. Clown Butterfly	55	65
29a.		30 c. Ghost Pipefish	30	90
30.		40 c. Blue Lined Surgeon	1·75	2·00
31.		$1 Meyers Butterfly	3·25	3·75

4. "Angel" (Mosaic).

5. "The Ansidei Madonna" (Raphael).

1969. Christmas.

No.	Type	Description	Unused	Used
32.	**4.**	5 c. multicoloured	30	45

1970. Christmas. Multicoloured.

No.	Type	Description	Unused	Used
33.		3 c. Type 5	12	25
34.		4 c. "The Virgin and Child, St. John the Baptist and an Angel" (Morando).	20	30

6. "The Adoration of the Shepherds" (ascr. to the School of Seville).

1971. Christmas. Multicoloured.

No.	Type	Description	Unused	Used
35.		6 c. Type 6	15	15
36.		20 c. "The Adoration of the Shepherds" (Reni)	40	40

7. H.M.S. "Flying Fish", 1887.

1972. Ships. Multicoloured.

No.	Type	Description	Unused	Used
37.		1 c. "Eagle", 1714	5	5
38.		2 c. HMS "Redpole", 1890	5	5
39.		3 c. M.V. "Hoi Houw", 1959	5	5
40.		4 c. "Pigot", 1771	5	5
41.		5 c. S.S. "Valetta", 1968	5	8
42.		6 c. Type 7	8	8
43.		7 c. "Asia", 1805	10	10
44.		8 c. T.S.S. "Islander", 1929-60	10	12
45.		9 c. H.M.S. "Imperieuse", 1888	10	12
46.		10 c. H.M.S. "Egeria", 1887	12	15
47.		20 c. "Thomas", 1615	25	30
48.		25 c. H.M.S. "Gordon", 1864	30	35
49.		30 c. "Cygnet", 1688	35	40
50.		35 c. S.S. "Triadic", 1945-73	45	50
51.		50 c. H.M.S. "Amethyst", 1857	60	70
52.		$1 "Royal Mary", 1843	1·25	1·40

8. Angel of Peace.

1972. Christmas. Multicoloured.

No.	Type	Description	Unused	Used
53.		3 c. Type 8	8	8
54.		3 c. Angel of Joy	8	8
55.		7 c. Type 8	15	15
56.		7 c. As No. 54	15	15

9. Virgin and Child, and Map.

1973. Christmas.

No.	Type	Description	Unused	Used
57.	**9.**	7 c. multicoloured	10	12
58.		25 c. multicoloured	35	40

10. Mary and Holy Child within Christmas Star.

1974. Christmas.

No.	Type	Description	Unused	Used
59.	**10.**	7 c. mauve and grey	10	10
60.		30 c. oran., yell. & grey	40	45

11. "The Flight into Egypt".

1975. Christmas.

No.	Type	Description	Unused	Used
61.	**11.**	10 c. yell., brn. & gold	12	15
62.		35 c. pink, blue & gold	40	45

12. Dove of Peace and Star of Bethlehem.

1976. Christmas.

No.	Type	Description	Unused	Used
63.	**12.**	10 c. red, yellow & mauve	15	15
64.	–	10 c. red, yellow & mauve	15	15
65.	**12.**	35 c. violet, blue & green	50	55
66.	–	35 c. violet, blue & green	50	55

DESIGNS: Nos. 64 and 66 are "mirror-images" of T 12.

CILICIA O1

A district in Asia Minor, occupied and temporarily controlled by the French between 1918 and 20 Oct. 1921. The territory was then returned to Turkey.

40 paras = 1 piastre.

1919. Various issues of Turkey optd. **CILICIE** in various types.

A. On 1901 issue optd. with Star and Crescent.

No.	Type	Description	Unused	Used
47.	**5.**	1 pi. blue (No. 170)	8	5

B. On 1909 issue optd. with Star and Crescent.

No.	Type	Description	Unused	Used
35.	**11.**	20 pa. pink (No. 263)	12	12
8.		1 pi. blue (No. 264)	1·10	90

C. On Pictorial issue of 1914.

No.	Type	Description	Unused	Used
37.	**14.**	2 pa. red	12	12
11.	–	4 pa. brown (No. 500)	12	12
12.	–	6 pa. blue (No. 502)	1·60	75
13.	–	1¾ pi. brn. & grey (No. 507)	55	55

D. On Postal Anniv. issue of 1916.

No.	Type	Description	Unused	Used
14.	**36.**	5 pa. green	28·00	10·00
39.		20 pa. blue	15	15
58.		1 pi. black and violet	15	15
59.		5 pi. black and brown	15	15

E. On Pictorial issues of 1916 and 1917.

No.	Type	Description	Unused	Used
60.	**45.**	5 pa. orange	40	40
18.	**46.**	10 pa. green	25	25
19.	**49.**	50 pa. blue	90	30
61.	**48.**	1 pi. blue	25	25
62.	**44.**	5 pi. on 2 pa. blue (No. 914)	60	55
21.	**40.**	25 pi. red	25	25
22.	**41.**	50 pi. red	25	25
63.		50 pi. green on yellow	4·00	3·75
23.		50 pi. blue	3·25	3·25

F. On Armistice issue of 1919 optd. with T **55** of Turkey.

No.	Type	Description	Unused	Used
24.	**49.**	50 pa. blue	1·10	65
25.	**38.**	2 pi. blue and brown	45	35
26.	**50.**	5 pi. black and green	1·00	40

G. On 1913 issue optd. with Star and Crescent.

No.	Type	Description	Unused	Used
53.	**12.**	5 pa. orange (No. 535)	40	40
36.		20 pa. red (No. 336)	15	15

H. On 1908 issue optd. with Star and Crescent.

No.	Type	Description	Unused	Used
50.	**9.**	20 pa. pink (No. 640a)	60	60

1919. Various issues of Turkey overprinted **T.E.O. Cilicie** in various types.

A. On 1892 issue optd. with Star and Crescent.

No.	Type	Description	Unused	Used
70.	**4.**	10 pa. on 20 pa. red (No. 630)	5	5

B. On 1909 issue optd. with Star and Crescent.

No.	Type	Description	Unused	Used
72.	**11.**	20 pa. rose (No. 572)	15	15

C. On 1909 issue optd. with Tougra and surch. in Arabic.

No.	Type	Description	Unused	Used
73.	**11.**	5 pa. on 2 pa. ol. (No. N 332)	5	5

D. On Pictorial stamp of 1914.

No.	Type	Description	Unused	Used
74.	–	1 pi. blue (No. 518)	8	5

E. On Postal Jubilee issue of 1916.

No.	Type	Description	Unused	Used
75.	**36.**	5 pa. green	45·00	15·00
76.		20 pa. blue	5	5
77.		1 pi. black and violet	10	10

F. On Postal Anniv. issue of 1916 optd. with Star and Crescent.

No.	Type	Description	Unused	Used
78.	**36.**	10 pa. red (No. 654)	5	5

H. On Pictorial issues of 1916 and 1917.

No.	Type	Description	Unused	Used
79.	**45.**	5 pa. orange	5	5
80.	**46.**	10 pa. green	8	8
81.	**47.**	20 pa. red	5	5
82.	**38.**	2 pi. blue and brown	5	5
83.	**50.**	5 pi. black and green	8	5
84.	**44.**	5 pi. on 2 pa. blue	60	50
85.	**40.**	25 pi. red	60	45
86.	**41.**	50 pi. green	10·00	90

G. On Charity stamp of 1917.

No.	Type	Description	Unused	Used
87.	**42.**	10 pa. purple	10	10

1920. "Mouchon" key-type of French Levant surch. **T.E.O. 20 PARAS.**

No.	Type	Description	Unused	Used
88.	B.	20 pa. on 10 c. red	5	5

1.

1920. Surch. **OCCUPATION MILITAIRE Francaise CILICIE** and value.

No.	Type	Description	Unused	Used
89.	**1.**	70 pa. on 5 pa. red	8	8
90.		3½ pi. on 5 pa. red	8	8

1920. Stamps of France surch. **O.M.F. Cilicie** and new value.

No.	Type	Description	Unused	Used
91.	**11.**	5 pa. on 2 c. claret	5	5
101.	**17.**	10 pa. on 5 c. green	5	5
102.		20 pa. on 10 c. red	5	5
103.		1 pi. on 25 c. blue	5	5
104.	**15.**	2 pi. on 15 c. green	8	8
105.	**13.**	5 pi. on 40 c. red & blue	10	10
106.		10 pi. on 50 c. brn. & lav.	10	10
107.		50 pi. on 1 f. red & yell	30	30
108.		100 pi. on 5 f. blue & yell.	2·00	2·00

1920. Stamps of France surch. **O.M.F. Cilicie SAND. EST** and new value.

No.	Type	Description	Unused	Used
109.	**11.**	5 pa. on 2 c. claret	75	
110.	**17.**	10 pa. on 5 c. green	75	
111.		20 pa. on 10 c. red	25	
112.		1 pi. on 25 c. blue	30	
113.	**15.**	2 pi. on 15 c. green	1·40	
114.	**13.**	5 pi. on 40 c. red and blue	11·00	
115.		20 pi. on 1 f. red & green	18·00	

POSTAGE DUE STAMPS

1919. Postage Due stamps of Turkey optd. **CILICIE** in various types.

No.	Type	Description	Unused	Used
D 27.	**D 2.**	5 pa. purple	30	25
D 28.	**D 3.**	20 pa. red	25	20
D 29.	**D 4.**	1 pi. blue	60	60
D 30.	**D 5.**	2 pi. grey	55	55

1921. Postage Due Stamps of France surch. **O.M.F. Cilicie** and value.

No.	Type	Description	Unused	Used
D 118.	**D 2.**	1 pi. on 10 c. brown	75	75
D 119.		2 pi. on 20 c. olive	75	75
D 120.		3 pi. on 30 c. red	80	80
D 121.		4 pi. on 50 c. purple	80	80

PRINTED MATTER STAMPS

1919. No. N161 of Turkey optd. **CILICIE** with Star and Crescent.

No.	Type	Description	Unused	Used
N46.	**4.**	5 pa. on 10 pa. green	20	20

1919. No. N161 of Turkey optd. **T.E.O. Cilicie** with Star and Crescent.

No.	Type	Description	Unused	Used
N69.	**4.**	5 pa. on 10 pa. green	8	8

COCHIN BC

A state of S.W. India. Now uses Indian stamps.

1892. 6 puttans = 5 annas. Later as India.

1. Emblems of State.

1892. Value in "puttans".

No.	Type	Description	Unused	Used
7a.	**1.**	½ put. orange	65	65
8.		1 put. purple	80	65
3.		2 put. violet	50	50

2. 3.

1898. Value in " pies " or "puttans ".
16. **2.** 3 pies, blue 10 5
17. ½ put. green (smaller) .. 25 5
18. **3.** 1 put. red 50 8
19. **2.** 2 put. violet 65 12

1909. Surch. **2.**
22. 2. "2" on 3 pies, mauve .. 12 12

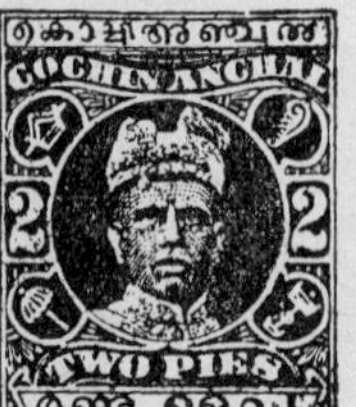

4. Raja Sir Sri Rama Varma I. **5.** Maharaja Sir Sri Rama Varma II.

1911. Value in "pies" or "annas".
26. **4.** 2 p. brown 10 5
27. 3 p. blue 8 5
28. 4 p. green 45 5
29. 9 p. red 65 5
30. 1 a. orange 65 5
31. 1½ a. purple .. .. 2·00 10
32. 2 a. grey .. .. .. 4·00 20
33. 3 a. red .. .. .. 20·00 9·00

1918. Various frames.
35b. **5.** 2 p. brown 30 5
36. 4 p. green 55 5
37. 6 p. brown 40 5
38. 8 p. brown 80 5
39. 9 p. red .. .. .. 3·25 8
40. 10 p. blue 60 5
41a. 1 a. orange 45 5
42. 1½ a. purple .. .. 1·25 5
43. 2 a. grey .. .. .. 2·25 10
44. 2¼ a. green .. .. 2·10 30
45. 3 a. red .. .. .. 7·00 30

1922. Surch. with figure and words.
46. **4.** 2 p. on 3 p. blue .. 12 5

1928. Surch. in words in English and native characters and **ANCHAL & REVENUE.**
50. **5.** 1 a. on 2¼ a. green .. 3·25 6·00

1932. Surch. in figures and words both in English and in native characters.
51. **5.** 3 p. on 4 p. green .. 55 12
52. 3 p. on 8 p. brown .. 55 8
53. 9 p. on 10 p. blue .. 80 20

6. Maharaja Sir Sri Rama Varma III. **7.** Maharaja Sri Kerala Varma I.

1933.
54. **6.** 2 p. brown 35 5
55. 4 p. green 45 5
56. 6 p. claret 50 5
57. 1 a. orange 50 5
58. 1 a. 8 p. red .. .. 2·00 45
59. 2 a. grey .. .. .. 1·00 5
60. 2¼ a. green .. .. 1·00 5
61. 3 a. orange .. .. 2·00 10
62. 3 a. 4 p. violet 65 5
63. 6 a. 8 p. sepia .. .. 1·10 45
64. 10 a. blue .. .. .. 2·00 55

1934. Surch. with figure and words.
65. **5.** 6 p. on 8 p. brown .. 65 25
66. 6 p. on 10 p. blue .. 1·60 30

1939. Optd. **ANCHAL.**
75. **6.** 1 a. orange .. .. 1·00 5

1939. Surch. in words only.
72. **6.** 3 p. on 1 a. 8 p. red .. 13·00 11·00
74. 6 p. on 1 a. 8 p. red .. 65 25

1943. Surch. **SURCHARGED** and value in words.
77. **6.** 3 p. on 4 p. green .. 4·00 20
73. 3 p. on 1 a. 8 p. red .. 1·50 40
76. 1 a. 3 p. on 1 a. 8 p. red.. 65 8

1943. Surch. **ANCHAL SURCHARGED NINE PIES.**
82. **6.** 9 p. on 1 a. orange .. 4·00 8

1943. Surch. **ANCHAL** and value in words.
79. **6.** 6 p. on 1 a. orange .. 6·50 4·00
80. 9 p. on 1 a. orange .. 8·00 8·00

1943.
85. **7.** 2 p. brown 20 5
87. 4 p. green .. .. 2·00 30
88. 6 p. brown 55 5
89. 9 p. blue .. .. .. 1·60 30
90. 1 a. orange .. .. 16·00 7·00
91. 2¼ a. green .. .. 1·25 5

1944. Surch. with value in words only.
93. **7.** 2 p. on 6 p. brown .. 20 5
94. 3 p. on 4 p. green .. 45 5
96. 3 p. on 6 p. brown .. 10 5
97. 4 p. on 6 p. brown .. 40 8

1944. Surch. **SURCHARGED** and value in words.
95. **7.** 3 p. on 4 p. green .. 30 5
92c. 1 a. 3 p. on 1 a. orange..

1944. Surch. **ANCHAL NINE PIES.**
92a. **7.** 9 p. on 1 a. orange .. 3·00 45

1944. Surch. **ANCHAL SURCHARGED NINE PIES.**
92b. **7.** 9 p. on 1 a. orange .. 10 5

8. Maharaja Sri Ravi Varma. **9.**

1944.
98a. **8.** 9 p. blue 80 8
99. 1 a. 3 p. mauve .. 4·00 8
100. 1 a. 9 p. blue .. .. 6·00 45

1946.
101. **9.** 2 p. brown 20 5
102. 3 p. red .. .. .. 1·50 5
103. 4 p. green .. .. — 3·50
104. 6 p. brown .. .. 2·75 10
105. 9 p. blue .. .. 1·25 5
106. 1 a. orange .. .. 2·75 1·00
107. 2 a. black .. .. 6·00 5
108. 3 a. orange .. .. 6·00 20

For No. 106. overprinted "U.S.T.C." or "T.-C." with or without surcharge, see Travancore-Cochin.

10. Maharaja Sri Kerala Varma II.

1948.
109. **10.** 2 p. brown .. .. 1·00 5
110. 3 p. red 65 5
111. 4 p. green .. .. 1·00 5
112. 6 p. brown .. .. 1·00 5
113. 9 p. blue 65 5
114. 2 a. black .. .. 5·50 5
115. 3 a. orange .. .. 6·50 5
115b. 3 a. 4 p. violet.. .. 15·00 20·00

11. Chinese Nets.

1949.
117. **11.** 2 a. black 25 30
118. – 2¼ a. green (Dutch palace) 25 30

SIX PIES

ആറു പൈ

(12.)

1949. Surch. as T **12.**
121. **9.** 3 p. on 9 p. blue .. 3·25 1·25
125. **10.** 3 p. on 9 p. blue .. 90 10
126. 6 p. on 9 p. blue .. 1·25 45
119. **8.** 6 p. on 1 a. 3 p. mauve 40 5
122. **9.** 6 p. on 1 a. 3 p. mauve 30 5
120. **9.** 1 a. on 1 a. 9 p. blue .. 1·00 5
123. **9.** 1 a. on 1 a. 9 p. blue 2·25 5

1949. Surch. **SIX PIES** or **NINE PIES** only.
127. **9.** 6 p. on 1 a. orange .. 22·00 22·00
128. 9 p. on 1 a. orange .. 16·00 16·00

OFFICIAL STAMPS

1913. Optd. **ON G C S.**
O 1. **4.** 3 p. blue .. .. 11·00 5
O 2. 4 p. green .. .. 2·75 5
O 3. 9 p. red .. .. 7·00 5
O 4. 1½ a. purple .. .. 8·00 5
O 5. 2 a. grey .. .. 7·00 5
O 6. 3 a. red .. .. 7·00 8
O 7. 6 a. violet .. .. 7·00 1·25
O 8. 12 a. blue .. .. 9·00 2·75
O 9. 1½ r. green .. .. 9·00 9·00

1919. Optd. **ON C G S.**
O 10. **5.** 4 p. green .. .. 2·00 5
O 11. 6 p. brown .. .. 2·60 5
O 12. 8 p. brown .. .. 1·75 5
O 13. 9 p. red .. .. 2·25 5
O 14. 10 p. blue .. .. 3·00 5
O 15. 1½ a. purple .. .. 2·75 5
O 16. 2 a. grey .. .. 3·00 5
O 17. 2¼ a. green .. .. 2·75 5
O 29. 3 a. red .. .. 4·50 10
O 19. 6 a. violet .. .. 7·00 40
O 19a. 12 a. blue .. .. 8·00 1·50
O 19b. 1½ r. green .. .. 9·00

1923. Official stamps surch. in figures and words.
O 32. **5.** 6 p on 8 p. brown .. 80 10
O 33. 6 p. on 10 p. blue .. 2·75 5
O 20. **4.** 8 p. on 9 p. red .. 35·00 5
O 21. **5.** 8 p. on 9 p. red .. 35·00 5
O 23. **7.** 10 p. on 9 p. red .. 55·00 4·50
O 22. **5.** 10 p. on 9 p. red .. 35·00 5

1933. Optd. **ON C G S.**
O 34. **6.** 4 p. green 40 5
O 51. 6 p. claret 30 5
O 52. 1 a. orange .. .. 1·00 5
O 37. 1 a. 8 p. red .. .. 2·00 5
O 50. 2 a. grey .. .. 1·25 5
O 39. 2¼ a. green .. .. 2·00 5
O 53. 3 a. orange .. .. 2·00 5
O 41. 3 a. 4 p. violet .. 2·25 5
O 42. 6 a. 8 p. sepia .. 2·25 8
O 43. 10 a. blue .. .. 2·75 10

1943. Official stamp surch. **NINE PIES.**
O 57. **5.** 9 p. on 1½ a. purple .. 32·00 65

1943. Official stamps surch. **SURCHARGED** and value in words.
O 63. **6.** 3 p. on 4 p. green .. 30·00 11·00
O 58. 3 p. on 1 a. 8 p. red .. 10 5
O 66. 1 a. 3 p. on 1 a. orange.. 20·00 11·00
O 61. 1 a. 9 p. on 1 a. 8 p. red 50 10

1943. Official stamps surch. in words.
O 62. **6.** 3 p. on 4 p. green .. 1·25 10
O 64. 3 p. on 1 a. orange .. 55 5
O 65. 9 p. on 1 a. orange .. 16·00 30
O 59. 9 p. on 1 a. 8 p. red .. 18·00 4·00
O 60. 1 a. 9 p. on 1 a. 8 p. red 50 5

1944. Optd. **ON C G S.**
O 68. **7.** 4 p. green 55 5
O 69. 6 p. brown 5 5
O 70. 1 a. orange .. .. £275 20·00
O 71. 2 a. black 5 5
O 72. 2¼ a. green 80 8
O 73. 3 a. red 65 20

1944. Official stamps surch. **SURCHARGED** and value in words.
O 75. **7.** 3 p. on 4 p. green .. 1·75 30
O 78. 9 p. on 6 p. brown .. 10 5
O 80. 1 a. 3 p. on 1 a. orange 1·00 5

1944. Official stamps surch. in words.
O 74. **7.** 3 p. on 4 p. green .. 30 5
O 76. 3 p. on 1 a. orange .. 1·25 5
O 77. 9 p. on 6 p. brown .. 1·25 5
O 79. 1 a. 3 p. on 1 a. orange 1·25 5

1944. Optd. **ON C G S.**
O 81. **8.** 9 p. blue 15 5
O 82. 1 a. 3 p. mauve .. 15 5
O 83. 1 a. 9 p. blue 15 10

1948. Optd. **ON C.G.S.**
O 84. **9.** 3 p. red 5 5
O 85. 4 p. green .. .. 8·00 3·00
O 86. 6 p. brown 20 5
O 87. 9 p. blue 65 5
O 88. 1 a. 3 p. mauve .. 35 5
O 89. 1 a. 9 p. blue 25 20
O 90. 2 a. black 20 5
O 91. 2¼ a. green 65 20

1949. Optd. **ON C.G.S.**
O 92. **10.** 3 p. red 10 5
O 93. 4 p. green 10 5
O 94. 6 p. brown 10 5
O 95. 9 p. blue 20 5
O 96. 2 a. black 30 5
O 97. 2¼ a. green 65 5
O 98. 3 a. orange 65 5
O 99. 3 a. 4 p. violet .. 2·75 2·00

1949. Official stamps surch. as T **12.**
O 103. **10.** 6 p. on 3 p. red .. 12 5
O 104. 9 p. on 4 p. green .. 25 8
O 100. **8.** 1 a. on 1 a. 9 p. blue 35 5
O 101. **9.** 1 a. on 1 a. 9 p. blue 1·50 75

1949. Optd. **SERVICE**
O 105. **10.** 3 p. on 9 p. (No. 125) 30 12

For later issues see under Travancore-Cochin

COCHIN-CHINA O2

A former French colony in the extreme S. of Indo-China, subsequently incorporated into French Indo-China.

1886. Stamps of French Colonies.
1. **9.** 5 on 25 c. brn. on yellow .. 32·00 20·00
2. 5 on 2 c. brown on buff .. 1·75 1·75
3. 5 on 25 c. brn. on yellow .. 1·75 1·75
4. 5 on 25 c. black on red .. 5·50 4·50

No. 1 is Surch. with numeral only: No. 3 is additionally optd. **C. CH.**

COCOS (KEELING) ISLANDS BC

Islands in the Indian Ocean formerly administered by Singapore and transferred to Australian administration in 1955.

1. Dukong (sailboat).

2. White Tern.

1963.
1. – 3d. chocolate 45 35
2. – 5d. blue 45 40
3. – 8d. red 75 75
4. – 1 s. green .. .. 2·50 2·50
5. **1.** 2s. purple .. .. 4·00 3·50
6. **2.** 2s. 3d. green .. .. 6·00 5·00

DESIGNS—As T **1**, HORIZ. 3d. Copra industry. 1s. Palms. VERT. 8d. Map of islands. As T **2**: 5d. Super Constellation airliner.

1965. Gallipoli Landing. 50th Anniv. As T **147** of Australia, but slightly larger (22×34½ mm.).
7. 5d. brown, black and green 30 30

With the introduction of decimal currency on 14th February, 1966, Australian stamps were used in Cocos Islands until the 1969 issue.

3. Turbo mollusc.

1969. Decimal Currency. Multicoloured.
8. 1 c. Type **3** 8 8
9. 2 c. Burrowing clam .. 8 8
10. 3 c. Reef clam 8 8
11. 4 c. Blenny (fish) .. 8 8
12. 5 c. Coral 8 10
13. 6 c. Flying Fish .. 10 12
14. 10 c. Land Rail .. 10 12
15. 15 c. Java Sparrow .. 20 25
16. 20 c. Red-tailed Tropic Bird 25 30
17. 30 c. Sooty Tern .. 35 40
18. 50 c. Reef Heron .. 90 1·00
19. **$1** Frigate Bird .. 1·75 2·00

4. " Dragon ".

1976. Multicoloured.

20. 1 c. Type **4** 5 5
21. 2 c. H.M.S. "Juno", 1857 (horiz.) 5 5
22. 5 c. H.M.S. "Beagle", 1836 (horiz.) 5 8
23. 10 c. H.M.A.S. "Sydney", 1914 (horiz.) 12 12
24. 15 c. S.M.S. "Emden", 1907 (horiz.) 20 20
25. 20 c. "Ayesha", 1907 (horiz.) 25 25
26. 25 c. T.S.S. "Islander", 1927 .. .. .. 30 35
27. 30 c. M.V. "Cheshire", 1951 35 40
28. 35 c. Jukung (sailboat) (horiz.) 40 45
29. 40 c. C.S. "Scota", 1900 (horiz.) 45 50
30. 50 c. R.M.S. "Orontes", 1929 .. .. .. 60 70
31. $1 Royal Yacht "Gothic", 1954 .. .. .. 1·25 1·40

COLOMBIA O1

A republic in the N.W. of South America. Formerly part of the Spanish Empire, Colombia became independent in 1819. The constituent states became the Granadine Confederation in 1858. The name was changed to the United States of New Granada in 1861 and the name Colombia was adopted later the same year.

100 centavos = 1 peso.

Prices. For the early issues prices in the used column are for postmarked copies, pen-cancellations are generally worth less.

1. 2.

1859. Imperf.

1. **1.** 2½ green .. .. .. 10·00 8·00
2. 5 c. blue .. .. .. 11·00 11·00
8b. 5 c. slate .. .. .. 10·00 9·00
4. 10 c. yellow .. .. .. 8·00 7·00
5. 20 c. blue .. .. .. 5·00 5·00
6. 1 p. red .. .. .. 5·00 5·00

1861. Imperf.

11. **2.** 2½ c. black £250 £100
12. 5 c. yellow .. .. 45·00 15·00
13. 10 c. blue .. .. .. 60·00 25·00
14. 20 c. red .. .. .. £100 50·00
15. 1 p. rose .. .. .. £130 70·00

3. 4. 5.

1862. Imperf.

16. **3.** 10 c. blue .. .. .. 25·00 15·00
17. 20 c. red £400 £130
18. 50 c. green .. .. .. 60·00 20·00
19. 1 p. lilac .. .. .. 75·00 40·00

1862. Imperf.

21. **4.** 5 c. yellow .. .. .. 8·00 6·00
22. 10 c. blue .. .. .. 10·00 4·00
23. 20 c. red .. .. .. 12·00 10·00
25. 50 c. green .. .. .. 15·00 12·00

1863. Imperf.

26. **5.** 5 c. yellow .. .. .. 7·00 4·00
27. 10 c. blue .. .. .. 5·00 2·50
28. 20 c. red .. .. .. 10·00 4·50
29. 50 c. green .. .. .. 10·00 4·50
30. 1 p. mauve .. .. .. 45·00 20·00

6. 7. 8.

1865. Imperf.

31. **6.** 1 c. red .. .. .. 2·00 1·50
32. **7.** 2½ c. black on lilac .. 2·50 2·50
33. **8.** 5 c. orange .. .. .. 3·00 2·00
34. 10 c. violet .. .. .. 2·00 90
35. 20 c. blue .. .. .. 2·75 1·60
36. 50 c. green .. .. .. 8·00 3·00
38. 1 p. red .. .. .. 8·00 2·00

9. 10. 16.

1865. Imperf.

39. **9.** 25 c. black on blue .. 8·00 22·00
40. 50 c. black on yellow .. 10·00 30·00
41. 1 p. black on rose .. 12·00 25·00

1866. Imperf. Various Arms Designs.

44. **10.** 5 c. orange .. .. 3·50 1·75
45. – 10 c. lilac 90 65
46. – 20 c. blue .. .. .. 5·50 2·75
47. – 50 c. green .. .. 2·25 1·75
48. – 1 p. red .. .. .. 4·00 1·75
49. – 5 p. black on green .. 55·00 28·00
50. – 10 p. black on red .. 45·00 20·00

1868. Arms (various frames) inscr. "ESTADOS UNIDOS DE COLOMBIA". Imperf.

51. **16.** 5 c. yellow .. .. 10·00 7·00
52. 10 c. lilac .. .. .. 1·00 25
54. 20 c. blue .. .. .. 1·25 60
55. 50 c. green .. .. 1·50 60
57. 1 p. red .. .. .. 1·50 75

17. 18.

19. 20.

21. 22.

1869. Imperf.

58. **17.** 2½ c. black on violet .. 2·50 2·50

1870. Imperf.

59a. **18.** 1 c. green 60 45
60. 1 c. red 40 40
61. **19.** 2 c. brown 40 40
62. **20.** 5 c. yellow 40 40
65a. **21.** 10 c. mauve 60 30
67. 25 c. black on blue .. 5·00 4·00
87. 25 c. green .. .. 5·00 5·00

1870. Different frames. Imperf.

68. **22.** 5 p. black on green .. 10·00 3·00
71. 10 p. black on red .. 10·00 2·50

See also Nos. 118/9.

23. 24. 26.

1876. On papers of various colours. Imperf.

84a. **23.** 5 c. violet 50 15
85. **24.** 10 c. brown 40 15
86. – 20 c. blue 40 25

DESIGN: 20 c. as T **24** but with different frame.

1881. Imperf.

93. **26.** 1 c. green 40 35
99. 2 c. red 25 25
100. 5 c. blue 25 20
101. 10 c. purple 60 30
97. 20 c. black .. .. 1·00 75

27. 28.

1881. Imperf.

102. **27.** 1 c. black on green .. 40 40
103. 2 c. black on rose .. 40 40
104. 5 c. black on lilac .. 60 40

1883. Inscr. "CORREOS NACIONALES DE LOS E.E. U.U. DE COLOMBIA".

106. **28.** 1 c. yell.-grn. on green 20 20
107. 2 c. red on pink .. 30 20
109. 5 c. blue on blue .. 40 25
111. 10 c. orange on yellow 45 30
112. 20 c. mauve on lilac .. 50 40
113. **28.** 50 c. brown on buff .. 60 40
114. 1 p. lake .. .. 1·25 60
115. 5 p. brown on yellow .. 3·00 1·50
116. 10 p. black on rose .. 3·00 1·75

1886. Perf.

118. **22.** 5 p. brown .. .. 3·00 1·10
119. 10 p. black on lilac .. 3·00 1·10

29. 30. Gen. Sucre.

31. Bolivar. 33. Gen. Narino.

1886.

120. **29.** 1 c. green 15 15
121. **30.** 2 c. red on pink .. 30 30
124. **31.** 5 c. blue on blue .. 30 12
125. – 10 c. orge. (Pres. Nunez) 40 20
126. **33.** 20 c. violet on lilac ("REPULICA") .. 60 30
137. 20 c. violet on lilac ("REPUBLICA") .. 15 15
130. **29.** 50 c. brown on buff .. 20 20
132. 1 p. mauve 40 30
133. 5 p. brown .. .. 1·75 1·60
134. 5 p. black .. .. 1·10 1·10
135. 10 p. black on pink .. 1·75 1·25

See also Nos. 162/4a.

34. 35. 36.

1890.

143. **34.** 1 c. green on green .. 20 15
144. **35.** 2 c. red on pink .. 20 15
145. **36.** 5 c. blue on blue .. 15 10
147. **35.** 10 c. brown on yellow .. 15 10
148. 20 c. violet 40 30

See also Nos. 149, etc.

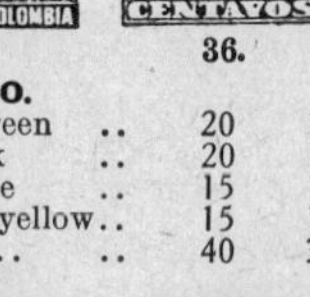

37. 38. 39.

40. 41. 42.

1892.

149. **34.** 1 c. red on yellow .. 10 8
150. **37.** 2 c. red on rose .. 70 55
151. 2 c. green 10 8
152a. **36.** 5 c. black on brown .. 10 8
153. **38.** 5 c. brown on brown .. 12 8
155. **35.** 10 c. brown on rose .. 12 10
156. **39.** 20 c. brown on blue .. 12 8
159. **29.** 50 c. purple 25 12
161. **40.** 1 p. blue on green .. 25 15
162. **29.** 5 p. red on pink .. 1·00 30
164a. 10 p. blue .. .. 1·75 60

1898.

171. **41.** 1 c. red on yellow .. 10 8
172. 5 c. brown on brown .. 10 8
173. 10 c. brown on rose .. 25 15
174. 50 c. blue on lilac .. 25 20

For stamps showing map of Panama and inscr. "COLOMBIA" see Panama Nos. 5/18.

For provisionals issued at Cartagena during the Civil War, 1899–1902, see list in Gibbon's Overseas Catalogue, Volume 2.

1902. Arms in various frames. Imperf. or perf.

259. **42.** ½ c. brown 20 20
260. 1 c. green 20 15
192. 2 c. black on rose .. 10 8
261. 2 c. blue 12 12
193. 4 c. red on green .. 8 8
194. 4 c. blue on green .. 8 8
195. 5 c. green on green .. 8 8
196. 5 c. blue on blue .. 12 12
262. 5 c. rose 20 20
197. 10 c. black on pink .. 10 10
263. 10 c. mauve 30 30
198. 20 c. brown on brown .. 10 10
199. 20 c. blue on brown .. 12 12
200. 50 c. green on rose .. 12 12
201. 50 c. blue on rose .. 35 35
202. 1 p. purple on brown .. 12 12

43. 44. River Magdalena.

1903. Imperf. or perf.

203. **43.** 5 p. green on blue .. 1·00 1·00
204. 10 p. green on green .. 1·00 1·00
205. 50 p. orange on rose .. 26·00 26·00
206. 100 p. blue on rose .. 23·00 23·00

Nos. 205/6 are larger (31 × 38 mm.).

1902. Imperf. or perf.

212. **44.** 2 c. green 15 15
213. 2 c. blue 15 20
214. 2 c. rose 70 70
215. – 10 c. red 10 10
216. – 10 c. pink 12 12
219. – 10 c. orange 75 75
242. – 10 c. blue on brown .. 20 20
243. – 10 c. blue on green .. 45 45
244. – 10 c. blue on rose .. 20 20
245. – 10 c. blue on lilac .. 25 25
220. – 20 c. violet 12 12
221. – 20 c. blue 50 50
224. – 20 c. red .. .. 1·50 1·50

DESIGNS: 10 c. Iron Quay, Savanilla, with eagle above. 20 c. Hill of La Popa.

45. Cruiser "Cartagena". 46. Bolivar.

47. General Pinzon. 48. 49.

1903. Imperf. or perf.

225. **45.** 5 c. blue 10 10
226. 5 c. brown 15 15
227. **46.** 50 c. green 20 20
228. 50 c. brown 20 20
230. 50 c. orange 12 12
231. 50 c. red 25 25
233. **47.** 1 p. brown 12 12
234. 1 p. red 15 15
235. 1 p. blue 30 30
237. **48.** 5 p. brown 25 25
238. 5 p. purple 30 30
239. 5 p. green 40 40
240. **49.** 10 p. green 60 60
241. 10 p. purple 80 80

ILLUSTRATIONS British Commonwealth and all overprints and surcharges are FULL SIZE. Foreign Countries have been reduced to ¾-LINEAR.

50.

1902.

248. **50.** 1 c. green on yellow .. 8 8
249. 2 c. red on pink .. 8 8
250. 5 c. blue 10 10
251. 10 c. brown on yellow .. 10 10
252. 20 c. mauve on pink .. 10 10
253. 50 c. red on green .. 12 12
254. 1 p. black on yellow .. 35 30
255. 5 p. blue on blue .. 4·50 4·00
256. 10 p. brown on pink .. 4·00 3·25

51. 52. 53. President Marroquin.

1904.

270. **51.** ½ c. yellow 12 8
274. 1 c. green 8 5
278. 2 c. red 20 5
281. 5 c. blue 25 5
283. 10 c. violet 15 5
284. 20 c. black 30 8
286. **52.** 1 p. brown .. .. 1·10 25
287. **53.** 5 p. black and red .. 7·50 7·50
288. 10 p. black and blue .. 8·00 7·50

54. Camilo Torres.

55. Narino Demanding Liberation of Slaves.

1910. Independence Cent.

345. **54.** ½ c. black and purple .. 30 20
346. – 1 c. green 30 20
347. – 2 c. red 25 15
348. – 5 c. blue 25 15
349. – 10 c. purple .. .. 3·00 1·25
350. – 20 c. brown .. .. 5·00 1·75
351. **55.** 1 p. purple .. .. 9·00 5·00
352. – 10 p. lake .. .. 48·00 40·00

DESIGNS—As T **54**: 1 c. P. Salvarrieta. 2 c. Narino. 5 c. Bolivar. 10 c. Caldas. 20 c. Santander. As T **55**: 10 p. Narino in group.

56. C. Torres. **57.** Arms. **58.** Boyaca Monument.

59. Sabana Station. **60.** Cartagena.

1917. Portraits as T **56.**

357. **56.** ½ c. yellow (Caldas) .. 25 5
358. 1 c. green (Torres) .. 10 5
393. **57.** 1½ c. brown 12 10
359. **56.** 2 c. red (Narino) .. 10 8
380. **57.** 3 c. red on yellow .. 20 5
394. 3 c. blue 10 5
360. **56.** 4 c. purple (Santander) 30 8
395. 4 c. blue (Santander) .. 10 5
361. 5 c. blue (Bolivar) .. 40 5
396. 5 c. claret (Bolivar) .. 20 5
397. **57.** 8 c. blue 12 5
362. **56.** 10 c. grey (Cordoba) .. 50 5
398. 10 c. blue (Cordoba) .. 1·00 10
363. **58.** 20 c. red 75 10
399. **57.** 30 c. bistre (Caldas) .. 1·40 12
400. **59.** 40 c. brown .. .. 2·25 15
364. **60.** 50 c. red 75 8
606. 50 c. red (San Pedro Alejandrino) .. 1·40 30
365a. **56.** 1 p. blue (Sucre) .. 1·75 20
366. 2 p. orange (Cuervo) .. 2·50 30
367. 5 p. grey (Ricaurte) .. 7·50 2·00
401. 5 p. violet (Ricaurte) .. 5·50 45
368. **57.** 10 p. brown .. .. 18·00 6·00
402. 10 p. green .. .. 12·00 2·50

For similar 40 c. see No. 541.

1918. Surch. **Especie Provisional** and value.

374. **51.** 0·00½ c. on 20 c. black .. 90 25
376. 0·03 c. on 10 c. violet .. 1·25 60

61.

62.

1918.

378. **61.** 3 c. red 20 5

1918. Air. Optd. **1 er Servicio Postal Aereo 6-18-19.**

379. – 2 c. red (No. 359) .. £600 £275

1920. As T **42**, **51** and **57**, but with "PROVISIONAL" added in label across design.

381. **51.** ½ c. yellow 30 12
382. 1 c. green 12 5
383. 2 c. red 8 8
384. **57.** 3 c. green 10 8
385. **51.** 5 c. blue 20 5
386. 10 c. violet 50 25
387. 10 c. blue .. .. 1·10 75
388. 20 c. green .. .. 2·25 60
389. **42.** 50 c. red .. .. 3·00 1·25

1921. No. 360 surch. **PROVICIONAL $003.**

390. **57.** $0.03 on 4 c. purple .. 20 8

1921. No. 360 surch. **PROVISIONAL $0.03.**

391. **57.** $0.03 on 4 c. purple .. 1·25 60

1924.

403. **62.** 1 c. red 12 5
404. 3 c. blue 20 5

1925. Large fiscal stamps surch. **CORREOS 1 CENTAVO** or optd. **CORREOS PROVISIONAL.**

405. 1 c. on 3 c. brown .. 8 5
406. 4 c. purple 12 5

63.

65. Death of Bolivar.

1926.

410. **63.** 1 c. green 15 10
411. 4 c. blue 15 10

1930. Bolivar Death Cent.

412. **65.** 4 c. black and blue .. 20 12

66. **67.**

1932. Air. Optd. **CORREO AEREO.**

413. **66.** 5 c. yellow .. .. 4·25 4·00
414. 10 c. maroon 75 20
415. 15 c. green 75 40
416. 20 c. red 30 8
417. 30 c. blue 35 8
418. 40 c. lilac 50 35
419. 50 c. olive 90 75
420. 60 c. brown 55 50
421. 80 c. green .. .. 5·50 5·50
422. **67.** 1 p. blue .. .. 4·00 1·10
423. 2 p. red .. .. 10·00 6·00
424. 3 p. mauve .. .. 16·00 17·00
425. 5 p. olive .. .. 32·00 35·00

These and similar stamps without the "CORREO AEREO" overprint were issues of a private air company which we do not list.

1932. Stamps of 1917 surch.

427. **57.** 1 c. on 4 c. blue .. 5 5
428. 20 c. on 30 c. bistre .. 2·75 20

68. Coffee Plantation. **69.** Oil Wells.

70. Gold Mining. **71.** Columbus.

1932. 1 c. is vert., 8 c. is horiz.

429. – 1 c. green (Emeralds) 10 5
430. **69.** 2 c. red (Oil) .. 10 5
431. **68.** 5 c. brown (Coffee) .. 15 5
432. – 8 c. blue (Platinum) 60 15
485. **70.** 10 c. yellow (Gold) .. 25 5
486. **71.** 20 c. blue 70 10

72. Coffee. **73.** Gold.

1932. Air.

435. **72.** 5 c. brown and orange 12 5
436. – 10 c. black and lake .. 8 5
437. – 15 c. violet and green .. 12 8
438. – 15 c. violet and red .. 75 5
439. – 20 c. green and red .. 20 5
440. – 20 c. olive and green .. 1·75 12
441. **72.** 30 c. brown and blue .. 25 5
442. – 40 c. yellow and violet .. 30 5
443. – 50 c. brown and green .. 1·75 10
444. – 60 c. violet and brown .. 40 8
445. **72.** 80 c. brown and green .. 1·60 40
446. **73.** 1 p. yellow and blue .. 3·00 20
447. – 2 p. yellow and lake .. 4·50 60
448. – 3 p. green and violet .. 7·00 1·00
449. – 5 p. green and olive .. 16·00 3·50

DESIGNS—As T **72**: 10 c., 50 c. Cattle. 15 c., 60 c. Oil Wells. 20 c., 40 c. Bananas. As T **73**: 3 p. 5 p. Emeralds.

74. Pedro de Heredia. **75.** Coffee Plantation.

76. Oil Wells. **77.** Runners.

1934. Cartagena. 4th Cent.

451. **74.** 1 c. green 80 25
452. 5 c. brown 70 15
453. 8 c. blue 75 20

1934. Air. Cartagena. 4th Cent. Surch. **CARTAGENA 1533-1933** and value.

454. – 10 c. on 50 c. brown and green (No. 443) .. 1·25 1·50
455. **72.** 15 c. on 80 c. brn. & grn. 1·25 1·50
456. **73.** 20 c. on 1 p. yell. & blue 1·50 1·50
457. 30 c. on 2 p. yell. & lake 2·25 2·50

1934.

458. **75.** 2 c. red 20 5
459. **76.** 5 c. brown 75 5
460. – 10 c. orange 75 5

DESIGN: 10 c. Gold miner facing left.

1935. 3rd National Olympiad. Inscr. "III OLIMPIADA BARRANQUILLA 1935".

461. – 2 c. orange and green .. 1·00 70
462. – 4 c. green .. .. 1·00 70
463. – 5 c. yellow and brown .. 1·00 70
464. **77.** 7 c. red .. .. 1·40 1·00
465. – 8 c. mauve and black .. 1·40 1·00
466. – 10 c. blue and brown .. 1·40 1·00
467. – 12 c. blue .. .. 1·75 1·50
468. – 15 c. red and blue .. 2·75 1·75
469. – 18 c. yellow and purple 3·25 2·10
470. – 20 c. green and violet .. 3·75 2·50
471. – 24 c. blue and green .. 4·25 3·50
472. – 50 c. orange and blue .. 6·00 6·00
473. – 1 p. blue and olive .. 22·00 15·00
474. – 2 p. blue and green .. 50·00 40·00
475. – 5 p. blue and violet .. £110 £100
476. – 10 p. blue and black .. £170 £150

DESIGNS—VERT. 2 c. Footballers. 4 c. Discus thrower. 1p. G.P.O. 2 p. "Flag of the Race" Monument. 5 p. Arms. 10 p. Condor. HORIZ. 5 c. Allegory of 1935 Olympiad. 8 c. Tennis player. 10 c. Hurdler. 12 c. Puerto Pier. 15 c. Athlete. 18 c. Baseball. 20 c. Seashore. 24 c. Swimmer. 50 c. Aerial view Barranquilla.

80. Nurse and Sick.

1935. Obligatory Tax. Red Cross.

477. **80.** 5 c. red and green .. 1·50 40

1935. Surch. **12 CENTAVOS.**

478. 12 c. on 1 p. blue (No. 365a) 75 30

81. Bolivar. **82.** Tequendama Falls.

1937.

487. **81.** 1 c. green 10 5
488. **82.** 10 c. red 12 5
489. 12 c. blue 50 20

83. Footballer. **84.** Discus Thrower.

1937. 4th National Olympiad.

490. **83.** 3 c. green 85 25
491. **84.** 10 c. red .. .. 2·75 60
492. – 1 p. black .. .. 14·00 7 50

DESIGN: 1 p. Runner (20½ × 27 mm.).

85. Exhibition Palace. **87.** Mother and Child.

1937. Barranquilla Industrial Exn. Inscr. "EXPOSICION NACIONAL BARRANQUILLA, 1936 1937".

493. **85.** 5 c. purple 30 20
494. – 15 c. blue .. .. 1·50 40
495. – 50 c. brown .. .. 3·00 1·75

DESIGNS—HORIZ. 15 c. Stadium. VERT. 50 c. Monument.

1937. Obligatory Tax. Red Cross.

509. **87.** 5 c. red 30 12

1937. Surch. in figures and words.

510. **83.** 1 c. on 3 c. green .. 35 20
511. **82.** 2 c. on 12 c. blue .. 12 10
512. – 5 c. on 8 c. (No. 432) .. 15 8
513. – 5 c. on 8 c. bl. (No. 397) 12 5
514. **82.** 10 c. on 12 c. blue .. 25 10

88. Entrance to Church of the Rosary. **90.** "Bochica" (Indian god).

1938. Bogota. 4th Cent. Insc. "1538 1938 IV CENTENARIO BOGOTA".

515. – 1 c. green 5 5
516. **88.** 2 c. red 10 8
517. – 5 c. black 12 10
518. – 10 c. brown 20 10
519. **90.** 15 c. blue 60 25
520. – 20 c. mauve 65 50
521. – 1 p. brown .. .. 6·00 4·50

DESIGNS—VERT. 1 c. "Calle del Arco" ("Street of the Arch") Old Bogota. 5 c. Bogota Arms. 10 c. G. J. de Quesada. HORIZ. (larger): 20 c. Convent of S. Domingo. 1 p. First Mass on Site of Bogota.

92. Proposed P.O., Bogota.

1939. Obligatory Tax. P.O. Rebuilding Fund.

522. **92.** ¼ c. blue 5 5
564. ¼ c. maroon 5 5
523. ½ c. red 5 5
524. 1 c. violet 5 5
567. 1 c. orange 5 5
525. 2 c. green 10 10
526. 20 c. brown 75 30

1939. Air. Surch. **5 cts.** or **15 cts** and bar.

527. 5 c. on 20 c. (No. 439) 15 10
528. 5 c. on 40 c. (No. 442) 15 10
530. 15 c. on 30 c. (No. 441) 50 10
531. 15 c. on 40 c. (No. 442) 50 10

93. Bolivar. **94.** Coffee Plantation. **95.** Arms of Colombia.

96. Columbus. **97.** Caldas. **98.** Sabana Station.

1939.

533. **93.** 1 c. green 5 5
535. **94.** 5 c. brown 8 5
536. 5 c. blue 5 5
538. **95.** 15 c. blue 30 5
539. **96.** 20 c. black 45 8
540. **97.** 30 c. olive 60 15
541. **98.** 40 c. brown .. .. 1·50 30

For similar 40 c. see No. 400.

99. Proposed new P.O., Bogota.

1940. Obligatory Tax. P.O. Rebuilding Fund.

542. **99.** ¼ c. blue 5 5
543. ½ c. red 5 5
544. 1 c. violet 5 5
545. 2 c. green 5 5
546. 20 c. brown 45 15

100. General Santander. **101.** Victorious Army at Zamora.

1940. Gen. Santander. Death Cent. Dated "1840 1940".

547. **100.** 1 c. olive 20 15
548. – 2 c. red 20 15
549. – 5 c. brown 25 12
550. – 8 c. red 30 20
551. – 10 c. yellow 40 20
552. – 15 c. blue 60 25
553. – 20 c. green 80 45
554. – 50 c. violet .. .. 1·10 90
555. – 1 p. red .. .. 3·25 2·50
556. **101.** 2 p. orange .. .. 13·00 10·00

DESIGNS—VERT. 2 c. "Arms and the Law". 5 c. Medallion of Santander by David. 8 c. Santander's statue, Cucuta. 15 c. Church at Rosario. HORIZ. 10 c. Santander's birthplace, Rosario. 20 c. Battlefield at Paya. 50 c. Bridge at Boyaca. 1 p. Death of Santander.

102. Tobacco Plant. **103.** Garcia Rovira. **104.** Galan.

105. General Sucre. **106.** Allegory of Protection.

1940.

557. **102.** 8 c. green and red .. 75 35
558. – 15 c. blue (Santander) 15 8
559. **103.** 20 c. grey 60 10
560. **104.** 40 c. brown 50 8
561. **105.** 1 p. black .. .. 1·50 20
562. 1 p. violet 75 8

1940. National Red Cross.

563. **106.** 5 c. red 10 5

107. Pre-Colombian Monument. **108.** Proclamation of Independence.

1941. Air.

568. **107.** 5 c. grey 5 5
691. 5 c. yellow 8 5
742. 5 c. ultramarine .. 10 5
747. 5 c. red 12 5
569. – 10 c. orange 8 5
692. – 10 c. vermilion .. 8 5
743. – 10 c. ultramarine .. 10 5
748. – 10 c. red 12 5
570. – 15 c. red 10 5
693. – 15 c. blue 8 5
744. – 15 c. ultramarine .. 12 5
571. – 20 c. green 8 5
694. – 20 c. violet 10 5
745. – 20 c. ultramarine .. 40 10
749. – 20 c. red 25 5
572. **107.** 30 c. blue 20 5
695. 30 c. green 15 5
746. 30 c. ultramarine .. 40 10
750. 30 c. red 30 5
573. – 40 c. maroon 25 5
696. – 40 c. grey 20 5
574. – 50 c. green 30 5
697. – 50 c. claret 25 5
575. – 60 c. purple 30 5
698. – 60 c. olive 30 5
576. **107.** 80 c. olive 50 8
699. 80 c. brown 40 5
577. **108.** 1 p. black and blue .. 90 12
700. 1 p. brown and olive 50 8
578. – 2 p. black and red 1·75 25
701. – 2 p. blue and green .. 1·10 15
579. **108.** 3 p. black and violet .. 3·00 1·40
702. 3 p. black and red .. 2·50 1·00
580. – 5 p. black and green .. 7·00 4·00
703. – 5 p. green and sepia .. 6·00 2·50

DESIGNS: As T **107**: 10 c., 40 c., "El Dorado" Monument. 15 c. 50 c. Spanish Fort, Cartagena. 20 c., 60 c. Street in Old Bogota. As T **108**: 2 p., 5 p. National Library, Bogota.

109. Arms of Palmira. **110.** Home of Jorge Isaacs (author).

1942. 8th National Agricultural Exn., Palmira.

581. **109.** 30 c. claret 65 25

1942. Honouring J. Isaacs.

582. **110.** 50 c. green 75 25

ILLUSTRATIONS British Commonwealth and all overprints and surcharges are FULL SIZE. Foreign Countries have been reduced to ¾-LINEAR

111. Peace Conference Delegates.

1942. Wisconsin Peace Treaty ending Civil War. 40th Anniv.

583. **111.** 10 c. orange 40 15

1943. Surch. $0.0½ **MEDIO CENTAVO.**

584. **92.** ½ c. on 1 c. violet .. 5 5
585. ½ c. on 2 c. green .. 5 5
586. ½ c. on 20 c. brown .. 12 10

1944. Surch. **5 Centavos.**

587. – 5 c. on 10 c. orge. (No. 460) 8 5

112. National Shrine. **113.** San Pedro, Alejandrino.

1944.

592. **112.** 30 c. olive 50 12
593. **113.** 50 c. red 60 15

1944. Surch. with new values in figures and words.

594. **94.** 1 c. on 5 c. brn. (No. 535) 5 5
595. 2 c. on 5 c. brn. (No. 535) 5 5

114. Banner. **115.** Murillo Toro.

116. Virrey Solis. **117.** Murillo Toro.

1944. General Benefit Assn. of Cundinamarca. 75th Anniv.

596. **114.** 2 c. blue and yellow .. 12 8
597. – 5 c. blue and yellow .. 12 10
598. **115.** 20 c. black and green .. 50 30
599. – 40 c. black and red .. 1·25 1·10
600. **116.** 1 p. black and red .. 3·25 3·00

DESIGNS: 5 c. as T **114**, Arms of the Association. 40 c. as T **116**. St. Juan de Dios Maternity Hospital.

1944.

602. **117.** 5 c. olive 12 5

118. Proposed P.O., Bogota. (**119.** Stalin, Roosevelt and Churchill.)

1945. Obligatory Tax. P.O. Rebuilding Fund.

609. **118.** ½ c. blue 5 5
610. ½ c. brown 5 5
611. ½ c. red 5 5
612. ½ c. mauve 5 5
613. 1 c. violet 5 5
614. 1 c. orange 5 5
615. 1 c. olive 5 5
616. 2 c. green 5 5
617. 20 c. brown 15 5

1945. Victory. Optd. with T **119.**

618. **94.** 5 c. brown 20 5

119a. Clock Tower, Cartagena. **120.** Fort San Sebastian Cartagena.

121. Tequendama Falls. **122.** Sierra Nevada of Santa Maria.

1945.

621. **119a.** 50 c. olive .. .. 1·40 20

1945. Air. Inscr. "SOBREPORTE AEREO—".

622. **120.** 5 c. grey 5 5
623. **121.** 10 c. orange 5 5
624. – 15 c. red 8 5
625. **120.** 20 c. green 12 5
626. **121.** 30 c. blue 15 5
627. – 40 c. claret 25 5
628. **120.** 50 c. green 25 5
629. 60 c. purple 70 15
630. – 80 c. grey 80 20
631. – 1 p. blue .. .. 1·40 25
632. – 2 p. red .. .. 2·50 35

DESIGNS—As T **120/1**: 15 c., 40 c., 80 c. Santa Marta Bay. HORIZ. (larger): 1 p., 2 p. Capitol, Bogota.

1945. 1st Air Mail Service in America. 25th Anniv. Inscr. as in T **122.**

633. **122.** 20 c. green 40 30
634. – 30 c. blue 50 25
635. – 50 c. red 85 25

DESIGNS: 30 c. Seaplane "Tolima". 50 c. San Sebastian Fortress, Cartagena.

1946. Surch. **1** above **UN CENTAVO.**

636. **68.** 1 c. on 5 c. brown .. 5 5

123. Gen. Sucre. **124.** Map of South America. **125.** Bogota Observatory.

1946.

638. **123.** 1 c. blue and brown .. 5 5
639. 2 c. red and violet .. 5 5
640. 5 c. blue and olive .. 5 5
641. 9 c. red and green .. 40 40
642. 10 c. orange and blue .. 30 15
643. 20 c. orange and black 30 15
644. 30 c. green and red .. 35 15
645. 40 c. claret and green 35 15
646. 50 c. violet and purple 50 25

The 5 c. to 50 c. are larger (23½ × 32 mm.).

1946. Obligatory Tax. Red Cross Fund. Optd. with red cross.

647. **94.** 5 c. brown (No. 535) .. 12 5

1946.

648. **124.** 15 c. blue 12 5

1946.

649. **125.** 5 c. brown 20 5
650. 5 c. blue 5 5

126. Andres Bello. **127.** Joaquin de Cayzedo y Cuero.

1946. Andres Bello (poet and teacher). 80th Death Anniv.

651. **126.** 3 c. brown (postage) .. 8 5
652. 10 c. orange 20 8
653. 15 c. black 20 10
654. 5 c. blue (air) .. 10 8

1946.

655. **127.** 2 p. blue-green .. 2·25 40
656. 2 p. green 70 15

128. Proposed New P.O., Bogota. **129.** Coffee Plant.

1946. Obligatory Tax. P.O. Rebuilding Fund.

657. **128.** 3 c. blue 5 5

1946. 5th Olympic Games, Barranquilla. As No. 621 optd. **V JUEGOS C. A. Y DEL C. 1946.**

658. – 50 c. red .. .. 2·50 1·25

1947.

659. **129.** 5 c. multicoloured .. 35 15

130. "Masdevallia Nicterina". **131.** Antonio Narino.

1947. Orchids. Multicoloured.

660. 1 c. Type **130** .. 40 12
661. 2 c. "Miltonia Vexillaria" 40 10
662. 5 c. "Cattleya Dowiana Aurea" 50 10
663. 5 c. "Cattleya Chocoensis" 40 8
664. 5 c. "Odontoglossum Crispum" 50 10
665. 10 c. "Cattleya Labiata Trianae" 80 25

1947. Obligatory Tax. Optd. **SOBRETASA** in fancy letters.

666. **103.** 20 c. grey (No. 559) .. 60 15
676. **71.** 20 c. blue (No. 434) .. 2·25 2·25

1947. 4th Pan-American Press Conf., Bogota.

667. **131.** 5 c. blue on blue (post.) 10 5
668. – 10 c. brown on blue .. 15 5
669. – 5 c. blue on blue (air) 20 8
670. – 10 c. red on blue .. 30 15

PORTRAITS: No. 667, A. Urdaneta y Urdaneta. 669, F. J. de Caldas. 670, M. del Socorro Rodriguez.

133. Arms of Colombia and Cross. **134.** J. C. Mutis and J. J. Triana.

135. M. A. Caro and R. J. Cuervo.

1947. Obligatory Tax. Red Cross Fund.

671. **133.** 5 c. lake 8 5
704. 5 c. vermilion 8 5

1947.

672. **134.** 25 c. green 15 5
673. 25 c. olive 20 5
674. **135.** 3 p. slate-purple .. 1·75 70
675. 3 p. purple 90 30

DESIGNS—No. 678, National Capitol. 679, Foreign Office. 680, Chancellery. 681, Raphael Court, Capitol.

136. Bogota Cathedral.

1948. 9th Pan-American Congress, Bogota. Inscr. as in T **136.**

677. **136.** 5 c. brown (postage) .. 8 5
678. – 10 c. orange 25 20
679. – 15 c. blue 30 30
680. – 5 c. brown (air) .. 10 5
681. – 15 c. blue 80 70

1948. Obligatory Tax. Savings Bank stamps surch. **COLOMBIA SOBRETASA 1 CENTAVO.** various designs.

682. 1 c. on 5 c. brown .. 5 5
683. 1 c. on 10 c. violet .. 5 5
684. 1 c. on 25 c. red .. 5 5
685. 1 c. on 50 c. blue .. 5 5

1948. Optd. C(= "CORREOS"). No gum.

686. **92.** 1 c. orange 5 5

1948. Optd. **CORREOS.**

687. **118.** 1 c. olive 5 5
688. 2 c. green 5 5
689. 20 c. brown 20 5

137. Simon Bolivar. **139.** C. M. Silva

138. Proposed New P.O., Bogota.

1948.
690. 137. 15 c. green 12 5

1948. Obligatory Tax. P.O. Rebuilding Fund.
705. 138. 1 c. red 5 5
706. 2 c. green 5 5
707. 3 c. blue 5 5
708. 5 c. grey 5 5
709. 10 c. violet 8 5
See also Nos. 756 and 758/62.

1949.
710. 139. 40 c. red 25 5

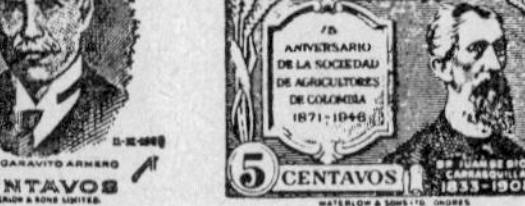

140. J. G. Armero. 141. Dr. Juan de Dios Carrasquilla.

1949. J. G. Armero (mathematician).
711. 140. 4 c. green 10 5

1949. National Agricultural Society. 75th Anniv.
712. 141. 5 c. bistre 5 5

143. Arms of Colombia. 144. Allegory of Justice.

1949. New Constitution.
713. 143. 15 c. blue (postage) .. 10 5
714. 144. 5 c. green (air) .. 5 5
715. – 10 c. orange 8 5
DESIGN: 10 c. Allegory of Constitution.

145. Tree and Shield. 146. F. J. Cisneros.

1949. 1st Forestry Congress, Bogota.
716. 145. 5 c. olive 5 5

1949. Francisco Javier Cisneros (engineer). 50th Death Anniv.
717. 146. 50 c. blue and brown 35 12
718. 50 c. violet and green 35 12
719. 50 c. yellow and purple 35 12

146a. Mother and Child.

1950. Red Cross Fund. Surch. with new value and date as in T **146a.**
720. 146a. 5 on 2 c. multicoloured 50 20

1950. Obligatory Tax. Optd. **SOBRETASA.**
721. 94. 5 c. blue 8 5

147. "Masdevallia Chimaera". 148. Santo Domingo Palace.

1950. U.P.U. 75th Anniv. Inscr. "1874 U.P.U. 1949".
722. 147. 1 c. brown 12 5
723. – 2 c. violet 12 5
724. – 3 c. magenta 15 5
725. – 4 c. green 20 5
726. – 5 c. orange 40 5
727. – 11 c. red 70 70
728. 148. 18 c. blue 60 20
DESIGNS: 2 c. to 11 c. Various orchids as T **147.**

149. A. Baraya (patriot). 150. Farm.

1950.
729. 149. 2 c. red 5 5

1950.
730. 150. 5 c. red and buff .. 10 5
731. 5 c. green and turquoise 10 5
732. 5 c. blue and light blue 10 5

151. Arms of Bogota. 152. Map and Badge.

1950.
733. 151. 5 p. green .. .. 1·90 40
734. – 10 p. orange (Arms of Colombia) .. .. 3·50 80

1951. Colombian Society of Engineers. 60th Anniv.
735. 152. 20 c. red, yellow & blue 15 5

153. Arms of Colombia and Cross. 154. Fray Bartolome de Las Casas.

1951. Obligatory Tax. Red Cross Fund.
736. 153. 5 c. red 10 5
737. 154. 5 c. red 10 5
738. 5 c. green and red .. 10 5

155. D. G. Valencia. 156. Dr. J. M. Lombana.

1951. 8th Death Anniv. of D. G. Valencia (poet and orator).
739. 155. 25 c. black 15 5

1951. Surch.
740. 138. 1 c. on 3 c. blue .. 5 5

1951. Nationalization of Barranca Oilfields. Optd. **REVERSION CONCESION MARES 25 Agosto 1951.**
741. 78. 2 c. red 5 5

1952. Colombian Doctors.
751. – 1 c. blue (N. Osorio) 5 5
752. – 1 c. blue (P. Martinez) 5 5
753. – 1 c. bl. (E. Uriocoechea) 5 5
754. 156. 1 c. blue 5 5

157. Proposed New P.O. Bogota. 158. Manizales Cathedral. 159. Queen Isabella and Columbus Monument.

1952.
755. 157. 5 c. blue 5 5
756. 138. 20 c. brown .. .. 1·75 5
757. 118. 25 c. grey .. .. 3·50 75
758. 138. 25 c. green 40 5
759. 50 c. orange .. .. 3·25 1·75
760. 1 p. red .. .. 1·40 8
761. 2 p. purple .. .. 5·00 1·00
762. 2 p. violet 70 15
Owing to a shortage of postage stamps the above obligatory tax types were issued for ordinary postal use.

1952. Obligatory Tax. No. 759 surch.
763. 138. 8 c. on 50 c. orange 5 5

1952. Manizales. Cent.
764. 158. 23 c. black and blue 20 8

1952. 1st Latin-American Congress of Iron Specialists. Surch. **1952 1° CONFERENCIA SIDERURGICA LATINO-AMERICANA** and new value.
765. 134. 15 c. on 25 c. green (postage) 20 8
766. 107. 70 c. on 80 c. red (air) 40 25

1953. Isabella the Catholic. 500th Birth Anniv.
767. 159. 23 c. black and blue .. 20 12

1953. Air. Optd. **CORREO AEREO** or surch. also
768. 138. 5 c. on 8 c. blue .. 5 5
769. 15 c. on 20 c. brown .. 12 5
770. 15 c. on 25 c green .. 30 5
771. 25 c. green 15 5

1953. Air. Optd. **AEREO.**
772. 82. 10 c. red 5 5

EXTRA RAPIDO. Stamps bearing this overprint or inscription were used to prepay the additional cost of air carriage of inland mail handled by the National Postal Service from 1953 to 1964. Subsequently remaining stocks of these stamps were used for other classes of correspondence. Since the 1920's regular air service for inland and foreign mail has been provided by the Air Postal Service, a separate undertaking which is administered by the Avianca airline and for which the regular air stamps are used.

1953. Air. No. 727 surch. **CORREO EXTRA RAPIDO 5 5.**
773. 5 c. on 11 c. red 30 15

159a.

1953. Air. Fiscal stamps optd. as in **159a** or surch. also.
774. 159a. 1 c. on 2 c. green .. 5 5
775. 50 c. red 25 15

159b.

1953. Air. Real Estate Tax stamps optd. as in **159b.**
776. 159b. 5 c. red 5 5
777. 20 c. brown .. 12 8

1953. Surch.
778. 138. 40 c. on 1 p. red .. 20 10
779. 127. 50 c. on 2 p. green .. 20 10

160. Don M. Ancizar. 161.

1953. Colombian Chorographical Commission Cent. Portraits inscr. as in T **160.**
780. 160. 14 c. red and black .. 15 15
781. – 23 c. blue and black .. 12 5
782. – 30 c. sepia and black .. 25 8
783. – 1 p. green and black .. 45 12
PORTRAITS: 23 c. J. J. Triana. 30 c. M. Ponce de Leon. 1 p. A. Codazzi.

1953. 2nd National Philatelic Exn., Bogota. Real Estate Tax stamps surch. as in T **161.**
784. 161. 5 c. on 5 p. mult. (post.) 10 5
785. – 15 c. on 10 p. multicoloured (air) 30 20
DESIGN: 15 c. Map of Colombia.

1953. Air. Optd. **CORREO EXTRA-RAPIDO** or surch. also.
786. 138. 2 c. on 8 c. blue .. 5 5
787. 10 c. violet 10 5

162. Fountain, Tunja. 164. Map of Colombia.

163. Pastelillo Fort, Cartagena.

1954. Air.
788. – 5 c. purple 8 5
789. – 10 c. black 8 5
790. – 15 c. red 10 5
791. – 15 c. vermilion .. 12 5
792. – 20 c. brown 12 5
793. – 25 c. blue 12 5
794. – 25 c. purple 12 5
795. – 30 c. chestnut .. 12 5
796. – 40 c. blue 15 5
797. – 50 c. purple 20 5
798. 162. 60 c. sepia 25 5
799. – 80 c. lake 40 8
800. – 1 p. black and blue .. 80 5
801. 163. 2 p. black and green .. 1·00 10
802. – 3 p. black and red .. 1·75 40
803. – 5 p. green and brown 3·00 70
804. 164. 10 p. olive & vermilion 2·75 1·90
DESIGNS. As T **162**—VERT. 5 c., 30 c. Galeras volcano, Pasto. 15 c. red, 50 c. Bolivar Monument, Boyaca. 15 c. verm., 25 c. (2) Sanctuary of the Rocks, Narino. 20 c., 80 c. Nevado del Ruiz Mts., Manizales. 40 c. J. Isaacs Monument, Cali. HORIZ. 10 c. San Diego Monastery, Bogota. As T **163**—HORIZ. 1 p. Girardot Stadium, Medellin. 3 p. Santo Domingo Gateway and University, Popayan. As T **164**—HORIZ. 5 p. Sanctuary of the Rocks, Narino.

1954. Surch.
805. 160. 5 c. on 14 c red & blk. 10 5
806. 158. 5 c. on 23 c. blk. & blue 10 5

164a. 165.

1954. Air.
807. 164a. 5 c. purple 15 5

1954. Franciscan Community in Colombia. 400th Anniv.
808. 165. 5 c. brown, grn. & sepia 10 5

1954. Obligatory Tax. Red Cross Fund. No. 807 optd. with cross and bar in red.
809. 164a. 5 c. purple 25 10

166. Soldier, Flag and Arms of Republic. 167.

1954. National Army Commem.
810. 166. 5 c. blue (postage) .. 5 5
811. 15 c. red (air) .. 15 5

1954. 7th National Athletic Games, Cali. Inscr. "VII JUEGOS ATLETICOS", etc.
812. – 5 c. blue (postage) .. 15 5
813. 167. 10 c. red 25 5
814. – 15 c. brown (air) .. 20 5
815. 167. 20 c. green 60 10
DESIGN: 5 c., 15 c. Badge of the Games.

168. 169. Saint's Convent and Cell.

1954. Colombian Academy of History. 50th Anniv.
816. 168. 5 c. green and blue .. 8 5

1954. San Pedro Claver. Tercent. Inscr. "1654–1954".
817. 169. 5 c. green (postage) .. 10 5
819. – 15 c. brown (air) .. 15 5
DESIGN: 15 c. San Pedro Claver Church, Cartagena

170. Mercury.

170a. Archbishop Mosquera.

1954. 1st Int. Fair, Bogota.

821. 170. 5 c. orange (postage) 15 5
822. 15 c. blue (air) .. 15 5
823. 50 c. red ("EXTRA RAPIDO") .. 25 5

1954. Air. Archbishop Mosquera. Death Cent.

824. 170a. 2 c. green 5 5

170b. Virgin of Chiquinquira.

1954. Air.

825. 170b. 5 c. mult. (brown frame) 10 5
826. 5 c. mult. (violet frame) 10 5

171. Tapestry presented by Queen Margaret of Austria.

1954. Senior College of Our Lady of the Rosary Bogota. Tercent. Inscr. "1653 1953".

827. 171. 5 c. black and orange (postage) 12 5
828. – 10 c. blue 12 5
829. – 15 c. brown 15 8
830. – 20 c. brown and black 30 10
832. 171. 15 c. black & red (air) 20 5
833. – 20 c. blue 25 8
834. – 25 c. brown 25 10
835. – 50 c. red and black .. 60 30

DESIGNS—VERT. Nos. 828, 833, Friar Cristobal de Torres (founder). HORIZ. 829, 834, Cloisters and statue. 830, 835, Chapel and coat of arms.

172. Paz de Rio Steel Works.

173. J. Marti.

1954. Paz del Rio Steel Plant. Inaug.

837. 172. 5 c. black & blue (post.) 5 5
838. 20 c. black & grn. (air) 35 12

1955. Marti (Cuban revolutionary). Birth Cent.

839. 173. 5 c. red (postage) .. 5 5
840. 15 c. green (air) .. 15 5

174. Badge, Flags and Korean Landscape.

1955. Colombian Forces in Korea.

841. 174. 10 c. purple (postage) 15 5
842. 20 c. green (air) .. 25 8

175. Ship's Wheel and Map.

175a. M. Fidel Suarez.

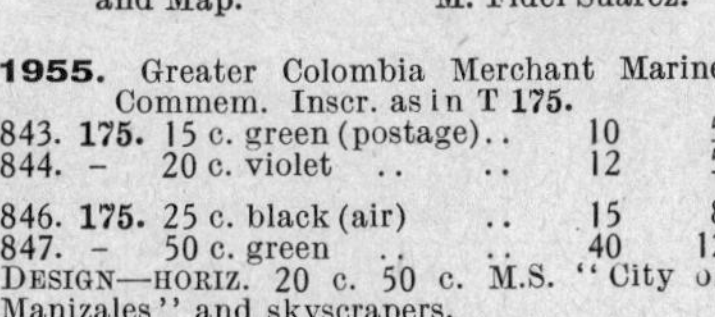

1955. Greater Colombia Merchant Marine Commem. Inscr. as in T 175.

843. 175. 15 c. green (postage).. 10 5
844. – 20 c. violet 12 5
846. 175. 25 c. black (air) .. 15 8
847. – 50 c. green 40 12

DESIGN—HORIZ. 20 c. 50 c. M.S. "City of Manizales" and skyscrapers.

1955. Air. Pres. Suarez. Birth Cent.

849. 175a. 10 c. blue 5 5

176. San Pedro Claver Feeding Slaves.

1955. Obligatory Tax. Red Cross Fund and 300th Anniv. of San Pedro Claver.

850. 176. 5 c. maroon and red.. 10 5

177. Hotel Tequendama and San Diego Church.

1955.

851. 177. 5 c. blue and pale blue (postage) 5 5
852. 15 c. lake and pink (air) 15 5

178. Bolivar's Country House.

1955. Rotary Int. 50th Anniv.

853. 178. 5 c. blue (postage) .. 5 5
854. 15 c. red (air) .. 15 5

179. Belalcazar, De Quesada and Balboa.

180. J. E. Caro.

1955. 7th Postal Union Congress of the Americas and Spain. Inscr. as in T 179.

855. 179. 2 c. brn. & grn. (post.) 5 5
856. – 5 c. brown and blue .. 5 5
857. – 23 c. black and blue .. 15 10
859. – 15 c. black and red (air) 8 5
860. – 20 c. black and brown 10 5
862. – 2 c. black and brown ("EXTRA RAPIDO") 5 5
863. – 5 c. sepia and yellow 8 5
864. – 1 p. brown and slate.. 1·60 1·50
865. – 2 p. black and violet.. 1·00 50

DESIGNS—HORIZ. 2 c. (No. 855), T 179. 2 c. (No. 862), Atahualpa, Tisquesuza, Moctezuma. 5 c. (No. 856), San Martin, Bolivar and Washington. 5 c. (No. 863), King Ferdinand, Queen Isabella and coat of arms. 15 c. O'Higgins, Santander and Sucre. 20 c. Marti, Hidalgo and Petion. 23 c. Colombus, "Santa Maria", "Pinta" and "Nina". 1 p. Artigas, Lopez and Murillo. 2 p. Calderon, Baron de Rio Branco and De La Mar.

1955. Caro's Death Cent.

866. 180. 5 c. brown (postage).. 5 5
867. 180. 15 c. green (air) .. 15 5

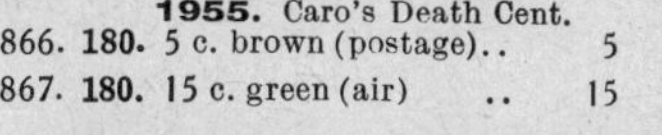

180a. Salamanca University.

181. Gold Mining, Narino.

1955. Air. Salamanca University. 7th Cent.

868. 180a. 20 c. brown 10 8

1956. Regional Industries. Inscr. "DEPARTAMENTO", "PROVIDENCIA" (No. 874), "INTENDENCIA" (2 p. to 5 p.) or "COMISARIA" (10 p.).

869. – 2 c. green and red .. 5 5
870. – 3 c. black and purple.. 5 5
871. – 3 c. brown and blue .. 5 5
872. – 3 c. violet and green.. 5 5
873. – 4 c. black and green.. 5 5
874. – 5 c. black and blue .. 10 5
875. – 5 c. slate and red .. 10 5
876. – 5 c. olive and brown.. 10 5
877. – 5 c. brown and olive.. 25 5
878. – 5 c. brown and blue .. 15 5
879. – 10 c. black and yellow 25 5
880. – 10 c. brown and green 5 5
881. – 10 c. brown and blue.. 5 5
882. – 15 c. black and blue .. 12 5
883. – 20 c. blue and brown.. 15 5
884. – 23 c. vermilion & blue 20 15
885. – 25 c. black and olive.. 20 5
886. 181. 30 c. brown and blue.. 15 5
887. – 40 c. brown and purple 20 8
888. – 50 c. black and green.. 15 8
889. – 60 c. green and sepia.. 20 10
890. – 1 p. slate and purple.. 40 12
891. – 2 p. brown and green.. 45 25
892. – 3 p. black and red .. 90 20
893. – 5 p. blue and brown .. 1·40 40
894. – 10 p. green and brown 2·75 1·10

DESIGNS—As T 181. HORIZ. 2 c. Barranquilla naval workshops, Atlantico. 4 c. Fishing' Cartagena Port, Bolivar. 5 c. (No. 875) View of Port, San Andres. 5 c. (876) Cocoa, Cauca. 5 c. (877) Prize cattle, Cordoba. 23 c. Rice harvesting, Huila. 25 c. Bananas Magdalena. 40 c. Tobacco, Santander. 50 c. Oil wells of Catatumbo, Norte de Santander. 60 c. Cotton harvesting, Tolima. VERT. 3 c. (3), Allegory of Industry, Antioquia. 5 c. (874) Map of San Andres Archipelago. 5 c. (878) Steel plant, Boyaca. 10 c. (3), Coffee, Caldas. 15 c. Cathedral at Sal Salinas de Zipaquira, Cundinamarca. 20 c. Platinum and map, Choco. LARGER ($37\frac{1}{2}$ × 27 mm.)—HORIZ. 1 p. Sugar factory, Valle del Cauca. 2 p. Cattle fording river, Meta. 3 p. Statue and R. Amazon, Leticia. 5 p. Landscape, La Guajira. VERT. 10 p. Rubber tapping, Vaupes.

182. Henri Dunant and S. Samper Brush.

1956. Obligatory Tax. Red Cross Fund.

895. 182 5 c. brown 10 5

1956. Air. No. 783 optd. **EXTRA-RAPIDO**.

896. 1 p. green and black .. 40 25

183. Columbus and Lighthouse.

1956. Columbus Memorial Lighthouse.

897. 183. 3 c. black (postage) .. 5 5
898. 15 c. blue (air) .. 12 5
899. 3 c. green ("EXTRA RAPIDO") .. 5 5

184. The Altar of St. Elisabeth, Primada Basilica, Bogota.

185. St. Ignatius of Loyola.

1956. St. Elisabeth of Hungary. 7th Cent.

900. 184. 5 c. purple (postage) . 8 5
901. 15 c. brown (air) .. 15 5

1956. St. Ignatius of Loyola. 4th Death Cent.

902. 185. 5 c. blue (postage) .. 8 5
903. 5 c. brown (air) .. 15 5

186. Javier Pereira.

187. Dairy Farm.

1956. Pereira Commem.

904. 186. 5 c. blue (postage) .. 5 5
905. 20 c. red (air) .. 10 5

1957. Air. No. 874 optd. **EXTRA-RAPIDO.**

906. 5 c. black and blue 5 5

1957. Air. As No. 580 (colours changed) optd. **EXTRA-RAPIDO.**

907. 5 p. black and buff .. 1·75 90

1957. Agricultural Credit Bank. 25th Anniv. Inscr. "CAJA DE CREDITO AGRARIO".

908. 187. 1 c. olive (postage) .. 5 5
909. – 2 c. brown 5 5
910. – 5 c. blue 5 5
911. 187. 5 c. orange (air) .. 5 5
912. – 10 c. green 25 5
913. – 15 c. black 8 5
914. – 20 c. red 35 10
915. – 5 c. brown ("EXTRA RAPIDO") .. 5 5

DESIGNS: 2 c., 10 c. Farm tractor. 5 c. (No. 910), 15 c. Emblem of agricultural prosperity. 5 c. (No. 915), Livestock. 20 c. Livestock.

187a. Racing Cyclist.

1957. Air. 7th Round Colombia Cycle Race.

916. 187a. 2 c. brown .. 5 5
917. 5 c. blue 8 5

188. Arms and Gen. Rayes (founder).

189. Father J. M. Delgado.

1957. Military Cadet School. 50th Anniv. Inscr. as in T 188.

918. 188. 5 c. blue (postage) .. 5 5
919. – 10 c orange 5 5
921. 188. 15 c. red (air).. .. 8 5
922. – 20 c. brown 12 5

DESIGN: 10 c., 20 c. Arms and Military Cadet School.

1957. Father Delgado Commemoration.

923. 189. 2 c. lake (postage) .. 5 5
924. 189. 10 c. blue (air) .. 10 5

190. St. Vincent de Paul with Children.

192. Fencer.

191. Signatories to Bogota Postal Convention of 1838, and U.P.U. Monument, Berne.

1957. Colombian Order of St. Vincent de Paul. Cent.
925. **190.** 1 c. green (postage) .. 5 5
926. 5 c. brown-red (air) .. 10 5

1957. 14th U.P.U. Congress, Ottawa and Int. Correspondence Week.
927. **191.** 5 c. green (postage) .. 5 5
928. 10 c. grey 5 5
929. **191.** 15 c. brown (air) .. 10 5
930. 25 c. blue 12 5

1957. 3rd S. American Fencing Championships.
931. **192.** 4 c. purple (postage) .. 5 5
932. 20 c. chocolate (air) .. 15 5

193. Discovery of Hypsometry by F. J. de Caldas.

194. Nurses with Patient, and Ambulance.

1958. Int. Geophysical Year.
933. **193.** 10 c. black (postage) 25 5
934. 25 c. green (air) .. 25 5
935. 1 p. violet ("EXTRA RAPIDO") .. 30 8

1958. Obligatory Tax. Red Cross Fund.
936. **194.** 5 c. red & black .. 5 5

1958. Nos. 882 and 884 surch.
937. 5 c. on 15 c. black & blue 5 5
938. 5 c. on 23 c. verm. & blue 10 5

1958. Air. No. 888 optd. **AEREO.**
939. – 50 c. black and green 15 8

195. Father R. Almanza and San Diego Church, Bogota.

196. Mons. Carrasquilla and Rosario College, Bogota.

1958. Father Almanza Commem.
940. **195.** 10 c. lilac (postage) .. 5 5
941. 25 c. grey (air) .. 12 5
942. 10 c. green ("EXTRA RAPIDO") .. 5 5

1958. Nos. 780/2 surch. **CINCO** (5 c.) or **VEINTE** (20 c.).
943. **160.** 5 c. on 14 c. red & blk. 15 5
944. – 5 c. on 30 c. sepia & blk. 5 5
945. – 20 c. on 23 c. bl. & blk. 8 5

1959. Mons. R. M. Carrasquilla. Birth Cent.
946. **196.** 10 c. brown (postage) 5 5
947. 25 c. red (air) .. 8 5
948. 1 p. blue 30 10

1959. Surch. **20. c.** and ornament.
949. **159.** 20 c. on 23 c. blk. & bl. 8 5

1959. As No. 826 but with "CORREO EXTRA RAPIDO" obliterated.
950. 170b 5 c. multicoloured .. 5 5

1959. No. 794 surch.
951. 10 c. on 25 c. purple .. 5 5

197. Luz Marina Zuluaga ("Miss Universe 1959").

198. J. E. Gaitan. (political leader).

1959. "Miss Universe 1959" Commem.
952. **197.** 10 c. mult. (postage).. 8 5
953. 1 p. 20 mult. (air) .. 30 25
954. 5 p. mult. ("EXTRA RAPIDO").. .. 10·00 10·00

1959. No. 873 surch.
955. 2 c. on 4 c. black and green 5 5

1959. J. E. Gaitan Commem. Nos. 956 and 958 are surch. on T **198.**
956. **198.** 10 c. on 3 c. grey .. 5 5
957. 30 c. purple 15 5
958. 2 p. on 1 p. black ("EXTRA RAPIDO") 30 25

1959. Air. Surch.
960. **162.** 50 c. on 60 c. sepia .. 35 10

199. Capitol, Bogota.

200. Santander.

1959.
961. **199.** 2 c. brn. & blue (post.) 5 5
962. 3 c. violet and black .. 5 5
963. **200.** 5 c. chocolate & yellow 5 5
964. – 5 c. ultramarine & blue 5 5
965. – 10 c. black and red .. 5 5
966. **200.** 10 c. black and green 5 5
967. – 35 c. blk. & grey (air) 25 8
PORTRAIT (as T **200**): Nos. 964/5, 967, Bolivar.

1959. Air. Unification of Airmail Rates. Optd. **UNIFICADO** within outline of aeroplane.
968. **185.** 5 c. brown 30 20
969. **187.** 5 c. orange 15 10
970. **190.** 5 c. brown-red .. 30 20
971. **82.** 10 c. red (No. 772) .. 20 5
972. – 10 c. black (No. 789) 15 5
973. **188.** 15 c. red 25 5
974. – 20 c. brown (No. 792) 15 5
975. – 20 c. brown (No. 922) 15 5
976. **192.** 20 c. chocolate .. 20 5
977. – 25 c. blue (No. 793) 15 5
978. – 25 c. purple (No. 794) 10 5
979. **195.** 25 c. grey 12 5
980. **196.** 25 c. red 15 5
981. – 30 c. chestnut (No. 795) 20 5
982. **162.** 50 c. on 60 c. sepia (No. 960) .. 25 5
983. **196.** 1 p. blue 30 5
984. **197.** 1 p. 20 brown, blue, red and green .. 55 8
985. **163.** 2 p. black and green .. 50 8
986. – 3 p. blk. & red (No. 802) 1·10 15
987. – 5 p. grn. & brn. (No. 803) 1·25 20
988. **164.** 10 p. olive & vermilion 2·00 60

201. Colombian 2½c. stamp of 1859 and Postman with Mule.

202. Colombian 2 c. Air Stamp of 1918, Seaplane and "Super Constellation" Airliner.

1959. Colombian Stamp Cent. Inscr. "1859 1959".
989. **201.** 5 c. grn. & orge. (post.) 5 5
990. – 10 c. blue and lake .. 5 5
991. **201.** 15 c. green and red .. 10 10
992. – 25 c. brown and blue 12 8
993. – 25 c. red & brown (air) 10 5
994. – 50 c. blue and red .. 20 8
995. – 1 p. 20 chest. & green 35 20
996. – 10 c. lilac and bistre "EXTRA-RAPIDO") 5 5
DESIGNS—VERT. Colombian stamps of 1859 (except No. 993): No. 990, 5 c. and river steamer. 992, 10 c. and railway train. 1093, Postal decree of 1859 and Pres. M. Ospina. 996, 10 c. and map of Colombia. HORIZ. 994, 20 c. and seaplane. 995, 1 p. and "Super Constellation" airliner over valley.

1959. Air. Colombian "AVIANCA" Air Mail Services. 40th Anniv. Inscr. as in T **202.**
998. **202.** 35 c. red, black & blue 15 8
999. – 60 c. black and green 20 10
DESIGN: 60 c. As T **202** but without Colombian 2 c. stamp.

203. Eldorado Airport, Bogota.

204. A. von Humboldt (naturalist).

1960. Air.
1002. **203.** 35 c. orange and black 25 5
1003. 60 c. red and grey .. 15 8
1004. **203** 1 p. blue and grey ("EXTRA RAPIDO") 20 12

1960. Alexander von Humboldt. Death Cent. Animals.
1005. – 5 c. brn. & turq. (post.) 5 5
1006. **204.** 10 c. sepia and red .. 12 5
1007. – 20 c. slate-purple and olive-yellow .. 12 5
1008. – 35 c. brown (air) .. 40 5
1009. – 1 p. 30 brown and rose 60 25
1010. – 1 p. 45 lemon and blue 60 35
DESIGNS—VERT. 5 c. Sloth. 20 c. Monkey. HORIZ. 35 c. Anteater. 1 p. 30, Armadillo. 1 p. 45 Parrot fish.

205. "Anthurium andreanum".

206. Refugee Family.

1960. Colombian Flowers.
1011. **205.** 5 c. mult. (postage).. 5 5
1012. A. 20 c. yell., grn. & sep. 8 5
1013. B. 5 c. mult. (air) .. 5 5
1014. 5 c. multicoloured .. 5 5
1015. A. 10 c. yell., grn. & blue 8 5
1016. C. 20 c. multicoloured 12 5
1017. D. 25 c. multicoloured .. 20 5
1018. C. 35 c. multicoloured .. 15 5
1019. B. 60 c. multicoloured .. 15 5
1020. **205.** 60 c. multicoloured .. 15 5
1021. 1 p. 45, multicoloured 30 20
1022. C. 5 c. mult. ("EXTRA RAPIDO") .. 5 5
1023. D. 10 c. multicoloured .. 5 5
1024. **205.** 1 p. multicoloured .. 40 35
1025. A. 1 p. yellow, green & sepia .. 40 35
1026. B. 1 p. multicoloured .. 40 35
1027. C. 1 p. multicoloured .. 40 35
1028. D. 1 p. multicoloured .. 40 35
1029. C. 2 p. multicoloured .. 40 25
FLOWERS: A. "Espelitia grandiflora". B. "Passiflora mollissma". C. "Ondontoglossum luteo purpureum". D. "Stanhopea tigrina".

1960. Air. World Refugee Year.
1030. **206.** 60 c. grey and green 25 10

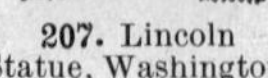

207. Lincoln Statue, Washington.

208. "House of the Flower Vase".

1960. Abraham Lincoln. 150th Birth Anniv.
1032. **207.** 20 c. blk. & mve. (post.) 10 5
1033. 40 c. black & choc. (air) 25 10
1034. 60 c. black and red 20 5

1960. Independence. 150th Anniv. Inscr. "INDEPENDENCIA NACIONAL 1810-1960".
1035. – 5 c. brn. & grn. (post.) 8 5
1036. **208.** 20 c. purple & brown 5 5
1037. – 20 c. yellow, blue and magenta 5 5
1038. – 5 c. multicoloured (air) 8 5
1039. – 5 c. sepia and violet.. 10 5
1040. – 35 c. multicoloured .. 10 5
1041. – 60 c. green & chestnut 12 8
1042. – 1 p. green and red .. 20 10
1043. – 1 p. 20 indigo & blue 25 12
1044. – 1 p. 30 black & orge. 25 15
1045. – 1 p. 45, multicoloured 30 20
1046. – 1 p. 65 brown & green 30 12
DESIGNS—VERT. No. 1035, Cartagena coins of 1811–13. 1038, Arms of Cartagena. 1037, Arms of Mompos. 1043, Statue of A. Galan. HORIZ. 1039, J. Camacho, J. T. Lozano and J. M. Pey. 1040, 1045, Colombian Flag. 1041, A. Rosillo, A. Villavicencio and J. Caicedo. 1042, B. Alvares and J. Gutierrez. 1044, Front page of "La Bagatela" (newspaper). 1046, A. Santos, J. A. Gomez and L. Mejia.

209. St. Luisa de Marillac and Sanctuary.

210. St. Isidro Labrador.

1960. Obligatory Tax. Red Cross Fund.
1048. **209.** 5 c. red and brown .. 8 5
1049. – 5 c. red and violet-blue 8 5
DESIGN: No. 1049, H. Dunant and battle scene.

1960. St. Isidro Labrador Commem. (1st issue).
1050. **210.** 10 c. mult. (postage).. 8 5
1051. – 20 c. multicoloured .. 10 5
1052. **210.** 35 c. multicoloured (air) 12 5
DESIGN: 20c. "The Nativity" (after Vasquez). See also Nos. 1126/8.

211. U.N. Headquarters, New York.

212. Highway Map, Northern Colombia.

1960. U.N. Day.
1054. **211.** 20 c. red and black.. 8 5

1961. 8th Pan-American Highway Congress.
1056. **212.** 20 c. brn. & blue (post.) 25 15
1057. 10 c. pur. & grn. (air) 20 12
1058. 20 c. red and blue .. 20 12
1059. 30 c. black and green.. 20 15
1060. 10 c. blue and green ("EXTRA RAPIDO") 20 15

213. Alfonso Lopez (statesman).

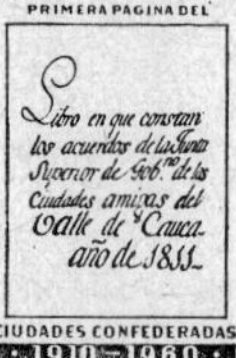

214.

216. Arms of Barranquilla.

215. Arms and View of Cucuta.

1961. Alfonso Lopez Commem.
1061. **213.** 10 c. brn. & red (post.) 5 5
1062. 20 c. brown and violet 5 5
1063. 35 c. brn. & blue (air) 12 5
1064. 10 c. brown and green ("EXTRA RAPIDO") 5 5

1961. Valle del Cauca. 50th Anniv.
1066. – 10 c. brown blue, green and red (postage) .. 5 5
1067. **214.** 20 c. brown and black 5 5

1068. – 35 c. choc. & olive (air) 10 5
1069. – 35 c. brown & emerald 15 5
1070. – 1 p. 30 sepia & maroon 20 10
1071. – 1 p. 45 green & chest. 20 10

1072. – 10 c. choc. & yell.-ol. ("EXTRA RAPIDO") 10 5

DESIGNS—HORIZ. 10 c. (No. 1066), La Ermita Church, bridge and arms of Cali. 35 c. (No. 1068), St. Francis' Church, Cali. 1 p. 30, Conservatoire. 1 p. 45, Agricultural College, Palmira. VERT. 10 c. (No. 1072), Aerial view of Cali. 35 c. (No. 1069), University emblem.

1961. North Santander. 50th Anniv.
1073. – 20 c. multicoloured (post.) 5 5
1074. **215.** 20 c. multicoloured .. 5 5

1075. – 35 c. grn. & bistre (air) 20 5

1076. – 10 c. purple & green ("EXTRA RAPIDO") 10 5

DESIGNS—HORIZ. No. 1073, Arms of Ocana and Pamplona. No. 1075, Panoramic view of Cucuta. VERT. No. 1076, Villa del Rosario, Cucuta.

1961. Air. Optd. **Aereo** or **AEREO** and 'plane or surch. also.
1077. **205.** 5 c. multicoloured .. 5 5
1078. – 5 c. brown & turquoise (No. 1005) 5 5
1079. – 10 c. on 20 c. slate-pur. & olive-yell. (No. 1007) 5 5

1961. Atlantico Tourist Issue.
1080. 10 c. yellow, blue, green, red and silver (postage) 5 5
1081. 20 c. red, blue and yellow 5 5
1082. 20 c. yellow, blue, green, red and gold 5 5

1083. 35 c. sepia and red (air) .. 12 5
1084. 35 c. red, yellow and green 15 5
1085. 35 c. blue and gold .. 15 5
1086. 1 p. 45 brown and green .. 25 8

1087. 10 c. yellow and brown ("EXTRA RAPIDO") 5 5

DESIGNS—VERT. No. 1080, Arms of Popayan. 1081, T **216**. 1082, Arms of Bucaramanga. 1083, Courtyard of Tourist Hotel. 1087, Holy Week procession, Popayan. HORIZ. 1084, View of San Gil. 1085, Barranquilla Port. 1086, View of Velez.

217. Nurse M. de la Cruz.

218. Boxing.

1961. Red Cross Fund. Cross in red.
1090. **217.** 5 c. chocolate .. 5 5
1091. 5 c. purple .. 5 5

1961. 4th Bolivar Games. Inscr. as in T **218**. Multicoloured.
1092. 20 c. T **218** (postage) .. 8 5
1093. 20 c. Basket-ball 5 5
1094. 20 c. Running 5 5
1095. 25 c. Football 10 5

1096. 35 c. Diving (air) 15 5
1097. 35 c. Tennis 15 5
1098. 1 p. 45 Baseball 25 15

1099. 10 c. Statue and flags ("EXTRA RAPIDO") 5 5
1100. 10 c. Runner with Olympic torch 5 5

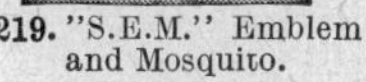
219. "S.E.M." Emblem and Mosquito.

220. Society Emblem.

1962. Malaria Eradication.
1102. **219.** 20 c. red & ochre (post.) 5 5
1103. – 50 c. blue and ochre .. 12 5

1104. **219.** 40 c. red & yell. (air) 12 5
1105. – 1 p. 45 blue and grey 15 10

1106. – 1 p. blue and green ("EXTRA RAPIDO") 70 60

DESIGN: 50 c., 1 p., 1 p. 45, Campaign emblem and mosquito.

1962. 6th National Engineers' Congress, 1961, and 75th Anniv. of Colombian Society of Engineers.
1107. **220.** 10 c. black, yellow, red and blue (postage) 5 5

1108. – 5 c. red and blue (air) 5 5
1109. – 10 c. brown and green 5 5
1110. – 15 c. brown & purple 8 5

1111. **220.** 2 p. black, yellow, red and blue ("EXTRA RAPIDO") .. 30 12

DESIGNS: No. 1108, A. Ramos and Engineering Faculty, Cauca University, Popayan. 1109, M. Triana, A. Arroyo and Monserrate cable and funicular railways. 1110, D. Sanchez and first Society H.Q., Bogota.

221. O.E.A. Emblem.

222. Mother Voting and Statue of Policarpa Salavarrieta.

1962. Organization of American States (O.E.A.). 70th Anniv. Flags mult. Background colours given.
1112. **221.** 25 c. red & blk. (post.) 5 5
1114. 35 c. blue & black (air) 12 5

1962. Women's Franchise.
1115. **222.** 5 c. black, grey and chestnut (postage) 5 5
1116. 10 c. blk., grey & blue 5 5

1117. **222.** 5 c. black, grey and pink (air) 5 5
1118. 35 c. black, grey & buff 10 5
1119. 45 c. blk., grey & grn. 10 5
1120. 45 c. blk., grey & mve. 10 5

223. Scouts in Camp.

224. St. Isidro Labrador.

1962. Colombian Boy Scouts. 30th Anniv. and Colombian Girl Scouts. 25th Anniv. As T **223** but without "EXTRA RAPIDO".
1121. **223.** 10 c. brn. & turq. (post.) 5 5

1122. 15 c. brn. & red (air) 10 5
1123. – 40 c. lake and red 10 5
1124. – 1 p. blue and salmon 25 5

1125. **223.** 1 p. violet & yellow ("EXTRA RAPIDO") 80 70

DESIGN: 40 c., 1 p. Girl Scouts.

1962. St. Isidro Labrador Commem. (2nd issue).
1126. **224.** 10 c. multicoloured .. 5 5
1127. – 10 c. mult. (air—"EXTRA RAPIDO") 5 5
1128. **224.** 2 p. multicoloured .. 30 20

DESIGN: 10 c. (No. 1127), "The Nativity" (after G. Vasquez).

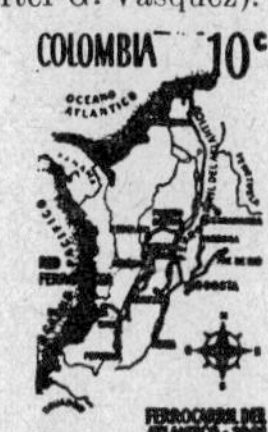

225. Railway Map.

226. Posthorn.

1962. Completion of Colombia Atlantic Railway.
1129. **225.** 10 c. red, green and olive (postage) .. 5 5

1130. – 5 c. myrtle & sepia (air) 5 5
1131. **225.** 10 c. red, turq. & bistre 8 5
1132. – 1 p. chocolate & purple 30 8

1133. – 5 p. brn., blue & green ("EXTRA RAPIDO") 60 25

DESIGNS—HORIZ. 5 c. 1854 and 1961 locomotives. 1 p., 5 p. Pres. A. Parra and R. Magdalena railway bridge.

1962. Postal Union of the Americas and Spain. 50th Anniv.
1134. **226.** 20 c. gold & indigo (post.) 5 5

1135. – 50 c. gold and grey-green (air) 12 5
1136. **226.** 60 c. gold and purple .. 10 5

DESIGN: 50 c. Posthorn, dove and map.

227. Virgin of the Mountain, Bogota.

228. Centenary Emblem.

1963. Ecumenical Council, Vatican City.
1137. **227.** 60 c. multicoloured (postage) 10 5

1138. – 60 c. red, yellow and gold (air) 12 8

DESIGN: No. 1138, Pope John XXIII.

1963. Obligatory Tax. Red Cross Cent.
1139. **228.** 5 c. red and bistre .. 5 5

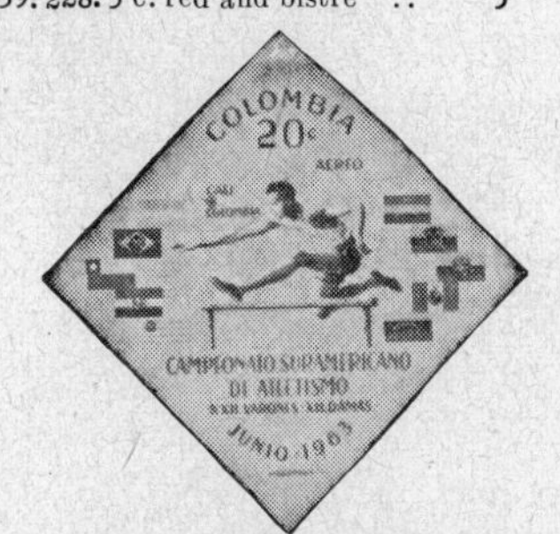

229. Hurdling and Flags.

1963. Air. South American Athletic Championships. Cali.
1140. **229.** 20 c. multicoloured .. 10 5
1141. 80 c. multicoloured .. 8 5

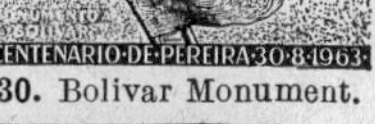

230. Bolivar Monument.

231. Tennis-player.

233. Veracruz Church.

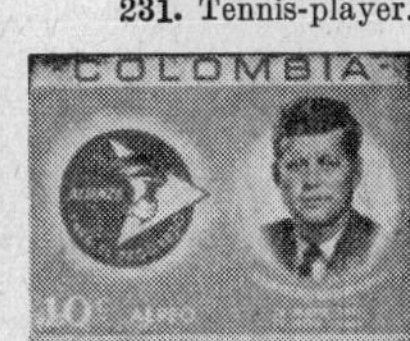

232. Pres. Kennedy and Alliance Emblem.

1963. Air. Centenary of Pereira.
1142. **230.** 1 p. 90 brown and blue 20 5

1963. Air. South American Tennis Championships, Medellin.
1143. **231.** 55 c. multicoloured .. 10 5

1963. Air. "Alliance for Progress".
1144. **232.** 10 c. multicoloured .. 5 5

1964. Air. National Pantheon, Veracruz Church. Multicoloured.
1145. 1 p. Type **233** 10 5
1146. 2 p. "The Crucifixion" .. 20 8

234. Cartagena.

235. Eleanor Roosevelt.

1964. Air. Cartagena Commemoration.
1147. **234.** 3 p. multicoloured .. 65 15

1964. Air. Declaration of Human Rights. 15th Anniv.
1148. **235.** 20 c. brown and olive 5 5

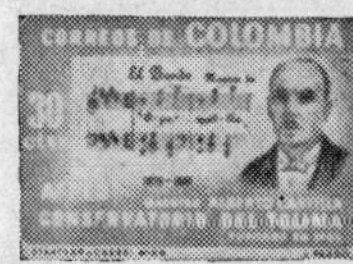

236. A. Castilla (composer and founder) and Music.

1964. Air. Tolima Conservatoire Commem.
1149. **236.** 30 c. blue-green & bistre 5 5

237. Manuel Mejia and Coffee Growers' Flag Emblem.

238. Nurse with Patient.

1965. Manuel Mejia Commem.
1150. **237.** 25 c. sepia & red (post.) 5 5

1151. – 45 c. sepia & brown (air) 12 5
1152. – 5 p. black and green .. 40 20
1153. – 10 p. black and blue .. 80 25

DESIGNS: 45 c. Gathering coffee-beans. 5 p. Mule transport. 10 p. Freighter "Manuel Mejia" at Buenaventura Port. Each design includes a portrait of M. Mejia, director of the National Coffee Growers' Association.

1965. Obligatory Tax. Red Cross Fund.
154. **238.** 5 c. indigo and red .. 5 5

239. I.T.U. Emblem and "Waves".

240. Orchid ("Cattleya trianae").

1965. Air. I.T.U. Cent.
1155. **239.** 80 c. indigo, red & blue 8 5

1965. Air. 5th Philatelic Exn., Bogota.
1156. **240.** 20 c. multicoloured .. 5 5

241. Satellites, Telegraph Pole and Map.

1965. Air. Colombian Telegraphs Cent. Multicoloured.
1157. 60 c. Type **241** 15 5
1158. 60 c. Statue of Pres. Murrilo Toro, Bogota (vert.) .. 5 5

242. Junkers "F-13" Seaplane (1920).

1965. Air. "History of Colombian Aviation". Multicoloured.
1159. 5 c. Type **242** 5 5
1160. 10 c. Dornier "Wal" (1924) 5 5
1161. 20 c. Dornier "Mercury" sea-plane (1926) .. 10 5
1162. 50 c. Ford "Trimotor" (1932) 5 5
1163. 60 c. De Havilland "Moth" (1930) 8 5
1164. 1 p. Douglas "DC-4" (1947) 15 5
1165. 1 p. 40 Douglas "DC-3" (1944) 10 5
1166. 2 p. 80 Super Constellation (1951) 20 8
1167. 3 p. Boeing "720 B" jet-liner (1961) 35 15

See also No. E 1168.

243. Badge, and Car on Mountain Road.

1966. Air. Colombian Automobile Club. 25th Anniv. (1965).
1168. 243. 20 c. multicoloured .. 5 5

244. J. Arboleda (writer). 245. Red Cross and Children as Nurse and Patient.

1966. Julio Arboleda Commem.
1169. 244. 5 c. multicoloured .. 5 5

1966. Obligatory Tax. Red Cross Fund.
1170. 245. 5 c.+5 c. mult. .. 5 5

246. 16th-century Galleon.

1966. History of Maritime Mail. Mult.
1171. 5 c. Type 246 .. .. 5 5
1172. 15 c. Riohacha brigantine (1850) 5 5
1173. 20 c. Uraba Schooner .. 5 5
1174. 40 c. Magdalena steamboat and barge (1900) .. 5 5
1175. 50 c. Modern motor-ship 8 5

247. Hogfish.

1966. Fishes. Multicoloured.
1176. 80 c. Type 247 (postage) 8 5
1177. 10 p. "Flying Fish" .. 1·10 50
1178. 2 p. "Angel Fish" (air) 15 10
1179. 2 p. 80 "Electric Ray" .. 25 20
1180. 20 p. "Spanish Mackerel" 2·40 2·00

248. Arms of Colombia, Venezuela and Chile. 249. C. Torres (patriot).

1966. Visits of Chilean and Venezuelan Presidents.
1181. 248. 40 c. mult. (postage) 5 5
1182. 1 p. multicoloured (air) 12 5
1183. 1 p. 40 multicoloured 15 8

1967. Famous Colombians.
1184. 249. 25 c. vio. & yell. (post.) 5 5
1185. – 60 c. maroon & yellow 5 5
1186. – 1 p. green and yellow 15 5
1187. – 80 c. indigo & yell. (air) 8 5
1188. – 1 p. 70 black & yellow 12 8

PORTRAITS: 60 c. J. T. Lozano (naturalist). 80 c. Father F. R. Mejia (scholar). 1 p. F. A. Zea (writer). 1 p. 70. J. J. Casas (diplomat).

250. Map of Signatory Countries.

1967. "Declaration of Bogota".
1189. 250. 40 c. mult. (postage) 8 5
1190. 60 c. multicoloured .. 8 5
1191. 3 p. multicoloured (air) 20 15

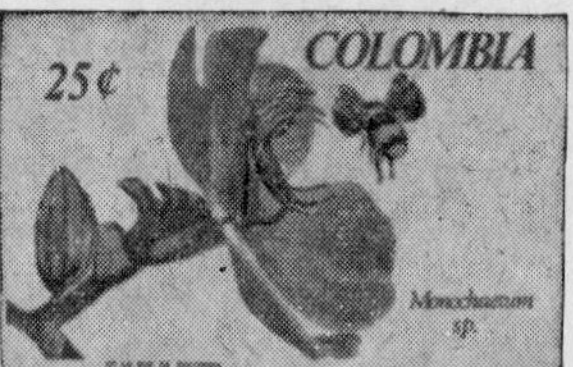

251. "Monochaetum" and Bee.

1967. National Orchid Congress and Tropical Flora and Fauna Exn., Medellin. Multicoloured.
1192. 25 c. Type 251 (postage) .. 5 5
1193. 25 p. "Passiflora vitifolia" and butterfly .. 20 15
1194. 1 p. "Cattleya dowiana" (air) 15 5
1195. 1 p. 20 "Masdevallia coccinea" 12 5
1196. 5 p. "Catasetum macrocarpum" and bee .. 50 20
Nos. 1194/5 are vert.

252. Nurse's Cap. 253. Lions Emblem.

1967. Obligatory Tax. Red Cross Fund.
1198. 252. 5 c. red and blue .. 5 5

1967. Lions Int. 50th Anniv.
1199. 253. 10 p. mult. (postage) 75 30
1200. 253. 25 c. multicoloured (air) 5 5

254. "Caesarian Operation, 1844" (from painting by Grau). 255. S.E.N.A. Emblem.

1967. Air. 6th Colombian Surgeons' Congress, Bogota, and National University. Cent.
1201. 254. 80 c. multicoloured .. 5 5

1967. National Apprenticeship Service. 10th Anniv.
1202. 255. 5 p. black, gold and green (postage) .. 35 20
1203. 255. 2 p. black, gold and red (air) 35 5

256. Calima Diadem. 257. Radio Antenna.

1967. Administrative Council of U.P.U. Consultative Commission of Postal Studies. Main design and lower inscr. in brown and gold.
1204. 256. 1 p. 60 purple (post.) 10 8
1205. – 3 p. blue 20 15
1206. – 30 c. vermilion (air) 10 5
1207. – 5 p. red 60 12
1208. – 20 p. violet .. .. 1·75 80

DESIGNS (Colombian archaeological treasures) VERT. 30 c. Chief's head-dress. 5 p. Cauca breastplate. 20 p. Quimbaya jug. HORIZ. 3 p. Tolima anthropomorphic figure and postal "pigeon on globe" emblem.

1968. "21 Years of National Telecommunications Services". Inscr. "1947-1968".
1210. 257. 50 c. mult. (postage) 5 5
1211. – 1 p. multicoloured .. 12 5
1212. – 50 c. mult. (air) .. 8 5
1213. – 1 p. yell., grey & blue 12 5

DESIGNS: No. 1211, Communications network. No. 1212, Diagram. No. 1213, Satellite.

258. The Eucharist. 259. St. Augustine (Vasquez).

1968. 39th Int. Eucharistic Congress, Bogota. (1st Issue).
1214. 258. 60 c. multicoloured (postage) 5 5
1215. 80 c. multicoloured (air) 8 5
1216. 3 p. multicoloured .. 20 8

1968. 39th International Eucharistic Congress, Bogota (2nd Issue). Multicoloured.
1217. 25 c. Type 259 (postage) 5 5
1218. 60 c. "Gathering Manna" (Vasquez) 5 5
1219. 1 p. "Betrothal of the Virgin and St. Joseph" (B. de Figueroa) .. 8 5
1220. 5 p. "La Lechuga" (Jesuit Statuette) .. 35 20
1221. 10 p. "Pope Paul VI" (painting by Franciscan Missionary Mothers) .. 65 50
1222. 80 c. "The Last Supper" (Vasquez) (air) .. 10 5
1223. 1 p. "St. Francis Xavier's Sermon" (Vasquez) 12 5
1224. 2 p. "Elijah's Dream" (Vasquez) 15 10
1225. 3 p. As No. 1220 .. .. 25 5
1226. 20 p. As No. 1221 .. 1·50 60
No. 1222 is horiz.

260. Pope Paul VI. 261. University Arms.

1968. Pope Paul's Visit to Colombia. Multicoloured.
1228. 25 c. Type 260 (postage) 5 5
1229. 80 c. Reception podium (air) 5 5
1230. 1 p. 20 Pope Paul giving Blessing 10 5
1231. 1 p. 80 Cathedral, Bogota 15 5
No. 1229 is horiz.

1968. National University. Cent.
1232. 261. 80 c. mult. (postage) 8 5
1233. – 20 c. red, green and yellow (air) .. 5 5

DESIGN: 20 c. Computer symbols.

262. Antioquia $2\frac{1}{2}$ c. Stamp of 1868. 263. Institute Emblem & Split Leaf.

1968. 1st Antioquia Stamps. Cent.
1234. 262. 30 c. blue & emerald 5 5

1969. Inter-American Agricultural Sciences Institute. 25th Anniv. (1967).
1236. 263. 20 c. black, yellow, grn. & blue (postage) 5 5
1237. 263. $1 black, yellow, grn. & grey (air) .. 8 5

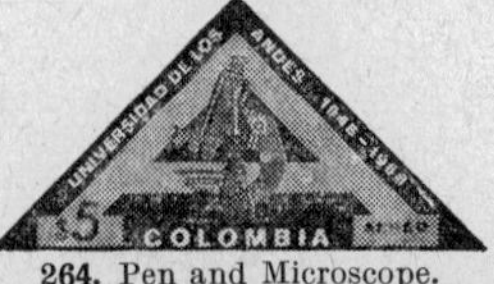

264. Pen and Microscope.

1969. Air. University of the Andes. 20th Anniv.
1238. 264. 5 p. multicoloured .. 30 8

265. Von Humboldt and Andes (Quindio Region).

1969. Air. Alexander von Humboldt (naturalist). Birth Bicent.
1239. 265. 1 p. green & chocolate 10 5

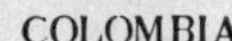

266. Junkers "F-13" Seaplane and Map. 267. Red Cross.

1969. Air. 1st Colombian Airmail Flight. 50th Anniv. Multicoloured.
1240. 1 p. Type 266 .. .. 10 5
1241. 1 p. 50 Boeing "720-B" and Globe 12 5
See also Nos. 1249/50.

1969. Obligatory Tax. Colombian Red Cross.
1243. 267. 5 c. red and violet .. 5 5

268. "The Battle of Boyaca" (J. M. Espinosa).

1969. Independence. 150th Anniv. Mult.
1244. 20 c. Type 268 (postage) 5 5
1245. 30 c. "Death on the Pisba" (F. A. Caro) .. 8 5
1246. 2 p. 30 "Entry into Santa Fe" (I. Castillo-Cervantes) (air) 15 8

269. Institute Emblem. 270. Cranial Diagram.

1969. Air. Colombian Social Security Institute. 20th Anniv.
1247. 269. 20 c. green and black 5 5

1969. Air. 13th Latin-American Neurological Congress, Bogota.
1248. 270. 70 c. multicoloured 5 5

271. Boeing "720-B" and Globe. 272. Child posting Christmas Card.

1969. Air. "Avianca" Airline. 50th Anniv. Multicoloured.
1249. 2 p. Junkers "F 13" seaplane and Puerto Colombia .. 15 5
1250. 3 p. 50 Type 271 .. 25 8

1969. Air. Christmas. Multicoloured.
1252. 60 c. Type 272 .. .. 5 5
1253. 1 p. Type 272 .. .. 15 5
1254. 1 p. 50 Child with Christmas presents 15 5

273. "Poverty".

275. National Sports Institute Emblem.

274. Dish Aerial and Ancient Head.

1970. Colombian Social Welfare Institute and Children's Rights Law. 10th Anniv.

1255. **273.** 30 c. multicoloured .. 5 5

1970. Air. Opening of Satellite Earth Station, Choconta.

1256. **274.** 1 p. black, red & grn. 12 5

1970. Air. 9th National Games, Ibague (1st issue).

1257. **275.** 1 p. 50 blk., yell. & grn. 12 5

1258. – 2 p. 30 red, black, yellow and blue .. 15 8

DESIGN: 2 p. 30 Dove and rings (Games emblem).

276. "A B C" of Art.

277. Dr. E. Santos (founder) and Buildings.

1970. Air. 2nd Fine Arts Biennial, Medellin.

1259. **276.** 30 c. multicoloured 5 5

1970. Air Territorial Credit Institute (1969). 30th Anniv.

1260. **277.** 1 p. yellow, blue and ultramarine .. 10 5

278. U.N. Emblem, Scales and Dove.

279. Hands protecting Child.

1970. Air. United Nations. 25th Anniv.

1261. **278.** 1 p. 50 yellow, blue and ultramarine . 10 5

1970. Obligatory Tax. Colombian Red Cross.

1262. **279.** 5 c. red and blue .. 5 5

280. Theatrical Mask.

1970. Latin-American University Theatre Festival, Manizales.

1263. **280.** 30 c. brown, orange & black 5 5

281. Postal Emblem, Letter and Stamps.

1970. Philatelic Week.

1264. **281.** 2 p. multicoloured .. 12 8

282. Discus-thrower and Ibague Arms.

283. "St. Teresa" (B. de Figueroa).

1970. Ninth National Games, Ibague (2nd issue).

1265. **282.** 80 c. brn., grn. & yell. 5 5

1970. St. Teresa of Avila's Elevation to Doctor of the Universal Church. No. 1267 optd. **AEREO.**

1266. **283.** 2 p. mult. (postage).. 12 5

1267. **283.** 2 p mult. (air) .. 10 5

284. Int. Philatelic Federation Emblem.

285. Napanga Costume.

1970. Air. "EXFILCA 70" Stamp Exhibition, Caracas, Venezuela.

1268. **284.** 10 p. multicoloured.. 65 25

1970. Folklore Dances and Costumes. Mult.

1269. 1 p. Chicha Maya dance (postage) 12 5

1270. 1 p. 10 Currulao dance.. 12 5

1271. 60 c. Type **285** (air) .. 12 5

1272. 1 p. Joropo dance .. 15 5

1273. 1 p. 30 Guabina dance .. 15 5

1274. 1 p. 30 Bambuco dance.. 15 5

1275. 1 p. 30 Cumbia dance .. 12 5

286. Stylised Athlete.

287. G. Alzate Avendano.

1971. Air. 6th Pan-American Games. Cali. (1st issue).

1277. **286.** 1 p. 50 multicoloured 15 8

1278. – 2 p. orange green and black 25 8

DESIGN: 2 p. Games Emblem.

1971. Air. Gilberto Alzate Avendano (politician). 10th Death Anniv.

1279. **287.** 1 p. multicoloured .. 10 5

288. Priest's House, Guacari.

1971. Guacari (town). 400th Anniv.

1280. **288.** 1 p. 10 multicoloured 8 5

289. Commemorative Medal.

1971. Air. Bank of Bogota. Cent.

1281. **289.** 1 p. gold, brn. & grn. 10 5

290. Sports Centre.

291. Weightlifting.

1971. Air. 6th Pan-American Games (2nd issue) and "EXFICALI 71" Stamp Exhibition, Cali. Multicoloured.

1282. 1 p. 30 Type **290** (yellow emblem) 12 5

1283. 1 p. 30 Football.. .. 12 5

1284. 1 p. 30 Wrestling .. 12 5

1285. 1 p. 30 Cycling .. 12 5

1286. 1 p. 30 Volleyball .. 12 5

1287. 1 p. 30 Diving 12 5

1288. 1 p. 30 Fencing 12 5

1289. 1 p. 30 Type **290** (green emblem) 12 5

1290. 1 p. 30 Sailing 12 5

1291. 1 p. 30 Show-jumping .. 12 5

1292. 1 p. 30 Athletics .. 12 5

1293. 1 p. 30 Rowing 12 5

1294. 1 p. 30 Cali emblem .. 12 5

1295. 1 p. 30 Netball 12 5

1296. 1 p. 30 Type **290** (blue emblem) 12 5

1297. 1 p. 30 Stadium.. .. 12 5

1298. 1 p. 30 Baseball.. .. 12 5

1299. 1 p. 30 Hockey 12 5

1300. 1 p. 30 Type **291** .. 12 5

1301. 1 p. 30 Medals 12 5

1302. 1 p. 30 Boxing 12 5

1303. 1 p. 30 Gymnastics .. 12 5

1304. 1 p. 30 Rifle-shooting .. 12 5

1305. 1 p. 30 Type **290** (red emblem) 12 5

Nos. 1282/1305 come se-tenant in sheets of 25, No. 1296, occurring twice in the sheet.

292. "Bolivar at Congress". (after S. Martinez-Delgado).

1971. Great Colombia Constituent Assembly, Rosario del Cucuta. 150th Anniv.

1306. **292.** 80 c. multicoloured 5 5

293. "Battle of Carabobo" (M. Tovar y Tovar).

1971. Air. Battle of Carabobo. 150th Anniv.

1307. **293.** 1 p. 50 multicoloured 12 5

COLOMBIA $0.60

1952·CIME·1972

294. C.I.M.E. Emblem. 295. I.C.E.T.E.X. Emblem.

1972. Inter-Governmental Committee on European Migration. 20th Anniv.

1308. **294.** 60 c. black and grey.. 5 5

1972. Institute of Educational Credit and Technical Training Abroad. 20th Anniv.

1309. **295.** 1 p. 10 brown and grn. 5 5

296. Rev. Mother F. J. del Castillo.

297. Soldier and Frigate "Almirante Padilla".

1972. Reverend Mother Francisca J. del Castillo. 300th Birth Anniv.

1310. **296.** 1 p. 20 multicoloured 8 5

1972. Colombian Troops' Participation in Korean War. 20th Anniv.

1311. **297.** 1 p. 20 multicoloured 8 5

298. Hat and Ceramics.

299. "Maxillaria triloris" (orchid).

1972. Colombian Crafts and Products. Multicoloured.

1312. 1 p. 10 Type **298** (postage) 10 5

1313. 50 c. Woman in shawl (air) 5 5

1314. 1 p. Male doll 8 5

1315. 3 p. Female doll.. .. 25 10

1972. National, Stamp Exn., and 7th World Orchid-growers Congress, Medellin Conference. Multicoloured.

1316. 20 p. Type **299** (postage) 1·00 90

1317. 1 p. 30 "Mormodes rolfeanum" (orchid) (horiz.) (air) 12 5

300. Uncut Emeralds and Pendant.

302. Congo Dance.

301. Pres. Narino's House.

1972. "Colombia Emeralds".

1318. **300.** 1 p. 10 multicoloured 8 5

1972. Leyva (town). 400th Anniv.

1319. **301.** 1 p. 10 multicoloured 8 5

1972. Air. Barranquilla Int. Carnival.

1320. **302.** 1 p. 30 multicoloured 12 5

303. Island Scene.

304. "Pres. L. Gomez" (R. Cubillos).

1972. Annexation of San Andres and Providencia Islands. 150th Anniv.

1321. **303.** 60 c. multicoloured 8 5

1972. Air. No. 1142 surch.

1322. **230.** 1 p. 30 on 1 p. 90 brown and blue .. 25 8

1972. Air. Pres. Gomez Commem.

1323. **304.** 1 p. 30 multicoloured 10 5

305. Postal Administration Emblem. 306. Colombian Family.

1972. National Postal Administration.

1324. **305.** 1 p. 10 green .. 5 5

1972. "Social Front for the People" Campaign.

1325. **306.** 60 c. orange .. 5 5

307. Pres. G. L. Valencia. **308.** B. Juarez.

1972. Air. Pres. Valencia Commem.
1326. **307.** 1 p. 30 multicoloured 10 5

1972. Air. Benito Juarez (Mexican Statesman). Death Cent.
1327. **308.** 1 p. 50 multicoloured 10 5

309. " La Rebeca " Monument. **310.** " 350 " and Arms of Bucaramanga.

1972. Air. " La Rebeca " Monument, Centenary Park, Bogota.
1328. **309.** 80 c. multicoloured .. 5 5
1329. 1 p. multicoloured .. 8 5

1972. Air. Bucaramanga. 350th Anniv.
1330. **310.** 5 p. multicoloured .. 35 10

311. University Buildings. **312.** League Emblems.

1973. Air. Javeriana University. 350th Anniv.
1331. **311.** 1 p. 30 brown and green 8 5
1332. 1 p. 50 brown and blue 8 5

1973. Colombian Radio Amateurs League. 40th Anniv.
1333. **312.** 60 c. red, new blue and blue 5 5

313. Tamalameque Vessel. **314.** Battle Scene.

1973. Museum of Pre-Colombian Antiques, Bogota. Inaug. Multicoloured.
1334. 60 c. Type **313** (postage) 5 5
1335. 1 p. Tairona axe-head .. 10 5
1336. 1 p. 10 Muisca jug 8 8
1337. 1 p. As No. 1335 (air) .. 10 5
1338. 1 p. 30 Sinu vessel 12 5
1339. 1 p. 70 Quimbaya vessel 15 5
1340. 3 p. 50 Tumaco figurine 35 10

1973. Air. Naval Battle of Maracaibo. 150th Anniv.
1341. **314.** 10 p. multicoloured .. 85 20

315. Banknote Emblem.

1973. Air. Republican Bank. 50th Anniv.
1342. **315.** 2 p. multicoloured .. 15 5

1973. Air. No. 1306 optd. **AEREO.**
1343. **292.** 80 c. multicoloured .. 5 5

316. " Pres. Ospina " (C Leudo). **317.** Arms of Toro.

1973. Air. Ministry of Communications. 50th Anniv.
1344. **316.** 1 p. 50 multicoloured 12 5

1973. Air. Toro. 400th Anniv.
1345. **317.** 1 p. multicoloured .. 8 5

318. Bolivar at Bombona.

1973. Air. Battle of Bombona. 150th Anniv.
1346. **318.** 1 p. 30 multicoloured 12 5

319. " General Narino " (J. M. Espinosa). **320.** Young Child.

1973. General Antonio Narino. 150th Death Anniv.
1347. **319.** 60 c. multicoloured .. 5 5

1973. Child Welfare Campaign.
1348. **320.** 1 p. 10 multicoloured 5 5

321. Fiscal Emblem.

1974. Republic's General Comptrollership. 50th Anniv.
1349. **321.** 80 c. black, brn. & blue 5 5

322. Copernicus. **323.** Andes Communications and Map.

1974. Air. Copernicus. 500th Birth Anniv.
1350. **322.** 2 p. 50 multicoloured 20 8

1974. Air. Meeting of Communications Ministers, Andean Group, Cali.
1351. **323.** 2 p. multicoloured .. 15 8

324. Laura Montoya and Cross. **325.** Television Set.

1974. Revd. Mother Laura Montoya (missionary). Birth Cent.
1352. **324.** 1 p. multicoloured .. 5 5

1974. Air. Inravision (National Institute of Radio and Television). 20th Anniv.
1353. **325.** 1 p. 30 blk., brn. & orge. 12 5

326. Athlete.

1974. Tenth National Games, Pereira.
1354. **326.** 2 p. brown, red & yell. 15 8

327. Jose Rivera (author) and Monument.

1974. Novel "La Voragine". 50th Anniv.
1355. **327.** 10 p. multicoloured .. 60 25

328. Aquatic Emblem.

1974. Air. 2nd World Swimming Championships, Cali. (1975).
1356. **328.** 4 p. 50 bl., turq. & blk. 25 8

329. Condor Emblem.

1974. Air. Bank of Colombia. Cent.
1357. **329.** 1 p. 50 multicoloured 8 5

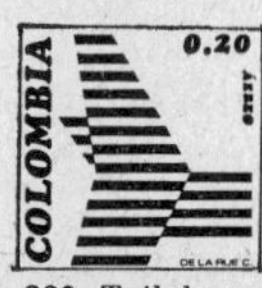

330. Tailplane.

1974. Air.
1358. **330.** 20 c. brown 5 5

331. U.P.U. "Letter".

1974. Air. Universal Postal Union. Cent. (1st issue).
1359. **331.** 20 p. red, bl. & blk... 1·00 35

332. General Jose Cordoba. **333.** " Progress and Expansion ".

1974. Air. Battles of Junin and Ayacucho. 150th Anniv.
1360. **332.** 1 p. 30 multicoloured 8 5

1974. Colombian Insurance Company. Cent.
1361. **333.** 1 p. 10 mult. (postage) 8 5
1362. **333.** 3 p. mult. (air) .. 15 5

334. " Trogon viridis " and U.P.U. " Letter ". **335.** La Quiebra Tunnel.

1974. Air. Universal Postal Union. Cent. (2nd issue). Colombian Birds. Multicoloured.
1363. 1 p. Type **334** 5 5
1364. 1 p. 30 " Ramphastos sulfuratus " (horiz.) .. 8 5
1365. 2 p. " Rupicola peruviana s." (horiz.) 12 5
1366. 2 p. 50 " Ara macao " .. 15 5
Nos. 1364/6 also depict the U.P.U. " letter ".

1974. Antioquia Railway. Centenary.
1367. **336.** 1 p. 10 multicoloured 8 5

336. Boy with Ball.

1974. Christmas. Multicoloured.
1368. 80 c. Type **336** 5 5
1369. 1 p. Girl with racquet .. 5 5

337. " Protect the Trees ".

1975. Air. Colombian Ecology. Mult.
1370. 1 p. Type **337** .. 5 5
1371. 6 p. " Protect the Amazon " 30 12

338. " Wood No. 1 " (R. Roncancio).

1975. Air. Colombian Art. Multicoloured.
1372. 2 p. Type **338** .. 10 5
1373. 3 p. " The Market " (M. Diaz Vargas) 15 5
1374. 4 p. " Child with Thorn " (G. Vazquez) 20 8
1375. 5 p. " The Annunciation " (Santaferena School) .. 25 10

339. Gold Cat.

1975. Pre-Colombian Archaeological Discoveries. Sinu Culture. Multicoloured.
1376. 80 c. Type **339** (postage) 5 5
1377. 1 p. 10, Gold necklace .. 8 5
1378. 2 p. Nose Pendant (air) .. 10 5
1379. 10 p. " Alligator " staff ornament 50 20

340. Marconi. **341.** Santa Marta Cathedral.

1975. Guglielmo Marconi (radio pioneer). Birth Cent.
1380. **340.** 3 p. multicoloured .. 15 5

1975. Santa Marta. 450th Anniv. Mult.
1381. 80 c. Type **341** (postage) 5 5
1382. 2 p. "El Rodadero" (seafront), Santa Marta (horiz.) air) 10 5

342. Maria de J. Paramo (teacher). **343.** Pres. R. Nunez.

1975. International Women's Year.
1383. **342.** 4 p. multicoloured .. 20 8

1975. President Rafael Nunez. 150th Birth Anniv.
1384. **343.** 1 p. 10 multicoloured 8 5

344. Arms of Medellin. **345.** Sugar Cane.

1975. Medellin. 300th Anniv.
1385. **344.** 1 p. multicoloured .. 5 5
See also Nos. 1386, 1388 and 1394.

1976. Reconstruction of Cucuta. Centenary. As T **344.**
1386. 1 p. 50 multicoloured 8 5

1976. Surch.
1387. **339.** 1 p. 20 on 80 c. mult. 5 5

1976. Arms of Cartagena. As T **344.**
1388. 1 p. 50 multicoloured .. 8 5

1976. 4th Cane Sugar Export and Production Congress, Cali.
1389. **345.** 5 p. green and black 25 10

346. Bogota.

1976. HABITAT. U.N. Conference on Human Settlements. Multicoloured.
1390. 10 p. Type **346** 50 30
1391. 10 p. Barranquilla .. 50 30
1392. 10 p. Cali 50 30
1393. 10 p. Medellin 50 30

1976. Arms of Ibague. As T **344.**
1394. 1 p. 20 multicoloured .. 8 5

PRIVATE AIR COMPANIES

The "LANSA" and Avianca Companies operated inland and foreign air mail services on behalf of the Government and issued the following stamps. Later only the Avianca Company performed this service and the regular air stamps were used on the mail without overprints.

Similar issues were also made by Compania Colombiana de Navegacion Aerea during 1920. These are very rare and will be found listed in the Stanley Gibbons' Overseas Catalogue, Volume 1.

A. "LANSA" (Lineas Aereas Nacionales Sociedad Anonima).

1. Wing.

1950. Air.
1. **1.** 5 c. yellow 15 12
2. 10 c. red 20 12
3. 15 c. blue 25 12
4. 20 c. green 40 25
5. 30 c. purple 60 45
6. 60 c. brown .. .. .. 1·25 1·25

With background network colours in brackets.
7. **1.** 1 p. grey (buff) .. .. 3·25 3·00
8. 2 p. blue (green .. .. 6·50 6·00
9. 5 p. claret (claret) .. 14·00 12·00
The 1 p. was also issued without the network.

1950. Air. Nos. 691 etc. optd. **L.**
10. 5 c. yellow 8 5
11. 10 c. vermilion 10 5
12. 15 c. blue 10 5
13. 20 c. violet 12 5
14. 30 c. green 15 5
15. 40 c. grey 25 5
16. 50 c. claret 25 8
17. 1 p. purple and green .. 90 25
18. 2 p. blue and green .. 1·50 25
19. 3 p. black and red .. .. 4·00 3·25
20. 5 p. turquoise & sepia .. 7·50 7·00

1951. As Nos. 696 etc. but colours changed and optd. **L.** at bottom right.
21. 40 c. orange 35 20
22. 50 c. blue 40 15
23. 60 c. grey 35 15
24. 80 c. red 45 15
25. 1 p. red and vermilion .. 85 70
26. 2 p. blue and red .. .. 1·60 1·00
27. 3 p. green and chocolate .. 3·25 2·75
28. 5 p. grey and yellow .. 8·50 8·50

B. Avianca Company.

1950. Air. Nos. 691/703 optd. **A.**
1. 5 c. yellow 5 5
2. 10 c. vermilion 8 5
3. 15 c. blue 10 5
4. 20 c. violet 12 5
5. 30 c. green 15 5
6. 40 c. grey 20 5
7. 50 c. claret 25 5
8. 60 c. olive 30 5
9. 80 c. brown 40 8
10. 1 p. purple and green .. 90 5
11. 2 p. blue and green .. 1·40 25
12. 3 p. black and red .. .. 2·50 1·40
13. 5 p. turquoise and sepia .. 5·50 4·50

1951. Air. As Nos. 696 etc. but colours changed and optd. **A** at bottom right.
14. 40 c. orange 35 10
15. 50 c. blue 60 10
16. 60 c. grey 80 12
17. 80 c. red 60 12
18. 1 p. red and vermilion .. 1·40 10
19. 1 p. brown and green .. 1·00 12
20. 2 p. blue and red .. .. 1·60 25
21. 3 p. green and chocolate .. 2·75 60
22. 5 p. grey and yellow .. 5·50 80
The 60 c. also comes with the A in the centre.
All values except the 2 p. and 3 p. exist without the overprint.

ACKNOWLEDGMENT OF RECEIPT STAMPS

A 1. A 2.

1894.
AR 169. A 1. 5 c. red 30 20

1902. Similar to Type A 1. Imperf. or perf.
AR 265. 5 c. blue 45 45
AR 211. 10 c. blue on blue .. 20 20

1903. No. 197 optd. **Habilitado Medellin A R.**
AR 258. **42.** 10 c. black on pink .. 12·00

1904. No. 262 optd. **A R.**
AR 266. **42.** 5 c. rose .. .. 3·75 3·75

1904.
AR 290. A **2.** 5 c. blue 30 15

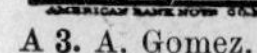

A 3. A. Gomez. A 4. Map of Colombia.

1910.
AR 354. A **3.** 5 c. green & orange 2·00 2·00

1917. Inscr. "AR".
AR 371. **59.** 4 c. brown .. 75 75
AR 372. A **4.** 5 c. brown .. 1·10 1·10

SPECIAL DELIVERY STAMPS

E 1. Express Messenger.

1917.
E 373. E **1.** 5 c. green .. .. 90 1·00

E 2.

1958. Air.
E 936. E **2.** 25 c. red and blue .. 15 5

1959. Air. Unification of Air Mail Rates. Optd. **UNIFICADO** within outline of aeroplane.
E 989. E **2.** 25 c. red and blue .. 20 5

E **3.** Jetliner on Back of "Express" Letter.

1963. Air.
E 1143. E **3.** 50 c. black & red .. 10 5

1966. Air. "History of Colombian Aviation". As T **242.** Inscr. "EXPRESO". Multicoloured.
E 1168. 80 c. Boeing "727" jetliner (1966) 15 5

OFFICIAL STAMPS

1937. Optd. **OFICIAL.**
O 496. – 1 c. green (No. 429) 5 5
O 497. **69.** 2 c. red (No. 430) 8 5
O 498. – 5 c. brown (No. 482) 5 5
O 499. – 10 c. orange (No. 485) 25 5
O 500. **82.** 12 c. blue 15 10
O 501. **71.** 20 c. blue 15 8
O 502. **56.** 30 c. bistre 70 25
O 503. **59.** 40 c. brown 60 20
O 504. **60.** 50 c. red 50 20
O 505. **56.** 1 p. blue 90 40
O 506. 2 p. orange .. .. 1·90 1·00
O 507. 5 p. grey .. .. 5·50 2·75
O 508. **57.** 10 p. brown .. .. 18·00 15·00

REGISTRATION STAMPS

R 1. R 2.

1865. Imperf.
R 42. R **1.** 5 c. black .. .. 9·00 9·00

1865. Type similar to R 1, but letter "R" in star. Imperf.
R 43. 5 c. black .. .. 9·00 9·00

1870. Imperf.
R 73. R **2.** 5 c. black .. .. 1·50 1·50

1870. Type similar to R 2 but with "R" in centre and inscr. "REJISTRO". Imperf.
R 74. 5 c. black .. 1·50 1·50

1881. Eagle and arms in oval frame, inscr. "RECOMENDADA" at foot. Imperf. or pin-perf.
R 105. 10 c. lilac .. .. 5·00 5·00

R 4. R 5.

1883. Perf.
R 117. R **4.** 10 c red on orange .. 60 40

1889.
R 141. R **5.** 10 c. red 30 25
R 166. 10 c. brown 20 20

R 6.

1902. Imperf. or perf.
R 264. R **6.** 10 c. purple .. 50 50
R 207. 20 c. red on blue .. 40 20
R 208. 20 c. blue on blue .. 20 20

R 7.

1904. Perf.
R 289. R **7.** 10 c. purple .. 40 30

R 8.

1904.
R 308. R **8.** 10 c. purple 60 25

R **9.** Execution of 24th Feb., 1810.

1910.
R 353. R **9.** 10 c. black and red 8·00 8·00

R **10.** Port of Colombia.

1917.
R 369. R **10.** 4 c. blue and green 75 75
R 370. – 10 c. blue 50 20
DESIGN: 10 c. Tequendama Falls.

R 12.

1925.
R 409. R **12.** (10 c.) blue .. 1·25 1·25

1932. Air. Air stamps of 1932 optd. **R.**
R 426. **66.** 20 c. red .. .. 5·00 3·75
R 450. — 20 c. grn. & red (439) 3·00 80

TOO LATE STAMPS

T 1. T 2.

1888. Perf.
L 136. T 1. 2½ c. black on lilac .. 30 15

1892. Perf.
L 167. T 2. 2½ c. blue on rose .. 30 12

T 3. T 4.

1902. Imperf. or perf.
L 209. T 3. 5 c. violet on red .. 5 5

1914. Perf.
L 335. T 4. 2 c. brown 40 40
L 336. 5 c. green 40 40

COMORO ISLANDS

01

An archipelago N.W. of Madagascar comprising Anjouan, Great Comoro, Mayotte and Moheli.

1. Anjouan Bay.

2. Native Woman.

3. Mutsamudu Village.

1950.
1. 1. 10 c. blue (postage) .. 5 5
2. 50 c. green 5 5
3. 1 f. brown.. .. .. 5 5
4. 2. 2 f. emerald 5 5
5. 5 f. violet 5 5
6. 6 f. purple 8 8
7. – 7 f. red 8 8
8. – 10 f. green 8 8
9. – 11 f. blue 10 10
10. – 15 f. brown 12 10
11. – 20 f. lake 15 10
12. – 40 f. indigo and blue .. 1·50 1·25
13. 3. 50 f. lake and green (air) 55 25
14. – 100 f. chocolate and red 1·10 25
15. – 200 f. lake, grn. & violet.. 4·50 2·25
DESIGNS (as T 1)—HORIZ. 7 f., 10 f., 11 f. Mosque at Moroni. 40 f. Coelacanth. VERT. 15 f.. 20 f. Ouani Mosque, Anjouan. (As T 3) HORIZ. 100 f. Natives and Mosque. 200 f. Ouani Mosque.

1952. Military Medal Cent. As T 27 of Cameroun.
16. 15 f. blue, yellow and green 5·50 5·50

1954. Air. Liberation. 10th Anniv. As T 29 of Cameroun.
17. 15 f. red and brown .. 5·00 5·00

4. Village Pump.

1956. Economic and Social Development.
18. 4. 9 f. violet 20 15

5. "Human Rights".

1958. Declaration of Human Rights. 10th Anniv.
19. 5. 20 f. green and blue .. 1·90 1·90

1959. Tropical Flora. As T 21 of French Equatorial Africa.
20. 10 f. red, yell., grn. & blue 90 65

6. Radio Station, Dzaoudzi.

1960. Comoro Broadcasting Service Inaug.
21. 6. 20 f. grn., violet & claret.. 25 25
22. – 25 f. green, brown & blue 35 35
DESIGN: 25 f. Radio mast and map.

7. Bull Mouth Helmet.

8. Marine Plants.

1962. Multicoloured. (a) Postage. Seashells.
23. 50 c. T 7 .. .. .. 10 10
24. 1 f. Conoidal harp .. 10 10
25. 2 f. White murex 10 10
26. 5 f. Green turban 20 20
27. 20 f. Scorpion conch .. 50 50
28. 25 f. Pacific triton.. .. 60 60
(b) Air. Marine plants.
29. 100 f. T 8 .. .. 1·10 1·10
30. 500 f. Stoney coral .. 5·00 4·00

1962. Malaria Eradication. As T 45 of Cameroun.
31. 25 f. + 5 f. red 85 85

1962. Air. 1st Trans-Atlantic T.V. Satellite Link. As Type F 13 of Andorra.
32. 25 f. mauve, purple & violet 1·10 65

9. Emblem in Hands and Globe.

1963. Freedom from Hunger.
33. 9. 20 f. slate-blue and choc. 85 85

1963. Red Cross Cent. As Type F 2 of New Hebrides.
34. 50 f. red, grey and green .. 85 85

10. Globe and Scales of Justice.

1963. Declaration of Human Rights. 15th Anniv.
35. 10. 15 f. green and red .. 85 85

11. Tobacco Pouch.

12. Pirogue.

1963. Handicrafts. (a) Postage as T 11.
36. 11. 3 f. ochre, red & emerald 5 5
37. – 4 f. myrtle, maroon & orge. 5 5
38. – 10 f. choc., green & chest. 10 10
(b) Air. Size 27 × 48 mm.
39. – 65 f. red, brown & green 65 55
40. – 200 f. claret, red & turq. 1·90 1·90
DESIGNS: 4 f. Perfume-burner. 10 f. Lamp bracket. 65 f. Baskets. 200 f. Filigree pendant.

1964. "PHILATEC 1964" Int. Stamp Exn., Paris. As T 481 of France.
41. 50 f. red, green and blue .. 60 60

1964. Native Craft. Multicoloured.
42. 15 f. Type 12 (postage) .. 25 25
43. 30 f. Boutre felucca.. .. 40 40
44. 50 f. Mayotte pirogue (air) 55 25
45. 85 f. Schooner 80 55
Nos. 44/5 are larger, 27 × 48½ mm.

13. Boxing (Ancient bronze plaque).

14. Medal.

1964. Air. Olympic Games, Tokyo.
46. 13. 100 f. grn., brown & choc. 85 65

1964. Air. Star of Grand Comoro.
47. 14. 500 f. multicoloured .. 4·00 2·75

15. "Syncom" Communications Satellite, Telegraph Poles and Morse Key.

16. Hammer-head Shark.

17. Lake Sale.

1965. Air. I.T.U. Cent.
48. 15. 50 f. blue, olive and slate 3·50 2·75

1965. Marine Life.
49. – 1 f. green, orange & violet 5 5
50. 16. 12 f. black, indigo and red 15 12
51. – 20 f. red and green .. 20 20
52. – 25 f. brown, red and green 25 20
DESIGNS—VERT. 1 f. Spiny lobster. 25 f. Grouper. HORIZ. 20 f. Scaly turtle.

1966. Air. Launching of 1st French Satellite. As Nos. 1696/7 (plus se-tenant label) of France.
53. 25 f. plum, violet & ultram. 65 65
54. 30 f. plum, violet & ultram. 1·00 1·00

1966. Air. Launching of Satellite "D1". As T 521 of France.
55. 30 f. maroon, green & orge. 65 55

1966. Comoro Views. Multicoloured.
56. 15 f. Type 17 (postage) .. 12 12
57. 25 f. Itsandra Hotel, Moroni 20 12
58. 50 f. The Battery, Dzaoudzi (air) 45 25
59. 200 f. Ksar Fort, Mutsamudu (vert.) .. .. .. 1·40 80
Nos. 58/9 are larger, 48 × 27 mm. and 27 × 48 mm. respectively.

18. Comoro Sunbird.

19. Nurse tending Child.

1967. Birds. Multicoloured.
60. 2 f. Type 18 (postage) .. 10 10
61. 10 f. Kingfisher 15 15
62. 15 f. Fody 25 25
63. 30 f. Cuckoo-roller 40 40
64. 75 f. Flycatcher (air) .. 65 25
65. 100 f. Blue-cheeked bee-eater 80 40
Nos. 64/5 are vert. and also larger 27 × 48 mm.

1967. Comoro Red Cross.
66. 19. 25 f. + 5 f. maroon, red and green 30 30

20. Slalom Skiing.

21. Bouquet, Sun and W.H.O. Emblem.

1968. Air. Winter Olympic Games, Grenoble.
67. 20. 70 f. brown, blue & green 55 35

1968. W.H.O. 20th Anniv.
68. 21. 40 f. crimson, vio. & grn. 40 35

22. Powder Blue Surgeon.

23. Human Rights Emblem.

1968. Fishes.
69. 22. 20 f. blue, yell. & red (postage) 25 25
70. – 25 f. ultram., orge. & turq. 30 25
71. – 50 f. ochre, indigo and purple (air) 40 25
72. – 90 f. ochre, grn. & emer. 70 45
DESIGNS: 25 f. Imperial Angelfish. LARGER 48 × 27 mm. 50 f. Moorish Idol. 90 f. Yellow-banded sweetlips.

1968. Human Rights Year.
73. 23. 60 f. green, choc. & orge. 45 45

24. Swimming.

1968. Air. Olympic Games, Mexico.
74. 24. 65 f. multicoloured .. 40 25

25. Prayer Mat and Worshipper.

1969. Msoila Prayer Mats.
75. 25. 20 f. red, green and violet 10 8
76. – 30 f. green, violet and red 15 12
77. – 45 f. violet, red and green 25 20
DESIGNS: As T 25, but worshipper stooping (30 f.) or kneeling upright (45 f.).

26. Vanilla Flower.

1969. Flowers. Multicoloured.
78. 10 f. Type 26 (postage) .. 8 5
79. 15 f. Ylang-ylang blossom 12 10
80. 50 f. "Heliconia" (air) .. 25 20
81. 85 f. Tuberose 55 35
82. 200 f. Orchid .. .. 1·10 75
Nos. 80/2 are vert, size 27 × 49 mm.

27. "Concorde" in Flight.

1969. Air. 1st Flight of "Concorde".
83. 27. 100 f. plum and brown.. 1·60 1·40

28. I.L.O. Building, Geneva.

1969. Int. Labour Organization. 50th Anniv.
84. **28.** 5 f. grey, emerald & orge. 5 5

29. Poinsettia. **30.** "EXPO" Panorama.

1970. Flowers.
85. **29.** 25 f. multicoloured .. 20 15

1970. New U.P.U. Headquarters Building, Berne. As T **127** of Cameroun.
86. 65 f. brown, green and violet 45 35

1970. Air. World Fair "EXPO 70", Osaka, Japan. Multicoloured.
87. 60 f. Type **30** 55 35
88. 90 f. Geisha and map of Japan 55 35

31. Chiromani Costume, Anjouan. **32.** Mosque de Vendredi.

1970. Comoro Costumes. Multicoloured.
89. 20 f. Type **31** 15 12
90. 25 f. Bouiboui, Great Comoro 20 15

1970.
91. **32.** 5 f. turq., grn. and red 5 5
92. 10 f. violet, green & pur. 8 5
93. 40 f. brn., green and red 25 20

33. White Egret.

1971. Birds. Multicoloured.
94. 5 f. Type **33** 5 5
95. 10 f. Comoro pigeon .. 5 5
96. 15 f. Green-backed heron .. 8 5
97. 25 f. Sganzin's wart pigeon 15 12
98. 35 f. "Humblotia flavirostris" 20 15
99. 40 f. Allen's gallinule .. 25 20

34. Sunset, Moutsamoudou (Anjouan).

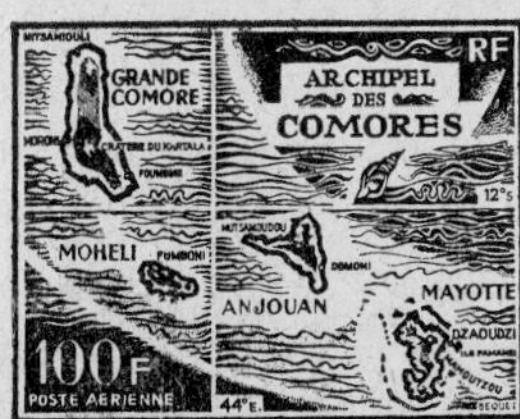

35. Map of Comoros Archipelago.

1971. Air. Comoro Landscapes. Mult.
100. **34.** 15 f. multicoloured .. 10 5
101. – 20 f. multicoloured .. 15 8
102. – 65 f. multicoloured .. 40 20
103. – 85 f. multicoloured .. 50 20
104. **35.** 100 f. brn., grn. & blue 80 40
DESIGNS—(As T **34**). 20 f. Sanda village (Mayotte). 65 f. Ruined palace, Iconi (Great Comoro). 85 f. Off-shore islands, Mounatchoua (Moheli).
See also Nos. 124/8, 132/6, 157/60 and 168/71.

36. "Allamanda cathartica".

1971. Tropical Plants. Multicoloured.
105. 1 f. "Pyrostegia venusta" (vert.) (postage) .. 5 5
106. 3 f. Type **36** 5 5
107. 20 f. "Plumeria rubra" (vert.) 10 8
108. 60 f. "Hibiscus schizopetalus" (vert.) (air) .. 45 20
109. 85 f. "Acalypha sanderii" (vert.) 55 25

37. "Gonus lithoglyphus".

1971. Seashells. Multicoloured.
110. 5 f. Type **37** 5 5
111. 10 f. "Conus litteratus" .. 5 5
112. 20 f. "Conus aulicus" .. 12 8
113. 35 f. "Nerita polita" .. 15 12
114. 60 f. "Cypraea caput-serpentis" 30 25

1971. Charles de Gaulle. 1st Death Anniv. Designs as Nos. 1939 and 1940 of France.
115. 20 f. black and purple .. 15 12
116. 35 f. black and purple .. 20 20

38. Airport Buildings.

1972. Air. New Airport, Moroni. Inaug.
117. – 65 f. multicoloured .. 25 15
118. – 85 f. multicoloured .. 40 20
119. **38.** 100 f. green, brn. & blue 55 25
DESIGNS: 65 f., 85 f. show different, but similar, designs of the airport's buildings abstract interior decor.

39. Eiffel Tower, Paris and Telecommunications Centre, Moroni.

1972. Air. Paris-Moroni Radio-Telephone Link. Inaug.
120. **39.** 35 f. red, purple & blue 15 8
121. – 75 f. brn., violet and blue 40 15
DESIGN: 75 f. Telephone conversation.

40. Underwater Spear-fishing.

1972. Air. Aquatic Sports.
122. **40.** 70 f. brn., green & blue 35 15

41. Pasteur, Crucibles and Microscope.

1972. Louis Pasteur. 150th Birth Anniv.
123. **41.** 65 f. blue, brn. & orge. 25 20

1972. Air. Anjouan Landscapes. As Types **34**. Multicoloured.
124. 20 f. Fortress wall, Cape Sima 8 5
125. 35 f. Bambao Palace .. 12 8
126. 40 f. Palace, Domoni .. 20 8
127. 60 f. Gomajou island .. 25 12

(b). As Type **35**.
128. – 100 f. grn., blue & brn. 50 20
DESIGN: 100 f. Map of Anjouan.

42. Pres. Said Mohamed Cheikh.

43. Bank.

1973. Air. Said Mohamed Cheikh, President of Comoro Council, Commem.
129. **42.** 20 f. multicoloured .. 10 5
130. 35 f. multicoloured .. 15 10

1973. Air. Int. Coelacanth Study Expedition. No. 72 surch. **Mission Internationale pour l'etude du Coelacanthe** and value.
131. 120 f. on 90 f. brn., grn. & emerald 50 40

1973. Great Comoro Landscapes. (a) As T **34**. Multicoloured.
132. 10 f. Goulaivoini 5 5
133. 20 f. Mitsamiouli .. 8 5
134. 35 f. Foumbouni 15 10
135. 50 f. Moroni 20 15

Air. (b) As Type **35**.
136. – 135 f. pur., grn. & violet 65 45
DESIGN—VERT. 135 f. Map of Great Comoro.

1973. Moroni Buildings. Multicoloured.
137. 5 f. Type **43** 5 5
138. 15 f. Post Office 5 5
139. 20 f. Prefecture 8 5

44. Volcanic Eruption.

1973. Air. Karthala Volcanic Eruption (Sept. 1972).
140. **44.** 120 f. multicoloured .. 60 50

45. Dr. G. A. Hansen.

47. Zaouiyat Chaduli Mosque.

46. Picasso.

1973. Air. Hansen's Identification of Leprosy Bacillus. Cent.
141. **45.** 100 f. grn., pur. & blue 50 35

1973. Air. Nicholas Copernicus. 500th Birth Anniv. As Type **45**.
142. – 150 f. pur., grn. & blue 70 50
DESIGN: Copernicus and Solar System.

1973. Air. Picasso Commem.
143. **46.** 200 f. multicoloured .. 90 60

1973. Mosques. Multicoloured.
145. 20 f. Type **47** 8 8
146. 35 f. Salimata Hamissi Mosque (horiz.) 15 12

48. Star and Ribbon.

49. Said Omar Ben Soumeth (Grand Mufti of the Comoros).

1974. Air. Order of the Star of Anjouan.
147. **48.** 500 f. gold, blue & brown 2·25 1·60

1974. Air. Multicoluored.
148. 135 f. Type **49** 60 45
149. 200 f. Ben Soumeth seated (vert.) 90 65

50. Doorway of Mausoleum.

51. Wooden Combs.

1974. Mausoleum of Shaikh Said Mohamed.
150. **50.** 35 f. brn., blk. & grn... 12 10
151. – 50 f. brn., blk. & grn... 20 15
DESIGN: 50 f. Mausoleum.

1974. Comoro Handicrafts (1st series). Mult.
152. 15 f. Type **51** 5 5
153. 20 f. Three-legged table .. 5 5
154. 35 f. Koran lectern (horiz.) 12 8
155. 75 f. Sugar-cane press (horiz.) 25 20
See also Nos. 164/7.

52. Mother and Child.

1974. Comoros Red Cross Fund.
156. **52.** 35 f.+10 f. brn. & red .. 15 15

1974. Air. Mayotte Landscapes. (a) As Type **34**. Multicoloured.
157. 20 f. Moya beach 8 5
158. 35 f. Chiconi 15 10
159. 90 f. Mamutzu harbour .. 40 40

(b). Air. As Type **35**.
160. 120 f. green and blue .. 55 45
DESIGN:—VERT. Map of Mayotte.

53. U.P.U. Emblem and Globe.

1974. Universal Postal Union. Centenary.
161. 53. 30 f. red, brown & green 10 8

54. Aircraft taking off.

1975. Air. Direct Moroni-Hahaya-Paris Air Service. Inaug.
162. 54. 135 f. blue, green and red 50 45

55. Rotary Emblem, Moroni Clubhouse and Map.

1975. Air. Rotary International 70th Anniv and 10th Anniv. of Motoni Rotary Club.
163. 55. 250 f. multicoloured .. 1·00 75

56. Bracelet.

1975. Comoro Handicrafts (2nd series).
164. 56. 20 f. brown and purple 8 5
165. – 35 f. brown and green .. 12 10
166. – 120 f. brown and blue .. 45 35
167. – 135 f. brown and red .. 50 45
DESIGNS: 35 f. Diadem. 120 f. Sabre. 125 f. Dagger.

1975. Moheli Landscapes (a) As T 34. Mult.
168. 30 f. Mohani Village .. 10 8
169. 50 f. Djoezi Village .. 20 15
170. 55 f. Chirazian tombs .. 20 15

(b) Air. As Type 35.
171. 230 f. grn., blue & brown .. 80 60
DESIGN: 230 f. Map of Moheli.

57. Coelacanth and Skin-diver.

1975. Coelacanth Expedition.
172. 57. 50 f. bistre, blue & brn. 20 15

58. Tambourine-player.

1976. Folklore Dances. Multicoloured.
173. 100 f. Type 58 .. .. 40 30
174. 150 f. Folk-dancers .. 60 45

POSTAGE DUE STAMPS

D 1. Mosque in Anjouan.

D 2. Coelacanth.

1950.
D 16. D 1. 50 c. green 5 5
D 17. 1 f. chocolate .. 5 5

1954.
D 18. D 2. 5 f. sepia and green .. 5 5
D 19. 10 f. violet and brown 10 10
D 20. 20 f. indigo and blue 15 15

CONGO (Kinshasa) O4

This Belgian colony in Central Africa became independent in 1960. There were separate issues for the province of Katanga (q.v.).

In 1971 the country was renamed ZAIRE REPUBLIC and later issues will be found under that heading.

1967. 100 sengi = 1 (li)kuta; 100 (ma) kuta = 1 zaire.

1960. Various stamps of Belgian Congo optd. **CONGO** or surch. also. (a) Flowers issue of 1952. Multicoloured.
360. 10 c. "Dissotis" 5 5
361. 10 c. on 15 c. "Protea" .. 5 5
362. 20 c. "Vellozia" 5 5
363. 40 c. "Ipomoea" 5 5
364. 50 c. on 60 c. "Euphorbia" 5 5
365. 50 c. on 75 c. "Ochna" .. 5 5
366. 1 f. "Hibiscus" 5 5
367. 1 f. 50 "Schizoglossum" .. 5 5
368. 2 f. "Ansellia" 5 5
369. 3 f. "Costus" 10 8
370. 4 f. "Nymphaea" .. 12 12
371. 5 f. "Thunbergia" .. 12 5
372. 6 f. 50 "Thonningia" .. 20 8
373. 8 f. "Gloriosa" 25 12
374. 10 f. "Silene" 35 12
375. 20 f. "Aristolochia" .. 80 30
376. 50 f. "Eulophia" .. .. 4·00 2·10
377. 100 f. "Cryptosepalum" .. 4·25 2·50

(b) Wild animals issue of 1959.
378. 10 c. brown, sepia & blue 5 5
379. 20 c. grey-blue & verm. 5 5
380. 40 c. brown and blue .. 5 5
381. 50 c. red, olive, black and blue 5 5
382. 1 f. black, green & brn. 5 5
383. 1 f. 50 black and yellow 5 5
384. 2 f. black, brown & red 5 5
385. 3 f. 50 on 3 f. black, pur. and slate 10 5
386. 5 f. brown, green & sepia 12 5
387. 6 f. 50 brown, yellow and blue 15 5
388. 8 f. bistre, violet & chest. 20 15
389. 10 f. brown, black, orange and yellow .. 25 12

(c) Madonna.
390. 56. 50 c. brn., ochre & chest. 40 40

(d) African Technical Co-operation Commission. Inscr. in French or Flemish.
391. 57. 3 f. 50 on 3 f. salmon and slate 25 25

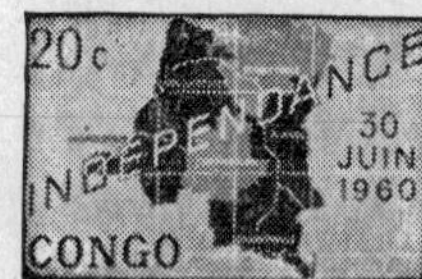

59. Congo Map.

1960. Independence Commem.
392. 59. 20 c. bistre-brown .. 5 5
393. 50 c. red 5 5
394. 1 f. green 5 5
395. 1 f. 50 red-brown .. 5 5
396. 2 f. magenta 5 5
397. 3 f. 50 violet 5 5
398. 5 f. blue 8 5
399. 6 f. 50 black 10 5
400. 10 f. orange 15 12
401. 20 f. ultramarine .. 30 20

60. Congo Flag and People breaking Chain.

61. Pres. Kasavubu.

1961. Congo Independence Agreement. 2nd Anniv. Flag in yellow and blue.
402. 60. 2 f. violet 5 5
403. 3 f. 50 vermilion .. 5 5
404. 6 f. 50 brown .. 12 5
405. 10 f. emerald .. 15 10
406. 20 f. magenta .. 30 20

1961 Coquilhatville Conf. Optd. **CONFERENCE COQUILHATVILLE AVRIL -MAI-1961.**
407. 59. 20 c. bistre-brown .. 20 20
408. 50 c. red 20 20
409. 1 f. green 20 20
410. 1 f. 50 red-brown .. 20 20
411. 2 f. magenta 20 20
412. 3 f. 50 violet 20 20
413. 5 f. blue 20 20
414. 6 f. 50 black 20 20
415. 10 f. orange 20 20
416. 20 f. ultramarine .. 20 20

1961. Independence. 1st Anniv. Inscr. as in T 61. Portraits and inscriptions in sepia.
417. 61. 10 c. yellow 5 5
418. 20 c. rose 5 5
419. 40 c. turquoise 5 5
420. 50 c. salmon 5 5
421. 1 f. lilac 5 5
422. 1 f. 50 brown 5 5
423. 2 f. green 5 5
424. – 3 f. 50 magenta .. 8 5
425. – 5 f. grey 50 8
426. – 6 f. 50 blue 15 5
427. – 8 f. olive 20 8
428. – 10 f. violet-blue .. 50 8
429. – 20 f. orange 50 10
430. – 50 f. blue 90 25
431. – 100 f. yellow-green .. 1·25 40
DESIGNS—HORIZ. 3 f. 50 to 8 f. Pres. Kasavubu and map of Congo Republic. VERT. 10 f. to 100 f. Pres. Kasavubu in full uniform and outline map.

1961. Re-opening of Parliament. Optd. **REOUVERTURE du PARLEMENT, JUILLET 1961.**
432. 61. 10 c. yellow 5 5
433. 20 c. rose 5 5
434. 40 c. turquoise 5 5
435. 50 c. salmon 15 15
436. 1 f. lilac 15 15
437. 1 f. 50 brown 40 40
438. 2 f. green 40 40
439. – 5 f. grey (No. 425) .. 40 40
440. – 10 f. violet-bl. (No. 428) 55 55

62. Dag Hammarskjoeld.

63. Campaign Emblem.

1962. Dag Hammarskjoeld Commemoration.
441. 62. 10 c. chocolate and grey 5 5
442. 20 c. slate-blue and grey 5 5
443. 30 c. bistre-brn. & grey 5 5
444. 40 c. blue and grey .. 5 5
445. 50 c. red and grey .. 5 5
446. 3 f. olive and grey .. 1·00 1·00
447. 6 f. 50 violet and grey 40 30
448. 8 f. brown and grey .. 45 30

1962. Malaria Eradication.
449. 63. 1 f. 50 brn., blk. & yell. 5 5
450. 2 f. blue-green, chocolate and green .. 20 10
451. 6 f. 50 lake, black & blue 12 5

1962. Reorganization of Adoula Ministry. Optd. **"Paix Travail, Austerite . . . , C. ADOULA 11 juillet 1962.**
452. 62. 10 c. chocolate and grey 5 5
453. 20 c. slate-blue & grey 5 5
454. 30 c. bistre-brn. & grey 5 5
455. 40 c. blue and grey .. 5 5
456. 50 c. red and grey .. 50 30
457. 3 f. olive and grey .. 10 5
458. 6 f. 50 violet and grey .. 12 5
459. 8 f. brown and grey .. 20 10

64.

1963. 1st Participation in U.P.U. Congress.
460. 64. 2 f. slate-violet .. 60 70
461. 4 f. red 5 5
462. 7 f. blue 8 5
463. 20 f. green 15 10

65. Emblem, Bearers and Tractor.

66. Shoebill Stork.

67. Strophanthus ("S. sarmentosus").

68. "Reconciliation".

1963. Freedom from Hunger.
464. 65. 5 f. + 2 f. violet & mauve 10 5
465. 9 f. + 4 f. green & yellow 20 12
466. 12 f. + 6 f. blue-violet and cobalt 25 20
467. 20 f. + 10 f. green & red 1·10 1·00

1963. Protected Birds.
468. – 10 c. multicoloured .. 5 5
469. – 20 c. blue, black and red 5 5
470. – 30 c. black, chest. & grn. 5 5
471. – 40 c. black, orge. & grey 5 5
472. 66. 1 f. blk., emerald & brn. 5 5
473. – 2 f. grey-bl., brn. & red 60 25
474. – 3 f. blk., pink & ol.-grn. 5 5
475. – 4 f. ultram., grn. & cerise 5 5
476. – 5 f. blk., brn.-red & blue 5 5
477. – 6 f. black, bistre & violet 60 25
478. – 7 f. indigo, blue & turq. 8 5
479. – 8 f. indigo, yell. & orge. 8 5
480. – 10 f. black, red and blue 10 5
481. – 20 f. black, verm. & yell. 15 5
BIRDS—VERT. 10 c. Pelicans. 30 c. Open-beak stork. 2 f. Marabou stork. 4 f. Congo peacock. 6 f. Secretary bird. 8 f. Sacred ibis. HORIZ. 20 c. Schouteden's guineafowl. 40 c. White-bellied storks. 3 f. Flamingoes. 5 f. Hartlaub's duck. 7 f. Hornbill. 10 f. Crowned crane. 20 f. African jabiru.

1963. Red Cross Cent. Cross in red.
482. 67. 10 c. grey-green & violet 5 5
483. A. 20 c. blue and claret .. 5 5
484. 67. 30 c. verm. & grey-green 5 5
485. A. 40 c. violet and blue .. 5 5
486. 67. 5 f. lake and olive .. 5 5
487. A. 7 f. slate-purple & orge. 8 8
488. B. 9 f. olive 8 8
489. 20 f. violet 80 80
DESIGNS—VERT. A, Cinchona ("C. ledgeriana"). HORIZ. B, Red Cross nurse.

1963. "National Reconciliation".
490. 68. 4 f. blk., yell., bl. & brn. 55 20
491. 5 f. blk., yell., bl. & grn. 5 5
492. 9 f. blk., yell., bl. & red 8 5
493. 12 f. blk., yell., bl. & pur. 10 5

DESIGNS: A, Tractor, bridge, etc. B, Construction of Ituri Road.

69. Kabambare Sewer, Leopoldville.

1963. European Economic Community Aid.
494. 69. 20 c. lake, bl., brn. & grn. 5 5
495. A. 30 c. brn., bl., lake & grn. 5 5
496. B. 50 c. lake, bl., brn. & grn. 5 5
497. 69 3 f. lake, grn., brn. & bl. 55 20
498. A. 5 f. brn., lake, grn. & bl. 5 5
499. B. 9 f. lake, brn., grn. & bl. 8 5
500. A. 12 f. brn., grn., bl. & lake 12 8

DESIGN: 5 f., 7 f. 50 f. Tailplane and control tower.

70. N'Djili Airport, Leopoldville.

1963. "Air Congo" Commemoration.
501. 70. 2 f. multicoloured .. 5 5
502. – 5 f. multicoloured .. 5 5
503. 70. 6 f. multicoloured .. 35 25
504. – 7 f. multicoloured .. 5 5
505. 70. 30 f. multicoloured .. 15 12
506. – 50 f. multicoloured .. 25 20

1963. Declaration of Human Rights. 15th Anniv. Optd. **10 DECEMBRE 1948 10 DECEMBRE 1963 15e anniversaire DROITS DE L'HOMME.**
507. 64. 2 f. slate-violet .. 5 5
508. 4 f. red 5 5
509. 7 f. blue 12 12
510. 20 f. green 12 12

71. Student in Laboratory.

1964. Lovanium University. 10th Anniv. Multicoloured.
511. 50 c. T **71** 5 5
512. 1 f. 50 University buildings 5 5
513. 8 f. Atomic and nuclear reactor symbols .. 1·10 1·00
514. 25 f. University arms and buildings 12 8
515. 30 f. Type **71** 15 12
516. 60 f. As 1 f. 50 .. .. 25 20
517. 75 f. As 8 f. 35 30
518. 100 f. As 25 f. 40 40

1964. Various stamps surch. over coloured metallic panels.

(a) Stamps of Belgian Congo surch. **REPUBLIQUE DU CONGO** and value.
519. – 1 f. on 20 c. (No. 340) .. 5 5
520. – 2 f. on 1 f. 50 (No. 306) 65 60
521. – 5 f. on 6 f. 50 (No. 348) 12 10
522. – 8 f. on 6 f. 50 (No. 311) 15 12

(b) Stamps of Congo (Kinshasa) surch.
523. – 1 f. on 20 c. (No. 379) . 5 5
524. – 1 f. on 6 f. 50 (No. 372) 5 5
525. – 2 f. on 1 f. 50 (No. 367) 5 5
530. **61.** 3 f. on 20 c. 10 8
531. 4 f. on 40 c. 10 10
526. – 5 f. on 6 f. 50 (No. 387) 12 10
528. **59.** 6 f. on 6 f. 50 .. .. 15 12
529. 7 f. on 20 c. 20 12

72. Pole-vaulting.

DESIGNS—VERT. 7 f., 20 f. Throwing the javelin. HORIZ. 8 f., 100 f. Hurdling.

1964. Olympic Games, Tokyo.
532. **72.** 5 f. sepia, grey and red 5 5
533. – 7 f. violet, red and green 50 25
534. – 8 f. brown, yellow & blue 5 5
535. **72.** 10 f. maroon, blue & pur. 5 5
536. – 20 f. brown, green & orge. 12 5
537. – 100 f. brown, mve. & grn. 50 12

OCCUPATION OF STANLEYVILLE

During the occupation of Stanleyville from 5th August to 24th November, 1964, stocks of a number of contemporary issues were overprinted **REPUBLIQUE POPULAIRE** and issued by the rebel authorities.

73. National Palace.

1964. National Palace, Leopoldville.
538. **73.** 50 c. magenta and blue 5 5
539. 1 f. blue and purple .. 5 5
540. 2 f. brown and violet .. 5 5
541. 3 f. green and brown .. 5 5
542. 4 f. orange & ultramarine 5 5
543. 5 f. slate-violet & green 5 5
544. 6 f. chocolate & orange 5 5
545. 7 f. olive and brown .. 5 5
546. 8 f. red and ultramarine 1·10 15
547. 9 f. violet and red .. 5 5
548. 10 f. olive-brown & green 5 5
549. 20 f. blue and chestnut 8 5
550. 30 f. claret and green .. 12 5
551. 40 f. ultramarine & pur. 15 5
552. 50 f. orge.-brown & grn. 20 5
553. 100 f. black and orange 40 8

74. Pres. Kennedy. **75.** Rocket and Unisphere.

1964. Pres. Kennedy Commem.
554. **74.** 5 f. blue and black .. 5 5
555. 6 f. purple and black .. 5 5
556. 9 f. brown and black .. 5 5
557. 30 f. violet and black 20 5
558. 40 f. green and black .. 1·25 40
559. 60 f. chestnut and black 30 15

1965. New York World's Fair.
560. **75.** 50 c. purple and black 5 5
561. 1 f. 50 blue and violet 5 5
562. 2 f. brown and green .. 5 5
563. 10 f. green and red .. 45 25
564. 18 f. ultram. and brown 5 5
565. 27 f. red and green .. 15 5
566. 40 f. grey and red .. 20 8

76. Football.

1965. 1st African Games, Leopoldville.
567. – 5 f. black, brown & blue 5 5
568. **76.** 6 f. red, black & grey-bl. 5 5
569. – 15 f. black, green & orge. 5 5
570. – 24 f. black, grn. & mve. 12 5
571. **76.** 40 f. blue, blk. & turq. 75 25
572. – 60 f. purple, black & bl. 25 10
SPORTS—VERT. 5 f., 24 f. Basketball. 15 f., 60 f. Volleyball.

77. Telecommunications Satellites.

1965. I.T.U. Cent. Multicoloured.
573. 6 f. Type **77** 5 5
574. 9 f. Telecommunications satellites (different view) 5 5
575. 12 f. Type **77** 5 5
576. 15 f. As 9 f. 5 5
577. 18 f. Type **77** 60 15
578. 20 f. As 9 f. 10 5
579. 30 f. Type **77** 15 5
580. 40 f. As 9 f. 15 8

78. Parachutist and troops landing.

1965. Independence. 5th Anniv.
581. **78.** 5 f. brown and blue .. 5 5
582. 6 f. brown and orange 5 5
583. 7 f. brown and green .. 25 12
584. 9 f. brown and magenta 5 5
585. 18 f. brown and yellow 8 5

79. Matadi Port.

1965. Int. Co-operation Year.
586. **79.** 6 f. blue, black & yellow 5 5
587. – 8 f. chestnut, blk. & blue 5 5
588. – 9 f. turq., black & brown 5 5
589. **79.** 12 f. mag., black & grey 50 20
590. – 25 f. olive, black & red 12 5
591. – 60 f. grey, black & yell. 25 5
DESIGNS: 8 f., 25 f. Katanga mines. 9 f., 60 f. Tshopo Barrage, Stanleyville.

80. Medical Care.

1965. Congolese Army.
592. **80.** 2 f. blue and vermilion 5 5
593. 5 f. brown, red and pink 5 5
594. – 6 f. brown and blue .. 5 5
595. – 7 f. green and yellow .. 5 5
596. – 9 f. brown and green .. 5 5
597. – 10 f. brown and green 25 25
598. – 18 f. violet and red .. 8 5
599. – 19 f. brown & turq. .. 35 20
600. – 20 f. brown and blue .. 10 5
601. – 24 f. multicoloured .. 12 10
602. – 30 f. multicoloured .. 15 5
DESIGNS—HORIZ. 6 f., 9 f. Feeding child. 7 f., 18 f. Bridge-building. VERT. 10 f., 20 f. Building construction. 19 f. Telegraph line maintenance. 24 f., 30 f. Soldier and flag.

1966. World Meteorological Day. Nos. 590/1 optd. **6e Journee Meteorologique Mondiale / 23.3.66** (on coloured metallic panel) and W.M.O. Emblem.
603. – 25 f. olive, black and red 35 35
604. – 60 f. grey, black & yellow 35 35

81. Carved Stool and Head.

1966. World Festival of Negro Arts, Dakar.
605. **81.** 10 f. black, red and grey 5 5
606. – 12 f. black, green & blue 8 8
607. – 15 f. black, blue & pur. 8 8
608. – 53 f. blk., claret & ultram. 65 50
DESIGNS—VERT. 12 f. Statuettes. 53 f. Statuettes of women. HORIZ. 15 f. Woman's head and carved goat.

82. Pres. Mobutu and Fish Workers.

1966. Pres. Mobutu Commem.
609. **82.** 2 f. brown and blue .. 5 5
610. – 4 f. brown and vermilion 5 5
611. – 6 f. brown and olive .. 40 40
612. – 8 f. brown and turquoise 5 5
613. – 10 f. brown and lake .. 5 5
614. – 12 f. brown and violet .. 5 5
615. – 15 f. brown and green .. 5 5
616. – 24 f. brown and magenta 12 12
DESIGNS (Pres. Mobutu and): 4 f. Harvesting pyrethrum. 6 f. Building construction. 8 f. Winnowing maize. 10 f. Cotton-picking. 12 f. Harvesting fruit. 15 f. Picking coffee-beans. 24 f. Harvesting pineapples.

1966. W.H.O. Headquarters, Geneva. Inaug. Nos. 550/3 optd. **O.M.S. Geneve 1966** and WHO Emblem.
618. **73.** 30 f. claret and green .. 40 40
619. 40 f. ultram. and purple 45 45
620. 50 f. orge.-brown & green 50 50
621. 100 f. black and orange 50 50

83. Footballer.

1966. World Cup Football Championships.
622. **83.** 10 f. green, violet & brn. 5 5
623. – 30 f. apple, violet & pur. 15 12
624. – 50 f. brown, blue & grn. 55 50
625. – 60 f. gold, sepia & emer. 30 25
DESIGNS: 30 f. Two footballers. 50 f. Three footballers. 60 f. Jules Rimet Cup and football.

1966. World Cup Football Championships Final. Nos. 622/5 optd. **FINALE. ANGLETERRE—ALLEMAGNE 4 - 2.**
626. **83.** 10 f. green, vio. & brn. 8 8
627. – 30 f. apple, violet & pur. 25 20
628. – 50 f. brown, blue & grn. 35 35
629. – 60 f. gold, sepia & emer. 45 35

1967. 4th African Unity Organisation (O.U.A.) Conf., Kinshasa. Nos. 538/43 surch. **4e Sommet OUA KINSHASA du 11 au 14-9-67** and value.
631. **73.** 1 k. on 2 f. 5 5
632. 3 k. on 5 f. 5 5
633. 5 k. on 4 f. 10 8
634. 6 k. 60 on 1 f. 12 10
635. 9 k. 60 on 50 c. .. 20 20
636. 9 k. 80 on 3 f. .. 30 25

1967. New Constitution. Nos. 609/10 and 592 surch. **1967 NOUVELLE CONSTITUTION** with coloured metallic panel obliterating old value.
639. **82.** 4 k. on 2 f. 10 8
640. **80.** 5 k. on 2 f. 12 10
641. – 21 k. on 4 f. 55 45

1967. 1st Congolese Games, Kinshasa. Nos. 567 and 569 surch. **1ers Jeux Congolais 25/6 au 2/7/67 Kinshasa** and value.
642. 1 k. on 5 f. 5 5
643. 9.6 k. on 15 f. 25 25

1967. 1st Flight by Air Congo BAC "One-Eleven." No. 504 surch. **1er VOL BAC ONE ELEVEN 14/5/67** and value.
644. 9.6 k. on 7 f. 30 12

1968. World Children's Day (8.10.67). Nos. 586 and 588 surch. **JOURNEE MONDIALE DE L'ENFANCE 8-10-67** and new value.
645. **79.** 1 k. on 6 f. 5 5
646. 9 k. on 9 f. 25 25

1968. Int. Tourist Year (1967). Nos. 538, 541 and 544 surch. **Annee Internationale du Tourisme 24-10-67** and new value.
647. **73.** 5 k. on 50 c. 12 12
648. 10 k. on 6 f. 25 25
649. 15 k. on 3 f. 40 40

1968. (a) No. 540 surch.
650. **73.** 1 k. on 2 f. 5 5

(b) Surch. (coloured panel obliterating old value, and new value surch. on panel. Panel colour given first, followed by colour of new value).

(i) Nos. 538 and 542.
651. **73.** 2 k. on 50 c. (Bronze and Black) 5 5
652. 2 k. on 50 c. (Ultram. & White) 5 5
653. 9.6 k. on 4 f. (Black & White) 30 25

(ii) No. 609.
654. **82.** 10 k. on 2 f. (Black & White) 25 8

84. Leaping Leopard.

1968.
655. **84.** 2 k. black on green .. 5 5
656. 9.6 k. black on red .. 25 8

1968. As Nos. 609, etc. but with colours changed and surch. in new value.
657. **82.** 15 s. on 2 f. brown & blu 5 5
658. – 1 k. on 6 f. brown & chestnut 5 5
659. – 3 k. on 10 f. brown and green 8 5
660. – 5 k. on 12 f. brown and orange 12 8
661. – 20 k. on 15 f. brown and green 50 40
662. – 50 k. on 24 f. brown and purple .. .. 1·25 85

85. Human Rights Emblem.

1968. Human Rights Year.
663. **85.** 2 k. green and blue .. 5 5
664. 9.6 k. red and green .. 25 20
665. 10 k. brown and lilac 25 20
666. 40 k. violet and brown 1·00 75

1969. 4th O.C.A.M. (Organisation Commune Africaine et Malgache) Summit Meeting, Kinshasa. Nos. 663/6 with colours changed optd. **4 EME SOMMET OCAM 27-1-1969 KINSHASA** and emblem.
667. **85.** 2 k. chestnut and green 5 5
668. 9.60 k. emerald and pink 25 20
669. 10 k. blue and grey .. 25 20
670. 40 k. violet and blue .. 1·00 75

86. Map of Africa and "Cotton".

1969. Int. Fair, Kinshasa. (1st Issue).
671. 86. 2 k. multicoloured .. 5 5
672. – 6 k. multicoloured .. 20 20
673. – 9.6 k. multicoloured .. 25 12
674. – 9.8 k. multicoloured .. 25 20
675. – 11.6 k. multicoloured .. 30 25
DESIGNS: Map of Africa and: 6 k. "Copper". 9,6 k. "Coffee". 9.8 k. "Diamonds". 11.6 k. "Palm-oil".

87. Fair Entrance.

1969. Int. Fair, Kinshasa (2nd Issue). Inaug.
676. 87. 2 k. purple and gold .. 5 5
677. – 3 k. blue and gold .. 5 5
678. – 10 k. green and gold .. 20 20
679. – 25 k. red and gold .. 50 40
DESIGNS: 3 k. "Gecomin" (mining company) pavilion. 10 k. Administration building. 25 k. African Unity Organization pavilion.

88. Congo Arms.

89. Pres. Mobutu.

1969.
680. 88. 10 s. red and black .. 5 5
681. 15 s. blue and black .. 5 5
682. 30 s. emerald and black 5 5
683. 60 s. purple and black 5 5
684. 90 s. bistre and black .. 5 5
685. 89. 1 k. multicoloured .. 5 5
686. 2 k. multicoloured .. 5 5
687. 3 k. multicoloured .. 8 5
688. 5 k. multicoloured .. 10 8
689. 6 k. multicoloured .. 12 10
690. 9.6 k. multicoloured .. 15 12
691. 10 k. multicoloured .. 20 15
692. 20 k. multicoloured .. 40 30
693. 50 k. multicoloured .. 1·00 90
694. 100 k. multicoloured .. 2·00 1·75

90. "The Well-sinker" (O. Bonnevalle).

1969. Int. Labour Organization. 50th Anniv. Paintings. Multicoloured.
695. 3 k. Type 90 .. .. 5 5
696. 4 k. "Cocoa Production" (J. van Noten) 8 8
697. 8 k. "The Harbour" (C. Meunier) 20 15
698. 10 k. "The Poulterer" (H. Evenepoel) .. 25 20
699. 15 k. "Industry" (C. Meunier) 35 30
No. 697 is vert., size 29 × 42 mm.

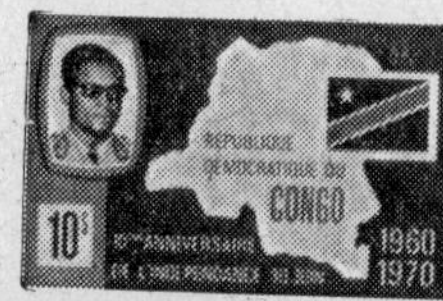

91. Pres. Mobutu, Map and Flag.

1970. Independence. 10th Anniv.
701. 91. 10 s. multicoloured .. 5 5
702. 90 s. multicoloured .. 5 5
703. 1 k. multicoloured .. 5 5
704. 2 k. multicoloured .. 5 5
705. 7 k. multicoloured .. 10 10
706. 10 k. multicoloured .. 20 20
707. 20 k. multicoloured .. 40 40

1970. Surch. (a) National Palace series.
708. 73. 10 s. on 1 f. 5 5
709. 20 s. on 2 f. 5 5
710. 30 s. on 3 f. 5 5
711. 40 s. on 4 f. 5 5
712. 60 s. on 7 f. 50 40
713. 90 s. on 9 f. 50 40
714. 1 k. on 6 f. 8 5
715. 3 k. on 30 f. 50 40
716. 4 k. on 40 f. 8 5
717. 5 k. on 50 f. .. .. 1·25 1·00
718. 10 k. on 100 f. .. 60 50

(b) Congolese Army series.
719. 90 s. on 9 f. (No. 596) 8 8
720. 1 k. on 7 f. (No. 595) .. 8 8
721. 2 k. on 24 f. (No. 601) 8 8

(c) Pres. Mobutu series.
722. 82. 20 s. on 2 f. 8 8
723. – 40 s. on 4 f. (No. 610).. 8 8
724. – 1 k. on 12 f. (No. 614) 50 40
725. – 2 k. on 24 f. (No. 616) 8 8

92. I.T.U. Headquarters, Geneva.

1970. United Nations Commemorations.
726. 92. 1 k. olive, grn. & pink .. 5 5
727. – 2 k. grey-grn., grn. & orge. 5 5
728. – 6 k. 60 red, pink & blue 15 15
729. 92. 9 k. 60 multicoloured .. 20 20
730. – 9 k. 80 sepia, brn. & bl. 20 20
731. – 10 k. sepia, brn. & lilac 20 20
732. – 11 k. sepia, brn. & pink 25 25
DESIGNS AND EVENTS: 1 k., 9 k. 60, (I.T.U. World Day). 2 k., 6 k. 60, New U.P.U. Headquarters, Berne (Inauguration). 9 k. 80, 10 k., 11 k. U.N. Headquarters, New York (25th anniversary).

93. Pres. Mobutu and Independence Arch.

1970. "New Regime". Fifth Anniv.
733. 93. 2 k. multicoloured .. 5 5
734. 10 k. multicoloured .. 25 20
735. 20 k. multicoloured .. 50 40

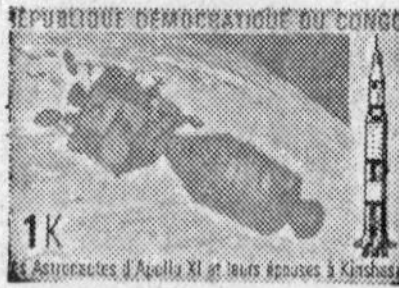

94. "Apollo II".

1970. Visit of "Apollo 11" Astronauts to Kinshasa.
736. 94. 1 k. bl., blk. & red .. 5 5
737. – 2 k. violet, blk. & red .. 5 5
738. – 7 k. blk., orge. & red .. 15 15
739. – 10 k. blk., pink & red .. 20 20
740. – 30 k. blk., grn. & red .. 60 60
DESIGNS: 2 k. Astronauts on Moon. 7 k. Pres. Mobutu decorating wives. 10 k. Pres. Mobutu with astronauts. 30 k. Astronauts after splashdown.

95. "Metopodontus savagei".

1971. Insects. Multicoloured.
741. 10 s. Type 95 .. .. 5 5
742. 50 s. "Cicindela regalis" .. 5 5
743. 90 s. "Magacephala catenulata" 5 5
744. 1 k. "Stephanorrhina guttata" 5 5
745. 2 k. "Pupuricenus congoanus" 5 5
746. 3 k. "Sagra tristis" .. 8 8
747. 5 k. "Steraspis subcalida" 15 15
748. 10 k. "Mecosaspis explanata" 30 30
749. 30 k "Goliathus meleagris" 80 80
750. 40 k. "Sternotomis virescens" 1·10 1·10

96. "Colotis protomedia".

1971. Butterflies and Moths. Multicoloured.
751. 10 s. Type 96 .. .. 5 5
752. 20 s. "Rhodophitus simplex" 5 5
753. 70 s. "Euphaedra overlaeti" 5 5
754. 1 k. "Argema bouvieri" .. 5 5
755. 3 k. "Cymothoe reginae-elisabethae" .. 8 8
756. 5 k. "Miniodes maculifera" 15 15
757. 10 k. "Salamis temora" .. 30 30
758. 15 k. "Eronia leda" .. 40 40
759. 25 k. "Cymothoe sangaris" 60 60
760. 40 k. "Euchloron megaera" 1·00 1·00

97. "Four Races" around Globe.

98. Pres. Mobutu and Obelisk.

1971. Racial Equality Year.
761. 97. 1 k. multicoloured .. 5 5
762. 4 k. multicoloured .. 8 8
763. 5 k. multicoloured .. 12 12
764. 10 k. multicoloured .. 40 40

1971. Popular Revolutionary Movement (M.P.R.). Fourth Anniv.
765. 98. 4 k. multicoloured .. 10 10

99. "Hypericum bequaertii".

1971. Tropical Plants. Multicoloured.
766. 1 k. Type 99 .. .. 5 5
767. 4 k. "Dissotis brazzae" 12 12
768. 20 k. "Begonia wollast" 50 50
769. 25 k. "Cassia alata" .. 60 60

100. I.T.U. Emblem (International Telecommunications Day).

1971. "Telecommunications and Space". Multicoloured.
770. 1 k. Type 100 .. .. 5 5
771. 3 k. Dish aerial (Satellite Earth Station, Kinshasa) 8 8
772. 6 k. Map of Pan-African telecommunications network 15 15

101. "Cercopithecus aethiops".

1971. Congo Monkeys. Multicoloured.
773. 10 s. Type 101 .. .. 5 5
774. 20 s. "Cercopithecus cephus" (vert.) .. 5 5
775. 70 s. "Cercopithecus neglectus" 5 5
776. 1 k. "Papio cynocephalus" 5 5
777. 3 k. "Pan paniscus" (vert.) 8 8
778. 5 k. "Cercocebus" (vert.) 15 12
779. 10 k. "Cercopithecus hamlyni" 30 25
780. 15 k. "Cercopithecus diana d." 50 40
781. 25 k. "Colobus polykomos" (vert.) 75 60
782. 40 k. "Cercopithecus l'hoesti" (vert.) .. 1·10 95

102. Hotel Inter-Continental.

1971. Opening of Hotel Inter-Continental, Kinshasa.
783. 102. 2 k. multicoloured .. 5 5
784. 12 k. multicoloured .. 25 20

103. "Reader".

1971. Literacy Campaign. Multicoloured.
785. 50 s. Type 103 .. .. 5 5
786. 2 k. 50 Open book and abacus 8 5
787. 7 k. Symbolic alphabet .. 20 15

For later issues see **ZAIRE REPUBLIC.**

CONGO (Brazzaville) O1

Formerly Middle Congo. An independent republic within the French Community.

1. "Birth of the Republic".

1959. Republic. 1st Anniv.
1. 1. 25 f. purple, yellow brown and bronze-green .. 20 5

1960. African Technical Co-operation Commission. 10th Anniv. As T 39 of Cameroun.
2. 50 f. lake and green .. 45 45

1960. Air. Olympic Games. No. 276 of French Equatorial Africa optd. with Olympic rings, **XVIIe OLYMPIADE 1960 REPUBLIQUE DU CONGO** and surch. **250 F.** and bars.
3. 250 f. on 500 f. blue, black and green .. .. 3·25 2·25

2. Pres. Youlou.

3. U.N. Emblem, Map and Flag.

1960.
4. 2. 15 f. green, red & turquoise 15 10
5. 85 f. blue and red .. 70 35

1961. Admission into U.N.O.
6. 3. 5 f. multicoloured 5 5
7. 20 f. multicoloured .. 15 12
8. 100 f. multicoloured .. 90 75

4. "Thesium tencio"

1961. Air.
9. – 100 f. purple, yell. & green 75 55
10. – 200 f. yell., turq. & brown 1·50 75
11. 4. 500 f. yell., myrtle & chest. 3·75 1·90
FLOWERS: 100 f. "Helicrysum mechowiam". 200 f. "Cogniauxia podolaena".

1961. Air. Foundation of "Air Afrique" Airline. As T **44** of Cameroun.
12. 50 f. purple, myrtle & green 40 25

5. "Elegatis bipinnulatus". 6. Brazzaville Market.

1961. Tropical Fish.
13. 5. 50 c. yell. grn., orge. & grn. 5 5
14. – 1 f. brown and green .. 5 5
15. – 2 f. brown and blue .. 5 5
15a. – 2 f. red, brown & green .. 5 5
16. 5. 3 f. green, orange & blue .. 5 5
17. – 5 f. sepia, chestnut & emer. 5 5
18. – 10 f. brown and turquoise 10 5
18a. – 15 f. mar., green & violet 15 10
FISH: 1 f., 2 f. (No. 15) "Chauliodus sloanei". 2 f. (No. 15a), "Lycoteuthis diadema". 5 f. "Argyropelecus gigas". 10 f. "Caulolepis longidens". 15 f. "Melanocetus johnsoni"

1962.
19. 6. 20 f. red, green and black 15 8

1962. Malaria Eradication. As T **45** of Cameroun.
20. 25 f.+5 f. brown 25 25

7. Export of Timber, Pointe Noire.

1962. Air. International Fair, Pointe Noire.
21. 7. 50 f. multicoloured .. 40 20

1962. Sports. As T **6** of Central African Republic.
22. 20 f. sepia, red & blk. (post.) 20 12
23. 50 f. sepia, red and black .. 40 25
24. 100 f. sepia, red & black (air) 75 55
DESIGNS—HORIZ. 20 f. Boxing. 50 f. Running. VERT. (26×47 mm.): 100 f. Basketball.

1962. Union of African and Malagasy States. 1st Anniv. As No. 328 of Cameroun.
25. 47. 30 f. violet .. 35 35

1962. Freedom from Hunger. As T **51** of Cameroun.
26. 25 f.+5 f. turquoise, brown and ultramarine .. 25 25

8. Town Hall, Brazzaville and Pres. Youlou.

1963. Air.
27. 8. 100 f. multicoloured .. 25·00 25·00

9. "Costus spectabilis (K. Schum)". 9a. King Makoko's Gold Chain.

1963. Air. Flowers. Mult.
28. 100 f. Type **9** 75 45
29. 250 f. "Acanthus montanus T. anders" .. .. 1·90 1·10

1963. Air African and Malagasian Posts and Telecommunications Union. As T **10** of Central African Republic.
30. 85 f. red, buff and violet .. 65 45

1963. Space Telecommunications. As Nos. 37/8 of Central African Republic.
31. 25 f. blue, orange and green 20 15
32. 100 f. violet, brown & blue 80 70

1963. Folklore and Tourism.
33. 9a. 10 f. bistre and black .. 8 5
34. – 15 f. mar., red. yell. & blue 12 5
DESIGN: 15 f. Kebekebe mask.
See also Nos. 45/6 and 62/4.

10. Airline Emblem.

1963. Air. "Air Afrique". 1st Anniv. and "DC-8" Service Inaug.
35. 10. 50 f. black, green, drab and blue 40 35

11. Liberty Square, Brazzaville.

1963. Air.
36. 11. 25 f. multicoloured .. 20 15
See also No. 56.

1963. Air. European-African Economic Convention. As T **16** of Central African Republic.
37. 50 f. brn., yell., ochre & drab 45 35

1963. Declaration of Human Rights. 15th Anniv. As T **18** of Central African Republic.
38. 25 f. blue, blue-grn. & brown 20 12

12. Statue of Hathor, Abu Simbel. 13. Barograph.

1964. Air. Nubian Monuments.
39. 12. 10 f.+5 f. vio. & brown 15 12
40. 25 f.+5 f. chest., & bl.-grn. 25 25
41. 50 f.+5 f. bl.-grn. & brn. 50 50

1964. World Meteorological Day.
42. 13. 50 f. brown, blue & green 40 40

14. Machinist. 15. Emblem and Implements of Manual Labour.

1964. "Technical Instruction".
43. 14. 20 f. choc., mag. & turq. 20 10

1964. Manual Labour Rehabilitation.
44. 15. 80 f. green, red and sepia 60 35

16. Diaboua Ballet. 18. Wood Carving.

17. Tree-felling.

1964. Folklore and Tourism. Multicoloured.
45. 30 f. Type **16** 25 12
46. 60 f. Kebekebe dance (vert.) 45 25

1964. Air.
47. 17. 100 f. sepia, red & green 75 45

1964. Congo Sculpture.
48. 18. 50 f. sepia and red .. 40 25

19. Boys in Classroom. 20. Sun, Ears of Wheat, and Globe within Cogwheel.

1964. Development of Education.
49. 19. 25 f. red, maroon & blue 20 10

1964. Air. Equatorial African Heads of State Conf. 5th Anniv. As T **23** of Central African Republic.
50. 100 f. multicoloured .. 75 45

1964. Air. Europafrique.
51. 20. 50 f. yellow, blue & red 25 15

21. Stadium, Olympic Flame and Throwing the Hammer.

1964. Air. Olympic Games, Tokyo. Sport and flame orange.
52. 21. 25 f. violet and brown .. 20 10
53. – 50 f. purple and olive .. 40 35
54. – 100 f. green and brown .. 75 65
55. – 200 f. olive and red .. 1·50 1·25
DESIGNS—Stadium, Olympic Flame and: VERT. 50 f. Weightlifting. 100 f. Volley-ball. HORIZ. 200 f. High-jumping.

1964. Revolution. 1st Anniv. and National Festival. As T **11** but inscr. "1er ANNIVERSAIRE DE LA REVOLUTION FETE NATIONALE 15 AOUT 1964".
56. 20 f. multicoloured 15 8

22. Posthorns, Envelope and Radio Mast.

1964. Air. Pan-African and Malagasy Posts and Telecommunications Congress, Cairo.
57. 22. 25 f. sepia & brown-red 20 15

1964. French, African and Malagasy Cooperation. As T **500** of France.
58. 25 f. chocolate, green & red 20 10

23. Dove, Envelope and Radio Mast.

1965. Establishment of Posts and Telecommunications Office, Brazzaville.
59. 23. 25 f. brown, olive, grey .. and black 20 12

24. Town Hall, Brazzaville.

1965. Air.
60. 24. 100 f. multicoloured .. 75 45

25. "Europafrique".

1965. Air. Europafrique.
61. 25. 50 f. multicoloured .. 40 20

26. Elephant. 28. Pres. Massamba-Debat.

27. Cadran de Breguet's Telegraph and "Telstar".

1965. Folklore and Tourism.
62. – 15 f. maroon, grn. & blue 12 5
63. 26. 20 f. black, blue & green 15 8
64. – 85 f. multicoloured .. 60 40
DESIGNS—VERT. 15 f. Antelope. 85 f. Dancer on stilts.

1965. Air. I.T.U. Cent.
65. 27. 100 f. brown and blue .. 75 50

1965. Portrait in sepia.
66. 28. 20 f. yellow, grn. & brn. 15 8
66a. 25 f. green, turq. & brn. 20 10
66b. 30 f. orange, turq. & brn. 25 12

29. Sir Winston Churchill. 30. Pope John XXIII.

1965. Air. Famous Men.
67. – 25 f. on 50 f. sepia & red 20 20
68. 29. 50 f. sepia and green .. 40 40
69. – 80 f. sepia and blue .. 60 60
70. – 100 f. sepia and yellow .. 75 75
PORTRAITS: 25 f. Lumumba. 80 f. Pres. Boganda. 100 f. Pres. Kennedy.

1965. Air. Pope John Commem.
71. 30. 100 f. multicoloured .. 75 65

31. Athletes and Map of Africa. 32. Natives hauling Log.

1965. 1st African Games, Brazzaville. Inscr. "PREMIERS JEUX AFRICAINS". Multicoloured.

72.	25 f. Type **31**	20	12
73.	40 f. Football	35	20
74.	50 f. Handball	40	25
75.	85 f. Running	65	45
76.	100 f. Cycling	80	55

Nos. 73/6 are larger 34½ × 34½ mm.

1965. Air. National Unity.

77. **32.**	50 f. brown and green	40	25

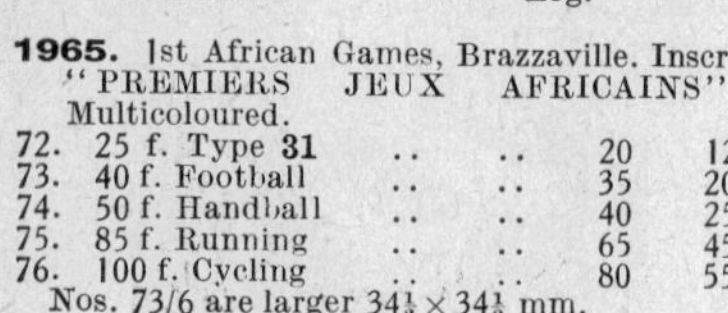

33. "World Co-operation".

1965. Air. Int. Co-operation Year.

78. **33.**	50 f. multicoloured	35	25

34. Arms of Congo. 36. Trench-digging.

35. Lincoln.

1965.

79. **34.**	20 f. multicoloured	15	8

1965. Air. Abraham Lincoln Death Cent.

80. **35.**	90 f. multicoloured	75	45

1966. Village Co-operation.

81. **36.**	25 f. multicoloured	15	8

1966. National Youth Day. As T **36** but showing Youth display.

82.	30 f. multicoloured	25	15

37. De Gaulle and Flaming Torch.

1966. Air. Brazzaville Conf. 22nd Anniv.

83. **37.**	500 f. brown, red & green	9·00	7·00

38. Weaving. 39. People and Clocks.

40. W.H.O. Building. 41. Satellite "D1" and Brazzaville Tracking Station.

1966. World Festival of Negro Arts, Dakar. Multicoloured.

84.	30 f. Type **38**	25	12
85.	85 f. Musical Instrument (horiz.)	65	40
86.	90 f. Mask	70	40

1966. Establishment of Shorter Working Day.

87. **39.**	70 f. multicoloured	60	30

1966. W.H.O. Headquarters, Geneva. Inaug.

88. **40.**	50 f. violet, yellow & blue	40	20

1966. Air. Launching of Satellite "D1".

89. **41.**	150 f. black, red & green	1·10	65

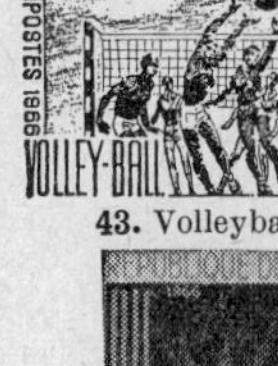

42. St. Pierre Claver Church. 43. Volleyball.

44. Jules Rimet Cup and Globe. 45. Corn, Atomic Emblem and Map.

1966.

90. **42.**	70 f. multicoloured	60	30

1966. Sports.

91. **43.**	1 f. brown, bistre & blue	5	5
92. –	2 f. brown, green & blue	5	5
93. –	3 f. brown, lake and green	5	5
94. –	5 f. brown, blue & emerald	5	5
95. –	10 f. violet, turq. & green	8	5
96. –	15 f. brown, violet & lake	10	5

DESIGNS—VERT. 2 f. Basketball. 5 f. Sportsmen. 10 f. Athlete. 15 f. Football. HORIZ. 3 f. Handball.

1966. World Cup Football Championships, England.

97. **44.**	30 f. gold, blk., blue & red	30	12

1966. Air. Europafrique.

98. **45.**	50 f. gold, grn., vio. & bl.	40	20

46. Pres. Massamba-Debat and Presidential Palace, Brazzaville.

1966. Air. Congolese Revolution. 3rd Anniv. Multicoloured.

99.	25 f. Type **46**	20	10
100.	30 f. Robespierre and Bastille, Paris	25	10
101.	50 f. Lenin and Winter Palace, St. Petersburg	40	25

1966. Air. "DC–8" Air Services Inaug. As T **45** of Central African Republic.

103.	30 f. yellow, black & violet	25	10

47. Dr. Albert Schweitzer.

1966. Air. Schweitzer Commem.

104. **47.**	100 f. multicoloured	75	50

48. Savorgnan de Brazza High School.

1966. Savorgnan de Brazza High School. Inaug.

105. **48.**	30 f. multicoloured	25	12

49. Pointe-Noire Railway Station. 50. Silhouette of Congolese, and U.N.E.S.C.O. Emblem.

1966.

106. **49.**	60 f. red, brown & green	45	20

1966. U.N.E.S.C.O. 20th Anniv.

107. **50.**	90 f. indigo, brn. & grn.	65	40

51. Balumbu Mask. 52. Cancer ("The Crab"), Microscope and Pagoda.

1966. Congolese Masks.

108. **51.**	5 f. sepia and red	5	5
109. –	10 f. brown and blue	8	5
110. –	15 f. blue, sepia & brown	10	5
111. –	20 f. red, blue, yellow and green	15	8

MASKS: 10 f. Kuyu. 15 f. Bakwele. 20 f. Bateke.

1966. Air. 9th Int. Cancer Congress, Tokyo.

112. **52.**	100 f. multicoloured	75	45

53. Social Weaver. 54. Medal, Ribbon and Map.

1967. Air. Birds. Multicoloured.

113.	50 f. Type **53**	35	20
114.	75 f. Bee-eater	55	25
115.	100 f. Lilac-breasted roller	75	30
116.	150 f. Regal sunbird	1·10	55
117.	200 f. Crowned crane	1·50	80
118.	250 f. Secretary bird	1·90	1·00
119.	300 f. Knysna lourie	2·25	1·10

1967. "Companion of the Revolution" Order.

120. **54.**	20 f. multicoloured	15	8

55. Learning the Alphabet (Educational Campaign). 56. Mahatma Gandhi.

1967. Education and Sugar Production Campaigns. Multicoloured.

121.	25 f. Type **55**	20	10
122.	45 f. Cutting sugar-cane	35	15

1967. Gandhi Commem.

123. **56.**	90 f. black and blue	65	35

57. Prisoner's Hands in Chains. 58. Ndumba, Lady of Fashion.

1967. Air. African Liberation Day.

124. **57.**	500 f. multicoloured	3·75	1·60

1967. Congolese Dolls. Multicoloured.

125.	5 f. Type **58**	5	5
126.	10 f. Fruit vendor	8	8
127.	25 f. Girl pounding saka-saka	20	10
128.	30 f. Mother and child	25	10

59. Congo Scenery. 60. "Europafrique".

1967. Int. Tourist Year.

129. **59.**	60 f. claret, orge. & grn.	45	25

1967. Europafrique.

130. **60.**	50 f. multicoloured	40	25

61. "Sputnik 1" and "Explorer 6".

1967. Air. Space Exploration.

131. **61.**	50 f. blue, violet & chest.	35	20
132. –	75 f. lake and slate	55	35
133. –	100 f. blue, red & turq.	75	55
134. –	200 f. verm., blue & lake	1·50	1·10

DESIGNS: 75 f. "Ranger 6" and "Lunik 2". 100 f. "Mars 1" and "Mariner 4". 200 f. "Gemini" and "Vostok".

62. Brazzaville Arms.

1967. Congo Revolution. 4th Anniv.

135. **62.**	30 f. multicoloured	20	8

1967. Air. African and Malagasy Posts and Telecommunications Union. 5th Anniv. As T **55** of Central African Republic.

136.	100 f. green, red and brown	75	45

63. Jamboree Emblem, Scouts and Tents.

1967. Air. World Scout Jamboree, Idaho.
137. 63. 50 f. blue, brown & chest. 40 20
138. – 70 f. red, green and blue 55 25
DESIGN: 70 f. Saluting hand, Jamboree camp and emblem.

64. Sikorsky "S–43" Flying-boat and Map.

1967. Air. Aeromaritime Airmail Link. 30th Anniv.
139. 64. 30 f. multicoloured .. 25 12

65. Dove, Human Figures and U.N. Emblem.
66. Young Congolese.

1967. U.N. Day and Campaign in Support of U.N.
140. 65. 90 f. multicoloured . 65 35

1967. U.N.I.C.E.F. 21st Anniv.
141. 66. 90 f. black, blue & brown 65 35

67. Albert Luthuli (winner of Nobel Peace Prize) and Dove.
69. Arms of Pointe Noire.

68. Global Dance.

1968. Luthuli Commem.
142. 67. 30 f. brown and green 20 10

1968. Air. "Friendship of the Peoples".
143. 68. 70 f. brown, green & blue 55 25

1968.
144. 69. 10 f. multicoloured .. 8 5

70. "Old Man and His Grandson" (Ghirlandaio).

1968. Air. Paintings. Multicoloured.
145. 30 f. Type 70 .. .. 25 12
146. 100 f. "The Horatian Oath" (J.–L. David) 70 45
147. 200 f. "The Negress with Peonies" (Bazille) .. 1·50 95
The 100 f. and 200 f. are horiz. designs.
See also Nos. 209/13.

71. "Mother and Child".
72. Train crossing Mayombe Viaduct.

1968. Mothers' Festival.
148. 71. 15 f. black, blue & lake 10 8

1968.
149. 72. 45 f. lake, blue & green 30 15

73. Beribboned Rope.

1968. Air. Europafrique. 5th Anniv.
150. 73. 50 f. red, yellow, green and sepia 35 15

74. Daimler, 1889.

1968. Veteran Motor Cars. Multicoloured.
151. 5 f. Type 74 (postage) .. 5 5
152. 20 f. Berliet, 1897 .. 12 5
153. 60 f. Peugeot, 1898 .. 45 20
154. 80 f. Renault, 1900 .. 55 25
155. 85 f. Fiat, 1902 .. 60 35
156. 150 f. Ford, 1915 (air) .. 1·10 55
157. 200 f. Citroen .. .. 1·40 75

1968. Petroleum Refinery, Port Gentil, Gaboon. Inaug. As T 69 of Central African Republic.
158. 30 f. blue, red, green and chestnut 12 5

75. Dr. Martin Luther King.
77. Robert Kennedy.

76. "The Barricade" (Delacroix).

1968. Air. Martin Luther King Commem.
159. 75. 50 f. black, green & emerald 35 15

1968. Air. Revolution Paintings. 5th Anniv. Multicoloured.
160. 25 f. Type 76 .. .. 20 8
161. 30 f. "Destruction of the Bastille" (H. Robert).. 25 12

1968. Air. Robert Kennedy Commem.
162. 77. 50 f. black, green & red 35 15

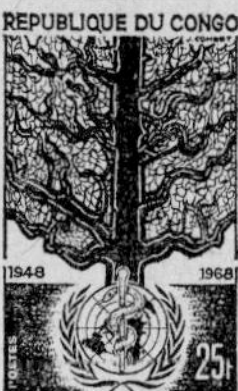

78. "Tree of Life" and W.H.O. Emblem.

1968. World Health Organization. 20th Anniv.
163. 78. 25 f. red, pur. & green 20 10

79. Start of Race.

1968. Air. Olympic Games, Mexico.
164. 79. 5 f. brown, blue & grn... 5 5
165. 20 f. green, brown & bl. 12 8
166. 60 f. brn., green & red 45 20
167. 85 f. brown red & slate 60 30
DESIGNS—VERT. 20 f. Football; 60 f. Boxing. HORIZ. 85 f. High-jumping.

1968. Air. "Philexafrique" Stamp Exn. Abidjan (1969) (1st issue). As T 74 of Central African Republic.
168. 100 f. multicoloured .. 75 70
DESIGN: 100 f. "G. de Gueidan writing" (N. de Largilliere).

1969. Air. "Philexafrique" Stamp Exn., Abidjan, Ivory Coast (2nd issue). As Type 110 of Cameroun.
169. 50 f. green, brown & mag. 40 35
DESIGN: 50 f. Pointe-Noire harbour, lumbering and Middle Congo stamp of 1933.

80. "Battle of Rivoli" (C. Vernet).

1969. Air. Napoleon Bonaparte. Birth Bicent. Multicoloured.
170. 25 f. Type 80 .. .. 25 15
171. 50 f. "Battle of Marengo" (Pajou) 45 35
172. 75 f. "Battle of Friedland" (H. Vernet) 65 30
173. 100 f. "Battle of Jena" (Thevenin) .. .. 1·10 55

81. "Che" Guevara.

1969. Air. Ernesto "Che" Guevara (Latin-American revolutionary) Commem.
174. 81. 90 f. brown, orge. & lake 60 30

82. Doll and Toys.

1969. Air. Int. Toy Fair, Nuremberg.
175. 82. 100 f. slate, mag. & orge. 65 35

83. Beribboned Bar.

1969. Air. Europafrique.
176. 83. 50 f. vio., blk. & turq. 35 20

1969. African Development Bank. 5th Anniv. As T 118 of Cameroun.
177. 25 f. brown, red & emerald 20 8
178. 30 f. brown, emerald & blue 20 10

84. Modern Bicycle.

1969. Cycles and Motor-cycles.
180. 84. 50 f. purple, orge. & brn. 30 12
181. – 75 f. black, lake & orge. 45 20
182. – 80 f. green, blue & pur. 45 25
183. – 85 f. green, slate & brn. 50 25
184. – 100 f. maroon, carmine, blue and black .. 65 35
185. – 150 f. brown, red & blk. 80 50
186. – 200 f. purple, deep green and green .. .. 1·40 60
187. – 300 f. emerald, pur. & blk. 1·90 1·00
DESIGNS: 75 f. "Hirondelle" cycle. 80 f. Folding cycle. 85 f. "Peugeot" cycle. 100 f. "Excelsior Manxman" motor-cycle. 150 f. "Norton" motor-cycle. 200 f. "Brough Superior" motor-cycle. 300 f. "Matchless and N.L.G.-J.A.P.S." motor-cycle.

85. Train crossing the Mayombe.

1969. African Int. Tourist Year. Multicoloured.
188. 40 f. Train entering Mbamba Tunnel (vert.) 25 12
189. 60 f. Type 85 .. .. 40 15

86. Mortar Tanks.

1969. Loutete Cement Works.
190. 86. 10 f. slate, brown & lake 5 5
191. – 15 f. violet, blue & brn. 10 8
192. – 25 f. blue, brown & red 15 10
193. – 30 f. indigo, violet and ultramarine .. 20 12
DESIGNS—VERT. 15 f. Mixing tower. 25 f. Cableway. HORIZ. 30 f. General view of works.

1969. A.S.E.C.N.A. 10th Anniv. As T 121 of Cameroun.
195. 100 f. brown 65 35

87. Harvesting Pineapples.

1969. Int. Labour Organization. 50th Anniv.
196. 87. 25 f. chest., grn. & blue 15 8
197. – 30 f. slate, purple & red 20 10
DESIGN: 30 f. Operating lathe.

88. Textile Plant.

1970. "SOTEXCO" Textile Plant, Kinsoundi.
198. 88. 15 f. black, vio. & emer. 10 5
199. – 20 f. green, carmine & purple 12 5
200. – 25 f. brn., bl. & new bl. 15 5
201. – 30 f. brown, red & slate 20 10
DESIGNS: 20 f. Spinning machines. 25 f. Printing textiles. 30 f. Checking finished cloth.

90. Cosmos Hotel, Brazzaville.

89. Linzolo Church.

91. Artist at work.

92. Diosso Gorges.

1970. Buildings.

202. **89.** 25 f. grn., choc. & indigo 15 8
203. **90.** 90 f. choc., green & blue 55 25

1970. Air. "Art and Culture".

204. **91.** 100 f. chest., plum & grn. 65 35
205. – 150 f. plum, lake & green 1·00 50
206. – 200 f. brn., choc. & ochre 1·40 75

DESIGNS: 150 f. Lesson in wood-carving. 200 f. Potter at wheel.

1970. Tourism.

207. **92.** 70 f. pur., choc. & green 45 20
208. – 90 f. pur., green & brown 60 25

DESIGN: 90 f. Foulakari Falls.

1970. Air. Paintings. As T **70**. Multicoloured.

209. 150 f. "Child with Cherries" (J. Russell) .. .. 1·00 50
210. 200 f. "Erasmus" (Holbein the younger) .. .. 1·40 65
211. 250 f. "Silence" (Bernadino Luini) .. .. 1·60 80
212. 300 f. "Scenes from the Scio Massacre" (Delacroix) 2·00 1·00
213. 500 f. "Capture of Constantinople" (Delacroix) .. 3·25 1·75

93. Aurichalcite.

94. "Volvaria esculenta".

1970. Air. Minerals. Multicoloured.

214. 100 f. Type **93** 65 35
215. 150 f. Dioptase .. .. 1·00 50

1970. Mushrooms. Multicoloured.

216. 5 f. Type **94** 5 5
217. 10 f. "Termitomyces entolomoides" 5 5
218. 15 f. "Termitomyces microcarpus" 10 5
219. 25 f. "Termitomyces aurantiacus" 15 8
220. 30 f. "Termitomyces mammiformis" 20 10
221. 50 f. "Tremella fuciformis" 35 15

95. Laying Cable.

96. Mother feeding Child

1970. Laying of Coaxial Cable, Brazzaville. Pointe-Noire.

222. **95.** 25 f. choc., brn. & blue 15 10
223. – 30 f. brown and green .. 20 10

DESIGN: 30 f. Diesel locomotive and cable-laying gang.

1970. New U.P.U. Headquarters Building, Berne. As T **126** of Cameroun.

224. 30 f. purple, slate and plum 20 10

1970. Mothers' Day. Multicoloured.

225. 85 f. Type **96** 55 35
226. 90 f. Mother suckling baby 60 35

97. U.N. Emblem and Trygve Lie.

98. Lenin in Cap.

1970. United Nations. 25th Anniv.

227. **97.** 100 f. blue, indigo & lake 65 50
228. – 100 f. lilac, carmine and lake 65 50
229. – 100 f. grn., bl.-grn. & lake 65 50

DESIGNS—VERT. No. 228, as Type **97**, but with portrait of Dag Hammarskjoeld. HORIZ. 229, as Type **97**, but with portrait of U Thant and arrangement reversed.

1970. Air. Lenin. Birth Cent.

231. **98.** 45 f. brown, yell. & grn. 30 12
232. – 75 f. brown, claret and ultramarine .. 50 25

DESIGN: 75 f. Lenin seated (after Vassiliev).

99. "Brillantaisia vogeliana".

100. Karl Marx.

1970. "Flora and Fauna". Multicoloured.

(a) Flowers. Horiz. designs.

233. 1 f. Type **99** 5 5
234. 2 f. "Plectranthus decurrens" 5 5
235. 3 f. "Myrianthemum mirabile" 5 5
236. 5 f. "Connarus griffonianus" 5

(b) Insects. Vert. designs.

237. 10 f. "Sternotomis variabilis" 5 5
238. 15 f. "Chelorrhina polyphemus" 10 5
239. 20 f. "Metopodontus savagei" 12 5

1970. Air. Founders of Communism.

240. **100.** 50 f. choc., grn. & lake 35 15
241. – 50 f. choc., blue & lake 35 15

DESIGN: No. 241, Friedrich Engels.

101. Kenthrosaurus.

1970. Prehistoric Creatures. Multicoloured.

242. 15 f. Type **101** 10 5
243. 20 f. Dinotherium .. 12 8
244. 60 f. Brachiosaurus .. 40 15
245. 80 f. Arsinoitherium .. 50 25

Nos. 243/4 are vert.

102. "Mikado 141" Steam Engine (1932).

1970. Locomotives of Congo Railways. (1st series).

246. **102.** 40 f. black, grn. & pur. 25 12
247. – 60 f. black, green & blue 40 20
248. – 75 f. black, red & blue 50 20
249. – 85 f. red, green & orge. 55 25

DESIGNS: 60 f. Type 130+032 Steam loco (1947). 75 f. Alsthom BB 1100 engine (1962). 85 f. C.E.M. C.A.F.L. "BB BB 302" diesel (1969).

See also Nos. 371/4.

103. Lilienthal's Glider, 1891.

1970. Air. History of Flight and Space Travel.

250. **103.** 45 f. brown, blue & red 30 15
251. – 50 f. green & brown .. 35 20
252. – 70 f. brown, lake & blue 50 25
253. – 90 f. brown, olive & blue 65 25

DESIGNS: 50 f. Lindbergh's "Spirit of St. Louis", 1927. 70 f. "Sputnik I". 90 f. First man on the Moon, 1969.

104. "Wise Man".

1970. Air. Christmas. Stained-glass Windows, Brazzaville Cathedral. Multicoloured.

254. 100 f. Type **104** 65 35
255. 150 f. "Shepherd" .. .. 1·00 50
256. 250 f. "Angels" .. .. 1·60 90

105. "Cogniauxia padolaena".

106. Marilyn Monroe.

1971. Tropical Flowers. Multicoloured.

258. 1 f. Type **105** 5 5
259. 2 f. "Celosia cristata" .. 5 5
260. 5 f. "Plumeria acutifolia" 5 5
261. 10 f. "Bauhinia variegata" 5 5
262. 15 f. "Euphorbia pulcherrima" 8 5
263. 20 f. "Thunbergia grandiflora" 10 5

See also D 264/9.

1971. Air. Great Names of the Cinema.

270. **106.** 100 f. brn., blue & grn. 60 25
271. – 150 f. mve., blue & pur. 90 40
272. – 200 f. brown and blue 1·20 50
273. – 250 f. plum, blue & grn. 1·50 65

PORTRAITS: 150 f. Martine Carol. 200 f. Eric K. von Stroheim. 250 f. Sergei Eisenstein.

107. "Carrying the Cross" (Veronese).

1971. Air. Easter. Religious Paintings. Multicoloured.

274. 100 f. Type **107** 60 30
275. 150 f. "Christ on the Cross" (Burgundian School c. 1500) (vert.) 90 45
276. 200 f. "Descent from the Cross" (Van der Weyden) 1·25 60
277. 250 f. "The Entombment" (Flemish School c.1500) (vert.) .. .. 1·50 75
278. 500 f. "The Resurrection" (Memling) (vert.) .. 3·00 1·50

108. Telecommunications Map.

1971. Air. Pan-African Telecommunications Network.

279. **108.** 70 f. multicoloured .. 45 20
280. 85 f. multicoloured .. 50 25
281. 90 f. multicoloured .. 55 30

109. Global Emblem.

1971. Air. World Telecommunications Day.

282. **109.** 65 f. multicoloured .. 40 20

110. Green Night Adder.

111. Afro-Japanese Allegory.

1971. Reptiles. Multicoloured.

283. 5 f. Type **110** 5 5
284. 10 f. African egg-eating snake (horiz.) 5 5
285. 15 f. Flap-necked chameleon 10 5
286. 20 f. Nile crocodile (horiz.) 15 10
287. 25 f. Rock python (horiz.) 20 15
288. 30 f. Gaboon viper .. 20 15
289. 40 f. Brown house snake (horiz.) 25 20
290. 45 f. Jameson's mamba .. 35 20

1971. Air. "Philatokyo 1971". Stamp Exhib., Tokyo.

291. **111.** 75 f. black, mve. & violet 45 25
292. – 150 f. brn., red & pur. 90 55

DESIGN: 150 f. "Tree of Life", Japanese girl and African in mask.

112. "Bunaea alcinoe". 113. Japanese Scout.

1971. Caterpillars. Multicoloured.

293. 10 f. "Pseudimbrasia deyrollei" (horiz.) .. 8 5
294. 15 f. Type **112** 10 8
295. 20 f. "Epiphora vacuna ploetzi" (horiz.) .. 15 10
296. 25 f. "Imbrasia eblis" (horiz.) 20 12
297. 30 f. "Imbrasia dione" .. 20 15
298. 40 f. "Holocera angelata" (horiz.) 35 20

1971. World Scout Jamboree, Asagiri, Japan (1st issue). On foil.

299. **113.** 90 f. silver (postage) .. 50
300. – 90 f. silver 50
301. – 90 f. silver 50
302. – 90 f. silver 50
303. – 1,000 f. gold (air) .. 6·50

DESIGNS—VERT. No. 300, French Scout No. 301, Congolese Scout. No. 302, Lord Baden-Powell. HORIZ. No. 303, Scouts and Lord Baden-Powell.

Nos. 299/302 were issued together se-tenant in blocks of four within the sheet.

114. Olympic Torch.

115. African and Japanese Mask.

1971. Air. Olympic Games, Munich.
304. **114.** 150 f. red, grn. & pur. 90 55
305. – 350 f. violet, grn. & brn. 2·10 1·10
DESIGN-HORIZ. 350 f. Sporting cameos within Olympic rings.

1971. Air. World Scout Jamboree, Asagiri, Japan (2nd issue).
306. – 85 f. pur., brn. & green 50 20
307. **115.** 90 f. brn., violet & lake 55 25
308. – 100 f. grn., lake & brn. 60 30
309. – 250 f. brn., red & grn. 1·50 75
DESIGNS—HORIZ. 85 f. Scout badge, dragon and Congolese wood carving. 250 f. Congolese mask, geisha and scout badge. VERT. 100 f. Japanese woman and African.

116. Running.

1971. Air. Modern Olympic Games. 75th Anniv.
310. **116.** 75 f. brn., blue & lake 45 20
311. – 85 f. brn., blue & red 50 25
312. – 90 f. brown & violet.. 50 25
313. – 100 f. brown and blue 60 30
314. – 150 f. brn., red & grn. 90 50
DESIGNS: 85 f. Hurdling. 90 f. Various events. 100 f. Wrestling. 150 f. Boxing.

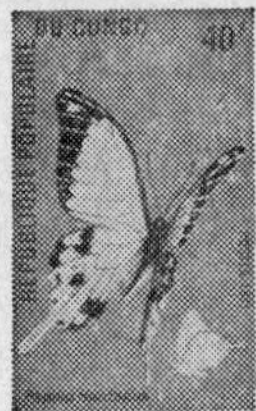

117. " Papilio dardanus ". **118.** African and European Workers.

1971. Butterflies. Multicoloured.
315. 30 f. " Cymothae sangaris " (horiz.) 20 10
316. 40 f. Type **117** 35 15
317. 75 f. " Iolaus timon " (horiz.) 45 25
318. 90 f. " Papilio phorcas ".. 65 40
319. 100 f. " Euchloron megaera " (horiz.) .. 90 55

1971. Racial Equality Year.
320. **118.** 50 f. multicoloured .. 30 15

119. De Gaulle and Congo 1966 Brazzaville Conference Stamp.

1971. Air. General De Gaulle. 1st Death Anniv.
321. **119.** 500 f. brn., grn. & red 3·00 2·00
322. – 1000 f. red & grn. on gold 6·50
323. – 1000 f. red & grn. on gold 6·50
DESIGNS—VERT. (29×38 mm.). No. 322, Tribute by Pres. Ngouabi. No. 323, De Gaulle and Cross of Lorraine.

1971. Air. African and Malagasy Posts and Telecommunications Union. 10th Anniv. Similar to T **153** of Cameroun. Multicoloured.
324. 100 f. U.A.M.P.T. H.Q. and Congolese woman .. 60 35

1971. Brazzaville-Pointe Noire Cable Link Inaug. Surch **REPUBLIQUE POPULAIRE DU CONGO INAUGURATION DE LA LIAISON COXIALE 18-11-71** and new value.
325. **95.** 30 f. on 25 f. chocolate, brown and blue .. 20 12
326. – 40 f. on 30 f. brown and green (No. 223) .. 25 15

120. Congo Republic Flag and Allegory of Revolution.

1971. Air. Revolution. 8th Anniv.
327. **120.** 100 f. multicoloured.. 60 35

121. Congolese with Flag.

1971. Air. Congolese Workers' Party. 2nd Anniv., and Adoption of New National Flag. Multicoloured.
328. 30 f. Type **121** 15 8
329. 40 f. National flag.. .. 20 10

122. Map and Emblems. **123.** Lion.

1971. " Work-Democracy-Peace ".
330. **122.** 30 f. multicoloured .. 20 12
331. 40 f. multicoloured .. 20 10
332. 100 f. multicoloured 60 30

1972. Wild Animals.
333. **123.** 1 f. brn., bl. and grn... 5 5
334. – 2 f. brn., grn. and red 5 5
335. – 3 f. brn., red and lake 5 5
336. – 4 f. brn., blue and vio. 5 5
337. – 5 f. brn., green and red 5 5
338. – 20 f. brn., bl. and orge. 15 8
339. – 30 f. grn., emer. & brn. 20 10
340. – 40 f. blk., grn. and blue 25 10
DESIGNS—HORIZ. 2 f. Elephants. 3 f. Leopard. 4 f. Hippopotamus. 20 f. Potto. 30 f. De Brazza's monkey. VERT. 5 f. Gorilla. 40 f. Chimpanzee.

124. Book Year Emblem. **125.** Team Captain with Cup.

1972. Air. Int. Book Year.
341. **124.** 50 f. grn., yellow & red 25 12

1973. Air. Congolese Victory in Africa Football Cup. Multicoloured.
342. 100 f. Type **125** 55 35
343. 100 f. Congolese team (horiz.) 55 35

126. Girl with Bird. **127.** Miles Davis.

1973. Air. U.N. Environmental Conservation Conf., Stockholm.
344. **126.** 85 f. grn., blue & orge. 40 25

1973. Air. Famous Negro Musicians.
345. **127.** 125 f. multicoloured 55 30
346. – 140 f. red, lilac & mauve 65 35
347. – 160 f. grn., emer. & orge. 75 40
348. – 175 f. pur., red & blue 90 45
DESIGNS: 140 f. Ella Fitzgerald. 160 f. Count Basie. 175 f. John Coltrane.

128. Hurdling.

1973. Air. Olympic Games, Munich (1972).
349. **128.** 100 f. violet & mauve 50 25
350. – 150 f. violet and green 75 40
351. – 250 f. red and blue .. 1·25 70
DESIGNS-VERT. 150 f. Pole-vaulting. HORIZ. 250 f. Wrestling.

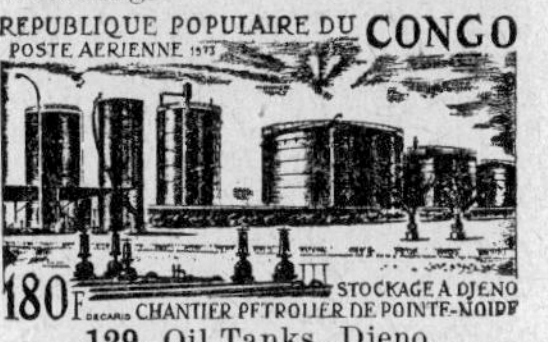

129. Oil Tanks, Djeno.

1973. Air. Oil Installations, Pointe Noire.
352. **129.** 180 f. indigo, red & blue 90 45
353. – 230 f. black, red & blue 1·00 55
354. – 240 f. maroon, blue & red 1·25 60
355. – 260 f. black, red and blue 1·40 70
DESIGNS-VERT. 230 f. Oil-well head. 240 f. Drill in operation. HORIZ. 260 f. Off-shore oil-well.

130. Lunar Module and Astronaut on Moon.

1973. Air. Moon Flight of " Apollo 17 ".
356. **130.** 250 f. multicoloured 1·25 80

131. " Telecommunications ".

1973. Air. World Telecommunications Day.
357. **131.** 120 f. multicoloured .. 50 25

132. Copernicus and Solar System.

1973. Air. Copernicus (astronomer). 500th Birth Anniv.
358. **132.** 50 f. grn., blue & light bl. 20 15

133. Rocket and African Scenes.

1973. Air. World Meteorological Organization. Centenary.
359. **133.** 50 f. multicoloured .. 20 15

134. W.H.O. Emblem. **136.** General View of Brewery.

135. " Study of a White Horse ".

1973. World Health Organization. 25th Anniv. Multicoloured.
360. 40 f. Type **134** 15 8
361. 50 f. Design similar to T **134** (horz.) 20 10

1973. Air. Paintings by Delacroix. Mult.
362. 150 f. Type **135** 65 45
363. 250 f. " Sleeping Lion " .. 1·10 75
364. 300 f. " Tiger and Lion ".. 1·40 90
See also Nos. 384/6 and 437/40.

1973. Congo Brewers Assn. Views of Kronenbourg Brewery.
365. **136.** 30 f. blue, red & bright bl. 12 5
366. – 40 f. grey, orge. & red 15 8
367. – 75 f. blue, red & black 30 12
368. – 85 f. multicoloured .. 35 20
369. – 100 f. multicoloured 45 30
370. – 250 f. green, brn. & red 1·10 65
DESIGNS: 40 f. Laboratory. 75 f. Regulating vats. 85 f. Control console. 100 f. Bottling plant. 250 f. Capping bottles.

1973. Locomotives of Congo Railways (2nd series). As T **102.** Multicoloured.
371. 30 f. Golwe steam locomotive c. 1935 .. .. .. 12 5
372. 40 f. Diesel-electric locomotive, 1935 .. .. 15 8
373. 75 f. Withcomb diesel-electric locomotive, 1946 .. 35 12
374. 85 f. CC/200 diesel-electric locomotive, 1973 .. 40 20

137. Stamp Map, Album, Dancer and Oil Rig. **138.** President Marien Ngouabi.

1973. Air. Int. Stamp Exhib., Brazzaville and 10th Anniv. of Revolution.
375. **137.** 30 f. grey, lilac and brn. 12 5
376. – 40 f. red, brn. & purple 15 8
377. **137.** 100 f. blue, brn. & pur. 45 35
378. – 100 f. lilac, mar. & red 45 35
DESIGNS: 40 f., 100 f. Map, album and Globes.

1973. Air.
379. **138.** 30 f. multicoloured .. 12 5
380. 40 f. mnlticoloured .. 15 8
381. 75 f. multicoloured .. 35 15

1973. Pan-African Drought Relief. No. 236 surch. **SECHERESSE SOLIDARITE AFRICAINE** and value.
382. 100 f. on 5 f. multicoloured 45 35

1973. African and Malagasy Posts and Telecommunications Union. 12th Anniv. As T **182** of Cameroun.
383. 100 f. violet, blue & purple 45 30

1973. Air. Europafrique. As T **135.** Mult.
384. 100 f. " Wild Dog " .. 45 35
385. 100 f. " Lion and Leopard " 45 35
386. 100 f. " Adam and Eve in Paradise " 45 35
Nos. 384/6 are details taken from J. Brueghel's " Earth and Paradise ".

139. " Apollo " and " Soyuz " Spacecraft.

1973. Air. International Co-operation in Space.
387. **139.** 40 f. brn., red & blue.. 15 10
388. – 80 f. blue, red & green 35 20
DESIGN: 80 f. Spacecraft docked.

140. U.P.U. Monument and Satellite.

1973. Air. U.P.U. Day.
389. **140.** 80 f. blue & ultramarine 35 20

1973. Air. " Skylab " Space Laboratory. As T **139.**
390. 30 f. grn., brn. & blue .. 12 8
391. 40 f. grn., red & orange .. 15 10
DESIGNS: 30 f. Astronauts walking outside " Skylab ". 40 f. " Skylab " and " Apollo " spacecraft docked.

141. Hive and Bees.

1973. " Labour and Economy ".
392. **141.** 30 f. grn., blue & red 12 5
393. 40 f. green, blue & grn. 15 8

142. Congo Family and Emblems.

1973. World Food Programme. 10th Anniv.
394. **142.** 30 f. brown and red .. 12 5
395. – 40 f. orge., green & blue 15 8
396. – 100 f. brn., grn. & orge. 45 35
DESIGNS—HORIZ. 40 f. Ears of corn and emblems. VERT. 100 f. Ear of corn, granary and emblems.

143. Goalkeeper. **144.** Runners.

1973. Air. World Football Cup Championships, West Germany (1974). (1st issue).
397. **143.** 40 f. grn., dark brown and brown 15 10
398. – 100 f. grn., red & violet 45 35
DESIGN: 100 f. Foward.
See also Nos. 403 and 408.

1973. Air. 2nd African Games, Lagos, Nigeria.
399. **144.** 40 f. red, green & brn. 15 10
400. 100 f. grn., red & brn. 45 35

145. Pres. Kennedy. **146.** Map and Flag.

1973. Air. Pres. Kennedy. 10th Anniv.
401. **145.** 150 f. black, gold & blue 65 50

1973. Air. Congo Worker's Party. 4th Anniv.
402. **146.** 40 f multicoloured .. 15 10

147. Players seen through Goalkeeper's Legs.

1974. Air. World Cup Football Championships, West Germany (2nd issue).
403. **147.** 250 f. grn., red & brn. 1·10 80

148. Globe, Flags and Names of Dead Astronauts.

1974. Air. Conquest of Space.
404. **148.** 30 f. brn., bl. & red .. 12 5
405. – 40 f. multicoloured .. 15 10
406. – 100 f. brn., bl. & red .. 45 35
DESIGNS: 40 f. Gagarin and Shepard. 100 f. Leonov in space, and Armstrong on Moon.

149. Amilcar Cabral. **150.** Spacecraft docking.

1974. Cabral (Guinea-Bissau guerilla leader). 1st Death Anniv.
407. **149.** 100 f. purple, red & bl. 40 35

1974. Air. West Germany's Victory in World Cup Football Championships. As T **147.**
408. 250 f. brn., pink & blue .. 1·10 80
DESIGN: Footballers within Ball.

1974. Air. Soviet-American Space Co-operation.
409. **150.** 200 f. bl., violet & red 80 65
410. – 300 f. blue, brn. & red 1·25 90
DESIGN—HORIZ. 300 f. Spacecraft on segments of globe.

151. "Sound and Vision".

1974. Air. U.P.U. Cent.
411. **151.** 500 f. black and red .. 2·25 1·50

152. Felix Eboue and Cross of Lorraine.

1974. Eboue (" Free French Leader). 30th Death Anniv.
412. **152.** 30 f. multicoloured .. 10 5
413. 40 f. multicoloured .. 15 5

153. Lenin.

1974. Air. Lenin. 50th Death Anniv.
414. **153.** 150 f. orge, red & grn. 60 45

1974. Churchill. Birth Cent. As T **152.** Mult.
415. 200 f. Churchill and Order of the Garter 75 55

1974. Gugliemo Marconi (radio pioneer). Birth Cent. As T **152.** Multicoloured.
416. 200 f. Marconi and early apparatus 75 55

1974. Air. Berne Convention. Cent. No. 411 surch. **9 OCTOBRE 1974**, and value.
417. **151.** 300 f. on 500 f. blk. & red 1·40 90

154. Pineapple.

1974. Congolese Fruits. Multicoloured.
418. 30 f. Type **154** 10 5
419. 30 f. Bananas 10 5
420. 30 f. Safous 10 5
421. 40 f. Avocado pears .. 15 8
422. 40 f. Mangoes 15 8
423. 40 f. Papaya 15 8
424. 40 f. Oranges 15 8

155. Gen. Charles De Gaulle.

1974. Brazzaville Conference. 30th Anniv.
425. **155.** 100 f. brown and green 40 35

1974. Central African Customs and Economic Union. 10th Anniv. As Nos. 734/5 of Cameroun.
426. 40 f. mult. (postage) .. 12 10
427. 100 f. multicoloured (air) 40 25

156. George Stephenson (railway pioneer) and Early and Modern Locomotives. (Illustration reduced. Actual size 77 × 23 mm.).

1974. Public Railways. 150th Anniv. (1975).
428. **156.** 75 f. olive and green .. 35 20

157. Irish Setter.

1974. Dogs. Multicoloured.
429. 30 f. Type **157** 12 5
430. 40 f. Borzoi 15 10
431. 75 f. Pointer 25 15
432. 100 f. Great Dane .. 40 30

1974. Cats. As T **157.** Multicoloured.
433. 30 f. Havana chestnut .. 12 5
434. 40 f. Red Persian .. 15 10
435. 75 f. British blue .. 25 15
436. 100 f. African serval .. 40 30

1974. Air. Impressionist Paintings. As T **135.** Multicoloured.
437. 30 f. " The Argenteuil Regatta " (Monet) .. 12 8
438. 40 f. " Seated Dancer " (Degas) (vert.) .. 15 10
439. 50 f. " Girl on Swing " (Renoir) (vert.) .. 20 15
440. 75 f. " Girl in Straw Hat " (Renoir) (vert.) .. 30 25

158. National Fair.

1974. Air. National Fair, Brazzaville.
441. **158.** 30 f. multicoloured .. 10 5

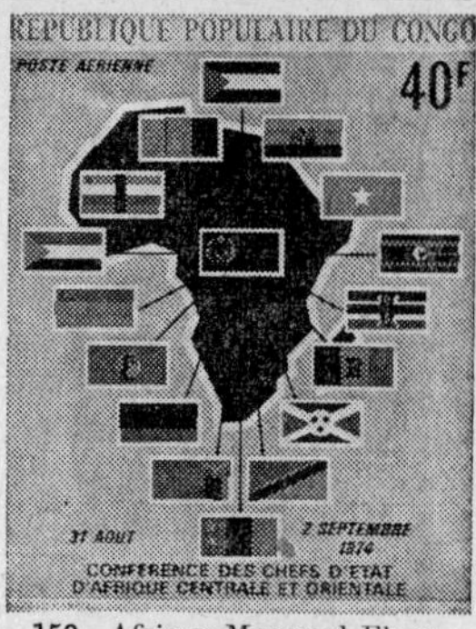

159. African Map and Flags.

1974. Air. African Heads-of-State Conference, Brazzaville.
442. **159.** 40 f. multicoloured .. 15 8

160. Flags and Dove.

1974. Congo Labour Party. Fifth Anniv.
443. **160.** 30 f. red, yellow & green 12 5
444. – 40 f. brown, red & yellow 15 10
DESIGN: 40 f. Hands holding flowers and hammer.

161. U Thant and U.N. Headquarters.

1975. U Thant (U.N. Secretary-General). 1st Death Anniv.
445. **161.** 50 f. multicoloured .. 15 10

1975. Paul G. Hoffman (U.N. Programme for Underdeveloped Countries administrator). 1st Death Anniv. As T **161.** Multicoloured.
446. 50 f. Hoffman and U.N. " Laurel Wreath " (vert.) 15 10

162. Workers and Development.

1975. National Economic Development.
447. **162.** 40 f. multicoloured .. 15 8

163. Mao Tse-tung and Map of China.

1975. Chinese People's Republic. 25th Anniv. (1974).
448. **163.** 75 f. red, mauve & blue 25 15

164. Women with Hoe.

1975. Revolutionary Union of Congolese Women. 10th Anniv.

449. **164.** 40 f. multicoloured .. 12 10

165. Paris-Brussels Line, 1890. (Illustration reduced, actual size 80×25 mm.)

1975. Air. Railway History. Multicoloured.

450. 50 f. Type **165** 15 8
451. 75 f. Santa Fe Line, 1880 .. 30 25

166. " Five Weeks in a Balloon ".

1975. Air. Jules Verne (novelist). 70th Death Anniv. Multicoloured.

452. 40 f. Type **166** 15 8
453. 50 f. " Around the World in 80 Days " 15 10

167. Line-up of Team.

1975. Victory of Cara Football Team in Africa Cup. Multicoloured.

454. 30 f. Type **167** 12 5
455. 40 f. Receiving trophy (vert.) 12 10

168. 1935 Citroen and Notre Dame Cathedral, Paris.

1975. Veteran Cars. Multicoloured.

456. 30 f. Type **168** 12 5
457. 40 f. 1911 Alfa Romeo and St. Peter's, Rome .. 12 10
458. 50 f. 1926 Rolls Royce and Houses of Parliament, London 20 15
459. 75 f. 1893 C. F. Duryea and Manhattan skyline, New York 30 25

169. " Soyuz " Spacecraft.

1975. Air. " Apollo-Soyuz " Space Test Project.

460. **169.** 95 f. black and red .. 40 25
461. – 100 f. blk., vio. & blue 40 25

DESIGNS: 100 f. " Apollo " Spacecraft.

170. Tipoye Carriage.

1975. Traditional Congo Transport. Mult.

462. 30 f. Type **170** 12 5
463. 40 f. Pirogue canoe .. 15 8

171. " Raising the Flag ".

1975. Institutions of Popular Tasks. 2nd Anniv.

464. **171.** 30 f. multicoloured .. 12 5

1975. Congolese National Conference. 3rd Anniv. As T **171**. Multicoloured.

465. 40 f. Conference Hall .. 15 8

172. Fishing with Wooden Baskets.

1975. Traditional Fishing. Multicoloured.

466. 30 f. Type **172** 12 5
467. 40 f. Fishing with line (vert.) 15 8
468. 60 f. Fishing with spear (vert.) 25 20
469. 90 f. Fishing with net .. 35 25

173. Chopping Firewood.

174. " Esanga ".

1975. Domestic Chores. Multicoloured.

470. 30 f. Type **173** 12 5
471. 30 f. Pounding meat .. 12 5
472. 40 f. Preparing manioc (horiz.) 15 8

1975. Traditional Musical Instruments. Multicoloured.

473. 30 f. Type **174** 12 5
474. 40 f. " Kalakwa " 15 8
475. 60 f. " Likembe " 25 20
476. 75 f. " Ngongui " 30 25

175. " Dzeke " Shell Money.

1975. Ancient Congolese Money.

477. **175.** 30 f. brown and red .. 12 5
478. – 30 f. brown and violet 12 5
479. – 40 f. brown and blue .. 15 8
480. – 50 f. blue and brown .. 20 15
481. – 60 f. brown and green 25 20
482. – 85 f. green and brown 35 25

DESIGNS: 30 f. " Okengo " iron money. 40 f. Gallic coin (60 BC). 50 f. Roman coin (37 BC). 60 f. Danubian coin (2nd century BC). 85 f. Greek coin (4th century BC).

176. Dr. Schweitzer.

178. Boxing.

177. " Moschops ".

1975. Dr. Albert Schweitzer. Birth Cent.

483. **176.** 75 f. grn., mve. & brn. 30 20

1975. Prehistoric Animals. Multicoloured.

484. 55 f. Type **177** 20 15
485. 75 f. " Tyrannosaurus " .. 30 20
486. 95 f. " Cryptocleidus " .. 35 35
487. 100 f. " Stegosauras " .. 40 25

1975. Air. Olympic Games, Montreal (1976). Multicoloured.

488. 40 f. Type **178** 12 8
489. 50 f. Basketball 20 15
490. 85 f. Cycling (horiz.) .. 35 25
491. 95 f. High jumping (horiz.) 35 25
492. 100 f. Throwing the javelin (horiz.) 40 25
493. 150 f. Running (horiz.) .. 60 40

179. Alexander Fleming. (scientist) (20th Death Anniv.).

1975. Celebrities.

494. **179.** 60 f. black, green & red 25 20
495. – 95 f. black, blue & red 35 25
496. – 95 f. green, red & lilac 35 25

DESIGNS: No. 495, Clement Ader (aviation pioneer) (50th Death Anniv.). No. 496, Andre Marie Ampere (physicist) (Birth Bicent).

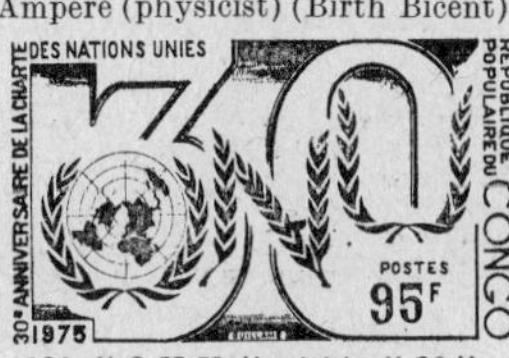

180. " O.N.U. " within " 30 ".

1975. United Nations Organisation. 30th Anniv.

497. **180.** 95 f. blue, lake & green 35 25

181. President and Crowd.

1975. Parti Congolais due Travail (P.C.T.). 6th Anniv. Multicoloured.

498. 30 f. Type **181** (postage) .. 12 8
499. 35 f. " Echo "–P.C.T. " man " with roll of newsprint and radio waves .. 12 8
500. 60 f. Party members with Flag (air). 25 20

SIZES: 35 f. 36×27 mm. 60 f. 26×38 mm.

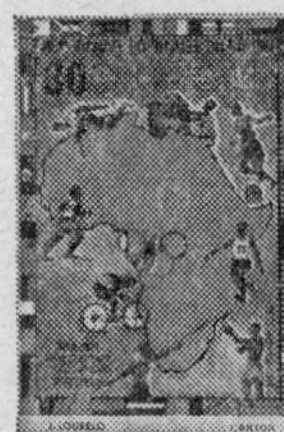

182. Map of Africa and Sportsmen.

1976. Air. 1st African Games, Brazzaville. 10th Anniv.

501. **182.** 30 f. multicoloured .. 15 10

183. Chained Women with Broken Link.

1976. International Women's Year. Multicoloured.

502. 35 f. Type **183** 15 10
503. 60 f. Global handclasp .. 30 20

184. Steamboat " Alphonse Fondere ".

1976. Air. Old-time Ships (1st series). Multicoloured.

504. 30 f. Type **184** 15 10
505. 40 f. Steam paddler " Hamburg ", 1839 .. .. 20 12
506. 50 f. Steam paddler " Gomer ", 1831 .. 25 15
507. 60 f. " Great Eastern ", 1858 .. .. .. 30 20
508. 95 f. Steamboat " J. M. White II ", 1878 .. 45 35

See also Nos. 515/18.

185. " The Peasant Family " (Le Nain).

1976. Air. Europafrique. Paintings. Multicoloured.

509. 60 f. Type **185** 30 20
510. 80 f. " Boy with spinning Top " (Chardin) .. 40 25
511. 95 f. " Venus and Aeneas " (Poussin) 45 35
512. 100 f. " The Sabines " (David) 45 35

186. A. Graham Bell and Early Telephone.

1976. Telephone Centenary.

513. **186.** 35 f. brown, light brown and yellow (postage) 15 10
514. **186.** 60 f. red, mauve and pink (air) 30 20

1976. Air. Old-time Ships (2nd series). As T **184**.

515. 5 f. green, blue and brown 5 5
516. 10 f. olive, blue and brown 5 5
517. 15 f. grn., blue & dark grn. 8 5
518. 20 f. dark blue, green blue and blue 10 5

SHIPS: HORIZ. 5 f. Steamboat " Alphonse Fondere ", 10 f. Steam paddler " Hamburg ", 1839, 15 f. Steam paddler " Gomer ", 1831, 20 f. " Great Eastern ", 1858.

187. Fruit Market.

1976. Market Scenes. Multicoloured.

519. 35 f. Type **187** 15 10
520. 60 f. Laying out produce .. 30 20

OFFICIAL STAMPS

O 1. Arms.

1968.

O 142.	O 1.	1 f. multicoloured ..	5	5
O 143.		2 f. multicoloured ..	5	5
O 144.		5 f. multicoloured ..	5	5
O 145.		10 f. multicoloured ..	8	8
O 146.		25 f. multicoloured ..	10	5
O 147.		30 f. multicoloured ..	12	5
O 148.		50 f. multicoloured ..	35	20
O 149.		85 f. multicoloured ..	65	35
O 150.		100 f. multicoloured	75	40
O 151.		200 f. multicoloured	1·50	90

POSTAGE DUE STAMPS

D 1. Letter-carrier.

1961. Transport designs.

D 19.	50 c. bistre, red and blue	5	5
D 20.	50 c. bistre, purple & blue	5	5
D 21.	1 f. brown, red and green	5	5
D 22.	1 f. green, red and lake ..	5	5
D 23.	2 f. brown, green and blue	5	5
D 24.	2 f. brown, green and blue	5	5
D 25.	5 f. sepia and violet ..	5	5
D 26.	5 f. sepia and violet ..	5	5
D 27.	10 f. chocolate, bl. & grn.	10	10
D 28.	10 f. chocolate and green	10	10
D 29.	25 f. choc., blue & turq.	20	20
D 30.	25 f. black and blue ..	20	20

DESIGNS: Nos. D 19, Type D 1. D 20 "Broussard" monoplane. D 21, Hammock-bearers. D 22. "Land Rover" car. D 23, Pirogue. D 24, River steamer of 1932. D 25, Cyclist. D 26, Motor lorry. D 27, Steam locomotive. D 28, Diesel locomotive. D 29, Seaplane of 1935. D 30, "Boeing 707" jet airliner.

1971. Tropical Flowers. Similar to T **105**, but inscr. "Timbre-Taxe". Multicoloured

D 264.	1 f. Stylised bouquet ..	5	5
D 265.	2 f. "Phaeomeria magnifica"	5	5
D 266.	5 f. "Millettia laurentii"	5	5
D 267.	10 f. "Polianthes tuberosa"	5	5
D 268.	15 f. "Pyrostegia venusta"	8	8
D 269.	20 f. "Hibiscus rosa sinensis"	10	10

COOK ISLANDS BC

A group of islands in the S. Pacific under New Zealand control, including Aitutaki, Niue, Penrhyn and Rarotonga. Granted Self-Government in 1965.

See also issues for Aitutaki and Penrhyn Island.

1967. 100 cents = 1 dollar.

1.

ILLUSTRATIONS
British Commonwealth and all overprints and surcharges are FULL SIZE. Foreign Countries have been reduced to ¾-LINEAR.

1892.

1.	1.	1d. black	8·00	10·00
2.		1½d. mauve	10·00	12·00
3.		2½d. blue	12·00	14·00
4.		10d. red	40·00	38·00

2. Torea or Wry-bill.

3. Queen Makea Takau.

1893.

11.	2.	½d. blue	1·50	2·00
28.		½d. green	60	1·25
13.	3.	1d. brown	1·50	2·75
12.		1d. blue	1·00	2·00
40.		1d. red	90	2·00
14a.		1½d. mauve	1·40	2·75
15a.	2.	2d. brown	1·50	2·75
16a.	3.	2½d. red	1·60	3·50
32.		2½d. blue	1·50	2·75
9.		5d. black	4·00	6·00
34.	2.	6d. purple	7·00	7·50
45.	3.	10d. green	7·50	9·50
46.	2.	1s. red	7·50	10·00

1899. Surch. **ONE HALF PENNY.**

21.	3.	½d. on 1d. blue	15·00	18·00

1901. Optd. with crown.

22.	3.	1d. brown	55·00	45·00

1919. New Zealand stamps (King George V.) surch. **RAROTONGA** and value in native language in words.

50.	43.	½d. green	8	12
51.	42.	1d. red	8	15
52.	43.	1½d. brown	25	55
53.		2d. yellow	35	55
55.		2½d. blue	60	60
54.		3d. brown	45	65
59.		4d. violet	75	1·50
61.		4½d. green	75	1·75
64.		6d. red	1·00	2·50
65.		7½d. brown	90	2·50
66.		9d. green	1·25	2·50
68.		1s. red	1·40	4·50

1921. New Zealand stamps optd. **RAROTONGA.**

70.	20.	2s. blue	16·00	20·00
71.		2s. 6d. brown	12·00	15·00
72.		5s. green	12·00	15·00
73.		10s. claret	24·00	29·00
74.		£1 red	32·00	40·00

4. Landing of Capt. Cook.

9. Harbour, Rarotoga and Mt. Ikurangi.

1920. Inscr. "RAROTONGA".

75.	4.	½d. black and green ..	90	1·60
82.	–	1d. black and red ..	85	50
77.	–	1½d. black and blue ..	1·75	2·50
83.	–	2½d. brown and blue ..	1·75	2·50
78.	–	3d. black and brown ..	2·25	3·00
84.	9.	4d. green and violet ..	2·50	3·50
79.	–	6d. brown and orange ..	2·50	3·00
80.	–	1s. black and violet ..	4·00	6·50

DESIGNS—VERT. 1d. Wharf at Avarua. 1½d. Capt. Cook. 2½d. Rarotongan chief. 3d. Palm tree. HORIZ. 6d. Huts at Arorangi. 1s. Avarua Harbour.

1926. "Admiral" type of New Zealand optd. **RAROTONGA.**

91.	52.	2s. blue	6·50	11·00
92.		3s. mauve	10·00	11·00

1931. No. 77 surch. **TWO PENCE.**

94.		2d. on 1½d. black & blue	50	80

1931. Arms type of New Zealand optd. **RAROTONGA.**

95.	56.	2s. 6d. brown	6·00	7·00
96.		5s. green	12·00	14·00
97.		10s. red	22·00	26·00
98.		£1 pink	32·00	35·00

12. Capt. Cook landing.

14. Double Maori Canoe.

1932. Inscr. "COOK ISLANDS".

106.	12.	½d. black and green ..	15	20
107.	–	1d. black and red ..	15	20
108.	14.	2d. black and brown ..	20	15
109.	–	2½d. black and blue ..	25	30
110.	–	4d. black and blue ..	25	25
111.	–	6d. black and orange ..	65	65
112.	–	1s. black and violet ..	3·75	4·50

DESIGNS—VERT. 1d. Capt. Cook and King George V. HORIZ. 2½d. Natives working cargo. 4d. Port of Avarua. 6d. R.M.S. "Monowai". 1 s. King George V.

1932. Stamps of New Zealand optd. **COOK ISLANDS.**

116.	52.	2s. blue	6·00	8·50
131.	56.	2s. 6d. brown	2·25	2·50
117.	52.	3s. mauve	8·00	9·50
132.	56.	5s. green	1·90	2·50
133.		10s. red	6·00	7·50
134.		£1 pink	7·00	9·50
135.		£3 green	22·00	26·00
136.		£5 blue	45·00	50·00

1935. Jubilee. As 1932, optd. **SILVER JUBILEE OF KING GEORGE V 1910-1935.**

113.		1d. red	12	35
114.		2½d. blue	30	60
115.		6d. green and orange ..	1·60	2·50

1937. Coronation T **80** of New Zealand optd. **COOK IS'DS.**

124.	80.	1d. red	5	5
125.		2½d. blue	8	10
126.		6d. orange	12	20

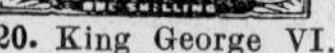

20. King George VI. 21. Native Village.

1938.

143.	20.	1s. black and violet ..	30	30
128.	21.	2s. black and orange ..	1·10	1·60
145.	–	3s. blue and green ..	1·40	1·75

DESIGN—HORIZ. 3s. Native canoe.

23. Tropical Landscape.

1940.

130.	23.	3d. on 1½d. black & pur.	5	8

1946. Peace. Peace stamps of New Zealand of 1946 optd. **COOK ISLANDS.**

146.	91.	1d. green	5	5
147.	–	2d. purple	5	8
148.	–	6d. brown and red ..	8	10
149.	94.	8d. black and red ..	12	15

24. Ngatangila Channel, Rarotonga.

1949.

150.	24.	½d. violet and brown ..	8	15
151.	–	1d. brown and green ..	25	25
152.	–	2d. brown and red ..	15	20
153.	–	3d. green and blue ..	12	20
154.	–	5d. green and violet ..	50	70
155.	–	6d. black and red ..	25	30
156.	–	8d. olive and orange ..	50	65
157.	–	1s. blue and brown ..	85	1·00
158.	–	2s. brown and red ..	2·00	2·25
159.	–	3s. blue and green ..	2·50	2·75

DESIGNS—HORIZ. 1d. Capt. Cook and map of Hervey Is. 2d. Rarotonga and Rev. John Williams. 3d. Aitutaki and palm trees. 5d. Rarotonga Airfield. 6d. Penrhyn village. 8d. Native hut. VERT. 1s. Map and statue of Capt. Cook. 2s. Native hut and palms. 3s. M.V. "Matua".

1953. Coronation. As Types of New Zealand but inscr. "COOK ISLANDS".

160.	106.	3d. brown	10	12
161.	108.	6d. grey	25	30

1960. No. 154 surch. **1/6.**

162.		1s. 6d. on 5d. green & violet	35	45

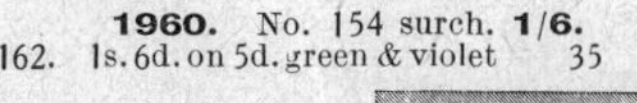

25. Tiare Maori.

26. Queen Elizabeth II.

27. Rarotonga.

1963.

163.	25.	1d. emerald and yellow	5	5
164.	–	2d. brown-red & yellow	5	5
165.	–	3d. yellow, grn. & violet	5	5
166.	–	5d. blue and black ..	8	10
167.	–	6d. red, yellow and green	10	12
168.	–	8d. black and blue ..	15	15
169.	–	1s. yellow & yellow-grn.	20	20
170.	26.	1s. 6d. violet	65	55
171.	–	2s. brown and grey-blue	1·10	80
172.	–	3s. black & yellow-green	1·40	1·10
173.	27.	5s. brown and blue ..	2·40	2·25

DESIGNS—As T **25**. VERT. 2d. Fishing God. 8d. Bonito (fish). HORIZ. 3d. Frangipani (plant). 5d. Love tern. 6d. Hibiscus. 1s. Oranges. As T **27**: 2s. Island scene. 3s. Administration Centre, Mangalia.

28. Eclipse and Palm.

1965. Solar Eclipse Observation, Manuae Island.

174.	28.	6d. black, yellow & blue	15	20

29. N.Z. Ensign and Map.

1965. Internal Self-Government.

175.	29.	4d. red and blue ..	12	12
176.	–	10d. multicoloured ..	25	25
177.	–	1s. multicoloured ..	30	30
178.	–	1s. 9d. multicoloured ..	45	45

DESIGNS: 10d. London Missionary Society Church. 1s. Proclamation of Cession, 1900. 1s. 9d. Nikao School.

1966. Churchill Commem. Nos. 171/3 and 175/7 optd. **In Memoriam SIR WINSTON CHURCHILL 1874-1965.**

179.	29.	4d. red and blue ..	12	12
180.	–	10d. multicoloured ..	35	40
181.	–	1s. multicoloured ..	40	45
182.	–	2s. brown and grey-blue	90	1·10
183.	–	3s. black & yellow-green	1·40	1·60
184.	27.	5s. brown and blue ..	2·25	2·25

1966. Air. Various stamps optd. **Airmail** and aeroplane or surch. in addition.

185.	–	6d. red, yellow & green (No. 167)	12	15
186.	–	7d. on 8d. black & blue (No. 168)	12	15
187.	–	10d. on 3d. yellow-green and violet (No. 165) ..	20	20
188.	–	1s. yellow & yellow-grn. (No. 169)	25	25
189.	26.	1s. 6d. violet	30	30
190.	–	2s. 3d. on 3s. black and yellow-green (No. 172)	45	50
191.	27.	5s. brown and blue ..	95	1·10
192.	–	10s. on 2s. brown, and grey-blue (No. 171) ..	2·25	3·00
193.	–	£1 pink (No. 143) ..	5·00	5·50

30. "Adoration of the Wise Men" (Fra Angelico).

1966. Christmas. Multicoloured.

194.	1d. Type **30**	5	5
195.	2d. "The Nativity" (Memling)	8	8
196.	4d. "Adoration of the Wise Men" (Velazquez) ..	15	15
197.	10d. "Adoration of the Wise Men" (H. Bosch) ..	35	35
198.	1s. 6d. "Adoration of the Shepherds" (J. de Ribera)	70	55

31. Tennis and Queen Elizabeth II.

1967. 2nd South Pacific Games, Noumea. Multicoloured.

199.	½d. Type **31** (postage) ..	5	5
200.	1d. Basketball and Games Emblem	5	5

201. 4d. Boxing and Cook Islands Team Badge 10 10
202. 7d. Football and Queen Elizabeth II 15 15
203. 10d. Running and Games Emblem (air) 20 20
204. 2s. 3d. Running and Cook Islands' Team Badge .. 45 45

1967. Decimal currency. Various stamps surch.

205. **25.** 1 c. on 1d. 20 20
206. – 2 c. on 2d. (No. 164) .. 5 5
207. – $2\frac{1}{2}$ c. on 3d. (No. 165) .. 5 5
209. **29.** 3 c. on 4d. 5 5
210. – 4 c. on 5d. (No. 166 .. 10 10
211. – 5 c. on 6d. (No. 167) .. 8 8
212. **28.** 5 c. on 6d. 40 40
213. – 7 c. on 8d. (No. 168) .. 10 10
214. – 10 c. on 1s. (No. 169) .. 12 15
215. **26.** 15 c. on 1s. 6d... .. 75 75
216. – 30 c. on 3s. (No. 172) .. 3·75 2·75
217. **27.** 50 c. on 5s. .. .. 2·75 2·75
218. – $1 and 10s. on 10d. (No. 176) .. .. 6·50 5·50
219. – $2 on £1 (No. 143) .. 85·00 85·00
220. – $6 on £3 (No. 144) .. £110 £110
221. – $10 on £5 (No. 145) .. £110 £110

32. Village Scene, Cook Islands 1d. Stamp of 1892 and Queen Victoria (from "Penny Black").

1967. 1st Cook Island Stamps. 75th Anniv.

222. **32.** 1 c. (1d.) multicoloured 5 5
223. – 3 c. (4d.) multicoloured 8 8
224. – 8 c. (10d.) multicoloured 15 20
225. – 18 c. (1s. 9d.) mult. .. 30 40

DESIGNS: 3 c. Post Office, Avarua, Rarotonga and Queen Elizabeth II. 8 c. Avarua, Rarotonga, and Cook Islands 10d. stamp of 1892. 18 c. S.S. "Moana Roa", "DC-3" Aircraft, Map and Captain Cook.

The stamps are expressed in decimal currency and in the sterling equivalent.

33. Hibiscus.

34. Queen Elizabeth and Flowers.

1967. Flowers. Multicoloured.

227. $\frac{1}{2}$ c. Type **33** 5 5
228. 1 c. "Hibiscus syriacus" 5 5
229. 2 c. Frangipani 5 5
230. $2\frac{1}{2}$ c. "Clitoria ternatea" 5 5
231. 3 c. "Suva Queen" .. 5 5
232. 4 c. Water Lily (wrongly inscr. "Walter Lily") 30 30
233. 4 c. Water Lily 5 5
234. 5 c. "Bauhinia bipinnata rosea" 8 8
235. 6 c. Yellow Hibiscus .. 8 8
236. 8 c. "Allamanda cathartica" 10 10
237. 9 c. Stephanotis 12 12
238. 10 c. "Poinciana regia flamboyant" 12 12
239. 15 c. Frangipani .. 20 20
240. 20 c. Thunbergia .. 25 25
241. 25 c. Canna Lily .. 30 30
242. 30 c. "Euphorbia pulcherrima poinsettia" 35 40
243. 50 c. "Gardenia taitensis" 55 60
244. $1 Queen Elizabeth II 1·25 1·25
245. $2 Queen Elizabeth II 2·25 2·50
246. $4 Type **34** .. 4·25 4·50
247. $6 As No. 246 .. 6·50 7·00
247a. $8 As No. 246 .. 8·50 9·00
248. $10 As No. 246 .. 10·00 11·00

35. "Ia Orana Maria".

1967. Gaugin's Polynesian Paintings.

249. **35.** 1 c. multicoloured .. 5 5
250. – 3 c. multicoloured .. 5 5
251. – 5 c. multicoloured .. 8 8
252. – 8 c. multicoloured .. 12 12
253. – 15 c. multicoloured .. 25 25
254. – 22 c. multicoloured .. 35 40

DESIGNS: 3 c. "Riders on the Beach". 5 c. "Still Life with Flowers" and inset portrait of Queen Elizabeth. 8 c. "Whispered Words". 15 c. "Maternity". 22 c. "Why are you angry?".

36. "The Holy Family" (Rubens).

1967. Christmas. Renaissance Paintings.

256. **36.** 1 c. multicoloured .. 5 5
257. – 3 c. multicoloured .. 5 5
258. – 4 c. mulitcoloured .. 8 8
259. – 8 c. multicoloured .. 15 15
260. – 15 c. multicoloured .. 30 30
261. – 25 c. multicoloured .. 50 50

DESIGNS: 3 c. "The Epiphany" (Durer). 4 c. "The Lucca Madonna" (J. Van Eyck). 8 c. "The Adoration of the Shepherds" (J. da Bassano). 15 c. "The Nativity" (El Greco). 25 c. "The Madonna and Child" (Correggio).

1968. Hurricane Relief. Nos. 231, 233, 251, 238, 241 and 243/4 optd. **HURRICANE RELIEF** plus value.

262. 3 c.+1 c. multicoloured .. 5 5
263. 4 c.+1 c. multicoloured .. 8 8
264. 5 c.+2 c. multicoloured .. 10 10
265. 10 c.+2 c. multicoloured 20 20
266. 25 c.+5 c. multicoloured 65 65
267. 50 c.+10 c. multicoloured 1·25 1·25
268. $1+10 c. multicoloured .. 2·00 2·00

On No. 264 silver blocking obliterates the design area around the lettering.

37. "Matavai Bay, Tahiti" (S. Parkinson).

1968. Captain Cook's 1st Voyage of Discovery. Bicent.

269. **37.** $\frac{1}{2}$ c. multicoloured (post.) 5 5
270. – 1 c. multicoloured .. 5 5
271. – 2 c. multicoloured .. 10 10
272. – 4 c. multicoloured .. 15 15
273. – 6 c. multicoloured (air) 15 15
274. – 10 c. multicoloured .. 20 20
275. – 15 c. multicoloured .. 30 30
276. – 25 c. multicoloured .. 55 60

DESIGNS—VERT. 1 c. "Island of Huaheine" (John Cleveley). 2 c. "Town of St. Peter and St. Paul, Kamchatka" (J. Webber). 4 c. "The Ice Islands" (Antarctica: W. Hodges). HORIZ. 6 c. "Resolution and Discovery" (J. Webber). 10 c. "The Island of Tahiti" (W. Hodges). 15 c. "Karakakooa, Hawaii" (J. Webber). 25 c. "The Landing at Middleburg" (W. Hodges).

38. Sailing.

1968. Olympic Games, Mexico. Multicoloured.

277. 1 c. Type **38** 5 5
278. 5 c. Gymnastics 8 8
279. 15 c. High-jumping .. 20 20
280. 20 c. High-diving .. 25 25
281. 30 c. Cycling 40 40
282. 50 c. Hurdling 65 65

39. "Virgin and Child" (Titian).

1968. Christmas. Multicoloured.

283. 1 c. Type **39** 5 5
284. 4 c. "The Holy Family of the Lamb" (Raphael) 5 5
285. 10 c. "The Madonna of the Rosary" (Murillo) .. 15 15
286. 20 c. "Adoration of the Magi" (Memling) .. 30 30
287. 30 c. "Adoration of the Magi" (Ghirlandaio) .. 45 45

40. Camp-fire Cooking.

1969. Diamond Jubilee of New Zealand Scout Movement and 5th National (New Zealand) Jamboree. Multicoloured.

289. $\frac{1}{2}$ c. Type **40** 5 5
290. 1 c. Descent by rope .. 5 5
291. 5 c. Semaphore 8 8
292. 10 c. Tree-planting .. 15 15
293. 20 c. Constructing a Shelter 30 30
294. 30 c. Lord Baden-Powell and Island Scene .. 50 50

41. Footballer.

1969. 3rd South Pacific Games. Port Moresby. Multicoloured.

295. $\frac{1}{2}$ c. Pole-vaulter 5 5
296. $\frac{1}{2}$ c. Type **41** 5 5
297. 1 c. Long-jumper 5 5
298. 1 c. Weightlifter 5 5
299. 4 c. Tennis-player .. 5 5
300. 4 c. Hurdler 5 5
301. 10 c. Javelin-thrower .. 15 15
302. 10 c. Runner 15 15
303. 15 c. Golfer 30 30
304. 15 c. Boxer 30 30

42. Flowers, Map and Premier Albert Henry. (Illustration reduced. Actual size 72 × 26 mm).

1969. South Pacific Conf., Noumea. Multicoloured.

306. 5 c. Type **42** 8 8
307. 10 c. Captain Cook, map and flowers 15 15
308. 25 c. Flowers, map and arms of New Zealand .. 35 35
309. 30 c. Queen Elizabeth II, map and flowers .. 50 50

43. "Madonna and Child with Saints" (Lippi).

1969. Christmas. Multicoloured.

310. 1 c. Type **43** 5 5
311. 4 c. "The Holy Family" (Fra. B. Della Porta) .. 5 5
312. 10 c. "Virgin and Child with Saints" (Memling) .. 15 15
313. 20 c. "Virgin and Child with Saints" (Robert Campin) 30 30
314. 30 c. "Virgin and Child" (Correggio) .. 55 55

44. "The Resurrection of Christ" (Raphael).

1970. Easter.

316. **44.** 4 c. multicoloured .. 5 5
317. – 8 c. multicoloured .. 10 10
318. – 20 c. multicoloured .. 35 35
319. – 25 c. multicoloured .. 45 45

DESIGNS: "The Resurrection of Christ" by Dirk Bouts (8 c.), Altdorfer (20 c.), Murillo (25 c.).

1970. "Apollo 13". Nos. 233, 236, 239/40, 242, and 245/6, optd. **KIA ORANA APOLLO 13 ASTRONAUTS Te Atua to Tatou Irinakianga.**

321. 4 c. multicoloured .. 5 5
322. 8 c. multicoloured .. 10 10
323. 15 c. multicoloured .. 20 20
324. 20 c. multicoloured .. 25 25
325. 30 c. multicoloured .. 35 35
326. $2 multicoloured .. 2·25 2·25
327. $4 multicoloured .. 6·00 6·00

45. The Royal Family.

1970. Royal Visit to New Zealand. Multicoloured.

328. 5 c. Type **45** 8 8
329. 30 c. Captain Cook and H.M.S. "Endeavour" 50 50
330. $1 Royal Visit Commem. Coin .. .. 1·50 1·50

1970. Self-Government. 5th Anniv. Nos. 328/30, optd. **FIFTH ANNIVERSARY SELF-GOVERNMENT AUGUST 1970.**

332. **45.** 5 c. multicoloured .. 5 8
333. – 30 c. multicoloured .. 75 75
334. – $1 multicoloured .. 2·00 2·00

On No. 332, the opt. is arranged in one line around the frame of the stamp.

1970. Surch.

335. **34.** $4 on $8 multicoloured 8·00 8·00
336. $4 on $10 multicoloured 8·00 8·00

46. Mary, Joseph, and Christ in Manger.

1970. Christmas. Multicoloured.

337. 1 c. Type **46** 5 5
338. 4 c. Shepherds and Apparition of the Angel 5 5
339. 10 c. Mary showing Child to Joseph 20 20
340. 20 c. The Wise Men bearing Gifts 35 35
341. 30 c. Parents wrapping Child in swaddling clothes 50 50

1971. Surch. **PLUS 20c. UNITED KINGDOM SPECIAL MAIL SERVICE.**

343. 30 c. + 20 c. (No. 242) .. 2·00 2·50
344. 50 c. + 20 c. (No. 243) .. 4·00 5·00

The premium of 20 c. was to prepay a private delivery service fee in Great Britain during the postal strike. The mail was sent by air to a forwarding address in the Netherlands. No. 343 was intended for ordinary airmail ½ oz. letters, and No. 344 included registration fee.

No. 343 was issued on 25 Feb, and No. 344 on 8 March. The strike ended on 8 March and both stamps were withdrawn on 12 March.

47. Wedding of Princess Elizabeth and Prince Philip.

1971. Royal Visit of Duke of Edinburgh. Multicoloured.

345. 1 c. Type **47** 5 5
346. 4 c. Queen Elizabeth, Prince Philip, Prince Charles and Princess Anne at Windsor 5 5
347. 10 c. Prince Philip sailing 20 20
348. 15 c. Prince Philip in polo gear 40 40
349. 25 c. Prince Philip in Naval uniform, and Royal Yacht, "Britannia" 60 60

1971. Fourth South Pacific Games, Tahiti, Nos. 238, 241 and 242 optd. **Fourth South Pacific Games Papeete** and emblem or surch. also.

351. 10 c. multicoloured .. 20 20
352. 10 c. + 1 c. multicoloured .. 20 20
353. 10 c. + 3 c. multicoloured .. 20 20
354. 25 c. multicoloured .. 50 60
355. 25 c. + 1 c. multicoloured .. 50 60
356. 25 c. + 3 c. multicoloured .. 50 60
357. 30 c. multicoloured .. 75 85
358. 30 c. + 1 c. multicoloured .. 75 85
359. 30 c. + 3 c. multicoloured .. 75 85

The stamps additionally surcharged 1 c. or 3 c. helped to finance the Cook Islands' team at the games.

1971. Nos. 230, 233, 236/7 and 239 surch.

360. 10 c. on 2½ c. multicoloured 20 20
361. 10 c. on 4 c. multicoloured 20 20
362. 10 c. on 8 c. multicoloured 20 20
363. 10 c. on 9 c. multicoloured 20 20
364. 10 c. on 15 c. multicoloured 20 20

48. "Virgin and Child" (Bellini). **49.** Mary Magdalen.

1971. Christmas.

365. **48.** 1 c. multicoloured .. 8 8
366. – 4 c. multicoloured .. 8 8
367. – 10 c. multicoloured .. 20 25
368. – 20 c. multicoloured .. 40 45
369. – 30 c. multicoloured .. 60 75

DESIGNS: Various paintings of the "Virgin and Child" by Bellini. Similar to T **48.**

1972. South Pacific Commission. 25th Anniv. No. 244 optd. **SOUTH PACIFIC COMMISSION FEB. 1947-1972.**

372. $1 multicoloured .. .. 2·00 2·25

1972. Easter. Multicoloured.

373. 5c. Type **49** 10 10
374. 10c. Christ on the Cross .. 20 25
375. 30c. Mary, Mother of Jesus 60 65

1972. Hurricane Relief.

(a). Nos. 239, 241 and 243 optd. **HURRICANE RELIEF PLUS** premium.

379. 15c. + 5c. multicoloured .. 30 30
380. 25c. + 5c. multicoloured .. 50 50
382. 50c. + 10c. multicoloured .. 1·00 1·25

(b). Nos. 373/5 optd. **Hurricane Relief Plus** premium.

377. 5c. + 2c. multicoloured .. 10 10
378. 10c. + 2c. multicoloured .. 20 20
381. 30c. + 5c. multicoloured .. 60 60

50/51. Rocket in Moon Orbit. (Nos. 383/4). (Illustration reduced. Actual size 62 × 30 mm.)

1972. The Apollo Moon Exploration Flights. Multicoloured.

383. 5 c. Type **50** 8 8
384. 5 c. Type **51** 8 8
385. 10 c. } Astronauts on Moon 15 15
386. 10 c. } 15 15
387. 25 c. } Moon River and 45 45
388. 25 c. } astronaut working 45 45
389. 30 c. } Splashdown and 55 55
390. 30 c. } helicopter 55 50

These were issued in horizontal se-tenant pairs of each value, forming one composite design.

1972. Hurricane Relief. Nos. 383/390 surch. **HURRICANE RELIEF Plus** and premium.

392. 5 c. + 2 c. multicoloured .. 8 8
393. 5 c. + 2 c. multicoloured .. 8 8
394. 10 c. + 2 c. multicoloured 20 20
395. 10 c. + 2 c. multicoloured 20 20
396. 25 c. + 2 c. multicoloured 50 50
397. 25 c. + 2 c. multicoloured 50 50
398. 30 c. + 2 c. multicoloured 60 60
399. 30 c. + 2 c. multicoloured 60 60

52. High-jumping. **53.** "The Rest in Egypt". (Caravaggio).

1972. Olympic Games, Munich. Mult.

401. 10 c. Type **52** 20 20
402. 25 c. Running 75 75
403. 30 c. Boxing 75 75

1972. Christmas. Multicoloured.

406. 1 c. Type **53** 5 5
407. 5 c. "Virgin of the Swallow" (Guercino) 10 10
408. 10 c. "Virgin with Green Cushion" (Solario) .. 20 20
409. 20 c. "Virgin and Child" (di Credi) 40 40
410. 30 c. "Virgin and Child" (Bellini) 75 75

54. Marriage Ceremony.

1972. Royal Silver Wedding. Each black and silver.

413. 5 c. Type **54** 10 10
414. 10 c. Leaving Westminster Abbey 25 25
415. 15 c. Bride and Bridegroom (40 × 41 mm.) 35 35
416. 30 c. Family group (67 × 40 mm.) 75 75

55. Taro Leaf.

1973. Silver Wedding Coinage.

417 **55.** 1 c. gold, mve. & black 5 5
418. – 2 c. gold, blue & black .. 5 5
419. – 5 c. silver, grn. & black 5 5
420. – 10 c. silver, blue & black 20 20
421. – 20 c. silver, grn. & black 45 45
422. – 50 c. silver, mauve & blk. 85 85
423. – $1 silver, blue & black 1·75 1·75

DESIGNS—HORIZ. (37 × 24 mm.). 2 c. Pineapple. 5 c. Hibiscus Flower. (46 × 30 mm.). 10 c. Oranges. 20 c. Fairy Tern. 50 c. Bonito. VERT. (32 × 55 mm.). $1 Tangaroa.

56. "Noli me Tangere" (Titian).

1973. Easter. Multicoloured.

424. 5 c. Type **56** 5 5
425. 10 c. "The Descent from the Cross" (Rubens) .. 15 15
426. 30 c. "Christ weeping for His People" (Durer) .. 45 45

57. Queen Elizabeth II in Coronation Regalia.

1973. Queen Elizabeth's Coronation. 20th Anniv.

429. **57.** 10 c. multicoloured .. 1·00 1·00

1973. Treaty Banning Nuclear Testing 10th Anniv. Nos. 234, 236, 238 and 240/42. optd. **TENTH ANNIVERSARY CESSATION OF NUCLEAR TESTING TREATY.**

431. 5 c. multicoloured 8 8
432. 8 c. multicoloured 12 12
433. 10 c. multicoloured .. 15 15
434. 20 c. multicoloured .. 30 30
435. 25 c. multicoloured .. 40 40
436. 30 c. multicoloured .. 50 55

58. Tipairua.

1973. Maori Exploration of the Pacific. Sailing Craft. Multicoloured.

437. ½ c. Type **58** 5 5
438. 1 c. Wa'a Kaulua 5 5
439. 1½ c. Tainui 5 5
440. 5 c. War canoe 8 8
441. 10 c. Pahi 15 15
442. 15 c. Amatasi 20 25
443. 25 c. Vaka 35 40

59. The Annunciation.

1973. Christmas. Scenes from a 15th-cent. prayer-book. Multicoloured.

444. 1 c. Type **59** 5 5
445. 5 c. The Visitation 8 8
446. 10 c. Announcement to the Shepherds 15 15
447. 20 c. Epiphany 30 30
448. 30 c. The Slaughter of the Innocents 45 45

60. Princess Anne.

1973. Royal Wedding. Multicoloured.
450. 25 c. Type **59** 35 40
451. 30 c. Capt. Mark Phillips 50 60
452. 50 c. Princess Anne and Capt. Phillips 80 90

61. Running.

1974. British Commonwealth Games, Christchurch. Multicoloured.
455. 1 c. Diving (vert.) .. 5 5
456. 3 c. Boxing (vert.) .. 5 5
457. 5 c. Type **61** 8 8
458. 10 c. Weightlifting .. 12 15
459. 30 c. Cycling 40 50

62. " Jesus bearing the Cross" (Raphael).

1974. Easter. Multicoloured.
461. 5 c. Type **62** 5 8
462. 10 c. " Christ in the Arms of God " (El Greco) .. 12 15
463. 30 c. " The Descent from the Cross " (Caravaggio) 35 40

63. "Pallicuim glaucum".

64. Queen Elizabeth II.

1974 Multicoloured.
466. ½ c. Type **63** 5 5
467. 1 c. "Vasum turbinellus" 5 5
468. 1½ c. "Corculum cardissa" 5 5
469. 2 c. "Terebellum terebellum" 5 5
470. 3 c. "Aulica vespertilio" .. 5 5
471. 4 c. "Strombus gibberulus" 5 5
472. 5 c. "Cymatium pileare" .. 5 5
473. 6 c. "Cypraea caputserpentis" 5 5
474. 8 c. "Bursa granularis" .. 8 8
475. 10 c. "Tenebra muscaria" 10 10
476. 15 c. "Mitra mitra" .. 15 15
477. 20 c. "Natica alapapillonis" 20 20
478. 25 c. "Gloripallium pallium" 25 25
479. 30 c. "Conus miles" .. 30 35
480. 50 c. "Conus textile" .. 50 55
481. 60 c. "Oliva senicea" .. 60 70
482. $1 Type **64** .. .. 95 1·10
483. $2 Type **64** .. .. .. 1·90 2·10
484. $4 Queen Elizabeth II and sea shells .. .. 3·75 4·00
485. $6 As $4 .. .. .. 5·75 6·00
486. $8 As $4 .. .. .. 7·50 8·00
487. $10 As $4 .. .. .. 9·50 10·00
Nos. 484/7 are horiz. 60×39 mm.

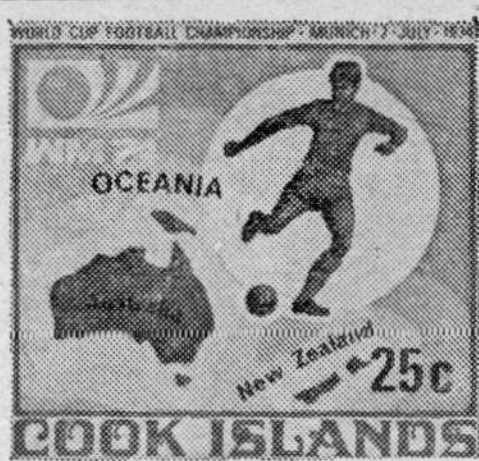

65. Footballer and Australasian Map.

1974. World Cup Football Championships. Multicoloured.
488. 25 c. Type **65** 30 35
489. 50 c. Map and Munich Stadium 60 65
490. $1 Footballer, stadium and World Cup .. .. 1·25 1·40

66. Obverse and Reverse of Commemorative $2·50 Silver Coin.

1974. Capt. Cook's Second Voyage of Discovery. Bicent.
492. **66.** $2·50 silver, blk. & vio. 3·50 3·75
493. – $7·50 silver, blk. & grn. 10·00 11·00
DESIGN: $7·50 As Type **66** but showing $7·50 coin.

67. Early Stamps of Cook Islands.

1974. U.P.U. Centenary. Multicoloured.
495. 10 c. Type **67** 15 15
496. 25 c. Old landing strip, Rarotonga, and stamp of 1898 .. .. .. 35 35
497. 30 c. Post Office, Rarotonga, and stamp of 1920 .. 40 40
498. 50 c. U.P.U. emblem and stamps 65 65

68. "Madonna of the Goldfinch" (Raphael).

1974. Christmas. Multicoloured.
500. 1 c. Type **68** 5 5
501. 5 c. "The Holy Family" (Andrea del Sarto) .. 5 5
502. 10 c. "Virgin and Child" (Correggio) 10 12
503. 20 c. "The Holy Family" (Rembrandt) 20 25
504. 30 c. "The Nativity" (Rogier Van Der Weyden) .. 35 40

69. Churchill and Blenheim Palace.

1974. Sir Winston Churchill. Birth Centenary. Multicoloured.
506. 5 c. Type **69** 8 8
507. 10 c. Churchill and Houses of Parliament 20 15
508. 25 c. Churchill and Chartwell 35 40
509. 30 c. Churchill and Buckingham Palace 45 45
510. 50 c. Churchill and St. Paul's Cathedral 90 80

70. Vasco Nunez de Balboa and Discovery of Pacific Ocean (1513).

1975. Pacific Explorers. Multicoloured.
513. 1 c. Type **70** 5 5
514. 5 c. Fernando de Magallanes and map (1520) .. 8 8
515. 10 c. Juan Sebastian de Elcano and " Vitoria " .. (1520) 12 12
516. 25 c. Friar Andres de Urdaneta & ship (1564-67) 30 35
517. 30 c. Miguel Lopez de Legazpi and ship (1564-67) 35 40

71. " Apollo " Capsule.

1975. " Apollo-Soyuz " Space Project. Mult.
518. 25 c. Type **71** 25 30
519. 25 c. " Soyuz " capsule .. 25 30
520. 30 c. " Soyuz " crew .. 30 35
521. 30 c. " Apollo " crew .. 30 35
522. 50 c. Cosmonaut within " Soyuz " 50 60
523. 50 c. Astronauts within " Apollo " 50 60
These were issued in horiz. se-tenant pairs of each value, forming one composite design.

72. $100 Commemorative Gold Coin.

1975. Captain Cook's 2nd Voyage. Bicent.
525. **72.** $2 brown, gold and vio. 2·00 2·25

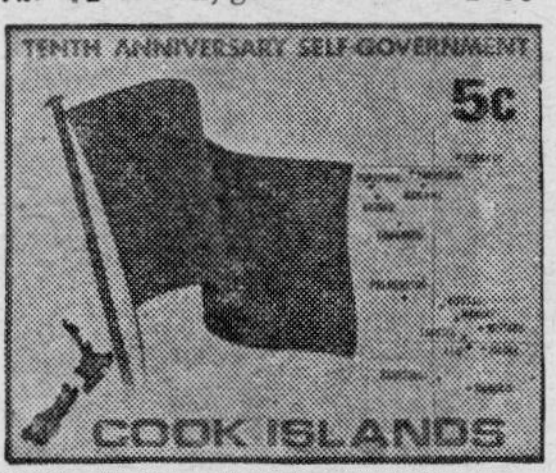

73. Cook Island's Flag and Map.

1975. Self-Government 10th Anniv.
526. 5 c. Type **73** 5 5
527. 10 c. Premier Sir Albert Henry and flag (vert.) .. 10 12
258. 25 c. Rarotonga and flag .. 25 30

74. " Virgin and Child " (Flemish Master).

1975. Christmas. Multicoloured.
529. 6 c. Type **74** 5 8
530. 10 c. " Madonna of the Meadow " (Raphael) .. 10 12
531. 15 c. " Holy Family of Oak " (Raphael) 15 20
532. 20 c. " Adoration of the Shepherds " (J. B. Mayno) 20 25
533. 35 c. " The Annunication " (Murillo) 30 35

75. " The Descent " (Raphael).

1976. Easter. Multicoloured.
536. 7 c. Type **75** 8 8
537. 15 c. " Pieta " (Veronese) 15 20
538. 35 c. " Pieta " (El Greco) 40 45

76. Benjamin Franklin and " Resolution ".

1976. American Revolution. Bicent. Multicoloured.
541. $1 Type **76** .. .. 1·10 1·25
542. $2 Capt. Cook and " Resolution " .. .. .. 2·25 2·50

1976. Visit of Queen Elizabeth to U.S.A. Nos. 541/2 optd. **Royal Visit July 1976.**
544. **76.** $1 multicoloured .. 1·10 1·25
545. $2 multicoloured .. 2·25 2·50

77. Hurdling.

1976. Olympic Games, Montreal. Multicoloured.
547. 7 c. } Type **77** 8 8
548. 7 c. } 8 8
549. 15 c. } Hockey 15 20
550. 15 c. } 15 20
551. 30 c. } Fencing 35 40
552. 30 c. } 35 40
553. 35 c. } Football 40 45
554. 35 c. } 40 45

78. " The Visitation ".

1976. Christmas. Renaissance sculptures. Multicoloured.

556. 6 c. Type 78 .. .. 5 5
557. 10 c. " Adoration of the Shepherds " 10 12
558. 15 c. " Adoration of the Shepherds " (different) 15 20
559. 20 c. " The Epiphany " .. 20 20
560. 35 c. " The Holy Family " 35 40

OFFICIAL STAMPS

1975. Nos. 227, etc., optd. **O.H.M.S.** or surch. also.

O 1. 1 c. multicoloured ..
O 2. 2 c. multicoloured ..
O 3. 3 c. multicoloured ..
O 4. 4 c. multicoloured ..
O 5. 5 c. on $2\frac{1}{2}$ c. multicoloured
O 6. 8 c. multicoloured ..
O 7. 10 c. on 6 c. multicoloured
O 8. 18 c. on 20 c. multicoloured
O 9. 25 c. on 9 c. multicoloured
O 10. 30 c. on 15 c. multicoloured
O 11. 50 c. multicoloured ..
O 12. $1 multicoloured ..
O 13. $2 multicoloured ..
O 14. $4 multicoloured ..
O 15. $6 multicoloured ..
O 1/15 .. .. Set of 15 + 15·00

These stamps were only sold to the public cancelled to order and not in unusual condition.

CORFU E2

(ITALIAN OCCUPATION)

One of the Greek Ionian Islands situated off the coast of Albania temporarily occupied by Italy during a dispute with Greece in 1923. For later Occupation Issues see Corfu & Paxos below.

1923. Stamps of Italy optd. **CORFU.**

1. **24.** 5 c. green 15 15
2. 10 c. red 15 15
3. 15 c. grey 15 15
4. **25.** 20 c. orange 15 15
5. **26.** 30 c. brown 15 15
6. 50 c. mauve 15 15
7. 60 c. blue 15 15
8. **23.** 1 l. brown and green .. 15 15

1923. Stamps of Italy surch. **CORFU** and value.

9. **24.** 25 l. on 10 c. red .. 85 45
10. **26.** 60 l. on 25 c. blue .. 50
11. 70 l. on 30 c. brown .. 50
12. 1 d. 20 on 50 c. mauve .. 65 40
13. **23.** 2 d. 40 on 1 l. brn. & grn. 65 40
14. 4 d. 75 on 2 l. grn. & orge. 50

CORFU AND PAXOS E2

Greek Ionian Islands occupied by Italy in 1941.

1941. Stamps of Greece optd. **CORFU.**

(a) On postage stamps of 1937.

1. **69.** 5 l. blue and brown .. 85 65
2. – 10 l. brown and blue .. 12 12
4. – 20 l. green and black .. 12 12
5. – 40 l. black and bgreen .. 15 15
6. – 50 l. black and brown .. 12 12
7. – 80 l. brown and violet .. 15 15
8. **72.** 1 d. green 20 25
9. **72a.** 1 d. 50 green .. 1·25 85
10. – 2 d. blue 65 20
11. **72.** 3 d. brown 25 30
12. – 5 d. red 65 40
13. – 6 d. olive 85 50
14. – 7 d. brown 95 70
15. **72.** 8 d. blue 65 65
16. – 10 d. brown .. .. 60·00 27·00
17. – 15 d. green .. .. 3·00 2·50
18. – 25 d. blue .. .. 2·10 1·50
19. **72a.** 30 d. red .. .. 11·00 6·00
20. **72.** 100 d. red .. .. 26·00 17·00

(b) On air stamps of 1938 and 1935.

21. **D 2.** 50 l. brown (No. 521) .. 35 25
23. **66.** 1 d. red .. .. .. 75·00 29·00
24. 2 d. blue 85 50
25. 5 d. mauve 85 50
26. 7 d. blue .. .. .. 1·00 65
27. 10 d. brown .. .. 70·00 32·00
28. 10 d. orange .. .. 6·50 4·25
29. 25 d. red .. .. 12·00 8·50
30. 30 d. green .. .. 18·00 15·00
31. 50 d. mauve .. .. 15·00 12·00
32. 100 d. brown £450 £200

(c) On Charity Tax stamps of 1939.

33. **C 7.** 10 l. red 25 20
34. 50 l. green 35 30
35. 1 d. blue .. .. 3·25 1·90

(d) On Postage Due stamps of 1902 and 1913.

36. **D 2.** 10 l. red 25 25
37. 25 l. blue 50 50
38. 80 l. purple .. .. 75·00 30·00
39. 1 d. blue £450 £140
40. 2 d. red .. .. .. 1·25 80
41. 5 d. blue .. .. 4·25 3·25
42. 10 d. green .. .. 2·50 2·00
43. 15 d. brown .. .. 2·50 2·00
44. 25 d. rose .. .. 2·50 2·00
45. 50 d. orange .. .. 3·25 2·50
46. 100 d. green .. .. £140 85·00

COSTA RICA O1

A Republic of Central America. Independent since 1821.

1863. 8 reales = 1 peso.
1881. 100 centavos = 1 peso.
1901. 100 centimos = 1 colon.

1. 2. General P. Fernandez. 3. President B. Soto.

1863.

1. **1.** $\frac{1}{2}$ r. blue 20 40
3. 2 r. red 40 70
4. 4 r. green .. .. 2·50 2·75
5. 1 p. orange .. .. 7·00 7·50

1881. Surch.

6. **1.** 1 c. on $\frac{1}{2}$ r. blue .. .. 90 1·75
8. 2 c. on $\frac{1}{2}$ r. blue .. .. 70 1·50
9. 5 c. on $\frac{1}{2}$ r. blue .. .. 2·00 3·00

1882. Surch. **U.P.U.** and value.

10. **1.** 5 c. on $\frac{1}{2}$ r. blue .. .. 30·00 30·00
11. 10 c. on 2 r. red .. .. 14·00 16·00
12. 20 c. on 4 r. green .. .. 32·00 30·00

1883.

13. **2.** 1 c. green 40 30
14. 2 c. red 40 30
15. 5 c. violet 60 25
16. 10 c. orange .. .. 5·50 1·40
17. 40 c. blue 40 35

1887.

18. **3.** 5 c. violet .. .. .. 1·40 35
19. 10 c. orange 70 50

1887. Fiscal stamps similar to T 2/3 optd. **CORREOS.**

20. 1 c. red 75 75
21. 5 c. brown 60 50

4. President B. Soto. 5.

1889. Various frames.

22. **4.** 1 c. brown 15 15
23. 2 c. green 12 12
24. 5 c. orange 25 15
25. 10 c. lake 12 12
26. 20 c. green 12 12
27. 50 c. red 40 40
28. 1 p. blue 50 50
29. 2 p. violet .. .. .. 2·75 2·75
30. 5 p. olive .. .. .. 10·00 9·00
31. 10 p. black .. .. 16·00 14·00

1892. Various frames.

32. **5.** 1 c. blue 12 12
33. 2 c. orange 12 12
34a. 5 c. mauve 12 12
35. 10 c. green 25 15
36. 20 c. red .. .. .. 1·75 12
37. 50 c. blue .. .. .. 1·90 1·90
38. 1 p. green on yellow .. 50 40
39. 2 p. red on grey 75 50
40. 5 p. blue on blue 75 50
41a. 10 p. brown on buff .. 1·90 1·75

6. Juan Santamaria. 9. View of Puerto Limon.

1901. Various designs dated "1900".

42. **6.** 1 c. black and green .. 12 20
43. – 2 c. black and red .. 35 20
52. – 4 c. black and purple .. 70 35
44. **9.** 5 c. black and blue .. 12 5
53. – 6 c. black and olive .. 1·90 75
45. – 10 c. black and brown .. 40 5
46. – 20 c. black and lake .. 1·00 12
54. – 25 c. brown and lilac .. 1·25 8
47. – 50 c. blue and claret .. 1·00 35
48. – 1 col. black and olive .. 4·50 1·10
49. – 2 col. black and red .. 2·40 65
50. – 5 col. black and brown .. 4·50 65
51. – 10 col. red and green .. 6·00 1·00

DESIGNS—VERT. 2 c. Juan Mora F. 4 c. Jose M. Canas. 6 c. Julian Volio. 10 c. Braulio (wrongly inscr. "BRANLIO") Carrillo. 25 c. Eusebio Figueroa. 50 c. Jose M. Castro. 1 col. Puente de Birris. 2 col. Juan Rafael Mora. 5 col. Jesus Jimenez. HORIZ. 20 c. National Theatre. 10 col. Arms.

1905. No. 46 surch. **UN CENTIMO** in ornamental frame.

55. 1 c. on 20 c. black & lake 25 25

19 Juan Santamaria. 20. Juan Mora.

1907. Dated "1907".

57. **19.** 1 c. blue and brown .. 20 8
58. **20.** 2 c. black and green .. 35 10
69. – 4 c. blue and red .. 2·00 75
60. – 5 c. blue and orange .. 25 10
71. – 10 c. black and blue .. 25 12
72. – 20 c. black and olive .. 1·50 60
63. – 25 c. slate and lavender 90 30
74. – 50 c. blue and claret .. 10·00 3·25
75. – 1 col. black and brown .. 3·50 2·50
76. – 2 col. green and claret .. 15·00 8·00

PORTRAITS: 4 c. Jose M. Canas. 5 c. Mauro Fernandez. 10 c. Braulio Carrillo. 20 c. Julian Volio. 25 c. Eusebio Figueroa. 50 c. Jose M. Castro. 1 col. Jesus Jimenez. 2 col. Juan Rafael Mora.

29. Juan Santamaria. 30. Julian Volio.

1910. Various frames.

77. **29.** 1 c. brown 5 5
78. – 2 c. green (Juan Mora F.) 5 5
79. – 4 c. red (Jose M. Canas) .. 8 5
80. – 5 c. orange (Mauro Fernandez) 10 5
81. – 10 c. blue (B. Carrillo) .. 5 5
82. **30.** 20 c. olive 15 12
83. – 25 c. purple (Eusebio Figueroa) .. .. 1·10 25
84. – 1 col. brown (Jesus Jimenez) 55 35

1911. Optd. **1911** between stars.

85. **6.** 1 c. black and green .. 25 20
86. **19.** 1 c. blue and brown .. 30 20
88. **20.** 2 c. black and green .. 30 20

1911. Optd. **Habilitado 1911.**

93. 4 c. black & purple (No. 52) 40 30
90. 5 c. blue & orange (No. 60) 20 10
91. 10 c. black & blue (No. 71) 75 50

31. 32.

1911. Surch. **Correos Un centimo** or **Correos 5 centimos.**

94. **31.** 1 c. on 10 c. blue .. 12 10
95. 1 c. on 25 c. violet .. 10 10
96. 1 c. on 50 c. brown .. 10 10
97. 1 c. on 1 col. brown .. 15 15
98. 1 c. on 5 col. red .. 20 20
99. 1 c. on 10 col. brown .. 40 30
100. 5 c. on 5 c. orange .. 40 30

1912. Surch. **Correos Dos centimos 2.**

102. **32.** 2 c. on 5 c. brown .. 1·25 1·25
109. 2 c. on 10 c. blue .. 20·00 15·00
110. 2 c. on 50 c. claret .. 20 20
105. 2 c. on 1 col. brown .. 35 35
112. 2 c. on 2 col. red .. 45 40
107. 2 c. on 5 col. green .. 35 40
108. 2 c. on 10 col. maroon 35 35

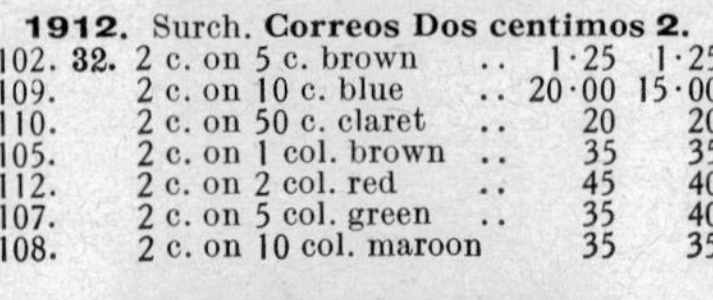

33.

1921. Coffee Cultivation Cent.

115. **33.** 5 c. black and blue .. 65 65

34. Bolivar. 35.

1921.

116. **34.** 15 c. violet 15 10

1921. Independence Cent.

117. **35.** 5 c. violet 40 20

36. Juan Mora and Julio Acosta.

1921. Independence Cent.

118. **36.** 2 c. black and orange .. 70 45
119. 3 c. black and green .. 70 45
120. 6 c. black and red .. 90 65
121. 15 c. black and blue .. 2·25 1·75
122. 30 c. black and brown 4·50 4·00

1922. Coffee Publicity. Nos. 77/81 and 116. Optd. with a sack inscr. "CAFE DE COSTA RICA".

123. **29.** 1 c. brown 10 5
124. **30.** 2 c. green 12 5
125. 4 c. red 15 10
126. 5 c. orange 15 12
127. 10 c. blue 25 20
128. **34.** 15 c. violet 90 60

1922. Optd. **CORREOS 1922.**

129. **35.** 5 c. violet 25 15

1922. Surch. with red cross and **5 c.**

130. **30.** 5 c. + 5 c. orge. (No. 80) 60 20

1923. Optd. **COMPRE UD. CAFE DE COSTA RICA** in circular frame.

131. **30.** 5 c. orange (No. 80) .. 25 15

37.

ILLUSTRATIONS
British Commonwealth and all overprints and surcharges are FULL SIZE. Foreign Countries have been reduced to $\frac{3}{4}$-LINEAR.

1923. J. Jimenez Cent.

132. **37.** 2 c. brown 10 8
133. 4 c. green 12 10
134. 5 c. blue 20 12
135. 20 c. red 12 12
136. 1 col. violet 25 20

38. National Monument. 39. Coffee-growing.

1923.

137. **38.** 1 c. purple 5 5
138. **39.** 2 c. yellow 15 5
139. – 4 c. green 25 20
140. – 5 c. blue 30 5
141. – 5 c. green 10 5
142. – 10 c. brown 60 12
143. – 10 c. red 12 5
144. – 12 c. red .. .. 1·10 80
145. – 20 c. blue .. .. 1·50 70
146. – 40 c. orange .. .. 3·50 1·40
147. – 1 col. olive 90 45

All the above are inscr. "U.P.U. 1923." except the 10 c. and 12 c. which are inscr. "1921 EN COMMEMORACION DEL PRIMER CONGRESO POSTAL", etc.

DESIGNS—HORIZ. 5 c. P.O., San Jose, 10 c. Columbus and Isabella I. 12 c. Columbus. 20 c. Columbus at Cariari. 40 c. Map of Costa Rica. VERT. 4 c. Banana-growing. 1 col. M. Gutierrez.

41. Don R. A. Maldonado y Velasco. **42.** Map of Guanacaste.

1924.

148. **41.** 2 c. green 10 5

For 3 c. green see No. 211 and for other portraits as T **41** see Nos. 308/12.

1924. Incorporation of Province of Nicoya (Guanacaste). Cent. Dated "1824 1924".

149. **42.** 1 c. red 30 20
150. 2 c. purple 30 20
151. 5 c. green 30 15
152. 10 c. orange .. .. 1·90 40
153. – 15 c. blue 55 35
154. – 20 c. grey 70 60
155. – 25 c. brown .. .. 1·50 1·00

DESIGN: 15 c., 20 c. 25 c. Church at Nicoya.

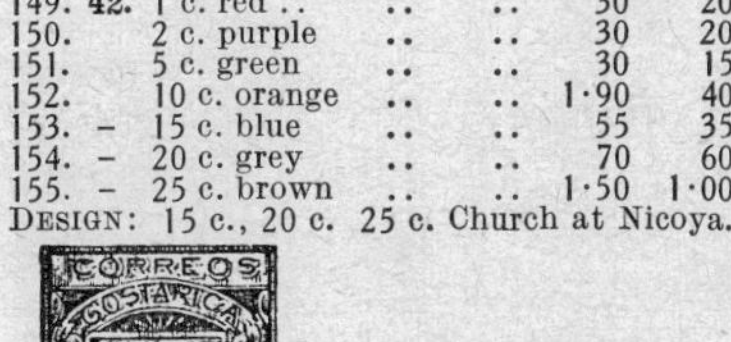

44. Discus Thrower. **47.**

1925. Inscr. "JUEGOS OLIMPICOS". Imperf. or perf.

156. **44.** 5 c. green .. .. 3·00 2·50
157. – 10 c. red .. .. 3·00 2·50
158. – 20 c. blue .. .. 5·50 4·25

DESIGNS—VERT. 10 c. Trophy. HORIZ. 20 c. Parthenon.

1926. Surch. with values in ornamental designs.

159. 3 c. on 5 c. (No. 140) .. 15 15
160. 6 c. on 10 c. (No. 142) .. 20 20
161. 30 c. on 40 c. (No. 146) 30 25
162. 45 c. on 1 col. (No. 147) 50 30

1926. Surch. with value between bars.

163. 10 on 12 c. red (No. 144) 70 12

1926. Air.

164. **47.** 20 c. blue 85 20

DESIGNS: 3 c. St. Louis College, Cartago. 6 c. Chapui Asylum, San José. 45 c. Ruins of Ujarras.

48. Heredia Normal School.

1926. Dated "1926".

165. – 3 c. blue 12 10
166. – 6 c. brown 20 12
167. **48.** 30 c. orange 25 15
168. – 45 c. violet 35 20

1928. Lindbergh Good Will Tour of Central America. Surch. with aeroplane, **LINDBERGH ENERO 1928** and new value.

169. 10 c. on 12 c. red (No. 144) 2·75 2·25

1928. Surcharged with new value.

170. **32.** 5 c. on 15 c. violet .. 20 5

1929. Surch. **CORREOS** and value.

171. **32.** 5 c. on 2 col. red .. 8 8
173. 13 c. on 40 c. green .. 10 5

49. Post Office. **50.** Juan Rafael Mora.

1930. Types of 1923 reduced in size and dated "1929" as T **49**.

174. – 1 c. purple (as No. 137) 8 5
175. **49.** 5 c. green 8 5
176. – 10 c. red (as No. 143) 25 5

1930. Air. No. O 178 surch. **CORREO 1930 AEREO**, aeroplane and value.

177. **O 1.** 8 c. on 1 col. 40 35
178. 20 c. on 1 col. .. 50 40
179. 40 c. on 1 col. .. 1·00 75
180. 1 col. on 1 col. .. 1·10 90

1930. Air. Optd. **CORREO AEREO** or surch. also.

182. **32.** 5 c. on 10 c. brown .. 12 10
181. – 10 c. red (No. 143) .. 35 10
183. **32.** 20 c. on 50 c. blue .. 15 10
184. 40 c. on 50 c. blue .. 20 10
185. 1 col. orange 60 15

1931.

186. **50.** 13 c. red 20 12

1931. Air. Fiscal stamps (Arms design) inscr. "TIMBRE 1929" (or "1930", 3 col.), surch. **Habilitado 1931 Correo Aereo** and new value.

190. 2 col. on 2 col. green .. 7·50 7·50
191. 3 col. on 5 col. brown .. 7·50 7·50
192. 5 col. on 10 col. black .. 7·50 7·50

1932. Air. Telegraph stamp optd. with wings inscr. **CORREO CR AEREO.**

193. **32.** 40 c. green .. .. 1·25 20

51.

1932. 1st National Philatelic Exn.

194. **51.** 3 c. orange 12 12
195. 5 c. green 20 20
196. 10 c. red 20 20
197. 20 c. blue 25 25

See also Nos. 231/4.

DESIGN: 1, 2 5, 10 col. Flying figure and winged wheel.

52. Landing ground. San Jose.

1934. Air.

198. **52.** 5 c. green 12 5
507. 5 c. deep blue 5 5
508. 5 c. pale blue 5 5
199. 10 c. red 12 5
509. 10 c. yellow-green .. 5 5
510. 10 c. blue-green .. 5 5
200. 15 c. brown 30 12
511. 15 c. red 8 5
201. 20 c. blue 30 5
202. 25 c. orange 40 12
512. 35 c. violet 15 8
203. 40 c. brown 70 8
204. 50 c. black 50 10
205. 60 c. yellow .. .. 1·40 25
206. 75 c. violet .. .. 1·50 35
207. – 1 col red .. .. 1·10 8
208. – 2 col. blue .. .. 1·75 30
209. – 5 col. black .. .. 3·00 2·00
210. – 10 col. brown .. .. 5·00 3·75

1934.

211. **41.** 3 c. green 5 5

54. Nurse at Altar. **55.** Image of the Virgin.

1935. Costa Rican Red Cross Jubilee.

212. **54.** 10 c. red 25 15

1935. Apparition of Our Lady of the Angels. Tercent. Inscr. "III CENTENARIO DE NTRA. SRA.DE LOS ANGELES", etc.

213. – 5 c. green 20 10
214. **55.** 10 c. red 30 12
215. – 30 c. orange 60 20
216. – 45 c. violet .. .. 1·40 30
217. **55.** 50 c. black .. .. 2·00 70

DESIGNS: 5 c., 30 c. Aerial view of Cartago. 45 c. Allegory of the Apparition.

56. Cocos Island.

1936.

218. **56.** 4 c. brown 20 10
219. 8 c. violet 25 12
220. 25 c. orange 30 20
221. 35 c. brown 30 20
222. 40 c. brown 40 25
223. 50 c. yellow 50 30
224. 2 col. green .. .. 3·00 1·10
225. 5 col. green .. .. 10·00 5·00

57. Cocos Is. and Fleet of Columbus.

1936.

226. **57.** 5 c. green 10 5
227. 10 c. red 10 5

58. Aeroplane over Mt. Poas.

1937. Air. 1st Annual Fair.

228. **58.** 1 c. black 10 8
229. 2 c. brown 10 8
230. 3 c. violet 10 8

1937. 2nd National Philatelic Exn. As T **51**, but inscr. "DICIEMBRE 1937".

231. **51.** 2 c. purple 10 10
232. 3 c. black 10 10
233. 5 c. green 12 12
234. 10 c. orange 15 12

59. Tunny.

DESIGN — As T **60**: 5 c. Native and donkey carrying bananas.

60. Coffee gathering.

61. Puntarenas.

1937. National Exn., San Jose. 1st issue.

235. **59.** 2 c. black (postage) .. 25 12
236. – 5 c. green 30 12
237. **60.** 10 c. red 40 25
238. **61.** 2 c. black (air) .. 5 5
239. 5 c. green 10 8
240. 20 c. blue 25 20
241. 1 col. 40 brown .. 2·50 2·00

62. Purple Guaria Orchid.

DESIGN—As T **62**: 3 c. Cocoa-bean.

63. National Bank.

1938. National Exn., San Jose. 2nd Issue.

242. **62.** 1 c. violet & grn. (post) 20 20
243. – 3 c. brown 25 15
244. **63.** 1 c. violet (air) .. 5 5
245. 3 c. red 5 5
246. 10 c. red 10 10
247. 75 c. brown .. 1·60 1·60

1938. No. 145 optd. **1938.**

248. 20 c. blue 15 12

64. La Sabana Airport.

1940. Air. Opening of San Jose Airport.

249. **64.** 5 c. green 5 5
250. 10 c. red 10 8
251. 25 c. blue 12 10
252. 35 c. brown 20 20
253. 60 orange 40 30
254. 85 c. violet .. .. 1·10 85
255. 2 col. 35 green .. 5·50 5·00

1940. No. 168 variously surch. **15 CENTIMOS** in ornamental frame.

256. – 15 c. on 45 c. violet .. 20 15

There are five distinct varieties of this surcharge.

1940. Pan-American Health Day. Unissued stamps prepared for the 8th Pan-American Child Welfare Congress optd. **DIA PANAMERICANO DE LA SALUD 2 DICIEMBRE 1940** and bars.

(a) Postage. Allegorical design.

261. 5 c. green 15 10
262. 10 c. red 20 12
263. 20 c. blue 25 15
264. 40 c. brown 45 40
265. 55 c. orange .. .. 1·25 50

(b) Air. View of Duran Sanatorium.

266. 10 c. red 10 8
267. 15 c. violet 12 10
268. 25 c. blue 25 15
269. 35 c. brown 35 30
270. 60 c. green 45 40
271. 75 c. olive 90 80
272. 1 col. 35 orange .. .. 3·75 3·50
273. 5 col. brown .. .. 12·00 12·00
274. 10 col. mauve .. .. 26·00 26·00

1940. Air. Pan-American Aviation Day. Surch. **AERO Aviacion Panamericana Dic. 17 1940** and value.

275. 15 c. on 50 c. yellow .. 35 35
276. 30 c. on 50 c. yellow .. 35 35

1941. Surch. **15 CENTIMOS 15** and ornamental rule.

277. **56.** 15 c. on 25 c. orange .. 20 15
278. 15 c. on 35 c. brown .. 20 15
279. 15 c. on 40 c. brown .. 20 15
280. 15 c. on 2 col. green .. 20 15
281. 15 c. on 5 col. green .. 30 25

65. Stadium and Flag.

66. Football Match.

1941. Central American and Caribbean Football Championship.

282. **65.** 5 c. green (postage) .. 80 20
283. 10 c. orange 75 20
284. 15 c. red .. .. 1·10 25
285. 25 c. blue .. .. 1·75 40
286. 40 c. brown .. .. 4·00 1·25
287. 50 c. violet .. .. 5·00 1·40
288. 75 c. orange .. .. 10·00 2·75
289. 1 col. red .. .. 16·00 5·00
290. **66.** 15 c. red (air) 65 15
291. 30 c. blue 75 20
292. 40 c. brown 75 25
293. 50 c. violet .. .. 1·00 60
294. 60 c. green .. .. 1·25 70
295. 75 c. yellow .. .. 2·10 90
296. 1 col. mauve .. .. 3·75 2·25
297. 1 col. 40 red .. .. 7·00 4·50
298. 2 col. green .. .. 15·00 13·00
299. 5 col. black .. .. 32·00 30·00

1941. Air. Costa Rica–Panama Boundary Treaty. Optd. **MAYO 1941 TRATADO LIMITROFE COSTA RICA-PANAMA** or surch. also.

300. **52.** 5 c. on 20 c. blue .. 10 8
301. 15 c. on 20 c. blue .. 15 8
302. 40 c. on 75 c. violet .. 25 15
303. – 65 c. on 1 col. red (No. 207) 45 35
304. – 1 col. 40 on 2 col. blue (No. 208) .. .. 2·00 1·75
305. – 5 col. black (No. 209) .. 8·00 7·00
306. – 10 col. brown (No. 210) 9·00 9·00

1941. As Type **41** but with new portraits.

308. – 3 c. orange 8 5
309. – 3 c. maroon 8 5
310. – 3 c. red 8 5
310a. – 3 c. blue 8 5
311. – 5 c. violet 8 5
312. – 5 c. black 8 5

PORTRAITS: 3 c. (Nos. 308/10) C. G. Viquez. 3 c. (No. 310a) Mgr. B. A. Thiel. 5 c. J. J. Rodriguez.

67. New Decree and Restored University.

1941. Restoration of National University.

313. – 5 c. green (postage) .. 20 10
314. **67.** 10 c. orange 20 10
315. – 15 c. red 30 8
316. **67.** 25 c. blue 45 15
317. – 50 c. brown .. .. 1·50 1·00
318. **67.** 15 c. red (air) 12 8
319. – 30 c. blue 20 8
320. **67.** 40 c. orange 30 15
321. – 60 c. blue 45 30
322. **67.** 1 col. violet .. .. 1·25 90
323. – 2 col. black .. .. 2·75 2·25
324. **67.** 5 col. purple .. .. 9·00 8·00

DESIGN—(Nos. 313, 315, 317, 319, 321 and 323): The origina Decree and University.

1941. Surch.
325. 5 c. on 6 c. brn. (No. 166).. 12 8
326. 15 c. on 20 c. blue (No. 248) 15 12

68. "V", Torch and Flags.
69. Francisco Morazan.

1942. War Effort.
327. 68. 5 c. red 15 8
328. 5 c. orange 15 8
329. 5 c. green 15 8
330. 5 c. blue 15 8
331. 5 c. violet 15 8

1942. Portraits and dates.
332. A. 1 c. lilac (postage) .. 5 5
333. B. 2 c. black 5 5
334. C. 3 c. blue 5 5
335. D. 5 c. blue-green .. 5 5
336. 5 c. emerald 5 5
337. 69. 15 c. red 8 5
338. E. 25 c. blue 20 10
339. F. 50 c. violet 35 20
340. G. 1 col. black .. .. 1·00 60
341. H. 2 col. orange .. .. 1·50 1·10
341a. I. 5 c. brown (air) .. 8 5
342. A. 10 c. red 8 5
342a. 10 c. olive-black .. 8 5
342b. J. 15 c. violet 10 5
343. K. 25 c. blue 15 8
344. L. 30 c. brown 12 10
345. D. 40 c. blue 15 8
346. 40 c. red 15 10
347. 69. 45 c. purple 25 15
348. M. 45 c. black 15 12
349. E. 50 c. green 90 15
350. 50 c. orange 25 20
351. N. 55 c. purple 20 12
352. F. 60 c. blue 35 12
353. 60 c. green 15 12
354. G. 65 c. red 45 15
355. 65 c. blue 15 12
356. O. 75 c. green 30 20
357. H. 85 c. orange 50 25
358. 85 c. violet 75 30
359. P. 1 col. black 80 30
360. 1 col. red 30 15
361. Q. 1 col. 5 sepia 40 30
362. R. 1 col. 15 brown .. 1·00 90
363. 1 col. 15 green .. 1·60 70
364. B. 1 col. 40 violet .. 1·75 1·10
365. 1 col. 40 yellow .. 90 75
366. C. 2 col. black .. .. 2·50 60
367. 2 col. olive 75 25

PORTRAITS: A, J. Mora Fernandez. B, B. Carranza. C, T. Guardia. D, M. Aguilar. E, J. M. Alfaro. F, F. M. Oreamuno. G, J. M. Castro. H, J. R. Mora. I, S. Lara. J, C. Duran. K, A. Esquivel. L, V. Herrera. M, J. R. de Gallegos. N, P. Fernandez. O, B. Soto. P, J. M. Montealegre. Q, B. Carrillo. R, J. Jimenez.

1943. Air. Optd. **Legislacion Social 15 Setiembre 1943.**
368. 5 col. black (No. 209) .. 2·25 1·50
369. 10 col. brown (No. 210) 3·75 2·50

70. San Ramon.

71. Allegory of Flight.

1944. San Ramon. Cent.
370. 70. 5 c. green (postage) .. 8 5
371. 10 c. orange 10 5
372. 15 c. red 15 8
373. 40 c. grey 40 30
374. 50 c. blue 60 50
375. 71. 10 c. orange (air) .. 10 8
376. 15 c. red 15 10
377. 40 c. blue 30 15
378. 45 c. red 35 20
379. 60 c. green 40 30
380. 1 col. brown 80 70
381. 1 col. 40 grey .. 5·00 3·50
382. 5 col. violet .. 10·00 10·00
383. 10 col. black .. 23·00 22·00

1944. Ratification of Costa Rica and Panama Boundary Treaty. Optd. **La entrevista ...1944.**
384. 63 5 c. orange 8 5
385. 5 c. green 8 5
386. 5 c. blue 8 5
387. 5 c. violet 8 5

1944. Air. No. 207 optd. **1944.**
388. 1 col. red 45 20

1945. Air. Official Air stamps of 1934 optd. **1945**, in oblong network frame.
389. 52. 5 c. green 40 40
390. 10 c. red 40 40
391. 15 c. brown 40 40
392. 20 c. blue 25 25
393. 25 c. orange 40 40
394. 40 c. brown 35 35
395. 50 c. black 45 45
396. 60 c. yellow 60 30
397. 75 c. violet 60 50
398. – 1 col. red (No. O 220).. 45 35
399. – 2 col. blue (No. O 221) 3·50 3·00
400. – 5 col. black (No. O 222) 4·50 4·50
401. – 10 col. brown (No. O 223) 7·50 7·50

1945. Air stamps. Telegraph stamps as Type 32 optd. **CORREO AEREO 1945** and bar.
402. 32. 40 c. green 15 8
403. 50 c. blue 15 8
404. 1 col. orange 35 20

72. Mauro Fernandez.
73. Coffee Gathering.

1945. Fernandez. Birth Cent.
405. 72. 20 c. green 12 8

1945.
406. 73. 5 c. black and green .. 10 5
407. 10 c. black and orange.. 15 8
408. 20 c. black and red .. 20 10

74. Florence Nightingale and Nurse Cavell.

1945. Air. National Red Cross Society. 60th Anniv.
409. 74. 1 col. black 30 15

1946. Air. Central American and Caribbean Football Championship. As Type 66, but inscribed "FEBRERO 1946".
410. 66. 25 c. green 75 60
411. 30 c. orange 75 60
412. 55 c. blue 90 60

1946. Surch. **15 15.**
413. 72. 15 c. on 20 c. green .. 10 5

75. San Juan de Dios, Hospital.
76. Ascension Esquivel.

1946. Air. San Juan de Dios Hospital Cent.
414. 75. 5 c. black and green .. 5 5
415. 10 c. black and brown.. 5 5
416. 15 c. black and red .. 5 5
417. 25 c. black and blue .. 10 8
418. 30 c. black and orange 25 20
419. 40 c. black and olive 10 8
420. 50 c. black and violet 20 15
421. 60 c. black and green .. 45 35
422. 75 c. black and brown 35 20
423. 1 col. black and blue .. 50 25
424. 2 col. black and brown 60 40
425. 3 col. black and purple 1·40 1·40
426. 5 col. black and yellow 1·90 1·90

1947. Air. Former Presidents.
427. – 2 col. black and blue 70 60
428. 76. 3 col. black and red 1·10 1·00
429. – 5 col. black and green 1·60 1·25
430. – 10 col. black & orange.. 3·25 2·75

PORTRAITS: 2 col. Rafael Iglesias. 5 col. Cleto Gonzalez Viquez. 10 col. Ricardo Jimenez.

1947. No. O 228 optd. **CORREOS 1947.**
431. 57. 5 c. green 8 5

1947. Air. Nos. 410/2 surch. **Habilitado para ₡0.15 Decreto No. 16 de 28 abril de 1947.**
432. 66. 15 c. on 25 c. green .. 70 55
433. 15 c. on 30 c. orange .. 70 55
434. 15 c. on 55 c. blue .. 70 55

77. Columbus at Cariari.
78. Franklin D. Roosevelt.

1947. Air.
435. 77. 25 c. black and green 15 10
436. 30 c. black and blue .. 15 10
437. 40 c. black and orange 25 12
438. 45 c. black and violet 30 15
439. 50 c. black and red .. 40 15
440. 65 c. black and brown 60 40

1947. Air. Stamps of 1942 surch. **₡0.15.**
441. E. 15 c. on 50 c. orange .. 12 12
442. F. 15 c. on 60 c. green .. 12 12
443. O. 15 c. on 75 c. green .. 12 12
444. P. 15 c. on 1 col. red .. 12 12
445. Q. 15 c. on 1 col. 5 sepia .. 12 12

1947.
446. 78. 5 c. green (postage) .. 5 5
447. 10 c. red 8 5
448. 15 c. blue 10 8
449. 25 c. orange 15 12
450. 30 c. claret 25 20
451. 15 c. green (air) .. 8 5
452. 30 c. red 20 10
453. 45 c. brown 20 20
454. 65 c. orange 20 20
455. 75 c. blue 20 20
456. 1 col. green 40 35
457. 2 col. black .. .. 1·00 90
458. 5 col. red .. .. 2·60 1·75

79. Cervantes.
80. Early Steam Locomotive.

1947. Cervantes. 4th Birth Cent.
459. 79. 30 c. blue 15 8
460. 55 c. red 25 15

1947. Air. Electrication of Pacific Railway. 50th Anniv.
461. 80. 35 c. black and green.. 50 20

81. National Theatre.
82. Rafael Iglesias.

1948. Air. National Theatre. 50th Anniv.
462. 81. 15 c. black and blue .. 8 5
463. 20 c. black and red .. 12 8
464. 82. 35 c. black and green.. 15 15
465. 81. 45 c. black and violet.. 15 12
466. 50 c. black and red .. 20 15
467. 75 c. black and purple.. 45 30
468. 1 col. black and green.. 60 35
469. 2 col. black and lake .. 85 75
470. 82. 5 col. black and yellow 2·00 1·60
471. 10 col. black and blue.. 3·50 3·00

1948. Air. Surch. **HABILITADO PARA ₡0.35.**
472. 77. 35 c. on 40 c. black and orange 25 20

1949. Air. Annexation of Guanacaste. 125th Anniv. Nos. 361, 409, 363 and 365 variously surch. **1824-1949 125 Aniversario de la Anexion Guanacaste** and value.
473. Q. 35 c. on 1 col. 5 sepia.. 12 10
474. 74. 50 c. on 1 col. black .. 20 15
475. R. 55 c. on 1 col. 15 green 40 35
476. B. 55 c. on 1 col. 40 yellow 40 35

83. Globe and Dove.

1950. Air. U.P.U. 75th Anniv.
477. 83. 15 c. red 10 5
478. 25 c. blue 12 8
479. 1 col. green 25 12

84. Battle of El Tejar, Cartago.
85. Dr. C. L. Valverde.

1950. Air. Inscr. "GUERRA DE LIBERACION NACIONAL 1948".
480. 84. 15 c. black and red .. 8 5
481. – 20 c. black and green .. 12 10
482. – 25 c. black and blue .. 15 12
483. – 35 c. black and brown 25 12
484. – 55 c. black and violet.. 35 15
485. – 75 c. black and orange 55 20
486. 85. 80 c. black and grey .. 60 25
487. 1 col. black and orange 75 35

DESIGNS—VERT. 20 c. Bayonet charge. HORIZ. 25. c La Lucha Ranch. 35 c. Trench of San Isidro Battalion. 55 c., 75 c. Observation post.

86. Bull.
87. Queen Isabella and Caravels.

1950. Air. National Agriculture and Industries Fair. Centres in black.
488. 86. 1 c. green 12 10
489. A. 2 c. blue 12 10
490. B. 3 c. brown 12 10
491. C. 5 c. blue 12 10
492. 86. 10 c. green 30 10
493. A. 30 c. violet 25 10
494. D. 45 c. orange 30 12
495. C. 50 c. grey 40 12
496. B. 65 c. blue 50 25
497. D. 80 c. red 75 40
498. 86. 2 col. orange .. .. 2·00 1·10
499. A. 3 col. blue .. .. 2·25 1·75
500. C. 5 col. red .. .. 4·50 4·00
501. D. 10 col. claret .. .. 5·00 4·50

DESIGNS—VERT. A. Fishing. B. Pineapple. C. Bananas. D. Coffee.

1952. Air. Isabella the Catholic. 500th Birth Anniv.
502. 87. 15 c. red 8 5
503. 20 c. orange 8 8
504. 25 c. blue 12 5
505. 55 c. green 30 15
506. 2 col. violet 80 40

1953. Air. Surch.
513. 78. 15 c. on 30 c. red .. 12 10
514. 15 c. on 45 c. brown .. 12 5
515. 15 c. on 65 c. orange .. 12 5

1953. Air. Surch. **HABILITADO PARA CINCO CENTIMOS 1953.**
515a. 77. 5 c. on 30 c. blk. & blue 70 50
516. 5 c. on 40 c. blk. & orge. 8 8
517. 5 c. on 45 c. blk. & vio. 8 8
518. 5 c. on 65 c. blk. & brn. 15 12

88.

1953. Fiscal stamps surch. as in T 88.
519. 88. 5 c. on 10 c. green .. 10 5

89. "Vegetable Oil".
90.

1954. Air. National Industries. Horiz. designs as T 89. Centres in black.
520. 5 c. red (T 89) 5 5
520a. 5 c. blue (as No. 520) .. 10 5
521. 10 c. indigo (Pottery) .. 10 5
521a. 10 c. blue (Pottery) .. 15 5
522. 15 c. green (Sugar) .. 10 5
522a. 15 c. yellow (Sugar) .. 12 5
523. 20 c. violet (Soap) .. 10 5
524. 25 c. lake (Timber) .. 10 5
525. 30 c. lilac (Matches) .. 30 15
526. 35 c. purple (Textiles) .. 15 8
527. 40 c. black (Leather) .. 25 12
528. 45 c. green (Tobacco) .. 40 15
529. 50 c. maroon (Confectionery) 30 10
530. 55 c. yellow (Canning) .. 20 10
531. 60 c. brown (General Industries) 45 25
532. 65 c. red (Metals) .. 55 25
533. 75 c. violet (Pharmaceutics).. .. .. 85 30
533a. 75 c. red (as No. 533) .. 20 12
533b. 80 c. violet (as No. 533).. 35 20
534. 1 col. turq. (Paper) .. 25 15
535. 2 col. magenta (Rubber) 75 40
536. 3 col. green (Aircraft) .. 1·10 75
537. 5 col. black (Marble) .. 1·75 80
538. 10 col. yellow (Beer) .. 5·00 4·00

1955. Fiscal stamps optd. for postal use as in T **90**.

539. **90.** 5 c. on 2 c. green .. 5 5
540. 15 c. on 2 c. green .. 10 5

91. Rotary Emblem over Central America. **92.** Map of Costa Rica.

1956. Air. Rotary International. 50th Anniv. Inscr. as in T **91**.

542. **91.** 10 c. green 8 5
543. – 25 c. blue 15 10
544. – 40 c. brown 25 15
545. – 45 c. red 20 15
546. – 60 c. purple 20 15
547. – 2 col. orange 50 35

DESIGNS: 25 c. Emblem, hand and boy. 40 c., 2 col. Emblem and hospital. 45 c. Emblem, leaves and C. America. 60 c. Emblem and lighthouse.

1957. Air. War of 1856–67. Cent. Inscr. as in T **92**.

548. **92.** 5 c. blue 5 5
549. – 10 c. green 5 5
550. – 15 c. orange 5 5
551. – 20 c. brown 5 5
552. – 25 c. blue 8 8
553. – 30 c. violet 12 10
554. – 35 c. red 12 8
555. – 40 c. black 12 10
556. – 45 c. red 15 12
557. – 50 c. blue 15 12
558. – 55 c. ochre 20 12
559. – 60 c. red 25 15
560. – 65 c. red 25 15
561. – 70 c. yellow 30 20
562. – 75 c. emerald 25 20
563. – 80 c. sepia 35 25
564. – 1 col. black 45 30

DESIGNS: 10 c. Map of Guanacaste. 15 c. War-time inn. 20 c. Santa Rosa house. 25 c. Gen. D. J. M. Quiros. 30 c. Old Presidential Palace. 35 c. Minister D. J. B. Calvo. 40 c. Minister L. Molina. 45 c. Gen. D. J. J. Mora. 50 c. Gen. D. J. M. Canas. 55 c. Juan Santamaria Monument. 60 c. National Monument. 65 c. A. Vallerriestra. 70 c. Pres. R. Castilla Marquesado of Peru. 75 c. San Carlos Fortress. 80 c. Vice-President D. F. M. Oreamuno of Costa Rica. 1 col. Pres. D. J. R. Mora of Costa Rica.

1958. Obligatory Tax. Juvenile Delinquents' Fund. Nos. 489 and 521a surch. **SELLO DE NAVIDAD PRO-CIUDAD DE LOS NINOS 5 5.**

565. A. 5 c. on 2 c. black & blue 8 5
566. – 5 c. on 10 c. black & blue 8 5

93. Pres. C. Gonzalez. **94.** Pres. R. J. Oreamuno and Electric Train.

1959. Air. Birth Centenaries of Presidents Gonzalez (1958) and Oreamuno (1959).

567. **93.** 5 c. blue and pink .. 5 5
568. – 10 c. slate and red .. 5 5
569. – 15 c. black and slate .. 5 5
570. – 20 c. brown and red .. 10 8
571. – 35 c. blue and purple .. 12 12
572. – 55 c. violet and brown 15 12
573. – 80 c. blue 30 25
574. **94.** 1 col. lake and orange 40 25
575. – 2 col. lake and black .. 70 60

DESIGNS—As T **93**: 10 c. Pres. Oreamuno. As T **94**: Pres. Gonzalez and: 15 c. Highway bridge. 55 c. Water pipe-line. 80 c. National Library. Pres. Oreamuno and: 20 c. Puntarenas Quay. 35 c. Post Office, San Jose. 2 col. Both presidents and open book inscr. "PROBIDAD" ("Honesty").

95. Father Flanagan. **96.** Goal Attack.

1959. Obligatory Tax. Christmas. Inscr. "SELLO DE NAVIDAD".

576. **95.** 5 c. green 15 8
577. – 5 c. magenta 15 8
578. – 5 c. olive 15 8
579. – 5 c. black 15 8

PAINTINGS: No. 577, "Girl with braids" (after Modigliani). 578, "Boy with a club-foot" (after Ribera). 579, "The boy blowing on charcoal" (after "El Greco").

1960. Air. 3rd Pan-American Football Games.

580. **96.** 10 c. indigo 10 8
581. – 25 c. blue 15 10
582. – 35 c. red 20 15
583. – 50 c. brown 25 15
584. – 85 c. turquoise 50 30
585. – 5 col. purple .. .. 1·90 1·50

DESIGNS: 25 c. Player heading ball. 35 c. Defender tackling forward. 50 c. Referee bouncing ball. 85 c. Goalkeeper seizing ball. 5 col. Player kicking high ball.

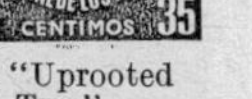

97. "Uprooted Tree". **98.** Prof. J. A. Facio.

1960. Air. World Refugee Year.

586. **97.** 35 c. blue and yellow .. 20 12
587. 85 c. black and rose .. 30 25

1960. Professor Justo A. Facio. Birth Cent.

588. **98.** 10 c. lake-red 5 5

99.

1960. Air. 6th and 7th Chancellors' Reunion Conference, Organization of American States, San Jose. As T **99**. Multicoloured.

589. 25 c. T **99** 12 10
590. 35 c. "OEA" within oval chains 20 15
591. 55 c. Clasped hands and chains 30 25
592. 5 col. Flags in form of flying bird .. .. 2·25 2·00
593. 10 col. "OEA" on map of Costa Rica, and flags .. 4·00 3·00

100. St. Louise de Marillac, Sister of Charity & Children. **101.** Father Peralta.

1960. Air. St. Vincent de Paul. Death Tercent. Inscr. as in T **100**.

594. **100.** 10 c. green 5 5
595. – 25 c. lake 8 5
596. – 50 c. blue 15 12
597. – 1 col. yellow-brown .. 35 25
598. – 5 col. sepia .. .. 1·60 1·25

DESIGNS—HORIZ. St. Vincent de Paul, and: 25 c. Two-storey building. 1 col. Modern building. 50 c. As T **100**, but scene shows Sister at bedside. VERT. 5 col. Stained-glass window picturing St. Vincent de Paul with children.

1960. Obligatory Tax. Christmas. Inscr. "SELLO DE NAVIDAD".

599. **101.** 5 c. chocolate .. 25 5
600. – 5 c. orange 25 5
601. – 5 c. claret 25 5
602. – 5 c. grey-blue 25 5

DESIGNS: No. 600. "Girl" (after Renoir). 601. "The Drinkers" (after Velasquez). 602. "Children Singing" (sculpture, after Zuniga).

102. Running.

1960. Air. Olympic Games Rome Centres and inscriptions in black.

603. 1 c. greenish yell. (T **102**) 5 5
604. 2 c. cobalt (Diving) .. 5 5
605. 3 c. red (Cycling) .. 5 5
606. 4 c. yellow (Weightlifting) 5 5
607. 5 c. yellow-grn. (Tennis) .. 5 5
608. 10 c. vermilion (Boxing) .. 5 5
609. 25 c. blue-green (Football) 10 8
610. 85 c. mauve (Basketball) .. 60 50
611. 1 col. grey (Baseball) .. 75 60
612. 10 col. lavender (Pistol-shooting) .. .. 6·00 5·00

1961. Air. 15th World Amateur Baseball Championships. No. 533a optd. **XV Campeonato Mundial de Beisbol de Aficionados** or surch. in figs. also.

613. 25 c. on 75 c. black and red 10 5
614. 75 c. black and red .. 30 15

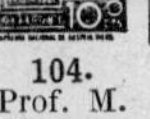

103. M. Aguilar. **104.** Prof. M. Obregon. **105.** Granary (F.A.O.).

1961. Air. First Continental Lawyers' Conference.

615. **103.** 10 c. blue 5 5
616. – 10 c. maroon 5 5
617. – 25 c. violet 8 5
618. – 25 c. sepia 8 5

PORTRAITS: No. 616, A. Brenes. 617, A. Gutierrez. 618, V. Herrera.
See also Nos. 628/31.

1961. Air. Obregon's Birth Cent.

619. **104.** 10 c. turquoise .. 5 5

1961. Air. United Nations Commem.

620. **105.** 10 c. green 5 5
621. – 20 c. orange 10 5
622. – 25 c. slate 15 10
623. – 30 c. indigo 15 10
624. – 35 c. red 65 15
625. – 45 c. violet 25 15
626. – 85 c. blue 50 35
627. – 10 col. black .. 3·50 3·00

DESIGNS: 20 c. "Medical Care" (W.H.O.). 25 c. Globe and workers (I.L.O.). 30 c. Globe and communications satellite. "Correo 1B" (I.T.U.). 35 c. Compass and rocket (W.M.O.). 45 c. "The Thinker" (statue) and open book (U.N.E.S.C.O.) 85 c. Airliner and globe (I.C.A.O.). 10 col. "Spiderman" on girder (International Bank).

1961. Air. 9th Central American Medical Congress. As T **103** but inscr. "NOVENO CONGRESO MEDICO", etc.

628. 10 c. violet 5 5
629. 10 c. turquoise 5 5
630. 25 c. sepia 10 5
631. 25. c. maroon 10 5

PORTRAITS. No. 628, Dr. E. J. Roman. 629, Dr. J. M. S. Alfaro. 630, Dr. A. S. Llorente. 631, Dr. J. J. U. Giralt.

1961. Air. Children's City Christmas issue. No. 522 surch. **SELLO DE NAVIDAD PRO-CIUDAD DE LOS NINOS** and value.

632. 5 c. on 15 c. black & green 12 5

1962. Air. Surch. in figures.

633. 10 c. on 15 c. black & green (No. 522) 5 5
634. 25 c. on 15 c. black & green (No. 522) 10 8
635. 35 c. on 50 c. blk. & maroon (No. 529) 15 8
636. 85 c. on 80 c. blue (No. 573) 35 30

1962. Air. 2nd Central American Philatelic Convention. Optd. **11 CONVENCION FILATELICA CENTROAMERICANA SETIEMBRE 1962.**

637. 30 c. indigo (No. 623) .. 25 20
638. 2 col. lake & black (No. 575) 70 60

1962. Air. No. 522 surch.

639. 10 c. on 15 c. blk. & green 5 5

1962. Air. Fiscal stamps as T **90** optd. **CORREO AEREO** and surch. with new value for postal use.

640. 25 c. on 2 c. green .. 5 5
641. 35 c. on 2 c. green .. 8 8
642. 45 c. on 2 c. green .. 15 12
643. 85 c. on 2 c. green .. 30 25

106. "Virgin and Child" (after Bellini). **107.** Jaguar.

1962. Obligatory Tax. Christmas.

644. **106.** 5 c. sepia 25 5
645. A. 5 c. green 25 5
646. B. 5 c. blue 25 5
647. C. 5 c. claret 25 5

DESIGNS: A, "Angel with Violin" (after Mellozo). B, Mgr. Ruben Odio. C, "Child's Head" (after Rubens).
See also Nos. 674/7.

1963. Air.

648. – 5 c. brown and olive .. 5 5
649. – 10 c. grey-bl. and orge. 5 5
650. **107.** 25 c. yellow and blue .. 10 5
651. – 30 c. brown & yell.-grn. 15 12
652. – 35 c. chestnut & bistre 20 10
653. – 40 c. blue and green .. 30 20
654. – 85 c. black and green .. 50 30
655. – 5 col. choc. & ol.-grn. 2·00 1·50

ANIMALS (As T **107**): 5 c Paca. 10 c. Tapir. 30 c. Ocelot. 35 c. Deer. 40 c. Manatee. 85 c. Cebus monkey. 5 col. Peccary.

108. Arms and Campaign Emblem. **109.** Anglo-Costa Rican Bank.

1963. Air. Malaria Eradication.

656. **108.** 25 c. red 10 5
657. 35 c. chestnut 12 8
658. 45 c. blue 20 12
659. 85 c. green 30 20
660. 1 col. grey-blue .. 40 30

1963. Obligatory Tax Fund for Children's Village. Nos. 644/7 surch. **1963 10 CENTIMOS.**

661. **106.** 10 c. on 5 c. sepia .. 12 10
662. A. 10 c. on 5 c. green .. 12 10
663. B. 10 c. on 5 c. blue .. 12 10
664. C. 10 c. on 5 c. claret .. 12 10

1963. Anglo-Costa Rican Bank Centenary.

665. **109.** 10 c. indigo 5 5

110. ½ real Stamp of 1863 and Packet-ship "William le Lacheur".

1963. Air. Stamp Cent.

666. **110.** 25 c. blue and purple .. 5 5
667. – 2 col. orange and grey 75 45
668. – 3 col. green and ochre 1·10 80
669. – 10 col. brown and green 3·50 2·50

DESIGNS: 2 col. 2 reales stamp of 1863 and Postmaster-General R. B. Carrillo. 3 col. 4 reales stamp of 1863, and mounted postman and pack-mule of 1839. 10 col. 1 peso stamp of 1863 and mule-drawn mail-car.

1963. Unissued animal designs as T **107**. Surch.

670. 10 c. on 1 c. brown & green 8 5
671. 25 c. on 2 c. sepia & brown 8 5
672. 35 c. on 3 c. brown & myrtle 10 8
673. 85 c. on 4 c. brown and lake 20 12

ANIMALS: 1 c. Little anteater. 2 d. Grey fox. 3 c. Armadillo. 4 c. Great anteater.

1963. Obligatory Tax. Christmas. As Nos. 644/7 but inscr. "1963" and new colours.

674. **106.** 5 c. blue 15 5
675. A. 5 c. claret 15 5
676. B. 5 c. black 15 5
677. C. 5 c. sepia 15 5

111. Pres. Orlich (Costa Rica). **112.** Puma (clay) statuette).

1963. Air. Presidential Reunion, San Jose. Portraits in black-brown.

678. 111. 25 c. purple 8 5
679. – 30 c. magenta .. 12 10
680. – 35 c. ochre 12 12
681. – 85 c. grey-blue .. 20 15
682. – 1 col. chestnut .. 35 20
683. – 3 col. olive-green .. 1·40 1·00
684. – 5 col. slate .. 2·50 1·75

PRESIDENTS: 30 c. Rivera (Salvador). 35 c. Ydigoras (Guatemala). 85 c. Villeda (Honduras). 1 col. Somoza (Nicaragua). 3 col. Chiari (Panama). 5 col. Kennedy (U.S.A.).

1963. Air. Archaeological Discoveries.

685. 112. 5 c. turq. & apple-green 5 5
686. – 10 c. blue-green and light yellow .. 5 5
687. – 25 c. sepia and red .. 8 5
688. – 30 c. blue-green & buff 10 5
689. – 35 c. bronze-green and salmon 10 10
690. – 45 c. brown and blue .. 10 10
691. – 50 c. brown and blue .. 15 10
692. – 55 c. brown and green 15 10
693. – 75 c. chocolate & buff 20 12
694. – 85 c. chestnut & yellow 35 20
695. – 90 c. brown and yellow 50 25
696. – 1 col. brown and blue 25 20
697. – 2 col. blue-green & yell. 40 25
698. – 3 col. brown and green 70 50
699. – 5 col. brn. & apple-yell. 1·75 1·00
700. – 10 col. myrtle & mauve 2·25 2·00

DESIGNS—HORIZ. 10 c. Ceremonial stool. 1 col. Twin beakers. 2 col. Alligator. VERT. 25 c. Man (statuette). 30 c. Dancer. 35 c. Vase 45 c. Deity. 50 c. Simian effigy. 55 c. "Eagle" bell. 75 c. Multi-limbed deity. 85 c. Kneeling effigy. 90 c. "Bird" jug. 3 col. Twin-tailed lizard. 5 col. Child. 10 col. Stone effigy of woman.

113. Flags.

114. Mgr. R. Odio and Children.

1964. Air. "Centro America".

701. 113. 30 c. multicoloured .. 25 20

1964. Air. Surch.

702. – 5 c. on 30 c. (No. 683) 5 5
703. 113. 15 c. on 30 c. 5 5
704. – 15 c. on 85 c. (No. 694) 5 5

See Nos. 745/9.

1964. Paris Postal Conf. No. 695 surch. C **0.15 CONFERENCIA POSTAL DE PARIS-1864.**

705. 15 c. on 90 c. brn. & yellow 8 5

1964. Obligatory Tax. Christmas. Inscr. "SELLO DE NAVIDAD" etc.

706. 114. 5 c. brown 12 5
707. A. 5 c. blue 12 5
708. B. 5 c. purple 12 5
709. C. 5 c. green 12 5

DESIGNS: A, Teacher and child. B, Children at play. C, Children in class.

115. A. Gonzalez F.

116. Handfuls of grain.

1965. Air. National Bank. 50th Anniv.

710. 115. 35 c. green 10 5

1965. Air. Chapui Hospital. 75th Anniv. No. 697 surch. **75 ANIVERSARIO ASILO CHAPUI 1890-1965.**

711. 2 col. blue-green & yellow 45 30

1965. Air. Freedom from Hunger.

712. – 15 c. blk., grey & brn. 5 5
713. 116. 35 c. black and buff .. 10 5
714. – 50 c. green and blue .. 15 10
715. – 1 col. silver, blk. & grn. 25 15

DESIGNS—HORIZ. 15 c. Map and grain silo. 1 col. Jetliner over map. VERT. 50 c. Children and population graph.

117. National Children's Hospital.

118. L. Briceno B.

1965. Christmas Charity. Obligatory Tax. Inscr. "SELLO DE NAVIDAD", etc.

716. 117. 5 c. green 10 5
717. A. 5 c. brown 10 5
718. B. 5 c. red 10 5
719. C. 5 c. blue 10 5

DESIGNS—As T 117: A, Father Casiano. B. Poinsettia. DIAMOND: C, Father Christmas with children.

1965. Air. Incorporation of Nicoya District.

720. 118. 5 c. slate, blk. & chest. 5 5
721. – 10 c. slate and blue .. 5 5
722. – 15 c. slate and bistre 5 5
723. – 35 c. slate and blue .. 8 5
724. – 50 c. violet and grey .. 10 8
725. – 1 col. slate and ochre .. 25 20

DESIGNS: 10 c. Nicoya Church. 15 c. Incorporation scroll. 35 c. Map of Guanacaste Province. 50 c. Provincial dance. 1 col. Guanacaste map and produce.

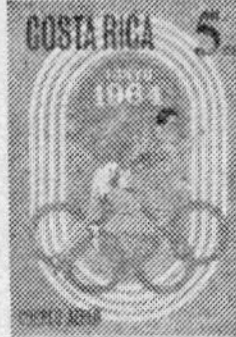

119. Running.

120. Pres. Kennedy and Capsule encircling Globe.

1965. Air. Olympic Games (1964). Mult.

726. 5 c. Type 119 .. .. 5 5
727. 10 c. Cycling 5 5
728. 40 c. Judo 20 12
729. 65 c. Handball 20 15
730. 80 c. Football 25 25
731. 1 col. Olympic torches .. 30 30

1965. Air. Pres. Kennedy. 2nd Death Anniv. Multicoloured.

732. 45 c. Type 120 .. .. 12 10
733. 55 c. Kennedy in San Jose Cathedral 20 15
734. 85 c. President with son .. 25 25
735. 1 col. Facade of White House, Washington .. 30 30

Nos. 732/5 are vert.

121. Fire Engine.

122. Angel.

1966. Air. Fire Brigade. Cent.

736. 121. 5 c. red and black .. 5 5
737. – 10 c. red and yellow .. 5 5
738. – 15 c. black and red .. 5 5
739. – 35 c. yellow and black 8 5
740. – 50 c. red and blue .. 12 8

DESIGNS—VERT. 10 c. Fire engine of 1866. 15 c. Firemen with hoses. 35 c. Brigade badge. 50 c. Emblem of Central American Fire Brigades Confederation.

1966. Obligatory Tax. Christmas. Inscr. "SELLO DE NAVIDAD", etc.

741. 122. 5 c. blue 10 5
742. – 5 c. red (Trinkets) .. 10 5
743. – 5 c. green (Church) .. 10 5
744. – 5 c. brown (Reindeer) 10 5

1966. Air (a) Surch.

745. 15 c. on 30 c. (No. 688) 5 5
746. – 15 c. on 45 c. (No. 690) 5 5
747. – 35 c. on 75 c. (No. 693) 8 5
748. – 35 c. on 55 c. (No. 733) 8 5
749. – 50 c. on 85 c. (No. 734) 12 10

(b) Revenue stamps (as T 90) surch.

750. – 15 c. on 5 c. blue .. 5 5
751. – 35 c. on 10 c. claret .. 5 5
752. – 50 c. on 20 c. vermilion 12 8

123. Central Bank, San Jose.

124. Telecommunications Building, San Pedro.

1967. Obligatory Tax. Social Plan for Postal Workers.

753. – 10 c. blue (postage) .. 5 5

DESIGN as T 123 (34×26 mm.): 10 c. Post Office, San Jose.

1967. Air. Central Bank. 50th Anniv.

754. 123. 5 c. green 5 5
755. 15 c. brown 5 5
756. 35 c. red 8 5

1967. Air. Costa Rican Electrical Industry.

757. – 5 c. black 5 5
758. 124. 10 c. magenta .. 5 5
759. – 15 c. orange .. 5 5
760. – 25 c. ultramarine .. 5 5
761. – 35 c. green .. 8 5
762. – 50 c. brown 12 10

DESIGNS—VERT. 5 c. Electric pylons. 15 c. Central Telephone Exchange, San Jose, HORIZ. 25 c. La Garita Dam. 35 c. Rio Macho Reservoir. 50 c. Cachi Dam.

125. "Chondrorhyncha aromatica".

126. O.E.A. Emblem and Split Leaf.

1967. Air. University Library. Orchids. Multicoloured.

763. 5 c. Type 125 .. .. 5 5
764. 10 c. "Miltonia endresii" 5 5
765. 15 c. "Stanhopea cirrhata" 5 5
766. 25 c. "Trichopilia suavis" 8 5
767. 35 c. "Odontoglossum schlieperianum" .. 10 8
768. 50 c. "Cattleya skinneri" 12 10
769. 1 col. "Cattleya dowiana" 25 15
770. 2 col. "Odontoglossum chiriquense" 50 35

1967. Air. Inter-American Institute of Agricultural Science. 25th Anniv.

771. 126. 50 c. ultramarine & blue 10 5

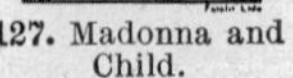

127. Madonna and Child.

128. L.A.C.S.A. Emblem.

1967. Obligatory Tax. Christmas.

772. 127. 5 c. green 5 5
773. 5 c. magenta 5 5
774. 5 c. blue 5 5
775. 5 c. turquoise-blue .. 5 5

1967. Air. Lineas Aereas Costaricenses (L.A.C.S.A. – Costa Rica Airlines). 20th Anniv. (1966). Multicoloured.

776. 40 c. Type 128 .. .. 8 8
777. 45 c. L.A.C.S.A. emblem and jetliner 8 8
778. 50 c. Wheel and emblem .. 10 8

The 45 c. is a horiz. design.

129. Church of Solitude.

130. Scouts in Camp.

1967. Air. Churches and Cathedrals. (1st series).

779. 129. 5 c. green 5 5
780. – 10 c. blue 5 5
781. – 15 c. purple 5 5
782. – 25 c. ochre 5 5
783. – 30 c. brown 5 5
784. – 35 c. blue 8 5
785. – 40 c. orange 10 8
786. – 45 c. green 10 8
787. – 50 c. olive 12 8
788. – 55 c. brown 12 8
789. – 65 c. magenta 12 8
790. – 75 c. sepia 15 12
791. – 80 c. yellow 15 12
792. – 85 c. purple 20 15
793. – 90 c. green 20 15
794. – 1 col. slate 20 12
795. – 2 col. green 45 30
796. – 3 col. orange .. .. 1·10 50
797. – 5 col. blue .. .. 1·50 70
798. – 10 col. red .. .. 2·00 1·75

DESIGNS: 10 c. Santo Domingo Basilica, Heredia. 15 c. Tilaran Cathedral. 25 c. Alajuela Cathedral. 30 c. Church of Mercy. 35 c. Our Lady of the Angels Basilica. 40 c. San Rafael Church, Heredia. 45 c. Ruins, Ujarras. 50 c. Ruins of Parish Church, Cartago. 55 c. San Jose Cathedral. 65 c. Parish Church, Puntarenas. 75 c. Orosi Church. 80 c. Cathedral of San Isidro the General. 85 c. San Ramon Church. 90 c. Church of the Forsaken. 1 col. Coronado Church. 2 col. Church of St. Teresita. 3 col. Parish Church, Heredia. 5 col. Carmelite Church. 10 col. Limon Cathedral.

See also Nos. 918/33.

1968. Air. Scout Movement in Costa Rica. Golden Jubilee (1966). Multicoloured.

799. 15 c. Scout on traffic control 5 5
800. 25 c. Scouts tending camp-fire 5 5
801. 35 c. Scout badge and flags 10 5
802. 50 c. Type 130 .. .. 12 10
803. 65 c. First scout troop on parade (1916) 15 12

The 15 c., 25 c. and 35 c. are vert. designs.

131. "Madonna and Child".

132. Running.

1968. Christmas Charity. Obligatory Tax.

805. 131. 5 c. black 5 5
806. 5 c. maroon 5 5
807. 5 c. chestnut 5 5
808. 5 c. red 5 5

1969. Air. Olympic Games, Mexico. Multi-coloured.

809. 30 c. Type 132 .. .. 5 5
810. 40 c. Woman breasting tape 8 5
811. 55 c. Boxing 12 10
812. 65 c. Cycling 15 10
813. 75 c. Weightlifting .. 15 12
814. 1 col. High-diving .. 20 15
815. 3 col. Rifle-shooting .. 75 50

133. Postal Emblems.

134. Arms of San Jose.

1969. Air. "Costa Rica 69" Philatelic Exn.

816. 133. 35 c. multicoloured .. 5 5
817. 40 c. multicoloured .. 5 5
818. 50 c. multicoloured .. 10 8
819. 2 col. multicoloured .. 35 25

1969. Coats of Arms. Multicoloured.

820. 15 c. Type 134 .. .. 5 5
821. 35 c. Cartago 8 5
822. 50 c. Heredia 12 10
823. 55 c. Alajuela 12 10
824. 65 c. Guanacaste .. 15 12
825. 1 col. Puntarenas .. 30 12
826. 2 col. Limon 45 25

135. I.L.O. Emblem.

136. Map of Central America on Football.

1969. Air. Int. Labour Organization. 50th Anniv.

827. 135. 35 c. turquoise & black 5 5
828. 50 c. red and black .. 10 8

1969. Air. 4th CONCACAF Football Championships. Multicoloured.

829. 65 c. Type 136 .. .. 12 10
830. 75 c. Goal mouth melee .. 12 10
831. 85 c. Players with ball .. 15 12
832. 1 col. Two players with ball 20 15

137. Madonna and Child.

138. Stylised Crab.

1969. Christmas. Charity. Obligatory Tax.

833. 137. 5 c. bluish green .. 5 5
834. 5 c. lake 5 5
835. 5 c. blue 5 5
836. 5 c. orange 5 5

1970. Air. 10th Inter-American Cancer Congress, San Jose.

837. 138. 10 c. black and magenta 5 5
838. 15 c. black and yellow 5 5
839. 50 c. black and orange 10 8
840. 1 col. 10 black & green 20 15

139. Costa Rican stamps and Magnifier. **140.** Japanese Vase and Flowers.

1970. Air. "Costa Rica 70" Philatelic Exhibition.
843. **139.** 1 col. red and blue .. 20 15
844 2 col. mauve and blue 35 25

1970. Air. Expo 70. Multicoloured.
845. 10 c. Type **140** 5 5
846. 15 c. Ornamental cart .. 5 5
847. 35 c. Sun tower 5 5
848. 40 c. Tea-ceremony .. 8 5
849. 45 c. Coffee-picking .. 10 8
850. 55 c. Earth from the Moon 12 10
The 15 c., 35 c. and 40 c. are horiz.

141. "Irazu" (R. A. Garcia). **142.** 'Holy Child'.

1970. Air. Costa Rican Paintings. Multicoloured.
851. 25 c. Type **141** 5 5
852. 45 c. "Escazu Valley" (M. Bertheau) 8 5
853. 80 c. "Estuary Landscape" (T. Quiros) .. 12 5
854. 1 col. "The Other Face" (C. Valverde) 15 12
855. 2 col. 50 "Madonna" (L. Daell) 40 35
The 2 col. 50 is vert.

1970. Christmas Charity. Obligatory Tax.
856. **142.** 5 c. magenta 5 5
857. 5 c. brown 5 5
858. 5 c. olive 5 5
859. 5 c. violet 5 5

143. Arms of 21 October 1964. **144.** National Theatre, San Jose.

1971. Air. Various Costa Rican Coats of Arms (with dates). Multicoloured.
860. 5 c. Type **143** 5 5
861. 10 c. 27 November 1906 .. 5 5
862. 15 c. 29 September 1848 .. 5 5
863. 25 c. 21 April 1840 .. 5 5
864. 35 c. 22 November 1824 .. 8 5
865. 50 c. 2 November 1824 .. 10 5
866. 1 col. 6 March 1824 .. 20 15
867. 2 col. 10 May 1823 .. 35 30

1971. Air. O.E.A. General Assembly. San Jose.
868. **144.** 2 col. purple 35 25

145. J. M. Delgado and M. J. Arce (Salvador).

1971. Air. Central-American Independence. 150th Anniv. Multicoloured.
869. 5 c. Type **145** 5 5
870. 10 c. M. Larreinaga and M. A. de la Cerda (Nicaragua) 5 5
871. 15 c. J. C. del Valle and D. de Herrera (Honduras) 5 5
872. 35 c. P. Alvarado and F. del Castillo (Costa Rica) 5 5
873. 50 c. A. Larrazabal and P. Molina (Guatemala) .. 10 8
874. 1 col. O.D.E.C.A. flag (vert.) 20 15
875. 2 col. O.D.E.C.A. emblem (vert.) 35 30
O.D.E.C.A. = Organisation of Central American States.

146. Cradle on "PAX". **147.** Federation Emblem.

1971. Christmas Charity. Obligatory Tax.
876. **146.** 10 c. orange 5 5
877. 10 c. brown 5 5
878. 10 c. green 5 5
879. 10 c. blue 5 5

1971. Air. Costa Rican Football Federation. 50th Anniv.
880. **147.** 50 c. multicoloured .. 10 8
881. 60 c. multicoloured .. 10 8

148. "Children of the World". **149.** Tree of Guanacaste.

1972. Air. U.N.I.C.E.F. 25th Anniv.
882. **148.** 50 c. multicoloured .. 10 8
883. 1 col. 10 multicoloured 20 15

1972. Air. Liberia City. Bicent. Multicoloured.
884. 20 c. Type **149** 5 5
885. 40 c. Hermitage, Liberia .. 8 5
886. 55 c. Mayan petroglyph .. 10 8
887. 60 c. Clay head (vert.) .. 12 10

150. Farmer's Family and Farm. **151.** Latin-American Stamp Exhibitions.

1972. Air. OEA Institute of Agricultural Sciences (IICA). 30th Anniv.
892. **150.** 20 c. multicoloured .. 5 5
893. – 45 c. multicoloured .. 8 8
894. – 50 c. yell., grn. & blk. 10 8
895. – 10 col. multicoloured 1·90 1·40
DESIGNS—HORIZ. 45 c. Cattle. VERT. 50 c. Tree-planting. 10 col. Agricultural worker and map.

1972. Air. "Exfilbra 72" Stamp Exhib.
896. **151.** 50 c. brown and orange 10 8
897. 2 col. violet and blue .. 35 25

152. Madonna and Child. **153.** First Book printed in Costa Rica.

1972. Christmas Charity. Obligatory Tax.
898. **152.** 10 c. red 5 5
899. 10 c. lilac 5 5
900. 10 c. blue 5 5
901. 10 c. green 5 5

1972. Air. Int. Book Year. Mult.
902. 20 c. Type **153** 5 5
903. 50 c. National Library, San Jose (horiz.) 10 8
904. 75 c. Type **153** 12 10
905. 5 col. As 50 c. 80 70

154. View near Irazu. **155.** Madonna and Child.

1972. Air. American Tourist Year. Mult.
906. 5 c. Type **154** 5 5
907. 15 c. Entrance to Culebra Bay 5 5
908. 20 c. Type **154** 5 5
909. 25 c. As 15 c. 5 5
910. 40 c. Manuel Antonio Beach 8 5
911. 45 c. Costa Rican Tourist Institute emblem .. 8 5
912. 50 c. Lindora Lake .. 10 8
913. 60 c. Post Office Building, San Jose (vert.) 10 8
914. 80 c. As 40 c. 15 10
915. 90 c. As 45 c. 20 12
916. 1 col. As 50 c. 20 12
917. 2 col. As 60 c. 35 25

1973. Air. Churches and Cathedrals. (2nd series). As Nos. 779/94 but colours changed.
918. **129** 5 c. grey 5 5
919. – 10 c. green 5 5
920. – 15 c. orange 5 5
921. – 25 c. brown 5 5
922. – 30 c. purple 5 5
923. – 35 c. violet 8 5
924. – 40 c. green 8 5
925. – 45 c. brown 10 8
926. – 50 c. red 10 8
927. – 55 c. blue 10 8
928. – 65 c. black 12 10
929. – 75 c. red 15 12
930. – 80 c. green 15 12
931. – 85 c. lilac 15 12
932. – 90 c. red 20 15
933. – 1 col. blue 20 15

1973. Obligatory Tax. Christmas Charity.
934. **155.** 10 c. red 5 5
935. 10 c. purple 5 5
936. 10 c. black 5 5
937. 10 c. brown 5 5

156. Flame Emblem. **157.** O.E.A. Emblem.

1973. Air. Declaration of Human Rights. 25th Anniv.
938. **156.** 50 c. red and blue .. 12 8

1973. Air. O.E.A. (Organisation of American States). 25th Anniv.
939. **157.** 20 c. red and blue .. 5 5

158. J. Vargas Calvo. **159.** Telephone Centre, San Pedro.

1974. Air. Costa Rican Composers. Mult.
940. 20 c. Type **158** 5 5
941. 20 c. Alejandro Monestel .. 5 5
942. 20 c. Julio Mata 5 5
943. 60 c. Julio Fonseca .. 12 10
944. 2 col. Rafael Chaves .. 35 25
945. 5 col. Manuel Gutierrez .. 80 60

1974. Air. Fiscal stamps as Type **90** (but without surcharge) optd. **HABILITADO PARA CORREO AEREO.**
946. 50 c. brown 10 8
947. 1 col. violet 20 15
948. 2 col. orange 40 30
949. 5 col. green .. .. 1·00 70

1974. Air. Costa Rican Electrical Institute. 25th Anniv. Multicoloured.
950. 50 c. Type **159** 10 8
951. 65 c. Control Room, Rio Macho (horiz.) 12 10
952. 85 c. Powerhouse, Rio Macho 15 12
953. 1 col. 25 Cachi Dam, Rio Macho (horiz.) 25 20
954. 2 col. Institute H.Q. Building 35 25

160. "Exfilmex" Emblem. **162.** R. B. Mesen.

161. Couple on Map.

1974. Air. "Exfilmex" Stamp Exhibition, Mexico City.
955. **160.** 65 c. green 12 10
956. 3 col. pink 55 35

1974. Air. 4-S Clubs. 25th Anniv.
957. **161.** 20 c. emerald & green 5 5
958. – 50 c. multicoloured .. 10 8
DESIGN: 50 c. Young agricultural workers.

1974. Air. R. B. Mesen (educator). Birth Cent.
959. **162.** 20 c. black and brown 5 5
960. – 85 c. black and red .. 15 12
961. – 5 col. brown and black 1·00 70
DESIGNS—VERT. 85 c. Mesen's "Poems of Love and Death". HORIZ. 5 col. Mesen's hands.

163. R. J. Oreamuno and T. S. Gill (founders).

1974. Air. Costa Rican Insurance Institute. 50th Anniv.
962. **163.** 20 c. multicoloured .. 5 5
963. – 50 c. multicoloured .. 8 5
964. – 65 c. multicoloured .. 12 10
965. – 85 c. multicoloured .. 15 12
966. – 1 col. 25 black & gold .. 25 15
967. – 2 col. multicoloured .. 35 25
968. – 2 col. 50 multicoloured 45 35
969. – 20 col. multicoloured .. 3·50 3·00
DESIGNS—HORIZ. 50 c. Spade ("Harvest Insurance"). VERT. 65 c. Child's and adult's hands ("Life Insurance"). 85 c. Paper boat within hand ("Maritime Insurance"). 1 col. 25 Institute emblem. 2 col. Arm in brace ("Workers' Rehabilitation"). 2 col. 50 Hand holding spanner ("Risks at Work"). 20 col. House in protective hands ("Fire Insurance").

164. W.P.Y. Emblem. **165.** "Boys eating Cakes". (Murillo).

1974. Air. World Population Year.
970. **164.** 2 col. red and blue .. 35 25

1974. Obligatory Tax. Christmas.
971. **165.** 10 c. red 5 5
972. – 10 c. purple 5 5
973. – 10 c. black 5 5
974. – 10 c. blue 5 5
DESIGNS: No. 972, "The Beautiful Gardener" (Raphael). No. 973, "Maternity" (J. R. Bonilla). No. 974 "The Prayer" (J. Reynolds)

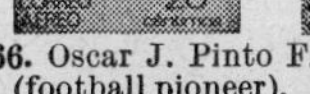

166. Oscar J. Pinto F. (football pioneer). **167.** "Mormodes buccinator".

1974. Air. First Central American Olympic Games, Guatemala (1973). Each grey and blue.
975. 20 c. Type **166** 5 5
976. 50 c. D. A. Montes de Oca (shooting champion) 10 8
977. 1 col. U. E. Garnier (promoter of athletics) 25 15

1975. Air. First Central American Orchids Exhibition. Multicoloured.
978. 25 c. Type **167** 5 5
979. 25 c. " Gongora claviodora" 5 5
980. 25 c. " Masdevallia ephippium " 5 5
981. 25 c. " Encyclia spondiadum" 5 5
982. 65 c. " Lycaste skinneri alba " 12 10
983. 65 c. " Peristeria elata " 12 10
984. 65 c. " Miltonia roezelii " 12 10
985. 65 c. " Brassavola digbyana" 12 10
986. 80 c. " Epidendrum mirabile " 15 12
987. 80 c. " Barkeria lindleyana" 15 12
988. 80 c. " Cattleya skinneri " 15 12
989. 80 c. " Sobralia macrantha splendens " 15 12
990. 1 col. 40, " Lycaste cruenta " 30 25
991. 1 col. 40, " Oncidium obryzatum " 30 25
992. 1 col. 40, " Gongora armeniaca " 30 25
993. 1 col. 40, " Stevekingia suavis " 30 25
994. 1 col. 75, " Hexisea imbricata " 40 30
995. 2 col. 15, " Warcewiczella discolor " 45 35
996. 2 col. 50, " Oncidium kramerianum " 50 40
997. 3 col. 25, " Cattleya dowiana " 70 60

168. Emblem of Costa Rica Radio Club.

1975. Air. 16th Convention of Costa Rican Radio Amateurs Federation, San José.
998. **168.** 1 col. purple & black 25 15
999. – 1 col. 10, scar. & ultram. 25 15
1000. – 2 col. blue & black 45 35
DESIGNS—VERT. 1 col. 10, Federation emblem within " V " of Flags. HORIZ. 2 col. Federation emblem.

169. Nicoyan Beach.

1975. Air. Annexation of Nicoya. 150th Anniv. Multicoloured.
1001. 25 c. Type **169** 5 5
1002. 75 c. Cattle-drive 15 12
1003. 1 col. Colonial church 25 15
1004. 3 col. Savannah riders (vert.) 70 60

170. 3 c. Philatelic Exhibition Stamp of 1932.

1975. Air. 6th National Philatelic Exhibition, San Jose.
1005. **170.** 2 col. 20 orange & blk. 45 35
1006. – 2 col. 20 green & blk. 45 35
1007. – 2 col. 20 red & black 45 35
1008. – 2 col. 20 blue & black 45 35
DESIGNS: Stamps of 1932. No. 1006, 5 c. stamp No. 1007, 10 c. stamp. No. 1008, 20 c. stamp.

171. I.W.Y. Emblem. 172. U.N. Emblem.

1975. Air. International Women's Year.
1009. **171.** 40 c. red and blue 8 5
1010. 1 col. 25 blue & black 25 15

1975. Air. United Nations. 30th Anniv.
1011. **172.** 10 c. blue and black 5 5
1012. – 60 c. multicoloured 12 8
1013. – 1 col. 20 multicoloured 25 15
DESIGNS—HORIZ. 60 c. General Assembly. VERT. 1 col. 20 U.N. Headquarters, New York.

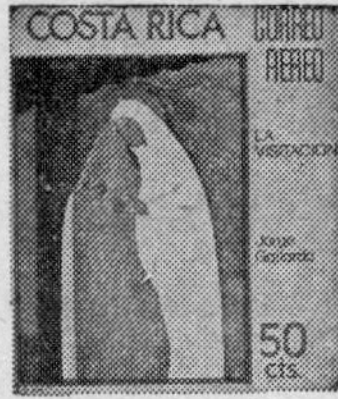

173. " The Visitation ". 174. " Children with Tortoise " (F. Amighetti).

1975. Air. " The Christmas Tradition ". Paintings by Jorge Gallardo. Mult.
1014. 50 c. Type **173** 10 8
1015. 1 col. " The Nativity and the Comet " 25 15
1016. 5 col. " St. Joseph in his workshop " 1·00 70

1975. Obligatory Tax. Christmas. Children's Village. Multicoloured.
1017. **174.** 10 c. brown 5 5
1018. – 10 c. purple 5 5
1019. – 10 c. grey 5 5
1020. – 10 c. blue 5 5
DESIGNS: No. 1018. " The Virgin of the Carnation " (Da Vinci). No. 1019. " Happy Dreams " (child in bed—Sonia Romero). No. 1020. " Child with Pigeon " (Picasso).

175. Schoolboy and Flags. 176. Prof. A. M. Brenes Mora.

1976. Air. " 20–30 " Youth Clubs in Costa Rica. 20th Anniversary.
1021. **175.** 1 col. multicoloured 20 10

1976. Professor A. M. Brenes Mora (botanist). Birth Centenary (1970).
1022. **176.** 1 col. violet (postage) 20 10
1023. – 5 c. multicoloured (air) 5 5
1024. – 30 c. multicoloured 5 5
1025. 55 c. multicoloured 10 5
1026. 2 col. multicoloured 40 20
1027. – 10 col. multicoloured 2·00 1·75
DESIGNS: 5 c. " Quercus brenesii ". 30 c. " Maxillaria albertii ". 55 c. " Calathea brenesii ". 2 col. " Brenesia costaricensis ". 10 col. " Philodendron brenesii ".

177. Open Book as " Flower ". 179. Early and Modern Telephones.

178. Mounted Postman with Pack Mule.

1976. Air. Costa Rican Literature. Multicoloured.
1028. 15 c. Type **177** 5 5
1029. 1 col. 10 Reader with " TV eye " 20 10
1030. 5 col. Book and flag (horiz.) 1·00 90

1976. Universal Postal Union. Centenary (1974).
1032. **178.** 20 c. black and yellow 5 5
1033. – 50 c. multicoloured 10 5
1034. – 65 c. multicoloured 12 8
1035. – 85 c. multicoloured 15 10
1036. – 2 col. black and blue 40 20
DESIGNS—HORIZ. 50 c. 5 c. U.P.U. stamp of 1882. 65 c. 10 c. U.P.U. stamp of 1882. 85 c. 20 c. U.P.U. stamp of 1882. VERT. 2 col. U.P.U. Monument, Berne.

1976. Telephone Centenary.
1037. **179.** 1 col. black and blue 20 10
1038. – 2 col. blk., brn. & grn. 40 20
1039. – 5 col. black & yellow 1·00 90
DESIGNS: 2 col. Costa Rica's first telephone. 5 col. Alexander Graham Bell.

EXPRESS DELIVERY STAMPS

E 1. New U.P.U. Headquarters Building and Emblem.

1970. Air. New U.P.U. Headquarters Building.
E 841. **E 1.** 35 c. multicoloured 5 5
E 842. 60 c. multicoloured 10 8
In Type E 1, **" ENTREGA INMEDIATA "** is in the form of a perforated tab. No. E 842 has the same main design, but the tab is inscr. **" EXPRESS ".**

E 2. Winged Letter.

1972.
E 888. **E 2.** 75 c. brn. and red 15 12
E 889. 75 c. green and red 15 12
E 890. 75 c. mauve and red 15 12
E 891. 1 col. 50 blue and red 30 20

E 3. " Concorde ".

1976.
E 1031. **E 3.** 1 col. multicoloured 20 10

OFFICIAL STAMPS

Various issues optd. **OFICIAL** except where otherwise stated.

1883. Stamps of 1883.
O 35. **2.** 1 c. green 30 30
O 36. 2 c. red 30 30
O 22. 5 c. violet 1·75 1·75
O 37. 10 c. orange 1·75 1·75
O 38. 40 c. blue 40 45

1887. Stamps of 1887.
O 39. **3.** 5 c. violet 1·25 1·25
O 40. 10 c. orange 30 30

1889. Stamps of 1889.
O 41. **4.** 1 c. brown 12 15
O 42. 2 c. blue 12 15
O 43. 5 c. orange 12 15
O 44. 10 c. lake 12 15
O 45. 20 c. green 12 15
O 46. 50 c. red 60 65

1892. Stamps of 1892.
O 47. **5.** 1 c. blue 15 15
O 48. 2 c. orange 15 15
O 49. 5 c. mauve 15 15
O 50. 10 c. green 65 65
O 51. 20 c. red 10 10
O 52. 50 c. blue 30 30

1901. Stamps of 1901 (Nos. 42/48).
O 53. 1 c. black and green 20 20
O 54. 2 c. black and red 20 20
O 61. 4 c. black and purple 65 65
O 55. 5 c. black and blue 20 20
O 62. 6 c. black and olive 75 75
O 56. 10 c. black and brown 35 35
O 57. 20 black and lake 50 50
O 63. 25 c. brown and lilac 3·50 2·25
O 58. 50 c. blue and claret 1·50 1·50
O 59. 1 col. black and olive 3·25 3·25

1903. Stamp of 1901 optd. **PROVISORIO OFICIAL.**
O 60. – 2 c. blk. & red (No. 43) 1·50 1·50

1908. Stamps of 1907 (Nos. 57/76).
O 77. 1 c. blue and brown 5 5
O 78. 2 c. black and green 5 5
O 79. 4 c. blue and red 8 8
O 80. 5 c. blue and orange 10 10
O 81. 10 c. black and blue 20 12
O 82. 25 c. slate and lavender 20 15
O 83. 50 c. blue and claret 20 20
O 84. 1 col. black and brown 50 45

1917. Stamps of 1910 optd. **OFICIAL 15. VI. 1917.**
O 115. 5 c. orange (No. 80) 15 15
O 116. 10 c. blue (No. 81) 12 12

1920. No. 82 surch. **OFICIAL 15 CENTIMOS.**
O 117. 15 c. on 20 c. olive 30 30

1921. Official stamps of 1908 optd. **1921-22** or surch. also.
O 123. – 4 c. bl. & red (No. 69) 25 20
O 124. **19.** 6 c. on 1 c. blue & brn. 25 25
O 125. – 20 c. on 25 c. (No. 63) 25 25
O 126. – 50 c. bl. & claret (74) 1·50 1·50
O 127. – 1 col. blk. & brn. (75) 2·25 2·25

1921. No. O 115 surch. **10 CTS.**
O 128. 10 c. on 5 c. orange 25 25

1923. Stamps of 1923.
O 137. **87.** 2 c. brown 20 20
O 138. 4 c. green 10 10
O 139. 5 c. blue 20 20
O 140. 20 c. red 12 12
O 141. 1 col. violet 25 25

C 1.

ILLUSTRATIONS British Commonwealth and all overprints and surcharges are FULL SIZE. Foreign Countries have been reduced to ¾-LINEAR.

1926.
O 169. **O 1.** 2 c. black and blue 5 5
O 231. 2 c. black and lilac 5 5
O 170. 3 c. black and red 5 5
O 232. 3 c. black and brown 5 5
O 171. 4 c. black and blue 5 5
O 233. 4 c. black and red 5 5
O 172. 5 c. black and green 5 5
O 173. 6 c. black and yellow 5 5
O 235. 8 c. black and choc. 5 5
O 174. 10 c. black and red 5 5
O 175. 20 c. black and green 5 5
O 237. 20 c. black and blue 5 5
O 176. 30 c. black and orange 10 10
O 238. 40 c. black and orange 10 12
O 177. 45 c. black and brown 12 12
O 239. 55 c. black and lilac 15
O 178. 1 col. black and lilac 20 20
O 240. 1 col. black and brown 20 20
O 241. 2 col. black and blue 35 40
O 242. 5 col. black & yellow 1·25 1·25
O 243. 10 col. blue and black 5·00 5·00

1934. Air. Air stamps of 1934.
O 211. **52.** 5 c. green 20 20
O 212. 10 c. red 20 20
O 213. 15 c. brown 35 35
O 214. 20 c. blue 45 45
O 215. 25 c. orange 45 45
O 216. 40 c. brown 50 50
O 217. 50 c. black 50 50
O 218. 60 c. yellow 65 65
O 219. 75 c. violet 65 65
O 220. – 1 col. red 90 90
O 221. – 2 col. blue 3·25 3·25
O 222. – 5 col. black 6·00 6·00
O 223. – 10 col. brown 7·00 7·00

1936. Stamps of 1936.
O 228. – 5 c. green 5 5
O 229. **57.** 10 c. red 5 5

POSTAGE DUE STAMPS

D 1. D 2.

1903.
D 55. **D 1.** 5 c. blue 2·40 70
D 56. 10 c. brown 2·40 70
D 57. 15 c. green 1·10 85
D 58. 20 c. red 1·50 90
D 59. 25 c. blue 1·60 1·25
D 60. 30 c. brown 2·75 1·60
D 61. 40 c. olive 2·75 1·60
D 62. 50 c. claret 2·75 1·40

1915.
D 115. **D 2.** 2 c. orange 5 5
D 116. 4 c. blue 5 5
D 117. 8 c. green 25 25
D 118. 10 c. violet 10 10
D 119. 20 c. brown 15 15

CRETE E1

Former Turkish island in the E. Mediterranean under the joint protection of Gt. Britain, France, Italy and Russia from 1898 to 1908, when the island was united to Greece. This was recognised by Turkey in 1913. Greek stamps now used.

100 lepta = 1 drachma.

1. Hermes.

2. Hera.

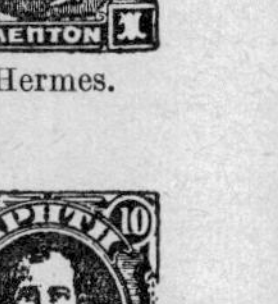
3. Prince George of Greece.

4. Talos.

1900.

1. 1. 1 l. brown 15 8
12. 1 l. yellow 25 25
2. 2. 5 l. green 50 10
3. 3. 10 l. red 30 10
4. 2. 20 l. red .. .. .. 2·75 50
13. 20 l. orange .. .. 1·60 35
15. 3. 25 l. blue .. .. 4·00 45
14. 1. 50 l. blue .. .. 2·50 1·60
16. 50 l. lilac .. .. .. 5·00 2·50
17. 4. 1 d. violet .. .. 9·00 4·50
18. – 2 d. brown .. .. 6·50 4·50
19. – 5 d. black and green .. 8·50 7·00

DESIGNS (as T 4): 2 d. Minos. 5 d. St. George and Dragon.

ΠΡΟΣΩΡΙΝΟΝ
(7.)

1900. Optd. as T 7.

5. 3. 25 l. blue .. .. 1·75 35
6. 1. 50 l. lilac .. .. 1·40 1·25
7. 4. 1 d. violet .. .. 2·50 1·50
8. – 2 d. brown (No. 18) .. 4·50 2·50
9. – 5 d. black & grn. (No. 19) 12·00 12·00

1904. Surch. **5** twice.

20. 2. 5 on 20 l. orange .. 1·00 50

8. Rhea.

10. Prince George of Greece.

14. Europa and Jupiter.

DESIGNS (As T 8): 5 l. Britomartis. 20 l. Miletus. 25 l. Triton. 50 l. Ariadne. (As T 14): 3 d. Minos Ruins. (44 × 28½ mm.): 5 d. Mt. Ida.

1905.

21. 8. 2 l. lilac 75 15
22. – 5 l. green .. .. 1·75 8
23. 10. 10 l. red .. .. 2·50 8
24. – 20 l. green .. .. 4·25 50
25. – 25 l. blue .. .. 4·25 40
26. – 50 l. brown .. .. 5·00 2·00
27. 14. 1 d. sepia and red .. 35·00 24·00
28. – 3 d. black and orange .. 12·00 9·00
29. – 5 d. black and olive .. 11·00 8·00

21. High Commissioner A. T. A. Zaimis.

23. Hermes.

1907. Various designs.

30. 21. 25 l. black and blue .. 4·50 55
31. – 1 d. black and green .. 4·50 3·50

DESIGN—HORIZ. (larger). 1 d. Landing of Prince George of Greece at Suda.

ΕΛΛΑΣ
(24.)

1908. Optd. **HELLAS** as T 24 in various sizes and styles.

32. 1. 1 l. brown 15 8
33. 8. 2 l. lilac 15 8
34. – 5 l. green (No. 22) .. 30 5
35. 3. 10 l. red 40 5
36. 23. 10 l. red 50 20
37. – 20 l. green (No. 24) .. 1·25 40
38. 21. 25 l. black and blue .. 2·25 45
63. – 25 l. blue (No. 25) .. 85 20
39. – 50 l. brown (No. 26) .. 2·25 1·25
40. 14. 1 d. sepia and red .. 35·00 24·00
52. – 1 d. blk. & grn. (No. 31) 4·50 4·25
41. – 2 d. brown (No. 18) .. 3·75 2·00
42. – 3 d. blk. & or (No. 28) 7·50 6·00
43. – 5 d. blk. & olive (No. 29) 9·00 6·50

1909. Optd. with T 7 and 24 or surcharged with new value also.

44. 1. 1 l. yellow (No. 12) .. 25 25
45. D 1. 1 l. red (No. D 10) .. 20 20
46. 2 on 20 l. red (No. D 73) 30 30
47. 2 on 20 l. red (No. D 13) 25 25
48. 2. 5 on 20 l. red (No. 4) .. 40·00 40·00
49. 5 on 20 l. orange (No. 13) 35 35

OFFICIAL STAMPS

O 1.

1908.

O 32. O 1. 10 l. claret .. .. 10·00 55
O 33. 30 l. blue .. .. 12·00 55

In the 30 l. the central figures are in an oval frame.

1908. Optd. with T 24.

O 68. O 1. 10 l. claret 40 25
O 69. 30 l. blue 40 25

POSTAGE DUE STAMPS

D 1.

1901.

D 10. D 1. 1 l. red 20 20
D 11. 5 l. red .. .. 1·40 1·40
D 12. 10 l. red .. .. 1·60 1·60
D 13. 20 l. red .. .. 2·50 1·75
D 14. 40 l. red .. .. 3·25 2·75
D 15. 50 l. red .. .. 4·25 3·50
D 16. 1 d. red .. .. 20·00 18·00
D 17. 2 d. red .. .. 6·50 6·00

1901. Surch. " 1 drachma " in Greek characters.

D 18. D 1. 1 d. on 1 d. red .. 4·50 4·50

1908. Optd. with T 24.

D 70. D 1. 1 l. red 30 30
D 71. 5 l. red 95 60
D 72. 10 l. red .. .. 1·10 60
D 73. 20 l. red .. .. 3·50 3·25
D 74. 40 l. red .. .. 3·50 3·25
D 75. 50 l. red .. .. 3·50 3·25
D 76. 1 d. red .. .. 22·00 22·00
D 51. 1 d. on 1 d. red (No. D 18) .. .. 15·00 12·00
D 77. 2 d. red .. .. 8·50 7·50

REVOLUTIONARY ASSEMBLY. 1905.

In March, a revolt in favour of union with Greece began, organised by Venizelos with Headquarters at Theriso. South of Canea. The revolt collapsed in Nov., 1905.

R 1.

R 2. Crete enslaved.

1905. Imperf.

R 1. R 1. 5 l. green and red .. 2·50 2·00
R 2. 10 l. red and green .. 2·50 2·00
R 3. 20 l. red and blue .. 2·50 2·00
R 4. 50 l. violet and green 2·50 2·00
R 5. 1 d. blue and red .. 2·50 2·00

1905.

R 6. R 2. 5 l. orange 30 35
R 7. 10 l. grey 30 35
R 8. 20 l. mauve 50 60
R 9. 50 l. blue 50 60
R 10. – 1 d. violet and red .. 60 70
R 11. – 2 d. brown and green 60 70

DESIGN: 1 d., 2 d. King George of Greece.

CROATIA E1

Part of Yugoslavia made semi-autonomous after German-Italian intervention in 1941. Liberated by partisans and Russian troops in early 1945 when the area reverted to Yugoslavia.

100 paras = 1 dinar
100 banicas = 1 kuna

NEZAVISNA
DRŽAVA
HRVATSKA
IIIIII
(1.)

(2.)

1941. Stamps of Yugoslavia optd. as T 1 (" Independent Croat State ").

1. 63. 50 p. orange 35 40
2. 1 d. green 35 40
3. 1 d. 50 red 35 40
4. 2 d. mauve 35 40
5. 3 d. brown .. .. 1·50 1·60
6. 4 d. blue .. .. 1·50 1·60
7. 5 d. blue .. .. 1·50 1·60
8. 5 d. 50 violet .. .. 1·50 1·60

1941. Stamps of Yugoslavia optd. as T 2.

9. 63. 25 p. black 8 8
10. 50 p. orange 8 8
11. 1 d. green 8 8
12. 1 d. 50 red 8 8
13. 2 d. mauve 8 8
14. 3 d. brown 8 8
15. 4 d. blue 8 8
16. 5 d. blue 15 15
17. 5 d. 50 violet 20 25
18. 6 d. blue 20 25
19. 8 d. brown 20 25
20. 12 d. violet 20 25
21. 16 d. purple 50 50
22. 20 d. blue 80 80
23. 30 d. pink .. .. 1·00 1·00

NEZAVISNA
1
DIN
DRŽAVA
HRVATSKA
(2a.)

10. IV. 1941
NEZAVISNA
DRŽAVA
HRVATSKA
(2b.)

1941. Stamps of Yugoslavia surch. as T 2a.

24. 83. 1 d. on 3 d. brown .. 5 8
25. 2 d. on 4 d. blue .. 5 8

1941. Founding of Croatian Army. Nos. 414/26 of Yugoslavia optd. with T 2b.

25a. 63. 25 p. black
25b. 50 p. orange
25c. 1 d. green
25d. 1 d. 50 red
25e. 2 d. mauve
25f. 3 d. brown
25g. 4 d. blue
25h. 5 d. blue
25i. 5 d. 50 violet
25j. 6 d. blue
25k. 8 d. brown
25l. 12 d. violet
25m. 16 d. purple
25n. 20 d. blue
25o. 30 d. pink
Set of 15 .. .. £100 £100

Sold at double face value.

1941. Stamps of Yugoslavia optd. as T 2 but without shield.

26. 69. 1 d. 50 + 1 d. 50 black .. 3·25 3·25
27. – 4 d. + 3 d. brn. (No. 457) 3·25 3·25

1941. Postage Due stamps of Yugoslavia optd. **NEZAVISNA DRZAVA HRVATSKA** and **FRANCO.**

28. D 10. 50 p. violet 5 5
29. 2 d. blue 8 8
30. 5 d. orange 8 8
31. 10 d. brown 12 15

3. Mt. Ozalj.

4. Banjaluka.

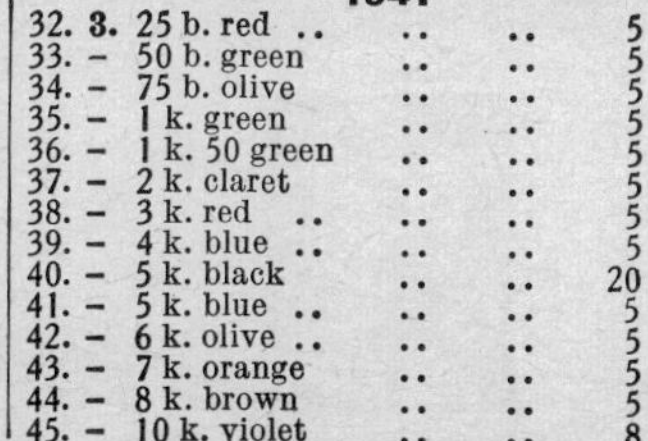

1941

32. 3. 25 b. red 5 5
33. – 50 b. green 5 5
34. – 75 b. olive 5 5
35. – 1 k. green 5 5
36. – 1 k. 50 green 5 5
37. – 2 k. claret 5 5
38. – 3 k. red 5 5
39. – 4 k. blue 5 5
40. – 5 k. black 20 5
41. – 5 k. blue 5 5
42. – 6 k. olive 5 5
43. – 7 k. orange 5 5
44. – 8 k. brown 5 5
45. – 10 k. violet 8 5
46. – 12 k. brown 12 5
47. – 20 k. brown 8 5
48. – 30 k. brown 10 5
49. – 50 k. green 20 5
50. 4. 100 k. violet 35 35

DESIGNS: 50 b. Waterfall at Jajce. 75 b. Varazdin. 1 k. Mt. Velebit. 1 k. 50, Zelenjak. 2 k. Zagreb Cathedral. 3 k. Church at Osijek. 4 k. River Drina. 5 k. (No. 40), Konjic Bridge. 5 k. (No. 41), Modern building at Zemun. 6 k. Dubrovnik. 7 k. R. Save in Slavonia. 8 k. Mosque at Sarajevo. 10 k. Lake Plitvice. 12 k. Klis Fortress near Split. 20 k. Hvar. 30 k. Harvesting in Syrmia. 50 k. Senj.

5. Croat (Sinj) Costume.

6. Emblems of Germany, Croatia and Italy.

1941. Red Cross.

51. 5. 1 k. 50 + 1 k. 50 blue .. 5 8
52. – 2 k. + 2 k. brown .. 8 12
53. – 4 k. + 4 k. claret .. 15 20

COSTUMES: 2 k. Travnik. 4 k. Turopolje.

1941. Eastern Front Volunteer Fund.

54. 6. 4 k. + 2 k. blue 40 65

7.

1941-1942
10-IV
(8.)

1942. Aviation Fund. Designs showing aeroplane in flight as T 7.

55. 7. 2 k. + 2 k. brown 8 8
56. – 2 k. 50 b. + 2 k. 50 b. green 10 10
57. – 3 k. + 3 k. red 15 15
58. – 4 k. + 4 k. blue 20 20

The 2 k. and 3 k. are vert.

1942. Croat Independence. 1st Anniv. Optd. with T 8.

59. 2 k. brown (as No. 37) .. 5 5
60. 5 k. red (as No. 40) .. 5 5
61. 10 k. green (as No. 45) .. 10 10

1942. Banjaluka Philatelic Exn. Inscr. " F.I." in top right corner.

62. 4. 100 k. violet 25 30

1942. Surch. **O. 25 Kn.** and bar.

63. 25 b. on 2 k. claret (No. 37) 5 5

9. Trumpeters.

10. M. Gubec.

1942. National Relief Fund.

64. 9. 3 k. + 1 k. red 15 15
65. – 4 k. + 2 k. brown 15 15
66. – 5 k. + 5 k. blue 15 15

DESIGNS—HORIZ. 4 k. Procession beneath triumphal archways. VERT. 5 k. Mother and child.

1942. Croat (" USTASCHA ") Youth Fund.

72. 10. 3 k. + 6 k. red 5 5
73. – 4 k. + 7 k. brown .. 5 5

PORTRAIT: 4 k. A. Starcevic.

11. Sestine (Croatia).

11a.

1942. Red Cross Fund. Peasant girls in provincial costumes.

67. 11. 1 k. 50 + 50 b. brown .. 12 15
68. – 3 k. + 1 k. violet .. 12 15
69. – 4 k. + 2 k. blue 12 15
70. – 10 k. + 5 k. bistre .. 25 40
71. 11. 13 k. + 6 k. claret .. 65 80

COSTUMES: 3 k. Slavonia. 4 k. Bosnia. 10 k. Dalmatia.

1942. Charity Tax. Red Cross Fund. Cross in red.

71a. 11a. 1 k. green 12 12

12. 13. Arms of Zagreb.

1943. Labour Front. Vert. designs showing workers as T **12**.
74. **12.** 2 k. + 1 k. brown & olive 30 35
75. – 3 k. + 3 k. brn. & purple 30 35
76. – 7 k. + 4 k. brown & grey 30 35

1943. Zagreb. 7th Cent.
77. **13.** 3 k. 50 (+ 6 k. 50) blue 25 25

1943. Pictorial designs as T **4**, but with views surrounded by frame line.
78. 3 k. 50 brown 10 8
79. 12 k. 50 black 15 10
DESIGNS: 3 k. 50, Trakoscan Castle, 12 k. 50, Veliki Tabor.

14. A. Pavelitch. 15. Krsto Frankopan.

1943. Croat ("Ustascha") Youth Fund.
80. **14.** 5 k. + 3 k. red 5 8
81. 7 k. + 5 k. green .. 5 8

1943. Famous Croats.
82. – 1 k. blue 5 5
83. **15.** 2 k. olive 5 5
84. – 3 k. 50 red 5 5
PORTRAITS: 1 k. Katarina Zrinska. 3 k. 50, Peter Zrinski.

17. Croat Sailor.

1943. Croat Legion. Relief Fund.
85. **17.** 1 k.+50 b. green .. 5 5
86. – 2 k.+1 k. red .. 5 5
87. – 3 k. 50+1 k. 50 blue .. 5 5
88. – 9 k.+4 k. 50 brown .. 5 5
DESIGNS: 2 k. Pilot and aeroplane. 3 k. 50, Infantrymen. 9 k. Mechanized column.

18. St. Mary's Church and Cistercian Monastery, 1650.

1943. Philatelic Exhibition, Zagreb.
89. **18.** 18 k.+9 k. blue.. .. 55 60

1943. Return of Sibenik to Croatia. Optd. **HRVATSKO MORE/8, IX./1943.**
90. **18.** 18 k.+9 k. blue.. .. 90 90

19. Nurse and Patient. 19a.

1943. Red Cross Fund.
91. – 1 k.+50 b. blue .. 8 8
92. – 2 k.+1 k. red .. 8 8
93. – 3 k. 50+1 k. 50 blue .. 8 8
94. **19.** 8 k.+3 k. brown .. 8 8
95. 9 k.+4 k. green .. 8 8
96. – 10 k.+ 5 k. violet .. 8 8
97. **19.** 12 k.+6 k. blue .. 8 8
98. – 12 k. 50+6 k. brown .. 8 8
99. **19.** 18 k.+8 k. orange .. 15 15
100. 32 k.+12 k. grey .. 20 20
DESIGN: 1 k., 2 k., 3 k. 50, 10 k., 12 k. 50, Mother and children.

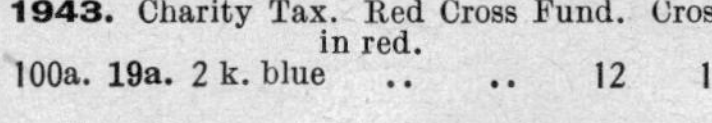

1943. Charity Tax. Red Cross Fund. Cross in red.
100a. **19a.** 2 k. blue 12 12

20. Pavelitch. 21. Ruder Boskovic.

1943.
101. **20.** 25 b. red 5 5
105. 50 b. blue 5 5
102. 75 b. green 5 5
106. 1 k. green 5 5
107. 1 k. 50 violet 5 5
108. 2 k. red 5 5
109. 3 k. red 5 5
110. 3 k. 50 blue 5 5
111. 4 k. purple 5 5
103. 5 k. blue 5 5
112. 8 k. brown 5 5
113. 9 k. red 5 5
114. 10 k. maroon 5 5
115. 12 k. brown 5 5
116. 12 k. 50 black 5 5
117. 18 k. brown 5 5
104. 32 k. brown 5 5
118. 50 k. green 5 5
119. 70 k. orange 5 5
120. 100 k. violet 10 10
The design of the 25 b., 75 b., 5 k., and 32 k. is $20\frac{1}{2} \times 26$ mm., the rest are 22×28 mm.

1943. R. Boskovic (astronomer). Commem.
121. **21.** 3 k. 50 red 5 5
122. 12 k. 50 purple .. 8 8

22. Posthorn. 23. St. Sebastian.

1944. Postal and Railway Employees' Relief Fund.
123. **22.** 7 k.+3 k. 50 brn., red & bis. 5 5
124. – 16 k.+8 k. blue .. 8 8
125. – 24 k.+12 k. red .. 12 12
126. – 32 k.+16 k. blk. & red 20 20
DESIGNS—VERT. 16 k. Dove, aeroplane and globe. 24 k. Mercury. HORIZ. 32 k. Winged wheel.

1944. War Invalids' Relief Fund.
127. **23.** 7 k.+3 k. 50 clar. & red 8 10
128. – 16 k.+8 k. green .. 15 20
129. – 24 k.+12 k. yellow, brown and red .. 15 20
130. – 32 k.+16 k. blue .. 15 20
DESIGNS—HORIZ. 16 k. Blind man and cripple. 32 k. Death of Peter Svacic, 1094. VERT. 24 k. Mediaeval statuette.

24. The Legion in Action. 25. Jure Ritter Francetic.

1944. Croat Youth Fund. No. 134 perf. others imperf.
131. **24.** 3 k. 50 + 1 k. 50 brown 5 5
132. – 12 k. 50 + 6 k. 50 blue.. 5 5
134. **25.** 12 k. 50 + 287 k. 50 black 70 90
133. 18 k + 9 k. brown .. 5 8
DESIGN: No. 132, Sentries on the Drina.

26.

1944. Labour Front. Inscr. "D.R.S."
135. **26.** 3 k. 50+1 k. red .. 5 5
136. – 12 k. 50+6 k. brown .. 5 5
137. – 18 k.+8 k. blue .. 5 5
138. – 32 k.+16 k. green .. 5 5
DESIGNS: 12 k. 50, Digging. 18 k. Instruction. 32 k. "On Parade".

27. Bombed Home. 28. War Victim.

1944. Charity Tax. War Victims.
138b. **27.** 1 k. green 5 5
138c. **28.** 2 k. red 5 5
138d. 5 k. green 8 8
138e. 10 k. blue 12 12
138f. 20 k. brown 25 25

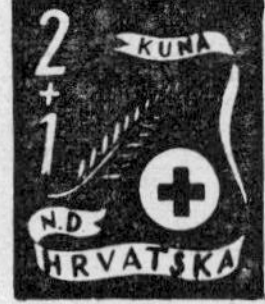

29. 30. Storm Division Soldiers.

1944. Red Cross. Cross in red.
139. **29.** 2 k.+1 k. green .. 5 5
140. 3 k. 50+1 k. 50 red .. 5 5
141. 12 k. 50+6 k. blue .. 5 8

1945. Creation of Croatian Storm Division.
142. **30.** 50 k.+50 k. red and grey 28·00 30·00
143. – 70 k.+70 k. sepia & grey 28·00 30·00
144. – 100 k.+100 k. bl. & grey 28·00 30·00
DESIGNS: 70 k. Storm Division soldiers in action. 100 k. Division emblem.

31. 32.

1945. Postal Employees' Fund.
145. **31.** 3 k. 50+1 k. 50 grey .. 5 5
146. – 12 k. 50+6 k. purple .. 5 5
147. – 24 k.+12 k. green .. 5 5
148. – 50 k.+25 k. purple .. 8 8
DESIGNS: 12 k. 50, Telegraph linesman. 24 k. Telephone switchboard. 50 k. The postman calls.

1945.
149. **32.** 3 k. 50 brown .. 12 15

OFFICIAL STAMPS

O 1. O 2.

1942.
O 55. **O 1.** 25 b. claret 5 5
O 56. 50 b. grey 5 5
O 57. 75 b. green 5 5
O 58. 1 k. brown 5 5
O 59. 2 k. blue 5 5
O 60. 3 k. red 5 5
O 61. 3 k. 50 red 5 5
O 62. 4 k. purple 5 5
O 63. 5 k. blue 10 10
O 64. 6 k. violet 5 5
O 65. 10 k. green 5 5
O 66. 12 k. red 5 5
O 67. 12 k. 50 orange .. 5 5
O 68. 20 k. blue 5 5
O 69. **O 2.** 30 k. grey and brown 5 5
O 70. 40 k. grey and violet 8 5
O 71. 50 k. grey and red .. 15 8
O 72. 100 k. salmon & black 15 8

POSTAGE DUE STAMPS

1941. Nos. D 259/63 of Yugoslavia optd. **NEZAVISNA/DRZAVA/HRVATSKA** in three lines above a chequered shield.
D 26. **D 10.** 50 p. violet.. .. 5 5
D 27. 1 d. rose 5 5
D 28. 2 d. blue .. .. 2·10 2·40
D 29. 5 d. orange .. 10 10
D 30. 10 d. brown .. 45 50

D 1. D 2.

1941.
D 51. **D 1.** 50 b. claret 5 5
D 52. 1 k. claret 5 5
D 53. 2 k. claret 10 12
D 54. 5 k. claret 10 12
D 55. 10 k. claret 30 30

1942.
D 67. **D 2.** 50 b. olive and blue 5 5
D 68. 1 k. olive and blue .. 5 5
D 69. 2 k. olive and blue .. 5 5
D 76. 4 k. olive and blue .. 5 5
D 70. 5 k. olive and blue .. 5 5
D 78. 6 k. olive and blue .. 5 5
D 79. 10 k. blue and indigo 10 10
D 80. 15 k. blue and indigo 10 10
D 72. 20 k. blue and indigo 30 30

CUBA O1

An island in the W. Indies, ceded by Spain to the United States in 1898. A republic under U.S. protection until 1901 when the island became independent. The issues to 1871, except Nos. 13, 14, 19, 20/7, 32, 44 and 48, were for Puerto Rico also.

8 reales Plata Fuerte (strong silver reales) = 1 peso.
1866. 100 centesimos = 1 escudo.
1871. 100 centesimos = 1 peseta.
1881. 1000 milesimas = 100 centavos = 1 peso.
1899. 100 cents = $1 U.S.A.
1899. 100 centavos = 1 peso.

A. SPANISH OCCUPATION

1855. As T **7** of Spain, but currency changed. Imperf.
6. ½ r. green 25 15
9. ½ r. blue 25 10
10. 1 r. green 20 10
11. 2 r. red 50 25

1855. No. 11 surch. Y¼.
12. Y¼ on 2 r. red .. .. 12·00 6·00

1862. As T **8** of Spain, but currency changed. Imperf.
13. ¼ r. black .. .. .. 2·50 1·50

1864. As T **10** of Spain but currency changed and without date. Imperf.
14. ¼ r. black .. .. .. 2·50 1·25
15. ½ r. green 30 10
16. ½ r. green on rose .. 1·50 15
17. 1 r. blue on brown .. 30 10
18a. 2 r. red on rose .. .. 3·00 1·25

1866. No. 14 optd. **66.** Imperf.
19. ¼ r. black .. .. .. 8·00 4·50

1866. As 1864 issue, but dated "1866" and currency changed. Imperf.
20. 5 c. mauve .. .. .. 4·00 2·00
21. 10 c. blue 40 15
22. 20 c. green 25 15
23. 40 c. red .. .. .. 1·20 1·00

1867. As last, but dated "1867". Perf.
24. 5 c. mauve .. .. .. 2·50 1·50
25. 10 c. blue 75 15
26. 20 c. green 75 15
27. 40 c. red .. .. .. 1·00 75

1.

ILLUSTRATIONS
British Commonwealth and all overprints and surcharges are FULL SIZE. Foreign Countries have been reduced to ¾-LINEAR.

1868.
28. **1.** 5 c. lilac .. .. .. 2·50 1·50
29. 10 c. blue 45 15
30. 20 c. green .. .. .. 1·00 40
31. 40 c. red .. .. .. 1·00 75

1869. As T **1** but dated "1869".
32. **1.** 5 c. red .. .. .. 3·00 1·50
33. 10 c. brown 50 25
34. 20 c. orange 75 30
35. 40 c. lilac .. .. .. 3·00 1·25
Nos. 44/84 are as Types of Spain but with different inscriptions and dates.

1870. Inscr. "CORREOS" and currency changed.
44. **16.** 5 c. blue .. .. .. 12·00 5·00
45. 10 c. green 15 10
46. 20 c. brown 15 10
47. 40 c. red .. .. .. 15·00 4·00

1871. Inscr. "ULTRAMAR 1871".
48. **21.** 12 c. lilac .. .. 1·75 75
49. 25 c. blue 20 10
50. 50 c. green 20 10
51. 1 p. brown .. .. 3·00 1·00

1873. Inscr. "ULTRAMAR 1873".
52. **19.** 12½ c. green .. .. 3·50 2·00
53. 25 c. lilac 20 10
54. 50 c. brown 15 10
55. 1 p. brown .. .. 25·00 7·00

1874. Inscr. "ULTRAMAR 1874".

56. 21. 12½ c. brown 1·75 80
57. 25 c. blue 10 10
58. 50 c. lilac 12 10
59. 1 p. red 10·00 3·50

1875. Inscr. "ULTRAMAR 1875".

60. 23. 12½ c. mauve 15 10
61. 25 c. blue 8 8
62. 50 c. green 8 8
63. 1 p. brown 75 60

1876. Inscr. "ULTRAMAR 1876".

64. 24. 12½ c. green 30 12
65a. 25 c. lilac 10 8
66. 50 c. blue 8 8
67. 1 p. black 1·00 60

1877. Inscr. "CUBA 1877".

68. 24. 10 c. green 4·00 3·00
69. 12½ c. lilac 50 20
70. 25 c. green 10 5
71. 50 c. black 10 5
72. 1 p. brown 3·00 1·75

1878. Inscr. "CUBA 1878".

73. 24. 5 c. blue 8 8
74. 10 c. black 6·00 4·00
75. 12½ c. brown 20 20
76. 25 c. green 10 5
77. 50 c. green 5 5
78. 1 p. red 1·00 80

1879. Inscr. "CUBA 1879".

79. 24. 5 c. black 10 8
80. 10 c. orange 12·00 8·00
81. 12½ c. red 10 8
82. 25 c. blue 8 8
83. 50 c. grey 8 8
84. 1 p. grey 2·00 1·25

1880. "Alfonso XII" key-type inscr. "CUBA 1880".

85. X. 5 c. green 8 5
86. 10 c. red 6·50 3·50
87. 12½ c. grey 8 5
88. 25 c. lilac 8 5
89. 50 c. brown 8 5
90. 1 p. brown 75 30

1881. "Alfonso XII" key-type inscr. "CUBA 1881".

91. X. 1 c. green 8 5
92. 2 c. red 3·50 2·50
93. 2½ c. brown 15 5
94. 5 c. lilac 8 5
95. 10 c. brown 8 5
96. 20 c. brown 75 60

1882. "Alfonso XII" key-type inscr. "CUBA".

97. X. 1 c. green 10 8
98. 2 c. red 40 8
120. 2½ c. brown 50 30
119. 2½ c. mauve 10 5
100. 5 c. lilac 40 8
123. 5 c. grey 40 8
101. 10 c. brown 8 5
126. 10 c. blue 20 15
121. 20 c. brown 1·50 60
122. 20 c. lilac 1·50 60

1883. "Alfonso XII" key-type inscr. "CUBA" and optd. with fancy pattern.

103. X. 5 c. lilac 50 45
104. 10 c. brown 1·00 85
105. 20 c. brown 7·00 5·00

1883. "Alfonso XII" key-type inscr. "CUBA" and surch. with fancy pattern with value in figures in centre.

106. X. 5 c. lilac 30 25
113. 10 c. brown 75 45
111. 20 c. brown 3·00 3·00

1890. "Baby" key-type inscr. "ISLA DE CUBA".

135. Y. 1 c. brown 1·50 55
147. 1 c. grey 75 20
159. 1 c. blue 50 10
169. 1 c. purple 20 10
136. 2 c. blue 75 35
148. 2 c. brown 25 10
160. 2 c. pink 2·00 50
170. 2 c. claret 1·00 10
137. 2½ c. green 1·25 45
149. 2½ c. orange 3·00 60
161. 2½ c. mauve 40 10
171. 2½ c. rose 15 10
138. 5 c. grey 20 15
150. 5 c. green 15 10
172. 5 c. blue 10 10
139. 10 c. purple 50 20
151. 10 c. rose 25 10
173. 10 c. green 50 10
140. 20 c. purple 20 15
152. 20 c. blue 1·50 60
162. 20 c. brown 1·75 50
175. 40 c. brown 4·50 2·50
176. 80 c. brown 7·00 4·00

1898. "Curly Head" key-type inscr. "CUBA 1898 Y 99".

183. Z. 1 m. brown 10 10
184. 2 m. brown 10 10
185. 3 m. brown 10 10
186. 4 m. brown 50 25
187. 5 m. brown 10 10
188. 1 c. violet 10 10
189. 2 c. blue 10 10
190. 3 c. brown 10 10
191. 4 c. orange 1·25 45
192. 5 c. red 20 10
193. 6 c. blue 10 10
194. Z. 8 c. brown 25 15
195. 10 c. red 25 15
196. 15 c. olive 45 15
197. 20 c. claret 15 10
198. 40 c. mauve 40 15
199. 60 c. black 40 15
200. 80 c. brown 1·50 1·25
201. 1 p. green 2·00 1·50
202. 2 p. blue 3·50 1·75

PRINTED MATTER STAMPS

Nos. P 129/33, P141/6, P153/8, P163/8 and P177/82 are key-types inscribed "CUBA IMPRESOS".

1888. "Alfonso XII."

P 129. X. ½ m. black 10 10
P 130. 1 m. black 10 10
P 131. 2 m. black 10 10
P 132. 3 m. black 30 20
P 133. 4 m. black 40 25
P 134. 8 m. black 1·00 60

1890. "Baby."

P 141. Y. ½ m. brown 15 15
P 142. 1 m. brown 15 20
P 143. 2 m. brown 25 20
P 144. 3 m. brown 25 20
P 145. 4 m. brown 1·25 45
P 146. 8 m. brown 1·25 55

1892. "Baby".

P 153. Y. ½ m. violet 10 10
P 154. 1 m. violet 10 10
P 155. 2 m. violet 15 10
P 156. 3 m. violet 30 10
P 157. 4 m. violet 50 30
P 158. 8 m. violet 1·25 40

1894. "Baby."

P 163. Y. ½ m. pink 10 10
P 164. 1 m. pink 15 10
P 165. 2 m. pink 15 10
P 166. 3 m. pink 40 15
P 167. 4 m. pink 50 20
P 168. 8 m. pink 75 40

1896. "Baby."

P 177. Y. ½ m. blue 10 10
P 178. 1 m. blue 10 10
P 179. 2 m. blue 10 10
P 180. 3 m. blue 40 20
P 181. 4 m. blue 75 75
P 182. 8 m. blue 1·50 75

B. UNITED STATES ADMINISTRATION.

1899. Stamps of United States of 1894 surch. **CUBA** and value.

246. 1 c. on 1 c. green (No. 283) 65 15
247. 2 c. on 2 c. red (No. 284 C) 65 20
248. 2½ c. on 2 c. red (No. 284 C) 50 25
249. 3 c. on 3 c. violet (No. 271) 1·00 45
250. 5 c. on 5 c. blue (No. 286) 1·25 35
251. 10 c. on 10 c. brn. (No. 289) 3·50 1·75

DESIGNS: 2 c. Palms. 3 c. Statue of "La India" (Woman). 5 c. Liner (Commerce). 10 c. Ploughing Sugar Plantation.

2. Statue of Columbus.

1899.

307. 2. 1 c. green 80 5
308. – 2 c. red 80 5
303. – 3 c. purple 75 10
304. – 5 c. blue 70 15
310. – 10 c. brown 1·60 20

POSTAGE DUE STAMPS

1899. Postage Due stamps of United States of 1894 surch. **CUBA** and value.

D 253. D 2. 1 c. on 1 c. red 4·25 1·50
D 254. 2 c. on 2 c. red 4·25 1·25
D 255. 5 c. on 5 c. red 1·75 75
D 256. 10 c. on 10 c. red 1·00 50

SPECIAL DELIVERY STAMP

1899. No. E 224 of United States surch. **CUBA** and value.

E 252. S 1. 10 c. on 10 c. blue 25·00 25·00

C. INDEPENDENT REPUBLIC.

1902. Surch. **UN CENTAVO HABILITADO OCTUBRE 1902** and figure **1.**

306. – 1 c. on 3 c. pur. (No. 303) 1·25 20

7. Major-General Antonio Maceo.

8. B. Maso.

1907.

311. 7. 50 c. black and slate 80 40
318. 50 c. black and violet 70 20

1910.

312. 8. 1 c. violet and green 20 5
320. 1 c. green 55 5
313. – 2 c. green and red 80 5
321. – 2 c. red 55 5
314. – 3 c. blue and violet 45 10
315. – 5 c. green and blue 4·50 45
322. – 5 c. blue 1·10 5
323. – 8 c. violet and olive 55 12
316. – 8 c. black and olive 80 25
317. – 10 c. blue and sepia 1·90 12
319. – 1 p. black and slate 4·00 2·25
324. – 1 p. black 2·50 1·10

PORTRAITS: 2 c. M. Gomez. 3 c. J. Sangully. 5 c. I. Agramonte. 8 c. C. Garcia. 10 c. Mayia. 1 p. C. Roloff.

9. Map of W. Indies.

10. Gertrudis Gomez de Avellaneda (poetess).

1914.

325. 9. 1 c. green 20 5
326. 2 c. red 20 5
328. 3 c. violet 1·50 20
329. 5 c. blue 1·50 10
330. 8 c. olive 1·50 50
331. 10 c. brown 2·75 25
332. 10 c. olive 1·60 20
333. 50 c. orange 14·00 9·00
334. $1 slate 16·00 10·00

1914. Gertrudis Gomez de Avellaneda. Cent

335. 10. 5 c. blue 1·50 65

11. Jose Marti.

13.

1917.

336. 11. 1 c. green (Marti) 20 5
337. – 2 c. red (Gomez) 20 5
338. – 3 c. violet (La Luz) 30 5
339. – 5 c. blue (Garcia) 35 5
340. – 8 c. brown (Agramonte) 1·75 5
341. – 10 c. brown (Palma) 55 5
351. – 20 c. green (Saco) 1·10 20
343. – 50 c. rose (Maceo) 2·75 35
344. – 1 p. black (Cespedes) 2·25 12

1927. Republic. 25th Anniv.

352. 13. 25 c. violet 5·50 2·25

14. Flying Boat over Havana Harbour.

1927. Air.

353. 14. 5 c. blue 1·60 75

15. T. Estrada Palma.

1928. 6th Pan-American Conf. As T 15.

354. 1 c. green 15 12
355. 2 c. red 15 12
356. 5 c. blue 25 20
357. 8 c. brown 45 40
358. 10 c. brown 45 20
359. 13 c. orange 90 40
360. 20 c. olive 95 45
361. 30 c. purple 1·60 40
362. 50 c. red 2·75 1·00
363. 1 p. black 5·50 2·25

DESIGNS: 2 c. Gen. G. Machado. 5 c. El Morro, Havana. 8 c. Railway Station, Havana. 10 c. President's Palace. 13 c. Tobacco plantation. 20 c. Treasury Secretariat. 30 c. Sugar Mill. 50 c. Havana Cathedral. 1 p. Galician Immigrants' Centre, Havana.

1928. Air. Lindbergh Commem. Optd. **LINDBERGH FEBRERO 1928.**

364. 14. 5 c. red 1·60 75

17. The Capitol, Havana.

18. Hurdler.

1929. Inaug. of Capitol.

365. 17. 1 c. green 20 15
366. 2 c. red 20 15
367. 5 c. blue 30 20
368. 10 c. brown 65 30
369. 20 c. purple 2·50 1·10

1930. 2nd Central American Games, Havana.

370. 18. 1 c. green 45 20
371. 2 c. red 45 25
372. 5 c. blue 55 25
373. 10 c. brown 75 55
374. 20 c. purple 3·75 2·00

1930. Air. Surch. **CORREO AEREO NACIONAL 10 C.**

375. 13. 10 c. on 25 c. violet 1·90 95

19. 'Plane over Cuban Coast.

1931. Air.

376. 19. 5 c. green 12 5
377. 8 c. red 75 45
378. 10 c. blue 20 5
379. 15 c. red 45 20
380. 20 c. brown 50 5
381. 30 c. purple 75 5
382. 40 c. orange 1·40 20
383. 50 c. olive 1·60 45
384. $1 black 3·25 55

20.

1931. Air.

385. 20. 5 c. purple 15 5
386. 10 c. black 20 5
387. 20 c. red 1·00 12
388. 20 c. pink 1·25 65
389. 50 c. blue 2·25 20
390. 50 c. greenish blue 1·60 75

21. Mangos of Baragua.

22. Maceo, Gomez and Zayas.

1933. War of Independence. 35th Anniv.

391. 21. 3 c. chocolate 75 20
392. – 5 c. blue 40 15
393. – 10 c. green 75 20
394. 22. 13 c. red 1·90 25
395. – 20 c. black 2·75 1·60

DESIGNS—HORIZ. 5 c. Battle of Mal Tiempo. 10 c. Battle of Coliseo. VERT. 20 c. Campaign Monument.

1933. Establishment of Revolutionary Govt. Stamps of 1917 optd. **GOBIERNO REVOLUCIONARIO 4-9-1933** or surch. also.

396. 11. 1 c. green 35 15
397. – 2 c. on 3 c. vio. (No. 338) 35 15

23. Dr. Carlos J. Finlay.

24. Matanzas Bay and Free Zone.

1934. C. J. Finlay ("yellow-fever" researcher). 101st Birth Anniv.

398. 23. 2 c. red 20 8
399. 5 c. blue 1·10 35

1935. Air. Havana-Miami "Air Train". Surch. **PRIMER TREN AEREO INTERNACIONAL. 1935 O'Meara y du Pont+10 cts.** Imperf. or perf.

400. 19. 10 c.+10 c. red 1·25 1·25

1936. Free Port of Matanzas. Inscr. as in T 24. Perf. or imperf. (same prices).

401. – 1 c. green (postage) 12 8
402. 24. 2 c. red 25 8
403. – 4 c. purple 40 15
404. – 5 c. blue 55 15
405. – 8 c. brown 90 20
406. – 10 c. green 1·10 40
407. – 20 c. brown 1·60 80
408. – 50 c. slate 2·75 2·25
409. – 5 c. violet (air) 25 12
410. – 10 c. orange 55 25
411. – 20 c. green 1·40 75
412. – 50 c. black 3·25 1·60

DESIGNS—POSTAGE: 1 c. Map of Caribbean. 4 c. S.S. "Rex" in Matanzas Bay. 5 c. Ships in the Free Zone. 8 c. Bellamar Caves. 10 c. Yumuri Valley. 20 c. Yumuri River. 50 c. Sailing vessel and steamboat. AIR: 5 c. Aerial panorama. 10 c. Airship "Macon" over Concord Bridge. 20 c. Aeroplane "Cuatro Vientos" over Matanzas. 50 c. San Severino Fortress.

25. President J. M. Gomez. 26. Gen. J. M. Gomez Monument.

1936. Gomez Monument. Inaug. Inscr. "CORREOS 1936".

413. **25.** 1 c. green .. .. 1·10 35
414. **26.** 2 c. red .. .. 1·40 55

27. "Peace and Labour". 28. Maximo Gomez Monument.

1936. Maximo Gomez Monument. Inaug. Inscr. "18 NOV. 1935" or "18 DE NOVIEMBRE 1935".

415. **27.** 1 c. green (postage) .. 25 8
416. **28.** 2 c. red 25 8
417. – 4 c. purple 35 12
418. – 5 c. blue .. .. 1·10 35
419. – 8 c. olive .. .. 1·90 70
420. – 5 c. violet (air) .. .. 1·60 80
421. – 10 c. brown .. .. 2·75 1·40

DESIGNS—VERT. 4 c. Flaming torch. 8 c. Dove of Peace. HORIZ. 5 c. (No. 418) Army of Liberation. 5 c. (No. 420) Lightning. 10 c. "Flying Wing".

DESIGNS (each with caravel in upper triangle)—VERT. 1 c. Cane plant. HORIZ. 2 c. Primitive sugar mill.

29. Caravel and Modern Sugar Mill.

1937. Cane Sugar Industry. 4th Cent.

422. – 1 c. green 65 35
423. – 2 c. red 35 15
424. **29.** 5 c. blue 65 35

30. Mountain View (Bolivia). 31. Camilo Henriquez (Chile).

1937. American Writers and Artists Assn.

424a. – 1 c. green (postage) .. 25 25
424b. **69.** 1 c. green 25 25
424c. – 2 c. red 25 25
424d. – 2 c. red 25 25
424e. **70.** 3 c. violet 55 55
424f. – 3 c. violet 55 55
424g. – 4 c. brown 70 70
424h. – 4 c. brown .. .. 1·40 1·40
424i. – 5 c. blue 80 80
424j. – 5 c. blue 80 80
424k. – 8 c. green .. .. 1·50 1·50
424l. – 8 c. green .. .. 1·10 1·10
424m. – 10 c. brown .. .. 1·25 1·25
424n. – 10 c. brown .. .. 1·25 1·25
424o. – 25 c. lilac .. .. 11·00 11·00
424p. – 5 c. red (air) .. .. 2·25 2·25
424q. – 5 c. red .. .. 2·25 2·25
424r. – 10 c. blue .. .. 2·25 2·25
424s. – 10 c. blue .. .. 2·25 2·25
424t. – 20 c. green .. .. 3·75 3·25
424u. – 20 c. green .. .. 3·75 3·25

DESIGNS-VERT. No. 424a, Arms of the Republic (Argentina). 424c, Arms (Brazil). No. 424f, Gen. F. de Paula Santander (Colombia). No. 424g, Autograph of Jose Marti (Cuba). No. 424j, Juan Montalvo (Ecuador). No. 424k, Abraham Lincoln (U.S.A.). No. 424l, Quetzal and scroll (Guatemala). No. 424m, Arms (Haiti). No. 424n, Francisco Morazan (Honduras). No. 424r, Inca gate, Cuzco (Peru). No. 424s, Atlacatl (Indian warrior) (El Salvador). No. 424t, Simon Bolivar (Venezuela). No. 424u, Jose Rodo (Uruguay). HORIZ. No. 424d, River scene (Canada). No. 424h, National Monument (Costa Rica). No. 424i, Columbus Lighthouse (Dominican Republic). No. 424o, Ships of Columbus. No. 424p, Arch (Panama). No. 424q. Carlos Lopez (Paraguay).

1937. Cuban Railway Cent. Surch. **1837 1937 PRIMER CENTENARIO FERROCARRIL EN CUBA** and value either side of an early engine and coach.

425. **13.** 10 c. on 25 c. violet .. 3·75 1·50

1938. Air. D. Rosillo's Overseas Flight from Key West to Havana. 25th Anniv. Optd. **1913 1938 ROSILLO Key West-Habana.**

426. **14.** 5 c. orange .. .. 2·25 1·10

33. Pierre and Marie Curie. 34. Allegory of Child Care.

1938. Int. Anti-Cancer Fund. 40th Anniv. of Discovery of Radium.

427. **33.** 2 c.+1 c. red .. .. 1·60 65
428. 5 c.+1 c. blue .. .. 1·60 65

1938. Obligatory Tax. Anti-T.B. Fund.

429. **34.** 1 c. green 10 5

35. Native and Cigar. 36. Calixto Garcia.

1939. Havana Tobacco Industry.

430. **35.** 1 c. green 10 5
431. – 2 c. red 20 5
432. – 5 c. blue 55 5

DESIGNS: 2 c. Cigar, globe and wreath of leaves. 5 c. Tobacco plant and box of cigars.

1939. Air. Experimental Rocket Post. Optd. **EXPERIMENTO DEL/COHETE/Postal/AÑO DE 1939.**

433. **20.** 10 c. green .. .. 19·00 3·75

1939. Gen. Calixto Garcia. Birth Cent. Perf. or imperf.

434. **36.** 2 c. red 35 15
435. – 5 c. blue 65 35

DESIGN: 5 c. Garcia on horseback.

37. Nurse and Child. 38. Gonzalo de Quesada and Union Flags. 39. Rotarian Symbol, Flag and Tobacco Plant.

1939. Obligatory Tax. Anti-T.B.

436. **37.** 1 c. red 10 5

1940. Pan-American Union. 50th Anniv.

437. **38.** 2 c. red 65 35

1940. Rotary Int. Convention.

438. **39.** 2 c. red .. .. 1·40 65

40. Lions, Emblem, Flag and Palms. 41. Dr. N. G. Gutierres.

1940. Lions Int. Convention, Havana.

439. **40.** 2 c. red .. .. 1·00 50

1940. Publication of First Cuban Medical Review. Cent.

440. **41.** 2 c. red 65 35
441. 5 c. blue 80 35

42. Sir Rowland Hill and G.B. 1d. of 1840 and Cuba Issues of 1855 and 1899.

1940. Air. 1st Adhesive Postage Stamps Cent.

443. **42.** 10 c. brown .. .. 2·75 1·40

43. "Health" protecting Children. 44. Heredia and Niagara Falls.

1940. Obligatory Tax. Children's Hospital and Anti-T.B. Funds.

444. **43.** 1 c. blue 10 5

1940. Air. J. M. Heredia y Campuzano (poet). Death Cent.

446. – 5 c. emerald .. .. 1·25 65
447. **44.** 10 c. grey .. .. 1·90 1·00

DESIGN: 5 c. Heredia and palms.

45. Major-Gen. Moncada and Sword. 46. Moncada riding into Battle.

1941. H. Moncada. Birth Cent.

448. **45.** 3 c. brown 65 35
449. **46.** 5 c. blue 80 40

46a. Mother and Child. 47. "Labour, Wealth of America".

1941. Obligatory Tax. Anti-T.B.

450. **46a.** 1 c. brown 10 5

1942. American Democracy. Imperf. or perf.

451. – 1 c. green 20 5
452. – 3 c. brown 25 10
453. **47.** 5 c. blue 50 20
454. – 10 c. mauve .. .. 1·10 45
455. – 13 c. red .. .. 1·25 55

DESIGNS: 1 c. Western Hemisphere. 3 c. Cuban Arms and portraits of Maceo, Bolivar, Juarez and Lincoln. 10 c. Tree of Fraternity, Havana. 13 c. Statue of Liberty.

48. Gen. I. A. Loynaz. 49. Rescue of Sanguily.

1942. Gen. I. A. Loynaz. Birth Cent.

456. **48.** 3 c. brown 55 20
457. **49.** 5 c. blue .. .. 1·00 35

50. "Victory". 51. "Unmask Fifth Columnists".

1942. Obligatory Tax. Red Cross Fund.

458. **50.** ½ c. orange 12 5
459. ½ c. grey 12 5

1942. Obligatory Tax. Anti-T.B. Fund. Optd. **1942.**

460. **46a.** 1 c. red 12 5

1943. Anti-Fifth Column.

461. **51.** 1 c. green 20 10
462. – 3 c. red 35 10
463. – 5 c. blue 35 12
464. – 10 c. brown 75 35
465. – 13 c. purple .. .. 1·60 95

DESIGNS—HORIZ. (45×25 mm). 5 c. Woman in snake's coils ("The Fifth Column is like the Serpent – destroy it"). 10 c. Men demolishing column with battering-ram ("Fulfil your patriotic duty by destroying the Fifth Column"). As T **51**. 13 c. Woman with monster "Don't be afraid of the Fifth Column. Attack it". VERT. Girl with finger to lips "Be Careful! The Fifth Column is spying on you".

52. Eloy Alfaro, Flags of Eucador and Cuba.

1943. E. Alfaro (former President of Ecuador). Birth Cent.

466. **52.** 3 c. green 75 35

53. "Road to Retirement". 54. Mother protecting Child.

1943. Postal Employees' Retirement Fund.

467. **53.** 1 c. green 55 25
470. 3 c. red 55 20
471. 5 c. blue 55 25

1943. Obligatory Tax. Anti-Tuberculosis.

473. **54.** 1 c. brown 12 5

55. Columbus. 56. Mountains of Gibara.

1944. Discovery of America. 450th Anniv.

474. **55.** 1 c. green (postage) .. 15 10
475. – 3 c. brown 25 10
476. – 5 c. blue 40 15
477. – 10 c. violet 80 45
478. – 13 c. red .. .. 1·60 80
479. **56.** 5 c. olive (air) 45 20
480. – 10 c. grey .. .. 1·10 35

DESIGNS—VERT. 3 c. Bartolome de as Casas. 5 c. (No. 476), Statue of Columbus. HORIZ. 10 c. (No. 477), Xeres Torres discovering tobacco. 10 c. (No. 480), Columbus Light house. 13 c. Columbus at Pinar del Rio.

57. Carlos Roloff. 58. American Continents and Brazilian "Bull's Eyes" stamps.

1944. Major-Gen. Roloff. Birth Cent.

481. **57.** 3 c. violet 45 12

1944. 1st American Postage stamps. Cent.

482. **58.** 3 c. brown .. .. 1·10 45

59. Arms. 60. Governor Las Casas and Bishop Penalver.

1945. Economic Society of Friends of Havana. 150th Anniv.

483. **59.** 1 c. green 20 10
484. **60.** 2 c. red 25 10

61. Old Age Pensioners.

1945. Postal Employees' Retirement Fund.

485. **61.** 1 c. green 10 5
487. 2 c. red 20 5
489. 5 c. blue 45 20

62. "Valdes".

1946. Gabriel de la Concepcion Valdes (poet). Death Cent.

491. **62.** 2 c. red 55 25

63. Manuel M. Sterling.

64.

1946. Founding of "Manuel Marquez Sterling" Professional School of Journalism.
492. **63.** 2 c. red 55 25

1946. Int. Red Cross. 80th Anniv.
493. **64.** 2 c. red 55 25

65. Prize Cattle and Dairymaid.

66. Franklin D. Roosevelt.

1947. National Cattle Show.
494. **65.** 2 c. red 65 25

1947. Pres. Roosevelt. 2nd Death Anniv.
495. **66.** 2 c red 55 25

67. Antonio Oms and Pensioners.

1947. Postal Employees' Retirement Fund.
496. **67.** 1 c. green 10 10
497. 2 c. red 20 10
498. 5 c. blue 45 20

68. Marta Abreu.

69. "Charity".

1947. M. Abreu (philanthropist). Birth Cent.
499. **68.** 1 c. green 20 10
500. **69.** 2 c. red 35 10
501. – 5 c. blue 55 20
502. – 10 c. violet .. .. 1·10 55
DESIGNS: 5 c. Monument. 10 c. Allegory of Patriotism.

70. Dr. G. A. Hansen and Isle of Pines.

1948. Int. Leprosy Relief Congress, Havana.
503. **70.** 2 c. red 45 20

71. Initial Council of War.

1948. Air. War of Independence. 50th Anniv.
504. **71.** 8 c. black and yellow .. 1·25 65

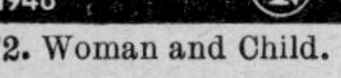

72. Woman and Child.

73. Death of Marti.

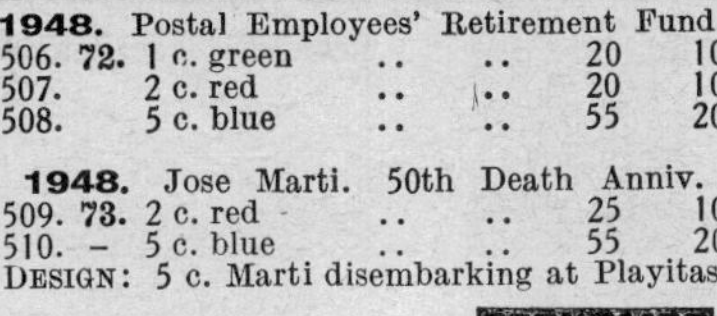
1948. Postal Employees' Retirement Fund.
506. **72.** 1 c. green 20 10
507. 2 c. red 20 10
508. 5 c. blue 55 20

1948. Jose Marti. 50th Death Anniv.
509. **73.** 2 c. red 25 10
510. – 5 c. blue 55 20
DESIGN: 5 c. Marti disembarking at Playitas.

74. Gathering Tobacco.

75. Gen. Maceo.

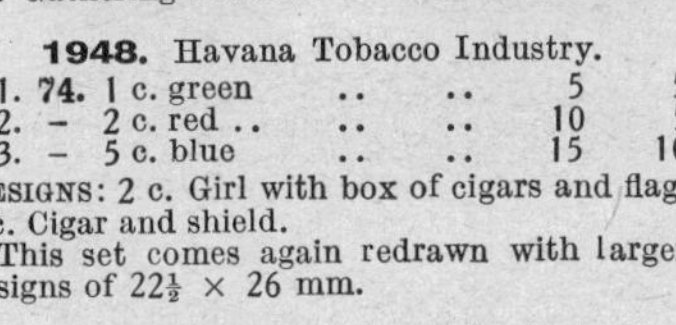
1948. Havana Tobacco Industry.
511. **74.** 1 c. green 5 5
512. – 2 c. red 10 5
513. – 5 c. blue 15 10
DESIGNS: 2 c. Girl with box of cigars and flag. 5 c. Cigar and shield.

This set comes again redrawn with larger designs of $22\frac{1}{2} \times 26$ mm.

1948. Gen. Maceo. Birth Cent.
514. – 1 c. green 5 5
515. **75.** 2 c. red 10 5
516. – 5 c. blue 12 10
517. – 8 c. brown and black .. 20 15
518. – 10 c. green and brown .. 30 10
519. – 20 c. blue and red .. 80 55
520. – 50 c. blue and red .. 2·25 1·25
521. – 1 p. violet and black .. 4·50 1·90
DESIGNS—VERT. 1 c. Equestrian statue of Maceo. 5 c. Mausoleum at El Cacahual. HORIZ. 8 c. Maceo and raised swords. 10 c. Maceo leading charge. 20 c. Maceo at Peralejo. 50 c. Declaration at Baragua. 1 p. Death of Maceo at San Pedro.

76. Symbol of Medicine.

77. Morro Lighthouse.

1948. 1st Pan-American Pharmaceutical Congress.
522. **76.** 2 c. red 45 20

1949. El Morro Lighthouse. Cent.
523 **77.** 2 c. red 35 20

78. Jagua Castle.

1949. Newspaper "Hoja Economica" Cent. and Bicentenary of Jagua Fortress.
524. **78.** 1 c. green 25 10
525. 2 c. red 55 20

79. M. Sanguily.

80. Isle of Pines.

1949. Manuel Sanguily y Garritte (post). Birth Cent.
526. **79.** 2 c. red 25 10
527. 5 c. blue 55 20

1949. Return of Isle of Pines to Cuba. 20th Anniv.
528. **80.** 5 c. blue 25 12

81. Ismael Cespedes.

82. Woman and Child.

1949. Postal Employees' Retirement Fund.
529. **81.** 1 c. green 20 10
530. 2 c. red 20 10
531. 5 c. blue 55 20

1949. Obligatory Tax. Anti-Tuberculosis.
532. **82.** 1 c. blue 12 5
547. 1 c. red 12 5
No. 547 is dated "1950".

83. General E. Collazo.

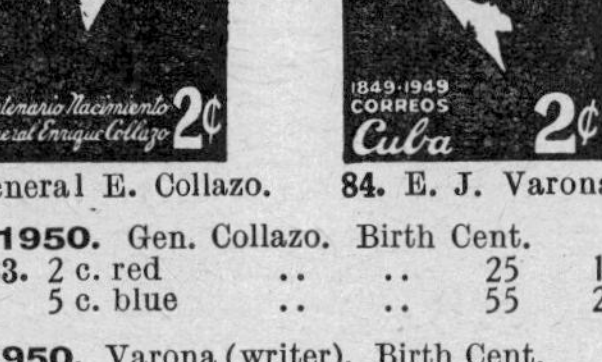

84. E. J. Varona.

1950. Gen. Collazo. Birth Cent.
533. **83.** 2 c. red 25 10
534. 5 c. blue 55 20

1950. Varona (writer). Birth Cent.
535. **84.** 2 c. red 25 10
536. 5 c. blue 55 20

1950. National Bank Opening. No. 512 optd. **BANCO NACIONAL DE CUBA INAUGURACION 27 ABRIL 1950.**
540. – 2 c. red 55 25

1950. U.P.U. 75th Anniv. Optd. **U.P.U. 1874 1949.**
541. **74.** 1 c. emerald 20 10
542. – 2 c. pink (As No. 512) .. 35 10
543. – 5 c. blue (As No. 513) .. 55 20

85. Balanzategui Pausa and Railway Crash.

86. F. Figueredo.

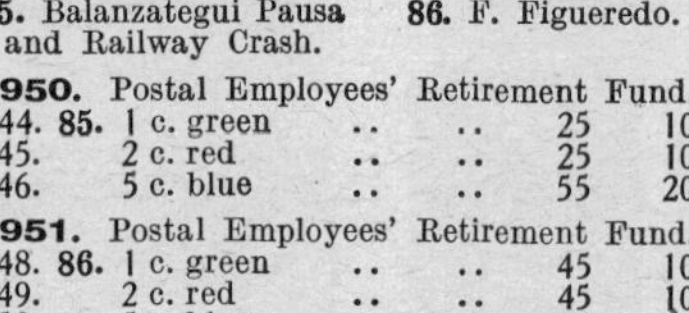
1950. Postal Employees' Retirement Fund.
544. **85.** 1 c. green 25 10
545. 2 c. red 25 10
546. 5 c. blue 55 20

1951. Postal Employees' Retirement Fund.
548. **86.** 1 c. green 45 10
549. 2 c. red 45 10
550. 5 c. blue 65 35

87. Foundation Stone.

88. Narciso Lopez.

89. Raising the Flag.

1951. Obligatory Tax. P.O. Rebuilding Fund.
551. **87.** 1 c. violet 5 5

1951. Cuban Flag Cent. Inscr. "CENTENARIO DE LA BANDERA CUBANA".
552. – 1 c. red, bl. & grn. (post.) 20 10
553. **88.** 2 c. black and red .. 35 10
554. – 5 c. red and blue .. 65 35
555. – 10 c. red, blue & violet 1·00 45
556. – 5 c. red, bl. & olive (air) 80 35
557. **89.** 8 c. red, blue & brown .. 1·10 50
558. – 25 c. red, blue and black 1·60 80
DESIGNS—VERT. 1 c. Miguel Teurbe Tolon. 5 c. (No. 554) Emilia Teurbe Tolon. 10 c. Flag. 25 c. Flag and lighthouse. HORIZ. 5 c. (No. 556) Lopez landing at Cardenas.

90. Clara Maass and Hospitals.

1951. Clara Maass (nurse). 50th Death Anniv.
559. **90.** 2 c. red 55 25

91. J. R. Capablanca.

92. Chess-board.

1951. World Chess Championship. 30th Anniv. Inscr. as in T **91.**
562. **91.** 1 c. orge. & grn. (post.) 90 25
563. – 2 c. brown and red .. 1·10 55
564. E **8.** 5 c. blue and black .. 2·25 1·10
565. **92.** 5 c. yellow & green (air) 1·10 45
566. – 8 c. purple and blue .. 1·60 65
567. **91.** 25 c. sepia and brown .. 2·75 1·10
DESIGN—VERT. 2 c., 8 c. Capablanca playing chess.

93. Dr. Antonio Guiteras Holmes.

94. Morrillo Fortress.

1951. Death of Dr. A. Guiteras Holmes in skirmish at Morrillo. 16th Anniv.
568. **93.** 1 c. green (postage) .. 35 10
569. – 2 c. rose 55 20
570. **94.** 5 c. blue 65 35
571. **93.** 5 c. mauve (air) .. 1·10 90
572. – 8 c. green .. 1·60 1·25
573. **94.** 25 c. black .. .. 2·75 2·25
DESIGN—HORIZ. 2 c., 8 c. Guiteras framing social laws.

95. Mother and Child.

96. Christmas Emblems.

1951. Obligatory Tax. Anti-Tuberculosis.
575. **95.** 1 c. brown 15 5
576. 1 c. red 15 5
577. 1 c. green 15 5
578. 1 c. blue 15 5

1951. Christmas Greetings.
579. **96.** 1 c. red and green .. 75 40
580. 2 c. green and red .. 1·20 60

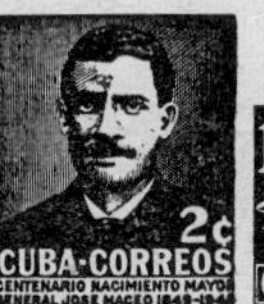

96a. Gen. J. Maceo.

97. General Post Office.

98. Isabella the Catholic.

1952. Gen. Maceo. Birth Cent.
581. **96a.** 2 c. brown 35 10
582. 5 c. blue 55 20

1952. Obligatory Tax. P.O. Rebuilding Fund.
583. **97.** 1 c. blue 5 5
584. 1 c. red 5 5

1952. Isabella the Catholic. 5th Birth Cent.
585. **98.** 2 c. red (postage) .. 55 25
586. **98.** 25 c. purple (air) .. 1·90 80

1952. As No. 549 surch. with new value.

(a) Postage.
588. **86.** 10 c. on 2 c. brown .. 75 35

(b) Air. Optd. **AEREO** in addition.
589. **86.** 5 c. on 2 c. brown .. 45 20
590. 8 c. on 2 c. brown .. 55 20
591. 10 c. on 2 c. brown .. 65 20
592. 25 c. on 2 c. brown .. 80 45
593. 50 c. on 2 c. brown .. 2·45 1·10
594. 1 p. on 2 c. brown .. 4·00 1·90

99. Proclamation of Republic.

100. Statue, Havana University.

1952. Republic. 50th Anniv. Inscr. "1902 1952".
595. **99.** 1 c. blk. & grn. (postage) 20 10
596. – 2 c. black and red .. 20 10
597. – 5 c. black and blue .. 35 10
598. – 8 c. black and brown 35 10
599. – 20 c. black and olive .. 90 45
600. – 50 c. black and orange 1·25 65
601. – 5 c. green & violet (air) 55 20
602. **100.** 8 c. green and red .. 55 35
603. – 10 c. emerald and blue 65 35
604. – 25 c. emerald and purple 1·25 65
DESIGNS—HORIZ.—POSTAGE: 2 c. Estrada Palma and Esteuez Romero. 5 c. Barnet, Finlay, Guiteras and Nuney. 8 c. The Capitol. 20 c. Map. 50 c. Sugar factory. AIR: 5 c. Rural school. 10 c. Presidential Palace. 25 c. Banknote.

101. Route of Flight. 102. Coffee Beans.

1952. Air. Florida-Cuba Flight by A. Parla. 39th Anniv. Inscr. "1913 1952".
605. 101. 8 c. black 65 20
606. – 25 c. blue .. .. 1·25 65
DESIGN—HORIZ. 25 c. Parla Orduna and biplane.

1952. Coffee Cultivation. Bicent.
608. 102. 1 c. green 20 10
609. – 2 c. red 35 20
610. – 5 c. green and blue .. 55 25
DESIGNS: 2 c. Plantation worker and map. 5 c. Coffee plantation.

103. Col. C. Hernandez.

ILLUSTRATIONS British Commonwealth and all overprints and surcharges are FULL SIZE. Foreign Countries have been reduced to ¾-LINEAR.

1952. Postal Employees' Retirement Fund.
611. 103. 1 c. green (postage) .. 10 8
612. 2 c. red 20 10
613. 5 c. blue 20 12
614. 8 c. black 45 20
615. 10 c. red 65 30
616. 20 c. brown .. .. 2·25 75
617. 5 c. orange (air) .. 25 5
618. 8 c. green 45 5
619. 10 c. brown 45 10
620. 15 c. green 55 15
621. 20 c. turquoise .. 55 25
622. 25 c. red 75 35
623. 30 c. violet .. .. 1·50 40
624. 45 c. mauve .. .. 1·75 1·25
625. 50 c. blue .. .. 1·25 80
626. 1 p. yellow .. .. 3·50 1·90

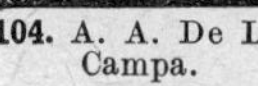

104. A. A. De La Campa. 105. Statue, Havana University.

106. Dominguez, Estebanez and Capoevila. (defence lawyers)

1952. Execution of Eight Rebel Medical Students. 81st Anniv.
627. 104. 1 c. black and green (post). 5 5
628. – 2 c. black and red .. 12 5
629. – 3 c. black and violet.. 12 5
630. – 5 c. black and blue .. 25 8
631. – 8 c. black and sepia .. 25 12
632. – 10 c. black and brown 45 10
633. – 13 c. black and purple 75 20
634. – 20 c. black and olive.. 1·20 45
635. 105. 5 c. blue and indigo (air) 55 35
636. 106. 25 c. green and orange 1·60 75
PORTRAITS: 2 c. C. A. de la Torre. 3 c. A. Bermudez. 5 c. E. G. Toledo. 8 c. A. Laborde. 10 c. J. De M. Medina. 13 c. P. Rodriguez. 20 c. C. Verdugo.

107. Child's Face. 108. Christmas Tree.

1952. Obligatory Tax. Anti-Tuberculosis.
637. 107. 1 c. orange 15 5
638. 1 c. red 15 5
639. 1 c. green 15 5
640. 1 c. blue 15 5

1952. Christmas.
641. 108. 1 c. red and green .. 1·90 1·10
642. 3 c. green and violet.. 1·90 1·10

109. Marti's Birthplace. 110. Dr. Rafael Montoro.

1953. Jose Marti. Birth Cent. Inscr. "CENTENARIO DE MARTI".
643. 109. 1 c. brn. & grn. (post.) 5 5
644. – 1 c. brown and green 5 5
645. – 3 c. brown and violet 15 5
646. – 3 c. brown and violet 15 5
647. – 5 c. brown and blue .. 25 10
648. – 5 c. brown and blue .. 25 10
649. – 10 c. black and brown 65 20
650. – 10 c. black and brown 65 20
651. – 13 c. brown and green 75 35
652. – 13 c. brown and green 75 35
653. – 5 c. black & red (air) 20 10
654. – 5 c. black and red .. 20 10
655. – 8 c. black and green 20 10
656. – 8 c. black and green 20 10
657. – 10 c. red and blue .. 20 10
658. – 10 c. blue and red .. 20 10
659. – 15 c. black and violet 45 20
660. – 15 c. black and violet 45 20
661. – 25 c. red and brown .. 1·10 45
662. – 25 c. red and brown .. 1·10 55
663. – 50 c. blue and yellow 1·60 65
DESIGNS—HORIZ. No. 644, Marti before Council of War. No. 645, Prison building. No. 647, "El Abra" ranch. No. 652, First edition of "Patria". No. 656, House of Maximo Gomez, Montecristi. No. 658, Marti as an orator. No. 663, "Fragua Martiana" (modern building). VERT. No. 646, Marti in prison. No. 648, Allegory of Marti's poems. No. 649, Marti and Bolivar Statue, Caracas. No. 650, Marti writing. No. 651, Revolutionaries' meeting-place. No. 653, Marti in Kingston. No. 654, Marti in Ibor City. No. 655, Manifesto of Montecristi. No. 657, Marti's portrait. No. 659, Marti's first tomb. No. 660, Obelisk at Des Rios. No. 661, Monument in Havana. No. 662, Marti's present tomb.

1953. Montoro (statesman). Birth Cent.
664. 110. 3 c. purple 55 25

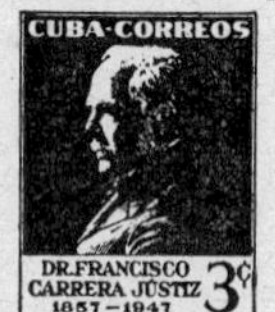

111. Dr. F. Carrera Justiz. 112. Lockheed "Constellation" Airliner.

1953.
665. 111. 3 c. red 55 25

1953. Air.
666. 112. 8 c. brown 35 20
667. 15 c. red 75 55
668. – 2 p. brown and green 6·50 3·75
670. – 2 p. myrtle and blue.. 5·50 2·75
669. – 5 p. brown and blue .. 14·00 6·50
671. – 5 p. myrtle and rose .. 12·00 6·50
DESIGN: Nos. 669/71, "Constellation" facing right.

1953. No. 512 surch.
672. 3 c. on 2 c. red 35 15

113. Congress Building. 114.

1953. 1st Int. Accountancy Congress, Havana.
673. 113. 3 c. blue (postage) .. 35 15
674. – 8 c. red (air) 90 45
675. – 25 c. green .. .. 1·25 65
DESIGNS: 8 c. Congress building and "Cuba". 25 c. Aerial view of building and 'plane.

1953. Obligatory Tax. Anti-T.B.
676. 114. 1 c. red 10 5

115. M. C. Llanguno. 116.

1954. Postal Employees' Retirement Fund. Inscr. "1953".
677. 115. 1 c. green (postage) .. 20 5
678. – 3 c. red 20 5
679. 116. 5 c. blue 45 10
680. – 8 c. claret 75 35
681. – 10 c. sepia .. .. 1·10 55
682. – 5 c. indigo (air) .. 45 20
683. – 8 c. purple 55 20
684. – 10 c. orange 65 20
685. 116. 1 p. grey .. .. 2·25 1·25
PORTRAITS—VERT. Nos. 678, 680, F. L. C. Hensell. 681, 683, A. G. Rojas. 684, G. H. Saez. HORIZ. 682, M. C. Llaguno.

117. Jose Marti. 118. Aeroplane over Tractor.

1954. Portraits. Roul. (Nos. 1180a/b) or perf. (others).
686. 117. 1 c. green 5 5
990. 1 c. red 5 5
1680. – 1 c. blue 5 5
687. – 2 c. red (Gomez) .. 5 5
991. – 2 c. green (Gomez) .. 10 5
1681. – 2 c. yellow-green (Gomez) .. 10 5
688. – 3 c. violet (de la Luz Caballero) .. 5 5
1180a. – 3 c. orange (Cabaltero) 5 5
689. – 4 c. mauve (Aldama) 5 5
690. – 5 c. blue (Garcia) .. 8 5
691. – 8 c. lake (Agramonte) 12 5
692. – 10 c. sepia (Palma) 15 5
693. – 13 c. red (Finlay) .. 20 5
1180b. – 13 c. chestnut (Finlay) 25 15
694. – 14 c. grey (Sanchez) 35 5
695. – 20 c. olive (Saco) .. 80 8
1682. – 20 c. violet (Saco) .. 45 8
696. – 50 c. ochre (Maceo) 1·10 20
697. – 1 p. orange (Cespedes) 1·90 35

1954. Air. Sugar Industry.
698. – 5 c. yellow-green .. 20 8
699. – 8 c. brown 65 35
700. 118. 10 c. green 65 35
701. – 15 c. chestnut .. 25 8
702. – 20 c. blue 30 8
703. – 25 c. red 50 10
704a. – 30 c. purple 80 30
705. – 40 c. blue .. .. 1·10 25
706. – 45 c. violet .. .. 1·25 30
707. – 50 c. blue .. .. 1·25 40
708. – 1 p. indigo .. .. 2·75 1·00
DESIGNS—VERT. 5 c. Sugar cane. 1 p. A. Reinoso. HORIZ. 8 c. Sugar harvesting. 15 c. Tram-load of sugar cane. 20 c. Modern sugar factory. 25 c. Evaporators. 30 c. Stacking sugar in sacks. 40 c. Loading sugar on ship. 45 c. Ox-cart. 50 c. Primitive sugar factory.

119. Major-Gen. J. M. Rodriguez. 120. Sanatorium.

1954. Rodriguez. Birth Cent.
709. 119. 2 c. sepia and lake .. 35 10
710. – 5 c. sepia and blue .. 55 20
DESIGN: 5 c. Rodriguez on horseback.

1954. General Batista Sanatorium.
711. 120. 3 c. blue (postage) .. 55 25
712. 9 c. green (air) .. 1·00 55

121. 122. Father Christmas. 123. Maria Luisa Dolz.

1954. Obligatory Tax. Anti-T.B.
713. 121. 1 c. red 10 5
714. 1 c. green 10 5
715. 1 c. blue 10 5
716. 1 c. violet 10 5

1954. Christmas Greetings.
717. 122. 2 c. green and red .. 1·90 1·10
718. 4 c. red and green .. 1·90 1·10

1954. Maria Dolz (educationist). Cent.
719. 123. 4 c. blue (postage) .. 55 25
720. 12 c. magenta (air) .. 1·10 55

124. Boy Scouts and Cuban Flag. 126. Major-Gen. F. Carrillo.

125. P. P. Harris and Rotary Emblem.

1954. 3rd National Scout Camp.
721. 124. 4 c. green 55 25

1954. Rotary Int. 50th Anniv.
722. 125. 4 c. blue (postage) .. 55 25
723. 12 c. red (air) .. .. 1·10 55

1955. Carrillo's Birth Cent.
724. 126. 2 c. blue and red .. 35 10
725. – 5 c. sepia and blue .. 55 20
DESIGN: 5 c. Half-length portrait.

127. 1855 Stamp and "La Volanta".

1955. First Cuban Postage Stamps Cent. and First Republican Stamps. 50th Anniv.
726. – 2 c. blue & pur. (post.) 20 10
727. 127. 4 c. green and buff .. 35 20
728. – 10 c. red and blue .. 80 45
729. – 14 c. orange and green 2·25 90
730. – 8 c. green & blue (air) 35 10
731. – 12 c. red and green .. 55 15
732. – 24 c. blue and red .. 80 35
733. – 30 c. brown & orange 1·25 55
DESIGNS (a) With 1855 stamp: 2 c. Old Square and Convent of St. Francis. 10 c. Havana in 19th century. 14 c. Captain-General's residence and Plaza de Armas. (b) With 1855 and 1905 stamps: 8 c. Palace of Fine Arts. 12 c. Plaza de la Fraternidad. 24 c. Aerial view of Havana. 30 c. Plaza de la Republica.

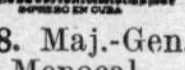

128. Maj.-Gen. Menocal. 129. Mariel Bay.

1955. Postal Employees' Retirement Fund.
734. 128. 2 c. green (postage) .. 35 10
735. 4 c. mauve 45 15
736. – 10 c. blue 55 20
737. – 14 c. grey 90 45
738. 129. 8 c. green & red (air).. 55 20
739. – 12 c. blue and brown.. 1·10 55
740. – 1 p. ochre and green .. 2·25 1·25
DESIGNS—As T 128: HORIZ. 4 c. Gen. E. Nunez. 14 c. Dr. A. de Bustamante. VERT. 10 c. J. Gomez. As T 129: HORIZ. 12 c. Varadero Beach. 1 p. Vinales Valley.

130. Cuban Academy. 131. Route of 1944 Flight.

1955. Air. Tampa, Florida. Cent.
741. 130. 12 c. brown and red .. 1·10 55

1955. Air. Crocier (aviator). 35th Death Anniv.
742. 131. 12 c. green and red .. 55 20
743. – 30 c. mauve and green 1·10 45
DESIGN: 30 c. Crocier in aircraft cockpit.

132. 133. Wright Brothers' Biplane.

1955. Obligatory Tax. Anti-T.B.
744. 132. 1 c. orange 20 10
745. 1 c. yellow 20 10
746. 1 c. blue 20 10
747. 1 c. mauve 20 10

1955. Air. Int. Philatelic Exn., Havana.
748. 133. 8 c. black, red and blue 55 25
749. – 12 c. black, green & red 55 25
750. – 24 c. blk., violet & red 80 45
751. – 30 c. blk., blue & orge. 1·90 90
752. – 50 c. blk., olive & orge. 2·25 1·10
DESIGNS: 12 c. "Spirit of St. Louis", 24 c. "Graf Zeppelin". 30 c. "Super Constellation" aircraft. 50 c. "Convair" delta-wing plane.

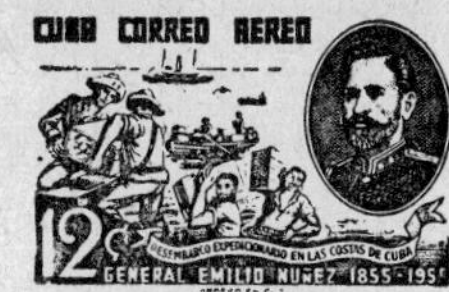

134. Turkey. **135.** Expedition Disembarking.

1955. Christmas Greetings.
754. **134.** 2 c. green and red .. 1·90 1·10
755. 4 c. lake and green .. 1·90 1·10

1955. General Nunez. Birth Cent.
756. – 4 c. lake (postage) .. 55 25
757. – 8 c. blue and red (air) 65 35
758. **135.** 12 c. green and brown 1·10 55
DESIGNS—VERT. (22½ + 32½ mm.): 4 c. Portrait of Nunez. HORIZ. As T **135**: 8 c. "Three Friends" (ship).

136. Bishop Morell de Santa Cruz. **137.** J. del Casal.

1956. Cuban Postal Service. Bicent.
759. – 4 c. blue & brn. (post.) 55 25
760. **136.** 12 c. green & brn. (air) 75 35
PORTRAIT: 4 c. F. C. de la Vega.

1956. Postal Employees' Retirement Fund.
761. **137.** 2 c. blk. & green (post.) 20 10
762. – 4 c. black and mauve .. 35 15
763. – 10 c. black and blue .. 55 15
764. – 14 c. black and violet .. 1·40 40
765. – 8 c. black & brown (air) 35 12
766. – 12 c. black and ochre .. 55 35
767. – 30 c. black and indigo 80 40
PORTRAITS: 4 c. Luisa Perez de Zambrana. 8 c. Gen. J. Sanguily. 10 c. J. Clemente Zena. 12 c. Gen. J. M. Aguirre. 14 c J. J. Palma. 30 c. Col. E. Fonts Sterling.

138. Victor Munoz. **139.** Mother and Baby.

1956. Munoz Commem.
768. **138.** 4 c. brown and green .. 55 25

1956. Air Mothers' Day.
769. **139.** 12 c. blue and red .. 75 35

140. Aerial View of Temple. **141.** Hawk.

1956. Masonic Grand Lodge of Cuba Temple, Havana.
770. – 4 c. blue (postage) .. 55 25
771. **140.** 12 c. green (air) .. 55 25
DESIGN: 4 c. Ground level view of Temple.

1956. Air. Birds.
772. – 8 c. blue 35 12
773. – 12 c. grey 55 35
783. – 12 c. green 35 20
774. **141.** 14 c. olive 55 15
775. – 19 c. brown 55 15
776. – 24 c. magenta 55 15
777. – 29 c. green 75 20
778. – 30 c. brown .. .. 1·10 20
779. – 50 c. slate .. .. 2·25 25
780. – 1 p. red .. .. 3·25 80
784. – 1 p. blue .. .. 1·25 90
781. – 2 p. purple .. .. 5·50 1·40
785. – 2 p. red .. .. 3·25 2·25
782. – 5 p. red .. .. 12·00 3·25
786. – 5 p. purple .. .. 8·00 5·50
DESIGNS—HORIZ. 8 c. Wild duck. 12 c. Pigeon. 29 c. Wild geese. 30 c. Quails. 2 p. (2), Sand pipers. VERT. 19 c. Seagulls. 24 c. Pelicans. 50 c. Herons. 1 p. (2), Black vulture. 5 p. (2), Woodpeckers.

142. H. de Blanck (composer). **143.** Church of Our Lady of Charity.

1956. Air. H. De Blanck. Birth Cent.
787. **142.** 12 c. blue 55 25

1956. Air. Inaug. of Philatelic Club of Cuba Building. No. 776 but colour changed and surch. "**Inauguracion Edificio Club Filatelico de la Republica de Cuba Julio 13 de 1956**" and value.
788. – 8 c. on 24 c. orange .. 1·00 50

1956. Inscr. "NTRA. SRA. DE LA CARIDAD", etc.
789. – 4 c. blue & yellow (post.) 55 25
790. **143.** 12 c. grn. and red (air) 65 35
DESIGN: 4 c. Our Lady of Charity over landscape.

144. **145.**

1956. Air. Benjamin Franklin. 250th Birth Anniv.
792. **144.** 12 c. brown .. .. 1·00 45

1956. "Gritto de Yara" (War of Independence). Commem.
793. **145.** 4 c. sepia and green .. 55 25

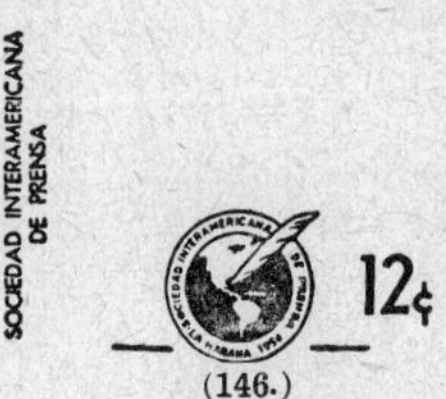

(**146.**) **147.**

1956. Air. 12th Inter-American Press Assn. Meeting. As No. 781 but colour changed and surch with T **146**.
794. – 12 c. on 2 p. grey .. 1·10 55

1956. Obligatory Tax. Anti-T.B.
795. **147.** 1 c. red 10 5
796. 1 c. green 10 5
797. 1 c. blue 10 5
798. 1 c. brown 10 5

148. **149.** Prof. Menocal.

1956. Christmas Greetings.
799. **148.** 2 c. red and green .. 1·90 1·10
800. 4 c. green and red .. 1·90 1·10

1956. Prof. R. G. Menocal. Birth Cent.
801. **140.** 4 c. brown 35 5

149a. Martin M. Delgado (patriot). **150.** Scouts around Camp Fire.

1957. Delgado. Birth Cent.
802. **149a.** 4 c. green 55 25

1957. Lord Baden-Powell. Birth Cent.
803. **150.** 4 c. green & red (post.) 55 25
804. – 12 c. slate (air) .. 1·00 45
DESIGN—VERT. 12 c. Lord Baden-Powell.

151. "The Art Critics" (Melero). **152.** Hanabanilla Falls.

1957. Postal Employees' Retirement Fund.
805. – 2 c. olive & brn. (post.) 20 10
806. **151.** 4 c. red and brown .. 20 10
807. – 10 c. olive and brown 45 20
808. – 14 c. blue and brown .. 75 20
809. **152.** 8 c. blue and red (air) 35 15
810. – 12 c. green and red .. 55 25
811. – 30 c. olive and violet .. 90 45
DESIGNS—HORIZ. As T **151** (Paintings): 2 c. "The Blind" (Vega). 10 c. "Carriage in the Storm" (Menocal). 14 c. "The Convalescent" (Romanach). As T **152**: 12 c. Sierra de Cubitas. 30 c. Puerto Boniato.

153. Posthorn Emblem of Cuban Philatelic Society. **154.** Juan F. Steegers.

1957. Stamp Day. Cuban Philatelic Exn.
812. **153.** 4 c. blue, brown and red (postage) .. 55 25
813. – 12 c. brown, yellow and green (air) .. 65 35
DESIGN: 12 c. Philatelic Society Building, Havana.

1957. Steegers (fingerprint pioneer). Birth Cent.
814. **154.** 4 c. blue (postage) .. 55 25
815. – 12 c. chocolate (air) .. 65 35
DESIGN: 12 c. Thumbprint.

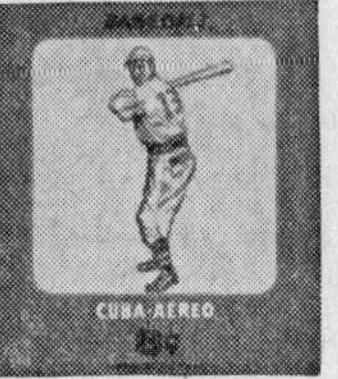

155. Baseball Player. **156.** Nurse V. B. Sanchez.

1957. Air. Youth Recreation. Centres in brown.
816. **155.** 8 c. green on green .. 40 20
817. – 12 c. lilac on lavender 65 35
818. – 24 c. blue on blue .. 1·00 55
819. – 30 c. flesh on orange 1·25 55
DESIGNS—12 c. Ballet dancer. 24 c. Diver. 30 c. Boxers.

1957. Nurse Victoria Bru Sanchez Commem.
820. **156.** 4 c. indigo 55 25

157. J. de Aguero leading Patriots. **158.** Youth with Dogs and Cat. **159.** Col. R. Manduley del Rio.

1957. Joaquin de Aguero (patriot) Commem.
821. **157.** 4 c. green (postage) .. 55 25
822. – 12 c. blue (air) (portrait) 65 35

1957. Young Helpers' League. 50th Anniv.
823. **158.** 4 c. green (postage) .. 65 20
824. – 12 c. brown (air) .. 65 35
DESIGN: 12 c. Jeanette Ryder (founder).

1957. Col. R. Manduley del Rio (patriot). Commem.
825. **159.** 4 c. green 55 25

160. J. M. Heredia y Girard. **161.** Palace of Justice, Havana.

1957. Air. J. M. Heredia y Girard (poet). Commem.
826. **160.** 8 c. violet 55 20

1957. Palace of Justice Inaug.
827. **161.** 4 c. grey (postage) .. 55 25
828. 12 c. green (air) .. 65 35

162. Army Leaders of 1856. **163.** J. R. Gregg.

1957. Cuban Army of Liberation. Cent.
829. **162.** 4 c. chestnut and green 25 10
830. 4 c. brown and blue .. 25 10
831. 4 c. brown and pink .. 25 10
832. 4 c. brown and yellow 25 10
833. 4 c. brown and lilac .. 25 10

1957. Air. J. R. Gregg (shorthand pioneer) Commem.
834. **163.** 12 c. green 65 35

164. Cuba's First Publication, 1723. **165.** "Jose Marti" Public Library.

1957. "Jose Marti" Public Library. Inscr. "BIBLIOTECA NACIONAL".
835. **164.** 4 c. slate (postage) .. 55 25
836. – 8 c. blue (air) .. 35 15
837. **165.** 12 c. sepia 55 35
DESIGN—VERT. As T **165**: 8 c. D. F. Caneda, first Director.

166. U.N. Emblem and Map of Cuba. **167.** Aeroplane and Map.

1957. Air. U.N. Day.
838. **166.** 8 c. brown and green .. 55 20
839. 12 c. green and red .. 90 35
840. 30 c. magenta and blue 1·60 65

1957. Air. Inaug. of Air Mail Service between Havana and Key West. Florida. 30th Anniv.
841. **167.** 12 c. blue & brown-pur. 65 35

168. **169.** Courtyard.

1957. Obligatory Tax. Anti-Tuberculosis.
842. **168.** 1 c. red 8 5
843. 1 c. emerald 8 5
844. 1 c. blue 8 5
845. 1 c. grey 8 5

1957. First Cuban Normal School Cent. Inscr. "CENTENARIO DE LA PRIMERA ESCUELA NORMAL DE CUBA".
846. **169.** 4 c. brn. & grn. (post.) 55 25
847. – 12 c. buff & indigo (air) 65 35
848. – 30 c. sepia and red .. 80 40
DESIGNS—VERT. 12 c. School facade. HORIZ. 30 c. General view of school.

170. Street Scene, Trinidad. **171.** Christmas Crib.

1957. Postal Employees' Retirement Fund. Inscr. "RETIRO DE COMUNICACIONES 1957".

849. **170.** 2 c. brn. & ind. (post.) 10 5
850. – 4 c. green and brown .. 20 5
851. – 10 c. sepia and red .. 25 10
852. – 14 c. green and red .. 40 15

853. – 8 c. black and red (air) 45 20
854. – 12 c. black and brown 65 25
855. – 30 c. chestnut and grey 80 45

DESIGNS—VERT. 4 c. Sentry-box on old wall of Havana. 10 c. Calle Padre Pico (street), Santiago de Cuba. 12 c. Sancti Spiritus Church. 14 c. Church and street scene, Camaguey. HORIZ. 8 c. "El Viso" Fort, El Caney. 30 c. Concordia Bridge, Matanzas.

1957. Christmas. Multicoloured centres.

856. **171.** 2 c. sepia .. .. 1·60 80
857. 4 c. black .. .. 1·60 80

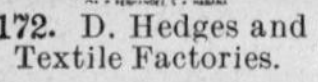

172. D. Hedges and Textile Factories. **173.** Dr. F. D. Roldan.

1958. Dayton Hedges (founder of Cuban Textile Industry) Commem.

858. **172.** 4 c. blue (postage) .. 55 25
859. 8 c. green (air) .. 45 20

1958. Dr. Francisco D. Roldan (physiotherapy pioneer) Commem.

861. **173.** 4 c. green 40 20

174. "Diario de la Marina".

1958. "Diario de la Marina" Newspaper. 125th Anniv.

862. – 4 c. olive (postage) .. 45 20
863. **174.** 29 c. black (air) .. 1·25 65

PORTRAIT—VERT. 4 c. J. I. Rivero y Alonso (Director 1919-44).

175. Map of Cuba showing Postal Routes of 1756. **178.** Gen. J. M. Gomez.

1958. Stamp Day and National Philatelic Exn. Havana. Inscr. as in T **175.**

864. **175.** 4 c. myrtle, buff and blue (postage) .. 45 20
865. – 29 c. indigo, buff and blue (air) .. .. 1·25 65

DESIGN: 29 c. Ocean map showing sea-postal routes of 1765.

1958. Gen. J. M. Gomez. Birth Cent. Inscr. "1858-CENTENARIO NACIMIENTO Gral. JOSE MIGUEL GOMEZ-1958".

866. **176.** 4 c. indigo (postage) .. 45 20
867. – 12 c. myrtle (air) .. 55 25

DESIGN: 12 c. Gen. Gomez in action at Arroyo Blanco.

177. Dr. T. R. Chacon. **178.** Dr. C. de la Torre.

179. "Polymita picta" (Snail).

1958. Famous Cubans. Portraits as T **177.**

(a) Doctors. With emblem of medicine.

868. 2 c. brown and green .. 20 10
869. 4 c. black and green .. 20 5
870. 10 c. red and green .. 20 10
871. 14 c. blue and green .. 35 12

(b) Lawyers. With emblem of law.

872. 2 c. sepia and red .. 20 5
873. 4 c. black and red .. 20 10
874. 10 c. green and red .. 35 12
875. 14 c. blue and red .. 20 12

(c) Composers. With lyre emblem of music.

876. 2 c. brown and indigo .. 20 5
877. 4 c. grey-pur and indigo .. 20 12
878. 10 c. green and indigo .. 25 12
879. 14 c. red and indigo .. 35 12

PORTRAITS—Doctors: 2 c. T **177.** 4 c. A. A. Aballi 10 c. F. G. del Valle. 14 c. V. A. de Castro. Lawyers: 2 c. J. M. G. Montes. 4 c. J. A. G. Lanuza. 10 c. J. B. H. Barreiro. 14 c. P. G. Llorente. Composers: 2 c. N. R. Espadero. 4 c. I. Cervantes. 10 c. J. White. 14 c. B de Salas.

1958. De la Torre (archaeologist). Birth Cent.

880. **178.** 4 c. blue (postage) .. 45 20

881. **179.** 8 c. red, yell. & blk. (air) 1·10 55
882. – 12 c. sepia on green .. 2·25 1·10
883. – 30 c. green on pink .. 2·75 1·40

DESIGNS—As T **179**: 12 c. "Megalocnus rodens". 30 c. "Ammonite".

180. Felipe Poey (naturalist). **181.** "Papilio caiguanabus" (butterfly).

1958. Poey Commem. Designs as T **180/1** inscr. "1799-FELIPE POEY-1891".

884. – 2 c. black and lavender (postage) 20 10
885. **180.** 4 c. sepia 45 20

886. **181.** 8 c. sepia, yellow, black and r.d (air) .. 50 20
887. – 12 c. orge. black & gr.. 1·00 25
888. – 14 c. yellow, black, orange and purple .. 1·25 25
889. – 19 c. yellow, sepia, black and blue .. 1·60 40
890. – 24 c. pink, yellow, slate and black .. 2·25 65
891. – 29 c. blue, brn. & black 3·25 1·50
892. – 30 c. brn., grn. & black 5·00 2·25

DESIGNS—VERT. 2 c. Cover of Poey's book. 12 c. "Teria gundlachia". 14 c. "Teria ebriola". 19 c. "Nathalis felicia" (all butterflies). HORIZ. 24 c. Jacome. 29 c. Anil. 30 c. Diana (all fishes).

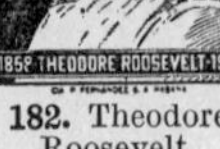

182. Theodore Roosevelt. **183.** National Tuberculosis Hospital.

1958. Roosevelt. Birth Cent. No. 894 inscr. "LOS ROUGH RIDERS", etc.

893. **182.** 4 c. grey-grn. (postage) 45 20

894. – 12 c. sepia (air) .. 45 20

DESIGN—HORIZ. 12 c. Roosevelt leading Rough Riders at San Juan, 1898.

1958. Obligatory Tax. Anti-T.B.

895. **183.** 1 c. brown 8 5
896. 1 c. green 8 5
897. 1 c. red 8 5
898. 1 c. grey 8 5

184. U.N.E.S.C.O. Headquarters, Paris. **185.** "Cattleyopsis lindenii" (orchid).

1958. Air. U.N.E.S.C.O. Headquarters. Inaug.

899. **184.** 12 c. green 65 45
900. – 30 c. blue .. .. 1·25 65

DESIGN: 30 c. Facade composed of letters "UNESCO" and map of Cuba.

1958. Christmas. Orchids.

901. **185.** 2 c. yellow, purple, green and black .. .. 1·60 70
902. – 4 c. yellow, red, blue and black .. .. 1·60 70

DESIGN: 4 c. "Oncidium guibertianum".

186. "The Revolutionary". **187.** Gen. A. F. Crombet.

1959. Liberation Day.

903. **186.** 2 c. black and red .. 15 10

1959. Gen. Crombet Commem.

904. **187.** 4 c. myrtle 40 25

188. Posta Notice of 1765. **189.** Hand Supporting Sugar Factory.

1959. Air. Stamp Day and National Philatelic Exn., Havana.

905. **188** 12 c. sepia and blue .. 65 35
906. – 30 c. blue and sepia .. 1·10 55

DESIGN: 30 c. Administrative postal book of St. Cristobal, Havana, 1765.

1959. Agricultural Reform.

907. **189.** 2 c.+1 c. blue and red (postage) 25 10

908. – 12 c.+3 c. green & red (air) 25 15

DESIGN (42 × 30 mm.): 12 c. Farm workers and factory plant.

190. Red Cross Nurse.

1959. "For Charity".

909. **190.** 2 c.+1 c. red .. 20 10

191. Pres. C. M. de Cespedes. **192.** Teresa G. Montes (founder).

1959. Cuban Presidents.

910. 2 c. slate (T **191** .. 20 8
911. 2 c. green (Betancourt) .. 20 8
912. 2 c. violet (Calvar) .. 20 8
913. 2 c. chestnut (Maso) .. 20 8
914. 4 c. red (Spotorno) .. 35 15
915. 4 c. chocolate (Palma) .. 35 15
916. 4 c. blk. (F. J. de Cespedes) 35 15
917. 4 c. violet (Garcia) .. 35 15

1959. Air. American Society of Travel Agents Convention, Havana. No. 780 (colour changed) surch. **CONVENCION ASTA OCTUBRE 17 1959 12 c.** and bar.

918. 12 c. on 1 p. emerald .. 65 35

1959. Musical Arts Society Festival, Havana.

919. **192.** 4 c. brown (postage) .. 35 15

920. – 12 c. green (air) .. 55 35

DESIGN—HORIZ. 12 c. Society Headquarters, Havana.

193. Rebel Attack at Moncada Barracks. **194.** T. Estrada Palma Monument, Havana.

1960. Cuban Revolution. 1st Anniv.

921. **193.** 1 c. green, red and blue (postage) .. 12 5
922. – 2 c. green, sepia & blue 12 5
923. – 10 c. green, red & blue 55 25
924. – 12 c. green, mar. & blue 55 30

925. – 8 c. green, red and blue (air) 35 20
926. – 12 c. grn., mar. & brn. 70 35
927. – 29 c. red, blk. & grn. 1·10 55

DESIGNS: 2 c. Rebels disembarking from "Granma". 8 c. Battle of Santa Clara. 10 c. Battle of the Uvero. 12 c. postage, "The Invasion" (Rebel and map of Cuba). 12 c. air, Rebel Army entering Havana. 29 c. Passing on propaganda ("Clandestine activities in the towns").

1960. Surch. **HABILITADO PARA** and value (No. 932 without **PARA**).

928. **189.** 2 c. on 2 c.+1 c. blue and red (postage) 35 10
929. – 2 c. on 4 c. mauve (No. 689) 25 12
930. – 2 c. on 5 c. blue (No.690) 25 12
931. – 2 c. on 13 c. red (No.693) 25 12
932. – 10 c. on 20 c. ol (No.695) 45 12

933. – 12 c. on 12 c.+3 c. grn. & red (No.908) (air) 65 35

1960. Surch in figures.

934. – 1 c. on 4 c. (No. 869) (postage) 12 10
935. – 1 c. on 4 c. (No. 873) .. 12 10
936. – 1 c. on 4 c. (No. 877) .. 12 10
937. **178.** 1 c. on 4 c. blue .. 12 10
938. – 1 c. on 4 c. (No. 902) .. 12 10
939. **187.** 1 c. on 4 c. myrtle .. 12 10
940. **192.** 1 c. on 4 c. brown .. 12 10
941. – 2 c. on 14 c. (No. 694) 35 10

942. **19.** 12 c. on 40 c. orge. (air) 65 35
943. – 12 c. on 45 c. (No. 706) 65 35

1960. Postal Employees' Retirement Fund.

944. **194.** 1 c. brn. & blue (post.) 10 5
945. – 2 c. green and red .. 10 5
946. – 10 c. brown and red .. 35 15
947. – 12 c. bronze-grn. & vio. 45 20

948. – 8 c. grey and red (air) 35 15
949. – 12 c. blue and red .. 35 15
950. 30 c. violet and claret 1·00 45

MONUMENTS—VERT. 2 c. "Mambi Victorisoo.", 8 c. Marti. 10 c. Marta Abreu. 12 c. postage. Agramonte. 12 c. air, Heroes of Cacarajicara. HORIZ. 30 c. Dr. C. de la Torriente.

(**195.**)

197. C. Cienfuegos and View of Escolar. **196.** Pistol-shooting.

1960. Air. Stamp Day and National Philatelic Exn., Havana. Nos. 772/3 in new colours optd. with T **195.**

951. 8 c. yellow 45 20
952. 12 c. red 55 25

1960. Olympic Games.

954. – 1 c. violet (Sailing) (postage) 20 10
955. **196.** 2 c. orange 35 15

956. – 8 c. blue (Boxing) (air) 45 20
957. – 12 c. red (Running) .. 55 35

1960. Cienfuegos (revolutionary leader). 1st Death Anniv. Centre multicoloured.

959. **197.** 2 c. sepia 10 5

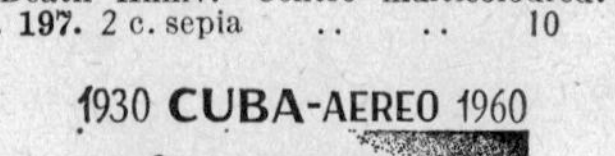

198. Air Stamp of 1930, 'Plane and "Sputnik".

1960. Air. National Airmail Service. 30th Anniv. Centre multicoloured.

960. **198.** 8 c. violet .. .. 1·10 65

199. Aguinaldo.

199a. Tobacco.

1960. Christmas. Inscr. "NAVIDAD 1960–61".

(a) T **199.**

961. 1 c. multicoloured .. 25 25
962. 2 c. multicoloured . 25 25
963. 10 c. multicoloured .. 55 55

(b) As T **199a.**

964. 1 c. multicoloured .. 25 25
965. 2 c. multicoloured .. 1·10 1·10
966. 10 c. multicoloured .. 2·75 2·25

Nos. 961 and 964, 962 and 965, 963 and 966 were printed together in three sheets of 25, each comprising nine stamps of T **199** forming a centre cross and four blocks of four different stamps as T **199a** in each corner. The four-stamp design incorporates various floral subjects with an oval border of music (the "Christmas Hymn").

Designs — HORIZ. 2 c. Graph and symbols. 6 c. Cogwheels. 12 c. Workers holding lever. 30 c. Maps. VERT. 8 c. Hand holding machets. 50 c. Upraised hand.

200.

1960. Sub-Industrialized Countries Conf.

967. **200.** 1 c. black yellow and red (postage) .. 10 5
968. – 2 c. red grey, black and blue 10 5
969. – 6 c. red black & cream 45 20
970. – 8 c. black, green, yellow, red and brown (air) 20 10
971. – 12 c. turquoise, buff, black and blue .. 35 12
972. – 30 c. red and grey .. 65 40
973. – 50 c. red, pale blue, blue and black .. 1·00 55

201. J. Menendez. **202.** "Declaration of Havana".

1961. Jesus Menendez Commem.

974. **201.** 2 c. sepia and green .. 20 10

1961. Air. Declaration of Havana.

975. **202.** 8 c. red, black & yellow 35 35
976. 12 c. violet, blk. & buff 65 65
977. 30 c. brown, blk. & blue 1·25 1·25

The above were issued with part of background text of the declaration in English, French and Spanish. Prices the same for each language.

203. U.N. Emblem within Dove of Peace.

1961. U.N.O. 15th Anniv.

979. **203.** 2 c. brn. & apple (post.) 20 10
980. 10 c. green and purple 20 20
982. 8 c. red & yellow (air) 20 10
983. 12 c. blue and orange .. 55 25

204. Cuban 10 c. Revolutionary Label of 1874 and "CUBA MAMBISA" "Postmark".

1961. Stamp Day. Inscr. "24 DE ABRIL DIA DEL SELLO".

985. **204.** 1 c. red, green & black 10 5
986. – 2 c. orge., slate & black 10 8
987. – 10 c. turq., red & black 35 12

Designs: 2 c. Cuban 50 c. stamp of 1907 and "CUBA REPUBLICANA" "postmark". 10 c. Cuban 2 c. stamp of 1959 and "CUBA REVOLUCIONARIA" "postmark".

1961. May Day. Optd. **PRIMERO DE MAYO 1961 ESTAMOS VENCIENDO** in red.

988. **201.** 2 c sepia and green .. 20 10

205.

1961. "For Peace and Socialism".

989. **205.** 2 c. red., blk., yell. & grey 20 10

No. 989 is lightly printed on back with pattern of wavy lines and multiple inscr. "CORREOS CUBA" in buff.

1961. 1st Official Philatelic Exn. No. 987 optd. **primera exposicion filatelica oficial oct. 7-17, 1961.**

990. 10 c. turq., red and black 35 15

1961. Air. Surch. **HABILITADO PARA 8 cts.**

992. **112.** 8 c. on 15 c. red .. 40 20
993. **19.** 8 c. on 20 c. brown .. 40 20

The 2, 10 and 12 c. show the letters "U", "B" and "A" on the book forming the word "CUBA".

206. Book and Lamp.

1961. Education Year.

995. **206.** 1 c. red, black & green 5 5
996. 2 c. red, black & blue 12 5
997. 10 c. red, black & violet 25 10
998. 12 c. red., black & orge. 30 15

207. "Polymita S. Flammulata T." (snail).

207a. "Polymita P. Fulminata T" (snail).

1961. Christmas. Inscr. "NAVIDAD 1961–62". Multicoloured.

(a) Various designs as T **207.**

999. 1 c. Type **207** 15 8
1000. 2 c. Bird (vert.) 20 10
1001. 10 c. Butterfly (horiz.) .. 60 20

(b) Various designs as T **207a.**

1002. 1 c. Snails (horiz.) .. 15 8
1003. 2 c. Birds (vert.) .. 20 10
1004. 10 c. Butterflies (horiz.) .. 60 20

Nos. 999 and 1002, 1000 and 1003, 1001 and 1004 were printed together in three sheets of 25, each comprising four stamps as T **207** plus five se-tenant stamp-size labels showing pealing bells, and a star forming a centre cross and four blocks of four different stamps as T **207a** in each corner. The four-stamp design incorporates different subjects, which together form a composite picture.

208. Castro Emblem.

209. Hand with Machete.

1962. Cuban Revolution. 3rd Anniv. Emblem in yellow, red, grey and blue. Colours of background and inscriptions given.

1005. **208.** 1 c. green & pink (post.) 20 10
1006. 2 c. black and orange 35 15
1007. 8 c. brn. & blue (air) 25 10
1008. 12 c. ochre and green 55 20
1009. 30 c. violet and yellow 1·10 55

1962. Air. Socialist Republic's First Sugar Harvest. 1st Anniv.

1010. **209.** 8 c. sepia and red .. 35 10
1011. 12 c. black and lilac .. 45 20

210. Armed Peasant and Tractor.

1962. National Militia.

1012. **210.** 1 c. black and green .. 10 5
1013. – 2 c. black and blue .. 20 8
1014. – 10 c. black and orange 25 15

Designs: 2 c. Armed worker and welder. 10 c. Armed woman and sewing-machinist.

211. Globe and Music Emblem.

1962. Air. Int. Radio Service. Inscr. and aerial yellow; musical notation black; lines on globe brown, background colours given.

1015. **211.** 8 c. grey 20 10
1016. 12 c. blue 35 15
1017. 30 c. green 55 40
1018. 1 p. lilac .. .. 1·25 1·00

212. Soldiers, Aircraft and Burning Ship.

1962. "Playa Giron" (Sea Invasion Attempt of Cuban Exiles). 1st Anniv.

1019. **212.** 2 c. multicoloured .. 10 5
1020. 3 c. multicoloured .. 15 8
1021. 10 c. multicoloured .. 25 15

213. Arrival of First Mail from the Indies.

1962. Stamp Day.

1022. **213.** 10 c. black & red on cream 35 20

214. Clenched Fist Salute.

ILLUSTRATIONS
British Commonwealth and all overprints and surcharges are FULL SIZE. Foreign Countries have been reduced to ¾-LINEAR

1962. Labour Day.

1023. **214.** 2 c. black on buff .. 10 5
1024. 3 c. black on red .. 20 10
1025. 10 c. black on blue .. 25 10

215. Wrestling.

1962. National Sports Institute (I.N.D.E.R.) Commem. As T **215.** On cream paper.

1026. 1 c. brown and red .. 5 5
1027. 2 c. lake and green .. 5 5
1028. 3 c. blue and lake .. 5 5
1029. 9 c. maroon and blue .. 12 8
1030. 10 c. orange and purple 12 10
1031. 13 c. black and red .. 20 10

The above were each printed in five different sports designs repeated five times in the sheet.

216. A. Santamaria and Soldiers.

217. Dove and Festival Emblem.

1962. "Rebel Day". 9th Anniv.

1032. **216.** 2 c. lake and blue .. 10 8
1033. – 3 c. blue and lake .. 20 10

Design: 3 c. Santamaria and children.

1962. World Youth Festival, Helsinki.

1034. **217.** 2 c. multicoloured .. 20 10
1035. – 3 c. multicoloured .. 25 12

Design: 3 c. As T **217** but with "clasped hands" instead of dove.

218. Czech 5 k. "Praga 1962" stamp of 1961.

1962. Air. Int. Stamp Exn., Prague.

1037. **218.** 31 c. multicoloured .. 1·10 55

Designs: Rings and: 2 c. Tennis rackets. 3 c. Baseball bats. 13 c. Rapiers and mask.

219. Rings and Boxing Gloves.

1962. 9th Central American and Caribbean Games, Jamaica.

1039. **219.** 1 c. ochre and red .. 5 5
1040. – 2 c. ochre and blue .. 10 5
1041. – 3 c. ochre and purple 10 5
1042. – 13 c. ochre and green 55 20

Design — vert. 13 c. Mother and child, and Globe.

220. "Cuban Women".

1962. 1st Cuban Women's Federation National Congress.

1043. **220.** 9 c. red, green & black 35 10
1044. – 13 c. black, blue & grn. 45 20

221. Running.

1962. 1st Latin-American University Games. Multicoloured.

1045. 1 c. Type **221** 8 5
1046. 2 c. Baseball 10 5
1047. 3 c. Netball 12 8
1048. 13 c. Globe 45 20

222. Microscope and Parasites.

1962. Malaria Eradication. Mult.

1049. 1 c. Type **222** 10 5
1050. 2 c. Mosquito and pool .. 10 5
1051. 3 c. Cinchona plant and formulae 20 10

223. " Epicrates angulifer B." (snake).

223a. " Cricolepis typica " (lizard).

1962. Christmas. Inscr. " NAVIDAD 1962–63 ". Multicoloured.

(a) Various designs as **T 223.**

1052. 2 c. Type **223** 10 5
1053. 3 c. Beetle (vert.) .. 15 5
1054. 10 c. Bat (horiz.) .. 80 45

(b) Various designs as **T 223a.**

1055. 2 c. Reptiles (horiz.) .. 10 5
1056. 3 c. Insects (vert.) .. 15 5
1057. 10 c. Mammals (horiz.) .. 80 45

Nos. 1052 and 1055, 1053 and 1056, 1054 and 1057 were printed together in three sheets of 25, each comprising four stamps as **T 223** plus five se-tenant stamp-size labels showing pealing bells, and a star forming a centre cross and four blocks of four different stamps as **T 223a** in each corner. The four-stamp design incorporates different subjects, which together form a composite picture.

224. " Vostok-2 " and Titov.

1963. Cosmic Flights (1st issue).

1058. – 1 c. blue, lake & yellow 5 5
1059. **224.** 2 c. grn., mar. & yellow 20 10
1060. – 3 c. violet, red & yellow 20 10

DESIGNS: 1 c. " Vostok-1 " and Gagarin. 3 c. " Vostoks-3 and 4 " and Nicolaev and Popovich.

See also Nos. 1133/4.

DESIGNS: 13 c. Rodriguez. C. Servia, Machado and Westbrook. 30 c. J. Echeverria and M. Mora.

225. Attackers.

1963. Attack on Presidential Palace. 6th Anniv.

1061. **225.** 9 c. black and red .. 20 10
1062. – 13 c. maroon and blue 45 20
1063. – 30 c. green & orge.-red 65 45

226. Baseball.

1963. 4th Pan-American Games, Sao Paulo.

1064. **226.** 1 c. green 20 10
1065. – 13 c. red (Boxing) .. 65 20

227. " Mask " Letter Box.

1963. Stamp Day.

1066. **227.** 3 c. black & chestnut 20 10
1067. – 10 c. black and violet 45 20

DESIGN: 10 c. 19th-century Post Office, Cathedral Square, Havana.

228. Revolutionaries and Statue. **229.** Child.

1963. Labour Day. Multicoloured.

1068. 3 c. **T 228.** 20 10
1069. 13 c. Celebrating Labour Day 45 20

1963. Children's Week.

1070. **229.** 3 c. brown and blue.. 10 5
1071. 30 c. red and blue .. 55 20

230. Ritual Effigy. **231.** " Breaking chains of old regime ".

1963. Montane Anthropological Museum. 60th Anniv.

1072. **230.** 2 c. chocolate & salmon 20 10
1073. – 3 c. maroon and blue 25 15
1074. – 9 c. grey and claret.. 35 15

DESIGNS—HORIZ. 3 c. Carved chair. VERT. 9 c. Statuette.

1963. " Rebel Day ". 10th Anniv.

1075. **231.** 1 c. black and pink .. 8 5
1076. – 2 c. maroon & pale blue 8 5
1077. – 3 c. sepia and lilac .. 12 5
1078. – 7 c. purple and emerald 12 5
1079. – 9 c. purple and yellow 15 8
1080. – 10 c. green and ochre.. 25 15
1081. – 13 c. blue and buff .. 50 20

DESIGNS: 2 c. Palace attack. 3 c. " The Insurrection ". 7 c. " Strike of April 9th " (defence of radio station). 9 c. " Triumph of the Revolution " (upraised flag and weapons). 10 c. " Agrarian Reform and Nationalization " (artisan and peasant). 13 c. " Victory of Giron " (soldiers in battle).

232. Caimito (plum). **233.** " Roof and Window ".

1963. Cuban Fruits. Multicoloured.

1082. 1 c. **T 232** 8 5
1083. 2 c. Chiromoya 10 5
1084. 3 c. Cashew nut.. .. 10 5
1085. 10 c. Custard apple .. 25 20
1086. 13 c. Mango 50 30

1963. 7th Int. Architects Union Congress, Havana.

1087. 3 c. red, carmine, deep blue and bistre 10 5
1088. 3 c. orange, black, purple, violet, red and green .. 10 5
1089. 3 c. black, blue and bistre 10 5
1090. 3 c. bistre, purple, blue and black 10 5
1091. 13 c. blue, purple, orange, grey, black and bistre.. 45 20
1092. 13 c. black, blue, purple, and red 45 20
1093. 13 c. red, olive and black.. 45 20
1094. 13 c. black, blue, purple, red and orange.. .. 45 20

DESIGNS—VERT. No. 1087, T **233.** Nos. 1090, 1091 and 1092, Symbols of building construction as T **233.** HORIZ. Nos. 1089/90 and 1093, Sketches of urban buildings. No. 1094, as T **233** (girders and outline of house).

234. Hemingway and Scene from " The Old Man and the Sea ".

1963. Ernest Hemingway Commemoration.

1095. **234.** 3 c. brown and blue .. 10 5
1096. – 9 c. blue-green & mauve 20 10
1097. – 13 c. blk. & yellow-grn. 45 20

DESIGNS—Hemingway and: 9 c. Scene from " For Whom the Bell Tolls ". 13 c. Residence at San Francisco de Paula, near Havana.

DESIGNS—VERT. (32 × 42½ mm.): 3 c. "The Rape of the Mulattos" (after C. Enriquez). 9 c. Greek amphora. 13 c. "Dilecta Mea" (bust, after J. A. Houdon).

235. " Zapateo " (dance) after V. P. de Landaluze.

1964. National Museum. 50th Anniv.

1098. **235.** 2 c. multicoloured .. 10 5
1099. – 3 c. multicoloured .. 15 8
1100. – 9 c. orange, brown, buff and black 25 10
1101. – 13 c. black and violet.. 45 20

236. B. J. Borrell (revolutionary). **237.** Fish in Net.

1964. Revolution. 5th Anniv.

1102. **236.** 2 c. black, orge. & grn. 10 5
1103. – 3 c. black, orge. & red 15 8
1104. – 10 c. black, orge. & pur. 25 12
1105. – 13 c. black, orge. & bl. 45 20

PORTRAITS: 3 c. M. Salado 10 c. O. Lucero. 13 c. S. Gonzalez (revolutionaries).

1964. Giron Victory. 3rd Anniv.

1106. **237.** 3 c. orange, brown, black & turquoise .. 10 5
1107. – 10 c. black, grey & bis. 25 15
1108. – 13 c. slate, black & orge. 40 20

DESIGNS—HORIZ. 10 c. Victory Monument. VERT. 13 c. Fallen eagle.

238. V. M. Pera (1st Director of Military Posts. 1868-71).

1964. Stamp Day.

1109. **238.** 3 c. grey-blue & brown 12 8
1110. – 13 c. green and lilac .. 45 20

DESIGN: 13 c. Cuba's first (10 c.) military stamp.

239. Symbolic "1". **240.** Chinese Monument, Havana.

1964. Labour Day.

1111. **239.** 3 c. multicoloured .. 12 8
1112. – 13 c. multicoloured .. 45 20

DESIGN: 13 c. As T **239** but different symbols within " 1 ".

1964. Cuban-Chinese Friendship.

1113. **240.** 1 c. grey, blk., grn. & red 8 5
1114. – 2 c. red, olive & black 10 5
1115. – 3 c. multicoloured .. 12 8

DESIGNS—HORIZ. 2 c. Cuban and Chinese. VERT. 3 c. Flags of Cuba and China.

DESIGNS: 30 c. H. von Stephan (founder of U.P.U.). 50 c. U.P.U. Monument, Berne.

241. Globe.

1964. U.P.U. Congress, Vienna.

1116. **241.** 13 c. brn., grn. & red 35 10
1117. – 30 c. black, bistre & red 65 35
1118. – 30 c. black, blue & red 1·25 55

242. Fish.

1964. Popular Savings Movement. Multicoloured.

1119. 1 c. Type **242** 10 5
1120. 2 c. Cow 12 5
1121. 13 c. Poultry 40 20

243. " Rio Jibacoa ".

1964. Cuban Merchant Fleet. Multicoloured.

1122. 1 c. Type **243** 8 5
1123. 2 c. " Camilo Cienfuegos " 10 5
1124. 3 c. " Sierra Maestra " .. 12 8
1125. 9 c. " Bahia de Siguanea " 20 10
1126. 10 c. " Oriente " 45 20

244. Viet-Namese Fighter. **245.** Raul Gomez Garcia and Poem.

1964. " Unification of Vietnam " Campaign. Multicoloured.

1127. 2 c. Type **244** 10 5
1128. 3 c. Viet-Namese shaking hands across map .. 12 8
1129. 10 c. Hand and mechanical ploughing 25 12
1130. 13 c. Viet-Namese, Cuban and flags 50 20

1964. " Rebel Day ". 11th Anniv.

1131. **245.** 3 c. black, red & ochre 10 5
1132. – 13 c. ochre, red, black and blue 45 20

DESIGN: 13 c. Inscr. " LA HISTORIA ME ABSOLVERA " (Castro's book).

1964. Cosmic Flights (2nd issue). As T **224.**

1133. 9 c. yellow, violet and red 20 10
1134. 13 c. yellow, claret & green 40 15

DESIGNS: 9 c. " Vostok-5 " and Bykovksy. 13 c. " Vostok-6 " and Tereshkova.

246. Start of Races.

1964. Olympic Games, Tokyo.

1135. – 1 c. yellow, blue & pur. 10 5
1136. – 2 c. multicoloured .. 10 5
1137. – 3 c. brown, blk. & red 15 5
1138. **246.** 7 c. violet, blue & orge. 20 10
1139. – 10 c. yellow, pur. & bl. 45 20
1140. – 13 c. multicoloured.. 50 25

DESIGNS—VERT. 1 c. Gymnastics. 2 c. Rowing. 3 c. Boxing. HORIZ. 10 c. Fencing. 13 c. Games symbols.

247. Satellite and Globe.

247a. Rocket and part of Globe.

1964. Cuban Postal Rocket Experiment. 25th Anniv. Various rockets and satellites.

(a) Horiz. designs as T **247**.

1141. **247.** 1 c. multicoloured .. 10 5
1142. – 2 c. multicoloured .. 20 10
1143. – 3 c. multicoloured .. 35 15
1144. – 9 c. multicoloured .. 90 20
1145. – 13 c. multicoloured .. 1·10 55

(b) Horiz. designs as T **247a**.

1146. – 1 c. multicoloured .. 10 5
1147. – 2 c. multicoloured .. 20 10
1148. – 3 c. multicoloured .. 35 15
1149. – 9 c. multicoloured .. 90 20
1150. – 13 c. multicoloured .. 1·10 55

(c) Larger 44 × 28 mm.

1151. – 50 c. green and black 50 30

Nos. 1141 and 1146, 1142 and 1147, 1143 and 1148, 1144 and 1149, 1145 and 1150 were printed together in five sheets of 25, each comprising four stamps as T **247** plus five se-tenant stamp-size labels inscribed overall "1939-COHETE POSTAL CUBANO–1964" forming a centre cross and four blocks of four different stamps as T **247a** in each corner. The four-stamp design incorporates different subjects, which together form a composite design around globe. DESIGN: 50 c. Cuban Rocket Post. 10 c. stamp of 1939.

1964. 1st Three-Manned Space Flight. As No. 1151 but colours changed. Optd. **VOSJOD-1 octubre 12 1964 PRIMERA TRIPULACION DEL ESPACIO** and large rocket.

1153. 50 c. green and brown .. 1·10 55

248. Lenin addressing Meeting. **249.** Leopard.

1964. Lenin's Death. 40th Anniv.

1154. **248.** 3 c. black and orange .. 10 5
1155. – 13 c. rose and violet .. 20 15
1156. – 30 c. black and blue .. 45 20

DESIGNS—HORIZ. 13 c. Lenin mausoleum. VERT. 30 c. Lenin and hammer and sickle emblem.

1964. Havana Zoo Animals. Multicoloured.

1157. 1 c. Type **249** 5 5
1158. 2 c. Elephant (vert.) .. 5 5
1159. 3 c. Fallow deer (vert.) .. 8 5
1160. 4 c. Kangaroo 8 5
1161. 5 c. Lions 8 5
1162. 6 c. Eland 10 5
1163. 7 c. Zebra 10 5
1164. 8 c. Hyena 15 5
1165. 9 c. Tiger 15 5
1166. 10 c. Guanaco 20 5
1167. 13 c. Chimpanzees .. 20 8
1168. 20 c. Peccary 20 10
1169. 30 c. Raccoon (vert.) .. 45 25
1170. 40 c. Hippopotamus .. 75 40
1171. 50 c. Tapir 90 50
1172. 60 c. Dromedary (vert.) 1·00 60
1173. 70 c. Bison .. .. 1·10 55
1174. 80 c. Bear (vert.) .. 1·25 75
1175. 90 c. Water buffalo .. 1·40 90
1176. 1 p. Deer at Zoo Entrance 1·60 90

250. Jose Marti.

1964. "Liberators of Independence". Multicoloured. Each showing portraits and campaigning scenes.

1177. 1 c. Type **250** 10 5
1178. 2 c. A. Maceo 12 8
1179. 3 c. M. Gomez 15 10
1180. 13 c. C. Garcia 40 20

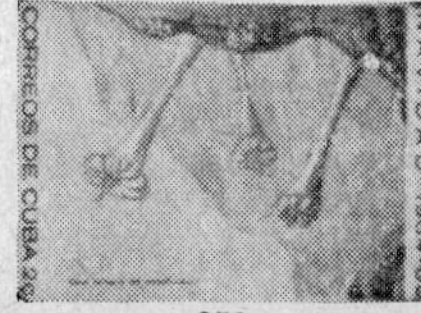

251.

251a.

1964. Christmas. Inscr. "NAVIDAD 1964–65". Horiz. designs showing marine life.

(a) As T **251**.

1181. **251.** 2 c. multicoloured .. 15 5
1182. – 3 c. multicoloured .. 25 8
1183. – 10 c. multicoloured .. 45 30

(b) As T **251a**.

1184. – 2 c. multicoloured .. 15 5
1185. – 3 c. multicoloured .. 25 8
1186. – 10 c. multicoloured .. 45 30

Nos. 1181 and 1184, 1182 and 1185, 1183 and 1186 were printed together in three sheets of 25, each comprising four stamps as T **251** plus five se-tenant stamp-size labels showing pealing bells, and a star forming a centre cross and four blocks of four different stamps as T **251a** in each corner. The four-stamp design incorporates different subjects, which together form a composite marine picture.

252. Dr. Tomas Romay. **253.** Map of Latin America and Part of Declaration.

1964. Dr. Tomas Romay (scientist). Birth Bicent. Inscr. "TOMAS ROMAY".

1187. **252.** 1 c. black and bistre .. 10 5
1188. – 2 c. sepia and brown .. 10 5
1189. – 3 c. brown and bistre .. 10 5
1190. – 10 c. black and bistre .. 35 20

DESIGNS—VERT. 2 c. First vaccination against smallpox. HORIZ. 3 c. Dr. Romay and extract from his treatise on the vaccine. 10 c. Dr. Romay's statue.

1964. 2nd Declaration of Havana. Multicoloured.

1191. 3 c. Type **253** 35 20
1192. 13 c. Map of Cuba and native receiving revolutionary message .. 1·10 65

The two stamps have the declaration superimposed in tiny print across each horiz. row of five stamps, thus requiring strips of five to show the complete declaration.

254. "Maritime Post" (diorama).

1965. Cuban Postal Museum. Inaug. Multicoloured.

1193. 13 c. Type **254** 45 20
1194. 30 c. "Insurgent Post" (diorama) 75 35

255. Lydia Doce.

1965. Int. Women's Day. Multicoloured.

1202. 3 c. Type **255** 10 5
1203. 13 c. Clara Zetkin .. 55 20

256. Schooner.

1965. Cuban Fishing Fleet. Multicoloured. Fishing crafts.

1196. 1 c. Type **256** 5 5
1197. 2 c. "Omicron" 8 5
1198. 3 c. "Victoria" 10 8
1199. 9 c. "Cardenas" 15 10
1200. 10 c. "Sigma" 20 15
1201. 13 c. "Lambda" 45 20

257. Jose Antonio Echeverria University City.

1965. "Technical Revolution". Inscr. "REVOLUCION TECNICA".

1204. **257.** 3 c. blk., brn. & chest. 10 5
1205. – 13 c. black, yellow, violet and blue .. 55 20

DESIGN: 13 c. Scientific symbols.

258. Leonov.

1965. "Voskhod 2", Space flight.

1206. **258.** 30 c. brown and blue 55 35
1207. – 50 c. blue and magenta 1·10 55

DESIGN: 50 c. Beliaiev, Leonov and "Voskhod 2".

259. "Figure" (after E. Rodrigues). **260.** Lincoln Statue, Washington.

1965. National Museum Treasures. Multicoloured.

1208. 2 c. Type **259** (27 × 42 mm) 10 5
1209. 3 c. "Landscape with sunflowers" (V. Manuel) (31 × 42 mm.) .. 15 10
1210. 10 c. "Abstract" (W. Lam) (42 × 31 mm.) 45 20
1211. 13 c. "Children" (E. Ponce) (39 × 33½ mm.) .. 45 20

1965. Abraham Lincoln. Death Cent.

1212. – 1 c. brown, grey & yell. 5 5
1213. – 2 c. ultramarine & blue 10 5
1214. **260.** 3 c. black, red and blue 20 10
1215. – 13 c. black, orge. & blue 45 20

DESIGNS—HORIZ. 1 c. Cabin at Hodgenville, Kentucky (Lincoln's birthplace). 2 c. Lincoln Monument, Washington. VERT. 13 c. Abraham Lincoln.

261. Sailing Packet and Old Postmarks (Maritime Mail bicent).

1965. Stamp Day.

1216. **261.** 3 c. bistre and red .. 10 5
1217. – 13 c. red, black & blue 45 20

DESIGN: 13 c. Cuban. 10 c. "Air Train" stamp of 1935 and glider train over Capitol, Havana.

262. Sun and Earth's Magnetic Pole.

1965. Int. Quiet Sun Year. Multicoloured.

1218. 1 c. Type **262** 5 5
1219. 2 c. I.Q.S.Y. emblem (vert.) 10 5
1220. 3 c. Earth's magnetic fields 15 5
1221. 6 c. Solar rays 20 8
1222. 30 c. Effect of solar rays on various atmospheric layers 55 25
1223. 50 c. Effect of solar rays on satellite orbits .. 80 45

Nos. 1221/3 are larger, 47 × 20 mm. or 20 × 47 mm. (30 c.).

263. Telecommunications Station.

1965. I.T.U. Cent. Multicoloured.

1225. 1 c. Type **263** 5 5
1226. 2 c. Satellite (vert.) .. 8 5
1227. 3 c. "Telstar" 15 5
1228. 10 c. "Telstar" and receiving station (vert.) .. 25 8
1229. 30 c. I.T.U. emblem .. 55 35

264. Festival Emblem and Flags.

1965. World Youth and Students Festival. Multicoloured.

1230. 13 c. Type **264** 45 20
1231. 30 c. Soldiers of three races and flags 65 35

265. M. Perez (pioneer balloonist), Balloon and Satellite.

1965. Matias Perez Commem.

1232. **265.** 3 c. black and rose .. 20 10
1233. – 13 c. black and blue 45 25

DESIGN: 13 c. As T **265**, but with rocket in place of satellite.

266. Rose (Europe).

1965. Flowers of the World. Multicoloured.

1234. 1 c. Type **266** 5 5
1235. 2 c. Chrysanthemum (Asia) 5 5
1236. 3 c. Strelitzia (Africa) .. 10 5
1237. 4 c. Dahlia (N. America) .. 12 5
1238. 5 c. Orchid (S. America) .. 20 8
1239. 13 c. "Grevillea banksii" (Oceania) 55 35
1240. 30 c. "Brunfelsia nitida" (Cuba) 80 55

267. Swimming.

1965. First National Games.

1241. **267.** 1 c. orge., bl., blk. & grey 5 5
1242. – 2 c. black, red, orange and grey .. 8 5
1243. – 3 c. black, red & grey 12 5
1244. – 30 c. black, red & grey 45 25

SPORTS: 2 c. Basketball. 3 c. Gymnastics. 30 c. Hurdling.

268. Anti-tank gun.

1965. Museum of the Revolution. Multicoloured.

1245. 1 c. Type **268** 5 5
1246. 2 c. Tank 5 5
1247. 3 c. Bazooka 12 5
1248. 10 c. Rebel Uniform .. 20 12
1249. 13 c. Launch "Granma" and compass .. 45 20

269. C. J. Finlay (malaria researcher). **270.** "Anetia numidia" (butterfly).

1965. Carlos J. Finlay. 50th Death Anniv.

1250. – 1 c. blk., grn. & blue 5 5
1251. – 2 c. brown, ochre & blk. 10 5
1252. **269.** 3 c. chestnut and black 12 5
1253. – 7 c. black and lilac .. 20 8
1254. – 9 c. bronze and black 20 10
1255. – 10 c. black and blue .. 25 12
1256. – 13 c. multicoloured .. 45 25

DESIGNS—HORIZ. 1 c. Finlay's signature. VERT. 2 c. Mosquito. 7 c. Finlay's microscope. 9 c. Dr. C. Delgado. 10 c. Finlay's monument. 13 c. Finlay demonstrating his theories, after painting by Valderrama.

1965. Cuban Butterflies. Multicoloured.

1257. 2 c. Type **270** 5 5
1258. 2 c. "Carathis gortynoides" 5 5
1259. 2 c. "Hymenitis cubana" 5 5
1260. 2 c. "Eubaphe heros" .. 5 5
1261. 2 c. "Dismorphia cubana" 5 5
1262. 3 c. "Siderone nemesis" .. 5 5
1263. 3 c. "Syntomidopsis variegata" 5 5
1264. 3 c. "Ctenuchidia virgo" 5 5
1265. 3 c. "Lycorea ceres" .. 5 5
1266. 3 c. "Eubaphe disparilis" 5 5
1267. 13 c. "Anetia cubana" .. 55 30
1268. 13 c. "Prepona antimache" 55 30
1269. 13 c. "Sylepta reginalis" 55 30
1270. 13 c. "Chlosyne perezi" 55 30
1271. 13 c. "Anaea clytemnestra" 55 30

The five designs in each value were issued in sheets of 25 (5×5) arranged se-tenant horiz. and vert.

271. 20 c. Coin of 1962.

1965. Cuban Coinage. 50th Anniv. Multicoloured.

1273. 1 c. Type **271** 5 5
1274. 2 c. 1 p. coin of 1934 .. 5 5
1275. 3 c. 40 c. coin of 1962 .. 8 5
1276. 8 c. 1 p. coin of 1915 .. 15 8
1277. 10 c. 1 p. coin of 1953 .. 35 12
1278. 13 c. 20 p. coin of 1915 45 20

272. Oranges.

1965. Tropical Fruits. Multicoloured.

1279. 1 c. Type **272** 5 5
1280. 2 c. Custard-apples .. 10 5
1281. 3 c. Papayas 15 5
1282. 4 c. Bananas 15 5
1283. 10 c. Avocado pears .. 20 5
1284. 13 c. Pineapples .. 20 10
1285. 20 c. Guavas 45 15
1286. 50 c. Mameys 80 50

273. **273a.**

1965. Christmas. Inscr. "NAVIDAD 1965–66". Vert. designs showing bird life.

(a) As T **273**.

1287. **273.** 3 c. multicoloured .. 10 5
1288. – 5 c. multicoloured .. 20 10
1289. – 13 c. multicoloured 75 40

(b) As T **273a**.

1290. – 3 c. multicoloured .. 10 5
1291. – 5 c. multicoloured .. 20 10
1292. – 13 c. multicoloured 75 40

Nos. 1287 and 1290, 1288 and 1291, 1289 and 1292 were printed together in three sheets of 25, each comprising four stamps as T **273** plus five se-tenant stamp-size labels showing pealing bells, and a star forming a centre cross and four blocks of four different stamps as T **273a** in each corner. The four-stamp design incorporates different subjects which together form a composite picture

274. Hurdling.

1965. Int. Athletics, Havana. 7th Anniv. Multicoloured.

1293. 1 c. Type **274** 8 5
1294. 2 c. Throwing the discus 10 5
1295. 3 c. Putting the shot .. 12 8
1296. 7 c. Throwing the javelin 20 10
1297. 9 c. High-jumping .. 25 15
1298. 10 c. Throwing the hammer 35 20
1299. 13 c. Running 50 25

275. Shark-sucker.

1965. National Aquarium. Multicoloured.

1300. 1 c. Type **275** 10 5
1301. 2 c. Bonito 10 5
1302. 3 c. Sergeant Major .. 10 5
1303. 4 c. Sailfish 10 5
1304. 5 c. Nassau grouper .. 20 5
1305. 10 c. Muttonfish .. 20 10
1306. 13 c. Yellowtail snapper 35 15
1307. 30 c. Atlantic squirrelfish 75 45

276. A. Voisin, Cuban and French Flags.

1965. Prof. Andre Voisin (scientist). 1st Death Anniv.

1308. **276.** 3 c. multicoloured .. 20 10
1309. – 13 c. multicoloured .. 45 20

DESIGN: 13 c. Similar to T **276** but with microscope and plant in place of cattle.

277. "Skoda Omnibus".

1965. Cuban Transport. Multicoloured.

1310. 1 c. Type **277** 8 5
1311. 2 c. "Ikarus" omnibus .. 8 5
1312. 3 c. "Leyland" omnibus .. 10 5
1313. 4 c. "Tem-4" diesel locomotive 10 5
1314. 7 c. "BB.69,000" disel locomotive 15 5
1315. 10 c. Tugboat "Remolcador" 20 8
1316. 13 c. Freighter "15 de Marzo" 20 15
1317. 20 c. Ilyushin "Il-18" airliner 50 20

278. Infantry Column.

1966. Revolution. 7th Anniv. Inscr. "1966 VII ANIVERSARIO". Multicoloured.

1318. 1 c. Type **278** 10 5
1319. 2 c. Soldier and tank .. 10 5
1320. 3 c. Sailor and torpedo-boat 10 5
1321. 10 c. MiG-21 jet fighter .. 20 10
1322. 13 c. Rocket missile .. 45 20

SIZES—As T **278**: 2 c., 3 c. HORIZ. (38½ × 23½ mm.): 10 c., 13 c.

279. Conference Emblem.

1966. Tricontinental Conf., Havana.

1323. **279.** 2 c. multicoloured .. 8 5
1324. – 3 c. multicoloured .. 12 5
1325. – 13 c. multicoloured .. 45 20

DESIGNS: 3 c., 13 c. As T **279** but re-arranged.

280. Guardalabarca Beach.

1966. Tourism. Multicoloured.

1326. 1 c. Type **280** 5 5
1327. 2 c. La Gran Piedra (mountain resort) .. 10 5
1328. 3 c. Guama, Las Villas (country scene) .. 12 5
1329. 13 c. Waterfall, Soroa (vert.) 45 25

281. Congress Emblem and "Treating Patient" (old engraving).

1966. Medical and Stomachal Congresses, Havana. Multicoloured.

1330. 3 c. Type **281** 10 5
1331. 13 c. Congress emblem and children receiving treatment 45 20

282. Afro-Cuban Doll.

1966. Cuban Handicrafts. Multicoloured.

1332. 1 c. Type **282** 5 5
1333. 2 c. Sombreros 5 5
1334. 3 c. Vase 5 5
1335. 7 c. Gourd lampshades .. 10 5
1336. 9 c. Rare-wood Lampstand 12 8
1337. 10 c. "Horn" shark (horiz.) 25 12
1338. 13 c. Snail-shell necklace and earrings (horiz.) .. 45 20

283. "Chelsea College" (after Canaletto).

1966. National Museum Exhibits. Inscr. "1966". Multicoloured.

1339. 1 c. Ming Dynasty vase (vert.) 8 5
1340. 2 c. Type **283** 10 5
1341. 3 c. "Portrait of a Young Girl" (after Goya) (vert.) 20 10
1342. 13 c. Portrait of Fayum (vert.) 50 20

284. Cosmonauts in Training. **285.** Tank in Battle.

1966. 1st Manned Space Flight. 5th Anniv. Multicoloured.

1343. 1 c. Tsiolkovsky and diagram 5 5
1344. 2 c. Type **284** 5 5
1345. 3 c. Gagarin, rocket and globe 8 5
1346. 7 c. Nikolaev and Popovich 12 5
1347. 9 c. Tereshkova and Bykovsky 20 8
1348. 10 c. Komarov, Feoktistov and Yegorov .. 25 10
1349. 13 c. Leonov in space .. 50 12

Nos. 1343, 1345 and 1347/9 are horiz.

1966. Giron Victory. 5th Anniv.

1350. **285.** 2 c. blk., grn. & bistre 5 5
1351. – 3 c. black, blue & red 8 5
1352. – 9 c. blk., brown & grey 20 8
1353. – 10 c. blk., blue & apple 20 10
1354. – 13 c. black, brn. & blue 45 12

DESIGNS: 3 c. Sinking ship. 9 c. Disabled tank and poster-hoarding. 10 c. Young soldier. 13 c. Operations map.

286. Interior of Postal Museum (1st anniv.).

1966. Stamp Day.

1355. **286.** 3 c. green and red .. 10 8
1356. – 13 c. brown, blk. & red 45 20

DESIGN: 13 c. Stamp collector and Cuban 2 c. stamp of 1959.

287. Bouquet and Anvil. **288.** W.H.O. Building.

1966. Labour Day. Multicoloured.

1357. 2 c. Type **287** 8 5
1358. 3 c. Bouquet and Machete 10 5
1359. 10 c. Bouquet and Hammer 20 10
1360. 13 c. Bouquet and parts of globe and cogwheel .. 45 25

1966. W.H.O. Headquarters, Geneva. Inaug.

1361. **288.** 2 c. blk., grn. & yellow 8 5
1362. – 3 c. blk., blue & yell. 10 5
1363. – 13 c. blk., yell. & blue 40 20

DESIGNS (W.H.O. Building on): 3 c. Flag. 13 c. Emblem.

289. Athletics.

290. Makarenko Pedagogical Institute.

1966. 10th Central American and Caribbean Games.

No.	Type	Description	Unused	Used
1364.	289.	1 c. sepia and green	8	5
1365.	–	2 c. sepia and orange	10	5
1366.	–	3 c. brown and yellow	8	5
1367.	–	7 c. blue and magenta	10	8
1368.	–	9 c. black and blue ..	20	10
1369.	–	10 c. black and brown	20	10
1370.	–	13 c. blue and red ..	45	12

DESIGNS—HORIZ. 2 c. Rifle-shooting. VERT. 3 c. Baseball. 7 c. Volleyball. 9 c. Football. 10 c. Boxing. 13 c. Basketball.

1966. Educational Development.

No.	Type	Description	Unused	Used
1371.	290.	1 c. black and green ..	5	5
1372.	–	2 c. blk., ochre & yell.	8	5
1373.	–	3 c. black, ultram. & bl.	10	5
1374.	–	10 c. black, brn. & grn.	20	10
1375.	–	13 c. blk., red, bl. & pur.	40	12

DESIGNS: 2 c. Alphabetisation Museum. 3 c. Lamp (5th anniv. of National Alphabetisation Campaign). 10 c. Open-air class. 13 c. "Farmers' and Workers' Education".

291. "Agrarian Reform".

1966. Air. "Conquests of the Revolution". Multicoloured.

No.	Description	Unused	Used
1376.	1 c. Type **291**	10	5
1377.	2 c. "Industrialisation" ..	10	5
1378.	3 c. "Urban Reform" ..	15	5
1379.	7 c. "Eradication of Unemployment" ..	20	8
1380.	9 c. "Education" ..	20	10
1381.	10 c. "Public Health" ..	25	10
1382.	13 c. Paragraph from Castro's book, "La Historia me Absolvera"	55	30

292. Workers with Flag.

1966. 12th Revolutionary Workers' Union Congress, Havana.

No.	Type	Description	Unused	Used
1383.	292.	3 c. multicoloured ..	12	8

293. Flamed Tree Snail.

1966. Cuban Shells. Multicoloured.

No.	Description	Unused	Used
1384.	1 c. Type **293**	8	5
1385.	2 c. Measled Cowrie ..	10	5
1386.	3 c. Fighting Conch ..	12	8
1387.	7 c. Scallops ..	15	10
1388.	9 c. Striped Tree Snail ..	20	10
1389.	10 c. Atlantic Triton ..	20	15
1390.	13 c. Banded Tree Snail	40	20

HAVE YOU READ THE NOTES AT THE BEGINNING OF THIS CATALOGUE?

These often provide answers to the enquiries we receive.

294. Pigeon and Breeding Pen.

295. Arms of Pinar del Rio.

1966. Pigeon-breeding. Multicoloured.

No.	Description	Unused	Used
1391.	1 c. Type **294**	5	5
1392.	2 c. Pigeon and time-clock	5	5
1393.	3 c. Pigeon and pigeon-loft	10	5
1394.	7 c. Pigeon and breeder tending pigeon-loft ..	15	8
1395.	9 c. Pigeon and pigeon-yard	20	10
1396.	10 c. Pigeon and breeder placing message in capsule	35	15
1397	13 c. Pigeons in flight over map of Cuba (44½ × 28 mm.)	55	25

1966. National and Provincial Arms. Multicoloured.

No.	Description	Unused	Used
1398.	1 c. Type **295**	5	5
1399.	2 c. Arms of Havana ..	5	5
1400.	3 c. Arms of Matanzas ..	10	5
1401.	4 c. Arms of Las Villas ..	15	5
1402.	5 c. Arms of Camaguey ..	20	8
1403.	9 c. Arms of Oriente ..	35	25
1404.	13 c. National Arms (26 × 44 mm.) ..	55	25

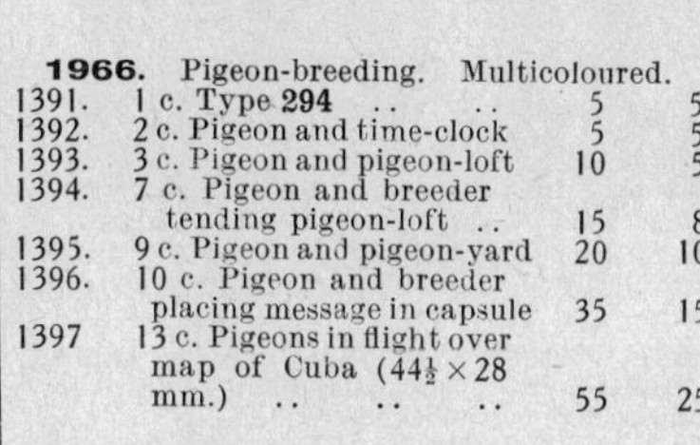
296. " Queen " and Mass Games.

1966. World Chess Olympiad, Havana.

No.	Type	Description	Unused	Used
1405.	–	1 c. black and green .	5	5
1406.	–	2 c. black and grey-blue	5	5
1407.	–	3 c. black and red ..	10	5
1408.	–	9 c. black and ochre ..	15	8
1409.	296.	10 c. black & magenta	20	10
1410.	–	13 c. blk., bl. & turq.	50	10

DESIGNS—VERT. 1 c. " Pawn ". 2 c. " Rook ". 3 c. " Knight ". 9 c. " Bishop ". HORIZ. 13 c. Olympiad Emblem and " King ".

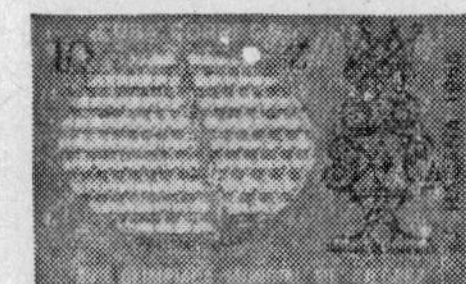

297. Lenin Hospital.

1966. Cuban-Soviet Friendship. Multicoloured.

No.	Description	Unused	Used
1412.	2 c. Type **297**	8	5
1413.	3 c. World map and oil tanker	10	5
1414.	10 c. Cuban and Soviet technicians	12	10
1415.	13 c. Cuban fruit-pickers and Soviet tractor technicians	45	25

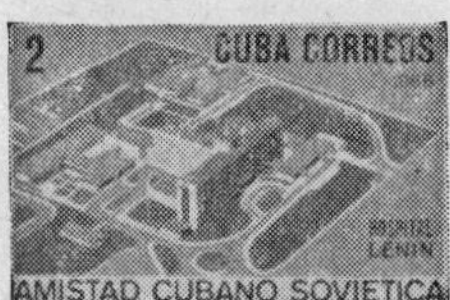

298. A. Roldan and Music of "Fiesta Negra".

1966. Song Festival.

No.	Type	Description	Unused	Used
1416.	298.	1 c. brn., blk. & grn.	5	5
1417.	–	2 c. brn., blk. & mag.	5	5
1418.	–	3 c. brown, black & bl.	10	5
1419.	–	7 c. brown, blk. & vio.	15	5
1420.	–	9 c. brown, blk. & yell.	20	10
1421.	–	10 c. brn., blk. & orge.	25	12
1422.	–	13 c. brown, blk. & bl.	50	25

CUBAN COMPOSERS AND WORKS: 2 c. E. S. de Fuentes and " Tu " (habanera, Cuban dance). 3 c. M. Simons and " El Manisero ". 7 c. J. Anckermann and " El arroyo que murmura ". 9 c. A. G. Caturla and " Pastoral Lullaby ". 10 c. E. Grenct and " Ay Mama Ines ". 13 c. E. Lecuona and " La Comparsa " (dance).

299. Bacteriological Warfare.

300. A. L. Fernandez (" Nico ") and Beach Landing.

1966. " Genocide in Viet-Nam ". Each black, red, yellow and blue.

No.	Description	Unused	Used
1423.	2 c. Type **299**	5	5
1424.	3 c. Gas warfare ..	10	5
1425.	13 c. " Conventional " bombing	45	20

1966. 1956 Revolutionary Successes. 10th Anniv. Portrait in black and brown.

No.	Type	Description	Unused	Used
1426.	300.	1 c. brown and green	8	5
1427.	–	2 c. brown and purple	8	5
1428.	–	3 c. brown and purple	10	5
1429.	–	7 c. brown and blue ..	12	8
1430.	–	9 c. brown & turquoise	15	8
1431.	–	10 c. brown and olive	25	10
1432.	–	13 c. brown & orange	50	25

HEROES AND SCENES: 2 c. C. Gonzalez and beach landing. 3 c. J. Tey and street fighting. 7 c. T. Aloma and street fighting. 9 c. O. Parellada and street fighting. 10 c. J. M. Marquez and beach landing. 13 c. F. Pais and trial scene.

301. Globe and Recreational Activities.

1966. Int. Leisure Time and Recreation Seminar. Multicoloured.

No.	Description	Unused	Used
1433.	3 c. Type **301**	10	5
1434.	9 c. Clock, eye and world map	15	8
1435.	13 c. Seminar poster ..	45	20

302. Arrow and Telecommunications Symbols.

1966. 1st National Telecommunications Forum. Multicoloured.

No.	Description	Unused	Used
1436.	3 c. Type **302**	8	5
1437.	10 c. Target and satellites	20	5
1438.	13 c. Shell and satellites (28½ × 36 mm.)	50	20

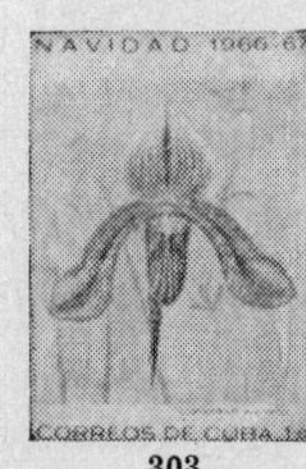

303.

304.

1966. Christmas. Inscr. "NAVIDAD 1966–67". Vert. designs showing orchids.

(a) As T 303.

No.	Type	Description	Unused	Used
1440.	301.	1 c. multicoloured ..	8	5
1441.	–	3 c. multicoloured ..	20	5
1442.	–	13 c. multicoloured ..	50	20

(b) As T 304.

No.	Type	Description	Unused	Used
1443.	–	1 c. multicoloured ..	5	5
1444.	–	3 c. multicoloured ..	5	5
1445.	–	13 c. multicoloured ..	65	35

Nos. 1440 and 1443, 1441 and 1444, 1442 and 1445 were printed together in three sheets of 24, each comprising four stamps as T **303** plus se-tenant stamp-size labels showing pealing bells, and four blocks of four different stamps as T **304**. The four-stamp design incorporates different subjects, which together form a composite picture.

305. Flag and Hands ("1959—Liberation").

1967. Revolution. 8th Anniv. Multicoloured.

No.	Description	Unused	Used
1446.	3 c. Type **305**	10	5
1447.	3 c. Clenched fist ("1960—Agrarian Reform") ..	10	5
1448.	3 c. Hands holding pencil ("1961—Education") ..	10	5
1449.	3 c. Hand protecting plant ("1965—Agriculture")	10	5
1450.	13 c. Head of Rodin's statue, "The Thinker", and arrows ("1962—Planning" ..	35	15
1451.	13 c. Hands moving lever ("1963—Organisation")	35	15
1452.	13 c. Hand holding plant within cogwheel ("1964—Economy") ..	35	15
1453.	13 c. Hand holding rifle-butt, and part of globe ("1966—Solidarity") ..	35	15

Nos. 1450/3 are vert.

Nos. 1446/9 and 1450/3 were issued respectively together se-tenant in rows of four (vert., 3 c., horiz., 13 c.) in the sheets.

306. " Spring " (after J. Arche).

1967. National Museum Exhibits. Paintings. (1st Series.) Multicoloured.

No.	Description	Unused	Used
1454.	1 c. " Coffee-pot " (A. A. Leon)	10	5
1455.	2 c. " Peasants " (E. Abela)	20	8
1456.	3 c. Type **306** ..	35	10
1457.	13 c. " Still Life " (Amelia Pelaez) ..	70	20
1458.	30 c. " Landscape " (G. Escalante)	1·60	55

The 1, 2 and 13 c. are vert.

See also Nos. 1648/54, 1785/91, 1871/7, 1900/906, 2005/11, 2047/53 and 2104/9.

307. Menelo Mora, Jose A. Echeverria and Attack on Presidential Palace.

1967. National Events of 13th March, 1957.

No.	Type	Description	Unused	Used
1459.	307.	3 c. green and black	10	5
1460.	–	13 c. brown and black	35	12
1461.	–	30 c. blue and black	55	25

DESIGNS (36½ × 24½ mm.): 13 c. Calixto Sanchez and "Corynthia" landing. 30 c. Dionisio San Roman and Cienfuegos revolt.

308. " Homo habilus ".

1967. " Prehistoric Man ". Multicoloured.

No.	Description	Unused	Used
1462.	1 c. Type **308**	8	5
1463.	2 c. " Australopithecus "	10	5
1464.	3 c. " Pithecanthropus erectus "	12	5
1465.	4 c. Peking man	20	8
1466.	5 c. Neandertal man ..	25	10
1467.	13 c. Cro-Magnon man carving ivory tusk ..	50	25
1468.	20 c. Cro-Magnon man painting on wall of cave	70	40

309. Victoria.

1967. Stamp Day. Carriages. Multicoloured.

1469. 3 c. Type **309** 12 5
1470. 9 c. Volanta 25 10
1471. 13 c. Quitrin 45 20

310. Cuban Pavilion.

1967. "Expo 67" Montreal.

1472. **310.** 1 c. multicoloured .. 5 5
1473. – 2 c. multicoloured .. 8 5
1474. – 3 c. multicoloured .. 10 5
1475. – 13 c. multicoloured .. 45 20
1476. – 20 c. multicoloured .. 60 25

DESIGNS: 2 c. Bathysphere, satellite and met. balloon ("Man as Explorer"). 3 c. Ancient rock-drawing and tablet ("Man as Creator"). 13 c. Tractor, ear of wheat and electronic console ("Man as Producer"). 20 c. Olympic athletes ("Man in the Community").

311. "Eugenia malaccencis". **312.** "Giselle".

1967. Cuban Botanical Gardens. 150th Anniv. Multicoloured.

1477. 1 c. Type **311** 5 5
1478. 2 c. "Jacaranda filicifelia" 5 5
1479. 3 c. "Coroupita guianensis" 8 5
1480. 4 c. "Spathodea campanulata" 10 8
1481. 5 c. "Cassia fistula" .. 12 10
1482. 13 c. "Plumieria alba" .. 40 25
1483. 20 c. "Erythrina poeppigiana" 70 30

1967. Int. Ballet Festival, Havana. Multicoloured.

1484. 1 c. Type **312** 10 5
1485. 2 c. "Swan Lake" .. 10 5
1486. 3 c. "Don Quixote" .. 20 5
1487. 4 c. "Calaucan" .. 20 8
1488. 13 c. "Swan Lake" (different) 45 25
1489. 20 c. "Nutcracker" .. 90 45

313. Baseball.

1967. 5th Pan-American Games, Winnipeg. Multicoloured.

1490. 1 c. Type **313** 5 5
1491. 2 c. Swimming 8 5
1492. 3 c. Basketball (vert.) .. 10 5
1493. 4 c. Gymnastics (vert.) .. 12 5
1494. 5 c. Water-polo (vert.) .. 20 10
1495. 13 c. Weight-lifting .. 45 25
1496. 20 c. Hurling the javelin 70 40

314. L. A. Turcios Lima, Map and OLAS Emblem. **316.** Octopus.

315. "Portrait of Sonny Rollins" (Alan Davie).

1967. 1st Conf. of Latin-American Solidarity Organisation (OLAS), Havana.

1497. 13 c. black, red and blue 45 20
1498. 13 c. black, red and brown 45 20
1499. 13 c. black, red and lilac 45 20
1500. 13 c. black, red and green 45 20

DESIGNS: No. 1497, Type **314**. 1498, Fabricio Ojidia. 1499, L. de La Puente Uceda. 1500, Camilo Torres. Martyrs of Guatemala, Venezuela, Peru and Colombia respectively. Each with map and OLAS emblem.

1967. "Contemporary Art" (Havana Exn. from the Paris "Salon de Mayo"). Various designs showing modern paintings. Sizes given in millimetres. Multicoloured.

1501. 1 c. Type **315** 5 5
1502. 1 c. "Twelve Selenites (F. Labisse) (39 × 41) .. 5 5
1503. 1 c. "Night of the Drinker" (F. Hundertwasser) (53 × 41) 5 5
1504. 1 c. "Figure" (Mariano) (48 × 41) 5 5
1505. 1 c. "All-Souls" (W. Lam) (45 × 41) 5 5
1506. 2 c. "Darkness and Cracks" (A. Tapies) (37 × 54) .. 5 5
1507. 2 c. "Bathers" (G. Singier) (37 × 54) 5 5
1508. 2 c. "Torso of a Muse" (J. Arp) (37 × 46) .. 5 5
1509. 2 c. "Figure" (M. W. Svanberg) (57 × 54) .. 5 5
1510. 2 c. "Oppenheimer's Information" (Erro) (37 × 41) 5 5
1511. 3 c. "Where Cardinals are Born" (Max Ernst) (37 × 52) 10 5
1512. 3 c. "Havana Landscape" (Portocarrero) (37 × 41) 10 5
1513. 3 c. "EG 12" (V. Vasarely) (37 × 42) 10 5
1514. 3 c. "Frisco" (A. Calder) (37 × 50) 10 5
1515. 3 c. "The Man with the Pipe" (Picasso) (37 × 52) 10 5
1516. 4 c. "Abstract Composition" (S. Poliakoff) (36 × 50) 12 8
1517. 4 c. "Painting" (Bram van Velde) (36 × 68) .. 12 8
1518. 4 c. "Sower of Fires" (detail, Matta) (36 × 47) 12 8
1519. 4 c. "The Art of Living" (R. Magritte) (36 × 50) 12 8
1520. 4 c. "Poem" (J. Miro) (36 × 56) 12 8
1521. 13 c. "Young Tigers" (J. Messagier) (50 × 33) .. 55 25
1522. 13 c. "Painting" (Vieira da Silva) (50 × 36) .. 55 25
1523. 13 c. "Live Cobra" (P. Alechinsky) (50 × 35) .. 55 25
1524. 13 c. "Stalingrad" (detail, A. Jorn) (50 × 46) .. 55 25
1525. 30 c. "Warriors" (E. Pignon) (55 × 32) .. 1·25 40

The stamps in each denomination were issued together vert. or horiz. se-tenant in sheets of 20.

1967. World Underwater Fishing Championships. Multicoloured.

1527. 1 c. Green Moray eel .. 5 5
1528. 2 c. Type **316** .. 5 5
1529. 3 c. Great barracuda .. 8 5
1530. 4 c. Bull shark 10 5
1531. 5 c. Spotted Jewfish .. 35 8
1532. 13 c. Ray 45 20
1533. 20 c. Green turtle .. 65 35

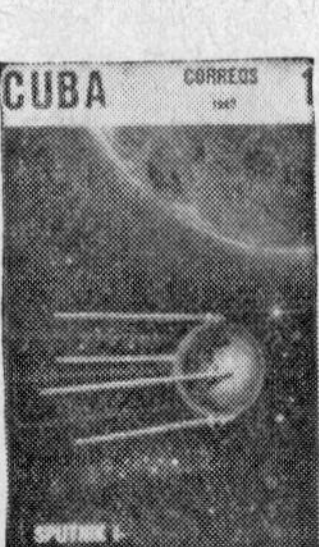

317. "Sputnik 1".

1967. Soviet Space Achievements. Multicoloured.

1534. 1 c. Type **317** 5 5
1535. 2 c. "Lunik 3" 8 5
1536. 3 c. "Venusik" 10 5
1537. 4 c. "Cosmos" 12 5
1538. 5 c. "Mars 1" 20 5
1539. 9 c. "Electron 1, 2" .. 20 8
1540. 10 c. "Luna 9" 35 20
1541. 13 c. "Luna 10" .. 50 35

318. "Storming the Winter Palace" (from painting by Sokolov, Skalia and Miasnikova).

1967. October Revolution. 50th Anniv. Multicoloured. Designs showing paintings. Sizes given in millimetres.

1543. 1 c. Type **318** 5 5
1544. 2 c. "Lenin addressing 2nd Soviet Congress" (Serov) (48 × 36) .. 8 5
1545. 3 c. "Lenin in the year 1919" (Nalbandian) (35 × 37) 12 8
1546. 4 c. "Lenin explaining the GOELRO Map" (Schmatko) (48 × 36) .. 15 10
1547. 5 c. "Dawn of the Five-Year Plan" construction work (Romas) (50 × 36) 20 15
1548. 13 c. "Kusnetzkroi steel Furnace No. 1" (Kotov) (36 × 51) 40 15
1549. 30 c. "Victory Jubilation" (rebels in the Palace, Krivonogov) (50 × 36) .. 80 40

319. Royal Force Castle, Havana.

1967. Historic Cuban Buildings. Multicoloured. Sizes given in millimetres.

1550. 1 c. Type **319** 5 5
1551. 2 c. Iznaga Tower, Trinidad ($26\frac{1}{2} \times 47\frac{1}{2}$) .. 8 5
1552. 3 c. Castle of Our Lady of the Angels, Cienfuegos ($41\frac{1}{2} \times 29$) 12 5
1553. 4 c. Church of St. Francis of Paula, Havana ($41\frac{1}{2} \times 29$) 20 5
1554. 13 c. Convent of St. Francis, Havana (39 × 13) .. 40 25
1555. 30 c. Morro Castle, Santiago de Cuba (43 × 26) .. 90 50

320. Ostrich. **321.** Golden Pheasant.

1967. Christmas. Inscr. "NAVIDAD 1967-68". Vert. designs showing birds of Havana Zoo.

(a) As T **320**.

1556. 1 c. multicoloured .. 5 5
1557. 3 c. multicoloured .. 10 5
1558. 13 c. multicoloured .. 55 25

(b) As T **321**.

1559. 1 c. multicoloured .. 5 5
1560. 3 c. multicoloured .. 10 5
1561. 13 c. multicoloured .. 55 25

Nos. 1556 and 1559, 1557 and 1560, 1558 and 1561 were printed together in three sheets of 24, each comprising four stamps as **T 320** plus se-tenant stamp-size labels showing pealing bells and four blocks of four different stamps as **T 321**. The four-stamp design incorporates different bird subjects, which together form a composite picture (Price for three sheets un. £3.)

322. "Che" Guevara.

1968. Major Ernesto "Che" Guevara Commem.

1562. **322.** 13 c. black and red .. 45 20

323. Man and Tree ("Problems of Artistic Creation, Scientific and Technical Work").

1968. Cultural Congress, Havana. Multicoloured.

1563. 3 c. Chainbreaker cradling flame ("Culture and Independence") .. 10 5
1564. 3 c. Hand with spanner and rifle ("Integral Formation of Man") .. 10 5
1565. 13 c. Demographic emblems ("Intellectual Responsibility") 45 25
1566. 13 c. Hand with communications emblems ("Culture and Mass-Communications Media") .. 45 25
1567. 30 c. Type **323** .. 90 40

The 3 and 13 c. values are all vert.

324. Canaries. **325.** "The Village Postman" (after J. Harris).

1968. Canary-breeding.

1568. **324.** 1 c. multicoloured .. 5 5
1569. – 2 c. multicoloured .. 8 5
1570. – 3 c. multicoloured .. 10 5
1571. – 4 c. multicoloured .. 12 5
1572. – 5 c. multicoloured .. 20 8
1573. – 13 c. multicoloured .. 45 25
1574. – 20 c. multicoloured .. 60 30

DESIGNS: Canaries and breeding cycle—mating, eggs, incubation and rearing young.

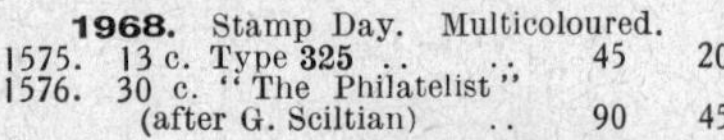

1968. Stamp Day. Multicoloured.

1575. 13 c. Type **325** 45 20
1576. 30 c. "The Philatelist" (after G. Sciltian) .. 90 45

326. Nurse tending Child ("Anti-Polio Campaign"). **327.** "Children".

1968. W.H.O. 20th Anniv.

1577. **326.** 13 c. black, red & olive 45 20
1578. – 30 c. blk., blue & olive 90 45

DESIGN: 30 c. Two doctors ("Hospital Services").

1968. Int. Children's Day.

1579. **327.** 3 c. multicoloured .. 15 8

328. "Four Wings" Aircraft and Route-map.

1968. Seville–Camaguey Flight by Barberan and Collar. 35th Anniv. Multicoloured.
1580. 13 c. Type **328** 45 15
1581. 30 c. Captain M. Barberan and Lieut. J. Collar 65 25

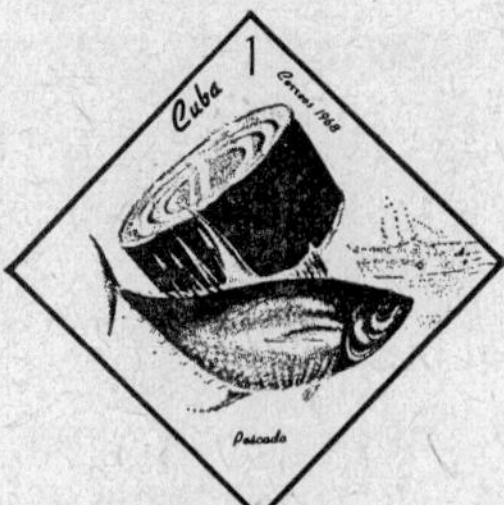
329. "Canned Fish".

1968. Cuban Food Products. Multicoloured.
1582. 1 c. Type **329** 8 8
1583. 2 c. "Milk Products" .. 10 5
1584. 3 c. "Poultry and Eggs" 12 15
1585. 13 c. "Cuban Rum" .. 35 15
1586. 20 c. "Canned Shell-fish" 55 25

330. Siboney Farmhouse. **331.** Committee Members and Emblem.

1968. Attack on Moncado Barracks. 15th Anniv. Multicoloured.
1587. 3 c. Type **330** 10 5
1588. 13 c. Map of Santiago de Cuba and assault route 35 15
1589. 30 c. Students and school buildings (on site of Moncado Barracks) .. 65 35

1968. Revolutionary Defence Committee. 8th Anniv.
1590. **331.** 3 c. multicoloured .. 15 8

332. Che Guevara and Rifleman.

1968. Day of the Guerrillas.
1591. **332.** 1 c. black grn. & gold 5 5
1592. – 3 c. black, brn. & gold 8 5
1593. – 9 c. blk., red, orange and gold 15 8
1594. – 10 c. blk., grn. & gold 35 12
1595. – 13 c. blk., pink & gold 45 20
DESIGNS—"Che" Guevara and: 3 c. Machine-gunners. 9 c. Riflemen. 10 c. Soldiers cheering. 13 c. Map of Caribbean and South America.

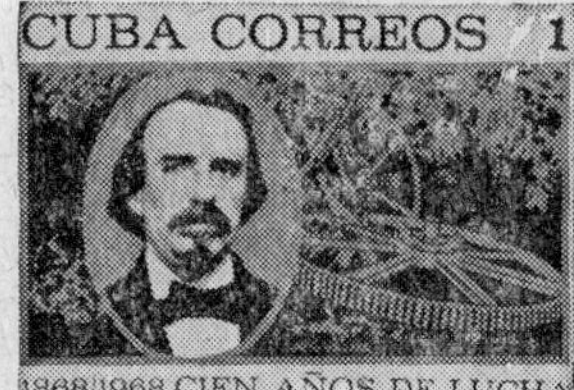

333. C. M. de Cespedes and Broken Wheel.

1968. Cuban War of Independence. Cent. Multicoloured.
1596. 1 c. Type **333** 5 5
1597. 1 c. E. Betances and horsemen 5 5
1598. 1 c. I. Agramonte and monument 5 5
1599. 1 c. A. Maceo and "The Protest" .. 5 5
1600. 1 c. J. Marti & patriots 5 5
1601. 3 c. M. Gomez and "Invasion" 5 5
1602. 3 c. J. A. Mella and declaration 5 5
1603. 3 c. A. Guiteras and monument 5 5
1604. 3 c. A Santamaria and riflemen 5 5
1605. 3 c. F. Pais & graffiti .. 5 5
1606. 9 c. J. Echeverria and students 12 8
1607. 13 c. C. Cienfuegos and rebels 35 20
1608. 30 c. "Che" Guevara and Castro addressing meeting 65 35
Nos. 1596/1600 and 1601/5 were respectively issued together in se-tenant strips of five within the sheet.

334. Parade of Athletes, Olympic Flag and Flame.

1968. Olympic Games, Mexico. Multicoloured.
1610. 1 c. Type **334** 5 5
1611. 2 c. Basketball 5 5
1612. 3 c. Throwing the hammer 8 5
1613. 4 c. Boxing 10 5
1614. 5 c. Water-polo .. 12 5
1615. 13 c. Pistol-shooting .. 35 20
1616. 30 c. Calendar-stone .. 70 35
The 2, 3 and 30 c. are vert., but the 30 c. and 50 c are larger, 32½ × 50 mm. and 50 × 30 mm. respectively.

335. Aerial Crop-spraying.

1968. Civil Activities of Cuban Armed Forces. Multicoloured.
1618. 3 c. Type **335** 5 5
1619. 9 c. "Che Guevara" Brigade 15 5
1620. 10 c. Road-building Brigade 20 10
1621. 13 c. Agricultural Brigade 45 20

336. "Manrique de Lara's Family" (J.-B. Vermay).

1968. San Alejandro Painting School. 150th Anniv. Multicoloured. Sizes given in millimetres.
1622. 1 c. Type **336** 8 5
1623. 2 c. "Seascape" (L. Romanach) (48×37) .. 10 5
1624. 3 c. "Wild Cane" (A. Rodriguez) (40×48) .. 10 10
1625. 4 c. "Self-portrait" (M Melero) (40×50) .. 15 12
1626. 5 c. "The Lottery List" (J. J. Tejada) (48×37) 20 15
1627. 13 c. "Portrait of Nina" (A. Menocal) (40×50) 55 15
1628. 30 c. "Landscape" (E. S. Chartrand) (54×37) .. 75 40

337. Cuban Flag and Rifles. **339.** Mariana Grajales, Rose and Statue.

338. Gutierrez and Sanchez.

1969. "The Triumph of the Rebellion". 10th Anniv.
1630. **337.** 13 c. multicoloured 25 15

1969. Villaclarenos Patriots Rebellion. Cent.
1631. **338.** 3 c. multicoloured .. 20 10

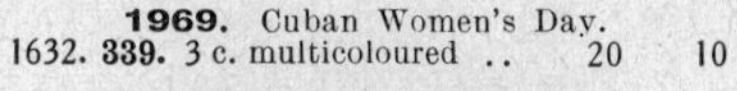
1969. Cuban Women's Day.
1632. **339.** 3 c. multicoloured .. 20 10

340. Cuban Pioneers.

1969. Cuban Pioneers and Young Communist Unions. Multicoloured.
1633. 3 c. Type **340** 12 8
1634. 13 c. Young Communists 40 20

341. Guaimaro Assembly.

1969. Guaimaro Assembly. Cent.
1635. **341.** 3 c. brown and sepia 20 8

342. "The Postman" (J. C. Cazin).

1969. Cuban Stamp Day. Multicoloured.
1636. 13 c. Type **342** 35 20
1637. 30 c. "Portrait of a Young Man" (George Romney) (36×44 mm.). 65 30

343. Agrarian Law, Headquarters, Eviction of Family, and Tractor.

1969. Agrarian Reform. 10th Anniv.
1638. **343.** 13 c. multicoloured 35 20

344. Hermit Crab.

1969. Crustaceans. Multicoloured.
1639. 1 c. Type **344** 10 5
1640. 2 c. Spiny shrimp .. 10 5
1641. 3 c. Spiny lobster .. 10 5
1642. 4 c. Blue crab 12 8
1643. 5 c. Land crab 12 10
1644. 13 c. Freshwater prawn 25 25
1645. 30 c. Pebble crab .. 60 25

345. Factory and Peasants.

1969. Int. Labour Organization. 50th Anniv. Multicoloured.
1646. 3 c. Type **345** 10 8
1647. 13 c. Worker breaking chain 40 15

346. "Flowers" (R. Milian).

1969. National Museum Paintings (2nd Series). Multicoloured.
1648. 1 c. Type **346** 8 5
1649. 2 c. "The Annunciation" (A. Eiriz) 10 5
1650. 3 c. "Factory" (M. Pogolotti) .. 10 5
1651. 4 c. "Territorial Waters" (L. M. Pedro) 10 5
1652. 5 c. "Miss Sarah Gale" (John Hoppner) .. 12 10
1653. 13 c. "Two Women wearing Mantillas" (I. Zuloaga) 25 15
1654. 30 c. "Virgin and Child" (F. Zurbaran) .. 55 35

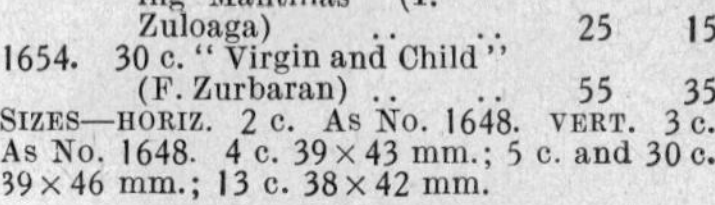
SIZES—HORIZ. 2 c. As No. 1648. VERT. 3 c. As No. 1648. 4 c. 39×43 mm.; 5 c. and 30 c. 39×46 mm.; 13 c. 38×42 mm.

347. Television Cameras and Emblem.

1969. Cuban Radiodiffusion Institute. Multicoloured.
1655. 3 c. Type **347** 10 10
1656. 13 c. Broadcasting tower and "Globe" 35 15
1657. 1 p. TV Reception diagram 1·25 55

348. Spotted Cardinal.

1969. Cuban Pisciculture. Multicoloured.
1658. 1 c. Type **348** 5 5
1659. 2 c. Spanish hogfish .. 5 5
1660. 3 c. Yellowtail damsel fish 8 5
1661. 4 c. Royal gramma .. 10 8
1662. 5 c. Blue chromis .. 12 8
1663. 13 c. Squirrel fish .. 25 12
1664. 30 c. Portuguese man-of-war fish (vert.) . 60 35

349. "Cuban Film Library".

1969. Cuban Cinema Industry. 10th Anniv. Multicoloured.

1665. 1 c. Type **349** .. 5 5
1666. 3 c. "Documentaries" .. 10 5
1667. 13 c. "Cartoons" .. 40 12
1668. 30 c. "Full-length Features" 75 40

350. "Napoleon in Milan" (A. Appiana–"El Viejo").

1969. Paintings in Napoleonic Museum, Havana. Multicoloured.

1669. 1 c. Type **350** 5 5
1670. 2 c. "Hortensia de Beauharnais" (F. Gerard) .. 10 5
1671. 3 c. "Napoleon-First Consul" (J. B. Regnault) 10 5
1672. 4 c. "Elisa Bonaparte" (R. Lefevre) 10 5
1673. 5 c. "Napoleon planning the Coronation" (J. G. Vibert) 20 10
1674. 13 c. "Corporal of Cuirassiers" (J. Meissonier) .. 35 15
1675. 30 c. "Napoleon Bonaparte" (R. Lefevre) .. 70 35

SIZES—VERT. 2 c. 42½×55½ mm.; 3 c. 46×56½ mm.; 4 c., 13 c., 44×13 mm.; 30 c. 45½×60 mm. HORIZ. 5 c. 64×47 mm.

351. Baseball Players.

1969. Cuba's Victory in World Amateur Baseball Championships, Dominican Republic.

1676. **351.** 13 c. multicoloured 35 15

352. Von Humboldt and Condors.

1969. Alexander von Humboldt. Birth Bicent. Multicoloured.

1677. 3 c. Von Humboldt and Surinam Eel 5 5
1678. 13 c. Von Humboldt and Monkey 35 20
1679. 30 c. Type **352** 70 35

353. Ancient Egyptians in Combat.

1969. World Fencing Championships, Havana. Multicoloured.

1683. 1 c. Type **353** 5 5
1684. 2 c. Roman Gladiators .. 5 5
1685. 3 c. Norman and Viking .. 8 5
1686. 4 c. Medieval tournament 10 5
1687. 5 c. French musketeers .. 12 10
1688. 13 c. Japanese samurai .. 35 15
1689. 30 c. Mounted Cubans, War of Independence .. 70 35

INDEX

Countries can be quickly located by referring to the index at the end of this volume.

354. Militiaman. **355.** Major Cienfuegos and Wreath on Sea.

1969. National Revolutionary Militias. 10th Anniv.

1691. **354.** 3 c. multicoloured .. 15 8

1969. Major Camilo Cienfuego. 10th Anniv. of Disappearance.

1692. **355.** 13 c. multicoloured .. 35 15

356. Strawberries and Grapes.

1969. Agriculture and Livestock Projects. Multicoloured.

1693. 1 c. Type **356** 5 5
1694. 1 c. Onion and asparagus 5 5
1695. 1 c. Rice 5 5
1696. 1 c. Bananas 5 5
1697. 3 c. Pineapple 8 5
1698. 3 c. Tobacco plant .. 8 5
1699. 3 c. Citrus fruits .. 8 5
1700. 3 c. Coffee 8 5
1701. 3 c. Rabbits 8 5
1702. 10 c. Pigs 20 8
1703. 13 c. Sugar-cane .. 45 20
1704. 30 c. Bull 75 30

Nos. 1696/1702 are vert.

Nos. 1693/96 and 1796/1701 were respectively arranged in horizontal se-tenant strips within the sheets.

357. Stadium and Map of Cuba (2nd National Games).

1969. "Sporting Events of 1969". Multicoloured.

1705. 1 c. Type **357** 5 5
1706. 2 c. Throwing the discus (9th Anniv. Games) .. 5 5
1707. 3 c. Running (Barrientos commemoration) (vert.) 8 5
1708. 10 c. Basketball (2nd Olympic Trial Games) (vert.) 20 5
1709. 13 c. Cycling (6th Cycle Race) (vert.) 40 15
1710. 30 c. Chessmen and Globe (Capablanca commemoration) (vert.) .. 65 40

358. "Plumbago capensis". **359.** "Petrea volubilis".

1969. Christmas. Inscr. "NAVIDAD 1969/70". Vert. designs showing flowers.

(a) As T **358.**

1711. **358.** 1 c. multicoloured .. 8 5
1712. – 3 c. multicoloured .. 15 5
1713. – 13 c. multicoloured .. 35 25

(b) As T **359.**

1714. – 1 c. multicoloured .. 8 5
1715. – 3 c. multicoloured .. 15 5
1716. – 13 c. multicoloured 35 25

Nos. 1711 and 1714, 1712 and 1715, 1713 and 1716, were printed together in three sheets of 24, each comprising four stamps as Type **358** plus se-tenant stamp-size labels and four blocks of four different stamps as Type **359**. The four-stamp design incorporates different flower subjects, which together form a composite picture.

360. River Snake.

1969. Swamp Fauna. Multicoloured.

1717. 1 c. Type **360** 5 5
1718. 2 c. Banana frog 5 5
1719. 3 c. Manjuari (fish) .. 8 5
1720. 4 c. Cuban dwarf rat (vert.) 10 5
1721. 5 c. Alligator 12 5
1722. 13 c. Parrot 35 15
1723. 30 c. Mayito (bird) .. 60 30

Nos. 1720 and 1722/3 are vertical designs.

361. "Jibacoa Beach" (J. Hernandez). **362.** Yamagua.

1970. Tourism. Multicoloured.

1724. 1 c. Type **361** 5 5
1725. 3 c. "Trinidad City" .. 8 5
1726. 13 c. Santiago de Cuba .. 35 20
1727. 30 c. Vinales Valley .. 60 35

1970. Medicinal Plants. Multicoloured.

1728. 1 c. Type **362** 5 5
1729. 3 c. Albahaca Morada .. 5 5
1730. 10 c. Curbana 15 5
1731. 13 c. Romerillo 25 10
1732. 30 c. Marilope 60 35
1733. 50 c. Aguedita .. .. 1·10 45

363. Weightlifting.

1970. 11th Central American and Caribbean Games. Multicoloured.

1734. 1 c. Type **363** 5 5
1735. 3 c. Boxing 5 5
1736. 10 c. Gymnastics .. 12 10
1737. 13 c. Athletics 25 15
1738. 30 c. Fencing 70 30

364. "Enjoyment of Life".

1970. "EXPO 70" World Fair, Osaka, Japan. Multicoloured.

1740. 1 c. Type **364** 5 5
1741. 2 c. "Uses of nature" .. 5 5
1742. 3 c. "Better Living Standards" 5 5
1743. 13 c. "International Co-operation" .. 40 15
1744. 30 c. Cuban Pavilion, Expo 70 .. .. 65 35

Nos. 1741 and 1743 are vert.

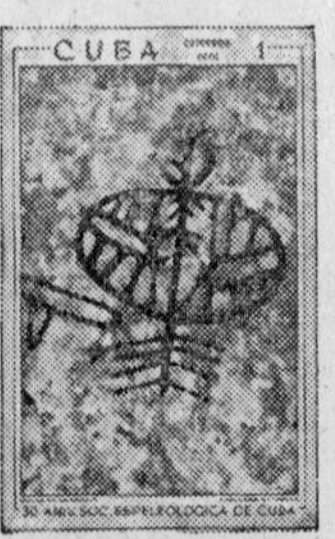

365. Oval Pictograph, Ambrosio Cave.

1970. Cuban Spelaeological Society. 30th Anniv.

1745. **365.** 1 c. red and brown .. 5 5
1746. – 2 c. black and brown 5 5
1747. – 3 c. red and brown .. 5 5
1748. – 4 c. black and brown 10 5
1749. – 5 c. blackish brown, red and brown .. 10 8
1750. – 13 c. blackish brown and brown .. 40 10
1751. – 30 c. red and brown 65 25

PICTOGRAPHS—HORIZ. (42×32½ mm.): 2 c. Cave 1, Punta del Este, Isle of Pines. 5 c. As 2 c. (different). 30 c. Stylised fish, Cave 2, Punta del Este. VERT. 3 c. Stylised mask, Pichardo Cave, Sierra de Cubitas. 4 c. Conical complex, Ambrosio Cave, Varadero. 13 c. Human face, Garcia Robiou Cave, Catalina de Guines.

366. J. D. Blino, Balloon and Spacecraft.

1970. Aviation Pioneers. Multicoloured.

1752. 3 c. Type **366** 15 10
1753. 13 c. A. Teodore, balloon and satellite .. 40 35

367. "Lenin in Kazan" (Vishniakov).

1970. Lenin. Birth Cent. Paintings. Multicoloured.

1754. 1 c. Type **367** 5 5
1755. 2 c. "Lenin's Youth" (Prager) 5 5
1756. 3 c. "The 2nd Socialist Party Congress" (Vinagradov) 5 5
1757. 4 c. "The First Manifesto" (Golubkov) 8 8
1758. 5 c. "The First Day of Soviet Power" (Babasiu) 15 10
1759. 13 c. "Lenin in the Smolny Institute" (Sokolov) .. 35 15
1760. 30 c. "Autumn in Gorky" (Varlamov) 65 30

SIZES: 4 c., 5 c. As T **367**: 2 c., 3 c., 13 c., 30 c. 70×34 mm.

368. "The Letter", after J. Arche.

1970. Cuban Stamp Day. Paintings. Multicoloured.

1762. 13 c. Type **368** .. 35 20
1763. 30 c. "Portrait of a Cadet" (anonymous) (35×49 mm.) 55 35

369. Da Vinci's Anatomical Drawing, Earth and Moon.

1970. World Telecommunications Day.

1764. **369.** 30 c. multicoloured .. 55 35

370. Pres. Ho Chi Minh.

1970. Ho Chi Minh's 80th Birthday. Multicoloured.

1765. 1 c. Fisherman 5 5
1766. 3 c. Cultivating-rice-fields 10 5
1767. 3 c. Two Vietnamese children 10 5
1768. 3 c. Children entering air-raid shelter 10 5
1769. 3 c. Camouflaged machine-shop 10 5
1770. 3 c. Rice harvest .. 10 5
1771. 13 c. Type **370** 35 15

SIZES: No. 1765, 32 × 49 mm. Nos. 1766/7 33 × 44½ mm. Nos. 1768, 1770, 33½ × 46 mm. No. 1769, 35 × 42 mm.

371. Tobacco Plantation and "Eden" Cigar band.

1970. "Cuban Cigar Industry". Multicoloured.

1772. 3 c. Type **371** 5 5
1773. 13 c. 19th century cigar factory and "El Mambi" band 40 20
1774. 30 c. Packing cigars (19th-century) and "Gran Pena" band 65 35

372. Automatic Cane crushing Machinery.

1970. Cuban Sugar Harvest Target. "Over 10 Million Tons". Multicoloured.

1775. 1 c. Type **372** 5 5
1776. 2 c. Sowing and air-spraying 5 5
1777. 3 c. Cutting sugar-cane .. 5 5
1778. 10 c. Ox-cart and diesel locomotive 12 5
1779. 13 c. Modern cane cutting machine 20 15
1780. 30 c. Cane-cutters and Globe (vert.) 65 25
1781. 1 p. Sugar Warehouse .. 1·60 80

373. P. Figueredo and National Anthem (modern version).

1970. Perucho Figueredo (composer of National Anthem). Death Cent. Multicoloured.

1782. 3 c. 1898 version of anthem 5 5
1783. 20 c. Type **373** 45 25

374. Cuban Girl, Flag and Federation Badge.

1970. Cuban Women's Federation. 10th Anniv.

1784. **374.** 3 c. multicoloured .. 35 20

375. "Peasant Militia" (S. Cabrera Moreno).

1970. National Museum Paintings (3rd series). Multicoloured.

1785. 1 c. Type **375** 5 5
1786. 2 c. "Washerwoman" (A. Fernandez) 5 5
1787. 3 c. "Puerta del Sol, Madrid" (L.P. Alcazar) 5 5
1788. 4 c. "Fishermen's Wives" (J. Sorolla) 5 5
1789. 5 c. "Portrait of a Lady" (T. de Keyser) .. 10 5
1790. 13 c. "Mrs. Edward Foster" (Lawrence) .. 35 12
1791. 30 c. "Tropical Gipsy" (V. Manuel Garcia) .. 60 20

SIZES—HORIZ. 2 c., 3 c. 46 × 42 mm. SQUARE. 4 c. 41 × 41 mm. VERT. 5 c., 13 c., 30 c. 39 × 46 mm.

376. Crowd in Jose Marti Square, Havana. (Illustration reduced. Actual size 75 × 26 mm.)

1970. Havana Declaration. 10th Anniv.

1792. **376.** 3 c. bl., carmine & blk. 5 5

377. C. D. R. Emblem.

1970. Revolution Defence Committees. 10th Anniv.

1793. **377.** 3 c. multicoloured .. 10 5

378. Laboratory, Emblem and Microscope.

1970. 39th A.T.A.C. (Sugar Technicians Assn.) Conference.

1794. **378.** 30 c. multicoloured .. 65 35

379. Grey-breasted Guineafowl.

1970. Wildlife. Multicoloured.

1795. 1 c. Type **379** 5 5
1796. 2 c. Whistling tree-duck 5 5
1797. 3 c. Ring-necked pheasant 5 5
1798. 4 c. Mourning dove .. 5 5
1799. 5 c. Bobwhite quail .. 5 5
1800. 13 c. Wild boar .. 35 12
1801. 30 c. Virginia deer .. 70 25

380. "Black Magic Parade" (M. Puente).

1970. Afro-Cuban Folklore Paintings. Multicoloured.

1802. 1 c. Type **380** 5 5
1803. 3 c. "Zapateo Hat Dance" (V. P. Landaluze) .. 5 5
1804. 10 c. "Los Hoyos Conga Dance" (D. Ravenet) .. 15 10
1805. 13 c. "Climax of the Rumba" (E. Abela) .. 35 20

SIZES—HORIZ. 10 c. 45 × 44 mm. VERT. 3 c., 13 c. 37 × 49 mm.

381. Zebra on Road Crossing.

1970. Road Safety Week. Multicoloured.

1806. 3 c. Type **381** 8 5
1807. 9 c. Prudence the Bear on point duty 20 10

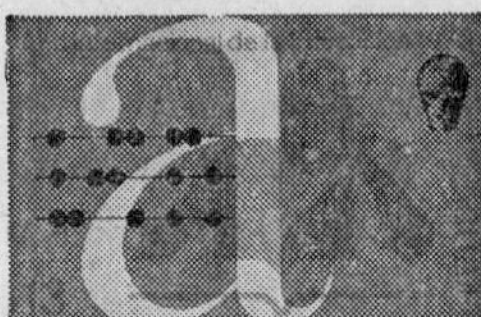

382. Letter 'a' and Abacus.

1970. International Education Year. Mult.

1808. 13 c. Type **382** 25 10
1809. 30 c. Microscope and cow 55 35

383. Cuban Oriole. **384.** Cuban Pigmy Owl.

1970. Christmas. Inscr. "NAVIDAD 1970/71" Vert. designs showing birds of Cuba.

(a) As T **383.**

1810. **383.** 1 c. multicoloured .. 5 5
1811. – 3 c. multicoloured .. 10 5
1812. – 13 c. multicoloured 35 15

(b) As T **384.**

1813. **384.** 1 c. multicoloured .. 5 5
1814. – 3 c. multicoloured .. 10 5
1815. – 13 c. multicoloured .. 35 15

Nos. 1810 and 1813, 1811 and 1814, 1812 and 1815 were printed together in three sheets of 24, each comprising four stamps as T **383** plus se-tenant stamp-size labels showing pealing bells, and four blocks of four different stamps as T **384**. The four-stamp design incorporates different bird subjects which together form a composite picture.

385. School Badge and Cadet Colour-party.

1970. "Camilo Cienfuegos" Military School.

1816. **385.** 3 c. multicoloured .. 10 5

386. "Reporter" with Pen.

1971. 7th Journalists International Organisation Congress, Havana.

1817. **386.** 13 c. multicoloured .. 25 12

387. Lockheed "Altair" Aircraft.

1971. Camaguey-Seville Flight by Menendez Pelaez. 35th Anniv. Multicoloured.

1818. 13 c. Type **387** 25 10
1819. 30 c. Lieut. Menendez Pelaez and map .. 55 35

388. Meteorological Class. **389.** Games Emblem.

1971. World Meteorological Day. Multicoloured.

1820. 1 c. Type **388** 5 5
1821. 3 c. Hurricane map (40 × 36 mm.) 5 5
1822. 8 c. Meteorological equipment 35 12
1823. 30 c. Weather radar systems (horiz.) .. 75 45

1971. 6th Pan-American Games. Cali, Colombia. Multicoloured.

1824. 1 c. Type **389** 5 5
1825. 2 c. Athletics 5 5
1826. 3 c. Rifle-shooting (horiz.) 5 5
1827. 4 c. Gymnastics 5 5
1828. 5 c. Boxing 5 5
1829. 13 c. Water-polo (horiz.) 25 10
1830. 30 c. Baseball (horiz.) .. 60 35

390. Paris Porcelain, 19th-century. **391.** Woman and Child.

1971. Porcelain and Mosaics in Metropolitan Museum, Havana. Mult.

1831. 1 c. Type **390** 5 5
1832. 3 c. Mexican pottery bowl, 17th-century .. 5 5
1833. 10 c. 19th-century Paris porcelain (similar to T **390**) 12 5
1834. 13 c. "Colosseum", Italian mosaic, 19th-century .. 15 5
1835. 20 c. 17th-century Mexican pottery dish (similar to 3 c.) 40 15
1836. 30 c. "St. Peter's Square" (Italian mosaic 19th-cent.) 65 30

SIZES—VERT. 3 c. 46 × 54 mm. 10 c. as T **390.** 20 c. 43 × 49 mm. HORIZ. 13 c., 30 c. 50 × 33 mm.

1971. Cuban Infant Centres. 10th Anniv.

1837. **391.** 3 c. multicoloured .. 5 5

392. Cosmonaut in training.

1971. First Manned Space Flight. 10th Anniv. Multicoloured.

1838. 1 c. Type **392** 5 5
1839. 2 c. Speedometer test .. 5 5
1840. 3 c. Medical examination 5 5
1841. 4 c. Acceleration tower .. 5 5
1842. 5 c. Pressurisation test .. 5 5
1843. 13 c. Cosmonaut in gravity chamber .. 20 10
1844. 30 c. Crew in flight simulator 65 30

393. Cuban and Burning Ship.

1971. Giron Victory. Tenth Anniv.

1846. **393.** 13 c. multicoloured 25 10

394. " Windsor Castle " attacked by " Jeune Richard " (1807).

1971. Stamp Day. Multicoloured.

1847. 13 c. Type **394** 25 10
1848. 30 c. Steam-packet " Orinoco ". 1851 .. 55 25

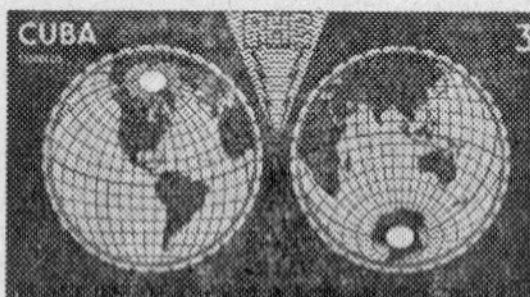

395. Transmitter and Hemispheres.

1971. Cuban Int. Broadcasting Services. 10th Anniv.

1849. **396.** 3 c. multicoloured .. 5 5
1850. 50 c. multicoloured .. 75 40

396. " Cattleya skinnerii". **398.** Larvae and Pupae.

397. Loynaz del Castillo and " Invasion Hymn ".

1971. Tropical Orchids (1st series). Multicoloured.

1851. 1 c. Type **396** 5 5
1852. 2 c. " Vanda hibrida " .. 5 5
1853. 3 c. " Cypripedium callossum " 5 5
1854. 4 c. " Cypripedium glaucophullum " .. 5 5
1855. 5 c. " Vanda tricolor " .. 5 5
1856. 13 c. " Cypripedium mowgh " 30 8
1857. 30 c. "Cypripedium solum" 65 35

See also Nos. 1908/14 and 2012/18.

1971. Enrique Loynaz del Castillo (composer) Birth Cent.

1858. **397.** 3 c. multicoloured .. 8 5

1971. Apiculture. Multicoloured.

1859. 1 c. Type **398** 5 5
1860. 3 c. Working bee .. 5 5
1861. 9 c. Drone .. 10 5
1862. 13 c. Defending the hive 15 5
1863. 30 c. Queen bee 45 20

399. " The Ship " (Lydia Rivera).

1971. Exhibition of Children's Drawings, Havana. Multicoloured.

1864. 1 c. Type **399** 5 5
1865. 3 c. " Little Train " (Yuri Ruiz) 5 5
1866. 9 c. "Sugar-cane Cutter" (Horacio Carracedo) .. 10 5
1867. 10 c. " Return of Cuban Fishermen " (Angela Munoz and Lazaro Hernandez) 12 5
1868. 13 c. " The Zoo " (Victoria Castillo) 15 8
1869. 20 c. " House and Garden" (Elsa Garcia) 45 20
1870. 30 c. " Landscape " (Orestes Rodriguez) (vert.) .. 60 25

SIZES: 9 c., 13 c. 45 × 35 mm. 10 c. 45 × 38 mm. 20 c. 47 × 42 mm. 30 c. 39 × 49 mm.

1971. National Museum Paintings (4th series). As T **375**. Multicoloured.

1871. 1 c. " St. Catherine of Alexandria " (Zurbaran) 5 5
1872. 2 c. " The Cart " (F. Americo) (horiz.) 5 5
1873. 3 c. " St. Christopher and the Child " (J. Bassano) 5 5
1874. 4 c. " Little Devil " (R. Portocarrero) .. 5 5
1875. 5 c. " Portrait of a Lady " (M. Maes) 5 5
1876. 13 c. " Phoenix " (R. Martinez) .. 25 5
1877. 30 c. " Sir William Pitt " (Gainsborough) .. 50 25

SIZES: 1 c., 3 c. 30 × 56 mm. 2 c. 48 × 37 mm. 4 c., 5 c. 37 × 49 mm. 13 c., 30 c. 39 × 49 mm.

400. Macabi.

1971. Sport Fishing. Multicoloured.

1878. 1 c. Type **400** 5 5
1879. 2 c. Great amberjack .. 5 5
1880. 3 c. Large-mouth black bass 5 5
1881. 4 c. Dorado 5 5
1882. 5 c. Tarpon 5 5
1883. 13 c. Waho 20 10
1884. 30 c. Swordfish 45 20

401. Ball within " C ".

1971. World Amateur Baseball Championships. Multicoloured.

1885. 3 c. Type **401** 5 5
1886. 1 p. Hand holding globe within " C " .. .. 1·25 65

402. " Dr. F. Valdes Dominguez " (artist unknown).

1971. Medical Students' Execution. Cent. Multicoloured.

1887. 3 c. Type **402** 5 5
1888. 13 c. " Students Execution " (M. Mesa) .. 15 10
1889. 30 c. " Captain Federico Capdevila " (unknown artist) 45 20

The 13 c. is horiz. and larger, 62 × 47 mm.

403. American Sparrowhawk.

1971. Ramon de la Sagra (naturalist). Death Cent. Cuban Birds. Multicoloured.

1890. 1 c. Type **403** 5 5
1891. 2 c. Pygmy owl .. 5 5
1892. 3 c. Cuban trogon .. 5 5
1893. 4 c. Lizard cuckoo .. 5 5
1894. 5 c. Red-crowned woodpecker 8 5
1895. 13 c. Flycatcher (horiz.) .. 20 10
1896. 30 c. Tyrant flycatcher (horiz.) 55 25
1897. 50 c. Emerald and ruby-throated hummingbirds (horiz. 56 × 30 mm.) .. 75 35

404. Baseball Player and Global Emblem.

1971. Cuba's Victory in World Amateur Baseball.

1898. **404.** 13 c. multicoloured .. 20 10

405. "Children of the World".

1971. U.N.I.C.E.F. 25th Anniv.

1899. **405.** 13 c. multicoloured .. 25 12

1972. National Museum Paintings (5th series). As T **375**. Multicoloured.

1900. 1 c. "The Reception of an Ambassadors " (V. Carpaccio) 5 5
1901. 2 c. "Senora Malpica" (G. Collazo) 5 5
1902. 3 c. "La Chorrera Fortress" (E. Chartrand) .. 5 5
1903. 4 c. "Creole Landscape" (C. Enriquez) 5 5
1904. 5 c. "Sir William Lemon" (G. Romney) 5 5
1905. 13 c. "La Tajona Beach" (H. Gleenewerk) .. 30 10
1906. 30 c. "Valaneia Beach" (J. Sorolla y Bastida) .. 55 25

SIZES: 1 c., 3 c. 51 × 33 mm. 2 c. 28 × 53 mm. 4 c., 5 c. 36 × 44 mm. 13 c., 30 c. 43 × 34 mm.

406. " Capitol " Stamp of 1929. (now Natural History Museum).

1972. Academy of Sciences. 10th Anniv.

1907. **406.** 13 c. maroon and yell. 25 12

1972. Tropical Orchids (2nd series). As T **396**. Multicoloured.

1908. 1 c. " Brasso Cattleya sindorossiana " .. 5 5
1909. 2 c. " Cypripedium doraeus" 5 5
1910. 3 c. " Cypripedium exul " 5 5
1911. 4 c. " Cypripedium 'rosydawn' " 5 5
1912. 5 c. " Cypripedium champolliom " 8 5
1913. 13 c. " Cypripedium bucolique " 35 10
1914. 30 c. " Cypripedium sullanum " 55 25

407. " Eduardo Agramonte ". (F. Martinez).

1972. Dr. E. Agramonte (surgeon and patriot). Death Cent.

1915. **407.** 3 c. multicoloured .. 8 5

408. Human Heart and Thorax. **410.** " V. M. Pera " (Postmaster General, War of Independence) (R. Loy).

409. " Sputnik 1 ".

1972. World Health Day.

1916. **408.** 13 c. multicoloured .. 20 10

1972. " History of Space ". Multicoloured.

1917. 1 c. Type **409** 5 5
1918. 2 c. " Vostok 1 " .. 5 5
1919. 3 c. Valentina Tereshkova in capsule 5 5
1920. 4 c. Leonov in space .. 5 5
1921. 5 c. " Lunokhod 1 " moon Vehicle 10 5
1922. 13 c. Linking of " Soyuz " Capsules 20 10
1923. 30 c. Dobrovolsky, Volkov & Pataiev, victims of " Soyuz 11 " disaster .. 55 25

1972. Stamp Day. Multicoloured.

1924. 13 c. Type **410** 25 10
1925. 30 c. Mambi Mail cover of 1897 (48 × 39 mm.) .. 45 25

411. Cuban Workers. **412.** Jose Marti and Ho Chi Minh.

1972. Labour Day.

1926. **411.** 3 c. multicoloured .. 8 5

1972. 3rd Symposium on Indo-China War. Mult.

1927. 3 c. Type **412** 5 5
1928. 13 c. Bombed house (38 × 39 mm.) 20 8
1929. 30 c. Symposium emblem 55 25

1972. Paintings from the Metropolitan Museum, Havana. (6th series). As T **346**. Multicoloured.

1930. 1 c. " Salvador de Muro " (J. del Rio) 5 5
1931. 2 c. " Louis de las Casas " (J. del Rio) 5 5

1932. 3 c. "Christopher Columbus" (anonymous) .. 5 5
1933. 4 c. "Tomas Gamba" (V. Escobar) 5 5
1934. 5 c. "Maria Galarraga" (V. Escobar) 10 5
1935. 13 c. "Isabella II of Spain" (F. Madrazo).. 20 10
1936. 30 c. "Carlos III of Spain" (M. Melero) .. 55 25
SIZES—VERT. (35×44 mm.). 1930/34. (34×52 mm.). 1935/6.

413. Children in Boat.

1972. Children's Song Competition.
1937. **413.** 3 c. multicoloured .. 8 5

414. Airliner, Map and Flags.

1972. Air. Havana-Santiago de Chile Air Service. 1st Anniversary.
1938. **414.** 25 c. multicoloured.. 45 20

415. Tarpan.

1972. Thoroughbred Horses. Multicoloured.
1939. 1 c. Type **415** 5 5
1940. 2 c. Kertag 5 5
1941. 3 c. Criollo 5 5
1942. 4 c. Andalusian 5 5
1943. 5 c. Arabe 8 5
1944. 13 c. Quarter-horse .. 20 10
1945. 30 c. Pursang 55 25

416. Frank Pais.

1972. Frank Pais. 15th Death Anniv.
1946. **416.** 13 c. multicoloured 20 10

417. Athlete and Emblem.

1972. Olympic Games, Munich.
1947. **417.** 1 c. orange and brown 5 5
1948. – 2 c. purple, blue and orange 5 5
1949. – 3 c. grn., yell. & blk. 5 5
1950. – 4 c. blue, yell. & brn. 5 5
1951. – 5 c. red, black & yell. 8 5
1952. – 13 c. lilac, green & blue 20 10
1953. – 30 c. blue, red & green 55 25
DESIGNS—HORIZ. 2 c. "M" and boxing. 3 c. "U" and weightlifting. 4 c. "N" and fencing. 5 c. "I" and rifle-shooting. 13 c. "C" and running. 30 c. "H" and basketball.

418. Landscape with Tree-trunks" (D. Ramos).

1972. Int. Hydrological Decade. Mult.
1955. 1 c. Type **418** 5 5
1956. 3 c. "Cyclone" (T. Lorenzo) 5 5
1957. 8 c. "Vineyards" (D. Ramos) 10 5
1958 30 c. "Forest and Stream" (A. R. Morey) (vert.) .. 45 30

419. "Papilio thoas oviedo".

1972. Butterflies from the Gundlach Collection. Mult.
1959. 1 c. Type **419** 5 5
1960. 2 c. "Papilio devilliers" 5 5
1961. 3 c. "Papilio polixenes polixenes" .. 5 5
1962. 4 c. "Papilio androgeus epidaurus" .. 5 5
1963. 5 c. "Papilio cayguanabus" 8 5
1964. 13 c. "Papilio andraemon hernandezi" .. 20 10
1965. 30 c. "Papilio celadon" 55 25

420. "In La Mancha" (A. Fernandez).

1972. Cervantes. 425th Birth Anniv. Paintings by A. Fernandez. Mult.
1966. 3 c. Type **420** 5 5
1967. 13 c. "Battle with the Wine Skins" (horiz.).. 20 10
1968. 30 c. "Don Quixote of La Mancha" 45 25

421. E. "Che" Guevara and Map of Bolivia.

1972. Guerillas' Day. 5th Anniv. Mult.
1970. 3 c. Type **421** 5 5
1971. 13 c. T. "Tania" Bunke and map of Bolivia .. 20 10
1972. 30 c. G. "Inte" Peredo and map of Bolivia .. 50 25

422. "Abwe" (shakers).

1972. Folklore Musical Instruments. Mult.
1973. 3 c. Type **422** 5 5
1974. 13 c. "Bonko enchemiya" (drum) 10 8
1975. 30 c. "Iya" (drum) .. 40 20

423. Cuban 2 c. Stamp of 1951.

1972. National Philatelic Exhib., Matanzas. Multicoloured.
1976. 13 c. Type **423** 20 10
1977. 30 c. Cuban 25 c. airmail stamp of 1951 .. 45 20

424. Viking Longship.

1972. Maritime History. Ships Through the Ages. Multicoloured.
1978. 1 c. Type **424** 5 5
1979. 2 c. Caravel (vert.) .. 5 5
1980. 3 c. Galley 5 5
1981. 4 c. Galleon (vert.) .. 5 5
1982. 5 c. Clipper 5 5
1983. 13 c. Steam Packet-boat 20 5
1984. 30 c. Atomic ice-breaker "Lenin" (53×29 mm.) 45 25

425. Lion of St. Mark.

1972. U.N.E.S.C.O. "Save Venice" Campaign. Multicoloured.
1985. 3 c. Type **425** 5 5
1986. 13 c. Bridge of Sighs (vert.) 20 8
1987. 30 c. St. Mark's Cathedral 45 20

426. Baseball Coach (poster.) **427.** Bronze Medal (women's 100 metres).

1972. "Cuba, World Amateur Baseball Champions of 1972".
1988. **426.** 3 c. violet and orange 8 5

1972. Sports events of 1972.
1989. – 1 c. multicoloured .. 5 5
1990. – 2 c. multicoloured .. 5 5
1991. **426.** 3 c. blk., orge. & grn. 5 5
1992. – 4 c. red, black & blue 5 5
1993. – 5 c. orge., bl. & light bl. 5 5
1994. – 13 c. multicoloured.. 15 12
1995. – 30 c. violet, blk. & blue 50 25
DESIGNS AND EVENTS: 1 c. Various sports (Tenth National Scholars' Games). 2 c. Pole vaulting (Barrientos Memorial Athletics). 3 c. As T **426**, but inscription changed to read "XI serie nacional de beisbol aficionado" and colours changed (11th National Amateur Baseball Series). 4 c. Wrestling (Cerro Pelado International Wrestling Championships). 5 c. Foil (Central American and Caribbean Fencing Tournament). 13 c. Boxing (Giraldo Cordova Boxing Tournament). 30 c. Fishes (Ernest Hemingway National Marlin Fishing Contest).

1972. Cuban Successes in Olympic Games, Munich. Multicoloured.
1996. 1 c. Type **427** .. 5 5
1997. 2 c. Bronze (women's 4×100 m. relay) .. 5 5
1998. 3 c. Bronze (boxing, 51 kg.) 5 5
1999. 4 c. Silver (boxing, 81 kg.) 5 5
2000. 5 c. Bronze (boxing, 54 kg.) 5 5
2001. 13 c. Gold (boxing, 67 kg.) 15 8
2002. 30 c. Gold (boxing, 81 kg.) and Silver Cup (boxing Teofilo Stevenons) .. 45 25

428. Gertrude de Avellaneda" (Esquivel).

1973. Gertrude Gomez de Avellaneda (poetess). Death Cent.
2004. **428.** 13 c. multicoloured .. 20 10

1973. National Museum Paintings (6th Series). As T **375**. Multicoloured.
2005. 1 c. "Bathers in the Lagoon" (C. Enriquez) (vert.) 5 5
2006. 2 c. "Still Lfe" (W. C. Heda) (vert.) 5 5
2007. 3 c. "Scene of Gallantry" (V. de Landaluse) (vert.) 5 5
2008. 4 c. "Return at Evening" (C. Troyon) (vert.) .. 5 5
2009. 5 c. "Elizabetta Mascagni" (F. X. Fabre) (vert.) .. 5 5
2010. 13 c. "The Picador" (E. de Lucas Padilla) (horiz.) 15 8
2011. 30 c. "In the Garden" (J. A. Morell) (vert.) .. 45 25

1973. Tropical Orchids (3rd Series). As Type **396**. Multicoloured.
2012. 1 c. "Dendrobium" (hybrid) 5 5
2013. 2 c. "Cypripedium exul. O' Brien" 5 5
2014. 3 c. "Vanda miss. Joaquin" 5 5
2015. 4 c. "Phalaenopsia scilleriana Reichb" .. 5 5
2016. 5 c. "Vanda gilbert tribulet" 5 5
2017. 13 c. "Dendrobium" (hybrid) (different) .. 15 8
2018. 30 c. "Arachnis catherine" 45 25

429. Medical Examination. **431.** "Soyuz" Rocket on Launch-pad.

430. Children and Vaccine.

1973. World Health Organization. 25th Anniv.
2019. **429.** 10 c. multicoloured .. 12 5

1973. Freedom from Polio Campaign.
2020. **430.** 3 c. multicoloured .. 5 5

1973. Cosmonautics Day. Russian Space Exploration. Multicoloured.
2021. 1 c. Type **431** 5 5
2022. 2 c. "Luna 1" in moon orbit (horiz.) 5 5
2023. 3 c. "Luna 16" leaving moon 5 5
2024. 4 c. "Venus" probe (horiz.) 5 5
2025. 5 c. "Molnia 1" communications satellite 5 5
2026. 13 c. "Mars 3" probe (horiz.) 15 5
2027. 30 c. Research ship Yuri Gargarin (horiz.) .. 45 20

432. "Cuba" Postmark, 1939.

1973. Stamp Day. Multicoloured.
2028. 13 c. Type **432** 15 5
2029. 30 c. "Havana" postmark, 1760 .. .. 40 20

433. " Ignacio Agramonte " (A. Espinosa).

1973. Maj.-Gen. Ignacio Agramonte. Death Cent.

2030. **433.** 13 c. multicoloured .. 20 8

434. Copernicus' Birthplace and Instruments.

1973. Copernicus. 500th Birth Anniv. Multicoloured.

2031. 3 c. Type **434** 5 5
2032. 13 c. Copernicus and " spaceship " .. 15 5
2033. 30 c. " De Revolutionibus Orbium Celestium " and Frombork Tower .. 45 25

435. Emblem of Basic Schools.

1973. Educational Development.

2035. **435.** 13 c. multicoloured .. 20 8

436. Jersey Breed. **437.** Festival Emblem.

1973. Cattle Breeds. Multicoloured.

2036. 1 c. Type **436** 5 5
2037. 2 c. Charolais 5 5
2038. 3 c. Creole 5 5
2039. 4 c. Swiss.. .. 5 5
2040. 5 c. Holstein 5 5
2041. 13 c. St. Gertrude's .. 15 5
2042. 30 c. Brahman Cebu .. 45 20

1973. 10th World Youth and Students Festival, East Berlin.

2043. **437.** 13 c. multicoloured .. 12 5

438. Siboney Farmhouse. **440.** " Amalia de Sajonia " (J. K. Rossler).

439. Midshipman and Warship.

1973. Revolution. 20th Anniv. Multicoloured.

2044. 3 c. Type **438** 5 5
2045. 13 c. Moncada Barracks 12 5
2046. 30 c. Revolution Square, Havana 35 20

1973. Revolutionary Navy. 10th Anniv.

2047. **439.** 3 c. multicoloured .. 5 5

1973. National Museum Paintings (7th series). Multicoloured.

2048. 1 c. Type **440** 5 5
2049. 2 c. " Interior " (M. Vicens) (horiz.) 5 5
2050. 3 c. " Margaret of Austria " (J. Pantoja de la Cruz) 5 5
2051. 4 c. " Syndic of the City Hall " (anon.) .. 5 5
2052. 5 c. " View of Santiago de Cuba " (J. H. Giro) (horiz.) 5 5
2053. 13 c. " The Catalan " (J. J. Tejada) 15 8
2054. 30 c. " Guayo Alley " (J. J. Tejada) 45 20

441. " Spring ".

1973. World Meteorological Organization. Cent. Paintings by J. Madrazo. Mult.

2055. 8 c. Type **441** 10 8
2056. 8 c. " Summer " 10 8
2057. 8 c. " Autumn " 10 8
2058. 8 c. " Winter " 10 8

442. Weightlifting. **443.** "Erythrina standleyana".

1973. 27th Pan-American World Weightlifting Championships, Havana. Designs showing various stages of weightlifting exercise.

2059. **442.** 1 c. multicoloured .. 5 5
2060. – 2 c. multicoloured .. 5 5
2061. – 3 c. multicoloured .. 5 5
2062. – 4 c. multicoloured .. 5 5
2063. – 5 c. multicoloured .. 5 5
2064. – 13 c. multicoloured .. 15 5
2065. – 30 c. multicoloured .. 45 20

1973. Wild Flowers (1st series). Mult.

2066. 1 c. Type **443** 5 5
2067. 2 c. " Lantana camara " 5 5
2068. 3 c. " Canavalia maritima " 5 5
2069. 4 c. " Dichromena colorata " 5 5
2070. 5 c. " Borrichia arborescens " 5 5
2071. 13 c. " Anguria pedata " 15 8
2072. 30 c. " Cordia sebestena " 40 20

See also Nos. 2152/6.

444. Congress Emblem.

1973. 8th World Trade Union Congress, Varna, Bulgaria.

2073. **444.** 13 c. multicoloured .. 15 8

445. Ballet Dancers. **446.** " Liguus fasciatus f.".

1973. Cuban National Ballet. 25th Anniv.

2074. **445.** 13 c. bright blue, blue and gold 15 8

1973. Sea-shells. Multicoloured.

2075. 1 c. Type **446** 5 5
2076. 2 c. " Liguus fasciatus guitarti " 5 5
2077. 3 c. " L. fasciatus whartoni " 5 5
2078. 4 c. " L. fasciatus angelae " 5 5
2079. 5 c. " L. fasciatus trinidadense " 5 5
2080. 13 c. " L. fasciatus blainianus " 15 8
2081. 30 c. " L. vittatus " .. 40 20

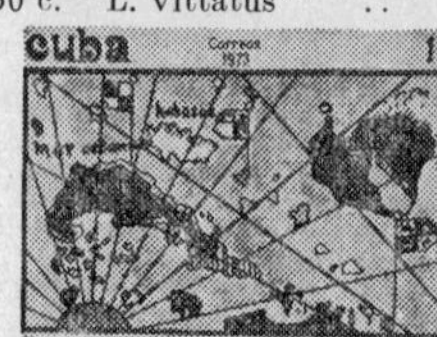

447. Juan de la Cosa's Map, 1502.

1973. Maps of Cuba. Multicoloured.

2082. 1 c. Type **447** 5 5
2083. 3 c. Ortelius's map, 1572 5 5
2084. 13 c. Bellini's map, 1762 .. 15 8
2085. 40 c. Cartographic survey map, 1973 .. 50 30

448. 1 c. Stamp of 1960.

1974. Revolution. 15th Anniv. Revolution stamps of 1960. Mult.

2086. 1 c. Type **448** 5 5
2087. 3 c. 2 c. stamp 5 5
2088. 13 c. 8 c. air stamp .. 15 8
2089. 40 c. 12 c. air stamp .. 65 35

449. " Head of a Woman " (F. Ponce de Leon).

1974. Paintings in Camaguey Museum. Multicoloured.

2090. 1 c. Type **449** 5 5
2091. 3 c. " Mexican Children " (J. Arche) 5 5
2092. 8 c. " Portrait of a Young Woman " (A. Menocal) 8 5
2093. 10 c. " Mulatto Woman with Coconut " (L. Romanach) 12 8
2094. 13 c. " Head of Old Man " (J. Arburu) .. 15 8

450. A. Cabral. **451.** " Lenin ". (after J. Kosmin).

1974. Amilcar Cabral (Guinea-Bissau guerilla leader). 1st Death Anniv.

2095. **450.** 13 c. multicoloured .. 15 8

1973. Lenin's Death. 50th Anniv.

2096. **451.** 30 c. multicoloured .. 35 20

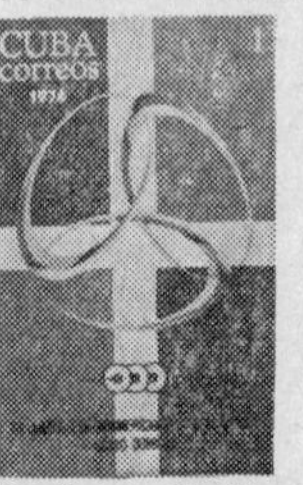

452. Games Emblem. **453.** " C. M. de Cespedes." (F. Mantinez).

1974. 12th Central American and Caribbean Games, Santo Domingo. Multicoloured.

2097. 1 c. Type **452** 5 5
2098. 2 c. Throwing the javelin 5 5
2199. 3 c. Boxing 5 5
2100. 4 c. Baseball player (horiz.) 5 5
2101. 13 c. Handball player (horiz.) 15 8
2102. 30 c. Volleyball (horiz.) .. 35 20

1974. Carlos M. de Cespedes (patriot). Death Centenary.

2103. **453.** 13 c. multicoloured .. 15 8

454. "Portrait of a Man" (J. B. Vermay). **455.** "Comecon" H.Q., Moscow.

1974. National Museum Paintings (8th series). Multicoloured.

2104. 1 c. Type **454** 5 5
2105. 2 c. " Nodriza " (C. A. Van Loo) 5 5
2106. 3 c. " Cattle by a River " (R. Morey) 5 5
2107. 4 c. " Village Landscape " (R. Morey) 5 5
2108. 13 c. " Faun and Bacchus " (Rubens) 15 8
2109. 30 c. " Playing Patience " (R. Madrazo) 35 20

Nos. 2106/7 are horiz. designs, size 46 × 32 mm.

1974. Council for Mutual Economic Aid. 25th Anniv.

2110. **455.** 30 c. multicoloured .. 15 8

456. Jose Marti and Lenin.

1974. Visit of Leonid Brezhnev (General Secretary of Soviet Communist Party). Mult.

2111. 13 c. Type **456** 15 8
2112. 30 c. Brezhnev with Castro 35 20

457. "Martian Crater".

1974. Cosmonautics Day. Science Fiction paintings by Sokolov. Multicoloured.

2113. 1 c. Type **457** 5 5
2114. 2 c. " Fiery Labyrinth " 5 5
2115. 3 c. " Amber Wave " .. 5 5
2116. 4 c. " Space Navigators" 5 5
2117. 13 c. " Planet in the Nebula " 15 8
2118. 30 c. " The World of the Two Suns " 35 20

See also Nos. 2196/201.

458. Cuban Letter of 1874.

1974. Universal Postal Union. Cent.

2119. **458.** 30 c. multicoloured .. 15 8

459. "Havana" Postmark.

1974. Stamp Day. Postal Markings of Pre-Stamp Era. Multicoloured.

2120. 1 c. Type **459** 5 5
2121. 3 c. "Matanzas" postmark 5 5
2122. 13 c. "Trinidad" postmark 15 8
2123. 20 c. "Guana Vacoa" postmark 20 12

460. Congress Emblem.

1974. 18th Sports' Congress of "Friendly Armies".
2124. **460.** 3 c. multicoloured .. 5 5

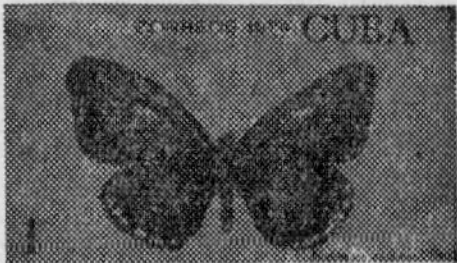

461. "Eumaeus atala atala" (butterfly).

1974. Felipe Poey (naturalist). 175th Birth Anniv. Multicoloured.
2125. 1 c. Type **461** 5 5
2126. 2 c. "Pineria terebra" (shell) 5 5
2127. 3 c. "Chaetodon sedenterius" (fish) 5 5
2128. 4 c. "Eurema dina dina" (butterfly) 5 5
2129. 13 c. "Hemitrochus fusco-labiata" (shell) .. 15 8
2130. 30 c. "Eupomacentrus partitus" (fish) .. 35 20

462. A. Mompo and Cello.

1974. Havana Philharmonic Orchestra. 50th Anniv. Leading Personalities. Multicoloured.
2132. 1 c. Type **462** 5 5
2133. 3 c. C. P. Sentenat and piano 5 5
2134. 5 c. P. Mercado and trumpet 5 5
2135. 10 c. P. Sanjuan and emblem 8 5
2136. 13 c. R. Ondina and woodwind 15 8

463. "Heliconia humilis".

464. Boxers and Global Emblem.

1974. Garden Flowers. Multicoloured.
2137. 1 c. Type **463** 5 5
2138. 2 c. "Anthurium andraeanum" 5 5
2139. 3 c. "Canna generalis" .. 5 5
2140. 4 c. "Alpinia purpurata" 5 5
2141. 13 c. "Gladiolus grandiflorus" 15 8
2142. 30 c. "Amomum capitatum" 35 20

1974. World Amateur Boxing Championships.
2143. **464** 1 c. multicoloured 5 5
2144. – 3 c. multicoloured 5 5
2145. – 13 c. multicoloured 15 8
DESIGNS: 3 c., 13 c. Stages of Boxing matches similar to Type **464**.

465. Dodo.

467. "Suriana maritima".

466. Salvador Allende.

1974. Extinct Birds. Multicoloured.
2146. 1 c. Type **465** .. 5 5
2147. 3 c. Cuban parrot .. 5 5
2148. 8 c. Passenger pigeon .. 8 5
2149. 10 c. Moa 8 5
2150. 13 c. Great auk 15 8

1974. Pres. Allende of Chile. 1st Death Anniv.
2151. **466.** 13 c. multicoloured .. 15 8

1974. Wild Flowers. (2nd series). Mult.
2152. 1 c. Type **467** 5 5
2153. 3 c. "Cassia ligustrina" .. 5 5
2154. 8 c. "Flaveria linearis" .. 8 5
2155. 10 c. "Stachytarpheta jamaicensis" 8 5
2156. 13 c. "Bacopa monnieri" 15 8

468. Flying Model Aircraft.

469. Indians playing Ball.

1974. Civil Aeronautical Institute. Tenth Anniv. Multicoloured.
2157. 1 c. Type **468** 5 5
2158. 3 c. Parachutist 5 5
2159. 8 c. Glider in flight (horiz.) 5 5
2160. 10 c. Crop-spraying aircraft (horiz.) 8 5
2161. 13 c. "Cubana" jetliner in flight (horiz.) 15 8

1974. History of Baseball in Cuba. Mult.
2162. 1 c. Type **469** 5 5
2163. 3 c. Players of 1874 (First official game) 5 5
2164. 8 c. Emilio Sabourin .. 8 5
2165. 10 c. Modern players .. 8 5
2166. 13 c. Latin-American Stadium, Havana .. 15 8
Nos. 2165/6 are horiz. size, 44 × 27 mm.

470. Stamp, Cachet and Horseman.

1974. "Mambi" Revolutionary Stamp. Cent.
2167. **470.** 13 c. multicoloured .. 15 8

471. Comecon Building, Moscow and Emblem.

1974. 16th Socialist Countries' Customs Conference.
2168. **471.** 30 c. blue and gold .. 35 20

472. Maj. C. Cienfuegos (revolutionary).

1974. Camilo Cienfuegos. 15th Anniv. of Disappearance.
2169. **472.** 3 c. multicoloured .. 5 5

473. Miner's Helmet.

1974. 8th World Mining Congress.
2170. **473.** 13 c. multicoloured .. 15 8

474. Oil Refinery.

1974. Cuban Petroleum Institute. 15th Anniv.
2171. **474.** 3 c. multicoloured .. 5 5

475. Earth Station.

1974. "Inter-Sputnik" Satellite Earth Station. Inauguration. Multicoloured.
2172. 3 c. Type **475** 5 5
2173. 13 c. Satellite and aerial .. 12 8
2174. 1 p. Satellite and flags .. 1·00 75

476. Emblem and Magnifying Glass.

1974. Cuban Philatelic Federation. Tenth Anniv.
2175. **476.** 30 c. multicoloured .. 15 8

477. F. Joliot-Curie (1st president).

1974. World Peace Congress. 25th Anniv.
2177. **477.** 30 c. multicoloured .. 35 20

478. R. M. Villena.

1974. Ruben Martinez Villena (revolutionary). 75th Birth Anniv.
2178. **478.** 3 c. red and yellow .. 5 5

479. "The Word" (M. Pogolotti).

1975. National Museum Paintings (9th series). Multicoloured.
2180. 1 c. Type **479** 5 5
2181. 2 c. "The Silk-Cotton Tree" (H. Cleenewerk) 5 5
2182. 3 c. "Landscape" (G. Collazo) 5 5
2183. 5 c. "Still Life" (F. Peralta) 5 5
2184. 13 c. "Maria Wilson" (F. Martinez) (vert.) .. 15 8
2185. 30 c. "The Couple" (M. Fortuny) 35 20

480. Bouquet and Women's Head.

1975. International Woman's Year.
2186. **480.** 13 c. multicoloured .. 15 8

481. Bonito and Fishing-boat.

1975. Cuban Fishing Industry. Mult.
2187. 1 c. Type **481** 5 5
2188. 2 c. Tunny 5 5
2189. 3 c. Grouper 5 5
2190. 8 c. Hake 5 5
2191. 13 c. Prawn 15 8
2192. 30 c. Lobster 35 20

482. Nickel.

1975. Cuban Minerals. Multicoloured
2193. 3 c. Type **482** 5 5
2194. 13 c. Copper 15 8
2195. 30 c. Chromium 35 20

1975. Cosmonautics Day. Science Fiction paintings as T **457**. Multicoloured.
2196. 1 c. "Cosmodrome" .. 5 5
2197. 2 c. "Exploration craft" (vert.) 5 5
2198. 3 c. "Earth eclipsing the Sun" 5 5
2199. 5 c. "On the Threshold" 5 5
2200. 13 c. "Cosmonauts on Mars" 15 8
2201. 30 c. "Cosmonauts' view of Earth" 35 20

483. Letter and "Correos" Postmark.

1975. Stamp Day. Multicoloured.
2202. 3 c. Type **483** 5 5
2203. 13 c. Letter and steamship postmark 15 8
2204. 30 c. Letter and "N.A." postmark 35 20

484. Hoisting Red Flag over Reichstag, Berlin.

1975. "Victory over Fascism". 30th Anniv.
2205. **484.** 30 c. multicoloured .. 35 20

485. Sevres Vase.

1975. National Museum Treasures. Mult.
2206. 1 c. Type **485** 5 5
2207. 2 c. Meissen "Shepherdess and Dancers" 5 5
2208. 3 c. Chinese Porcelain Dish—"Lady with Parasol" (horiz.) 5 5

2209. 5 c. Chinese Bamboo Screen— "The Phoenix" .. 5 5
2210. 13 c. "Allegory of Music" (F. Boucher) 15 8
2211. 30 c. "Portrait of a Lady" (L. Toque) 35 20

486. Coloured Balls and Globe "Man".

1975. International Children's Day.
2213. **486.** 3 c. multicoloured .. 5 5

487. "Vireo gundlachi".

1975. Birds (1st series). Multicoloured.
2214. 1 c. Type **487** 5 5
2215. 2 c. "Gymnoglaux l. lawrenci" 5 5
2216. 3 c. "Aratinga eoups" .. 5 5
2217. 5 c. "Starnoenas cyanocephala" 5 5
2218. 13 c. "Chondrohierax wilsoni" 15 8
2219. 30 c. "Cyanolimnas cerverai" 35 20
See also Nos. 2301/6.

488. View of Centre.

1975. National Scientific Investigation Centre. 10th Anniv.
2220. **488.** 13 c. multicoloured .. 15 8

489. Commission Emblem and Drainage Equipment.

1975. International Commission on Irrigation and Drainage.
2221. **489.** 13 c. multicoloured .. 15 8

490. "Cedre a mexicana". **491.** Women cultivating Young Plants.

1975. Reafforestation. Multicoloured.
2222. 1 c. Type **490** 5 5
2223. 3 c. "Swietonia mahagoni" 5 5
2224. 5 c. "Calophyllum brasiliense" 5 5
2225. 13 c. "Hibiscus tiliaceus" 15 8
2226. 30 c. "Pinus caribaea" .. 35 20

1975. Cuban Women's Federation. 15th Anniv.
2227. **491.** 3 c. multicoloured .. 5 5

492. Conference Emblem and Broken Chains. **493.** Baseball.

1975. International Conference on the Independence of Puerto Rico.
2228. **492.** 13 c. multicoloured .. 15 8

1975. Seventh Pan-American Games, Mexico. Multicoloured.
2229. 1 c. Type **493** 5 5
2230. 3 c. Boxing 5 5
2231. 5 c. Handball 5 5
2232. 13 c. High jumping .. 15 8
2233. 30 c. Weightlifting .. 35 20

494. Emblem and Crowd.

1975. Revolutionary Defence Committees. 15th Anniv.
2235. **494.** 3 c. multicoloured .. 5 5

495. Institute Emblem.

1975. Cuban "Friendship Amongst the Peoples" Institute. 15th Anniv.
2236. **495.** 3 c. multicoloured .. 5 5

496. Silver 1 Peso Coin, 1913.

1975. Nationalization of Bank of Cuba. 15th Anniv. Multicoloured.
2237 13 c. Type **496** 15 8
2238. 13 c. 1 peso banknote, 1934 15 8
2239. 13 c. 1 peso banknote, 1946 15 8
2240. 13 c. 1 peso banknote, 1964 15 8
2241. 13 c. 1 peso banknote, 1973 15 8

497. "La Junta", Cuba's first locomotive (1837).

1975. "Evolution of Railways". Mult.
2242. 1 c. Type **497** 5 5
2243. 3 c. Steam locomotive .. 5 5
2244. 5 c. Soviet "TEM-4" diesel locomotive .. 5 5
2245. 13 c. Hungarian "DVM-9" diesel locomotive .. 15 8
2246. 30 c. Soviet "M-62K" diesel locomotive .. 35 20

498. Bobbins and Flag.

1975. Textile Industry.
2247. **498.** 13 c. multicoloured .. 15 8

499. Sheep and Diagram.

1975. Development of Veterinary Medicine. Animals and Disease Cycles. Mult.
2248. 1 c. Type **499** 5 5
2249. 2 c. Dog 5 5
2250. 3 c. Cockerel 5 5
2251. 5 c. Horse 5 5
2252. 13 c. Pig 15 8
2253. 30 c. Ox 35 20

500. Manuel Domenech. **502.** Communists with Flags within Figure "1".

501. "Irrigation".

1975. Manuel Domenech Educational Detachment.
2254. **500.** 3 c. multicoloured .. 5 5

1975. Agriculture and Water-supply.
2255. **501**. 13 c. multicoloured .. 15 8

1976. 1st Cuban Communist Party Congress. Multicoloured.
2256. 3 c. Type **502** 5 5
2257. 13 c. Workers with banner (horiz.) 15 8
2258. 30 c. Jose Marti and Cuban leaders (horiz.) .. 35 20

503. Pre-natal Exercises.

1976. 8th Latin-American Obstetrics and Gynaecology Congress, Havana.
2259. **503.** 3 c. multicoloured .. 5 5

504. "Seated Woman" (V. Manuel). **505.** Conference Emblem and Building.

1976. National Museum Paintings (11th series). Mult.
2260. 1 c. Type **504** 5 5
2261. 2 c. "Garden" (S. Rusinol) (horiz.) 5 5
2262. 3 c. "Guadalquivir River" (M. Barron y Carrillo) (horiz.) 5 5
2263. 5 c. "Self-portrait" (Jan Steen) 5 5
2264. 13 c. "Portrait of Woman" (L. M. van Loo) .. 15 8
2265. 30 c. "La Chula" (J. A. Morell) (27 × 44 mm.) .. 35 20

1976. Socialist Communications Ministers' Conference, Havana.
2266. **505.** 13 c. multicoloured .. 25 12

506. American Foxhound.

1976. Hunting Dogs. Multicoloured.
2267. 1 c. Type **506** 5 5
2268. 2 c. Labrador retriever .. 5 5
2269. 3 c. Borzoi 5 5
2270. 5 c. Irish setter 10 5
2271. 13 c. Pointer 25 12
2272. 30 c. Cocker Spaniel .. 60 45

507. Flags, Arms and Anthem.

1976. Socialist Constitution, 1976.
2273. **507.** 13 c. multicoloured .. 25 12

508. Ruy Lopez Segura.

1976. History of Chess. Multicoloured.
2274. 1 c. Type **508** 5 5
2275. 2 c. Francois Philidor .. 5 5
2276. 3 c. Wilhelm Steinitz .. 5 5
2277. 13 c. Emanuel Lasker .. 25 12
2278. 30 c. Jose Raul Capablanca 60 45

509. Radio Aerial and Map.

1976. Cuban International Broadcasting Services. 15th Anniv.
2279. **509.** 50 c. multicoloured .. 1·00 85

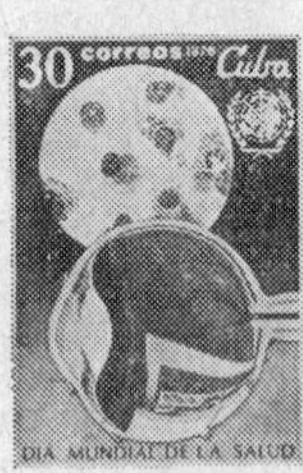

510. Section of Human Eye and Microscope Slide. **511.** Children and Creche.

1976. World Health Day.
2280. **510.** 30 c. multicoloured .. 60 45

1976. Infant Welfare Centres. 15th Anniv.
2281. **511.** 3 c. multicoloured .. 5 5

512. Y. Gagarin in Space-suit.

1976. First Manned Space Flight. 15th Anniversary. Multicoloured.
2282. 1 c. Type 512 .. .. 5 5
2283. 2 c. V. Tereshkova and rockets 5 5
2284. 3 c. Cosmonaut on " space walk " (vert.) . 5 5
2285. 5 c. Spacecraft and Moon (vert.) .. 10 5
2286. 13 c. Spacecraft in manoeuvre (vert.) 25 12
2287. 30 c. Space link 60 45

513. Cuban Machine-gunner.

1976. Giron Victory. 15th Anniv. Mult.
2288. 3 c. Type 513 .. .. 5 5
2289. 13 c. Cuban pilot and fighters attacking ship 25 12
2290. 30 c. Cuban soldier wielding rifle (vert.) .. 60 45

514. Heads of Farmers.

1976. Nat. Assn. of Small Farmers (ANAP). 15th Anniv.
2291. **514.** 3 c. multicoloured .. 5 5

515. Volleyball.

1976. Olympic Games, Montreal. Mult.
2292. 1 c. Type **515** 5 5
2293. 2 c. Basketball 5 5
2294. 3 c. Long-jumping .. 5 5
2295. 4 c. Boxing .. 8 5
2296. 5 c. Weightlifting .. 10 5
2297. 13 c. Judo .. 25 12
2298. 30 c. Swimming 60 45

516. Modern Secondary School.

1976. Rural Secondary Schools.
2300. **516.** 3 c. black and red .. 5 5

517. " Teretistris fornsi ".

1976. Birds (2nd series). Multicoloured.
2301. 1 c. Type **517** 5 5
2302. 2 c. " Glaucidium siju " 5 5
2303. 3 c. " Nesoceleus fernandinae " 5 5
2304. 5 c. " Todus multicolor " 10 5
2305. 13 c. " Accipiter gundlachi " 25 12
2306. 30 c. " Priotelus temnurus " 60 45

518. Medical Treatment. **519.** " El Inglesito ".

1976. " Expo ", Havana. Soviet Science and Technology. Multicoloured.
2307. 1 c. Type **518** 5 5
2308. 3 c. Child and deer (" Environmental Protection ") 5 5
2309. 10 c. Cosmonauts on launch-pad (" Cosmos Investigation ") .. 20 10
2310. 30 c. Tupolev supersonic aircraft (" Soviet Transport ") (horiz.) .. 60 45

1976. Henry M. Reeve (patriot). Death Cent.
2311. **519.** 13 c. multicoloured .. 25 12

520. G. Collazo (J. Dabour).

1976. Cuban Paintings. Multicoloured.
2312. 1 c. Type **520** 5 5
2313. 2 c. " The Art Lovers " (G. Collazo) (horiz.) .. 5 5
2314. 3 c. " Patio " (G. Collazo) 5 5
2315. 5 c " Cocotero " (G Collazo) .. 10 5
2316. 13 c. " New York Studio " (G Collazo) (horiz).. 25 12
2317. 30 c. " Emerlina Collazo " (G. Collazo) (horiz.) .. 60 45

POSTAGE DUE STAMPS

D 1.

1914.
D 335. D 1. 1 c. red .. .. 1·25 65
D 337. 2 c. red .. .. 1·10 55
D 340. 5 c. red .. .. 2·25 1·10

SPECIAL DELIVERY STAMPS

E 1. Cyclist Messenger.

1900. As Type E 1, but inscr. " immediata ".
E 306. E 1. 10 c. orange .. 3·25 2·25

1902. Inscribed " inmediata ".
E 307. E 1. 10 c. orange .. 1·75 75

E 2. Cyclist Messenger and J. B. Zayas.

1910.
E 320. E 2. 10 c. blue and orange 1·60 55

E 3. Plane and Morro Castle.

1914.
E 352a. E 3. 10 c. blue .. .. 2·25 1·10

E 4. Mercury.

1936. Free Port of Matanzas. Inscr. as T **24** Perf. or imperf. (same prices).
E 409. E **4.** 10 c. purple (Express) 2·75 2·75
E 413. – 15 c. blue (Air express) 2·25 50
DESIGN: 15 c. Maya Lighthouse.

E 5. Triumph of the Revolution.

1936. Maximo Gomez Monument.
E 422. E **5.** 10 c. orange .. 2·75 2·25

E 6. Temple of Quetzalcoatl (Mexico).

1937. American Writers and Artists Assn.
E 424v. E **6.** 10 c. orange .. 1·60 1·60
E 424w. – 10 c. orange .. 1·60 1·60
DESIGN: No. 424w. Ruben Dario (Nicaragua).

E 7.

1945.
E 485. E 7. 10 c. brown .. 1·10 15

E 8. Government House, Cardenas. E 9. Capablanca Club, Havana.

1951. Cuban Flag Cent.
E 559. E **8.** 10 c. red, bl. & orge. 1·60 75

1951. World Chess Championship. 30th Anniv.
E 568. E **9.** 10 c. purple & green 3·25 1·25

1952. As No. 549 surch. **10 c. E. ESPECIAL.**
E 595. **86.** 10 c. on 2 c. brown.. 1·60 75

E 10. Nationa Anthem and Arms. E 11.

1952. Republic. 50th Anniv.
E 605. E **10.** 10 c. blue & orange 1·60 75

1952. Postal Employees' Retirement Fund. Inscr. " ENTREGA ESPECIAL ".
E 627. **103.** 10 c. olive .. .. 1·60 75

1953.
E 673. E **11.** 10 c. blue .. .. 1·25 65

1954. Postal Employees' Retirement Fund Portrait of G. H. Saez as No. 684, inscr. " ENTREGA ESPECIAL ".
E 686. 10 c. olive .. .. 1·25 65

1955. Postal Employees' Retirement Fund. Vert. portrait (F. Varela) as T **128**, inscr. " ENTREGA ESPECIAL ".
E 741. 10 c. lake .. .. 1·25 65

1956. Postal Employees' Retirement Fund. Vert. portrait (J. J. Milanes) as T **137**, inscr. " ENTREGA ESPECIAL ".
E 768. 10 c. black and red .. 1·25 65

1957. Postal Employees' Retirement Fund. As T **151** but inscr. " ENTREGA ESPECIAL ".
E 812. 10 c. turquoise & brown 1·25 65
PAINTING: 10 c. " Yesterday " (Cabrera).

1957. Postal Employees' Retirement Fund. As T **170** but inscr. " ENTREGA ESPECIAL "
E 856. 10 c. violet and brown.. 1·25 65
DESIGN—HORIZ. 10 c Statue of Gen. A. Maceo, Independen. Park, Pinar del Rio.

E 12. Motor-cyclist in Havana.

1958.
E 858. E **12.** 10 c. blue .. .. 1·10 55
E 954. 10 c. violet .. 1·10 55
E 955. 10 c. orange .. 1·10 55
E 859. 20 c. green .. 1·10 55

1958. Poey Commem. As Nos. 890/2 but inscr. " ENTREGA ESPECIAL ".
E 893. 10 c. red, yell., bl. & blk. 3·25 2·25
E 894. 20 c. red, blue & black.. 5·50 3·25
DESIGNS—HORIZ. Fish: 10 c. Rabiche. 20 c. Guajacon.

1960. Surch. **HABILITADO ENTREGA ESPECIAL 10 c.**
E 961. **20.** 10 c. on 20 c. pink .. 35 20
E 962. 10 c. on 50 c. greenish blue 35 20

1962. Stamp Day. As T **213** but inscr. " ENTREGA ESPECIAL "
E 1023. 10 c. brn. & bl. on yell. 1·10 45
DESIGN: 10 c. 18-century sailing packet.

CUNDINAMARCA O1

One of the states of the Granadine Confederation.

A Department of Colombia from 1886, now uses Colombian stamps.

1. 2.

1870. Imperf.
1. 1. 5 c. blue .. .. .. 1·50 1·50
2. 2. 10 c. red .. .. .. 6·50 6·50

3. 4.

1877. Imperf.
5. 3. 10 c. red .. .. .. 1·10 1·10
6. 4. 20 c. green .. .. 2·00 2·00
7. – 50 c. mauve .. .. 2·75 2·75
8a.– 1 p. brown .. .. 4·50 4·50

The 50 c. and 1 p. are in larger Arms designs.

6. 7.

1884. Imperf.
14. 6. 5 c. blue 50 60

1885. Imperf.
17. 7. 5 c. blue 30 30
18. 10 c. red .. .. 1·25 1·25
19. 10 c. red on lilac .. 90 90
20. 20 c. green .. .. 1·25 1·25
21. 50 c. mauve .. .. 1·50 1·50
22. 1 p. brown .. .. 2·00 2·00

8. 9.

1904. Imperf. or perf. Various frames.

23. 8. 1 c. orange 15 15
24. 2 c. blue 15 15
35a. 2 c. grey .. .. .. 1·90 1·90
25. 9. 3 c. red 20 20
26. 5 c. green 20 20
27 10 c. brown 20 20
28. 15 c. pink 25 25
29. 20 c. blue on green .. 20 20
32. 20 c. blue 40 40
42. 40 c. blue 30 30
30. 50 c. mauve 25 25
31. 1 p. green 25 25

The illustrations show the main type. The frames and position of the arms in T **9** differ for each value.

REGISTRATION STAMP

R 1.

1904. Imperf. or perf.

R 46. R 1. 10 c. brown 60 60

CURACAO

A Netherlands colony consisting of two groups of islands in the Caribbean Sea, N. of Venezuela. Later part of Netherlands Antilles.

1. 2. 3.

1873.

13. 1. 2½ c. green .. .. 60 1·75
7. 3 c. bistre .. .. .. 9·00 26·00
14. 5 c. red .. .. .. 1·10 1·50
15. 10 c. blue .. .. .. 9·00 2·25
32. 12½ c. yellow .. .. 14·00 5·50
22. 15 c. grey .. .. .. 4·00 2·50
16. 25 c. brown .. .. 6·50 1·75
24. 30 c. grey .. .. .. 5·50 9·00
17. 50 c. lilac 45 60
26. 60 c. olive .. .. .. 6·00 1·75
35. 1 g. 50 blue .. .. 16·00 15·00
36. 2 g. 50 mauve and bistre 6·00 6·00

1889.

37. 2. 1 c. grey 20 20
38. 2 c. mauve 12 25
39. 2½ c. green 60 35
40. 3 c. brown 55 70
41. 5 c. red .. .. .. 1·75 25

1891. Surch. **25 CENT.**

42. 1. 25 c. on 30 c. grey .. 1·90 3·00

1892.

43. 3. 10 c. blue 20 30
44. 12½ c. green .. .. 4·50 1·50
45. 15 c. red 60 75
46. 25 c. brown .. .. 15·00 1·40
47. 30 c. grey .. .. .. 60 1·90

1895. Surch. **2½ CENT.**

48. 1. 2½ c. on 10 c. blue .. 1·25 1·10
50. 2½ c. on 30 c. grey .. 15·00 75

1899. 1898 stamps of Netherlands surch. **CURACAO** and value.

51. 11. 12½ c. on 12½ c. blue .. 7·50 1·50
52. 25 c. on 25 c. blue & red 20 25
53. 12. 1 g. 50 on 2½ g. lilac .. 4·50 6·00

4. 5. 6.
(Shaded background.)

1903.

54. 4. 1 c. olive 25 20
55. 2 c. brown .. .. .. 2·25 80
56. 2½ c. green .. .. .. 2·00 80
57. 3 c. orange .. .. .. 1·25 80
58. 5 c. red .. .. .. 1·10 10
59. 7½ c. grey .. .. .. 6·00 1·40
60. 5. 10 c. slate .. .. .. 3·00 1·00
61. 12½ c. blue 30 8
62. 15 c. brown .. .. .. 3·25 2·25
63. 22½ c. olive and brown .. 3·75 1·50
64. 25 c. violet .. .. .. 3·25 55
65. 30 c. brown .. .. .. 7·50 3·00
66. 50 c. brown .. .. .. 7·50 1·75
67. 6. 1½ g. brown .. .. .. 9·00 6·00
68. 2½ g. blue .. .. .. 9·00 6·00

7. 8. 9.
(Unshaded background.)

1915.

69. 7. ½ c. lilac 10 20
70. 1 c. olive 5 5
71. 1½ c. blue 5 5
72. 2 c. brown 30 35
73. 2½ c. green 25 5
74. 3 c. yellow 20 30
75. 3 c. green 40 50
76. 5 c. red 25 5
77. 5 c. green 50 55
78. 5 c. mauve 20 5
79. 7½ c. bistre 50 50
80. 8. 10 c. red .. .. .. 2·25 55
81. 7. 10 c. lilac 60 60
82. 10 c. red 70 30
83. 8. 12½ c. blue 35 12
84. 12½ c. red 35 40
85. 15 c. olive 15 20
86. 15 c. blue 60 50
87. 20 c. blue .. .. .. 1·10 60
88. 20 c. olive 55 55
89. 8. 22½ c. orange 40 60
90. 25 c. mauve 60 20
91. 30 c. slate 70 15
92. 35 c. slate and orange .. 60 70
93. 9. 50 c. green 80 12
94a. 1½ g. violet .. .. .. 3·00 2·50
95. 2½ g. red .. .. .. 6·00 6·50

1918. Provisional. Type-set inscription: "CURACAO 1 CENT".

96. 1 c. black on buff .. 90 60

1919. Surch. **5 CENT.**

97. 8. 5 c. on 12½ c. blue .. 1·10 60

10. Queen Wilhelmina. 11.

1923 Queen's Silver Jubilee.

98. 10. 5 c. green 25 60
99. 7½ c. olive 30 40
100. 10 c. red 35 60
101. 20 c. blue 60 90
102. 1 g. purple .. .. 8·00 6·50
103. 2 g. 50 black .. .. 15·00 38·00
104. 5 g. brown .. .. 18·00 55·00

1927. Unissued Marine Insurance stamps, as Type M 1 of Netherlands, inscr. "CURACAO", surch. **FRANKEERZEGEL** and value.

105. 3 c. on 15 c. green .. 5 8
106. 10 c. on 60 c. red .. 8 12
107. 12½ c. on 75 c. brown .. 8 12
108. 15 c. on 1 g. 50 blue .. 1·00 90
109. 25 c. on 2 g. 25 brown 1·60 1·60
110. 30 c. on 4½ g. black .. 2·25 2·25
111. 50 c. on 7½ g. red .. 1·75 1·75

1928.

112. 11. 6 c. orange 35 8
113. 7½ c. orange 20 12
114. 10 c. red 50 15
115. 12½ c. brown 50 45
116. 15 c. blue 45 15
117. 20 c. blue 95 15
118. 21 c. green .. .. 2·50 3·00
119. 25 c. purple 75 45
120. 27½ c. black .. .. 3·25 4·00
121. 30 c. green .. .. 1·10 15
122. 35 c. black 60 75

1929. Air. Surch. **LUCHTPOST** and value.

123. 8. 50 c. on 12½ c. red .. 3·75 4·50
124. 1 g. on 20 c. blue .. 3·75 4·50
125. 2 g. on 15 c. olive .. 14·00 15·00

1929. Surch. **6ct.** and bars.

126. 11. 6 c. on 7½ c. orange .. 30 25

12.

ILLUSTRATIONS
British Commonwealth and all overprints and surcharges are FULL SIZE. Foreign Countries have been reduced to ¾-LINEAR.

1931. Air.

126a. 12. 10 c. green 5 5
126b. 15 c. slate 5 8
127. 20 c. red 20 8
127a. 25 c. olive 15 15
127b. 30 c. yellow 12 10
128. 35 c. blue 25 20
129. 40 c. green 15 8
130. 45 c. orange 65 75
130a. 50 c. red 15 20
131. 60 c. purple 20 12
132. 70 c. black .. .. 1·50 60
133. 1 g. 40 brown .. .. 1·50 1·50
134. 2 g. 80 bistre .. .. 1·50 1·60

1931. Surch.

134a. 7. 1½ on 2½ c. green .. 55 65
135. 2½ on 3 c. green .. 20 30

1933. William I of Orange. 400th Birth Anniv. As T **50** of Netherlands.

136. 6 c. orange 50 45

13. Frederik Hendrik. 14. "Johannes Van Walbeeck".

1934. Dutch Colonization. 300th Anniv. Inscr. "1634 1934".

137. – 1 c. black 35 40
138. – 1½ c. mauve 20 15
139. – 2 c. orange 35 40
140. 13. 2½ c. green 30 45
141. 5 c. brown 30 30
142. 6 c. blue 30 12
143. – 10 c. red 75 30
144. – 12½ c. brown .. .. 2·25 2·25
145. – 15 c. blue 60 30
146. 14. 20 c. black 95 60
147. 21 c. chocolate .. 2·50 3·25
148. 25 c. green .. .. 2·25 2·10
149. – 27½ c. purple .. .. 3·25 4·00
150. – 30 c. red .. .. 2·40 1·10
151. 50 c. yellow .. .. 2·40 1·90
152. – 1 g. 50 blue .. .. 12·00 13·00
153. – 2 g. 50 green .. .. 14·00 9·00

PORTRAITS: 1 c. to 2 c. Willem Usselinx. 10 c. to 15 c. Jacob Binckes. 27½ c. to 50 c. Cornelis Evertson de Jongste. 1 g. 50, 2 g. 50, Louis Brion.

1934. Air. Surch. **10 CT.**

154. 12. 10 c. on 20 c. red .. 5·50 3·75

16. 17. Dutch Flags and Arms.

1936.

155. 16. 1 c. brown 5 5
156. 1½ c. blue 5 5
157. 2 c. orange 8 10
158. 2½ c. green 8 8
159. 5 c. red 5 5

1936. As T **4** of Surinam.

160. 6 c. purple 15 5
161. 10 c. red 30 8
162. 12½ c. green 50 30
163. 15 c. blue 30 12
164. 20 c. orange 30 12
165. 21 c. black 60 75
166. 25 c. red 35 30
167. 27½ c. brown 60 75
168. 30 c. bistre 20 8
169. 50 c. green 90 8
170. 1 g. 50 brown .. .. 6·00 4·50
171a. 2 g. 50 red .. .. 3·25 2·25

1938. Coronation. 40th Anniv. As T **71** of Netherlands.

172. 1½ c. violet 8 12
173. 6 c. red 20 20
174. 15 c. blue 40 40

1941. Air. Prince Bernhard and Bomber Funds. Centres in red, blue and orange.

175. 17. 10 c.+10 c. red .. .. 4·50 3·50
176. 15 c.+25 c. blue .. .. 4·50 3·50
177. 20 c.+25 c. brown .. 4·50 3·50
178. 25 c.+25 c. violet .. 4·50 3·50
179. 30 c.+50 c. orange .. 4·50 3·50
180. 35 c.+50 c. green .. 4·50 3·50
181. 40 c.+50 c. brown .. 4·50 3·50
182. 50 c.+1 g. blue .. .. 4·50 3·50

1941. As Type **78** of Netherlands.

248. – 6 c. violet 30 45
249. – 10 c. red 30 45
250. – 12½ c. green 30 35
251. – 15 c. blue 35 50
187. – 20 c. orange 15 20
253. – 21 c. grey 35 55
254. – 25 c. red 8 5
255. – 27½ c. brown 25 30
256. – 30 c. bistre 30 15
257. – 50 c. green 35 5
192. – 50 c. green .. .. 3·00 5
193. – 1½ g. brown .. .. 3·25 35
194. – 2½ g. purple .. .. 3·00 45

Nos. 192/4 are larger, 21 × 26 mm.
See also Nos. 258/61.

18. Aruba. 19. Queen Wilhelmina and Aeroplane over Atlantic Ocean.

1942.

195. – 1 c. brown and violet .. 5 5
196. – 1½ c. green and blue .. 5 5
197. – 2 c. brown and black .. 12 12
198. – 2½ c. yellow and green 8 10
199. 18. 5 c. black and red .. 25 5
200. – 6 c. blue and purple .. 20 25

DESIGNS—HORIZ. 1 c. Bonaire. 2 c. Saba. 2½ c. St. Maarten. 6 c. Curacao. VERT. 1½ c. St. Eustatius.

1942. Air.

201. 19. 10 c. blue and green .. 5 5
202. – 15 c. green and red .. 10 5
203. – 20 c. green and brown 10 5
204. – 25 c. brown and blue .. 8 8
205. – 30 c. violet and red .. 12 12
206. 19. 35 c. olive and violet .. 15 12
207. – 40 c. brown and olive .. 20 15
208. – 45 c. black and red .. 20 10
209. – 50 c. black and violet .. 30 5
210. – 60 c. blue and brown .. 30 20
211. 19. 70 c. green and brown 35 25
212. – 1 g. 40 green and blue 1·60 50
213. – 2 g. 80 blue .. .. 1·90 1·00
214. – 5 g. green and claret .. 4·00 4·00
215. – 10 g. brown and green 5·50 6·00

DESIGNS: 15 c., 40 c., 1 g. 40 c. Aeroplane over coast. 20 c., 45 c., 2 g. 80 c. Map of Netherlands West Indies. 25 c., 50 c., 5 g. Side view of aeroplane. 30 c., 60 c., 10 g. Front view of aeroplane.

20. Dutch Royal Family. 21. Princess Juliana

1943. Birth of Princess Margriet.

216. 20. 1½ c. orange 5 5
217. 2½ c. red 5 5
218. 6 c. black 25 20
219. 10 c. blue 30 30

1943. Air. Dutch Prisoners of War Relief Fund. Nos. 212/5 surch. **Voor Krijgsgevangenen** and new value.

220. – 40 c.+50 c. on 1 g. 40 green and blue .. 2·10 1·75
221. – 45 c.+50 c. on 2 g. 80 bl. 1·75 1·60
222. – 50 c.+75 c. on 5 g. green and claret .. 1·75 1·60
223. – 60 c.+100 c. on 10 g. brown and green .. 1·75 1·60

1944. Air. Red Cross Fund. Cross in red; frame in red and blue.

224. 21. 10 c.+10 c. brown .. 70 60
225. 15 c.+25 c. green .. 70 60
226. 20 c.+25 c. black .. 70 60
227. 25 c.+25 c. grey .. 70 60
228. 30 c.+50 c. purple .. 70 60
229. 35 c.+50 c. brown .. 70 60
230. 40 c.+50 c. green .. 70 60
231. 50 c.+100 c. violet .. 90 85

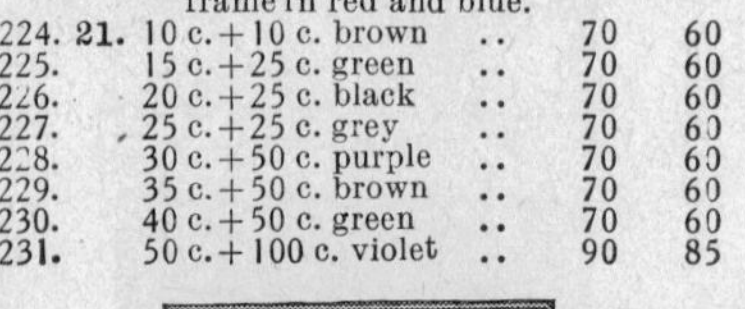

22. Map of Netherlands.

1946. Air. Netherlands Relief Fund. Value in black.

232. 22. 10 c.+10 c. orge. & grey 45 50
233. 15 c.+25 c. grey and red 45 50
234. 20 c.+25 c. orge. & grn. 45 50
235. 25 c.+25 c. grey & violet 45 50
236. 30 c.+50 c. buff & green 45 60
237. 35 c.+50 c. orge. & clar. 45 60
238. 40 c.+75 c. buff & blue 45 70
239. 50 c.+100 c. buff & vio. 45 70

1946. Air. National Relief Fund. As T **22** but showing map of Netherlands Indies and inscr. "CURACAO HELPT ONZEOOST". Value in black.

240. 10 c.+10 c. buff & violet 45 50
241. 15 c.+25 c. buff & blue 45 50
242. 20 c.+25 c. orge. & clar. 45 50
243. 25 c.+25 c. buff & grn. 45 50
244. 30 c.+50 c. grey & violet 45 60
245. 35 c.+50 c. orge & grn. 45 60
246. 40 c.+75 c. grey & red 45 70
247. 50 c.+100 c. orge. & grey 45 70

1947. As T **95** of Netherlands.

258. **95.** 1½ g. brown 40 20
259. 2½ g. purple .. .. 4·75 1·50
260. 5 g. olive .. .. 16·00 22·00
261. 10 g. orange .. .. 21·00 30·00

23. Aeroplane and Posthorn. **24.** Aeroplane and Waves.

1947. Air.

262. **23.** 6 c. black 5 5
263. 10 c. red 5 5
264. 12½ c. purple 8 5
265. 15 c. blue 5 5
266. 20 c. green 8 8
267. 25 c. orange 8 5
268. 30 c. violet 12 12
269. 35 c. red 12 15
270. 40 c. green 15 20
271. 45 c. violet 15 25
272. 50 c. red 15 5
273. 60 c. blue 20 15
274. 70 c. brown 50 35
275. **24.** 1 g. 50 black 45 20
276. 2 g. 50 red .. .. 3·00 1·25
277. 5 g. green .. .. 6·00 2·25
278. 7 g. 50 blue .. .. 17·00 18·00
279. 10 g. violet .. .. 11·00 4·50
280. 15 g. red .. .. 18·00 21·00
281. 25 g. brown .. .. 19·00 19·00

1947. Netherlands Indies. Social Welfare Fund. Surch. **NIWIN** and value.

282. 1½ c.+2½ c. on 6 c. pur. (No. 160) 20 30
283. 2½ c.+5 c. on 10 c. red (No. 16) 20 30
284. 5 c.+7½ c. on 15 c. blue (No. 163) 20 30

1948. Portrait of Queen Wilhelmina as T **38** of Netherlands Indies.

285. 6 c. purple 20 30
286. 10 c. red 20 40
287. 12½ c. green 20 20
288. 15 c. blue 20 30
289. 20 c. orange 20 45
290. 21 c. black 25 55
291. 25 c. magenta 12 5
292. 27½ c. brown .. .. 3·50 3·50
293. 30 c. olive .. .. 2·75 30
294. 50 c. green .. .. 2·75 8
295. 1 g. 50 c. brown .. .. 4·25 1·10

No. 295 is larger, 21½×28½ mm.

1948. Queen Wilhelmina's Golden Jubilee. As T **104** of Netherlands.

296. 6 c. orange 12 15
297. 12½ c. blue 15 20

25. Queen Juliana. **26.**

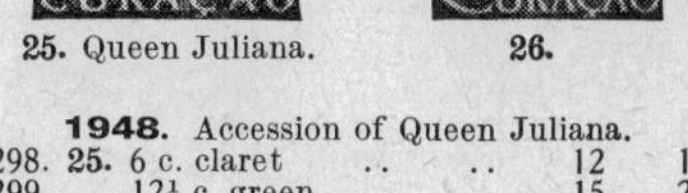

1948. Accession of Queen Juliana.

298. **25.** 6 c. claret 12 15
299. 12½ c. green 15 20

1948. Child Welfare Fund. Inscr. "VOOR HET KIND".

300. **26.** 6 c.+10 c. brown .. 40 55
301. – 10 c.+15 c. red .. 45 55
302. – 12½ c.+20 c. green .. 45 55
303. **26.** 15 c.+25 c. blue .. 54 60
304. – 20 c.+30 c. brown .. 50 70
305. – 25 c.+35 c. violet .. 55 70

DESIGNS: 10 c., 20 c. Boy. 12½ c., 25 c. Girl.

POSTAGE DUE STAMPS.

For stamps as Nos. D42/61 and D96/105 in other colours see Postage Due stamps of Netherlands Indies and Surinam.

D 1.

D 2.

1889.

D 42. **D 1.** 2½ c. black and green 45 90
D 43. 5 c. black and green 20 35
D 44. 10 c. black and green 5·50 6·00
D 45. 12½ c. black and green 60·00 30·00
D 46. 15 c. black and green 3·25 3·75
D 47. 20 c. black and green 1·50 1·60
D 48. 25 c. black and green 24·00 19·00
D 49. 30 c. black and green 1·50 1·60
D 50. 40 c. black and green 1·50 1·60
D 51. 50 c. black and green 7·50 8·50

1892.

D 52. **D 2.** 2½ c. black and green 8 5
D 53. 5 c. black and green 20 15
D 54. 10 c. black and green 20 12
D 55. 12½ c. black and green 25 12
D 56. 15 c. black and green 25 25
D 57. 20 c. black and green 40 25
D 58. 25 c. black and green 25 20
D 59. 30 c. black and green 1·90 1·50
D 60. 40 c. black and green 2·25 1·60
D 61. 50 c. black and green 2·75 1·75

1915.

D 96. **D 2.** 2½ c. green 15 15
D 97. 5 c. green 15 15
D 98. 10 c. green 15 15
D 99. 12½ c. green 15 15
D 100. 15 c. green 30 35
D 101. 20 c. green 15 30
D 102. 25 c. green 8 5
D 103. 30 c. green 50 55
D 104. 40 c. green 50 60
D 105. 50 c. green 45 55

For later issues see **NETHERLANDS ANTILLES.**

CYPRUS BC

An island in the E. Mediterranean. A Br. colony which became a republic within the Br. Commonwealth in 1960.

1881. 40 paras=1 piastre. 180 piastres=£1. 1955. 1000 mils=£1.

1880. Stamps of Gt. Britain (Queen Victoria) optd. **CYPRUS.**

1. **8.** ½d. red .. .. 28·00 32·00
2. **9.** 1d. red .. .. 4·00 7·00
3. **29.** 2½d. mauve .. .. 90 1·25
4. – 4d. green (No. 153) .. 60·00 65·00
5. – 6d. grey (No. 161) .. £110 £100
6. – 1s. green (No. 150) .. £300 £150

1881. Stamps of Gt. Britain (Queen Victoria), surch. with new values.

9. **9.** ½d. on 1d. red .. 9·00 11·00
10. 30 par. on 1d. red .. 25·00 28·00

1.

4.

1881.

16a. **1.** ½ pi. green .. .. 1·60 30
40. ½ pi. green and red .. 1·00 20
32. 30 par. mauve .. 1·10 90
41. 30 par. mauve and green 1·00 20
33. 1 pi. red .. .. 3·25 1·10
42. 1 pi. red and blue .. 1·40 25
34. 2 pi. blue .. .. 5·00 60
43. 2 pi. blue and purple .. 1·40 30
35a. 4 pi. olive .. .. 8·00 3·00
44. 4 pi. olive and purple .. 3·00 1·40
21. 6 pi. grey .. .. 12·00 6·00
45. 6 pi. olive and green .. 3·00 2·25
46. 9 pi. brown and red .. 6·00 3·00
22. 12 pi. brown .. .. 40·00 12·00
47. 12 pi. brown and black .. 5·50 9·00
48. 18 pi. grey and brown .. 14·00 9·00
49. 45 pi. purple and blue .. 25·00 25·00

1882. T **1** surch.

25. **1.** ½ pi. on ½ pi. green .. 20·00 5·00
24. 30 par. on 1 pi. red .. £250 70·00

1903. As T **1** but portrait of King Edward VII.

60. 5 par. brown and black .. 20 40
61. 10 par. orange and green .. 50 65
62. ½ pi. green and red .. 40 15
51. 30 par. violet and green .. 65 65
64. 1 pi. red and blue .. 65 30
65. 2 pi. blue and purple .. 1·40 30
66. 4 pi. olive and purple .. 6·50 2·50
67. 6 pi. olive and green .. 6·00 3·00
68. 9 pi. brown and red .. 2·75 3·25
57. 12 pi. brown and black .. 6·00 7·50
70. 18 pi. black and brown .. 16·00 6·00
71. 45 pi. purple and blue .. 26·00 23·00

1912. As T **1** but portrait of King George V.

74. 10 par. orange and green 55 65
86. 10 par. grey and yellow .. 2·00 2·25
75. ½ pi. green and red .. 65 55
76. 30 par. violet and green .. 65 50
88. 30 par. green .. 1·00 60
77. 1 pi. red and blue .. 90 1·10
90. 1 pi. violet and red .. 2·00 2·25
91. 1½ pi. yellow and black .. 1·10 1·75
78. 2 pi. blue and purple .. 1·75 75
93. 2 pi. red and blue .. 3·25 4·00
94. 2¾ pi. blue and purple .. 4·00 5·00
79. 4 pi. olive and purple .. 1·75 80
80. 6 pi. olive and green .. 1·75 1·10
81. 9 pi. brown and red .. 8·00 6·00
82. 12 pi. brown and black .. 3·25 3·50
83. 18 pi. black and brown .. 7·50 7·50
84. 45 pi. purple and blue .. 22·00 22·00
100. 10s. green and red on yell. £120 £130
101. £1 purple and black on red £500 £600

1924.

103. **4.** ¼ pi. grey and brown .. 20 25
104. ½ pi. black 40 65
118. ½ pi. green 40 65
105. ¾ pi. green 40 30
119. ¾ pi. black 40 10
106. 1 pi. purple and brown .. 25 25
107. 1½ pi. orange and black 55 80
120. 1½ pi. red 65 45
108. 2 pi. red and green .. 1·10 1·40
121. 2 pi. yellow and black .. 1·40 1·75
122. 2½ pi. blue .. .. 1·10 40
109. 2¾ pi. blue and purple .. 55 1·10
110. 4 pi. olive and purple .. 1·00 1·40
111. 4½ pi. blk. & orge. on grn. 1·90 2·50
112. 6 pi. brown and green .. 1·75 2·75
113. 9 pi. brown and purple .. 1·75 2·75
114. 12 pi. brown and black .. 2·50 7·00
115. 18 pi. black and orange 6·00 6·00
116. 45 pi. purple and blue .. 10·00 13·00
117. 90 pi. green & red on yell. 35·00 45·00
102. £1 purple & black on red 80·00 90·00
117a. £5 black on yellow .. £1500 £1750

5. Silver coin of Amathus.

1928. British Rule. 50th Anniv. Dated "1878 1928".

123. **5.** ¾ pi. violet 45 25
124. – 1 pi. black and blue .. 60 65
125. – 1½ pi. red .. .. 1·40 1·10
126. – 2½ pi. blue .. .. 55 1·00
127. – 4 pi. brown .. .. 2·50 3·50
128. – 6 pi. blue .. .. 3·25 4·00
129. – 9 pi. purple .. .. 2·75 2·75
130. – 18 pi. black and brown .. 5·50 6·50
131. – 45 pi. violet and blue .. 12·00 15·00
132. – £1 blue and brown .. 55·00 65·00

DESIGNS—VERT. 1 pi. Philosopher Zeno. 2½ pi. Discovery of body of St. Barnabas. 4 pi. Cloister, Abbey of Bella Paise. 9 pi. Tekke of Umm Haram. 18 pi. Statue of Richard I, London. 45 pi. St. Nicholas Famagusta. £1 King George V. HORIZ. 1½ pi. Map of Cyprus. 6 pi. Badge of Cyprus.

15. Vouni Palace.

21. St. Sophia, Nicosia.

DESIGNS—HORIZ. ½ pi. Salamis. ¾ pi. Peristerona Church. 1 pi. Soli Theatre. 1½ pi. Kyrenia Harbour. 2½ pi. Kolossi Castle. 45 pi. Forest scene. VERT. 6 pi. Bairakdar Mosque. 9 pi. Queen's Window. St. Hilarion Castle. 18 pi. Buyuk Khan, Nicosia.

1934.

133. **15.** ¼ pi. blue and brown .. 12 30
134. – ½ pi. green 12 30
135. – ¾ pi. black and violet .. 15 10
136. – 1 pi. black and brown 40 55
137. – 1½ pi. red 35 25
138. – 2½ pi. blue 40 55
139. **21.** 4½ pi. black and red .. 2·00 85
140. – 6 pi. black and blue .. 1·75 2·75
141. – 9 pi. brown and violet 1·50 1·75
142. – 18 pi. black & olive-grn. 6·50 4·50
143. – 45 pi. green and black 14·00 13·00

The ¼ pi. to 2½ pi. values have a medallion portrait of King George V.

1935. Silver Jubilee. As T **11** of Antigua.

144. ¾ pi. blue and grey .. 12 10
145. 1½ pi. blue and red .. 1·00 1·00
146. 2½ pi. brown and blue 2·25 2·75
147. 9 pi. grey and purple .. 4·50 5·50

1937. Coronation. As T **2** of Aden.

148. ¾ pi. grey 20 5
149. 1½ pi. red 40 20
150. 2½ pi. blue 80 70

26. Cyprus.

27. Citadel (Othello's Tower), Famagusta.

28. King George VI.

1938.

151. **15.** ¼ pi. blue and brown .. 10 8
152. – ½ pi. green 8 5
152a. – ½ pil violet 20 8
153. – ¾ pi. black and violet .. 60 5
154. – 1 pi. orange 20 5
155. – 1½ pi. red 35 25
155a. – 1½ pi. violet 10 8
155ab. 1½ pi. green 50 12
155b. – 2 pi. black and red .. 12 5
156. – 2½ pi. blue .. .. 1·10 1·60
156a. – 3 pi. blue 15 5
156b. – 4 pi. blue 60 10
157. **26.** 4½ pi. grey 12 5
158. – 6 pi. black and blue .. 40 30
159. **27.** 9 pi. black and purple .. 25 10
160. – 18 pi. black and olive .. 50 35
161. – 45 pi. green and black .. 1·25 60
162. **28.** 90 pi. mauve and black 5·00 6·50
163. £1 red and blue .. 11·00 11·00

DESIGNS: 2 pi. Peristerona Church. 3 pi., 4 pi. Kolossi Castle. All other values except 4½ pi., 9 pi., 90 pi. and £1 have designs as 1934 issue but portrait of King George VI.

1946. Victory. As T **4** of Aden.

164. 1½ pi. violet 8 5
165. 3 pi. blue 8 5

1948. Silver Wedding. As T **5/6** of Aden.

166. 1½ pi. violet 10 10
167. £1 blue .. .. 17·00 20·00

1948. U.P.U. As T **14/17** of Antigua.

168. 1½ pi. violet 25 30
169. 2 pi. red 40 55
170. 3 pi. blue 75 90
171. 9 pi. purple .. .. 1·50 1·40

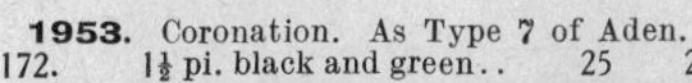

1953. Coronation. As Type **7** of Aden.

172. 1½ pi. black and green .. 25 25

29. Carobs.

30. Copper Pyrites Mine.

31. St. Hilarion Castle.

32. Arms of Byzantium. Lusignan, Ottoman Empire and Venice.

1955.

173. **29.** 2 m. brown 8 10
174. – 3 m. violet 8 10
175. – 5 m. orange 8 5
176. **30.** 10 m. brown and green 10 5
177. – 15 m. olive and indigo.. 15 15
178. – 20 m. brown and blue.. 20 15
179. – 25 m. turquiose .. 30 25
180. – 30 m. black and lake.. 25 15
181. – 35 m. chestnut & turq. 30 25
182. – 40 m. green and brown 35 25
183. **31.** 50 m. blue and brown.. 55 30
184. – 100 m. magenta & green 1·40 60
185. – 250 m. blue and brown 3·75 2·25
186. – 500 m. slate and purple 8·50 6·50
187. **32.** £1 lake and slate .. 16·00 13·00

DESIGNS—As T **29**: 3 m. Grapes. 5 m. Oranges. As T **30**: 15 m. Troodos Forest. 20 m. Beach of Aphrodite. 25 m. Ancient coin of Paphos. 30 m. Kyrenia. 35 m. Harvest in Messaoria. 40 m. Famagusta harbour. As T **31**: 100 m. Hala Sultan Tekke. 250 m. Kanakaria Church. As T **32**; 500 m. Coins of Salamis, Paphos, Citium and Idalium.

ΚΥΠΡΙΑΚΗ ΔΗΜΟΚΡΑΤΙΑ KIBRIS CUMHURIYETI
33.

34. Map of Cyprus.

1960. Nos. 173/87 optd. as T **33** ("CYPRUS REPUBLIC" in Greek and Turkish).

188. **29.** 2 m. brown 15 25
189. – 3 m. violet 15 25
190. – 5 m. orange 12 10
191. **30.** 10 m. brown and green 20 10
192. – 15 m. olive and indigo.. 40 40
193. – 20 m. brown and blue.. 40 35
194. – 25 m. turquoise .. 65 45
195. – 30 m. black and lake.. 65 30
196. – 35 m. chestnut & turq. 75 55
197. – 40 m. green and brown 85 65
198. **31.** 50 m. blue and brown.. 1·00 65
199. – 100 m. magenta & grn. 3·50 2·50
200. – 250 m. blue and brown 7·50 6·50
201. – 500 m. slate and purple 23·00 19·00
202. **32.** £1 lake and slate .. 65·00 65·00

1960. Constitution of Republic.

203. **34.** 10 m. sepia and green.. 30 30
204. 30 m. blue and brown.. 80 80
205. 100 m. purple and slate 2·00 1·75

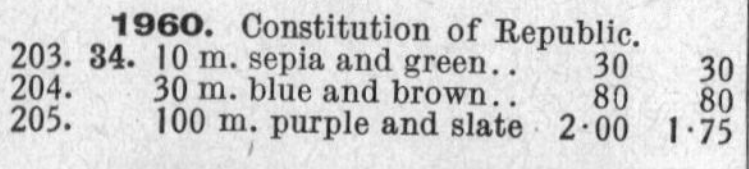

35. Doves.

1962. Europa.

206. **35.** 10 m. purple and mauve 8 8
207. 40 m. ultram. and cobalt 30 30
208. 100 m. emerald & grn. 60 60

36. Campaign Emblem.

1962. Malaria Eradication.

209. **36.** 10 m. black & ol.-green 15 15
210. 30 m. black and brown 55 55

37. St. Barnabas' Church.

1962.

211. – 3 m. brown & orge.-brn. 10 10
212. – 5 m. purple & grey-green 10 10
213. – 10 m. black & yell.-grn. 10 10
214. – 15 m. black and purple 12 10
215. **37.** 25 m. brown & chestnut 25 20
216. – 30 m. dp. blue & lt. blue 30 25
217. – 35 m. green and blue .. 35 25
218. – 40 m. black & viol-blue 45 35
219. – 50 m. bronze and bistre 60 40
220. – 100 m. brown & yell.-brn. 1·25 50
221. – 250 m. black & cinnamon 3·50 1·50
222. – 500 m. brown and green 9·50 5·00
223. – £1 bronze and grey .. 20·00 15·00

DESIGNS—VERT. 3 m. Iron Age jug. 5 m. Grapes. 10 m. Bronze head of Apollo. 15 m. St. Sophia Church. 35 m. Head of Aphrodite. 100 m. Hala Sultan Tekke. 500 m. Cyprus Moufflon. HORIZ. 30 m. Temple of Apollo Hylates. 40 m. Skiing at Troodos. 50 m. Salamis Gymnasium. 250 m. Bellapais Abbey. £1, St. Hilarion Castle.

38. Europa "Tree".

1963. Europa.

224. **38.** 10 m. blue and black .. 10 10
225. 40 m. red and black .. 60 60
226. 150 m. emerald & black 1·40 1·40

39. Harvester.

40. Wolf Cub in Camp.

1963. Freedom from Hunger.

227. **39.** 25 c. ochre, sepia & blue 30 30
228. – 75 m. grey, black & lake 75 80

DESIGN: 75 m. Demeter, Goddess of Corn.

1963. Cyprus Scout Movement. 50th Anniv. and 3rd Commonwealth Scout Conference, Platres. Inscr. "1911–1963". Multi-coloured.

229. 3 m. Type **40** 8 8
230. 20 m. Sea Scout 30 30
231. 150 m. Scout with Moufflon 1·40 1·50

The 10 m. is vert.

41. Children's Home, Kyrenia.

1963. Red Cross Cent. Inscr. "1863-1963". Multicoloured.

232. 10 m. Nurse tending child 12 12
233. 100 m. Type **41** .. .. 1·40 1·50

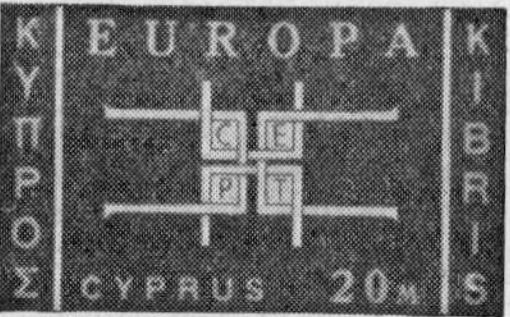

42. "Co-operation".

1963. Europa.

234. **42.** 20 m. buff, blue & violet 25 20
235. 30 m. grey, yell. & blue 40 35
236. 150 m. buff, blue & brown 1·60 1·60

1964. U.N. Security Council's Cyprus Resolutions, March, 1964. Nos. 213, etc., optd. with U.N. emblem and **1964.**

237. 10 m. black & yellow-green 12 12
238. 30 m. deep blue & light blue 20 25
239. 40 m. black and violet-blue 30 30
240. 50 m. bronze and bistre.. 40 40
241. 100 m. brown & yellow-brn. 70 70

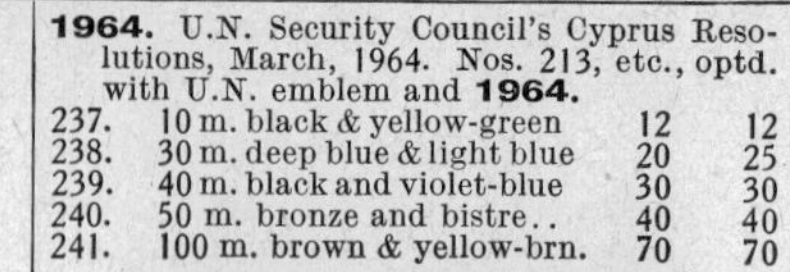

43. Soli Theatre.

1964. 400th Anniv. of Shakespeare's Birth. Multicoloured.

242. 15 m. Type **43** 10 20
243. 35 m. Curium Theatre .. 35 35
244. 50 m. Salamis Theatre .. 50 45
245. 100 m. Othello Tower, and scene from Shakespeare's "Othello" 85 80

44. Running.  **45.** Europa "Flower".

1964. Olympic Games, Tokyo.

246. **44.** 10 m. brown, blk. & yell. 12 12
247. – 25 m. brown, bl. & slate 20 20
248. – 75 m. brn., blk. & chest. 50 50

DESIGNS—HORIZ. 25 m. Boxing. 75 m. Charioteers.

1964. Europa.

249. **45.** 20 m. chestnut & ochre 12 12
250. 30 m. ultramarine & blue 25 25
251. 150 m. olive and green 1·50 1·50

46. Dionysus and Acme.

1964. Cyprus Wines. Multicoloured.

252. 10 m. Type **46** 5 5
253. 40 m. Silenus (satyr) .. 35 35
254. 50 m. Commandaria Wine 45 45
255. 100 m. Wine factory .. 90 90

Nos. 253/4 are vert.

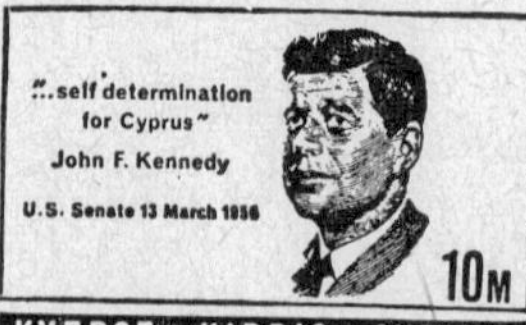

47. Pres. Kennedy.

1965. Pres. Kennedy Commem.

256. **47.** 10 m. blue 5 5
257. 40 m. green 30 30
258. 100 m. red 85 90

48. "Old Age".

DESIGNS—As T **48**: 45 m. "Accident". LARGER (23 × 48 mm.): 75 m. "Maternity".

1965. Social Insurance Law.

259. **48.** 30 m. drab and green .. 25 25
260. – 45 m. grey-green, blue and ultramarine .. 40 40
261. – 75 m. chestnut & flesh .. 85 90

49. I.T.U. Emblem and Symbols.

1965. I.T.U. Cent.

262. **49.** 15 m. black, brn. & yell. 12 12
263. 60 m. blk., grn. & lt.-grn. 50 55
264. 75 m. blk., indigo & blue 70 75

50. I.C.Y. Emblem.

1965. Int. Co-operation Year.

265. **50.** 50 m. brown and green 45 45
266. 100 m. purple and green 80 80

51. Europa "Sprig".

1965. Europa.

267. **51.** 5 m. black, brn. & orge. 8 8
268. 45 m. black, brown & grn. 40 40
269. 150 m. black, brn. & grey 1·10 1·10

1966. U.N. General Assembly's Cyprus Resolution, Nos. 211, 213, 216 and 221 optd. **U.N. Resolution on Cyprus 18 Dec. 1965.**

270. 3 m. brown & orge.-brown 5 5
271. 10 m. black & yell.-green 8 8
272. 30 m. deep blue & lt. blue 25 25
273. 250 m. black and cinnamon 1·25 1·25

52. Discovery of St. Barnabas' Body.

1966. St. Barnabas. 1900th Death Anniv.

274. **52.** 15 m. multicoloured .. 20 20
275. – 25 m. drab, blk. & blue 30 30
276. – 100 m. multicoloured .. 1·25 1·40

DESIGNS—HORIZ. 25 m. St. Barnabas' Chapel. VERT. 100 m. St. Barnabas (icon).

1966. No. 211 surch.

278. – 5 m. on 3 m. brown and orange-brown .. 10 10

53. General K. S. Thimayya and U.N. Emblem.

1966. Gen. Thimayya Commem.

279. **53.** 50 m. blk. & orge.-brown 25 25

54. Europa "Ship".

56. Silver Coin of Evagoras I.

55. Stavrovouni Monastery.

1966. Europa.

280. 54. 20 m. green and blue .. 15 15
281. 30 m. purple and blue 25 25
282. 150 m. bistre and blue 1·10 1·10

1966. Multicoloured.

283. 3 m. Type 55 .. .. 5 5
284. 5 m. Church of St. James (Tricomo) 5 5
285. 10 m. Zeno of Citium (marble bust) 5 8
286. 15 m. Ancient ship (painting) 8 8
287. 20 m. Type **56** 8 10
288. 25 m. Sleeping Eros (marble statue) 12 12
289. 30 m. St. Nicholas' Cathedral, Famagusta 25 12
290. 35 m. Gold sceptre from Curium 30 25
291. 40 m. Silver disc of 7th century 30 12
292. 50 m. Silver coin of Alexander the Great .. 35 20
293. 100 m. 7th century jug .. 1·00 40
294. 250 m. Bronze ingot-stand 1·50 80
295. 500 m. "The Rape of Ganymede" (mosaic) .. .. 5·00 2·50
296. £1 Aphrodite (marble statue) .. .. 8·00 8·00

DESIGNS—As T **55**—VERT. 5 m. and 10 m. As T **56**—HORIZ. 15 m. 25 m. and 50 m. VERT. 30 m., 35 m., 40 m. and 100 m. Nos. 294/6 are as T **56** but larger, 28×40 mm.

57. Power Station, Limassol.

58. Cogwheels.

1967. 1st Development Programme. Multicoloured.

297. 10 m. Type **57** 10 10
298. 15 m. Arghaka-Maghounda Dam 10 10
299. 35 m. Troodos Highway .. 20 20
300. 50 m. Hilton Hotel, Nicosia 25 25
301. 100 m. Famagusta Harbour 45 45

Nos. 298/301 are vert.

1967. Europa.

302. 58. 20 m. olive, grn. & apple 12 12
303. 30 m. violet, lilac & mve. 20 20
304. 150 m. sepia, brn. & chest. 60 60

59. Throwing the Javelin.

1967. Athletic Games, Nicosia. Multicoloured.

305. 15 m. Type **59** 8 8
306. 35 m. Running 20 20
307. 100 m. High-jumping .. 45 55

60. Ancient Monuments.

1967. Int. Tourist Year. Multicoloured.

309. 10 m. Type **60** 8 8
310. 40 m. Famagusta Beach 20 20
311. 50 m. Comet at Nicosia Airport 30 30
312. 100 m. Skier and Youth Hostel 55 55

61. St. Andrew Mosaic.

1967. St. Andrew's Monastery. Cent.

313. 61. 25 m. multicoloured .. 15 15

62. The Crucifixion.

1967. Cyprus Art Exn., Paris.

314. 62. 50 m. multicoloured .. 25 25

63. The Three Magi.

1967. U.N.E.S.C.O. 20th Anniv.

315. 63. 75 m. multicoloured .. 30 35

64. Human Rights Emblem over Stars.

1968. Human Rights Year. Multicoloured.

316. 50 m. Type **64** 25 25
317. 90 m. Human Rights and U.N. Emblems .. 40 40

65. Europa Key.

1968. Europa.

319. 65. 20 m. multicoloured .. 8 8
320. 30 m. multicoloured .. 20 20
321. 150 m. multicoloured .. 75 75

66. U.N. Children's Fund Symbol and Boy drinking Milk.

1968. U.N.I.C.E.F. 21st Anniv.

322. 66. 35 m. brn., red & black 20 20

67. Aesculapius.

68. Throwing the Discus.

1968. W.H.O. 20th Anniv.

323. 67. 50 m. blk., grn. & olive 25 25

1968. Olympic Games, Mexico. Multicoloured.

324. 10 m. Type **68** 12 12
325. 25 m. Runners breasting Tape 20 20
326. 100 m. Olympic Stadium 65 65

69. I.L.O. Emblem.

1969. Int. Labour Organisation. 50th Anniv.

327. 69. 50 m. brown and blue 20 20
328. 90 m. brown, black & grey 45 45

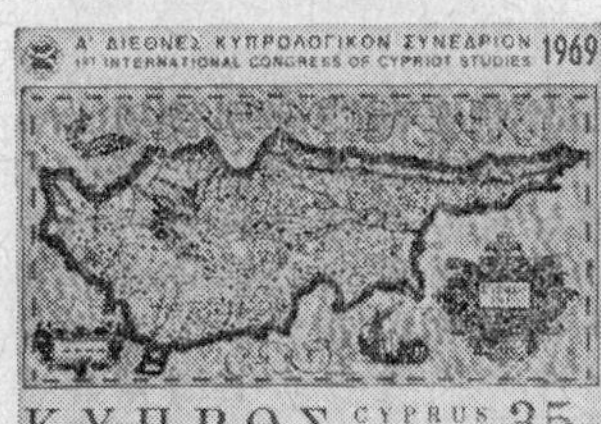

70. Mercator's Map of Cyprus, 1554.

1969. 1st Int. Congress of Cypriot Studies.

329. 70. 35 m. multicoloured .. 25 25
330. – 50 m. multicoloured .. 25 25

DESIGN: 50 m. Blaeu's map of Cyprus.

71. Colonnade.

1969. Europa.

331. 71. 20 m. multicoloured .. 10 10
332. 30 m. multicoloured .. 20 20
333. 150 m. multicoloured .. 65 65

72. Roller.

1969. Birds of Cyprus. Multicoloured.

334. 5 m. Type **72** 8 8
335. 15 m. Audouin's Gull .. 10 10
336. 20 m. Cyprus Warbler .. 12 12
337. 30 m. Cyprus Jay 20 20
338. 40 m. Hoopoe 25 25
339. 90 m. Eleonora's Falcon .. 80 80

Nos. 337/339 are vert.

73. "The Nativity" (14th Century Wall Painting).

1969. Christmas. Multicoloured.

340. 20 m. "The Nativity" (12th Cent. Wall Painting) 15 15
341. 45 m. Type **73** 40 40

74. Mahatma Gandhi.

1970. Mahatma Gandhi. Birth Cent.

343. 74. 25 m. blue, drab & black 12 12
344. 75 m. brown, drab & blk. 45 45

75. "Flaming Sun".

1970. Europa.

345. 75. 20 m. brown, yell. & orge. 10 10
346. 30 m. blue, yell. & orge. 25 25
347. 150 m. pur., yell. & orge. 65 65

76. Gladioli.

1970. Nature Conservation Year. Multicoloured.

348. 10 m. Type **76** 5 5
349. 50 m. Poppies 25 25
350. 90 m. Giant Fennel .. 55 55

77. I.E.Y. Emblem. **78.** Virgin and Child.

1970. International Events.

351. **77.** 5 m. black and brown .. 5 5
352. – 15 m. multicoloured .. 8 8
353. – 75 m. multicoloured 35 35

DESIGNS AND EVENTS: 5 m. Int. Education Year. 15 m. Mosaic (50th General Assembly of Int. Vine and Wine Office). 75 m. Globe, Dove and U.N. Emblem (United Nations 25th Anniv.).

1970. Christmas. Multicoloured.

354. 25 m. Archangel (facing right) 12 12
355. 25 m. Type **78** 12 12
356. 25 m. Archangel (facing left) 12 12
357. 75 m. Virgin and Child between Archangels (42 × 30 mm.) 45 45

79. Cotton Napkin.

1971. Multicoloured.

358. 3 m. Type **79** 5 5
359. 5 m. St. George and Dragon (19th-cent. bas-relief) .. 5 5
360. 10 m. Woman in festival costume 5 5
361. 15 m. Archaic Bychrome Kylix (cup) (horiz.) .. 5 5
362. 20 m. A pair of Donors, Church of St. Mamas .. 8 5
363. 25 m. "The Creation" (6th-cent. mosaic) .. 8 10
364. 30 m. Athena and Horse-drawn Chariot (5th-cent. B.C. terracotta) (horiz.) .. 8 5
365. 40 m. Shepherd playing pipe (14th-cent. fresco) .. 12 15
366. 50 m. Hellenistic bust (3rd-cent. B.C.) 15 20
367. 75 m. Detail of Apse Mosaic 25 25
368. 90 m. Mycenaean silver bowl (horiz.) 30 30
369. 250 m. Moufflon (detail of 3rd-cent. mosaic) (horiz.) 75 80
370. 500 m. Ladies and Sacred Tree (detail of 6th-cent. amphora) (horiz.) .. 1·40 1·60
371. £1 Horned God from Enkomi (12th-cent. bronze statue) 2·75 3·00

SIZES: 24 × 37 or 37 × 24 10 m. to 90 m. 41 × 28 or 28 × 41 250 m. to £1.

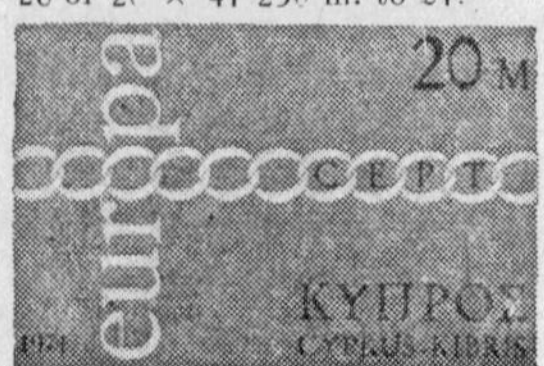

80. Europa Chain.

1971. Europa.

372. **80.** 20 m. blue, ultram. & blk. 12 12
373. 30 m. grn., myrtle-grn. and black 20 20
374. 150 m. yell., grn. & blk. 65 65

81. Archbishop Kyprianos.

1971. Greek War of Independence. 150th Anniv. Multicoloured.

375. 15 m. Type **81** 8 8
376. 30 m. "Taking the Oath" (horiz.) 20 20
377. 100 m. Bishop Paleon Patron Germanos, flag and freedom-fighters .. 50 50

82. Harbour Castle.

1971. Tourism. Multicoloured.

378. 15 m. Type **82** 8 8
379. 25 m. Gourd on sunny beach (vert.) 10 10
380. 60 m. Mountain scenery (vert.) 35 35
381. 100 m. Church and blue sky 50 50

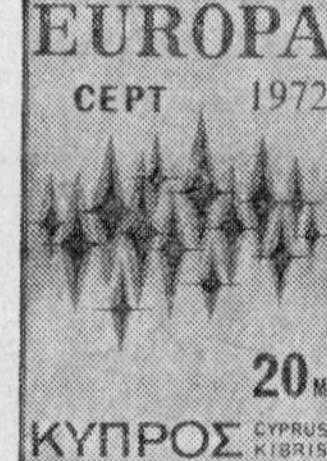

83. Madonna and Child in Stable. **85.** "Communications".

84. Heart.

1971. Christmas. Multicoloured.

382. 10 m. Type **83** 8 8
383. 50 m. The Three Wise Men 25 25
384. 100 m. The Shepherds .. 50 50

The 50, 10 and 100 m. (in that order) were printed horizontally se-tenant within each sheet.

1972. World Heart Month.

385. **84.** 15 m. multicoloured .. 8 8
386. 50 m. multicoloured .. 25 25

1972. Europa.

387. **85.** 20 m. orange, brown and grey-brown 5 5
388. 30 m. orge., ultram. & bl. 10 10
389. 150 m. orge., myrtle & grn. 55 55

86. Archery.

1972. Olympic Games. Multicoloured.

390. 10 m. Type **86** 5 5
391. 40 m. Wrestling 15 15
392. 100m. Football 45 45

87. Stater of Marion.

1972. Ancient Coins of Cyprus.

393. **87.** 20 m. blue, blk. & silver 5 5
394. – 30 m. blue, blk. & silver 15 15
395. – 40 m. brn., blk. & silver 20 20
396. – 100 m. pink, blk. & silver 60 60

COINS: 30 m. Stater of Pahhos. 40 m. Stater of Lapithos. 100 m. Stater of Idalion.

88. Bathing the Child Jesus.

1972. Christmas. Detail of mural in Holy Cross Church, Agiasmati. Multicoloured.

397. 10 m. Type **88** 5 5
398. 20 m. the Magi 8 8
399. 100 m. The Nativity .. 45 45

89. Snow-covered Landscape.

1973. 29th Int. Ski Federation Congress. Multicoloured.

401. 20 m. Type **89** 5 5
402. 100 m. Congress emblem .. 45 45

90. Europa "Posthorn".

1973. Europa.

403. **90.** 20 m. multicoloured .. 5 5
404. 30 m. multicoloured .. 8 8
405. 150 m. multicoloured .. 55 55

91. Archbishopric Palace, Nicosia.

1973. Traditional Architecture. Multicoloured.

406. 20 m. Type **91** 5 5
407. 30 m. Konak of Hajigeorgajis Cornessios, Nicosia (vert.) 10 10
408. 50 m. House at Gourri, 1850 (vert.) 20 20
409. 100 m. House at Rizokarpaso, 1772 .. .. 45 45

1973. No. 361 surch.

410. 20 m. on 15 m. multicoloured 12 12

MINIMUM PRICE

The minimum price quoted is 5p which represents a handling charge rather than a basis for valuing common stamps. For further notes about prices see introductory pages.

92. Scout Emblem.

1973. Anniversaries.

411. **92.** 10 m. green and brown 8 8
412. – 25 m. blue and lilac .. 10 10
413. – 35 m. grn., cream & grn. 12 12
414. – 50 m. blue and indigo .. 20 20
415. – 100 m. brown & sepia .. 50 50

DESIGNS AND EVENTS—VERT. 10 m. (Cyprus Boy Scouts. 60th anniv.). 50 m. Airline emblem (Cyprus Airways. 25th anniv.). 100 m. Interpol emblem (Interpol. 50th anniv.). HORIZ. 25 m. Outlines of Cyprus and the E.E.C. (Association of Cyprus with "Common Market"). 35 m. F.A.O. emblem (F.A.O. 10th anniv.).

93. Archangel Gabriel.

1973. Christmas. Multicoloured.

416. 10 m. Type **93** 5 5
417. 20 m. Madonna and Child 5 5
418. 100 m. Arakas Church (horiz.) 45 45

94. Grapes. **95.** "The Rape of Europa" (Silver Stater of Marion).

1974. Products of Cyprus. Multicoloured.

419. 25 m. Type **94** 8 10
420. 50 m. Grapefruit .. 25 25
421. 50 m. Oranges 25 25
422. 50 m. Lemons 25 25

1974. Europa.

423. **95.** 10 m. multicoloured .. 5 5
424. 40 m. multicoloured .. 15 15
425. 150 m. multicoloured .. 40 45

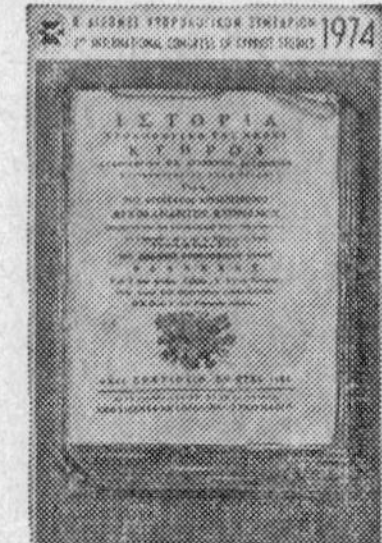

96. Title Page of A. Kyprianos' "History of Cyprus" (1788).

1974. Second Int. Congress of Cypriot Studies. Multicoloured.

426. 10 m. Type **96** 5 5
427. 25 m. Solon (philosopher) in mosaic (horiz.) .. 10 10
428. 100 m. "St. Neophytos" (wall painting) 35 35

1974. Obligatory Tax. Refugee Fund. No. 359 surch. **REFUGEE FUND** in English, Greek and Turkish.

430. 10 m. on 5 m. multicoloured 8 8

1974. U.N. Security Council Resolution 353. Nos. 360, 365, 366 and 369 optd. with **SECURITY COUNCIL RESOLUTION 353 20 JULY 1974.**

431. 10 m. multicoloured .. 5 5
432. 40 m. multicoloured .. 12 10
433. 50 m. multicoloured .. 12 15
434. 250 m. multicoloured .. 70 75

97. " Refugees ".

1974. Obligatory Tax. Refugee Fund.

435. **97.** 10 m. black and grey 8 8

98. " Virgin and Child between Two Archangels ".

1974. Christmas. Church Wall-paintings. Multicoloured.

436. 10 m. Type **98** 5 5
437. 50 m. " Adoration of the Magi " (vert.) 15 15
438. 100 m. " Flight to Egypt " 25 30

99. First Cyprus Mail-coach.

1975. International Events.

439. **99.** 20 m. multicoloured .. 5 5
440. – 30 m. blue and orange .. 8 8
441. **99.** 50 m. multicoloured .. 15 15
442. – 100 m. multicoloured .. 30 30

DESIGNS AND EVENTS—HORIZ. 20 m., 50 m. Universal Postal Union. Cent. VERT. 30 m. " Disabled Persons " (Eighth European Meeting of International Society for the Rehabilitation of Disabled Persons). 100 m. Council flag (Council of Europe. 25th anniv.).

100. " The Distaff " (M. Kashalos).

1975. Europa. Multicoloured.

443. 20 m. Type **100** 5 5
444. 30 m. " Nature Morte " (C. Savva) 8 8
445. 150 m. " Virgin and Child of Liopetri " (G. P. Georghiou) 45 50

101. Red Cross Flag over Map.

1975. International Events. Multicoloured.

446. 25 m. Type **101** 5 5
447. 30 m. Nurse and Lamp (horiz.) 8 8
448. 75 m. Woman's Steatite idol (horiz.) .. 20 25

EVENTS: 25 m. 25th anniv. of Red Cross. 30 m. International Nurses' Day. 75 m. International Women's Year.

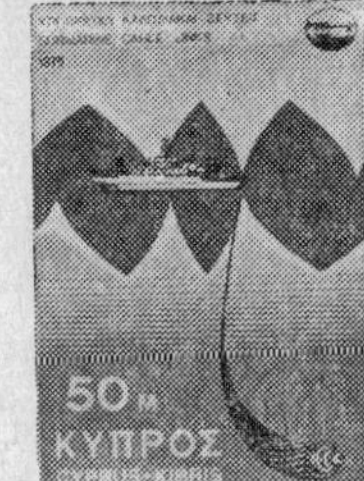

102. Submarine Cable Links.

1976. Telecommunications Achievements.

449. **102.** 50 m. multicoloured .. 15 20
450. – 100 m. yell., vio. & lilac 30 35

DESIGN—HORIZ. 100 m. International subscriber dialling.

1976. Surch.

451. **79.** 10 m. on 3 m. mult. .. 5 5

103. Human-figured Vessel, 19th-Century.

1976. Europa. Multicoloured.

452. 20 m. Type **103** 5 5
453. 60 m. Composite vessel, 2100–2000 B.C. .. 15 20
454. 100 m. Byzantine goblet .. 30 35

104. Self-help housing.

1976. Economic Reactivation. Mult.

455. 10 m. Type **104** 5 5
456. 25 m. Handicrafts .. 8 8
457. 30 m. Reafforestation .. 8 10
458. 60 m. Air Communications 15 20

105. Terracotta Statue. **106.** Olympic Symbol.

1976. Cypriot Treasures.

459. **105.** 5 m. multicoloured .. 5 5
460. – 10 m. multicoloured .. 5 5
461. – 20 m. red, yell., & blk. 5 5
462. – 25 m. multicoloured .. 5 8
463. 30 m. multicoloured .. 8 8
464. – 40 m. grn., brn. & blk. 10 10
465. – 50 m. light brown, brown and black .. 12 12
466. – 60 m. multicoloured .. 15 20
467. – 100 m. multicoloured 25 30
468. – 250 m. blue, grey & blk. 60 65
469. – 500 m. blk., brn. & grn. 1·25 1·40
470. – £1 multicoloured .. 2·50 2·75

DESIGNS—VERT. 10 m. Limestone head (23 × 34 mm.). 20 m. Gold necklace (24 × 37 mm.). 25 m. Terracotta warrior (24 × 37 mm.). 30 m. Statue of a priest (24 × 37 mm.). 250 m Silver dish (28 × 41 mm.). 500 m. Bronze stand (28 × 41 mm.). £1 Statue of Artemis (28 × 41 mm.). HORIZ. 40 m. Bronze tablet (37 × 24 mm.). 50 m. Mycenaean crater (37 × 24 m..). 60 m. Limestone sarcophagus (37 × 24 mm.). 100 m. Gold bracelet (As T **105**).

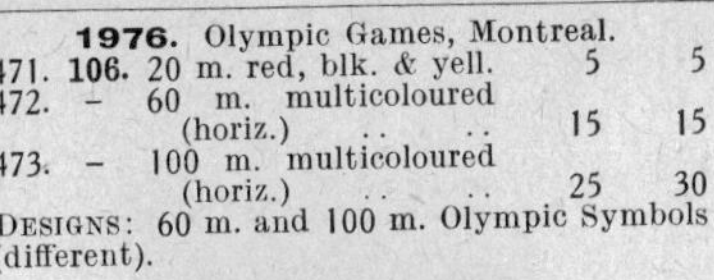

1976. Olympic Games, Montreal.

471. **106.** 20 m. red, blk. & yell. 5 5
472. – 60 m. multicoloured (horiz.) 15 15
473. – 100 m. multicoloured (horiz.) 25 30

DESIGNS: 60 m. and 100 m. Olympic Symbols (different).

107. George Washington.

1976. American Revolution. Bicent.

474. **107.** 100 m. multicoloured 25 30

108. Children in Library.

1976. International Events.

475. **108.** 40 m. multicoloured .. 12 12
476. – 50 m. brown and black 15 20
477. – 80 m. multicoloured .

DESIGNS AND EVENTS: 40 m. Type 108 (Promotion of Children's Books). 50 m. Low-cost housing (HABITAT Conference, Vancouver). 80 m. Eye protected by hands (World Health Day).

109. Archangel Michael.

1976. Christmas. Multicoloured.

478. 10 m. Type **109** 5 5
479. 15 m. Archangel Gabriel .. 5 5
480. 150 m. The Nativity .. 45 50

Designs show icons from Ayios Neophytis Monastry.

TURKISH CYPRIOT POSTS

After the inter-communal clashes during December, 1963, a separate postal service was established on 6th January, 1964, between some of the Turkish Cypriot areas, using handstamps inscribed " KIBRIS TURK POSTALARI ". During 1964, however, an agreement was reached between representatives of the two communities for the restoration of postal services. This agreement, to which the United Nations representatives were a party, was ratified in November 1966 by the Republic's Council of Ministers. Under the scheme postal services were provided for the Turkish Cypriot communities in Famagusta, Limassol, Lefka and Nicosia, staffed by Turkish Cypriot employees of the Cypriot Department of Posts.

On 8th April, 1970, 5 m. and 15 m. locally-produced labels, originally designated " Social Aid Stamps ", were issued by the Turkish Cypriot community and these can be found on commercial covers. These local stamps are outside the scope of this catalogue.

On 29th October, 1973 Nos. 1/7 were placed on sale, but were again used only on mail between the Turkish Cypriot areas.

Following the intervention by the Republic of Turkey in July 1974 these stamps replaced issues of the Republic of Cyprus in that part of the island, north and east of the Attila Line, controlled by the Autonomous Turkish Cypriot Administration.

1. 50th Anniversary Emblem.

1974. Republic of Turkey. 50th Anniv.

1. – 3 m. multicoloured ..
2. – 5 m. multicoloured ..
3. – 10 m. multicoloured ..
4. **1.** 15 m. red and black ..
5. – 20 m. multicoloured ..
6. – 50 m. multicoloured ..
7. – 70 m. multicoloured ..

1/7, Set of 7 .. .. .. 45·00 45·00

DESIGNS—VERT. 3 m. Woman sentry. 10 m. Man and woman with Turkish flags. 20 m. Ataturk statue, Kyrenia Gate, Nicosia. 50 m. " The Fallen ". HORIZ. 5 m. Military parade, Nicosia. 70 m. Turkish flag and map of Cyprus.

These were first issued in 1973 for local use.

1975. Proclamation of the Turkish Federated State of Cyprus. Nos. 3 and 5 surch. **KIBRIS TURK FEDERE DEVLETI 13.2.1975.**

8. 30 m. on 20 m. multicoloured 1·40 1·60
9. 100 m. on 10 m. multicoloured 5·00 5·50

2. Namik Kemal's Bust, Famagusta.

1975. Multicoloured.

10. 3 m. Type **2** 5 5
11. 10 m. Ataturk Statue, Nicosia 5 5
12. 15 m. St. Hilarion Castle .. 5 8
13. 20 m. Ataturk Square, Nicosia 10 12
14. 25 m. Famagusta Beach .. 10 12
15. 30 m. Kyrenia Harbour .. 15 20
16. 50 m. Lala Mustafa Pasha Mosque, Famagusta (vert.) 20 25
17. 100 m. Interior, Kyrenia Castle 35 40
18. 250 m. Castle walls, Kyrenia 85 95
19. 500 m. Othello Tower, Famagusta (vert.) .. 1·75 2·00

See also Nos. 37, etc.

3. Map of Cyprus.

1975. " Peace in Cyprus ". Multicoloured.

20. 30 m. Type **3** 8 8
21. 50 m. Map, laurel and broken chain 12 15
22. 150 m. Map and laurel-sprig on globe (vert.) 40 45

4. " Pomegranates " (I. V. Guney).

1975. Europa. Paintings. Multicoloured.

23. 90 m. Type **4** 20 20
24. 100 m. " Harvest Time " (F Direkoglu) 25 25

1976. Nos. 16/17 surch.

25. 10 m. on 50 m. multicoloured 1·25 1·25
26. 30 m. on 100 m. multicoloured .. .. .. 3·75 3·75

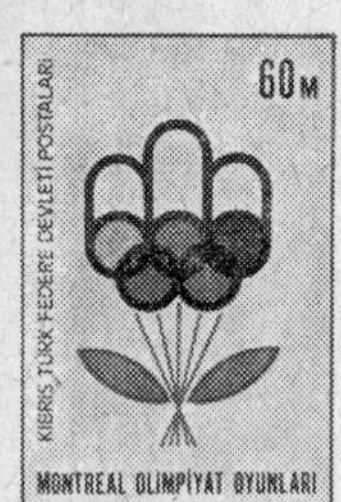

5. " Expectation " (ceramic statuette). 7. Olympic Symbol " Flower ".

6. Carob.

1976. Europa. Multicoloured.
27. 60 m. Type 5 .. .. 15 20
28. 120 m. " Man in Meditation " 35 40

1976. Export Products. Fruits. Mult.
29. 10 m. Type 6 .. .. 8 10
30. 25 m. Mandarin 15 20
31. 40 m. Strawberry 20 25
32. 60 m. Orange 30 35
33. 80 m. Lemon 40 45

1976. Olympic Games, Montreal. Mult.
45. 60 m. Type 7 .. .. 15 20
35. 100 m. Olympic symbol and doves 25 25

8. Kyrenia Harbour.

1976. Multicoloured.
37. 5 m. Type 8 .. .. 5 5
38. 15 m. St. Hilarion Castle.. 5 5
39. 20 m. Ataturk Square, Nicosia 5 5

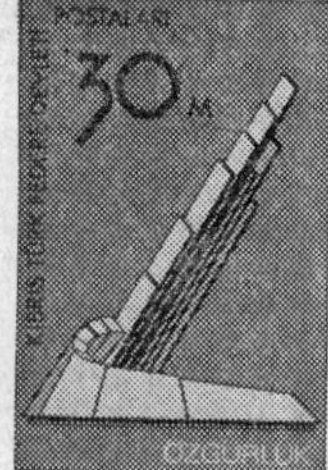

9. Liberation Monument, Nicosia.

1976. Liberation Monument.
47. **9.** 30 m. blue, pink and black 8 10
48. – 150 m. red, pink and black 30 35
DESIGN: 150 m. Liberation Monument (different view).

CYRENAICA O3

Part of the former Italian colony of Libya, N. Africa. Allied Occupation, 1942-49. Independent Administration, 1949-52. Then part of independent Libya.

Stamps optd. **BENGASI** formerly listed here will be found under Italian P.Os. in the Levant, Nos. 169/70.

Stamps of Italy optd. **CIRENAICA.**

1923. Propagation of the Faith Tercentenary.
1. **44.** 20 c. orange and green.. 90 1·50
2. 30 c. orange and red .. 90 1·50
3. 50 c. orange and violet.. 70 1·25
4. 1 l. orange and blue .. 70 1·25

1923. Fascist March on Rome stamps.
5. **45.** 10 c. green 20 35
6. 30 c. violet 25 40
7. 50 c. red 30 50
8. **46.** 1 l. blue 30 60
9. 2 l. brown 35 70
10. **47.** 5 l. black and blue .. 1·50 2·10

1924. Manzoni stamps (Nos. 155/60).
11. **49.** 10 c. black and red 25 45
12. – 15 c. black and green .. 25 45
13. – 30 c. black 25 45
14. – 50 c. black and brown .. 25 45
15. – 1 l. black and blue .. 6·50 9·00
16. – 5 l. black and purple .. 90·00 £110

1925. Holy Year stamps.
17. – 20 c.+10 c. brown & grn. 20 35
18. **51.** 30 c.+15 c. brn. & choc. 20 35
19. – 50 c.+25 c. brn. & violet 20 35
20. – 60 c.+30 c. brown & red 20 35
21. – 1 l.+50 c. purple & blue 35 55
22. – 5 l.+2 l. 50 purple & red 55 90

1925. Royal Jubilee stamps.
23. **53.** 60 c. red 10 20
24. 1 l. blue 10 20
24a. 1 l. 25 blue 30 60

1926. St. Francis of Assisi stamps.
25. **54.** 20 c. green 20 20
26. – 40 c. violet 20 30
27. – 60 c. red 20 30
28. – 1 l. 25 blue 20 30
29. – 5 l.+2 l. 50 olive (as No. 196) .. .. 70 1·10

1. 2.

1926. Colonial Propaganda.
30. **1.** 5 c.+5 c. brown.. .. 8 12
31. 10 c.+5 c. olive.. .. 8 12
32. 20 c.+5 c. green .. 8 12
33. 40 c.+5 c. red 8 12
34. 60 c.+5 c. orange .. 8 12
35. 1 l.+5 c. blue 8 12

1927. First National Defence stamps optd. **CIRENAICA.**
36. **60.** 40+20 c. black & brown 25 55
37. – 60+30 c. brown and red 30 55
38. – 1 l. 25+60 c. black & blue 35 70
39. – 5 l.+2 l. 50 black & green 70 1·10

1927. Volta Centenary stamps optd. **Cirenaica.**
40. **61.** 20 c. violet .. .. 3·25 3·00
41. 50 c. orange 20 20
42. 1 l. 25 blue 70 90

1928. 45th Anniv. of Italian-African Society.
43. **2.** 20 c.+5 c. green .. 15 35
44. 30 c.+5 c. red 15 35
45. 50 c.+10 c. violet .. 15 35
46. 1 l. 25+20 c. blue .. 15 35

Stamps of Italy optd. **CIRENAICA.** Colours changed in some instances.

1929. Second National Defence stamps.
47. **60.** 30 c.+10 c. black and red 25 40
48. – 50 c.+20 c. black & lilac 25 40
49. – 1 l. 25+50 c. bl. & brown 45 70
50. – 5 l.+2 l. black and olive 45 90

1929. Montecassino stamps.
51. **75.** 20 c. green 20 35
52. – 25 c. orange 20 35
53. – 50 c.+10 c. red 25 45
54. – 75 c.+15 c. brown .. 25 60
55. **75.** 1 l. 25+25 c. purple .. 1·10 1·40
56. – 5 l.+1 l. blue .. .. 1·10 1·75
57. – 10 l.+2 l. brown .. 1·10 2·00

1930. Marriage of Prince Humbert and Princess Marie Jose stamps. (optd. **Cirenaica**).
58. **80.** 20 c. green 15 25
59. 50 c.+10 c. orange .. 25 40
60. 1 l. 25+25 c. red .. 45 70

1930. Ferrucci stamps (optd. **Cirenaica**).
61. **85.** 20 c. violet 15 15
62. – 25 c. green 15 15
63. – 50 c. black 15 15
64. – 1 l. 25 blue 15 15
65. – 5 l.+2 l. red .. .. 90 1·00

1930. Third National Defence stamps.
66. **60.** 30 c.+10 c. green & olive 40 55
67. 50 c.+10 c. violet & olive 35 50
68. 1 l. 25+30 c. brown .. 70 1·00
69. 5 l.+1 l. 50 green & blue 5·00 7·00

3.

5.

1930. Italian Colonial Agricultural Institute. 25th Anniv. (1929).
70. **3.** 50 c.+20 c. brown .. 25 35
71. 1 l. 25+20 c. blue .. 25 35
72. 1 l. 75+20 c. green .. 25 35
73. 2 l. 55+50 c. violet .. 90 1·10
74. 5 l.+1 l. red .. .. 90 1·10

1930. Virgil Bimillenary stamps.
75. **89.** 15 c. violet 5 10
76. 20 c. brown 5 10
77. 25 c. green 5 10
78. 30 c. brown 5 10
79. 50 c. purple 5 10
80. 75 c. red 5 10
81. 1 l. 25 blue 5 10
82. 5 l.+1 l. 50 purple .. 65 1·00
83. 10 l.+2 l. 50 brown .. 65 1·25

1931. St. Anthony of Padua stamps.
84. **92.** 20 c. brown 12 20
85. – 25 c. green 12 20
86. – 30 c. brown 12 20
87. – 50 c. violet 12 20
88. – 75 c. grey (as No. 308) 12 20
89. – 1 l. 25 blue 12 20
90. – 5 l.+2 l. 50 brown (as No. 310) .. .. 1·00 1·75

1932. Air stamps of Tripolitania optd. **Cirenaica.**
91. **5.** 50 c. red 15 10
92. 60 c. orange 25 25
93. 80 c. purple 30 55

1932. Air stamps of Tripolitania of 1931 optd. **CIRENAICA** and bars.
94. **5.** 50 c. red 15 8
95. 80 c. purple 25 40

1932. Air.
96. – 50 c. violet 25 45
97. – 75 c. red 20 25
98. – 80 c. blue 25 25
99. **5.** 1 l. black.. .. .. 20 8
100. 2 l. green.. .. .. 20 20
101. 5 l. red 50 45
DESIGN—VERT. 50 c. to 80 c. Arab on Camel.

6. "Graf Zeppelin".

DESIGNS: 5 l., 12 l. "Graf Zeppelin" and ancient galley. 10 l., 20 l. "Graf Zeppelin" and giant archer.

1933. Air. "Graf Zeppelin". Inscr. "CROCIERA ZEPPELIN".
102. **6.** 3 l. brown .. .. 3·25 7·00
103. – 5 l. violet .. .. 3·25 7·00
104. – 10 l. green .. .. 3·25 7·00
105. – 12 l. blue .. .. 3·25 7·00
106. **6.** 15 l. red .. .. 3·25 7·00
107. – 20 l. black .. .. 3·25 7·00

7. Air Squadron.

1933. Air. Balbo Transatlantic Mass Formation Flight.
108. **7.** 19 l. 75 blue and green .. 13·00 35·00
109. 44 l. 75 blue and red .. 13·00 35·00

1934. Air. Optd. with Aeroplane and **PRIMO VOLO DIRETTO ROMA-BUENOS-AYRES TRIMOTORE LOMBARDI MAZZOTTI** or surch. also.
110. **5.** 2 l. on 5 l. brown .. 1·25 3·50
111. 3 l. on 5 l. green .. 1·25 3·50
112. 5 l. brown .. .. 1·25 3·50
113. 10 l. on 5 l. red .. .. 1·25 3·50

8. Arab Horseman.

DESIGNS: 25 c. to 75 c. Arrival of Mail 'plane. 80 c. to 2 l. Aeroplane and Venus of Cyrene.

1934. 2nd Int. Colonial Exn., Naples.
114. **8.** 5 c. brn. and grn. (post) 45 1·10
115. 10 c. black and brown.. 45 1·10
116. 20 c. slate and red .. 45 1·10
117. 50 c. brown and violet.. 45 1·10
118. **8.** 60 c. slate and brown .. 45 1·10
119. 1 l. 25 green and blue .. 45 1·10
120. – 25 c. orange & blue (air) 45 1·10
121. – 50 c. slate and green .. 45 1·10
122. – 75 c. orange and brown.. 45 1·10
123. – 80 c. green and brown .. 45 1·10
124. – 1 l. green and red .. 45 1·10
125. – 2 l. grown and blue .. 45 1·10

9.

1934. Air. Rome—Mogadiscio Flight.
126. **9.** 25 c.+10 c. green .. 45 2·50
127. 50 c.+10 c. brown .. 45 2·50
128. 75 c.+15 c. red .. .. 45 2·50
129. 80 c.+15 c. brown .. 45 2·50
130. 1 l.+20 c. brown-red .. 45 2·50
131. 2 l.+20 c. blue .. .. 45 2·50
132. 3 l.+25 c. violet .. 10·00 14·00
133. 5 l.+25 c. orange .. 10·00 14·00
134. 10 l.+30 c. purple .. 10·00 14·00
135. 25 l.+2 l. green.. .. 10·00 14·00

10. Mounted Warrior. 11.

1950.
136. **10.** 1 m. brown 5 5
137. 2 m. red 5 5
138. 3 m. yellow 5 5
139. 4 m. green 40 50
140. 5 m. grey 8 8
141. 8 m. orange 10 10
142. 10 m. violet 12 12
143. 12 m. red 12 12
144. 20 m. blue 15 15
145. **11.** 50 m. blue and brown.. 70 90
146. 100 m. red and black .. 2·75 2·75
147. 200 m. violet and blue.. 4·25 4·25
148. 500 m. yellow and green 14·00 14·00

POSTAGE DUE STAMPS

D 1.

1950.
D 1. **D 1.** 2 m. brown .. .. 10·00 11·00
D 2. 4 m. green .. .. 10·00 11·00
D 3. 8 m. red .. .. 10·00 11·00
D 4. 10 m. orange .. .. 10·00 11·00
D 5. 20 m. yellow .. .. 10·00 11·00
D 6. 40 m. blue .. .. 10·00 11·00
D 7. 100 m. brown.. .. 10·00 11·00

CZECHOSLOVAKIA E1

Formerly part of Austrian Empire; became an independent Republic in 1918. Occupied by Germany in 1939. Independence restored 1944/5. See note after No. 393c.

100 haleru = 1 koruna.

1.

2. Hradcany, Prague.

1918. Scouts' Post. Roul.
1. **1.** 10 h. blue .. .. .. 10·00 10·00
2. 20 h. red .. .. .. 12·00 12·00

1918. (a) Imperf.
4. **2.** 3 h. mauve 5 5
9. 30 h. olive.. .. .. 10 5
10. 40 h. orange 10 5
12. 100 h. brown 30 5
14. 400 h. violet 75 8

(b) Imperf. or perf.
5a. 5 h. green 5 5
6. 10 h. red 5 5
7. 20 h. green 5 5
8. 25 h. blue 8 5
13. 200 h. blue 35 5

3.

ILLUSTRATIONS
British Commonwealth and all overprints and surcharges are FULL SIZE. Foreign Countries have been reduced to ¾-LINEAR.

1919. Imperf. or perf.
3. **3.** 1 h. brown 5 5
38. 5 h. green 5 5
39. 10 h. green 95 10
40. 15 h. red 5 5
41. 20 h. red .. .. .. 1·10 15
42. 25 h. purple 20 5
49. 30 h. mauve 5 5
11. 50 h. purple 15 5
30. 50 h. blue 10 5
50. 60 h. orange 30 5
32. 75 h. green 15 5
33. 80 h. olive 15 5
34. 120 h. black 45 5
35. 300 h. green .. .. 1·40 5
36. 500 h. brown .. .. 1·00 5
37. 1000 h. purple .. .. 2·75 30

4. **5.**

1919. Czechoslovak Legion and 1st Anniv. of Independence. Perf.
61. **4.** 15 h. green 5 5
62. 25 h. brown 5 5
63. 50 h. blue 5 5
64. **5.** 75 h. black 5 5
65. 100 h. purple 5 5
66. 120 h. violet on yellow 5 5

1919. Charity. Stamps of Austria optd. **POSTA CESKOSLOVENSKA 1919.**
A. Postage stamp issue of 1916.
67. **26.** 3 h. violet 5 5
68. 5 h. green 5 5
69. 6 h. orange 20 20
70. 10 h. claret 30 45
71. 12 h. blue 25 30
72. **30.** 15 h. red 5 5
73. 20 h. green 5 5
75. 25 h. blue 10 10
76. 30 h. violet 10 12
77. **28.** 40 h. olive 10 12
78. 50 h. green 8 10
79. 60 h. blue 12 15
80. 80 h. brown 8 10
81. 90 h. purple 25 30
82. 1 k. red on yellow .. 15 20
83a.**29.** 2 k. blue .. .. .. 1·00 1·00
85aa. 3 k. red .. .. .. 3·50 3·25
87a. 4 k. green .. .. 4·00 3·50
89a. 10 k. violet £120 £110

B. Air stamps of 1918 optd. **FLUGPOST** or surch. also.
91. **29.** 1 k. 50 on 2 k. mauve .. 80·00 75·00
92. 2 k. 50 on 3 k. yellow .. 80·00 75·00
93. 4 k. grey £300 £275

C. Newspaper stamp of 1908. Imperf.
94. N **8.** 10 h. red £700 £700

D. Newspaper stamps of 1916. Imperf.
95. N **9.** 2 h. brown 5 5
96. 4 h. green 12 15
97. 6 h. blue 10 10
98. 10 h. orange .. .. 1·75 1·75
99. 30 h. claret 65 75

E. Express Newspaper stamps of 1916.
100. N **10.** 2 h. red on yellow .. 9·00 7·00
101. 5 h. green on yellow £425 £400

F. Express Newspaper stamps of 1917.
102. N **11.** 2 h. red on yellow .. 5 5
103. 5 h. green on yellow 5 8

G. Postage Due stamps of 1908.
104. D **2.** 2 h. red £1200 £1100
105. 4 h. red .. .. 7·00 7·00
106. 6 h. red .. .. 3·25 3·50
108. 14 h. red .. .. 20·00 21·00
109. 25 h. red .. .. 16·00 14·00
110. 30 h. red £140 £140
111. 50 h. red £375 £375

H. Postage Due stamps of 1916.
112. D **3.** 5 h. red 5 10
113. 10 h. red 8 10
114. 15 h. red 5 10
115. 20 h. red 80 80
116. 25 h. red 50 50
117. 30 h. red 20 30
118. 40 h. red 60 70
119. 50 h. red £140 £140
120. D **4.** 1 k. blue .. .. 3·00 3·25
121. 5 k. blue .. .. 17·00 17·00
122. 10 k. blue £140 £150

I. Postage Due stamps of 1916 (optd. **PORTO** or surch. **15** also).
123. **18.** 1 h. black .. .. 6·50 7·00
124. – 15 h. on 2 h. violet .. 55·00 55·00

J. Postage Due stamps of 1917 (surch. **PORTO** and value.)
125. **27.** 10 h. on 24 h. blue .. 42·00 40·00
126. 15 h. on 36 h. violet .. 30 30
127. 20 h. on 54 h. orange .. 42·00 40·00
128. 50 h. on 42 h brown .. 40 40

1919. Various stamps of Hungary optd. **POSTA CESKOSLOVENSKA 1919.**
A. Postage stamp issue of 1900 ("Turul" type).
129. **3.** 1 f. grey £600 £600
130. 2 f. yellow .. .. 1·40 1·40
131. 3 f. orange .. .. 12·00 14·00
132. 6 f. olive .. .. 1·75 1·90
133. 50 f. lake on blue .. 35 40
134. 60 f. green on red .. 12·00 14·00
135. 70 f. brown on green £500 £500

B. Postage stamp issue of 1916 ("Harvester" and "Parliament" types).
136. **11.** 2 f. brown (No. 245) .. 5 5
137. 3 f. claret 5 5
138. 5 f. green 5 5
139. 6 f. blue 25 30
140. 10 f. red (No. 250) .. 90 90
141. 10 f. red (No. 243) .. £110 £100
142. 15 f. violet (No. 251) .. 8 10
143. 15 f. violet (No. 244) .. 45·00 45·00
144. 20 f. brown .. .. 2·75 2·50
145. 25 f. blue 30 40
146. 35 f. brown .. .. 2·75 2·50
147. 40 f. olive 85 85
148. **12.** 50 f. purple 45 45
149. 75 f. blue 35 35
150. 80 f. green 60 60
151. 1 k. lake 80 80
152. 2 k. brown .. .. 2·75 3·25
153. 3 k. grey and violet .. 17·00 17·00
154. 5 k. brown .. .. 45·00 45·00
155. 10 k. lilac and brown .. £375 £375

C. Postage stamp issue of 1918 ("Karl" and "Zita" types).
156. **13.** 10 f. red 5 5
157. 20 f. brown 8 8
158. 25 f. blue 35 35
159. **14.** 40 f. olive 95 95
160. 50 f. purple .. .. 14·00 15·00

D. War Charity stamps of 1916.
161. **6.** 10+2 f. red 35 35
162. – 15+2 f. violet (No. 265) 45 45
163. **8.** 40+2 f. lake .. .. 1 75 1·75

E. Postage stamps of 1919 ("Harvester" type inscr. "MAGYAR POSTA").
164. **11.** 10 f. red (No. 305) .. 3·50 3·50
165. 20 f. brown £1400 £1400

F. Newspaper stamp of 1900.
166. N **3.** 2 f. orange (No. N 136) 5 5

G. Express Letter stamp of 1916.
167. E **1.** 2 f. olive & red (No. E 245) 5 5

H. Postage Due stamps of 1903 with figures in black.
170. D **1.** 1 f. green (No. D 170) £225 £225
173. 2 f. green £140 £140
174. 5 f. green £300 £300
168. 12 f green £1200 £1200
172. 50 f. green .. .. 90·00 90·00

I. Postage Due Stamps of 1915 with figures in red.
176. D **1.** 1 f. green (No. D 190) 80·00 75·00
177. 2 f. green 40 40
178. 5 f. green .. .. 4·50 4·25
179. 6 f. green 85 85
180. 10 f. green 25 25
181. 12 f. green .. .. 1·25 1·25
182. 15 f. green .. .. 3·00 3·00
183. 20 f. green 55 55
184. 30 f. green .. .. 17·00 17·00

6. President Masaryk. **7.** **8.** Allegories of Republic.

9. Hussite. **10.**

1920.
185. **6.** 125 h. blue 60 8
186. 500 h. black .. .. 2·50 1·00
187. 1,000 h. brown .. .. 5·50 2·50

1920.
188. **7.** 5 h. blue 5 5
189. 5 h. violet 5 5
190. 10 h. green 5 5
191. 10 h. olive 5 5
192. 15 h. brown 5 5
196. **8.** 20 h. red 5 5
193b. **7.** 20 h. orange 5 5
197. **8.** 25 h. brown 5 5
194a. **7.** 25 h. green 10 5
198. **8.** 30 h. purple 5 5
195. **7.** 30 h. purple .. .. 1·40 5
199. **8.** 40 h. brown 8 5
200. 50 h. red 10 5
201. 50 h. green 8 5
202. 60 h. blue 10 5
203. **9.** 80 h. violet 12 8
204. 90 h. sepia 20 20
205. **10.** 100 h. green 30 5
206. **8.** 100 h. brown 25 5
227. **10.** 100 h. red on yellow .. 90 5
207. **8.** 150 h. red .. .. 2·50 45
208. 185 h. orange 60 10
209. **10.** 200 h. purple 45 5
228. 200 h. blue on yellow .. 4·00 5
210. **8.** 250 h. green .. .. 2·75 12
211. **10.** 300 h. red .. .. 1·25 5
229. 300 h. purple on yellow 2·25 5
212. 400 h. brown .. .. 4·25 30
213. 500 h. green .. .. 4·00 25
214. 600 h. purple .. .. 5·00 25

1920. Air. Surch with aeroplane and value. Imperf. or perf.
215. **2.** 14 k. on 200 h. blue (No. 13) .. .. 13·00 12·00
216. **3.** 24 k. on 500 h. brown (No. 36) .. .. 27·00 25·00
217. 28 k. on 1,000 h. purple (No. 37) .. .. 25·00 25·00

1920. Red Cross Fund. Surch. with new value, etc.
221. **2.** 40 h.+20 h. yellow .. 60 60
222. **3.** 60 h.+20 h. green .. 60 60
223. **6.** 125 h.+25 h. blue .. 1·60 1·60

1922. Air. Surch. with aeroplane and value.
224. **10.** 50 on 100 h. green .. 1·25 1·25
225. 100 on 200 h. purple .. 1·90 1·90
226. 250 on 400 h. brown .. 4·25 4·25

11. President Masaryk. **12.** **13.**

1923. Republic. 5th Anniv.
230. **11.** 50 h. (+50 h.) green .. 50 35
231. 100 h. (+100 h.) red .. 65 40
232. 200 h. (+200 h.) blue .. 3·50 3·00
233. 300 h. (+300 h.) brown 3·25 2·40

1925.
234. **12.** 40 h. orange 70 5
235. 50 h. green .. .. 1·10 5
236. 60 h. purple .. .. 1·25 5
244c.**11.** 1 k. red 65 5
238. 2 k. blue .. .. 1·60 10
245. 3 k. brown .. .. 3·00 5
240. 5 k. green .. .. 1·10 20
The 1, 2 and 3 k. (which with the 5 k. differ slightly in design from the haleru values) come in various sizes, differing in some cases in the details of the designs.

1925. Int. Olympic Congress. Optd. **CONGRES OLYMP. INTERNAT. PRAHA 1925.**
246. **11.** 50 h. (+50 h.) green .. 10·00 8·00
247. 100 h (+100 h.) red .. 12·00 10·00
248. 200 h. (+200 h.) blue .. 85·00 80·00

1926.
254b. **13.** 50 h. green 10 5
254c. 60 h. purple 45 5
254d. 1 k. red 15 5

1926. 8th All-Sokol Display. Prague. Optd. **VIII SLET VSESOKOLSKY PRAHA 1926.**
249. **11.** 50 h. (+50 h.) green .. 4·50 3·75
250. 100 h. (+100 h.) red .. 4·75 3·75
251. 200 h. (+200 h.) blue .. 25·00 20·00
252. 300 h. (+300 h.) brown 40·00 30·00

14. Karluv Tyn Castle. **15.** Strahov. **16.** Pernstyn Castle.

17. Orava Castle. **18.** Hradcany, Prague.

1926. Perf or imperf. × perf.
255. **14.** 20 h. red 45 20
256. **16.** 30 h. green 25 5
258. **17.** 40 h. brown 30 5
259. **14.** 1 k. 20 purple 55 25
260. **15.** 1 k. 20 purple .. .. 3·25 1·00
261. **14.** 1 k. 50 red 40 5
270. **16.** 2 k. green 20 5
272. **18.** 2 k. blue 30 5
262. **14.** 2 k. 50 blue .. .. 2·10 20
273b. **17.** 3 k. brown 40 5
275. **18.** 3 k. red .. .. 1·40 5
265. – 4 k. purple } Upper 2·75 20
277. – 5 k. green } Tatra 4·25 30

20. Hradek Castle. **21.** Pres. Masaryk.

1928. Independence. 10th Anniv.
278. **20.** 30 h. black 5 5
279. – 40 h. red-brown .. 8 5
280. – 50 h. green 10 5
281. – 60 h. red 10 5
282. – 1 k. red 15 5
283. – 1 k. 20 purple 25 20
284. – 2 k. blue 35 10
285. – 2 k. 50 blue .. .. 1·00 75
286. **21.** 3 k. sepia .. .. 1·25 80
287. – 5 k. violet .. .. 1·25 80

DESIGNS—HORIZ. 40 h. Town Hall, Levoca. 50 h. Telephone Exchange, Prague. 60 h. Village of Jasina. 1 k. Hluboka Castle. 1 k. 20 Pilgrim's House, Velehrad. 2 k. 50 The Grand Tatra. VERT. 2 k. Brno Cathedral. 5 k. Town Hall, Prague.

22. National Arms. **23.** St. Wenceslas.

1929. Perf. or imperf. × perf.
287a.**22.** 5 h. blue 5 5
287b. 10 h. brown 5 5
288. 20 h. red 5 5
289. 25 h. green 5 5
290. 30 h. purple 5 5
291a. 40 h. brown 12 5

1929. St. Wenceslas. Death Millenary.
293. **23.** 50 h. green 10 5
294. – 60 h. violet 25 5
295. – 2 k. blue 60 20
296. – 3 k. brown 70 5
297. – 5 k. purple .. .. 3·50 1·25
DESIGNS: 2 k. Foundation of St. Vitus's Church. 3 k., 5 k. Martyrdom of St. Wenceslas.

24. Statue of St. Wenceslas, Prague. **25.** Brno Cathedral.

1929.
273a. **24.** 2 k. 50 blue 20 5

1929.
298. **25.** 3 k. brown .. .. 1·50 5
299. – 4 k. blue .. .. 3·50 35
300. – 5 k. green .. .. 4·00 20
301. – 10 k. violet .. .. 4·50 1·10
DESIGNS: 4 k. Tatra Mountains. 5 k. Town Hall, Prague. 10 k. St. Nicholas Church, Prague.

26. **27.**

1930. Perf. or imperf. × perf.
302a. **26.** 50 h. green 8 5
303. 60 h. purple 55 5
304. 1 k. red 12 5
See also No. 373.

1930. President Masaryk's 80th Birthday.
305. **27.** 2 k. green 45 12
306. 3 k. claret 70 12
307. 5 k. blue .. .. 2·25 45
308. 10 k. black .. .. 5·50 2·10

28. Fokker FVIII b. **29.** Smolik S 19.

1930. Air.
394. **28.** 30 h. violet 5 8
309. 50 h. green 5 5
310. 1 k. red 12 10
311. **29.** 2 k. green 35 20
312. 3 k. purple 70 65
313. – 4 k. blue 45 40
314. – 5 k. brown 85 65
315. – 10 k. blue .. .. 2·40 2·25
316a. – 20 k. violet .. .. 2·10 2·10
DESIGNS—HORIZ. as T **29.** 4 k., 5 k. Smolik S 19 with tree in foreground. 10 k., 20 k. Fokker F VIII b over Prague.

31. Krumlov. **32.** Dr. Miroslav Tyrs.

1932. Views.
317. – 3 k. 50 pur (Krivoklat) 90 50
318. – 4 k. blue (Orlik) .. 1·10 10
319. **31.** 5 k. green .. .. 1·25 10

1932. Dr. Tyrs. (founder of the "Sokol" Movement). Birth Cent.
320. **32.** 50 h. green 25 5
321. 1 k. red 40 5
322. – 2 k. blue .. .. 4·00 15
323. – 3 k. red-brown .. 7·50 15
On the 2 k. and 3 k. the portrait faces left.

34. Dr. M. Tyrs. **35.** Church and Episcopal Palace, Nitra.

1933.
324. **34.** 60 h. violet 8 5

1933. 1st Christian Church at Nitra. 1100th Anniv.
325. **35.** 50 h. green 25 5
326. – 1 k. red (Church gateway) .. .. .. 1·75 5

36. Frederick Smetana. **37.** Consecrating Colours at Kiev.

1934. Smetana. 50th Death Anniv.
327. **36.** 50 h. green 15 5

1934. Czechoslovak Foreign Legions. 20th Anniv.
328. **37.** 50 h. green 15 5
329. – 1 k. red 20 5
330. – 2 k. blue 90 12
331. – 3 k. brown .. .. 1·50 12
DESIGNS—HORIZ. 1 k, French battalion enrolling at Bayonne. VERT. 2 k. Standard of the Russian Legion. 3 k. French, Russian and Serbian legionaries.

39. Antonin Dvorak. **40.** "Where is my Fatherland?"

1934. Dvorak. 30th Death Anniv.
332. **39.** 50 h. green 15 5

1934. Czech National Anthem. Cent.
333. **40.** 1 k. purple 25 5
334. 2 k. blue 75 15

41. President Masaryk. **42.**

1935. President Masaryk's 85th Birthday.
335. **41.** 50 h. green 10 5
336. 1 k. red 20 5
337. **42.** 2 k. blue 55 15
338. 3 k. brown .. .. 1·25 20

43. Czech Monument Arras. **44.** Gen. M. R. Stefanik.

1935. Battle of Arras. 20th Anniv.
339. **43.** 1 k. red 30 5
340. 2 k. blue 75 15

1935. Gen. Stefanik. 16th Death Anniv.
341. **44.** 50 h. green 8 5

45. St. Cyril and St. Methodius. **46.** J. A. Komensky.

47. Dr. Bens. **48.** Gen. M.R. Stefanik. **49.** Pres. Masaryk.

1935. Prague Catholic Church.
342. **45.** 50 h. green 10 5
343. 1 k. claret 20 5
344. 2 k. blue 50 15

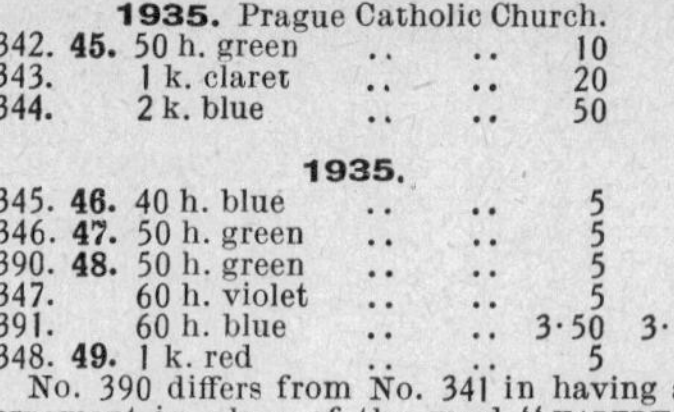

1935.
345. **46.** 40 h. blue 5 5
346. **47.** 50 h. green 5 5
390. **48.** 50 h. green 5 5
347. 60 h. violet 5 5
391. 60 h. blue .. .. 3·50 3·50
348. **49.** 1 k. red 5 5
No. 390 differs from No. 341 in having an ornament in place of the word "HALERU".

50. "Infancy". **51.** K. H. Macha.

1936. Child Welfare.
349. – 50 h.+50 h. green .. 25 20
350. **50.** 1 k.+50 h. claret .. 40 35
351. – 2 k.+50 h. blue .. 80 80
DESIGN: 50 h., 2 k. Grandfather, mother and child from centre of T **50** (enlarged).

1936. Macha (poet). Death Cent.
352. **51.** 50 h. green 8 5
353. 1 k. claret 15 5

52. Banska Bystrica. **53.** Podebrady.

1936.
354. – 1 k. 20 purple .. 5 5
355. **52.** 1 k. 50 red .. 5 5
355a. – 1 k. 60 olive .. 5 5
356. – 2 k. green .. 5 5
357. – 2 k. 50 blue .. 10 5
358. – 3 k. chocolate .. 12 5
359. – 3 k. 50 violet .. 45 15
360. **53.** 4 k. violet .. 20 5
361. – 5 k. green .. 20 5
362. – 10 k. blue .. 45 20
DESIGNS—AS T **51**: 1 k. 20 Palanok Castle. 1 k. 60 St. Barbara's Church, Kutna Hora. 2 k. Zvikov Castle. 2 k. 50 Strecno Castle. 3 k. Hruba Skala Castle (Cesky Raj). 3 k. 50, Slavkov Castle. 5 k. Town Hall, Olomouc (23½ × 29½ mm.). As T **52**: 10 k. Bratislava and Danube.

ILLUSTRATIONS
British Commonwealth and all overprints and surcharges are FULL SIZE. Foreign Countries have been reduced to ¾-LINEAR.

54. President Benes.

1937.
363. **54.** 50 h. green 5 5

55. Mother and Child. **56.** "Lullaby".

1937. Child Welfare.
364. **55.** 50 h+50 h green .. 25 20
365. 1 k.+50 h. claret .. 40 35
366. **56.** 2 k.+1 k. blue.. .. 65 55

57. Czech Legionaries. **58.** Prague.

1937. Battle of Zborov. 20th Anniv.
367. **57.** 50 h. green 10 5
368. 1 k. claret 15 5

1937. Little Entente. 16th Anniv.
369. **58.** 2 k. green 30 5
370. 2 k. 50 blue 50 10

59. J. E. Purkyne. **60.** Falcon.

1937. J. E. Purkyne (physiologist). 150th Birth Anniv.
371. **59.** 50 h. green 5 5
372. 1 k. red 10 5

1937. Mourning for President Masaryk. As T **26** and **42**, but panels of T **42** dated "14.ix.1937".
373. **26.** 50 h. black 5 5
374. **42.** 2 k. black 15 5

1937. Labour Congress, Prague. Optd. **B.I.T. 1937.**
375. **54.** 50 h. green 5 5
376. **52.** 1 k. 50 red 10 5
377. – 2 k. green (No. 356) .. 20 20

1938. 10th Int. Sokol Display, Prague.
378. **60.** 50 h. green 8 5
379. 1 k. claret 15 5

61. Pres. Masaryk and Slovak Girl. **62.** Czech Legionaries at Bachmac.

1938. Child Welfare.
380. **61.** 50 h.+50 h. green .. 20 20
381. 1 k.+50 h. claret .. 30 30

1938. Battles in Russia, Italy and France. 20th Anniv. Inscr. "1918 1938".
382. **62.** 50 h. green 5 5
383. – 50 h. green 5 5
384. – 50 h. green 5 5
DESIGNS: Czech Legionaries at Doss Alto (No. 383) and at Vouziers (No. 384).

63. J. Fugner. **64.** Armament Factories. Pilsen.

1938. Sokol Summer Games.
385. **63.** 50 h. green 5 5
386. 1 k. red 5 5
387. 2 k. blue 12 5

1938. Provincial Economic Council Meeting, Pilsen.
388. **64.** 50 h. green 5 5

65. St. Elisabeth's Cathedral, Kosice. **66.** "Peace".

1938. Kosice Cultural Exhibition.
389. **65.** 50 h. green 5 5

1938. Czech Republic. 20th Anniv.
392. **66.** 2 k. blue 15 5
393. 3 k. brown 20 8

1939. Inaug. of Slovak Parliament. No. 362 of Czechoslovakia surch. **Otvorenie slovenskecho Snemu 18.1.1939** and **300 h.** between bars.
393b. 300 h. on 10 k. blue .. 20 50
No. 393b was only issued in Slovakia. It was formerly listed there, but was withdrawn prior to the establishment of the Slovak state. The used price is for cancelled to order stamps.

66a. Jasina.

1939. Carpatho-Ukrainian Parliament. Inaug.
393c. **66a.** 3 k. blue .. .. 1·25 32·00
The used price is for stamp on cover.

From mid-1939 until 1945, Czechoslovakia was divided into the German Protectorate of Bohemia and Moravia and the independent state of Slovakia. Both these countries issued their own stamps. Germany had already occupied Sudetenland where a number of unauthorised local issues were made at Asch, Karlsbad, Konstantinsbad, Hiklasdorf, Reichenberg-Maffersdorf and Rumburg. Hungary occupied Carpatho-Ukraine and the stamps of Hungary were used there. In 1945, upon liberation, stamps of Czechoslovakia were once again issued.

67. Clasped Hands. **68.** Arms and Soldier.

1945. Kosice Issue. Imperf.
396. **67.** 1 k. 50 maroon .. 1·40 1·40
397. **68.** 2 k. red 10 10
398. 5 k. slate 95 95
399. 6 k. blue 25 25
400. **67.** 9 k. red 30 30
401. 13 k. brown 40 40
402. 20 k. blue .. .. 1·25 1·25

69. Arms and Linden Leaf. **70.** Linden in bud. **71.** Linden in flower.

1945. Bratislava Issue. Imperf.
403. **69.** 50 h. green 5 5
404. 1 k. purple 5 5
405. 1 k. 50 red 5 5
406. 2 k. blue 5 5
407. 2 k. 40 red 15 10
408. 3 k. brown 5 5
409. 4 k. green 5 5
410. 6 k. violet 5 5
411. 10 k. brown 12 5

1945. Prague Issue.
412. **70.** 10 h. black 5 5
413. 30 h. brown 5 5
414. 50 h. green 5 5
415. 60 h. blue 5 5
416. **71.** 60 h. blue 5 5
417. 80 h. orange 5 5
418. 120 h. red 5 5
419. 300 h. purple 5 5
420. 500 h. green 5 5

72. Pres. Masaryk. **73.** Staff Capt. Ridky.

1945. Moscow Issue. Perf.
421. **72.** 5 h. violet 5 5
422. 10 h. yellow 5 5
423. 20 h. brown 5 5
424. 50 h. green 5 5
425. 1 k. red 5 5
426. 2 k. blue 12 12

1945. War Heroes.
427. **72.** 5 h. grey 5 5
428. – 10 h. brown 5 5
429. – 20 h. red 5 5
430. – 25 h. red 5 5
431. – 30 h. violet 8 5
432. – 40 h. brown 5 5
433. – 50 h. green 5 5
434. – 60 h. violet 10 5
435. **73.** 1 k. red 5 5
436. – 1 k. 50 claret 5 5
437. – 2 k. blue 5 5
438. – 2 k. 50 violet 5 5
439. – 3 k. brown 5 5
440. – 4 k. mauve 10 5
441. – 5 k. green 10 5
442. – 10 k. blue 20 5
PORTRAITS: 10 h., 1 k. 50, Dr. Novak. 20 h., 2 k. Capt. O. Jaros. 25 h., 2 k. 50 h. Staff Capt. Cimprick. 30 h., 3 k. Lt. J. Kral. 40 h., 4 k. J. Gabelk (parachutist). 50 h., 5 k. Staff Capt. Vasatko. 60 h., 10 k. Fr. Adamek.

74. Allied Flags.

75. Russian Soldier and Czech Partisan.

1945. Partisan Issue.

443. 74. 1 k. 50 red 5 5
444. – 2 k. blue 5 5
445. 75. 4 k. brown 12 12
446. – 4 k. 50 violet .. 12 12
447. – 5 k. green 20 20

DESIGNS—VERT. 2 k. Banska Bystrica. HORIZ. 4 k. 50, Silabina. 5 k. Strecno and partisan.

76. Pres. Masaryk.

77. Pres. Benes.

78.

1945.

452. – 30 h. purple 5 5
448. 76. 50 h. brown 5 5
453. 77. 60 h. blue 5 5
449. – 80 h. green 5 5
454. – 1 k. orange 5 5
455. 76. 1 k. 20 red 8 5
456. 1 k. 20 mauve 5 5
450. 77. 1 k. 60 green 5 5
457. – 2 k. 40 red 5 5
458. 77. 3 k. purple 12 5
459. 76. 4 k. blue 8 5
460. 5 k. green 12 5
461. 77. 7 k. black 15 5
462. – 10 k. blue 30 5
451. 76. 15 k. purple 40 5
462a. – 20 k. brown 70 8

PORTRAIT: 30 h., 80 h., 1 k., 2 k. 40, 10 k. 20 k. Gen. M. R. Stefanik.

1945. Students' World Congress, Prague.

463. 78. 1 k. 50+1 k. 50 red .. 5 5
464. 2 k. 50+2 k. 50 blue .. 10 12

79. J. S. Kozina Monument.

80. St. George and Dragon.

1945. Execution of Jan Stadky Kozina, 1695.

465. 79. 2 k. 40 red 8 8
466. 4 k. blue 15 15

1946. Victory Issue.

467. 80. 2 k. 40+2 k. 60 red .. 12 8
468. 4 k.+6 k. blue.. .. 25 8

80a. Douglas DC4 over Charles' Bridge, Prague.

1946. Air. First Prague-New York Flight.

468b. 80a. 24 k. blue on buff .. 55 50

81. Captain Novak.

82. Aeroplane over Bratislava.

1946. Air.

469. 81. 1 k. 50 red 10 8
470. 5 k. 50 blue 25 10
471. 9 k. purple 65 10
472. 82. 10 k. green 55 25
473. 81. 16 k. violet 85 30
474. 82. 20 k. blue .. .. 1·00 30
475. 80a. 24 k. claret .. .. 1·10 50
476. 50 k. blue .. .. 1·90 1·10

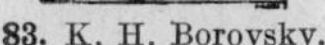
83. K. H. Borovsky.

84. Brno.

1946. Borovsky (Independence advocate). 90th Death Anniv.

477. 83. 1 k. 20 h. grey .. 10 5

1946.

478. 84. 2 k. 40 claret .. 15 8
479. – 7 k. 40 violet (Hodonin) 25 5

85. Emigrants.

86. President Benes.

1946. Repatriation Fund.

480. – 1 k. 60+1 k. 40 brown 12 12
481. 85. 2 k. 40+2 k. 60 red .. 15 10
482. – 4 k.+4 k. blue.. .. 25 15

DESIGNS: 1 k. 60, Emigrants' departure. 4 k. Emigrants' return.

1946. Independence Day.

483. 86. 60 h. blue 5 5
484. 1 k. 60 green 5 5
485. 3 k. purple 5 5
486. 8 k. violet 15 5

87. Flag and Symbols.

88. St. Adalbert.

1947. Two Year Plan.

487. 87. 1 k. 20 green 5 5
488. 2 k. 40 red 8 5
489. 4 k. blue 25 10

1947. St. Adalbert (Bishop of Prague). 950th Death Anniv.

490. 88. 1 k. 60 black 30 20
491. 2 k. 40 red 55 40
492. 5 k. green 45 20

89. "Grief".

90. Rekindling Flame of Remembrance.

1947. Destruction of Lidice. 5th Anniv.

493. 89. 1 k. 20 black 20 15
494. 1 k. 60 black 15 12
495. 90. 2 k. 40 mauve 30 20

91. Congress Emblem.

92. Pres. Masaryk.

1947. Youth Festival.

496. 91. 1 k. 20 purple 15 10
497. 4 k. grey 25 20

1947. Pres. Masaryk. 10th Death Anniv.

498. 92. 1 k. 20 black on buff .. 10 10
499. 4 k. blue on cream .. 20 12

93. Stefan Moyses.

94. "Freedom".

1947. Stefan Moyses. (Slavonic Society Organizer). 150th Birth Anniv.

500. 93. 1 k. 20 purple 12 12
501. 4 k. blue 20 10

1947. Russian Revolution. 30th Anniv.

502. 94. 2 k. 40 red 10 10
503. 4 k. blue 30 10

95. Pres. Benes.

96. "Athletes paying Homage to Republic".

97. Dr. J. Vanicek.

1948.

504. 95. 1 k. 50 brown 5 5
505. 2 k. purple 5 5
506. 5 k. blue 10 5

The 2 k. and 5 k. are larger, 19 × 23 mm.

1948. 11th Sokol Congress, Prague. (a) 1st issue.

507. 96. 1 k. 50 brown 5 5
508. 3 k. red 10 5
509. 5 k. blue 20 5

(b) 2nd issue. Inscr. "XI. VSESOKOLSKY SLET V PRAZE 1948".

515. 97. 1 k. green 8 5
516. – 1 k. 50 violet 8 5
517. – 2 k. blue 15 5
518. 97. 3 k. mauve 20 5

PORTRAIT: 1 k. 50, 2 k. Dr. J. Scheiner.

98. Charles IV.

99. St. Wenceslas and Charles IV.

1948. Charles IV University, Prague. 6th Cent.

510. 98. 1 k. 50 sepia 8 5
511. 99. 2 k. brown 10 5
512. 3 k. lake 10 5
513. 98. 5 k. blue 25 8

100. Insurgents.

101. Fr. Palacky and Dr. F. L. Rieger.

102. M. J. Hurban.

103. President Benes.

1948. Abolition of Serfdom. Cent.

514. 100. 1 k. 50 black 8 5

1948. Constituent Assembly at Kromeriz. Cent.

519. 101. 1 k. 50 violet 8 5
520. 3 k. claret 10 5

1948. Slovak Insurrection. Cent.

521. 102. 1 k. 50 brown.. .. 8 5
522. – 3 k. red (L. Stur) .. 10 5
523. – 5 k. blue (M. Hodza).. 20 8

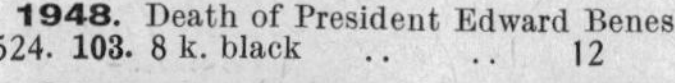
1948. Death of President Edward Benes.

524. 103. 8 k. black 12 5

104. "Independence".

105. President Gottwald.

1948. Independence. 30th Anniv.

525. 104. 1 k. 50 blue 5 5
526. 3 k. red 12 10

1948.

772. 105. 15 h. green 20 5
773. 20 h. brown 30 5
526a. 1 k. green 5 5
774. 1 k. lilac 50 5
527. 1 k. 50 brown 5 5
528. 3 k. red 12 5
528b. 3 k. claret 5 5
528a. 3 k. black 15 5
529. 5 k. blue 12 5
530. 20 k. violet (larger).. 55 5

106. Czech and Russian Workers.

107. Girl and Bird-drawings.

1948. Russian Alliance. 5th Anniv.

531. 106. 3 k. red 8 5

1948. Child Welfare.

532. – 1 k. 50+1 k. purple .. 8 5
533. – 2 k.+1 k. blue .. 8 5
534. 107. 3 k.+1 k. red .. 15 5

DESIGNS: 1 k. 50, Boy and bird-drawings. 2 k. Mother and child.

108. V. I. Lenin.

109. Pres. Gottwald Addressing Rally.

1949. Lenin. 25th Death Anniv.

535. 108. 1 k. 50 purple .. 15 10
536. 5 k. blue 25 12

1949. Gottwald Government. 1st Anniv.

537. 109. 3 k. brown 5 5

1949. As T 105 but larger. Inscr. "UNOR 1948".

538. 105. 10 k. green 30 10

110. P. O. Hviezdoslav.

111. Mail-coach and Train.

1949. Poets.

539. 110. 50 h. purple 5 5
540. – 80 h. red 5 5
541. – 1 k. green 5 5
542. – 2 k. blue 20 5
543. – 4 k. purple 20 5
544. – 8 k. black 25 5

PORTRAITS: 80 h. V. Vancura. 1 k. J. Sverma. 2 k. Julius Fucik. 4 k. Jiri Wolker. 8 k. Alois Jirasek.

1949. U.P.U. 75th Anniv.

545. 111. 3 k. red .. .. 1·50 1·25
546. – 5 k. blue 40 25
547. – 13 k. green 90 40

DESIGNS: 5 k. Mounted postman and mail-van. 13 k. Sailing ship and aeroplane.

112. Girl Agricultural Worker.

113. Industrial Worker.

1949. Czechoslovak Communist Party. 9th Meeting.

548. 112. 1 k. 50 green 25 20
549. – 3 k. red 12 12
550. 113. 5 k. blue 35 30

DESIGN—HORIZ. 3 k. Workers and flag.

114. F. Smetana and National Theatre, Prague.

115. F. Chopin and Warsaw Conservatoire.

1949. Smetana (composer). 125th Birth Anniv.

551. 114. 1 k. 50 green 12 5
552. 5 k. blue 30 15

1949. Chopin (composer). Death Cent.

554. 115. 3 k. claret 20 15
555. 8 k. purple 45 25

116. A. S. Pushkin.

117. Globe and Ribbon.

1949. A. S. Pushkin (poet). 150th Birth Anniv.
553. **116.** 2 k. green 15 10

1949. 50th Sample Fair, Prague.
556. **117.** 1 k. 50 purple .. 15 15
557. 5 k. blue 35 30

ILLUSTRATIONS British Commonwealth and all overprints and surcharges are FULL SIZE. Foreign Countries have been reduced to ¾-LINEAR

119a. Zvolen Castle.

1949.
558. **119a.** 10 k. lake 40 5

1949. Air. Surch. in figures and bars.
559. **81.** 1 k. on 1 k. 50 red .. 5 5
560. 3 k. on 5 k. 50 blue .. 12 8
561. 6 k. on 9 k. purple .. 25 8
562. 7 k. 50 on 16 k. violet 35 12
563. **82.** 8 k. on 10 k. green .. 35 20
564. 12 k. 50 on 20 k. blue .. 60 20
565. **80a.** 15 k. on 24 k. claret .. 70 30
566. 30 k. on 50 k. blue .. 1·25 45

118. Mediaeval Miners.

119. Modern Miner.

1949. Czechoslovak Mining Industry. 700th Anniv. and Introduction of Miners' Laws. 150th Anniv.
567. **118.** 1 k. 50 violet 60 55
568. **119.** 3 k. red .. .. 1·75 90
569. – 5 k. blue .. .. 2·25 90
DESIGN—HORIZ. 5 k. Miner with cutting machine.

120. Carpenters.

121. Dove and Buildings.

1949. 2nd T.U.C., Prague. Inscr. "1949".
570. **120.** 1 k. green .. .. 1·10 50
571. – 2 k. pur. (Mechanic) .. 60 20

1949. Red Cross Fund. Inscr. "CS CERVENY KRIZ".
572. **121.** 1 k. 50 h. + 50 h. claret 1·40 65
573. – 3 k. + 1 k. red .. 1·40 80
DESIGN—VERT. 3 k. Dove and globe.

122. Mother and Child.

123. Joseph Stalin.

1949. Child Welfare Fund. Inscr. "DETEM 1949".
574. **122.** 1 k. 50 + 50 h. grey .. 1·40 65
575. – 3 k. + 1 k. claret .. 2·00 80
DESIGN: 3 k. Father and child.

1949. Stalin's 70th Birthday. Inscr. "21 XII 1879-1949".
576. **123.** 1 k. 50 green 35 30
577. – 3 k. claret .. .. 1·40 70
PORTRAIT: 3 k. Stalin facing left.

124. Skier.

125. Efficiency Badge.

1950. Tatra Cup Ski Championship.
578. **124.** 1 k. 50 blue .. .. 1·10 35
579. **125.** 3 k. claret and buff .. 1·10 70
580. **124.** 5 k. ultramarine .. 1·25 75

126. V. Mayakovsky (poet).

127. Soviet Tank Driver and Hradcany, Prague.

128. Factory and Workers.

129. S. K. Neumann (writer).

1950. Mayakovsky. 20th Death Anniv.
581. **126.** 1 k. 50 purple .. .. 1·25 65
582. 3 k. red .. .. 1·25 65

1950. Republic. 5th Anniv. 1st issue.
583. **127.** 1 k. 50 green 20 15
584. – 2 k. purple 55 20
585. – 3 k. red 20 15
586. – 5 k. blue 30 10
DESIGNS: 2 k. "Hero of Labour" medal. 3 k. Workers and Town Hall. 5 k. "The Kosice Programme".

1950. Republic. 5th Anniv. 2nd issue.
587. **128.** 1 k. 50 green 55 45
588. – 2 k. brown 90 45
589. – 3 k. red 25 15
590. – 5 k. blue 40 15
DESIGNS: 2 k. Crane and Tatra Mts. 3 k. Labourer and tractor. 5 k. Three workers.

1950. Neumann. 75th Birth Anniv.
591. **129.** 1 k. 50 blue 12 8
592. 3 k. purple 55 55

130. B. Nemcova (authoress).

131. "Liberation of Colonial Nations".

132. Miner, Soldier and Farmer.

133. Z. Fibich.

1950. Nemcova. 130th Birth Anniv.
593. **130.** 1 k. 50 blue 65 50
594. 7 k. purple 20 12

1950. 2nd Int. Students' World Congress, Prague. Inscr. "II KONGRES MSS".
595. **131.** 1 k. 50 green 8 5
596. – 2 k. purple 65 30
597. – 3 k. red 12 10
598. – 5 k. blue 30 15
DESIGNS—HORIZ. 2 k. Woman, globe and dove. 3 k. Students. 5 k. Students and banner.

1950. Army Day. Inscr. "6.x.1950 DEN CS. ARMADY".
599. **132.** 1 k. 50 blue 40 35
600. – 3 k. red 20 12
DESIGN: 3 k. Czechoslovak and Russian soldiers.

1950. Fibich (composer). Birth Cent.
601. **133.** 3 k. claret 55 40
602. 8 k. green 20 10

134. "Communications".

135. J. G. Tajovsky.

1950. League of P.T.T. Employees. 1st Anniv.
603. **134.** 1 k. 50 brown .. 8 5
604. 3 k. claret 30 20

1950. Tajovsky (writer). 10th Death Anniv.
605. **135.** 1 k. 50 brown .. 45 30
606. 5 k. blue 45 40

136. Reconstruction of Prague.

1950. Philatelic Exhibition, Prague.
607. **136.** 1 k. 50 blue 20 8
608. 3 k. claret 35 30

137. Czech and Russian Workers.

138. Dove (after Picasso).

1950. Czechoslovak-Soviet Friendship.
609. **137.** 1 k. 50 brown 25 15
610. 5 k. blue 40 35

1951. Czechoslovak Peace Congress.
611. **138.** 2 k. blue .. .. 1·60 1·10
612. 3 k. claret .. .. 1·60 1·10

139. Julius Fucik.

140. Mechanical Hammer.

1951. Peace Propaganda.
613. **139.** 1 k. 50 grey 30 25
614. 5 k. blue 60 50

1951. Five Year Plan (heavy industry).
615. **140.** 1 k. 50 black 5 5
616. – 3 k. brown 5 5
617. **140.** 4 k. blue 45 25
DESIGN—HORIZ. 3 k. Installing machinery.

141. Industrial Workers.

142. Miners.

1951. Int. Women's Day. Dated "8.iii.1951".
618. **141.** 1 k. 50 olive 15 5
619. – 3 k. claret 55 40
620. – 5 k. blue 25 15
DESIGNS: 3 k. Woman driving tractor. 5 k. Korean woman and group.

1951. Mining Industry.
625. **142.** 1 k. 50 grey 25 12
626. 3 k. claret 10 5

143. Karlovy Vary.

144. Ploughing.

1951. Air. Spas.
621. **143.** 6 k. green 75 30
622. – 10 k. purple .. .. 1·10 40
623. – 15 k. blue .. .. 1·75 40
624. – 20 k. brown .. .. 4·00 1·25
SPAS. 10 k. Piestany. 15 k. Marianske Lazne. 20 k. Silac.

1951. Agriculture.
627. **144.** 1 k. 50 brown 40 35
628. – 2 k. green (Woman and cows) 40 35

145. Tatra Mountains.

146. Partisan and Soviet Soldier.

1951. Recreation Centres. Inscr. "ROH".
629. **145.** 1 k. 50 green 12 8
630. – 2 k. brown 40 30
631. – 3 k. red 8 5
DESIGNS: 2 k. Beskydy Mts. 3 k. Krkonose Mts.

1951. Czechoslovak Communist Party. 30th Anniv. Inscr. "30 LET" etc.
635. – 1 k. 50 grey 40 20
632. – 2 k. lake 12 8
633. **146.** 3 k. lake 20 5
636. – 5 k. blue .. .. 1·40 75
634. – 8 k. black 40 20
DESIGNS—HORIZ. 1 k. 50, 5 k. Gottwald and Stalin. 8 k. Marx, Engels, Lenin and Stalin. VERT. 2 k. Factory militiaman.

147. Dvorak.

148. Gymnast.

1951. Prague Musical Festival.
637. **147.** 1 k. brown 8 8
638. – 1 k. 50 grey (Smetana) 30 15
639. **147.** 2 k. chocolate 40 30
640. – 3 k. purple (Smetana) 8 8

1951. 9th Sokol Federation Congress.
641. **148.** 1 k. green 30 15
642. – 1 k. 50 brown (Woman discus-thrower) .. 30 15
643. – 3 k. red (Footballers) 55 20
644. – 5 k. blue (Skier) .. 1·25 60

1951. Bohumir Smeral. 10th Death Anniv. As T **135**, but portrait of Smeral.
645. 1 k. 50 grey 25 20
646. 3 k. lake 20 12

150. A. Jirasek.

149. Scene from "Fall of Berlin".

151. "Fables and Fates".

1951. Int. Film Festival, Karlovy Vary. Inscr. "SE SOVETSKYM FILMEN", etc.
647. **149.** 80 h. claret 20 15
648. – 1 k. 50 grey 25 20
649. **149.** 4 k. blue 70 55
DESIGN: 1 k. 50. Scene from 'The Great Citizen'.

1951. J. Hybes (politician). 30th Death Anniv. As T **135**, but portrait of Hybes.
650. 1 k. 50 brown 8 8
651. 2 k. red 25 20

1951. Jirasek (author). Birth Cent.
652. **150.** 1 k. 50 black 12 8
653. **151.** 3 k. red 20 10
654. – 4 k. black 25 10
655. **150.** 5 k. blue 85 60
DESIGN—As T **151**: 4 k. "The Region of Tabor".

152. Miner and Pithead. 153. Soldiers Parading.

1951. Miners' Day.
656. 152. 1 k. 50 brown 8 5
657. – 3 k. claret (miners drilling) 8 5
658. 152. 5 k. blue 60 35

1951. Army Day. Inscr. "DEN CS ARMADY 1951".
659. 153. 80 h. brown 10 8
660. – 1 k. green 15 12
661. – 1 k. 50 black 20 12
662. – 3 k. purple 30 15
663. – 5 k. blue 80 50

DESIGNS—VERT. 1 k. Gunner and field-gun. 1 k. 50 h. Pres. Gottwald. 3 k. Tank driver and tank. 5 k. Two pilots and aeroplanes.

154. Stalin and Gottwald. 155. P. Jilemnicky.

1951. Czechoslovak-Soviet Friendship.
664. 154. 1 k. 50 black 8 5
665. – 3 k. claret 5 5
666. 154. 4 k. blue 40 30
DESIGN (23½×31 mm.): 3 k. Lenin, Stalin and Russian soldiers.

1951. Jilemnicky (writer). 50th Birth Anniv.
667. 155. 1 k. 50 purple 15 12
668. 2 k. blue 35 30

156. L. Zapotocky. 157. J. Kollar.

1952. Zapotocky (socialist pioneer). Birth Cent.
669. 156. 1 k. 50 red 8 5
670. 4 k. black 30 25

1952. Kollar (poet). Death Cent.
671. 157. 3 k. lake 10 5
672. 5 k. blue 40 30

158. Lenin Hall, Prague. 159. Explorer.

1952. 40th Anniv. of 6th All-Russian Party Conference.
673. 158. 1 k. 50 claret 8 5
674. 5 k. blue 30 25

1952. Dr. Holub (explorer). 50th Death Anniv.
675. 159. 3 k. lake 20 15
676. 5 k. blue 85 70

160. Electric Welding.

DESIGNS: 2 k. Foundry. 3 k. Chemical plant.

1952. Industrial Development.
677. 160. 1 k. 50 black 8 8
678. – 2 k. brown 60 50
679. – 3 k. red 8 5

161. Factory and Farm Workers. 162. Woman and Children.

1952. Int. Women's Day.
680. 161. 1 k. 50 blue on cream 70 35

1952. Child Welfare.
690. 162. 2 k. purple 50 35
691. 3 k. red 12 8

163. Young Workers. 164. Otakar Sevcik.

1952. Int. Youth Week.
681. 163. 1 k. 50 blue 8 5
682. – 2 k. green 12 8
683. 163. 3 k. red 40 35
DESIGN: 2 k. Three heads and globe (badge of Democratic Youth World Federation).

1952. Sevcik (composer). Birth Cent.
684. 164. 2 k. brown 25 20
685. 3 k. claret 10 5

165. J. A. Komensky. 166. Anti-fascist.

1952. Komensky (philosopher). 360th Birth Anniv.
686. 165. 1 k. 50 brown .. 70 30
687. 11 k. blue 20 8

1952. "Fighters Against Fascism" Day.
688. 166. 1 k. 50 brown 5 5
689. 2 k. blue 35 25

167. Combine Harvester.

1952. Agriculture Day.
692. 167. 1 k. 50 blue 45 30
693. 2 k. brown 12 12
694. – 3 k. red (Combine Drill) 12 12

168. May Day Parade.

1952. Labour Day.
695. 168. 3 k. red 30 25
696. 4 k. brown 40 30

169. Russian Tank and Crowd.

1952. Liberation. 7th Anniv.
697. 169. 1 k. 50 red 30 25
698. 5 k. blue 50 45

170. Boy Pioneer and Children. 171. J. V. Myslbek (sculptor).

1952. Int. Children's Day.
699. 170. 1 k. 50 sepia 5 5
700. 2 k. green 40 20
701. – 3 k. red (Pioneers and Teacher) 5 5

1952. Myslbek. 30th Death Anniv. No. 704 inscr. "JOS. V. MYSELBEK HUDBA".
702. 171. 1 k. 50 chestnut .. 12 5
703. 2 k. chocolate 65 45
704. – 8 k. green 15 5
DESIGN: 8 k. "Music" (statue).

172. Beethoven. 173. " Rebirth of Lidice ".

1952. Int. Music Festival, Prague. No. 705 inscr. "PRAZSKE JARO 1952", etc.
705. 172. 1 k. 50 brown .. 15 12
706. – 3 k. lake 15 12
707. 172. 5 k. blue 60 45
DESIGN—HORIZ. 3 k. The House of Artists.

1952. Destruction of Lidice. 10th Anniv.
708. 173. 1 k. 50 black 8 5
709. 5 k. blue 40 35

174. Jan Hus. 175. Bethlehem Chapel, Prague.

1952. Renovation of Bethlehem Chapel and 550th Anniv. of Installation of Hus as Preacher.
710. 174. 1 k. 50 brown 5 5
711. 175. 3 k. lake 5 5
712. 174. 5 k. black 50 45

176. Testing Blood-pressure. 177. Running.

1952. National Health Service.
713. 176. 1 k. 50 brown .. 40 25
714. – 2 k. violet 5 5
715. 176. 3 k. red 12 5
DESIGN—HORIZ. 2 k. Doctor examining baby.

1952. Physical Culture Propaganda.
716. 177. 1 k. 50 sepia 40 35
717. – 2 k. green (Canoeing) 60 50
718. – 3 k. brown (Cycling) .. 25 20
719. – 4 k. blue (Ice-hockey) 1·25 1·10

178. F. L. Celakovsky.

ILLUSTRATIONS British Commonwealth and all overprints and surcharges are FULL SIZE. Foreign Countries have been reduced to ¾-LINEAR

1952. Celakovsky (poet). Death Cent.
720. 178. 1 k. 50 sepia 5 5
721. 2 k. green 25 15

179. M. Ales. 180. Hussite Warrior.

1952. Ales (painter). Birth Cent.
722. 179. 1 k. 50 green 25 15
737. 180. 2 k. brown 40 30
738. – 3 k. slate-green .. 8 5
723. 179. 6 k. lake .. .. 1·10 85
DESIGN—As T 180: 3 k. Warrior fighting dragon.

181. Mining in 17th Century.

DESIGNS: 1 k. 50 Mining machinery. 2 k. Ostrava mine. 3 k. Mechanical excavator.

1952. Miners' Day.
724. 181. 1 k. slate-purple .. 55 30
725. – 1 k. 50 blue 5 5
726. – 2 k. olive-black .. 8 5
727. – 3 k. purple 5 5

182. Jan Zizka. 183. "Fraternization" (after Pokorny).

1952. Army Day.
728. 182. 1 k. 50 lake 5 5
729. 183. 2 k. olive 8 5
730. – 3 k. red 10 5
731. 182. 4 k. black 60 50
DESIGN: 3 k. Soldiers marching with flag.

184. R. Danube, Bratislava. 185. Lenin, Stalin and Revolutionaries.

1952. National Philatelic Exn., Bratislava.
732. 184. 1 k. 50 sepia 10 5

1952. Russian Revolution. 35th Anniv.
733. 185. 2 k. sepia 40 30
734. 3 k. red 8 5

186. Nurses and Red Cross Flag. 187. Flags.

1952. 1st Czechoslovak Red Cross Conf.
735. 186. 2 k. brown 40 30
736. 3 k. red 8 5

1952. Peace Congress, Vienna.
739. 187. 3 k. red 10 5
740. 4 k. blue 40 30

188. " Dove of Peace " (after Picasso). 189. Smetana Museum, Prague.

1953. 2nd Czechoslovak Peace Congress, Prague.
741. 188. 1 k. 50 sepia 5 5
742. – 4 k. blue 30 20
DESIGN: 4 k. Workman woman and child (after Lev Haas).

1953. Prof. Z. Nejedly (museum founder). 75th Birth Anniv.
743. 189. 1 k. 50 chocolate .. 5 5
744. – 4 k. black 40 30
DESIGN: 4 k. Jirasek Museum, Prague.

190. Marching Soldiers. 191. M. Kukucin.

192. Torch and Open Book.

193. Woman Revolutionary.

1953. Communist Govt. 5th Anniv.
745. **190.** 1 k. 50 blue 5 5
746. – 3 k. red 5 5
747. – 8 k. brown 70 40
DESIGNS—VERT. 3 k. Pres. Gottwald addressing meeting. HORIZ. 8 k. Stalin, Gottwald and crowd with banners.

1953. Czech Writers and Poets.
748. **191.** 1 k. grey 5 5
749. – 1 k. 50 brown 5 5
750. – 2 k. lake 5 5
751. – 3 k. brown 5 5
752. – 5 k. blue 85 60
PORTRAITS—VERT. 1 k. 50, J. Vrchlicky. 2 k. E. J. Erben. 3 k. V. M. Kramerius. 5 k. J. Dobrovsky.

1953. Vaclavek (writer). 10th Death Anniv.
753. **192.** 1 k. brown 30 25
754. – 3 k. chestnut (Vaclavek) 10 8

1953. Int. Women's Day.
755. – 1 k. 50 blue 5 5
756. **193.** 2 k. red 25 15
DESIGN—VERT. 1 k. 50, Mother and baby.

194. Stalin.

195. Pres. Gottwald.

1953. Death of Stalin.
757. **194.** 1 k. 50 black 10 10

1953. Death of President Gottwald.
758. **195.** 1 k. 50 black 8 5
759. 3 k. black 5 5

196. Pecka, Zapotocky and Hybes.

197. Cyclists.

1953. 1st Czech Social Democratic Party Congress. 75th Anniv.
760. **196.** 2 k. chocolate .. 8 5

1953. 6th Int. Cycle Race.
761. **197.** 3 k. blue 25 15

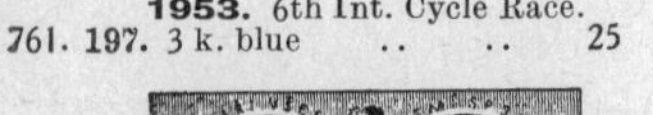

198. 1890 May Day Medal.

199. Marching Crowds.

1953. Labour Day.
762. **198.** 1 k. brown 65 60
763. – 1 k. 50 blue 5 5
764. **199.** 3 k. red 5 5
765. – 8 k. green 12 8
DESIGNS—As T **198**: 1 k. 50, Lenin and Stalin. 8 k. Marx and Engels.

200. Hydro-Electric Barrage.

201. Seed-drills.

1953.
766. **200.** 1 k. 50 grey-green .. 40 25
767. – 2 k. blue 5 5
768. – 3 k. brown 5 5
DESIGNS—VERT. 2 k. Welder and blast-furnaces, Kuncice. HORIZ. 3 k. Gottwald Foundry, Kuncice.

1953.
769. **201.** 1 k. 50 brown 20 5
770. – 7 k. green (Combine-harvester) 80 70

202. President Zapotocky. 203.

1953.
776. **202.** 30 h. blue 40 5
780c. **203.** 30 h. blue 20 5
777. **202.** 60 h. red 30 5
781. **203.** 60 h. red 35 5

204. J. Slavik.

205. L. Janacek.

1953. Prague Music Festival. (a) 120th Death Anniv. of Slavik (violinist).
778. **204.** 75 h. blue 20 5

(b) Janacek (composer). 25th Death Anniv.
779. **205.** 1 k. 60 brown 60 5

206. Charles Bridge, Prague.

1953.
782. **206.** 5 k. grey .. .. 1·40 5

207. J. Fucik.

208. Book, Carnation and Laurels.

1953. Fucik (writer). 10th Death Anniv.
783. **207.** 40 h. sepia 15 5
784. **208.** 60 h. mauve 30 15

209. Miner and Banner.

210. Volley-ball.

1953. Miner's Day.
785. **209.** 30 h. black 10 5
786. – 60 h. plum 30 20
DESIGN: 60 h. Miners and colliery shafthead.

1953. Sports.
787. **210.** 30 h. lake .. .. 1·10 70
788. – 40 h. slate .. .. 1·50 70
789. – 60 h. purple .. .. 1·50 70
DESIGNS—HORIZ. 40 h. Motor-cycling. VERT. 60 h. Throwing the javelin.

211. Hussite Warrior.

212. "Friendship" (after I. Bartfay).

1953. Army Day.
790. **211.** 30 h. sepia 10 5
791. – 60 h. claret 20 8
792. – 1 k. red 55 50
DESIGNS: 60 h. Soldier presenting arms. 1 k. Czechoslovak Red Army soldiers.

1953. Czechoslovak-Korean Friendship.
793. **212.** 30 h. sepia .. .. 2·25 95

213. Hradcany, Prague and Kremlin, Moscow.

1953. Czechoslovak-Soviet Friendship: Inscr. "MESIC CESKOSLOVENSKO-SOVETSKEHO", etc.
794. **213.** 30 h. slate 90 60
795. – 60 h. sepia .. .. 1·00 65
796. – 1 k. 20 blue .. .. 1·25 90
DESIGNS: 60 h. Lomonosov University, Moscow. 1 k. 20, Lenin Ship-Canal.

214. Ema Destinnova (Opera singer).

215. National Theatre, Prague.

1953. National Theatre, Prague. 70th Anniv.
797. **214.** 30 h. black 35 20
798. **215.** 60 h. brown 25 5
799. – 2 k. sepia .. .. 1·10 40
PORTRAIT—As T **214**: 2 k. E. Vojan (actor).

216. J. Manes (painter).

217. V. Hollar (etcher).

1953.
800. **216.** 60 h. lake 20 5
801. 1 k. 20 blue 60 40

1953. Inscr. "1607 1677".
802. **217.** 30 h. black 10 5
803. – 1 k. 20 sepia 60 35
PORTRAIT: 1 k. 20 Hollar and engraving tools.

218. Leo Tolstoy.

219. Locomotive.

1953. Tolstoy. 125th Birth Anniv.
804. **218.** 60 h. green 20 8
805. 1 k. sepia 65 35

1953. Transport Propaganda.
806. **219.** 60 h. indigo and brown 20 5
807. – 1 k. blue and brown .. 80 50
DESIGN: 1 k. Loading mail-plane (30th anniv. Czech airmails).

220. Lenin (after J. Lauda).

221. Lenin Museum, Prague.

1954. Lenin. 30th Death Anniv.
808. **220.** 30 h. sepia 25 10
809. **221.** 1 k. 40 brown 75 60

222. Gottwald Speaking.

223. Gottwald Mausoleum, Prague.

224. Gottwald and Stalin.

1954. 5th Czechoslovak Communist Party Congress. 25th Anniv. Inscr. "1929 1954".
810. **222.** 60 h. brown 25 5
811. – 2 k. 40 lake 90 85
DESIGN: 2 k. 40, Revolutionary and flag.

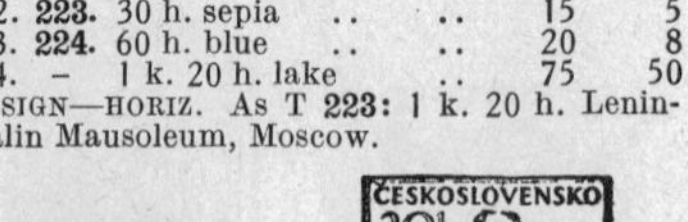
1954. Deaths of Stalin and Gottwald. 1st Anniv.
812. **223.** 30 h. sepia 15 5
813. **224.** 60 h. blue 20 8
814. – 1 k. 20 h. lake 75 50
DESIGN—HORIZ. As T **223**: 1 k. 20 h. Lenin-Stalin Mausoleum, Moscow.

225. Girl and Sheaf of Corn.

226. Athletics.

1954.
815. – 15 h. green 10 5
816. – 20 h. lilac 10 5
817. – 40 h. brown 12 5
818. – 45 h. blue 15 5
819. – 50 h. grey-green .. 20 5
820. – 75 h. blue 20 5
821. – 80 h. chocolate .. 20 5
822. **225.** 1 k. green 35 5
823. – 1 k. 20 blue 25 5
824. – 1 k. 60 grey 60 5
825. – 2 k. chestnut 70 5
826. – 2 k. 40 blue 60 5
827. – 3 k. claret 80 5
DESIGNS: 15 h. Labourer. 20 h. Nurse. 40 h. Postwoman. 45 h. Foundry Worker. 50 h. Soldier. 75 h. Metal worker. 80 h. Mill girl. 1 k. 20, Scientist. 1 k. 60, Miner. 2 k. Doctor and baby. 2 k. 40, Woman engine-driver. 3 k. Chemist.

1954. Sports.
828. **226.** 30 h. sepia .. .. 1·10 50
829. – 80 h. green .. .. 1·60 1·50
830. – 1 k. blue 90 30
DESIGNS—HORIZ. 80 h. Hiking. VERT. 1 k. Girl diving.

227. Dvorak.

228. Prokop Divis (physicist).

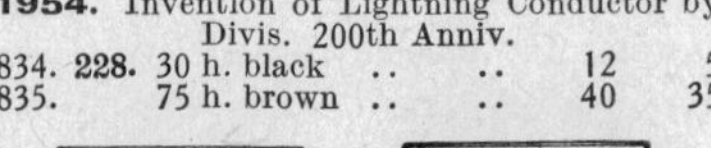
1954. Czechoslovak Musicians. Inscr. as in T **227**.
831. **227.** 30 h. brown 65 12
832. – 40 h. red (Janacek) .. 85 12
833. – 60 h. blue (Smetana) 60 10

1954. Invention of Lightning Conductor by Divis. 200th Anniv.
834. **228.** 30 h. black 12 5
835. 75 h. brown 40 35

229. Partisan.

230. A. P. Chekhov.

1954. Slovak National Uprising. 10th Anniv. Inscr. "1944–29. 8.–1954".
836. **229.** 30 h. red 10 5
837. – 1 k. 20 blue (Woman partisan) 60 50

1954. Chekhov (playwright). 50th Death Anniv.
838. 230. 30 h. green 10 5
839. 45 h. brown 45 35

231. Soldiers in Battle. 232. Farm Workers in Cornfield.

1954. Army Day. 2 k. inscr. "ARMADY 1954".
840. 231. 60 h. green 20 5
841. – 2 k. brown 80 65
DESIGN—VERT. 2 k. Soldier carrying girl.

1954. Czechoslovak-Russian Friendship.
842. 232. 30 h. brown 10 5
843. – 60 h. blue 25 5
844. – 2 k. salmon 80 50
DESIGNS: 60 h. Factory workers and machinery. 2 k. Group of girl Folk dancers.

233. J. Neruda. 234. Ceske Budejovice.

1954. Czechoslovak Poets.
845. 233. 30 h. blue 60 5
846. – 60 h. red .. .. 1·10 25
847. – 1 k. 60 h. slate-purple 60 8
PORTRAITS—VERT. 60 h. J. Jesensky. 1 k. 60 h. J. Wolker.

1954. Czechoslovak Architecture. Horiz. views. Background in buff.
848. – 30 h. black (Telc) .. 25 5
849. – 60 h. brown (Levoca) 30 5
850. 234. 3 k. indigo .. .. 1·25 85

235. President Zapotocky. 236. "Spirit of the Games".

1954. Pres. Zapotocky's 70th Birthday.
851. 235. 30 h. sepia 25 10
852. 60 h. blue 25 10
See also Nos. 1006/7.

1955. 1st National Spartacist Games (1st Issue). Inscr. as in T 236.
853. 236. 30 h. red .. .. 1·00 15
854. – 45 h. blk. & blue (Skier) 65 8

DESIGN: 75 h. Comenius Medal (after O. Spaniel).

237. University Building.

1955. Comenius University, Bratislava. 35th Anniv. Inscr. as in T 237.
855. 237. 60 h. green 20 5
856. – 75 h. chocolate .. 35 25

238. Cesky Krumlov.

1955. Air.
857. 238. 80 h. green 85 5
858. – 1 k. 55 sepia 70 20
859. – 2 k. 35 blue .. .. 1·10 12
860. – 2 k. 75 purple .. 1·40 25
861. – 10 k. blue .. .. 2·50 1·10
DESIGNS: 1 k. 55, Olomouc. 2 k. 35, Banska Bystrica. 2 k. 75, Bratislava. 10 k. Prague.

239. Skoda Motor Car. 240. Russian Tank-driver.

1955. Czechoslovak Industries.
862. 239. 45 h. green 40 25
863. – 60 h. blue 20 5
864. – 75 h. black 30 5
DESIGNS: 60 h. Shuttleless jet boom. 75 h. Skoda Machine-tool.

1955. Liberation. 10th Anniv. Inscr. as in T 240.
865. – 30 h. blue 10 5
866. 240. 35 h. brown 35 25
867. – 60 h. red 15 5
868. – 60 h. black-brown .. 15 5
DESIGNS—VERT. 30 h. Girl and Russian soldier. No. 867, Children and Russian soldier. HORIZ. No. 868, Stalin Monument, Prague.

241. Agricultural Workers. 242. "Music and Spring".

1955. 3rd Trades' Union Congress. Inscr. as in T 241.
869. – 30 h. blue 5 5
870. 241. 45 h. green 30 25
DESIGN: 30 h. Foundry worker.

1955. International Music Festival, Prague. Inscr. as in T 242.
371. 242. 30 h. indigo and blue .. 12 15
372. – 1 k. indigo and pink .. 55 35
DESIGN: 1 k. "Music" playing a lyre.

243. A. S. Popov. 244. Folk Dancers.

1955. Cultural Anniversaries. Vert. portraits as T 243.
873. – 20 h. brown (J. Arbes) 12 5
874. – 30 h. black (J. Stursa) 12 5
875. – 40 h. grn. (E. Marothy-Soltesova) .. 25 5
876. – 60 h. blk. (J. V. Sladek) 12 5
877. 243. 75 h. maroon 45 35
878. – 1 k. 40 black on yellow (J. Holly) 30 10
879. – 1 k. 60 blue (P. J. Safarik) 35 5

1955. 1st National Spartacist Games 2nd Issue). Inscr. as in T 244.
880. – 20 h. blue 35 25
881. 244. 60 h. green 15 5
882. – 1 k. 60 red 50 12
DESIGNS: 20 h. Girl athlete. 1 k. 60, Male athlete.

245. "Friendship". 246. Ocova Woman, Slovakia.

1955. 5th World Youth Festival, Warsaw.
883. 245. 60 h. blue 20 5

1955. National Costumes (1st series).
884. 246. 60 h. sepia, rose & red 3·75 2·50
885. – 75 h. sep., orge. & lake 1·75 1·50
886. – 1 k. 60 sepia, blue and orange .. .. 3·50 2·40
887. – 2 k. sepia, yell. & rose 4·00 3·25
DESIGNS: 75 h. Detva man, Slovakia. 1 k. 60, Chodsko man, Bohemia. 2 k. Hana woman, Moravia.
See also Nos. 952/5 and 1008/11.

247. Swallow-tail Butterfly.

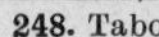

248. Tabor. 249. Motor-cyclists and Trophy.

1955. Animals and Insects. Horiz. designs as T 247.
888. – 20 h. black & bl. (Carp) 35 5
889. – 30 h. brown and rose (Stag beetle) .. 25 5
890. – 35 h. brown and buff (Partridge) 25 5
891. 247. 1 k. 40 black & yellow 1·10 90
892. – 1 k. 50 black and green (Hare) 35 10

1955. Towns of Southern Bohemia.
893. 248. 30 h. chocolate .. 8 5
894. – 45 h. red 25 20
895. – 60 h. green 12 5
TOWNS: 45 h. Prachatice. 60 h. Jindrichuv Hradec.

1955. 30th Int. Motor-cycle Six-Day Trial.
896. 249. 60 h. chocolate .. 90 20

250. Soldier and Family. 251. Hans Andersen.

1955. Army Day. Inscr. as in T 250.
897. 250. 30 h. brown 10 5
898. – 60 h. grn. (Tank attack) 65 60

1955. Famous Writers. Vert. portraits.
899. 251. 30 h. red 10 5
900. – 40 h. blue (Schiller) .. 40 35
901. – 60 h. pur. (Mickiewicz) 12 5
902. – 75 h. blk. (Walt Whitman) 15 5

DESIGNS: 30 h. Railway tracks. 60 h. Railway tunnel. 1 k. 60, Block of flats.

252. Viaduct.

1955. Building Progress. Insc. "STAVBA SOCIALISMU".
903. 252. 20 h. green 10 10
904. – 30 h. brown 8 5
905. – 60 h. blue 15 5
906. – 1 k. 60 h. red .. 40 5

253. "Electricity". 254. Karlovy Vary.

1956. Five Year Plan. Inscr. "1956–1960".
907. 253. 5 h. chocolate .. 10 5
908. – 10 h. black 12 5
909. – 25 h. red 20 5
910. – 30 h. green 12 5
911. – 60 h. blue 12 5
DESIGNS—HORIZ. 10 h. "Mining". 25 h. "Building". 30 h. "Agriculture". 60 h. "Industry".

1956. Czechoslovak Spas (1st series).
912. 254. 30 h. green 45 5
913. – 45 h. brown 45 10
914. – 75 h. maroon .. .. 2·40 2·00
915. – 1 k. 20 blue 40 5
SPAS: 45 h. Marianske Lazne. 75 h. Piestany. 1 k. 20, Vysne Ruzbachy, Tatra Mountains.
See also Nos. 1043/8.

255. Jewellery. 256. "We serve our People" (after J. Cumpelik).

1956. Czechoslovak Products.
916. 255. 30 h. green 20 5
917. – 45 h. blue (Glassware) 1·25 1·10
918. – 60 h. mar. (Ceramics) 15 5
919. – 75 h. black (Textiles) .. 20 5

1956. Defence Exn.
920. 256. 30 h. brown 8 5
921. – 60 h. red 12 5
922. – 1 k. blue .. .. 1·90 1·60
DESIGNS: 60 h. Liberation Monument, Berlin. 1 k. Tank driver holding flag.

DESIGNS—As T 257: VERT. 30 h. (9th Int. Cycle Race). 45 h. Basketball (European Women's Championships). HORIZ. 60 h. Horsemen jumping (Pardubice Steeple-chase). 80 h. Runners (Int. Marathon, Kosice).

257. Cyclists.

258. Discus Thrower, Hurdler and Runner (Olympic Games, Melbourne).

1956. Sport Events of 1956.
923. 257. 30 h. green and blue .. 90 12
924. – 45 h. blue and red .. 55 12
925. – 60 h. indigo and buff .. 65 20
926. 258. 75 h. brown and yellow 55 12
927. – 80 h. maroon & lavender 48 8
928. 258. 1 k. 20 green & orange 35 10

259. Mozart. 260.

1956. 200th Anniv. of Birth of Mozart and Prague Music Festival. Centres in black.
929. 259. 30 h. yellow 20 10
930. – 45 h. green .. .. 3·50 3·50
931. – 60 h. purple 20 5
932. – 1 k. salmon 20 5
933. – 1 k. 40 blue 30 15
934. – 1 k. 60 lemon .. 35 5
DESIGNS: 45 h. J. Myslivecek. 60 h. J. Benda. 1 k. "Bertramka" (Mozart's villa). 1 k. 40, Mr. and Mrs. Dushek. 1 k. 60, Nostic Theatre.

1956. 1st National Meeting of Home Guard.
935. 260. 60 h. blue 20 5

261. J. K. Tyl. 262. Naval Guard.

1956. Czech Writers.
936. – 20 h. purple (Stur) .. 12 5
937. – 30 h. blue (Sramek) .. 12 5
938. 261. 60 h. black 12 5
939. – 1 k. 40 mar. (Borovsky) 85 70
See also Nos. 956/9.

1956. Frontier Guards' Day.
940. 262. 30 h. blue 35 15
941. – 60 h. green 12 5
DESIGN: 60 h. Military guard and watchdog.

263. Picking Grapes. 264. "Kladno", 1855.

1956. National Products.

942. 263. 30 h. lake 15 5
943. – 35 h. green 15 8
944. – 80 h. blue 15 5
945. – 95 h. brown 70 65

DESIGNS—VERT. 35 h. Picking hops. HORIZ. 80 h. Fishing. 95 h. Logging.

1956. European Timetable Conf. for Freight Services. Czechoslovak Locomotives.

946. – 10 h. brown 50 5
947. 264. 30 h. sepia 15 5
948. – 40 h. green 85 5
949. – 45 h. claret .. .. 3·75 3·00
950. – 60 h. indigo 25 5
951. – 1 k. blue 30 5

DESIGNS—VERT. 10 h. "Zbraslav", 1846. HORIZ. 40 h. "Rady 534.0", 1945. 45 h. "Rady 556.0", 1952. 60 h. "Rady 477.0", 1955. 1 k. Electric locomotive "E 499.0", 1954.

1956. National Costumes (2nd series). As T **246**.

952. 30 h. sepia, red and blue .. 55 20
953. 1 k. 20 sepia, blue and red 55 15
954. 1 k. 40 brown, yell. & red 1·25 80
955. 1 k. 60 sepia, green & red 55 20

DESIGNS: 30 h. Slovacko woman. 1 k. 20 Blata woman. 1 k. 40, Cicmany woman. 1 k. 60, Novohradsko woman.

1957. Czech Writers. As T **261**. On buff paper.

956. 15 h. brown (Olbracht) .. 15 5
957. 20 h. green (Toman) .. 10 5
958. 30 h. sepia (Salda) .. 10 5
959. 1 k. 60 blue (Vansova) .. 35 5

265. Forestry Academy, Banska Stiavnica.

266. Girl Harvester.

268. J. A. Komensky (Comenius). 267. Komensky's Mausoleum.

1957. Towns and Monuments Anniversaries.

960. – 30 h. blue 10 5
961. 265. 30 h. purple 10 5
962. – 60 h. red 15 5
963. – 60 h. sepia 15 5
964. – 60 h. green 15 5
965. – 1 k. 25 grey 65 60

DESIGNS: No. 960, Kolin. 962, Uherske Hradiste. 963, Charles' Bridge, Prague. 964, Karlstejn Castle. 965, Moravska Treyova.

1957. 3rd Collective Farming Agricultural Congress, Prague.

966. 266. 30 h. turquoise .. 15 5

1957. Publication of Komensky's "Opera Didactica Omnia". 300th Anniv.

967. 267. 30 h. drab 10 5
968. – 40 h. green 10 5
969. 268. 60 h. brown 50 30
970. – 1 k. red 30 5

DESIGNS—As T **267**: 40 h. Komensky at work. 1 k. Illustration from the work.

269. Racing Cyclists.

270. J. B. Foerster.

272. Young Collector Blowing Posthorn. 271. J. Bozek (founder).

1957. Sports Events of 1957.

971. 269. 30 h. slate-pur. & blue 15 5
972. 60 h. green and bistre 90 50
973. – 60 h. violet and brown 20 5
974. – 60 h. slate-pur. & chest. 20 5
975. – 60 h. black and green 20 5
976. – 60 h. black and blue .. 30 5

DESIGNS—HORIZ. Nos. 971/2 (10th Int. Cycle Race). 973, Rescue squad (Mountain climbing Rescue Service). 975, Archer (World Archery Championships, Prague). VERT. No. 974, Boxers (European Boxing Championships, Prague). 976, Motor-cyclists (32nd Int. Motor-cycle meeting).

1957. Int. Music Festival Jubilee. Musicians.

977. – 60 h. violet (Stamic) .. 10 5
978. – 60 h. black (Laub) .. 10 5
979. – 60 h. blue (Ondricek) 10 5
980. 270. 60 h. sepia 10 5
981. – 60 h. brown (Novak) 20 5
982. – 60 h. turquoise (Suk) .. 10 5

1957. Polytechnic Engineering Schools, Prague. 250th Anniv.

983. 271. 30 h. grey 5 5
984. – 60 h. brown 10 5
985. – 1 k. brown-purple .. 20 5
986. – 1 k. 40 violet 30 5

DESIGNS—VERT. 60 h. F. J. Gerstner. 1 k. R. Skuhersky. HORIZ. 1 k. 40, The Building.

1957. Junior Philatelic Exn., Pardubice.

987. 272. 30 h. orange and green 40 5
988. – 60 h. blue and brown .. 80 65

DESIGN: 60 h. Girl sending letter by pigeon.

273. "Rose of Friendship and Peace". 274. Karel Klic and Printing Press.

1957. Destruction of Lidice. 15th Anniv.

989. – 30 h. black 10 5
990. 273. 60 h. red and black .. 30 10

DESIGN: 30 h. Veiled woman.

1957. Czech Inventors.

991. 274. 30 h. black 10 5
992. – 60 h. blue 15 5

DESIGN: 60 h. Joseph Ressel and propeller.

275. Chamois. 276. Marycka Magdonova.

1957. Tatra National Park.

993. 275. 20 h. black and green 25 20
994. – 30 h. brown and blue 20 5
995. – 40 h. blue and brown 25 5
996. – 60 h. green and yellow 20 5
997. – 1 k. 25 black and ochre 1·25 65

DESIGNS—VERT. 30 h. Bear. HORIZ. 40 h. Gentian. 60 h. Edelweiss. 1 k. 25 (49 × 29 mm.) Tatra Mountains.

1957. 90th Birthday of Peter Bezruc (poet).

998. 276. 60 h. black and red .. 15 5

277. Worker with Banner. 279. Television Tower and Aerials.

278. "Paris—Prague—Moscow".

1957. 4th World T.U.C., Leipzig.

999. 277. 75 h. red 20 5

1957. Opening of Czechoslovak Airlines.

1000. 278. 75 h. blue and red .. 45 5
1001. – 2 k. 35 blue and yellow 55 12

DESIGN: 2 k. 35 "Prague—Cairo—Beirut—Damascus".

1957. Television Development.

1002. 279. 40 h. blue and red .. 10 5
1003. – 60 h. brown and green 15 5

DESIGN: 60 h. Family watching television.

280. Youth, Globe and Lenin.

1957. Russian Revolution. 40th Anniv.

1004. 280. 30 h. lake 8 5
1005. – 60 h. blue 20 5

DESIGN: 60 h. Lenin, industrial scene and Russian emblem.

1957. Death of President Zapotocky. As T **235** but dated "19 XII 1884–13 XI 1957".

1006. 30 h. black 8 5
1007. 60 h. black 12 5

1957. National Costumes (3rd Series). As T **246**.

1008. 45 h. sepia, red and blue 85 40
1009. 75 h. sepia, red and green 50 12
1010. 1 k. 25 sepia, red & yellow 50 10
1011. 1 k. 95 sepia, blue and red 1·40 60

DESIGNS—VERT. 45 h. Pilsen woman. 75 h. Slovacko man. 1 k. 25 Hana woman. 1 k. 95, Tesin woman.

281. Artificial Satellite ("Sputnik" II). 282. Figure-skating (European Championships, Bratislava).

1957. Int. Geophysical Year. Design showing globe and dated "1957–1958".

1012. – 30 h. lake and yellow 1·00 30
1013. – 45 h. sepia and blue 35 15
1014. 281. 75 h. lake and blue .. 1·95 55

DESIGNS—HORIZ. 30 h. Radio-telescope and observatory. VERT. 45 h. Lomnicky Stit meteorological station.

1958. Sports Events of 1958.

1015. 283. 30 h. purple 20 12
1016. – 40 h. blue (Canoeing) 10 5
1017. – 60 h. brn. (Volley-ball) 15 5
1018. – 80 h. vio. (Parachuting) 70 20
1019. – 1 k. 60 green (Football) 40 8

EVENTS: 40 h. Canoeing (World Canoeing Championships, Prague). 60 h. Volley-ball (European Volley-ball Championship, Prague). 80 h Parachuting (4th World Parachute-jumping Championship, Bratislava). 1 k. 60, Football (World Football Championship, Stockholm).

DESIGN—HORIZ. 60 h. Bethlehem Chapel, Prague.

283. Litomysl Castle (birthplace of Nejedy).

1958. 80th Birthday of Nejedly (musician).

1020. 283. 30 h. green 5 5
1021. – 60 h. brown 15 5

DESIGNS—VERT. 30 h. Giant mine-excavator. HORIZ. 1 k. 60, Combine-harvester.

284. Soldiers guarding Shrine of "Victorious February".

1958. Communist Govt. 10th Anniv.

1022. – 30 h. blue and yellow 10 5
1023. 284. 60 h. brown and red 12 5
1024. – 1 k. 60 green & orange 40 8

286. George of Podebrady and his Seal.

285. Jewellery.

287. Hammer and Sickle. 288. "Towards the Stars" (after sculpture by G. Postnikov).

1958. Brussels Int. Exhibition. Inscr. "Bruxelles 1958".

1025. 285. 30 h. lake and blue .. 8 5
1026. – 45 h. red and lilac .. 10 5
1027. – 60 h. violet and green 15 5
1028. – 75 h. blue and orange 80 30
1029. – 1 k. 20 turquoise & mag. 45 5
1030. – 1 k. 95 brown and blue 80 10

DESIGNS—VERT. 45 h. Toy dolls. 60 h., Draperies. 75 h. Kaplan turbine. 1 k. 20, Glassware. HORIZ. (48½ × 29½ mm.), 1 k. 95. Czech pavilion.

1958. National Exhibition of Archive Documents. Inscr. as in T **286**.

1031. 286. 30 h. red 8 5
1032. – 60 h. violet 15 5

DESIGN: 60 h. Prague, 1628 (from engraving).

1958. 11th Czech Communist Party Congress and Czech-Soviet Friendship Treaty. 15th Anniv. 45 h. inscr. as in T **287** and 60 h. inscr. "15. VYROCI UZAVRENI", etc.

1033. 287. 30 h. red 5 5
1034. – 45 h. green 8 5
1035. – 60 h. indigo 15 5

DESIGNS: 45 h. Map of Czechoslovakia, with hammer and sickle. 60 h. Atomic reactor, Rez (near Prague).

1958. Cultural and Political Events. 45 h. inscr. "IV. KONGRES MEZINARODNI", etc., and 60 h. inscr. "I. SVETOVA ODBOROVA", etc.

1036. 288. 30 h. red 25 15
1037. – 45 h. purple 15 8
1038. – 60 h. blue 12 5

DESIGNS—VERT. 45 h. Three women of different races and globe (4th Int. Democratic Women's Federation Congress, Vienna). HORIZ. 60 h. Boy and girl with globes (1st World T.U. Conference of Working Youth, Prague). T **288** represents the Society for the Dissemination of Cultural and Political Knowledge.

289. Pres. Novotny. 290. Telephone Operator.

1958.

1039. 289. 30 h. violet 8 5
1039a. 30 h. purple 10 5
1040. 60 h. red 12 5

1958. Communist Postal Conference. Prague. Inscr. as in T **290**.
1041. **290.** 30 h. sepia and chest. 12 5
1042. – 45 h. black and green 20 10
DESIGN: 45 h. Aerial mast.

SPAS. 40 h. Podebrady. 60 h. Marianske Lazne (150th Anniv.). 80 h. Luhacovice. 1 k. 20, Strbske Pleso. 1 k. 60, Trencianske.

291. Karlovy Vary (600th Anniv.).

1958. Czech Spas (2nd series).
1043. **291.** 30 h. lake 5 5
1044. – 40 h. brown 8 5
1045. – 60 h. green 12 5
1046. – 80 h. sepia 15 5
1047. – 1 k. 20 blue 25 5
1048. – 1 k. 60 violet .. 85 40

292. "The Poet and the Muse" (after Max Svabinsky). **293.** S. Cech.

1958. Dr. Max Svabinsky (artist). 85th Birthday.
1049. **292.** 1 k. 60 sepia .. .. 1·25 35

1958. Cultural Anniversaries.
1050. – 30 h. red (J. Fucik) 5 5
1051. – 45 h. violet (G. K. Zechenter) .. 50 15
1052. – 60 h. ind. (K. Capek) 12 5
1053. **293.** 1 k. 40 black 25 5

294. Children's Hospital, Brno. **295.** "Lepiota procera".

1958. National Stamp Exn., Brno. Inscr. as in T **294**.
1054. **294.** 30 h. violet 8 5
1055. – 60 h. red 12 5
1056. – 1 k. sepia 25 5
1057. – 1 k. 60 myrtle .. 1·00 80
DESIGNS: 60 h. New Town Hall, Brno. 1 k. St. Thomas's Church, Red Army Square. 1 k. 60 (50×28½ mm.), Brno view.

1958. Mushrooms.
1058. **295.** 30 h. buff, green & brn. 12 5
1059. – 40 h. buff, red & brown 12 5
1060. – 60 h. red, buff and black 20 5
1061. – 1 k. 40 red, grn. & brn. 30 10
1062. – 1 k. 60 red, grn. & blk. 1·00 40
DESIGNS—VERT. 40 h. "Boletus edulis". 60 h. "Krombholzia rufescens". 1 k. 40, "Amanita muscaria L.". 1 k. 60, "Armillariella mellea".

296. Children sailing. **297.** Bozek's Steam Car of 1815.

1958. Inaug. of U.N.E.S.C.O. Headquarters Building, Paris. Inscr. "ZE SOUTEZE PRO UNESCO".
1063. **296.** 30 h. red, yell. & blue 12 5
1064. – 45 h. red and blue .. 20 5
1065. – 60 h. blue, yell. & brn. 25 5
DESIGNS: 45 h. Mother, child and bird. 60 h. Child skier.

1958. Czech Motor Industry Commem.
1066. **297.** 30 h. slate and yellow 8 5
1067. – 45 h. sepia and green 10 5
1068. – 60 h. green and salmon 12 5
1069. – 80 h. lake and green .. 15 5
1070. – 1 k. brown and green 20 5
1071. – 1 k. 25 green & yellow 1·00 25
DESIGNS: 45 h. "President" car of 1897. 60 h. Skoda "450" car. 80 h. Tatra "603" car. 1 k. Skoda "706" motor-coach. 1 k. 25, Tatra "III" and Praga "VS 3" motor trucks in Tibet.

298. Garlanded Women ("Republic") with First Czech Stamp. **299.** Ice Hockey Goalkeeper.

1958. 1st Czech Postage Stamps. 40th Anniv.
1072. **298.** 60 h. indigo 25 5

1959. Sports Events of 1959.
1073. – 20 h. chocolate & grey 20 5
1074. – 30 h. brown & orange 20 5
1075. **299.** 60 h. blue and green .. 12 5
1076. – 1 k. lake and yellow .. 20 5
1077. – 1 k. 60 slate-violet and blue 35 5
1078. – 2 k. brown and blue .. 1·10 50
DESIGNS: 20 h. Ice hockey player (50th Anniv. of Czech Ice Hockey Assn.). 30 h. Throwing the javelin. 60 h. (T **299**) World Ice Hockey Championships, 1959. 1 k. Hurdling. 1 k. 60 Rowing. 2 k. High-jumping.

300. U.A.C. Emblem. **301.** "Equal Rights".

1959. 4th National Unified Agricultural Co-operatives Congress, Prague.
1079. **300.** 30 h. lake and blue .. 5 5
1080. – 60 h. indigo & yellow 12 5
DESIGN: 60 h. Artisan shaking hand with farmer.

1959. Human Rights. 10th Anniv. Inscr. "DEN LIDSKYCH PRAV", etc.
1081. **301.** 60 h. slate-green .. 12 5
1082. – 1 k. sepia 20 5
1083. – 2 k. indigo .. 1·00 25
DESIGNS: 1 k. "World Freedom" (girl with Dove of Peace). 2 k. "Freedom for Colonial Peoples" (native woman with child).

302. Girl with Doll. **303.** F. Joliot-Curie (scientist).

1959. Young Pioneers' Movement. 10th Anniv.
1084. **302.** 30 h. vio.-bl. & yellow 5 5
1085. – 40 h. black and blue 12 5
1086. – 60 h. black and purple 20 5
1087. – 80 h. brown and green 35 10
DESIGNS: 40 h. Boy hiker. 60 h. Young radio technician. 80 h. Girl planting tree.

1959. Peace Movement. 10th Anniv.
1088. **303.** 60 h. slate-purple .. 55 10

304. Man in outer space and Moon Rocket. **305.** Pilsen Town Hall.

1959. 2nd Czech Political and Cultural Knowledge Congress, Prague.
1089. **304.** 30 h. blue 50 12

1959. Skoda Works Cent. and National Stamp Exn., Pilsen. Inscr. "PILSEN 1959".
1090. **305.** 30 h. brown 5 5
1091. – 60 h. violet and green 12 5
1092. – 1 k. blue 20 5
1093. – 1 k. 60 black & yellow 80 40
DESIGNS: 60 h. Part of steam turbine. 1 k. St. Bartholomew's Church, Pilsen. 1 k. 60, Part of SR-1200 lathe.

306. Congress Emblem and Industrial Plant.

307. Zvolen Castle. **308.** F. Benda.

1959. 4th W.F.T.U. Congress, Prague. Inscr. "IV VSEODBOROVY SJEZD 1959".
1094. **306.** 30 h. red and yellow 5 5
1095. – 60 h. brn.-olive & blue 10 5
DESIGN: 60 h. Dam.

1959. Slovak Stamp Exhibition.
1096. **307.** 60 h. olive and yellow 15 5

1959. Cultural Anniversaries.
1097. **308.** 15 h. blue 5 5
1098. – 30 h. chestnut .. 5 5
1099. – 40 h. green 8 5
1100. – 60 h. chocolate .. 12 5
1101. – 60 h. violet-black .. 12 5
1102. – 80 h. violet 20 5
1103. – 1 k. sepia 30 5
1104. – 3 k. chocolate .. 65 25
PORTRAITS: 30 h. Klicpera. 40 h. Stodola. 60 h. (No. 1100), Rais. 60 h. (No. 1101), Haydn. 80 h. Slavicek. 1 k. Bezruc. 3 k. Darwin.

DESIGNS: 30 h. View of Fair. 60 h. Fair emblem and world map.

309. "Z" Pavilion.

1959. Int. Fair, Brno. Inscr. "BRNO 6-20. IX. 1959".
1105. – 30 h. purple & yellow .. 5 5
1106. – 60 h. blue 12 5
1107. **309.** 1 k. 60 blue & yellow 40 5

310. Revolutionary (after A. Holly).

1959. Slovak National Uprising. 15th Anniv. and Republic. 40th Anniv. Inscr. "1944 29.8.1959".
1108. **310.** 30 h. black & magenta 5 5
1109. – 60 h. claret 12 5
1110. – 1 k. 60 indigo & yell. 40 5
DESIGNS—VERT. 60 h. Revolutionary with upraised rifle (after sculpture "Forward" by L. Snopka). HORIZ. 1 k. 60, Factory, sun and linden leaves.

311. Moon Rocket. **312.** Lynx.

1959. Landing of Russian Rocket on Moon.
1111. **311.** 60 h. red and blue .. 35 5

1959. Tatra National Park. 10th Anniv. Inscr. "1949 TATRANSKY NARODNY PARK 1959".
1112. – 30 h. black and grey 15 5
1113. – 40 h. chocolate & turq. 20 5
1114. **312.** 60 h. brn.-red & yell. 12 5
1115. – 1 k. olive-brn. & blue 90 30
1116. – 1 k. 60 brown .. 35 5
DESIGNS—HORIZ. 30 h. Marmots. 40 h. European bison. 1 k. Wolf. 1 k. 60, Stag.

313. Stamp Printing Works, Peking.

1959. Chinese People's Republic. 10th Anniv.
1117. **313.** 30 h. brown-red and yellow-green .. 10 5

DESIGN: 1 k. 80. Jan Kaspar and 'plane in flight.

314. Bleriot-type 'Plane of First Czech Aviation School.

1959. Air. 1st Flight by Jan Kaspar. 50th Anniv. Inscr. as in T **314**.
1118. **314.** 1 k. black and yellow 20 5
1119. – 1 k. 80 black & blue 50 8

BIRDS: 30 h. Blue tit. 40 h. Nuthatch. 60 h. Oriole. 80 h. Goldfinch. 1 k. Bullfinch. 1 k. 20. Kingfisher.

315. Woodpecker.

1959. Birds.
1120. **315.** 20 h. red, brown, blue and black 15 5
1121. – 30 h. blue, yellow brown and black .. 10 5
1122. – 40 h. slate, orange, brown and sepia .. 70 40
1123. – 60 h. red, brown, yellow and black .. 15 5
1124. – 80 h. yellow, chestnut, red and black .. 15 5
1125. – 1 k. red, blue & black 20 5
1126. – 1 k. 20 chestnut, blue and black 25 15

316. Tesla and Electrical Apparatus. **317.** Exercises.

1959. Radio Inventors.
1127. **316.** 25 h. black and rose 30 5
1128. – 30 h. black & chestnut 10 5
1129. – 35 h. black and lilac 10 5
1130. – 60 h. black and blue 15 5
1131. – 1 k. black and green 20 5
1132. – 2 k. black and bistre 85 30
INVENTORS (each with sketch of invention): 30 h. Popov. 35 h. Branly. 60 h. Marconi. 1 k. Hertz. 2 k. Armstrong.

1960. 2nd National Spartacist Games (1st issue). Inscr. as in T **317**.
1133. **317.** 30 h. sepia & turquoise 5 5
1134. – 60 h. indigo and blue 20 5
1135. – 1 k. 60 sepia & bistre 45 8
DESIGNS: 60 h. Skiing. 1 k. 60, Basketball. See also Nos. 1160/2.

SHIPS: 30 h. Dredger. 60 h. Ocean tug-boat "Komarno". 1 k. Tourist M.V. "Komarno".

318. Freighter "Lidice".

1960. Czech Ships.
1136. – 30 h. green and red .. 8 5
1137. – 60 h. lake & turquoise 15 5
1138. – 1 k. violet and yellow 25 5
1139. **318.** 1 k. 20 purple & green 60 40

DESIGN: 1k 80, Skating pair. See also Nos. 1163/5.

319. Ice-hockey.

1960. Winter Olympic Games. Inscr. as in T 319.
1140. **319.** 60 h. sepia and blue 25 5
1141. – 1 k. 80 black & green 1·75 90

320. Trencin Castle. **321.** Lenin. **322.** Soldier and Child.

1960. Czechoslovak Castles.
1142. 5 h. violet-blue (T **320**).. 5 5
1143. 10 h. black (Bezdez) .. 5 5
1144. 20 h. chestnut (Kost) .. 5 5
1145. 30 h. green (Pernstyn) .. 8 5
1146. 40 h. brown (Kremnice) 10 5
1146a. 50 h. black (Krivoklat).. 15 5
1147. 60 h. red (Karluv Tyn).. 15 5
1148. 1 k. purple (Smolenice).. 20 5
1149. 1 k. 60 blue (Kokorin) .. 35 5

1960. Lenin. 90th Birth Anniv.
1150. **321.** 60 h. olive 25 5

1960. Liberation. 15th Anniv.
1151. **322.** 30 h. lake and blue .. 8 5
1152. – 30 h. grn. & lavender 5 5
1153. – 30 h. red and pink .. 8 5
1154. – 60 h. blue and buff .. 12 5
1155. – 60 h. maroon & green 12 5
DESIGNS—VERT. No. 1152, Soldier with liberated political prisoner. 1153, Child eating pastry. HORIZ. 1154, Welder. 1155, Tractor-driver.

DESIGN: 60 h. Country woman and child.

323. Smelter.

1960. Parliamentary Elections.
1156. **323.** 30 h. red and grey .. 8 5
1157. – 60 h. green and blue 15 5

324. Red Cross Woman with Dove.

1960. 3rd Czechoslovak Red Cross Congress.
1158. **324.** 30 h. red and blue .. 8 5

325. Fire-prevention team with Hose.

1960. 2nd Firemen's Union Congress.
1159. **325.** 60 h. blue and pink.. 12 5

1960. 2nd National Spartacist Games (2nd issue). As Type **317.**
1160. 30 h. red and green.. 8 5
1161. 60 h. black and pink 12 5
1162. 1 k. blue and orange 20 5
DESIGNS: 30 h. Ball exercises. 60 h. Stick exercises. 1 k. Girls with hoops.

1960. Summer Olympic Games.
1163. 1 k. black and orange 20 5
1164. 1 k. 80 black and red 40 10
1165. 2 k. black and blue .. 1·10 40
DESIGNS: 1 k. Sprinting. 1 k. 80, Gymnastics. 2 k. Rowing.

326. Czech 10 k. Stamp of 1936.

327. Stalin Mine, Ostrava-Hermanice.

328. V. Cornelius of Vsehra (historian).

1960. National Philatelic Exn., Bratislava (1st issue).
1166. – 60 h. black and yellow 12 5
1167. **326.** 1 k. black and blue.. 25 5
DESIGN: 60 h. Hand of philatelist holding stamp T **326.**
See also Nos. 1183/4.

1960. 3rd Five Year Plan (1st issue).
1168. **327.** 10 h. black and green 5 5
1169. – 20 h. lake and blue .. 5 5
1170. – 30 h. indigo and rose 5 5
1171. – 40 h. green and lilac.. 8 5
1172. – 60 h. blue and yellow 15 5
DESIGNS: 20 h. Hodonin Power Station. 30 h. Klement Gottwald Iron Works, Kuncice. 40 h. Excavator. 60 h. Naphtha refinery.
See also Nos. 1198/1200.

1960. Cultural Anniversaries.
1173. **328.** 10 h. black 5 5
1174. – 20 h. chocolate .. 8 5
1175. – 30 h. red 5 5
1176. – 40 h. green 8 5
1177. – 60 h. violet 12 5
PORTRAITS: 20 h. K. M. Capek Chod (writer). 30 h. Hana Kvapilova (actress). 40 h. Oskar Nedbal (composer). 60 h. Otakar Ostricil (composer).

329. Aircraft flying upside-down.

330. "New Constitution". **331.** Worker with "Rude Pravo".

1960. 1st World Aviation Aerobatic Championships, Bratislava.
1178. **329.** 60 h. violet and blue 30 5

1960. Proclamation of New Constitution.
1179. **330.** 30 h. blue and red .. 8 5

1960. Czechoslovak Press Day (30 h.) and 40th Anniv. of Newspaper "Rude Pravo".
1180. – 30 h. indigo & orange 8 5
1181. **331.** 60 h. black and red .. 12 5
DESIGN—HORIZ. (inscr. "DEN TISKU"): 30 h. Steel-workers with newspaper.

332. Globes.

1960. W.F.T.U. 15th Anniv.
1182. **332.** 30 h. grey-blue & bistre 8 5

333. Mail Coach and Airliner.

1960. Air. National Philatelic Exn., Bratislava (2nd issue).
1183. **333.** 1 k. 60 blue and grey 1·60 60
1184. – 2 k. 80 green & cream 1·60 1·00
DESIGN: 2 k. 80, Helicopter over Bratislava.

334. Mallard Duck. **335.** "Doronicum clusii tausch".

1960. Water Birds.
1185. – 25 h. black and blue 8 5
1186. – 30 h. black and green 20 5
1187. – 40 h. black & turquoise 8 5
1188. – 60 h. black and pink 12 5
1189. – 1 k. black and yellow 20 5
1190. **334.** 1 k. 60 black & lilac 90 35
BIRDS—VERT. 25 h. Night heron. 30 h. Great crested grebe. 40 h. Lapwing. 60 h. Grey heron. HORIZ. 1 k. Grey-lag goose.

1960. Flowers. Inscr. in black.
1191. **335.** 20 h. yell., orge. & grn. 5 5
1192. – 30 h. red and green .. 5 5
1193. – 40 h. yellow and green 10 5
1194. – 60 h. pink and green 15 5
1195. – 1 k. blue, violet & grn. 25 5
1196. – 2 k. yell., grn. & pur. 1·00 45
FLOWERS: 30 h. "Cyclamen europaeum L". 40 h. "Primula auricula L". 60 h. "Sempervivum mont. L". 1 k. "Gentiana clusii perr, et song". 2 k. "Pulsatilla slavica reuss".

336. Alfons Mucha (painter and stamp designer). **337.** Automatic Machinery ("Automation").

1960. Stamp Day and Mucha's Birth Cent.
1197. **336.** 60 h. indigo 15 5

1961. 3rd Five Year Plan (2nd issue).
1198. **337.** 20 h. blue 8 5
1199. – 30 h. red 8 5
1200. – 60 h. green 15 5
DESIGNS: 30 h. Turbo-generator and control desk ("Atomic Power"). 60 h. Excavator ("Mechanisation").

338. Motor-cycling (Int. Grand Prix. Brno).

339. Exhibition Emblem.

341. J. Mosna. **340.** Sputnik III.

1961. Sports Events of 1961.
1201. **338.** 30 h. indigo and mag. 5 5
1202. – 30 h. red and blue .. 5 5
1203. – 40 h. black and red.. 20 5
1204. – 60 h. purple and blue 15 5
1205. – 1 k. blue and yellow 20 5
1206. – 1 k. 20 green & salmon 25 5
1207. – 1 k. 60 brown and red 80 35
DESIGNS—VERT. No. 1202, Athletes with banners (40th Anniv. of Czech Physical Culture). 60 h. Figure-skating (World Figure-skating Championships, Prague). 1 k. Rugger (35th Anniv. of Rugby Football in Czechoslovakia). 1 k. 20, Football (60th Anniv. of Football in Czechoslovakia). 1 k. 60, Running (65th Anniv. of Bechovice-Prague Marathon Race). HORIZ. 40 h. Rowing (European Rowing Championships, Prague).

1961. "PRAGA 1962" Int. Stamp Exn. (1st issue).
1208. **339.** 2 k. red and blue .. 85 5
See also Nos. 1250/70, 1297/300 and 1311/5.

1961. Cosmic Space Research (1st issue).
1209. – 20 h. red and violet.. 20 5
1210. **340.** 30 h. turquoise & buff 8 5
1211. – 40 h. red and green.. 10 5
1212. – 60 h. violet & yellow 15 5
1213. – 1 k. 60 blue & green 40 8
1214. – 2 k. claret and blue.. 1·40 45
DESIGNS—VERT. 20 h. Launching cosmic rocket. 40 h. Venus rocket. HORIZ. 60 h. Lunik I. 1 k. 60, Lunik III and Moon. 2 k. "Space Man" in flight.
See also Nos. 1285/90 and 1349/54.

1961. Cultural Anniversaries.
1215. **341.** 60 h. green 15 5
1216. – 60 h. black (Uprka).. 15 5
1217. – 60 h. bl. (Hviezdoslav) 15 5
1218. – 60 h. lake (Mrstik) 15 5
1219. – 60 h. sepia (Hora) .. 15 5

342. Man in Space.

1961. World's 1st Manned Space Flight.
1220. **342.** 60 h. red & turquoise 20 5
1221. 3 k. blue and yellow 1·10 30

343. Kladno Steel Mills. **344.** "Instrumental. Music".

1961.
1222. **343.** 3 k. red 70 5

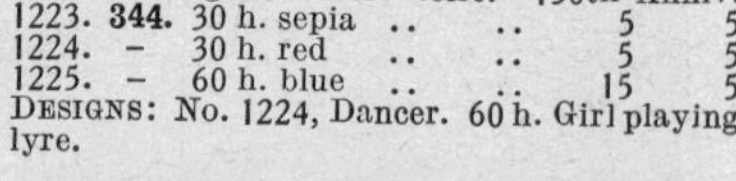

1961. Prague Conservatoire. 150th Anniv.
1223. **344.** 30 h. sepia 5 5
1224. – 30 h. red 5 5
1225. – 60 h. blue 15 5
DESIGNS: No. 1224, Dancer. 60 h. Girl playing lyre.

345. "People's House" (Lenin Museum), Prague.

346. Manasek Doll.

347. Gagarin waving Flags. **348.** Woman's Head and Map of Africa.

1961. Czech Communist Party. 40th Anniv.
1226. **345.** 30 h. chocolate .. 5 5
1227. – 30 h. indigo 5 5
1228. – 30 h. violet 5 5
1229. – 60 h. red 15 5
1230. – 60 h. myrtle .. 15 5
1231. – 60 h. vermilion .. 15 5
DESIGNS—HORIZ. No. 1227, Gottwald's Museum, Prague. VERT. 1228, Workers in Wenceslas Square, Prague. 1229, Worker, star and factory plant. 1230, Woman wielding hammer and sickle. 1231, May Day procession, Wenceslas Square.

1961. Czech Puppets.
1232. **346.** 30 h. red and yellow.. 8 5
1233. – 40 h. sepia & turquoise 10 5
1234. – 60 h. ultram. & salmon 15 5
1235. – 1 k. green and blue .. 25 5
1236. – 1 k. 60 red and blue.. 1·10 20
PUPPETS: 40 h. "Dr. Faustus and Caspar". 60 h. "Spejbl and Hurvinek". 1 k. Scene from "Difficulties with the Moon" (Askenazy). 1 k. 60, "Jasanek" of Brno.

1961. Gagarin's Visit to Prague.
1237. **347.** 60 h. black and red .. 12 5
1238. – 1 k. 80 black and blue 45 8
DESIGN: 1 k. 80, Yuri Gagarin in space helmet, rocket and dove.

1961. Czecho-African Friendship.
1239. **348.** 60 h. red and blue .. 15 5

349. Map of Europe and Fair Emblem.

350. Clover and Cow.

351. Prague. **352.** Orlik Dam.

1961. Int. Trade Fair, Brno. Inscr. "M.V.B. 1961".

1240. 349. 30 h. blue and green 10 5
1241. – 60 h. green & salmon 12 5
1242. – 1 k. chocolate & blue 20 5

DESIGNS—VERT. 60 h. Horizontal drill. HORIZ. 1 k. Scientific discussion group.

1961. Agricultural Produce.

1243. – 20 h. purple & indigo 5 5
1244. 350. 30 h. ochre and purple 5 5
1245. – 40 h. orange & choc. 8 5
1246. – 60 h. bistre and green 12 5
1247. – 1 k. 40 chest. & choc. 30 5
1248. – 2 k. blue & slate-pur. 1·00 25

DESIGNS: 20 h. Sugar beet; cup and saucer. 40 h. Wheat and bread. 60 h. Hops and beer. 1 k. 40, Maize and cattle. 2 k. Potatoes and factory.

1961. 26th Session of Red Cross Societies League Governors' Council, Prague.

1249. 351. 60 h. violet and red.. 40 5

1961. "Praga 1962" Int. Stamp Exn. (2nd issue).

1250. 352. 20 h. black and blue 20 5
1251. – 30 h. blue and red .. 5 5
1252. – 40 h. blue and green 20 5
1253. – 60 h. slate and bistre 20 5
1267. – 1 k. maroon and green 30 25
1254. – 1 k. 20 myrtle & pink 40 25
1268. – 1 k. 60 brown & violet 45 40
1269. – 2 k. black and orange 55 50
1255. – 3 k. blue and yellow 85 65
1256. – 4 k. violet and orange 1·10 90
1270. – 5 k. multicoloured .. 7·50 6·50

DESIGNS—As T 352: 30 h. Prague. 40 h. Hluboka Castle from lake. 60 h. Karlovy Vary. 1 k. Pilsen. 1 k. 20, North Bohemian landscape. 1 k. 60, High Tatras. 2 k. Ironworks, Ostrava-Kuncice. 3 k. Brno. 4 k. Bratislava. (50 × 29 mm.): 5 k. Prague and flags.

No. 1270 was only issued in sheets of four.

353. "Anthocharis cardamines L.".

354. Congress Emblem and World Map.

1961. Czech Butterflies. Multicoloured.

1257. 15 h. T 353 5 5
1258. 20 h. "Zerynthia hypsipyle Sch." 5 5
1259. 30 h. "Parnassius apollo L." 5 5
1260. 40 h. "Papilio machaon L." 8 5
1261. 60 h. "Nymphalis Io L." 12 5
1262. 80 h. "Nymphalis antiopa L." 20 8
1263. 1 k. "Catocala fraxini L." 20 10
1264. 1 k. 60 "Vanessa atalanta L." 35 15
1265. 2 k. "Gonepteryx rhamni L." 1·75 45

1961. 5th W.F.T.U. Congress, Moscow.

1266. 354. 60 h. blue and red .. 15 5

355. Racing Cyclists (Berlin-Prague-Warsaw Cycle Race).

356. Karel Kovarovic (composer).

1962. Sports Events of 1962.

1271. 355. 30 h. blk. & vio.-blue 5 5
1272. – 40 h. black and yellow 8 5
1273. – 60 h. slate and blue.. 12 5
1274. – 1 k. black and pink.. 20 5
1275. – 1 k. 20 black & green 25 5
1276. – 1 k. 60 black & green 85 20

DESIGNS: 40 h. Gymnastics (15th World Gymnastic Championships, Prague). 60 h. Figure-skating (World Figure-skating Championships, Prague). 1 k. Bowling (World Bowling Championships, Bratislava). 1 k. 20, Football (World Football Championships, Chile). 1 k. 60, Discus-throwing (7th European Athletic Championships, Belgrade).

See also No. 1306.

1962. Cultural Anniversaries.

1277. 356. 10 h. chestnut .. 5 5
1278. – 20 h. blue 5 5
1279. – 30 h. brown 5 5
1280. – 40 h. purple 5 5
1281. – 60 h. black 12 5
1282. – 1 k. 60 myrtle .. 40 5
1283. – 1 k. 80 indigo .. 50 5

DESIGNS—As T 356: 20 h. F. Skroup (composer). 30 h. Bezena Nemcova (writer). 60 h. Rod of Aesculapius and Prague Castle (Czech Medical Association Cent.). 1 k. 60 L. Celakovsky (founder, Czech Botanical Society). HORIZ. (41 × 22½ mm.): 40 h. F. Zaviska and K. Petr. 1 k. 80, M. Valouch and J Hronec. (These two commemorate Czech Mathematics and Physics Union Cent.)

357. Miner holding Lamp.

358. "Man Conquers Space".

360. Dove and Nest.

359. Elephants.

1962. Miners' Strike, Most. 30th Anniv.

1284. 357. 60 h. indigo and red.. 12 5

1962. Cosmic Space Research (2nd issue).

1285. 358. 30 h. red and blue .. 8 5
1286. – 40 h. blue and orange 8 5
1287. – 60 h. blue and pink.. 12 5
1288. – 80 h. purple and green 15 5
1289. – 1 k. indigo and yellow 20 5
1290. – 1 k. 60 green & yellow 1·00 35

DESIGNS—VERT. 40 h. Launching of Soviet rocket. 1 k. Automatic station on Moon. HORIZ. 60 h. "Vostok-II". 80 h. Multi-stage automatic rocket. 1 k. 60, Television satellite station.

1962. Animals of Prague Zoos.

1291. – 20 h. black & turq. 8 5
1292. – 30 h. black and violet 8 5
1293. – 60 h. black and yellow 12 5
1294. 359. 1 k. black and green 30 5
1295. – 1 k. 40 blk. & magenta 30 8
1296. – 1 k. 60 black & brown 1·00 35

ANIMALS—VERT. 20 h. Polar bear. 30 h. Chimpanzee. 60 h. Bactrian camel. HORIZ. 1 k. 40, Leopard. 1 k. 60, Przewalski's horses.

1962. Air. "Praga 1962" Int. Stamp Exn. (3rd issue).

1297. 80 h. yell., red, brn. & blk. 15 15
1298. 1 k. 40 red, blue and black 65 65
1299. 2 k. 80 yell., red, brn. & blk. 95 95
1300. 4 k. 20 red, blk., yell. & brn. 1·60 1·60

DESIGNS: 80 h. T 360. 1 k. 40, Dove. 2 k. 80, Flower and bird. 4 k. 20, Plant and bird. All designs feature "Praga 62" emblem. The 80 h. and 2 k. 80 are inscr. in Slovakian and the others in Czech.

361. Girl of Lidice.

362. Klary's Fountain, Teplice.

1962. Destruction of Lidice and Lezaky. 20th Anniv.

1301. 361. 30 h. black and red.. 5 5
1302. – 60 h. black and blue.. 15 5

DESIGN: 60 h. Flowers and Lezaky ruins.

1962. Teplice Springs Discovery. 12th Cent.

1303. 362. 60 h. myrtle & yellow 20 5

HAVE YOU READ THE NOTES AT THE BEGINNING OF THIS CATALOGUE?

These often provide answers to the enquiries we receive.

363. Campaign Emblem.

364. Swimmer with Rifle.

1962. Malaria Eradication.

1304. 363. 60 h. red and black .. 12 5
1305. – 3 k. blue and yellow.. 85 30

DESIGN: 3 k. Campaign emblem and dove.

1962. Participation in World Football Championships' Final, Chile. As No. 1275 but inscr. "CSSR VE FINALE" and value.

1306. 1 k. 60 green and yellow.. 55 12

1962. 2nd Military Spartacist Games. Inscr. as in T 364.

1307. 364. 30 h. myrtle and blue 8 5
1308. – 40 h. violet and yellow 10 5
1309. – 60 h. brown and green 12 5
1310. – 1 k. indigo and red .. 20 5

DESIGNS: 40 h. Soldier mounting obstacle. 60 h. Footballer. 1 k. Relay Race.

365. "Sun" and Field (Socialized Agriculture).

366. Swallow, "Praga 62" and Congress Emblems.

1962. "Praga 1962" Int. Stamp Exn. (4th issue).

1311. 365. 30 h. multicoloured.. 50 50
1312. – 60 h. multicoloured.. 20 20
1313. – 80 h. multicoloured.. 65 65
1314. – 1 k. multicoloured .. 90 90
1315. – 1 k. 40 multicoloured 1·00 1·00

DESIGNS—VERT. 60 h. Astronaut in "spaceship". 1 k. 40, Children playing under "tree". HORIZ. 80 h. Boy with flute, and peace doves. 1 k. Workers of three races. All have "Praga 62" emblem.

1962. F.I.P. Day (Federation Internationale de Philatelie).

1316. 366. 1 k. 60 multicoloured 1·10 1·10

368. Cruiser "Aurora".

367. Zinkovy Sanatorium and Sailing Boat.

369. Astronaut and Worker.

1962. Czech Workers' Social Facilities.

1317. – 30 h. black and blue 5 5
1318. 367. 60 h. sepia and ochre 12 5

DESIGN—HORIZ. 30 h. Children in day nursery, and factory.

1962. Russian Revolution. 45th Anniv.

1319. 368. 30 h. sepia and blue 5 5
1320. 60 h. black and pink 15 5

1962. U.S.S.R. 40th Anniv.

1321. 369. 30 h. red and blue .. 5 5
1322. – 60 h. black and pink 15 5

DESIGN—VERT. 60 h. Lenin.

370. Crane ("Building Construction").

1962. 12th Czech Communist Party Congress Prague. Inscr. as in T 370.

1323. 370. 30 h. lake and yellow 8 5
1324. – 40 h. slate-bl. & yell. 8 5
1325. – 60 h. lake and slate-vio. 15 5

DESIGNS—VERT. 40 h. Produce ("Agriculture"). HORIZ. 60 h. Factory plants ("Industry").

371. Stag Beetle ("Lucanus cervus L.").

372. Table Tennis (World Championships, Prague).

1962. Beetles.

1326. 20 h. blue, red, green, olive-yellow and chestnut .. 5 5
1327. 30 h. red, green and black 8 5
1328. 60 h. choc., brown & myrtle 12 8
1329. 1 k. mar., ochre, grn. & bl. 20 8
1330. 1 k. 60 chocolate, blue, turquoise and apple .. 35 10
1331. 2 k. indigo and apple .. 1·25 40

BEETLES—HORIZ. 20 h. Sycophant ("Calosoma sycophanta L."). 30 h. Cardinal ("Pyrochoa coccinea L."). 1 k. Great water-beetle ("Dytiscus marginalis L."). VERT. 60 h. T 371. 1 k. 60, Alpine longhorn ("Rosalis alpina L."). 2 k. Ground-beetle ("Carabus intricatus L.").

1963. Sports Events of 1963.

1332. 372. 30 h. black and green 8 5
1333. – 60 h. black & orange 15 5
1334. – 80 h. black and blue.. 20 5
1335. – 1 k. black and violet 25 5
1336. – 1 k. 20 black & brown 30 8
1337. – 1 k. 60 black and red 45 5

DESIGNS: 60 h. Cycling (80th Anniv. of Czech Cycling). 80 h. Ski-ing (1st Czech Winter Games). 1 k. Motor-cycle dirt track racing (15th Anniv. of "Golden Helmet" Race, Pardubice). 1 k. 20, Weightlifting (World Championships, Prague). 1 k. 60, Hurdling (1st Czech Summer Games).

373. Industrial Plant.

374. Guild Emblem.

1963. 15th Anniv. of "Victorious February" and 5th T.U. Congress.

1338. 373. 30 h. red and blue .. 5 5
1339. – 60 h. red and black.. 12 5
1340. – 60 h. black and verm. 12 5

DESIGNS—VERT. No. 1339, Sun and campfire. HORIZ. No. 1340, Industrial plant and annual "stepping stones".

1963. Cultural Anniversaries.

1341. 374. 20 h. black and blue 5 5
1342. – 30 h. red 5 5
1343. – 30 h. red and blue .. 5 5
1344. – 60 h. black 12 5
1345. – 60 h. maroon & blue 12 5
1346. – 60 h. myrtle .. 12 5
1347 – 1 k. 60 brown .. 40 5

DESIGNS—VERT. No. 1341, (Artists' Guild Cent.). 1342, E. Urx (journalist). 1343, J. Janosik (national hero). 1344, J. Palkovic (author). 1346, Woman with book, and children (Cent. of Slovak Cultural Society, Slovenska Matice). 1347, M. Svabinsky (artist; after self-portrait). HORIZ. 1345, Allegorical figure and National Theatre, Prague (80th Anniv.).

375. Young People.

376. TV Cameras and Receiver.

377. Broadcasting Studio and Receiver.

378. Ancient Ring and Moravian Settlements Map.

1963. 4th Czech Youth Federation Congress, Prague.
1348. **375.** 30 h. indigo and red 10 5

1963. Cosmic Space Research (3rd issue). As T **340** but inscr. "1963" at foot.
1349. 30 h. maroon, red & yellow 8 5
1350. 50 h. blue & turq.-green 10 5
1351. 60 h. blue-green & yellow 12 5
1352. 1 k. black and brown .. 20 5
1353. 1 k. 60 sepia and green .. 35 5
1354. 2 k. violet and yellow .. 90 35
DESIGNS—HORIZ. 30 h. Rocket circling Sun. 50 h. Rockets and Sputniks leaving Earth. 60 h. Spacecraft and Moon. 1 k. "Mars 1" rocket and Mars. 1 k. 60, Rocket heading for Jupiter. 2 k. Spacecraft returning from Saturn.

1963. Czech Television Service. 10th Anniv. Inscr. as in T **376**.
1355. **376.** 40 h. blue and orange 5 5
1356. – 60 h. red and blue .. 10 15
DESIGN—VERT. 60 h. TV transmitting aerial.

1963. Czech Radio Service. 40th Anniv. Inscr. as in T **377**.
1357. **377.** 30 h. maroon & blue 5 5
1358. – 1 k. purple & turquoise 25 5
DESIGN—VERT. 1 k. Aerial mast, globe and doves.

1963. Moravian Empire. 1100th Anniv. Inscr. as in T **378**.
1359. **378.** 30 h. black and green 8 5
1360. – 1 k. 60 black & yellow 40 5
DESIGN: 1 k. 60. Ancient silver plate showing falconer with hawk.

379. Tupolev "Tu-104" Jetliner. **380.** Singer.

1963. Czech Airlines. 40th Anniv.
1361. **379.** 80 h. violet and blue 20 5
1362. – 1 k. 80 indigo & green 45 8
DESIGN: 1 k. 80, Il-18 turbo-prop. airliner.

1963. Moravian Teachers' Singing Club. 60th Anniv.
1363. **380.** 30 h. red 20 5

381. Nurse and Child. **382.** Wheatears and Kromeriz Castle.

1963. Red Cross Cent.
1364. **381.** 30 h. indigo and red .. 20 5

1963. Nat. Agricultural Exn.
1365. **382.** 30 h. green and yellow 20 5

383. Bee, Honeycomb and Congress Emblem.

1963. 19th Int. Bee-keepers' Congress ("Apimondia '63").
1366. **383.** 1 k. brown and yellow 25 5

384. "Vostok 5" and Bykovsky. **385.** "Modern Fashion".

1963. Second "Team" Manned Space Flights.
1367. **384.** 80 h. pink and slate .. 15 5
1368. – 2 k. 80 blue & brn.-pur. 70 10
DESIGN: 2 k. 80, "Vostok 6" and Valentina Tereshkova.

1963. Liberec Consumer Goods Fair.
1369. **385.** 30 h. black & magenta 20 5

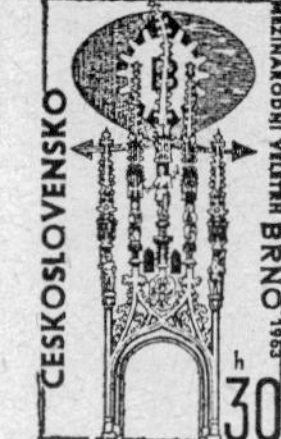

386. Portal of Brno Town Hall. **387.** Cave and Stalagmites.

1963. Brno. Int. Fair.
1370. **386.** 30 h. brn.-pur. & blue 8 5
1371. – 60 h. blue and salmon 15 5
DESIGN: 60 h. Tower of Brno Town Hall.

1963. Czech Scenery. (a) Moravia.
1372. **387.** 30 h. brown and blue 8 5
1373. – 80 h. sepia & light pink 20 5

(b) Slovakia.
1374. – 30 h. deep blue & green 8 5
1375. – 60 h. blue and yellow 15 5
DESIGNS: No. 1373, Macocha Chasm. 1374, Pool, Hornad Valley. 1375, Waterfall, Great Hawk Gorge.

388. Mouse.

391. Dolls.

389. Blast Furnace.

390. "Aid for Farmers Abroad".

1963. 2nd Int. Pharmacological Congress, Prague.
1376. **388.** 1 k. red and black .. 20 5

1963. 30th Int. Foundry Congress, Prague.
1377. **389.** 60 h. black and blue .. 15 5

1963. Freedom from Hunger.
1378. **390.** 1 k. 60 sepia 40 5

1963. U.N.E.S.C.O. Commem. Folklore. Multicoloured.
1379. 60 h. Type **391** 12 5
1380. 80 h. Rooster 15 5
1381. 1 k. Vase of flowers 20 8
1382. 1 k. 20 Detail of glass-painting "Janasik and his Men" 25 8
1383. 1 k. 60 Stag 35 10
1384. 2 k. Horseman .. .. 1·10 40

392. Canoeing. **393.** Linden Tree.

1963. Olympic Games, Tokyo, 1964, and Czech Canoeing 50th Anniv. (30 h.).
1385. **392.** 30 h. grey-blue & green 5 5
1386. – 40 h. brown and blue 8 5
1387. – 60 h. lake and yellow 12 5
1388. – 80 h. violet and red .. 15 5
1389. – 1 k. blue and red .. 20 5
1390. – 1 k. 60 ultram. & blue 1·00 40
DESIGNS: 40 h. Volleyball. 60h. Wrestling. 80 h. Basketball. 1 k. Boxing. 1 k. 60, Gymnastics.

1963. Czech-Soviet Treaty of Friendship.
1391. **393.** 30 h. brown and blue 8 5
1392. – 60 h. red & grey-green 15 5
DESIGN: 60 h. Hammer, sickle and star.

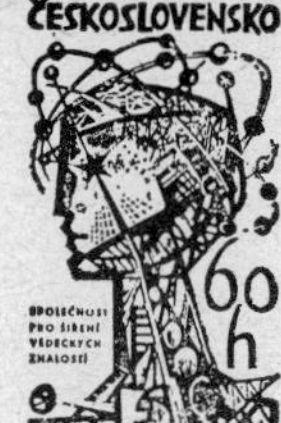

394. "Human Reason and Technology." **395.** Chamois.

1963. Technical and Scientific Knowledge Society Congress.
1393. **394.** 60 h. slate-violet .. 20 5

1963. Mountain Animals.
1394. **395.** 30 h. black, yellow, purple and blue .. 15 5
1395. – 40 h. black, brown, red and slate .. 25 8
1396. – 60 h. sepia, yell. & grn. 30 10
1397. – 1 k. 20 black, brown, red and green .. 45 10
1398. – 1 k. 60 black, chestnut, red and green .. 60 15
1399. – 2 k. chestnut, orange and green .. .. 1·60 85
ANIMALS: 40 h. Ibex, 60 h. Moufflon. 1 k. 20, Roebuck. 1 k. 60, Fallow deer. 2 k. Stag.

396. Figure-skating. **397.** Ice Hockey.

1964. Sports Events of 1964.
1400. **396.** 30 h. violet and yellow 5 5
1401. – 80 h. blue and orange 20 5
1402. – 1 k. chocolate and lilac 25 5
DESIGNS—VERT. 30 h. T **396** (Czech Students Games). 1 k. Handball (World Handball Championships). HORIZ. 80 h. Cross-country skiing (Students' Games).

1964. Winter Olympic Games, Innsbruck.
1403. **397.** 1 k. purple & turquoise 30 25
1404. – 1 k. 80 slate-grn. & lav. 65 60
1405. – 2 k. blue and green .. 1·25 85
DESIGNS—VERT. 1 k. 80. Tobogganing. HORIZ. 2 k. Ski-jumping.

398. Belanske Tatra Mountains, Skiers and Tree.

1964. Tourist Issue.
1406. **398.** 30 h. maroon & blue 5 5
1407. – 60 h. indigo and red .. 15 5
1408. – 1 k. brown and olive 25 5
1409. – 1 k. 80 bronze-green and orange .. 45 12
DESIGNS: 60 h. Telc (Moravia) and motor-camp. 1 k. Spis Castle (Slovakia) and angler. 1 k. 80, Cesky Krumlov (Bohemia) and boating. Each design includes a tree.

399. Magura Hotel, Zdiar, High Tatra.

DESIGN: 80 h. "Slovak Insurrection" Hotel, Lower Tatra.

1964. Trade Union Recreation Hotels.
1410. **399.** 60 h. green and yellow 15 5
1411. – 80 h. blue and pink .. 20 5

400. Statuary (after Michelangelo).

1964. U.N.E.S.C.O. Cultural Anniversaries.
1412. **400.** 40 h. black and green 8 5
1413. – 60 h. black and red .. 12 5
1414. – 1 k. black and blue .. 20 5
1415. – 1 k. 60 black & yellow 45 8
DESIGNS—HORIZ. 40 h. T **400** (400th Anniv. of Michelangelo's death). 60 h. Bottom, "Midsummer Night's Dream" (400th Anniv. of Shakespeare's birth). 1 k. 60, King George of Podebrady (500th Anniv. of his mediation in Europe). VERT. 1 k. Galileo Galilei (400th anniv. of birth).

401. Gagarin.

1964. "Space Exploration". On cream paper.
1416. **401.** 30 h. ultram. & black 20 5
1417. – 60 h. crimson & green 15 5
1418. – 80 h. blue-violet & lake 25 5
1419. – 1 k. violet and blue .. 30 10
1420. – 1 k. 20 bronze & verm. 35 12
1421. – 1 k. 40 blue-grn. & blk. 55 20
1422. – 1 k. 60 turq. & violet 90 50
1423. – 2 k. red and blue .. 60 25
ASTRONAUTS—HORIZ. 60 h. Titov. 80 h. Glenn. 1 k. 20, Popovich and Nikolaev. VERT. 1 k. Carpenter. 1 k. 40, Schirra. 1 k. 60, Cooper,. 2 k. Tereshkova and Bykovsky.

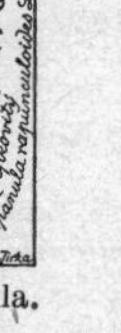

402. Campanula. **403** Miner of 1764 (Bicentenary of Banska Stiavnica Mining School).

1964. Wild Flowers.
1424. **402.** 60 h. pur., orge. & grn. 30 10
1425. – 80 h. purple, red, grn. and black 35 12
1426. – 1 k. blue, pink & grn. 35 12
1427. – 1 k. 20 yellow, orange, green and black .. 35 15
1428. – 1 k. 60 violet & green 45 20
1429. – 2 k. red, turq. & violet 2·00 90
FLOWERS: 80 h. Thistle. 1 k. Chicory. 1 k. 20. Iris. 1 k. 60, Gentian. 2 k. Poppy.

1964. Czech Anniversaries.
1430. – 30 h. black and yellow 12 5
1431. – 60 h. red and blue .. 15 5
1432. **403.** 60 h. sepia and green 15 5
DESIGNS—HORIZ. (30½ × 22½ mm.): 30 h. Silesian coat of arms (stylised) (150th Anniv. of Silesian Museum, Opava). (41½ × 23 mm.): No. 1431, Skoda ASC-16 fire engine (Centenary of Voluntary Fire Brigades).

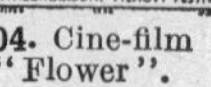

404. Cine-film "Flower". **405.** Hradcany, Prague and Seagulls.

1964. 14th Int. Film Festival, Karlovy Vary.
1433. **404.** 60 h. black, blue & red 30 5

1964. 4th Czech Red Cross Congress, Prague.
1434. **405.** 60 h. slate-violet and red 20 5

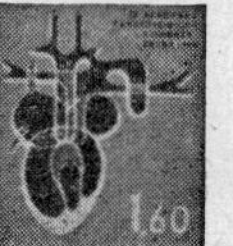

406. Human Heart. **407.** Slovak Girl and Workers.

1964. 4th European Cardiological Congress, Prague.
1435. **406.** 1 k. 60 red and blue .. 45 5

1964. Slovak Rising and Dukla Battles. 20th Anniv.
1436. **407.** 30 h. red and brown . . 5 5
1437. – 60 h. blue and red . . 15 5
1438. – 60 h. sepia and red . . 15 5
DESIGNS: No. 1437, Armed Slovaks. No. 1438, Soldiers in battle at Dukla Pass.

408. Hradcany, Prague.

409. Cycling.

411. Brno Engineering Works (150th Anniv.). **410.** Redstart.

1964. Prague, Millenary.
1439. **408.** 60 h. sepia and red 20 5

1964. Olympic Games, Tokyo. Multicoloured.
1440. 60 h. Type **409** 15 5
1441. 80 h. Throwing the Discus and Pole-vaulting . . 20 5
1442. 1 k. Football 25 10
1443. 1 k. 20 Rowing 30 15
1444. 1 k. 60 Swimming . . 40 15
1445. 2 k. 80 Weight-lifting . . 2·00 90
Nos. 1441/3 are vert., the others horiz.

1964. Birds. Multicoloured.
1446. 30 h. Type **410** 5 5
1447. 60 h. Green woodpecker 12 5
1448. 80 h. Hawfinch 15 5
1449. 1 k. Black woodpecker . . 20 10
1450. 1 k. 20 Robin 25 15
1451. 1 k. 60 Roller 50 25

1964. Czech Engineering.
1452. **411.** 30 h. brown 8 5
1453. – 60 h. green and salmon 12 5
DESIGN: 60 h. Diesel-electric shunter.

412. "Dancing Girl". **413.** Mountain Rescue Service (10th Anniv.).

1965. 3rd National Spartacist Games.
1454. **412.** 30 h. red and blue . . 8 5
See also Nos. 1489/92.

1965. Sports Events of 1965.
1455. **413.** 60 h. violet and blue 15 5
1456. – 60 h. lake and orange 15 5
1457. – 60 h. green and red . . 15 5
1458. – 60 h. green and yellow 15 5
SPORTS: No. 1456, Exercising with hoop (1st World Artistic Gymnastics Championships, Prague). 1457, Cycling (World Indoor Cycling Championships, Prague). 1458, Hurdling (Czech University Championships, Brno).

414. Domazlice. **415.** Exploration of Mars.

1965. Six Czech Towns. 700th Anniv. and Terezin Concentration Camp (No. 1465). 20th Anniv.
1459. **414.** 30 h. reddish violet and yellow . . 10 5
1460. – 30 h. violet and blue 10 5
1461. – 30 h. ultram. & olive 10 5
1462. – 30 h. sepia and olive 10 5
1463. – 30 h. green and buff . . 10 5
1464. – 30 h. slate and drab . . 10 5
1465. – 30 h. red and black . . 10 5
TOWNS: No. 1460, Beroun. 1461, Zatec. 1462, Policka. 1463, Linnik and Becvou. 1464, Frydek-Mistek. 1465, Terezin concentration camp.

1965. Int. Quiet Sun Years and Space Research.
1466. – 20 h. purple and red 5 5
1467. – 30 h. yellow and red 8 5
1468. – 60 h. indigo and yellow 12 5
1469. – 1 k. violet & turquoise 20 8
1470. – 1 k. 40 slate and salmon 30 8
1471. **415.** 1 k. 60 black and pink 35 10
1472. – 2 k. indigo & turquoise 55 40
DESIGNS—HORIZ. 20 h. Maximum sun-spot activity. 30 h. Minimum sun-spot activity ("Quiet Sun"). 60 h. Moon exploration. 1 k. 40, Artificial satellite and space station. 2 k. Soviet "Kosmos" and U.S. "Tiros" satellites. VERT. 1 k. Space-ships rendezvous.

416. Horse-jumping (Amsterdam, 1928).

DESIGNS (each with city feature): 30 h. Throwing the discus (Paris, 1900). 60 h. Marathon (Helsinki, 1952). 1 k. Weight-lifting (Los Angeles, 1932). 1 k. 40, Gymnastics (Berlin, 1936). 1 k. 60, Rowing (Rome, 1960). 2 k. Gymnastics (Tokyo, 1964).

1965. Czechoslovakia's Olympic Victories.
1473. **416.** 20 h. brown and gold 5 5
1474. – 30 h. violet and green 8 5
1475. – 60 h. blue and gold . . 12 5
1476. – 1 k. chestnut and gold 20 5
1477. – 1 k. 40 green and gold 40 20
1478. – 1 k. 60 black and gold 45 25
1479. – 2 k. red and gold . . 50 25

417. Leonov in Space.

1965. Space Achievements.
1480. **417.** 60 h. slate-pur. & blue 12 10
1481. – 60 h. blue and mauve 12 10
1482. – 3 k. slate-pur. & blue 75 55
1483. – 3 k. blue and mauve 75 55
DESIGNS: Nos. 1481, Grissom, Young and "Gemini 3". 1482, Leonov leaving space-ship "Voskhod 2". 1483. "Gemini 3" on launching pad at Cape Kennedy. Nos. 1480 and 1482, and 1481 and 1483 were issued together in the sheets with each design in alternate rows.

418. Soldier.

419. Children's Exercises. **420.** Slovak "Kopov".

1965. Liberation. 20th Anniv. Inscr. "20 LET CSSR".
1484. **418.** 30 h. olive, blk. & red 8 5
1485. – 30 h. violet, bl. & red 8 5
1486. – 60 h. black, red & blue 12 5
1487. – 1 k. violet, brn. & orge. 20 5
1488. – 1 k. 60 black, purple, red, orge. & yellow 40 8
DESIGNS: 30 h. (No. 1485), Workers. 60 h. Mechanic. 1 k. Building worker. 1 k. 60, Peasant.

1965. 3rd National Spartacist Games. Inscr. "III CELOSTATNI SPARTAKIADA".
1489. **419.** 30 h. ultramarine & red 8 5
1490. – 60 h. brown and blue 15 5
1491. – 1 k. indigo and yellow 25 5
1492. – 1 k. 60 brown & drab 45 12
DESIGNS: 60 h. Young gymnasts. 1 k. Women's exercises. 1 k. 60, Start of race.

1965. Various Canine Events.
1493. **420.** 30 h. black and red . . 8 5
1494. – 40 h. black & yellow 10 5
1495. – 60 h. black and red . . 15 5
1496. – 1 k. black and claret 20 8
1497. – 1 k. 60 black & yellow 40 10
1498. – 2 k. black and orange 50 30
DOGS: 30 h. T **420**. 1 k. Poodle (Int. Dog-breeders' Congress, Prague). 40 h. German sheepdog. 60 h. Czech "fousek" (retriever), (both World Dog Exn., Brno). 1 k. 60, Czech terrier. 2 k. Afghan hound (both Plenary Session of F.C.I.—Int. Federation of Cynology, Prague).

421. U.N. Emblem and Inscription "Twentieth Anniversary of the Signing of the U.N. Charter".

1965. U.N. Commem. and Int. Co-operation Year.
1499. **421.** 60 h. brown & yellow 12 5
1500. – 1 k. blue and turquoise 25 5
1501. – 1 k. 60 red and gold . . 40 15
DESIGNS: 1 k. U.N. Headquarters ("20th Anniv. of U.N."). 1 k. 60, I.C.Y. emblem.

422. "SOF" and Linked Rings. **423.** Women of Three Races.

1965. World Federation of Trade Unions. 20th Anniv.
1502. **422.** 60 h. red and blue . . 15 5

1965. Int. Democratic Women's Federation. 20th Anniv.
1503. **423.** 60 h. blue 15 5

424. Children's House. **425.** Marx and Lenin.

1965. Prague Castle (1st series). Inscr. "PRAHA HRAD".
1504. **424.** 30 h. green 8 5
1505. – 60 h. sepia 15 5
DESIGN—VERT. 60 h. Mathias Gate.
See also Nos. 1572/3, 1656/7, 1740/1, 1827/8, 1892/3, 1959/60, 2037/8, 2103/4 and 2163/4.

1965. Postal Ministers' Congress, Peking.
1506. **425.** 60 h. red and gold . . 15 5

426. Jan Hus (reformer—550th death anniv.). **427.** "Fourfold Aid".

1965. Various Anniversaries and Events (1st issue).
1507. **426.** 60 h. black and red . . 15 5
1508. – 60 h. ultramarine & red 15 5
1509. – 60 h. lilac and gold . . 15 5
1510. – 1 k. blue and orange 30 5
DESIGNS—VERT. No. 1508, G. J. Mendel (publication cent. in Brno of his study of heredity). HORIZ. (30½ × 23 mm.): No. 1509, Jewellery emblems ("Jablonec 65" Jewellery Exn). No. 1510, Early telegraph and telecommunications satellite (I.T.U. cent.).

1965. Various Anniversaries and Events (2nd issue).
1512. 30 h. black and green . . 8 5
1513. 30 h. black and brown . . 8 5
1514. 60 h. black and red . . 15 5
1515. 60 h. brown on cream . . 15 5
1516. 1 k. black and orange . . 30 5
DESIGNS—As T **426**: HORIZ No. 1512, L. Stur (nationalist; 150th birth anniv.). No. 1513, J. Navratil (painter; death cent.). VERT. No. 1514, B. Martinu (composer: 75th birth anniv.). LARGER—VERT. (23½ × 30½ mm.): No. 1515, Allegoric figure (Academia Istropolitana, Bratislava. 500th anniv.). HORIZ. (30 × 22½ mm.): No. 1516. Emblem (IUPAC Macromolecular Symposium, Prague).

1965. Flood Relief.
1517. **427.** 30 h. blue 5 5
1518. – 2 k. black and olive . . 50 40
DESIGN—HORIZ. 2 k. Rescue by boat.

428. Dotterel. **429.** Levoca.

1965. Mountain Birds. Multicoloured.
1519. 30 h. Type **428** 5 5
1520. 60 h. Wall-creeper (vert.) 12 5
1521. 1 k. 20 Redpoll 25 5
1522. 1 k. 40 Golden eagle (vert.) 30 10
1523. 1 k. 60 Ring ouzel . . 35 12
1524. 2 k. Nutcracker (vert.) . . 50 55

1965. Czech Towns. (a) Size 23 × 19 mm.
1525. **429.** 5 h. black and yellow 5 5
1526. – 10 h. blue and bistre 5 5
1527. – 20 h. sepia and blue 5 5
1528. – 30 h. ultram. & green 8 5
1529. – 40 h. sepia and blue 8 5
1530. – 50 h. black and buff . . 10 5
1531. – 60 h. red and blue . . 12 5
1532. – 1 k. violet and green 25 5

(b) Size 30½ × 23½ mm.
1533. – 1 k. 20 olive and blue 25 5
1534. – 1 k. 60 blue and yellow 40 5
1535. – 2 k. bronze & yell.-grn. 45 5
1536. – 3 k. maroon & yellow 65 5
1537. – 5 k. black and pink . . 1·10 5
TOWNS: 10 h. Jindrichuv Hradec. 20 h. Nitra. 30 h. Kosice. 40 h. Hradec Kralove. 50 h. Telc. 60 h. Ostrava. 1 k. Olomouc. 1 k. 20, Ceske Budejovice. 1 k. 60, Cheb. 2 k. Brno. 3 k. Bratislava. 5 k. Prague.

430. Coltsfoot. **432.** "Music".

431. Panorama of "Stamps".

1965. Medicinal Plants. Multicoloured.
1538. 30 h. Type **430** 5 5
1539. 60 h. Meadow saffron . . 10 5
1540. 80 h. Poppy 12 5
1541. 1 k. Foxglove 20 5
1542. 1 k. 20 Arnica 25 5
1543. 1 k. 60 Cornflower . . 35 15
1544. 2 k. Dog-rose 55 25

1965. Stamp Day.
1545. **431.** 1 k. red and green . . 1·10 1·10

1966. Czech Philharmonic Orchestra. 70th Anniv.
1546. **432.** 30 h. black and gold . . 25 10

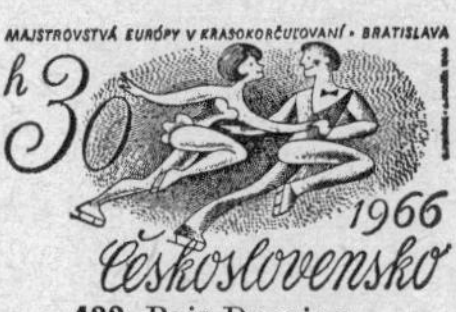

433. Pair Dancing. **434.** S. Sucharda (sculptor).

1966. Sports Events of 1966.
(a) European Figure Skating Championships, Bratislava.
1547. **433.** 30 h. red and pink . . 8 5
1548. – 60 h. emerald & green 12 5
1549. – 1 k. 60 brown & yellow 35 10
1550. – 2 k. blue and turquoise 1·00 15
DESIGNS: 60 h. Male skater leaping. 1 k. 60, Female skater leaping. 2 k. Pair-skaters taking bows.

(b) World Volleyball Championships, Prague.
1551. – 60 h. red and buff . . 12 5
1552. – 1 k. violet and blue . . 20 5
DESIGNS—VERT. 60 h. Player leaping to ball. 1 k. Player falling.

1966. Cultural Anniversaries.
1553. **434.** 30 h. green 5 5
1554. – 30 h. blue 5 5
1555. – 60 h. red 15 5
1556. – 60 h. brown 15 5
PORTRAITS: No. 1554, I. J. Pesina (veterinary). No. 1555, R. Rolland (writer). No. 1556, Donatello (sculptor).

435. "Ajax", 1841. 436. Trout.

1966. Czech Locomotives.

No.	Type	Description	Unused	Used
1557.	435.	20 h. sepia on cream	5	5
1558.	–	30 h. violet on cream	8	5
1559.	–	60 h. plum on cream	15	5
1560.	–	1 k. ultram. on cream	20	8
1561.	–	1 k. 60 blue on cream	30	12
1562.	–	2 k. lake on cream ..	90	40

LOCOMOTIVES: 30 h. "Karlstejn", 1865. 60 h. 423.0 type, 1946. 1 k. 498.0 type, 1946. 1 k. 60, E699.0 (electric) type, 1964. 2 k. T669.0 (diesel-electric) type, 1964.

1966. World Angling Championships, Svit. Multicoloured.

No.	Description	Unused	Used
1564.	30 h. Type 436	8	5
1565.	60 h. Perch	15	5
1566.	1 k. Carp..	20	5
1567.	1 k. 20 Pike	25	5
1568.	1 k. 40 Grayling	35	15
1569.	1 k. 60 Eel	1·10	35

Nos. 1565/9 are horiz.

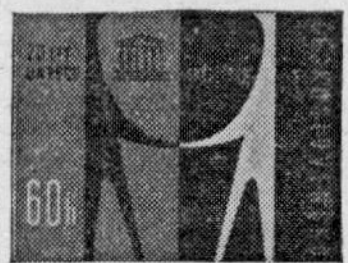

437. "Solidarity of Mankind".

1966. U.N.E.S.C.O. 20th Anniv.

1570. 437. 60 h. black and yellow 15 5

438. W.H.O. Building.

1966. W.H.O. Headquarters, Geneva. Inaug.

1571. 438. 1 k. ultram. and blue 25 5

439. Belvedere Palace.

1966. Prague Castle (2nd series).

No.	Type	Description	Unused	Used
1572.	439.	30 h. blue	10	5
1573.	–	60 h. black and yellow	20	5

DESIGN: 60 h. Wood triptych, "Virgin and Child" (St. George's Church).

440. Swallowtail.

1966. Butterflies. Multicoloured.

No.	Description	Unused	Used
1575.	30 h. Type 440	5	5
1576.	60 h. Alpine Clouded Yellow	15	5
1577.	80 h. Purple Emperor ..	20	5
1578.	1 k. Apollo	20	8
1579.	1 k. 20 Tiger (moth) ..	30	10
1580.	2 k. Cream-spot Tiger (moth)	1·10	55

441. Flags.

1966. Czech Communist Party Congress.

No.	Type	Description	Unused	Used
1581.	441.	30 h. red and blue ..	8	5
1582.	–	60 h. red and blue ..	15	5
1583.	–	1 k. 60 red and blue..	35	8

DESIGNS: 60 h. Hammer and sickle. 1 k. 60 Girl.

442. Indian Village. 443. Atomic Symbol.

1966. "North American Indians". Naprstek's Ethnographic Museum, Prague. Cent.

No.	Type	Description	Unused	Used
1584.	442.	20 h. blue and orange	5	5
1585.	–	30 h. black & cinnamon	5	5
1586.	–	40 h. sepia and blue..	5	5
1587.	–	60 h. green & yellow	12	5
1588.	–	1 k. purple & emerald	15	5
1589.	–	1 k. 20 indigo & mauve	25	8
1590.	–	1 k. 40 multicoloured	80	35

DESIGNS—VERT. 30 h. Tomahawk. 40 h. Haida totem poles. 60 h. Katchina, "good spirit" of Hopi tribe. 1 k. 20, Dakota calumet (pipe of peace). 1 k. 40, Dakota Indian chief. HORIZ. 1 k. Buffalo-hunting.

1966. Czech Chemical Society. Cent.

1591. 443. 60 h. black and blue.. 15 5

444. "Guernica", after Picasso.

1966. Int. Brigade's War Service in Spain. 30th Anniv.

1592. 444. 60 h. black and blue 80 70

445. Pantheon Bratislava. 446. Fair Emblem.

1966. "Cultural Anniversaries".

No.	Type	Description	Unused	Used
1593.	444.	30 h. lilac	5	5
1594.	–	60 h. ultramarine ..	15	5
1595.	–	60 h. green	15	5
1596.	–	60 h. sepia	15	5

DESIGNS: T 445 (Liberation of Bratislava. 21st anniv.). 1594, L. Stur (Slovak leader) and Devin Castle. 1595, Nachod (700th anniv.). 1596, Arms, globe, books and view of Olomouc (State Science Library. 400th anniv.).

1966. Brno Int. Fair.

1597. 446. 60 h. black and red.. 15 5

447. "Atomic Age". 448 Olympic Coin.

449. Missile Carrier, Tank and "Mig-21" Fighter. 450. Moravian Silver Thaler (reverse and obverse).

1966. Jachymov (source of pitchblende).

1598. 447. 60 h. black and red.. 15 5

1966. Olympic Committee. 70th Anniv.

No.	Type	Description	Unused	Used
1599.	448.	60 h. black and gold..	15	5
1600.	–	1 k. blue and red ..	25	5

DESIGN: 1 k. Olympic flame and rings.

1966. Military Manoeuvres.

1601. 449. 60 h. black and yellow 15 5

1966. Brno Stamp Exn.

No.	Type	Description	Unused	Used
1602.	450.	30 h. black and red ..	5	5
1603.	–	60 h. black & orange	15	5
1604.	–	1 k. 60 black and green	40	10

DESIGNS—HORIZ. 60 h. "Mercury". 1 k. 60. Brno buildings and crest.

451. First Space Rendezvous.

1966. Space Research.

No.	Type	Description	Unused	Used
1606.	451.	20 h. violet and green	5	5
1607.	–	30 h. green & orange	8	5
1608.	–	60 h. indigo & mauve	15	5
1609.	–	80 h. purple and blue	20	5
1610.	–	1 k. black and violet	25	8
1611.	–	1 k. 20 red and blue..	60	25

DESIGNS: 30 h. Satellite and "back" of Moon. 60 h. "Mariner 4" and first pictures of Mars. 80 h. Satellite making "soft" landing on Moon. 1 k. Satellite, laser beam and binary code. 1 k. 20, "Telstar", Earth and tracking station.

452. Badger.

1966. Game Animals. Multicoloured.

No.	Description	Unused	Used
1612.	30 h. Type 452	5	5
1613.	40 h. Red deer (vert.) ..	5	5
1614.	60 h. Lynx	12	5
1615.	80 h. Hare	15	5
1616.	1 k. Fox	20	5
1617.	1 k. 20 Brown bear (vert.)	25	8
1618.	2 k. Wild boar	1·10	30

453. "Spring", after V. Hollar.

1966. Czech Paintings (1st series).

No.	Type	Description	Unused	Used
1619.	453.	1 k. black	1·25	1·00
1620.	–	1 k. multicoloured ..	1·25	1·00
1621.	–	1 k. multicoloured ..	1·25	1·00
1622.	–	1 k. multicoloured ..	1·25	1·00
1623.	–	1 k. multicoloured ..	5·00	4·50

PAINTINGS: No. 1620, "Mrs. F. Wussin" (J. Kupecky). 1621, "Snowy Owl" (K. Purkyne). 1622, "Buoquet" (V. Spale). 1623, "Recruit" (L. Fulla).

See also Nos. 1669, 1699/1703, 1747, 1753, 1756, 1790/4, 1835/8, 1861/5, 1914/18, 1999/2003, 2067/71, 2134/9, 2194/8 and 2256/60.

454. "Carrier Pigeon".

1966. Stamp Day.

1624. 454. 1 k. ultramarine & yell. 45 45

455. "Youth" (5th Youth Congress). 456. Distressed Family.

1967. Czech Congresses.

No.	Type	Description	Unused	Used
1625.	455.	30 h. red and blue ..	8	5
1626.	–	30 h. red and yellow..	8	5

DESIGN: No. 1626, Rose and T.U. emblem (6th Trade Union Congress).

1967. "Peace for Viet-Nam".

1627. 456. 60 h. black and salmon 15 5

457. Jihlava.

1967. Int. Tourist Year.

No.	Type	Description	Unused	Used
1628.	457.	30 h. maroon ..	5	5
1629.	–	40 h. red ..	8	5
1630.	–	1 k. 20 blue ..	25	12
1631.	–	1 k. 60 black ..	70	25

DESIGNS—As T 457: 40 h. Brno (76 × 30 mm.): 1 k. 20. Bratislava. 1 k. 60, Prague.

458. Black-tailed Godwit. 460. Gothic Art (after painting by Theodoric).

459. Sun and Satellite.

1967. Water Birds. Multicoloured.

No.	Description	Unused	Used
1632.	30 h. Type 458	5	5
1633.	40 h. Shoveler (horiz.) ..	8	5
1634.	60 h. Purple heron ..	12	5
1635.	80 h. Penduline tit ..	20	5
1636.	1 k. Avocet	25	5
1637.	1 k. 40 Black stork ..	35	10
1638.	1 k. 60 Tufted duck (horiz.)	1·00	50

1967. Space Research.

No.	Type	Description	Unused	Used
1639.	459.	30 h. red and yellow..	5	5
1640.	–	40 h. ultram. and grey	8	5
1941.	–	60 h. green and violet	15	5
1642.	–	1 k. blue and mauve	25	5
1643.	–	1 k. 20 black and blue	30	5
1644.	–	1 k. 60 lake and grey	40	35

DESIGNS: 40 h. Space vehicles in orbit. 60 h. "Man on the Moon" and orientation systems. 1 k. "Exploration of the planets". 1 k. 20, Lunar satellites. 1 k. 60, Lunar observatory and landscape.

1967. World Fair, Montreal. Multicoloured.

No.	Description	Unused	Used
1645.	30 h. Type 460	8	5
1646.	40 h. Jena Codex-ancient manuscript, "Burning of John Hus" ..	8	8
1647.	60 h. Lead crystal glass..	12	10
1648.	80 h. "The Shepherdess and the Chimney Sweep" (Andersen's Fairy Tales), after painting by J. Trnka	15	12
1649.	1 k. Atomic diagram ("Technical Progress")	20	15
1650.	1 k. 20 Dolls by P. Rada ("Ceramics") ..	50	20

461. Bicycle Wheels and Dove.

1967. Sports Events of 1967.

No.	Type	Description	Unused	Used
1652.	461.	60 h. black and verm.	12	5
1653.	–	60 h. black & turquoise	12	5
1654.	–	60 h. black and blue	12	5
1655.	–	1 k. 60 black and violet	50	20

DESIGNS—HORIZ. T 461 (20th Warsaw-Berlin-Prague Cycle Race). No. 1654, Canoeist in kayak (5th World Canoeing Championships). VERT. 1653, Basketball players (World Women's Basketball Championships). 1655. Canoeist (10th World Water-slalom Championships).

1967. Prague Castle (3rd Series). As Type 439.

No.	Description	Unused	Used
1656.	30 h. lake	8	5
1657.	60 h. slate	15	5

DESIGNS: 30 h. "Golden Street". 60 h. St. Wenceslas' Hall.

462. "PRAZSKE 1967". 463. Synagogue Curtain (detail).

1967. Prague Music Festival.
1659. **462.** 60 h. violet and green 20 5

1967. Jewish Culture.
1660. **463.** 30 h. red and blue .. 10 5
1661. – 60 h. black & emerald 20 5
1662. – 1 k. blue and mauve 20 12
1663. – 1 k. 20 lake & brown 25 20
1664. – 1 k. 40 black & yellow 30 20
1665. – 1 k. 60 green & yellow 1·60 70
DESIGNS: 60 h. Printers' imprint (1530). 1 k. Mikulov jug. (1801). 1 k. 20, "Old-New" Synagogue, Prague (1268). 1 k. 40, Jewish memorial candelabra. Pinkas Synagogue (1536) (The memorial is for Czech victims of Nazi persecution). 1 k. 60, David Gans' tombstone (1613).

464. Lidice Rose. **465.** "Architecture".

1967. Destruction of Lidice. 25th Anniv.
1666. **464.** 30 h. black and red .. 10 5

1967. 9th Int. Architects' Union Congress, Prague.
1667. **465.** 1 k. black and gold .. 25 10

466. Petr Bezruc (poet).

1967. Petr. Bezruc. Birth Cent.
1668. **466.** 60 h. black and red .. 15 5

1967. Publicity for "Praga 68" Stamp Exn. As Type **453**. Multicoloured.
1669. 2 k. "Henri Rousseau" (self-portrait) 70 50

467. Skalica.

1967. Czech Towns.
1670. **467.** 30 h. blue 8 5
1671. – 30 h. lake (Presov) .. 8 5
1672. – 30 h. green (Pribram) 8 5

468. Thermal Fountain and Colonnade, Karlovy Vary.

1967. Postal Employees' Games.
1673. **468.** 30 h. violet and gold 15 5

469. Ondrejov Observatory and Universe. **470.** "Miltonia spectabilis".

1967. 13th Int. Astronomic Union Congress, Prague.
1674. **469.** 60 h. silver, blue & pur. 45 8

1967. Botanical Garden Flowers. Multicoloured.
1675. 20 h. Type **470** 5 5
1676. 30 h. "Cobaea scandens" 5 5
1677. 40 h. "Lycaste deppei" 5 5
1678. 60 h. "Glottiphyllum davisii" 12 5
1679. 1 k. "Anthurium andreanum" 20 10
1680. 1 k. 20, "Rhodocactus bleo" 25 12
1681. 1 k. 40 "Dendrobium phalaenopsis" 80 25

471. Red Squirrel. **472.** Military Vehicles.

1967. Fauna of Tatra National Park.
1682. **471.** 30 h. blk., orge. & yell. 5 5
1683. – 60 h. black and buff .. 12 5
1684. – 1 k. black and blue .. 20 5
1685. – 1 k. 20 blk., yell. & grn. 20 5
1686. – 1 k. 40 blk., yell. & pink 30 10
1687. – 1 k. 60 blk., orge. & yell. 65 20
DESIGNS: 60 h. Wild cat. 1 k. Ermine. 1 k. 20, Dormouse. 1 k. 40, Hedgehog. 1 k. 60, Pine marten.

1967. Army Day.
1688. **472.** 30 h. green 12 5

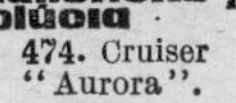
473. Prague Castle ("PRAGA 62").

1967. Air. "PRAGA 1968" Int. Stamp Exn. (1st Issue).
1689. **473.** 30 h. multicoloured .. 5 5
1690. – 60 h. multicoloured .. 12 5
1691. – 1 k. multicoloured .. 20 5
1692. – 1 k. 40 multicoloured 30 15
1693. – 1 k. 60 multicoloured 35 20
1694. – 2 k. multicoloured .. 40 20
1695. – 5 k. multicoloured .. 1·25 1·10
DESIGNS (Sites of previous Int. Stamp Exns.): 60 h. St. Sophia, Istanbul ("ISTANBUL 1963"). 1 k. Notre Dame, Paris ("PHILATEC 1964"). 1 k. 40, Hofburg Palace, Vienna ("WIPA 1965"). 1 k. 60, White House, Washington ("SIPEX 1965"). 2 k. Amsterdam ("AMPHILEX 1967"). (40×55 mm.) 5 k. Prague ("PRAGA 1968").
See also Nos. 1718/20, 1743/8, 1749/54, and 1756.

476. "L-13" Glider.

1967. Czech Aircraft. Multicoloured.
1706. 30 h Type **476** 5 5
1707. 60 h. "L-40" Meta-Sokol Sports 12 5
1708. 80 h. "L-200" Morava Aerotaxi 15 5
1709. 1 k. Jet "Z-37" Cmelak Crop-sprayer 20 5
1710. 1 k. 60 Zlin "Z-526" Trener (Trainer) 30 5
1711. 2 k. "L-29" Delfin Jet-trainer 80 45

477. Czech Stamps of 1920.

1967. Stamp Day.
1712. **477.** 1 k. lake and silver .. 45 45

478. "CESKOSLOVENSKO 1918-1968".

1968. Republic. 50th Anniv. (1st Issue).
1713. **478.** 30 h. red, blue & ult. 8 5
See Nos. 1780/1.

479. Skater and Stadium.

1968. Winter Olympic Games, Grenoble.
1714. **479.** 60 h. blk., yell. & ochre 12 5
1715. – 1 k. brown, bistre & bl. 20 8
1716. – 1 k. 60 blk., grn. & lilac 30 15
1717. – 2 k. blk., blue & yell. 50 30
DESIGNS: 1 k. Bob-sleigh run. 1 k. 60, Ski-jump. 2 k. Ice-hockey.

480. Charles' Bridge, Prague, and Balloon. **481.** Industrial Scene and Red Sun.

1968. "PRAGA 1968" Int. Stamp Exn. (2nd Issue). Multicoloured.
1718. 60 h. Type **480** 12 5
1719. 1 k. Royal Summer-house, Belvedere, and aircraft 20 8
1720. 2 k. Prague Castle and airship 40 20

1968. "Victorious February". 20th Anniv.
1721. **481.** 30 h. red and blue .. 5 5
1722. – 60 h. red and blue .. 12 5
DESIGN: 60 h. Workers and banner.

482. Battle Plan. **483.** Human Rights Emblem.

1968. Sokolovo Battles. 25th Anniv.
1723. **482.** 30 h. red, blue & green 10 5

1968. Human Rights Year.
1724. **483.** 1 k. claret 20 10

484. Liptovsky Mikulás (town) and Janko Král (writer). **486.** Athlete and Statuettes.

485. "Radio" (45th anniv.).

1968. Various Commems.
1725. **484.** 30 h. green .. 10 5
1726. – 30 h. blue and orange 10 5
1727. – 30 h. red and gold .. 10 5
1728. – 30 h. purple 10 5
1729. – 1 k. multicoloured .. 20 5
DESIGNS—VERT. No. 1726, Allegorical figure of woman (150th anniv. of Prague National Museum). No. 1727, Girl's head (cent. of Prague National Theatre). No. 1728, Karl Marx (150th anniv. of birth). No. 1729, Diagrammatic skull (20th anniv. of W.H.O.).

1968. Czech Radio and Television Annivs.
1730. **485.** 30 h. black, red & blue 8 5
1731. – 30 h. black, red & blue 8 5
DESIGN: No. 1731, "Television" (15th anniv.).

1968. Olympic Games, Mexico. Multicoloured.
1732. 30 h. Type **486** 5 5
1733. 40 h. Runner and seated figure (Quetzalcoatl) .. 8 5
1734. 60 h. Netball and ornaments 12 5
1735. 1 k. Altar and Olympic emblems 20 5
1736. 1 k. 60 Football and ornaments 30 5
1737. 2 k. Prague Castle and key 90 35

487. Pres. Svoboda. **488.** "Bretislav I" (from tomb in St. Vitus' Cathedral).

1968.
1738. **487.** 30 h. blue 5 5
1738a. 50 h. green 10 5
1739. 60 h. red 12 5
1739a. 1 k. red 20 5

1968. Prague Castle (4th series).
1740. **488.** 30 h. black, yellow, red and green .. 5 5
1741. – 60 h. black, grn. & red 12 5
DESIGN: 60 h. Knocker on door of St. Wenceslas' Chapel.

489. "Business" (sculpture by O. Gutfreund).

474. Cruiser "Aurora". **475.** Pres. Novotny.

1967. October Revolution. 50th Anniv.
1696. **474.** 30 h. red and black .. 5 5
1697. – 60 h. red and black .. 12 5
1698. – 1 k. red and black .. 20 5
DESIGNS—VERT. 60 h. Hammer and sickle emblems. 1 k. "Reaching hands".

1967. Czech Paintings (2nd Series). As T **453**. Multicoloured.
1699. 60 h. "Conjurer with Cards" (F. Tichy) .. 15 12
1700. 80 h. "Don Quixote" (C. Majernik) 20 15
1701. 1 k. "Promenade in the Park" (N. Grund) .. 20 20
1702. 1 k. 20 "Self-Portrait" (P. J. Brandl) 25 25
1703. 1 k. 60 "Epitaph to Jan of Jeren" (Czech master) 2·00 1·75
All in National Gallery, Prague.

1967.
1704. **475.** 2 k. green 40 5
1705. 3 k. brown 60 5

1968. "PRAGA 1968" Int. Stamp Exn. (3rd Issue). Multicoloured.

1743. 30 h. Type **489** 5 5
1744. 40 h. Broadcasting building, Prague 8 5
1745. 60 h. Parliament Building 12 5
1746. 1 k. 40 "Prague" (Gobelin tapestry by Jan Bauch) 25 10
1747. 2 k. "The Cabaret Artiste" (painting by F. Kupka) (size 40 × 50 mm.) .. 85 75
1748. 3 k. Presidential standard 60 25

1968. "PRAGA 1968" Int. Stamp Exn. (4th Issue).

1749. 30 h. green, yell. & grey 5 5
1750. 60 h. violet, gold & grn. 12 5
1751. 1 k. indigo, pink and blue 20 8
1752. 1 k. 60 pink, gold, blue & olive 30 12
1753. 2 k. multicoloured .. 65 55
1754. 3 k. blk., blue, pink & yell. 60 25

DESIGNS—As T **489**: 30 h. St. George's Basilica, Prague Castle. 60 h. Renaissance fountain. 1 k. Dvorak's Museum. 1 k. 60, "Three Violins" insignia (18th-cent. house). 3 k. Prague emblem of 1475. As T **473**: 2 k. "Josefina" (painting by Josef Manes, National Gallery, Prague).

1968. "PRAGA 1968" (5th Issue—F.I.P. Day).

1756. 5 k. multicoloured .. 1·90 1·90

DESIGN: 5 k. "Madonna of the Rosary" (detail from painting by Albrecht Durer in National Gallery, Prague).

490. Horse-drawn Coach on Rails (140th Anniv. of Ceske Budejovice-Linz Railway).

491. Symbolic "S".

1968. Railway Annivs.

1757. **490.** 60 h. multicoloured .. 12 5
1758. – 1 k. multicoloured .. 20 5

DESIGN: 1 k. Early steam and modern electric locomotives (Ceske Budejovice-Pilsen Railway Cent.).

1968. 6th Int. Slavonic Congress, Prague.

1759. **491.** 30 h. red and blue .. 8 5

492. Adrspach Rocks and Ammonite.

1968. 23rd Int. Geological Congress, Prague.

1760. **492.** 30 h. black & yellow 8 5
1761. – 60 h. black and mauve 15 5
1762. – 80 h. blk., pink & lav. 20 5
1763. – 1 k. black and blue .. 25 8
1764. – 1 k. 60 black & yellow 55 25

DESIGNS: 60 h. Basalt columns and fossilised frog. 80 h. Bohemian "Paradise" and agate. 1 k. Tatra landscape and shell. 1 k. 60, Barrandien (Bohemia) and limestone.

493. M. J. Hurban and Standard-bearer.

1968. Slovak Insurrection, 120th Anniv., Slovak National Council, 25th Anniv.

1765. **493.** 30 h. blue 5 5
1766. – 60 h. red 15 5

DESIGN: 60 h. Partisans (Slovak Insurrection, 120th Anniv.).

494. "Man and Child" (Jiri Beutler, aged 10).

495. Banska Bystrica.

1968. Munich Agreement. Drawings by children in Terezin concentration camp. Multicoloured.

1767. 30 h. Type **494** .. 5 5
1768. 60 h. "Butterflies" (Kitty Brunnerova, aged 11) 12 5
1769. 1 k. "The Window" (Jiri Schlessinger, aged 10) 20 5

The 1 k. is larger (40 × 23 mm.).

1968. Arms of Czech Regional Capitals (1st Series). Multicoloured.

1770. 60 h. Type **495** .. 12 5
1771. 60 h. Bratislava 12 5
1772. 60 h. Brno 12 5
1773. 60 h. Ceske Budejovice 12 5
1774. 60 h. Hradec Kralove .. 12 5
1775. 60 h. Kosice 12 5
1776. 60 h. Ostrava 12 5
1777. 60 h. Pilsen 12 5
1778. 60 h. Usti nad Labem 12 5
1779. 1 k. Prague (vert.) .. 25 10

See also Nos. 1855/60, 1951/6, 2106/8 and 2214/15.

496. National Flag.

497. Ernest Hemingway.

1968. Republic 50th Anniv. (2nd Issue).

1780. **496.** 30 h. blue and red .. 8 5
1781. – 60 h. black, red, blue, and gold 15 5

DESIGN: 60 h. Prague and Bratislava within outline "map".

1968. U.N.E.S.C.O. "Cultural Personalities of the 20th century in Caricature" (1st Series).

1783. **497.** 20 h. black and red .. 5 5
1784. – 30 h. black, green, red and yellow .. 8 5
1785. – 40 h. red, black & lilac 10 5
1786. – 60 h. blk., grn. & blue 12 5
1787. – 1 k. blk., brn. & yell. 20 5
1788. – 1 k. 20, black, violet and carmine .. 25 5
1789. – 1 k. 40 blk., brn. & orange 90 30

PERSONALITIES: 30 h. Karel Capek (dramatist); 40 h. George Bernard Shaw; 60 h. Maxim Gorky; 1 k. Picasso; 1 k. 20, Taikan Yokoyama (painter); 1 k. 40, Charlie Chaplin.

See also Nos. 1829/34.

1968. Czech Paintings (3rd Series). Designs as T **453**, showing paintings in National Gallery, Prague. Multicoloured.

1790. 60 h. "Cleopatra II" (J. Zrzavy). 12 12
1791. 80 h. "The Black Lake" (J. Preisler) 20 20
1792. 1 k. 20, "Giovanni Francisci as a Volunteer" (P. Bohun) 30 30
1793. 1 k. 60, "Princess Hyacinth" (A. Mucha) .. 40 40
1794. 3 k. "Madonna and Child" (altar detail, Master Paul of Levoca) .. 1·75 1·75

498. "Cinder Boy".

1968. Slovak Fairy Tales. Multicoloured.

1795. 30 h. Type **498** .. 5 5
1796. 60 h. "The Proud Lady" 12 5
1797. 80 h. "The Knight who ruled the World" .. 15 5
1798. 1 k. "Good Day, Little Bench" 20 5
1799. 1 k. 20 "The Enchanted Castle" 20 8
1800. 1 k. 80 "The Miraculous Hunter" .. .. 1·00 30

499. 5 h. and 10 h. Stamps of 1918.

1968. Stamp Day and 50th Anniv. of 1st Czech Stamps.

1801. **499.** 1 k. gold and blue .. 50 45

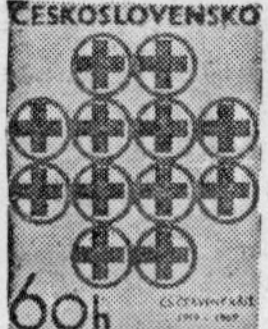

500. Red Crosses forming Cross.

501. I.L.O. Emblem.

1969. Czech Red Cross and League of Red Cross Societies.

1802. **500.** 60 h. red, gold & sepia 10 5
1803. – 1 k. red, ult. & black 20 5

DESIGN: 1 k. Red Cross symbols within heart-shaped "dove".

1969. Int. Labour Organization. 50th Anniv.

1804. **501.** 1 k. black and grey .. 20 5

502. Wheel-lock Pistol, *circa* 1580.

1969. Early Pistols. Multicoloured.

1805. 30 h. Type **502** 5 5
1806. 40 h. Italian horse-pistol, c. 1600 .. .. .. 8 5
1807. 60 h. Kubik wheel-lock carbine, c. 1720 .. 12 5
1808. 1 k. Flint-lock pistol, c. 1760 .. .. 15 8
1809. 1 k. 40 Lebeda duelling pistols, c. 1830 .. 20 10
1810. 1 k. 60 Derringer pistols, c. 1865 .. .. .. 65 15

503. University Emblem and Symbols. (50th Anniv. of Brno University).

1969. Anniversaries.

1811. **503.** 60 h. black, bl. & gold 12 5
1812. – 60 h. ultramarine .. 12 5
1813. – 60 h. red, gold, black and blue 12 5
1814. – 60 h. black and red .. 12 5
1815. – 60 h. red, silver & blue 12 5
1816. – 60 h. black and gold .. 12 5

DESIGNS and ANNIVERSARIES:—No. 1812, Bratislava Castle, open book and head of woman (50th Anniv. Comenius University, Bratislava); No. 1813, Harp and symbolic eagle (50th Anniv. Brno Conservatoire); No. 1814, Theatrical allegory (50th Anniv. Slovak National Theatre (1970); No. 1815, Arms and floral emblems (Slovak Republican Council. 50th Anniv.) No. 1816, Grammar school and allegories of Learning (Zniev Grammar School. Cent.).

504. Veteran Cars of 1900-05.

1969. Motor Vehicles. Multicoloured.

1817. 30 h. Type **504** 5 5
1818. 1 k. 60 Veteran Cars of 1907 .. .. .. 25 5
1819. 1 k. 80 Prague Buses of 1907 and 1967 .. .. 70 25

505. "Peace" (after L. Guderna).

1969. Peace Movement. 20th Anniv.

1820. **505.** 1 k. 60 multicoloured 45 15

506. Engraving by H. Goltzius.

1969. Horses. Works of Art.

1821. **506.** 30 h. sepia on cream 5 5
1822. – 80 h. purple on cream 15 5
1823. – 1 k. 60 slate on cream 25 5
1824. – 1 k. 80 black on cream 30 10
1825. – 2 k. 40 mult. on cream 95 20

DESIGNS—HORIZ. 80 h. Engraving by M. Merian. VERT. 1 k. 60 Engraving by V. Hollar. 1 k. 80 Engraving by A. Durer. 2 k. 40 Painting by J. E. Ridinger.

507. Dr. M. R. Stefanik as Civilian and Soldier.

1969. General Stefanik. 50th Death Anniv.

1826. **507.** 60 h. claret 15 5

508. "St. Wenceslas" (detail of mural by the Master of Litomerice, 1511, St. Wenceslas Chapel).

1969. Prague Castle. (5th series). Multicoloured.

1827. 3 k. Type **508** 90 75
1828. 3 k. Coronation Banner of the Czech Estates, 1723 90 75

See also Nos. 1892/3, 1959/60, 2037/8, 2103/4, 2163/4 and 2253/4.

1969. U.N.E.S.C.O. "Cultural Personalities of the 20th Century in Caricature" (2nd Series). Designs as Type **497**.

1829. 30 h. black, red and blue 5 5
1830. 40 h. black, violet & blue 10 5
1831. 60 h. black, red & yellow 10 5
1832. 1 k. multicoloured .. 15 5
1833. 1 k. 80 black, blue & orge. 25 8
1834. 2 k. black, yellow & green 90 25

DESIGNS: 30 h. P. O. Hviezdoslav (poet). 40 h. G. K. Chesterton (writer). 60 h. V. Mayakovsky (poet). 1 k. Henri Matisse (painter). 1 k. 80 A. Hrdlicka (anthropologist). 2 k. Franz Kafka (novelist).

509. "Music".

510. Astronaut, Moon and Aerial View of Manhattan.

1969. "Woman and Art". Paintings by Alfons Mucha. Multicoloured.

1835. 30 h. Type **509** 5 5
1836. 60 h. "Painting" .. 10 5
1837. 1 k. "Dance" 20 5
1838. 2 k. 40 "Ruby and Amethyst" (39 × 51 mm.) 80 60

1969. 1st Man on the Moon.

1839. **510.** 60 h. black, blue, yellow and silver 12 5

1840. – 3 k. black, blue, orange and silver 65 20

DESIGN: 3 k. "Eagle" module and aerial view of J. F. Kennedy Airport.

511. Soldier and Civilians.

1969. Slovak Rising and Battle of Dukla. 25th Annivs.

1841. **511.** 30 h. blue and red on cream 5 5

1842. – 30 h. green and red on cream 5 5

DESIGN: No. 1842. General Svoboda and partisans.

512. Ganek (actual size 71 × 33½ mm.).

1969. Tatra National Park. 20th Anniv.

1843. **512.** 60 h. purple 12 5

1844. – 60 h. blue 12 5

1845. – 60 h. green 12 5

1846. – 1 k. 60 multicoloured 75 25

1847. – 1 k. 60 multicoloured 20 5

1848. – 1 k. 60 multicoloured 20 5

DESIGNS: No. 1844, Mala Valley. 1845, Bielovodska Valley. (SMALLER. 45 × 28 mm.): 1846, Velka Valley and Gentian. 1847, Mountain Stream, Mala Valley and Gentian, 1848: Krivan Peak and autumn crocus.

513. Bronze Belt Fittings. (8th-9th century).

1969. Archaeological Discoveries. Multicoloured.

1849. 20 h. Type **513** 5 5

1850. 30 h. Decoration showing masks (6th-8th century) 5 5

1851. 1 k. Gold Ear-rings (8th-9th century) 20 5

1852. 1 k. 80 Metal Crucifix (obverse and reverse) (9th century) 40 5

1853. 2 k. Gilt ornament with figure (9th century) 60 30

514. "Focal Point"—Tokyo.

1969. 16th U.P.U. Congress, Tokyo.

1854. **514.** 3 k. 20 red, orange, green and black .. 80 40

1969. Arms of Czech Regional Capitals (2nd Series). As T **495.** Multicoloured.

1855. 50 h. Bardejov 10 5

1856. 50 h. Hranice 10 5

1857. 50 h. Kezmarok 10 5

1858. 50 h. Krnov 10 5

1859. 50 h. Litomerice .. 10 5

1860. 50 h. Manetin 10 5

1969. Czech Paintings (4th Series). As T **453.** Multicoloured.

1861. 60 h. "Great Requiem" (F. Muzika) 12 12

1862. 1 k. "Resurrection" (Master of Trebon) .. 20 20

1863. 1 k. 60 "Crucifixion" (V. Hloznik) 35 35

1864. 1 k. 80 "Girl with Doll" (J. Bencur) 40 40

1865. 2 k. 20 "St. Jerome" (Master Theodoric) .. 90 90

All stamps show paintings in National Gallery, Prague.

515. Emblem and "Stamps".

1969. Stamp Day.

1866. **515.** 1 k. mar., gold & blue 25 12

516. Ski-jumping.

1970. World Skiing Championships, High Tatras. Multicoloured.

1867. 50 h. Type **516** .. 10 5

1868. 60 h. Cross-country skiing 12 5

1869. 1 k. Ski-jumper "taking-off" 20 8

1870. 1 k. 60 Woman Skier .. 45 15

517. J. A. Comenius (300th Death Anniv.). **518.** Bells.

1970. U.N.E.S.C.O. Anniversaries of World Figures.

1871. **517.** 40 h. black 8 5

1872. – 40 h. grey 8 5

1873. – 40 h. brown 8 5

1874. – 40 h. red 8 5

1875. – 40 h. red 8 5

1876. – 40 h. brown 8 5

DESIGNS: No. 1872, Ludwig van Beethoven (Birth Bicent). No. 1873, Josef Manes (150th Birth Anniv.). No. 1874, Lenin (Birth Cent.). No. 1875, Friedrich Engels (150th Birth Anniv.). No. 1876, Maximilian Hell (250th Birth Anniv.).

1970. World Fair, Osaka, Japan. "Expo 70". Multicoloured.

1877. 50 h. Type **518** 10 5

1878. 80 h. Heavy Machinery .. 15 5

1879. 1 k. Beehives (folk sculpture) 20 5

1880. 1 k. 60 "Angels and Saints" (17th-century icon) 30 20

1881. 2 k. "Orlik Castle, 1787" (F. K. Wolf) 40 30

1882. 3 k. "Fujiyama" (Hokusai) 1·00 1·00

Nos. 1880/2 are larger, 51 × 35 mm.

519. Town Hall, Kosice. **521.** Lenin.

520. "Autumn, 1955".

1970. Kosice Reforms. 25th Anniv.

1883. **519.** 60 h. blue, gold & red 12 5

1970. Paintings by Joseph Lada. Multicoloured.

1884. 60 h. Type **520** 12 5

1885. 1 k. "The Magic Horse" 20 5

1886. 1 k. 80 "The Water Demon" 30 8

1887. 2 k. 40 "Children in Winter, 1943" .. 85 30

Nos. 1885/6 are vert.

1970. Lenin. Birth Cent.

1888. **521.** 30 h. red and gold .. 5 5

1889. – 60 h. black and gold 10 5

DESIGN: 60 h. Lenin (bareheaded).

522. Prague Panorama and Hand giving "V" Sign.

1970. Prague Rising and Liberation of Czechoslovakia. 25th Anniv.

1890. **522.** 30 h. mar., gold & blue 5 5

1891. – 30 h. green, gold & red 5 5

DESIGN: No. 1891, Soviet tank arriving in Prague.

1970. Prague Castle. Art Treasures (6th series). As Type **508.** Multicoloured.

1892. 3 k. "Hermes and Athena" (painting by B. Spranger) 75 60

1893. 3 k. "St. Vitus" (bust) .. 75 60

523. Compass and "World Capitals".

1970. United Nations. 25th Anniv.

1894. **523.** 1 k. multicoloured .. 20 10

524. Thirty Years War Cannon and "Baron Munchausen".

1970. Historic Artillery. Multicoloured.

1895. 30 h. Type **524** .. 5 5

1896. 60 h. Hussite bombard and St. Barbara 10 5

1897. 1 k. 20, Austro-Prussian War field-gun and Hradec Kralove .. 20 5

1898. 1 k. 80 Howitzer (1911) and Verne's "Colombiad" 30 8

1899. 2 k. 40 Mountain-gun (1915) and "Good Soldier Schweik" .. 70 30

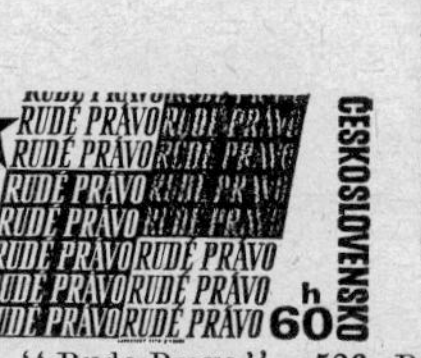

525. "Rude Pravo". **526.** Bridge-tower and "Golden Sun", Prague.

1970. "Rude Pravo" (newspaper). 50th Anniv.

1900. **525.** 60 h. red, drab & blk. 12 5

1970. Ancient Buildings and House-signs from Prague, Brno and Bratislava. Multicoloured.

1901. 40 h. Type **526** .. 5 5

1902. 60 h. "Blue Lion" and Town Hall tower, Brno 12 5

1903. 1 k. Gothic bolt and Town Hall tower, Bratislava 20 5

1904. 1 k. 40 Coat of arms and Michael Gate, Bratislava 65 20

1905. 1 k. 60 "Moravian Eagle" and Town Hall gate, Brno 25 5

1906. 1 k. 80 "Black Sun", "Green Frog" and bridge-tower, Prague .. 25 8

527. World Cup Emblem and Flags.

1970. World Cup Football Championships. Mexico. Multicoloured.

1907. 20 h. Type **527** 5 5

1908. 40 h. Two players and badges of Germany and Uruguay 8 5

1909. 60 h. Two players and badges of England and Czechoslovakia .. 12 5

1910. 1 k. Three players and badges of Rumania and Czechoslovakia .. 20 5

1911. 1 k. 20 Three players and badges of Brazil and Italy 25 5

1912. 1 k. 80 Two players and badges of Brazil and Czechoslovakia .. 50 25

528. "S.S.M." and Flags. **529.** Dish Aerial.

1970. Czechoslovak Socialist Youth Federation's First Congress.

1913. **528.** 30 h. multicoloured .. 5 5

1970. Czech Paintings (5th Series). As T **453.** Multicoloured.

1914. 1 k. "Mother and Child" (M. Galanda) 20 20

1915. 1 k. 20, "The Bridesmaid" (K. Svolinsky) .. 20 20

1916. 1 k. 40 "Walk by Night" (F. Hudecek) 25 25

1917. 1 k. 80 "Banska Bystrica Market" (detail, D. Skutecky) 30 30

1918. 2 k. 40 "Adoration of the Kings" (Vysehrad Codex) 90 90

1970. "Intercosmos". Space Research Programme. Multicoloured.

1919. 20 h. Type **529** 5 5

1920. 40 h. Experimental satellite 8 5

1921. 60 h. Meteorological satellite 12 5

1922. 1 k. Astronaut ("medical research") 20 5

1923. 1 k. 20 Solar research .. 25 5

1924. 1 k. 60 Rocket on Launch-pad 50 20

See also No. 1993.

530. "Adam and Eve with Archangel Michael" (16th-century).

1970. Slovak Icons. Multicoloured.

1925. 60 h. Type **530** .. 12 12

1926. 1 k. "Mandylon" (16th-century) (horiz.) .. 20 20

1927. 2 k. "St. George slaying the Dragon" (18th-century) (horiz.) 40 40

1928. 2 k. 80 "St. Michael the Archangel" (18th-century) 90 90

531. Czech 5 h. Stamps of 1920.

1970. Stamp Day.
1929. **531.** 1 k. red, black & green 20 20

532. "Songs from the Walls" (frontispiece, K. Stika). **533.** Saris Church.

1971. Czechoslovak Graphic Art. (1st series).
1930. **532.** 40 h. brown 8 5
1931. – 50 h. multicoloured .. 10 5
1932. – 60 h. grey 12 5
1933. – 1 k. grey 20 5
1934. – 1 k. 60 blk. & cream 30 8
1935. – 2 k. multicoloured .. 60 25
DESIGNS: 50 h. "The Fruit Trader" (C. Bouda). 60 h. "Moon searching for Lilies-of-the-valley" (J. Zrzavy). 1 k. "At the End of the Town" (K. Sokol). 1 k. 60 "Summer" (V. Hollar). 2 k. "Shepherd and Gamekeeper, Orava Castle" (P. Bohun).

1971. Regional Buildings.
1936. – 1 k. blk., red & blue 20 5
1937. **533.** 1 k. 60 blk., vio. & grn. 30 5
1938. – 2 k. multicoloured .. 40 5
1939. – 2 k. 40 multicoloured 40 5
1940. – 3 k. multicoloured .. 50 5
1941. – 3 k. 60 multicoloured 60 5
1942. – 5 k. multicoloured .. 80 5
1943. – 5 k. 40 multicoloured 1·00 5
1944. – 6 k. multicoloured .. 1·10 5
1945. – 9 k. multicoloured .. 1·75 5
1946. – 10 k. multicoloured .. 1·75 5
1947. – 14 k. multicoloured .. 2·40 8
1948. – 20 k. multicoloured .. 3·50 10
DESIGNS—HORIZ. 2 k. 40 House, Jicinsko. 3 k. 60 Church, Chrudimsko. 5 k. 40 Southern Bohemia baroque house, Posumavi. 10 k. Wooden houses, Liptov. 14 k. House and belfry, Valassko. 20 k. Decorated house, Cicmany. (22×19 mm.) 3 k. Half-timbered house, Melnicko. 6 k. Cottages Orava. 9 k. Cottage, Turnovsko. VERT. (19×22 mm.). 1 k. Ornamental roofs, Horacko. 2 k. Belltower, Hronsek. 5 k. Watch-tower, Nachodsko.

534. "The Paris Commune" (allegory).

1971. U.N.E.S.C.O. World Annivs. Multicoloured.
1949. 1 k. Type **534** 20 5
1950. 1 k. "World Fight against Racial Discrimination" (allegory) 20 5

1971. Arms of Czech Regional Capitals (3rd series). As Type **495**. Multicoloured.
1951. 60 h. Ceska Trebova .. 12 5
1952. 60 h. Karlovy Vary .. 12 5
1953. 60 h. Levoca 12 5
1954. 60 h. Trutnov 12 5
1955. 60 h. Uhersky Brod .. 12 5
1956. 60 h. Zilina 12 5

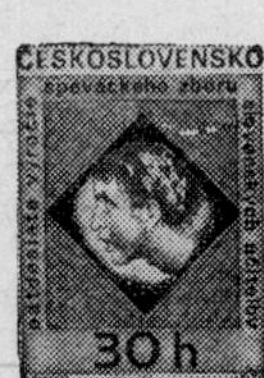

535. Chorister. **536.** Lenin.

1971. 50th Annivs. Multicoloured.
1957. 30 h. Type **535** (Slovak Teachers' Choir) .. 8 5
1958. 30 h. Edelweiss, ice-pick and mountain (Slovak Alpine Organisation) (19×48 mm.) 8 5

1971. Prague Castle (seventh series). Art Treasures. As Type **508**. Multicoloured.
1959. 3 k. sepia, buff and black 70 65
1960. 3 k. multicoloured .. 70 65
DESIGNS. No. 1959 "Music" (16th cent. wall-painting). No. 1960, Head of 16th cent. crozier.

1971. Czech Communist Party. 50th Anniv. Multicoloured.
1961. 30 h. Type **536** 5 5
1962. 40 h. Hammer and sickle emblems 8 5
1963. 60 h. Clenched fists .. 12 5
1964. 1 k. Emblem on pinnacle 20 5

537. "50" Star Emblem.

1971. 14th Czech Communist Party Congress. Multicoloured.
1965. 30 h. Type **537** 5 5
1966. 60 h. Clenched fist, worker and emblems (vert.) .. 12 5

538. Pheasant.

1971. World Hunting Exhib., Budapest. Multicoloured.
1967. 20 h. Type **538** 5 5
1968. 60 h. Trout 12 5
1969. 80 h. Mouflon 15 5
1970. 1 k. Chamois 20 5
1971. 2 k. Stag 40 8
1972. 2 k. 60 Wild boar .. 90 35

539. Motorway Junction (diagram). **540.** Diesel Locomotives.

1971. World Road Congress.
1973. **539.** 1 k. multicoloured .. 20 5

1971. Prague C.K.D. Locomotive Works. Cent.
1974. **540.** 30 h. blk., red & blue 5 5

541. Gymnasts.

1971. Proletarian Physical Federation. 50th Anniv.
1975. **541.** 30 h. multicoloured .. 5 5

542. "Procession" (from "The Miraculous Bamboo Shoot" by K. Segawa).

1971. Biennale of Book Illustrations for Children, Bratislava. Multicoloured.
1976. 60 h. "Princess" (Chinese Folk Tales, E. Bednarova) (vert.) 8 5
1977. 1 k. "Tiger" (Animal Fairy Tales, Hanak) (vert.) 15 5
1978. 1 k. 60 Type **542** 30 20

543. Coltsfoot and Canisters.

1971. Int. Pharmaceutical Congress, Prague. Medicinal Plants and Historic Pharmaceutical Utensils. Multicoloured.
1979. 30 h. Type **543** .. 5 5
1980. 60 h. Dog rose and glass jars 10 5
1981. 1 k. Spring Adonis and hand scales 15 5
1982. 1 k. 20 Valerian, pestle and mortar 20 5
1983. 1 k. 80 Succory and crucibles 30 5
1984. 2 k. 40 Henbane and grinder 85 30

544. "Co-operation in Space".

1971. "Intersputnik" Day.
1997. **544.** 1 k. 20 multicoloured 20 5

545. "The Krompachy Revolt". (J. Nemcik). (Actual size 76×29 mm.)

1971. The Krompachy Revolt. 50th Anniv.
1998. **545.** 60 h. multicoloured .. 12 5

1971. Czech Paintings (sixth issue). As Type **453**. Multicoloured.
1999. 1 k. "Waiting" (I. Weiner-Kral) .. 15 15
2000. 1 k. 20 "The Resurrection" (unknown 14th century artist) 20 20
2001. 1 k. 40 "Woman with Jug" (M. Bazovsky) 25 25
2002. 1 k. 80 "Woman in National Costume" (J. Manes) 30 30
2003. 2 k. 40 "Festival of the Rosary" (Durer) .. 90 90

546. Wooden Dolls and Birds. **547.** Ancient Greek Runners.

1971. U.N.I.C.E.F. 25th Anniv. Czech and Slovak Folk Art. Multicoloured.
2004. 60 h. Type **546** (frame and U.N.I.C.E.F. emblem in bl.) 10 5
2005. 60 h. Type **546** (frame and and U.N.I.C.E.F. emblem in black) 10 5
2006. 80 h. Decorated handle 15 5
2007. 1 k. Horse and rider .. 20 5
2008. 1 k. 60 Shepherd .. 30 8
2009. 2 k. Easter eggs and rattle 40 10
2010. 3 k. Folk hero .. 60 20

1971. Czechoslovak Olympic Committee. 75th Anniv., and 1972 Games at Sapporo and Munich. Multicoloured.
2011. 30 h. Type **547** 5 5
2012. 40 h. Modern runner .. 5 5
2013. 1 k. 60 Skiers 25 5
2014. 2 k. 60 Discus-throwers, ancient and modern .. 80 25

548. Posthorns.

1971. Stamp Day.
2015. **548.** 1 k. multicoloured .. 20 5

549. Figure-skating.

1972. Winter Olympic Games, Sapporo, Japan. Multicoloured.
2016. 40 h. Type **549** .. 5 5
2017. 50 h. Skiing 8 5
2018. 1 k. Ice-hockey .. 15 5
2019. 1 k. 60 Bobsleighing .. 30 15

550. Sentry. **551.** Book Year Emblem.

1972. 30th Annivs.
2020. – 30 h. black & brown 5 5
2021. – 30 h. blk., red & yell. 5 5
2022. **550.** 60 h. multicoloured .. 12 5
2023. – 60 h. blk., red & yell. 12 5
ANNIVERSARIES: No. 2020, Child and barbed wire (Terezin Ghetto). No. 2021, Widow and buildings (Destruction of Lezaky). No. 2022, Type **550** (Czechoslovak Unit in Russian Army). No. 2023, Hand and ruined building (Destruction of Lidice).

1972. Int. Book Year.
2024. **551.** 1 k. black and red .. 15 5

552. Steam and Electric Locomotives. **553.** Cycling.

1972. Kosice-Bohumin Railway. Cent.
2025. **552.** 30 h. multicoloured .. 5 5

1972. Czechoslovak Graphic Art (2nd series). As Type **532**. Multicoloured.
2026. 40 h. "Pasture" (V. Sedlacek) 5 5
2027. 50 h. "Dressage" (F. Tichy) 8 5
2028. 60 h. "Otakar Kubin" (V. Fiala) 10 5
2029. 1 k. "The Three Kings" (E. Zmetak) 15 10
2030. 1 k. 60 "Toilet" (L. Fulla) 50 50

1972. Olympic Games, Munich. Multicoloured.
2031. 50 h. Type **553** 5 5
2032. 1 k. 60 Diving 25 5
2033. 1 k. 80 Kayak-canoeing 30 8
2034. 2 k. Gymnastics 90 20

554. Players in Tackle. **555.** A. Sladkovic (poet, Death cent.).

1972. World and European Ice-hockey Championships, Prague. Multicoloured.
2035. 60 h. Type **554** 10 5
2036. 1 k. Attacking goal .. 20 5

1972. Prague Castle (8th series). Roof Decorations. As T **508**. Multicoloured.
2037. 3 k. Heraldic emblem (roof-boss), Royal Palace .. 50 50
2038. 5 k. "Adam and Eve" (bracket), St. Vitus' Cathedral .. .. 1·00 90

1972. Czech Victory in Ice-hockey Championships. Nos. 2035/6, optd. CSSR MAJSTROM SVETA (World Champions).

2039. 555. 60 h. multicoloured .. 3·75 3·75
2040. – 1 k. multicoloured .. 3·75 3·75

1972. Cultural Anniversaries.

2041. – 40 h. multicoloured .. 8 5
2042. – 40 h. multicoloured .. 8 5
2043. – 40 h. grn., yell. & bl. 8 5
2044. – 40 h. multicoloured .. 8 5
2045. 555. 40 h. violet, bl. & grn. 8 5
2046. – 40 h. grn., brn. & orge. 8 5

DESIGNS: No. 2041, Frantisek Bilek (sculptor: birth cent.). No. 2042, Antonin Hudecek (painter: birth cent.) No. 2043, Janko Kral (poet: 150th birth anniv.). No. 2044, Ludmila Podjavorinska (writer: birth cent.). No. 2046, Jan Preisler (painter: birth cent.).

556. Workers with Banners. 557. Wire Coil and Cockerel.

1972. 8th Trade Union Congress, Prague.

2047. 556. 30 h. violet, red & yell. 5 5

1972. Slovak Wireworking. Multicoloured.

2048. 20 h. Type 557 .. .. 5 5
2049. 60 h. Aeroplane and rosette 10 5
2050. 80 h. Dragon and gilded ornament 12 5
2051. 1 k. Locomotive and pendant 20 8
2052. 2 k. 60 Owl and tray .. 70 25

558. "Jiskra" at Basra.

1972. Czechoslovak Ocean-going Ships. Multicoloured.

2053. 50 h. Type 558 .. .. 5 5
2054. 60 h. "Mir" 8 5
2055. 80 h. "Republika" .. 10 5
2056. 1 k. "Kosice" 12 5
2057. 1 k. 60 "Dukla" .. 25 8
2058. 2 k. "Kladno" 60 20

Nos. 2056/58 are size 49 × 30 mm.

559. "Hussar" (ceramic tile).

1972. "Horsemanship". Ceramics and Glass. Multicoloured.

2059. 30 h. Type 559 .. .. 5 5
2060. 60 h. "Turkish Janissary" (enamel on glass) .. 8 5
2061. 80 h. "St. Martin" (painting on glass) 10 5
2062. 1 k. 60 "St. George" (enamel on glass) .. 25 5
2063. 1 k. 80 "Nobleman's Guard, Bohemia" (enamel on glass) 30 8
2064. 2 k. 20 "Cavalryman, c. 1800" (ceramic tile) .. 80 20

560. Revolutionary and Red Flag.

1972. Russian October Revolution. 55th Anniv. and U.S.S.R. 50th Anniv.

2065. 560. 30 h. multicoloured .. 5 5
2066. – 60 h. red and gold .. 12 5

DESIGN: 60 h. Soviet star emblem.

1972. Czech Paintings (7th issue). As T 453.

2067. 1 k. multicoloured .. 15 5
2068. 1 k. 20 multicoloured .. 20 15
2069. 1 k. 40 brown and cream 25 20
2070. 1 k. 80 multicoloured .. 30 25
2071. 2 k. 40 multicoloured .. 90 75

DESIGN: 1 k. "Nosegay" (M. Svabinsky). 1 k. 20 "St. Ladislav fighting a Nomad" (14th century painter). 1 k. 40 "Lady with Fur Cap" (V. Hollar). 1 k. 80 "Midsummer Night's Dream" (J. Liesler). 2 k. 40 "Self-portrait" (P. Picasso).

561. Warbler feeding young Cuckoo.

1972. Songbirds. Multicoloured.

2072. 60 h. Type 561 .. .. 10 5
2073. 80 h. Cuckoo 12 5
2074. 1 k. Magpie 20 5
2075. 1 k. 60 Bullfinch 25 5
2076. 2 k. Goldfinch 30 8
2077. 3 k. Young thrush .. 75 25

SIZES: 1 k. 60, 2 k., 3 k. 30 × 23 mm.

562. "Thoughts into Letters".

1972. Stamp Day.

2078. 562. 1 k. black, gold & pur. 20 15

1973. Czechoslovak Graphic Art (3rd series). As Type 532. Multicoloured.

2079. 30 h. "Flowers in the Window" (J. Grus) .. 5 5
2080. 60 h. "Quest for Happiness" (J. Balaz) 8 5
2081. 1 k. 60 "Balloon" (K. Lhotak) 30 10
2082. 1 k. 80 "Woman with Viola" (R. Wiesner) .. 60 30

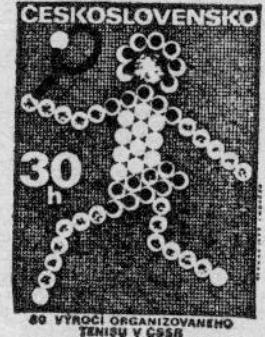

563. "Tennis Player". 534. Red Star and Factory Buildings.

1973. Sports Events. Multicoloured.

2083. 30 h. Type 563 .. .. 5 5
2084. 60 h. Figure-skating .. 10 5
2085. 1 k. Spartakiad emblem .. 20 5

EVENTS: 30 h. Lawn Tennis in Czechoslovakia. 80th Anniv. 60 h. World Figure-skating Championships, Bratislava. 1 k. 3rd Warsaw Pact Armies Summer Spartakiad.

1973. "Victorious February" and People's Militia (60 h.). 25th Anniv.

2086. 564. 30 h. multicoloured .. 5 5
2087. – 60 h. blue, red & gold 10 5

DESIGN: 60 h. Militiaman and banners.

565. V. Clementis and K. Smidke.

1973. Czechoslovak Martyrs during World War II.

2088. – 30 h. black, red and gold on cream .. 5 5
2089. – 40 h. black, red and green on cream .. 5 5
2090. 565. 60 h. black, red and gold on cream .. 8 5
2091. – 80 h. black, red and green on cream .. 12 5
2092. – 1 k. black, pink and green on cream .. 15 5
2093. – 1 k. 60 black, red and silver on cream .. 50 15

DESIGNS: 30 h. Jan Nalepka and Antonin Sochor. 40 h. Evzen Rosicky and Mirko Nespor. 80 h. Jan Osoha and Josef Molak. 1 k. Marie Kuderikova and Jozka Jaburkova. 1 k. 60 Vaclav Sinkule and Eduard Urx.

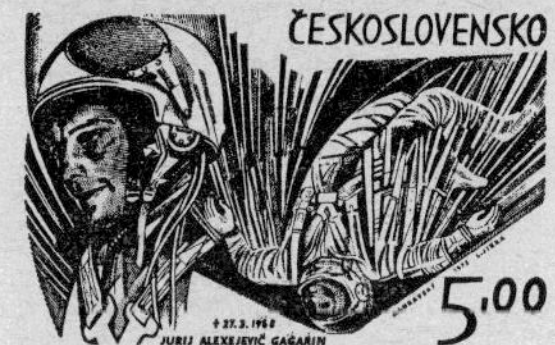

566. Death of Yuri Gagarin (first cosmonaut).

1973. Cosmonautics Day. Multicoloured.

2094. 20 h. Russian "Venera" Space-probe 5 5
2095. 30 h. "Cosmos" Satellite 5 5
2096. 40 h. "Lunokhod" on Moon 5 5
2097. 3 k. American astronauts Grissom, White and Chaffee 45 12
2098. 3 k. 60 Russian cosmonaut Komarov, and crew of "Soyuz II" 50 15
2099. 5 k. Type 566 .. .. 1·75 1·25

Nos. 2094/5 are size 41 × 23 mm.

567. Radio Aerial and Receiver. 568. Czech Arms.

1973. Telecommunications Annivs.

2100. 567. 30 h. multicoloured .. 5 5
2101. – 30 h. multicoloured .. 5 5
2102. – 30 h. red, blk. & blue 5 5

DESIGNS AND ANNIVERSARIES: No. 2100, (Czech broadcasting. 50th anniv.). No. 2101, T.V. colour chart (Czech television service. 20th anniv.). No. 2102, Map and telephone (nationwide telephone system. 20th anniv.).

1973. Prague Castle (9th series). As Type 508. Multicoloured.

2103. 3 k. Gold seal of Charles IV 70 55
2104. 3 k. "Royal Legate" (from illuminated manuscript) 60 45

1973. May 9th Constitution. 25th Anniv.

2105. 568. 60 h. multicoloured 10 5

1973. Arms of Czech Regional Capitals (4th series). As T 495.

2106. 60 h. multicoloured (Mikulov) 10 5
2107. 60 h. multicoloured (Smolenice) 10 5
2108. 60 h. black and gold (Zlutice) 10 5

569. "Learning." 570. Tulip.

1973. Olomouc University. 400th Anniv.

2109. 569. 30 h. multicoloured .. 5 5

1973. Olomouc Flower Show. Multicoloured.

2110. 60 h. Type 570 .. .. 25 25
2111. 1 k. Rose 20 20
2112. 1 k. 60 Anthurium .. 15 5
2113. 1 k. 80 Iris 20 12
2114. 2 k. Chrysanthemum .. 1·10 1·10
2115. 3 k. 60 Boat orchid .. 40 20

Nos. 2112/3 and 2115 are smaller, size 23 × 40 mm.

571. Irish Setter.

1973. Czechoslovak Hunting Organization. 50th Anniv. Hunting Dogs. Multicoloured.

2116. 20 h. Type 571 .. .. 5 5
2117. 30 h. Czech whisker .. 5 5
2118. 40 h. Bavarian mountain bloodhound 5 5
2119. 60 h. German pointer .. 8 5
2120. 1 k. Golden cocker spaniel 15 5
2121. 1 k. 60 Dachshund .. 60 20

572. "St. John the Baptist". 573. Congress Emblem.

1973. Max Svabinsky (artist and designer). Birth Cent.

2122. 572. 20 h. black & green .. 5 5
2123. – 60 h. black & yellow .. 8 5
2124. – 80 h. black 12 5
2125. – 1 k. green 15 5
2126. – 2 k. 60 multicoloured 75 60

DESIGNS: 60 h. "August Noon". 80 h. "Marriage of True Minds". 1 k. "Paradise Sonata I". 2 k. 60 "The Last Judgement" (stained glass window).

1973. 8th World Trade Union Congress, Varna (Bulgaria).

2127. 573. 1 k. multicoloured .. 15 5

574. "TU-104A" over Bitov Castle.

1973. Czechoslovak Airlines. 50th Anniv. Multicoloured.

2128. 30 h. Type 574 .. .. 5 5
2129. 60 h. "IL-62" and Bezdez Castle 5 5
2130. 1 k. 40 "TU-134A" and Orava Castle 20 5
2131. 1 k. 90 "IL-18" and Veveri Castle 25 5
2132. 2 k. 40 "IL-14" and Pernstejn Castle .. 1·10 80
2133. 3 k. 60 "TU-154" and Trencin Castle 40 15

1973. Czech Paintings (8th series). As Type 453.

2134. 1 k. multicoloured .. 80 80
2135. 1 k. 20 multicoloured .. 80 80
2136. 1 k. 80 black and buff .. 25 25
2137. 2 k. multicoloured .. 30 30
2138. 2 k. 40 multicoloured .. 35 35
2139. 3 k. 60 multicoloured .. 55 55

DESIGNS: 1 k. "Boy from Martinique" (A. Pelc). 1 k. 20 "Fortitude" (M. Benka). 1 k. 80 Self-portrait (Rembrandt). 2 k. "Pierrot" (B. Kubista), 2 k. 40 "Ilona Kubinyiova" (P. Bohun). 3 k. 60 Madonna and Child" (unknown artist, c. 1350).

575. Mounted Postman.

1973. Stamp Day.

2140 575. 1 k. multicoloured .. 15 5

576. "CSSR 1969-1974". 577. Bedrich Smetana.

1974. Federal Constitution. 5th Anniv.

2141. 576. 30 h. red, blue and gold 5 5

1974. Celebrities' Birth Anniversaries.

2142. 577. 60 h. multicoloured 10 5
2143. – 60 h. multicoloured .. 10 5
2144. – 60 h. brown, blue & red 10 5

DESIGNS AND ANNIVERSARIES: No. 2142, (composer, 150th birth anniv.). No. 2143, Josef Suk (composer, birth anniv.). No. 2144, Pablo Neruda (Chilean poet, 70th birth Anniv.).

578. Council Building, Moscow. 580. Oskar Benes and Vaclau Prochazka.

579. Allegory of Exhibition.

1974. Communist Bloc Council of Mutual Economic Assistance. 25th Anniv.

2145. **578.** 1 k. violet, red & gold 20 5

1974. "Brno 74" National Stamp Exhibition. (1st issue).

2146. **579.** 3 k. 60 multicoloured 70 15

1974. Czech Paintings (9th series). As Type **453**. Inscr. "1974". Multicoloured.

2147. 60 h. "Tulips" (J. Broz) 12 5
2148. 1 k. "Structures" (O. Dubay) 20 5
2149. 1 k. 60 "Golden Sun-Glowing Day" (A. Zubransky) 30 8
2150. 1 k. 80 "Artificial Flowers" (F. Gross) 35 8

1974. Czechoslovak Partisan Heroes. Multicoloured.

2151. 30 h. Type **580** 5 5
2152. 40 h. Milos Uher and Anton Sedlacek 5 5
2153. 60 h. Jan Hajecek and Marie Sedlackova 12 5
2154. 80 h. Jan Sverma and Albin Grznar 15 5
2155. 1 k. Jaroslav Neliba and Alois Hovorka 20 5
2156. 1 k. 60 Ladislav Exnar and Ludovit Kukorelli 30 10

581. "Water-Source of Energy".

1974. International Hydrological Decade. Multicoloured.

2157. 60 h. Type **581** 12 12
2158. 1 k. "Water for Agriculture" 20 20
2159. 1 k. 20 "Study of the Oceans" 25 25
2160. 1 k. 60 Decade emblem 30 30
2161. 2 k. "Keeping water pure" 40 40

582. "Telecommunications". 583. Sousaphone.

1974. Inauguration of Czechoslovak Satellite Telecommunications Earth Station.

2162. **582.** 30 h. multicoloured 5 5

1974. Prague Castle (10th series). As Type **508**. Multicoloured.

2163. 3 k. "Golden Cock" enamel locket 60 60
2164. 3 k. Bohemian glass monstrance 60 60

1974. Musical Instruments. Multicoloured.

2165. 20 h. Type **583** 5 5
2166. 30 h. Bagpipes 5 5
2167. 40 h. Benka violin 5 5
2168. 1 k. Sauer pyramid piano 20 5
2169. 1 k. 60 Hulinsby tenor quinton 35 10

584. Child and Flowers (book illustration). 585. "Stamp Collectors".

1974. 25th International Children's Day.

2170. **584.** 60 h. multicoloured 12 5

1974. "Brno 74" National Stamp Exhibition. Multicoloured.

2171. 30 h. Type **585** 5 5
2172. 6 k. "Rocket Post" 1·25 45

586. Slovak Partisan. 587. "Hero and Leander".

1974. Czechoslovakia Anniversaries. Mult.

2173. 30 h. Type **586** 5 5
2174. 30 h. Folk-dancer 5 5
2175. 30 h. Actress holding masks 5 5

EVENTS: No. 2173, Slovak National Uprising. 30th anniv. No. 2174, Sluk Folk Song and Dance Ensemble of Slovakia. 25th anniv. No. 2175, Bratislavia Academy of Music and Dramatic Arts. 25th anniv.

1974. Bratislava Tapestries, "Hero and Leander" (1st series). Multicoloured.

2176. 2 k. Type **587** 40 40
2177. 2 k. 40 "Leander swimming across the Hellespont" 50 50

See also Nos. 2227/8.

588. "Soldier On Guard". 590. Bridge Tower and Posthorn.

589. U.P.U. Emblem and Postilion.

1974. Old Shooting Targets. Multicoloured.

2178. – 30 h. Type **588** 5 5
2179. – 60 h. "Pierrot and Owl", 1828 12 12
2180. – 1 k. "Diana awarding Marksman's Crown", 1832 20 20
2181. – 1 k. 60 "Still Life with Guitar", 1839 35 35
2182. – 2 k. 49 "Stag", 1834 45 45
2183. – 3 k. "Turk and Giraffe", 1831 60 60

1974. Universal Postal Union. Cent. Mult.

2184. 30 h. Type **589** 5 5
2185. 40 h. Early mail-coach 8 5
2186. 60 h. Early railway carriage 12 5
2187. 80 h. Modern mobile post-office 15 5
2188. 1 k. Mail-plane 20 5
2189. 1 k. 60 Dish aerial, earth station 30 8

1974. Czechoslovak Postal Services.

2190. **590.** 20 h. multicoloured 5 5
2191. – 30 h. red, brn. & blue 5 5
2192. – 40 h. multicoloured 8 5
2193. – 60 h. yell., blue & red 12 5

DESIGNS: 30 h. PTT emblem within letter. 40 h. Postilion blowing posthorn. 60 h. PTT emblem on dove's wing.

1974. Czech Paintings (9th series). As Type **453**. Multicoloured.

2194. 1 k. "Self-portrait" (L. Kuba) 20 20
2195. 1 k. 20, "Frantisek Ondricek" (V. Brozik) 25 25
2196. 1 k. 60, "Pitcher with Flowers" (O. Khubin) 30 30
2197. 1 k. 80, "Woman with Pitcher" (J. Alexy) 35 35
2198. 2 k. 40, "Bacchanalia" (K. Streba) 50 50

591. Stylised Posthorn.

1974. Stamp Day.

2199. **591.** 1 k. multicoloured 20 10

592. "Still Life with Hare" (V. Hollar). 593. "Woman".

1975. Hunting Scenes. Old Engravings.

2200. **592.** 60 h. brown & cream 12 5
2201. – 1 k. brown and cream 20 5
2202. – 1 k. 60 brown & green 30 10
2203. – 1 k. 80 brown 35 12

ENGRAVINGS: 1 k. "The Lion and the Mouse" (V. Hollar). 1 k. 60 "Deer Hunt" (detail—P. Galle). 1 k. 80 "Grand Hunt" (detail—J. Callot).

1975. International Women's Year.

2204. **593.** 30 h. multicoloured 5 5

594. Village Family. 595. Winged Emblem.

1975. Villages Destruction. 30th Anniv. Multicoloured.

2205. 60 h. Type **593** 12 5
2206. 1 k. Women and flames 20 5
2207. 1 k. 20 Villagers and flowers 25 5

1975. Coil Stamps.

2208. **595.** 30 h. blue 5 5
2209. 60 h. red 12 12

596. "Little Queens" (Moravia).

1975. Czech and Slovak Customs. Mult.

2210. 60 h. Type **596** 12 12
2211. 1 k. Slovak "straw men" 20 20
2212. 1 k. 40, "Maid Dorothea" 30 30
2213. 2 k. Effigy commemorating "The Drowning of Morena" 40 40

1975. Arms of Czech Regional Capitals (5th series). As T **495**.

2214. 60 h. black, gold and red 12 8
2215. 60 h. multicoloured 12 8

ARMS: No. 2214, Nymburk, No. 2215, Znojmo.

597. Partisans at Barricade. (Actual size 70×34 mm.)

1975. Czechoslovak Anniversaries.

2216. **597.** 1 k. multicoloured 20 5
2217. 1 k. sepia and cream 20 5
2218. 1 k. multicoloured 20 5

DESIGNS and ANNIVERSARIES: No. 2216, Type **597** (30th anniv. of Czech Rising), No. 2217, Liberation celebrations (30th anniv. of Liberation by Soviet Army), No. 2218, Czech-Soviet fraternity (5th anniv. of Czech-Soviet Treaty).

598. Youth Exercises.

1975. National Spartacist Games.

2219. **598.** 30 h. pur., bl. & pink 5 5
2220. – 60 h. rose, lilac & yell. 12 5
2221. – 1 k. vio., red and yell. 20 8

DESIGNS: 60 h. Children's exercises; 1 k. Adult exercises.

599. "Datrioides microlepis" and "Hippocampus erentus".

1975. Aquarium Fishes. Multicoloured.

2222. 60 h. Type **599** 12 5
2223. 1 k. "Betasplendensregan" and "Pterophyllum scalare" 20 8
2224. 1 k. 20, "Carassius auratus" 25 8
2225. 1 k. 60, "Amphiprion percula" and "Chaetodon sp." 30 12
2226. 2 k. "Pomacanthodes semicirculatus", "Pomacanthus maculosus" and "Paracanthorus Hepatus" 40 15

1975. Bratislava Tapestries (2nd series). As T **587**. Multicoloured.

2227. 3 k. "Leander's Arrival" 60 60
2228. 3 k. 60 "Hermione" 75 75

600. "Pelicans". (N. Charushin). 601. "CZ-150" Motorcycle (1951).

1975. Children's Book Illustrations Biennial. Multicoloured.

2229. 20 h. Type **600** 5 5
2230. 30 h. "Sleeping Hero" (L. Schwarz) 5 5
2231. 40 h. "Horseman" (V. Munteau) 8 5
2232. 60 h. "Peacock" (K. Ensikat) 12 5
2233. 80 h. "The Stone King" (R. Dubravec) 20 10

1975. Czechoslovak Motorcycles. Mult.

2234. 20 h. Type **601** 5 5
2235. 40 h. "Jawa 250" (1945) 8 5
2236. 60 h. "Jawa 175" (1935) 12 5
2237. 1 k. Janatka "Itar" (1921) 20 8
2238. 1 k. 20 Michi "Orion" (1903) 25 10
2239. 1 k. 80 Laurin and Klement (1898) 35 15

602. "Solar Radiation". 603. President Gustav Husak.

1975. Co-operation in Space Research.

2240. **602.** 30 h. violet, yell. & red 5 5
2241. – 60 h. red, lilac & yell. 12 5
2242. – 1 k. pur., yell. & blue 20 8
2243. – 2 k. multicoloured 40 15
2244. – 5 k. multicoloured 1·00 50

DESIGNS—HORIZ. 60, Aurora Borealis, 1 k. Cosmic radiation measurement, 2 k. Copernicus and solar radiation. VERT (40×50 mm.). 5 k. Apollo-Soyuz" space link.

1975.

2245. **603.** 30 h. blue 5 5
2246. 60 h. red 12 5

604. Oil Refinery.

1975. Liberation. 30th Anniv. Multicoloured.

2247. 30 h. Type **604** 5 5
2248. 60 h. Atomic power complex 12 5
2249. 1 k. Underground Railway, Prague 20 8
2250. 1 k. 20 Laying oil pipe-lines 25 8
2251. 1 k. 40 Combine-harvesters and granary 30 10
2252. 1 k. 60 Building construction 30 10

1975. Prague Castle. Art Treasures. (11th series). As T **508**. Multicoloured.
2253. 3 k. Late 9th-cent. gold earring.. .. .. 60 60
2254. 3 k. 60 Leather Bohemian Crown case (1347) .. 75 75

1975. Czech Paintings (10th series). As T **453**.
2256. 1 k. red, brown and black 20 20
2257. 1 k. 40 multicoloured .. 30 30
2258. 1 k. 80 multicoloured .. 35 35
2259. 2 k. 40 multicoloured .. 55 55
2260. 3 k. 40 multicoloured .. 75 75
PAINTINGS—VERT. 1 k. "May" (Z. Slenar), 1 k. 40, "Girl in National Costume" (E. Nevan), 2 k. 40, "Fire" (J. Capek), 3 k. 40, "Prague, 1828" (V. Morstadt). HORIZ: 1 k. 80, "Liberation of Prague" (A. Cermakova).

605. Posthorn Motif.

1975. Stamp Day.
2261. **605.** 1 k. multicoloured .. 20 8

606. F. Halas (poet).

1975. Celebrities' Anniversaries.
2262. **606.** 60 h. multicoloured.. 12 5
2263. – 60 h. multicoloured.. 12 5
2264. – 60 h. multicoloured.. 12 5
2265. – 60 h. blue, red & yell. 12 5
2266. – 60 h. multicoloured.. 12 5
DESIGNS: No. 2263, W. Pieck (statesman). No. 2264, F. Leta (scholar). No. 2265, J. Jindrich (ethrographer). No. 2266, L. Krasko (poet).

607. Ski-jumping.

1976. Winter Olympic Games, Innsbruck. Multicoloured.
2267. 1 k. Type **607** 20 5
2268. 1 k. 40, Figure-skating.. 30 10
2269. 1 k. 60, Ice-hockey .. 30 12

608. Throwing the Javelin.

1976. Olympic Games, Montreal. Multicoloured.
2270. 2 k. Type **608** 40 15
2271. 3 k. Relay-racing .. 60 30
2272. 3 k. 60, Putting the Shot 70 35

609. Table-tennis Player.

1976. European Table-tennis Championships, Prague. Organized Table-tennis in Czechoslovakia. 50th Anniv.
2273. **609.** 1 k. multicoloured .. 20 8

610. Star Emblem and Workers. 611. Microphone and Musical Instruments.

1976. 15th Czechoslovak Communist Party Congress, Prague. Multicoloured.
2274. 30 h. Type **610** 5 5
2275. 60 h. Furnace and monolith 12 5

1976. Cultural Events and Anniversaries.
2276. **611.** 20 h. multicoloured.. 5 5
2277. – 20 h. multicoloured.. 5 5
2278. – 20 h. multicoloured.. 5 5
2279. – 30 h. multicoloured.. 5 5
2280. – 30 h. violet, red & blue 5 5
DESIGNS—HORIZ: Type **611** (Czechoslovak Radio Symphony Orchestra, 50th Anniv.). No. 2279, Folk dancers, Wallachia (International Folk Song and Dance Festival, Straznice). No. 2278, Stage revellers (Nova Scena Theatre, Bratislava, 30th Anniv.). VERT: No. 2277, Ballerina, violin and mask (Prague Academy of Music and Dramatic Art, 30th Anniv.). No. 2280, Film profile (20th Film Festival, Karlovy Vary).

1976. Bratislava Tapestries. Hero and Leander. (3rd series). As T **587**. Multicoloured.
2281. 3 k. "Hero with Leander's body" 60 60
2282. 3 k. 60 "Eros grieving" 70 70

612. Hammer, Sickle and Red Flags.

1976. Czechoslovak Communist Party. 55th Anniv.
2283. **612.** 30 h. blue, gold and red 5 5
2284. – 60 h. multicoloured.. 12 5
DESIGN: 60 h. Hammer and Sickle on flag.

613. Manes Hall. Czechoslovakia Artists' Union.

1976. Air. "PRAGA 78" International Stamp Exhibition. Prague Architecture. Multicoloured.
2286. 60 h. Type **613** 12 5
2287. 1 k. 60, Congress Hall, Old Town (vert.) .. 30 8
2288. 2 k. Powder Tower, Old Town (vert.) 40 12
2289. 2 k. 40, Charles Bridge and Old Bridge Tower 50 25
2290. 4 k. Old Town Square and Town Hall (vert.) 80 40
2291. 6 k. Prague Castle and St. Vitus' Cathedral (vert.) .. .. .. 1·25 60

614. "Warship" (Frans Huys). 615. "UNESCO" Plant.

1976. Ship Engravings.
2292. **614.** 40 h. blk., cream & drab 8 5
2293. – 60 h. blk., cream & grey 12 5
2294. – 1 k. blk., cream & grn. 20 8
2295. – 2 k. blk., cream & blue 75 30
DESIGNS: 60 h. "Dutch Merchantman" (V. Hollar). 1 k. "Ship at Anchor" (N. Zeeman). 2 k. "Galleon under Full Sail" (F. Chereau).

1976. UNESCO. 30th Anniv.
2296. **615.** 2 k. multicoloured .. 40 15

616. Merino Ram. 617. "Stop Smoking".

1976. "Bountiful Earth" Agricultural Exhibition. Multicoloured.
2298. 30 h. Type **616** 5 5
2299. 40 h. Berna-Hana Cow.. 8 5
2300. 1 k. 60, Kladruby stallion 30 8

1976. WHO Campaign against Smoking.
2301. **618.** 2 k. multicoloured .. 40 15

EXPRESS STAMPS FOR PRINTED MATTER

E 1.

1918. Imperf. On yellow or white paper.
E 24. **E 1.** 2 h. purple 5 5
E 25. 5 h. green 5 5
E 26. 10 h. brown 25 25

NEWSPAPER STAMPS

N 1. N 2. Dove. N 3. Messenger.

1918. Imperf.
N 24. **N 1.** 2 h. green 5 5
N 25. 5 h. green 5 5
N 26. 6 h. red 12 12
N 27. 10 h. lilac 5 5
N 28. 20 h. blue 5 5
N 29. 30 h. brown 5 5
N 30. 50 h. orange 12 5
N 31. 100 h. brown .. 20 5

1925. Surch. with new value and stars.
N 249. **N 1.** 5 on 2 h. green .. 45 30
N 250. 5 on 6 h. red .. 30 20

1926. Express stamps. optd. **NOVINY** or surch. also.
N 251. **E 1.** 5 h. on 2 h. purple on yellow 5 5
N 253. 5 h. green on yellow 20 15
N 254. 10 h. brown on yellow 10 10

1934. Optd. O.T.
N 332. **N 1.** 10 h. lilac .. 5 5
N 333. 20 h. blue 5 5
N 334. 30 h. brown .. 8 5

1937. Imperf.
N 364. **N 2.** 2 h. brown 5 5
N 365. 5 h. blue 5 5
N 366. 7 h. orange 5 5
N 367. 9 h. green 5 5
N 368. 10 h. lake 5 5
N 369. 12 h. blue 5 5
N 370. 20 h. green 5 5
N 371. 50 h. brown 5 5
N 372. 1 k. olive 5 5

1946. Imperf.
N 467. **N 3.** 5 h. blue 5 5
N 468. 10 h. red 5 5
N 469. 15 h. green 5 5
N 470. 20 h. green 5 5
N 471. 25 h. purple 5 5
N 472. 30 h. brown 5 5
N 473. 40 h. red 5 5
N 474. 50 h. brown 5 5
N 475. 1 k. grey 5 5
N 476. 5 k. blue 10 10

OFFICIAL STAMPS

O 1. O 2.

1945.
O 463. **O 1.** 50 h. green .. 5 5
O 464. 1 k. blue 5 5
O 465. 1 k. 20 purple .. 8 5
O 466. 1 k. 50 red 5 5
O 467. 2 k. 50 blue .. 10 10
O 468. 5 k. purple .. 15 20
O 469. 8 k. red 25 40

1947.
O 490. **O 2.** 60 h. red 5 5
O 491. 80 h. olive .. 5 5
O 492. 1 k. blue 5 5
O 493. 1 k. 20 maroon .. 5 5
O 494. 2 k. 40 red 5 5
O 495. 4 k. blue 10 10
O 496. 5 k. purple .. 12 12
O 497. 7 k. 40 violet .. 20 20

PERSONAL DELIVERY STAMPS

P 1.

1937. For Prepayment. "V" in each corner.
P 363. **P 1.** 50 h. blue 8 8

1937. For Payment on Delivery. "D" in each corner.
P 364. **P 1.** 50 h. red 8 8

P 2.

1946.
P 469. **P 2.** 2 k. blue 12 12

POSTAGE DUE STAMPS

D 1.

ILLUSTRATIONS
British Commonwealth and all overprints and surcharges are FULL SIZE. Foreign Countries have been reduced to ¾-LINEAR.

1919. Imperf.
D 24. **D 1.** 5 h. olive 5 5
D 25. 10 h. olive 5 5
D 26. 15 h. olive 5 5
D 27. 20 h. olive 5 5
D 28. 25 h. olive 12 5
D 29. 30 h. olive 10 5
D 30. 40 h. olive 20 10
D 31. 50 h. olive 15 5
D 32. 100 h. brown .. 40 5
D 33. 250 h. orange .. 4·50 45
D 34. 400 h. red .. .. 5·00 45
D 35. 500 h. green .. 1·25 5
D 36. 1000 h. violet .. 1·60 5
D 37. 2000 h. blue .. 10·00 10

1922. Postage stamps surch. **DOPLATIT** and new value. Imperf. or perf.
D 229. **2.** 10 on 3 h. mauve .. 5 5
D 224. 20 on 3 h. mauve .. 10 5
D 230. 30 on 3 h. mauve .. 5 5
D 257. **3.** 30 on 15 h. red .. 20 8
D 231. **2.** 40 on 3 h. mauve .. 5 5
D 260. **3.** 40 on 15 h. red .. 20 8
D 225. 50 on 75 h. green .. 20 5
D 263. 60 on 50 h. blue .. 90 35
D 262. 60 on 50 h. purple .. 75 35
D 232. 60 on 75 h. green .. 30 5
D 226. 60 on 80 h. olive .. 15 5
D 227. 100 on 80 h. olive .. 15 5
D 233. 100 on 120 h. black .. 55 5
D 264. **2.** 100 on 400 h. violet .. 25 5
D 265. **3.** 100 on 1000 h. purple 60 5
D 228. **2.** 200 on 400 h. violet .. 30 5

1924. Postage Due stamp surch.
D 249. **D 1.** 10 on 5 h. olive .. 5 5
D 250. 20 on 5 h. olive .. 5 5
D 251. 30 on 15 h. olive 8 5
D 252. 40 on 15 h. olive 10 5
D 253. 50 on 250 h. orange 30 5
D 234. 50 on 400 h. red .. 20 5
D 254. 60 on 250 h. orange 50 10
D 235. 60 on 400 h. red .. 1·10 20
D 255. 100 on 250 h. orange 80 5
D 236. 100 on 400 h. red .. 90 8
D 256. 200 on 500 h. green 1·50 75

1926. Postage stamps optd. **DOPLATIT** or surch. also.
D 266. **10.** 30 on 100 h. green .. 5 5
D 279. **8.** 40 on 185 h. orange 5 5
D 267. **10.** 40 on 200 h. purple 10 5
D 268. 40 on 300 h. red .. 50 10

D 280. 8. 50 on 20 h. red .. 8 5
D 281. 50 on 150 h. red .. 8 5
D 269. 10. 50 on 500 h. green .. 25 5
D 282. 8. 60 on 25 h. brown .. 15 5
D 283. 60 on 185 h. orange 10 5
D 270. 10. 60 on 400 h. brown.. 20 5
D 278. 8. 100 h. brown .. 30 5
D 284. 100 on 25 h. brown 25 5
D 271. 10. 100 on 600 h. purple 1·10 10

D 2. D 3.

1928.

D 285. D 2. 5 h. red 5 5
D 286. 10 h. red 5 5
D 287. 20 h. red 5 5
D 288. 30 h. red 5 5
D 289. 40 h. red 5 5
D 290. 50 h. red 5 5
D 291. 60 h. red 5 5
D 292. 1 k. blue 8 5
D 293. 2 k. blue 15 5
D 294. 5 k. blue 45 5
D 295. 10 k. blue .. .. 1·10 5
D 296. 20 k. blue .. .. 2·00 5

1946.

D 467. D 3. 10 h. blue 5 5
D 468. 20 h. blue 5 5
D 469. 50 h. blue 10 5
D 470. 1 k. red 20 5
D 471. 1 k. 20 red 25 5
D 472. 1 k. 50 red 30 5
D 473. 1 k. 60 red 30 5
D 474. 2 k. red 40 5
D 475. 2 k. 40 red 45 5
D 476. 3 k. red 55 5
D 477. 5 k. red 90 5
D 473. 6 k. red .. .. 1·10 5

D 4. D 5.

1954.

D 845. D 4. 5 h. green 5 5
D 846. 10 h. green 5 5
D 847. 30 h. green 10 5
D 848. 50 h. green 10 5
D 849. 60 h. green 12 5
D 850. 95 h. green 25 5
D 851. D 5. 1 k. violet 25 5
D 852. 1 k. 20 violet .. 25 5
D 865. 1 k. 50 violet .. 55 5
D 854. 1 k. 60 violet .. 35 5
D 855. 2 k. violet 60 5
D 866. 3 k. violet 90 5
D 857. 5 k. violet .. .. 1·10 10

D 6. Stylized Plant.

1971.

D 1985. – 10 h. pink and blue 5 5
D 1986. – 20 h. blue & purple 5 5
D 1987. – 30 h. pink & green 5 5
D 1988. – 60 h. green & pur. 10 5
D 1989. – 80 h. blue & orange 12 5
D 1990. – 1 k. green & red .. 15 5
D 1991. – 1 k. 20 orange & grn. 20 5
D 1992. – 2 k. red and blue .. 30 5
D 1993. – 3 k. yellow & black 50 5
D 1994. – 4 k. blue & brown 65 5
D 1995. D 6. 5 k. 40 lilac and red 90 5
D 1996. – 6 k. yellow and red 1·00 5

DESIGNS: Various Stylised Plants as Type D 6.

DAHOMEY O2

A French colony on the W. Coast of Africa, incorporated in French West Africa in 1944. In 1958 it became an antonomous republic within the French Community, and in 1960 was proclaimed fully independent.

The area used the issues of French West Africa from 1944 until 1960.

1899. "Tablet" key-type inscr. "DAHOMEY ET DEPENDANCES".

1. D. 1 c. black on blue .. 5 5
2. 2 c. brown on yellow .. 10 10
3. 4 c. brown on grey .. 20 20
4. 5 c. green .. 25 25
5. 10 c. red .. 50 45
6. 15 c. grey .. 30 20
7. 20 c. red on green .. 2·40 2·40
8. 25 c. black on red .. 2·10 1·60
9. 25 c. blue .. 2·25 1·90
10. 30 c. brown on drab .. 2·40 2·40
11. 40 c. red on yellow .. 2·75 2·75
12. 50 c. brown on blue (A) 2·75 2·10
13. 50 c. brown on blue (B) 3·75 3·75
14. 75 c. brown on orange .. 11·00 11·00
15. 1 f. olive .. 5·50 5·00
16. 2 f. violet on red .. 13·00 13·00
17. 5 f. mauve on blue .. 24·00 20·00

(A) has the name in red and (B) in blue.

1906. "Faidherbe", "Palms" and "Balay" key-types inscr. "DAHOMEY".

18. I. 1 c. slate 5 5
19. 2 c. brown 10 10
20. 4 c. brown on blue .. 20 20
21. 5 c. green .. 1·10 20
22. 10 c. red .. .. 2·75 25
23. J. 20 c. black on blue .. 1·75 1·40
24. 25 c. blue .. 1·60 1·40
25. 30 c. brown on pink .. 1·60 1·40
26. 35 c. black on yellow .. 15·00 1·60
27. 45 c. brown on green .. 2·25 1·40
28. 50 c. violet .. 2·50 2·50
29. 75 c. green and orange.. 2·25 1·90
30. K. 1 f. black on blue .. 2·75 2·25
31. 2 f. blue on red .. .. 19·00 18·00
32. 5 f. red on yellow .. 15·00 14·00

1912. Surch. in figures.

33. D. 05 on 2 c. brown on buff.. 5 5
34. 05 on 4 c. brown on grey.. 10 10
35. 05 on 15 c. grey 5 5
36. 05 on 20 c. red on green.. 5 5
37. 05 on 25 c. blue 5 5
38. 05 on 30 c. brown on drab 10 10
39. 10 on 40 c. red on yellow 8 8
40. 10 on 50 c. brn. & bl. on blue (A) 15 15
40a. 10 on 50 c. brn. and red on blue (B) £160 £190
41. 10 on 75 c. brown on orge. 80 80

1. Native Climbing Palm. 2. Rene Caillie.

1913.

42. 1. 1 c. black and violet .. 5 5
43. 2 c. red and brown .. 5 5
44. 4 c. brown and black .. 5 5
45. 5 c. green and yellow-green 5 5
60. 5 c. violet and purple .. 5 5
46. 10 c. red and orange .. 8 8
61. 10 c. green and pale-green 5 5
75. 1. 10 c. olive and red .. 5 5
47. 15 c. purple and brown .. 5 5
48. 20 c. brown and grey .. 5 5
77. 20 c. black and claret .. 5 5
76. 20 c. green 5 5
49. 25 c. blue and ultramarine 8 8
62. 25 c. orange and purple .. 5 5
50. 30 c. violet and chocolate 25 25
63. 30 c. red and orange .. 15 15
78. 30 c. violet and yellow .. 5 5
79. 30 c. green and olive .. 5 5
51. 35 c. black and brown .. 10 10
80. 35 c. green and blue .. 5 5
52. 40 c. orange and black .. 5 5
53. 45 c. blue and grey .. 5 5
54. 50 c. brown & chocolate.. 45 45
64. 50 c. blue & ultramarine.. 5 5
81. 50 c. blue and red .. 5 5
82. 55 c. chocolate and green 5 5
83. 60 c. violet on rose .. 5 5
84. 65 c. olive and brown .. 5 5
55. 75 c. violet and blue .. 5 5
85. 80 c. ultram. and brown 5 5
86. 85 c. red and blue .. 8 8
87. 90 c. orange and claret .. 5 5
87a. 90 c. red and brown .. 5 5
56. 1 f. black and green .. 10 10
88. 1 f. blue 8 8
89. 1 f. red and brown .. 12 8
90. 1 f. red and brown-red .. 5 5
91. 1 f. 10 brown & violet .. 30 30
92. 1 f. 25 brown and blue .. 1·75 90
93. 1 f. 50 blue and indigo .. 5 5
94. 1 f. 75 orange and brown 40 30
94a. 1 f. 75 blue 5 5
57. 2 f. brown and yellow .. 12 12
95. 3 f. mauve on pink .. 20 20
58. 5 f. blue and violet .. 25 25

1915. Surch. **5 c.** and red cross.

59. 1. 10 c.+5 c. red and orange 12 10

1922. Surch. in figures and bars.

65. 1. 25 c. on 2 f. brown & yell 5 5
66. 60 on 75 c. violet on rose 5 5
67. 65 on 15 c. purple & brown 8 8
68. 85 on 15 c. purple & brown 8 8
69. 90 c. on 75 c. orge. & claret 20 20
70. 1 f. 25 on 1 f. blue .. 5 5
71. 1 f. 50 on 1 f. blue .. 20 20
72. 3 f. on 5 f. red and olive 1·10 1·10
73. 10 f. on 5 f. brown & blue 90 90
74. 20 f. on 5 f. green and red 90 90

1931. "Colonial Exn." key-types inscr. "DAHOMEY".

96. E. 40 c. green 65 65
97. F. 50 c. mauve 65 65
98. G. 90 c. red 65 65
99. H. 1 f. 50 blue 65 65

1937. Paris Int. Exn. As Nos. 110/15 of Cameroun.

100. 20 c. violet 10 10
101. 30 c. green 10 10
102. 40 c. red 15 15
103. 50 c. brown 15 15
104. 90 c. red 15 15
105. 1 f. 50 blue 15 15

1938. Int. Anti-Cancer Fund. As T **10** of Cameroun.

106. 1 f. 75+50 c. blue .. 1·60 1·60

1939. R. Caillie (explorer). Death Cent.

107. 2. 90 c. orange 20 20
108. 2 f. violet 20 20
109. 2 f. 25 blue 20 20

1939. New York World's Fair. As T **11** of Cameroun.

110. 1 f. 25 red.. .. .. 12 12
111. 2 f. 25 blue 12 12

1939. French Revolution. 150th Anniv. As T **16** of Cameroun.

112. 45 c.+25 c. green .. 1·10 1·10
113. 70 c.+30 c. brown .. 1·10 1·10
114. 90 c.+35 c. orange .. 1·10 1·10
115. 1 f. 25+1 f. red .. .. 1·10 1·10
116. 2 f. 25+2 f. blue.. .. 1·00 1·10

3. African Landscape. 4. Native Poling Canoe.

1940. Air.

117. 3. 1 f. 90 blue 5 5
118. 2 f. 90 red 5 5
119. 4 f. 50 green 5 5
120. 4 f. 90 olive 8 8
121. 6 f. 90 orange 15 15

1941.

122. 4. 2 c. red 5 5
123. 3 c. blue 5 5
124. 5 c. violet 5 5
125. 10 c. green 5 5
126. 15 c. black 5 5
127. – 20 c. brown 5 5
128. – 30 c. violet 5 5
129. – 40 c. red 5 5
130. – 50 c. green 5 5
131. – 60 c. black 5 5
132. – 70 c. mauve 5 5
133. – 80 c. black 5 5
134. – 1 f. violet 8 8
135. – 1 f. 30 violet 8 8
136. – 1 f. 40 green 10 10
137. – 1 f. 50 red 10 10
138. – 2 f. orange 20 20
139. – 2 f. 50 blue 10 10
140. – 3 f. red 20 20
141. – 5 f. green 10 10
142. – 10 f. brown 15 15
143. – 20 f. black 20 20

DESIGNS—HORIZ. 20 c., 70 c. Village on Piles. VERT. 80 c. to 2 f. Boat on Lake Nokoue. 2 f. 50 to 20 f. Dahomey warrior.

1941. National Defence Fund. Surch. **SECOURS NATIONAL** and value.

143a. 1. +1 f. on 50 c. blue & red 10 10
143b. +2 f. on 80 c. ultram. and chestnut.. .. 1·00 1·00
143c. +2 f. on 1 f. 50 blue and indigo .. .. 1·10 1·10
143d. +3 f. on 2 f. brn. & yell. 1·10 1·10

4a. Village on Piles and Marshal Petain.

1942. Marshal Petain Issue.

143e 4a. 1 f. green 5 5
143f. 2 f. 50 blue 5 5

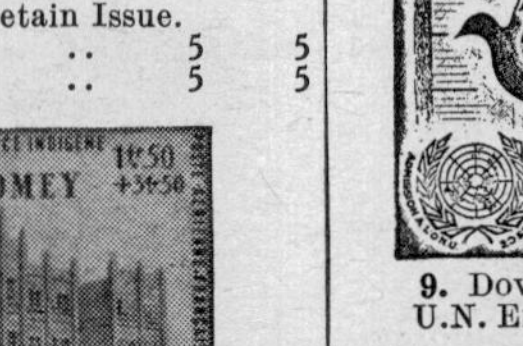

4b. Maternity Hospital, Dakar.

1942. Air. Colonial Child Welfare Fund.

143g. 4b. 1 f. 50+3 f. 50 green.. 8
143h. – 2 f.+6 f. brown .. 8
143i. – 3 f.+9 f. red .. 8

DESIGNS: 2 f. Dispensary, Mopti. (48½×27 mm.). 3 f. "Child welfare".

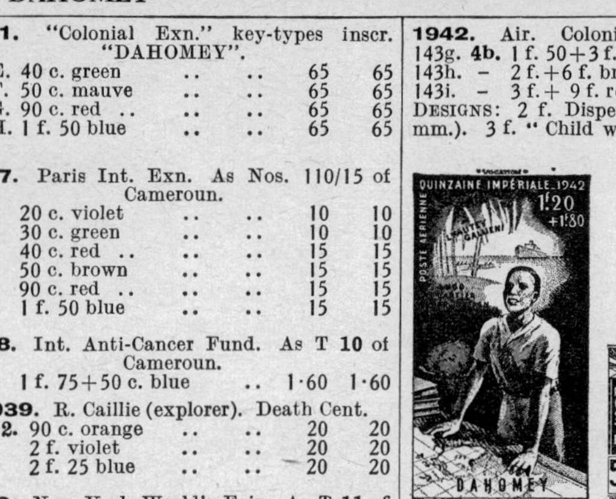

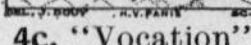

4c. "Vocation".

4d. Camel Caravan.

1942. Air. "Imperial Fortnight".

143j. 4c. 1 f. 20+1 f. 80 bl. & red 5

1942. Air.

143k. 4d. 50 f. blue and green .. 25 25

5. Ganvie Village.

1960.

144. 5. 25 f. chocolate, red and blue (postage) .. 15 5
145. – 100 f. chocolate, ochre and indigo (air) .. 75 20
146. – 500 f. red bistre & green 3·25 80

DESIGNS: 100 f. Somba fort. 500 f. Royal Court, Abomey.

1960. African Technical Co-operation Commission. 10th Anniv. As T **39** of Cameroun.

147. 5 f. blue and purple .. 15 15

6. Conseil de l'Entente Emblem. 7. Prime Minister Maga. 8. Weaver.

1960. Conseil de l'Entente. 1st Anniv.

148. 6. 25 f. multicoloured .. 30 25

1960. Independence Proclamation.

149. 7. 85 f. purple and sepia .. 65 40

1961. Artisans.

150. 8. 1 f. purple and orange .. 5 5
151. – 2 f. chocolate and brown 5 5
152. – 3 f. orange and green .. 5 5
153. – 4 f. lake and bistre .. 5 5
154. 8. 6 f. vermilion and lilac .. 5 5
155. – 10 f. myrtle and blue .. 8 5
156. – 15 f. violet and purple .. 10 5
157. – 20 f. turquoise and blue.. 15 8

DESIGNS—VERT. 2 f., 10 f. Wood-carver. HORIZ. 3 f., 15 f. Fisherman casting net. 4 f., 20 f. Potter.

1961. Independence. 1st Anniv. No. 149 surch. **100 F** and **President de la 'Republique**.

158. 7. 100 f. on 85 f. pur. & sepia 80 80

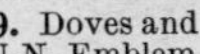

9. Doves and U.N. Emblem. 10. Wrecked Car and Fort.

1961. Admission into U.N.O. 1st Anniv.

159. 9. 5 f. multicoloured (postage) 15 10
160. 60 f. multicoloured .. 50 45
161. 200 f. multicoloured (air) 1·60 1·40

1961. Abidjan Games. Optd. **JEUX SPORTIFS D'ABIDJAN 24 AU 31 DECEMBRE 1961.**
162. **5.** 25 f. choc., red and blue 25 25

1962. Air. Foundation of "Air Afrique" Airline. As T **44** of Cameroun.
163. 25 f. blue, chestnut & black 25 20

1962. Malaria Eradication. As T **45** of Cameroun.
164. 25 f.+5 f. brown .. 25 25

1962. Portuguese Evacuation from Fort Ouidah. 1st. Anniv.
165. **10.** 30 f. multicoloured .. 25 15
166. 60 f. multicoloured .. 50 25

1962. Union of African and Malagasy States. 1st Anniv. As No. 328 of Cameroun.
167. **47.** 30 f. multicoloured .. 40 20

11. Map, Nurses and Patients.

1962. Red Cross.
168. **11.** 5 f. red, blue & maroon 5 5
169. 20 f. red, blue & green.. 15 12
170. 25 f. red, blue & sepia 20 15
171. 30 f. red, blue & brown 25 20

12. Peuhl Herd-boy. **13.** Boxing.

1963. Dahomey Tribes.
172. A. 2 f. violet and blue .. 5 5
173. B. 3 f. black and blue .. 5 5
174. **12.** 5 f. grn., brn. & blk. .. 5 5
175. C. 15 f. brn., chest. & turq. 10 5
176. D. 20 f. black, red & green 15 10
177. E. 25 f. turq., choc. & blue 20 5
178. D. 30 f. chocolate, magenta and brown-red .. 20 8
179. E. 40 f. blue, choc. & green 30 15
180. C. 50 f. brown, black & grn. 40 20
181. **12.** 60 f. orge., red & purple 45 20
182. B. 65 f. chocolate & brn.-red 50 25
183. A. 85 f. chocolate and blue 70 35
DESIGNS—VERT. A Ganvie girl in pirogue. B, Bariba chief of Nikki. C, Ouidah witch-doctor and python. D, Nessoukoue witch-doctors of Abomey. HORIZ. E, Dahomey girl.

1963. Freedom from Hunger. As T **51** of Cameroun.
184. 25 f.+5 f. lake, brn. & olive 25 25

1963. Dakar Games.
185. **13.** 50 c. black and emerald 5 5
186. – 1 f. black, bistre & brn. 5 5
187. – 2 f. choc., blue & bronze 5 5
188. – 5 f. black, red & brown 5 5
189. **13.** 15 f. maroon and violet 12 10
190. – 20 f. black, green & red 15 12
DESIGNS—HORIZ. 1 f., 20 f. Football. VERT. 2 f., 5 f. Running.

14. U. A. M. Palace.

1963. Air. Meeting of Heads of State of African and Malagasy Union.
191. **14.** 250 f. multicoloured .. 1·60 1·00

15. Presidential Palace, Cotonou.

1963. Independence. 3rd Anniv.
192. **15.** 25 f. multicoloured .. 20 12

1963. Air. African and Malagasy Posts and Telecommunications Union. As T **10** of Central African Republic.
193. 25 f. red, buff, brown & blue 20 15

16. Boeing "707" Airliner.

1963. Air.
194. **16.** 100 f. bistre, grn. & vio. 55 20
195. – 200 f. vio. chest. & green 1·10 50
196. – 300 f. mar., emer. & blue 1·60 80
197. – 500 f. mar., chest. & blue 2·75 1·10
DESIGNS: 200 f. Aerial views of Boeing "707". 300 f. Cotonou Airport. 500 f. Boeing "707" in flight.

17. Toussaint L'Ouverture. (Haitian statesman). **18.** Flame on U.N. Emblem.

1963. Toussaint L'Ouverture (Haitian statesman). 150th Death Anniv.
198. **17.** 25 f. multicoloured .. 20 15
199. 30 f. multicoloured .. 20 20
200. 100 f. multicoloured .. 75 60

1963. Declaration of Human Rights. 15th Anniv. Multicoloured. Background colours given.
201. **18.** 4 f. blue 5 5
202. 6 f. brown 5 5
203. 25 f. green 20 12

19. Sacred Boat of Isis, Philae.

1964. Air. Nubian Monuments Preservation.
204. **19.** 25 f. brown and violet 35 20

20. Somba Dance (Tancka Coco).

DANCES—HORIZ. 3 f. Nago (Pobe-Ketou). 15 f. Nago (Ouidah). 30 f. Nessou houessi (Abomey). VERT. 10 f. Baton (Paysbariba). 25 f. Sakpatassi (Abomey).

1964. Native Dances.
205. **20.** 2 f. black, red & green.. 5 5
206. – 3 f. red, green and blue 5 5
207. – 10 f. black, red & violet 8 5
208. – 15 f. sepia, lake & green 10 8
209. – 25 f. blue, brown & orge. 20 10
210. – 30 f. red, orange & choc. 20 15

21. Running.

1964. Olympic Games, Tokyo.
211. **21.** 60 f. green and brown.. 45 30
212. – 85 f. purple and blue.. 65 50
DESIGN: 85 f. Cycling.

1964. French, African and Malagasy Co-operation. As T **500** of France.
213. 25 f. chocolate, violet & orge. 20 10

22. Mother and Child. **23.** Satellite and Sun.

1964. U.N.I.C.E.F. 18th Anniv.
214. **22.** 20 f. black, green & red 15 10
215. – 25 f. black, blue & red.. 20 12
DESIGN: 25 f. Mother and child different).

1964. Int. Quiet Sun Year.
216. **23.** 25 f. green and yellow .. 20 10
217. – 100 f. yellow and purple 75 50
DESIGN: 100 f. Another satellite and Sun.

24. "Weather".

1965. Air. World Meteorological Day.
218. **24.** 50 f. multicoloured .. 40 25

25. Rug Pattern.

1965. Abomey Rug-weaving. Mult.
219. 20 f. Bull, tree, etc. (vert.) 15 8
220. 25 f. Witch-doctor, etc. (vert.) 20 12
221. 50 f. Type **25** 40 25
222. 85 f. Ship, tree, etc. .. 65 45

26. Baudot's Telegraph and Ader's Telephone. **27.** Sir Winston Churchill.

1965. I.T.U. Cent.
223. **26.** 100 f. blk., purple & orge. 75 55

1965. Air. Churchill Commem.
224. **27.** 100 f. multicoloured .. 90 65

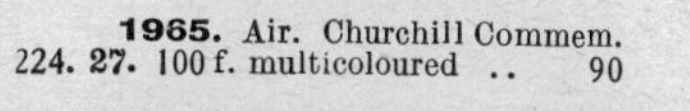

28. Heads of Three Races within I.C.Y. Emblem.

1965. Air. Int. Co-operation Year.
225. **28.** 25 f. lake, green & violet 20 10
226. 85 f. lake, green & blue 65 45

29. Lincoln.

1965. Air. Abraham Lincoln. Death Cent.
227. **29.** 100 f. multicoloured .. 75 60

30. Cotonou Port.

1965. Cotonou Port Inaug. Multicoloured.
228. 25 f. Type **30** 20 12
229. 100 f. Cotonou Port .. 75 50

The two stamps joined together form a complete design and were issued se-tenant in the sheets.

31. Spanish Mackerel. **32.** Independence Monument.

1965. Fishes.
230. **31.** 10 f. blk., greenish blue and blue 8 5
231. – 25 f. orge., grey & blue 20 12
232. – 30 f. ultram. & turquoise 20 12
233. – 50 f. grey, orge. & blue 40 20
FISHES: 25 f. Sea bream. 30 f. Sailfish. 50 f. Tripletail.

1965. 28th October Revolution. 2nd Anniv.
234. **32.** 25 f. red, grey and black 20 10
235. 30 f. red, blue and black 20 12

1965. No. 177 surch. **1 f.**
236. 1 f. on 25 f. turq., choc., & bl. 5 5

33. Arms and Pres. Kennedy.

1965. Air. Kennedy. 2nd Death Anniv.
237. **33.** 100 f. brown and green 85 65

34. Dr. Schweitzer and Hospital Scene.

1966. Air. Schweitzer Commem.
238. **34.** 100 f. multicoloured .. 85 65

35. Porto-Novo Cathedral. **36.** Beads, Bangles and Anklets.

1966. Dahomey Cathedrals.
239. **35.** 30 f. mar., blue & green 20 15
240. – 50 f. brown, blue & mar. 40 20
241. – 70 f. maroon, blue & grn. 55 30
DESIGNS—VERT. 50 f. Ouidah Church (old Pro-Cathedral). HORIZ. 70 f. Cotonou Cathedral.

1966. World Festival of Negro Arts, Dakar.
242. **36.** 15 f. maroon and black 10 5
243. – 30 f. red, maroon & blue 20 10
244. – 50 f. blue and chocolate 35 20
245. – 70 f. lake and black .. 55 35
DESIGNS: 30 f. Building construction. 50 f. Craftsman. 70 f. Religious carvings.

1966. France-Dahomey Treaty. 5th Anniv. Nos. 228/9 surch. **ACCORD DE CO-OPERATION FRANCE - DAHOMEY 5e Anniversaire - 24 Avril 1966.**

246. **30.** 15 f. on 25 f. mult. .. 10 5
247. – 15 f. on 100 f. mult. .. 10 5

37. W.H.O. Building and Emblem.

1966. W.H.O. Headquarters, Geneva. Inaug.

248. **37.** 30 f. multicoloured (post.) 20 12
249. – 100 f. multicoloured (air) 75 50

DESIGN (48×27 mm.): 100 f. W.H.O. building (different view) and emblem.

38. Pygmy Goose. **39.** Industrial Emblems.

1966. Air. Birds. Multicoloured.

250. 50 f. Type **38** 45 20
251. 100 f. "Malaconotus cruentus" 70 25
252. 500 f. "Coccyoliusiris" .. 1·50 1·60

See also Nos. 271/2.

1966. Air. "Europafrique".

253. **39.** 100 f. multicoloured .. 75 45

40. Pope Paul and St. Peter's.

1966. Air. Pope Paul's Visit to U.N.

254. **40.** 50 f. red, brown & green 40 20
255. – 70 f. red, green and blue 55 30
256. – 100 f. purple and indigo 75 50

DESIGNS—HORIZ. 70 f. Pope Paul and New York. VERT. (36×48 mm.). 100 f. Pope Paul and U.N. General Assembly.

1966. Air. "DC-8" Air Services Inaug. As T **45** of Central African Republic.

258. 30 f. grey, black and purple 20 12

41. Scout signalling with flags.

1966. Scouting.

259. **41.** 5 f. red, ochre and brown 5 5
260. – 10 f. magenta, grn & blk. 8 5
261. – 30 f. orange, red & violet 20 12
262. – 50 f. chocolate, grn & bl. 35 25

DESIGNS—VERT. 10 f. Tent-pole and banners. 30 f. Scouts, camp-fire and map. HORIZ. 50 f. Constructing bridge.

42. Scientific Emblem.

1966. Air. U.N.E.S.C.O. 20th Anniv.

264. **42.** 30 f. plum, ult. & purple 20 12
265. – 45 f. lake and green .. 35 20
266. – 100 f. blue, lake & black 75 45

DESIGNS—VERT. 45 f. Cultural Emblem. HORIZ. 100 f. Educational emblem.

43. "The Nativity" (15th-cent. Beaune Tapestry). **44.** Broad-billed Roller.

1966. Air. Christmas. Multicoloured.

268. 50 f. Type **43** .. .. 1·00 75
269. 100 f. "The Adoration of the Shepherds" (after Jose Ribera) .. .. 2·10 1·60
270. 200 f. "Madonna and Child" (after A. Baldovinetti) .. 3·75 2·75

See also Nos. 311/14, 348/51, 384/7 and 423/6.

1967. Air. Birds. Multicoloured.

271. 200 f. Type **44** .. .. 1·50 70
272. 250 f. Emerald cuckoo .. 2·00 90

45. "Clappertonia ficifolia". **46.** Bird bearing Lions Emblem.

1967. Flowers. Multicoloured.

273. 1 f. Type **45** 5 5
274. 3 f. "Hewittia sublobata" .. 5 5
275. 5 f. "Clitoria ternatea" .. 5 5
276. 10 f. "Nymphaea micrantha" 8 5
277. 5 f. "Commelina forskalaei" 10 5
278. 30 f. "Eremomastax speciosa" 20 12

1967. Nos. 182/3 surch.

279. 30 f. on 65 f. chocolate and brown-red 25 15
280. 30 f. on 85 f. choc. & blue 25 12

1967. Lions Int. 50th Anniv.

281. **46.** 100 f. blue, green & vio. 75 30

47. "Ingres" (self-portrait).

1967. Air. Ingres (painter). Death Cent. Multicoloured.

282. 100 f. Type **47** .. .. 1·10 90
283. 100 f. "Oedipus and the Sphinx" (after Ingres) 1·10 90

See also Nos. 388/90, 429/30, 431/2 and 486/7.

48. "Suzanne" (barque).

1967. Air. French Sailing ships. Mult.

284. 30 f. Type **48** 25 15
285. 45 f. "Esmeralda" (schooner) (vert.) .. 30 25
286. 80 f. "Marie Alice" (schooner) (vert.) .. 60 30
287. 100 f. "Antonin" (barque) 70 50

1967. Air. Pres. Kennedy. 50th Birth Anniv. Nos. 227 and 237 surch. **29 MAI 1967 50e Anniversaire de la naissance de John F. Kennedy.**

288. **29.** 125 f. on 100 f. mult... 95 55
289. **33.** 125 f. on 100 f. brown and green 95 55

49. "Man in the City" Pavilion.

1967. World Fair, Montreal.

290. **49.** 30 f. choc. & grn. (post.) 20 10
291. – 70 f. red and green .. 55 40
292. – 100 f. blue & brown (air) 75 40

DESIGNS—HORIZ. 70 f. "New Africa" pavilions. VERT. (27×48 mm.). 100 f. "Man Examines the Universe".

50. Dr. Konrad Adenauer (from painting by O. Kokoschka). **51.** "Economic Association".

1967. Air. Dr. Adenauer Commem.

294. **50.** 70 f. multicoloured .. 50 40

1967. Europafrique.

296. **51.** 30 f. multicoloured .. 20 8
297. – 45 f. multicoloured .. 35 12

52. Scouts Climbing.

1967. World Scout Jamboree, Idaho.

298. **52.** 30 f. ind., brn. & bl. (post.) 20 8
299. – 70 f. purple, green & blue 50 30
300. – 100 f. pur., grn. & bl. (air) 65 45

DESIGNS—HORIZ. 70 f. Scouts with canoe. VERT. (27×48 mm.). 100 f. Jamboree emblem, rope and map.

1967. Air. Riccione Stamp Exn. No. 270 surch. **RICCIONE 12 - 29 Aout 1967** and value.

302. 150 f. on 200 f. mult. .. 1·25 1·00

53. Rhone at Grenoble.

1967. Winter Olympic Games, Grenoble.

303. **53.** 30 f. blue, brn. & grn... 20 5
304. – 45 f. ultram., grn. & brn. 35 10
305. – 100 f. purple, grn. & bl. 75 50

DESIGNS—VERT. 45 f. View of Grenoble. HORIZ. 100 f. Rhone Bridge, Grenoble, and Pierre de Coubertin.

1967. Air. U.A.M.P.T. 5th Anniv. As T **95** of Cameroun.

307. 100 f. green, scarlet & pur. 75 55

54. Currency Tokens. **55.** Pres. de Gaulle.

1967. West African Monetary Union. 5th Anniv.

308. **54.** 30 f. black, red & green 20 12

1967. Air. "Homage to General de Gaulle". President Soglo of Dahomey's visit to Paris.

309. **55.** 100 f. multicoloured .. 1·25 1·00

56. "The Adoration" (Master of St. Sebastian).

1967. Air. Christmas. Multicoloured paintings.

311. 30 f. "Virgin and Child" (M. Grunewald) (vert.).. 20 15
312. 50 f. Type **56** 35 25
313. 100 f. "The Adoration of the Magi" (Ulrich Apt the Elder) (vert.) .. 70 40
314. 200 f. "The Annunciation" (M. Grunewald) (vert.).. 1·50 70

58. Buffalo.

57. Venus de Milo and "Mariner 5". **59.** W.H.O. Emblem.

1968. Air. "Exploration of the Planet Venus". Multicoloured.

315. 70 f. Type **57** 55 30
316. 70 f. Venus de Milo and "Venus 4" 55 30

1968. Fauna (1st Series). Multicoloured.

318. 15 f. Type **58** 10 5
319. 30 f. Lion 20 8
320. 45 f. Antelope 30 15
321. 70 f. Crocodile 50 20
322. 100 f. Hippopotamus .. 70 40

See also Nos. 353/7.

1968. W.H.O. 20th Anniv.

323. **59.** 30 f. brn., blue & ultram. 20 15
324. 70 f. multicoloured .. 50 25

60. Gutenberg Memorial, Strasbourg. **61.** Dr. Martin Luther King.

1968. Air. Johann Gutenberg. 500th Death Anniv.

325. **60.** 45 f. green and orange.. 30 20
326. – 100 f. deep blue & blue 70 40

DESIGNS: 100 f. Gutenberg statue Mainz, and printing-press.

1968. Air. Martin Luther King Commem.

328. – 30 f. black, brn. & yell. 20 8
329. – 55 f. multicoloured .. 35 20
330. **61.** 100 f. multicoloured .. 70 40

DESIGNS: 55 f. Dr. King receiving Nobel Peace Prize. LARGER (25×46 mm.). 30 f. Inscription "We must meet hate with creative love" (also in French and German).

62. Schuman.

1968. Air. Europafrique. 5th Anniv.
332. **62.** 30 f. multicoloured .. 20 8
333. – 45 f. mar., olive & orge. 30 12
334. – 70 f. multicoloured .. 50 25
DESIGNS: 45 f. De Gasperi. 70 f. Dr. Adenauer.

63. "Battle of Montebello" (Philippoteaux).

1968. Air. Red Cross. Designs showing paintings. Multicoloured.
335. 30 f. Type **63** 20 10
336. 45 f. "2nd Zouaves at Magenta" (Riballier) .. 30 15
337. 70 f. "Battle of Magenta" (Charpentier) 50 25
338. 100 f. "Battle of Solferino" (Charpentier) .. 70 35

64. Mail Van.

1968. Air. Rural Mail Service. Multicoloured.
339. 30 f. Type **64** 15 8
340. 45 f. Rural Post Office and mail van 30 15
341. 55 f. Collecting mail at river-side 30 15
342. 70 f. Loading mail on train 40 25

65. Aztec Stadium.

1968. Air. Olympic Games, Mexico.
343. **65.** 30 f. green and purple .. 20 15
344. – 45 f. lake and ultram... 30 15
345. – 70 f. choc. and green .. 40 25
346. – 150 f. choc. and red .. 90 65
DESIGNS—VERT. 45 f. "Pelota-player" (Aztec figure); 70 f. "Uxpanapan wrestler" (Aztec figure). HORIZ. 150 f. Olympic Stadium.

1968. Air. Christmas Paintings by Foujita. Multicoloured as T **56**.
348. 30 f. "The Nativity" .. 20 10
349. 70 f. "The Visitation" .. 50 20
350. 100 f. "Virgin and Child" 70 30
351. 200 f. "Baptism of Christ" 1·40 75
No. 348 is horiz.

1968. Air. "Philexafrique" Stamp Exn., Abidjan (Ivory Coast, 1969). As T **109** of Cameroun. Multicoloured.
352. 100 f. "Diderot" (L. M. Vanloo) 70 70

66. Warthog.

1969. Fauna (2nd series). Multicoloured.
353. 5 f. Type **66** 5 5
354. 30 f. Leopard 20 8
355. 60 f. Spotted hyena .. 40 15
356. 75 f. Baboon 50 20
357. 90 f. Hartebeest 65 35

1969. Air. "Philexafrique" Stamp Exn., Abidjan, Ivory Coast (2nd issue). As T **110** of Cameroun.
358. 50 f. violet, sepia and blue 35 35
DESIGN: 50 f. Cotonou harbour and stamp of 1941.

67. Heads and Globe.

1969. Int. Labour Organisation. 50th Anniv.
359. **67.** 30 f. multicoloured .. 20 8
360. 70 f. multicoloured .. 50 25

68. "The Virgin of the Scales" (C. da Sesto —Da Vinci School).

1969. Air. Leonardo da Vinci Commem. Multicoloured.
361. 100 f. Type **68** 65 30
362. 100 f. "The Virgin of the Rocks" (Da Vinci) .. 65 30

69. "General Bonaparte" (J. L. David).

1969. Air. Napoleon Bonaparte. Birth Bicent. Multicoloured.
363. 30 f. Type **69** 45 40
364. 60 f. "Napoleon I in 1809" (Lefevre) 85 70
365. 75 f. "Napoleon at the Battle of Eylau" (Gros) (horiz.) .. .. .. 1·10 90
366. 200 f. "General Bonaparte at Arcola" (Gros) .. 2·50 1·75

70. Arms of Dahomey.

1969.
367. **70.** 5 f. multicoloured (post) 5 5
368. 30 f. multicoloured .. 20 15
369. 50 f. multicoloured (air) 30 15

71. "Apollo 8" over Moon.

1969. Air. Moon flight of "Apollo 8". Embossed on gold foil.
370. **71.** 1,000 f. gold .. .. 7·00

1969. Air. 1st Man on the Moon (1st issue). Nos. 315/6 surch. **ALUNISSAGE APOLLO XI JUILLET 1969** with "Apollo 11" and value.
371. **57.** 125 f. on 70 f. (No. 315) 80 65
372. – 125 f. on 70 f. (No. 316) 80 65

72. Bank Emblem. and Cornucopia.

74. "Cotonou" Rotary Emblem.

73. Kenaf Plant and Mill, Bohicon.

1969. African Development Bank. 5th Anniv.
373. **72.** 30 f. multicoloured .. 20 8

1969. "Europafrique". Multicoloured.
374. 30 f. Type **73** (postage) .. 20 8
375. 45 f. Cotton plant & Mill, Parakou 30 15
376. 100 f. Coconut and Palm-oil Plant, Cotonou (air) .. 65 35

1969. Air. Rotary International Organization.
378. **74.** 50 f. multicoloured .. 30 20

1969. Air. No. 250 Surch.
379. **38.** 10 f. on 50 f. mult. .. 5 5

75. Sakpata Dance. **76.** F. D. Roosevelt.

1969. Dahomey Dances. Multicoloured.
380. 10 f. Type **75** (postage) .. 8 5
381. 30 f. Guelede dance .. 20 8
382. 45 f. Sato dance 30 15
383. 70 f. Teke dance (air) .. 45 20

1969. Air. Christmas. Paintings. Multicoloured. As T **43**.
384. 30 f. "The Annunciation" (Van der Stockt) .. 25 15
385. 45 f. "The Nativity" (15th-cent. Swabian School) 40 25
386. 110 f. "Virgin and Child" (Masters of the Gold Brocade) .. .. 1·00 70
387. 200 f. "The Adoration of the Magi" (Antwerp School, c. 1530) .. .. 1·90 1·40

1969. Air. Old Masters. Multicoloured. As T **47**.
388. 100 f. "The Painter's Studio" (G. Courbet) 65 50
389. 100 f. "Self-portrait with Gold Chain" (Rembrandt) 65 50
390. 150 f. "Hendrickje Stoffels" (Rembrandt) .. .. 1·00 80

1970. Air. Franklin D. Roosevelt. 25th Death Anniv.
391. **76.** 100 f. black, grn. & blue 60 35

77. Rocket and Men on Moon.

78. "U.N. in War and Peace".

1970. Air. 1st Man on Moon (2nd issue).
392. **77.** 30 f. multicoloured .. 20 10
The 50, 70, 110 f. values were only issued in miniature sheet form.

1970. U.N. 25th Anniv.
394. **78.** 30 f. indigo, blue & verm. 20 10
395. 40 f. green, blue & brown 25 15

79. Walt Whitman and African Village.

1970. Air. Walt Whitman (American poet). 150th Birth Anniv.
396. **79.** 100 f. brown, blue & grn. 65 25

1970. Air. Space Flight of "Apollo 13". No. 392 surch. **40 f.** and **APOLLO 13 SOLIDARITE SPATIALE INTERNATIONALE.**
397. **77.** 40 f. on 30 f. mult. .. 25 30

80. Footballers and Globe.

1970. Air. World Cup Football Championships, Mexico. Multicoloured.
398. 40 f. Type **80** 25 15
399. 50 f. Goalkeeper saving goal 30 20
400. 200 f. Player kicking ball .. 1·25 65

1970. Aerial Navigation Security Agency for Africa and Madagascar. (A.S.E.C.N.A.) (1969). 10th Anniv. As T **121** of Cameroun.
401. 40 f. red and purple .. 25 15

81. Mt. Fuji and Expo Emblem. **82.** "La Justice" and "La Concorde".

1970. World Fair "EXPO 70", Osaka, Japan. Multicoloured.
402. 5 f. Type **81** (postage) .. 5 5
403. 70 f. Dahomey Pavilion (air) 45 20
404. 120 f. Mt. Fuji and temple 80 40

1970. Ardres Embassy to Louis XIV of France. 300th Anniv.
405. **82.** 40 f. brn., blue & green 25 12
406. – 50 f. red, brown & green 30 15
407. – 70 f. brown, slate & bistre 45 20
408. – 200 f. brown, blue & red 1·25 65
DESIGNS: 50 f. Matheo Lopes. 70 f. King Alkemy of Ardres. 200 f. Louis XIV of France.

1970. Air. Brazil's Victory in World Cup Football Championships. No. 400 surch. **BRESIL-ITALIE 4-1** and value.
409. 100 f. on 200 f. multicoloured 65 40

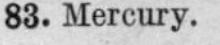

83. Mercury. **84.** Order of Independence.

1970. Air. Europafrique
410. **83.** 40 f. multicoloured .. 25 15
411. 70 f. multicoloured .. 45 20

1970. Independence. 10th Anniv.
412. **84.** 30 f. multicoloured .. 20 8
413. 40 f. multicoloured .. 25 12

85. Bariba Horseman. **86.** Beethoven.

1970. Bariba Horsemen. Multicoloured.
414. 1 f. Type **85** 5 5
415. 2 f. Two horsemen .. 5 5
416. 10 f. Horseman facing left 5 5
417. 40 f. Type **85** 25 12
418. 50 f. As 2 f. 30 12
419. 70 f. as 10 f. 45 15

1970. Air. Birth Bicentenary of Beethoven.
420. **86.** 90 f. violet and blue .. 60 25
421. 110 f. brown and green 70 40

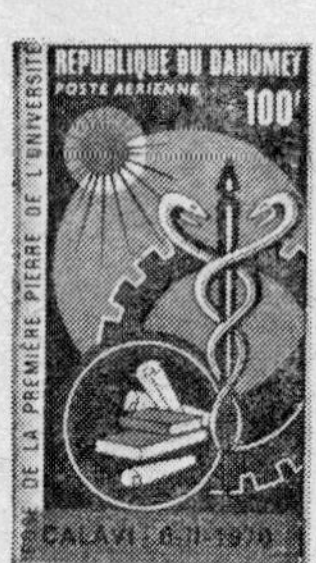

87. Emblems of Learning. **88.** " The Annunciation ".

1970. Air. Laying of Foundation Stone, Calavi University.
422. **87.** 100 f. multicoloured .. 65 30

1970. Air. Christmas. Miniatures of the Rhenish School c.1340. Multicoloured.
423. 40 f. Type **88** 25 12
424. 70 f. " The Nativity " .. 45 20
425. 110 f. " The Adoration of the Magi " .. 70 30
426. 200 f. " The Presentation in the Temple " .. 1·25 65

89. De Gaulle and Arc de Triomphe. **90.** " The Dandy " (" L'Indifferent ").

1971. Air. Gen. Charles de Gaulle. 1st Death Anniv. Multicoloured.
427. 40 f. Type **89** 25 15
428. 500 f. De Gaulle and Notre Dame, Paris .. .. 3·00 1·60

1971. Air. Watteau. 250th Death Anniv. Paintings. Multicoloured.
429. 100 f. Type **90** 65 50
430. 100 f. " Girl with lute " (" La Finette ") .. 65 50

91. Durer's Self-portrait, 1498.

1971. Air. Durer. 500th Birth Anniv. Multicoloured.
431. 100 f. Type **91** 65 50
432. 200 f. Self-portrait, 1500 1·25 1·10

92. " Heart " on Globe.

1971. Racial Equality Year.
433. – 40 f. red, brn. & green 25 12
434. **92.** 100 f. red, blue & green 60 30
DESIGN—VERT. 40 f. Hands supporting heart.

93. "The Twins" (wood-carving) and Lottery Ticket.

1971. National Lottery. Fourth Anniv.
435. **93.** 35 f. multicoloured .. 20 10
436. 40 f. multicoloured .. 25 12

94. Kepler, Earth and Planets.

1971. Air. Johannes Kepler (astronomer). 400th Birth Anniv.
437. **94.** 40 f. blk., pur. & blue.. 25 12
438. – 200 f. green, red & indigo 1·10 65
DESIGN: 200 f. Kepler, globe, satellite and rocket.

95. Boeing " 747 " Airliner linking Europe and Africa.

1971. Air. Europafrique.
439. **95.** 50 f. orge., blue & black 30 15
440. – 100 f. multicoloured .. 60 30
DESIGN: 100 f. Mail-boat and maps of Europe and Africa.

96. Cockerel and Drum (King Ganyehousson).

1971. Emblems of Dahomey Kings. Mult.
441. 25 f. Leg, saw and hatchet (Agoliagbo) 15 8
442. 35 f. Type **96** 20 10
443. 40 f. Fish and egg (Behanzin) (vert.) 25 12
444. 100 f. Cow, tree and birds (Guezo) (vert.) .. 60 25
445. 135 f. Fish and hoe (Ouegbadja) 80 35
446. 140 f. Lion and sickle (Glele) 85 40

1971. Air. U.A.M.P.T. 10th Anniv. As T **153.** of Cameroun. Multicoloured.
447. 100 f. U.A.M.P.T. H.Q., Brazzaville and Arms of Dahomey 60 30

97. " Adoration of the Shepherds " (Master of the Hausbuch).

1971. Air. Christmas. Paintings. Mult.
448. 40 f. Type **97** 25 15
449. 70 f. " Adoration of the Magi " (Holbein) .. 50 25
450. 100 f. " Flight into Egypt " (Van Dyck) (horiz.) .. 60 30
451. 200 f. " Birth of Christ " (Durer) (horiz.).. .. 1·10 60

98. " Prince Balthazar " (Velazquez).

1971. Air. U.N.I.C.E.F. 25th Anniv. Paintings of Children. Multicoloured.
452. 40 f. Type **98** 25 15
453. 100 f. " The Maids of Honour " (detail, Velazquez) 60 30

1972. No. 395. Surch. in figures.
454. **78.** 35 f. on 40 f. grn., bl. & brown 20 10

99. Cross-country Skiing. **100.** Scout taking Oath.

1972. Winter Olympic Games, Sapporo, Japan.
455. **99.** 35 f. maroon, brown and green (postage) .. 20 10
456. – 150 f. purple, blue and brown (air) 90 45
DESIGN: 150 f. Ski-jumping.

1972. Air. Int. Scout Seminar, Cotonou. Multicoloured.
457. 35 f. Type **100** 15 8
458. 40 f. Scout playing " xylophone ".. .. 20 12
459. 100 f. Scouts working on the land (26 × 47 mm.).. 60 30

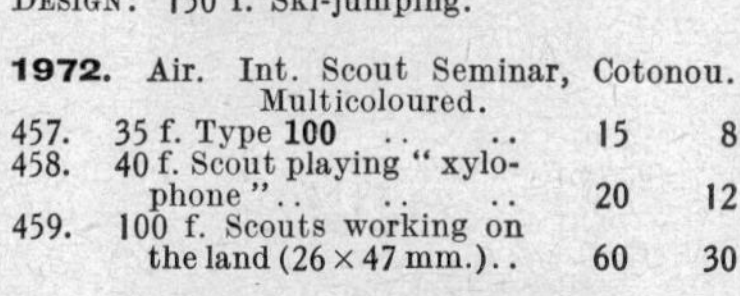

101. Institute Building and F. Naumann.

1972. Air. Laying of Foundation Stone for National Workers Education Institute. Multicoloured.
461. **101.** 100 f. multicoloured.. 55 30
462. – 250 f. Pres. Heuss of West Germany and Institute .. .. 1·40 75

102. Stork with Serpent.

1972. Air. U.N.E.S.C.O. "Save Venice" Campaign. Mosaics in St. Mark's Basilica. Multicoloured.
463. 35 f. Type **102** 20 10
464. 40 f. Cockerels carrying fox 25 12
465. 65 f. Noah releasing dove.. 40 20

193. Exhibition Emblem and Dancers.

1972. Air. 12th International Philatelic Exhib., Naples.
466. **103.** 100 f. multicoloured .. 55 35

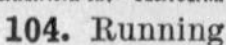

104. Running. **106.** Brahms, and Clara Schumann at Piano.

105. Bleriot and Early Aircraft.

1972. Air. Olympic Games. Munich.
467. **104.** 20 f. brn., grn. & blue 10 8
468. – 85 f. brn., blue & green 45 25
469. – 150 f. brn., blue & grn. 80 50
DESIGNS: 85 f. High-jumping. 150 f. Putting the shot.

1972. Air. Louis Bleriot (pioneer airman). Birth Cent.
471. **105.** 10 f. blue, violet & red 55 40

1972. Johannes Brahms (composer). 75th Death Anniv.
472. – 30 f. blk., brn. & violet 15 10
473. **106.** 65 f. blk., violet & lake 35 25
DESIGN—VERT. Brahms and opening bars of " Soir d'Ete ".

107. " The Hare and the Tortoise ".

1972. Fables of Jean de la Fontaine.
474. **107.** 10 f. grey, blue & lake 5 5
475. – 35 f. blue, lake & purple 20 12
476. – 40 f. indigo, blue & pur. 20 15
DESIGNS—VERT. 35 f. " The Fox and the Stork ". HORIZ. 40 f. " The Cat, the Weasel and the Little Rabbit ".

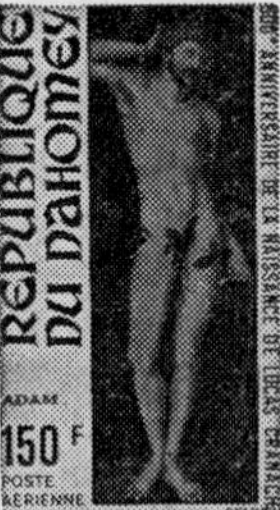

108. " Adam " (Cranach).

1972. Air. Lucas Cranach (painter). 500th Birth Anniv. Multicoloured.
477. 150 f. Type **108** 80 55
478. 200 f. " Eve " (Cranach).. 1·10 65

109. Africans and 500 f. Coin.

1972. West African Monetary Union. 10th Anniv.

479. 109. 40 f. brown, grey & yell. 20 12

110. "Pauline Borghese" (Canova).

1972. Air. Antonio Canova 150th Death Anniv.

480. 110. 250 f. multicoloured.. 1·25 80

1972. Air. Olympic Medal Winners. Nos. 467/9 optd. as listed below.

481. 104. 20 f. brn., blue & grn. 10 8
482. – 85 f. brn., blue & green 45 25
483. – 150 f. brn., blue & grn. 80 45

OVERPRINTS: 20 f. **5,000 M.-10,000 M. VIREN 2 MEDAILLES D'OR.** 85 f. **HAUT-EUR DAMES MEYFARTH MEDAILLE D'OR.** 150 f. **POIDS KOMAR MEDAILLE D'OR.**

111. Pasteur and Apparatus.

1972. Air. Louis Pasteur (scientist). 150th Birth Anniv.

485. 111. 100 f. mar., violet & grn. 55 30

112. "The New born Child".

1972. Air. Paintings by G. de la Tour. Multicoloured.

486. 35 f. "Hurdy-gurdy Player" (vert.) 20 10
487. 150 f. Type 112 .. .. 80 55

113. "The Annunciation" (School of Agnolo Gaddi).

1972. Air. Christmas. Religious Paintings. Multicoloured.

488. 35 f. Type 113 .. .. 20 10
489. 125 f. "The Nativity" (Simone dei Crociffissi) 70 35
490. 140 f. "The Adoration of the Shepherds" (P. di Giovanni) 80 45
491. 250 f. "Adoration of the Magi" (Giotto) .. 1·40 75

114. Dr. Hansen, Microscope and Bacillus.

116. Arms of Dahomey.

115. Statue and Basilica, Lisieux.

1973. Identification of Leprosy Bacillus by Hansen. Cent.

492. 114. 35 f. brown, purple-brown and blue .. 15 8
493. – 85 f. brn., orge. & green 35 25

DESIGN: 85 f. Dr. Gerhard Armauer Hansen.

1973. Air. St. Theresa of Lisieux. Birth Cent. Multicoloured.

494. 40 f. Type 115 .. .. 15 10
495. 100 f. St. Theresa of Lisieux (vert.) 45 30

1973. ..

496. 116. 5 f. multicoloured .. 5 5
497. 35 f. multicoloured .. 12 8
498. 40 f. multicoloured .. 15 8

117. Scouts in Boat.

1973. Air. 24th World Scouting Congress, Nairobi, Kenya.

499. 117. 15 f. mar., grn. & blue 5 5
500i – 20 f. blue and brown.. 8 5
501. – 40 f. blue, grn. & brn. 15 8

DESIGNS—VERT. 20 f. Lord Baden-Powell. HORIZ. 40 f. Bridge-building.

118. Interpol Emblem and Web.

1973. Int. Criminal Police Organization (Interpol). 50th Anniv.

503. 118. 35 f. brn., grn. & red.. 12 8
504. – 50 f. grn., brown & red 20 12

DESIGN-VERT. 50 f. Interpol badge and "Communications".

119. "Education in Nutrition".

1973. World Health Organization. 25th Anniv. Multicoloured.

505. 35 f. Type 119 .. .. 15 8
506. 100 f. Pre-natal examination 40 30

1973. Pan-African Drought Relief. No. 321 surch. **SECHERESSE SOLIDARITE AFRICAINE** and value.

507. 100 f. on 70 f. multicoloured 40 30

120. Copernicus and Solar System.

1973. Air. Copernicus. 500th Birth Anniv.

508. 120. 65 f. blk., maroon & yell. 35 25
509. – 125 f. grn., blue & pur. 55 40

DESIGN-VERT. 125 f. Copernicus.

1973. U.A.M.P.T. As Type 182 of Cameroun.

510. 100 f. violet, red & black 45 30

1973. Air. African Fortnight, Brussels. As Type 183 of Cameroun.

511. 100 f. black, green & blue 45 30

121. Grouper.

1973. Fishes.

512. 121. 5 f. steel-blue and blue 5 5
513. – 15 f. black and blue .. 5 5
514. – 35 f. cinnamon, brn. and green 15 8

DESIGNS: 15 f. Sickle Fish. 35 f. Sea Bream.

122. W.M.O. Emblem and World Map.

1973. Air. I.M.O./W.M.O. Cent.

515. 122. 100 f. brown and green 45 30

123. "Europafrique".

1973. Air. Europafrique.

516. 123. 35 f. blue, grn. & yell. 15 8
517. – 40 f. brn., ultram. & bl. 15 12

DESIGN. 40 f. Europafrique, plant and cogwheels.

124. President Kennedy. 126. Chameleon.

125. Footballers.

1973. Air. President Kennedy. 10th Death Anniv.

518. 124. 200 f. grn., violet & grn. 90 65

1973. Air. World Football Championship Cup.

520. 125. 35 f. grn., brn. & bistre 15 10
521. – 40 f. brown, blue and orange-brown .. 15 12
522. – 100 f. grn., brn. & blue 45 30

DESIGNS: 40 f., 100 f. Football scenes similar to T 125.

1973. 26th October Revolution. 1st Anniv. Multicoloured.

523. 35 f. Type 126 .. .. 15 8
524. 40 f. Arms of Dahomey (vert.) 15 8

127. "The Annunciation" (Dirk Bouts).

128. "The Elephant, the Chicken and the Dog.

1973. Air. Christmas. Paintings by Old Masters. Multicoloured.

525. 35 f. Type 127 .. .. 14 10
526. 100 f. "The Nativity" (Giotto).. .. .. 45 30
527. 150 f. "The Adoration of the Magi" (Botticelli) 65 50
528. 200 f. "The Adoration of the Shepherds" (Le Bassan) (horiz.) .. 90 65

1974. Air. "Skylab". No. 515 surch. **OPERATION SKYLAB 1973-1974** and value.

529. 122. 200 f. on 100 f. brn. & grn. 90 75

1974. Dahomey Folk Tales. Multicoloured.

530. 5 f. Type 128 .. .. 5 5
531. 10 f. "The Sparrowhawk and the Dog" 5 5
532. 25 f. "The Windy Tree" (horiz.) 10 8
533. 40 f. "The Eagle, the Snake and the Chicken" (horiz.) 20 10

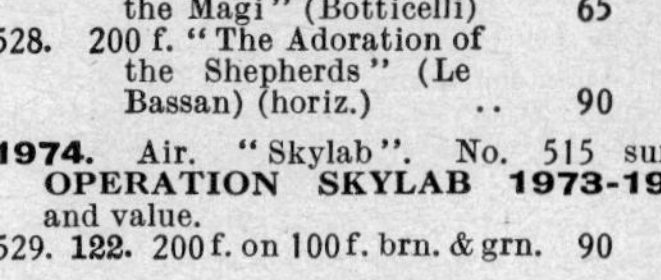

129. Snow Crystal and Skiers.

1974. Air. Winter Olympic Games. 50th Anniv.

534. 129. 100 f. blue, brn. and vio. 45 30

130. Alsatian Dog.

1974. Breeds of Dogs. Multicoloured.

535. 40 f. Type 130 .. .. 15 10
536. 50 f. Boxer 20 15
537. 100 f. Saluki 40 25

131. Map of Member Countries.

1974. Council of Accord. 15th Anniv.

538. 131. 40 f. multicoloured .. 15 10

132. Sir Winston Churchill (Birth Cent.).

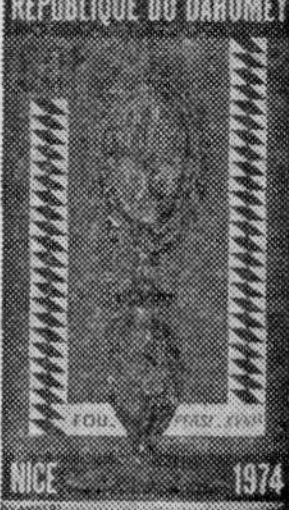

133. Bishop (18th-century Persian).

1974. Air. Celebrities' Anniversaries.

539. – 50 f. purple and red .. 20 12
540. – 125 f. brown & green.. 50 30
541. 132. 150 f. blue & purple .. 60 95

DESIGNS AND ANNIVERSARIES: 50 f. Lenin (50th death anniv.). 125 f. Marie Curie (40th death anniv.).

1974. Air. Chess Olympics, Nice. Ancient Chess-pieces. Multicoloured.

542. 50 f. Type 133 .. .. 20 12
543. 200 f. Queen (Siamese 19th-century) 90 55

134. Beethoven.

135. Earth seen through Astronaut's Legs.

1974. Air. Famous Composers.

544. 134. 150 f. red and black .. 60 45
545. – 150 f. red and black .. 60 45

DESIGN: No. 545, Chopin.

1974. Air. Fifth Anniv. of 1st Manned Moon Landing.
546. 135. 150 f. brn., blue & red 60 55

Sets commemorating the World Cup, U.P.U. Centenary, Treaty of Berne, Space Exploration and West Germany's World Cup Victory appeared in 1974. Their status is uncertain.

1974. Air. 11th Pan-Arab Scout Jamboree, Batroun, Lebanon. Nos. 499/500 surch. **XIe JAMBOREE PANARABE DE BATROUN—LIBAN** and value.
547. 117. 100 f. on 15 f. maroon, green and blue .. 45 30
548. – 140 f. on 20 f. bl. & brn. 55 40

1974. Air. West Germany's Victory in World Cup Football Championships. Nos. 521/2 surch. **R F A 2 HOLLANDE 1** and value.
549. 100 f. on 40 f. brown, blue and orange brown .. 45 30
550. 150 f. on 100 f. grn., brn. & bl. 60 50

136. U.P.U. Emblem and Globe.

1974. Air. Universal Postal Union. Cent.
551. 136. 35 f. violet and red .. 15 8
552. – 65 f. blue and red .. 25 15
553. – 125 f. grn., bl. & lt. bl. 50 40
554. – 200 f. blue, yell. & brn. 85 55
DESIGNS: 65 f. "Concorde" in flight over African village. 125 f. French mobile post office, circa 1860. 200 f. Drummer and mail-van.

137. Bartholdi's "Lion of Belfort".

1974. Air. F. Bartholdi (sculptor). 70th Death Anniv.
555. 137. 100 f. brown 45 30

138. "Young Girl with Falcon" (Philippe de Champaigne).

1974. Air. Philippe de Champaigne (painter). 300th Death Anniv.
556. 138. 250 f. multicoloured .. 1·00 75

139. 2-3-2 Locomotive (1911).

1974. Steam Locomotives.
557. 139. 35 f. multicoloured .. 15 8
558. – 40 f. grey, blk. & red .. 15 8
559. – 100 f. multicoloured .. 45 30
560. – 200 f. multicoloured .. 85 55
DESIGNS: 40 f. 0-3-0 Goods loco (1877). 100 f. "Crampton" loco (1849). 200 f. "Stephenson" loco (1846).

140. Rhamphorhynchus.

1974. Air. Prehistoric Animals. Multicoloured.
561. 35 f. Type 140 .. .. 15 8
562. 150 f. Stegosaurus .. 60 45
563. 200 f. Tyrannosaurus .. 85 55

141. Globe, Notes and Savings Bank.

1974. World Savings Day.
564. 141. 35 f. brn., myrtle & grn. 15 8

142. Europafrique Emblem on Globe.

1974. Air. Europafrique.
565. 142. 250 f. multicoloured .. 95 70

143. "The Annunciation" (Schongauer).

1974. Air. Christmas. Paintings by Old Masters. Multicoloured.
566. 35 f. Type 143 .. .. 15 8
567. 40 f. "The Nativity" (Schongauer) 15 10
568. 100 f. "The Virgin of the Rose Bush" (Schongauer) 95 30
569. 250 f. "The Virgin, Infant Jesus and St. John the Baptist" (Botticelli) 95 70

144. "Apollo" and "Soyuz" Spacecraft.

1975. Air. "Apollo-Soyuz" Space Link. Mult.
570. 35 f. Type 144 .. .. 15 8
571. 200 f. Rocket launch and flags of Russia and U.S.A. 85 55
572. 500 f. "Apollo" and "Soyuz" docked together 2·00 1·50

145. Dompago Dance, Hissi.

146. Flags on Map of Africa.

1975. Dahomey Dances and Folklore. Mult.
573. 10 f. Type 145 .. .. 5 5
574. 25 f. Fetish dance, Vaudou-Tchinan 12 8
575. 40 f. Bamboo dance, Agbehoun 15 10
576. 100 f. Somba dance, Sandoua (horiz.) 40 30

1975. "Close Co-operation with Nigeria." Multicoloured.
577. 65 f. Type 146 .. .. 25 15
578. 100 f. Arrows linking maps of Dahomey and Nigeria (horiz.) 40 30

147. Community Emblem and Pylons.

1975. Benin Electricity Community. Mult.
579. 40 f. Type 147 .. .. 15 10
580. 150 f. Emblem and pylon (vert.) 60 40
C.E.B. = "Communate Electrique du Benin".

148. Head of Ceres.

1975. Air. "Arphila 75" International Stamp Exhibition, Paris.
581. 148. 100 f. pur., ind. & blue 40 30

149. Rays of Light and Map.

150. Dr. Schweitzer.

1975. "New Dahomey Society".
582. 149. 35 f. multicoloured .. 15 10

1975. Air. "Apollo-Soyuz" Space Link. Project. Nos. 570/1 surch. **RENCONTRE APOLLO-SOYOUZ 17 Juil. 1975** and value.
583. 144. 100 f. on 35 f. mult... 40 30
584. – 300 f. on 200 f. mult... 1·40 80

1975. Dr. Albert Schweitzer. Birth Cent.
585. 150. 200 f. olive, brn. & grn. 85 65

151. "The Holy Family" (Michelangelo).

152. Woman and I.W.Y. Emblem.

1975. Air. Europafrique.
586. 151. 300 f. multicoloured .. 1·40 80

1975. International Women's Year.
587. 152. 50 f. blue and violet .. 20 12
588. – 150 f. orge., brn. & grn. 60 40
DESIGN: 150 f. I.W.Y. emblem within ring of bangles.

153. Continental Infantry.

155. "Allamanda cathartica".

154. Diving.

1975. Air. American Revolution. Bicent.
589. 153. 75 f. lilac red & green 30 20
590. – 135 f. brn., pur. & bl... 60 40
591. – 300 f. brn. red & bl... 1·40 80
592. – 500 f. brn. red & grn. 2·00 1·50
DESIGNS: 135 f. "Spirit of 76". 300 f. Artillery battery. 500 f. Cavalry.

1975. Air. Olympic Games, Montreal.
593. 154. 40 f. brn., bl. and vio. 20 12
594. – 250 f. brn., grn. & red 1·00 75
DESIGN: 250 f. Football.

1975. Flowers. Multicoloured.
595. 10 f. Type 155 .. .. 5 5
596. 35 f. "Ixora coccinea" .. 15 10
597. 45 f. "Hibiscus rosa-sinensis" 20 12
598. 60 f. "Phaemeria magnifica" 25 15

156. "The Nativity" (Van Leyden).

1975. Air. Christmas. Multicoloured.
599. 40 f. Type 156 .. .. 20 12
600. 85 f. "Adoration of the Magi" (Rubens) (vert.) 40 25
601. 140 f. "Adoration of the Shepherds" (Le Brun) 60 40
602. 300 f. "The Virgin of the Blue Diadem" (Raphael) (vert.) .. .. 1·40 80
For later issues see **BENIN**.

POSTAGE DUE STAMPS

1906. "Natives" key-type inscr. "DAHOMEY".
D 33. L. 5 c. green 30 30
D 34. 10 c. claret 55 55
D 35. 15 c. blue on blue .. 1·10 1·10
D 36. 20 c. black on yellow 60 60
D 37. 30 c. red on cream .. 1·00 1·00
D 38. 50 c. violet .. .. 3·00 3·00
D 39. 60 c. black on buff .. 1·60 1·60
D 40. 1 f. black on pink .. 3·75 3·75

1914. "Figure" key-type inscr. "DAHOMEY".
D 59. M. 5 c. green 5 5
D 60. 10 c. red 5 5
D 61. 15 c. grey 5 5
D 62. 20 c. brown 5 5
D 63. 30 c. blue 10 10
D 64. 50 c. black 12 12
D 65. 60 c. orange 15 15
D 66. 1 f. violet 15 15

1927. Surch. in figures.
D 96. M. 2 f. on 1 f. mauve .. 40 40
D 97. 3 f. on 1 f. brown .. 45 45

D 1. Native Head.

D 2. Panther attacking African.

1941.
D 143. D 1. 5 c. black 5 5
D 144. 10 c. red 5 5
D 145. 15 c. blue 5 5
D 146. 20 c. green 5 5
D 147. 30 c. orange 5 5
D 148. 50 c. brown 5 5
D 149. 60 c. green 8 8
D 150. 1 f. red 10 10
D 151. 2 f. yellow 12 12
D 152. 3 f. purple 15 15

1963.
D 191. D 2. 1 f. red and green .. 5 5
D 192. 2 f. green & brown 5 5
D 193. 5 f. blue and orange 5 5
D 194. 10 f. black and purple 8 8
D 195. 20 f. orange & blue 12 12

D 3. Pirogue.

1967.

D 308. D 3. 1 f. plum, bl. & brn.	5	5
D 309. A. 1 f. brn., bl. & plum	5	5
D 310. B. 3 f. grn., orge. & choc.	5	5
D 311. C. 3 f. choc., orge. & grn.	5	5
D 312. D. 5 f. pur., blue & brn.	5	5
D 313. E. 5 f. brn., blue & pur.	5	5
D 314. F. 10 f. grn., vio. & brn.	8	8
D 315. G. 10 f. brn., grn. & vio.	8	8
D 316. H. 30 f. vio., crim. & bl.	15	15
D 317. I. 30 f. bl., crim. & vio.	15	15

DESIGNS: A, Heliograph. B, Old morse receiver. C, Cycle-postman. D, Old telephone. E, Modern rail-car. F, Citroen "2-CV" mail-van. G, Radio station. H, Douglas "DC-8F" airliner. I, "Early Bird" satellite. The two designs in each value are arranged in tete-beche pairs.

PARCEL POST STAMPS

1967. Surch. **COLIS POSTAUX** and value.

P 271. 8. 5 f. on 1 f. (postage)..	5	5
P 272. – 10 f. on 2 f. (No. 151)..	10	10
P 273. 8. 20 f. on 6 f. ..	15	15
P 274. – 25 f. on 3 f. (No. 152)..	25	25
P 275. – 30 f. on 4 f. (No. 153)..	25	25
P 276. – 50 f. on 10 f. (No. 155)	45	65
P 277. – 100 f. on 20 f. (No. 157)	90	65
P 278. – 200 f. on 200 f. (No. 195) (air)	1·75	1·10
P 279. 16. 300 f. on 100 f.	2·50	1·90
P 280. – 500 f. on 300 f. (No. 196)	2·25	2·75
P 281. – 1000 f. on 500 f. (No. 197)	8·50	7·50
P 282. – 5000 f. on 100 f. (No. 145)	32·00	22·00

DANISH WEST INDIES O2

A group of islands in the West Indies formerly belonging to Denmark and purchased in 1917 by the United States, whose stamps they now use. Now known as the United States Virgin Islands.

1855. 100 cents = 1 dollar.
1905. 100 bit = 1 franc.

1.

2.

3.

1855. Imperf.

4. 1. 3 c. red	12·00	12·00

1872. Perf.

6. 1. 3 c. red	28·00	30·00
7. 4 c. blue	50·00	70·00

1873.

31. 2. 1 c. claret and green ..	1·40	1·40
32. 3 c. red and blue ..	1·40	1·40
33. 4 c. blue and brown ..	1·40	1·40
19. 5 c. grey and green ..	5·00	4·25
21. 7 c. orange and lilac ..	6·50	7·00
25. 10 c. brown and blue ..	6·00	4·25
27. 12 c. green and lilac ..	5·00	6·00
28. 14 c. lilac and green ..	£120	£130
30. 50 c. lilac	20·00	27·00

1887. Handstamped **1 CENT.**

37. 2. 1 c. on 7 c. orange & lilac	12·00	15·00

1895. Surch. **10 CENTS 1895.**

38. 2. 10 c. on 50 c. lilac ..	4·00	5·00

1900.

39. 3. 1 c. green	30	30
40. 2 c. red	1·75	1·75
41. 5 c. blue	1·90	1·90
42. 8 c. brown	5·00	5·00

1902. Surch. **2** (or **8**) **CENTS 1902.**

43. 2. 2 c. on 3 c. red and blue..	1·60	1·75
44. 8 c. on 10 c. brown & blue	2·75	2·75

1905. Surch. **5 BIT 1905.**

48. 2. 5 b. on 4 c. blue & brown	4·50	7·00
49. 3. 5 b. on 5 c. blue	2·75	4·75
50. 5 b. on 8 c. brown ..	2·75	4·75

4. King Christian IX.

5. St. Thomas Harbour and Cruiser "Ingolf".

1905.

51. 4. 5 b. green	2·00	1·00
52. 10 b. red	2·00	1·00
53. 20 b. blue and green ..	3·25	3·00
54. 25 b. blue	3·00	2·40
55. 40 b. grey and red ..	2·50	2·50
56. 50 b. grey and yellow ..	2·75	3·25
57. 5. 1 f. blue and green ..	4·75	7·00
58. 2 f. brown and red ..	8·00	12·00
59. 5 f. brown and yellow ..	15·00	32·00

6. King Frederick.

7. King Christian X.

1907.

60. 6. 5 b. green	65	30
61. 10 b. red	50	30
62. 15 b. brown and violet ..	1·00	1·25
63. 20 b. blue and green ..	5·50	3·50
64. 25 b. blue	50	40
65. 30 b. black and claret ..	8·50	4·00
66. 40 b. grey and red ..	90	2·25
67. 50 b. brown and yellow ..	1·10	2·50

1915.

68. 7. 5 b. green	50	1·10
69. 10 b. red	60	10·00
70. 15 b. brown and lilac ..	75	10·00
71. 20 b. blue and green ..	75	10·00
72. 25 b. blue	75	3·00
73. 30 b. black and claret ..	75	10·00
74. 40 b. grey and red ..	75	10·00
75. 50 b. brown and yellow ..	75	10·00

POSTAGE DUE STAMPS

D 1.

D 2.

1902.

D 43. D 1. 1 c. blue	1·60	3·00
D 44. 4 c. blue	2·40	3·75
D 45. 6 c. blue	8·00	12·00
D 46. 10 c. blue	6·50	8·50

1905.

D 60. D 2. 5 b. red and grey ..	60	1·25
D 61. 20 b. red and grey ..	2·25	3·50
D 62. 20 b. red and grey	60	1·40
D 63. 50 b. red and grey ..	1·60	2·75

DANZIG E1

A Baltic seaport, from 1920-1939 (with the surrounding district) a free state under the protection of the League of Nations. Later incorporated in Germany. Now part of Poland.

1920. 100 pfennige = 1 mark.
1923. 100 pfennige = 1 Danzig gulden.

Stamps of Germany inscr. "DEUTSCHES REICH" optd. or surch.

1920. Optd. **Danzig** horiz.

1. 8. 5 pf. green	8	8
2. 10 pf. red	8	8
3. 13. 15 pf. brown	8	8
4. 8. 20 pf. blue	8	8
5. 30 pf. blk. & orge. on buff	8	8
6. 40 pf. red	8	8
7. 50 p.f blk. & pur. on buff	8	8
8. 9. 1 m. red	20	25
9. 1 m. 25 green	20	25
10. 1 m. 50 brown	35	40
11. 10. 2 m. blue	35	55
12. 2 m. 50 claret	85	1·40
13. 11. 3 m. black	1·45	2·75
14. 8. 4 m. red and black ..	1·90	2·10
15a. 12. 5 m. red and black ..	35	65

1920. Surch. **Danzig** horiz. and large figures of value.

16. 8. 5 on 30 pf. black and orange on buff ..	5	5
17. 10 on 20 pf. blue ..	5	5
18. 25 on 30 pf. black and orange on buff ..	5	5
19. 60 on 30 pf. black and orange on buff ..	20	20
20. 80 on 30 pf. black and orange on buff ..	20	20

1920. Optd. **Danzig** diagonally and bar.

21. 13. 2 pf. grey	50·00	50·00
22. 2½ pf. grey	70·00	85·00
23. 8. 3 pf. brown	4·25	4·75
24. 5 pf. green	8	8
25. 13. 7½ pf. orange	12·00	14·00
26. 8. 10 pf. red	1·40	1·90
27. 13. 15 pf. violet	15	20
28. 8. 20 pf. blue	15	20
29. 25 pf. blk. & red on yell.	15	20
30. 30 pf. blk. & oran. on buff	19·00	21·00
31. 40 pf. black and red ..	55	80
32. 50 pf. lbk. & pur. on buff	70·00	80·00
32a. 60 pf. purple	£700	£800
33. 75 pf. black and green ..	15	20
34. 80 pf. blk. & red on rose	1·10	1·40
34a. 9. 1 m. red	£225	£300

1920. Optd. **DANZIG** three times in semi-circle.

34b. 10. 2 m. blue	£325	£375

1920. Surch. **Danzig** and new value.

40a. 8. 1 m. on 30 pf. black and orange on buff ..	50	55
36. 1¼ m. on 3 pf. brown ..	50	60
37. 13. 2 m. on 35 pf. brown ..	50	60
40d. 3 m. on 7½ pf. orange ..	60	70
40e. 5 m. on 2 pf. grey ..	60	70
40f. 10 m. on 7½ pf. orange..	60	70

1920. Air. No. 6 of Danzig surch. with aeroplane or wings and value.

41. 8. 40 on 40 pf. red	1·00	1·10
42. 60 on 40 pf. red	1·00	1·10
43. 1 m. on 40 pf. red ..	1·00	1·10

1. "Kogge", a Hanse sailing vessel.

ILLUSTRATIONS
British Commonwealth and all overprints and surcharges are FULL SIZE. Foreign Countries have been reduced to ¾-LINEAR.

1921. Roul. (Nos. 48, 55 and 43, also perf.).

44. 1. 5 pf. purple and brown ..	12	12
45. 10 pf. violet and orange..	12	12
46. 25 pf. red and green ..	20	25
55. 40 pf. red	50	50
48. 80 pf. blue	15	15
49. – 1 m. black and red ..	55	80
50. – 2 m. olive and blue ..	1·90	2·25
51. – 3 m. green and black ..	55	90
52. – 5 m. red and black ..	55	90
53. – 10 m. brown and olive ..	1·10	2·40

The mark values are as T 1, but larger.

1921. No. 33 of Danzig surch. **60** and bars.

57. 8. 60 on 75 pf. black & green	10	15

2. Aeroplane over Danzig.

3.

1921. Air.

112. 2. 40 pf. green	12	65
113. 60 pf. purple	12	65
114. 1 m. red	12	65
115. 2 m. brown	12	68
116. 3. 5 m. violet	12	25
117. 10 m. green	12	20
118. 20 m. brown	12	20
119. 2. 25 m. blue	10	15
120. 3. 50 m. orange	10	25
121. 100 m. red	10	25
122. 250 m. brown	10	25
123. 500 m. red	10	25

Nos. 120 to 123 are similar to T 3, but larger.

4.

5.

1921.

64. 4. 5 pf. orange	10	10
65. 10 pf. brown	5	5
66. 15 pf. green	5	5
67. 20 pf. grey	5	5
68. 25 pf. green	5	5
69. 30 pf. red and blue ..	8	5
70. 40 pf. red and green ..	5	5
71. 4. 50 pf. red and green ..	5	5
72. 60 pf. red	5	12
73. 75 pf. purple	5	8
74. 80 pf. red and black ..	8	20
75. 80 pf. green	5	8
76. 1 m. red and orange ..	5	5
77. 1.20 m. blue	40	40
78. 1.25 m. red and purple ..	5	8
79. 1.50 m. grey	5	5
80. 2 m. red and grey ..	95	1·10
81. 2 m. red	5	8
82. 2.40 m. red and brown ..	20	40
83a. 3 m. red and purple ..	3·25	3·75
84. 3 m. red	5	8
106. 4 m. blue	5	8
86. 5 m. green	5	8
87. 6 m. red	5	8
88. 8 m. blue	10	25
89. 10 m. orange	5	8
90. 20 m. brown	5	10
110. 40 m. blue	5	10
111. 80 m. red	5	10

1921. Rouletted.

91. 5. 5 m. green, black and red	50	90
91a. 9 m. orange and red ..	2·00	3·00
92. 10 m. blue, black and red	50	90
93. 20 m. black and red ..	50	90

6.

7.

1921. Charity. Tuberculosis Week.

93a. – 30 pf. (+30 pf.) grn. & orge.	12	15
93b. – 60 pf. (+60 pf.) red & yell.	55	60
93c. 6. 1.20 m (+1.20 m.) indigo and orange	1·00	1·00

Nos. 93a/b are smaller.

1922.

94a. 7. 50 m. red and gold ..	80	1·40
95. 100 m. red and green ..	1·60	2·00

1922. Surch. in figures.

96. 4. 6 on 3 m. red	5	5
97. 8 on 4 m. indigo ..	8	20
98. 20 on 8 m. blue ..	8	15

8.

9.

1923.

99. 8. 50 m. red and blue ..	5	8
129. 50 m. blue	5	10
100. 100 m. red and olive ..	5	8
130. 100 m. olive	5	10
101. 150 m. red and purple ..	5	8
131. 200 m. orange	5	10
102. 9. 250 m. red and purple ..	8	10
103. 500 m. red and olive ..	8	10
104. 1000 m. red and brown	8	10
105. 5000 m. red and silver ..	45	2·00
132. 10,000 m. red and orange	12	15
133. 20,000 m. red and blue..	15	30
134. 50,000 m. red and green	12	25

10.

1923. Charity. Poor People's Fund.

123b. 10. 50+20 m. red	10	15
123c. 100+30 m. purple ..	10	15

11.

12.

1923.

124. 11. 250 m. red and purple..	5	10
125. 300 m. red and green..	5	10
126. 500 m. red and grey ..	5	10
127. 1000 m. red and brown	8	10
135. 1000 m. brown.. ..	5	8
128. 3000 m. red and violet..	8	10
136. 5000 m. red	5	8
137. 20,000 m. blue.. ..	5	8
138. 50,000 m. green ..	5	8
139. 100,000 m. blue ..	5	8
140. 250,000 m. purple ..	5	8
141. 500,000 m. grey ..	5	8

1923. Surch. **100000** and bar.

157. 9. 100,000 on 20,000 m. red and blue (No. 133) ..	55	1·50

1923. Surch. with figure of value and **Tausend** (T.) or **Million** or **Millionen** (M.)

142. 8. 40 T. on 200 m. orange..	20	60
143. 100 T. on 200 m. orange	20	60
144. 250 T. on 200 m. orange	2·20	5·50
145. 400 T. on 100 m. olive..	10	15
146. 11. 500 T. on 50,000 m. green	10	15

147. 1 M. on 10,000 m. orange 1·00 2·10
148. 1 M. on 10,000 m. red .. 5 12
149. 2 M. on 10,000 m. red .. 5 12
150. 3 M. on 10,000 m. red .. 5 12
151. 5 M. on 10,000 m. red .. 5 12
152. 10 M. on 10,000 m. lav. 8 15
158. 9. 10 M. on 1,000,000 m. orange 8 15
153. 11. 20 M. on 10,000 m. lav. 5 12
154. 25 M. on 10,000 m. lav. 5 12
155. 40 M. on 10,000 m. lav. 5 12
156. 50 M. on 10,000 m. lav. 5 12
159. 100 M. on 10,000 m. lav. 5 12
160. 300 M. on 10,000 m. lav. 5 12
161. 500 M. on 10,000 m. lav. 5 12

1923. Air.
162. 12. 250,000 m. red 12 55
163. 500,000 m. red 12 55

1923. Surch. in **Millionen.**
164. 12. 2 M. on 100,000 m. red .. 12 45
165. 5 M. on 50,000 m. red .. 12 45

1923. Surch. with new currency. **Pfennige** or **Gulden.**
166. 8. 5 pf. on 50 m. red .. 10 15
167. 10 pf. on 50 m. red .. 10 15
168. 20 pf. on 100 m. red .. 10 15
169. 25 pf. on 50 m. red .. 1·60 3·50
170. 30 pf. on 50 m. red .. 50 55
171. 40 pf. on 100 m. red .. 50 55
172. 50 pf. on 100 m. red .. 65 80
173. 75 pf. on 100 m. red .. 2·50 5·50
174. 9. 1 g. on 1,000,000 m. red .. 1·60 2·25
175. 2 g. on 1,000,000 m. red .. 5·00 7·00
176. 3 g. on 1,000,000 m. red .. 9·00 20·00
177. 5 g. on 1,000,000 m. red .. 9·00 20·00

13. 14.

1924.
177b. 13. 3 pf. brown 65 15
178b. 5 pf. orange .. .. 1·10 5
178e. 7 pf. green 60 70
178f. 8 pf. green .. .. 1·25 1·60
270. 10 pf. green 50 20
180. 15 pf. grey 75 12
180a. 15 pf. red .. .. 1·25 5
181. 20 pf. red & carmine .. 1·00 5
182. 20 pf. grey 90 80
183. 20 pf. red and grey .. 5·50 20
272. 25 pf. red .. .. 1·25 2·00
185. 30 pf. red and green .. 2·00 5
186. 30 pf. purple .. .. 85 1·25
186a. 35 pf. blue 65 20
187. 40 pf. blue and indigo 1·75 5
188. 40 pf. red and brown .. 4·25 5·00
189. 40 pf. blue 85 65
274. 50 pf. red and blue .. 1·25 2·40
190a. 55 pf. red and purple .. 3·25 1·50
191. 60 pf. red and green .. 2·50 3·50
192. 70 pf. red and green .. 80 90
193. 75 pf. red and purple .. 1·60 1·25
194. 80 pf. red and brown .. 1·25 1·40

1924. Air.
195. 14. 10 pf. orange .. .. 9·00 1·25
196. 20 pf. red 80 60
197. 40 pf. brown .. .. 2·00 95
198. 1 g. green .. .. 2·00 95
199. 2½ g. chocolate .. .. 11·00 13·00
The 2½ g. is larger (22 × 40 mm.).

15. Oliva. 16. St. Mary's Church.

1924.
200. 15. 1 g. black and green .. 12·00 10·00
275. 1 g. black and orange .. 2·50 3·00
201. – 2 g. black and purple .. 27·00 27·00
206. – 2 g. black and red .. 1·40 1·40
202. – 3 g. black and blue .. 1·75 1·75
203. 16. 5 g. black and lake .. 1·90 1·90
204. – 10 g. black and brown .. 12·00 15·00
DESIGNS—HORIZ. 2 g. Krantor and River Mortlau. 3 g. Zoppot. VERT. 10 g. Town Hall and Langemarkt.

17. Fountain of Neptune. 18. 19.

1929. Int. Philatelic Exn. Various frames.
207. 17. 10 pf. (+10 pf.) black and green 80 90
208. 15 pf. (+15 pf.) blk. & red 80 90
209. 25 pf. (+25 pf.) blk. & bl. 3·25 2·75

1930. Constitution of Free City of Danzig. 10th Anniv. Optd. **1920 15** November **1930.**
210. 13. 5 pf. orange 70 55
211. 10 pf. green .. .. 1·25 80
212. 15 pf. red .. .. 1·60 1·25
213. 20 pf. red 80 85
214. 25 pf. red and black .. 2·00 1·40
215. 30 pf. red and green .. 3·50 4·50
216. 35 pf. blue .. .. 13·00 14·00
217. 40 pf. blue and indigo 4·00 4·50
218. 50 pf. red and blue .. 13·00 14·00
219. 75 pf. red and purple .. 13·00 14·00
220. 15. 1 g. black and orange .. 13·00 14·00

1932. Danzig Int. Air Post Exn. ("Luposta"). Nos. 200/4 surch. **Luftpost-Ausstellung 1932** and value.
221. 15. 10 pf. + 10 pf. on 1 g. black and green .. 5·00 4·25
222. 15 pf. + 15 pf. on 2 g. black and purple .. 5·00 4·25
223. – 20 pf. + 20 pf. on 3 g. black and blue .. 5·00 4·25
224. 16. 25 pf. + 25 pf. on 5 g. black and lake .. 5·00 4·25
225. – 30 pf. + 30 pf. on 10 g. black and brown .. 5·00 4·25

1934. "Winter Relief Work" Charity. Surch. **5 W.H.W.** in gothic characters.
226. 13. 5 pf. + 5 pf. orange .. 5·50 5·00
227. 10 pf. + 5 pf. green .. 12·00 11·00
228. 15 pf. + 5 pf. red .. 6·50 6·50

1934. Surch.
229. 13. 6 pf. on 7 pf. green .. 40 45
230b. 8 pf. on 7 pf. green .. 50 55
231. 30 pf. on 35 pf. blue .. 4·25 5·50

1935. Air.
233. 18. 10 pf. red 70 15
234. 15 pf. yellow .. .. 1·00 55
235. 25 pf. green .. .. 1·00 55
236. 50 pf. blue .. .. 3·50 3·00
237. 19. 1 g. purple .. .. 1·90 4·50

20. Stockturm, 1346. 21. Brosen Beach.

1935. Charity. Inscr. "Fur das Winterhilfswerk".
238. 20. 5 pf. + 5 pf. orange .. 40 40
239. – 10 pf. + 5 pf. green .. 65 65
240. – 15 pf. + 10 pf. red .. 1·25 1·25
DESIGNS—HORIZ. 10 pf. Lege Tor. VERT. 15 pf. Georgshalle, 1487.

1936. Brosen. 125th Anniv. Inscr. "125 JAHRE OSTSEEBAD BROSEN".
241. 21. 10 pf. green 40 40
242. – 25 pf. red 80 90
243. – 40 pf. blue .. .. 1·40 1·50
DESIGNS—HORIZ. 25 pf. Zoppot end of Brosen Beach. VERT. 40 pf. Brosen War Memorial.

23. Frauentor and Observatory. 24. D(anziger) L(uftschutz) B(und). 25. Danziger Dorf, Magdeburg.

1936. Winter Relief. Inscr. "WINTERHILFE".
244. – 10 pf. + 5 pf. blue .. 80 80
245. 23. 15 pf. + 5 pf. green .. 80 80
246. – 25 pf. + 10 pf. claret .. 1·00 1·00
247. – 40 pf. + 20 pf. brown & claret .. .. 1·25 1·40
248. – 50 pf. + 20 pf. blue .. 1·75 1·75
DESIGNS—VERT. 10 pf. Milchkannenturm, 25 pf. Krantor. HORIZ 40 pf. Langgartertor. 50 pf. Hohestor.

1937. Air. Defence League.
249. 24. 10 pf. blue 55 55
250. 15 pf. purple 65 65

1937. 1st National Philatelic Exn., Danzig. Designs in miniature sheets inscr. "DAPOSTA 1937" above and "I DANZIGER/LANDES. POSTWERTZEICHEN/AUSSTELLUNG" below.
MS 251. 50 pf. + 50 pf. grn. (post) 60 60
MS 252. 50 pf. + 50 pf. blue (air) 60 60

1937. Charity. Foundation of Danzig Community, Magdeburg. Inscr. "DANZIGER DORF IN MAGDEBURG".
253. 25. 25 pf. red .. .. 1·75 2·25
254. – 40 pf. red and blue .. 1·75 2·25
DESIGN—HORIZ. 40 pf. Village and Arms of Danzig and Magdeburg.

26. Madonna and Child. 27. Schopenhauer.

1937. Winter Relief. Statues inscr. "WINTERHILFE" or "WINTERHILFSZUSCHLAG".
255. 26. 5 pf. + 5 pf. violet .. 75 60
256. – 10 pf. + 5 pf. brown .. 1·75 1·60
257. – 15 pf. + 5 pf. orge. & blue 2·00 2·25
258. – 25 pf. + 10 pf. grn. & bl. 2·25 2·25
259. – 40 pf. + 25 pf. bl. & red 3·50 4·25
DESIGNS: 10 pf. Mercury. 15 pf. "Golden Knight". 25 pf. Fountain of Neptune. 40 pf. St. George and Dragon.

1938. Schopenhauer. 150th Birth. Anniv. Portraits inscr. as in T 27.
260. – 15 pf. blue (as old man) 1·00 1·00
261. – 25 pf. brown (as youth) 2·50 2·50
262. 27. 40 pf. red .. .. 1·10 1·10

28. Yacht "Peter von Danzig" (1936). 29. Teutonic Knights.

1938. Winter Relief. Ship types inscr. "W H W".
276. 28. 5 pf. + 5 pf. green .. 90 90
277. – 10 pf. + 5 pf. brown .. 1·10 1·10
278. – 15 pf. + 10 pf. olive .. 1·25 1·25
279. – 25 pf. + 10 pf. blue .. 1·75 1·75
280. – 40 pf. + 15 pf. maroon .. 1·90 1·90
DESIGNS: 10 pf. Dredger "Fu Shing". 15 pf. Steamship "Columbus". 25 pf. Steamship "Hansestadt Danzig". 40 pf. Sailing vessel "Peter von Danzig" (1472).

1939. Prussian Annexation. 125th Anniv.
281. 29. 5 pf. green 55 80
282. – 10 pf. brown .. .. 65 1·10
283. – 15 pf. blue .. .. 90 1·25
284. – 25 pf. purple .. .. 1·10 1·75
DESIGNS: 10 pf. Danzig-Swedish treaty of neutrality. 1630. 15 pf. Danzig united to Prussia. 2.1.1814. 25 pf. Stephen Batori's defeat at Weichselmunde, 1577.

30. Gregor Mendel.

1939. Anti-Cancer Campaign.
285. 30. 10 pf. brown 35 35
286. – 15 pf. black (Koch) .. 50 45
287. – 25 pf. green (Rontgen) .. 70 1·00

OFFICIAL STAMPS

1921. Stamps of Danzig optd. **D M.**
O 94. 4. 5 pf. orange 8 8
O 95. 10 pf. brown 5 8
O 96. 15 pf. green 5 8
O 97. 20 pf. grey 5 8
O 98. 25 pf. olive 5 8
O 99. 30 pf. red and blue .. 15 20
O 100. 40 pf. red and green .. 5 8
O 101. 50 pf. red and olive .. 5 8
O 102. 60 pf. red 5 8
O 103. 75 pf. purple 5 10
O 104. 80 pf. red and black .. 50 55
O 105. 80 pf. green 5 10
O 106. 1 m. red and orange .. 5 5
O 107. 1 m. 20 blue 50 55
O 108. 4. 1 m. 25 red and purple 5 10
O 109. 1 m. 50 grey 5 10
O 110. 2 m. red and grey .. 5·00 6·50
O 111. 2 m. red 5 10
O 112. 2 m. 40 red and sepia 70 90
O 113. 3 m. red and purple .. 4·50 5·50
O 114. 3 m. red 5 10
O 122. 4 m. indigo 5 5
O 116. 5 m. green 5 10
O 117. 6 m. red 5 10
O 121. 6 on 3 m. red (No. 96) .. 5 15
O 118. 10 m. orange 5 10
O 119. 20 m. brown 5 10

1922. Stamps of Danzig optd. **D M.**
O 120. 5. 5 m. green, black and red (No. 91) .. 1·50 2·25
O 126. 8. 50 m. red and blue .. 5 8
O 135. 50 m. blue 5 12
O 127. 100 m. red and olive .. 5 8
O 136. 100 m. olive 5 10
O 137. 200 m. orange 5 10
O 138. 11. 300 m. red and green 5 8
O 139. 500 m. red and grey .. 5 12
O 140. 1,000 m. red and brown 5 12

1924. Optd. **Dienst-marke.**
O 195. 13. 5 pf. orange 50 45
O 196. 10 pf. green 50 45
O 197. 15 pf. grey 50 45
O 198. 15 pf. red .. .. 6·00 1·75
O 199. 20 pf. red 50 45
O 200. 25 pf. red and black .. 6·00 6·50
O 201. 30 pf. red and green .. 1·00 65
O 202. 35 pf. blue .. .. 15·00 13·00
O 203. 40 pf. blue and indigo 2·00 2·10
O 204. 50 pf. red and blue .. 6·00 5·50
O 205. 75 pf. red and purple .. 14·00 26·00

POSTAGE DUE STAMPS

D 1. D 2.

1921. Value in "pfennige" (figures only).
D 94. D 1. 10 pf. purple .. 8 15
D 95. 20 pf. purple .. 8 15
D 96. 40 pf. purple .. 8 15
D 97. 60 pf. purple .. 8 15
D 98. 75 pf. purple .. 8 15
D 99. 80 pf. purple .. 8 15
D 112. 100 pf. purple .. 12 25
D 100. 120 pf. purple .. 8 15
D 101. 200 pf. purple .. 25 45
D 102. 240 pf. purple .. 8 15
D 114. 300 pf. purple .. 12 25
D 115. 400 pf. purple .. 12 25
D 116. 500 pf. purple .. 12 25
D 117. 800 pf. purple .. 15 35
Value in "marks" ("M" after figure).
D 118. D 1. 10 m. purple .. 12 25
D 119. 20 m. purple .. 12 25
D 120. 50 m. purple .. 12 25
D 121. 100 m. purple .. 10 15
D 122. 500 m. purple .. 10 15

1923. Surch. with figures and bar.
D 162. D 1. 1,000 on 100 m. purple 45·00 55·00
D 163. 5,000 on 50 m. purple 10 12
D 164. 10,000 on 20 m. pur. 10 12
D 165. 50,000 on 500 m. pur. 10 12
D 166. 100,000 on 20 m. pur. 35 35

1924.
D 178. D 2. 5 pf. blue and black .. 25 20
D 179. 10 pf. blue and black 20 12
D 180. 15 pf. blue and black 30 25
D 181. 20 pf. blue and black 40 40
D 182. 30 pf. blue and black 3·00 25
D 183. 40 pf. blue and black 70 65
D 184. 50 pf. blue and black 70 15
D 185. 60 pf. blue and black 5·50 5·00
D 186. 100 pf. blue and black 5·50 1·90
D 187. 3 g. blue and red .. 3·00 5·00

1932. Surch. in figures over bar.
D 226. D 2. 5 on 40 pf. blue & blk. 70 1·25
D 227. 10 on 60 pf. blue and black .. .. 13·00 1·75
D 228. 20 on 100 pf. blue and black .. .. 70 1·40

DEDEAGATZ E3

Former French Post Office, closed in Aug. 1914. Dedeagatz was part of Turkey to 1913, then a Bulgarian town.

100 centimes = 1 franc.
40 paras = 1 piastre.

1893. Stamps of France optd. **Dedeagh** or surch. also in figures and words.
59. 10. 5 c. green .. .. 1·10 1·10
60. 10 c. black on lilac .. 1·60 1·40
62a. 15 c. blue .. .. 2·75 1·60
63. 1 pi. on 25 c. black on red 3·25 2·75
64. 2 pi. on 50 c. red .. 7·00 5·00
65. 4 pi. on 1 f. olive .. 7·00 5·00
66. 8 pi. on 2 f. brn. on blue 12·00 12·00

1902. "Blanc", "Mouchon" and "Merson" key-types inscr. "DEDEAGH". Some surch. in figures and words.

67. A. 5 c. green 15 12
68. B. 10 c. red 15 12
69. 15 c. orange 20 15
71. 1 pi. on 25 c. blue .. 30 20
72. C. 2 pi. on 50 c. brown & lav. 70 70
73. 4 pi. on 1 f. red and green 1·40 1·25
74. 8 pi. on 2 f. lilac & yellow 2·25 1·90

DENMARK E1

A kingdom in N. Europe, on a peninsula between the Baltic and the N. Sea.

1851. 96 rigsbank skilling = 1 rigsdaler.
1875. 100 ore = 1 krone.

1. 2. 3.

1851. Imperf.
3. 1. 2 R.B.S. blue £1100 £450
4b. 2. 4 R.B.S. brown .. .. £225 18·00

1854. Dotted background. Impef.
8. 3. 2 s. blue .. .. .. 35·00 26·00
10. 4 s. brown .. .. .. 95·00 5·00
12. 8 s. green .. .. .. £120 24·00
14. 16 s. lilac .. .. .. £180 55·00

4. 5. 6.

1958. Background of wavy lines. Imperf.
15. 4. 4 s. brown .. .. .. 23·00 2·75
18. 8 s. green .. .. .. £130 18·00

1863. Roul.
20. 4. 4 s. brown .. .. .. 27·00 6·00
21. 3. 16 s. mauve £375 £180

1864. Perf.
22. 5. 2 s. blue .. .. .. 23·00 10·00
24. 3 s. mauve .. .. 35·00 19·00
27. 4 s. red .. .. .. 24·00 4·50
29. 8 s. bistre .. .. .. £200 23·00
30a. 16 s. olive .. .. .. £180 35·00

1870. Value in "skilling".
38. 6. 2 s. blue and grey .. .. 38·00 12·00
41. 3 s. mauve and grey .. 65·00 30·00
43. 4 s. red and grey .. .. 50·00 4·50
46. 8 s. brown and grey .. 60·00 21·00
47. 16 s. green and grey .. £130 45·00
37. 48 s. lilac and brown .. £190 75·00

1875. As T 6, but value in "ore".
80. 6. 3 ore grey and blue .. 1·10 60
81. 4 ore blue and grey .. 1·50 8
56. 5 ore blue and red .. 20·00 20·00
82. 8 ore red and grey .. 2·75 8
83. 12 ore lilac and grey .. 2·75 70
84. 16 ore brown and grey .. 9·00 75
72. 20 ore grey and red .. 25·00 4·25
85. 25 ore green and grey .. 6·50 1·50
86. 50 ore purple and brown 9·00 3·50
87. 100 ore orange and grey .. 9·00 3·50

7. 8. King Christian IX. 9.

1882.
96. 7. 1 ore orange 20 20
97. 5 ore green .. .. 1·00 8
98. 10 ore red .. .. 1·10 8
99. 15 ore mauve .. .. 4·00 12
95. 20 ore blue .. .. 5·60 75
101. 24 ore brown .. .. 5·50 2·50

1904. Surch. **4** (white figure in black oval) **ORE.**
102 6. 4 ore on 8 ore red and grey 75 75

1904. Surch. **15 ORE.**
103. 7. 15 ore on 24 ore brown .. 1·50 1·50

1904.
119. 8. 5 ore green .. .. 1·50 8
104. 10 ore red .. .. 1·00 8
105. 20 ore blue .. .. 5·00 30
106. 25 ore brown .. .. 6·00 75
107. 50 ore lilac .. .. 11·00 11·00
108. 100 ore brown .. .. 7·50 7·50

1905.
173. 9. 1 ore yellow 12 8
174. 2 ore red 20 8
175. 3 ore grey 60 8
176. 4 ore blue 90 8
178. 5 ore green 40 8
114. 10 ore pink .. .. 1·50 8
115. 15 ore mauve .. .. 3·15 8
116. 20 ore blue .. .. 8·00 20
See also Nos. 177, etc., and 265, etc.

10. King Frederick VIII. 11. G.P.O. Copenhagen.

1907.
121. 10. 5 ore green 40 8
122. 10 ore red 90 8
123. 20 ore blue .. .. 1·50 10
125. 25 ore sepia .. .. 2·25 15
126. 35 ore yellow .. .. 2·75 1·60
129. 50 ore purple .. .. 7·50 90
130. 100 ore brown .. .. 21·00 45

1912. Surch. **35 ORE.**
131. 6. 35 ore on 16 ore (No. 84) 5·50 7·00
132. 35 ore on 20 ore (No. 72) 4·75 6·00

1912. No. O 98 surch. **35 ORE FRIMAERKE.**
133. O 1. 35 ore on 32 ore green 6·00 10·00

1912.
134. 11. 5 k. red .. .. £150 35·00

12. King Christian X. 13.

1913.
135. 12. 5 ore green 30 8
136. 7 ore orange .. .. 3·75 3·75
137. 8 ore grey .. .. 2·75 75
138. 10 ore red 30 8
139. 12 ore olive .. .. 2·25 1·75
141a. 15 ore lilac 45 8
142. 20 ore blue .. .. 1·50 8
145. 25 ore brown .. .. 1·75 15
146. 25 ore black and brown 9·00 50
149. 27 ore black and red .. 8·50 8·50
150. 30 ore black and green .. 2·50 20
153. 35 ore orange .. .. 2·50 30
154. 35 ore black and yellow 1·10 25
155. 40 ore black and violet 2·40 20
158. 50 ore claret .. .. 6·00 90
159. 50 ore black and claret 8·50 15
161. 60 ore blue and brown .. 5·50 30
163. 70 ore green and brown 2·10 20
164. 80 ore blue-green .. 12·00 3·75
165. 90 ore red and brown .. 2·00 20
166. 13. 1 k. brown .. .. 14·00 12
168. 2 k. black .. .. 17·00 1·25
170. 5 k. violet .. .. 5·50 95
For other stamps of T 12, see Nos. 143, etc.

1915. No. O 94 surch. **DANMARK 80 ORE POSTFRIM.**
186. O 1. 80 ore on 8 ore red .. 16·00 27·00

1915. Surch. **80 ORE.**
187. 6. 80 ore on 12 ore (No. 83) 14·00 25·00

1918. Newspaper Stamps Surch. **POSTFRIM ORE 27 ORE DANMARK.**
197. N 1. 27 ore on 1 ore olive .. 1·10 1·75
198. 27 ore on 5 ore blue .. 3·75 5·50
199. 27 ore on 7 ore red .. 1·10 1·50
200. 27 ore of 8 ore green .. 2·75 4·00
201. 27 ore on 10 ore lilac 1·90 2·25
202. 27 ore on 20 ore green 1·75 2·75
203. 27 ore on 29 ore orange 1·60 1·90
204. 27 ore on 38 ore orange 7·50 12·00
205. 27 ore on 41 ore brown 2·40 3·75
194. 27 ore on 68 ore brown 3·75 6·50
206. 27 ore on 1 k. claret and green .. 1·25 1·25
195. 27 ore on 5 k. (N 139) 1·90 2·25
196. 27 ore on 10 k. (N 140) 3·00 6·00

1919. Surch. **2 ORE.**
207. 12. 2 ore on 5 ore green .. £300 £150

14. Castle of Kronborg, Elsinore. 15. Roskilde Cathedral.

1920. Recovery of Northern Schleswig.
208. 14. 10 ore red 90 12
209. 10 ore green .. .. 1·00 15
210. – 20 ore slate .. .. 1·10 8
211. 15. 40 ore brown .. .. 3·00 1·75
212. 40 ore blue .. .. 12·00 2·25
DESIGN—HORIZ. 20 ore Sonderborg Castle.

1921 Surch. **8.**
216. 9. 8 ore on 3 ore grey .. 90 90
217. 12. 8 ore on 7 ore orange .. 90 90
213. 8 ore on 12 ore olive .. 1·10 1·10

1921. Red Cross. Surch. with figure of value between red crosses.
214. 14. 10 ore + 5 ore green .. 6·00 6·00
215. – 20 ore + 10 ore (No. 210) 9·00 9·00

1921.
177. 9. 5 ore brown 25 8
179. 7 ore green 95 12
180. 7 ore violet .. .. 1·25 60
181. 8 ore grey .. .. 1·25 30
182. 10 ore green 30 8
183. 10 ore brown 50 8
184. 12 ore lilac .. .. 2·75 40
143. 12. 20 ore brown 35 8
144. 20 ore red 90 12
147. 25 ore red .. .. 1·10 15
148. 25 ore green 95 12
151. 30 ore orange 90 30
152. 30 ore blue .. .. 1·10 20
156. 40 ore blue .. .. 1·90 60
157. 40 ore yellow .. .. 1·10 20
160a. 50 ore grey .. .. 1·25 8
162. 60 ore blue .. .. 1·50 20
167. 1 k. blue and brown .. 10·00 35
169. 2 k. claret and grey .. 19·00 2·25
171. 5 k. brown and mauve 3·50 1·75
225b. 10 k. green and red .. 85·00 17·00

16. Christian IV. 17. Christian X.

1924. Danish Post Tercent.
218. 16. 10 ore green .. .. 2·00 90
219. 17. 10 ore green .. .. 2·00 90
220. 16. 15 ore mauve .. .. 2·00 90
221. 17. 15 ore mauve .. .. 2·00 90
222. 16. 20 ore brown .. .. 2·00 90
223. 17. 20 ore brown .. .. 2·00 90
Each type and value exists with portrait facing to right or to left.

18.

ILLUSTRATIONS
British Commonwealth and all overprints and surcharges are FULL SIZE.
Foreign Countries have been reduced to ¾-LINEAR

1925. Air.
224. 18. 10 ore green .. .. 9·00 9·00
225. 15 ore lilac .. .. 14·00 14·00
226. 25 ore red .. .. 12·00 12·00
227. 50 ore grey .. .. 40·00 40·00
228. 1 k. brown .. .. 35·00 35·00

1926. Surch.
234. 9. 7 on 8 ore grey .. 75 75
235. 12. 7 on 20 ore red .. 35 20
236. 7 on 27 ore black & red 2·40 2·50
237. 12 on 15 ore lilac .. 75 75
229. 20 on 30 ore orange .. 1·50 1·50
230. 20 on 40 ore blue .. 1·90 1·90

19. 20. 21. Caravel.

1926. First Danish stamps. 75th Anniv.
231. 19. 10 ore olive 70 8
232. 20. 20 ore red 70 8
233. 30 ore blue .. .. 3·50 20

1926. Official stamps surch. **DANMARK 7 ORE POSTFRIM.**
238. O 1. 7 ore on 1 ore orange .. 1·90 2·40
239. 7 ore on 3 ore grey .. 4·50 6·50
240. 7 ore on 4 ore blue .. 1·60 2·50
241. 7 ore on 5 ore green .. 19·00 23·00
242. 7 ore on 10 ore green .. 2·25 3·00
243. 7 ore on 15 ore lilac .. 1·60 2·10
244. 7 ore on 20 ore blue .. 7·00 9·00

1927. Solid background.
246. 21. 15 ore red .. .. 1·25 8
247. 20 ore grey .. .. 1·40 10
248. 25 ore blue 60 8
249. 30 ore orange 60 8
250. 35 ore brown .. .. 2·25 10
251. 40 ore green .. .. 1·75 8
See also Nos. 272, etc.

22. 23. King Christian X. 24.

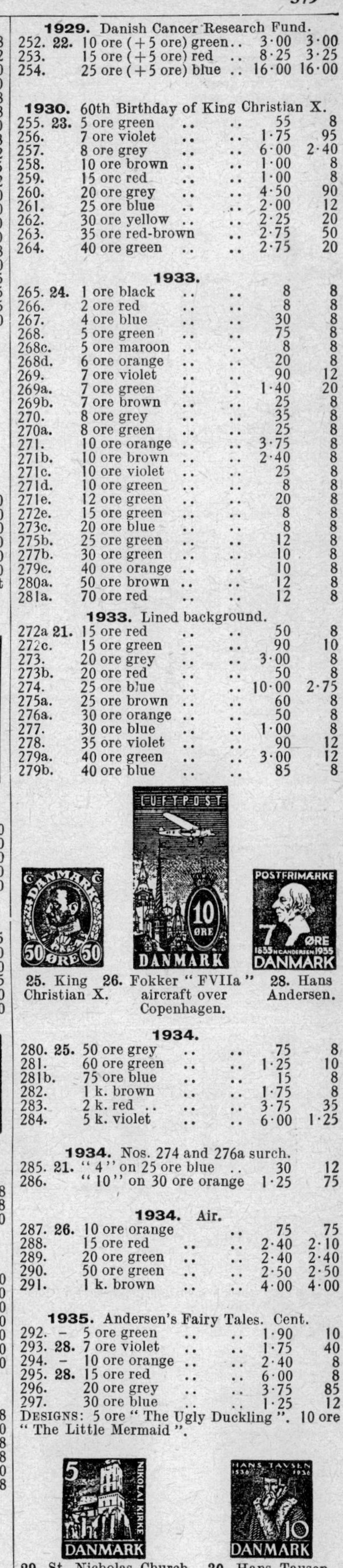

1929. Danish Cancer Research Fund.
252. 22. 10 ore (+5 ore) green .. 3·00 3·00
253. 15 ore (+5 ore) red .. 8·25 3·25
254. 25 ore (+5 ore) blue .. 16·00 16·00

1930. 60th Birthday of King Christian X.
255. 23. 5 ore green 55 8
256. 7 ore violet .. .. 1·75 95
257. 8 ore grey .. .. 6·00 2·40
258. 10 ore brown .. .. 1·00 8
259. 15 ore red .. .. 1·00 8
260. 20 ore grey .. .. 4·50 90
261. 25 ore blue .. .. 2·00 12
262. 30 ore yellow .. .. 2·25 20
263. 35 ore red-brown .. 2·75 50
264. 40 ore green .. .. 2·75 20

1933.
265. 24. 1 ore black 8 8
266. 2 ore red 8 8
267. 4 ore blue 30 8
268. 5 ore green 75 8
268c. 5 ore maroon 8 8
268d. 6 ore orange 20 8
269. 7 ore violet 90 12
269a. 7 ore green .. .. 1·40 20
269b. 7 ore brown 25 8
270. 8 ore grey 35 8
270a. 8 ore green 25 8
271. 10 ore orange .. .. 3·75 8
271b. 10 ore brown .. .. 2·40 8
271c. 10 ore violet 25 8
271d. 10 ore green 8 8
271e. 12 ore green 20 8
272e. 15 ore green 8 8
273c. 20 ore blue 8 8
275b. 25 ore green 12 8
277b. 30 ore green 10 8
279c. 40 ore orange 10 8
280a. 50 ore brown 12 8
281a. 70 ore red 12 8

1933. Lined background.
272a 21. 15 ore red 50 8
272c. 15 ore green 90 10
273. 20 ore grey .. .. 3·00 8
273b. 20 ore red 50 8
274. 25 ore blue .. .. 10·00 2·75
275a. 25 ore brown 60 8
276a. 30 ore orange 50 8
277. 30 ore blue .. .. 1·00 8
278. 35 ore violet 90 12
279a. 40 ore green .. .. 3·00 12
279b. 40 ore blue 85 8

25. King Christian X. 26. Fokker "FVIIa" aircraft over Copenhagen. 28. Hans Andersen.

1934.
280. 25. 50 ore grey 75 8
281. 60 ore green .. .. 1·25 10
281b. 75 ore blue 15 8
282. 1 k. brown .. .. 1·75 8
283. 2 k. red .. .. 3·75 35
284. 5 k. violet .. .. 6·00 1·25

1934. Nos. 274 and 276a surch.
285. 21. "4" on 25 ore blue .. 30 12
286. "10" on 30 ore orange 1·25 75

1934. Air.
287. 26. 10 ore orange 75 75
288. 15 ore red .. .. 2·40 2·10
289. 20 ore green .. .. 2·40 2·40
290. 50 ore green .. .. 2·50 2·50
291. 1 k. brown .. .. 4·00 4·00

1935. Andersen's Fairy Tales. Cent.
292. – 5 ore green .. .. 1·90 10
293. 28. 7 ore violet .. .. 1·75 40
294. – 10 ore orange .. .. 2·40 8
295. 28. 15 ore red .. .. 6·00 8
296. 20 ore grey .. .. 3·75 85
297. 30 ore blue .. .. 1·25 12
DESIGNS: 5 ore "The Ugly Duckling". 10 ore "The Little Mermaid".

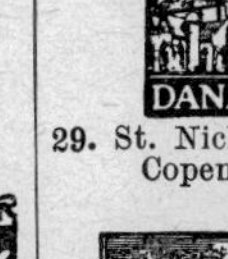
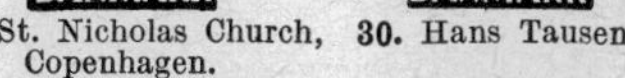

29. St. Nicholas Church, Copenhagen. 30. Hans Tausen.

31. Ribe Cathedral. 32. Dybbol Mill.

1936. Reformation. 400th Anniv.
298. **29.** 5 ore green .. .. 1·40 8
299. 7 ore mauve .. .. 1·25 40
300. **30.** 10 ore brown .. .. 1·50 8
301. 15 ore red .. .. 1·50 8
302. **31.** 30 ore blue .. .. 6·00 40

1937. H. P. Hansen (North Schleswig patriot). Memorial Fund.
303. **32.** 5 ore+5 ore green .. 60 60
304. 10 ore+5 ore brown.. 1·60 1·60
305. 15 ore+5 ore red .. 1·60 1·60

33. Marselisborg Castle. **34.** King Christian X.

1937. King's Silver Jubilee.
306. **33** 5 ore green .. .. 1·40 20
307. **34.** 10 ore brown .. .. 1·40 8
308. – 15 ore red 90 8
309. **34.** 30 ore blue .. .. 6·00 75
DESIGN—HORIZ. 15 ore Amalienborg.

1937. "K.P.K." Exn. and Silver Jubilee. Optd. **K.P.K. 17.-26. SEPT. 1937.**
310. **24.** 10 ore brown .. .. 1·10 1·10

35. Emancipation Monument. **36.** R. Thorwaldsen. **38.** Queen Alexandrine.

1938. Abolition of Villeinage. 150th Anniv.
311. **35.** 15 ore red 45 8

1938. Return of Sculptor Thorwaldsen to Denmark. Cent.
312. **36.** 5 ore maroon .. 45 10
313. – 10 ore violet 45 10
314. **36.** 30 ore blue .. .. 1·25 20
DESIGN: 10 ore Statue of Jason.

1939. Red Cross Fund. Cross in red.
314a. **38.** 5 ore+3 ore claret.. 12 12
315. 10 ore+5 ore violet.. 20 12
316. 15 ore+5 ore red .. 40 30

1940. Surch. with value in large figures.
317. **24.** 6 ore on 7 ore green .. 15 15
318. 6 ore on 8 ore grey .. 30 30
319a. **21.** 15 ore on 40 ore green 70 60
320. 20 ore on 15 ore red .. 60 8
321. 40 ore on 30 ore blue .. 90 15

39. Queen Ingrid and Princess Margrethe. **40.** Bering's Ship.

1941. Child Welfare.
322. **39.** 10 ore+5 ore violet .. 20 12
323. 20 ore+5 ore red .. 20 15

1941. Vitus Bering (explorer). Death Bicent.
324. **40.** 10 ore violet 30 10
325. 20 ore brown 45 30
326. 40 ore blue 45 25

41. King Christian X. **42.** Round Tower of Trinity Church.

1942.
327. **41.** 10 ore violet 20 8
328. 15 ore green 20 8
329. 20 ore red 30 8
330. 25 ore brown 20 8
331. 30 ore orange 20 8
332. 35 ore purple 35 8
333. 40 ore blue 30 8
333a. 45 ore olive 45 8
334. 50 ore grey 40 8
335. 60 ore green 40 8
335a. 75 ore blue 40 8

1942. Building of the Round Tower. Tercent.
336. **42.** 10 ore violet 12 8

43. Focke-wulf "FW200 Condor" Aeroplane. **44.** Osterlars Church.

1943. "D.D.L." (Danish Aviation Co.). 25th Anniv.
337. **43.** 20 ore red 20 10

1944. Red Cross Fund. Surch. **+5.**
338. **42.** 10 ore+5 ore vio. & red 8 8

1944.
339. – 10 ore violet 15 10
340. **44.** 15 ore green 45 40
341. – 20 ore red 15 10
DESIGNS: 10 ore Ejby Church. 20 ore Hvidbjerg Church.

45. Ole Romer. **46.** King Christian X. **47.** Arms.

1944. Romer (astronomer). Birth Tercent.
342. **45.** 20 ore brown 30 12

1945. King Christian's 75th Birthday.
343. **46.** 10 ore mauve 12 8
344. 20 ore red 20 8
345. 40 ore blue 35 12

1946.
346. **47.** 1 k. brown 20 8
346a. 1 k. 10 purple 55 20
346b. 1 k. 20 grey 45 8
346c. 1 k. 20 blue 25 8
346d. 1 k. 25 orange 45 8
346e. 1 k. 30 green 50 10
346f. 1 k. 50 purple 35 8
346g. 2 k. red 45 8
347. 2 k. 20 orange 70 8
347a. 2 k. 50 violet 55 12
347b. 2 k. 80 grey 85 10
347c. 2 k. 80 brown 65 10
347d. 2 k. 90 violet 75 8
347e. 3 k. green 70 8
347f. 3 k. 10 violet 70 8
347g. 3 k. 50 violet 75 10
348. 4 k. grey 90 8
348a. 4 k. 10 brown .. .. 1·00 8
348b. 4 k. 50 brown .. .. 1·00 10
348c. 5 k. blue .. .. 1·10 8
348f. 25 k. green .. .. 5·00 30

48. Tycho Brahe. **49.** Wreath and Torch. **50.** Bombed Railways.

1946. Tycho Brahe. 400th Birth Anniv.
349. **48.** 20 ore red 25 8

1947. Liberation.
350. **49.** 15 ore+5 ore green .. 30 30
351. **50.** 20 ore+5 ore red .. 30 30
352. – 40 ore+5 ore blue (Flag) 75 75

51. Steam Train. **52.** I. C. Jacobsen.

1947. Danish Railways Cent. Dated "1847 1947".
353. – 15 ore green 40 12
354. **51.** 20 ore red 35 12
355. – 40 ore blue 75 40
DESIGNS—HORIZ. 15 ore Primitive locomotive, "Odin". 40 ore Electric train.

1947. Jacobsen. 60th Death Anniv. and Carlsberg Foundation for Scientific Research Cent.
356. **52.** 20 ore red 25 8

53. King Frederick IX. **54.** "Constituent Assembly of the kingdom" after Constantine Hansen".

1948.
357a. **53.** 15 ore green 40 5
358. 15 ore violet 30 5
359a. 20 ore red 40 5
360. 20 ore brown 20 5
361. 25 ore brown 60 5
362. 25 ore red 75 5
362a. 25 ore blue 90 5
362b. 25 ore violet 30 5
363. 30 ore orange .. .. 5·50 5
363b. 30 ore red 45 5
364. 35 ore myrtle 55 10
365. 40 ore blue .. .. 1·90 30
366. 40 ore grey 45 8
367. 45 ore olive 80 8
368. 50 ore grey 80 8
369. 50 ore blue .. .. 1·10 8
369a. 50 ore green 20 8
370. 55 ore brown .. .. 3·25 1·25
371. 60 ore blue-green 75 8
371a. 60 ore blue 40 8
371b. 65 ore grey 35 10
372. 70 ore green 80 8
373. 75 ore magenta 50 8
373a. 80 ore orange 35 8
373b. 90 ore bistre .. .. 1·10 8
373c. 95 ore vermilion 75 15

1949. Danish Constitution Cent.
374. **54.** 20 ore brown 35 8

55. Globe. **56.** Kalundborg Transmitter.

1949. U.P.U. 75th Anniv.
375. **55.** 40 ore blue 60 25

1950. State Broadcasting. 25th Anniv.
376. **56.** 20 ore brown 35 8

57. Princess Anne-Marie. **58.** Sailing Ship. **59.** H. C. Oersted.

1950. National Children's Welfare Assn.
377. **57.** 25 ore+5 ore lake .. 55 50

1951. Naval Officers' College. 250th Anniv.
378. **58.** 25 ore brown 60 12
379. 50 ore blue .. .. 2·10 90

1951. Oersted (physicist). Death Cent.
380. **59.** 50 ore blue .. .. 1·10 25

60. Mail-coach. **61.** Hospital ship "Jutlandia".

1951. Danish Stamp Cent.
381. **60.** 15 ore violet 75 8
382. 25 ore red 75 8

1951. Danish Red Cross Fund.
383. **61.** 25 ore+5 ore red .. 60 50

62. "Life-Saving". **63.** Memorial Stone, Skamlingsbanken. **64.** Runic Stone at Jelling.

1952. Danish Life-Saving Service. Cent.
384. **62.** 25 ore red 35 8

1953. Netherlands Flood Relief Fund. Surch. **NL+10.**
385. **53.** 30 ore+10 ore red .. 1·25 1·25

1953. Danish Border Union Fund.
386. **63.** 30 ore+5 ore red .. 1·10 90

1953. 1,000 years of Danish History. Inscr. "KONGERIGE I 1000 AR". (a) 1st series.
387. **64.** 10 ore green 15 5
388. – 15 ore lilac 15 5
389. – 20 ore brown 20 5
390. – 30 ore red 25 5
391. – 60 ore blue 45 5
DESIGNS: 15 ore Vikings' camp Trelleborg. 20 ore Kalundborg Church. 30 ore Nyborg Castle. 60 ore Goose Tower, Vordinborg.

(b) 2nd series.
392. – 10 ore green 15 5
393. 15 ore lilac 15 5
394. – 20 ore brown 20 5
395. – 30 ore red 25 8
396. – 60 ore blue 60 8
DESIGNS: 10 ore Spottrup Castle. 15 ore Hammershus Castle. 20 ore Copenhagen Stock Exchange. 30 ore King Frederick V Statue. 60 ore Soldier's Statue (H. V. Bissen).

65. Telegraph Table, 1854. **66.** Head of Statue of King Frederick V at Amalienborg.

67. S. Kierkegaard (philosopher). **68.** Ellehammer's Aircraft.

1954. Telecommunications in Denmark. Cent.
397. **65.** 30 ore chestnut .. 45 8

1954. Royal Academy of Fine Arts. Bicent.
398. **66.** 30 ore red 75 10

1955. Liberty Fund. Surch.
399. **49.** 20+5 on 15 ore+5 ore green .. .. 1·00 1·00
400. **50.** 30+5 on 20 ore+5 ore red .. .. 1·00 1·00

1955. Nos. 268d, 269b, 359a, and 362 surch.
401. **24.** 5 ore on 6 ore orange.. 10 10
402. 5 ore on 7 ore brown .. 10 10
403. **53.** 30 ore on 20 ore red .. 20 8
404. 30 ore on 25 ore red .. 55 8

1955. Kierkegaard. Death Cent.
405. **67.** 30 ore red 40 8

1956. 1st Flight by J. C. H. Ellehammer. 50th Anniv.
406. **68.** 30 ore red 45 8

69. Flying Swans. **70.** National Museum.

1956. Northern Countries' Day.
407. **69.** 30 ore red .. .. 2·25 15
408. 60 ore blue .. .. 1·00 50

1957. Danish Red Cross Hungarian Relief Fund. Surch. **Ungarns-hjælpen** and value.
409. **53.** 30+5 ore on 95 ore verm. 40 40

1957. National Museum. 150th Anniv. Inscr. as in T **70.**
410. **70.** 30 ore red .. .. 1·25 8
411. – 60 ore blue 90 40
DESIGN: 60 ore "Sun-God's Chariot".

71. Harvester. **72.** King Frederick IX. **73.** Dancer in "Les Sylphides".

1958. Danish Royal Veterinary and Agricultural College. Cent.
412. **71.** 30 ore red 25 8

1959. Greenland Fund. Surch. **Gronlandsfonden+10.**
413. **53.** 30 ore+10 ore red .. 75 75
The Fund was for the relatives of the crew and passengers of the "Hans Hedtoft", lost on her maiden voyage after striking an iceberg on January 30th, 1959.

1959. King Frederick IX. 60th Birthday.
414. **72.** 30 ore red 60 8
415. 35 ore purple 45 10
416. 60 ore blue 45 10

1959. Danish Ballet and Music Festival, 1959.
417. **73.** 35 ore mauve 20 8
See also Nos. 445 and 467.

74.

75. "Wheel of Agriculture".

1959. Red Cross Commem.
418. **74.** 30 ore+5 ore red .. 35 15
419. – 60 ore+5 ore red & blue 75 55

1960. World Refugee Year. Surch. **30** uprooted tree and **Verdensflygtningeаret 1950-60.**
420. **53.** 30 ore on 15 ore violet.. 20 10

1960. 1st Danish Food Fair.
421. **75.** 12 ore green 12 8
422. – 30 ore red 15 8
423. – 60 ore blue 20 15
DESIGNS: 30 ore Combine-harvester. 60 ore Plough.

76. King Frederick and Queen Ingrid.

77. Ancient Bascule Light.

1960. Royal Silver Wedding.
424. **76.** 30 ore red 70 8
425. 60 ore blue 35 10

1960. Danish Lighthouse Service. 400th Anniv.
426. **77.** 30 ore red 25 8

78. N. Finsen (physician).

79. Mother and Child.

80. Queen Ingrid.

1960. Niels R. Finsen. Birth Cent.
427. **78.** 30 ore red 30 8

1960. W.H.O. 10th European Regional Committee Meeting.
428 **79.** 60 ore blue 55 20

1960. Europa. 1st Anniv. As T **279** of Belgium but size 28 × 20 mm.
429. 60 ore blue 30 12

1960. 25th Year of Queen Ingrid's Service as a Girl Guide.
430. **80.** 30 ore+10 ore red .. 55 55

81. "Jet Flight".

82. Coastal Scene.

1961. Scandinavian Airlines System (SAS). 10th Anniv.
431. **81.** 60 ore blue 30 10

1961. Society for Preservation of Danish National Amenities. 50th Anniv.
432. **82.** 30 ore red 15 8

83. King Frederick IX.

84. Old Mill.

85. African Mother and Child.

1961.
433. **83.** 20 ore brown 35 5
434. 25 ore brown 15 5
435. 30 ore red 35 5
436. 35 ore grey-green .. 75 15
437. 35 ore red 15 5
438. 40 ore grey 30 5
438a. 40 ore brown 15 5
439. 50 ore turquoise .. 20 5
439a. 50 ore red 15 5
439b. 50 ore brown 15 5
440. 60 ore blue 25 8
440a. 60 ore red 20 8
441. 70 ore green .. .. 1·10 10
442. 80 ore orange 30 8
442a. 80 ore blue 30 8
442b. 80 ore green 25 8
443. 90 ore olive .. .. 1·10 8
443a. 90 ore blue 25 8
444. 95 ore purple 50 25

1962. Danish Ballet and Music Festival, 1962. As T **73** but inscr. "15–31 MAJ".
445. 60 ore blue.. .. .. 25 8

1962. Abolition of Mill Monopolies. Cent.
446. **84.** 10 ore red-brown .. 8 5

1962. Aid for Under-developed Countries.
447. **85.** 30 ore+10 ore brn.-red 65 65

86. M.S. "Selandia".

87. "Tivoli".

1962. M.S. "Selandia". 50th Anniv.
448. **86.** 60 ore blue .. .. 1·50 70

1962. George Carstensen (founder of Tivoli Pleasure Gardens, Copenhagen). 150th Birth Anniv.
449. **87.** 35 ore purple 20 8

88. Cliffs, Island of Mon.

89. Wheat.

1962. "Dansk Fredning" (Preservation of Danish Natural Amenities and Ancient Monuments).
450. **88.** 20 ore brown 12 8

1963. Freedom from Hunger.
451. **89.** 35 ore red 15 8

90. Rail and Sea Symbols.

91. 19th-century Mail Transport.

1963. Opening of Denmark-Germany Railway ("Bird-flight Line").
452. **90.** 15 ore green 10 5

1963. Paris Postal Conference Cent.
453. **91.** 60 ore blue 35 12

92. Hands.

93. Prof. Niels Bohr.

1963. Danish Cripples Foundation Fund.
454. **92.** 35 ore+10 ore red .. 75 75

1963. Bohr's Atomic Theory. 50th Anniv.
455. **93.** 35 ore red 25 8
456. 60 ore blue 30 8

94. Ancient Bridge.

95. "Going to School". (child's slate).

1964. Danish Border Union.
457. **94.** 35 ore+10 ore red .. 70 70

1964. Institution of Primary Schools. 150th Anniv.
458. **95.** 35 ore red 15 8

96. Princesses Margrethe, Benedikte and Anne-Marie.

97. "Exploration of the Sea".

1964. Danish Red Cross Fund.
459. **96.** 35 ore+10 ore red .. 50 50
460. 60 ore+10 ore blue & red 85 85

1964. Int. Council for the Exploration of the Sea Conference, Copenhagen.
461. **97.** 60 ore ultramarine .. 40 8

98. Danish Stamp "Watermarks, Perforations and Varieties".

99. Landscape.

1964. Stamp Day. 25th Anniv.
462. **98.** 35 ore rose 20 8

1964. "Dansk Fredning" (Preservation of Danish Natural Amenities and Ancient Monuments).
463. **99.** 25 ore brown 12 8

100. Office Equipment.

101. Morse Key, Teleprinter Tape and I.T.U. Emblem.

1965. Handelsskolen (Commercial School) Cent.
464. **100.** 15 ore olive 12 8

1965. I.T.U Cent.
465. **101.** 80 ore blue 30 10

102. C. Nielsen (composer).

103. Child in Meadow.

104. Bogo Windmill.

1965. Carl Nielsen. Birth Cent.
466. **102.** 50 ore red 15 8

1965. Danish Ballet and Music Festival, 1965. As T **73** but inscr. "15–31 MAJ".
467. 50 ore red 20 8

1965. Child Welfare.
468. **103.** 50 ore+10 ore red .. 35 35

1965. "Dansk Fredning" (Preservation of Danish Natural Amenities and Ancient Monuments).
469. **104.** 40 ore brown 15 8

105. Titles of International Red Cross Organisations.

106. Heathland.

1966. Danish Red Cross Fund.
470. **105.** 50 ore+10 ore red .. 40 30
471. 80 ore+10 ore bl. & red 50 45

1966. Danish Heath Society.
472. **106.** 25 ore olive-green .. 12 8

107. C. Kold.

108. Almshouses.

109. Trees at Bregentved.

110. G. Jensen.

111. Fund Emblem.

1966. Christen Kold (educationist). 150th Birth Anniv.
473. **107.** 50 ore red 15 8

1966. "Dansk Fredning" (Preservation of Danish Natural Amenities and Ancient Monuments).
474. **108.** 50 ore red 15 8
475. **109.** 80 ore blue 30 8

1966. Georg Jensen (silversmith) Birth Cent.
476. **110.** 80 ore blue 40 10

1966. "Refugee 66" Fund.
477. **111.** 40 ore+10 ore brown 60 60
478. 50 ore+10 ore red 60 60
479. 80 ore+10 ore blue 1·00 1·00

112. Barrow in Jutland.

113. Musical Instruments.

1966. "Dansk Fredning" (Preservation of Danish Natural Amenities and Ancient Monuments).
480. **112.** 1 k. 50 green 50 5

1967. Royal Danish Academy. Cent.
481. **113.** 50 ore red 15 5

114. Cogwheels.

115. Old City and Windmill.

1967. European Free Trade Assn.
482. **114.** 80 ore blue 20 8

1967. Copenhagen. 800th Anniv.
483. **115.** 25 ore green 8 5
484. – 40 ore brown 15 8
485. – 50 ore lake 15 8
486. – 80 ore blue 50 15
DESIGNS: 40 ore, Ancient building and ship's masts. 50 ore, Old Town Hall. 80 ore, Building construction.

116. Princess Margrethe and Prince Henri de Monpezat.

117. H. C. Sonne (founder of Danish Co-operative Movement).

1967. Royal Wedding.
487. **116.** 50 ore red 15 8

1967. Hans Sonne. 150th Birth Anniv.
488. **117.** 60 ore red 10 5

118. "Rose".

119. Porpoise and Cross-anchor.

1967. The Salvation Army.
489. **118.** 60 ore+10 ore red .. 35 35

1967. Danish Seamen's Church in Foreign Ports. Cent.
490. **119.** 90 ore ultramarine .. 25 10

120. Esbjerg Harbour.

121. Koldinghus Castle.

1968. Esbjerg Harbour Construction Act. Cent.
491. **120.** 30 ore green 20 8

1968. Koldinghus Castle. 700th Anniv.
492. **121.** 60 ore red 12 8

122. "The Children in the Round Tower" (Greenlandic legend). **123.** Shipbuilding.

1968. Child Welfare.
493. **122.** 60 ore + 10 ore red .. 50 50

1968. Danish Industries.
494. **123.** 30 ore green 8 8
495. – 50 ore brown 12 8
496. – 60 ore red 15 8
497. – 90 ore blue 20 15
INDUSTRIES: 50 ore Chemical. 60 ore, Electric power. 90 ore, Engineering.

124. "The Sower". **125.** Viking Ships.

1969. Danish Royal Agricultural Society. Bicent.
498. **124.** 30 ore green 8 8

1969. Northern Countries' Union. 50th Anniv.
499. **125.** 60 ore red 12 8
500. 90 ore blue 30 15

126. King Frederick IX. **127.** Colonnade.

1969. King Frederick's 70th Birthday.
501. **126.** 50 ore brown 12 8
502. 60 ore red 15 8

1969. Europa.
503. **127.** 90 ore blue 20 12

128. Kronborg Castle. **129.** Fall of Danish Flag.

1969. "Danes Living Abroad" Assn. 50th Anniv.
504. **128.** 50 ore brown 12 8

1969. "Danish Flag Falling from Heaven". 750th Anniv.
505. **129.** 60 ore red, blue & black 20 8

130. M. A. Nexo. **131.** Niels Stensen (geologist).

1969. Martin Anderson Nexo (poet). Birth Cent.
506. **130.** 80 ore green 15 8

1969. Stensen's "On Solid Bodies". 300th Anniv.
507. **131.** 1 k. sepia 20 8

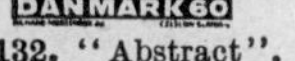

132. "Abstract". **133.** Symbolic "P".

1969. "Non-figurative" stamp.
508. **132.** 60 ore red, rose and blue 12 8

1969. Valdemar Poulsen (inventor). Birth Cent.
509. **133.** 30 ore green 8 8

134. Princess Margrethe, Prince Henri and Prince Frederik (baby). **135.** "Postgiro".

1969. Danish Red Cross.
510. **134.** 50 ore + 10 ore brown and red .. 30 30
511. 60 ore + 10 ore red .. 35 35

1970. Danish Postal Giro Service. 50th Anniv.
512. **135.** 60 ore red and orange 15 8

136. School Safety Patrol. **137.** Child appealing for help.

1970. Road Safety.
513. **136.** 50 ore brown 12 8

1970. Save the Children Fund. 25th Anniv.
514. **137.** 60 ore + 10 ore red .. 35 35

138. Candle in window. **139.** Deer in Park.

1970. Liberation. 25th Anniv.
515. **138.** 50 ore black, yell. & blue 12 8

1970. Jaegersborg Deer Park. 300th Anniv.
516. **139.** 60 ore brown, red and green 12 8

140. Ship's Figurehead. **141.** "The Reunion".

1970. "Royal Majesty's Model Chamber" (Danish Naval Museum). 300th Anniv.
517. **140.** 30 ore multicoloured.. 12 5

1970. North Schleswig's Reunion with Denmark. 50th Anniv.
518. **141.** 60 ore violet, yellow and olive 12 8

142. Electromagnetic Apparatus.

1970. Oersted's Discovery of Electro-magnetism. 150th Anniv.
519. **142.** 80 ore green 20 8

143. Bronze-age Ship (from engraving on razor).

1970. Danish Shipping.
520. **143.** 30 ore purple and brn. 8 5
521. – 50 ore brn. and purple 10 5
522. – 60 ore brown & green.. 12 8
523. – 90 ore blue and green.. 20 12
DESIGNS: 50 ore, Viking shipbuilders (Bayeux Tapestry). 60 ore, Thuroe schooner. 90 ore, Tanker.

144. Strands of Rope. **145.** B. Thorvaldsen (after Scholer).

1970. United Nations. 25th Anniv.
524. **144.** 90 ore red, green & blue 20 15

1970. Bertel Thorvaldsen (sculptor). Birth Bicent.
525. **145.** 2 k. blue 45 10

146. Mathilde Fibiger (suffragette). **147.** Refugees.

1971. Danish Women's Association ("Kvindesamfund"). Cent.
526. **146.** 80 ore green 20 8

1971. Aid for Refugees.
527. **147.** 50 ore brown 10 5
528. 60 ore red 12 5

148. Danish Child. **149.** Hans Egede.

1971. National Children's Welfare Association.
529. **148.** 60 ore + 10 ore red .. 30 20

1971. Hans Egede's Arrival in Greenland. 250th Anniv.
530. **149.** 1 k. brown 20 5

150. Swimming. **151.** Georg Brandes.

1971. Sports.
531. **150.** 30 ore green & blue .. 8 5
532. – 50 ore brown and lake 10 5
533. – 60 ore yell., blue & grey 12 5
534. – 90 ore violet, grn. & bl. 20 5
DESIGNS: 50 ore Hurdling. 60 ore Football. 90 ore Yachting.

1971. First Lectures by Georg Brandes (writer). Cent.
535. **151.** 90 ore blue 20 5

152. Beet Harvester.

1972. Danish Sugar Production. Cent.
536. **152.** 80 ore green 15 5

153. Meteorological Symbols.

1972. Danish Meteorological Office. Cent.
537. **153.** 1 k. 20 mauve, bl. & brn. 25 5

154. King Frederick IX. **155.** "N. F. S. Grundtvig" (pencil sketch P. Skovgaard).

1972. King Frederick IX – In Memorium.
538. **154.** 60 ore red 12 5

1972. N. F. S. Gruntvig (poet and clergyman). Death Cent.
539. **155.** 1 k. brown 20 5

156. Early Locomotive, Ship and Passengers. **157.** Rebild Hills.

1972. Danish State Railways. 125th Anniv.
540. **156.** 70 ore red 15 5

1972. Nature Protection.
541. **157.** 1 k. grn., brn. & blue.. 20 8

158. Marsh Marigold. **159.** "The Tinker" (from Holberg's satire).

1972. "Vanforefhjemmet" (Home for the Disabled). Cent.
542. **158.** 70 ore + 10 ore yell. & bl. 20 15

1972. Theatre in Denmark and Holberg's Comedies. 250th Anniv.
543. **159.** 70 ore red 15 5

160. W.H.O. Building, Copenhagen. **161.** Little Belt Bridge.

1972. W.H.O. Building, Copenhagen. Inaug.
544. **160.** 2 k. blk., brn. & blue.. 45 8

1972. Danish Construction Projects.
545. **161.** 40 ore green 8 5
546. – 60 ore brown 12 5
547. – 70 ore red 15 8
548. – 90 ore green 20 10
DESIGNS: 60 ore Hanstholm Port. 70 ore Liim Fiord Tunnel. 90 ore Knudshoved port.

162. Farmhouse, East Bornholm. **163.** J. V. Jensen.

1972. Danish Architecture.
549. – 40 ore blk., brn. & red 8 5
550. **162.** 60 ore bl., grn. & brn... 12 5
551. – 70 ore brn., red & verm. 15 8
552. – 1 k. 20 grn., lake & brn. 30 12
DESIGNS—VERT. 40 ore House, Aeroskobing. (21 × 37 mm.). 70 ore House, Christianshavn. HORIZ. (37 × 21 mm.). 1 k. 20 Farmhouse, Hvide Sande.

1973. Johannes V. Jensen (writer). Birth Cent.
553. **163.** 90 ore green 20 5

164. Cogwheels and Guard-rails. **165.** P. C. Abilgaard (founder).

1973. 1st Danish Factory Act. Cent.
554. **164.** 50 ore brown 10 5

1973. Royal Veterinary College, Christianshavn. Bicent.
555. **165.** 1 k. blue 20 5

166. "Rhododendron impeditum". **167.** Stella Nova and Sextant. **168.** "St. Mark the Evangelist" (Book of Dalby).

1973. Jutland Horticultural Society. Cent.
556. **166.** 60 ore blue, grn. & brn. .. 12 5
557. – 70 ore red, grn. & brn. .. 15 5
DESIGN: 70 ore "Queen of Denmark" rose.

1973. Nordic Countries' Postal Co-operation. As T **198** of Sweden.
558. 70 ore multicoloured .. 12 5
559. 1 k. multicoloured .. 20 5

1973. Tycho Brahe's "De Nove Stella". 400th Anniv.
560. **167.** 2 k. blue 45 10

1973. Royal Library. 300th Anniv.
561. **168.** 1 k. 20 multicoloured .. 25 12

169. Heimaey Eruption. **170.** "Devil and Scandalmongers" (Fanefjord Church).

1973. Aid for Victims of Heimaey (Iceland) Eruption.
562. **169.** 70 ore+20 ore red & bl. 20 12

1973. Kalkmalerier Frescoes. Each red, blue and yellow on cream.
563. 70 ore Type **170** 15 5
564. 70 ore "Queen Esther and King Xerxes" (Tirsted Church) 15 5
565. 70 ore "The Harvest Miracle" (Jetsmark Church) 15 5
566. 70 ore "The Crowning with Thorns" (Biersted Church) 15 5
567. 70 ore "The Creation of Eve" (Fanefjord Church) 15 5

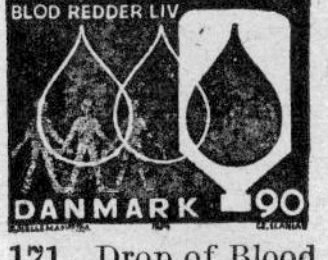

171. Drop of Blood and Donors. **172.** Queen Margrethe.

1974. Blood Donors Campaign.
568. **171.** 90 ore red and violet .. 20 5

1974.
569. **172.** 60 ore brown 12 5
570. 60 ore red 12 5
571. 70 ore red 15 5
572. 70 ore brown 15 5
573. 80 ore green 20 5
575. 90 ore purple 20 5
576. 90 ore red 20 5
578. 100 ore blue 25 5
579. 100 ore grey 25 5
581. 120 ore grey 25 5
582. 130 ore blue 30 5

173. Theatre Facade. **174.** Hverringe.

1974. Tivoli Pantomime Theatre, Copenhagen. Cent.
583. **173.** 1 k. blue 25 5

1974. Provincial Series.
584. **174.** 50 ore brn., dark brn. and violet 12 5
585. – 60 ore grn. and violet .. 15 5
586. – 70 ore multicoloured .. 15 5
587. – 90 ore brn., grn. & dark green 20 5
588. – 1 k. 20 grn., orge. & red 30 10
DESIGNS—HORIZ. 60 ore Carl Nielsen's birthplace, Norre Lyndelse. 70 ore Hans Christian Andersen's birthplace, Odense. 1 k. 20 Hindsholm. VERT. 90 ore Hesselagergard.

175. Orienteering. **176.** "Iris spuria"

1974. World Orienteering Championships.
589. **175.** 70 ore blue and brown 15 5
590. – 80 ore brown and blue 20 5
DESIGN: 80 ore Compass.

1974. Botanical Gardens, Copenhagen. Cent.
591. **176.** 90 ore bl., grn. & brn. .. 20 5
592. – 1 k. 20 grn., pur. & bl. 30 8
DESIGN: 1 k. 20 "Dactylorhiza purpurella" (orchid).

177. Mail-carriers of 1624 and 1780. **178.** Pigeon with Letter.

1974. Danish Post Office. 350th Anniv.
593. **177.** 70 ore bistre & brown 15 5
594. – 90 ore green & brown .. 20 5
DESIGN. 90 ore Postal transport of 1624.

1974. Universal Postal Union. Cent.
595. **178.** 1 k. 20 blue 30 5

179. Radio Equipment of 1925. **180.** Queen Margrethe and IWY Emblem.

1975. "Danish Broadcasting". 50th Anniv.
597. **179.** 90 ore red 20 5

1975. International Women's Year.
598. **180.** 90 ore+20 ore red & yell. 30 30

181. Floral Decorated Plate. **182.** Moravian Brethren Church Christiansfeld.

1975. Danish Porcelain.
599. **181.** 50 ore green 15 5
600. – 90 ore red 25 5
601. – 130 ore blue 30 15
DESIGNS: 90 ore Floral decorated tureen. 130 ore Floral decorated vase and tea-caddy.

1975. European Architectural Heritage Year.
602. **182.** 70 ore sepia 15 5
603. – 120 ore green 35 15
604. – 150 ore blue 35 15
DESIGNS—HORIZ. 120 ore farmhouse, Lejre. VERT. 150 ore Anna Queenstraede street, Helsingor.

183. "Numskull Jack" (V. Pederson). **184.** Watchman's Square, Aabenraa.

1975. Hans Christian Andersen. 170th Birth Anniv.
605. **183.** 70 ore black & brown .. 10 5
606. – 90 ore brown and lake 15 5
607. – 130 ore brown and blue 20 10
DESIGNS: 90 ore Hans Andersen. 130 ore "The Marshking's Daughter" (L. Frolich).

1975. Provincial Series. South Jutland. Mult.
608. 70 ore Type **184** 15 5
609. 90 ore Haderslev Cathedral (vert.) 25 5
610. 100 ore Mogeltonder polder 25 5
611. 120 ore Estuary of Vidaaen at Hojer floodgates .. 30 10

185. Kingfisher.

1975. Animal Protection.
612. **185.** 50 ore blue 10 5
613. – 70 ore brown 15 5
614. – 90 ore brown 20 5
615. – 130 ore blue 30 15
616. – 200 ore black 45 25
DESIGNS: 70 ore Hedgehog. 90 ore Cats. 130 ore Avocets. 200 ore Otter.
The 90 ore also commemorates the centenary of the Danish Society for the Prevention of Cruelty to Animals.

186. Viking Long-Ship.

1976. American Independence. Bicent.
618. **186.** 70 ore+20 ore brown 20 20
619. – 90 ore+20 ore red .. 25 25
620. – 100 ore+20 ore green 30 30
621. – 130 ore+20 ore blue .. 35 35
DESIGNS: 90 ore S.S. "Thingvalla". 100 ore S.S. "Frederik VIII". 130 ore Training-ship "Danmark".

187. "Humanity". **188.** Old Copenhagen.

1976. Danish Red Cross. Centenary.
622. **187.** 100 ore +20 ore black and red 30 30
623. 130 ore+20 ore black, blue and red .. 35 35

1976. Provincial Series. Copenhagen.
624. **188.** 60 ore multicoloured .. 15 5
625. – 80 ore multicoloured .. 20 5
626. – 100 ore lake and red .. 25 10
627. – 130 ore grn., brn. & red 30 15
DESIGNS—VERT. 80 ore View from the Round Tower. 100 ore Interior of the Central Railway Station. HORIZ. 130 ore The Harbour.

189. Handicapped Person In Wheel-chair. **190.** Mail-coach Driver (detail from "A String of Horses outside an Inn" (O. Bache)).

1976. Danish Foundation for the Disabled.
628. **189.** 100 ore+20 ore black and red 30 30

1976. "Hafnia 1976" Stamp Exhibition.
629. **190.** 130 ore multicoloured 30 30

191. Prof. Emil Hansen.

1976. Carlsberg Foundation. Centenary
631. **191.** 100 ore red 25 10

MILITARY FRANK STAMPS

1917. Stamps of 1913 optd. **S.F.**
M 188. **12.** 5 ore green .. .. 4·50 5·50
M 189. 10 ore red .. .. 3·00 3·75

NEWSPAPER STAMPS

N 1.

ILLUSTRATIONS
British Commonwealth and all overprints and surcharges are FULL SIZE. Foreign Countries have been reduced to ¾-LINEAR.

1901.
N 185. **N 1.** 1 ore olive .. .. 1·40 20
N 132. 5 ore blue .. .. 4·50 2·50
N 187. 7 ore red .. .. 2·25 25
N 188. 8 ore green .. .. 5·50 35
N 189. 10 ore lilac .. 5·50 20
N 135. 20 ore green .. 4·50 20
N 199. 29 ore orange .. 11·00 60
N 136. 38 ore orange .. 6·00 30
N 193. 41 ore brown .. 7·50 45
N 137. 68 ore brown .. 8·50 3·00
N 138. 1 k. claret and green 4·75 25
N 139. 5 k. green and rose 22·00 5·00
N 140. 10 k. blue and bistre 27·00 4·75

OFFICIAL STAMPS

O 1.

1871. Value in "skilling".
O 51. **O 1.** 2 s. blue .. .. 45·00 30·00
O 52. 4 s. red .. .. 23·00 5·00
O 53. 16 s. green .. .. £120 75·00

1875. Value in "ore".
O 99. **O 1.** 1 ore orange .. 75 75
O 100. 3 ore mauve .. 75 75
O 185. 3 ore grey .. .. 2·25 3·75
O 101. 4 ore blue 75 75
O 187. 5 ore green .. 45 12
O 188. 5 ore brown .. 2·25 4·50
O 94. 8 ore red .. .. 1·75 35
O 104. 10 ore red 75 55
O 191. 10 ore green .. 70 45
O 192. 15 ore lilac .. 7·00 7·00
O 193. 20 ore blue .. 2·75 2·25
O 98. 32 ore green .. 7·50 7·50

PARCEL POST STAMPS

Postage stamps overprinted **POSTFAERGE.**

1919. Various types.
P 209. **9.** 10 ore green .. 5·50 4·25
P 210. 10 ore brown .. 5·00 2·25
P 208. **12.** 10 ore red .. 14·00 14·00
P 211. 15 ore lilac .. 6·00 6·00
P 252. **21.** 15 ore red .. 5·00 3·00
P 212. **12.** 30 ore orange .. 6·00 6·00
P 213. 30 ore blue .. 1·75 2·10
P 253. **21.** 30 ore orange .. 5·00 3·00
P 254. 40 ore green .. 2·00 2·25
P 214. **12.** 50 ore black and claret 38·00 38·00
P 215a. 50 ore grey .. .. 8·50 2·50
P 216. **13.** 1 k. brown .. 30·00 30·00
P 217. **12.** 1 k. blue and brown .. 15·00 5·50
P 218. 5 k. brown and mauve 1·75 1·60
P 219. 10 k. green and red .. 42·00 38·00

1936. Stamps of 1933.
P 299. **24.** 10 ore orange .. 7·00 5·50
P 300. 10 ore brown .. 90 90
P 301. 10 ore violet .. 20 20
P 302. 10 ore green .. 20 20
P 303. **21.** 15 ore red (No. 272) .. 45 45
P 304. 30 ore blue (No. 277) 1·50 1·50
P 305. 30 ore orge. (No. 276a) 45 45
P 306. 40 ore green (No. 279a) 1·50 1·50
P 307. 40 ore blue (No. 279b) 45 45
P 308. **25.** 50 ore grey 60 55
P 309. 1 k. brown 60 55

1945. Stamps of 1942.
P 346. **41.** 30 ore orange .. 45 35
P 347. 40 ore blue 45 35
P 348. 50 ore grey 45 35

1949. Stamps of 1946 and 1948.
P 376. **53.** 30 ore orange .. 70 70
P 377. 30 ore red 60 60
P 378. 40 ore blue 60 60
P 779. 40 ore grey 50 50
P 380. 50 ore grey 70 70
P 381. 50 ore green .. 60 60
P 382. 70 ore green .. 30 30
P 384. **47.** 1 k. 25 orange .. 1·90 1·90

1967. Optd. **POSTFAERGE.**
P 488. **83.** 40 ore brown .. 30 30
P 489. 80 ore blue 40 40

1967. Optd. **POSTFAERGE.**
P 491. 24. 5 ore maroon 5 5
P 492. 83. 50 ore brown 10 10
P 493. – 90 ore blue 20 20
P 494. 47. 1 k. brown 20 20
P 495 2 k. red 45 45
P 496. 5 k. blue .. .. 1·10 1·10

No. P 491 has the overprint at the top of the stamp, No. P 492/3 at the foot and No. 494/5 across the centre.

1975. Overprinted **POSTAERGE.**
P 597. 172. 100 ore blue .. 25 15

POSTAGE DUE STAMPS.

1921. Stamps of 1905 optd. **PORTO.**
D 214. 9. 1 ore orange 60 60
D 215. 12. 5 ore green 70 70
D 216. 7 ore orange .. 70 70
D 217. 10 ore red .. .. 4·25 3·75
D 218. 20 ore blue .. .. 2·10 1·50
D 219. 25 ore black & brown 2·10 1·10
D 220. 50 ore black & claret 1·10 55

D 1.

1921. Solid background.
D 221. D 1. 1 ore orange .. 20 20
D 222. 4 ore blue 95 95
D 223. 5 ore brown .. 50 20
D 224. 5 ore green .. 40 20
D 225. 7 ore green .. 3·75 3·75
D 226. 7 ore violet .. 5·50 5·50
D 227. 10 ore green .. 50 15
D 228. 10 ore brown .. 50 15
D 229. 20 ore blue .. 75 20
D 230. 20 ore grey .. 1·10 45
D 231. 25 ore red .. .. 1·25 45
D 232. 25 ore lilac .. 1·25 70
D 233. 25 ore blue .. 1·25 1·00
D 234. 1 k. blue .. .. 7·50 4·00
D 285. 1 k. blue and brown 3·50 1·50
D 286. 5 k. violet .. .. 7·50 4·50

1921. Military Frank stamp optd. **PORTO.**
D 227. 12. 10 ore red (No. M 161) 1·00 1·00

1934. Same type. Lined background.
D 285. D 1. 1 ore black .. 8 8
D 286. 2 ore red 8 8
D 287. 5 ore green .. 8 8
D 288. 6 ore olive .. 20 10
D 289. 8 ore mauve .. 1·25 1·25
D 290. 10 ore orange .. 12 8
D 291. 12 ore blue .. 12 10
D 292. 15 ore violet .. 12 8
D 293. 20 ore grey .. 15 8
D 294. 25 ore blue .. 15 8
D 295. 30 ore green .. 20 10
D 296. 40 ore claret .. 20 12
D 297. 1 k. brown 45 10

1934. Surch. **PORTO 15.**
D 298. 9. "15" on 12 ore lilac 70 35

SPECIAL FEE STAMPS

1923. No. D 217 optd. **GEBYR** twice.
S 218. D 1. 10 ore green .. 1·40 45

S 1.

1926.
S 285. S 1. 5 ore green .. 20 8
S 229. 10 ore green .. 75 15
S 230. 10 ore brown .. 75 15
S 286. 10 ore orange .. 12 8

DHAR BC

A state of Central India. Now uses Indian stamps.

4 pice = 1 anna.

1. 2.

1897. Imperf.
1. 1. ½ pice black on red .. 15 15
2. ¼ a. black on orange .. 30 40
3. ½ a. black on mauve .. 30 30
4. 1 a. black on green .. 80 80
5. 2 a. black on yellow .. 4·50 6·00

1898. Perf.
6. 2. ½ a. red 40 40
7. 1 a. purple 40
9. 2 a. green .. .. .. 1·50

DIEGO-SUAREZ O3

A port in N. Madagascar. A separate colony till 1896, when it was incorporated with Madagascar.

1890. Stamps of French Colonies. "Commerce" type, surch. **15** sideways.
1. 9. 15 on 1 c. black on blue .. 30·00 8·50
2. 15 on 5 c. green .. 65·00 7·50
3. 15 on 10 c. black on lilac .. 30·00 7·50
4. 15 on 20 c. red on green .. 65·00 8·50
5. 15 on 25 c. black on red .. 11·00 3·25

1. 2.

1890 Various designs.
6. 1. 1 c. black .. .. .. £130 35·00
7. 5 c. black .. .. .. £130 22·00
8. 15 c. black .. .. .. 32·00 9·50
9. 25 c. black .. .. .. 32·00 14·00

1891.
10. 2. 5 c. black .. .. .. 27·00 11·00

1891. Stamps of French Colonies. "Commerce" type surch. **1891. DIEGO-SUAREZ 5 c.**
13. 9. 5 c. on 10 c. black on lilac 19·00 11·00
14. 5 c. on 20 c. red on green 19·00 6·50

1892. Stamps of French Colonies, "Commerce" type, optd. **DIEGO-SUAREZ.**
15. 9. 1 c. black on blue .. 4·25 2·25
16. 2 c. brown on yellow .. 4·25 2·25
17. 4 c. claret on grey .. 5·50 3·75
18. 5 c. green .. .. 13·00 11·00
19. 10 c. black on red .. 4·25 3·25
20. 15 c. blue .. .. 3·75 2·25
21. 20 c. red on green .. 4·50 2·75
22. 25 c. black on red .. 3·00 2·10
23. 30 c. brown £160 £130
24. 35 c. black on orange .. £190 £150
25. 75 c. red .. .. 8·50 5·50
26. 1 f. olive .. .. 8·50 5·50

1892. "Tablet" key-type inscr. "DIEGO-SUAREZ ET DEPENDANCES".
38. D. 1 c. black on blue .. 30 30
39. 2 c. brown on yellow .. 30 30
40. 4 c. claret on grey .. 12 12
41. 5 c. green 45 30
42. 10 c. black on lilac .. 65 45
43. 15 c. blue .. .. 1·10 60
44. 20 c. red on green .. 1·90 1·25
45. 25 c. black on red .. 1·25 1·10
46. 30 c. brown .. .. 1·00 75
47. 40 c. red on yellow .. 2·75 2·00
48. 50 c. red .. .. 5·50 3·25
49. 75 c. brown on yellow .. 4·25 2·75
50. 1 f. olive .. .. 7·50 5·50

1894. "Tablet" key-type inscr. "DIEGO-SUAREZ".
51. D. 1 c. black on blue .. 8 8
52. 2 c. brown on yellow .. 20 20
53. 4 c. claret on grey .. 20 20
54. 5 c. green 25 20
55. 10 c. black on lilac .. 45 30
56. 15 c. blue 50 35
57. 20 c. red on green .. 1·00 60
58. 25 c. black on red .. 45 25
59. D. 30 c. brown 70 35
60. 40 c. red on yellow .. 80 70
61. 50 c. red .. .. 1·60 80
62. 75 c. brown on yellow .. 50 40
63. 1 f. olive .. .. 2·00 70

POSTAGE DUE STAMPS

D 1.

1891.
D 11. D 1. 5 c. violet .. .. 16·00 7·00
D 12. 50 c. black on yellow 16·00 7·00

1892. Postage Due stamps of French Colonies overprinted **DIEGO-SUAREZ.**
D 27. D 1. 1 c. black .. .. 15·00 8·00
D 28. 2 c. black .. .. 15·00 8·00
D 29. 3 c. black .. .. 11·00 5·00
D 30. 4 c. black .. .. 11·00 5·00
D 31. 5 c. black .. .. 11·00 5·00
D 32. 10 c. black .. .. 3·75 3·50
D 33. 15 c. black .. .. 5·00 3·50
D 34. 20 c. black .. .. 25·00 12·00
D 35. 30 c. black .. .. 11·00 8·00
D 36. 60 c. black .. .. £100 70·00
D 37. 1 f. brown £200 £140

DJIBOUTI O2

A port in French Somaliland S. of the Red Sea. Now capital of French Territory of the Afars and the Issas.

1893. "Tablet" key-type stamp of Obock optd. **DJ.**
83. D. 5 c. green .. .. .. 22·00 20·00

1894. Same type surch. in figures and **DJIBOUTI.**
85. D. 25 on 2 c. brown on buff 50·00 32·00
86. 50 on 1 c. black on blue .. 60·00 42·00

1894. Triangular stamp of Obock optd. **DJIBOUTI** or surch. **1** also.
87. 1. 1 f. on 5 f. red £130 £110
88. 5 f. red £300 £275

1. Djibouti. (The apparent perforation is part of the design.)

2. Gunboat.

3. Desert Scene.

1894. Imperf.
89. 1. 1 c. claret and black .. 25 25
90. – 2 c. black and claret .. 25 25
91. – 4 c. blue and brown .. 1·40 1·10
92. – 5 c. red and green .. 90 65
93. – 5 c. green .. .. 1·25 1·10
94. – 10 c. green and brown .. 2·75 1·10
95. – 15 c. green and lilac .. 1·75 1·10
96. – 25 c. blue and red .. 2·75 1·75
97. – 30 c. red and brown .. 2·50 2·00
98. – 40 c. blue and yellow .. 7·50 6·50
99. – 50 c. red and blue .. 2·25 1·75
100. – 75 c. orange and mauve 6·50 5·50
101. – 1 f. black and olive .. 2·75 2·40
102. – 2 f. red and brown .. 15·00 12·00
103. 2. 5 f. blue and red .. 22·00 20·00
104. 3. 25 f. blue and red .. £140 £130
105. 50 f. red and blue .. £140 £130

DESIGNS—As T 1.: 2 c. to 75 c. Different views of Djibouti. 1 f., 2 f. Port of Djibouti.

1899. As last, surch.
108. – 0.05 on 75 c. orge & mve. 8·00 6·00
109. – 0.10 on 1 f. blk. & olive 14·00 9·50
106. – 0.40 on 4 c. blue & brown £550 3·25
110. – 0.40 on 2 f. red & brown £100 65·00
111. 2. 0.75 on 5 f. blue and red £110 95·00

1902. Rectangular stamp of Obock surch. **0.05.**
107. 2. 0.05 on 75 c. lilac & orge. £275 £160

1902. Triangular stamps of Obock surch.
112. 3. 5 c. on 25 f. blue & brown 10·00 8·00
113. 10 c. on 50 f. grn. & lake 14·00 11·00

1902. Nos. 98/9 surch.
114. 5 c. on 40 c. blue and yellow 75 65
115. 10 c. on 50 c. red and blue 3·25 3·25

1902. Stamps of Obock surch. **DJIBOUTI** and value.
120. 2. 5 c. on 30 c. yell. & grn. 2·00 1·75
116. 10 c. on 25 c. black & blue 2·25 1·75
117. 3. 10 c. on 2 f. orange & lilac 9·00 8·00
119. 10 c. on 10 f. lake and red 5·50 5·00

For later issues see **FRENCH SOMALI COAST** and **FRENCH TERRITORY OF THE AFARS AND ISSAS.**

MORE DETAILED LISTS

are given in the Stanley Gibbons Catalogues referred to in the country headings:

BC	British Commonwealth
E1, E2, E3	Europe 1, 2, 3
O1, O2, O3, O4	Overseas 1, 2, 3, 4

DOMINICA BC

Until Dec. 31st, 1939, one of the Leeward Is., but then transferred to the Windward Is. Used Leeward Is. stamps concurrently with Dominican issues from 1903 to above date.

1949. 100 cents = 1 West Indian dollar.

1.

1874.
15. 1. ½d. yellow .. .. 2·00 3·75
20. ½d. green .. .. 60 2·50
5. 1d. lilac .. .. 2·75 2·00
22a. 1d. red .. .. 1·00 1·75
16. 2½d. brown .. .. 35·00 6·00
23. 2½d. blue .. .. 2·75 2·25
7. 4d. blue .. .. 35·00 4·50
24. 4d. grey .. .. 2·00 2·00
8. 6d. green .. .. 50·00 11·00
25. 6d. orange .. .. 7·00 9·50
3. 1s. mauve .. .. £120 38·00

1882. No. 5 bisected and surch. with small ½.
10. 1. ½(d.) on half 1d. lilac .. 42·00 17·00

1882. No. 5 bisected and surch. with large ½.
11. 1. ½(d.) on half 1d. lilac .. 13·00 13·00

1883. No. 5 bisected and surch. **HALF PENNY** vert.
14. 1. ½d. on half 1d. lilac .. 15·00 17·00

1886. Nos. 8 and 3 surch in words and bar.
17. 1. ½d. on 6d. green .. .. 4·50 6·50
18. 1d. on 6d. green £6000 £5000
19. 1d. on 1s. mauve .. 6·00 7·50

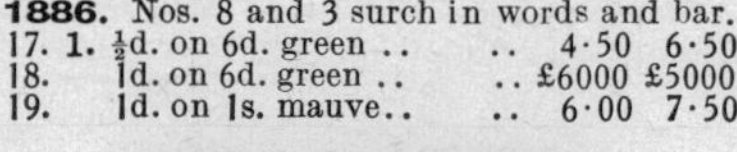

2. View of Dominica from the Sea.

3.

1903.
47. 2. ½d. green .. .. 80 1·10
28. 1d. grey and red .. .. 1·40 85
29. 2d. green and brown .. 6·00 6·00
30. 2½d. grey and blue .. 7·00 5·50
31. 3d. purple and black .. 7·50 7·50
32. 6d. grey and brown .. 9·00 9·00
33. 1s. mauve and green .. 13·00 14·00
34. 2s. black and purple .. 14·00 15·00
35. 2s. 6d. green and orange 15·00 17·00
46. 3. 5s. black and brown .. 32·00 35·00

1908.
48. 2. 1d. red .. .. 1·00 65
64. 1½d. orange .. .. 2·00 3·00
65. 2d. grey .. .. 4·00 4·00
50a. 2½d. blue .. .. 2·50 3·75
51a. 3d. purple on yellow .. 4·75 6·00
52a. 6d. purple .. .. 7·00 8·00
53. 1 s. black on green .. 4·50 5·00
53a. 2s. pur. and blue on blue 9·50 14·00
53b. 2s. 6d. black & red on blue 15·00 18·00

1914. As T 3, but portrait of King George V.
54. 5 s. red and green on yellow 23·00 27·00

1916. Surch. **WAR TAX ONE HALF-PENNY.**
55. 2. ½d. on ½d. green .. 15 60

1918. Optd. **WAR TAX** in small letters.
56. 2. ½d. green .. .. .. 40 1·75

1918. Optd. **WAR TAX** in large letters.
57. 2. ½d. green 8 45
58. 3d. purple on yellow .. 12 1·10

1919. Surch. **WAR TAX 1½D.**
59. 2. 1½d. on 2½d. orange .. 8 85

1920. Surch. **1½D.**
60. 2. 1½d. on 2½d. orange .. 80 2·25

5. Seal of the Colony and King George V.

1923.
71. 5. ½d. black and green .. 25 35
72. 1d. black and violet .. 50 90
73. 1d. black and red .. 1·00 1·10
74. 1½d. black and red .. 65 65
75. 1½d. black and brown .. 1·60 1·25
76. 2d. black and grey .. 65 90
77. 2½d. black and yellow .. 1·00 1·75
78. 2½d. black and blue .. 1·25 1·75
79. 3d. black and blue .. 1·25 1·75
80. 3d. black & red on yellow 80 1·10
81. 4d. black and brown .. 80 2·00
82. 6d. black and mauve .. 1·50 3·00
83. 1s. black on green .. 1·75 3·00
84. 2s. black & blue on blue.. 3·75 6·00
85. 2s. 6d. blk. & red on blue 7·00 9·50
86. 3s black & purple on yell. 6·00 9·50
87. 4s. black and red on green 7·50 12·00
88. 5s. black & green on yell. 12·00 17·00
91. £1 black and purple on red 95·00 £150

1935. Silver Jubilee. As T **11** of Antigua.
92. 1d. blue and red 25 35
93. 1½d. blue and grey .. 30 45
94. 2½d. brown and blue .. 1·50 2·00
95. 1s. grey and purple .. 2·75 3·50

1937. Coronation. As T **2** of Aden.
96. 1d. red 15 25
97. 1½d. brown 15 15
98. 2½d. blue 30 60

6. Fresh Water Lake. 7. King George VI.

1938.
99. 6. ½d. brown and green .. 8 5
100. – 1d. black and red .. 10 10
101. – 1½d. green and purple .. 25 12
102. – 2d. red and black .. 15 20
103a.– 2½d. purple and blue .. 10 12
104. – 3d. olive and brown .. 12 20
104a.– 3½d. blue and mauve .. 35 25
105. 6. 6d. green and violet .. 20 25
105a. 7d. green and brown .. 30 30
106. – 1s. violet and olive .. 55 35
106a.– 2s. grey and purple .. 1·25 1·40
107. 6. 2s. 6d. black and red .. 1·00 1·40
108. – 5s. blue and brown .. 2·25 2·50
108a.– 10s. black and orange .. 5·50 7·50
DESIGNS—As T **6**: 1d., 3d., 2s. 5s. Layon River. 1½d., 2½d., 3½d. Picking Limes. 2d., 1s., 10s. Boiling Lake.

1940.
109. 7. ¼d. brown 5 5

1946. Victory. As Type **4** of Aden.
110. 1d. red 8 5
111. 3½d. blue 10 8

1948. Silver Wedding. As T **5/6** of Aden.
112. 1d. red 8 5
113. 10s. brown .. .. 4·00 7·00

1949. U.P.U. As T **14/17** of Antigua.
114. 5 c. blue 12 20
115. 6 c. brown 25 30
116. 12 c. purple 45 70
117. 24 c. olive 60 75

1951. Inaug. of B.W.I. University College. As T **18/19** of Antigua.
118. 3 c. green and violet .. 25 15
119. 12 c. green and red .. 45 35

8. Drying Cocoa.

1951. New Currency.
120. 7. ½ c. brown 12 15
121. 8. 1 c. black and vermilion 12 12
122. – 2 c. brown and green .. 10 20
123. – 3 c. green and purple .. 12 20
124. – 4 c. orange and sepia .. 15 30
125. – 5 c. black and red .. 20 30
126. – 6 c. olive and brown .. 15 30
127. – 8 c. green and blue .. 20 40
128. – 12 c. black and green .. 20 45
129. – 14 c. blue and purple .. 20 45
130. – 24 c. purple and red .. 35 45
131. – 48 c. green and orange.. 70 2·00
132. – 60 c. red and black .. 1·10 2·00
133. – $1.20 green and black .. 2·75 4·50
134. – $2.40 orange and black 7·00 7·50
DESIGNS—As T **8**—HORIZ. 2 c., 60 c. Carib baskets. 3 c., 48 c. Lime plantation. 4 c. Picking oranges. 5 c. Bananas. 6 c. Botanical Gardens. 8 c. Drying vanilla beans. 12 c., $1.20 Fresh Water Lake. 14 c. Layou River. 24 c. Boiling Lake. VERT. $2.40 Picking oranges.

1951. New Constitution. Stamps of 1951 optd. **NEW CONSTITUTION 1951.**
135. 3 c. green and violet .. 8 15
136. 5 c. black and red .. 10 25
137. 8 c. green and blue .. 15 20
138. 14 c. blue and violet .. 20 25

1953. Coronation. As T **7** of Aden.
139. 2 c. black and green .. 12 12

1954. As Nos. 120/34 but with portrait of Queen Elizabeth II.
140. ½ c. brown 5 8
141. 1 c. brown and vermilion 5 5
142. 2 c. brown and green .. 5 5
143. 3 c. green and purple .. 12 12
144. 3 c. black and red .. 5 5
145. 4 c. orange and sepia .. 5 5
146. 5 c. black and red .. 20 20
147. 5 c. blue and sepia .. 5 5
148. 6 c. olive and brown .. 8 8
149. 8 c. green and blue .. 8 8
150. 10 c. green and brown .. 25 25
151. 12 c. black and green .. 12 12
152. 14 c. blue and purple .. 12 12
153. 24 c. purple and red .. 25 20
154. 48 c. green and orange .. 4·50 6·50
155. 48 c. brown and violet .. 2·50 3·00
156. 60 c. red and black .. 75 95
157. $1.20 green and black .. 2·75 3·25
158. $2.40 orange and black .. 4·50 5·00
DESIGNS (New)—HORIZ. Nos. 144, 155, Matmaking. No. 147, Canoe making. No. 150, Bananas.

1958. British Caribbean Federation. As T **21** of Antigua.
159. 3 c. green 8 8
160. 6 c. blue 20 20
161. 12 c. red 25 25

9. Seashore at Rosalie.

1963.
162. 9. 1 c. green, blue and sepia 5 5
163. – 2 c. blue 5 5
164. – 3 c. brown and blue .. 5 5
200. – 4 c. grn., sep. & slate-vio. 5 5
166. – 5 c. magenta 5 5
201. – 6 c. green, bistre & violet 5 5
168. – 8 c. green, sepia & black 10 10
169. – 10 c. sepia and pink .. 10 12
170. – 12 c. green, blue & sepia 12 15
171a.– 14 c. multicoloured .. 12 12
172. – 15 c. yellow, green & brn. 15 15
173. – 24 c. multicoloured .. 40 40
174. – 48 c. green, blue & black 60 65
175. – 60 c. orange, green & blk. 65 80
176. – $1.20 multicoloured .. 2·25 1·60
177. – $2.40 blue, turq. & brown 2·25 2·75
178. – $4.80 green, blue & brown 5·50 6·00
DESIGNS—VERT. 2 c., 5 c. Queen Elizabeth II (after Annigoni). 14 c. Traditional costume. 24 c. Sisserou parrot. $2.40 Trafalgar Falls. $4.80 Coconut palm. HORIZ. 3 c. Sailing canoe. 4 c. Sulphur springs. 6 c. Road making. 8 c. Dug-out canoe. 10 c. Crapaud (frog). 12 c. Scotts Head. 15 c. Bananas. 48 c. Goodwill. 60 c. Cocoa tree. $1.20 Coat of Arms.

1963. Freedom from Hunger. As T **10** of Aden.
179. 15 c. violet 35 35

1963. Red Cross Cent. As T **24** of Antigua.
180. 5 c. red and black .. 12 12
181. 15 c. red and blue .. 45 45

1964. Shakespeare. 400th Birth Anniv. As T **25** of Antigua.
182. 15 c. purple 35 40

1965. I.T.U. Cent. As T **26** of Antigua.
183. 2 c. green and blue .. 5 5
184. 48 c. turquoise and grey .. 45 50

1965. I.C.Y. As T **27** of Antigua.
185. 1 c. purple and turquoise .. 5 5
186. 15 c. green and lavender .. 25 25

1966. Churchill Commem. As T **28** of Antigua.
187. 1 c. blue 5 5
188. 5 c. green 8 8
189. 15 c. brown 25 25
190. 24 c. violet 40 40

1966. Royal Visit. As T **29** of Antigua.
191. 5 c. black and blue .. 10 10
192. 15 c. black and magenta .. 25 25

1966. World Cup Football Championships. As T **30** of Antigua.
193. 5 c. vio., grn., lake & brn. 8 8
194. 24 c. chocolate, turquoise, lake and brown 25 25

1966. W.H.O. Headquarters, Geneva. Inaug. As T **31** of Antigua.
195. 5 c. black, green and blue .. 8 10
196. 24 c. black, purple & ochre 30 30

1966. U.N.E.S.C.O. 20th Anniv. As T **33/5** of Antigua.
197. 5 c. violet red, yell. & orge. 8 10
198. 15 c. yellow, violet & olive 20 20
199. 24 c. black, purple & orge. 30 35

10. Children of Three Races.

1967. National Day. Multicoloured.
205. 5 c. Type **10** 5 5
206. 10 c. The "Santa Maria" and Motto 5 8
207. 15 c. Hands holding Motto Ribbon 10 10
208. 24 c. Belaire Dancing .. 20 20

11. John F. Kennedy.

1968. Human Rights Year. Multicoloured.
209. 1 c. Type **11** 5 5
210. 10 c. Cecil E. A. Rawle .. 5 8
211. 12 c. Pope John XXIII .. 8 8
212. 48 c. Florence Nightingale 30 30
213. 60 c. Albert Schweitzer .. 40 45

1968. Associated Statehood. Nos. 162, etc. optd. **ASSOCIATED STATEHOOD.**
214. 1 c. grn., blue and sepia.. 5 5
215. 2 c. blue 5 5
216. 3 c. brown and blue .. 5 5
217. 4 c. green, sepia and violet 5 5
218. 5 c. magenta 5 5
219. 6 c. green, bistre and violet 5 5
220. 8 c. green, sepia and black 5 8
221. 10 c. sepia and pink .. 8 8
222. 12 c. green, blue and brown 8 8
224. 14 c. multicoloured .. 8 10
225. 15 c. yellow, green & brn. 12 12
226. 24 c. multicoloured .. 20 20
227. 48 c. green, blue and black 45 60
228. 60 c. orange, green and blk. 50 50
229. $1.20 multicoloured .. 1·10 85
230. $2.40 blue, turq. & brown 1·50 1·60
231. $4.80 green, blue & brown 2·75 3·00

1968. National Day. Nos. 162/4, 171a and 176 optd. **NATIONAL DAY 3 NOVEMBER 1968.**
232. 1 c. grn., blue and sepia.. 5 5
233. 2 c. blue 5 5
234. 3 c. brown and blue .. 10 10
235. 14 c. multicoloured .. 15 15
236. $1.20 multicoloured .. 70 70

12. Forward shooting at Goal.

1968. Olympic Games, Mexico. Multicoloured.
237. 1 c. Type **12** 5 5
238. 1 c. Goalkeeper attempting to save ball 5 5
239. 5 c. Swimmers preparing to dive 8 8
240. 5 c. Swimmers diving .. 8 8
241. 48 c. Javelin-throwing .. 30 35
242. 48 c. Hurdling 30 35
243. 60 c. Basketball 35 40
244. 60 c. Basketball players 35 40
Nos. 237/44 were issued in sheets of 40 containing two panes of se-tenant pairs.

13. "The Small Cowper Madonna" (Raphael).

1968. Christmas.
245. 13. 5 c. multicoloured .. 5 5

14. "Venus and Adonis" (Rubens).

1969. World Health Organisation. 20th Anniv.
246. 14. 5 c. multicoloured .. 5 5
247. – 15 c. multicoloured .. 12 12
248. – 24 c. multicoloured .. 15 15
249. – 50 c. multicoloured .. 25 35
DESIGNS: 15 c. "The Death of Socrates" (David). 24 c. "Christ and the Pilgrims of Emmaus" (Velasquez). 50 c. "Pilate washing his hands" (Rembrandt).

15. Picking Oranges.

1969. Tourism. Multicoloured.
250. 10 c. Type **15** 8 8
251. 10 c. Woman, child and ocean scene 8 8
252. 12 c. Fort Yeoung Hotel .. 10 10
253. 12 c. Parrots 10 10
254. 24 c. Calypso band .. 20 25
255. 24 c. Women dancing .. 20 25
256. 48 c. Underwater life .. 35 40
257. 48 c. Skin-diver and turtle 35 40

16. "Strength in Unity" Emblem and Fruit trees.

1969. 1st Anniv. of C.A.R.I.F.T.A. (Caribbean Free Trade Area). Multicoloured.

258. 5 c. Type **16** 5 5
259. 8 c. "HS 748" aircraft, emblem and island .. 10 10
260. 12 c. Chart of Caribbean Sea and emblem .. 12 12
261. 24 c. Steamship unloading, tug and emblem .. 25 25

17. "Spinning" (J. Millet).

1969. Int. Labour Organisation. 50th Anniv. Multicoloured.

262. 15 c. Type **17** 10 10
263. 30 c. "Threshing" (J. Millet) 20 20
264. 38 c. "Flax-pulling" (J. Millet) 25 25

18. Mahatma Gandhi weaving and Clock Tower, Westminster.

1969. Mahatma Gandhi. Birth Cent. Multicoloured.

265. 6 c. Type **18** 5 5
266. 38 c. Gandhi, Nehru, and Mausoleum 25 25
267. $1.20 Gandhi and Taj Mahal 85 85

NOTE: All stamps are incorrectly inscribed "Ghandi".

19. "Saint Joseph".

1969. National Day. Multicoloured.

268. 6 c. Type **19** 5 5
269. 8 c. "Saint John" .. 10 10
270. 12 c. "Saint Peter" .. 15 15
271. 60 c. "Saint Paul" .. 60 60

20. Queen Elizabeth II.

21. Humming Bird and flower.

1969. Centres multicoloured; colours of "D" given.

272. **20.** ½ c. black and silver .. 5 5
273. **21.** 1 c. black and yellow .. 5 5
274. – 2 c. black and yellow. .. 5 5
275. – 3 c. black and yellow .. 5 5
276. – 4 c. black and yellow .. 5 5
277. – 5 c. black and yellow .. 5 5
278. – 6 c. black and chestnut 5 8
279. – 8 c. black and brown .. 8 8
280. – 10 c. black and yellow 8 10
281. – 12 c. black and yellow 10 8
282. – 15 c black and blue .. 8 10
283. – 25 c. black and red 10 12
284. – 30 c. black and olive .. 20 20
285. – 38 c. black and purple 12 15
286. – 50 c. black and chestnut 20 20
287. – 60 c. black and yellow 30 35
288. – $1.20 black and yellow 55 60
289. – $2.40 black and gold .. 1·00 1·10
290. – $4.80 black and gold .. 2·00 2·25

DESIGNS—HORIZ. As T **21**: 2 c. Poinsettia. 3 c. Ramier Pigeon. 4 c. Sisserou Parrot. 5 c. Swallowtail Butterfly. 6 c. Julia Butterfly. 8 c. Shipping bananas. 10 c. Portsmouth Harbour. 12 c. Copra Processing Plant. 15 c. Straw Workers. 25 c. Timber Plant. 30 c. Pumice Mine. 38 c. Grammar School and Playing Fields. 50 c. Roseau Cathedral. 60 c. Government Headquarters (38 × 26½ mm.). $1.20 Melville Hall Airport (38 × 26½ mm.). $2.40 Coat of Arms (39½ × 26 mm.). VERT. $4.80 As T **20** but larger (26 × 39 mm.).

22. "The Virgin and the Child" (Lippi).

1969. Christmas. Paintings multicoloured; frame colours given.

291. **22.** 6 c. blue 10 10
292. – 10 c. brown and flesh .. 12 12
293. – 15 c. violet and lilac .. 20 20
294. – $1.20 green .. .. 80 1·10

DESIGNS: 10 c. "Holy Family with the Lamb" (Raphael). 15 c. "Virgin and Child" (Perugino). $1.20 "Madonna of the Rose Hedge" (Botticelli).

23. Astronaut's First Step on the Moon.

1970. Moon Landing. Multicoloured; frame colours given.

296. **23.** ½ c. lilac 8 8
297. – 5 c. blue 10 10
298. – 8 c. red 15 15
299. – 30 c. blue 20 20
300. – 50 c. brown 35 35
301. – 60 c. pink 40 40

DESIGNS: 5 c. Scientific experiment on the Moon, and flag. 8 c. Astronauts collecting rocks. 30 c. Module over the Moon. 50 c. Moon plaque. 60 c. Astronauts.

24. Giant Green Turtle.

1970. Flora and Fauna. Multicoloured.

303. 6 c. Type **24** 8 8
304. 24 c. Flying fish .. 20 20
305. 38 c. Anthurium lily .. 25 25
306. 60 c. Imperial and Red-Necked parrots .. 35 35

25. 18th-Century National Costume.

1970. National Day. Multicoloured.

308. 5 c. Type **25** 5 5
309. 8 c. Carib basketry .. 5 5
310. $1 Flag and chart of Dominica 55 55

26. Scrooge and Marley's Ghost.

1970. Christmas and Charles Dicken's Death Cent. Scenes from "A Christmas Carol". Multicoloured.

312. 2 c. Type **26** 8 8
313. 15 c. Fezziwig's Ball .. 15 15
314. 24 c. Scrooge and his Nephew's Party .. 25 25
315. $1.20 Scrooge and the Ghost of Christmas Present 95 95

27. "The Doctor" (Sir Luke Fildes).

1970. British Red Cross Cent. Multicoloured.

317. 8 c. Type **27** 10 10
318. 10 c. Hands and Red Cross 12 12
319. 15 c. Flag of Dominica and Red Cross emblem .. 15 15
320. 50 c. "The Sick Child" (E. Munch) 50 50

28. Marigot School.

1971. Int. Education Year. Multicoloured.

322. 5 c. Type **28** 5 5
323. 8 c. Goodwill Junior High School 8 8
324. 14 c. University of West Indies (Jamaica) .. 15 15
325. $1 Trinity College, Cambridge 60 60

29. Waterfall.

1971. Tourism. Multicoloured.

327. 5 c. Type **29** 8 8
328. 10 c. Boat-building .. 10 10
329. 30 c. Sailing 20 20
330. 50 c. Yacht and motor launch 30 35

30. U.N.I.C.E.F. Symbol in "D".

1971. U.N.I.C.E.F. 25th Anniv.

332. **30.** 5 c. violet, blk., & gold 8 8
333. 10 c. yell., blk. & gold .. 10 10
334. 38 c. grn., blk. & gold .. 20 20
335. $1.20 orge., blk. & gold 70 70

31. German Boy Scout.

1971. World Scout Jamboree, Asagiri, Japan, Various designs showing Boy Scouts from the nations listed. Multicoloured.

337. 20 c. Type **31** 12 12
338. 24 c. Great Britain .. 15 15
339. 30 c. Japan 20 25
340. $1 Dominica 60 60

32. Groine at Portsmouth.

1971. National Day. Multicoloured.

342. 8 c. Type **32** 8 8
343. 15 c. Carnival scene .. 8 10
344. 20 c. Carifta Queen (vert.) 15 15
345. 50 c. Rock of Atkinson (vert.) 30 35

33. Eight Reals Piece, 1761.

1972. Coins.

347. **33.** 10 c. black, sil. & vio. 10 10
348. – 30 c. black, sil. & grn... 20 20
349. – 35 c. black, sil. & blue.. 25 25
350. – 50 c. black, silver & red 30 30

DESIGNS—HORIZ. 30 c. Eleven and three bitt pieces, 1798. VERT. 35 c. Two reals and two bitt pieces, 1770. 50 c. Mocos, Pieces of eight and eight reals-eleven bitts piece, 1798.

34. Manicou.

1972. U.N. Conf. on the Human Environment, Stockholm. Multicoloured.

352. ½ c. Type **34** 5 5
353. 35 c. Agouti (rodent) .. 15 15
354. 60 c. Orchid 30 35
355. $1·20 Hibiscus .. .. 1·00 1·00

35. Sprinter.

1972. Olympic Games, Munich. Multicoloured.

357. 30 c. Type **35** 15 15
358. 35 c. Hurdler 20 20
359. 58 c. Hammer-thrower (vert.) 30 30
360. 72 c. Long-jumper (vert.) .. 50 50

36. General Post Office.

1972. National Day. Multicoloured.

362. 10 c. Type **36** 8 8
363. 20 c. Morne Diablotin .. 12 12
364. 30 c. Rodney's Rock .. 20 20

1972. Royal Silver Wedding. As T **19** of Ascension, but with Bananas and Sisserou Parrot in background.

366. 5 c. green 8 10
367. $1 green 60 65

37. "Madonna and Child and Shepherds" (Boccaccino).

1972. Christmas. Multicoloured.

368. 8 c. Type **37** 5 5
369. 14 c. "Madonna and Child" (Rubens) 5 5
370. 30 c. "Madonna and Child" (Gentileschi) 15 15
371. $1 "Visit of the Magi" (Mastaert) 70 70

38. Launching of Weather Satellite.

1973. I.M.O./W.M.O. Cent. Multicoloured.

373. ½ c. Type **38** .. 5 5
374. 1 c. Nimbus satellite .. 5 5
375. 2 c. Radiosonde balloon .. 5 5
376. 30 c. Radarscope (horiz.) 15 20
377. 35 c. Diagram of pressure zones (horiz.) .. 20 20
378. 50 c. Hurricane shown by satellite (horiz.) .. 30 35
379. $1 Computer weather-map (horiz.) 55 65

39. Going to Hospital.

1973. W.H.O. 25th Anniv. Multicoloured.

381. ½ c. Type **39** 5 5
382. 1 c. Maternity care .. 5 5
383. 2 c. Smallpox inoculation 5 5
384. 30 c. Emergency service 15 20
385. 35 c. Waiting for the doctor 20 20
386. 50 c. Medical examination 25 30
387. $1 Travelling doctor .. 45 50

40. Cyrique Crab.

1973. Flora and Fauna. Multicoloured.

389. ½ c. Type **40** 5 5
390. 22 c. Blue Land-crab .. 10 10
391. 25 c. Bread Fruit .. 15 15
392. $1·20 Sunflower .. 75 75

41. Princess Anne and Captain Mark Philips.

1973. Royal Wedding.

394. **41.** 25 c. multicoloured .. 12 12
395. – $2 multicoloured .. 1·25 1·25

DESIGN: $2 As T **41**, but with different frame.

42. Painting by Brueghel.

1973. Christmas. "The Adoration of the Shepherds" by the artists listed. Mult.

397. ½ c. Type **42** 5 5
398. 1 c. Botticelli 5 5
399. 2 c. Durer 5 5
400. 12 c. Botticelli 5 5
401. 22 c. Rubens 10 12
402. 35 c. Durer 20 20
403. $1 Giorgione 80 85

43. Carib Basket-Weaving.

1973. National Day. Multicoloured.

405. 5 c. Type **43** 5 5
406. 10 c. Staircase of the Snake 5 5
407. 50 c. Miss Caribbean Queen 1973 .. .. .. 25 30
408. 60 c. Miss Carifta Queen 1973 30 35
409. $1 Dance Group 45 50

Nos. 407/8 are vert.

44. University of Dominica.

1973. West Indies University. 25th Anniv. Multicoloured.

411. 12 c. Type **44** 5 5
412. 30 c. Graduation ceremony 12 15
413. $1 University coat of arms 50 55

45. Dominican 1d. Stamp of 1874 and Map.

1974. Stamp Centenary. Multicoloured.

415. ½ c. Type **45** 5 5
416. 1 c. 6d. stamp of 1874 and posthorn 5 5
417. 2 c. 1d. stamp of 1874 and arms 8 8
418. 10 c. Type **45** 12 12
419. 50 c. As 1 c. 25 30
420. $1.20 As 2 c. 55 60

46. Footballer and Flag of Brazil.

1974. World Cup Football Championships. Multicoloured.

422. ½ c. Type **46** 5 5
423. 1 c. West Germany .. 5 5
424. 2 c. Italy 5 5
425. 30 c. Scotland 15 20
426. 40 c. Sweden 20 25
427. 50 c. Netherlands 25 30
428. $1 Yugoslavia 45 50

47. Indian Hole.

1974. National Day. Multicoloured.

430. 10 c. Type **47** 5 5
431. 40 c. Teachers' Training College 20 25
432. $1 Bay Oil distillery plant, Petite Savanne 45 50

48. Churchill with "Colonist".

1974. Sir Winston Churchill Birth Cent. Multicoloured.

434. ½ c. Type **48** 5 5
435. 1 c. Churchill and Eisenhower 5 5
436. 2 c. Churchill and Roosevelt 5 5
437. 20 c. Churchill and troops on assault-course .. 10 10
438. 45 c. Painting at Marrakesh 25 30
439. $2 Giving the "V" sign .. 90 1·00

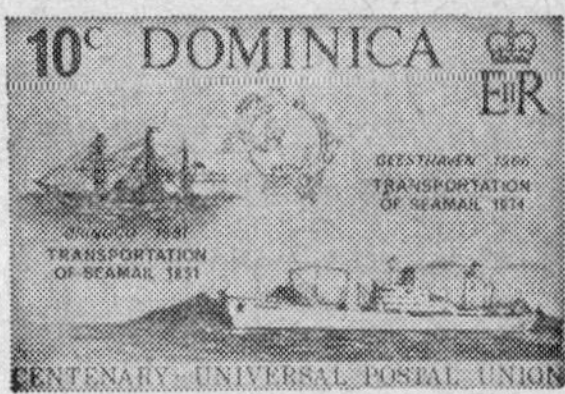

49. Mailboats "Orinoco" (1851) and "Geesthaven" (1974).

1974. Universal Postal Union. Cent. Mult.

441. 10 c. Type **49** 5 5
442. $2 Mailplanes—De Havilland "4" (1918) and Boeing "747" (1974) .. 90 1·00

50. "The Holy Family" (Tiso).

1974. Christmas. Multicoloured.

444. ½ c. Type **50** 5 5
445. 1 c. "Virgin and Child" (Costa) 5 5
446. 2 c. "Virgin, Child and Mary Magdalen" (unknown) .. 5 5
447. 10 c. "The Holy Family" (Romanelli) .. 5 5
448. 25 c. "Nativity" (de Sermoneta) 12 15
449. 45 c. "The Nativity" (Guido Reni) .. 25 30
450. $1 "The Adoration of the Kings" (Caselli) .. 45 50

51. Old Wife.

1975. Fishes. Multicoloured.

452. ½ c. Type **51** 5 5
453. 1 c. Cola 5 5
454. 2 c. Billfish 5 5
455. 3 c. Vayway 5 5
456. 20 c. Bechine 10 12
457. $2 Grouper 85 90

52. "Myscelia antholia".

1975. Dominican Butterflies. Multicoloured.

459. ½ c. Type **52** 5 5
460. 1 c. "Lycorea ceres" .. 5 5
461. 2 c. "Siderone nemesis" .. 5 5
462. 6 c. "Battus polydamus" 5 5
463. 30 c. "Anartia lytrea" .. 15 20
464. 40 c. "Morpho peleides" 20 25
465. $2 "Dryas julia" .. 85 90

53. R.M.S. "Yare".

1975. "Ships tied to Dominicas' History". Multicoloured.

467.	½ c. Type **53**	5	5
468.	1 c. R.M.S. "Thames" ..	5	5
469.	2 c. S.S. "Lady Nelson" ..	5	5
470.	20 c. S.S. "Lady Rodney"	10	12
471.	45 c. M.V. "Statesman" ..	25	30
472.	50 c. M.V. "Geestecape"	25	30
473.	$2 M.V. "Geestestar" ..	85	90

54. "Women in Agriculture".

1975. International Women's Year. Mult.

475.	10 c. Type **54**	5	5
476.	$2 "Women in Industry and Commerce" ..	85	95

55. Miss Caribbean Queen, 1975.

1975. National Day. Multicoloured.

477.	5 c. Type **55**	5	5
478.	10 c. Public Library (horiz.)	5	5
479.	30 c. Citrus Factory (horiz.)	12	15
480.	$1 National Day Trophy ..	40	45

56. "Virgin and Child" (Mantegna).

1975. Christmas. "Virgin and Child" paintings by Artists named. Mult.

482.	½ c. Type **56**	5	5
483.	1 c. Fra Filippo Lippi ..	5	5
484.	2 c. Bellini	5	5
485.	10 c. Botticelli	5	5
486.	25 c. Bellini	12	12
487.	45 c. Correggio	20	25
488.	$1 Durer	40	45

57. Hibiscus.

1975. Multicoloured.

490.	½ c. Type **57**	5	5
491.	1 c. African Tulip	5	5
492.	2 c. Castor Oil Tree ..	5	5
493.	3 c. White Cedar Flower ..	5	5
494.	4 c. Egg Plant	5	5
495.	5 c. Gare	5	5
496.	6 c. Ochro	5	5
497.	8 c. Mountain Dove ..	5	5
498.	10 c. Screw Pine	5	5
499.	20 c. Mango Longue ..	8	8
500.	25 c. Crayfish	10	10
501.	30 c. Manicou	10	12
502.	40 c. Bay Leaf Groves ..	12	15
503.	50 c. Tomatoes	20	20
504.	$1 Lime Factory	35	40
505.	$2 Rum Distillery ..	70	80
506.	$5 Bay Oil Distillery ..	1·75	2·00
507.	$10 Queen Elizabeth II ..	3·50	4·00

Nos. 502/7 are larger, 44×28 mm.

58. American Infantry.

1976. American Revolution. Bicent. Multicoloured.

508.	½ c. Type **58**	5	5
509.	1 c. English three-decker, 1782	5	5
510.	2 c. George Washington ..	5	5
511.	45 c. British sailors ..	20	20
512.	75 c. British ensign ..	30	35
513.	$2 Admiral Hood ..	80	90

59. Rowing.

1976. Olympic Games, Montreal. Multicoloured.

515.	½ c. Type **59**	5	5
516	1 c. Shot putting	5	5
517.	2 c. Swimming	5	5
518.	40 c. Relay	15	20
519.	45 c. Gymnastics	20	20
520.	60 c. Sailing	25	30
521.	$2 Archery	80	90

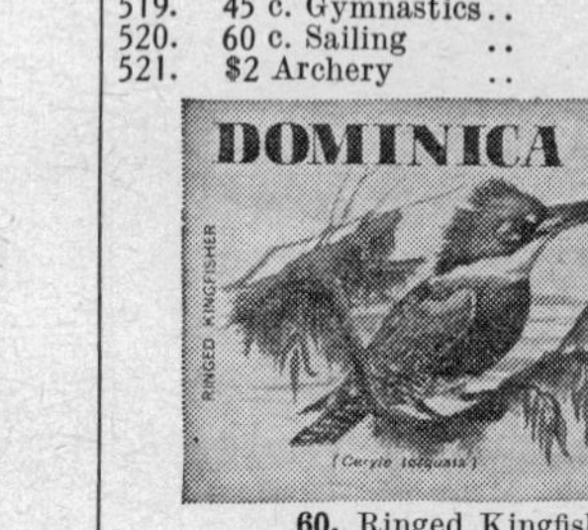

60. Ringed Kingfisher.

1976. Wild Birds. Multicoloured.

523.	½ c. Type **60**	5	5
524.	1 c. Mourning Dove ..	5	5
525.	2 c. Green Heron	5	5
526.	15 c. Blue-winged Hawk ..	5	8
527.	30 c. Blue-headed Hummingbird ..	12	15
528.	45 c. Bananaquit	20	20
529.	$2 Imperial Parrot ..	80	90

1976. West Indian Victory in World Cricket Cup. As Nos. 559/60 of Barbados.

531.	15 c. Map of the Caribbean	5	8
532.	25 c. Prudential Cup ..	10	12

61. Viking Spacecraft System.

1976. Viking Space Mission. Multicoloured.

533.	½ c. Type **61**	5	5
534.	1 c. Launching pad ..	5	5
535.	2 c. Titan IIID and Centaur DII	5	5
536.	3 c. Obriter and lander capsule	5	5
537.	45 c. Capulse, parachute unopened	20	20
538.	75 c. Capsule, parachute opened	30	35
539.	$1 Lander descending ..	40	45
540.	$2 Space vehicle on Mars	80	90

62. "Virgin and Child" (Giorgione).

1976. Christmas. "Virgin and Child" paintings by artists named. Multicoloured.

542.	½ c. Type **62**	5	5
543.	1 c. Bellini	5	5
544.	2 c. Mantegna	5	5
545.	6 c. Mantegna (different) ..	5	5
546.	25 c. Memling	10	12
547.	45 c. Corregio	20	25
548.	$3 Raphael	1·25	1·40

DOMINICAN REPUBLIC O2

The Eastern portion of the island of San Domingo in the W. Indies finally became independent of Spain in 1865.

1865. 8 reales = 1 peso.
1880. 100 centavos = 1 peso.
1883. 100 centimos = 1 franco.
1885. 100 centavos = 1 peso.

1.

2.

1865. Imperf.

1.	1.	½ r. black on rose ..	70·00	65·00
3.		½ r. black on green ..	£100	£100
2.		1 r. black on green ..	£180	£170
4.		1 r. black on yellow ..	£325	£275

1865. Imperf.

5.	2.	½ r. black on buff ..	35·00	30·00
7.		½ r. black on rose ..	10·00	10·00
12.		½ r. black on grey ..	30·00	30·00
18.		½ r. black & blue on rose	12·00	12·00
19.		½ r. black on yellow ..	6·00	6·00
20.		1 r. black on green ..	13·00	13·00
9.		1 r. black on blue ..	9·00	9·00
15.		1 r. black on flesh ..	25·00	25·00
21.		1 r. black on lilac ..	5·50	5·50

3.

4.

5.

1879. Perf.

22.	3.	½ r. violet	45	45
24.		1 r. red	45	45

1880. Rouletted.

35.	4.	1 c. green	20	20
36.		2 c. red	20	20
28.		5 c. blue	25	20
38.		10 c. pink	20	20
39.		20 c. bistre	25	25
40.		25 c. mauve	35	30
32.		50 c. orange	40	30
33.		75 c. blue	75	75
34.		1 p. gold	1·10	1·10

1883. Surch.

44.	4.	5 c. on 1 c. green ..	35	30
73.		10 c. on 2 c. red	50	50
46.		25 c. on 5 c. blue	1·00	90
47.		50 c. on 10 c. pink ..	3·25	1·90
58.		1 f. on 20 c. bistre ..	2·00	2·00
51.		1 f. 25 on 25 c. mauve ..	3·00	3·00
52.		2 f. 50 c. on 50 c. orange ..	3·00	3·00
53.		3 f. 75 c. on 75 c. blue ..	4·00	4·00
64.		5 f. on 1 p. gold	25·00	25·00

1885. Figures in lower corner only.

77.	5.	1 c. green	15	12
78.		2 c. red	15	12
79.		5 c. blue	20	12
80.		10 c. orange	30	15
81.		20 c. brown	45	25
82.		50 c. violet	1·25	1·00
83.		1 p. red	3·00	2·50
84.		2 p. brown	3·50	3·25

1895. As T **5** but figures in four corners.

85.		1 c. green	25	20
86.		2 c. red	25	20
87.		5 c. blue	25	20
88.		10 c. orange	25	25

6. Voyage of Mendez from Jamaica to Santo Domingo.

7. Sarcophagus of Columbus with Date of Discovery.

1899. Columbus Mausoleum Fund.

98.	7.	½ c. black	25	25
99.	–	½ c. black	25	25
89.	6.	1 c. purple	1·25	1·25
90.		1 c. green	30	25
91.	–	2 c. red	30	30
92.	7.	5 c. blue	40	30
93.	–	10 c. orange	75	45
94.	–	20 c. brown	1·10	1·10
95.	–	50 c. green	1·10	1·10
96.	–	1 p. black on blue ..	3·50	3·00
97.	–	2 p. brown on cream ..	6·00	6·00

DESIGNS—As T **6**: ½ c. (No. 99), 1 p. Columbus at Salamanca assembly. 2 c. Enriquillo's rebellion. 20 c. Toscanelli replying to Columbus. 50 c. Las Casas defending Indians. As T 7: 10 c. Hispaniola guarding remains of Columbus. 2 p. Columbus Mausoleum, Santo Domingo Cathedral.

8. Island of Hispaniola.

9.

1900.

100.	8.	½ c. blue	30	25
101.		½ c. rose	30	20
102.		1 c. olive	30	20
103.		2 c. green	30	20
104.		5 c. brown	30	20
105.		10 c. orange	30	20
106.		20 c. purple	85	85
107.		50 c. black	75	70
108.		1 p. brown	75	70

1901.

109.	9.	½ c. lilac and red ..	12	12
110.		1 c. lilac and olive ..	15	10
111.		2 c. lilac and green ..	20	10
112.		5 c. lilac and brown ..	20	12
113.		10 c. lilac and orange ..	20	15
114.		20 c. lilac and chocolate	45	30
115.		50 c. lilac and black ..	1·10	85
116.		1 p. lilac and brown ..	2·50	2·25

10. Sanchez.

11. Fortress of Santo Domingo.

1902. Santo Domingo. 400th Anniv.

125.	10.	1 c. blk. & grn. ..	15	15
126.		2 c. blk. & red (Duarte)	15	15
127.		5 c. blk. & blue (Duarte)	15	15
128.		10 c. blk. & or. (Sanchez)	15	15
129.		12 c. blk. & violet (Mella)	15	15
130.		20 c. black & rose (Mella)	15	15
131.	11.	50 c. black and brown ..	20	20

1904. Surch. with new value.

132.	9.	2 c. on 50 c. lilac & black	1·90	1·25
133.		2 c. on 1 p. lilac & brown	2·10	1·90
134.		5 c. on 50 c. lilac & black	55	55
135.		5 c. on 1 p. lilac and brown	75	75
136.		10 c. on 50 c. lilac & black	1·25	1·25
137.		10 c. on 1 p. lilac & brown	1·25	1·25

1904. Official stamps optd. **16 de Agosto 1904** or surch. with figure **1** also.

138.	O 1.	1 c. on 20 c. blk. & yell	75	75
139.		2 c. black and red ..	1·00	1·00
140.		5 c. black and blue ..	75	75
141.		10 c. black and green	85	85

1904. Postage Due stamps optd. **REPUBLICA DOMINICANA CENTAVOS CORREOS** or surch. with figure **1** also.

142.	D 1.	1 c. on 2 c. sepia ..	40	25
143.		1 c. on 4 c. sepia ..	15	15
145.		2 c. sepia	15	10

1905. Surch. **1905.** and new value.

146.	5.	2 c. on 20 c. brown ..	1·00	1·00
147.		5 c. on 20 c. brown ..	60	50
148.		10 c. on 20 c. brown ..	1·00	1·00

1905.

149.	9.	½ c. orange and black ..	25	20
150.		1 c. blue and black ..	25	15
151.		2 c. mauve and black ..	25	12
152.		5 c. claret and black ..	35	20
153.		10 c. green and black ..	60	30
154.		20 c. olive and black ..	1·50	1·25
155.		50 c. brown and black ..	7·00	4·00
156.		1 p. grey and black ..	42·00	42·00

1906. Postage Due stamps surch. **REPUBLICA DOMINICANA** and new value.

157.	D 1.	1 c. on 4 c. sepia ..	25	15
158.		1 c. on 10 c. sepia ..	30	15
159.		2 c. on 5 c. sepia ..	30	15

1906.

168. 9. ½ c. black and green .. 10 8
169. 1 c. black and red .. 10 5
170. 2 c. black and brown .. 12 5
171. 5 c. black and blue .. 15 12
164. 10 c. black and purple .. 20 15
165. 20 c. black and olive .. 85 60
166. 50 c. black and brown .. 1·10 1·10
167. 1 p. black and violet .. 2·00 2·00

12. 13. J. P. Duarte.

1911. No. O 178 optd. **HABILITADO. 1911**
182. O 1. 2 c. black and red .. 40 20

1911

183. 12. ½ c. black and orange .. 8 5
184. 1 c. black and green .. 8 5
185. 2 c. black and red .. 8 5
186. 5 c. black and blue .. 12 8
187. 10 c. black and purple .. 30 15
188. 20 c. black and olive .. 1·75 1·25
189. 50 c. black and brown .. 70 70
190. 1 p. black and violet .. 1·10 1·00

For stamps in other colours see Nos. 235/8 and for stamps in similar type see No. 240/6.

1914. Duarte. Birth Cent. Background in red, white and blue.

195. 13. ½ c. black and orange .. 15 15
196. 1 c. black and green .. 15 15
197. 2 c. black and red .. 15 15
198. 5 c. black and grey .. 15 15
199. 10 c. black and mauve .. 25 25
200. 20 c. black and olive .. 40 40
201. 50 c. black and brown .. 70 70
202. 1 p. black and lilac .. 1·10 1·10

1915. Nos. O 177/181 optd. **Habilitado 1915** or surch. **MEDIO CENTAVO** also.

203. O 1. ½ c. on 20 c. blk. & yell. 20 15
204. 1 c. black and green .. 20 15
205. 2 c. black and red .. 20 15
206. 5 c. black and blue .. 20 15
207. 10 c. black and green .. 65 65
208. 20 c. black and yellow 1·75 1·60

1915. Optd. **1915.**

209. 12. ½ c. black and mauve .. 15 10
210. 1 c. black and brown .. 12 5
211. 2 c. black and olive .. 40 12
213. 5 c. black and claret .. 40 8
214. 10 c. black and blue .. 50 20
215. 20 c. black and red .. 1·40 50
216. 50 c. black and green .. 1·75 1·00
217. 1 p. black and orange .. 3·00 1·25

1916. Optd. **1916.**

218. 12. ½ c. black and mauve .. 10 8
219. 1 c. black and green .. 30 8

1917. Optd. **1917.**

220. 12. ½ c. black and mauve .. 30 8
221. 1 c. black and green .. 30 5
222. 2 c. black and olive .. 20 5
223. 5 c. black and claret .. 2·25 25

1919. Optd. **1919.**

224. 12. 2 c. black and olive .. 1·25 5

1920. Optd. **1920.**

225. 12. ½ c. black and mauve .. 15 5
226. 1 c. black and green .. 10 5
227. 2 c. black and olive .. 10 5
228. 5 c. black and claret .. 1·25 10
229. 10 c. black and blue .. 60 8
230. 20 c. black and red .. 1·10 20
231. 50 c. black and green .. 10·00 3·00

1921. Optd. **1921.**

233. 12. 1 c. black and green .. 35 10
234. 2 c. black and olive .. 65 12

1922.

235. 12. ½ c. black and claret .. 8 5
236. 1 c. green 10 5
237. 2 c. red 35 5
238. 5 c. blue 70 10

14. 15. Exhibition Pavilion.

1924. Straight top to shield.

240. 14. 1 c. green 10 5
241. 2 c. red 15 5
242. 5 c. blue 15 5
244. 10 c. black and blue .. 3·00 20
245. 50 c. black and green .. 8·00 6·00
246. 1 p. black and orange .. 2·00 1·25

1927. National and West Indian Exn. Santiago.

248. 15. 2 c. red 35 15
249. 5 c. blue 40 15

16. Air Mail Routes.

1928. Air.

256. 16. 10 c. deep blue .. .. 2·00 1·50
280. 10 c. pale blue 75 50
271. 10 c. yellow .. .. 1·60 1·40
272. 15 c. red .. .. 3·00 2·00
281. 15 c. blue-green .. 1·75 60
273. 20 c. green .. .. 1·50 25
282. 20 c. chestnut .. .. 1·75 25
274. 30 c. violet .. .. 3·00 2·00
283. 30 c. brown .. .. 2·25 65

17. Ruins of Fortress of Columbus. 18. Horacio Vasquez.

1928.

258. 17. ½ c. claret 8 8
259. 1 c. green 12 8
260. 2 c. red 15 8
261. 5 c. blue 40 12
262. 10 c. blue 35 12
263. 20 c. red 60 15
264. 50 c. green .. .. 2·50 1·50
265. 1 p. yellow .. .. 5·00 4·00

1929. Frontier Agreement with Haiti.

266. 18. ½ c. claret 15 10
267. 1 c. green 15 10
268. 2 c. red 20 10
269. 5 c. blue 30 15
270. 10 c. blue 50 15

19. Jesuit Convent of San Ignacio de Loyola. 20. After the Hurricane.

1930.

275. 19. ½ c. red-brown 15 10
276. 1 c. green 15 10
277. 2 c. red 20 10
278. 5 c. blue 35 15
279. 10 c. blue 80 30

1930. Hurricane Relief.

284. – 1 c. green and red .. 8 12
285. – 2 c. red 10 15
286. 20. 5 c. blue and red .. 15 25
287. 10 c. yellow and red .. 20 30

DESIGN: 1 c., 2 c. Riverside.

1931. Air. Hurricane Relief. Surch. **HABILITADO PARA CORREO AEREO** premium and aeroplane. Imperf. or perf.

288. 20. 5 c. + 5 c. blue and red 3·00 3·00
289. 5 c. + 5 c. black and red 6·00 3·75
290. 10 c. + 10 c. yellow & red 3·00 3·00
291. 10 c. + 10 c. black & red 6·00 6·00

21. Cathedral of Santo Domingo.

1931.

294. 21. 1 c. green 25 8
295. 2 c. red 25 8
296. 3 c. purple 30 8
297. 7 c. blue 50 8
298. 8 c. brown 80 30
299. 10 c. blue .. .. 1·25 35

22. Sun Dial, 1754.

1931. Air.

300. 22 10 c. red .. .. 1·75 25
301. 10 c. blue 90 25
302. 10 c. green .. .. 3·00 1·00
303. 15 c. mauve .. .. 1·50 30
304. 20 c. blue .. .. 3·00 65
306. 30 c. green .. .. 1·40 25
307. 50 c. brown .. .. 3·00 45
308. 1 p. orange .. .. 5·00 1·40

23. Fort Ozama.

ILLUSTRATIONS
British Commonwealth and all overprints and surcharges are FULL SIZE. Foreign Countries have been reduced to ¾-LINEAR

1932.

309. 23. 1 c. green 15 8
310. 1 c. green 20 5
311. 3 c. violet 25 5

No. 310 is inscribed "CORREOS".

1932. Red Cross stamps inscr. "CRUZ ROJA DOMINICANA", with cross in red and optd. **HABILITADO Dic. 20-1932 En. 5-1933 CORREOS** or surch. also.

312. 1 c. green 20 12
313. 3 c. on 2 c. violet .. 30 15
314. 5 c. blue 35 30
315. 7 c. on 10 c. blue .. 75 50

24. F. A. de Merino. 25. Cathedral of Santo Domingo.

1933. F. A. de Merino. Birth Cent.

316. – ½ c. violet 15 12
317. 24. 1 c. green 20 10
318. – 2 c. red 30 25
319. 24. 3 c. violet 25 12
320. – 5 c. blue 30 12
321. – 7 c. blue 50 20
322. 8 c. green 50 30
323. 24. 10 c. orange 50 15
324. – 20 c. red 85 50
325. 25. 50 c. olive .. .. 2·50 1·75
326. 1 p. sepia .. .. 7·00 4·50

DESIGNS—VERT. ½ c., 5 c., 8 c. Merino's Tomb. 2 c., 7 c., 30 c. Merino in uniform.

1933. Portraits as T 24.

327. 1 c. black and green .. 30 15
328. 3 c. black and violet .. 35 12
329. 7 c. black and ultram. .. 80 30

DESIGNS: 1 c., 7 c. Pres. Trujillo in uniform. 3 c. Pres. Trujillo in evening dress.

1933. Air. Optd. **CORREO AEREO INTERNO.**

330. 21. 2 c. red 15 10

28. Fort Ozama.

1933. Air.

331. 28. 10 c. blue .. .. 1·60 30

29. San Rafael Suspension Bridge.

1934.

332. 29. ½ c. mauve 25 10
333. 1 c. green 35 10
334. 3 c. violet 40 10

30. Trujillo Bridge.

1934. (a) Postage. As T 30 but without aeroplane, inscr. "CORREOS".

335. ½ c. brown 25 8
336. 1 c. green 35 5
337. 3 c. violet 45 5

(b) Air.

338. 30. 10 c. blue .. .. 1·60 30

32. National Palace.

1935. For obligatory use on mail addressed to the President.

339. 32. 25 c. orange .. .. 1·25 10

1935. Opening of Ramfis Bridge. As T 30 but view of Ramfis Suspension Bridge.

340. 1 c. green 15 5
341. 3 c. brown 20 5
342. 5 c. purple 45 20
343. 10 c. pink 80 35

33. Aeroplane and Carrier Pigeon.

1935. Air.

344. 33. 10 c. light blue and blue 1·00 1·25

34. President Trujillo.

1935. Frontier Agreement.

352. 34. 3 c. brown and yellow .. 15 10
353. – 5 c. brown and orange .. 15 5
354. – 7 c. brown and blue .. 30 5
355. – 10 c. brown and purple .. 40 8

RECTANGULAR DESIGNS: Portrait as T 34. Red, white and blue ribbons in side panels on 7 c. or diagonally across 5 c. and 10 c.

36. Post Office, Santiago de los Caballeros.

1936.

356. 36. ½ c. violet 20 8
357. 1 c. green 20 5

37.

1936. Air.

358. 37. 10 c. blue .. 1·25 25

38. George Washington Avenue. Ciudad Trujillo.

1936. Dedication of George Washington Av.

359. 38. ½ c. brown 20 15
360. 2 c. brown and red .. 20 10
361. 3 c. brown and yellow .. 35 12
362. 7 c. brown and blue .. 45 25

39. Gen. A. Duverge. 40. "Flight".

1936. National Archives and Library Fund. Inscr. "PRO ARCHIVO Y BIBLIOTECA NACIONALES".

363. – ½ c. lilac 10 5
364. – 1 c. green 10 5
365. – 2 c. red 10 8
366. – 3 c. violet 12 5
367. – 5 c. blue 15 12
368. 39. 7 c. blue 35 15
369. – 10 c. orange 40 25
370. – 20 c. olive .. .. 1·25 70
371. – 25 c. purple 80 65
372. – 30 c. red .. .. 1·50 1·10
373. – 50 c. brown .. .. 2·00 1·40
374. – 1 p. black .. .. 2·75 2·50
375. – 2 p. brown .. .. 8·00 7·00

DESIGNS—As T 39: ½ c. J. N. de Caceres. 1 c. Grn. G. Luperon. 2 c. E. Tejera. 3 c. Pres. Trujillo. 5 c. Jose Reyes. 10 c. Felix M. Del Monte. 25 c. F. J. Peynado. 30 c. Salome Urena. 50 c. Gen. Jose Ma. Cabral. 1 p. Manuel Js. Galvan. 2 p. Gaston F. Deligne TRIANGULAR: 20 c. National Library.

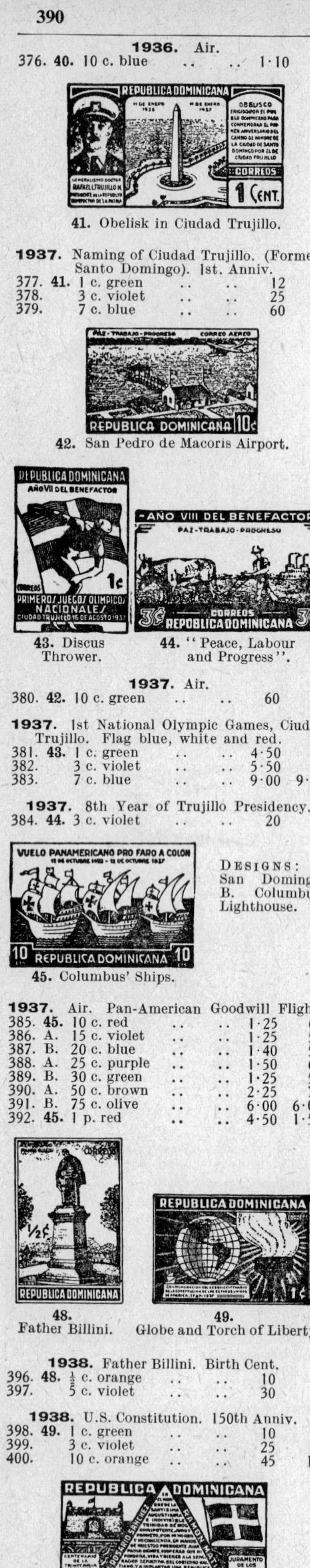

1936. Air.
376. **40.** 10 c. blue .. .. 1·10 20

41. Obelisk in Ciudad Trujillo.

1937. Naming of Ciudad Trujillo. (Formerly Santo Domingo). 1st. Anniv.
377. **41.** 1 c. green 12 5
378. 3 c. violet 25 10
379. 7 c. blue 60 15

42. San Pedro de Macoris Airport.

43. Discus Thrower. **44.** "Peace, Labour and Progress".

1937. Air.
380. **42.** 10 c. green 60 10

1937. 1st National Olympic Games, Ciudad Trujillo. Flag blue, white and red.
381. **43.** 1 c. green .. .. 4·50 35
382. 3 c. violet .. .. 5·50 70
383. 7 c. blue .. .. 9·00 9·60

1937. 8th Year of Trujillo Presidency.
384. **44.** 3 c. violet 20 8

DESIGNS: A. San Domingo. B. Columbus' Lighthouse.

45. Columbus' Ships.

1937. Air. Pan-American Goodwill Flight.
385. **45.** 10 c. red .. .. 1·25 65
386. A. 15 c. violet .. .. 1·25 50
387. B. 20 c. blue .. .. 1·40 50
388. A. 25 c. purple .. .. 1·50 65
389. B. 30 c. green .. .. 1·25 50
390. A. 50 c. brown .. .. 2·25 75
391. B. 75 c. olive .. .. 6·00 6·00
392. **45.** 1 p. red .. .. 4·50 1·50

48. Father Billini. **49.** Globe and Torch of Liberty.

1938. Father Billini. Birth Cent.
396. **48.** ½ c. orange 10 5
397. 5 c. violet 30 8

1938. U.S. Constitution. 150th Anniv.
398. **49.** 1 c. green 10 5
399. 3 c. violet 25 5
400. 10 c. orange 45 15

50. Bastion, Oath and Flag.

1938. Trinitarian Rebellion. Cent.
401. **50.** 1 c. green 20 15
402. 3 c. violet 30 15
403. 10 c. orange 55 25

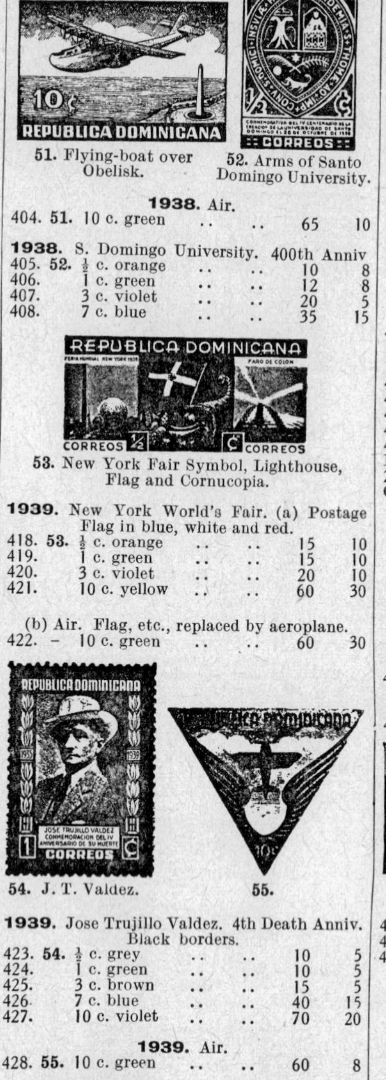

51. Flying-boat over Obelisk. **52.** Arms of Santo Domingo University.

1938. Air.
404. **51.** 10 c. green 65 10

1938. S. Domingo University. 400th Anniv
405. **52.** ½ c. orange 10 8
406. 1 c. green 12 8
407. 3 c. violet 20 5
408. 7 c. blue 35 15

53. New York Fair Symbol, Lighthouse, Flag and Cornucopia.

1939. New York World's Fair. (a) Postage Flag in blue, white and red.
418. **53.** ½ c. orange 15 10
419. 1 c. green 15 10
420. 3 c. violet 20 10
421. 10 c. yellow 60 30

(b) Air. Flag, etc., replaced by aeroplane.
422. – 10 c. green 60 30

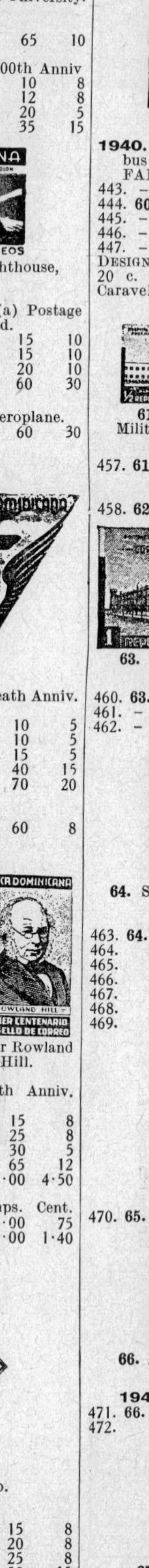

54. J. T. Valdez. **55.**

1939. Jose Trujillo Valdez. 4th Death Anniv. Black borders.
423. **54.** ½ c. grey 10 5
424. 1 c. green 10 5
425. 3 c. brown 15 5
426. 7 c. blue 40 15
427. 10 c. violet 70 20

1939. Air.
428. **55.** 10 c. green 60 8

56. Western Hemisphere and Union Flags. **57.** Sir Rowland Hill.

1940. Pan-American Union. 50th Anniv. Flags in national colours.
429. **56.** 1 c. green 15 8
430. 2 c. red 25 8
431. 3 c. violet 30 5
432. 10 c. orange 65 12
433. 1 p. brown .. .. 7·00 4·50

1940. 1st Adhesive Postage Stamps. Cent.
434. **57.** 3 c. mauve .. .. 5·00 75
435. 7 c. blue .. .. 9·00 1·40

58. Julia Molina de Trujillo.

1940. Mother's Day.
436. **58.** 1 c. green 15 8
437. 2 c. red 20 8
438. 3 c. orange 25 8
439. 7 c. blue 50 15

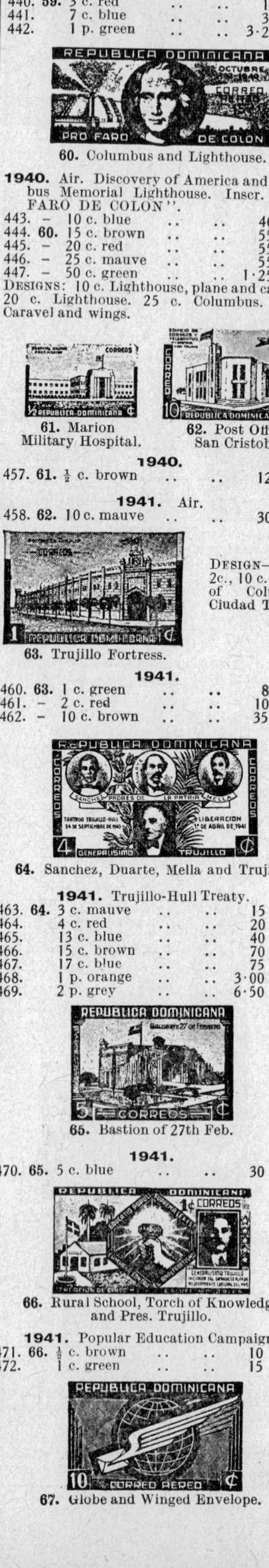

59. Central America and Arms.

1940. 2nd Caribbean Conf., Trujillo City.
440. **59.** 3 c. red 15 8
441. 7 c. blue 30 12
442. 1 p. green .. .. 3·25 2·10

60. Columbus and Lighthouse.

1940. Air. Discovery of America and Columbus Memorial Lighthouse. Inscr. "PRO FARO DE COLON".
443. – 10 c. blue 40 30
444. **60.** 15 c. brown 55 45
445. – 20 c. red 55 45
446. – 25 c. mauve 55 25
447. – 50 c. green .. .. 1·25 90

DESIGNS: 10 c. Lighthouse, plane and caravels. 20 c. Lighthouse. 25 c. Columbus. 50 c. Caravel and wings.

61. Marion Military Hospital. **62.** Post Office, San Cristobal.

1940.
457. **61.** ½ c. brown 12 10

1941. Air.
458. **62.** 10 c. mauve 30 12

DESIGN—VERT. 2c., 10 c. Statue of Columbus, Ciudad Trujillo.

63. Trujillo Fortress.

1941.
460. **63.** 1 c. green 8 5
461. – 2 c. red 10 5
462. – 10 c. brown 35 8

64. Sanchez, Duarte, Mella and Trujillo.

1941. Trujillo-Hull Treaty.
463. **64.** 3 c. mauve 15 8
464. 4 c. red 20 8
465. 13 c. blue 40 12
466. 15 c. brown 70 30
467. 17 c. blue 75 40
468. 1 p. orange .. .. 3·00 1·60
469. 2 p. grey .. .. 6·50 3·00

65. Bastion of 27th Feb.

1941.
470. **65.** 5 c. blue 30 15

66. Rural School, Torch of Knowledge and Pres. Trujillo.

1941. Popular Education Campaign.
471. **66.** ½ c. brown 10 5
472. 1 c. green 15 5

67. Globe and Winged Envelope.

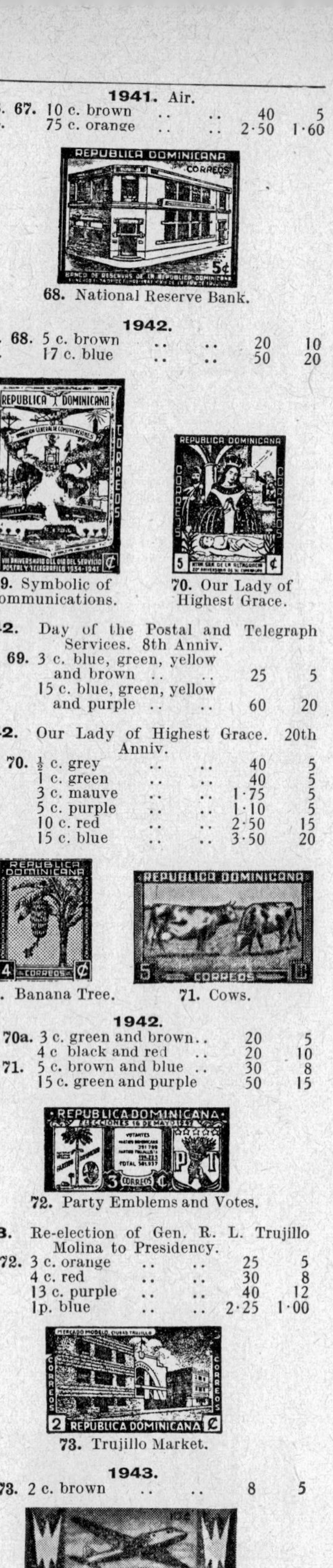

1941. Air.
473. **67.** 10 c. brown 40 5
474. 75 c. orange .. .. 2·50 1·60

68. National Reserve Bank.

1942.
475. **68.** 5 c. brown 20 10
476. 17 c. blue 50 20

69. Symbolic of Communications. **70.** Our Lady of Highest Grace.

1942. Day of the Postal and Telegraph Services. 8th Anniv.
477. **69.** 3 c. blue, green, yellow and brown .. 25 5
478. 15 c. blue, green, yellow and purple .. 60 20

1942. Our Lady of Highest Grace. 20th Anniv.
479. **70.** ½ c. grey 40 5
480. 1 c. green 40 5
481. 3 c. mauve .. .. 1·75 5
482. 5 c. purple .. .. 1·10 5
483. 10 c. red .. .. 2·50 15
484. 15 c. blue .. .. 3·50 20

70a. Banana Tree. **71.** Cows.

1942.
494. **70a.** 3 c. green and brown.. 20 5
495. 4 c. black and red .. 20 10
496. **71.** 5 c. brown and blue .. 30 8
497. 15 c. green and purple 50 15

72. Party Emblems and Votes.

1943. Re-election of Gen. R. L. Trujillo Molina to Presidency.
498. **72.** 3 c. orange 25 5
499. 4 c. red 30 8
500. 13 c. purple 40 12
501. 1p. blue .. .. 2·25 1·00

73. Trujillo Market.

1943.
502. **73.** 2 c. brown 8 5

74. Mail plane.

1943. Air.
503. **74.** 10 c. mauve 30 5
504. 20 c. blue 35 10
505. 25 c. olive .. .. 3·00 1·75

75. Bastion of 27 Feb. **76.** Monument and Dates.

1944. Independence Cent. (a) Postage. Flag in blue and red.

506. 75. ½ c. ochre 5 5
507. 1 c. green 5 5
508. 2 c. red 8 5
509. 3 c. purple 10 5
510. 5 c. orange 12 5
511. 7 c. blue 15 12
512. 10 c. brown 25 12
513. 20 c. olive 45 25
514. 50 c. blue .. .. 1·10 75

(b) Air. Flag in grey, blue and red.

515. 76. 10 c. yellow, grey, brown blue and violet .. 25 5
516. 20 c. yellow, grey, brown, blue and red 40 10
517. 1 p. yellow, grey, brown, blue and green .. 1·60 1·10

77. Dr. Martos Sanatorium.

78. Nurse and Battlefield.

1944. Tuberculosis Relief Fund.

518. 77. 1 c. blue and red .. 8 5

1944. International Red Cross. 80th Anniv.

519. 78. 1 c. green, red and yellow 10 5
520. 2 c. brown, red and yellow 15 8
521. 3 c. blue, red and yellow 15 5
522. 10 c. red and yellow .. 35 10

79. Communications Building, Ciudad Trujillo.

1944. Air.

523. 79. 9 c. blue and green .. 15 5
524. 13 c. red and brown .. 20 5
525. 25 c. red and orange .. 40 8
526. 30 c. blue and black .. 65 50

80. Municipal Palace, San Cristobal.

81. Emblem of Communications.

1945. 1st Constitution of Dominican Republic Cent.

527. 80. ½ c. blue 5 5
528. 1 c. green 8 5
529. 2 c. orange 8 5
530. 3 c. brown 10 5
531. 10 c. blue 30 15

1945. Centres in blue and red.

532. 81. 3 c. orange (postage) .. 8 5
533. 20 c. green 50 12
534. 50 c. blue .. .. 1·00 30

535. 7 c. green (air) 15 15
536. 12 c. orange 20 12
537. 13 c. blue 20 8
538. 25 c. brown 45 12

82. Flags and National Anthem.

83. Law Courts, Ciudad Trujillo.

1946. Air. National Anthem.

540. 82. 10 c. red 30 20
541. 15 c. blue 45 40
542. 20 c. brown 60 40
543. 35 c. orange 80 35
544. – 1 p. green .. .. 7·00 6·00

DESIGN: 1 p. As T 82, but horiz.

1946.

545. 83. 3 c. brown and buff .. 10 5

84. Caribbean Air Routes.

1946. Santo Domingo. 450th Anniv.

546. 84. 10 c. multicoloured (post.) 25 10
547. 10 c. multicoloured (air) 25 8
548. 13 c. multicoloured .. 40 10

85. Jimenoa Waterfall.

ILLUSTRATIONS
British Commonwealth and all overprints and surcharges are FULL SIZE. Foreign Countries have been reduced to ¾-LINEAR.

1947. Centres multicoloured, frame colours given.

549. 85. 1 c. green (postage) .. 8 5
550. 2 c. red 8 5
551. 3 c. blue 10 5
552. 13 c. purple 25 15
553. 20 c. brown 40 12
554. 50 c. yellow .. .. 1·00 50

555. 18 c. blue (air) 35 30
556. 23 c. red 40 40
557. 50 c. violet 60 35
558. 75 c. brown 80 60

86. Nurse and Child.

87. State Building, Ciudad Trujillo.

1947. Tuberculosis Relief Fund.

559. 86. 1 c. blue and red .. 8 5

1948.

560. 87. 1 c. green (postage) .. 5 5
561. 3 c. blue 8 5

562. 37 c. brown (air) .. 50 40
563. 1 p. orange .. .. 1·50 1·00

88. Ruins of San Francisco Church, Ciudad Trujillo.

89. El Santo Socorro Sanatorium.

1949.

564. 88. 1 c. green (postage) .. 8 5
565. 3 c. blue 8 5

566. 7 c. olive (air) 10 8
567. 10 c. brown 12 5
568. 15 c. red 35 15
569. 20 c. green 50 35

1949. Tuberculosis Relief Fund.

570. 89. 1 c. blue and red .. 8 5

90. General Pedro Santana.

91. Monument.

1949. Battle of Las Carreras. Cent.

571. 90. 3 c. blue (postage) .. 10 5
572. 91. 10 c. red (air) 15 5

92. Bird and Globe.

94. Hotel Jimani.

93. Youth Holding Banner.

95. St. Nicholas of Bari Church.

1949. 75th Anniv. of U.P.U.

573. 92. 1 c. brown and green .. 8 5
574. 2 c. brown and yellow 10 5
575. 5 c. brown and blue .. 15 5
576. 7 c. brown and blue .. 25 8

1950. Tuberculosis Relief Fund.

584. 93. 1 c. blue and red .. 8 5

1950. Various Hotels.

585. 94. ½ c. brown (postage) .. 5 5
586. – 1 c. green (Hamaca) .. 5 5
587. – 2 c. orange (Hamaca) 5 5
588. – 5 c. blue (Montana) .. 12 5
589. – 15 c. orge. (San Cristobal) 25 8
590. – 20 c. lilac (Maguana) .. 40 12
591. 94. $1 yellow and brown .. 1·75 75

592. – 12 c. bl. (Montana) (air) 15 5
593. – 37 c. red (San Cristobal) 1·10 65

1950. 13th Pan-American Sanitary Congress. Inscr. as T 95.

595. 95. 2 c. brown & grn. (post) 10 5
596. – 5 c. brown and blue .. 15 5

597. – 12 c. orange & brn. (air) 25 5

DESIGNS—VERT. 5 c. Medical school. 12 c. Map and aeroplane.

96.  96a.  96b.
"Suffer Little Children to Come Unto Me".

96c. "Suffer Little Children to Come Unto Me."

97. Isabella the Catholic.

1950. Child Welfare.

(a) Child at left with light hair.

598. 96. 1 c. pale light blue .. 12 5

(b) Child at left with dark hair.

599. 96. 1 c. pale light blue .. 20 5

(c) Child at left with dark hair.

627. 96a. 1 c. blue 12 5

(d) Child at left with light hair.

628. 96b. 1 c. blue 10 5

(e) Dark hair, smaller figures and square value tablet.

629. 96c. 1 c. blue 8 5

There are two versions of Nos. 628/9. See also Nos. 835 and 907.

1951. Isabella the Catholic. 500th Birth Anniv.

600. 97. 5 c. brown and blue .. 12 5

98. Santiago Tuberculosis Sanatorium.

1952. Tuberculosis Relief Fund.

601. 98. 1 c. blue and red .. 8 5

99. Dr. S. B. Gautier Hospital.

1952.

602. 99. 1 c. green (postage) .. 5 5
603. 2 c. red 5 5
604. 5 c. blue 12 5

605. 23 c. blue (air) .. 35 25
606. 29 c. red 75 60

100.

101. Columbus Lighthouse and Flags.

1952. Anti-Cancer Fund. No. 608 has "1 c" larger with line through "c" and no stop. No 609 is as 608 but with smaller "c".

607. 100. 1 c. red 8 5
608. 1 c. red 8 5
609. 1 c. red 8 5

See also Nos. 1029/30.

1952. Columbus's Discovery of Santo Domingo. 460th Anniv. (a) Postage

610. 101. 2 c. green 8 5
611. 5 c. blue 12 5
612. 10 c. red 20 8

(b) Air. Similar design inscr. "S./S.A.S./XMY", etc.

613. 12 c. brown 15 12
614. 14 c. blue 25 15
615. 20 c. sepia 30 15
616. 23 c. purple 40 25
617. 25 c. indigo 40 30
618. 29 c. green 50 35
619. 1 p. brown .. .. 1·50 1·25

DESIGN—Nos. 613/19: Aeroplane over Columbus Lighthouse.

101a. T.B. Children's Dispensary.

1953. Tuberculosis Relief Fund.

621. 101a. 1 c. blue and red .. 8 5

There are two versions of this design.

102. Treasury.

104. Jose Marti.

105. Monument to Trujillo Peace.

103. Rio Haina Sugar Factory.

1953.

622. 102. ½ c. brown 5 5
623. 2 c. blue 5 5
624. 103. 5 c. brn. and blue .. 10 5
625. 102. 15 c. orange 30 10

1953. Marti (Cuban revolutionary). Birth Cent.

626. 104. 10 c. sepia and blue .. 20 8

1954.

630. 105. 2 c. green 5 5
631. 7 c. blue 12 5
632. 20 c. orange 40 8

There are two versions of No. 631.

106.

107. Rotary Emblem.

1954. Air. Marian Year.
633. **106.** 8 c. purple 12 8
634. 11 c. blue 15 5
635. 33 c. orange .. 50 30

1955. Rotary International. 50th Anniv.
636. **107.** 7 c. blue (postage) .. 20 8
637. 11 c. red (air).. .. 20 10

108. Pres. R. Trujillo.

109.

110. Angelita Trujillo.

1955. 25th Year of Trujillo Era.
638. **108.** 2 c. vermilion (postage) 5 5
639. – 4 c. green 8 5
640. – 7 c. indigo 12 5
641. – 10 c. brown 20 8
642. – 11 c. red, yell. & bl. (air) 15 5
643. – 25 c. purple 30 15
644. – 33 c. brown 45 25
DESIGNS: 4 c. Pres. R. Trujillo in civilian clothes. 7 c. Equestrian statue. 10 c. Allegory of Prosperity. 11 c. National flags. 25 c. Pres. R. Trujillo in evening clothes. 33 c. Pres. R. Trujillo in uniform.

1955. Obligatory Tax. Tuberculosis Relief Fund.
645. **109.** 1 c. black, red & yellow 8 5

1955. Child Welfare.
654. **110.** 1 c. violet 10 5

111. Gen. R. Trujillo.

112. Angelita Trujillo.

1955. Peace and Brotherhood Fair, Ciudad Trujillo.
656. **111.** 7 c. maroon (postage) 12 5
657. 10 c. blue 20 8
655. **112.** 10 c. blue and ultram 25 8
658. **111.** 11 c. red (air).. .. 15 5

113. "B.C.G." = "Bacillus" Calmette-Guerin.

114. Punta Caucedo Airport.

1956. Obligatory Tax, Tuberculosis Relief Fund.
659. **113.** 1 c. multicoloured .. 8 5

1956. 3rd Caribbean Region Aerial Navigation Conf.
660. **114.** 1 c. brown (postage).. 5 5
661. 2 c. orange 8 5
662. 11 c. blue (air) .. 15 5

115. Cedar Tree.

116. Fanny Blankers-Koen and Dutch Flag.

1956. Re-afforestation. Inscr. "REPOBLACION FORESTAL".
664. **115.** 5 c. green, brown and red (postage) .. 12 5
665. – 6 c. green and purple.. 15 5
666. – 13 c. grn. & orge. (air) 25 10
DESIGNS: 6 c. Pine tree. 13 c. Mahogany tree.

1957. Olympic Games (1st issue). Famous Athletes. Flags in national colours.
667. **116.** 1 c. brn., pur., chestnut and blue (postage).. 5 5
668. – 2 c. sepia, purple & blue 5 5
669. – 3 c. purple and red .. 8 5
670. – 5 c. orge., pur. & blue.. 12 5
671. – 7 c. green and purple.. 15 10
673. – 11 c. blue and red (air) 20 15
674. – 16 c. red and green .. 25 25
675. – 17 c. black and purple 30 30
DESIGNS—(each with national flag of athlete): 2 c. Jesse Owens. 3 c. Kee Chung Sohn. 5 c. Lord Burghley. 7 c. Bob Mathias. 11 c. Paavo Nurmi. 16 c. Ugo Frigerio. 17 c. Mildred Didrickson.
See also Nos. 689/96, 713/21, 748/56 and 784/91.

117. Horse's Head and Globe.

118.

1957. 2nd Int. Livestock Fair, Ciudad Trujillo.
677. **117.** 7 c. blue, brown & red 15 8

1957. Hungarian Refugees Fund. Nos. 667/75 surch. with red cross in circle surrounded by **ASISTENCIA REFUGIADOS HUNGAROS 1957** and **+2c.**
678. 1 c.+2 c. (postage) .. 8 8
679. 2 c.+2 c. 8 8
680. 3 c.+2 c. 10 10
681. 5 c.+2 c. 15 15
682. 7 c.+2 c. 12 12
684. 11 c.+2 c. (air) .. 20 20
685. 16 c.+2 c. 25 25
686. 17 c.+2 c. 30 30

1956. Obligatory Tax. Tuberculosis Relief Fund.
688. **113.** 1 c. multicoloured .. 5 5

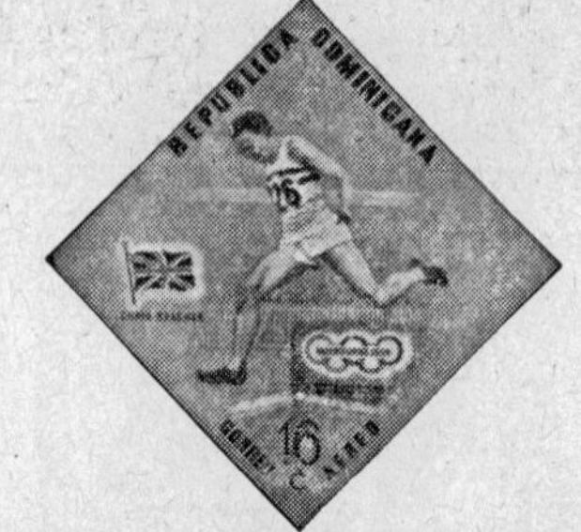

119. Chris Brasher and Union Jack (steeplechase).

1957. Olympic Games (2nd issue). Winning Athletes. Inscr. "MELBOURNE 1956". Flags in national colours.
689. – 1 c. brown & blue (post.) 5 5
690. – 2 c. vermilion and blue 5 5
691. – 3 c. blue 5 5
692. – 5 c. olive and blue .. 10 8
693. – 7 c. red and blue .. 20 12
694. – 11 c. grn. & blue (air) 15 12
695. **119.** 16 c. purple and blue 25 20
696. – 17 c. sepia and green 25 25
DESIGNS—(each with national flag of athlete): 1 c. Lars Hall (Sweden; pentathlon). 2 c. Betty Cuthbert (Australia; 100 and 200 metres). 3 c. Egil Danielson (Norway; javelin-throwing). 5 c. Alain Mimoum (France; marathon). 7 c. Norman Read (New Zealand; 50 km. walk). 11 c. Robert Morrow (U.S.A.; 100 and 200 metres). 17 c. A. Ferreira da Silva (Brazil; hop, step and jump).

1957. Boy Scout Movement 50th Anniv. and Lord Baden-Powell. Birth Cent. Nos. 689/96 surch. **CENTENARIO LORD BADEN-POWELL. 1857-1957+2 c.** surrounding scout badge.
699. 1 c.+2 c. brn. & blue (post.) 5 5
700. 2 c.+2 c. vermilion & blue 8 8
701. 3 c.+2 c. blue 8 8
702. 5 c.+2 c. olive and blue .. 10 10
703. 7 c.+2 c. red and blue .. 15 15
704. 11 c.+2 c. grn. & blue (air) 20 20
705. 16 c.+2 c. purple and blue 30 30
706. 17 c.+2 c. sepia and green 40 40

120. Mahogany Flower.

1957.
709. **120.** 2 c. claret and green.. 8 5
710. 4 c. red and mauve .. 8 5
711. 7 c. green and blue .. 12 5
712. 25 c. orange and brown 35 15

121. Gerald Ouellette and Canadian Flag (rifle-shooting).

1957. Olympic Games (3rd issue). More winning athletes. Flags in national colours.
713. **121.** 1 c. brown (postage).. 5 5
714. – 2 c. sepia 5 5
715. – 3 c. violet 5 5
716. – 5 c. orange 10 8
717. – 7 c. slate 12 12
719. – 11 c. blue (air) .. 15 15
720. – 16 c. red 20 20
721. – 17 c. purple 25 25
DESIGNS—(each with national flag of athlete): 2 c. Ron Delaney (Ireland; 1500 metres). 3 c. Tenley Albright (U.S.A.; figure-skating). 5 c. J. Capilla (Mexico; high-diving). 7 c. Ercole Baldini (Italy; cycle-racing). 11 c. Hans Winkler (Germany; horse-jumping). 16 c. Alfred Oerter (U.S.A.; discus-throwing). 17 c. Shirley Strickland (Australia; 80 metres hurdles). The designs of Nos. 714, 716 and 720 are arranged with the long side of the triangular format uppermost.

122.

123. Cervantes, Open Book, Marker and Globe.

1958. Tuberculosis Relief Fund.
723. **122.** 1 c. red and claret .. 5 5
See also No. 773.

1958. 4th Latin-American Book Fair.
724. **123.** 4 c. green 8 5
725. 7 c. mauve 10 5
726. 10 c. bistre 15 8

124. Gen. R. Trujillo and Arms of Republic.

125. S.S. "Rhadames".

1958. Gen. Trujillo's designation as "Benefactor of the Country". 25th Anniv.
743. **124.** 2 c. mauve and yellow 5 5
744. 4 c. green and yellow.. 8 5
745. 7 c. sepia and yellow.. 12 5

1958. Merchant Marine Day.
747. **125.** 7 c. blue 15 10

127.

126. Gillian Sheen and Union Jack (fencing). 128. Dominican Republic Pavilion.

1958. Olympic Games (4th issue). More winning athletes. Flags in national colours.
748. **126.** 1 c. slate, blue and rose (postage) 5 5
749. – 2 c. brown and blue .. 5 5
750. – 3 c. brown, black, violet and grey 10 10
751. – 5 c. brown, slate, red and lake 12 12
752. – 7 c. brn., bl., red & buff 15 15
754. – 11 c. sepia, olive and blue (air) 20 15
755. – 16 c. blue, orge. & grn. 30 25
756. – 17 c. blue, yell. & red 40 35
DESIGNS (each with national flag of athlete)—VERT. 2 c. Milton Campbell (U.S.A., decathlon). HORIZ. 3 c. Shozo Sasahara (Japan, feather-weight wrestling). 5 c. Madeleine Berthod (Switzerland, skiing). 7 c. Murray Rose (Australia, 400 m. and 1,500 m. free-style). 11 c. Charles Jenkins and Thomas Courtney (U.S.A., 400 m. and 800 m., and 1,600 m. relay). 16 c. Indian team in play (India, hockey). 17 c. Swedish yachts (Sweden, yachting).

1958. Inaug. of U.N.E.S.C.O. Headquarters Building, Paris.
758. **127.** 7 c. blue and red .. 12 8

1958. Brussels International Exhibition.
759. **128.** 7 c. green (postage).. 12 8
760. 9 c. grey (air).. .. 15 10
761. 25 c. violet 35 25

1959. I.G.Y. Nos. 748/56 surch. with globe and **ANO GEOFISICO INTERNACIONAL 1957-1958 + 2 c.**
763. 1 c.+2 c. (postage) .. 12 12
764. 2 c.+2 c. 20 20
765. 3 c.+2 c. 20 20
766. 5 c.+2 c. 30 30
767. 7 c.+2 c. 35 35
769. 11 c.+2 c. (air) .. 35 35
770. 16 c.+2 c. 50 50
771. 17 c.+2 c. 70 70

1959. Obligatory Tax. Tuberculosis Relief Fund. As T **122** but inscr. "1959".
773. **122.** 1 c. red and lake .. 5 5

129. Leonidas R. Trujillo (Team Captain).

130. Gen. Trujillo before National Shrine.

1959. Jamaican-Dominican Republic Polo Match, Trujillo City. Inscr. as in T **129**.
774. **129.** 2 c. violet (postage) .. 5 5
775. – 7 c. brown 20 10
776. – 10 c. green 20 12
777. – 11 c. orange (air) .. 25 15
DESIGNS—HORIZ. 7 c. Jamaican team. 10 c. Dominican Republic team's captain on horseback. 11 c. Dominican Republic team.

1959. Trujillo Era. 29th Year.
778. **130.** 9 c. sepia, bistre, red and green 15 8

131. Gen. Trujillo and Cornucopia.

1959. National Census of 1960. Centres in black, red and blue. Frame colours given.
780. **131.** 1 c. pale blue .. 5 5
781. 9 c. green 12 10
782. 13 c. orange 20 15

132. Trujillo Stadium.

1959. 3rd Pan-American Games, Chicago.
783. **132.** 9 c. black and green .. 20 10

1959. Third Pan-American Games, Chicago. Nos. 667/71 and 673/5, surch. **III JUEGOS DEPORTIVOS PANAMERICANOS + 2** and runner.
784. **116.** 1 c. brn., blue, red, pur. & brn.-red (postage) 5 5
785. – 2 c. brn., bl., red & pur. 8 8
786. – 3 c. purple and red .. 10 10
787. – 5 c. orge., bl., red & pur. 10 10
788. – 7 c. grn., bl., red & pur. 20 20
789. – 11 c. bl., red & orge.-red (air) 20 20
790. – 16 c. red, grn. & carmine 25 25
791. – 17 c. blk., bl., red & pur. 30 30

133. Emperor Charles V.

134. Rhadames Bridge.

1959. Emperor Charles V. 4th Death Cent.
792. **133.** 5 c. mauve 10 5
793. 9 c. blue 15 8

1959. Opening of Rhadames Bridge.
794. – 1 c. black and green .. 5 5
795. **134.** 2 c. black and blue .. 8 5
796. – 2 c. black and red .. 5 5
797. **134.** 5 c. brown and bistre 10 5
DESIGN—Nos. 794, 796, Close-up view of Rhadames Bridge.

135. Douglas DC-4 Airliner, "San Cristobal".

1960. Air. Dominican Civil Aviation.
798. **135.** 13 c. black, green, blue and orange 20 10

136. Sosua Refugee Colony.

1960. World Refugee Year. Inscr. "ANO MUNDIAL DE LOS REFUGIADOS". Centres in black.
799. **136.** 5 c. grn. & brn. (post) 8 5
800. 9 c. blue, maroon & red 15 8
801. 13 c. grn., brn. & orge. 20 12
802. – 10 c. green, maroon and purple (air) 25 20
803. – 13 c. green and grey .. 30 25
DESIGN: Nos. 802/803, Refugee children.

1960. World Refugee Year Fund. Nos. 799/803 surch. **+ 5** with **c** below.
804. **136.** 5 c. + 5 c. green and brown (postage) .. 12 12
805. 9 c. + 5 c. bl., mar. & red 20 20
806. 13 c. + 5 c. green, brown and orange 30 30
807. – 10 c. + 5 c. grn., maroon and purple (air) .. 20 20
808. – 13 c. + 5 c. grn. & grey 25 25

137.

1960. Obligatory Tax. Tuberculosis Relief Fund.
810. **137.** 1 c. red, blue & cream 8 5

138. G.P.O., Ciudad Trujillo.

1960.
811. **138.** 2 c. black and blue .. 8 5

139. Cattle in Street.

1960. Agricultural and Industrial Fair, San Juan de la Maquana.
812. **139.** 9 c. black and red .. 15 8

140. Gholam Takhti (Persia; lightweight wrestling).

141.

1960. Olympic Games, 1960. More Winning Athletes of Olympic Games, Melbourne, 1956. Flags in national colours.
813. **140.** 1 c. black, green and red (postage) .. 5 5
814. – 2 c. brn., turq. & orge. 5 5
815. – 3 c. blue & brown-red 8 8
816. – 5 c. brown and blue .. 10 10
817. – 7 c. brn.-red, bl. & grn. 12 12
819. – 11 c. brown, grey and blue (air) 15 15
820. – 16 c. bronze-green, brn. and red 20 20
821. – 17 c. ochre, blue and black 25 25
DESIGNS (each with national flag of athlete): 2 c. Mauru Furukawa (Japan 200 m. breaststroke swimming). 3 c. Mildred McDaniel (U.S.A., high jump). 5 c. Terence Spinks (spelt "Terrence" on stamp) (Great Britain, featherweight boxing). 7 c. Carlo Pavesi (Italy, fencing). 11 c. Pat McCormick (U.S.A., high diving). 16 c. Mithat Bayrack (Turkey, Greco-Roman welterweight wrestling). 17 c. Ursula Happe (Germany, women's 200 m. breaststroke swimming).

1961. Surch. **HABILITADA PARA** and value.
823. – 2 c. on 1 c. black and green (No. 794) .. 8 5
824. **120.** 9 c. on 4 c. red & mauve 30 8
825. 9 c. on 7 c. green & blue 30 8
826. **102.** 36 c. on ½ c. brown .. 90 30
827. **85.** 1 p. on 50 c. yellow .. 2·00 1·00

1961. Obligatory Tax. Tuberculosis Relief Fund.
828. **141.** 1 c. red and blue .. 5 5
See also No. 876.

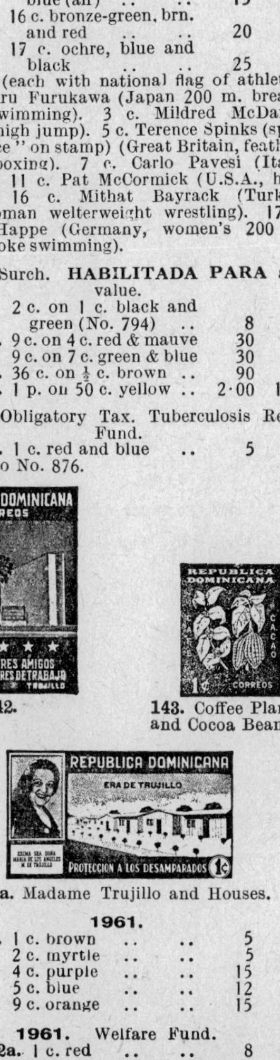

142.

143. Coffee Plant and Cocoa Beans.

142a. Madame Trujillo and Houses.

1961.
829. **142.** 1 c. brown 5 5
830. 2 c. myrtle 5 5
831. 4 c. purple 15 12
832. 5 c. blue 12 5
833. 9 c. orange 15 8

1961. Welfare Fund.
834. **142a.** 1 c. red 8 5

1961. Obligatory Tax. Child Welfare. As Nos. 628/9 but with "ERA DE TRUJILLO" omitted.
(a) Size $23\frac{1}{2} \times 32$ mm.
835. **96b.** 1 c. blue 5 5
(b) Size $21\frac{3}{4} \times 32$ mm.
907. **96c.** 1 c. blue 8 5

1961.
836. **143.** 1 c. green (postage) .. 5 5
837. 2 c. brown 5 5
838. 4 c. violet 5 5
839. 5 c. blue 8 5
840. 9 c. grey 12 8
841. 13 c. red (air) 15 8
842. 33 c. yellow 35 12

1961. U.N.E.S.C.O. 15th Anniv. Nos. 813/21 surch. **XV ANIVERSARIO DE LA UNESCO + 2c.**
843. 1 c. + 2 c. (postage) .. 5 5
844. 2 c. + 2 c. 5 5
845. 3 c. + 2 c. 8 8
846. 5 c. + 2 c. 10 10
847. 7 c. + 2 c. 12 12
849. 11 c. + 2 c. (air) 15 15
850. 16 c. + 2 c. 25 25
851. 17 c. + 2 c. 25 25

144. Mosquito and Dagger.

145. Plantation.

1962. Malaria Eradication.
853. **144.** 10 c. mauve (postage) 12 10
854. 10 c. + 2 c. mauve .. 15 12
855. 20 c. sepia 25 20
856. 20 c. + 2 c. sepia .. 25 20
857. 25 c. green 35 25
858. 13 c. red (air) 15 10
859. 13 c. + 2 c. red .. 20 15
860. 33 c. orange 30 25
861. 33 c. + 2 c. orange .. 40 35

1962. Farming and Industrial Development. Flag in red and blue.
863. **145.** 1 c. green and blue .. 5 5
864. 2 c. red and blue .. 5 5
865. 3 c. brown and blue .. 5 5
866. 5 c. blue 8 5
867. 15 c. orange and blue 15 10

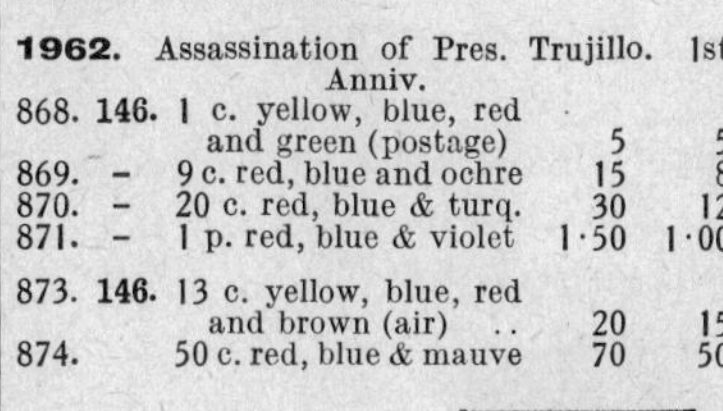

146. Laurel Sprig and Broken Link.

DESIGNS — VERT. 9 c., 1 p. "Justice" on map. HORIZ. 20 c., 50 c. Flag and flaming torch.

1962. Assassination of Pres. Trujillo. 1st Anniv.
868. **146.** 1 c. yellow, blue, red and green (postage) 5 5
869. – 9 c. red, blue and ochre 15 8
870. – 20 c. red, blue & turq. 30 12
871. – 1 p. red, blue & violet 1·50 1·00
873. **146.** 13 c. yellow, blue, red and brown (air) .. 20 15
874. 50 c. red, blue & mauve 70 50

147. Map and Laurel.

148. U.P.A.E. Emblem.

1962. Martyrs of June 1959 Revolution.
875. **147.** 1 c. black 12 8

1962. Tuberculosis Relief Fund. As No. 828 but inscr. "1962".
876. **141.** 1 c. red and blue .. 5 5

1962. Postal Union of the Americas and Spain. 50th Anniv.
877. **148.** 2 c. red (postage) .. 5 5
878. 9 c. orange 15 8
879. 14 c. turquoise .. 20 12
880. 13 c. blue (air) .. 20 12
881. 22 c. brown 30 20

149. Archbishop Nouel.

150. Globe, Riband and Campaign Emblem.

1962. Archbishop Adolfo Nouel. Birth Cent.
882. **149.** 2 c. myrtle & grn. (post) 5 5
883. 9 c. brown and orange 15 8
884. 13 c. mar. & brown-pur. 20 10
885. – 13 c. blue (air) .. 20 10
886. – 25 c. violet 30 20
DESIGN: Air stamps as T **149** but different frame.

1963. Freedom from Hunger. Riband in red and blue.
888. **150.** 2 c. green 5 5
891. 2 c. + 1 c. green .. 5 5
889. 5 c. mauve 8 5
892. 5 c. + 2 c. mauve .. 10 8
890. 9 c. orange 12 8
893. 9 c. + 2 c. orange .. 15 15

151. Duarte.

152. Espaillat, de Rojas and Bono.

1963. Separation from Haiti. 120th Anniv.
895. **151.** 2 c. blue (postage) .. 5 5
896. – 7 c. green (Sanchez) .. 10 8
897. – 9 c. purple (Mella) .. 12 10
898. – 15 c. salmon (air) .. 20 15
DESIGN—HORIZ. 15 c. Sanchez, Duarte and Mella.

1963. "Restoration Cent.".
899. **152.** 2 c. green 5 5
900. – 4 c. red 5 5
901. – 5 c. brown 8 5
902. – 9 c. blue 12 20
DESIGNS: 4 c. Rodriguez, Cabrera and Moncion. 5 c. Capotillo Monument. 9 c. Polanco, Luperon and Salcedo.

153. Nurse tending Patient.

154.

1963. Red Cross Cent. Cross in red.
904. **153.** 3 c. grey (postage) .. 5 5
905. 6 c. green 10 5
906. – 10 c. grey (air) .. 15 12
DESIGN—HORIZ. 10 c. Map of continents bordering Atlantic.

1963. Obligatory Tax. T.B. Relief Fund.
908. **154.** 1 c. red and blue .. 8 5

155. Scales of Justice and Globe.

1963. Declaration of Human Rights. 15th Anniv.
911. **155.** 6 c. red (postage) .. 10 5
912. 50 c. green 55 40
913. 7 c. brown (air) .. 15 10
914. 10 c. blue 20 12

156. Rameses II in War Chariot, Abu Simbel.

1964. Nubian Monuments Preservation. Designs as T **156**, also surch. **2c** in circle.
915. **156.** 3 c. red (postage) .. 5 5
916. 3 c.+2 c. red 8 8
917. – 6 c. blue 10 8
918. – 6 c.+2 c. blue .. 12 10
919. **156.** 9 c. brown 15 10
920. 9 c.+2 c. brown .. 15 12

921. – 10 c. violet (air) .. 15 12
922. – 10 c.+2 c. violet .. 15 15
923. – 13 c. yellow 20 12
924. – 13 c.+2 c. yellow .. 25 20
DESIGNS—HORIZ. 6 c. Heads of Rameses II. VERT. 10 c., 13 c. As T **156**

157. M. Gomez (founder). **158.** Palmchat.

1964. Bani Foundation. Bicent.
925. **157.** 2 c. blue & light blue .. 5 5
926. 6 c. brn.-pur. and brn. 10 5

1964. Dominican Birds. Multicoloured.
927. 1 c. Narrow-billed tody (postage) 5 5
928. 2 c. Swainson's emerald hummingbird 5 5
929. 3 c. Type **158** 5 8
930. 6 c. Parrot 12 8
931. 6 c. Trogons 10 8

932. 10 c. Woodpecker (air) 12
The 1 c., 2 c. and 6 c. (No. 931) are smaller (26×37½ mm.); the 10 c. is horiz. (43½×27½ mm.).

159. Rocket. **160.** Pres. Kennedy.

1964. "Conquest of Space".
933. – 1 c. blue (postage) .. 5 5
934. **159.** 2 c. green 5 5
935. – 3 c. ultramarine .. 10 5
936. **159.** 6 c. blue 15 8

937. **159.** 7 c. green (air) .. 15 12
938. – 10 c. ultramarine .. 25 20
DESIGNS—VERT. 1 c. Rocket launching. HORIZ. 3 c., 10 c. Capsule in orbit.

1964. Air. Pres. Kennedy Commem.
940. **160.** 10 c. brown and buff .. 25 15

161. U.P.U. Monument, Berne.

1964. 15th U.P.U. Congress, Vienna.
941. **161.** 1 c. red (postage) .. 5 5
942. 4 c. green 8 5
943. 5 c. orange 10 5

944. **161.** 7 c. blue (air) 10 8

162. I.C.Y. Emblem. **163.** Hands and Lily.

1965. Int. Co-operation Year.
945. **162.** 2 c. blue and light-blue (postage) .. 5 5
946. 3 c. green and emerald 5 5
947. 6 c. red and pink .. 10 8
948. 10 c. violet & lilac (air) 15 10

1965. 4th Mariological and 11th Int. Marian Congresses. Multicoloured.
949. 2 c. Type **163** (postage) .. 5 5
950. 6 c. Virgin of the Altagracia 20 15
951. 10 c. Aircraft over Basilica of Virgin of Altagracia (horiz.) (39½×31½ mm.) (air) 20 12

164. Flags Emblem. **165.** Lincoln.

1965. Organisation of American States. 75th Anniv.
952. **164.** 2 c. multicoloured .. 5 5
953. 6 c. multicoloured .. 10 5

1965. Air. Abraham Lincoln. Death Cent.
954. **165.** 17 c. grey-blue and blue 25 15

166. ½ r. Stamp of 1865. **167.** Hibiscus.

1965. Stamp Cent.
955 **166.** 1 c. multicoloured (post.) 5 5
956. 2 c. multicoloured .. 5 5
957. 6 c. multicoloured .. 10 8

958. – 7 c. multicoloured (air) 15 12
959. – 10 c. multicoloured .. 20 15
DESIGN: 7 c., 10 c., As T **166**, but showing 1 f. stamp of 1865.

1966. Obligatory Tax. Tuberculosis Relief Fund.
963. **167.** 1 c. red and green .. 5 5
996. – 1 c. mauve, lilac & red 5 5
1015. – 1 c. multicoloured .. 5 5
1016. – 1 c. multicoloured .. 5 5
1017. – 1 c. multicoloured .. 5 5
DESIGN: (21½×30 mm.). No. 996, Orchid. (20×28 mm.). No. 1015, Dogbane. No. 1016, Violets. No. 1017, "Eeanthus capitatus".

168. I.T.U. Emblem and symbols. **169.** W.H.O. Building.

1966. Air. I.T.U. Cent. (1965).
964. **168.** 28 c. red and pink .. 30 20
965. 45 c. green & emerald 45 35

1966. W.H.O. Headquarters, Geneva. Inaug.
966. **169.** 6 c. blue 8 5
967. 10 c. purple 15 8

170. Man supporting "Republic". **171.** "Ascia monuste".

1966. General Elections.
968. **170.** 2 c. black and emerald 5 5
969. 6 c. black and red .. 8 5

1966. Butterflies. Multicoloured.
970. 1 c. Type **171** (postage) .. 5 5
971. 2 c. "Heliconius chariton-ius" 5 5
972. 3 c. "Phoebis sennae sennae" 5 5
973. 6 c. "Anteos clorinde clorinde" 8 5
974. 8 c. "Siderone nemesis" .. 12 8
975. 10 c. "Eurema gundlachia" (air) 20 12
976. 50 c. "Clothilda pantherata pantherata" 75 40
977. 75 c "Papilio androgeus epidaurus" .. .. 1·25 75
Nos. 975/7 are larger, 35×24½ mm.

1966. Hurricane Inez Relief. Nos. 970/77. surch. **PRO DAMNIFICADOS CICLON INES** and value.
978. **171.** 1 c.+2 c. mult. (post.) 5 5
979. – 2 c.+2 c. multicoloured 5 5
980. – 3 c.+2 c. multicoloured 5 5
981. – 6 c.+4 c. multicoloured 10 8
982. – 8 c.+4 c. multicoloured 12 10

983. – 10 c.+5 c. mult. (air) .. 20 15
984. – 50 c.+10 c. mult. .. 70 60
985. – 75 c.+10 c. mult. .. 1·00 90

172. National Shrine. **173.** Emblem and Map.

1967. (a) Postage.
986. **172.** 1 c. blue 5 5
987. 2 c. red 5 5
988. 3 c. green 5 5
989. 4 c. grey 5 5
990. 5 c. yellow 5 5
991. 6 c. orange 8 5

(b) Air. Size 20½ × 25 mm.
992. **172.** 7 c. olive 10 8
993. 10 c. lilac 12 8
994. 20 c. brown 25 15

1967. Development Year. Emblem and map in black and blue.
997. **173.** 2 c. orange and yellow 5 5
998. 6 c. orange 10 5
999. 10 c. green 15 5

174. Civil Defence Emblem. **175.** Castle and Knight (chess pieces).

1967. Obligatory Tax. Civil Defence Fund.
1000. **174.** 1 c. multicoloured .. 8 5

1967. 5th Central American Chess Championships, Santo Domingo.
1001. **175.** 25 c. black, green, blue & yellow (postage) 35 20

1002. – 10 c. blk. & olive (air) 15 12
DESIGN: 10 c. Bishop and pawn.

176. Alliance Emblem. **177.** Institute Emblem.

1967. "Alliance for Progress". 6th Anniv.
1004. **176.** 1 c. green (postage) .. 5 5
1005. **176.** 8 c. grey (air) .. 10 5
1006. 10 c. blue 15 10

1964. Inter-American Agricultural Institute. 25th Anniv.
1007. **177.** 3 c. green (postage) .. 5 5
1008. 6 c. pink 8 5

1009. – 12 c. mult. (air) .. 15 10
DESIGN: 12 c. Emblem and cornucopia.

178. Child and Children's Home. **179.** Hand Holding Invalid.

1967. Obligatory Tax. Child Protection.
1010. **178.** 1 c. red 8 5
1011. 1 c. violet 5 5
See also Nos. 1036/7.

1968. Obligatory Tax. Rehabilitation of the Handicapped.
1012. **179.** 1 c. yellow and green 5 5
1013. 1 c. blue 5 5
1014. 1 c. bright purple .. 5 5
1015. 1 c. brown 5 5

180. W.M.O. Emblem.

1968. World Meteorological Day.
1019. **180.** 6 c. mult. (postage) .. 10 8

1020. 10 c. multicoloured (air) 15 10
1021. 15 c. multicoloured 25 15

181. Ortiz v. Cruz. **182.** "Lions" Emblem.

1968. World Lightweight Boxing Championships. Designs showing similar scenes of the contest.
1024. **181.** 6 c. purple & red (post.) 8 8

1025. – 7 c. green & yellow (air) 10 8
1026. – 10 c. blue and agate .. 15 10

1968. Lions Int.
1027. **182.** 6 c. mult. (postage) .. 10 5

1028. 10 c. multicoloured (air) 15 8

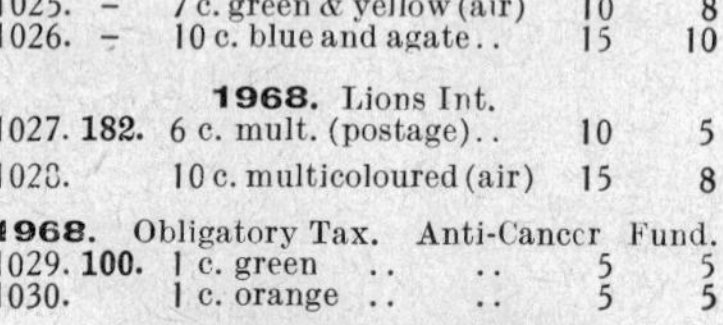

1968. Obligatory Tax. Anti-Cancer Fund.
1029. **100.** 1 c. green 5 5
1030. 1 c. orange 5 5

183. Wrestling.

1968. Olympic Games, Mexico. Multicoloured.
1031. 1 c. Type **183** (postage) .. 5 5
1032. 6 c. Running 10 5
1033. 25 c. Boxing 35 20

1034. 10 c. Weightlifting (air) .. 15 8
1035. 33 c. Pistol-shooting .. 50 30

1968. Obligatory Tax. Child Protection. As T **178**.
1036. **178.** 1 c. orange 8 5
1037. 1 c. green 5 5

184. Map of Americas and House. **185.** Carved Stool.

1969. 7th Inter-American Savings and Loans Congress, Santo Domingo. Multicoloured.
1038. 6 c. Type **184** (postage) .. 8 5

1039. 10 c. Latin-American flags (air) 12 8

1969. Taino Art. Multicoloured.
1040. 1 c. Type **185** (postage) .. 5 5
1041. 2 c. Female idol 5 5
1042. 3 c. Three-cornered foot-stone 5 5
1043. 4 c. Stone axe 8 5
1044. 5 c. Clay pot 10 5

1045. 7 c. Spatula and carved handles (air) 10 5
1046. 10 c. Breast-shaped vessel 15 10
1947. 20 c. Figured vase .. 30 20
The 2, 4, 7 and 20 c. are vert.

186. School Playground and Torch. **187.** Community Emblem.

1969. Obligatory Tax. Education Year.
1048. **186.** 1 c. blue 5 5

1969. Community Development Day.
1049. **187.** 6 c. gold and green .. 10 5

189. C.O.T.A.L. Emblem. **190.** I.L.O. Emblem.

1969. 12th C.O.T.A.L. (Confederation of Latin American Tourist Organizations) Congress, Santo Domingo.
1050. **189.** 1 c. blue, red and light blue (post.) .. 5 5
1051. – 2 c. bright grn. & grn. 5 5
1052. – 6 c. red 8 5
1053. – 10 c. brown (air) .. 12 8
DESIGNS—VERT. 2 c. Boy with flags. HORIZ. (39 × 31 mm.): 6 c. C.O.T.A.L. Building and emblem. 10 c. "Airport of the Americas", Santo Domingo

1969. Int. Labour Organization. 50th Anniv.
1054. **190.** 6 c. black & turq. (post.) 15 5
1055. 10 c. black and red (air) 12 8

191. Baseball Player Taking a Catch. **192.** Las Damas Hydro-electric Scheme.

1969. World Baseball Championships Santo Domingo.
1056. **191.** 1 c. grey & grn. (post.) 5 5
1057. – 2 c. green .. 5 5
1058. – 3 c. brown and violet 5 5
1059. – 7 c. orge. & pur. (air) 10 8
1060. – 10 c. red 15 10
1061. – 1 p. brown and blue 1·25 90
DESIGNS—VERT. 3 c. Making for base. 10 c. Player making strike. HORIZ. (43 × 30½ mm.): 2 c. Cibao Stadium. 7 c. Tetelo Vargas Stadium. 1 p. Quisqueya Stadium.

1969. National Electrification Plan.
1062. **192.** 2 c. mult. (postage) .. 5 5
1063. – 3 c. multicoloured .. 5 5
1064. – 6 c. purple 8 5
1065. – 10 c. red (air) .. 15 8
DESIGNS—HORIZ. 3 c. Las Damas Dam. 6 c. Arroyo Hondo substation. 10 c. Haina River power station.

193. Tavera Dam. **194.** Caduceus and Crab.

1969. Completion of Dam Projects. Multicoloured.
1066. 6 c. Type **193** (postage) .. 8 5
1067. 10 c. Valdesia Dam (air) 15 8

1969. Obligatory Tax. Anti-Cancer Fund.
1068. **194.** 1 c. purple 5 5
1069. 1 c. green 5 5

195. Juan Pablo Duarte. **196.** Outline Map, Arms of Census Office and Family.

1970. Juan Pablo Duarte (patriot). Commem.
1070. **195.** 1 c. green (postage) .. 5 5
1071. 2 c. red 5 5
1072. 3 c. purple 5 5
1073. 6 c. blue 8 5
1074. 10 c. brown (air) .. 15 8

1970. National Census.
1075. **196.** 5 c. blk. & grn. (post.) 8 5
1076. – 6 c. ultram. and blue 8 5
1077. – 10 c. multicoloured (air) 15 10
DESIGNS: 6 c. Arms and quotation. 10 c. Arms and buildings.

197. Open Book and Emblem. **198.** A. R. Urdaneta.

1970. Obligatory Tax. Int. Education Year.
1078. **197.** 1 c. purple 5 5

1970. A. R. Urdaneta (sculptor). Birth Cent.
1079. **198.** 3 c. blue (postage) .. 5 5
1080. – 6 c. green 8 5
1081. – 10 c. blue (air) .. 15 8
DESIGNS—HORIZ. (39½ × 27 mm.). 6 c. "One of Mary" (sculpture.) VERT. (25 × 39 mm.). 10 c. Prisoner (statue).

199. Masonic Symbols. **201.** New U.P.U. Building.

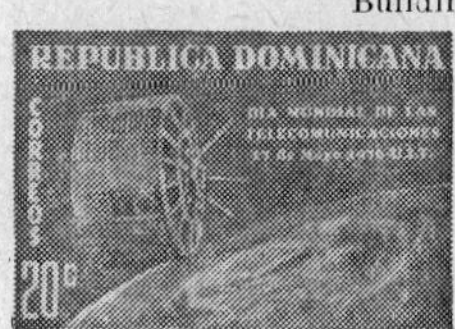

200. Telecommunications Satellite.

1970. 8th Inter-American Masonic Conf. Santo Domingo.
1082. **199.** 6 c. green (postage) .. 8 5
1083. 10 c. brown (air) .. 12 8

1970. World Telecommunications Day.
1084. **200.** 20 c. grey and olive (postage) 30 15
1085. 7 c. grey and blue (air) 10 8

1970. New U.P.U. Headquarters Building Berne.
1086. **201.** 6 c. brown and grey (postage) 8 5
1087. 10 c. brn. & yell. (air) 12 8

202. I.E.Y. Emblem. **203.** P. A. Pina.

1970. Int. Education Year.
1088. **202.** 4 c. purple (postage) 5 5
1089. 15 c. magenta (air) 15 12

1970. Pedro A. Pina (writer). 150th Birth Anniv., and Death Cent.
1090. **203.** 6 c. black & brown 8 5

204. Children with Book. **205.** Emblem and Stamp Album.

1970. 1st World Book Exhib. and Cultural Festival, Santo Domingo.
1091. **204.** 5 c. green (postage) .. 8 5
1092. – 7 c. multicoloured (air) 10 5
1093. – 10 c. multicoloured .. 15 8
DESIGNS: 7 c. Dancers. 10 c. U.N. emblem within "wheel".

1970. Air. "EXFILICA 70" Inter-American Philatelic Exn, Caracas, Venezuela.
1094. **205.** 10 c. multicoloured .. 15 8

206. Virgin of Altagracia. **207.** C.A.R.E. Parcel, Emblem and Map.

1971. Our Lady of Altagracia Basilica. Inaug. Multicoloured.
1095. 3 c. Type **206** (postage) .. 5 5
1096. 17 c. Basilica (22½ × 36 mm.) (air) 25 15

1971. Air. C.A.R.E. (Cooperative for American Relief Everywhere). 25th Anniv.
1097. **207.** 10 c. green and blue 12 8

208. M. R. Objio. **209.** Communications Emblems.

1971. Manuel Rodriguez Objio (poet). Death Cent.
1098. **208.** 6 c. blue 8 5

1971. Obligatory Tax. For Postal and Telecommunications School.
1099. **209.** 1 c. blue and red .. 5 5
1100. 1 c. brown, red and blue 5 5

210. Boxing and Canoeing. **211.** Goat and Fruit.

1971. 2nd National Games.
1101. **210.** 2 c. brown and orange (postage) 5 5
1102. – 5 c. brown and green 8 5
1103. – 7 c. purple & grey (air) 10 5
DESIGNS: 5 c. Basketball. 7 c. Volleyball.

1971. 6th National Agricultural Census. Multicoloured.
1104. 1 c. Type **211** (postage) .. 5 5
1105. 2 c. Cow and goose .. 5 5
1106. 3 c. Cocoa pods and horse 5 5
1107. 6 c. Bananas, coffee beans and pig 10 5
1108. 25 c. Cockerel and grain (air) 35 20

212. Jose Nunez de Caceres. **213.** Shepherds and Star.

1971. 1st Declaration of Independence 150th Anniv.
1109. **212.** 6 c. b ., vio. & pale bl. (postage) 8 5
1110. – 10 c. bl., red & yellow (air) 12 8
DESIGN: 10 c. Flag of the Santo Domingo-Colombia Union.

1971. Christmas.
1111. **213.** 6 c. brn. yell. & bl. (post) 8 5
1112. – 10 c. red, blk. & yell. (air) 12 8
DESIGN: 10 c. Spanish bell of 1493.

214. Child on Beach. **215.** Book Year Emblem.

1971. U.N.I.C.E.F. 25th Anniv.
1113. **214.** 6 c. multicoloured (postage) 8 5
1114. **214.** 15 c. multicoloured (air) 15 12

1971. Int. Book Year.
1115. **215.** 1 c. grn, red & blue (postage) 5 5
1116. 2 c. brn., red and blue 5 5
1117. **215.** 12 c. pur., red & blue (air) 15 10

216. Magnifier on Map. **217.** Orchid.

1972. Air. "Exfilima 71" Inter American Philatelic Exn., Lima, Peru.
1118. **216.** 10 c. multicoloured .. 15 10

1972. Obligatory Tax. Tuberculosis Relief Fund.
1119. **217.** 1 c. multicoloured .. 5 5

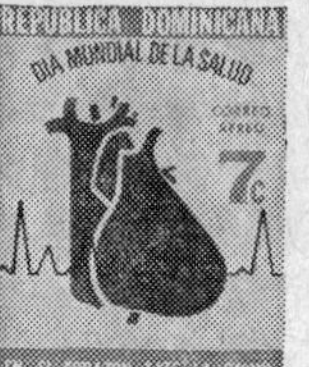

218. Heart Emblem. **219.** Mask.

1972. Air. World Health Day.
1120. **218.** 7 c. multicoloured .. 10 5

1972. Taino Arts and Crafts. Multicoloured.
1121. 2 c. Type **219** (postage) 5 5
1122. 4 c. Spoon and amulet 5 5
1123. 6 c. Nasal aspirator .. 8 5
1124. 8 c. Ritual vase (air) .. 10 5
1125. 10 c. Couch trumpet .. 15 8
1126. 25 c. Ritual spatulas .. 30 15
Nos. 1123/5 on horiz.

220. Globe.

1972. World Tele-communications Day.
1127. **220.** 6 c. mult. (postage) .. 8 5
1128. **220.** 21 c. multicoloured (air) 25 15

221. Map and "Stamps".

1972. 1st Nat. Stamp Exhib., Santo Domingo.
1129. **221.** 2 c. mult. (postage) .. 5 5
1130. **221.** 33 c. mult. (air) .. 45 25

222. Basketball.

1972. Olympic Games, Munich. Multicoloured.
1131. 2 c. Type **222** (postage) .. 5 5
1132. 33 c. Running (air) .. 45 25

223. Club Badge.

1972. Int. Activo 20–30 Club. 50th Anniv.
1133 223. 1 c. mult. (postage) .. 5 5
1134. 223. 20 c. mult. (air) .. 30 15

224. Emilio A. Morel and Quotation.

1972. Morel (poet and journalist). Commem.
1135. 224. 6 c. mult. (postage) .. 8 5
1136. 224. 10 c. mult. (air) .. 12 8

225. Bank Building.

1972. Central Bank. 25th Anniv. Mult.
1137. 1 c. Type 225 .. .. 5 5
1138. 5 c. One-peso banknote .. 8 5
1139. 25 c. 1947 50 c. Coin and Mint 30 20

226. Nativity Scene.

277. Student and Letter-box.

1972. Christmas. Multicoloured.
1140. 2 c. Type 226 (postage) .. 5 5
1141. 6 c. Poinsettia (horiz.) .. 8 5
1142. 10 c. "La Navidad" Fort 1492 (horiz.) (air) .. 12 10

1972. Publicity for Correspondence Schools.
1143. 227. 2 c. red and pink .. 5 5
1144. 6 c. blue and light blue 8 5
1145. 10 c. grn. and yellow-grn. 12 8

288. View of Dam.

289. Invalid in Wheel-chair.

1973. Tavera Dam. Inaug.
1146. 288. 10 c. multicoloured .. 12 8

1973. Obligatory Tax. Dominican Rehabilitation Assn.
1147. 289. 1 c. green 5 5

290. Boxing, football, wrestling and shooting.

291. Hibiscus.

1973. 12th Central American and Caribbean Games, Santo Domingo. Multicoloured.
1148. 2 c. Long-jumping, Diving, Running, Cycling and Weightlifting (postage) 5 5
1149. 2 c. Type 290 .. .. 5 5
1150. 2 c. Fencing, tennis, high-jumping and sprinting 5 5
1151. 2 c. Putting the shot, throwing the javelin and show-jumping .. 5 5
1152. 25 c. Type 290 .. .. 30 20
1153. 25 c. As No. 1149 .. .. 30 20
1154. 25 c. As No. 1150 .. .. 30 20
1155. 25 c. As No. 1151 .. .. 30 20
1156. 8 c. Type 290 (air) .. 10 8
1157. 8 c. As No. 1149 .. .. 10 8
1158. 8 c. As No. 1150 .. .. 10 8
1159. 8 c. As No. 1151 .. .. 10 8
1160. 10 c. Type 290 .. .. 12 8
1161. 10 c. As No. 1149 .. .. 12 8
1162. 10 c. As No. 1150 .. .. 12 8
1163. 10 c. As No. 1151 .. .. 12 8

1973. Obligatory Tax. Tuberculosis Relief Fund.
1164. 291. 1 c. multicoloured .. 5 5

292. "Christ carrying the Cross".

293. Global Emblem.

1973. Easter. Multicoloured
1165. 2 c. Type 292 (postage) 5 5
1166. 6 c. Belfry, Church of Our Lady of Carmen (vert.) 8 5
1167. 10 c. Belfry, Chapel of Our Lady of Succour (air) 12 8

1973. Air. Pan-American Health Organisation. 70th Anniv.
1168. 293. 7 c. multicoloured .. 10 8

294. Weather Zones.

1973. World Meteorological Organization Centenary.
1169. 294. 6 c. mult. (postage) .. 8 5
1170. 294. 7 c. multicoloured (air) 10 8

295. "Maguey" Drum.

1973. Opening of Museum of Dominican Man, Santo Domingo. Multicoloured.
1171. 1 c. Type 295 (postage) .. 5 5
1172. 2 c. Amber carvings .. 5 5
1173. 4 c. Cibao mask (vert.) .. 5 5
1174. 6 c. Pottery (vert.) .. 8 5
1175. 7 c. Model ship in mosaic (vert.) (air) .. 8 5
1176. 10 c. Maracas rattles .. 12 8

296. Forensic Scientist.

1973. Air. Interpol. 50th Anniv.
1177. 296. 10 c. bl., grn. & light bl. 12 8

297. Nativity Scene.

1973. Christmas. Multicoloured.
1178. 2 c. Type 297 (postage) .. 5 5
1179. 6 c. "Prayer" (stained-glass window) (vert.) .. 8 5
1180. 10 c. Angels beside Crib (air) 12 8

298. Scout Badge.

1973. Dominican Boy Scouts. 50th Anniv. Multicoloured.
1181. 1 c. Type 298 (postage) .. 5 5
1182. 5 c. Scouts and flag .. 5 5
1183. 21 c. Scouts cooking, and Lord Baden Powell (inset) (air) 25 15

No. 1182 is smaller, size 26 + 36 mm.

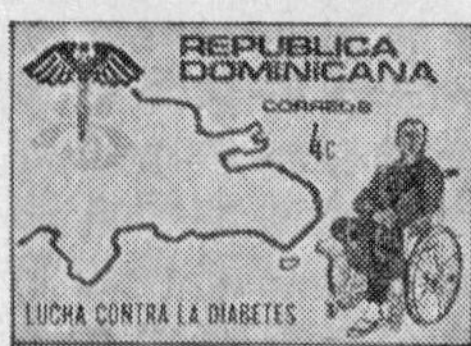
299. Stadium and Basketball Players.

300. Belfry of Santo Domingo Cathedral.

1974. 12th Central American and Caribbean Games, Santo Domingo. Multicoloured.
1184. 2 c. Type 299 (postage) .. 5 5
1185. 6 c. Arena and cyclist .. 8 5
1186. 10 c. Swimming pool and diver (air) 12 10
1187. 25 c. Stadium, soccer players and discus-thrower 30 20

1974. Holy Week.
1188. 300. 2 c. multicoloured (postage) 5 5
1189. – 6 c. pur., grn. & olive 8 5
1190. – 10 c multicoloured (air) 12 10

DESIGN—VERT: 6 c. "Sorrowful Mother" (D. Bouts). HORIZ. 10 c. "The Last Supper" (R. M. Budi).

301. Francisco del Rosario Sanchez Bridge

1974. Dominican Bridges. Multicoloured.
1191. 6 c. Type 301 (postage) .. 8 5
1192. 10 c. Higuamo Bridge (air) 12 10

302. Emblem and Patient.

1974. Anti-Diabetes Campaign. Multicoloured.
1193. 4 c. Type 302 (postage) .. 5 5
1194. 5 c. Emblem and pancreas 5 5
1195. 7 c. Emblem and kidney (air) 8 5
1196. 33 c. Emblem, eye and heart 35 25

303. Steam Train.

1974. Universal Postal Union. Centenary. Multicoloured.
1197. 2 c. Type 303 (postage) .. 5 5
1198. 6 c. Stage-coach .. 8 5
1199. 7 c. Packet-steamer (air) 8 5
1200. 33 c. Boeing "727" of Dominicana Airways .. 35 25

304. Emblems of World Amateur Golf Council and Dominican Golf Association.

1974. World Amateur Golf Championships.
1202. 304. 2 c. black and yellow (postage) 5 5
1203. – 6 c. multicoloured .. 8 5
1204. – 10 c. multicoloured (air) 12 10
1205. – 20 c. multicoloured .. 25 20

DESIGNS—VERT. 6 c. Golfers teeing-off. HORIZ. 10 c. Council emblem and golfers. 20 c. Dominican Golf Association emblem, golfer and hand with ball and tee.

305. Christmas Decorations.

307. Dr. Defillo.

306. Tomatoes.

1974. Christmas. Multicoloured.
1206. 2 c. Type 305 (postage) .. 5 5
1207. 6 c. Virgin and Child .. 8 5
1208. 10 c. Hand holding dove (horiz.) (air) 12 10

1974. World Food Programme. Tenth Anniv. Multicoloured.
1209. 2 c. Type 306 (postage) .. 5 5
1210. 3 c. Avocado pears .. 5 5
1211. 5 c. Coconuts 8 5
1212. 10 c. Bee, hive and cask of honey (air) 12 10

1975. Dr. Fernando Defillo (medical scientist). Birth Cent.
1213. 307. 1 c. brown 5 5
1214. 6 c. green 8 5

308. "I am the Resurrection and the Life".

309. Spanish 6-cuartos Stamp of 1850.

1975. Holy Week. Multicoloured.
1215. 2 c. Type 308 (postage) .. 5 5
1216. 6 c. Bell tower, Nuestra Senora del Rosario convent 8 5
1217. 10 c. Catholic emblems (air) 12 10

1975. Air. "Espana 75" International Stamp Exhibition, Madrid.
1218. 309. 12 c. blk., red & yell. 15 12

310. Hands supporting "Agriculture" and Industry.

311. Earth Station.

1975. 16th Meeting of Industrial Development Bank Governors, Santo Domingo.
1219. **310.** 6 c. mult. (postage) .. 8 5
1220. **310.** 10 c. mult. (air) 12 10

1975. Satellite Earth Station Opening.
1221. 5 c. Type **311** (postage) .. 8 5
1222. 15 c. Hemispheres and satellites (horiz.) (air) .. 20 15

311. "Apollo" Spacecraft with Docking Tunnel.

313. Father Castellanos.

1975. "Apollo-Soyuz" Space Link. Mult.
1223. 1 c. Type **312** (postage) .. 5 5
1224. 4 c. "Soyuz" spacecraft 5 5
1225. 2 p. Docking manoeuvre (air) .. .. .. 2·50 2·25
The 2 p. is larger, 42×28 mm.

1975. Father Rafael C. Castellanos. Birth Cent.
1226. **313.** 6 c. brown and buff 8 5

314. Women encircling I.W.Y. Emblem.

315. Guacanagarix.

1975. International Women's Year.
1227. **314.** 3 c. multicoloured .. 5 5

1975. Indian Chiefs. Mult.
1228. 1 c. Type **315** (postage) .. 5 5
1229. 2 c. Guarionex 5 5
1230. 3 c. Caonabo 5 5
1231. 4 c. Bohechio 5 5
1232. 5 c. Cayacoa 8 5
1233. 6 c. Anacaona 8 5
1234. 9 c. Hatuey 10 8
1235. 7 c. Mayobanex (air) .. 8 5
1236. 8 c. Cotubanama with Juan de Esquivel 10 8
1237. 10 c. Enriquillo and wife, Mencia 12 10

316. Basketball.

1975. 7th Pan-American Games, Mexico City. Multicoloured.
1238. 2 c. Type **316** (postage) .. 5 5
1239. 6 c. Baseball 8 5
1240. 7 c. Volleyball (horiz.) (air) 8 5
1241. 10 c. Weightlifting (horiz.) 12 10

317. Carol-singers.

1975. Christmas. Multicoloured.
1242. 2 c. Type **317** (postage) .. 5 5
1243. 6 c. "Dominican" Nativity 5 5
1244. 10 c. Dove and Peace message (air) 10 8

318. "Abudefdul marginatus".

1976. Fishes. Multicoloured.
1245. 10 c. Type **318** 10 0
1246. 10 c. "Halichoeres radiata" 10 8
1247. 10 c. "Holocentrus ascensionis" 10 8
1248. 10 c. "Angelichthys ciliaris" 10 8
1249. 10 c. "Lutianus aya" .. 10 8

319. Valdesia Dam.

1976. Air. Inauguration of Valdesia Dam.
1250. **319.** 10 c. multicoloured .. 12 10

320. "Magdalene" (E. Godoy).

321. Schooner "Separacion Dominicana".

1976. Holy Week. Multicoloured.
1251. 2 c. Type **320** (postage) .. 5 5
1252. 6 c. "The Ascension" (V. Priego) 8 5
1253. 10 c. "Mount Calvary" (E. Castillo) (air) .. 12 10

1976. Navy Day.
1254. **321.** 20 c. multicoloured .. 25 20

322. Orchid.

324. Dominican and Spanish Flags.

323. National Flower.

1976. Obligatory Tax. Tuberculosis Relief Fund.
1255. **322.** 1 c. multicoloured .. 5 5

1976. American Revolution. Bicentenary, and "Interphil '76" Int. Stamp Exn., Philadelphia.
1256. **317.** 6 c. multicoloured (postage) 8 5
1257. 9 c. multicoloured .. 10 8
1258. 10 c. multicoloured (air) 12 10
1259. – 75 c. black and orange 80 60
DESIGNS—HORIZ. 9 c. Maps within cogwheels. 10 c. Maps within hands. VERT. 75 c. George Washington and Philadelphia buildings.

1976. Visit of King and Queen of Spain. Multicoloured.
1260. 6 c. Type **324** (postage) .. 8 5
1261. 21 c. King Juan Carlos I and Queen Sofia (air) .. 25 15

325. Various Telephones.

1976. Telephone Centenary. Multicoloured.
1262. 6 c. Type **325** (postage) .. 8 5
1263. 10 c. A. Graham Bell. (horiz.) (air) 12 10

326. "Duarte's Vision" (L. Desangles).

1976. Juan Duarte (patriot). Death Cent. Multicoloured.
1264. 2 c. Type **326** (postage) .. 5 5
1265. 6 c. "Juan Duarte" (R. Mejia) (vert.) 8 5
1266. 10 c. Text of Duarte's Declaration (vert.) (air) 12 10
1267. 33 c. "Duarte Sailing to Exile" (E. Godoy) .. 40 35

327. Fire Hydrant.

1976. Dominican Fire Service. Multicoloured.
1268. 4 c. Type **327** (postage) .. 5 5
1269. 6 c. Fire Service emblem 8 5
1270. 10 c. Fire engine (horiz.) (air) 12 10

EXPRESS DELIVERY STAMPS

E 1.

1920.
E 232. **E 1.** 10 c. blue .. .. 1·50 45

E 2.

1925. Inscr. "ENTREGA ESPECIAL".
E 247. **E 2.** 10 c. blue .. .. 2·50 60

1927. Inscr. "EXPRESO".
E 250. **E 2.** 10 c. brown .. 2·00 50
E 459a. 10 c. green 50 20

E 3.

1945.
E 539. **E 3.** 10 c. blue, red and carmine 25 12

E 4. Shield, Hand and Letter.

1950.
E 594. **E 4.** 10 c. red, grn. & blue 20 10

E 5.

1956.
E 663. **E 5.** 25 c. green 35 25

E 6. Pigeon and Letter.

1967.
E 995. **E 6.** 25 c. blue 35 25

OFFICIAL STAMPS

O 1. Bastion of 27th Feb.

O 2. Columbus Lighthouse.

1902.
O 121. **O 1.** 2 c. black and red .. 15 10
O 122. 5 c. black & blue .. 20 12
O 123. 10 c. black & green .. 25 20
O 124. 20 c. black & yellow 30 25

1910. As Type O 1, but inscr. "27 DE FEBRERO 1844" and "10 DE AGOSTO 1865" at sides.
O 177. **O 1.** 1 c. black & green .. 10 10
O 178. 2 c. black & red .. 12 12
O 179. 5 c. black and blue .. 15 12
O 180. 10 c. black & green .. 30 25
O 181. 20 c. black & yellow 45 40

1928.
O 251. **O 2.** 1 c. green 5 5
O 252. 2 c. red 5 5
O 253. 5 c. blue 8 8
O 254. 10 c. blue 10 10
O 255. 20 c. yellow .. 15 15

1931. Air. Optd. **CORREO AEREO.**
O 292. **O 2.** 10 c. blue .. .. 8·00 8·00
O 293. 20 c. yellow .. 8·00 8·00

O 3. Columbus Lighthouse.

1937. White letters and figures.
O 393. **O 3.** 3 c. violet 15 8
O 394. 7 c. blue 20 15
O 395. 10 c. yellow .. 30 20

O 4. Columbus Lighthouse.

1939. Coloured letters and figures.
O 409. **O 4.** 1 c. green 5 5
O 410. 2 c. red 5 5
O 411. 3 c. violet 5 5
O 412. 5 c. blue 15 10
O 414. 7 c. blue 15 8
O 415. 10 c. orange .. 20 10
O 416. 20 c. brown .. 45 20
O 577. 50 c. magenta .. 75 30
O 417. 50 c. claret .. 80 50
No. O 417 has smaller figures of value than No. O 577.

1950. Values inscr. "CENTAVOS ORO".
O 578. **O 4.** 5 c. blue 8 5
O 581. 7 c. blue 10 5
O 579. 10 c. yellow .. 15 10
O 582. 20 c. brown .. 25 15
O 583. 50 c. purple .. 60 40

POSTAGE DUE STAMPS

D 1.

D 2.

1901.

D 117. D 1. 2 c. sepia 10 8
D 118. 4 c. sepia 12 8
D 119. 5 c. sepia 30 15
D 175. 6 c. sepia 30 25
D 120. 10 c. sepia 45 25

1913.

D 239. D 1. 1 c. olive 8 8
D 191. 2 c. olive 10 8
D 192. 4 c. olive 12 10
D 193. 6 c. olive 15 15
D 194. 10 c. olive 25 25

1942. Size 20½ × 25½ mm.

D 485. D 2. 1 c. red 5 5
D 486. 2 c. blue 5 5
D 487. 2 c. blue 5 5
D 488. 4 c. green 5 5
D 489. 6 c. brown & buff .. 8 8
D 490. 8 c. orange & yellow 12 12
D 491. 10 c. magenta & pink 15 15

1966. Size 21 × 25½ mm. Inscr. larger and in white.

D 492. D 2. 1 c. red 8 8
D 493. 2 c. blue 8 8

REGISTRATION STAMPS

1935. De Merino stamps of 1933 surch. **PRIMA VALORES DECLARADOS SERVICIO INTERIOR** and value in figures and words.

R 345. – 8 c. on ½ c. (No. 316) 50 35
R 346. – 8 c. on 7 c. blue .. 20 10
R 348. 24. 15 c. on 10 c. orange .. 35 8
R 349. – 30 c. on 8 c. green .. 70 25
R 350. – 45 c. on 20 c. red .. 1·00 20
R 351. 25. 70 c. on 50 c. olive .. 1·50 40

R 1. National Coat of Arms. R 2.

1940.

R 448. R 1. 8 c. black and red .. 15 5
R 449. 15 c. black & orange 25 8
R 450. 30 c. black and green 40 8
R 451. 70 c. black & maroon 1·00 30

1944. Redrawn. Larger figures of value and "c" as in Type R 2.

R 452. 45 c. black and blue 60 30
R 453. 70 c. black & olive .. 1·00 35

1953.

R 454. R 2. 8 c. black & red .. 20 8
R 455. 10 c. black & lake 15 8
R 456. 15 c. black & orange 30 10

R 3.

R 4.

1955.

R 646. R 3. 10 c. black and red .. 15 5
R 647. 15 c. black & orange 45 25
R 648. 20 c. black & orange 30 20
R 649. 30 c. green 40 15
R 650. 40 c. black & green 50 35
R 651. 45 c. black & blue .. 80 40
R 652. 70 c. black & maroon 1·00 75

1963. Redrawn as Type R 2.

R 909. 10 c. black & orange 15 8
R 910. 20 c. black & orange 25 20

1965.

R 961. R 4. 10 c. black & lilac .. 12 12
R 962. 40 c. black & yellow 60 40

MINIMUM PRICE

The minimum price quoted is 5p which represents a handling charge rather than a basis for valuing common stamps. For further notes about prices see introductory pages.

DUBAI

O2

One of the Trucial States in the Persian Gulf. Formerly used the stamps of Muscat. British control of the postal services ceased in 1963.

On 2 December, 1971, Dubai and six other Gulf Shaikhdoms formed the State of the United Arab Emirates. U.A.E. issues commenced in 1973.

100 naye paise = 1 rupee.
1966. 100 dirhams = 1 riyal.

IMPERF STAMPS. Some of the following issues exist imperf. from limited printings.

1. Hermit Crab.

2. Shaikh Rashid bin Said.

1963.

1. 1. 1 n.p. red & grey-bl. (post.) 5 5
2. A. 2 n.p. orange-brn. & blue 5 5
3. B. 3 n.p. sepia and green .. 5 5
4. C. 4 n.p. orange and purple 5 5
5. D. 5 n.p. black and violet .. 5 5
6. E. 10 n.p. blk. & orge.-brn. 5 5
7. 1. 15 n.p. red and drab .. 5 5
8. A. 20 n.p. orange-brn. & red 8 8
9. B. 25 n.p. brown and apple 8 8
10. C. 30 n.p. red and grey .. 10 10
11. D. 35 n.p. deep blue & lilac 12 12
12. E 50 n.p. sepia and orange 15 15
13. F. 1 r. salmon and blue .. 25 25
14. G. 2 r. brown and bistre .. 50 50
15. H. 3 r. black and red .. 90 90
16. I. 5 r. brown & blue-green .. 2·00 2·00
17. 2. 10 r. black, turq. & purple 3·50 3·50

18. J. 20 n.p. blue & choc. (air) 5 5
19. K. 25 n.p. dull pur. & yellow 8 8
20. J. 30 n.p. black & vermilion 10 10
21. K. 40 n.p. slate-purple & brn. 12 12
22. J. 50 n.p. claret & emerald 15 15
23. K. 60 n.p. black & orge.-brn. 20 20
24. J. 75 n.p. green and violet .. 30 30
25. K. 1 r. brown and yellow .. 45 45

DESIGNS (Postage)—HORIZ. A, Lobster. B, Sea snail. C, Crab. D, Sea anemone. E, Mollusc. F, Mosque. G, Buildings. H, Ancient wall and tower. I, Dubai view. (Air)—HORIZ. J, Falcon in flight over bridge. VERT. K, Falcon.

3. Dhows.

4. Mosquito.

1963. Red Cross Cent. Crescent in red.

26. 3. 1 n.p. blue & yell. (post.) 8 8
27. – 2 n.p. brown and yellow .. 8 8
28. – 3 n.p. brown and orange .. 8 8
29. – 4 n.p. brown and green .. 8 8

30. 3. 20 n.p. brown & yell. (air) 20 20
31. – 30 n.p. blue and orange .. 30 30
32. – 40 n.p. black and yellow .. 40 40
33. – 50 n.p. violet, red & turq. 50 50

DESIGNS: 2, 30 n.p., First Aid field post. 3, 40 n.p. Camel train. 4, 50 n.p. Butterfly.

1963. Malaria Eradication.

34. 4. 1 n.p. chocolate & red (post.) 5 5
35. 1 n.p. brown and green .. 5 5
36. 1 n.p. red and blue .. 5 5
37. – 2 n.p. blue and red .. 5 5
38. – 2 n.p. vermilion & choc. .. 5 5
39. – 3 n.p. blue and chestnut 5 5

40. 4. 30 n.p. green & purple (air) 10 10
41. – 40 n.p. grey and red .. 12 12
42. – 70 n.p. yellow & slate-pur. 20 20

DESIGNS: 2, 40 n.p. Mosquito and snake emblem. 3, 70 n.p. Mosquitoes and swamp.

5. Ears of Wheat.

7. Scout Gymnastics.

6. U.S. Seal and Pres. Kennedy.

1963. Air. Freedom from Hunger.

43. 5. 30 n.p. brown and violet .. 8 8
44. – 40 n.p. olive and red .. 10 10
45. – 70 n.p. orange and green 20 25
46. – 1 r. blue and chestnut .. 30 30

DESIGNS: 40 n.p. Palm and campaign emblem. 70 n.p. Emblem within hands. 1 r. Woman bearing basket of fruit.

1964. Air. 1st Pres. Kennedy Memorial Issue.

47. 6. 75 n.p. blk., grn. & pale grn. 20 20
48. 1 r. blk., orange-brown & buff 25 25
49. 1½ r. blk. & red grey .. 30 30

1964. World Scout Jamboree Marathon (1963).

50. 7. 1 n.p. yellow-brown and chocolate (postage) .. 5 5
51. – 2 n.p. brown and red .. 5 5
52. – 3 n.p. chestnut and blue 5 5
53. – 4 n.p. blue and magenta .. 5 5
54. – 5 n.p. turquoise & indigo .. 5 5

55. 7. 20 n.p. brown & grn. (air) 8 8
56. – 30 n.p. chestnut & violet .. 10 10
57. – 40 n.p. green and blue .. 12 12
58. – 70 n.p. grey and green .. 20 20
59. – 1 r. vermilion and blue .. 30 30

DESIGNS: 2, 30 n.p. Bugler. 3, 40 n.p. Wolf cubs. 4, 70 n.p. Scouts on parade. 5 n.p., 1 r. Scouts with standard.

8. "Atlas" Rocket.

10. Flame of Freedom. and Scales of Justice.

9. Globe, New York and Dubai Harbours.

1964. Air. "Honouring Astronauts". Multicoloured.

60. 1 n.p. Type 8 .. .. 5 5
61. 2 n.p. "Mercury" capsule 5 5
62. 3 n.p. Space craft 5 5
63. 4 n.p. Twin space craft .. 5 5
64. 5 n.p. Type 8 .. .. 5 5
65. 1 r. "Mercury" capsule .. 30 30
66. 1½ r. Space craft 50 50
67. 2 r. Twin space craft .. 85 85

Nos. 62/3 and 66/7 are horz.

1964. New York World's Fair.

68. 9. 1 n.p. red & dp. bl. (post) 5 5
69. – 2 n.p. blue, red and mag. 5 5
70. 9. 3 n.p. deep green & brown 5 5
71. – 4 n.p. red, yellow-green and blue-green 5 5
72. 9. 5 n.p. violet, olive & green 5 5
73. – 10 n.p. black, brn. & red 5 5
74. – 75 n.p. black, green and ultramarine (air) .. 30 30
75. – 2 r. ochre, blue-green and sepia 55 55
76. – 3 r. orge., bl.-grn. & olive 85 85

DESIGNS: 2, 4, 10 n.p. New York skyline and Dubai hotel. 75 n.p., 2 r., 3 r. Statue of Liberty, New York, and harbour scene Dubai.

1964. Air. Human Rights Declaration. 15th Anniv. Flame in red.

77. 10. 35 n.p. brown and blue .. 10 10
78. 50 n.p. olive-green & blue 12 12
79. 1 r. black & greenish blue 25 25
80. 3 r. ultramarine and blue 80 80

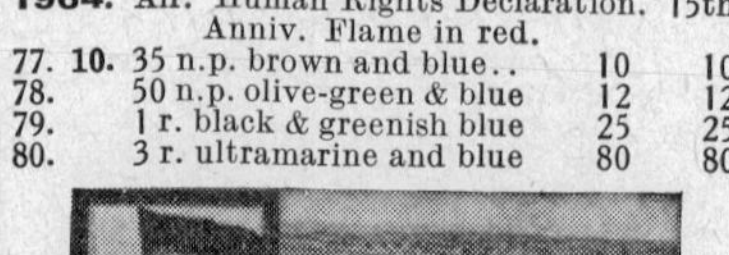

11. Shaikh Rashid bin Said and View of Dubai.

1964.

81. 11. 10 n.p. olive, red & brown (postage) 5 5
82. A. 20 n.p. brown, red & grn. 5 5
83. 11. 30 n.p. black, red & blue 8 8
84. A. 40 n.p. indigo, red & cer. 10 10
85. B. 1 r. olive, red & brn. (air) 20 20
86. C. 2 r. brown, red & green .. 50 50
87. B. 3 r. black, red and blue .. 75 75
88. C. 5 r. indigo, red and cerise 1·25 1·25

SCENES: A, Waterfront. B, Waterside buildings. C, Harbour.

1964. Air. Winter Olympic Games, Innsbruck. Nos. 55/9 optd. with Olympic Rings, Games Emblem and **INNSBRUCK 1964.**

98. 7. 20 n.p. brown and green 30 30
90. – 30 n.p. chestnut and violet 35 35
91. – 40 n.p. green and blue .. 50 50
92. – 70 n.p. black and grey .. 80 80
93. – 1 r. vermilion and blue .. 1·40 1·40

1964. Air. 48th Birth Anniv. of Pres. Kennedy. Op.d. **MAY 29** (late President's birthday).

94. 6. 75 n.p. blk. & grn. on grn. 60 60
95. 1 r. black & chest. on buff 85 85
96. 1½ r. black and red on grey 1·25 1·25

1964. Air. Anti-T.B. Campaign. Crescent in red. Optd. **ANTI TUBERCULOSE** in English and Arabic, and Cross of Lorraine. Perf. or roul.

101. 3. 20 n.p. brown & yell. .. 2·00 2·00
102. – 30 n.p. blue and orange .. 2·00 2·00
103. – 40 n.p. black and yellow 2·00 2·00
104. – 50 n.p. violet, red & turq. 2·00 2·00

12. Gymnastics.

1964. Olympic Games, Tokyo.

105. 12. 1 n.p. chestnut & olive 5 5
106. – 2 n.p. sepia & turquoise 5 5
107. – 3 n.p. ultram. and brown 5 5
108. – 4 n.p. violet and yellow 5 5
109. – 5 n.p. ochre and slate .. 5 5
110. – 10 n.p. blue and buff .. 10 10
111. – 20 n.p. olive and cerise 15 15
112. – 30 n.p. blue and yellow 20 20
113. – 40 n.p. green and buff .. 35 35
114. – 1 r. purple and blue .. 75 75

DESIGNS: 2 n.p. to 1 r. Various gymnastic exercises as T 12, each with portrait of Ruler.

1964. Air. U.N. 19th Anniv. Nos 43/6 optd. **U N O 19TH ANNIVERSARY** in English and Arabic.

115. 5. 30 n.p. brown and violet 25 25
116. – 40 n.p. olive and red .. 55 55
117. – 70 n.p. orange and green 80 80
118. – 1 r. blue and chestnut .. 1·10 1·10

13. Shaikh Rashid and Shaikh Ahmad of Qatar.

14. Globe and Rockets.

1964. "Educational Progress". Portraits in black; torch orange

119. 13. 5 n.p. purple (postage) 5 5
120. 10 n.p. rose 5 5
121. 15 n.p. blue 5 5
122. – 20 n.p. olive 5 5
123. – 30 n.p. red (air) 12 12
124. – 40 n.p. brown 20 20
125. – 50 n.p. ultramarine .. 25 25
126. – 1 r. green 45 45

DESIGNS: 20, 30, 40 n.p. Shaikh Rashid and Shaikh Abdullah of Kuwait. 50 n.p., 1 r. Shaikh Rashid and Pres. Nasser of Egypt.

1964. Air. Outer Space Achievements 1964. Optd. **OUTER SPACE ACHIEVEMENTS 1964** in English and Arabic, **RANGER 7** and space capsule motif.

127. 1 r. multicoloured (No. 65) 1·10 1·10
128. 1½ r. multicoloured (No. 66) 1·10 1·10
129. 2 r. multicoloured (No. 67) 1·10 1·10

1964. Achievements in Outer Space. Multicoloured.

130. 10 n.p. on 75 n.p. "Man on Moon" .. .. 1·40 1·40
131. 20 n.p. on 1 r. 50 Type 14 .. 1·50 1·50
132. 30 n.p. on 2 r. "Universe" 1·60 1·60

Nos. 130 and 132 are larger, 25 × 78 mm.

1964. Air. 1st Death Anniv. of Pres. J. Kennedy. As No. 47 with colours changed, optd. **22 NOVEMBER.**
133. **6.** 75 n.p. black and green .. 6·00 6·00

15. Telephone Handset.

1966. Opening of Dubai Automatic Telephone Exchange.
134. **15.** 10 n.p. brn. & grn. (post). 5 5
135. 15 n.p. red and plum .. 5 5
136. 25 n.p. green and blue .. 5 5
137. – 40 n.p. blue & grn. (air) 10 10
138. – 60 n.p. orange and sepia 20 20
139. – 75 n.p. violet and black 25 25
140. – 2 r. green and red .. 65 65
DESIGN: Nos. 137/40, As T **15** but showing telephone dial.

16. Sir Winston Churchill and Catafalque.

1966. Churchill Commem. (a) Postage.
142. **16.** 1 r. black and violet .. 20 20
143. 1 r. 50 black and olive 35 35
144. 3 r. black and blue .. 70 70
145. 4 r. black and claret .. 85 85

(b) Air. Nos. 142/5 optd. **AIR MAIL** in English and Arabic and with black borders.
147. **16.** 1 r. black and violet .. 20 20
148. 1 r. 50 black and olive 35 35
149. 3 r. black and blue .. 70 70
150. 4 r. black and claret .. 85 85

17. Ruler's Palace. **18.** Bridge.

1966.
152. **17.** 5 n.p. brown and blue .. 5 5
153. 10 n.p. black & orange .. 5 5
154. 15 n.p. blue and brown 5 5
155. A. 20 n.p. blue and brown 5 5
156. 25 n.p. red and blue .. 5 5
157. B. 35 n.p. violet & emerald 8 8
158. 40 n.p. turquoise & blue 10 12
159. **18.** 60 n.p. green and red .. 15 15
160. 1 r. ultramarine and blue 25 25
161. C. 1 r. 25 chestnut & black 30 30
162. D. 1 r. 50 purple & green .. 35 35
163. 3 r. brown and violet .. 65 70
164. E. 5 r. red .. .. .. 1·00 1·10
165. 10 r. indigo .. .. 2·25 2·25
DESIGNS—HORIZ. (28×21 mm.): A, Waterfront, Dubai. B, Bridge and dhow. As T **18**: C, Minaret (Ruler's portrait on right). D, Fort Dubai. VERT. (32½×42½ mm.): E, Shaikh Rashid bin Said.

19. Oil Rig. **20.** Ocean Oil Rig.

1966. Air. Oil Exploration.
(a) "Land" series as T **19.**
166. – 5 n.p. black and lilac .. 5 5
167. – 15 n.p. black and bistre 5 5
168. – 25 n.p. black and blue .. 5 5
169. – 35 n.p. black & vermilion 8 8
170. – 50 n.p. black and brown 12 12
171. **19.** 70 n.p. black and rose .. 20 20
DESIGNS—HORIZ. 5 n.p. Map of Dubai. 15 n.p. Surveying 25 n.p. Dubai Petroleum Company building. 35 n.p. Oil drilling. VERT. 50 n.p. Surveying with level.

(b) "Sea" series as T **20.**
173. **20.** 10 n.p. purple and blue 5 5
174. – 20 n.p. magenta & green 5 5
175. **20.** 30 n.p. brown and green 5 5
176. – 40 n.p. lilac and agate .. 10 10
177. **20.** 50 n.p. ultram. & olive 10 10
178. – 60 n.p. blue and violet .. 12 12
179. **20.** 75 n.p. green & brown .. 20 20
180. – 1 r. green and blue .. 25 25
DESIGN: 20, 40, 60 n.p. and 1 r. Ocean well-head.

21. Rulers of Gulf Arab States (reduced size illustration. Actual size 77×20 mm.).

1966. Gulf Arab States Summit Conf.
182. **21.** 35 p. multicoloured .. 12 12
183. 60 p. multicoloured .. 20 20
184. 150 p. multicoloured .. 40 40

22. Jules Rimet Cup.

1966. World Cup Football Championships. Multicoloured.
185. 40 d. Type **22** 12 8
186. 60 d. } Various 20 12
187. 1 r. } football 30 20
188. 1 r. 25 } scenes. 40 30
189. 3 r. Wembley Stadium, London 90 60

1966. England's World Cup Victory. Nos. 185/9 optd. **ENGLAND WINNERS.**
191. **22.** 40 d. multicoloured .. 12 8
192. – 60 d. multicoloured .. 20 12
193. – 1 r. multicoloured .. 30 20
194. – 1 r. 25 multicoloured .. 40 30
195. – 3 r. multicoloured .. 90 60

23. Rulers of Dubai and Kuwait, and I.C.Y. Emblem.

1966. Int. Co-operation Year (1965). Currency expressed in rupees.
197. **23.** 1 r. brown and green .. 30 25
198. A. 1 r. green and brown .. 30 25
199. B. 1 r. blue and violet .. 30 25
200. C. 1 r. blue and violet .. 30 25
201. D. 1 r. turquoise and red .. 30 25
202. E. 1 r. turquoise and red .. 30 25
203. F. 1 r. violet and blue .. 30 25
204. G. 1 r. violet and blue .. 30 25
205. H. 1 r. red and turquoise .. 30 25
206. I. 1 r. red and turquoise .. 30 25
HEADS OF STATE AND POLITICAL LEADERS (Ruler of Dubai and): A. Pres. John F. Kennedy. B, Prime Minister Harold Wilson. C. Pres. Helou of the Lebanon. D, Pres. De Gaulle. E, Pres. Nasser. F, Pope Paul VI. G, Ruler of Bahrain. H, Pres. Lyndon Johnson. I, Ruler of Qatar.

24. "Gemini" Capsules manoeuvring.

1966. "Gemini" Space Rendezvous. Multicoloured.
208. 35 d. Type **24** 12 8
209. 40 d. "Gemini" capsules linked 12 8
210. 60 d. "Gemini" capsules separating 20 12
211. 1 r. Schirra and Stafford in "Gemini 6" 30 20
212. 1 r. 25 "Gemini" orbits .. 40 30
213. 3 r. Borman and Lovell in "Gemini 7" 90 60

1967. Nos. 197/206 surch. **Riyal** in English and Arabic.
215. **23.** 1 r. on 1 r. 30 20
216. A. 1 r. on 1 r. 30 20
217. B. 1 r. on 1 r. 30 20
218. C. 1 r. on 1 r. 30 20
219. D. 1 r. on 1 r. 30 20
220. E. 1 r. on 1 r. 30 20
221. F. 1 r. on 1 r. 30 20
222. G. 1 r. on 1 r. 30 20
223. H. 1 r. on 1 r. 30 20
224. I. 1 r. on 1 r. 30 20

1967. Gemini Flight Success. Nos. 208/13 optd. **SUCCESSFUL END OF GEMINI FLIGHT.**
226. **24.** 35 d. multicoloured .. 12 8
227. – 40 d. multicoloured .. 12 8
228. – 60 d. multicoloured .. 20 12
229. – 1 r. multicoloured .. 30 20
230. – 1 r. 25 multicoloured .. 40 30
231. – 3 r. multicoloured .. 90 60

1967. Nos. 152/61, 163/5 with currency names changed by overprinting in English and Arabic (except Nos. 244/5 which have the currency name in Arabic only).
233. **17.** 5 d. on 5 n.p. 5 5
234. 10 d. on 10 n.p. .. 5 5
235. 15 d. on 15 n.p. .. 5 5
236. A. 20 d. on 20 n.p. .. 5 5
237. 25 d. on 25 n.p. .. 5 5
238. B. 35 d. on 35 n.p. .. 8 8
239. 40 d. on 40 n.p. .. 10 10
240. **18.** 60 d. on 60 n.p. .. 15 15
241. 1 r. on 1 r. 25 25
242. C. 1 r. 25 on 1 r. 25 .. 30 30
243. D. 3 r. on 3 r. 75 75
244. E. 5 r. on 5 r. .. .. 1·25 1·25
245. 10 r. on 10 r. .. .. 2·50 2·50

25. "The Moving Finger writes . . .".

1967. Rubaiyat of Omar Khayyam. Multicoloured.
246. 60 d. Type **25** 20 12
247. 60 d. "Here with a Loaf of Bread . . ." 20 12
248. 60 d. "So, while the Vessels. . ." 20 12
249. 60 d. "Myself when young . . ." 20 12
250. 60 d. "One Moment in Annihilation's Waste . . ." .. 20 12
251. 60 d. "And strange to tell . . ." 20 12

26. "The Straw Hat" (Rubens).

1967. Paintings. Multicoloured.
253. 1 r. Type **26** 30 15
254. 1 r. "Thomas, Earl of Arundel" (Rubens) .. 30 15
255. 1 r. "A peasant boy leaning on a sill" (Murillo) .. 30 15
See also Nos. 273/5.

27. Ruler and Falcon. **28.** Arab Dhow.

1967.
257. **27.** 5 d. red and orange .. 5 5
258. 10 d. sepia and green .. 5 5
259. 20 d. purple and blue .. 5 5
260. 35 d. turquoise & mag. 10 10
261. 60 d. ultram. & green .. 15 15
262. 1 r. green and purple .. 20 20
263. **28.** 1 r. 25 purple and blue 25 25
264. 3 r. purple and blue .. 65 65
265. 5 r. violet and green .. 1·10 1·10
266. 10 r. green and magenta 2·25 2·25

29. Globe and Scout Badge.

1967. World Scout Jamboree, Idaho. Mult.
267. 10 d. Type **29** 5 5
268. 20 d. Dubai scout & camels 5 5
269. 35 d. Bugler 10 12
270. 60 d. Jamboree emblem and U.S. flags. 12 12
271. 1 r. Lord Baden-Powell .. 25 20
272. 1 r. 25 Idaho on U.S. Map 30 25

1967. Goya's Paintings in National Gallery, London. As T **26.** Multicoloured.
273. 1 r. "Dr. Peral" 25 15
274. 1 r. "Dona Isabel Cobos de Porcel" 25 15
275. 1 r. "Duke of Wellington" 25 15

30. "Teinopalpus imperialis".

1968. Butterflies. Multicoloured.
277. 60 d. Type **30** 12 5
278. 60 d. "Erasmia pulchella" 12 5
279. 60 d. "Euthalia indica" .. 12 5
280. 60 d. "Attacus atlas syltheticus" 12 5
281. 60 d. "Dysphania militaris" 12 5
282. 60 d. "Neochera Butleri" 12 5
283. 60 d. "Danais chrysippus" 12 5
284. 60 d. "Danais Tytia" .. 12 5

31. "Madonna and Child". (Ferruzi).

1968. Arab Mothers Day. Multicoloured.
285. 60 d. "Games in the Park" (Zandomeneghi) 15 10
286. 1 r. Type **31** 25 15
287. 1 r. 25 "Mrs. Cookburn and Children" (Reynolds) .. 30 20
288. 3 r. "Self-portrait with Daughter" (Vigee-Lebrun) 75 50

32. "Althea rosea".

1968. Flowers. Multicoloured.
289. 60 d. Type **32** 12 5
290. 60 d. "Geranium Lancastriense" 12 5
291. 60 d. "Catharanthus roseus" 12 5
292. 60 d. "Convolvulus minor" 12 5
293. 60 d. "Opuntai" 12 5
294. 60 d. "Gaillardia aristata" 12 5
295. 60 d. "Heliopsis" 12 5
296. 60 d. "Centaurea moschata" 12 5

33. Running.

1968. Olympic Games, Mexico. Multicoloured.

297.	15 d. Type **33**	5	5
298.	20 d. Swimming	5	5
299.	25 d. Boxing	5	5
300.	35 d. Water-polo	10	5
301.	40 d. High jump	10	5
302.	60 d. Gymnastics ..	12	8
303.	1 r. Football	20	10
304.	1 r. 25 Fencing	25	12

34. "Young Girl with Kitten". (Perronneau).

1968. Children's Day. Multicoloured.

306.	60 d. "Two Boys with Mastiff" (Goya) ..	15	8
307.	1 r. Type 34	25	12
308.	1 r. 25 "Soap Bubbles" (Manet)	30	15
309.	3 r. "The Fluyder Boys" (Lawrence)	20	35

35. Pheasant.

1968. Arabian Gulf Birds. Multicoloured.

310.	60 d. Type **35**	15	5
311.	60 d. Turtle dove ..	15	5
312.	60 d. Red-footed falcon ..	15	5
313.	60 d. Bee-eater	15	5
314.	60 d. Hoopoe	15	5
315.	60 d. Common egret ..	15	5
316.	60 d. Little terns	15	5
317.	60 d. Lesser black-backed gulls	15	5

36. S.S. "Bamora", 1914.

1969. Dubai Postal Services. 60th Anniv. Multicoloured.

318.	25 d. Type **36**	5	5
319.	35 d. De Havilland "66", 1930	10	5
320.	60 d. "Sirdhana", 1947 ..	12	8
321.	1 r. Armstrong Whitworth "Atlanta", 1938 ..	20	10
322.	1 r. 25 "Chandpara", 1949	25	12
323.	3 r. Short "Sunderland", 1943	65	30

37. "Madonna and Child" (Murillo).

1969. Arab Mothers' Day. Multicoloured.

325.	60 d. Type **37**	12	12
326.	1 r. "Mother and Child" (Muzzuoli)	20	15
327.	1 r. 25 "Mother and Children" (Rubens) ..	25	20
328.	3 r. "Madonna and Child" (Correggio)	60	30

38. Pork Fish.

1969. Fishes. Multicoloured.

329.	60 d. Type **38**	12	10
330.	60 d. Spotted Grouper ..	12	10
331.	60 d. Moonfish	12	10
332.	60 d. Sweetlips	12	10
333.	60 d. Blue angel ..	12	10
334.	60 d. Texas Skate ..	12	10
335.	60 d. Striped butterfly Fish	12	10
336.	60 d. Imperial angelfish ..	12	10

39. Burton, Doughty, Burckhardt, Thesiger and Map.

1969. Explorers of Arabia.

337.	**39.**	25 d. brown and green	10	8
338.		60 d. blue and brown ..	15	10
339.		1 r. green and blue ..	20	15
340.		1 r. 25 black and red ..	25	20

40. Construction of Storage Tank.

1969. Oil Industry. Multicoloured.

341.	5 d. Type **40**	5	5
342.	20 d. Floating-out storage tank	5	5
343.	35 d. Underwater tank in operation	10	8
344.	60 d. Ruler, drilling platform and monument ..	12	10
345.	1 r. Fateh marine oil field ..	20	15

41. Astronauts on Moon.

1969. 1st Man on the Moon. Multicoloured.

346.	60 d. Type **41** (postage) ..	12	10
347.	1 r. Astronaut and ladder ..	25	20
348.	1 r. 25 Astronauts planting U.S. flag on Moon (air)	30	25

No. 348 is horiz., size 62×38 mm.

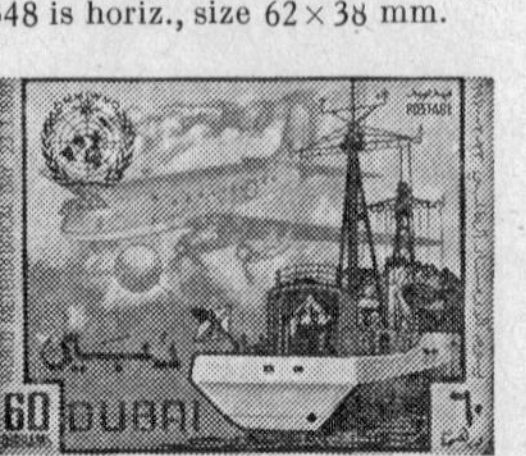

42. Weather-ship, launching Radio-Sonde and Hastings Reconnaissance Aircraft.

1970. World Meteorological Day. Multicoloured.

349.	60 d. Type **42**	12	10
350.	1 r. Kew-type radio-sonde and dish aerial	25	20
351.	1 r. 25 "Tiros" satellite and rocket	30	25
352.	3 r. "Ariel" satellite and rocket	65	55

43. New Headquarters Building.

1970. New U.P.U. Headquarters Building, Berne. Multicoloured.

353.	5 d. Type **43**	5	5
354.	60 d. U.P.U. Monument, Berne	12	10

44. Charles Dickens.

1970. Charles Dickens. Death Cent. Mult.

355.	60 d. Type **44**	15	12
356.	1 r. Signature, quill and London sky-line (horiz.)	25	20
357.	1 r. 25 Dickens and Victorian street	30	25
358.	3 r. Dickens and books ..	65	50

45. "The Graham Children" (Hogarth).

1970. Children's Day. Multicoloured.

359.	35 d. Type **45**	8	5
360.	60 d. "Caroline Murat and Children" (Gerard) (vert.)	12	10
361.	1 r. "Napoleon as Uncle" (Ducis)	25	20

46. Dubai National Bank.

1970. Multicoloured.

362.	5 d. Shaikh Rashid (vert.)	5	5
363.	10 d. Dhow building ..	5	5
364.	20 d. Al Maktum Bridge	5	5
365.	35 d. Great Mosque (vert.)	5	5
366.	60 d. Type **46**	10	8
367.	1 r. International airport	20	15
368.	1 r. 25 Harbour project	30	20
369.	3 r. Hospital	60	50
370.	5 r. Trade school ..	1·00	90
371.	10 r. Television and "Intelsat 4" (vert.)	2·00	1·75

The riyal values are larger, 40×25 or 25×40 mm.

47. Terminal Building and Control Tower.

1971. Dubai Int. Airport Opening. Mult.

372.	1 r. Type **47**	25	20
373.	1 r. 25 Airport Entrance	30	25

48. Telecommunications Map and Satellites.

1971. Outer Space Telecommunications Congress, Paris. Multicoloured.

374.	60 d. Type **48** (postage) ..	12	10
375.	1 r. Rocket and "Intelstat 4" (air)	25	20
376.	5 r. Eiffel Tower and Goonhilly aerial ..	1·10	85

49. Scout Badge, Japanese Fan and Map. **50.** Durer.

1971. 13th World Scout Jamboree, Asagiri (Japan). Multicoloured.

377.	60 d. Type **49**	12	10
378.	1 r. Canoeing	25	20
379.	1 r. 25 Rock-climbing ..	30	25
380.	3 r. Scouts around campfire (horiz.)	65	50

1971. Famous People. (1st issue). Mult.

381.	60 d. Type **50** (postage) ..	12	10
382.	1 r. Sir Isaac Newton (air)	25	20
383.	1 r. 25 Avicenna	30	25
384.	3 r. Voltaire	65	45

See also Nos. 388/91.

51. Boy in Meadow.

1971. U.N.I.C.E.F. 25th Anniv. Multicoloured.

385.	60 d. Type **51** (postage) ..	12	10
386.	5 r. Children with toys (horiz.)	1·00	75
387.	1 r. Mother and children (air)	25	20

1972. Famous People (2nd issue). As Type **50**. Multicoloured.

388.	10 d. Leonardo da Vinci (postage)	5	5
389.	35 d. Beethoven	8	5
390.	75 d. Khalil Gibran (poet) (air)	20	12
391.	5 r. Charles De Gaulle ..	1·00	75

52. Doctor treating baby.

1972. Air. World Health Day. Multicoloured.

392.	75 d. Nurse supervising children (vert.)	20	12
393.	1 r. 25 Type **52**	30	20

53. Gymnastics.

1972. Olympic Games, Munich. Multicoloured.

399.	35 d. Type **53** (postage) ..	5	5
400.	40 d. Fencing	10	5
401.	65 d. Hockey	12	10
402.	75 d. Water-polo (air) ..	20	12
403.	1 r. Horse-jumping ..	25	15
404.	1 r. Athletics	30	20

POSTAGE DUE STAMPS

1963. Designs as T 1 but inscr. "DUE".

D 26.	1 n.p. red & greenish grey	5	5
D 27.	2 n.p. blue and bistre ..	5	5
D 28.	3 n.p. green and claret ..	5	5
D 29.	4 n.p. red and green ..	5	5
D 30.	5 n.p. black and vermilion	5	5
D 31.	10 n.p. violet & yellow-ol.	5	5
D 32.	15 n.p. red and ultramarine	5	5
D 33.	25 n.p. bronze-green and yellow-brown	10	10
D 34.	35 n.p. orange and blue ..	12	12

DESIGNS—HORIZ. 1 n.p. to 35 n.p. Various seashells (three types).

D 1. Shaikh Rashid.

1972.

No.	Type	Description	Unused	Used
D 394.	D 1.	5 d. grey, blue & brn.	5	5
D 395.		10 d. brn., ochre & bl.	5	5
D 396.		20 d. brn., red and blue	5	5
D 397.		30 d. violet, lilac & blk.	5	5
D 398.		50 d. brn., ochre & pur.	10	10

DUTTIA (DATIA) BC

A state of Central India. Now uses Indian stamps.

1. Ganesh.

2.

1893. Imperf.

No.	Type	Description		Unused
1.	1.	¼ a. black on orange	..	£800
2.		½ a. black on green	..	£800
4.		2 a. black on yellow	..	£800
5.		4 a. black on red	..	£800

Stamps of T 1 come with or without the circular handstamp as shown on T 2. Prices are the same for either state.

1897 (?). Imperf.

No.	Type	Description		Unused
6.	2.	½ a. black on green	..	6·00
3.		1 a. red	..	£800
7b.		1 a. black	..	4·00
8.		2 a. black on yellow	..	7·00
10.		4 a. black on red ..	..	7·00

3.

4.

1897. Imperf.

No.	Type	Description		Unused
12.	3.	½ a. black on green	..	16·00
13.		1 a. black ..	..	17·00
14.		2 a. black on yellow	..	22·00
15.		4 a. black on red	..	22·00

1899. Imperf., roul. or perf.

No.	Type	Description		Unused	Used
16.	4.	¼ a. red	..	25	
29.		¼ a. blue	..	60	1·50
37.		¼ a. black ..	..	1·50	
17b.		½ a. black on green	..	35	
30.		½ a. green ..	..	1·25	3·00
35.		½ a. blue	..	35	
39.		½ a. pink ..	..	60	75
18.		1 a. black ..	..	40	
31.		1 a. purple ..	..	1·50	
36.		1 a. pink	..	40	
19c.		2 a. black on yellow	..	60	
32.		2 a. brown ..	..	3·00	
33.		2 a. lilac	..	3·50	
20.		4 a. black on red ..	..	60	
34.		4 a. brown ..	..	7·00	

EAST AFRICA BC

The following stamps were issued by the East African Postal Administration for use in Uganda, Kenya and Tanganyika (renamed Tanzania in 1965).

100 cents = 1 shilling.

1. East African "Flags".

1964. Olympic Games, Tokyo.

No.	Type	Description	Unused	Used
1.	–	30 c. yellow and maroon ..	8	8
2.	–	50 c. maroon and yellow ..	12	12
3.	1.	1s. 30 yellow, green & blue	30	30
4.		2s. 50 magenta, vio. & blue	50	50

DESIGNS—VERT. 30 c., 50 c. Chrysanthemum Emblem.

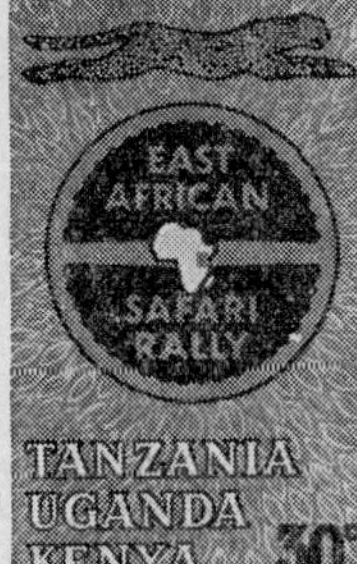

2. Rally Badge.

DESIGN: Nos. 7/8 Cars on Rally and Badge.

1965. 13th East African Safari Rally.

No.	Type	Description	Unused	Used
5.	2.	30 c. black, yell. & turquoise	10	8
6.		50 c. black, yellow & brown	12	10
7.	–	1s. 30 green, ochre & blue..	25	25
8.	–	2s. 50 green, red and blue..	50	55

3. I.T.U. Emblem and Symbols.

1965. I.T.U. Cent. "I.T.U." and symbols in gold.

No.	Type	Description	Unused	Used
9.	3.	30 c. chocolate & magenta	8	8
10.		50 c. chocolate and grey..	12	12
11.		1s 30 chocolate and blue	15	15
12.		2s. 50 chocolate & turquoise	40	45

4. I.C.Y. Emblem.

1965. Int. Co-operation Year.

No.	Type	Description	Unused	Used
13.	4.	30 c. green and gold ..	8	8
14.		50 c. black and gold ..	12	12
15.		1s. 30 blue and gold ..	15	15
16.		2s. 50 red and gold ..	40	45

5. Game Park Lodge, Tanzania.

1966. Tourism. Multicoloured.

No.	Type	Description	Unused	Used
17.		30 c. Type 5	8	8
18.		50 c. Murchison Falls, Uganda	12	12
19.		1 s. 30 Flamingoes, Lake Nakuru, Kenya ..	15	15
20.		2s 50 Deep Sea Fishing Tanzania	40	45

6. Games Emblem.

1966. 8th British Empire and Commonwealth Games, Jamaica.

No.	Type	Description	Unused	Used
21.	6.	30 c. blk., gold, grn. & grey	8	8
22.		50 c. blk., gold, cobalt & cerise	12	12
23.		1s. 30 blk., gold, red & grn.	15	15
24.		2 s. 50 blk., gold, lake & bl.	40	45

7. U.N.E.S.C.O. Emblem.

1966. U.N.E.S.C.O. 20th Anniv.

No.	Type	Description	Unused	Used
25.	7.	30 c. black, green and red	8	8
26.		50 c. black, green & brown	12	12
27.		1 s. 30 black, green & grey	15	15
28.		2 s. 50 blk., green & yellow	40	45

8. D. H. Dragon Rapide.

1967. East African Airways. 21st Anniv. Multicoloured.

No.	Type	Description	Unused	Used
29.		30 c. Type 8	8	8
30.		50 c. Super VC-10 ..	12	12
31.		1 s. 30 Comet 4 ..	15	15
32.		2 s. 50 F-27 Friendship ..	60	50

9. Pillar Tomb.

1967. Archaeological Relics.

No.	Type	Description	Unused	Used
33.	9.	30 c. ochre, black & purple	8	8
34.	–	50 c. red, black and brown	12	12
35.	–	1 s. 30 black, yell. & green	15	15
36.	–	2 s. 50 black, ochre & red	40	45

DESIGNS: 50 c. Rock painting. 1 s. 30, Clay head. 2. s. 50 Proconsul skull.

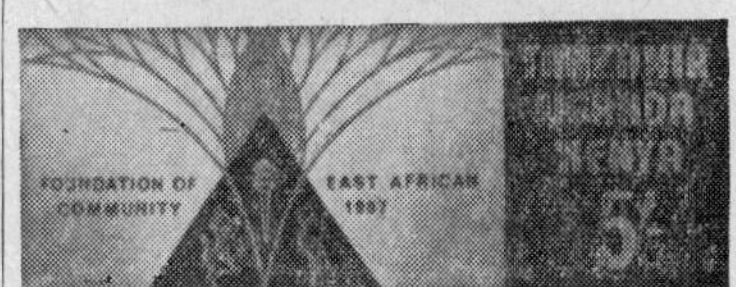

10. Unified Symbols of Kenya, Tanzania, and Uganda. (Illustration reduced. Actual size 58×21 mm.).

1967. Foundation of East African Community.

No.	Type	Description	Unused	Used
37.	10.	5s. gold, black and grey..	65	70

11. Mountaineering.

1968. Mountains of East Africa. Multi-coloured.

No.	Type	Description	Unused	Used
38.		30 c. Type 11	10	10
39.		50 c. Mount Kenya	15	15
40.		1 s. 30 Mount Kilimanjaro	20	20
41.		2s. 50 Ruwenzori Mountains	40	60

12. Family and Rural Hospital.

1968. World Health Organization.

No.	Type	Description	Unused	Used
42.	12.	30 c. green, lilac & choc.	5	5
43.	–	50 c. slate, lilac & black	8	8
44.	–	1 s. 30 brn., lilac & choc.	15	15
45.	–	2 s. 50 grey, black & lilac	40	60

DESIGNS: 50 c. Family and Nurse. 1 s. 30, Family and Microscope. 2 s. 50, Family and Hypodermic Syringe.

13. Olympic Stadium, Mexico City.

1968. Olympic Games, Mexico.

No.	Type	Description	Unused	Used
46.	13.	30 c. green and black ..	5	5
47.	–	50 c. green and black ..	8	8
48.	–	1 s. 30 red, black & grey	15	15
49.	–	2 s. 50 sepia and brown	40	60

DESIGNS—HORIZ. 50 c. High-diving Boards. 1 s. 30, Running Tracks. VERT. 2 s. 50, Boxing Ring.

14. M.V. Umoja.

1969. Water Transport.

No.	Type	Description	Unused	Used
50.	14.	30 c. blue and grey ..	10	10
51.	–	50 c. multicoloured ..	15	15
52.	–	1 s. 30, green and blue	20	20
53	–	2 s. 50, orange and blue	50	55

DESIGNS: 50 c. S.S. Harambee, 1 s. 30, M.V. Victoria. 2 s. 50, St. Michael.

15. I.L.O. Emblem and Agriculture.

1969. Int. Labour Organisation. 50th Anniv.

No.	Type	Description	Unused	Used
54.	15.	30 c. black, green & yell.	5	5
55.	–	50 c. black, plum, cerise and red	8	8
56.	–	1 s. 30 blk., brn. & orge.	15	15
57.	–	2 s. 50 blk., ult. & turq.	45	45

DESIGNS—I.L.O. Emblem and: 50 c. Building-work. 1 s. 30, Factory-workers. 2 s. 50, Shipping.

16. Pope Paul VI and Ruwenzori Mountains.

17. Euphorbia Tree shaped as Africa, and Emblem.

1969. Visit of Pope Paul VI to Uganda.

No.	Type	Description	Unused	Used
58.	16.	30 c. black, gold and blue	5	5
59.		70 c. black, gold and red	15	12
60.		1 s. 50 black, gold & blue	30	30
61.		2 s. 50 black, gold & violet	45	60

1969. African Development Bank. 5th Anniv.

No.	Type	Description	Unused	Used
62.	17.	30 c. green and gold ..	5	5
63.		70 c. green, gold & violet	10	10
64.		1 s. 50 green, gold & blue	20	20
65.		2 s. 50 green, gold & brn.	40	45

18. Marimba.

1970. Musical Instruments.

66.	18.	30 c. buff and brown ..	5	5
67.	–	70 c. green, brown & yellow	10	10
68.	–	1 s. 50 chocolate & yellow	20	20
69.	–	2 s. 50 orange, yell. & choc.	40	55

DESIGNS: 70 c. Amadinda. 1 s. 50 Nzomari. 2 s. 50 Adeudeu.

19. Satellite Earth Station.

1970. Satellite Earth Station. Inaug.

70.	19.	30 c. multicoloured ..	5	5
71.	–	70 c. multicoloured ..	10	10
72.	–	1 s. 50 black, violet & orge.	20	20
73.	–	2 s. 50 multicoloured ..	40	55

DESIGNS: 70 c. Transmitter—Daytime. 1 s. 50, Transmitter—Night. 2 s. 50, Earth and satellite.

20. Athlete.

1970. 9th Commonwealth Games.

74.	20.	30 c. brown and black ..	5	5
75.		70 c. green, brown and black	10	10
76.		1 s. 50 lilac, brown and black	20	20
77.		2 s. 50 blue, brown and black	55	40

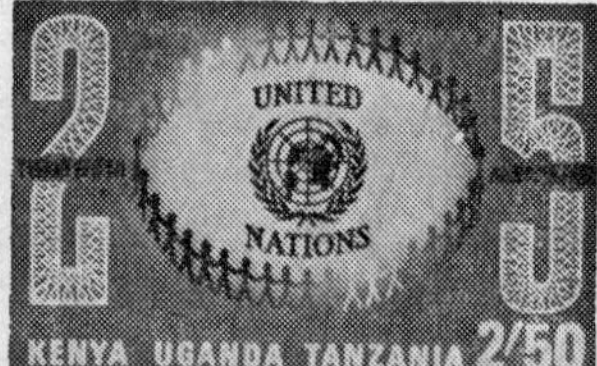

21. "25" and U.N. Emblem.

1970. United Nations. 25th Anniv.

78.	21.	30 c. multicoloured ..	5	5
79.		70 c. multicoloured ..	10	10
80.		1 s. 50 multicoloured ..	20	20
81.		2 s. 50 multicoloured ..	55	55

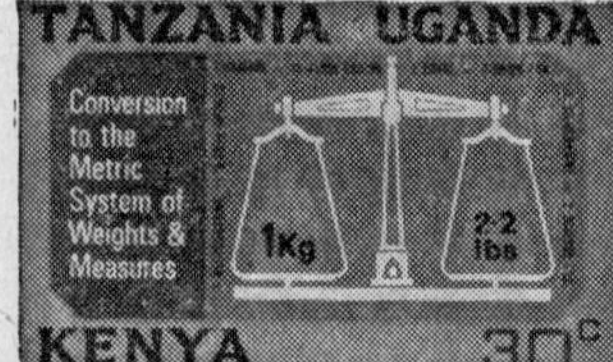

22. Balance and Weight Equivalents.

1970. Conversion to Metric System. Multicoloured

82.	30 c. Type 22	5	5
83.	70 c. Fahrenheit and Centigrade thermometers ..	10	10
84.	1 s. 50 Petrol pump and liquid capacities ..	20	20
85.	2 s. 50 Surveyors and land measures	40	40

23. 11 Class Locomotive.

1971. Railway Transport. Multicoloured.

86.	30 c. Type 23	10	5
87.	70 c. 90 Class Locomotive ..	15	15
88.	1 s. 50 59 Class Locomotive	30	30
89.	2 s. 50 30 Class Locomotive	50	60

24. Syringe and Cow.

1971. O.A.U. Rinderpest Campaign.

91.	24.	30 c. blk., brown & grn.	5	5
92.	–	70 c. blk., blue & brown	10	10
93.	24.	1 s. 50 blk., pur., & brn.	20	20
94.	–	2 s. 50 blk., red & brown	45	45

DESIGN: 70 c., 2 s. 50, As T 24 but with bull facing right.

25. Livingstone meets Stanley.
(Illustration reduced: actual size 58 × 22 mm.)

1971. Livingstone and Stanley meeting at Ujiji. Cent.

95.	25.	5 s. multicoloured ..	1·00	1·00

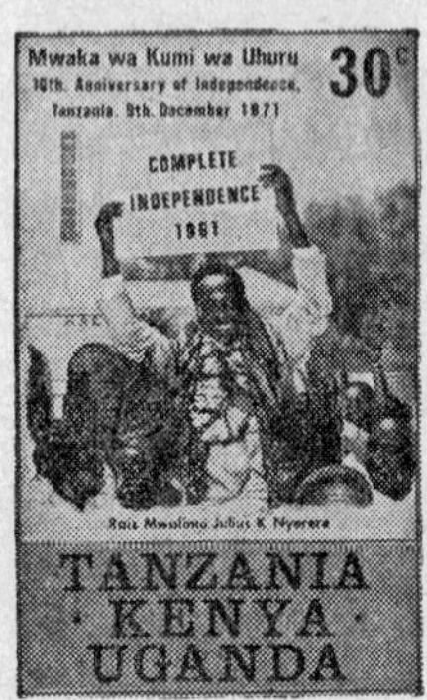

26. Pres. Nyerere and Supporters.

1971. Tanzanian Independence. 10th Anniv. Multicoloured.

96.	30 c. Type 26	8	8
97.	70 c. Ujamaa village ..	10	12
98.	1 s. 50 Dar-es-Salaam University	25	30
99.	2 s. 50 Kilimanjaro airport ..	45	45

27. Flags and Trade Fair Emblem.

1972. 1st All-Africa Trade Fair, Nairobi.

100.	27.	30 c. multicoloured ..	8	8
101.		70 c. multicoloured ..	10	12
102.		1 s. 50 multicoloured ..	25	30
103.		2 s. 50 multicoloured ..	45	45

28. Child with cup.

1972. U.N.I.C.E.F. 25th Anniv. Multicoloured.

104.	30 c. Type 28	8	8
105.	70 c. Children with ball ..	10	12
106.	1 s. 50 Child at blackboard	25	30
107.	2 s 50 Child and tractor ..	45	45

29. Hurdling.

1972. Olympic Games, Munich, Multicoloured.

108.	40 c. Type 29	8	8
109.	70 c. Running	10	10
110.	1 s. 50 Boxing	20	20
111.	2 s. 50 Hockey	50	50

30. Ugandan Kobs.

1972. Ugandan Independence. 10th Anniv. Multicoloured.

113.	40 c. Type 30	5	5
114.	70 c. Conference Centre ..	8	8
115.	1 s. 50 Makere University	20	20
116.	2 s. 50 Coat of Arms ..	45	45

31. Community Flag.
(Illustration reduced. Actual size 58 × 21½ mm.)

1972. East African Community. 5th Anniv.

118.	31.	5 s. multicoloured ..	70	75

32. Run-of-the-wind Anemometer.

1972. IMO/WMO Cent. Multicoloured.

119.	40 c. Type 32	10	10
120.	70 c. Weather balloon (vert.)	12	12
121.	1 s. 50 Meteorological rocket	20	20
122.	2 s. 50 Satellite receiving aerial	45	45

33. "Learning by Serving".

1973. 24th World Scouting Conference, Nairobi.

123.	33.	40 c. multicoloured ..	10	10
124.	–	70 c. red, violet & blk.	12	12
125.	–	1 s. 50 blue, violet & blk.	20	25
126.	–	2 s. 50 multicoloured ..	45	45

DESIGNS: 70 c. Baden-Powell's grave, Nyeri. 1 s. 50, World Scout emblem. 2 s. 50, Lord Baden-Powell.

34. Kenyatta Conference Centre.

1973. I.M.F./World Bank Conference.

127.	34.	40 c. grn., grey and blk.	10	10
128.	–	70 c. brn., grey & black	12	12
129.	–	1 s. 50 multicoloured ..	35	35
130.	–	2 s. 50 orge. grey & blk.	30	35

DESIGNS: Nos. 128/30 show different arrangements of Bank emblems and the Conference Centre the 1 s. 50 being, vertical.

35. Police Dog-handler.

1973. Interpol. 50th Anniv.

132.	35.	40 c. yell., blue & black	8	8
133.	–	70 c. grn., yellow & blk.	10	10
134.	–	1 s. 50 violet, yell. & blk.	20	25
135.	–	2 s. 50 grn., orge. & blk.	30	35
136.	–	2 s. 50 grn., orge. & blk.	30	35

DESIGNS: 70 c. East African policemen. 1 s. 50, Interpol emblem. 2 s. 50 (2), Interpol H.Q. No. 135 is inscribed "St. Clans" and No. 136, "St. Cloud".

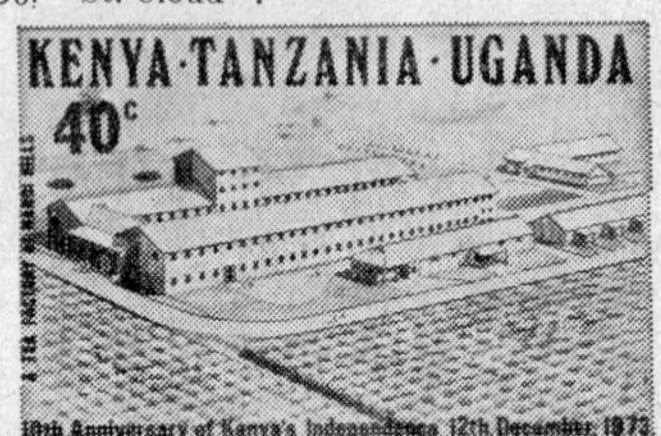

36. Tea Factory.

1973. Kenya's Independence. 10th Anniv. Multicoloured.

137.	40 c. Type 36	8	8
138.	70 c. Kenyatta Hospital	10	10
139.	1 s. 50 Nairobi Airport ..	20	25
140.	2 s. 50 Kindaruma hydro-electric scheme	45	45

37. Party H.Q.

1973. Zanzibar's Revolution. 10th Anniv. Multicoloured.

141.	40 c. Type 37	8	8
142.	70 c. Housing scheme ..	10	10
143.	1 s. 50 Colour T.V. ..	20	25
144.	2 s. 50 Amaan Stadium ..	45	45

38. "Symbol of Union".

1974. Tanzania-Zanzibar Union. 10th Anniv. Multicoloured.

145.	40 c. Type 38	8	8
146.	70 c. Handclasp	10	10
147.	1 s. 50 "Communications"	20	25
148.	2 s. 50 Flags of Tanu, Tanzania and Afro-Shirazi Party	30	35

39. East African Family ("Stability of the Home").

1974. 17th Social Welfare Conf., Nairobi.
149. **39.** 40 c. yell., brn. & blk... 8 8
150. – 70 c. multicoloured .. 10 10
151. – 1 s. 50 yell., grn. & blk. 20 25
152 – 2 s. 50 red, vio. & blk... 30 35

DESIGNS: 70 c. Dawn and Drummer (U.N. Second Development Plan). 1 s. 50, Agricultural scene (Rural Development Plan). 2 s. 50, Transport and Telephone ("Communications").

40. New Postal H.Q., Kampala.

1974. U.P.U. Centenary. Multicoloured.
153. 40 c. Type **40** 5 5
154. 70 c. Mail-train and post-van 8 10
155. 1 s. 50 U.P.U. Building, Berne 20 25
156. 2 s. 50 Loading mail into "VC-10".. .. .. 30 35

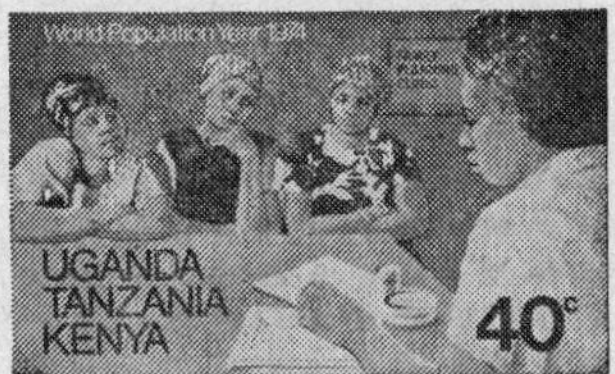

41. Family Planning Clinic.

1974. World Population Year.
157. **41.** 40 c. multicoloured .. 8 8
158. – 70 c. mauve and red .. 10 10
159. – 1 s. 50 multicoloured .. 20 25
160. – 2 s. 50 blue, emer & grn. 30 35

DESIGNS: 70 c. " Tug of war ". 1 s. 50, Population " scales ". 2 s. 50, W.P.Y. emblem.

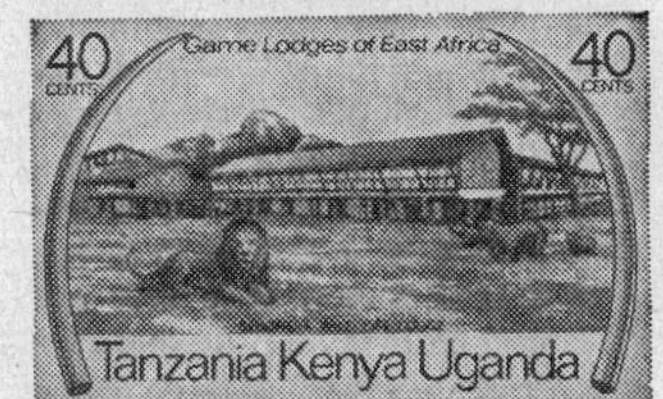

42. Seronera Wildlife Lodge, Tanzania.

1975. East African Game Lodges. Mult.
161. 40 c. Type **42** 8 8
162. 70 c. Mweya Safari Lodge, Uganda 10 10
163. 1 s. 50 " Ark "—Aberdare Forest Lodge, Kenya .. 20 25
164. 2 s. 50 Paraa Safari Lodge, Uganda 30 35

43. Kitana (wooden comb), Bajun of Kenya.

1975. African Arts. Multicoloured.
165. 50 c. Type **43** 5 8
166. 1 s. Earring, Chaga of Tanzania 12 15
167. 2 s. Okoco (armlet), Acholi of Uganda 25 30
168. 3 s. Kitete, Kamba gourd, Kenya 40 45

44. International Airport, Entebbe.

1975. O.A.U. Summit Conference, Kampala, Multicoloured.
169. 50 c. Type **44** 5 8
170. 1 s. Map of Africa and flag (vert.) 12 15
171. 2 s. Nile Hotel, Kampala 25 30
172. 3 s. Martyrs' Shrine, Namugongo (vert.) 35 40

45. Ahmed (" Presidential " Elephant).

1975. Rare Animals. Multicoloured.
173. 50 c. Type **45** 5 8
174. 1 s. Albino buffalo .. 12 15
175. 2 s. Ahmed in grounds of National Museum .. 25 30
176. 3 s. Abbott's duiker .. 35 40

46. Masai Manyatta (animal slaughter), Kenya.

1975. 2nd World Black and African Festival of Arts and Culture. Multicoloured.
177. 50 c. Type **46** 5 8
178. 1 s. " Heartbeat of Africa " (Ugandan dancers) .. 12 15
179. 2 s. Makonde sculpture, Tanzania 25 30
180. 3 s. " Early Man and Technology " (skinning animal) 35 40

47. Fokker " Friendship " at Nairobi Airport.

1975. East African Airways. 30th Anniv. Multicoloured.
181. 50 c. Type **47** 5 8
182. 1 s. " DC 9 " at Kilimanjaro Airport 12 15
183. 2 s. Super " VC 10 " at Entebbe Airport .. 25 30
184. 3 s. East African Airways Crest 35 40

Further commemorative sets were released from 1976 onwards; using common designs, but each valid in one republic only. See Kenya, Tanzania and Uganda.

EAST SILESIA E1

Special overprints were applied to Czechoslovakian and Polish stamps prior to a plebiscite. The plebiscite was never held, due to disorders and the area was divided between Czechoslovakia and Poland in 1920.

1920. Stamps of Czechoslovakia optd. **SO 1920.** Imperf. or perf.
23. **3.** 1 h. brown 5 5
2. **2.** 3 h. mauve 5 5
24. **3.** 5 h. green 8 8
25. 10 h. green 5 5
26. 15 h. red 5 5
6. **2.** 20 h. green 5 5
27. **3.** 20 h. red 15 15
28. 25 h. purple 15 15
9. **2.** 30 h. olive 10 10
35. **3.** 30 h. mauve 15 15
10. **2.** 40 h. orange 10 10
11. **3.** 50 h .purple 20 20
12. 50 h. blue 70 70
36. 60 h. orange 20 20
14. 75 h. green 15 20
15. 80 h. olive 15 20
16. **2.** 100 h. brown 30 30
17. **3.** 120 h. black 70 70
18. **2.** 200 h. blue 60 60
19. **3.** 300 h. green .. .. 1·00 1·00
20. **2.** 400 h. violet 75 75
21. **3.** 500 h. brown .. .. 2·00 2·00
22. 1000 h. purple .. .. 4·00 4·00

1920. Stamps of Poland of 1919 optd. **S.O. 1920** Perf.
57. **6.** 5 f. green 5 5
58. 10 f. purple 5 5
59. 15 f. red 5 5
60. **7.** 25 f. olive 5 5
61. 50 f. green 5 5
62. **8.** 1 k. green 5 5
63. 1 k. 50 brown 5 5
64. 2 k. blue 5 5
65. **9.** 2 k. 50 purple 5 5
66. **10.** 5 k. blue 5 5

EXPRESS STAMPS FOR PRINTED MATTER

1920. Express stamps of Czechoslovakia optd. **SO 1920.**
E 39. E **1.** 2 h. purple on yellow 5 5
E 40. 5 h. green on yellow .. 5 5

NEWSPAPER STAMPS

1920. Newspaper stamps of Czechoslovakia optd. **SO 1920** Imperf.
N 41. N **1.** 2 h. green 5 5
N 42. 6 h. red 5 5
N 43. 10 h. lilac 15 15
N 44. 20 h. blue 15 15
N 45. 30 h. brown 15 15

POSTAGE DUE STAMPS

1920. Postage Due stamps of Czechoslovakia optd. **SO 1920.** Imperf.
D 46. D **1.** 5 h. olive 5 5
D 47. 10 h. olive 5 5
D 48. 15 h. olive 5 5
D 49. 20 h. olive 8 8
D 50. 25 h. olive 10 10
D 51. 30 h. olive 10 10
D 52. 40 h. olive 20 20
D 53. 50 h. olive 20 20
D 54. 100 h. brown 30 30
D 55. 500 h. green .. .. 1·40 1·40
D 56. 1000 h. violet .. .. 3·25 3·25

EASTERN ROUMELIA (SOUTH BULGARIA) E1

This area, part of the Turkish Empire, situated south of the Balkan Mts., became semi-autonomous after 1878. In 1885 the population revolted against the Turks, changing the district's name to South Bulgaria. Incorporation into Bulgaria followed in 1886.

40 paras = 1 piastre.

A. EASTERN ROUMELIA.

1880. Stamps of Turkey optd. **RO.**
1. **2.** ½ pre. on 20 pa. green (No. 78) .. .. 8·50 8·50
2. **3.** 20 pa. pur. & grn. (No. 83) 11·00 11·00
3. 2 pi. blk. & orge. (No. 85) 27·00 27·00
4. 5 pi. red & blue (No. 86) 55·00 55·00

1881. Stamp of Turkey optd. **R.O.** and **ROUMELIE ORIENTALE.**
5. **3.** 10 pa. black and mauve.. 9·00 9·00

1881. As T **3** of Turkey, but inscr. "ROUMELIE ORIENTALE" at left.
6. **3.** 5 pa. black and olive .. 70 20
11. 5 pa. lilac 10 10
7. 10 pa. black and green .. 1·00 20
12. 10 pa. green 5 20
8. 20 pa black and red .. 12 20
9. 1 pi. black and blue .. 1·00 1·10
10. 5 pi. red and blue .. 4·25 11·00

B. SOUTH BULGARIA.

1885. As T **3** of Turkey, but inscr. " ROUMELIE ORIENTALE " at left and optd. with lion.
13. **3.** 5 pa. black and olive .. — 40·00
29. 5 pa. lilac .. .. 1·40 3·75
14. 10 pa. black and green .. — £130
30. 10 pa. green .. .. 4·00 6·00
15. 20 pa. black and red .. 30·00
34. 20 pa. red .. .. 2·75 4·50
18. 1 pi. black and blue .. 2·75 5·50
26. 5 pi. red and blue .. .. 80·00

1885. As T **3** of Turkey, but inscr. " ROUMELIE ORIENTALE " and optd. with lion and inscription in frame.
43. **3.** 5 pa. black and olive .. 70·00 70·00
48a. 5 pa. lilac .. .. 2·50 3·00
44. 10 pa. black and green .. 70·00 70·00
49. 10 10 pa. green .. .. 3·25 4·00
45. 20 20 black and red .. 12·00 15·00
50. 20 pa. red.. .. .. 3·00 4·00
46. 1 pi. black and blue .. 12·00 15·00
47. 5 pi. red and blue .. £150 £180

ECUADOR O2

A Republic on the W. Coast of S. America. Independent since 1830.

1865. 8 reales = 1 peso.
1881. 100 centavos = 1 sucre.

1.

2.

1865. Imperf.
1b. **1.** ½ r. blue .. .. .. 2·50 3·00
2c. 1 r. yellow .. .. 4·50 5·00
3. 1 r. green .. .. .. 20·00 9·00
4. **2.** 4 r. red .. .. .. 45·00 35·00

3.

4.

5.

1872.
10. **3.** ½ r. blue .. .. .. 2·50 50
11. **4.** 1 r. orange .. .. 2·40 65
12. **3.** 1 p. red .. .. .. 30 1·40

1881. Various frames.
13. **5.** 1 c. brown 5 5
14. 2 c. lake 5 5
15. 5 c. blue 55 20
16. 10 c. orange 5 5
17. 20 c. violet 10 10
18. 50 c. green 15 30

1883. Surch. **DIEZ CENTAVOS.**
19. **5.** 10 c. on 50 c. green .. 8·00 8·00

6.

7. Pres. J. Flores.

8. Pres. Rocofuerte.

1887. Various frames.
26. **6.** 1 c. green 8 8
27. 2 c. red 8 8
28. 5 c. blue 10 10
29. 80 c. olive.. .. .. 35 1·75

1892.
34. **7.** 1 c. orange 5 5
35. 2 c. brown 5 5
36. 5 c. red 5 5
37. 10 c. green 5 5
38. 20 c. brown 5 5
39. 50 c. claret 5 15
40. 1 s. blue 10 50
41. 5 s. violet 15 75

1893. Surch. **5 CENTAVOS.**
53. **7.** 5 c. on 50 c. claret .. 20 20
49. 5 c. on 1 s. blue 25 25
50. 5 c. on 5 s. violet .. .. 1·00 90

1894. Dated "1894".
57. **8.** 1 c. blue 8 8
58. 2 c. brown 8 8
59. 5 c. green 12 12
60. 10 c. red 30 15
61. 20 c. black 25 12
62. 50 c. orange .. .. 1·50 40
63. 1 s. red .. .. .. 1·75 75
64. 5 s. blue .. .. .. 2·40 1·40

1895. Dated "1895".
74. **8.** 1 c. blue 25 25
75. 2 c. brown 25 22
76. 5 c. green 12 12
77. 10 c. red 10 10
78. 20 c. black 30 30
79. 50 c. orange .. .. 1·10 50
80. 1 s. red .. .. .. 3·50 2·10
81. 5 s. blue .. .. .. 2·10 95

These two series were re-issued in 1897 optd. "1897-1898".

9.

10.

1896. Arms designs, inscr. "U.P.U. 1896".

89. **9.** 1 c. green 25 10
90. 2 c. red 25 10
91. 5 c. blue 25 10
92. 10 c. brown 25 10
93. 20 c. orange 40 20
94. 50 c. blue 25 30
95. 1 s. brown .. .. 1·25 60
96. 5 s. lilac .. .. .. 1·75 1·00

This series was re-issued in 1897 optd. "1897-1898".

1896. Dated "1887 1888". Surch.

112. **10.** 5 c. on 10 c. orange .. 20 15
113. 10 c. on 4 c. brown .. 30 25

1896. As T 10, but dated "1891 1892". Surch.

114. **10.** 10 c. on 4 c. brown .. 2·40 2·40

1896. As T 10, but dated "1893 1894". Surch.

115. **10.** 1 c. on 1 c. red .. 15 15
116. 2 c. on 2 c. blue.. .. 50 50
117. 5 c. on 10 c. orange .. 1·25 1·25

11. V. Roca, D. Noboa and J. Olmedo. (**12.**)

1896. Triumph of Liberal Party. Dated "1845-1895".

118. **11.** 1 c. red 15 15
119. – 2 c. blue 12 12
120. **11.** 5 c. green 15 15
121. – 10 c. yellow 20 20
122. **11.** 20 c. red 25 50
123. – 50 c. lilac 30 60
124. **11.** 1 s. orange .. .. 50 1·00

DESIGN: 2 c., 10 c., 50 c. Gen. Elizalde.

This series was re-issued in 1897 optd. "1897-1898".

1896. Surch.

125. **9.** 5 c. on 20 c. orange .. 2·50 2·25
126. 10 c. on 50 c. blue .. 2·50 2·50

1897. 1896 Jubilee issue optd. with T 12.

162. **11.** 1 c. red 25 25
164. – 2 c. blue (No. 119) .. 40 40
165. **11.** 5 c. green 60 60
166. – 10 c. yellow (No. 121) .. 40 40

14. **15.** L. V. Torres.

1897.

173. **14.** 1 c. green 5 5
174. 2 c. red 5 5
175. 5 c. lake 5 5
176. 10 c. brown 5 5
177. 20 c. yellow 8 8
178. 50 c. blue 10 10
179. 1 s. grey 20 20
180. 5 s. purple 30 30

1899. Surch.

191. **14.** 1 c. on 2 c. red .. 20 15
192. 5 c. on 10 c. brown .. 15 12

1899.

193. **15.** 1 c. black and grey .. 8 5
205. 1 c. black and red .. 5 5
194. – 2 c. black and brown .. 8 5
206. – 2 c. black and green .. 8 5
195. – 5 c. black and red .. 10 5
207. – 5 c. black and lilac .. 8 5
196. – 10 c. black and lilac .. 10 5
208. – 10 c. black and blue .. 8 5
197. – 20 c. black and green .. 10 8
209. – 20 c. black and grey .. 10 8
198. – 50 c. black and red .. 35 30
210. – 50 c. black and blue .. 30 25
199. – 1 s. black and yellow .. 1·00 70
211. – 1 s. black and brown .. 90 60
200. – 5 s. black and lilac .. 2·25 1·60
212. – 5 s. black and grey .. 1·60 1·25

PORTRAITS: 2 c. A. Calderon. 5 c. J. Montalvo. 10 c. Mejia. 20 c. Espejo. 50 c. Carbo. 1 s. J.J. Olmedo. 5 s. Moncayo.

24. Capt. A. Calderon. **26.**

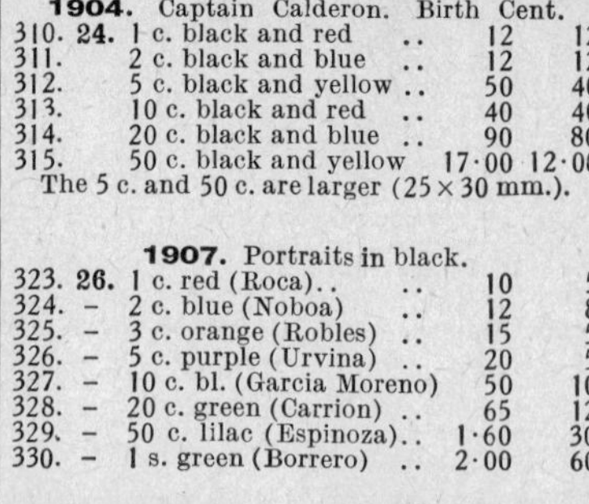

1904. Captain Calderon. Birth Cent.

310. **24.** 1 c. black and red .. 12 12
311. 2 c. black and blue .. 12 12
312. 5 c. black and yellow .. 50 40
313. 10 c. black and red .. 40 40
314. 20 c. black and blue .. 90 80
315. 50 c. black and yellow 17·00 12·00

The 5 c. and 50 c. are larger (25 × 30 mm.).

1907. Portraits in black.

323. **26.** 1 c. red (Roca).. .. 10 5
324. – 2 c. blue (Noboa) .. 12 8
325. – 3 c. orange (Robles) .. 15 5
326. – 5 c. purple (Urvina) .. 20 5
327. – 10 c. bl. (Garcia Moreno) 50 10
328. – 20 c. green (Carrion) .. 65 12
329. – 50 c. lilac (Espinoza).. 1·60 30
330. – 1 s. green (Borrero) .. 2·00 60

27.

29. Mount Chimborazo.

28. Garcia Moreno.

1908. Opening of Guayaquil to Quito Railway.

331. **27.** 1 c. brown 25 15
332. **28.** 2 c. black and blue .. 50 25
333. – 5 c. black and red .. 1·10 70
334. – 10 c. black and yellow 40 30
335. – 20 c. black and green .. 40 30
336. – 50 c. black and grey .. 40 30
337. **29.** 1 s. black 80 55

PORTRAITS—As T 28: 5 c. Gen. E. Alfaro. 10 c. A. Moncayo. 20 c. A. Harman. 50 c. Sivewright.

30. J. M. Vallejo.

31. Exhibition Buildings.

1909. National Exn. Portraits as T 30.

340. **30.** 1 c. green (Vallejo) .. 8 12
341. – 2 c. blue (Espejo) .. 8 12
342. – 3 c. orange (Ascasubi).. 8 12
343. – 5 c. lake (Salinas) .. 8 12
344. – 10 c. brown (Alegre) .. 8 12
345. – 20 c. grey (Montufar) .. 8 15
346. – 50 c. red (Morales) .. 10 20
347. – 1 s. olive (Quiroga) .. 10 30
348. **31.** 5 s. violet 20 50

1909. Surch. **CINCO CENTAVOS.**

349. – 5 c. on 50 c. red (No. 346) 30 30

32. Pres. Roca.

33. Pres. Dr. Noboa.

34. Robles.

35. Valdez. **36.** Pres. Gen. Urvina.

37. Pres. Dr. Garcia Moreno.

38. Espinoza.

39. Dr. Borrero.

1911.

354. **32.** 1 c. black and red .. 8 5
366. 1 c. orange 5 5
355. **33.** 2 c. black and blue .. 15 5
367. 2 c. green 5 5
356. **34.** 3 c. black and orange.. 60 15
368. 3 c. black 8 5
369. **35.** 4 c. black and red .. 10 5
357. **36.** 5 c. black and red .. 25 5
370. 5 c. violet 10 5
358. **37.** 10 c. black and blue .. 40 5
371. 10 c. blue 30 5
373. **38.** 50 c. black and violet.. 90 20
359. **39.** 1 s. black and green .. 1·50 40

See also Nos. 413/6b.

1912. Large Fiscal stamps inscr. "TIMBRE CONSULAR" at top. Surch. **POSTAL** and new value.

362. 1 c. on 1 s. green .. 25 25
363. 2 c. on 2 s. red.. .. 35 35
364. 2 c. on 5 s. blue .. 35 35
365. 2 c. on 10 s. yellow .. 60 60

1920. Optd. **CASA de CORREOS.**

374. **32.** 1 c. orange 10 8

40.

41.

42.

1920. Optd. **CASA de CORREOS** or surch. also. Dated as shown.

375. **40.** 1 c. bl. & red (no date) 8 5
376. 1 c. bl. ("1919–1920") 15 5
379. 1 c. on 2 c. grn. ("1917–1918") 15 10
380. 1 c. on 5 c. grn. ("1911–1912") 10 10
380a. 1 c. on 5 c. grn. ("1913–1914") .. .. 1·10 45
377. 20 c. bl. ("1913–1914") 75 35
378. 20 c. ol. ("1917–1918") 90 70

1920. Liberation of Guayaquil. Cent. Portraits as T 41.

381. **41.** 1 c. green (Olmedo) .. 10 5
382. – 2 c. red (Ximena) .. 5 5
383. – 3 c. bistre (Roca) .. 8 8
384. – 4 c. green (Vivero) .. 12 10
385. – 5 c. blue (Cordero) .. 12 5
386. – 6 c. orange (Lavayen).. 20 20
387. – 7 c. brown (Elizalde) .. 35 30
388. – 8 c. green (Garcia) .. 25 15
389. – 9 c. red (Antepara) .. 35 30
390. **42.** 10 c. blue 25 5
391. – 15 c. black (Urdaneta) 35 20
392. – 20 c. purple (Villamil) 45 12
393. – 30 c. violet (Letamendi) 65 60
394. – 40 c. sepia (Escobedo) 1·40 1·00
395. – 50 c. green (Sucre) .. 90 20
396. – 60 c. blue (Illingworth) 1·40 1·00
397. – 70 c. grey (Roca) .. 2·00 1·60
398. – 80 c. yellow (Rocafuerte) 1·60 1·50
399. – 90 c. green (Star and wreath) .. .. 2·00 1·75
400. – 1 s. blue (Bolivar) .. 3·50 2·50

43. Post Office, Quito.

44.

1920.

401. **43.** 1 c. olive 5 5
402. 2 c. green 12 5
403. 20 c. brown 40 12
404. 2 s. violet 54 45
405. 5 s. blue .. .. 1·50 1·40

1921. Obligatory Tax. Surch. **CASA DE CORREOS. VEINTE CTS. 1921 1922.**

505a. **40.** 20 c. on 1 c. blue .. 10·00 2·00
405b. 20 c. on 2 c. green .. 10·00 2·00

1924. Obligatory Tax. Surch. **DOS CENTAVOS -2-.**

406. **43.** 2 c. on 20 c. brown .. 10 5

1924. Oblong Tobacco Tax stamps optd. **CASA-CORREOS.**

407. 1 c. red (Loco.) .. 10 10
408. 2 c. blue (Arms) .. 12 8

1924. Telegraph stamps as T 40, but inscr. "TELEGRAFOS DEL ECUADOR" optd. **CASA—CORREOS.**

(a) Inscr. "TIMBRE FISCAL".

409. 1 c. yellow 50 40
410. 2 c. blue 15 10

(b) Inscr. "REGION ORIENTAL".

411. 1 c. yellow 15 8
412. 2 c. blue 15 8

1925.

413. **32.** 1 c. blue 5 5
414. **33.** 2 c. violet 5 5
415. **36.** 5 c. red 8 5
415a. 5 c. brown 15 5
416. **37.** 10 c. green 10 5
416a. 10 c. black 30 5
416b. **39.** 1 s. black and orange.. 1·00 5

1925. Optd. **POSTAL** over ornament.

417. **43.** 20 c. brown 50 25

1926. Opening of Quito-Esmeraldas Railway. Optd. **QUITO** and railway train and **ESMERALDAS 1926.**

418. **32.** 1 c. blue .. .. 1·40 1·40
419. **33.** 2 c. violet .. .. 1·40 1·40
420. **34.** 3 c. black .. .. 1·40 1·40
421. – 4 c. green (No. 384) .. 1·40 1·40
422. **36.** 5 c. red .. .. .. 1·40 1·40
423. **37.** 10 c. green .. .. 1·40 1·40

1927. Optd. **POSTAL.**

424. **43.** 1 c. olive 5 5
425. 2 c. green 5 5
426. 20 c. brown 30 5

1927. Opening of new Post Office. Quito.

427. **44.** 5 c. orange 5 5
428. 10 c. green 8 5
429. 20 c. purple 15 12

1928. Opening of Quito-Cayambe Railway. Stamps of 1920 issue surch. **Frril. Norte Julio 8 de 1928 Est. Cayambe** and value.

431. 10 c. on 30 c. (No. 393) 75 75
432. 50 c. on 70 c. (No. 397) 75 75
433. 1 s. on 80 c. (No. 398).. 75 75

1928. National Assembly. Stamps of 1920 surch. **ASAMBLEA NCNAL, 1928** and value.

434. **41.** 1 c. on 1 c. green (381).. 3·25 3·25
435. – 1 c. on 2 c. red (382) .. 8 8
436. – 2 c. on 3 c. bistre (383).. 40 40
437. – 2 c. on 4 c. green (384).. 35 35
438. – 2 c. on 5 c. (No. 385) .. 12 12
440. – 5 c. on 6 c. (No. 386) .. 8 8
441. – 10 c. on 2 c. on 7 c. (387) 8 8
442. – 10 c. on 7 c. (No. 387).. 25 25
443. – 20 c. on 8 c. (No. 388).. 8 8
444. **42.** 40 c. on 10 c. (No. 390).. 50 50
445. – 40 c. on 15 c. (No. 391).. 25 25
446. – 50 c. on 20 c. (No. 392).. 2·50 2·50
447. – 1 s. on 40 c. (No. 394).. 70 70
448. – 5 s. on 50 c. (No. 395).. 90 90
449. – 10 s. on 60 c. (No. 395).. 3·50 3·50

1928. Opening of Railway at Otavalo, Consular Service stamps inscr. "TIMBRE-CONSULAR" surch. **Postal — Frril Norte Est. OTAVALO** and value.

450. 5 c. on 20 c. lilac 40 25
451. 10 c. on 20 c. lilac .. 40 25
452. 20 c. on 1 s. green .. 40 25
453. 50 c. on 1 s. green .. 55 20
454. 1 s. on 1 s. green 60 25
455. 5 s. on 2 s. red .. .. 2·00 1·00
456. 10 s. on 2 s. red .. .. 2·50 2·50

45. Aeroplane over R. Guayas.

46. Ploughing.

1929. Air.

458. **45.** 2 c. black 8 5
459. 5 c. red 8 5
460. 10 c. brown 10 5
461. 20 c. purple 15 5
462. 50 c. green 30 10
463. 1 s. blue 90 75
467. 1 s. red .. .. .. 1·50 25
709. 1 s. green 25 8
464. 5 s. yellow .. .. 3·75 3·50
468. 5 s. olive .. .. 2·00 1·60
710. 5 s. violet 50 5
465. 10 s. red .. .. 27·00 25·00
469. 10 s. black .. .. 6·00 1·50
711. 10 s. blue .. .. 1·00 5

1929. As T 40, but inscr. "MOVILES" and optd. **POSTAL.**

466. **40.** 1 c. blue 5 5

1930. Air. Official Air stamps of 1929 optd. **MENDEZ BOGOTA-QUITO Junio 4 de 1930.**

470. **45.** 1 s. red .. .. .. 5·00 5·00
471. 5 s. olive .. .. 5·00 5·00
472. 10 s. black .. .. 5·00 5·00

1930. Independence Cent. Dated "1830 1930".
473. 46. 1 c. red and yellow .. 10 5
474. – 2 c. green and yellow .. 10 5
475. – 5 c. purple and green .. 12 8
476. – 6 c. red and yellow .. 15 5
477. – 10 c. olive and orange.. 15 8
478. – 16 c. green and red .. 20 15
479. – 20 c. yellow and blue .. 25 10
480. – 40 c. sepia and yellow.. 25 10
481. – 50 c. sepia and yellow.. 30 10
482. – 1 s. black and green .. 65 12
483. – 2 s. black and deep blue 1·10 15
484. – 5 s. black and purple .. 2·00 30
485. – 10 s. black and red .. 9·00 2·10
DESIGNS—As T 46: 1 c. Labourer and oxen, ploughing. 2 c. Cocoa cultivation. 6 c. Tobacco plantation. 10 c. Exportation of fruit. 10 s. Bolivar's monument (41×37½ mm.). LARGER (27×42½ mm.): 5 c. Cocoa bean. 20 c. Sugar plantation. 1 s. Olmedo. 2 s. Sucre. 5 s. Bolivar (41½×28 mm.): 16 c. Mountaineer, locomotive and aeroplane. 40 c., 50 c. Views of Quito.

1933. Optd. **CORREOS.**
486. 40. 10 c. brown 8 5

1933. Optd. **CORREOS—Emision Junio 1933—Dcto. No. 200.**
487. 40. 10 c. brown 8 5

1933. Nos. 476 and 478 surch.
488. 5 c. on 6 c. red and yellow 8 5
489. 10 c. on 16 c. green and red 8 5

1934. Obligatory Tax. Optd. **CASA de Correos y Telegrafos de Guayaquil.**
(a) Fiscal stamp as T 40, but inscr. "MOVILES" (instead of dates at top).
490. 40. 2 c. green 5 5
(b) Centenary stamp of 1930 (No. 479).
491. 20 c. yellow and blue .. 10 5
(c) Telegraph stamp as T 40, but inscr. "TELEGRAFOS DEL ECUADOR" surch **2 ctvos.** also.
492. 40. 2 c. on 10 c. brown .. 5 5

50. Mount Chimborazo. 51. Mount Chimborazo.

1934.
493. 50. 5 c. mauve 8 5
494. 5 c. blue 8 5
495. 5 c. brown 8 5
495a. 5 c. grey 8 5
496. 10 c. red 8 5
497. 10 c. green 8 5
498. 10 c. orange 8 5
499. 10 c. brown 8 5
500. 10 c. olive 8 5
500a. 10 c. black 5 5
500b. 10 c. lilac 5 5

1934.
501. 51. 1 s. red 55 30

1934. Optd. **CASA de Correos y Teleg. de Guayaquil.**
502. 43. 2 c. green (No. 425) .. 5 5

52. Symbol of Telegraphy. 54. Galapagos Islands.

1934. G.P.O. Rebuilding Fund.
503. 52. 2 c. green 5 5
504. – 20 c. red 8 5
The symbolic design of the 20 c. is 38×18½ mm.

1935. Unveiling of Bolivar Monument, Quito. Optd. **INAUGURACION MONUMENTO A BOLIVAR QUITO,** etc., or surch. also.
(a) Postage. On 1930 Independence Issue.
505. 5 c. on 6 c. red and yellow 15 10
506. 10 c. on 6 c. red and yellow 15 8
507. 20 c. yellow and blue .. 20 10
508. 40 c. sepia and yellow .. 25 15
509. 50 sepia and yellow .. 35 25
510. $1 on 5 s. black and purple 80 45
511. $2 on 5 s. black and purple 1·40 65
512. $5 on 10 s. black and red 2·25 1·60
(b) Air. On Official stamps of 1929.
513. 45. 50 c. green .. .. 2·00 2·00
514. 50 c. brown .. .. 2·00 2·00
515. $1 on 5 s. olive .. .. 2·00 2·00
516. $2 on 10 s. black.. .. 2·00 2·00

1935. Fiscal stamp, but without dates and inscr. "TELEGRAFOS DEL ECUADOR", optd. **POSTAL.**
517. 40. 10 c. brown 5 5

1935. Rural Workers Social Insurance Fund. No. 503 surch. **Seguro Social del Campesino Quito, 16 de Otbre.—1935** and value.
518. 52. 3 c. on 2 c. green .. 5 5

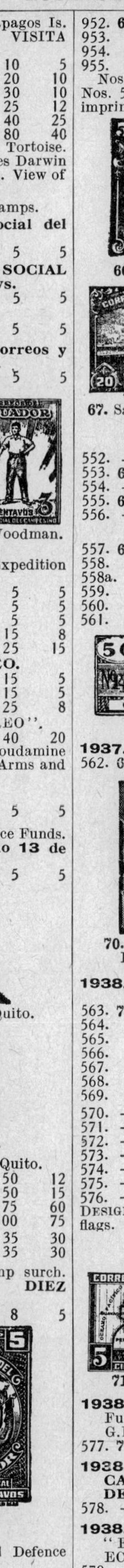
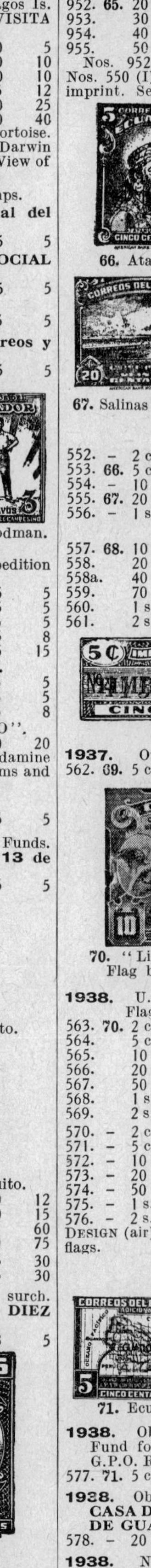
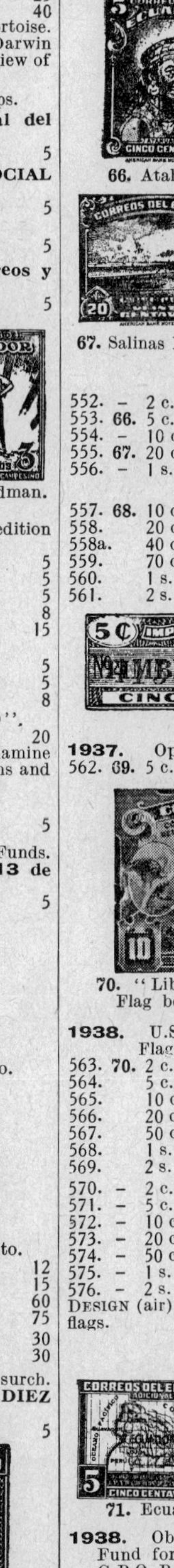

1936. Darwin's Visit to the Galapagos Is. Cent. Inscr. "CENTENARIO VISITA DARWIN".
519. 54. 2 c. black 10 5
520. – 5 c. olive 20 10
521. – 10 c. brown 30 10
522. – 20 c. purple 25 12
523. – 1 s. red 40 25
524. – 2 s. blue 80 40
DESIGNS—HORIZ. 10 c. Galapagos Tortoise. VERT. 5 c. Giant Lizard. 20 c. Charles Darwin and "Beagle". 1 s. Columbus. 2 s. View of Galapagos Is.

1936. Oblong Tobacco Tax Stamps.
(a) Charity. Surch. **Seguro Social del Campesino 3 ctvs.**
525. – 3 c. on 1 c. red .. 5 5
(b) Charity. Surch. **SEGURO SOCIAL DEL CAMPESINO 3 ctvs.**
526. – 3 c. on 1 c. red .. 5 5
(c) Optd. **POSTAL.**
527. – 1 c. red .. 5 5

1936. No. 479 optd. **Casa de Correos y Telegrafos de Guayaquil.**
528. – 20 c. yellow and blue.. 5 5

60. Ulloa, La Condamine and Juan. 61. Woodman.

1936. La Condamine Scientific Expedition Bicent. (a) Postage.
529. – 2 c. blue 5 5
530. 60. 5 c. green 5 5
531. – 10 c. orange 5 5
532. 60. 20 c. violet 15 8
533. – 50 c. red 25 15
(b) Air. Nos. 531/3 optd. **AEREO.**
534. – 10 c. orange 15 5
535. 60. 20 c. violet 15 5
536. – 50 c. red 25 8
(c) Air. Inscr. "CORREO AEREO".
537. – 70 c. grey 40 20
DESIGNS: 2 c. 10 c., 50 c. Godin. La Coudamine and Bouguer. 70 c. La Condamine, Arms and Maldonado.

1936. Social Insurance.
540. 61. 3 c. blue.. .. 5 5

1936. Building and National Defence Funds. Surch. **5 Centavos Dect. Junio 13 de 1936.**
539. 61. 5 c. on 3 c. blue .. 5 5

62. Independence Monument, Quito.

63. Condor and Aeroplane.

1936. 1st Int. Philatelic Exn., Quito.
542. 62. 5 c. purple (postage) .. 50 12
543. 10 c. red 50 15
544. 50 c. blue 75 60
545. 1 s. red .. .. 1·00 75
546. 63. 70 c. brown (air) .. 35 30
547. 1 s. violet 35 30

1936. Oblong Tobacco Tax stamp surch. **TIMBRE PATRIOTICO DIEZ CENTAVOS.**
541. – 10 c. on 1 c. red .. 8 5

64. Symbolical of Defence. 65.

1937. Obligatory Tax. National Defence Fund. (a) Without surch.
549. 64. 10 c. blue .. 8 5
(b) Surch. **POSTAL ADICIONAL** and value in figures.
548. 64. 5 on 10 c. blue .. 5 5

1937. Fiscal stamps inscr. "MOVILES" at top optd. **POSTAL** or surch. also.
550. 65. 5 c. olive (I) 10 5
955a. 5 c. olive (II) 8 5
551. 10 c. blue 10 5
819. 10 c. orange 30 5
952. 65. 20 c. on 30 c. blue .. 5 5
953. 30 c. blue 5 5
954. 40 c. on 50 c. purple .. 10 5
955. 50 c. purple 20 5
Nos. 952/3 are smaller (19½×25½ mm.). Nos. 550 (I) with imprint. 955a (II) without imprint. See also No. 685.

DESIGNS — VERT. 2 c. Andean landscape. 1 s. Gold washer. HORIZ. 10 c. Straw-hat makers.

66. Atahualpa.

67. Salinas Beach. 68. Condor over El Altar.

1937.
(a) Postage.
552. – 2 c. green 5 5
553. 66. 5 c. red 8 5
554. – 10 c. blue 10 5
555. 67. 20 c. red 20 12
556. – 1 s. olive 30 10
(b) Air.
557. 68. 10 c. brown 5 5
558. 20 c. olive 8 5
558a. 40 c. red 8 5
559. 70 c. brown 12 8
560. 1 s. slate 15 12
561. 2 s. violet 35 15

69.

1937. Optd. **TIMBRE PATRIOTICO.**
562. 69. 5 c. brown 8 5

70. "Liberty" supporting Ecuadorian Flag between Eagle and Condor.

1938. U.S. Constitution. 150th Anniv. Flags in yellow, blue and red.
563. 70. 2 c. blue (postage) .. 8 5
564. 5 c. violet 10 5
565. 10 c. black 12 5
566. 20 c. purple 15 8
567. 50 c. black 20 10
568. 1 s. olive 35 15
569. 2 s. brown 75 25
570. – 2 c. olive (air) .. 5 5
571. – 5 c. black 5 5
572. – 10 c. brown 8 5
573. – 20 c. blue 12 5
574. – 50 c. purple 30 10
575. – 1 s. black 50 12
576. – 2 s. violet .. .. 1·10 30
DESIGN (air): Washington portrait, eagle and flags.

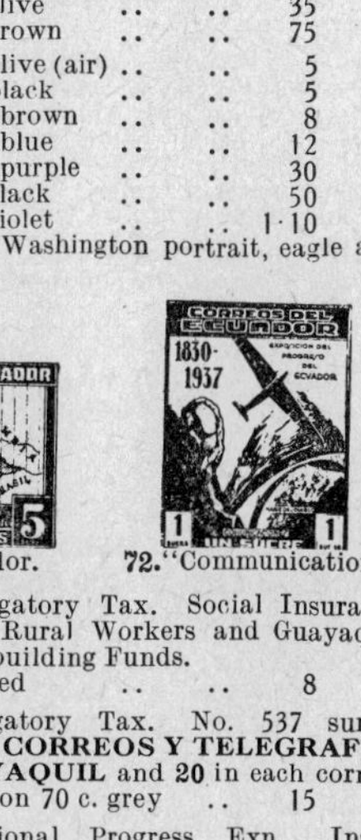
71. Ecuador. 72. "Communication".

1938. Obligatory Tax. Social Insurance Fund for Rural Workers and Guayaquil G.P.O. Rebuilding Funds.
577. 71. 5 c. red 8 5

1938. Obligatory Tax. No. 537 surch. **CASA DE CORREOS Y TELEGRAFOS DE GUAYAQUIL** and **20** in each corner.
578. – 20 c. on 70 c. grey .. 15 5

1938. National Progress Exn. Inscr. "EXPOSICION DEL PROGRESO DEL ECUADOR".
579. – 10 c. blue 5 5
580. – 50 c. purple 10 5
581. 72. 1 s. red 15 5
582. – 2 s. green 30 5
DESIGNS—VERT. 10 c. "Road Transport" (winged figure holding globe). 50 c. "Railways" (winged wheel). HORIZ. 2 s. "Building" (inscr. "CONSTRUCCION").

1938. Air. Surch. **AEREO SEDTA** and value.
582a. 61. 65 c. on 3 c. blue .. 8 5

1938. Obligatory Tax. Int. Anti-Cancer Fund. No. 476 surch. **CAMPANA. CONTRA EL CANCER 5 5.**
583. 5 c. on 6 c. red and yellow 5 5

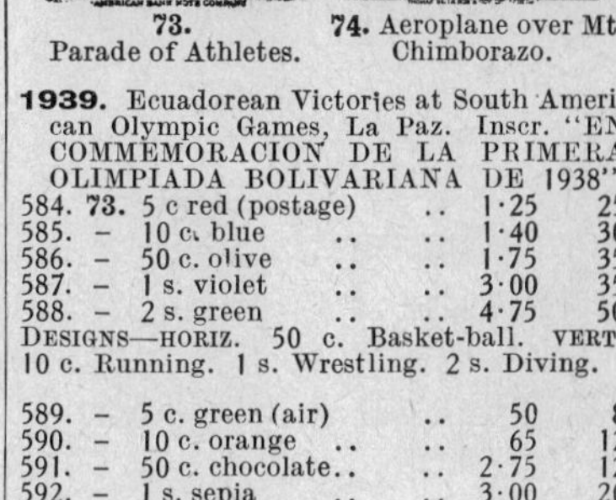
73. Parade of Athletes. 74. Aeroplane over Mt. Chimborazo.

1939. Ecuadorean Victories at South American Olympic Games, La Paz. Inscr. "EN COMMEMORACION DE LA PRIMERA OLIMPIADA BOLIVARIANA DE 1938".
584. 73. 5 c red (postage) .. 1·25 25
585. – 10 c. blue .. .. 1·40 30
586. – 50 c. olive .. .. 1·75 35
587. – 1 s. violet .. .. 3·00 35
588. – 2 s. green .. .. 4·75 50
DESIGNS—HORIZ. 50 c. Basket-ball. VERT. 10 c. Running. 1 s. Wrestling. 2 s. Diving.
589. – 5 c. green (air) .. 50 8
590. – 10 c. orange 65 12
591. – 50 c. chocolate.. .. 2·75 12
592. – 1 s. sepia .. .. 3·00 20
593. – 2 s. red .. .. 5·00 20
DESIGNS—HORIZ. 5 c. Riding. 1 s. Boxing. VERT. 10 c. Running. 50 c. Tennis. 2 s. Olympic flame.

1939. Air.
594. 74. 1 s. brown 20 5
595. 2 s. purple 30 5
596. 5 s. black 85 5

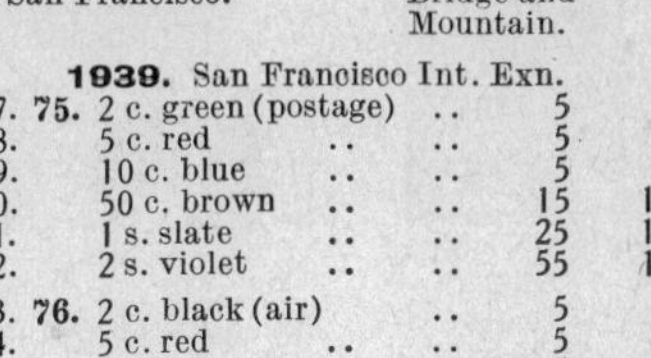
75. Dolores Mission, San Francisco. 76. Suspension Bridge and Mountain.

1939. San Francisco Int. Exn.
597. 75. 2 c. green (postage) .. 5 5
598. 5 c. red 5 5
599. 10 c. blue 5 5
600. 50 c. brown 15 10
601. 1 s. slate 25 12
602. 2 s. violet 55 15
603. 76. 2 c. black (air) .. 5 5
604. 5 c. red 5 5
605. 10 c. blue 5 5
606. 50 c. purple 8 5
607. 1 s. brown 10 8
608. 2 s. brown 20 8
609. 5 s. green 50 12

77. Symbol of N.Y. World's Fair. 78. Building and Mountain.

1939. New York World's Fair.
610. 77. 2 c. olive (postage) .. 5 5
611. 5 c. orange 5 5
612. 10 c. blue 8 5
613. 50 c. grey 15 8
614. 1 s. red 25 10
615. 2 s. brown 50 12
616. 78. 2 c. brown (air) .. 5 5
617. 5 c. red 5 5
618. 10 c. blue 5 5
619. 50 c. olive 8 5
620. 1 s. orange 12 5
621. 2 s. mauve 20 8
622. 5 s. black 45 5

1939. Obligatory Tax. Social Insurance Fund for Rural Workers. Oblong Tobacco Tax stamps surch. **POSTAL ADICIONAL CINCO CENTAVOS** and value.
623. – 5 c. on 1 c. pink .. 5 5

1940. Obligatory Tax. G.P.O. Rebuilding Fund. Oblong Tobacco Tax stamps surch. **CASAS DE CORREOS Y TELEGRAFOS CINCO CENTAVOS.** and value.
624. – 5 c. on 1 c. pink .. 5 5

1940. Obligatory Tax. Guyaquil G.P.O. Rebuilding Fund. No. 567 surch. **CASA DE CORREOS y TELEGRAFOS DE GUAYAQUIL 20 20.**
625. 70. 20 c. on 50 c. yellow, blue pink and black .. 8 5

1940. Obligatory Tax. National Defence Fund. Oblong Tobacco Tax stamps surch. **TIMBRE PATRIOTICO VEINTE CENTAVOS** and value.
625a. – 20 c. on 1 c. pink .. 8 5

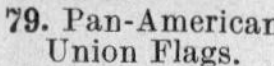

79. Pan-American Union Flags. 80. Allegory of Union.

1940. Pan-American Union. 50th Anniv.
626. **79.** 5 c. black & red (post.) 8 5
627. 10 c. black and blue .. 8 5
628. 50 c. black and green .. 20 8
629. 1 s. black and violet .. 30 12
630. **80.** 10 c. blue & orange (air) 10 5
631. 70 c. blue and purple .. 12 5
632. 1 s. blue and brown .. 20 8
633. 10 s. blue and black .. 1·00 15

81. Ploughing. 82. Symbolic of Communications.

1940. Obligatory Tax. Social Insurance Fund for Rural Workers and Guayaquil G.P.O. Rebuilding Funds.
634. **81.** 5 c. red 5 5

1940. Obligatory Tax. G.P.O. Rebuilding Fund.
635. **82.** 5 c. brown 5 5
636. 5 c. green 5 5

83. Pursuit 'Planes. 84. Dr. de Santa Cruz y Espejo.

86. Early Map of S. America. 85. Guayaquil.

1941. Obligatory Tax. National Defence Fund.
637. **83.** 20 c. blue 12 5

1941. 1st National Periodical Exn.
638. **84.** 30 c. blue (postage) .. 12 5
639. 1 s. orange 30 8
640. 3 s. red (air) 75 10
641. 10 s. orange .. .. 1·50 20

1942. Discovery of R. Amazon. 4th Cent.
642. – 10 c. brown (postage) .. 8 5
643. – 40 c. red 15 5
644. **85.** 1 s. violet 25 8
645. – 2 s. blue 40 15
646. **86.** 40 c. bistre & black (air) 15 10
647. – 70 c. olive 30 8
648. – 2 s. green 50 20
649. – 5 s. red .. .. 1·00 40

DESIGNS—VERT. 10 c., 40 c. (No. 643). 70 c. Portraits of F. Orellana, G. Pizarro and G. Diaz de Pineda. 2 s. (No. 645) Quito. 5 s. Expedition leaving Quito. HORIZ. 2 s. (No. 648) Relief map of R. Amazon.

87. R. Crespo Tora. 88. Mt. Chimborazo.

1942.
650. **87.** 10 c. green (postage) .. 5 5
651. 50 c. brown 12 5
652. 10 c. violet (air) .. 15 5

1942. As T **87.** but portrait of Pres. A. B. Moreno.
653. 10 c. green 5 5

1942.
654. **88.** 30 c. brown 8 5
654a. 30 c. blue 8 5
654b. 30 c. orange 8 5
654c. 30 c. green 10 5

88a. "Defence". 89. Guayaquil Riverside.

1942. Obligatory Tax. National Defence Fund.
655. **88a.** 20 c. blue 8 5
655a. 40 c. brown 8 5

1942. Obligatory Tax. National Defence Fund. As T **69** surch.
655b. **69.** 20 c. on 5 c. pink .. — 2·25
655c. 20 c. on 1 s. brown .. — 2·25
655d. 20 c. on 2 s. green .. — 2·25

1942. Obligatory Tax. Guayaquil G.P.O. Rebuilding Fund, No. 567 surch. **CASA DE CORREOS Y TELEGRAFOS DE GUAYAQUIL VEINTE CENTAVOS.**
655e. – 20 c. on 50 c. mult. .. 10 5

1943.
656. **89.** 20 c. red 5 5
656a. 20 c. blue 5 5

1943. Guayaquil G.P.O. Rebuilding Fund. Surch. **ADICIONAL CINCO CENTAVOS 5 Centavos CASA DE CORREOS DE GQUIL. y.**
657. **61.** 5 c.+5 c. on 3 c. blue.. 5 5

1943. Surch. **ADICIONAL CINCO CENTAVOS.**
658. **61.** 5 c. on 3 c. blue .. 5 5

90. Gen. Alfaro. 91. Alfaro's Birthplace.

1943. Alfaro Birth Cent.
659. **90.** 10 c. black & red (post.) 8 5
660. – 20 c. brown and olive.. 10 5
661. – 30 c. green and olive .. 12 8
662. **91.** 1 s. red and grey .. 30 12
663. **90.** 70 c. black and red (air) 30 15
664. – 1 s. brown and olive .. 30 25
665. – 3 s. green and olive .. 60 40
666. **91.** 5 s. red and grey .. 75 50

DESIGNS—HORIZ 20 c., 1 s. Devil's Nose Zigzag, Guayaquil-Quito Rly. 30 c., 3 s. Alfaro Military College.

92. Labourers. 93. Arms of Ecuador.

1943. Obligatory Tax. Social Insurance Fund for Rural Workers and Guayaquil G.P.O. Rebuilding Funds.
667. **92.** 5 c. blue 5 5

1943. Welcome to Henry A. Wallace Vice-President of U.S.A Optd. **BIENVENIDO-WALLACE Abril 15-1943.**
668. **70.** 50 c. black, yellow, blue and red (postage) .. 15 15
669. 1 s. olive, yellow, blue and red .. 35 35
670. 2 s. brn., yell., blue & red 60 60
671. – 50 c. purple, yellow, blue & red (No. 574) (air) 35 35
672. – 1 s. black, yellow, blue and red (No. 575) .. 40 40
673. – 2 s. violet, yellow, blue and red (No. 576) .. 65 65

1943. Obligatory Tax. National Defence Fund. Fiscal stamp optd. **TIMBRE PATRIOTICO.**
674. 20 c. orange .. 3·00 15

1943 Air. Visits of Presidents of Bolivia, Paraguay and Venezuela to Ecuador.

(a) Optd. **AEREO LOOR A BOLIVIA JUNIO 11-1943.**
675. – 50 c. purple (No. 580).. 12 12
676. **73.** 1 s. red 20 15
677. – 2 s. green (No. 582) .. 30 25

(b) Optd. **AEREO LOOR AL PARAGUAY JULIO 5-1943.**
678. – 50 c. purple (No. 580).. 12 12
579. **73.** 1 s. red 20 20
680. – 2 s. green (No. 582) .. 30 25

(c) Optd. **AEREO LOOR A VENEZUELA JULIO 23-1943.**
681. – 50 c. purple (No. 580).. 12 12
682. **73.** 1 s. red 20 20
683. – 2 s. green (No. 582) .. 30 30

1943. Obligatory Tax National Defence Fund. Fiscal stamp surch. **TIMBRE PATRIOTICO VEINTE CENTAVOS.**
684. – 20 c. on 10 c. orange 35 5

1943. Fiscal stamp as T **65.** surch. **POSTAL 30 Centavos** with or without bars.
685. **65.** 30 c. on 50 c. brown .. 8 5

As No. 685 but surch. **POSTAL 30 Ctvs.**
780. **65.** 30 c. on 50 c. brown .. 5 5

1943. Obligatory Tax. National Defence Fund.
686. **93.** 20 c. red 5 5

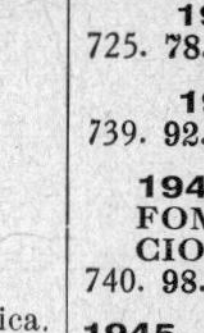

94. Arms of Ecuador and Central America.

95. Pres. Arroyo del Rio at Washington.

1943. President's Visit to Washington.
687. **94.** 10 c. violet (postage) .. 12 10
698. 10 c. green 8 15
688. 20 c. brown 12 12
699. 20 c. pink 10 8
689. 30 c. orange 15 12
700. 30 c. brown 12 10
690. 50 c. olive 20 12
701. 50 c. purple 20 15
691. 1 s. violet 25 15
702. 1 s. grey 20 20
692. 10 s. brown .. .. 1·60 90
703. 10 s. orange .. .. 1·60 1·25
693. **95.** 50 c. brown (air) .. 25 25
704. 50 c. purple 25 20
694. 70 c. red 30 25
705. 70 c. brown 40 25
695. 3 s. blue 40 40
706. 3 s. green 40 20
696. 5 s. green 85 50
707. 5 s. blue 65 50
697. 10 s. olive .. .. 3·00 2·75
708. 10 s. red 80 75

1944. Nos. 698/708 surch. **Hospital Mendez** and new value.
708a. **94.** 10 c.+10 c. grn. (post.) 12 12
708b. 20 c.+20 c. pink .. 15 15
708c. 30 c.+20 c. brown .. 15 15
708d. 50 c.+20 c. purple .. 20 20
708e. 1 s.+50 c. grey .. 40 40
708f. 10 s.+2 s. orange .. 1·25 1·25
708g. **95.** 50 c.+50 c. pur. (air) 2·00 2·00
708h. 70 c.+30 c. brown .. 2·00 2·00
708i. 3 s.+50 c. green .. 2·00 2·00
708j. 5 s+1 s. blue.. .. 2·00 2·00
708k. 10 s.+2 s. red.. .. 2·25 2·25

1944. No. 600. Surch. **30 Centavos.**
712. **75.** 30 c. on 50 c. brown .. 10 5

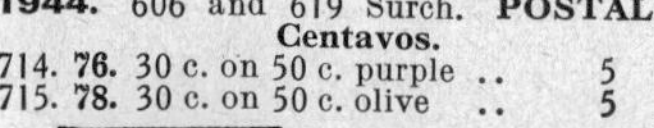

1944. Obligatory Tax. National Defence Fund. No. 686 surch. **POSTAL 30 Centavos.**
713. **93.** 30 c. on 20 c. red .. 5 5

1944. 606 and 619 Surch. **POSTAL 30 Centavos.**
714. **76.** 30 c. on 50 c. purple .. 5 5
715. **78.** 30 c. on 50 c. olive .. 5 5

96. F. G. Suarez. 97. Cathedral.

1944. F. G. Suarez. Birth Cent.
716. **96.** 10 c. blue (postage) .. 5 5
717. 20 c. green 8 5
718. 30 c. purple 12 5
719. 1 s. violet 25 10
720. **97.** 70 c. green (air) .. 25 25
721. 1 s. olive 25 25
722. 3 s. red 80 40
723. 5 s. red 80 50

1944. Surch. **CINCO Centavos.**
724. **75.** 5 c. on 2 c. green .. 5 5

98. Government Palace, Quito. 99. Red Cross Symbol.

1944.
726. **98.** 10 c. green (postage) .. 5 5
727. 30 c. blue 5 5
728. 3 s. orange (air) .. 25 5
729. 5 s. brown 35 5
730. 10 s. red 75 5
730a. 10 s. violet 80 5

1945. Int. Red Cross. 80th Anniv. Cross in red.
731. **99.** 30 c. brown (postage).. 35 12
732. 1 s. brown 45 15
733. 5 s. green 80 50
734. 10 s. red .. .. 1·75 1·25
735. 2 s. blue (air) .. 50 45
736. 3 s. green 60 50
737. 5 s. violet 80 75
738. 10 s. red .. .. 2·25 2·00

1945. Surch. **CINCO Centavos.**
725. **78.** 5 c. on 2 c. green .. 5 5

1945. Air. Surch. **AERO 40 Ctvs.**
739. **92.** 40 c. on 5 c. blue .. 10 5

1945. Obligatory Tax. Air. Surch. **FOMENTO - AERO - COMUNICACIONES 20 Ctvs.**
740. **98.** 20 c. on 10 c. green .. 12 5

1945. Air. Victory. Optd. **V SETIEMBRE 5 1945.**
742. **98.** 3 s. orange 35 35
743. 5 s. brown 45 45
744. 10 s. red .. .. 1·40 1·40

1945. Visit of Pres. Juan Antonio Rios of Chile. Optd. **LOOR A CHILE OCTUBRE 2 1945** and five-pointed star. Flags in yellow, blue and red.
745. **70.** 50 c. black (postage) .. 12 10
746. 1 s. olive 20 12
747. 2 s. brown 40 40
748. – 50 c. pur. (No. 574) (air) 35 30
749. – 1 s. black (No. 575) .. 35 30
750. – 2 s. violet (No. 576) .. 40 30

100. Marshal Sucre. 101. Pan-American Highway.

1945. Marshal Sucre. 150th Birth Anniv. Inscr. as in T **100.**
751. **100.** 10 c. green (postage).. 5 5
752. 20 c. brown 5 5
753. 40 c. grey 8 5
754. 1 s. green 15 12
755. 2 s. brown 35 20
756. – 30 c. blue (air) .. 10 5
757. – 40 c. red 12 8
758. – 1 s. violet 25 20
759. – 3 s. black 50 40
760. – 5 s. purple 75 50

DESIGN—Air stamps: Liberty Monument.

1945. Surch. **c VEINTE CENTAVOS.**
761. **98.** 20 c. on 10 c. green .. 5 5

1946. Completion of Pan-American Highway.
762. **101.** 20 c. brown (postage) 5 5
763. 30 c. green 8 5
764. 1 s. blue 12 12
765. 5 s. purple 70 40
766. 10 s. red .. .. 1·60 1·25
767. 1 s. red (air) .. 20 15
768. 2 s. violet 35 20
769. 3 s. green 55 25
770. 5 s. orange 60 40
771. 10 s. blue .. .. 1·25 30

102. Torch of Democracy. 103. Popular Suffrage.

1946. Revolution. 2nd Anniv.
772. **102.** 5 c. blue (postage) .. 5 5
773. **103.** 10 c. green 5 5
774. – 20 c. red 12 5
775. – 30 c. brown 15 8
776. **102.** 40 c. claret (air) .. 8 5
777. **103.** 1 s. brown 12 5
778. – 2 s. blue 30 12
779. – 3 s. green 50 20

DESIGNS—VERT. 20 c., 2 s. Ecuador flag. 30 c., 3 s. Pres. Ibarra.

1946. Nos. O 567/8 optd. **POSTAL.**
781. **68.** 10 c. brown 5 5
782. 20 c. olive 5 5

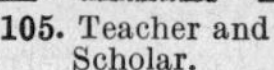

105. Teacher and Scholar. 106. Initials and Quill Pen.

1946. Adult Instruction Campaign.
783. **105.** 10 c. blue (postage) .. 8 5
784. 20 c. brown 8 5
785. 30 c. green 10 5
786. 50 c. black 12 8
787. 1 s. red 25 10
788. 10 s. purple .. .. 1·60 50

789. **106.** 50 c. violet (air) .. 20 15
790. 70 c. green 20 20
791. 3 s. red 35 25
792. 5 s. blue 50 35
793. 10 s. brown .. .. 1·60 45

107. "Liberty", "Mercury" and Aeroplanes. **108.** Mariana de Jesus Paredes y Flores.

1946. Obligatory Tax. Air. National Defence Fund.
794. **107.** 20 c. brown 10 5

1946. Blessed Mariana de Jesus Paredes y Flores. Death Tercent. Inscr. as in T **108.**
795. **108.** 10 c. brown (postage) .. 10 5
796. 20 c. green 12 5
797. 30 c. violet 15 8
798. – 1 s. brown (Urn) .. 30 15

799. – 40 c. brown (air) .. 20 8
800. – 60 c. blue 25 20
801. – 3 s. yellow 55 50
802. – 5 s. green 90 60

DESIGNS: 40 c., 60 c. Blessed Mariana teaching children. 3 s., 5 s. Cross and lilies.

109. Vicente Rocafuerte. **110.** Jesuit Church, Quito. **111.** Andres Bello.

1947.
803. **109.** 5 c. brown (postage) .. 5 5
804. 10 c. purple 5 5
805. 15 c. black 5 5
806. **110.** 20 c. lake 8 5
807. 30 c. mauve 8 8
808. 40 c. blue 10 8
809. – 45 c. green 12 5
810. – 50 c. grey 12 8
811. – 80 c. red 15 8

PORTRAIT: 45 c. to 80 c. F. J. E. de Santa Cruz y Espejo.

812. – 60 c. green (air) .. 8 5
813. – 70 c. violet 10 5
814. – 1 s. brown 12 5
815. – 1 s. 10 red 10 8
816. – 1 s. 30 blue 12 10
817. – 1 s. 90 brown 25 12
818. – 2 s. olive 25 8

DESIGNS: 60 c. to 1 s. 10, Father J. de Velasco. 1 s. 30 to 1 s. Riobamba Irrigation Canal.

1948. Andres Belle (educationalist). 83rd Death Anniv.
820. **111.** 20 c. blue (postage) .. 5 5
821. 30 c. pink 8 5
822. 40 c. green 10 5
823. 1 s. black 20 10

824. 60 c. mauve (air.) .. 15 8
825. 1 s. 30 green 30 15
826. 1 s. 90 red 25 15

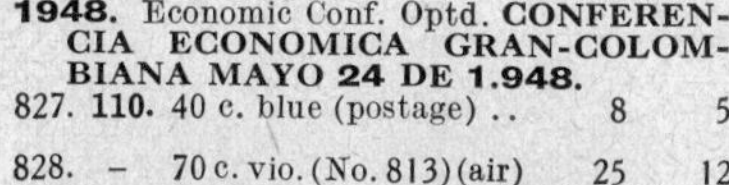

1948. Economic Conf. Optd. **CONFERENCIA ECONOMICA GRAN-COLOMBIANA MAYO 24 DE 1.948.**
827. **110.** 40 c. blue (postage) .. 8 5

828. – 70 c. vio. (No. 813) (air) 25 12

112. The "Santa Maria". **113.** Christopher Columbus.

1948. Completion of Columbus Memorial Lighthouse.
829. **112.** 10 c. green (postage) .. 8 5
830. 20 c. brown 10 5
831. 30 c. violet 12 5
832. 50 c. claret 15 5
833. 1 s. blue 25 8
834. 5 s. red 75 15

835. **113.** 50 c. green (air) .. 10 8
836. 70 c. red 15 12
837. 3 s. blue 30 25
838. 5 s. brown 60 25
839. 10 s. violet .. .. 1·10 30

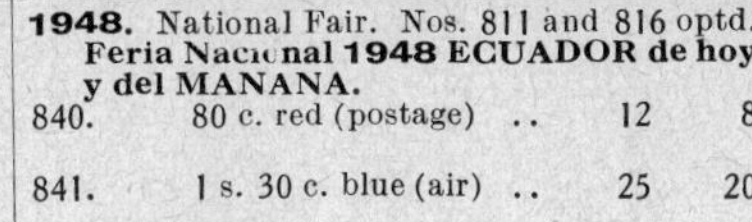

1948. National Fair. Nos. 811 and 816 optd. **Feria Nacional 1948 ECUADOR de hoy y del MANANA.**
840. 80 c. red (postage) .. 12 8

841. 1 s. 30 c. blue (air) .. 25 20

114. Aeroplane in Flight. **115.** Pilot and Aeroplane.

1948. First Ecuadorian Postal Flight. 25th Anniv.
842. **114.** 30 c. orange (postage) 10 5
843. 40 c. mauve 10 5
844. 60 c. blue 10 5
845. 1 s. brown 15 8
846. 3 s. brown 30 15
847. 5 s. black 50 25

848 **115.** 60 c. red (air) .. 20 15
849. 1 s. green 20 20
850. 1 s. 30 claret .. 25 25
851. 1 s. 90 violet .. 25 20
852. 2 s. brown 30 25
853. 5 s. blue 65 40

116. "Reading and Writing". **117.** "Education For All".

1948. National Education Campaign.
854. **116.** 10 c. claret (postage) 5 5
855. 20 c. brown 5 5
856. 30 c. green 8 5
857. 50 c. red 12 5
858. 1 s. violet 20 8
859. 10 s. blue .. .. 1·10 25

860. **117.** 50 c. violet (air) .. 20 12
861. 70 c. blue 20 15
862. 3 s. green 30 25
863. 5 s. red 40 25
864. 10 s. brown 75 30

118. "Freedom from Fear". **119.** "Freedom of Religion".

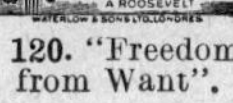

120. "Freedom from Want". **121.** "Freedom of Speech and Expression".

1948. Homage to Franklin D. Roosevelt.
865. **118.** 10 c. clar. & grey (post.) 8 8
866. 20 c. olive and blue .. 10 8
867. **119.** 30 c. olive and red .. 15 10
868. 40 c. purple and sepia 20 10
869. 1 s. brown and red .. 30 20

870. **121.** 60 c. grn. & brn. (air) .. 10 8
871. 1 s. red and black .. 12 10
872. **120.** 1 s. 50 green & brown 20 12
873. 2 s. red and black .. 45 12
874. 5 s. blue and black .. 70 15

122. Riobamba Aqueduct.

123. Maldonado at Academy of Sciences, Paris. **124.** P. V. Maldonado.

1948. Maldonado (geographer and scientist). Death Bicent.
875. **123.** 5 c. red & blk. (post.) .. 8 5
876. **122.** 10 c. black and red .. 10 5
877. – 30 c. blue and brown 12 5
878. **122.** 40 c. violet and green 15 5
879. **123.** 50 c. red and green .. 20 8
880. **124.** 1 s. blue and brown .. 25 8

881. – 60 c. red & orge. (air) 20 8
882. **124.** 90 c. black and red .. 20 10
883. – 1 s. 30 orange & mauve 30 15
884. **124.** 2 s. green and blue .. 30 15

DESIGN—VERT. 30 c., 60 c., 1 s. 30, Maldonado making road to Esmeraldas.

125. Cervantes, Don Quixote and Windmill. **126.** Don Quixote and Sheep.

1949. Birth of Cervantes. 400th Anniv.
885. – 30 c. blue & pur. (post.) 10 5
886. **125.** 60 c. brown & purple .. 20 8
887. – 1 s. red and green .. 25 10
888. **125.** 2 s. black and red .. 40 15
889. – 5 s. green and brown 1·00 30

890. – 1 s. 30 sep. & blue (air) 25 15
891. **126.** 1 s. 90 red and green .. 25 15
892. – 3 s. violet and red .. 25 12
893. **126.** 5 s. black and red .. 75 15
894. – 10 s. purple and green 1·10 12

DESIGNS—HORIZ. 30 c., 1 s., 5 s. (No. 889) Cervantes, Don Quixote and Sancho Panza. 1 s. 30, 3 s., 10 s. Don Juan Montalvo and Cervantes.

1949. 2nd Eucharistic Congress. Stamps of 1947 surch. **II CONGRESO Junio 1949 Eucaristico Ncl.** and values.

(a) Postage. No. 808 surch.
895. **110.** 10 c. on 40 c. blue .. 8 5
896. 20 c. on 40 c. blue .. 10 5
897. 30 c. on 40 c. blue .. 12 5

(b) Air. No. 815 surch.
898. 50 c. on 1 s. 10 red .. 10 8
899. 60 c. on 1 s. 10 red .. 12 12
900. 90 c. on 1 s. 10 red .. 15 15

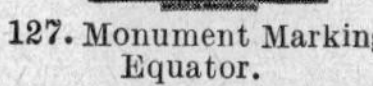

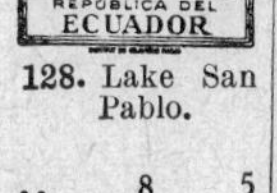

127. Monument Marking Equator. **128.** Lake San Pablo.

1949.
901. **127.** 10 c. purple 8 5

1949. U.P.U. 75th Anniv. Surch. **75 ANIVERSARIO** (or **Aniversario**—air stamps) **U.P.U.** and value.
902. **128.** 10 c. on 50 c. grn. (post.) 10 5
903. 20 c. on 50 c. green .. 12 5
904. 30 c. on 50 c. green .. 20 5

905. **98.** 60 c. on 3 s. orge. (air) 30 25
906. 90 c. on 3 s. orange .. 25 20
907. 1 s. on 3 s. orange .. 35 25
908. 2 s. on 3 s. orange .. 70 35

For unoverprinted stamp T **128**, see No. 926.

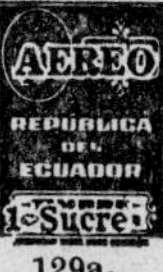

129. **129a.**

1949. Consular Service stamps optd. or surch. for postal use.

I. On T **129.**

A. Postage.

(a) Vert. surch. **POSTAL** and value before **ct.**
908a. **129.** 5 c. on 10 c. red .. 5 5
909. 20 c. on 25 c. brown 5 5
910. 30 c. on 50 c. black .. 5 5

(b) Optd. **CORREOS** diag.
927. **129.** 10 c. red 5 5

(c) Optd. **POSTAL** diag.
929. **129.** 10 c. red 5 5

(d) Vert. surch. with figs. before and after **Ctvs.**

(i) **CORREOS** upwards.
928. **129.** 30 c. on 50 c. black .. 8 5

(ii) **POSTAL** upwards.
930. **129.** 20 c. on 25 c. brown .. 5 5
931. 30 c. on 50 c. black .. 5 5

(e) Surch. **POSTAL centavos** with figs. between.
969. **129.** 10 c. on 20 s. blue .. 5 5
970. 20 c. on 10 s. grey .. 5 5
971. 20 c. on 20 s. blue .. 5 5
972. 30 c. on 10 s. grey .. 8 5
973. 30 c. on 20 s. blue .. 8 5

B. Air. Surch. **AEREO** and value.
913. **129.** 60 c. on 50 c. black .. 8 5
913a. 60 c. on 2 s. brown .. 8 5
913b. 1 s. on 2 s. brown (D.) 12 5
913c. 1 s. on 2 s. brown (U.) 15 5
913d. 2 s. on 2 s. brown .. 25 5
913e. 3 s. on 5 s. violet .. 40 12

In No. 913b the surch. reads down and in No. 913c it reads up.

II. On T **129a.**

A. Postage. Surch. **POSTAL** and value.
935. **129a.** 30 c. on 50 c. red .. 8 5
934. 40 c. on 25 c. blue .. 5 5
936. 50 c. on 25 c. blue .. 10 5

B. Air. Surch. **AEREO** and value.
913f. **129a.** 60 c. on 1 s. green .. 5 5
913g. 60 c. on 5 s. sepia .. 8 5
913h. 70 c. on 5 s. sepia .. 10 5
913i. 90 c. on 50 c. red .. 15 5
913j. 1 s. on 1 s. green .. 12 5

1950. Optd. **POSTAL.**
911. **83.** 5 c. green 5 5
912. **92.** 5 c. blue 5 5

1950. Air. (a) Nos. 816/7 surch. **90 ctvs. 90.**
914. 90 c. on 1 s. 30 blue .. 10 5
914a. 90 c. on 1 s. 90 brown .. 12 5

(b) No. 816 surch. **90 CENTAVOS.**
914b. 90 c. on 1 s. 30 blue .. 8 5

1950. Adult Education Campaign. Optd. **ALFABETIZACION.** Four also surch. with new values and No. 920 also optd. **POSTAL.** (a) Postage.
915. **127.** 10 c. purple 5 5
916. **122.** 20 c. on 40 c. (878) .. 5 5
917. 30 c. on 40 c. (878) .. 5 5
918. **123.** 50 c. red and green .. 10 5
919. **124.** 1 s. blue and brown .. 15 5
920. **98.** 10 s. violet .. .. 1·00 35

(b) Air.
921. – 50 c. on 1 s. 10 (No. 815) 12 10
922. – 70 c. on 1 s. 10 (No. 815) 15 12
923. **98.** 3 s. orange 30 25
924. 5 s. brown 55 35
925. 10 s. violet .. .. 1·00 30

1950.
926. **128.** 50 c. green 8 5

1951. Air. Panagra Airlines' 20,000th Flight across Equator. Optd. **20,000 Cruce** etc., in four lines.
932. **98.** 3 s. orange 40 40
933. 5 s. brown 75 50

1951. Adult Education. Surch. **CAMPANA Alfabetizacion** and values. (a) Postage.
937. **129a.** 20 c. on 25 c. blue .. 5 5
938. 30 c. on 25 c. blue .. 8 5

(b) Air.
939. – 60 c. on 1 s. 30 (No. 890) 12 8
940. **126.** 1 s. on 1 s. 90 (891) .. 12 8

130. Reliquary. **131.** St. Mariana de Jesus.

1952. Canonization of St. Mariana de Jesus.
941. **130.** 10 c. grn. & lake (post) 8 5
942. 20 c. blue and violet .. 10 8
943. 30 c. red and green .. 15 8

944. **131.** 60 c. clar. & turq. (air) 25 12
945. 90 c. green and blue .. 30 12
946. 1 s. red and green .. 30 12
947. 2 s. blue and mauve .. 35 10

132. Presidents Plaza and Truman.

1952. Visit of President of Ecuador to U.S.A.
948. 132. 1 s. blk. & red (postage) 15 8
949. – 2 s. sepia and blue .. 30 10

950. 132. 3 s. green & lilac (air) 35 30
951. – 5 c. olive and brown .. 70 60
DESIGN: 2 s. 5 s. Pres. Plaza addressing U.S. Congress.

1952. Consular Service stamps surch. TIMBRE ESCOLAR 20 ctvs. 20.
957. 129. 20 c. on 1 s. red .. 5 5
958. 20 c. on 2 s. brown .. 5 5
959. 20 c. on 5 s. violet .. 5 5

133. Pres. Urvina, Slave and "Liberty".

133a. Teacher and Scholars.

1952. Abolition of Slavery in Ecuador. Cent. Roul.
960. 133. 20 c. grn. & red (post.) 10 5
961. 30 c. red and blue .. 12 5
962. 50 c. blue and red .. 20 5

963. – 60 c. red & blue (air) 50 20
964. – 90 c. lilac and red .. 50 20
965. – 1 s. orange and green 50 12
966. – 2 s. brown and blue .. 50 15
DESIGN—VERT. Nos. 963/6, Pres. Urvina, condor and freed slave.

1952. Obligatory Tax. Literacy Campaign.
967. 133a. 20 c. green 8 5

1952. Obligatory Tax. Public Health Fund. Fiscal stamp optd. **PATRIOTICO y SANITARIO.**
968. 65. 40 c. olive 8 5

134. Old People learning Alphabet.

134a. Flag-bearer and Health Emblem.

1953. Literacy Campaign. Inscr. "UNP LAE".
974. – 5 c. blue (postage) .. 12 5
975. – 10 c. red 15 5
976. – 20 c. orange 20 5
977. – 30 c. purple 25 5

978. – 1 s. blue (air) 35 8
979. 134. 2 s. vermilion 55 8
DESIGNS: 5 c. Teacher and pupils. 10 c. Instructor and student. 1 s. Hand and torch. HORIZ. 20 c. Men and ballot-box. 30 c. Teaching the alphabet.

1953. Obligatory Tax. Public Health Fund.
980. 134a. 40 c. blue 8 5

135.

136. Equatorial Line Monument.

1953. Air. Crossing of Equator by Pan-American Highway.
981. 135. 60 c. yellow 15 15
982. 90 c. blue 20 15
983. 3 s. red 40 25

1953.
984. – 5 c. blue and black .. 5 5
985. 136. 10 c. green and black 5 5
986. – 20 c. lilac and black .. 5 5
987. – 30 c. brown and black 8 5
988. – 40 c. orange and black 12 5
989. – 50 c. red and black .. 15 5
DESIGNS: 5 c. Cuicocha Lagoon. 20 c. Quininde landscape. 30 c. River Tomebamba. 40 c. La Chilintosa rock. 50 c. Iliniza Mountains.

137. Cardinal de la Torre.

138.

1954. 1st Anniv. of Elevation to Cardinal.
990. 137. 30 c. blk. & verm. (post.) 8 5
991. 50 c. black and purple 10 5

992. 138. 60 c. blk. & pur. (air) 12 5
993. 90 c. black and green 15 8
994. 3 s. black and orange 25 15

139. Isabella the Catholic.

140.

1954. Isabella the Catholic. 500th Birth Anniv.
995. 139. 30 c. blk. & bl. (post.) 8 5
996. 50 c. black and yellow 10 5

997. 140. 60 c. green (air) .. 8 8
998. 90 c. purple 10 10
999. 1 s. black and pink .. 12 10
1000. 2 s. black and blue .. 15 15
1001. 5 s. black and flesh .. 45 25

141.

1954. Air. Silver Jubilee of Panagra Air Lines. Unissued stamp surch. as in T 141.
1002. 141. 80 c. on 20 c. vermilion 12 10
1003. 1 s. on 20 c. vermilion 15 10

1954. Obligatory Tax. Literacy Campaign. Telegraph stamp (18½×22½ mm.) surch. **ESCOLAR 20 Centavos.**
1004. 20 c. on 30 c. brown .. 8 5

1954. Obligatory Tax. Literacy Campaign. Fiscal stamp as T 65 (19½×25½ mm.) optd. **EXCOLAR.**
1004a. 65. 20 c. olive-black .. 5 5

1954. Obligatory Tax. Tourist Promotion Fund.

(a) Telegraph stamp as No. 1004 but surch. **Pro Turismo 1954 10 ctvs. 10.**
1005. 10 c. on 30 c. brown .. 5 5

(b) Judicial stamp as T 35 (19½ × 25½ mm.) optd. **PRO TURISMO 1954.**
1006. 10 c. red 5 5

(c) Fiscal stamp as T 65 (19½ × 25½ mm.) surch. **PRO TURISMO 1954 10 ctvs. Diez Centavos.**
1006a. 65. 10 c. on 50 c. red .. 5 5

(d) Consular Service stamp surch. **PRO TURISMO 1954 10 ctvs.**
1007. 129a. 10 c. on 25 c. blue .. 5 5

1954. Consular Service stamp surch. **0.20 0.20 ESCOLAR Veinte centavos.**
1007a. 129. 20 c. on 10 s. grey .. 5 5

142. Message Carrier.

143. Aeroplane over Building.

1954. Postal Employees' Day.
1008. 142. 30 c. sepia (postage) 8 5
1009. 143. 80 c. blue (air) .. 10 5

144. Bananas.

145. San Pablo Lake.

1954.
1010. 144. 10 c. orange (post.) .. 5 5
1011. 20 c. vermilion .. 5 5
1012. 30 c. magenta .. 8 5
1013. 40 c. myrtle 10 5
1014. 50 c. brown 15 5

1015. 145. 60 c. orange (air) .. 8 5
1016. 70 c. magenta .. 10 5
1017. 90 c. green 10 5
1018. 1 s. myrtle 12 5
1019. 2 s. blue 20 8
1020. 3 s. brown 25 10

145a. Young Student.

146. Death on Battlefield.

1954. Obligatory Tax. Literacy Fund.
1020a. 145a. 20 c. red 5 5

1954. Air. Captain A. C. Garaicoa. 150th Death Anniv.
1021. 146. 80 c. magenta .. 15 10
1022. – 90 c. blue 15 10
PORTRAIT—VERT. 90 c. Captain Calderon.

147. "El Cebollar" College.

148. "Transport."

1954. Air. F. F. Cordero. Birth Cent.
1023. 147. 70 c. myrtle 8 5
1024. – 80 c. sepia 10 5
1025. – 90 c. blue 10 5
1026. – 2 s. 50 slate 20 12
1027. – 3 s. lilac 30 20
DESIGNS—VERT. 80 c. Cordero and boys. 90 c. Cordero. 2 s. 50, Tomb. HORIZ. 3 s. Monument.

1954. Obligatory Tax. Tourist Promotion Fund.
1028. 148. 10 c. magenta .. 5 5

149. Kissing the Flag.

150. La Rotonda, Guayaquil.

1955. Obligatory Tax. National Defence Fund.
1029. 149. 40 c. blue 5 5

1955. Air. World Press Exn. No. 730a surch. **E. M. P. 1955** and value.
1030. 98. 1 s. on 10 s. violet .. 12 5
1031. 1 s. 70 on 10 s. violet .. 20 10
1032. 4 s. 20 on 10 s. violet .. 40 35

1955. Air. Rotary Int. 50th Anniv.
1033. 150. 80 c. brown 20 20
1034. – 90 c. green 25 20
DESIGN: 90 c. Eugenio Espejo Hospital, Quito.

151. J. A. Castillo.

152. River Babahoyo.

1955. Castillo (pioneer aviator). Birth Cent.
1035. – 30 c. bistre (postage) 5 5
1036. – 50 c. black 8 5

1037. 151. 60 c. chocolate (air) 15 10
1038. 90 c. green 15 10
1039. 1 s. mauve 20 12
1040. – 2 s. red 20 12
1041. – 5 s. blue 45 35
DESIGNS—VERT. 30 c., 50 c. Bust of Castillo. HORIZ. 2 s., 5 s. Castillo and map.

1955. Air. Surch. **1 SUCRE** over ornamental bar.
1042. 45. 1 s. on 5 s. violet .. 15 15

1956. Pictorial designs as T 152.
1043. A. 5 c. green (postage) .. 5 5
1043a. 5 c. blue 5 5
1043b. B. 5 c. bronze-green .. 5 5
1044. C. 10 c. blue 5 5
1044a. 10 c. brown 5 5
1044b. B. 10 c. brown 5 5
1045. 152. 20 c. brown 5 5
1045a. 20 c. pink 5 5
1045b. 20 c. green 5 5
1045c. B. 20 c. plum 5 5
1046. D. 30 c. black 5 5
1046a. 30 c. red 5 5
1046b. B. 30 c. blue 5 5
1046c. E. 40 c. grey-blue .. 10 5
1047. F. 50 c. green 5 5
1047a. 50 c. violet 5 5
1048. E. 70 c. olive 12 5
1049. G. 80 c. violet 15 5
1049a. B. 80 c. crimson .. 5 5
1049b. G. 90 c. blue 20 5
1050. H. 1 s. orange 15 5
1050a. 1 s. sepia 10 5
1050b. I. 1 s. black 10 5
1051. J. 2 s red 20 10
1051a. 2 s. brown 15 10

1052. K. 50 c. slate (air) .. 15 5
1052a. 50 c. green 10 5
1053. L. 1 s. blue 20 5
1053a. 1 s. orange 15 5
1054. M. 1 s. 30 red 20 8
1055. N. 1 s. 50 green 12 5
1056. O. 1 s. 70 brown .. 12 8
1057. P. 1 s. 90 olive 20 15
1058. Q. 2 s. 40 vermilion .. 25 12
1059. R. 2 s. 50 violet .. 25 15
1060. S. 4 s. 20 black .. 30 25
1061. T. 4 s. 80 yellow .. 35 30
DESIGNS—POSTAGE: A. Las Palmas. B. "The Virgin of Quito" (after L. y del Arco). C. Manta fisherman. D. Guayaquil. E. Cactus. F. River Pital. G. Orchids. H. Aguacate Mission. I. San Pablo. J. Jibaro Indian. AIR: K. Rumichaca Grotto. L. San Pablo. M. "The Virgin of Quito". N. Cotopaxi Volcano. O. Tungurahua Volcano. P. Llamas. Q. Selling mats. R. Ingapirca ruins. S. El Carmen, Cuenca. T. Santo Domingo Church.

153. Vazquez in 1883.

154. J. A. Schwarz.

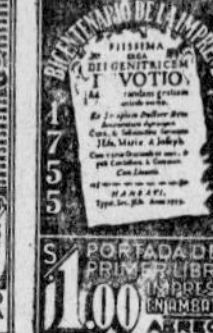
155.

1956. Air. Vazquez. Birth Cent.
1062. 153. 1 s. green 12 5
1063. – 1 s. 50 red 15 12
1064. – 1 s. 70 blue 15 12
1065. – 1 s. 90 slate 20 12
PORTRAITS OF VAZQUEZ: 1 s. 50, 1905. 1 s. 70, 1910. 1 s. 90, 1931.

1956. Printing in Ecuador. Bicent.
1066. 154. 5 c. green (postage) .. 5 5
1067. 10 c. red 5 5
1068. 20 c. violet 5 5
1069. 30 c. green 5 5
1070. 40 c. blue 5 5
1071. 50 c. blue 8 5
1072. 70 c. orange 10 5

1073. 155. 1 s. black (air) .. 10 8
1074. 1 s. 70 slate 15 10
1075. 2 s. sepia 20 15
1076. 3 s. brown 25 15

156.

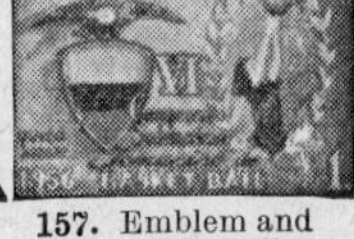
157. Emblem and Girl with Ball.

1956. Air. U.N.O. 10th Anniv.
1077. 156. 1 s. 70 red 30 15
For stamp as T 156 see No. 1095.

1956. Air. 6th S. American Women's Basketball Championships.
1078. 157. 1 s. mauve 15 5
1079. – 1 s. 70 green 25 10
DESIGN: 1 s. 70, Map, flags and players.

158. Marquis of Canete.

159. Cuenca Cathedral.

1957. Cuenca. 400th Anniv.
1082. 158. 5 c. blue on flesh (post.) 5 5
1083. – 10 c. bronze on green .. 5 5
1084. – 20 c. chocolate on buff 5 5

1085. – 50 c. sep. on cream (air) 8 5
1086. 159. 80 c. red on blue .. 10 8
1087. – 1 s. violet on yellow .. 12 8

DESIGNS—HORIZ. 10 c. Scene from D'Avalos legend. 50 c. Early plan of Cuenca. 1 s. Municipal Palace. VERT. 20 c. Father Vicente Solano.

160. Delegates to the 1838 Postal Congress.
161. Gabriela Mistral (poet).

1957. 7th U.P.A.E. Postal Congress, 1955.
1088. **160.** 40 c. yellow 5 5
1089. 50 c. blue 5 5
1090. 2 s. red 15 12

1957. Air. Gabriela Mistral Commem.
1091. **161.** 2 s. grey, black & red 15 12

162. Arms of Espejo.
163. Parakeet.

1957. Air. Carchi Cantonal Arms. Inscr. "PROVINCIA DEL CARCHI". Arms mult.
1092. **162.** 1 s. red 10 5
1093. – 2 s. black (Montufar) 12 10
1094. – 4 s. 20 blue (Tulcan) 30 25
For other Arms as T **162** see Nos. 1125/8, 1147/51, 1155/9, 1197 and 1220/3.

1957. Air. United Nations Day. As T **156** but without dates.
1095. 2 s. blue 25 20

1958. Tropical Birds. Birds in natural colours
(a) As T **163**.
1096 **163.** 10 c. brown 5 5
1097. – 20 c. grey and buff .. 10 5
1098. – 30 c. green 12 5
1099. – 40 c. orange .. 15 5
BIRDS: 20 c. Toucan. 30 c. Condor. 40 c. Humming-birds.

(b) As T **163** but "ECUADOR" at top in black.
1120. – 20 c. turquoise and red 5 5
1121. – 30 c. blue and yellow 5 5
1122. – 50 c. orange and green 10 5
1123. – 60 c. pink & turquoise 12 5
BIRDS: 20 c. Cardinal. 30 c. Rock cockerel. 50 c. Blackbird. 60 c. Parakeets.

164. The Virgin of Sorrows.
165. Vice-Pres. Nixon and Flags of Ecuador and the U.S.A.

1958. Air. 50th Anniv. of the Miracle of the Virgin of Sorrows of St. Gabriel College, Quito.
1100. **164.** 30 c. purple on purple 12 8
1101. – 30 c. purple on purple 12 8
1102. – 1 s. blue on blue .. 15 10
1103. **164.** 1 s. 70 blue on blue .. 20 12
DESIGN: Nos. 1101/2, Gateway of St. Gabriel College, Quito.
The above designs are arranged alternately in the sheet se-tenant (30 c. and 30 c., 1 s. and 1 s. 70).

1958. Visit of Vice-Pres. of the United States. Flags in red, blue and yellow.
1104. **165.** 2 s. salmon and myrtle 20 10

1958. Visit of Pres. Morales of Honduras. As T **165**, but with portrait of Pres. Morales, flags of Ecuador and Honduras, and inscriptions changed. Flags in red, blue and yellow.
1105. 2 s. brown 20 10

166. Dr. C. Sanz de Santamaria (Chancellor).

1958. Visit of Chancellor of Colombia.
1106. **166.** 1 s. 80 violet, red, blue and yellow 15 10

167. Dr. R. M. Arizaga.
168 Gonzalo I. Cornejo Bridge.

1958. Air. Arizaga (diplomat). Birth Cent.
1107. **167.** 1 s. multicoloured .. 10 8
See also Nos. 1135, 1142 and 1241.

1958. Air. Gonzalo I. Cornejo Bridge Inaug.
1108. **168.** 1 s. 30 green 15 10

169. Pioneer Locomotive.
170. Basketball Player.

1958. Opening of Guayaquil-Quito Railway. 50th Anniv.
1109. **169.** 30 c. black 5 5
1110. – 50 c. red 8 5
1111. – 5 s. brown 45 30
DESIGNS—HORIZ. 50 c. Diesel-electric train. DIAMOND. 5 s. Four founders of the railway.

1958. Air. South American Basketball Champions' Tournament, Quito.
1112. **170.** 1 s. 30 green & brown 30 20

171. J. C. de Macedo Soares.
172. Monstrance and Doves.

1958. Visit of Brazilian Chancellor.
1113. **171.** 2 s. 20 multicoloured 20 12

1958. Air. 3rd National Eucharistic Congress, Guayaquil. Inscr. as in T **173**.
1114. **172.** 10 c. violet and yellow 5 5
1115. 60 c. violet and salmon 5 5
1116. **172.** 1 s. sepia and turquoise 10 8
DESIGN: 60 c. Guayaquil Cathedral.

173. T 2 and stamp of 1920.

1958. Air. National Stamp Exn., Guayaquil.
1117. **173.** 1 s. 30 red and green .. 20 12
1118. – 2 s. violet and blue .. 30 20
1119. – 4 s. 20 sepia 50 40
DESIGNS: 2 s. Reproduction of T **42** and T **11**[illegible]. 4 s. 20, Guayaquil Municipal Library and Museum.

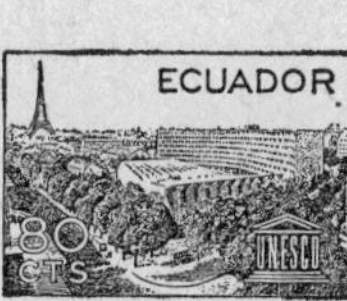

174. U.N.E.S.C.O. Headquarters, Paris.
175. Emperor Charles V (after Titian).

1958. Air. Imbabura Cantonal Arms. As T **162**. Inscr. "PROVINCIA DE IMBABURA". Arms multicoloured.
1124. 50 c. red and black .. 5 5
1125. 60 c. blue, red and black .. 8 5
1126. 80 c. yellow and black .. 10 5
1127. 1 s. 10 red and black .. 12 8
ARMS: 50 c. Cotacachi. 60 c. Antonio Ante. 80 c. Otavalo. 1 s. 10, Ibarra.

1958. Inaug. of U.N.E.S.C.O. Headquarters Building.
1128. **174.** 80 c. brown 15 8

1958. Air. Emperor Charles V. 4th Death Cent.
1129. **175.** 2 s. sepia and claret .. 15 12
1130. 4 s. 20 brown & black 35 30

176.
177. Paul Rivet (scientist).

1958. I.G.Y.
1131. **176.** 1 s. 80 blue 60 20

1958. Air. Rivet Commem.
1132. **177.** 1 s. sepia 10 5
See also No. 1134.

178. Front page of "El Telegrafo".

1959. Air. "El Telegrafo" (newspaper). 75th Anniv.
1133. **178.** 1 s. 30 black and green 15 10

1959. Air. Alexander von Humboldt (naturalist). Death Cent. Portrait in design as T **177**.
1134. 2 s. slate 15 10

1959. Air. Dr. Jose L. Tamayo (statesman). Birth Cent. Portrait in design as T **167**.
1135. 1 s. 30 multicoloured .. 12 8

179. House of M. Canizares.
180. Pope Pius XII.

1959. Air. Independence. 150th Anniv.
1136. **179.** 20 c. brown and blue 5 5
1137. – 80 c. chestnut and blue 8 5
1138. – 1 s. myrtle and brown 10 5
1139. – 1 s. 30 orange and blue 12 8
1140. – 2 s. brown and blue .. 15 10
1141. – 4 s. 20 blue and red .. 35 25
DESIGNS—HORIZ. 80 c. St. Augustine's chapter-house. 1 s. The Constitution. VERT. 1 s. 30, Condor with broken chains. 2 s. Royal Palace. 4 s. 20, "Liberty" (statue).

1959. Air. Dr. A. B. Moreno (statesman). Birth Cent. Portrait in design as T **167**.
1142. 1 s. multicoloured .. 10 5

1959. Air. Pope Pius XII Commem.
1143. **180.** 1 s. 30 multicoloured 15 12

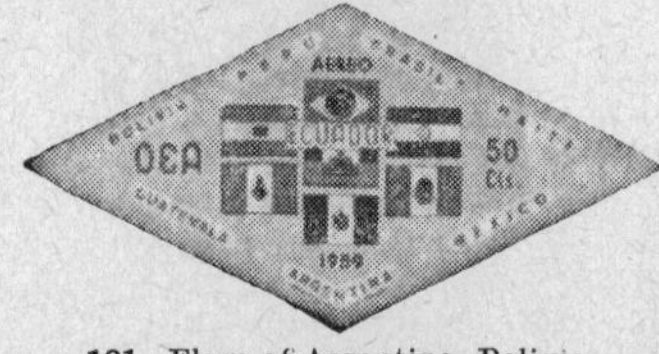

181. Flags of Argentina, Bolivia, Brazil, Guatemala, Haiti, Mexico and Peru.

1959. Air. Organization of American States Commem. Flag designs inscr. "OEA".
1144. **181.** 50 c. red, yellow, blue, green & light blue .. 8 5
1145. – 80 c. red, blue & yellow 10 5
1146. – 1 s. 30 red, blue, yellow and light green .. 15 12
FLAGS: 80 c. Chile, Costa Rica, Cuba, Dominican Republic, Panama, Paraguay and U.S.A. 1 s. 30, Colombia, Ecuador, Honduras, Nicaragua, Salvador, Uruguay and Venezuela.

1959. Air. Pichincha Cantonal Arms. As T **162**. Inscr. "PROVINCIA DE PICHINCHA". Arms multicoloured.
1147. 10 c. red and black .. 5 5
1148. 40 c. yellow and black .. 5 5
1149. 1 s. brown and black .. 10 5
1150. 1 s. 30 green and black .. 12 10
1151. 4 s. 20 yellow and black .. 30 25
ARMS: 10 c. Ruminahui. 40 c. Pedro Moncayo. 1 s. Mejia 1 s. 30, Cayambe. 4 s. 20. Quito.

182. Arms of Quito and Flags.
183. "Uprooted Tree".

1960. Air. 11th Inter-American Conference, Quito (1st issue). Centres multicoloured within red circle.
1152. **182.** 1 s. 30 turquoise .. 10 8
1153. 2 s. light sepia .. 15 12

1960. World Refugee Year.
1154. **183.** 80 c. green and lake .. 12 8

1960. Air. Cotopaxi Cantonal Arms. As T **162**. Inscr. "PROVINCIA DE COTOPAXI". Arms multicoloured.
1155. 40 c. red and black .. 5 5
1156. 60 c. blue and black .. 5 5
1157. 70 c. turquoise and black 8 5
1158. 1 s. red and black .. 10 5
1159. 1 s. 30 orange and black .. 12 5
ARMS: 40 c. Pangua. 60 c. Pujili. 70 c. Saquisili 1 s. Salcedo. 1 s. 30. Latacunga.

DESIGNS: 40 c. Tapir. 80 c. Spectacled bear. 1 s. Puma.

184. Ant Eaters.

1960. 4th Cent. of Baeza. Inscr. as in T **184**.
1160. **184.** 20 c. blk., orge. & grn. 5 5
1161. – 40 c. chocolate, green and blue-green .. 8 5
1162. – 80 c. blk., blue & brn. 12 8
1163. – 1 s. orge., blue & mar. 20 10

185. Quito Airport.

1960. 11th Inter-American Conference, Quito. (2nd issue). Views of Quito. Inscr. as in T **185**.
1164. **185.** 1 s. blue and deep blue 10 5
1165. – 1 s. violet and black .. 10 5
1166. – 1 s. lake and violet .. 10 5
1167. – 1 s. green and blue .. 10 5
1168. – 1 s. slate-blue & violet 10 5
1169. – 1 s. brown and blue .. 10 5
1170. – 1 s. red-brown & violet 10 5
1171. – 1 s. red and black .. 10 5
1172. – 1 s. olive-brown & blk. 10 5
VIEWS No. 1165, Legislative Palace. 1166, Southern approach motorway and flyover. 1167, Government Palace. 1168, Foreign Ministry. 1169, Students' Quarters, Catholic University. 1170, Hotel Quito. 1171, Students' Quarters, Central University. 1172, Security Bank.

186. Ambato Railway Bridge.
187. "Liberty of Expression".

1960. Air. New Bridges.
1173. – 1 s. 30 chocolate .. 10 5
1174. – 1 s. 30 green 10 5
1175. **186.** 2 s. brown 15 10
DESIGNS—No. 1173, Bridge of the Juntas. No. 1174, Saracay Bridge.

1960. Five Year Development Plan (1st issue). (a) Postage.
1176. **187.** 5 c. blue 5 5
1177. – 10 c. violet 5 5
1178. – 20 c. orange 5 5
1179. – 30 c. turquoise .. 5 5
1180. – 40 c. brown and blue 5 5
DESIGNS—VERT. 10 c. Mother voting. 20 c. People at bus-stop. 30 c. Coins. HORIZ. (37×22 mm.): 40 c. Irrigation project Manabi.

188. Bahia Road at Chone.

(b) Air.

1181. 188. 1 s. 30 black and ochre 10 5
1182. – 4 s. 20 lake and green 25 20
1183. – 5 s. chocolate & lemon 30 25
1184. – 10 s. indigo and blue 65 50

DESIGNS—As T 188: 4 s. 20, Ministry of Works and Communications, Cuenca. 5 s. El Coca Airport. 10 s. New port of Guayaquil under construction

189. Pres. Ponce and Constitution.

1960. Air. Construction. 5th Anniv.
1185. 189. 2 s. black and brown 1·10 25

190. H. Dunant and Red Cross Buildings, Quito.
191. "El Belen" Church, Quito.

1960. Air. Red Cross Commem.
1186. 190. 2 s. purple and red .. 25 12

1961. Air. 1st Int. Philatelic Congress, Barcelona.
1187. 191. 3 s. pale blue, deep blue, yellow and olive .. 25 15

192. Map of River Amazon.

1961. Air. "Amazon Week". Map in green.
1188. 192. 80 c. purple and brown 12 8
1189. 1 s. 30 indigo and grey 15 12
1190. 2 s. red and grey .. 25 15

193. J. Montalvo, J. L. Mera and J. B. Vela.

1961. Air. Tungurahua Province Cent.
1191. 193. 1 s. 30 black & salmon 12 8

194. 1 s. Philatelic Exn. Air Stamp of 1930.
195. Statue of H. Ortiz Garces.

1961. Air. 3rd Int. Philatelic Exn., Quito.
1192. 194. 80 c. violet and orange 12 10
1193. – 1 s. 30 multicoloured 20 15
1194. – 2 s. black and red .. 25 20

DESIGNS: 1 s. 30, San Lorenzo-Belem route map of S. America and 1 r. stamp of 1865 (41 × 33½ mm.). 2 s., 10 s. Independence stamp of 1930 postmarked "QUITO" (41 × 36 mm.).

1961. Air. H. Ortiz Garces (national hero). Commem. Multicoloured.
1195. 1 s. 30 T 195 .. .. 12 8
1196. 1 s. 30 Portrait 12 8

1961. Air. Los Rios Province Cent. As T 162. Inscr. "LOS RIOS".
1197. 2 s. multicoloured .. 20 12

196. "Graphium pausianus" (butterfly).
197. Peccary (Mexican hog) ("Pecari tajacu").

1961. Butterflies.
1198. 196. 20 c. yellow, green, black and salmon .. 5 5
1198a. 20 c. yellow, grey, black and green .. 5 5
1199. – 30 c. yell., black & blue 5 5
1200. – 50 c. black, grn. & yell. 8 5
1200a. – 50 c. blk., grn. & salmon 5 5
1201. 80 c. brown yellow, black and turquoise 12 8
1201a. – 80 c. turquoise yellow black and brown .. 8 5

BUTTERFLIES: 30 c. "Papilio torquatus leptalea". 50 c. "Graphium molops molops". 80 c. "Battus lycidas".

1961. Tena. 4th Cent.
1202. 197. 10 c. indigo, grn. & red 8 5
1203. – 20 c. brn., violet & blue 8 5
1204. – 80 c. orge., blk. & bis. 10 5
1205. – 1 s. brn., orge. & emer. 15 10

ANIMALS: 20 c. Kinkajou. 80 c. Jaguar. 1 s. Coati.

198. G. G. Moreno.
199. R. C. Toral.

1961. Air. Re-establishment of "National Integrity". Cent.
1206. 198. 1 s. brown, buff & blue 12 8

1961. Opening of Marine Biology Station on Galapagos Is. and 15th Anniv. of U.N.E.S.C.O. Nos. 1/6 of Galapagos Is. optd. **UNESCO 1961 Estacion de Biologia Maritima de Galapagos.**
1207. 1. 20 c. brown (postage) .. 5 5
1208. – 50 c. violet 10 8
1209. – 1 s. green 20 12
1210. – 1 s. blue (air) 15 12
1211. – 1 s. 80 purple 20 12
1212. – 4 s. 20 black 40 30

1961. Air. R. C. Toral. Birth Cent.
1213. 199. 50 c. multicoloured .. 5 5

200. Soldier and Flag.
200a. Daniel Enrique Proana School Quito.

1961. Obligatory Tax. National Defence Fund.
1213a. 200a. 40 c. blue 5 5

1961. Five-Year Development Plan. Inscr. "1956-1960".
1214. 200. 50 c. black and blue .. 5 5
1215. – 60 c. black and olive 5 5
1216. – 80 c. black and red .. 8 5
1217. – 1 s. black and claret .. 10 8

DESIGNS—VERT. 60 c. Loja-Zamora Highway. HORIZ. 80 c. Aguirre Abad College, Guayaquil. 1 s. Epiclachima Barracks, Quito.

201. Pres. C. Arosemena and Duke of Edinburgh.

1962. Air. Visit of Duke of Edinburgh.
1218. 201. 1 s. 30 multicoloured 15 10
1219. 2 s. multicoloured .. 20 12

1962. Air. Tungurahua Cantonal Arms. As T 162. Inscr. "PROVINCIA DE TUNGURAHUA". Arms mult.
1220. 50 c. black (Pillaro) .. 5 5
1221. 1 s. black (Pelileo) .. 8 5
1222. 1 s. 30 black (Banos) .. 10 5
1223. 2 s. black (Ambato) .. 15 8

202. Mt. Chimborazo and Spade in Field.
203. Mosquito.

1963. Air. Freedom from Hunger.
1224. 202. 30 c. blk., emer. & yell. 5 5
1225. 3 s. black, red & orge. 20 12
1226. 4 s. 20 blk., bl. & yell. 30 25

1963. Air. Malaria Eradication.
1227. 203. 50 c. black, olive-yellow and red .. 5 5
1228. 80 c. blk., emer. & red 8 5
1229. 2 s. blk., pink & mar. 15 15

204. Mail-coach and Aircraft.
205. Pres. Arosemena and Flags of Ecuador.

1963. Air. Paris Postal Conf. Cent.
1230. 204. 2 s. red and orange .. 15 12
1231. 4 s. 20 blue and purple 30 25

1963. Air. Unissued Galapagos Is. stamps in designs as Ecuador T 161 optd. vert. **ECUADOR** and surch.
1232. 161. 5 s. on 2s. grey, black, blue and red .. 30 25
1233. 10 s. on 2 s. grey, black, blue and red .. 65 50

1963. Air. Red Cross Cent. Optd. **1863-1963 Centenario de la Fundacion de la Cruz Roja Internacional.**
1234. 190. 2 s. purple and red .. 15 12

1963. Presidential Goodwill Tour. Multicoloured.
1235. 10 c. Type 205 (postage) 5 5
1236. 20 c. Ecuador & Panama flags 5 5
1237. 60 c. Ecuador & U.S.A. flags 5 5
1238. 70 c. Type 205 (air) .. 5 5
1239. 2 s. Ecuador and Panama flags 15 10
1240. 4 s. Ecuador & U.S.A. flags 30 25

1963. Air. Dr. M. Cueva (statesman). 150th Birth Anniv. Portrait in design as T 167.
1241. 2 s. multicoloured .. 12 8

206. "Shield of Security".
207. Terminal Building.

1963. Social Insurance Scheme. 25th Anniv. Multicoloured.
1242. 10 c. Type 206 (postage) 5 5
1243. 10 s. "Statue of Security" (air) 50 40

1963. Air. Simon Bolivar Airport, Guayaquil. Inaug.
1244. 207. 60 c. black 5 5
1245. 70 c. black and blue .. 8 5
1246. 5 s. maroon and black 30 20

208. Nurse and Child.
209. "Commerce".

1963. Air. 7th Pan-American Pediatrics Congress, Quito.
1247. 208. 1 s. 30 blue, black and orange 12 10
1248. 5 s. lake, red and grey 30 20

1963. Postal Employees' Day. No. 1049a optd. **1961 DIA DEL EMPLEADO POSTAL** and posthorn or surch. also.
1249. B. 10 c. on 80 c. crimson 5 5
1250. 20 c. on 80 c. crimson 5 5
1251. 50 c. on 80 c. crimson 5 5
1252. 60 c. on 80 c. crimson 5 5
1253. 80 c. crimson .. 8 5

1964. Nos. 1164, etc., surch.
1254. 10 c. on 1 s. sl.-blue & vio. 5 5
1255. 10 c. on 1 s. red-brn. & vio. 5 5
1256. 20 c. on 1 s. green & blue 5 5
1257. 20 c. on 1 s. brown & blue 5 5
1258. 30 c. on 1 s. lake & violet 5 5
1259. 40 c. on 1 s. ol.-brn. & blk. 5 5
1260. 60 c. on 1 s. red and black 5 5
1261. 80 c. on 1 s. bl. & deep blue 8 5
1262. 80 c. on 1 s. violet & black 8 5

1964. Optd. **1961** and ornaments.
1263. 182. 80 c. green and lake 1·00 20

1964. Air. Optd. **AEREO.** Honduras flag in red, blue and yellow.
1264. 166. 1 s. 80 violet .. 30 20
1265. – 2 s. brown (No. 1105) 30 25
1266. 171. 2 s. 20 sepia and green 30 25

1964. "Columbus Lighthouse". Optd. **FARO DE COLON.**
1267. 176. 1 s. 80 blue (postage) 1·10 45
Optd. **FARO DE COLON AEREO.**
1268. 176. 1 s. 80 blue (air) .. 1·60 75

1964. Air. Nos. 1144/6 optd. **1961.**
1269. 181. 50 c. red, yellow, blue, green & light blue 35 20
1270. – 80 c. red, blue & yell. 35 20
1271. – 1 s. 30 red, blue, yellow and light green .. 35 25

1964. O.E.A. Commemoration. Optd. **OEA** with decorative frame across a block of four stamps.
1272. 182. 80 c. green and lake .. 1·00 12
The unused price is for the block of four.

1964. "Alliance for Progress".
1273. – 40 c. bistre and violet 5 5
1274. – 50 c. red and black .. 5 5
1275. 209. 80 c. blue and brown 8 5

DESIGNS: 40 c. "Agriculture". 50 c. "Industry".

1964. Air. Declaration of Human Rights. 15th Anniv. Optd. **DECLARATION DERECHOS HUMANOS 1964 XV-ANIV.**
1276. 156. 1 s. 70 red 12 10

210. Banana Tree and Map.

1964. Banana Conf., Quito.
1277. 210. 50 c. olive, brown and grey (postage) .. 5 5
1278. 80 c. olive, blk. & orge. 8 5
1279. 4 s. 20 olive, black and ochre (air) .. 25 20
1280. 10 s. olive, blk. & red 60 40

211. Pres. Kennedy and son.

1964. Air. Pres. Kennedy Commem. Flag in blue and red.
1281. 211. 4 s. 20 brn., blue & grn. 50 40
1282. 5 s. brown, blue & vio. 60 50
1283. 10 s. brown, bl. & mag. 1·00 70

112. Old Map of Ecuador and Philip II of Spain.

DESIGNS: As T 212 but portrait of Juan de Salinas Loyola (20 c.), Hernando de Santillan (30 c.).

1964. Superior Court, Quito. 4th Cent.
1284. 212. 10 c. black, buff & red 5 5
1285. – 20 c. black, buff & grn. 5 5
1286. – 30 c. black, buff & bl. 5 5

213. Pole vaulting.
214. Sloth and P. Fleming (missionary).

1964. Olympic Games, Tokyo. Multicoloured.
1287. 80 c. Type 213 (postage) 8 5
1288. 1 s. 30 Gymnastics (air) .. 12 10
1289. 1 s. 80 Hurdling 15 12
1290. 2 s. Basketball 15 15
The 1 s. 30 is vert.

1965. Death of Missionaries in Ecuador's Eastern Forests. Multicoloured.

1291. 20 c. Armadillo & J. Elliot .. 5 5
1292. 30 c. Squirrel & E. McCully .. 5 5
1293. 40 c. Deer & R. Youderian .. 5 5
1294. 60 c. Aircraft over Napo River, and N. Saint .. 5 5
1295. 80 c. Type **214** 8 5

215. Dr. J. B. Vazquez (founder) and College Buildings.

1965. Benigno Malo College Cent.

1296. **215.** 20 c. multicoloured .. 5 5
1297. 60 c. multicoloured .. 5 5
1298. 80 c. multicoloured .. 8 5

216. J. L. Mera (wrongly inscr. "MERAN"), A. Neumane and Part of Anthem.

1965. National Anthem Cent.

1299. **216.** 50 c. black and rose .. 5 5
1300. 80 c. black and green 8 5
1301. 5 s. black and ochre .. 30 20
1302. 10 s. black and blue .. 55 45

217. "Olympic" Flame and Athletic Events.

1965. 5th Bolivar Games, Quito. Flame in gold and black; athletes in black.

1303. **217.** 40 c. orange (postage) 5 5
1304. – 50 c. red 5 5
1305. – 60 c. blue 5 5
1306. **217.** 80 c. green 5 5
1307. – 1 s. violet 8 5
1308. – 1 s. 50 magenta .. 10 8
1309. – 2 s. blue (air) .. 12 10
1310. – 2 s. 50 orange .. 15 10
1311. – 3 s. magenta .. 20 12
1312. – 3 s. 50 violet .. 25 15
1313. – 4 s. green 25 20
1314. – 5 s. red 30 20

DESIGNS: 50 c., 1 s. Running. 60 c., 1 s. 50, Football. 2 s., 3 s. Diving, gymnastics, etc. 2 s. 50, 4 s. Cycling. 3 s. 50, 5 s. Pole-vaulting, long-jumping, etc.

218. ½ r. and Two 1 r. Stamps of 1865. **219.** "Pharomachrus auriceps".

1965. Stamp Cent.

1315. **218.** 80 c. multicoloured .. 5 5
1316. 1 s. 30 multicoloured 10 8
1317. 2 s. multicoloured .. 15 10
1318. 4 s. multicoloured .. 25 15

1966. Birds. Multicoloured.

1320. 40 c. Type **219** (postage) 5 5
1321. 50 c. "Momotus momota" 5 5
1322. 60 c. "Tangara chilensis" 5 5
1323. 80 c. "Cirrhipipra filicauda" 5 5
1324. 1 s. "Pheucticus chrysopeplus" (air) .. 5 5
1325. 1 s. 30 "Pionites melanocephala" .. 8 5
1326. 1 s. 50 "Piranga erythromelas" .. 8 5
1327. 2 s. "Osculatia saphirina" 10 8
1328. 2 s. 50 "Aglaiocercus kingi coelestis" .. 12 10
1329. 3 s. "Capito richardsoni" 15 12
1330. 4 s. "Icterus mesomelas" 20 15
1331. 10 s. "Bucco capensis" 50 45

1967. Various stamps surch. (a) Postage.

1332. 30 c. on 1 s. 10 (No. 1128) 5 5
1332a. 40 c. on 1 s. 70 (No. 1056) 5 5
1333. 40 c. on 3 s. 50 (No. 1312) 5 5
1334. 80 c. on 1 s. 50 (No. 1308) 5 5
1335. 80 c. on 2 s. 50 (No. 1328) 5 5
1336. 1 s. on 4 s. (No. 1330) .. 5 5

(b) Air.

1337. 80 c. on 1 s. 50 (No. 1326) 5 5
1338. 80 c. on 2 s. 50 (No. 1310) 5 5

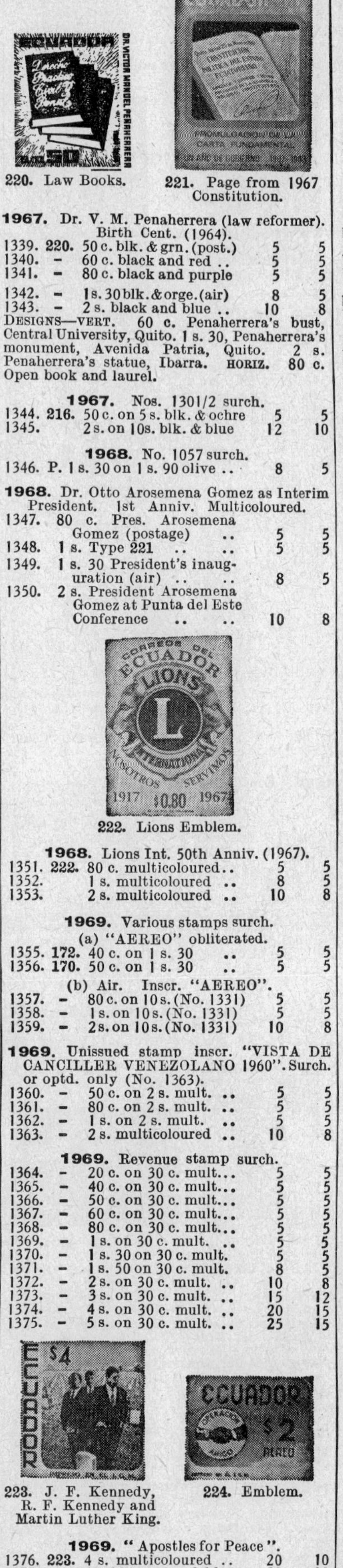

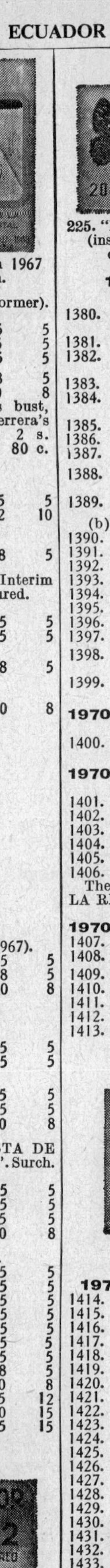

220. Law Books. **221.** Page from 1967 Constitution.

1967. Dr. V. M. Penaherrera (law reformer). Birth Cent. (1964).

1339. **220.** 50 c. blk. & grn. (post.) 5 5
1340. – 60 c. black and red .. 5 5
1341. – 80 c. black and purple 5 5
1342. – 1 s. 30 blk. & orge. (air) 8 5
1343. – 2 s. black and blue .. 10 8

DESIGNS—VERT. 60 c. Penaherrera's bust, Central University, Quito. 1 s. 30, Penaherrera's monument, Avenida Patria, Quito. 2 s. Penaherrera's statue, Ibarra. HORIZ. 80 c. Open book and laurel.

1967. Nos. 1301/2 surch.

1344. **216.** 50 c. on 5 s. blk. & ochre 5 5
1345. 2 s. on 10 s. blk. & blue 12 10

1968. No. 1057 surch.

1346. P. 1 s. 30 on 1 s. 90 olive .. 8 5

1968. Dr. Otto Arosemena Gomez as Interim President. 1st Anniv. Multicoloured.

1347. 80 c. Pres. Arosemena Gomez (postage) .. 5 5
1348. 1 s. Type **221** 5 5
1349. 1 s. 30 President's inauguration (air) 8 5
1350. 2 s. President Arosemena Gomez at Punta del Este Conference 10 8

222. Lions Emblem.

1968. Lions Int. 50th Anniv. (1967).

1351. **222.** 80 c. multicoloured .. 5 5
1352. 1 s. multicoloured .. 8 5
1353. 2 s. multicoloured .. 10 8

1969. Various stamps surch.

(a) "AEREO" obliterated.

1355. **172.** 40 c. on 1 s. 30 .. 5 5
1356. **170.** 50 c. on 1 s. 30 .. 5 5

(b) Air. Inscr. "AEREO".

1357. – 80 c. on 10 s. (No. 1331) 5 5
1358. – 1 s. on 10 s. (No. 1331) 5 5
1359. – 2 s. on 10 s. (No. 1331) 10 8

1969. Unissued stamp inscr. "VISTA DE CANCILLER VENEZOLANO 1960". Surch. or optd. only (No. 1363).

1360. – 50 c. on 2 s. mult. .. 5 5
1361. – 80 c. on 2 s. mult. .. 5 5
1362. – 1 s. on 2 s. mult. .. 5 5
1363. – 2 s. multicoloured .. 10 8

1969. Revenue stamp surch.

1364. – 20 c. on 30 c. mult... 5 5
1365. – 40 c. on 30 c. mult... 5 5
1366. – 50 c. on 30 c. mult... 5 5
1367. – 60 c. on 30 c. mult... 5 5
1368. – 80 c. on 30 c. mult... 5 5
1369. – 1 s. on 30 c. mult. .. 5 5
1370. – 1 s. 30 on 30 c. mult. 5 5
1371. – 1 s. 50 on 30 c. mult. 8 5
1372. – 2 s. on 30 c. mult. .. 10 8
1373. – 3 s. on 30 c. mult. .. 15 12
1374. – 4 s. on 30 c. mult. .. 20 15
1375. – 5 s. on 30 c. mult. .. 25 15

223. J. F. Kennedy, R. F. Kennedy and Martin Luther King. **224.** Emblem.

1969. "Apostles for Peace".

1376. **223.** 4 s. multicoloured .. 20 10
1377. 4 s. blk., green & blue 20 10

1969. Air. "Operation Friendship". Multicoloured. Emblem's background colour given.

1378. **22.** 2 s. blue 10 8
1379. 2 s. yellow 10 8

225. "Papilio zabreus" (inscr. "zagreus" on stamp). **226.** Arms of Zamora Chinchipe.

1970. Butterflies. Multicoloured.

(a) Coloured backgrounds.

1380. 10 c. "Thecla coronata" (postage) 5 5
1381. 20 c. Type **225** 5 5
1382. 30 c. "Heliconius chestertoni" 5 5
1383. 40 c. "Papilio pausanias" 5 5
1384. 50 c. "Pereute leucodrosime" 5 5
1385. 60 c. "Metemorpha dido" 5 5
1386. 80 c. "Morpho cypris" 5 5
1387. 1 s. "Catagramma astarte" 5 5
1388. 1 s. 30 "Morpho peleides" (air) 5 5
1389. 1 s. 50 "Anartia amathea" 8 5

(b) White backgrounds. As Nos. 1380/9.

1390. – 10 c. mult. (post.) .. 5 5
1391. **225.** 20 c. multicoloured .. 5 5
1392. – 30 c. multicoloured .. 5 5
1393. – 40 c. multicoloured .. 5 5
1394. – 50 c. multicoloured .. 5 5
1395. – 60 c. multicoloured .. 5 5
1396. – 80 c. multicoloured .. 5 5
1397. – 1 s. multicoloured .. 5 5
1398. – 1 s. 30 multicoloured (air) 5 5
1399. – 1 s. 50 multicoloured 8 5

1970. Air. No. 1104 surch. **AEREO** and new value.

1400. **165.** 5 s. on 2 s. multicoloured 25 15

1970. Public Works Fiscal Stamps surch. "POSTAL" and value.

1401. 1 s. on 1 s. blue 5 5
1402. 1 s. 30 on 1 s. blue .. 5 5
1403. 1 s. 50 on 1 s. blue .. 8 5
1404. 2 s. on 1 s. blue 12 8
1405. 5 s. on 1 s. blue 25 15
1406. 10 s. on 1 s. blue .. 50 30

The basic stamps are inscr. "TIMBRE DE LA RECONSTRUCCION".

1970. Provincial Arms and Flags. Mult.

1407. 50 c. Type **226** (postage) 5 5
1408. 1 s. Esmeraldas 5 5
1409. 1 s. 30 El Oro (air) .. 8 5
1410. 2 s. Loja 10 5
1411. 3 s. Manabi 15 8
1412. 5 s. Pichincha 25 15
1413. 10 s. Guayas 50 30

227. **228.** "Presentation of the Virgin".

1971. Revenue stamps surch. for postal use.

1414. **227.** 60 c. on 1 s. violet .. 5 5
1415. 80 c. on 1 s. violet .. 5 5
1416. 1 s. on 1 s. violet .. 5 5
1417. 1 s. 10 on 1 s. violet 5 5
1418. 1 s. 10 on 2 s. green .. 5 5
1419. 1 s. 30 on 1 s. violet 5 5
1420. 1 s. 30 on 2 s. green 5 5
1421. 1 s. 50 on 1 s. violet 5 5
1422. 1 s. 50 on 2 s. green 5 5
1423. 2 s. on 1 s. violet .. 8 5
1424. 2 s. on 2 s. green .. 8 5
1425. 2 s. 20 on 1 s. violet 10 5
1426. 3 s. on 1 s. violet .. 15 5
1427. 3 s. on 5 s. blue .. 15 8
1428. 3 s. 40 on 2 s. green 20 5
1429. 5 s. on 2 s. green .. 25 8
1430. 5 s. on 5 s. blue .. 25 8
1431. 10 s. on 2 s. green .. 50 15
1432. 10 s. on 40 s. orange 50 15
1433. 20 s. on 2 s. green .. 1·00 30
1434. 50 s. on 2 s. green .. 2·50 60

1971. **Air.** Quito Religious Art. Multicoloured.

1435. 1 s. 30 Type **228** 5 5
1436. 1 s. 50 "St. Anne" .. 8 5
1437. 2 s. "St. Teresa of Jesus" 10 8
1438. 2 s. 50 Retable, Carmen altar (horiz.) 12 10
1439. 3 s. "Descent from the Cross" 15 12
1440. 4 s. "Christ of St. Mary" 20 15
1441. 5 s. St. Anthony Shrine .. 30 20
1442. 10 s. Cross of San Diego .. 60 35

229. Flags of Chile and Ecuador.

230. Emblem on Globe.

1971. Visit of Pres. Allende of Chile. Mult.

1443. 1 s. 30 Type **229** (postage) 8 5
1444. 2 s. Pres. Allende (horiz.) (air) 10 8
1445. 2 s. 10 Pres. Ibarra of Ecuador and Pres. Allende (horiz.) .. 10 8

1971. Air. Opening of Postal Museum, Quito.

1446. **230.** 5 s. blue and black .. 30 20
1447. 5 s. 50 maroon and blk. 30 20

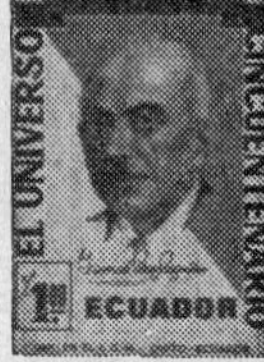

231. I. P. Paznino (founder).

232. Punch-card and Map.

1971. "El Universo" (newspaper). 50th Anniv.

1448. **231.** 1 s. multicoloured (postage) 5 5
1449. **231.** 1 s. 50 multicoloured (air) 8 5
1450. 2 s. 50 multicoloured 12 10

1971. Air. Pan-American Road Conference.

1451. **232.** 5 s. multicoloured .. 25 20
1452. – 10 s. black and orange 50 40
1453. – 20 s. black, red & blue 1·00 70
1454. – 50 s. blk., lilac & blue 2·50 1·90

DESIGNS: 10 s. Converging roads. 20 s. Globe and equator. 50 s. Mountain road.

233. C.A.R.E. Package.

234. Flags of Ecuador and Argentina.

1972. C.A.R.E. Organisation. 25th Anniv.

1455. **233.** 30 c. purple 5 5
1456. 40 c. green 5 5
1457. 50 c. blue 5 5
1458. 60 c. red 5 5
1459. 80 c. brown 5 5

1972. State Visit of Pres. Lanusse of Argentine Republic. Multicoloured.

1460. 1 s. Type **234** (postage) .. 5 5
1461. 3 s. Arms of Ecuador and Argentina (air) .. 15 10
1462. 5 s. Presidents Velasco Ibarra and Lanusse .. 25 20

235. "Jesus giving Keys to St. Peter" (M. de Santiago).

236. Map in Flame, and Scales of Justice.

1972. Religious Paintings of 18th-century Quito School. Multicoloured.

1463. 50 c. Type **235** (postage) 5 5
1464. 1 s. 10 "Virgin of Mercy" (Quito School) 5 5
1465. 2 s. "The Immaculate Conception" (M. Samaniego) .. 12 8
1466. 3 s. "Virgin of the Flowers" (M. de Santiago) (air) .. 20 12
1467. 10 s. "Virgin of the Rosary" (Quito School) 65 40

1972. Air. Inter-American Lawyers' Federation Congress, Quito.
1469. 236. 1 s. 30 blue and red 8 5

237. "The Nativity" (Quito School).

1972. 18th century Ecuador Statues. Multicoloured.
1470. 50 c. "Our Lady of Sorrow" (Caspicara) (vert.) (postage) 5 5
1471. 1 s. 10 Type 237 .. 8 5
1472. 2 s. "Virgin of Quito" (anon) (vert.) 12 8
1473. 3 s. "St. Dominic" (Quito School) (vert.) (air) .. 15 10
1474. 10 s. "St. Rosa of Lima" (B. de Legarda) (vert.) 65 40

238. Juan Ignacio Pareja. 239. Woman in Poncho.

1972. Battle of Pichincha. 150th Anniv. (1st issue). Multicoloured.
1476. 30 c. Type 238 (postage) 5 5
1477. 40 c. Juan Jose Flores .. 5 5
1478. 50 c. Leon de Febres Cordero 5 5
1479. 60 c. Ignacio Torres .. 5 5
1480. 70 c. F. de Paula Santander 5 5
1481. 1 s. Jos M. Cordova .. 5 5
1482. 1 s. 30 Jose M. Saenz (air) 8 5
1483. 3 s. Tomas Wright .. 15 8
1484. 4 s. Antonio Farfan .. 25 12
1485. 5 s. A. Jose de Sucre .. 40 25
1486. 10 s. Simon Bolivar .. 65 40
1487. 20 s. Arms of Ecuador.. 1·25 75
See also Nos. 1508/19.

1972. Ecuador Handicrafts and Costumes. Multicoloured.
1488. 2 s. Type 239 (postage) .. 12 5
1489. 3 s. Girl in striped poncho 15 8
1490. 5 s. Girl in embroidered poncho.. .. 25 12
1491. 10 s. Copper urn 55 25
1492. 2 s. Woman in floral poncho (air) 12 5
1493. 3 s. Girl in banded poncho 15 8
1494. 5 s. Woman in rose poncho 25 20
1495. 10 s. "Sun" sculpture .. 55 35

240. Epidendrum (orchid).

1972. Air. Ecuador Flowers. Mult.
1497. 4 s. Type 240 .. .. 25 12
1498. 6 s. Canna 30 20
1499. 10 s. Simson weed .. 55 45

241. Oil Rigs. 242. Arms of Ecuador.

1972. Air. Oil Industry.
1501. 241. 1 s. 30 multicoloured 8 5

1972. Air. Civic and Armed Forces Day.
1502. 242. 2 s. multicoloured .. 12 5
1503. 3 s. multicoloured .. 15 12
1504. 4 s. multicoloured .. 20 12
1505. 4 s. 50 multicoloured 25 20
1506. 6 s. 30 multicoloured 35 25
1507. 6 s. 90 multicoloured 40 30

243. Sucre's Statue, Santo Domingo. 244. Presidents Lara and Caldera.

1972. Battle of Pichincha. 150th Anniv. (2nd issue). Multicoloured.
1508. 1 s. 20 Type 243 (post.) 8 5
1509. 1 s. 80 San Agustin Monastery 10 8
1510. 2 s. 30 Independence Square 12 10
1511. 2 s. 50 Bolivar's statue, La Alameda 15 10
1512. 4 s. 75 Carved chapel doors 25 20
1513. 2 s. 40 Cloister, San Augustin Monastery (air) .. 12 10
1514. 4 s. 50 La Merced Monastery 25 20
1515. 5 s. 50 Chapel column .. 30 20
1516. 6 s. 30 Altar, San Agustin Monastery 30 25
1517. 6 s. 90 Ceiling, San Augustin Monastery 35 30
1518. 7 s. 40 Crucifixion, Cantuna Chapel 45 30
1519. 7 s. 90 Ceiling detail, San Agustin Monastery .. 45 35

1973. Air. Visit of Pres. Caldera of Venezuela.
1520. 244. 3 s. multicoloured .. 15 10

245. Dish Aerial. 246. U.N. Emblem.

1973. Earth Satellite Station. Inaug. (1972).
1521. 245. 1 s. multicoloured .. 8 5

1973. Air. U.N. Economic Committee for Latin America (C.E.P.A.L.). 25th Anniv.
1522. 246. 1 s. 30 black and blue 8 5

247. O.E.A. Emblem. 248. Young Sea Birds.

1973. "Day of the Americas".
1523. 247. 1 s. 50 multicoloured 10 8

1973. Formation of Galapagos Islands Province. Multicoloured.
1524. 30 c. Type 248 (postage) 5 5
1525. 40 c. Gulls 5 5
1526. 50 c. Oyster-catcher .. 5 5
1527. 60 c. Basking seals .. 5 5
1528. 70 c. Giant tortoise .. 5 5
1529. 1 s. Sea-lion 5 5
1530. 1 s. 30 Sea birds (air) .. 8 5
1531. 3 s. Pelican 15 10

249. Gold Coin of 1928. 250. Black-chinned Mountain Tanager.

1973. Air. Coins. Multicoloured.
1532. 5 s. Silver Coin of 1934 .. 25 15
1533. 10 s. Reverse of silver coin, showing arms .. 45 30
1534. 50 s. Type 249 .. .. 2·25 1·25

1973. Birds of Ecuador. Multicoloured.
1536. 1 s. Type 250 .. .. 5 5
1537. 2 s. Moriche oriole .. 10 8
1538. 3 s. Toucan barbet (vert.) 15 10
1539. 5 s. Masked crimson tanager (vert.) 25 15
1540. 10 s. Blue-necked tanager (vert.) 50 40

251. OPEC Emblem. 252. Dr. Marco T. Varea Quevedo (botanist).

1974. Air. OPEC (Oil exporters) Meeting, Quito.
1542. 251. 2 s. multicoloured .. 10 8

1974. Ecuadorian Personalities. (1st series).
1543. 252. 1 s. blue 5 5
1544. – 1 s. orange 5 5
1545. – 1 s. green 5 5
1546. – 1 s. brown 5 5
PERSONALITIES: No. 1544. Dr. J. M. Carbo Noboa (medical scientist). No. 1545, Dr. A. J. Valenzuela (physician). No. 1546 Capt. E. Chiriboga (national hero).
See also Nos. 1551/6 and 1565/9.

253. Ecuador Flag and U.P.U. Emblem. 254. Airborne Postman with Letter.

1974. Air. Universal Postal Union. Cent.
1548. 253. 1 s. 30 multicoloured 8 5

1974. Ecuadorian Personalities (2nd series). As Type 252.
1551. 60 c. red (postage) .. 5 5
1552. 70 c. lilac.. .. 5 5
1553. 1 s. 20 green 8 5
1554. 1 s. 80 blue 10 8
1555. 1 s. 30 blue and black (air) 8 5
1556. 1 s. 50 grey on pale grey.. 5 5
PERSONALITIES: 60 c. Dr. Pio Jaramillo Alvarado (sociologist). 70 c. Prof. Luciano Andrade Marin (naturalist). 1 s. 20, Dr. Francisco Campos Ruiadaneira (entomologist). 1 s. 30, Teodore Wolf (geographer). 1 s. 50, Capt. Edmundo Chiriboga G. (national hero). 1 s. 80, Luis Vernaza Lazarte (philanthropist).

1974. Air. 8th Inter-American Postmasters' Congress, Auibo.
1557. 254. 5 s. multicoloured .. 25 15

255. Map of the Americas and F.I.A.F. Emblem. 256. Colonnade.

1974. Air. "Exfigua" Stamp Exhibition and Inter-American Philatelic Federation 5th General Assembly, Guayaquil (1973).
1558. 255. 3 s. multicoloured .. 15 10

1974. Colonial Monastery, Tilipulo, Cotopaxi Province. Multicoloured.
1559. 20 c. Type 256 .. .. 5 5
1560. 30 c. Entrqnce 5 5
1561. 40 c. Church 5 5
1562. 50 c. Archway (vert.) .. 5 5
1563. 60 c. Chapel (vert.) .. 5 5
1564. 70 c. Cemetery (vert.) .. 5 5

1975. Ecuadorian Personalities (3rd series). As T 252.
1565. 80 c. blue (postage) .. 5 5
1566. 80 c. red and pink .. 5 5
1567. 5 s. red (air) 25 15
1568. 5 s. grey 25 15
1569. 5 s. violet 25 15
PORTRAITS: No. 1565, Angel Polibio Chaves (statesman). No. 1566, Emilio Estrada Ycaza (archaeologist). No. 1567, Manuel J. Calle (journalist). No. 1568, Leopoldo Benites Vinueza (statesman). No. 1569, Adolfo H. Simmonds G. (journalist).

257. President Lara.

1975. Air. State Visits of President Lara to Algeria, Rumania and Venezuela.
1570. 257. 5 s. black and red .. 25 15

258. Ministerial Greetings. 259. "The Sacred Heart".

1975. Meeting of Public Works' Ministers of Ecuador and Colombia, Quito. Multicoloured.
1571. 1 s. Type 258 (postage) .. 5 5
1572. 1 s. 50 Ministers at opening ceremony (air) . .. 8 5
1573. 2 s. Ministers signing treaty 10 8

1975. Air. Third Bolivian Eucharistic Congress, Quito. Multicoloured.
1574. 1 s. 30 Type 259 .. .. 8 5
1575. 2 s. Golden monstrance .. 10 8
1576. 3 s. Quito Cathedral .. 15 10

260. President Mera. 261. J. Delgado Panchana (swimming champion) with Trophy.

1975. Air. Juan de Dios Martinez Mera, former President of Ecuador. Birth Cent.
1577. 260. 5 s. red and black .. 25 15

1975. Air. Jorge Delgado Panchana Commemoration. Multicoloured.
1578. 1 s. 30 Type 261 .. .. 8 5
1579. 3 s. Delgado Panchana in water 15 10

262. "Women of Peace". 263. "Armed Forces".

1975. International Women's Year. Mult.
1580. 1 s. Type 262 .. .. 5 5
1581. 1 s. "Women of Action" 5 5

1975. 15th February Revolution. Third Anniv.
1582. 263. 2 s. multicoloured .. 10 8

264. Hurdling. 265. "Phragmipedum candatum".

1975. 3rd Ecuadorian Games, Quito.

1583. 264. 20 c. black and orange (postage) 5 5
1584. – 20 c. black and yellow 5 5
1585. – 30 c. black and magenta 5 5
1586. – 30 c. black and buff 5 5
1587. – 40 c. black and yellow 5 5
1588. – 40 c. black and mauve 5 5
1589. – 50 c. black and green 5 5
1590. – 50 c. black and red 5 5
1591. – 60 c. black and green 5 5
1592. – 60 c. black and pink 5 5
1593. – 70 c. black and drab 5 5
1594. – 70 c. black and grey 5 5
1595. – 80 c. black and blue 5 5
1596. – 80 c. black and orange 5 5
1597. – 1 s. black and olive 5 5
1598. – 1 s. black and brown 5 5
1599. – 1 s. 30 black and orange (air) 8 5
1600. – 2 s. black and yellow 10 8
1601. – 2 s. 80, black and red 12 10
1602. – 3 s. black and blue 15 12
1603. – 5 s. black and purple 25 15

DESIGNS: No. 1584, Chess. No. 1585, Boxing. No. 1586, Basketball. No. 1587, Show jumping. No. 1588, Cycling. No. 1589, Football. No. 1590, Fencing. No. 1591, Golf. No. 1592, Gymnastics. No. 1593, Wrestling. No. 1594, Judo. No. 1595, Swimming. No. 1596, Weight-lifting. No. 1597, Handball. No. 1598, Table tennis. No. 1599, Squash. No. 1600, Rifle shooting. No. 1601, Volleyball. No. 1602, Inca raft. No. 1603, Inca mask.

1975. Orchids and Cacti. Multicoloured.

1604. 20 c. Type **265** (postage) .. 5 5
1605. 30 c. " Genciana " (horiz.) 5 5
1606. 40 c. " Bromeliacae cactacceae " 5 5
1607. 50 c. " Cachlioda volcanica " (horiz.) 5 5
1608. 60 c. " Odontoglossum hallii (horiz.) 5 5
1609. 80 c. " Cactacceae sp. " (horiz.) 5 5
1610. 1 s. " Odontoglossum sp. " (horiz.) 5 5
1611. 1 s. 30 " Pitcairnia pungens " (horiz.) (air) .. 8 5
1612. 2 s. " Salvia sp. " (horiz.) 10 8
1613. 3 s. " Bomarea " (horiz.) 15 10
1614. 4 s. " Opuntia quitense " (horiz.) 20 12
1615. 5 s. " Bomarea " (different) (horiz.) 25 15

266. Aircraft Tail-fins. **267.** Benalcazar Statue.

1976. Air. TAME Airline. 23rd Anniv. Multicoloured.

1616. 1 s. 30 Type **266** .. 8 5
1617. 3 s. Planes encircling map 15 10

1976. Air. Sebastian de Benalcazar Commem.

1618. 267. 2 s. multicoloured .. 10 8
1619. 3 s. multicoloured .. 15 10

268. " Venus " (Chorrera Culture). **269.** Strawberries.

1976. Archaeological Discoveries. Multi.

1620. 20 c. Type **268** (postage) 5 5
1621. 30 c. " Venus " (Valdivia) 5 5
1622. 40 c. Seated monkey (Chorrera) 5 5
1623. 50 c. Man wearing poncho (Panzaleo Tardio) .. 5 5
1624. 60 c. Mythical figure (Cashaloma) 5 5
1625. 80 c. Musician (Tolita) .. 5 5
1626. 1 s. Chief priest (censer-Mantema) 5 5
1627. 1 s. Female mask (Tolita) 5 5
1628. 1 s. Gold and platinum brooch (Tolita) 5 5
1629. 1 s. " Angry person " mask (Tolita) 5 5
1630. 1 s. 30 Coconut-dealer (Carchi) (air) 8 5
1631. 2 s. Funerary urn (Tuncahuan) 10 8
1632. 3 s. Priest (Bahia de Caraquez) 15 10
1633. 4 s. seashell (Cuasmal) .. 20 12
1634. 5 s. Bowl supported by figurines (Guangala) .. 25 15

1976. Flowers and Fruits Festival, Ambato. Multicoloured.

1635. 1 s. Type **269** (postage) .. 8 5
1636. 2 s. Apples (air) 10 8
1637. 5 s. Rose 15 10

270. S. Cueva Celi. **271.** Lufthansa Airliner crossing " 50 ".

1976. Musical Celebrities. Multicoloured.

1638. 1 s. Type **270** 8 5
1639. 1 s. C. Ojeda Davila .. 8 5
1640. 1 s. S. Maria Duran .. 8 5
1641. 1 s. C. Amable Ortiz .. 8 5
1642. 1 s. L. Alberto Valencia 8 5

1976. Air. Lufthansa Airline. 50th Anniv.

1643. 271. 10 s. multicoloured .. 50 30

272. " Cerros del Carmen y Santa Ana ". **273.** New Post Office Building.

1976. Air. Guayaquil. 441st Anniv. Multicoloured.

1644. 1 s. 30 Type **272** .. 8 5
1645. 1 s. 30 " Pregonero " (vert.) 8 5
1646. 1 s. 30 " Estibador " (vert.) 8 5
1647. 2 s. " Sebastian de Benalcazar " (vert.) .. 10 8
1648. 2 s. " Francisco de Orellana " (vert.) .. 10 8
1649. 2 s. " Guayas y Quil " (vert.) 10 8

1976. Air. Post Office Building Project.

1650. 273. 1 s. 30 multicoloured 8 5

274. Emblem and Wreath. **275.** The Americas on Globe.

1976. Air. Bolivar Society. 50th Anniv.

1651. 274. 1 s. 30 multicoloured 8 5

1976. Air. 3rd Pan-American Ministers' Conference on Transport Infrastructure, Quito.

1652. 275. 2 s. multicoloured .. 10 8

276. George Washington.

1976. Air. American Revolution Bicent. Multicoloured.

1654. 3 s. Type **276** 15 10
1655. 5 s. Naval battle, Sept. 1779 (horiz.) 25 15

EXPRESS LETTER STAMPS

1928. Oblong Tobacco Tax stamp surch. **CORREOS EXPRESO** and new value.

E 457. 2 c. on 2 c. blue .. 50 2·75
E 458. 5 c. on 2 c. blue .. 50 2·75
E 459. 10 c. on 2 c. blue .. 50 2·75
E 460. 20 c. on 2 c. blue .. 80 2·75
E 461. 50 c. on 2 c. blue .. 80 2·75

1945. Surch. **EXPRESO 20 Ctvs.**

E 742. 83. 20 c. on 5 c. green 5 5

LATE FEE STAMP

1945. Surch. **U H 10 Ctvs.**

L 742. 83. 10 c. on 5 c. green .. 8 5

OFFICAL STAMPS

1886. Stamps of 1881 optd. **OFICIAL.**

O 20. 5. 1 c. brown 25 25
O 21. 2 c. lake 35 35
O 22. 5 c. blue 55 55
O 23. 10 c. orange 25 25
O 24. 20 c. violet 25 25
O 25. 50 c. green .. .. 1·10 1·10

1887. Stamps of 1887 optd. **OFICIAL.**

O 30. 6. 1 c. green 40 40
O 31. 2 c. red 40 40
O 32. 5 c. blue 25 25
O 33. 80 c. olive .. .. 1·10 1·00

1892. Stamps of 1892 optd. **FRANQUEO OFICIAL.**

O 42. 7. 1 c. blue 5 12
O 43. 2 c. blue 5 12
O 44. 5 c. blue 5 12
O 45. 10 c. blue 5 12
O 46. 20 c. blue 5 12
O 47. 50 c. blue 5 25
O 48. 1 s. blue 12 25

1894. Stamps of 1894 (dated " 1894") optd. **FRANQUEO OFICIAL.**

O 65. 8. 1 c. grey 12 25
O 66. 2 c. grey 12 12
O 67. 5 c. grey 10 12
O 68. 10 c. grey 5 10
O 69. 20 c. grey 15 12
O 70. 50 c. grey 75 75
O 71. 1 s. grey .. .. 1·00 1·00

This series was re-issued in 1897 optd. "1897–1898".

1894. Postal Fiscals as T 12, but dated "1891-1892", optd. **OFICIAL 1894 y 1895.**

O 72. 12. 1 c. grey 80 80
O 73. 2 c. lake 80 80

1895. Stamps of 1895 (dated " 1895") optd. **FRANQUEO OFICIAL.**

O 82. 8. 1 c. grey .. .. 1·10 1·10
O 83. 2 c. grey .. .. 1·60 1·60
O 84. 5 c. grey 25 25
O 85. 10 c. grey .. .. 1·60 1·60
O 86. 20 c. grey .. .. 2·25 2·25
O 87. 50 c. grey .. .. 6·00 6·00
O 88. 1 s. grey 75 75

This series was re-issued in 1897 optd. "1897–1898".

1896. Stamps of 1896 optd. **FRANQUEO OFICIAL** in oval.

O 97. 11. 1 c. bistre 20 15
O 98. 2 c. bistre 20 15
O 99. 5 c. bistre 25 15
O 100. 10 c. bistre 25 15
O 101. 20 c. bistre 25 15
O 102. 50 c. bistre 25 15
O 103. 1 s. bistre 40 35
O 104. 5 s. bistre 85 75

O 1.

O 2. Government Building, Quito.

1898. Fiscal stamps as Type O 1, surch. **CORREOS OFICIAL** and value in frame.

O 181. O 1. 5 c. on 50 c. purple 15 15
O 184. 10 c. on 20 s. orange 40 40
O 185. 20 c. on 50 c. purple 1·25 1·25
O 187. 20 c. on 50 s. green 1·10 1·10

1899. Stamps as 1899 optd. **OFICIAL.**

O 201. 2 c. black and orange 12 10
O 202. 10 c. black and orange 12 10
O 203. 20 c. black and orange 12 12
O 204. 50 c. black and orange 12 12

1913. Stamps of 1911 (except No. O 396) optd. **OFICIAL.**

O 374. 32. 1 c. black and red .. 30 30
O 387. 1 c. orange 10 8
O 388. 33. 2 c. black and blue .. 20 15
O 424. 2 c. green 5 5
O 368. 34. 3 c. black and orange 20 20
O 390. 3 c. black 8 8
O 437. 35. 4 c. black and red .. 8 8
O 369. 36. 5 c. black and red .. 35 35
O 393. 5 c. violet 15 10
O 370. 37. 10 c. black and blue 35 25
O 395 10 c. blue 10 10
O 396. 26. 20 c. black and green (No. 328) 50 20
O 429. 39. 1 s. black and green .. 45 45

1920. Stamps of 1920 (Nos. 381/400) optd. **OFICIAL.**

O 401. 41. 1 c. green 8 8
O 402. – 2 c. red 8 8
O 403. – 3 c. bistre 8 8
O 404. – 4 c. green 10 10
O 405. – 5 c. blue 10 10
O 406. – 6 c. orange 8 8
O 407. – 7 c. brown 10 10
O 408. – 8 c. green 12 12
O 409. – 9 c. red 15 15
O 410. 42. 10 c. blue 10 10
O 411. – 15 c. black 50 50
O 412. – 20 c. purple 40 40
O 413. – 30 c. violet 70 60
O 414. – 40 c. sepia .. .. 1·00 50
O 415. – 50 c. green 60 60
O 416. – 60 c. blue 75 70
O 417. – 70 c. grey 75 70
O 418. – 80 c. yellow 80 80
O 419. – 90 c. green .. .. 1·00 1·00
O 420. – 1 s. blue .. .. 1·50 1·40

1924. Fiscal stamps of 1919 optd. **OFICIAL.**

O 421. 40. 1 c. blue 12 10
O 422. 2 c. green 75 70

1924. No. O 204 optd. **Acuerdo No. 4,228.**

O 430. 50 c. black and orange 45 45

1925. Stamps of 1925 optd. **OFICIAL.**

O 457. 32. 1 c. blue 8 5
O 439. 36. 5 c. red 15 15
O 440. 37. 10 c. green 10 10

1928. Stamp of 1927 optd. **OFICIAL.**

O 463. 44. 20 c. purple 8 8

1929. Official Air stamps. Air stamps of 1929 optd. **OFICIAL.**

O 466. 45. 2 c. black 25 25
O 467. 5 c. red 25 25
O 468. 10 c. brown 25 25
O 469. 20 c. purple 25 25
O 470. 50 c. green 75 70
O 474. 50 c. brown 75 70
O 471. 1 s. blue 75 70
O 475. 1 s. red .. .. 1·10 1·10
O 472. 5 s. yellow .. .. 3·00 3·00
O 476. 5 s. olive .. .. 2·50 2·50
O 473. 10 s. red .. .. 60·00 55·00
O 477. 10 s. black .. .. 3·75 3·75

1936. Stamps of 1936 (Nos. 520/4) optd. **OFICIAL.**

O 525. 5 c. olive 15 5
O 526. 10 c. brown 15 5
O 527. 20 c. purple 10 5
O 528. 1 s. red 25 20
O 529. 2 s. blue 40 25

1937. Stamps of 1937 optd. **OFICIAL.**

O 562. – 2 c. green (postage) .. 5 5
O 563. 66. 5 c. red 5 5
O 564. – 10 c. blue 5 5
O 565. 67. 20 c. red 5 5
O 566. – 1 s. olive 12 10
O 567. 68. 10 c. brown (air) .. 8 8
O 568. 20 c. olive 12 10
O 569. 70 c. brown 15 10
O 570. 1 s. slate 20 15
O 571. 2 s. violet 25 20

1941. Air stamp of 1939 optd. **OFICIAL.**

O 638. 77. 5 s. green 35 30

1946. Oblong Tobacco Tax stamp optd. **CORRESPONDENCIA OFICIAL.** Roul.

O 803. 1 c. red 5 5

1947.

O 804. O 2. 30 c. blue 8 5
O 805. 30 c. brown 8 5
O 806. 30 c. violet 8 5

1964. Air. Nos. 1269/71 optd. **Oficial.**
O 1272. **181.** 50 c. red, yellow, bl., green and light blue 50 50
O 1273. – 80 c. red, bl. & yell. 50 50
O 1274. 1 s. 30 red, blue, yell. & light green 50 50

1964. No. 1272 optd. **oficial** on each stamp.
O 1275. **182.** 80 c. green and lake 1·00 12

The "OEA" overprint is across four stamps, the "oficial" overprint is on each stamp.

The unused price is for a block of four.

POSTAGE DUE STAMPS

D 1. D 2.

1896.
D 105. **D 1.** 1 c. green 70 1·00
D 106. 2 c. green 20 40
D 107. 5 c. green 65 70
D 108. 10 c. green 40 50
D 109. 20 c. green 20 50
D 110. 50 c. green 20 50
D 111. 100 c. green 30 80

1929.
D 466. **D 2.** 5 c. blue 5 5
D 467. 10 c. yellow 8 5
D 468. 20 c. red 10 10

D 3.

1958.
D 1128. **D 3.** 10 c. violet 5 5
D 1129. 50 c. green 5 5
D 1130. 1 s. brown 8 8
D 1131. 2 s. red 12 12

EGYPT O2; BC

Formerly a kingdom of N.E. Africa. Turkish till 1914, when it became a British Protectorate. Independent from 1922. A republic from 1953.

In 1958 the United Arab Republic was formed, comprising Egypt and Syria, but separate stamps continued to be issued for each territory as they have different currencies. In 1961 Syria became an independent Arab republic and left the U.A.R. but the title was retained by Egypt until a new federation was formed with Libya and Syria in 1971, when the country's name was changed to Arab Republic of Egypt.

1866. 40 paras = 1 piastre.
1888. 1000 milliemes = 100 piastres = £1 (Egyptian).

1. 2. Sphinx and Pyramid.

1866. Designs as T 1. Imperf. or perf.
1. **1.** 5 pa. grey 7·00 7·00
2. 10 pa. brown 12·00 8·00
3. 20 pa. blue 16·00 10·00
4. 1 pi. mauve 10·00 1·75
5. 2 pi. yellow 18·00 9·00
6. 5 pi. red 80·00 70·00
7. 10 pi. blue 95·00 90·00

1867.
11. **2.** 5 pa. yellow 4·00 2·25
12b. 10 pa. violet 9·00 2·75
13a. 20 pa. green 10·00 2·50
14. 1 pi. red 2·00 65
15. 2 pi. blue 18·00 3·50
16. 5 pi. brown 75·00 40·00

On the piastre values the letters "P" and "E" appear on the upper corners.

3. 4.

1872.
28. **3.** 5 pa. brown 3·00 2·00
36. 10 pa. mauve 2·50 1·50
30. 20 pa. blue 7·00 1·50
37. 20 pa. grey 1·50 1·25
38. 1 pi. red 1·50 50
39. 2 pi. yellow 2·00 2·00
40. 2½ pi. violet 2·50 1·75
41. 5 pi. green 14·00 5·50

1875. As T 3, but "PARA" inscr. left-hand side and figure "5" inverted.
35. – 5 pa. brown 1·50 1·25

1879. Surch. in English and Arabic.
42. **3.** 5 pa on 2½ pi. violet 3·00 2·25
43. 10 pa. on 2½ pi. violet 3·00 2·25

1879. Various frames.
44. **4.** 5 pa. brown 10 8
45. 10 pa. mauve 9·00 1·40
50. 10 pa. rose 14·00 1·50
51. 10 pa. grey 3·00 35
52. 10 pa. green 10 5
46. 20 pa. blue 16·00 65
53a. 20 pa. red 2·00 15
47a. 1 pi. red 5·00 10
69a. 1 pi. blue 75 5
70a. 2 pi. orange 3·75 30
70. 2 pi. brown 3·50 5
49a. 5 pi. green 22·00 2·00
55a. 5 pi. grey 4·50 12

1884. Surch. in English and Arabic.
56. **4.** 20 pa. on 5 pi. green 3·00 60

5.

1888. Various frames.
64a. **5.** 1 m. brown 8 5
58. 2 m. green 25 5
61. 3 m. claret 1·00 35
66. 3 m. yellow 40 5
67. 4 m. red 30 5
59. 5 m. red 45 5
60. 10 pi. mauve 5·00 20

6. Native boats on Nile. 9. Pylon of Karnak Temple, Luxor.

7. Statue of Rameses II. 8. (Arabic inscriptions differ.)

1914.
73. **6.** 1 m. sepia 5 5
74. 2 m. green 12 5
86. 2 m. red 15 10
75. 3 m. orange 20 10
76. 4 m. red 35 20
88. 4 m. green 65 50
77. 5 m. lake 25 5
90. 5 m. pink 40 5
78. 10 m. blue 55 5
92. 10 m. lake 65 12
96. **7.** 15 m. blue 50 10
97. **8.** 15 m. blue 3·00 35
79. **9.** 20 m. olive 1·10 5
80. 50 m. purple 1·90 20
81. 100 m. grey 4·00 30
82. 200 m. claret 8·50 50

DESIGNS—As T 6: 2 m. Cleopatra in headdress of Isis. 3 m. Ras-el-Tin Palace, Alexandria. 4 m. Pyramids, Giza. 5 m. Sphinx. 10 m. Colossi of Thebes. As T 9: 50 m. Citadel, Cairo. 100 m. Rock Temples, Abu Simbel. 200 m. Assouan Dam.

1915. Surch. **2 Milliemes** in English and Arabic.
83. **6.** 2 m. on 3 m. orge. (No. 75) 12 12

(10. "The Kingdom of Egypt, 15 March, 1922".) 11. King Fuad I.

1922. Stamps of 1914 optd. with T **10.**
98. **6.** 1 m. sepia 15 5
99. 2 m. red 20 5
100. 3 m. orange 35 15
101. 4 m. green 25 15
102. 5 m. pink 25 5
103. 10 m. lake 40 5
104. **7.** 15 m. blue 90 5
105. **8.** 15 m. blue 50 10
106. **9.** 20 m. olive 90 8
107. 50 m. purple 1·25 12
108. 100 m. grey 3·50 30
110. 200 m. claret 3·50 30

1923.
111. **11.** 1 m. orange 5 5
112. 2 m. black 8 5
113. 3 m. brown 15 10
114. 4 m. green 15 10
115. 5 m. brown 8 5
116. 10 m. rose 15 5
117. 15 m. blue 20 5
118. – 20 m. green 65 5
119. – 50 m. green 1·60 5
120. – 100 m. purple 2·75 12
121. – 200 m. mauve 6·00 50
122. – £1 violet and blue 30·00 3·75

The 20 m. to £1 values are larger (22½ × 28 mm.).

12. Thoth writing name of King Fuad. 14. King Farouk.

13. Ploughing with Oxen.

1925. Int. Geographical Congress, Cairo.
123. **12.** 5 m. brown 2·00 2·00
124. 10 red 3·00 3·00
125. 15 m. blue 3·50 3·50

1926. 12th Agricultural Exn., Cairo.
126. **13.** 5 m. brown 50 40
127. 10 m. red 50 40
128. 15 m. blue 50 40
129. 50 m. green 2·25 1·60
130. 100 m. purple 5·00 4·00
131. 200 m. violet 7·00 6·50

1926. King's 58th Birthday.
132. **14.** 50 pi. purple 18·00 4·00

15. De Haviland "DH 34" over Nile.

1926. Air.
133. **15.** 27 m. violet 4·50 3·25
134. 27 m. brown 1·50 1·25

1926. Surch.
135. **13.** 5 m. on 50 m. green 50 50
136. 10 m. on 100 m. purple 50 50
137. 15 m. on 200 m. violet 50 50

16. Ancient Egyptian Ship.

1926. Int. Navigation Congress.
138. **16.** 5 m. black and brown 80 50
139. 10 m. black and red 80 50
140. 15 m. black and blue 80 50

1926. Port Fuad Inaug. Optd. **PORT FOUAD.**
141. **16.** 5 m. black and brown 30·00 20·00
142. 10 m. black and red 30·00 20·00
143. 15 m. black and blue 30·00 20·00
144. **14.** 50 pi. purple £300 £250

17. Cotton Plant.

1927. Int. Cotton Congress, Cairo.
145. **17.** 5 m. green and brown 70 60
146. 10 m. green and red 80 60
147. 15 m. green and blue 90 60

18. 19.

20.

1927.
148. **18.** 1 m. orange 5 5
149. 2 m. black 8 5
150. 3 m. brown 8 5
151. 3 m. green 12 5
153. 4 m. green 25 8
154. 4 m. brown 25 10
156a. 5 m. brown 12 5
157a. 10 m. red 30 5
158. 10 m. violet 75 5
159. 13 m. red 25 5
160a. 15 m. blue 50 5
161. 15 m. purple 1·10 5
162. 20 m. blue 1·60 5
163a. **19.** 20 m. olive 60 5
164. 20 m. blue 1·00 5
165. 40 m. brown 65 5
166a. 50 m. blue 50 5
167a. 100 m. purple 1·50 5
168a. 200 m. mauve 2·00 20
171. **20.** 500 m. blue and brown 14·00 2·50
172. – £1 brown and green 14·00 2·25

DESIGN—VERT. As T **20:** £1 King Fuad I.

See also Nos. 233/9.

22. Amenhotep. 23. Imhotep.

1927. Statistical Congress.
173. **22.** 5 m. brown 30 25
174. 10 m. red 40 30
175. 15 m. blue 50 45

1928. Medical Congress.
176. **23.** 5 m. brown 25 20
177. – 10 m. red 25 20

DESIGN: 10 m. Mohammed Ali Pasha.

25. King Farouk as Crown Prince. 26. Tillers of the Soil.

1929. Prince's 9th Birthday.
178. **25.** 5 m. grey and purple 35 35
179. 10 m. grey and red 35 35
180. 15 m. grey and blue 35 35
181. 20 m. grey & turquoise 35 35

1931. Agricultural and Industrial Exhibition, Cairo.
182. **26.** 5 m. brown 35 30
183. 10 m. red 35 30
184. 15 m. blue 45 40

1931. Air. Surch. **GRAF ZEPPELIN AVRIL 1931** and value in English and Arabic.
185. **15.** 50 m. on 27 m. brown 9·00 9·00
186. 100 m. on 27 m. brown 9·00 9·00

1932. Surch. in English and Arabic.
187. **14.** 50 m. on 50 pi. purple 1·90 70
188. – 100 m. on £1 violet and blue (No. 122) 45·00 42·00

27.

1933. Int. Railway Congress. Locomotive types inscr. as in T **27.**
189. **27.** 5 m. black and brown . . 1·10 1·10
190. – 13 m. black and red . . 4·25 3·25
191. – 15 m. black and violet . 4·25 3·25
192. – 20 m. black and blue . . 4·25 3·25
DESIGNS: 13 m. 2-2-2 locomotive, 1859. 15 m. 2-2-2 locomotive, 1862. 20 m. 4-4-2 locomotive, 1932.

28. Handley Page " HP 42 " over Pyramids.

1933. Air.
193. **28.** 1 m. black and orange . . 5 5
194. 2 m. black and grey . . 30 30
195. 2 m. black and orange . . 60 50
196. 3 m. black and brown . . 10 10
197. 4 m. black and green . . 30 30
198. 5 m. black and brown . . 10 5
199. 6 m. black and green . . 35 30
200. 7 m. black and blue . . 30 25
201. 8 m. black and violet . . 12 8
202. 9 m. black and red . . 45 40
203. 10 m. brown and violet 25 8
204. 20 m. brown and green 15 5
205. 30 m. brown and blue 50 20
206. 40 m. brown and red . . 3·00 30
207. 50 m. brown and orange 2·25 5
208. 60 m. brown and grey . . 1·00 10
209. 70 m. green and blue . . 75 10
210. 80 m. green and sepia . . 75 10
211. 90 m. green and orange 85 12
212. 100 m. green and violet 1·10 12
213. 200 m. green and red . . 3·00 50
See also Nos. 285/8.

Armstrong-Whitworth " Atlanta " of Imperial Airways.

1933. Int. Aviation Congress. Inscr. as in T **29.**
214. **29.** 5 m. brown . . . . 1·25 1·25
215. 10 m. violet . . . . 3·25 2·25
216. – 13 m. red . . . . 3·25 2·25
217. – 15 m. purple . . . . 3·25 2·25
218. – 20 m. blue . . . . 3·25 3·00
DESIGNS: 13 m., 15 m. Dornier " Do 10 " Flying-boat. 20 m. Airship " Graf Zeppelin ".

30. Khedive Ismail Pasha. **31.**

1934. 10th Universal Postal Union Congress, Cairo.
219. **30.** 1 m. orange 12 12
220. 2 m. black 12 12
221. 3 m. brown 12 12
222. 4 m. green 15 15
223. 5 m. red 20 10
224. 10 m. violet 35 20
225. 13 m. red 55 35
226. 15 m. purple 40 20
227. 20 m. blue 60 20
228. 50 m. blue . . . . 1·90 30
229. 100 m. olive . . . . 3·50 65
230. 200 m. violet . . . . 9·00 2·00
231. **31.** 50 p. brown . . . . 35·00 20·00
232. £1 blue . . . . 70·00 30·00

1936. As T **18** but inscribed "POSTES".
233. **18.** 1 m. orange 8 5
234. 2 m. black 12 5
235. 4 m. green 20 5
236. 5 m. brown 15 5
237. 10 m. violet 50 5
238. 15 m. purple 75 5
239. 20 m. blue 90 5

32. Exhibition Entrance. **33.** Palace of Agriculture.

1936. 15th Agricultural and Industrial Exn., Cairo.
240. **32.** 5 m. brown 30 25
241. **33.** 10 m. violet 45 35
242. 13 m. red 55 50
243. – 15 m. purple 50 35
244. – 20 m. blue . . . . 1·50 1·00
DESIGN—HORIZ. 15 m., 20 m. Palace of Industry.

34. Nahas Pasha and Treaty Delegates.

1936. Anglo-Egyptian Treaty.
245. **34.** 5 m. brown 30 30
246. 15 m. purple 35 35
247. 20 m. blue 50 40

35. King Farouk. **36.**

1937. Investiture of King Farouk.
248. **35.** 1 m. orange 5 5
249. 2 m. red 5 5
250. 3 m. brown 5 5
251. 4 m. green 5 5
252. 5 m. brown 5 5
253. 6 m. green 10 5
254. 10 m. violet 10 5
255. 13 m. red 12 5
256. 15 m. purple 12 5
257. 20 m. blue 15 5
258. 20 m. violet 20 5

1937. Abolition of Capitulations.
259. **36.** 5 m. brown 25 20
260. 15 m. purple 40 35
261. 20 m. blue 50 40

37. Nekhbet, Sacred Eye of Horus and Buto.

1937. 15th Ophthalmological Congress, Cairo.
262. **37.** 5 m. brown 35 30
263. 15 m. purple 35 30
264. 20 m. blue 35 30

38. King Farouk and Queen Farida.

1938. Royal Wedding.
265. **38.** 5 m. brown . . . . 1·75 1·40

39. Gathering Cotton. **40.** Pyramids of Giza and Colossus of Thebes.

1938. 18th Int. Cotton Congress, Cairo.
266. **39.** 5 m. brown 35 35
267. 15 m. purple 80 75
268. 20 m. blue 65 60

1938. Int. Telecommunications Conf.. Cairo
269. **40.** 5 m. brown 50 50
270. 15 m. purple 65 60
271. 20 m. blue 65 60

1938. King Farouk's 18th Birthday. Portrait similar to T **38** with inscr. " 11 FEVRIER 1938 " at foot.
272. – £E 1 brown and green . . 35·00 32·00

41. Hydnocarpus. **42.** King Farouk and Pyramids.

43. King Farouk. **44.**

1938. Leprosy Research Congress.
273. **41.** 5 m. brown 70 50
274. 15 m. purple 70 50
275. 20 m. blue 70 50

1939.
276. **42.** 30 m. grey 20 5
277. 30 m. green 15 5
278. – 40 m. brown 25 5
279. – 50 m. blue 30 5
280. – 100 m. purple 40 5
281. – 200 m. violet . . . . 1·40 5
282. **43.** 50 p. brown and green 2·00 25
283. **44.** £E 1 brown and blue . . 4·00 50
DESIGNS (As T **42**): 40 m. Mosque. 50 m. Cairo Citadel. 100 m. Aswan Dam. 200 m. Fuad I University, Giza.

For similar issue with portrait looking to left, see 1947 issue.

45. Princess Ferial. **46.** King Fuad I.

1940. Child Welfare. Princess Ferial when 18 months old.
284. **45.** 5 m.+5 m. brown . . 30 25

1941. Air.
285. **28.** 5 m. brown 12 8
286. 10 m. violet 20 10
287. 25 m. purple 25 12
288. 30 m. green 25 10

1943. 5th Birthday of Princess Ferial. Optd. **1943.** in English and Arabic.
289. **45.** 5 m.+5 m. brown . . 2·00 2·00

1944. King Fuad I. 8th Death Anniv.
290. **46.** 10 m. purple 10 10

47. King Farouk. **48.** King Farouk. **49.** Khedive Ismail Pasha.

1944.
291. **47.** 1 m. orange 5 5
292. 2 m. red 5 5
293. 3 m. brown 5 5
294. 4 m. green 10 8
295. 5 m. brown 5 5
296. 10 m. violet 8 5
297. 13 m. red . . . . 1·00 75
298. 15 m. purple 12 5
299. 17 m. olive 12 5
300. 20 m. violet 15 5
301. 22 m. blue 25 5

1945. 25th Birthday of King Farouk.
302. **48.** 10 m. violet 10 10

1945. Ismail Pasha. 50th Death Anniv.
303. **49.** 10 m. olive 10 10

50. Flags of the Arab Union. **51.** Flags of Egypt and Saudi Arabia.

1945. Arab Union.
304. **50.** 10 m. violet 8 8
305. 22 m. green 15 15

1946. Visit of King Abdel-Aziz Al Sa'oud.
306. **51.** 10 m. green 8 8

DESIGNS: 2 m. Khedive Ismail Pasha. 17 m. King Fuad. 22 m. King Farouk.

52. Reproduction of First Stamp.

1946. First Egyptian Postage stamp. 80th Anniv. Inscr. "LXXX ANNIVERSAIRE DE 1er TIMBRE POSTE 1866 1946". Perf. or imperf.
307. **52.** 1 m.+1 m. grey . . 5 5
308. – 10 m.+10 m. purple . . 8 8
309. – 17 m.+17 m. brown . . 12 12
310. – 22 m.+22 m. green . . 15 15

53. Cairo Citadel.

1946. Evacuation of Cairo Citadel.
313. **53.** 10 m. brown and green 12 12

1946. Air. Cairo Aviation Congress. Optd. **Le Caire 1946** and Arabic characters.
314. **28.** 30 m. green (No. 288) . . 20 10

54. King Farouk and Inshas Palace.

DESIGNS: 2 m Prince Abdullah of Yemen. 3 m. President of Lebanon. 4 m. King of Saudi Arabia. 5 m. King of Iraq. 10 m. King of Jordan. 15 m. Pres. of Syria.

1946. Arab League Congress. Portraits.
315. **54.** 1 m. green 5 5
316. – 2 m. brown 5 5
317. – 3 m. blue 5 5
318. – 4 m. orange 5 5
319. – 5 m. brown 8 8
320. – 10 m. grey 10 10
321. – 15 m. violet 12 12

55. Tutankhamun. **56.** King Farouk, and Douglas " Dakota ".

57. Egyptian Parliament Buildings. **58.** King Farouk hoisting Flag.

1947. Air.
322. **56.** 2 m. red 5 5
323. 3 m. brown 5 5
324. 5 m. red 5 5
325. 7 m. orange 5 5
326. 8 m. green 8 5
327. 10 m. violet 8 5
328. 20 m. blue 12 8
329. 30 m. purple 15 10
330. 40 m. red 25 10
331. 50 m. blue 40 20
332. 100 m. olive 75 30
333. 200 m. grey . . . . 1·25 80

1947. Int. Exhibition of Fine Arts. Inscr. "EXPOSITION INTERNATIONALE D'ART CONTEMPORAIN".

334. – 5 m.+5 m. grey .. 15 25
335. – 15 m.+15 m. blue .. 30 50
336. – 30 m.+30 m. red .. 50 70
337. **55.** 50 m.+50 m. brown .. 70 1·25

DESIGNS—VERT. 5 m. Triad of Mykerinus. 30 m. Queen Nefertiti. HORIZ. 15 m. Temple of Rameses.

1947. 36th Int. Parliamentary Union Conference, Cairo.

338. **57.** 10 m. green 10 10

1947. Withdrawal of British Troops from Nile Delta.

339. **58.** 10 m. purple and green 10 10

59. King Farouk and Mosque.

59a. King Farouk.

1947. Designs as 1939 issue but with portrait altered as T **59** and **59a.**

340. – 30 m. olive 15 5
341. **59.** 40 m. brown 20 5
342. – 50 m. blue 30 5
343. – 100 m. purple 85 5
344. – 200 m. violet .. .. 2·00 50
345. **59a.** 50 p. brown and green.. 3·50 2·00
346. – £E1 brown and blue .. 7·00 60

60. Cotton Plant.

61. Egyptian Soldiers Entering Palestine.

1948. Int. Cotton Congress.

347. **60.** 10 m. green 20 15

1948. Arrival of Egyptian Troops in Gaza.

348. **61.** 10 m. green 20 20

1948. Air. Air Mail Service to Athens and Rome. Surch. **S.A.I.D.E. 23-8-1948** and values in English and Arabic.

349. **56.** 13 m. on 100 m. olive.. 20 20
350. 22 m. on 200 m. grey .. 25 25

62. Ibrahim Pasha and Fighting Ships.

1948. Ibrahim Pasha (statesman and general). Death Cent.

351. **62.** 10 m. green and red .. 15 15

63. Reclining Male Figure symbolising River Nile.

64. Soldier and Workers.

65. Mohammed Ali and Map.

1949. 16th Agricultural and Industrial Exn., Cairo.

352. **63.** 1 m. green 5 5
353. 10 m. violet 10 10
354. 17 m. red 12 12
355. 22 m. blue 15 15
356. **64.** 30 m. sepia 25 25

1949. Mohammed Ali (statesman and general). Death Cent.

358. **65.** 10 m. green and brown 15 15

66. Globe.

67. Scales of Justice.

1949. Universal Postal Union. 75th Anniv.

359. **66.** 10 m. red 15 10
360. 22 m. violet 30 25
361. 30 m. blue 40 35

1949. Abolition of Mixed Courts.

362. **67.** 10 m. green 12 10

68. Camels by Water-hole.

1950. Fuad I Desert Institute. Inaug.

363. **68.** 10 m. brown and violet 15 15

69. University.

1950. Fuad I University. 25th Anniv.

364. **69.** 22 m. purple and green 20 15

70. Khedive Ismail and Globe.

71. Girl and Cotton.

1950. Royal Egyptian Geographical Society. 75th Anniv.

365. **70.** 30 m. green and purple 25 20

1951. Int. Cotton Congress.

366. **71.** 10 m. olive 12 10

72. King Farouk and Queen Narriman.

1951. Royal Wedding.

367. **72.** 10 m. brown and green 60 50

73. Triumphal Arch.

1951. 1st Mediterranean Games. Inscr. "ALEXANDRIE 1951".

369. **73.** 10 m. brown 15 12
370. – 22 m. green 25 25
371. – 30 m. blue and green .. 30 25

DESIGNS—VERT. 22 m. Badge. HORIZ. 30 m. King Farouk and waves.

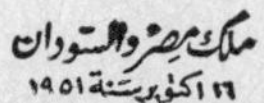

74. (" King of Egypt and the Sudan.")

1952. Optd. as T **74.**

373. **47.** 1 m. orange (postage).. 5 5
374. 2 m. red 5 5
375. **35.** 3 m. brown 5 5
376. **47.** 4 m. green 5 5
377. **35.** 6 m. green 15 8
378. **47.** 10 m. violet 10 5
379. 13 m. red 12 8
380. 15 m. purple 30 15
381. 17 m. olive 45 10
382. 20 m. violet 50 10
383. 22 m. blue 85 50
385. – 30 m. olive (No. 340).. 25 5
386. **59.** 40 m. brown 25 10
387. – 50 m. blue (No. 342) .. 35 5
388. – 100 m. purple (No. 343) 60 15
389. – 200 m. violet (No. 344) 1·40 20
390. **59a.** 50 p. brown and green 3·25 2·25
391. – £E1 brown and blue (No. 346) .. .. 9·00 3·00

392. **56.** 2 m. red (air) 5 5
393. 3 m. brown 8 5
394. 5 m. red 8 5
395. 7 m. orange 25 12
396. 8 m. green 10 8
397. 10 m. violet 12 12
398. 20 m. blue 95 40
399. 30 m. purple 30 25
400. 40 m. red .. .. 1·50 50
401. 50 m. blue 70 60
402. 100 m. olive .. .. 1·40 1·25
403. 200 m. grey .. .. 2·50 2·00

75. "Egypt".

76. Egyptian Flag.

1952. Abrogation of Anglo-Egyptian Treaty of 1936. Inscr. "16 Oct. 1951".

404. **75.** 10 m. green 12 10
405. – 22 m. green and maroon 25 20
406. – 30 m. green and brown 30 25

DESIGNS: 22 m. King Farouk and map of Nile Valley. 30 m. King Farouk and flag.

1952. Birth of Crown Prince Ahmed Fuad.

408. **76.** 10 m. green, yell. & blue 12 12

77. " Freedom, Hope and Peace ".

1952. Revolution of 23rd July, 1952. Inscr. "23 JUILLET 1952".

410. **77.** 4 m. orange and green .. 5 5
411. – 10 m. chestnut & green 8 5
412. – 17 m. brown and green 15 15
413. – 22 m. green & chocolate 25 25

DESIGNS—HORIZ. 10 m. Allegory of Egyptian freedom. VERT. 17 m. Map of Nile Valley, and Egyptian citizens. 22 m. Rejoicing crowd and Egyptian flag.

78. "Agriculture".

79. "Defence".

80. Mosque.

81. Queen Nefertiti.

1953. Inscr. "DEFENCE" (A) or "DEFENSE" (B).

414. **78.** 1 m. brown 5 5
415. 2 m. purple 5 5
416. 3 m. blue 5 5
417. 4 m. green 5 5
418. **79.** 10 m. sepia (A) .. 8 5
419. 10 m. sepia (B) .. 5 5
420. 15 m. grey (B).. .. 8 5
421. 17 m. turquoise (B) .. 10 5
422. 20 m. violet (B) .. 10 5
423. **80.** 30 m. green 10 5
424. 32 m. blue 12 5
425. 35 m. violet 20 5
426. 37 m. brown 25 5
427. 40 m. brown 15 5
428. 50 m. purple 25 5
429. **81.** 100 m. chestnut .. 40 5
430. 200 m. turquoise .. 75 12
431. 500 m. violet .. .. 1·75 45
432. £E1 red and green .. 3·50 50

See also Nos. 619 and 634.

82. Douglas " Dakota " Aircraft over Delta Barrage.

1953. Air.

433. **82.** 5 m. brown 5 5
434. 15 m. green 10 8

1953. Various issues of King Farouk with portrait obliterated by three horiz. bars.

(i) Stamps of 1937.

435. **35.** 1 m. orange .. .. 1·25 1·25
436. 3 m. brown 5 5
437. 6 m. green 5 5

(ii) Stamps of 1944.

438. **47.** 1 m. orange 5 5
439. 2 m. red 5 5
440. 3 m. brown 5 5
441. 4 m. green 5 5
442. 10 m. violet 8 5
443. 13 m. red 10 8
444. 15 m. purple 10 5
445. 17 m. olive 10 8
446. 20 m. violet 12 5
447. 22 m. blue 15 12

(iii) Stamps of 1947.

448. – 30 m. olive (No. 340).. 25 12
449. **59.** 40 m. brown .. .. 5·50 5·50
450. – 50 m. blue (No. 342) .. 30 12
451. – 100 m. purple (No. 343) 65 15
452. – 200 m. violet (No. 344) 1·40 25
453. **59a.** 50 p. brown and green.. 3·00 80
454. – £E1 brown and blue (No. 346) .. .. 6·50 1·25

(iv) Air stamps of 1947.

455. **56.** 2 m. red 12 10
456. 3 m. brown 25 20
457. 5 m. red 5 5
458. 7 m. orange 8 8
459. 8 m. green 10 10
460. 10 m. violet .. .. 3·00 3·00
461. 20 m. blue 12 10
462. 30 m. purple 20 15
463. 40 m. red 25 20
464. 50 m. blue 30 25
465. 100 m. olive 50 40
466. 200 m. grey .. .. 8·00 8·00

(v) Stamps of 1952 with "Egypt-Sudan" opt. T **74.** (a) Postage.

467. **47.** 1 m. orange 75 75
468. 2 m. red 12 10
469. **35.** 3 m. brown 75 75
470. **47.** 4 m. green 75 75
471. **35.** 6 m. green .. .. 1·00 1·00
472. **47.** 10 m. violet 50 40
473. 13 m. red 25 20
474. 15 m. purple .. .. 3·00 3·00
475. 17 m. olive .. .. 3·00 3·00
476. 20 m. violet .. .. 3·00 3·00
477. 22 m. blue .. .. 11·00 11·00
478. **59.** 40 m. brown 35 20
479. – 200 m. violet (No. 389) 1·25 30

(b) Air.

480. **56.** 2 m. red 5 5
481. 3 m. brown 8 8
482. 5 m. red 5 5
483. 7 m. orange .. .. 1·60 1·60
484. 8 m. green 10 10
485. 10 m. violet 12 12
486. 20 m. blue .. .. 6·00 6·00
487. 30 m. purple 20 20
488. 40 m. red .. .. 7·50 7·50
489. 50 m. blue 25 20
490. 100 m. olive 50 35
491. 200 m. grey .. .. 1·00 85

83.

1953. Electronics Exn., Cairo.
492. **83.** 10 m. blue 15 12

84. "Young Egypt".

85. "Agriculture".

1954. Republic. 1st Anniv. Inscr. "18 JUIN 1953–1954".
493. **84.** 10 m. brown 8 8
494. – 30 m. blue 25 15
DESIGN: 30 m. Marching crowd, Egyptian flag and eagle.

1954.
495. **85.** 1 m. brown 5 5
496. 2 m. purple 5 5
497. 3 m. blue 5 5
498. 4 m. green 8 5
499. 5 m. red 20 5

86. Egyptian Flag over Suez Canal.

87.

1954. Evacuation of British Troops from Suez Canal. Inscr. "EVACUATION".
500. **86.** 10 m. purple and green 10 8
501. – 35 m. green and red .. 25 20
DESIGN: 35 m. Egyptian army bugler, machine-gunner and map.

1955. Arab Postal Union.
502. **87.** 5 m. brown 5 5
503. 10 m. green 10 10
504. 37 m. violet 30 25

88. P. P. Harris and Rotary Emblem.

مؤتمر البريد العربي
القاهرة ١٩٥٥/٣/١٥
(89.)

1955. Rotary Int. 50th Anniv. Inscr. "1905 1955".
505. **88.** 10 m. claret 15 8
506. – 35 m. blue 30 20
DESIGN: 35 m. Globe and emblem.

1955. Arab Postal Union Conf., Cairo. Optd. with T **89.**
507. **87.** 5 m. brown 5 5
508. 10 m. green 12 10
509. 37 m. violet 30 25

90. Scout Badge.

91.

1956. 2nd Arab Scout Jamboree, Aboukir (Alexandria). Inscr. "2EME JAMBOREE ARABE", etc.
510. **90.** 10 m.+10 m. green .. 15 15
511. – 20 m.+10 m. ultram... 25 25
512. – 35 m.+15 m. blue .. 35 30
DESIGNS: 20 m. Sea Scout badge. 35 m. Air Scout badge.

1956. Afro-Asian Festival, Cairo. Inscr. "FESTIVAL ASIATICO-AFRICAIN".
515. **91.** 10 m. green and brown 12 8
516. – 35 m. purple and yellow 25 20
DESIGN—VERT. 35 m. Globe, lamp, dove and ear of corn.

92. Map of Suez Canal.

93. Queen Nefertiti.

1956. Nationalisation of Suez Canal.
517. **92.** 10 m. blue and buff .. 25 20

1956. Int. Museum Week.
518. **93.** 10 m. green 25 20

94. Defence of Port Said.

1956. "Port Said, Nov. 1956".
519. **94.** 10 m. maroon 15 10

1957. Evacuation of British and French Troops from Port Said. Optd. **EVACUATION 22.12.56** in English and Arabic.
520. **94.** 10 m. maroon 15 12

95. Early Locomotive and Modern Express Train.

1957. Egyptian Railways Cent.
521. **95.** 10 m. purple and sepia .. 10 8

96. Mother and Children.

1957. Mothers' Day.
522. **96.** 10 m. red 10 8

97. Battle Scene.

1957. Victory over British at Rosetta. 150th Anniv.
523. **97.** 10 m. blue 8 8

1957. Re-opening of Suez Canal. As T **92** but with inscriptions in English instead of French and also inscr. "PORT SAID" and "REOPENING 1957".
524. 100 m. blue and green .. 40 30

98. Al-Azhar University.

100. Motor Ambulance.

99. Map of Gaza.

1957. Millenary of Al-Azhar University, Cairo. Unissued stamps of 1942 as T **98** optd. with the present Arabic year (1376).
525. **98.** 10 m. violet 8 8
526. 15 m. purple 10 10
527. 20 m. grey 12 12

1957. Re-occupation of Gaza Strip.
528. **99.** 10 m. blue 10 10

1957. Public Aid Society. 50th Anniv.
529. **100.** 10 m.+5 m. red .. 12 10

101. Shepheard's Hotel.

102. Egyptian Parliament Buildings.

1957. Re-opening of Shepheard's Hotel, Cairo.
530. **101.** 10 m. violet 10 8

1957. Opening of National Assembly.
531. **102.** 10 m. brown & yellow 10 8

103. Avaris, 1580 B.C.

1957. 1952 Revolution. 5th Anniv. Inscr. "EGYPT TOMB OF THE AGGRESSORS 1957".
532. **103.** 10 m. red 10 5
533. – 10 m. green 10 5
534. – 10 m. maroon 10 5
535. – 10 m. blue 10 5
536. – 10 m. brown 10 5
DESIGNS—HORIZ. No. 533, Saladin at Hitteen, A.D. 1187. 534, Ein Galout, A.D. 1260 (Middle East map). 536, Evacuation of Port Said, 1956. VERT. 534, Louis IX in chains at Mansourah, A.D. 1250.

104. Ahmed Arabi addressing Revolutionaries.

105. Rameses II.

1957. Arabi Revolution. 75th Anniv.
537. **104.** 10 m. violet 10 5

1957.
538. – 1 m. turquoise 5 5
541. – 5 m. sepia 5 5
539. **105.** 10 m. violet 8 5
DESIGNS: 1 m. "Agriculture" (farmer's wife). 5 m. "Industry" (factory skyline).
See also Nos. 553/9, 603/19, and 669/72.

106. Ahmed Shawky.

107. Vickers "Viscount" Airliner and Airline Badge.

108. Pyramids, Dove of Peace and Globe.

109. Racing Cyclists.

1957. Ahmed Shawky and Ibrahim Hafez (poets). 25th Death Anniv.
543. **106.** 10 m. olive 8 8
544. – 10 m. brown (Hafez) 8 8
Nos. 543/4 are printed alternately throughout the sheet.

1957. Egyptian Civil Airlines "MISRAIR", and Air Force. 25th Anniv.
545. **107.** 10 m. green 8 8
546. – 10 m. blue 8 8
DESIGN: No. 546, Ilyushin bomber, two Mig fighters and Air Force emblem.
Nos. 545/6 are printed alternately throughout the sheet.

1957. Afro-Asian People's Conference. Cairo.
547. **108.** 5 m. brown 5 5
548. 10 m. green 8 5
549. 15 m. violet 12 10

1958. 5th Egyptian Int. Cycle Race.
550. **109.** 10 m. brown 8 5

110. Mustapha Kamal (patriot).

ILLUSTRATIONS British Commonwealth and all overprints and surcharges are FULL SIZE. Foreign Countries have been reduced to ¾-LINEAR.

1958. Mustapha Kamal. 50th Death Anniv.
551. **110.** 10 m. slate 10 8

UNITED ARAB REPUBLIC

For stamps inscribed "UAR" but with value in piastres, see under Syria.

111. Congress Emblem.

112. Princess Nofret.

1958. 1st Afro-Asian Ophthalmology Congress.
552. **111.** 10 m. + 5 m. orange .. 30 30

1958. Inscr. "U A R EGYPT".
553. – 1 m. red (as No. 538) 5 5
554. – 2 m. blue 5 5
555. **112.** 3 m. brown 5 5
556. – 4 m. green 5 5
557. – 5 m. sepia (as No. 541) 5 5
558. **105.** 10 m. violet 5 5
559. – 35 m. blue 75 5
DESIGNS—VERT. 2 m. Ibn Tulun's Mosque. 4 m. Glass lamp and mosque. 35 m. Ship and crate on hoist.
See also Nos. 603/19 and 669/72.

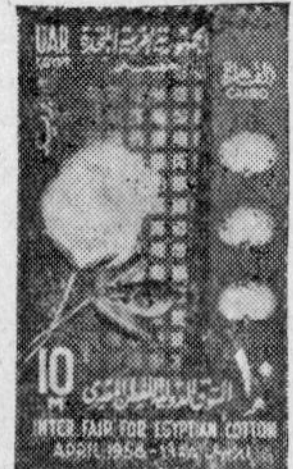

113. Union of Egypt and Syria. **114.** Cotton Plant.

1958. Birth of United Arab Republic.
560. **113.** 10 m. grn.& yell.(post). 8 5
561. 15 m. brn. & blue (air) 10 10

1958. Int. Cotton Fair, Cairo.
562. **114.** 10 m. blue-green .. 8 5

115. Qasim Amin (reformer). **116.** Dove of Peace.

1958. Qasim Amin. 50th Death Anniv.
563. **115.** 10 m. blue 10 5

1958. Republic. 5th Anniv.
564. **116.** 10 m. violet 8 5

117. 'Iron and Steel'.  **118.** Sayed Darwich.

1958. Egyptian Industries.
565. – 10 m. brown 5 5
566. – 10 m. green 5 5
567. **117.** 10 m. red 5 5
568. – 10 m. myrtle 5 5
569. – 10 m. blue 5 5
DESIGNS: Industrial views representing: No. 565, "Cement". 566, "Textiles". 568, "Petroleum". 569, "Electricity and Fertilizers".

The above stamps are issued together in sheets of 25, and arranged se-tenant in horiz. rows in the order of listing.

1958. Sayed Darwich. 35th Death Anniv.
580. **118.** 10 m. maroon .. 8 5

119. **120.** Cogwheels, Maps and Emblems of Productivity.

1958. Republic of Iraq Commem.
581. **119.** 10 m. red 8 5

1958. Afro-Asian Economic Conf., Cairo.
582. **120.** 10 m. blue 10 5

1958. Industrial and Agricultural Fair, Cairo. As No. 582 but colour changed, optd. **INDSTRIAL & AGRICULTURAL PRODUCTION FAIR** in Arabic and English.
583. **120.** 10 m. brown 10 5

121. Dr. Mahmoud Azmy (Egyptian U.N.O. representative).

1958. Declaration of Human Rights. 10th Anniv.
584. **121.** 10 m. slate-violet .. 10 5
585. 35 m. green .. 30 25

122. "Learning".  **123.** Egyptian Postal Emblem.

1958. Cairo University. 50th Anniv.
586. **122.** 10 m. grey-green .. 8 5

1959. Post Day and Postal Employees Social Fund.
587. **123.** 10 m.+5 m. red, black and turquoise .. 10 5

1959. Surch. **UAR 55** and bars and equivalent in Arabic.
588. **81.** 55 m. on 100 m. chestnut 25 15

124. **126.**

125. Nile Hilton Hotel.

1959. Afro-Asian Youth Conf., Cairo.
589. **124.** 10 m. bronze-green .. 8 5

1959. Opening of Nile Hilton Hotel.
590. **125.** 10 m. olive-brown .. 8 5

1959. United Arab Republic. 1st Anniv.
591. **126.** 10 m. red, black & grn. 8 5

127. "Telecommunications".

1959. Arab Telecommunications Union Commem.
592. **127.** 10 m. violet 8 5

128. U.A.R. and Yemeni Flags.  **129.** Oil Derrick and Pipe-lines.

131. 'Migration". **130.** "Railways" (Diesel-electric Train).

1959. Proclamation of United Arab States (U.A.R. and Yemen). 1st Anniv.
593. **128.** 10 m. red and green .. 8 5

1959. 1st Arab Petroleum Congress.
594. **129.** 10 m. blue 8 5

1959. 7th Anniv. of Revolution of Transport and Communications Commem. Frames in slate. Centre colours given.
595. **130.** 10 m. lake 5 5
596. – 10 m. green 5 5
597. – 10 m. blue 5 5
598. – 10 m. violet 5 5
599. – 10 m. plum 5 5
600. – 10 m. red 5 5
DESIGNS—No. 596, "Highways" (Bus passing bridge.) 597, "Seaways" (Ocean liner). 598, "Nile Transport" (River Barge). 599, "Telecommunications" (Telephone and radio mast). 600, "Postal Services" (Post office H.Q., Cairo).

1959. 3rd Arab Emigrants' Association Convention, Middle East.
602. **131.** 10 m. lake 5 5

1959. As Types **82**, **105** and **112**, but inscr. "U A R" only. No. 659 is optd. **UAR** in English and Arabic in red.
603. – 1 m. verm. (as No. 553) 5 5
604. – 2 m. blue (as No. 554) 5 5
605. **112.** 3 m. claret 5 5
606. – 4 m green (as No. 556) 5 5
607. – 5 m. black (as No. 557) 5 5
608. **105.** 10 m. bronze-green .. 5 5
609. – 15 m. maroon.. .. 8 5
610. – 20 m. red 10 5
611. – 30 m. purple .. 15 5
612. – 35 m. blue (as No. 559) 20 5
613. – 40 m. sepia 20 5
614. – 45 m. slate 30 15
615. – 55 m. green 50 8
616. – 60 m. violet 30 8
617. – 100 m. green & orange 50 8
618. – 200 m. brown and blue 80 15
619. **81.** 500 m. red and indigo 2·00 30
634. £E1 red and green .. 4·00 90
DESIGNS—VERT. 15 m. Omayad Mosque. 20 m. Lotus flower vase. 40 m. Statue. 55 m. Cotton and ears of corn. 60 m. Barrage and plant. 100 m. Egyptian eagle and hand holding agricultural products. HORIZ. 30 m. Stone archway. 45 m. Fort. 200 m. Temple ruins.

See also Nos. 669/72 etc., and No. 739.

132. 'Plane over Pyramids.

133. "Shield against Aggression".

134. Children and U.N. Emblem. **135.** Cairo Museum.

1959. Air.
620. **132.** 5 m. vermilion .. 5 5
621. – 15 m. purple .. 8 8
758. – 50 m. brown and blue 25 20
622. – 60 m. green 25 25
760. – 80 m. slate-pur. & blue 35 25
623. – 90 m. maroon.. .. 35 25
761. – 115 m yellow and sepia 50 35
762. – 140 m. red and violet.. 60 45
DESIGNS—Plane over: 15 m. Colossi of Thebes. 50 m. Cairo Tower and Arch. 60 m., 80 m. Al-Azhar University. 90 m. St. Catherine Monastery, Sinai. 115 m. Nefertari. 140 m. Rameses II.

See also Nos. 658 and 741/3.

1959. Army Day.
624. **133.** 10 m. red 8 5

1959. U.N. Day and UNICEF Commem.
625. **134.** 10 m.+5 m. maroon.. 10 5
626. 35 m.+10 m. blue .. 25 15

1959. Cairo Museum Cent.
627. **135.** 10 m. olive-brown .. 8 5

136. Rock Temples of Abu Simbel.

1959. U.N.E.S.C.O. Campaign for Preservation of Nubian Monuments (1st issue).
628. **136.** 10 m. red-brown .. 10 5
650. – 10 m. yellow-brown .. 8 5
DESIGN—No. 650, Rock Temples of Abu Simbel (different view).

See also Nos. 676, 728, 754/6, 825/7, 664/6 and 878/9.

137. Mounted Postman.

1960. Post Day.
629. **137.** 10 m. blue 8 5

138.

139. View of projected Aswan High Dam.

1960. Laying of Foundation Stone of Aswan High Dam.
630. **138.** 10 m. lake 8 5
631. **139.** 35 m. lake 25 12

Nos. 630/1 were issued together in sheets with the two designs arranged in alternate horiz. rows.

140. Aswan Dam Hydro-Electric Power station.  **141.**

1960. Projected Aswan Dam Hydro-Electric Power Station.
632. **140.** 10 m. black 8 5

1960. 2nd Industrial and Agricultural Fair.
633. **141.** 10 m. grey-green .. 8 5

142. **143.**

1960. United Arab Republic. 2nd Anniv.
635. **142.** 10 m. red, black & green 8 5

1960. 3rd Fine Arts Biennale. Alexandria.
636. **143.** 10 m. sepia 8 5

144. Arab League Centre, Cairo.

1960. Inaug. of Arab League Centre, Cairo.
637. **144.** 10 m. green and black 8 5

145. Refugee Children. 146. Weight-lifting.

1960. World Refugee Year.
638. **145.** 10 m. vermilion .. 5 5
639. 35 m. turquoise .. 20 15

1960. Sports Campaign and Olympic Games.
640. 5 m. grey (T **146**) 5 5
641. 5 m. brown (Basketball) .. 5 5
642. 5 m. maroon (Football) .. 5 5
643. 10 m. red (Fencing) .. 8 5
644. 10 m. green (Rowing) .. 8 5
645. 30 m. vio. (Horse jumping) 20 10
646. 35 m. blue (Swimming) .. 25 15
Nos. 640/4 are vert. and arranged together "se-tenant" in the sheet. Nos. 645/6 are horiz.

147. U.N. Emblem within 15 candles.

1960. U.N.O. 15th Anniv. Inscr. as in T **147**.
648. – 10 m. violet 8 5
649. **147.** 35 m. red 20 12
DESIGN—VERT. 10 m. Dove and U.N. Emblem.

148. Modern Post Office. 149.

1961. Post Day.
651. **148.** 10 m. red 8 5

1961. U.A.R. 3rd. Anniv.
652. **149.** 10 m. purple 8 5

150. Globe, Flags and Wheat. 151. Patrice Lumumba and Map.

1961. Int. Agricultural Exn., Cairo.
653. **150.** 10 m. red 8 5

1961. 3rd All African Peoples' Conf., Cairo.
654. **151.** 10 m. black 8 5

152. Hands "reading" Braille. 153. Tower of Cairo.

1961. World Health Organization Day.
655. **152.** 10 m. brown 8 5
656. 35 m. + 15 m. yellow & brown 25 25

1961. Tower of Cairo Inaug.
657. **153.** 10 m. turquoise .. 8 5

1961. Air. As No. 657, but with aircraft replacing inscr. in upper corners and inscr. "AIR MAIL" in English and Arabic.
658. **153.** 50 m. blue 25 20

154. Refugee Mother and Child, and Map. 155. "Transport and Communications".

1961. Palestine Day.
659. **154.** 10 m. green 8 5

1961. 9th Anniv. of Revolution and Five Year Plan. Inscr. "1961".
660. **155.** 10 m. maroon .. 5 5
661. – 10 m. red 5 5
662. – 10 m. blue 5 5
663. – 35 m. myrtle 15 8
664. – 35 m. violet 15 8
DESIGNS: No. 661, Worker turning cogwheel, and pylons ("Industry and Electricity"). 662, Apartment houses ("Housing"). 663, Cotton plant and dam ("Agriculture and Irrigation"). 664, Family moving towards lighted candle ("Public Services").

157. Mehalla El Kobra Buildings.

156. Ships and Map of Suez Canal. 158.

1961. Nationalization of Suez Canal. 5th Anniv.
666. **156.** 10 m. olive 8 5

1961. Misr Bank Organization and Talaat Harb. 20th Death Anniv.
667. **157.** 10 m. brown 8 5

1961. Navy Day.
668. **158.** 10 m. blue 8 5

1961. As Nos. 553, etc. Inscr. "UAR" only (in English). New colours.
669. 1 m. turquoise (as No. 603) 5 5
670. 4 m. olive (as No. 606) .. 5 5
671. 10 m. violet 5 5
672. 35 m. slate (as No. 612) .. 15 5
NEW DESIGN: 10 m. Eagle of Saladin.
See also No. 739.

159. "Industrial Worlds".

1961. U.N. Technical Co-operation. Programme and 16th Anniv. of U.N.O.
674. – 10 m. black and brown 5 5
675. **159.** 35 m. choc. and green 15 12
DESIGN—VERT. 10 m. Corncob, wheel and book ("Agriculture, Industry and Education").

160. Philae Temple.

1961. 15th Anniv. of U.N.E.S.C.O. and Preservation of Nubian Monuments Campaign (2nd issue).
676. **160.** 10 m. blue 10 8

161. "Fine Arts". 162. "Arts and Sciences".

1961. 4th Fine Arts Biennale, Alexandria.
677. **161.** 10 m. brown 8 5

1961. Education Day.
678. **162.** 10 m. purple 8 5

163. State Emblem, Torch and Olive Branch. 164. Sphinx and Pyramid.

1961. Victory Day.
679. **163.** 10 m. green and red .. 8 5

1961. "Son et Lumiere" Display.
680. **164.** 10 m. black 8 5

165. Postal Authority Press Building, El Nasr. 166. King Mohammed V of Morocco and Map.

1962. Post Day.
681. **165.** 10 m. brown 8 5

1962. African Charter of Casablanca. 1st Anniv.
682. **166.** 10 m. slate-blue .. 8 5

167. Guide and Badge. 168. Gaza Family and Egyptian Flag.

1962. Egyptian Girl Guides' Association. Silver Jubilee.
683. **167.** 10 m. blue 8 5

1962. Egyptian Occupation of Gaza. 5th Anniv.
684. **168.** 10 m. myrtle 8 5

169. Mother and Child. 170. Arab League Centre, Cairo, and Emblem.

1962. Mothers' Day.
694. **169.** 10 m. maroon .. 8 5

1962. Arab League Week.
695. **170.** 10 m. + 5 m. black .. 12 10

171. W.M.O. Emblem and Weather-vane.

172. Posthorn on North Africa.

174. Campaign Emblem. 173. Cadets on Parade.

1962. World Meteorological Day.
696. **171.** 60 m. blue and yellow 25 25

1962. African Postal Union Commem.
697. **172.** 10 m. brown and red .. 5 5
698. 50 m. brown and blue 20 15

1962. Military Academy. 150th Anniv.
699. **173.** 10 m. green 8 5

1962. Malaria Eradication.
700. **174.** 10 m. red and sepia .. 5 5
701. – 35 m. blue and myrtle 15 15
DESIGN: 35 m. As T **174** but with laurel and inscription around emblem.

175. Bilharz and Microscope. 176. Patrice Lumumba.

1962. Dr. Theodore Bilharz (discoverer of parasitic disease: bilharzia). Death Cent.
702. **175.** 10 m. brown 8 5

1962. Lumumba Commem.
703. **176.** 10 m. red (postage) .. 8 5
704. – 35 m. slate, red, yellow, and green (air) .. 15 15
DESIGN: 35 m. Lumumba with laurel sprays and flaming torch.

177. "The Charter". 178. "Birth of the Revolution".

1962. Proclamation of National Charter.
705. **177.** 10 m. brown and blue 8 5

1962. 1952 Revolution. 10th Anniv.
706. **178.** 10 m. brown and pink 8 5
707. A. 10 m. sepia and blue .. 8 5
708. B. 10 m. blue and sepia .. 8 5
709. C. 10 m. blue and olive .. 8 5
710. D. 10 m. red, black & grn. 8 5
711. E. 10 m. slate and brown 8 5
712. F. 10 m. purple and brown 8 5
713. G. 10 m. sepia and orange 8 5
DESIGNS: A, Scroll and book. B, Agricultural Scene. C, Globe and dove. D, Flag and eagle emblem. E, Industrial scene and cogwheel. F, Dam construction. G, Eagle, building, cogwheel and ear of corn.

179. M. Moukhtar (sculptor) and "La Vestale de Secrets".

1962. Moukhtar Museum Inaug.
716. **179.** 10 m. olive and blue .. 5 5

180. Algerian Flag.

181. Rocket.

1962. Independence of Algeria.
717. 180. 10 m. red, green & pink 8 5

1962. Launching of U.A.R. Rocket.
718. 181. 10 m. red, black & green 10 5

182. Table Tennis Bat, Ball and Net.

1962. 1st African Table Tennis Tournament, Alexandria, and 38th World Shooting Championships, Cairo.
719. 182. 5 m. red and green .. 5 5
720. – 5 m. red and green .. 5 5
721. 182. 10 m. blue and ochre .. 8 5
722. – 10 m. blue and ochre .. 8 5
723. 182. 35 m. red and blue .. 15 12
724. – 35 m. red and blue .. 15 12
DESIGN: Nos. 720, 722, 724, Rifle and target. The two designs in each value were issued together se-tenant in sheets.

183. Dag Hammarskjoeld and U.N. Emblem.

184. Coronation of Queen Nefertari (from small temple of Abu Simbel).

185. College Emblem and Aircraft.

1962. U.N.O. 17th Anniv. and Hammarskjoeld Commem.
725. 183. 5 m. indigo and violet 5 5
726. 10 m. indigo and olive 8 5
727. 35 m. indigo and blue 15 15

1962. U.N.E.S.C.O. Campaign for Preservation of Nubian Monuments (3rd issue).
728. 184. 10 m. brown and blue 8 5

1962. Silver Jubilee of U.A.R. Air Force College.
729. 185. 10 m. red and blue .. 8 5

186. Postal Authority Emblem.

1963. Post Day and 1966 Int. Stamp Exn. Insc. "1866 1966".
736. 186. 20 m. + 10 m. red & grn. 25 25
737. – 40 m. + 20 m. sepia and chestnut 40 40
738. – 40 m. + 20 m. chestnut and sepia 40 40
DESIGNS—TRIANGULAR (in se-tenant pairs): Egyptian stamps of 1866 – No. 737, 5 paras. No. 738, 10 paras.

1963. As No. 670 but inscr. "1963" in English and Arabic and new colours.
739. 4 m. red, green and sepia .. 5 5

187. Yemeni Republican Flag and Torch.

188. Maritime Station, Alexandria.

1963. Proclamation of Yemeni Arab Republic.
740. 187. 10 m. red and olive .. 5 5

1963. Air.
741. 188. 20 m. sepia 8 5
742. – 30 m. magenta .. 12 10
743. – 40 m. black 15 12
DESIGNS: 30 m. International Airport, Cairo. 40 m. Railway Station, Luxor.

189. Tennis-player.

1963. 51st Int. Lawn Tennis Championships held in U.A.R.
744. 189. 10 m. brown and black 5 5

190. Cow and Emblems.

1963. Freedom from Hunger.
745. 190. 5 m. chestnut & violet 5 5
746. – 10 m. yellow and blue 5 5
747. – 35 m. yellow, blue & blk. 15 12
DESIGNS—VERT. 10 m. Corncob and ear of wheat. HORIZ. 35 m. Corncob, ear of wheat and U.N. and F.A.O. emblems.

191. Centenary Emblem within Red Crescent.

192. "Arab Socialist Union".

1963. Red Cross Cent.
748. 191. 10 m. red, maroon & bl. 5 5
749. – 35 m. red and blue .. 15 12
DESIGN: 35 m. Emblem, Red Crescent, olive branches and Globe.

1963. 11th Anniv. of Revolution.
750. 192. 10 m. mag. & slate-blue 5 5

193. TV Buildings, Cairo, and TV Receiver.

194. Queen Nefertari.

195. Swimmer and Map.

196. Ministry Building.

1963. 2nd Int. Television Festival, Alexandria.
753. 193. 10 m. yellow and blue 5 5

1963. U.N.E.S.C.O. Campaign for preservation of Nubian Monuments (4th issue).
754. 194. 5 m. yellow and blue .. 5 5
755. – 10 m. orange and black 5 5
756. – 35 m. yellow and black 15 12
DESIGNS—(28 × 61 mm.): 10 m. Great Hall o Pillars, Abu Simbel. As T 194: 35 m. Heads of Colossi, Abu Simbel.

1963. Suez Canal Int. Long-distance Swimming Race.
757. 195. 10 m. red and blue .. 5 5

1963. 50th Anniv. of Egyptian Ministry o Agriculture.
763. 196. 10 m. blue and brown 5 5

197. Map and Tenements.

198. Globe and Scales of Justice.

199. Statuette and Palette.

1963. Afro-Asian Housing Congress.
764. 197. 10 m. blue, blk. & brn. 5 5

1963. Declaration of Human Rights. 15th Anniv.
765. 198. 5 m. yellow and green 5 5
766. – 10 m. black, drab & bl. 8 5
767. – 35 m. black, pink & red 20 15
DESIGNS: 10 m. 35 m. As T 198 but arranged differently.

1963. 5th Fine Arts Biennale, Alexandria.
768. 199. 10 m. brown and blue 5 5

199a. El Mitwali Gate, Cairo.

200. Glass and Enamel Urn.

201. King Osircaf.

1964.
769. – 1 m. blue and olive .. 5 5
770. – 2 m. bistre and purple 5 5
771. – 3 m. bl., orge. & salmon 5 5
772. – 4 m. brown, blk. & blue 5 5
773. – 5 m. brown and blue 5 5
774. – 10 m. brown and green 5 5
775. – 15 m. yellow and blue 5 5
776. – 20 m. chestnut & indigo 5 5
777. 199a. 20 m. yellow-olive .. 5 5
778. 200. 30 m. brown & yellow 8 5
779. – 35 m. brn., bl. & salmon 10 5
780. – 40 m. blue and yellow 10 5
781. – 55 m. violet 15 5
782. – 60 m. brown and blue 15 5
783. 201. 100 m. slate-blue and slate-purple .. 25 10
784. – 200 m. brown & indigo 70 20
785. – 500 m. orange & blue 1·75 40
DESIGNS—As T 199a. 55 m. Kiosk, Sultan Hassan's Mosque. As T 200—VERT. 1 m. 14th-century glass vase. 4 m. Minaret and archway. 10 m. Eagle emblem and pyramids. 35 m. Queen Nefertari. 40 m. Nile near Agouza. 60 m. Azhar Mosque. HORIZ. 2 m. Ancient Egyptian head-rest. 3 m. Alabaster (funerary) barge. 5 m. Aswan High Dam. 15 m. Window, Ahmed ibn Toulon Mosque. 20 m. (No. 776), Nile Hilton Hotel and Kasr el Nile Bridge. As T 201: 200 m. Rameses. 500 m. Tutankhamun.

For the 4 m. in different colours, and with date "1964" added to design, see No. 791.

Stamps as Nos. 777 and 781 but larger and in different colours, were issued in 1969. See Nos. 1042, 1044, 1131/4 and 1136/7.

202. Eagle and Pyramids.

203. Emblems on Map.

1964. Post Day.
786. 202. 10 m. + 5 m. grn. & yell. 30 30
787. 80 m. + 40 m. blk. & bl. 75 75
788. 115 m. + 55 m. black and chestnut .. 1·00 1·00

1964. 1st Health, Sanitation and Nutrition Commission Conference, Cairo.
789. 203. 10 m. yellow and blue 5 5

204. League Emblem and Links.

1964. Arab League Heads of State Council, Cairo.
790. 204. 10 m. black and green 5 5

205. Arch and Minaret.

206. Map and Old and New Houses.

1964. Ramadan Festival.
791. 205. 4 m. green, red & black 5

1964. Nubians' Resettlement.
792. 206. 10 m. yellow & slate-pur. 5 5

207. King Akhnaton and Family (Tutankhamun's tomb).

208. Diesel Train and Afro-Asian Map.

1964. Mothers' Day.
793. 207. 10 m. brown and blue 5 5

1964. Asian Railways Conference.
794. 208. 10 m. yellow and blue 5 5

209. Office Emblem.

210. W.H.O. Emblem.

1964. Arab Postal Union's Permanent Office. 10th Anniv.
795. 209. 10 m. blue & chestnut 5 5

1964. World Health Day.
796. 210. 10 m. indigo and red .. 5 5

211. Statue of Liberty, U.A.R. Pavilion and Pyramids.

1964. New York World's Fair.

797. **211.** 10 m. emerald, olive brown and olive .. 5 5

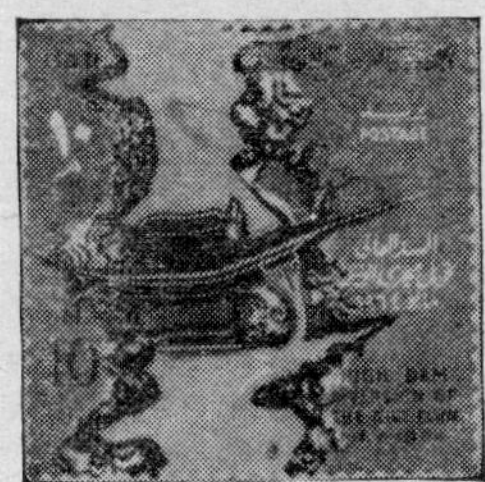

212. Site of Diversion.

1964. Nile High Dam (Diversion of Flow).

798. **212.** 10 m. black and blue.. 5 5

213. Map of Africa and Flags.

1964. O.A.U. Assembly, Cairo.

799. **213.** 10 m. black, bl. & brn. 5 5

DESIGN: No. 801, "Land Reclamation" (tractor and symbols of land cultivation).

214. "Electricity".

1964. Aswan Dam Projects.

800. **214.** 10 m. indigo and green 5 5
801. – 10 m. green and yellow 5 5

215. Jamboree Badge.

1964. 6th Pan Arab Scout Jamboree, Alexandria.

803. **215.** 10 m. green and red .. 5 5
804. – 10 m. red and green .. 5 5

DESIGN: No. 804, Air Scout's badge.

The two designs were issued together se-tenant in the sheets.

216. Algerian Flag.

1964. 2nd Arab League Heads of State Council. Flags in national colours; inscr. in green (except Sudan, in blue). Each with country name at foot.

805. 10 m. T 216 .. .. 5 5
806. 10 m. Iraq 5 5
807. 10 m. Jordan 5 5
808. 10 m. Kuwait 5 5
809. 10 m. Lebanon 5 5
810. 10 m. Libya 5 5
811. 10 m. Morocco 5 5
812. 10 m. Saudi Arabia .. 5 5
813. 10 m. Sudan 5 5
814. 10 m. Syria 5 5
815. 10 m. Tunisia 5 5
816. 10 m. U.A.R. 5 5
817. 10 m. Yemen 5 5

217. Globe, Dove and Pyramids.

1964. Non-aligned Countries Conf., Cairo.

818. **217.** 10 m. yell. & slate-blue 5 5

218. Emblem and Map. 219. Gymnastics.

1964. 1st Afro-Asian Medical Congress.

819. **218.** 10 m. violet & yellow.. 5 5

1964. Olympic Games, Tokyo.

820. – 5 m. orange and green 5 5
821. **219.** 10 m. ochre & slate-blue 5 5
822. – 35 m. ochre & slate-pur. 20 15
823. – 50 m. brown and blue 20 20

DESIGNS—As T **219** – HORIZ. 5 m. Gymnastics. VERT. 35 m. Wrestling. LARGER (61 × 28 mm.): 50 m. Charioteer hunting lions.

220. Emblems of Posts and Telecommunications and Map. 221. Rameses II.

1964. Pan-African and Malagasy Posts and Telecommunications Congress, Cairo.

824. **220.** 10 m. sepia and green 5 5

1964. U.N.E.S.C.O. Campaign for Preservation of Nubian Monuments (5th issue).

825. – 5 m. brown and blue.. 5 5
826. **221.** 10 m. yellow and sepia 5 5
827. – 35 m. indigo & brown 20 15

DESIGNS—SQUARE (40 × 40 mm.): 5 m. Horus and facade of Abu Simbel. 35 m. Wall sculpture, Abu Simbel.

222. Handicrafts and Weaving. 223. U.N. Emblem UNESCO Emblems.

1964. Ministry of Social Affairs. 25th Anniv.

829. **222.** 10 m. blue and yellow 5 5

1964. U,N.E.S.C.O. Day.

830. **223.** 10 m. yellow and blue 5 5

224. Emblem and Posthorn.

1965. Post Day and 1966 Int. Stamp Exn.

831. **224.** 10 m. + 5 m. red, maroon and green .. 8 8
832 – 10 m. + 5 m. red, black and blue 8 8
833. – 80 m. + 40 m. black, green and red .. 60 60

DESIGNS—As T **224**: No. 832, Posthorn over emblem. As T **186**: 80 m. Bird carrying letter, inscr. "STAMP CENTENARY EXHIBITION".

1965. Ramadan Festival.

834. – 4 m. brown and blue.. 5 5

DESIGN: As T **200**. 4 m. Mardani Mosque minaret.

225. Police Emblem. 226. Oil Derrick.

1965. Police Day.

835. **225.** 10 m. yellow and sepia 5 5

1965. 5th Arab Petroleum Congress and 2nd Petroleum Exn.

836. **226.** 10 m. sepia and yellow 5 5

227. Arab League Emblem and Flags. 228. W.M.O. Emblem and Weather Vane.

1965. Arab League. 20th Anniv.

837. **227.** 10 m. green and red .. 8 8
838. – 20 m. brown and blue 8 8

DESIGN—HORIZ. 20 m. Arab League emblem.

1965. Air. World Meteorological Day.

839. **228.** 80 m. mauve and blue 35 25

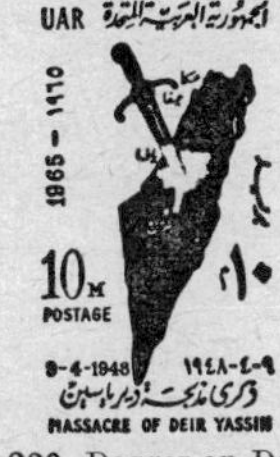

229. W.H.O. Emblem within Red Crescent. 230. Dagger on Deir Yasin, Palestine.

1965. World Health Day.

840. **229.** 10 m. red and blue 5 5

1965. Deir Yasin Massacre.

841. **230.** 10 m. red and sepia .. 5 5

231. I.T.U. Emblem and Symbols.

1965. I.T.U. Cent.

842. **231.** 5 m. slate-pur., yellow and black-purple .. 5 5
843. 10 m. rose, yellow & red 5 5
844. 35 m. blue, yellow and deep blue 15 12

232. Lamp and Burning Library.

233. Chess-table of 1350 B.C.  234. Shaikh Mohamed Abdo.

1965. Reconstitution of Algiers University Library.

845. **232.** 10 m. green, red & black 5 5

1965. Air. Re-establishment of Egyptian Civil Airlines, "MISRAIR".

846. **233.** 10 m. blue and yellow 5 5

1965. Shaikh Abdo (mufti). 60th Death Anniv.

847. **234.** 10 m. brown and blue 5 5

235. "Housing".

1965. Revolution. 13th Anniv.

848. **235.** 10 m. black and brown 5 5
849. – 10 m. brown & yellow 5 5
850. – 10 m. indigo and blue 5 5
851 – 100 m. black and green 75 75

DESIGNS—SQUARE: No. 849, "Heavy Industry" (ladle and furnace). No. 850, "Petroleum and Mining" (refinery and off-shore drilling rig). LARGER ($3\frac{1}{2} \times 3\frac{1}{2}$ in.): No. 851. President Nasser.

236. Stadium, Flag and Torch.

1965. 4th Pan-Arab Games.

857. **236.** 5 m. blue & red on blue 5 5
858. – 10 m. orange-brn & blue 8 5
859. – 35 m. brown and green 15 12

DESIGNS—As T **236**: 35 m. Horse "Saadoon". DIAMOND (56 × 56 mm): 10 m. Map and emblems of Arab countries.

237. Swimmers Zeitun and Abd el Gelil.

1965. Long-Distance Swimming Championships, Alexandria.

860. **237.** 10 m. sepia and blue.. 8 5

238. Map and Arab League Emblem. 239. Land Forces Emblem.

1965. 3rd Arab Summit Conf., Casablanca.

861. **238.** 10 m. sepia and yellow 5 5

1965. Land Forces Day.

862. **239.** 10 m. black and brown 5 5

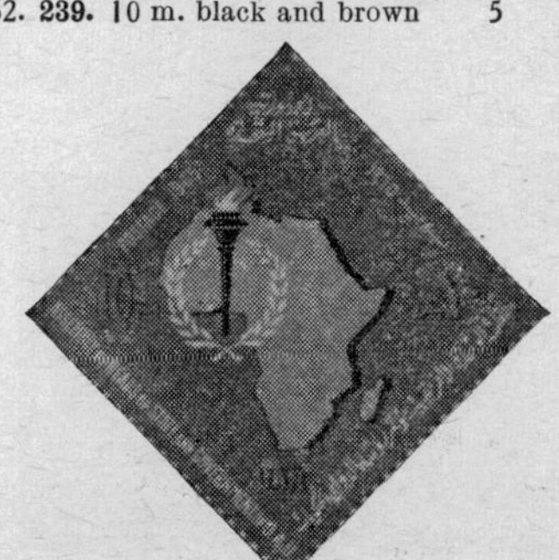

240. Flaming Torch on Africa.

1965. O.A.U. Assembly, Accra.
863. **240.** 10 m. slate-purple & red 5 5

241. Rameses II, Abu Simbel.

1965. U.N.E.S.C.O. Campaign for Preservation of Nubian Monuments (6th Issue).
864. **241.** 5 m. indigo and yellow 5 5
865. – 10 m. black and blue . . 8 8
866. – 35 m. violet and yellow 15 12
DESIGNS—As T **241**: 35 m. Colossi, Abu Simbel. VERT. (28×61½ mm.): 10 m. Hall of Pillars, Abu Simbel.

242. Al-Maqrizi, Scrolls and Books. **243.** Bust and Flag.

1965. Al-Maqrizi (historian). 600th Birth Anniv.
868. **242.** 10 m. blue and olive . . 5 5

1965. 6th Fine Arts Biennale, Alexandria.
869. **243.** 10 m. green, red, pink and black . . 5 5

244. Pigeon, Parchment and Horseman. **5.** Glass Lamp.

1966. Post Day. Multicoloured.
870. 10 m. Type **244** (postage) . . 5 5
871. 80 m.+40 m. Pharaonic messengers (air) . . 40 35
872. 115 m.+55 m. Jet aircraft and 27 m. air stamp of 1926 . . . . 50 40
Nos. 871/2 were arranged together se-tenant in the sheets.

1966. Ramadan Festival.
874. **245.** 4 m. orange and violet 5 5

246. Exhibition Emblem. **247.** Arab League Emblem.

1966. Industrial Exn., Cairo.
875. **246.** 10 m. black and blue 5 5

1966. Arab Publicity Week.
876. **247.** 10 m. violet and yellow 5 5

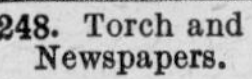

248. Torch and Newspapers. **250.** Traffic Signals.

249. Rock Temples of Abu Simbel.

1966. Egyptian National Press. Cent.
877. **248.** 10 m. slate and orange 5 5

1966. Air. U.N.E.S.C.O. Campaign for Preservation of Nubian Monuments. (7th issue.)
878. **249.** 20 m. multicoloured . . 8 5
879. 80 m. multicoloured . . 25 15

1966. Traffic Day.
880. **250.** 10 m. red, emer. & grn. 5 5

251. Torch. **252.** "Labourers".

1966. U.A.R.—Iraq Union Agreement.
881. **251.** 10 m. red, emer. & mar. 5 5

1966. I.L.O. Conf. 50th Session.
882. **252.** 5 m. black & turquoise 5 5
883. 10 m. green and purple 5 5
884. 35 m. black and orange 15 12

253. Emblem, People and City. **254.** Shipbuilding.

1966. 1st Population Census.
885. **253.** 10 m. purple and brown 5 5

1966. Revolution. 14th Anniv. Multicoloured.
886. 10 m. Type **254** 5 5
887. 10 m. Transfer of first stones at Abu Simbel 5 5
888. 10 m. Map (development of Sinai) 5 5
889. 10 m. El Mahdi Hospital, nurse and patient . . 5 5

255. Suez Canal HQ, Ships and Map.

1966. Suez Canal Nationalisation. 10th Anniv.
891. **255.** 10 m. red and blue . . 8 5

256. Jamboree Emblem and Camp.

1966. Air. 7th Pan-Arab Scout Jamboree, Libya.
892. **256.** 20 m. red and olive . . 8 5

257. Cotton.

1966. Peasants' Day.
893. **257.** 5 m. violet, yell. & blue 5 5
894. – 10 m. brn. & grn. (Rice) 5 5
895. – 35 m. orge. & bl. (Onions) 15 12

258. W.H.O. Building.

1966. U.N. Day.
896. **258.** 5 m. violet and olive . . 5 5
897. – 10 m. violet & orange 5 5
898. – 35 m. violet and blue . . 15 12
DESIGNS: 10 m. U.N.R.W.A. (Refugees) emblem. 35 m. U.N.I.C.E.F. emblem.

259. Globe and Festival Emblem.

1966. 5th Int. Television Festival.
899. **259.** 10 m. violet and yellow 5 5

260. St. Catherine's Monastery.

1966. Air. St. Catherine's Monastery. 1,400th Anniv.
900. **260.** 80 m. multicoloured . . 25 15

261. Eagle and Torch.

1966. Victory Day.
901. **261.** 10 m. red and green . . 5 5

262. Anubis (God).

1967. Post Day. Designs showing items from Tutankhamen's Tomb. Multicoloured.
902. 10 m. Type **262** 10 5
903. 35 m. Alabaster head of Tutankhamen 15 10
904. 80 m.+20 m. Jewelled sarcophagus 45 45
905. 115 m.+40 m. Statue of Tutankhamen 70 70
The 80 m. and 115 m. are 28½×62 mm.

263. Carnations. **264.** Tree-planting.

1967. Ramadan Festival.
906. **263.** 4 m. violet and olive . . 5 5

1967. Tree Festival.
907. **264.** 10 m. lilac and green 5 5

265. Gamal el-Dine el-Afghani and Arab League Emblem. **266.** Workers, Factories and Census Symbol.

1967. Arab Publicity Week.
908. **265.** 10 m. brown and green 5 5

1967. 1st Industrial Census.
909. **266.** 10 m. green & orange 5 5

267. "Comet" Airliner at Cairo Airport.

1967. Air.
910. **267.** 20 m. blue and brown 8 5

268. "Workers" (rock-carvings).

1967. Labour Day.
911. **268.** 10 m. orange and olive 5 5

269. Rameses and Queen.

1967. Int. Tourist Year. Multicoloured.
912. 10 m. Type **269** (postage) . . 10 5
913. 35 m. Duck-shooting . . 15 12
914. 20 m. Hotel, El Alamein (air) 10 5
915. 80 m. Virgin's Tree . . 40 15
916. 115 m. Hotel and fishes, Red Sea 75 35
The 20, 80 and 115 m. are 40 × 40 mm.

270. Pres. Nasser and Map.

1967. Arab Solidarity for Palestine Defence.
917. **270.** 10 m. ol., yell. & orge. 25 15

271. "Petroleum" (oil rigs).

1967. Air. Revolution. 15th Anniv.
930. **271.** 50 m. blk., orge. & blue 15 12

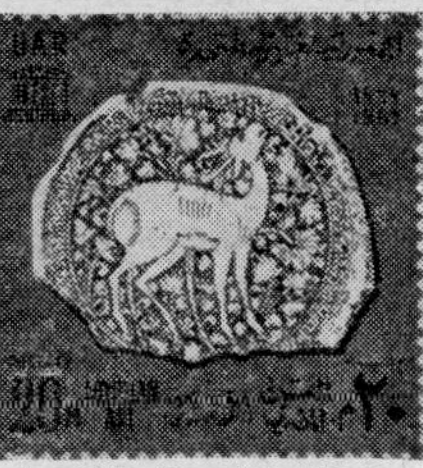

272. Salama Higazi (lyric stage impresario). **273.** Porcelain Dish.

1967. Higazi (lyric stage impresario). 50th Death Anniv.
932. **272.** 20 m. brown and blue .. 8 5

1967. U.N. Day. Egyptian Art.
933. 20 m. blue & red (postage) 8 5
934. 55 m. multicoloured .. 20 12
935. 80 m. multicoloured (air).. 25 15
DESIGNS: 20 m. T **273**. 55 m. "Christ in Glory" (painting). 80 m. Painting on back of Tutankhamun's throne.

274. Savings Bank "Coffer".

1967. World Savings Day.
936. **274.** 20 m. blue and pink 8 5

275. Ca d'Oro Palace (Venice) and Santa Maria Cathedral (Florence).

1967. "Save the Monuments of Florence and Venice".
937. **275.** 80 m.+20 m. brown, yellow and green .. 35 35
938. – 115 m.+30 m. blue, yellow and olive .. 50 50
DESIGN: 115 m. Palace of the Doges and Campanile (Venice) and Vecchio Palace (Florence).

276. Rose. **277.** Isis.

1967. Ramadan Festival.
939. **276.** 5 m. purple and green 5 5

1968. Post Day. Pharaonic Dress.
940. **277.** 20 m. sepia, green & yell. 8 5
941. – 55 m. brn., yell. & grn. 15 12
942. – 80 m. cerise, bl. & blk. 25 20
DESIGNS: 55 m. Nefertari. 80 m. Isis (different).
See also Nos. 970/3.

278. High Dam and Power Station.

1968. Electrification of High Dam.
943. **278.** 20 m. multicoloured .. 5 5

279. Alabaster Vessel (Tutankhamen). **280.** Head of Woman.

1968. Int. Museums Festival. Multicoloured.
944. 20 m. Type **279** 8 5
945. 80 m. Capital of Coptic limestone pillar (39×39 mm.) 25 15

1968. 7th Fine Arts Biennale, Alexandria.
946. **280.** 20 m. black and blue.. 5 5

281. "The Glorious Koran". (Illustration reduced. Actual size 75×36 mm.).

1968. Air. The Holy Koran. 1400th Anniv.
947. **281.** 30 m. violet, blue & yell. 12 8
948. 80 m. violet, blue & yell. 35 20

282. Tending Cattle.

1968. Arab Veterinary Congress.
949. **282.** 20 m. brn., grn. & yell. 5 5

283. St. Mark and St. Mark's Cathedral.

1968. Air. Martyrdom of St. Mark 1900th Anniv.
950. **283.** 80 m. sep., cerise & emer. 25 15

284. Human Rights Emblem. **285.** Open Book and Symbols.

1968. Human Rights Year.
951. **284.** 20 m. red, emer. & olive 8 5
952. 60 m. red, emerald & bl. 20 15

1968. Revolution. 16th Anniv.
953. **485.** 20 m. green and red .. 8 5

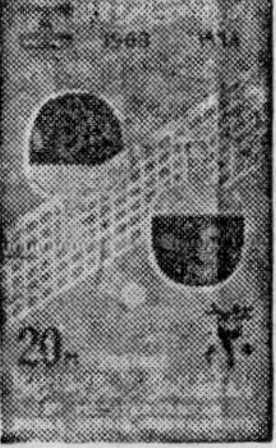

286. W.H.O. Emblem and Imhotep. **287.** Table-tennis Bats and Net.

1968. W.H.O. 20th Anniv.
955. **286.** 20 m. sepia, yell. & bl. 8 5
956. – 20 m. turquoise, sepia and yellow 8 5
DESIGN: No. 956, W.H.O. emblem and Avicenna.

1968. 1st Mediterranean Table-tennis Tournament.
957. **287.** 20 m. brown & emerald 8 5

288. Industrial Skyline.

1968. Int. Industrial Fair, Cairo.
958. **288.** 20 m. red, indigo and blue 8 5

289. Philae Temple. **290.** Scout Badge.

1968. United Nations Day.
959. – 20 m. salmon, vio. & bl. 8 5
960. – 30 m. ultramarine, orange and yellow .. 12 10
961 **289.** 55 m. purple, yell. & bl. 25 12
DESIGNS (62×29 mm.): 20 m. Philae Temples (aerial view). (As T **289**): 30 m. Refugee women and children.

1968. Egyptian Scout Movement. 50th Anniv.
962. **290.** 10 m. ultram. & orge. 5 5

291. Ancient Games.

1968. Olympic Games, Mexico.
963. **291** 20 m. violet, olive & orge 5 5
964. – 30 m. violet, bl. & buff 12 8
DESIGN: 30 m. Ancient Games (different).

292. Boeing Jetliner and Route Map. **293.** Ali Moubarek (educator).

1968. Air. 1st United Arab Air'ines Boeing Flight, Cairo—London.
965. **292.** 55 m. red, blue & orge. 15 12

1968. Ali Moubarek. 75th Death Anniv.
966. **293.** 20 m. multicoloured 8 5

294. Boy and Girl. **295.** Lotus.

1968. World Children's Day.
967. 20 m.+10 m. red, blue and chestnut 10 10
968. 20 m.+10 m. ultram., brown & green .. 10 10
DESIGNS: No. 967, T **294**. 968, Group of children.

1968. Ramadan Festival.
969. **295.** 5 m. yellow, bl. & grn 5 5

1968. Post Day. Pharaonic Dress. As T **277**. Multicoloured.
970. 5 m. Son of Rameses III 5 5
971. 20 m. Rameses III .. 8 5
972. 20 m. Maiden carrying offering 8 8
973. 55 m. Queen 15 15

296. H. Nassef (poet and writer). **298.** Teacher at Blackboard.

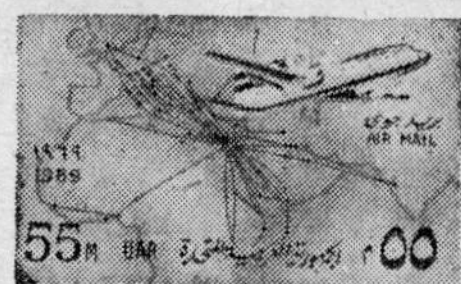

297. Ilyushin "Il-18" and Route Map.

1969. Hefni Nassef and Mohamed Farid. 50th Death Anniv.
974. **296.** 20 m. brown and violet 8 5
975. – 20 m. brn. & emerald 8 5
DESIGN: No. 975, M. Farid (politician).

1969. Air. Inaug. of Ilyushin "Il-18" Aircraft by United Arab Airlines.
976. **297.** 55 m. mar., yell. & blue 15 12

1969. Arab Teachers' Day.
977. **298.** 20 m. black, orange, violet and grey .. 8 5

299. Flags of Arab Nations. **300.** I.L.O. Emblem and Factory Stacks.

1969. Arab Publicity Week.
978. **299.** 20 m. + 10 m. mult.. 10 10

1969. Int. Labour Organization. 50th Anniv.
979. **300.** 20 m. multicoloured .. 8 5

301. Zambian Flag.

1969. African Tourist Year. Flags of African Nations.
980. – 10 m. red and green 8 8
981. – 10 m. blk., blue & grn. 8 8
982. – 10 m. red and green.. 8 8
983. – 10 m. red, yell. & grn. 8 8
984. – 10 m. multicoloured.. 8 8
985. – 10 m. yell., red & blue 8 8
986. – 10 m. brn., red & grn. 8 8
987. – 10 m. red, yellow & bl. 8 8
988. – 10 m. brn., red & grn. 8 8
989. – 10 m. grn., red & blk. 8 8
990. – 10 m. multicoloured.. 8 8
991. – 10 m. multicoloured 8 8
992. – 10 m. yell., grn. & blue 8 8
993. – 10 m. bl., red & green 8 8
994. – 10 m. multicoloured 8 8
995. – 10 m. brn., red & grn. 8 8
996. – 10 m. orange & green 8 8
997. – 10 m. blk., red & green 8 8
998. – 10 m. blue, red & grn. 8 8
999. – 10 m. red and blue .. 8 8
1000. – 10 m. blk., red & green 8 8
1001. – 10 m. red and green .. 8 8
1002. – 10 m. red, blk. & grn. 8 8
1003. – 10 m. brn., red & grn. 8 8
1004. – 10 m. yellow & green 8 8
1005. – 10 m. multicoloured.. 8 8
1006. – 10 m. green and red 8 8
1007. – 10 m. orange & green 8 8
1008. – 10 m. green 8 8
1009. – 10 m. multicoloured 8 8
1010. – 10 m. grn., brn. & red 8 8

1011. – 10 m. blue and green 8 8
1012. – 10 m. blue and green 8 8
1013. – 10 m. yell., grn. & blue 8 8
1014. – 10 m. multicoloured 8 8
1015. – 10 m. multicoloured 8 8
1016. – 10 m. yell., grn. & red 8 8
1017. – 10 m. red and green .. 8 8
1018. – 10 m. blk., yell. & red 8 8
1019. – 10 m. blk., red & grn. 8 8
1020. **301.** 10 m. multicoloured 8 8

FLAGS: No. 980, Algeria. No. 981, Botswana. No. 982, Burundi. No. 983, Cameroun. No. 984, Central African Republic. No. 985, Chad. No. 986, Congo-Brazzaville. No. 987, Congo-Kinshasa. No. 988, Dahomey. No. 989, Egypt-U.A.R. No. 990, Equatorial Guinea. No. 991, Ethiopia. No. 992, Gabon. No. 993, Gambia. No. 994, Ghana. No. 995, Guinea. No. 996, Ivory Coast. No. 997, Kenya. No. 998, Lesotho. No. 999, Liberia. No. 1000, Libya. No. 1001, Malagasy Republic. No. 1002, Malawi. No. 1003, Mali. No. 1004, Mauritania. No. 1005, Mauritius. No. 1006, Morocco. No. 1007, Niger. No. 1008, Nigeria. No. 1009, Rwanda. No. 1010, Senegal. No. 1011, Sierra Leone. No. 1012, Somalia. No. 1013, Sudan. No. 1014, Swaziland. No. 1015, Tanzania. No. 1016, Togo. No. 1017, Tunisia. No. 1018, Uganda. No. 1019, Upper Volta.

302. El Fetouh Gate. **303.** Development Bank Emblem.

1969. Cairo Millenary.

1021. **302.** 10 m. brn., yell. & blue 5 5
1022. – 10 m. multicoloured .. 5 5
1023. – 10 m. pink and blue .. 5 5
1024. – 20 m. multicoloured .. 8 5
1025. – 20 m. pur., yell. & blue 8 5
1026. – 20 m. blue, yell. & brn. 8 5

DESIGNS—As T **302**. No. 1022, Al-Azhar University. No. 1023, Citadel. (57½ × 24½ mm.). No. 1024, Two sculptures from Pharaonic period. No. 1025, Carved decorations, Coptic era. No. 1026, Glassware, Fatimid dynasty.

1969. African Development Bank. 5th Anniv.

1028. **303.** 20 m. grn., vio. & yell. 8 5

304. Mahatma Gandhi. **305.** Egyptian ship (I.M.C.O.).

1969. Air. Mahatma Gandi. Birth Cent.

1029. **304.** 80 m. brn., yell. & blue 35 20

1969. United Nations Day.

1030. – 5 m. yell., blue & brn. 5 5
1031. **305.** 20 m. ultram. & yellow 8 5
1032. – 30 m + 10 m. mult. .. 10 10
1033. – 55 m. multicoloured 15 12

DESIGNS-VERT. 5 m. "King and Queen", Abu Simbel (U.N.E.S.C.O.). SQUARE: 30 m. + 10 m. Arab refugees (U.N.R.W.A.). 55 m. Partly submerged temple, Philae (U.N.E.S.C.O.).

306. Demonstrators.

1969. Anniversaries.

1034. **306.** 20 m. purple, red & grn. 8 5
1035. – 20 m. brn., yell. & blue 8 5
1036. – 20 m. multicoloured .. 8 5

DESIGNS AND EVENTS: No. 1034, (1919 Revolution. 50th anniv.). LARGER. (58 × 25 mm.). No. 1035, Labourers, ships and map (Suez Canal Cent.). No. 1036, Performance of "Aida" (Cairo Opera-house Cent.).

307. "Ancient Egyptian Accountants".

1969. Int. Scientific Accounts Congress, Cairo.

1037. **307.** 20 m. multicoloured 8 5

308. Poinsettia.

1969. Ramadan Festival.

1038. **308.** 5 m. multicoloured 5 5

309. "Step" Pyramid, Sakkara. **310.** Pres. Nasser.

1969.

1039. **309.** 1 m. multicoloured .. 5 5
1040. – 5 m. multicoloured .. 5 5
1041. – 10 m. multicoloured 5 5
1042. **199a.** 20 m. brown 8 5
1043. – 50 m. multicoloured 15 10
1044. – 55 m. green .. 15 10
1045. **310.** 200 m. blue & purple 60 35
1046. 500 m. blk. & blue .. 1·75 1·00
1047. – £E1 green & orange .. 3·25 2·25

DESIGNS—HORIZ. As T **319**. 5 m. Al-Azhar Mosque, Cairo. 10 m. Temple, Luxor. 50 m. Quaitbay Citadel, Alexandria. VERT. (22 × 27½ mm.). 20 m. Type **199a**. 55 m. As No. 781. SQUARE. As T **336**. £E1 Khafre.

See also Nos. 1131/41 and 1198/9.

311. Imam Mohamed El Boukhary. **312.** Azzahir Beybars Mosque.

1969. Air. Imam El Boukhary (philospher and writer). 1,100th Death Anniv.

1048. **311.** 30 m. brown and olive 10 8

1969. Air. Azzahir Beybars Mosque. 700th Anniv.

1049. **312.** 30 m. purple 10 8

313. "Three Veiled Women" (M. Said).

1970. Post Day.

1050. **313.** 100 m. multicoloured 35 25

314. Parliament Building and Emblems.

1970. Int. Conf. on Middle East Crisis, Cairo.

1051. **314.** 20 m. multicoloured 8 5

315. Human Rights Emblem and "Three Races".

1970. Int. Day for the Elimination of Racial Discrimination.

1052. **315.** 20 m. + 10 m. yellow, brown and green .. 10 8

316. Arab League Flag, Arms and Map.

1970. Arab League. 25th Anniv.

1053. **316.** 20 m. + 10 m. green, brown and blue .. 10 10
1054. 30 m. grn., plum & orge. 10 5

317. Mina House Hotel, Giza, and Sheraton Hotel, Cairo.

1970. Mina House Hotel Cent. and Opening of Sheraton Hotel.

1055. **317.** 20 m. multicoloured 8 5

318. Pharmacists.

1970. Egyptian Pharmaceutical Industry. 30th Anniv.

1056. **318.** 20 m. multicoloured 8 5

319. Mermaid. **320.** Lenin.

1970. 8th Fine Arts Biennale, Alexandria.

1057. **319.** 20 m. blk., bl. & orge. 8 5

1970. Air. Lenin. Birth Cent.

1058. **320.** 80 m. brown and green 25 20

321. Emblem and Bombed Factory.

1970. Air. Attack on Abu Zaabal Factory.

1059. **321.** 80 m. purple, blue and yellow 25 20

322. Talaat Harb Founder) and Bank. **323.** I.T.U. Emblem.

1970. Misr Bank. 50th Anniv.

1060. **322.** 20 m. multicoloured 8 5

1970. World Telecommunications Day.

1061. **323.** 20 m. multicoloured 8 5

324. New H.Q.'s Building. **325.** Basketball Player, Cup and Map.

1970. New U.P.U. Headquarters Building, Berne.

1062. **324.** 20 m. mult. (postage) 8 5
1063. 80 m. mult. (air) .. 25 15

1970. 5th Africa Men's Basketball Championships.

1064. **325.** 20 m. multicoloured 8 5

326. Emblems of U.P.U., U.N. and African Postal Union.

1970. U.P.A.F. (African Postal Union) Seminar.

1065. **326.** 20 m. grn. violet & orge. 8 5

327. Footballer and Cup. **328.** Clenched Fists and Dove.

1970. Africa Cup Football Championships.

1066. **327.** 20 m. multicoloured 8 5

1970. Revolution. 18th Anniv.

1067. **328.** 20 m. orange, black and emerald .. 8 5

329. Mosque in Flames.

1970. Burning of Al Aqsa Mosque, Jerusalem. 1st Anniv.

1069. **329.** 20 m. multicoloured 8 5
1070. 60 m. multicoloured 15 12

330. Globe, Wheat and Cogwheel.

1970. World Standards Day.

1071. **330.** 20 m. brn., blue & grn. 8 5

331. "Peace, Justice and Progress".

1970. United Nations Day.
1072. **331.** 5 m. blk., pur. & blue 5 5
1073. – 10 m. blue, brn. & stone 5 5
1074. – 20 m. multicoloured 8 5
1075. – 20 m.+10 m. mult... 10 10
1076. – 55 m. multicoloured.. 15 12
1077. – 55 m. multicoloured.. 15 12
DESIGNS AND EVENTS: 5 m. (U.N.25th Anniv.). SQUARE. (37×37 mm.). 10 m. U.N. emblem. 55 m. (2) Philae Temple (composite design) (U.N.E.S.C.O. Campaign to preserve Nubian Monuments). (36×36 mm.) 20 m. Frightened child and bombed school (Int. Education Year). HORIZ. (43×26 mm.). 20 m×10 m. Palestinian guerillas and refugees ("Int. support for Palestinians").

332. President Nasser. **333.** Medical Association Building.

1970. Pres. Gamal Nasser Memorial Issue.
1078. **332.** 5 m. black and blue (postage) 5 5
1079. – 20 m. black and grn. 8 5
1080. – 30 m. blk. & yell. (air) 12 8
1081. – 80 m. black & brown 30 20
DESIGN-HORIZ. (46×27 mm.) 30 m., 80 m. Pres. Nasser and tomb.

1970. Egyptian Anniversaries.
1082. **333.** 20 m. brn., grn. & yell. 8 5
1083. – 20 m. multicoloured.. 8 5
1084. – 20 m. brown and blue 8 5
1085. – 20 m. multicoloured.. 8 5
1086. – 20 m. multicoloured.. 8 5
DESIGNS AND EVENTS: No. 1082 (Egyptian Medical Assn. 50th anniv.). No. 1083, Old and new library buildings (Nat. Library cent.). No. 1084, "The most significant victory . . ." Pres. Nasser text ("Egyptian Credo"). No. 1085, Old and new printing works (Govt. Printing Office. 150th anniv.). No. 1086, Old and new headquarters (Egyptian Engineering Society. 50th anniv.).

334. Map of Egypt, Libya and Sudan.

1970. Signing of Tripoli Charter.
1087. **334.** 20 m. green, blk. & red 8 5

335. Minaret, Qalawun Mosque. **337.** Fair Emblem.

1970. Post Day. Mosque Minarets. Multicoloured.
1088. 5 m. Type **335** 5 5
1089. 10 m. As-Salem Mosque 5 5
1090. 20 m. Isna Mosque .. 8 5
1091. 55 m. Al-Hakim Mosque 20 12
See also Nos. 1142/5 and 1189/92.

1971. Cairo International Fair.
1093. **337.** 20 m. yell., blk. & pur. 8 5

338. Map of Arab States and A.P.U. Emblem.

1971. 9th Arab Postal Union Congress, Cairo.
1094. **338.** 20 m. multicoloured (postage) 8 5
1095. 30 m. multicoloured (air) 12 8

339. Globe and Cotton Symbols.

1971. Egyptian Cotton Production.
1096. **339.** 20 m. brn., bl. & grn. 8 5

340. Army Emblem. **341.** Hesy Ra (ancient physician) and Papyrus.

1971. Forces' Mail.
1097. **340.** 10 m. violet 5 5
The above stamp was issued for civilian use on letters addressed to servicemen and is not valid for any other purpose.

1971. World Health Day.
1098. **341.** 20 m. purple and yell. 8 5

342. Pres. Nasser. **343.** Map and I.T.U. Emblem.

1971.
1099. **342.** 20 m. blue & maroon 8 5
1100. 55 m. plum and blue 20 12

1971. Pan-African Telecommunications Year.
1101. **343.** 20 m. multicoloured 8 5

334. El Rifaei and Sultan Hassan Mosques.

1971. Air. Multicoloured.
1102. 30 m. Type **344** 10 8
1103. 85 m. Rameses Square, Cairo 25 20
1104. 110 m. Sphinx and pyramids 35 25

345. "Industrial Progress". **346.** A.P.U. Emblem.

1971. 23rd July Revolution. 19th Anniv. Multicoloured.
1105. 20 m. Type **245** 8 5
1106. 20 m. Ear of Wheat ("Land Reclamation") 8 5

1971. Sofar Conference and founding of Arab Postal Union. 25th Anniv.
1108. **346.** 20 m. green, yellow & blackish green (postage) 8 5
1109. **346.** 30 m. mult. (air) .. 12 8

347. Federal Links. **348.** Pres. Gamal Nasser.

1971. Confederation of Arab Republics. Inaug.
1110. **347.** 20 m. brn., blk. and purple (postage) .. 8 5
1111. **347.** 30 m. green, blk. and purple (air) .. 12 8

1971. Pres. Nasser's First Death Anniv.
1112. **348.** 5 m. blue & maroon 5 5
1113. 20 m. purple & blue 8 5
1114. 30 m. blue and brown 10 8
1115. 55 m. brown & green 20 12

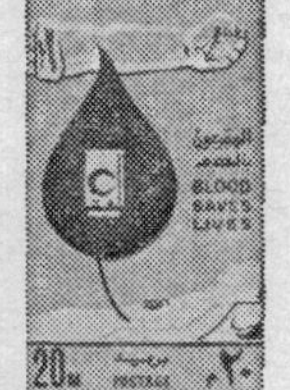
349. "Princess and Child" (statue). **350.** "Blood Saves Lives".

1971. United Nations Day.
1116. **349.** 5 m. blk., brn. & red (postage) 5 5
1117. – 20 m. multicoloured.. 8 5
1118. – 55 m. multicoloured.. 20 12
1119. – 30 m. mult. (air) .. 12 8
DESIGNS—As T **349**. VERT. 5 m. (U.N.I.C.E.F.). HORIZ. 20 m. Emblem and four heads (Racial Equality Year). SQUARE—(36×36 mm.). 30 m. Refugee and Al-Aqsa Mosque (U.N.R.W.A.). VERT. (24×58 mm.). 55 m. Partly submerged pillar, Philae (U.N.E.S.C.O. 25th Anniv.).

1971. Blood Donors.
1120. **350.** 20 m. red and green 8 5

351. New Post Office. **352.** Sunflower.

1971. Opening of New Head Post Office, Alexandria.
1121. **351.** 20 m. brown and blue 8 5

1971. Ramadan Festival.
1122. **352.** 5 m. multicoloured.. 5 5

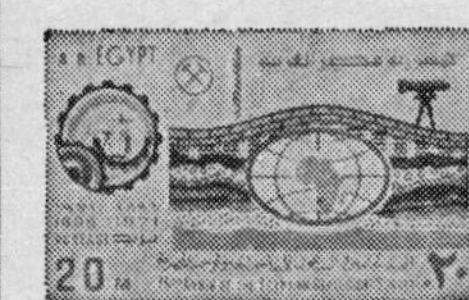
353. Abdallah El Nadim. **354.** Globe and Earth's Strata.

1971. Abdallah El Nadim (poet and journalist). 75th Death Anniv.
1123. **353.** 20 m. brown & green 5 5

1971. Egyptian Geological Survey. 75th Anniv.
1124. **354.** 20 m. multicoloured 5 5

355. A.P.U. Emblem and Dove with Letter.

1971. African Postal Union. 10th Anniv.
1125. **355.** 5 m. mult. (postage).. 5 5
1126. 20 m. grn., orge. & blk. 8 5
1127. – 55 m. blk., bl. & red 20 12
1128. – 30 m. mult. (air) .. 12 8
DESIGN: 30 m., 55 m. A.P.U. emblem and airmail envelope.

356. "Savings Bank".

1971. Postal Savings Bank. 70th Anniv.
1129. **356.** 20 m. multicoloured.. 8 5

357. "Victory Parade" (Scene from "Aida"). **358.** Cairo Citadel.

1971. Air. First Performance of Verdi's Opera, "Aida", in Cairo. Cent.
1130. **357.** 110 m. yell., grn. & brn. 40 25

1972. Inscr. "A.R. EGYPT".
1131. **309.** 1 m. grn., brn. & blue 5 5
1131a. 1 m. brown 5 5
1132. – 5 m. multicoloured (As No. 1040) .. 5 5
1132a. – 5 m. green 5 5
1133. – 10 m. multicoloured (As No. 1041) .. 5 5
1133a. – 10 m. brown .. 5 5
1134. **199a.** 20 m. green (22×27½ mm.) 8 5
1135. 20 m. purple (22×27½ mm.).. .. 5 5
1136. – 50 m. multicoloured (As No. 1043) .. 20 12
1136a. – 50 m. blue 12 8
1137. – 55 m. purple (As No. 1044) 20 15
1137a. – 55 m. green.. .. 15 10
1138. **358.** 100 m. blk., red & bl. 25 15
1139. – 200 m. brn. & green 55 40
1140. – 500 m. blk. & blue (As No. 1046) .. 1·40 85
1141. £E1 green & orange (As No. 1047) .. 2·75 2·10
DESIGNS—As T **358.** 5 m. Rameses II. 10 m. Head of Seti I. 50 m. Goddess Hathar. 55 m. Sphinx and pyramid. As T **310.** 200 m. Head of Userkaf.

1972. Post Day. Mosque Minarets. As T **335.** Multicoloured.
1142. 5 m. Western minaret, An-Nasir Mosque 5 5
1143. 20 m. Eastern minaret, An-Nasir Mosque .. 10 5
1144. 30 m. Al-Gawli Mosque .. 12 8
1145. 55 m. Ibn Tulun Mosque 20 12
The note under No. 1091 also applies here.

359. Police Emblem and Activities.

1972. Police Day.
1146. **359.** 20 m. yell., bl. & brn. 8 5

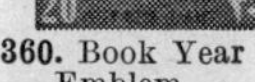

360. Book Year Emblem. **361.** Globe, Glider, Rocket and Emblem.

1972. Int. Book Year.
1147. **360.** 20 m. vio., yell. & grn. 8 5

1972. Air. Int. Aerospace Education Conference, Cairo.
1148. **361.** 30 m. brn., bl. & yell. 12 8

362. Monastery Aflame. **363.** "Palette" (Seif Wanli).

1972. Air. Burning of St. Catherine's Monastery, Sinai.
1149. 362. 110 m. multicoloured 40 25

1972. 9th Fine Arts Biennale, Alexandria.
1150. 363. 20 m. red, yell. & blk. 8 5

364. Fair Emblem. 365. Brig.-Gen. Abd El M. Riad.

1972. Int. Fair, Cairo.
1151. 364. 20 m. multicoloured 8 5

1972. Brig. Abdel Moniem Riad. 2nd Death Anniv.
1152. 365. 20 m. multicoloured. 8 5

366. Birds in Tree.

1972. Mother's Day.
1153. 366. 20 m. multicoloured.. 8 5

367. Head of Tutankhamun.

1972. Discovery of Tutankhamun's Tomb. 50th Anniv.
1154. 367. 20 m. mult. (postage) 8 5
1155. – 55 m. multicoloured.. 15 12
1156. – 110 m. grn., brn. & bl. (air) 35 20
1157 – 110 m. grn. brn. & bl. 35 20
DESIGNS—As T 367. 55 m. Decorated chair-back. (68×62 mm.). 110 m. (No. 1156), Tutankhamun. 110 m. (No. 1157), Ankhesenamun.

368. Nefertiti. 369. Map of Africa.

1972. Society of Friends of Art. 50th Anniv.
1159. 368. 20 m. blk., gold & red 5 5

1972. Africa Day.
1160. 369. 20 m. brn., bl. & pur. 5 5

370. Eagle Emblem.

1972. Revolution. 20th Anniv.
1167. 370. 20 m. gold, blk. & grn. 5 5
1168. 20 m. red, blk. & blue 5 5

371. Temple Abu Simbel.

1972. Air. Multicoloured.
1170. 30 m. Al-Azhar Mosque and St. George's Church, Cairo .. 10 5
1171. 85 m. Type 371 .. .. 25 15
1172. 110 m. Pyramids, Giza 30 20

372. Boxing.

1972. Olympic Games, Munich.
1173. 372. 5 m. mult. (postage) 5 5
1174. – 10 m. yell., blk. & red 5 5
1175. – 20 m. red, grn. & orge. 5 5
1176. – 30 m. yellow, green and red (air) .. 10 5
1177. – 30 m. red, mauve & bl. 10 5
1178. – 50 m. bl., blk. & grn. 12 10
1179. – 55 m. green, red & bl. 15 10
DESIGNS—HORIZ. 10 m. Wrestling. 20 m. Basketball. VERT. 30 m. (No. 1176), Weightlifting. 30 m. (No. 1177), Handball. 50 m. Swimming. 55 m. Gymnastics.

373. Confederation Flag.

1972. Confederation of Arab Republics. 1st Anniv.
1180. 373. 20 m. multicoloured.. 5 5

374. J.-F. Champollion and Rosetta Stone.

1972. Air. Champollion's Translation of Hieroglyphics. 150th Anniv.
1181. 374. 110 m. grn., blk. & brn. 35 20

375. Heart Motif (World Health Day).

1972. United Nations Day. Multicoloured.
1182. 10 m. Health Emblems (14th Regional T.B. Conf.) 5 5
1183. 20 m. Type 375 (World Health Day) .. 5 5
1184. 30 m. Palestinian refugees (U.N.R.W.A.).. 10 5
1185. 55 m. Flooded temple, Philae (U.N.E.S.C.O. Preservation Campaign of Nubian monuments) 15 12

376. Hibiscus. 377. Work Day Emblem.

1972. Ramadan Festival.
1186. 376. 10 m. pur., grn. & brn. 5 5

1972. Social Work Day.
1187. 377. 20 m. multicoloured.. 5 5

378. "Rowing Fours" on Nile.

1972. 3rd Nile Rowing Festival, Luxor.
1188. 378. 20 m. brown and blue 5 5

1973. Post Day. Mosque Minarets. As T 335. Multicoloured.
1189. 10 m. Al-Maridani Mosque 5 5
1190. 20 m. Bashtak Mosque .. 5 5
1191. 30 m. Qusun Mosque .. 10 5
1192. 55 m. Al-Gashankir Mosque 15 5

379. Ears of Corn and Globe within Cogwheel. 380. Symbolic Family.

1973. Int. Fair, Cairo.
1193. 379. 20 m. multicoloured.. 5 5

1973. Family Planning Week.
1194. 380. 20 m. blk., orge. & grn. 5 5

381. Telecommunications Map.

1973. Air. Fifth Int. Telecommunications Day.
1195. 381. 30 m. blue, blk. & blue 5 5

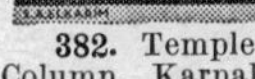

382. Temple Column, Karnak. 383. Bloody Hand and Airliner.

1973. Air. "Son et Lumiere", Karnak Temples, Luxor.
1196. 382. 110 m. blk., pink & bl. 30 20

1973. Air. Attack on Libyan Airliner over Sinai.
1197. 383. 110 m. red, blk. & brn. 30 20

384. Rifaa el Tahtawi. 385. Mrs. Hoda Sharawi and Sania Girls Secondary School.

1973. Rifaa el Tahtawi (educationalist). Death Cent.
1200. 384. 20 m. brn., myrt. & grn. 5 5
See also Nos. 1245/6 and 1277/9.

1973. Female Education. Cent., and Women's Union. 50th Anniv.
1201. 385. 20 m. grn., brn. & blue 5 5

386. Mohamed Korayem. 387. Refugees and Map of Palestine.

1973. Revolution. 21st Anniv. Leaders of the 1798 Resistance Movement.
1202. 386. 20 m. brn., bl. & grn. 5 5
1203. – 20 m. brn., blue & grn. 5 5
1204. – 20 m. choc., pink & brn. 5 5
DESIGNS: No. 1203, Omar Makram. No. 1204, Abdel Rahman el Gaberti.

1973. Air. Palestinian Refugees.
1206. 387. 30 m. multicoloured.. 8 5

388. Rose. 389. "Light and Hope for the Blind".

1973. Ramadan Festival.
1207. 388. 10 m. multicoloured.. 5 5

1973. World Health Organization. 25th Anniv.
1208. 390. 20 m. + 10 m. bl. & gold 8 8

390. Bank Building. 391. Emblem and Weather-vane.

1973. National Bank of Egypt. 75th Anniv.
1209. 390. 20 m. blk., grn. & orge. 5 5

1973. Air. World Meteorological Organization Cent.
1210. 391. 110 m. gold, vio. & bl. 30 20

392. Global Emblem.

1973. World Food Programme. 10th Anniv.
1211. 392. 10 m. bl., grn. & brn. 5 5

393. Philae Temples.

1973. U.N.E.S.C.O. Campaign for the Preservation of Nubian Monuments.
1212. 393. 55 m. orge., blue & violet 15 10

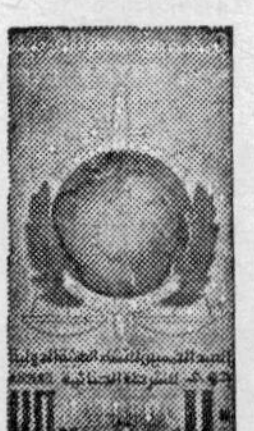
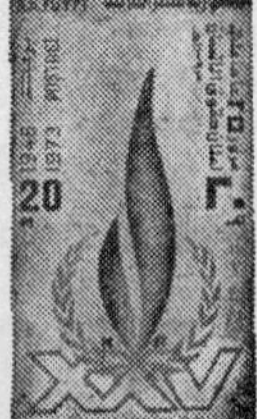

394. Interpol Emblem. 395. Flame Emblem.

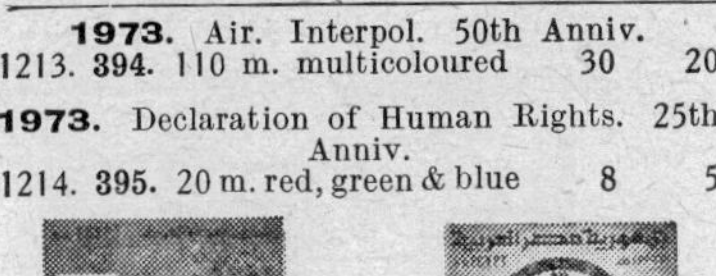

1973. Air. Interpol. 50th Anniv.
1213. **394.** 110 m. multicoloured 30 20

1973. Declaration of Human Rights. 25th Anniv.
1214. **395.** 20 m. red, green & blue 8 5

396. Laurel and Map of Africa.

397. " Donation ".

1973. O.A.U. 10th Anniv.
1215. **396.** 55 m. +20 m. multi 25 15

1973. Social Work Day.
1216. **397.** 20 m.+10 m. blue, pink and red .. 10 8

398. Dr. Taha Hussein (scholar).

400. Postal Services Emblem.

399. Pres. Sadat and Flag.

1973. Hussein Commemoration.
1217. **398.** 20 m. brn., blue & grn. 5 5

1973. Crossing of the Suez Canal, 6 October 1973.
1218. **399.** 20 m. multicoloured.. 5 5
See also No. 1233.

1973. Air. Post Day. Multicoloured.
1219. 20 m. Type **400** 5 5
1220. 30 m. A.P.U. emblem .. 8 5
1221. 55 m. A.F.P.U. emblem.. 15 10
1222. 110 m. U.P.U. monument, Berne (37×37 mm.) .. 30 20

401. Cogwheel, Ear of Corn and Fair Emblem.

403. Emblem and Graph.

402. Madame Sadat with Patient.

1974. International Fair, Cairo.
1223. **401.** 20 m. multicoloured.. 5 5

1974. Society of Faith and Hope (for rehabilitation of the disabled).
1224. **402.** 20 m.+10 m. purple, gold and green .. 10 8

1974. World Population Year.
1225. **403.** 55 m. multicoloured.. 15 10

404. Solar Barque of Cheops.

1974. Air. Inauguration of Solar Barque Museum.
1226. **404.** 110 m. brn., gold & bl. 30 20

405. " Ancient Egyptian Workers " (carving from Queen Tee's tomb, Sakara).

1974. Labour Day (1st May).
1227. **405.** 20 m. blk., yell. & blue 8 5

406. Nurse with Syringe.

407. Map of Suez Canal ("Reconstruction").

1974. Nurses' Day.
1228. **406.** 55 m. multicoloured.. 15 10

1974. Revolution. 22nd Anniv.
1229. **407.** 20 m. gold, blk. & bl. 8 5
1230. – 20 m. silver, grey & pur. 8 5
1231. – 20 m. multicoloured 8 5
DESIGNS—SQUARE (36×36 mm.). No. 1230, Aluminium sheet (" Aluminium production "). VERT.—As T **407** No. 1231, Troops crossing Barlev Line during October War.

408. Pres. Sadat and Flag.

1974. Suez Crossing. First Anniv.
1233. 408. 20 m. multicoloured.. 8 5
See also No. 1218.

409. Teachers' Badge.

410. Artist's Palette.

1974. Teachers' Day.
1234. **409.** 20 m. brn., blk. & blue 8 5

1974. Sixth Plastic Arts Exhibition.
1235. **410.** 30 m. blk., yell. & vio. 12 8

411. Meridian Hotel.

1974. Opening of Meridian Hotel, Cairo.
1236. **411.** 110 m. multicoloured 30 20

412. Child and Emblems.

1974. Social Work Day.
1238. **412.** 30 m. grn., brn. & bl. 12 8

413. Emblems of Standardisation.

1974. World Standards Day.
1239. **413.** 10 m. oran., bl. & blk. 5 5

414. " Aggression Registers ".

415. Philae Temples.

1974. Refugees Propaganda.
1240. **414.** 20 m. red, bl. & black 8 5

1974. U.N.E.S.C.O. Campaign for Preservation of Nubian Monuments.
1241. **415.** 55 m. yell., brn. & bl. 15 10

416. Arum Lily.

417. Pile of Coins.

1974. Ramadan Festival.
1242. **416.** 10 m. yell., grey & bl. 5 5

1974. International Savings Day.
1243. **417.** 20 m. grey, blue & grn. 8 5

418. Organisation Emblems and Cameos.

419. Abbas Mahmoud El Akkad (writer).

1974. Health Insurance Organisation.
1244. **418.** 30 m. grey, red & mve. 12 8

1974. Famous Egyptians.
1245. **419.** 20 m. blue and brown 8 5
1246. – 20 m. brown and blue 8 5
PORTRAITS AND ANNIVERSARIES: No. 1245 (10th death anniv.). No. 1246, Mustafa Lutfy El Manfalouty (journalist). 50th death anniv.

420. Sacred Ibis.

1975. Post Day. Ancient Treasures.
1247. **420.** 20 m. brn., grn. & silv. 8 5
1248. – 30 m. orge., bl. & pur. 8 5
1249. – 55 m. brn., gold & grn. 15 10
1250. – 110 m. yell., brn. & bl. 30 20
DESIGNS—HORIZ. 30 m. Glass " fish " vase. VERT. 55 m. Pharaonic gold vase. 110 m. Mirror shaped as " Sign of Life ".

421. Om Kolthoum (Arab singer).

422. Crescent and Globe.

1975. Om Kolthoum Commemoration.
1251. **421.** 20 m. brown 8 5

1975. Mohammed's Birthday.
1252. **422.** 20 m. multicoloured 8 5

423. Fair Emblem.

424. Kasr El Ainy Hospital.

1975. Cairo International Fair.
1253. **423.** 20 m. multicoloured 8 5

1975. World Health Day.
1254. **424.** 20 m. brown & blue.. 8 5

425. Children Reading Book.

427. Belmabgoknis Flower.

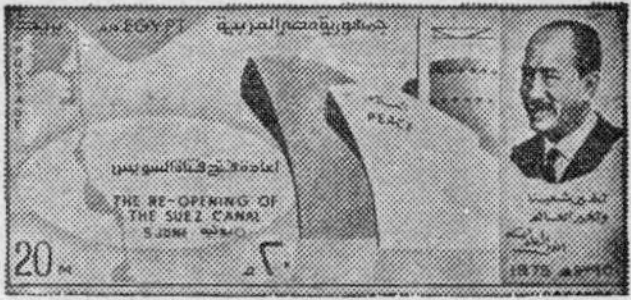

426. President Sadat, Ships and Map.

1975. Science Day. Multicoloured.
1255. 20 m. Type **425** .. 8 5
1256. 20 m. Pupils and graph.. 8 5

1975. Suez Canal Re-opening.
1257. **426.** 20 m. blk., brn. & blue (postage) 8 5
1258. 30 m. deep blue, blue and green (air) .. 12 8
1259. 110 m. deep blue, blue and green 30 20

1975. Festivals.
1260. **427.** 10 m. blue, grey & grn. 5 5

428. I.C.I.D. Emblem. **429.** Spotlight on Village.

1975. Air. International Irrigation and Drainage Commission, 25th Anniv.
1261. **428.** 110 m. bl., grn. & orge. 30 20

1975. Revolution. 23rd Anniv.
1262. **429.** 20 m. blue & brown.. 8 5
1263. – 20 m. orge., blk. & grn. 8 5
1264. – 110 m. multicoloured 30 20
DESIGNS: (38 × 22 mm.). No. 1263, "Tourism", pyramids and sphinx (70 × 79 mm.). No. 1264, Tourist map of Egypt.

430. Volleyball. **431.** Egyptian Flag and Tanks.

1975. Sixth Arab School Sports Tournament. Multicoloured.
1265. 20 m. Type **430** 8 5
1266. 20 m. Running 8 5
1267. 20 m. Tournament emblem 8 5
1268. 20 m. Basketball .. 8 5
1269. 20 m. Football 8 5

1975. Battle of 6 October. 2nd Anniv.
1270. **431.** 20 m. multicoloured.. 8 5

1975. October War International Symposium, Cairo University. As T **431**, but with additional line of Arabic inscr. at foot and "M" placed above face value.
1271. 20 m. multicoloured .. 8 5

432. "Treatment of Schistosomiasis". **433.** University Emblem.

1975. United Nations Day. Multicoloured.
1272. 20 m. Type **432** (postage) 8 5
1273. 55 m. Wall motif (27 × 48 mm.) 15 10
1274. 30 m. Refugees and barbed wire (48 × 40 mm.) (air) 12 8
1275. 110 m. Egyptian woman 30 20
EVENTS: 20 m. International Schistosomiasis Conference, Cairo. 55 m. U.N.E.S.C.O. campaign to save Nubian temples. 30 m. U.N.R.W.A. 110 m. International Women's Year.

1975. Ein Shams University. 25th Anniv.
1276. **433.** 20 m. multicoloured 8 5

MINIMUM PRICE

The minimum price quoted is 5p which represents a handling charge rather than a basis for valuing common stamps. For further notes about prices see introductory pages.

434. Al Kanady (philosopher). **435.** Ibex.

1975. Arab Philosophers.
1277. **434.** 20 m. brn., grn. & bl. 8 5
1278. – 20 m. brn., grn. & bl. 8 5
1279. – 20 m. brn., grn. & bl. 8 5
DESIGNS: No. 1278. Al Farabi, with lute. No. 1279. Al Biruni, with open book.

1976. Post Day. Ancient Treasures. Mult.
1280. 20 m. Type **435** 8 5
1281. 30 m. Lioness 12 8
1282. 55 m. Sacred cow .. 15 10
1283. 110 m. Hippopotamus .. 30 20

436. High Dam and Industrial Potential. **437.** Fair Emblem.

1976. Filling of High Dam Lake.
1284. **436.** 20 m. multicoloured.. 8 5

1976. Cairo Int. Fair.
1285. **437.** 20 m. violet & orange 8 5
1286. – 20 m. yell., blk. & orge. 8 5
DESIGN: No. 1286, Biennale commemorative emblem.

438. Protective Hands.

1976. Faith and Hope Society. Inauguration.
1287. **438.** 20 m. multicoloured.. 8 5

439. "Pharaonic" Eye and Emblem. **440.** Scales of Justice.

1976. World Health Day.
1288. **439.** 20 m. multicoloured.. 8 5

1976. Rectification Movement. 5th Anniv.
1289. **440.** 20 m. blk., grn. & red 8 5

441. Emblem and Pres. Sadat.

1976. Arbitration Service. Cent.
1290. **441.** 20 m. multicoloured.. 8 5

442. Front Page of First Issue.

1976. Al-Ahram Newspaper. Centenary.
1291. **442.** 20 m. multicoloured.. 8 5

443. Pres. Sadat and World Map.

1976. Revolution. 24th Anniv.
1292. **443.** 20 yell., blue & black 8 5

444. "Vollota speciosa". **445.** Red Sea Map and Pres. Sadat with Abu Redice Oil Refinery.

1976. Festivals.
1294. **444.** 10 m. multicoloured.. 5 5

1976. Suez Crossing. 3rd Anniv. Mult.
1295. 20 m. Type **456** .. 8 5
1296. 20 m. "Water and ear of wheat" (redevelopment of Sinai) (48 × 41 mm.) 8 5
1297. 110 m. Monument to Martyrs and "Unknown Soldier" (65 × 80 mm.) 30 20

457. Animals on Papyrus Leaf. ("Literature for Children").

1976. United Nations Day. Multicoloured.
1298. 20 m. Type **457** .. 8 5
1299. 30 m. Dome of the Rock (Palestinian Refugees) 12 8
1300. 55 m. Philae Temple (Nubian Temples preservation) (vert.) .. 15 10
1301. 110 m. UNESCO. Emblem (30th Anniv.).. .. 30 20
The 30 m. and 110 m. values are 39 × 22 mm.

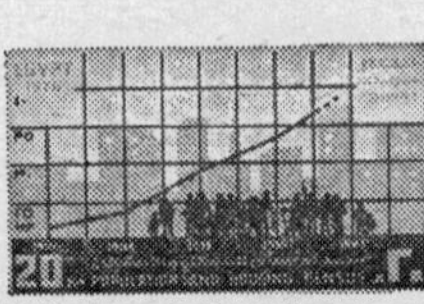

458. Population Graph and Skyline. **459.** Society Medal and Map of Nile.

1976. Population and Housing Census.
1302. **458.** 20 m. sepia, brn. & bl. 8 5

1976. Egyptian Geographical Society. Cent.
1303. **459.** 20 m. brown and green 8 5

EXPRESS LETTER STAMPS

E 1. Postman on Motor-cycle.

1926.
E 138. **E 1.** 20 m. green .. 2·25 1·00
E 139. 20 m. black and red 35 20

1943. As Type E 1, but inscr. "POSTES EXPRES".
E 289. **E 1.** 26 m. black and red 45 45
E 290. 40 m. black and brown 30 15

1952. No. E 4 optd. as T 74.
E 404. **E 1.** 40 m. black & brown 25 20

OFFICIAL STAMPS

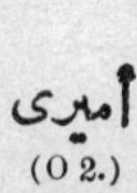

O 1. (O 2.) O 3.

1893.
O 64. **O 1.** brown 10 5

1907. Stamps of 1879 and 1888 optd. **O.H.H.S.** and Arabic equivalent.
O 73. **5.** 1 m. brown 5 5
O 74. 2 m. green 10 5
O 75. 3 m. yellow 8 5
O 86. 4 m. red 12 10
O 76. 5 m. red 8 5
O 77. **4.** 1 pl. blue 15 5
O 78. 5 pl. grey .. .. 1·10 10

1913. Optd. **O.H.H.S.** in English only.
O 79. **5.** 5 m. red (No. 59) .. 12 8

1915. Stamps of 1914 optd. **O.H.H.S.** and Arabic equivalent.
O 83. **6.** 1 m. sepia 8 8
O 99. 2 m. red .. .. 1·10 70
O 85. 3 m. orange 8 8
O 87. 5 m. lake 10 5
O 101. 5 m. pink .. .. 1·10 60

1922. Stamps of 1914 optd. **O.H.E.M.S.** and Arabic equivalent.
O 111. **6.** 1 m. sepia 12 12
O 112. 2 m. red 15 15
O 113. 3 m. orange 40 40
O 114. 4 m. green 75 75
O 115. 5 m. pink 25 15
O 116. 10 m. blue 50 45
O 117. 10 m. lake 65 60
O 118. **7.** 15 m. blue 65 65
O 119. **8.** 15 m. blue .. .. 22·00 22·00
O 120. **9.** 50 m. purple .. .. 2·10 1·90

1923. Stamps of 1923 optd. with Type O 2.
O 123. **11.** 1 m. orange 25 12
O 124. 2 m. black 35 20
O 125. 3 m. brown 50 35
O 126. 4 m. green 75 45
O 127. 5 m. brown 30 15
O 128. 10 m. rose 60 25
O 129. 15 m. blue 75 30
O 130. – 50 m. green .. .. 2·50 90

1926.
O 138. **O 3.** 1 m. orange 5 5
O 139. 2 m. black 5 5
O 140. 3 m. brown 5 5
O 141. 4 m. green 5 5
O 142. 5 m. brown 8 5
O 143. 10 m. lake 25 5
O 144. 10 m. violet 15 5
O 145. 15 m. blue 30 5
O 146. 15 m. purple 15 5
O 148. 20 m. olive 90 20
O 147. 20 m. blue 20 8
O 149. 50 m. green 60 12
Nos. O 148/9 are larger ($22\frac{1}{2} \times 27\frac{1}{2}$ mm.).

O 4. O 5.

1938.
O 276. **O 4.** 1 m. orange 5 5
O 277. 2 m. red 5 5
O 278. 3 m. brown.. .. 5 5
O 279. 4 m. green 5 5
O 280. 5 m. brown.. .. 5 5
O 281. 10 m. violet 5 5
O 282. 15 m. purple .. 10 5
O 283. 20 m. blue 12 8
O 284. 50 m. green .. 25 10

1952. Optd. as T 74.
O 404. **O 4.** 1 m. orange .. 5 5
O 405. 2 m. red 5 5
O 406. 3 m. brown.. .. 5 5
O 407. 4 m. green 5 5

O 408. O 4. 5 m. brown 5 5
O 409. 10 m. violet .. 5 5
O 410. 15 m. purple .. 8 5
O 411. 20 m. blue 10 10
O 412. 50 m. green .. 25 25

1958.

O 685. O 5. 1 m. orange .. 5 5
O 686. 4 m. green 5 5
O 687. 5 m. brown 5 5
O 571. 10 m. purple .. 5 5
O 572. 35 m. blue 10 5
O 689. 35 m. violet .. 12 10
O 690. 50 m. green .. 20 12
O 691. 100 m. lilac 40 20
O 692. 200 m. red 80 40
O 693. 500 m. black .. 2·00 1·00

O 6. Eagle. O 7. Eagle.

1967.

O 918. O 6. 1 m. blue 5 5
O 919. 4 m. brown 5 5
O 920. 5 m. olive 5 5
O 921. 10 m. brown .. 5 5
O 922. 10 m. purple .. 5 5
O 923. 20 m. purple .. 5 5
O 924. 35 m. violet .. 10 10
O 925. 50 m. orange .. 12 12
O 926. 55 m. violet .. 15 12
O 927. 100 m. verm. & grn. 25 20
O 928. 200 m. verm. & blue 50 35
O 929. 500 m. verm. & olive 1·25 1·00

1972.

O 1161. O 7. 1 m. blue & black .. 5 5
O 1162. 10 m. red & black .. 5 5
O 1163. 20 m. green & black 5 5
O 1164. 20 m. brn. & violet 5 5
O 1165. 50 m. orange & blk. 15 12
O 1166. 55 m. violet & blk. 15 12

POSTAGE DUE STAMPS

D 1. D 2. D 3.

1884.

D 62. D 1. 10 pa. red .. .. 1·10 50
D 58. 20 pa. red .. .. 7·50 1·50
D 64. 1 pi. red 80 40
D 65. 2 pi. red 80 15
D 61. 5 pi. red .. .. 3·25 3·25

1888. As Type D 1, but values in "Millemes" and "Piastres".

D 66. D 1. 2 m. green 50 35
D 67. 5 m. red 80 35
D 68. 1 p. blue .. .. 8·50 3·50
D 69. 2 p. orange .. .. 7·50 1·50
D 70. 5 p. grey .. .. 42·00 30·00

1889. Inscr. "A PERCEVOIR POSTES EGYPTIENNES".

D 71. D 2. 2 m. green 25 5
D 72. 4 m. maroon 20 5
D 73. 1 p. blue 40 5
D 74. 2 p. orange 45 15

1898. Surch. **3 Milliemes** in English and Arabic.

D 75. D 2. 3 m. on 2 p. orange .. 12 12

1921. As Type D 2, but inscr. "POSTAGE DUE EGYPT POSTAGE".

D 98. D 2. 2 m. green 8 8
D 99. 2 m. red 5 5
D 100. 4 m. red 60 35
D 101. 4 m. green 10 5
D 102. 10 m. blue 50 45
D 103. 10 m. lake 12 5

1922. Optd. with T 10 inverted.

D 111. D 2. 2 m. red (No. D 99) 10 10
D 112. 4 m. grn. (No. D 101) 15 15
D 113. 10 m. lake (No. D 103) 25 15
D 114. 2 pi. orge. (No. D 74) 1·00 70

1927.

D 173. D 3. 2 m. black 8 5
D 174. 2 m. orange .. 5 5
D 175. 4 m. green 10 5
D 176. 4 m. sepia 25 10
D 177. 5 m. brown 30 5
D 178. 6 m. green 5 5
D 179. 8 m. purple 8 5
D 180. 10 m. lake 12 5
D 732. 10 m. chestnut .. 15 10
D 181. 12 m. red 10 8
D 182. 20 m. brown .. 8 5
D 183. 30 m. violet .. 15 8
The 30 m. is larger, 22×27½ mm.

1952. Optd. as T **74.**

D 404. D 3. 2 m. orange .. 5 5
D 405. 4 m. green 5 5
D 406. 6 m. green 8 8
D 407. 8 m. purple 8 10
D 408. 10 m. lake 20 12
D 410. 12 m. red 12 8
D 411. 30 m. violet 30 20

ILLUSTRATIONS
British Commonwealth and all overprints and surcharges are FULL SIZE. Foreign Countries have been reduced to ¾-LINEAR.

D 4.

1965.

D 852. D 4. 2 m. violet on orange 5 5
D 853. 8 m. blue on pale bl. 5 5
D 854. 10 m. grn. on yellow 5 5
D 855. 20 m. vio. on pale bl. 8 5
D 856. 40 m. grn. on orge. 12 10

SPECIAL SEALS AND STAMPS FOR THE USE OF BRITISH FORCES IN EGYPT.

A. SEALS.

A 1. A 2.

1932. (a) Inscr. "POSTAL SEAL".

A 1. A 1. 1 p. blue and red .. 4·00 2·50

(b) Inscr. "LETTER SEAL".

A 2. A 1. 1 p. blue and red .. 4·00 1·60

1932. Christmas Seals.

A 3. A 2. 3 m. black on blue .. 6·00 6·00
A 4. 3 m. brown-lake .. 2·50 2·25
A 5. 3 m. blue .. .. 1·60 1·60
A 6. 3 m. vermilion .. 85 85

A 3.

1934.

A 9. A 3. 1 p. red 55 30
A 8. 1 p. green .. .. 1·25 80

1935. Silver Jubilee. Optd. **JUBILEE COMMEMORATION 1935.**

A 10. A 3. 1 p. blue .. .. 20·00 20·00

1935. Provisional Christmas Seal. Optd. **Xmas 1935 3 Milliemes.**

A 11. A 3. 3 m. on 1 p. red .. 6·50 4·00

B. POSTAGE STAMPS.

A 4. King Fuad I. A 5.

1936.

A 12. A 4. 3 m. green 20 20
A 13. 10 m. red 40 20

1939.

A 14. A 5. 3 m. green 12 12
A 15. 10 m. red 12 12

EGYPTIAN OCCUPATION OF PALESTINE O2

1948. Various stamps of Egypt optd. **PALESTINE** in English and Arabic.

1. 47. 1 m. orange (postage) .. 5 5
2. 2 m. red 5 5
3. 35. 3 m. brown 8 8
4. 47. 4 m. green 5 5
5. 5 m. brown 8 8
6. 35. 6 m. green 10 10
7. 47. 10 m. violet 10 10
8. 35. 13 m. red 10 10
9. 47. 15 m. purple 10 10
10. 17 m. olive 10 10
11. 20 m. violet 12 12
12. 20 m. blue 15 15
13. – 30 m. olive (No. 340) .. 15 15
14. 59. 40 m. brown 25 25
15. – 50 m. blue (No. 342) .. 25 25
16. – 100 m. pur. (No. 280) .. 1·50 1·40
17. – 200 m. violet (No. 281) .. 2·75 2·50
18. 43. 50 p. brown and green .. 4·00 3·75
19. 44. £E1 brown and blue .. 6·50 6·00
20. 56. 2 m. red (air) 5 5
21. 3 m. brown 5 5
22. 5 m. red 5 5
23. 7 m. orange 5 5
24. 8 m. green 5 5
25. 10 m. violet 10 10
26. 20 m. blue 12 12
27. 30 m. purple 20 20
28. 40 m. red 30 30
29. 50 m. blue 40 40
30. 100 m. olive 70 70
31. 200 m. grey .. .. 3·75 3·75

1953. Stamps of 1948 with portrait obliterated by three horiz. bars. (a) Postage.

32. 47. 1 m. orange 5 5
33. 2 m. red 5 5
34. 35. 3 m. brown 5 5
35. 47. 4 m. green 5 5
36. 5 m. brown 5 5
37. 35. 6 m. green 10 10
38. 47. 10 m. violet 12 12
39. 35. 13 m. red 15 15
40. 47. 15 m. purple 15 15
41. 17 m. olive 20 20
42. 20 m. violet 20 20
43. 22 m. blue 25 25
44. – 30 m. olive (No. 13) .. 30 30
45. 59. 40 m. brown 35 35
46. – 50 m. blue (No. 15) .. 55 50
47. – 100 m. pur. (No. 16) .. 1·10 90
48. – 200 m. violet (No. 17) .. 3·00 2·75
49. 43. 50 p. brown and green .. 7·00 6·50
50. 44. £E1 brown and blue .. 12·00 10·00

(b) Air.

51. 56. 2 m. red 45 45
52. 3 m. brown 8 8
53. 5 m. red .. .. .. 2·10 2·10
54. 7 m. orange 12 12
55. 8 m. green 20 20
56. 10 m. violet 12 12
57. 20 m. blue 20 20
58. 30 m. purple 30 30
59. 40 m. red 45 45
60. 50 m. blue .. .. 2·75 2·75
61. 100 m. olive .. .. 8·50 8·50
62. 200 m. grey .. .. 4·00 4·00

(c) Air. Stamps of 1948 additionally optd. with T 74 of Egypt.

63. 56. 2 m. red 5 5
64. 3 m. brown .. .. 1·10 1·10
65. 5 m. red 15 15
66. 10 m. violet .. .. 2·00 2·00
67. 50 m. blue .. .. 1·10 1·10
68. 100 m. olive .. .. 4·00 4·00

1955. Stamps of Egypt, 1953/4, optd. **PALESTINE** in English and Arabic.

69. 85. 1 m. brown (postage) .. 5 5
70. 2 m. purple 5 5
71. 3 m. blue 5 5
72. 4 m. green 5 5
73. 5 m. red 5 5
74. 79. 10 m. sepia (B) 8 8
75. 15 m. grey 20 15
76. 17 m. turquoise .. 10 10
77. 20 m. violet 10 10
78. 80. 30 m. green 12 10
79. 32 m. blue 20 15
80. 35 m. violet 15 10
81. 40 m. brown 25 20
82. 50 m. purple 25 20
83. 81. 100 m. chestnut 70 65
84. 200 m. turquoise .. 1·60 1·50
85. 500 m. violet .. .. 5·00 4·50
86. £E1 red and green .. 9·00 9·00
86a. 83. 5 m. brown (air) .. 55 55
86b. 15 m. green 75 75

Types of Egypt (sometimes with colours changed) overprinted **PALESTINE** in English and Arabic.

1957. Re-occupation of Gaza Strip.

87. 99. 10 m. green 75 75

1958. Stamps of 1957.

88. – 1 m. turq. (No. 538) .. 5 5
89. – 5 m. sepia (No. 541) .. 5 5
90. 105. 10 m. violet 8 8

UNITED ARAB REPUBLIC

1958. Stamps of 1958 (inscr. "U A R EGYPT").

91. – 1 m. red (No. 553) .. 5 5
92. – 2 m. blue (No. 554) .. 5 5
93. 112. 3 m. brown 5 5
94. – 4 m. green (No. 556) .. 5 5
95. – 5 m. sepia (No. 557) .. 5 5
96. 105. 10 m. violet (No. 558) 5 5
96a. – 35 m. blue (No. 559) .. 35 15

1958. Republic. 5th Anniv.

97. 116. 10 m. brown 65 65

1958. Human Rights. 10th Anniv.

98. 121. 10 m. purple 65 65
99. 35 m. brown .. .. 1·50 1·50

1959. No. 588.

100. 81. 55 m. on 100 m. chest. 75 60

Types of Egypt with some colours changed and additionally inscribed "PALESTINE" in English and Arabic.

1960. As Nos. 603, etc.

101. 105. 1 m. chestnut 5 5
104. – 4 m. brown 5 5
105. – 5 m. violet 5 5
106. – 10 m. bronze-green .. 5 5

1960. World Refugee Year.

109. 145. 10 m. chestnut .. 12 8
110. 35 m. black 55 45

1961. World Health Day.

111. 152. 10 m. blue 15 8

1961. Palestine Day.

112. 154. 10 m. violet 10 5

1961. U.N. Technical Co-operation Programme and 16th Anniv. of U.N.O.

113. – 10 m. blue & orange 12 10
114. 150. 35 m. purple and red 30 20

1961. Education Day.

115. 162. 10 m. brown 12 8

1961. Victory Day.

116. 163. 10 m. brown & chest. 12 8

1962. Egyptian Occupation of Gaza. 5th Anniv.

117. 168. 10 m. brown 8 5

1962. Arab League Week.

118. 170. 10 m. maroon 8 5

1962. Malaria Eradication.

119. 174. 10 m. red & brown .. 8 8
120. 35 m. yellow & black .. 35 25

1962. U.N.O. 17th Anniv. and Hammarskjoeld Commem.

121. 183. 5 m. indigo and pink .. 8 5
122. 10 m. indigo & brown 10 8
123. 35 m. indigo & blue .. 35 30

1963. As No. 739.

124. 4 m. bl., orge & blk. 5 5

1963. Freedom from Hunger.

125. 190. 5 m. chestnut & green 5 5
126. – 10 m. yellow & olive .. 10 8
127. – 35 m. yell., vio. & blk. 60 40

1963. Red Cross Centenary.

128. 191. 10 m. red, pur. & ult. 12 8
129. – 35 m. ult., blue & red 40 25

1963. U.N.E.S.C.O. Campaign for Preservation of Nubian Monuments (4th issue).

130. 194. 5 m. yell. & slate-pur. 5 5
131. – 10 m. yellow and blk. 5 5
132. – 35 m. yellow & violet .. 25 20

1963. Air. As Nos. 758, 760 and 761/2.

133. 50 m. slate-pur. and blue .. 25 20
134. 80 m. indigo and blue .. 30 25
135. 115 m. yellow and black .. 55 50
136. 140 m. red and blue .. 80 70

1963. Human Rights.

137. 198. 5 m. yellow & sepia .. 5 5
138. – 10 m. blk., grey & pur. 5 5
139. – 35 m. black, green and turquoise .. 30 25

1964. As No. 769, etc.

140. – 1 m. violet and olive .. 5 5
141. – 2 m. indigo & orange 5 5
142. – 3 m. blue and brown 5 5
143. – 4 m. grn., brn. & pink 5 5
143a. – 4 m. brown and green 5 5
144. – 5 m. red and blue .. 5 5
145. – 10 m. red, brn. & olive 5 5
146. – 15 m. yellow & violet .. 8 8
147. – 20 m. olive & violet .. 10 8
148. 200. 30 m. slate-blue & orge. 10 8
149. – 35 m. brown, green and salmon .. 15 10
150. – 40 m. blue and green .. 15 8
151. – 60 m. chest. and blue .. 30 20
152. 201. 100 m. brn. & indigo .. 65 45

1964. Arab League Congress.

153. 204. 10 m. black and olive .. 8 5

1964. Ramadan Festival.

154. 205. 4 m. olive, red & lake .. 5 5

1964. Arab P.U.'s Permanent Office.

155. 209. 10 m. blue & green .. 8 5

1964. World Health Day.

156. 210. 10 m. slate-pur. & red 5 5

1965. Ramadan Festival. As No. 834.

157. – 4 m. brown and green 5 5

1965. Arab League. 20th Anniv.

158. 226. 10 m. green and red .. 5 5
159. – 20 m. brown & green .. 8 5

1965. World Meteorological Day.

160. 227. 80 m. orange and blue 50 45

1965. World Health Day.

161. 229. 10 m. red and green .. 8 5

1965. Deir Yasin Massacre.

162. 230. 10 m. red & slate-blue 5 5

1965. I.T.U. Cent.

163. 231. 5 m. slate-blue, yellow and green .. 5 5
164. 10 m. rose, blue & red 8 5
165. 35 m. blue, yellow and ultramarine .. 20 12

1965. Air. Re-establishment of Egyptian Civil Airlines. "MISRAIR".

166. 233. 10 m. green & orange .. 5 5

1966. U.N. Day.

167. 258. 5 m. violet and red .. 5 5
168. – 10 m. violet & brown .. 5 5
169. – 35 m. violet and green 15 12

1966. Victory Day.

170. 261. 10 m. red and olive .. 5 5

1967. Arab Publicity Week.

171. 265. 10 m. brown and blue 5 5

1967. Labour Day.

172. 268. 10 m. sepia and olive .. 5 5

EXPRESS LETTER STAMP

1948. Express Letter stamp of Egypt optd. **PALESTINE** in English and Arabic.

E 32. E 1. 40 m. black & brown 40 40

POSTAGE DUE STAMPS

1948. Postage Due stamps of Egypt optd. **PALESTINE** in English and Arabic.

D 32. D 3. 2 m. orange 5 5
D 33. 4 m. green 5 5
D 34. 6 m. green 5 5
D 35. 8 m. purple 5 5
D 36. 10 m. lake 5 5
D 37. 12 m. red 8 8
D 38. 30 m. violet 30 30

This area was occupied by Israel on 6th June 1967. Post Offices were opened in July 1967 and Israeli stamps are now used.

ELOBEY, ANNOBON AND CORISCO O2

A group of Spanish islands off the W. Coast of Africa in the Gulf of Guinea. Became part of Spanish Guinea until 1960, when the area was united into one postal area using stamps of Fernando Poo.

1903. "Curly Head" key-type inscr. "ELOBEY, ANNOBON Y CORISCO".

1. Z. ¼ c. red 35 15
2. ½ c. purple 35 15
3. 1 c. black 35 15
4. 2 c. red 35 12
5. 3 c. green 35 15
6. 4 c. green 35 15
7. 5 c. lilac 35 15
8. 10 c. red 60 30
9. 15 c. orange 1·75 40
10. 25 c. blue 2·50 1·00
11. 50 c. brown 3·50 1·50
12. 75 c. black 3·50 1·75
13. 1 p. orange 5·50 2·50
14. 2 p. brown 12·00 5·00
15. 3 p. grey 20·00 7·00
16. 4 p. claret 42·00 12·00
17. 5 p. green 45·00 13·00
18. 10 p. blue 85·00 16·00

1905. "Curly Head" key-type inscr. "ELOBEY, ANNOBON Y CORISCO" and dated "1905".

19. Z. 1 c. red 60 15
20. 2 c. purple 1·50 15
21. 3 c. black 60 15
22. 4 c. red 60 15
23. 5 c. green 60 12
24. 10 c. green 1·60 30
25. 15 c. lilac 2·50 1·00
26. 25 c. red 2·50 1·00
27. 50 c. orange 3·25 1·25
28. 75 c. blue 4·00 1·25
29. 1 p. brown 8·00 3·00
30. 2 p. grey 9·00 3·25
31. 3 p. red 9·00 3·50
32. 4 p. brown 60·00 16·00
33. 5 p. green 60·00 16·00
34. 10 p. red £1·50 50·00

1906. Preceding issue surch. **1906** and value in figures and words in ornamental frame.

35. Z. 10. c. on 1 c. red 4·00 2·75
36. 15 c. on 2 c. purple 4·00 2·75
38. 25 c. on 3 c. black 4·50 2·50
40. 50 c. on 4 c. red 4·00 2·50

ILLUSTRATIONS British Commonwealth and all overprints and surcharges are FULL SIZE. Foreign Countries have been reduced to ¾-LINEAR.

1. King Alfonso XIII.

1907.

41. 1. 1 c. purple 30 20
42. 2 c. black 30 20
43. 3 c. red 30 20
44. 4 c. green 30 20
45. 5 c. green 30 20
46. 10 c. lilac 3·00 1·25
47. 15 c. red 1·25 50
48. 25 c. orange 1·25 50
49. 50 c. blue 1·25 40
50. 75 c. brown 3·00 80
51. 1 p. grey 5·00 1·25
52. 2 p. red 7·50 1·75
53. 3 p. brown 7·50 1·75
54. 4 p. green 7·50 1·75
55. 5 p. red 9·50 1·75
56. 10 p. rose 20·00 4·25

1908. Surch. **HABILITADO PARA 05 CTMS.**

57. 1. 05 c. on 1 c. purple 1·10 60
58. 05 c. on 2 c. black 1·10 60
59. 05 c. on 3 c. red 1·10 60
60. 05 c. on 4 c. green 1·10 60
61. 05 c. on 10 c. lilac 2·00 2·00
62. 25 c. on 10 c. lilac 11·00 6·00

For later issues see **FERNANDO POO.**

EL SALVADOR O2

A republic of C. America, Independent since 1838.

1867. 8 reales = 100 centavos = 1 peso.
1912. 100 centavos = 1 colon.

1. San Miguel Volcano. 2.

1867.

1. 1. ½ r. blue 30 35
2. 1 r. red 30 30
3. 2 r. green 1·00 1·25
4. 4 r. brown 1·90 1·50

1874. Optd. **CONTRA SELLO 1874.** and Arms in circle.

5. 1. ½ r. blue 1·10 1·10
6. 1 r. red 1·10 1·10
7. 2 r. green 1·50 1·50
8. 4 r. brown 3·50 3·50

1879.

9. 2. 1 c. green 45 30
15. 2 c. red 80 80
16. 5 c. blue 1·25 75
12. 10 c. black 2·50 1·50
13. 20 c. purple 3·00 1·90

3. 4. 5.

1887.

18. 3. 3 c. brown (perf.) 20 20
19. 4. 5 c. blue (roul.) 20 15
20. 5. 10 c. orange (perf.) 2·50 80

1889. Surch. **1 centavo.**

21. 3. 1 c. on 3 c. brown 50 30

A number of postage stamps listed above are found overprinted **1889.**

1889. As T **3**, but with bar at top. Perf.

22. 3. 1 c. green 25 25

6. 7. 8. Landing of Columbus.

1890.

30. 6. 1 c. green 8 10
31. 2 c. brown 8 12
32. 3 c. yellow 8 12
33. 5 c. blue 8 12
34. 10 c. violet 8 12
35. 20 c. orange 8 25
36. 25 c. red 8 30
37. 50 c. maroon 8 70
38. 1 p. red 8 1·60

1891.

39. 7. 1 c. red 8 8
40. 2 c. green 8 8
41. 3 c. violet 8 10
42. 5 c. red 8 10
43. 10 c. blue 8 10
44. 11 c. violet 8 30
45 20 c. green 8 40
46. 25 c. brown 8 45
47. 50 c. blue 8 90
48. 1 p. brown 8 1·50

1891. Surch. **1 centavo.**

49. 7. 1 c. on 2 c. green 90 90

1891. Surch. **UN CENTAVO.**

50. 7. 1 c. on 2 c. green 80 80

1891. Surch. **5 CENTAVOS.**

51. 7. 5 c. on 3 c. violet 1·10 1·10

1892.

52. 8. 1 c. green 8 8
53. 2 c. brown 8 8
54. 3 c. blue 8 8
55. 5 c. grey 8 8
56. 10 c. red 8 10
57. 11 c. brown 8 45
58. 20 c. orange 8 45
59. 25 c. maroon 8 55
60. 50 c. yellow 8 90
61. 1 p. red 8 1·40

1892. Surch.

62a. 8. 1 c. on 5 c. grey 25 30
64. 1 c. on 20 c. orange 50 55
66. 1 c. on 25 c. maroon 65 65

9. Gen. Ezeta. 10. Founding the City of Isabella.

1893. Dated "1893".

67. 9. 1 c. blue 8 10
68. 2 c. red 8 10
69. 3 c. violet 8 10
70. 5 c. brown 8 12
71. 10 c. brown 8 12
72. 11 c. red 8 30
73. 20 c. green 8 30
74. 25 c. black 8 40
75. 50 c. orange 8 60
76. 1 p. black 8 80
77. 10. 2 p. green 35
78. – 5 p. violet 35
79. – 10 p. red 35

DESIGNS—VERT. 5 p. Statue of Columbus at Genoa. 10 p. Departure from Palos.

1893. Surch. **UN CENTAVO.**

80. 9. 1 c. on 2 c. red 25 30

13. Liberty. 14. Columbus before the Council.

1894. Dated "1894".

81. 13. 1 c. brown 8 10
82. 2 c. blue 8 10
83. 3 c. maroon 8 10
84. 5 c. brown 8 15
85. 10 c. violet 8 15
86. 11 c. red 8 30
87. 20 c. blue 8 40
88. 25 c. orange 8 50
89. 50 c. black 8 70
90. 1 p. blue 8 95
91. 14. 2 p. blue 25
92. – 5 p. red 30
93. – 10 p. brown 30

DESIGNS—HORIZ. 5 p. Columbus protecting hostages. 10 p. Columbus received by King and Queen.

1894. Surch. **1 Centavo.**

94. 13. 1 c. on 11 c. red 65 30

17. 18. Arms.

1895. Optd. with Arms obliterating portrait. Various frames.

95. 17. 1 c. olive 8 10
96. 2 c. green 8 10
97. 3 c. brown 8 12
98. 5 c. blue 8 12
99. 10 c. orange 8 10
100. 12 c. claret 8 30
101. 15 c. red 8 35
102. 20 c. yellow 8 45
103. 24 c. violet 8 50
104. 30 c. blue 8 60
105. 50 c. red 8 65
106. 1 p. black 8 90

1895. Various frames.

115. 18. 1 c. olive 45 50
116. 2 c. green 10 10
117. 3 c. brown 10 10
118. 5 c. blue 10 10
119. 10 c. orange 70 30
120. 12 c. rose 70 30
121. 15 c. red 12 35
122. 20 c. green 15 50
123. 24 c. lilac 20 50
124. 30 c. blue 12 45
125. 50 c. red 1·00 1·25
126. 1 p. brown 1·25 1·90

1895. Surch.

132. 18. 1 c. on 12 c. rose 70 70
133. 1 c. on 24 c. lilac 70 70
134. 1 c. on 30 c. blue 70 70
135. 2 c. on 20 c. green 70 70
136. 3 c. on 30 c. blue 90 90

19. 20. 21. Government Buildings.

1896.

137. 19. 1 c. brown 8 8
138. 2 c. brown 8 15
139. 3 c. green 8 20
140. 5 c. olive 8 15
141. 10 c. yellow 8 25
142. 12 c. blue 60 80
143. 15 c. violet 9 25
144. 20 c. claret 33 55
145. 24 c. red 8 25
146. 30 c. orange 8 45
147. 50 c. black 8 60
148. 1 p. red 8 90

1896. Dated "1896".

158. 20. 1 c. green 8 8
159. 21. 2 c. lake 8 8
160. – 3 c. brown 8 8
161. – 5 c. blue 8 8
162. – 10 c. brown 8 12
163. – 12 c. grey 8 15
164. – 15 c. green 8 25
165. – 20 c. red 8 30
166. – 24 c. violet 8 45
167. – 30 c. green 8 45
168. – 50 c. orange 8 45
169. – 100 c. blue 8 90

DESIGNS: 3 c. Locomotive. 5 c. Mt. San Miguel. 10 c., 12 c. Steamship. 15 c. Post Office. 20 c. Lake Ilopango. 24 c. Magra Falls. 30 c., 50 c. Arms. 100 c. Columbus.

1896. No. 166 surch. **Quince centavos.**

218. 15 c. on 24 c. violet 2·75 2·75

1897. As Nos. 158/69. New colours.

220. 1 c. red 8 8
221. 2 c. green 8 8
222. 3 c. brown 8 8
223. 5 c. orange 8 8
224. 10 c. green 8 10
225. 12 c. blue 30 25
226. 15 c. black 2·00 1·10
227. 20 c. slate 8 20
228. 24 c. yellow 8 25
229. 30 c. rose 8 20
230. 50 c. violet 12 50
231. 100 c. lake 1·90 1·90

32. 33.

1897. Federation of Central America.

270. 32. 1 c. blue, rose, gold and green 30 1·25
271. 5 c. rose, blue, gold and green 30 1·40

1897. Nos. 228/31 surch. **TRECE centavos.**

272. 13 c. on 24 c. yellow 1·90 1·90
273. 13 c. on 30 c. rose 1·90 1·90
274. 13 c. on 50 c. violet 1·90 1·90
275. 13 c. on 100 c. lake 2·25 2·25

1898.

276. 33. 1 c. red 5 8
277. 2 c. red 5 8
278. 3 c. green 8 8
279. 5 c. green 8 8
280. 10 c. blue 10 10
281. 12 c. violet 15 20
282. 13 c. lake 8 10
283. 20 c. bue 8 20
284. 24 c. blue 8 25
285. 26 c. brown 8 30
286. 50 c. orange 10 65
287. 1 p. yellow 12 80

Some values of the above set exist optd. with a wheel as T 35.

34. (35.)

1899. Optd. with T **35.**

318. 34. 1 c. brown 20 10
319. 2 c. green 25 5
320. 3 c. blue 30 15
321. 5 c. orange 20 8
322. 10 c. brown 20 10
323. 12 c. green 50 35
324. 13 c. red 45 40
325. 24 c. blue 4·00 4·00
326. 26 c. rose 1·10 1·00
327. 50 c. red 1·10 1·00
328. 100 c. violet 1·40 75

1899. Optd. **1900.**

398. 33. 1 c. red 50 50

1900. Stamps of 1898 surch. **1900** and new value, with or without wheel opt., T **35.**

400. 33. 1 c. on 10 c. blue 2·50 2·50
401. 1 c. on 13 c. lake £170
414. 2 c. on 12 c. violet 1·25 1·10
403. 2 c. on 13 c. lake 1·25 1·25
404. 2 c. on 20 c. blue 1·25 1·25
406. 3 c. on 12 c. violet 28·00 28·00
407. 3 c. on 50 c. orange 10·00 11·00
419. 5 c. on 12 c. violet 13·00 13·00
409. 5 c. on 24 c. blue 10·00 10·00
410. 5 c. on 26 c. brown 32·00 32·00
411. 5 c. on 1 p. yellow 12·00 12·00

1900. Stamps of 1899 surch. **1900** and new value, with or without wheel opt., T 35.

424. 34. 1 c. on 2 c. green 12 10
420. 1 c. on 13 c. red 20 20
426. 2 c. on 12 c. green 65 65
422. 2 c. on 13 c red 40 25
423. 3 c. on 12 c. green 40 25
429. 5 c. on 24 c. blue 1·50 75
430. 5 c. on 26 c. rose 50 50

(36.) 37. Columbus Monument.

1900. T **34** with date altered to "1900" and optd. as T **36.**

438. 34. 1 c. green 8 8
468. 2 c. rose 10 10
469. 3 c. black 10 10
470. 5 c. blue 8 5
471. 10 c. blue 20 12
472. 12 c. green 20 20
473. 13 c. brown 10 10
474. 24 c. black 15 15
475. 26 c. brown 25 25
447. 50 c. rose 1·00 1·00

1902. Nos. 468, 469 & 472 surch. **1 centavo.**

483. **34.** 1 c. on 2 c. rose .. .. 1·50 1·25
484. 1 c. on 3 c. black .. 1·00 90
485. 1 c. on 5 c. blue .. 90 75

1903.

486. **37.** 1 c. green 15 15
487. 2 c. red 15 15
488. 3 c. orange 45 35
489. 5 c. blue 15 15
490. 10 c. purple 15 15
491. 12 c. grey 20 15
492. 13 c. brown 20 15
493. 24 c. red 85 75
494. 26 c. brown 75 60
495. 50 c. yellow 50 45
496. 100 c. blue .. .. 1·90 1·25

1905. Surch. in words or figures and words.

514. **37.** 1 c. on 2 c. red 15 15
517. 5 c. on 12 c. grey .. 55 45

1905. Surch. in figures only and two black circles.

515. **37.** 1 c. on 13 c. brown .. 45 15
516. 3 c. on 13 c. brown .. 15 15

1905. Surch. in figures twice.

527. **37.** 5 c. on 12 c. grey .. 1·25 1·00

1905. Surcharged in figures repeated four times.

529. **37.** 5 c. on 12 c. grey .. 1·50 1·50

1905. Surch. with new value: **1 1** at top of stamp and **1 CENTAVO 1** at foot.

523. **37.** 1 c. on 2 c. red .. 15 15
524. 1 c. on 10 c. purple .. 15 15
525. 1 c. on 12 c. grey .. 45 45
526. 1 c. on 13 c. brown .. 2·75 2·75
530. 6 c. on 12 c. grey .. 25 20
531. 6 c. on 13 c. brown .. 35 30

1905. Stamps dated "1900", with or without opt. T **36**, and optd. **1905** or **01905**.

552. **34.** 1 c. green .. .. 2·00 2·00
546. 2 c. rose 20 20
543. 3 c. black .. .. 4·00 1·40
547. 5 c. blue 80 40
548. 10 c. blue 40 40

1906. Stamps dated "1900", with or without opt. T **36**, and optd. **1906** or surch. also.

560. **34.** 2 c. on 26 c. brown .. 25 25
562. 3 c. on 26 c. brown .. 1·25 1·25
564. 10 c. blue 65 65

38. Pres. Pedro Jose Escalon. **39.** President's Palace.

1906.

570. **38.** 1 c. black and green .. 8 8
571. 2 c. black and red .. 8 8
572. 3 c. black and yellow .. 8 8
573. 5 c. black and blue .. 8 8
574. 6 c. black and red .. 8 8
575. 10 c. black and violet .. 8 8
576. 12 c. black and violet .. 8 8
577. 13 c. black and brown 8 8
578. 24 c. black and red .. 10 15
579. 26 c. black and brown 15 25
580. 50 c. black and yellow 15 35
581. 100 c. black and blue .. 35 75

1907. Nos. 570/2 optd. as T **36**.

592. **38.** 1 c. black and green .. 15 15
593. 2 c. black and red .. 15 15
594. 3 c. black and yellow .. 15 15

1906. Surch. with new value and black circles and optd. with shield, T **36**.

595. **38.** 1 c. on 5 c. blk. & blue .. 8 8
596. 1 c. on 6 c. black and red 10 10
597. 2 c. on 6 c. black and red 1·00 50
598. 10 c. on 6 c. black & red 25 20

1907. Optd. with shield, T **36**.

599. **39.** 1 c. black and green .. 8 8
600. 2 c. black and red .. 8 8
601. 3 c. black and yellow .. 10 8
602. 5 c. black and blue .. 10 8
603. 6 c. black and red .. 10 8
604. 10 c. black and violet .. 10 8
605. 12 c. black and violet .. 10 8
606. 13 c. black and sepia .. 8 8
607. 24 c. black and rose .. 10 8
608. 26 c. black and brown .. 20 12
609. 50 c. black and yellow .. 30 25
610. 100 c. black and blue .. 50 40

1908. Surch. **UN CENTAVO** and one black circle.

621. **39.** 1 c. on 2 c. black and red 12 12

1909. Optd. **1821. 15 Septiembre 1909.**

633. **39.** 1 c. black and green .. 1·00 65

1909. Surch. with new value and **1909.**

634. **39.** 2 c. on 13 c. blk. & sep. 80 80
635. 3 c. on 26 c. blk. & brn. 1·00 80

40. Gen. Figueroa. **41.** M. J. Arce.

1910.

642. **40.** 1 c. black and brown .. 8 8
643. 2 c. black and green .. 10 10
644. 3 c. black and orange .. 10 10
645. 4 c. black and red .. 10 10
646. 5 c. black and violet .. 10 10
647. 6 c. black and red .. 10 10
648. 10 c. black and violet .. 12 12
649. 12 c. black and blue .. 12 12
650. 17 c. black and green .. 12 12
651. 19 c. black and brown .. 12 12
652. 29 c. black and brown .. 12 12
653. 50 c. black and yellow .. 12 12
654. 100 c. black and blue .. 12 12

1911. Insurrection Cent.

655. – 5 c. brown and blue .. 8 8
656. **41.** 6 c. brown and orange .. 8 8
657. – 12 c. black and mauve .. 8 8

DESIGNS: 5 c. J. M. Delgado. 12 c. Centenary Monument.

1911. T **39** without shield opt. T **36.**

658. **39.** 1 c. red 5 5
659. 2 c. brown 20 20
660. 13 c. green 8 8
661. 24 c. yellow 10 10
662. 50 c. brown 10 10

42. Jose Matias Delgado. **48.** Independence Monument.

49. National Palace. **51.** National Arms.

1912.

663. **42.** 1 c. black and blue .. 8 8
664. – 2 c. black and brown .. 12 10
665. – 5 c. black and red .. 12 10
666. – 6 c. black and green .. 10 8
667. – 12 c. black and olive .. 25 12
668. – 17 c. grey and purple .. 20 10
669. **48.** 19 c. grey and red .. 45 12
670. **49.** 29 c. grey and orange .. 60 12
671. – 50 c. grey and blue .. 70 25
672. **51.** 1 col. grey and black .. 1·25 60

DESIGNS—As T **42**: 2 c. M. J. Arce. 5 c. F. Morazan. 6 c. R. Campo. 12 c. T. Cabanas. 17 c. Barrios Monument. As T **49**: 50 c. Rosales Hospital.

52. J. M. Rodriguez.

ILLUSTRATIONS
British Commonwealth and all overprints and surcharges are FULL SIZE. Foreign Countries have been reduced to ¾-LINEAR.

1914.

673. **52.** 10 c. brown and orange 80 25
674. – 25 c. brown and violet .. 80 25

PORTRAIT: 25 c. Dr. M. E. Araujo.

1915. Re-issue of T **39.** No shield. Optd. **1915.**

675. **39.** 1 c. grey 10 8
676. 2 c. red 10 8
677. 5 c. blue 10 8
678. 6 c. blue 10 8
679. 10 c. yellow 35 20
680. 12 c. brown 20 10
681. 50 c. purple 15 12
682. 100 c. brown .. .. 1·00 75

53. National Theatre. **54.** Pres. Carlos Melendez.

1916. Various frames.

683. **53.** 1 c. green 5 5
684. 2 c. red 8 8
685. 5 c. blue 8 8
686. 6 c. violet 10 10
687. 10 c. brown 10 10
688. 12 c. purple 70 40
689. 17 c. orange 15 10
690. 25 c. brown 40 25
691. 29 c. black 90 40
692. 50 c. grey 75 50
693. **54.** 1 col. black and blue .. 30 30

1917. Official stamps of 1915, with word "OFICIAL" cancelled with five bars.

694. **39.** 2 c. red (No. O 686) .. 15 12
695. 5 c. blue (No. O 687) .. 20 15

1918. Official stamps of 1915 optd. **CORRIENTE** and bar.

696. **39.** 1 c. grey (No. O 685) .. 1·10 1·10
697. 2 c. red .. .. .. 1·25 1·25
698. 5 c. blue .. .. 5·00 5·00
699. 6 c. blue 25 25
700. 10 c. yellow 50 40
701. 12 c. brown 40 40
702. 50 c. purple 25 25

1918. Official stamps of 1916 optd. **Corriente** and bar or surch. also.

704. **53.** 1 c. on 6 c. vio. (No. O 696) 45 45
705. 5 c. blue 75 75
706. 6 c. violet .. .. 3·00 3·00

1919. Surch. with new value and square or circles or bars.

710. **53.** 1 c. on 6 c. violet .. 45 45
711. 1 c. on 12 c. purple .. 10 10
712. 1 c. on 17 c. orange .. 12 8
713. 2 c. on 10 c. brown .. 20 12
714. 5 c. on 50 c. grey .. 15 12
715. 6 c. on 25 c. brown .. 25 20
716. 15 c. on 29 c. black .. 55 20
717. 26 c. on 29 c. black .. 65 30
719. 35 c. on 50 c. grey .. 45 30
720. 60 c. on 1 col. blk. & bl. 25 25

1919. No. O 699 surch. **1 Centavo 1** and black squares.

721. **53.** 1 c. on 12 c. purple .. 60 60

1920. Municipal stamps (Arms) surch. **Correos Un centavo 1919.**

722. 1 c. on 1 c. olive 5 5
723. 1 c. on 5 c. yellow 5 5
724. 1 c. on 10 c. blue 10 8
725. 1 c. on 25 c. green 5 5
726. 1 c. on 50 c. olive 12 12
727. 1 c. on 1 p. black 12 15

55. F. Menendez. **56.**

57. Delgado addressing Crowd. **58.**

59. Independence Monument. **60.** J. S. Canas.

1921. Portraits are as T **55.**

728. **55.** 1 c. green 10 5
729. – 2 c. black (M. J. Arce) 12 5
730. **56.** 5 c. orange 30 12
731. **57.** 6 c. red 25 10
732. **58.** 10 c. blue 30 10
733. – 25 c. grn. (F. Morazan) 80 12
734. **59.** 60 c. violet .. .. 2·25 25
735. – 1 col. sepia (Columbus) 2·75 30

1921. Independence. Cent. Nos. 728/31 optd. **CENTENARIO.**

735a. **55.** 1 c. green .. .. 1·75 1·40
735b. – 2 c. black .. .. 1·75 1·40
735c. **56.** 5 c. orange .. .. 1·75 1·40
735d. **57.** 6 c. red .. .. 1·75 1·40

1923. As last, surch.

745. **56.** 1 c. on 5 c. orange .. 20 15
741. – 1 c. on 25 c. green .. 8 8
746. **56.** 2 c. on 5 c. orange .. 25 25
737. **57.** 5 c. on 6 c. red .. 12 8
747. **58.** 6 c. on 10 c. blue .. 25 25
742. – 6 c. on 25 c. green .. 12 10
738. – 10 c. on 2 c. black .. 25 15
739. **57.** 20 c. on 6 c. red .. 25 25
743. – 20 c. on 25 c. green .. 30 20
744. – 20 c. on 1 col. sepia .. 40 30

1923. Abolition of slavery.

740. **60.** 5 c. blue 25 15

1924. U.P.U. Commem. Surch. **15 Sept. 1874-1924 5 5 U.P.U. CINCO CENTAVOS.**

749. **59.** 5 c. on 60 c. violet .. 2·10 2·10

61. Daniel Hernandez. **66.** Central America.

67.

1924.

750. **61.** 1 c. purple 8 8
751. – 2 c. red 12 10
752. – 3 c. brown 10 8
753. – 5 c. black 10 8
754. – 6 c. blue 12 8
755. **66.** 10 c. orange 30 15
756. – 20 c. green 35 25
757. – 35 c. green and rose .. 75 30
758. – 50 c. brown 90 25
759. **67.** 1 col. blue and green .. 1·25 30

DESIGNS—VERT. 2 c. National Gymnasium. 3 c. Atlacatl. 20 c. Balsam tree. 35 c. Senora T. S. Morazan. HORIZ. 5 c. Conspiracy of 1811. 6 c. Bridge over R. Lempa. 50 c. Columbus at La Rabida.

1925. San Salvador. 4th Cent. Surch. **1525 2 2 1925 Dos centavos.**

760. **59.** 2 c. on 60 c. violet .. 80 80

70. View of San Salvador.

1925.

761. **70.** 1 c. blue 60 80
762. 2 c. green 60 80
763. 3 c. red 60 80

72. Dr. P. R. Bosque and Gen. L. Chacon.

1928. Artistic Industrial Exn. Surch. **Exposicion Santaneca Julio de 1928** and value in figures.

764. 3 c. on 10 c. orange .. 60 50

1928. No. 753 surch.

765. 1 c. on 5 c. black 25 15

1930. Connection of Railways between Salvador and Guatemala.

766. **72.** 1 c. purple and mauve 30 20
767. 3 c. purple and brown .. 30 20
768. 5 c. purple and green .. 30 20
769. 10 c. purple and orange 30 20

1930. Air. Nos. 755/759 optd **Servicio Aereo** or surch. also.

770. **66.** 15 c. on 10 c. orange 50 50
771. – 20 c. green 50 50
772. – 25 c. on 35 c. grn. & rose 50 50
773. – 40 c. on 50 c. brown .. 50 40
774. **71.** 50 c. on 1 col. bl. & grn. 1·00 1·00

73. Aeroplane over San Salvador.

1930. Air.

775. **73.** 15 c. red 20 8
776. 20 c. green 25 10
777. 25 c. purple 25 8
778. 40 c. blue 30 8

74. Tomb of Menendez. **75.** Simon Bolivar.

1930. Menendez. Birth Cent.

779. **74.** 1 c. violet .. .. 2·50 2·50
780. 3 c. brown .. .. 2·50 2·50
781. 5 c. green .. .. 2·50 2·50
782. 10 c. orange .. .. 2·50 2·50

1930. Air. Bolivar. Death Cent.

783. **75.** 15 c. red .. .. 3·00 3·00
784. 20 c. green .. .. 3·00 3·00
785. 25 c. purple .. .. 3·00 3·00
786. 40 c. blue .. .. 3·00 3·00

1931. Air. Optd. with aeroplane.

787. **71.** 1 col. blue and green .. 2·25 2·25

1931. New G.P.O. Building Fund. Nos. 756 and 758 surch. **EDIFICIOS POSTALES** and value.

788.		1 c. on 20 c. green	10	5
789.		1 c. on 50 c. brown	10	5
790.		2 c. on 20 c. green	10	5
791.		2 c. on 50 c. brown	10	5

76. Church of Mercy, San Salvador.

77. Jose Matias Delgado.

1931. Air. Independence. 120th Anniv.

792.	**76.**	15 c. red	3·00	3·00
793.		20 c. green	3·00	3·00
794.		25 c. purple	3·00	3·00
795.		40 c. blue	3·00	3·00

1932. Issues of 1924 and 1926 optd. **1932.**

796.	**61.**	1 c. purple	8	8
797.	–	2 c. red	12	8
798.	–	3 c. brown	15	10
799.	–	5 c. black	15	8
800.	–	6 c. blue	20	8
801.	**66.**	10 c. orange	50	15
802.	–	20 c. green	60	30
803.	–	35 c. green and red	80	45
804.	–	50 c. brown	1·50	70
805.	**71.**	1 col. blue and green	2·75	1·50

1932. Air. J. M. Delgado. Death Cent.

806.	**77.**	15 c. red and violet	1·10	1·00
807.		20 c. green and blue	1·50	1·40
808.		25 c. violet and red	1·50	1·40
809.		40 c. blue and green	1·50	1·40

78. Columbus' Ships and Aeroplane.

79. Police Headquarters.

1933. Air. Departure of Columbus from Palos. 441st Anniv.

810.	**78.**	15 c. orange	1·10	1·10
811.		20 c. green	2·25	2·25
812.		25 c. mauve	2·25	2·25
813.		40 c. blue	2·25	2·25
814.		1 col. bronze	2·25	2·25

1934. Issues of 1924 and 1926 surch.

815.	–	2 on 5 c. blk. (No. 753)	10	5
816.	–	2 on 50 c. brn. (No. 758)	20	12
817.	**66.**	3 on 10 c. orange	12	8
818.	**71.**	8 on 1 col. blue & green	10	10
819.	–	15 on 35 c. green and rose (No. 757)	20	20

1934.

820.	**79.**	2 c. brown	12	5
821.		5 c. red	12	5
822.		8 c. blue	12	5

1934. Air. Inscr. "SERVICIO AEREO".

823.	**79.**	25 c. violet	30	15
824.		30 c. brown	50	25
825.		1 col. black	1·50	40

81. Discus Thrower.

82. Runner breaking the Tape.

1935. 3rd Central American Athletic Games.

826.	**81.**	5 c. red (postage)	3·50	2·40
827.		8 c. blue	3·50	2·40
828.		10 c. orange	4·75	3·00
829.		15 c. bistre	5·50	3·50
830.		37 c. green	9·00	5·50
831.	**82.**	15 c. red (air)	4·00	3·50
832.		25 c. violet	4·00	3·50
833.		30 c. brown	2·50	3·00
834.		55 c. blue	19·00	14·00
835.		1 col. black	13·00	11·00

These also exist optd. **HABILITADO.**

83. National Flag.

84. The Settlers' Oak.

1935.

846.	**83.**	1 c. blue (postage)	8	5
847.		2 c. grey	10	5
848.		3 c. purple	12	10
849.		5 c. red	20	10
850.		8 c. blue	20	10
851.		15 c. brown	30	12
852.		30 c. black (air)	40	12

1935. San Vicente Tercent. Value in black.

853.	**84.**	2 c. grn. & choc. (post.)	25	15
854.		3 c. green	30	15
855.		5 c. green and red	40	25
856.		8 c. green and blue	40	25
857.		15 c. green and brown	45	30
858.		10 c. grn. & yellow (air)	1·25	90
859.		15 c. green and brown	1·25	90
860.		20 c. green	1·25	90
861.		25 c. green and violet	1·25	90
862.		30 c. green & chocolate	1·25	90

86. Cutuco Harbour

87. D Vasoncelos.

88. Sugar Refinery.

89. Coffee Cargo.

1935.

863.	–	1 c. violet	8	5
864.	**86.**	2 c. brown	8	5
865.	**87.**	3 c. green	8	5
866.	–	5 c. red	12	8
867.	–	8 c. blue	10	5
868.	**88.**	10 c. yellow	12	8
869.	**89.**	15 c. bistre	25	10
870.	–	50 c. blue	70	45
871.	–	1 col. black	2·75	2·00

DESIGNS—As T **86**: 1 c. Mt. Izalco. 5 c. Campo de Marte playing-fields. As T **87**: 8 c. T. G. Palomo. 1 col. Manuel Araujo. As T **88**: 50 c. Balsam tree.

1937. Air. Optd. **AEREO** in frame.

872.	**89.**	15 c. bistre	35	20

1937. Air. Surch. **30** in frame and **HABILITADO.**

873.	**82.**	30 c. on 55 c. blue	1·75	65

90. Panchimalco Church.

1937. Air.

874.	**90.**	15 c. orange	20	12
875.		20 c. green	20	12
876.		25 c. violet	25	15
877.		30 c. brown	20	5
878.		40 c. blue	35	25
879.		1 col. black	75	20
880.		5 col. red	3·00	2·10

1938. Surch.

881.	**86.**	1 c. on 2 c. brown	10	5
882.	–	1 c. on 5 c. (No. 866)	10	8
883.	**88.**	3 c. on 10 c. yellow	10	8
884.	**89.**	8 c. on 15 c. bistre	10	5

1938. J. Simeon Canas. Death Cent. Surch. **3.**

885.	**60.**	3 c. on 5 c. blue	15	12

91. Flags and Book of Constitution.

1938. U.S. Constitution. 150th Anniv.

(a) Postage (without air liner).

886.	**91.**	8 c. red, yellow and blue	35	30

(b) Air.

887.	**91.**	30 c. pink, red yellow & brown	80	80

92. J. S. Canas.

93. Women at Washing Pool.

1938. Air. J. S. Canas. Death Cent.

888.	**92.**	15 c. orange	1·10	1·00
889.		20 c. green	1·10	1·00
890.		30 c. brown	1·10	1·00
891.		1 col. black	4·50	3·75

1938.

892.	–	1 c. violet	8	5
893.	**93.**	2 c. green	8	5
894.	–	3 c. brown	10	5
895.	–	5 c. red	12	5
896.	–	8 c. blue	25	5
897.	–	10 c. orange	20	5
898.	–	20 c. brown	30	10
899.	–	50 c. violet	65	30
900.	–	1 col. black	90	50

DESIGNS: 1 c. Native sugar-mill. 3 c. Girl at spring. 5 c. Native ploughing. 8 c. Yucca plant. 10 c. Champion cow. 20 c. Extraction of Peruvian balsam. 50 c. Maquilishuat tree in flower. 1 col. G.P.O., San Salvador.

94. Golden Gate Bridge.

1939. Air. Golden Gate Int. Exn., San Francisco.

901.	**94.**	15 c. black and yellow	25	12
902.		30 c. black and brown	35	12
903.		40 c. black and blue	45	20

1939. Battle of San Pedro Perulapan. Cent. Surch. **BATALLA SAN PEDRO PERULAPAN** and value.

904.	–	8 c. on 50 c. bl. (No. 870)	15	12
905.	–	10 c. on 1 col. black (No. 871)	20	15
906.	**71.**	50 c. on 1 col. bl. & grn.	1·50	1·50

95. Sir Rowland Hill.

97. Coffee Tree in Bloom.

96. "Peace" and Western Hemisphere.

1940. First Postage Stamps. Cent.

907.	**95.**	8 c. black & blue (post.)	3·50	70
908.		30 c. black & brown (air)	6·00	2·00
909.		80 c. black and red	15·00	12·00

1940. Air. 50th Anniv. of Pan-American Union.

910.	**96.**	30 c. blue and brown	35	30
911		80 c. black and red	75	65

1940. Air.

912.	**97.**	15 c. orange	80	15
913.		20 c. green	1·00	10
914.		25 c. violet	1·90	30
915.	–	30 c. brown	1·75	5
916.	–	1 col. black	6·50	20

DESIGN: 30 c., 1 col. Coffee tree in fruit.

98. Dr. Lindo, Gen. Mallespin and New National University of El Salvador.

1941. Air. El Salvador University. Cent.

917.	**98.**	20 c. red and green	80	65
918.	–	40 c. orange and blue	80	65
919.	–	60 c. brown and violet	80	65
920.	–	80 c. green and red	2·20	2·00
921.	–	1 col. orange and black	2·20	2·00
922.	**98.**	2 col. purple and orange	2·50	2·25

PORTRAITS: 40 c., 80 c. Dr. N. Monterey and A. J. Canas. 60 c., 1 col. Dr. I. Menendez and Dr. C. Salazar.

DESIGN: 8 c. Patron Saint and Cathedral of San Salvador, in medallions.

99. Map of El Salvador.

1942. 1st National Eucharistic Congress. Inscr. "NOVIEMBRE 1942".

923.	–	8 c. blue (postage)	50	20
924.	**99.**	30 c. orange (air)	55	40

1943. Air. Surch in large figures.

925.	**94.**	15 on 15 c. black & yell.	25	15
926.		20 on 30 c. blk. & brown	35	20
927.		25 on 40 c. black & blue	75	40

1944. Air. Surch. in small figures.

928.	**94.**	15 on 15 c. black & yell.	30	30
929.		20 on 30 c. black & brn.	50	30
930.		25 on 40 c. black & blue	75	35

100. Cuscatlan Bridge.

1944. Optd. with small shield.

931.	**100.**	8 c. blk. & blue (post)	15	8
932.		30 c. blk. & red (air)	35	15

101. Presidential Palace.

102. General J. J. Canas.

1944. Air.

933.	**101.**	15 c. mauve	12	5
934.	–	20 c. green	20	5
935.	–	25 c. purple	30	5
936.	–	30 c. red	25	5
937.	–	40 c. blue	35	20
938.	–	1 col. black	80	45

DESIGNS: 20 c. National Theatre. 25 c. National Palace. 30 c. Mayan Pyramid. 40 c. Public Gardens. 1 col. Aeronautics School.

1945. General J. J. Canas (author of National Anthem).

939.	**102.**	8 c. blue	10	5

1945. No. 893 surch. **1.**

940.		1 c. on 2 c. green	8	5

1945. Air. Optd. **Aereo.**

942.		1 col. black (No. 900)	75	25

103. Juan Ramon Uriarte.

104. Alberto Masferrer.

1945. Air. J. R. Uriarte, former Director General of Posts.
943. **103.** 12 c. blue 15 8
944. 14 c. orange 15 5

1945. Air. Alberto Masferrer (writer).
945. **104.** 12 c. red 15 8
946. 14 c. green 15 5

105. Lake of Ilapango. **106.** Osidro Menendez.

1946.
947. **105.** 1 c. blue 5 5
948. – 2 c. green 12 8
949. – 5 c. red 10 5
DESIGNS: 2 c. Ceiba tree. 5 c. Water carriers (larger).

1947.
950. **106.** 1 c. red 5 5
951. – 2 c. yellow (Salazar) .. 5 5
952. – 3 c. violet (Bertis) .. 5 5
953. – 5 c. grey (Duenas) .. 5 5
954. – 8 c. blue (Belloso) .. 5 5
955. – 10 c. bistre (Trigueros) 10 5
956. – 20 c. green (Gonsalez) 15 10
957. – 50 c. black (Castaneda) 50 25
958. – 1 col. red (Castro) .. 1·00 25

107. A. Espino. **108.** M. J. Arce.

1947. Air.
959. – 12 c. brown (F. Soto) 15 8
960. **107.** 14 c. blue 10 5

1948. M. J. Arce. Death Cent.
961. **108.** 8 c. blue (postage) .. 15 10
962. 12 c. green (air) .. 15 10
963. 14 c. red 15 10
964. 1 col. purple .. 1·90 1·60

109. Mackenzie King, Roosevelt and Churchill.

110. F. D. Roosevelt.

DESIGNS—HORIZ. 5 c., 14 c. Pres. Roosevelt bestowing distinguished service decorations. 8 c., 25 c. Pres. and Mrs. Roosevelt. 20 c. (2) Pres. Roosevelt and Secretary Hull. 50 c., 2 col. Pres. Roosevelt's funeral.

1948. Franklin D. Roosevelt. 3rd Death Anniv. Inscr. "12 DE ABRIL DE 1945 12 DE ABRIL DE 1948".
965. – 5 c. blk. & bl. (post.) 8 5
966. – 8 c. black and green .. 12 8
967. **110.** 12 c. black and violet 20 10
968. **109.** 15 c. black and red .. 20 12
969. – 20 c. black and lake .. 20 15
970. – 50 c. black and grey .. 50 30

971. **110.** 12 c. blk. & grn. (air) 30 15
972. – 14 c. black and olive .. 30 20
973. – 20 c. black and brown 30 25
974. – 25 c. black and red .. 30 25
975. **109.** 1 col. black and purple 1·40 90
976. – 2 col. black and lilac .. 2·25 1·25

1948. Air. Optd. **Aereo.**
977. 5 c. grey (No. 953) .. 10 5
978. 10 c. bistre (No. 955) .. 12 8
979. 1 col. red (No. 958) .. 70 50

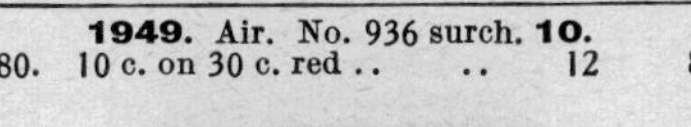

1949. Air. No. 936 surch. **10.**
980. 10 c. on 30 c. red 12 8

111. Torch and Wings.

1949. U.P.U. 75th Anniv.
981. **111.** 8 c. blue (postage) .. 40 15
982. 5 c. brown (air) .. 10 8
983. 10 c. black 15 5
984. 1 col. violet .. .. 7·00 6·50

112. Civilian and Soldier. **113.** Flag and Arms of Salvador.

1949. Revolution. 1st Anniv. (a) Postage.
985. **112.** 8 c. blue 15 10

(b) Air. Centres in blue and yellow.
986. **113.** 5 c. brown 10 5
987. 10 c. green 15 5
988. 15 c. violet 25 5
989. 1 col. red 60 45
990. 5 col. purple .. 4·50 4·00

ILLUSTRATIONS
British Commonwealth and all overprints and surcharges are FULL SIZE. Foreign Countries have been reduced to ¾-LINEAR.

114. Isabella the Catholic.

1951. Air. Isabella the Catholic. 500th Birth Anniv. Backgrounds in blue, red and yellow.
991. **114.** 10 c. green 30 8
992. 20 c. violet 30 15
993. 40 c. red 40 20
994. 1 col. brown .. 1·10 50

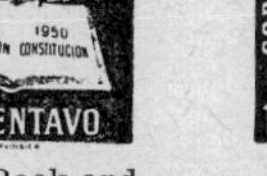

115. Book and Laurel Wreath. **116.** Flag and Scroll.

1952. 1948 Revolution and 1950 Constitution. (a) Postage. Wreath in green.
995. **115.** 1 c. emerald 5 5
996. 2 c. purple 5 5
997. 5 c. brown 5 5
998. 10 c. yellow 8 8
999. 20 c. green 15 12
1000. 1 col. red 80 50

(b) Air. Flag in blue.
1001. **116.** 10 c. blue 10 5
1002. 15 c. chocolate .. 15 8
1003. 20 c. blue 15 8
1004. 25 c. grey 20 10
1005. 40 c. violet 30 25
1006. 1 col. orange .. 60 45
1007. 2 col. brown .. 2·00 1·75
1008. 5 col. indigo .. 2·25 90

1952. Surch. in figures and words (No. 1009) or in figures only (remainder). (a) Postage.
1009. – 2 c. on 3 c. violet (952) 5 5
1010. – 2 c. on 8 c. blue (954) 5 5
1011. – 2 c. on 12 c. brn. (959) 10 5
1012. **107.** 2 c. on 14 c. blue .. 10 4
1013. – 3 c. on 8 c. blue (954) 10 5
1014. – 5 c. on 8 c. blue (954) 10 5
1015. – 5 c. on 12 c. brn. (959) 10 8
1016. – 7 c. on 8 c. blue (954) 10 8
1017. **107.** 10 c. on 14 c. blue .. 12 8
1018. – 10 c. on 50 c. blk. (957) 12 8

(b) Air.
1019. 20 c. on 25 c. pur. (935) 20 15

117. J. Marti. **118.** Signing Act of Independence.

119. Campanile of Our Saviour. **120.** General Barrios.

1953. Marti. Birth Cent.
1020. **117.** 1 c. red (postage) .. 5 5
1021. 2 c. green 8 5
1022. 10 c. blue 10 8

1023. 10 c. violet (air) .. 15 10
1024. 20 c. brown 25 15
1025. 1 col. orange 65 40

1953. 4th Pan-American Social Medicine Congress. Nos. 952 and 953 optd. "**IV Congreso Medico Social Panamericano 16/19 Abril, 1953**".
1026. 3 c. violet (postage) .. 12 5

1027. 25 c. purple (air) .. 25 20

1953. Independence.
1028. **118.** 1 c. red (postage) .. 5 5
1029. 2 c. blue-green .. 5 5
1030. 3 c. violet 5 5
1031. 5 c. blue 8 5
1032. 7 c. brown 8 8
1033. 10 c. ochre 12 10
1034. 20 c. orange 20 15
1035. 50 c. green 35 30
1036. 1 col. grey 70 60

1037. **119.** 5 c. red (air) .. 8 8
1038. 10 c. blue-green .. 8 8
1039. 20 c. blue 15 12
1040. 1 col violet 60 45

1953. Optd. **C de C.**
1041. **120.** 1 c. green 5 5
1042. 2 c. blue 5 5
1043. – 3 c. green 5 5
1044. **120.** 5 c. red 8 5
1045. – 7 c. blue 10 5
1046. – 10 c. red 12 8
1047. **120.** 20 c. violet 20 15
1048. – 22 c. violet 25 20
PORTRAIT: 3 c., 7 c., 10 c., 22 c. Gen. Morazan.

121. **122.**

123. General Barrios Square. **124.** Balboa Park.

1954.
1049. A. 1 c. red & olive (post) 8 5
1050. **123.** 1 c. violet 8 5
1051. B. 1 c. olive and green .. 8 5
1052. **121.** 2 c. vermilion .. 10 5
1053. **122.** 2 c. red 10 5
1054. **123.** 2 c. green and blue .. 10 5
1055. F. 3 c. slate and blue .. 10 5
1056. C. 3 c. green and blue .. 12 5
1057. I. 3 c. lake 10 5
1058. F. 5 c. violet and blue .. 10 5
1059. I. 5 c. green 10 5
1060. C. 7 c. chestnut and buff 12 5
1061. B. 7 c. green and blue .. 12 5
1062. **124.** 7 c. crimson and choc. 12 5
1063. G. 10 c. blue, brown & red 12 5
1064. **122.** 10 c. turquoise .. 12 5
1065. D. 10 c. lake and pink .. 12 5
1066. H. 20 c. orange and buff 20 10
1067. E. 22 c. blue 25 15
1068. J. 50 c. black and drab .. 50 25
1069. G. 1 col. blue, brown and chestnut 90 45
1070. E. 1 col. blue 90 45
1071. **121.** 5 c. red (air) 15 5
1072. B. 5 c. chestnut and buff 15 5
1073. G. 10 c. blue, green and emerald 20 5
1074. **123.** 10 c. olive and grey .. 20 5
1075. E. 10 c. red 20 5
1076. **124.** 10 c. violet & chocolate 20 5
1077. I. 10 c. blue 20 5
1078. D. 15 c. slate and blue .. 30 10
1079. A. 20 c. violet and slate 30 12
1080. E. 25 c. green and blue .. 30 15
1081. H. 30 c. crimson and pink 35 15
1082. J. 40 c. chestnut & brown 50 25
1083. **122.** 80 c. lake .. .. 1·10 80
1084. C. 1 col. crimson & pink 1·40 80
1085. **122.** 2 col. orange .. 2·75 1·00
DESIGNS—HORIZ. (32½ × 22½ mm.): A. Litoral Bridge. B. Fishing boats. C. Izalco Volcano and Atecosol Baths. D. Lake Ilopango and Apulo Baths. E. Coastguard cutter. (37½ × 22½ mm.): F. Guayabo Dam. G. Six Prime Ministers and flag of O.D.E.C.A. H. Workers' houses. VERT. (22½ × 32½ mm.): I. Gen. Arce. (21 × 25½ mm.): J. Sonsonate-Puerto Acajutla Highway.

125. Captain General Barrios. **126.** Gathering Coffee Beans.

1956.
1086. **125.** 1 c. red (postage) .. 5 5
1087. 2 c. green 8 5
1088. 3 c. blue 10 5
1089. 20 c. violet 15 10

1090. 20 c. brown (air) .. 20 12
1091. 30 c. lake 25 15

1956. Santa Ana. Cent.
1092. **126.** 3 c. brown (postage) .. 5 5
1093. 5 c. orange 8 5
1094. 10 c. blue 10 5
1095. 2 col. red .. .. 1·40 90

1096. 5 c. chestnut (air) .. 5 5
1097. 10 c. green 5 5
1098. 40 c. purple 25 15
1099. 80 c. green 55 45
1100. 5 col. slate .. .. 3·00 2·10

127. **128.** Arms of Nueva San Salvador.

1956. Chalatenango Centenary.
1101. **127.** 2 c. blue (postage) .. 10 5
1102. 7 c. red 25 15
1103. 50 c. brown 40 25

1104. 10 c. red (air) .. 8 5
1105. 15 c. orange 12 8
1106. 20 c. olive 12 8
1107. 25 c. lilac 30 15
1108. 50 c. chestnut .. 40 25
1109. 1 col. blue 75 60

1957. Nueva San Salvador Centenary.
1110. **128.** 1 c. red (postage) .. 5 5
1111. 2 c. green 5 5
1112. 3 c. violet 5 5
1113. 7 c. orange 25 20
1114. 10 c. blue 10 8
1115. 50 c. brown 30 25
1116. 1 col. red 55 50

1117. 10 c. salmon (air) .. 10 5
1118. 20 c. red 15 8
1119. 50 c. red 35 25
1120. 1 col. green 60 45
1121. 2 col. red .. .. 1·50 90

1957. Surch.
1121a. **128.** 1 c. on 2 c. green .. 8 8
1121b. 5 c. on 7 c. orange .. 10 8
1122. C. 6 c. on 7 c. chestnut & buff (No. 1060) .. 20 12
1123. B. 6 c. on 7 c. green and blue (No. 1061) .. 20 12
1124. **127.** 6 c. on 7 c. red .. 12 8
1125. **128.** 6 c. on 7 c. orange .. 12 10

129. Salvador Hotel.

1958. Salvador Hotel Commem. Centre mult., frame colour below.
1126. 129. 3 c. brown 5 5
1127. 6 c. red 5 5
1128. 10 c. blue 8 5
1129. 15 c. green 10 8
1130. 20 c. violet 12 8
1131. 30 c. apple-green .. 15 12

130. Presidents Eisenhower and Lemus.

1959. Visit of Pres. Lemus to U.S. Flags in red and blue. Portraits in brown.
1132. 130. 3 c. pink & blue (post.) 8 5
1133. 6 c. green and blue .. 10 5
1134. 10 c. red and blue .. 12 8
1135. 15 c. orge. & blue (air) 15 10
1136. 20 c. green and blue.. 20 12
1137. 30 c. red and blue .. 25 20

1960. Salvador Philatelic Society. 20th Anniv. Optd. **5 Enero 1960 XX Aniversario Fundacion Sociedad Filatelica de El Salvador.**
1138. 128. 2 c. green 8 5

1960. Air. World Refugee Year. Optd. **ANO MUNDIAL DE LOS REFUGIADOS 1959-1960.**
1139. 126. 10 c. green 20 15

131. Block of Flats. **132.** Poinsettias.

1960. "I.V.U." Building Project. Centres multicoloured.
1140. 131. 10 c. red 8 5
1141. 15 c. purple 12 8
1142. 25 c. green 15 10
1143. 30 c. turquoise .. 20 12
1144. 40 c. olive 25 20
1145. 80 c. indigo .. 50 40

1960. Christmas Issue. Flowers in yellow, red and green. Background colours given.
1146. 132. 3 c. yellow (postage) 8 5
1147. 6 c. orange .. 10 5
1148. 10 c. blue 15 5
1149. 15 c. violet-blue .. 20 8
1150. 20 c. mauve (air) .. 25 12
1151. 30 c. blue-grey .. 30 20
1152. 40 c. grey 50 30
1153. 50 c. salmon .. 70 35

133. Fathers Nicolas, Vincent and Manuel Aguilar.

1961. Patriots' Revolution against Spaniards. 150th Anniv. Inscr. as in T **133.**
1154. 133. 1 c. sepia and grey .. 5 5
1155. 2 c. brown and pink.. 5 5
1156. – 5 c. bronze-grn. & brn. 5 5
1157. – 6 c. sepia and magenta 5 5
1158. – 10 c. sepia and blue.. 8 5
1159. – 20 c. sepia and violet 12 10
1160. – 30 c. mauve and blue 15 12
1161. – 40 c. sepia & chestnut 20 15
1162. – 50 c. sepia & turquoise 30 20
1163. – 80 c. blue and grey.. 40 35
DESIGNS: 5 c., 6 c. Manuel Arce, Jose Delgado and Juan Rodriguez. 10 c., 20 c. Pedro Castillo, Domingo de Lara and Santiago Celis. 30 c., 40 c. Parochial Church of San Salvador, 1808. 50 c., 80 c. Monument, Plaza Libertad.

1962. Nos. 1161/2, 1141 and 1070 surch.
1169. – 6 c. on 40 c. sepia and chestnut .. 10 5
1170. – 6 c. on 50 c. sepia and turquoise .. 12 5
1164. 131. 10 c. on 15 c. purple.. 8 5
1171. E. 10 c. on 1 col. blue .. 12 5

1962. 3rd Central American Industrial Exn. Nos. 1048, 1069, 1116 and 1121 optd. "**III Exposicion Industrial Centroamericana Diciembre de 1962**". Nos. 1166/7 additionally optd. **AEREO.**
1165. – 22 c. violet (postage) 15 10
1166. G. 1 col. blue, brown and chestnut (air) .. 45 35
1167. 128. 1 col. red 45 35
1168. 2 col. red 90 70

1963. Surch. in figures.
1172. 131. 6 c. on 15 c. pur. (post.) 12 5
1173. – 10 c. on 50 c. sepia and turquoise (No. 1162) 12 5
1174. – 10 c. on 80 c. blue and grey (No. 1163) (air) 12 5
1175. 128. 10 c. on 1 col. green.. 80 10
1176. 132. 10 c. on 30 c. blue-grey 12 10
1177. 128. 10 c. on 1 col. red (No. 1167).. .. 12 10
1178. 128. 10 c. on 2 col. red (No. 1168).. .. 80 10

1963. Freedom from Hunger. No. 1161 optd. **CAMPANA MUNDIAL CONTRA EL HAMBRE** and Campaign emblem.
1179. 40 c. sepia and chestnut 25 20

134. Coyote. **135.** Statue of Christ on Globe.

1963. Fauna. Multicoloured.
1180. 1 c. Type **134** (postage) .. 5 5
1181. 2 c. Monkey 5 5
1182. 3 c. Raccoon 5 5
1183. 5 c. King vulture.. 5 5
1184. 6 c. Coati 5 5
1185. 10 c. Kinkajou .. 8 5
1186. 5 c. As No. 1183 (air: birds) 5 5
1187. 6 c. Yellow-headed amazon 5 5
1188. 10 c. Spot-breasted oriole.. 10 5
1189. 20 c. Turquoise-browed motmot 15 10
1190. 30 c. Boat-tailed grackle.. 25 15
1191. 40 c. "Craxglobicera" .. 35 20
1192. 50 c. "Calocitta formosa pompata" 45 25
1193. 80 c. Golden-fronted woodpecker 75 45
The 2 c. and 5 c. postage and 5 c., 6 c., 40 c. and 80 c. air stamps are vert.

1964. 2nd National Eucharistic Congress, San Salvador.
1194. 135. 6 c. bl. & brn. (post.) 5 5
1195. 10 c. blue and bistre.. 8 5
1196. 10 c. slate-bl. & bl. (air) 8 5
1197. 25 c. blue and red .. 15 10

136. President Kennedy. **137.** Water-lily.

1964. Pres. Kennedy Commem.
1198. 136. 6 c. black & stone (post.) 5 5
1199. 10 c. black and drab.. 10 5
1200. 50 c. black and pink 35 20
1201. 15 c. black & grey (air) 12 8
1202. 20 c. black and green 20 12
1203. 40 c. black and yellow 30 20

1965. Flora. Multicoloured.
1204. 3 c. Type **137** (postage) .. 5 5
1205. 5 c. "Maquilishuat" .. 5 5
1206. 6 c. "Cinco Negritos" .. 5 5
1207. 30 c. Hydrangea .. 25 15
1208. 50 c. "Maguey" .. 40 20
1209. 60 c. Geranium .. 50 25
1210. 10 c. Rose (air) .. 8 5
1211. 15 c. "Platanillo" .. 10 8
1212. 25 c. "San Jose" .. 20 12
1213. 40 c. Hibiscus .. 30 20
1214. 45 c. Bougainvillea .. 35 25
1215. 70 c. "Flor de Fuego" .. 45 35

138. I.C.Y. Emblem. **139.** F. A. Gavidia (philosopher).

1965. Int. Co-operation Year. Laurel in gold.
1216. 138. 5 c. brn. & yell. (post.) 5 5
1217. 6 c. brown and rose 5 5
1218. 10 c. brown and grey 8 5
1219. 138. 15 c. brown & blue (air) 12 8
1220. 30 c. brown and violet 20 12
1221. 50 c. brown and orange 30 20

1965. Captain General Barrios. Death Cent. No. 1163 optd. **1 er. Centenario Muerte Cap. Gral. Gerardo Barrios 1865 29 de Agosto 1965.**
1222. 80 c. blue and grey .. 55 30

1965. Gavidia Commem.
1223. 139. 2 c. multicoloured (post.) 5 5
1224. 3 c. multicoloured .. 8 5
1225. 6 c. multicoloured .. 8 5
1226. 10 c. multicoloured (air) 8 5
1227. 20 c. multicoloured.. 12 8
1228. 1 col. multicoloured.. 60 30

1965. Dr. M. E. Araujo. Birth Cent. Optd. **1865 12 de Octubre 1965 Dr. Manuel Enrique Araujo.** Laurel in gold.
1229. 138. 10 c. brn. & grey (post.) 8 5
1230. 50 c. brown & orge. (air) 35 20

140. Fair Emblem. **141.** W.H.O. Building.

1965. Int. Fair, Salvador.
1231. 140. 6 c. mult. (postage).. 5 5
1232. 10 c. multicoloured.. 10 5
1233. 20 c. multicoloured.. 15 10
1234. 20 c. multicoloured (air) 12 8
1235. 80 c. multicoloured.. 50 35
1236. 5 col. multicoloured.. 2·40 2·00

1966. W.H.O. Headquarters, Geneva. Inaug.
1237. 141. 15 c. mult. (postage) 12 8
1238. 50 c. multicoloured (air) 35 20

1966. Air. St. Juan Bosco. 150th Birth Anniv. No. 1197 optd. **1816 1966 150 anos Nacimiento San Juan Bosco.**
1239. 135. 25 c. blue and red .. 20 15

1966. Civic Commem. of Independence Month No. 1163 optd. **Mes de Conmemoracion Civica de la Independencia. Centroamericana 15 Sept. 1821 1966.**
1240. 80 c. ultramarine and grey 50 35

142. U.N.E.S.C.O. Emblem.

1966. U.N.S.C.O.. 20th Anniv.
1241. 142. 20 c. blue, grey and black (postage) .. 12 10
1242. 1 col. blue, green and black 65 40
1243. 142. 30 c. blue, brown and black (air).. .. 25 12
1244. 2 col. blue, green and black .. .. 1·25 80

143. Map, Cogwheels and Flags.

1966. 2nd Int. Fair, El Salvador.
1245. 143. 6 c. mult. (postage).. 8 5
1246. 10 c. multicoloured.. 8 5
1247. 15 c. multicoloured (air) 12 8
1248. 20 c. multicoloured.. 15 10
1249. 60 c. multicoloured.. 40 25

1967. Air. 9th Int. Catholic Education Congress No. 1197 optd. **IX-Congreso Interamericano de Educacion Catolica 4 Enero 1967.**
1250. 135. 25 c. blue and red .. 25 15

144. Father Canas pleading for Slaves.

1967. Father J. S. Canas y Villacorta (slavery emancipator). Birth Cent.
1251. 144. 6 c. mult. (postage).. 8 5
1252. 10 c. multicoloured.. 8 5
1253. 144. 5 c. mult. (air) .. 5 5
1254. 45 c. multicoloured.. 35 25

1967. 15th Lions Convention El Salvador. No. 1161 optd. "**XV Convencion de Clubes de Leones etc.**".
1255. 40 c. sepia and chestnut 30 15

145. Central Design of First El Salvador Stamp.

1967. Stamp Cent.
1256. 145. 70 c. brn. & mve. (post.) 50 30
1257. 145. 50 c. brn. & ol.-brn. (air) 40 25

1967. 8th Central-American Pharmaceutical and Biochemical Congress. Nos. 1237/8 optd. **VIII CONGRESO CENTROAMERICANO,** etc.
1258. 141. 15 c. mult. (postage) 12 8
1259. 141. 50 c. mult. (air) .. 30 20

1967. 1st Central American and Caribbean Basket-ball Games, San Salvador. Nos. 1204 and 1212 optd. **1 Juegos Centroamericanoes,** etc.
1260. 137. 3 c. mult. (postage).. 8 5
1261. – 25 c. mult. (air) .. 15 12

1968. Human Rights Year. Nos. 1216, 1220 optd. **1968 ANO INTERNACIONAL DE LOS DERECHOS HUMANOS.**
1262. 138. 5 c. mult. (postage).. 8 5
1263. 30 c. mult. (air) .. 25 15

146. Weather Map, Satellite and W.M.O. Emblem.

1968. World Meteorological Day.
1264. 146. 1 c. multicoloured .. 5 5
1265. 30 c. multicoloured.. 20 12

1968. W.H.O. 20th Anniv. Nos. 1237/8 optd. **1968 XX ANIVERSARIO DE LA ORGANIZACION MUNDIAL DE LA SALUD.**
1266. 141. 15 c. mult. (postage) 15 8
1267. 50 c. mult. (air) .. 40 20

1968. Rural Credit Year. Nos. 1231, 1235 optd. **1968 Ano del Sistema de Credito Rural.**
1268. 140. 6 c. mult. (postage).. 8 5
1269. 80 c. mult. (air) .. 50 30

147. A. Masferrer (philosopher). **148.** Building Construction ("Service to the Community").

1968. Alberto Masferrer. Birth Cent.
1270. 147. 2 c. mult. (postage).. 5 5
1271. 6 c. multicoloured .. 5 5
1272. 25 c. multicoloured.. 20 12
1273. 5 c. multicoloured (air) 5 5
1274. 15 c. multicoloured.. 12 8

1968. 7th Inter-American Scout Conf., San Salvador.
1275. 148. 25 c. mult. (postage) 15 10
1276. – 10 c. multicoloured (air) 8 5
DESIGN—HORIZ. 10 c. Scouts and Conference emblem.

149. Map, Presidents and Flags.

1968. Meeting of President Lyndon B. Johnson (U.S.A.) with Central American Presidents, San Salvador.
1277. **149.** 10 c. mult. (postage) 8 5
1278. 15 c. multicoloured.. 10 5
1279. 20. multicoloured (air) 10 8
1280. 1 cor. multicoloured.. 55 40

150. "Heliconius charithonius".

1969. Butterflies. Multicoloured.
1281. 5 c. Type **150** (postage).. 5 5
1282. 10 c. "Diaethria astala" 8 5
1283. 30 c. "Heliconius hortense" 20 12
1284. 50 c. "Pyrrhogyra arge".. 30 15
1285. 20 c. "Ageronia amphinome" (air) 12 5
1286. 1 col. "Smyrna karkwinskii" 55 35
1287. 2 col. "Papilio photinus" 1·40 65
1288. 10 col. "Papilio consus".. 6·00 3·50

151. Red Cross Activities.

1969. League of Red Cross Societies. 50th Anniv. Multicoloured.
1289. 10 c. Type **151** (postage) 5 5
1290. 20 c. Type **151** 10 8
1291. 40 c. Type **151** 20 12
1292. 30 c. Red Cross emblems (air) 15 10
1293. 1 col. As No. 1292 .. 60 35
1294. 4 col. As No. 1292 .. 2·50 1·50
Nos. 1292/4 are smaller size 34×25 mm.

1969. 1st Man on the Moon. Nos. 1200 and 1203 (Kennedy) optd. **"Alunzaje Apolo-11 21 Julio 1969".**
1295. **136.** 50 c. black & pink (post.) 30 25
1297. 40 c. blk. & yellow (air) 25 20

152. Social Security Hospital.

153. I.L.O. Emblem.

1969. Salvador Hospitals. Multicoloured.
1299. 6 c. Type **152** (postage).. 5 5
1300. 10 c. Type **152** 8 5
1301. 30 c. Type **152** 20 12
1302. 1 col. Benjamin Bloom Children's Hospital, San Salvador (air) 70 50
1303. 2 col. As No. 1302 .. 1·25 1·10
1304. 5 col. As No. 1302 .. 3·25 2·25

1969. Int. Labour Organization. 50th Anniv.
1305. **153.** 10 c. mult. (postage) 8 5
1306. 50 c. multicoloured (air) 30 25

154. Los Chorros Baths.

1969. Tourism. Multicoloured.
1307. 10 c. Type **154** (postage) 5 5
1308. 40 c. Jaltepeque estuary 25 20
1309. 80 c. Amapulapa Fountains 55 40
1310. 20 c. Devil's Gate (air) .. 15 8
1311. 35 c. Gardens, Ichanmichen 20 15
1312. 60 c. Port of Acajutla .. 40 25

155. "Euchroma gigantea" (beetle).

1970. Insects. Multicoloured.
1313. 5 c. Type **155** (postage).. 5 5
1314. 25 c. Grasshopper .. 15 12
1315. 30 c. Wasp 20 12
1316. 2 col. Bee (air) .. .. 1·25 1·00
1317. 3 col. "Elaterida" (beetle) 2·00 1·40
1318. 4 col. Praying mantis .. 2·75 2·00

156. Map, Emblem and Arms.

1970. "Human Rights".
1319. **156.** 10 c. mult. (postage) 5 5
1320. 40 c. multicoloured.. 25 20
1321. – 20 c. multicoloured (air) 10 8
1322. – 80 c. multicoloured.. 65 40
DESIGNS—VERT. Nos. 1321/2, Similar to, T **156.**

157. Infantry with National Flag.

1970. Army Day. Multicoloured.
1323. 10 c. Type **157** (postage) 5 5
1324. 30 c. Anti-aircraft gun position 20 10
1325. 20 c. Fighter aircraft (air) 10 8
1326. 40 c. Artillery gun and crew 30 20
1327. 50 c. Coastguard patrol-boat 35 25

158. Brazilian Team.

1970. Air. World Cup Football Championships, Mexico. National Teams. Mult.
1328. 1 col. Belgium 70 50
1329. 1 col. Type **158** 70 50
1330. 1 col. Bulgaria 70 50
1331. 1 col. Czechoslovakia .. 70 50
1332. 1 col. El Salvador .. 70 50
1333. 1 col. England 70 50
1334. 1 col. West Germany .. 70 50
1335. 1 col. Israel 70 50
1336. 1 col. Italy 70 50
1337. 1 col. Mexico 70 50
1338. 1 col. Morocco 70 50
1339. 1 col. Peru 70 50
1340. 1 col. Rumania 70 50
1341. 1 col. Russia 70 50
1342. 1 col. Sweden 70 50
1343. 1 col. Uruguay 70 50

159. Lottery Building.

160. Education Year and U.N. Emblems.

1970. National Lottery. Cent.
1344. **159.** 20 c. multicoloured (postage) 12 8
1345. 80 c. multicoloured (air) 55 30

1970. Int. Education Year.
1346. **160.** 50 c. multicoloured (postage) 30 20
1347. 1 col. multicoloured.. 65 50
1348. 20 c. multicoloured (air) 12 10
1349. 2 col. multicoloured.. 1·60 75

161. Globe and Fair Symbols.

1970. Fourth International Fair, El Salvador.
1350. **161.** 5 c. multicoloured (postage) 5 5
1351. 10 c. multicoloured .. 10 5
1352. 20 c. multicoloured (air) 15 8
1353. 30 c. multicoloured.. 25 12

1970. National Library. Cent. Nos. 1272/3 optd. **Ano del Centenario de la Biblioteca Nacional 1970.**
1354. **147.** 25 c. mult. (postage) 15 12
1355. 5 c. mult. (air) .. 5 5

162. Beethoven and Music.

1971. 2nd Int. Music Festival. San Salvador.
1356. **162.** 50 c. brn., yell & green (postage) .. 25 20
1357. – 40 c. multicoloured (air) 25 20
DESIGN: 40 c. Bach, manuscript and harp.

163. Maria Elena Sol.

164. Michelangelo's "Pieta".

1971. Maria Elena Sol's Election as "World Tourism Queen", Punta del Este, Uruguay.
1358. **163.** 10 c. mult. (postage) 5 5
1359. 30 c. multicoloured.. 20 12
1360. **163.** 20 c. mult. (air) .. 12 10
1361. 60 c. multicoloured.. 45 30

1971. Mothers' Day.
1362. **164.** 10 c. purple and pink (postage) 5 5
1363. **164.** 40 c. pur. & grn (air) 25 20

1971. Nat. Police Force. 104th Anniv. Nos. 1320/1 optd. **1867, C. I. V. Aniversario Fundacion de La Policia Nacional 6-Julio, 1971.**
1364. **156.** 40 c. mult. (postage) 25 20
1365. – 20 c. mult. (air) .. 20 15

165. Tiger Shark.

1971. Fishes. Multicoloured.
1366. 10 c. Type **165** (postage) 5 5
1367. 40 c. Swordfish 15 10
1368. 30 c. Sawfish (air) .. 15 10
1369. 1 col. Sailfish 65 45

166. Izalco Church.

1971. Churches. Multicoloured.
1370. 20 c. Type **166** (postage) 20 12
1371. 30 c. Sonsonate Church .. 30 15
1372. 15 c. Metapan Church (air) 12 8
1373. 70 c. Panchimalco Church 60 35

1971. Air. El Salvador Navy. 20th Anniv. No. 1327 optd. **1951-12 Octubre-1971 XX Aniversario MARINA NACIONAL.**
1374. 50 c. multicoloured .. 40 25

167. Declaration of Independence.

1971. Central American Independence. 150th Anniversary.
1375. **167.** 5 c. blk. & grn. (post.) 5 5
1376. – 10 c. black and pur. 8 5
1377. – 15 c. black and red.. 10 5
1378. – 20 c. black & mauve 12 10
1379. – 30 c. blk. & blue (air) 20 15
1380. – 40 c. black & brown.. 30 20
1381. – 50 c. black & yellow.. 40 25
1382. – 60 c. black and grey.. 45 30
DESIGNS: Nos. 1376/82 as Type **167**, but showing different manuscripts.

1972. Air. Fifth Int. Fair, El Salvador. No. 1235 optd. **V Feria Internacional 3-20 Noviembre de 1972.**
1384. **140.** 80 c. multicoloured.. 70 40

1972. American Tourist Year. No. 1359 optd. **1972. Ano del Tourismo de las Americas.**
1385. **163.** 30 c. multicoloured. 20 15

1972. Air. Inter-American Agricultural Science Institute. 30th Anniv. No. 1221 optd. **1972 - XXX Anniversario Creacion Instituto Interamericano de Ciencias Agricolas.**
1386. **138.** 50 c. multicoloured 40 25

1973. 3rd Int. Music Festival. Nos. 1356/7 optd. **III Festival Internacional de Musica 9 - 25 Febrero - 1973.**
1387. **162.** 50 c. brn., yell. & grn. (postage) 25 20
1388. – 40 c. multicoloured (air) 25 15

168. Lions Emblem.

170. Institute Emblem.

169. Hurdling.

1973. Lions Int. District. 31st Convention.
1389. **168.** 10 c. mult. (post.) .. 5 5
1390. 25 c. multicoloured .. 12 10
1391. – 20 c. mult. (air) .. 12 8
1392. – 40 c. multicoloured.. 20 15
DESIGN: 20 c., 40 c., Map of Central America.

1973. El Salvador Air Force. 50th Anniv. No. 1324 optd. **1923 1973 50 ANOS FUNDACION AEREA.**
1393. 30 c. multicoloured .. 15 12

1973. Olympic Games, Munich (1972). Multicoloured.
1394. 5 c. Type **169** (postage).. 5 5
1395. 10 c. High-jumping .. 5 5
1396. 25 c. Running 12 8
1397. 60 c. Pole-vaulting .. 30 25
1398. 20 c. Throwing the javelin (air) 12 10
1399. 80 c. Throwing the discus 55 25
1400. 1 col. Throwing the hammer 75 50
1401. 2 col. Putting the shot 1·50 90

1973. Nos. 1256/7 surch.
1402. **145.** 10 c. on 70 c. brown and mauve (post.) 5 5
1403. **145.** 25 c. on 50 c. brown and olive-brn. (air) 12 8

1973. Slaves' Liberation in Central America. 150th Anniv. Nos. 1251 and 1254 surch. **1823—1973 150 Aniversario Liberacion Esclavos en Centroamerica** and value.
1404. **144.** 5 c. on 6 c. multicoloured 5 5
1405. 10 c. on 45 c. multicoloured 5 5
No. 1405 has the word "AEREO" obliterated.

1974. Nos. 1198 and 1238 surch.
1407. **136.** 5 c. on 6 c. black and stone (postage) .. 5 5
1408. **141.** 25 c. on 50 c. multi-coloured (air) .. 12 8

1974. Institute for the Rehabilitation of Invalids. 10th Anniv.
1409. **170.** 10 c. multicoloured (post.) 5 5
1410. **170.** 25 c. multicoloured (air) 12 8

1974. Air. No. 1235 surch.
1411. **140.** 10 c. on 80 c. multicoloured 5 5

1974. Air. West Germany's Victory in World Cup Football Championships. Nos. 1328/43 optd. **ALEMANIA 1974.**
1412. 1 col. Belgium 50 40
1413. 1 col. Type **158** 50 40
1414. 1 col. Bulgaria 50 40
1415. 1 col. Czechoslovakia 50 40
1416. 1 col. El Salvador 50 40
1417. 1 col. England 50 40
1418. 1 col. West Germany 50 40
1419. 1 col. Israel 50 40
1420. 1 col. Italy 50 40
1421. 1 col. Mexico 50 40
1422. 1 col. Morocco 50 40
1423. 1 col. Peru 50 40
1424. 1 col. Rumania 50 40
1425. 1 col. Russia 50 40
1426. 1 col. Sweden 50 40
1427. 1 col. Uruguay 50 40

1974. No. 1271 surch.
1428. **147.** 5 c. on 6 c. multicoloured 5 5

171. Interpol H.Q., Paris. **172.** F.A.O. and W.F.P. Emblems.

1974. Int. Criminal Police Organization (Interpol). 50th Anniv.
1429. **171.** 10 c. multicoloured (post.) 5 5
1430. **171.** 25 c. multicoloured (air) 12 8

1974. World Food Programme. Tenth Anniv.
1431. **172.** 10 c. gold, turquoise & blue (postage) 5 5
1432. **172.** 25 c. gold, turquoise & blue (air) 12 8

1974. Surch.
1432a. **142.** 25 c. on 1 col. blue, grn. & blk. (postage) 12 8
1433. **145.** 10 c. on 50 c. brown & olive-brown (air) 5 5
1434. **142.** 25 c. on 2 col. blue, green and black 12 8

1974. 12th Central American and Caribbean Chess Tournament. Surch. **XII Serie Ajedrez de Centro America y del Caribe Oct. 1974.**
1435. **139.** 5 c. on 6 c. mult. 5 5

1974. Surch.
1436. **152.** 5 c. on 6 c. multicoloured (postage) 5 5
1437. **139.** 10 c. on 3 c. mult. 5 5
1438. – 10 c. on 45 c. multicoloured (No. 1214) (air) 5 5
1439. – 10 c. on 70 c. multicoloured (No. 1215) 5 5
1440. – 25 c. on 2 col. multicoloured (No. 1287) 12 10
1441. – 25 c. on 1 col. multicoloured (No. 1293) 12 10
1442. – 25 c. on 4 col. multicoloured (No. 1294) 12 10
1443. – 25 c. on 5 col. multicoloured (No. 1304) 12 10

173. 25-cent Silver Coin, 1914.

1974. El Salvador Coins. Multicoloured.
1445. 10 c. Type **173** (postage) 5 5
1446. 15 c. 50-cent silver coin, 1953 8 5
1447. 25 c. 25-cent silver coin, 1943 10 8
1448. 30 c. 1-centavo copper coin, 1892 12 10
1449. 20 c. 1-peso silver coin, 1892 (air) 8 5
1450. 40 c. 20-cent silver coin, 1828 15 8
1451. 50 c. 20-peso gold coin, 1892 20 15
1452. 60 c. 20-col gold coin, 1925 25 20

174. U.P.U. Emblem.

1975. Universal Postal Union. Centenary.
1453. **174.** 10 c. mult. (postage) 5 5
1454. 60 c. multicoloured 25 20
1455. **174.** 25 c. mult. (air) 10 8
1456. 30 c. multicoloured 12 10

175. Harbour, Acajutla. **176.** Central Post Office, San Salvador.

1975. Opening of Acajutla Port.
1457. **175.** 10 c. mult. (post.) 5 5
1458. **175.** 15 c. mult. (air) 8 5

1975.
1459. **176.** 10 c. mult. (postage) 5 5
1460. **176.** 25 c. mult. (air) 12 10

177. Map of Salvador and the Americas.

1975. "Miss Universe" Contest.
1461. **177.** 10 c. mult. (postage) 5 5
1462. 40 c. multicoloured 20 15
1463. **177.** 25 c. mult. (air) 12 10
1464. 60 c. multicoloured 30 25

178. Claudia Lars (poet). **179.** Nurse tending Patient.

1975. International Women's Year.
1465. **178.** 10 c. blue & yellow (post.) 5 5
1466. **178.** 15 c. blue & light blue (air) 8 5
1467. – 25 c. blue & green 15 10
DESIGN: 25 c. I.W.Y. emblem.

1975. Honouring Nursing Profession.
1468. **179.** 10 c. mult. (postage) 5 5
1469. **179.** 25 c. mult. (air) 15 10

180. Conference Emblem. **181.** Congress Emblem and Flags.

1975. 15th Conference of Inter-American Security Printers Federation, San Salvador.
1470. **180.** 10 c. mult. (postage) 5 5
1471. **180.** 30 c. mult. (air) 10 5

1975. 16th Central American Medical Congress, San Salvador. Optd. **XVI CONGRESO MEDICO CENTRO-AMERICANO SAN SALVADOR, EL SALVADOR DIC. 10–13, 1975.**
1472. **141.** 15 c. multicoloured 5 5

1975. 8th Ibero-Latin-American Dermatological Congress, El Salvador.
1473. **181.** 15 c. mult. (postage) 5 5
1474. 50 c. multicoloured 20 12
1475. **181.** 20 c. mult. (air) 10 5
1476. 30 c. multicoloured 10 5

182. Congress Emblem. **183.** U.N.I.C.E.F. Emblem.

1975. 7th Latin-American Charity Congress, San Salvador.
1477. **182.** 10 c. brn. & red (post.) 5 5
1478. **182.** 20 c. light bl. & bl. (air) 10 5

1975. Air. U.N.I.C.E.F. 25th Anniv. (1971).
1479. **183.** 15 c. silver & green 5 5
1480. 20 c silver and red 10 5

1976. Air. Nos. 1316/18 surch.
1481. 25 c. on 2 col. mult. 10 5
1482. 25 c. on 3 col. mult. 10 5
1483. 25 c. on 4 col. mult. 10 5

184. "Caularthron bilamellatum". **185.** Map of El Salvador.

1976. Air. Orchids. Multicoloured.
1484. 20 c. Type **184** 15 12
1485. 25 c. "Oncidium oliganthum" 15 12
1486. 25 c. "Epidendrum radicans" 15 12
1487. 25 c. "Cyrtopodium punctatum" 15 12
1488. 25 c. "Epidendrum vitellinum" 15 12
1489. 25 c. "Pleurothallis schiedei" 15 12
1490. 25 c. "Lycaste cruenta" 15 12
1491. 25 c. "Spireanthes speciosa" 15 12

1976. "Cencamex '76" 3rd Nurses' Congress. **III CONGRESO ENFERMERIA CENCAMEX '76.**
1493. **179.** 10 c. multicoloured 5 5

1976. Central Inter-American Tax-collectors Association. 10th Anniv.
1494. **185.** 10 c. multicoloured (postage) 5 5
1495. **185.** 50 c. multicoloured (air) 30 25

186. Torch and Flags of El Salvador and U.S.A.

1976. American Revolution. Bicent. Mult.
1496. 10 c. Type **186** (postage) 5 5
1497. 40 c. "Spirit of '76" (A. M. Willard) (vert.) 20 15
1498. 25 c. Type **186** (air) 15 12
1499. 5 col. As 40 c. 3·00 2·50

187. "Crocodylus Acutus".

1976. Reptiles. Multicoloured.
1499. 10 c. Type **185** (postage) 5 5
1500. 20 c. "Iguana rhinolopha" 10 8
1501. 30 c. "Ctenosaura similis" 15 12
1502. 15 c. "Sceloporus malachiticus" (air) 8 5
1503. 25 c. "Basiliscus villatus" 15 12
1504. 60 c. "Anolis sp." 30 25

ACKNOWLEDGMENT OF RECEIPT STAMP

ILLUSTRATIONS
British Commonwealth and all overprints and surcharges are FULL SIZE. Foreign Countries have been reduced to ¾-LINEAR.

A 1.

1897.
AR 264. A 1. 5 c. green 5

OFFICIAL STAMPS

1896. Stamps of 1896 (first issue) optd. **FRANQUEO OFICIAL** in oval.
O 170. **19.** 1 c. blue 5
O 171. 2 c. brown 5
O 172. 3 c. green 30
O 173. 5 c. olive 5
O 174. 10 c. yellow 5
O 175. 12 c. blue 10
O 176. 15 c. violet 5
O 177. 20 c. claret 30
O 178. 24 c. red 5
O 179. 30 c. orange 30
O 180. 50 c. black 20
O 181. 1 p. red 12

1896. Stamps of 1896 (second issue) optd **FRANQUEO OFICIAL** in oval.
O 182. **20.** 1 c. green 5
O 183. **21.** 2 c. lake 5
O 184. 3 c. orange 5
O 185. 5 c. blue 12
O 186. 10 c. brown 5
O 187. 12 c. grey 15
O 188. 15 c. green 15
O 189. 20 c. rose 15
O 190. 24 c. violet 15
O 191. 30 c. green 10
O 192. 50 c. orange 15
O 193. 100 c. blue 20

1896. Stamps of 1895 (first issue) optd. **CORREOS DE EL SALVADOR DE OFICIO** in circle and band.
O 194. **19.** 1 c. blue 6·00
O 195. 2 c. brown 6·00
O 196. 3 c. green 6·00
O 197. 5 c. olive 6·00
O 198. 10 c. yellow 7·50
O 199. 12 c. blue 8·50
O 200. 15 c. violet 8·50
O 201. 20 c. claret 8·50
O 202. 24 c. red 8·50
O 203. 30 c. orange 8·50
O 204. 50 c. black 11·00
O 205. 1 p. red 11·00

1896. Stamps of 1896 (second issue) optd. **CORREOS DE EL SALVADOR DE OFICIO** in circle and band.
O 206. **20.** 1 c. green 6·00
O 207. **21.** 2 c. lake 6·00
O 208. 3 c. orange 6·00
O 209. 5 c. blue 6·00
O 210. 10 c. brown 6·00
O 211. 12 c. grey 8·00
O 212. 15 c. green 9·00
O 219. 15 c. on 24 c. violet (No. 218) 9·00
O 213. 20 c. red 9·00
O 214. 24 c. violet 9·00
O 215. 30 c. green 9·00
O 216. 50 c. orange 9·00
O 217. 100 c. blue 9·00

1897. Stamps of 1897 optd. **FRANQUEO OFICIAL** in oval.
O 232. 1 c. red 5 5
O 233. 2 c. green 30 1·10
O 234. 3 c. brown 10 35
O 235. 5 c. orange 10 12
O 236. 10 c. green 12 40
O 237. 12 c. blue 15
O 238. 15 c. black 20 25
O 239. 20 c. grey 8
O 240. 24 c. yellow 12 20
O 241. 30 c. red 12 35
O 242. 50 c. violet 55 1·10
O 243. 100 c. lake 45 1·00

1897. Stamps of 1897 optd. **CORREOS DE EL SALVADOR DE OFICIO** in circle and band.
O 244. 1 c. red 6·00 6·00
O 245. 2 c. green 6·00 6·00
O 246. 3 c. brown 6·00 6·00
O 247. 5 c. orange 6·00 6·00
O 248. 10 c. green 6·00 6·00
O 249. 12 c. blue 8·00
O 250. 15 c. black 8·00
O 251. 20 c. grey 8·00
O 252. 24 c. yellow 9·00
O 253. 30 c. red 12·00
O 254. 50 c. violet 13·00
O 255. 100 c. lake 14·00

1898. Stamps of 1898 optd. **FRANQUEO OFICIAL** in oval.
O 288. **33.** 1 c. red 5
O 289. 2 c. rose 8
O 290. 3 c. green 1·50
O 291. 5 c. green 8
O 292. 10 c. blue 5
O 293. 12 c. violet 1·50
O 294. 13 c. lake 8
O 295. 20 c. blue 8
O 296. 24 c. blue 5
O 297. 26 c. brown 8
O 298. 50 c. orange 8
O 299. 1 p. yellow 8

1899. Stamps of 1899, with wheel opt. T **35** optd. **FRANQUEO OFICIAL** in fancy letters.
O 329. **34.** 1 c. brown 25 25
O 330. 2 c. green 40 40
O 331. 3 c. blue 25 25
O 332. 5 c. orange 25 25
O 333. 10 c. brown 30 30
O 334. 12 c. green
O 335. 13 c. red 65 65
O 336. 24 c. blue 10·00 10·00
O 337. 26 c. rose 30 30
O 338. 50 c. red 70 70
O 339. 100 c. violet 70 70

1900. Federation issue of 1897 optd **CORREOS DE EL SALVADOR DE OFICIO** in circle and band.
O 355. **32.** 1 c. blue, rose, gold and green 12·00 12·00
O 356. 5 c. rose, blue, gold and green 12·00 12·00

1900. Stamps of 1900, dated "1900", optd. **FRANQUEO OFICIAL** in oval, and with or without shield optd. T **36.**
O 448. **34.** 1 c. green (No. 438) 25 25
O 449. 2 c. rose 30 25
O 450. 3 c. black 20 20
O 451. 5 c. blue 20 20
O 452. 10 c. blue 45 45
O 453. 12 c. green 45 45

O 454. 13 c. brown 45 45
O 455. 24 c. black 35 45
O 461. 26 c. brown 35 35
O 462. 50 c. red 40 40

1903. As T **37,** but inscr. "FRANQUEO OFICIAL" across statue.
O 497. 1 c. green 25 15
O 498. 2 c. red 25 12
O 499. 3 c. orange 75 60
O 500. 5 c. blue 25 12
O 501. 10 c. purple 35 25
O 502. 13 c. brown 35 25
O 503. 15 c. brown .. .. 1·75 90
O 504. 24 c. red 25 25
O 505. 50 c. brown 25 20
O 506. 100 c. blue 30 60

1905. Nos. O 500/502 surch. with new value and two black circles.
O 518. 2 c. on 5 c. blue .. 2·00 2·00
O 519. 3 c. on 5 c. blue ..
O 520. 3 c. on 10 c. purple .. 2·50 2·50
O 521. 3 c. on 13 c. brown .. 35 35

1905. No. O 450 optd. **1905.**
O 558. **34.** 3 c. black 50 50

1906. Nos. O 249/50 optd. **1906.**
O 567. **34.** 2 c. rose .. ..
O 568. 3 c. black 35 35

1906. As T **38**, but inscr. "FRANQUEO OFICIAL" at foot of portrait.
O 582. 1 c. black and green .. 10 8
O 583. 2 c. black and red .. 10 8
O 584. 3 c. black and yellow .. 10 8
O 585. 5 c. black and blue .. 10 35
O 586. 10 c. black and violet.. 10 8
O 587. 13 c. black and brown 10 8
O 588. 15 c. black and red .. 12 8
O 589. 24 c. black and red .. 15 15
O 590. 50 c. black and orange 15 80
O 591. 100 c. black and blue .. 15 2·00

1908. As T **39**, but inscr. "FRANQUEO OFICIAL" below building.
O 611. 1 c. black and green .. 8 8
O 612. 2 c. black and red .. 8 8
O 613. 3 c. black and yellow .. 8 8
O 614. 5 c. black and blue .. 8 8
O 615. 10 c. black and violet.. 8 8
O 616. 13 c. black and violet.. 10 10
O 617. 15 c. black and sepia .. 10 10
O 618. 24 c. black and rose .. 10 10
O 619. 50 c. black and yellow.. 10 10
O 620. 100 c. black and blue .. 15 10
These stamps also exist optd. with shield, T **36.**

1910. As T **40** but inscr. "OFICIAL" below portrait
O 655. 2 c. black and green .. 8 8
O 656. 3 c. black and orange .. 8 8
O 657. 4 c. black and red .. 8 8
O 658. 5 c. black and violet .. 8 8
O 659. 6 c. black and red .. 8 8
O 660. 10 c. black and violet .. 8 8
O 661. 12 c. black and blue .. 8 8
O 662. 17 c. black and green .. 8 8
O 663. 19 c. black and brown.. 8 8
O 664. 29 c. black and brown.. 8 8
O 665. 50 c. black and yellow.. 8 8
O 666. 100 c. black and blue .. 8 8

1911. Stamps of 1900, dated "1900", optd. **OFICIAL** and black circles or surch. also.
O 667. **34.** 1 c. green 8 8
O 668. 3 c. on 13 c. brosn .. 8 8
O 669. 5 c. on 10 c. green .. 8 8
O 670. 10 c. green 8 8
O 671. 12 c. green 8 8
O 672. 13 c. brown 8 8
O 673. 50 c. on 10 c. green.. 8 8
O 674. 1 col. on 13 c. brown 8 8

O 1. O 2.

1914. Words of background in green, shield and word "PROVISIONAL" in black.
O 675. **O 1.** 2 c. brown 8 8
O 676. 3 c. yellow 8 8
O 677. 5 c. blue 8 8
O 678. 10 c. red 8 8
O 679. 12 c. green 8 8
O 680. 17 c. violet 8 8
O 681. 50 c. brown 8 8
O 682. 100 c. brown 8 8

1915.
O 683. **O 2.** 2 c. green 5 5
O 684. 3 c. orange 5 5

1915. Stamps of 1915, with optd. **1915** optd. **OFICIAL.**
O 685. **39.** 1 c. grey (No. 675) .. 12 12
O 686. 2 c. red 12 12
O 687. 5 c. blue 12 15
O 688. 6 c. blue 25 20
O 689. **39.** 10 c. yellow 25 20
O 690. 12 c. brown 35 30
O 691. 50 c. purple 35 35
O 692. 100 c. brown.. .. 80 80

1916. Stamps of 1916 optd. **OFICIAL.**
O 694. **53.** 1 c. green 8 8
O 695. 2 c. red 20 15
O 696. 5 c. blue 15 15
O 697. 6 c. violet 8 8
O 698. 10 c. brown 8 8
O 699. 12 c. purple 25 25
O 700. 17 c. orange 8 8
O 701. 25 c. brown 8 8
O 702. 29 c. black 8 8
O 703. 50 c. grey 8 8

1922. Stamps of 1921 optd. **OFICIAL.**
O 736. **55.** 1 c. green 8 8
O 737. – 2 c. black 8 8
O 738. **56.** 5 c. orange 10 10
O 739. **57.** 6 c. red 10 8
O 740. **58.** 10 c. blue 15 15
O 741. – 25 c. green 30 20
O 742. **59.** 60 c. sepia 40 30
O 743. – 1 col. sepia 45 45

1925. Stamps of 1924 optd. **OFICIAL.**
O 768. **61.** 1 c. purple 8 8
O 769. – 2 c. red 8 8
O 770. – 5 c. black 5 5
O 765. – 6 c. blue .. .. 2·10 2·10
O 766. **66.** 10 c. orange 25 12
O 767. **71.** 1 col. blue and green 1·25 55

1947. Stamps of 1947 optd. **OFICIAL.**
O 959. **106.** 1 c. red .. .. 20·00 12·00
O 960. – 2 c. yellow .. .. 20·00 12·00
O 961. – 5 c. grey .. .. 20·00 12·00
O 962. – 10 c. yellow .. .. 20·00 12·00
O 963. – 20 c. green .. .. 22·00 14·00
O 964. – 50 c. black .. .. 22·00 14·00

1964. No. O 963 further surch. **1 CTS XX.**
O 1198. 1 c. on 20 c. green ..

PARCEL POST STAMPS

P 1. Hermes.

1895.
P 127. **P 1.** 5 c. orange .. 12 20
P 128. 10 c. blue 12 20
P 129. 15 c. red 12 30
P 130. 20 c. orange .. 12 30
P 131. 50 c. green 12 30

POSTAGE DUE STAMPS

D 1. D 2. Columbus Monument.

1895.
D 107. **D 1.** 1 c. green 5 8
D 108. 2 c. green 5 8
D 109. 3 c. green 5 8
D 110. 5 c. green 5 10
D 111. 10 c. green .. 5 10
D 112. 15 c. green .. 5 12
D 113. 25 c. green .. 5 25
D 114. 50 c. green .. 20 25

1896.
D 150. **D 1.** 1 c. red 5 8
D 151. 2 c. red 5 8
D 152. 3 c. red 5 8
D 153. 5 c. red 5 8
D 154. 10 c. red 5 10
D 155. 15 c. red 8 15
D 156. 25 c. red 8 15
D 157. 50 c. red 8 20

1897.
D 256. **D 1.** 1 c. blue 5 8
D 257. 2 c. blue 5 8
D 258. 3 c. blue 5 10
D 259. 5 c. blue 5 10
D 260. 10 c. blue 10 12
D 261. 15 c. blue 8 12
D 262. 25 c. blue 5 15
D 263. 50 c. blue 5 20

1898.
D 302. **D 1.** 1 c. violet 8 8
D 303. 2 c. violet 8 8
D 304. 3 c. violet 8 8
D 305. 5 c. violet 8 8
D 306. 10 c. violet 15 20
D 307. 15 c. violet 8 10
D 308. 25 c. violet 8 12
D 309. 50 c. violet 20 20

1899. Optd. with T **35.**
D 347. **D 1.** 1 c. orange 30 30
D 348. 2 c. orange 30 30
D 349. 3 c. orange 30 30
D 350. 5 c. orange 55 55
D 351. 10 c. orange 75 75
D 352. 15 c. orange 75 75
D 353. 25 c. orange 90 90
D 354. 50 c. orange .. 1·10 1·10

1903.
D 507. **D 2.** 1 c. green 70 70
D 508. 2 c. red .. .. 1·10 1·10
D 509. 3 c. orange .. 1·10 1·10
D 510. 5 c. blue .. .. 1·10 1·10
D 511. 10 c. purple .. 1·10 1·10
D 512. 25 c. green .. 1·10 1·10

1908. Stamps of 1907 optd. **Deficiencia de franques.**
D 623. A **39.** 1 c. black and green 30 30
D 624. A 2 c. black and red 35 35
D 625. A 3 c. black & yellow 35 35
D 626. A 5 c. black & blue.. 40 40
D 627. A 10 c. blk. & violet.. 75 75

1908. Stamps of 1907 optd. **DEFICIENCIA DE FRANQUEO.**
D 628. B **39.** 1 c. black and green 30 30
D 629. B 2 c. black and red .. 25 25
D 630. B **39.** 5 c. black and blue 60 60
D 631. B 10 c. black & mauve 45 45
D 632. B 3 c. black & yellow (No. O 613) .. 25 25

1910. As T **40**, but inscr. "FRANQUEO DEFICIENTE" below portrait.
D 655. 1 c. black and brown .. 10 10
D 656. 2 c. black and green .. 10 10
D 657. 3 c. black and yellow .. 10 10
D 658. 4 c. black and red .. 10 10
D 659. 5 c. black and violet .. 10 10
D 660. 12 c. black and blue .. 10 10
D 661. 24 c. black and red .. 10 10

REGISTRATION STAMP

R 1. Gen. R. A. Gutierrez.

1897.
R 266. **R 1.** 10 c. lake 8 10

OFFICIAL REGISTRATION STAMP

1897. Registration stamp optd. **FRANQUEO OFICIAL** in oval.
OR 268. **R 1.** 10 c. blue .. 8

EQUATORIAL GUINEA O2

The former Spanish Overseas Provinces of Fernando Poo and Rio Muni united on 12th October, 1968, to become the Republic of Equatorial Guinea.

1968. 100 centimos = 1 peseta.

1. Clasped Hands. **2.** President F. M. Nguema.

1968. Independence.
1. **1.** 1 p. sepia, gold and blue .. 5 5
2. 1 p. 50 sepia gold & green 5 5
3. 6 p. sepia, gold and red .. 15 8

1970. Independence. 1st Anniv. (12.10.69).
4. **2.** 50 c. red, maroon & orange 5 5
5. 1 p. purple, green & mauve 5 5
6. 1 p. 50 green and maroon 5 5
7. 2 p. green and buff .. 5 5
8. 2 p. 50 blue and green .. 5 5
9. 10 p. purple, blue & brown 20 8
10. 25 p. brown, black and grey 50 20

3. Pres. Nguema and Cockerel.

1971. Independence. 2nd Anniv.
11. **3.** 3 p. multicoloured .. 5 5
12. 5 p. multicoloured .. 8 5
13. 10 p. multicoloured .. 15 10
14. 25 p. multicoloured .. 40 30

4. Flaming Torch.

1972. 3rd Year of Independence.
17. **4.** 50 p. multicoloured .. 75 25

EXPRESS LETTER STAMPS

E 1. Guinea Archer.

1971. Independence. 3rd Anniv.
E 15. **E 1.** 4 p. multicoloured .. 8 5
E 16. 8 p. multicoloured .. 12 8

ERITREA O2

A former Italian colony on the Red Sea, N.E. Africa. Under British Administration from 1942 to Sept. 1952, when Eritrea was federated with Ethiopia whose stamps are now used. See also Middle East Forces.

100 centesimi = 1 lira.
1948. 100 cents = 1 shilling.

Stamps of Italy with curved or straight opt. **COLONIA ERITREA.**

1893.
1. **4.** 1 c. green 40 20
2. **5.** 2 c. brown 15 10
3. **14.** 5 c. green .. .. 4·00 60
4. **9.** 10 c. red .. .. 2·50 25
5. 20 c. orange .. .. 16·00 30
6. 25 c. blue .. .. 38·00 2·50
7. **11.** 40 c. brown 45 45
8. 45 c. grey-green.. .. 55 60
9. 60 c. mauve 70 75
10. 1 l. brown and orange .. 1·50 60
11. **19.** 5 l. red and blue .. 45·00 25·00

1895.
12. **12.** 1 c. brown 55 70
13. **13.** 2 c. brown 10 10
14. **15.** 5 c. green 10 10
15. **16.** 10 c. lake 12 10
16. **17.** 20 c. orange 12 10
17. **18.** 25 c. blue 25 20
18. 45 c. olive 50 70

1903. Stamps of Italy with straight opt. **Colonia Eritrea.**
19. **20.** 1 c. brown 5 5
20. **21.** 2 c. brown 5 5
21. 5 c. green .. .. 2·50 12
22. **22.** 10 c. red .. .. 2·75 8
30. 15 c. on 20 c. orange .. 1·60 15
23. 20 c. orange 15 8
24. 25 c. blue .. .. 25·00 1·00
25. 40 c. brown .. .. 15·00 70
26. 45 c. olive 20 25
27. 50 c. violet .. .. 11·00 70
28. **23.** 1 l. brown and green .. 20 15
29. 5 l. blue and red .. 1·10 55

1908. Stamps of Italy with straight opt. **Colonia Eritrea,** except 20 c. optd. **ERITREA.**
31. **24.** 5 c. green 5 5
32. 10 c. red 5 5
41. 15 c. grey 20 15
42. **25.** 20 c. orange 20 25
33. **26.** 25 c. blue.. .. 10 8
43. 40 c. brown 30 20
44. 50 c. mauve 25 10
45. 60 c. red 50 50
46. **23.** 10 l. olive and red .. 28·00 35·00

1. Ploughing.

DESIGN: 15 c., 25 c. Government Palace, Massawa.

1910.
34. **1.** 5 c. green 10 8
35. 10 c. red 30 10
36. – 15 c. black .. .. 10·00 40
37. – 25 c. blue 25 20

Various issues of Italy optd. **ERITREA** or **Eritrea.** Colours changed in some instances.

1916. Red Cross.
47. **34.** 10 c.+5 c. red 25 25
48. **35.** 15 c.+5 c. grey .. 1·10 1·10
49. 20 c.+5 c. orange .. 1·10 1·10
50. 20 on 15 c.+5 c. grey .. 45 55

1916. No. 41 surch. with new value and bars or crosses.
51. 5 c. on 15 c. black .. 1·10 1·10
52. 20 c. on 15 c. black .. 10 8

1922. Victory.
34. **40.** 5 c. green 10 8
35. 10 c. red 30 10
36. 15 c. grey .. .. 10·00 40
37. 25 c. blue 25 20

1922. Stamps of Somalia optd. **ERITREA** and bars.
57. **1.** 2 c. on 1 b. brown .. 25 50
58. 5 c. on 2 b. green .. 20 30
59. **2.** 10 c. on 1 a. red .. 15 8
60. 15 c. on 2 a. orange .. 20 10
61. 25 c. on 2½ a. blue .. 30 10
62. 50 c. on 5 a. yellow .. 45 15
63. 1 l. on 10 a. lilac .. 1·10 60

1923. Propagation of the Faith.
64. **44.** 20 c. orange and green .. 1·00 1·75
65. 30 c. orange and red .. 1·00 1·75
66. 50 c. orange and violet.. 80 1·50
67. 1 l. orange and blue .. 80 1·50

1923. Fascisti stamps.
68. **45.** 10 c. green 25 45
69. 30 c. violet 30 50
70. 50 c. red 30 50
71. **46.** 1 l. blue 35 65
72. 2 l. brown 40 70
73. **47.** 5 l. black and blue .. 1·60 2·50

1924. Manzoni.
74. **49.** 10 c. black and red .. 25 70
75. – 15 c. black and green .. 25 70
76. – 30 c. black 25 70
77. – 50 c. black and brown .. 25 70
78. – 1 l. black and blue .. 6·50 11·00
79. – 5 l. black and purple .. £1·00 £1·40

1924. Postage stamps.
80. **20.** 1 c. brown 20 40
81. **21.** 2 c. brown 12 20
82. 5 c. green 35 15

1925. Holy Year.
90. – 20 c.+10 c. brn. & green 30 55
91. **51.** 30 c.+15 c. brn. & choc. 30 55
92. – 50 c.+25 c. brn. & violet 30 55
93. – 60 c.+30 c. brown & red 30 55
94. – 1 l.+50 c. pur. and blue 40 70
95. – 5 l.+2 l. 50 purple & red 55 1·00

1925. Stamps of Italy optd. **Colonia Eritrea**
123. **61.** 7½ c. brown .. .. 90 1·10
124. **26.** 20 c. purple 20 20
96. 20 c. green 15 15
97. 30 c. grey 20 15
125. **61.** 50 c. mauve 90 90
126. **26.** 60 c. orange .. .. 3·50 9·50
127. **23.** 75 c. red 50 45
128. 1 l. 25 blue 40 20
98. 2 l. green and orange .. 85 80
129. 2 l. 50 green and orange 3·50 1·10

1925. Royal Jubilee.
99. **53.** 60 c. red 15 30
100. 1 l. blue 10 25
101. 1 l. 25 blue 25 40

1926. St. Francis of Assisi.
102. **54.** 20 c. green 20 35
103. – 40 c. violet 20 35
104. – 60 c. red 20 35
105. – 1 l. 25 blue 20 35
106. – 5 l.+2 l. 50 brown .. 85 1·50

1926. Colonial Propaganda stamps as T 1 of Cyrenaica, but inscr. "ERITREA".
107. 5 c.+5 c. brown .. 10 20
108. 10 c.+5 c. olive .. 10 20
109. 20 c.+5 c. green .. 10 20
110. 40 c.+5 c. red 10 20
111. 60 c.+5 c. orange .. 10 20
112. 1 l.+5 c. blue 10 20

1926. Postage stamps.
113. **23.** 75 c. red 70 25
114. 1 l. 25 blue 55 10
115. 2 l. 50 green & orange.. 4·25 1·00

1927. 1st National Defence issue.
116. **59.** 40 c.+20 c. black & brn. 30 55
117. 60 c.+30 c. brown & red 35 70
118. 1 l. 25+60 c. black and blue 45 90
119. 5 l.+2 l. 50 blk. & grn. 70 1·50

1927. Volta Centenary.
120. **63.** 20 c. violet 55 70
121. 50 c. orange 70 90
122. 1 l. 25 blue .. .. 1·25 1·75

1928. 45th Anniv. of the Italian-African Society. As T 2 of Cyrenaica but inscr. "ERITREA".
133. 20 c.+5 c. green .. 20 45
134. 30 c.+5 c. red 20 45
135. 50 c.+10 c. violet .. 20 45
136. 1 l. 25+20 c. blue .. 20 45

1929. Postage stamps.
131. **61.** 50 c. mauve .. .. 1·75 2·00
130. **62.** 50 c. grey and brown .. 30 10
132. 1 l. 75 brown .. .. 1·40 60

1929. 2nd National Defence issue.
137. **59.** 30 c.+10 c. blk. & red.. 30 70
138. 50 c.+20 c. blk. & lilac 30 70
139. 1 l. 25+50 c. blue and brown .. .. 55 1·10
140. 5 l.+2 l. black & olive.. 55 1·10

1929. Montecassino.
141. **75.** 20 c. green 20 40
142. – 25 c. orange 20 40
143. – 50 c.+10 c. red .. 30 55
144. – 75 c.+15 c. brown .. 35 70
145. **75.** 1 l. 25+25 c. purple .. 1·75 2·50
146. – 5 l.+1 l. blue .. .. 1·75 2·50
147. – 10 l.+2 l. brown .. 1·75 2·50

1930. Royal Wedding stamps.
148. **80.** 20 c. green 20 30
149. 50 c.+10 c. orange .. 30 55
150. 1 l. 25+25 c. red .. 45 90

4. Railway Bridge.

6. King Victor Emmanuel III.

5.

1930.
151. – 2 c. black and blue .. 5 5
152. – 5 c. black and violet .. 5 5
153. – 10 c. black and brown .. 5 5
154. – 15 c. black and green .. 5 5
155. – 25 c. black and green .. 5 5
156. – 35 c. black and brown .. 12 15
157. – 1 l. black and blue .. 8 5
158. **4.** 2 l. black and brown .. 55 25
159. – 5 l. black and olive .. 90 95
160. – 10 l. black and blue .. 1·25 1·60

DESIGNS—VERT. 2 c., 35 c. Lancer. 5 c., 10 c. Postman. 15 c. Telegraph linesman. 25 c. Rifleman. HORIZ. 1 l. Massawa. 5 l. Asmara Deghe Selam. 10 l. Camel transport.

1930. Ferrucci.
161. **85.** 20 c. violet 20 20
162. – 25 c. green (283) .. 20 20
163. – 50 c. black (284) .. 20 20
164. – 1 l. 25 c. blue (285) .. 20 20
165. – 5 l.+2 l. red (286) .. 90 1·10

1930. 3rd National Defence issue.
166. **59.** 30 c.+10 c. grn. & olive 50 90
167. 50 c.+10 c. vio. & olive 50 90
168. 1 l. 25+30 c. brown .. 70 1·50
169. 5 l.+1 l. 50 grn. & blue 5·50 9·00

1930. 25th Anniv. (1929) of Italian Colonial Agricultural Institute.
170. **5.** 50 c.+20 c. brown .. 25 50
171. 1 l. 25+20 c. blue .. 25 50
172. 1 l. 75+20 c. green .. 25 50
173. 2 l. 55+50 c. violet .. 90 1·50
174. 5 l.+1 l. red .. .. 90 1·50

1930. Virgil Bimillenary. As Italy Nos. 290/8.
175. 15 c. violet 8 15
176. 20 c. brown 8 15
177. 25 c. green 8 15
178. 30 c. brown 8 15
179. 50 c. purple 8 15
180. 75 c. red 8 15
181. 1 l. 25 blue 8 15
182. 5 l.+1 l. 50 purple .. 75 1·75
183. 10 l.+2 l. 50 brown .. 80 1·75

1931. St. Anthony of Padua.
184. **92.** 20 c. brown 15 25
185. – 25 c. green 15 25
186. – 30 c. brown 15 25
187. – 50 c. purple 15 25
188. – 75 c. grey 15 25
189. – 1 l. 25 blue 15 25
190. – 5 l.+2 l. 50 brown .. 1·25 2·50

1931.
191. **6.** 7½ c. brown 5 8
192. 20 c. red and blue .. 5 5
193. 30 c. purple and olive .. 5 5
194. 40 c. green and blue .. 5 5
195. 50 c. olive and brown .. 5 5
196. 75 c. red 15 5
197. 1 l. 25 blue and purple .. 30 5
198. 2 l. 50 green 65 10

7. Camel.

1933.
199. **7.** 2 c. blue 5 5
200. – 5 c. black 5 5
201. **7.** 10 c. brown 5 5
202. – 15 c. brown 8 5
203. – 25 c. green 8 5
204. – 35 c. violet 12 8
205. – 1 l. blue 10 5
206. – 2 l. olive 70 8
207. – 5 l. red 95 12
208. – 10 l. orange .. .. 1·10 15

DESIGNS—HORIZ. 5 c., 15 c. Fish wharf. 25 c. Baobab tree. 35 c. Native village. 2 l. African Elephant. VERT. 1 l. Ruins at Cholloe. 5 l. Eritrean man. 10 l. Eritrean woman.

1934. Honouring the Duke of the Abruzzi. Optd. **ONORANZE AL DUCA DEGLI ABRUZZI.** Designs as Nos. 201/2 and 204/8.
209. 10 c. blue 50 70
210. 15 c. blue 50 70
211. 35 c. green 50 70
212. 1 l. red 50 70
213. 2 l. red .. .. 1·10 1·75
214. 5 l. violet .. .. 1·10 1·75
215. 10 l. green .. .. 1·10 1·75

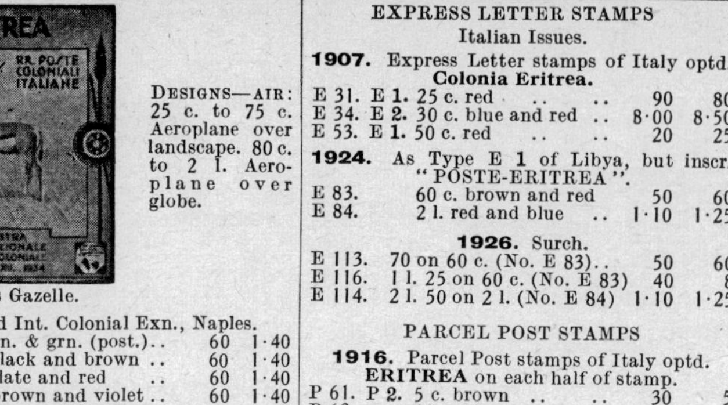

8. Grant's Gazelle.

DESIGNS—AIR: 25 c. to 75 c. Aeroplane over landscape. 80 c. to 2 l. Aeroplane over globe.

1934. 2nd Int. Colonial Exn., Naples.
216. **8.** 5 c. brn. & grn. (post.).. 60 1·40
217. 10 c. black and brown .. 60 1·40
218. 20 c. slate and red .. 60 1·40
219. 50 c. brown and violet .. 60 1·40
220. 60 c. slate and brown .. 60 1·40
221. 1 l. 25 green and blue .. 60 1·40
222. – 25 c. orge. and blue (air) 60 1·40
223. – 50 c. slate and green .. 60 1·40
224. – 75 c. orange and brown 60 1·40
225. – 80 c. green and brown .. 60 1·40
226. – 1 l. green and red .. 60 1·40
227. – 2 l. brown and blue .. 60 1·40

9.

1934. Air. Rome-Mogadiscio Flight.
228. . 25 c.+10 c. green .. 60 2·50
229. 50 c.+10 c. brown .. 60 2·50
230. 75 c.+15 c. red .. 60 2·50
231. 80 c.+15 c. brown .. 60 2·50
232. 1 l.+20 c. red .. .. 60 2·50
233. 2 l.+20 c. blue .. 60 2·50
234. 3 l.+25 c. violet .. 14·00 17·00
235. 5 l.+25 c. orange .. 14·00 17·00
236. 10 l.+30 c. purple .. 14·00 17·00
237. 25 l.+2 l. green .. 14·00 17·00

DESIGNS: 25 c., 1 l. 50, Zebu drawing plough. 50 c., 2 l. Section of Massawa-Asmara rly. 60 c., 5 l. Dom palm trees. 75 c. 10 l. Roadway through cactus trees.

10. Aeroplane and bridge.

1936. Air.
238. – 25 c. green 8 8
239. – 50 c. brown 5 5
240. – 60 c. orange 15 25
241. – 75 c. brown 12 8
242. **10.** 1 l. blue 8 5
243. – 1 l. 50 violet .. 12 5
244. – 2 l. blue 15 5
245. **10.** 3 l. lake.. .. 1·60 60
246. – 5 l. green .. .. 1·40 12
247. – 10 l. red .. .. 3·50 20

BRITISH MILITARY ADMINISTRATION

1948. Stamps of Great Britain surch. **B.M.A. ERITREA** and value in cents or shillings.
E 1. **103.** 5 c. on ½d. pale green 8 12
E 2. 10 c. on 1d. pale red 12 35
E 3. 20 c. on 2d. pale orge. 20 50
E 4. 25 c. on 2½d. light blue 8 25
E 5. 30 c. on 3d. pale violet 25 35
E 6. **104.** 40 c. on 5d. brown .. 10 35
E 7. 50 c. on 6d. purple .. 10 30
E 7a. **105.** 65 c. on 8d. red 25 50
E 8. 75 c. on 9d. olive .. 20 35
E 9. 1s. on 1s. brown .. 20 25
E 10. **106.** 2s. 50 on 2s. 6d. green 1·00 2·75
E 11. 5s. on 5s. red .. 2·50 3·75
E 12. – 10s. on 10s. bright blue (No. 478a) .. 3·50 5·00

BRITISH ADMINISTRATION

1950. Stamps of Great Britain surch. **B.A. ERITREA** and value in cents or shillings.
E 13. **103.** 5 c. on ½d. pale green 5 20
E 26. 5 c. on ½d. orange .. 8 25
E 14. 10 c. on 1d. pale red 5 20
E 27. 10 c. on 1d. blue .. 8 20
E 15. 20 c. on 2d. pale orge. 5 30
E 28. 20 c. on 2d. brown .. 8 25
E 16. 25 c. on 2½d. light blue 5 25
E 29. 25 c. on 2½d. red .. 8 20
E 17. 30 c. on 3d. pale violet 5 25
E 18. **104.** 40 c. on 5d. brown .. 10 25
E 19. 50 c. on 6d. purple .. 12 25
E 20. **105.** 65 c. on 8d. red 25 45
E 21. 75 c. on 9d. olive .. 12 20
E 22. 1s. on 1s. brown .. 15 20
E 23. **106.** 2s. 50 on 2s. 6d. green 1·00 1·75
E 24. 5s. on 5s. red .. 2·25 3·50
E 25. – 10s. on 10s. bright blue (No. 478a) 5·50 6·50

1951. Nos. 509/11 of Great Britain surch. **B.A. ERITREA** and value in cents or shillings.
E 30. **116.** 2s. 50 on 2s. 6d. green 1·40 2·50
E 31. – 5s. on 5s. red.. 4·00 4·50
E 32. – 10s. on 10s. blue 5·00 5·50

EXPRESS LETTER STAMPS

Italian Issues.

1907. Express Letter stamps of Italy optd. **Colonia Eritrea.**
E 31. E **1.** 25 c. red 90 80
E 34. E **2.** 30 c. blue and red .. 8·00 8·50
E 53. E **1.** 50 c. red 20 25

1924. As Type E 1 of Libya, but inscr. "POSTE-ERITREA".
E 83. 60 c. brown and red 50 60
E 84. 2 l. red and blue .. 1·10 1·25

1926. Surch.
E 113. 70 on 60 c. (No. E 83).. 50 60
E 116. 1 l. 25 on 60 c. (No. E 83) 40 8
E 114. 2 l. 50 on 2 l. (No. E 84) 1·10 1·25

PARCEL POST STAMPS

1916. Parcel Post stamps of Italy optd. **ERITREA** on each half of stamp.
P 61. P **2.** 5 c. brown 30 5
P 62. 10 c. blue 15 5
P 63. 20 c. black 15 5
P 64. 25 c. red 15 5
P 65. 50 c. orange 20 5
P 66. 1 l. violet 20 5
P 67. 2 l. green 25 5
P 68. 3 l. yellow 35 5
P 69. 4 l. grey 70 8
P 70. 10 f. purple .. .. 6·00 15
P 71. 12 l. brown .. .. 13·00 25
P 72. 15 l. olive .. .. 15·00 30
P 73. 20 l. purple .. .. 18·00 50

1927. Parcel Post stamps of Italy optd. **ERITREA** on each half of stamp.
P 123. P **3.** 10 c. blue .. .. £800 3·00
P 124. 25 c. red .. .. 38·00 15
P 125. 30 c. blue 8 12
P 126. 50 c. orange .. .. 42·00 15
P 127. 60 c. red 5 5
P 128. 1 l. violet .. .. 17·00 5
P 129. 2 l. green .. .. 4·25 5
P 130. 3 l. yellow 15 5
P 131. 4 l. grey 25 5
P 132. 10 l. mauve .. .. 18·00 30
P 133. 20 l. purple.. .. 22·00 40

The prices unused are for the complete stamp

POSTAGE DUE STAMPS

1903. Postage Due stamps of Italy optd. **Colonia Eritrea.**
D 53. D **3.** 5 c. purple & orange 15 15
D 54. 10 c. purple & orange 15 25
D 32. 20 c. purple & orange 30 35
D 33. 30 c. purple & orange 35 45
D 57. 40 c. purple & orange 80 1·10
D 58. 50 c. purple & orange 80 1·10
D 36. 60 c. purple & orange 70 85
D 116. 60 c. brown & orange 3·50 4·50
D 37. 1 l. purple and blue 75 25
D 38. 2 l. purple and blue 75 85
D 62. 5 l. purple and blue 12·00 14·00
D 63. 10 l. purple and blue 1·50 2·50
D 41. D **4.** 50 l. yellow .. .. 40·00 15·00
D 42. 100 l. blue .. .. 14·00 4·25

1934. Postage Due stamps of Italy optd. **ERITREA.**
D 216. D **6.** 5 c. brown 10 15
D 217. 10 c. blue 10 15
D 218. 20 c. red 10 15
D 219. 25 c. green 15 15
D 220. 30 c. orange 20 20
D 221. 40 c. brown 20 20
D 222. 50 c. violet 20 20
D 223. 60 c. blue 30 35
D 224. D **7.** 1 l. orange 35 25
D 225. 2 l. green .. .. 3·50 4·25
D 226. 5 l. violet .. .. 4·50 5·50
D 227. 10 l. blue .. .. 6·00 7·00
D 228. 20 l. red .. .. 9·00 10·00

1948. Postage Due stamps of Great Britain surch. **B.M.A. ERITREA** and new value in cents or shillings.
ED 1. D **1.** 5 c. on ½d. green .. 1·40 2·75
ED 2. 10 c. on 1d. red .. 1·40 2·75
ED 3. 20 c. on 2d. black .. 1·40 2·75
ED 4. 30 c. on 3d. violet .. 1·75 3·25
ED 5. 1s. on 1s. blue .. 4·00 5·50

1950. Postage Due stamps of Great Britain surch. **B.A. ERITREA** and new value in cents or shillings.
ED 6. D **1.** 5 c. on ½ d. green 2·25 2·75
ED 7. 10 c. on 1d. red .. 2·25 2·75
ED 8. 20 c. on 2d. black 2·25 2·25
ED 9. 30 c. on 3d. violet 2·75 2·50
ED 10. 1s. on 1s. blue 4·00 3·50

ESTONIA E1

A district on the S. Coast of the Gulf of Finland. Under Russian rule until 1917, when it became an independent republic. The area was incorporated into the Soviet Union during 1940.

1918. 100 kopecks = 1 rouble.
1919. 100 penni = 1 Estonian mark.
1928. 100 senti = 1 kroon.

1.

2. Seagulls.

1918. Imperf.
1. 1. 5 k. pink 10 10
2. 15 k. blue 10 10
3. 35 k. brown 20 25
4. 70 k. olive 35 30

1919. Imperf.
5. 2. 5 p. yellow 35 35

3. 4. 5.

7. Viking Galley. 8.

1919. Imperf. (10 p., 15 m. and 25 m., also perf.).
6. 3. 5 p. orange 5 5
7a. 10 p. green 5 5
8. 4. 15 p. red 8 8
9. 5. 35 p. blue 8 8
10. 70 p. lilac 8 8
11. 7. 1 m. blue and sepia .. 10 20
12. 5 m. yellow and black .. 10 35
13. 15 m. green and violet .. 50 35
14. 25 m. blue and sepia .. 75 45

1920. Air. Imperf.
15. 8. 5 m. black, blue & yellow 70 85

9. Tallinn. 10. War Invalids. 11.

1920. Imperf.
16. 9. 25 p. green 12 5
17. 25 p. yellow 5 5
18. 35 p. red 20 5
19. 50 p. green 10 5
20. 1 m. red 40 8
21. 2 m. blue 20 8
23. 2 m. 50 blue 40 5

1920. Charity. Imperf.
24. 10. 35+10 p. green and red 10 30
25. 11. 70+15 p. brown & blue 10 30

1920. Surch.
26. 4. 1 m. on 15 p. red .. 10 5
27. 9. 1 m. on 35 p. red .. 10 5
29. 10. 1 m. on 35+10 p. green and red 20 15
28. 5. 2 m. on 70 p. lilac .. 20 10
30. 11. 2 m. on 70+15 p. brown and blue 20 15

12. 13. Weaver. 14. Blacksmith.

1921. Red Cross. Imperf. or perf.
31. 12. 2½—3½ m. brown, red and orange 40 65
32. 5—7 m. brn., red & blue 40 65

1922. Imperf. or perf.
35. 13. ½ m. orange 25 5
36. 1 m. brown 60 5
37. 2 m. green .. .. 1·00 5
38. 2½ m. claret .. .. 1·25 5
39. 3 m. green 90 5
40. 14. 5 m. red .. .. 1·25 5
41. 9 m. red .. .. 1·10 15
42. 10 m. blue .. .. 1·10 5
72. 10 m. grey .. .. 1·10 65
42a. 12 m. red .. .. 1·75 45
42b. 15 m. purple .. .. 1·50 20
42c. 20 m. blue .. .. 4·00 10

* An asterisk after the date indicates that stamps have network backgrounds in colour.

15. Map of Estonia.

1923.*
43. 15. 100 m. blue and olive .. 5·50 85
43a. 300 m. blue and brown .. 8·50 1·10

1923. Air. No. 15 optd. **1923** or surch. **15 Marks 1923.**
44. 8. 5 m. black, blue & yellow 2·10 3·25
45. 15 m. on 5 m. black, blue and yellow .. .. 2·50 4·25

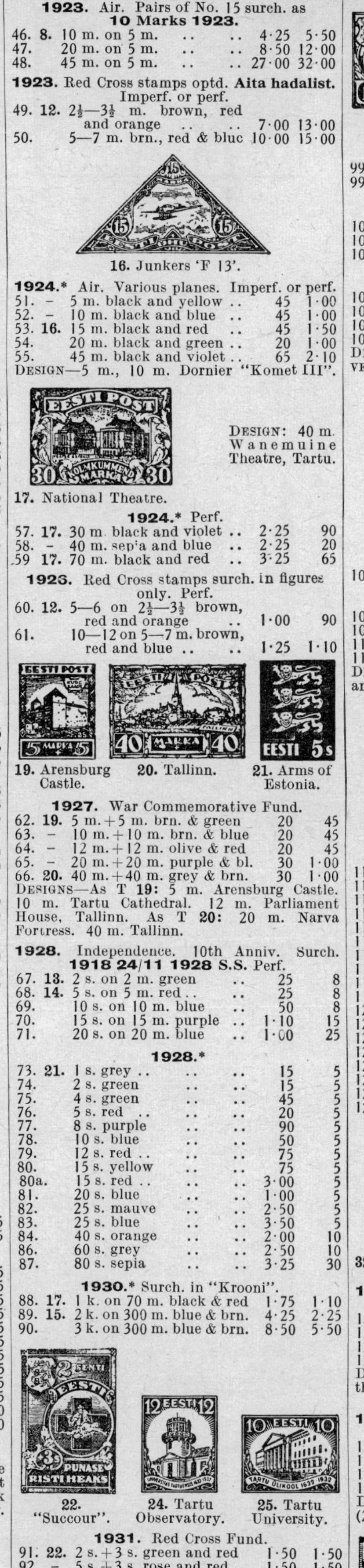

1923. Air. Pairs of No. 15 surch. as **10 Marks 1923.**
46. 8. 10 m. on 5 m. .. .. 4·25 5·50
47. 20 m. on 5 m. .. .. 8·50 12·00
48. 45 m. on 5 m. .. .. 27·00 32·00

1923. Red Cross stamps optd. **Aita hadalist.** Imperf. or perf.
49. 12. 2½—3½ m. brown, red and orange .. .. 7·00 13·00
50. 5—7 m. brn., red & blue 10·00 15·00

16. Junkers 'F 13'.

1924.* Air. Various planes. Imperf. or perf.
51. – 5 m. black and yellow .. 45 1·00
52. – 10 m. black and blue .. 45 1·00
53. 16. 15 m. black and red .. 45 1·50
54. 20 m. black and green .. 20 1·00
55. 45 m. black and violet .. 65 2·10
DESIGN—5 m., 10 m. Dornier "Komet III".

DESIGN: 40 m. Wanemuine Theatre, Tartu.

17. National Theatre.

1924.* Perf.
57. 17. 30 m. black and violet .. 2·25 90
58. – 40 m. sepia and blue .. 2·25 20
59. 17. 70 m. black and red .. 3·25 65

1926. Red Cross stamps surch. in figures only. Perf.
60. 12. 5—6 on 2½—3½ brown, red and orange .. 1·00 90
61. 10—12 on 5—7 m. brown, red and blue .. 1·25 1·10

19. Arensburg Castle. 20. Tallinn. 21. Arms of Estonia.

1927. War Commemorative Fund.
62. 19. 5 m.+5 m. brn. & green 20 45
63. – 10 m.+10 m. brn. & blue 20 45
64. – 12 m.+12 m. olive & red 20 45
65. – 20 m.+20 m. purple & bl. 30 1·00
66. 20. 40 m.+40 m. grey & brn. 30 1·00
DESIGNS—As T 19: 5 m. Arensburg Castle. 10 m. Tartu Cathedral. 12 m. Parliament House, Tallinn. As T 20: 20 m. Narva Fortress. 40 m. Tallinn.

1928. Independence. 10th Anniv. Surch. **1918 24/11 1928 S.S.** Perf.
67. 13. 2 s. on 2 m. green .. 25 8
68. 14. 5 s. on 5 m. red .. 25 8
69. 10 s. on 10 m. blue .. 50 8
70. 15 s. on 15 m. purple .. 1·10 15
71. 20 s. on 20 m. blue .. 1·00 25

1928.*
73. 21. 1 s. grey 15 5
74. 2 s. green 15 5
75. 4 s. green 45 5
76. 5 s. red 20 5
77. 8 s. purple 90 5
78. 10 s. blue 50 5
79. 12 s. red 75 5
80. 15 s. yellow 75 5
80a. 15 s. red .. .. 3·00 5
81. 20 s. blue .. .. 1·00 5
82. 25 s. mauve .. .. 2·50 5
83. 25 s. blue .. .. 3·50 5
84. 40 s. orange .. .. 2·00 10
86. 60 s. grey .. .. 2·50 10
87. 80 s. sepia .. .. 3·25 30

1930.* Surch. in "Krooni".
88. 17. 1 k. on 70 m. black & red 1·75 1·10
89. 15. 2 k. on 300 m. blue & brn. 4·25 2·25
90. 3 k. on 300 m. blue & brn. 8·50 5·50

22. "Succour". 24. Tartu Observatory. 25. Tartu University.

1931. Red Cross Fund.
91. 22. 2 s.+3 s. green and red 1·50 1·50
92. – 5 s.+3 s. rose and red .. 1·50 1·50
93. – 10 s.+3 s. blue and red 1·50 1·50
94. 22. 20 s.+3 s. blue and red 3·00 3·00
DESIGN: 5 s., 10 s. Lighthouse.

1932.* Founding of University. Tercent.
95. 24. 5 s. red .. .. 1·50 5
96. 25. 10 s. blue 85 5
97. 24. 12 s. red .. .. 2·10 55
98. 25. 20 s. blue .. .. 3·25 12

26. Narva Falls. 27. Ancient Bard. 28. Invalid and Nurse.

1933.
99. 26. 1 k. black .. .. 1·50 10
99a. 1 k. green .. .. 20 1·25

1933.* 10th Estonian Choral Festival.
100. 27. 2 s. green 55 10
101. 5 s. red 70 10
102. 10 s. blue .. .. 1·25 5

1933.* Anti-tuberculosis Fund.
103. 28. 5 s.+3 s. red .. .. 1·75 1·25
104. – 10 s.+3 s. blue .. 1·75 1·25
105. – 12 s.+3 s. red .. .. 2·25 2·25
106. – 20 s.+3 s. blue .. 3·25 2·75
DESIGNS—HORIZ. 10 s., 20 s. Sanatorium. VERT. 12 s. Lorraine Cross.

29. Harvesting. 30. Arms of Narva.

1935.
107. 29. 3 k. brown 40 40

1936.* Charity.
108. 30. 10 s.+10 s. blue & green 1·10 1·60
109. – 15 s.+15 s. blue and red 1·50 2·10
110. – 25 s.+25 s. orge. & blue 2·00 2·50
111. – 50 s.+50 s. yell. & blk. 4·00 5·50
DESIGNS—Arms of Parnu (15 s.), Tartu (25 s.), and Tallinn (50 s.).

31. Pres. Konstantin Pats. 31a. Tallinn Harbour.

1936.
112. 31. 1 s. brown 20 5
113. 2 s. green 20 5
113a. 3 s. orange .. .. 1·10 50
114. 4 s. purple 30 5
115. 5 s. green 20 5
116. 6 s. red 20 5
117. 6 s. green .. .. 5·50 5·50
118. 10 s. blue 40 5
119. 15 s. red 90 5
119a. 15 s. blue .. .. 1·75 10
120. 18 s. red .. .. 4·75 80
121. 20 s. mauve 60 5
122. 25 s. blue .. .. 2·10 5
123. 30 s. yellow .. .. 2·25 5
123a. 30 s. blue .. .. 3·25 12
124. 50 s. brown .. .. 1·25 10
125. 60 s. mauve .. .. 2·50 30
127. 31a. 2 k. blue .. .. 30 1·25

32. St. Brigitte Abbey. 33. Paide.

1936.* Founding St. Brigitte Abbey. 500th Anniv.
128. 32. 5 s. green 20 5
129. – 10 s. blue 30 8
130. – 15 s. red 45 55
131. – 25 s. blue 80 80
DESIGNS: 5 s. Restored portal. 10 s. Ruins of the Abbey. 15 s. Ruined facade. 25 s. Old seal.

1937.* Social Relief Fund. Inscr. "CARITAS 1937".
132. 33. 10 s.+10 s. green .. 1·25 1·90
133. – 15 s.+15 s. red .. 1·25 1·90
134. – 25 s.+25 s. blue .. 1·75 2·50
135. – 50 s.+50 s. purple .. 3·50 5·00
DESIGNS—Arms of Rakvere (15 s.). Valga (25 s.). Viljandi (50 s.).

34. Paldiski (Port Baltic). 35. Dr. F. R. Faehlmann. 36. Arms of Viljandi.

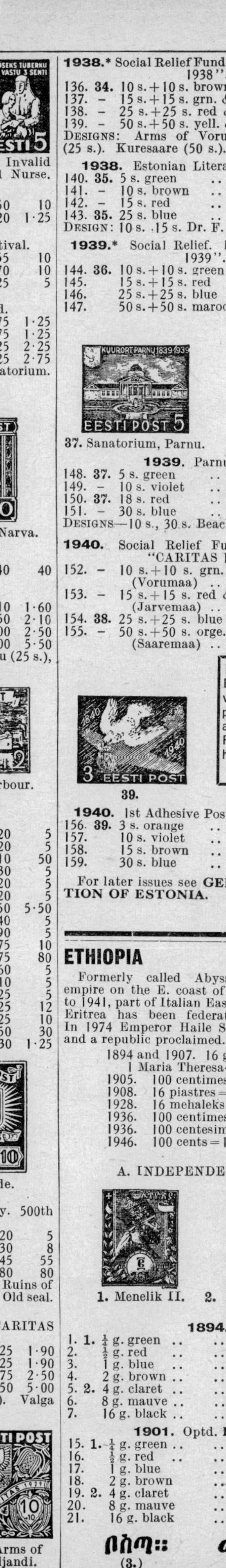

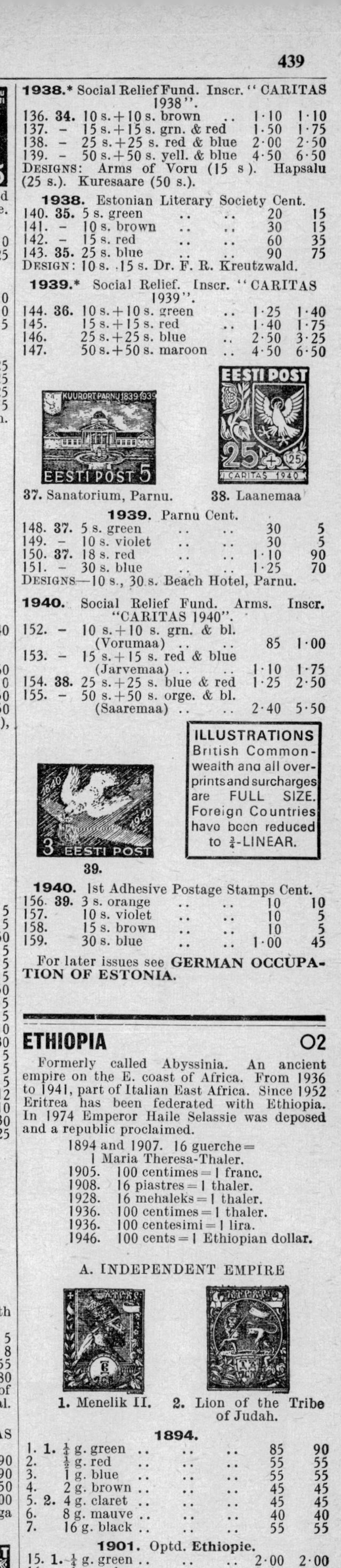

1938.* Social Relief Fund. Inscr. "CARITAS 1938".
136. 34. 10 s.+10 s. brown .. 1·10 1·10
137. – 15 s.+15 s. grn. & red 1·50 1·75
138. – 25 s.+25 s. red & blue 2·00 2·50
139. – 50 s.+50 s. yell. & blue 4·50 6·50
DESIGNS: Arms of Voru (15 s). Hapsalu (25 s.). Kuresaare (50 s.).

1938. Estonian Literary Society Cent.
140. 35. 5 s. green 20 15
141. – 10 s. brown 30 15
142. – 15 s. red 60 35
143. 35. 25 s. blue 90 75
DESIGN: 10 s. 15 s. Dr. F. R. Kreutzwald.

1939.* Social Relief. Inscr. "CARITAS 1939".
144. 36. 10 s.+10 s. green .. 1·25 1·40
145. 15 s.+15 s. red .. 1·40 1·75
146. 25 s.+25 s. blue .. 2·50 3·25
147. 50 s.+50 s. maroon .. 4·50 6·50

37. Sanatorium, Parnu. 38. Laanemaa

1939. Parnu Cent.
148. 37. 5 s. green 30 5
149. – 10 s. violet 30 5
150. 37. 18 s. red .. .. 1·10 90
151. – 30 s. blue .. .. 1·25 70
DESIGNS—10 s., 30 s. Beach Hotel, Parnu.

1940. Social Relief Fund. Arms. Inscr. "CARITAS 1940".
152. – 10 s.+10 s. grn. & bl. (Vorumaa) .. .. 85 1·00
153. – 15 s.+15 s. red & blue (Jarvemaa) .. .. 1·10 1·75
154. 38. 25 s.+25 s. blue & red 1·25 2·50
155. – 50 s.+50 s. orge. & bl. (Saaremaa) .. .. 2·40 5·50

ILLUSTRATIONS British Commonwealth and all overprints and surcharges are FULL SIZE. Foreign Countries have been reduced to ¾-LINEAR.

39.

1940. 1st Adhesive Postage Stamps Cent.
156. 39. 3 s. orange 10 10
157. 10 s. violet 10 5
158. 15 s. brown 10 5
159. 30 s. blue .. .. 1·00 45

For later issues see **GERMAN OCCUPATION OF ESTONIA.**

ETHIOPIA O2

Formerly called Abyssinia. An ancient empire on the E. coast of Africa. From 1936 to 1941, part of Italian East Africa. Since 1952 Eritrea has been federated with Ethiopia. In 1974 Emperor Haile Selassie was deposed and a republic proclaimed.

1894 and 1907. 16 guerche = 1 Maria Theresa-Thaler.
1905. 100 centimes = 1 franc.
1908. 16 piastres = 1 thaler.
1928. 16 mehaleks = 1 thaler.
1936. 100 centimes = 1 thaler.
1936. 100 centesimi = 1 lira.
1946. 100 cents = 1 Ethiopian dollar.

A. INDEPENDENT EMPIRE

1. Menelik II. 2. Lion of the Tribe of Judah.

1894.
1. 1. ¼ g. green 85 90
2. ½ g. red 55 55
3. 1 g. blue 55 55
4. 2 g. brown 45 45
5. 2. 4 g. claret 45 45
6. 8 g. mauve 40 40
7. 16 g. black 55 55

1901. Optd. **Ethiopie.**
15. 1. ¼ g. green .. .. 2·00 2·00
16. ½ g. red .. .. 2·00 2·00
17. 1 g. blue .. .. 2·25 2·25
18. 2 g. brown .. .. 2·25 2·25
19. 2. 4 g. claret .. .. 2·25 2·25
20. 8 g. mauve .. .. 2·75 2·75
21. 16 g. black .. .. 3·50 3·75

ቦስጣ። (3.) መልክት። (4.)

1902. Optd. with T 3.
22. 1. ¼ g. green .. .. .. 1·00 1·10
23. ½ g. red .. .. .. 1·10 1 10
24. 1 g. blue .. .. .. 1·50 1·50
25. 2 g. brown .. .. 1·50 1·50
26. 2. 4 g. claret .. .. 2·25 2·25
27. 8 g. mauve .. .. 3·00 3·25
28. 16 g. black .. .. 5·50 5·50

1903. Optd. with T 4.
29. 1. ¼ g. green .. .. 1·10 1·10
30. ½ g. red .. .. .. 1·10 1·10
31. 1 g. blue .. .. 1·60 1·60
32. 2 g. brown .. .. 2·25 2·25
33. 2. 4 g. claret .. .. 3·25 3·25
34. 8 g. mauve .. .. 3·75 3·75
35. 16 g. black .. .. 5·00 5·50

ምልክት (5.) ምኒልክ (6.)

1904. Optd. with T 5.
36. 1. ¼ g. green .. .. .. 1·00 1·10
37. ½ g. red .. .. .. 1·60 1·60
38. 1 g. blue .. .. 2·75 2·75
39. 2 g. brown .. .. 3·25 3·25
40. 2. 4 g. claret .. .. 3·50 3·50
41. 8 g. mauve .. .. 7·00 7·50
42. 16 g. black .. .. 11·00 12·00

1905. Surch. in figures.
43. 1. 05 on ¼ g. green .. .. 1·10 1·10
44. 10 on ½ g. red .. .. 1·25 1·25
45. 20 on 1 g. blue .. .. 1·60 1·60
46. 40 on 2 g. brown .. .. 2·10 2·10
47. 2. 80 on 4 g. claret .. 2·75 2·75
48. 1.60 on 8 g. mauve .. 3·00 3·00
49. 3.20 on 16 g. black .. 6·50 6·50
The above surcharge was also applied to some stamps optd. with **Ethiopie** and T 3, 4 and 5.

1905. Surch. in figures and words.
90. 2. 5 c. on 16 g. black (No. 28) 19·00 19·00

1905. No. 2 divided diagonally and surch. **5c/m.**
86. 1. 5 c. on half of ½ g. red .. 1·50 1·75

1906. Surch. **5c/m.**
88. 1. 5 c. on ¼ g. green (No. 22)

1906. Optd. with T 6 and surch. in figures.
94. 1. 05 on ¼ g. green .. .. 1·60 1·60
95. 10 on ½ g. red .. .. 1·90 1·90
96. 20 on 1 g. blue .. .. 2·25 2·25
97. 40 on 2 g. brown .. .. 2·00 2·00
98. 2. 80 on 4 g. claret .. .. 2·75 2·75
99. 1.60 on 8 g. mauve .. 2·75 2·75
100. 3.20 on 16 g. black .. 6·50 6·50

1906. Surch. with figures and native word.
101. 1. 05 on ¼ g. green .. .. 1·75 1·75
102. 10 on ½ g. red .. .. 1·75 1·75
103. 20 on 1 g. blue .. .. 2·25 2·25
104. 40 on 2 g. brown .. .. 2·75 2·75
105. 2. 80 on 4 g. claret .. .. 2·75 2·75
106. 1.60 on 8 g. mauve .. 3·25 3·25
107. 3.20 on 16 g. black .. 8·00 8·00

ዳግማዊ።

(8.)

1907. Optd. with T 8 and surch. in figures between stars.
115. 1. ¼ on ¼ g. green .. .. 1·10 1·25
116. ½ on ½ g. red .. .. 1·50 1·60
117. 1 on 1 g. blue .. .. 2·00 2·00
118. 2 on 2 g. brown .. .. 2·50 2·50
119. 2. 4 on 4 g. claret .. .. 2·50 2·50
120. 8 on 8 g. mauve .. .. 4·00 4·00
121. 16 on 16 g. black .. .. 5·00 5·50

1908. Entry into U.P.U. Nos. 1/7 surch. in figures and words.
133. 1. ¼ pi. on ¼ g. green .. 40 40
134. ½ pi. on ½ g. red 40 40
129. 1 pi. on ½ g. red .. .. 1·60 1·60
135. 1 pi. on 1 g. blue 50 50
136. 2 pi. on 2 g. brown .. 80 80
137. 2. 4 pi. on 4 g. claret .. 1·00 2·75
138. 8 pi. on 8 g. mauve .. 2 50 2·75
139. 16 pi. on 16 g. black .. 3·50 3·50

9. Throne of Solomon. **10.** Emperor Menelik.

1909.
147. 9. ¼ g. green 20 20
148. ½ g. red 20 25
149. 1 g. orange and green .. 50 50
150. 10. 2 g. blue 75 65
151. 4 g. claret and green .. 1·10 1·10
152. – 8 g. grey and red .. 2·25 1·60
153. – 16 g. red .. .. 3·25 2·75
DESIGN: 8 g., 16 g. Another portrait.

1911. T 1 and 2 optd. **AFF EXCEP FAUTE TIMB** and surch. in manuscript.
154. 1. ¼ g. on ¼ g. green .. 22·00 8·00
155. ½ g. on ½ g. red .. 22·00 8·00
156. 1 g. on 1 g. blue .. 22·00 8·00
157. 2 g. on 2 g. brown .. 22·00 8·00
158. 2. 4 g. on 4 g. claret .. 22·00 8·00
159. 8 g. on 8 g. mauve .. 22·00 8·00
160. 16 g. on 16 g. black .. 22·00 8·00

11-2-1917
12.

ተፈሪ።
11/2/1917.
(13.)

1917. Coronation. Optd. with T 12 (and similar type).
161. 9. ¼ g. green 85 90
162. ½ g. red 85 90
163. 10. 2 g. blue 85 90
164. 4 g. claret and green .. 1·60 1·75
165. – 8 g. grey and red (No. 152) 2·50 2·50
166. – 16 g. red (No. 153) .. 4·50 4·50

1917. Optd. with T 13 (and similar type).
168. 9. ¼ g. green 10 10
169. ½ g. red 12 12
170. 1 g. orange and green .. 75 75
171. 10. 2 g. blue 15 15
174. 4 g. claret and green .. 30 30
175. – 8 g. grey & red (No. 152) 30 30
176. – 16 g. red (No. 153) .. 45 45

1917. Nos. 175/6 surch. with large figure.
177. ¼ on 8 g. grey and red .. 75 40
178. ½ on 8 g. grey and red .. 75 1·00
179. 1 on 16 g. red .. .. 1·75 1·90
180. 2 on 16 g. red .. .. 1·75 1·90

14. Gazelle. **15.** Ras Taffari, later Emperor Haile Selassie.

16. Buffalo.

1919.
181. 14. ⅛ g. brown and violet .. 5 5
182. – ¼ g. grey and green .. 5 5
183. – ½ g. green and red .. 5 5
184. – 1 g. black and purple .. 5 5
185. 15. 2 g. brown and blue .. 5 5
186. – 4 g. orange and blue .. 5 8
187. – 6 g. orange and blue .. 5 8
188. – 8 g. black and olive .. 15 15
189. – 12 g. grey and purple .. 20 25
190. – $1 black and red .. 35 40
191. 16. $2 brown and black .. 80 75
192. – $3 red and green .. 1·10 85
193. – $4 pink and brown .. 1·25 1·00
194. – $5 grey and red .. 1·75 1·50
195. – $10 yellow and olive .. 2·50 2·25
DESIGNS—VERT. As T **14**: ¼ g. Giraffes. ½ g. Leopard. As T **15**: 1 g. Crown Prince Taffari (later Haile Selassie). 4 g. ditto (different portrait). $4, $5, $10 Empress Waizeru Zauditu (different portraits). HORIZ. As T **16**: 6 g. St. George's Cathedral, Addis Ababa. 8 g. Rhinoceros. 12 g. Ostriches. $1 Elephant. $3 Lions.

1919. Stamps of 1919 variously surch.
197. 14. ½ g. on ⅛ g. brn. & violet 20 20
208c. – ½ g. on 8 g. blk. & olive 20 25
202. – ½ g. on $1 black and red 15 15
203. – ½ g. on $5 grey and red 20 20
198. – 1 g. on ¼ g. grey & green 30 35
204. – 1 g. on 6 g. orge. & blue 20 20
208. – 1 g. on 12 g. grey & pur. 40 40
205. – 1 g. on $3 red and green 25 25
206. – 1 g. on $10 yell. & olive 25 25
198c. – 2 g. on 1 g. black & pur. 30 30
199. – 2 g. on $4 pink & brown 40 40
200. – 2 g. ½ on ½ g. grn. & red 30 30
201. 15. 4 g. on 2 g. brn. & blue 30 30
196. – 4 g. on $4 pink & brown 35 35

17. Ras Taffari.

18. Empress Zauditu.

ም፡ ቴ፡ ቴ፡
የተመረቀበት፡
ቀን፡ መታሰቢያ፡
(19.)

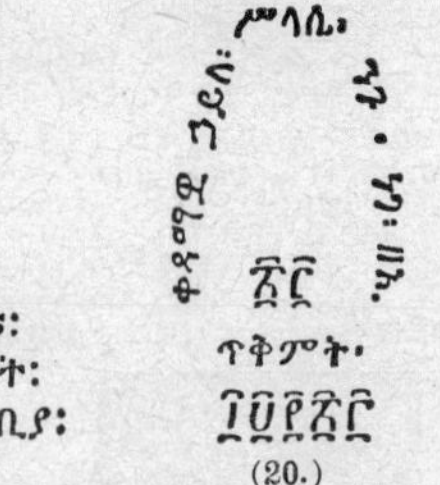
(20.)

1928. Opening of P.O. at Addis Ababa. Optd. with T 19.
213. 17. ⅛ m. blue and orange .. 30 30
214. 18. ¼ m. red and blue .. 30 30
215. 17. ½ m. black and green .. 30 30
216. 18. 1 m. black and red .. 30 30
217. 17. 2 m. black and blue .. 30 30
218. 18. 4 m. olive and yellow .. 30 30
219. 17. 8 m. olive and mauve .. 30 30
220. 18. 1 t. mauve and brown .. 30 30
221. 17. 2 t. brown and green .. 50 50
222. 18. 3 t. green and purple .. 75 75

1928.
223. 17. ⅛ m. blue and orange .. 30 30
224. 18. ¼ m. red and blue .. 25 25
225. 17. ½ m. black and green .. 25 30
226. 18. 1 m. black and red .. 20 20
227. 17. 2 m. black and blue .. 20 20
228. 18. 4 m. olive and yellow .. 20 20
229. 17. 8 m. olive and mauve .. 40 45
230. 18. 1 t. mauve and brown .. 60 65
231. 17. 2 t. brown and green .. 1·00 1·00
232. 18. 3 t. green and purple .. 1·40 1·40

1928. Elevation of Ras Taffari to Negus. Optd. with Crown and **NEGOUS TEFERI.**
233. 17. ⅛ m. blue and orange .. 45 55
234. ½ m. black and green .. 45 55
235. 2 m. black and blue .. 45 55
236. 8 m. olive and mauve .. 45 55
237. 2 t. brown and green .. 45 55

1929. Arrival of First Aeroplane of the Ethiopian Government. Air. Optd. with aeroplane and native inscriptions.
238. 17. ⅛ m. blue and orange .. 25 30
239. 18. ¼ m. red and blue .. 25 30
240. 17. ½ m. black and green .. 25 30
241. 18. 1 m. black and red .. 25 30
242. 17. 2 m. black and blue .. 25 30
243. 18. 4 m. olive and yellow .. 25 30
244. 17. 8 m. olive and mauve .. 30 40
245. 18. 1 t. mauve and brown .. 50 50
246. 17. 2 t. brown and green .. 60 60
247. 18. 3 t. green and purple .. 60 65

1930. Accession of Ras Taffari as Emperor Haile Selassie. Optd. **HAYLE** (or **HAILE**) **SELASSIE 1er 3 Avril 1930** and native inscriptions.
248. 17. ⅛ m. blue and orange .. 10 12
249. 18. ¼ m. red and blue .. 12 15
250. 17. ½ m. black and green .. 12 15
261. 18. 1 m. black and red .. 12 15
262. 17. 2 m. black and blue .. 15 15
263. 18. 4 m. olive and yellow .. 20 20
264. 17. 8 m. olive and mauve .. 30 35
265. 18. 1 t. mauve and brown .. 80 80
266. 17. 2 t. brown and green .. 90 1 00
267. 18. 3 t. green and purple .. 1·25 1·25

1930. Coronation of Emperor Haile Selassie (1st issue). Optd. with T 20.
268. 17. ⅛ m. blue and orange .. 20 20
269. 18. ¼ m. red and blue .. 20 20
270. 17. ½ m. black and green .. 20 20
271. 18. 1 m. black and red .. 20 20
272. 17. 2 m. black and blue .. 20 20
273. 18. 4 m. olive and yellow .. 20 20
274. 17. 8 m. olive and mauve .. 25 25
275. 18. 1 t. mauve and brown .. 30 30
276. 17. 2 t. brown and green .. 55 55
277. 18. 3 t. green and purple .. 80 80

21. The Ethiopian Lion and Royal Symbols.

ILLUSTRATIONS
British Commonwealth and all overprints and surcharges are FULL SIZE. Foreign Countries have been reduced to ¾-LINEAR

1930. Coronation of Emperor Haile Selassie (2nd issue).
278. 21. 1 g. orange 12 12
279. 2 g. blue 12 12
280. 4 g. purple 12 12
281. 8 g. green 20 20
282. 1 t. brown 30 30
283. 3 t. green 35 35
284. 5 t. brown 40 40
REPRINTS. Our unused prices for Nos. 278/84 and 296/312 are for reprints which are not practicably distinguishable from the originals.

1931. Issue of 1928 surch. in Mehaleks.
285. 18. ⅛ m. on 1 m. blk. & red 15 20
286. 17. ⅛ m. on 2 m. blk. & blue 15 20
287. 18. ⅛ m. on 4 m. olive & yell. 15 20
288. ¼ m. on 1 m. blk. & red 15 20
289. 17. ¼ m. on 2 m. blk. & blue 20 25
290. 18. ¼ m. on 4 m. olive & yell. 20 25
291. ½ m. on 1 m. blk. & red 25 30
292. 17. ½ m. on 2 m. blk. & blue 25 30
293. 18. ½ m. on 4 m. olive & yell. 25 30
294. ½ m. on 3 t. grn. & pur. 1·60 1·75
295. 17. 1 m. on 2 m. blk. & blue 25 30

22. Potez "25 A2" Aircraft over Map of Ethiopia. **23.** Ras Makonnen

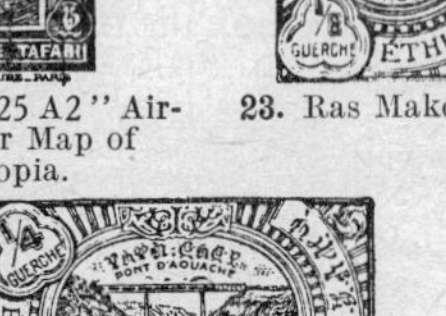
24. Railway Bridge across R. Hawash.

1931. Air.
296. 22. 1 g. red 10 10
297. 2 g. blue 10 10
298. 4 g. mauve 10 10
299. 8 g. green 35 35
300. 1 t. brown 75 75
301. 2 t. red .. .. 1·40 1·40
302. 3 t. green .. .. 2·25 2·25
Reprints. See note below No. 284.

1931.
303. 23. ⅛ g. red 10 10
304. 24. ¼ g. olive 10 10
305. 23. ½ g. purple 12 12
306. – 1 g. orange 12 12
307. – 2 g. blue 15 15
308. – 4 g. lilac 20 20
309. – 8 g. green 50 50
310. – 1 t. brown 90 90
311. – 3 t. green .. .. 1·40 1·40
312. – 5 t. brown .. .. 2·00 2·00
PORTRAITS as T **23**: 1 g. Empress Waizeru Menen (profile). 2 g., 8 g. Haile Selassie (profile). 4 g., 1 t. Statue of Menelik II. 3 t. Empress Waizeru Menen (full face). 5 t. Haile Selassie (full face).
Reprints. See note below No. 284.

1936. Red Cross. As T 23/24 optd. with red cross.
313. 1 g. green 20 20
314. 2 g. pink 20 20
315. 4 g. blue 20 20
316. 8 g. brown 25 30
317. 1 t. violet 25 30

1936. As T 23/24 surch. with value and native inscription.
318. 23. 1 c. on ⅛ g. red 50 30
319. 24. 2 c. on ¼ g. olive .. 50 30
320. 23. 3 c. on ½ g. purple .. 55 30
321. – 5 c. on 1 g. orange .. 65 45
322. – 10 c. on 2 g. blue .. 1·00 55

25. King Victor Emmanuel III.

28. Haile Selassie I in Coronation Robes.

B. ITALIAN COLONY

1936. Annexation of Ethiopia.
322a. 25. 10 c. brown 12 10
322b. 20 c. violet 25 12
322c. – 25 c. green 15 8
322d. – 30 c. brown 30 30
322e. – 50 c. red 25 8
322f. 25. 75 c. orange 30 8
322g. 1 l. 25 blue 50 40

DESIGNS—VERT. 25 c., 30 c., 50 c. Victor Emmanuel III. HORIZ. Victor Emmanuel III and 20 c. Mountain scenery. 75 c. Gonder Castle. 1 l. 25 Tomb of Scec Hussen and Dordola Hills.

C. INDEPENDENCE RESTORED

1942. 1st issue. "Centimes" with capital initial and small letters.
323. **28.** 4 c. black and green .. 20 20
324. 10 c. black and red .. 55 40
325. 20 c. black and blue .. 1·25 55

1942. 2nd issue. "CENTIMES" in block capital letters.
326. **28.** 4 c. black and green .. 15 10
327. 8 c. black and orange .. 20 12
328. 10 c. black and red .. 25 15
329. 12 c. black and violet .. 30 20
330. 20 c. black and blue .. 45 25
331. 25 c. black and green .. 65 40
332. 50 c. black and brown .. 1·00 55
333. 60 c. black and mauve .. 1·40 80

1943. Restoration of Obelisk and 13th Anniv. of Coronation of Haile Selassie. Stamps of 1942 inscr. "CENTIMES" surch. **OBELISK 3 NOV. 1943** and value.
334. **28.** 5 c. on 4 c. black & grn. 8·50 8·50
335. 10 c. on 8 c. blk. & orge. 8·50 8·50
336. 15 c. on 10 c. blk. & red 8·50 8·50
337. 20 c. on 12 c. blk. & vio. 8·50 8·50
338. 30 c. on 20 c. blk. & bl. 8·50 8·50
In No. 338 the figure "3" is surcharged on the "2" of "20" to make "30" and this value is confirmed by the Amharic characters.

29. Royal Palace, Addis Adaba. **30.** Nenelik II.

1944. Emperor Menelik II. Birth Cent. Inscr. "1844 1944 CENTENAIRE MENELIK II". No gum.
339. **29.** 5 c. green 25 15
340. **30.** 10 c. red 35 20
341. – 20 c. blue 65 25
342. – 50 c. violet 65 35
343. – 65 c. orange .. .. 1·50 60
DESIGNS—VERT. 20 c. Equestrian statue of Menelik II. 65 c. Menelik in royal robes. HORIZ. 50 c. Menelik's mausoleum.

31. Patient and Nurse. **32.** Lion of the Tribe of Judah.

33. Postal Transport by Mule and by Bus.

1945. Victory. Optd. **V** in red.
344. – 5 c. green 20 20
345. – 10 c. red 20 20
346. **31.** 25 c. blue 25 25
347. – 50 c. brown .. .. 1·00 1·00
348. – 1 t. violet .. .. 1·50 1·50
DESIGNS: 5 c. Nurse and baby. 10 c. Native soldier. 50 c. Nurse and child. 1 t. "Supplication". The above stamps without the "V" were not issued for postal purposes.

1946. Air. Resumption of National Air Mail Services. (a) Surch. at sides and top in Amharic, with **20-4-39** and value below.
349. **28.** 12 c. on 4 c. blk. & grn. 10·00 10·00

(b) Surch. **REPRISE POSTE AERIENNE ETHIOPIENNE** at sides and top, with **29.12.46** and values below.
350. **28.** 0.50 on 25 c. blk. & grn. 10·00 10·00
351. $2 on 60 c. blk. & mve. 22·00 20·00

1947. Postal Service. 50th Anniv. Inscr. "1894 1944".
352. **32.** 10 c. yellow 40 25
353. – 20 c. blue 55 40
354. **33.** 30 c. brown .. .. 1·00 55
355. – 50 c. green .. .. 1·75 1·00
356. – 70 c. magenta .. .. 2·50 1·75
DESIGNS—VERT. 20 c. Menelik II (as in T 1). HORIZ. 50 c. G.P.O., Addis Ababa. 70 c. Menelik and Haile Selassie.

34. Negus Sahle Selassie.

1947. Selassic Dynasty. 150th Anniv.
357. **34.** 20 c. blue 60 30
358. – 30 c. purple 80 40
359. – $1 green .. .. 2·00 1·10
DESIGNS—HORIZ. 30 c. View of Ancober. VERT. $1 Negus Sahle Selassie.

35. Emperor Haile Selassie and Pres. Roosevelt.

1947. Pres. Roosevelt Commem.
360. **35.** 12 c. grn. & lake (post.) 15 15
361. 25 c. red and blue .. 35 30
362. – 65 c. blue, red and black 70 65
363. – $1 sepia & purple (air) 3·25 2·75
364. – $2 blue and red .. 4·50 3·75
DESIGNS—HORIZ. 65 c. Pres. Roosevelt and U.S. flags. VERT. $1, Pres. Roosevelt. $2, Haile Selassie.

1947. Surch. **12 centimes** in French and Amharic with six bars.
365. **29.** 12 c. on 25 c. blk. & grn. 5·50 5·50

36. Trinity Church, Addis Ababa.

1947. Views with medallion portrait of Haile Selassie inset. (a) Postage.
366. – 1 c. purple 5 5
367. **36.** 2 c. violet 5 5
368. – 4 c. green 10 8
369. – 5 c. green 10 5
370. – 8 c. orange 12 8
371. – 12 c. red 20 12
371a. – 15 c. grey-olive .. 15 15
372. – 20 c. blue 25 20
373. – 30 c. brown 50 25
373a. – 60 c. red 75 45
374. – 70 c. magenta .. 1·00 40
375. – $1 red .. .. 2·00 50
376. – $3 blue .. .. 5·00 1·40
377. – $5 olive .. .. 7·50 2·50
DESIGNS: 1 c. Amba Alagi. 4 c. Debra Sina. 5 c. Mecan mountain pathway, near Ashangi. 8 c. Lake Tana. 12 c., 15 c. Parliament Buildings. Addis Ababa. 20 c. Aiba mountain scenery, near Mai Chio. 30 c. Nile Bridge. 60 c., 70 c. Canoe on Lake Tana. $1 Omo Falls. $3 Mt. Alamata. $5 Ras Dashan Mountains.

37. Douglas "DC 3" Aircraft over Zoquala Volcano.

(b) Air.
378. – 8 c. purple 10 5
379. **37.** 10 c. green 15 8
379a. – 25 c. purple 20 10
380. – 30 c. orange 30 10
380a. – 35 c. blue 40 12
380b. – 65 c. purple 55 20
381. – 70 c. red 65 25
382. – $1 blue 80 30
383. – $3 magenta .. .. 3·25 2·10
384. – $5 brown .. .. 5·50 2·75
385. – $10 violet .. .. 10·10 6·00
DESIGNS: 8 c. Ploughing with oxen. 30 c., 35 c. Tehis Isat Falls, Blue Nile. 65 c., 70 c. Amba Alagi. $1 Sacula source of River Nile. $3 Gorgora and Dembia on Lake Tana. $5 Magdala Fort. $10 Ras Dasnan Mountains and Lake.

38. Emperor, Empress, Lion and Map.

1949. Liberation. 8th Anniv. Inscr. "5/5/49".
386. – 20 c. blue 30 20
387. **38.** 30 c. orange 35 25
388. – 50 c. violet 65 45
389. – 80 c. green .. .. 1·10 55
390. – $1 red .. .. 2·00 1·00
DESIGNS—20 c. Emperor and Empress with sceptres and orb. 50 c. Coat of arms. 80 c. Shield and spears. $1, Star of Solomon.

1949. Industrial and Agricultural Exn. Nos. 370/1 and 373/5 surch. **EXPOSITION 1949** and new value and two lines of Amharic characters.
391. 8 c.+8 c. orange .. 35 35
392. 12 c.+5 c. red 35 35
393. 30 c.+15 c. brown .. 75 75
394. 70 c.+70 c. magenta .. 3·00 3·00
395. $1+80 c. red .. .. 3·75 3·75

39. Emperor and U.P.U. Monument, Berne.

1950. Air. U.P.U. 75th Anniv.
396. **39.** 5 c. red and green .. 15 15
397. 15 c. red and blue .. 20 20
398. 25 c. green and yellow 30 30
399. 50 c. blue and red .. 60 60

1950. Red Cross Fund. As Nos. 344/8 but without V opt. and surch. + **10 ct.** below a cross.
399a. 5 c.+10 c. green .. 30 30
399b. 10 c.+10 c. red .. 55 55
399c. 25 c.+10 c. blue .. 90 90
399d. 50 c.+10 c. brown .. 1·60 1·60
399e. $1+10 c. violet .. 2·25 2·25

40. Lion of the Tribe of Judah. **41.** Emperor and Bridge.

1950. Coronation. 20th Anniv. Dated "2.11.30".
400. – 5 c. violet 25 15
401. – 10 c. magenta 30 20
402. – 20 c. red 55 40
403. **40.** 30 c. green .. .. 1·10 70
404. – 50 c. blue .. .. 2·10 1·50
DESIGNS—HORIZ. 5 c. Dejach Balcha Hospital. 50 c. Emperor, Empress and palace. VERT. 10 c. Abuna Petros. 20 c. Emperor hoisting flag.

1951. Opening of Abbayo Bridge.
405. **41.** 5 c. brown and green .. 55 20
406. 10 c. black and orange .. 1·00 30
407. 15 c. brown and blue .. 1·40 40
408. 30 c. magenta and olive 2·50 55
409. 60 c. blue and brown .. 3·50 70
410. 80 c. green and violet .. 5·50 1·60

1951. Battle of Adwa. 55th Anniv. As T **41**, but Emperor and Tomb of Ras Makonnen.
411. 5 c. black and green .. 30 12
412. 10 c. black and blue .. 50 20
413. 15 c. black and blue .. 55 35
414. 30 c. black and claret .. 1·60 70
415. 80 c. black and red .. 2·25 1·10
416. $1 black and brown .. 2·50 2·00

1951. Industrial and Agricultural Exhibition. Nos. 391/3 further optd. **1951** and Amharic characters above.
417. 8 c.+8 c. orange .. 30 30
418. 12 c.+5 c. red 30 30
419. 30 c.+15 c. brown .. 55 55
420. 70 c.+70 c. magenta .. 2·40 2·40
421. $1+80 c. red .. .. 3·00 3·00

42. "Tree of Health". **43.** Haile Selassie.

1951. Anti-Tuberculosis Fund. Cross and inscr. in red.
422. **42.** 5 c.+2 c. green .. 8 8
423. 10 c.+3 c. orange .. 12 12
424. 15 c.+3 c. blue .. 15 15
424a. 20 c.+3 c. purple .. 10 5
424b. 25 c.+4 c. green .. 12 8
425. 30 c.+5 c. vermilion .. 30 30
425a. 35 c.+5 c. purple .. 15 10
426. 50 c.+7 c. brown .. 70 70
426a. 60 c.+7 c. blue .. 25 20
436b. 65 c.+7 c. violet .. 50 30
426c. 80 c.+9 c. red .. 60 50
427. $1+10 c. purple .. 1·60 1·60

1952. Emperor Haile Selassie's 60th Birthday.
428. **43.** 5 c. green 10 8
429. 10 c. orange 20 10
430. 15 c. black 20 15
431. 25 c. blue 30 20
432. 30 c. violet 40 25
433. 50 c. red 70 40
434. 65 c. sepia .. .. 1·10 70

44. Ethiopian Flag over the Sea.

1952. Celebration of Federation of Eritrea with Ethiopia.
435. – 15 c. lake 45 20
436. – 25 c. brown 55 30
437. – 30 c. brown 95 50
438. – 50 c. purple .. .. 1·40 60
439. – 65 c. black .. .. 1·60 80
440. – 80 c. green .. .. 2·25 1·10
441. – $1 red .. .. 2·25 1·40
442. **44.** $2 blue .. .. 5·50 2·25
443. – $3 magenta .. .. 10·00 3·75
DESIGNS: 15 c., 30 c. Port Assab. 25 c., 50 c. Port Massawa. 65 c. Map. 80 c. Allegory of Federation. $1 Emperor raising flag. $3 Emperor in 1936.

45. Emperor and Massawa Harbour.

DESIGN—HORIZ. 15 c., 30 c. Emperor aboard ship at sea.

1953. Federation of Ethiopia and Eritrea. 1st Anniv. Inscr. "1ST ANNIVERSARY".
444. **45.** 10 c. brown and red .. 45 30
445. – 15 c. green and blue .. 65 35
446. **45.** 25 c. brown and orange 1·00 55
447. – 30 c. green and brown 1·40 70
448. **45.** 50 c. brown and purple 2·25 1·25

46. Princess Tsahai tending sick Child.

1952. Ethiopian Red Cross Society. 20th Anniv. Cross in red.
449. **46.** 15 c. blue and chocolate 35 25
450. 20 c. orange and green .. 60 35
451. 30 c. green and blue .. 75 65

47. Promulgating the Constitution. **48.** Emperor Haile Selassie.

1955. Silver Jubilee of Emperor. Inscr. "1930-1955".
452. **47.** 5 c. brown and green .. 15 8
453. – 20 c. green and red .. 30 15
454. – 25 c. black and magenta 40 20
455. – 35 c. red and brown .. 50 30
456. – 50 c. blue and brown .. 90 40
457. – 65 c. red and lilac .. 1·10 50
DESIGNS—HORIZ. 20 c. Bishop's consecration. 25 c. Emperor presenting standard to troops. 50 c. Emperor, Empress and symbols of progress. 65 c. Emperor and Empress in coronation robes. VERT. 35 c. Allegory of re-union of Ethiopia and Eritrea.

1955. Silver Jubilee Fair, Addis Ababa.
458. **48.** 5 c. olive and green .. 15 10
459. 10 c. blue and red .. 20 15
460. 15 c. green and black .. 30 20
461. 50 c. lake and magenta 65 40

49. " Convair " Airliner.

50. Promulgating the Constitution.

52. Amharic " A ". 51. Aksum.

1955. Air. Ethiopian Airlines. 10th Anniv.
462. 49. 10 c. multicoloured .. 20 15
463. 15 c. multicoloured .. 25 20
464. 20 c. multicoloured .. 40 20

1956. Air. Constitution. 25th Anniv.
465. 50. 10 c. blue and brown .. 25 15
466. 15 c. green and red .. 30 20
467. 20 c. orange and blue .. 45 30
468. 25 c. green and lilac .. 60 40
469. 30 c. brown and green .. 75 50

1957. Air. Ancient Capitals of Ethiopia. Centres in green.
470. 51. 5 c. brown 15 12
471. – 10 c. red (Lalibela) .. 25 15
472. – 15 c. orange (Gondar) .. 30 20
473. – 20 c. blue (Makalle) .. 45 30
474. – 25 c. mauve (Ankober) 50 30

1957. Air. Addis Ababa. 70th Anniv. Amharic characters in red and miniature views of buildings as in T 52.
475. 52. 5 c. blue on salmon .. 12 8
476. – 10 c. green on flesh .. 15 12
477. – 15 c. purple on buff .. 20 12
478. – 20 c. green on buff .. 25 15
479. – 25 c. mauve on lavender 40 20
480. – 30 c. chestnut on emer. 55 25
AMHARIC CHARACTERS: 10 c. " DDI ". 15 c. " S ". 20 c. " A ". 25 c. " BE ". 30 c. " BA ". The set spells out "Addis Ababa" in Amharic

53. Emperor Haile Selassie, Map of Africa, Building and Monument.

1958. Air. Conf. of Independent African States, Accra.
481. 53. 10 c. green 15 8
482. 20 c. red 25 15
483. 30 c. blue 50 25

1958. Anti-tuberculosis Fund. As Nos. 422/7 but new values.
483a. 42. 20 c.+3 c. pur. & red .. 15 10
483b. 25 c.+4 c. green & red 20 12
483c. 35 c.+5 c. reddish purple and red .. 25 20
484d. 60 c.+7 c. blue and red 50 30
485e. 65 c.+7 c. violet & red 1·00 80
486f. 80 c.+9 c. carmine & red 1·60 1·10

54. Emperor Haile Selassie, Map of Africa, and U.N. Emblem. 55. Woman with Torch.

1958. Air. 1st Session of U.N. Economic Conf. for Africa, Addis Ababa.
484. 54. 5 c. green 10 8
485. 20 c. red 15 12
486. 25 c. blue 25 20
487. 50 c. purple 45 35

1959. Red Cross Commem. Surch. **RED CROSS CENTENARY 1859-1959** in English and Amharic and premium. Colours changed. Cross in red.
488. 46. 15 c.+2 c. red & brown 20 20
489. 20 c.+3 c. green & violet 25 25
490. 30 c.+5 c. blue and red 40 40

1959. Air. Air Mail Service in Ethiopia. 30th Anniv. Nos. 378/81 optd. **30th Airmail Ann. 1929-1959.**
491. 8 c. purple 12 12
492. 10 c. green 15 15
493. 25 c. purple 25 15
494. 30 c. orange 30 20
495. 35 c. blue 40 30
496. 65 c. violet 60 50
497. 70 c. red 75 50

1960. World Refugee Year. Optd. **World Refugee Year 1959-1960** in English and Amharic.
498. 20 c. blue (No. 372) .. 20 20
499. 60 c. red (No. 373a) .. 45 45

1960. Ethiopian Red Cross Society's Silver Jubilee. As Nos. 344/8 but without V opt. surch. **Silver Jubilee 1960** in English and Amharic and premium.
500. 5 c.+1 c. green 12 12
501. 10 c.+2 c. red 15 12
502. 25 c.+3 c. blue 40 30
503. 50 c.+4 c. brown 70 55
504. $1+5 c. violet .. .. 1·40 1·10

1960. 2nd Independent African States Conf., Addis Ababa.
505. 55. 20 c. green and red .. 25 15
506. 80 c. violet and red .. 80 45
507. $1 lake and red .. 1·10 55

56. Emperor Haile Selassie. 57. Africa Hall, Addis Ababa.

1960. Emperor's Coronation. 30th Anniv.
508. 56. 10 c. brown and blue .. 12 12
509. 25 c. violet and green .. 25 20
510. 50 c. blue and buff .. 55 50
511. 65 c. myrtle and salmon 75 60
512. $1 indigo and purple .. 1·10 75

1961. Africa Day.
513. 57. 80 c. blue 55 35

58. Emperor Haile Selassie and Map of Ethiopia.

1961. Liberation. 20th Anniv.
514. 58. 20 c. green 15 12
515. 30 c. blue 20 15
516. $1 brown 80 50

59. Wild Ass.

DESIGNS: 15 c. Eland. 25 c. Elephant. 35 c. Giraffe. 50 c. Beisa. $1 Lion and lioness.

1961. Ethiopian Fauna.
517. 59. 5 c. black and green .. 8 5
518. – 15 c. brown & emerald .. 15 8
519. – 25 c. sepia and green .. 20 10
520. – 35 c. chestnut & emer. 25 15
521. – 50 c. red and green .. 35 20
522. – $1 brown and green .. 90 40
See also Nos. 641/5.

60. Emperor Haile Selassie I and Empress Waizeru Menen.

1961. Golden Wedding of Emperor and Empress.
523. 60. 10 c. green 15 12
524. 50 c. blue 30 25
525. $1 red 65 55

DESIGNS: 15 c Ganna (Ethiopian hockey). 20 c. Cycling. 30 c. Football (3rd Africa Cup game). 50 c. Abbebe Bikila (Marathon winner Olympic Games Rome, 1960).

61. Guks (jousting).

1962. Sports.
526. 61. 10 c. red and green .. 10 8
527. – 15 c. brown and rose .. 15 12
528. – 20 c. black and red .. 20 15
529. – 30 c. purple and blue .. 30 20
530. – 50 c. green and buff .. 50 25

62. Global Map and Mosquito.

1962. Malaria Eradication.
531. 62. 15 c. black 15 10
532. 30 c. purple 20 15
533. 60 c. brown 50 30

63. Abyssinian ground Hornbill. 64. " Collective Security ".

1962. Ethiopian Birds (1st series). Multicoloured.
534. 5 c. Type 63 (postage) .. 12 5
535. 15 c. Abyssinian Roller .. 15 8
536. 30 c. Bateleur Eagle .. 25 12
537. 50 c. Double-toothed Barbet 55 25
538. $1 Emerald Cuckoo .. 1·40 55

539. 10 c. Black-headed Forest Oriole (air) 12 5
540. 15 c. Broad-tailed Paradise Whydah 15 10
541. 20 c. Bearded Vulture .. 20 20
542. 50 c. White-checked Touraco .. 40 25
543. 80 c. Purple Indigo-bird .. 75 40
Nos. 536/7 and 540/1 are vert.
See also Nos. 633/7 and 673/7.

1962. Air. Ethiopian U.N. Forces in Congo. 2nd Anniv. and 70th Birthday of Emperor.
544. 64. 15 c. multicoloured .. 15 8
545. 50 c. multicoloured .. 40 25
546. 60 c. multicoloured .. 35 25

DESIGNS: 15 c. Assab school. 20 c. Massawa church. 50 c. Massawa mosque. 60 c. Assab port.

65. Assab Hospital.

1962. Federation of Ethiopia and Eritrea. 10th Anniv.
547. 65. 3 c. purple 5 5
548. – 15 c. blue 10 8
549. – 20 c. green 15 10
550. – 50 c. brown 30 20
551. – 60 c. red 50 25

66. Bazan, " The Nativity " and Bethlehem. 67. Telephone and Communications Map.

1962. Ethiopian Rulers (1st issue). Mult.
552. 10 c. Type 66 .. .. 12 8
553. 15 c. Ezana and monuments, Aksum 12 8
554. 20 c. Kaleb and fleet in Adulis port 15 10
555. 50 c. Lalibela, Christian figures from Lalibela churches (vert.) .. 30 20
556. 60 c. Yekuno Amlak and Abuna Tekle Haimanot preaching in Ankober .. 40 20
557. 75 c. Zara Yacob and ceremonial pyre .. 45 30
558. $1 Lebna Bengel and battle against Mohammed Gragn 65 50

1963. Ethiopian Imperial Telecommunications Board. 10th Anniv.
559. 67. 10 c. red 12 8
560. – 50 c. blue 45 25
561. – 60 c. brown 55 25
DESIGNS: 50 c. Radio aerial. 60 c. Telegraph pole.

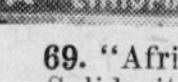

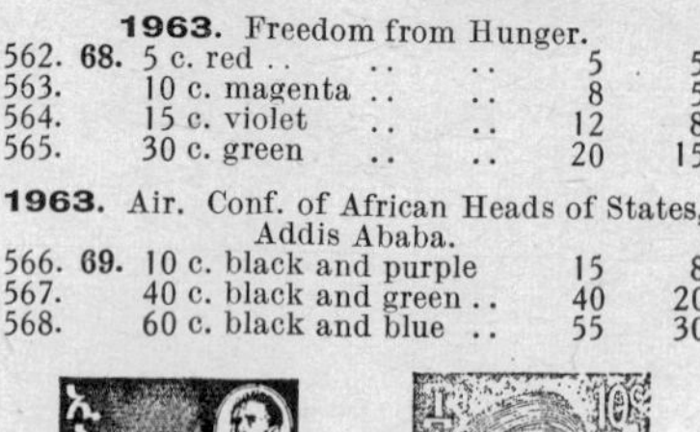

68. Campaign Emblem. 69. "African Solidarity".

1963. Freedom from Hunger.
562. 68. 5 c. red 5 5
563. 10 c. magenta 8 5
564. 15 c. violet 12 8
565. 30 c. green 20 15

1963. Air. Conf. of African Heads of States, Addis Ababa.
566. 69. 10 c. black and purple 15 8
567. 40 c. black and green .. 40 20
568. 60 c. black and blue .. 55 30

70. Disabled Boy. 71. Bishop Abuna Salama.

1963. "Aid for the Disabled" Fund.
569. 70. 10 c.+2 c. blue .. 12 12
570. 15 c.+3 c. red 20 15
571. 50 c.+5 c. green .. 50 40
572. 60 c.+5 c. purple .. 80 55

1964. Ethiopian Spiritual Leaders.
573. 71. 10 c. blue 12 8
574. – 15 c. green (Abuna Aregawi) 20 10
575. – 30 c. lake (Abuna Tekle Haimanot) .. 25 20
576. – 40 c. indigo (Yared) .. 40 25
577. – 60 c. brn. (Zara Yacob) 65 50

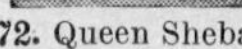

72. Queen Sheba. 73. Priest teaching Alphabet.

1964. Ethiopian Empresses. Multicoloured.
578. 10 c. Type 72 .. .. 12 8
579. 15 c. Helen 20 10
580. 50 c. Seble Wongel .. 45 20
581. 60 c. Mentiwab 50 30
582. 80 c. Taitu 90 40

1964. " Education ".
583. 73. 5 c. brown 8 5
584. – 10 c. green 10 5
585. – 15 c. purple 15 8
586. – 40 c. violet-blue .. 30 15
587. – 60 c. slate-purple .. 50 25
DESIGNS—HORIZ. 10 c. Pupils in classroom. VERT. 15 c. Teacher with pupil. 40 c. Students in laboratory. 60 c. Graduates in procession.

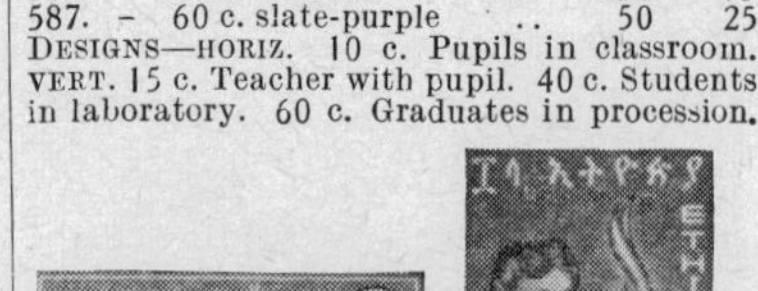

74. Swimming. 75. Eleanor Roosevelt.

1964. Air. Olympic Games, Tokyo. Multicoloured.
588. 5 c. Type 74 .. .. 5 5
589. 10 c. Basketball (vert.) .. 8 5
590. 15 c. Throwing the javelin 15 10
591. 80 c. Football at Addis Ababa stadium 70 30

1964. Eleanor Roosevelt Commem.
592. 75. 10 c. indigo and bistre 5 5
593. 60 c. indigo and chestnut 30 25
594. 80 c. indigo, gold & grn. 45 35

1964. Ethiopian Rulers (2nd issue). As T 66. Multicoloured.

595. 5 c. Serse Dengel and view of Gondar, 1563 .. .. 5 5
596. 10 c. Fasiladas and Gondar, 1632 .. .. .. 8 5
597. 20 c. Yassu the Great and Gondar, 1682 .. .. 12 8
598. 25 c. Theodore II and map of Ethiopia 15 10
599. 60 c. John IV and Battle of Gura, 1876 .. .. 40 25
600. 80 c. Menelik II and Battle of Adwa, 1896 .. .. 55 35

76. Queen Elizabeth II and Emperor Haile Selassie.

1965. Air. Visit of Queen Elizabeth II.

601. **76.** 5 c. multicoloured .. 10 5
602. 35 c. multicoloured .. 30 15
603. 60 c. multicoloured .. 50 30

77. Abyssinian Rose. **78.** I.T.U. Emblem and Symbols.

1965. Ethiopian Flowers. Multicoloured.

604. 5 c. Type **77** 5 5
605. 10 c. Kosso tree 5 5
606. 25 c. St. John's wort .. 12 8
607. 35 c. Parrot tree 30 15
608 60 c Maskal daisy .. 45 25

1965. I.T.U. Cent.

609. **78.** 5 c. yell., indigo & blue 8 5
610. 10 c. orge., indigo & blue 10 5
611. 60 c. mag., indigo & blue 45 25

79. Laboratory Technicians **80.** I C Y Emblem

1965. Multicoloured

612. 3 c. Type **79** (postage) .. 5 5
613. 5 c. Textile mill 5 5
614. 10 c. Sugar factory .. 5 5
615. 20 c. Mountain highway .. 20 5
616. 25 c. Motor coach .. 10 5
617. 30 c. Diesel locomotive .. 25 12
618. 35 c. Railway Station Addis Ababa 30 15
619. 15 c Sisal (inscr "SUGAR CANES") (air) .. 10 5
620. 40 c. Koka Dam 25 12
621. 50 c. Blue Nile Bridge .. 30 15
622. 60 c. Gondar castles .. 45 20
623. 80 c. Coffee tree 45 30
624. $1 Cattle 60 35
625. $3 Camels .. .. .. 1·90 1·00
626. $5 Boeing jetliner of E.A.L. 4·00 1·60

1965. I.C.Y.

627. **80.** 10 c. red and greenish bl. 8 5
628. 50 c. red and blue .. 35 25
629. 80 c. red and violet blue 50 35

81. Commercial Bank's Seal.

1965. Ethiopian National and Commercial Banks.

630. **81.** 10 c. black, indigo & red 10 5
631. – 30 c. black, ind. & ultram. 30 12
632. – 60 c. yellow, ind. & black 45 25

DESIGNS: 30 c. National Bank's Seal. 60 c. Banking halls and main building.

1966. Air. Ethiopian Birds (2nd series). As T 63. Multicoloured.

633. 10 c. White-collared kingfisher 12 5
634. 15 c. Blue-breasted bee-eater 20 8
635. 25 c. Paradise flycatcher .. 25 12
636. 40 c. Black-headed weaver 45 20
637. 60 c. White-necked pigeon 65 25

82. Press Building.

1966. "Light and Peace" Printing Press, Addis Ababa. Inaug.

638. **82.** 5 c. black and red .. 5 5
639. 15 c. black and green .. 15 5
640. 30 c. black and yellow .. 25 12

83. Rhinoceros. **84.** Kebero Drum.

1966. Air. Animals.

641. **83.** 5 c. black, grey & green 8 5
642. – 10 c. ochre, black & grn. 12 5
643. – 20 c. black, green & olive 20 8
644. – 30 c. ochre, black & grn. 25 12
645. – 60 c. brown, black & olive 65 20

ANIMALS: 10 c. Leopard. 20 c. Colobus monkey. 30 c. Nyala. 60 c. Ethiopian ibex.

1966. Musical Instruments.

646. **84.** 5 c. black and green .. 5 5
647. – 10 c. black and blue .. 8 5
648. – 35 c. black and orange 30 12
649. – 50 c. black and yellow 45 20
650. – 60 c. black and red .. 50 25

INSTRUMENTS: 10 c. Begena harp. 35 c. Mosenko stringed instrument. 50 c. Krar lyre. 60 c. Washent flutes.

85. Emperor Haile Selassie.

1966. "Fifty Years of Leadership".

651. **85.** 10 c. blk., grey, gold & grn. 8 5
652. 15 c. blk., grey, gold & red 12 5
653. 40 c. black, grey & gold 35 25

86. U.N.E.S.C O. Emblem and Map of Africa.

1966. U.N.E.S.C.O. 20th Anniv.

654. **86.** 15 c. red, black & blue .. 15 5
655. 60 c. ult., chest. & green 40 25

87. W.H.O. Building. **88.** Ethiopian Pavilion.

1966 W.H.O. Headquarters, Geneva. Inaug.

656. **87.** 5 c. green, sepia & blue 8 5
657. 40 c. sepia, green & vio. 25 15

1967. World Fair, Montreal.

658. **88.** 30 c. multicoloured .. 20 12
659. 45 c. multicoloured .. 30 15
660. 80 c. multicoloured .. 65 25

89. Diesel Train and Route-Map.

1967. Completion of Djibouti—Addis Ababa Railway. 50th Anniv.

661. **89.** 15 c. multicoloured .. 15 8
662. 30 c. multicoloured .. 30 15
663. 50 c. multicoloured .. 50 25

90. "Papilio aethiops" (inscr. "Papilionidae").

1967. Butterflies. (1st series). Multicoloured.

664. 5 c. Type **90** 5 5
665. 10 c. "Charaxes epijasius" 8 5
666. 20 c. "Charaxes varans" 15 8
667. 35 c. "Euphaedra neophron" 30 10
668. 40 c. "Salamis aethiops" 45 15

See also Nos. 915/19.

91. Haile Selassie I.

1967. Emperor Haile Selassies' 75th Birthday.

669. **91.** 10 c. multicoloured .. 8 5
670. 15 c. multicoloured .. 12 8
671. $1 multicoloured .. 90 35

1967. Air. Birds (3rd series). As T 68. Multicoloured.

673. 10 c. Abyssinian blue-winged goose 10 5
674. 15 c. Yellow-billed duck .. 12 8
675. 20 c. Wattled ibis 15 8
676. 25 c. Abyssinian striped swallow 25 12
677. 40 c. Black-winged lovebird 55 20

The 10 c. and 40 c. are vert.

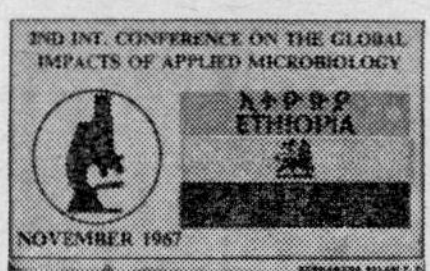

92. Microscope and Flag.

1967. 2nd Int. Conf. on Global Impacts of Applied Microbiology, Addis Ababa.

678. **92.** 5 c .multicoloured .. 8 5
679. 30 c. multicoloured .. 20 10
680. $1 multicoloured .. 80 35

93. Wall Painting, Gondar.

1967. Int. Tourist Year. Multicoloured.

681. 15 c. Type **93** 15 10
682. 25 c. Ancient votive stone and statuary, Atsbe Dera 25 15
683. 35 c. Cave paintings of animals, Harrar Province 35 20
684. 50 c. Prehistoric stone tools, Melke Kontoure .. 50 30

The 25 c. and 50 c. are vert. designs.

94. Cross of Biet-Maryam (bronze). **95.** Emperor Theodore with Lions.

1967. Crosses of Lalibela (1st series). Crosses in black and silver.

685. **94.** 5 c. black and lemon .. 5 5
686. – 10 c. black and orange 8 5
687. – 15 c. black and violet .. 12 5
688. – 20 c. black and cerise .. 15 8
689. – 50 c. black and yellow .. 50 20

CROSSES: 10 c. "Zagwe King's" cross. 15 c. Copper, Biet-Maryam. 20 c. Typical cross of Lalibela region. 50 c. Copper, Medhani Alem.

See also Nos. 737/40.

1968. Emperor Theodore. Death Cent.

690. – 10 c. brn., lilac & yellow 8 5
691. **95.** 20 c. lilac, brn. & mauve 12 8
692. – 50 c. red, orge. & green 40 15

DESIGNS—VERT. 10 c. Emperor Theodore. 50 c. Imperial crown.

96. Human Rights Emblem.

1968. Human Rights Year.

693. **96.** 15 c. black and red .. 15 5
694. $1 black and blue .. 80 25

97. Shah of Iran and Haile Selassie I.

1968. State Visit of Shah of Iran.

695. **97.** 5 c. multicoloured .. 5 5
696. 15 c. multicoloured .. 10 5
697. 30 c. multicoloured .. 30 10

98. Haile Selassie I and Addressing League of Nations, 1936.

1968. "Ethiopia's Struggle for Peace".

698. **98.** 15 c. multicoloured .. 12 5
699. – 35 c. multicoloured .. 25 12
700. – $1 multicoloured .. 90 40

HAILE SELASSIE and: 35 c. Africa Hall. 1 t. World map ("International Relations").

99. W.H.O. Emblem.

1968. World Health Organization. 20th Anniv.

701. **99.** 15 c. black and green .. 12 5
702. 60 c. black and purple 45 20

100. Running. **101.** Arrussi Costume.

1968. Olympic Games, Mexico. Multicoloured.

703. 10 c. Type **100** 8 5
704. 15 c. Football 12 5
705. 20 c. Boxing 15 5
706. 40 c. Basketball 30 12
707. 50 c. Cycling 50 15

1968. Ethiopian Costume. (1st series). Multicoloured.

708. 5 c. Type **101** 5 5
709. 15 c. Gemu Gofa 8 5
710. 20 c. Godjam 12 5
711. 30 c. Kaffa 15 8
712. 35 c. Harar 20 10
713. 60 c. Illubabor 30 15
714. 60 c. Eritrea 35 15

102. Postal Service Emblem and Initials.

1969. Ethiopian Postal Service. 75th Anniv.

715. **102.** 10 c. blk., brn. & green 10 5
716. 15 c. blk., brn. & yell. 12 5
717. 35 c. black, brn. & red 40 20

103. I.L.O. Emblem.

104. Red Cross Emblems. 105. Silver Coin of Endybis (3rd cent.).

1969. Int. Labour Organization. 50th Anniv.
718. **103.** 15 c. orange and black .. 10 5
719. 60 c. green and black .. 40 25

1969. League of Red Cross Societies. 50th Anniv.
720. **104.** 5 c. red, black and blue 5 5
721. 15 c. red, green & blue 12 5
722. 30 c. red, ultram & blue 25 12

1969. Ancient Ethiopian Coins.
723. **105.** 5 c. silver, black & blue 5 5
724. – 10 c. gold, black & red 8 5
725. – 15 c. gold, blk. & brown 12 5
726. 30 c. bronze, blk. & red 25 8
727. – 40 c. bronze, blk. & grn. 30 12
728. – 50 c. silver, blk. & violet 40 15
COINS: 10 c. Gold coin of Ezana (4th century). 15 c. Gold coin of Kalob (6th century). 30 c. Bronze coin of Armah (7th century) 40 c. Bronze coin of Wazena (7th century). 50 c. Silver coin of Gersem (8th century)

106. "Hunting".

1969. African Tourist Year. Multicoloured.
729. 5 c. Type **106** 5 5
730. 10 c. "Camping" 8 5
731. 15 c. "Fishing" 12 5
732. 20 c. "Watersports" .. 20 8
733. 25 c. "Mountaineering" (vert.) 25 8

107. Dove of Peace.

1969. United Nations. 25th Anniv. Mult.
734. 10 c. Type **107** 8 5
735. 30 c. Stylised flowers (vert.) 25 10
736. 60 c. Peace dove and emblem 55 25

108. Ancient Cross, and "Holy Family".

1969. Ancient Ethiopian Crosses (2nd series).
737. **108.** 5 c. black, yell. & green 5 5
738. – 10 c. black and yellow 8 5
739. – 25 c. black, grn. & yell. 25 12
740. – 60 c. black and yellow 50 25
DESIGNS—VERT. 10 c., 25 c. and 60 c. show different crosses and drawings similar to T **108**.

109. Ancient Figurines.

1970. Ancient Ethiopian Pottery. Multicoloured.
741. 10 c. Type **109** 8 5
742. 20 c. Decorated jar, Yeha 15 5
743. 25 c. Axum Pottery .. 20 8
744. 35 c. "Bird" jug, Matara 25 10
745. 60 c. Christian pottery, Adulis 30 15

110. Medhane Alem.

1970. Rock Churches of Lalibela. Multicoloured.
746. 5 c. Type **110** 5 5
747. 10 c. Bieta Amanuel .. 8 5
748. 15 c. Four churches .. 12 5
749. 20 c. Bieta Mariam .. 15 8
750. 50 c. Bieta Giorgis .. 40 20

111. Sail-finned Surgeon.

1970. Fishes. Multicoloured.
751. 5 c. Type **111** 5 5
752. 10 c. Undulate triggerfish 8 5
753. 15 c. Red striped butterfly 12 5
754. 25 c. Ghost butterfly .. 20 8
755. 50 c. Imperial angelfish .. 40 20

112. I.E.Y. Emblem. 114. Haile Selassie I.

113. O.A.U. Emblem.

1970. International Education Year.
756. **112.** 10 c. multicoloured .. 8 5
757. 20 c. multicoloured .. 20 8
758. 50 c. multicoloured .. 40 20

1970. Organisation of African Unity. Multicoloured.
759. 20 c. Type **113** 12 5
760. 30 c. O.A.U. flag .. 20 10
761. 40 c. O.A.U. Headquarters, Addis Ababa 25 12

1970. Haile Selassie's Coronation. 40th Anniv.
762. **114.** 15 c. multicoloured .. 10 5
763. 50 c. multicoloured .. 30 15
764. 60 c. multicoloured .. 40 25

115. Ministry Buildings.

1970. New Posts and Telecommunications Buildings, Addis Ababa. Inaug.
765. **115.** 10 c. multicoloured .. 8 5
766. 50 c. multicoloured .. 35 12
767. 80 c. multicoloured .. 45 20

1971. Ethiopian Costumes (2nd Series). Multicoloured designs similar to T 101.
768. 5 c. Begemedir and Semain Costume 5 5
769. 10 c. Bale 8 5
770. 15 c. Wolega 10 5
771. 20 c. Showa 15 5
772. 25 c. Sidamo 20 8
773. 40 c. Tigre 25 15
774. 50 c. Wello 45 20

116. Aircraft. Tail-fin. 117. "The Fountain of Life".

1971. Air. Ethiopian Airlines. 25th Anniv. Multicoloured.
775. 5 c. Type **116** 5 5
776. 10 c. "Ethiopian Life" .. 8 5
777. 20 c. Aircraft nose and control tower 15 5
778. 60 c. Airliner's flight deck and jet engine 40 15
779. 80 c. Route map 60 25

1971. Ethiopian Paintings. Multicoloured.
780. 5 c. Type **117** 5 5
781. 10 c. "King David" (15th-cent. manuscript) .. 8 5
782. 25 c. "St. George" (17th-cent. canvas) .. 15 5
783. 50 c. "King Kaleb" (18th-cent. triptych, Lalibela) 35 12
784. 60 c. "Yared singing to King Kaleb" (18th-cent. mural, Axum) 45 15

118. Black and White Heads.

1971. Racial Equality Year.
785. **118.** 10 c. blk., red & orange 8 5
786. – 60 c. multicoloured .. 30 15
787. – 80 c. multicoloured .. 45 20
DESIGN: 60 c. Black and white hands holding Globe. 80 c. Heads of four races.

119. Emperor Menelik II and Proclamation.

1971. Victory of Adwa. 75th Anniv. Multicoloured.
788. 10 c. Type **119** 8 5
789. 30 c. Ethiopian army on the march 15 8
790. 50 c. Battle of Auwa .. 25 12
791. 60 c. Ethiopian soldiers .. 40 20

120. Emperor Menelik II, Ras Makonnen and Early Telephones.

1971. Ethiopian Telecommunications. 75th Anniv. Multicoloured.
792. 5 c. Type **120** 5 5
793. 10 c. Emperor Haile Selassie and radio masts .. 8 5
794. 30 c. T.V. set & Ethiopians 20 8
795. 40 c. Microwave equipment 25 10
796. 60 c. Telephone dial and part of Globe 45 20

121. Mother and Child.

1971. U.N.I.C.E.F. 25th Anniv. Multicoloured.
797. 5 c. Type **121** 5 5
798. 10 c. Refugee children .. 8 5
799. 15 c. Man embracing child 10 5
800. 30 c. Children with toys .. 20 10
801. 50 c. Students 35 20

122. Lion's Head.

1971. Tourism. Embossed on gold foil.
802. **122.** $15 gold .. ..
803. – $15 gold .. ..
DESIGN: No. 803, Visit of Queen of Sheba to King Solomon.

1972. 1st U.N. Security Council Meeting in Africa (1st issue). Nos. 615/8 Optd. **U.N. SECURITY COUNCIL FIRST MEETING IN AFRICA 1972.**, in English and Amharic.
804. 20 c. multicoloured .. 15 8
805. 25 c. multicoloured .. 20 10
806. 30 c. multicoloured .. 30 12
807. 35 c. multicoloured .. 40 15
See also Nos. 832/4.

123. Reed Raft, Lake Haik.

1972. Ethiopian River Craft. Multicoloured.
808. 10 c. Type **123** 5 5
809. 20 c. Canoes, Lake Abaya 12 8
810. 30 c. Punts, Lake Tana .. 20 12
811. 60 c. Dugout canoes, Baro River 45 25

124. Cuneiform Proclamation of Cyrus the Great.

1972. Persian Empire. 2,500th Anniv.
812. **124.** 10 c. multicoloured .. 8 5
813. 60 c. multicoloured .. 45 20
814. 80 c. multicoloured .. 65 30

125. "Beehive" Hut, Sidamo Province.

1972. Architecture of Ethiopian Provinces.
815. **125.** 5 c. multicoloured .. 5 5
816. – 10 c. blk., grey & brn. 10 5
817. – 20 c. multicoloured .. 15 8
818. – 40 c. multicoloured .. 25 15
819. – 80 c. multicoloured .. 55 25
DESIGNS: 10 c. Two-storey houses, Tigre Province. 20 c. House with veranda, Eritrea Province. 40 c. Town house, Addis Ababa. 80 c. Thatched huts, Shoa Province.

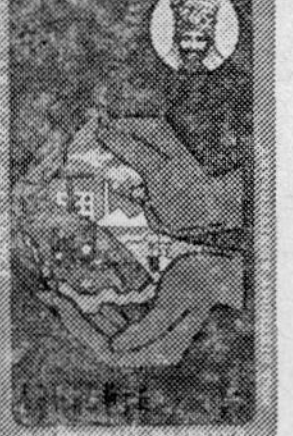

126. "Development" within Cupped Hands. 127. Running.

1972. Emperor Haile Selassie's 80th Birthday. Multicoloured.

820. 5 c. Type **126** 5 5
821. 10 c. Ethiopians within cupped hands 5 5
822. 25 c. Map, hands and O.A.U. emblem 12 8
823. 50 c. Handclasp and U.N. emblem 30 12
824. 60 c. Peace dove within hands 35 20

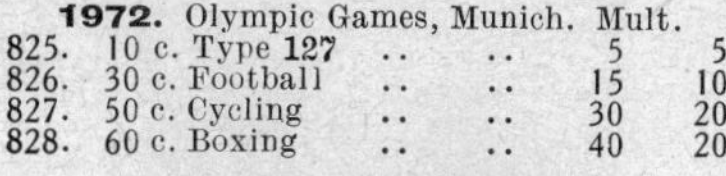

1972. Olympic Games, Munich. Mult.

825. 10 c. Type **127** 5 5
826. 30 c. Football 15 10
827. 50 c. Cycling 30 20
828. 60 c. Boxing 40 20

128. Cross and Open Bible.

1972. World Assembly of United Bible Societies, Addis Ababa. Multicoloured.

829. 20 c. Type **128** 12 5
830. 50 c. First office of B.F.B.S., and new H.Q. (vert.) .. 30 15
831. 80 c. Amharic Bible .. 50 25

129. Council in Session.

1972. 1st U.N. Security Council Meeting in Africa (2nd issue). Multicoloured.

832. 10 c. Type **129** 5 5
833. 60 c. Africa Hall, Addis Ababa 30 15
834. 80 c. Map of Africa and flags 50 25

130. " Polluted Waters ".

1973. World Campaign against Sea Pollution. Multicoloured.

835. 20 c. Type **130** 10 5
836. 30 c. Fishing in polluted sea 20 15
837. 80 c. Beach pollution .. 45 25

131. Interpol and Ethiopian Police Badges.

1973. Int. Criminal Police Organization (Interpol). 50th Anniv.

838. **131.** 40 c. black and orange 20 10
839. – 50 c. blk., brown & blue 25 12
840. – 60 c. black and red .. 35 15

DESIGNS: 50 c. Interpol badge and Headquarters, Paris. 60 c. Interpol badge.

132. " The Virgin and Child " (Fere Seyoum Zana Yacob period).

1973. Ethiopian Fine Arts. Multicoloured.

841. 5 c. Type **132** 5 5
842. 15 c. " The Crucifixion " (Zara Yacob (period) .. 8 5
843. 30 c. " St. Mary " (Entoto Mariam church painting) 15 8
844. 40 c. " Saint " mosaic (Addis Ababa Art School) 20 10
845. 80 c. Sculptured relief (Addis Ababa Art School) 45 20

133. African Colonial Maps, 1963 and 1973. **134.** Ethiopian Scout Flags.

1973. Organization of African Unity. 10th Anniv. Multicoloured.

846. 5 c. Type **133** 5 5
847. 10 c. Map, Headquarters and flags 5 5
848. 20 c. Map and emblems .. 10 5
849. 40 c. Map and "population" ranks 20 10
850. 80 c. Map on globe, O.A.U. and U.N. emblems .. 45 20

1973. Scouting in Ethiopia. 40th Anniv. Multicoloured.

851. 5 c. Type **134** 5 5
852. 15 c. " Scout " sign on highway 10 5
853. 30 c. Guide teaching old man to read 15 8
854. 40 c. " First Aid " 20 10
855. 60 c. Ethiopian scout .. 35 15

135. W.M.O. Emblem. **136.** Old Wall, Harar.

1973. World Meteorological Organization Cent.

856. **135.** 40 c. black, blue & new bl. 20 10
857. – 50 c. black and blue .. 25 12
858. – 60 c. multicoloured .. 35 15

DESIGNS: 50 c. Wind gauge and emblem. 60 c. Weather satellite.

1973. Prince Makonnen Memorial Hospital. Inaug. Multicoloured.

859. 5 c. Type **136** 5 5
860. 10 c. Prince Makonnen, equipment and patients 5 5
861. 20 c. Operating Theatre .. 8 5
862. 40 c. Scouts giving first-aid 15 10
863. 80 c. Prince Makonen .. 40 20

137. Haile Selassie I **138.** Flame Emblem.

1973.

864. **137.** 5 c. multicoloured .. 5 5
865. 10 c. multicoloured .. 5 5
866. 15 c. multicoloured .. 8 5
867. 20 c. multicoloured .. 8 5
868. 25 c. multicoloured .. 10 5
869. 30 c. multicoloured .. 12 8
870. 35 c. multicoloured .. 15 10
871. 40 c. multicoloured .. 15 10
872. 45 c. multicoloured .. 20 12
873. 50 c. multicoloured .. 25 15
874. 55 c. multicoloured .. 25 15
875. 60 c. multicoloured .. 30 15
876. 70 c. multicoloured .. 35 20
877. 90 c. multicoloured .. 40 25
878. $1 multicoloured .. 45 30
879. $2 multicoloured .. 90 60
880. $3 multicoloured .. 1·25 75
881. $5 multicoloured .. 2·25 1·40

1973. Declaration of Human Rights. 25th Anniv.

882. **138.** 40 c. gold, grn. & yell. 15 10
883. 50 c. gold, grn. & emerald 25 15
884. 60 c. gold, grn. & orge. 30 20

MINIMUM PRICE

The minimum price quoted is 5p which represents a handling charge rather than a basis for valuing common stamps. For further notes about prices see introductory pages.

139. Wicker Furniture. **140.** Cow, Calf and Syringe.

1974. Ethiopian Wicker-work. Various Wicker handicrafts.

885. **139.** 5 c. multicoloured .. 5 5
886. 10 c. multicoloured .. 5 5
887. 30 c. multicoloured .. 12 8
888. 50 c. multicoloured .. 25 15
889. 60 c. multicoloured .. 30 20

1974. Campaign Against Rinderpest. Mult.

890. 5 c. Type **140** 5 5
891. 15 c. Inoculation 8 5
892. 20 c. Bullock and syringe 8 5
893. 50 c. Laboratory technician 25 15
894. 60 c. Symbolic map .. 30 15

141. Umbrella Manufacture.

1974. Haile Selassie I Foundation. 20th Anniv. Multicoloured.

895. 10 c. Type **141** 5 5
896. 30 c. Weaving 12 8
897. 50 c. Children with books and toys 25 15
898. 60 c. Foundation building 30 15

142. Bitwoded Robe.

1974. Traditional Ceremonial Robes. Multicoloured.

899. 15 c. Type **142** 8 5
900. 25 c. Wageyoum 20 8
901. 35 c. Ras 20 10
902. 40 c. Leol Ras 25 15
903. 60 c. Negusenegest .. 30 20

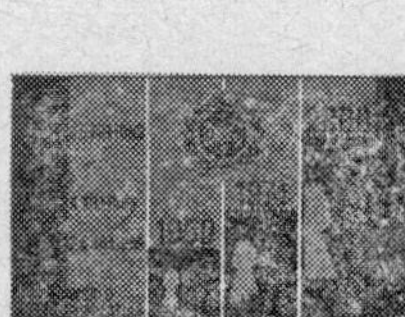

143. " Population Growth ". **144.** U.P.U. and Ethiopian P.T.T. Emblems.

1974. World Population Year. Multicoloured.

904. 40 c. Type **143** 20 12
905. 50 c. Diagram with large family 25 15
906. 60 c. " Rising Population " 30 20

1974. Universal Postal Union. Centenary. Multicoloured.

907. 15 c. Type **144** 8 5
908. 50 c. Emblem and letters .. 25 15
909. 60 c. U.P.U. emblem .. 30 20
910. 70 c. U.P.U. emblem and H.Q., Berne 35 20

145. Ethiopian Landscape. **146.** "Nymphalidae precis clelia CR."

1974. Meskel Festival.

911. **145.** 5 c. multicoloured .. 5 5
912. – 10 c. multicoloured .. 5 5
913. – 20 c. multicoloured .. 10 8
914. – 80 c. multicoloured .. 40 25

DESIGNS: Nos. 912/4, Various festive scenes similar to Type **145**.

1975. Butterflies (2nd series). Mult.

915. 10 c. Type **146** 5 5
916. 25 c. " Nymphalidae charaxes achaemenes F " .. 12 10
917. 45 c. " Papilionidae P. learanus " 20 12
918. 50 c. " Nymphalidae charaxes druceanus B " 25 15
919. 60 c. " Papilionidae P. demodocus " 30 20

147. " The Three Wise Men ". **148.** Warthog.

1975. Paintings in Ethiopian Churches' Multicoloured.

1975. Religious Paintings in Ethiopian Churches. Multicoloured.

920. 5 c. Type **147** 5 5
921. 10 c. " The Entombment " 5 5
922. 15 c. " Christ with the Apostles " 10 8
923. 30 c. " The Miracle of the Blind " 20 15
924. 40 c. " The Crucifixion " .. 25 20
925 80 c. "Christ in Majesty " 50 40

1975. Animals. Multicoloured.

926. 5 c. Type **148** 5 5
927. 10 c. Aardvark 5 5
928. 20 c. Semien wolf 12 10
929. 40 c. Gelada baboon .. 25 20
930. 80 c. Civet 50 40

149. Dove crossing Globe. **150.** Reception Desk.

1975. International Women's Year. Mult.

931. 40 c. Type **149** 25 20
932. 50 c. I.W.Y. emblem and symbols .. 30 25
933. 90 c. " Equality " .. 55 50

1975. Opening of National Postal Museum.

934. **150.** 10 c. multicoloured .. 5 5
935. – 30 c. multicoloured .. 20 15
936. – 60 c. multicoloured .. 40 30
937. – 70 c. multicoloured .. 45 35

DESIGNS: 30 c. to 70 c. Views of museum display area.

151. Map Emblem. **152.** U.N. Emblem.

1975. " Ethiopian Tikdem " (Socialism). 1st Anniv.

938. **151.** 5 c. multicoloured .. 5 5
939. 10 c. multicoloured .. 5 5
940. 25 c. multicoloured .. 15 12
941. 50 c. multicoloured .. 30 25
942. 90 c. multicoloured .. 55 50

1975. United Nations. 30th Anniv.

943. **152.** 40 c. multicoloured .. 25 20
944. 50 c. multicoloured .. 30 25
945. 90 c. multicoloured .. 55 50

HAVE YOU READ THE NOTES AT THE BEGINNING OF THIS CATALOGUE?

These often provide answers to the enquiries we receive.

153. Illubabor.

154. " Delphinium wellbyi ".

1975. Regional Hair-styles. Mult.
946. 5 c. Type 153 .. .. 5 5
947. 15 c. Arussi 8 5
948. 20 c. Eritrea 10 8
949. 30 c. Bale 20 15
950. 35 c. Kaffa 20 15
951. 50 c. Begemder 30 25
952. 60 c. Shoa 40 30

1975. Ethiopian Flowers. Multicoloured.
953. 5 c. Type 154 .. .. 5 5
954. 10 c. " Plectocephalus varians " 5 5
955. 20 c. " Brachystelma asmarensis " (horiz.) .. 10 8
956. 40 c. " Ceropegia inflata " 25 20
957. 80 c. " Erythrina brucei " 50 40

155. Goalkeeper diving.

156. Early and Modern Telephones.

1976. Tenth African Football " Cup of Nations " Championships. Multicoloured.
958. 5 c. Type 155 .. .. 5 5
959. 10 c. Footballers in tackle 5 5
960. 25 c. Player shooting at goal 15 12
961. 50 c. Defender clearing ball 30 25
962. 90 c. Ball and Ethiopian flag 55 50

1976. Telephone Cent. Multicoloured.
963. 30 c. Type 156 .. .. 20 15
964. 60 c. A. Graham Bell .. 40 30
965. 90 c. Aerial complex .. 55 50

157. Amulets.

158. Boxing.

1976. Ethiopian Jewellery.
966. 157. 5 c. multicoloured .. 5 5
967. – 10 c. multicoloured .. 5 5
968. – 20 c. multicoloured .. 10 8
969. – 40 c. multicoloured .. 25 20
970. – 80 c. multicoloured .. 50 40
Nos 967/70 are similar to T 157 showing models with jewellery.

1976. Olympic Games, Montreal. Multicoloured.
971. 10 c. Type 158 .. .. 5 5
972. 80 c. Shot-putting .. 50 40
973. 90 c. Cycling 55 45

159. Campaign Emblem.

160. Map Emblem.

1976. " Development Through Co-operation " Campaign.
974. 159. 5 c. multicoloured .. 5 5
975. 10 c. multicoloured .. 5 5
976. 50 c. multicoloured .. 30 25
977. 90 c. multicoloured .. 55 45

1976. Ethiopian Tikdem (Socialism). 2nd Anniv.
978. 160. 5 c. multicoloured .. 5 5
979. 10 c. multicoloured .. 5 5
980. 25 c. multicoloured .. 15 12
981. 50 c multicoloured .. 30 25
982. 90 c. multicoloured .. 55 45

161. Donkey Boy and Aircraft.

1976. Ethiopian Airlines. 30th Anniv. Multicoloured.
983. 5 c. Type 161 .. .. 5 5
984. 10 c. Crescent on globe .. 5 5
985. 25 c. " Star " of crew and passengers 15 12
986. 50 c. Propeller and jet engines 30 25
987. 90 c. Aircraft converging on map 55 45

POSTAGE DUE STAMPS

(D 1.)

D 2.

1896. Optd. with Type D 1.
D 8. 1. ¼ g. green 40
D 9. ½ g. red 40
D 10. 1 g. blue 40
D 11. 2 g. brown 40
D 12. 4 g. claret 20
D 13. 8 g. mauve 20
D 14. 16 g. black 20

1905. Optd. **Taxe a Percevoir T.**
D 108. 1. ¼ g. green .. .. 2·00 2·00
D 109. ½ g. red .. .. 2·00 2·00
D 110. 1 g. blue .. .. 2·00 2·00
D 111. 2 g. brown .. .. 1·90 1·90
D 112. 4 g. claret .. .. 2·10 2·10
D 113. 8 g. mauve .. .. 2·75 2·75
D 114. 16 g. black .. .. 3·25 3·25

1907. As above further optd. with value in figures between stars.
D 122. 1. ¼ g. green .. .. 3·25 3·25
D 123. ½ g. red .. .. 3·25 3·25
D 124. 1 g. blue .. .. 3·25 3·25
D 125. 2 g. brown .. .. 3·25 3·25
D 126. 2. 4 g. claret .. .. 3·25 3·25
D 127. 8 g. mauve .. .. 3·25 3·25
D 128. 16 g. black .. .. 1·75 1·75

1908. Optd. with Amharic inscription and large T in triangle.
D 140. 1. ¼ g. green 30 30
D 141. ½ g. red 30 30
D 142. 1 g. blue 30 30
D 143. 2 g. brown 35 35
D 144. 2. 4 g. claret 55 55
D 145. 8 g. mauve .. .. 1·40 1·40
D 146. 16 g. black .. .. 2·50 2·50

1913. Stamps of 1909 and the 1 g. of 1919 optd. with Amharic inscription and large T in triangle.
D 161. 9. ¼ g. green 70 70
D 162. ½ g. red 70 70
D 163. 1 g. orange and green 60 60
D 210. – 1 g. black and purple (No. 184) 40 40
D 164. 10. 2 g. blue 75 75
D 165. 4 g. claret and green 1·00 1·00
D 166. – 8 g. grey and red (No. 152) .. .. 1·60 1·60
D 167. – 16 g. red (No. 153) .. 4·25 4·25

1951.
D 417. D 2. 1 c. green 5 5
D 418. 5 c. red 8 8
D 419. 10 c. violet .. 12 10
D 420. 20 c. brown .. 20 15
D 421. 50 c. blue .. 45 40
D 422. $1 purple .. 80 75

EXPRESS LETTER STAMPS

E 1. Motor-cycle Messenger.

DESIGN: 50 c. G.P.O., Addis Ababa.

1947. Inscr. " EXPRESS ".
E 357. E1. 30 c. brown .. 35 20
E 358. – 50 c. blue .. 75 55

FALKLAND ISLANDS BC

A Br. colony in the S. Atlantic.

1.

2.

1878.
8. 1. ½d. green 35 45
16. 1d. claret to brown .. 2·00 2·00
17. 1d. red .. .. .. 2·00 2·00
20. 2d. purple .. .. 2·00 5·00
24. 2½d. blue .. .. 2·75 6·00
28. 4d. black .. .. .. 5·00 8·50
3. 6d. green .. .. .. 10·00 13·00
29. 6d. yellow .. .. 5·50 11·00
31. 9d. red .. .. .. 5·00 13·00
34. 1s. brown .. .. .. 5·50 11·00
41. – 2s. 6d. blue .. .. 42·00 45·00
42. 2. 5s. red .. .. .. 35·00 40·00
DESIGN: 2s. 6d. As T 2, but different frame.

1891. No. 16 bisected diagonally and each half surch. **½d.**
39. 1. ½d. on half of 1d. brown .. 75·00 42·00

4.

5.

1904.
43. 4. ½d. green .. .. .. 65 1·10
47. 1d. red .. .. .. 1·50 1·40
50. 2d. purple .. .. 2·25 10·00
52. 2½d. blue .. .. .. 7·00 7·00
54. 6d. orange .. .. 9·00 11·00
55. 1s. brown .. .. .. 7·00 10·00
57. 5. 3s. green .. .. .. 23·00 28·00
58. 5s. red .. .. .. 45·00 45·00

1912. As T 4/5 but portrait of King George V.
98. ½d green .. .. .. 65 1·00
100. 1d. red 40 65
104. 2d. purple .. .. 80 1·10
74. 2½d. blue .. .. .. 1·60 3·25
106. 2½d. purple on yellow .. 1·10 2·00
111. 6d. orange .. .. 1·25 1·90
113. 1s. brown .. .. 5·50 9·00
81. 3s. green .. .. .. 12·00 14·00
82. 5s. red .. .. .. 22·00 24·00
83a. 5s. purple .. .. 18·00 20·00
84. 10s. red on green .. 60·00 75·00
85. £1 black on red £100 £120

1918. As 1912, optd. **WAR STAMP.**
86. ½d. green .. .. 50 2·25
92. 1d. red .. .. .. 25 1·00
95. 1s. brown .. .. 2·40 10·00

1928. No. 104 surch. **2½d.**
115. 2½d. on 2d. purple .. £250 £350

8. Whale and Penguins.

ILLUSTRATIONS
British Commonwealth and all overprints and surcharges are FULL SIZE. Foreign Countries have been reduced to ¾-LINEAR.

1929.
116. 8. ½d. green 15 30
117. 1d. red 25 25
118. 2d. grey 25 50
119. 2½d. blue 25 70
120. 4d. orange .. .. 1·10 2·25
121. 6d. purple .. .. 1·50 2·25
122. 1s. black on green .. 3·00 4·00
123. 2s. 6d. red on blue .. 9·50 12·00
124. 5s. green on yellow .. 13·00 18·00
125. 10s. red on green .. 27·00 45·00
126. £1 black on red £100 £130

9. Romney Marsh Ram.

1933. British Occupation Cent. Inscr. " 1833-1933 ".
127. 9. ½d. black and green .. 70 1·00
128. – 1d. black and red .. 60 75
129. – 1½d. black and blue .. 70 1·60
130. – 2d. black and brown .. 1·40 2·25
131. – 3d. black and violet .. 1·75 3·00
132. – 4d. black and orange .. 3·00 5·00
133. – 6d. black and grey .. 11·00 13·00
134. – 1s. black and olive .. 14·00 20·00
135. – 2s. 6d. black and violet 35·00 45·00
136. – 5s. black and yellow .. £130 £150
137. – 10s. black and brown .. £170 £200
138. – £1 black and red .. £500 £550
DESIGNS—HORIZ. 1d. Iceberg. 1½d. Whale-catcher. 2d. Port Louis. 3d. Map of Falkland Is. 4d. S. Georgia. 6d. Whale. 1s. Government House, Stanley. VERT 2s. 6d. Battle Memorial. 5s. King Penguin. 10s. Arms. £1 King George V.

1935. Silver Jubilee. As T **11** of Antigua.
139. 1d. blue and red .. 20 12
140. 2½d. brown and blue .. 40 65
141. 4d. green and blue .. 50 70
142. 1s. grey and purple .. 1·25 2·25

1937. Coronation. As T **2** of Aden.
143. ½d. green 12 12
144. 1d. red 15 12
145. 2½d. blue 20 30

21. Whale's Jaw Bones.

1938.
146. 21. ½d. black and green .. 10 10
147a. A. 1d. black and red .. 50 50
148. B. 1d. black and violet .. 10 12
149. 2d. black and violet .. 55 80
150. A. 2d. black and red .. 10 12
151. C. 2½d. black and blue .. 35 50
152. D. 2½d. black and blue .. 45 80
153. C. 3d. black and blue .. 25 20
154. D. 4d. black and purple .. 40 40
155. E. 6d. black and brown .. 1·75 2·25
156. 6d. black .. .. 80 1·25
157. F. 9d. black and blue .. 55 55
158a. G. 1s. blue .. .. 1·00 1·00
159. H. 1s. 3d. black and red .. 40 55
160. I. 2s. 6d. black .. .. 8·50 9·00
161. J. 5s. blue and orange .. 5·00 5·50
162. K. 10s. black and orange .. 6·50 7·00
163. L. £1 black and violet .. 11·00 12·00
DESIGNS—HORIZ. A. Black-necked swan. B. Battle memorial. C. Flock of sheep. D. Upland goose. E. R.R.S. " Discovery II ". F. R.R.S. " William Scoresby G. Mount Sugar Top. H. Turkey vultures. I. Gentoo penguins. J. Sea lion. K. Deception Is. L. Arms of the Colony.

1946. Victory. As T **4** of Aden.
164. 1d. mauve 10 12
165. 3d. blue 10 15

1948. Silver Wedding. As T **5/6** of Aden.
166. 2½d. blue 10 12
167. £1 mauve .. .. 14·00 22·00

1949. U.P.U. As T **14/17** of Antigua.
168. 1d. violet 12 20
169. 3d. blue 20 25
170. 1s. 3d. green 55 90
171. 2s. blue .. .. .. 85 1·60

22. Sheep.

1952.
172. 22. ½d. green 25 25
173. – 1d. red 30 25
174. – 2d. violet 45 55
175. – 2½d. black and blue .. 20 30
176. – 3d. blue 20 35
177. – 4d. purple 25 40
178. – 6d. brown 50 55
179. – 9d. yellow .. .. 1·00 1·10
180. – 1s. black .. .. 1·10 95
181. – 1s. 3d. orange .. .. 55 1·10
182. – 2s. 6d. olive .. .. 1·60 2·25
183. – 5s. purple .. .. 2·25 3·00
184. – 10s. grey .. .. 4·00 5·50
185. – £1 black .. .. 7·00 7·50
DESIGNS—HORIZ. 1d. R.M.S. " Fitzroy ". 2d. Upland goose. 2½d. Map. 4d. Auster aircraft. 6d. M.S.S. " John Biscoe ". 9d. View of " Two Sisters ". 1s. 3d. Kelp goose and gander. 10s. Sea-lion and female. £1 Hulk of " Great Britain ". VERT. 3d. Arms. 1s. Gentoo penguins. 2s. 6d. Sheep shearing. 5s. Memorial.

1953. Coronation. As T **7** of Aden.
186. 1d. black and red .. 45 50

1955. As 1952 issue but with portrait of Queen Elizabeth II.

187. ½d. green 12 12
188. 1d. red 15 15
189. 2d. violet 30 40
190. 6d. brown .. .. 1·40 1·60
191. 9d. yellow .. .. 2·40 3·00
192. 1s. black .. .. 2·40 3·00

23. Falkland Island Thrush.

1960. Birds.

227. **23.** ½d. black and green .. 25 25
194. – 1d. black and red .. 15 15
195. – 2d. black and blue .. 12 12
196. – 2½d. black & yell.-brown 15 15
197. – 3d. black and olive .. 15 20
198. – 4d. black and carmine 15 20
199. – 5½d. black and violet .. 20 25
200. – 6d. black and sepia .. 30 25
201. – 9d. black and vermilion 30 30
202. – 1s. black and maroon .. 20 25
203. – 1s. 3d. black and blue 60 1·75
204. – 2s. black and chestnut 70 85
205. – 5s. black and turquoise 2·50 3·00
206. – 10s. black and purple .. 5·00 6·00
207. – £1 black and yellow .. 10·00 11·00

BIRDS: 1d. Dominican gull. 2d. Gentoo penguins. 2½d. Falkland Is. marsh starling. 3d. Upland geese. 4d. Steamer ducks. 5½d. Rockhopper penguins. 6d. Black-browed albatross. 9d. Silver grebe. 1s. Pied oystercatchers. 1s. 3d. Yellow-billed teal. 2s. Kelp geese. 5s. King cormorants. 20s. Carancho. 20s. Black-necked swan.

24. Morse Key. **25.** Battle Memorial.

1962. Establishment of Radio Communications. 50th Anniv.

208. **24.** 6d. red and orange .. 40 40
209. – 1s. green and olive .. 90 90
210. – 2s. violet and blue .. 1·75 1·75

DESIGNS: 1s. One-valve receiver. 2s. Rotary Spark transmitter.

1963. Freedom from Hunger. As T **10** of Aden.

211. 1s. blue .. .. .. 3·00 3·00

1963. Red Cross Cent. As T **24** of Antigua.

212. 1d. red and black .. 75 75
213. 1s. red and blue .. 3·00 4·50

1964. Shakespeare. 400th Birth Anniv. As T **25** of Antigua.

214. 6d. black 50 55

1964. Battle of the Falkland Islands. 50th Anniv.

215. – 2½d. black and red .. 30 30
216. – 6d. black and blue .. 30 30
217. – 1s. black and red .. 60 70
218. **25.** 2s. black and blue .. 1·25 1·40

SHIPS—HORIZ. 2½d. H.M.S. "Glasgow". 6d. H.M.S. "Kent". 1s. H.M.S. "Invincible".

1965. I.T.U. Cent. As T **26** of Antigua.

219. 1d. light blue & deep blue 15 15
220. 2s. lilac and yellow .. 1·75 1·75

1965. I.C.Y. As T **27** of Antigua.

221. 1d. purple and turquoise .. 15 15
222. 1s. green and lavender .. 90 1·10

1966. Churchill Commem. As T **28** of Antigua.

223. ½d. blue 10 10
224. 1d. green 15 15
225. 1s. brown .. .. .. 80 1·10
226. 2s. violet .. .. .. 1·60 2·25

26. Globe and Human Rights Emblem.

1968. Human Rights Year.

228. **26.** 2d. multicoloured .. 10 10
229. 6d. multicoloured .. 25 25
230. 1s. multicoloured .. 40 40
231. 2s. multicoloured .. 70 70

27. Dusty Miller.

1968. Flowers Multicoloured.

232. ½d. Type **27** 5 5
233. 1½d. Pig Vine 5 5
234. 2d. Pale Maiden 5 5
235. 3d. Dog Orchid 5 8
236. 3½d. Sea Cabbage .. 10 12
237. 4½d. Vanilla Daisy .. 12 15
238. 5½d. yellow, brown and grn. (Arrowleaf Marigold) .. 15 20
239. 6d. red, black and green (Diddle Dee) 15 20
240. 1s. Scurvy Grass 25 30
241. 1s. 6d. Prickly Burr .. 40 1·10
242. 2s. Fachine 70 75
243. 3s. Lavender .. .. 90 1·10
244. 5s. Felton's Flower .. 1·25 1·50
245. £1 Yellow Orchid .. 1·75 2·00

Nos. 233, 236, 238/40 and 244 are horiz.

28. DHC—2 Beaver Floatplane.

1969. Government Air Services. 21st Anniv. Multicoloured.

246. 2d. Type **28** 10 10
247. 6d. "Norseman" 15 15
248. 1s. "Auster" 30 35
249. 2s. Arms of the Falkland Islands 60 70

29. Holy Trinity Church 1869.

1969. Bishop Stirling's Consecration. Cent.

250. **29.** 2d. black, grey & green 8 8
251. – 6d. black, grey and red 12 12
252. – 1s. black, grey & lilac .. 20 25
253. – 2s. multicoloured .. 40 50

DESIGNS: 6d. Christ Church Cathedral, 1969. 1s. Bishop Stirling. 2s. Bishop's Mitre.

30 Mounted Volunteer.

1970. Defence Force. Golden Jubilee. Multicoloured.

254. 2d. Type **30** 5 8
255. 6d. Defence Post .. 12 12
256. 1s. Corporal in No. 1 Dress uniform 30 30
257. 2s. Badge 50 55

Nos. 255 and 257 are horiz.

31. S.S. "Great Britain" (1843).

1970. S.S. "Great Britain" Restoration. Stamps show S.S. "Great Britain" in year given. Multicoloured.

258. 2d. Type **31** 10 10
259. 4d. 1845 .. .. .. 20 25
260. 9d. 1876 .. .. .. 25 30
261. 1s. 1886 .. .. .. 40 50
262. 2s. 1970 .. .. .. 80 1·00

1971. Decimal Currency. Nos. 232/44 surch.

263. ½p. on ½d. multicoloured 15 15
264. 1p. on 1½d. multicoloured 5 5
265. 1½p. on 2d. multicoloured 5 5
266. 2p. on 3d. multicoloured 8 8
267. 2½p. on 3½d. multicoloured 10 12
268. 3p. on 4½d. multicoloured 12 15
269. 4p. on 5½d. yellow, brown and green 20 25
270. 5p. on 6d. red, blk. & grn. 25 30
271. 6p. on 1s. multicoloured .. 25 35
272. 7½p. on 1s. 6d. multicoloured 40 50
273. 10p. on 2s. multicoloured .. 45 55
274. 15p. on 3s. multicoloured .. 65 80
275. 25p. on 5s. multicoloured .. 1·50 1·75

1972. Decimal Currency. Nos. 232/44 inscr. in decimal currency.

276. ½p. multicoloured .. 8 10
277. 1p. multicoloured .. 5 5
278. 1½p. multicoloured .. 5 5
279. 2p. multicoloured .. 10 10
280. 2½p. multicoloured .. 5 5
281. 3p. multicoloured .. 5 8
282. 4p. yellow, brown & green 10 10
283. 5p. red, black and green .. 12 12
284. 6p. multicoloured .. 20 25
285. 7½p. multicoloured .. 15 20
286. 10p. multicoloured .. 20 25
287. 15p. multicoloured .. 25 30
288. 25p. multicoloured .. 45 50

1972. Royal Silver Wedding. As T **19** of Ascension but with Romney Marsh Sheep and Giant Sea Lions in background.

289. 1p. green 12 20
290. 10p. blue .. .. .. 75 1·10

1973. Royal Wedding. As Type **26** of Anguilla. Background colour given. Mult.

291. 5p. mauve 12 15
292. 15p. brown 45 50

32. Fur Seal.

1974. Tourism. Multicoloured.

306. 2p. Type **32** 8 8
307. 4p. Trout-Fishing 12 12
308. 5p. Rockhopper Penguins 15 20
309. 15p. Military Starling .. 45 50

33. 19th-century Mail-coach.

1974. U.P.U. Multicoloured.

310. 2p. Type **33** 8 8
311. 5p. Packet ship, 1841 .. 15 15
312. 8p. First U.K. aerial post, 1911 .. .. .. 20 25
313. 16p. Ship's catapult mail, 1920's 45 45

34. Churchill and Houses of Parliament.

1974. Sir Winston Churchill. Birth Cent Multicoloured.

314. 16p. Type **34** 40 45
315. 20p. Churchill and warships 45 50

35. H.M.S. "Exeter".

1974. Battle of the River Plate. 35th Anniv. Multicoloured.

317. 2p. Typ **35** 10 10
318. 6p. H.M.N.Z. "Achilles" 20 25
319. 8p. "Admiral Graf Spee" 25 30
320. 16p. H.M.S. "Ajax" .. 40 45

36. Seal and Flag Badge.

1975. Heraldic Arms, 50th Anniv. Mult.

321. 2p. Type **36** 5 5
322. 7½p. Coat of arms, 1925 .. 20 20
323. 10p. Coat of arms, 1948 .. 25 25
324. 16p. Arms of the Dependencies, 1952 .. .. 35 40

37. ½p Coin and Trout.

1975. New Coinage. Multicoloured.

338. 2p. Type **37** 5 5
339. 5½p. p coin and Gentoo penguin 12 15
340. 8p. 2p coin and Upland goose 20 25
341. 10p. 5 p coin and albatross 25 25
342. 16p. 10p coin and sea lion 40 45

38. Gathering Sheep.

1976. Sheep Farming Industry. Multicoloured.

343. 2p. Type **38** 5 5
344. 7½p. Shearing 15 15
345. 10p. Dipping 20 20
346. 20p. Shipping 40 45

FALKLAND ISLANDS DEPENDENCIES BC

Four groups of Islands situated between the Falkland Is. and the South Pole. In 1946 the four groups ceased issuing separate issues which were replaced by a single general issue. In 1963 the stamps of Br. Antarctic Territory were used in all these islands except South Georgia and South Sandwich for which separate stamps were issued (q.v.).

GRAHAM LAND

1944. Stamps of Falkland Is. of 1938 optd. **GRAHAM LAND DEPENDENCY OF.**

A 1. **11.** ½d. black and green .. 12 15
A 2. – 1d. black and violet .. 12 20
A 3. – 2d. black and red .. 12 20
A 4. – 3d. black and blue .. 15 25
A 5. – 4d. black and purple .. 20 40
A 6. – 6d. black and brown .. 65 75
A 7. – 9d. black and blue .. 45 60
A 8. – 1s. blue 50 65

SOUTH GEORGIA

1944. Stamps of Falkland Is. of 1938 optd. **SOUTH GEORGIA DEPENDENCY OF.**

B 1. **21.** ½d. black and green .. 12 12
B 2. – 1d. black and violet .. 12 12
B 3. – 2d. black and red .. 12 15
B 4. – 3d. black and blue .. 15 20
B 5. – 4d. black and purple .. 20 25
B 6. – 6d. black and brown .. 70 80
B 7. – 9d. black and blue .. 45 40
B 8. – 1s. blue 45 60

SOUTH ORKNEYS

1944. Stamps of Falkland Is. of 1938 optd. **SOUTH ORKNEYS DEPENDENCY OF.**

C 1. **21.** ½d. black and green .. 12 20
C 2. – 1d. black and violet .. 12 20
C 3. – 2d. black and red .. 12 20
C 4. – 3d. black and blue .. 15 25
C 5. – 4d. black and purple .. 20 25
C 6. – 6d. black and brown .. 70 80
C 7. – 9d. black and blue .. 45 70
C 8. – 1s. blue 45 70

SOUTH SHETLANDS

1944. Stamps of Falkland Is. of 1938 optd. **SOUTH SHETLAND DEPENDENCY OF.**

D 1. **11.** ½d. black and green .. 12 20
D 2. – 1d. black and violet .. 12 20
D 3. – 2d. black and red .. 12 20
D 4. – 3d. black and blue .. 15 20
D 5. – 4d. black and purple .. 20 40
D 6. – 6d. black and brown .. 70 70
D 7. – 9d. black and blue .. 45 60
D 8. – 1s. blue 45 70

GENERAL ISSUES

1.

1946.

G 1. **1.** ½d. black and green .. 10 12
G 2. 1d. black and violet .. 10 15
G 3. 2d. black and red .. 10 15
G 11a. 2½d. black and blue .. 30 60
G 4. 3d. black and blue .. 12 15
G 5. 4d. black and claret .. 15 25
G 6. 6d. black and orange .. 20 40
G 7. 9d. black and brown .. 20 40
G 8. 1s. black and purple .. 40 65

1946. Victory. As T. 4 of Aden.

G 17. 1d. violet 10 10
G 18. 3d. blue 10 12

1949. Silver Wedding. As T 5/6 of Aden.

G 19. 2½d. blue 10 15
G 20. 1s. deep blue .. .. 1·10 1·40

1949. U.P.U. As T 14/17 of Antigua.

G 21. 1d. violet 20 30
G 22. 2d. red 30 50
G 23. 3d. blue 55 65
G 24. 6d. orange .. .. 80 1·10

1953. Coronation. As T 7 of Aden.

G 25. 1d. black and violet .. 50 50

2. "Trepassey", 1945-47.

1954. Ships.

G 26. – ½d. black and green .. 12 12
G 27. **2.** 1d. black and sepia .. 12 12
G 28. – 1½d. black and olive .. 12 15
G 29. – 2d. black and red .. 12 15
G 30. – 2½d. black and yellow .. 12 15
G 31. – 3d. black and blue .. 15 20
G 32. – 4d. black and purple .. 30 35
G 33. – 6d. black and lilac .. 40 45
G 34. – 9d. black .. 45 60
G 35. – 1s. black and brown .. 70 80
G 36. – 2s. black and red .. 1·75 2·00
G 37. – 2s. 6d. black & turquoise 2·00 2·25
G 38. – 5s. black and violet .. 5·00 6·00
G 39. – 10s. black and blue .. 9·00 11·00
G 40. – £1 black .. .. 20·00 22·00

SHIPS—VERT. ½d. "John Biscoe". 6d. "Discovery". 9d. "Endurance". 2s. 6d. "Francais". 5s. "Scotia". £1, "Belgica". HORIZ. 1½d. "Wyatt Earp". 2d. "Eagle". 2½d. "Penola". 3d. "Discovery II". 4d. "William Scoresby". 1s. "Deutschland". "Pourquois Pas?". 10s. "Antarctic"

1956. Trans-Antarctic Expedition. Nos. G 27, G 30/1 and G 33 optd. **TRANS-ANTARCTIC EXPEDITION 1955-1958.**

G 41. **2.** 1d. black and sepia .. 10 10
G 42. – 2½d. black and yellow 15 25
G 43. – 3d. black and blue .. 20 25
G 44. – 6d. black and lilac .. 35 45

For later issues see **BRITISH ANTARCTIC TERRITORIES** and **SOUTH GEORGIA.**

FARIDKOT BC

A state of the Punjab, India. Now uses Indian stamps.

1 folus = 1 paisa = ¼ anna. Later, as India.

1.

2.

1879. Imperf.

N 5. **1.** 1 f. blue 40 60
N 6. **2.** 1 p. blue 50 70

1887. Stamps of India (Queen Victoria) optd. **FARIDKOT STATE.**

17. **25.** 3 p. red 15 30
1. **14.** ½ a. blue-green 5 5
2. – 1 a. purple 10 25
4. – 2 a. blue 50 50
6. – 3 a. orange 45 50
8. – 4 a. green (No. 96) .. 45 50
11. – 6 a. brown (No 80) .. 65 70
12. – 8 a. mauve .. .. 1·10 1·10
14. – 12 a. purple on red .. 4·00 4·00
15. – 1 r. grey .. .. .. 4·00 4·00
16. **26.** 1 r. green and red .. 4·00 4·00

OFFICIAL STAMPS

1886. Stamps of India (Queen Victoria) optd. **SERVICE FARIDKOT STATE.**

O 1. **14.** ½ a. blue-green .. 5 10
O 2. – 1 a. purple 25 30
O 4. – 2 a. blue 50 50
O 6. – 3 a. orange 40 80
O 8. – 4 a. green (No. 96) .. 50 65
O 11. – 6 a. brown (No. 80) .. 1·25 1·50
O 12. – 8 a. mauve 60 75
O 14. – 1 r. grey .. .. 4·00 5·00
O 15. **26.** 1 r. green and red .. 6·50 8·00

FAROE ISLANDS E1

A Danish possession in the North Atlantic Ocean.

Under British Administration during the German Occupation of Denmark, 1940/5.

1940. Stamps of Denmark surch. in figures and bar or bars.

2. **24.** 20 ore on 1 ore black .. 20·00 20·00
3. 20 ore on 5 ore maroon .. 20·00 15·00
1. **21.** 20 ore on 15 ore red .. 25·00 8·00
4. **25.** 50 ore on 5 ore maroon .. 80·00 22·00
5. 60 ore on 6 ore orange .. 60·00 55·00

1. Map of the Faroe Islands.

2. "Vidoy and Svinoy" (E. Mohr).

1975.

(a) As Type **1.**

6. **1.** 5 ore brown 5 5
7. – 10 ore blue and green .. 5 5
8. **1.** 50 ore blue 12 12
9. – 60 ore blue and brown .. 15 15
10. – 70 ore black and blue .. 15 15
11. – 80 ore blue and brown .. 20 20
12. **1.** 90 ore red 20 20
13. – 120 ore indigo and blue .. 30 30
14. – 200 ore black and blue .. 45 45
15. – 250 ore blue, green & black 55 55
16. – 300 ore blue, green & black 70 70

(b) As Type **2.**

17. **2.** 350 ore multicoloured .. 80 80
18. – 450 ore multicoloured .. 1·10 1·10
19. – 500 ore multicoloured .. 1·25 1·25

DESIGNS—HORIZ. 10 ore, 60 ore, 80 ore, 120 ore Northern map (A. Ortelius). 70 ore, 200 ore West Sandoy. 250 ore, 300 ore Streymoy and Vagar. 450 ore "Nes" (R. Smith). 500 ore "Hvitanes and Skalafordur" (S. Joensen-Mikines).

3. Faroese Boat.

1976. Faroese Post Office Inauguration.

20. **3.** 125 ore red 30 30
21. – 160 ore multicoloured .. 40 40
22. – 800 ore green .. .. 1·90 1·90

DESIGNS—24 × 34 mm. 160 ore Faroese flag. As T **3.** 800 ore Faroese postman.

FEDERATED MALAY STATES BC

A Br. protectorate in S.E. Asia, comprising the States of Negri Sembilan (with Sungei Ujong), Pahang, Perak and Selangor.

Separate issues for each of these states appeared in 1936.

100 cents = $1 (Straits).

1900. Stamps of Negri Sembilan optd **FEDERATED MALAY STATES** and bar.

1. **1.** 1 c. purple and green .. 80 1·10
2. 2 c. purple and brown .. 6·50 6·50
3. 3 c. purple and black .. 1·10 1·25
4. 5 c. purple and yellow .. 8·00 10·00
5. 10 c. purple and orange .. 80 3·00
6. 20 c. green and olive .. 8·00 10·00
7. 25 c. green and red .. 18·00 20·00
8. 50 c. green and black .. 9·00 11·00

1900. Stamps of Perak optd. **FEDERATED MALAY STATES** and bar.

9. **2.** 5 c. purple and yellow .. 5·00 7·00
10. 10 c. purple and orange .. 8·00 10·00
11. **3.** $1 green .. .. 14·00 16·00
12. $2 green and red .. .. 13·00 16·00
13. $5 green and blue .. .. 50·00 45·00
14. $25 green and orange .. £1400

1. Tiger.

2. Elephants.

1900.

15. **1.** 1 c. black and green .. 12 15
29. 1 c. green 30 15
30. 1 c. brown .. .. 1·00 50
53. 1 c. black 20 15
55. 2 c. green 15 12
54. 2 c. brown 60 55
16. 3 c. black and brown .. 65 15
58. 3 c. brown 15 15
34. 3 c. red 85 12
56. 3 c. grey .. .. 1·25 90
57. 3 c. green .. .. .. 2·00 80
17. 4 c. black and red .. 80 30
59. 4 c. red 40 15
60. 4 c. orange 12 12
39. 5 c. green & red on yellow 1·10 40
61. 5 c. mauve on yellow .. 15 20
62. 5 c. brown 30 12
63. 6 c. orange 20 20
64. 6 c. red 20 15
19. 8 c. black and blue .. 4·50 80
42a. 8 c. blue .. .. .. 2·25 50
43. 10 c. black and mauve .. 1·00 15
65. 10 c. blue 35 30
66. 10 c. black and blue .. 40 40
67. 10 c. purple on yellow .. 2·50 40
68. 12 c. blue 65 15
45. 20 c. mauve and black .. 40 15
70. 25 c. purple and mauve .. 95 40
71. 30 c. purple and orange .. 1·75 35
46. 35 c. red on yellow .. 4·00 2·75
73. 35 c. red and purple .. 4·50 3·50
74a. 50 c. black and orange .. 2·00 20
75. 50 c. black on green .. 3·00 80
76. **2.** $1 green .. .. 6·50 3·50
77. **1.** $1 black and red on blue .. 6·00 80
78. **2.** $2 green and red .. 4·50 5·50
79. **1.** $2 green & red on yellow 10·00 8·00
80. **2.** $5 green and blue .. 24·00 18·00
81. **1.** $5 green and red on green 45·00 22·00
82. **2.** $25 green and orange .. £200 £110

POSTAGE DUE STAMPS

D 1.

1924.

D 1. **D 1.** 1 c. violet 50 12
D 2. 2 c. black 12 15
D 3. 4 c. green 65 60
D 4. 8 c. red 65 80
D 5. 10 c. orange 80 85
D 6. 12 c. blue .. .. 1·25 1·25

FERNANDO POO O2

A Spanish island off the W. coast of Africa, in the Gulf of Guinea. Administered as part of Spanish Guinea, but resumed issuing stamps in 1960. On 12th October, 1968, became independent and joined Rio Muni to become Equatorial Guinea.

1. Queen Isabella II. 2. King Alfonso XIII.

1868.

1. **1.** 20 c. de e. brown .. £110 42·00

1879. "Alfonso XII" key-type inscr. "FERNANDO POO".

5. **X.** 1 c. green .. .. 4·50 1·10
6. 2 c. red .. .. 5·00 1·40
2. 5 c. green .. .. 12·00 1·90
7. 5 c. lilac .. .. 9·00 2·00
3. 10 c. red .. .. 12·00 1·90
8. 10 c. brown .. .. 11·00 1·40
4. 50 c. blue .. .. 12·00 2·50

The face value of No. 1 is expressed in centimos de escudo. It was in use until Dec. 1868. Stamps of Cuba were then used until 1879.

Nos. 2, 3 and 4 have face values expressed in centimos de peseta and the remainder are in centavos de peso.

1884. Nos. 5, 6 and 7 surch. **HABILITADO PARA CORREOS 50 CENT-PTA.**

9. **X.** 50 c. on 1 c. green .. 12·00 4·50
10. 50 c. on 2 c red .. 5·50 1·60
11. 50 c. on 5 c. lilac .. 12·00 4·75

1894. "Baby" key-type inscr. "FERNANDO POO".

13. **Y.** ½ c. grey .. .. 6·00 1·00
14. 2 c. red .. .. 3·75 60
15. 5 c. green .. .. 4·25 60
16. 6 c. purple .. .. 4·00 60
18. 10 c. red .. .. 7·00 1·75
19. 10 c. brown .. .. 3·00 60
20. 12½ c. grey .. .. 3·75 60
21. 20 c. blue .. .. 3·75 60
22. 25 c. red .. .. 4·75 60

1896. Nos. 13, etc., surch. **HABILITADO 5 c. DE PESO** in circle.
23. Y. 5 c. on ½ c. grey .. 8·00 8·00
24. 5 c. on 2 c. red .. .. 4·50 90
25. 5 c. on 6 c. purple .. 12·00 2·75
26. 5 c. on 10 c. brown .. 13·00 8·00
28. 5 c. on 12½ c. grey .. 2·00 2·00
29. 5 c. on 20 c. blue .. 8·00 7·00
30. 5 c. on 25 c. red .. 13·00 13·00

1897. Nos. 13, etc., surch. **5 cen.** in circle.
31a. Y. 5 c. on ½ c. grey .. 2·00 2·00
32a. 5 c. on 2 c. red .. .. 1·75 1·25
33b. 5 c. on 5 c. green .. 8·00 8·00
39. 5 c. on 6 c. purple .. 8·00 8·00
35. 5 c. on 10 c. red .. 12·00 4·50
36. 5 c. on 10 c. brown .. 17·00 6·00
37a. 5 c. on 12½ c. grey .. 16·00 9·00
39b. 5 c. on 20 c. blue .. 1·75 1·75
40. 5 c. on 25 c. red .. 4·00 3·50

1898. Nos. 13, etc., surch. **HABILITADO PARA CORREOS 50 CENT-PTA.**
41. Y. 50 c. on ½ c. grey .. 5·00 4·50
42. 50 c. on 2 c. red .. .. 7·00 6·00
43. 50 c. on 5 c. green .. 15·00 4·50
46a. 50 c. on 10 c. brown .. 8·00 4·50
47a. 50 c. on 12½ c. grey .. 10·00 4·50
48. 50 c. on 25 c. red .. .. 14·00 6·00

1899. "Curly Head" key-type inscr. "FERNANDO POO 1899".
66. Z. 1 m. brown .. .. 1·25 30
67. 2 m. brown .. .. 1·25 30
68. 3 m. brown .. .. 1·25 30
69. 4 m. brown .. .. 1·25 30
70. 5 m. brown .. .. 1·25 30
71. 1 c. purple .. .. 1·25 30
72. 2 c. green .. .. 1·25 30
73. 3 c. brown .. .. 1·25 30
74. 4 c. orange .. .. 4·00 50
75. 5 c. red .. .. 1·25 30
76. 6 c. blue .. .. 1·25 30
77. 8 c. brown .. .. 4·00 30
78. 10 c. red .. .. 1·50 30
79. 15 c. grey .. .. 1·50 30
80. 20 c. claret .. .. 6·50 55
81. 40 c. lilac .. .. 35·00 6·00
82. 60 c. black .. .. 35·00 6·00
83. 80 c. brown .. .. 35·00 6·00
84. 1 p. green .. .. £150 30·00
85. 2 p. blue .. .. £150 30·00

1900. Nos. 74 and 80 surch. **HABILITADO PARA CORREOS 50 CENT-PTA.**
116. Z. 50 c. on 4 c. orange .. 4·50 1·75
117. 50 c. on 20 c. claret .. 5·00 2·00

1900. No. 80 surch. **HABILITADO 5 c. DE PESO.**
86. Z. 5 c. on 20 c. claret .. 8·00 1·60

1900. No. 80 surch. **5 cen.** in circle.
87. Z. 5 c. on 20 c. claret .. 6·00 1·40

1900. "Curly Head" key-type inscr. "FERNANDO POO 1900".
91. Z. 1 m. black .. .. 1·75 30
92. 2 m. black .. .. 1·75 30
93. 3 m. black .. .. 1·75 30
94. 4 m. black .. .. 1·75 30
95. 5 m. black .. .. 1·75 30
96. 1 c. green .. .. 1·75 30
97. 2 c. lilac .. .. 1·75 30
98. 3 c. pink .. .. 1·75 30
99. 4 c. brown .. .. 1·75 30
100. 5 c. blue .. .. 1·75 30
101. 6 c. orange .. .. 1·90 50
102. 8 c. green .. .. 1·90 50
103. 10 c. claret .. .. 1·75 30
104. 15 c. purple .. .. 1·75 30
105. 20 c. brown .. .. 1·75 30
106. 40 c. brown .. .. 3·00 70
107. 60 c. green .. .. 5·00 70
108. 80 c. blue .. .. 6·00 1·00
109. 1 p. brown .. .. 30·00 5·00
110. 2 p. orange .. .. 50·00 11·00

1900. No. 105 surch. **HABILITADO PARA CORREOS 50 CENT-PTA.**
88. Z. 50 c. on 20 c. brown .. 4·50 90

1901. "Curly Head" key-type inscr. "FERNANDO POO 1901".
124. Z. 1 c. black .. .. 1·25 30
125. 2 c. brown .. .. 1·25 30
126. 3 c. purple .. .. 1·25 30
127. 4 c. lilac .. .. 1·25 30
128. 5 c. orange 90 30
129. 10 c. brown 90 30
130. 25 c. blue 90 30
131. 50 c. claret .. .. 1·25 30
132. 75 c. grey .. .. 1·25 30
133. 1 p. green .. .. 6·00 1·25
134. 2 p. brown .. .. 7·50 1·75
135. 3 p. grey .. .. 8·50 2·50
136. 4 p. orange .. .. 8·50 2·50
137. 5 p. green .. .. 11·00 2·50
138. 10 p. brown .. .. 21·00 5·50

1902. "Curly Head" key-type inscr. "FERNANDO POO 1902".
140. Z. 5 c. green .. .. 1·25 20
141. 10 c. grey .. .. 1·25 20
142. 25 c. claret .. .. 2·50 40
143. 50 c. brown .. .. 4·50 1·00
144. 75 c. lilac .. .. 4·75 1·00
145. 1 p. red .. .. 7·00 1·25
146. 2 p. green .. .. 13·00 2·50
147. 5 p. orange .. .. 20·00 5·00

1903. "Curly Head" key-type inscr. "FERNANDO POO PARA 1903".
154. Z. ¼ c. purple 20 10
155. ½ c. black 20 10
156. 1 c. red 20 10
157. 2 c. green 20 10
158. 3 c. green 20 10
159. 4 c. lilac 20 10
160. 5 c. red 25 12
161. 10 c. orange 30 15
162. 15 c. blue .. .. 1·25 50
163. 25 c. brown .. .. 1·40 65
164. 50 c. grey .. .. 2·00 1·00
165. 75 c. red .. .. 6·00 1·50
166. 1 p. brown .. .. 9·00 2·25
167. 2 p. green .. .. 12·00 3·00
168. 3 p. claret .. .. 12·00 4·00
169. 4 p. blue .. .. 15·00 5·25
170. 5 p. blue .. .. 20·00 6·50
171. 10 p. orange .. .. 40·00 9·00

1905. "Curly Head" key-type inscr. "FERNANDO POO PARA 1905".
172. Z. 1 c. purple 20 15
173. 2 c. black 20 15
174. 3 c. red 20 15
175. 4 c. green 20 15
176. 5 c. green 25 15
177. 10 c. lilac 75 30
178. 15 c. red 75 30
179. 25 c. orange .. .. 3·50 50
180. 50 c. green .. .. 3·50 70
181. 75 c. brown .. .. 4·00 1·75
182. 1 p. grey .. .. 4·25 2·00
183. 2 p. red .. .. 7·50 3·25
184. 3 p. brown .. .. 10·00 4·00
185. 4 p. green .. .. 14·00 4·50
186. 5 p. red .. .. 25·00 7·00
187. 10 p. blue .. .. 35·00 9·00

1907.
188. 2. 1 c. black 10 15
189. 2 c. red 10 5
190. 3 c. purple 10 5
191. 4 c. black 10 5
192. 5 c. orange 15 10
193. 10 c. claret 55 25
194. 15 c. grey 25 10
195. 25 c. brown .. .. 7·50 3·00
196. 50 c. green 15 10
197. 75 c. red 20 10
198. 1 p. blue .. .. 1·00 30
199. 2 p. brown .. .. 3·00 1·25
200. 3 p. red .. .. 3·00 1·25
201. 4 p. lilac .. .. 3·00 1·25
202. 5 p. grey .. .. 3·00 1·25
203. 10 p. brown .. .. 3·00 1·25

1908. Surch. **HABILITADO PARA 05 CTMS.**
204. 2. 05 c. on 10 c. claret .. 1·50 90

1929. Seville and Barcelona Exhibition stamps of Spain (Nos. 504, etc.) optd. **FERNANDO POO.**
209. 5 c. red 5 5
210. 10 c. green 5 5
211. 15 c. blue 12 5
212. 20 c. violet 5 5
213. 25 c. red 5 5
214. 30 c. brown 10 10
215. 40 c. blue 15 15
216. 50 c. orange 30 30
217. 1 p. grey 55 55
218. 4 p. red .. .. 1·50 2·50
219. 10 p. brown .. .. 3·50 3·50

3. Woman at Prayer.
4. De Falla (composer).
5. Whale.
6. "The Blessing".

1960.
220. 3. 25 c. violet-grey .. 5 5
221. 50 c. drab 5 5
222. 75 c. chocolate .. 5 5
223. 1 p. red 5 5
224. 1 p. 50 turquoise .. 5 5
225. 2 p. purple 5 5
226. 3 p. blue .. .. 1·50 30
227. 5 p. brown 10 8
228. 10 p. olive 20 10

1960. Child Welfare. Inscr. "PRO-INFANCIA 1960".
229. 4. 10 c.+5 c. maroon .. 5 5
230. – 15 c.+5 c. bistre .. 5 5
231. – 35 c. myrtle .. 8 5
232. 4. 80 c. green .. 12 10
DESIGNS—VERT. (representing ballets): 15 c. Spanish dancer ("Love, the Magician"). 35 c. Tricorne, stick and windmill ("Three-cornered Hat").

1960. Stamp Day. Inscr. "DIA DEL SELLO 1960".
233. 5. 10 c.+5 c. lake .. 5 5
234. – 20 c.+5 c. myrtle .. 5 5
235. 5. 30 c.+10 c. olive-brown 5 5
236. – 50 c.+20 c. sepia .. 10 5
DESIGN: 20 c., 50 c. Natives harpooning whale.

1961. Child Welfare. Inscr. "PRO-INFANCIA 1961".
237. 6. 10 c.+5 c. lake .. 5 5
238. – 25 c.+10 c. violet .. 5 5
239. 6. 80 c.+20 c. green .. 8 8
DESIGN: 25 c. African kneeling before Cross.

7.

DESIGNS—VERT. 25 c. Map. 70 c. St. Isabel Cathedral.

1961. Gen. Franco as Head of State. 25th Anniv.
240. – 25 c. violet-grey .. 5 5
241. 7. 50 c. olive-brown .. 5 5
242. – 70 c. green 5 5
243. 7. 1 p. orange 10 10

8. Great Turtle.

DESIGN: 25 c. 1 p. Native porters, palm trees and shore.

1961. Stamp Day. Inscr. "DIA DEL SELLO 1961".
244. 8. 10 c.+5 c. red .. 5 5
245. – 25 c.+10 c. plum .. 5 5
246. 8. 30 c.+10 c. maroon .. 5 5
247. – 1 p.+10 c. orange .. 10 10

9. Modern Spanish Freighter.

1962. Child Welfare. Inscr. "PRO-INFANCIA 1962".
248. 9. 25 c. violet 5 5
249. – 50 c. olive 5 5
250. 9. 1 p. chestnut 8 5
DESIGN: 50 c. Spanish Colonial Steamer, "San Francisco".

10. Postman. 11. Native Shrine. 12. Sister and Child.

1962. Stamp Day. Inscr. "DIA DEL SELLO 1962".
251. 10. 15 c. green 5 5
252. – 35 c. magenta .. 5 5
253. 10. 1 p. brown 8 5
DESIGN—HORIZ. 35 c. Mail transport.

1963. Seville Flood Relief.
254. 11. 50 c. olive 5 5
255. 1 p. purple 5 5

1963. Child Welfare.
256. – 25 c. purple 5 5
257. 12. 50 c. green 5 5
258. – 1 p. salmon 8 5
DESIGN—HORIZ. 25 c., 1 p. Two sisters.

13. Child and Arms.

1963. "For Barcelona".
259. 13. 50 c. olive 5 5
260. 1 p. red 5 5

14. Governor Chacon.

15. Canoe.

16. Partridge.

17. "The Three Kings".

1964. Stamp Day. Inscr. "DIA DEL SELLO 1963".
261. 14. 25 c. violet 5 5
262. – 50 c. olive 5 5
263. 14. 1 p. brown 8 5
DESIGN—VERT. 50 c. Orange blossom.

1964. Child Welfare. Inscr. "PRO-INFANCIA 1964".
264. 15. 25 c. violet 5 5
265. – 50 c. olive (Pineapple) 5 5
266. 15. 1 p. brown-purple .. 5 5

1964. Birds.
267. 16. 15 c. brown 5 5
268. – 25 c. violet (Wild duck) 5 5
269. – 50 c. olive (Crested parrot) .. 5 5
270. 16. 70 c. green 5 5
271. – 1 p. chest. (Wild duck) 5 5
272. – 1 p. 50 turquoise (Crested parrot) .. 10 5
273. 16. 3 p. grey-blue .. 35 12
274. – 5 p. maroon (Wild duck) 80 20
275. – 10 p. emerald (Crested parrot) .. 1·25 25

1964. Stamp Day.
276. – 50 c. green 5 5
277. 17. 1 p. red 8 8
278. – 1 p. 50 green 8 8
279. 17. 3 p. blue 90 45
DESIGNS—VERT. 50 c., 1 p. 50, King presenting gift to Infant Jesus.

18. Native.

19. "Metopondontus savagei"

1965. End of Spanish Civil War. Inscr. "XXV ANOS DE PAZ". 25th Anniv.
280. 18. 50 c. indigo 5 5
281. – 1 p. red 5 5
282. – 1 p. 50 turquoise .. 8 5
DESIGNS: 1 p. "Agriculture" (fruit farming). 1 p. 50, "Education" (child writing).

1965. Child Welfare. Insects.
283. – 50 c. olive 5 5
284. 19. 1 p. red 5 5
285. – 1 p. 50 blue 8 5
DESIGN—VERT. 50 c., 1 p. 50, "Plectrocneria cruciata".

20. Pole-vaulting.

1965. Stamp Day.
286. 20. 50 c. green 5 5
287. – 1 p. chestnut 5 5
288. 20. 1 p. 50 blue 8 5
DESIGN—VERT. 1 p. Arms of Fernando Poo.

21. European and African Women.

1966. Child Welfare.
289. **21.** 50 c. green 5 5
290. 1 p. red 5 5
291. – 1 p. 50 blue 8 5
DESIGN—VERT. 1 p. 50, St. Isabel of Hungary.

22. Greater White-nosed Guenon.
23. Flowers.

1966. Stamp Day.
292. **22.** 10 c. blue and yellow .. 5 5
293. – 40 c. blue and brown .. 5 5
294. **22.** 1 p. 50 olive and brown 8 8
295. – 4 p. brown and green .. 10 10
DESIGN—VERT. 40 c., 4 p. Moustached Monkey.

1967. Child Welfare and similar floral design.
296. **23.** 10 c. cerise and green . 5 5
297. – 40 c. brown and orange 5 5
298. **23.** 1 p. 50 purple & brown 5 5
299. – 4 p. blue and green .. 8 8

24. Civet-cat.

26. Scales (Libra).

25. Arms of San Carlos and Stamp of 1868.

1967. Stamp Day.
300. **24.** 1 p. black and bistre .. 5 5
301. – 1 p. 50 brown and olive 5 5
302. – 3 p. 50 maroon & green 8 8
DESIGNS—VERT. 1 p. 50, Bush-baby. HORIZ. 3 p. 50, Flying squirrel.

1928. Stamp Cent.
303. **25.** 1 p. brown and purple.. 5 5
304. – 1 p. 50 brown and blue 5 5
305. – 2 p. 50 brown & red-brn. 8 8
DESIGNS: Each with stamp of 1868. 1 p. 50, Arms of Santa Isabel. 2 p. 50, Arms of Fernando Poo.

1968. Child Welfare. Signs of the Zodiac.
306. **26.** 1 p. magenta on yellow 5 5
307. – 1 p. 50 brown on pink.. 5 5
308. – 2 p. 50 violet on yellow 8 8
DESIGNS: 1 p. 50, Lion (Leo). 2 p. 50, Waterman (Aquarius).

For later issues see **EQUATORIAL GUINEA.**

FEZZAN O3

A desert territory in N. Africa taken from Turkey by Italy and captured by French forces in 1943. Algerian stamps used from April 1944, until 1946, and then under French control until the end of 1951 when it was incorporated in the independent kingdom of Libya.

1943. Issues for Fezzan and Ghadames. Optd. **FEZZAN Occupation Francaise** or surch. in addition with bars obliterating old inscr. and values.

(a) Postage.
No. 247 of Italy optd.
1943. Issues for Fezzan and Ghadames.
1. **74.** 50 c. violet .. .. 9·50 9·50

Stamps of Libya surch.
2. **1.** 0 f. 50 on 5 c. grn. & black 30·00 27·00
3. **2.** 1 f. on 10 c. red and black 45·00 42·00
4. **4.** 2 f. on 30 c. brown & black 80·00 70·00
5. **3.** 3 f. on 20 c. green .. 13·00 13·00
6. **2.** 3 f. 50 on 25 c. blue .. 19·00 16·00
7. **4.** 5 f. on 50 c. olive & black 2·75 2·75
8. 10 f. on 1 l. 25 blue .. £300 £275
9. **3.** 20 f. on 1 l. 75 orange .. £800 £700
10. **5.** 50 f. on 75 c. red and violet £900 £900

(b) Air.
No. 271 of Italy optd.
11. **81.** 50 c. brown .. .. 15·00 14·00

No. 72 of Libya surch.
12. **5.** 7 f. 50 on 50 c. red .. 16·00 16·00

1943. Handstamped locally. (a) Postage.

No. 247 of Italy handstamped **R.F. 0, 50 FEZZAN** around circle and within dotted circle.
13. **74.** 0 f. 50 on 50 c. violet .. — 75·00

No. 27 of Libya handstamped **R.F. 1 Fr FEZZAN** in two lines.
14. **2.** 1 f. on 25 c. blue.. .. — 70·00

(b) Air.
No. 271 of Italy handstamped as No. 13.
15. **81.** 0 f. 50 on 50 c. brown — £190

1943. Parcel Post stamps of Libya handstamped across each half as No. 14.
16. 1 f. on 5 c. brown (No. P 1) — £100
17. 1 f. on 10 c. blue (No. P 15) — £100
18. 1 f. on 50 c. orge. (No. P 18) — £100
19. 1 f. on 1 l. violet (No. P 20) — £100
20. 1 f. on 2 l. green (No. P 21) — £700
21. 1 f. on 3 l. yellow (No. P 22) — £700
22. 1 f. on 4 l. grey (No. P 23) .. — £700
The prices are for each half of the Parcel Post stamps.

1. Fort of Sebha.

2. Turkish Fort and Mosque at Mourzouk.

1946. Issues for Fezzan and Ghadames.
23. **1.** 10 c. black 5 5
24. 50 c. red 5 5
25. 1 f. brown.. .. .. 5 5
26. 1 f. 50 green 5 5
27. 2 f. blue 5 5
28. **2.** 2 f. 50 violet 5 5
29. 3 f. red 8 10
30. 5 f. brown.. .. .. 8 8
31. 6 f. green 8 8
32. 10 f. blue 8 10
33. – 15 f. violet 12 12
34. – 20 f. red 15 20
35. – 25 f. brown 15 20
36. – 40 f. green 20 25
37. – 50 f. blue 25 30
DESIGN: 15 f. to 50 f. Map and Fort of Sebha.

3. Fezzan Airfield.

DESIGN — VERT. 200 f. Aeroplane over Fezzan.

1948 Air.
38. **3.** 100 f. red 75 75
39. – 200 f. blue .. .. 1·40 1·40

4. Djerma.

5. Well at Gorda.

1949.
40. **4.** 1 f. black 5 5
41. 2 f. pink 5 5
42. – 4 f. brown.. .. .. 15 15
43. – 5 f. emerald 20 20
44. **5.** 8 f. blue 20 20
45. 10 f. brown 55 55
46. 12 f. green 95 95
47. – 15 f. red .. .. 1·00 1·00
48. – 20 f. black 40 40
49. – 25 f. blue 40 40
50. – 50 f. red 45 45
DESIGNS—HORIZ. 4 f., 5 f. Beni Khettab tombs. 15 f., 20 f. Col. Colonna d'Ornano and fort. 25 f., 50 f. Gen. Leclare and map of Europe and N. Africa.

6. "Charity".

7. Mother and Child.

1950. Charity.
51. **6.** 15 f.+5 f. lake 40 50
52. **7.** 25 f.+5 f. blue 40 50

8. Camel Breeding.
9. Ahmed Bey.

1951.
59. **8.** 30 c. brown (postage) .. 5 5
60. 1 f. blue 8 8
61. 2 f. red 8 8
62. – 4 f. red-brown 8 8
63. – 5 f. green 8 8
64. – 8 f. blue 15 15
65. – 10 f. black 60 60
66. – 12 f. green 65 65
67. – 15 f. red 90 90
68. **9.** 20 f. grey 90 90
69. **9.** 25 f. blue and indigo .. 75 75
70. 50 f. brown and black .. 1·00 1·00
71. – 100 f. blue (air) .. .. 1·40 1·40
72. – 200 f. red .. .. .. 2·25 2·25
DESIGNS—HORIZ. 4 f. to 8 f. Arab hoeing. 100 f. Brak Oasis. 200 f. Sebha Fort. VERT. 10 f. to 15 f. Artesian Well.

POSTAGE DUE STAMPS

1943. Postage Due stamps of Libya optd. **FEZZAN Occupation Francaise** or surch. in addition with bars obliterating old inscr. and values.
D 13. **D 6.** 0 f. 50 on 5 c. brown.. £325 £325
D 14. 1 f. on 10 c. blue .. £325 £325
D 15. 2 f. on 25 c. green .. £325 £325
D 16. 3 f. on 50 c. violet .. £325 £325
D 17. **D 7.** 5 f. on 1 l. orange .. £1600 £1600

D 1. Brak Oasis.

ILLUSTRATIONS British Commonwealth and all overprints and surcharges are FULL SIZE. Foreign Countries have been reduced to ¾-LINEAR.

1950.
D 53. **D 1.** 1 f. black 8 8
D 54. 2 f. green 8 8
D 55. 3 f. lake 10 10
D 56. 5 f. violet 12 12
D 57. 10 f. red 35 35
D 58. 20 f. blue 45 45

FIJI BC

A Br. colony in the S. Pacific which became independent within the Commonwealth during Oct., 1970.

1969. 100 cents = 1 dollar.

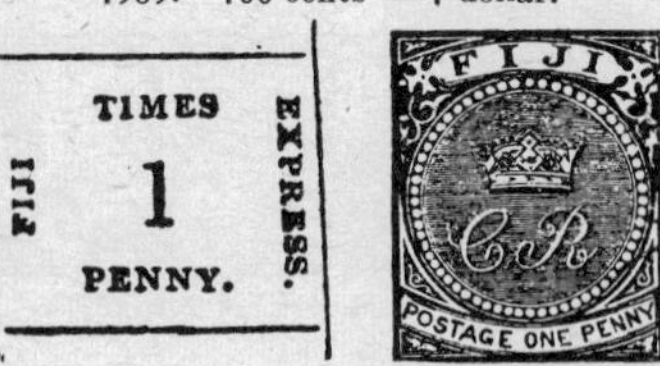

1.
2. Cypher of King Cakobau.

1870.
5. **1.** 1d. black on pink £225 £275
6. 3d. black on pink £325 £400
7. 6d. black on pink £225 £275
8. 9d. black on pink £325 £400
9. 1s. black on pink £225 £275

1871.
10. **2.** 1d. blue .. .. .. 26·00 35·00
11. 3d. green .. .. .. 45·00 70·00
12. 6d. red .. .. .. 55·00 80·00

1872. Surch. in words.
13. **2.** 2 c. on 1d. blue .. .. 8·00 9·00
14. 6 c. on 3d. green .. 9·50 12·00
15. 12 c. on 6d. red .. .. 14·00 13·00

V.R. (3.)
(4.)

1874. Optd. as T 3.
19. **2.** 2 c. on 1d. blue .. .. 85·00 35·00
17. 6 c. on 3d. green £160 £130
18. 12 c. on 6d. red .. .. 80·00 35·00

1875. Nos. 17 and 18 surch. **2d.**
22. **2.** 2d. on 6 c. on 3d. green .. 45·00 20·00
27. 2d. on 12 c. on 6d. red .. 90·00 70·00

1876. Optd. with T **4**, and the 3d. surch. in words also.
31. **2.** 1d. blue .. .. .. 3·50 4·00
29. 2d. on 3d. green .. 8·00 8·00
33. 4d. on 3d. mauve .. 6·50 6·50
34. 6d. red .. .. .. 9·00 9·00

5. Cypher of Queen.

6.

1878. Surcharges on Nos. 92, 102, 100 in words.
53. **5.** 1d. blue 65 90
40. 2d. green.. .. .. 1·60 90
36. 2d. on 3d. green .. 1·50 1·60
58a. 4d. mauve .. .. 1·60 1·90
41. 4d. on 1d. mauve .. 2·50 2·00
42. 4d. on 2d. mauve .. 5·25 2·00
55. 6d. red .. .. .. 1·90 1·60
65. **6.** 1s. brown .. .. 9·00 6·50
69. 5 s. red and black .. 18·00 20·00

1891. Surch. in figures or words.
72a. **5.** ½d. on 1d. blue .. 6·50 5·25
70. 2½d. on 2d. green .. 8·00 8·00
73a. 5d. on 4d. mauve .. 13·00 13·00
74a. 5d. on 6d. red .. .. 11·00 11·00

7

8. Native Canoe.

1891.
76. **7.** ½d. grey .. .. 1·10 90
87. **8.** 1d. black.. .. .. 65 65
101. 1d. mauve 80 35
89. 2d. green.. .. .. 1·00 65
90. **5.** 2½d. brown .. .. 1·90 1·90
85. **8.** 5d. blue .. .. .. 2·00 2·75

9.

ILLUSTRATIONS British Commonwealth and all overprints and surcharges are FULL SIZE. Foreign Countries have been reduced to ¾-LINEAR.

1903.
118. **9.** ½d. green.. .. .. 35 55
116. 1d. purple & black on red 55 25
119. 1d. red 35 55
106. 2d. purple and orange 60 1·00
107. 2½d. purple & blue on blue 4·00 5·50
120. 2½d. blue.. .. .. 1·60 2·75
108. 3d. purple .. .. 1·40 2·25
109. 4d. purple and black .. 1·60 2·25
110. 5d. purple and green .. 1·60 2·25
111. 6d. purple and red .. 2·50 3·50
121. 6d. purple .. .. 1·60 3·00
112. 1s. green and red .. 5·50 8·00
122. 1s. black on green .. 3·25 3·50
113. 5s. green and black .. 24·00 28·00
123. 5s. green and red on yellow 23·00 28·00
114. £1 black and blue .. £150 £180
124. £1 purple and black on red £110 £140

1912. As T **9**, but portrait of King George V.
125. ¼d. brown 15 40
138. ½d. green 12 35
127. 1d. red 60 15
231. 1d. violet 35 12
232. 1½d. red .. .. .. 1·00 1·25
233. 2d. grey 50 12
129. 2½d. blue .. .. .. 1·75 2·50
130. 3d. purple on yellow .. 1·75 2·25
234. 3d. blue .. .. .. 65 1·00
235. 4d. black & red on yellow 1·40 1·90
236. 5d. purple and olive .. 1·25 1·75
237. 6d. purple .. .. 85 1·25
134. 1s. black on green .. 2·25 3·50
239. 2s. purple and blue on blue 8·00 11·00
135. 2s. 6d. black & red on blue 9·00 11·00
136. 5s. green and red on yellow 19·00 24·00
137. £1 purple and black on red £100 £120

1916. Nos. 229 and 210 optd. **WAR STAMP.**
138. ½d. green 12 25
139a. 1d. red .. .. .. 40 1·10

1935. Silver Jubilee. As T **11** of Antigua.
242. 1½d. blue and red .. 20 40
243. 2d. blue and grey .. 35 45
244. 3d. brown and blue .. 95 1·25
245. 1s. grey and purple .. 1·75 3·00

1937. Coronation. As T **2** of Aden.
246. 1d. violet 20 20
247. 2d. grey 25 20
248. 3d. blue 25 30

11. Sailing Canoe.

12. Native Village.

13. Government House.

1938.

249b. **11.** ½d. green 15 15
250. **12.** 1d. brown and blue .. 12 12
252c. – 1½d. red 15 20
254. – 2d. brown and green .. 65 1·40
255. **13.** 2d. green and mauve 12 15
256b. – 2½d. brown and green 12 12
257. – 3d. blue 15 15
258. – 5d. blue and red .. 8·00 6·50
259. – 5d. green and red .. 30 35
261. – 6d. black .. .. 1·10 30
261d. – 8d. red 30 70
262. – 1s. black and yellow 40 35
263. – 1s. 5d. black and red 35 40
263a. – 1s. 6d. blue .. 50 70
264. – 2s. violet and orange 40 65
265. – 2s. 6d. green and brown 75 1·10
266. – 5s. green and purple 1·10 1·10
266a. – 10s. orange and green 6·00 7·00
266b. – £1 blue and red .. 7·50 8·00

DESIGNS—HORIZ. As T **13**: 1½d. Canoe. 2d. (No. 254), 2½d., 6d. Map of Fiji Is. HORIZ. As T **12**: 3d. Canoe and Arms. 8d., 1s. 5d., 1s. 6d. Arms. 2 s. Suva Harbour. 2s. 6d. River scene. 5s. Chief's hut. VERT. As T **12**: 5d. (Nos. 258/9) Sugar cane. 1s. Spearing fish. 10s. Paw-Paw tree. £1 Police bugler.

1941. No. 254 surch.
267. – 2½d. on 2d. brown & green 5 5

1946. Victory. As T **4** of Aden.
268. 2½d. green 8 5
269. 3d. blue 15 10

1948. Silver Wedding. As T **5/6** of Aden.
270. 2½d. green 8 5
271. 5s. blue .. .. .. 2·25 4·00

1949. U.P.U. As T **14/17** of Antigua.
272. 2d. purple 12 15
273. 3d. blue 20 30
274. 8d. red 35 50
275. 1s. 6d. blue 65 60

14. Children Bathing.

1951. Health stamps. Inscr. "HEALTH".
276. **14.** 1d. + 1d. brown .. 20 25
277. – 2d. + 1d. green .. 25 30
DESIGN—VERT. 2d. Rugby footballer.

1953. Coronation. As T **7** of Aden.
278. 2½d. black and green .. 35 30

1953. Royal Visit. As No. 261d. but with portrait of Queen Elizabeth II and inscr. "ROYAL VISIT 1953".
279. 8d. red 20 25

15. Queen Elizabeth II (after Annigoni).

16. Loading Copra.

1954. Queen Elizabeth II. (I) inscr. "FIJI". (II) inscr. "Fiji".
280. **11.** ½d. green 5 5
298. **15.** ½d. green 5 5
281. 1d. turquoise (I) .. 5 5
311. 1d. blue (II) 5 5
282. 1½d. sepia (I) 8 8
300. 1½d. sepia (II) 8 8
283. **13.** 2d. green and mauve .. 10 10
312. **15.** 2d. red (I) 5 5
284. 2½d. violet (I) 12 15
302. 2½d. orange brown (I) .. 8 8
285. **16.** 3d. brown and purple .. 12 10
287. – 6d. black (As No. 261) 20 20
314. A. 6d. red and black .. 10 10
288. – 8d. red (As No. 261d) 25 25
316. B. 10d. brown and red .. 15 15
289. – 1s. black & yell. (As 262) 30 30
317. C. 1s. blue 20 15
290. D. 1s. 6d. blue and green 90 60
291. E. 2s. black and red .. 70 60
292. – 2s. 6d. grn. & brn. (As 265) 70 70
320. F. 2s. 6d. black and purple 50 50
293. G. 5s. ochre and blue .. 2·00 2·25
294. – 10s. orange and green (As 266a) .. .. 13·00 13·00
324. H. 10s. green and sepia .. 2·25 2·25
295. – £1 blue and red (As 266b) .. .. 10·00 11·00
325. I. £1 black and orange .. 4·50 5·00

DESIGNS—HORIZ. As T **16**: A, Fijian beating lali. B, Yaqona ceremony. C, Locating map. D, Sugar cane train. E, Preparing bananas for export. F, Nadi Airport. G, Gold industry. H, Cutting sugar-cane. I, Arms of Fiji.

17. River Scene.

1954. Health stamps.
296. **17.** 1½d. + ½d. brown & grn. 15 20
297. – 2½d. + ½d. orge. & black 20 25
DESIGN: 2½d. Queen's portrait and Cross of Lorraine inscr. "FIJI WAR MEMORIAL" and "ANTI-TUBERCULOSIS CAMPAIGN".

18. Hibiscus.

DESIGNS — HORIZ. 1s. 6d. International date line. 4s. Kandavu parrot. 5s. Orange dove. VERT. 2s. White orchid. SMALLER (23 × 28 mm.): 3d. Queen Elizabeth II.

1959.
313. – 3d. multicoloured .. 8 8
304. **18.** 8d. red, yell., grn. & blk. 30 35
315. – 9d. red, yell., grn. & blue 15 15
318. – 1s. 6d. red, yellow, gold, black and blue .. 35 35
319. – 2s. yellow-green, green and copper 60 60
322. – 4s. red, yellow-green, blue and myrtle .. 1·00 1·75
321. – 4s. red, yellow-green, blue and green .. 1·10 1·10
323. – 5s. red, yellow and grey 1·10 1·10

1963. Royal Visit. Optd. **ROYAL VISIT 1963.**
326. – 3d. mult. (No. 313) .. 15 20
327. C. 1s. blue (No. 317) .. 45 50

1963. Freedom from Hunger. As T **10** of Aden.
328. – 2s. blue .. .. .. 1·50 1·75

19. Running.

1963. 1st South Pacific Games, Suva, Inscr. as in T **19**.
329. **19.** 3d. brn., yellow & black 15 20
330. – 9d. brown, violet & black 35 40
331. – 1s. brown, green & black 35 35
332. – 2s. 6d. brown, blue & blk. 1·10 1·25
DESIGNS—VERT. 9d. Throwing the discus. 1s. Hockey. HORIZ. 2s. 6d. High-jumping.

1963. Red Cross Cent. As T **24** of Antigua.
333. 2d. red and black 12 12
334. 2s. red and blue .. .. 1·40 1·60

1963. Opening of COMPAC (Trans-Pacific Telephone Cable). No. 317 optd. **COMPAC CABLE IN SERVICE DECEMBER 1963** and ship.
335. C. 1s. blue 60 65

20. Jamborette Emblem.

21. Flying-boat "Aotearoa".

1964. Fijian Scout Movement. 50th Anniv.
336. **20.** 3d. red, gold, blue & grn. 12 15
337. – 1s. violet and brown .. 55 60
DESIGN: 1s. Scouts of three races.

1964. 1st Fiji-Tonga Airmail Service. 25th Anniv.
338. **21.** 3d. black and vermilion 15 15
339. – 6d. vermilion and blue 30 30
340. – 1s. black and turquoise 60 65
DESIGNS—VERT. 6d. Fiji Airways "Heron". HORIZ. (37½ × 25 mm.): 1s. "Aotearoa" and map.

1965. I.T.U. Cent. As T **26** of Antigua.
341. 3d. blue and red 12 15
342. 2s. yellow and bistre .. 80 85

1965. I.C.Y. As T **27** of Antigua.
343. 2d. purple and turquoise .. 8 10
344. 2s. 6d. green and lavender 60 70

1966. Churchill Commem. As T **23** of Antigua.
345. 3d. blue 8 8
346. 9d. green 30 35
347. 1s. brown 45 50
348. 2s. 6d. violet .. .. 1·40 1·60

1966. World Cup Football Championships. As T **30** of Antigua.
349. 2d. vio., grn., lake & brn. 10 10
350. 2s. choc., turq., lake & brn. 50 60

22. H.M.S. "Pandora" approaching Split Island, Rotuma.

1966. Discovery of Rotuma. 175th Anniv. Multicoloured.
351. 3d. Type **22** 10 10
352. 10d. Rotuma Chiefs .. 30 35
353. 1s. 6d. Rotumans welcoming H.M.S. "Pandora" .. 60 60

1966. W.H.O. Headquarters, Geneva. Inaug. As T **31** of Antigua.
354. 6d. black, green and blue .. 15 20
355. 2s. 6d. black, purple & ochre 70 75

23. Running.

1966. 2nd South Pacific Games.
356. **23.** 3d. black, brown & green 10 10
357. – 9d. black, brown & blue 25 30
358. – 1s. multicoloured .. 30 35
DESIGNS: 9d. Putting the shot. 1s. Diving.

24. Military Forces Band.

1967. Int. Tourist Year. Multicoloured.
360. 3d. Type **24** 10 10
361. 9d. Reef diving 25 25
362. 1s. Beqa Fire Walkers .. 30 35
363. 2s. Cruise Liner at Suva .. 40 45

25. Bligh (bust), H.M.S. "Providence" and Chart.

1967. Admiral Bligh. 150th Death Anniv.
364. **25.** 4d. multicoloured .. 8 8
365. – 1s. multicoloured .. 20 20
366. – 2s. 6d. multicoloured .. 40 45
DESIGNS—(As T **25**): 2s. 6d. Bligh's Tomb. (54 × 20 mm.) 1s. "Bounty's longboat being chased in Fiji waters".

26. Simmonds Spartan Seaplane.

1968. Kingsford Smith's Pacific Flight via Fiji. 40th Anniv.
367. **26.** 2d. black and green .. 8 8
368. – 6d. blue, black and lake 15 15
369. – 1s. violet and green .. 25 25
370. – 2s. brown and blue .. 45 50
DESIGNS: 6d. "HS 748" aircraft. 1s. "Southern Cross" and Crew. 2s. Lockheed Altair Monoplane.

27. Bure Huts.

1968.
371. ½d. multicoloured 5 5
372. 1d. blue, red & yellow .. 5 5
373. 2d. blue, brown & ochre .. 5 5
374. 3d. green, blue & ochre .. 8 8
375. 4d. multicoloured 8 8
376. 6d. multicoloured 10 10
377. 9d. multicoloured 15 20
378. 10d. blue, orange & brown 20 20
379. 1s. blue and red 25 30
380. 1s. 6d. multicoloured .. 50 60
381. 2s. turq., black & red .. 50 65
382. 2s. 6d. multicoloured .. 70 60
383. 3s. multicoloured .. .. 1·00 1·50
384. 4s. ochre, black and olive 1·00 1·25
385. 5s. multicoloured .. .. 1·00 1·25
386. 10s. brown, black & ochre 2·25 2·50
387. £1 multicoloured .. .. 5·00 6·00

DESIGNS—HORIZ. ½d. Type **27**. 1d. Passion Flowers. 2d. "Nautilus pompilius". 4d. Hawk Moth. 6d. Angel Fish. 9d. Bamboo Raft. 10d. Tiger Moth. 2s. Sea Snake. 2s. 6d. Outrigger Canoes. 3s. Golden Cowrie Shell. 5s. Bamboo Orchids. £1 Queen Elizabeth and Arms of Fiji. VERT. 3d. Reef Heron. 1s. Black Marlin. 1s. 6d. "Sun Birds" (Orange Breasted Honeyeaters). 4s. Mining Industry. 10s. Ceremonial Whale's Tooth.

28. Map of Fiji, W.H.O. Emblem and Nurses.

1968. W.H.O. 20th Anniv. Multicoloured.
388. 3d. Type **28** 8 8
389. 9d. Transferring Patient to Medical Ship "Vuniwai" 20 25
390. 3s. Recreation 50 60

29. Passion Flowers.

1969. Decimal Currency. Designs as T **27** etc., but with values inscr. in decimal currency as in T **29**.
391. **29.** 1 c. bl., red & yell. .. 5 5
392. – 2 c. bl., brn. & ochre (As 373) 5 5
393. – 3 c. green, blue & ochre (As 374) 5 5
394. – 4 c. multicoloured (As 375) 8 8

395. – 5 c. multicoloured (As 376) 10 10
396. 27. 6 c. multicoloured .. 12 12
397. – 8 c. multicoloured (As 377) 15 15
398. – 9 c. blue, orange and brown (As 378) .. 15 15
399. – 10 c. blue & red (As 379) 20 20
400. – 15 c. mult. (As 380) .. 30 40
401. – 20 c. turq., blk. & red (As 381) 40 45
402. – 25 c. mult. (As 382) .. 45 35
403. – 30 c. mult. (As 383) .. 60 80
404. – 40 c. ochre, blk. & olive (As 384) 75 80
405. – 50 c. mult. (As 385) .. 1·00 75
406. – $1 brn. blk. & ochre (As 386) .. .. 2·00 1·75
407. – $2 mult. (As 387) .. 4·50 5·50

30. Fijian Soldiers overlooking the Solomon Islands.

1969. Fijian Military Forces' Solomons Campaign. 25th Anniv.
408. 30. 3 c. multicoloured .. 5 5
409. – 10 c. multicoloured .. 15 15
410. – 25 c. multicoloured .. 40 45
DESIGNS: 10 c. Regimental flags and soldiers in full dress and battledress. 25 c. Fijian soldier and Victoria Cross.

31. Javelin Throwing.

1969. 3rd South Pacific Games, Port Moresby.
411. 31. 4 c. blk., brown & verm. 5 5
412. – 8 c. black, grey & blue 15 15
413. – 20 c. multicoloured .. 30 35
DESIGNS: 8 c. Yachting. 20 c. Games medal and winner's rostrum.

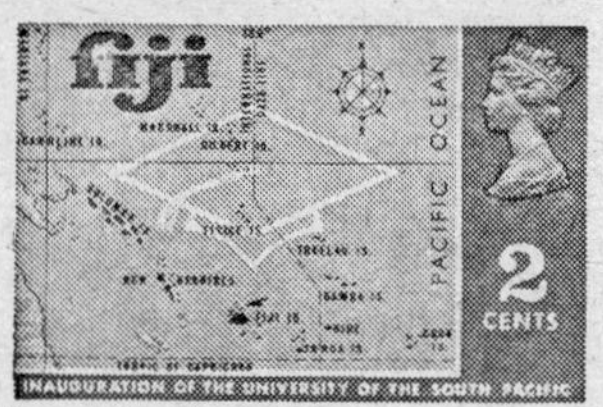

32. Map of South Pacific and "Mortar-board."

1969. University of the South Pacific. Inaug. Multicoloured.
414. 2 c. Type 32 .. .. 5 5
415. 8 c. R.N.Z.A.F. Badge and "Sunderland" Flying-Boat over Laucala Bay (Site of University) .. 15 20
416. 25 c. Science Students at work 40 45

1970. Royal Visit. Nos. 392, 399 and 402 optd. **ROYAL VISIT 1970.**
417. 2 c. blue, brown and ochre 5 5
418. 10 c. blue and red .. 20 20
419. 25 c. multicoloured .. 45 45

33. Chaulmugra Tree, Makogai.

1970. Closing of Leprosy Hospital, Makogai.
420. 33. 2 c. multicoloured .. 5 5
421. – 10 c. green and black .. 20 20
422. – 10 c. blue, black & mag. 20 20
423. – 30 c. multicoloured .. 45 45
DESIGNS: 10 c. (No. 421) "Cascade" (Semisi Maya). 10 c. (No. 422) "Gasagasau" (Semisi Maya). 30 c. Makogai Hospital.
Nos. 421/2 are vert., and were printed se-tenant throughout the sheet.

34. Abel Tasman and Log, 1643.

1970. Explorers and Discoverers.
424. 34. 2c. blk., brn. & turquoise 5 5
425. – 3 c. multicoloured .. 8 8
426. – 8 c. multicoloured .. 25 25
427. – 25 c. multicoloured .. 55 55
DESIGNS: 3 c. Captain Cook and "Endeavour". 8 c. Captain Bligh and Longboat, 1789. 25 c. Fijian and Ocean-going Canoe.

35. King Cakobau and Cession Stone.

1970. Independence. Multicoloured.
428. 2 c. Type 35 .. .. 5 5
429. 3 c. Children of the World 8 8
430. 10 c. Prime Minister and Fijian Flag 20 20
431. 25 c. Dancers in Costume 45 45

36. 1d. and 6d. Stamps of 1870.

1970. Stamp Cent. Multicoloured.
432. 4 c. Type 36 .. .. 8 8
433. 15 c. Fijian Stamps of all Reigns (61 × 21 mm.) .. 25 25
434. 20 c. "Fiji Times" Office and modern G.P.O. .. 35 35

37. Grey-backed White-eye.

38. Women's Basketball.

1971. Birds and Flowers. Multicoloured.
435. 1 c. "Cirrhopetalum umbellatum" 5 5
436. 2 c. Cardinal Honey-eater 5 5
460. 3 c. "Calanthe furcata" 8 8
461. 4 c. "Bulbophyllum sp. nov." 8 8
462. 5 c. Type 37 .. 10 10
463. 6 c. "Phaius tancarvilliae" 8 10
464. 8 c. Blue-crested Broadbill 10 12
442. 10 c. "Acanthephippium vitiense" 15 15
466. 15 c. "Dendrobium tokai" 20 25
467. 20 c. Slaty Flycatcher .. 25 30
468. 25 c. Kandavu Honey-eater 30 35
446. 30 c. "Dendrobium gordonii" 40 45
447. 40 c. Yellow-breasted Musk Parrot 55 60
448. 50 c. White-throated pigeon 85 90
472. $1 Collared Lory .. .. 1·25 1·40
473. $2 "Dendrobium platygastrium" .. 2·50 2·75
The 25c. to $2 are larger ($22\frac{1}{2} \times 35\frac{1}{2}$ mm.).

1971. Fourth South Pacific Games, Tahiti.
451. 38. 8 c. multicoloured .. 12 15
452. – 10 c. blue, blk., & brn.. 20 20
453. – 25 c. green, blk. & brn. 40 45
DESIGNS: 10 c. Running. 25 c. Weightlifting.

39. Community Education.

1972. South Pacific Commission. 25th Anniv. Multicoloured.
454. 2 c. Type 39 .. .. 8 8
455. 4 c. Public Health .. 10 10
456. 50 c. Economic Growth .. 75 85

40. "Native Canoe".

1972. South Pacific Festival of Arts, Suva.
457. 40. 10 c. blk., orge. and bl. 15 20

41. Flowers, Conch and Ceremonial Whale's Tooth.

1972. Royal Silver Wedding. Multicoloured. Background colours given.
474. 41. 10 c. green 15 20
475. 25 c. purple 35 35

1972. Hurricane Relief. Nos. 400 and 403 surch **HURRICANE RELIEF +** and premium.
476. 15 c. + 5 c. multicoloured .. 35 40
477. 30 c. + 10 c. multicoloured 70 80

42. "Line Out".

1973. Diamond Jubilee of Rugby Union. Multicoloured.
478. 2 c. Type 42 .. .. 8 8
479. 8 c. Body tackle 12 15
480. 25 c. Conversion 35 40

43. Forestry Development.

1973. Development Projects. Multicoloured.
481. 5 c. Type 43 .. .. 8 8
482. 8 c. Rice irrigation scheme 12 15
483. 10 c. Low income housing 15 15
484. 25 c. Highway construction 35 40

44. Christmas.

1973. Festivals of Joy. Multicoloured.
485. 3 c. Type 44 .. .. 10 10
486. 10 c. Diwali 20 20
487. 20 c. Id-ul-Fitar 30 30
488. 25 c. Chinese New Year .. 40 40

45. Athletics.

1973. Commonwealth Games, Christchurch, New Zealand. Multicoloured.
489. 3 c. Type 45 .. .. 5 5
490. 8 c. Boxing 15 20
491. 50 c. Bowling 70 80

46. Bowler.

1973. Cricket Cent. Multicoloured.
492. 3 c. Type 46 .. .. 5 5
493. 25 c. Batsman and wicket-keeper 40 40
494. 40 c. Fielder (horiz.) .. 60 65

47. Fiji Postman.

1974. Universal Postal Union. Cent. Mult.
495. 3 c. Type 47 .. .. 5 8
496. 8 c. Loading mail onto ship 12 15
497. 30 c. Fijian post office and mailbus 40 45
498. 50 c. Modern aircraft .. 70 80

48. Cubs lighting Fire.

1974. First National Scout Jamboree, Lautoka. Multicoloured.
499. 3 c. Type **48** 5 5
500. 10 c. Scouts reading map 15 20
501. 40 c. Scouts and Fijian flag (vert.) 60 65

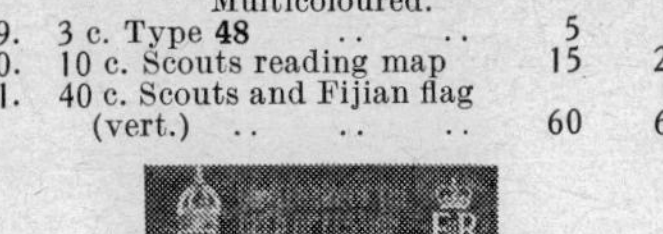

49. Cakobau Club and Flag.

1974. Cent. of Deed of Cession and Fourth Anniv. of Independence. Multicoloured.
502. 3 c. Type **49** 5 5
503. 8 c. King Cakobau and Queen Victoria 12 15
504. 50 c. Raising the Royal Standard at Nasova Ovalau 65 70

50. " Diwali " (Hindu Festival).

1975. " Festivals of Joy ". Multicoloured.
521. 3 c. Type **50** 5 5
522. 15 c. " Id-Ul-Fitar " (Muslim Festival).. .. .. 20 20
523. 25 c. Chinese New Year .. 30 35
524. 30 c. Christmas 40 45

51. Steam Loco. No. 21.

1975. Sugar Trains. Multicoloured.
526. 4 c. Type **51** 5 5
527. 15 c. Diesel Loco. No. 8 .. 20 20
528. 20 c. Diesel Loco. No. 1 .. 25 30
529. 30 c. Free Passenger Train 35 40

52. Fiji Blind Society and Rotary Symbols.

1976. Rotary in Fiji. 40th Anniversary.
530. **52.** 10 c. blue, grn. and blk. 12 12
531. – 25 c. multicoloured .. 30 35
DESIGN: 25 c. Ambulance and Rotary Symbol.

53. D.H. " Drover ".

(Illustration reduced. Actual size 57×21 mm.)

1976. Air Services. 25th Anniversary. Multicoloured.
532. 4 c. Type **53** 5 5
533. 15 c. B.A.C. " 1-11 " .. 20 25
534. 25 c. H.S. " 748 " .. 30 35
535. 30 c. Britten-Norman " Trislander " 40 45

POSTAGE DUE STAMPS

D 1. D 2.

1917.
1. D **1.** ½d. black .. .. £100 90·00
D 2. 1d. black .. .. 32·00 20·00
D 3. 2d. black .. .. 32·00 17·00
D 4. 3d. black .. .. 42·00 22·00
D 5. 4d. black .. .. £100 80·00

1918.
D 6. D **2.** ½d. black 55 55
D 7. 1d. black 55 55
D 8. 2d. black 60 70
D 9. 3d. black .. .. 1·10 1·25
D 10. 4d. black .. .. 1·60 1·75

D 3.

ILLUSTRATIONS British Commonwealth and all overprints and surcharges are FULL SIZE. Foreign Countries have been reduced to ¾-LINEAR.

1940.
D 11. D **3.** 1d. green 20 40
D 12. 2d. green 30 50
D 13. 3d. green 30 60
D 14. 4d. green 55 70
D 15. 5d. green 80 90
D 16. 6d. green .. .. 1·10 1·25
D 17. 1s. red .. .. 1·60 2·00
D 18. 1s. 6d. red .. .. 3·00 4·00

FINLAND E1

A country to the E. of Scandinavia: a Russian Grand-Duchy until 1917, then a Republic.

100 kopecks = 1 rouble.
1865. 100 penni = 1 Finnish markka.
1963. 100 (old marks) = 1 (new) mark.

1. 2.

1856. Imperf.
1. **1.** 5 k. blue £3250 £800
2. 10 k. red £2500 £400

1860. Roul. Values in " Kopecks ".
11. **2.** 5 k. blue on blue .. .. £200 85·00
13. 10 k. rose on rose.. .. £180 26·00

1866. As T **2**, but values in " Pen. " and " Mark. " Roul.
29. **2.** 5 p. brown on grey .. 80·00 60·00
46. 8 p. black on green .. 85·00 65·00
30. 10 p. black on buff .. £140 45·00
38. 20 p. blue on blue.. .. 95·00 27·00
42. 40 p. rose .. .. .. £110 35·00
49. 1 m. brown £600 £450

3. 4.

1875. Perf.
81. **3.** 2 p. grey .. .. .. 5·00 6·00
83. 5 p. yellow .. .. 15·00 3·25
97. 5 p. green .. .. 10·00 20
71. 8 p. green .. .. 70·00 32·00
85. 10 p. brown .. .. 38·00 6·00
99. 10 p. red .. .. .. 14·00 80
86. 20 p. blue .. .. 21·00 1·25
102. 20 p. yellow .. .. 10·00 20
89. 25 p. red .. .. .. 20·00 2·75
103. 25 p. blue .. .. 18·00 50
79. 32 p. red .. .. .. £100 12·00
90. 1 m. mauve .. .. 85·00 18·00
105. 1 m. grey and rose .. 7·50 6·00
106. 5 m. green and rose .. £170 £120
107. 10 m. brown and rose .. £225 £200

1889.
108. **4.** 2 p. grey 25 25
148. 5 p. green 20 8
149. 10 p. red 20 8
150. 20 p. yellow 20 8
151. 15 p. blue 45 10
119. 1 m. grey and rose .. 1·25 75
120a. 5 m. green and rose .. 18·00 19·00
122. 10 m. brown and rose .. 20·00 24·00

5. 6. 7.

8. 9.

1891. Similar to Russian types, but with circles added in designs.
133. **5.** 1 k. yellow .. .. 2·25 2·50
134. 2 k. green .. .. 3·00 3·75
135. 3 k. rose .. .. .. 3·75 5·00
136. **6.** 4 k. rose .. .. .. 4·75 5·50
137. **5.** 7 k. blue .. .. .. 3·00 80
138. **6.** 10 k. blue .. .. 5·00 3·75
139. **7.** 14 k. red and blue .. 7·00 6·00
140. **6.** 20 k. red and blue .. 6·00 6·00
141. **7.** 35 k. green and purple .. 9·00 10·00
142. **6.** 50 k. green and purple .. 9·50 10·00
143. **8.** 1 r. orange and brown .. 29·00 27·00
144. **9.** 3½ r. yellow and black .. 95·00 £130
145. 7 r. yellow and black .. 70·00 80·00

10. 11.

12. 13.

1901. Similar to Russian types, but value in Finnish currency.
161. **10.** 2 p. orange 45 35
162b. 5 p. green 70 8
169a. **11.** 10 p. red 20 5
170. **10.** 20 p. blue 20 5
165a. **12.** 1 m. green and purple 40 10
166. **13.** 10 m. grey and black 35·00 11·00

14. 15. 16.

1911.
176. **14.** 2 p. orange 5 8
177. 5 p. green 5 5
180. 10 p. red 8 5
181. 20 p. blue 15 5
182. **15.** 40 p. blue and claret .. 8 5

1917.
187a. **16.** 5 p. green 5 5
188. 5 p. grey 5 5
189a. 10 p. red 5 5
190. 10 p. green 45 5
191a. 10 p. blue 5 5
192. 20 p. orange 5 5
194. 20 p. brown 15 15
193. 20 p. red 15 5
195a. 25 p. blue 12 5
196. 25 p. brown 5 5
197. 30 p. green 15 5
198a. 40 p. purple 5 5
199a. 40 p. green 5 15
200. 50 p. brown 15 5
201. 50 p. blue .. .. 1·00 8
234. 50 p. green 5 5
235. 60 p. purple 10 5
204. 75 p. yellow 5 8
205. 1 m. black and rose .. 3·75 5
250. 1 m. orange 5 5
207. 1½ m. purple and green 5 8
208a. 2 m. black and green.. 90 15
252. 2 m. blue 5 8
253. 3 m. black and blue .. 5 5
242. 5 m. black and purple 5 5
212. 10 m. black and brown 50 30
213. 25 m. yellow & orange 40 3·00

17. 18. 19.

1918.
214. **17.** 5 p. green 15 30
215. 10 p. red 12 20
216. 30 p. grey 20 45
217. 40 p. lilac 12 25
218. 50 p. brown 20 60
219. 70 p. brown .. .. 1·10 2·40
220. 1 m. grey and red .. 20 40
221. 5 m. grey and lilac .. 27·00 40·00

1919. Surch.
222. **16.** 10 on 5 p. green .. 15 10
223. 20 on 10 p. red .. 15 10
224. 50 on 25 p. blue .. 30 15
225. 75 on 20 p. orange .. 8 8

1921. Surch. with value, **P** and bars.
226. **16.** 30 p. on 10 p. green .. 30 5
227. 60 p. on 40 p. purple .. 90 25
228. 90 p. on 20 p. red .. 5 8
229. 1½ m. on 50 p. blue .. 15 10

1922. Red Cross.
230. **18.** 1 m.+50 p. red & grey 40 1·50

1927. Independence. 10th Anniv.
245. **19.** 1½ m. mauve 5 12
246. 2 m. blue 10 45

1928. Philatelic Exn. Optd. **Postim. naytt. 1928. Frim. utstalln.**
258. **16.** 1 m. orange .. .. 3·75 6·00
259. 1½ m. purple and green 3·75 6·00

20. S.S. " Bore " leaving Turku (Abo).

DESIGNS—VERT. 1½ m. Abo Cathedral. HORIZ. 2 m. Abo Castle.

1929. Abo. 7th Cent.
260. **20.** 1 m. olive 90 60
261. – 1½ m. chocolate .. 1·75 75
262. – 2 m. grey 30 85

23. **24.** Olavinlinna. 27.

1930.
263. **23.** 5 p. chocolate .. 5 5
264. 10 p. lilac 5 5
265. 20 p. green 15 15
266. 25 p. brown 5 5
267. 40 p. green .. .. 1·25 12
268. 50 p. yellow 15 12
268a. 50 p. green 5 5
269. 60 p. grey 15 12
270. 1 m. orange 15 5
271. 1 m. 20 red 20 30
271a. 1 m. 25 yellow .. 8 5
272. 1½ m. mauve .. .. 1·50 5
272a. 1½ m. red 12 5
272b. 1½ m. slate 5 5
272c. 1 m. 75 yellow .. 40 5
273. 2 m. blue 12 8
273a. 2 m. mauve .. .. 4·25 5
273b. 2 m. red 12 5
273c. 2½ m. blue 90 5
273d. 2 m. 75 purple .. 5 5
274. 3 m. olive .. .. 11·00 5
274a. 3½ m. blue .. .. 2·75 5
275. **24.** 5 m. blue 12 5
276b. – 10 m. lilac 35 5
410. **24.** 15 m. purple 60 5
277. – 25 m. sepia 75 5
456. **24.** 35 m. violet .. .. 1·25 5
457. – 40 m. brown 45 5
DESIGNS—As T **24**: 10 m. Lake Saimaa. 25 m., 40 m. Wood cutter.
For further issues in T **23**, see Nos. 371/455a.

1930. Red Cross. Various designs.
278. **27.** 1 m.+10 p. red & orange 95 2·50
279. – 1½ m.+15 p. red & grn. 75 2·50
280. – 2 m.+20 p. red & blue 1·50 5·50

1930. Air. No. 276b optd. **ZEPPELIN 1930.**
281. – 10 m. lilac .. .. 70·00 70·00

30. Church at Hattula.

31. Elias Lonnroth.

32. Finn. Lit. Soc. Seal.

33.

1931. Red Cross.
282. **30.** 1 m.+10 p. grn. & red 1·50 3·75
283. – 1½ m.+15 p. brn. & red 4·25 3·00
284. – 2 m.+20 p. blue & red 80 4·25
DESIGNS: 1½ m. Hameen Castle. 2 m. Viipuri Castle.

1931. Finnish Literary Society's Centenary.
285. **31.** 1 m. brown .. .. 1·75 1·00
286. **32.** 1½ m. blue .. .. 3·75 1·00

1931. First Finnish Stamps. 75th Anniv.
287. **33.** 1½ m. red .. .. 1·25 2·10
288. 2 m. blue .. .. 1·25 2·10

34.

35.

1931. Granberg Collection Fund.
289. **34.** 1 m.+4 m. black .. 12·00 14·00

1931. President Svinhufvud's 70th Birthday.
290. **35.** 2 m. black and blue .. 90 75

1932. Surch.
291. **23.** 50 p. on 40 p. green .. 50 5
292. 1 m. 25 on 50 p. yellow 1·50 30

36. University Library, Helsinki.

37. Magnus Tawast.

1932. Red Cross.
293. **36.** 1¼ m.+10 p. red & bistre 90 3·75
294. – 2 m.+20 p. red & purple 60 1·60
295. – 2½ m.+25 p. red & blue 70 4·50
DESIGNS—VERT. 2 m. St. Nicholas Cathedral. HORIZ. 2½ m. Houses of Parliament.

1933. Red Cross.
296. **37.** 1¼ m.+10 p. red & sepia 1·00 1·25
297. – 2 m.+20 p. red & pur. 40 50
298. – 2½ m.+25 p. red & blue 40 50
DESIGNS: 2 m. Michael Agricola. 2½ m. Isacus Rothovius.

38. Evert Horn.

39. Aleksis Kivi

1934. Red Cross. Men in armour.
299. **38.** 1¼ m.+10 p. red & brn. 60 60
300. – 2 m.+20 p. red & mve. 90 1·25
301. – 2½ m.+25 p. red & blue 60 60
DESIGNS: 2 m. Torsten Stalhandske. 2½ m. Jacob de la Gardie.

1934. Kivi (poet). Birth Cent.
302. **39.** 2 m. purple .. .. 1·00 75

40. M. Calonius.

41. Finnish Bards.

1935. Red Cross. Cross in red.
303. **40.** 1¼ m.+15 p. brown .. 30 35
304. – 2 m.+20 p. purple .. 70 90
305. – 2½ m.+25 p. blue .. 30 45
PORTRAITS: 2 m. H. G. Porthan. 2½ m. A. Chydenius.

1935. Publication of "Kalevala" (Finnish National Poems). Cent. Inscr. "1835 KALEVALA 1935".
306. **41.** 1¼ m. red 80 45
307. – 2 m. brown .. .. 1·25 20
308. – 2½ m. blue .. .. 2·10 60
DESIGNS: 2 m. Louhi's failure to recover the "Sampo" from Vainamoinen. 2½ m. Kullervo's departure to war.

42. R. H. Rehbinder.

43. "Turunmaa."

44. Marshal Mannerheim.

1936. Red Cross.
309. **42.** 1¼ m.+15 p. red & brn. 45 60
310. – 2 m.+20 p. red & pur. 2·00 2·00
311. – 2½ m.+25 p. red & bl. 45 60
PORTRAITS: 2 m. G. M. Armfelt. 2½ m. A. Horn.

1937. Red Cross. Men-of-war. Cross in red.
312. – 1¼ m.+15 p. brown .. 60 60
313. **43.** 2 m.+20 p. red .. .. 11·00 2·10
314. – 3½ m.+35 p. blue .. 45 60
DESIGNS—HORIZ. 1¼ m. "Uusimaa". 3½ m. "Hameenmaa".

1937. Surch. **2 MARKHAA** and bars.
315. **23.** 2 m. on 1½ m. red .. 2·00 12

1937. Marshal Mannerheim's 70th Birthday.
316. **44.** 2 m. blue 50 35

45. A. Makipeska.

46. Long distance Skiing.

47. War Veteran.

1938. Red Cross. Cross in red.
317. **45.** 50 p.+5 p. green .. 35 40
318. – 1¼ m.+15 p. brown .. 60 65
319. – 2 m.+20 p. red .. 6·00 1·75
320. – 3½ m.+35 p. blue .. 45 65
PORTRAITS: 1¼ m. R. I. Orn. 2 m. E. Bergenheim. 3½ m. J. M. Nordenstam.

1938. Int. Skiing Contest, Lahti. Inscr. as in T **43**.
321. **46.** 1 m. 25+75 p. black .. 3·00 4·50
322. – 2 m.+1 m. red .. 3·00 4·50
323. – 3 m. 50+1 m. 50 blue 3·00 4·50
DESIGNS: 2 m. Ski-jumping. 3 m. 50, Downhill skiing contest.

1938. Disabled Soldiers' Relief Fund. Independence. 20th Anniv.
324. **47.** 2 m.+½ m. blue .. 1·00 90

48. Colonizers felling Trees.

49. Ahvenkoski P.O. 1787.

1938. Scandinavian Settlement in America. Tercent.
325. **48.** 3½ m. brown 90 50

1938. Finnish Postal Service. Tercent. Dated "1638-1938".
326. **49.** 50 p. green 12 15
327. – 1¼ m. blue 50 50
328. – 2 m. red 60 25
329. – 3½ m. slate .. .. 2·50 1·60
DESIGNS: 1¼ m. Sledge-boat. 2 m. Junkers "JU-52" mail-plane. 3½ m. G.P.O., Helsinki.

50. Battlefield of Solferino.

51. G.P.O., Helsinki.

1939. Int. Red Cross. 75th Anniv. Cross in red.
330. **50.** 50 p.+5 p. green .. 55 60
331. 1¼ m.+15 p. brown .. 50 60
332. 2 m.+20 p. red .. 11·00 2·10
333. 3½ m.+35 p. blue .. 50 60

1939.
334. **51.** 4 m. brown 10 5
See also Nos. 382/4.

52. Crossbowman.

53. Lion of Finland.

1940. Red Cross Fund. Cross in red.
335. **52.** 50 p.+5 p. green .. 40 55
336. – 1¼ m.+15 p. brown .. 60 70
337. – 2 m.+20 p. red 75 75
338. – 3½ m.+35 p. blue .. 50 60
DESIGNS: Mounted (1¼ m.) and unmounted cavalrymen (2 m.). 3½ m. Officer and infantryman.

1940. National Defence Fund.
339. **53.** 2 m.+2 m. blue .. 30 50

54. Helsinki University.

55. Builder.

1940. Founding of Helsinki University. 300th Anniv.
340. **54.** 2 m. blue 45 30

1940. Surch.
341. **23.** 1 m. 75 on 1 m. 25 yellow 40 20
342. 2 m. 75 on 2 m. red .. 1·10 8

1941. Red Cross Fund. Cross in red.
343. **55.** 50 p.+5 p. green .. 20 25
344. – 1 m. 75+15 p. sepia .. 70 75
345. – 2 m. 75+25 p. brown .. 3·00 2·75
346. – 3 m. 50+35 p. blue .. 60 75
DESIGNS: 1 m. 75, "Farmer". 2 m. 75, Mother and child. 3 m. 50, Flag.

56. Farewell Review.

57. Crusader.

1941. President Kallio Memorial.
347. **56.** 2 m. 75 black 45 30

1941. "Brothers-in-Arms" Welfare Fund.
348. **57.** 2 m. 75+25 p. blue .. 45 30

58. Viipuri Castle.

1941. Reconquest of Viipuri.
349. **58.** 1 m. 75 orange 30 35
350. 2 m. 75 purple 30 35
351. 3 m. 50 blue 45 45

59. Pres. Risto Ryti.

60. Marshal Mannerheim.

1941.
352. **59.** 50 p. green 20 20
353. 1 m. 75 brown 20 20
354. 2 m. red 15 15
355. 2 m. 75 violet 25 25
356. 3 m. 50 blue 20 20
357. 5 m. grey 20 20

1941.
358. **60.** 50 p. green 20 20
359. 1 m. 75 brown 20 20
360. 2 m. red 20 20
361. 2 m. 75 violet 25 25
362. 3 m. 50 blue 15 15
363. 5 m. grey 15 15

61. Aland.

62. Tampere.

1942. Red Cross Fund. Cross in red.
364. **61.** 50 p.+5 p. green .. 15 20
365. – 1 m. 75+15 p. brown .. 60 65
366. – 2 m. 75+25 p. red .. 75 75
367. – 3 m. 50+35 p. blue .. 75 75
368. – 4 m. 75+45 p. grey .. 45 50
ARMS: 1 m. 75, Uusimaa (Nyland). 2 m. 75, Finland Proper. 3 m. 50, Karelia. 4 m. 75, Satakunta.

1942.
369. **62.** 50 m. violet 90 8
370. – 100 m. blue 75 5
DESIGN: 100 m. Helsinki Harbour.
See also No. 557b.

1942.
371. **23.** 75 p. orange 5 5
372. 1 m. green 5 5
373. 2 m. orange 12 5
373a. 2 m. green 8 5
374. 2½ m. red 12 5
439. 2½ m. green 5 5
375. 3 m. red 12 5
375a. 3 m. yellow 15 15
440. 3 m. grey 5 5
441. 3 m. green 35 5
376. 3½ m. olive 5 5
377. 4 m. olive 5 5
378. 4½ m. blue 5 5
379. 5 m. blue 12 5
379b. 5 m. yellow 15 5
379a. 5 m. violet 12 5
379c. 6 m. red 12 5
442. 6 m. orange 30 5
443. 6 m. green 25 15
444. 7 m. red 5 5
379d. 8 m. violet 5 5
445. 8 m. green 15 20
446. 9 m. red 5 5
447. 9 m. orange 10 10
379e. 10 m. blue 15 5
448. 10 m. violet .. .. 1·25 5
449. 10 m. brown .. .. 1·50 5
449a. 10 m. green 30 5
450. **23.** 12 m. blue 50 5
451. 12 m. red 12 5
452. 15 m. blue .. .. 1·25 5
453. 15 m. purple .. .. 3·75 5
453a. 15 m. red 70 5
454. 20 m. blue .. .. 1·90 5
455. 24 m. claret 15 10
455a. 25 m. blue 75 5

63. New Testament.

64. Mediaeval Press.

65. Lapland.

1942. Introduction of Printing into Finland. Tercent.
380. **63.** 2 m. 75 brown .. 20 30
381. **64.** 3 m. 50 blue 35 50

1942.
382. **51.** 7 m. brown 30 5
383. 9 m. mauve 30 5
384. 20 m. brown 75 5

1943. Red Cross Fund. Cross in red.
385. **65.** 50 p.+5 p. green .. 20 30
386. – 2 m.+20 p. brown .. 40 45
387. – 3 m. 50+35 p. red .. 45 45
388. – 4 m. 50+45 p. blue .. 60 90
ARMS: 2 m. Hame (Tavastland). 3 m. 50, Pohjanmaa (Oesterbotten). 4 m. 50, Savo (Savolaks).

1943. Surch **3½ mk** over bars.
389. **23.** 3½ m. on 2 m. 75 purple 8 5

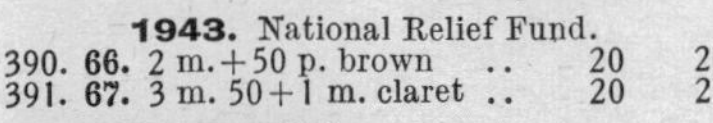

66. Military Emblems. 67. Widow and Orphans.

1943. National Relief Fund.
390. 66. 2 m.+50 p. brown .. 20 20
391. 67. 3 m. 50+1 m. claret .. 20 25

68. Red Cross Train.

DESIGNS: 2 m. Ambulance. 3 m. 50, Hospital. 4 m. 50, Aeroplane.

1944. Red Cross Fund. Inscr. "1944". Cross in red.
392. 68. 50 p.+25 p. green .. 15 15
393. – 2 m.+50 p. violet .. 15 15
394. – 3 m. 50+75 p. red .. 15 15
395. – 4 m. 50+1 m. blue .. 50 75

69. Minna Canth. 70. Douglas "DC3" Mail 'Plane.

1944. Minna Canth (author). Birth Cent.
396. 69. 3 m. 50 olive 15 20

1944. Air. Air Mail Service. 20th Anniv.
397. 70. 3 m. 50 brown .. 20 20

71. Pres. Svinhufvud. 72. 73. Pres. Stahlberg.

1944. Mourning for Pres. Svinhufvud.
398. 3½ m. black 12 15

1944. National Relief Fund.
399. 72. 3 m. 50+1 m. 50 brown 12 15

1945. Red Cross Fund. As Nos. 343/6, but dated "1945". Cross in red.
405. 1 m.+25 p. green .. 8 8
406. 2 m.+50 p. brown .. 10 10
407. 3 m. 50+75 p. brown .. 10 10
408. 4 m. 50+1 m. blue .. 20 25

1945. Pres. Stahlberg. 80th Birth Anniv.
409. 73. 3 m. 50 violet 10 12

74. Wrestling. 75. Sibelius. 76. Trawling.

1945. Sports Fund.
400. 74. 1 m.+50 p. green .. 12 25
401. – 2 m.+1 m. red .. 12 25
402. – 3 m. 50+1 m. 75 vio.. 12 25
403. – 4 m. 50+2 m. 25 blue 12 25
404. – 7 m.+3 m. 50 brown 30 45
DESIGNS: 2 m. Vaulting. 3 m. 50, Running. 4 m. 50, Ski-ing. 7 m. Throwing the javelin.

1945. Sibelius (composer). 80th Birthday.
411. 75. 5 m. green 12 15

1946. Red Cross. Dated "1946". Cross in red.
412. 76. 1 m.+25 p. green .. 25 20
413. – 3 m.+75 p. purple .. 8 8
414. – 5 m.+1 m. 25 red .. 8 8
415. – 10 m.+2 m. 50 blue .. 10 12
DESIGNS: 3 m. Butter-making. 5 m. Harvesting. 10 m. Logging.

1946. Surch. with bold figures and bars.
416. 23. 8 m. on 5 m. violet .. 5 5
416a. 12 m. on 10 m. violet .. 35 5

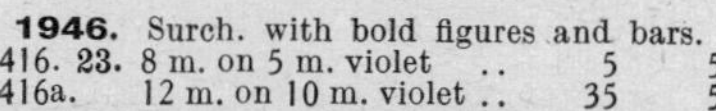

77. Athletes. 78. Nurse and Children. 79. Lighthouse, and Sailing Ship.

1946. National Games.
417. 77. 8 m. purple 15 15

1946. Tuberculosis Fund. Dated "1946".
418. 78. 5 m.+1 m. green .. 12 15
419. – 8 m.+2 m. red .. 12 15
DESIGN: 8 m. Lady doctor examining child.

1946. Pilotage Institution. 250th Anniv.
420. 79. 8 m. violet 15 15

80. Postal Motor Coach. 81. Museum.

1946.
421. 80. 16 m. black 12 15
421a. 30 m. black 45 5

1946. Porvoo (Borga). 600th Anniv.
422. 81. 5 m. black 12 15
423. – 8 m. purple 12 15
DESIGN—VERT. 8 m. View of bridge and church.

82. Tammisaari. 83. J. K. Paasikivi.

1946. Tammisaari (Ekenas). 4th Cent.
424. 82. 8 m. green 12 15

1947.
425. 83. 10. m black 12 15

1947. Tuberculosis Fund. 1946 issue surch.
426. 78. 6+1 on 5 m.+1 m. grn. 8 15
427. – 10+2 on 8 m.+2 m. red 12 20

84. Savings Bank Emblem. 85. Athletes.

1947. Finnish Postal Savings Bank. 60th Anniv.
428. 84. 10 m. claret 12 15

1947. National Sports Festival.
429. 85. 10 m. blue 15 15

86. Ilmaringen Ploughing. 87. Emblem of Savings Bank Association.

1947. Conclusion of Peace Treaty.
430. 86. 10 m. black 12 15

1947. Savings Bank Assn. 125th Anniv.
431. 87. 10 m. brown 12 15

88. Physical Exercise. 89. Sower.

1947. Tuberculosis Fund. Dated "1947".
432. 88. 2 m. 50+1 m. green .. 12 15
433. – 6 m.+1 m. 50 red .. 15 20
434. – 10 m.+2 m. 50 brown.. 12 20
435. – 12 m.+3 m. blue .. 15 20
436. – 20 m.+5 m. mauve .. 15 25
DESIGNS—VERT. 6, 10, 20 m. Various child-exercises. HORIZ. 12 m. Mme. Paasikivi and child.

1947. League of Agricultural Societies. 150th Anniv.
437. 89. 10 m. grey 12 15

90. Heights of Koil. 91. Z. Topelius.

92. Michael Agricola. 93. Sveaborg Fortress.

1947. Tourist Society. 60th Anniv.
438. 90. 10 m. blue 12 15

1948. Red Cross Fund. Dated "1948". Cross in red.
460. 91. 3 m.+1 m. green .. 12 12
461. – 7 m.+2 m. red.. .. 12 15
462. – 12 m.+3 m. blue .. 30 20
463. – 20 m.+5 m. violet .. 25 25
PORTRAITS: 7 m. Fr. Pacius. 12 m. J. L. Runeburg. 20 m. F. R. Cygnaeus.

1948. Anti-Tuberculosis Fund. Surch. with figures and bars.
464. 7 m.+2 m. on 6 m.+1 m. 50 red (No. 433) .. 70 70
465. 15 m.+3 m. on 10 m.+ 2 m. 50 brn. (No. 434) .. 20 35
466. 24 m.+6 m. on 20 m.+ 5 m. mauve (No. 436) .. 20 35

1948. Translation of New Testament into Finnish. 400th Anniv.
467. 92. 7 m. purple 25 35
468. – 12 m. blue 25 35
DESIGN: 12 m. Agricola translating New Testament.

1948. Founding of Suomenlinna (Sveaborg). Bicent.
469. 93. 12 m. green 45 40

94. Finnish Mail-carrier's Badge. 95. Girl Bundling Twigs. 96. Anemone.

1948. Helsinki Philatelic Exn.
470. 94. 12 m. green .. 7·50 10·00
Sold only at the Exn., at 62 m. (including 50 m. entrance fee).

1949. Red Cross Fund. Inscr. "SAUNA BASTU 1949". Cross in red.
471. 95. 5 m.+2 m. green .. 15 20
472. – 9 m.+3 m. red .. 15 20
473. – 15 m.+5 m. blue .. 15 20
474. – 30 m.+10 m. brown .. 30 50
DESIGNS: 9 m. Bathing scene. 15 m. Steaming bath-house. 30 m. Bathers running to plunge in lake.

1949. Tuberculosis Relief Fund.
475. 96. 5 m.+2 m. green .. 20 25
476. – 9 m.+3 m. red.. .. 20 25
477. – 15 m.+5 m. brown .. 20 25
DESIGNS: 9 m. Rose. 15 m. Coltsfoot.

97. Trees and Paper-Mill. 98. Girl with Torch.

1949. 3rd World Forestry Congress. Inscr. "IIIE CONGRES FORESTIER MONDIAL 1949".
478. 97. 9 m. brown 65 60
479. – 15 m. green (Tree and Globe) .. 65 60

1949. Labour Movement. 50th Anniv. Inscr. as in T 98.
480. 98. 5 m. green .. .. 1·25 2·25
481. – 15 m. red (Man with mallet) .. .. 1·25 2·25

99. Kristinestad. 100. Lappeenranta.

1949. Kristiinankaupunki (Kristinestad), Tercent.
482. 99. 15 m. blue 45 45

1949. Tercent of Lappeenranta.
483. 100. 5 m. green 20 15

101. Church Raahe. 102. Allegory of Work and Learning. 103. Hannes Gebhard.

1949. Tercent of Raahe.
484. 101. 9 m. purple 35 25

1949. Technical High School. Cent.
485. 102. 15 m. blue 35 30

1949. Finnish Co-operative Movement. 50th Anniv.
486. 103. 15 m. green 35 30

104. 105. Douglas "DC4" Skymaster. 106. Nymphaea Candida.

1949. U.P.U. 75th Anniv
487. 104. 15 m. blue 35 30

1950. Air. (a) With "mk".
488. 105. 300 m. blue .. .. 1·75 1·40

(b) "mk" omitted.
585. 105. 300 m. blue .. .. 3·25 55
See also No. 676.

1950. T.B. Fund. Dated "1950".
489. 106. 5 m.+2 m. green .. 1·25 1·25
490. – 9 m.+3 m. magenta.. 25 40
491. – 15 m.+5 m. blue .. 40 45
DESIGNS: 9 m. "Pulsatilla vernalis". 15 m. "Campanula gomerata".

107. Plan of Helsinki, 1550. 108. President Paasikivi.

1950. Helsinki. 400th Anniv.
492. 107. 5 m. green 20 15
493. – 9 m. brown 25 25
494. – 15 m. blue 25 15
DESIGNS: 9 m. J. A. Ehrenstrom and C. L. Engel. 15 m. Town Hall.

1950. President's 80th Birthday.
495. 108. 20 m. blue 25 15

109. Hospital. 110. Town Hall, Kajaani. 111. Capercailzie.

1951. Red Cross. Cross in red.
496. 109. 7 m.+2 m. brown .. 15 20
497. – 12 m.+3 m. violet .. 15 30
498. – 20 m.+5 m. red .. 60 60
DESIGNS: 12 m. Blood donor and nurse. 20 m. Blood donor's badge.

1951. Kajaani. 300th Anniv.
499. 110. 20 m. brown 25 15

1951. T.B. Fund. Dated "1951".
500. 111. 7 m.+2 m. green .. 60 70
501. – 12 m.+3 m. lake .. 50 50
502. – 20 m.+5 m. blue .. 50 50
DESIGNS: 12 m. Cranes. 20 m. Caspian terns.

112. Diving.

113. Marshal Mannerheim.

114. Arms of Pietarsaari.

1951. 15th Olympic Games, Helsinki.
503. **112.** 12 m.+2 m. red .. 15 20
504. – 15 m.+2 m. green .. 20 25
505. – 20 m.+3 m. blue .. 20 25
506. – 25 m.+4 m. brown .. 20 25
DESIGNS—HORIZ. 15 m. Football. 25 m. Running. VERT. 20 m. Stadium.

1952. Red Cross. Cross in red.
507. **113.** 10 m.+2 m. black .. 35 45
508. 15 m.+3 m. purple .. 45 50
509. 25 m.+5 m. blue .. 60 65

1952. Pietarsaari (Jakobstad). 300th Anniv.
510. **114.** 25 m. blue 30 15

115. Vaasa.

116. Knight, Castle and Chessboard.

117. Continental Great Tit.

1952. Fire of Vaasa. Cent.
511. **115.** 25 m. brown 25 15

1952. 10th Chess Olympiad, Helsinki.
512. **116.** 25 m. black 50 40

1952. Tuberculosis Fund. Dated "1952".
513. **117.** 10 m.+2 m. green .. 50 50
514. – 15 m.+3 m. claret .. 50 50
515. – 25 m.+5 m. blue .. 70 70
BIRDS: 15 m. Spotted Flycatchers. 25 m. Swifts.

118. "Flame of Temperance".

119. Aerial view of Hamina.

1953. Finnish Temperance Movement. Cent.
516. **118.** 25 m. blue 25 15

1953. Hamina (Fredrikshamn). 300th Anniv.
517. **119.** 25 m. slate 25 15

DESIGNS: 15 m. Brown bear. 25 m. Elk.

120. Squirrel.

1953. Tuberculosis Fund. Dated "1953".
518. **120.** 10 m.+2 m. brown .. 50 55
519. – 15 m.+3 m. violet .. 55 60
520. – 25 m.+5 m. green .. 60 65

121. I. Wilskman.

122. Mother and Children.

1954. Wilskman (gymnast). Birth Cent.
521. **121.** 25 m. blue 25 15

1954. Red Cross. Cross in red. Inscr. "1954".
522. **122.** 10 m.+2 m. green .. 40 40
523. – 15 m.+3 m. blue .. 45 45
524. – 25 m.+5 m. brown .. 60 60
DESIGNS: 15 m. Old lady knitting. 25 m. Blind man and dog.

123.

124. "In the Outer Archipelago" (Edelfelt).

1954.
525. **123.** 1 m. brown 15 5
526. 2 m. green 15 5
527. 3 m. orange 15 5
527a. 4 m. grey 12 5
528. 5 m. lavender 40 5
529. 10 m. green 20 5
530. 15 m. red .. .. 1·10 5
530a. 15 m. buff .. .. 1·50 5
531. 20 m. purple .. .. 1·25 5
531a. 20 m. red 35 5
532. 25 m. blue .. .. 1·10 5
532a. 25 m. purple .. .. 1·40 5
532b. 30 m. blue 20 5
See also Nos. 647, etc.

1954. A. Edelfelt (painter). Birth Cent.
533. **124.** 25 m. black 35 15

125. Bees Collecting Pollen.

126. J. J. Nervander (astronomer and poet).

1954. Tuberculosis Fund. Dated "1954". Cross in red.
534. **125.** 10 m.+2 m. brown .. 50 50
535. – 15 m.+3 m. red .. 50 50
536. – 25 m.+5 m. blue .. 55 55
DESIGNS: 15 m. Butterfly and wild rose. 25 m. Dragonfly.

1955. Nervander. 150th Birth Anniv.
537. **126.** 25 m. blue 35 15

127. St. Henry.

128. Parliament Building.

1955. Establishment of Christianity in Finland. 800th Anniv. Inscr. "1155 1955".
539. **127.** 15 m. purple 35 15
540. – 25 m. green 35 15
DESIGN: 25 m. Arrival of Christian preachers in 1155.

1955. National Philatelic Exn., Helsinki.
538. **128.** 25 m. grey .. .. 8·50 8·50
Sold only at the Exn., at 125 m. (including 100 m. entrance fee.).

129. Conference in Session.

130. Sailing Ship and Cargo.

1955. Interparliamentary Conf., Helsinki.
541. **129.** 25 m. green 35 15

1955. Oulu (Uleaborg). 350th Anniv.
542. **130.** 25 m. brown 30 15

131. Perch.

132. Town Hall, Lahti.

1955. Tuberculosis Fund. Cross in red.
543. **131.** 10 m.+2 m. green .. 35 35
544. – 15 m.+3 m. brn. (Pike) 50 45
545. – 25 m.+5 m. bl. (Salmon) 60 55

1955. Lahti. 50th Anniv.
546. **132.** 25 m. blue 35 15

133. J. Z. Duncker.

134. "Telegraphs".

1955. Red Cross. Cross in red. Inscr. "1955".
547. – 10 m.+2 m. blue .. 35 35
548. **133.** 15 m.+3 m. brown .. 50 45
549. – 25 m.+5 m. green .. 60 55
DESIGNS: 10 m. Van Dobeln on horseback. 25 m. Boy soldier.

1955. Cent. of Telegraphs in Finland. Inscr. "1855-1955 Telegrafin".
550. **134.** 10 m. green 30 15
551. – 15 m. violet 30 12
552. – 25 m. blue 35 15
DESIGNS: 15 m. Otto Nyberg. 25 m. Telegraph pole.

135. Lighthouse at Porkkala.

136. Lammi Church.

1956. Return of Porkkala to Finland.
553. **135.** 25 m. blue 35 15

1956.
553a. – 5 m. green (postage) .. 12 5
554. **136.** 30 m. olive 15 5
555. – 40 m. lilac 30 5
556. **136.** 50 m. olive .. .. 1·00 5
557. – 60 m. purple .. .. 1·00 5
557a. – 75 m. black 30 5
557b. – 100 m. blue-green .. 3·25 5
557c. – 125 m. myrtle .. 1·00 15
593. – 34 m. blue (air) .. 50 30
594. – 45 m. blue 50 15
DESIGNS: 5 m. View of lake. 34 m., 45 m. Convair 440 "Metropolitan" Airliner over lakes. 40 m. Houses of Parliament. 60 m. Olavinlinna. 75 m. Pyhakoski Dam. 100 m. Helsinki Harbour. 125 m. Turku Castle.
No. 557b differs from No. 370 in that "FINLAND" is without the scroll, the figures "100" are upright and "mk" is omitted.
See also Nos. 647 etc.

137. J. V. Snellman.

138. Athletes.

1956. Snellman (statesman). 150th Birth Anniv.
558. **137.** 25 m. chocolate .. 35 15

1956. Finnish Games.
559. **138.** 30 m. blue 45 12

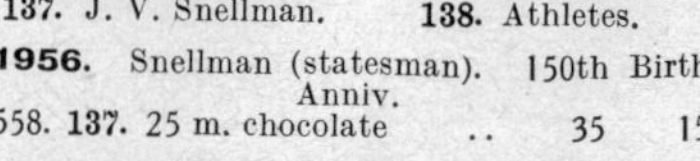

139.

140. Waxwing.

1956. Finnish Stamp Cent. and Int. Philatelic Exn., Helsinki. Roul.
560. **139.** 30 m. blue .. .. 1·75 2·25
Sold at face value plus 125 m. entrance fee to Exhibition.

1956. Tuberculosis Fund. Inscr. "1956". Cross in red.
561. **140.** 10 m.+2 m. brown .. 40 35
562. – 20 m.+3 m. grn. (Owl) 50 40
563. – 30 m.+5 m. bl. (Swan) 60 55

141. Vaasa Town Hall.

142. P. Aulin.

HAVE YOU READ THE NOTES AT THE BEGINNING OF THIS CATALOGUE?
These often provide answers to the enquiries we receive.

144. Scout Badge and Saluting Hand.

143. University Hospital, Helsinki.

1956. Vaasa. 350th Anniv.
564. **141.** 30 m. blue 35 15

1956. Northern Countries' Day. As T **89** of Denmark.
565. 20 m. red .. .. 1·40 20
566. 30 m. blue .. .. 1·90 20

1956. Red Cross. Inscr. "1956". Cross in red.
567. **142.** 5 m.+1 m. green .. 25 15
568. – 10 m.+2 m. brown .. 30 25
569. – 20 m.+3 m. claret .. 45 30
570. – 30 m.+5 m. blue .. 55 40
PORTRAITS: 10 m. L. von Pfaler. 20 m. G. Johansson. 30 m. V. M. von Born.

1956. National Health Service. Bicent.
571. **143.** 30 m. green 50 15

1957. Boy Scout Movement. 50th Anniv.
572. **144.** 30 m. blue 50 20

145. "In Honour of Work".

146. "Lex" (sculpture by W. Runeberg).

147. Glutton.

148. Factories within Cogwheel.

1957. Finnish Trade Union Movement. 50th Anniv.
573. **145.** 30 m. red 30 15

1957. Finnish Parliament. 50th Anniv.
574. **146.** 30 m. olive 45 15

1957. Tuberculosis Relief Fund. Inscr. "1957". Cross in red.
575. **147.** 10 m.+2 m. purple .. 30 30
576. – 20 m.+3 m. sepia .. 45 35
577. – 30 m.+5 m. blue .. 60 50
DESIGNS: 20 m. Lynx. 30 m. Reindeer.
See also Nos. 642/4.

1957. Central Federation of Finnish Employers. 50th Anniv.
578. **148.** 20 m. blue 30 15

149. Red Cross Flag.

150. Ida Aalberg.

1957. Red Cross Fund and Finnish Red Cross. 80th Anniv. Cross in red.
579. **149.** 10 m.+2 m. green .. 75 75
580. 20 m.+3 m. lake .. 75 75
581. 30 m.+5 m. blue .. 75 75

1957. Ida Aalberg (actress). Birth Cent.
582. **150.** 30 m. maroon & purple 40 15

151. Arms of Finland.

152. Sibelius.

1957. Independence. 40th Anniv.
583. **151.** 30 m. blue 50 15

1957. Death of Sibelius (composer).
584. **152.** 30 m. black 50 15

153. Ski-jumping.

154. "March of the Bjorneborglenses" (after Edelfelt).

1958. World's Ski Championships. Inscr. "MM-VM 1958".
586. 153. 20 m. green 35 30
587. – 30 m. blue 55 25
DESIGN—VERT. 30 m. Skier, walking.

1958. Founding of Pori (Bjorneborg). 400th Anniv.
588. 154. 30 m. slate-purple .. 50 15

155. Lily of the Valley.

156. Lyceum Seal.

158. Missionary Emblem and Globe.

157. Cloudberry.

1958. Tuberculosis Relief Fund. Inscr. "1958". Cross in red.
589. 155. 10 m.+2 m. green .. 50 40
590. – 20 m.+3 m. crimson 50 45
591. – 30 m.+5 m. blue .. 60 55
DESIGNS: 20 m. Red clover. 30 m. Anemone.

1958. Jyvaskyla Lyceum (secondary school). Cent.
592. 156. 30 m. red 70 15

1958. Red Cross Fund. Inscr. "1958". Cross in red.
595. 157. 10 m.+2 m orange .. 55 50
596. – 20 m.+3 m. red .. 60 50
597. – 30 m.+5 m. blue .. 65 60
DESIGNS: 20 m. Cowberry. 30 m. Blueberry.

1959. Finnish Missionary Society Cent.
598. 158. 30 m. slate-purple .. 35 15

159. Opening of Diet, 1809.

160. Multiple Saws.

1959. Re-convening of Finnish Diet at Porvoo. 150th Anniv.
599. 159. 30 m. indigo 35 12

1959. Air. No. 593 surch.
600. 45 m. on 34 m. blue .. 95 95

1959. Kestila Sawmill Cent. (10 m.) and Finnish Forestry Department (30 m.). Inscr." 1859-1959".
601. 160. 10 m. chocolate .. 25 12
602. – 30 m. grn. (Forest firs) 40 12

1959. Tuberculosis Relief Fund. As T 155 but inscr. "1959". Cross in red.
603. 10 m.+2 m. green .. 75 45
604. 20 m.+3 m. brown .. 80 50
605. 30 m.+5 m. blue .. 90 55
DESIGNS: 10 m. Marguerite. 20 m. Cowslip. 30 m. Cornflower.

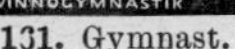

131. Gymnast.

162. Oil Lamp.

1959. Finnish Women's Gymnastics (Elin Oihonna Kallio Cent.).
606. 161. 30 m. purple 45 12

1959. Trade Freedom in Finland. Cent.
607. 162. 30 m. blue 30 12

ILLUSTRATIONS
British Commonwealth and all overprints and surcharges are FULL SIZE. Foreign Countries have been reduced to ¾-LINEAR.

163. Arms of the Towns.

1960. Extra Privileges for Finnish Towns—Hyvinkaa, Kouvola, Riihimaki, Rovaniemi, Salo and Seinajoki.
608. 163. 30 m. violet 35 10

No. 609 was only on sale at 150 m. including entrance fee.

164. 5 k. "Serpentine Roulette" Stamp of 1860.

1960. Stamp Exn., Helsinki, and Cent. of "Serpentine Roulette" stamps. Roul.
609. 164. 30 m. blue and grey .. 2·75 2·75

165. Refugees and Symbol.

166. J. Gadolin.

167. H. Nortamo.

168. Bird on Tree.

1960. World Refugee Year.
610. 165. 30 m. claret 35 8
611. 40 m. blue 35 8

1960. Johan Gadolin (chemist). Birth Bicent.
612. 166. 30 m. brown 30 5

1960. H. Nortamo (writer). Birth Cent.
613. 167. 30 m. green 30 8

1960. Karelian National Festival, Helsinki.
614. 168. 30 m. red 35 8

169. "Geodesy" (Geodetic instrument).

170. Pres. Kekkonen.

171. Pastor Cygnaeus.

172. Reindeer.

1960. 12th Int. Geodesy and Geophysics Union Assembly, Helsinki. Inscr. "1960 Helsinki".
615. 169. 10 m. sepia and blue .. 30 10
616. – 30 m. orn., red & verm. 35 5
DESIGN: 30 m. "Geophysics" (represented by Northern Lights).

1960. President Kekkonen's 60th Birthday.
617. 170. 30 m. blue 50 5

1960. Europa. As T 279 of Belgium but size 31×20½ mm.
618. 30 m. blue and ultramarine 30 8
619. 40 m. maroon and sepia .. 80 20

1960. Pastor Uno Cygnaeus (founder of elementary schools). 150th Birth Anniv.
620. 171. 30 m. violet 30 8

1960. Red Cross. Inscr. "1960". Cross in red.
621. 172. 10 m.+2 m. black .. 50 40
622. – 20 m.+3 m. violet .. 55 50
623. – 30 m.+5 m. maroon .. 60 55
DESIGNS: 20 m. Hunter with lasso. 30 m. Mountain and lake.

173. "Pommern".

174. Savings Bank Emblem.

1961. Mariehamn (town) Cent.
624. 173. 30 m. turquoise .. 40 8

1961. Postal Savings Bank. 75th Anniv.
625. 174. 30 m. turquoise .. 25 8

175. Symbol of Standardization.

176. J. Aho.

177. Public Buildings.

178. A. Jarnefelt.

1961. General Assembly of Int. Organization for Standardization, Helsinki.
626. 175. 30 m. green & orange .. 25 8

1961. Tuberculosis Relief Fund. As T 147. Inscr. "1961". Cross in red.
627. 10 m.+2 m. claret .. 40 30
628. 20 m.+3 m. indigo .. 50 40
629. 30 m.+5 m. blue-green .. 60 50
ANIMALS: 10 m. Musk-rat. 20 m. Otter. 30 m. Seal.

1961. Aho (writer). Birth Cent.
630. 176. 30 m. brown 25 8

1961. Finnish Central Building Board. 150th Anniv.
631. 177. 30 m. black 25 8

1961. Arvid Jarnefelt (writer). Birth Cent.
632. 178. 30 m. purple 30 8

179. Bank Facade.

180. First locomotive, "Ilmarinen".

1961. Bank of Finland. 150th Anniv.
633. 179. 30 m. maroon 35 8

1962. Finnish Railways Cent.
634. 180. 10 m. green 35 8
635. – 30 m. blue 50 8
636. – 40 m. maroon 60 8
LOCOMOTIVES: 30 m. Class Hr 1 steam locomotive. 40 m. Class Hr 12 diesel.

181. Mora Stone.

182. Senate Place, Helsinki.

1962. Finnish People's Political Rights. 600th Anniv.
637. 181. 30 m. slate-purple .. 25 8

1962. Proclamation of Helsinki as Finnish Capital. 150th Anniv.
638. 182. 30 m. chocolate .. 25 8

183. Customs Board Crest.

184. Emblem of Commerce.

1962. Finnish Customs Board. 150th Anniv.
639. 183. 30 m. red 25 8

1962. 1st Finnish Commercial Bank. Cent.
640. 184. 30 m. turquoise .. 25 8

185. S. Alkio.

186. Finnish Labour Emblem on Conveyor Belt.

1962. S. Alkio (writer and founder of Young People's Societies' Movement). Birth Cent.
641. 185. 30 m. maroon 25 8

1962. Tuberculosis Relief Fund. As T 147 inscr. "1962". Cross in red.
642. 10 m.+2 m. sepia .. 35 30
643. 20 m.+3 m. maroon .. 45 30
644. 30 m.+5 m. blue 55 45
DESIGNS: 10 m. Hare. 20 m. Marten. 30 m. Ermine.

1962. Home Production.
645. 186. 30 m. purple .. 25 5

187. Aerial Survey.

138.

1962. Finnish Land Survey Board. 150th Anniv.
646. 187. 30 m. green 25 8
New currency. 100 (old) markka or pennia = 1 (new) markka.

1963. (a) Lion Type.

647.	188.	1 p. brown	5	5
648.		2 p. green	5	5
649.		4 p. grey	5	5
650.		5 p. blue	5	5
651a.		10 p. green	5	5
652.		15 p. brown	5	5
653a.		20 p. red	5	5
654a.		25 p. purple	5	5
655.		30 p. blue	15	5
656.		30 p. grey-blue ..	12	5
657.		35 p. blue	12	5
657a.		35 p. yellow	12	5
658.		40 p. blue	30	5
658b.		40 p. orange	12	5
659.		50 p. blue	15	5
659aa.		50 p. purple	15	5
659a.		60 p. blue	20	5

(b) Views.

660.	–	5 p. green (As No. 553a) (postage)	5	5
661.	–	25 p. multicoloured ..	15	5
662.	–	30 p. multicoloured ..	30	5
663.	–	40 p. lilac (As No. 555)	20	5
664.	136.	50 p. olive	25	5
665.	–	60 p. plum (As No. 557)	30	5
666.	–	65 p. plum (As No. 557)	35	5
667.	–	75 p. blk. (As No. 557a)	35	5
668.	–	80 p. multicoloured ..	40	5
669.	–	90 p. multicoloured ..	45	8
670.	–	1 m. grn. (As No. 557b)	35	5
671.	–	1 m. 25 grn. (As No. 557c)	60	5
672.	–	1 m. 30 multicoloured	65	5
673.	–	1 m. 50 green ..	55	5
674.	–	1 m. 75 blue ..	85	5
675.	–	2 m. green	70	5
676.	–	2 m. 50 bl. & yellow	1·50	15
677.	–	5 m. green	2·40	40
678.	–	45 p. blue (594) (air) ..	20	5
678a.	–	57 p. blue (594)	30	5
679.	–	3 m. blue (585) ..	1·60	20

NEW DESIGNS: As T 136: VERT.—30 p. Nasinneula Tower, Tampere. 80 p. Keuruu church. 1 m. 30 Helsinki Railway Station. HORIZ.—25 p. Country mail bus. 70 p., 90 p. Hameen Bridge, Tampere. 1 m. 50, Loggers afloat. 1 m. 75, Perainen Bridge. 2 m. Country house by lake. 2 m. 50, Aerial view of Punkaharju. 5 m. Ristikallio gorge.

No. 679 is as No. 585, but with a comma after "3".

189. Mother and Child.

190. Hands reaching for Red Cross.

1963. Freedom from Hunger.
680. 189. 40 p. brown 25 8

1963. Red Cross Cent.
681. 190. 10 p.+2 p. red & brn. 40 25
682. 20 p.+3 p. red & violet 45 30
683. 30 p.+5 p. red & grn. 45 40

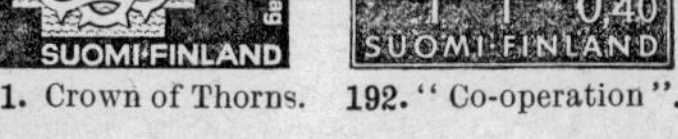

191. Crown of Thorns.

192. "Co-operation".

1963. Lutheran World Federation Assembly, Helsinki.
684. 191. 10 p. lake 25 5
685. – 30 p. green 35 8
DESIGN: 30 p. Head of Christ.

1963. Europa.
686. 192. 40 p. purple .. 35 8

193. House of Estates, Helsinki.

194. Convair "Metropolitan" CV440 Airliner.

1963. Finnish Representative Assembly. Cent.
687. **193.** 30 p. purple 25 5

1963. 40 Years of Finnish Civil Aviation.
688. **194.** 35 p. green 30 5
689. – 40 p. blue 30 5
DESIGN: 40 p. Sud-Aviation "Caravelle" SE210 in flight.

195. M. A. Castren. **196.** Soapstone Elk's Head.

1963. M. A. Castren (explorer and scholar). 150th Birth Anniv.
690. **195.** 35 p. violet-blue .. 40 5

1964. "For Art" (Finnish Artists' Society Cent).
691. **196.** 35 p. green and buff .. 45 12

197. E. N. Setala. **198.** Doctor tending Patient on Sledge.

1964. Emil Setala (philologist and statesman). Birth Cent.
692. **197.** 35 p. brown .. 45 5

1964. Red Cross Fund. Inscr. "CONVENTION DE GENEVE 1864–1964". Cross in red.
693. **198.** 15 p.+3 p. violet .. 30 25
694. – 25 p.+4 p. green .. 30 30
695. – 35 p.+5 p. purple .. 40 35
696. – 40 p.+7 p. myrtle .. 50 50
DESIGNS: 25 p. Red Cross Ship. 35 p. Military sick parade. 40 p. Distribution of Red Cross parcels.

199. Emblem of Medicine. **200.** Ice-hockey Players.

1964. World Medical Association. 18th General Assembly.
697. **199.** 40 p. green 30 8

1965. World Ice-hockey Championships.
698. **200.** 35 p. blue 30 5

201. Centenary Medal. **202.** K. J. Stahlberg and Runeberg's sculpture, "Lex".

1965. Finnish Communal Self-Government Cent.
699. **201.** 35 p. green 30 8

1965. K. J. Stahlberg (statesman). Birth Cent.
700. **202.** 35 p. brown 35 5

203. I.C.Y. Emblem. **204.** "The Fratricide"

1965. Int. Co-operation Year.
701. **203.** 40 p. black, green, red and buff 35 10

1965. A. Gallen-Kallela (artist). Birth Cent Multicoloured.
702. 25 p. Type **204** 45 10
703. 35 p. "Head of a Young Girl" 45 10

205. Spitz. **206.** Sibelius' Profile, Music and Piano.

1965. Tuberculosis Relief Fund. Dogs.
704. **205.** 15 p.+3 p. brn., & red 40 30
705. – 25 p.+4 p. blk. & red 40 35
706. – 35 p.+5 p. sep. & red 50 40
FINNISH DOGS: 25 p. Karelian bear dog. 35 p. Retriever.

1965. Sibelius (composer). Birth Cent.
707. **206.** 25 p. violet 45 12
708. – 35 p. green 45 12
DESIGN: 35 p. Fragment of music and dove.

207. Radio Aerial. **208.** "Winter Day" (after P. Halonen).

210. "Kiss of Life". **209.** Europa "Sprig".

1965. I.T.U. Cent.
709. **207.** 35 p. blue 40 5

1965. Pekka Halonen (painter). Birth Cent.
710. **208.** 35 p. multicoloured .. 55 8

1965. Europa.
711. **209.** 40 p. multicoloured .. 30 8

1966. Red Cross Fund. Multicoloured.
712. 15 p.+3 p. Type **210** .. 25 20
713. 25 p.+4 p. Diver rescuing car occupants under water 30 25
714. 35 p.+5 p. Red Cross helicopter on emergency mission 45 35

211. "Growing Up". **212.** Old Post Office.

213. Globe and U.N.E.S.C.O. Emblem. **214.** Police Emblem.

1966. Finnish Elementary School Decree Cent.
715. **211.** 35 p. blue & ultramarine 25 5

1966. "Nordia 1966" Stamp Exn., Helsinki, and 1st Postage Stamps in Finnish Currency. Cent.
716. **212.** 35 p. blue, brown and buff .. .. .. 3·00 3·00

1966. U.N.E.S.C.O. Commem.
717. **213.** 40 p. blue, brown, yellow and green .. 25 5

1966. Finnish Police Force. 150th Anniv.
718. **214.** 35 p. silver, black & blue 30 5

215. Anniversary Medal (after K. Kallio). **216.** U.N.I.C.E.F Emblem.

1966. Finnish Insurance. 150th Anniv.
719. **215.** 35 p. olive and lake .. 25 5

1966. U.N.I.C.E.F. Commem.
720. **216.** 15 p. violet, grn. & blue. 20 5

217. FINEFTA Symbol. **218.** Windmill.

1967. Finnish E.F.T.A. Agreement.
721. **217.** 40 p. blue 35 5

1967. Uusikaupunki (Nystad). 350th Anniv.
722. **218.** 40 p. multicoloured .. 30 5

219. Birch Tree and Foliage. **220.** Mannerheim Statue.

1967. Tuberculosis Relief Fund. Trees.
723. **219.** 20 p.+3 p. mult. .. 25 20
724. – 25 p.+4 p. mult. .. 30 20
725. – 40 p.+7 p. mult. .. 40 25
FINNISH FOREST TREES: 25 p. Pine and foliage. 40 p. Spruce and foliage.
See also Nos. 753/5.

1967. Marshal Mannerheim. Birth Cent.
726. **220.** 40 p. multicoloured .. 25 5

221. "Solidarity". **222.** Watermark of Thomasbole Factory.

1967. Finnish Settlers in Sweden.
727. **221.** 40 p. multicoloured .. 27 5

1967. Finnish Paper Industry. 300th Anniv.
728. **222.** 40 p. blue and bistre .. 25 5

223. Martin Luther (from painting by Lucas Cranach the Elder). **224.** Horse-drawn Ambulance.

1967. Reformation. 450th Anniv.
729. **223.** 40 p. chocolate, brown, black & bistre .. 25 5

1967. Red Cross Fund. Multicoloured.
730. 20 p.+3 p. Type **224** .. 25 30
731. 25 p.+4 p. Modern ambulance 30 25
732. 40 p.+7 p. Red Cross emblem 40 35

225. "Wood and Water". **226.** Z. Topelius and "Bluebird".

1967. Independence. 50th Anniv.
733. **225.** 20 p. green and blue .. 25 5
734. – 25 p. blue 25 5
735. – 40 p. magenta and blue 25 5
DESIGNS: 25 p. Flying swan. 40 p. Ear of wheat.

1968. Zacharias Topelius (writer). 150th Birth Anniv.
736. **226.** 25 p. multicoloured .. 30 5

227. Skiing.

1968. Winter Tourism.
737. **227.** 25 p. multicoloured .. 30 5

228. "Paper-making" (from wood relief by H Autere). **229.** W.H.O. Emblem.

1968. Tervakoski Paper Factory. 150th Anniv.
738. **228.** 45 p. sepia, buff & red 25 5

1968. W.H.O. 20th Anniv.
739. **229.** 40 p. multicoloured .. 30 5

230. "Infantryman" (statue, Vaasa). **231.** Holiday Camp.

1968. "National Defence". Multicoloured.
740. 20 p. Type **230** 25 5
741. 25 p. Memorial Bieteniemi cemetery 25 5
742. 40 p. Modern soldier .. 25 5

1968. Tourism.
743. **231.** 25 p. multicoloured .. 30 5

232. Pulp Bale (with outline of tree in centre) and Paper Reel. **233.** O. Merikanto (composer).

1968. Finnish Wood-processing Industry.
744. **232.** 40 p. black, salmon, yellow and green .. 25 5

1968. Oskar Merikanto. Birth Cent.
745. **233.** 40 p. sepia, brown, violet and grey 25 5

234. Mustola Lock. **235.** Dock Cranes, Ships and Chamber of Commerce Emblem.

1968. Opening of Saima Canal.
746. **234.** 40 p. multicoloured .. 25 5

1968. "Finnish Economic Life". Finnish Central Chamber of Commerce. 50th Anniv.
747. **235.** 40 p. black, indigo, green and blue .. 25 5

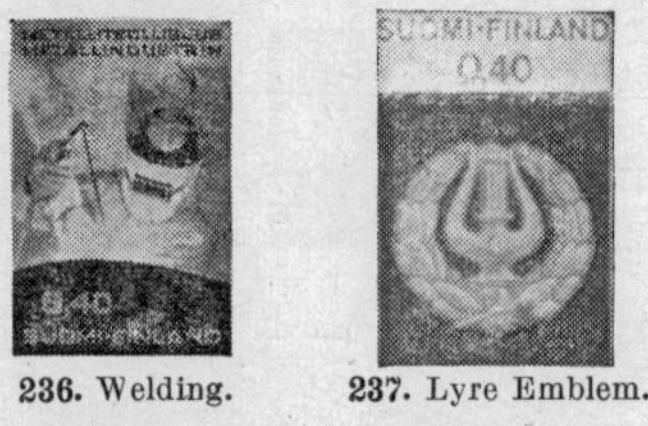

236. Welding. **237.** Lyre Emblem.

1968. Finnish Metal Industry.
748. **236.** 40 p. multicoloured .. 25 5

1968. Finnish Students Unions.
749. **237.** 40 p. brn., bl. & ultram. 25 5

1969. Northern Countries' Union. 50th Anniv. As T **125** of Denmark.
750. 40 p. blue 25 5

238. City Hall and Arms, Kemi. **239.** Colonnade.

1969. Cent. of Kemi.
751. **238.** 40 p. multicoloured .. 25 5

1969. Europa.
752. **239.** 40 p. multicoloured .. 35 5

240. Juniper and Berries.

241. I.L.O Emblem.

243. Fairs Symbol.

242. A. Jarnefelt.

1969. Tuberculosis Relief Fund. Multicoloured.
753. 20 p.+3 p. Type **240** .. 25 20
754. 25 p.+4 p. Aspen and catkins 30 25
755. 40 p.+7 p. Wild cherry and flowers 40 35

1969. Int. Labour Organisation. 50th Anniv.
756. **241.** 40 p. blue and red .. 25 5

1969. Armas Jarnefelt (composer). Birth Cent.
757. **242.** 40 p. multicoloured .. 25 5

1969. Finnish National and Int. Fairs.
758. **243.** 40 p. multicoloured .. 25 5

244. J. Linnankoski.

245. Board Emblems.

1969. Johannes Linnankoski. Birth Cent.
759. **244.** 40 p. multicoloured .. 25 5

1969. Central School Board. Cent.
760. **245.** 40 p. violet, grn. & grey 25 5

246. Douglas "DC-8 62-CF" and Helsinki Airport.

247. Golden Eagle and Eyrie.

1969.
761. **246.** 25 p. multicoloured .. 30 5

1970. Nature Conservation Year.
762. **247.** 30 p. multicoloured .. 30 5

248. "Fabric" Factories.

249. Molecular Structure and Factories.

1970. Finnish Textile Industry.
763. **248.** 50 p. multicoloured .. 30 5

1970. Finnish Chemical Industry.
764. **249.** 50 p. multicoloured .. 25 5

250. U.N.E.S.C.O. Emblem and Lenin.

251. "The Seven Brothers".

1970. Finnish Co-operation with United Nations.
765. **250.** 30 p. multicoloured .. 30 5
766. – 30 p. multicoloured .. 30 5
767. – 50 p. gold, ultram. & bl. 30 5

DESIGNS—VERT. 30 p. (No. 765), T **250** (Lenin Symposium of U.N.E.S.C.O., Tampere). 30 p. (No. 766), "Nuclear data" (Int. Atomic Energy Agency Conference, Otaniemi). HORIZ. 50 p. U.N. emblem and globe (United Nations 25th Anniv.).

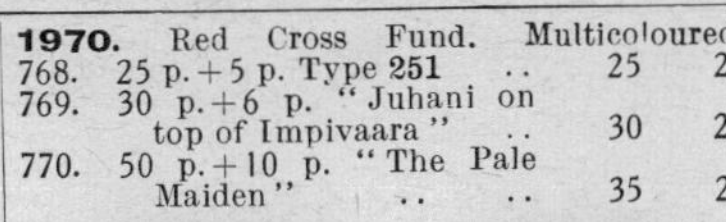

1970. Red Cross Fund. Multicoloured.
768. 25 p.+5 p. Type **251** .. 25 20
769. 30 p.+6 p. "Juhani on top of Impivaara" .. 30 20
770. 50 p.+10 p. "The Pale Maiden" 35 25

252. Invalid playing Handball.

253. "Aurora Society Meeting" (from painting by E. Jarnefelt).

1970. Finnish Invalids.
771. **252.** 50 p. multicoloured .. 25 5

1970. "Aurora" Society. Bicent.
772. **253.** 50 p. multicoloured .. 25 5

254. City Hall and Church, Uusikaarlepyy.

255. Pres. Kekkonen.

1970. Uusikaarlepyy and Kokkola (towns). 350th Anniv. Multicoloured.
773. 50 p. Type **254** 25 5
774. 50 p. Kokkola and arms 25 5

1970. President Urho Kekkonen's 70th Birthday.
775. **255.** 50 p. silver and blue .. 25 5

260. "S.A.L.T." and Globe.

261. Pres. Paasikivi (after sculpture by E. Renvall).

1970. Strategic Arms Limitation Talks, Helsinki.
776. **260.** 50 p. multicoloured .. 25 5

1970. President Paasikivi. Birth Cent.
777. **261.** 50 p. blk. blue & gold .. 25 5

262. Cogwheels.

263. Felling Trees.

1971. Finnish Industry.
778. **262.** 50 p. multicoloured .. 25 5

1971. Tuberculosis Relief Fund. Timber Industry. Multicoloured.
779. 25 p.+5 p. Type **263** .. 25 20
780. 30 p.+6 p. Floating log-"train" 30 20
781. 50 p.+10 p. Sorting logs .. 40 35

264. Europa Chain.

265. Tornio Church.

1971. Europa.
782. **264.** 50 p. yell., pink & blk. 30 5

1971. Tornio. 350th Anniv.
783. **265.** 50 p. multicoloured .. 25 5

266. "Front-page News".

267. Hurdling, High-jumping and Discus-throwing

1971. Finnish Press. Bicent.
784. **266.** 50 p. multicoloured .. 25 5

1971. European Athletic Championships, Helsinki. Multicoloured.
785. 30 p. Type **267** 45 5
786. 50 p. Throwing the javelin and running 45 5

These two designs form a composite picture when placed side by side.

268. "Lightning" Class Yachts.

269. Silver Pot, Seal and Tools.

1971. Int. "Lightning" Class Sailing Championships, Helsinki.
787. **268.** 50 p. multicoloured .. 35 5

1971. Jewellery and Precious-metal Crafts. 600th Anniv.
788. **269.** 50 p. multicoloured .. 25 5

270. Plastic Buttons.

271. "Communications".

1971. Finnish Plastics Industry.
789. **270.** 50 p. multicoloured .. 30 5

1972. Europa.
790. **271.** 30 p. multicoloured .. 30 5
791. 50 p. multicoloured .. 45 5

272. National Theatre Building.

273. Globe.

1972. Finnish National Theatre. Cent.
792. **272.** 50 p. multicoloured .. 25 5

1972. Conclusion of the Strategic Arms Limitation Talks, Helsinki.
793. **273.** 50 p. multicoloured .. 25 5

274. Map and Arms.

275. Training-ship "Suomen Joutsen".

1972. Self-government of the Aland Islands. 50th Anniv.
794. **274.** 50 p. multicoloured .. 25 5

1972. Start of the Tall Ships' Race, Helsinki.
795. **275.** 50 p. multicoloured .. 35 5

276. Post Office, Tampere.

277. Blood Donation.

1972. Multicoloured.
797. 40 p. Type **276** 20 5
798. 60 p. National Museum (25×37 mm.) 20 5
799. 70 p. Market Place, Helsinki (39×27 mm.) 25 5
800. 80p. As 70p. 30 8

1972. Red Cross Fund. Blood Service. Multicoloured.
820. 25 p.+5 p. Type **277** .. 20 25
821. 30 p.+6 p. Laboratory research (vert.) 25 20
822. 50 p.+10 p. Blood transfusion 35 30

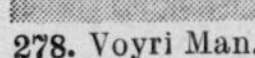

278. Voyri Man.

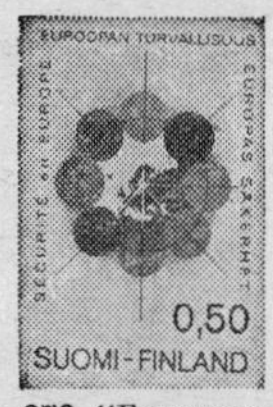

279. "European Co-operation".

1972. Ancient and National Costumes. Multicoloured.
823. 50 p. Pernio woman .. 15 5
824. 50 p. Married couple, Tenhola 15 5
825. 50 p. Nastola girl .. 15 5
826. 50 p. Type **278** 15 5
827. 50 p. Lapp winter costumes 15 5
828. 60 p. Kaukola girl .. 20 5
829. 60 p. Jaaski woman .. 20 5
830. 60 p. Koivisto couple .. 20 5
831. 60 p. Mother and son, Sakyla 20 5
832. 60 p. Heinavesi girl .. 20 5

1972. European Security and Co-operation Conf., Helsinki.
833. **279.** 50 p. multicoloured .. 50 5

280. "Treaty" and National Colours.

281. Pres. K. Kallio.

1973. Friendship Treaty with Russia. 25th Anniv.
834. **280.** 60 p. multicoloured .. 20 5

1973. Pres. Kyosti Kallio. Birth Cent.
835. **281.** 60 p. multicoloured .. 20 5

282. Europa "Posthorn".

283. "E.U.R.O.P.A." on Map.

1973. Europa.
836. **282.** 60 p. green, greenish blue and blue .. 30 5

1973. Nordic Countries' Postal Co-operation. As T **198** of Sweden.
837. 60 p. multicoloured .. 20 5
838. 70 p. multicoloured .. 25 8

1973. European Security and Co-operation Conf., Helsinki.
839. **283.** 70 p. multicoloured .. 25 5

284. Canoe Paddle.

285. Radiosonde Balloon.

1973. World Paddling Championships. Tampere.
840. **284.** 60 p. multicoloured .. 20 5

1973. World Meteorological Organization. Cent.
841. **285.** 60 p. multicoloured .. 20 5

286. E. Saarinen.

287. "Young Girl with Lamb" (H. Simberg).

1973. Eliel Saarinen (architect). Birth Cent.
842. **286.** 60 p. multicoloured .. 20 5

1973. Tuberculosis Relief Fund. Artists' Birth Centenaries. Multicoloured.
843. 30 p.+5 p. Type **287** .. 20 20
844. 40 p.+10 p. "Summer Evening" (W. Sjostrom) 30 30
845. 60 p.+15 p. "At a Mountain Spring" (J. Rissanen) 45 45

288. Finnair "DC-10/30" Jetliner.

289. Santa Claus.

1973. Finnair (airline) and Regular Air Services in Finland. 50th Anniv.
846. 288. 60 p. multicoloured .. 20 5

1973. Christmas.
847. 289. 30 p. multicoloured .. 10 5

290. Scene from "The Barber of Seville".

1973. Finnish State Opera Company. Centenary.
848. 290. 60 p. multicoloured .. 20 5

291. Porcelain Products. 292. "Paavo Nurmi" (Statue by W. Aaltonen).

1973. Finnish Porcelain Industry.
849. 291. 60 p. grn., blk. & bl.. 20 5

1973. Nurmi (Olympic athlete). Commemoration.
850. 292. 60 p multicoloured .. 20 5

293. Hanko Casino, Harbour and Map. 294. Arms of Finland, 1581.

1974. Hanko. Centenary.
851. 493. 60 p. multicoloured .. 20 5

1974.
852. 294. 10 p. multicoloured .. 3·50 90

295. Ice-hockey Players.

1974. World and European Ice-hockey Championships.
853. 295. 60 p. multicoloured .. 20 5

296. Seagulls.

1974. Baltic Area Marine Environmental Conference, Helsinki.
854. 296. 60 p. multicoloured .. 20 5

297. "Goddess of Victory bestowing Wreath of Youth" (W. Aaltonen). 298. "Umari Kianto".

1974. Europa.
855. 297. 70 p. multicoloured .. 35 5

1974. Ilmari Kianto ("Iki Kianto") (writer). Birth Centenary.
856. 298. 60 p. multicoloured .. 20 5

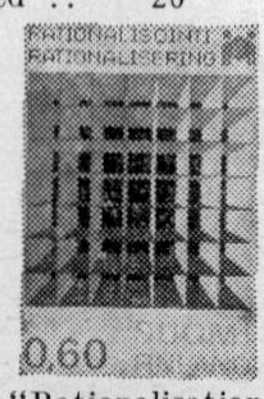

299. Society Emblem. 300. "Rationalisation".

1974. Finnish Rationalisation in Social Development.
858. 299. 60 p. multicoloured .. 20 5

1974. Popular Education Society. Centenary.
857. 300. 60 p. multicoloured .. 20 5

301. "Gyromitra Esculenta". 302. U.P.U. Emblem.

1974. Red Cross Fund. Mushrooms. Multicoloured.
859. 35 p.+5 p. Type 301 .. 20 20
860. 50 p.+10 p. "Cantharellus cibarius" 30 30
861. 60 p.+15 p. "Boletus edulis" 45 45

1974. Universal Postal Union. Cent.
862. 302. 60 p multicoloured .. 20 5
863. 70 p multicoloured .. 20 5

303. Christmas Gnomes. 304. Aunessilta Granibe Bridge and Modern Reinforced Concrete Bridge.

1974. Christmas.
864. 303. 35 p. multicoloured .. 12 5

1974. Finnish Road and Waterways Board. 175th Anniv.
865. 304. 60 p. multicoloured .. 20 5

305. National Coat of Arms. 306. Finnish 32 p. Stamp of 1875.

1975.
866. 305. 40 p. orange 15 5
867. 50 p. green 15 5
861. 60 p. blue 20 5
869. 70 p. brown 25 5
870. 80 p. red and green .. 30 5

1975. "Nordia 1975" Stamp Exhibition.
876. 306. 70 p. brn., blk. & buff 25 60

307. "A Girl Combing Her Hair" (M. Enckell). 308. Office Seal.

1975. Europa. Multicoloured.
877. 70 p. Type 307 .. .. 25 5
878. 90 p. "Washerwomen" (T. Sallinen) 35 8

1975. State Economy Controller's Office 150th Anniv.
879 308. 70 p. multicoloured .. 25 5

309. Salvage Tug and Sinking Ship.

1975. 12th International Salvage Conference Helsinki.
880. 309. 70 p. multicoloured .. 25 5

310. "Pharmacology". 311. Olavinlinna Castle.

1975. 6th International Pharmacological Congress, Helsinki.
881. 310. 70 p. multicoloured .. 25 5

1975. Olavinlinna Castle. 500th Anniv.
882. 311. 70 p. multicoloured .. 25 5

312. Finlandia Hall (Conference Headquarters) and Swallows. 313. "Echo" (Thesleff).

1975. European Security and Co-operation Conference, Helsinki.
883. 312. 90 p. multicoloured .. 30 8

1975. Anti-Tuberculosis Fund. Paintings by women artists. Multicoloured.
884. 40 p.+10 p. Type 313 .. 20 20
885. 60 p.+15 p. "Hild Wiik" (Maria Wiik) 25 25
886. 70 p.+20 p. "At Home" (Helene Schjerfbeck) .. 30 30

314. Women supporting Globe. 315. Graphic Quarter-circle.

1975. International Women's Year.
887. 314. 70 p. multicoloured .. 25 5

1975. Finnish Society of Industrial Art Centenary.
888. 315. 70 p. multicoloured .. 25 5

316. Nativity Play. 317. State Debenture.

1975. Christmas.
889. 316. 40 p. multicoloured .. 15 5

1975. Finnish State Treasury. Centenary.
890. 317. 80 p. multicoloured .. 30 8

318. Finnish Glider. 319. Disabled Ex-servicemen's Association Emblem.

1976. 15th World Gliding Championships, Rayskala.
891. 318. 80 p. multicoloured .. 30 8

1976. Finnish War Invalids Fund.
892. 319. 70 p.+30 p. mult. .. 40 35

320. Cheese-frames. 321. H. Klemetti.

1976. Traditional Finnish Arts. Multicoloured.
893. 1 m. 50 Rusko drinking bowl, 1542 (vert.) .. 60 20
894. 2 m. 50 Type 320 .. 90 30
895. 4 m. 50 Spinning distaffs .. 1·60 50

1976. Professor Heikki Klemetti (composer). Birth Cent.
900. 321. 80 p. multicoloured .. 30 5

322. Diagramatic Map of Finland. 323. "Aino Ackte in Paris" (A. Edelfelt).

1976. Finnish Language Society. Cent.
901. 322. 80 p. multicoloured .. 30 5

1976. Aino Ackte (opera singer). Birth Cent.
902. 323. 70 p. multicoloured .. 25 5

324. Ancient Knives and Belt. 325. "Radio Broadcasting".

1976. Europa.
903. 324. 80 p. multicoloured .. 30 5

1976. Finland Radio Broadcasting. 50th Anniv.
904. 325. 80 p. multicoloured .. 30 5

326. Wedding Procession.

1976. Tuberculis Relief Fund. Traditional Wedding Customs. Multicoloured.
905. 50 p.+10 p. Type 326 .. 20 20
906. 70 p.+15 p. Wedding dance (vert.) 30 30
907. 80 p.+20 p. Wedding breakfast 40 40

327. Sleigh arriving at Church.

1976. Christmas.
908. 327. 50 p. multicoloured .. 20 5

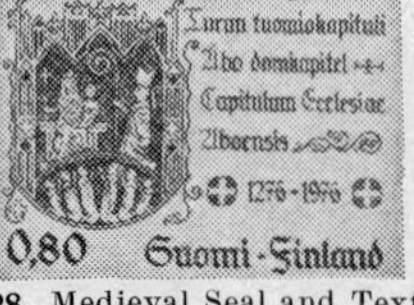

328. Medieval Seal and Text.

1976. Cathedral Chapter, Turku. 700th Anniv.
909. 328. 80 p. multicoloured .. 30 5

MILITARY FIELD POST.

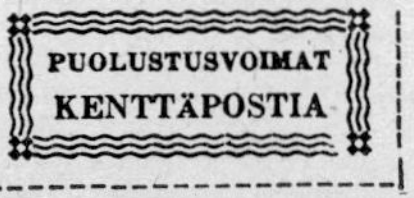

M 1.

1941. No value indicated. Imperf.
M 352. M 1. (–) black on red .. 30 30

M 2. M 3.

1943. No value indicated.
M 392. M 2. (–) green 8 15
M 393. (–) purple .. 8 15

1943. Optd. **KENTTA-POSTIA FALTPOST.**
M 394. 23. 2 m. orange .. 5 15
M 395. 3½ m. blue .. 5 12

1944. As Type M 2, but smaller (20 × 16 mm.) and inscr. "1944".
M 396. (–) purple 5 8
M 397. (–) green 5 8

1963. No value indicated.
M 688. M 3. (–) violet .. .. 30·00 35·00

PARCEL POST STAMPS

P 1.

1949. Printed in black on coloured backgrounds. Roul.
P 471. P 1. 1 m. green .. .. 50 1·60
P 472. 5 m. red .. .. 2·75 2·75
P 473. 20 m. orange .. 3·50 3·50
P 474. 50 m. blue .. .. 1·00 2·40
P 475. 100 m. brown .. 1·00 2·75

P 2. P 3.

1952.
P 507. P 2. 5 m. red 20 35
P 508. 20 m. orange .. 25 30
P 509. 50 m. blue .. .. 45 1·00
P 510. 100 m. brown .. 75 1·75

1963. Figures of value in black.
P 647. P 3. 5 p. magenta .. 5 5
P 648. 20 p. orange .. 5 8
P 649. 50 p. blue 15 15
P 650. 1 m. sepia 35 40

FINNISH OCCUPATION OF EASTERN KARELIA E3

Part of Russia, extending East to Lake Onega occupied by Finland from 1941 to 1944.

1941. Types of Finland in unissued colour variously optd. **ITA-KARJALA Sot. hallinto.**

(a) Arms and pictorial issue.
8. 23. 50 p. green 8 10
9. 1 m. 75 grey 8 12
10. 2 m. orange 15 30
11. 2 m. 75 yellow 8 12
5. 3½ m. blue 35 40
13. 24. 5 m. purple 55 65
14. – 10 m. brown (as No. 276b) 75 90
15. – 25 m. green (as No. 277) 90 1·00

(b) President Ryti.
16. 59. 50 p. green 5 8
17. 1 m. 75 slate 8 10
18. 2 m. red 5 8
19. 2 m. 75 brown 12 15
20. 3 m. 50 blue 12 15
21. 5 m. purple 12 15

(c) Marshal Mannerheim.
22. 60. 50 p. green 12 15
23. 1 m. 75 slate 12 15
24. 2 m. red 12 12
25. 2 m. 75 brown 8 18
26. 3 m. 50 blue 5 8
27. 5 m. purple 5 5

1. Arms of E. Karelia.

1943. National Relief Fund.
28. 1. 3 m. 50+1 m. 50 olive .. 15 35

FIUME E1

A seaport and territory on the Adriatic Sea formally belonging to Hungary, which was occupied by the Allies in 1918/19. Between 1919 and 1924 the territory was a Free State, controlled by D'Annunzio and his legionaries, until annexation to Italy in 1924. For later issues see Fiume and Kupa Zone; Venezia Giulia. Ceded to Yugoslavia in 1947.

1918. 100 filler = 1 krone.
1919. 100 centesimi = 1 corona.
1920. 100 centesimi = 1 lira.

1918. Various issues of Hungary optd. **FIUME.**

On "Harvesters" and "Parliament" issue of 1916.
1. 11. 2 f. brown 20 10
2. 3 f. claret 20 10
3. 5 f. green 20 10
4. 6 f. green 20 10
5. 10 f. red (No. 250) .. 12·00 5·50
6. 10 f. red (No. 243) .. 12·00 6·00
7. 15 f. violet (No. 251) .. 20 15
8. 15 f. violet (No. 244) .. 8·00 3·75
9. 20 f. brown 20 15
10. 25 f. blue 30 20
11. 35 f. brown 40 30
12. 40 f. olive .. .. 3·75 2·25
13. 12. 50 f. purple 40 30
14. 75 f. blue 95 50
15. 80 f. green 40 30
16. 1 k. lake .. .. 3·75 90
17. 2 k. brown 30 30
18. 3 k. grey and violet .. 1·75 90
19. 5 k. brown .. .. 4·50 2·25
20. 10 k. lilac and brown .. 42·00 28·00

On "Charles" and "Zita" issue of 1918.
21. 13. 10 f. red 20 12
22. 20 f. brown 20 12
23. 14. 40 f. olive .. .. 2·25 70

On War charity issue of 1916.
24. 6. 10+2 f. red 45 25
25. – 15+2 f. violet 45 25
26. 8. 40+2 f. lake 70 35

On Newspaper issue of 1900.
27. N 3. (2 f.) orange 12 8

On Express Letter stamp of 1916.
28. E 1. 2 f. olive and red .. 12 8

On Saving Bank stamp and surch. **FRANCO** and value.
29. B 1. 15 on 10 f. purple .. 1·25 45

On Postage Due stamps of 1915 with figures in red and surch. **FRANCO** and value.
30. D 1. 45 on 6 f. green .. 1·25 35
31. 45 on 20 f. green .. 1·25 35

1. Liberty.

2. Clock Tower over Market in Fiume.

3.

4. Port of Fiume.

1919. Inscr. "FIUME".
32. 1. 2 c. blue 5 5
33. 3 c. brown 5 5
34. 5 c. green 5 5
36. 2. 10 c. red 5 5
37. 15 c. violet 5 5
39. 20 c. green 5 5
41. 3. 25 c. blue 5 5
60. 4. 30 c. violet 5 5
42. 3. 40 c. brown 5 5
45. 45 c. orange 8 8
63. 4. 50 c. green 8 8
46. 60 c. lake 10 8
65. 1 cor. brown 8 8
66. 2 cor. blue 8 8
67. 3 cor. red 12 8
68. 5 cor. brown 15 12
69. 10 cor. olive 60 40

INDEX

Countries can be quickly located by referring to the index at the end of this volume.

5. Statue, Romulus, Remus and Wolf.

8. Dr. Grossich.

1919. Students' Education Fund. 200th day of peace.
71. 5. 5 c.+5 l. green .. .. 1·00 50
72. 10 c.+5 l. red .. .. 1·00 50
73. 15 c.+5 l. grey .. .. 1·00 50
74. 20 c.+5 l. orange .. 1·00 50
75. – 45 c.+5 l. olive .. .. 1·00 50
76. – 60 c.+5 l. red .. .. 1·00 50
77. – 80 c.+5 l. violet .. 1·00 50
78. – 1 cor.+5 l. grey .. 1·00 50
79. – 2 cor.+5 l. red .. 1·00 50
80. – 3 cor.+5 l. brown .. 1·00 50
81. – 5 cor.+5 l. brown .. 1·00 50
82. – 10 cor.+5 l. violet .. 1·00 50

DESIGNS—HORIZ. 45 c., 60 c., 80 c., 1 cor. Venetian galley. 2, 3, 5, 10 cor. Piazza of St. Mark, Venice.

1919. As T 1 to 4, but inscr. "POSTA FIUME".
83. 1. 5 c. green 5 5
84. 2. 10 c. red 5 5
85. 4. 30 c. violet 10 10
86. 3. 40 c. brown 25 20
87. 45 c. orange 8 5
88. 4. 50 c. green 10 5
89. 60 c. lake 10 5
90. 10 cor. olive 50 40

1919. Dr. Grossich Foundation.
91. 8. 25 c.+2 l. blue 15 8

1919. Stamps of 1919 inscr. "FIUME" and surch. **FRANCO** and value.
92. 2. 5 on 20 c. green 5 5
93. 3. 10 on 45 c. orange .. 5 5
94. 4. 25 on 50 c. green .. 25 25
95. 55 on 1 cor. brown .. 40 30
96. 55 on 2 cor. blue .. 55 40
97. 55 on 3 cor. red .. 55 40
98. 55 on 5 cor. brown .. 55 40

1919. Stamps of 1919 inscr. "POSTA FIUME" surch. **FRANCO** and value.
99. 3. 5 on 25 c. blue 5 5
100. 4. 15 on 30 c. violet .. 5 5
101. 3. 15 on 45 c. orange .. 5 5
102. 4. 15 on 60 c. lake .. 5 5
103. 25 on 50 c. green .. 5 5
104. 55 on 10 cor. olive .. 70 70

1919. Charity stamps of 1919 surch. **Valore globale** and value.
118. 5 c. on 5 c. green .. 5 5
119. 10 c. on 10 c. red .. 5 5
120. 15 c. on 15 c. grey .. 5 5
121. 20 c. on 20 c. orange .. 5 5
122. 25 c. on 25 c. blue .. 5 5
123. 45 c. on 45 c. olive .. 5 5
110. 60 c. on 60 c. red .. 5 5
111. 80 c. on 80 c. violet .. 5 5
112. 1 cor. on 1 cor. grey .. 8 8
113. 2 cor. on 2 cor. red .. 15 15
114. 3 cor. on 3 cor. brown .. 20 20
115. 5 cor. on 5 cor. brown .. 40 40
130. 10 cor. on 10 cor. violet .. 12 12

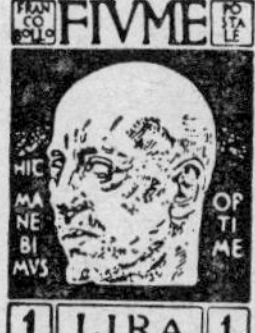

9. Gabriele d'Annunzio.

10. Severing the Gordian Knot.

1920.
131. 9. 5 c. green 5 5
132. 10 c. red 5 5
133. 15 c. grey 8 5
134. 20 c. orange 10 5
135. 25 c. blue 20 5
136. 30 c. brown 20 5
137. 45 c. olive 20 5
138. 50 c. lilac 20 5
139. 55 c. yellow 20 8
140. 1 l. black 45 35
141. 2 l. claret .. .. 1·25 40
142. 3 l. green .. .. 1·40 45
143. 5 l. brown .. .. 1·40 55
144. 10 l. lilac .. .. 1·60 90

1920. Military Post. 1st Anniv. of capture of Fiume by d'Annunzio's "legionaries".
M 145. 10. 5 c. green .. .. 3·25 1·60
M 146. – 10 c. red 80 30
M 147. – 20 c. brown .. 1·25 30
M 148. – 25 c. blue .. .. 5·00 2·50

DESIGNS: 10 c. Arms of Fiume. 20 c. "Crown of Thorns". 25 c. Daggers raised in clenched fists.

1920. Nos. M 145/8 optd. **Reggenza Italiana del Carnaro** or surch. also.
146. 1 on 5 c. green .. 5 5
147. 2 on 25 c. blue .. 5 5
148. 5 c. green 5 5
149. 10 c. red 5 5
150. 15 on 10 c. red .. 5 5
151. 15 on 20 c. brown .. 5 5
152. 15 on 25 c. blue .. 8 8
153. 20 c. brown 5 5
154. 25 c. blue 5 5
155. 25 on 10 c. red 60 40
156. 50 on 20 c. brown .. 5 5
157. 55 on 5 c. green .. 5 5
158. 1 l. on 10 c. red .. 1·00 60
159. 1 l. on 25 c. blue .. 80·00 42·00
160. 2 l. on 5 c. green .. 2·10 80
161. 5 l. on 10 c. red .. 4·50 1·75
162. 10 l. on 20 c. brown .. 42·00 11·00

1921. Issue of d'Annunzio optd. **Governo Provvisorio** or also surch. **LIRE UNA** (No. 173).
163. 9. 5 c. green 5 5
164. 10 c. red 5 5
165. 15 c. grey 5 5
166. 20 c. orange 5 5
167. 25 c. blue 8 8
168. 30 c. brown 8 8
169. 45 c. olive 8 8
170. 50 c. lilac 10 8
171. 55 c. yellow 12 8
172. 1 l. black .. .. 13·00 13·00
173. 1 l. on 30 c. brown .. 20 12
174. 2 l. claret 40 25
175. 3 l. green 80 50
176. 5 l. brown 80 35
177. 10 l. lilac .. .. 1·40 1·10

1921. Charity stamps of 1919 optd. **24-IV-1921 Costituente Fiumana 1922** and L over "Cor" in high values.
178. 5 c. green 20 8
191. 10 c. red 5 8
180. 15 c. grey 15 5
193. 20 c. orange 5 8
194. 45 c. olive 5 8
195. 60 c. red 5 8
196. 80 c. violet 5 8
197. 1 l. on 1 cor. grey .. 5 8
198. 2 l. on 2 cor. red .. 8 8
199. 3 l. on 3 cor. brown .. 8 12
200. 5 l. on 5 cor. brown .. 12 12
189. 10 l. on 10 cor. violet .. 4·25 3·25

14.

DESIGNS. 20 c., 25 c. 30 c. Roman Arch. 50 c. 60 c. 1 l. St. Vitus. 2 l., 3 l., 5 l. Tarsabic Column.

1923.
201. 14. 5 c. green 5 5
202. 10 c. mauve 5 5
203. 15 c. brown 5 5
204. – 20 c. red 5 5
205. – 25 c. grey 5 5
206. – 30 c. green 5 5
207. – 50 c. blue 5 5
208. – 60 c. red 5 5
209. – 1 l. blue 5 5
210. – 2 l. chocolate .. 60 20
211. – 3 l. olive .. .. 3·75 1·50
212. – 5 l. brown .. .. 1·10 45

1924. Issue of 1923 optd. **REGNO D'ITALIA** in frame.
213. 5 c. green 5 8
214. 10 c. mauve 5 8
215. 15 c. brown 5 8
216. 20 c. red 5 8
217. 25 c. grey 5 8
218. 30 c. green 5 8
219. 50 c. blue 5 8
220. 60 c. red 5 8
221. 1 l. blue 5 8
222. 2 l. chocolate .. 20 25
223. 3 l. olive 30 45
224. 5 l. brown 45 65

1924. Issue of 1923 optd. **ANNESSIONE ALL' ITALIA** in frame with **22 Febb 1924** below.
225. 5 c. green 5 8
226. 10 c. mauve 5 8
227. 15 c. brown 5 8
228. 20 c. red 5 8
229. 25 c. grey 5 8
230. 30 c. green 5 8
231. 50 c. blue 5 8
232. 60 c. red 5 8
233. 1 l. blue 5 8
234. 2 l. chocolate .. 10 15
235. 3 l. olive 15 20
236. 5 l. brown 20 30

EXPRESS LETTER STAMPS

E 1.

1920.
E 145. E 1. 30 c. blue 25 12
E 146. 50 c. red 25 12

1920. Nos. M147 and M145 surch. **ESPRESSO** and new value.
E 163. 30 c. on 20 c. brown .. 17·00 5·50
E 164. 50 c. on 5 c. green .. 4·00 1·25

1921. Optd. **Governo Provvisorio.**
E 178. E 1. 30 c. blue 20 10
E 179. 50 c. red 20 10

E 2. Fiume in 16th Century.

1923.
E 213. E 2. 60 c. red 8 8
E 214. 2 l. blue 10 15

1924. Optd. **ANNESSIONE ALL'ITALIA** in frame with **22 Febbraio 1924** below.
E 225. E 2. 60 c. red 8 10
E 226. 2 l. blue 10 15

1924. Optd. **REGNO D'ITALIA** in frame, with cross between the two words.
E 237. E 2. 60 c. red 5 8
E 238. 2 l. blue 8 10

NEWSPAPER STAMPS

N 1.

1919.
N 92. N 2. 2 c. brown 8 8

N 2.

1920.
N 145. N 2. 1 c. green 8 8

POSTAGE DUE STAMPS

1918. Postage Due stamps of Hungary of 1903 (figures in black), optd. **FIUME.**
D 29. D 1. 6 f. green (D 21) .. 27·00 6·50
D 30. 12 f. green (D 31) .. 25·00 7·50
D 31. 50 f. green (D 33) .. 20·00 8·75

1918. Postage Due stamps of Hungary of 1915 (figures in red), optd. **FIUME.**
D 32. D 1. 1 f. green .. .. 4·25 2·10
D 33. 2 f. green 15 10
D 34. 5 f. green .. .. 1·75 65
D 35. 6 f. green 15 10
D 36. 10 f. green .. .. 3·00 85
D 37. 12 f. green 15 10
D 38. 15 f. green .. .. 3·25 2·10
D 39. 20 f. green 20 10
D 40. 30 f. green .. .. 3·25 1·75

ILLUSTRATIONS British Commonwealth and all overprints and surcharges are FULL SIZE. Foreign Countries have been reduced to ¾-LINEAR.

D 1.

1919.
D 91. D 1. 2 c. brown 5 5
D 92. 5 c. brown 5 8

1921. Charity stamps of 1919, surch. **"Segnatasse"**, new value, and device obliterating old surch.
D 191. 5. 2 c. on 15 c. (No. 120) 15 15
D 192. 4 c. on 10 c. (No. 119).. 5 5
D 193. 8. 5 c. on 25 c. (No. 122).. 8 8
D 194. 5. 6 c. on 20 c. (No. 121).. 8 8
D 195. 10 c. on 20 c. (No. 121) 30 25
D 188. – 20 c. on 45 c. (No. 123) 20 20
D 183. – 30 c. on 1 cor. (No. 112) 20 25
D 184. – 40 c. on 80 c. (No. 111) 12 12
D 185. – 50 c. on 60 c. (No. 110) 15 15
D 189. – 60 c. on 45 c. (No. 123) 20 20
D 190. – 80 c. on 45 c. (No. 123) 20 20
D 201. – 1 l. on 2 cor. (No. 113) 40 40

For stamps of Italy surch. **3-V-1945 FIUME RIJEKE** and new value, see Venezia Giulia and Istria, Nos. 18/24.

FIUME AND KUPA ZONE E3

The zone comprised Fiume (Rijeka), Susak and Kupa River area.

100 pares = 1 dinar.

1941. Nos. 414, etc. of Yugoslavia optd. **ZONA OCCUPATA FIUMANO KUPA.**
1. 63. 25 p. black 60 60
2. 50 p. orange 5 5
3. 1 d. green 20 20
4. 1 d. 50 red 5 5
5. 3 d. brown 20 20
6. 4 d. blue 60 60
7. 5 d. blue .. .. 1·00 1·00
8. 5 d. 50 violet .. .. 1·00 1·00
9. 6 d. blue .. .. 2·50 2·50
10. 8 d. chocolate .. .. 2·10 2·10
11. 12 d. violet .. .. 25·00 25·00
12. 16 d. purple .. .. 8·00 8·00
13. 20 d. blue £120 £120
14. 30 d. pink £1800 £1300

1941. Maternity and Child Welfare Fund. Nos. 2/4 further optd. **O.N.M.I.** (=Opera Nazionale Maternita e Infanzia).
15. 63. 50 p. orange 15 15
16. 1 d. green 15 15
17. 1 d. 50 red 15 15

1941. Italian Naval Exploit at Buccari (Bakar) 1918. No. 415 of Yugoslavia surch. **MEMENTO AVDERE** and value etc.
18. 63. 1 l. on 50 p. orange .. 65 75

1942. Maternity and Child Welfare. Nos. 15/17 further optd. **Pro Maternita—Infanzia.**
19. 63. 50 p. orange 15 15
20. 1 d. green 15 15
21. 1 d. 50 red 15 15

Nos. 1/21 were valid until 26.5.42 after which unoverprinted Italian stamps were used until the Italian Occupation ended.

FRANCE E1

A republic in the W. of Europe. France, together with many of its former colonies, forms the French Community.

100 centimes = 1 franc.

NOTE. Stamps in types of France up to the 1877 issue were also issued for the French Colonies and where the values and colours are the same they can only be distinguished by their shade or postmark or other minor differences which are outside the scope of this Catalogue. They are priced here by whichever is the lower of the quotations under France or French Colonies in the Stanley Gibbons Europe Catalogue, Vol 1.
Nos. 18* and 19* are French Colonies numbers.

1. Ceres. 2. Louis Napoleon, President. 3. Napoleon III, Emperor of the French.

1349. Imperf.
160. 1. 10 c. yellow .. .. £250 22·00
4. 15 c. green £2750 £375
6. 20 c. black .. .. 90·00 15·00
18.* 25 c. blue .. .. 50·00 4·25
19.* 40 c. orange .. .. 70·00 4·25
17. 1 f. orange £1200 £4500
19. 1 f. carmine £1600 £275

For 15 c. yellow, imperf., see French Colonies No. 16.

1852. Imperf.
37a. 2. 10 c. yellow £5500 £160
39. 25 c. blue .. .. £600 16·00

1853. Imperf.
42. 3. 1 c. olive .. .. 30·00 19·00
45. 5 c. green .. .. £130 19·00
50a. 10 c. yellow .. .. £110 2·25
59. 20 c. blue .. .. 70·00 35·00
63. 25 c. blue £550 £100
64. 40 c. orange .. .. £550 4·50
70. 80 c. red .. .. £850 12·00
72. 1 f. red £950 £750

1862. Perf.
86. 3. 1 c. olive .. .. 22·00 11·00
89. 5 c. green .. .. 35·00 2·25
91. 10 c. yellow .. .. £190 1·25
95. 20 c. blue .. .. 30·00 25
97. 40 c. orange .. .. £225 1·75
98. 80 c. red .. .. £200 12·00

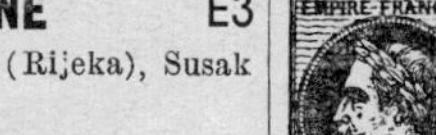

4. 5. Head with Laurel Wreath. 7. Ceres.

1863. Perf.
102. 4. 1 c. olive .. .. 5·50 4·00
104. 2 c. brown .. .. 12·00 8·50
109. 4 c. grey .. .. 40·00 16·00
112. 5. 10 c. yellow .. .. 50·00 1·50
114. 20 c. blue .. .. 40·00 50
116. 30 c. brown .. .. £120 5·50
119. 40 c. orange .. .. £150 4·00
121. 80 c. red .. .. £140 6·00
131. – 5 f. lilac £1300 £300

The 5 f. is 38 × 22 mm. with the same portrait.
For 1 c. green, 30 c. brown and 80 c. red all imperf. see French Colonies, Nos. 7, 9 and 10.

1870. Imperf.
146. 7. 1 c. olive .. .. 21·00 21·00
152. 2 c. brown .. .. 65·00 60·00
154. 4 c. grey .. .. 80·00 80·00
157. 1. 5 c. green .. .. 75·00 45·00
171. 20 c. blue .. .. £275 6·50
175. 30 c. brown .. .. £120 85·00
182. 80 c. red .. .. £150 95·00

For 1 c. green on blue, 2 c. brown on yellow and 5 c. green as T 7 and imperf. see French Colonies, Nos. 11, 12 and 14a.

1870. Perf.
185. 7. 1 c. olive .. .. 8·00 3·75
187. 2 c. brown .. .. 15·00 3·00
189. 4 c. grey .. .. 55·00 9·00
191. 5 c. green .. .. 23·00 1·90
135. 1. 10 c. yellow .. .. £110 20·00
202. 10 c. yellow on rose .. 42·00 2·25
203. 15 c. yellow .. .. 40·00 1·25
137. 20 c. blue .. .. 42·00 2·25
206. 25 c. blue .. .. 22·00 25
140. 40 c. orange .. .. £100 1·40

9. Ceres. 10. Peace and Commerce.

1872. Larger figures of value.
194. 9. 10 c. yellow on rose .. 60·00 2·50
195. 15 c. yellow .. .. 60·00 1·00
198. 30 c. brown .. .. 95·00 1·40
199. 80 c. red .. .. £120 3·75

For Nos. 194/5 and 198/9 but imperf. see French Colonies Nos. 20/3.

1876.
212. 10. 1 c. green .. .. 30·00 14·00
225. 2 c. green .. .. 22·00 5·50
214. 4 c. green .. .. 25·00 10·00
228. 5 c. green .. .. 5·00 10·00
216. 10 c. green .. .. £150 6·50
232. 15 c. lilac .. .. £100 50·00
219. 20 c. brown on yellow £110 4·50
234. 25 c. blue .. .. 85·00 12
237. 30 c. brown .. .. 9·00 15
269. 40 c. red on yellow .. 12·00 50
223. 75 c. red .. .. £150 5·00
239. 1 f. green .. .. 15·00 20

1877.
243. 10. 1 c. black on blue .. 60 12
247. 2 c. brown on yellow .. 1·00 25
249. 3 c. yellow .. .. 35·00 12·00
251. 3 c. grey 60 35
252. 4 c. lilac on grey .. 85 50
282. 5 c. yellow-green .. 2·10 10
255. 10 c. black on lilac .. 7·50 25
257. 15 c. blue .. .. 5·00 12
260. 20 c. red on green .. 7·50 66
262. 25 c. black on red .. £160 6·00
263. 25 c. yellow .. .. 60·00 1·10
266. 25 c. black on pink .. 7·50 20
268. 35 c. brown on yellow 95·00 10·00
272. 50 c. red .. .. 28·00 30
275. 75 c. brown on orange 40·00 9·00
287. 2 f. brown on blue .. 23·00 10·00
278. 5 f. mauve on lilac .. £130 25·00

For other stamps as T 10 but imperf. see French Colonies, Nos. 24/44.

11. "Blanc". 12. "Mouchon".

13. "Merson".

1900.
288. 11. 1 c. grey 5 5
289. 2 c. claret 5 5
290. 3 c. red 12 5
292a. 4 c. brown 40 12
293. 5 c. green 20 5
300. 12. 10 c. red .. .. 8·50 20
301. 15 c. orange .. .. 1·45 5
297. 20 c. claret .. .. 22·00 2·50
302. 25 c. blue .. .. 35·00 30
299. 30 c. mauve .. .. 25·00 1·75
303. 13. 40 c. red and blue .. 4·25 10
304. 45 c. green and blue .. 4·25 20
305. 50 c. brown and lavender 32·00 20
306. 1 f. red and green .. 8·50 5
307. 2 f. lilac and yellow .. £300 12·00
308. 5 f. blue and yellow .. 19·00 85

14. 15. Sower.

1902.
309. 14. 10 c. red .. .. 7·50 8
310. 15 c. red .. .. 1·90 5
311. 20 c. claret .. .. 25·00 4·25
312. 25 c. blue .. .. 32·00 35
313. 30 c. mauve .. .. 75·00 3·00

1903.
314. 15. 10 c. red .. .. 2·50 5
316. 15 c. green 60 5
317. 20 c. claret .. .. 15·00 35
319. 25 c. blue .. .. 23·00 30
321. 30 c. lilac .. .. 55·00 1·60

16. Ground below Feet. 17. No Ground. 18.

1906.
325. 16. 10 c. red .. .. 1·25 15

1906.
332. 17. 5 c. green 12 5
334. 10 c. red 10 5
337. 20 c. chocolate 55 5
339. 25 c. blue 20 5
343. 30 c. orange .. .. 3·75 20
346. 35 c. violet .. .. 3·25 12

1914. Red Cross Fund. Surch. with red cross and **5 c.**
351. 17. 10 c. + 5 c. red .. .. 1·10 80

1914. Red Cross Fund.
352. 18. 10 c. + 5 c. red .. 10·00 1·10

19. War Widow. 24. Spirit of War.

21. Woman replaces Man. 25. Sinking of Hospital Ship, and Bombed Hospital.

1917. "War Orphans" Issue. Inscr. "ORPHELINS DE LA GUERRE".
370. 19. 2 c. + 3 c. claret .. 70 45
371. – 5 c. + 5 c. green .. 2·50 1·60
372. 21. 15 c. + 10 c. grey .. 8·00 6·00
373. 25 c. + 15 c. blue .. 35·00 20·00
374. – 35 c. + 25 c. vio. & grey 50·00 35·00
375. – 50 c. + 50 c. brown .. 65·00 55·00
376. 24. 1 f. + 1 f. red .. .. £120 80·00
377. 5 f. + 5 f. blue & black .. £550 £400

DESIGNS—VERT. 5 c. Orphans. HORIZ. as T 24 35 c. Front line trench. 50 c. Lion of Belfort.
See also Nos. 450/3.

1918. Red Cross Fund.
378. 25. 15 c. + 5 c. red & green .. 35·00 12·00

1919. Surch. ½ **centime.**
379. 11. ½ c. on 1 c. grey .. 5 5
515a. 17. ½ c. on 1 c. olive .. 12 12
515b. ½ c. on 1 c. brown .. 12 12

1920.
497. 17. 1 c. olive 5 5
497a. 1 c. brown 5 5
498. 2 c. green 5 5
499. 3 c. red 5 5
380. 5 c. orange 35 5
500. 5 c. cerise 5 5
413. 11. 7½ c. mauve* 10 5
381. 17. 10 c. green 8 5
501. 10 c. blue 5 5
413a. 11. 10 c. lilac 95 5
414. 17. 15 c. claret 5 5
415. 20 c. mauve 5 5
415b. 25 c. brown 5 5
503. 30 c. red 5 5
382a. 30 c. cerise 10 5
416. 30 c. blue 25 5
505. 35 c. green 25 8
417. 40 c. olive 15 5
418. 40 c. red 40 5
418a. 40 c. violet 65 5
418b. 40 c. blue 30 5

419. **15.** 45 c. lilac 70 15
383. 50 c. blue .. .. 4·25 8
420. 50 c. green 60 5
421. 50 c. red 5 5
384. **13.** 60 c. violet and blue .. 25 8
385. **15.** 60 c. violet 60 8
385a. 65 c. red .. .. 1·00 25
422. 65 c. green .. .. 1·00 20
423. 75 c. mauve 35 5
424. 80 c. red .. .. 20·00 1·75
386. 85 c. red .. .. 5·50 10
425. 1 f. blue .. .. 1·10 5
426. **17.** 1 f. 05 red .. .. 1·75 60
427. 1 f. 10 red .. .. 3·25 40
428. 1 f. 40 red .. .. 4·50 3·00
387. **13.** 2 f. orange and green .. 6·00 8
428a. **17.** 2 f. green .. .. 2·10 12
429. **13.** 3 f. violet and blue .. 6·50 1·40
430. 3 f. mauve and red .. 13·00 30
431. 10 f. green and red .. 30·00 8·25
432. 20 f. red and green .. 65·00 6·50

***PRECANCEL.** No. 413 was issued only pre-cancelled. The "unused" price is for stamps with full gum and the used price for stamps without gum.

1922. "War Orphans" issues surch with new value, cross and bars.

388. **19.** 1 c. on 2 c+3 c. claret .. 5 5
389. – 2½ c. on 5 c.+5 c. grn... 12 12
390. **21.** 5 c. on 15 c.+10 c. grey 25 15
391. 5 c. on 25 c.+15 c. blue 35 25
392. – 5 c. on 35 c.+25 c. violet and grey .. 70 40
393. – 10 c. on 50 c.+50 c. brn. 2·50 1·50
394. **24.** 25 c. on 1 f.+1 f. red .. 7·00 5·00
395. – 1 f. on 5 f.+5 f. blue and black .. .. 38·00 27·00

26. Pasteur. **27.** Stadium and Arc de Triomphe.

1923.

396. **26.** 10 c. green 12 5
396a. 15 c. green 20 5
396b. 20 c. green 20 5
397. 30 c. red 8 5
397a. 30 c. green 8 5
398. 45 c. red 30 30
399. 50 c. blue 65 5
400. 75 c. blue 70 5
400a. 90 c. red .. .. 2·00 65
400b. 1 f. blue .. .. 4·50 5
400c. 1 f. 25 blue .. .. 5·00 1·10
400d. 1 f. 50 blue .. .. 1·75 5

1923. Optd. **CONGRES PHILATELIQUE DE BORDEAUX 1923.**

400e. **13.** 1 f. red and green .. £120 £150

1924. Olympic Games. Inscr. "VIIIe OLYMPIADE, PARIS. 1924".

401. **27.** 10 c. green 40 20
402. – 25 c. red 55 5
403. – 30 c. red and black .. 4·00 3·50
404. – 50 c. blue .. .. 5·00 60

DESIGNS—HORIZ. 25 c. Notre Dame and Pont Neuf. VERT. 30 c. Milan de Gotone (statue). 50 c. The victor.

31. Ronsard. **32.** Allegory of "Light and Liberty".

1924. Ronsard. 400th Birth Anniv.

405. **31.** 75 c. blue 30 25

1924. Int. Exn. of Modern Decorative Arts. Dated "1925".

406. **32.** 10 c. yellow and green 15 12
407. – 15 c. green .. 15 12
408. – 25 c. claret and purple.. 10 5
409. – 25 c. mauve and blue .. 25 8
410. – 75 c. blue and grey 80 40
411. **32.** 75 c. blue .. 4·25 1·40

DESIGNS—HORIZ. 25 c. (No. 408), 75 c. (No. 410) Potter decorating vase. 25 c. (No. 409), Chateau terrace. VERT. 15 c. Ornate vase.

1925. Paris Int. Philatelic Exn.

412. **10.** 5 f. red .. .. .. 48·00 30·00

1926. Surch. with new value and bars.

433. **17.** 25 c. on 30 c. blue .. 5 5
434. 25 c. on 35 c. violet .. 5 5
436. **15.** 50 c. on 60 c. violet .. 25 10
437. 50 c. on 65 c. red .. 12 5
438. **26.** 50 c. on 75 c. blue .. 40 12
439. **15.** 50 c. on 80 c. red .. 20 5
440. 50 c. on 85 c. red .. 15 10
441. **17.** 50 c. on 1 f. 05 red .. 40 8
442. **26.** 50 c. on 1 f. 25 blue .. 25 12
443. **15.** 55 c. on 60 c. violet* .. 45·00 18·00
444. **17.** 90 c. on 1 f. 05 red .. 1·40 90
445. 1 f. 10 on 1 f. 40 red .. 25 10

***PRECANCEL.** See note below No. 432.

1926. War Orphans Fund.

450. **19.** 2 c.+1 c. claret .. 12 12
451. – 50 c.+10 c. brown (No. 375) .. .. 3·75 1·10
452. **24.** 1 f.+25 c. red .. 8·50 5·00
453. 5 f.+1 f. blue & black 28·00 20·00

1927. Strasburg Philatelic Exn.

454. **17.** 5 f. blue .. .. £100 90·00
454a. 10 f. red .. .. £100 90·00

1927. Air. 1st Int. Display of Aviation and Navigation, Marseilles. Optd. with aeroplane and **Poste Aerienne.**

455. **13.** 2 f. red and green .. 65·00 65·00
456. 5 f. blue and yellow .. 65·00 65·00

36. Marcelin Berthelot. **37.** Lafayette, Washington, S.S. "Paris" and Lindbergh 'plane.

1927. Berthelot. Birth Cent.

457. **36.** 90 c. red 15 5

1927. Visit of American Legion.

458. **37.** 90 c. red 35 25
459. 1 f. 50 blue 65 40

1927. "Sinking Fund". Surch. **Caisse d'Amortissement** or **C A** and premium.

460. **17.** 40 c.+10 c. blue .. 1·25 95
461. **15.** 50 c.+25 c. green .. 1·75 1·25
462. **26.** 1 f. 50+50 c. orange .. 1·75 1·50

See also Nos. 466/8, 476/8, 485/7 and 494/6.

38. **39.** Joan of Arc.

1928. "Sinking Fund".

463. **38.** 1 f. 50+8 f. 50 blue .. 55·00 55·00

1928. Air ("Ile de France"). Surch. **10. FR.** and bars.

464. **36.** 10 f. on 90 c. red .. £650 £650
465. **26.** 10 f. on 1 f. 50 blue .. £3250 £3250

1928. "Sinking Fund". Surch as Nos. 460/2.

466. **17.** 40 c.+10 c. violet .. 3·75 3·00
467. **15.** 50 c.+25 c. red.. .. 7·00 6·00
468. **26.** 1 f. 50+50 c. mauve .. 10·00 9·00

1929. Relief of Orleans. 500th Anniv.

469. **39.** 50 c. blue 15 5

1929. Optd. **EXPOSITION LE HAVRE 1929. PHILATELIQUE.**

470. **13.** 2 f. red and green .. £160 £120

40. Reims Cathedral. **41.** Mont St. Michel.

1929. Views.

470a. – 90 c. mauve .. .. 1·40 10
471. – 2 f. brown .. .. 9·50 10
472c. **40.** 3 f. blue.. .. .. 35·00 90
473. **41.** 5 f. chocolate .. .. 7·00 10
474b. – 10 f. blue .. .. 30·00 1·90
475b. – 20 f. brown .. .. 75·00 11·00

DESIGNS—HORIZ. 90 c. Le Puy-en-Velay. 2 f. Arc de Triomphe. 10 f. Port de la Rochelle. 20 f. Pont du Gard.

1929. "Sinking Fund". Surch. as Nos. 460/2.

476. **17.** 40 c.+10 c. green .. 6·00 3·50
477. **15.** 50 c.+25 c. mauve .. 7·50 5·50
478. **26.** 1 f. 50+50 c. brown .. 14·00 10·00

42. Bay of Algiers.

1930. French Conquest of Algeria. Cent.

479. **42.** 50 c. red and blue .. 80 5

43. "Le Sourire de Reims".

1930. "Sinking Fund".

480. **43.** 1 f. 50+3 f. 50 purple.. 26·00 26·00

1930. I.L.O. Session, Paris. Optd. **CONGRES du B.I.T. 1930.**

481. **15.** 50 c. red 50 50
482. **26.** 1 f. 50 blue .. .. 5·00 5·00

44. Notre Dame de la Garde, Marseilles.

1930. Air.

483. **44.** 1 f. 50 red .. .. 6·00 55
484. 1 f. 50 blue .. .. 6·00 20

1930. "Sinking Fund". Surch. as Nos. 460/2.

485. **17.** 40 c.+10 c. red .. 6·00 4·50
486. **15.** 50 c.+25 c. brown .. 11·00 8·00
487. **17.** 1 f. 50+50 c. violet .. 15·00 9·50

45. Woman of the Fachi tribe. **46.** "French Colonies".

1930. Int. Colonial Exn.

488. **45.** 15 c. black 5 5
489. 40 c. brown 20 5
490. 50 c. red 5 5
491. 1 f. 50 blue .. .. 4·00 10
492. **46.** 1 f. 50 blue .. .. 9·00 25

47. "French Provinces".

1931. "Sinking Fund".

493. **47.** 1 f. 50+3 f. 50 green .. 50·00 50·00

1931. "Sinking Fund". Surch as Nos. 460/2.

494. **17.** 40 c.+10 c. sage-green 13·00 9·50
495. **15.** 50 c.+25 c. violet .. 30·00 19·00
496. **17.** 1 f. 50+50 c. red .. 30·00 19·00

48. Peace. **49.** A. Briand. **50.** J. M. Jacquard.

1932.

502. **48.** 30 c. green 12 5
506. 40 c. mauve 5 5
507. 45 c. brown 40 25
508. 50 c. red 5 5
508d. 55 c. violet 15 5
508e. 60 c. bistre 5 5
509. 65 c. purple 12 5
509a. 65 c. blue 8 5
510. 75 c. green 5 5
510a. 80 c. orange 5 5
511. 90 c. red .. .. 10·00 60
511a. 90 c. green 5 5
511b. 90 c. blue 5 5
512. 1 f. orange 30 5
512a. 1 f. pink 30 5
513. 1 f. 25 olive .. .. 17·00 75
513a. 1 f. 25 red 50 25
513b. 1 f. 40 mauve .. .. 1·50 1·00
514. 1 f. 50 blue 5 5
515. 1 f. 75 mauve 75 5

1933. Portraits.

516. **49.** 30 c. green .. .. 7·50 3·25
517. – 75 c. mauve (Doumer) 9·50 15
518. – 1 f. 25 clar. (Victor Hugo) 75 15

1934. Jacquard. Death Cent.

520. **50.** 40 c. blue 90 25

51. "Dove of Peace". **52.** Jacques Cartier.

1934.

519. **51.** 1 f. 50 c. blue .. .. 15·00 3·25

1934. Discovery of Canada. 4th Cent.

521. **52.** 75 c. mauve .. .. 8·50 35
522. 1 f. 50 blue .. .. 17·00 90

53. Bleriot's monoplane.

1934. Air. Channel Flight. 25th Anniv.

523. **53.** 2 f. 25 violet .. .. 8·00 1·50

1934. Surch. in figures and bars.

524. **48.** 50 c. on 1 f. 25 olive .. 1·10 8
524a. 80 c. on 1 f. orange .. 15 15

54. Breton River Scene.

1935.

525. **54.** 2 f. green .. .. 11·00 12

55. S.S. "Normandie".

1935. Maiden Trip of S.S. "Normandie".

526. **55.** 1 f. 50 blue .. .. 5·50 40

56. Benjamin Delessert. **57.** Victor Hugo.

1935. Int. Savings Bank Congress.

528. **56.** 75 c. green .. .. 8·00 20

1935. Victor Hugo. 50th Death Anniv.

529. **57.** 1 f. 25 purple .. .. 1·10 40

58. Cardinal Richelieu. **59.** St. Trophime, Arles.

1935. French Academy Tercent.

530. **58.** 1 f. 50 red .. .. 6·00 35

1935.

527. **59.** 3 f. 50 brown .. .. 11·00 85

60. Jacques Callot. **61.** French help for Intellectuals.

1935. Tercent of Callot's Death.

531. **60.** 75 c. red .. .. 5·50 8

1935. Unemployed Intellectuals' Relief Fund. Inscr. "POUR L'ART ET LA PENSEE".

532. **61.** 50 c.+10 c. blue .. 2·00 5
533. – 50 c.+2 f. red .. 22·00 18·00

DESIGN: No. 533, Symbolic of Art.

62. Aeroplane over Paris.

1936. Air.

534. **62.** 85 c. green .. .. 1·00 20
535. 1 f. 50 blue .. .. 2·25 75
536. 2 f. 25 violet .. .. 5·50 2·25
537. 2 f. 50 red .. .. 4·50 2·25
538. 3 f. blue .. .. 1·75 12
539. 3 f. 50 brown .. .. 11·00 2·75
540. 50 f. green .. .. £275 90·00

63. Statue of Liberty.

64. Andre-Marie Ampere.

1936. Nansen (Refugee) Fund.
541a. 63. 50 c.+25 c. blue .. 2·00 1·40
542. 75 c.+50 c. violet .. 4·50 3·25

1936. Ampere. Death Cent.
543. 64. 75 c. brown .. .. 8·00 25

65. Daudet's Mill, Fontvieille.

1936.
544. 65. 2 f. blue 75 5

66. Aeroplane over Paris.

1936. Air.
541. 66. 50 f. blue .. .. £250 90·00

67. Children of the Unemployed.

68. Pilatre de Rozier.

1936. Unemployed (Children's) Fund.
545. 67. 50 c.+10 c. red .. 2·75 2·00

1936. Pilatre de Rozier. 150th Death Anniv.
546. 68. 75 c. blue .. .. 8·50 50

69. Rouget de Lisle.

71. Canadian War Memorial, Vimy.

1936. Rouget de Lisle (composer of the "Marseillaise"). Death Cent.
547. 69. 20 c. green 40 25
548. – 40 c. brown .. .. 2·25 75
DESIGN—HORIZ. 40 c. Female figure inscr. "LA MARSEILLAISE".

1936. Unveiling of Canadian War Memorial.
549. 71. 75 c. red .. .. 2·50 25
550. 1 f. 50 blue .. .. 4·00 1·75

The 1 f. 50 has a head and shoulders portrait of Jaures.

72. Jean Jaures as an Orator.

1936. Jean Jaures Commemoration.
551. 72. 40 c. brown 95 20
552. – 1 f. 50 blue .. .. 4·75 60

DESIGN — VERT. 1 f. 50, Aeroplane and old-time sailing ship.

75. S. Atlantic Flight.

1936. 100th Flight between France and S. America.
553. – 1 f. 50 blue .. .. 5·00 50
554. 75. 10 f. green .. .. 75·00 27·00

76. Herald.

77. "World Exhibition".

1936. Paris Int. Exn.
555. 76. 20 c. mauve 5 5
556. 30 c. green 30 15
557. 40 c. blue 12 5
558. 50 c. orange 10 5
559. 77. 90 c. red .. .. 3·75 3·00
560. 1 f. 50 blue .. .. 5·50 50

78. "Vision of Peace".

1936. Universal Peace Propaganda.
561. 78. 1 f. 50 blue .. .. 6·50 30

1936. Unemployed Intellectuals' Fund. No. 533 surch. **+20 c.** over former surcharge.
562. – 20 c. on 50 c.+2 f. red 1·90 1·50

DESIGNS: 40 c. Berlioz. 50 c. Victor Hugo. 1 f. 50, Pasteur.

79. Jacques Callot.

1936. Unemployed Intellectuals' Fund. Inscr. as in T 79.
563. 79. 20 c.+10 c. lake .. 1·25 1·00
564. – 40 c.+10 c. green .. 1·25 1·00
565. – 50 c.+10 c. red .. 2·00 1·10
566. – 1 f. 50+50 c. blue .. 8·00 5·00

80. Ski-jumper.

1937. Chamonix-Mont Blanc Ski-ing Week.
567. 89. 1 f. 50 blue .. .. 3·25 30

81. Pierre Corneille.

82. France and Minerva.

83. Jean Mermoz.

84. Jean Mermoz Memorial.

1937. First Performance of "Le Cid". 300th Anniv.
568. 81. 75 c. red 65 20

1937. Paris Int. Exn.
569. 82. 1 f. 50 blue 75 20

1937. Mermoz Commem.
570. 83. 30 c. green 10 8
571. 84. 3 f. violet .. .. 2·25 85

DESIGN. 1 f. 50, Stream-lined locomotive.

85. Electric Train.

1937. 13th Int. Railway Congress, Paris
572. 85. 30 c. green 30 25
573. – 1 f. 50 blue .. .. 3·75 2·50

86. Rene Descartes.

1937. Publication of "Discours". 300th Anniv. (a) Wrongly inscr. "DISCOURS SUR LA METHODE".
574. 86. 90 c. red 45 30

(b) Corrected to "DISCOURS DE LA METHODE".
575. 86. 90 c. red 80 30

PORTRAIT—VERT. 30 c. Anatole France.

88. Auguste Rodin.

1937. Unemployed Intellectuals' Relief Fund.
576. – 30 c.+10 c. green .. 1·10 85
577. 88. 90 c.+10 c. red .. 2·50 1·75

DESIGNS—HORIZ. 40 c. Runners and discus thrower. VERT. 50 c. Ramblers.

89. Tug-of-War.

1937. Postal Workers' Sports Fund.
578. 89. 20 c.+10 c. brown .. 1·00 80
579. – 40 c.+10 c. lake .. 1·00 80
580. – 50 c.+10 c. purple .. 1·00 80

1937. Int. Philatelic Exn., Paris. As T 1 printed in miniature sheets of four inscr. "PEXIP PARIS 1937" between stamps.
MS 581. 1. 5 c. bistre and blue
15 c. red .. ..
30 c. red and blue
50 c. bistre and red
Sheet of 4 .. .. 60·00 50·00

91. Pierre Loti and Constantinople.

92. "Victory of Samothrace".

1937. Pierre Loti Memorial.
585. 91. 50 c.+20 c. red .. 1·75 1·40

1937. National Museums Propaganda.
586. 92. 30 c. green .. .. 28·00 16·00
587. 55 c. red .. .. 28·00 16·00

93. "France" and Child.

1937. Public Health Fund.
588. 93. 65 c.+25 c. purple .. 65 45
588a. 90 c.+30 c. blue .. 60 45

94. France congratulating U.S.A.

1937. U.S. Constitution. 150th Anniv.
589. 94. 1 f. 75 blue 75 50

95. Iseran Pass.

96. Ceres.

1937. Opening of Col de l'Iseran Road.
590. 95. 90 c. green 20 5

1938.
591. 96. 1 f. 75 blue 40 8
591a. 2 f. red 5 5
591b. 2 f. 25 blue .. 1·25 5
591c. 2 f. 50 green .. 60 5
591d. 2 f. 50 blue .. 35 10
591e. 3 f. lilac 30 5

1938. Charity. Shipwrecked Mariners Society. As T 81 but portrait of Jean Charcot.
593. 65 c.+35 c. green .. 65 65
593a. 90 c.+35 c. purple .. 3·75 3·00

1938. Gambetta. Birth Cent. As T 81 but portrait of Leon Gambetta.
594. 55 c. violet 25 13

97. Beaune Hospital, 1443.

1938. As T 40, 41 and 97 (provincial types and views).
594a. – 90 c. red on blue .. 50 25
595. – 1 f. 75 blue .. .. 1·75 75
596. – 2 f. sepia 50 40
597. – 2 f. 15 purple 50 5
598. – 3 f. brown .. .. 3·25 90
599. – 5 f. blue 25 5
700. 97. 5 f. sepia 10 5
600. – 10 f. purple on blue .. 80 50
701. – 10 f. violet 5 5
702. 97. 15 f. red 5 5
601. – 20 f. green .. .. 14·00 4·50
703. – 20 f. sepia 35 35
DESIGNS—VERT. 1 f. 75, Champagne girl. 2 f. 15, Coal miners. 10 f. (No. 600) Vincennes. HORIZ. 90 c. Chateau de Pau. 2 f. Arc de Triomphe at Orange. 3 f. Papal Palace, Avignon. 5 f. (No. 599), Carcassonne. 10 f. (No. 701), Angers. 20 f. (No. 601), St. Malo. 20 f. (No. 703), Ramparts of St. Louis, Aigues-Mortes.

99. Clement Aden.

1938. Aviation Pioneer.
612a. 99. 50 f. blue .. .. 40·00 26·00

1938. Unemployed Intellectuals' Relief Fund. As Nos. 563/6 and 576/7, inscr. "POUR LES CHOMEURS INTELLECTUELS".
602. 30 c.+10 c. red .. .. 1·25 1·00
603. 35 c.+10 c. green .. 1·25 1·00
604. 55 c.+10 c. violet .. 2·25 1·00
605. 65 c.+10 c. blue .. 2·25 1·00
606. 1 f.+10 c. red .. .. 2·25 1·00
607. 1 f. 75+25 c. blue .. 3·25 1·60
PORTRAITS—As T 79: 35 c. Callot. 55 c. Berlioz. 65 c. Victor Hugo. 1 f. 75, Louis Pasteur. As T 88: 1 f. Auguste Rodin. As T 81, 30 c. Anatole France.

100. Palais de Versailles.

1938. French National Music Festivals.
608. 100. 1 f. 75+75 c. blue .. 8·00 6·00

101. Soldier in Trench.

102. Medical Corps Monument at Lyons.

1938. Charity. Infantry Monument Fund.
609. 101. 55 c.+70 c. purple .. 1·25 1·25
610. 65 c.+1 f. 10 blue .. 1·25 1·25

1938. Military Medical Corps' Monument Fund.
611. 102 55 c.+45 c. red .. 4·25 3·25

103. Saving a Goal.

104. Jean de La Fontaine.

1938. World Football Cup.

612. **103.** 1 f. 75 blue .. .. 3·75 1·90

1938. La Fontaine (writer of fables) Commem.

613. **104.** 55 c. green 30 30

1938. Rheims Cathedral Restoration Fund. As T **40**, but inscr. "REIMS 10.VII.1938".

614. – 65 c.+35 c. blue .. 3·50 2·75

105. Houses of Parliament, "Friendship" and Arc de Triomphe.

106. "France" welcoming repatriated Frenchmen.

1938. Visit of King George VI and Queen Elizabeth to France.

615. **105.** 1 f. 75 blue.. .. 50 35

1938. French Refugees' Fund.

616. **106.** 65 c.+60 c. red .. 2·45 1·75

106a. Pierre and Marie Curie.

1938. Int. Anti-Cancer Fund. Discovery of Radium. 40th Anniv.

617. **106a.** 1 f. 75+50 c. blue .. 3·25 2·50

107. Arc de Triomphe and Allied Soldiers.

108. Mercury.

1938. 1918 Armistice. 20th Anniv.

618. **107.** 65 c.+35 c. red .. 2·00 1·75

1938. Inscr. "REPUBLIQUE FRANCAISE".

618a. **108.** 1 c. brown 5 5
619. 2 c. green 5 5
620. 5 c. red 5 5
621. 10 c. blue 5 5
622. 15 c. orange .. 5 5
622a. 15 c. brown .. 12 5
623. 20 c. mauve .. 5 5
624. 25 c. green 5 5
625. 30 c. red 5 5
626. 40 c. violet 5 5
627. 45 c. green .. 25 10
627a. 50 c. blue 60 5
627b. 50 c. green .. 10 5
628. 60 c. orange .. 5 5
629. 70 c. mauve .. 10 5
629a. 75 c. brown .. 1·75 60

For similar stamps inscr. "POSTES FRANCAISES", see Nos. 750/3.

109. Nurse and Patient.

110. Blind Radio-listener.

1938. Students' Fund.

630. **109.** 65 c.+60 c. blue .. 2·25 1·75

1938. "Radio for the Blind" Fund.

631. **110.** 90 c.+25 c. purple .. 2·00 1·60

111. Monument to Civilian War Victims, Lille.

112. Paul Cezanne.

1939. War Victims Monument Fund.

632. **111.** 90 c.+ 35 c. brown .. 2·25 2·00

1939. Cezanne Birth Cent.

633. **112.** 2 f. 25 blue .. .. 1·50 75

113. Red Cross Nurse.

114. Military Engineer.

1939. Red Cross Society. 75th Anniv. Cross in red.

634. **113.** 90c.+35c. bl. & blk... 2·00 1·50

1939. French Military Engineers.

635. **114.** 70 c.+50 c. red .. 2·25 2·00

115. Ministry of Posts, Telegraphs and Telephones.

1939. P.T.T. Orphans' Fund.

636. **115.** 90 c.+35 c. green .. 3·75 3·25

116. "Clemenceau".

1939. Laying down Keel of Battleship "Clemenceau".

637. **116.** 90 c. bluo 25 20

117. French Pavilion, New York Exn.

1939. New York World's Fair.

638. **117.** 2 f. 25 blue .. .. 1·25 70
638a. 2 f. 50 blue .. .. 1·00 80

118. Mother and Child.

119. Niepce and Daguerre.

1939. Children of the Unemployed Fund.

639. **118.** 90 c.+35 c. red .. 1·00 80

1939. Photographic Cent.

640. **119.** 2 f. 25 blue .. .. 1·75 95

120. Eiffel Tower.

121. Iris.

1939. Eiffel Tower. 50th Anniv.

641. **120.** 90 c.+50 c. purple .. 2·75 1·60

1939.

642. **121.** 80 c. brown 5 5
643. 1 f. green 12 5
643a. 1 f. red 5 5
643b. 1 f. 30 blue 5 5
643c. 1 f. 50 orange.. .. 8 8

See also Nos. 861/8.

122. Marly Water Works.

124. St. Gregory of Tours.

125. Mother and Children.

123. Balzac.

1939. Int. Water Exn. Liege.

644. **122.** 2 f. 25 blue .. .. 1·90 75

1939. Unemployed Intellectuals' Fund.

645. – 40 c.+10 c. red .. 80 60
646. – 70 c.+10 c. purple .. 1·10 70
647. **123.** 90 c.+10 c. magenta .. 1·10 70
648. – 2 f. 25+25 c. blue .. 1·40 95

PORTRAITS—VERT. 40 c. Puvis de Chavannes. HORIZ. 70 c. Claude Debussy. 2 f. 25, Claude Bernard.

See also Nos. 667b/d.

1939. St. Gregory of Tours. 1400th Birth Anniv.

649. **124.** 90 c. red 30 20

1939. Birth-rate Development Fund.

650. – 70 c.+80 c. violet, blue and green .. 1·10 1·10
651. **125.** 90 c.+60 c. brown, purple and sepia .. 1·10 1·10

DESIGN: 70 c. Mother and children admiring infant in cot.

126. "Oath of the Tennis Court".

127. Strasbourg Cathedral.

1939. French Revolution. 150th Anniv.

652. **126.** 90 c. green 20 20

1939. Strasbourg Cathedral Spire. 5th Cent.

653. **127.** 70 c. red 30 15

128. Porte Chaussee, Verdun.

129. "The Letter".

130. Statue to Sailors lost at Sea.

131. Languedoc.

1939. Battle of Verdun. 23rd Anniv.

654. **128.** 90 c. grey 45 35

1939. Postal Museum Fund.

655. **129.** 40 c.+60 c. brown and purple .. .. 1·60 1·25

1939. Boulogne Monument Fund.

656. **130.** 70 c.+30 c. plum .. 2·25 2·00

1939.

657. **131.** 70 c. black on blue .. 20 20

132. Lyons.

1939.

658. **132.** 90 c. purple 20 20

133. French Soldier and Strasbourg Cathedral.

DESIGN: 1 f. Veteran French Colonial Soldier and African village.

1940. Soldiers' Comforts Fund. Inscr. "POUR NOS SOLDATS".

659. **133.** 40 c.+60 c. purple .. 50 40
660. – 1 f.+50 c. blue .. 50 40

134. French Colonial Empire.

1990. Overseas Propaganda Fund.

661. **134.** 1 f.+25 c. red .. 1·25 95

135. Marshal Joffre.

DESIGNS — HORIZ. 1 f. 50, General Gallieni. 2 f. 50, Ploughing. VERT. 1 f. Marshal Foch.

1940. War Charities. Inscr. as in T **135.**

662. **135.** 80 c.+45 c. brown .. 60 60
663. – 1 f.+50 c. violet .. 60 60
664. – 1 f. 50+50 c. red .. 70 70
665. – 2 f. 50+50 c. blue .. 80 70

136. Nurse and Wounded Soldier.

DESIGN — HORIZ. 80 c. Doctor, nurse, soldier and family.

1940. Red Cross. Inscr. "CROIX ROUGE FRANCAISE". Cross in red.

666. – 80 c.+1 f. green .. 1·25 1·25
667. **136.** 1 f.+2 f. sepia .. 1·25 1·25

137. G. Guynemar (pilot).

138. Nurse, wounded Solider and Family.

1940.

667a. **137.** 50 f. blue .. .. 4·25 3·00

1940. Unemployed Intellectuals' Fund. As T **123**, inscr. "POUR LES CHOMEURS INTELLECTUELS".

667b. 80 c.+10 c. brown .. 50 50
667c. 1 f.+10 c. purple .. 50 50
667d. 2 f. 50+25 c. blue .. 50 50

PORTRAITS: 80 c. Debussy. 1 f. Balzac. 2 f. 50 c. Bernard.

1940. War Victims.

667e. **138.** 1 f.+2 f. violet .. 30 30

138a. Harvesting.

DESIGNS: 1 f. Sowing. 1 f. 50, Gathering grapes. 2 f. 50, Cattle.

1940. National Relief Fund. Inscr. "SECOURS NATIONAL".

668. **138a.** 80 c.+2 f. sepia .. 50 50
669. – 1 f.+2 f. brown .. 50 50
670. – 1 f. 50+2 f. violet .. 50 50
671. – 2 f. 50+2 f. green .. 50 50

1940. Surch. with new value and with bars. on all except T **96.**

672. **17.** 30 c. on 35 c. green. .. 5 5
673. **48.** 50 c. on 55 c. violet .. 5 5
674. 50 c. on 65 c. blue .. 5 5
675. 50 c. on 75 c. green .. 5 5
676. **108.** 50 c. on 75 c. brown .. 5 5
677. **48.** 50 c. on 80 c. orange .. 5 5
678. 50 c. on 90 c. blue .. 5 5
679. 1 f. on 1 f. 25 red .. 5 5
680. 1 f. on 1 f. 40 mauve .. 5 5
681. 1 f. on 1 f. 50 blue .. 5 5
682. **96.** 1 f. on 1 f. 75 blue .. 5 5

683. – 1 f. on 2 f. 15 purple (No. 597) 5 5
684. 96. 1 f. on 2 f. 25 blue .. 5 5
685. 1 f. on 2 f. 50 green .. 5 5
686. – 2 f. 50 on 5 f. blue (No. 599) 8 8
687. – 5 f. on 10 f. purple on blue (No. 600) 1·00 1·00
688. – 10 f. on 20 f. green (No. 601) .. 40 40
689. 99. 20 f. on 50 f. blue .. 11·00 11·00

139. Marshal Petain. 140. Prisoners of War.

1940.
690. 139. 40 c. brown 20 15
691. 80 c. green 30 20
692. 1 f. red 5 5
693. 2 f. 50 blue 45 45

1940. Prisoners of War Fund. Inscr. as in T 140.
696. 140. 80 c.+5 f. green .. 60 60
697. – 1 f.+5 f. red .. 60 60
DESIGN: 1 f. Group of soldiers.

141. Frederic Mistral. 142. Science against Cancer.

1941. Mistral (poet) Commem.
698. 141. 1 f. red 8 8

1941. Anti-Cancer Fund.
699. 142. 2 f. 50+50 c. black and brown 60 60

1941. National Relief Fund. Surch. +10 c.
704. 139. 1 f.+10 c. red .. 8 8

143.

DESIGN: 2 f. 50, "Charity" helping a pauper.

1941. Winter Relief Fund. Inscr. as in T 143.
705. 143. 1 f.+2 f. purple .. 30 25
706. – 2 f. 50+7 f. 50 blue.. 45 35

144. Liner "Pasteur".

1941. Charity. Surch.
707. 144. 1 f.+1 f. on 70 c. green 10 10

1941. As No. 661, but without "R.F." and dated "1941".
708. 134. 1 f.+1 f. green, purple, blue and mauve 10 10

144a. 145. Marshal Petain. 146.

1941. Frame in T 145 is 17×20½ mm.
709. 144a. 20 c. purple 5 5
710. 30 c. red 5 5
711. 40 c. blue 5 5
712. 145. 50 c. green 5 5
713. 60 c. violet 5 5
714. 70 c. blue 5 5
715. 70 c. orange 5 5
716. 80 c. brown 5 5
717. 80 c. green 5 5
718. 1 f. red 5 5
719. 1 f. 20 brown 5 5
720. 146. 1 f. 50 brown 5 5
721. 1 f. 50 red 5 5
722. 2 f. green 5 5
723. 2 f. 40 red 5 5
724. 2 f. 50 blue 25 10
725. 3 f. orange 5 5
725a. 145. 4 f. blue 5 5
725b. 4 f. 50 green 20 8

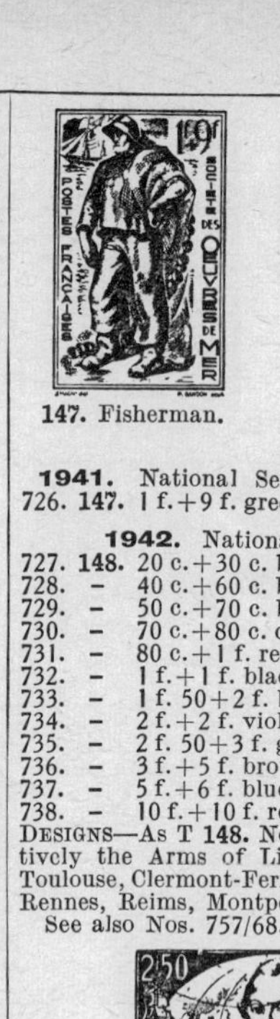

147. Fisherman. 148. Arms of Nancy.

1941. National Seamen's Relief Fund.
726. 147. 1 f.+9 f. green .. 50 50

1942. National Relief Fund.
727. 148. 20 c.+30 c. black .. 70 70
728. – 40 c.+60 c. brown .. 70 70
729. – 50 c.+70 c. blue .. 70 70
730. – 70 c.+80 c. claret .. 70 70
731. – 80 c.+1 f. red .. 70 70
732. – 1 f.+1 f. black .. 70 70
733. – 1 f. 50+2 f. blue .. 70 70
734. – 2 f.+2 f. violet .. 70 70
735. – 2 f. 50+3 f. green .. 70 70
736. – 3 f.+5 f. brown .. 70 70
737. – 5 f.+6 f. blue .. 70 70
738. – 10 f.+10 f. red .. 70 70
DESIGNS—As T 148. Nos. 728/38 show respectively the Arms of Lille, Rouen, Bordeaux, Toulouse, Clermont-Ferrand, Marseilles, Lyons, Rennes, Reims, Montpellier and Paris.
See also Nos. 757/68.

149. Jean-Francois de La Perouse.

1942. La Perouse (navigator and explorer). Birth Bicent. and National Relief Fund.
739. 149. 2 f. 50+7 f. 50 blue .. 50 50

1942. As T 145. Frame 18 × 21½ mm.
740. 145. 4 f. blue 8 5
741. 4 f. 50 green 5 5

150. Potez 63–11 Bombers.

1942. Air Force Dependants Relief Fund.
742. 150. 1 f. 50+3 f. 50 violet.. 20 20

151. Alexis Emmanuel Chabrier.

1942. Chabrier (composer). Birth Cent. and Musicians' Mutual Assistance Fund.
743. 151. 2 f.+3 f. brown .. 45 45

152. Symbolical of French Colonial Empire

1942. Empire Fortnight and National Relief Fund.
744. 152. 1 f. 50+8 f. 50 black.. 40 40

153. Marshal Petain. 154. Marshal Petain.

1942.
745. 153. 5 f. green 5 5
746. 154. 50 f. black .. .. 1·10 85

155. Jean de Vienne. 156. Jules Massenet.

1942. Jean de Vienne (admiral). 600th Birth Anniv. and Seamen's Relief Fund.
748. 155. 1 f. 50+8 f. 50 brown 50 50

1942. Massenet (composer). Birth Cent.
749. 156. 4 f. green 5 5

1942. As T 108, but inscr. "POSTES FRANCAISES".
750. 10 c. blue 5 5
751. 30 c. red 5 5
752. 40 c. violet 5 5
753. 50 c. blue 5 5

1942. National Relief Fund. Surch. +50 S N.
754. 146. 1 f. 50+50 c. blue .. 5 5

157. Stendhal (Marie Henri Beyle). 158. Andre Blondel.

1942. Stendhal (novelist) Death Cent.
755. 157. 4 f. brown and red .. 20 20

1942. Andre Blondel (physicist).
756. 158. 4 f. blue 15 15

1942. National Relief Fund. Arms of French towns as T 148.
757. 50 c.+60 c. black .. 70 70
758. 60 c.+70 c. green .. 70 70
759. 80 c.+1 f. red .. 70 70
760. 1 f.+1 f. 30 green .. 70 70
761. 1 f. 20+1 f. 50 claret .. 70 70
762. 1 f. 50+1 f. 80 blue .. 70 70
763. 2 f.+2 f. 30 red .. 70 70
764. 2 f. 40+2 f. 80 green .. 70 70
765. 3 f.+3 f. 50 violet .. 70 70
766. 4 f.+5 f. blue .. 70 70
767. 4 f. 50+6 f. red .. 70 70
768. 5 f.+7 f. lilac .. 70 70
DESIGNS: Nos. 757/68 respectively show the Arms of Chambery, La Rochelle, Poitiers, Orleans, Grenoble, Angers, Dijon, Limoges, Le Havre, Nantes, Nice and St. Etienne.

159. Legionary and Grenadiers. 160. Belfry Arras Town Hall.

1942. Tricolor Legion.
769. 159. 1 f. 20+8 f. 80 blue .. 1·00 1·00
770. 1 f. 20+8 f. 80 red .. 1·00 1·00

1942.
771. 160. 10 f. green .. 10 8

1943. National Relief Fund.
772. 147a. 1 f.+10 f. blue .. 1·60 1·60
773. 1 f.+10 f. red .. 1·60 1·60
774. 138. 2 f.+12 f. blue .. 1·60 1·60
775. 2 f.+12 f. red .. 1·60 1·60
Strip of 4 .. 7·00 7·00

162. Arms of Lyonnais. 163. "Work". 164. Marshal Petain.

1943. Provincial Coats of arms.
776. 162. 5 f. red, blue & yellow 5 5
777. – 10 f. black and brown 8 5
778. – 15 f. yellow, blue & red 70 60
779. – 20 f. yell., blue & brn. 50 40
ARMS: "Bretagne" (10 f.), "Provence" (15 f.), "Ile-de-France" (20 f.).
For other provinces in this series, see Nos. 814/7, 971/4, 1049/53, 1121/5, 1178/83, 1225/31, 1270/3. For arms of French towns, see Nos. 1403/10, etc.

1943. National Relief Fund.
780. – 1 f. 20+1 f. 40 purple 3·00 3·00
781. 163. 1 f. 50+2 f. 50 red .. 3·00 3·00
782. – 2 f. 40+7 f. brown .. 3·00 3·00
783. – 4 f.+10 f. violet .. 3·00 3·00
784. 164. 5 f.+15 f. brown .. 3·00 3·00
Strip of 5 .. .. 16·00 16·00
DESIGNS: 1 f. 20, Marshal Petain bare-headed. 2 f. 40, inscr. "Famille". 4 f. inscr. "Patrie".

165. Lavoisier (chemist). 166. Lake Lerie and the Meije Peak.

1943. Lavoisier. Birth Bicent.
785. 165. 4 f. blue 10 10

1943.
786. 166. 20 f. green 30 30

167. Nicholas Rolin and Guisone de Salins.

168. Victims of Bombed Towns.

170. Bayard. 169. Prisoners' Families' Relief Work.

1943. Beaune Hospital. 500th Anniv.
787. 167. 4 f. blue 12 15

1943. National Relief Fund.
788. 168. 1 f. 50 +3 f. 50 black 35 35

1943. Prisoners' Families Relief Fund. Inscr. as in T 169.
789. – 1 f. 50+8 f. 50 brown.. 40 40
790. 169. 2 f. 40+7 f. 60 green.. 40 40
DESIGN—VERT. 1 f. 50, Prisoner's family.

1943. National Relief Fund.
791. – 60 c.+80 c. green .. 70 70
792. – 1 f. 20+1 f. 50 black.. 70 70
793. – 1 f. 50+3 f. blue .. 70 70
794. 170. 2 f. 40+4 f. red .. 70 70
795. – 4 f.+6 f. brown .. 70 70
796. – 5 f+10 f. green .. 70 70
PORTRAITS: 60 c. Montaigne. 1 f. 20, Francois Clouet. 1 f. 50, Ambroise Pare. 4 f. Sully. 5 f. Henri IV.

171. Picardy. 177. Admiral de Tourville.

1943. National Relief Fund. Provincial costumes.
797. 171. 60 c.+1 f. 30 brown .. 70 70
798. – 1 f. 20+2 f. violet .. 70 70
799. – 1 f. 50+4 f. blue .. 70 70
800. – 2 f. 40+5 f. red .. 70 70
801. – 4 f.+6 f. blue.. .. 70 70
802. – 5 f.+7 f. red 70 70
DESIGNS: Inscribed "Bretagne" (1 f. 20), "Ile de France" (1 f. 50), "Bourgogne" (2 f. 40), "Auvergne" (4 f.) and "Provence" (5 f.).

The stamps issued by the French Committee of National Liberation, formerly listed here, will now be found under Nos. 82/89 of French Colonies.

1944. Admiral de Tourville. 300th Birth Anniv.
810. 177. 4 f.+6 f. red 35 35

178. Branly. 179. Gounod.

1944. Branly (physicist). Birth Cent.
811. 178. 4 f. blue 10 5

1933. Gounod (composer). 50th Death Anniv.
812. 179. 1 f. 50+3 f. 50 brown 5 5

181. Marshal Petain.

180. Flanders.

182. " Petain gives France Workers' Charter ".

1944. Provincial Coats of arms.
814. **180.** 5 f. black, orge. & red 5 5
815. – 10 f. yellow, red & brn. 5 5
816. – 15 f. yellow, blue & brn. 30 30
817. – 20 f. yellow, red & blue 30 30
ARMS: " Languedoc " (10 f.), " Orleanais " (15 f.) and " Normandie " (20 f.).
For other provinces in this series, see Nos. 776/9, 971/4, 1049/53, 1121/5, 1178/83, 1225/31, 1270/3. For arms of French towns, see Nos. 1403/10, etc.

1944. Marshal Petain's 88th Birthday.
818. **181.** 1 f. 50+3 f. 50 brown 1·40 1·40
819. – 2 f.+3 f. blue.. .. 30 30
820. **182.** 4 f.+6 f. red 30 30
DESIGN—As T **182**: 2 f. inscr. " Le Marechal institua la Corporation Paysanne " (Trans. " The Marshal set up the Peasant Corporation ").

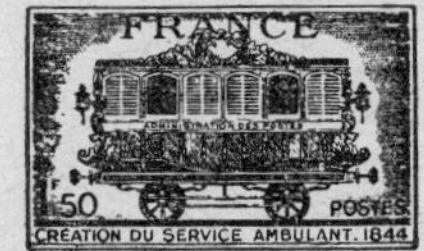
183. Mobile Post Office.

1944. Mobile Post Office. Cent.
821. **183.** 1 f. 50 green 5 5

184. Chateau of Chenonceaux.

1944.
822. **184.** 15 f. brown 20 20
823. 25 f. black 20 20
The 15 f. is inscr. ' FRANCE ".

185. Louis XIV.

186. Old and Modern Locomotives.

1944. National Relief Fund.
824. – 50 c.+1 f. 50 red .. 25 25
825. – 80 c.+2 f. 20 green .. 25 25
826. – 1 f. 20+2 f. 80 black 25 25
827. – 1 f. 50+3 f. 50 blue .. 25 25
828. – 2 f.+4 f. brown .. 25 25
829. **185.** 4 f.+6 f. orange .. 25 25
DESIGNS: 50 c. Moliere. 80 c. Hardouin-Mansart. 1 f. 20, Pascal. 1 f. 50, Le Grand Condé. 2 f. Colbert.

1944. National Relief Fund. Cent. of Paris-Orleans and Paris-Rouen Railways.
830. **186.** 4 f.+6 f. black .. 20 20

187. Claude Chappe.

188. Gallic Cock.

189. " Marianne ".

1944. Invention of Semaphore Telegraph 150th Anniv.
831. **187.** 4 f. blue 10 10

1944.
832. **188.** 10 c. green 5 5
833. 30 c. lilac 5 5
834 40 c. blue 5 5
835. 50 c. red 5 5
836. **189.** 60 c. brown 5 5
837. 70 c. mauve 5 5
838. 80 c. green 12 12
839. 1 f. violet 5 5
840. 1 f. 20 red 5 5
841. 1 f. 50 blue 5 5
842. **188.** 2 f. blue 5 5
843. **189.** 2 f. 40 red 25 25
844. 3 f. green 5 5
845. 4 f. blue 5 5
846. 4 f. 50 black 5 5
847. 5 f. blue 55 55
848. **188.** 10 f. violet 55 55
849. 15 f. brown 55 55
850. 20 f. green 60 60

190. Arc de Triomphe, Paris.

191. "Marianne".

1944.
851. **190.** 5 c. purple 5 5
852. 10 c. grey 5 5
853. 25 c. brown 5 5
936. 30 c. orange and black 5 5
937. 40 c. grey and black .. 5 5
854. 50 c. yellow 5 5
938. 50 c. olive and black .. 5 5
939. 60 c. violet and black 5 5
940. 80 c. green and black.. 5 5
855. 1 f. green 5 5
941. 1 f. 20 brown & black 5 5
856. 1 f. 50 red 5 5
942. 1 f. 50 red and black.. 5 5
943. 2 f. yellow and black.. 5 5
944. 2 f. 40 red and black .. 5 5
857. 2 f. 50 violet 5 5
945. 3 f. purple and black.. 5 5
858. 4 f. blue 5 5
859. 5 f. black 5 5
860. 10 f. orange .. .. 3·75 3·75

1944. New colours and values.
861. **121.** 80 c. green 5 5
862. 1 f. blue 5 5
863. 1 f. 20 violet 5 5
864. 1 f. 50 brown 5 5
865. 2 f. brown 5 5
866. 2 f. 40 red 5 5
867. 3 f. orange 5 5
868. 4 f. blue 5 5

1944.
869. **191.** 10 c. blue 5 5
870. 30 c. brown 5 5
871. 40 c. blue 5 5
872. 50 c. orange 5 5
873. 60 c. blue 5 5
874. 70 c. brown 5 5
875. 80 c. green 5 5
876. 1 f. lilac 5 5
877. 1 f. 20 green 5 5
878. 1 f. 50 red 5 5
879. 2 f. brown 5 5
880. 2 f. 40 red 5 5
881. 3 f. olive 5 5
882. 4 f. blue 5 5
883. 4 f. 50 grey 5 5
884. 5 f. orange 5 5
885. 10 f. green 8 5
886. 15 f. claret 12 10
887. 20 f. orange 40 25
888. 50 f. violet 85 55

192. St. Denis Basilica.

1944. St. Denis Basilica. 8th Cent.
889. **192.** 2 f. 40 brown 5 5

193. Marshal Bugeaud.

194. Angouleme Cathedral.

1944. Battle of Isly. Cent.
890. **193.** 4 f. green 8 8

1944. Cathedrals of France. 1st Issue.
891. **194.** 50 c.+1 f. 50 black .. 8 12
892. – 80 c.+2 f. 20 purple.. 10 12
893. – 1 f. 20+2 f. 80 red .. 20 20
894. – 1 f. 50+3 f. 50 blue .. 25 25
895. – 4 f.+6 f. red 15 15
DESIGNS: Cathedrals of Chartres (80 c.), Amiens (1 f. 20), Beauvais (1 f. 50) and Albi (4 f.).

1944. Nos. 750/3 optd. **RF.**
896. 10 c. blue 5 5
897. 30 c. red 5 5
898. 40 c. violet 5 5
899. 50 c. blue 5 5

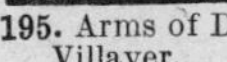
195. Arms of De Villayer.

196. " France " exhorting Resistance Forces.

1944. Stamp Day.
900. **195.** 1 f. 50+3 f. 50 brown 5 5

1945. Liberation.
901. **196.** 4 f. blue 5 5

197. Shield and broken Chains.

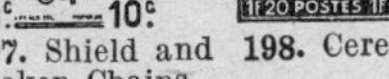
198. Ceres.

199. Marianne.

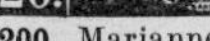
200. Marianne.

201. Arms of Strasbourg.

1945. Frame in T **199** is $17\frac{1}{2} \times 21$ mm.
902. **197.** 10 c. brown 5 5
903. 30 c. green 5 5
904. 40 c. magenta .. 5 5
905. 50 c. blue 5 5
906. **198.** 60 c. blue 5 5
907. 80 c. green 5 5
908. 90 c. green* 5 5
909. 1 f. red 5 5
910. 1 f. 20 black .. 5 5
997. 1 f. 30 blue 8 8
911. 1 f. 50 lilac .. 5 5
912. **199.** 1 f. 50 red 5 5
913. 2 f. green 5 5
914. **198.** 2 f. green 5 5
915. **199.** 2 f. 40 red 5 5
916. **198.** 2 f. 50 brown .. 5 5
997a. **199.** 2 f. 50 brown* .. 85 50
917. 3 f. brown 5 5
918. 3 f. red 5 5
998. 3 f. green 5 5
999. 3 f. magenta.. .. 5 5
1000. 3 f. 50 red 8 5
919. 4 f. blue 5 5
920. 4 f. violet 5 5
1001. 4 f. green 10 5
1001a. 4 f. orange 12 5
1002. 4 f. 50 blue 5 5
921. 5 f. green 5 5
1003. 5 f. red 5 5
1004. 5 f. blue 5 5
1004b. 5 f. violet 20 5
922. 6 f. blue 5 5
923. 6 f. red 5 5
1005a. 6 f. green .. .. 1·50 10
1006. 8 f. blue 10 5
924. 10 f. orange 5 5
925. 10 f. blue 10 5
1007. 10 f. violet 12 5
1007a. 12 f. blue 15 5
1007b. 12 f. orange 20 5
926. 15 f. purple 50 30
1007c. 15 f. pink 12 5
1007d. 15 f. blue 12 5
1007e. 18 f. red .. .. 2·00 20
932. **200.** 20 f. green 30 15
933. 25 f. violet 50 35
934. 50 f. brown .. 50 25
935. 100 f. red .. .. 1·10 75

Frame 18×22 mm.
927. **199.** 4 f. blue 5 5
928. 10 f. blue 12 5
929. 15 f. purple .. 55 15
930. 20 f. green 20 5
931. 25 f. red 30 15
***PRECANCELS.** See note below No. 432.

1945. Liberation of Metz and Strasbourg.
946. – 2 f. 40 blue 5 5
947. **201.** 4 f. brown 5 5
DESIGN: 2 f. 40, Arms of Metz.

202. Patient in Deck Chair.

203. Refugee Employee and Family.

1945. Anti-Tuberculosis Fund.
948. **202.** 2 f.+1 f. orange .. 5 5

1945. Postal Employees War Victims Fund.
949. **203.** 4 f.+6 f. brown .. 5 5

204. Sarah Bernhardt.

205. Alsatian and Lorrainer in Native Dress.

1945. Sarah Bernhardt (actress). Birth Cent.
950. **204.** 4 f.+1 f. brown .. 8 8

1945. Liberation of Alsace-Lorraine.
951. **205.** 4 f. brown 8 8

206. Children in Country.

207. Destruction of Oradour.

1945. Fresh Air Crusade.
952. **206.** 4 f.+2 f. green .. 5 5

1945. As No. 661 but inscr. "LA FRANCE D'OUTREMER 1945".
953. **134.** 2 f. blue 5 5

1945. Destruction of Oradour-sur-Glane.
954. **207.** 4 f.+2 f. brown .. 8 8

208. Louis XI.

1945. Stamp Day.
955. **208.** 2 f.+3 f. blue .. 10 10

209. Dunkirk.

210. Alfred Fournier.

1945. Devastated Towns.
956. **209.** 1 f. 50+1 f. 50 red .. 8 8
957. – 2 f.+2 f. violet .. 8 8
958. – 2 f. 40+2 f. 60 blue .. 8 8
959. – 4 f.+4 f. black .. 8 8
DESIGNS: 2 f. Rouen. 2 f. 40 c. Caen. 4 f. St. Malo.

1946. Prophylaxis Fund.
960. **210.** 2 f.+3 f. red 8 8
961. 2 f.+3 f. blue.. .. 12 12

211. Henri Becquerel.

212. " Les Invalides ".

1946.
962. **211.** 2 f.+3 f. violet .. 8 8

1946. Surcharged **3F.**
963. **202.** 3 f. on 2 f.+1 f. orange 5 5

1946. War Invalids' Relief Fund.
964. **212.** 4 f.+6 f. brown .. 10 10

213. Warships.

214. "The Letter".

215. Iris.

216. Apollo and Chariot.

1946. Naval Charities.
965. **213.** 2 f.+3 f. black 10 10

1946. Postal Museum Fund.
966. **214.** 2 f.+3 f. red 20 20

1946. Air.
967. – 40 f. green 25 5
968. **215.** 50 f. pink 25 5
969. – 100 f. blue 50 5
970. **216.** 200 f. red 85 25
DESIGNS—VERT. 40 f. Centaur. HORIZ. 100 f. Jupiter carrying off Egine.

217. Arms of Corsica.
218. Fouquet de la Varane.
219. "Peace".

1946. Provincial Coats of arms.
971. **217.** 10 c. black and blue .. 5 5
972. – 30 c. blk., red and yell. 5 5
973. – 50 c. brn., yell. & red 5 5
974. – 60 c. red, blue & black 5 5
DESIGNS: Arms of Alsace (30 c.), Lorraine (50 c.) and Nice (60 c.).
For other provinces in this series, see Nos. 776/9, 814/7, 1049/53, 1121/5, 1178/83, 1225/31, 1270/3. For arms of French towns, see Nos. 1403/10, etc.

1946. Stamp Day.
975. **218.** 3 f.+2 f. brown .. 20 20

1946. Peace Conf.
983. **219.** 3 f. green 5 5
984. – 10 f. blue 8 5
DESIGN: 10 f. Woman releasing dove.

221. Luxembourg Palace.

222. Roc-Amadour.

1946. Views.
976. – 5 f. mauve 5 5
977. – 6 f. red 5 5
1101. – 8 f. brown 12 12
978. **221.** 10 f. blue 5 5
979. 12 f. red 5 5
1102. – 12 f. brown 15 15
1142. – 12 f. brown 45 35
980. **222.** 15 f. purple 10 5
980a. **221.** 15 f. red 10 10
1021. – 15 f. red 8 5
1149. – 15 f. blue 12 12
1022. – 18 f. blue 10 5
1160. – 18 f. maroon .. 65 55
1160a. – 18f. indigo, bl. & sepia 2·00 1·25
981. – 20 f. blue 5 5
1067. – 20 f. red 10 5
1144. – 20 f. violet 15 5
982. – 25 f. sepia 15 5
982a. – 25 f. blue 35 12
1068. – 25 f. blue 12 5
1068a. – 30 f. blue .. .. 1·10 80
1068b. – 30 f. indigo 30 5
1069. – 40 f. slate 45 5
1070. – 50 f. purple .. 50 5
DESIGNS—HORIZ. 5 f. Vezelay. 6 f. Cannes. 8 f. Chateaudun. 12 f. No. (1102), Palace of Fontainebleau. 15 f. (1149), Garabit Viaduct. 18 f. (1160/a), Versailles Gateway. 20 f. (981), Pointe du Raz. (1067), St. Bertrand de Comminges Abbey. (1144), Chambord Chateau. 25 f. (982/a), Stanislas Square, Nancy. 25 f., 30 f. (1068/a), St. Wandrille Abbey. 30 f. (1068b), Arbois. 40 f. Valley of the Meuse. 50 f. Mt. Gerbier de Jonc. VERT. 12 f. (1142), Gate of France, Vaucouleurs. 15 f. (1021), 18 f. (1022), Conques Abbey.

224. Francois Villon.

225.

1946. National Relief Fund. 15th century Figures.
985. **224.** 2 f.+1 f. blue .. 30 30
986. – 3 f.+1 f. blue .. 30 30
987. – 4 f.+3 f. red .. 30 30
988. – 5 f.+4 f. blue .. 30 30
989. – 6 f.+5 f. brown .. 30 30
990. – 10 f.+6 f. orange .. 40 40
DESIGNS: 3 f. Jean Fouquet. 4 f. Phillipe de Commynes. 5 f. Joan of Arc. 6 f. Jean Gerson. 10 f. Charles VII.

1946. U.N.E.S.C.O. Conf.
991. **225.** 10 f. blue 15 12

226. St. Julien Cathedral, Le Mans.
227. Louvois.

1947. National Relief Fund. Cathedrals of France (2nd issue).
992. – 1 f.+1 f. red .. 8 8
993. – 3 f.+2 f. black .. 10 10
994. – 4 f.+3 f. red .. 20 20
995. **226.** 6 f.+4 f. blue .. 25 25
996. – 10 f.+6 f. green .. 35 35
DESIGNS—VERT. 1 f. St. Sernin, Toulouse. 3 f. Notre-Dame du Port, Clermont-Ferrand. 10 f. Notre-Dame, Paris. HORIZ. 4 f. St. Front, Perigueux.

1947. Stamp Day.
1008. **227.** 4 f. 50+5 f. 50 red .. 75 75

228. The Louvre Colonnade.

229. Seagull over "Ile de la Cite".

1947. 12th U.P.U. Congress.
1009. **228.** 3 f. 50 purple (postage) 20 20
1010. – 4 f. 50 grey 20 20
1011. – 6 f. red 25 25
1012. – 10 f. blue 25 25
1013. **229.** 500 f. green (air) .. 8·00 5·50
DESIGNS—HORIZ. as T 228: 4 f. 50, "La Conciergerie". 6 f. "La Cite". 10 f. "Place de la Concorde".

230. Auguste Pavie.
231. Fenelon.

1947. Auguste Pavie (explorer). Birth Cent.
1014. **230.** 4 f. 50 purple .. 8 8

1947. Fenelon, Archbishop of Cambrai.
1015. **231.** 4 f. 50 brown .. 8 8

232. St. Nazaire Monument.
233.

1947. British Commando Raid on St. Nazaire. 5th Anniv.
1016. **232.** 6 f.+4 f. blue .. 12 12

1947. Boy Scouts' Jamboree.
1017. **233.** 5 f. brown 15 15

234. Milestone on Road of Liberty.
235. "Resistance."

1947. Road Maintenance Fund.
1018. **234.** 6 f.+4 f. green .. 15 15

1947. Resistance Movement.
1019. **235.** 5 f. purple 10 10

1947. No. 997 surch. **1 F.**
1020. 1 f. on 1 f. 30 blue .. 5 5

236. Louis Braille.
237. A. de St.-Exupery (pilot and writer).

1948. Louis Braille Commem.
1023. **236.** 6 f.+4 f. violet .. 15 15

1948. Air. Famous Airmen.
1026. – 40 f.+10 f. blue .. 35 30
1024. **237.** 50 f.+30 f. purple .. 50 45
1025. – 100 f.+70 f. blue .. 85 75
DESIGNS: 40 f. Aeroplane and "Aeolus" inscr. "ADER". 100 f. Dagnaux.

238. Etienne Arago.
239. Lamartine.

1948. Stamp Day and French Postage Stamp Cent.
1027. **238.** 6 f.+4 f. violet .. 20 20

1948. National Relief Fund and Cent. of 1848 Revolution. Dated "1848 1948".
1028. **239.** 1 f.+1 f. green .. 25 25
1029. – 3 f.+2 f. red .. 25 25
1030. – 4 f.+3 f. purple .. 25 25
1031. – 5 f.+4 f. blue .. 35 35
1032. – 6 f.+5 f. blue .. 35 35
1033. – 10 f.+6 f. red .. 35 35
1034. – 15 f.+7 f. blue .. 80 80
1035. – 20 f.+8 f. violet .. 1·00 1·00
PORTRAITS—Nos. 1029/35 in order of value: Ledru-Rollin; Louis Blanc; A. M. Albert; P. J. Proudhon; Blanqui; Barbes, and Mgr. Affre.

240. Dr. Calmette.

1948. 1st Int. B.C.G. (Vaccine) Congress.
1036. **240.** 6 f.+4 f. slate .. 12 10

241. Gen. Leclerc.

1948. Gen. Leclerc Memorial.
1037. **241.** 6 f. black 5 5
See also Nos. 1177/a.

242. Chateaubriand.

1948. Chateaubriand. Death Cent.
1038. **242.** 18 f. blue 15 15

243. Genissiat Barrage.

1948. Genissiat Barrage. Inaug.
1039. **243.** 12 f. red 15 15

244. Aerial View of Chaillot Palace.
245. Paul Langevin.

1948. United Nations Meeting.
1040. – 12 f. red 20 20
1041. **244.** 18 f. blue 20 20
DESIGN: 12 f. Ground level view of Chaillot Palace.

1948. Transfer of Ashes of Paul Langevin and Jean Perrin to the Pantheon.
1042. **245.** 5 f. brown 10 8
1043. – 8 f. green (Perrin) .. 10 8

1949. Surch.
1044. **200.** 5 f. on 6 f. red .. 5 5
1193. 15 f. on 18 f. red .. 20 15

246. Agricultural Worker.
247. Arms of Burgundy.

1949. Craftsmen.
1045. **246.** 3 f.+1 f. purple .. 10 10
1046. – 5 f.+3 f. blue .. 12 10
1047. – 8 f.+4 f. blue .. 25 20
1048. – 10 f.+6 f. red .. 30 25
DESIGNS: 5 f. Fisherman. 8 f. Miner. 10 f. Industrial worker.

1949. Provincial Coats of Arms.
1049. **247.** 10 c. red, yellow & blue 5 5
1050. – 50 c. yellow, red & blue 5 5
1051. – 1 f. red and brown .. 5 5
1052. – 2 f. red, yellow & green 8 5
1053. – 4 f. blue, yellow & red 15 5
ARTS: "Guyenne" (50 c.). "Savoie" (1 f.), "Auvergne" (2 f.) and "Aniou" (4 f.).
For other provinces in this series, see Nos. 776/9, 814/7, 971/4, 1121/5, 1178/83, 1225/31, 1270/3. For arms of French towns, see Nos. 1403/10, etc.

248. Duc de Choiseul.
249. Lille.

1949. Stamp Day.
1054. **248.** 15 f.+5 f. green .. 60 60

1949. Air. Views.
1055. **249.** 100 f. purple 40 5
1056. – 200 f. green .. .. 1·50 20
1057. – 300 f. violet .. .. 4·25 2·00
1058. – 500 f. red .. .. 11·00 1·25
DESIGNS: 200 f. Bordeaux. 300 f. Lyons. 500 f. Marseilles.

250. Polar Scene. **251.** Collegiate Church of St. Barnard, Romans.

1949. French Polar Expeditions.
1060. **250.** 15 f. blue 25 20

1949. French Stamp Cent. (a) Imperf.
1061. **1.** 15 f. red .. .. 1·25 1·25
1062. 25 f. blue .. .. 1·25 1·25
(b) Perf.
1063. **200.** 15 f. red .. .. 1·25 1·25
1064. 25 f. blue .. .. 1·25 1·25
Strip of 4 (Nos. 1061/4) .. 5·50 5·50

1949. Cession of Dauphiny to France. 6th Cent.
1065. **251.** 12 f. brown 15 12

252. Emblems of U.S.A. and France. **253.** Jean Racine.

1949. Franco-American Amity.
1066. **252.** 25 f. blue and red .. 40 35

1949. Racine (dramatist). 250th Death Anniv.
1071. **253.** 12 f. purple 20 20

254. Claude Chappe. **256.** Allegory of Commerce.

255. Alexander III Bridge and "Petit Palais".

1949. Int. Telephone and Telegraph Congress, Paris. Inscr. as in T **254**.
1072. **254.** 10 f. red (postage) .. 50 30
1073. – 15 f. black 75 40
1074. – 25 f. claret .. .. 1·25 1·10
1075. – 50 f. blue .. .. 1·40 85
1076. **255.** 100 f. claret (air) .. 2·00 1·75
PORTRAITS—As T **254**: 15 f. Arago and Ampere. 25 f. Emile Baudot. 50 f. Gen. Ferrie.

1949. Assembly of Presidents of Chambers of Commerce. 500th Anniv.
1077. **256.** 15 f. red 15 12

257. Allegory. **258.** Montesquieu.

1949. U.P.U. 75th Anniv.
1078. **257.** 5 f. green 10 10
1079. 15 f. red 20 15
1080. 25 f. blue 60 35

1949. National Relief Fund.
1081. **258.** 5 f.+1 f. green .. 1·25 1·25
1082. – 8 f.+2 f. black .. 1·25 1·25
1083. – 10 f.+3 f. brown .. 1·25 1·25
1084. – 12 f.+4 f. violet .. 1·25 1·25
1085. – 15 f.+5 f. red .. 1·25 1·25
1086. – 25 f.+10 f. blue .. 1·90 1·90
PORTRAITS: 8 f. Voltaire. 10 f. Watteau. 12 f. Buffon. 15 f. Dupleix. 25 f. Turgot.

DESIGNS: 8 f. "Summer". 12 f. "Autumn". 15 f. "Winter".

259. "Spring".

1949. National Relief Fund. Seasons.
1087. **259.** 5 f.+1 f. green .. 75 75
1088. – 8 f.+2 f. yellow .. 75 75
1089. – 12 f.+3 f. violet .. 1·00 1·00
1090. – 15 f.+4 f. blue .. 1·00 1·00

260. Paris.

1950. Air.
1059. **260.** 1,000 f. purple & black 30·00 8·00

261. Postman. **262.** Raymond Poincare.

1950. Stamp Day.
1091. **162.** 12 f.+3 f. blue .. 1·75 1·40

1950. Honouring Poincare.
1092. **262.** 15 f. blue 20 15

263. Charles Peguy. **264.** Francois Rabelais.

1950. Charles Peguy (writer).
1093. **263.** 12 f. purple 20 15

1950. Francois Rabelais (writer).
1094. **264.** 12 f. lake 20 20

265. Andre Chenier. **266.** Madame Recamier.

1950. National Relief Fund. Frames in blue.
1095. **265.** 5 f.+2 f. purple .. 2·25 2·25
1096. – 8 f.+3 f. sepia .. 2·25 2·25
1097. – 10 f.+4 f. red .. 2·50 2·50
1098. – 12 f.+5 f. brown .. 2·50 2·50
1099. – 15 f.+6 f. green .. 2·50 2·50
1100. – 20 f.+10 f. blue .. 2·50 2·50
PORTRAITS: 8 f. Louis David. 10 f. Lazare Carnot. 12 f. Danton. 15 f. Robespierre. 20 f. Hoche.

1950.
1103. **266.** 12 f. green 20 20
1104. – 15 f. blue 20 20
PORTRAIT: 15 f. Madame de Sevigne.

267. "L'Amour". **268.** T.P.O. Sorting Van.

1950. Red Cross. Cross in red.
1105. – 8 f.+2 f. blue .. 1·25 1·25
1106. **267.** 15 f.+3 f. purple .. 1·25 1·25
DESIGN: 8 f. Bust of A. Brongniart.

1951. Stamp Day.
1107. **268.** 12 f.+3 f. violet .. 1·60 1·60

269. J. Ferry (statesman). **270.** Shuttle.

272. Anchor and Map. **271.** De La Salle.

1951.
1108. **269.** 15 f. red 30 25

1951. Textile Industry.
1109. **270.** 25 f. blue 50 45

1951. Jean Baptiste de la Salle (educator). Birth Tercent.
1110. **271.** 15 f. brown 25 20

1951. Colonial Troops. 50th Anniv.
1111. **272.** 15 f. blue 30 25

273. Vincent D'Indy.

1951. Vincent D'Indy (composer). Birth Cent.
1112. **273.** 25 f. green .. .. 1·00 60

274. A de Musset. **275.** Nocard, Bouley and Chauveau.

276. Picue, Roussin and Villemin. **277.** St. Nicholas.

1951. National Relief Fund. Frames in sepia.
1113. **274.** 5 f.+1 f. green .. 2·25 2·25
1114. – 8 f.+2 f. purple .. 2·25 2·25
1115. – 10 f.+3 f. green .. 2·40 2·40
1116. – 12 f.+4 f. brown .. 2·40 2·40
1117. – 15 f.+5 f. red .. 2·40 2·40
1118. – 30 f.+10 f. blue .. 4·00 4·00
PORTRAITS: 8 f. Delacoix. 10 f. Gay-Lussac. 12 f. Surcouf. 15 f. Talleyrand. 30 f. Napoleon.

1951. French Veterinary Research.
1119. **275.** 12 f. magenta .. 40 30

1951. Military Health Service.
1120. **276.** 15 f. purple 40 25

1951. Provincial Coats of arms as T **247.**
1121. 10 c. yellow, blue and red 5 5
1122. 50 c. black, red and green 8 5
1123. 1 f. red, yellow and blue.. 10 5
1124. 2 f. yellow, blue and red.. 15 5
1125. 3 f. yellow, blue and red.. 45 8
ARMS: "Artois" (10 c.), "Limousin" (50 c.), "Bearn" (1 f.), "Touraine" (2 f.) and "Franche-Comte" (3 f.).

1951. Popular Pictorial Art Exn., Epinal. Multicoloured centre.
1126. **277.** 15 f. blue 35 25

278. Seal of Mercantile Guild. **279.** Nogues.

1951. Bimillenary of Paris.
1127. **278.** 15 f. brn., blue & red 30 20

1951. M. Nogues (aviator).
1128. **279.** 12 f. indigo and blue 35 25

280. C. Baudelaire.

281. Eiffel Tower and Chaillot Palace. **282.** Clemenceau (statesman).

1951. French Poets.
1129. **280.** 8 f. violet 20 20
1130. – 12 f. lav. (Verlaine).. 25 25
1131. – 15 f. grn. (Rimbaud) 30 30

1951. U.N.O. General Assembly.
1132. **281.** 18 f. red 50 40
1133. 30 f. blue 60 45

1951. Clemenceau. 110th Birth Anniv. and Armistice. 33rd Anniv.
1134. **282.** 15 f. sepia 20 20

283. Chateau Clos-Vougeot **284.** 15th century Child.

1951. Chateau Clos-Vougeot. 400th Anniv.
1135. **283.** 30 f. brown 90 45

1951. Red Cross. Cross in red.
1136. **284.** 12 f.+3 f. brown .. 1·50 1·50
1137. – 15 f.+5 f. blue .. 1·50 1·50
DESIGN: 15 f. 18th cent. child.

285. Church of St. Etienne, Caen. **286.** 19th-cent. Mail Coach.

1951.
1138. – 40 f. violet 90 5
1139. **285.** 50 f. brown .. .. 1·00 5
VIEW—HORIZ. 40 f. Observatory, Pic du Midi de Bigorre.

1952. Stamp Day.
1140. **286.** 12 f.+3 f. green .. 2·00 1·50

287. Marshal de Lattre de Tassigny.

1952.
1140a. **287.** 12 f. indigo and blue 1·10 65
1141. 15 f. purple.. .. 50 20

288. French Monument, Narvik.

1952. Battle of Narvik.
1143. **288.** 30 f. blue .. .. 1·25 60

289. Council of Europe Building, Strasbourg.

1952. Council of Europe Assembly.
1145. **289.** 30 f. green .. .. 3·50 2·25

290. Bir Hakeim Monument.

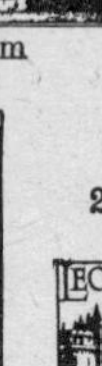

291. Abbey of the Holy Cross, Poitiers.

292. Medaille Militaire, in 1852 and 1952.

293. Leonardo, Amboise Chateau and Town of Vinci.

1952. Battle of Bir Hakeim. 10th Anniv.
1146. **290.** 30 f. lake .. .. 1·40 90

1952. Abbey of the Holy Cross, Poitiers. 14th Cent.
1147. **291.** 15 f. red 25 20

1952. Medaille Militaire. Cent.
1148. **292.** 15 f. brn., yell. & grn. 30 20

1952. Leonardo da Vinci. 5th Birth Cent.
1150. **293.** 30 f. blue .. .. 2·25 1·50

294. Flaubert (after E. Giraud).

295. R. Laennec (physician).

1952. National Relief Fund. Frames in sepia.
1151. **294.** 8 f.+2 f. blue .. 1·75 1·75
1152. – 12 f.+3 f. ultramarine 1·75 1·75
1153. – 12 f.+4 f. green .. 1·75 1·75
1154. – 18 f.+5 f. sepia .. 1·75 1·75
1155. – 20 f.+6 f. red .. 2·10 2·10
1156. – 30 f.+7 f. violet .. 2·10 2·10
PORTRAITS: 12 f. Manet. 15 f. Saint-Saens. 18 f. H. Poincare. 20 f. Haussmann (after Yvon). 20 f. Thiers.

1952.
1157. **295.** 12 f. green 25 20

296. "Cherub" (bas-relief).

297. Count D'Argenson.

1952. Red Cross Fund. Sculptures from Basin of Diana, Versailles. Cross in red.
1158. **296.** 12 f.+3 f. green .. 1·40 1·40
1159. – 15 f.+5 f. blue .. 1·40 1·40
DESIGN: 15 f. "Cherub" (facing left).

1953. Stamp Day.
1161. **297.** 12 f.+3 f. violet .. 1·75 1·75

299. "Gargantua" (Rabelais).

300. Mannequin and Place Vendome, Paris.

1953. Literary Figures and National Industries.
1162. **299.** 6 f. lake and red .. 5 5
1163. – 8 f. blue and indigo .. 8 5
1164. – 12 f. green and brown 8 5
1165. – 18 f. sepia and purple 35 20
1166. – 25 f. sepia, red & brn. 1·25 5
1166a. – 25 f. blue and black .. 35 5
1167 **300.** 30 f. violet and indigo 40 8
1167a. – 30 f. indigo & blue-grn. 12 5
1168. – 40 f. brown & chocolate 25 5
1169. – 50 f. brown, blue-green and blue 35 5
1170. – 75 f. lake and red .. 1·90 15
DESIGNS—As T **299/300**: 8 f. "Celimene" (Moliere). 12 f. "Figaro" (Beaumarchais). 18 f. "Hernani" (Victor Hugo). 25 f. (No. 1166) Tapestry. 25 f. (1166a) Mannequin modelling gloves. 30 f. (1168a) Rare books and book-binding. 40 f. Porcelain and glass. 50 f. Gold cut plate and jewellery. 75 f. Flowers and perfumes.

1953. General Leclerc. As T **241** but inscr. "GENERAL LECLERC MARECHAL DE FRANCE".
1171. **241.** 8 f. brown 35 25
1171a. 12 f. blue-green & grn. 1·10 60

301 Olivier de Serres.

302. Cyclists and Map.

303. Swimming.

304. Mme. Vigee-Lebrun and Daughter (self-portrait).

1953. National Relief Fund.
1172. – 8 f.+2 f. blue .. 2·10 2·10
1173. **301.** 12 f.+3 f. green .. 2·10 2·10
1174. – 15 f.+4 f. lake .. 2·10 2·10
1175. – 18 f.+5 f. blue .. 2·10 2·10
1176. – 20 f.+6 f. violet .. 2·10 2·10
1177. – 30 f.+7 f. brown .. 2·25 2·25
PORTRAITS: 8 f. St. Bernard. 15 f. Rameau. 18 f. Monge. 20 f. Michelet. 30 f. Marshal Lyautey.

1953. Provincial Coats of arms as T **247**.
1178. 50 c. yellow, red and blue 15 10
1179. 70 c. yellow, blue and red 12 8
1180. 80 c. yellow, red and blue 12 8
1181. 1 f. yellow, red and black 5 5
1182. 2 f. yellow, blue and brown 5 5
1183. 3 f. yellow, blue and red .. 12 5
ARMS: "Picardie" (50 c.), "Gascogne" (70 c.), "Berri" (80 c.), "Poitou" (1 f.), "Champagne" (2 f.) and "Dauphine" (3 f.).

1953. "Tour de France" Cycle Race. 50th Anniv.
1184. **302.** 12 f. black, blue & lake 35 25

1953. Sports.
1185. **303.** 20 f. brown and red 35 5
1186. – 25 f. brown and green 75 5
1187. – 30 f. brown and blue 35 5
1188. – 40 f. indigo and brown 90 10
1189. – 50 f. brown and green 75 5
1190. – 75 f. lake and orange 6·50 4·00
SPORTS: 25 f. Running. 30 f. Fencing. 40 f. Canoeing. 50 f. Rowing. 75 f. Horse-jumping.

1953. Red Cross Fund. Cross in red.
1191. **304.** 12 f.+3 f. brown .. 1·90 1·90
1192. – 15 f.+5 f. blue .. 2·50 2·50
DESIGN: 15 f. "The Return from the Baptism" (L. Le Nain).

305. Magister.

AEROPLANES: 100 f. Mystere IV (jet fighter). 200 f. Noratlas (cargo). 1,000 f. Provence (transport).

1954. Air.
1194. – 100 f. brown & blue .. 60 5
1195. – 200 f. purple & blue .. 1·25 5
1196. **305.** 500 f. red & orange .. 40·00 3·75
1197. – 1000 f. blue, maroon and turquoise .. 32·00 4·25
See also No. 1457.

306. Harvester.

307. Gallic Cock.

308. Lavallette.

1954.
1198. **306.** 4 f. turquoise* .. 15 5
1198a. **307.** 5 f. sepia* 15 5
1198b. **306.** 6 f. brown 5 5
1199. 8 f. lake* .. .. 2·00 5
1199a. **307.** 8 f. violet* 20 5
1199b. 10 f. blue* 20 8
1199c. **306.** 10 f. green .. 30 5
1200. **307.** 12 f. red* .. .. 1·50 20
1200a. **306.** 12 f. mauve .. 12 5
1200b. **307.** 15 f. purple* .. 50 25
1200c. 20 f. green* .. 50 20
1201. 24 f. green* .. 4·25 1·50
1201a. 30 f. orange* .. 1·50 20
1201b. 40 f. brown-red* .. 2·50 1·10
1201c. 45 f. green* .. 6·00 2·40
1201d. 55 f. emerald* .. 5·00 2·50
*PRECANCELS. See note below No. 432.
See also Nos. 1470, etc.

1954. Stamp Day.
1202. **308.** 12 f.+3 f. grn. & brn. 2·50 2·25

309. Exhibition Buildings.

310. "D-Day".

311. Lourdes.

312. Jumieges Abbey.

1954. Paris Fair. 50th Anniv.
1203. **309.** 15 f. lake and blue .. 25 20

1954. Liberation. 10th Anniv.
1204. **310.** 15 f. vermilion & blue 25 15

1954. Views.
1205. **311.** 6 f. indigo, blue & grn. 12 5
1206. – 8 f. green and blue .. 5 5
1207. – 10 f. chestnut and blue 5 5
1208. – 12 f. lilac and violet .. 5 5
1209. – 12 f. brown and purple 60 45
1250. – 12 f. black 35 20
1210. – 18 f. indigo, blue & grn. 12 10
1211. – 20 f. chestnut, blue-grn. and sepia .. 10 5
1211a. **311.** 20 f. olive & turq. .. 20 5
VIEWS—HORIZ. 8 f. Seine Valley at Andelys. 10 f. Royan Beach. 12 f. (No. 1209), Limoges. 18 f. Cheverny Chateau. 20 f. (No. 1211), Ajaccio Bay. VERT. 12 f. (No. 1208), Quimper. 12 f. (No. 1250), "The Jacquemart" (Campanile), Moulins.

1954. Jumieges Abbey. 13th Cent.
1212. **312.** 12 f. indigo, bl. & grn. 65 50

313. Abbey Church of St. Philibert, Tournus.

314. Stenay.

1954. 1st Conference of Romanesque Studies. Tournus.
1213. **313.** 30 f. blue and indigo 4·00 2·50

1954. Return of Stenay to France. Tercent.
1214. **314.** 15 f. brown and sepia 50 30

315. St. Louis.

316. Villandry Chateau.

1954. National Relief Fund.
1215. **315.** 12 f.+4 f. blue .. 7·50 7·50
1216. – 15 f.+5 f. violet .. 7·50 7·50
1217. – 18 f.+6 f. sepia .. 7·50 7·50
1218. – 20 f.+7 f. red .. 8·50 8·50
1219. – 25 f.+8 f. indigo .. 8·50 8·50
1220. – 30 f.+10 f. maroon 8·50 8·50
PORTRAITS: 15 f. Bossuet. 18 f. Sadi Carnot. 20 f. A. Bourdelle. 25 f. Dr. E. Roux. 30 f. Paul Valery.

1954. Four Centuries of Renaissance Gardens.
1221. **316.** 18 f. green and blue .. 2·25 1·50

317. Cadet and Flag.

1954. St. Cyr Military Academy. 150th Anniv.
1222. **317.** 15 f. indigo, blue & red 75 35

318. Napoleon Conferring Decorations.

319. "Basis of Metric System."

1954. First Legion of Honour Presentation. 150th Anniv.
1223. **318.** 12 f. red 75 35

1954. Metric System. 150th Anniv.
1224. **319.** 30 f. sepia and indigo 3·00 2·25

1954. Provincial Coats of arms as T **247**.
1225. 50 c. yellow, bl., red & blk. 5 5
1226. 70 c. yellow, red and green 5 5
1227. 80 c. yellow, blue and red 10 8
1228. 1 f. yellow, blue and red .. 5 5
1229. 2 f. yellow, red and black .. 5 5
1230. 3 f. yellow, red and brown 5 5
1231. 5 f. yellow and blue .. 5 5
ARMS: 50 c. "Maine". 70 c. "Navarre". 80 c. "Nivernais". 1 f. "Bourbonnais". 2 f. "Angoumois". 3 f. "Aunis". 5 f. "Saintonge".

320. "Young Girl with Doves" (J.-B. Greuze).

321. Saint-Simon.

1954. Red Cross Fund. Cross in red.
1232. – 12 f.+3 f. blue .. 2·00 2·00
1233. **320.** 15 f.+5 f. brown .. 2·00 2·00
DESIGN: 12 f. "The Sick Child" (E. Carriere).

1955. Saint-Simon (writer). Death Bicent.
1234. **32.** 12 f. purple and sepia 55 30

322. "Industry", "Agriculture" and Rotary Emblem.

323. "France".

1955. Rotary International. 50th Anniv.
1235. **322.** 30 f. orange and blue 50 40

1955.
1236. **323.** 6 f. brown .. .. 1·25 85
1237. 12 f. green .. .. 1·00 75
1238. 15 f. red 12 5
1238a. 18 f. green 12 5
1238b. 20 f. blue 15 5
1238c. 25 f. red 20 5

324. Thimonnier and Sewing-machines.

1955. French Inventors (1st series).

1239. – 5 f. blue 30 20
1240. **324.** 10 f. choc. & chestnut 30 20
1241. – 12 f. green 40 35
1242. – 18 f. blue and grey .. 95 80
1243. – 25 f. violet and plum 95 50
1244. – 30 f. vermilion and red 80 50

DESIGNS: 5 f. Le Bon (gaslight). 12 f. Appert (food canning). 18 f. Sainte-Claire Deville (aluminium). 25 f. Martin (steel). 30 f. Chardonnet (artificial silk).

325. Paris Balloon Post, 1870.

1955. Stamp Day.

1245. **325.** 12 f.+3 f. chocolate, green and blue .. 3·00 2·50

326. Florian and Pastoral scene.

1955. Florian (fabulist). Birth Bicent.

1246. **326.** 12 f. turquoise .. 40 25

327. Eiffel Tower and T.V. Aerials.

1955. Television Development.

1247. **327.** 15 f. blue and dp. blue. 30 20

328. Observation Tower and Fence.

1955. Liberation of Concentration Camps. 10th Anniv.

1248. **328.** 12 f. sepia and blue.. 25 20

329. Electric Train.

1955. Electrification of Valenciennes-Thionville Railway Line.

1249. **329.** 12 f. chocolate and blue 35 25

330. Jules Verne and Capt. Nemo on the "Nautilus".

1955. Jules Verne (author). 50th Death Anniv.

1251. **330.** 30 f. blue .. .. 3·00 2·50

331. Maryse Bastie (airwoman).

332. Vauban.

1955. Air. Maryse Bastie Commemoration.

1252. **331.** 50 f. claret and red .. 2·75 1·90

1955. National Relief Fund.

1253. – 12 f.+5 f. violet .. 5·50 5·50
1254. – 15 f.+6 f. blue .. 5·50 5·50
1255. **322.** 18 f.+7 f. green .. 5·50 5·50
1256. – 25 f.+8 f. slate .. 6·00 6·00
1257. – 30 f.+9 f. lake .. 6·00 6·00
1258. – 50 f.+15 f. turquoise 6·00 6·00

PORTRAITS: 12 f. King Phillippe-Auguste. 15 f. Malherbe. 25 f. Vergennes. 30 f. Laplace. 50 f. Renoir.

333. A. and L. Lumiere.

1955. French Cinema Industry. 60th Anniv.

1259. **333.** 30 f. lake .. .. 2·50 1·75

334. Jacques Cœur (merchant prince).

1955.

1260. **334.** 12 f. violet .. .. 1·10 50

335. "La Capricieuse".

1955. Cent. of Voyage of "La Capricieuse".

1261. **335.** 30 f. blue & turquoise 2·75 1·75

336. Marseilles.

337. Gerard de Nerval.

1955. Views.

1262. – 6 f. lake 5 5
1263. **336.** 8 f. indigo 5 5
1264. – 10 f. blue 5 5
1265. – 12 f. brown & violet 5 5
1284. – 12 f. brn., green & blk. 85 50
1265a. – 15 f. indigo and blue 20 15
1266. – 18 f. indigo and green 10 5
1267. – 20 f. mauve & violet.. 10 5
1268. – 25 f. maroon & chest. 15 5
1268a. – 35 f. blue-grn. & grn. 30 15
1268b. – 70 f. black and green 1·10 25

DESIGNS—HORIZ. 6 f., 35 f. Bordeaux. 10 f. Nice. 12 f. (No. 1265). 70 f. Valentre Bridge, Cahors. 12 f. (No. 1284) Grand Trianon, Versailles. 18 f. Uzerche. 20 f. Mount Pele, Martinique. 25 f. Ramparts of Brouage. VERT. 15 f. Douai Belfry.

1955. De Nerval (writer). Death Cent.

1269. **337.** 12 f. sepia and red 30 20

1955. Provincial Coats of arms as T **247**.

1270. 50 c. yell., red, grn. & blk. 5 5
1271. 70 c. yellow, blue and red 5 5
1272. 80 c. yellow, red and brown 5 5
1273. 1 f. yellow, red and blue.. 5 5

ARMS: 50 c. "Comte de Foix". 70 c. "Marche". 80 c. "Roussillon". 1 f. "Comtat Venaissin".

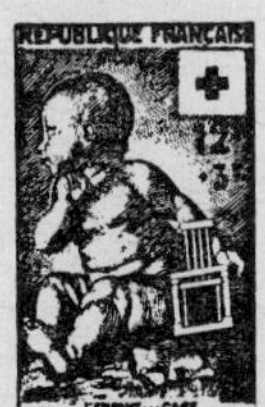

338. "Child and Cage (after Pigalle).

339.

1955. Red Cross Fund. Cross in red.

1274. **338.** 12 f.+3 f. lake .. 1·50 1·50
1275. – 15 f.+5 f. blue .. 1·50 1·50

DESIGN: 15 f. "Child and goose" (Greek sculpture).

1956. National Deportation Memorial.

1276. **339.** 15 f. brown and lake 15 15

340. Colonel Driant.

341. Trench Warfare.

1956. Col. Driant. Birth Cent.

1277. **340.** 15 f. blue 20 20

1956. Battle of Verdun. 40th Anniv.

1278. **341.** 30 f. blue and brown 50 35

342. Francis of Taxis.

1956. Stamp Day.

1279. **342.** 12 f.+3 f. brown, green and blue 80 80

343. J. H. Fabre (entomologist).

DESIGNS: 15 f. C. Tellier (refrigeration expert). 18 f. C. Flammarion (astronomer). 30 f. P. Sabatier (chemist).

1956. French Scientists.

1280. **343.** 12 f. chest. & maroon 20 20
1281. – 15 f. blue and black 30 20
1282. – 18 f. blue 80 60
1283. – 30 f. green 80 60

344. "Latin America" and "France".

1956. Franco-Latin American Friendship.

1285. **344.** 30 f. chestnut & sepia 95 55

345. "Reims" and "Florence".

347. St. Yves de Treguier.

346. Order of Malta and Leper Colony.

1956. Reims-Florence Friendship.

1286. **345.** 12 f. green and black 50 20

1956. Order of Malta Leprosy Relief.

1287. **346.** 12 f. red, chest. & sep. 25 20

1956. St. Yves de Treguier Commemoration.

1288. **347.** 15 f. black and grey.. 20 20

348. Marshal Franchet d'Esperey.

349. Monument.

1956. Marshal d'Esperey. Birth Cent.

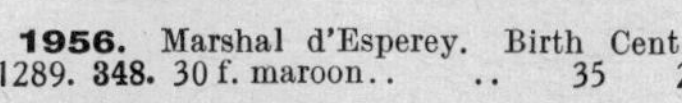

1289. **348.** 30 f. maroon.. .. 35 25

1956. Montreau-les-Mines. Cent.

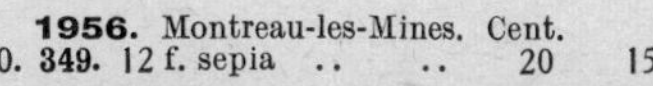

1290. **349.** 12 f. sepia 20 15

350. Bude.

351. Pelota.

1956. National Relief Fund.

1291. **350.** 12 f.+3 f. blue .. 1·25 1·25
1292. – 12 f.+3 f. grey .. 1·25 1·25
1293. – 12 f.+3 f. red .. 1·25 1·25
1294. – 15 f.+5 f. green .. 1·25 1·25
1295. – 15 f.+5 f. chocolate 1·25 1·25
1296. – 15 f.+5 f. violet .. 1·25 1·25

PORTRAITS: No. 1292, Goujon. 1293, Champlain. 1294, Chardin. 1295, Barres. 1296, Ravel.

1956. Sports.

1297. – 30 f. black and grey.. 20 5
1298. **351.** 40 f. maroon & sepia 25 5
1299. – 50 f. violet & purple 30 5
1300. – 75 f. grn., bl. & indigo 75 25

DESIGNS: 30 f. Basket-ball. 50 f. Rugby. 75 f. Mountaineering.

1956. Europe. As T **230** of Belgium.

1301. 15 f. lake and pink .. 50 5
1302. 30 f. blue and indigo .. 90 20

352. Donzere-Mondragon Barrage.

DESIGNS—VERT. 18 f. Aiguille du Midi cable railway. HORIZ. 30 f. Port of Strasbourg.

1956. Technical Achievements.

1303. **352.** 12 f. grey & chocolate 30 20
1304. – 18 f. indigo 45 25
1305. – 30 f. blue and indigo 75 35

353. A. A. Parmentier (agronomist).

354. Petrarch.

1956. Parmentier Commemoration.

1306. **353.** 12 f. chestnut & sepia 30 20

1956. Famous men.

1307. **354.** 8 f. green 20 15
1308. – 12 f. maroon (Lully) 20 15
1309. – 15 f. red (Rousseau) 25 20
1310. – 18 f. blue (Franklin) 1·00 60
1311. – 20 f. violet (Chopin) 75 35
1312. – 30 f. turq. (Van Gogh) 1·00 75

355. Pierre de Coubertin.

356. "Jeune Paysan" (after Le Nain).

1956. Pierre de Coubertin (reviver of Olympic Games).

1313. **355.** 30 f. purple and grey 75 50

1956. Red Cross Fund. Cross in red.

1314. **356.** 12 f.+3 f. olive .. 85 85
1315. – 15 f.+5 f. lake .. 85 85

DESIGN: 15 f. "Gillies" (after Watteau).

357. Pigeon and Loft.

358. "Caravelle".

359. Victor Schoelcher.

1957. Pigeon-fanciers' Commemoration.

1316. **357.** 15 f. blue, pur. & blk. 25 20

1957. Air.

1318. – 300 f. olive & turq... 2·00 85

1319. **358.** 500 f. black & blue .. 7·50 75

1320. – 1000 f. black, violet and sepia .. .. 16·00 5·00

DESIGNS: 300 f. "Paris" (jet training aircraft) 1000 f. "L'Alouette" (helicopter).

See also Nos. 1458/60.

1957. Schoelcher Commem. (slavery abolitionist).

1321. **358.** 18 f. magenta .. 20 15

360. 18th Cent. Felucca.

1957. Stamp Day.

1322. **360.** 12 f.+3 f. sep. & slate 1·00 75

361. Statuette (after Falconet), and Sevres Porcelain.

1957. National Porcelain Industry at Sevres. Bicent.

1323. **361.** 30 f. blue 35 25

DESIGNS: 12 f. Beclere (radiology). 18 f. Terrillon (asepsis). 30 f. Oehmichen (helicopter).

362. Plante and Accumulators.

1957. French Inventors (2nd series).

1324. **362.** 8 f. maroon and sepia 25 25

1325. – 12 f. blk., blue & grn. 25 25

1326. – 18 f. lake and red .. 80 80

1327. – 30 f. myrtle & green 80 80

363. Uzes Chateau.

364. Jean Moulin.

366. Joinville.

365. Emblems of Auditing.

1957.

1334. – 8 f. green 5 5

1328. **363.** 12 f. sepia & grey-blue 20 12

1344. – 12 f. green and brown 25 20

1335. – 15 f. brown and green 5 5

DESIGNS—VERT. 8 f., 15 f. Le Quesnoy (bridge). HORIZ. 12 f. (No. 1344), Port of Brest.

1957. Heroes of the Resistance (1st issue). Inscr. as in T **364.**

1329. **364.** 8 f. chocolate & brn. 25 20

1330. – 10 f. blue and black.. 20 20

1331. – 12 f. green and brown 25 20

1332. – 18 f. black and violet 85 70

1333. – 20 f. blue & turquoise 30 25

PORTRAITS: 10 f. H. d'Estienne d'Orves. 12 f. R. Keller. 18 f. P. Brossolette. 20 f. J.-B. Lebas.

See also Nos. 1381/4, 1418/22, 1478/82 and 1519/22.

1957. Court of Accounts. 150th Anniv.

1336. **365.** 12 f. blue and brown 15 15

1957. National Relief Fund.

1337. **366.** 12 f.+3 f. olive & sage 55 55

1338. – 12 f.+3 f. black and turquoise .. 60 60

1339. – 15 f.+5 f. lake and vermilion .. 70 70

1340. – 15 f.+5 f. blue and ultramarine .. 70 70

1341. – 18 f.+7 f. blk. & grn. 1·10 1·10

1342. – 18 f.+7 f. chocolate and brown .. 1·10 1·10

PORTRAITS: No. 1338, Bernard Palissy. 1339, Quentin de la Tour. 1340, Lamennais. 1341, George Sand. 1342, Jules Guesde.

See also Nos. 1390/5.

367. "Public Works".

1957. French Public Works.

1343. **367.** 30 f. brn., mar. & grn. 25 20

368. Leo Lagrange (founder) and Stadium.

369. Auguste Comte.

1957. Universities World Games.

1345. **368.** 18 f. black and grey.. 25 20

1957. Auguste Comte (philosopher). Death Cent.

1346. **369.** 35 f. sepia and brown 35 30

370. "Agriculture and Industry".

371. Roman Theatre, Lyons.

1957. Europa.

1347. **370.** 20 f. green and brown 20 5

1348. 35 f. blue and sepia.. 30 15

1957. Lyons Bimillenary.

1349. **371.** 20 f. maroon & chest. 25 20

372. Sens River, Guadeloupe.

373. Copernicus.

1957. Tourist Publicity Series.

1350. **372.** 8 f. brown & green.. 5 5

1351. – 10 f. brown & bistre 5 5

1351a. – 15 f. sepia, grn. & blue 15 10

1352. – 18 f. brown & indigo 12 5

1353. – 25 f. brown and grey 12 5

1353a. – 30 f. myrtle.. .. 20 5

1354. – 35 f. magenta and red 15 5

1355. – 50 f. sepia and green 20 5

1356. – 65 f. blue and indigo 35 5

1356a. – 85 f. maroon .. 55 5

1356b. **372.** 100 f. violet .. 1·25 5

DESIGNS—HORIZ. 10 f., 30 f. Palais de l'Elysee, Paris. 15 f. Chateau de Foix. 25 f. Chateau de Valencay. 50 f. Les Antiques, Saint Remy. 65 f., 85 f. Evian-les-Bains. VERT. 18 f. Beynac-Cazenac (Dordogne). 35 f. Rouen Cathedral.

1957. Famous Men.

1357. **373.** 8 f. brown 20 12

1358. – 10 f. green (Michelangelo) 15 15

1359. – 12 f. violet (Cervantes) 20 15

1360. – 15 f. brn. (Rembrandt) 20 15

1361. – 18 f. blue (Newton).. 45 30

1362. – 25 f. maroon and purple (Mozart) .. 35 20

1363. – 35 f. blue (Goethe) .. 50 35

See also Nos. 1367/74.

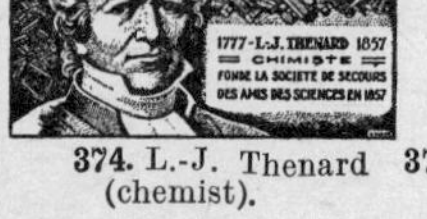

374. L.-J. Thenard (chemist).

375. "The Blind Man and the Beggar" (after J. Callot).

1957. Thenard. Death Cent.

1364. **374.** 15 f. green and bistre 20 20

1957. Red Cross Fund. Cross in red.

1365. **375.** 15 f.+7 f. blue .. 75 75

1366. – 20 f.+8 f. brown .. 75 75

DESIGN: 20 f. "The Beggar and the One-eyed Woman" (after J. Callot).

1958. French Doctors. As T **373.**

1367. 8 f. brown 20 15

1368. 12 f. violet 20 15

1369. 15 f. blue 25 20

1370. 35 f. black 40 25

PORTRAITS: 8 f. Dr. Pinel. 12 f. Dr. Wida. 15 f. Dr. C. Nicolle. 35 f. Dr. R. Leriche.

1958. French Scientists. As T **373.**

1371. 8 f. violet and blue .. 20 15

1372. 12 f. grey and sepia .. 20 15

1373. 15 f. bronze and green .. 25 20

1374. 35 f. red and lake .. 35 25

PORTRAITS: 8 f. Lagrange (mathematician). 12 f. Le Verrier (astronomer). 15 f. Foucault (physicist). 35 f. Berthollet (chemist).

376. Rural Postal Services.

1958. Stamp Day.

1375. **376.** 15 f.+5 f. olive, brown, green and red .. 55 45

DESIGNS—VERT. 15 f. Maubeuge. 18 f. Saint-Die. HORIZ. 25 f. Sete.

377. Le Havre.

1958. Municipal Reconstruction.

1376. **377.** 12 f. red and olive .. 20 20

1377. – 15 f. brown and violet 30 20

1378. – 18 f. indigo and blue 20 15

1379. – 25 f. brn., turq. & blue 25 25

378. French Pavilion.

1958. Brussels Int. Exn.

1380. **378.** 35 f. grn., blue & brn. 25 20

1958. Heroes of the Resistance (2nd issue). Portraits inscr. as in T **364.**

1381. 8 f. black and violet .. 15 15

1382. 12 f. green and blue .. 15 15

1383. 15 f. grey and sepia .. 55 35

1384. 20 f. blue and brown .. 40 30

PORTRAITS: 8 f. Jean Cavailles. 12 f. Fred Scamaroni. 15 f. Simone Michel Levy. 20 f. Jacques Bingen.

379. Bowls.

380. Senlis Cathedral.

1958. French Local Games.

1385. **379.** 12 f. brown and red.. 15 15

1386. – 15 f. bronze, grn. & bl. 20 15

1387. – 18 f. brown and green 35 30

1388. – 25 f. indigo & brown 30 25

DESIGNS—HORIZ. 15 f. Nautical jousting. VERT. 18 f. Archery. 25 f. Breton wrestling.

1958. Senlis Cathedral Commem.

1389. **380.** 15 f. blue and indigo 20 20

1958. Red Cross Fund. French Celebrities as T **366.**

1390. 12 f.+4 f. yellow green 45 45

1391. 12 f.+4 f. blue .. 55 55

1392. 15 f.+5 f. claret .. 60 60

1393. 15 f.+5 f. blue .. 60 60

1394. 20 f.+8 f. vermilion .. 75 75

1395. 35 f.+15 f. blue green .. 75 75

PORTRAITS: No. 1390, J. du Bellay. 1391, Jean Bart. 1392, D. Diderot. 1393, G. Courbet. 1394, J. B. Carpeaux. 1395, Toulouse-Lautrec.

381. Fragment of the Bayeux Tapestry.

1958.

1396. **381.** 15 f. red and blue .. 30 15

1958. Europa. As T **254** of Belgium. Size 22×36 mm.

1397. 20 f. red 35 5

1398. 35 f. blue 45 15

382. Town Halls of Paris and Rome.

1958. Paris-Rome Friendship.

1399. **382.** 35 f. grey, blue & red 35 20

383. U.N.E.S.C.O. Headquarters, Paris.

384. Flanders Grave.

386. St. Vincent de Paul.

385. Arms of Marseilles.

1958. Inaug. of U.N.E.S.C.O. Building.

1400. **383.** 20 f. bistre and turq. 12 5

1401. – 35 f. red and myrtle.. 20 20

DESIGN: 35 f. Different view of building.

1958. First World War Armistice. 40th Anniv.

1402. **384.** 15 f. blue and green.. 12 12

1958. Arms of French Towns.

1403. **385.** 50 c. blue 5 5

1404. – 70 c. red, yellow & bl. 5 5

1405. – 80 c. red, yellow & bl. 5 5

1406. – 1 f. red, yellow & blue 5 5

1407. – 2 f. red, green & blue 5 5

1408. – 3 f. red, yellow, green and black 5 5

1409. – 5 f. red and sepia .. 5 5

1410. – 15 f. red, blue, yellow and green 10 5

ARMS: 70 c. "Lyon". 80 c. "Toulouse". 1 f. "Bordeaux". 2 f. "Nice". 3 f. "Nantes". 5 f. "Lille". 15 f. "Alger".

See also Nos. 1452, 1454 and 1498a, etc.

1958. Red Cross Fund. Cross in red.

1411. **386.** 15 f.+7 f. grey-grn... 50 50

1412. – 20 f.+8 f. violet .. 55 55

PORTRAIT: 20 f. J. H. Dunant (founder).

387. Arc de Triomphe and Flowers.

388. Symbols of Learning and "Academic Palms".

1959. Paris Flower Festival.

1413. **387.** 15 f. multicoloured.. 15 8

1959. "Academic Palms". 150th Anniv.

1414. **388.** 20 f. blk., vio. & lake 12 8

389. Father Charles de Foucauld (missionary).

1959. Charles de Foucauld Commem.

1415. **389.** 50 f. maroon, chestnut, blue and black .. 50 40

390. Mail 'plane making Night-landing.

1959. Stamp Day.
1416. **390.** 20 f. + 5 f. red, sepia, green and myrtle .. 35 35
See also No. 1644.

391. Miner's Lamp, Picks and School Building.

392. "Five Martyrs".

1959. School of Mines. 175th Anniv.
1417. **391.** 20 f. turq., blk. & red 15 12

1959. Heroes of the Resistance (3rd Issue). Portraits inscr. as in T **364**.
1418. **392.** 15 f. black and violet 20 12
1419. – 15 f. violet & purple 20 15
1420. – 20 f. brown & chestnut 35 25
1421. – 20 f. turquoise & green 25 20
1422. – 30 f. violet and purple 40 25
PORTRAITS: No. 1419, Yvonne Le Roux. 1420, L. Martin Bret. 1421, G. Mederic-Vedy. 1422, G. Moutardier.

393. Foum el Gherza (Dam).

1959. French Technical Achievements.
1423. **393.** 15 f. turq. & ol. brn. 15 15
1424. – 20 f. pur., red & chest. 25 20
1425. – 30 f. brn., turq. & bl. 25 20
1426. – 50 f. blue & ol.-green 35 20
DESIGNS—VERT. 20 f. Marcoule Atomic Power Station. 30 f. Oil derrick and pipe-line at Hassi-Massaoud, Sahara. HORIZ. 50 f. National Centre of Industry and Technology, Paris.

394. C. Goujon and C. Rozanoff (test pilots).

1959. Goujon and Rozanoff Commem.
1427. **394.** 20 f. chest., red & blue 20 20

395. Villehardouin (chronicler).

1959. Red Cross Fund.
1428. **395.** 15 f. + 5 f. violet-blue 50 50
1429. – 15 f. + 5 f. myrtle .. 50 50
1430. – 20 f. + 10 f. bistre .. 55 55
1431. – 20 f. + 10 f. grey .. 55 55
1432. – 30 f. + 10 f. lake .. 55 55
1433. – 30 f. + 10 f. chestnut 55 55
PORTRAITS: No. 1429, Le Notre (Royal gardener). 1430, Alembert (philosopher). 1431, Angers (sculptor). 1432, Bichat (physiologist). 1433 Bartholdi (sculptor).

396. M. Desbordes-Valmore (poet).

397. "Marianne in Ship of State".

1959. Marceline Desbordes-Valmore. Death Cent.
1434. **396.** 30 f. choc., bl. & grn. 15 12

1959.
1437. **397.** 25 f. red and black .. 20 5
See also No. 1456.

398. Tancarville Bridge.

1959. Tancarville Bridge Inaug.
1438. **398.** 30 f. grn., choc. & blue 20 12

399. Jean Jaures (Socialist leader).

400. "Giving Blood".

401. Clasped Hands of Friendship.

402. Youth throwing away Crutches.

1959. Jean Jaures. Birth Cent.
1439. **399.** 50 f. chocolate .. 25 20

1959. Europa. As T **268** of Belgium but size 22 × 36 mm.
1440. 25 f. green 25 8
1441. 50 f. violet 35 15

1959. Blood Donors' Commem.
1442. **400.** 20 f. grey and lake .. 10 8

1959. Treaty of the Pyrenees. Tercent.
1443. **401.** 50 f. chest., red & blue 30 20

1959. Infantile Paralysis Relief Campaign.
1444. **402.** 20 f. blue 12 8

403. Henri Bergson.

404. Avesnes-sur-Helpe.

406. N.A.T.O. Headquarters, Paris.

405. Abbe C. M. de l'Epee (teacher of deaf mutes).

1959. Bergson (philosopher). Birth Cent.
1445. **403.** 50 f. chestnut .. 25 20

1959.
1446. **404.** 20 f. bl., choc. & blk. 10 8
1447. – 30 f. choc., pur. & bl. 15 12
DESIGN: 30 f. Perpignan Castle.

1959. Red Cross Fund. Cross in red.
1448. **405.** 20 f. + 10 f. purple and black .. 60 60
1449. – 25 f. + 10 f. blk. & bl. 60 60
PORTRAIT: 25 f. V. Hauy (teacher of the blind).

1959. N.A.T.O. 10th Anniv.
1450. **406.** 50 f. choc., grn. & blue 60 40

1959. Frejus Disaster Fund. Surch. **FREJUS + 5 f.**
1451. **397.** 25 f. + 5 f. red & blk. 25 20
(New currency. 100 (old) francs = 1 (new) franc.

407. Sower.

408. Laon Cathedral.

1960. T **407** and previous designs but new currency.
1452. – 5 c. red & sep. (1409) 2·25 5
1470. **307.** 8 c violet* 50 5
1453. **306.** 10 c. green 10 5
1454. – 15 c. red, blue, yellow and green (1410) .. 10 5
1455. **407.** 20 c. red and turq. .. 12 5
1471. **307.** 20 c. green* .. .. 1·40 5
1456. **397.** 25 c. blue and red .. 75 5
1456a. **407.** 30 c. violet & indigo .. 95 15
1472. **307.** 40 c. brown-red* .. 2·25 50
1473. 55 c. emerald* .. 5·00 3·00
***PRECANCELS.** See note below No. 432.

1960. Air. As previous designs but new currency. New design (No. 1457b).
1457. – 2 f. pur. & bl. (1195) 80 5
1457b. – 2 f. indigo and blue .. 1·25 5
1458. – 3 f. ol. & turq (1318) 80 5
1459. **358.** 5 f. black and blue .. 1·90 15
1460. – 10 f. black, violet and sepia (1320) .. 3·15 60
DESIGN: No. 1457b, Mystere "20" jetliner.

1960. Tourist Publicity.
1461. **408.** 15 c. indigo and blue 10 5
1462. – 30 c. mar., grn. & blue 20 5
1463. – 45 c. vio., pur. & sep. 25 5
1464. – 50 c. maroon and bronze-green .. 30 5
1465. – 65 c. brown, grey-green and blue .. 25 5
1466. – 85 c. sep., grn. & blue 35 5
1467. – 1 f. vio., grn. & turq. 35 5
DESIGNS—HORIZ. 30 c. Fougeres Chateau. 65 c. Valley of the Sioule. 85 c. Chaumont Viaduct. VERT. 45 c. Kerrata Gorges, Algeria. 50 c. Tlemcen Mosque, Algeria. 1 f. Cilaos Church and Great Benard Mountains, Reunion.
See also Nos. 1485/7.

409. Pierre de Nolhac.

1960. P. de Nolhac (historian). Birth Cent.
1468. **409.** 20 c. brown 15 8

410. St. Etienne Museum.

1960. Museum of Art and Industry St. Etienne.
1469. **410.** 30 c. choc., red & blue 15 10

411. Assembly Emblem and View of Cannes.

1960. 5th Meeting of European Mayors Assembly.
1474. **411.** 50 c. chestnut & green 65 35

412. Cable-laying Ship.

413. Girl of Savoy.

414. Child Refugee.

1960. Stamp Day.
1475. **412.** 20 c. + 5 c. blue and turquoise 35 35

1960. Cent. of Attachment of Savoy and Nice to France.
1476. **413.** 30 c. bronze-green .. 25 15
1477. – 50 c. choc., red & yell. (Girl of Nice) .. 35 20

1960. Heroes of the Resistance (4th issue). Portraits inscr. as in T **364**.
1478. 20 c. black and bistre .. 45 20
1479. 20 c. lake and red .. 45 20
1480. 30 c. red-violet & violet .. 45 20
1481. 30 c. blue and indigo .. 45 20
1482. 50 c. brown & bronze-grn. 55 35
PORTRAITS: No. 1478, E. Debeaumarche. 1479, P. Masse. 1480, M. Ripoche. 1481, L. Vieljeux. 1482, Abbe Rene Bonpain.

1960. World Refugee Year.
1483. **414.** 25 c. + 10 c. indigo, brown and green .. 25 15

415. "The Road to Learning".

1960. Normal School of Strasbourg. 150th Anniv.
1484. **415.** 20 c. vio., pur. & blk. 12 8

1960. Views as T **408**.
1485. 15 c. sepia, grey and blue 12 10
1485a. 20 c. blue, green and buff 15 8
1486. 30 c. sepia, green and blue 20 12
1487. 50 c. brown, green & red 30 20
DESIGNS: 15 c. Lisieux Basilica. 20 c. Bagnoles de l'Orne. 30 c. Chateau de Blois. 50 c. La Bourboule.

416. L'Hospital (statesman).

417. "Marianne".

1960. Red Cross Fund.
1488. **416.** 10 c. + 5 c. violet and crimson 75 75
1489. – 20 c. + 10 c. blue-grn. and green 95 95
1490. 20 c. + 10 c. olive and chocolate 95 95
1491. – 30 c. + 10 c. blue and violet 95 95
1492. – 30 c. + 10 c. crimson and red 95 95
1493. – 50 c. + 15 c. indigo and slate .. .. 1·10 1·10
DESIGNS: No. 1489, Boileau (poet). 1490, Turenne (military leader). 1491, Bizet (composer). 1492, Charcot (neurologist). 1493, Degas (painter).

1960.
1494. **417.** 25 c. grey and claret 8 5

418. Cross of Lorraine.

419. Jean Bouin and Olympic Stadium.

421. Gen. Estienne, Plane and Tank.

420. Madame de Stael (after Gerard).

1960. De Gaulle's Appeal of 18th June, 1940.
1495. **418.** 20 c. brn., grn. & sepia 12 10

1960. Olympic Games.
1496. **419.** 20 c. sep., lake & blue 15 8

1960. Europa. As T **279** of Belgium, but size 36 × 22½ mm.
1497. 25 c. turquoise & emerald 15 5
1498. 50 c. purple and crimson 25 12

1960. Arms type as T **385**.
1498a. 1 c. blue and yellow .. 5 5
1498b. 2 c. yellow, green & blue 5 5
1499. 5 c. red, yell., bl. & grn. .. 10 5
1499a. 5 c. red, yellow and blue 5 5
1700. 5 c. red and blue .. 5 5
1499b. 10 c. bl., yell. & brn.-red 5 5
1499c. 12 c. red, yellow & black 5 5
1499d. 15 c. yellow, blue & red .. 5 5
1499e. 18 c. grn., bl., yell. & red 8 5
1735. 20 c. multicoloured .. 5 5
1701. 20 c. blue and brown .. 5 5
1499f. 30 c. red and blue .. 12 5
ARMS: 1 c. "Niort". 2 c. "Gueret". 5 c. (No. 1499), "Oran". 5 c. (No. 1499a), "Amiens". 5 c. (No. 1700), Auch. 10 c. "Troyes". 12 c. "Agen". 15 c. "Nevers". 18 c. "Saint-Denis (Reunion". 20 c. Saint-Lo. 25 c. Mont-de-Marsan. 30 c. "Paris".
Nos. 1700/1 and 1735 are larger, 17 × 23 mm.

1960. Madame de Stael (writer). Commem.
1500. **420.** 30 c. olive brn. & mar. 20 12

1960. Gen. Estienne. Birth Cent.
1501. **421.** 15 c. sepia and lilac .. 8 8

422. Marc Sangnier (patriot).

423. Order of the Liberation.

1960. Marc Sangnier Commem.
1502. **422.** 20 c. blk., violet & bl. 10 8

1960. Order of the Liberation. 20th Anniv.
1503. **423.** 20 c. green and black 15 10

DESIGN: 50 c. Bee-eaters of Camargue.

424. Puffins at Les Sept. Iles.

1960. Nature Protection.

1504. **424.** 30 c. multicoloured .. 20 10
1505. – 50 c. multicoloured .. 45 20

425. A. Honnorat.

426. Mace of St. Martin's Brotherhood.

1960. Andre Honnorat (philanthropist). 10th Death Anniv.

1506. **425.** 30 c. blk., grn. & blue 20 10

1960. Red Cross Fund. Cross in red.

1507. **426.** 20 c.+10 c. lake .. 60 60
1508. – 25 c.+10 c. blue .. 60 60

DESIGN: 25 c. St. Martin (after 16th-cent. wood-carving).

427. St. Barbe and College.

1960. St. Barbe College. 500th Anniv.

1509. **427.** 30 c. red, blue, sepia and bistre 20 10

DESIGN: 45 c. European green winged teal.

428. Lapwings.

1960. Study of Bird Migration. Inscr. "ETUDE DES MIGRATIONS".

1510. **428.** 20 c. multicoloured .. 20 5
1511. – 45 c. multicoloured .. 50 45

429. "Mediterranean" (after Maillol).

430. "Marianne".

1961. Aristide Maillol (sculptor). Birth Cent.

1512. **429.** 20 c. indigo and red .. 12 8

1961.

1513. **430.** 20 c. red and blue .. 5 5

431. Orly Airport.

1961. Opening of New Installations at Orly Airport.

1514. **431.** 50 c. turq., blue & blk. 25 15

432. Georges Melies.

433. Postman of Paris "Little Post" 1760.

435. Father Lacordaire (after Chasseriau).

434. Jean Nicot and Tobacco Flowers and Leaves.

1961. Georges Melies (cinematograph pioneer). Birth Cent.

1515. **432.** 50 c. indigo, ol. & vio. 45 30

1961. Stamp Day and Red Cross Fund.

1516. **433.** 20 c.+5 c. green, red and chestnut .. 20 15

1961. Introduction of Tobacco into France 4th Cent.

1517. **434.** 30 c. red, chestnut & green 15 12

1961. Father Lacordaire. Death Cent.

1518. **435.** 30 c. sepia and brown 15 12

1961. Heroes of the Resistance (5th issue). Portraits inscr. as in T **364**.

1519. 20 c. violet and blue .. 25 20
1520. 20 c. blue & bronze-green 35 25
1521. 30 c. black and chestnut .. 25 15
1522. 30 c. blue-black and blue 60 35

PORTRAITS: No. 1519, J. Renouvain. 1520, L. Dubray. 1521, P. Gateaud. 1522, Mother Elisabeth.

436. Dove, Globe and Olive Branch.

437. Deauville, 1861.

438. Du Guesclin (Constable of France).

439. Champmesle ("Roxane").

1961. World Federation of Old Soldiers Meeting, Paris.

1523. **436.** 50 c. lake, blue & green 25 15

1961. Deauville. Cent.

1524. **437.** 50 c. lake 45 35

1961. Red Cross Fund.

1525. 15 c.+5 c. blk. & maroon 55 55
1526. 20 c.+10 c. myrtle & bl. 55 55
1527. 20 c.+10 c. crim. & red .. 75 75
1528. 30 c.+10 c. blk. & chest. 75 75
1529. 45 c.+10 c. chocolate & myrtle 85 85
1530. 50 c.+15 c. violet & lake 85 85

PORTRAITS: No. 1525, T **438**. 1526, Puget (sculptor). 1527, Coulomb (physicist). 1528, Drouot. 1529, Daumier (caricaturist). 1530, Apollinaire (writer).

1961. French Actors and Actresses. Frames in crimson.

1531. **439.** 20 c. chocolate & grn. 15 10
1532. – 30 c. brown and red .. 20 15
1533. – 30 c. myrt. & yell.-grn. 20 15
1534. – 50 c. chestnut & turq. 40 25
1535. – 50 c. chocolate & olive 40 25

PORTRAITS: No. 1532, Talma ("Oreste"). 1533, Rachel ("Phedre"). 1534, Raimu ("Cesar"). 1535, Gerard Philipe ("Le Cid").

440. Mont Dore, Snow Crystal and Cable Rly.

441. Thann.

442. Pierre Fauchard.

1961. Mont Dore Commem.

1536. **440.** 20 c. purple & orange 15 10

1961. 8th Cent. of Thann.

1537. **441.** 20 c. violet, chocolate and myrtle .. 30 15

1961. Fauchard (dentistry pioneer). Bicent.

1538. **442.** 50 c. black and green 25 20

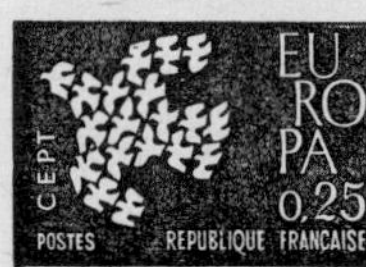

443. Doves.

1961. Europa.

1539. **443.** 25 c. vermilion .. 10 5
1540. 50 c. blue 20 12

444. Sully-sur-Loire.

1960. Tourist Publicity.

1541. – 15 c. slate, pur. & turq. 5 5
1542. – 20 c. brown and green 12 5
1543. – 30 c. bl., myrt. & sepia 12 5
1544. – 30 c. blk., grey & grn. 20 12
1545. **444.** 45 c. chest., grn. & bl. 20 5
1546. – 50 c. myrt., turq. & grn. 20 5
1547. – 65 c. bl., chest. & myrt. 20 5
1548. – 85 c. ind., chest. & myrt. 30 5
1549. – 1 f. brn., blue & myrt. 1·25 5
1550. – 1 f. chest., grn. & blue 45 5

VIEWS—HORIZ. 15 c. Saint-Paul. 30 c. (No. 1543), Arcachon. 30 c. (No. 1544), Law Courts, Rennes. 50 c. Cognac. 65 c. Dinan. 85 c. Calais. 1 f. (No. 1549), Medea, Algeria. 1 f. (No. 1550), Le Touquet-Paris-Plage, golf-bag and aircraft. VERT. 20 c. Laval, Mayenne.

See also Nos. 1619/23, 1654/7, 1684/8, 1755/61, 1794, 1814/18, 1883/5, 1929/33, 1958/61, 2005/8, 2042/4, 2062/4 and 2115/20.

445. "14th July" (R. de la Presnaye).

1961. Modern French Art.

1551. 50 c. blk., brn., grey & bl. 1·50 85
1552. 65 c. blue, green & violet 1·50 90
1553. 85 c. red, bistre and blue 2·10 1·40
1554. 1 f. multicoloured .. 2·10 1·60

PAINTINGS: 50 c. "The Messenger" (Braque). 65 c. "Blue Nudes" (Matisse). 85 c. "The Cardplayers" (Cezanne).

See also Nos. 1590/2, 1603/6, 1637/9, 1671/4, 1710/4, 1742/5, 1786/9, 1819/22, 1877/80, 1908/10, 1944/7, 1985/8, 2033/6 and 2108/13.

446. "It is so sweet to love" (Wood-carving from Roualt's "Miserere").

447. Liner "France".

1961. Red Cross Fund. Cross in red.

1555. **446.** 20 c.+10 c. black and maroon .. 80 80
1556. – 25 c.+10 c. black and maroon .. 80 80

DESIGN: 25 c. "The blind leading the blind" (from Roualt's "Miserere").

1962. Maiden Voyage of Liner "France".

1557. **447.** 30 c. blk., red & blue 20 20

448. Skier at Speed.

449. M. Bourdet.

1962. World Ski Championships, Chamonix.

1558. **448.** 30 c. violet and blue 20 20
1559. – 50 c. grn., blue & vio. 30 20

DESIGN: 50 c. Slalom-racer.

1962. Maurice Bourdet (journalist and radio commentator). 60th Birth Anniv.

1560. **449.** 30 c. grey 15 12

450. Dr. P.-F. Bretonneau.

451. Gallic Cock.

1962. Dr. Pierre-Fidele Bretonneau (medical scientist). Death Cent.

1561. **450.** 50 c. violet and blue 25 15

1962.

1562. **451.** 25 c. red, blue & brn. 10 5
1562a. 30 c. red, grn. & brn. 15 5

452. Royal Messenger of late Middle Ages.

453. Vannes.

1962. Stamp Day.

1563. **452.** 20 c.+5 c. brown, blue and red .. 30 25

1962.

1564. **453.** 30 c. blue 20 12

454. Globe and Stage Set.

455. Harbour Installations.

457. Emblem and Swamp.

456. Mount Valerien Memorial.

1962. World Theatre Day.

1565. **454.** 50 c. lake, grn. & ochre 30 25

1962. Cession of Dunkirk to France. Tercent.

1566. **455.** 95 c. pur., bis. & grn. 50 10

1962. Resistance Fighters' Memorials. (1st issue).

1567. **456.** 20 c. myrtle and drab 15 12
1568. – 30 c. indigo 20 20
1569. – 50 c. indigo and blue 25 20

MEMORIALS—VERT. 30 c. Vercors. 50 c. Ile de Sein.

See also Nos. 1609/10.

1962. Malaria Eradication.

1570. **457.** 50 c. red, blue & green 25 20

458. Nurses and Child.

459. Glider and Stork.

461. "Selecting a Tapestry".

460. Emblem and School of Horology.

1962. National Hospitals Week.

1571. **458.** 30 c. brn., grey & grn. 15 12

1962. Civil and Sports Aviation.

1572. **459.** 15 c. choc. & chest.. 8 8
1573. – 20 c. crimson & purple 12 10

DESIGN: 20 c. Early aircraft and modern light 'planes.

1962. School of Horology, Besançon. Cent.

1574. **460.** 50 c. vio., brown & red 30 25

1962. Manufacture of Gobelin Tapestries. Tercent.

1575. **461.** 50 c. blue-green, red and yellow-green .. 25 20

462. Pascal (philosopher).

463. Denis Papin (inventor).

464. "Modern" Rose.

465. Europa "Tree".

1962. Pascal. Death Tercent.

1576. **462.** 50 c. red & grey-green 25 20

1962. Red Cross Fund.

1577. 15 c.+5 c. sepia & bl.-grn. 50 50
1578. 20 c.+10 c. brn. & claret 55 55
1579. 20 c.+10 c. sl.-bl. & grey 55 55
1580. 30 c.+10 c. indigo & bl. 55 55
1581. 45 c.+15 c. mar. & chest. 55 55
1582. 50 c.+20 c. black & blue 90 90

DESIGNS: No. 1577, T **463**. 1578, Edme Bouchardon (sculptor). 1579, Joseph Lakanal (politician). 1580, Gustave Charpentier (composer). 1581, Edouard Estaunie (writer). 1582, Hyacinthe Vincent (scientist).

1962. Rose Culture.

1583. **464.** 20 c. red, green & olive 15 12
1584. – 30 c. rose, myrtle & ol. 25 20

DESIGN: 30 c. "Old fashioned" rose.

1962. Europa.

1585. **465.** 25 c. violet 12 5
1586. 50 c. chestnut 25 12

466. Telecommunications Centre, Pleumeur Bodou.

1962. 1st Trans-Atlantic Telecommunications Satellite Link.

1587. **466.** 25 c. buff, green & grey 12 5
1588. – 50 c. bl., grn. & indigo 25 20
1589. – 50 c. chocolate and blue 25 20

DESIGN: 50 c. (1588), "Telstar" satellite, globe and television receiver. 50 c. (1589), Radio telescope, Nancay (Cher).

1962. French Art. As T **445**.

1590. 50 c. multicoloured .. 1·60 1·00
1591. 65 c. multicoloured .. 1·25 85
1592. 1 f. multicoloured .. 2·25 1·60

PAINTINGS—HORIZ. 50 c. "Bonjour, Monsieur Courbet" (Courbet). 65 c. "Madame Manet on a Blue Sofa" (Manet). VERT. 1 f. "Officer of the Imperial Horse Guards" (Gericault).

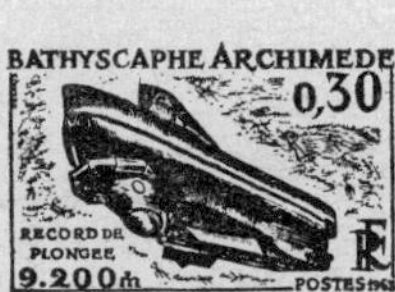

467. "Rosalie Fragonard" (Fragonard).

468. Bathyscaphe "Archimede".

1962. Red Cross Fund. Cross in red.

1593. **467.** 20 c.+10 c. choc. .. 50 50
1594. – 25 c.+10 c. green .. 50 50

PORTRAIT: 25 c. "Child as Pierrot" (after Fragonard).

1963. Record Undersea Dive.

1595. **468.** 30 c. black and blue .. 20 15

469. Flowers and Nantes Chateau.

1963. Nantes Flower Show.

1596. **469.** 30 c. blue, red & green 20 10

470. Jacques Amyot (Bishop of Auxerre).

DESIGNS: No. 1597, T **470**. 1598, Etienne Mehul (composer). 1599, Pierre de Marivaux (dramatist). 1600, N.-L. Vauquelin (chemist). 1601, Jacques Daviel (oculist). 1602, Alfred de Vigny (poet).

1963. Red Cross Fund.

1597. 20 c.+10 c. mar., slate-purple and red-violet 35 35
1598. 20 c.+10 c. maroon, orange and blue .. 35 35
1599. 30 c.+10 c. green and maroon .. 35 35
1600. 30 c.+10 c. black, purple and drab 35 35
1601. 50 c.+20 c. olive, ochre and blue 40 40
1602. 50 c.+20 c. black, slate-blue and chocolate .. 45 45

1963. French Art. As T **445**.

1603. 50 c. multicoloured .. 1·90 1·25
1604. 85 c. multicoloured .. 1·25 80
1605. 95 c. multicoloured .. 70 45
1606. 1 f. multicoloured .. 3·75 2·75

DESIGNS—VERT. 50 c. "Jacob's Struggle with the Angel" (Delacroix). 85 c. "The Married Couple of the Eiffel Tower" (Chagall). 95 c. "The Fur Merchants" (stained glass window, Chartres Cathedral). 1 f. "St. Peter and the Miracle of the Fishes" (stained glass window, Church of St. Foy de Conches).

471. Roman Post Chariot.

472. Woman reaching for Campaign Emblem.

473. Glieres Memorial.

1963. Stamp Day.

1607. **471.** 20 c.+5 c. dull purple and yellow-brown 20 20

1963. Freedom from Hunger.

1608. **472.** 50 c. chestnut & myrtle 30 25

1963. Resistance Fighters' Memorials (2nd issue).

1609. **473.** 30 c. olive & chocolate 20 20
1610. – 50 c. blue-black .. 25 25

DESIGN: 50 c. Deportees Memorial, Ile de la Cite (Paris).

474. Beethoven (West Germany).

1963. Celebrities of European Economic Community Countries.

1611. **474.** 20 c. ind., brn. & grn. 25 20
1612. – 20 c. blk., vio. & clar. 20 20
1613. – 20 c. ind., mar. & olive 20 20
1614. – 20 c. choc., pur. & brn. 20 20
1615. – 30 c. sep., vio. & brn. 25 25

PORTRAITS AND VIEWS: No. 1611, (Birthplace and Modern Bonn). No. 1612, Emile Verhaeren (Belgium: Family grave and residence, Roisin). 1613, Giuseppe Mazzini (Italy: Marcus Aurelius statue and Appian way, Rome). 1614, Emile Mayrisch (Luxembourg: Colpach Chateau and Steel Plant, Esch). 1615, Hugo de Groot (Netherlands: Palace of Peace, The Hague, and St. Agatha's Church, Delft).

475. Hotel des Postes, Paris.

476. College Building.

1963. Paris Postal Conf. Cent.

1616. **475.** 50 c. sepia 25 15

1963. Louis the Great College, Paris. 4th Cent.

1617. **476.** 30 c. myrtle 15 12

477. St. Peter's Church and Castle Keep, Caen.

1963. 36th French Philatelic Societies' Federation Congress, Caen.

1618. **477.** 30 c. brown & grey-bl. 20 15

1963. Tourist Publicity. As T **444**. Inscr. "1963".

1619. 30 c. ochre, indigo & green 12 5
1620. 50 c. red, blue & blue-green 15 5
1621. 60 c. red, blue-green & bl. 25 5
1622. 85 c. maroon, blue-green and yellow-green .. 40 5
1623. 95 c. black 40 12

DESIGNS—HORIZ. 30 c. Amboise Chateau. 50 c. Cote d'Azur, Var. 85 c. Vittel. VERT. 60 c. Saint-Flour. 95 c. Church and cloisters, Moissac.

478. Water-skiing.

1963. World Water-skiing Championships, Vichy.

1624. **478.** 30 c. blk., red & bl.-grn. 12 8

479. "Co-operation".

480. "Child with Grapes" (Angers).

1963. Europa.

1625. **479.** 25 c. red-brown .. 15 10
1626. 50 c. emerald .. 25 15

1963. Red Cross Fund. Cross in red.

1627. **480.** 20 c.+10 c. black .. 35 35
1628. – 25 c.+10 c. green .. 35 35

DESIGN: 25 c. "The Piper" (Manet).

481. "Philately".

1963. "PHILATEC 1964" Int. Stamp Exn., Paris (1st issue).

1629. **481.** 25 c. red, green & grey 12 5

See also Nos. 1640/3 and 1651.

482. Radio—T.V. Centre.

1963. Opening of Radio—T.V. Centre, Paris.

1630. **482.** 20 c. slate, olive and chestnut 10 5

483. Emblems of C.P. Services.

484. Paralytic at Work in Invalid Chair.

486. "Deportation".

485. 18th-century Courier.

1964. Civil Protection.

1631. **483.** 30 c. blue, red & orge. 12 8

1964. Professional Rehabilitation of Paralytics.

1632. **484.** 30 c. brown, chestnut and green 12 8

1964. Stamp Day.

1633. **485.** 20 c.+5 c. myrtle .. 20 12

1964. Liberation. 20th Anniv. (1st issue).

1634. **486.** 20 c.+5 c. slate .. 15 15
1635. – 50 c.+5 c. green .. 25 25

DESIGN: 50 c. "Resistance" (memorial). See also Nos. 1652/3 and 1658.

487. Pres. Rene Coty.

488. "Blanc" 2 c. Stamp of 1900.

1964. Pres. Coty Commem.

1636. **487.** 30 c.+10 c. sep. & lake 20 20

1964. French Art. As T **445**.

1637. 1 f. multicoloured .. 1·90 1·00
1638. 1 f. blue, grn., sepia & buff 1·60 80
1639. 1 f. multicoloured 60 45

DESIGNS—VERT. No. 1637, Jean le Bon (attributed to Girard of Orleans). 1638, Tomb plaque of Geoffrey IV (12th-century "champleve" (grooved) enamel from Limousin). 1639, "The Lady with the Unicorn" (15th-century tapestry).

1964. "PHILATEC 1964" Int. Stamp Exn., Paris (2nd issue).

1640. – 30 c. blue, sep. & chest. 15 15
1641. **488.** 25 c. claret and bistre 15 15
1642. – 25 c. blue and bistre 15 15
1643. – 30 c. red, sepia & turq. 15 15

DESIGNS: No. 1640, "Postal Mechanization" (letter-sorting equipment and parcel conveyor). No. 1642, "Mouchon" 25 c. stamp of 1900. No. 1643, "Telecommunications" (telephone dial, teleprinter and T.V. tower).

1964. Night Airmail Service. 25th Anniv. As T **390** but additionally inscr. "25E ANNIVERSAIRE" and colours changed.

1644. **390.** 25 c. black, brown-red, green and blue .. 12 5

489. Stained Glass Window.

490. Calvin.

1964. Notre Dame, Paris. 800th Anniv.

1645. **489.** 60 c. multicoloured .. 55 45

1964. Calvin (reformer). 400th Death Anniv.

1646. **490.** 30 c.+10 c. brown, sepia and blue-green 20 20

491. Gallic Coin.

492. Pope Sylvester II.

1964.

1647. **91.** 10 c. brown & green* 50 5
1647a. 15 c. brown & orange* 20 5
1647b. 22 c. violet & green* .. 15 5
1647c. 25 c. brown & violet* .. 25 5
1647d. 26 c. brown & purple* 8 5
1647e. 30 c. brn. & light brn.* 10 5
1647f. 35 c. bl. & red* .. 20 5
1647g. 42 c. red and orange* .. 12 5
1648. 45 c. brown & green* .. 12 5
1648a. 48 c. brn. & bl.* .. 12 5
1648b. 50 c. brown & blue* .. 45 5

1648c. 50 c. brn. & grn.* .. 10 5
1648d. 52 c. brn. & red* .. 10 5
1648e. 60 c. brn. & lilac* .. 12 5
1648f. 62 c. brn. & mve.* .. 15 8
1648g. 70 c. brn. & bl.* .. 70 15
1649. 70 c. red & mve.* .. 15 5
1649a. 90 c. brn. & red* .. 35 12
1649b. 90 c. brn. & pink* .. 20 12
1649c. 95 c. brn. & dark brn.* 25 12
1649d. 1 f. 35, brn. & grn.* .. 35 12
1649e. 1 f. 60, brn. & violet* 35 15
1649f. 1 f. 70, brn. & blue* .. 40 20
*PRECANCELS. See note below No. 432.

1964. Pope Sylvester II Commemoration.
1650. **492.** 30 c.+10 c. pur. & grey 25 25

493. Rocket and Horseman.

1964. "PHILATEC 1964" Int. Stamp Exn., Paris (3rd issue).
1651. **493.** 1 f. blue, red & brown 7·50 7·50
No. 1651 issued in sheets of 8 stamps (2×4) with stamp-size *se-tenant* labels bearing the "PHILATEC" emblem. Sold only at 4 francs incl. entrance fee to the Exhibition.

494. Landings in Normandy and Provence.

1964. Liberation. 20th Anniv. (2nd issue).
1652. **494.** 30 c.+5 c. sep., chestnut & slate-blue 15 15
1653. – 30 c.+5 c. claret, sepia & chestnut 25 25
DESIGN: No. 1653, Taking prisoners in Paris, and tank in Strasbourg.

1964. Tourist Publicity. As T **444**. Inscr. "1964".
1654. 40 c. brn., grn. & chest... 15 5
1655. 70 c. maroon, blue-green and indigo .. 25 5
1656. 1 f. 25 myrtle, blue & bistre 55 15
1657. 1 f. 30 chestnut, chocolate and brown 45 8
DESIGNS—HORIZ. 40 c., 1 f. 25, Notre-Dame Chapel, Haut-Ronchamp (Haut-Saone). VERT. 70 c. Caesar's Tower, Provins. 1 f. 30, Joux Chateau (Doubs).

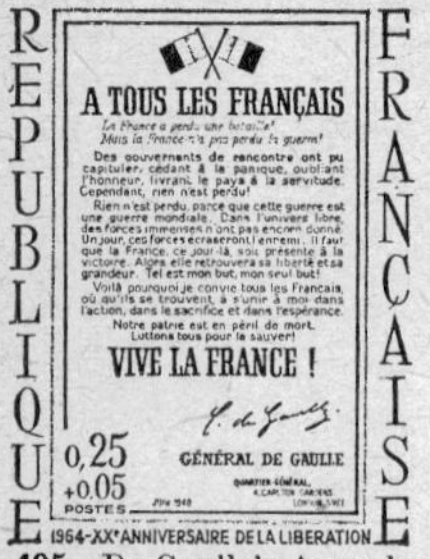

495. De Gaulle's Appeal of 18th June, 1940.

496. Judo.

1964. Liberation. 20th Anniv. (3rd issue).
1658. **495.** 25 c.+5 c. black, red and blue .. 20 20

1964. Olympic Games. Tokyo.
1659. **496.** 50 c. maroon and blue 20 12

497. G. Mandel (statesman).

498. Soldiers departing for the Marne by taxi-cab.

1964. Georges Mandel. 20th Death Anniv.
1660. **497.** 30 c. brown-purple .. 15 15

1964. Victory of the Marne. 50th Anniv.
1661. **498.** 30 c. black, red & blue 20 12

499. Europa "Flower".

500. Co-operation.

1964. Europa.
1662. **499.** 25 c. lake, brn. & grn. 12 5
1663. 50 c. lake, grn. & vio. 20 10

1964. French, African and Malagasy Co-operation.
1664. **500.** 25 c. choc., blue & brn. 8 5

501. J. N. Corvisart (physician). **502.** La Rochefoucauld.

1964. Red Cross Fund.
1665. **501.** 20 c.+10 c. black and red 25 15
1666. – 25 c.+10 c. black and red .. 25 15
DESIGN: 25 c. D. Larrey (military surgeon).

1965. Red Cross Fund. Inscr. "1965".
1667. **502.** 30 c.+10 c. blue and chestnut .. 30 25
1668. – 30 c.+10 c. brown and red .. 30 25
1669. – 40 c.+10 c. slate and brown .. 35 35
1670. – 40 c.+10 c. brown, blue & chestnut 35 35
PORTRAITS: No. 1668, Nicolas Poussin (painter). 1669, Paul Dukas (composer). 1670. Charles d'Orleans.

1965. French Art. As T **445**.
1671. 1 f. multicoloured .. 45 35
1672. 1 f. multicoloured .. 35 25
1673. 1 f. multicoloured .. 35 25
1674. 1 f. black, rose and red .. 35 25
DESIGNS—VERT. No. 1671, "L'Anglaise du 'Star' au Havre" (Toulouse-Lautrec). 1673, "The Apocalypse" (14th-century tapestry). HORIZ. 1672, "Hunting with Falcons" (miniature from manuscript "Les Tres Riches Heures du Duc de Berry", by the Limbourg brothers). 1674, "The Red Violin" (R. Dufy).

503. Packet-steamer "La Guienne".

504. Deportees.

1965. Stamp Day.
1675. **503.** 25 c.+10 c. black, green and blue .. 30 30

1965. Return of Deportees. 20th Anniv.
1676. **504.** 40 c. green 25 15

505. Youth Club.

506. Girl with Bouquet.

507. Allied Flags and Broken Swastika. **508.** I.T.U. Emblem, "Syncom", Morse Key and Pleumeur-Bodou Centre.

1965. Youth Clubs ("Maisons des Jeunes et de la Culture"). 20th Anniv.
1677. **505.** 25 c. indigo, brn. & grn. 20 8

1965. "Welcome and Friendship" Campaign.
1678. **506.** 60 c. red, orge. & grn. 25 20

1965. Victory in World War II. 20th Anniv.
1679. **507.** 40 c. red, blue & black 12 5

1965. I.T.U. Cent.
1680. **508.** 60 c. brown, blk. & bl. 20 15

509. Croix de Guerre. **510.** Bourges Cathedral.

1965. Croix de Guerre. 50th Anniv.
1681. **509.** 40 c. brown, red & grn. 15 12

1965. National Congress of Philatelic Societies, Bourges.
1682. **510.** 40 c. brown and blue 20 8

511. Stained Glass Window.

1965. Sens Cathedral. 800th Anniv.
1683. **511.** 1 f. multicoloured .. 35 25

1965. Tourist Publicity. As T **444**. Inscr. "1965".
1684. 50 c. blue, green and bistre 20 5
1685. 60 c. brown and blue .. 25 5
1686. 75 c. chocolate, grn. & blue 60 12
1687. 95 c. brown, green & blue 35 8
1688. 1 f. grey, green and brown 35 8
DESIGNS—HORIZ. 50 c. Moustiers Ste. Marie (Basses-Alpes). 95 c. Landscape, Vendee. 1 f. Monoliths, Carnac. VERT. 60 c. Yachting, Aix-les-Bains. 75 c. Tarn gorges.

512. Mont Blanc from Chamonix.

513. Europa "Sprig".

1965. Opening of Mont Blanc Road Tunnel.
1689. **512.** 30 c. violet, blue & plum 20 5

1965. Europa.
1690. **513.** 30 c. red 15 5
1691. 60 c. grey 25 15

514. Etienne Regnault and "Le Taureau".

515. "One Million Hectares".

1965. Colonisation of Reunion. Tercent.
1692. **514.** 30 c. blue and red .. 10 5

1965. Reafforestation.
1693. **515.** 25 c. brown, yellow-green and green .. 8 5

516. Atomic Reactor and Emblems. **517.** Aviation School, Salon-de-Provence.

1965. Atomic Energy Commission. 20th Anniv.
1694. **516.** 60 c. black and blue.. 20 15

1965. Aviation School. 30th Anniv.
1695. **517.** 25 c. green ind. & blue 8 5

518. Rocket "Diamant".

1965. Launching of 1st French Satellite.
1696. **518.** 30 c. blue, greenish blue and indigo .. 12 12
1697. – 60 c. blue, greenish blue and indigo .. 25 15
DESIGN: 60 c. Satellite "A1". Nos. 1696/7 were printed in sheets of 16 (2×8) giving 8 horiz. strips with a halfstamp size "se tenant" label in the centre inscr. "MISE SUR ORBITE DU PREMIER SATELLITE FRANCAIS 26 NOVEMBER 1965".

519. "Le Bebe a la Cuiller".

520. St. Pierre Fourier and Basilica, Mattaincourt (Vosges).

1965. Red Cross Fund. Paintings by Renoir.
1698. **519.** 25 c.+10 c. indigo and red 20 15
1699. – 30 c.+10 c. brown and red 20 15
DESIGN: 30 c. "Coco ecrivant" (portrait of Renoir's small son writing).

1966. Red Cross Fund.
1702. **520.** 30 c.+10 c. sepia and green .. 15 15
1703. – 30 c.+10 c. maroon and emerald .. 15 15
1704. – 30 c.+10 c. indigo, brown and green 15 15
1705. – 30 c.+10 c. bl. & brn. 15 15
1706. – 30 c.+10 c. brown and green .. 20 20
1707. – 30 c.+10 c. black and brown .. 20 20
DESIGNS: No. 1703, F. Mansard (architect) and Carnavalet House, Paris. 1704, M. Proust (writer) and St. Hilaire Bridge, Illiers (Eure-et-Loir). 1705, G. Faure (composer), statuary and music. 1706, Hippolyte Taine (philosopher) and birthplace. 1707, Elie Metchnikoff (scientist), microscope and Pasteur Institute.

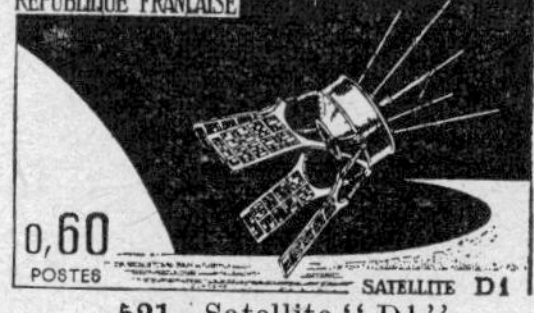

521. Satellite "D1".

1966. Launching of Satellite "D1".
1708. **521.** 60 c. red, blue & grn. 20 15

522. Engraving a die.

523. "Knight" and chess-board.

1966. Stamp Day.
1709. **522.** 25 c.+10 c. choc., slate and brown 20 20

1966. French Art. As T **445**.
1710. 1 f. bronze, green & mar. 30 25
1711. 1 f. multicoloured .. 35 35
1712. 1 f. multicoloured .. 30 25
1713. 1 f. multicoloured .. 35 25
1714. 1 f. multicoloured .. 35 25
DESIGN—HORIZ. No. 1710, Detail of Vix Crater (wine-bowl). 1711, "The New-born Child" (G. de la Tour). 1712, "Baptism of Judas" (stained glass window, Sainte Chapelle, Paris). 1714, "Crispin and Scapin" (after H. Daumier). VERT. 1713, "The Moon and the Bull" (Lurcat tapestry).

1966. Int. Chess Festival, L. Havre.
1715. **523.** 50 c. grey, brn. & violet 30 15

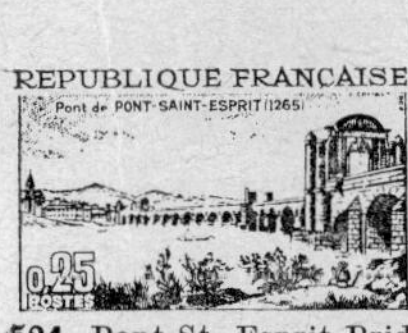

524. Pont St. Esprit Bridge. 525. St. Michel.

1966. Pont St. Esprit. 700th Anniv.
1716. 524. 25 c. black and blue . . 10 5

1966. Mont St. Michel. Millenary.
1717. 525. 25 c. brown, red, green and yellow 12 5

526. King Stanislas, Arms and Palace.

1966. Reunion of Lorraine and Barrois with France. Bicent.
1718. 526. 25 c. brown, grn. & bl. 10 5

527. Niort. 528. "Angel of Verdun".

1966. National Congress of Philatelic Societies, Niort.
1719. 527. 40 c. slate, green & blue 20 10

1966. Verdun Victory. 50th Anniv.
1720. 528. 50 c. + 5 c. slate, blue and green 15 15

529. Fontenelle.

1966. Academy of Sciences. Tercent.
1721. 529. 60 c. chocolate & lake 25 12

530. William the Conqueror, Castle and Landings.

1966. Battle of Hastings. 900th Anniv.
1722. 530. 60 c. chestnut and blue 25 20

531. Globe and Railway Track.

532. Oleron Bridge. 533. Europa "Ship".

1966. 19th Int. Railway Congress, Paris.
1723. 531. 60 c. brown, blue & lake 20 15

1966. Oleron Bridge. Opening.
1724. 532. 25 c. brn., grn. & blue 10 5

1966. Europa.
1725. 533. 30 c. blue 10 5
1726. 60 c. red 20 12

534. Vercingetorix.

1966. History of France. (1st Series). Inscr. "1966".
1727. 534. 40 c. brn., blue & grn. 12 8
1728. – 40 c. brown and black 12 8
1729. – 60 c. cerise, brn. & vio. 20 10

DESIGNS—VERT. 40 c. (1728), Clovis. 60 c. Charlemagne.

See also Nos. 1769/71, 1809/11, 1850/2, 1896/8, 1922/4, 1975/7 and 2017/19.

535. Route Map. 536. Chateau de Val.

1966. Paris Pneumatic Post. Cent.
1730. 535. 1 f. 60 blue, lake & brn. 70 40

1966. Chateau de Val.
1731. 536. 2 f. 30 brn., grn. & bl. 80 5

537. Rance Barrage. 538. Nurse tending wounded soldier (1859).

1966. Rance River Tidal Power Station. Inaug.
1732. 537. 60 c. slate, grn. & brn. 25 10

1966. Red Cross Fund. Cross in red.
1733. 538. 25 c. + 10 c. green . . 25 25
1734. – 30 c. + 10 c. indigo . . 25 25

DESIGN: 30 c. Nurse tending young girl (1966).

539. Beaumarchais (playwright). 540. Congress Emblem.

1967. Red Cross Fund.
1736. 539. 30 c. + 10 c. violet and lake . . 15 12
1737. – 30 c. + 10 c. bl. & ind. 15 12
1738. – 30 c. + 10 c. purple and chestnut . . 15 12
1739. – 30 c. + 10 c. violet and bluish violet 15 12

PORTRAITS: No. 1737, Emile Zola (writer). 1738, A. Camus (writer). 1739, St. Francois de Sales (reformer).

1967. 3rd Int. Congress of European Broadcasting Union (U.E.R.).
1740. 540. 40 c. red and blue . . 15 5

541. Postman of the Second Empire. 542. Winter Olympics Emblem.

1967. Stamp Day.
1741. 541. 25 c. + 10 c. green, red and blue . . 20 20

1967. French Art. As T 445.
1742. 1 f. multicoloured . . 35 25
1743. 1 f. multicoloured . . 35 25
1744. 1 f. brown, blue and black 35 25
1745. 1 f. multicoloured . . 35 25

DESIGNS—HORIZ. No. 1742, "Old Juniet's Trap" (after H. Rousseau). 1745, "The Window-makers" (stained glass window, St. Madeleine's Church, Troyes). VERT. 1743, "Francois I" (after Jean Clouet). 1744, "The Bather" (Ingres).

1967. Publicity for Winter Olympic Games, Grenoble (1968).
1746. 542. 60 c. red and blue . . 20 12

543. French Pavilion.

545. Nungesser and Coli, and "The White Bird" (aircraft). 544. Cogwheels.

1967. World Fair, Montreal.
1747. 543. 60 c. green and blue 20 10

1967. Europa.
1748. 544. 30 c. blue and grey . . 10 5
1749. 60 c. brown and blue 20 12

1967. Trans-Atlantic Flight Attempt by Nungesser and Coli. 40th Anniv.
1750. 545. 40 c. bl., brn. & mar. 15 10

546. Great Bridge, Bordeaux. 547. Gouin Mansion, Tours.

1967. Great Bridge, Bordeaux. Inaug.
1751. 546. 25 c. black, olive & brn. 8 5

1967. National Congress of Philatelic Societies, Tours.
1752. 547. 40 c. brown, blue & red . 15 8

548. Gaston Ramon (vaccine pioneer) and College Gates.

1967. Alfort Veterinary School, Bicent.
1753. 548. 25 c. brown, grn. & bl. 10 5

549. Esnault-Pelterie, Rocket and Satellite.

1967. Robert Esnault-Pelterie (rocket pioneer). 10th Death Anniv.
1754. 549. 60 c. indigo and blue 25 15

1967. Tourist Publicity. As T 444. Inscr. "1967".
1755. 50 c. sepia, slate and blue 15 5
1756. 60 c. chocolate and blue 20 5
1757. 70 c. brown, blue and red 25 5
1758. 75 c. blue, lake & chestnut 25 10
1759. 95 c. violet, green & blue 30 15
1760. 1 f. indigo 30 5
1761. 1 f. 50 red, blue and green 40 5

DESIGNS—VERT. 50 c. Town Hall, St. Quentin (Aisne). 60 c. Clock-tower and gateway, Vire (Calvados). 1 f. Rodez Cathedral. 1 f. 50, Morlaix—views and carved buttress. HORIZ. 70 c. St. Germain-en-Laye Chateau. 75 c. La Baule. 95 c. Boulogne-sur-Mer.

550. Orchids. 551. Scales of Justice.

1967. Orleans Flower Show.
1762. 550. 40 c. red, pur. & violet 15 8

1967. 9th Int. Accountancy Congress, Paris.
1763. 551. 60 c. chest., bl. & mar. 20 12

552. Servicemen and Cross of Lorraine. 553. Marie Curie and Pitchblende.

1967. Battle of Bir-Hakeim. 25th Anniv.
1764. 552. 25 c. ult., blue & brn. 8 5

1967. Marie Curie. Birth Cent.
1765. 553. 60 c. ultramarine & bl. 20 12

554. Lions Emblem. 555. "Republique".

1967. Lions Int. 50th Anniv.
1766. 554. 40 c. violet and lake 12 5

1967.
1767. 555. 25 c. blue 35 5
1768. 30 c. purple 45 5
1843. 30 c. green 15 5
1768b. 40 c. cerise 12 5

See also No. 1882.

1967. History of France (2nd Series). As T 534, but inscr. "1967".
1769. 40 c. ultram., slate & blue 12 10
1770. 40 c. black and slate . . 12 10
1771. 60 c. green and chocolate 20 10

DESIGNS—HORIZ. No. 1769, Hugues Capet elected King of France. VERT. 1770, Philippe Auguste at Bouvines. 1771, Saint-Louis receiving poor.

556. "Flautist". 557. Anniversary Medal.

1967. Red Cross Fund. Ivories in Dieppe Museum. Cross in red.
1772. 556. 25 c. + 10 c. maroon and violet . . 20 20
1773. – 30 c. + 10 c. maroon and green . . 20 20

DESIGN: 30 c. "Violinist".

1968. Postal Cheques Service. 50th Anniv.
1774. 557. 40 c. bistre and green 15 10

558. Cross-country Skiing and Ski-jumping. 559. Road Signs.

1968. Winter Olympic Games, Grenoble.
1775. 30 c. + 10 c. brown, slate and vermilion . . 12 12
1776. 40 c. + 10 c. purple and bistre 20 20
1777. 60 c. + 20 c. vermilion, purple and green . . 25 25
1778. 75 c. + 25 c. maroon, green and purple . . 40 40
1779. 95 c. + 35 c. brown, magenta and blue . . 55 55

DESIGNS: 30 c. T 558. 40 c. Ice-hockey. 60 c. Olympic flame. 75 c. Figure-skating. 95 c. Slalom.

1968. Road Safety.
1780. 559. 25 c. red, blue and purple 8 5

560. Rural Postman of 1830. **561.** F. Couperin (composer) and Concert Instruments.

1968. Stamp Day.
1781. **560.** 25 c.+10 c. indigo, blue and red .. 20 20

1968. Red Cross Fund. Inscr. "1968".
1782. **561.** 30 c.+10 c. lilac and violet 20 20
1783. – 30 c.+10 c. brown and green .. 20 20
1784. – 30 c.+10 c. red and brown 20 20
1785. – 30 c.+10 c. maroon and lilac .. 20 20
DESIGN: No. 1783, General Desaix, and death scene at Marengo. 1784, Saint Pol-Roux (poet) and "Evocation of Golgotha". 1785, Paul Claudel (poet) and "Joan of Arc".

1968. French Art. As T **445.**
1786. 1 f. multicoloured .. 40 25
1787. 1 f. multicoloured .. 45 25
1788. 1 f. olive and red .. 45 25
1789. 1 f. multicoloured .. 45 25
DESIGNS—HORIZ. No. 1786, Wall painting, Lascaux. 1787, "Arearea" (Gauguin). VERT. 1788, "La Danse" (relief by Bourdelle in Champs-Elysees Theatre, Paris). 1789, "Portrait of a Model" (Renoir).

562. Congress Palace, Royan. **564.** Alain R. Le Sage.

563. Europa "Key".

1968. World Co-operation Languages Conf., Royan.
1790. **562.** 40 c. blue, brn. & grn. 15 8

1968. Europa.
1791. **563.** 30 c. brown and purple 10 5
1792. 60 c. claret and brown 20 12

1968. Le Sage (writer). 300th Birth Anniv.
1793. **564.** 40 c. purple and blue 15 5

1968. Tourist Publicity. As T **444,** but inscr. "1968".
1794. 60 c. blue, purple & green 20 10
DESIGN—HORIZ. 60 c. Langeais Chateau.

565. Pierre Larousse (encyclopedist). **566.** Forest Trees.

1968. Larousse Commem.
1795. **565.** 40 c. brown & violet 15 5

1968. Link of Black and Rambouillet Forests.
1796. **566.** 25 c. brn., grn. & blue 8 5

567. Presentation of the Keys, and Map.

1968. Papal Enclave, Vaireas. 650th Anniv.
1797. **567.** 60 c. vio., bistre & brn. 20 12

568. Louis XIV, and Arms of Flanders and France.

1968. (First) Treaty of Aix-la-Chapelle. 300th Anniv.
1798. **568.** 40 c. lake, bistre & grey 15 5

569. Martrou Bridge, Rochefort.

1968. Martrou Bridge. Inaug.
1799. **569.** 25 c. blk., choc. & bl. 8 5

570. Letord "Lorraine" Military Biplane and Route-map. **571.** Tower of Constance, Aigues-Mortes.

1968. 1st Regular Internal Airmail Service. 50th Anniv.
1800. **570.** 25 c. indigo, blue & red 8 5

1968. Release of Huguenot Prisoners Bicent.
1801. **571.** 25 c. mar., brn. & bl. 10 5

572. Cathedral and Old Bridge, Beziers.

1968. National Congress of Philatelic Societies, Beziers.
1802. **572.** 40 c. ochre, grn. & ind. 15 5

573. "Victory" and White Tower, Salonika. **574.** Louis XV and Arms of Corsica and France.

1968. Armistice on Salonika Front. 50th Anniv.
1803. **573.** 40 c. pur. & bright pur. 15 5

1968. Union of Corsica and France. Bicent.
1804. **574.** 25 c. bl., grn. & blk. 10 5

575. Relay-racing. **577.** "Ball of the Little White Beds" (Paris Opera), Leon Bailby and Hospital Beds.

576. Polar Landscape.

1968. Olympic Games, Mexico.
1805. **575.** 40 c. bl., grn. & brn. 20 12

1968. French Polar Exploration.
1806. **576.** 40 c. turq., red & blue 20 8

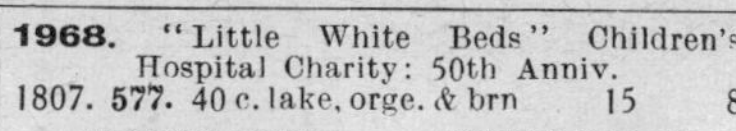

1968. "Little White Beds" Children's Hospital Charity: 50th Anniv.
1807. **577.** 40 c. lake, orge. & brn 15 8

578. "Angel of Victory" over Arc de Triomphe. **579.** "Spring".

1968. Armistice on Western Front. 50th Anniv.
1808. **578.** 25 c. blue & carmine 10 5

1968. History of France (3rd Series). Designs as T **534,** but inscr. "1968".
1809. 40 c. grn., grey & red .. 12 5
1810. 40 c. blue, grn. & brown 12 5
1811. 60 c. brown, blue & ultram. 25 10
DESIGNS—HORIZ. No. 1809, Philip the Good presiding over States-General. VERT. 1810, Death of Du Guesclin; 1811, Joan of Arc.

1968. Red Cross Fund. Cross in red.
1812. **579.** 25 c.+10 c. indigo and violet .. 20 20
1813. – 30 c.+10 c. red and brown 25 25
DESIGN: 30 c. "Autumn".
See also Nos. 1853/4.

1969. Tourist Publicity. Similar to T **444,** but inscr. "1969".
1814. 45 c. olive, chestnut & blue 20 5
1815. 70 c. brown, indigo & blue 30 12
1816. 80 c. brown, maroon & bistre 30 5
1817. 85 c. grey, blue and green 30 5
1818. 1 f. 15 brown and blue .. 45 15
DESIGNS—HORIZ. 45 c. Brou Church, Bourg-en-Bresse (Ain). 70 c. Hautefort Chateau. 80 c. Vouglans Dam, Jura. 85 c. Chantilly Chateau. 1 f. 15 La Trinite-sur-Mer, Morbihan.

1969. French Art. As T **445.**
1819. 1 f. brown and black .. 50 25
1820. 1 f. multicoloured .. 50 25
1821. 1 f. multicoloured .. 50 25
1822. 1 f. multicoloured .. 50 25
DESIGNS—VERT. No. 1819, "February" (bas-relief, Amiens Cathedral). 1820, "Philippe le Bon" (Rogier de la Pasture, called Van der Weyden). 1822, "The Circus" (Georges Seurat). HORIZ. 1821, "Savin and Cyprien appearing before Ladicius" (Romanesque painting, Church of St. Savin, Vienne).

580. "Concorde" in Flight. **582.** A. Roussel (composer).

581. Postal Horse-bus of 1890.

1969. Air. 1st Flight of "Concorde".
1823. **580.** 1 f. indigo and blue 1·25 15

1969. Stamp Day.
1824. **581.** 30 c. + 10 c. green, brown and black 20 15

1969. Red Cross Fund. Celebrities.
1825. **582.** 50 c.+10 c. ultram. 30 30
1826. – 50 c.+10 c. red .. 30 30
1827. – 50 c.+10 c. grey .. 30 30
1828. – 50 c.+10 c. chocolate 30 30
1829. – 50 c.+10 c. purple 30 30
1830. – 50 c.+10 c. green 30 30
PORTRAITS: No. 1826, General Marceau. 1827, C. A. Sainte-Beuve (writer). 1828, Marshal Lannes. 1829, G. Cuvier (anatomist and naturalist). 1830, A. Gide (writer).

583. Irises.

1969. Int. Flower Show, Paris.
1831. **583.** 45 c. multicoloured .. 20 12

584. Colonnade.

1969. Europa.
1832. **584.** 40 c. magenta .. 15 5
1833. 70 c. blue 25 12

585. Battle of the Garigliano (Italy).

1969. "Resistance and Liberation". 25th Annivs.
1834. **585.** 45 c. black & violet 20 8
1835. – 45 c. ultram., bl. & slate 20 8
1836. – 45 c. slate, bl. & grn. 20 8
1837. – 45 c. brown and slate 20 8
1838. – 45 c. ind., bl. & red 20 15
1839. – 45 c.+10 c. olive and slate .. 25 20
1840. – 70 c.+10 c. mult., 35 30
DESIGNS—VERT. No. 1835 Parachutists and Commandos ("D-Day Landings"). 1836, Memorial and Resistance fighters (Battle of Mont Mouchet). HORIZ. 1837, Troops storming Beach (Provence Landings). 1838, French Pilot, Soviet Mechanic and Fighter Aircraft (Normandy-Niemen Squadron). 1839, General Leclerc soldiers and Les Invalides (Liberation of Paris). 1840, As No. 1839, but showing Strasbourg Cathedral (Liberation of Strasbourg).

586. "Miners" (I.L.O. Monument, Geneva) and Albert Thomas (founder). **587.** Chalons-sur-Marne.

1969. Int. Labour Organisation. 50th Anniv.
1841. **586.** 70 c. brown and blue 25 10

1969. National Congress of Philatelic Societies, Chalons-sur-Marne.
1842. **587.** 45 c. ochre, blue & grn. 20 8

588. Canoeing. **590.** "Diamond Crystal" in Rain Drop.

589. Napoleon as Young Officer, and Birthplace.

1969. World Kayak-Canoeing Championships, Bourg-St. Maurice.
1844. **588.** 70 c. brown, olive & bl. 35 10

1969. Napoleon Bonaparte. Birth Bicent.
1845. **589.** 70 c. grn., violet & blue 40 12

1969. European Water Charter.
1846. **590.** 70 c. black, grn. & bl. 30 12

591. Mouflon. **592.** Aerial View of College.

1969. Nature Conservation.
1847. **591.** 45 c. black, brn. & grn. 20 8

1969. College of Arts and Manufactures, Chatenay-Malabry.
1848. **592.** 70 c. yell., orge. & grn. 30 10

593. "Le Redoutable".

1969. 1st French Nuclear Submarine, "Le Redoutable".
1849. **593.** 70 c. green and blue.. 25 12

1969. History of France (4th Series). As T **534** but inscr. "1969".
1850. 80 c. green and brown .. 35 12
1851. 80 c. brown, black & ochre 35 12
1852. 80 c. ultram., black and violet 35 12
DESIGNS—HORIZ. No. 1850, Louis XI and Charles the Bold. 1852, Henry IV and Edict of Nantes. VERT. 1851, Bayard at the Battle of Brescia.

1969. Red Cross Fund. As T **579**. Cross in red.
1853. 40 c.+15 c. brn. & choc. 30 30
1854. 40 c.+15 c. bl. & violet 30 30
DESIGNS: No. 1835, "Summer". 1836, "Winter".

594. Gerbault aboard "Firecrest". **596.** L. Le Vau (architect).

595. Gendarmerie Badge and Activities.

1970. Alain Gerbault's World Voyage.
1855. **594.** 70 c. indigo, grey & blue 35 12

1970. National Gendarmerie.
1856. **595.** 45 c. blue, grn. & brown 25 8

1970. Red Cross Fund.
1857. **596.** 40 c.+10 c. lake .. 30 30
1858. – 40 c.+10 c. blue .. 30 30
1859. – 40 c.+10 c. green.. 30 30
1860. – 40 c.+10 c. brown 30 30
1861. – 40 c.+10 c. slate.. 30 30
1862. – 40 c.+10 c. ultram. 30 30
DESIGNS: No. 1858, Prosper Merimee (writer). 1859, Philibert de l'Orme (architect). 1860, E. Branly (scientist). 1861, M. de Broglie (physicist). 1862, Alexandre Dumas (pere) (writer).

597. Handball Player. **599.** Hovertrain "Orleans" I-80.

598. Marshal Alphonse Juin and Les Invalides, Paris.

1970. 7th World Handball Championship.
1863. **597.** 80 c. green 40 15

1970. Marshal Juin Commem.
1864. **598.** 45 c. chocolate & blue 25 8

1970. 1st "Hovertrain" in Service.
1865. **599.** 80 c. drab and violet 30 15

600. Postman of 1830 and Paris Scene.

1970. Stamp Day.
1866. **600.** 40 c.+10 c. black, ultram. and red 30 15

601. P. J. Pelletier and J. B. Caventou with Formula.

1970. Discovery of Quinine. 150th Anniv.
1870. **601.** 50 c. green, mag. & blue 35 8

602. Flamingo. **603.** Rocket and Dish-aerial.

1970. Nature Conservation Year.
1871. **602.** 45 c. mag., slate & grn. 25 8

1970. "Diamant B" Rocket from Guyana. Launching.
1872. **603.** 45 c. green 25 8

604. "Health and Sickness". **605.** "Flaming Sun".

1970. W.H.O. "Fight Cancer" Day (7th April).
1873. **604.** 40 c.+10 c. magenta, brown and blue 25 12

1970. Europa.
1875. **605.** 40 c. carmine .. 15 5
1876. 80 c. blue 30 15

606. Marshal de Lattre de Tassigny and Armistice Meeting.

1970. Berlin Armistice. 25th Anniv.
1877. **606.** 40 c.+10 c. blue and greenish blue .. 25 20

1970. French Art. As T **445**.
1878. 1 f. multicoloured .. 50 25
1879. 1 f. chestnut .. 50 25
1880. 1 f. multicoloured .. 50 25
1881. 1 f. multicoloured .. 50 25
DESIGNS—VERT. No. 1874, 15th-cent Savoy Primitive painting on wood. No. 1877, "The Ballet-dancer" (Degas). HORIZ. No. 1875, "The Triumph of Flora" (sculpture by J. B. Carpeaux). No. 1876, "Diana's Return from the Hunt" (F. Boucher).

607. Arms of Lens, Miner's Lamp and Pithead.

1970. 43rd French Federation of Philatelic Societies Congress, Lens.
1881. **607.** 40 c. red 20 5

608. "Republique" and Perigueux. **609.** Javelin-thrower in Wheel-chair.

1970. Transfer of French Govt. Printing Works to Perigueux.
1882. **608.** 40 c. red 45 25
The above stamp and label were issued together se-tenant in sheets, for which special printing plates were laid down. The stamp is virtually indistinguishable from the normal 40 c. definitive No. 1768b.

1970. Tourist Publicity. As T **444**, but inscr. "1970".
1883. 50 c. purple, blue & green 20 5
1884. 95 c. choc., red & olive 30 15
1885. 1 f. green, blue & carmine 35 5
DESIGNS: 50 c. Diamond Rock, Martinique. 95 c. Chancelade Abbey (Dordogne). 1 f. Gosier Island, Guadaloupe.

1970. World Games for the Physically Handicapped, St-Etienne.
1886. **609.** 45 c. red, grn. & blue 20 8

610. Hand and Broken Chain. **611.** Observatory and Nebula.

1970. Liberation from Concentration Camps. 25th Anniv.
1887. **610.** 45 c. brown, ultramarine and blue .. 15 8

1970. Haute-Provence Observatory.
1888. **611.** 1 f. 30 vio., bl. & grn. 50 15

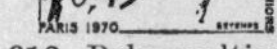

612. Pole-vaulting. **614.** Bath-House, Arc-et-Senans (Doubs).

613. Daurat and Vanier, and plane making night-landing.

1970. First European Junior Athletic Championships, Paris.
1889. **612.** 45 c. indigo, blue & pur. 20 8

1970. Air. Pioneer Aviators.
1890. **613.** 5 f. brn., grn. & blue 1·10 12
1891. – 10 f. grey, vio. & red 2·50 60
1892. – 15 f. grey, mve. & brn. 3·25 1·10
1893. – 20 f. indigo and blue 4·25 95
DESIGNS: 10 f. Helene Boucher, Maryse Hilsz and aircraft. 15 f. Henri Guillaumet, Paul Codos and flying-boat. 20 f. Jean Mermoz, A. de Saint-Exupery and "Concorde".

1970. Royal Salt Springs, Chaux (founded by N. Ledoux).
1895. **614.** 80 c. brn., green & blue 35 12

1970. History of France (5th Series). As T **534**, but inscr. "1970".
1896. 45 c. mauve, grey & black 20 12
1897. 45 c. brown, green & yell. 20 12
1898. 45 c. grey, brn. & orange 20 12
DESIGNS: No. 1896, Richelieu. No. 1897, Louis XIV. No. 1898, Louis XV at Battle of Fontenoy (after painting by H. Vernet).

615. U.N. Emblem, Headquarters, New York and Palais des Nations, Geneva.

1970. United Nations. 25th Anniv.
1899. **615.** 80 c. vio., grn. & blue 35 15

616. Bordeaux and "Ceres" Stamp.

1970. Bordeaux "Ceres" Stamp Issue. Cent.
1900. **616.** 80 c. violet and blue 40 15

617. Col. Denfert-Rochereau and "Lion of Belfort" (after Bartholdi).

1970. Belfort Siege. Cent.
1901. **617.** 45 c. blue, brn. & grn. 20 8

618. "Lord and Lady", circa 1500.

1970. Red Cross Fund. Frescoes from Dissay Chapel, Vienne. Cross in red.
1902. **618.** 40 c.+15 c. green .. 60 55
1903. – 40 c.+15 c. red .. 60 55
DESIGN: No. 1896, "Angel with instruments of mortification".

619. "Marianne." **620.** Balloon leaving Paris.

1971.
1904. **619.** 45 c. blue 12 5
1905. 50 c. red 12 5
1904a. 60 c. green 15 5
1905bp. 80 c. red 15 5
1904b. 80 c. green 12 5
1906a. 1 f. red 20 10

1971. Air. Paris Balloon Post. Cent.
1907. **620.** 95 c. multicoloured.. 75 50

1971. French Art. As T **445**.
1908. 1 f. brown 60 25
1909. 1 f. multicoloured .. 60 25
1910. 1 f. multicoloured .. 60 25
DESIGNS: No. 1908, "St. Matthew" (sculpture, Strasbourg Cathedral). No. 1909, "The Winnower" (Millet). No. 1910, "Songe Creux" (G. Rouault).

621. Ice-skaters. **622.** Diver and Underwater Craft.

1971. World Ice-skating Championships, Lyon.
1911. **621.** 80 c. ultram., bl. & ind. 35 20

1971. "Oceanexpo" Exhibition, Bordeaux.
1912. **622.** 80 c. turq. & indigo.. 35 15

623. General D. Brosset, and Fourviere Basilica, Lyon.

1971. Red Cross Fund. Celebrities.

1913. **623.** 50 c.+10 c. brn. & grn. 65 35
1914. – 50 c.+10 c. brn. & choc. 65 35
1915. – 50 c.+10 c. brn. & red 65 35
1916. – 50 c.+10 c. lilac & bl. 65 35
1917. – 50 c.+10 c. pur. & plum 65 35
1918. – 50 c.+10 c. bl. & indigo 65 35

DESIGNS: No. 1914, Esprit Auber (composer), and manuscript of "Fra Diavolo". No. 1915, Victor Grignard (chemist), and Nobel Prize for Chemistry. No. 1916, Henri Farman (aviation pioneer), and early flight. No. 1917, General C. Delestraint (Resistance leader), and "Secret Army" proclamation. No. 1918, J. Robert-Houdin (magician), and levitation act.

624. Field Post Office, World War I.

1971. Stamp Day.

1919. **624.** 50 c. + 10 c. blue, brown and bistre 35 15

625. Cape-Horner "Antoinette".

1971. French Merchant Marine. Sailing-ship era.

1920. **625.** 80 c. violet, ind. & bl. 40 25

See also Nos. 1967 and 2011.

626. Isard (Pyrenean chamois).

627. Basilica of Santa Maria, Venice.

1971. Western Pyrenees National Park. Inaug.

1921. **626.** 65 c. brn., bl. & choc. 35 15

1971. History of France (Sixth Series). As T **534** but inscr. "1971".

1922. 45 c. purple, blue & red 20 10
1923. 45 c. red, brown & blue.. 20 10
1924. 65 c. brn., purple & blue.. 25 12

DESIGNS: No. 1922, Cardinal, noble and commoner (Opening of the States-General, 1789). No. 1923, Battle of Valmy, 1792. No. 1924, Fall of the Bastille, 1789.

1971. Europa.

1925. **627.** 50 c. brown and blue 20 8
1926. – 80 c. purple 30 15

DESIGN: 80 c. Europa chain.

628. View of Grenoble. 629. A.F.R. Emblem and Town.

1971. 44th French Federation of Philatelic Societies Congress, Grenoble.

1927. **628.** 50 c. red, pink & brown 20 5

1971. Rural Family Aid. 25th Anniv. (1970).

1928. **629.** 40 c. blue, vio. & green 15 5

1971. Tourist Publicity. As T **444**, but inscr. "1971".

1929. 60 c. blk., blue & green.. 20 5
1930. 65 c. blk., violet & brown 25 5
1931. 90 c. brn., green & ochre.. 30 5
1932. 1 f. 10 brown, blue & grn. 35 8
1933. 1 f. 40 maroon, bl. & grn. 50 12

DESIGNS—VERT. 60 c. Sainte Chapelle, Riom. 65 c. Church and fountain, Dole. 90 c. Gatetower and houses, Riquewihr. 1 f. 40 Ardeche gorges. HORIZ. 1 f. 10 Fortress, Sedan.

630. Bourbon Palace, Paris.

1971. 50th Inter-Parliamentary Union Conference, Paris.

1934. **630.** 90 c. blue 35 12

631. Embroidery and Instrument-making.

1971. 1st Meeting of Crafts Guilds Assn. 40th Anniv.

1935. **631.** 90 c. purple and red.. 50 15

632. Reunion Chameleon. 633. De Gaulle in Uniform (June 1940).

1971. Nature Conservation.

1936. **632.** 60 c. grn., brn. & yell. 50 20

1971. General Charles de Gaulle Commem. and 1st Death Anniv.

1937. **633.** 50 c. black 15 10
1938. – 50 c. blue 15 10
1939. – 50 c. red 15 10
1940. – 50 c. black 15 10

DESIGNS: No. 1938, De Gaulle at Brazzaville, 1944. No. 1939, Liberation of Paris, 1944. No. 1940, De Gaulle as President of the French Republic, 1970.

Nos. 1937/40 were issued in se-tenant strips of four within the sheet, with a stamp size label showing the Cross of Lorraine in the centre of each horiz. strip.

634. Baron Portal (1st President) and First Assembly.

1971. National Academy of Medicine. 150th Anniv.

1941. **634.** 45 c. plum and purple 20 10

635. "Young Girl with Little Dog" (Greuze).

1971. Red Cross Fund. Cross in red.

1942. **635.** 30 c.+10 c. blue .. 50 50
1943. – 50 c.+10 c. brown .. 60 60

DESIGN: No. 1943, "The Dead Bird" (Greuze).

1972. French Art. As T **445**. Multicoloured.

1944. 1 f. "L'Etude" (portrait of a young girl) (Fragonard) 60 25
1945. 1 f. "Women in a Garden" (Monet) 60 25
1946. 2 f. "St. Peter presenting Pierre de Bourbon" (Master of Moulins) .. 1·10 35
1947. 2 f. "The Barges" (A. Derain).. .. .. 1·10 35

No. 1947 is horiz. the rest are vert.

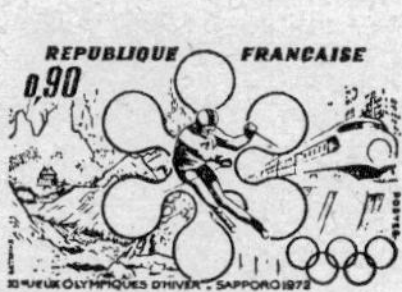

636. Penguin, Map and Ships. 637. Skier and Emblem.

1972. Discovery of Crozet Islands and Kerguelen (French Southern and Antarctic Territories). Bicent.

1948. **636.** 90 c. black, blue and orange-brown .. 60 25

1972. Winter Olympic Games, Sapporo, Japan.

1949. **637.** 90 c. red and deep olive 50 20

638. Aristide Berges (hydro-electric engineer). 639. Rural Postman of 1894.

1972. Red Cross Fund. Celebrities.

1950. **638.** 50 c. +10 c. black, grn. and emerald .. 60 60
1951. – 50 c.+10 c. black, blue and ultram. .. 60 60
1952. – 50 c.+10 c. blk., pur. and plum 60 60
1953. – 50 c.+10 c. blk., red and crimson .. 60 60
1954. – 50 c.+10 c. black, chestnut & brown 60 60
1955. – 50 c.+10 c. black, orange and red .. 60 60

DESIGNS: No. 1951, Paul de Chomedey, Sieur de Maisonneuve (founder of Montreal). No. 1952, Edouard Belin (communications scientist). No. 1953, Louis Bleriot (pioneer airman). No. 1954, Theophile Gautier (writer). No. 1955, Admiral Francois de Grasse.

1972. Stamp Day.

1956. **639.** 50 c.+10 c. blue, drab and yellow 35 30

640. Heart and W.H.O. Emblems. 641. Great Horned Owl.

1972. World Heart Month.

1957. **640.** 45 c. red, orge. & slate 25 10

1972. Tourist Publicity. As Type **444**, but inscr. "1972".

1958. 1 f. brown and yellow .. 35 5
1959. 1 f. 20 multicoloured .. 45 8
1960. 2 f. maroon & green .. 55 5
1961. 3 f. 50 multicoloured .. 1·25 15

DESIGNS—VERT. 1 f. Stag and forest, Sologne Nature Reserve. HORIZ. 1 f. 20 Charlieu Abbey. 2 f. Bazoches-du-Morvand Chateau. 3 f. 50, St. Just Cathedral, Narbonne.

1972. Nature Conservation.

1962. – 60 c. multicoloured . 45 20
1963. **641.** 65 c. brn., bistre & grey 45 20

DESIGN—HORIZ. 60 c. Salmon.

64.. "Communications". 643. "Tree of Hearts".

1972. Europa.

1964. – 50 c. purple, yell. & brn. 20 5
1965. **642.** 90 c. multicoloured.. 35 15

DESIGN: 50 c. Aix-la-Chapelle Cathedral.

1972. Post Office Employees' Blood-Donors Association. 20th Anniv.

1966. **643.** 40 c. red 20 8

644. "Cote d'Emeraude" Newfoundland Banks Fishing-boat.

1972. French Merchant Marine. Deep-sea Fishing Fleet.

1967. **644.** 90 c. blue, grn. & orge. 50 20

645. St.-Brieuc Cathedral (from lithograph of 1840).

1972. 45th French Federation of Philatelic Societies Congress, St.-Brieuc.

1968. **645.** 50 c. red 20 8

646. Hand and Code Emblems. 647. Old and New Communications.

1972. Postal Code Campaign.

1969. **646.** 30 c. red, blk. & grn. 12 5
1970. 50 c. yell., blk. & red 15 5

1972. 21st World Congress of Post Office Trade Union Federation (I.P.T.T.), Paris.

1971. **647.** 45 c. blue and grey.. 15 8

648. Hurdling. 649. Hikers on Road.

1972. Olympic Games, Munich.

1972. **648.** 1 f. green 50 15

1972. "Walking Tourism Year".

1973. **649.** 40 c. multicoloured.. 60 15

650. Cycling. 653. Nicholas Desgenettes (military physician).

652. J.-F. Champollion and Hieroglyphics.

1972. World Cycling Championships.

1974. **650.** 1 f. brn., pur. & grey 90 35

1972. History of France (7th Series). As T **534** but inscr. "1972".

1975. 45 c. purple, olive & grn. 20 10
1976. 60 c. blue, red and black.. 25 12
1977. 65 c. pur.-brn., brn. & blue 25 12

DESIGNS—VERT. 45 c. "Incroyables and Merveilleuses" (fashionable Parisians), 1794. 60 c. Napoleon Bonaparte at the Bridge of Arcole, 1796. 65 c. Discovery of antiquities, Egyptian Expedition, 1798.

1972. Translation of Egyptian Hieroglyphics by J.-F. Champollion. 150th Anniv.
1978. **652.** 90 c. brn., blue & blk. 35 15

1972. Red Cross Fund. Doctors of the 1st. Empire. Cross in red.
1979. **653.** 30 c.+10 c. green and bronze-green.. 45 35
1980. – 50 c.+10 c. red & brn. 45 35
DESIGN: No. 1980, Francois Broussuis (pathologist).

654. St. Theresa and Porch of Notre Dame, Alencon.

655. Anthurium.

1973. St. Theresa of Lisieux. Birth Cent.
1981. **654.** 1 f. indigo and blue.. 55 20

1973. Martinique Flower Cultivation.
1982. **655.** 50 c. multicoloured .. 20 5

656. National Colours of France and West Germany.

1973. Franco-German Co-operation Treaty. Tenth Anniv.
1983. **656.** 50 c. multicoloured .. 20 8

657. Polish Immigrants.

1973. Polish Immigration. 50th Anniv.
1984. **657.** 40 c. red, green & brn. 20 5

1973. French Art. As T **445.**
1985. 2 f. multicoloured .. 95 35
1986. 2 f. red and yellow .. 95 35
1987. 2 f. maroon and brown .. 95 35
1988. 2 f. multicoloured .. 80 30
DESIGNS: No. 1985, "The Last Supper" (carved capital, St. Austremoine Church, Issoire). No. 1986, "Study of a Kneeling Woman" (Charles le Brun). No. 1987, Wood-carving, Moutier d'Ahun. No. 1988, "La Finette" (girl with lute) (Watteau).

658. Admiral G. de Coligny (Protestant leader).

659. Mail Coach, circa 1835.

1973. Red Cross Fund. Celebrities' Anniversaries.
1989. **658.** 50 c.+10 c. blue, brown & purple .. 50 50
1990. – 50 c.+10 c. mauve, grey and orange .. 50 50
1991. – 50 c.+10 c. green, purple and yellow 50 50
1992. – 50 c.+10 c. brown, purple and bistre.. 50 50
1993. – 50 c.+10 c. grey, purple and brown 50 50
1994. – 50 c.+10 c. brown, lilac and blue .. 50 50
1995. – 50 c.+10 c. blue, purple and brown.. 50 50
DESIGNS: No. 1989, (400th death anniv. (1972)). No. 1990, Ernest Renan (philologist and writer) (150th birth nniv.). No. 1991, Santos-Dumont (pioneer aviator) (birth cent.). No. 1992, Colette (writer) irth cent.). No. 1993, Duguay-Trouin (naval hero) (300th birth anniv.). No. 1994, Louis Pasteur (scientist (150th birth anniv.) (1972)). No. 1995, Tony Garnier (architect) (25th death anniv.).

1973. Stamp Day.
1996. **659.** 50 c.+10 c. blue .. 25 20

660. Tuileries Palace and New Telephone Exchange.

661. Town Hall, Brussels.

1973. French Technical Achievements.
1997. **660.** 45 c. blue, grey & green 20 5
1998. – 90 c. blk., bl. & pur... 80 10
1999. – 3 f. blk., bl. & grn. .. 1·25 35
DESIGNS: 90 c. Francois I Lock, Le Havre. 3 f. European "A 300 B" airbus.

1973. Europa.
2000. **661.** 50 c. brown and red .. 20 5
2001. – 90 c. multicoloured .. 35 12
DESIGN—HORIZ. 90 c. Europa "Posthorn".

662. Guadeloupe Raccoon.

1973. Nature Conservation.
2002. **662.** 40 c. maroon, pur. & olive 12 8
2003. – 60 c. blk., bl. & red .. 25 12
DESIGN: 60 c. Alsace storks.

663. Masonic Emblem.

664. Globe and "Heart".

1973. Masonic Grand Orient Lodge of France. Bicent.
2004. **663.** 90 c. blue and purple 35 15

1973. Tourist Publicity. As T **444** but inscr. "1973".
2005. 60 c. purple, grn. & blue 20 5
2006. 65 c. violet and red .. 20 8
2007. 90 c. purple, green & blue 25 8
2008. 1 f. green, brown & blue.. 30 10
DESIGNS—VERT. 60 c. Waterfall, Doubs. 1 f. Clos-Luce, Amboise. HORIZ. 65 c. Palace of the Dukes of Burgundy, Dijon. 90 c. Gien Chateau.

1973. Academy of Overseas Sciences. 50th Anniv.
2009. **664.** 1 f. green, brn. & pur. 35 12

665. Racing-car at Speed.

667. Bell-tower, Toulouse.

666. Five-masted Barque "France II".

1973. Le Mans 24-hour Endurance Race. 50th Anniv.
2010. **665.** 60 c. blue and brown 25 12

1973. French Merchant Marine. Sailing-ship era.
2011. **666.** 90 c. green, vio. & blue 35 12

1973. 46th French Federation of Philatelic Societies Congress, Toulouse.
2012. **667.** 50 c. brown & violet.. 25 5

668. Dr. G. Hansen.

669. E. Ducretet (radio pioneer).

1973. Hansen's Identification of Leprosy Bacillus. Cent.
2013. **668.** 45 c. brn., olive & grn. 15 5

1973. 1st Eiffel Tower-Pantheon Experimental Radio Link. 75th Anniv.
2014. **669.** 1 f. green and red .. 35 8

670. Moliere in role of "Sganarelle".

671. P. Bourgoin (parachutist) and P. Kieffer (Marine commando).

1973. Moliere (playwright). 300th Death Anniv.
2015. **670.** 1 f. brown and red .. 35 12

1973. Heroes of World War II.
2016. **671.** 1 f. claret, blue & red 30 12

1973. History of France (8th Series). As Type **534**, but inscr. "1973".
2017. 45 c. maroon, grey & blue 15 8
2018. 60 c. brn., bistre & green 20 12
2019. 1 f. red, brown and green 35 12
DESIGNS—HORIZ. 45 c. Napoleon and Portalis (Preparation of Civil Code, 1800–1804). 60 c. Paris Industrial Exhibition, Les Invalides, 1806. VERT. 1 f. "The Coronation of Napoleon, 1804" (David).

672. Eternal Flame, Arc de Triomphe.

673. "Mary Magdalene".

1973. Tomb of the Unknown Soldier, Arc de Triomphe. 50th Anniv.
2020. **672.** 40 c. red, blue and lilac 15 5

1973. Red Cross Fund. Tomb Figures, Tonnerre.
2021. **673.** 30 c.+10 c. grn. & red 25 20
2022. – 50 c.+10 c. blk. & red 30 20
DESIGN: 50 c. Female saint.

674. Weathervane.

675. Figure and Human Rights Emblem.

1973. French Chambers of Agriculture. 50th Anniv.
2023. **674.** 65 c. blk., blue & grn. 20 10

1973. Declaration of Human Rights. 25th Anniv.
2024. **675.** 45 c. brn., orge. & red 15 5

676. Facade of Museum.

677. Exhibition Emblem.

1973. Opening of New Postal Museum Building.
2025. **676.** 50 c. bistre, brn. & red 10 5

1974. "ARPHILA 75" Stamp Exhibition, Paris.
2026. **677.** 50 c. brn., blue & pur. 12 5

678. St. Louis-Marie Grignion de Montfort.

679. Automatic Letter-sorting.

1974. Red Cross Fund. Celebrities' Anniversaries.
2027. **678.** 50 c.+10 c. brn., grn. and red .. 55 55
2028. – 50 c.+10 c. purple, red and blue .. 45 45
2029. – 80 c.+15 c. mve., pur. and blue .. 40 40
2030. – 80 c.+15 c. ind., bl. and purple .. 40 40
DESIGNS: No. 2028, Francis Poulenc (composer). No. 2029, Jean Giraudoux (writer). No. 2030, Jules Barbey d'Aurevilly (writer).

1974. Stamp Day.
2031. **679.** 50 c.+10 c. brn., red and green 25 15

680. "Concorde" over Airport.

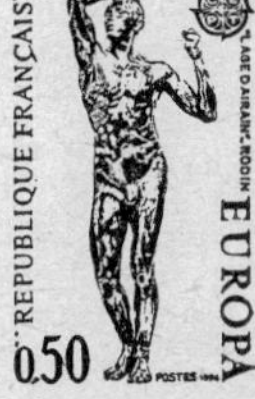

682. "The Brazen Age" (Rodin).

681. French Alps and Edelweiss.

1974. Opening of Charles de Gaulle Airport, Roissy.
2032. **680.** 60 c. violet and brown 25 12

1974. "Arphila 1975" Stamp Exhibition. French Art. As Type **445.** Multicoloured.
2033. 2 f. "Cardinal Richelieu" (P. de Champaigne) .. 75 40
2034. 2 f. "Abstract after Original Work" (J. Miro) .. 65 30
2035. 2 f. "Loing Canal" (A. Sisley) 65 30
2036. 2 f. "Homage to Nicolas Fouquet" (E. de Mathieu) 65 30

1974. French Alpine Club. Centenary.
2037. **681.** 65 c. vio., grn. & blue 25 10

1974. Europa. Sculptures.
2038. **682.** 50 c. black & purple 15 5
2039. – 90 c. brown and bistre 35 25
DESIGN—HORIZ. 90 c. "The Expression" (reclining woman) (A. Maillol).

683. Shipwreck and Modern Lifeboat.

1974. French Lifeboat Service.
2040. **683.** 90 c. blue, red & bistre 35 12

684. Council Headquarters, Strasbourg.

1974. Council of Europe. 25th Anniv.
2041. **684.** 45 c. bl., bright bl. & brn. 20 8

685. "Cornucopia of St. Florent" (Corsica). 687. General Koenig and Liberation Monuments.

686. European Bison.

1974. Tourist Publicity.

2042. – 65 c. brown & green 15 5
2043. – 1 f. 10 brown & green 30 10
2044. – 2 f. purple and blue 45 10
2045. **685.** 3 f. grn., blue & red 55 5

DESIGNS—As Type **444.** HORIZ. 65 c. Salers. 1 f. 10 Lot Valley. VERT. 2 f. Basilica of St. Nicholas-de-Port.

1974. Nature Conservation.

2046. **686.** 40 c. mar., bl. & brn. 25 5
2047. – 65 c. grey, grn. & blk. 25 12

DESIGN: 65 c. Giant Armadillo of Guiana.

1974. Liberation. 30th Anniv.

2048. – 45 c. red, blk. & grn. 15 5
2049. **687.** 1 f. red, brn. & purple 30 12
2050. – 1 f. brn., blk. and red 40 30
2051. – 1 f.+10 c. brn., grn. & bl. 40 15

DESIGNS—HORIZ. 45 c. Normandy landings 1 f. (No. 2050), Resistance medal and torch. 1 f.+10 c. Order of Liberation and towns.

688. Colmar. 689. "Chess".

1974. 47th Congress of Philatelic Societies.

2052. **688.** 50 c. red, pur. & mar. 15 5

1974. World Chess Championships, Nice.

2053. **689.** 1 f. red, brn., & blue 35 12

690. Commemorative Medallion.

1974. "Hotel des Invalides". 300th Anniv.

2054. **690.** 40 c. brn., bl. & indigo 20 5

691. French Turbotrain.

1974. Completion of Turbotrain T.G.V.001. Project.

2055. **691.** 60 c. red, black & blue 45 10

692. "Nuclear Power".

1974. Completion of Phenix Nuclear Generator.

2056. **692.** 65 c. brn., mve. & red 20 8

691. Peacocks with Letter.

1974. Universal Postal Union. Cent.

2057. **691.** 1 f. 20 red, grn. & blue 40 20

692. Copernicus and Heliocentric System.

1974. Copernicus. 500th Birth Anniv. (1973).

2058. **692.** 1 f. 20 mve., brn. & blk. 40 15

693. Children playing on Beach. 694. Dr. Schweitzer.

1974. Red Cross Fund. Seasons. Cross in red.

2059. **693.** 60 c.+15 c. brn., blue and red 25 15
2060. – 80 c.+15 c. blue, brown. and red 30 25

DESIGN: 80 c. Child in garden looking through window.

See also 2098/9.

1975. Dr. Albert Schweitzer. Birth Centenary.

2061. **694.** 80 c.+20 c. brown, red and green 35 35

1975. Tourist Publicity. As Type **444,** but inscr. "1975".

2062. 85 c. blue and brown .. 20 10
2063. 1 f. 20 brn., bistre & blue 25 10
2064. 1 f. 40 blue, brown & green 30 12

DESIGNS—HORIZ. 85 c. Palace of Justice, Rouen. 1 f. 40 Chateau de Rochechouart. VERT. 1 f. 20 St. Pol-de-Leon.

695. Herons. 696. Edmond Michelet (politician).

1975. Nature Conservation.

2065. **695.** 70 c. brown and blue 30 15

1975. Red Cross Fund. Celebrities.

2066. **696.** 80 c.+20 c. ind. & bl. 35 35
2067. – 80 c.+20 c. blk. & bl. 35 35
2068. – 80 c.+20 c. blk. & bl. 35 35
2069. – 80 c.+20 c. blk., turq. and blue 20 20

DESIGNS—VERT. No. 2067, Robert Schuman (statesman). No. 2068, Eugene Thomas (former Telecommunications Minister). HORIZ. No. 2069, Andre Siegfried (geographer and humanist).

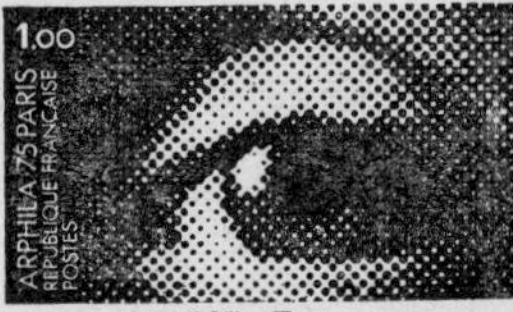

697. Eye.

1975. "Arphila 75" International Stamp Exhibition, Paris.

2070. **697.** 1 f. orge., vio. & red .. 25 12
2071. – 2 f. blk., red & grn... 55 20
2072. – 3 f. grn., slate & brn. 80 30
2073. – 4 f. grn., red & orge. 1·10 45

DESIGNS: 2 f. Capital. 3 f. "Arphila Paris". 4 f. Head of Ceres.

698. Postman's Badge. 699. Pres. G. Pompidou.

1975. Stamp Day.

2075. **698.** 80 c.+20 c. blk., yell. and blue 30 30

1975. Pres. George Pompidou Commemoration.

2076. **699.** 80 c. black and blue.. 20 5

700. "Paul as Harlequin" (Picasso).

1975. Europa. Multicoloured.

2077. 80 c. Type **700** 25 8
2078. 1 f. 20 "In the Square" (or "Woman leaning on Balcony"—Van Dongen) (horiz.) .. 30 15

701. Machine-Tools and Emblem.

1975. 1st World Machine-Tools Exhibition, Paris.

2079. **701.** 1 f. 20 blk., red & blue 30 10

702. First Assembly, Luxembourg Palace.

1975. French Senate. Cent.

2080. **702.** 1 f. 20 bistre, brn. and lake 30 10

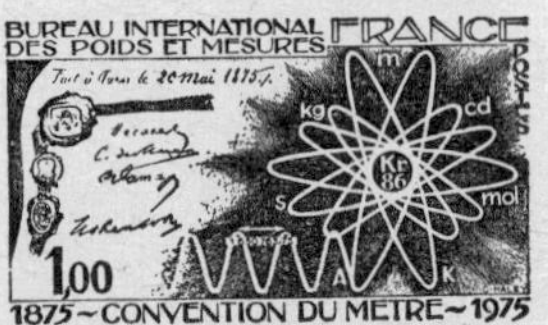

703. Seals, Signatures and Symbols.

1974. Metre Convention. Cent.

2081. **703.** 1 f. lilac, mauve & red 25 10

704. "Gazelle" Helicopter. 705. Youth and Health Symbols.

1975. Development of "Gazelle" Helicopter.

2082. **704.** 1 f. 30 green and blue 35 15

1975. Students' Health Foundation.

2083. **705.** 70 c. blk., pur. & red 25 8

FRANCE 1,00 METRO REGIONAL

706. Underground Train.

1975. Metro Regional Express Service. Opening.

2084. **706.** 1 f. deep blue and blue 30 10

707. M. Pottecher (founder) and Brussang Theatre. 708. Loire Scene.

1975. People's Theatre, Brussang. 80th Anniv.

2085. **707.** 85 c. orge., turq. & blue 20 5

1975. Regions of France.

2086. – 85 c. orge., turq. & blue 20 5
2087. – 1 f. lake, red & yellow 20 5
2088. **708.** 1 f. 15 grn., bl. & ochre 25 8
2089. – 1 f. 30 blk., red & bl. 30 10
2090. – 1 f. 90 bl., bistre & blk. 40 12
2091. – 2 f. 80 bl., red, & blk. 70 15

DESIGNS—VERT. 85 c. Picardy rose. 1 f. Bourgogne agriculture emblems. 1 f. 30 Auvergne (bouquet of carnations). 1 f. 90 Allegory, Poitou-Charentes. HORIZ. 2 f. 80 "Nord-Pas-de-Calais".

See also Nos. 2102/6.

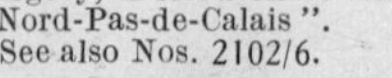

709. Concentration Camp Victims. 710. Mine-clearers' Monument, Ballon d'Alsace.

1975. Liberation of Concentration Camps. 30th Anniv.

2092. **709.** 1 f. grey, red and blue 25 12

1975. Mine Clearance Service. 30th Anniv.

2093. **710.** 70 c. grn., brn. & blue 20 5

711. "Urban Development".

1975. New Towns.

2094. **711.** 1 f. 70 bl., grn. & brn. 45 15

712. St. Nazaire Bridge. 713. Rainbow over Women's Faces.

1975. Opening of St. Nazaire Bridge.

2095. **712.** 1 f. 40 blk., bl. & grn. 35 12

1975. International Women's Year.

2096. **713.** 1 f. 20 multicoloured 30 12

714. French and Russian Flags. 715. Frigate "La Melpomene".

1975. Franco-Soviet Diplomatic Relations. 50th Anniv.

2097. **714.** 1 f. 20 yell., red & bl. 20 8

1975. Red Cross Fund. "The Seasons". As T 693.
2098. 60 c.+15 c. red & grn. .. 25 15
2099. 80 c.+20 c. brn., orge. & red 30 20
DESIGNS: 60 c. Child on swing. 80 c. Rabbits under umbrella.

1975. French Sailing Ships.
2100. **715.** 90 c. bl., orge. & red .. 20 10

716. "Concorde". **717.** French Stamp Design of 1876.

1976. Air. "Concorde's" First Commercial Flight, Paris–Rio de Janeiro.
2101. **716.** 1 f. 70 blk., bl. & red 45 20

1976. Regions of France. As T **708.**
2102. 25 c. green and blue .. 5 5
2103. 60 c. green, blue & mar... 12 5
2104. 70 c. blue, grn., & black.. 15 5
2105. 1 f. 25 blue, brn. & grn... 25 10
2106. 2 f. 20 multicoloured .. 50 12
DESIGNS—HORIZ. 25 c. Industrial complex in the Central Region. 60 c. Aquitaine 2 f. 20 Scene in Pyrenees. VERT. 70 c. "Limousin". 1 f. 25 "Guyane".

1976. French Art. As T **445.**
2108. 2 f. grey and blue .. 45 25
2109. 2 f. yellow and brown .. 45 25
2110. 2 f. multicoloured .. 45 25
2111. 2 f. multicoloured .. 45 25
2112. 2 f. multicoloured .. 45 25
2113. 2 f. multicoloured .. 45 25
DESIGNS—VERT. No. 2108, "The Two Saints", St.-Genis-des-Fontaines (wood-carving). No. 2109, "Venus of Brassempouy" (ivory sculpture). No. 2110, "La Joie de Vivre" (Robert Delaunay). HORIZ. No. 2111, Rameses II in war-chariot (wall-carving). No. 2112, Painting by Carzou. No. 2113, "Still Life with Fruit" (Maurice de Vlaminck).

1976. International Stamp Day.
2114. **717.** 80 c.+20 c. lilac & blk. 20 5

1976. Tourist Publicity. As T **444,** but but dated "1976".
2115. 1 f. brn., grn. & red .. 20 5
2116. 1 f. 10 blue .. 20 8
2117. 1 f. 40 blue, grn. & brn... 30 10
2118. 1 f. 70 pur., grn. & blue.. 35 10
2119. 2 f. magenta, lake & brn. 40 12
2120. 3 f. brn., blue & green .. 60 15
DESIGNS—HORIZ. 1 f. Chateau Bunaguil. 1 f. 40 Basque coast, Biarritz. 3 f. Chateau Malmaison. VERT. 1 f. 10 Lodeve Cathedral. 1 f. 70 Thiers. 2 f. Ussel.

719. Old Rouen. **720.** Naval Emblem and Warships.

1976. 49th Congress of French Philatelic Societies.
2121. **719.** 80 c. green and brown 15 8

1976. Central Marine Officers' Reserve Assn. 50th Anniv.
2122. **720.** 1 f. blue, yellow & red 20 8

721. Youth. **722.** Strasbourg Jug.

1976. "Juvarouen '76" Youth Stamp Exn. Rouen.
2123. **721.** 60 c. dp. bl., bl. & red 15 5

1976. Europa. Multicoloured.
2124. 80 c. Type **722** 15 5
2125. 1 f. 20 Sevres plate .. 25 10

723. Vergennes and Franklin.

1976. American Revolution. Bicent.
2126. **723.** 1 f. 20 blk., red & blue 25 10

724. Marshal Moncey. **725.** People talking.

1976. Red Cross. Celebrities.
2127. **724.** 80 c.+20 c. purple, black and brown.. 20 15
2128. – 80 c.+20 c. grn. & brn. 20 15
2129. – 80 c.+20 c. mve. & grn. 20 15
2130. – 1 f.+20 c. blk., pale blue and blue .. 25 20
2131. – 1 f.+20 c. blue, mauve and purple .. 25 20
2132. – 1 f.+20 c. grey & red 25 20
DESIGNS: No. 2128, Max Jacob (poet). 2129, Mounet-Sully (tragedian). 2130, General Daumesnil. 2131, Eugene Fromentin (writer and painter). 2132, Anna de Noailles.

1976. Communication.
2133. **725.** 1 f. 20 blk., red & yell. 25 12

726. Verdun Memorial. **727.** Troncais Forest.

1976. Verdun Offensive. 60th Anniv.
2134. **726.** 1 f. red, brown & green 20 10

1976. Nature Conservation.
2135. **727.** 70 c. brn., grn. & blue 15 5

728. Cross of Lorraine Emblem. **729.** Satellite "Symphonie".

1976. Free French Association. 30th Anniv.
2136. **728.** 1 f. red, deep bl. & bl. 20 10

1976. Launch of "Symphonie No. 1" Satellite.
2137. **729.** 1 f. 40 grn., brn. & vio. 30 12

730. Carnival Figures. **731.** Sailing.

1976. "La Fete" (Summer Festivals Exhibition, Tuileries, Paris).
2138. **730.** 1 f. red, green & blue 20 10

1976. Olympic Games, Montreal.
2139. **731.** 1 f. 20 violet, bright blue and blue .. 25 12

732. Officers in Military and Civilian Dress.

1976. Reserve Officers Corps. Cent.
2140. **732.** 1 f. grey, red & blue .. 20 8

733. Early and Modern Telephones.

1976. Telephone Centenary.
2141. **733.** 1 f. grey, brn. & blue 20 8

734. Bronze Statue and Emblem. **735.** Police and Emblems.

1976. International Tourist Film Association. 10th Anniv.
2142. **734.** 1 f. 40 brn., red & grn. 30 12

1976. National Police Force. 10th Anniv.
2143. **735.** 1 f. 10 grn., red & blue 25 8

736. Diagram of Accelerator.

1976. CERN. Atomic Particle Accelerator. Inaug.
2144. **736.** 1 f. 40, multicoloured 30 12

COUNCIL OF EUROPE STAMPS

Until March 25th, 1960, these stamps could only be used by delegates and permanent officials of the Council of Europe on official correspondence at Strasbourg. From that date they could be used on all correspondence posted within the Council of Europe building.

1958. No. 1354 optd. **CONSEIL DE L'EUROPE.**
C 1. 35 f. magenta and red .. 1·10 2·00

C 1. Council Flag.

1958.
C 2. **C 1.** 8 f. bl., orge. & maroon 12 12
C 3. 20 f. blue, yell. & brn. 20 15
C 4. 25 f. bl., pur. & myrtle 25 20
C 5. 35 f. blue and red .. 35 35
C 6. 50 f. blue and purple.. 60 60

(New currency. 100 (old) francs = 1 (new) franc.)

1963.
C 7. **C 1.** 20 c. blue, yell. & brown 10 10
C 8. 25 c. blue, pur. & myrtle 30 25
C 9. 25 c. blue, yellow, red and green .. 12 10
C 10. 30 c. blue, yellow & red 20 15
C 11. 40 c. ultram., yellow, red and black .. 10 10
C 12. 50 c. blue and purple.. 45 35
C 13. 50 c. blue, yellow, red and green .. 12 10
C 14. 60 c. blue, yellow, red and violet .. 35 30
C 15. 60 c. bl., yell., red & grn. 10 10
C 16. 70 c. ultram., yellow, red and brown .. 70 25
C 17. 80 c. blue, yell. & mauve 15 15
C 18. 1 f. 20, ultram., yellow, red and blue .. 20 20

UNESCO STAMPS

For use on correspondence posted within the UNESCO Headquarters building.

U 1. Buddha and Hermes.

1961.
U 1. **U 1.** 20 c. bistre, blue & sep. 15 12
U 2. 25 c. mar., grn. & blk. 20 15
U 3. 30 c. brown and sepia 25 20
U 4. 50 c. red, violet & blk. 65 50
U 5. 60 c. chest., mag. & turq. 30 30

U 2. Open Book and Globe. **U 3.** "Human Rights".

1966.
U 6. **U 2.** 25 c. brown 12 12
U 7. 30 c. red 15 15
U 8. 60 c. green 30 30

1969.
U 9. **U 3.** 30 c. red, grn. & choc. 10 8
U 10. 40 c. red, magenta and chocolate .. 12 10
U 11. 50 c. red, grn. & brn. 10 8
U 12. 60 c. red, grn. & pur. 10 10
U 13. 70 c. red, vio. & blue 12 12
U 14. 80 c. red, brn. & lake 15 20
U 15. 1 f. 20, red, blue & lake 15 15

MILITARY FRANK STAMPS

1901. Optd. **F.M.**
M 327. **15.** 10 c. red .. .. 6·00 2·25
M 348. **17.** 10 c. red 15 5
M 309. **12.** 15 c. orange .. 12·00 1·75
M 310. **14.** 15 c. red .. .. 8·00 1·50
M 311. **15.** 15 c. green .. .. 8·50 1·75
M 471. 50 c. red 95 30
M 516. **48.** 50 c. red 35 10
M 517. 65 c. blue 5 5
M 518. 90 c. blue 12 12

1939. Optd. **F.**
M 519. **48.** 90 c. blue 95 95

M 1. **M 2.** Flag.

1946. No value indicated.
M 967. **M 1.** Green 15 12
M 968. Red 12 8

1964. No value indicated.
M 1661. **M 2.** Blue, red, yell. & brn. 20 12

POSTAGE DUE STAMPS

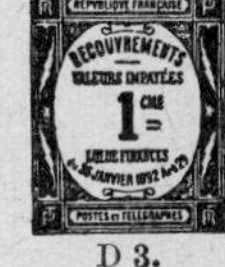

D 1. **D 2.** **D 3.**

1859.
D 87. **D 1.** 10 c. black .. .. 6·50 3·25
D 88. 15 c. black .. .. 6·50 3·25
D 212. 25 c. black .. .. 25·00 11·00
D 213. 30 c. black .. .. 45·00 30·00
D 214. 40 c. blue .. .. 80·00 £100
D 215. 60 c. yellow .. £140 £300
D 217. 60 c. blue .. .. 17·00 35·00

1882.
D 279. **D 2.** 1 c. black 12 12
D 280. 2 c. black .. .. 2·75 4·00
D 281. 3 c. black .. .. 3·75 4·25
D 282. 4 c. black .. .. 4·25 4·25
D 283. 5 c. black .. .. 11·00 2·50
D 284. 10 c. black .. .. 9·00 35
D 285. 15 c. black .. .. 6 00 1·50
D 286. 20 c. black .. .. 28·00 19·00
D 287. 30 c. black .. .. 18·00 7·00
D 288. 40 c. black .. .. 12·00 8·00
D 289. 50 c. black .. .. 60·00 25·00
D 290. 60 c. black .. .. 60·00 8·00
D 291. 1 f. black .. .. 95·00 60·00
D 293. 2 f. black £150 £130
D 295. 5 f. black £300 £275

1884.

No.	Type	Description		
D 297.	D 2.	5 c. blue	5	5
D 298.		10 c. brown	5	5
D 299.		15 c. green	1·40	15
D 300.		20 c. olive	50	5
D 301.		25 c. red	70	50
D 302.		30 c. red	5	5
D 304.		40 c. red	1·50	50
D 305.		45 c. green	60	35
D 306.		50 c. purple ..	10	5
D 307.		60 c. green	12	5
D 292.		1 f. brown	50·00	18·00
D 308.		1 f. red on yellow ..	90·00	70·00
D 310.		1 f. claret	25	5
D 294.		2 f. brown	32·00	30·00
D 311.		2 f. red	30·00	11·00
D 312.		2 f. violet	15	10
D 313.		3 f. red	15	10
D 296.		5 f. brown	60·00	55·00
D 314.		5 f. orange	35	20

1908.

No.	Type	Description		
D 348.	D 3.	1 c. olive	5	5
D 349.		10 c. violet	5	5
D 350.		20 c. bistre	65	8
D 351.		30 c. bistre	30	8
D 352.		50 c. red	35·00	7·00
D 353.		60 c. red	25	20

1917. Surch.

No.	Type	Description		
D 378.	D 3.	20 c. on 30 c. bistre	1·10	50
D 379.		40 c. on 50 c. red ..	1·25	30
D 433.		50 c. on 10 c. violet	65	20
D 434.		60 c. on 1 c. olive ..	1·00	40
D 435.		1 f. on 60 c. red ..	3·25	95
D 436.		2 f. on 60 c. red ..	3·25	1·40

D 4. D 5. Wheat Sheaves. D 6.

1927.

No.	Type	Description		
D 454.	D 4.	1 c. green	10	8
D 455.		10 c. red	12	5
D 456.		30 c. bistre	15	5
D 457.		60 c. red	12	5
D 458.		1 f. violet	1·10	20
D 459.		1 f. blue	2·25	5
D 460.		2 f. blue	4·50	2·10
D 461.		2 f. brown	14·00	1·75

1929. Surch.

No.	Type	Description		
D 471.	D 4.	1 f. 20 on 2 f. blue	2·25	60
D 472.		5 f. on 1 f. violet ..	4·50	60

1931. Surch. **UN FRANC.**

No.	Type	Description		
D 494.	D 4.	1 f. on 60 c. red ..	1·00	10

1943. Inscr. "CHIFFRE-TAXE".

No.	Type	Description		
D 787.	D 5.	10 c. brown	5	5
D 788.		30 c. purple	5	5
D 789.		50 c. green	5	5
D 790.		1 f. blue	5	5
D 791.		1 f. 50 red	5	5
D 792.		2 f. blue	5	5
D 793.		3 f. red	5	5
D 794.		4 f. violet	75	50
D 795.		5 f. red	12	10
D 796.		10 f. orange	75	12
D 797.		20 f. bistre	1·00	15

1946. As Type D 5 but inscr. "TIMBRE TAXE".

No.	Type	Description		
D 985.		10 c. brown	60	35
D 986.		30 c. purple	45	30
D 987.		50 c. green	1·10	60
D 988.		1 f. blue	5	5
D 989.		2 f. blue	5	5
D 990.		3 f. red	5	5
D 991.		4 f. violet	5	5
D 992.		5 f. magenta	5	5
D 993.		10 f. red	10	5
D 994.		20 f. brown	45	10
D 995.		50 f. slate-green ..	90	40
D 996.		100 f. green	6·00	25

1960. New currency.

No.	Type	Description		
D 1474.	D 6.	5 c. magenta	60	10
D 1475.		10 c. red	70	10
D 1476.		20 c. brown	1·10	12
D 1477.		50 c. slate-green ..	4·00	30
D 1478.		1 f. green	5·00	30

ILLUSTRATIONS
British Commonwealth and all overprints and surcharges are FULL SIZE. Foreign Countries have been reduced to ¾-LINEAR.

D 7. Poppies.

1964.

No.	Type	Description		
D 1650.	–	5 c. red, grn. & pur.	5	5
D 1651.	–	10 c. bl., grn. & pur.	5	5
D 1652.	D 7.	15 c. red, grn. & brn.	5	5
D 1653.	–	20 c. pur., grn. & turq.	5	5
D 1654.	–	30 c. bl., grn. & brn.	5	5
D 1655.	–	40 c. yell., red. & turq.	10	5
D 1656.	–	50 c. red, grn. & bl.	12	5
D 1657.	–	1 f. vio., grn. & bl.	25	10

DESIGNS: 5 c. Knapweed. 10 c. Gentian. 20 c. Little periwinkle. 30 c. Forget-me-not. 40 c. Columbine. 50 c. Clover. 1 f. Soldanella.

FREE FRENCH FORCES IN THE LEVANT O4

After British and Free French troops had occupied Syria and Lebanon in June 1941 the following stamps were issued for the use of Free French forces in those areas.

100 centimes = 1 franc.

1942. Surch. with Lorraine Crosses, **FORCES FRANCAISES LIBRES LEVANT** and value.

(i) On No. 252 of Syria.

No.	Type	Description		
1.	–	50 c. on 4 p. orange ..	65	65

(ii) On Nos. 251 and 212 of Lebanon.

No.	Type	Description		
2.	7.	1 f. on 5 p. blue	65	65
3.	13.	2 f. 50 on 12½ p. blue ..	65	65

1942. Air. Nos. 269/70 of Syria surch. with Lorraine Crosses, **LIGNES AERIENNES F.A.F.L.** and value.

No.	Type	Description		
4.		4 f. on 50 p. black ..	45	45
5.		6 f. 50 on 50 p. black ..	45	45
6.		8 f. on 50 p. black ..	45	45
7.		10 f. on 100 p. mauve ..	45	45

1. Camelry and Ruins at Palmyra.

2. Wings bearing Lorraine Crosses.

1942.

No.	Type	Description		
8.	1.	1 f. red (postage) ..	5	5
9.		1 f. 50 violet	5	5
10.		2 f. orange	5	5
11.		2 f. 50 brown	5	5
12.		3 f. blue	5	5
13.		4 f. green	5	5
14.		5 f. purple	5	5
15.	2.	6 f. 50 red (air) ..	15	15
16.		10 f. purple and blue ..	15	15

1942. Air. No. 15 such.

No.	Type	Description		
17.	2.	4 f. on 6 f. 50 red ..	20	20

1943. Surch. **RESISTANCE** and premium.

No.	Type	Description		
18.	1.	1 f.+9 f. red (postage) ..	90	90
19.		5 f.+20 f. purple ..	90	90
20.	2.	6 f. 50+48 f. 50 red (air)	3·25	3·25
21.		10 f.+100 f. pur. & bl...	3·25	3·25

1943. Air. No. 12 surch. with aeroplane and value.

No.	Type	Description		
22.	1.	4 f. on 3 f. blue ..	20	20

FRENCH COLONIES E1

General issues for use in French Colonies which had no special stamps.

NOTE. For other stamps issued for the French Colonies see the note at the beginning of France.

1. Eagle. 2. Laureated. 4. Laureated.

1859. Imperf.

No.	Type	Description		
1.	1.	1 c. green	5·50	6·50
2.		5 c. green	6·00	5·00
3.		10 c. brown	7·00	2·25
4.		20 c. blue	9·00	4·50
5.		40 c. orange	4·50	3·00
6.		80 c. red	20·00	17·00

1871. Imperf.

No.	Type	Description		
7.	2.	1 c. green	20·00	15·00
9.	4.	30 c. brown	42·00	11·00
10.		80 c. red	£225	30·00

5. Ceres. 6. Ceres (small figures).

1871. Imperf.

No.	Type	Description		
11.	5.	1 c. green on blue ..	4·50	4·50
12.		2 c. brown on yellow ..	£120	£225
14a.		5 c. green	5·00	3·00
16.	6.	15 c. yellow	80·00	4·00

7. Ceres (large figures). 8. Peace and Commerce. 9. Commerce.

1872. Imperf.

No.	Type	Description		
20.	7.	10 c. brown and red ..	60·00	5·00
21.		15 c. yellow	£160	38·00
22.		30 c. brown	28·00	6·00
23.		80 c. red	£110	50·00

1877. Imperf.

No.	Type	Description		
24.	8.	1 c. green	11·00	12·00
25.		2 c. green	5·00	3·75
26.		4 c. green	6·00	4·75
27.		5 c. green	6·00	1·50
28.		10 c. green	30·00	3·75
29.		15 c. grey	80·00	25·00
30.		20 c. brown on yellow ..	17·00	2·25
31a.		25 c. blue	12·00	3·00
32.		30 c. brown	13·00	13·00
33.		35 c. black on yellow ..	15·00	9·50
3 .		40 c. red on yellow ..	9·00	7·50
35.		75 c. red	22·00	20·00
36.		1 f. olive	11·00	6·50

1878. Imperf.

No.	Type	Description		
37.	8.	1 c. black on blue ..	7·00	6·50
38.		2 c. brown	6·00	5·00
39.		4 c. claret on grey ..	7·50	7·50
40.		10 c. black on lilac ..	30·00	8·50
41.		15 c. blue	11·00	5·50
42.		20 c. red on green ..	25·00	4·00
43.		25 c. black on red ..	£160	£110
44.		25 c. yellow	£190	10·00

1881 Perf.

No.	Type	Description		
45.	9.	1 c. black on blue ..	50	50
46.		2 c. brown on yellow ..	60	50
47.		4 c. claret on grey ..	60	50
48.		5 c. green	75	35
49.		10 c. black on lilac ..	1·50	75
50.		15 c. blue	2·25	35
51.		20 c. red on green ..	7·50	3·25
52.		25 c. yellow	2·00	80
53.		25 c. black on red ..	2·25	35
54.		30 c. brown	6·00	4·25
55.		35 c. black on yellow ..	7·50	6·50
56.		40 c. red on yellow ..	8·00	5·50
57.		75 c. red	18·00	10·00
58.		1 f. olive	11·00	6·50

10. Map of France.

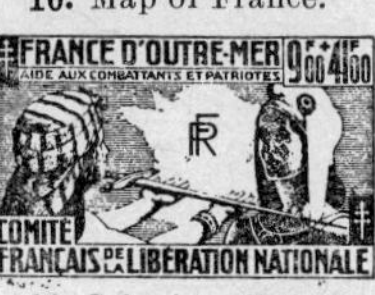

11. Colonies offering France Aid.

12. Resisters.

1943. Aid to Resistance Movement.

No.	Type	Description		
82.	10.	50 c.+4 f. 50 green ..	20	25
83.		1 f. 50+8 f. 50 red ..	20	25
84.		3 f.+12 f. blue	20	25
85.		5 f.+15 f. grey	20	25
86.	11.	9 f.+41 f. purple ..	20	25

1943. Aid to Resistance Movement. Roul.

No.	Type	Description		
87.	12.	1 f. 50+98 f. 50 bl. & grey	4·25	4·25

13. 14.

1943. French Solidarity Fund.

No.	Type	Description		
88.	13.	10 f.+40 f. blue ..	80	80

1944. Air. Aviation Fund.

No.	Type	Description		
89.	14.	10 f.+40 f. green ..	90	90

INDEX

Countries can be quickly located by referring to the index at the end of this volume.

POSTAGE DUE STAMPS

D 1. D 2.

1884. Imperf.

No.	Type	Description		
D 59.	D 1.	1 c. black	75	75
D 60.		2 c. black	70	70
D 61.		3 c. black	75	60
D 62.		4 c. black	85	85
D 63.		5 c. black	1·00	85
D 64.		10 c. black	1·90	1·50
D 65.		15 c. black	2·50	1·90
D 66.		20 c. black	2·50	2·50
D 67.		30 c. black	3·00	1·50
D 68.		40 c. black	5·00	1·90
D 69.		60 c. black	8·00	4·50
D 70.		1 f. brown	6·50	5·50
D 71.		2 f. brown	5·00	4·25
D 72.		5 f. brown	19·00	17·00

1893. Imperf.

No.	Type	Description		
D 73.	D 1.	5 c. blue	12	12
D 74.		10 c. brown	12	12
D 75.		15 c. green	12	12
D 76.		20 c. olive	12	12
D 77.		30 c. red	25	20
D 78.		50 c. claret	25	20
D 79.		60 c. brown on yellow	60	50
D 81.		1 f. red on yellow ..	85	75

1945. Perf.

No.	Type	Description		
D 90.	D 2.	10 c. blue	5	5
D 91.		15 c. green	5	5
D 92.		25 c. orange	5	5
D 93.		50 c. black	15	15
D 94.		60 c. brown	15	15
D 95.		1 f. claret	5	5
D 96.		2 f. red	15	15
D 97.		4 f. grey	35	35
D 98.		5 f. blue	35	35
D 99.		10 f. violet	1·50	1·50
D 100.		20 f. brown.. ..	60	60
D 101.		50 f. green	4·00	4·00

FRENCH CONGO O1

A French colony in C. Africa, afterwards divided into Gabon, Middle Congo, Oubangui Chari and Chad.

1891. Stamps of French Colonies, "Commerce" type, surch. **Congo francais** and value in figures.

No.	Type	Description		
2.	9.	5 c. on 1 c. black on blue	17·00	10·00
3.		5 c. on 15 c. blue	28·00	12·00
4.		5 c. on 25 c. black on red ..	10·00	4·00
11.		10 c. on 25 c. black on red	16·00	5·00
12.		15 c. on 25 c. black on red	18·00	5·00

1892. Stamps of French Colonies, "Commerce" type, surch. **Congo Francais** and value in figures.

No.	Type	Description		
5.	9.	5 c. on 20 c. red on green..	£125	60·00
6.		5 c. on 25 c. black on red..	10·00	4·00
7.		10 c. on 25 c. black on red	18·00	6·00
8.		10 c. on 40 c. red on yellow	£250	50·00
9.		15 c. on 25 c. black on red	20·00	4·00

1892. Postage Due stamps of French Colonies surch. **Congo francais Timbre poste** and value in figures.

No.	Type	Description		
13.	D 1.	5 c. on 5 c. black ..	10·00	9·00
14.		5 c. on 20 c. black ..	10·00	8·00
15.		5 c. on 30 c. black ..	12·00	9·00
16.		10 c. on 1 f. brown ..	12·00	7·00

1892. "Tablet" key-type inscr. "CONGO FRANCAIS".

No.	Type	Description		
17.	D.	1 c. black on blue ..	8	8
18.		2 c. brown on yellow ..	10	10
19.		4 c. claret on grey ..	12	12
20.		5 c. green	30	30
21.		10 c. black on lilac ..	1·10	80
22.		10 c. red	15	10
23.		15 c. blue	5·00	1·10
24.		15 c. grey	55	50
25.		20 c. red on green ..	1·75	1·25
26.		25 c. black on red ..	1·50	85
27.		25 c. blue	85	70
28.		30 c. brown	1·60	85
29.		40 c. red on yellow ..	4·00	2·00
30.		50 c. red	4·00	2·00
31.		50 c. brown on blue ..	80	70
32.		75 c. brown on orange ..	4·00	3·00
33.		1 f. olive	5·00	2·50

1. Leopard in Ambush. 2. Woman of the Bakalois Tribe.

1900.

36. 1. 1 c. purple and brown .. 5 5
37. 2 c. brown and yellow .. 5 5
38. 4 c. red and grey 5 5
39. 5 c. green 12 5
40. 10 c. red 35 20
41. 15 c. violet and green .. 12 5
42. 2. 20 c. green and orange .. 8 5
43. 25 c. blue 12 12
44. 30 c. red and yellow .. 15 10
45. 40 c. brown and green .. 20 15
46. 50 c. violet and lilac .. 65 65
47. 75 c. purple and yellow .. 1·40 1·25
48. – 1 f. grey and green .. 2·50 2·25
49. – 2 f. red and brown .. 3·75 3·50
50. – 5 f. orange and black .. 11·00 10·00

DESIGN—VERT. (LARGER): 1 f., 2 f., 5 f. Grove of coconut palms, Libreville.

1903. Surch. in figures.

51. 2. 5 c. on 30 c. red & yellow .. 50·00 25·00
52. – 0, 10 on 2 f. red and brown (No. 66).. .. .. 65·00 25·00

PARCEL POST STAMPS

1891. Type-set. Inscribed " Congo francais—COLIS POSTAUX " and value.

P 13. 10 c. black on blue .. 12·00 6·00

1893. Receipt stamp of France optd. **Congo Francais—COLIS POSTAUX.**

P 34. 10 c. grey .. .. 5·00 4·00

For later issues see **MIDDLE CONGO** and **CONGO REPUBLIC.**

FRENCH EQUATORIAL AFRICA O2

Consists of Gabon, Middle Congo, Ubangui-Chari and Chad. These territories were each proclaimed Republics within the French Community in 1958. Middle Congo becoming Congo Republic and Ubangui-Chari being renamed Central African Republic.

1936. Middle Congo Stamps of 1933 optd. **AFRIQUE EQUATORIALE FRANCAISE.**

1. 4. 1 c. brown 5 5
2. 2 c. blue 5 5
3. 4 c. green 5 5
4. 5 c. red 5 5
5. 10 c. green 20 15
6. 15 c. purple 20 15
7. 20 c. red on pink .. 10 10
8. 25 c. orange 35 25
9. 40 c. brown 45 30
10. 50 c. purple 30 12
11. 75 c. black on pink .. 55 45
12. 90 c. red 35 25
13. 1 f. blue 15 12
14. 5 f. grey .. .. 6·50 5·50
15. 10 f. black .. .. 5·00 4·50
16. 20 f. brown .. .. 5·00 4·50

1936. Gabon Stamps of 1933 optd. **AFRIQUE EQUATORIALE FRANCAISE.**

17. 5. 1 c. red 5 5
18. 2 c. black and pink .. 5 5
19. 4 c. green 5 5
20. 5 c. blue 8 5
21. 10 c. red on yellow .. 10 5
22. 6. 40 c. purple 20 12
23. 50 c. brown 15 10
24. 1 f. green on blue .. 4·75 2·25
25. 1 f. 50 blue 15 8
26. 2 f. red .. .. 3·25 2·00

1937. Int. Exn., Paris. As Nos. 110/15 of Cameroun.

27. 20 c. violet 40 40
28. 30 c. green 40 40
29. 40 c. red 40 40
30. 50 c. brown 20 20
31. 90 c. red 40 40
32. 1 f. 50 blue 40 40

1. Logging near Mayumba.

2. Chad Family.

3. Count de Brazza.

4. Savoia " S 73 " Aircraft over Stanley Pool.

1937.

34. 1. 1 c. brown & yellow (post) 5 5
35. 2 c. violet and green .. 5 5
36. 3 c. blue and yellow .. 5 5
37. 4 c. mauve and blue .. 5 5
38. 5 c. green 5 5
39. 2. 10 c. mauve and blue .. 5 5
40. 15 c. blue and pink .. 5 5
41. 20 c. brown and yellow .. 5 5
42. 25 c. red and blue .. 12 12
44. 3. 30 c. green 5 5
45. 30 c. blue and pink .. 5 5
46. 2. 35 c. green 12 8
47. 3. 40 c. red and blue .. 5 5
48. 45 c. blue and green .. 75 45
49. 45 c. green 10 5
50. 50 c. brown and yellow .. 5 5
51. 55 c. violet and blue .. 10 5
52. 60 c. purple and blue .. 5 5
53. A. 65 c. blue and green .. 5 5
54. A. 70 c. violet and orange .. 8 5
55. A. 75 c. black and yellow .. 90 60
56. A. 80 c. brown and yellow .. 5 5
57. A. 90 c. red and orange .. 5 5
58. A. 1 f. violet and green .. 15 12
59. 3. 1 f. red and orange .. 25 12
60. A. 1 f. green and blue .. 5 5
61. B. 1 f. 25 red and orange .. 20 20
62. B. 1 f. 40 brown and green .. 5 5
63. B. 1 f. 50 blue 15 12
64. B. 1 f. 60 violet and orange .. 5 5
65. B. 1 f. 75 brown and yellow .. 15 12
66. A. 1 f. 75 blue 5 5
67. B. 2 f. green 20 10
68. C. 2 f. 15 violet and yellow .. 5 5
69. C. 2 f. 25 blue 15 15
70. C. 2 f. 50 purple and orange .. 5 5
71. C. 3 f. blue and pink .. 8 5
72. C. 5 f. green 15 12
73. C. 10 f. violet and blue .. 40 25
74. 20 f. black and yellow .. 40 30
75. D. 1 f. 50 black & lemon (air) 5 8
76. 2 f. mauve and blue .. 5 5
77. 2 f. 50 green and pink .. 5 5
78. 3 f. 75 brown and green .. 8 8
79. 4. 4 f. 50 red and blue .. 5 5
80. 6 f. 50 blue and green .. 15 15
81. 8 f. 50 red and orange .. 15 15
82. 10 f. 75 violet and green .. 20 20

DESIGNS: A, Emile Gentil. B, Paul Crampel. C, Liotard. D, Flying-boat over Pointe Noire.

1938. Anti-Cancer Fund. As T 10 of Cameroun.

94. – 1 f. 75+50 c. blue .. 2·75 2·75

1938. Social Welfare. Surch. with premium in figures.

95. A. 65 c.+35 c. (No. 52) .. 40 30
96. – 1 f. 75+50 c. (No. 64) .. 40 30

5. Bouet-Willaumez and " La Malouine ".

1938. Landing of Bouet-Willaumez in Gabon. Cent.

97. 5. 65 c. brown 25 25
98. 1 f. red 25 25
99. 1 f. 75 blue 30 30
100. 2 f. violet 35 35

1939. New York World's Fair. As T 11 of Cameroun.

101. 1 f. 25 red 25 25
102. 2 f. 25 blue 25 25

1939. French Revolution. 150th Anniv. As T 16 of Cameroun.

103. 45 c.+25 c. green (post.) 2·25 2·25
104. 70 c.+30 c. brown .. 2·25 2·25
105. 90 c.+35 c. orange .. 2·25 2·25
106. 1 f. 25+1 f. red .. .. 2·25 2·25
107. 2 f. 25+2 f. blue .. .. 2·25 2·25
108. 4 f. 50+4 f. black (air) .. 4·25 4·25

1940. Adherence to General de Gaulle.

A. Postage stamps of 1937.

(a) Optd. **AFRIQUE FRANCAISE LIBRE** or **Afrique Francaise Libre.**

109. 1. 1 c. brown and yellow .. 10 10
110. 2 c. violet and green .. 10 10
111. 3 c. blue and yellow .. 15 15
112. 5 c. green 15 15
113. 2. 10 c. mauve and blue .. 15 15
114. 15 c. blue and pink .. 15 12
115. 20 c. brown and yellow .. 20 20
153. 25 c. red and blue .. 65 40
117. 35 c. green 15 15

(b) Optd. **LIBRE.**

120. 3. 30 c. blue and pink .. 1·50 1·25
119. 30 c. green 25 25
121. 40 c. red and blue .. 8 5
122. 45 c. green 10 8
123. 50 c. brown and yellow 45 40
124. 55 c. violet and blue .. 15 12
125. 60 c. purple and blue .. 5 5
126. A. 65 c. blue and green 5 5
127. 70 c. violet and orange .. 10 10
128. 75 c. black and yellow .. 6·00 5·50
129. 80 c. brown and yellow .. 5 5
130. 90 c. red and orange .. 12 12
131. 3. 1 f. red and orange .. 30 20
132. A. 1 f. green and blue .. 70 70
133. B. 1 f. 40 brown and green .. 5 5
134. 1 f. 50 blue 12 12
135. 1 f. 60 violet and orange 5 5
136. 1 f. 75 brown and yellow 15 10
137. C. 2 f. 15 violet and yellow 12 8
138. 2 f. 25 blue 25 25
139. 2 f. 50 purple and orange 12 12
140. 3 f. blue and pink .. 20 15
141. 5 f. green 55 40
142. 10 f. violet and blue .. 30 25
143. 20 f. black and yellow .. 35 20

(c) Surch. **LIBRE** and values in figures and two bars.

144. 3. 75 c. on 50 c. brn. & yell. 5 5
145. A. 1 f. on 65 c. blue & green 5 5

B. Air stamps of 1937.

(a) Optd. **Afrique Francaise Libre.**

155. D. 1 f. 50 black and lemon .. 42·00 38·00
156. 2 f. 50 green and pink .. 15 15
157. 3 f. 75 brown and green .. 35·00 32·00
158. 4. 4 f. 50 red and blue .. 20 20
159. 6 f. 50 blue and green .. 25 25
160. 8 f. 50 red and orange .. 25 25

(b) Optd. as last and surch. also.

161. D. 10 f. on 2 f. 50 grn. & pink 15·00 15·00
162. 4. 50 f. on 10 f. 75 violet and green 85 85

No. 71 of Middle Congo optd. **AFRIQUE FRANCAISE LIBRE.**

163. 4. 4 c. olive .. .. 7·50 6·00

1940. Arrival of Gen. de Gaulle in Brazzaville. Optd. **LIBRE 24-10-40.**

164. A. 80 c. brown and yellow .. 2·25 1·75
165. 3. 1 f. red and orange .. 2·25 1·75
166. A. 1 f. green and blue .. 2·25 1·75
167. B. 1 f. 50 blue and pale blue 2·25 1·75

6. Phoenix.

ILLUSTRATIONS British Commonwealth and all overprints and surcharges are FULL SIZE. Foreign Countries have been reduced to ¾-LINEAR.

1941. Free French Issue. (a) Postage.

168. 6. 5 c. brown 5 5
169. 10 c. blue 5 5
170. 25 c. green 5 5
171. 30 c. orange 5 5
172. 40 c. green 5 5
173. 80 c. maroon 5 5
174. 1 f. mauve 5 5
175. 1 f. 50 red 5 5
176. 2 f. black 5 5
177. 2 f. 50 blue 5 5
178. 4 f. violet 8 5
179. 5 f. yellow 5 5
180. 10 f. brown 8 8
181. 20 f. green 20 15

(b) Air. As T 18 of Cameron.

182. 6. 1 f. orange 5 5
183. 1 f. 50 red 5 5
184. 5 f. maroon 12 8
185. 10 f. black 12 8
186. 25 f. blue 12 10
187. 50 f. green 15 12
188. 100 f. claret 30 25

6a. Count Savorgnan de Brazza and Stanley Pool.

1941. De Brazza Memorial Fund.

189. 6a. 1 f.+2 f. brown and red 12 12

1943. Free French Funds. Nos. 69, 73 and 82 surch. **Afrique Francaise Combattante,** cross and value.

190. 2 f. 25+50 f. blue and pale blue (postage) .. .. 1·10 1·10
191. 10 f.+100 f. violet and blue 5·00 5·00
192. 10 f. 75+200 f. violet and green (air) .. .. 28·00 28·00

1944. French Aid Fund. Various stamps surch. **RESISTANCE** and value.

195. 6. 5 c.+10 f. brown (No. 168) 1·00 1·00
196. 10 c.+10 f. blue (No. 169) 1·00 1·00
197. 25 c.+10 f. grn. (No. 170) 1·00 1·00
198. 30 c.+10 f. orge. (No. 171) 1·00 1·00
199. 40 c.+10 f. grn. (No. 172) 1·00 1·00
193. A. 80 c.+10 f. brown and yellow (No. 164) .. 1·90 1·90
200. 6. 1 f.+10 f. mve. (No. 174) 1·00 1·00
194. B. 1 f. 50+15 f. blue and pale blue (No. 167) .. 1·90 1·90
201. 6. 2 f.+20 f. black (No. 176) 1·00 1·00
202. 2 f. 50+25 f. blue (No. 177) 1·00 1·00
203. 4 f.+40 f. violet (No. 178) 1·00 1·00
204. 5 f.+50 f. yell. (No. 179) 1·00 1·00
205. 10 f.+100 f. brn. (No. 180) 1·00 1·00
206. 20 f.+200 f. grn. (No. 181) 1·00 1·00

1944. French Aid Fund. Nos. 164, 167, 168/72. 174 and 176/7 surch. **LIBERATION** and value.

209. 6. 5 c.+10 f. brown .. 1·00 1·00
210. 10 c.+10 f. blue .. .. 1·00 1·00
211. 25 c.+10 f. green .. 1·00 1·00
212. 30 c.+10 f. orange .. 1·00 1·00
213. 40 c.+10 f. green .. 1·00 1·00
207. A. 80 c.+10 f. brown & yell. 2·40 2·40
214. 6. 1 f.+10 f. mauve .. 1·00 1·00
208. B. 1 f. 50+15 f. bl. & pale bl. 2·40 2·40
215. 6. 2 f.+20 f. black .. .. 1·00 1·00
216. 2 f. 50+25 f. blue .. 1·00 1·00

1944. Mutual Aid and Red Cross Funds. As T 19 of Cameroun.

217. 5 f.+20 f. blue .. 12 12

1945. Surch. with new values and bars.

218. 6. 50 c. on 5 c. brown .. 5 5
219. 60 c. on 5 c. brown .. 5 5
220. 70 c. on 5 c. brown .. 5 5
221. 1 f. 20 on 5 c. brown .. 5 5
222. 2 f. 40 on 25 c. green .. 8 8
223. 3 f. on 25 c. green .. 20 20
224. 4 f. 50 on 25 c. green .. 20 20
225. 15 f. on 2 f. 50 blue .. 20 20

1945. Eboue. As T 20 of Cameroun.

226. 2 f. black 5 5
227. 25 f. green 30 30

1946. Air. Victory. As T 21 of Cameroun.

228. 8 f. red 10 10

1946. Air. From Chad to the Rhine. As T 22 of Cameroun.

229. 5 f. purple 10 10
230. 10 f. green 10 10
231. 15 f. blue 20 20
232. 20 f. red 25 25
233. 25 f. black 25 25
234. 50 f. claret 35 35

7. Rhinoceros. 8. African Boatman.

9. Aeroplane over Beach.

1947.

235. 7. 10 c. blue (postage) .. 5 5
236. 30 c. violet 5 5
237. 40 c. orange 5 5
238. 50 c. blue 5 5
239. – 60 c. red 5 5
240. – 80 c. green 5 5
241. – 1 f. orange 5 5
242. – 1 f. 20 claret 12 12
243. – 1 f. 50 green 15 12
244. – 2 f. brown 5 5
245. – 3 f. red 5 5
246. – 3 f. 60 brown 30 30
247. – 4 f. blue 5 5
248. 8. 5 f. purple 10 5
249. 6 f. blue 5 5
250. – 10 f. black 12 5
251. – 15 f. brown 30 5
252. – 20 f. claret 20 5
253. – 25 f. black 25 5
254. – 50 f. brown (air) .. 45 12
255. 9. 100 f. green 85 15
256. – 200 f. blue .. .. 1·50 30

DESIGNS (SMALL SIZE)—VERT. 50 c. to 80 c. Palms and cataract. 1 f. to 1 f. 50 River view. 2 f. to 4 f. Tropical forest. 15 f. to 25 f. Bakongo girl. (LARGE SIZE)—HORIZ. 50 f. Aeroplane over village. 200 f. Aeroplane over column of porters.

1949. Air. U.P.U. 75th Anniv. As T 25 of Cameroun.

267. 25 f. green .. .. 1·75 1·75

1950. Colonial Welfare Fund. As T 26 of Cameroun.

268. 10 f.+2 f. purple & grn. 65 65

10. De Brazza and Landscape.

1951. De Brazza Birth Cent.

269. – 10 f. grn. & blue (post.) 20 5
270. 10. 15 f. red, bl. & choc. (air) 25 5

PORTRAIT (22×31½ mm.): 10 f. De Brazza.

11. Monseigneur Augouard.

1952. Air. Mgr. Augouard (First Bishop of the Congo). Birth Cent.
271. 11. 15 f. sepia, purple & olive 75 45

1952. Military Medal Cent. As T 27 of Cameroun.
272. 15 f. multicoloured 65 55

1954. Air. Liberation. 10th Anniv. As T 29 of Cameroun.
277. 15 f. maroon and violet 65 65

12. Lieut.-Governor Cureau.

1954.
278. 12. 15 f. brown and green 30 10

13. Native Craft.

1955. Air.
273. – 50 f. brn., green & blue 35 8
274. 13. 100 f. grn., turq. & sepia 65 12
275. – 200 f. red and lake 1·25 25
276. – 500 f. blue, blk. & grn. 5·50 55
DESIGNS: 50 f. Logs in river. 200 f. Native driver and docks. 500 f. Anhingas (Snake-birds).

14. Felix Eboue.

1955. Air. Governor General Eboue Commem.
279. 14. 15 f. sepia, brn. & blue 60 35

15. Lizard.

1955. Nature Protection.
280. 15. 8 f. green and lake 25 8

DESIGNS: 10 f. Cotton production, Chad. 15 f. Brazzaville Hospital, Middle Congo. 20 f. Libreville harbour, Gabon.

16. Boali Waterfall and Power Station.

1956. Economic and Social Development Fund.
281. 16. 5 f. maroon and sepia 5 5
282. – 10 f. green and black 8 5
283. – 15 f. grey and indigo 10 5
284. – 20 f. vermilion and red 12 5

1956. Coffee. As T 15 of New Caledonia.
285. 10 f. violet and lilac 12 5

17. Riverside Hospital.

19. Lion and Lioness. 18. Gen. Faidherbe and African Trooper.

1957. Order of Malta Leprosy Relief.
286. 17. 15 f. turquoise, grn. & red 25 10

1957. Air. African Troops. Cent.
287. 18. 15 f. brown & chestnut 40 30

1957.
288. – 1 f. brown and green 5 5
289. 19. 2 f. olive and green 5 5
290. – 3 f. black, blue & green 5 5
291. – 4 f. brown and grey 5 5
DESIGNS—HORIZ. 1 f. Eland. VERT. 3 f. Elephant. 4 f. Greater Kudu.

20. Regional Bureau, Brazzaville. 21. "Euadania".

1958. W.H.O. 10th Anniv.
292. 20. 20 f. chestnut and green 15 12

1958. Tropical Flora.
293. 21. 10 f. yell., grn. & violet 8 5
294. – 25 f. red, yellow & green 20 8
DESIGN: 25 f. "Spathodea".

1958. Declaration of Human Rights. 10th Anniv. As T 5 of Comoro Is.
295. 20 f. turquoise and blue 35 20

POSTAGE DUE STAMPS

D 1. D 2.

1937.
D 83. D 1. 5 c. blue and purple 5 5
D 84. 10 c. red 5 5
D 85. 20 c. green 5 5
D 86. 25 c. pink and brown 5 5
D 87. 30 c. blue and red 5 5
D 88. 45 c. green and mauve 5 5
D 89. 50 c. pink and olive 8 8
D 90. 60 c. yellow & purple 12 12
D 91. 1 f. yellow and brown 10 10
D 92. 2 f. pink and blue 25 25
D 93. 3 f. blue and brown 30 30

1947.
D 257. D 2. 10 c. red 5 5
D 258. 30 c. orange 5 5
D 259. 50 c. black 5 5
D 260. 1 f. red 5 5
D 261. 2 f. green 5 5
D 262. 3 f. mauve 5 5
D 263. 4 f. blue 5 5
D 264. 5 f. brown 5 8
D 265. 10 f. blue 8 12
D 266. 20 f. brown 12 12

FRENCH GUIANA O2

Formerly a French colony on the N.E. coast of S. America, now an overseas department using the stamps of France.

Nos. 1 to 32 and 51 are all stamps of French Colonies surcharged or overprinted.

1886. "Peace and Commerce" and "Commerce" types, surch. **Dec. 1886. GUY. FRANC. Of. 05.**
2. 8. 0 f. 05 on 2 c. green 70·00 70·00
5. 9. 0 f. 05 on 2 c. brown 60·00 60·00

1887. "Ceres" and "Peace and Commerce" types, surch. **Avril 1887 GUY. FRANC.** and value.
6. 8. 0 f. 05 on 2 c. green 16·00 15·00
7b. 0 f. 20 on 35 c. blk. on yell. 6·50 6·50
8. 7. 0 f. 25 on 30 c. brown 5·50 5·00

1887. "Ceres" and "Peace and Commerce" types, surch. **DEC. 1887 GUY. FRANC. 5c.**
9. 7. 5 c. on 30 c. brown 19·00 18·00
10. 8. 5 c. on 30 c. brown £250 £225

1888. "Ceres" and "Peace and Commerce" types, surch. **Fevrier 1888 GUY. FRANC** and value.
11. 7. 5 on 30 c. brown 19·00 19·00
12. 8. 10 on 75 c. red 32·00 30·00

1892. "Ceres", "Peace and Commerce" and "Commerce" types, optd. **GUYANE.**
20. 9. 1 c. black on blue 6·50 4·50
15. 8. 2 c. green £140 £130
21. 9. 2 c. brown on yellow 5·00 4·50
22. 4 c. lilac on grey 5·00 4·50
23. 5 c. green 5·00 4·50
24. 10 c. black on lilac 8·50 6·00
25. 15 c. blue 6·50 5·50
26. 20 c. red on green 6·50 6·00
27. 25 c. black on red 10·00 4·00
14. 7. 30 c. brown 18·00 18·00
28. 9. 30 c. brown 5·50 4·50
16. 8. 35 c. black on yellow £400 £325
29. 9. 35 c. black on yellow 28·00 30·00
17. 8. 40 c. red on yellow 16·00 15·00
30. 9. 40 c. red on yellow 19·00 16·00
18. 8. 75 c. red 16·00 15·00
31. 9. 75 c. red 17·00 15·00
19. 8. 1 f. olive 22·00 20·00
32. 9. 1 f. olive 32·00 30·00

1892. "Commerce" type, surch. **DEC. 92. Of 05 GUYANE.**
51. 9. 0 f. 05 on 15 c. blue 3·25 3·25

1892. "Tablet" key-type inscr. "GUYANE".
38. D. 1 c. black on blue 15 12
39. 2 c. brown on yellow 15 12
40. 4 c. lilac on grey 15 10
52. 5 c. green 5 5
42. 10 c. black on lilac 1·10 50
53. 10 c. red 50 15
43. 15 c. blue 3·25 25
54. 15 c. grey 16·00 13·00
44. 20 c. red on green 2·50 1·75
45. 25 c. black on red 1·75 35
55. 25 c. blue 2·25 2·50
46. 30 c. brown 2·25 1·60
47. 40 c. red on yellow 2·25 1·60
48. 50 c. red 3·25 1·90
56. 50 c. brown on blue 2·75 2·25
49. 75 c. brown on yellow 4·50 2·75
50. 1 f. olive 2·25 1·60
57. 2 f. violet on red 32·00 95

1. Ant-eater. 2. Gold-washer.

3. Plantation of Coco-nut palms, Cayenne.

1904.
58. 1. 1 c. black 5 5
59. 2 c. blue 5 5
60. 4 c. chocolate 5 5
61. 5 c. green 8 5
83. 5 c. orange 5 5
62. 10 c. red 5 5
84. 10 c. green 5 5
104. 10 c. orange 5 5
63. 15 c. violet 10 10
64. 2. 20 c. chocolate 5 5
65. 25 c. blue 15 8
85. 25 c. violet 8 8
66. 30 c. black 8 5
86. 30 c. red 5 5
105. 30 c. orange 5 5
106. 30 c. green 5 5
66a. 35 c. black on yellow 5 5
67. 40 c. red 5 5
87. 40 c. black 8 8
68. 45 c. olive 5 5
69. 50 c. lilac 30 25
88. 50 c. blue 5 5
107. 50 c. grey 5 5
108. 60 c. mauve 5 5
109. 65 c. green 5 5
70. 75 c. green 5 5
110. 85 c. purple 20 15
71. 3. 1 f. red 5 5
111. 1 f. blue 5 5
112. 1 f. blue on green 30 25
113. 1 f. 10 red 10 10
72. 2 f. blue 5 5
114. 2 f. red on yellow 10 10
73. 5 f. black 60 55
115. 10 f. green on yellow 1·90 1·90
116. 20 f. red 2·00 2·00

1912. "Tablet" key-type surch. in figures.
74. D. 05 on 2 c. brn. on yellow 5 5
75. 05 on 4 c. lilac on grey 5 5
76. 05 on 20 c. red on green 5 5
77. 05 on 25 c. black on red 25 25
78. 05 on 30 c. brown 10 10
79. 10 on 40 c. red on yellow 8 8
80. 10 on 50 c. red 20 20

1915. Red Cross surch. with red cross over **5.**
81. 1. 10 c.+5 c. red 1·75 1·25

1915. Red Cross surch. **5 c.** and red cross.
82. 1. 10 c.+5 c. red 5 5

1922. Surch. in figures with bars.
89. 1. 0. 01 on 15 c. violet 5 5
90. 0. 02 on 15 c. violet 5 5
91. 0. 04 on 15 c. violet 5 5
92. 0. 05 on 15 c. violet 5 5
95. 25 c. on 15 c. violet 5 5
96. 3. 25 c. on 2 f. blue 5 5
97. 2. 65 on 45 c. olive 8 8
98. 85 on 45 c. olive 8 8
99. 90 on 75 c. red 10 10
100. 3. 1 f. 05 on 2 f. brown 10 10
101. 1 f. 25 on 1 f. blue 8 [illegible]
102. 1 f. 50 on 1 f. blue 10 10
103. 3 f. on 5 f. mauve 12 12

1924. Surch. in words.
93. 3. 10 f. on 1 f. green on yell. 1·60 1·60
94. 20 f. on 5 f. mauve on red 1·60 1·60

4. Carib Archer. 5. Shooting the Rapids, R. Maroni.

6. Government Building, Cayenne.

1929.
117. 4. 1 c. green and lilac 5 5
118. 2 c. green and red 5 5
119. 3 c. green and violet 5 5
120. 4 c. mauve and brown 5 5
121. 5 c. red and blue 5 5
122. 10 c. brown and mauve 5 5
123. 15 c. red and yellow 5 5
124. 20 c. olive and blue 5 5
125. 25 c. brown and red 5 5
126. 5. 30 c. green 5 5
127. 30 c. brown and green 5 5
128. 35 c. green and blue 5 5
129. 40 c. olive and brown 5 5
130. 45 c. brown and green 5 5
131. 45 c. green and olive 5 5
132. 50 c. olive and blue 5 5
133. 55 c. red and blue 8 5
134. 60 c. green and red 5 5
135. 65 c. green and red 5 5
136. 70 c. green and blue 5 5
137. 75 c. blue 12 12
138. 80 c. blue and black 5 5
139. 90 c. red 5 5
140. 90 c. brown and mauve 5 5
141. 1 f. brown and mauve 10 8
142. 1 f. red 12 10
143. 1 f. blue and black 5 5
144. 6. 1 f. 05 green and red 60 55
145. 1 f. 10 mauve and olive 60 55
146. 1 f. 25 green and brown 8 8
147. 1 f. 25 red 5 5
148. 1 f. 40 mauve and brown 5 5
149. 1 f. 50 blue 5 5
150. 1 f. 60 green and brown 5 5
151. 1 f. 75 brown and red 20 15
152. 1 f. 75 blue 8 8
153. 2 f. red and green 5 5
154. 2 f. 25 blue 5 5
155. 2 f. 50 brown and red 5 5
156. 3 f. mauve and red 5 5
157. 5 f. green and violet 5 5
158. 10 f. blue and olive 8 8
159. 20 f. red and blue 12 12

1931. "Colonial Exhibition" key types inscr. "GUYANE FRANCAISE".
160. E. 40 c. green 55 55
161. F. 50 c. mauve 55 55
162. G. 90 c. red 55 55
163. H. 1 f. 50 blue 55 55

7. Cayenne.

1933. Air.
164. 7. 50 c. brown 5 5
165. 1 f. green 5 5
166. 1 f. 50 blue 5 5
167. 2 f. orange 5 5
168. 3 f. black 5 5
169. 5 f. violet 5 5
170. 10 f. olive 5 5
171. 20 f. red 8 8

8. Cayenne recaptured by D'Estrees, 1676.

9. Local Products.

1935. West Indies Tercent.
172. 8. 40 c. brown 65 50
173. 50 c. red .. .. 1·50 1·00
174. 1 f. 50 blue 65 60
175. 9. 1 f. 75 red .. .. 1·90 1·75
176. 5 f. brown .. .. 1·75 1·40
177. 10 f. green .. .. 1·75 1·40

1937. International Exhibition, Paris. As Nos. 110/15 of Cameroun.
178. 9. 20 c. violet 10 10
179. 30 c. green 10 10
180. 40 c. red 10 10
181. 50 c. brown 10 10
182. 90 c. red 12 12
183. 1 f. 50 blue 12 12

1936. Int. Anti-Cancer Fund. As T **10** of Cameroun.
184. 1 f. 75+50 c. blue .. 1·50 1·50

1939. New York World's Fair. As T **11** of Cameroun.
185. 1 f. 25 red 10 10
186. 2 f. 25 blue 10 10

1939. 150th Anniv. of French Revolution. As T **16** of Cameroun.
187. 45 c.+25 c. grn. & blk. (post) .. .. .. 1·10 1·10
188. 70 c.+30 c. brn. & blk.. . 1·10 1·10
189. 90 c.+35 c. orge. & blk. 1·10 1·10
190. 1 f. 25+1 f. red & black 1·10 1·10
191. 2 f. 25+2 f. blue & black 1·10 1·10
192. 5 f.+4 f. black & orange (air) .. .. .. 2·50 2·50

1941. Marshal Petain Issue. As T **4a** of Dahomey.
192a. 1 f. purple 5 5
192b. 2 f. 50 blue 5 5
DESIGN—HORIZ. View of Cayenne and Marshal Petain.

1944. Mutual Aid and Red Cross Funds. As T **19** of Cameroun.
193. 5 f.+20 f. maroon .. 8 8

1945. Felix Eboue. As T **20** of Cameroun.
194. 2 f. black 5 5
195. 25 f. green 8 8

10. Arms of French Guiana.

1945.
196. 10. 10 c. blue 5 5
197. 30 c. brown 5 5
198. 40 c. blue 5 5
199. 50 c. purple 5 5
200. 60 c. yellow 5 5
201. 70 c. brown 5 5
202. 80 c. green 5 5
203. 1 f. blue 5 5
204. 1 f. 20 lilac 5 5
205. 1 f. 50 orange 8 8
206. 2 f. black 8 8
207. 2 f. 40 red 5 5
208. 3 f. pink 8 8
209. 4 f. blue 10 10
210. 4 f. 50 green 10 10
211. 5 f. brown 10 10
212. 10 f. violet 10 10
213. 15 f. red 8 8
214. 20 f. olive 12 12

1945. Air. As T **18** of Cameroun.
215. 50 f. green 15 15
216. 100 f. claret 30 30

1946. Air. Victory. As T **21** of Cameroun.
217. 8 f. black 15 15

1946. Air. From Chad to the Rhine. As T **22** of Cameroun.
218. 5 f. blue 8 8
219. 10 f. red 10 10
220. 15 f. purple 15 15
221. 20 f. green 15 15
222. 25 f. purple 15 15
223. 50 f. mauve 20 20

11. Hammoc... 12. Toucans.

13. Eagles.

1947.
224. 11. 10 c. green (postage) .. 5 5
225. 30 c. red 5 5
226. 50 c. purple 5 5
227. – 60 c. grey 5 5
228. – 1 f. lake 5 5
229. – 1 f. 50 brown 5 5
230. – 2 f. green 5 5
231. – 2 f. 50 blue 5 5
232. – 3 f. lake 8 8
233. – 4 f. brown 12 12
234. – 5 f. blue 12 12
235. – 6 f. lake 12 12
236. 12. 10 f. blue 45 40
237. 15 f. brown 55 45
238. 20 f. lake 75 60
239. – 25 f. green 85 75
240. – 40 f. brown .. .. 1·00 90
241. 13. 50 f. green (air) .. 1·75 1·75
242. – 100 f. lake .. .. 1·75 1·75
243. – 200 f. blue .. .. 3·00 3·00
DESIGNS—As T **11/12**—HORIZ. 60 c. to 1 f. 50, Riverside village. 2 f. to 3 f. Pirogue. 25 f., 40 f. Macaws. VERT. 4 f. to 6 f. Girl. As T **13**—VERT. 100 f. 'Plane over Peccary and palms. HORIZ. 200 f. 'Plane and toucans.

POSTAGE DUE STAMPS

1925. Postage Due stamps of France optd. **GUYANE FRANCAISE** or surch. also **centimes a percevoir** and value in figures.
D 117. D 2. 5 c. blue 5 5
D 118. 10 c. brown 5 5
D 119. 15 c. on 20 c. olive .. 5 5
D 120. 20 c. olive 5 5
D 121. 25 c. on 5 c. blue .. 5 5
D 122. 30 c. on 20 c. olive 5 5
D 123. 45 c. on 10 c. brown 5 5
D 124. 50 c. claret .. 8 8
D 125. 60 c. on 5 c. blue .. 10 10
D 126. 1 f. on 20 c. olive 12 15
D 127. 2 f. on 50 c. claret.. 20 20
D 128. 3 f. magenta .. 1·00 1·00

D 1. Palm trees.

D 1.

1929.
D 160. D 1. 5 c. blue 5 5
D 161. 10 c. blue and yellow 5 5
D 162. 20 c. red and green 5 5
D 163. 30 c. red and brown 5 5
D 164. 50 c. brown & mauve 5 5
D 165. 60 c. brown and red 8 8
D 166. – 1 f. brown and blue 12 12
D 167. – 2 f. green and red .. 20 20
D 168. – 3 f. grey and mauve 30 30
DESIGN: 1 f. to 3 f. Creole girl.

1947.
D 244. D 2. 10 c. red 5 5
D 245. 30 c. green 5 5
D 246. 50 c. black 5 5
D 247. 1 f. blue 5 5
D 248. 2 f. lake 5 5
D 249. 3 f. violet 5 5
D 250. 4 f. red 8 8
D 251. 5 f. purple 10 10
D 252. 10 f. green 15 15
D 253. 20 f. purple 20 20

FRENCH GUINEA O2

A French colony on the W. coast of Africa incorporated in French West Africa in 1944. Became completely independent in 1958 (see Guinea).

1892. "Tablet" key-type inscr. "GUINEE FRANCAISE".
1. D. 1 c. black on blue .. 10 10
2. 2 c. brown on yellow .. 10 10
3. 4 c. lilac on grey 20 20
4. 5 c. green .. .. 1·00 90
5. 10 c. black on lilac .. 65 35
14. 10 c. red .. .. 6·00 5·50
6. 15 c. blue 75 40
15. 15 c. grey .. .. 18·00 17·00
7. 20 c. red on green .. 2·25 1·75
8. 25 c. black on red .. 1·60 1·10
16. 25 c. blue .. .. 2·75 2·25
9. 30 c. brown .. .. 4·50 3·50
10. 40 c. red on yellow .. 4·50 3·00
11. 50 c. red .. .. 6·50 9·00
17. 50 c. olive on blue .. 4·00 3·50
12. 75 c. olive on yellow .. 9·00 7·00
13. 1 f. olive .. .. 6·50 5·50

1. Fulas Shepherd.

2. Ford at Kitim.

1904.
18. 1. 1 c. black on green .. 10 8
19. 2 c. brown on yellow .. 10 10
20. 4 c. red on blue 20 15
21. 5 c. green 20 12
22. 10 c. red 40 20
23. 15 c. lilac .. .. .. 1·00 60
24. 20 c. red on green .. 2·25 1·75
25. 25 c. blue .. .. .. 2·25 1·75
26. 30 c. brown .. .. 3·75 3·25
27. 40 c. red on yellow .. 5·00 3·75
28. 50 c. olive on green .. 5·00 4·50
29. 75 c. blue on yellow .. 5·50 5·00
30. 1 f. olive .. .. .. 7·00 5·50
31. 2 f. red on yellow .. 14·00 12·00
32. 5 f. blue on green .. 20·00 18·00

1906. "Faidherbe", "Palms" and "Balay" key-types inscr. "GUINEE".
33. I. 1 c. slate 5 5
34. 2 c. brown 10 8
35. 4 c. brown on blue .. 12 12
36. 5 c. green 45 30
37. 10 c. red .. .. 2·50 25
38. J. 20 c. black on blue .. 45 40
39. 25 c. blue .. .. 1·10 75
40. 30 c. brown on pink .. 65 60
41. 35 c. black on yellow .. 25 20
43. 45 c. brown on green .. 55 50
44. 50 c. violet .. .. 1·50 1·40
45. 75 c. green on orange .. 55 50
46. K. 1 f. black on blue .. 2·75 2·50
47. 2 f. blue on pink .. .. 6·00 6·00
48. 5 f. red on yellow .. 8·50 7·50

1912. Surch. in figures.
49. D. 05 on 2 c. brown on yellow 12 12
50. 05 on 4 c. lilac on grey .. 8 8
51. 05 on 15 c. blue 8 8
52. 05 on 20 c. red on green .. 40 40
53. 05 on 30 c. brown.. .. 50 50
54. 10 on 40 c. red on yellow.. 12 12
55. 10 on 75 c. brown on yell. 75 75

1912. Surch. on figures.
56. 1. 05 on 2 c. brown on yellow 10 10
57. 05 on 4 c. red on blue .. 10 10
58. 05 on 15 c. lilac 10 10
59. 05 on 20 c. red on green.. 10 10
60. 05 on 25 c. blue 10 10
61. 05 on 30 c. brown 12 12
62. 10 on 40 c. red on yellow.. 15 15
63. 10 on 50 c. olive on green 25 25

1913.
64. 2. 1 c. blue on violet .. 5 5
65. 2 c. brown 5 5
66. 4 c. black and grey .. 5 5
67. 5 c. green 5 5
83. 5 c. green and purple .. 5 5
68. 10 c. purple and red .. 5 5
84. 10 c. green 5 5
85. 10 c. red and lilac .. 5 5
69. 15 c. red and purple .. 5 5
86. 15 c. green 5 5
87. 15 c. purple and brown 5 5
70. 20 c. violet and brown .. 5 5
88. 20 c. green 5 5
89. 20 c. brown and red .. 5 5
71. 25 c. deep blue and blue 8 8
90. 25 c. violet and black .. 5 5
72. 30 c. green and purple .. 5 5
91. 30 c. rose and red .. 5 5
92. 30 c. green and red .. 5 5
93. 30 c. green and olive .. 20 12
73. 35 c. red and blue .. 5 5
74. 40 c. grey and green .. 8 5
75. 45 c. red and brown .. 8 8
76. 50 c. black and blue .. 65 45
94. 50 c. blue 5 5
95. 50 c. olive and brown .. 5 5
96. 60 c. violet 5 5
97. 65 c. blue and brown .. 12 10
77. 75 c. blue and red .. 10 8
98. 75 c. blue 5 5
99. 75 c. green and purple .. 15 5
100. 85 c. claret and green .. 8 8
101. 90 c. mauve and red .. 90 75
78. 1 f. black and violet .. 12 5
102. 1 f. 10 brown and violet 95 95
103. 1 f. 25 orange and violet 15 12
104. 1 f. 50 blue 45 35
105. 1 f. 75 purple and brown 20 20
79. 2 f. brown and orange .. 20 8
106. 3 f. purple 90 60
80. 5 f. violet and black .. 1·25 1·10
107. 5 f. black and blue .. 25 20

1915. Surch. **5 c.** and red cross.
81. 2. 10 c.+5 c. purple and red 12 8

1922. Surch. in figures and bars.
108. 2. 25 c. on 2 f. brn. & oran. 5 5
109. 25 c. on 5 f. black & blue 5 5
110. 60 on 75 c. violet .. 5 5
111. 65 on 75 c. blue and red 8 8
112. 85 on 75 c. blue and red 8 8
113. 90 c. on 75 c. pur. & red 20 20
114. 1 f. 25 on 1 f. blue .. 5 5
115. 1 f. 50 on 1 f. blue .. 20 20
116. 3 f. on 5 f. slate & purple 55 55
117. 10 f. on 5 f. green & blue 95 95
118. 20 f. on 5 f. brown & pur. 2·50 2·50

1931. "Colonial Exhibition" key-types inscr. "GUINEE FRANCAISE".
119. E. 40 c. black and green .. 55 55
120. F. 50 c. black and purple .. 55 55
121. G. 90 c. black and red .. 50 40
122. H. 1 f. 50 black and blue .. 30 30

1937. Int. Exn. Paris. As Nos. 110/15 of Cameroun.
123. 20 c. violet 20 20
124. 30 c. green 20 20
125. 40 c. red 20 20
126. 50 c. brown 20 20
127. 90 c. red 20 20
128. 1 f. 50 blue 20 20

3. Native Village.

1938.
129. 3. 2 c. red 5 5
130. 3 c. blue 5 5
131. 4 c. green 5 5
132. 5 c. red 5 5
133. 10 c. blue 5 5
134. 15 c. purple 5 5
135. – 20 c. red 5 5
136. – 25 c. blue 5 5
137. – 30 c. blue 5 5
138. – 35 c. green 5 5
139. – 40 c. brown 5 5
140. – 45 c. green 5 5
141. – 50 c. red 5 5
142. – 55 c. blue 5 5
143. – 60 c. blue 5 5
144. – 65 c. green 8 5
145. – 70 c. green 10 10
146. – 80 c. purple 5 5
147. – 90 c. purple 12 12
148. – 1 f. red 20 15
149. – 1 f. brown 5 5
150. – 1 f. 25 red 12 12
151. – 1 f. 40 brown 10 10
152. – 1 f. 50 brown 12 12
153. – 1 f. 60 red 8 8
154. – 1 f. 75 blue 5 5
155. – 2 f. mauve 8 8
156. – 2 f. 25 blue 15 15
157. – 2 f. 50 brown 12 12
158. – 3 f. blue 5 5
159. – 5 f. purple 5 5
160. – 10 f. green 10 8
161. – 20 f. brown 15 10
DESIGNS—HORIZ. 20 c. to 50 c. Wooden pot makers. 55 c. to 1 f. 50 Waterfall. VERT. 1 f. 60 to 20 f. Native women.

1938. Int. Anti-Cancer Fund. As T **10** of Cameroun.
162. 1 f. 75+50 c. blue .. 1·25 1·25

1939. R. Caillie. Death Cent. As T **2** of Dahomey.
163. 90 c. orange 8 8
164. 2 f. violet 10 10
165. 2 f. 25 blue 10 10

1939. New York World's Fair. As T **11** of Cameroun.
166. 1 f. 25 red 10 10
167. 2 f. 25 blue 10 10

1939. French Revolution. 150th Anniv. As T **16** of Cameroun.
168. 45 c.+25 c. green & black 75 75
169. 70 c.+30 c. brown & black 75 75
170. 90 c.+35 c. orange & black 75 75
171. 1 f. 25+1 f. red & black 75 75
172. 2 f. 25+2 f. blue & black 75 75

1940. Air. As T **3** of Dahomey.
173. 1 f. 90 blue 5 5
174. 2 f. 90 red 5 5
175. 4 f. 50 green 8 8
176. 4 f. 90 olive 8 8
177. 6 f. 90 orange 12 12

1941. National Defence Fund. Surch. **SECOURS NATIONAL** and value.
178. +1 f. on 50 c. (No. 141) .. 10 10
179. +2 f. on 80 c. (No. 146) .. 70 70
180. +2 f. on 1 f. 50 (No. 152).. 70 70
181. +3 f. on 2 f. (No. 155) .. 70 70

1941. Marshal Petain Issue. As T **4a** of Dahomey.
182. 1 f. green 5 5
183. 2 f. 50 blue 5 5
DESIGN—VERT. Ford at Kitim and Marshal Petain.

1942. Air. Colonial Child Welfare. As Nos. 143g/i of Dahomey.
184. 1 f. 50+3 f. 50 green .. 5
185. 2 f.+6 f. brown 5
186. 3 f.+9 f. red 5

1942. Air. As T **4d** of Dahomey.
187. 50 f. olive and green .. 25 25

POSTAGE DUE STAMPS

D 1. Fulas Woman of Futa Jallon. **D 2.** Native Idol.

1905.
D 33. D 1. 5 c. blue 20 20
D 34. 10 c. brown 35 35
D 35. 15 c. green 75 55
D 36. 30 c. red 90 45
D 37. 50 c. black .. .. 1·10 1·00
D 38. 60 c. orange .. .. 1·75 1·40
D 39. 1 f. lilac .. .. 6·00 5·50

1906. "Natives" key-type inscr. "GUINEE".
D 49. L. 5 c. green .. .. 3·25 1·75
D 50. 10 c. claret 95 65
D 51. 15 c. blue 45 45
D 52. 20 c. black on yellow .. 45 45
D 53. 30 c. red .. .. 4·50 3·75
D 54. 50 c. violet .. .. 4·00 3·25
D 55. 60 c. black on buff .. 3·25 3·00
D 56. 1 f. black .. .. 2·00 1·75

1914. "Figure" key-type inscr. "**GUINEE**".
D 81. M. 5 c. green 5 5
D 82. 10 c. red 5 5
D 83. 15 c. grey 5 5
D 84. 20 c. brown 5 5
D 85. 30 c. blue 5 5
D 86. 50 c. black 8 8
D 87. 60 c. orange 20 20
D 88. 1 f. violet 25 25

1927. Surch. in figures.
D 119. M. 2 F. on 1 f. mauve .. 65 65
D 120. 3 F. on 1 f. brown .. 65 65

1938.
D 162. D 2. 5 c. violet 5 5
D 163. 10 c. red 5 5
D 164. 15 c. green 5 5
D 165. 20 c. brown 5 5
D 166. 30 c. purple 5 5
D 167. 50 c. chocolate 5 5
D 168. 60 c. blue 5 5
D 169. 1 f. red 8 8
D 170. 2 f. blue 12 12
D 171. 3 f. black 12 12

For later issues see **GUINEA**.

FRENCH LEVANT E3

General issues for the French Post Offices in the Turkish Empire.

40 paras = 1 piastre.
1902. 100 centimes = 1 franc.

1885. Stamps of France surch. in figures and words.
1. 10. 1 pi. on 25 c. yellow .. 60·00 1·60
4a. 1 pi. on 25 c. black on red 35 10
5. 2 pi. on 50 c. red .. 1·75 20
2. 3 pi. on 75 c. red .. 3·25 1·50
3. 4 pi. on 1 f. olive .. 2·75 1·10
7. 8 pi. on 2 f. brn. on blue .. 5·00 3·25
8. 20 pi. on 5 f. mauve .. 11·00 6·50

1902. "Blanc", "Mouchon" and "Merson" key-types inscr. "LEVANT".
9. A. 1 c. grey 5 5
10. 2 c. claret 5 5
11. 3 c. red 5 5
12. 4 c. brown 20 20
13. 5 c. green 8 5
14. B. 10 c. red 10 5
15. 15 c. orange 25 15
16. 20 c. claret 25 15
17. 30 c. mauve 50 25
18. C. 40 c. red and blue .. 50 25

1902. Surch. in figures and words.
19. B. 1 pi. on 25 c. blue .. 10 5
20. C. 2 pi. on 50 c. brn. & lav. 20 10
21. 4 pi. on 1 f. red & green 35 20
22. 8 pi. on 2 f. lilac & yellow 2·25 2·00
23. 20 pi. on 5 f. blue & yell. 55 50

1905. Surch. **1 Piastre Beyrouth.**
24. B. 1 pi. on 15 c. orange .. £225 38·00

1906. For use in Ethiopia.
25. A. 25 c. blue .. .. 7·00 6·00
26. B. 50 c. brown and lavender 27·00 22·00
27. 1 f. red and green .. 60·00 60·00

1921. Stamps of France surch. in figures and words.
28. 17. 30 par. on 5 c. green .. 5 5
29. 30 par. on 5 c. orange .. 5 5
30. 1 pi. 20 on 10 c. red .. 10 10
31. 1 pi. 20 on 10 c. green .. 10 5
39. 3 pi. 30 on 15 c. green .. 2·75 2·75
32. 3 pi. 30 on 25 c. blue .. 5 5
33. 4 pi. 20 on 30 c. orange .. 8 8
40. 7 pi. 20 on 35 c. violet .. 2·75 2·75
34. 15. 7 pi. 20 on 50 c. blue .. 8 5
35. 13. 15 pi. on 1 f. red & green 20 15
36. 30 pi. on 3 f. red & green 1·40 1·10
37. 75 pi. on 5 f. blue & yell. 1·10 45

For stamps issued by the Free French forces during 1942/3 see under **FREE FRENCH FORCES IN THE LEVANT.**

FRENCH MOROCCO O3

Part of the Sultanate of Morocco which was a French protectorate from 1912 until independence was granted on 2 March 1956. For issues before 1912, see French P.O's. in Morocco, and for stamps used in the International Zone French P.O's. in Tangier.

100 centimes = 1 franc

1914. "Blanc", "Mouchon" and "Merson" optd. **PROTECTORAT FRANCAIS.**
40. A. 1 c. on 1 c. grey 5 5
41. 2 c. on 2 c. claret .. 5 5
42. 3 c. on 3 c. orange .. 10 10
43. 5 c. on 5 c. green 5 5
44. B. 10 c. on 10 c. red 5 5
45. 15 c. on 15 c. orange .. 5 5
46. 20 c. on 20 c. claret .. 50 50
47. 25 c. on 25 c. blue .. 10 5
48. 25 c. on 25 c. brown .. 8 5
49. 30 c. on 30 c. brown .. 1·60 1·60
50. 35 c. on 35 c. lilac .. 45 12
51. C. 40 c. on 40 c. red and blue 1·75 75
52. 45 c. on 45 c. green & blue 4·75 4·50
53. 50 c. on 50 c. brn. & lilac .. 5 5
54. 1 p. red and green .. 12 5
55. 2 p. lilac and yellow .. 45 12
56. 5 p. blue and yellow .. 1·10 65

1914. Same types surch. 5 c. and red cross.
(a) Without Arabic opt.
63. A. 5 c.+5 c. green 20 20

(b) With Arabic opt.
58. B. 10 c.+5 c. red 35 35

(c) Without **PROTECTORAT FRANCAIS.**
64. B. 10 c.+5 c. red 35 35

(d) With Arabic and optd. **MAROC.**
63. 18. 10 c.+5 c. red 70 65

1.

1915. Optd. **PROTECTORAT FRANCAIS** and surch. also.
65. 1. 10 c.+5 c. red 30 30

2. Rabat.

3. Fez.

1917.
76. 2. 1 c. black 5 5
77. 2 c. purple 5 5
78. 3 c. brown 5 5
79. 3. 5 c. green 5 5
80. 10 c. red 5 5
81. 15 c. grey 5 5
82. – 20 c. claret 60 60
83. – 25 c. blue 50 8
84. – 30 c. lilac 60 45
85. – 35 c. orange 45 30
86. – 40 c. blue 12 8
87. – 45 c. green .. .. 2·25 1·60
88. – 50 c. brown 90 55
89. – 1 f. grey .. .. 1·00 55
90. – 2 f. brown .. .. 27·00 19·00
91. – 5 f. black .. .. 5·00 4·75
92. – 10 f. black .. .. 5·00 4·75
DESIGNS—HORIZ. 50 c., 1 f. Mekes. 2, 5, 10 f. Volubilis. VERT. 20 c. to 30 c. Chella. 35 c. to 45 c. Marrakesh.

8. Aeroplane over Casablanca.

1922. Air.
112. 8. 5 c. orange 5 5
113. 25 c. blue 5 5
114. 50 c. blue 5 5
115. 75 c. blue .. .. 10·00 1·90
116. 75 c. green 5 5
117. 80 c. claret 15 8
118. 1 f. red 5 5
119. 1 f. 40 red 15 15
120. 1 f. 90 blue 20 20
121. 2 f. violet 12 10
122. 3 f. black 25 15

1923. Types of 1917 re-drawn and inscr. "HELIO VAUGIRARD" below the designs.
123. 2. 1 c. olive 5 5
124. 2 c. claret 5 5
125. 3 c. brown 5 5
126. 3. 5 c. yellow 5 5
127. 10 c. green 5 5
128. 15 c. black 5 5
129. – 20 c. plum 5 5
130. – 20 c. claret 5 5
131. – 25 c. blue 5 5
132. – 30 c. red 5 5
133. – 30 c. blue 10 5
134. – 35 c. purple 5 5
135. – 40 c. orange 5 5
136. – 45 c. green 5 5
137. – 50 c. green 5 5
138. – 50 c. blue 5 5
139. – 60 c. mauve 8 5
140. – 75 c. purple 8 5
141. – 1 f. brown 8 5
142. – 1 f. 05 brown 15 15
143. – 1 f. 40 red 8 8
144. 1 f. 50 blue 8 5
145. – 2 f. brown 12 12
146. – 3 f. red 15 12
147. – 5 f. green 55 25
148. – 10 f. black .. .. 1·50 95
DESIGNS—HORIZ. 50 c. (No. 137) to 1 f. 50 c. Meknes. 2 f. to 10 f. Volubilis. VERT. 20 c. to 30 c. Cheila. 35 c. to 50 c. (No. 136) Marrakesh.

9. Ploughing with Camel and Donkey.

1928. Air. Flood Relief.
149. – 5 c. blue 45 45
150. 9. 25 c. orange 45 45
151. – 50 c. red 45 45
152. – 75 c. brown 45 45
153. – 80 c. green 45 45
154. – 1 f. orange 45 45
155. – 1 f. 50 blue 45 45
156. – 2 f. brown 45 45
157. – 3 f. purple 45 45
158. – 5 f. black 45 45
DESIGNS: 5 c. Moorish tribesmen. 50 c. Caravan nearing Safi. 75 c. Walls of Marrakesh. 80 c. Sheep grazing at Azrou. 1 f. Gateway at Fez. 1 f. 50, Tangier. 2 f. Casablanca. 3 f. Storks at Rabat. 5 f. "La Hedia", a Moorish entertainment.

1930. Stamps of 1923 surch.
163. 15 c. on 40 c. orange .. 8 8
164. 25 c. on 30 c. blue .. 30 30
165. 50 c. on 60 c. mauve .. 8 5
166. 1 f. on 1 f. 40 red .. 30 20

1931. Air. Surch.
167. 8. 1 f. on 1 f. 40 red .. 25 25
168. 1 f. 50 on 1 f. 90 blue .. 25 25

10. Sultan's Palace, Tangier.

11. Saadian Tombs, Marrakesh.

1933.
169. 10. 1 c. black 5 5
170. 2 c. mauve 5 5
171. – 3 c. brown 5 5
172. – 5 c. lake 5 5
173. – 10 c. green 5 5
174. – 15 c. black 5 5
175. – 20 c. maroon 5 5
176. – 25 c. blue 5 5
177. – 30 c. green 5 5
178. – 40 c. sepia 5 5
179. – 45 c. purple 5 5
180. – 50 c. green 5 5
181. – 65 c. red 5 5
182. – 75 c. purple 5 5
183. – 90 c. red 5 5
184. – 1 f. brown 5 5
185. – 1 f. 25 black 10 5
186. – 1 f. 50 blue 15 5
187. – 1 f. 75 green 8 5
188. – 2 f. brown 40 5
189. – 3 f. red .. .. 5·50 1·10
190. 11. 5 f. lake 80 15
191. 10 f. black .. .. 1·10 90
192. 20 f. grey .. .. 1·25 1·10
DESIGNS—HORIZ. 3 c., 5 c. Agadir Bay. 10 c. to 20 c. G.P.O., Casablanca. 25 c. to 40 c. Moulay Idriss. 45 c. to 65 c. Rabat. 1 f. 50 to 3 f. Quarzazat. VERT. 75 c. to 1 f. 25, Attarine College, Fez.

12. Hassan Tower, Rabat.

13. Marshal Lyautey.

1933. Air.
193. 12. 50 c. blue 10 8
194. 80 c. brown 8 5
195. 1 f. 50 lake 8 5
196. 2 f. 50 red 70 5
197. – 5 f. violet 45 25
198. – 10 f. green 15 8
DESIGN: 2 f. 50 to 10 f. Casablanca.

1935. Lyautey Memorial Fund.
199. 18. 50 c.+50 c. red (post.) 85 85
200. 1 f.+1 f. green .. 85 85
201. 5 f.+5 f. brown .. 7·00 6·50
202. – 1 f. 50+1 f. 50 blue (air) 3·25 3·25
DESIGN—HORIZ. 1 f. 50, Lyautey in profile.

1938. Charity. Stamps of 1933 surch. **O.S.E.** and value.
203. 10. 2 c.+2 c. mauve (post.) 50 50
204. – 3 c.+3 c. brown .. 50 50
205. – 20 c.+20 c. maroon .. 50 50
206. – 40 c.+40 c. sepia .. 50 50
207. – 65 c.+65 c. red .. 50 50
208. – 1 f. 25+1 f. 25 black .. 50 50
209. – 2 f.+2 f. brown .. 50 50
210. 11. 5 f.+5 f. lake .. 50 50
211. 12. 50 c.+50 c. blue (air) .. 80 80
212. – 10 f.+10 f. green .. 80 80

1939. No. 180 surch.
213. 4 c. on 50 c. green .. 5 5

15. Mosque at Sale.

16. Shepherd and Arganier Trees.

18. Aeroplane over Morocco.

1939.
214. 15. 1 c. mauve (postage) .. 5 5
215. A. 2 c. green 5 5
216. 3 c. blue 5 5
217. 15. 5 c. green 5 5
218. A. 10 c. purple 5 5
219. B. 15 c. green 5 5
220. 20 c. brown 5 5
221. 16. 30 c. blue 5 5
222. 40 c. brown 5 5
223. 45 c. green 5 5
224. E. 50 c. red 12 8
225. 50 c. green 5 5
226. 60 c. blue 12 8
227. 60 c. brown 5 5
228. C. 70 c. violet 5 5
229. F. 75 c. green 5 5
230. 80 c. blue 5 5
231. 80 c. green 5 5
232. E. 90 c. blue 5 5
233. B. 1 f. brown 5 5
234. F. 1 f. 20 mauve 5 5
295. 1 f. 20 brown 5 5
235. 1 f. 25 red 5 5
296. A. 1 f. 30 blue 8 8
236. F. 1 f. 40 purple 5 5
237. E. 1 f. 50 pink 5 5
297. 1 f. 50 red 5 5
239. D. 2 f. green 5 5
240. 2 f. 25 blue 5 5
241. 15. 2 f. 40 red 5 5
242. 2 f. 50 red 5 5
243. 2 f. 50 blue 5 5
299. D. 3 f. brown 5 5
300. 16. 3 f. 50 red 8 5
245. 15. 4 f. blue 5 5
246. F. 4 f. 50 green 5 5
301. C. 4 f. 50 mauve 5 5
247. 5 f. blue 5 5
303. F. 6 f. blue 5 5
248. C. 10 f. red 10 8
305. 15 f. green 20 8
250. 20 f. purple 20 20
307. 25 f. brown 20 20
DESIGNS—VERT. A, Mosque at Sefrou. B, Horseman and Cedar tree. C, Gazelles. D, Fez. HORIZ. E. Ramparts at Sale. F, Draa Valley.

251. G. 80 c. green (air) .. 5 5
252. 1 f. brown 5 5
253. 18. 1 f. 90 blue 5 5
254. 2 f. purple 5 5
255. 3 f. brown 5 5
256. G. 5 f. violet 15 15
257. 18. 10 f. blue 10 10
DESIGN—VERT. G, Storks and Mosque at Chella.

1940. Alternate horiz. rows of No. 183 surch.
258. 35 c. on 65 c. red .. 20 12
Price is for vertical pair with normal.

1942. French Child Refugees in Morocco Fund. Types of 1939 surch. **Enfants de France au Maroc** and premium.
259. 16. 45 c.+2 f. green .. 25 25
260. E. 90 c.+4 f. blue .. 25 25
261. F. 1 f. 25+6 f. red .. 25 25
262. 15. 2 f. 50+8 f. blue .. 25 25

1943. As T 19 of Algeria.
263. 1 f. 50 blue 5 5

ILLUSTRATIONS
British Commonwealth and all overprints and surcharges are FULL SIZE. Foreign Countries have been reduced to ¾-LINEAR.

19. Tower of Hassan.

1943.
264. 19. 10 c. lilac 5 5
265. 30 c. blue 5 5
266. 40 c. red 5 5
267. 50 c. green 5 5
268. 60 c. brown 5 5
269. 70 c. lilac 5 5
270. 80 c. green 5 5
271. 1 f. red 5 5
272. 1 f. 20 violet 5 5
273. 1 f. 50 red 5 5
274. 2 f. green 5 5
275. 2 f. 40 red 5 5
276. 3 f. brown 5 5
277. 4 f. blue 5 5
278. 4 f. 50 black 5 5
279. 5 f. blue 5 5
280. 10 f. brown 5 5
281. 15 f. green 12 5
282. 20 f. purple 15 5

20. Aeroplane over Desert.
21. Aeroplane over Minarets.

1944. Air.
283. 20. 50 c. green 5 5
284. 2 f. blue 5 5
285. 5 f. red 5 5
286. 10 f. violet 5 5
287. 50 f. black 15 15
288. 100 f. blue and red .. 40 40

1944. Air. Mutual Help Fund. Surch. **ENTR'AIDE FRANCAISE +98 f. 50.**
289. 20. 1 f. 50+98 f. 50 red & bl. 20 25

1945. Air.
290. 21. 50 f. brown 15 15

1945. Anti-Tuberculosis Fund. No. 239 surch. **AIDES LES TUBERCULEUX +1 f.** or **3 fr.** and bars also.
308. D. 2 f.+1 f. green.. .. 5 5
310. 3 f. on 2 f.+1 f. green.. 5 5

22. Mausoleum.
23 Marshal Lyautey Statue, Casablanca.

1945. Solidarity Fund. Marshal Lyautey's Mausoleum.
309. 22. 2 f.+3 f. blue 5 5

1946. Air. Gen. De Gaulle's Call to Arms. 6th Anniv. Surch. **+5 F 18 Juin 1940-18 Juin 1946.**
311. 20. 5 f.+5 f. red 10 10

1946. Solidarity Fund.
312. 23. 2 f.+10 f. black (post.) 20 20
313. 3 f.+15 f. red.. .. 25 25
314. 10 f.+20 f. blue .. 50 50
315. 23. 10 f. +30 f. green (air).. 30 30

1947. Stamp Day. Surch. **JOURNEE DU TIMBRE 1947 +5 F 50.**
316. C. 4 f. 50+5 f. 50 mauve (No. 301) 20 20

24. Coastline and Symbols of Prosperity.

1947. Sherifian Phosphates Office. 25th Anniv.
317. 24. 3 f. 50+5 f. 50 green .. 10 10

25. The Terraces.
26. Coastal Fortress.
28. La Medina Barracks.
27. Barracks in the Mountains.

1947. (a) Postage.
318. 25. 10 c. brown 5 5
319. 30 c. red 5 5
320. 30 c. purple 5 5
321. 50 c. blue 5 5
322. 60 c. purple 5 5
323. 26. 1 f. black 5 5
324. 1 f. 50 blue 5 5
325. 27. 2 f. green 5 5
325a. 26. 2 f. purple 5 5
326. 27. 3 f. lake 5 5
327. – 4 f. violet 5 5
328. – 4 f. green 5 5
329. – 5 f. green 8 5
329a. – 5 f. emerald 5 5
330 – 6 f. red 5 5
330a. – 8 f. orange 5 5
331. – 10 f. blue 5 5
332a. – 10 f. red 8 5
333. 26. 12 f. red 10 5
334. – 15 f. green 12 5
334a. – 15 f. red 10 5
335. – 18 f. blue 12 8
336. – 20 f. red 10 5
337. – 25 f. violet 20 8
337a. – 25 f. blue 15 5
337b. – 25 f. violet 10 10
337c. – 30 f. blue 20 5
337d. – 35 f. brown 15 5
337e. – 50 f. slate 15 5
DESIGNS—HORIZ. 4 f., 6 f. Marrakesh. 5 f. (No. 329), 8 f. 10 f. blue, The Gardens, Fez. 5 f. (No. 329a), Fortified oasis. 15 f. red 25 f. (Nos. 337a/b), Walled city. 30 f., 35 f., 50 f. Todra Valley. VERT. 10 f. red, 15 f. 18 f., 20 f., 25 f. (No. 337), Barracks in oasis.

(b) Air.
338. – 9 f. red 5 5
339. – 40 f. blue 15 5
340. – 50 f. purple 15 5
341. 28. 100 f. blue 60 10
342. 200 f. red 90 20
342a. – 300 f. violet .. .. 4·00 2·75
DESIGNS—VERT. 9 f., 40 f., 50 f. Aeroplane over Moulay Idriss. HORIZ. 300 f. Oudayas Kasbah, Rabat.

29. "Energy".
30. "Supplies".

1947. Solidarity Fund. Inscr. "SOLIDARITE 1947".
343. 29. 6 f.+9 f. red (postage) 25 25
344. – 10 f.+20 f. blue .. 25 25
345. 30. 9 f.+16 f. green (air) .. 25 25
346. – 20 f.+35 f. brown .. 25 25
DESIGNS—VERT. 10 f. Red Cross unit ("Health"). HORIZ. 20 f. Aeroplane over landscape ("Agriculture").

1948. Stamp Day. View of Meknes (as No. 80) inscr. "JOURNEE DU TIMBRE 1948" below central vignette.
347. 6 f.+4 f. brown .. 12 12

30a. Marshal Lyautey's Mausoleum.
31. P.T.T. Clubhouse Ifrane.

1948. Air. Lyautey Exn., Paris.
348. 30a. 10 f.+25 f. green .. 20 20

1948. Air. P.T.T. Employees' Holiday Camp Fund.
349. 31. 6 f.+34 f. green .. 25 25
350. 9 f.+51 f. red 25 25

31a. Warship and Coastline.

1948. Naval Charities.
351. 31a. 6 f.+9 f. purple .. 25 25

1948. No. 250 surch.
352. C. 8 f. on 20 f. purple .. 8 5

32. Wheat and View of Meknes.
33. Aeroplane over Agadir.
35. Soldiers with Flag.
34. Gazelle Hunter.

1949. Solidarity Fund. Inscr. "SOLIDARITE 1948".
353. 32. 1 f.+2 f. orange (post).. 15 15
354. – 2 f.+5 f. red 15 15
355. – 3 f.+7 f. blue 15 15
356. – 5 f.+10 f. purple .. 15 15
357. 33. 5 f.+5 f. green (air) .. 15 15
358. – 6 f.+9 f. red 15 15
359. – 9 f.+16 f. brown .. 15 15
360. – 15 f.+25 f. slate .. 15 15
DESIGNS—HORIZ. 2 f. Olive grove, Taraoudant. 3 f. Trawling. 5 f. Plums at Marrakesh. VERT. 6 f. Fez. 9 f. Atlas Mountains. 15 f. Draa Valley.

1949. Stamp Day and Mazagan-Marrakesh Local Postage Stamp. 50th Anniv.
361. 34. 10 f.+5 f. red and purple 15 15

1949. Army Welfare Fund.
362. 35. 10 f.+10 f. red.. .. 25 25

36. Oudayas Gate, Rabat.
37. Nejjarine Fountain, Fez.
38. Gardens at Meknes.

1949.
363. 36. 10 c. black 5 5
364. 50 c. lake 5 5
365. 1 f. violet 5 5
366. 37. 2 f. claret 5 5
367. 3 f. blue 5 5
368. 5 f. emerald 5 5
369. 38. 8 f. green 5 5
370. 10 f. red 5 5

39. Post Office, Meknes.
40. Aeroplane over Globe.
41. Carpets.
42. N. E. Morocco.

1949. U.P.U. 75th Anniv.
371. 39. 5 f. green 25 25
372. 15 f. red 30 30
373. 25 f. blue 45 45

1950. Air. Stamp Day.
374. 40. 15 f.+10 f. green & red 20 20

1950. Solidarity Fund. Inscr. "SOLIDARITE 1949".
375. 41. 1 f.+2 f. red (postage) 25 25
376. – 2 f.+5 f. blue .. 25 25
377. – 3 f.+7 f. violet .. 30 30
378. – 5 f.+10 f. brown .. 30 30
379. – 5 f.+5 f. blue (air) .. 20 20
380. 42. 6 f.+9 f. green .. 20 20
381. – 9 f.+16 f. brown .. 20 20
382. – 15 f.+25 f. brown .. 20 20
DESIGNS—VERT. Postage: 2 f. Pottery. 3 f. Books. 5 f. Copperware, HORIZ. Air—(Maps of Morocco): 5 f. N.W. 9 f. S.W., 15 f. S.E.

43. Ruins of Sala-Colonia.

1950. Army Welfare Fund. Inscr. "ŒUVRES SOCIALES DE L'ARMEE".
383. 43. 10 f.+10 f. claret (post.) 20 20
384. 15 f.+15 f. slate .. 20 20
385. – 10 f.+10 f. sepia (air).. 15 15
386. – 15 f.+15 f. green .. 15 15
DESIGN: 10 f., 15 f. Triumphal Arch of Caracalla, Volubilis.

1950. Surch. with new value and bars or wavy lines.
387. F. 1 f. on 1 f. 20 brown (No. 295) 5 5
388. A. 1 f. on 1 f. 30 blue (No. 296) 5 5
427. 26. 1 f. on 1 f. 50 blue .. 5 5
389. – 5 f. on 6 f. red (No. 330) 5 5
428. – 15 f. on 18 f. blue (No. 335) 8 8

44. General Leclerc.
45. New Hospital Meknes.

1951. Gen. Leclerc Monument, Casablanca.
390. 44. 10 f. green (postage) .. 20 20
391. 15 f. red 20 20
392. 25 f. blue 25 25
393. 50 f. violet (air) .. 35 35

1951. Solidarity Fund. Inscr. "SOLIDARITE 1950".
394. – 10 f. violet & ind. (post) 12 12
395. 45. 15 f. brown and green.. 20 20
396. – 25 f. blue and brown .. 25 25
397. – 50 f. green & violet (air) 35 35
DESIGNS: 10 f. Loustau Hospital, Oujda. 25 f. New Hospital Rabat. 50 f. Sanatorium, Ben Smine.

46. Fountain and Doves.

47. Karaouine Mosque, Fez.

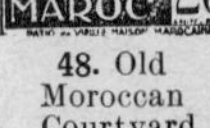

48. Old Moroccan Courtyard.

1951.

398. 46. 5 f. purple (A) .. 5 5
434. 5 f. purple (B) .. 5 5
399. 47. 6 f. emerald 5 5
400. 46. 8 f. brown 5 5
401. 47. 10 f. red 8 5
402. 12 f. blue 10 5
403. – 15 f. brown (A) .. 30 5
404. – 15 f. brown (B) .. 8 5
405. – 15 f. violet (A) .. 10 5
435. – 15 f. violet (B) .. 10 8
406a. 46. 15 f. green .. 10 5
407. – 18 f. red 20 15
408. 48. 20 f. blue 15 5

DESIGNS—As T 46/7: 15 f. brown (2) Oudayas Courtyard. 15 f. violet (2), 18 f. Oudayas Point, Rabat.

Two types each of 5 f. (A) 18×22 mm., (B) 17×21½ mm.; 15 f. brown (A) "MAROC" indistinct, (B) "MAROC" clearly legible in white tablet and 15 f. violet (A) 18×22½ mm., (B) 16½×21½ mm.

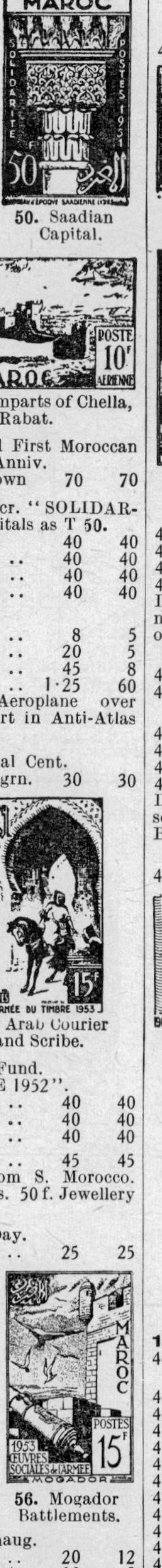

49. Casablanca P.O. and Reproduction of T 8.

50. Saadian Capital.

52. War Memorial, Casablanca.

51. Ramparts of Chella, Rabat.

1952. Air. Stamp Day and First Moroccan Air Stamps. 30th Anniv.

409. 49. 15 f.+5 f. blue & brown 70 70

1952. Solidarity Fund. Inscr. "SOLIDARITE 1951". Column capitals as T 50.

410. – 15 f. blue (Omeiyad) 40 40
411. – 20 f. red (Almohad) .. 40 40
412. – 25 f. violet (Merinid) .. 40 40
413. 50. 50 f. green 40 40

1952. Air.

414. 51. 10 f. green 8 5
415. – 40 f. red 20 5
416. – 100 f. brown 45 8
417. – 200 f. violet .. .. 1·25 60

DESIGNS—HORIZ. 40 f. Aeroplane over Marrakesh. VERT. 100 f. Fort in Anti-Atlas Mts. 200 f. Fez.

1952. Military Medal Cent.

418. 52. 15 f. brown, yellow & grn. 30 30

53. Jewellery from Fez

54. Arab Courier and Scribe.

1953. Solidarity Fund. Inscr. "SOLIDARITE 1952".

419. – 15 f. red (postage) .. 40 40
420. 53. 20 f. brown 40 40
421. – 25 f. blue 40 40
422. – 50 f. green (air) 45 45

DESIGNS: 15 f. Daggers from S. Morocco. 25 f. Jewellery from Anti-Atlas. 50 f. Jewellery from N. Morocco.

1953. Stamp Day.

423. 54. 15 f. purple 25 25

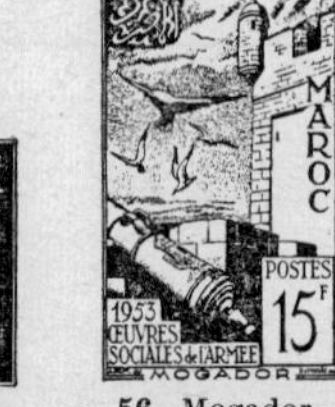

55. Bine el Ouidane Barrage.

56. Mogador Battlements.

1953. Barrage Inaug.

424. 55. 15 f. indigo 20 12
424a. 15 f. blue and chocolate 10 5

1953. Army Welfare Fund. Inscr. "ŒUVRES SOCIALES de l'ARMEE 1953".

425. 56. 15 f. green 25 25
426. – 30 f. brown 25 25

DESIGN: 30 f. Moorish horsemen.

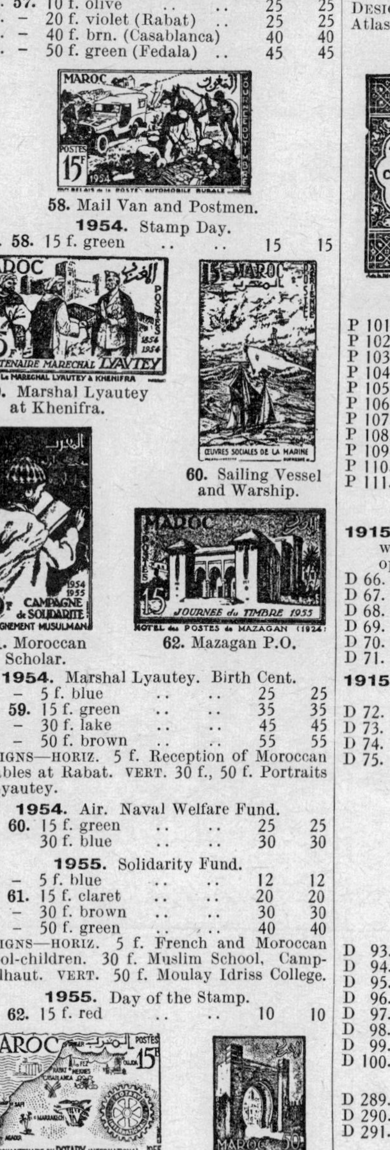

57. Meknes.

1954. Air. Solidarity Fund. Inscr. "1953".

429. 57. 10 f. olive 25 25
430. – 20 f. violet (Rabat) .. 25 25
431. – 40 f. brn. (Casablanca) 40 40
432. – 50 f. green (Fedala) .. 45 45

58. Mail Van and Postmen.

1954. Stamp Day.

433. 58. 15 f. green 15 15

59. Marshal Lyautey at Khenifra.

60. Sailing Vessel and Warship.

61. Moroccan Scholar.

62. Mazagan P.O.

1954. Marshal Lyautey. Birth Cent.

438. – 5 f. blue 25 25
439. 59. 15 f. green 35 35
440. – 30 f. lake 45 45
441. – 50 f. brown 55 55

DESIGNS—HORIZ. 5 f. Reception of Moroccan notables at Rabat. VERT. 30 f., 50 f. Portraits of Lyautey.

1954. Air. Naval Welfare Fund.

436. 60. 15 f. green 25 25
437. 30 f. blue 30 30

1955. Solidarity Fund.

442. – 5 f. blue 12 12
443. 61. 15 f. claret 20 20
444. – 30 f. brown 30 30
445. – 50 f. green 40 40

DESIGNS—HORIZ. 5 f. French and Moroccan school-children. 30 f. Muslim School, Camp-Boulhaut. VERT. 50 f. Moulay Idriss College.

1955. Day of the Stamp.

446. 62. 15 f. red 10 10

63. Map of Morocco.

64. Bab el Mrissa, Sale.

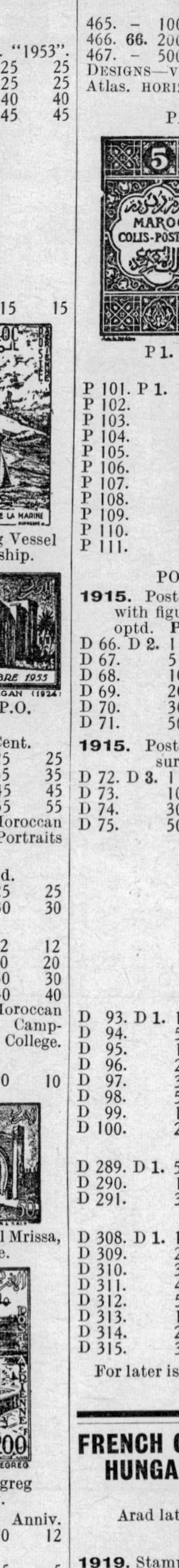

65. Mahakma, Casablanca.

66. Bou Regreg Estuary.

1955. Rotary International. 50th Anniv.

447. 63. 15 f. blue and brown .. 20 12

1955.

448. 64. 50 c. maroon 5 5
449. 1 f. blue 5 5
450. 2 f. purple 5 5
451. 3 f. indigo 5 5
452. – 5 f. red 5 5
453. – 6 f. green 5 5
454. – 8 f. brown 5 5
455. – 10 f. purple 15 5
456. – 12 f. turquoise 5 5
457. – 15 f. lake 15 5
458. 65. 18 f. myrtle 10 5
459. 20 f. lake 5 5
460. – 25 f. blue 25 5
461. – 30 f. green 15 5
462. – 40 f. red 10 5
463. – 50 f. sepia 75 5
464. – 75 f. turquoise 15 5

DESIGNS—As T 64. 5 f., 6 f., 8 f. Bab Chorfa, Fez. 10 f., 12 f., 15 f. Chella Minaret, Rabat. As T 65—HORIZ. 25 f. Coastal castle, Safi. 30 f. Menara, Marrakesh. 40 f. Tafraout. 50 f. Portuguese cistern, Mazagan. VERT. 75 f. Oudaya gardens, Rabat.

1955. Air.

465. – 100 f. violet 20 5
466. 66. 200 f. red 50 15
467. – 500 f. blue .. .. 1·50 65

DESIGNS—VERT. 100 f. Village in the Anti-Atlas. HORIZ. 500 f. Ksar es Souk.

PARCEL POST STAMPS

P 1.

ILLUSTRATIONS British Commonwealth and all overprints and surcharges are FULL SIZE. Foreign Countries have been reduced to ¾-LINEAR.

1917.

P 101. P 1. 5 c. green 8 5
P 102. 10 c. red 10 5
P 103. 20 c. brown 10 5
P 104. 25 c. blue 15 10
P 105. 40 c. brown 20 10
P 106. 50 c. red 45 10
P 107. 75 c. grey 45 20
P 108. 1 f. blue 55 5
P 109. 2 f. grey 65 5
P 110. 5 f. violet .. .. 1·10 5
P 111. 10 f. black .. .. 1·75 5

POSTAGE DUE STAMPS

1915. Postage Due stamps of France surch. with figure and Arabic word, and further optd. **PROTECTORAT FRANCAIS.**

D 66. D 2. 1 c. on 1 c. black .. 5 5
D 67. 5 c. on 5 c. blue .. 10 10
D 68. 10 c. on 10 c. brown 20 20
D 69. 20 c. on 20 c. green .. 20 20
D 70. 30 c. on 30 c. red .. 55 55
D 71. 50 c. on 50 c. purple 85 35

1915. Postage Due stamps of France with surch. and optd. as above.

D 72. D 3. 1 c. on 1 c. olive .. 5 5
D 73. 10 c. on 10 c. violet 30 20
D 74. 30 c. on 30 c. bistre 30 25
D 75. 50 c. on 50 c. red .. 35 25

D 1.

1917.

D 93. D 1. 1 c. black 5 5
D 94. 5 c. blue 5 5
D 95. 10 c. brown 5 5
D 96. 20 c. green 15 15
D 97. 30 c. red 5 5
D 98. 50 c. brown 5 5
D 99. 1 f. claret on yellow 10 8
D 100. 2 f. violet 50 35

1944. Surch.

D 289. D 1. 50 c. on 30 c. red .. 20 20
D 290. 1 f. on 10 c. brown .. 30 30
D 291. 3 f. on 10 c. brown .. 75 55

1945.

D 308. D 1. 1 f. brown 10 5
D 309. 2 f. violet 12 5
D 310. 3 f. blue 5 5
D 311. 4 f. orange 5 5
D 312. 5 f. green 10 5
D 313. 10 f. brown 8 5
D 314. 20 f. red 20 12
D 315. 30 f. sepia 30 25

For later issues see **MOROCCO.**

FRENCH OCCUPATION OF HUNGARY E2

ARAD

Arad later became part of Rumania.

100 filler = 1 korona.

1919. Stamps of Hungary Optd. **Occupation francaise** or surch. also.

(a) War Charity stamps of 1916.

1. 6. 10 f. (+2 f.) red .. .. 3·75 3·75
2. – 15 f. (+2 f.) violet .. 25 25
3. 8. 40 f. (+2 f.) lake 25 25

(b) Harvesters and Parliament Types.

4. 11. 2 f. brown 5 5
5. 3 f. claret 5 5
6. 5 f. green 15 15
7. 6 f. blue 5 5
8. 10 f. red 5 5
9. 15 f. violet 5 5
10. 15 f. violet (No. 244) .. 17·00 17·00
11. 20 f. brown .. .. 2·75 2·75
12. 35 f. brown .. .. 2·75 2·75
13. 40 f. olive .. .. 2·75 2·75
14. 11. 45 on 2 f. brown .. 10 10
15a. 45 on 3 f. claret .. 6·00
16. 50 on 3 f. claret .. 10 10
18. 12. 50 f. purple 10 10
19. 75 f. blue 5 5
20. 80 f. green 8 8
21. 1 k. lake 30 30
22. 2 k. brown 30 30
23. 3 k. grey and violet .. 45 45
24. 5 k. brown 55 55
25. 10 k. lilac and brown .. 3·25 3·25

(c) Charles and Zita stamps.

26. 13. 10 f. red .. .. 2·10 2·10
27. 20 f. brown 5 5
28. 25 f. blue 5 5
29. 14. 40 f. olive 5 5

(d) Harvester stamps inscr. "MAGYAR POSTA".

30. 11. 5 f. green 10 10
31. 10 f. red 8 8
32. 20 f. brown .. .. 1·60 1·60

The following (Nos. 33/46) are also optd. **KOZTARSASAG.**

(e) Harvesters and Parliament Types.

33. 11. 2 f. brown 5 5
34. 3 f. claret 10 10
35. 4 f. slate 5 5
36. 5 f. green 5 5
37. 6 f. blue 10 10
38. 10 f. red .. .. 3·25 3·25
39. 20 f. brown 20 20
40. 40 f. olive 8 8
41. 12. 1 k. lake 12 12
42. 3 k. grey and violet .. 55 55
43. 10 (k.) on 1 k. lake .. 1·60 1·60

(f) Charles and Zita stamps.

44. 13. 25 f. blue 8 8
45. 14. 40 f. olive .. .. 5·00 5·00
46. 50 f. violet 12 12

NEWSPAPER STAMP

1919. No. N 136 optd. **Occupation francaise.**

N 47. N 3. (2 f.) orange .. 10 10

EXPRESS LETTER STAMP

1919. No. E 245 optd. as above.

E 48. E 1. 2 f. olive and red .. 10 10

POSTAGE DUE STAMPS

1919. Nos. D 191, etc.

(a) Optd. as above, in blue.

D 49. D 1. 2 f. red and green .. 20 20
D 50. 10 f. red and green .. 20 20
D 51. 12 f. red and green .. 45 45
D 52. 15 f. red and green .. 55 55
D 53. 20 f. red and green .. 65 65

(b) No. N 47 (of Arad) optd. as above, and further surch. **Porto** and new value in blue.

D 54. N 3. 12 on (2 f.) orange .. 20 20
D 55. 15 on (2 f.) orange .. 20 20
D 56. 30 on (2 f.) orange .. 20 20
D 57. 50 on (2 f.) orange .. 20 20
D 58. 100 on (2 f.) orange 20 20

FRENCH POLYNESIA O2

The French Settlements in the E. Pacific, formerly called Oceanic Settlements.

1. Girl playing Guitar.

2. Polynesian.

3. "The Women of Tahiti" (after Gauguin).

1958.

1. 1. 10 c. brown, green and blue-green (postage) .. 5 5
2. 25 c. maroon, red & green 5 5
3. 1 f. sepia, red and blue .. 5 5
4. 2 f. violet, choc. & brown 8 5
5. 2. 4 f. myrtle, green & yellow 12 10
6. – 5 f. brown, violet & green 12 10
7. 2. 7 f. chestnut, grn. & oran. 25 15
8. 9 f. maroon, grn. & oran. 40 20
9 – 10 f. red, blue & chocolate 45 15
10 – 16 f. claret, yellow-green, blue-green and blue .. 50 40
11. – 17 f. brown, bl & bl-green 55 35
12. – 20 f. brown, violet & pink 65 40
13. – 13 f. brn, grn & drab (air) 45 25
14. 3. 50 f. multicoloured .. 1·75 60
15. – 100 f. multicoloured .. 2·75 1·10
16. – 200 f. slate and lilac .. 4·50 1·75

DESIGNS: As T 1/2—VERT. 5 f. Spear-fishing. 10 f., 20 f. Polynesian girl on beach. HORIZ. 16 f. Post Office, Papeete. 17 f. Tahitian dancers. As T 3—VERT. 13 f. Mother-of-Pearl engraver. 100 f. "The White Horse" (after Gauguin). HORIZ. 200 f. Night-fishing off Moorea.

1958. Declaration of Human Rights. 10th Anniv. As T 5 of Comoro Is.

17.		7 f. grey and blue	2·00	2·00

1959. Tropical Flora. As T 21 of French Equatorial Africa. Multicoloured.

18.		4 f. " Artocarpus " ..	50	35

4. Airliner over Papeete Airport.

1960. Air. Inaug. of Papeete Airport.

19.	4.	13 f. violet, purple & green	40	25

5. "Saraca indica". 7. Squirrel Fish.

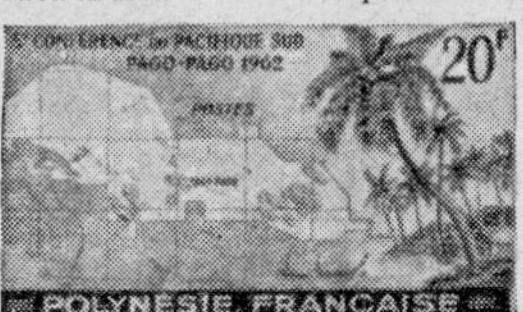

6. Pacific Map and Palms.

1962. Flowers.

20.		15 f. Type 6	60	50
21.		25 f. Hibiscus	1·00	80

1962. 5th South Pacific Conference, Pago-Pago.

22.	6.	20 f. multicoloured ..	1·25	1·00

1962. Air. 1st Trans-Atlantic TV Satellite Link. As T 18 of Andorra.

23.		50 f. blue, maroon & purple	1·40	90

1962. Fishes. Multicoloured.

24.		5 f. Type 7	30	15
25.		10 f. One Spot Butterfly ..	40	25
26.		30 f. Scorpion Fish	1·00	65
27.		40 f. Cowfish	1·50	1·10

8. Football.

1962. 1st South Pacific Games, Suva.

28.	8.	20 f. brown and blue ..	70	55
29.	–	50 f. blue and cerise ..	1·50	80

DESIGN: 50 f. Throwing the javelin.

1963. Red Cross Cent. As Type F 2 of New Hebrides.

30.		15 f. red, grey and maroon	1·25	1·25

1963. Declaration of Human Rights. 15th Anniv. As T 10 of Comoro Islands.

31.		7 f. violet and green ..	1·60	1·60

1964. " PHILATEC 1964 " Int. Stamp Exn., Paris. As T 481 of France.

32.		25 f. red, black & emerald	1·60	1·60

9. Dancer. 10. Tahitian Volunteers.

1964. Tahitian Dancers.

33.	9.	1 f. orange, sepia, bistre and blue (postage)	8	8
34.		3 f. orange, sepia & purple	15	12
35.	–	15 f. multicoloured (air) ..	45	25

DESIGN—VERT. (27 × 46½ mm.): 15 f. Dancer in full costume.

1964. Polynesia's War Effort in World War II. Multicoloured.

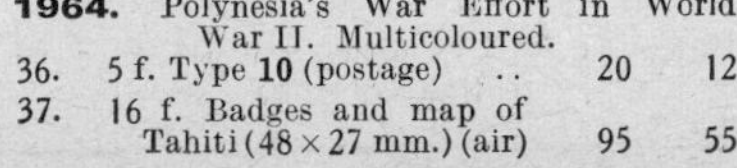

36.		5 f. Type 10 (postage) ..	20	12
37.		16 f. Badges and map of Tahiti (48 × 27 mm.) (air)	95	55

11. Tuamotu Lagoon (after J. D. Lajoux).

1964. Landscapes. Multicoloured.

38.		2 f. Type 11 (postage) ..	8	5
39.		4 f. Bora-Bora (after J. D. Lajoux)	12	10
40.		7 f. Pepecte (after A. Sylvain)	25	15
41.		8 f. Marquesas (Gauguin's grave)	25	15
42.		20 f. Gambler (after Mazellier)	70	50
43.		23 f. Moorea (after A. Sylvain) (48 × 27 mm.) (air) ..	50	30

1965. Air. I.T.U. Cent. As T 15 of Comoro Islands.

44.		50 f. chestnut, blue & violet	4·75	2·75

12. Museum Buildings.

1965. Air. Gauguin Museum.

45.	12.	25 f. green	80	40
46.	–	40 f. turquoise	1·10	80
47.	–	75 f. chestnut	2·00	1·25

DESIGNS: 40 f. Statues and hut. 75 f. Gauguin.

13. Skin-diver with Harpoon.

1965. Air. World Under-water Swimming Championships, Tuamoto.

48.	13.	50 f. blue, chestnut & grn.	3·00	2·25

14. Tropical Foliage. 15. Aerial, Globe and Palm.

1965. Schools Canteen Art.

49.	14.	20 f. red, green and brown (postage)	65	55
50.	–	80 f. red, blue and brown (27 × 48 mm.) (air) ..	2·00	1·40

DESIGN: 80 f. Totem, and garland in harbour.

1965. Air. 1st Radio Link with France. 50th Anniv.

51.	15.	60 f. brn., green & orange	1·75	1·10

1966. Air. Launching of 1st French Satellite. As Nos. 1696/7 (plus se-tenant label) of France.

52.		7 f. brown, purple & green	60	60
53.		10 f. brown, purple & green	90	90

1966. Air. Launching of Satellite "D1". As T 521 of France.

54.		20 f. claret, brown and green	85	50

16. Papeete Port.

1966. Air.

55.	16.	50 f. multicoloured ..	1·25	70

17. Pirogue.

1966. Polynesian Boats.

56.	17.	10 f. lake, green and blue	20	12
57.	–	11 f. lake, green and blue	25	20
58.	–	12 f. purple, green & blue	30	20
59.	–	14 f. brown, blue & green	35	25
60.	–	19 f. green, red and blue	45	25
61.	–	22 f. green, blue & purple	55	40

DESIGNS—VERT. 11 f. Schooner. 19 f. Early schooner. HORIZ. 12 f. Fishing launch. 14 f. Pirogues. 22 f. Coaster, " Oiseau des Iles II ".

18. Tahitian Dancer and Band.

1966. Air. " Vive, Tahiti! " (tourist publicity).

62.	18.	13 f. multicoloured ..	40	25

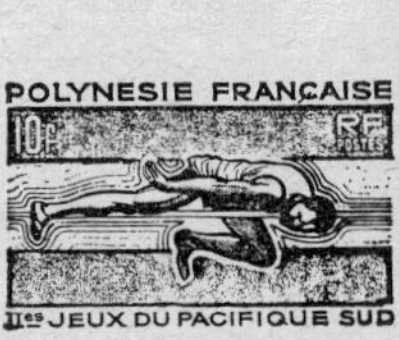

19. High-jumping. 20. Stone Pestle.

1966. 2nd South Pacific Games, Noumea.

63.	19.	10 f. bistre and red ..	20	10
64.	–	20 f. green and blue ..	30	20
65.	–	40 f. purple and emerald	65	45
66.	–	60 f. blue and brown ..	1·00	70

DESIGNS—VERT. 20 f. Pole-vaulting. 40 f. Basket-ball. HORIZ. 60 f. Hurdling.

1967. Oceanic Studies Society. 50th Anniv.

67.	20.	50 f. indigo and orange	85	55

21. Spring Dance.

1967. July Festival.

68.	21.	5 f. ult., maroon & drab	12	8
69.	–	13 f. purple, violet & grn.	25	10
70.	–	15 f. brown, purple & grn.	30	12
71.	–	16 f. purple, grn. & blue	30	15
72.	–	21 f. brown, green & blue	45	30

DESIGNS—VERT. 13 f. Javelin-throwing. 16 f. Fruit-porters' race. HORIZ. 15 f. Horse-racing. 21 f. Pirogue-racing.

22. Ear-ring.

1967. Ancient Art of the Marquesas Islands.

73.	–	10 f. blue, red & purple	20	12
74.	–	15 f. black and green ..	25	20
75.	22.	20 f. brown, green & lake	40	25
76.	–	23 f. brown and ochre ..	50	30
77.	–	25 f. brown, purple & blue	55	40
78.	–	30 f. brown and purple ..	65	45
79.	–	35 f. blue and brown ..	75	45
80.	–	50 f. brown, blue & green	1·00	55

DESIGNS: 10 f. Sculpture on mother-of-pearl. 15 f. Paddle-blade. 23 f. Receptacle for anointing oil. 25 f. Hunting stirrups. 30 f. Fan handles. 35 f. Tattooed man. 50 f. " Tikis ".

23. Ship's Stern and Canoe (" Wallis, 1767 ").

1968. Air. Discovery of Tahiti. Bicent.

81.	23.	40 f. brown, blue & green	90	50
82.	–	60 f. orge., black & blue	1·25	70
83.	–	80 f. salmon, lake & pur.	1·50	90

DESIGNS—HORIZ. 60 f. Ship and witch-doctor (" Cook, 1769 "). VERT. 80 f. " Bougainville, 1768 " (portrait).

1968. W.H.O. 20th Anniv. As T 21 of Comoro Islands, but inscr. "POLYNESIE FRANCAISE".

85.		15 f. violet, crimson & green	25	20
86.		16 f. green, purple and orge.	30	20

24. " The Meal " (Gauguin).

1968. Air.

87.	24.	200 f. multicoloured ..	5·00	3·25

1968. Human Rights Year. As T 23 of Comoro Islands.

88.		15 f. red, blue and brown	25	15
89.		16 f. ultram., choc. & pur.	35	20

25. Putting the Shot. 26. Tiare Apetahi.

1968. Air. Olympic Games, Mexico.

90.	25.	35 f. grn., pur. & lake	90	50

1969. Flowers. Multicoloured.

91.		9 f. Type 26	20	10
92.		17 f. Tiare Tahiti	40	20

1969. Air. 1st Flight of "Concorde". As T 27 of Comoro Islands.

93.		40 f. chestnut and cerise ..	1·50	1·00

27. Polynesian with Guitar.

1969. Air. Pacific Area Travel Association (P.A.T.A.) Congress, Tahiti.

94.	27.	25 f. multicoloured ..	55	30

28. Diver and Fish.

1969. Air. World Underwater Hunting Championships.

95.	28.	48 f. black, purple & turq.	1·10	70
96.	–	52 f. black, red and blue	1·25	75

DESIGN—VERT. 52 f. " Flag " Fish.

29. Boxing.

1969. 3rd South Pacific Games, Port Moresby, New Guinea.

97.	29.	9 f. brown and violet ..	15	8
98.	–	17 f. brown & vermilion	30	15
99.	–	18 f. brown and blue ..	45	20
100.	–	22 f. maroon & emerald	55	30

DESIGNS—VERT.: 17 f. High-jumping. 18 f. Running. 22 f. Long-jumping.

1969. Air. Napoleon Bonaparte. Birth Bicent. As T 116 of Cameroun.

101.		100 f. " Bonaparte as Commander-in-Chief, Italy " (Rouillard)	6·50	6·00

1969. Int. Labour Organization. 50th Anniv. As T 28 of Comoro Islands.
102. 17 f. drab, emerald & orge. 40 15
103. 18 f. ultram., brown & orge. 40 15

30. Territorial Assembly Building.

1969. Polynesian Buildings. Multicoloured.
104. 13 f. Type 30 .. .. 20 10
105. 14 f. Governor's residence 25 10
106. 17 f. Tourist offices .. 25 15
107. 18 f. Maeva Hotel .. 35 15
108. 24 f. Taharaa Hotel .. 50 25

31. Globe, Airliner and "Tourists".

1970. "P.A.T.A. 1970" (Pacific Area Tourist Assn.) Congress (2nd issue).
109. – 20 f. blue, brown & pur. 35 15
110. 31. 40 f. ultram., pur. & grn. 1·00 30
111. – 60 f. choc., blue & brown 1·10 60
DESIGNS—VERT. 20 f. "Tiki" holding P.A.T.A. emblem. 60 f. "Polynesian" holding globe.

1970. New U.P.U. Headquarters Building. As T 126 of Cameroun.
112. 18 f. brn., violet & red-brn. 30 15
113. 20 f. blue, brown & purple 35 20

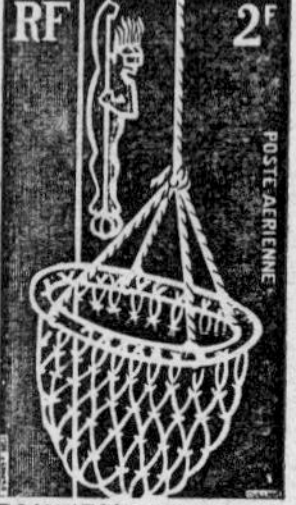
32. Tower of the Sun and Mt. Fuji.

1970. Air. "Expo 70" World Fair, Osaka, Japan. Multicoloured.
114. 30 f. Type 32 .. .. 55 30
115. 50 f. Eiffel Tower and Torii Gate (vert.) .. .. 1·00 55

33. Diver and Basket.

1970. Air. Pearl-diving.
116. 33. 2 f. brown, indigo & blue 8 5
117. – 5 f. ultram. orge. & blue 12 8
118. – 18 f. grey, orge. & pur. 40 15
119. – 27 f. mauve, brn. & pur. 55 25
120. – 50 f. orange, grey & brn. 1·00 55
DESIGNS—VERT. 5 f. Diver gathering oysters. 27 f. Pearl in opened oyster. 50 f. Woman with pearl jewellery. HORIZ. 18 f. Opening oyster-shell.

34. I.E.Y. Emblem, Open Book and "The Thinker" (statue).

1970. Air. International Education Year
121. 34. 50 f. blue, brn. & new bl. 95 50

35. "Polynesian Woman". (Y. de St. Front).

1970. Air. Paintings by Polynesian Artists (1st Series). Multicoloured.
122. 20 f. Type 35 .. .. 50 20
123. 40 f. "Harbour scene" (F. Fay).. .. .. 1·10 35
124. 60 f. "Niu" (abstract, J. Guillois) .. .. .. 1·40 55
125. 80 f. "Beach Hut" (J. Masson) 1·60 65
126. 100 f. "Polynesian Girl" (J. G. Bouloc) (vert.) .. 2·25 1·00
See also Nos. 147/51, 160/4 and 189/93.

36. Games Emblem. 37. Flame of Remembrance.

1971. Air. 4th South Pacific Games.
127. 36. 20 f. multicoloured .. 45 25

1971. Air. Erection of General de Gaulle Monument.
128. 37. 5 f. multicoloured .. 15 10

38. Volunteer, Crest and Tricolour.

1971. Air. Departure of Tahitian "Free French" Volunteers. 30th Anniv.
129. 38. 25 f. multicoloured .. 50 30

39. Marara Fisherman.

1971. Water Sports. Multicoloured.
130. 10 f. Type 39 (postage) .. 20 10
131. 15 f. Surfing (vert.) (air).. 25 15
132. 16 f. Skin-diving (vert.) . 30 15
133. 20 f. Water-skiing with kite 30 20

40. Hibiscus.

1971. "Day of the 1,000 Flowers". Multicoloured.
134. 8 f. Red flower (vert.) .. 15 8
135. 12 f. Type 40 .. .. 20 12
136. 22 f. "Porcelain rose" (vert.) 45 20

41. Yachting.

1971. Air. Fourth South Pacific Games, Tahiti (2nd issue). Multicoloured.
137. 15 f. Type 41 .. .. 30 20
138. 18 f. Golf 45 25
139. 27 f. Archery 55 30
140. 53 f. Tennis 70 50

42. Water-skiing.

1971. 1st World Water-ski Championships, Papeete.
142. 42. 10 f. red, green & brown 15 8
143. – 20 f. red, brown & green 30 15
144. – 40 f. purple, brn. & grn. 65 35
DESIGNS—VERT.: 20 f. Ski-jumping. HORIZ.: 40 f. Acrobatics on one ski.

1971. General de Gaulle. 1st Death Anniv. As Nos. 1937 and 1940 of France.
145. 30 f. black and purple .. 55 30
146. 50 f. black and purple .. 95 60

1971. Air. Paintings by Polynesian Artists (Second Series). As T 35. Multicoloured.
147. 20 f. "Polynesian Village" (I. Wolf) 40 25
148. 40 f. "Lagoon" (A. Dobrowolski) 70 40
149. 60 f. "Polynesian Woman" (F. Seli) (vert.) .. .. 1·10 70
150. 80 f. "The Holy Family" (P. Heymann) (vert.) .. 1·60 80
151. 100 f. "Faces in a Crowd" (N. Michoutouchkine) .. 1·75 1·10

43. Cross Emblem.

1971. 2nd French Pacific Scouts and Guides Rally, Taravao.
152. 43. 28 f. multicoloured .. 50 30

44. Harbour Scene, Papeete.

1972. Air. Autonomous Port of Papeete. 10th Anniv.
153. 44. 28 f. multicoloured .. 55 40

45. Figure-skating. 47. Alcoholic behind bars.

46. Commission H.Q., Noumea, New Caledonia.

1972. Air. Winter Olympic Games, Sapporo, Japan.
154. 45. 20 f. claret, grn. & vio. 50 30

1972. Air. South Pacific Commission. 25th Anniv.
155. 46. 21 f. multicoloured .. 40 25

1972. Campaign Against Alcoholism.
156. 47. 20 f. multicoloured .. 45 45

48. Floral Emblem.

1972. Air. South Pacific Arts Festival, Fiji.
157. 48. 36 f. orge., grn. & blue 65 40

49. Raft "Kon-Tiki" and Route-map.

1972. Air. Arrival of "Kon-Tiki" Expedition in French Polynesia. 25th Anniv.
158. 49. 16 f. multicoloured .. 30 25

50. General De Gaulle.

1972. Air. Completion of De Gaulle Monument.
159. 50. 100 f. grey .. .. 1·75 1·10

1972. Air. Paintings by Polynesian Artists (3rd Series). As Type 35. Multicoloured.
160. 20 f. "Horses" (G. Bovy) 40 25
161. 40 f. "Harbour" (R. Juventin) (vert.) .. 70 40
162. 60 f. "Landscape" (A. Brooke) .. .. 1·10 70
163. 80 f. "Polynesians" (D. Adam) (vert.) .. .. 1·60 80
164. 100 f. "Dancers" (A. Pilioko) (vert.) .. .. 1·75 1·10

51. St. Theresa and Lisieux Basilica.

1973. Air. St. Theresa of Lisieux. Birth Cent.
165. 51. 85 f. multicoloured .. 1·75 1·10

52. Copernicus and Planetary System.

1972. Air. Nicolas Copernicus (astronomer) 500th Birth Anniv.
166. 52. 100 f. violet, brn. & pur. 1·60 1·10

53. Aeroplane and Flying Fish.

1973. Air. "Air France" Round-the-World Service via Tahiti. Inaug.
167. 53. 80 f. multicoloured .. 1·40 1·00

54. "DC-10" in Flight.

1973. Air. "DC-10" Service. Inaug.
168. 54. 20 f. blue, grn. & light bl. 30 15

INDEX

Countries can be quickly located by referring to the index at the end of this volume.

55. " Ta Matete " (Gauguin).

1973. Air. Gauguin. 125th Birth Anniv.
169. **55.** 200 f. multicoloured .. 3·25 2·25

56. Loti, Fishermen and Polynesian Girl.

1973. Air. Pierre Loti (writer). 50th Death Anniv.
170. **56.** 60 f. multicoloured .. 95 65

57. Polynesian Mother and Child. **58.** "Teeing Off".

1973. Tahitian Women's Union Creche. Opening.
171. **57.** 28 f. multicoloured .. 45 30

1973. Air. Paintings by Polynesian Artists (4th Series). As Type **35.** Multicoloured.
172. 20 f. " Sun God " (J.-F. Favre) (vert.) 35 15
173. 40 f. " Polynesian Girl " (E. de Gennes) (vert.) .. 65 35
174. 60 f. " Abstract " (A. Sidet) (vert.) 75 60
175. 80 f. " Bus Passengers " (F. Ravello) (vert.) .. 1·40 85
176. 100 f. " Boats " (J. Bourdin) 1·75 1·10

1974. Atimaono Golf-Course, Tahiti. Multicoloured.
177. 16 f. Type **58** 30 15
178. 24 f. View of golf-course .. 45 30

59. "A Helping Hand".

1974. Polynesian Animal Protection Society
179. **59.** 21 f. multicoloured .. 35 15

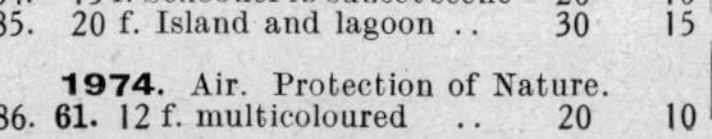

60. Mountains and Lagoon. **61.** Bird, Fish and Flower.

1974. Polynesian Landscapes. Multicoloured.
180. 2 f. Type **60** 5 5
181. 5 f. Beach games 5 5
182. 6 f. Canoe fishing 8 5
183. 10 f. Mountain peak (vert.) 15 8
184. 15 f. Schooner in sunset scene 20 10
185. 20 f. Island and lagoon .. 30 15

1974. Air. Protection of Nature.
186. **61.** 12 f. multicoloured .. 20 10

62. Catamarans. **63.** Polynesian Woman

1974. Air. 2nd World Catamaran Sailing Championships, Papeete.
187. **62.** 100 f. multicoloured .. 1·40 75

1974. Universal Postal Union. Centenary.
188. **63.** 65 f. multicoloured .. 70 55

1974. Air. Paintings by Polynesian Artists (5th Series). As Type **35.** Multicoloured.
189. 20 f. Flower arrangement (R. Temarui-Masson) (vert.) 25 12
190. 40 f. Palms on beach (M. Chardon) (vert.) .. 55 30
191. 60 f. Portrait of man (M. F. Avril) (vert.) 70 55
192. 80 f. Polynesian girl (H. Robin) (vert.) .. .. 1·10 65
193. 100 f. Lagoon at night (D. Farsi) .. .. .. 1·25 75

64. " Travelling Gods ".

1975. Air. " 50 Years of Tahitian Aviation ".
194. **64.** 50 f. violet, lake & brown 60 35
195. – 75 f. blue, red and green 1·00 60
196. – 100 f. brown, red & green 1·25 75

DESIGNS: 75 f. Tourville flying-boat. 100 f. Tourist airliner.

65. French " Ceres " Stamp of 1870 and Polynesian. **66.** Tahiti " Lions " Emblem.

1975. Air. " Arphila 75 " International Stamp Exhibition, Paris.
197. **65.** 32 f. red, brn. & blk. .. 40 25

1975. Tahiti Lions' Club. 15th Anniv.
198. **66.** 26 f. multicoloured .. 35 20

67. " Protect Nature ".

1975. Nature Protection.
199. **67.** 19 f. blue and green .. 25 15

68. Putting the Shot. **69.** Athlete and View of Montreal.

1975. Air. Fifth South Pacific Games, Guam. Multicoloured.
200. 25 f. Type **68** 35 20
201. 30 f. Volleyball 40 25
202. 40 f. Swimming 50 30

1975. Air. Olympic Games, Montreal (1976).
203. **69.** 44 f. brown, blue & red 60 36

70. Airliner and Letters.

1975. Air. World U.P.U. Day.
204. **70.** 100 f. bl., ol. and brn. 1·25 75

71. " Tropical Waters " (J. Steimetz).

1975. Air. Paintings by Polynesian Artists (6th series). Multicoloured.
205. 20 f. " Beach Scene " (R. Marcel Marius) (horiz.) 25 15
206. 40 f. " Rooftop Aerials " (M. Anglade) (horiz.) .. 50 30
207. 60 f. " Street Scene " (J. Day) (horiz.) 75 45
208. 80 f. Type **71** .. .. 1·00 60
209. 100 f. " Portrait of Woman " (A. van der Heyde) .. 1·25 75

72. " Concorde ".

1975. Air. " Concorde's " First Commercial Flight.
210. **72.** 100 f. bl., light bl. & mve. 1·25 75

73. President Pompidou. **75.** King Pomare I.

74. Battle of the Saints.

1976. Pompidou Commemoration.
211. **73.** 49 f. grey and blue .. 60 30

1976. Air. American Revolution. Bicent.
212. **74.** 24 f. blue, brown & black 35 20
213. – 31 f. red and brown .. 40 25

DESIGN: 31 f. The Chesapeake (sea-battle).

1976. Air. Pomare Dynasty. Multicoloured.
214. 18 f. Type **75** 25 15
215. 21 f. King Pomare II .. 25 15
216. 26 f. Queen Pomare IV .. 30 20
217. 30 f. King Pomare V .. 40 25

76. Gerbault and " Firecrest ".

1976. Alain Gerbault's Arrival at Bora-Bora. 50th Anniv.
218. **76.** 90 f. multicoloured .. 1·25 70

77. Turtle (" Chelonia mydas ").

1976. World Ecology Day. Multicoloured
219. 18 f. Type **80** 25 15
220. 42 f. Doves in hand .. 55 30

78. Legs of Runner.

1976. Air. Olympic Games, Montreal.
221. **78.** 26 f. brn., mar. and blue 30 20
222. – 34 f. mar., brn. and blue 45 30
223. – 50 f. brn., blue and mar. 70 40

DESIGNS: 34 f. Hurdlers. 50 f. Olympic Flame and flowers.

79. A. Graham Bell, early Telephone and Aerial.

1976. Telephone Centenary.
225. **79.** 37 f. blue, brn. and mar. 50 30

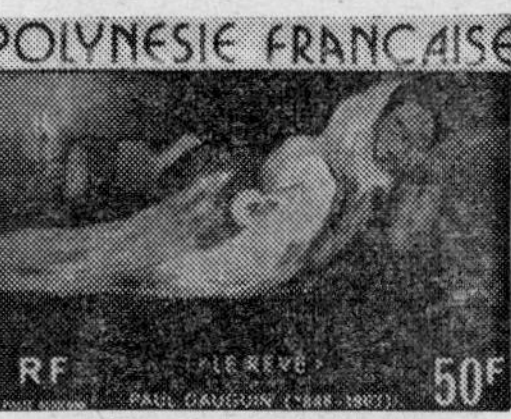

80. " The Dream " (Gauguin).

1976.
226. **80.** 50 f. multicoloured .. 50 30

POSTAGE DUE STAMPS

D 1. Polynesian Mask.

1958.
D 17. **D 1.** 1 f. green and brown 5 5
D 18. 3 f. red and indigo .. 8 8
D 19. 5 f. blue and brown .. 10 10

FRENCH POST OFFICES IN CHINA O1

General issues for the French post offices in China, which were closed in 1922.

1894. 100 centimes = 1 franc.
1907. 100 cents = 1 piastre.

1894. Stamps of France optd. **Chine.**

1. 10. 5 c. deep green 25 20
2. 5 c. yellow-green 20 15
5. 10 c. black on lilac .. 50 35
6. 15 c. blue 40 40
8. 20 c. red on green .. 50 30
9. 25 c. black on red .. 45 20
10. 30 c. brown 55 40
11. 40 c. red on yellow .. 65 50
12a. 50 c. red .. .. 2·25 1·25
14. 75 c. brown on orange .. 11·00 7·50
15. 1 f. green .. .. 1·10 35
16. 2 f. brown on blue .. 3·75 3·25
17a. 5 f. mauve on lilac .. 9·00 6·00

1900. Stamp of France surch. **Chine 25.**

18. 10. 25 on 1 f. green .. .. 9·00 5·50

1901. Stamp of France surch. **Chine** and value in figures and words.

19. 10. 2 c. on 25 c. black on red £150 45·00
20. 4 c. on 25 c. black on red £120 45·00
21. 6 c. on 25 c. black on red £170 55·00
22. 16 c. on 25 c. black on red 42·00 28·00

1902. Stamps of Indo-China "Tablet" key-type surch. **CHINE** and value in Chinese.

49. D. 1 c. black on blue .. 15 12
24. 2 c. brown on yellow .. 30 25
51. 4 c. claret on grey .. 25 25
52. 5 c. green 30 25
27. 10 c. red 30 25
28. 15 c. grey 55 40
29. 20 c. red on green .. 1·10 75
55. 25 c. black on red .. 1·25 1·10
56. 25 c. blue 60 50
57. 30 c. brown 60 50
58. 40 c. red on yellow .. 3·50 3·00
33. 50 c. red on rose .. 8·00 6·50
59. 50 c. brown on blue .. 1·25 75
60. 75 c. brown on orange .. 3·75 3·25
61. 1 f. green .. .. 4·25 3·50
36. 5 f. mauve on lilac .. 11·00 9·00

1902. "Blanc", "Mouchon" and "Merson" key-types inscr. "CHINE".

37. A. 5 c. green 12 10
38. B. 10 c. red 15 10
39. 15 c. orange 15 10
40. 20 c. claret 50 40
41. 25 c. blue 30 12
42. 30 c. mauve 40 30
43. C. 40 c. red and blue .. 1·25 1·10
44. 50 c. brown and lavender 1·50 1·10
45. 1 f. red and green .. 1·50 1·00
46. 2 f. lilac and yellow .. 5·50 5·00
47. 5 f. blue and yellow .. 10·00 6·50

1903. Surch. with large **5.**

48. B. 5 on 15 c. orange .. 1·75 90

1904. Stamps of Indo-China surch. **CHINE** and value in Chinese.

63. 1. 1 c. olive 10 10
64. 2 c. claret on yellow .. 12 12
65. 4 c. chocolate on grey .. £170 £130
66. 5 c. green 20 20
67. 10 c. red 25 25
68. 15 c. brown on blue .. 20 20
70. 20 c. red on green .. 1·50 1·50
71. 25 c. blue 55 55
72. 40 c. black on grey .. 55 55
73. 1 f. green .. .. 50·00 32·00
74. 2 f. brown on yellow .. 2·50 2·50
75. 10 f. red on green .. 27·00 27·00

1907. Types as for 1902 surch. in figures and words and also with value in Chinese.

92. A. 1 c. on 5 c. orange .. 40 20
76. 2 c. on 5 c. green .. 5 5
93. B. 2 c. on 10 c. green .. 1·10 55
94. 3 c. on 15 c. orange .. 1·25 1·00
77. 4 c. on 10 c. red .. 10 10
95. 4 c. on 20 c. claret .. 2·10 1·25
96. 5 c. on 25 c. purple .. 75 50
78. 6 c. on 15 c. orange .. 12 12
97. 6 c. on 30 c. red .. 2·00 1·60
87. 8 c. on 20 c. claret .. 15 5
80. 10 c. on 25 c. blue .. 5 5
98. 10 c. on 50 c. blue .. 2·50 1·60
81. C. 20 c. on 50 c. brown & lav. 25 15
89. B. 20 c. on 50 c. blue .. 6·50 6·00
99. C. 20 c. on 1 f. red and green 5·00 3·25
90. 40 c. on 1 f. red and green 30 20
100. 40 c. on 2 f. red and green 5·00 3·25
101. 1 pi. on 5 f. blue and yellow 25·00 25·00
83. 2 pi. on 5 f. blue & yellow 2·75 2·00
91. $2 on 5 f. blue and yellow 30·00 26·00

POSTAGE DUE STAMPS

1901. Postage Due stamps of France optd. **Chine.**

D 23. D 2. 5 c. blue 50 50
D 24. 10 c. brown .. .. 1·00 75
D 25. 15 c. green .. .. 1·00 75
D 26. 20 c. olive 70 60
D 27. 30 c. red .. .. 1·60 1·10
D 28. 50 c. claret .. .. 1·40 1·10

1911. Postage Due stamps of France surch. in figures and words and also with value in Chinese.

D 102. D 2. 1 c. on 5 c. blue .. 9·00 7·00
D 92. 2 c. on 5 c. blue .. 25 15
D 103. 2 c. on 10 c. brown 14·00 11·00
D 93. 4 c. on 10 c. brown 25 15
D 104. 4 c. on 20 c. olive .. 14·00 11·00
D 94. 8 c. on 20 c. olive .. 30 25
D 105. 10 c. on 50 c. claret 14·00 11·00
D 95. 20 c. on 50 c. claret 30 25

For stamps provisionally optd. **A PERCEVOIR** at Tientsin and Peking, see Stanley Gibbons' Overseas Stamp Catalogue, Vol. 1.

FRENCH POST OFFICES IN CRETE E1

These offices were closed in 1914.

1902. "Blanc", "Mouchon" and "Merson" key-types inscr. "CRETE".

1. A. 1 c. grey 30 30
2. 2 c. claret 35 35
3. 3 c. red 30 30
4. 4 c. brown 25 25
5. 5 c. green 15 12
6. B. 10 c. red 40 25
7. 15 c. orange 40 35
8. 20 c. claret 65 50
9. 25 c. blue 70 60
10. 30 c. mauve 90 75
11. C. 40 c. red and blue .. 1·75 1·25
12. 50 c. brown and lavender 2·25 1·40
13. 1 f. red and green .. 2·75 2·25
14. 2 f. lilac and buff .. 3·75 3·00
15. 5 f. blue and buff .. 5·00 4·50

1903. Surch. in figures and words.

16. B. 1 pi. on 25 c. blue .. 4·00 4·00
17. C. 2 pi. on 50 c. brown & lav. 7·50 7·50
18. 4 pi. on 1 f. red and green 14·00 12·00
19. 8 pi. on 2 f. lilac and buff 18·00 17·00
20. 20 pi. on 5 f. blue and buff 25·00 21·00

FRENCH POST OFFICES IN MOROCCO O3

French Post Offices were first established in Morocco in 1862, using the stamps of France. For stamps used by French Post Offices in Tangier after 1912 see under that heading.

100 centimos = 1 peseta.

1891. Stamps of France surch. in Spanish currency in figures and words. (Centimos on equivalent centime values).

1. 10. 5 c. on 5 c. deep green .. 85 45
2. 5 c. on 5 c. yellow-green .. 4·00 3·75
5. 10 c. on 10 c. blk. on lilac 3·25 30
6. 20 c. on 20 c. red on grn. 5·00 3·75
7. 25 c. on 25 c. blk. on red 3·25 10
8. 50 c. on 50 c. red .. 14·00 4·50
10. 1 p. on 1 f. olive .. 12·00 10·00
11. 2 p. on 2 f. brn. on blue .. 35·00 35·00

1893. Postage Due stamps of France optd. **TIMBRE POSTE** and bar.

12. D 2. 5 c. black £275 £140
13. 10 c. black £225 £100

1902. "Blanc", "Mouchon" and "Merson" key types inscr. "MAROC" and surch. in Spanish currency in figures and words.

14. A. 1 c. on 1 c. grey 5 5
15. 2 c. on 2 c. claret .. 10 10
16. 3 c. on 3 c. red 12 12
17. 4 c. on 4 c. brown .. 1·40 1·10
18. 5 c. on 5 c. green .. 55 10
19. B. 10 c. on 10 c. red 40 5
20. 20 c. on 20 c. claret .. 2·25 1·40
21. 25 c. on 25 c. blue .. 2·50 10
22. 35 c. on 35 c. lilac .. 4·50 2·75
23. C. 50 c. on 50 c. brn. & lilac .. 4·50 1·15
24. 1 p. on 1 f. red and green .. 12·00 10·00
25. 2 p. on 2 f. lilac & yellow .. 14·00 10·00

1903. Optd. **P.P.** in box.

26. D 2. 5 c. on 5 c. blue .. £120
27. 10 c. on 10 c. brown .. £275

1911. Same type surch. with figure of value and Arabic word.

28. A. 1 c. on 1 c. grey 5 5
29. 2 c. on 2 c. claret .. 5 5
30. 3 c. on 3 c. orange .. 5 5
31. 5 c. on 5 c. green .. 8 5
32. B. 10 c. on 10 c. red 5 5
33. 15 c. on 15 c. orange .. 25 20
34. 20 c. on 20 c. claret .. 45 40
35. 25 c. on 25 c. blue .. 25 8
36. 35 c. on 35 c. lilac .. 70 20
37. C. 40 c. on 40 c. red and blue 70 70
38. 50 c. on 50 c. brn. & lilac .. 2·75 2·00
39. 1 p. on 1 f. red and green .. 1·75 12

POSTAGE DUE STAMPS

1896. Postage Due stamps of France surch. in Spanish currency in figures and words.

D 14. D 2. 5 c. on 5 c. blue .. 55 55
D 15. 10 c. on 10 c. brown 1·10 55
D 16. 30 c. on 30 c. red .. 1·90 1·75
D 17. 50 c. on 50 c. red .. 2·00 1·75
D 18. 1 p. on 1 f. brown .. 42·00 35·00

1909. Postage Due stamps of France surch. in Spanish currency in figures.

D 28. D 8. 1 c. on 1 c. olive .. 25 25
D 29. 10 c. on 10 c. violet 4·00 4·00
D 30. 30 c. on 30 c. bistre 5·00 5·00
D 31. 50 c. on 50 c. red .. 7·00 7·00

1911. Postage Due stamps of France surch. with figure and Arabic word.

D 40. D 2. 5 c. on 5 c. blue .. 45 45
D 41. 10 c. on 10 c. brown 1·10 1·10
D 42. 50 c. on 50 c. purple 1·50 1·50

1911. Postage Due stamps of France surch. in figures and Arabic.

D 43. D 3. 1 c. on 1 c. olive .. 10 10
D 44. 10 c. on 10 c. violet 65 65
D 45. 30 c. on 30 c. bistre 75 75
D 46. 50 c. on 50 c. red .. 1·10 1·10

For later issues see **FRENCH MOROCCO.**

FRENCH POST OFFICES IN TANGIER O3

By Franco-Spanish Treaty of 27 November 1912, Tangier was given a special status outside the protectorates. After the Tangier Convention of 1924 the zone was administered by an international commission. Tangier was occupied by Spain in 1940 and the French P.O's. closed in 1942.

100 centimes = 1 franc.

1918. "Blanc", "Mouchon" and "Merson" key-types optd. **TANGER.**

1. A. 1 c. grey 5 5
2. 2 c. claret 5 5
3. 3 c. orange 5 5
4. 5 c. green 5 5
5. 5 c. orange 10 10
6. B. 10 c. red 8 8
7. 10 c. green 5 5
8. 15 c. orange 12 12
9. 20 c. claret 20 20
10. 25 c. blue 15 15
11. 30 c. red 20 20
12. 35 c. lilac 25 25
13. C. 40 c. red and blue .. 25 25
14. 50 c. brown and lilac .. 1·60 1·50
15. B. 50 c. blue .. .. .. 1·60 1·50
16. C. 1 f. red and green .. 65 55
17. 2 f. red and green .. 8·00 8·00
18. 5 f. blue and yellow .. 8·00 8·00

1928. Air. Nos. 149/58 of French Morocco optd. **Tanger.**

30. 5 c. blue 45 45
31. 25 c. orange 45 45
32. 50 c. red 45 45
33. 75 c. brown 45 45
34. 80 c. green 45 45
35. 1 f. orange 45 45
36. 1 f. 50 blue 45 45
37. 2 f. brown 45 45
38. 3 f. purple 45 45
39. 5 f. black 45 45

POSTAGE DUE STAMPS

1918. Postage Due stamps of France optd. **TANGER.**

D 19. D 2. 1 c. black 5 5
D 20. 5 c. blue 8 8
D 21. 10 c. brown 12 12
D 22. 15 c. green 45 45
D 23. 20 c. olive 50 50
D 24. 30 c. red .. .. 1·25 1·25
D 25. 50 c. purple .. .. 2·00 2·00

1918. Postage Due stamps of France optd. **TANGER.**

D 26. D 3. 1 c. olive 5 5
D 27. 10 c. violet 10 10
D 28. 20 c. bistre 85 85
D 29. 40 c. red .. .. 1·60 1·60

FRENCH POST OFFICES IN ZANZIBAR O4

The French post office in Zanzibar closed when Great Britain took over control.

16 annas = 1 rupee.
Stamps of France surcharged.

1894. Surch. in figures and words.

1. 10. ½ a. on 5 c. green .. 35 30
3. 1 a. on 10 c. black on lilac 65 35
4. 1½ a. on 15 c. blue .. 1·25 65
6. 2 a. on 20 c. red on green 1·00 65
7. 2½ a. on 25 c. black on red 50 25
8. 3 a. on 30 c. brown .. 1·00 65
9. 4 a. on 40 c. red on yellow 1·10 65
10. 5 a. on 50 c. red .. 1·50 1·25
11. 7½ a. on 75 c. brn. on orge. 32·00 30·00
12. 10 a. on 1 f. olive .. 2·50 2·00
14. 50 a. on 5 f. mve. on lilac 30·00 25·00

1894. Surch. in Indian and French currency in figures.

15. 10. ½ a. & 5 on 1 c. blk. on bl. 11·00 11·00
16a. 1 a. & 10 on 3 c. grey .. 11·00 11·00
17. 2½ a. and 25 on 4 c. lilac on grey .. .. 17·00 17·00
18. 5 a. and 50 and 20 c. red on green .. .. 17·00 17·00
19. 10 a. and 1 f. on 40 c. red on yellow .. .. 32·00 32·00

1896. Optd. **ZANZIBAR** and surch. in figures and words.

23. 10. ½ a. on 5 c. green .. 35 35
25. 1 a. on 10 c. black on lilac 35 35
26. 1½ a. on 15 c. blue .. 25 25
28. 2 a. on 20 c. red on green 25 25
29. 2½ a. on 25 c. black on red 25 25
30. 3 a. on 30 c. brown .. 35 35
31. 4 a. on 40 c. red on yellow 30 30
33. 5 a. on 50 c. red .. 1·50 1·25
35. 10 a. on 1 f. olive .. 70 65
37. 20 a. on 2 f. brown on blue 1·25 95
38. 50 a. on 5 f. mve. on lilac 2·40 1·75

1897. Nos. 1/4 and 8/9 further surch. with new figures of value in French and Indian currency and optd. **ZANZIBAR** vert.

42. 10. 2½ and 25 on ½ a. on 5 c. 80·00 15·00
43. 2½ and 25 on 1 a. on 10 c. £300 80·00
44. 2½ and 25 on 1½ a. on 15 c. £300 80·00
45. 5 and 50 on 3 a. on 30 c. £300 65·00
46. 5 and 50 on 4 a. on 40 c. £300 80·00

1902. "Blanc", "Mouchon" and "Merson" key-types inscr. "ZANZIBAR" and surch. in figures and words.

53. A. ½ a. on 5 c. green .. 25 25
54. B. 1 a. on 10 c. red .. 35 30
55. 1½ a. on 15 c. orange .. 75 60
56. 2 a. on 20 c. claret .. 90 65
57. 2½ a. on 25 c. blue .. 75 60
58. 3 a. on 30 c. mauve .. 45 45
59. C. 4 a. on 40 c. red and blue 1·40 1·10
60. 5 a. on 50 c. brown & lav. 90 80
61. 10 a. on 1 f. red and green 1·50 1·25
62. 20 a. on 2 f. lilac & yellow 3·25 3·00
63. 50 a. on 5 f. blue & yellow 6·00 6·00

1904. Surch. with both currencies in figures on either side of bars.

65. 10. "25 c. 2½" on 4 a. on 40 c. (No. 31) .. .. — £100
66. "50 5" on 4 a. on 40 c. (No. 31) .. .. — £100
67. "50 5" on 3 a. on 30 c. (No. 30) .. .. — £100
68. "1 fr 10" on 3 a. on 30 c. (No. 30) .. .. — £150
69. "1 fr 10" on 4 a. on 40 c. (No. 31) .. .. — £150

1904. "Blanc" key-type surch. with both currencies in large figures.

70. A. "2 25" on ½ a. on 5 c. green (No. 53) .. .. — 8·00

1904. "Mouchon" key-type surch. with both currencies in figures or in figures and words.

71. B. "25 c 2½" on 1 a. on 10 c. red (No. 54) .. .. — 8·00
72. "25 c 2½" on 3 a. on 30 c. mauve (No. 58) .. — £120
73. "50 c cinq" on 3 a. on 30 c. mauve (No. 58) .. — 80·00
74. "1 fr dix" on 3 a. on 30 c. mauve (No. 58) .. — £110

POSTAGE DUE STAMPS

1897. Postage Due stamps of France surch. **ZANZIBAR** and value in figures and words.

D 1. D 2. ½ a. on 5 c. blue .. 70 50
D 2. 1 a. on 10 c. brown .. 60 40
D 3. 1½ a. on 15 c. green .. 85 70
D 4. 3 a. on 30 c. red .. 85 70
D 5. 5 a. on 50 c. purple .. 1·25 95

FRENCH SOMALI COAST O2

A French colony on the Gulf of Aden, E. coast of Africa. Now known as French Territory of the Afars and the Issas.

1. Mosque at Tajurah.

2. Mounted Somalis. 3. Somali Warriors.

1902.

121. 1. 1 c. orange and purple .. 5 5
137. 1 c. black and purple .. 5 5
122. 2 c. green and brown .. 5 5
138. 2 c. black and brown .. 8 8
123. 4 c. red and blue 12 10
139. 4 c. black and red .. 10 10
124. 5 c. green 10 10
140. 5 c. black and green .. 30 15
125. 10 c. orange and red .. 90 65
141. 10 c. black and red .. 1·10 35
126. 15 c. blue and orange .. 70 50
142. 15 c. black and brown .. 2·25 1·00
127. 2. 20 c. green and lilac .. 1·50 1·25
143. 20 c. black and lilac .. 3·25 2·75
129. 25 c. blue .. .. .. 2·10 2·10
144. 25 c. black and blue .. 1·10 85
130. 30 c. black and red .. 55 45
131. 40 c. blue and yellow .. 1·75 1·40
145. 40 c. black and orange .. 1·10 1·00
132. 50 c. red and green .. 6·50 6·50
146. 50 c. black and green .. 2·50 1·75
133. 75 c. mauve and orange .. 45 45
147. 75 c. black and brown .. 1·10 1·00
134. 3. 1 f. purple and orange .. 3·25 3·25
148. 1 f. black and orange .. 1·75 1·60
135. 2 f. red and green .. 5·00 4·50
149. 2 f. black and green .. 1·25 1·10
136. 5 f. blue and orange .. 3·25 2·75
150. 5 f. black and orange .. 2·00 1·75

4. Mosque at Tajurah. **5.** Mounted Somalis.

1909.
151. **4.** 1 c. brown and claret .. 5 5
152. 2 c. olive and violet .. 5 5
153. 4 c. blue and brown .. 15 10
154. 5 c. olive and green .. 25 5
155. 10 c. orange and red .. 45 20
156. 20 c. brown and black .. 1·10 75
157. **5.** 25 c. blue .. 55 35
158. 30 c. red and brown .. 70 55
159. 35 c. green and violet .. 90 75
160. 40 c. violet and red .. 75 70
161. 45 c. green and brown .. 1·10 1·00
162. 50 c. brown and claret .. 1·10 1·00
163. 75 c. green and red .. 2·25 2·25
164. **3.** 1 f. brown and violet .. 3·25 2·75
165. 2 f. red and brown .. 5·50 5·50
166. 5 f. green and claret .. 8·00 9·00

1915. Surch **5 c.** and red cross.
167. 10 c.+5 c. red .. 1·40 1·40

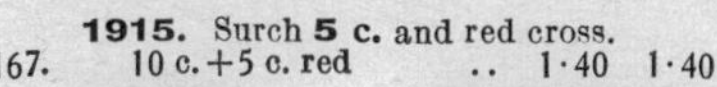

6. Drummer. **7.** Somali Woman.

8. Railway Bridge at Holl-Holli.

1915.
168. **6.** 1 c. brown and violet .. 5 5
169. 2 c. blue and orange .. 5 5
170. 4 c. red and brown .. 5 5
171. 5 c. green .. 8 8
195. 5 c. red and orange .. 8 8
172. **7.** 10 c. red .. 8 8
196. 10 c. green .. 8 8
214. 10 c. green and red .. 5 5
173. 15 c. red and purple .. 8 8
174. 20 c. brown and orange .. 5 5
215. 20 c. green .. 5 5
216. 20 c. red and green .. 5 5
175. 25 c. blue .. 5 5
197. 25 c. green and black .. 12 12
176. 30 c. green and black .. 15 12
198. 30 c. brown and red .. 8 8
217. 30 c. green and violet .. 5 5
218. 30 c. green .. 5 5
177. 35 c. red and green .. 5 5
178. 40 c. purple and blue .. 5 5
179. 45 c. blue and brown .. 12 10
180. 50 c. black and red .. 1·00 80
199. 50 c. blue and violet .. 12 12
219. 50 c. purple and brown .. 5 5
220. 60 c. purple and olive .. 5 5
221. 65 c. olive and red .. 5 5
181. 75 c. brown and purple .. 5 5
222. 75 c. blue .. 5 5
223. 75 c. brown and mauve .. 10 10
224. 85 c. green and claret .. 8 8
225. 90 c. red .. 90 90
182. **8.** 1 f. red and brown .. 12 10
226. 1 f. 10 blue and brown .. 55 55
227. 1 f. 25 brown and blue .. 1·10 70
228. 1 f. 50 blue .. 8 8
229. 1 f. 75 orange and olive .. 60 60
183. 2 f. black and violet .. 25 15
230. 3 f. magenta .. 80 75
184. 5 f. black and red .. 55 25

1922. Surch. **1922** and value in figures in frame.
193. **6.** 10 on 5 c. green .. 5 5
194. **7.** 50 on 25 c. blue and lilac 5 5

1922. Surch. in figures.
200. **7.** 0.01 on 15 c. red & purple 5 5
201. 0.02 on 15 c. red & purple 5 5
202. 0.04 on 15 c. red & purple 5 5
203. 0.05 on 15 c. red & purple 5 5
204. **8.** 25 c. on 5 f. black & red 10 10
205. **7.** 60 on 75 c. violet & olive 5 5
206. 65 on 15 c. red & purple 8 8
207. 85 on 40 c. purple & blue 8 8
208. 90 on 75 c. red .. 55 55
209. **8.** 1 f. 25 on 1 f. blue .. 10 10
210. 1 f. 50 on 1 f. blue .. 20 20
211. 3 f. on 5 f. mauve & red 55 55
212. 10 f. on 5 f. brown & red 1·10 1·10
213. 20 f. on 5 f. mauve & grn. 1·75 1·75

1931. "Colonial Exhibition" key-types inscr. "COTE FR. DES SOMALIS".
233. E. 40 c. green 80 80
234. F. 50 c. mauve 80 80
235. G. 90 c. red 80 80
236. H. 1 f. 50 blue 80 80

1937. Int. Exn., Paris. As Nos. 110/15 of Cameroun.
237. 20 c. violet 20 20
238. 30 c. green 25 25
239. 40 c. red 20 20
240. 50 c. brown 25 25
241. 90 c. red 20 20
242. 1 f. 50 blue 25 25

1938. Int. Anti-Cancer Fund. As T **10** of Cameroun.
244. 1 f. 75+50 c. blue .. 1·00 1·00

9. Mosque at Djibouti. **10.** Somali Warriors.

12. Djibouti.

1938.
245. **9.** 2 c. purple 5 5
246. 3 c. olive 5 5
247. 4 c. brown 5 5
248. 5 c. red 5 5
249. 10 c. blue 5 5
250. 15 c. black 5 5
251. 20 c. orange 5 5
252. **10.** 25 c. brown 5 5
253. 30 c. blue 5 5
254. 35 c. olive 5 5
255. **9.** 40 c. brown 5 5
256. 45 c. green 5 5
257. **10.** 50 c. red 5 5
258. 55 c. purple 8 5
259. 60 c. black 8 8
260. 65 c. brown 5 5
261. 70 c. violet 20 20
262. – 80 c. black 20 15
263. **10.** 90 c. mauve 20 20
264. – 1 f. red 20 15
265. – 1 f. black 5 5
266. – 1 f. 25 red 8 8
267. – 1 f. 40 blue 12 12
268. – 1 f. 50 green 5 5
269. – 1 f. 60 red 8 8
270. – 1 f. 75 blue 5 5
271. – 2 f. orange 5 5
272. – 2 f. 25 blue 8 8
273. – 2 f. 50 brown 15 15
274. – 3 f. purple 8 8
275. **12.** 5 f. brown 25 25
276. 10 f. blue 25 25
277. 20 f. blue and red .. 25 25
DESIGN—VERT. 80 c. and 1 f. to 3 f. Governor L. Lagarde.

1939. New York World's Fair. As T **11** of Cameroun.
288. 1 f. 25 red 12 12
289. 2 f. 25 blue 12 12

1939. 150th Anniv. of French Revolution. As T **16** of Cameroun.
290. 45 c.+25 c. green .. 1·25 1·25
291. 70 c.+30 c. brown .. 1·25 1·25
292. 90 c.+35 c. orange .. 1·25 1·25
293. 1 f. 25+1 f. red .. 1·25 1·25
294. 2 f. 25+2 f. blue .. 1·25 1·25

1941. Air. Free French Issue. As T **18** of Cameroun, but inscr. "DJIBOUTI".
295. **18.** 1 f. orange 5 5
296. 1 f. 50 red 5 5
297. 5 f. maroon 8 8
298. 10 f. black 8 8
299. 25 f. blue 20 20
300. 50 f. green 25 25
301. 100 f. claret 45 45

1943. Optd. **FRANCE LIBRE.**
302. **6.** 1 c. brown and violet .. 8 8
303. 2 c. blue and orange .. 10 10
304. **9.** 2 c. purple 12 12
305. 3 c. olive 15 15
306. **6.** 4 c. red and brown .. 2·75 2·75
307. **9.** 4 c. brown 12 12
308. **6.** 5 c. red and orange .. 10 10
309. **9.** 5 c. red 12 12
310. 10 c. blue 8 8
311. **7.** 15 c. red and purple .. 55 55
312. **9.** 15 c. black 12 12
313. **7.** 20 c. red and green .. 12 12
314. **9.** 20 c. orange 12 12
315. **10.** 25 c. brown 12 12
316. **7.** 30 c. green 15 15
317. **10.** 30 c. blue 5 5
318. 35 c. olive 10 10
319. **9.** 40 c. brown 5 5
320. 45 c. green 8 8
321. **7.** 50 c. purple and brown 8 8
322. **10.** 50 c. on 65 c. brown .. 5 5
323. 55 c. purple 15 15
324. 60 c. black 5 5
325. **7.** 65 c. olive and red .. 12 12
326. **10.** 70 c. violet 5 5
327. – 80 c. black (No. 262) .. 5 5
328. – 90 c. mauve (No. 263) 5 5
329. – 1 f. 25 red (No. 266) .. 5 5
330. – 1 f. 40 blue (No. 267) .. 5 5
331. **8.** 1 f. 50 blue 8 8
332. – 1 f. 50 green (No. 268) .. 8 8
333. – 1 f. 60 red (No. 269) .. 5 5
334. **8.** 1 f. 75 orange and olive 80 80
335. – 1 f. 75 blue (No. 270) .. 35 35
336. – 2 f. orange (No. 271) .. 5 5
337. – 2 f. 25 blue (No. 272) .. 8 8
338. – 2 f. 50 brn. (No. 273) .. 5 5
339. – 3 f. purple (No. 274) .. 5 5
340. **12.** 5 f. brown 30 30
341. 10 f. blue .. .. 20·00 20·00
342. 20 f. blue and red .. 30 30

13. Symbolical of Djibouti.

1943. Free French issue.
361. **13.** 5 c. blue 5 5
362. 10 c. red 5 5
363. 25 c. green 5 5
364. 30 c. black 5 5
365. 40 c. violet 5 5
366. 80 c. maroon 5 5
367. 1 f. blue 5 5
368. 1 f. 50 red 5 5
369. 2 f. bistre 5 5
370. 2 f. 50 blue 5 5
371. 4 f. orange 8 5
372. 5 f. mauve 5 5
373. 10 f. blue 8 8
374. 20 f. green 10 10

1944. Mutual Aid and Red Cross Funds. As T **19** of Cameroun.
375. 5 f.+20 f. green .. 20 20

1945. Eboue. As T **20** of Cameroun.
376. 2 f. black 5 5
377. 25 f. green 15 15

1945. Surch.
378. **13.** 50 c. on 5 c. blue .. 5 5
379. 60 c. on 5 c. blue .. 5 5
380. 70 c. on 5 c. blue .. 5 5
381. 1 f. 20 on 5 c. blue .. 5 5
382. 2 f. 40 on 25 c. green .. 5 5
383. 3 f. on 25 c. green .. 5 5
384. 4 f. 50 on 25 c. green .. 8 8
385. 15 f. on 2 f. 50 blue .. 12 12

1946. Air. Victory. As T **21** of Cameroun.
386. 8 f. blue 15 15

1946. Air. From Chad to the Rhine. As T **22** of Cameroun.
387. 5 f. black 15 15
388. 10 f. red 15 15
389. 15 f. brown 25 25
390. 20 f. mauve 25 25
391. 25 f. green 30 30
392. 50 f. blue 35 35

14. Outpost at Khor-Angar.

15. Danakil Tent. **16.** Somali.

17. Government Palace, Djibouti.

1947.
393. **15.** 10 c. orge. & vio. (post.) 5 5
394. 30 c. orange and green 5 5
395. 40 c. orange and purple 5 5
396. **14.** 50 c. orange and green 5 5
397. 60 c. yellow and brown 5 5
398. 80 c. orange and violet 5 5
399. – 1 f. brown and blue .. 5 5
400. – 1 f. 20 green and grey .. 8 8
401. – 1 f. 50 blue and orange 5 5
402. – 2 f. mauve and grey .. 5 5
403. – 3 f. blue and brown .. 5 5
404. – 3 f. 60 brown and red .. 20 20
405. – 4 f. brown and grey .. 12 8
406. – 5 f. orange and brown .. 5 5
407. – 6 f. blue and grey .. 8 8
408. – 10 f. purple and blue .. 10 5
409. – 15 f. brown, blue & buff 20 12
410. – 20 f. blue, orange & blue 20 12
411. – 25 f. claret, blue & pur. 30 20
412. **16.** 50 f. brown & blue (air) 65 35
413. – 100 f. yellow and green 1·10 55
414. **17.** 200 f. green, yell. & blue 2·25 80
DESIGNS—HORIZ. As T **14**: 1 f. to 1 f. 50, Obock Tajurah road. 2 f. to 4 f. Woman carrying dish. 5 f. to 10 f. Somali village. 15 f. to 25 f. Mosque, Djibouti. As T **17**: 100 f. Frontier post, Loyada.

1949. Air. U.P.U. As T **25** of Cameroun.
425. 30 f. multicoloured .. 1·40 1·40

1950. Colonial Welfare. As T **26** of Cameroun.
426. 10 f.+2 f. red and brown .. 65 65

1952. Military Medal Cent. As T **27** of Cameroun.
427. 15 f. violet, yellow & green 75 75

1954. Air. Liberation. As T **29** of Cameroun.
428. 15 f. violet and indigo .. 1·10 1·10

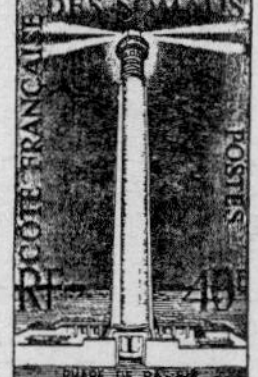

18. Ras-Bir Lighthouse. **20.** Djibouti.

19. Aerial Map of Djibouti.

1956.
429. **18.** 40 f. blue (postage) .. 45 30
430. **19.** 500 f. mve. & vio. (air) 7·50 5·50

1956. Economic and Social Development Fund.
431. **20.** 15 f. violet 15 8

21. Wart Hog.

1958. Animals, Fishes and Birds.
432. **21.** 30 c. brn. & red-brown (postage) 5 5
433. – 40 c. brown and bistre 5 5
434. – 50 c. maroon, grey & grn. 5 5
435. – 1 f. orge., blue & brown 5 5
436. – 2 f. multicoloured .. 5 5
437. – 3 f. brown and violet .. 8 5
438. – 4 f. brn., orange & blue 8 5
439. – 5 f. black and blue .. 10 8
440. – 10 f. red, brown & green 12 8
441. – 15 f. yell., grn. & mauve 20 12
442. – 20 f. pur., red and blue 30 15
443. – 25 f. blue, red & green .. 30 25
444. – 30 f. blk., red and blue 55 30
445. – 60 f. green and blue .. 80 60
446. – 75 f. yell., brn. and green 1·10 80
447. – 100 f. brn., grn. & bl. (air) 1·10 60
448. – 200 f. brn., blk. & orge. 1·90 1·10
449. – 500 f. multicoloured 3·75 2·00
DESIGNS—HORIZ. As T **21**. 40 c. Cheetah. 1 f. Parrot Fish. 3 f. Black Marlin. 4 f. Coffer Fish. 5 f. Eagle Ray. 15 f. Bee-eater. 20 f. Trigger-fish ("Balistapus undulatus"). 25 f. Trigger-fish ("Odonus niger"). 30 f. Ibis. 60 f. Hammerhead Shark (48×27 mm.). 100 f. Gazelles and aircraft. 200 f. Bustard. 500 f. Salt caravan. Lake Assal. VERT.—As T **21**. 50 c. Gerenuk Gazelles. 2 f. Angel-fish. 10 f. Flamingo. 75 f. Pelican.

1958. Tropical Flora. As T **21** of French Equatorial Africa.
450. 10 f. red, green and yellow 35 20
DESIGN—HORIZ. 10 f. "Haemanthus".

1958. Declaration of Human Rights. 10th Anniv. As T **5** of Comoro Is.
451. 20 f. violet and blue .. 30 30

23. Governor Bernard.

1960. Air. Governor Bernard. 25th Death Anniv.
452. 23. 55 f. choc., blue & red 55 30

25. Obock in 1862.

1962. Air. Obock Centenary.
453. 25. 100 f. brown and blue .. 75 60

26. Dragon Tree ("Dracena"). 27. "Meleagrina margaritifera".

1962. Fauna and Flora.
454. 2 f. grn., brn., red & yellow 12 12
455. 4 f. chocolate and ochre .. 12 12
456. 6 f. yellow, green orange, blue and maroon .. 20 15
457. 25 f. yellow-brown, green and brown-red .. 55 45
458. 40 f. chestnut, black & blue 80 75
459. 50 f. brown, maroon & blue 1·10 1·00
DESIGNS—HORIZ. 2 f. T 26. 4 f. Daman (marmot). 6 f. Large carangue (fish). 25 f. Fennecs. 40 f. Tawny vulture. VERT. 50 f. Mountain deer.

1962. Malaria Eradication. As T 45 of Cameroun.
460. 25 f.+5 f. blue .. .. 1·10 1·10

1962. Shells of the Red Sea. Multicoloured.
(a) Postage as T 27.
461. 8 f. Type 27 .. .. 10 8
462. 10 f. "Tridacna squamosa" 10 8
463. 25 f. "Strombus tricornis" 20 15
464. 30 f. "Trochus dentatus" 20 15
(b) Air. Horiz. (50×28 mm.).
465. 60 f. "Rostellaria magna" 50 25
466. 100 f. "Lambis bryonia" 65 30
The 10 f. and 25 f. are horiz. designs.

1962. Air. 1st Trans-Atlantic TV Satellite Link. As T 18 of Andorra.
467. 20 f. maroon and myrtle .. 15 15

1963. Red Cross Cent. As Type F 2 of New Hebrides.
468. 50 f. red, grey and brown 1·25 1·25

28. Madrepore. 29. Houri Sailing Boat.

1963. Coral Flowers. Multicoloured.
(a) Postage as T 28.
469. 5 f. Type 28 .. .. 12 12
470. 6 f. Tubipore 12 12
(b) Air. Horiz. (48×27 mm.).
471. 40 f. Millepore 30 20
472. 55 f. Meandrine 50 30
473. 200 f. Ramose polyp .. 1·40 80

1963. Declaration of Human Rights. 15th Anniv. As T 10 of Comoro Islands.
474. 70 f. blue and chocolate .. 1·25 1·25

1964. "PHILATEC 1964" Int. Stamp Exn., Paris. As T 481 of France.
475. 80 f. brown, green & purple 1·40 1·40

1964. Local Sailing Craft. Multicoloured.
(a) Postage as T 29.
476. 15 f. Type 29 .. .. 15 10
477. 25 f. Sambouk sailing ship 30 20
(b) Air. Horiz. Size 48×27 mm.
478. 50 f. Building sambouks .. 45 35
479. 85 f. Zaroug sailing ship .. 65 50
480. 300 f. Ziema .. .. 2·25 1·60

30. Rameses II and Nefertari Temple, Philae.

1964. Air. Nubian Monuments Preservation.
481. 30. 25 f.+5 f. brown, green and red .. .. 1·10 1·10

31. "The Discus Thrower". (Ancient Greece).

1964. Air. Olympic Games, Tokyo.
482. 31. 90 f. purple, red & black 1·25 1·00

1965. Air. I.T.U. Cent. As T 15 of Comoro Islands.
483. 95 f. blue, brown & purple 2·25 1·75

32. Ghoubet Kharab.

1965. Landscapes.
484. – 6 f. brown, ultramarine and green (postage) .. 10 8
485. – 20 f. green, ultram. & brown 15 12
486. – 45 f. brown & blue (air) 30 20
487. 32. 65 f. maroon, ochre & bl. 40 20
VIEWS (26×22 mm.): 6 f. Dadwayya. 20 f. Tajurah. As T 32: 45 f. Lake Abbe.

33. "Life and Death".

1965. Anti-Tuberculosis Campaign.
488. 33. 25 f.+5 f. brown, green and turquoise .. 30 30

1966. Air. Launching of 1st French Satellite. As Nos. 1696/7 (plus se-tenant label) of France.
489. 25 f. brn., bistre-brn. & red 25 20
490. 30 f. brn., bistre-brn. & red 25 25

34. Senna. 35. Feather Star and Flame Coral.

1966. Flowers.
491. 34. 5 f. orange, green and brown (postage) .. 8 5
492. – 8 f. orange, green & brn. 8 5
493. – 25 f. red, blue and green 20 12
494. – 55 f. lake, green & myrtle (air) 40 30
FLOWERS—VERT. 8 f. Poinciana. 25 f. Aloes. HORIZ. (48½×27 mm.); 55 f. Stapelia.

1966. Air. Marine Life. Multicoloured.
495. 8 f. Type 35 .. .. 12 12
496. 25 f. Regal angel fish .. 25 25
497. 40 f. Purple moon angel fish 50 50
498. 50 f. Cardinal coral fish .. 65 65
499. 70 f. Squirrel fish .. 80 80
500. 80 f. Majestic surgeon fish 85 85
501. 100 f. Scorpion fish .. 1·10 1·10

1966. Air. Launching of Satellite "D1". As T 521 of France.
502. 48 f. grn., chocolate & blue 40 30

36. Giant Lizard.

1967. Somali Fauna.
503. 36. 20 f. purple, chest. & brn. 20 15

POSTAGE DUE STAMPS

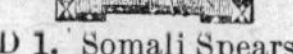

D 1. Somali Spears. D 2.

1915.
D 185. D 1. 5 c. blue 5 5
D 186. 10 c. red 5 5
D 280. 15 c. black 5 5
D 281. 20 c. violet 5 5
D 187. 30 c. yellow 5 5
D 190. 50 c. claret 40 40
D 283. 50 c. brown 5 5
D 284. 60 c. green 5 5
D 285. 1 f. blue 15 15
D 286. 2 f. red 5 5
D 287. 3 f. sepia 5 5

1927. Surch. in figures.
D 231. D 1. "2 F" on 1 f. red 50 50
D 232. "3 F" on 1 f. mve. 50 50

1942. (a) Optd. **FRANCE LIBRE.**
D 343. D 1. 5 c. blue 8 8
D 344. 10 c. red 8 8
D 345. 15 c. black 8 8
D 346. 20 c. violet 8 8
D 347. 30 c. yellow 8 8
D 348. 50 c. claret 8 8
D 349. 60 c. green 8 8
D 350. 1 f. blue 40 40

(b) Optd. **France Libre.**
D 351. D 1. 5 c. blue 5 5
D 352. 10 c. red 5 5
D 353. 15 c. black 5 5
D 354. 20 c. violet 5 5
D 355. 30 c. yellow 5 5
D 356. 50 c. brown 8 0
D 357. 60 c. green 10 18
D 358. 1 f. blue 5 5
D 359. 2 f. red 50 50
D 360. 3 f. sepia 75 75

1947.
D 415. D 2. 10 c. mauve .. 5 5
D 416. 30 c. brown .. 5 5
D 417. 50 c. green .. 5 5
D 418. 1 f. brown .. 5 5
D 419. 2 f. claret .. 5 5
D 420. 3 f. brown .. 5 5
D 421. 4 f. blue .. 5 5
D 422. 5 f. red .. 5 5
D 423. 10 f. green .. 8 8
D 424. 20 f. blue .. 12 12

For later issues see **FRENCH TERRITORY OF THE AFARS AND THE ISSAS.**

FRENCH SOUTHERN AND ANTARCTIC TERRITORIES O2

Stamps issued for use in the French settlements in the southern Indian Ocean and in the Antarctic.

1955. No. 324 of Madagascar optd. **TERRES AUSTRALES ET ANTARCTIQUE FRANCAISES.**
1. 14. 15 f. blue and green .. 9·00 9·00

1. Gorfous Penguins. 3. Polar Camp and Meteorologist.

2. Emperor Penguins and South Pole.

1956.
2. – 30 c. brn., grn. & bl. (post.) 10 10
3. – 40 c. blk., purple and blue 10 10
4. 1. 50 c. blue, ochre & brn. 10 10
5. 1 f. blue, orange and grey 10 12
6. – 2 f. black, brown & blue 10 10
7. – 4 f. brown, green & blue 10 10
8. – 5 f. blue and light blue 15 20
9. – 8 f. brown and grey .. 2·25 2·50
10. – 10 f. blue 25 25
11. – 12 f. black and blue .. 20 20
12. – 15 f. purple and blue .. 45 50
13. – 20 f. blue. yell. & pale blue 1·25 1·40
14. – 25 f. blk., brown & green 50 60
15. – 85 f. orge., blue and black 2·25 2·50
16. 2. 50 f. green and olive (air) 12·00 12·00
17. 100 f. indigo and blue .. 12·00 12·00
18. – 200 f. black, blue & purple 5·50 5·50
DESIGNS—VERT. As T 1. 30 c. Sooty albatross. 2 f. Sheathbills. 12 f. Cormorants. 20 f. Territorial arms. 85 f. King penguin. HORIZ. (36×22 mm.). 40 c. Skuas. 4 f. Sea leopard. 5 f., 8 f. Sea-lion and settlement. 10 f., 15 f. Sea-elephant. 25 f. Kerguelen seal. As T 2. 200 f. Albatross.
See also Nos. 26/34.

1957. Int. Geophysical Year.
19. 3. 5 f. black and violet .. 1·25 1·40
20. 10 f. red .. .. .. 1·25 1·40
21. 15 f. blue .. .. .. 1·25 1·40

1959. Tropical Flora. As T 21 of French Equatorial Africa.
22. 10 f. green, yellow, black and salmon .. 55 55
DESIGN—HORIZ. 10 f. "Pringlea".

4. Yves-Joseph Kerguelen-Tremarec and Ships.

1960. Kerguelen Archipelago Discovery Commem.
23. 4. 25 f. choc., chestnut & blue 2·00 2·00

5. Jean Charcot, Compass and Ship.

1962. Disappearance of Jean Charcot. 25th Anniv.
24. 5. 25 f. chocolate, red & green 2·00 2·00

1962. Air. 1st Trans-Atlantic TV Satellite Link. As T 18 of Andorra.
25. 50 f. green, olive and blue 3·75 3·75

1963. Designs as T 1/2.
26. 5 f. violet and blue (postage) 65 65
35. 5 f. brown, black and blue .. 55 55
27. 8 f. indigo, purple and blue 40 30
28. 10 f. black, blue and brown 1·50 1·50
29. 12 f. green, blue and brn. 1·60 1·60
30. 15 f. blue, black and brown 55 55
31. 20 f. grey, orange and green 2·10 1·90
32. 45 f. green, brown and blue 30 30
33. 25 f. pur., brn. & blue (air) 3·50 3·50
34. 50 f. black, purple and blue 2·50 2·50
DESIGNS—HORIZ. As T 1. 5 f. (No. 26) Great blue whale. 5 f. (No. 35) Crozet Archipelago. 8 f. Sea-lions in combat. 12 f. Phylica (tree), New Amsterdam island. 15 f. Killer whale, Crozet islands. As T 2. 50 f. Adelie penguins. VERT. As T 1. 10 f. Great skuas. 20 f. Black-browed albatross. 45 f. Kerguelen cabbage. As T 2. 25 f. Ionospheric research pylon, Adelie Land.

6. Observation Station.

1963. "Int. Year of the Quiet Sun".
36. 6. 20 f. slate, chestnut and violet (postage) .. 7·00 7·00
37. – 100 f. red, blue & blk. (air) 15·00 15·00
DESIGN—VERT. (27×48 mm.): 100 f. Pylons and penguins.

TERRES AUSTRALES ET ANTARCTIQUES FRANÇAISES
7. Landfall of Dumont d'Urville.

1965. Air. Discovery of Adelie Land, 1840.
38. 7. 50 f. indigo and blue .. 8·00 8·00

1965. Air. I.T.U. Cent. As T **15** of Comoro Islands.
39. 30 f. brn., mag. & blue .. 28·00 28·00

1966. Air. Launching of 1st French Satellite. As Nos. 1696/7 (plus se-tenant label) of France.
40. 25 f. blue, green and brown 4·00 4·00
41. 30 f. blue, green and brown 4·00 4·00

1966. Air. Launching of Satellite "D1". As T **521** of France.
42. 50 f. violet, purple & orange 4·50 4·50

8. Space Probe.

9. Dumont D'Urville and Ships.

1967. Launching of 1st Space Probe, Adelie Land.
43. 8. 20 f. black, purple & blue 1·25 1·25

1968. Dumont D'Urville Commem.
44. 9. 30 f. brn., dp. blue & lt. bl. 1·10 1·10

10. Port, Man and Penguin.

1968. Air. Port-aux-Francais, Kerguelen.
45. – 40 f. slate and blue .. 80 80
46. 10. 50 f. black, green & blue 1·60 1·60
DESIGN: 40 f. Aerial View of St. Paul Island.

11. Kerguelen and Rocket.

1968. Air. Launching of "Dragon" Space Rockets.
47. 11. 25 f. brown, green & blue 2·25 2·25
48. – 30 f. blue, brown & green 2·25 2·25
DESIGN: 30 f. Adelie Land and rocket.
Nos. 47/8 were issued together in horiz. pairs separated by a half stamp-size se-tenant label inscr. "ETUDE DE L'ENVIRONNEMENT SPATIAL PAR FUSEES SONDES IONOSPHERIQUES DRAGON 1967-1968".

1968. W.H.O. 20th Anniv. As T **21** of Comoro Islands, but inscr. "TERRES AUSTRALIS ET ANTARCTIQUES FRANCAISES".
49. 30 f. blue, yellow and red .. 1·25 1·25

1968. Human Rights Year. As T **23** of Comoro Islands.
50. 30 f. red, blue and brown .. 1·10 1·10

12. Eiffel Tower, Paris, and Ship in Antarctica.

1969. Air. 5th Antarctic Treaty Consultative Meeting, Paris.
51. 12. 50 f. blue .. .. 1·00 1·00

13. Antarctic Scene.

1969. French Polar Exploration.
52. 13. 25 f. blue and greenish-blue 75 75

1969. Air. 1st Flight of "Concorde". As Type **27** of Comoro Islands.
53. 85 f. blue .. .. .. 3·25 3·25

14. Possession Island, Crozet Archipelago.

1969.
54. 14. 50 f. green, red and blue 55 55
55. – 100 f. black, grey and blue 1·00 1·00
56. – 200 f. brn., green and blue 2·25 2·25
57. – 500 f. blue .. .. 4·25 4·25
DESIGNS—HORIZ. 100 f. Relief Map of Kerguelen. VERT. 200 f. Cape Geology Archipelago map. 500 f. Territorial arms.

1970. Int. Labour Organization. 50th Anniv. As T **28** of Comoro Islands.
58. 20 f. maroon, blue and red 55 55

15. Relief Map of New Amsterdam Island.

1970. Air. Meteorological Station, New Amsterdam Island. 20th Anniv.
59. 15. 30 f. brown 55 55

1970. New U.P.U. Headquarters Building. As T **126** of Cameroun.
60. 50 f. brown, purple and blue 90 90

16. "Chaenichthys rhinoceratus".

1971. Fishes.
61. 16. 5 f. blue, yell. and green 8 8
62. – 10 f. brn., violet and blue 10 10
63. – 20 f. grn., orge. & maroon 15 15
64. – 22 f. red, violet & brown 20 20
65. – 25 f. blue, yell. & green .. 25 25
66. – 30 f. grey, blue & brown 40 40
67. – 35 f. multicoloured .. 30 30
68. – 135 f. red, brn. and blue 1·00 1·00
DESIGNS: 10 f. "Notothenia rossii". 20 f. "Notothenia coriiceps". 22 f. "Trematomus hansoni". 25 f. "Notothenia macrocephala". 30 f. "Notothenia ctanobrancha". 35 f. "Trematomus bernacchii". 135 f. "Zanchlorhynchus spinifer".

17. Port-aux-Francais, 1950.

1971. Air. Port-aux-Francais, Kerguelen. 20th Anniv.
69. 17. 40 f. brown, green & blue 45 45
70. – 50 f. green, blue & brown 55 55
DESIGN: 50 f. Port-aux-Francais, 1970.

18. Treaty Emblem.

19. "Christiansenia dreuxi".

1971. Antarctic Treaty. 10th Anniv.
71. 18. 75 f. red .. .. .. 5·50 5·50

1971. Insects.
72. 19. 15 f. brn. pur. and red .. 10 10
73. – 22 f. yell. blue and green 15 15
74. – 25 f. violet, purple & grn. 20 20
75. – 30 f. multicoloured .. 25 25
76. – 40 f. black, brn. & choc. 30 30
77. – 140 f. brn., green & blue 1·25 1·25
DESIGNS: 22 f. "Phtirocoris antarcticus". 25 f. "Microzetia mirabilis". 30 f. "Antarctophytosus atriceps". 40 f. "Paractora dreuxi". 140 f. "Pringlephaga kergueleonensis".

20. Landing on Crozet Islands.

1972. Air. Discovery of Crozet Islands and Kerguelen. Bicent.
78. 20. 100 f. black .. .. 1·00 1·00
79. – 250 f. black and brown 2·25 2·25
DESIGN: 250 f. Hoisting the flag on Kerguelen.

1972. De Gaulle Commemoration. As Nos. 1937 and 1940 of France.
80. 50 f. black and green .. 15 15
81. 100 f. black and green .. 30 30

21. M.S. "Gallieni".

1973. Air. Antarctic Voyages of the "Gallieni".
82. 21. 100 f. black and blue .. 2·00 2·25

22. "Azorella selago".

1973. Plants.
83. 22. 61 f. green, slate-green and brown .. 35 35
84. – 87 f. green, blue and red 45 45
DESIGN: 87 f. "Acaena ascendens".

23. "Le Mascarin", 1772.

1973. Air. Antarctic Ships.
85. 23. 120 f. brown 50 50
86. – 145 f. blue 65 65
87. – 150 f. blue 70 70
88. – 185 f. brown 85 85
DESIGNS: 145 f. "L'Astrolabe", 1840. 150 f. "Le Rolland", 1774. 185 f. "La Victoire", 1522.

24. Part of Alfred Faure Base.

1974. Air. Alfred Faure Base, Crozet Archipelago. 10th Anniv.
89. 24. 75 f. brn., blue & ultram. 40 40
90. – 110 f. brn., blue & ultram. 55 55
91. – 150 f. brn., blue & ultram. 65 65
Nos. 89/91 were issued together se-tenant within the sheet, making a composite picture of the base.

25. Penguin, Globe and Letters.

1974. Air. Universal Postal Union. Cent.
92. 25. 150 f. brown, blk. & blue 65 65

26. "La Francais" (1903–05).

1974. Air. Charcot's Antarctic Voyages.
93. 26. 100 f. blue 45 45
94. – 200 f. red 90 90
DESIGN: 200 f. "Le Pourquoi Pas?" (1908–10 voyage).

27. Packet-boat "Sapmer".

1974. Postal Service. 25th Anniv.
95. 27. 75 f. black, blue & mauve 30 30

28. Rockets over Kerguelen Islands.

1975. Air. "ARAKS" Franco-Soviet Magnetosphere Research Project.
96. 28. 45 f. red, blue and lilac .. 15 15
97. – 90 f. red, lilac and blue .. 35 35
DESIGN: 90 f. Map of North Coast of U.S.S.R.

29. Antarctic Tern.

1975. Antarctic Fauna.
98. 29. 40 c. blk., bl. & orge. .. 8 8
99. – 50 c. blk., light bl. & bl. 10 10
100. – 90 c. brown, & blue .. 15 15
101. – 1 f. brn., bl. and vio. .. 20 20
102. – 1 f. 20 grn., bl. & brn. 25 25
103. – 1 f. 40 bl., grn. & orge. 30 30
DESIGNS—HORIZ. 50 c. Antarctic petrel. 90 c. Seal. 1 f. Weddell's seal. VERT. 1 f. 20 Kerguelen cormorant. 1 f. 40 Penguin.

30. "La Curieuse".

1975. Air. Antarctic Ships.
104. 30. 1 f. 90 turq., bl. & brn... 50 50
105. – 2 f. 70 brn., bl. & ultram. 75 75
106. – 4 f. blue and red .. 1·00 1·00
SHIPS. 2 f. 70 "Commandant Charcot". 4 f. "Marion-Dufresne".

31. Dumont d'Urville Base, 1956.

1975. Air. Dumont d' Urville Base, Adelie Land. 20th Anniv.
107. 31. 1 f. 20 brn., orge. & blue 25 25
108. – 4 f. orge., blue & brown 1·00 1·00
DESIGNS: 4 f. Dumont d'Urville Base, 1976.

FRENCH SUDAN O2

A territory in C. Africa, incorporated in French West Africa in 1944 but in 1958 became a republic within the French Community and in 1959 joined the Mali Federation. In 1960 Mali became an independent republic.

1894. Stamps of French Colonies, "Commerce" type, surch. **SOUDAN Fais** and value.
1. 9. 0.15 on 75 c. red £600 £400
2. 0.25 on 1 f. olive £600 £325

1894. "Tablet" key-type inscr. "SOUDAN FRANCAIS".
3. D. 1 c. black on blue .. 12 12
4. 2 c. brown on yellow .. 25 25
5. 4 c. lilac on grey .. 45 30
6. 5 c. green .. .. 1·00 65
7. 10 c. black on lilac .. 2·25 2·25
18. 10 c. red 30 30
8. 15 c. blue 45 30
19. 15 c. grey 90 90
9. 20 c. red on green .. 3·75 2·75
10. 25 c. black on red .. 3·75 2·75
20. 25 c. blue 75 75
11. 30 c. brown .. .. 7·00 6·00
12. 40 c. red on yellow .. 4·50 3·75
13. 50 c. red on rose .. 8·00 7·00
21. 50 c. brown on blue .. 1·40 1·40
14. 75 c. brown on yellow .. 5·50 5·50
15. 1 f. olive .. .. 1·00 1·00

1921. Stamps of Upper Senegal and Niger optd. **SOUDAN FRANCAIS.**
85. 1. 1 c. violet and purple .. 5 5
86. 2 c. purple and grey .. 5 5
87. 4 c. blue and black .. 5 5
88. 5 c. chocolate and brown 5 5
89. 10 c. green 5 5
121. 10 c. blue and mauve .. 5 5
90. 15 c. yellow and claret .. 5 5
122. 15 c. green 5 5
123. 15 c. violet and brown .. 8 8
91. 20 c. black and purple .. 5 5
92. 25 c. green and black .. 5 5
93. 30 c. claret and orange .. 5 5
124. 30 c. black and green .. 5 5
125. 30 c. green 15 15
94. 35 c. violet and claret .. 5 5
95. 40 c. claret and grey .. 10 8
96. 45 c. brown and blue .. 5 5
97. 50 c. blue 8 5
126. 50 c. blue and orange .. 5 5
127. 60 c. violet 5 5
128. 65 c. blue and yellow .. 10 10
98. 75 c. brown and yellow .. 5 5
129. 90 c. red 80 80
99. 1 f. purple and brown .. 8 5
130. 1 f. 10 mauve and lilac .. 20 20
131. 1 f. 50 blue 85 85
100. 2 f. blue and green .. 20 15
132. 3 f. mauve .. .. 1·40 1·40
101. 5 f. black and violet .. 80 60

1922. Surch. in figures and bars.
110. 1. 25 c. on 45 c. brown & blue 5 5
111. 60 on 75 c. violet .. 5 5
112. 65 on 75 c. brown & yellow 8 8
113. 85 on 2 f. blue and green .. 8 8
114. 85 on 5 f. black and violet 8 8
115. 90 c. on 75 c. red .. 12 12
116. 1 f. 25 on 1 f. blue .. 10 10
117. 1 f. 50 on 1 f. blue .. 10 10
118. 3 f. on 5 f. yellow and red 35 20
119. 10 f. on 5 f. green and red 2·50 2·10
120. 20 f. on 5 f. red and violet 2·75 2·75

1. Sudanese Woman. 2. Bamako Gateway.

1931.
135. 1. 1 c. black and red .. 5 5
136. 2 c. orange and blue .. 5 5
137. 3 c. black and red .. 5 5
138. 4 c. red and lilac .. 5 5
139. 5 c. green and blue .. 5 5
140. 10 c. red and olive .. 5 5
141. 15 c. violet and black .. 5 5
142. 20 c. blue and brown .. 5 5
143. 25 c. red and mauve .. 5 5
144. 2. 30 c. green 5 5
145. 30 c. red and blue .. 5 5
146. 35 c. green and olive .. 5 5
147. 40 c. red and olive .. 5 5
148. 45 c. orange and blue .. 5 5
149. 45 c. green and olive .. 5 5
150. 50 c. black and red .. 5 5
151. 55 c. red and blue .. 5 5
152. 60 c. brown and blue .. 5 5
153. 65 c. black and violet .. 5 5
154. 70 c. red and blue .. 5 5
155. 75 c. brown and blue .. 15 8
156. 80 c. brown and red .. 12 5
157. 90 c. orange and brown 5 5
158. 90 c. black and violet .. 5 5
159. 1 f. green and blue .. 85 12
160. 1 f. red 40 5
161. 1 f. brown and red .. 5 5
162. – 1 f. 25 purple and mauve 5 5
163. – 1 f. 25 red 5 5
164. – 1 f. 40 black and violet .. 5 5
165. – 1 f. 50 blue 5 5
166. – 1 f. 60 blue and brown .. 5 5
167. – 1 f. 75 blue and brown .. 5 5
168. – 1 f. 75 blue 5 5
169. – 2 f. green and brown .. 5 5
170. – 2 f. 25 blue 5 5
171. – 2 f. 50 brown 5 5
172. – 3 f. brown and green .. 5 5
173. – 5 f. black and red .. 12 8
174. – 10 f. green and blue .. 20 20
175. – 20 f. brown and mauve.. 20 20
DESIGN: 1 f. 25 to 20 f. Niger boatman.

1931. "Colonial Exn." key-types inscr. "SOUDAN FRANCAIS".
186. E. 40 c. green 30 25
187. F. 50 c. mauve 30 25
188. G. 90 c. red 30 25
189. H. 1 f. 50 blue 30 25

1937. Int. Exn., Paris. As Nos. 110/15 of Cameroun.
190. 20 c. violet 20 20
191. 30 c. green 20 20
192. 40 c. red 20 20
193. 50 c. brown 20 20
194. 90 c. red 20 20
195. 1 f. 50 blue 20 20

1938. Int. Anti-Cancer Fund. As T 10 of Cameroun.
197. 1 f. 75+50 c. blue .. 1·75 1·75

1939. Caillie. As T 2 of Dahomey.
198. 90 c. orange 10 10
199. 2 f. violet 10 10
200. 2 f. 25 blue 8 8

1939. New York World's Fair. As T 11 of Cameroun.
201. 1 f. 25 red 12 12
202. 2 f. 25 blue 12 12

1939. 150th Anniv. of French Revolution. As T 16 of Cameroun.
203. 45 c.+25 c. green .. 1·00 1·00
204. 70 c.+30 c. brown .. 1·00 1·00
205. 90 c.+35 c. orange .. 1·00 1·00
206. 1 f. 25+1 f. red .. 1·00 1·00
207. 2 f. 25+2 f. blue .. 1·00 1·00

1940. Air. As T 3 of Dahomey.
208. 1 f. 90 blue 5 5
209. 2 f. 90 red 5 5
210. 4 f. 50 green 10 10
211. 4 f. 90 olive 8 8
212. 6 f. 90 orange 8 8

1941. National Defence Fund. Surch. **SECOURS NATIONAL** and value.
213. +1 f. on 50 c. (No. 150) 10 10
214. +2 f. on 80 c. (No. 156) 1·10 1·10
215. +2 f. on 1 f. 50 (No. 171) 1·10 1·10
216. +3 f. on 2 f. (No. 175) .. 1·10 1·10

1941. Marshal Petain Issue. As T 4a of Dahomey.
217. 1 f. green 5
218. 2 f. 50 blue 5
DESIGN—VERT. Gate at Djenne and Marshal Petain.

1942. Air. As T 4d of Dahomey.
219. 50 f. blue and green .. 20 25

POSTAGE DUE STAMPS

1921. Postage Due stamps of Upper Senegal and Niger optd. **SOUDAN FRANCAIS.**
D 102. M. 5 c. green 5 5
D 103. 10 c. red 5 5
D 104. 15 c. grey 5 5
D 105. 20 c. brown 8 8
D 106. 30 c. blue 10 10
D 107. 50 c. black 20 20
D 108. 60 c. orange 25 25
D 109. 1 f. violet 25 25

1927. Postage Due stamps of Upper Senegal and Niger surch. **SOUDAN FRANCAIS** and value.
D 133. M. "2 F." on 1 f. mauve 70 70
D 134. "3 F." on 1 f. brown 70 70

1931. "Figure" key-type inscr. "SOUDAN FRANCAIS".
D 176. M. 5 c. green 5 5
D 177. 10 c. red 5 5
D 178. 15 c. grey 5 5
D 179. 20 c. brown 5 5
D 180. 30 c. blue 5 5
D 181. 50 c. black 5 5
D 182. 60 c. orange 8 8
D 183. 1 f. violet 12 12
D 184. 2 f. mauve 10 10
D 185. 3 f. brown 12 12

MINIMUM PRICE

The minimum price quoted is 5p which represents a handling charge rather than a basis for valuing common stamps. For further notes about prices see introductory pages.

FRENCH TERRITORY OF THE AFARS AND THE ISSAS O2

Formerly French Somali Coast.

1. Grey-headed Kingfisher.

1967. Fauna.
504. 1. 10 f. brown, ochre, olive and blue (postage) .. 15 12
505. – 15 f. multicoloured .. 30 25
506. – 50 f. mar., chest. & grn. 55 50
507. – 55 f. blue, violet and grey 65 50
508. – 60 f. orge., emer. and grn. 1·00 65
509. – 200 f. sepia, bistre and blue (air) .. .. 2·10 1·00
DESIGNS—HORIZ. 15 f. Oyster-catcher. 50 f. Sandpipers. 55 f. Abyssinian roller. VERT. (22×36 mm.). 60 f. Ground-squirrel. (27×48 mm.) 200 f. Tawny eagles.

2. Footballers.

1967. Sports.
510. 2. 25 f. brn., grn. & bl. (post) 30 20
511. – 30 f. brown, blue & purple 45 30
512. – 48 f. mar., bl. & bistre (air) 45 25
513. – 85 f. brown, blue & bistre 75 55
DESIGNS—HORIZ. 30 f. Basketball. VERT. (27×48 mm.) 48 f. Parachute-jumping. 85 f. Aquatic sports.

1968. W.H.O. 20th Anniv. As T 21 of Comoro Islands.
514. 15 f. brown, yellow-orange, red-orange and blue .. 15 12

3. Damerdjog Fort.

1968. Administrative Outposts.
515. 3. 20 f. blue, brown & green 15 12
516. – 25 f. blue, green & brown 20 12
517. – 30 f. blue, bistre-brown and orange-brown .. 25 15
518. – 40 f. blue, brown & green 45 20
DESIGNS—FORTS. 25 f. Ali Adde. 30 f. Dorra. 40 f. Assamo.

1968. Human Rights Year. As T 23 of Comoro Islands.
519. 10 f. verm., violet & yellow 15 10
520. 70 f. purple, green & orange 45 35

4. Broadcasting Station.

5. Relief Map of Territory.

1968. Buildings and Landmarks.
521. 4. 1 f. blue & red (postage) 5 5
522. – 2 f. blue and green .. 5 5
523. – 5 f. brown, green & blue 5 5
524. – 8 f. choc., blue & green 8 5
525. – 15 f. sepia, green & blue 20 15
526. – 40 f. slate, chest., & turq. 25 15
527. – 60 f. purple, blue and grn. 45 30
528. – 70 f. brown, green & slate 55 45
529. – 85 f. green, blue & brown 65 45
530. – 85 f. slate, blue & green 55 20
531. – 100 f. green & blue (air) 70 40
532. – 200 f. blue, brown & pur. 1·50 70
533. 5. 500 f. orge., maroon and blue .. .. .. 3·50 1·75
DESIGNS—HORIZ. 2 f. Courts of Justice. 5 f. Chamber of Deputies. 8 f. Great Mosque. 40 f. G.P.O. Building, Djibouti. 60 f. Palace of High Commissariat, Djibouti. 70 f. Governor's Residence, Obock. 85 f. Harbour Administration Building, Djibouti. 85 f. (No. 527), Airport Building. VERT. 15 f. Liberation Forces' Monument (48 × 27 mm.) 100 f. Djibouti Cathedral. 200 f. Sayed Hassan Mosque.

1969. Air. 1st Flight of "Concorde". As T 27 of Comoro Islands.
534. 100 f. red and drab .. 1·50 80

6. "Schistocerca gregaria" (locust).

1969. Anti-Locust Campaign.
535. 6. 15 f. brn., slate & emer. 10 8
536. – 50 f. brn., green & blue 30 20
537. – 55 f. brown, blue & lake 35 25
DESIGNS: 50 f. Spraying by helicopter. 55 f. Spraying by light aircraft.

1969. Int. Labour Organization. 50th Anniv. As T 28 of Comoro Islands.
538. 30 f. mauve, slate and red 25 15

7. Afar Dagger.
8. Ionospheric Station, Arta. 9. Clay-pigeon Shooting.

1970.
543. 7. 10 f. brn., grn. & myrtle 8 5
544. 15 f. brown, green & blue 10 8
545. 20 f. brown, green & verm. 12 10
546. 25 f. brown, green & violet 15 10

1970. Air. Opening of Ionospheric Station, Arta.
547. 8. 70 f. carmine, emerald and blue 55 30

1970. New U.P.U. Headquarters Building. As T 127 of Cameroun.
548. 25 f. choc., green & bistre 20 12

1970. Sports.
549. 9. 30 f. brn., blue & green.. 20 15
550. – 48 f. brn., purple & blue 30 20
551. – 50 f. red, violet & blue.. 35 20
552. – 55 f. brn., bistre & blue.. 35 25
553. – 60 f. black, brn. & green 40 25
DESIGNS-HORIZ. 48 f. Speed-boat racing. 50 f. Show-jumping. 60 f. Pony-trekking. VERT. 55 f. Sailing.

10. "Fish" Sword-guard. 11. Car Ferry.

1970. Air. Expo 70.
554. 10. 100 f. violet, blue and green on gold .. 1·00 45
555. – 200 f. violet, green, red on gold .. .. 1·75 65
DESIGN: 200 f. "Horse" sword-guard.

1970. Inauguration of Car Ferry, Tajurah.
556. 11. 48 f. brown, blue and grn. 35 20

12. Diabase and Chrysolite.

1971. Geology. Multicoloured.
557. 10 f. Dolerite basalt .. 8 5
558. 15 f. Olivine basalt .. 8 8
559. 25 f. Volcanic geode .. 20 12
560. 40 f. Type 12 .. .. 30 15

13. " Manta birostris".

15. " Clanculus pharaonium".

14. Aerial View of Port.

1971. Marine Fauna. Multicoloured.
561. 4 f. Type **13** (postage) .. 5 5
562. 5 f. " Coryphaena hippurus" (vert.) 5 5
563. 9 f. " Pristis pectinatus" (vert.) 8 5
564. 30 f. " Scarus vetula" (horiz.) (46 × 27 mm.) (air) 25 12
565. 40 f. " Octopus macropus" 30 20
566. 60 f. " Halicore dugong" 50 30

1971. De Gaulle Commemoration. As Nos. 1937 and 1940 of France.
567. 60 f. black and blue .. 40 25
568. 85 f. black and blue .. 55 35

1971. Air. New Harbour, Djibouti.
569. **14.** 100 f. multicoloured .. 75 40

1972. Seashells. Multicoloured.
570. 4 f. Type **15** 5 5
571. 9 f. " Cypraea pantherina" 5 5
572. 20 f. " Cypraecassis rufa" .. 12 8
573. 50 f. " Melo aethiopicus" 30 20

16. Liechtenstein's Sandgrouse.

1972. Air. Birds. Multicoloured.
574. 30 f. Type **16** 20 15
575. 49 f. Hoopoe 30 20
576. 66 f. Great snipe .. 55 30
577. 500 f. Francolin .. 3·50 1·60

17. Swimming.

1972. Air. Olympic Games, Munich.
578. – 5 f. brn., grn. and violet 10 5
579. – 10 f. brn., grn. & lake .. 15 8
580. **17.** 55 f. brn., blue & green 45 25
581. – 60 f. violet, lake & green 60 30
DESIGNS-VERT. 5 f. Running. 10 f. Basketball. HORIZ. 60 f. Olympic flame, rings and ancient frieze.

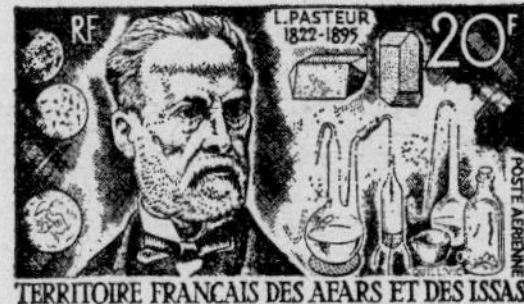

18. Pasteur and Equipment.

1972. Air. " Famous Medical Scientists".
582. **18.** 20 f. brn., green and red 15 10
583. – 100 f. brn., green & lake 65 40
DESIGN: 100 f. Calmette and Guerin.

19. Mosque, Map and Transport.

1973. Air. Visit of President Pompidou. Multicoloured.
584. 30 f. Type **19** 25 15
585. 200 f. Mosque and street scene, Djibouti (vert.) .. 1·50 90

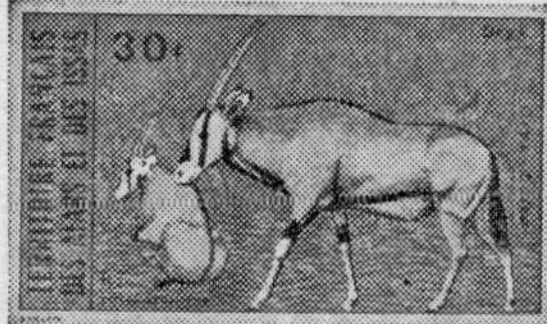
20. Oryx.

1973. Air. Wild Animals. Multicoloured.
587. 30 f. Type **20** 20 12
588. 50 f. Dik-dik 30 20
590. 66 f. Caracal 45 15
See also Nos. 603/5, 633/5, 648/9 and 651/3.

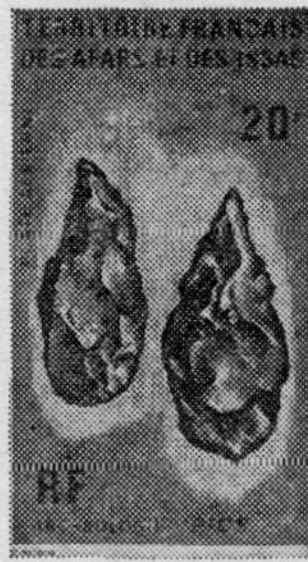
21. Flint Pick-heads.

23. Nicolas Copernicus (500th Birth Anniv.).

22. Shepherd watering Sheep.

1973. Air. Archeological Discoveries. Multicoloured.
592. 20 f. Type **21** 12 10
593. 40 f. Arrow-heads and blade (horiz.) 30 25
594. 49 f. Biface flint tool .. 40 30
595. 60 f. Flint axe-head and scraper (horiz.) .. 50 35

1973. Pastoral Economy. Multicoloured.
596. 9 f. Type **22** 8 5
597. 10 f. Camel herd .. 8 5

1973. Air. Celebrities' Anniversaries.
598. **23.** 8 f. blk., pur. and brn. 8 5
599. – 9 f. mar., orge. and brn. 8 5
600. – 10 f. mar., brn. & red .. 10 8
615. – 10 f. brn., blk. and pur. 8 5
601. – 49 f. maroon, green and bottle green 30 20
647. – 50 f. brn., bl. and grn. 35 25
611. – 55 f. deep bl., brn. & bl. 40 25
602. – 85 f. bl., blk. and violet 70 45
607. – 100 f. red., blue & green 80 55
646. – 150 f. bl., new bl. & brn. 90 65
645. – 250 f. brn., grn. & brze. 1·60 1·25
DESIGNS: 9 f. Wilhelm Rontgen (X-ray pioneer) (50th death anniv.). 10 f. Edward Jenner (smallpox vaccination pioneer) (150th death anniv.). 10 f. Marie Curie (physicist) (40th death anniv.). 49 f. Robert Koch (bacteriologist) (130th birth anniv.). 50 f. Clement Ader (aviation pioneer) (50th death anniv.). 55 f. G. Marconi (radio pioneer) (birth cent.). 85 f. Moliere (playwright) (300th death anniv.). 100 f. Henri Farman (aviator) (birth cent.). 150 f. Ampere (physicist) (birth cent.). 250 f. Michelangelo (500th birth anniv.).

1973. Air. Wild Animals (2nd series). As Type **20**. Multicoloured.
603. 20 f. Baboon (vert.) .. 15 10
604. 50 f. Genet 40 25
605. 66 f. Hare (vert.) 55 40

24. Afar Poignard.

1974.
606. **24.** 30 f. red and green .. 25 15

25. Flamingoes.

1974. Lake Abbe. Multicoloured.
608. 5 f. Type **25** 5 5
609. 15 f. Two flamingoes .. 10 8
610. 50 f. Flamingoes in flight 40 25

26. Underwater Hunting.

1974. Air. Third Underwater Hunting Trophy.
612. **26.** 200 f. blue, green & red 1·50 85
No. 612 has part of the original inscription blocked out.

27. Various Animals.

1974. Air. Balho Rock Paintings.
13. **27.** 200 f. green and red .. 1·50 85

28. Football and Emblem.

1974. World Cup Football Championships
614. **28.** 25 f. green and black .. 20 12

29. U.P.U. Emblem and Letters.

31. " Oleo chrysophylla".

30. Sunrise over Lake.

1974. Universal Postal Union. Centenary.
616. **29.** 20 f. violet, blue & ind. 15 8
617. – 100 f. brown, light brown and red 80 60

1974. Air. Lake Assal. Multicoloured.
618. 49 f. Type **30** 35 20
619. 50 f. Rocky shore .. 35 20
620. 85 f. Crysallisation on dead wood 65 45

1974. Forest Plants. Multicoloured.
621. 10 f. Type **31** 8 5
622. 15 f. " Ficus" (tree) .. 10 8
623. 20 f. " Solanum adoense" (shrub) 15 10

1975. Surch.
624. **24.** 40 f. on 30 f. red & green 30 15

32. Treasury Building.

1975. Administrative Buildings, Djibouti.
625. **32.** 8 f. grey, blue and red .. 5 5
626. – 25 f. grey, blue and red 15 10
DESIGN: 25 f. " Government City" complex.

33. " Darioconus textile".

1975. Seashells.
627. **33.** 5 f. brown and blue .. 5 5
628. – 10 f. brown and purple 8 5
629. – 15 f. brown and blue .. 12 8
630. – 20 f. yellow and violet .. 15 10
631. – 40 f. brown and yellow 30 20
632. – 45 f. brn., grn. and blue 30 20
632a. – 55 f. brown and blue .. 40 30
632b. – 60 f. black and brown .. 45 35
SEASHELLS: 10 f. " Conus sumatrensis". 15 f. " Cypraea pulcha". 20 f. " Murex scolopax". 40 f. " Ranella spinosa".

1975. Wild Animals (3rd series). As T **20.** Multicoloured.
633. 50 f. Ichneumon 30 20
634. 60 f. Porcupine (vert.) .. 35 25
635. 70 f. Zoril 40 30

34. " Hypolimnas misippus".

1975. Butterflies (1st series). Multicoloured.
636. 25 f. Type **34** 12 8
637. 40 f. " Papilio nereus" .. 25 15
639. 70 f. " Papilio demodocus" 40 30
641. 100 f. " Papilio dardanus" 60 50
See also No. 655/6.

35. " Vidua macroura".

36. " Wissmannia carinesis" (palms).

1975. Birds (1st series). Multicoloured.
640. 20 f. " Vidua macroua" (postage) 12 10
641. 50 f. " Cinnyris venutus" 35 25
642. 60 f. " Ardea goliath" .. 40 30
643. 100 f. " Scopus umbretta" 70 50
644. 500 f. Guinea Dove (air) .. 3·25 2·50
See also Nos. 657/9.

1975. Wild Animals (4th series). As T **20.** Multicoloured.
648. 15 f. Griverts (vert.) .. 10 8
649. 200 f. Anteaters .. .. 1·25 1·00

1975.
650. **36.** 20 f. multicoloured .. 12 10

1976. Wild Animals (5th series). As T **20.** Multicoloured.
651. 10 f. Hyena 8 5
652. 15 f. Wild ass (vert.) .. 12 8
653. 30 f. Antelope 15 10

37. A. Graham Bell and Satellite.

1976. Telephone Centenary.
654. 37. 200 f. blue, grn. & orge. 1·25 1·00

1976. Butterflies (2nd series). As T 34. Multicoloured.
655. 65 f. " Holocerina smilax menieri " .. 40 30
656. 100 f. " Balachowsky gonimbrasia " 70 50

1976. Birds (2nd series). As T 36. Multicoloured.
657. 25 f. " Psittacula krameri " 15 8
658. 100 f. " Oena capensis " .. 70 50
659. 300 f. African spoonbill .. 2·00 1·75

37. Basketball.

1976. Olympic Games, Montreal. Multicoloured.
660. 10 f. Type 37 .. .. 8 5
661. 15 f. Cycling 12 8
662. 40 f. Football 30 20
663. 60 f. Running 45 30

38. " Pterois radiata ".

1976. Marine Life.
664. 38. 45 f. multicoloured .. 35 25

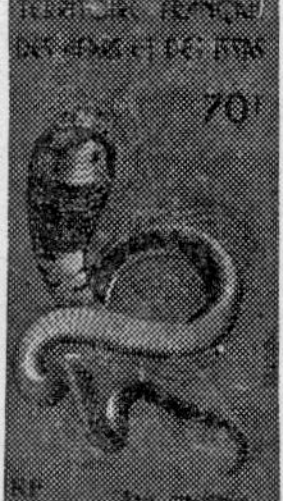
39. " Naja nigricollis ".

1976. Snakes. Multicoloured.
665. 70 f. Type 39 .. .. 55 40
666. 80 f. " Psammophis elegans " 60 40

POSTAGE DUE STAMPS

D 3. Nomadic Milk-jug.

1969.
D 539. D 3. 1 f. slate, brown & pur. 5 5
D 540. 2 f. slate, brn. & emer. 5 5
D 541. 5 f. slate, brown & blue 5 5
D 542. 10 f. slate, lake & brown 10 10

FRENCH WEST AFRICA O2

The territory in north-west Africa comprising Senegal, French Guinea, Ivory Coast, Dahomey, French Sudan, Mauritania, Niger and Upper Volta. French Sudan and Senegal became the Mali Federation and the rest independent republics.

1944. Mutual Aid and Red Cross Funds. As T 19 of Cameroun.
1. 5 f.+20 f. purple 45 45

1945. Eboue. As T 20 of Cameroun.
2. 2 f. black 5 5
3. 25 f. green 30 30

1. Soldiers.

ILLUSTRATIONS
British Commonwealth and all overprints and surcharges are FULL SIZE. Foreign Countries have been reduced to ¾-LINEAR.

1945.
4. 1. 10 c. blue and pink .. 5 5
5. 30 c. olive and cream .. 5 5
6. 40 c. blue and pink .. 5 5
7. 50 c. orange and grey .. 5 5
8. 60 c. olive and grey .. 5 5
9. 70 c. mauve and cream .. 5 5
10. 80 c. green and cream .. 5 5
11. 1 f. purple and olive .. 5 5
12. 1 f. 20 c. brown and olive 45 45
13. 1 f. 50 c. brown and red .. 5 5
14. 2 f. yellow and grey .. 8 5
15. 2 f. 40 c. red and grey .. 12 10
16. 3 f. red and olive 5 5
17. 4 f. blue and red 5 5
18. 4 f. 50 c. brown and olive 5 5
19. 5 f. violet and olive .. 5 5
20. 10 f. green and red .. 15 5
21. 15 f. brown and cream .. 30 12
22. 20 f. green and grey .. 30 12

1945. Stamp Day. As T 208 of France (Louis XI) but optd. **A O F.**
23. 2 f.+3 f. red 5 5

1945. Air. As T 18 of Cameroun.
24. 5 f. 50 c. blue 12 8
25. 50 f. green 50 8
26. 100 f. claret 50 8

1946. Air. Victory. As T 21 of Cameroun.
27. 8 f. mauve 15 15

1946. Air. From Chad to the Rhine. As T 22 of Cameroun.
28. 5 f. red 20 20
29. 10 f. blue 20 20
30. 15 f. mauve 30 30
31. 20 f. green 30 30
32. 25 f. brown 35 35
33. 50 f. brown 50 50

2. War Dance.

3. Sudanese Carving.

4. Africans and Aeroplane.

1947.
34. 2. 10 c. blue (postage) .. 5 5
35. – 30 c. brown 5 5
36. – 40 c. green 5 5
37. – 50 c. red 5 5
38. – 60 c. grey 8 8
39. – 80 c. lilac 8 8
40. – 1 f. claret 5 5
41. – 1 f. 20 c. green .. 10 10
42. – 1 f. 50 c. blue .. 12 12
43. 3. 2 f. orange 5 5
44. – 3 f. brown 5 5
45. – 3 f. 60 c. red .. 12 12
46. – 4 f. blue 5 5
47. – 5 f. green 5 5
48. – 6 f. blue 5 5
49. – 10 f. red 8 5
50. – 15 f. brown 15 5
51. – 20 f. brown 15 5
52. – 25 f. black 25 5
53. – 8 f. red (air) 12 8
54. – 50 f. violet 45 8
55. – 100 f. blue .. .. 1·25 30
56. 4. 200 f. grey .. .. 1·25 35

DESIGNS—As T 2/3—HORIZ. 30 c. Girl and bridge. 40 c. Canoe. 50 c. Niger landscape. 80 c. Dahomey weaver. 1 f. Donkey caravan. 1 f. 20, Crocodile and hippopotamus. 10 f. Dienne Mosque. 15 f. Railcar. VERT. 60 c. Coconuts. 1 f. 50, Palm trees. 3 f Togo girl. 3 f. 60, Sudanese market. 4 f. Dahomey labourer. 5 f. Mauritanian woman. 5 f. Guinea head-dress. 20 f. Ivory Coast girl. 25 f. Niger washerwomen. As T 4—VERT. 8 f. A. de St. Exupery. HORIZ. 50 f. Aeroplane over Dakar (Senegal). 100 f. Flight of storks (Niger).

1949. Air. U.P.U. 75th Anniv. As T 25 of Cameroun.
69. 25 f. blue, green, brn. & red 1·40 1·25

1950. Colonial Welfare Fund. As T 26 of Cameroun.
70. 10 f.+2 f. black and brown 1·10 1·10

5. Medical Research.

6. T. Laplene and Map of Ivory Coast.

7. Logging Camp.

1953.
71. – 8 f. blue and brown (post.) 20 8
72. 5. 15 f. grn., brown & sepia 20 5
73. – 20 f. myrtle and turquoise 20 5
74. – 25 f. sepia, bl. and maroon 20 5
75. 6. 40 f. red 30 5
76. 7. 50 f. brown and green (air) 30 5
77. – 100 f. choc., blue & green 65 8
78. – 200 f. green, turq. & lake 1·60 20
79. – 500 f. green, bl. and orange 3·75 50

DESIGNS—HORIZ. As T 6: 8 f. Gov.-Gen. Ballay. 20 f. Abidjan Bridge. 25 f. Africans, animals and sailing canoe. As T 7: 100 f. Telephonist, aeroplane and pylons. 200 f. Baobab trees. 500 f. Vridi Canal, Abidjan.

1952. Military Medal Cent. As T 27 of Cameroun.
80. 15 f. sepia, yellow & green 80 80

1954. Air. Liberation. 10th Anniv. As T 29 of Cameroun.
81. 15 f. blue and indigo .. 85 85

8. Chimpanzee.

9.

1955. Nature Protection. Inscr. as in T 8.
82. 8. 5 f. sepia and grey .. 12 5
83. – 8 f. sepia and green .. 12 5
DESIGN—HORIZ. 8 f. Scaly ant-eater.

1955. Rotary International. 50th Anniv.
84. 9. 15 f. blue 15 10

10. Mossi Railways.

DESIGNS — HORIZ. 1 f. Date palms. 2 f. Milo River bridge. 4 f. Herdsman and cattle. 15 f. Combine harvester. 17 f. Woman and aerial view. 20 f. Palm oil factory. 30 f. Abidjan-Abengourou road.

1955. Economic and Social Development Fund. Inscr. " F.I.D.E.S.".
85. – 1 f. green and myrtle .. 10 10
86. – 2 f. myrtle and turquoise 10 10
87. 10. 3 f. sepia and chestnut .. 12 12
88. – 4 f. red 12 12
89. – 15 f. blue and indigo .. 12 5
90. – 17 f. blue and indigo .. 15 8
91. – 20 f. maroon 15 8
92. – 30 f. maroon and lilac .. 15 8

1956. Coffee. As T 15 of New Caledonia.
93. 15 f. green and turquoise .. 8 5

11. Medical Station and Ambulance.

12. Map of Africa.

1957. Order of Malta Leprosy Relief.
94. 11. 15 f. claret, maroon & red 25 10

1957. Air. African Troops. Cent. As T 18 of French Equatorial Africa.
95. 15 f. blue and indigo .. 30 25

1958. 6th African Int. Tourist Congress.
96. 12. 20 f. red, turquoise & black 20 10

13. African and Symbols of Communication.

1958. Stamp Day.
97. 13. 15 f. choc., blue & orange 20 12

14. Isle of Goree and West African.

1958. Air. Dakar Cent. Inscr. " CENTENAIRE DE DAKAR ".
98. 14. 15 f. vio., grn., brn. & bl. 20 12
99. – 20 f. red, brown and blue 20 12
100. – 25 f. ochre, grn., lil. & brn. 20 12
101. – 40 f. brown, green & blue 20 15
102. – 50 f. violet, brown & green 30 15
103. – 100 f. green, blue & brown 55 20

DESIGNS: 20 f. Map of Dakar, ships and aircraft. 25 f. Town Construction. 40 f. Council House. 50 f. Ground-nuts, artisan and ship at quayside. 100 f. Bay of N'Gor.

15. Banana Plant and Fruit.

1958 Banana Production.
105. 15. 20 f. purple, bronze-green and olive 15 5

1958. Tropical Flora. As T 21 of French Equatorial Africa.
118. 10 f. red, yellow, green & blue 8 5
119. 25 f. yellow, green and red 15 5
120. 30 f. brown, green and blue 15 15
121. 40 f. yellow, green and sepia 25 20
122. 65 f. yellow, red, grn. & blue 40 20

DESIGNS—VERT. 10 f. " Gloriosa ". 25 f. " Adenopus ". 30 f. " Cyrtosperma ". 40 f. " Cistanche ". 65 f. " Crinum moorei ".

16. Moro Naba Sagha and Map of Upper Volta.

1958. Upper Volta Scheme. 10th Anniv.
123. 16. 20 f. sepia, violet, claret and red 12 10

17. Native Chief and Musician.

1958. Air. Nouakchott, Capital of Mauritania. Inaug.
124. 17. 20 f. sepia, chest. & grey 20 12

1958. Declaration of Human Rights. 10th Anniv. As T 5 of Comoro Is.
125. 20 f. maroon and blue .. 35 35

1959. Stamp Day. As T 13 but inscr. "DAKAR-ABIDJAN" in place of "AFRIQUE OCCIDENTALE FRANCAISE".

126. 20 f. green, blue and red .. 40 30

No. 126 was for use in Ivory Coast and Senegal.

OFFICIAL STAMPS.

O 1.

1958. Inscr. "OFFICIEL".

O 106. O 1. 1 f. brown 8 8
O 107. 3 f. green 8 8
O 108. 5 f. red 5 5
O 109. 10 f. blue 5 5
O 110. – 20 f. red 10 5
O 111. – 25 f. violet 15 5
O 112. – 30 f. green 20 12
O 113. – 45 f. black 25 10
O 114. – 50 f. red 30 5
O 115. – 65 f. blue 40 12
O 116. – 100 f. olive 70 8
O 117. – 200 f. green .. 1·60 20

DESIGNS—VERT. 20 f. to 45 f. Head as Type O 1 but with female face. 50 f. to 200 f. Head as Type O 1 but with hooped headdress, portrait being diagonal on stamp.

POSTAGE DUE STAMPS.

D 1.

1947.

D 57. D 1. 10 c. red 5 5
D 58. 30 c. orange 5 5
D 59. 50 c. black 5 5
D 60. 1 f. red 5 5
D 61. 2 f. green 5 5
D 62. 3 f. mauve 5 5
D 63. 4 f. blue 8 8
D 64. 5 f. brown 12 12
D 65. 10 f. blue 15 15
D 66. 20 f. brown 30 30

FUJEIRA O2

One of the Trucial States in the Persian Gulf. With six other shaikdoms formed the State of the United Arab Emirates on 18th July, 1971. Fujeira stamps were replaced by issues of United Arab Emirates on 1st January, 1973.

100 naye paise = 1 rupee.
1967. 100 dirhams = 1 riyal.

1. Shaikh Mohamed bin Hamad al Sharqi and Great Crested Grebe.

1964. Multicoloured.

(a) Size as T 1.

1. 1 n.p. Type 1 .. .. 5 5
2. 2 n.p. Arabian oryx .. 5 5
3. 3 n.p. Hoopoe 5 5
4. 4 n.p. Wild donkey .. 5 5
5. 5 n.p. Herons 5 5
6. 10 n.p. Arab horses .. 5 5
7. 15 n.p. Cheetah 5 5
8. 20 n.p. Dromedaries .. 8 8
9. 30 n.p. Falcon 10 10

(b) Size 42½ × 28½ mm.

10. 40 n.p. Type 1 .. .. 12 12
11. 50 n.p. Arabian oryx .. 15 15
12. 70 n.p. Hoopoe 20 20
13. 1 r. Wild donkey 30 30
14. 1 r. 50 Herons 40 40
15. 2 r. Arab horses 55 55

(c) Size 53½ × 35½ mm.

16. 3 r. Cheetah .. .. 1·10 1·10
17. 5 r. Dromedaries .. .. 1·60 1·60
18. 10 r. Falcon .. .. 3·25 3·25

2. Shaikh Mohamed and Putting the Shot.

1964. Olympic Games, Tokyo. Multicoloured.

(a) Size as T 2.

19. 25 n.p. Type 2 .. .. 10 10
20. 50 n.p. Throwing the discus 12 12
21. 75 n.p. Fencing 20 20
22. 1 r. Boxing 25 25
23. 1 r. 50 Relay-racing .. 40 40
24. 2 r. Football 55 55

(b) Size 53 × 35½ mm.

25. 3 r. High-jumping .. 1·10 1·10
26. 5 r. Hurdling .. .. 1·60 1·60
27. 7 r. 50 Horse-riding .. 3·25 2·75

3. Kennedy as a boy.

1965. Pres. Kennedy Commem. Each black and gold on coloured paper as given below.

28. 3. 5 n.p. pale blue 5 5
29. – 10 n.p. pale yellow .. 5 5
30. – 15 n.p. pale pink 5 5
31. – 20 n.p. pale green .. 8 8
32. – 25 n.p. pale blue .. 10 10
33. – 50 n.p. flesh 12 12
34. – 1 r. lavender 25 25
35. – 2 r. pale yellow .. 55 55
36. – 3 r. pale blue 90 90
37. – 5 r. pale buff .. 1·90 1·90

DESIGNS (Kennedy): 10 n.p. As student. 15 n.p. As cadet. 20 n.p. As Senator. 25 n.p. Sailing. 50 n.p. As President. LARGER (33 × 51 mm.): 1 r. With Mrs. Kennedy. 2 r. With Pres. Eisenhower. 3 r. With family. 5 r. Full face portrait.

1965. Air. Designs similar to Nos. 1/9, but with "FUJEIRA" and value transposed, and inscr. "AIR MAIL". Multicoloured.

(a) Size 43½ × 28½ mm.

39. 15 n.p. Type 1 .. .. 5 5
40. 25 n.p. Arabian oryx .. 8 8
41. 35 n.p. Hoopoe 10 10
42. 50 n.p. Wild donkey .. 15 15
43. 75 n.p. Herons 20 20
44. 1 r. Arab horses 30 30

(b) Size 53½ × 35½ mm.

45. 2 r. Cheetah 55 55
46. 3 r. Dromedaries .. .. 1·10 1·10
47. 5 r. Falcon .. .. 1·50 1·50

4. Queen Nefertiti.

1966. Stamp Cent. Exn., Cairo. Multicoloured.

57. 3 n.p. Type 4. .. .. 5 5
58. 5 n.p. Colossi, Abu Simbel .. 5 5
59. 10 n.p. Tutankhamen's mask 5 5
60. 15 n.p. Sphinx, Gezir .. 5 5
61. 25 n.p. Statues of seated figures 8 5
62. 50 n.p. Ancient church .. 12 10
63. 1 r. Colonnade, Great Temple of Isis, Philae 40 20
64. 2 r. Nile sphinxes 75 40
65. 5 r. Pyramids, Giza .. 2·22 1·25

The 50 n.p. to 5 r. are horiz.

5. Sir Winston Churchill as Harrow Schoolboy.

1966. Churchill Commem. Each design black and gold; frame in colours given.

67. 5. 10 n.p. yellow (postage) .. 5 5
68. – 15 n.p. blue 5 5
69. – 25 n.p. buff 8 5
70. – 50 n.p. blue 12 10
71. – 75 n.p. mauve 20 15
72. – 1 r. blue 30 20
73. – 2 r. gold (air) 60 30
74. – 3 r. gold .. .. .. 1·10 55

DESIGNS — CHURCHILL: 15 n.p. Wearing Hussars' uniform. 25 n.p. As Boer War correspondent. 50 n.p. In morning dress. 75 n.p. With Eisenhower. 1 r. Painting. 2 r. With grandson. 3 r. Giving "V" sign.

6. Lunar Satellite.

1966. Space Achievements. Multicoloured.

76. 5 n.p. Type 6 .. .. 5 5
77. 10 n.p. Satellite approaching Moon 5 5
78. 15 n.p. Satellite and planets 5 5
79. 25 n.p. Satellite and Solar System 8 5
80. 50 n.p. Communications satellite 12 10
81. 75 n.p. Venus probe .. 20 15
82. 1 r. "Telstar" 30 25
83. 2 r. "Relay" 55 40

1967. Various stamps with currency names changed by overprinting.

(i) Nos. 1/18 (Definitives).

85. 1 d. on 1 n.p. 5 5
86. 2 d. on 2 n.p. 5 5
87. 3 d. on 3 n.p. 5 5
88. 4 d. on 4 n.p. 5 5
89. 5 d. on 5 n.p. 5 5
90. 10 d. on 10 n.p. 5 5
91. 15 d. on 15 n.p. 8 8
92. 20 d. on 20 n.p. 10 10
93. 30 d. on 30 n.p. 12 12
94. 40 d. on 40 n.p. 15 15
95. 50 d. on 50 n.p. 20 20
96. 70 d. on 70 n.p. 25 25
97. 1 r. on 1 r. 40 40
98. 1 r. 50 on 1 r. 50 .. .. 65 65
99. 2 r. on 2 r. 80 80
100. 3 r. on 3 r. .. .. 1·25 1·25
101. 5 r. on 5 r. .. .. 2·00 2·00
102. 10 r. on 10 r. .. .. 4·00 4·00

(ii) Nos. 19/27 (Olympics).

103. 25 d. on 25 n.p. 10 10
104. 50 d. on 50 n.p. 20 20
105. 75 d. on 75 n.p. 30 30
106. 1 r. on 1 r. 45 45
107. 1 r. 50 on 1 r. 50 .. 65 65
108. 2 r. on 2 r. 90 90
109. 3 r. on 3 r. .. .. 1·25 1·25
110. 5 r. on 5 r. .. .. 2·00 2·00
111. 7 r. 50 on 7 r. 50 .. .. 3·00 3·00

(iv) Air. Nos. 39/47 (Airmails).

123. 15 d. on 15 n.p. 8 8
124. 25 d. on 25 n.p. 10 10
125. 35 d. on 35 n.p. 12 12
126. 50 d. on 50 n.p. 20 20
127. 75 d. on 75 n.p. 30 30
128. 1 r. on 1 r. 40 40
129. 2 r. on 2 r. 80 80
130. 3 r. on 3 r. .. .. 1·25 1·25
131. 5 r. on 5 r. .. .. 1·75 1·75

Nos. 19/37 and 57/83 were also surcharged in the new currency in limited quantities, but they had little local usage.

7. Butterfly.

1967. Butterflies. Various designs.

(a) Postage. (i) Size. As T 7.

167. 1 d. multicoloured .. 5 5
168. 2 d. multicoloured 5 5
169. 3 d. multicoloured 5 5
170. 4 d. multicoloured 5 5
171. 5 d. multicoloured 5 5
172. 10 d. multicoloured .. 5 5
173. 15 d. multicoloured .. 5 5
174. 20 d. multicoloured .. 5 5
175. 30 d. multicoloured .. 10 5

(ii) Size 40 × 40 mm.

176. 40 d. multicoloured .. 12 8
177. 50 d. multicoloured .. 15 10
178. 70 d. multicoloured .. 25 15
179. 1 r. multicoloured .. 30 20
180. 1 r. 50 multicoloured .. 45 20
181. 2 r. multicoloured .. 60 40

(iii) Size 42 × 42 mm.

182. 3 r. multicoloured 90 60
183. 5 r. multicoloured .. 1·50 1·00
184. 10 r. multicoloured .. 3·00 2·00

(b) Air. Size 45 × 45 mm.

185. 15 d. multicoloured .. 5 5
186. 25 d. multicoloured .. 8 5
187. 35 d. multicoloured .. 10 5
188. 50 d. multicoloured .. 15 5
189. 75 d. multicoloured .. 25 10
190. 1 r. multicoloured .. 30 15
191. 2 r. multicoloured .. 60 30
192. 3 r. multicoloured .. 90 40
193. 5 r. multicoloured .. 1·50 75

8. Shaikh Mohamed bin Hamad al Sharqi and Tropical Fish.

1971. Multicoloured.

194. 5 d. Type 8 (postage) .. 5 5
195. 20 d. Shaikh and fish (different) (air) 10 5
196. 35 d. Shaikh and fish (different) 12 5
197. 40 d. Shaikh and fish (different) 15 5
198. 60 d. Shaikh and daisy .. 20 10
199. 1 r. Shaikh and rose .. 25 12
200. 2 r. Shaikh and gentian .. 50 25
201. 3 r. Shaikh and wild rose 75 40

OFFICIAL STAMPS

1965. Designs similar to Nos. 1/9, but with "FUJEIRA" and value transposed, additionally inscr. "ON STATE'S SERVICE". Multicoloured.

(i) Postage. Size 43½ × 28½ mm.

O 48. 25 n.p. Type 1 .. 8 8
O 49. 40 n.p. Arabian oryx .. 10 10
O 50. 50 n.p. Hoopoe .. 12 12
O 51. 75 n.p. Wild donkey .. 20 20
O 52. 1 r. Herons 45 45

(ii) Air. (a) Size 43½ × 28½ mm.

O 53. 75 n.p. Arab horses .. 20 20

(b) Size 53½ × 35½ mm.

O 54. 2 r. Cheetah 55 55
O 55. 3 r. Dromedaries .. 80 80
O 56. 5 r. Falcon .. .. 1·25 1·25

1967. Nos. 48/56 with currency name changed by overprinting.

O 158. 25 d. on 25 n.p. (postage) 10 10
O 159. 40 d. on 40 n.p. 15 15
O 160. 50 d. on 50 n.p. .. 20 20
O 161. 75 d. on 75 n.p. 30 30
O 162. 1 r. on 1 r. 40 40
O 163. 75 d. on 75 n.p. (air) .. 30 30
O 164. 2 r. on 2 r. 80 80
O 165. 3 r. on 3 r. .. .. 1·25 1·25
O 166. 5 r. on 5 r. .. .. 2·00 2·00

FUNCHAL O3

A district of Madeira which used the stamps of Madeira from 1868 to 1881 and then the stamps of Portugal.

1892. As T **9** of Portugal inscr. "FUNCHAL".

85. 5 r. yellow 55 40
86. 10 r. mauve 55 50
87. 15 r. brown .. .. .. 1·50 75
89. 20 r. lilac .. .. .. 1·50 75
83. 25 r. green 85 30
91. 50 r. blue .. .. .. 1·50 40
92. 75 r. red .. .. .. 2·75 2·10
93. 80 r. green .. .. .. 3·50 3·25
95. 100 r. brown on buff .. 1·75 1·60
107. 150 r. red on rose .. .. 10·00 8·50
96. 200 r. blue on blue .. 11·00 10·00
97. 300 r. blue on brown .. 12·00 10·00

1897. "King Carlos" key-type inscr. "FUNCHAL".

110. S. 2½ r. grey 15 12
111. 5 r. orange 15 15
112. 10 r. green 15 15
113. 15 r. brown .. .. 1·00 70
126. 15 r. green 75 60
114. 20 r. lilac 30 25
115. 25 r. green 60 25
127. 25 r. red 15 12
128. 50 r. blue 25 20
129. 65 r. blue 25 20
117. 75 r. red 30 30
130. 75 r. brown on yellow .. 35 30
118. 80 r. mauve 30 30
119. 100 r. blue on blue .. 30 30
131. 115 r. red on pink .. 35 30
132. 130 r. brown on yellow .. 35 30
120. 150 r. brown on yellow .. 35 30
133. 180 r. black on pink .. 35 30
121. 200 r. purple on pink .. 85 75
122. 300 r. blue on pink .. 85 75
123. 500 r. black on blue .. 60 45

GABON O2

A French colony on the W. coast of equatorial Africa. Became part of Fr. Equatorial Africa in 1937 and a republic within the French Community in 1958.

1886. Stamps of French Colonies, "Commerce" type, surch. **GAB** surrounded by dots, and value in figures.

1. **9.** 5 on 20 c. red on green .. 80·00 80·00
2. 10 on 20 c. red on green .. 80·00 80·00
3. 25 on 20 c. red on green .. 8·50 7·50
4. 50 on 15 c. blue £300 £300
5. 75 on 15 c. blue £300 £300

1888. Stamps of French Colonies, "Commerce" type, surch. in figures.

6. **9.** 15 on 10 c. black on lilac £750 £180
7. 15 on 1 f. olive £300 £110
8. 25 on 5 c. green .. .. £170 30·00
9. 25 on 10 c. black on lilac .. £600 £200
10. 25 on 75 c. red £500 £190

1889. Postage Due stamps of French Colonies surch. **GABON TIMBRE** and value in figures.

11. D **1.** 15 on 5 c. black .. 28·00 25·00
12. 15 on 30 c. black .. £750 £700
13. 25 on 20 c. black .. 11·00 10·00

1.

1889. Imperf.

14. **1.** 15 c. black on pink .. £170 £110
15. 25 c. black on green .. £100 75·00

1904. "Tablet" key-type inscr. "GABON".

16. D. 1 c. black on blue .. 10 10
17. 2 c. brown on yellow .. 10 10
18. 4 c. claret on grey .. 12 12
19. 5 c. green 25 20
20. 10 c. red 85 70
21. 15 c. grey 85 80
22. 20 c. red on green .. 1·60 1·40
23. 25 c. blue 90 70
24. 30 c. brown .. .. 1·75 1·40
25. 35 c. black on yellow .. 3·25 3·00
26. 40 c. red on yellow .. 2·25 1·75
27. 45 c. black on green .. 5·00 4·50
28. 50 c. brown on blue .. 2·00 1·90
29. 75 c. brown on orange .. 2·25 2·10
30. 1 f. olive .. .. .. 5·50 5·00
31. 2 f. violet on red .. 12·00 10·00
32. 5 f. mauve on lilac .. 22·00 20·00

2. Warrior.

4. Bantou Woman.

3. Libreville.

1910.

33. **2.** 1 c. brown and orange .. 10 10
34. 2 c. black and brown .. 20 20
35. 4 c. violet and blue .. 12 12
36. 5 c. olive and green .. 20 20
37. 10 c. red and lake .. 30 30
38. 20 c. brown and violet .. 20 20
39. **3.** 25 c. brown and blue .. 15 15
40. 30 c. red and grey .. 2·75 2·75
41. 35 c. green and violet .. 1·10 1·10
42. 40 c. blue and brown .. 1·75 1·75
43. 45 c. violet and red .. 3·25 3·25
44. 50 c. grey and green .. 6·50 6·50
45. 75 c. brown and orange .. 12·00 12·00
46. **4.** 1 f. yellow and brown .. 12·00 12·00
47. 2 f. brown and red .. 50·00 50·00
48. 5 f. brown and blue .. 42·00 42·00

1910. As last but inscr. "AFRIQUE EQUATORIALE—GABON".

49. **2.** 1 c. brown and orange .. 5 5
50. 2 c. black and brown .. 5 5
51. 4 c. violet and blue .. 5 5
52. 5 c. olive and green .. 5 5
82. 5 c. black and yellow .. 5 5
53. 10 c. red and lake .. 5 5
83. 10 c. green 5 5
54. 15 c. purple and red .. 8 5
55. 20 c. brown and violet .. 1·25 1·10
56. **3.** 25 c. brown and blue .. 8 8
84. 25 c. black and green .. 12 12
57. 30 c. red and grey .. 5 5
85. 30 c. red 5 5
58. 35 c. green and violet .. 8 5
59. 40 c. blue and brown .. 5 5
60. 45 c. violet and red .. 5 5
86. 45 c. red and black .. 12 12
61. 50 c. grey and green .. 5 5
87. 50 c. blue 5 5
62. 75 c. brown and orange .. 70 60
63. **4.** 1 f. yellow and brown .. 30 25
64. 2 f. brown and red .. 50 45
65. 5 f. brown and blue .. 75 75

1912. "Tablet" key-type surch. in figures.

66. D. 05 on 2 c. brown on yellow 5 5
67. 05 on 4 c. claret on grey 5 5
68. 05 on 15 c. grey 5 5
69. 05 on 20 c. red on green .. 5 5
70. 05 on 25 c. blue 5 5
71. 05 on 30 c. brown .. 10 10
72. 10 on 40 c. red on yellow 8 8
73. 10 on 45 c. black on green 5 5
74. 10 on 50 c. brown on blue 10 10
75. 10 on 75 c. brown on orge. 10 10
76. 10 on 1 f. olive 10 10
77. 10 on 2 f. violet on red .. 10 10
78. 10 on 5 f. mauve on lilac .. 30 30

1915. Surch. with large red cross and **5 c.**

79. **2.** 10 c.+5 c. (No. 37) .. 2·25 2·00
80. 10 c.+5 c. (No. 53) .. 3·25 3·00

1917. Surch. **5 c.** and small red cross.

81. **2.** 10 c.+5 c. (No. 53) .. 10 8

1924. Inscr. "AFRIGUE EQUATORIALE —GABON" and optd. **AFRIQUE EQUATORIALE FRANCAISE.**

88. **2.** 1 c. brown and orange .. 5 5
89. 2 c. black and brown .. 5 5
90. 4 c. violet and blue .. 5 5
91. 5 c. black and yellow .. 5 5
92. 10 c. green 5 5
93. 10 c. blue and brown .. 5 5
94. 15 c. purple and red .. 5 5
95. 15 c. red and purple .. 5 5
96. 20 c. brown and violet .. 5 5
97. **3.** 25 c. black and green .. 8 8
98. 30 c. red 5 5
99. 30 c. yellow and black .. 5 5
100. 30 c. green 10 10
101. 35 c. green and violet .. 5 5
102. 40 c. blue and brown .. 5 5
103. 45 c. red and black .. 5 5
104. 50 c. blue 5 5
105. 50 c. green and red .. 5 5
106. 65 c. orange and blue .. 40 40
107. 75 c. brown and orange 10 10
108. 90 c. red 30 30
109. **4.** 1 f. yellow and brown .. 10 10
110. 1 f. 10 red and green .. 60 60
111. 1 f. 50 blue 10 10
112. 2 f. brown and red .. 10 10
113. 3 f. mauve 70 70
114. 5 f. brown and blue .. 50 50

1925. As last surch. in figures.

115. **4.** 65 on 1 f. brown & green 5 5
116. 85 on 1 f. brown & green 5 5
117. **3.** 90 c. on 75 c. red .. 25 25
118. **4.** 1 f. 25 on 1 f. blue .. 5 5
119. 1 f. 50 on 1 f. blue .. 10 10
120. 3 f. on 5 f. brown & mve. 50 50
121. 10 f. on 5 f. grn. & brown 1·75 1·75
122. 20 f. on 5 f. orge. & purple 1·60 1·60

1931. "Colonial Exn." key-types inscr. "GABON".

123. E. 40 c. green 40 40
124. F. 50 c. mauve 15 10
125. G. 90 c. orange 40 40
126. H. 1 f. 50 blue 40 35

5. Raft on the River Ogowe.

6. Count de Brazza.

1932.

127. **5.** 1 c. claret 5 5
128. 2 c. black on rose .. 5 5
129. 4 c. green 5 5
130. 5 c. blue 5 5
131. 10 c. red on yellow .. 5 5
132. 15 c. red on green .. 8 8
133. 20 c. red 10 10
134. 25 c. brown 5 5
135. **6.** 30 c. green 20 20
136. 40 c. purple 12 12
137. 45 c. black on green .. 20 20
138. 50 c. brown 12 12
139. 65 c. blue 65 65
140. 75 c. black on orange .. 40 40
141. 90 c. red 35 35
142. 1 f. green on blue .. 2·75 2·50
143. – 1 f. 25 violet 20 20
144. – 1 f. 50 blue 40 30
145. – 1 f. 75 green 20 20
146. – 2 f. red .. .. .. 2·75 2·50
147. – 3 f. green on blue .. 65 60
148. – 5 f. brown 90 85
149. – 10 f. black on orange .. 3·75 3·50
150. – 20 f. purple .. .. 5·50 4·50

DESIGN—HORIZ. 1 f. 25 to 20 f. Gabon Village.

7. Prime Minister Leon Mba.

1959. Republic. 1st Anniv.

161. **7.** 15 f. chocolate 12 5
162. – 25 f. green and sepia .. 20 5

PORTRAIT: 25 f. Prime Minister Mba (profile).

1960. African Technical Co-operation Commission. 10th Anniv. As T **39** of Cameroun.

163. 50 f. blue and purple .. 45 45

8. Dr. Schweitzer, Lambarene and Organ.

1960. Air. Dr. Albert Schweitzer Commem.

164. **8.** 200 f. choc., green & blue 1·75 80

1960. Air. Olympic Games. No. 192 of French Equatorial Africa optd. with Olympic rings, **XVIIe OLYMPIADE 1960 REPUBLIQUE GABONAISE** and surch. **250F** and bars.

165. 250 f. on 500 f. blue, black and green .. .. .. 2·75 2·75

9. Tree Felling.

1960. Air. 5th World Forestry Congress. Seattle.

166. **9.** 100 f. chest., black & grn. 80 55

10. Flag, Map and U.N. Emblem.

12. Combretum.

11. "Melichneutes robustus" in flight.

1961. Admission into U.N.O.

167. **10.** 15 f. multicoloured .. 20 10
168. 25 f. multicoloured .. 25 15
169. 85 f. multicoloured .. 90 55

1961. Air. Birds. Multicoloured.

170. 50 f. Type **11** 45 20
171. 100 f. "Cinnyris johannae" 80 40
172. 200 f. "Melittophagus mulleri" .. .. 1·60 85
173. 250 f. "Stephanoaetus coronatus" .. .. 2·00 1·00
174. 500 f. "Apaloderma narina" .. .. 3·75 1·75

The 200 f., 250 f. and 500 f. are vert. designs.

1961.

175. **12.** 50 c. red, maroon & grn. 5 5
176. – 1 f. red, bl.-grn. & bistre 5 5
177. – 2 f. yellow and green .. 5 5
178. – 3 f. yellow, green & olive 8 5
179. – 5 f. red, mar., grn. & bis. 8 5
180. **12.** 10 f. red, grn. & bl.-grn. 10 8

FLOWERS—VERT. 1 f., 5 f. Gabonese tulip (tree). HORIZ. 2 f., 3 f. Yellow cassia.

13. President Mba.

15. Capt. Ntchorere and Flags.

14. Breguet 14 Aircraft.

1962.

181. **13.** 15 f. indigo, red & grn. 12 5
182. 20 f. sepia, red & green 15 8
183. 25 f. brown, red & green 20 10

1962. Air. "Air Afrique" Airline. As T **44** of Cameroun.

184. 500 f. myrtle, ochre & blk. 3·75 2·25

1962. Malaria Eradication. As T **45** of Cameroun.

185. 25 f.+5 f. green 25 25

1962. Sports. As T **6** of Central African Republic. Inscr. "JEUX SPORTIFS".

186. 20 f. brown, ultramarine, blue and black (postage) 15 12
187. 50 f. brown, ultramarine, blue and black .. 40 25
188. 100 f. brown, ultramarine, blue and black (air) .. 1·10 55

DESIGNS—HORIZ. 20 f. Start of rqce. 50 f. Football. VERT. (26×47 mm.): 100 f. long-jump.

1962. Air. Evolution of Air Transport.

189. **14.** 10 f. indigo and claret .. 20 10
190. – 20 f. indigo, blue & brn. 25 15
191. – 60 f. grey-blue, maroon and myrtle 65 55
192. – 85 f. indigo, blue & orge. 1·10 1·10

AIRCRAFT: 20 f. D. H. Dragon-Rapide. 60 f. Caravelle airliner. 85 f. Rocket.

1962. Union of African and Malagasy States 1st Anniv. As No. 328 of Cameroun.

194. **47.** 30 f. emerald 45 30

1962. Capt. Ntchorere Commem.

195. **15.** 80 f. multicoloured .. 60 40

1963. Freedom from Hunger. As T **51** of Cameroun.

196. 25 f.+5 f. grn., brn. & red 25 25

1963. Air. 50th Anniv. of Arrival of Dr. Schweitzer in Gabon. Surch. **100 F JUBILE GABONAIS 1913-1963.**

197. **8.** 100 f. on 200 f. chocolate, green and blue .. 85 75

16. Libreville Post Office.

1963. Air. Gabon Postal Services Cent.
198. **16.** 100 f. multicoloured 75 60

1963. Air. African and Malagasy Posts and Telecommunications Union. As T 10 of Central African Republic.
199. 85 f. red, buff, magenta and carmine .. 65 50

1963. Space Telecommunications. As Nos. 37/8 of Central African Republic.
200. 25 f. orange, blue & green 20 15
201. 100 f. brown, green & blue 80 80

1963. Air. "Air Afrique". 1st Anniv. and "DC-8" Service. Inaug. As T 10 of Congo Republic.
202. 50 f. blk., grn., drab & vio. 40 30

1963. Air. European-African Economic Convention. As T 16 of Central African Republic.
203. 50 f. brn., yell., ochre & vio. 45 30

1963. Declaration of Human Rights. 15th Anniv. As T 18 of Central African Republic.
204. 25 f. slate green and brown 20 15

17. Rameses and Gods, Wadi-es-Sebua.

1964. Air. Nubian Monuments.
205. **17.** 10 f. + 5 f. brown & blue 25 25
206. 25 f. + 5 f. ultram. & crim. 40 40
207. 50 f. + 5 f. pur. & myrtle 55 55

1964. World Meterological Day. As T 13 of Congo Republic.
208. 25 f. green, blue and bistre 20 15

18. Arms of Gabon.

19. Tarpon.

20. Ear of Wheat, Cogwheel and Globe.

1964.
209. **18.** 25 f. multicoloured .. 20 12

1964. Air. Equatorial African Heads of State Conf. 5th Anniv. As T 23 of Central African Republic.
210. 100 f. multicoloured .. 85 60

1964. Gabon Fauna.
211. **19.** 30 f. black, blue & brown 20 12
212. – 60 f. brown, chest. & grn. 45 25
213. – 80 f. brown, green & blue 60 40
DESIGNS—VERT. 60 f. Gorilla. HORIZ. 80 f. Buffalo.

1964. Air. "Europafrique". 1st Anniv.
214. **20.** 50 f. blue, olive and red 40 30

21. Start of Race.

1964. Air. Olympic Games, Tokyo.
215. **21.** 25 f. green, brown & orge. 20 15
216. – 50 f. choc., orge. & green 40 25
217. – 100 f. violet, mar. & ol. 75 55
218. – 200 f. choc., pur. & red 1·60 1·10
DESIGNS—VERT. 50 f. Massaging athlete. 100 f. Anointing before the Games. HORIZ. 200 f. Athletes.

1964. Air. Pan-African and Malagasy Posts and Telecommunications Congress, Cairo. As T 22 of Congo Republic.
220. 25 f. sep., brn.-red & grn. 20 15

1964. French, African and Malagasy Co-operation. As T 500 of France.
221. 25 f. chocolate, blue & slate 20 15

22. "Dissotis rotundifolia".

23. Pres. Kennedy.

1964. Flowers. Multicoloured.
222. 3 f. Type **22** 5 5
223. 5 f. "Gloriosa superba" .. 5 5
224. 15 f. "Eulophia horsfallii" 10 8

1964. Air. Pres. Kennedy Commem.
225. **23.** 100 f. black, orge. & grn. 85 65

24. Women in Public Service.

1964. Air. Social Evolution of Gabonese Women.
227. **24.** 50 f. brown, blue & red 40 25

25. Sun and I.Q.S.Y. Emblem.

1965. Int. Quiet Sun Year.
228. **25.** 85 f. multicoloured .. 65 45

26. Globe and I.C.Y. Emblem.

1965. Air. Int. Co-operation Year.
229. **26.** 50 f. orge., turq. & blue 40 30

27. 17th-cent. Merchantman.

1965. Air. Old Ships. Multicoloured.
230. 25 f. 16th-cent. galleon .. 20 12
231. 50 f. Type **27** 40 20
232. 85 f. 18th-cent. frigate .. 70 40
233. 100 f. 19th-cent. brig .. 75 50
The 25 f. and 85 f. are vert.

82. Morse Telegraph Apparatus.

1965. I.T.U. Cent.
234. **28.** 30 f. green, orge. & blue 20 15

29. Manganese Mine, Moanda.

31. Football.

30. Nurse holding Child.

1965. "Mining Riches".
235. **29.** 15 f. red, violet and blue 10 8
236. – 60 f. red and blue .. 45 30
DESIGN: 60 f. Uranium mine, Mounana.

1965. Air. Gabon Red Cross.
237. **30.** 100 f. brown, red & grn. 75 50

1965. 1st African Games, Brazzaville.
238. **31.** 25 f. blk., red & grn. (post.) 20 15
239. – 100 f. purple, vermilion and brown (air) .. 80 50
DESIGN (27 × 48½ mm.): 100 f. Basketball.

32. "Globe", Pylon and "Sun".

1965. Air. "Europafrique".
240. **32.** 50 f. brn., red, orge. & bl. 85 20

33. President Mba.

1965. Air. Independence. 5th Anniv.
241. **33.** 25 f. multicoloured .. 20 12

34. Okoukoue Dance.

35. Abraham Lincoln.

1965. Gabon Dances.
242. **34.** 25 f. yellow, brown & grn. 20 12
243. – 60 f. black, red & brown 45 35
DESIGN: 60 f. Makudji dance.

1965. Abraham Lincoln. Death Cent.
244. **35.** 50 f. multicoloured .. 40 25

36. Sir Winston Churchill.

1965. Air. Churchill Commem.
245. **36.** 100 f. multicoloured .. 85 50

37. Dr. A. Schweitzer and Map.

1965. Air. Schweitzer Commem.
246. **37.** 1000 f. gold .. .. 17·00

38. Pope John XXIII.

1965. Air. Pope John Commem.
247. **38.** 85 f. multicoloured .. 65 45

39. Mail Carrier, Post Office and Van.

40. Nurse and Patients.

41. Balumbu Mask.

42. W.H.O. Building.

1965. Stamp Day.
248. **39.** 30 f. brown, green & blue 20 12

1966. Air. Red Cross. Multicoloured.
249. 50 f. Type **40** 45 25
250. 100 f. Bandaging patient 90 50

1966. World Festival of Negro Arts, Dakar. Multicoloured.
253. 5 f. Type **41** 5 5
254. 10 f. Statuette—"Ancestor of the Fang (tribe), Byeri" 8 5
255. 25 f. Fang mask 20 10
256. 30 f. Okuyi Myene mask .. 20 10
257. 85 f. Bakota copper mask 65 50

1966. W.H.O. Headquarters, Geneva. Inaug.
258. **42.** 50 f. black, yellow & blue 40 20

43. Satellite "A1" and Rocket.

1966. Air. "Conquest of Space".
259. **43.** 30 f. lake, plum and blue 25 15
260. – 90 f. plum, red and purple 75 45
DESIGN: 90 f. Satellite "FR1" and rocket.

44. "Learning the Alphabet".

45. Footballer.

1966. U.N.E.S.C.O. Literacy Campaign.
261. **44.** 30 f. multicoloured .. 20 10

1966. World Cup Football Championships, England.
262. **45.** 25 f. blue, green & lake (postage) 20 10
263. 90 f. maroon and blue .. 70 40
264. – 100 f. slate and red (air) 75 45
DESIGNS—VERT. 90 f. Footballer (different). HORIZ. 100 f. Footballers on world map (47½ × 27 mm.).

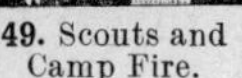

46. Industrial Scenes within leaves of "Plant".

48. Making Deposit.

49. Scouts and Camp Fire.

47. Paper Mill.

1966. Air. "Europafrique".
265. **46.** 50 f. multicoloured .. 40 20

1966. Economic Development.
266. **47.** 20 f. lake, purple & grn. 15 8
267. – 85 f. brown, blue & grn. 65 35
DESIGN: 85 f. Undersea oil-drilling rig.

1966. Air. "DC-8" Air Services Inaug. As T 45 of Central African Republic.
268. 30 f. grey, black and orange 20 10

1966. Savings Bank.
269. **48.** 25 f. brown, green & blue 20 10

1966. Scouting.
270. **49.** 30 f. brown, red & slate 20 8
271. – 50 f. brown, lake & blue 40 20
DESIGN—VERT. 50 f. Scouts taking oath.

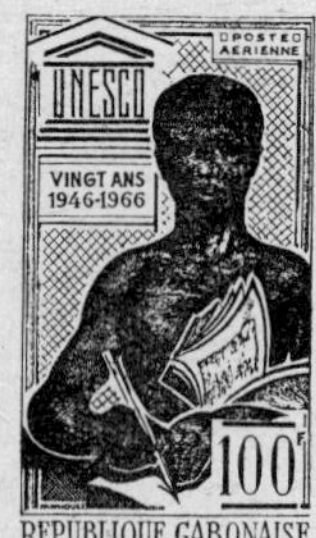

50. Gabonese Scholar.

ILLUSTRATIONS British Commonwealth and all overprints and surcharges are FULL SIZE. Foreign Countries have been reduced to ¾-LINEAR.

1966. Air. U.N.E.S.C.O. 20th Anniv.
272. **50.** 100 f. black, buff & blue 75 45

51. Libreville Airport.

1966. Air.
273. **51.** 200 f. brown, red & blue 1·50 55

52. Sikorsky "S-43" Flying-boat, Map and Flag (Aeromaritime's First Airmail Service, 1937).

1966. Stamp Day.
274. **52.** 30 f. multicoloured .. 20 8

53. Hippopotami.

1967. Gabon Fauna. Multicoloured.
275. 1 f. Type **53** 5 5
276. 2 f. Crocodiles 5 5
277. 3 f. Water chevrotains .. 5 5
278. 5 f. Chimpanzees 5 5
279. 10 f. Elephants 8 5
280. 20 f. Panthers 20 8

54. Lions Emblem and Anniversary Dates.

1967. Lions Int. 50th Anniv. Multicoloured.
281. 30 f. Type **54** 20 8
282. 50 f. Lions emblem, map and globe 40 20
Nos. 281/2 are separated by se-tenant stamp-size labels giving statistics of Lions Int.

55. Masked Faces.

56. I.T.Y. Emblem and Transport.

1967. Libreville Carnival.
283. **55.** 30 f. blue, brown & yell. 20 10

1967. Int. Tourist Year.
284. **56.** 30 f. multicoloured .. 20 10

57. Diving-board (Mexico City).

59. Atomic Symbol, Dove and Globe.

58. Farman "190".

1967. Publicity for 1968 Olympic Games, Mexico.
285. **57.** 25 f. turq., blue & violet 20 8
286. – 30 f. purple, lake & green 25 8
287. – 50 f. blue, green & mar. 40 25
DESIGNS: 30 f. Sun and snow crystal. 50 f. Ice rink, Grenoble.

1967. Air. Famous Aircraft.
288. **58.** 200 f. plum, bl. & turq. 1·50 50
289. – 300 f. blue, pur. & brn. 2·25 65
290. – 500 f. ind., mar. & grn. 3·75 1·75
AIRCRAFT: 300 f. De Havilland "Heron". 500 f. Potez "56".

1967. Int. Atomic Energy Agency.
291. **59.** 30 f. red, blue and green 20 8

60. Aircraft on Flight-paths.

1967. Air. I.O.A.O. Commem.
292. **60.** 100 f. pur., blue & green 75 45

61. Pope Paul VI.

62. Blood Donor and Bank.

63. Indigenous Emblems.

64. "Europafrique".

1967. Papal Encyclical "Populorum Progressio".
293. **61.** 30 f. black, blue & green 20 10

1967. Air. Red Cross.
294. **62.** 50 f. multicoloured .. 40 20
295. – 100 f. multicoloured .. 75 40
DESIGN: 100 f. Heart and blood-transfusion apparatus.

1967. World Fair, Montreal.
297. **63.** 30 f. choc., green & lake 20 10

1967. Europafrique.
298. **64.** 50 f. multicoloured .. 40 12

65. Orientation Diagram and Sun.

66. U.N. Emblem, Gabon Women and Child.

1967. Air. World Scout Jamboree, Idaho.
299. **65.** 50 f. green, orge. & blue 40 25
300. – 100 f. red, green & blue 75 45
DESIGN: 100 f. U.S. scout greeting Gabon scout on map.

1967. U.N. Status of Women Commission.
301. **66.** 75 f. blue, green & choc. 55 30

1967. Air. U.A.M.P.T. 5th Anniv. As T **55** of Central African Republic.
302. 100 f. red, blue and olive .. 75 45

67. Baraka Mission, Libreville.

1967. Air. American Missionaries Arrival. 125th Anniv.
303. **67.** 100 f. black, grn. & blue 75 45

68. U.N. Emblem and Book with Supporters.

70. "Mailboats of Yesterday".

69. "Draconea fragans".

1967. Air. U.N. Int. Rights Commission.
304. **68.** 60 f. multicoloured .. 45 25

1967. Gabon Trees.
305. **69.** 5 f. chocolate, green and blue (postage) .. 5 5
306. – 10 f. green, bronze & blue 8 5
307. – 20 f. red, green & brown 15 8
308. – 50 f. green, bistre and blue (air) .. 45 20
309. – 100 f. multicoloured .. 90 50
DESIGNS: 10 f. "Pycnanthus angolensis" 20 f. "Disthemonanthus benthamianus". (27 × 48 mm.). 50 f. "Baillonella toxisperma". 100 f. "Aucoumea klaineana".

1967. Stamp Day. Multicoloured.
311. 30 f. Type **70** 25 20
312. 30 f. "Mailboats of Today" 25 20
Nos. 311/2 were issued together se-tenant in sheets and form a composite design.

71. Chancellor Adenauer.

72. African W.H.O. Building.

1968. Air. Adenauer Commem.
313. **71.** 100 f. sepia, red & yellow 75 35

1968. W.H.O. 20th Anniv.
315. **72.** 20 f. purple, blue & grn. 12 5

73. Dam and Power-station.

74. President Bongo.

1968. Int. Hydrological Decade.
316. **73.** 15 f. blue, orange & lake 8 5

1968.
317. **74.** 25 f. black, yellow & grn. 15 5
318. – 30 f. black, turq. & pur. 15 8
DESIGN: 30 f. Pres. Bongo (half-length portrait).

75. "Madonna and Child with Rosary" (Murillo).

1968. Air. Religious Paintings. Multicoloured.
319. 60 f. Type **75** 45 20
320. 90 f. "Christ in Bonds" (Luis de Morales) .. 65 35
321. 100 f. "St. John at Patmos" (Juan Mates) (horiz.) .. 75 40

76. Beribboned Rope.

1968. Air. Europafrique. 5th Anniv.
322. **76.** 50 f. blue, yellow, green and ochre 35 15

1968. Petroleum Refinery, Port Gentil, Gabon. Inaug. As T **69** of Central African Republic.
323. 30 f. blue, red, green & chestnut 20 10

77. Distribution to the Needy.

1968. Air. Red Cross. Multicoloured.
324. 50 f. Type **77** 35 20
325. 100 f. "Support the Red Cross" 70 40

78. High-jumping.

1968. Air. Olympic Games, Mexico.
327. **78.** 25 f. choc., slate & cerise 15 8
328. – 30 f. choc., blue & red 20 10
329. – 100 f. choc., yellow & bl. 70 35
330. – 200 f. choc., slate & green 1·40 70
DESIGNS—VERT. 30 f. Cycling. 100 f. Judo. HORIZ. 200 f. Boxing.

79. Open Book. **80.** Coffee.

1968. Literacy Day.
332. **79.** 25 f. brown, red & ultram. 15 10

1968. Agricultural Produce.
333. **80.** 20 f. red, myrtle and green 12 5
334. – 40 f. orange, brn. & grn. 25 10
DESIGNS: 40 f. Cocoa.

81. Steam Packet "Junon". **83.** Advocate holding "Charter".

82. President Mba and Flag.

1968. Stamp Day.
335. **81.** 30 f. violet, grn. & orge. 20 10

1968. Air. 1st Death Anniv. of Pres. Mba.
336. **82.** 1,000 f. green, yellow, blue and gold .. 7·50

1968. Human Rights Year.
337. **83.** 20 f. black, grn. & red .. 12 5

84. Maps of Gabon and Owendo Port, and President Bongo.

1968. Air. "Laying of 1st Stone". Owendo Port. Multicoloured.
338. 25 f. Type **84** 15 8
339. 30 f. Harbour Project .. 20 8
Nos. 338/9 were issued together with an intervening se-tenant stamp-size label showing the Gabon arms and inscr. "PORT D'OWENDO C.E.E.—F.E.D. POSE DE LA PREMIERE PIERRE 24 JUIN 1968".

1969. Air. "Philexafrique" Stamp Exn., Abidjan, Ivory Coast (1st issue). As T **74** of Central African Republic.
340. 100 f. multicoloured .. 80 75
DESIGN: 100 f. "The Cloisters of Ste. Marie des Anges" (F. M. Granet).
See also No. 346.

85. Mahatma Gandhi. **86.** View of Okanda Gates.

1969. Air. "Apostles of Peace".
341. **85.** 25 f. black and pink .. 15 5
342. – 30 f. black and green .. 20 10
343. – 50 f. black and blue .. 30 15
344. – 100 f. black and mauve 65 30
DESIGNS: 30 f. J. F. Kennedy. 50 f. R. F. Kennedy. 100 f. Martin Luther King.

1969. Air. "Philexafrique" Stamp Exn., Abidjan, Ivory Coast (2nd Issue). As Type **110** of Cameroun.
346. 50 f. blue, red and green .. 40 40
DESIGN: 50 f. Oil refinery. Port Gentil and Gabon stamp of 1932.

1969. African Tourist Year.
347. **86.** 10 f. brown, grn. & blue 8 5
348. – 15 f. blue, green and red 10 5
349. – 25 f. pur., blue & brown 15 8
350. – 30 f. brn., choc. & blue 20 8
DESIGNS—HORIZ. 15 f. Barracuda. VERT. 25 f. Kinguele Falls. 30 f. Hunting Trophies.

87. "Battle of Rivoli" (Philippoteaux).

1969. Air. Napoleon Bonaparte. Bicent. Multicoloured.
351. 50 f. Type **87** 60 40
352. 100 f. "Oath of the Army" (J. L. David) .. .. 1·25 70
353. 250 f. "The Emperor Napoleon I on the Terrace at St. Cloud" (Ducis) .. 3·00 1·90

88. Mvet. **90.** "Aframomum polyanthum".

89. Refugees and Red Cross Plane.

1969. Traditional Musical Instruments from Folk Art Museum, Libreville.
354. **88.** 25 f. lake, drab & purple 15 10
355. – 30 f. choc., drab & red .. 20 10
356. – 50 f. lake, drab & purple 35 20
357. – 100 f. choc., drab & red 65 35
DESIGNS: 30 f. Ngombi harp. 50 f. Ebele and Mbe drums. 100 f. Medzang xylophone.

1969. Air. Red Cross. Aid for Biafra. Multicoloured.
359. 15 f. Type **89** 10 8
360. 20 f. Hospital and supplies van 12 8
361. 25 f. Doctor and nurse tending children 15 10
362. 30 f. Children and hospital 20 10

1969. Flowers. Multicoloured.
364. 1 f. Type **90** 5 5
365. 2 f. "Chlamydocola chlamydantha" 5 5
366. 5 f. "Costus dinklagei" .. 5 5
367. 10 f. "Cola rostrata" .. 8 5
368. 20 f. "Dischistocalyx grandifolius" 10 8

91. Astronauts and Module on Moon.

1969. Air. 1st Man on the Moon. Embossed on gold foil.
369. **91.** 1000 f. gold .. .. 7·50

92. Tree and Insignia. **93.** Oil Derrick.

1969. "National Renovation".
370. **92.** 25 f. multicoloured .. 15 8

1969. Elf/Spafe Petroleum Consortium. 20th Anniv.
371. 25 f. Type **93** 15 8
372. 50 f. Marine drilling-rigs .. 30 25

94. African Workers. **95.** Arms of Lambarene.

1969. Int. Labour Organization. 50th Anniv.
373. **94.** 30 f. green, blue and red 20 10

1969. Town Arms (1st series).
374. **95.** 20 f. multicoloured .. 10 5
375. – 25 f. gold, black & blue 15 5
376. – 30 f. multicoloured .. 20 8
ARMS: 25 f. Port-Gentil. 30 f. Libreville.
See also Nos. 405/7, 460/2, 504/2, 510/2 539/41 and 596/8.

96. Adoumas Mail Pirogue.

1969. Stamp Day.
377. **96.** 30 f. brown, emer. & grn. 20 10

97. Satellite and Globe.

1970. World Telecommunications Day.
378. **97.** 25 f. ultram., black & lake 15 8

1970. New U.P.U. Headquarters Building Berne. As T **127** of Cameroun.
379. 30 f. green, purple & brown 20 10

98. Japanese Geisha and African.

1970. "EXPO 70" World Fair, Osako, Japan.
380. **98.** 30 f. multicoloured .. 20 10

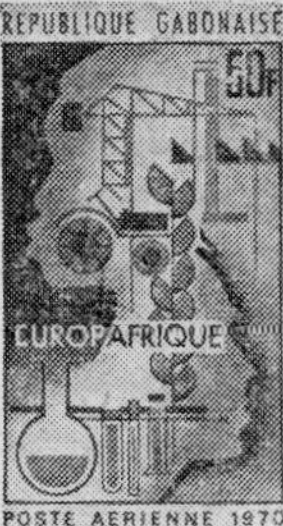

99. "Co-operation". **100.** Icarus and the Sun.

1970. Air. "Europafrique".
381. **99.** 50 f. multicoloured .. 30 15

1970. Air. History of Flight.
382. **100.** 25 f. blue, yell. and red 15 10
383. – 100 f. grn., brn. & pur. 65 30
384. – 200 f. blue, red & slate 1·40 65
DESIGNS: 100 f. Leonardo da Vinci's design for wings. 200 f. Jules Verne's rocket approaching Moon.

101. U.A.M.P.T. Emblem.

1970. Air. U.A.M.P.T. Conf., Libreville.
386. **101.** 200 f. gold, grn. & blue 1·40 90

102. Throwing-knives.

1970. Air. Gabonaise Weapons, Folk Art Museum, Libreville. All values indigo, red and green.
387. 25 f. Type **102** 15 8
388. 30 f. Assegai and crossbow 20 10
389. 50 f. War knives 30 15
390. 90 f. Dagger and sheath .. 60 13
Nos. 388/9 are vert.

103. Japanese Masks, Gateway and Mt. Fuji.

1970. Air. "Expo. 70" World Fair, Osaka, Japan. Embossed on gold foil.
392. **103.** 1000 f. red, black, green and gold .. 7·00

104. President Bongo. **105.** "Portrait of Young Man" (Raphael School).

1970. Air. Independence. 10th Anniv.
393. **104.** 200 f. gold, red bl. & grn. 1·40 90

1970. Aerial Navigation Security Agency for Africa and Madagascar. 10th Anniv. (1969). As T **121** of Cameroun.
394. 100 f. green and blue .. 65 45

1970. Air. Raphael. 450th Death Anniv. Multicoloured.
395. 50 f. Type **105** 30 15
396. 100 f. "Jeanne d'Aragon" (Raphael) 65 35
397. 200 f. "The Virgin of the Blue Diadem" (Raphael) 1·25 65

106. U.N. Emblem, Globe, Dove and Wheat.

1970. United Nations. 25th Anniv.
398. 106. 30 f. multicoloured .. 20 10

107. Harnessed or Spotted Bushbucks.

1970. Wild Fauna. Multicoloured.
399. 5 f. Type 107 .. .. 5 5
400. 15 f. Flying squirrel .. 10 5
401. 25 f. Grey-cheeked monkey (vert.) 15 8
402. 40 f. Leopard 25 10
403. 60 f. Civet-cat 40 15

108. Presidents Bongo and Pompidou.

1971. Air. Visit of Pres. Pompidou of France to Gabon.
404. 108. 50 f. multicoloured .. 40 20

1971. Arms (2nd Series). Vert. designs as T 95. Multicoloured.
405. 20 f. multicoloured .. 10 5
406. 25 f. black, green & gold 15 5
407. 30 f. multicoloured .. 15 8
ARMS: 20 f. Mouila. 25 f. Bitam. 30 f. Oyem.

109. Four Races and Emblem.

111. Freesias.

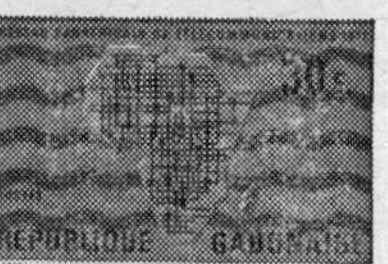
110. Telecommunications Map.

1971. Racial Equality Year.
408. 109. 40 f. black, orge. & yell. 25 12

1971. Pan-African Telecommunications Network.
409. 110. 30 f. multicoloured .. 15 10

1971. Air. "Flowers by Air". Multicoloured.
410. 15 f. Type 111 .. .. 8 5
411. 25 f. Carnations 15 8
412. 40 f. Roses 25 12
413. 55 f. Daffodils 30 15
414. 75 f. Orchids 45 20
415. 120 f. Tulips 70 35

112. Napoleon's Death Mask.

1971. Air. Napoleon. 150th Death Anniv. Multicoloured.
417. 100 f. Type 112 .. .. 60 35
418. 200 f. "Longwood House" (after Marchand) (horiz.) 1·25 65
419. 500 f. Napoleon's Tomb .. 3·25 1·75

113. "Charaxes smaragdalis".

114. Hertzien Communications Centre, Nkol Ogoum.

1971. Butterflies. Multicoloured.
420. 5 f. Type 113 .. .. 5 5
421. 10 f. "Euxanthe crossleyi" 10 5
422. 15 f. "Epiphora rectifascia" 12 5
423. 25 f. "Imbrasia bouvieri" 20 8

1971. World Telecommunications Day.
424. 114. 40 f. red, blue & green 25 12

115. Red Crosses.

1971. Air. Red Cross.
426. 115. 50 f. multicoloured .. 35 20

116. Uranium.

1971. Air. Minerals. Multicoloured.
427. 85 f. Type 116 .. .. 50 25
428. 90 f. Manganese.. .. 55 30

117. Landing Module above Moon's Surface.

1971. Air. Moon Flight of "Apollo 15". Embossed on gold foil.
429. 117. 1500 f. red, black, blue and gold .. .. 9·00

118. Mother feeding Child.

119. U.N. Emblem and New York Headquarters.

1971. Social Welfare Fund. 15th Anniv.
430. 118. 30 f. brown, bistre & mauve 15 10

1971. Gabon's Admission to United Nations. 10th Anniv.
431. 119. 30 f. multicoloured .. 15 10

120. Great White Heron.

1971. Birds. Multicoloured.
432. 30 f. Type 120 .. .. 15 12
433. 40 f. African Grey parrot 25 15
434. 50 f. Senegal kingfisher .. 30 15
435. 75 f. White-necked rockfowl 45 20
436. 100 f. Guinea touraco .. 60 25

1971. Air. African and Malagasy Posts and Telecommunications Union. 10th Anniv. As T 153 of Cameroun. Multicoloured.
439. 100 f. U.A.M.P.T. building & Bakota copper mask 65 30

121. Ski-jumping.

1972. Air. Winter Olympic Games, Sapporo. Japan.
440. 121. 40 f. violet, brn. & grn. 25 15
441. – 130 f. grn., violet & brn. 85 40
DESIGN: 130 f. Speed-skating.

122. "The Grand Canal" (detail, Vanvitelli).

1972. Air. U.N.E.S.C.O. "Save Venice" Campaign. Multicoloured.
443 60 f. Type 122 .. .. 30 5
444. 70 f. "Rialto Bridge" (Canaletto) (vert.) .. 45 20
445. 140 f. "Santa Maria della Salute" (Vanvitelli) (vert.) 90 45
On the stamp the design of No. 445 is wrongly attributed to Caffi.

123. Hotel Intercontinental.

1972. Air. Opening of Hotel Intercontinental, Gabon. Inaug.
447. 123. 40 f. brn., grn. and blue 25 15

1972. Air. Visit of the Grand Master, Sovereign Order of Malta. No. 289, surch. **VISITE OFFICIELLE GRAND MAITRE ORDRE SOUVERAIN DE MALTE 3 MARS 1972,** emblem and new value.
448. 50 f. on 300 f. blue, purple and brown 30 20

124. "Asystasia vogeliana".

1972. Flowers. Varieties of Acanthus. Multicoloured.
449. 5 f. Type 124 .. .. 5 5
450. 10 f. "Stenandriopsis guineensis" 8 5
451. 20 f. "Thomandersia hensii" 12 10
452. 30 f. "Thomandersia laurifolia" 20 12
453. 40 f. "Physacanthus batanganus" 25 20
454. 65 f. "Physacanthus nematosiphon" 35 25

125. "The Discus-thrower" (Alcamene).

126. Pasteur with Microscope.

1972. Air. Olympic Games, Munich. Ancient Sculptures.
455. 125. 30 f. grey and red .. 15 10
456. – 100 f. grey and red .. 55 30
457. – 140 f. grey and red .. 75 40
DESIGNS: 100 f. "Doryphoros" (Polyclete). 140 f. "Gladiator" (Agasias).

1972. Louis Pasteur (scientist). 150th Birth Anniv.
459. 126. 80 f. purple, grn. & red 45 30

1972. Town Arms (3rd series). Vert. designs as T 95. Multicoloured.
460. 30 f. multicoloured .. 15 8
461. 40 f. multicoloured .. 20 10
462. 60 f. silver, black & green 35 12
ARMS: 30 f. Franceville. 40 f. Makokou. 60 f. Tchibanga.

127. Global Emblem.

1972. World Telecommunications Day.
463. 127. 40 f. blk., orge. & yell. 20 10

128. Nat King Cole.

1972. Famous Negro Musicians. Mult.
464. 40 f. Type 128 .. .. 20 12
465. 60 f. Sidney Bechet .. 30 20
466. 100 f. Louis Armstrong .. 55 30

129. "Boiga blandingi".

1972. Reptiles. Multicoloured.
467. 1 f. Type 129 .. .. 5 5
468. 2 f. Sand snake 5 5
469. 3 f. Egg-eating snake .. 5 5
470. 15 f. Pit viper 10 5
471. 25 f. Jameson's tree asp.. 15 8
472. 50 f. Gabon viper .. 30 15

130. "The Adoration of the Kings in the Snow" (Bruegel the Elder).

1972. Air. Christmas. Multicoloured.
473. 30 f. Type 130 .. .. 20 12
474. 40 f. "Madonna and Child" (Basaiti) (vert.) .. 20 12

1972. Air. Olympic Gold Medal Winners. Nos. 455/7 surch. as listed below.
475. 125. 40 f. on 30 f. grey & red 20 12
476. – 120 f. on 100 f. grey & red 65 35
477. – 170 f. on 140 f. grey & red .. .. .. 1·00 60
SURCHARGES: No. 475, **MORELON**, No. 476, **KEINO.** No. 477, **SPITZ.**

131. Dr. G. A. Hansen and Hospital, Lambarene.

133. "Charaxes candiope".

132. "Thematic Collecting".

1973. Dr. Hansen's Discovery of Leprosy Bacillus. Cent.
478. **131.** 30 f. brn., grn. & blue .. 15 12

1973. Air. "PHILEXGABON 73" Int. Stamp Exhibition, Libreville.
479. **132.** 100 f. multicoloured .. 50 30

1973. Butterflies. Multicoloured.
481. 10 f. Type **133** 5 5
482. 15 f. "Eunica pechueli" 8 5
483. 20 f. "Cyrestis camillus" 12 5
484. 30 f. "Charaxes castor" .. 15 10
485. 40 f. "Charaxes ameliae" 20 10
486. 50 f. "Pseudacrea boisduvali" 25 15

134. "DC 10—30" over Libreville Airport.

1973. Air. Libreville-Paris Air Service by "Air Afrique" "DC 10 Libreville". No gum.
487. **134.** 40 f. multicoloured .. 20 12

135. Montgolfier's Balloon, 1783. 137. Interpol Emblem.

136. Power Station.

1973. History of Flight.
488. **135.** 1 f. green, myrtle & brn. 5 5
489. – 2 f. green and blue .. 5 5
490. – 3 f. new bl., bl. & orge. 5 5
491. – 4 f. vio. & reddish vio. 5 5
492. – 5 f. green and orange .. 5 5
493. – 10 f. purple and blue .. 5 5

DESIGNS—HORIZ. 2 f. Santos Dumont's airship, 1901. 3 f. Chanute's glider, 1896. 4 f. Clement Ader's "Avion III" flying-machine, 1897. 5 f. Bleriot's Cross-Channel flight, 1909. 10 f. Fabre's seaplane, 1910.

1973. Air. Kinguele Hydro-electric Project.
494. **136.** 30 f. green and brown 15 10
495. – 40 f. blue, green & brn. 20 12

DESIGN: 40 f. Dam.

1973. 50th Anniv. Int. Criminal Police Organisation (Interpol).
496. **137.** 40 f. blue and red .. 20 10

138. Dish Aerial and Station. 139. Gabon Woman.

1973. "2 Decembre" Satellite Earth Station. Inaug.
497. **138.** 40 f. brown, blue & grn. 20 10

1973. Air. M'Bigou Stone Sculptures.
498. **139.** 100 f. brown, bl. & blk. 45 30
499. – 200 f. green and brown 90 65

DESIGN: 200 f. Gabon man wearing head-dress.

1973. Air. Pan-African Drought Relief. No. 426 surch. **SECHERESSE SOLIDARITE AFRICAINE** and value.
500. **115.** 100 f. on 50 f. mult. .. 45 30

140. Party Headquarters.

1973. Gabonaise Democratic Party Headquarters, Libreville.
501. **140.** 30 f. multicoloured .. 12 8

141. Astronauts and Lunar Rover.

1973. Air. Moon Flight of "Apollo 17".
502. **141.** 500 f. multicoloured .. 2·25 1·40

1973. African and Malagasy Posts and Telecommunications Union. 10th Anniv. As T **182** of Cameroun.
503. 100 f. plum, purple & blue 45 30

1973. Town Arms (4th series). Vert. designs as T **95** dated "1973". Multicoloured.
504. 30 f. Kango 12 5
505. 40 f. Booue 15 8
506. 60 f. Koula-Moutou .. 25 10

142. "St. Theresa receiving Stigmata". 143. Flame Emblem.

1973. St. Theresa of Lisieux. Birth Cent. Stained-glass windows in the Basilica at Lisieux. Multicoloured.
507. 30 f. Type **142** 12 8
508. 40 f. "St. Theresa with Saviour" 20 12

1973. Declaration of Human Rights. 25th Anniv.
509. **143.** 20 f. red, blue & green 8 5

1974. Town Arms (5th series). Vert. designs as T **95** dated "1974". Multicoloured.
510. 5 f. Gamba 5 5
511. 10 f. Ogooue-Lolo .. 5 5
512. 15 f. Fougamou 5 5

144. White-collared Mangabey.

1974. Monkeys. Multicoloured.
513. 40 f. Type **144** 15 8
514. 60 f. Moustached Monkey 25 15
515. 80 f. Mona Monkey .. 35 25

145. De Gaulle and Houphouet-Boigny.

1974. Air. Brazzaville Conference. 30th Anniv.
516. **145.** 40 f. blue and purple .. 15 8

146. "Pleasure Boats" (Monet).

1974. Air. Impressionist Paintings. Multicoloured.
517. 40 f. Type **146** 15 8
518. 50 f. "End of an Arabesque" (Degas) (vert.) 20 12
519. 130 f. "Young Girl with Flowers" (Renoir) (vert.) 50 30

147. Eagle, and Astronaut on Moon. 148. Ogooue River, Lambarene.

1974. Air. First Manned Moon Landing. Fifth Anniv.
520. **147.** 200 f. blue, brn. & ind. 90 60

1974. Gabon Views. Multicoloured.
521. 30 f. Type **148** 12 8
522. 50 f. Cape Esterias .. 20 12
523. 75 f. Rope bridge, Poubara 30 20

149. U.P.U. Emblem and Letters.

1974. Air. Universal Postal Union. Cent.
524. **149.** 150 f. turq. and blue .. 60 40
525. – 300 f. red and orange 1·25 75

DESIGN: 300 f. Similar to T **149**, but with design reversed.

150. "Apollo" and "Soyuz" Spacecraft, Flight Badge and Maps of U.S.A. and U.S.S.R.

1974. Air. Soviet-American Co-operation in Space.
526. **150.** 1000 f. grn., red & blue 4·25 3·25

151. Ball and Footballers.

1974. Air. World Cup Football Championships, Munich.
527. **151.** 40 f. red, green & brown 15 10
528. – 65 f. green, brown & red 25 20
529. – 100 f. brown, red & grn. 40 30

DESIGNS: 65 f., 100 f. Football scenes similar to Type **151**.

152. Manioc Plantation.

1974. Agriculture. Multicoloured.
531. 40 f. Type **152** 15 10
532. 50 f. Palm-tree grove .. 20 12

1974. Central African Customs and Economic Union. 10th Anniv. As Nos. 734/5 of Cameroun.
533. 40 f. mult. (postage) .. 15 10
534. 100 f. multicoloured (air) .. 40 30

153. "The Visitation".

1974. Air. Christmas. Details from 15th-century tapestry of Notre Dame, Beaune. Multicoloured.
535. 40 f. Type **153** 15 10
536. 50 f. "The Annunciation" (horiz.) 20 15

154. Dr. Schweitzer and Lambarene Hospital.

1975. Air. Dr. Albert Schweitzer. Birth Centenary.
537. **154.** 500 f. grn., lilac & brn. 2·00 1·25

155. Dialogue Hotel.

1975. "Hotel du Dialogue", Libreville, Inauguration.
538. **155.** 50 f. multicoloured .. 20 12

1975. Town Arms (6th series). Vert. designs as Type **95** dated "1975". Multicoloured.
539. 5 f. Ogooue-Ivindo .. 5 5
540. 10 f. Moabi 5 5
541. 15 f. Moanda 5 5

156. "The Crucifixion".

1975. Air. Easter. Multicoloured.
542. 140 f. Type **156** 60 35
543. 150 f. "The Resurrection" (Burgundian School) (36 × 49 mm.) .. 60 35

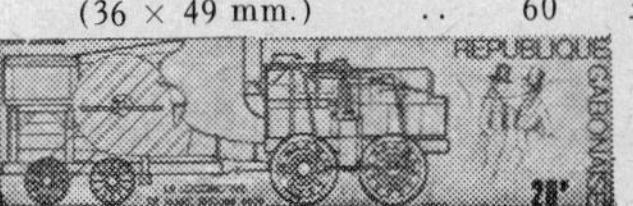

157. Locomotive "Marc Seguin".
(Illustration reduced. Actual size 100 × 27 mm.)

1975. Air. Scale Drawings of Steam Locomotives.
544. **157.** 20 f. bl., brn. & brt. bl. 10 5
545. – 25 f. red, yell. & blue .. 10 8
546. – 40 f. blue, pur. & grn. 15 10
547. – 50 f. pur., blue & grn. 20 12

Locomotives. 25 f. "Iron Duke" (1847). 40 f. "Thomas Rogers" (1895). 50 f. Soviet Type "LA-272" (1934).

158. Congress Emblem.

1975. 17th Lions Club Congress, Libreville.
548. **158.** 50 f. multicoloured .. 20 12

159. Aerial and Network Map.

1975. Gabonese Development of Hertzian Wave Radio Links.
549. **159.** 40 f. grn., brn. & bl... 20 12

160. Man and Woman and I.W.Y. Emblem.

1975. International Women's Year.
550. **160.** 50 f. brn., red and blue 20 12

161. Ange M'ba (founder of Gabonaise Scouts).

1975. "Nordjamb 75" World Scout Jamboree, Norway.
551. **161.** 40 f. blk., pur. and gn. 20 12
552. – 50 f. pur., grn. and red 20 12
DESIGN: 50 f. Scout camp.

162. "Lutjanus goreensis".

1975. Fishes. Multicoloured.
553. 30 f. Type **162** 15 10
554. 40 f. "Galeoides decadactylus" 20 12
555. 50 f. "Sardinella aurita" 20 12
556. 120 f. "Scarus hoefleri" 50 40

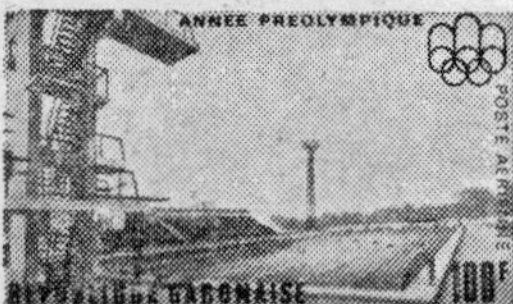

163. Swimming Pool.

1975. Air. Olympic Games, Montreal (1976). Multicoloured.
557. 100 f. Type **163** 45 30
558. 150 f. Boxing ring .. 70 50
559. 300 f. Aerial view of Games complex .. .. 1·40 1·00

1975. Air. "Apollo-Soyuz" Space Link. Optd. **JONCTION 17 Juillet 1975.**
561. **150.** 1000 f. grn., red & bl. 4·50 4·00

164. "The Annunciation" (M. Denis).

1975. Air. Christmas. Multicoloured.
562. 40 f. Type **164** 20 12
563. 50 f. "Virgin and Child with Two Saints" (Fra Filippo Lippi) 20 12

165. Franceville Complex.

1975. Agro-Industrial Complex, Franceville. Inauguration.
564. **165.** 60 f. multicoloured .. 30 20

166. "Concorde".

1975. Air. "Concorde" Commemoration.
565. **166.** 500 f. ultram., bl. & red 2·25 2·00

1975. Air. Concorde's First Commercial Flight. Surch. **21 Janv. 1976, 1 er Vol Commercial de CONCORDE** and value.
566. **166.** 1000 f. on 500 f. ultram., blue and red .. 4·50 4·00

167. Tchibanga Bridge.

1975. Gabon Bridges. Multicoloured.
567. 5 f. Type **167** 5 5
568. 10 f. Mouila Bridge .. 5 5
569. 40 f. Kango Bridges .. 20 12
570. 50 f. Lambarene Bridges (vert.) 20 12

168. A. G. Bell and Early and Modern Telephones.

1976. Telephone Centenary.
571. **168.** 60 f. grey, grn. & blue 30 20

169. Skiing (slalom).

1976. Air. Winter Olympic Games, Innsbruck.
572. **169.** 100 f. brn., blue & blk. 45 30
573. – 250 f. brn., blue & blk. 1·10 1·00
DESIGN: 250 f. Speed skating.

170. "The Crucifixion between Thieves" (wood-carving).

1976. Air. Easter. Multicoloured.
575. 120 f. Type **170** 50 40
576. 130 f. "Thomas placing finger in Jesus' wounds (wood-carving) .. 50 40

171. Monseigneur Jean-Remy Bessieux.

1976. Bessieux. Death Centenary.
577. **171.** 50 f. brn., blue & grn. 20 12

172. Boston Tea Party.

1976. Air. American Revolution. Bicent.
578. **172.** 100 f. brn., orge. & blue 45 30
579. – 150 f. brn., orge. & blue 70 50
580. – 200 f. brn., orge. & blue 90 60
DESIGNS: 150 f. Battle scenes at Hudson Bay and New York. 200 f. Wrecking of King George III's statue in New York.

173. Games Emblem.

1976. 1st Central African Games.
581. **173.** 50 f. multicoloured .. 20 12
582. 60 f. multicoloured .. 25 15

1976. Air. U.S. Independence Day. Nos. 578/80.

1976. Air. U.S. Independence Day. Nos. 578/80 optd. "**4 JUILLET 1976**".
583. **172.** 100 f. brn., orge. & blue 45 30
584. – 150 f. brn., orge. & blue 70 50
585. – 200 f. brn., orge. & blue 90 60

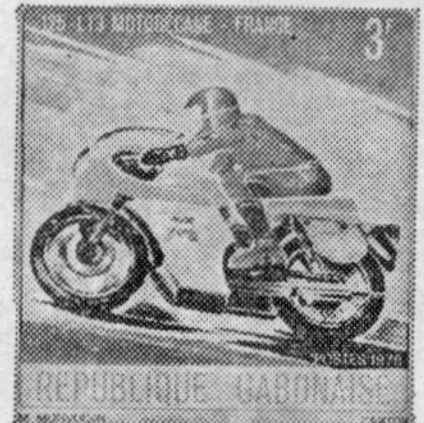

174. Motobecane 125–LT3 (France).

1976. Motorcycles.
586. **174.** 3 f. black, green & blue 5 5
587. – 5 f. blk., mve. & yell. 5 5
588. – 10 f. blk., grn. & blue 5 5
589. – 20 f. blk., grn. & red 10 5
MOTORCYCLES: 5 f. Bultaco 125 (Spain). 10 f. Suzuki 125 (Japan). 20 f. Kawasaki H2R (Japan). 100 f. Harley-Davidson 750–TX (USA).

175. Running.

1976. Air. Olympic Games, Montreal. Multicoloured.
591. 100 f. Type **175** 45 30
592. 200 f. Football 90 60
593. 260 f. High-jumping .. 1·10 90

176. Presidents Giscard d'Estaing and Bongo.

1976. Air. Visit of Pres. Giscard d'Estaing to Gabon.
594. **176.** 60 f. multicoloured .. 25 12

1976. Town Arms. (7th series). Vert. designs as T **95** dated "1976". Multicoloured.
596. 15 f. Nyanga 5 5
597. 25 f. Mandji 10 8
598. 50 f. Mekambo 20 12

OFFICIAL STAMPS

O 1. Map of Gabon River.

1968.
O 333. **O 1.** 1 f. multicoloured .. 5 5
O 334. 2 f. multicoloured .. 5 5
O 335. 5 f. multicoloured .. 5 5
O 336. 10 f. multicoloured 8 5
O 337. – 25 f. multicoloured 15 12
O 338. – 30 f. multicoloured 25 12
O 339. – 50 f. multicoloured 35 20
O 340. – 85 f. multicoloured 55 30
O 341. – 100 f. multicoloured 70 40
O 342. – 200 f. multicoloured 1·40 70
DESIGNS: 25 f., 30 f. Gabon flag. 50 f. to 200 f. Gabon coat of arms.

O 2. Gabonaise Flag.

1971.
O 437. **O 2.** 10 f. multicoloured 8 5
O 438. 40 f. multicoloured 30 12
O 438a. 50 f. multicoloured 20 12

POSTAGE DUE STAMPS

1928. Postage Due type of French Colonies optd. **GABON A.E.F.**
D 123. **D 1.** 5 c. blue 5 5
D 124. 10 c. brown .. 5 5
D 125. 20 c. olive 5 5
D 126. 25 c. red 15 15
D 127. 30 c. red 15 15
D 128. 45 c. green 20 20
D 129. 50 c. claret 20 20
D 130. 60 c. brown .. 20 20
D 131. 1 f. maroon .. 25 25
D 132. 2 f. red 30 30
D 133. 3 f. violet 40 40

D 1. Local Chief. **D 2.** Pahquin Woman.

1930.
D 134. **D 1.** 5 c. yellow and blue 8 8
D 135. 10 c. brown and red 10 10
D 136. 20 c. brown and grn. 15 15
D 137. 25 c. brown and blue 20 20
D 138. 30 c. green and brn. 25 25
D 139. 45 c. yellow and grn. 25 25
D 140. 50 c. brown and mve. 40 40
D 141. 60 c. black and lilac 70 70
D 142. – 1 f. black and brown 1·25 1·25
D 143. – 2 f. brown and mve. 1·40 1·40
D 144. – 3 f. brown and red .. 1·25 1·25
DESIGN—VERT. 1 f. to 3 f. Count de Brazza.

1932.
D 151. **D 2.** 5 c. blue on blue .. 10 10
D 152. 10 c. brown .. 15 15
D 153. 20 c. chocolate .. 30 30
D 154. 25 c. green on blue 20 20
D 155. 30 c. red 30 30
D 156. 45 c. red on yellow 75 75
D 157. 50 c. purple .. 20 20
D 158. 60 c. blue 25 25
D 159. 1 f. black on orange 60 60
D 160. 2 f. green .. .. 1·50 1·50
D 161. 3 f. claret 70 70

D 3. Pineapple.

1962. Fruits.
D 196. 50 c. red, yellow and grn. 5 5
D 197. 50 c. red, yellow and grn. 5 5
D 198. 1 f. magenta, yell. & grn. 5 5
D 199. 1 f. magenta, yell. & grn. 5 5
D 200. 2 f. yellow, brown & grn. 5 5
D 201. 2 f. yellow, brown & grn. 5 5
D 202. 5 f. yellow, green & brn. 5 5
D 203. 5 f. yellow, green & brn. 5 5
D 204. 10 f. multicoloured .. 8 8
D 205. 10 f. multicoloured .. 8 8

D 206. 25 f. yellow, green & mar. 20 20
D 207. 25 f. yellow, green & mar. 20 20

FRUITS: No. D 196, Type D 3. D 197, Mangoes. D 198, Mandarin oranges. D 199, Avocado pears. D 200, Grapefruit. D 201, Coconuts. D 202, Oranges. D 203, Papaws. D 204, Breadfruit. D 205, Guavas. D 206, Lemons. D 207. Bananas.

The two designs in each value are arranged in "tete-beche" pairs throughout the sheet.

GALAPAGOS ISLANDS O2

These islands, noted for their fauna and flora, were annexed by Ecuador, and later (1973) became a province of that country.

1. Seals.

DESIGNS—VERT. 50 c. Map of Ecuador coast-line. HORIZ. 1 s. (No. 3) Iguana. 1 s. (No. 4) Santa Cruz Island. 1 s. 80 c. Map of Galapagos Is. 4 s. 20 c. Giant tortoise.

1957. Inscr. "ISLAS GALAPAGOS".
1. 1. 20 c. brown (postage) .. 50 12
2. – 50 c. violet 20 12
3. – 1 s. green .. .. .. 1·25 25
4. – 1 s. blue (air) 20 15
5. – 1 s. 80 c. purple 40 25
6. – 4 s. 20 c. black .. .. 4·75 1·60

1959. Air. United Nations Commem. Triangular design as T 156 of Ecuador but insc. "ISLAS GALAPAGOS".
7. 2 s. green 25 25

GAMBIA BC

A Br. colony and protectorate on the W. coast of Africa. Granted full internal self-government on 4th October, 1963, and achieved independence on 18th February, 1965. Became a republic within the Commonwealth on 24th April, 1970.

1971. 100 bututs = 1 dalasy.

1.

2.

1869. Imperf.
6. 1. 4d. brown .. .. .. £225 85·00
8. 6d. blue .. .. .. £140 90·00

1880. Perf.
11. 1. ½d. orange .. .. .. 2·00 4·00
12. 1d. maroon .. .. .. 3·00 2·50
13. 2d. red .. .. .. 8·00 5·00
14. 3d. blue .. .. .. 10·00 12·00
31. 4d. brown .. .. .. 2·00 2·00
17. 6d. blue .. .. .. 20·00 12·00
19. 1s. green .. .. .. 85·00 50·00

1886.
21. 1. ½d. green 50 60
23. 1d. red .. .. .. 1·00 1·25
25. 2d. orange .. .. .. 1·75 2·00
27. 2½d. blue .. .. .. 2·50 2·00
28. 3d. grey .. .. .. 1·75 3·00
33. 6d. green .. .. .. 7·00 9·00
35. 1s. violet .. .. .. 4·50 7·00

1898.
37. 2. ½d. green .. .. .. 90 1·00
38. 1d. red .. .. .. 1·25 90
39. 2d. orange and mauve .. 1·25 2·00
40. 2½d. blue .. .. .. 1·60 2·40
41. 3d. purple and blue .. 3·50 5·00
42. 4d. brown and blue .. 3·00 5·50
43. 6d. green and red .. 5·00 8·50
44. 1s. mauve and green .. 7·00 11·00

1902. As T 2, but portrait of King Edward VII.
57. ½d. green 25 30
58. 1d. red 50 30
47. 2d. orange and mauve .. 1·90 2·50
60. 2½d. blue .. .. .. 1·60 1·75
61. 3d. purple and blue .. 3·25 3·75
62. 4d. brown and blue .. 4·00 5·50
63. 5d. grey and black .. 3·75 5·00
64. 6d. green and red .. 3·75 4·00
65. 7½d. green and red .. 3·25 4·50
66. 10d. olive and red .. 6·00 8·00
67. 1s. mauve and green .. 11·00 14·00
53. 1s. 6d. green & red on yell. 7·50 11·00
54. 2s. grey and orange .. 10·00 15·00
55. 2s. 6d. pur. & brn. on yell. 11·00 15·00
56. 3s. red & green on yellow 14·00 17·00

1906. Surch. in words.
69. ½d. on 2s. 6d. (No. 55) .. 15·00 17·00
70. 1d. on 3s. (No. 56) .. 20·00 21·00

1909. As T 2, but portrait King Edward VII.
74. 2d. grey .. .. .. 1·00 90
75. 3d. purple on yellow .. 1·90 1·60
76. 4d. black & red on yellow 1·00 1·10
77. 5d. orange and purple .. 1·75 1·60
78. 6d. purple .. .. .. 1·60 1·90
79. 7½d. brown and blue .. 1·75 1·90
80. 10d. green and red .. 1·75 1·40
81. 1s. black on green .. 1·75 2·50
82. 1s. 6d. mauve and green 6·50 6·00
83. 2s. purple & blue on blue 5·50 6·50
84. 2s. 6d. black & red on blue 11·00 10·00
85. 3s. yellow and green .. 14·00 14·00

1912. As T 2, but portrait of King George V.
86. ½d. green 30 35
109. 1d. red 30 35
88. 1½d. olive and green .. 40 65
89. 2d. grey 35 50
90a. 2½d. blue .. .. .. 1·25 1·10
91. 3d. purple on yellow .. 35 45
92b. 4d. black & red on yellow 1·90 2·50
93. 5d. orange and purple .. 55 1·00
94. 6d. purple 65 90
95. 7½d. brown and blue .. 85 1·10
116. 10d. green and red .. 1·60 3·25
97. 1s. black on green .. 75 1·60
98. 1s. 6d. violet and green .. 2·75 4·00
99. 2s. purple & blue on blue 2·75 4·00
100. 2s. 6d. black & red on blue 4·00 5·00
101. 3s. yellow and green .. 5·00 6·50
117. 4s. black and red .. 13·00 18·00
102. 5s. green & red on yellow 12·00 18·00

3.

4.

1922.
122. 3. ½d. black and green .. 20 15
124. 1d. black and brown .. 12 12
125. 1½d. black and red .. 25 15
126. 2d. black and grey .. 35 40
127. 2½d. black and orange .. 35 1·90
128. 3d. black and blue .. 40 35
118. 4d. black & red on yellow 45 85
130. 5d. black and olive .. 1·00 2·50
131. 6d. black and claret .. 75 75
119. 7½d. black & pur. on yell. 1·10 2·50
133. 10d. black and blue .. 1·90 3·25
134. 4. 1s. black & purple on yell. 1·00 1·25
135. 1s. 6d. black and blue .. 2·75 4·25
136. 2s. black & purple on blue 3·75 3·00
137. 2s. 6d. black and green .. 3·75 4·25
138. 3s. black and purple .. 5·50 7·50
140. 4s. black and brown .. 5·00 7·50
141. 5s. black & green on yell. 7·50 11·00
142. 10s. black and olive .. 20·00 25·00

1935. Silver Jubilee. As T 11 of Antigua.
143. 1½d. blue and red .. 25 25
144. 3d. brown and blue .. 90 80
145. 6d. blue and olive .. 1·00 1·10
146. 1s. grey and purple .. 1·10 1·25

1937. Coronation. As T 2 of Aden.
147. 1d. brown 10 12
148. 1½d. red 10 12
149. 3d. blue 20 30

5. Elephant.

1938.
150. 5. ½d. black and green .. 15 15
151. 1d. purple and brown .. 15 15
152a. 1½d. pink and red .. 12 15
152b. 1½d. blue and black .. 35 40
153. 2d. blue and black .. 20 35
153a. 2d. pink and red .. 15 20
154. 3d. blue 12 15
154a. 5d. green and purple .. 25 40
155. 6d. olive and claret .. 35 35
156. 1s. blue and purple .. 70 35
156a. 1s. 3d. purple and blue .. 35 50
157. 2s. red and blue .. .. 75 1·00
158. 2s. 6d. brown and green 1·60 1·25
159. 4s. red and purple .. 1·75 1·75
160. 5s. blue and red .. .. 2·40 2·40
161. 10s. orange and black .. 3·50 4·00

1946. Victory. As T 4 of Aden.
162. 1½d. black 25 10
163. 3d. blue 25 12

1948. Silver Wedding. As T 5/6 of Aden.
164. 1½d. black 10 10
165. £1 mauve .. .. .. 5·00 7·50

1949. U.P.U. As T 14/17 of Antigua.
166. 1½d. black 25 25
167. 3d. blue 30 30
168. 6d. magenta 45 65
169. 1s. violet 75 80

1953. Coronation. As T 7 of Aden.
170. 1½d. black and blue .. 10 12

6. Tapping for Palm Wine.

1953. Queen Elizabeth II.
171. 6. ½d. red and green .. 8 8
172. – 1d. blue and brown .. 8 8
173. – 1½d. brown and black .. 10 10
174. – 2½d. black and red .. 10 10
175. – 3d. indigo and lilac .. 12 12
176. – 4d. black and blue .. 12 15
177. 6. 6d. brown and purple .. 15 15
178. – 1s. brown and green .. 20 20
179. – 1s. 3d. ultram. and blue 30 20
180. – 2s. indigo and red .. 80 65
181. – 2s. 6d. green and brown 80 65
182. – 4s. blue and chestnut .. 1·40 1·40
183. – 5s. brown and blue .. 1·50 1·50
184. – 10s. blue and green .. 4·25 3·75
185. – £1 green and black .. 7·00 8·00

DESIGNS—HORIZ. 1d., 1s. 3d. Cutter (sailing ship). 1½d., 5s. Wollof woman. 2½d., 2s. Barra canoe. 3d., 10s. S.S. "Lady Wright" 4d., 4s. James Island. 1s., 2s. 6d. Woman hoeing. £1 as T 5.

7. Queen Elizabeth II and Palm.

1961. Royal Visit.
186. 7. 2d. green and purple .. 8 8
187. – 3d. turquoise and sepia. 12 12
188. – 6d. blue and red 15 15
189. 7. 1s. 3d. violet and green 30 35

DESIGN: 3d., 6d. Queen Elizabeth II and West African map.

1963. Freedom from Hunger. As T 10 of Aden.
190. 1s. 3d. red 50 50

1963. Red Cross Cent. As T 24 of Antigua.
191. 2d. red and black .. 8 10
192. 1s. 3d. red and blue .. 50 50

8. Beautiful Long-tailed Sunbird.

1963. Queen Elizabeth II. Multicoloured.
193. ½d. Type 8 .. .. 5 5
194. 1d. Yellow-mantled Whydah 5 5
195. 1½d. Cattle Egret .. 5 5
196. 2d. Yellow-bellied Parrot 8 8
197. 3d. Long-tailed Parakeet 10 10
198. 4d. Amethyst Starling .. 10 12
199. 6d. Village Weaver .. 12 12
200. 1s. Rufous-crowned Roller 25 20
201. 1s. 3d. Red-eyed Turtle Dove 80 90
202. 2s. 6d. Bush Fowl .. 1·25 1·25
203. 5s. Palm-nut Vulture .. 2·25 2·25
204. 10s. Orange-cheeked Waxbill .. .. 3·50 3·50
205. £1 Emerald Cuckoo .. 7·50 8·50

1963. New Constitution. Nos. 194, 197 and 200/1 optd. **SELF GOVERNMENT 1963.**
206. 1d. multicoloured .. 5 5
207. 3d. multicoloured .. 8 8
208. 1s. multicoloured .. 20 25
209. 1s. 3d. multicoloured .. 30 35

1964. Shakespeare. 400th Birth Anniv. As T 25 of Antigua.
210. 6d. blue 20 20

9. Gambia Flag and River.

1965. Independence. Multicoloured.
211. ½d. Type 9 .. .. 5 5
212. 2d. Arms 5 5
213. 7½d. Type 9 .. .. 15 20
214. 1s. 6d. Arms 25 30

1965. Nos. 193/205 optd. **INDEPENDENCE 1965.** Multicoloured.
215. ½d. Type 8 .. .. 5 5
216. 1d. Yellow-mantled Whydah 5 5
217. 1½d. Cattle Egret .. 5 5
218. 2d. Yellow-bellied Parrot 5 8
219. 3d. Long-tailed Parakeet 8 8
220. 4d. Amethyst Starling .. 8 10
221. 6d. Village Weaver .. 12 15
222. 1s. Rufous-crowned Roller 15 25
223. 1s. 3d. Red-eyed Turtle Dove 35 40
224. 2s. 6d. Bush Fowl .. 50 65
225. 5s. Palm-nut Vulture .. 1·10 1·10
226. 10s. Orange-cheeked Waxbill .. .. 2·25 3·25
227. £1 Emerald Cuckoo .. 5·00 7·00

10. I.T.U. Emblem and Symbols.

1965. I.T.U. Cent.
228. 10. 1d. silver and blue .. 5 5
229. 1s. 6d. gold and violet 25 25

11. Sir Winston Churchill and Houses of Parliament.

1966. Churchill Commem.
230. 11. 1d. multicoloured .. 5 5
231. 6d. multicoloured .. 10 15
232. 1s. 6d. multicoloured .. 30 40

12. Cordon Bleu.

1966. Birds. Multicoloured.
233. ½d. Type 12 .. .. 5 5
234. 1s. Whistling Teal .. 5 5
235. 1½d. Red-throated Bee-eater 5 5
236. 2d. Pied King-fisher .. 8 8
237. 3d. Napoleon Bishop .. 10 10
238. 4d. River Eagle 12 12
239. 6d. Yellow-bellied Fruit Pigeon 20 20
240. 1s. Blue-bellied Roller .. 25 25
241. 1s. 6d. Pigmy Kingfisher .. 30 30
242. 2s. 6d. Spur-winged Goose 30 50
243. 5s. Little Woodpecker .. 1·00 1·00
244. 10s. Violet Plantain-eater 1·75 1·75
245. £1 Pintailed Whydah (Size 25 × 39½ mm.) .. 3·25 3·50

13. Arms, Early Settlement and Modern Buildings (reduced size illustration. Actual size 58 × 21½ mm.).

1966. Bathurst. 150th Anniv.

No.	Type	Description	Unused	Used
246.	13.	1d. silver, brn. & orge..	5	5
247.		2d. silver, brown & blue	5	5
248.		6d. silver, brown & grn.	12	12
249.		1s. 6d. silver, brn. & mag.	25	25

14. I.T.Y. Emblem and Hotels (reduced size illustration. Actual size 57×21 mm.).

1967. Int. Tourist Year.

No.	Type	Description	Unused	Used
250.	14.	2d. silver, brown & green	5	5
251.		1s. silver, brown & orge.	15	15
252.		1s. 6d. silver, brn. & mag.	25	25

15 Handcuffs.

1968. Human Rights Year. Multicoloured.

No.	Description	Unused	Used
253.	1d. Type **15**	5	5
254.	1s. Fort Bullen	15	15
255.	5s. Methodist Church ..	70	75

16. Queen Victoria, Queen Elizabeth II and 4d. stamp of 1869.

1969. Gambia Stamp Cent.

No.	Type	Description	Unused	Used
256.	16.	4d. sepia and ochre ..	8	8
257.		6d. blue and green ..	12	15
258.	–	2s 6d. multicoloured ..	50	55

DESIGN: 2s. 6d. Queen Elizabeth II with 4d. and 6d. stamps of 1869.

17. Catapult-Ship "Westfalen" launching Dornier "Wal".

1969. Pioneer Air Service. 35th Anniv.

No.	Type	Description	Unused	Used
259.	17.	2d. blk., grey, flesh & red	10	10
260.	–	1s. black, grey, buff and ochre	20	25
261.	–	1s. 6d. blue, grey, black and ultramarine ..	25	35

DESIGNS: 1s. Dornier "Wal" Flying-Boat. 1s. 6d. Airship "Graf Zeppelin".

18. Athlete and Gambian Flag.

1970. 9th British Commonwealth Games, Edinburgh.

No.	Type	Description	Unused	Used
262.	18.	1d. multicoloured ..	5	5
263.		1s. multicoloured ..	15	20
264.		5s. multicoloured ..	70	75

19. President and State House.

1970. Republic Day. Multicoloured.

No.	Description	Unused	Used
265.	2d. Type **19.**	5	5
266.	1s. President Dauda Jawara	15	15
267.	1s. 6d. President and Flag of Gambia	20	25

The 1s. and 1s. 6d. are both vertical designs.

20. Methodist Church, Georgetown.

1971. Establishment of Methodist Mission. 150th Anniv. Multicoloured.

No.	Description	Unused	Used
268.	2d. Type **20**	5	5
269.	1s. Map of Africa and Gambian flag (vert.) ..	15	15
270.	1s. 6d. John Wesley and scroll	25	25

21. Yellowfin Tunny.

1971. New Currency. Multicoloured.

No.	Description	Unused	Used
271.	2 b. Type **21**	5	5
272.	4 b. Peters' Mormyrid ..	5	5
273.	6 b. Tropical Flying Fish	5	5
274.	8 b. African Sleeper Goby	5	5
275.	10 b. Yellowtail Snapper	5	5
276.	13 b. Rock Hind ..	5	8
277.	25 b. Gymnallabes ..	10	12
278.	38 b. Tiger Shark ..	15	20
279.	50 b. Electric Catfish ..	20	25
280.	63 b. Black Synbranchus	25	30
281.	1 d. 25 Smalltooth Sawfish	55	60
282.	2 d. 50 Barracuda ..	1·10	1·25
283.	5 d. Brown Bullhead ..	2·25	2·50

22. Mungo Park in Scotland.

1971. Mungo Park. Birth Cent. Multicoloured.

No.	Description	Unused	Used
284.	4 b. Type **22**	8	8
285.	25 b. Dug-out canoe ..	25	25
286.	37 b. Death of Mungo Park, Busa Rapids	40	40

23. Radio Gambia.

1972. Radio Gambia. 10th Anniv.

No.	Type	Description	Unused	Used
287.	23.	4 b. brown and black ..	8	8
288.	–	25 b. blue, orge. & blk.	20	20
289.	23.	37 b. green and black ..	25	25

DESIGN: 25 b. Broadcast-area map.

24. High-jumping.

1972. Olympic Games, Munich.

No.	Type	Description	Unused	Used
290.	24.	4 b. multicoloured ..	5	5
291.		25 b. multicoloured ..	20	20
292.		37 b. multicoloured ..	25	25

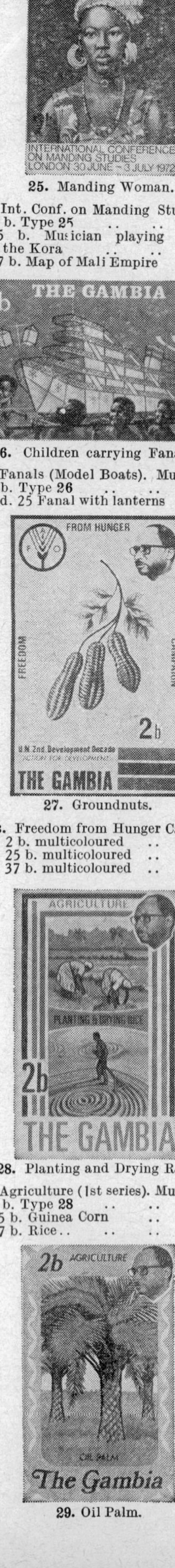

25. Manding Woman.

1972. Int. Conf. on Manding Studies. Mult.

No.	Description	Unused	Used
293.	2 b. Type **25**	5	5
294.	25 b. Musician playing the Kora	20	20
295.	37 b. Map of Mali Empire	25	25

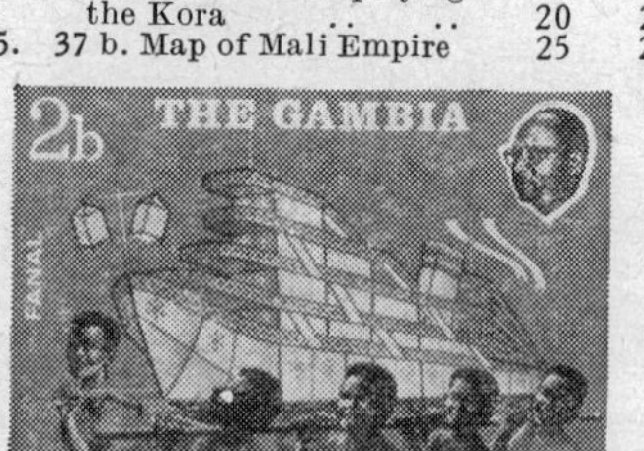

26. Children carrying Fanal.

1972. Fanals (Model Boats). Multicoloured.

No.	Description	Unused	Used
296.	2 b. Type **26**	5	5
297.	1 d. 25 Fanal with lanterns	75	85

27. Groundnuts.

1973. Freedom from Hunger Campaign.

No.	Type	Description	Unused	Used
298.	27.	2 b. multicoloured ..	5	5
299.		25 b. multicoloured ..	15	15
300.		37 b. multicoloured ..	25	25

28. Planting and Drying Rice.

1973. Agriculture (1st series). Multicoloured.

No.	Description	Unused	Used
301.	2 b. Type **28**	5	5
302.	25 b. Guinea Corn ..	15	15
303.	37 b. Rice	25	25

29. Oil Palm.

1973. Agriculture (2nd series). Multicoloured.

No.	Description	Unused	Used
304.	2 b. Type **29**	5	5
305.	25 b. Limes	15	15
306.	37 b. Oil Palm (fruits) ..	25	25

30. Cassava.

1973. Agriculture (3rd series). Multicoloured.

No.	Description	Unused	Used
307.	2 b. Type **30**	5	5
308.	50 b. Cotton	30	30

31. O.A.U. Emblem.

1973. O.A.U. 10th Anniv.

No.	Type	Description	Unused	Used
309.	31.	4 b. multicoloured ..	5	5
310.		25 b. multicoloured ..	15	15
311.		37 b. multicoloured ..	20	25

32. Red Cross.

1973. Gambian Red Cross. 25th Anniv.

No.	Type	Description	Unused	Used
312.	32.	4 b. red and black ..	5	5
313.		25 b. red black & blue	15	15
314.		37 b. red, black & green	20	25

33. Arms of Banjul.

1973. Change of Bathurst's Name to Banjul.

No.	Type	Description	Unused	Used
315.	33.	4 b. multicoloured ..	5	5
316.		25 b. multicoloured ..	15	15
317.		37 b. multicoloured ..	20	25

34. U.P.U. Emblem.

1974. U.P.U. Centenary.

No.	Type	Description	Unused	Used
318.	34.	4 b. multicoloured ..	5	5
319.		37 b. multicoloured ..	25	25

MINIMUM PRICE

The minimum price quoted is 5p which represents a handling charge rather than a basis for valuing common stamps. For further notes about prices see introductory pages.

35. Churchill as Harrow Schoolboy.

1974. Sir Winston Churchill. Birth Cent. Multicoloured.
320. 4 b. Type **35** 5 5
321. 37 b. Churchill as 4th Hussars officer 20 25
322. 50 b. Churchill as Prime Minister.. .. .. 30 30

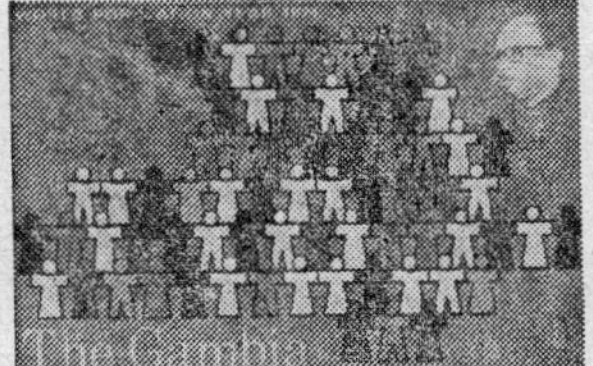

36. " Different Races ".

1974. World Population Year. Multicoloured.
323. 4 b. Type **36** 5 5
324. 37 b. " Multiplication and Division of Races " .. 20 25
325. 50 b. " World Population " 25 30

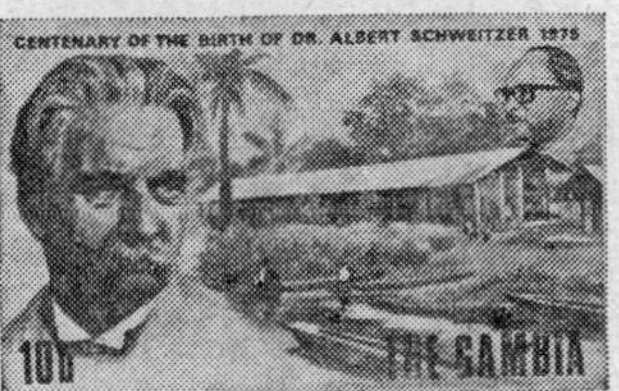

37. Dr. Schweitzer and River Scene.

1975. Dr. Albert Schweitzer. Birth Cent. Multicoloured.
326. 10 b. Type **37** 5 8
327. 50 b. Surgery scene .. 30 30
328. 1 d. 25 River journey .. 65 65

38. Dove of Peace.

1975. Independence. Tenth Anniv. Mult.
329. 4 b. Type **38** 5 5
330. 10 b. Gambian flag .. 5 5
331. 50 b. Gambian arms .. 30 30
332. 1 d. 25 Map of The Gambia 65 70

39. Development Graph.

1975. African Development Bank. Tenth Anniv. Multicoloured.
333. 10 b. Type **39** 5 8
334. 50 b. Symbolic plant .. 30 30
335. 1 d. 25 Bank emblem and symbols 65 70

40. " Statue of David " (Michelangelo).

1975. Michelangelo. 500th Birth Anniv. Multicoloured.
336. 10 b. Type **40** 5 8
337. 50 b. " Madonna of the Steps " 30 30
338. 1 d. 25 " Battle of the Centaurs " (horiz.) .. 65 70

41. School Building.

1975. Gambia High School. Cent. Multicoloured.
339. 10 b. Type **41** 5 8
340. 50 b. Pupil with scientific apparatus 30 30
341. 1 d. 50 School crest .. 75 80

42. " Teaching ".

1975. International Women's Year. Mult.
342. 4 b. Type **42** 5 5
343. 10 b. " Planting rice " .. 5 5
344. 50 b. " Nursing " 20 25
345. 1 d. 50 " Directing traffic " 65 75

43. Woman playing Golf.

1975. Independence. 11th Anniversary. Multicoloured.
346. 10 b. Type **43** 5 5
347. 50 b. Man playing golf .. 25 30
348. 1 d. 50 President playing golf 70 80

44. American Militiaman.

1976. American Revolution. Bicent. Multicoloured.
349. 25 b. Type **44** 12 15
350. 50 b. Soldier of the Continental Army 25 30
351. 1 d. 25 Independence Declaration 60 70

45. Mother and Child.

1976. Christmas.
353. **45.** 10 b. multicoloured .. 5 8
354. 50 b. multicoloured .. 25 30
355. 1 d. 25 multicoloured .. 65 75

46. Serval Cat.

1976. Abuko Nature Reserve (1st series). Multicoloured.
356. 10 b. Type **46** 5 5
357. 20 b. Harnessed Antelope 12 15
458. 50 b. Sitatunga (deer) .. 25 30
359. 1 d. 25 Leopard 60 70

GEORGIA E2

Formerly part of Transcaucasian Russia. Temporarily independent after the Russian revolution of 1917. Then one of the states of the Transcaucasian Federation which is now a part of Soviet Russia. Now uses Russian stamps.

1. St. George.

2. Queen Tamara (A.D. 1184-1212).

1919. Imperf. or perf.
10. **1.** 10 k. blue 5 55
1. 40 k. red 12 55
12. 50 k. green 5 55
13. 60 k. red 5 50
14. 70 k. purple 5 50
15. – 1 r. brown (20 × 25 mm.) 5 50
16. **2.** 2 r. brown.. .. .. 5 35
17a. 3 r. blue 5 50
18. 5 r. yellow 5 50

3. Soldier.

4. Industry and agriculture.

5.

1922. Perf.
28a. **3.** 500 r. red .. .. 1·40 2·00
29. – 1000 r. brown (Sower) .. 2·00 1·50
30. **4.** 2000 r. grey .. .. 2·25 1·60
31. 3000 r. brown .. .. 2·25 1·60
32. 5000 r. green .. .. 2·25 1·60

1922. Famine Relief. Designs as T **5**. Surch.
33. – 100 r. on 50 r. violet .. 10 1·50
34. – 3000 r. on 100 r. brown .. 10 1·50
35. – 5000 r. on 250 r. green .. 10 1·50
36. **5.** 10,000 r. on 25 r. blue .. 10 3·00

1923. Surch.
42. – 10,000 r. on 1000 r. (No. 20) 25 75
43. **4.** 15,000 r. on 2000 r. grey.. 1·00 2·00
44. **3.** 20,000 r. on 500 r. red .. 25 75
45. **4.** 40,000 r. on 5000 r. green 25 75
46. 80,000 r. on 3000 r. brown 70 80

1923. Arms types of Russia surch with hammer and sickle and value. Imperf. or perf.
50. **11.** 75,000 r. on 1 k. orange.. 1·25 2·25
52. 200,000 r. on 5 k. claret.. 1·50 3·00
53. **7.** 300,000 r. on 20 k. red and blue .. .. 1·10 2·25
51. **11.** 350,000 r. on 3 k. red .. 1·25 2·75
57. 700,000 r. on 2 k. green.. 90 3·50

GERMAN COMMANDS E2

EASTERN COMMAND

German occupation of Estonia, Latvia and Lithuania during the war of 1914-18.

100 pfennig = 1 mark.

1916. Stamps of Germany inscr. " DEUTSCHES REICH", optd. **Postgebiet Ob. Ost.**
1. **13.** 2½ pf. grey 5 8
2. **8.** 3 pf. brown 8 10
3. 5 pf. green 8 8
4. **13.** 7½ pf. orange 8 8
5. **8.** 10 pf. red 8 10
6. **13.** 15 pf. brown 75 75
7. 15 pf. violet 8 10
8. **8.** 20 pf. blue 25 25
9. 25 pf. black & red on yell. 8 20
10. 40 pf. black and red .. 30 40
11. 50 pf. black & pur. on buff 25 30
12a. **9.** 1 m. red .. .. .. 1·50 1·40

WESTERN COMMAND.

For Forces in Belgium and Northern France

100 centimes = 1 franc.

1916. Stamps of Germany surch with new values as **2 Cent. 1 F.** or **1 F. 25 Cent.**
1. **8.** 3 c. on 3 pf. brown .. 5 5
2. 5 c. on 5 pf. green .. 5 8
3. **13.** 8 c. on 7½ pf. orange .. 20 25
4. **8.** 10 c. on 10 pf. red .. 12 12
5. **13.** 15 c. on 15 pf. brown .. 5 5
6. **8.** 25 c. on 20 pf. blue .. 20 20
7. 40 c. on 30 pf. black and orange on buff .. 15 20
8. 50 c. on 40 pf. black & red 20 25
9. 75 c. on 60 pf. purple .. 35 55
10. 1 f. on 80 pf. black and red on rose 60 85
11a. **9.** 1 f. 25 on 1 m. red .. 3·75 3·75
12. **10.** 2 f. 50 on 2 m. blue .. 3·00 3·75

GERMAN OCCUPATION OF ALSACE E1

100 pfennig = 1 mark.

1940. Stamps of Germany optd. **Elsass.**
1. **53.** 3 pf. brown 8 12
2. 4 pf. slate 10 20
3. 5 pf. emerald 8 12
4. 6 pf. green 8 12
5. 8 pf. orange 8 12
6. 10 pf. chocolate .. 8 12
7. 12 pf. red 12 15
8. 15 pf. claret 20 25
9. 20 pf. blue 20 25
10. 25 pf. blue 20 30
11. 30 pf. olive 20 35
12. 40 pf. mauve 20 35
13. 50 pf. black and green .. 35 50
14. 60 pf. black and claret .. 60 65
15. 80 pf. black and blue .. 60 60
16. 100 pf. black and yellow 80 1·00

GERMAN OCCUPATION OF BELGIUM E1

German occupation of E. Belgium during the war of 1914–18.

100 centimes = 1 franc.

Stamps of Germany inscr. " DEUTSCHES REICH " surcharged.

1914. Surch. **Belgien** and value, thus: **3 Centimes,** or **1 Franc** or **1 Fr. 25 c.**
1. **8.** 3 c. on 3 pf. brown .. 5 5
2. 5 c. on 5 pf. green .. 5 5
3. 10 c. on 10 pf. red .. 10 5
4. 25 c. on 20 pf. blue .. 10 5
5. 50 c. on 40 pf. black & red 60 25
6. 5 c. on 60 pf. purple .. 20 25
7. 1 f. on 80 pf. black and red on rose 45 40
8. **9.** 1 f. 25 on 1 m. red .. 5·00 4·50
9. **10.** 2 f. 50 on 2 m. blue .. 5·00 4·50

1916. Surch. **Belgien** and value, thus: **2 Cent., 1 F.** or **1 F. 25 Cent.**

10.	13.	2 c. on 2 pf. grey ..	5	5
11.	8.	3 c. on 3 pf. brown ..	5	5
12.		5 c. on 5 pf. green ..	5	5
13.	13.	8 c. on 7½ pf. orange ..	5	5
14.	8.	10 c. on 10 pf. red ..	5	5
15.	13.	15 c. on 15 pf. brown ..	30	10
16.		15 c. on 15 pf. violet ..	5	5
17.	8.	20 c. on 25 pf. black and red on yellow	5	5
18.		25 c. on 20 pf. blue ..	5	5
19.		40 c. on 30 pf. black and orange on buff ..	10	5
20.		50 c. on 40 pf. blk. & red	12	5
21.		75 c. on 60 pf. purple ..	45	65
22.		1 f. on 80 f. black and red on rose ..	75	1·25
23.	9.	1 f. 25 on 1 m. red ..	9·00	8·00
24.	10.	2 f. 50 on 2 m. blue ..	11·00	11·00
25.	12.	6 f. 25 on 5 m. red & black	8·00	9·00

GERMAN OCCUPATION OF ESTONIA E1

1.

2. "The Long Hermann" Tower, Reval (Tallinn).

1941. Tartu issue.

3.	1.	15 (k.) brown	1·60
4.		20 (k.) green	1·50
5.		30 (k.) blue..	4·00

Originally issued for local use, the above were made available for use throughout Estonia from 29.9.41 to 30.4.42. However, not many were used since the German **OSTLAND**, stamps had already been issued on 4.11.41.

1941. Reconstruction Fund.

6.	2.	15+15 (k.) sepia & brown	8
7.	–	20+20 (k.) purple & brown	8
8.	–	30+30 (k.) indigo & brown	8
9.	–	50+50 (k.) green and brown	10
10.	–	60+60 (k.) red and brown	10
11.	–	100+100 (k.) slate & brown	15

DESIGNS—HORIZ. 20 k. Stone Bridge, Tartu. 30 k. Narva Castle. 50 k. View of Tallinn. VERT. 60 k. Tartu University. 100 k. Narva Castle.

German stamps optd. **OSTLAND** (see German Occupation of Russia, Nos. 1/20) were used from 4th November, 1941, till the Russian re-occupation of Estonia in 1944-45. Since then Russian stamps have been in use.

GERMAN OCCUPATION OF LATVIA E2

1941. Russian stamps of 1936-39 optd **LATVIJA 1941. I.VII.**

1.	5 k. red (No. 847a)	12	15
2.	10 k. blue (No. 727g) ..	12	15
3.	15 k. green (No. 847c) ..	4·00	5·50
4.	20 k. green (No. 727h) ..	12	15
5.	30 k. blue (No. 847d) ..	12	15
6.	50 k. brown (No. 727m) ..	25	90

German stamps optd. OSTLAND (see German Occupation of Russia Nos. 1/20) were used from 4th November, 1941, until the Russian re-occupation of Latvia in 1944-45. Since then Russian stamps have been in use.

GERMAN OCCUPATION OF LITHUANIA E2

1941. Russian stamps of 1936-40 optd. **NEPRIKLAUSOMA LIETUVA 1941-V1-23.**

1.	2 k. green (No. 542) ..	2·50	8·00
2.	5 k. red (No. 560da) ..	5	35
3.	10 k. blue (No. 558f) ..	5	35
4.	15 k. green (No. 558k) ..	5	35
5.	20 k. green (No. 558m) ..	5	35
6.	30 k. blue (No. 559b) ..	5	35
7.	50 k. brown (No. 560b) ..	15	90
8.	60 k. red (No. 560c) ..	60	2·40
9.	80 k. blue (No. 905) ..	60	2·40

1941. Issue for Vilna and South Lithuania Russian stamps of 1936-39 optd. **VILNIUS.**

10.	5 k. red (No. 560da) ..	8	8
11.	10 k. blue (No. 558f) ..	8	8
12.	15 k. green (No. 558k) ..	15	15
13.	20 k. green (No. 558m) ..	60	60
14.	30 k. blue (No. 559b) ..	40	40
15.	50 k. brown (No. 560b) ..	70	1·10
16.	60 k. red (No. 560c) ..	70	80
17.	80 k. red (No. 760) ..	60·00	40·00
18.	1 r. black & red (No. 767) ..	£120	£100

German stamps optd. OSTLAND (see German Occupation of Russia Nos. 1/20) were used from 4th November, 1941, till the Russian re-occupation of Lithuania in 1944. Since then Russian stamps have been in use.

GERMAN OCCUPATION OF LORRAINE E1

100 pfennig = 1 mark.

1940. Stamps of Germany optd. **Lothringen.**

1.	53.	3 pf. brown	8	20
2.		4 pf. slate	12	20
3.		5 pf. emerald	8	20
4.		6 pf. green	8	10
5.		8 pf. orange	8	20
6.		10 pf. chocolate ..	8	20
7.		12 pf. red	10	12
8.		15 pf. claret	15	20
9.		20 pf. blue	20	20
10.		25 pf. blue	20	25
11.		30 pf. olive	25	30
12.		40 pf. mauve	25	30
13.		50 pf. black and green ..	40	50
14.		60 pf. black and claret ..	50	60
15.		80 pf. black and blue ..	70	1·00
16.		100 pf. black and yellow	80	1·00

GERMAN OCCUPATION OF POLAND E2

German occupation of Poland, 1915-1918.

100 pfennig = 1 mark.

1915. Stamps of Germany inscr. "DEUTSCHES REICH" optd. **Russisch-Polen.**

1.	8.	3 pf. brown	8	8
2.		5 pf. green	10	10
3.		10 pf. red	20	12
4.		20 pf. blue	30	15
5.		40 pf. black and red ..	1·00	90

1916. Stamps of Germany inscr. "DEUTSCHES REICH" optd. **Gen.-Gouv. Warschau.**

6.	13.	2½ pf. grey	5	8
7.	8.	3 pf. brown	15	15
8.		5 pf. green	15	10
9.	13.	7½ pf. orange	10	8
10.	8.	10 pf. red	12	10
11.	13.	15 pf. brown	55	35
12.		15 pf. violet	10	10
13.	8.	20 pf. blue	25	15
14.		30 pf. blk. & orge. on buff	55	55
15.		40 pf. black and red ..	30	5
16.		60 pf. purple	30	5

GERMAN OCCUPATION OF RUMANIA E3

German occupation of Rumania, 1917-1918.

100 bani = 1 leu.

Stamps of Germany inscr. "DEUTSCHES REICH".

1917. Surch. **M.V.i.R.** in frame and value in "bani".

1.	13.	15 b. on 15 pf. violet ..	10	12
2.	8.	25 b. on 20 pf. blue ..	10	12
3.		40 b. on 30 pf. black and orange on buff ..	2·50	3·50

1917. Surch. **M.V.i.R.** (not in frame) and value in "bani".

4.	8.	10 b. on 10 pf. red ..	12	12
5.	13.	15 b. on 15 pf. violet ..	90	90
6.	8.	25 b. on 20 pf. blue ..	20	20
7.		40 b. on 30 pf. black and orange on buff ..	20	20

1918. Surch. **Rumanien** and value in "bani".

8.	8.	5 b. on 5 pf. green ..	5	5
9.		10 b. on 10 pf. red ..	5	5
10.	13.	15 b. on 15 pf. violet ..	5	5
11.	8.	25 b. on 20 pf. blue ..	5	5
12.		40 b. on 30 pf. black and orange on buff ..	8	8

1918. Stamps of Germany inscr. "DEUTSCHES REICH" optd. **Gultig 9 Armee** in frame.

13.	8.	10 pf. red..	2·50	3·50
14	13.	15 pf. violet	2·50	4·00
15	8.	20 pf. blue	30	45
16.		30 pf. blk. & orge. on buff	2·50	4·00

POSTAGE DUE STAMPS

1918. Postage Due stamps of Rumania optd. **M.V.i.R.** in frame.

D 1.	D 2.	5 b. blue on green ..	45	55
D 2.		10 b. blue on green ..	45	55
D 3.		20 b. blue on green ..	45	55
D 4.		30 b. blue on green ..	45	55
D 5.		50 b. blue on green ..	45	55

GERMAN OCCUPATION OF RUSSIA E3

1941. Issue for Ostland. Stamps of Germany of 1941 optd. **OSTLAND.**

1.	128.	1 pf. grey	5	5
2.		3 pf. brown	5	5
3.		4 pf. slate	5	5
4.		5 pf. green	5	5
5.		6 pf. violet	5	5
6.		8 pf. red	5	5
7.		10 pf. brown	12	12
9.		12 pf. red	12	12
11.		15 pf. red	5	5
12.		16 pf. green	5	5
13.		20 pf. blue	5	5
14.		24 pf. brown	5	5
15.		25 pf. blue	5	5
16.		30 pf. olive	5	5
17.		40 pf. mauve	5	5
18.		50 pf. green	5	5
19.		60 pf. brown	5	5
20.		80 pf. blue	5	5

1941. Issue for Ukraine. Stamps of Germany of 1941 optd. **UKRAINE.**

21.	128.	1 pf. grey	5	5
22.		3 pf. brown	5	5
23.		4 pf. slate	5	5
24.		5 pf. green	5	5
25.		6 pf. violet	5	5
26.		8 pf. red	5	5
27.		10 pf. brown	12	12
29.		12 pf. red	12	12
31.		15 pf. red	5	5
32.		16 pf. green	5	5
33.		20 pf. blue	5	5
34.		24 pf. brown	5	5
35.		25 pf. blue	5	5
36.		30 pf. olive	5	5
37.		40 pf. mauve	5	5
38.		50 pf. green	5	5
39.		60 pf. brown	5	5
40.		80 pf. blue	5	5

GERMAN POST OFFICES IN CHINA O1

German post offices in China, now closed.

1898. 100 pfennige = 1 mark.
1905. 100 cents = 1 dollar.

1898. Stamps of Germany optd. **China.**

7.	6.	3 pf. brown	90	1·10
8.		5 pf. green	70	70
9.	7.	10 pf. red	1·75	1·75
4.		20 pf. blue	4·50	1·75
11.		25 pf. orange	9·00	11·00
12.		50 pf. brown	4·00	2·75

1901. Stamps of Germany inscr. "REICHSPOST" optd. **China.**

22.	8.	3 pf. brown	45	55
23.		5 pf. green	45	25
24.		10 pf. red	60	25
25.		20 pf. blue	90	40
26.		25 pf. blk. & red on yell.	3·50	4·00
27.		30 pf. blk. & orge. on buff	3·50	3·75
28.		40 pf. black and red ..	3·50	2·40
29.		50 pf. blk. & pur. on buff	3·50	2·40
30.		80 pf. blk. & red on rose..	4·00	3·50
31.	9.	1 m. red	9·00	9·00
32.	10.	2 m. blue	8·00	8·00
33.	11.	3 m. black	13·00	18·00
35b.	12.	5 m. red and black ..	65·00	70·00

1905. Stamps of Germany inscr. "DEUTSCHES REICH" surch. **China** and new value.

46.	8.	1 c. on 3 pf. brown ..	15	35
47.		2 c. on 5 pf. green ..	15	20
48.		4 c. on 10 pf. red ..	15	20
39.		10 c. on 20 pf. blue ..	1·00	55
50.		20 c. on 40 pf. blk. & red	55	70
51.		40 c. on 80 pf. black and red on rose	55	9·00
52.	9.	½ dol. on 1 m. red ..	2·25	5·50
53.	10.	1 dol. on 2 m. blue ..	4·50	9·00
44a.	11.	1½ dol. on 3 m. black ..	6·00	11·00
55.	12.	2½ dol. on 5 m. red & blk.	11·00	22·00

GERMAN POST OFFICES IN MOROCCO O3

German Post Offices in Morocco, now closed.

100 centimos = 1 peseta.

Stamps of Germany surcharged **Marocco** (or **Marokko**) and new value.

1889. Spelt **Marocco.**

1.	6.	3 c. on 3 pf. brown ..	35	55
2.		5 c. on 5 pf. green ..	50	60
3.	7.	10 c. on 10 pf. red.. ..	1·40	1·40
4.		25 c. on 20 pf. blue ..	2·50	3·00
5.		30 c. on 25 pf. orange ..	6·00	8·00
6.		60 c. on 50 pf. brown ..	6·00	7·00

Marocco 3 Centimos (1.)   Marocco 5 Centimos (2.)

1900. Inscr. "REICHSPOST" surch. as T **1.**

7.	8.	3 c. on 3 pf. brown ..	45	45
8.		5 c. on 5 pf. green ..	45	25
9.		10 c. on 10 pf. red ..	60	25
10.		25 c. on 20 pf. blue ..	90	70
11.		30 c. on 25 pf. black and red on yellow ..	2·50	5·50
12.		35 c. on 30 pf. black and orange on buff ..	2·50	2·50
13.		50 c. on 40 pf. blk. & red	2·50	2·50
14.		60 c. on 50 pf. black and purple on buff ..	5·00	12·00
15.		1 p. on 80 pf. black and red on rose	4·00	4·00
16.	9.	1 p. 25 c. on 1 m. red ..	9·50	12·00
17.	10.	2 p. 50 c. on 2 m. blue ..	10·00	18·00
18.	11.	3 p. 75 c. on 3 m. black ..	14·00	23·00
19.	12.	6 p. 25 c. on 5 m. red and black	80·00	95·00

On Nos. 16 to 19a the word "Marocco" is vertical and the value also on No. 18.

1905. Inscr. "DEUTSCHES REICH" surch. as T **2.**

26.	8.	3 c. on 3 pf. brown ..	1·40	1·25
40.		5 c. on 5 pf. green ..	55	25
41.		10 c. on 10 pf. red ..	55	25
42.		25 c. on 20 pf. blue ..	90	70
43.		30 c. on 25 pf. black and red on yellow	3·00	2·75
44.		35 c. on 30 pf. black and orange on buff ..	2·10	2·10
32.		50 c. on 40 pf. black & red	3·50	2·75
46.		60 c. on 50 pf. black and purple on buff ..	4·00	3·25
34.		1 p. on 80 pf. black and red on rose	2·10	4·00
35.	9.	1 p. 25 on 1 m. red ..	27·00	27·00
49.	10.	2 p. 50 on 2 m. blue ..	14·00	35·00
37.	11.	3 p. 75 on 3 m. black ..	38·00	60·00
50.	12.	6 p. 25 on 5 m. red and black	29·00	48·00

On Nos. 30, 44, 32, 46, the word "Marocco" is vert., and the value also on No. 32.

1911. Inscr. "DEUTSCHES REICH". Spelt **Marokko.**

51.	8.	3 c. on 3 pf. brown ..	12	15
52.		5 c. on 5 pf. green ..	12	35
53.		10 c. on 10 pf. red ..	12	30
54.		25 c. on 20 pf. blue ..	25	55
55.		30 c. on 25 pf. black and red on yellow	55	4·50
56.		35 c. on 30 pf. black and orange on buff ..	55	3·00
57.		50 c. on 40 pf. black & red	35	1·40
58.		60 c. on 50 pf. black and purple on buff ..	70	9·00
59.		1 p. on 80 pf. black and red on rose	55	3·50
60.	9.	1 p. 25 c. on 1 m. red ..	50	11·00
61.	10.	2 p. 50 c. on 2 m. blue ..	1·40	11·00
62.	11.	3 p. 75 c. on 3 m. black..	4·00	28·00
63.	12.	6 p. 25 c. on 5 m. red and black	6·00	45·00

GERMAN POST OFFICES IN TURKEY E3

German Post Offices in Turkey, now closed.

1884. 40 para = 1 piaster.
1908. 100 centimes = 1 franc.

1884. Stamps of Germany surch. with new value. ("PFENNIG" without final "E".)

1.	4.	10 pa. on 5 pf. mauve ..	9·00	8·00
2.	5.	20 pa. on 10 pf. red ..	13·00	9·00
3.		1 pi. on 20 pf. blue ..	25·00	70
4.		1¼ pi. on 25 pf. brown ..	35·00	35·00
6.		2½ pi. on 50 pf. green ..	35·00	32·00

1889. Stamps of Germany surch.

10.	6.	10 pa. on 5 pf. green ..	55	15
11.	7.	20 pa. on 10 pf. red ..	1·40	45
12.		1 pi. on 20 pf. blue ..	1·40	25
14.		1¼ pi. on 25 pf. orange ..	7·00	4·50
16.		2½ pi. on 50 pf. brown ..	8·00	6·50

10 PARA 10 (1.)   20 Para 20 (2.)

1900. Stamps of Germany inscr. "REICHSPOST" surch. as T **1.**

17.	8.	10 pa. on 5 pf. green ..	45	35
18.		20 pa. on 10 pf. red ..	55	35
19.		1 pi. on 20 pf. blue ..	1·00	25
20.		1¼ pi. on 25 pf. black and red on yellow ..	2·50	1·75
21.		1½ pi. on 30 pf. black and orange on buff ..	2·50	1·75
22.		2 pi. on 40 pf. black & red	2·50	1·75
23.		2½ pi. on 50 pf. black and purple on buff ..	4·50	6·00
24.		4 pi. on 80 pf. black and red on rose	5·50	6·00
25.	9.	5 pi. on 1 m. red ..	11·00	12·00
26.	10.	10 pi. on 2 m. blue ..	11·00	11·00
27.	11.	15 pi. on 3 m. black ..	18·00	22·00
28b.	12.	25 pi. on 5 m. red & black	65·00	70·00

1905. Stamps of Germany inscr. "DEUTSCHES REICH", surch. as T **2**.

47.	8.	10 pa. on 5 pf. green ..	1·10	25
48.		20 pa on 10 pf. red ..	1·25	25
49.		1 pi on 20 pf. blue ..	2·00	25
38.		1¼ pi. on 25 pf. black and red and yellow ..	4·00	3·25
51.		1½ pi. on 30 pf. black and orange on buff	5·50	2·25
52.		2 pi. on 40 pf. blk. & red	5·50	2·25
53.		2½ pi. on 50 pf. black and purple on buff ..	5·50	4·50
54.		4 pi. on 80 pf. black and red on rose ..	5·50	4·00
55.	9.	5 pi. on 1 m. red ..	11·00	6·00
56.	10.	10 pi. on 2 m. blue ..	11·00	6·00
45.	11.	15 pi. on 3 m. black ..	18·00	18·00
58.	12.	25 pi. on 5 m. red & black	10·00	24·00

1908. Stamps of Germany inscr. "DEUTSCHES REICH", surch. in **Centimes**.

60.	8.	5 c. on 5 pf. green	40	45
61.		10 c. on 10 pf. red	70	90
62.		25 c. on 20 pf. blue	1·75	11·00
63.		50 c. on 40 pf. black & red	11·00	24·00
64.		100 c. on 80 pf. black and red on rose ..	18·00	32·00

GERMANY E2

A country in Northern Central Europe. A federation of states forming the German Reich. An empire till November 1918 and then a republic until the collapse of Germany in 1945. Until 1949 under Allied Military Control when the German Federal Republic was set up for W. Germany and the German Democratic Republic for E. Germany. See also notes before No. 899.

1872. Northern areas including Alsace and Lorraine: 30 groschen = 1 thaler. Southern areas: 90 kreuzer = 1 gulden.
1875. Throughout Germany: 100 pfennige = 1 mark.
1923. 100 renten-pfennige = 1 rentenmark (gold currency).
1928. 100 pfennige = 1 reichsmark.

1.

A.

1872. Arms embossed as Type A.

1.	1.	¼ g. mauve ..	80·00	32·00
2.		⅓ g. green ..	£140	12·00
3.		½ g. orange	£225	15·00
5.		1 g. red ..	£110	1·25
6.		2 g. blue	£200	3·75
7.		5 g. olive ..	£140	30·00
8.	1.	1 k. green	£150	21·00
10.		2 k. orange	16·00	55·00
11.		3 k. red	£160	3·00
12.		7 k. blue ..	£300	23·00
13.		18 k. olive ..	£225	£130

2.

B.

1872.

14.	2.	10 g. grey ..	38·00	45·00
15.	–	30 g. blue ..	60·00	£100
38d.	2.	2 m. purple	32·00	1·25

On the 30 g. the figures are in a rectangular frame.

1872. Arms embossed as Type B.

16.	1.	¼ g. mauve	24·00	24·00
17.		⅓ g. green ..	15·00	4·25
18.		½ g. orange	15·00	2·00
19.		1 g. red	15·00	50
20.		2 g. blue ..	10·00	1·90
21.		2½ g. brown	£600	20·00
22.		5 g. olive	15·00	10·00
23.		1 k. green	15·00	8·50
24.		2 k. orange	£150	£550
25.		3 k. red ..	10·00	2·00
26.		7 k. blue ..	16·00	20·00
27.		9 k. brown	£110	55·00
28.		18 k. olive	18·00	£600

1874. Surch. with bold figures over arms.

29.	1.	"2½" on 2½ g. brown	15·00	11·00
30.		"9" on 9 k. brown	38·00	90·00

4.

5.

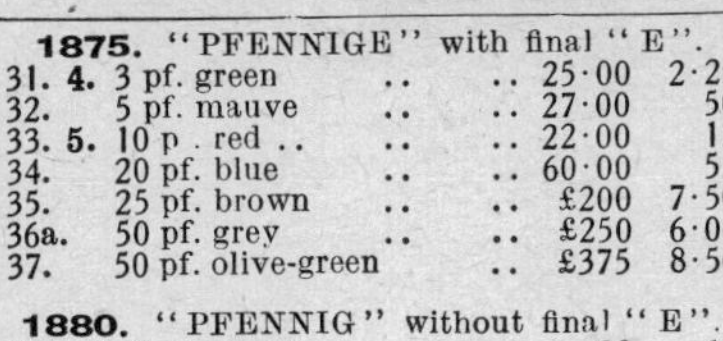

1875. "PFENNIGE" with final "E".

31.	4.	3 pf. green ..	25·00	2·25
32.		5 pf. mauve ..	27·00	50
33.	5.	10 pf. red ..	22·00	12
34.		20 pf. blue ..	60·00	55
35.		25 pf. brown ..	£200	7·50
36a.		50 pf. grey ..	£250	6·00
37.		50 pf. olive-green	£375	8·50

1880. "PFENNIG" without final "E".

39a.	4.	3 pf. green	90	15
40a.		5 pf. mauve	90	5
41b.	5.	10 pf. red	3·75	5
42a.		20 pf. blue	2·00	5
43b.		25 pf. brown	3·00	75
44c.		50 pf. green	20·00	1·75

6.

7.

1889.

45.	6.	2 pf. grey	25	25
46.		3 pf. brown	75	5
47a.		5 pf. green	35	5
48b.	7.	10 pf. red	90	5
49.		20 pf. blue	2·75	5
50b.		25 pf. orange	7·50	50
51b.		50 pf. brown	6·50	5

8. Germania.

9. General Post Office, Berlin.

10. Allegorical of Union of N. and S. Germany. (after Anton von Werner).

11. Unveiling of Kaiser Wilhelm I Memorial in Berlin (after W. Pape).

12. German Empire, 25th Anniv. Address by Wilhelm II (after W. Pape).

1899. T 8 to 12, inscr. "REICHSPOST".

52.	8.	2 pf. grey	25	5
53.		3 pf. brown	25	5
54.		5 pf. green	60	5
55.		10 pf. red	1·10	5
56.		20 pf. blue	3·75	5
57.		25 pf. blk. & red on yell.	5·00	50
58.		30 pf. blk. & orge. on buff	10·00	20
59.		40 pf. black and red ..	13·00	50
60.		50 pf. blk. & pur. on buff	13·00	30
61.		80 pf. blk. & red on rose	19·00	75
62.	9.	1 m. red ..	25·00	75
63.	10.	2 m. blue	30·00	2·00
64.	11.	3 m. black	38·00	18·00
65a.	12.	5 m. red and black	£120	£110

1902. T 8 to 12 inscr. "DEUTSCHES REICH".

82.	8.	2 pf. grey	60	1·10
83a.		3 pf. brown	5	10
84a.		5 pf. green	5	5
85.		10 pf. red	20	5
86d.		20 pf. blue	12	5
87.		25 pf. blk. & red on yell.	15	5
88a.		30 pf. blk. & orge. on buff	5	5
89a.		40 pf. black and red	25	5
90a.		50 pf. blk. & pur. on buff	10	5
91a.		60 pf. purple ..	55	15
92a.		80 pf. blk. & red on rose	30	25
113.	9.	1 m. red	80	20
94.	10.	2 m. blue	1·50	65
95.	11.	3 m. black	75	35
96.	12.	5 m. red and black	75	1·25

ILLUSTRATIONS British Commonwealth and all overprints and surcharges are FULL SIZE. Foreign Countries have been reduced to ¾-LINEAR.

13. Unshaded background.

1916. Inscr. "DEUTSCHES REICH".

97.	13.	2 pf. grey ..	5	15
98.		2½ pf. grey ..	5	5
140.	8.	5 pf. brown ..	5	5
99a.	13.	7½ pf. orange ..	5	5
141a.	8.	10 pf. orange ..	5	5
100.	13.	15 pf. brown ..	75	10
101.		15 pf. violet ..	5	5
102.		15 pf. purple ..	5	5
142.	8.	20 pf. green ..	5	10
143a.		30 pf. blue ..	5	5
103.	13.	35 pf. brown ..	5	5
144a.	8.	40 pf. red ..	5	5
145a.		50 pf. claret ..	30	30
146.		60 pf. olive ..	5	5
104.		75 pf. black and green	5	5
147a.		75 pf. purple ..	5	5
148a.		80 pf. blue ..	5	5
149.		1 m. green and lilac ..	5	8
150.		1¼ m. purple and red	5	12
114.	9.	1 m. 25 green	75	12
115.		1 m. 50 brown	10	12
151.	8.	2 m. blue and red	35	12
116a.	10.	2 m. 50 claret	5	10
152.	8.	4 m. red and black ..	5	12

1919. War Wounded Fund. Surch. **5 Pf. fur Kriegs-beschadigte.**

105.	8.	10 pf.+5 pf. (No. 85)	8	1·50
106.	13.	15 pf.+5 pf. (No. 101)	8	1·00

14.

15. 16.

1919. National Assembly, Weimar.

107.	14.	10 pf. red	8	12
108.	15.	15 pf. blue and brown	5	10
109.	16.	25 pf. red and green ..	8	15
110.		30 pf. red and purple ..	8	15

17.

18.

1919. Air.

111.	17.	10 pf. orange ..	5	15
112.	18.	40 pf. green ..	5	15

1920. Stamps of Bavaria optd. **Deutsches Reich.**

117.	12.	5 pf. green	5	15
118.		10 pf. orange	5	12
119.		15 pf. red	5	12
120.	13.	20 pf. violet	5	12
121.		30 pf. blue	5	12
122.		40 pf. brown	5	15
123.	14.	50 pf. red	5	15
124.		60 pf. green	5	15
125.		75 pf. claret	20	40
126.		80 pf. blue	5	20
127.	15.	1 m. red and grey	15	20
128.		1¼ m. blue and brown	15	20
129.		1½ m. green and grey ..	15	25
130.		2 m. violet and grey	25	25
131.		2½ m. black and grey ..	5	15
132.	16.	3 m. blue	60	1·25
133.		4 m. red	1·25	1·90
134.		5 m. orange	60	1·50
135.		10 m. green	1·00	2·25
136.		20 m. black	2·00	3·75

1920. Surch. with new value and stars.

137.	9.	1 m. 25 on 1 m. green ..	12	50
138.		1 m. 50 on 1 m. brown ..	12	50
139.	10.	2 m. 50 on 2 m. purple ..	5·00	50·00

1921. 1902 stamps surch.

172.	8.	1 m. 60 on 5 pf. brown ..	5	10
173.		3 m. on 1¼ m. pur. & red	5	10
174.		5 m. on 75 pf. purple ..	5	12
175.		10 m. on 75 pf. purple ..	15	20

19.

20. Blacksmiths.

21. Miners.

22. Reapers.

23.

24. Ploughman.

25. Posthorn.

1921.

153.	19.	5 pf. claret	5	5
154.		10 pf. olive	5	5
155.		15 pf. blue	5	5
179.		25 pf. brown	5	15
157.		30 pf. green	5	5
158.		40 pf. orange	5	5
182.		50 pf. purple	5	5
160.	20.	60 pf. claret	5	10
184.	19.	75 pf. blue	5	12
161.	20.	80 pf. red	5	20
186.	21.	100 pf. green	5	5
163.		120 pf. blue	5	12
188.	22.	150 pf. orange ..	5	5
165.		160 pf. green	5	35
193.	23.	5 m. orange	12	12
194.		10 m. red	35	25
195.	24.	20 m. blue and green ..	5	25

1921.

190.	25.	2 m. violet and rose ..	5	12
204.		2 m. purple	5	5
191.		3 m. red and yellow ..	12	12
205.		3 m. red	5	5
168.		4 m. grn. & yellow-green	5	15
206.		4 m. green	5	5
207.		5 m. orange and yellow	5	10
208.		5 m. orange	5	5
209.		6 m. blue	5	5
210.		8 m. olive	5	10
211.		10 m. red	5	10
212.		20 m. violet and red ..	5	12
213.		20 m. violet	5	10
214.		30 m. brown and yellow	5	10
215.		30 m. brown	10	1·25
216.		40 m. green	5	15
217.		50 m. green and purple	5	5

26. Arms of Munich.

27.

1922. Munich Exhibition.

198.	26.	1¼ m. red	12	12
199.		2 m. violet	12	12
200.		3 m. red	20	20
201.		4 m. blue	15	15
202.		10 m. brown on buff	30	30
203.		20 m. red on rose	1·25	1·25

1922. Air.

218.	27.	25 pf. brown	25	3·75
219.		40 pf. orange	25	6·00
220.		50 pf. purple	12	1·00
221.		60 pf. red	30	3·75
222.		80 pf. green	30	2·50
223.	–	1 m. green	10	50
224.	–	2 m. claret and grey	10	50
225.	–	3 m. blue and grey	10	65
226.	–	5 m. orange and yellow	1·10	50
227.	–	10 m. purple and rose ..	10	1·40
228.	–	25 m. brown and yellow	10	1·10
229.	–	100 m. olive and rose ..	10	2·00

The mark values are larger (21 × 27 mm.).

1922. New values.

235.	23.	50 m. blue	10	12
230.		100 m. purple and buff	15	15
237.		200 m. red on buff	5	5
238.		300 m. green on buff ..	5	5
239.		400 m. brown on buff	5	10
240.		500 m. orange on buff	5	5
241.		1000 m. grey	5	8
242.		2000 m. blue	5	10
243.		3000 m. brown ..	5	12
244.		4000 m. violet ..	5	12
245.		5000 m. green	12	20
246.		100,000 m. red	5	12

28. Allegory of Charity.

29. Miners.

30.

1922. Fund for the Old and for Children.
247. **28.** 6 m.+4 m. bl. & bistre 8 3·00
248. 12 m.+8 m. red & lilac 8 3·00

1923. Charity. For sufferers in occupied areas. Surch. **Rhein=Ruhr=Hilfe** and premium.
257. **29.** 5+100 m. orange .. 5 1·50
258. **22.** 25+500 m. brown .. 8 5·00
259. **24.** 20+1000 m. blue & grn. 1·10 45·00

1923. T=Tausend (thousand).
249. **29.** 5 m. orange 5 75
250. **22.** 10 m. blue 5 10
251. 12 m. red 5 10
252. **29.** 20 m. purple 5 10
253. **22.** 25 m. brown 5 10
254. **29.** 30 m. olive 5 10
255. **22.** 40 m. green 5 10
256. **29.** 50 m. blue .. .. 12 22·00
260. **30.** 100 m. purple 5 5
262. 200 m. red 5 5
263. 300 m. green 5 5
264. 400 m. brown 5 50
265. 500 m. orange 5 25
266. 1000 m. grey 5 5
312. 5 T. blue .. .. 5 2·75
313. 50 T. brown 5 5
314. 75 T. purple 5 55

1923. Air. As T **27**, but larger (21×27 mm.).
269. 5 m. orange .. .. 5 8·50
270. 10 m. purple .. .. 5 1·50
271. 25 m. brown .. .. 5 1·00
272. 100 m. deep green .. 5 75
273. 200 m. blue .. .. 5 8·50

31. Wartburg Castle. **33.**

1923.
267. **31.** 5000 m. blue 12 20
268. – 10,000 m. olive .. 10 20
DESIGN—VERT. 10,000 m. Cologne Cathedral.

1923. Surch. with new value in **Tausend** or **Millionen** (marks). Perf. or rouletted.
274. **19.** 5 T. on 40 pf. orange .. 5 25
275. 8 T. on 30 pf. green .. 5 5
276. **22.** 15 T. on 40 m. green .. 5 10
277. 20 T. on 12 m. red .. 5 10
278. 20 T. on 25 m. brown .. 5 25
279. **30.** 20 T. on 200 m. red .. 5 5
280. **22.** 25 T. on 25 m. bistre .. 5 75
281. 30 T. on 10 m. blue .. 5 5
282. **30.** 30 T. on 200 m. blue .. 5 10
283. 75 T. on 300 m. green .. 5 1·50
284. 75 T. on 400 m. green .. 5 5
285. 75 T. on 1000 m. green .. 5 5
286. 100 T. on 100 m. purple 5 15
287. 100 T. on 400 m. green .. 5 5
288. 125 T. on 1000 m. red .. 5 5
289. 250 T. on 200 m. red .. 5 45
290. 250 T. on 300 m. green .. 5 1·25
291. 250 T. on 400 m. brown 5 1·50
292. 250 T. on 500 m. pink .. 5 5
293. 250 T. on 500 m. orange 5 1·25
306. **19.** 400 T. on 15 pf. brown .. 5 60
307. 400 T. on 25 pf. olive .. 5 60
308. 400 T. on 30 pf. olive .. 5 60
309. 400 T. on 40 pf. olive .. 5 60
294. 800 T. on 5 pf. green .. 5 60
295. 800 T. on 10 pf. green .. 5 60
296. 800 T. on 200 m. red .. 5 7·50
297. **30.** 800 T. on 300 m. green 5 30
298. 800 T. on 400 m. green 5 30
299. 800 T. on 400 m. brown 5 2·50
300. 800 T. on 500 m. green 5 £300
301. 800 T. on 1000 m. green 5 5
302. 2 M. on 200 m. red .. 5 5
303. 2 M. on 300 m. green .. 5 5
304. 2 M. on 500 m. red .. 5 60
305. 2 M. on 5 T. red .. 5 5

1923. Perf. or rouletted.
315. **33.** 500 T. brown 5 20
316. 1 M. blue 5 5
317. 2 M. purple .. .. 5 5·00
318. 4 M. green 5 5
319. 5 M. red 5 5
320. 10 M. red 5 5
321. 20 M. blue 5 5
322. 30 M. purple .. .. 5 1·25
323. 50 M. green 5 5
324. 100 M. grey 5 5
325. 200 M. brown 5 5
326. 500 M. olive 5 5

1923. Surch. in **"Milliarden"**. Perf. or roul.
342. **30.** 1 Md. on 100 m. purple 5 4·50
343. **33.** 5 Md. on 2 M. purple .. 15 45·00
344. 5 Md. on 4 M. green .. 8 7·50
345. 5 Md. on 10 M. red .. 8 60
346. 10 Md. on 20 M. blue .. 15 60
347. 10 Md. on 50 M. green .. 5 60
348. 10 Md. on 100 M. grey .. 5 2·50

1923. As T **33**, but value in **"Milliarden"**. Perf. or roul.
327. **33.** 1 Md. brown 5 5
328. 2 Md. pink and green .. 5 10
329. 5 Md. orange and brown 5 10
330. 10 Md. green 5 10
331. 20 Md. green and brown 5 12
332. 50 Md. blue .. .. 25 7·50

1923. As T **33**, but without value in words and tablet blank.
352. **33.** 3 pf. brown 25 10
353. 5 pf. green 25 10
354. 10 pf. red 25 5
355. 20 pf. blue 60 10
356. 50 pf. orange 90 20
357. 100 pf. purple .. .. 2·75 30
The values of this and the following issues are expressed on the basis of the gold mark.

1924. Air.
358. **27.** 5 pf. green 75 75
359. 10 pf. red .. .. 75 1·25
360. 20 pf. blue .. .. 1·90 2·75
361. 50 pf. orange .. .. 5·00 7·50
362. 200 pf. purple .. .. 10·00 16·00
363. 200 pf. blue .. .. 21·00 32·00
364. 300 pf. grey .. .. 25·00 45·00

34. St. Elizabeth. **35.**

1924. Charity.
365. **34.** 5+15 pf. green .. 70 1·25
366. – 10+30 pf. red .. .. 70 1·10
367. – 20+60 pf. blue .. 2·75 3·50
368. – 50+1 m. 50 pf. brown .. 13·00 25·00
DESIGNS: St. Elizabeth feeding the hungry (5 pf.), giving drink to the thirsty (10 pf.), clothing the naked (20 pf.) and caring for the sick (50 pf.).

1924.
369. **35.** 3 pf. brown 12 5
370. 5 pf. green 20 5
371. 10 pf. red 25 5
372. 20 pf. blue 90 10
373. 30 pf. claret .. .. 1·40 15
374. 40 pf. olive .. .. 4·50 20
375. 50 pf. orange .. .. 4·50 50

36. Rheinstein.

DESIGNS: 2 m. Cologne. (A) inscr. "Zwei Mark"; (B) inscr. "ZWEI REICHSMARK". 3 m. Marienburg. 5 m. Speyer Cathedral.

1924.
376. **36.** 1 m. green .. .. 7·50 1·00
377. – 2 m. blue (A) .. .. 10·00 1·00
458. – 2 m. blue (B) .. .. 17·00 7·00
378. – 3 m. red .. .. 11·00 1·90
379. – 5 m. green .. .. 15·00 5·00

40. Dr. von Stephan. **41.** German Eagle and Rhine Valley. **42.**

1924. Postal Union Commem.
380. **40.** 10 pf. green 35 5
381. 20 pf. blue 75 15
382. – 60 pf. brown .. .. 3·50 15
383. – 80 pf. deep green .. 5·50 90
DESIGNS: Nos. 382/3. Similar to Type **40** but with border changed.

1925. German Rhineland Millenary.
384. **41.** 5 pf. green 30 10
385. 10 pf. red 55 10
386. 20 pf. blue .. .. 2·40 40

1925. Munich Exn.
387a. **42.** 5 pf. green .. .. 1·25 1·25
388. 10 pf. red .. .. 1·60 2·00

43. Arms of Prussia. **44.** **45.** Goethe.

1925. Charity. Arms dated "1925".
389. **43.** 5 pf.+5 pf. yellow black and green .. 25 30
390. – 10 pf.+10 pf. brown, blue and red .. 50 45
391. – 20 pf.+20 pf. brown, green and blue .. 3·75 6·00
ARMS: 10 pf. Bavaria. 20 pf. Saxony.
See also Nos. 413/16a, 446/50 and 451/4.

1926. Air.
392. **44.** 5 pf. green 35 30
393. 10 pf. red 35 30
394. 15 pf. purple 95 85
395. 20 pf. blue 95 85
396. 50 pf. orange .. .. 9·00 3·00
397. 1 m. red and black .. 7·50 3·00
398. 2 m. blue and black .. 7·50 11·00
399. 3 m. olive and black .. 17·50 38·00

1926. Portraits.
400. **45.** 3 pf. brown 25 5
402. – 5 pf. green (Schiller) .. 55 5
404. – 8 pf. green (Beethoven) 60 5
405. – 10 pf. red (Frederick the Great) 55 5
406. – 15 pf. red (Kant) .. 1·10 5
407. – 20 pf. deep green (Beethoven) .. .. 5·00 35
408. **45.** 25 pf. blue .. .. 1·50 20
409. – 30 pf. olive (Lessing) .. 2·75 10
410. – 40 pf. violet (Leibniz) .. 4·50 12
411. – 50 pf. brown (Bach) .. 4·75 1·50
412. – 80 pf. brown (Durer) .. 14·00 1·50

1926. Welfare Fund. As T **43**. Arms, dated "1926".
413. 5 pf.+5 pf. green, yellow, red and black 60 60
414. 10 pf.+10 pf. red, gold and rose .. .. 1·00 1·25
415. 25 pf.+25 pf. bl., yell. & red .. .. .. 6·00 7·00
416a. 50 pf.+50 pf. brn., yell., blue and red .. .. 25·00 25·00
ARMS: 5 pf. Wurttemberg. 10 pf. Baden. 25 pf. Thuringia. 50 pf. Hesse.

46. Pres. von Hindenburg. **47.** Pres. Ebert. **48.** Pres. von Hindenburg.

1927. Welfare Fund. President's 80th Birthday.
417. **46.** 8 pf.+7 pf. green .. 25 50
418. 15 pf.+15 pf. red .. 35 75
419. 25 pf.+25 pf. blue .. 4·25 7·50
420. 50 pf.+50 pf. brown .. 5·50 10·00

1927. International Labour Office Session, Berlin. Optd. **I.A.A. 10-15.10.1927.**
421. – 8 pf. green (No. 404) .. 12·00 14·00
422. – 15 pf. red (No. 406) .. 12·00 14·00
423. **45.** 25 pf. blue .. .. 12·00 15·00

1928.
424. **47.** 3 pf. brown 10 0
425. **48.** 4 pf. blue .. .. 1·10 1·15
426. 5 pf. green 15 5
427. **47.** 6 pf. olive 20 5
428. 8 pf. green 10 5
429. 10 pf. red 60 30
430. 10 pf. purple 55 10
431. **48.** 12 pf. orange 25 5
432. 15 pf. red 20 5
433. **47.** 20 pf. deep green .. 2·75 60
434. 20 pf. grey .. .. 2·75 10
435. **48.** 25 pf. blue .. .. 1·25 15
436. **47.** 30 pf. olive .. .. 1·25 15
437. **48.** 40 pf. violet .. .. 3·00 15
438. **47.** 45 pf. orange .. .. 2·50 30
439. **48.** 50 pf. brown .. .. 2·50 25
440. **47.** 60 pf. brown .. .. 4·25 25
441. **48.** 80 pf. brown .. .. 6·00 75
442. 80 pf. yellow .. .. 3·25 40

49. "Graf Zeppelin".

1928. Air.
443. **49.** 1 m. red .. .. 12·00 18·00
444. 2 m. blue .. .. 21·00 23·00
445. 4 m. brown .. .. 8·00 18·00

1928. Charity. As T **43**, dated "1928".
446. 5 pf.+5 pf. grn., red & yell. 30 40
447. 8 pf.+7 pf. green, black, red and yellow .. 30 40
448. 15 pf.+15 pf. red, blue and yellow 65 85
449. 25 pf.+25 pf. bl., red & yell. 6·50 6·50
450. 50 pf.+50 pf. brown, black red and yellow .. 23·00 30·00
ARMS: 5 pf. Hamburg. 8 pf. Mecklenburg-Schwerin. 15 pf. Oldenburg. 25 pf. Brunswick. 50 pf. Anhalt.

1929. Charity. As T **43**, dated "1929".
451. 5 pf.+2 pf. grn., red & yell. 35 60
452. 8 pf.+4 pf. grn., red & yell. 35 60
453. 15 pf.+5 pf. red, blk. & yell. 50 90
454. 25 pf.+10 pf. blue, black, red and yellow .. 7·00 12·00
455. 50 pf.+40 pf. brown, red and yellow .. .. 18·00 27·00
ARMS: 5 pf. Bremen. 8 pf. Lippe. 15 pf. Lubeck. 25 pf. Mecklenburg-Strelitz. 50 pf. Schaumburg-Lippe.

1930. Air. "Graf Zeppelin" 1st S. American Flight. T **49** inscr. "I. SUDAMERIKA FAHRT".
456. 2 m. blue .. .. 70·00 £100
457a. 4 m. brown 90 £110

1930. Allied Forces' evacuation of Rhineland Optd. **30 JUNI 1930.**
459. **47.** 8 pf. green 50 5
460. **48.** 15 pf. red 50 5

50. Aachen.

52. Heidelberg Castle.

1932. Welfare Fund.
465. **50.** 8 pf. (+4 pf.) green .. 20 20
466. – 15 pf. (+5 pf.) red .. 25 25
467. – 25 pf. (+10 pf.) blue .. 4·00 7·50
468. – 50 pf. (+40 pf.) brown 12·00 2·00
DESIGNS: 15 pf. Berlin. 25 pf. Marienwerder. 50 pf. Wurzburg.

1931. Air. "Graf Zeppelin" Polar Flight Optd. **POLAR-FAHRT 1931.**
469. **49.** 1 m. red .. .. 65·00 38·00
470. 2 m. blue .. .. 75·00 £100
471. 4 m. brown £170 £225

1931. Charity.
472. – 8 pf.+4 pf. green .. 20 30
473. – 15 pf.+5 pf. red .. 30 50
474. **52.** 25 pf.+10 pf. blue .. 5·50 10·00
475. – 50 pf.+40 pf. brown .. 18·00 24·00
DESIGNS—VERT. 8 pf. The Zwinger, Dresden. 15 pf. Town Hall, Breslau. 50 pf. The Holstentor, Lubeck.

1932. Charity. Nos. 472/3 surch.
476. 6+4 pf. on 8 pf.+4 pf. grn. 3·75 5·00
477. 12+3 pf. on 15 pf.+5 pf. red 3·00 3·75

53. President Hindenburg.

54. Nuremberg Castle.

55. Frederick the Great.

1932. Pres. Hindenburg. 85th Birthday.
478. **53.** 4 pf. blue 35 10
496. 5 pf. emerald 5 5
480. 12 pf. orange .. .. 1·75 3·75
481. 15 pf. red 75 20
503. 25 pf. blue 12 5
483. 40 pf. violet .. .. 6·00 50
484. 50 pf. brown .. .. 2·50 5·50
See also Nos. 493/509 and 545/50.

1932. Welfare Fund.
485. – 4 pf.+2 pf. blue .. 15 15
486. – 6 pf.+4 pf. olive .. 15 15
487. **54.** 12 pf.+3 pf. red .. 35 75
488. – 25 pf.+10 pf. blue .. 3·75 6·00
489. – 40 pf.+40 pf. purple .. 15·00 25·00
CASTLES: 4 pf. Wartburg. 6 pf. Stolzenfels. 25 pf. Lichtenstein. 40 pf. Marburg.

1933. Opening of Reichstag in Potsdam.
490. **55.** 6 pf. green 25 35
491. 12 pf. red 25 35
492. 25 pf. blue .. .. 12·00 10·00

1933.
493. **53.** 1 pf. black 5 5
494. 3 pf. brown 5 5
495. 4 pf. slate 5 5
497. 6 pf. green 5 5
498. 8 pf. orange 5 5
499. 10 pf. chocolate .. 5 5
500. 12 pf. red 5 5
501. 15 pf. claret 5 5
502. 20 pf. blue 8 5
504. 30 pf. olive 15 5
505. 40 pf. mauve 15 5
506. 50 pf. black and green .. 25 12
507. 60 pf. black and claret .. 25 12
508. 80 pf. black and blue .. 60 25
509. 100 pf. black and yellow 1·10 25

1933. Air. "Graf Zeppelin" Chicago World Exhibition Flight. Optd. **Chicagofahrt Weltausstellung 1933.**
510. **49.** 1 m. red £180 £120
511. 2 m. blue .. .. 26·00 50·00
512. 4 m. brown .. .. 20·00 45·00

56. Tannhauser.

OPERAS: 4 pf. The Flying Dutchman. 5 pf. Rhinegold. 6 pf. The Mastersingers. 8 pf. The Valkyries. 12 pf. Siegfried. 20 pf. Tristan and Isolde. 25 pf. Lohengrin. 40 pf. Parsifal.

1933. Welfare Fund. Wagner's Operas.
513. **56.** 3 pf.+2 pf. brown .. 75 1·10
514. – 4 pf.+2 pf. blue .. 45 35
515. – 5 pf.+2 pf. green .. 1·50 1·60
516. – 6 pf.+4 pf. green .. 50 35
517. – 8 pf.+4 pf. orange .. 80 70
518. – 12 pf.+3 pf. red .. 90 35
519. – 20 pf.+10 pf. light blue 50·00 50·00
520. – 25 pf.+15 pf. blue .. 12·00 10·00
521. – 40 pf.+35 pf. mauve .. 38·00 42·00

1933. Welfare Fund. Stamps as 1924, issued together in sheets of four, each stamp optd. **1923-1933.**
522. **34.** 5+15 pf. green .. 30·00 38·00
523. – 10+30 pf. red .. .. 30·00 38·00
524. – 20+60 pf. blue .. 30·00 38·00
525. – 50 pf.+1.50 m. brn. .. 30·00 38·00

57. Eagle, Globe and Swastika. **58.** Count Zeppelin and "Graf Zeppelin".

1934. Air.
526. **57.** 5 pf. green 25 15
527. 10 pf. red 25 30
528. 15 pf. blue 40 30
529. 20 pf. blue 65 50
530. 25 pf. brown 65 35
531. 40 pf. mauve 55 30
532. 50 pf. green .. .. 1·60 30
533. 80 pf. yellow .. .. 1·10 95
534. 100 pf. black .. .. 1·40 70
535. – 2 m. grey and green .. 4·50 5·50
536. **58.** 3 m. grey and blue .. 10·00 11·00
DESIGN—As T **58**: 2 m. Otto Lilienthal and glider.

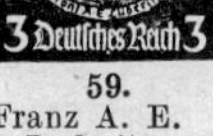

59. Franz A. E. Luderitz. **60.** "Saar Ownership". **61.** Nuremberg Castle.

1934. German Colonizers Jubilee.
537. **59.** 3 pf. brown and purple 1·50 1·50
538. – 6 pf. brown and green .. 65 50
539. – 12 pf. brown and red .. 1·10 30
540. – 25 pf. brown and blue .. 3·75 5·50
DESIGNS: 6 pf. Gustav Nachtigal. 12 pf. Karl Peters. 25 pf. Hermann von Wissmann.

1934. Saar Plebiscite.
541. **60.** 6 pf. green .. .. 1·00 8
542. – 12 pf. red .. .. 1·60 8
DESIGN: 12 pf. Eagle inscr. "Saar".

1934. Nuremberg Congress.
543. **61.** 6 pf. green .. .. 1·00 8
544. 12 pf. red .. .. 1·60 8

1934. Hindenburg Memorial. Portrait with black borders.
545. **53.** 3 pf. brown 25 15
546. 5 pf. green 30 20
547. 6 pf. green 45 12
548. 8 pf. orange .. .. 1·00 15
549. 12 pf. red .. .. 1·10 12
550. 25 pf. blue .. .. 3·25 2·50

62. Blacksmith. **63.** Friedrich von Schiller. **64.** "The Saar comes home."

1934. Welfare Fund.
551. – 3 pf.+2 pf. brown .. 40 50
552. **62.** 4 pf.+2 pf. black .. 30 25
553. – 5 pf.+2 pf. green .. 2·50 2·75
554. – 6 pf.+4 pf. green .. 20 25
555. – 8 pf.+4 pf. orange .. 30 35
556. – 12 pf.+3 pf. red .. 20 25
557. – 20 pf.+10 pf. deep grn. 6·00 8·50
558. – 25 pf.+15 pf. blue .. 6·00 8·50
559. – 40 pf.+35 pf. purple .. 17·00 25·00
DESIGNS: 3 pf. Merchant. 5 pf. Mason. 6 pf. Miner. 8 pf. Architect. 12 pf. Farmer. 20 pf. Scientist. 25 pf. Sculptor. 40 pf. Judge.

1934. Schiller. 175th Birth Anniv.
560. **63.** 6 pf. green .. .. 1·00 8
561. 12 pf. red .. .. 1·50 8

1935. Saar Restoration.
562. **64.** 3 pf. brown 30 35
563. 6 pf. green 45 10
564. 12 pf. red 60 10
565. 25 pf. blue .. .. 5·00 2·75

65. "Steel helmet". **66.** "Victor's Crown".

1935. War Heroes' Day.
566. **65.** 6 pf. green 60 40
567. 12 pf. red 50 40

1935. Apprentices' Vocational Contest.
568. **66.** 6 pf. green 45 30
569. 12 pf. red 45 30

67. Heinrich Schutz. **68.** Allenstein Castle.

1935. Musicians' Anniversaries.
570. **67.** 6 pf. green 25 15
571. – 12 pf. red (Bach) .. 30 15
572. – 25 pf. blue (Handel) .. 50 25

1935. Int. Philatelic Exn., Konigsberg. In miniature sheets.
573. **68.** 3 pf. brown .. .. 8·00 8·00
574. – 6 pf. green .. .. 8·00 8·00
575. – 12 pf. red .. .. 8·00 8·00
576. – 25 pf. blue .. .. 8·00 8·00
DESIGNS: 6 pf. Tannenberg Memorial. 12 pf. Konigsberg Castle. 25 pf. Heilsberg Castle.

72. "The Eagle." **73.** "Hitler Youth" Trumpeter.

1935. German Railway Cent. Locomotive types inscr. "1835–1935".
577. **72.** 6 pf. green 60 15
578. – 12 pf. red 60 10
579. – 25 pf. blue .. .. 5·00 75
580. – 40 pf. purple .. .. 6·00 75
DESIGNS: 12 pf. Steam. 25 pf. Diesel ("Flying Hamburger"). 40 pf. Stream-lined steam.

1935. "Hitler Youth" World Jamboree.
581. **73.** 6 pf. green 60 60
582. 15 pf. claret 85 70

74. Nuremberg. **75.** East Prussia.

1935. Nuremberg Congress.
583. **74.** 6 pf. green 35 8
584. 12 pf. red 60 8

1935. Welfare Fund. Provincial Costumes.
585. **75.** 3 pf.+2 pf. brown .. 5 5
586. – 4 pf.+3 pf. blue .. 25 25
587. – 5 pf.+3 pf. green .. 12 12
588. – 6 pf.+4 pf. olive .. 5 5
589. – 8 pf.+4 pf. brown .. 40 40
590. – 12 pf.+6 pf. red .. 15 15
591. – 15 pf.+10 pf. brown .. 2·25 1·90
592. – 25 pf.+15 pf. blue .. 2·00 2·40
593. – 30 pf.+20 pf. black .. 10·00 7·50
594. – 40 pf.+35 pf. purple .. 5·00 4·00
COSTUMES: 4 pf. Silesia. 5 pf. Rhineland. 6 pf. Lower Saxony. 8 pf. Kurmark. 12 pf. Black Forest. 15 pf. Hesse. 25 pf. Upper Bavaria. 30 pf. Friesland. 40 pf. Franconia.

76. S.A. Man and Feldherrnhalle, Munich. **77.** Skating.

1935. 12th Anniv. of Hitler Putsch.
595. **76.** 3 pf. brown 12 10
596. 12 pf. red 25 10

1935. Winter Olympic Games, Garmisch-Partenkirchen.
597. **77.** 6 pf.+4 pf. green .. 50 30
598. – 12 pf.+6 pf. red .. 1·00 45
599. – 25 pf.+15 pf. blue .. 4·50 4·00
DESIGNS: 12 pf. Ski-jumping. 25 pf. Bob-sleighing.

78. "Lufthansa" Monoplane. **79.** Gottlieb Daimler.

1936. "Lufthansa". 10th Anniv.
600. **78.** 40 pf. blue .. .. 2·25 60

1936. Berlin Motor Show. Invention of First Motor Car. 50th Anniv.
601. **79.** 6 pf. green 20 8
602. – 12 pf. red (Carl Benz) .. 35 8

80. "Hindenburg". **81.** Otto von Guericke.

1936. Air.
603. **80.** 50 pf. blue .. .. 2·00 20
604. 75 pf. green .. .. 2·40 25

1936. Otto von Guericke (scientist). 250th Death Anniv.
605. **81.** 6 pf. green 10 8

82. Gymnastics. **83.** Symbolical of Local Government.

1936. Summer Olympic Games, Berlin. Inscr. "OLYMPISCHE SPIELE 1936".
606. **82.** 3 pf.+2 pf. brown .. 12 10
607. – 4 pf.+3 pf. blue .. 12 10
608. – 6 pf.+4 pf. green .. 12 12
609. – 8 pf.+4 pf. red .. 55 25
610. – 12 pf.+6 pf. red .. 25 15
611. – 15 pf.+10 pf. claret .. 3·75 1·40
612. – 25 pf.+15 pf. blue .. 3·25 1·60
613. – 40 pf.+35 pf. violet .. 5·50 2·50
DESIGNS: 4 pf. Diver. 6 pf. Footballer. 8 pf. Javelin. 12 pf. Olympic torchbearer. 15 pf. Fencer. 25 pf. Double scullers. 40 pf. Show-jumper.

1936. VI Int. Local Government Congress.
614. **83.** 3 pf. brown 8 8
615. 5 pf. green 8 8
616. 12 pf. red 20 8
617. 25 pf. blue 60 30

84. "Brown Ribbon" Race. **85.** "Leisure Time".

1936. "Brown Ribbon of Germany". Single stamp in miniature sheet.
MS 618. **84.** 42 pf. brown .. 80 1·10

1936. Int. Recreational Congress, Hamburg.
619. **85.** 6 pf. green 25 12
620. 15 pf. claret 40 20

86. Saluting the Swastika. **87.** Luitpoldhain Heroes' Memorial, Nuremberg.

1936. Nuremberg Congress.
621. **86.** 6 pf. green 25 10
622. 12 pf. red 40 12

1936. Winter Relief Fund.
623. – 3 pf.+2 pf. brown .. 5 5
624. – 4 pf.+3 pf. black .. 10 12
625. **87.** 5 pf.+3 pf. green .. 8 8
626. – 6 pf.+4 pf. green .. 8 8
627. – 8 pf.+4 pf. brown .. 30 30
628. – 12 pf.+6 pf. red .. 10 8
629. – 15 pf.+10 pf. brown .. 2·40 1·75
630. – 25 pf.+15 pf. blue .. 1·90 1·50
631. – 40 pf.+35 pf. purple .. 3·00 2·00
DESIGNS: 3 pf. Munich frontier road. 4 pf. Air Ministry, Berlin. 6 pf. Bridge over R. Saale. 8 pf. Deutschlandhalle, Berlin. 12 pf. Alpine road. 15 pf. Fuhrerhaus, Munich. 25 pf. Bridge over R. Mangfall. 40 pf. German Art Museum, Munich.

88. R(eichs) L(uftschutz) B(und)=Civil Defence Union.

1937. Civil Defence Union. 4th Anniv.
632. **88.** 3 pf. brown 8 10
633. 6 pf. green 10 5
634. 12 pf. red 25 15

90. Fishing Smacks. **91.** Hitler Youth.

1937. Winter Relief Fund.
639. – 3 pf.+2 pf. brown .. 10 10
640. – 4 pf.+3 pf. black .. 25 20
641. **90.** 5 pf.+3 pf. green .. 10 10
642. – 6 pf.+4 pf. green .. 10 10
643. – 8 pf.+4 pf. orange .. 50 35
644. – 12 pf.+6 pf. red .. 25 8
645. – 15 pf.+10 pf. brown .. 2·25 1·00
646. – 25 pf.+15 pf. blue .. 2·50 1·00
647. – 40 pf.+35 pf. purple .. 3·25 2·00
DESIGNS: 3 pf. Lifeboat. 4 pf. Lightship "Elbe I". 6 pf. S.S. "Wilhelm Gustloff". 8 pf. Sailing ship. 12 pf. S.S. "Tannenberg". 15 pf. Train ferry "Schwerin". 25 pf. S.S. "Hamburg". 40 pf. S.S. "Europa".

1938. Hitler Culture Fund. 5th Anniv. of Hitler's Leadership.
648. **91.** 6 pf.+4 pf. green .. 45 30
649. 12 pf.+8 pf. red .. 80 50

92. "Unity". **93.** Adolf Hitler.

1938. Austrian Plebiscite.
650. **92.** 6 pf. green 12 12

1938. Hitler's Culture Fund and 49th Birthday.
652. **93.** 12 pf.+38 pf. red .. 1·25 70

94. Breslau Cathedral. **95.** Modern Airship Gondola.

1938. 16th German Sports Tournament. Breslau. Inscr. as in T **94.**
653. **94.** 3 pf. brown 12 5
654. – 6 pf. green 30 5
655. – 17 pf. red 40 5
656. – 15 pf. brown 65 30
DESIGNS: 6 pf. Hermann Goering Stadium. 12 pf. Breslau Town Hall. 15 pf. Centenary Hall.

1938. Air. Count Zeppelin. Birth Cent. Inscr. as in T **95.**
657. – 25 pf. blue .. .. 1·50 30
658. **95.** 50 pf. green .. .. 2·25 25
DESIGN: 25 pf. Count Zeppelin in early airship gondola.

96. Horsewoman. **97.** Saarpfalz Gautheater, Saarbrucken.

1938. "Brown Ribbon of Germany."
659. **96.** 42 pf.+108 pf. brown.. 22·00 12·00

1938. Nuremberg Congress and Hitler's Culture Fund. As No. 652, but inscr. "Reichsparteitag 1938".
660. **93.** 6 pf.+19 pf. green .. 1·75 1·25

1938. Opening of Gautheater and Hitler's Culture Fund.
661. **97.** 6 pf.+4 pf. green .. 90 80
662. 12 pf.+8 pf. red .. 1·25 1·10

98. Forchtenstein Castle, Burgenland. **99.** Sudeten Miner and Wife.

1938. Winter Relief. Inscr. "Winterhilfswerk".
663. **98.** 3 pf.+2 pf. brown .. 5 5
664. – 4 pf.+3 pf. blue .. 25 20
665. – 5 pf.+3 pf. green .. 8 8
666. – 6 pf.+4 pf. green .. 5 5
667. – 8 pf.+4 pf. red .. 55 30
668. – 12 pf.+6 pf. red .. 15 5
669. – 15 pf.+10 pf. claret .. 2·50 1·25
670. – 25 pf.+15 pf. blue .. 2·25 1·25
671. – 40 pf.+35 pf. mauve .. 6·00 2·10
DESIGNS: 4 pf. Flexenstrasse. 5 pf. Zell am See. 6 pf. Grossglockner. 8 pf. Augstein Castle, Wachau. 12 pf. Wien (Prince Eugene Statue, Vienna). 15 pf. Erzberg Steiermark. 25 pf. Halli. Tirol. 40 pf. Braunan.

1938. Acquisition of Sudetenland and Hitler's Culture Fund.
672. **99.** 6 pf.+4 pf. green .. 70 40
673. 12 pf.+8 pf. red .. 1·40 1·10

100. Racing Cars. **101.** Eagle and Laurel Wreath.

1939. Int. Motor Show, Berlin, and Hitler's Culture Fund. Inscr. "Internationale Automobil—und Motorrad—Ausstellung Berlin 1939".
674. – 6 pf.+4 pf. green .. 1·75 90
675. **100.** 12 pf.+8 pf. red .. 2·25 1·00
676. – 25 pf.+10 pf. blue .. 6·50 1·90
DESIGNS: 6 pf. Early Benz and Daimler cars. 25 pf. Volkswagen car.

1939. Apprentices' Vocational Contest.
677. **101.** 6 pf. green .. .. 1·00 1·00
678. 12 pf. red .. .. 1·10 1·00

102. Adolf Hitler in Braunau. **103.** Horticultural Exhibition Entrance and Arms of Stuttgart.

1939. Hitler's 50th Birthday and Culture Fund.
679. **102.** 12 pf.+38 pf. red .. 1·40 1·10

1939. Stuttgart Horticultural Exhibition and Hitler's Culture Fund.
680. **103.** 6 pf.+4 pf. green .. 70 70
681. 15 pf.+5 pf. claret .. 70 70

104. Adolf Hitler speaking. **105.** Racehorse "Investment".

1939. National Labour Day and Hitler's Culture Fund.
682. **104.** 6 pf.+19 pf. brown .. 1·50 1·25

1939. Nurburgring Races and Hitler's Culture Fund. Nos. 674/6 optd. **Nurburgring-Rennen.**
683. – 6 pf.+4 pf. green .. 12·00 10·00
684. **100.** 12 pf.+8 pf. red .. 12·00 10·00
685. – 25 pf.+10 pf. blue .. 12·00 10·00

1939. 70th Anniv. of German Derby. Hitler's Culture and Hamburg Training Establishment Funds.
686. **105.** 25 pf.+50 pf. blue .. 9·00 5·00

106. Trained Thoroughbred Horse. **107.** "Young Venetian Woman" after Durer.

1939. "Brown Ribbon of Germany" and Hitler's Culture Fund.
687. **106.** 42 pf.+108 pf. brown 10·00 8·00

1939. Day of German Art and Hitler's Culture Fund.
688. **107.** 6 pf.+19 pf. green .. 2·25 2·00

1939. Nuremberg Congress and Hitler's Culture Fund. As T **104**, but inscr. "REICHS-/PARTEITAG/1939".
689. 6 pf.+19 pf. brown .. 2·00 2·00

108. Mechanics at Work and Play. **109.** St. Mary's Church, Danzig.

1939. Postal Employees' and Hitler's Culture Funds. Inscr. "Kameradschaftsblock der Deutschen Reichspost".
690. – 3 pf.+2 pf. brown .. 1·40 1·60
691. – 4 pf.+3 pf. blue .. 1·25 1·50
692. **108.** 5 pf.+3 pf. green .. 35 40
693. – 6 pf.+4 pf. green .. 35 40
694. – 8 pf.+4 pf. orange .. 35 40
695. – 10 pf.+5 pf. brown .. 35 40
696. – 12 pf.+6 pf. red .. 70 70
697. – 15 pf.+10 pf. claret .. 70 70
698. – 16 pf.+10 pf. green .. 90 90
699. – 20 pf.+10 pf. blue .. 90 90
700. – 24 pf.+10 pf. olive .. 1·25 1·25
701. – 25 pf.+15 pf. blue .. 1·25 1·25
DESIGNS: 3 pf. Postal employees' rally. 4 pf. Review in Vienna. 6 pf. Youths on parade. 8 pf. Procession of flag-bearers. 10 pf. Distributing prizes. 12 pf. Motor-car race. 15 pf. Women athletes. 16 pf. Postal police march. 20 pf. Glider workshop. 24 pf. Mail coach. 25 pf. Sanatorium, Konigstein.
For further issues in this Type, see Nos. 761/6 and 876/81.

1939. Occupation of Danzig. Inscr. "DANZIG IST DEUTSCH".
702. **109.** 6 pf. green 10 10
703. – 12 pf. red (Crane Gate) 15 15

1939. Stamps of Danzig surch. **Deutsches Reich** and new values.
704. **13.** Rpf. on 3 pf. brown.. 50 60
705. 4 Rpf. on 35 pf. blue .. 50 60
706. Rpf. on 5 pf. orange 50 60
707. Rpf. on 8 pf. green .. 1·00 1·00
708. Rpf. on 10 pf. green 1·25 1·25
709. 12 Rpf. on 7 pf. green .. 60 70
710. Rpf. on 15 pf. red .. 1·50 1·75
711. Rpf. on 20 pf. grey .. 1·50 1·75
712. Rpf. on 25 pf. red .. 1·40 1·40
713. Rpf. on 30 pf. purple 1·00 1·10
714. Rpf. on 40 pf. blue .. 1·25 1·25
715. Rpf. on 50 pf. red and blue .. .. 2·00 1·90
716. **15.** 1 Rm. on 1 g. black and orange .. .. 7·00 7·00
717. 2 Rm. on 2 g. blk. & red 10·00 10·00

110. Elbogen Castle. **111.** Leipzig Library and Gutenberg.

1939. Winter Relief. Inscr. "Winterhilfswerk".
718. **110.** 3 pf.+2 pf. brown .. 10 5
719. – 4 pf.+3 pf. black .. 50 50
720. – 5 pf.+3 pf. green .. 12 10
721. – 6 pf.+4 pf. green .. 12 10
722. – 8 pf.+4 pf. orange .. 25 25
723. – 12 pf.+6 pf. red .. 20 12
724. – 15 pf.+10 pf. violet .. 1·10 1·10
725. – 25 pf.+15 pf. blue .. 1·40 1·10
726. – 40 pf.+35 pf. purple 2·00 1·75
DESIGNS: 4 pf. Drachenfels. 5 pf. Goslar Castle. 6 pf. Clock-tower, Graz. 8 pf. The Roemer, Frankfurt. 12 pf. City Hall, Klagenfurt. 15 pf. Ruins of Schreckenstein Castle. 25 pf. Salzburg Fortress. 40 pf. Hohentwiel Castle.

1940. Leipzig Fair. Inscr. "Leipziger Messe".
727. **111.** 3 pf. brown 12 12
728. – 6 pf. green 15 12
729. – 12 pf. red 15 8
730. – 25 pf. blue 25 35
DESIGNS: 6 pf. Augustusplatz, Leipzig. 12 pf. Old Town Hall, Leipzig. 25 pf. View of Leipzig Fair.

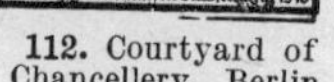

112. Courtyard of Chancellery, Berlin. **113.** Hitler and Child.

1940. 2nd Berlin Philatelic Exhibition.
731. **112.** 24 pf.+76 pf. green .. 3·00 3·75

1940. Hitler's 51st Birthday.
732. **113.** 12 pf.+38 pf. red .. 1·75 1·75

114. Wehrmacht Symbol. **115.** Horseman.

1940. Hitler's Culture Fund and National Fete Day.
733. **114.** 6 pf.+4 pf. green .. 20 20

1940. Hitler's Culture Fund and Hamburg Derby.
734. **115.** 25 pf.+100 pf. blue .. 2·40 2·40

116. Chariot. **117.** Malmedy.

1940. Hitler's Culture Fund and "Brown Ribbon" Race.
735. **116.** 42 pf.+108 pf. brown 9·00 10·00

1940. Eupen and Malmedy reincorporated in Germany, and Hitler's Culture Fund. Inscr. "Eupen-Malmedy wieder deutsch".
736. **117.** 6 pf.+4 pf. green .. 50 50
737. – 12 pf.+8 pf. red .. 50 50
DESIGN: 12 pf. View of Eupen.

118. Heligoland. **119.** Artushof, Danzig.

1940. 50th Anniv. of Cession of Heligoland to Germany and Hitler's Culture Fund.
738. **118.** 6 pf.+94 pf. red & grn. 2·00 2·00

1940. Winter Relief. Inscr. "Winterhilfswerk".
739. **119.** 3 pf.+2 pf. brown .. 5 5
740. – 4 pf.+3 pf. grey .. 15 15
741. – 5 pf.+3 pf. emerald .. 5 5
742. – 6 pf.+4 pf. green .. 5 5
743. – 8 pf.+4 pf. orange .. 15 15
744. – 12 pf.+6 pf. red .. 5 5
745. – 15 pf.+10 pf. purple 50 50
746. – 25 pf.+15 pf. blue .. 70 55
747. – 40 pf.+35 pf. claret .. 1·25 1·25
DESIGNS: 4 pf. Town Hall, Thorn. 5 pf. Kaub Castle. 6 pf. City Theatre, Posen. 8 pf. Heidelberg Castle. 12 pf. Porta Nigra, Trier. 15 pf. Prague Theatre. 25 pf. Town Hall, Bremen. 40 pf. Town Hall, Munster.

120. Emil von Behring. **121.** Postilion and Globe.

1940. Emil von Behring (bacteriologist).
748. **120.** 6 pf.+4 pf. green .. 20 20
749. 25 pf.+10 pf. blue .. 35 35

1941. Stamp Day.
750. **121.** 6 pf.+24 pf. green .. 30 30

122. Mussolini and Hitler. **123.** House of Nations, Leipzig.

1941. Hitler's Culture Fund.
751. **122.** 12 pf.+38 pf. red .. 75 75

1941. Leipzig Fair. Buildings. Inscr. "REICHSMESSE LEIPZIG 1941".
752. **123.** 3 pf. brown 12 12
753. – 6 pf. green 12 12
754. – 12 pf. red 20 12
755. – 25 pf. blue 30 30
DESIGNS: 6 pf. Cloth Hall. 12 pf. Exhibition Building. 25 pf. Railway Station.

124. Dancer. **125.** Adolf Hitler.

1941. Vienna Fair.
756. **124.** 3 pf. brown 10 12
757. – 6 pf. green 10 12
758. – 12 pf. red 20 15
759. – 25 pf. blue 55 50
DESIGNS: 6 pf. Arms and Exhibition Building. 12 pf. Allegory and Municipal Theatre. 25 pf. Prince Eugene's Equestrian Monument.

1941. Hitler's 52nd Birthday and Culture Fund.
760. **125.** 12 pf.+38 pf. red .. 80 75

1941. Postal Employees' and Hitler's Culture Funds. Inscr. "Kameradschaftsblock der Deutschen Reichspost" as Nos. 693/4, 696 and 698/700, but premium values and colours changed.
761. 6 pf.+9 pf. green .. 25 35
762. 8 pf.+12 pf. red.. .. 20 20
763. 12 pf.+18 pf. red .. 25 25
764. 16 pf.+24 pf. black .. 50 60
765. 20 pf.+30 pf. blue .. 50 60
766. 24 pf.+36 pf. violet .. 1·25 1·50

126. Racehorse. **127.** Two Amazons.

1941. Hamburg Derby. 72nd Anniv.
767. **126.** 25 pf.+100 pf. blue .. 2·00 2·25

1941. "Brown Ribbon of Germany".
768. **127.** 42 pf.+100 pf. brown 1·50 1·75

128. Adolf Hitler. **129.** Brandenburg Gate, Berlin.

1941.
769. **128.** 1 pf. grey 5 5
770. 3 pf. brown 5 5
771. 4 pf. slate 5 5
772. 5 pf. green 5 5

773. 128. 6 pf. violet 5 5
774. 8 pf. red 5 5
775. 10 pf. brown 5 5
776. 12 pf. red 5 5
779. 15 pf. brown 5 5
780. 16 pf. green 5 20
781. 20 pf. blue 5 5
782. 24 pf. brown 5 5
783. – 25 pf. blue 5 5
784. – 30 pf. olive 5 5
785. – 40 pf. mauve 5 5
786. – 50 pf. green 5 5
787. – 60 pf. brown 5 5
788. – 80 pf. blue 5 5
Nos. 783/8 are larger (21½ × 26 mm.).

1941. Berlin Grand Prix and Hitler's Culture Fund.
789. 129. 25 pf. + 50 pf. blue .. 80 1·00

130. Belvedere Palace, Vienna. **131.** Belvedere Gardens, Vienna.

1941. Vienna Fair and Hitler's Culture Fund.
790. 130. 12 pf.+8 pf. red .. 35 50
791. 131. 15 pf.+10 pf. violet .. 50 60

132. Marburg. **133.** Veldes.

1949. Union of Carinthia and Styria and Hitler's Culture Fund.
792. 132. 3 pf.+7 pf. brown .. 20 25
793. 133. 6 pf.+9 pf. violet .. 35 50
794. – 12 pf.+13 pf. red .. 50 65
795. – 25 pf.+15 pf. blue .. 90 1·10
DESIGNS: 12 pf. Pettau. 25 pf. Triglav.

134. Mozart. **135.** Philatelist.

1941. Mozart. 150th Death Anniv. and Hitler's Culture Fund.
796. 134. 6 pf.+4 pf. purple .. 5 10

1942. Stamp Day and Hitler's Culture Fund.
797. 135. 6 pf.+24 pf. violet .. 30 50

136. Symbolical of Heroism. **137.** Adolf Hitler.

1942. Heroes' Remembrance Day and Hitler's Culture Fund.
798. 136. 12 pf.+38 pf. slate .. 25 25

1942.
799. 137. 1 m. green 5 5
800. 2 m. violet 8 12
801. 3 m. red 20 50
802. 5 m. blue .. .. 85 1·25

138. Adolf Hitler. **139.** Jockey and Three-year-old Horse.

1942. Hitler's 53rd Birthday and Culture Fund.
803. 138. 12 pf.+38 pf. claret .. 90 90

1942. Hamburg Derby and Hitler's Culture Fund.
804. 139. 25 pf.+100 pf. blue .. 3·50 4·50

140. Equine Trio. **141.** Cream Jug and Loving Cup.

1942. "Brown Ribbon of Germany" and Hitler's Culture Fund.
805. 140. 42 pf.+108 pf. brown 1·50 1·75

1942. National Goldsmiths' Institution. 10th Anniv.
806. 141. 6 pf.+4 pf. red .. 15 15
807. 12 pf.+88 pf. green .. 20 25

142. Badge of Armed S.A. **143.** Peter Henlein.

1942. S.A. Military Training Month.
808. 142. 6 pf. violet 5 8

1942. Henlein (inventor of the watch). 400th Death Anniv.
809. 143. 6 pf.+24 pf. violet .. 20 25

DESIGNS—HORIZ. 3 pf. Postilion and map of Europe. VERT. 6 pf. Mounted postilion and globe.

144. Mounted Postilion.

1942. European Postal Congress, Vienna. Inscr. "EUROPAISCHER POSTKONGRESS WIEN 1942".
810. – 3 pf.+7 pf. blue .. 10 15
811. – 6 pf.+14 pf. brn. & bl. 15 25
812. 144. 12 pf.+38 pf. brown and red 30 40

1942. Signing of European Postal Union Agreement. Nos. 810/2 optd. **19. Okt. 1942.**
813. – 3 pf.+7 pf. blue .. 45 55
814. – 6 pf.+14 pf. brown and blue 45 55
815. 144. 12 pf.+38 pf. brown and red 60 65

145. Mail Coach. **146.** Brandenburg Gate and Torchlight Parade.

1943. Stamp Day and Hitler's Culture Fund.
816. 145. 6 pf.+24 pf. brown, yellow and blue .. 8 10

1943. Third Reich. 10th Anniv.
817. 146. 54 pf.+96 pf. red .. 15 25

147. **148.** Machine Gunners.

1943. Philatelic Cancellation Premium.
818. 147. 3 pf.+2 pf. bistre .. 5 5

1943. Armed Forces' and Heroes' Day.
819. – 3 pf.+2 pf. brown .. 8 12
820. 148. 4 pf.+3 pf. brown .. 8 12
821. – 5 pf.+4 pf. green .. 8 12
822. – 6 pf.+9 pf. violet .. 8 12
823. – 8 pf.+7 pf. red .. 8 12
824. – 12 pf.+8 pf. red .. 8 12
825. – 15 pf.+10 pf. brown .. 10 15
826. – 20 pf.+14 pf. blue .. 15 20
827. – 25 pf.+15 pf. blue .. 15 20
828. – 30 pf.+30 pf. green .. 25 50
829. – 40 pf.+40 pf. purple 25 50
830. – 50 pf.+50 pf. green .. 50 80
DESIGNS: 3 pf. Submarine. 5 pf. Armed motor-cyclists. 6 pf. Wireless operators. 8 pf. Engineers. 12 pf. Grenade thrower. 15 pf. Heavy artillery. 20 pf. Anti-aircraft gunners. 25 pf. Dive-bombers. 30 pf. Parachutists. 40 pf. Tank. 50 pf. Speedboat.

149. Hitler Youth. **150.** Adolf Hitler.

1943. Youth Dedication Day.
831. 149. 6 pf.+4 pf. green .. 10 12

1943. Hitler's 54th Birthday and Culture Fund.
832. 150. 3 pf.+7 pf. black .. 15 25
833. 6 pf.+14 pf. green 15 25
834. 8 pf.+22 pf. blue .. 15 25
835. 12 pf.+38 pf. red .. 15 25
836. 24 pf.+76 pf. purple 30 40
837. 40 pf.+160 pf. olive 25 60

151. Attestation. **152.** Huntsman.

1943. Labour Corps.
838. 151. 3 pf.+7 pf. brown .. 8 10
839. – 5 pf.+10 pf. green .. 8 10
840. – 6 pf.+14 pf. blue .. 8 10
841. – 12 pf.+18 pf. red .. 10 25
DESIGNS: 5 pf. Harvester sharpening scythe. 6 pf. Labourer wielding sledge-hammer. 12 pf. "Pick and shovel fatigue".

1943. "Brown Ribbon of Germany."
842. 152. 42 pf.+108 pf. brown 10 15

153. Birthplace of Peter Rosegger. **154.** Peter Rosegger.

1943. Peter Rosseger (poet). Birth Cent.
843. 153. 6 pf.+4 pf. green .. 5 5
844. 154. 12 pf.+8 pf. red .. 5 8

155. Racehorse. **156.** Mother and Children.

1943. Vienna Grand Prix.
845. 155. 6 pf.+4 pf. violet .. 5 8
846. 12 pf.+88 pf. red .. 8 10

1943. Winter Relief Fund. 10th Anniv.
847. 156. 12 pf.+38 pf. red .. 8 12

157. St. George and the Dragon. **158.** Lubeck.

1943. National Goldsmiths' Institution. 11th Anniv.
848. 157. 6 pf.+4 pf. green 5 5
849. 12 pf.+88 pf. purple 8 10

1943. Lubeck. 800th Anniv.
850. 158. 12 pf.+8 pf. red .. 8 12

159.

1943. Munich Rising. 20th Anniv.
851. 159. 24 pf.+26 pf. red .. 8 12

160. Dr. Robert Koch. **161.** Adolf Hitler.

1944. Dr. Robert Koch (bacteriologist). Birth Cent.
852. 160. 12 pf.+38 pf. sepia 8 12

1944. Third Reich. 11th Anniv.
853. 161. 54 pf.+96 pf. brown 10 12

162. Airport. **163.** Seaplane.

1944. Air Mail Services. 25th Anniv.
854. 162. 6 pf.+4 pf. green .. 5 8
855. 163. 12 pf.+8 pf. claret .. 5 8
856. – 45 pf.+108 pf. blue .. 12 15
DESIGN—VERT. 42 pf. Four-engined aeroplane seen from above.

164. Day Nursery. **165.** "Mother's Help".

1944. "Mother and Child" Organization. 10th Anniv.
857. 164. 3 pf.+2 pf. brown .. 5 5
858. 165. 6 pf.+4 pf. green .. 5 5
859. – 12 pf.+8 pf. red .. 5 5
860. – 15 pf.+10 pf. purple 5 8
DESIGNS: 12 pf. Child auscultation. 15 pf. Mothers at convalescent home.

166. Speedboat. **167.** Fulda Monument.

1944. Armed Forces' and Heroes' Day.
861. 166. 3 pf.+2 pf. brown .. 8 12
862. – 4 pf.+3 pf. blue .. 8 12
863. – 5 pf.+3 pf. green .. 8 12
864. – 6 pf.+4 pf. violet .. 8 12
865. – 8 pf.+4 pf. red .. 8 12
866. – 10 pf.+5 pf. brown .. 8 12
867. – 12 pf.+6 pf. red .. 8 12
868. – 15 pf.+10 pf. purple 8 12
869. – 16 pf.+10 pf. green .. 10 20
870. – 20 pf.+10 pf. blue .. 10 20
871. – 24 pf.+10 pf. brown 12 20
872. – 25 pf.+15 pf. blue .. 20 25
873. – 30 pf.+20 pf. olive .. 12 20
DESIGNS: 4 pf. Caterpillar tricar. 5 pf. Parachutists. 6 pf. Submarine officer. 8 pf. Mortar-firing party. 10 pf. Searchlight unit. 12 pf. Machine gunners. 15 pf. Tank. 16 pf. Speed launch. 20 pf. Seaplane. 24 pf. Armoured train. 25 pf. Rocket projectiles. 30 pf. Alpine trooper.

1944. Fulda. 1200th Anniv
874. 167. 12 pf.+38 pf. brown 5 8

168. Adolf Hitler. **169.** Postwoman.

1944. Hitler's 55th Birthday.
875. 168. 54 pf.+96 pf. red .. 12 15

1944. Postal Employees' and Hitler's Culture Funds. Inscr. "Kameradschaftsblock der Deutschen Reichspost".
876. **169.** 6 pf.+9 pf. blue .. 5 5
877. – 8 pf.+12 pf. green .. 5 5
878. – 12 pf.+18 pf. mauve 5 5
879. – 16 pf.+24 pf. green 5 5
880. – 20 pf.+30 pf. blue .. 5 8
881. – 24 pf.+36 pf. violet 5 8
DESIGNS: As T **108**—8 pf. Mail coach. 16 pf. Motor race. 20 pf. Police march. 24 pf. Glider workshop. As T **169**—12 pf. Field post on Eastern Front.

170. Riflemen. **171.** Duke Albert I of Prussia.

1944. 7th Innsbruck Shooting Competition.
884. **170.** 6 pf.+4 pf. green .. 5 5
885. 12 pf.+8 pf. red .. 5 5

1944. Albert University, Konigsberg. 400th Anniv.
886. **171.** 6 pf.+4 pf. green .. 5 10

172. Girl Worker. **173.** Labourer.

1944. Labour Corps.
882. **172.** 6 pf.+4 pf. green .. 5 5
883. **173.** 12 pf.+8 pf. red .. 5 5

ILLUSTRATIONS British Commonwealth and all overprints and surcharges are FULL SIZE. Foreign Countries have been reduced to $\frac{3}{4}$-LINEAR.

174. Racehorse and Foal.

1944. "Brown Ribbon of Germany".
887. **174.** 42 pf.+108 pf. brown 10 12

175. Racehorse and Laurel Wreath. **176.** Nautilus Beaker.

1944. Vienna Grand Prix.
888. **175.** 6 pf.+4 pf. green .. 5 5
889. 12 pf.+88 pf. red .. 5 5

1944. National Goldsmiths' Institution.
890. **176.** 6 pf.+4 pf. green .. 5 5
891. 12 pf.+88 pf. red .. 5 5

177. Posthorn. **178.** Eagle and Dragon.

1944. Stamp Day.
892. **177.** 6 pf.+24 pf. green .. 5 10

1944. Munich Rising. 21st Anniv.
893. **178.** 12 pf.+8 pf. red .. 5 10

179. Adolf Hitler. **180.** Count Anton Gunther.

1944.
894. **179.** 42 pf. green 5 20

1945. Oldenburg. 600th Anniv.
895. **180.** 6 pf.+14 pf. purple 5 8

181. "Home Guard." **182.** S.S. Troopers.

1945. Mobilization of "Home Guard".
896. **181.** 12 pf.+8 pf. red .. 8 15

1945. Third Reich. 12th Anniv.
897. **182.** 12 pf.+38 pf. red .. 1·00 4·00
898. – 12 pf.+38 pf. red .. 1·00 4·00
DESIGN: No. 898, S.A. man with torch.
For Nos. 899 onwards see after No. O 808.

MILITARY FIELDPOST STAMPS

M **1.** Junkers 52 Transport. M **2.**

1942. Air. No value indicated. Perf. or roul.
M 804. M **1.** (–) blue 5 5

1942. Parcel Post. Size 28×23 mm. No value indicated. Perf. or roul.
M 805. M **2.** (–) chestnut . 5 8
Nos. M 804/5 also exist overprinted **INSELPOST** in various types for use in Crete and the Aegean Islands and there are various other local field-post issues.

1944. Christmas Parcel Post. Size $22\frac{1}{2}\times$ 18 mm. No value indicated. Perf.
M 895. M **2.** (–) green 5 15

1944. For 2 kilo parcels. No value indicated. No. 785 optd. **FELDPOST 2 kg.**
M 896. (–) on 40 pf. mauve .. 5 15

NEWSPAPER STAMPS

N **1.** Newspaper Messenger and Globe.

1939.
N 727. N **1.** 5 pf. green 12 20
N 728. 10 pf. brown .. 12 20

OFFICIAL STAMPS

O **1.** O **2.**

1903.
O 82. O **1.** 2 pf. grey 50 75
O 83. 3 pf. brown 50 75
O 84. 5 pf. green 10 5
O 85. 10 pf. red 10 5
O 86. 20 pf. blue 10 5
O 87. 25 pf. black and red on yellow 10 35
O 88. 40 pf. black and red 25 35
O 89. 50 pf. black and purple on buff .. 10 25

1905.
O 90. O **2.** 2 pf. grey .. .. 20·00 20·00
O 91. 3 pf. brown .. .. 2·10 2·10
O 92. 5 pf. green .. .. 1·25 1·25
O 93. 10 pf. red 45 45
O 94. 20 pf. blue 85 70
O 95. 25 pf. black and red on yellow .. .. 8·50 8·50

O **3.** O **4.**

1920. Numeral designs as Types O **3** and O **4.**
O 117. 5 pf. green 12 20
O 118. 10 pf. red 35 30
O 119. 15 pf. brown .. 5 10
O 120. 20 pf. blue 12 12
O 121. 30 pf. orange on buff 5 12
O 122. 50 pf. violet on buff 20 12
O 123. 1 m. red on buff .. 2·40 75

1920. Similar designs but without figures "21".
O 124. 5 pf. green 25 75
O 125. 10 pf. red 5 5
O 126. 10 pf. orange .. 25 60·00
O 127. 15 pf. purple .. 5 5
O 128. 20 pf. blue 5 5
O 129. 30 pf. orange on rose 5 5
O 130. 40 pf. red 5 8
O 131. 50 pf. violet on buff 5 5
O 132. 60 pf. brown .. 5 12
O 133. 1 m. red on buff .. 5 5
O 134. 1 m. 25 blue on yellow 5 12
O 135a. 2 m. blue 5 5
O 136. 5 m. brown on yellow 5 5

1920. Official stamps of Bavaria optd. **Deutsches Reich.**
O 137. O **2.** 5 pf. green 5 12
O 138. 10 pf. orange .. 5 5
O 139. 15 pf. red 5 5
O 140. 20 pf. violet .. 5 5
O 141. 30 pf. blue 5 5
O 142. 40 pf. brown .. 5 5
O 143. O **3.** 50 pf. red 5 5
O 144. 60 pf. green .. 5 5
O 145. 70 pf. lilac 50 30
O 146. 75 pf. claret .. 5 20
O 147. 80 pf. blue 5 5
O 148. 90 pf. olive 45 35
O 149. O **4.** 1 m. brown 5 5
O 150. $1\frac{1}{4}$ m. green .. 5 5
O 151. $1\frac{1}{2}$ m. red 5 5
O 152. $2\frac{1}{2}$ m. blue 5 10
O 153. 3 m. red 5 20
O 154. 5 m. black .. .. 1·75 5·00

1920. Municipal Service stamps of Wurttemberg optd. **Deutsches Reich.**
O 155. M **1.** 5 pf. green .. .. 1·60 3·25
O 156. 10 pf. red .. .. 1·10 2·10
O 157. 15 pf. purple .. 85 1·90
O 158. 20 pf. blue .. .. 1·60 2·50
O 159. 50 pf. purple .. 2·00 4·25

1920. Official stamps of Wurttemberg optd. **Deutsches Reich.**
O 160. O **1.** 5 pf. green 20 70
O 161. 10 pf. red 5 20
O 162. 15 pf. purple .. 5 20
O 163. 20 pf. blue 5 20
O 164. 30 pf. black & orange 5 15
O 165. 40 pf. black and red 5 15
O 166. 50 pf. purple .. 8 30
O 167. 1 m. black and grey 8 75

O **5.** O **6.** O **7.**

1922. Figure designs.
O 220. O **5.** 75 pf. blue 5 25
O 218. – 3 m. brown on rose 5 5
O 219. O **6.** 10 m. green on rose 5 5
O 222. 20 m. violet on rose 5 5
O 223. 50 m. violet on rose 5 5
O 224. 100 m. red on rose .. 5 5

1923. Postage stamps optd. **Dienstmarke.**
O 274. **29.** 20 m. purple .. 5 1·00
O 275. 30 m. olive .. .. 5 6·00
O 276. **22.** 40 m. green 5 60
O 277. **30.** 200 m. red 5 12
O 278. 300 m. green .. 5 12
O 279. 400 m. brown .. 5 15
O 280. 500 m. orange .. 5 12
O 281. **33.** 100 M. grey .. .. 10 42·00
O 282. 200 M. brown .. 10 38·00
O 283. 2 MD. pink and green 10 35·00
O 284. 5 MD. orange & brown 10 11·00
O 285. 10 MD. green .. .. 1·90 38·00
O 286. 20 MD. green and brn. 1·40 45·00
O 287. 50 MD. blue .. .. 1·10 60·00

1923. Official stamps of 1920 and 1922 surch. **Tausend** or **Millionen** and figure.
O 312. – 5 T. on 5 m. brown on yellow 5 75
O 313. – 20 T. on 30 pf. orange on rose (No. O 129) 5 50
O 317. O **6.** 75 T. on 50 m. violet on rose 5 50
O 314. – 100 T. on 15 pf. pur. 5 75
O 315. – 250 T. on 10 pf. red (No. O 125) .. 5 35
O 318. – 400 T. on 15 pf. pur. 30 £100
O 319. – 800 T. on 30 pf. orge. on rose (No. O 129) 5 75
O 320. O **5.** 1 M. on 75 pf. blue .. 5 7·50
O 321. – 2 M. on 10 pf. red (No. O 125) .. 5 60
O 322. O **6.** 5 M. on 100 m. red on rose .. .. 5 1·25

1923. Nos. 352/7 optd. **Dienstmarke.**
O 358. **33.** 3 pf. brown 12 10
O 359. 5 pf. green 12 10
O 360. 10 pf. red 15 5
O 361. 20 pf. blue 40 5
O 362. 50 pf. orange .. 40 15
O 363. 100 pf. purple .. 1·25 1·75

1924. Optd. **Dienstmarke.**
O 376. **35.** 3 pf. brown 15 12
O 377. 5 pf. green 12 5
O 378. 10 pf. red 10 5
O 379. 20 pf. blue 15 5
O 380. 30 pf. claret 25 10
O 381. 40 pf. olive 30 12
O 382. 50 pf. orange .. 70 40
O 384. **40.** 60 pf. brown .. 60 50
O 385. 80 pf. deep green .. 2·75 7·50

1927.
O 424. O **7.** 3 pf. bistre 20 5
O 425. 4 pf. blue 10 5
O 426. 4 pf. grey 60 60
O 427. 5 pf. green 5 5
O 428. 6 pf. olive 12 5
O 429. 8 pf. green 12 5
O 430. 10 pf. red .. .. 3·25 2·10
O 433. 10 pf. brown .. 45 45
O 432. 10 pf. mauve .. 20 5
O 434. 12 pf. orange .. 15 5
O 435. 15 pf. red 60 8
O 437. 20 pf. green .. 1·00 45
O 438. 20 pf. grey 30 8
O 439. 30 pf. green .. 40 5
O 440. 40 pf. violet .. 40 5
O 441. 60 pf. brown .. 55 25

ILLUSTRATIONS British Commonwealth and all overprints and surcharges are FULL SIZE. Foreign Countries have been reduced to $\frac{3}{4}$-LINEAR.

O **8.**

1934.
O 526. O **8.** 3 pf. brown 5 5
O 527. 4 pf. blue 5 5
O 528. 5 pf. green 5 5
O 812. 6 pf. green 5 5
O 539. 6 pf. violet 5 5
O 530. 8 pf. red 15 5
O 531. 10 pf. brown .. 12 5
O 532. 12 pf. red 12 5
O 533. 15 pf. claret .. 35 55
O 534. 20 pf. blue 5 10
O 535. 30 pf. green .. 5 10
O 536. 40 pf. magenta .. 10 10
O 537. 50 pf. yellow .. 15 12
O 820. 50 pf. green .. 25 30

SPECIAL STAMPS FOR USE BY OFFICIALS OF THE NATIONAL SOCIALIST GERMAN WORKERS' PARTY.

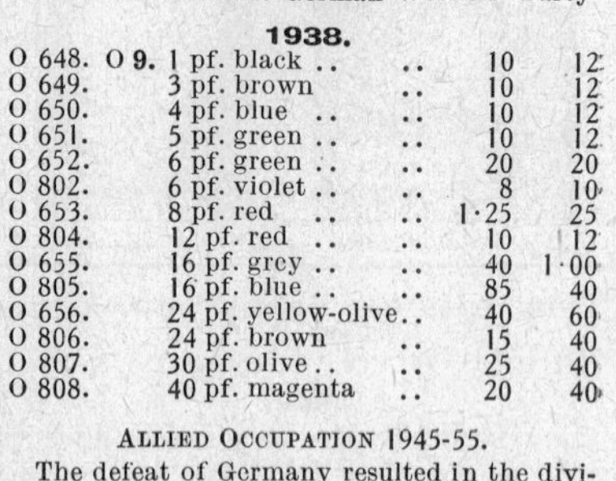

O **9.** N.S.D.A.P.
= National Socialist German Workers' Party

1938.
O 648. O **9.** 1 pf. black 10 12
O 649. 3 pf. brown .. 10 12
O 650. 4 pf. blue 10 12
O 651. 5 pf. green 10 12
O 652. 6 pf. green 20 20
O 802. 6 pf. violet 8 10
O 653. 8 pf. red .. .. 1·25 25
O 804. 12 pf. red 10 12
O 655. 16 pf. grey .. .. 40 1·00
O 805. 16 pf. blue 85 40
O 656. 24 pf. yellow-olive .. 40 60
O 806. 24 pf. brown .. 15 40
O 807. 30 pf. olive 25 40
O 808. 40 pf. magenta .. 20 40

ALLIED OCCUPATION 1945-55.

The defeat of Germany resulted in the division of the country into four zones of occupation (British, American, French and Russian), while Berlin was placed under joint allied control.

The territory occupied by the Anglo-American and French Zones was administered by the German Federal Republic (West Germany) which was set up in September 1949.

By the Nine Power Agreement of 3rd October 1954, the occupation of West Germany was ended and full sovereignty was granted to the German Federal Government as from 5th May, 1955.

The territory in the Russian Zone was administered by the German Democratic Republic (East Germany) which was set up on 7th October, 1949.

Separate issues for the Western Sectors of Berlin came into being in 1948. The Russian Zone issues inscribed "STADT BERLIN" were for use in the Russian sector of the city and Brandenburg and these were superseded first by the General Issues of the Russian Zone and then by the stamps of East Germany.

100 pfennige = 1 Reichsmark.
21.6.48. 100 pfennige = 1 Deutsche Mark (West).
24.6.48. 100 pfennige = 1 Deutsche Mark (East).

I. ALLIED OCCUPATION.

A. American, British and Russian Zones 1946-48.

These always used the same stamps (Nos. 899/956). It had been intended that these should be used throughout all four zones, but until the creation of the German Federal Republic, in Sept. 1949, the French Zone always had its own stamps, while after the revaluation of the currency in June 1948, separate stamps were again issued for the Russian Zone.

183. Numeral. 188. 1160: Leipzig obtains Charter.

1946.

899.	183.	1 pf. black	5	5
900.		2 pf. black	5	5
901.		3 pf. brown	5	5
902.		4 pf. blue	5	10
903.		5 pf. green	5	5
904.		6 pf. violet	5	5
905.		8 pf. red	5	5
906.		10 pf. brown	5	5
907.		12 pf. red	5	5
908.		12 pf. grey	5	5
909.		15 pf. claret	5	5
910.		15 pf. green	5	5
911.		16 pf. green	5	5
912.		20 pf. blue	5	5
913.		24 pf. brown	5	5
914.		25 pf. blue	5	12
915.		25 pf. orange	5	5
916.		30 pf. olive	5	5
917.		40 pf. purple	5	5
918.		42 pf. green	30	75
919.		45 pf. red	5	5
920.		50 pf. green	5	5
921.		60 pf. red	5	5
922.		75 pf. blue	5	5
923.		80 pf. blue	5	5
924.		84 pf. green	5	5
925.		1 m. ol. (24½ × 30 mm.)	5	5

1947. Leipzig Spring Fair. Inscr. "LEIPZIGER MESSE 1947".

926.	188.	24 pf. + 26 pf. brown ..	5	10
927.	–	60 pf. + 40 pf. blue ..	8	12

DESIGN: 60 pf. 1268: Foreign merchants at Leipzig Fair.

185. Gardener. 186. "Dove of Peace".

1947.

928.	185.	2 pf. black	5	5
929.		6 pf. violet	5	5
930.	A.	8 pf. red	5	5
931.		10 pf. green	5	5
932.	B.	12 pf. grey	5	5
933.	185.	15 pf. brown	5	5
934.	C.	16 pf. green	5	5
935.	A.	20 pf. blue	5	5
936.	C.	24 pf. brown	5	5
937.	185.	25 pf. yellow	5	5
938.	B.	30 pf. red	5	12
939.	A.	40 pf. mauve	5	5
940.	C.	50 pf. blue	5	12
941.	B.	60 pf. brown	5	5
943.		80 pf. blue	5	5
944.	C.	84 pf. green	5	10
945.	186.	1 m. olive	5	5
946.		2 m. violet	5	5
947.		3 m. lake	5	12
948.		5 m. blue	20	55

DESIGNS: A, Sower. B, Labourer. C, Bricklayer and reaper.

187. Dr. von Stephan.

1947. Von Stephan. 50th Death Anniv.

949.	187.	24 pf. brown	5	5
950.		75 pf. blue	5	10

1947. Leipzig Autumn Fair. As T 188.

951.	12 pf. red	5	5
952.	75 pf. blue	5	8

DESIGNS: 12 pf. 1497: Maximilian I granting Charter. 75 pf. 1365: Assessment and Collection of Ground Rents.

1948. Leipzig Spring Fair. As T 188 but dated "1948".

953.	50 pf. blue	5	5
954.	84 pf. green	5	8

DESIGNS: 50 pf. 1388: At the customs barrier. 84 pf. 1433: Bringing merchandise.

For similar types, dated "1948", "1949" or "1950", but with premium values, see Nos. R 31/2, R 51/2, R 60/1, E 7/8.

189. Weighing Goods.

1948. Hanover Trade Fair.

955.	189.	24 pf. red	5	5
956.		50 pf. blue	5	5

B. Anglo-American Zones.

(a) Military Government Issue, 1945-46.

A 1. (A 2.)

1945.

A 16.	A 1.	1 pf. black	5	5
A 1.		3 pf. violet	5	5
A 2.		4 pf. grey	5	5
A 3.		5 pf. green	5	5
A 4.		6 pf. yellow	5	5
A 5.		8 pf. orange	5	5
A 6.		10 pf. brown	5	5
A 7.		12 pf. purple	5	5
A 8.		15 pf. red	5	5
A 25.		16 pf. green	5	12
A 26.		20 pf. blue	5	5
A 27.		24 pf. brown	12	50
A 9.		25 pf. blue	5	5
A 29.	–	30 pf. olive	5	10
A 30.	–	40 pf. mauve	5	5
A 31.	–	42 pf. green	5	5
A 32.	–	50 pf. slate	5	10
A 33.	–	60 pf. plum	5	10
A 34.	–	80 pf. blue	5·00	8·50
A 35.	–	1 m. green	1·10	1·25

Values 30 pf. to 80 pf. are size 22 × 25 mm. and 1 m. size 25 × 29½ mm.

(b) Civil Government Issues, 1948-49.

1948. Currency Reform. Optd. I with Type A 2 or II with multiple posthorns over whole stamp.

(a) On Pictorial issue of 1947, Nos. 928/44.

		I.		II.	
A 36.	2 pf. black	5	5	30	60
A 37.	6 pf. violet	5	5	45	85
A 38.	8 pf. red ..	5	5	40	50
A 39.	10 pf. green	10	10	5	5
A 40.	12 pf. grey	10	5	35	35
A 41.	15 pf. brown	2·75	3·75	10	12
A 42.	16 pf. green	50	50	10	8
A 43.	20 pf. blue	25	35	10	8
A 44.	24 pf. brown	5	5	30	40
A 45.	25 pf. yellow	20	20	2·50	3·75
A 46.	30 pf. red ..	1·00	1·75	12	10
A 47.	40 pf. mauve	35	30	12	10
A 48.	50 pf. blue	35	30	15	15
A 49.	60 pf. brown	30	30	15	15
A 51.	80 pf. blue	55	75	20	15
A 52.	84 pf. green	1·75	2·25	45	30

(b) On Numeral issue of 1946, Nos. 899 to 924.

			I.		II.	
A 53.	183.	2 pf. blk	2·50	3·00	8·00	11·00
A 54.		8 pf. red	7·00	8·00	14·00	17·00
A 55.		10 pf. brn.	35	95	14·00	16·00
A 56.		12 pf. red	4·50	5·50	5·50	6·50
A 57.		12 pf. grey	75·00	95·00	£150	£190
A 58.		15 pf. clar.	4·00	5·00	4·50	5·50
A 59.		15 pf. grn.	1·75	2·25	30	95
A 60.		16 pf. grn.	17·00	21·00	15·00	19·00
A 61.		24 pf. brn.	21·00	25·00	21·00	25·00
A 62.		25 pf. blue	6·00	7·50	6·50	20·00
A 63.		25 pf. orge.	55	1·40	17·00	21·00
A 64.		30 pf. olive	90	1·40	75	1·10
A 65.		40 pf. pur.	22·00	27·00	28·00	32·00
A 66.		45 pf. red	1·10	1·50	1·50	1·90
A 67.		50 pf. grn.	1·10	1·50	1·50	1·75
A 68.		75 pf. blue	3·25	3·75	1·60	2·25
A 69.		84 pf. grn.	3·25	3·75	1·50	1·90

A 3. Crowned Head. A 4. Cologne Cathedral.

1948. 700th Anniv. of Cologne Cathedral and Restoration Fund. Dated "1248-1948".

A 70.	A 3.	6 pf. + 4 pf. brown .	35	50
A 71.	–	12 pf. + 8 pf. blue	70	1·10
A 72.	–	24 pf. + 16 pf. red	1·10	1·90
A 73.	A 4.	50 pf. + 50 pf. blue	4·75	7·00

DESIGNS—As T A 3. 12 pf. The Three Wise Men. 24 pf. Cologne Cathedral.

A 5. The Romer, Frankfurt-on-Main. A 6. Frauenkirche, Munich. A 7. Holstentor Lubeck.

1948. Various designs.

A 74.	A 5.	2 pf. black	5	5
A 75.	A 6.	4 pf. brown ..	12	5
A 76.	A.	5 pf. blue	12	5
A 77.	A 6.	6 pf. brown ..	5	12
A 78.		6 pf. orange ..	10	5
A 79.	A 5.	8 pf. yellow ..	12	25
A 80.	A 6.	8 pf. slate	12	5
A 81a.	A	10 pf. green ..	15	5
A 82.	A 6.	15 pf. orange ..	45	1·25
A 83.	A 5.	15 pf. violet ..	30	5
A 84.		16 pf. green ..	15	30
A 85.		20 pf. blue	35	75
A 86.	B.	20 pf. red	35	5
A 87.		24 pf. red	15	12
A 88.	A.	25 pf. red	45	5
A 89.	B.	30 pf. blue	65	5
A 90.	A 6.	30 pf. red	75	1·50
A 91.	A.	40 pf. mauve ..	95	5
A 92.	B.	50 pf. blue	60	75
A 93.	A 6.	50 pf. green ..	85	5
A 94.	A.	60 pf. purple ..	1·50	5
A 95.	B.	80 pf. mauve ..	2·00	5
A 96.	A 6.	84 pf. purple ..	50	1·90
A 97.	A.	90 pf. mauve ..	1·75	5
A 98.	A 7.	1 Dm. green ..	10·00	5
A 99.		2 Dm. violet ..	10·00	25
A 100.		3 Dm. magenta ..	10·00	45
A 101.		5 Dm. blue	15·00	1·50

DESIGNS—As Type A 5/7: A. Cologne Cathedral. B. Brandenburg Gate.

A 8. Brandenburg Gate, Berlin.

1948. Aid to Berlin.

A 102.	A 8.	10 pf. + 5 pf. grn. ..	1·75	2·50
A 103.		20 pf. + 10 pf. red ..	1·90	2·50

A 9. Herman Hillebrant Wedigh (after Holbein). A 10. Racing Cyclists.

1949. Hanover Trade Fair.

A 104.	A 9.	10 pf. green ..	1·25	65
A 105.		20 pf. red	1·25	65
A 106.		30 pf. blue ..	95	1·10

1949. Across Germany Cycle Race.

A 107.	A 10.	10 pf. + 5 pf. grn.	2·25	1·90
A 108.		20 pf. + 10 pf. brn.	5·00	7·00

A 11. Goethe in Italy. A 12. Goethe.

1949. Goethe (poet). Birth Bicent. Inscr. "1749 + 28 AUGUST + 1949".

A 109.	A 11.	10 pf. + 5 pf. grn.	1·75	1·60
A 110.	A 12.	20 pf. + 10 pf. red	2·25	2·25
A 111.	–	30 pf. + 15 pf. bl.	6·00	9·00

DESIGN—VERT. 30 pf. Profile portrait.

The Anglo-American Zones were incorporated in West Germany in September, 1949.

C. French Zone.

(a) General Issues, 1945-46.

F 1. Arms of the Palatinate. F 2. Goethe.

1945. Arms designs inscr. "ZONE FRANÇAISE BRIEFPOST".

F 1.	F 1.	1 pf. green, black & lem.	5	5
F 2.	–	3 pf. orge., black & red	5	5
F 3.	–	5 pf. blk., orge. & brn.	5	5
F 4.	–	8 pf. red, orge. & brn.	5	5
F 5.	F 1.	10 pf. grn., brn. & lem.	1·00	1·50
F 6.	–	12 pf. orge., blk. & red	5	5
F 7.	–	15 pf. bl., blk. & red	5	5
F 8.	–	20 pf. blk., orge. & red	5	5
F 9.	–	24 pf. bl., black & red	5	5
F 10.	–	30 pf. red, orge. & blk.	5	5

ARMS: 3 pf., 12 pf. Rhineland. 5 pf., 20 pf. Wurttemberg. 8 pf., 30 pf. Baden. 15 pf., 24 pf. Saar.

1945.

F 11.	F 2.	1 m. purple ..	40	1·00
F 12.	–	2 m. blue (Schiller) ..	35	1·25
F 13.	–	5 m. red (Heine) ..	45	1·25

(b) Baden, 1947-49.

FB 1. J. P. Hebel. FB 2. Rastatt Castle.

FB 3. Hollental Black Forest. FB 4. Freiburg Cathedral.

1947. Inscr. "BADEN".

FB 1.	FB 1.	2 pf. grey ..	5	5
FB 2.	–	3 pf. brown ..	5	5
FB 3.	–	10 pf. blue ..	5	5
FB 4.	FB 1.	12 pf. green ..	5	5
FB 5.	–	15 pf. violet ..	5	5
FB 6.	FB 2.	16 pf. green ..	5	25
FB 7.	–	20 pf. blue ..	5	5
FB 8.	FB 2.	24 pf. red ..	5	5
FB 9.	–	45 pf. magenta ..	5	12
FB 10.	FB 1.	60 pf. orange ..	5	5
FB 11.	–	75 pf. blue ..	5	12
FB 12.	FB 3.	84 pf. green ..	5	35
FB 13.	FB 4.	1 m. brown ..	5	8

DESIGNS—SMALL SIZE: 3 pf., 15 pf., 45 pf. Badensian girl and sailing boats. 10 pf., 20 pf., 75 pf. Hans Grien.

1948. Currency Reform. As 1947 issue.

(a) Value in pfennig.

FB 14.	FB 1.	2 pf. orange ..	12	12
FB 15.	–	6 pf. brown ..	12	5
FB 16.	–	10 pf. brown ..	15	5
FB 17.	FB 1.	12 pf. red ..	15	5
FB 18.	–	15 pf. blue ..	20	12
FB 19.	FB 2.	24 pf. green ..	35	5
FB 20.	–	30 pf. magenta ..	60	20
FB 21.	–	50 pf. blue ..	60	5

(b) New currency. Value in "D.PF" or "D.M." (= "Deutschpfennig" or "Deutschmark").

FB 22.	–	8 dpf. green ..	30	50
FB 23.	FB 2.	16 dpf. violet ..	45	50
FB 24.	–	20 dpf. brown ..	1·00	50
FB 25.	FB 1.	60 dpf. grey ..	2·00	10
FB 26.	FB 3.	84 dpf. red ..	2·75	95
FB 27.	FB 4.	1 dm. blue ..	2·75	95

DESIGNS: 6 pf., 15 pf. Badensian girl. 10 pf., 20 dpf. Hans Grien. 8 dpf., 30 pf. Black Forest girl in festive head-dress. 59 pf. Grandduchess Stephanie of Baden.

Nos. FB 14/21 were sold on the new currency basis though not inscribed "D.PF.".

1948. As 1947 issue, but "PF" omitted.

FB 28.	FB 1.	2 pf. orange ..	45	30
FB 29.	–	4 pf. violet ..	25	20
FB 30.	–	5 pf. blue ..	50	30
FB 31.	–	6 pf. brown ..	9·00	3·75
FB 32.	–	8 pf. claret ..	60	30
FB 33.	–	10 pf. green ..	60	10
FB 34.	–	20 pf. magenta ..	1·00	20

FB 35. – 40 pf. brown .. 30·00 35·00
FB 36. FB 1. 80 pf. red .. 6·00 2·50
FB 37. FB 3. 90 pf. claret .. 17·00 22·00
DESIGNS—SMALL SIZE: 4 pf., 40 pf. Rastatt. 5 pf., 6 pf. Badensian girl and sailing boats. 8 pf. Black Forest girl in festive head-dress. 10 pf., 20 pf. Portrait of Hans Baldung Grien.

FB 5. Cornhouse, Freiburg.

FB 6. Arms of Baden.

1949. Freiburg Rebuilding Fund.
FB 38. FB 5. 4 pf.+16 pf. vio. 2·25 3·00
FB 39. – 10 pf.+20 pf. grn. 2·50 3·25
FB 40. – 20 pf.+30 pf. red 3·50 4·50
FB 41. – 30 pf.+50 pf. blue 4·50 5·50
DESIGNS: 10 pf. Freiburg Cathedral. 20 pf. Trumpeting angel, Freiburg. 30 pf. "Fischbrunnen," Freiburg.

1949. Red Cross Fund.
FB 42. FB 6. 10 pf.+20 pf. grn. 9·50 14·00
FB 43. 20 pf.+40 pf. lilac 9·50 14·00
FB 44. 30 pf.+60 pf. bl. 9·50 14·00
FB 45. 40 pf.+80 pf. grey 9·50 14·00

FB 7. Seehof Hotel, Constance.

1949. Engineers' Congress, Constance.
FB 46. FB 7. 30 pf. blue .. 8·00 10·00

FB 8. Goethe.

FB 10. Conradin Kreutzer.

FB 9. Carl Schurz and Revolutionary Scene.

1949. Goethe. Birth Bicent. Inscr. "1749 GOETHE 1949".
FB 47. FB 8. 10 pf.+5 pf. grn. 4·25 5·00
FB 48. – 20 pf.+10 pf. red 4·25 5·00
FB 49. – 30 pf.+15 pf. blue 6·00 8·00

1949. Rastatt Insurrection. Cent.
FB 50. FB 9. 10 pf.+5 pf. grn. 3·75 5·00
FB 51. 20 pf.+10 pf. mag. 3·75 5·00
FB 52. 30 pf.+15 pf. bl. 3·75 5·00

1949. Conradin Kreutzer (composer). Death Cent.
FB 53. FB 10. 10 pf. green .. 1·00 1·25

FB 11. 1849 Mail-coach.

FB 12. Posthorn and Globe.

1949. 1st German Postage Stamps. Cent.
FB 54. FB 11. 10 pf. green .. 1·50 1·90
FB 55. – 20 pf. brown .. 1·50 1·90
DESIGN — HORIZ. 20 pf. Postal motor-coach and trailer.

1949. U.P.U. 75th Anniv.
FB 56. FB 12. 20 pf. red .. 2·50 4·00
FB 57. 30 pf. blue .. 2·50 2·00

(c) Rhineland Palatinate, 1947-49.

FR 1. "Porta Nigra" Trier.

FR 2. Karl Marx.

FR 3. Statue of Charlemagne.

FR 4. St. Martin.

1947. Inscr. "RHEINLAND-PFALZ".
FR 1. – 2 pf. grey .. 5 5
FR 2. – 3 pf. brown .. 5 5
FR 3. – 10 pf. blue .. 5 5
FR 4. FR 1. 12 pf. green .. 5 5
FR 5. FR 2. 15 pf. violet .. 5 5
FR 6. – 16 pf. green .. 5 5
FR 7. – 20 pf. blue .. 5 5
FR 8. – 24 pf. red .. 5 5
FR 9. – 30 pf. mauve .. 5 20
FR 10. – 45 pf. mauve .. 5 10
FR 11. – 50 pf. blue .. 5 25
FR 12. – 60 pf. orange .. 5 5
FR 13. – 75 pf. blue .. 5 5
FR 14. – 84 pf. green .. 8 25
FR 15. FR 3. 1 m. brown .. 5 12
DESIGNS—SMALL SIZE: 2 pf., 60 pf. Beethoven's death mask. 3 pf. Baron von Ketteler, Bishop of Mainz. 10 pf. Girl vintager. 16 pf. Rocks at Arnweiler. 20 pf. Palatinate village house. 24 pf. Worms Cathedral. 30 pf., 75 pf. Gutenberg (printer). 45 pf., 50 pf. Mainz Cathedral. LARGE SIZE—HORIZ. 84 pf. Gutenfels Castle and Rhine.

1948. Currency Reform. As 1947 issue.
(a) Value in pfennig.
FR 16. – 2 pf. orange .. 12 12
FR 17. – 6 pf. brown .. 12 12
FR 18. – 10 pf. brown .. 25 5
FR 19. FR 1. 12 pf. red .. 15 5
FR 20. FR 2. 15 pf. blue .. 50 20
FR 21. – 24 pf. green .. 20 5
FR 22. – 30 pf. magenta .. 50 5
FR 23. – 50 pf. blue .. 60 5

(b) New currency. Value in "D.PF." or "D.M." (= "Deutschpfennig" or "Deutschmark").
FR 24. FR 1. 8 dpf. green .. 25 55
FR 25. – 16 dpf. violet .. 25 25
FR 26. – 20 dpf. brown .. 60 30
FR 27. – 60 dpf. grey .. 3·75 12
FR 28. – 84 dpf. red .. 1·50 1·00
FR 29. FR 3. 1 dm. blue .. 1·50 85
DESIGNS—SMALL SIZE: 6 pf. Baron von Ketteler. 30 pf. Mainz Cathedral. 50 pf. Gutenberg (printer). Others as 1947 issue.
Nos. FR 16/23 were sold on the new currency basis though not inscribed "D.PF.".

1948. Ludwigshafen Explosion Relief Fund.
FR 30. FR 4. 20 pf.+30 pf. magenta .. 60 1·00
FR 31. – 30 pf.+50 pf. blue 60 1·00
DESIGN: 30 pf. St. Christopher.

1948. Inscr. "RHEINLAND-PFALZ". As 1947 issue, but "PF" omitted.
FR 32. – 2 pf. orange .. 10 10
FR 33. – 4 pf. violet .. 20 10
FR 34. FR 2. 5 pf. blue .. 30 12
FR 35. – 6 pf. brown .. 12·00 3·25
FR 36. FR 1. 8 pf. claret .. 25·00 30·00
FR 37. – 10 pf. green .. 35 12
FR 38. – 20 pf. magenta .. 35 12
FR 39. – 40 pf. brown .. 90 60
FR 40. FR 1. 80 pf. red .. 1·10 1·50
FR 41. – 90 pf. claret .. 1·60 4·50
DESIGNS—SMALL SIZE: 4 pf. Rocks at Arnweiler. 40 pf. Worms Cathedral. LARGE SIZE—HORIZ. 90 pf. Gutenfels Castle and Rhine. Others as 1947–48 issues.

1949. Red Cross Fund. As Type FB 5 of Baden, but Arms of Rhineland and inscr. "RHEINLAND/PFALZ".
FR 42. 10 pf.+20 pf. green .. 8·00 10·00
FR 43. 20 pf.+40 pf. lilac .. 8·00 10·00
FR 44. 30 pf.+60 pf. blue .. 8·00 10·00
FR 45. 40 pf.+80 pf. grey .. 8·00 10·00

1949. Goethe. Birth Bicent. As Nos. FB 47/9 of Baden.
FR 46. 10 pf.+5 pf. green .. 1·60 2·75
FR 47. 20 pf.+10 pf. red .. 1·60 2·75
FR 48. 30 pf.+15 pf. blue .. 4·00 5·00

1949. German Postage Stamp Cent. As Nos. FB 54/5 of Baden.
FR 49. 10 pf. green .. .. 4·00 5·50
FR 50. 20 pf. brown .. .. 4·00 5·50

1949. U.P.U. 75th Anniv. As Nos. FB 56/7 of Baden.
FR 51. 20 pf. red .. .. 2·25 4·00
FR 52. 30 pf. blue .. .. 2·25 2·00

(d) Saar, 1945–7.

The Saar District, from 1945 to 1947 part of the French Zone, also had its own stamps, but as it was in a different political category, we list its stamps for convenience of reference all together under SAAR.

(e) Wurttemberg, 1947-49.

FW 1. Fr. von Schiller.

FW 2. Bebenhausen Castle.

FW 3. Lichtenstein Castle.

1947. Inscr. "WURTTEMBERG".
FW 1. FW 1. 2 pf. grey .. 5 5
FW 2. – 3 pf. brown .. 5 5
FW 3. – 10 pf. blue .. 5 5
FW 4. FW 1. 12 pf. green .. 5 5
FW 5. – 15 pf. violet .. 5 5
FW 6. FW 2. 16 pf. green .. 5 15
FW 7. – 20 pf. blue .. 5 5
FW 8. FW 2. 24 pf. red .. 5 5
FW 9. – 45 pf. magenta .. 5 5
FW 10. FW 1. 60 pf. orange .. 5 15
FW 11. – 75 pf. blue .. 5 15
FW 12. FW 3. 84 pf. green .. 5 25
FW 13. – 1 m. brown .. 5 15
DESIGNS—SMALL SIZE: 3 pf., 15 pf., 45 pf. Holderlin (poet). 10 pf., 20 pf., 75 pf. Wangen Gate. LARGE SIZE—VERT. 1 m. Zwiefalten Monastery Church.

1948. Currency Reform. As 1947 issue.
(a) Value in pfennig.
FW 14. FW 1. 2 pf. orange .. 10 15
FW 15. – 6 pf. brown .. 10 8
FW 16. – 10 pf. brown .. 10 10
FW 17. FW 1. 12 pf. red .. 15 5
FW 18. – 15 pf. blue .. 30 15
FW 19. FW 2. 24 pf. green .. 40 5
FW 20. – 30 pf. magenta .. 50 5
FW 21. – 50 pf. blue .. 1·10 5

(b) New currency. Value in "D.PF." or "D.M." (= "Deutschpfennig" or "Deutschmark").
FW 22. – 8 dpf. green .. 30 60
FW 23. FW 2. 16 dpf. violet .. 30 60
FW 24. – 20 dpf. brown .. 80 25
FW 25. FW 1. 60 dpf. grey .. 5·50 10
FW 26. FW 3. 84 dpf. red .. 1·90 90
FW 27. – 1 dm. blue .. 1·90 75
DESIGNS—SMALL SIZE: 6 pf., 15 pf. Fr. Holderlin (poet). 8 dpf., 30 pf. Waldsee Castle. 50 pf. Ludwig Uhland (poet). Others as 1947 issue.
Nos. FW 14/21 were sold on the new currency basis though not inscribed "D.PF."

1948. Inscr. "WURTTEMBERG". As 1947 issue, but "PF" omitted.
FW 28. FW 1. 2 pf. orange .. 75 25
FW 29. FW 2. 4 pf. violet .. 75 25
FW 30. – 5 pf. blue .. 1·25 55
FW 31. – 6 pf. brown .. 2·75 2·00
FW 32. – 8 pf. claret .. 3·00 75
FW 33. – 10 pf. green .. 3·00 5
FW 34. – 20 pf. magenta .. 3·00 5
FW 35. FW 2. 40 pf. brown .. 12·00 10·00
FW 36. FW 1. 80 pf. red .. 25·00 6·50
FW 37. FW 3. 90 pf. claret .. 29·00 30·00
DESIGNS—SMALL SIZE: 5 pf., 6 pf. Holderlin. Others as 1947–48 issues.

FW 4. Isny and Coat of Arms.

FW 5. Gustav Werner.

1949. Ski Championships (Northern Combination) at Isny/Allgau.
FW 38. FW 4. 10 pf.+4 pf. grn. 1·60 2·00
FW 39. – 20 pf.+6 pf. lake 1·60 2·00
DESIGN: 20 pf. Skier and view of Isny.

1949. Red Cross Fund. As Type FB 5 of Baden, but Arms of Wurttemberg and inscr. "WURTTEMBERG".
FW 40. 10 pf.+20 pf. green .. 16·00 23·00
FW 41. 20 pf.+40 pf. lilac .. 16·00 23·00
FW 42. 30 pf.+60 pf. blue .. 16·00 23·00
FW 43. 40 pf.+80 pf. grey .. 16·00 23·00

1949. Goethe. Birth Bicent. As Nos. FB 47/9 of Baden.
FW 44. 10 pf.+5 pf. green .. 3·75 4·50
FW 45. 20 pf.+10 pf. red .. 4·50 7·00
FW 46. 30 pf.+15 pf. blue .. 6·00 8·50

1949. Christian Institution "Zum Bruderhaus" Cent.
FW 47. FW 5. 10 pf.+5 pf. grn. 1·75 2·50
FW 48. 20 pf.+10 pf. pur. 1·75 2·50

1949. German Postage Stamp Cent. As Nos. FB 54/5 of Baden.
FW 49. 10 pf. green .. .. 3·00 4·00
FW 50. 20 pf. brown .. .. 3·25 4·25

1949. U.P.U. 75th Anniv. As Nos. FB 56/7 of Baden.
FW 51. 20 pf. red .. .. 2·25 4·00
FW 52. 30 pf. blue .. .. 2·25 2·00
The French Zone was incorporated in West Germany in September, 1949.

D. Russian Zone.

For a list of the stamps issued by the Russian Zone Provincial Administrations of Berlin (Brandenburg), Mecklenburg - Vorpommern, Saxony (Halle, Leipzig and Dresden) and Thuringia, see Stanley Gibbons Europe Catalogue, volume 2.

General Issues.

In February 1946, the Provincial Issues were replaced by the General Issues, Nos. 899/956 until the revaluation of the currency in June 1948, when Nos. 928/44 were brought into use handstamped with District names and numbers as a control measure pending the introduction of the following overprinted stamps on 3rd July. There are over 1,900 different types of district handstamp.

R 1. Arms of Berlin.

R 2. Kathe Kollwitz.

1948. Optd. **Besatzungs Zone**.
(a) On Pictorial issue of 1947, Nos. 928/44.
R 1. 2 pf. black 5 5
R 2. 6 pf. violet 5 5
R 3. 8 pf. red 5 5
R 4. 10 pf. green 5 5
R 5. 12 pf. grey 5 5
R 6. 15 pf. brown 5 5
R 7. 16 pf. green 5 5
R 8. 20 pf. blue 5 5
R 9. 24 pf. brown 5 5
R 10. 25 pf. yellow 5 10
R 11. 30 pf. red 5 5
R 12. 40 pf. mauve 5 5
R 13. 50 pf. blue 12 12
R 14. 60 pf. brown 15 5
R 16. 80 pf. blue 20 25
R 17. 84 pf. green 20 25

(b) On Numerical issue of 1946, Nos. 903, etc.
R 18. 183. 5 pf. green 5 5
R 19. 30 pf. olive 12 25
R 20. 45 pf. red 5 12
R 21. 75 pf. blue 5 12
R 22. 84 pf. green 5 12

(c) On stamps inscr. "STADT BERLIN".
R 23. R 1. 5 pf. green 5 5
R 25. – 6 pf. violet 5 5
R 26. – 8 pf. orange 5 5
R 27. – 10 pf. brown 5 5
R 28. – 12 pf. red 10 15
R 29. – 20 pf. blue 5 12
R 30. – 30 pf. olive 5 15
DESIGNS: 6 pf. Bear with spade. 8 pf. Bear on shield. 10 pf. Bear holding brick. 12 pf. Bear carrying plank. 20 pf. Bear on small shield. 30 pf. Oak sapling amid ruins.

1948. Leipzig Autumn Fair. As T 188 but dated "1948".
R 31. 16 pf.+9 pf. purple .. 8 8
R 32. 50 pf.+25 pf. blue .. 12 12
DESIGNS: 16 pf. 1459: The first Spring Fair. 50 pf. 1469: Foreign merchants displaying cloth.

1948. Politicians, Artists and Scientists.
R 33. R 2. 2 pf. grey 5 5
R 34. – 6 pf. violet 5 5
R 35. – 8 pf. brown 12 5
R 36. – 10 pf. green 12 5
R 37. – 12 pf. blue .. .. 1·10 10
R 38. – 15 pf. brown 15 30
R 39. – 16 pf. blue 15 12
R 40. R 2. 20 pf. purple 15 15
R 41. – 24 pf. red .. .. 1·40 10
R 42. – 25 pf. olive 30 35
R 43. – 30 pf. red 20 15
R 44. – 40 pf. purple 30 20
R 45. – 50 pf. blue 30 12
R 46. – 60 pf. green 45 12
R 47. – 80 pf. blue 55 12
E 95. – 80 pf. red .. .. 2·00 3·00
R 48. – 84 pf. brown 75 30
PORTRAITS: 6 pf., 40 pf. Gerhardt Hauptmann. 8 pf., 50 pf. Karl Marx. 10 pf., 84 pf. August Bebel. 12 pf., 30 pf. Friedrich Engels. 15 pf., 60 pf. G. F. W. Hegel. 16 pf., 25 pf. Rudolf Virchow. 24 pf., 80 pf. Ernst Thaelmann.

R 3.

R 4. Liebknecht and Rosa Luxemburg.

1948. Stamp Day.
R 49. R 3. 12 pf.+3 pf. red .. 5 8

1949. Karl Liebknecht and Rosa Luxemburg (revolutionaries). 30th Death Anniv.
R 50. R 4. 24 pf. red 12 15

1949. Leipzig Spring Fair. As T **188**, but dated "1949".
R 51. 30 pf.+15 pf. red .. 55 90
R 52. 50 pf.+25 pf. blue .. 1·00 1·25
DESIGNS: 30 pf. 1st Neubau Town-hall bazaar, 1556. 50 pf. Italian merchants at Leipzig. 1536.

R 5. Dove.

R 6. Goethe.

1949. 3rd German Peoples' Congress.
R 53. R 5. 24 pf. red 25 30

1949. Optd. **3. Deutscher Volkskongress 29.-30 Mai 1949.**
R 54. R 5. 24 pf. red 25 30

1949. Goethe. Birth Bicent. Portraits of Goethe.
R 55. R 6. 6 pf.+4 pf. violet 55 55
R 56. – 12 pf.+8 pf. brn. 40 40
R 57. – 24 pf.+16 pf. lake 35 35
R 58. – 50 pf.+25 pf. blue 40 40
R 59. – 84 pf.+36 pf. grey 75 75

1949. Leipzig Autumn Fair. As T 188 but dated "1949".
R 60. 12 pf.+8 pf. slate .. 1·00 1·10
R 61. 24 pf.+16 pf. lake .. 1·00 1·40
DESIGNS: 12 pf. Russian merchants, 1650. 24 pf. Geothe at Fair, 1765.

The Russian Zone was incorporated in East Germany in October, 1949.

II. WEST GERMANY.

(Federal Republic.)

The German Federal Republic was set up on 23 May, 1949, and it administers the territory which formerly came under the British, American and French Zones.

202. Constructing Parliament Building.

203. Reproduction of T 1 of Bavaria.

1949. Opening of West German Parliament, Bonn.
1033. 202. 10 pf. green .. .. 20·00 17·00
1034. 20 pf. red .. .. 24·00 18·00

1949. Cent. of German Postage Stamps. Inscr. as in T **203**.
1035. 203. 10 pf.+2 pf. blk.& grn. 6·00 6·00
1036. – 20 pf. blue and red 13·00 12·00
1037. – 30 pf. brown and blue 24·00 30·00
DESIGNS: 20 pf., 30 pf. Reproductions of T 2 of Bavaria.

204. Dr. von Stephan, Old G.P.O., Berlin and Standehaus, Berne.

205. St. Elizabeth of Thuringia.

1949. U.P.U. 75th Anniv.
1038. 204. 30 pf. blue .. .. 24·00 24·00

1949. Refugees' Relief Fund. Inscr. as in T **205**.
1039. 205. 8 pf.+2 pf. purple .. 9·00 8·00
1040. – 10 pf.+5 pf. green 9·00 8·00
1041. – 20 pf.+10 pf. red .. 10·00 8·00
1042. – 30 pf.+15 pf. blue 40·00 45·00
PORTRAITS: 10 pf. Paracelsus von Hohenheim. 20 pf. F. W. A. Frebel. 30 pf. J. H. Wichern.

206. J. S. Bach's Seal.

207. Numeral and Posthorn.

1950. Bach's 200th Death Anniv.
1043. 206. 10 pf.+2 pf. green .. 30·00 25·00
1044. 20 pf.+3 pf. claret .. 30·00 25·00

1951.
1045. 207. 2 pf. green 30 15
1046. 4 pf. brown 30 5
1047. 5 pf. purple 90 5
1048. 6 pf. orange .. .. 3·50 25
1049. 8 pf. grey .. .. 7·00 1·75
1050. 10 pf. green 70 5
1051. 15 pf. violet .. .. 13·00 15
1052. 20 pf. red 70 5
1053. 25 pf. plum .. .. 32·00 70
1054. – 30 pf. blue .. .. 17·00 8
1055. – 40 pf. purple .. 38·00 5
1056. – 50 pf. grey .. 55·00 5
1057. – 60 pf. brown .. 25·00 5
1058. – 70 pf. yellow .. £160 3·00
1059. – 80 pf. red .. £100 40
1060. – 90 pf. green £180 75
The 30 pf. to 90 pf. are 20×24½ mm.

208. Figures.

209. Stamps under Magnifier.

1951. St. Mary's Church, Lubeck. 700th Anniv.
1065. 208. 10 pf.+5 pf. black and green .. 40·00 42·00
1066. 20 pf.+5 pf. black and claret .. 40·00 42·00

1951. National Philatelic Exn., Wuppertal.
1067. 209. 10 pf.+2 pf. yellow, black and green 22·00 22·00
1068. 20 pf.+3 pf. yellow, black and claret 22·00 22·00

210. St. Vincent de Paul.

211. W. C. Rontgen.

1951. Humanitarian Relief Fund. Inscr. "HELFER DER MENSCHHEIT".
1069. 210. 4 pf.+2 pf. brown 4·75 4·50
1070. – 10 pf.+3 pf. green 8·00 5·50
1071. – 20 pf.+5 pf. red .. 8·00 5·50
1072. – 30 pf.+10 pf. blue 50·00 55·00
PORTRAITS: 10 pf. F. Von Bodelschwingh. 20 pf. Elsa Brandstrom. 30 pf. J. H. Pestalozzi.

1951. 50th Anniv. of Award to Rontgen of 1st Nobel Prize for Physics.
1073. 211. 30 pf. blue .. .. 45·00 10·00

212. Mona Lisa.

213. Martin Luther.

1952. Leonardo de Vinci. 500th Birth Anniv. Multicoloured centre.
1074. 212. 5 pf. brown 90 30

1952. Lutheran World Federation Assembly, Hanover.
1075. 213. 10 pf. green .. .. 5·50 2·25

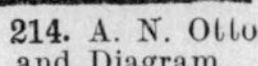

214. A. N. Otto and Diagram.

215. Nuremberg Madonna.

1952. 75th Anniv. of Otto Gas Engine.
1076. 214. 30 pf. blue .. .. 15·00 7·50

1952. Cent. of German National Museum, Nuremberg.
1077. 215. 10 pf.+5 pf. green .. 11·00 12·00

216. Trawler off Heligoland.

217. Carl Schurz.

1952. Rehabilitation of Heligoland.
1078. 216. 20 pf. red .. .. 5·50 3·50

1952. 100th Anniv. of Arrival of Schurz in America.
1079. 217. 20 pf. pink, blk. & bl. 10·00 4·00

218. Boy Hikers.

219. Elizabeth Fry.

1952. Youth Hostels Fund. Inscr. "JUGENDMARKE 1952".
1080. 218. 10 pf.+2 pf. green .. 9·00 9·00
1081. – 20 pf.+3 pf. red .. 10·00 10·00
DESIGN: 20 pf. Girl hikers.

1952. Humanitarian Relief Fund. Inscr. "HELFER DER MENSCHHEIT".
1082. 219. 4 pf.+2 pf. brown .. 5·00 3·50
1083. – 10 pf.+5 pf. green .. 4·00 3·00
1084. – 20 pf.+10 pf. lake .. 10·00 6·00
1085. – 30 pf.+10 pf. blue .. 45·00 35·00
PORTRAITS: 10 pf. Dr. C. Sonnenschein. 20 pf. T. Fliedner. 30 pf. H. Dunant.

220. Postman, 1852.

221. P. Reis.

1952. Thurn and Taxis Stamp Cent.
1086. 220. 10 pf. black, brown, yell., blue & green 2·00 1·00

1952. German Telephone Service. 75th Anniv.
1087. 221. 30 pf. blue .. .. 20·00 7·50

222. Road Accident Victim.

223.

1953. Road Safety Campaign.
1088. 222. 20 pf. blue, orange, brown, red & black 6·50 2·00

1953. Science Museum. 50th Anniv.
1089. 223. 10 pf.+5 pf. green .. 14·00 17·00

224. Red Cross and Compass.

225. Prisoner of War.

1953. Henri Dunant (founder of Red Cross). 125th Birth Anniv.
1090. 224. 10 pf. red and green .. 7·00 3·00

1953. Commemorating Prisoners of War.
1091. 225. 10 pf. grey .. .. 1·60 5

226. J. von Liebig.

227. "Rail Transport".

1953. Liebig (chemist). 150th Birth Anniv.
1092. 226. 30 pf. blue .. .. 20·00 8·50

1953. Transport Exn., Munich. Inscr. as in T **227**.
1093. 227. 4 pf. brown .. .. 3·50 3·50
1094. – 10 pf. green .. .. 5·50 5·50
1095. – 20 pf. red .. .. 8·50 6·00
1096. – 30 pf. blue .. .. 18·00 8·50
DESIGNS: 10 pf. "Air" (dove and aeroplanes). 20 pf. "Road" (traffic lights and cars). 30 pf. "Sea" (buoy and ships).

228. Gateway, Thurn and Taxis Palace.

229. A. H. Francke. 230. Pres. Heuss.

1953. Int. Philatelic Exhibition. Frankfurt-on-Main. Inscr. "IFRABA 1953".
1097. 228. 10 pf.+2 pf. chest., black and green .. 12·00 12·00
1098. – 20 pf.+3 pf. grey, indigo and red .. 12·00 12·00
DESIGN: 20 pf. Telecommunications Buildings, Frankfurt-on-Main.

1953. Humanitarian Relief Fund. Inscr. "HELFER DER MENSCHHEIT".
1099. 229. 4 pf.+2 pf. brown .. 3·50 3·50
1100. – 10 pf.+5 pf. green .. 6·50 3·50
1101. – 20 pf.+10 pf. red .. 6·50 4·25
1102. – 30 pf.+10 pf. blue .. 27·00 32·00
PORTRAITS: 10 pf. S. Kneipp. 20 pf. J. C. Senckenberg. 30 pf. F. Nansen.

1954. (a) Size 18½×22½ mm. or 18×22 mm.
1103. 230. 2 pf. olive-green .. 5 5
1104. 4 pf. brown .. 5 5
1105. 5 pf. mauve .. 5 5
1106. 6 pf. brown .. 5 30
1107. 7 pf. green .. 25 5
1108. 8 pf. grey .. 10 36
1109. 10 pf. green .. 10 5
1110. 15 pf. blue .. 35 5
1111. 20 pf. red .. 12 5
1112. 25 pf. maroon .. 70 15
1122a. 30 pf. green .. 50 10
1122c. 40 pf. blue .. 1·00 5
1122e. 50 pf. olive .. 65 5
1122f. 60 pf. brown .. 1·25 5
1122g. 70 pf. violet .. 2·75 5
1122h. 80 pf. orange .. 2·75 45
1122i. 90 pf. green .. 9·00 12

(b) Size 20×24 mm.
1113. 230. 30 pf. blue .. 7·50 60
1114. 40 pf. purple .. 1·75 5
1115. 50 pf. slate .. 90·00 12
1116. 60 pf. brown .. 22·00 5
1117. 70 pf. yellow-olive .. 6·50 20
1118. 80 pf. red .. 1·00 80
1119. 90 pf. green .. 4·50 30

(c) Size 25×30 mm.
1120. 230. 1 Dm. olive .. 1·10 5
1121. 2 Dm. lavender .. 1·50 25
1122. 3 Dm. crimson .. 2·50 40

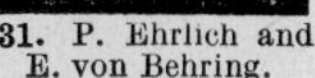

231. P. Ehrlich and E. von Behring.

232. Gutenberg and Printing-press.

1954. Ehrlich and Von Behring (bacteriologists). Birth Centenaries.
1123. **231.** 10 pf. green .. .. 4·50 1·90

1954. Gutenberg Bible. 500th Anniv.
1124. **232.** 4 pf. brown 40 12

233. Sword-pierced Mitre. **234.** Kathe Kollwitz.

1954. Martyrdom of St. Boniface. 1,200th Anniv.
1125. **233.** 20 pf. red and brown 2·25 1·40

1954. Humanitarian Relief Fund. Inscr. "HELFER DER MENSCHHEIT".
1126. **234.** 7 pf.+3 pf. brown .. 2·50 2·00
1127. – 10 pf.+5 pf. green .. 2·00 80
1128. – 20 pf.+10 pf. red .. 5·50 2·00
1129. – 40 pf.+10 pf. blue .. 20·00 21·00
PORTRAITS: 10 pf. L. Werthmann. 20 pf. J. F. Oberlin. 40 pf. Bertha Pappenheim.

235. C. F. Gauss. **236.** "Flight."

1955. Gauss (mathematician). Death Cent.
1130. **235.** 10 pf. green .. .. 1·50 15

1955. Re-establishment of "Lufthansa" Airways.
1131. **236.** 5 pf. magenta & black 60 50
1132. 10 pf. green and black 90 65
1133. 15 pf. blue and black 4·50 4·25
1134. 20 pf. red and black.. 8·00 4·75

237. O. von Miller. **238.** Schiller.

1955. Von Miller (electrical engineer). Birth Cent.
1135. **237.** 10 pf. emerald .. 1·90 80

1955. Schiller (poet). 150th Death Anniv.
1136. **238.** 40 pf. blue .. .. 7·50 8·00

239. Motor-coach 1906. **240.** Arms of Baden-Wurttemberg.

1955. Postal Motor Transport. 50th Anniv.
1137. **239.** 20 pf. black and red.. 5·50 3·25

1955. Baden-Wurttemberg Agricultural Exn. Stuttgart.
1138. **240.** 7 pf. blk. brn. & bistre 1·75 2·40
1139. 10 pf. blk. grn. & bistre 2·50 1·40

241. **242.** Refugees.

1955. Cosmic Research.
1140. **241.** 20 pf. lake .. .. 4·00 50

1955. Expulsion of Germans from beyond the Oder-Neisse Line. 10th Anniv.
1141. **242.** 20 pf. red .. .. 1·40 20
See also No. 1400.

243. Orb, arrows and waves. **244.** Magnifying Glass and Carrier Pigeon.

1955. Battle of Lechfeld. 1,000th Anniv.
1142. **243.** 20 pf. purple.. .. 3·75 1·40

1955. West European Postage Stamp Exn. Inscr. as in T **244.**
1143. **244.** 10 pf.+2 pf. green .. 2·75 3·75
1144. – 20 pf.+3 pf. red .. 6·00 7·50
DESIGN: 20 pf. Tweezers and posthorn.

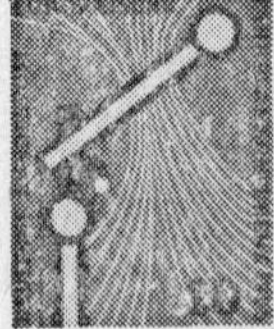

245. Railway Signal. **246.** Stifter Monument.

1955. European Railway Timetable Conf.
1145. **245.** 20 pf. black and red 3·50 60

1955. Stifter (Austrian poet). 150th Birth Anniv.
1146. **246.** 10 pf. green .. .. 1·40 1·00

247. U.N. Emblem. **248.** Amalie Sieveking.

1955. U.N. Day.
1147. **247.** 10 pf. green and red 75 75

1955. Humanitarian Relief Fund.
1148. **248.** 7 pf.+3 pf. brown 1·25 1·60
1149. – 10 pf.+5 pf. green 1·10 60
1150. – 20 pf.+10 pf. red 1·50 75
1151. – 40 pf.+10 pf. blue 16·00 17·00
PORTRAITS: 10 pf. A. Kolping. 20 pf. Dr. S. Hahnemann. 40 pf. Florence Nightingale.

249. **250.** Von Stephan's Signature.

1955.
1152. **249.** 1 pf. grey 5 5

1956. H. von Stephen. 125th Birth Anniv.
1153. **250.** 20 pf. red .. .. 3·00 1·25

251. Spinet and Opening Bars of Minuet. **252.** Heinrich Heine (poet).

1956. Mozart. Birth Bicent.
1154. **251.** 10 pf. black and lilac 12 12

1956. Heine. Death Cent.
1155. **252.** 10 pf. green and black 85 85

253. Old Houses and Crane. **254.**

1956. Millenary of Luneberg.
1156. **253.** 20 pf. red .. .. 3·50 3·50

1956. Olympic Year.
1157. **254.** 10 pf. green 12 12

255. Boy and Dove. **256.** Robert Schumann.

1956. Youth Hostels' Fund. Inscr. "JUGEND".
1158. **255.** 7 pf.+3 pf. grey, black & chestnut 1·40 1·75
1159. – 10 pf.+5 pf. grey, black and green 1·75 2·25
DESIGN: 10 pf. Girl playing flute and flowers.

1956. Schumann (composer). Death Cent.
1160. **256.** 10 pf. blk., red & bistre 20 12

257. **258.** T. Mann (author).

1956. Evangelical Church Convention, Frankfurt-on-Main
1161. **257.** 10 pf. green 65 65
1162. 20 pf. lake .. .. 1·50 1·50

1956. Thomas Mann Commem.
1163. **258.** 20 pf. claret .. 80 80

259. **260.** Ground Plan of Cologne Cathedral and Hand.

1956. Maria Laach Abbey. 800th Anniv.
1164. **259.** 20 pf. grey and lake.. 80 80

1956. 77th Meeting of German Catholics, Cologne.
1165. **260.** 10 pf. green & choc. 80 80

261. **262.** Nurse and Baby.

1956. Int. Police Exhibition, Essen.
1166. **261.** 20 pf. green, orange and black .. .. 1·00 1·00

1956. Europa. As T **230** of Belgium.
1167. 10 pf. green 35 5
1168. 40 pf. blue .. .. 3·00 40

1956. Humanitarian Relief Fund. Inscr. "HELFER DER MENSCHHEIT". Centres in black.
1169. **262.** 7 pf.+3 pf. brown .. 1·10 1·10
1170. – 10 pf.+5 pf. green .. 70 30
1171. – 20 pf.+10 pf. red .. 75 30
1172. – 40 pf.+10 pf. blue .. 6·00 8·00
DESIGNS: 10 pf. I. P. Semmelweis and cot. 20 pf. Mother, and baby in cradle. 40 pf. Nursemaid and children.

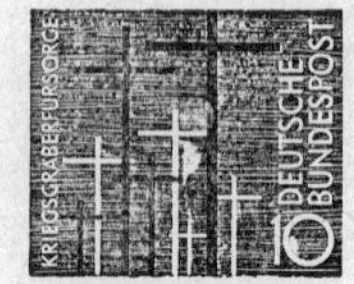

263. Carrier Pigeon. **264.** "Military Graves."

1956. Stamp Day.
1173. **263.** 10 pf. green 35 20

1956. War Graves Commission.
1174. **264.** 10 pf. grey 35 20

265. Arms. **266.** Children with Luggage.

1957. Return of the Saar to West Germany.
1175. **265.** 10 pf. brown & green 20 15

1957. Berlin Children's Holiday Fund.
1176. **266.** 10 pf.+5 pf. orge. and green .. 80 1·00
1177. – 20 pf.+10 pf. orge. and blue .. 1·50 1·75
DESIGN: 20 pf. Girl returning from holiday.

267. Heinrich Hertz. **268.** Paul Gerhardt.

1957. Hertz (physicist). Birth Cent.
1178. **257.** 10 pf. black and green 30 15

1957. Paul Gerhardt (hymn-writer). 350th Birth Anniv.
1179. **268.** 20 pf. lake 30 12

269. "Flora and Philately." **270.** Emblem of Aschaffenburg.

1957. Exhibition of 8th Congress of Int. Federation of "Constructive Philately".
1180. **269.** 20 pf. orange .. 30 12

1957. Millenary of Aschaffenburg.
1181. **270.** 20 pf. red and black.. 30 20

271. University Class.

1957. Freiburg University. 5th Cent.
1182. **271.** 10 pf. blk., grn. & red 20 12

272. Motor-ship.

1957. German Merchant Shipping Day.
1183. **272.** 15 pf. blk., red & blue 25 25

273. Justus Liebig University. **274.** Albert Ballin.

1957. Justus Liebig University, Giessen. 350th Anniv.
1184. **273.** 10 pf. green 15 12

1957. Albert Ballin, director of Hamburg-America Shipping Line. Birth Cent.
1185. **274.** 20 pf. black and lake 30 12

275. Television Screen.

276. " Europa " Tree.

1957. West German Television Service.
1186. 275. 10 pf. green and blue 15 12

1957. Europa.
1187. 276. 10 pf. green and blue 12 5
1188. 40 pf. blue .. .. 1·10 20

277. Young Miner.

278. Water Lily.

1957. Humanitarian Relief Fund.
1189. 277. 7 pf.+3 pf. blk. & brn. 80 80
1190. – 10 pf.+5 pf. blk. & grn. 35 20
1191. – 20 pf.+10 pf. blk. & red 75 20
1192. – 40 pf.+10 pf. blk. & bl. 6·50 8·00
DESIGNS: 10 pf. Miner drilling coal-face. 20 pf. Miner with coal-cutting machine. 40 pf. Operator at lift-shaft.

1957. Nature Protection Day.
1193. 278. 10 pf. orange, yellow and green 15 10
1194. – 20 pf. blue, black, red and bistre .. 30 15
DESIGN—VERT. 20 pf. Robin.

279. Carrier Pigeons.

280. Baron vom Stein.

1957. Int. Correspondence Week.
1195. 279. 20 pf. black and red.. 30 15

1957. Baron vom Stein (statesman). 200th Birth Anniv.
1196. 280. 20 pf. red 50 15

281. Dr. Leo Baeck (philosopher).

282. Wurttemberg Parliament House.

1957. Dr. Leo Baeck. 1st Death Anniv.
1197. 281. 20 pf. red 50 15

1957. First Wurttemberg Parliament. 500th Anniv.
1198. 282. 10 pf. olive and green 30 15

283. Stage Coach.

284. " Max and Moritz " (cartoon characters).

1957. Joseph von Eichendorff (novelist). Death Cent.
1199. 283. 10 pf. green 35 15

1958. Wilhelm Busch (writer and illustrator). 50th Death Anniv.
1200. 284. 10 pf. olive and black 15 10
1201. – 20 pf. red and black 30 15
DESIGN: 20 pf. Wilhelm Busch.

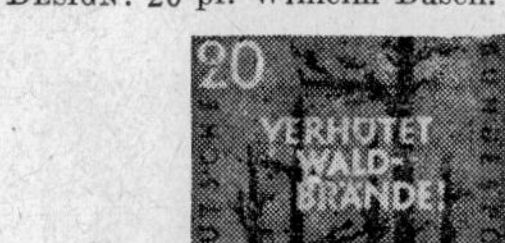

285. " Prevent Forest Fires ".

1958. Forest Fires Prevention Campaign.
1202. 285. 20 pf. black and red 35 15

286. Rudolf Diesel and First Oil Engine.

287. " The Fox who stole the Goose ".

1958. Rudolf Diesel (engineer). Birth Cent.
1203. 286. 10 pf. myrtle 15 12

1958. Berlin Students' Fund. Inscr. " Fur die Jugend ".
1204. 287. 10 pf.+5 pf. red black and green .. 50 75
1205. – 20 pf.+10 pf. brn. green and red .. 80 95
DESIGN: 20 pf. " A hunter from the Palatinate " (horseman).

288. Giraffe and Lion.

289. Old Munich.

1958. Frankfurt-am-Main Zoo. Cent.
1206. 288. 10 pf. black and green 20 15

1958. Munich. 8th Cent.
1207. 289. 20 pf. red 20 15

290. Trier and Market Cross.

291. Deutsche Mark (coin)

1958. Trier Market Millenary.
1208. 290. 20 pf. red and black.. 20 15

1958. Currency Reform. 10th Anniv.
1209. 291. 20 pf. black & orange 25 15

292. Emblem of Gymnastics.

293. H. Schulze-Delitzsch.

1958. German Gymnastics. 150th Anniv.
1210. 292. 10 pf. blk., grn. & grey 12 10

1958. Schulze-Delitzsch (pioneer of German co-operative movement). 150th Birth Anniv.
1211. 293. 10 pf. green 12 10

1958. Europa. As T 254 of Belgium. Size 24½ × 30 mm.
1212. 10 pf. blue and green .. 25 5
1213. 40 pf. red and blue .. 90 25

294. Friedrich Raiffeisen (philanthropist).

295. Dairymaid.

1958. Humanitarian Relief and Welfare Funds.
1214. 294. 7 pf.+3 pf. brown 15 25
1215. 295. 10 pf.+5 pf. red, yellow and green 25 12
1216. – 20 pf.+10 pf. blue, green and red .. 30 12
1217. – 40 pf.+10 pf. yellow, green and blue.. 2·10 2·50
DESIGNS: As T 295: 20 pf. Vine-dresser. 40 pf. Farm labourer.

296. Cardinal Nicholas of Cues (founder).

297. Jakob Fugger (merchant prince).

1958. Hospice of St. Nicholas. 500th Anniv.
1218. 296. 20 pf. black and lake 20 10

1959. As Type B 46 of West Berlin but without " BERLIN ".
1219. 7 pf. green 5 5
1220. 10 pf. green 5 5
1221. 20 pf. red 15 5
1222. 40 pf. blue 85 15
1223. 70 pf. violet .. .. 1·10 15

1959. Jakob Fugger. 500th Birth Anniv.
1224. 297. 20 pf. blk. & brn.-red 20 12

298. Adam Riese (mathematician).

299. A. von Humboldt (naturalist).

1959. Adam Riese. 400th Death Anniv.
1225. 298. 10 pf. blk. & sage-grn. 15 10

1959. Alexander von Humboldt. Death Cent.
1226. 299. 40 pf. blue 35 20

300. Hamburg Stamp of 1859.

301. Buxtehude.

1959. Hamburg Int. Stamp Exn. and Hamburg and Lubeck Stamp Centenaries. Inscr. " INTERPOSTA ".
1228. 300. 10 pf.+5 pf. brown and green .. 5 12
1230. – 20 pf.+10 pf. brn. and red .. 15 35
DESIGN: 20 pf. Lubeck stamp of 1859.

1959. Buxtehude. Millenary.
1231. 301. 20 pf. red and blue .. 15 12

302. Holy Tunic of Trier.

303. Congress Emblem.

1959. Holy Tunic of Trier Exn.
1232. 302. 20 pf. black and claret 15 12

1959. German Evangelical Church Day and Congress, Munich.
1233. 303. 10 pf. vio., grn. & blk. 10 10

1959. Europa. As T 268 of Belgium but size 24½ × 30 mm.
1234. 10 pf. olive-green .. 15 5
1235. 40 pf. grey-blue .. 55 20

304. " Feeding the Poor ".

305. " Uprooted Tree ".

1959. Humanitarian Relief and Welfare Funds.
1236. 304. 7 pf.+3 pf. sepia and yellow .. 12 20
1237. – 10 pf.+5 pf. green and yellow .. 15 12
1238. – 20 pf.+10 pf. red and yellow .. 30 12
1239. – 40 pf.+10 pf. black, ochre, grn. & yell. 1·40 1·75
DESIGNS: 10 pf. "Clothing the Naked". 20 pf. "Bounty from Heaven" (scenes from the Brothers Grimm story "The Star Thaler"). 40 pf. The Brothers Grimm.

1960. World Refugee Year.
1240. 305. 10 pf. blk., pur. & grn. 25 5
1241. 40 pf. blk., red & blue 1·10 60

306. P. Melanchthon.

307. Cross and Symbols of the Crucifixion.

1960. Philip Melanchthon (Protestant reformer). 400th Death Anniv.
1242. 306. 20 pf. blk. & crimson 55 25

1960. Oberammergau Passion Play.
1243. 307. 10 pf. grey, ochre and blue 8 8

308.

309. Wrestling.

1960. 37th World Eucharistic Congress, Munich.
1244. 308. 10 pf. grey-green .. 25 12
1245. 20 pf. claret .. 40 30

1960. Olympic Year. Inscr. as in T 309.
1246. 309. 7 pf. brown 12 12
1247. – 10 pf. olive-green .. 15 12
1248. – 20 pf. red 35 5
1249. – 40 pf. blue 55 65
DESIGNS: 10 pf. Running. 20 pf. Javelin and discus-throwing. 40 pf. Chariot-racing.

310. Hildesheim Cathedral.

311. Little Red Riding Hood meeting Wolf.

1960. Bishops St. Bernward and St. Godehard. Birth Millenary.
1250. 310. 20 pf. maroon .. 40 15

1960. Europa. As T 279 of Belgium.
1251. 10 pf. green & olive-green 5 5
1252. 20 pf. vermilion and red.. 35 10
1253. 40 pf. light blue and blue 40 65

1960. Humanitarian Relief and Welfare Funds.
1254. 311. 7 pf.+3 pf. black, red and bistre .. 10 12
1255. – 10 pf.+5 pf. black, red and green .. 10 5
1256. – 20 pf.+10 pf. black, green and red .. 15 12
1257. – 40 pf.+20 pf. black, red and blue .. 1·00 1·40
DESIGNS: 10 pf. Little Red Riding Hood and wolf disguised as grandmother. 20 pf. Woodcutter and dead wolf. 40 pf. Little Red Riding Hood with grandmother.

1960. Gen. George C. Marshall. 1st Death Anniv. Portrait as T 306.
1258. 40 pf. black and blue .. 1·10 40

312. Locomotive of 1835.

313. St. George and the Dragon.

1960. German Railway. 125th Anniv.
1959. 312. 10 pf. black and bistre 8 8

1961. Pathfinders (German Boy Scouts) Commem.
1260. 313. 10 pf. green 8 8

INDEX

Countries can be quickly located by referring to the index at the end of this volume.

1961. Famous Germans. As Nos. B 194, etc of West Berlin but without "BERLIN".
1261. 5 pf. olive 5 5
1262. 7 pf. brown 5 5
1263. 8 pf. violet 12 12
1264. 10 pf. green 5 5
1265. 15 pf. blue 5 5
1266. 20 pf. red 10 5
1267. 25 pf. chestnut .. 10 8
1268. 30 pf. sepia 20 5
1269. 40 pf. blue 20 5
1270. 50 pf. brown 35 5
1271. 60 pf. claret 30 5
1272a. 70 pf. green 35 5
1273. 80 pf. brown 35 5
1274. 90 pf. bistre 40 15
1275. 1 Dm. violet 40 12
1276. 2 Dm. green 50 20
PORTRAIT: 90 pf. Franz Oppenheimer (economist).

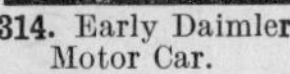

314. Early Daimler Motor Car. **315.** Nuremberg Messenger of 1700.

1961. Daimler-Benz Patent. 75th Anniv.
1277. **314.** 10 pf. green and black 5 5
1278. – 20 pf. red and black 12 12
DESIGN: 20 pf. Early Benz motor car.

1961. "The Letter during Five Centuries" Exhibition, Nuremberg.
1279. **315.** 7 pf. black & brn.-red 5 5

316. Speyer Cathedral. **317.** Doves.

1961. Speyer Cathedral. 9th Cent.
1280. **316.** 20 pf. red 12 12

1961. Europa.
1281. **317.** 10 pf. green 5 5
1282. 40 pf. blue 25 25

318. Hansel and Gretel in the Wood. **319.** Telephone Apparatus.

1961. Humanitarian Relief and Welfare Funds.
1283. 7 pf. + 3 pf. black, red, green and olive .. 8 12
1284. 10 pf. + 5 pf. black, red, blue and green .. 8 10
1285. 20 pf. + 10 pf. black, blue, green and red .. 12 10
1286. 40 pf. + 20 pf. black, red, olive and blue .. 85 1·00
DESIGNS: 7 pf. T **318.** 10 pf. Hansel, Gretel and the Witch. 20 pf. Hansel in the Witch's cage. 40 pf. Hansel and Gretel reunited with their father.

1961. Philipp Reis's Telephone. Cent.
1287. **319.** 10 pf. green 8 8

320. Baron W. E. von Ketteler. **321.** Drusus Stone.

1961. Baron W. E. von Ketteler (Catholic leader). 150th Birth Anniv.
1288. **320.** 10 pf. black & ol.-grn. 8 8

1962. Mainz. Bimillenary.
1289. **321.** 20 pf. maroon .. 12 10

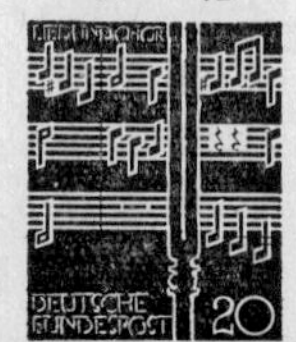

322. Apollo (butterfly). **323.** Part of "In Dulc Jubilo", from "Musæ Sionæ" (M. Praetorius).

1962. Child Welfare. Inscr. "JUGENDMARKEN 1962".
1290. **322.** 7 pf. + 3 pf. mult. .. 15 20
1291. – 10 pf. + 5 pf. mult. .. 15 15
1292. – 20 pf. + 10 pf. mult. .. 20 20
1293. – 40 pf. + 20 pf. mult. .. 75 90
BUTTERFLIES: 10 pf. Camberwell Beauty. 20 pf. Small Tortoiseshell. 40 pf. Swallowtail.

1962. "Song and Choir" (Summer Music Festivals).
1294. **323.** 20 pf. red and black 10 10

324. "Belief, Thanksgiving and Service". **325.** Open Bible.

1962. Catholics' Day.
1295. **324.** 20 pf. magenta .. 10 10

1962. "Wurttembergische Bibelanstalt" (publishers of the Bible in original languages). 150th Anniv.
1296. **325.** 20 pf. black and red .. 10 10

326. Europa "Tree". **327.** Snow White and Seven Dwarfs.

1962. Europa.
1297. **326.** 10 pf. green 5 5
1298. 40 pf. blue 25 25

1962. Humanitarian Relief and Welfare Funds. Scenes from "Snow White and the Seven Dwarfs" (Brothers Grimm). Multicoloured.
1299. 7 pf. + 3 pf. The "Magic Mirror" 10 10
1300. 10 pf. + 5 pf. T **327** .. 10 8
1301. 20 pf. + 10 pf. "The Poisoned Apple" .. 15 8
1302. 40 pf. + 20 pf. Snow White and Prince Charming 50 75

328. "Bread for the World". **329.** Relief Distribution.

1963. Freedom from Hunger.
1303. **328.** 20 pf. chestnut & black 10 10

1963. CRALOG and CARE Relief Organisations.
1304. **329.** 20 f. lake 10 10

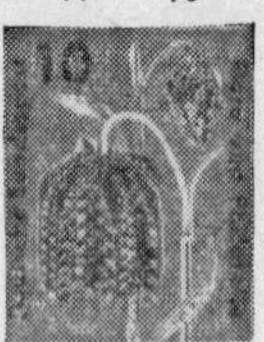

330. Ears of Wheat, Cross and Globe. **331.** Snake's Head Lily.

1963. Freedom from Hunger.
1305. **330.** 20pf. black, red & grey 10 10

1963. "Flora and Philately" Exhibition, Hamburg.
1306. **331.** 10 pf. pur., grn. & blk. 5 5
1307. – 15 pf. purple, turquoise, bistre and black .. 5 5
1308. – 20 pf. blue, yellow, turq., red and black 12 5
1309. – 40 pf. turquoise, purple-drab. blue and black 25 30
PLANTS: 15 pf. Lady's Slipper Orchid. 20 pf. Columbine. 40 pf. Sea Thistle.

332. "Heidelberger Catechismus". **333.** Cross, Sun and Moon.

1963. Heidelberg Catechism. 4th Cent.
1310. **332.** 20 pf. black, brown-red and red-orange 10 10

1963. Consecration of Regina Martyrum Church, Berlin.
1311. **333.** 10 pf. black, violet, red and blue-green 5 5

334. Emblems of Conference Participating Countries. **335.** Map and Flags.

1963. Paris Postal Conference Cent.
1312. **334.** 40 pf. ultramarine .. 20 20

1963. Opening of Denmark-Germany Railway ("Vogelfluglinie").
1313. **335.** 20 pf. red, olive, black and yellow .. 10 10

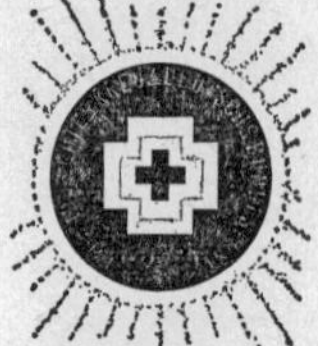

336. Red Cross Emblem. **337.** Common Hoopoe.

1963. Red Cross Cent.
1314. **336.** 20 pf. red, purple and olive-yellow .. 10 10

1963. Child Welfare. Bird designs inscr. "FUR DIE JUGEND 1963". Multicoloured.
1315. 10 pf. + 5 pf. T **337** .. 10 15
1316. 15 pf. + 5 pf. Golden oriole 15 20
1317. 20 pf. + 10 pf. Bullfinch 20 25
1318. 40 pf. + 20 pf. Kingfisher 65 85

338. Congress Emblem. **339.** "Co-operation".

1963. German Evangelical Church Day and Congress, Dortmund.
1319. **338.** 20 pf. blk. & orge.-brn. 15 15

1963. Europa.
1320. **339.** 15 pf. green 8 8
1321. 20 pf. red 8 8

340. Mother Goat warning kids. **341.** Herring.

1963. Humanitarian Relief and Welfare Funds.
1322. 10 pf. + 5 pf. black, red, green and bistre .. 5 10
1323. 15 pf. + 5 pf. black, red, yellow and green .. 5 5
1324. 20 pf. + 10 pf. black, yellow, green and red 10 5
1325. 40 pf. + 20 pf. black, red, olive and blue .. 45 60
DESIGNS: 10 pf. T **340.** 15 pf. Wolf entering house. 20 pf. Wolf in house, threatening kids. 40 pf. Mother Goat and kids dancing round wolf in well. From Grimm's "Wolf and the Seven Kids".

1964. Child Welfare. Fish designs inscr. "Fur die Jugend 1964". Multicoloured.
1326. 10 pf. + 5 pf. Type **341** .. 10 15
1327. 15 pf. + 5 pf. Red perch 12 15
1328. 20 pf. + 10 pf. Carp .. 15 15
1329. 40 pf. + 20 pf. Cod .. 65 80

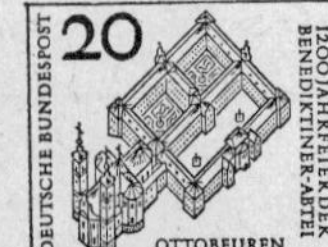

342. Old Town Hall, Hanover. **343.** Ottobeuren Abbey.

1964. Capitals of the Federal Lands. Multicoloured.
1330. 20 pf. Type **342** .. 12 12
1331. 20 pf. Hamburg 12 12
1332. 20 pf. Kiel 12 12
1333. 20 pf. Munich 12 12
1334. 20 pf. Wiesbaden .. 12 12
1335. 20 pf. Berlin 12 12
1336. 20 pf. Mainz 12 12
1337. 20 pf. Dusseldorf .. 12 12
1338. 20 pf. Bonn 12 12
1339. 20 pf. Bremen 12 12
1340. 20 pf. Stuttgart 12 12
1340a. 20 pf. Saarbrucken .. 12 12
DESIGNS: No. 1331, Ship and St. Michael's Church (775th Anniv.). 1332, Northern ferry. 1333, National Theatre. 1334, Kurhaus. 1335, Reichstag. 1336, Gutenberg Museum. 1337, Jan Wellen's Monument and Town Hall. 1338, Town Hall. 1339, Market Hall. 1340, Town view. 1340a, Ludwig's Church.

1964. Benedictine Abbey, Ottobeuren. 1200th Anniv.
1341. **343.** 20 pf. blk., red & pink 10 10

1964. Re-election of Pres. Lubke. As Type B **60** of West Berlin, inscr. "DEUTSCHE BUNDESPOST" only.
1342. 20 pf. red 8 5
1343. 40 pf. blue 20 12

343a. Sophie Scholl.

1964. Attempt on Hitler's Life. 20th Anniv. Anti-Hitlerite Martyrs. Each black and grey.
1343a. 20 pf. Type **343a** .. 75 1·25
1343b. 20 pf. Ludwig Beck .. 75 1·25
1343c. 20 pf. Dietrich Bonhoeffer 75 1·25
1343d. 20 pf. Alfred Delp .. 75 1·25
1343e. 20 pf. Karl Friedrich Goerdeler .. .. 75 1·25
1343f. 20 pf. Wilhelm Leuschner 75 1·25
1343g. 20 pf. Helmuth James (Von Moltke) .. .. 75 1·25
1343h. 20 pf. Claus Schenk (Von Stauffenberg) .. 75 1·25

344. Calvin. **345.** Diagram of Benzene Formula.

1964. World Council of Reformed Churches.
1344. **344.** 20 pf. black and red .. 15 10

1964. Scientific Anniversaries. (1st Series).
1345. 10 pf. green, black & choc. 5 5
1346. 15 pf. light blue, blue, black and green .. 5 5
1347. 20 pf. green, black and red 10 5
DESIGNS: 10 pf. T **345** (centenary of publication of Kekule's benzene formula). 15 pf. Diagram of nuclear reaction (25th anniv. of publication of Hahn-Strassman treatise on splitting the nucleus of the atom). 20 pf. Gas engine (centenary of Otto-Langen internal-combustion engine).
See also Nos. 1426/7 and 1451/3.

346. F. Lassalle. **347.** "The Sun".

1964. Ferdinand Lassalle (Socialist founder and leader). Death Cent.
1348. **346.** 20 pf. black and blue 10 10

1964. 80th Catholic's Day.
1349. **347.** 20 pf. red and grey .. 15 15

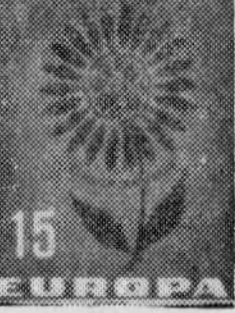

348. Europa "Flower". **349.** "The Sleeping Beauty".

1964. Europa.
1350. **348.** 15 pf. violet and green 10 5
1351. 20 pf. violet and red .. 10 5

1964. Humanitarian Relief and Welfare Funds.
1352. **349.** 10 pf. + 5 pf. mult. .. 5 5
1353. – 15 pf. + 5 pf. mult. .. 8 5
1354. – 20 pf. + 10 pf. mult... 12 8
1355. – 40 pf. + 20 pf. mult... 40 65
DESIGNS: 15 pf., 20 pf., 40 pf. Various scenes from Grimm's "The Sleeping Beauty".

350. Judo. **351.** Prussian Eagle.

1964. "Olympic Year".
1356. **350.** 20 pf. multicoloured 10 10

1964. German Court of Accounts. 250th Anniv.
1357. **351.** 20 pf. chest. and black 10 10

352. Pres. Kennedy. **353.** Castle Gateway Ellwangen (Jagst).

1964. Pres. Kennedy Commem.
1358. **352.** 40 pf. blue 20 20

1964. Twelve Centuries of German Architecture.
(a) Size 18½ × 22½ mm. Plain background.
1359. – 10 pf. brown 5 5
1360. – 15 pf. green 8 5
1361. – 20 pf. brown 10 5
1362. – 40 pf. blue 20 5
1363. **353.** 50 pf. brown 30 5
1364. – 60 pf. red 40 25
1365. – 70 pf. green 40 12
1366. – 80 pf. brown 40 15

(b) Size 19½ × 24 mm. Coloured background.
1367. – 5 pf. brown 5 5
1368. – 10 pf. maroon .. 5 5
1369. – 20 pf. green 12 5
1370. – 30 pf. green 30 5
1371. – 30 pf. red 20 5
1372. – 40 pf. brown 30 10
1373. – 50 pf. blue 35 5
1374. – 60 pf. red 60 30
1375. – 70 pf. brown 75 15
1376. – 80 pf. brown 75 30
1377. – 90 pf. black 70 15
1378. – 1 Dm. blue 70 8
1379. – 1 Dm. 10 brown .. 80 20
1380. – 1 Dm. 30 green .. 80 30
1381. – 2 Dm. purple .. 1·10 20
BUILDINGS: 5 pf. Berlin Gate, Stettin. 10 pf. Zwinger pavilion, Dresden. 15 pf. Tegel Castle, Berlin. 20 pf. Monastery Gate, Lorsch. 30 pf. North Gate, Flensburg. 40 pf. Trifels Castle (Palatinate). 60 pf. Treptow Portal, Neubrandenburg. 70 pf. Osthofen Gate, Soest. 80 pf. Ellingen Portal, Weissenburg (Bavaria). 90 pf. Zschlokk's Convent, Konigsberg. 1 Dm. Melanchthon House, Wittenberg. 1 Dm. 10, Trinity Hospital, Hildesheim. 1 Dm. 30, Tegel Castle, Berlin (diff.). 2 Dm. Burghers' Hall, Lowenburg Town Hall (Silesia).

354. Owl, Hat, Walking-stick and Satchel. **355.** Woodcock.

1965. Matthias Claudius (poet). 150th Death Anniv.
1383. **354.** 20 pf. black and red .. 10 10

1965. Child Welfare. Inscr. "FUR DIE JUGEND 1965". Multicoloured.
1384. 10 pf. + 5 pf. Type **355** .. 5 5
1385. 15 pf. + 5 pf. Pheasant .. 8 12
1386. 20 pf. + 10 pf. Black grouse 12 12
1387. 40 pf. + 20 pf. Capercaillie 25 60

356. Bismarck (statesman). **357.** Jetliner and Space Capsule.

1965. Otto von Bismarck. 150th Brith Anniv.
1388. **356.** 20 pf. black and red .. 10 10

1965. Int. Transport Exn., Munich. Multicoloured.
1389. 5 pf. Traffic lights and road signs 5 5
1390. 10 pf. "Syncom" satellite and tracking station .. 5 5
1391. 15 pf. Old and modern postal buses 5 5
1392. 20 pf. Old semaphore station and modern signal tower 5 5
1393. 40 pf. Old steam engine & modern electric loco .. 15 5
1394. 60 pf. Type **357** 30 25
1395. 70 pf. Early steamship and modern motorship .. 30 20
No. 1394 was also issued to mark the 10th anniv. of Lufthansa's renewed air services.

358. Bouquet. **359.** I.T.U. Emblem.

1965. "May 1st" (Labour Day). 75th Anniv.
1396. **358.** 15 pf. multicoloured 5 5

1965. I.T.U. Cent.
1397. **359.** 40 pf. black and blue 20 20

360. A Kolping. **361.** Sea-Rescue Vessel.

1965. Adolph Kopling (miners' padre). Death Cent.
1398. **360.** 20 pf. black, red & grey 5 5

1965. German Sea-Rescue Service. Cent.
1399. **361.** 20 pf. violet, blk. & red 5 5

1965. Influx of East German Refugees. 20th Anniv. As T **242** but inscr. "ZWANZIG JAHRE VERTREIBUNG 1945 1965".
1400. 20 pf. slate-purple .. 5 5

362. Evangelical Church Emblem. **363.** Radio Tower.

1965. German Evangelical Church Day and Synod, Cologne.
1401. **362.** 20 pf. black, turq. & bl. 5 5

1965. Radio Exn., Stuttgart.
1402. **363.** 20 pf. blk., blue & mag. 5 5

364. Thurn and Taxis 1, 2, and 5 sgr. Stamps of 1852. **365.** Europa "Sprig".

1965. 1st Postage Stamp. 125th Anniv.
1403. **364.** 20 pf. multicoloured 5 5

1965. Europa.
1404. **356.** 15 pf. green 8 8
1405. 20 pf. red 8 8

366. Cinderella with Birds. **367.** N. Soderblom.

1965. Humanitarian Relief Funds. Inscr. "WOHLFAHRTSMARKE". Multicoloured.
1406 10 pf. + 5 pf. Type **366** .. 5 12
1407. 15 pf. + 5 pf. Cinderella and birds with dress 10 10
1408. 20 pf. + 10 pf. Prince offering slipper to Cinderella 12 10
1409. 40 pf. + 20 pf. Cinderella and Prince on horse 45 60

1966. Nathan Soderblom. Archbishop of Uppsala. Birth Cent.
1410. **367.** 20 pf. black and lilac 8 8

369. Cardinal von Galen. **370.** Brandenburg Gate, Berlin.

1966. Cardinal Clemens von Galen. 20th Death Anniv.
1411. **369.** 20 pf. red, mag. & blk. 8 8

1966.
1412. **370.** 10 pf. chocolate .. 5 5
1413. 20 pf. green 12 12
1414. 30 pf. red 12 5
1415. 50 pf. blue 35 35
1415a. 100 pf. blue 90 35

371. Roebuck. **372.** Christ and Fishermen (Miracle of the Fishes).

1966. Child Welfare. Multicoloured.
1416. 10 pf. + 5 pf. Type **371** 5 10
1417. 20 pf. + 10 pf. Chamois 15 12
1418. 30 pf. + 15 pf. Fallow deer 25 15
1419. 50 pf. + 25 pf. Red deer 55 85

1966. Catholics' Day.
1420. **372.** 30 pf. black & salmon 15 10

373. 19th-cent. Postman. **374.** G. W. Leibniz.

1966. F.I.P. Meeting, Munich. Multicoloured
1421. 30 pf. + 15 pf. Bavarian mail-coach .. 30 40
1422. 50 pf. + 25 pf. Type **373** .. 35 40

1966. Gottfried Leibniz (scientist). 250th Death Anniv.
1423. **374.** 30 pf. black & magenta 15 10

375. Europa "Ship". **376.** Diagram of A.C. Transmission (75th Anniv.).

1966. Europa.
1424. **375.** 20 pf. multicoloured 12 5
1425. 30 pf. multicoloured 15 8

1966. Scientific Annivs. (2nd series). Multicoloured.
1426. 20 pf. Type **376** 10 8
1427. 30 pf. Diagram of electric dynamo (cent.) .. 15 8

377. Princess and Frog. **378.** U.N.I.C.E.F. Emblem.

1966. Humanitarian Relief Funds. Multicoloured.
1428. 10 pf. + 5 pf. Type **377** 8 10
1429. 20 pf. + 10 pf. Frog dining with Princess .. 12 12
1430. 30 pf. + 15 pf. Prince and Princess .. 20 12
1431. 50 pf. + 25 pf. In coach .. 50 75
Designs from Grimm's "The Frog Prince".

1966. U.N.I.C.E.F.
1432. **378.** 30 pf. sep., black & red 15 10

379. W. von Siemens (electrical engineer). **380.** Rabbit.

1966. Werner von Siemens (electrical engineer). Birth Anniv.
1433. **379.** 30 pf. lake 15 10

1967. Child Welfare. Multicoloured.
1434. 10 pf. + 5 pf. Type **380** 15 15
1435. 20 pf. + 10 pf. Weasel .. 15 15
1436. 30 pf. + 15 pf. Hamster 30 25
1437. 50 pf. + 25 pf. Fox .. 75 95
See also Nos. 1454/7.

381. Cogwheels. **382.** Francis of Taxis.

1967. Europa.
1438. **381.** 20 pf. multicoloured 15 10
1439. 30 pf. multicoloured 15 5

1967. Francis of Taxis. 450th Death Anniv.
1440. **382.** 30 pf. black & orange 15 10

383. Evangelical Symbols. **384.** F. von Bodelschwingh (founder's son).

1967. 13th German Evangelical Churches Day.
1441. **383.** 30 pf. black & magenta 15 10

1967. Bethel Institution. Cent.
1442. **384.** 30 pf. black & maroon 15 10

385. Frau Holle at Spinning-wheel. **386.** Wartburg (castle), Wittenberg.

1967. Humanitarian Relief Funds. Multicoloured.
1443. 10 pf. + 5 pf. Type **385** 5 10
1444. 20 pf. + 10 pf. In the clouds .. 12 12
1445. 30 pf. + 15 pf. With shopping-basket and cockerel .. 20 15
1446. 50 pf. + 25 pf. Covered with soot .. 55 75
Designs from Grimm's "Frau Holle" ("Mother Carey").

1967. Re-election of Pres. Lubke. As Type B 60 of West Berlin, but inscr. "DEUTSCHE BUNDESPOST".
1447. 30 pf. red 15 15
1448. 50 pf. blue 25 25

1967. Luther's "Theses" and the Reformation. 450th Anniv.
1449. 386. 30 pf. red 15 10

387. Cross on South American Map.

388. Koenig's Printing Machine.

1967. "Adveniat" (Aid for Catholic Church in Latin America).
1450. 387. 30 pf. multicoloured 15 10

1968. Scientific Annivs. (3rd Series). Multicoloured.
1451. 10 pf. Type 388 .. .. 5 5
1452. 20 pf. Ore Crystals .. 10 5
1453. 30 pf. Lens Refraction .. 15 10
ANNIVS.: 10 pf. 150th Anniv. 20 pf. Millenary of ore mining in Harz Mountains. 30 pf. Abbe-Zeiss Scientific Microscope. Cent.

1968. Child Welfare. As T 380 but inscr. "1968". Multicoloured.
1454. 10 pf.+5 pf. Wildcat .. 15 20
1455. 20 pf.+10 pf. Otter .. 25 25
1456. 30 pf.+15 pf. Badger .. 40 40
1457. 50 pf.+25 pf. Beaver .. 1·10 1·25

389. Trade Symbols.

1968. German Crafts and Trades.
1458. 389. 30 pf. multicoloured 10 5

390. Europa "Key".

391. Karl Marx.

1968. Europa.
1460. 390. 20 pf. yell., brn. & grn. 12 8
1461. 30 pf. yellow, brn. & red 15 8

1968. Karl Marx. 150th Birth Anniv.
1462. 391. 30 pf. red, blk & grey 15 10

392. F. von Langen (horseman).

1968. Olympic Games (1972) Promotion Fund (1st Series).
1463. 392. 10 pf.+5 pf. black and green .. 12 12
1464. – 20 pf.+10 pf. black and green. .. 25 25
1465. – 30 pf. black & lilac 15 5
1466. – 30 pf.+15 pf. black and red .. 25 25
1467. – 50 pf.+25 pf. black and blue .. 60 60
DESIGN: 20 pf. R. Harbig (runner). 30 pf. (No. 1465) Pierre de Coubertin (founder of Olympics). 30 pf. (No. 1466) Helene Mayer (fencer). 50 pf. Carl Diem (sports organiser).
See also Nos. 1493/6, 1524/7, 1589/92, 1621/4 and 1629/32.

393. Opening Bars of "The Mastersingers".

394. Dr. Adenauer.

1968. 1st Performance of Richard Wagner's Opera, "The Mastersingers". Cent.
1468. 393. 30 pf. multicoloured 20 10

1968. Adenauer Commem.
1469. 394. 30 pf. black & orange 20 10

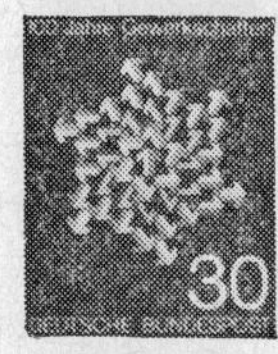
395. Cross, Dove and "The Universe".

396. Northern District 1 g. and Southern District 7 k. stamps of 1868.

1968. Catholics' Day.
1470. 395. 20 pf. violet, yellow and green 20 10

1968. Cent. of North German Postal Confederation and First Stamps.
1471. 396. 30 pf. red, ultramarine and black .. 15 10

397. Arrows.

398. Doll of 1878.

1968. German Trade Unions. Cent.
1472. 397. 30 pf. multicoloured 15 10

1968. Humanitarian Relief Funds. Multcoloured.
1473. 10 pf.+5 pf. Type 398 12 12
1474. 20 pf.+10 pf. Doll of 1850 12 12
1475. 30 pf.+15 pf. Doll of 1870 20 15
1476. 50 pf.+25 pf. Doll of 1885 55 75

399. Human Rights Emblem.

400. Pony.

1968. Human Rights Year.
1477. 399. 30 pf. multicoloured 15 10

1969. Child Welfare.
1478. 400. 10 pf.+5 pf. brown, black and yellow .. 15 15
1479. – 20 pf.+10 pf. chestnut, black and buff 15 15
1480. – 30 pf.+15 pf. brown, black and red .. 25 25
1481. – 50 pf.+25 pf. grey, yellow, black & blue 1·00 1·00
HORSES: 20 pf. Draught-horse. 30 pf. Saddle-horse. 50 pf. Thoroughbred.

401. Junkers "Ju-52" Aircraft.

1969. German Airmail Services. 50th Anniv.
1482. 401. 20 pf. multicoloured 15 8
1483. – 30 pf. multicoloured 20 8
DESIGN: 30 pf. Boeing "707" airliner.

402. Colonnade.

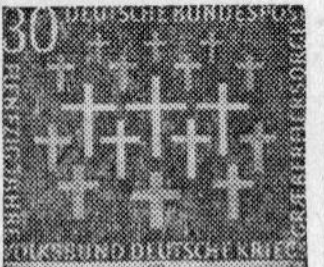
403. "The Five Continents".

1969. Europa.
1484. 402. 20 pf. yell., grn. & bl. 15 5
1485. 30 pf. yellow, brown, red and violet .. 15 10

1969. Int. Labour Organisation. 50th Anniv.
1486. 403. 30 pf. multicoloured 20 10

404. Eagle Emblems of Weimar and Federal Republics.

405. "War Graves".

1969. German Federal Republic. 20th Anniv.
1487. 404. 30 pf. black, gold & red 25 10

1969. German War Graves Commission. 50th Anniv.
1488. 405. 30 pf. blue and yellow 15 10

406. Lakeside Landscape.

407. "Racing Tracks".

1969. Nature Protection. Multicoloured.
1489. 10 pf. Type 406 .. 8 5
1490. 20 pf. Highland landscape 35 15
1491. 30 pf. Alpine landscape .. 15 12
1492. 50 pf. River landscape .. 30 30

1969. Olympic Games (1972). Promotion Fund (2nd Series). Multicoloured.
1493. 10 pf.+5 pf. Type 407 .. 12 10
1494. 20 pf.+10 pf. "Hockey" .. 25 25
1495. 30 pf.+15 pf. "Shooting target" 35 35
1496. 50 pf.+25 pf. "Sailing" .. 80 80

408. "Longing for Justice".

409. "Electro-magnetic Field".

1969. 14th German Protestant Congress, Stuttgart.
1497. 408. 30 pf. multicoloured 15 10

1969. German Radio Exn., Stuttgart.
1498. 409. 30 pf. multicoloured 15 10

410. Maltese Cross Symbol.

411. Bavaria 3 k. Stamp of 1867.

1969. "Malteser Hilfsdienst" (welfare organization).
1500. 410. 30 pf. red and black .. 15 10

1969. Philatelists' Day. German Philatelic Federation Congress and Exn., Garmisch-Partenkirchen.
1501. 411. 30 pf. red and slate .. 15 10

412. Map of Pipeline.

1969. Bad Reichenhall-Traunstein Brine Pipeline. 350th Anniv.
1502. 412. 20 pf. multicoloured 12 10

413. Rothenburg ob der Tauber.

1969. Tourism.
1503. 413. 30 pf. black and red .. 20 10
See also Nos. 1523, 1558, 1564, 1587, 1606, 1641/2, 1655/6 and 1680/2.

414. Mahatma Gandhi.

415. Pope John XXIII.

1969. Mahatma Gandhi. Birth Cent.
1504. 414. 20 pf. black & green 12 10

1969. Pope John XXIII Commem.
1505. 415. 30 pf. red 12 10

416. Locomotive (1835).

417. E. M. Arndt.

1969. Humanitarian Relief Funds. Pewter Figurines. Multicoloured.
(a) Inscr. "WOHLFAHRTSMARKE".
1506. 10 pf.+5 pf. Type 416 .. 5 5
1507. 20 pf.+10 pf. Woman watering flowers (1780) 15 15
1508. 30 pf.+15 pf. Bird salesman (1850) 25 25
1509. 50 pf.+25 pf. Mounted dignitary (1840) .. 60 60
(b) Christmas. Inscr. "WEIHNACHTSMARKE".
1510. 10 pf.+5 pf. "Child Jesus in crib" (1850) .. 12 12

1969. Ernst Arndt (writer). Birth Bicent.
1511. 417. 30 pf. lake and bistre 15 10

418. "H. von Rugge".

1970. Child Welfare. Minnesinger Themes. Multicoloured.
1512. 10 pf.+5 pf. Type 418 .. 10 10
1513. 20 pf.+10 pf. "W. von Eschenbach" 20 20
1514. 30 pf.+15 pf. "W. von Metz" 30 30
1515. 50 pf.+25 pf. "W. von der Vogelweide" .. 70 70

419. G. W. Hegel (philosopher).

420. Saar 1 m. Stamp of 1947.

1970. Birth Bicents.
1516. – 10 pf. black & blue .. 8 5
1517. 419. 20 pf. black & olive .. 12 10
1518. – 30 pf. black and pink 20 10
DESIGNS: 10 pf. Beethoven. 30 pf. F. Holderlin (poet).

1970. "Sabria 70" Stamp Exn., Saarbrucken.
1519. 420. 30 pf. grn., blk. & verm. 20 10

421. "Flaming Sun". 422. Von Munchhausen on Severed Horse.

1970. Europa.
1520. 421. 20 pf. green 12 5
1521. 30 pf. red 15 8

1970. Baron H. von Munchhausen. 250th Birth Anniv.
1522. 422. 20 pf. multicoloured 15 5

1970. Tourism. Horiz. design as T 413, but with view of Oberammergau.
1523. 30 pf. black and orange .. 20 10

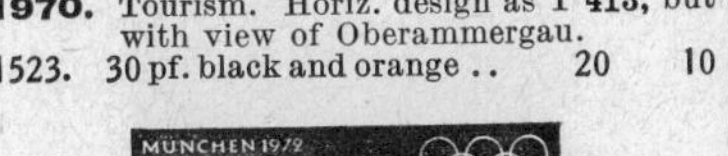

423. Royal Palace.

1970. Olympic Games (1972) Promotion Fund (3rd Series).
1524. 423. 10 pf. + 5 pf. brown.. 12 12
1525. – 20 pf. + 10 pf. turq... 25 25
1526. – 30 pf. + 15 pf. red .. 35 35
1527. – 50 pf. + 25 pf. blue .. 70 70
DESIGNS (Munich buildings): 20 pf. Propylaea. 30 pf. Glyptothek. 50 pf. "Bavaria" (statue and colonnade).

424. Ship and Road-tunnel. 425. Nurse with Invalid.

1970. Kiel Canal. 75th Anniv.
1528. 424. 20 pf. multicoloured 15 5

1970. Voluntary Relief Services. Multicoloured.
1529. 5 pf. Oxygen-lance operator 5 5
1530. 10 pf. Mountain rescue.. 5 5
1531. 20 pf. Type 425 .. 15 8
1532. 30 pf. Fireman with hose 20 8
1533. 50 pf. Road-accident casualty 30 20
1534. 70 pf. Rescue from drowning 45 35

426. President Heinemann. 427. Illuminated Cross.

1970.
1535. 426. 5 pf. black 5 5
1536. 10 pf. brown.. .. 5 5
1537. 20 pf. green 5 5
1538. 25 pf. green 10 5
1539. 30 pf. brown .. 12 5
1540. 40 pf. orange .. 20 10
1541. 50 pf. blue 20 8
1542. 60 pf. blue 25 12
1543. 70 pf. agate 30 15
1544. 80 pf. green 30 20
1545. 90 pf. red 70 20
1546. 1 Dm. green 45 15
1547. 110 pf. grey 50 25
1548. 120 pf. brown .. 50 30
1549. 130 pf. ochre .. 55 25
1550. 140 pf. green .. 65 30
1551. 150 pf. lake 70 30
1552. 160 pf. orange .. 70 40
1553. 170 pf. orange .. 75 30
1554. 190 pf. purple .. 90 30
1555. 2 Dm. violet.. .. 1·00 35

1970. Catholic Church World Mission.
1556. 427. 20 pf. yellow & green 12 10

428 Stylised Cross. 429. "Jester".

1970. Catholics Day and 83rd German Catholic Congress, Trier.
1557. 428. 20 pf. multicoloured 12 5

1970. Tourism. As T 413.
1558. 20 pf. black and green .. 15 5
DESIGN: 20 pf. View of Cochem.

1970. Humanitarian Relief Funds. Puppets. Multicoloured.
(a) Inscr. "WOHLFAHRTSMARKE".
1559. 10 pf. + 5 pf. Type 429 5 5
1560. 20 pf. + 10 pf. "Buffoon" 15 15
1561. 30 pf. + 15 pf. "Clown" 25 25
1562. 50 pf. + 25 pf. "Harlequin" 55 55
(b) Christmas. Inscr. "WEIHNACHTSMARKE".
1563. 10 pf. + 5 pf. "Angel" 12 12

1970. Tourism. Horiz. design as T 413, but with view of Freiburg im Breisgau.
1564. 20 pf. brown and green 15 5

430. A. J. Comenius (scholar). 431. Engels as Young Man.

1970. Int. Education Year, and Amos Comenius (Jan Komensky), 300th Death Anniv.
1565. 430. 30 pf. red and black.. 20 5

1970. Friedrich Engels. 150th Birth Anniv.
1566. 431. 50 pf. red and blue .. 30 15

432. German Eagle. 433. "Ebert" Stamp of 1928 and inscr. "To the German People".

1971. German Unification Cent.
1567. 432. 30 pf. blk., red & orge. 15 5

1971. Pres. Friedrich Ebert. Birth Cent.
1568. 433. 30 pf. grn., lake & blk. 15 5

434. "King of Blackamoors". 435. Molecular Chain.

1971. Child Welfare. Children's Drawings. Multicoloured.
1569. 10 pf. + 5 pf. Type 434 .. 12 12
1570. 20 pf. + 10 pf. "Flea" .. 20 20
1571. 30 pf. + 15 pf. "Puss-in-Boots" .. 30 30
1572. 50 pf. + 25 pf. "Serpent" 70 70

1971. 125 Years of Chemical Fibre Research.
1573. 435. 20 pf. black, red & grn. 12 5

436. Road-crossing Patrol. 437. Luther before Charles V.

1971. New Road Traffic Regulations (1st series).
1574. 436. 10 pf. blk., blue & red 5 5
1575. – 20 pf. blk., red & grn. 12 5
1576. – 30 pf. red, blk. & grey 15 5
1577. – 50 pf. blk., blue & red 30 20
ROAD SIGNS: 20 pf. "Right-of-way across junction". 30 pf. "STOP". 50 pf. "Pedestrian Crossing".
See also Nos. 1579/82.

1971. Diet of Worms. 450th Anniv.
1578. 437. 30 pf. black and red.. 15 8

1971. New Traffic Regulations. (2nd series). Horiz designs similar to T 436.
1579. 5 pf. red, black and blue.. 5 5
1580. 10 pf. multicoloured .. 5 5
1581. 20 pf. red, black & green 12 8
1582. 30 pf. yellow, black & red 25 8
NEW HIGHWAY CODE: 5 pf. Overtaking. 10 pf. Warning of obstruction. 20 pf. Lane discipline. 30 pf. Pedestrian Crossing.

438. Europa Chain. 439. Thomas a Kempis writing "The Imitation of Christ".

1971. Europa.
1583. 438. 20 pf. gold, grn. & blk. 10 5
1584. 30 pf. gold, red & blk. 20 5

1971. Thomas a Kempis (devotional writer). 500th Death Anniv.
1585. 439. 30 pf. black and red 15 5

440. Durer's Monogram. 441. Meeting Emblem.

1971. Albrecht Durer. 500th Birth Anniv.
1586. 440. 30 pf. brown & red .. 20 5

1971. Tourism. As T 413, but with view of Nuremburg.
1587. 30 pf. black and red.. 20 5

1971. Whitsun Ecumenical Meeting. Augsburg.
1588. 441. 30 pf. black, orange & red 20 5

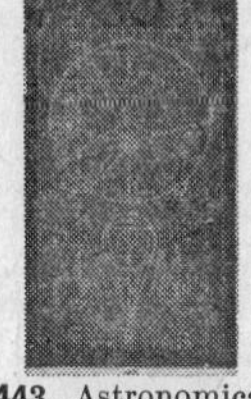

442. Ski-jumping. 443. Astronomical Calculus.

1971. Olympic Games (1972). Promotion Fund. (4th Series). Winter Games, Sapporo.
1589. 442. 10 pf. + 5 pf. blk. & brn. 15 15
1590. – 20 pf. + 10 pf. blk. & grn. 35 35
1591. – 30 pf. + 15 pf. blk. & red 50 50
1592. – 50 pf. + 25 pf. blk. & bl. 95 95
DESIGNS: 20 pf. Ice-dancing. 30 pf. Skiing-start. 50 pf. Ice-hockey.

1971. Johann Kepler (astronomer). 400th Birth Anniv.
1594. 443. 30 pf. gold, red & blk. 20 5

444. Dante. 445. Alcohol and front of Car. ("Don't Drink and Drive").

1971. Dante Allghieri. 650th Death Anniv.
1595. 444. 10 pf. black 5 5

1971. Coil Stamps. Accident Prevention.
1596. – 5 pf. orange 5 5
1597. – 10 pf. brown.. .. 5 5
1598. – 20 pf. violet 8 5
1599. 445. 25 pf. green 10 5
1600. – 30 pf. red 12 5
1601. – 40 pf. mauve .. 15 5
1602. – 50 pf. blue 20 5
1603. – 60 pf. blue .. .. 1·50 50
1603a. – 70 pf. blue and green 30 12
1604. – 1 Dm. green 45 12
1605. – 1 Dm. 50 brown .. 65 35
DESIGNS: 5 pf. Man within flame, and spent match ("Fire Prevention"). 10 pf. Fall from ladder. 20 pf. Unguarded machinery ("Factory Safety"). 30 pf. Falling brick and protective helmet. 40 pf. Faulty electric plug. 50 pf. Protruding nail in plank. 60 pf., 70 pf. Ball in front of car ("Child Road Safety"). 1 Dm. Crate on hoist. 1 Dm. 50 Open manhole.

1971. Tourism. As T 413, but with view of Goslar.
1606. 20 pf. black & green.. 15 5

446. Women churning Butter. 447. Deaconess and Nurse.

1971. Humanitarian Relief Funds. Wooden Toys. Multicoloured.
(a) Inscr. "WOHLFAHRTSMARKE".
1607. 20 pf. + 10 pf. Type 446 .. 15 15
1608. 25 pf. + 10 pf. Horseman on wheels 15 15
1609. 30 pf. + 15 pf. Nutcracker man 20 20
1610. 60 pf. + 30 pf. Dovecote .. 55 55
(b) Christmas. Inscr. "WEIHNACHTSMARKE".
1611. 20 pf. + 10 pf. Angel with three candles 15 15

1972. Johann Wilhelm Lohe (founder of Deaconesses Mission, Neuendettelsau). Death Cent.
1612. 447. 25 pf. slate, black & green 12 5

448. Ducks crossing Road. 449. Senefelder's Press.

1972. Child Welfare. Animal Protection. Multicoloured.
1613. 20 pf. + 10 pf. Type 448 .. 20 20
1614. 25 pf. + 10 pf. Hunter scaring deer 25 25
1615. 30 pf. + 15 pf. Child protecting bird from cat .. 35 35
1616. 60 pf. + 30 pf. Boy annoying swans 85 85

1972. "175 Years of Offset Lithography".
1617. 449. 25 pf. multicoloured 15 5

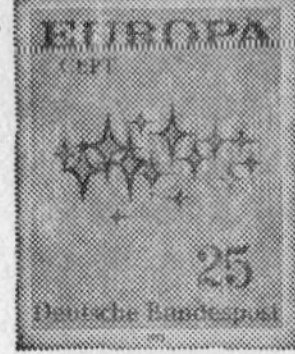

450. "Communications". 451. Lucas Cranach.

1972. Europa.
1618. 450. 25 pf. multicoloured 12 10
1619. 30 pf. multicoloured 15 12

1972. Lucas Cranach the Elder (painter). 500th Birth Anniv.
1620. 451. 25 pf. blk., stone & grn. 15 5

452. Wrestling. 453. Invalid Archer.

1972. Olympic Games, Munich (5th Series). Multicoloured.
1621. 20 pf. + 10 pf. Type 452 .. 25 25
1622. 25 pf. + 10 pf. Sailing .. 30 30
1623. 30 pf. + 15 pf. Gymnastics 30 30
1624. 60 pf. + 30 pf. Swimming 1·10 1·10
See also Nos. 1629/32.

1972. 21st Int. Games for the Paralysed, Heidelberg.
1626. 453. 40 pf. red, blk. & yell. 20 10

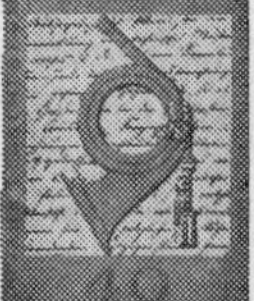

454. Posthorn and Decree. 455. K. Schumacher.

1972. German Postal Museum. Cent.
1627. 454. 40 pf. gold, blk. & red 20 5

1972. Kurt Schumacher (politician). 20th Death Anniv.
1628. 455. 40 pf. black and red .. 20 5

1972. Olympic Games, Munich (7th Series). As Type **452**. Multicoloured.

1629.	25 pf.+5 pf. Long-jumping	1·40	1·40
1630.	30 pf.+10 pf. Basketball	1·40	1·40
1631.	40 pf.+10 pf. Throwing the discus	1·40	1·40
1632.	70 pf.+10 pf. Canoeing ..	1·40	1·40

456. Open Book.

457. Music and Signature.

1972. Int. Book Year.
1634. **456.** 40 pf. multicoloured 20 5

1972. Heinrich Schutz (composer). 300th Death Anniv.
1635. **457.** 40 pf. multicoloured 20 5

458. Knight.

459. "The Three Wise Men".

1972. Humanitarian Relief Funds. Multicoloured.

(a) Chessmen. Inscr. "WOHLFAHRTSMARKE".

1636.	20 pf.+10 pf. Type **458**	15	15
1637.	30 pf.+15 pf. Castle ..	20	20
1638.	40 pf.+20 pf. Queen ..	30	30
1639.	70 pf.+35 pf. King ..	55	55

(b) Christmas. Inscr. "WEIHNACHTSMARKE".

1640. 30 pf.+15 pf. Type **459** 20 20

1972. Tourism. As T **413**.

1641.	30 pf. black and green ..	15	5
1642.	40 pf. black and orange ..	20	8

VIEWS: 30 pf. Heligoland. 40 pf. Heidelberg.

460. Revellers.

1972. Cologne Carnival. 150th Anniv.
1643. **460.** 40 pf. multicoloured 20 5

461. H. Heine.

1972. Heinrich Heine (poet). 175th Birth Anniv.
1644. **461.** 40 pf. blk., red & pink 20 5

462. "Brot fur die Welt".

463. Wurzburg Cathedral (seal).

1972. Freedom from Hunger Campaign.
1645. **462.** 30 pf. green, emerald and red 20 20

1972. Catholic Synod '72.
1646. **463.** 40 pf. blk., pur. & red 20 5

464. National Colours of France and Germany.

1973. Franco-German Treaty. Tenth Anniv.
1647. **464.** 40 pf. multicoloured 20 15

465. Osprey.

467. Radio Mast and Transmission.

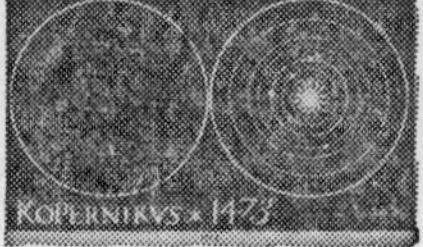

466. Copernicus.

1973. Youth Welfare. Birds of Prey. Multicoloured.

1648.	25 pf.+10 pf. Type **465**	15	15
1649.	30 pf.+15 pf. Buzzard ..	25	25
1650.	40 pf.+20 pf. Kite ..	40	40
1651.	70 pf.+35 pf. Montagu's Harrier	80	80

1973. Copernicus. 500th Birth Anniv.
1652. **466.** 40 pf. black and red 20 10

1973. Interpol. 50th Anniv.
1653. **467.** 40 pf. blk., red & grey 20 10

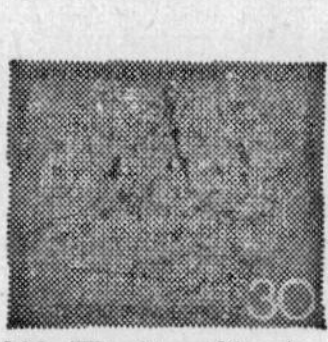

468. Weather Chart.

469. "Gymnast" (poster).

1973. Int. Meteorological Organisation. Cent.
1654. **468.** 30 pf. multicoloured 20 10

1973. Tourism. As T **413**.

1655.	40 pf. black and red ..	25	10
1656.	40 pf. black and orange ..	25	10

VIEWS: No. 1655, Hamburg. 1656. Rudesheim.

1973. Gymnastics Festival, Stuttgart.
1657. **469.** 40 pf. multicoloured 20 10

470. Kassel (Hesse) Sign.

472. "R" Motif.

471. Europa "Posthorn".

1973. "I.B.R.A. Munchen 73" Int. Stamp Exhib., Munich. F.I.P. Congress. Post-house Signs. Multicoloured.

1658.	40 pf.+20 pf. Type **470** ..	55	55
1659.	70 pf.+35 pf. Prussia ..	90	90

1973. Europa.

1661. **471.**	30 pf. yell., myrtle & grn.	20	10
1662.	40 pf. yell., lake & pink	20	10

1973. Roswitha von Gandersheim (poetess). 1,000th Death Anniv.
1663. **472.** 40 pf. multicoloured 20 10

473. M. Kolbe.

474. "Profile" (from poster).

1973. Father Maximilian Kolbe (Concentration camp victim). Commem.
1664. **473.** 40 pf. red, brn. & blk. 20 10

1973. 15th German Protestant Church Conference.
1665. **474.** 30 pf. multicoloured 15 10

475. Environmental Conference Emblem and Waste.

1973. "Protection of the Environment". Multicoloured.

1666.	25 pf. Type **475**	15	5
1667.	30 pf. Emblem and "Water"	15	8
1668.	40 pf. Emblem and "Noise"	20	10
1669.	70 pf. Emblem and "Air"	40	25

476. Schickard's Calculating Machine.

477. Otto Wels.

1973. Schickard's Calculating Machine. 350th Anniv.
1670. **476.** 40 pf. black, red and orange 20 20

1973. Otto Wels (Social Democratic Party leader). Birth Cent.
1671. **477.** 40 pf. purple and lilac 20 10

478. Lubeck Cathedral.

1973. Lubeck Cathedral. 800th Anniv.
1672. **478.** 40 pf. multicoloured 20 10

479. U.N. and German Eagle Emblems.

1973. Admission of German Federal Republic to U.N. Organization.
1673. **479.** 40 pf. multicoloured 20 10

480. 18th Century Pedal Grand Piano.

481. Christmas Star.

1973. Humanitarian Relief Funds. Multicoloured.

(a) Musical Instruments. Inscr. "WOHLFAHRTSMARKE".

1674.	25 pf.+10 pf. 19th century French horn	15	15
1675.	30 pf.+15 pf. Type **480** ..	20	20
1676.	40 pf.+20 pf. 18th century violin	30	30
1677.	70 pf.+70 pf. 18th century pedal harp ..	60	60

(b) Christmas. Inscr. "WEIHNACHTSMARKE".

1678. 30 pf.+15 pf. Type **481** .. 1·10 1·10

482. Radio set of 1923.

1973. "50 Years of German Broadcasting".
1679. **482.** 30 pf. multicoloured 15 8

1974. Tourism. As Type **413**.

1680.	30 pf. black and green ..	15	10
1681.	40 pf. black and red ..	20	10
1682.	40 pf. black and red ..	20	10

VIEWS: No. 1680, Saarbrucken. No. 1681, Aachen. No. 1682. Bremen.

483. Louise Otto-Peters.

1974. Women in German Politics. Each black and orange.

1683.	40 pf. Type **483**	20	12
1684.	40 pf. Helene Lange	20	12
1685.	40 pf. Rosa Luxemburg	20	12
1686.	40 pf. Gertrud Baumer ..	20	12

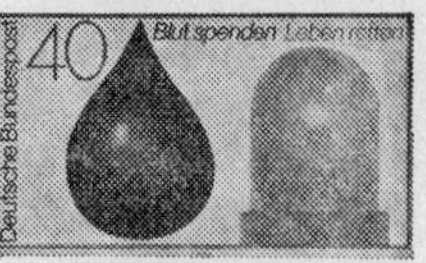

484. Drop of Blood and Emergency Light.

1974. Blood Donor and Accident/Rescue Services.
1687. **484.** 40 pf. red and blue 12 10

485. "Deer in Red" (Franz Marc).

1974. German Expressionist Paintings. Multicoloured.

1688.	30 pf. Type **485**	12	5
1689.	30 pf. "Girls under Trees" (A. Macke)	12	5
1690.	40 pf. "Portrait in Blue" (A. von Jawlensky) ..	15	8
1691.	50 pf. "Pechstein asleep" (E. Heckel) (vert.) ..	20	12
1692.	70 pf. "Still Life with Telescope" (Max Beckmann)	25	10
1693.	120 pf. "Old Peasant" (L. Kirchner) (vert.) ..	40	30

486. St. Thomas teaching Pupils.

1974. St. Thomas Aquinas. 700th Death Anniv.
1694. **486.** 40 pf. black and red .. 15 8

487. Disabled Persons in Outline.

1974. Rehabilitation of the Handicapped.
1695. **487.** 20 pf. red and black .. 25 12

488. Construction (Bricklayer).

489. "Ascending Youth". (W. Lehmbruck).

1974. Youth Welfare. Youth Activities. Multicoloured.

1696.	25 pf.+10 pf. Type **488** ..	20	20
1697.	30 pf.+15 pf. Folk-dancing	25	25
1698.	40 pf.+20 pf. Study ..	40	40
1699.	70 pf.+35 pf. Research ..	1·40	1·40

1974. Europa.

1700. **489.**	30 pf. blk., grn. & silver	20	12
1701. –	40 pf. blk., red & lilac	25	12

DESIGN: 40 pf. "Kneeling Woman" (W. Lehmbruck).

490. Imanuel Kant. **491.** Country Road.

1974. Imanuel Kant (philosopher). 250th Birth Anniv.

1702. **490.** 90 pf. red 40 30

1974. Rambling, and Birth Centenaries of Richard Schirrman and Wilhelm Munker (founders of Youth Hostelling Assn.).

1704. **491.** 30 pf. multicoloured 20 12

492. Friedrich Klopstock. **493.** "Crowned Cross" Symbol.

1974. Friedrich Gottlieb Klopstock (poet). 250th Birth Anniv.

1705. **492.** 40 pf. black and red .. 20 12

1974. German Protestant Church Diaconal Association (charitable organization). 125th Anniv.

1706. **493.** 40p. multicoloured .. 20 12

494. Goalkeeper saving Goal.

1974. World Cup Football Championships. Multicoloured.

1707. 30 pf. Type **494** 15 10
1708. 40 pf. Mid-field melee .. 20 12

495. Hans Holbein (self-portrait). **496.** Broken Prison Bars.

1974. Hans Holbein the Elder (painter). 450th Death Anniv.

1709. **495.** 50 pf. black and red .. 30 12

1974. Amnesty International Commemoration.

1710. **496.** 70 pf. black and blue 35 20

497. "Man and Woman Watching the Moon" (Friedrich).

1974. Casper Friedrich (painter). Birth Centenary.

1711. **497.** 50 pf. multicoloured 30 15

498. Campion. **499.** Old Letter-boxes.

1974. Humanitarian Relief Funds. Flowers. Multicoloured.

(a) Welfare Stamps. 25th Anniv. Inscr. "25 JAHRE WOHLFAHRTSMARKE".

1712. 30 pf. + 15 pf. Type **498** 20 20
1713. 40 pf. + 20 pf. Foxglove 30 30
1714. 50 pf. + 25 pf. Mallow .. 35 35
1715. 70 pf. + 35 pf. Campanula 55 55

(b) Christmas. Inscr. "WEIHNACHTSMARKE".

1716. 40 pf. + 20 pf. Poinsettia 30 30

1974. Universal Postal Union. Cent.

1717. **499.** 50 pf. multicoloured 35 20

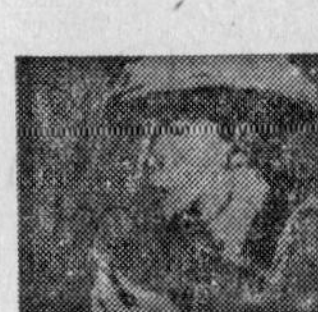 

500. Annette Kolb. **502.** Mother and Child and Emblem.

501. Dr. Schweitzer.

1975. "Important Women". German Writers. Multicoloured.

1718. 30 pf. Type **500** 20 12
1719. 40 pf. Ricarda Huch .. 25 12
1720. 50 pf. Else Lasker-Schuler 30 15
1721. 70 pf. Gertrud von le Fort 1·00 55

1975. Birth Centenaries.

1722. – 40 pf. black and green 20 12
1723. – 50 pf. black and red .. 25 12
1724. **501.** 70 pf. black and blue 35 20

DESIGNS: 40 pf. Hans Bockler (trade union leader). 50 f. Matthias Erzberger (statesman).

1975. Mothers' Rest Organization. 25th Anniv.

1725. **502.** 50 pf. multicoloured 35 20

503. Detail of Ceiling Painting (Sistine Chapel). **504.** Plan of St. Peter's, Rome.

1975. Michelangelo. 500th Birth Anniv.

1726. **503.** 70 pf. black and blue 25 12

1975. Holy Year ("Year of Reconciliation").

1727. **504.** 50 pf. multicoloured 35 20

505. Ice-hockey Players.

1975. World Ice-hockey Championships.

1728. **505.** 50 pf. multicoloured 25 12

506. Diesel Locomotive, Series 218.

1975. Youth Welfare. Railway Locomotives. Multicoloured.

1729. 30 pf. + 15 pf. Type **506** 25 12
1730. 40 pf. + 20 pf. Electric loco. Series 103 .. 30 30
1731. 50 pf. + 25 pf. Electric motortrain. Series 403 35 35
1732. 70 pf. + 35 pf. "Transrapid" hovertrain (model) 40 40

 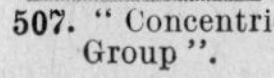 

507. "Concentric Group". **509.** "Neuss" (wood carving from Pfettisheim's "Burgundian Wars").

508. Morike's Silhouette and Signature.

1975. Europa. Paintings by Oskar Schlemmer. Multicoloured.

1733. 40 pf. Type **507** .. 12 12
1734. 50 pf. "Bauhaus Staircase" 20 15

1975. Eduard Morike (writer). Death Cent.

1735. **508.** 40 pf. multicoloured 25 15

1975. Siege of Neuss. 500th Anniv.

1736. **509.** 50 pf. multicoloured 20 12

510. Jousting Contest.

1975. Landshut Wedding. 500th Anniv.

1737. **510.** 50 pf. multicoloured 25 15

 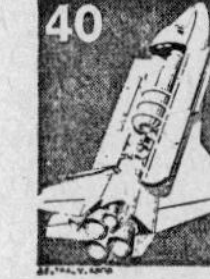

511. Mainz Cathedral. **512.** Space Laboratory.

1975. Mainz Cathedral. Millenary.

1738. **511.** 40 pf. multicoloured 25 15

1975. Industry and Technology.

1742. – 5 pf. green 5 5
1743. – 10 pf. purple .. 5 5
1744. – 20 pf. red 8 5
1745. – 30 pf. violet 10 10
1746. **512.** 40 pf. green 5 5
1747. – 50 pf. purple .. 5 5
1748. – 70 pf. blue 30 15
1749. – 80 pf. green 35 20
1750. – 100 pf. brown .. 45 20
1751. – 120 pf. blue 55 25
1752. – 140 pf. red 65 35
1753. – 160 pf. green .. 70 30
1754. – 200 pf. purple .. 90 35
1755. – 500 pf. black .. 2·25 2·25

DESIGNS: 5 pf. Telecommunications satellite. 10 pf. Rail motor-train. 20 pf. Lighthouse. 30 pf. Rescue helicopter. 50 pf. Earth station. 70 pf. Shipbuilding. 80 pf. Farm tractor. 100 pf. Lignite excavator. 120 pf. Chemical plant. 140 pf. Power station. 160 pf. Blast furnace. 200 pf. Drilling rig. 500 pf. Radio telescope.

513. Town Hall and Market, Alsfeld.

1975. European Architectural Heritage Year. Multicoloured.

1756. 50 pf. Type **513** 25 12
1757. 50 pf. Plonlein, Siebers Tower and Kobelzeller Gate, Rothenburg o. T. 25 12
1758. 50 pf. Town Hall, Trier 25 12
1759. 50 pf. Xanten 25 12

514. Stages of Addiction.

1975. "Fight Drug Abuse" Campaign.

1760. **514.** 40 pf. Multicoloured 25 12

515. Royal Prussian Posthouse Sign, c. 1776. **516.** Edelweiss.

1975. Stamp Day.

1761. **515.** 10 pf. multicoloured 25 12

1975. Humanitarian Relief Funds. Alpine Flowers.

1762. 30 pf. + 15 pf. Type **516** .. 25 12
1763. 40 pf. + 20 pf. Troll-flower 20 12
1764. 50 pf. + 25 pf. Alpine rose 5 5
1765. 70 pf. + 35 pf. Pasque-flower 25 25

1975. Christmas. As T **516** but inscr. "WEIHNACHTSMARKE 1975". Mult.

1766. **516.** 40 pf. + 20 pf. Christmas Rose 30 30

517. Ski-runners. **518.** Dr. Adenauer.

1975. Winter Olympic Games, Innsbruck.

1768. **517.** 50 pf. multicoloured 45 45

1975. Konrad Adenauer. Birth Cent.

1769. **518.** 50 pf. green 30 30

519. Title-pages of Hans Sachs' Books. **520.** Junkers "F-13" Aircraft.

1976. Hans Sachs (poet and composer). 400th Death Anniv.

1770. **519.** 40 pf. multicoloured 12 12

1976. Deutsche Lufthansa Airline. 50th Anniv.

1771. **520.** 50 pf. multicoloured 25 12

521. Commemorative Inscription. **522.** "E G".

1976. "25 Years of Federal Constitutional Court".

1772. **521.** 50 pf. multicoloured 25 12

1976. European Coal and Steel Community. 25th Anniv.

1773. **522.** 40 pf. multicoloured 20 10

523. Suspension Train. **524.** Basketball.

1976. Wuppertal Suspension Railway. 75th Anniv.

1774. **523.** 50 pf. multicoloured 25 12

1976. Youth Welfare. "Training for the Olympics". Multicoloured.
1775. 30 pf. + 15 pf. Type **524**.. 25 25
1776. 40 pf. + 20 pf. Rowing .. 30 30
1777. 50 pf. + 25 pf. Gymnastics 35 35
1778. 70 pf. + 35 pf. Volleyball 55 55

525. Swimming.

1976. Olympic Games, Montreal. Mult.
1779. 40 pf. + 20 pf. Type **525**.. 30 30
1780. 50 pf. + 25 pf. High-jumping 35 35

526. "Vendor of Trinkets". **527.** Dr. Sonnenschein.

1976. Europa. Ludwigsburg China. Multicoloured.
1782. 40 pf. Type **526** 20 12
1783. 50 pf. "Vendor of Prints" 25 15

1976. Dr. Carl Sonnenschein (The "Cosmopolitan Clergyman"). Birth Centenary.
1784. **527.** 50 pf. multicoloured 25 15

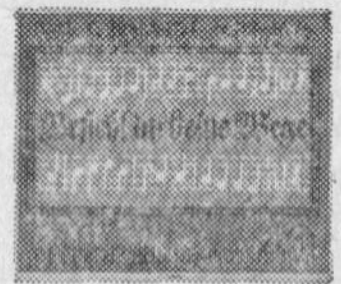

528. Opening Bars of Hymn "Entrust Yourself to God".

1976. Paul Gerhardt (hymn-writer). 300th Birth Anniv.
1785. **528.** 40 pf. multicoloured 20 12

529. "The Conductor" (contemporary lithograph).

1976. Carl Maria von Weber (composer) 150th Death Anniv.
1786. **529.** 50 pf. black & brown 25 15

530. Carl Schurz, Washington Capitol and U.S. Flag.

1976. American Revolution Bicent.
1787. **530.** 70 pf. multicoloured 35 20

531. Wagnerian Stage.

1976. Bayreuth Festival. Centenary.
1788. **531.** 50 pf. multicoloured 25 25

532. Bronze Ritual Chariot.

1976. Archaeological Cultural Heritage. Multicoloured.
1789. 30 pf. Type **532**.. 15 15
1790. 40 pf. Gold-ornamental bowl 20 20
1791. 50 pf. Silver necklet .. 25 25
1792. 120 pf. Roman cup with masks 60 60

533. Golden Plover. **534.** "Creature of Fable".

1976. Bird Protection.
1793. **533.** 50 pf. multicoloured

1976. J. J. C. von Grimmelshausen (writer). 300th Death Anniv.
1794. **534.** 40 pf. multicoloured 20 20

Type **534** is taken from Grimmelshausen's "Simpliciissimus Teutsch".

III. WEST BERLIN.

The Russian Government withdrew from the four-power control of Berlin on 1st July, 1948, and the Western Sectors remain under American, British and French control. West Berlin was constituted a "Land" of the Federal Republic on 1st September, 1950.

The Russian Zone issues inscribed "STADT BERLIN" (which we do not list unoverprinted in this Catalogue), were not intended for use throughout Berlin, but were for the Russian sector of the city and for Brandenburg.

The first stamps to be used in the Western Sectors were Nos. A 4/5 and A 7 of the Anglo-American Zones, followed by Nos. A 36/52, which were on sale from 24th June to 31st August, 1948, and remained valid until 19th September, 1948.

1948. 100 pfennige = 1 Deutsche Mark (East).
1949. 100 pfennige = 1 Deutsche Mark (West).

1948. Pictorial issue of 1947 (Nos. 928/48) optd. **BERLIN.**
B 1. 2 pf. black .. .. 70 1·90
B 2. 6 pf. violet 30 55
B 3. 8 pf. red 40 55
B 4. 10 pf. green 30 10
B 5. 12 pf. grey 30 40
B 25. 15 pf. brown .. .. 3·25 1·00
B 7. 16 pf. green 50 75
B 26. 20 pf. blue .. .. 1·60 25
B 9. 24 pf. brown 35 30
B 10. 25 pf. yellow .. .. 12·00 21·00
B 11. 30 pf. red.. .. .. 1·90 2·25
B 12. 40 pf. mauve .. .. 1·50 1·25
B 13. 50 pf. blue .. .. 4·50 12·00
B 14. 60 pf. brown .. .. 1·90 15·00
B 15. 80 pf. blue .. .. 4·50 7·50
B 16. 84 pf. green .. .. 9·00 32·00
B 17. 1 m. olive .. .. 18·00 50·00
B 18. 2 m. violet .. .. 30·00 £120
B 19. 3 m. lake .. .. 35·00 £180
B 20. 5 m. blue .. .. 38·00 £225

B 1. Stephan Monument and Globe. **B 2.** Heinrich von Stephan Monument.

1949. U.P.U. 75th Anniv.
B 35. **B 1.** 12 pf. grey .. .. 3·50 3·00
B 36. 16 pf. green .. .. 8·50 3·00
B 37. 24 pf. orange .. .. 7·50 15
B 38. 50 pf. olive .. .. 55·00 7·00
B 39. 60 pf. brown .. .. 55·00 7·00
B 40. **B 2.** 1 Dm. olive .. .. 25·00 24·00
B 41. 2 Dm. purple .. .. 30·00 12·00

B 3. Schoneberg. **B 4.** Aeroplane over Tempelhof.

1949. Inscr. "DEUTSCHE POST". Berlin Views. (a) Small size.
B 42. – 1 pf. grey 5 5
B 43. **B 3.** 4 pf. chestnut .. 15 5
B 43c. – 4 pf. brown .. 1·10 75
B 44. – 5 pf. green 30 5
B 45. – 6 pf. purple 35 35
B 46. **B 3.** 8 pf. orange 60 35
B 47. – 10 pf. emerald .. 50 5
B 48. **B 4.** 15 pf. brown .. 2·50 15
B 49. – 20 pf. red .. .. 2·40 5
B 49b. – 20 pf. red .. .. 20·00 10
B 50. – 25 pf. yellow .. 10·00 20
B 51. – 30 pf. blue .. .. 2·50 15
B 52. **B 3.** 40 pf. lake .. .. 5·00 5
B 53. – 50 pf. olive .. .. 6·00 5
B 54. – 60 pf. lake .. .. 22·00 5
B 55. – 80 pf. blue .. .. 4·50 25
B 56. – 90 pf. green .. .. 5·00 25

(b) Large size.
B 57. **B 4.** 1 Dm. olive .. 11·00 30
B 58. – 2 Dm. purple .. 18·00 30
B 59. – 3 Dm. red .. .. £100 2·00
B 60. – 5 Dm. blue .. 40·00 3·00

DESIGNS—SMALL SIZE: 1 pf. Brandenburg Gate. 4 pf. (No. 43b) Exhibition Bldg. 5 pf., 25 pf. "Tegel Schloss". 6 pf., 50 pf. Reichstag Bldg. 10 pf., 30 pf. "Kleistpark". 20 pf. (B 49), 80 pf., 90 pf. Technical High School. 20 pf. (B 49a) Olympia Stadium. 60 pf. National Gallery. LARGE SIZE: 2 Dm. "Gendarmenmarkt". 3 Dm. Brandenburg Gate. 5 Dm. "Tegel Schloss".

For similar views inscr. "DEUTSCHE POST BERLIN" see Nos. B 118/9.

B 5. Goethe and Scene from "Iphigenie". **B 6.** Alms Bowl and Bear.

1949. Goethe. Birth Bicent. Portraits of Goethe and scenes from his works.
B 61. **B 5.** 10 pf. green .. .. 60·00 18·00
B 62. – 20 pf. red .. .. 55·00 27·00
B 63. – 30 pf. blue .. .. 7·50 8·50

DESIGNS: Scenes from—20 pf. "Reineke Fuchs" or—30 pf. "Faust".

1949. Numeral and pictorial issues of 1946/7 surch. **BERLIN** and bold figures.
B 64. **183.** 5 pf. on 45 pf. red .. 1·25 10
B 65. **C.** 10 pf. on 24 pf. brn. 2·50 15
B 66. **B.** 20 pf. on 80 pf. blue 12·00 7·50
B 67. **186.** 1 m. on 3 m. lake .. 55·00 6·50

1949. Berlin Relief Fund.
B 68. **B 6.** 10 pf. + 5 pf. green .. 45·00 55·00
B 69. 20 pf. + 5 pf. red .. 45·00 55·00
B 70. 30 pf. + 5 pf. blue .. 45·00 55·00

B 7. **B 8.** Harp.

1950. European Recovery Programme.
B 71. **B 7.** 20 pf. red .. .. 30·00 22·00

1950. Berlin Philharmonic Orchestra. Inscr. as in Type **B 8.**
B 72. **B 8.** 10 pf. + 5 pf. green .. 13·00 13·00
B 73. – 30 pf. + 5 pf. blue .. 28·00 28·00

DESIGN: 30 pf. "Singing Angels" (painting).

B 9. G. A. Lortzing. **B 10.** Freedom Bell, Berlin.

1951. Lortzing (composer). Death Cent.
B 74. **B 9.** 20 pf. brown .. 25·00 24·00

1951. (a) Clapper at left.
B 75. **B 10.** 5 pf. sepia .. .. 2·25 2·00
B 76. 10 pf. blue-green .. 6·50 6·00
B 77. 20 pf. red .. .. 2·75 3·00
B 78. 30 pf. blue .. .. 18·00 19·00
B 79. 40 pf. purple .. 12·00 16·00

(b) Clapper at right.
B 82. **B 10.** 5 pf. olive .. .. 1·25 60
B 83. 10 pf. yellow-green 2·50 2·50
B 84. 20 pf. red .. .. 9·00 9·00
B 85. 30 pf. blue .. .. 19·00 18·00
B 86. 40 pf. claret .. 8·00 7·50

(c) Clapper in centre.
B 101. **B 10.** 5 pf. brown .. 60 35
B 102. 10 pf. blue-green 1·40 60
B 103. 20 pf. red .. .. 2·75 1·75
B 104. 30 pf. blue .. 5·00 4·50
B 105. 40 pf. lilac .. 20·00 10·00

B 11. Boy Stamp Collectors. **B 12.** Mask of Beethoven (taken from life, 1812).

1951. Stamp Day.
B 80. **B 11.** 10 pf. + 3 pf. green 8·00 8·50
B 81. 20 pf. + 2 pf. lake 10·00 11·00

1952. Beethoven. 125th Death Anniv.
B 87. **B 12.** 30 pf. blue .. 18·00 15·00

B 13. Olympic Torch. **B 14.** W. von Siemens.

1952. Olympic Games Festival, Berlin.
B 88. **B 13.** 4 pf. brown .. 60 60
B 89. 10 pf. green .. 3·50 4·00
B 90. 20 pf. red .. .. 6·00 6·50

1952. Famous Berliners.
B 91. – 4 pf. brown .. 20 10
B 92. – 5 pf. blue .. 30 20
B 93. – 6 pf. brown .. 2·25 3·75
B 94. – 8 pf. brown .. 1·00 1·10
B 95. – 10 pf. green .. 1·00 30
B 96. – 15 pf. lilac .. 5·00 5·50
B 97. **B 14.** 20 pf. lake .. 1·50 35
B 98. – 25 pf. olive .. 18·00 2·75
B 99. – 30 pf. purple .. 6·00 2·50
B 100. – 40 pf. black .. 10·00 1·50

PORTRAITS: 4 pf. Zelter (musician). 5 pf. Lilienthal (aviator). 6 pf. Rathenau (statesman). 8 pf. Fontane (writer). 10 pf. Von Menzel (artist). 15 pf. Virchow (pathologist). 25 pf. Schinkel (architect). 30 pf. Planck (physicist). 40 pf. W. von Humboldt (philologist).

B 15. Church before Bombing. **B 16.** Chainbreaker.

1953. Kaiser Wilhelm Memorial Church Reconstruction Fund.
B 106. **B 15.** 4 pf. + 1 pf. brown 15 20
B 107. 10 pf. + 5 pf. grn... 1·25 1·75
B 108. – 20 pf. + 10 pf. red.. 60 60
B 109. – 30 pf. + 15 pf. blue 16·00 18·00

DESIGN: 20 pf., 30 pf. Church after bombing.

1953. East German Uprising. Inscr. "17 JUNI 1953".
B 110. **B 16.** 20 pf. black .. 1·25 90
B 111. – 30 pf. red 10·00 10·00

DESIGN: 30 pf. Brandenburg Gate.

B 17. Ernst Reuter. **B 18.** Conference Buildings.

1954. Death of Ernst Reuter (Mayor of West Berlin).
B 112. **B 17.** 20 pf. brown .. 4·00 40

1954. Four Power Conference. Berlin.
B 113. **B 18.** 20 pf. red... .. 4·00 2·40

B 19. O. Mergenthaler and Linotype Machine. **B 20.** "Germany in Bondage".

1954. Merganthaler (inventor). Birth Cent.
B 114. **B 19.** 10 pf. green .. 75 80

1954. West German Presidential Election. No. B 103 optd. **Wahl des Bundespräsidenten in Berlin 17. Juli 1954.**
B 115. B **10.** 20 pf. red .. .. 1·40 1·75

1954. Attempt on Hitler's Life. 10th Anniv.
B 116. B **20.** 20 pf. grey and red 2·50 2·50

B **21.** Prussian Postilion, 1827.

B **22.** Memorial Library.

1954. National Stamp Exhibition.
B 117. B **21.** 20 pf. + 10 pf. blue red, yell. & blk. 6·00 7·00

1954. Berlin Views. As Type B **3** but inscr. "DEUTSCHE POST BERLIN".
B 118. 7 pf. green .. .. 2·50 12
B 119. 70 pf. olive .. .. 38·00 5·50
DESIGNS: 7 pf. Exhibition building. 70 pf. Grunewald hunting lodge.

1954.
B 120. B **22.** 40 pf. purple .. 7·50 70

B **23.** Richard Strauss.

B **24.** Blacksmiths at Work.

1954. Strauss (composer). 5th Death Anniv.
B 121. B **23.** 40 pf. blue .. 6·00 1·00

1954. A. Borsig (industrialist). Death Cent.
B 122. B **24.** 20 pf. brown .. 4·00 50

B **25.** M.S. "Berlin".

B **26.** Wilhelm Furtwangler (conductor).

1955.
B 123. B **25.** 10 pf. green .. 50 20
B 124. 25 pf. blue .. 2·10 2·00

1955. 1st Anniv. of Furtwangler's Death.
B 125. B **26.** 40 pf. blue .. 6·00 6·00

B **27.**

B **28.** Prussian Rural Postilion, 1760.

1955. Federal Parliament Session, Berlin.
B 126. B **27.** 10 pf. blk., yell. & red 12 12
B 127. 20 pf. blk., yell. & red .. .. 2·25 2·50

1955. Stamp Day and Philatelic Fund.
B 128. B **28.** 25 pf. + 10 pf. red, yell., bl. & brn. 3·00 3·75

B **29.** St. Otto.

B **30.** Radio Tower and Exhibition Hall.

1955. Berlin Bishopric. 25th Anniv.
B 129. B **29.** 7 pf. + 3 pf. brown 30 35
B 130. – 10 pf. + 5 pf. green 20 35
B 131. – 20 pf. + 10 pf. mag. 30 60
DESIGNS: 10 pf. St. Hedwig. 20 pf. St. Peter.

1956. Berlin Buildings and Monuments.
B 133. – 1 pf. grey 5 5
B 133b. – 3 pf. violet .. 5 5
B 134. – 5 pf. mauve .. 5 5
B 132. B **31.** 7 pf. turq. (A) .. 2·25 60
B 135. – 7 pf. turq. (B) .. 12 5
B 136. – 8 pf. grey 20 35
B 136a. – 8 pf. red 8 8
B 137. – 10 pf. green .. 5 5
B 138. – 15 pf. blue .. 20 8
B 139. – 20 pf. red 12 5
B 140. – 25 pf. brown .. 20 30
B 141. – 30 pf. grey .. 20 35
B 142. – 40 pf. blue .. 2·50 1·50
B 143. – 50 pf. olive .. 45 50
B 144. – 60 pf. brown .. 65 55
B 145. – 70 pf. violet .. 7·50 3·75
B 146. – 1 Dm. olive .. 1·00 65
B 146a. – 3 Dm. lake .. 2·50 3·75
(A) Type B **31**. (B) As Type B **31** but with inscription at top.
DESIGNS—As Type B **31**—HORIZ. 1 pf., 3 pf. Brandenburg Gate. 5 pf. P.O. Headquarters. 20 pf. Free University. 40 pf. Charlottenburg Castle. 60 pf. Chamber of Commerce and Bourse. 70 pf. Schiller Theatre. VERT. 8 pf. Town Hall, Neukolln. 10 pf. Emperor William Memorial Church. 15 pf. Air Lift Monument. 25 pf. Lilienthal Monument. 30 pf. Pfaueninsel Castle. 50 pf. Reuter Power station. LARGER (23 × 28 mm.): 1 Dm. "The Great Elector" (statue, after Schluter). (29½ × 25 mm.): 3 Dm. Congress Hall.

B **31.**

B **32.**

1956. Federal Council Meeting, Berlin.
B 147. B **30.** 10 pf. black, yellow and red .. 30 15
B 148. 25 pf. black, yellow and red .. 1·60 1·75

1956. German Engineers' Union. Cent.
B 149. B **32.** 10 pf. green .. 35 15
B 150. 20 pf. red .. 2·10 2·25

1956. Flood Relief Fund. As No. B 77 (colour changed) surch. **+10 Berlinhilfe für die Hochwassergeschädigten. DEUTSCHE BUNDESPOST BERLIN** and bar.
B 151. B **10.** 20 pf. + 10 pf. bistre 70 1·00

B **33.** P. Lincke.

B **34.** Wireless Transmitter.

1956. Lincke (composer). 10th Death Anniv.
B 152. B **33.** 20 pf. red .. 35 60

1956. Industrial Exhibition.
B 153. B **34.** 25 pf. chocolate .. 2·25 2·50

B **35.** Brandenburg Postilion, 1700.

B **36.** Spandau.

1956. Stamp Day and Philatelic Fund.
B 154. B **35.** 25 pf. + 10 pf. multicoloured .. 50 65

1957. 725th Anniv. of Spandau.
B 155. B **36.** 20 pf. olive and chestnut .. 12 20

B **37.** Model of Hansa District.

FR.K.v. SAVIGNY 1779-1861
30
DEUTSCHE
BERLIN
BUNDESPOST
B **38.** Friedrich K. von Savigny (jurist).

1957. Int. Building Exn., Berlin. Inscr. as in Type B **37.**
B 156. B **37.** 7 pf. chocolate .. 5 5
B 157. – 20 pf. red .. 15 12
B 158. – 40 pf. blue .. 30 60
DESIGNS—HORIZ. 20 pf. Aerial view of Exhibition. 40 pf. Exhibition Congress Hall.

1957. Portraits as Type B **38.**
B 159. 7 pf. brown and green 5 5
B 160. 8 pf. chocolate and grey 5 5
B 161. 10 pf. brown and green 5 5
B 162. 15 pf. sepia and blue .. 40 40
B 163. 20 pf. + 10 pf. sep. & red 20 20
B 164. 20 pf. brown and red 12 10
B 165. 25 pf. sepia and lake .. 40 50
B 166. 30 pf. sepia and green 55 65
B 167. 40 pf. sepia & grey-blue 20 25
B 168. 50 pf. sepia and olive .. 1·25 1·50
PORTRAITS—VERT. 7 pf. T. Mommsen (historian). 8 pf. H. Zille (painter). 10 pf. E. Reuter (Mayor of Berlin). 15 pf. E. Haber (chemist). 20 pf. (No. B 164), F. Schleiermacher (theologian). 20 pf. (B 163), L. Hock (zoologist). 25 pf. Max Reinhardt (theatrical producer). 30 pf. Type B **38.** 40 pf. A. von Humboldt (naturalist). 50 pf. C. D. Ranch (sculptor).
The premium on No. B 163 was for the Berlin Zoo.

B **39.** Uta von Naumburg (statue).

B **40.** "Unity Justice and Freedom."

1957. German Cultural Congress.
B 169. B **39.** 25 pf. brown .. 15 30

1957. 3rd Federal Parliament Assembly.
B 170. B **40.** 10 pf. black, ochre and red 15 15
B 171. 20 pf. black, ochre and red 70 95

B **41.** Postilion, 1897-1925.

B **42.** Torch of Remembrance.

1957. Stamp Day.
B 172. B **41.** 20 pf. multicoloured 35 35

1957. 7th World War Veterans Congress.
B 173. B **42.** 20 pf. myrtle, yellow and green .. 30 35

B **43.** Elly Heuss-Knapp (social worker).

B **44.** Christ and Symbols of the Cosmos.

1957. Mothers' Convalescence Fund.
B 174. B **43.** 20 pf. + 10 pf. red 30 40

1958. German Catholics' Day.
B 175. B **44.** 10 pf. blk. & grn. 12 12
B 176. 20 pf. blk. & mag. 25 40

B **45.** Otto Suhr.

B **46.** Pres. Heuss.

1958. Burgomaster Otto Suhr. 1st Death Anniv.
B 177. B **45.** 20 pf. red 25 30
See also Nos. B 187 and B 193.

1959.
B 178. B **46.** 7 pf. green .. 5 5
B 179. 10 pf. green .. 10 5
B 180. 20 pf. red 20 5
B 181. 40 pf. blue .. 90 90
B 182. 70 pf. violet .. 1·10 1·10

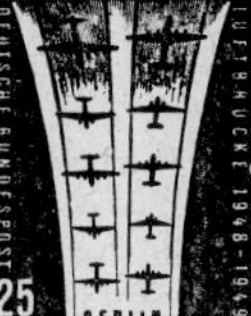

B **47.** Symbolic Airlift.

B **48.** Brandenburg Gate, Berlin.

1959. Berlin Airlift. 10th Anniv.
B 183. B **47.** 25 pf. black & brown 15 20

1959. 14th World Communities Congress, Berlin.
B 184. B **48.** 20 pf. blue and red 15 20

B **49.** Schiller.

B **50.** Robert Koch.

1959. Schiller (poet). Birth Bicent.
B 185. B **49.** 20 pf. brn. & red .. 10 12

1960. Robert Koch (bacteriologist). 50th Death Anniv.
B 186. B **50.** 20 pf. maroon .. 10 12

1960. Walther Shreiber (Mayor of Berlin, 1951-53). 5th Death Anniv. As Type B **45.**
B 187. 20 pf. red 15 20
DESIGN: Portrait of Schreiber.

B **51.** Boy at Window.

B **52.** Hans Boeckler.

1960. Berlin Children's Holiday Fund. Inscr. "FERIENPLATZE FUR BERLINER KINDER".
B 188. 7 pf. + 3 pf. sep. & brn. 10 10
B 189. 10 pf. + 5 pf. olive and yellow-green .. 5 10
B 190. 20 pf. + 10 pf. brown and pink .. 15 15
B 191. 40 pf. + 20 pf. ind. & bl. 45 70
DESIGNS: 7 pf. Type B **51.** 10 pf. Girl in street. 20 pf. Girl blowing on Alpine flower. 40 pf. Boy on beach.

1961. Hans Boeckler (politician). 10th Death Anniv.
B 192. B **52.** 20 pf. blk. & red .. 10 10

1961. Louise Schroeder (politician) 4th Death Anniv. As Type B **45.**
B 193. 20 pf. chocolate .. 10 12
DESIGN: Portrait of Schroeder.

B **53.** Durer.

B **54.** "Five Crosses" Symbol and St. Mary's Church.

B **55.** Exhibition Emblem.

1961. Famous Germans.
B 194. 5 pf. olive (Magnus) .. 5 5
B 195. 7 pf. brown (St. Elizabeth of Thuringia) .. 15 15
B 196. 8 pf. violet (Gutenberg) 12 15
B 197. 10 pf. green (Type B **53**) 5 5
B 198. 15 pf. blue (Luther) .. 15 20
B 199. 20 pf. red (Bach) .. 10 5
B 200. 25 pf. chest. (Neumann) 20 25
B 201. 30 pf. sepia (Kant) .. 20 30
B 202. 40 pf. blue (Lessing) .. 20 30
B 203. 50 pf. brown (Goethe) .. 25 35
B 204. 60 pf. claret (Schiller) .. 35 40
B 205. 70 pf. green (Beethoven) 35 35
B 206. 80 pf. brown (Kleist) .. 70 95
B 207. 1 Dm. violet (Annette von Droste-Hulshoff) 55 35
B 208. 2 Dm. grn. (Hauptmann) 1·10 75

1961. 10th Evangelical Churches' Day. Crosses in violet.
B 210. B 54. 10 pf. green .. 5 5
B 211. 20 pf. purple .. 12 12

1961. West Berlin Radio and Television Exn.
B 212. B 55. 20 pf. chocolate and brown-red .. 10 12

B 56. " Die Linden " (1650).

B 57. " Yellow Dog " of 1912 and Modern Jet Aircraft.

1962. " Old Berlin " series.
B 213. 7 pf. sepia and brown .. 5 5
B 214. 10 pf. sepia and green .. 5 5
B 215. 15 pf. black and ultram. 5 5
B 216. 20 pf. sepia & chestnut 5 5
B 217. 25 pf. sepia and olive .. 5 5
B 218. 40 pf. black and blue .. 15 12
B 219. 50 pf. sepia and maroon 15 15
B 220. 60 pf. sepia & magenta 15 25
B 221. 70 pf. black and purple 25 25
B 222. 80 pf. sepia and red .. 20 35
B 223. 90 pf. sepia and brown .. 25 45
B 224. 1 Dm. sepia and green .. 35 60

DESIGNS: 7 pf. Type B 56. 10 pf. " Waisenbrucke " (Orphans' Bridge), 1783. 15 pf. Mauerstrasse, 1780. 20 pf. Berlin Castle, 1703. 25 pf. Potsdamar Platz, 1825. 40 pf. Bellevue Castle, circa 1800. 50 pf. Fischer Bridge, 1830. 60 pf. Halle Gate, 1880. 70 pf. Parochial Church 1780. 80 pf. University, 1825. 90 pf. Opera House, 1780. 1 Dm. Grunewald Lake circa 1790.

1962. German Airmail Transport. 50th Anniv.
B 225. B 57. 60 pf. black & blue 30 35

B 58. Exhibition Emblem.

B 59. Town Hall Schoneberg.

1963. West Berlin Broadcasting Exn.
B 226. B 58. 20 pf. ultram., grey and blue .. 10 12

1964. Schoneberg. 700th Anniv.
B 227. B 59. 20 pf. chocolate .. 10 12

B 60. Pres. Lubke.

B 61. Kaiser Wilhelm Memorial Church.

1964. Re-election of Pres. Lubke.
B 228. B 60. 20 pf. red 8 8
B 229. 40 pf. blue .. 20 20
See also Nos. B 308/9.

WEST GERMAN DESIGNS. Except where illustrated the following are stamps of West Germany additionally inscr. " BERLIN ".

1964. Capitals of the Federal Lands. As No. 1335.
B 230. 20 pf. multicoloured. .. 10 12

1964. Humanitarian Relief and Welfare Funds. As Nos. 1352/5.
B 231. 10 pf. + 5 pf. mult. .. 8 10
B 232. 15 pf. + 5 pf. mult. .. 8 8
B 233. 20 pf. + 10 pf. mult. .. 15 10
B 234. 40 pf. + 20 pf. mult. .. 40 65

1964. Pres. Kennedy Commem. As Type 352.
B 235. 40 pf. blue 20 20

1964. Twelve Centuries of German Architecture.

(a) Size $18\frac{1}{2} \times 22\frac{1}{2}$ mm. As Nos. 1359/66. Plain backgrounds.
B 236. 10 pf. brown 5 5
B 237. 15 pf. green 5 5
B 238. 20 pf. chestnut 10 5
B 239. 40 pf. ultramarine .. 15 12
B 240. 50 pf. bistre .. .. 1·50 1·50
B 241. 60 pf. red 30 30
B 242. 70 pf. green 50 50
B 243. 80 pf. chocolate 35 35

(b) Size $19\frac{1}{2} \times 24$ mm. As Nos. 1367/81. Coloured backgrounds.
B 244. 5 pf. bistre 5 5
B 245. 8 pf. red 20 20
B 246. 10 pf. maroon 5 5
B 247. 20 pf. emerald 10 5
B 248. 30 pf. olive 30 20
B 249. 30 pf. red 20 5
B 250. 40 pf. bistre 25 25
B 251. 50 pf. blue 30 25
B 252. 60 pf. vermilion .. 50 45
B 253. 70 pf. bronze 55 45
B 254. 80 pf. brown 70 45
B 255. 90 pf. black 60 50
B 256. 1 Dm. blue 60 25
B 257. 1 Dm. 10 chestnut .. 75 40
B 258. 1 Dm. 30 green .. 90 90
B 259. 2 Dm. purple .. 1·00 60

BUILDINGS: 8 pf. Palatine Castle, Kaub. Others as Nos. 1359/81 of West Germany.

1965. Child Welfare. As Nos. 1384/7.
B 261. 10 pf. + 5 pf. mult. .. 5 10
B 262. 15 pf. + 5 pf. mult. .. 10 12
B 263. 20 pf. + 10pf. mult. .. 12 15
B 264. 40 pf. + 20 pf. mult. .. 35 45

1965. " New Berlin ". Multicoloured.
B 265. 10 p . Type B 61 .. 5 5
B 266. 15 pf. Opera House .. 5 5
B 267. 20 pf. Philharmonic Hall 5 5
B 268. 30 pf. Jewish Community Centre 12 5
B 269. 40 pf. Regina Martyrum Memorial Church .. 20 8
B 270. 50 pf. Ernst-Reuter Square 25 12
B 271. 60 pf. Europa Centre .. 30 12
B 272. 70 pf. Technical University, Charlottenburg 30 25
B 273. 80 pf. City Motorway .. 35 25
B 274. 90 pf. Planetarium .. 40 25
B 275. 1 Dm. Telecommunications, Tower .. 45 35
B 276. 1 Dm. 10, University Clinic, Steglitz .. 50 45
The 15 pf. to 50 pf. and 90 pf. are horiz.

1965. Humanitarian Relief Funds. As Nos. 1406/9.
B 277. 10 pf. + 5 pf. mult. .. 10 12
B 278. 15 pf. + 5 pf. mult. .. 8 8
B 279. 20 pf. + 10 pf. mult. .. 15 12
B 280. 40 pf. + 20 pf. mult. .. 45 65

1966. As Nos. 1412/5a.
B 281. 10 pf. chocolate .. 5 5
B 282. 20 pf. green 10 5
B 283. 30 pf. red 15 5
B 284. 50 pf. blue 30 25
B 284a. 100 pf. blue 75 70

1966. Child Welfare. As Nos. 1416/9.
B 285. 10 pf. + 5 pf. Type 371 5 5
B 286. 20 pf. + 10 pf. Chamois 12 15
B 287. 30 pf. + 15 pf. Fallow deer 20 20
B 288. 50 pf. + 25 pf. Red deer 50 75

1966. Humanitarian Relief Funds. As Nos. 1428/31.
B 289. 10 pf. + 5 pf. Type 377 12 10
B 290. 20 pf. + 10 pf. Frog dining with Princess .. 12 12
B 291. 30 pf. + 15 pf. Frog Prince and Princess .. 20 20
B 292. 50 pf. + 25 pf. In coach 55 75
Designs from Grimm's " The Frog Prince ".

1967. Child Welfare. As Nos. 1434/7.
B 293. 10 pf. + 5 pf. Rabbit .. 10 12
B 294. 20 pf. + 10 pf. Weasel .. 15 15
B 295. 30 pf. + 15 pf. Hamster 25 25
B 296. 50 pf. + 25 pf. Fox 65 85

B 62. " Bust of a Young Man " (after C. Meit).

B 63. Broadcasting Tower and TV Screen.

1967. Berlin Art Treasures.
B 297. B 62. 10 pf. sepia & bistre 5 5
B 298. – 20 pf. olive and blue 12 8
B 299. – 30 pf. brown & olive 15 12
B 300. – 50 pf. sepia and grey 30 30
B 301. – 1 Dm. black & blue 65 65
B 302. – 1 Dm. 10 brown and chestnut .. 70 70

DESIGNS: 20 pf. Head of " The Elector of Brandenburg " (statue by Schluter). 30 pf. " St. Mark " (statue by Riemenschneider). 50 pf. Head from Quadriga, Brandenburg Gate. 1 Dm. " Madonna " (carving by Feuchtmayer). ($22\frac{1}{2} \times 39$ mm.) 1 Dm. 10, " Christ and St. John " (after carving from Upper Swabia, circa 1320).

1967. West Berlin Broadcasting Exn.
B 303. B 63. 30 pf. multicoloured 15 15

1967. Humanitarian Relief Funds. As Nos. 1443/6.
B 304. 10 pf. + 5 pf. mult. .. 15 15
B 305. 20 pf. + 10 pf. mult. .. 15 12
B 306. 30 pf. + 15 pf. mult. .. 20 15
B 307. 50 pf. + 25 pf. mult. .. 55 75

1967. Re-election of President Lubke. As Type B 60.
B 308. B 60. 30 pf. red 15 12
B 309. 50 pf. blue .. 30 30

1968. Child Welfare. As Nos. 1457/7.
B 310. 10 pf. + 5 pf. Wildcat .. 15 15
B 311. 20 pf. + 10 pf. Otter .. 20 20
B 312. 30 pf. + 15 pf. Badger .. 35 40
B 313. 50 pf. + 25 pf. Beaver .. 1·00 1·10

B 64. Former Court-house.

B 65. Festival Emblems.

1968. Berlin Magistrate's Court. 500th Anniv.
B 314. B 64 30 pf. black .. 20 20

1968. Athletics Festival, Berlin.
B 315. B 65. 20 f. red, blk. & grey 12 15

1968. Humanitarian Relief Funds. As Nos. 1473/6.
B 316. 10 pf. + 5 pf. Doll of 1878 12 15
B 317. 20 pf. + 10 pf. Doll of 1850 15 12
B 318. 30 pf. + 15 pf. Doll of 1870 20 15
B 319. 50 pf. + 25 pf. Doll of 1885 55 70

B 66. " The Newspaper Seller " (C. W. Allers, 1889).

1969. 19th-Cent. Berliners. Contemporary Art.
B 320. – 5 pf. black .. 5 5
B 321. B 66. 10 pf. maroon .. 5 5
B 322. – 10 pf. brown .. 5 5
B 323. – 20 pf. green .. 12 12
B 324. – 20 pf. blue-green 12 12
B 325. – 30 pf. brown .. 20 20
B 326. – 30 pf. lake brown 15 15
B 327. – 50 pf. blue 50 50

DESIGNS—HORIZ. 5 pf. " The Cab-driver ". VERT. 10 pf. " The Bus-driver " (C. W. Allers). 20 pf. (No. B 323) " The Cobbler's Boy " (F. Kruger, 1839). 20 pf. (No. B 324) " The Cobbler " (A. von Menzel). 30 pf. (No. B 325) " The Borsig Forge ". 30 pf. (No. B 326) " Three Berlin Ladies " (F. Kruger). 50 pf. " At the Brandenburg Gate " (C. W. Allers, 1889.).

1969. Child Welfare. As Nos. 1478/81.
B 328. 10 pf. + 5 pf. 15 15
B 329. 20 pf. + 10 pf. 20 20
B 330. 30 pf. + 15 pf. 25 25
B 331. 50 pf. + 25 pf. 90 90

B 67. Postman.

B 68. J. Joachim (violinist & director; after A. von Menzel).

1969. Post Office Trade Union Federation (I.P.T.T.), Berlin. 20th Congress.
B 333. B 67. 10 pf. olive .. 5 5
B 334. – 20 pf. brown and buff 12 12
B 335. – 30 pf. vio. & ochre 15 15
B 336. – 50 pf. blue .. 30 30

DESIGNS: 20 pf. Telephonist. 30 pf. Technician. 50 pf. Airmail Handlers.

1969. Annivs. Multicoloured.
B 337. 30 pf. Type B 68 .. 20 20
B 338. 50 pf. Alexander von Humboldt (after J. Stieler) 30 30

ANNIVERSARIES: 30 pf. Berlin Academy of Music, Cent. 50 pf. Alexander von Humboldt, Birth Bicent.

B 69. Railway Carriage (1835).

B 70. T. Fontane.

1969. Humanitarian Relief Funds. Pewter Figurines. Multicoloured.

(a) Inscr. " WOHLFAHRTSMARKE ".
B 339. 10 pf. + 5 pf. Type B 69 5 5
B 340. 20 pf. + 10 pf. Woman feeding chicken (1850) 15 15
B 341. 30 pf. + 15 pf. Market stall (1850) .. 25 25
B 342. 50 pf. + 25 pf. Mounted postilion (1860) .. 55 55

(b) Christmas. Inscr. "WEIHNACHTSMARKE".
B 343. 10 pf. + 5 pf. "The Three Kings " .. 12 12

1970. Theodor Fontane (writer). 150th Birth Anniv.
B 344. B 70. 20 pf. multicoloured 15 15

B 71 " H. von Stretlingen ".

B 72. Film " Title ".

1970. Child Welfare. Minnesinger Themes. Multicoloured.
B 345. 10 pf. + 5 pf. Type B 71 12 12
B 346. 20 pf. + 10 pf. " M. von Levelingen " .. 20 20
B 347. 30 pf. + 15 pf. " B. von Hohenfels " .. 30 30
B 348. 50 pf. + 25 pf. "A. von Johannsdorf" .. 65 65

1970. 20th Int. Film Festival, Berlin.
B 349. B 72. 30 pf. multicoloured 20 20

1970. Pres. Heinemann. As Nos. 1535/1555.
B 350. 426. 5 pf. black 5 5
B 351. 8 pf. brown .. 50 40
B 352. 10 pf. brown .. 5 5
B 353. 15 pf. bistre .. 8 5
B 354. 20 pf. green .. 8 5
B 355. 25 pf. green .. 30 15
B 356. 30 pf. brown .. 12 5
B 357. 40 pf. orange .. 15 10
B 358. 50 pf. blue 20 5
B 359. 60 pf. blue 25 15
B 360. 70 pf. agate .. 30 15
B 361. 80 pf. green .. 30 20
B 362. 90 pf. red 70 40
B 363. 1 Dm. green .. 45 12
B 364. 1 Dm. 10 grey .. 55 25
B 365. 1 Dm. 20 brown .. 50 35
B 366. 1 Dm. 30 ochre .. 65 30
B 367. 1 Dm. 40 green .. 70 30
B 368. 1 Dm. 50 lake .. 80 35
B 369. 1 Dm. 60 orange .. 70 40
B 370. 1 Dm. 70 orange .. 90 35
B 371. 1 Dm. 90 purple .. 1·00 45
B 372. 2 Dm. violet .. 90 50

B 73. Allegory of Folklore.

B 74. " Caspar ".

1970. 20th Berlin Folklore Week.
B 373. B 73. 30 pf. multicoloured 20 20

1970. Humanitarian Relief Funds. Puppets. Multicoloured.

(a) Inscr. " WOHLFAHRTSMARKE ".
B 374. 10 pf. + 5 pf. Type B 74 5 5
B 375. 20 pf. + 10 pf. " Polichinelle " .. 15 15
B 376. 30 pf. + 15 pf. "Punch" 20 20
B 377. 50 pf. + 25 pf. " Pulcinella " .. 55 55

(b) Christmas. Inscr. " WEIHNACHTSMARKE ".
B 378. 10 pf. + 5 pf. " Angel " 12 12

75. L. von Ranke (after painting by J. Schrader). B 76. City Train (1933).

1970. Leopold von Ranke (historian). Birth Anniv.
B 379. B 75. 30 pf. multicoloured 20 20

1971. German Unification Cent. As No. 1562.
B 380. 432. 30 pf. blk., red & orge. 20 20

1971. Berlin Rail Transport. Multicoloured.
B 381. 5 pf. Local steam train (1925) 5 5
B 382. 10 pf. Electric Tramcars (1890) 5 5
B 383. 20 pf. Horse-drawn tram-car (1880) 12 10
B 384. 30 pf. Type B 76 .. 20 15
B 385. 50 pf. Electric tramcar (1950) 35 35
B 386. 1 Dm. Underground train (1971) 55 55

B 77. "Fly". B 78. "The Bagpiper" (copper engraving, Durer, c 1514).

1971. Child Welfare Children's Drawings. Multicoloured.
B 387. 10 pf.+5 pf. Type B 77 8 8
B 388. 20 pf.+10 pf. "Fish" .. 15 15
B 389. 30 pf.+15 pf. "Porcupine" 30 30
B 390. 50 pf.+25 pf. "Cockerel" 70 70

1971. Albrecht Durer. 500th Birth Anniv.
B 391. B 78. 10 pf. blk. & ochre 8 8

B 79. Communications Tower and Dish Aerials. B 80. Bach and part of 2nd Brandenburg Concerto.

1971. West Berlin Broadcasting Exhib.
B 392. B 79. 30 pf. ind., bl. & red 20 20

1971. Bach's Brandenburg Concertos. 250th Anniv.
B 393. B 80. 30 pf. black, green, red and flesh .. 20 20

B 81. H. von Helmholtz (from painting by K. Morell-Kramer). B 82. Dancing Men.

1971. Hermann von Helmholtz (scientist). 150th Anniv.
B 394. B 81. 25 pf. multicoloured 15 15

1972. Coil Stamps. Accident Prevention. As Nos. 1596/1605.
B 396. 5 pf. orange 25 12
B 397. 10 pf. brown 3 5
B 398. 20 pf. violet 8 5
B 399. 25 pf. green 10 5
B 400. 30 pf. red 12 5
B 401. 40 pf. mauve 15 5
B 402. 50 pf. blue 20 12
B 403. 60 pf. blue .. .. 1·10 50
B 404. 70 pf. blue and green .. 30 25
B 405. 1 Dm. green 45 20
B 406. 1 Dm. 50 brown .. 65 45

1971. Humanitarian Relief Funds. Wooden Toys. Multicoloured.

(a) Inscr. "WOHLFAHRTSMARKE".
B 407. 10 pf.+5 pf. Type B 82 5 5
B 408. 25 pf.+10 pf. Horseman on wheels 15 15
B 409. 30 pf.+15 pf. Acrobat .. 20 20
B 410. 60 pf.+30 pf. Nurse and babies 55 55

(b) Christmas. Inscr. "WEIHNACHTS MARKE".
B 411. 10 pf.+5 pf. Angel with two candles 10 10

B 83. Microscope. B 84. F. Gilly (after bust by Schadow).

1971. Material-Testing Laboratory, Berlin. Cent.
B 412. B 83. 30 pf. multicoloured 20 15

1972. Friedrich Gilly (architect). Birth Bicent.
B 413. B 84. 30 pf. black & blue 20 20

B 85. Boy raiding Bird's-nest. B 87. E. T. A. Hoffman.

B 86. "Grunewaldsee" (A. von Riesen).

1972. Child Welfare. Animal Protection. Multicoloured.
B 414. 10 pf.+5 pf. Type B 85 12 12
B 415. 25 pf.+10 pf. Care of kittens 15 15
B 416. 30 pf.+15 pf. Man beating watch-dog .. 30 30
B 417. 60 pf.+30 pf. Animals crossing road at night 80 80

1972. Paintings of Berlin Lakes. Multicoloured.
B 418. 10 pf. Type B 86 .. 5 5
B 419. 25 pf. "Wannsee" (Max Liebermann) .. 15 12
B 420. 30 pf. "Schlachtensee" (W. Leistikow) .. 20 20

1972. E. T. A. Hoffman (poet and musician). 150th Death Anniv.
B 421. B 87. 60 pf. blk. & violet 35 30

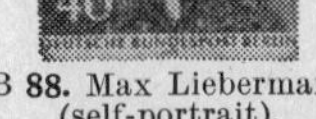

B 88. Max Liebermann (self-portrait). B 89. Stamp Printing-press.

1972. Max Liebermann (painter). 125th Birth Anniv.
B 422. B 88. 40 pf. multicoloured 25 25

1972. Stamp Day.
B 423. B 89. 20 pf. blue, blk. & red 12 12

B 90. Knight. B 91. "The Holy Family".

1972. Humanitarian Relief Funds. Multicoloured.

(a) Chessmen. Inscr. "WOHLFAHRTSMARKE".
B 424. 20 pf.+10 pf. Type B 90 15 15
B 425. 30 pf.+15 pf. Rook .. 20 20
B 426. 40 pf.+20 pf. Queen .. 30 30
B 427. 70 pf.+35 pf. King .. 60 60

(b) Christmas. Inscr. "WEIHNACHTSMARKE".
B 428. 20 pf.+10 pf. Type B 91 20 20

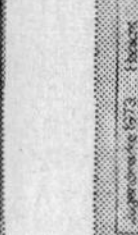

B 92. Prince of Hardenberg. B 93. Goshawk.

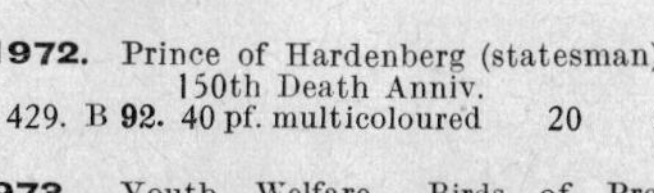

1972. Prince of Hardenberg (statesman). 150th Death Anniv.
B 429. B 92. 40 pf. multicoloured 20 20

1973. Youth Welfare. Birds of Prey. Multicoloured.
B 430. 20 pf.+10 pf. Type B 93 15 15
B 431. 30 pf.+15 pf. Peregrine falcon 20 20
B 432. 40 pf.+20 pf. Sparrowhawk 40 40
B 433. 70 pf.+35 pf. Golden eagle 70 70

B 94. Horse-bus, 1907.

1973. Berlin Buses. Multicoloured.
B 434. 20 pf. Type B 94 .. 12 12
B 435. 20 pf. Trolley bus, 1933 12 12
B 436. 30 pf. Motor bus, 1919 .. 15 15
B 437. 30 pf. Double-decker, 1970 .. .. 15 15
B 438. 40 pf. Double-decker motor bus, 1925 .. 25 25
B 439. 40 pf. "Standard" bus, 1973 .. .. .. 25 25

B 95. L. Tieck. B 96. J. J. Quantz.

1973. Ludwig Tieck (poet and writer) Birth Bicent.
B 440. B 95. 40 pf. multicoloured 25 20

1973. Johann Quantz (composer). Death Bicent.
B 441. B 96. 40 pf. black .. 25 20

B 97. 17th-Century Hurdy-Gurdy. B 98. Christmas Star.

1973. Humanitarian Relief Funds. Multicoloured.

(a) Musical Instruments. Inscr. "WOHLFAHRTSMARKE".
B 443. 20 pf.+10 pf. Type B 97 15 15
B 444. 30 pf.+15 pf. 16th century drum 25 25
B 445. 40 pf.+20 pf. 18th century lute 35 35
B 446. 70 pf.+35 pf. 16th century organ 60 60

(b) Christmas. Inscr. "WEIHNACHTSMARKE".
B 447. 20 pf.+10 pf. Type B 98 20 20

B 99. G. W. Knobelsdorff. B 100. G. R. Kirchhoff.

1974. Georg W. von Knobelsdorff (architect). 275th Birth Anniv.
B 448. B 99. 20 pf. brown .. 12 12

1974. Gustav R. Kirchhoff (physicist). 150th Birth Anniv.
B 449. B 100. 30 pf. grn. & grey 20 20

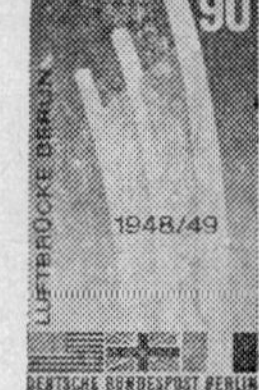

B 101. A. Slaby. B 102. Airlift Memorial.

1974. Adolf Slaby (radio pioneer). 125th Birth Anniv.
B 450. B 101. 40 pf. black & red 20 20

1974. Berlin Airlift. 25th Anniv.
B 451. B 102. 90 pf. multicoloured 45 45

B 103. Photography. B 104. School Seal.

1974. Youth Welfare. Youth Activities. Multicoloured.
B 452. 20 pf.+10 pf. Type B 103 15 15
B 453. 30 pf.+15 pf. Athletics .. 25 25
B 454. 40 pf.+20 pf. Music .. 35 35
B 455. 70 pf.+35 pf. Voluntary service (Nurse) .. 65 65

1974. Evangelical Grammar School, Berlin. 400th Anniv.
B 456. B 104. 50 pf. grey, brn. & gold 25 20

B 105. Spring Bouquet.

1974. Humanitarian Relief Funds. Flowers. Multicoloured.

(a) Welfare Stamps. 25th Anniv. Inscr. "25 JAHRE WOHLFAHRTSMARKE".
B 457. 30 pf.+15 pf. Type B 105 .. .. 20 20
B 458. 40 pf.+20 pf. Autumn bouquet 30 30
B 459. 50 pf.+25 pf. Bouquet of roses 35 35
B 460. 70 pf.+35 pf. Winter bouquet 60 60

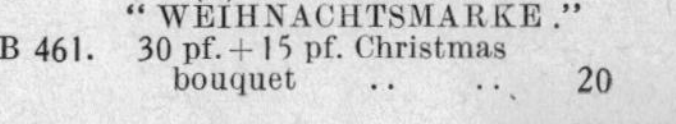

(b) Christmas. Inscr. "WEIHNACHTSMARKE."
B 461. 30 pf.+15 pf. Christmas bouquet 20 20

B 106. Aerial View of Tegel Airport. B 107. "Venus". (F. E. Meyer).

1974. Tegel Airport, Berlin. Inauguration.
B 462. B 106. 50 pf. vio., bl. & yell. 25 25

1974. Berlin Porcelain. Multicoloured.
B 463. 30 pf. Type B 107 .. 20 15
B 464. 40 pf. "Astronomy" (W. C. Meyer) .. 25 15
B 465. 50 pf. "Justice" (J. G. Muller) 30 20

B 108. G. Schadow. B 109. Steamboat "Princess Charlotte".

1975. Gottfried Schadow (sculptor). 125th Death Anniv.
B 466. B **108.** 50 pf. purple .. 25 25

1975. Berlin Pleasure Craft. Multicoloured.
B 467. 30 pf. Type B **109** .. 20 15
B 468. 40 pf. Steamboat "Siegfried" 20 15
B 469. 50 pf. Steamboat "Sperber" 25 30
B 470. 60 pf. MV "Vaterland" 30 25
B 471. 70 pf. MV "Moby Dick" 35 30

B **110.** "Drache" Locomotive of 1840.

1975. Youth Welfare. Railway Locomotives. Multicoloured.
B 472. 30 pf. + 15 pf. Type B **110** 25 25
B 473. 40 pf. + 20 pf. Tank loco. Series 89 (70–75) .. 30 30
B 474. 50 pf. + 25 pf. Steam loco. Series 050 .. 35 35
B 475. 70 pf. + 35 pf. Steam loco. Series 010 .. 55 55

B **111.** F. Sauerbruch (surgeon). B **112.** Gymnastics Emblem.

1975. Ferdinand Sauerbruch. Birth Cent.
B 476. B **111.** 50 pf. agate and chestnut .. 25 25

1975. Sixth Gymnaestrada (Gymnastic Games).
B 477. B **112.** 40 pf. multicoloured 20 20

1975. Industry and Technology. As Nos. 1742/55.
B 478. – 5 pf. green 5 5
B 479. – 10 pf. purple .. 5 5
B 480. – 20 pf. red 8 5
B 481. – 30 pf. violet .. 15 15
B 482. **512.** 40 pf. green .. 20 10
B 483. – 50 pf. red 25 10
B 484. – 70 pf. blue 30 15
B 485. – 80 pf. green .. 35 20
B 486. – 100 pf. brown .. 45 25
B 487. – 120 pf. blue .. 55 30
B 488. – 140 pf. red 65 40
B 489. – 160 pf. green .. 70 45
B 490. – 200 pf. purple .. 90 50
B 491. – 500 pf. black .. 2·25 2·25

B **113.** "Louis Corinth" (self-portrait). B **114.** Naunynstrasse Buildings, Berlin-Kreuzberg.

1975. Louis Corinth (painter). 50th Death Anniv.
B 492. B **113.** 50 pf. multicoloured 25 20

1975. European Architectural Heritage Year.
B 493. B **114.** 50 pf. multicoloured .. 25 20

B **115.** Yellow Gentian. B **116.** Paul Lobe.

1975. Humanitarian Relief Funds. Alpine Flowers. Multicoloured.
B 494. 30 pf. + 15 pf. Type B **115** 20 20
B 495. 40 pf. + 20 pf. Arnica .. 25 25
B 496. 50 pf. + 25 pf. Cyclamen 35 35
B 497. 70 pf. + 35 pf. Blue gentian 55 55

1975. Paul Lobe (politician). Birth Cent.
B 498. B **116.** 50 pf. red .. 20 20

1975. Christmas. As Type B **115**, inscr. "WEIHNACHTSMARKE". Mult.
B 499. 30 pf. + 15 pf. Snow heather 25 20

B **117.** "Grune Woche" Ears of Wheat. B **118.** Putting the Shot.

1976. International Green Week, Berlin.
B 500. B **117.** 70 pf. gr. & yell.. 30 30

1976. Youth Welfare. "Training for the Olympics" Mult.
B 501. 30 pf. + 15 pf. Type B **118** 20 20
B 502. 40 pf. + 20 pf. Hockey .. 25 25
B 503. 50 pf. + 25 pf. Handball 55 55
B 504. 70 pf. + 35 pf. Swimming 1·25 1·25

B **119.** Hockey-players.

1976. Women's World Hockey Championships.
B 505. B **119.** 30 pf. green .. 20 15

B **120.** Treble Clef. B **121.** Fire Service Emblem.

1976. German Choristers' Festival.
B 506. B **120.** 40 pf. multicoloured 25 20

1976. Berlin Fire Service. 125th Anniv.
B 507. B **121.** 50 pf. multicoloured 25 20

IV. EAST GERMANY.

(Democratic Republic.)

The German Democratic Republic was set up in October, 1949, and it administers the former Russian Zone. Its stamps are used in East Berlin.

E **7.** Pigeon and Globe. E **8.** Postal Workers and Globe.

1949. U.P.U. 75th Anniv.
E 1. E **7.** 50 pf. blue .. .. 3·00 3·00

1949. Postal Workers' Congress.
E 2. E **8.** 12 pf. blue 60 60
E 3. 30 pf. red .. .. 2·50 2·75

E **9.** T 1 of Bavaria and Magnifying Glass.

E **10.** Skier.

1949. Stamp Day.
E 4. E **9.** 12 pf. + 3 pf. black .. 40 60

1950. Leipzig Spring Fair. As T **188** but dated "1950".
E 5. 24 pf. + 12 pf. purple .. 1·00 1·00
E 6. 30 pf. + 14 pf. red .. 1·25 1·50
DESIGNS: 24 pf. First Dresden China Fair, 1710. 30 pf. First Sample Fair, 1894.

1950. First Winter Sports Meeting, Schierke.
E 7. E **10.** 12 pf. violet .. 1·25 1·60
E 8. – 24 pf. blue .. .. 1·60 1·90
DESIGN: 24 pf. Girl skater.

E **11.** Globe and Sun. E **12.** Wilhelm Pieck.

E **12a.** Wilhelm Pieck. E **13.** Shepherd Playing Pipes.

1950. Labour Day. 60th Anniv.
E 9. E **1.** 30 pf. red .. .. 2·25 2·50

1950.
E 68. E **12.** 5 pf. emerald .. 75 20
E 10. 12 pf. blue .. 3·00 20
E 70. 24 pf. brown .. 2·50 5
E 12. E **12a.** 1 Dm. olive .. 2·50 80
E 13. 2 Dm. red .. 2·00 1·10
E 14. 5 Dm. blue .. 90 30
For 1 and 2 Dm. with different portrait of president see Nos. E 320/1.

1950. Bach. Death Bicent. Inscr. "BACHJAHR 1950".
E 15. E **13.** 12 pf. + 4 pf. green .. 90 90
E 16. – 24 pf. + 6 pf. olive .. 90 80
E 17. – 30 pf. + 8 pf. red .. 2·25 1·50
E 18. – 50 pf. + 16 pf. blue .. 2·75 2·00
DESIGNS: 24 pf. Girl playing hand-organ 30 pf. Bach. 50 pf. Three singers.

E **14.** Dove and Stamp. E **15.** L. Euler.

1950. Philatelic Exhibition, Leipzig.
E 19. E **14.** 84 pf. + 41 pf. red .. 1·10 1·00

1950. Academy of Science, Berlin. 250th Anniv. Inscr. as in Type E **15.**
E 20. E **15.** 1 pf. grey 50 50
E 21. – 5 pf. green .. .. 1·75 1·75
E 22. – 6 pf. violet .. .. 1·75 1·75
E 23. – 8 pf. brown .. .. 2·75 2·75
E 24. – 10 pf. green .. 2·50 2·50
E 25. – 12 pf. blue 80 80
E 26. – 16 pf. blue .. .. 4·25 4·75
E 27. – 20 pf. purple .. 2·75 2·50
E 28. – 24 pf. red .. .. 3·75 60
E 29. – 50 pf. blue .. .. 5·00 4·75
PORTRAITS: 5 pf. A. von Humboldt. 6 pf. T. Mommsen. 8 pf. W. von Humboldt. 10 pf. H. von Helmholtz. 12 pf. M. Planck. 16 pf. J. Grimm. 20 pf. W. Nernst. 24 pf. G. W. Leibniz. 50 pf. A. von Harnack.

E **16.** Miner. E **17.** Ballot Box.

1950. Mansfeld Copper Mines. 750th Anniv.
E 30. E **16.** 12 pf. blue 50 60
F 31. – 24 pf. red .. .. 1·00 1·00
DESIGN: 24 pf. Copper smelting.

1950. East German Elections.
E 32. E **17.** 24 pf. brown .. 70 70

E **18.** Hand, Dove and Burning Buildings. E **19.** Tobogganing.

1950. Peace Propaganda. Inscr. "ERKAMPFT DEN FRIEDEN".
E 33. – 6 pf. violet .. 1·25 1·40
E 34. E **18.** 8 pf. brown .. 90 75
E 35. – 12 pf. blue .. .. 1·50 1·40
E 36. – 24 pf. red .. .. 1·25 75
DESIGNS (all include hand and dove): 6 pf. Tank. 12 pf. Atom bomb Explosion. 24 pf. Rows of gravestones.

1951. 2nd Winter Sports Meeting, Oberhof.
E 37. E **19.** 12 pf. blue .. .. 90 1·00
E 38. – 24 f. red (ski-jumper) .. .. 1·00 1·10

E **20.**

ILLUSTRATIONS
British Commonwealth and all overprints and surcharges are FULL SIZE. Foreign Countries have been reduced to ¾-LINEAR.

1951. Leipzig Spring Fair.
E 39. E **20.** 24 pf red .. .. 3·75 5·00
E 40. 50 pf. blue .. .. 3·75 2·50

E **21.** Presidents Pieck and Bierut.

1951. Visit of Polish President to Berlin.
E 41. E **21.** 24 pf. red .. .. 5·00 5·00
E 42. 50 pf. blue .. .. 5·00 5·00

E **22.** Mao Tse-tung.

E **23.** Chinese Land Reform.

1951. Friendship with China.
E 43. E **22.** 12 pf. green .. 9·00 7·50
E 44. E **23.** 24 pf. red .. .. 16·00 13·00
E 45. E **22.** 50 pf. blue .. .. 9·00 6·50

E **24.** Youth Hoisting Flag. E **25.** Symbols of Agriculture & Industry

1951. 3rd World Youth Festival. Inscr. as in Type E **24.** On coloured papers.
E 46. E **24.** 12 pf. brown .. 2·25 2·75
E 47. – 24 pf. green & red .. 2·75 1·40
E 48. E **24.** 30 pf. buff and green 2·75 2·50
E 49. – 50 pf. red and blue .. 3·50 2·50
DESIGN: 24 pf., 50 pf. Three girls dancing.

1951. Five Year Plan.
E 50. E **25.** 24 pf. yellow, red, black and lake .. 55 35

E **26.** K. Liebknecht. E **27.** Instructing Young Collectors.

1951. Liebknecht (revolutionary). 80th Birth Anniv.
E 51. E 26. 24 pf. slate and red 65 65

1951. Stamp Day.
E 52. E 27. 12 pf. blue 25 25

E 28. P. Bykow and E. Wirth.

1951. German-Soviet Friendship.
E 53. E 28. 12 pf. blue .. .. 1·00 1·10
E 54. – 24 pf. red .. .. 1·10 1·10
DESIGN: 24 pf. Stalin and Pres. Pieck.

E 29. Skier. E 30. Beethoven.

1952. 3rd Winter Sports Meeting, Oberhof.
E 55. E 29. 12 pf. green .. 60 65
E 56. – 24 pf. blue 70 95
DESIGN (inscr. "OBERHOF"): 24 pf. Ski-jumper.

1952. Beethoven. 125th Death Anniv.
E 57. – 12 pf. blue 20 5
E 58. E 30. 24 pf. brn. & grey .. 40 5
DESIGN: 12 pf. Full face portrait.

E 31. President Gottwald. E 32. Bricklayers.

1952. Czechoslovak-German Friendship.
E 59. E 31. 24 pf. blue 35 40

1952. National Reconstruction Fund.
E 60. – 12 pf.+3 pf. violet .. 5 5
E 61. E 32. 24 pf.+6 pf. red .. 8 15
E 62. – 30 pf.+10 pf. green 5 5
E 63. – 50 pf.+10 pf. blue 12 15
DESIGNS: 12 pf. Workers clearing debris. 30 pf. Carpenters. 50 pf. Architect and workmen.

E 33. Cyclists. E 34. Handel.

1952. Warsaw-Berlin-Prague Cycle Race.
E 64. E 33. 12 pf. blue 25 25

1952. Handel Festival, Halle.
E 65. E 34. 6 pf. brown .. 40 35
E 66. – 8 pf. red 40 35
E 67. – 50 pf. blue 70 45
COMPOSERS: 8 pf. Lortzing. 50 pf. Weber.

E 35. Victor Hugo E 36. Machinery Dove and Globe.

1952. Cultural Anniversaries.
E 73. E 35. 12 pf. brown .. 55 40
E 74. – 20 pf. green .. 50 75
E 75. – 24 pf. red 50 40
E 76. – 35 pf. blue 85 90
PORTRAITS: 20 pf. Leonardo da Vinci. 24 pf. N. Gogol. 35 pf. Avicenna.

1952. Leipzig Autumn Fair.
E 77. E 36. 24 pf. red 45 15
E 78. 35 pf. blue 45 70

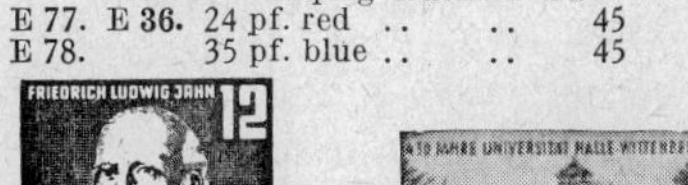

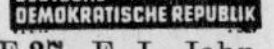

E 37. F. L. Jahn. E 38. University Building.

1952. Jahn (patriot). Death Cent.
E 79. E 37. 12 pf. blue 12 8

1952. Halle-Wittenberg University. 450th Anniv.
E 80. E 38. 24 pf. green .. 10 10

E 39. Dove, Stamp and Flag. E 40. Dove, Globe and St. Stephen's Cathedral, Vienna.

1952. Stamp Day.
E 81. E 39. 24 pf. brown .. 20 20

1952. Vienna Peace Congress.
E 97. E 40. 24 pf. red 30 25
E 98. 35 pf. blue 45 50

E 41. President Pieck. E 42. Karl Marx.

1953. President's Birthday.
E 320. E 41. 1 Dm. olive .. 30 15
E 321. 2 Dm. brown .. 70 30
For same values but different portrait of president, see Nos. E 12/13.

1953. Marx. 70th Death Anniv.
E 102. – 6 pf. red & green .. 15 5
E 103. – 10 pf. brn. & green 75 15
E 104. – 12 pf. red & green 15 10
E 105. – 16 pf. blue and red 70 70
E 106. – 20 pf. brown & yell. 20 25
E 107. E 42. 24 pf. brown & red 25 5
E 108. – 35 pf. yell. & purple 80 90
E 109. – 48 pf. brn. & green 25 25
E 110. – 60 pf. red & brown 1·00 1·00
E 111. – 84 pf. brown & blue 50 50
DESIGNS—VERT. 6 pf. Flag and foundry. 12 pf. Flag and Spasski Tower, Kremlin. 20 pf. Marx reading book. 35 pf. Marx addressing meeting. 48 pf. Marx and Engels. HORIZ. 10 pf. Marx, Engels and "Communist Manifesto". 16 pf. Marching crowd. 60 pf. Flag and workers. 84 pf. Marx in medallion and modern buildings. In each case the flag shows heads of Marx, Engels, Lenin and Stalin.

E 43. Maxim Gorki. E 44. Cyclists.

1953. Gorki (writer). 85th Birth Anniv.
E 112. E 43. 35 pf. brown .. 5 5

1953. 6th Int. Cycle Race.
E 113. E 44. 24 pf. green .. 30 25
E 114. – 35 pf. blue .. 25 25
E 115. – 60 pf. brown .. 45 35
DESIGNS—VERT. 35 pf. Cyclists and countryside. 60 pf. Cyclists in town.

E 45. H. Von Kleist. E 46. Miner.

1953. Frankfurt-on-Oder. 700th Anniv.
E 116. E 45. 16 pf. brown .. 15 30
E 117. – 20 pf. green .. 12 15
E 118. – 24 pf. red 15 8
E 119. – 35 pf. blue .. 30 30
DESIGNS—HORIZ. 20 pf. St. Mary's Church. 24 pf. Frankfurt from R. Oder. 35 pf. Frankfurt Town Hall and coat-of-arms.

1953. Five Year Plan. (a) Design in minute dots.
E 120. E 46. 1 pf. black .. 12 5
E 121. – 5 pf. green .. 25 15
E 122. – 6 pf. violet .. 20 12
E 123. – 8 pf. brown .. 35 20
E 124. – 10 pf. green .. 25 20
E 125. – 12 pf. blue .. 35 25
E 126. – 15 pf. mauve .. 40 30
E 127. – 16 pf. violet .. 50 70
E 128. – 20 pf. green .. 50 60
E 129. – 24 pf. red 40 10
E 130. – 25 pf. green .. 65 85
E 131. – 30 pf. red 65 85
E 132. – 35 pf. blue .. 65 85
E 133. – 40 pf. red 85 65
E 134. – 48 pf. mauve .. 1·25 90
E 135. – 60 pf. blue .. 1·25 1·00
E 136. – 80 pf. turquoise .. 1·90 1·00
E 137. – 84 pf. brown .. 2·40 1·50

(b) Design in lines.
E 153. E 46. 1 pf. black .. 12 5
E 310. – 5 pf. green .. 5 5
E 155. – 6 pf. violet .. 30 8
E 156. – 8 pf. chestnut .. 35 8
E 312. – 10 pf. green .. 5 5
E 311. – 10 pf. blue .. 5 5
E 159. – 12 pf. greenish blue 45 5
E 160. – 15 pf. mauve .. 60 15
E 313. – 15 pf. violet .. 5 5
E 162. – 16 pf. violet .. 65 25
E 163. – 20 pf. green .. 90 25
E 314. – 20 pf. red 5 5
E 165. – 24 pf. red 80 5
E 315. – 25 pf. green .. 5 8
E 316. – 30 pf. red 5 5
E 168. – 35 pf. blue .. 1·10 30
E 169. – 40 pf. red .. .. 1·10 30
E 317. – 40 pf. mauve .. 5 10
E 171. – 48 pf. mauve .. 2·00 50
E 318. – 50 pf. blue .. 5 25
E 173. – 60 pf. blue .. 2·25 50
E 319. – 70 pf. brown .. 5 25
E 175. – 80 pf. turquoise .. 2·50 60
E 176. – 84 pf. brown .. 3·50 60
DESIGNS—VERT. 5 pf. Woman turning wheel. 6 pf. Workmen shaking hands. 8 pf. Students. 10 pf. Engineers. 10 pf. bl. and 12 pf. Agricultural and industrial workers. 15 pf. mve. Tele-typist. 15 pf. vio. and 16 pf. Foundry worker. 20 pf. grn. Workers' health centre, Elster. 20 pf. red and 24 pf. Stalin Avenue, Berlin. 25 pf. Railway engineers. 30 pf. Folk dancers. 35 pf. Stadium. 40 pf. red, Scientist. 40 pf. mve., 48 pf. Zwinger, Dresden. 50 pf., 60 pf. Launching ship. 80 pf. Farm workers. 70 pf., 84 pf. Workman and family.

E 47. Mechanical Grab. E 48. G. W. von Knobelsdorff and Opera House, Berlin.

1953. Leipzig Autumn Fair.
E 138. E 47. 24 pf. brown .. 35 20
E 139. – 35 pf. green .. 60 60
DESIGN: 35 pf. Potato-harvester.

1953. German Architects.
E 140. E 48. 24 pf. magneta .. 25 10
E 141. – 35 pf. slate .. 55 50
DESIGN: 35 pf. B. Neumann and Wurzburg Palace.

E 49. Lucas Cranach. E 50. Nurse and Patient.

1953. Cranach (painter). 400th Death Anniv.
E 142. E 49. 24 pf. brown .. 25 30

1953. Red Cross.
E 143. E 50. 24 pf. red & brown 20 8

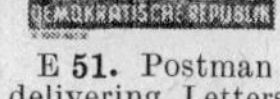

E 51. Postman delivering Letters. E 52. Lion and Lioness.

1953. Stamp Day.
E 144. E 51. 24 pf. slate .. 25 8

1953. Leipzig Zoo. 75th Anniv.
E 145. E 52. 24 pf. brown .. 25 5

E 53. Muntzer and Peasants. E 54. Franz Schubert.

1953. German Patriots.
E 146. E 53. 12 pf. brown .. 15 10
E 147. – 16 pf. brown .. 15 5
E 148. – 20 pf. red 25 5
E 149. – 24 pf. blue .. 30 5
E 150. – 35 pf. green .. 65 40
E 151. – 48 pf. sepia .. 65 25
DESIGNS: 16 pf. Baron vom Stein and scroll. 20 pf. Von Schill and cavalry. 24 pf. Blucher and infantry. 35 pf. Students marching. 48 pf. Barricade, 1848 Revolution.

1953. Schubert. 125th Death Anniv.
E 152. E 54. 48 pf. brown .. 25 30

E 55. G. E. Lessing (writer). E 56. Conference Table and Crowd.

1954. Lessing. 225th Birth Anniv.
E 177. E 55. 20 pf. green .. 15 8

1954. Four Power Conf. Berlin.
E 178. E 56. 12 pf. blue .. 10 5

E 57. Stalin. E 58. Racing Cyclists.

1954. Stalin. 1st Death Anniv.
E 179. E 57. 20 pf. brown, vermilion and grey 20 12

1954. 7th International Cycle Race.
E 180. E 58. 12 pf. brown .. 15 15
E 181. – 24 pf. green .. 25 25
DESIGN: 24 pf. Cyclists racing through countryside.

E 59. Folk-dancing. E 60. F. Reuter.

1954. 2nd German Youth Assembly
E 182. E 59. 12 pf. green .. 10 10
E 183. – 24 pf. lake .. 12 12
DESIGN: 24 pf. Young people and flag.

1954. Reuter (author). 80th Death Anniv.
E 184. E 60. 24 pf. sepia .. 15 5

E 61. Dam and Forest. E 62. E. Thalmann.

1954. Flood Relief Fund.
E 185. E 61. 24 pf.+6 pf. green 5 10

1954. Thalmann (Politician). 10th Death Anniv.
E 186. E 62. 24 pf. brown, blue and orange .. 8 8

ILLUSTRATIONS
British Commonwealth and all overprints and surcharges are FULL SIZE. Foreign Countries have been reduced to ⅔-LINEAR.

E 63. Exhibition Buildings.

1954. Leipzig Autumn Fair.
E 187. E 63. 24 pf. red 8 5
E 188. 35 pf. blue .. 12 5

1954. (a) Nos. E 155, etc., surch. in figures.
E 189. 5 pf. on 6 pf. violet .. 5 5
E 190. 5 pf. on 8 pf. chestnut 5 5
E 191. 10 pf. on 12 pf. grn'sh bl. 5 10
E 192. 15 pf. on 16 pf. violet .. 5 15
E 194. 20 pf. on 24 pf. red .. 10 12
E 195. 40 pf. on 48 pf. mauve 25 60
E 196. 50 pf. on 60 pf. blue .. 30 35
E 197. 70 pf. on 84 pf. brown .. 55 60

(b) No. E 129 similarly surch.
E 193a. 20 pf. on 24 pf red .. 10 15

E 64. President Pieck.

1954. German Democratic Republic. 5th Anniv.

E 198. E 64. 20 pf. brown .. 8 5
E 199. 35 pf. blue .. 15 12

E 65. Stamp of 1953. E 66. Russian Pavilion.

1954. Stamp Day.

E 200. E 65. 20 pf magenta .. 15 5

1955. Leipzig Spring Fair.

E 201. E 66. 20 pf. purple .. 5 5
E 202. – 35 pf. blue (Chinese Pavilion) .. 15 12

1955. Flood Relief Fund. Surch. in figures.

E 203. E 61. 20+5 pf. on 24 pf.+6 pf. green .. 5 5

E 67. "Women of All Nations".

1955. Int. Women's Day. 45th Anniv.

E 204. E 67. 10 pf. green .. 10 5
E 205. 20 pf. red 12 10

E 68. Parade of Workers. E 69. Monument to Fascist Victims, Brandenburg.

1955. Municipal Workers, Vienna. Int. Conf.

E 206. E 68. 10 pf. black & red .. 5 5

1955. Int. Liberation Day.

E 207. E 69. 10 pf. blue .. 10 5
E 208. 20 pf. magenta .. 12 5

E 70. Monument to Russian Soldiers, Treptow. E 71. Schiller (poet).

1955. Liberation. 10th Anniv.

E 209. E 70. 20 pf. magenta .. 8 5

1955. Schiller. 150th Death Anniv.

E 210. E 71. 5 pf. green .. 30 30
E 211. – 10 pf. blue .. 5 5
E 212. – 20 pf. brown .. 5 5

PORTRAITS OF SCHILLER: 10 pf. Full-face. 20 pf. Facing left.

E 72. Cyclists. E 73. Karl Liebknecht.

1955. 8th Int. Cycle Race.

E 213. E 72. 10 pf. turquoise .. 5 5
E 214. 20 pf. red 5 5

1955. German Labour Leaders.

E 215. E 73. 5 pf. green .. 5 5
E 216. – 10 pf. blue .. 5 5
E 217. – 15 pf. violet .. 1·10 60
E 218. – 20 pf. red 5 5
E 219. – 25 pf. blue .. 8 5
E 220. – 40 pf. red 8 5
E 221. – 60 pf. brown .. 8 5

PORTRAITS: 10 pf. A. Bebel. 15 pf. F. Mehring. 20 pf. E. Thalmann. 25 pf. Clara Zetkin. 40 pf. Wilhelm Liebknecht. 60 pf. Rosa Luxemburg.

E 74. Pottery. E 75. Workers and Charter.

1955. Leipzig Autumn Fair.

E 222. – 10 pf. blue .. 5 5
E 223. E 74. 20 pf. green .. 5 5

DESIGN: 10 pf. Camera and microscope.

1955. Land Reform. 10th Anniv.

E 224. E 75. 5 pf. green .. 50 60
E 225. – 10 pf. blue .. 5 5
E 226. – 20 pf. red 5 5

DESIGNS—VERT. 10 pf. Bricklayers at work. HORIZ. 20 pf. Combine-harvesters.

E 76. "Solidarity". E 77. Engels speaking.

1955. People's Solidarity Movement. 10th Anniv.

E 227. E 76. 10 pf. blue .. 5 5

1955. Engels. 135th Birth Anniv. Inscr. "FRIEDRICH ENGELS 1820-1955".

E 228. E 77. 5 pf. blue & yellow 5 5
E 229. – 10 pf. violet & yell. 5 5
E 230. – 15 pf. green & yell. 5 5
E 231. – 20 pf. lake & orge. 5 5
E 232. – 30 pf. brown & blue 1·90 1·90
E 233. – 70 pf. grey and red 8 8

DESIGNS: 10 pf. Engels and Marx. 15 pf. Engels and newspaper. 20 pf. Portrait facing right. 30 pf. Portrait facing left. 70 pf. 1848 Revolution scene.

E 78. Magdeburg Cathedral. E 79. Georg Agricola.

1955. Historic Buildings.

E 234. E 78. 5 pf. sepia 5 5
E 235. – 10 pf. green .. 5 5
E 236. – 15 pf. purple .. 5 5
E 237. – 20 pf. red 5 5
E 238. – 30 pf. brown .. 2·00 2·00
E 239. – 40 pf. blue .. 15 15

DESIGNS: 10 pf. State Opera House, Berlin. 15 pf. Old Town-hall, Leipzig. 20 pf. Town-hall, Berlin. 30 pf. Erfurt Cathedral. 40 pf. Zwinger, Dresden.

1955. Agricola (scholar). 400th Death Anniv.

E 240. E 79. 10 pf. brown .. 5 5

E 80. "Portrait of a Young Man" (Durer). E 81. Mozart.

1955. Paintings in the Dresden Gallery (1st series).

E 241. E 80. 5 pf. chocolate .. 5 5
E 242. – 10 pf. brown .. 5 5
E 243. – 15 pf. purple .. 3·50 2·25
E 244. – 20 pf. sepia .. 10 5
E 245. – 40 pf. green .. 15 5
E 246. – 70 pf. blue .. 20 10

PAINTINGS: 10 pf. "The Chocolate Girl" (Liotard). 15 pf. "Portrait of a Boy" (Pinturicchio). 20 pf. "Self-portrait with Saskia" (Rembrandt). 40 pf. "Maiden with Letter" (Vermeer). 70 pf. "Sistine Madonna" (Raphael). See also Nos. E 325/30 and E 427/31.

1956. Mozart. Birth Bicent.

E 247. E 81. 10 pf. green .. 55 55
E 248. – 20 pf. red 5 5

PORTRAIT: 20 pf. Facing left.

E 82. "Lufthansa" 'Plane. E 83. Heinrich Heine (poet).

1956. Establishment of East German "Lufthansa" Airways. Inscr. as in Type E 82.

E 249. – 5 pf. yellow, red, blue & black .. 1·10 1·10
E 250. E 82. 10 pf. green .. 5 5
E 251. – 15 pf. blue .. 5 5
E 252. – 20 pf. red 5 5

DESIGNS: 5 pf. "Lufthansa" flag. 15 pf. View of 'plane from below. 20 pf. 'Plane facing left.

1956. Heine. Death Cent. Inscr. as in Type E 83.

E 253. E 83. 10 pf. green .. 60 60
E 254. – 20 pf. red 5 5

PORTRAIT: 20 pf. Full-face.

E 84. Mobile Cranes. E 85. E. Thalmann.

1956. Leipzig Spring Fair.

E 255. E 84. 20 pf. red 5 5
E 256. 35 pf. blue .. 5 5

1956. Thalmann. 70th Birth Anniv.

E 257. E 85. 20 pf. red & brn.. .. 5 5

E 86. Hand, Laurels and Cycle Wheel. E 87. New Buildings, Old Market-place.

1956. 9th Int. Cycle Race. Inscr. as in Type E 86.

E 258. E 86. 10 pf. green .. 5 5
E 259. – 20 pf. red 5 5

DESIGN: 20 pf. Arms of Warsaw, Berlin and Prague and cycle wheel.

1956. Dresden. 750th Anniv. Inscr. "750 JAHRE DRESDEN".

E 260. E 87. 10 pf. green .. 5 5
E 261. – 20 pf. red .. 5 5
E 262. – 40 pf. violet .. 15 15

DESIGNS: 20 pf. Elbe Bridge. 40 pf. Technical High School.

E 88. Workman.

1956. Industrial Reforms. 10th Anniv.

E 263. E 88. 20 pf. red .. 5 5

E 89. Robert Schumann. E 89a.

1956. Schumann (composer). Death Cent.

(a) Type E 89 (wrong music).

E 264. E 89. 10 pf. green .. 20 20
E 265. 20 pf. red 5 5

(b) Type E 89a (correct music).

E 266. E 89a. 10 pf. green .. 15 15
E 267. 20 pf. red 5 5

E 90. Footballers. E 91. T. Mann (author).

1956. 2nd Sports Festival, Leipzig.

E 268. E 90. 5 pf. green .. 5 5
E 269. – 10 pf. blue .. 5 5
E 270. – 15 pf. purple .. 35 15
E 271. – 20 pf. red 5 5

DESIGNS: 10 pf. Javelin thrower. 15 pf. Hurdlers. 20 pf. Gymnast.

1956. 1st Anniv. of Death of Thomas Mann.

E 272. E 91. 20 pf. black .. 5 5

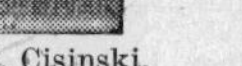

E 92. J. B. Cisinski. E 93. Lace.

1956. Cisinki (poet). Birth Cent.

E 273. E 92. 50 pf. chocolate .. 5 5

1956. Leipzig Autumn Fair. Inscr. as in Type E 93.

E 274. E 93. 10 pf. green & black 5 5
E 275. – 20 pf. red and black (Yacht) 5 5

E 94. Buchenwald Memorial.

1956. Concentration Camp Memorials Fund.

E 276. E 94. 20 pf.+80 pf. red.. 35 35

For similar stamp see No. E 390.

E 95. Torch and Olympic Rings. E 96.

1956. Olympic Games.

E 277. E 95. 20 pf. brown .. 5 5
E 278. – 35 pf. slate .. 5 5

DESIGN: 35 pf. Greek athlete.

1956. Greifswald University. 5th Cent.

E 279. E 96. 20 pf. lake .. 5 5

E 97. Postal Carrier, 1450. E 98. E. Abbe.

1956. Stamp Day.

E 280. E 97. 20 pf. red 5 5

1956. Zeiss Factory, Jena. 110th Anniv.

E 281. E 98. 10 pf. green .. 5 5
E 282. – 20 pf. brown .. 5 5
E 283. – 25 pf. indigo .. 5 5

DESIGNS—HORIZ. 20 pf. Factory buildings. 25 pf. Carl Zeiss.

E 99. "Negro". E 100. Elephants.

1956. Human Rights Day.

E 284. – 5 pf. green on olive 12 5
E 285. E 99. 10 pf. choc. on pink 5 5
E 286. – 25 pf. indigo on lav. 5 5

DESIGNS: 5 pf. "Chinese". 25 pf. "European".

1956. Berlin Zoological Gardens. Inscr. "TIERPARK BERLIN". Centres in grey.

E 287 E 100. 5 pf. black .. 5 5
E 288. – 10 pf. green .. 5 5
E 289. – 15 pf. purple .. 40 30
E 290. – 20 pf. chestnut .. 5 5
E 291. – 25 pf. sepia .. 5 5
E 292. – 30 pf. blue .. 5 5

DESIGNS: 10 pf. Flamingoes. 15 pf. Rhinoceros. 20 pf. Wild sheep. 25 pf. Bison. 30 pf. Polar bear.

1956. Egyptian Relief Fund. No. E 237 surch. **HELFT AGYPTEN+10.**

E 293. 20 pf.+10 pf. red .. 5 5

1956. Hungarian Socialists' Relief Fund. No. E 237 surch. **HELFT DEM SOZIALISTISCHEN UNGARN+10.**

E 294. 20 pf.+10 pf. red .. 5 5

E 101. Motor-ship.

DESIGN—HORIZ. 25 pf. Electric locomotive.

1957. Leipzig Spring Fair.

E 295. E 101. 20 pf. red .. 5 5
E 296. – 25 pf. blue .. 5 5

E 102. Silver Thistle.

E 103. Friedrich Froebel and Children.

1957. Nature Protection Week.

E 297. E 102. 5 pf. chocolate .. 5 5
E 298. – 10 pf. myrtle .. 20 12
E 299. – 20 pf. chestnut .. 5 5

DESIGNS: 10 pf. Emerald lizard. 20 pf. " Lady's Slipper " orchid.

1957. Froebel (educator). 175th Birth. Anniv. Inscr. "1782 1852".

E 300. – 10 pf. blk. & olive 12 10
E 301. E 103. 20 pf. blk. & chest. 5 5

DESIGN: 10 pf. Children at play.

E 104. Ravensbruck Memorial.

DESIGN—HORIZ. 20 pf. Memorial and environs.

E 105. Cycle Race Route.

1957. Concentration Camp Memorials Fund. Inscr. as in Type E 104.

E 302. E 104. 5 pf.+5 pf. green 5 5
E 303. – 20 pf.+10 pf. red 8 15

For similar stamp to No. E 303 see No. E 453.

1957. 10th Int. Cycle Race.

E 304. E 105. 5 pf. orange .. 5 5

E 106. Miner.

E 107. Henri Dunant and Globe.

1957. Coal Mining Industry.

E 305. – 10 pf. green .. 5 5
E 306. – 20 pf. brown .. 5 5
E 307. E 106. 25 pf. blue .. 20 12

DESIGNS: (39×21 mm.): 10 pf. Mechanical shovel. 20 pf. Gantry.

1957. Int. Red Cross Day. Insc. as in Type E 107. Cross in red

E 308. E 107. 10 pf. brown & grn. 5 5
E 309. – 25 pf. brn. & blue 5 5

DESIGN: 25 pf. H. Dunant wearing hat, and globe.

E 108. Joachim Jungius (botanist).

E 109. Clara Zetkin and Flower.

1957. Scientists' Anniversaries.

E 322. E 108. 5 pf. brown .. 10 8
E 323. – 10 pf. green .. 5 5
E 324. – 20 pf. chestnut .. 5 5

PORTRAITS: 10 pf. L. Euler (mathematician). 20 pf. H. Hertz (physicist).

1957. Various Paintings in the Dresden Gallery as Type E 80 (2nd series).

E 325. 5 pf. sepia 5 5
E 326. 10 pf. green 5 5
E 327. 15 pf. brown 5 5
E 328. 20 pf. red 5 5
E 329. 25 pf. purple 5 5
E 330. 40 pf. grey 35 30

PAINTINGS—VERT. 5 pf. " The Holy Family " (Mantegna). 10 pf. " The Dancer, Barbarina Campani " (Carriera). 15 pf. " Portrait of Morette " (Holbein the Younger). 20 pf. " The Tribute Money " (Titian). 25 pf. "Saskia with a Red Flower " (Rembrandt). 40 pf. " A Young Standard-bearer " (Piazzetta).

1957. Clara Zetkin (patriot). Birth Cent.

E 331. E 109. 10 pf. red & green 5 5

E 110. Bertolt Brecht (dramatist).

E 111. Congress Emblem.

1957. Bertolt Brecht. 1st Death Anniv.

E 332. E 110. 10 pf. green .. 5 5
E 333. 25 pf. blue .. 5 5

1957. 4th World Trade Unions Congress.

E 334. E 111. 20 pf. black & red 5 5

E 112. Fair Emblem.

E 113. Savings Bank Book.

1957. Leipzig Autumn Fair.

E 335. E 112. 20 pf. red .. 5 5
E 336. 25 pf. blue .. 5 5

1957. Savings Week.

E 337. E 113. 10 pf. black & grn. 15 10
E 338. 20 pf. black & mag. 5 5

E 114. Postrider of 1563.

E 115. Revolutionary's Rifle and Red Flag.

1957. Stamp Day.

E 339. E 114. 5 pf. blue on brown 5 5

1957. 40th Anniv. of Russian Revolution.

E 340. E 115. 10 pf. green & red 5 5
E 341. 25 pf. blue & red.. 5 5

E 116. Artificial Satellite.

E 117. Professor Ramin.

1957. Int. Geophysical Year. Inscr. as in Type E 116.

E 342. E 116. 10 pf. indigo .. 5 5
E 343. – 20 pf. red .. 5 5
E 344. – 25 pf. blue .. 25 20

DESIGNS: 20 pf. Stratosphere balloon. 25 pf. Ship using echo-sounder.

1957. " National Prize " Composers.

E 345. E 117. 10 pf. black & grn. 15 10
E 346. – 20 pf. black & orge 5 5

PORTRAIT: 20 pf. Professor Abendroth.

E 118. Ernst Thalmann.

PORTRAITS: 20 pf. Type E 118. 25 pf. R. Breitscheid. 40 pf. Father P. Schneider. For other stamps as Type E 118 see Nos. E 374/8, E 448/52, E 485/7, E 496/500, E 540/4 and E 588/92.

1957. National Memorials Fund. East German War Victims. Portraits in grey.

E 347. 20 pf.+10 pf. magenta 5 5
E 348. 25 pf.+15 pf. blue .. 5 5
E 349. 40 pf.+20 pf. violet .. 5 5

E 119.

E 120.

1957. Air.

E 350. E 119. 5 pf. black & grey 5 5
E 351. 20 pf. black & red 5 5
E 352. 35 pf. black & vio. 8 5
E 353. 50 pf. black & brn. 10 5
E 354. E 120. 1 Dm. olive & yell. 25 5
E 355. 3 Dm. brn. & yell. 90 5
E 356. 5 Dm. blue & yell. 1·50 5

E 121. Fair Emblem.

1958. Leipzig Spring Fair.

E 357. E 121. 20 pf. red .. 5 5
E 358. 25 pf. blue .. 5 5

E 122. Transmitting Aerial and Posthorn.

E 123. "Zille at play".

1958. Communist Postal Conf., Moscow.

E 359. E 122. 5 pf. black and grey 12 10
E 360. – 20 pf. red .. 5 5

DESIGN—HORIZ. 20 pf. Aerial as in 5 pf. but posthorn above figures of value.

1958. Heinrich Zille (painter). Birth Cent.

E 361. E 123. 10 pf. drab & grn. 15 12
E 362. – 20 pf. drab and red 5 5

DESIGN—VERT. 20 pf. Self-portrait of Zille.

E 124. Max Planck.

E 125. Breeding Cow.

1958. Max Planck (physicist). Birth Cent.

E 363. – 10 pf. olive .. 15 12
E 364. E 124. 20 pf. magenta .. 5 5

DESIGN—VERT. 10 pf. "h" (symbol of Planck's Constant).

1958. 6th Markkleeberg Agricultural Exn. Inscr. "6 Landwirtschaftausstellung der DDR in Markkleeberg".

E 365. E 125. 5 pf. grey .. 20 20
E 366. – 10 pf. green .. 5 5
E 367. – 20 pf. red .. 5 5

DESIGNS (39×22½ mm.): 10 pf. Chaff-cutter. 20 pf. Beet-harvester.

E 126. Charles Darwin.

E 127. Congress Emblem.

1958. Cent. of Darwin's Theory of Evolution and Bicent. of Linnaeus's Plant Classification System. Portraits in black.

E 368. E 126. 10 pf. green .. 15 10
E 369. – 20 pf. red .. 5 5

PORTRAIT—HORIZ. 20 pf. Linnaeus (Carl von Linne) inscr. "200 JAHRE SYSTEMA NATURAE".

1958. 5th German Socialist Unity Party Congress.

E 370. E 127. 10 pf. red .. 5 5

INDEX

Countries can be quickly located by referring to the index at the end of this volume.

E 128. " The Seven Towers of Rostock " and Ships.

E 129. Mare and Foal.

1958. Rostock Port Reconstruction. Inscr. as in Type E 123.

E 371. – 10 pf. green .. 5 5
E 372. E 128. 20 pf. orange .. 5 5
E 373. – 25 pf. blue .. 15 12

DESIGNS: 10 pf. Ship at quayside. 25 pf. Ships in Rostock harbour.

1958. " Resistance Fighters ". As Type E 118. Portraits in grey.

E 374. 5 pf.+5 pf. chocolate 5 5
E 375. 10 pf.+5 pf. green .. 5 5
E 376. 15 pf.+10 pf. violet .. 5 30
E 377. 20 pf.+10 pf. brown .. 5 5
E 378. 25 pf.+15 pf. black .. 25 50

PORTRAITS—VERT. 5 pf. A. Kuntz. 10 pf. R. Arndt. 15 pf. Dr. K. Adams. 20 pf. R. Renner. 25 pf. W. Stoecker.

1958. " Grand Prix of the D.D.R. " Horse Show. Inscr. as in Type E 129.

E 379. E 129. 5 pf. sepia .. 25 25
E 380. – 10 pf. green .. 5 5
E 381. – 20 pf. brown .. 5 5

DESIGNS: 10 pf. Horse-trotting. 20 pf. Racing horses.

130. J. A. Komensky (" Comenius ").

E 131. Camp Bugler.

1958. Komensky Commem. Inscr. as in Type E 130. Centres in black.

E 382. E 130. 10 pf. green .. 15 12
E 383. – 20 pf. brown .. 5 5

DESIGN: 20 pf. Komensky with pupils (from an old engraving).

1958. East German " Pioneer " Organisation. 10th Anniv. Inscr. as in Type E 131.

E 384. E 131. 10 pf.+5 pf. green 5 5
E 385. – 20 pf.+10 pf. red 5 5

DESIGN—VERT. 20 pf. Young Pioneer saluting.

E 132. University Seal.

DESIGN: 20 pf. University building.

1958. Friedrich Schiller University, Jena. 400th Anniv. Inscr. as in Type E 132.

E 386. E 132. 5 pf. black & grey 15 5
E 387. – 20 pf. grey and red 5 5

E 133. Model with Hamster-lined Coat, and Leipzig Railway Station.

E 134. Soldier climbing Wall.

1958. Leipzig Autumn Fair.

E 388. E 133. 10 pf. brn. & grn. 5 5
E 389. – 25 pf. black & blue 5 5

DESIGN: 25 pf. Model with Karakul fur coat, and Leipzig Old Town Hall.

1958. Concentration Camp Memorials Fund. As Type E 94 but additionally inscr. "14. SEPTEMBER 1958" in black.

E 390. 20 pf.+20 pf. red .. 12 8

1958. 1st Summer Military Games, Leipzig. Inscr. "20.–28. SEPTEMBER 1958".

E 391. E 134. 10 pf. brn. & green 20 20
E 392. – 20 pf. yell. & chest. 5 5
E 393. – 25 pf. red & blue 5 5

DESIGNS: 20 pf. Games emblem. 25 pf. Marching athletes with banner.

E 135. Warding off the Atomic Bomb. E 136. 17th-century Mailcart.

1958. Campaign against Atomic Warfare.
E 394. E 135. 20 pf. red .. 5 5
E 395. 25 pf. blue .. 5 5

1958. Stamp Day.
E 396. E 136. 10 pf. green .. 12 10
E 397. – 20 pf. lake .. 5 5
DESIGN: 20 pf. Modern Postal sorting train and aircraft.

E 137. Revolutionary and Soldier. E 138. Brandenburg Gate, Berlin.

E 140. Negro and European Youths. E 139. "Girl's Head" (bas-relief).

1958. November Revolution. 40th Anniv.
E 398. E 137. 20 pf. black, purple & red 2·50 3·00

1958. Brandenburg Gate Commem.
E 399. E 138. 20 pf. red .. 5 5
E 400. 25 pf. blue .. 20 15

1958. Antique Art Treasures.
E 401. E 139. 10 pf. black & grn. 20 12
E 402. – 20 pf. black & red 5 5
DESIGN: 20 pf. "Large Head" (from Pergamon frieze).
See also Nos. E 475/8.

1958. Declaration of Human Rights. 10th Anniv.
E 403. E 140. 10 pf. black & grn. 5 5
E 404. – 25 pf. black & blue 20 15
DESIGN: 25 pf. Chinese and European girls.

E 141. O. Nuschke. E 142. "The Red Flag" (Party Newspaper).

1958. Vice-Premier Otto Nuschke. 1st Death Anniv.
E 405. E 141. 20 pf. red .. 5 5

1958. German Communist Party. 40th Anniv.
E 406. E 142. 20 pf. red .. 5 5

E 143. Pres. Pieck. E 144. Rosa Luxemburg (revolutionary).

1959. Pres. Pieck's 83rd Birthday.
E 407. E 143. 20 pf. red .. 5 5
For 20 pf. black see No. E 517.

1959. Rosa Luxemburg and Karl Liebknecht. 40th Death Annivs. Centres in black.
E 408. E 144. 10 pf. green .. 20 20
E 409. – 20 pf. red .. 5 5
DESIGN—HORIZ. 20 pf. Liebknecht (revolutionary).

E 145. Concert Hall, Leipzig.

DESIGN—HORIZ. 25 pf. Opening theme of Symphony in A Major ("The Italian").

1959. Felix Mendelssohn-Bartholdy (composer). 150th Birth Anniv.
E 410. E 145. 10 pf. green on grn. 5 5
E 411. – 25 pf. blue on blue 20 15

E 146. "Schwarze Pumpe" plant. E 147. Boy holding Book for Girl.

1959. Leipzig Spring Fair. Inscr. as in Type E 146.
E 412. E 146. 20 pf. red .. 5 5
E 413. – 25 pf. blue .. 5 5
DESIGN—HORIZ. 25 pf. Various cameras.

1959. "Youth Consecration". 5th Anniv. Inscr. as in Type E 147.
E 414. E 147. 10 pf. black on grn. 15 12
E 415. – 20 pf. blk. on salm. 5 5
DESIGN: 20 pf. Girl holding book for boy.

E 148. Handel's Statue, Oboe and Arms of Halle. E 149. A. von Humboldt and Jungle Scene.

1959. Handel's Death Bicent. Inscr. "1685–1759". Centre in black.
E 416. E 148. 10 pf. green .. 15 12
E 417. – 20 pf. red .. 5 5
DESIGN: 20 pf. Portrait of Handel (after oil painting by Thomas Hudson).

1959. Alexander von Humboldt (naturalist). Death Cent.
E 418. E 149. 10 pf. green .. 15 12
E 419. – 20 pf. red .. 5 5
DESIGN: 20 pf. As Type E 149 but with view of sleigh in forest.

E 150. Posthorn. E 151. Heron.

1959. Postal Ministers' Conf., Berlin.
E 420. E 150. 20 pf. black, yellow and red 5 5
E 421. 25 pf. black, yellow & blue.. 25 20

1959. Nature Preservation.
E 422. E 151. 5 pf. lilac, black and blue .. 5 5
E 423. – 10 pf. chestnut, sepia & turq. .. 5 5
E 424. – 20 pf. blue, sepia, green & chest. 5 5
E 425. – 25 pf. yell.. black, brown & lilac.. 5 5
E 426. – 40 pf. yellow, black and grey 90 50
DESIGNS. 10 pf. Bittern. 20 pf. Lily of the Valley and Peacock butterfly. 25 pf. Beaver. 40 pf. Bee and willow catkin.

1959. Various paintings in the Dresden Gallery as Type E 80 (3rd series).
E 427. 5 pf. olive 5 5
E 428. 10 pf. green 5 5
E 429. 20 pf. chestnut 5 5
E 430. 25 pf. brown 5 5
E 431. 40 pf. lake 65 40
PAINTINGS—VERT. 5 pf. "The Vestal Virgin" (Kauffman). 10 pf. "The Needlewoman" (Metsu). 20 pf. "Mlle. Lavergne reading a letter" (Liotard). 25 pf. "Old woman with a brazier" (Rubens). 40 pf. "Young man in black coat" (Hals).

E 152. Cormorant. E 153.

1959. "Birds of the Homeland". Centres and inscriptions in black.
E 432. E 152. 5 pf. yellow .. 5 5
E 433. – 10 pf. green .. 5 5
E 434. – 15 pf. violet .. 70 45
E 435. – 20 pf. pink .. 5 5
E 436. – 25 pf. blue .. 5 5
E 437. – 40 pf. red .. 5 5
BIRDS: 10 pf. Black stork. 15 pf. Eagle owl. 20 pf. Black cock. 25 pf. Hoopoe. 40 pf. Hawk.

1959. 7th World Youth Festival, Vienna.
E 438. E 153. 20 pf. red .. 5 5
E 439. – 25 pf. blue .. 20 15
DESIGN—HORIZ. 25 pf. White girl embracing negro girl.

E 154. Hoop Exercises. E 155. Modern Leipzig Building.

1959. 3rd German Gymnastic and Sports Festival, Leipzig.
E 440. E 154. 5 pf. + 5 pf. chest 5 5
E 441. – 10 pf. + 5 pf. green 5 5
E 442. – 20 pf. + 10 pf. red 5 5
E 443. – 25 pf. + 10 pf. blue 5 5
E 444. – 40 pf. + 20 pf. pur. 65 35
DESIGNS: 10 pf. High-jumping. 20 pf. Vaulting. 25 pf. Club exercises. 40 pf. Fireworks over Leipzig Stadium.

1959. Leipzig Autumn Fair.
E 445. E 155. 20 pf. grey & red 5 5
See also Nos. E 483/4.

E 156. Glass Tea-set.

1959. 75 Years of Jena Glassware.
E 446. E 156. 10 pf. turquoise .. 5 5
E 447. – 25 pf. blue .. 15 12
DESIGN—VERT. 25 pf. Laboratory retorts.

1959. Ravensbruck Concentration Camp Victims. As Type E 118. Portraits in black.
E 448. 5 pf. + 5 pf. brown .. 5 5
E 449. 10 pf. + 5 pf. green .. 5 5
E 450. 15 pf. + 10 pf. violet .. 5 5
E 451. 20 pf. + 10 pf. magenta .. 5 5
E 452. 25 pf. + 15 pf. blue .. 20 35
PORTRAITS: 5 pf. T. Klose. 10 pf. K. Niederkirchner 15 pf. C. Eisenblatter. 20 pf. O. Benario-Prestes. 25 pf. M. Grollmuss.

1959. Concentration Camp Memorials Fund. As No. E 303 but inscr. "12. SEPTEMBER 1959" in black.
E 453. 20 pf. + 10 pf. red .. 5 5

E 158. "Russian Pennant on the Moon".

1959. Landing of Russian Rocket on the Moon.
E 454. E 158. 20 pf. red .. 5 5

E 159. E. German Flag & Combine-harvester. E 160. J. R. Becher.

1959. German Democratic Republic. 10th Anniv. Designs as Type E 159 showing E. German Flag in black, red and yellow. Inscriptions in black and red on coloured paper.
E 455. E 159. 5 pf. buff.. .. 5 5
E 456. – 10 pf. grey .. 5 5
E 457. – 15 pf. pale yellow 5 5
E 458. – 20 pf. grey-lilac.. 5 5
E 459. – 25 pf. pale olive.. 5 5
E 460. – 40 pf. yellow .. 5 5
E 461. – 50 pf. salmon .. 5 5
E 462. – 60 pf. blue-green 5 5
E 463. – 70 pf. pale green 10 5
E 464. – 1 Dm. brown .. 15 5
DESIGNS: 10 pf. "Fritz Heckert" convalescent home. 15 pf. Zwinger Palace, Dresden. 20 pf. Steel worker. 25 pf. Industrial chemist. 40 pf. Leipzig Stadium. 50 pf. Woman tractor-driver. 60 pf. Airliner. 70 pf. Shipbuilding. 1 Dm. East Germany's first atomic reactor.

1959. Becher (poet). 1st Death Anniv.
E 465. E 160. 20 pf. slate and red 10 5
The above was issued in sheets with alternate horiz. rows of labels inscr. "AUFERSTANDEN" etc. (part of E. German national anthem) and with Becher's signature, in slate on yellow.

E 161. Schiller. E 162. 18th-century Courier and Milestone.

1959. Schiller (poet). Birth Bicent.
E 466. – 10 pf. grey-green on green .. 30 15
E 467. E 161. 20 pf. lake on pink 5 5
DESIGN: 10 pf. Schiller's house, Weimar.

1959. Stamp Day.
E 468. E 162. 10 pf. green .. 15 12
E 469. – 20 pf. lake .. 5 5
DESIGN: 20 pf. Postwoman on motor-cycle.

E 163. Red Squirrels. E 164. Boxing.

1959. Forest Animals.
E 470. 163. 5 pf. brn.-red, brn. & grey 5 5
E 471. – 10 pf. yellow-brown brown and emerald 5 5
E 472. – 20 pf. bistre, blk. & red 5 5
E 473. – 25 pf. chestnut, brown, green and blue .. 5 5
E 474. – 40 pf. yellow, brown and violet-blue .. 1·25 55
ANIMALS: 10 pf. Brown hares. 20 pf. Roe deer. 25 pf. Red deer. 40 pf. Lynx.

1959. Antique Art Treasures. As Type E 139.
E 475. 5 pf. black and yellow .. 5 5
E 476. 10 pf. black and green .. 5 5
E 477. 20 pf. black and red .. 5 5
E 478. 25 pf. black and blue .. 55 20
DESIGNS—As Type E 139: 5 pf. Attic goddess (about 580 B.C.). 10 pf. Princess of Tell el-Amarna (about 1360 B.C.). 20 pf. Bronze horse of Toprak-Kale, Armenia (7th-cent B.C.). HORIZ. (49 × 28 mm.): 25 pf. Altar of Zeus, Pergamon (about 160 B.C.).

1960. Olympic Games. As Type E 164 inscr. "OLYMPISCHE SOMMERSPIELE 1960" or "WINTERSPIELE" etc. (20 pf.). Centres and inscriptions in yellow-brown.
E 479. E 164. 5 pf. brown .. 1·40 50
E 480. – 10 pf. green .. 5 5
E 481. – 20 pf. red .. 5 5
E 482. – 25 pf. blue .. 5 5
DESIGNS: 10 pf. Running. 20 pf. Ski-jumping 25 pf. Yachting.

1960. Leipzig Spring Fair. As Type E 155 but inscr. "LEIPZIGER FRUHJAHRSMESSE 1960".
E 483. 20 pf. grey and red .. 5 5
E 484. 25 pf. grey and blue .. 5 5
DESIGNS: 20 pf. Northern Entrance, Technical Fair. 25 pf. Ring Fair Building.

1960. Sachsenhausen Concentration Camp Victims (1st issue). As Type E 118. Portraits in black.
E 485. 5 pf. + 5 pf. drab .. 5 5
E 486. 10 pf. + 5 pf. myrtle .. 5 5
E 487. 20 pf. + 10 pf. purple .. 5 5
PORTRAITS: 5 pf. L. Erdmann. 10 pf. E. Schneller. 20 pf. L. Horn.
See also Nos. E 496/500.

E 165. Purple Foxglove.

E 166. Lenin.

1960. Medicinal Flowers. Background in pale drab.

E 488. 5 pf. red and green .. 5 5
E 489. 10 pf. olive and green .. 5 5
E 490. 15 pf. red and green .. 5 5
E 491. 20 pf. violet & turquoise 5 5
E 492. 40 pf. red, green & brn. 1·40 50

FLOWERS: 5 pf. Type **E 165.** 10 pf. Camomile. 15 pf. Peppermint. 20 pf. Poppy. 40 pf. Wild Rose.

1960. Lenin. 90th Birth Anniv.

E 493. **E 166.** 20 pf. lake .. 5 5

1960. Re-opening of Rostock Port. No. E 371. optd. **Inbetriebnahme des Hochsee-hofens 1. Mai 1960.**

E 494. 10 pf. green 5 5

E 167. Russian Soldier and Liberated Prisoner.

1960. Liberation. 15th Anniv.

E 495. **E 167.** 20 pf. red .. 5 5

1960. Sachsenhausen Concentration Camp. Victims (2nd issue). As Type **E 118.** Portraits in black.

E 496. 10 pf. + 5 pf. green .. 5 5
E 497. 15 pf. + 5 pf. violet .. 25 30
E 498. 20 pf. + 10 pf. lake .. 5 5
E 499. 25 pf. + 10 pf. blue .. 5 5
E 500. 40 pf. + 20 pf. brown .. 75 40

PORTRAITS: 10 pf. M. Lademann. 15 pf. L. Breunig. 20 pf. M. Thesen. 25 pf. G. Sandtner. 40 pf. H. Rothbarth.

E 168. Holiday Ship Model and Plans.

1960. Launching of F.D.G.B. Holiday Ship.

E 501. **E 168.** 5 pf. slate, red and yellow 5 5
E 502. – 10 pf. + 5 pf. black, red and yellow .. 5 5
E 503. – 20 pf. + 10 pf. black, red and blue .. 5 5
E 504. – 25 pf. black, yell. and cobalt .. 75 40

DESIGNS: 10 pf. Ship under construction at Wismar. 20 pf. Ship off Stubbenkammer. 25 pf. Ship and cruiser "Aurora" at Leningrad.

E 169. Lenin Statue, Eisleben.

E 170. Masked Dancer (statuette).

1960. Lenin-Thalmann Statues.

E 505. **E 169.** 10 pf. slate-grn. .. 5 5
E 506. – 20 pf. red .. 5 5

DESIGN: 20 pf. Thalmann Statue, Pushkin, U.S.S.R.

1960. Porcelain Industry, Meissen. 250th Anniv. Centres and inscriptions in grey-blue. Figures in colours given.

E 507. **E 170.** 5 pf. orange .. 5 5
E 508. – 10 pf. green .. 5 5
E 509. – 15 pf. purple .. 90 90
E 510. – 20 pf. red .. 5 5
E 511. – 25 pf. olive .. 5 5

DESIGNS: 10 pf. Dish inscr. with swords and years "1710 1960". 15 pf. Otter. 20 pf. Potter. 25 pf. Coffee-pot.

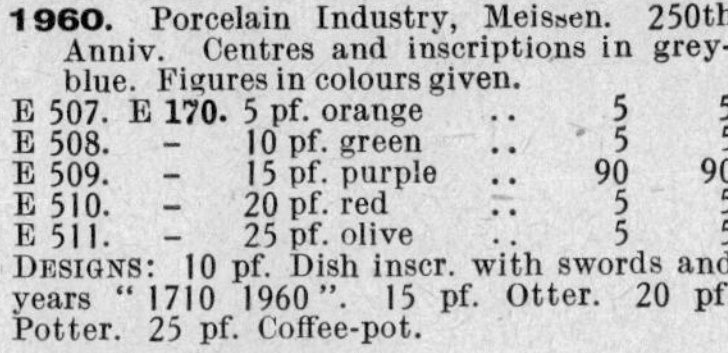

E 171. Racing Cyclist.

E 172. Opera House, Leipzig.

1960. World Cycling Championships. Inscr. as in Type **E 171.**

E 512. **E 171.** 20 pf. + 10 pf. red, blue, black, yellow and green .. 5 5
E 513. – 25 pf. + 10 pf. brn., drab and blue .. 40 30

DESIGN ($38\frac{1}{2} \times 21$ mm.): 25 pf. Racing cyclists on track.

1960. Leipzig Autumn Fair. Inscr. as in Type **E 172.**

E 514 **E 172.** 20 pf. grey and red 5 5
E 515. – 25 pf. brn. & blue 5 5

DESIGN: 25 pf. Export goods.

E 174. Rook.

E 173. Sachsenhausen Memorial.

E 175. Mail Vans.

1960. Concentration Camp Memorials Fund.

E 516. **E 173.** 20 pf. + 10 pf. red 5 5

1960. President Pieck Mourning issue.

E 517. **E 143.** 20 pf. black .. 5 5

1960. 14th Chess Olympiad, Leipzig.

E 518. **E 174.** 10 pf. + 5 pf. green 5 5
E 519. – 20 pf. + 10 pf. claret 5 5
E 520. – 25 pf. + 10 pf. blue 60 35

DESIGNS: 20 pf. Knight. 25 pf. Bishop.

1960. Stamp Day. Inscr. as in Type **E 175.**

E 521. **E 175.** 20 pf. yellow, blk. and magenta .. 5 5
E 522. – 25 pf. mauve, black and blue .. 40 35

DESIGN: 25 pf. 19th-cent. railway mail-coach.

E 176. Medal of 1518 showing Hans Burgkmair (painter).

E 177. Count N. von Gneisenau.

1960. Dresden Art Collections. 400th Anniv.

E 523. **E 176.** 20 pf. ochre, green and buff 5 5
E 524. – 25 pf. black & blue 40 40

DESIGN: 25 pf. "Dancing Peasants" (after Durer).

1960. Count N. von Gneisenau. Birth Bicent.

E 525. **E 177.** 20 pf. black & red 5 5
E 526. – 25 pf. blue .. 40 35

DESIGN: 25 pf. Similar portrait but vert.

E 178. R. Virchow.

E 179. Scientist with notebook.

1960. 250th Anniv. of Berlin Charity and 150th Anniv. of Humboldt University, Berlin. Centres in black.

E 527. **E 178.** 5 pf. ochre .. 5 5
E 528. – 10 pf. green .. 5 5
E 529. – 20 pf. chestnut .. 5 5
E 530. – 25 pf. blue .. 5 5
E 531. – 40 pf. red .. 55 40

DESIGNS—As Type **E 178** (Berlin Charity): 10 pf. Robert Koch. 40 pf. W. Griesinger. (Humboldt University): 20 pf. University building and statues of William and Alexander von Humboldt. 25 pf. Plaque with profiles of Von Humboldt brothers.

1960. Chemical Workers' Day.

E 532. **E 179.** 5 pf. grey & red 5 5
E 533. – 10 pf. green and orange 5 5
E 534. – 20 pf. red & bl. 5 5
E 535. – 25 pf. bl. & yell. 40 25

DESIGNS: 10 pf. Chemical worker with fertiliser. 20 pf. Girl worker with jar, and Trabant car. 25 pf. Laboratory assistant and synthetic dress.

E 180. "Young Socialists' Express" (double-decker train).

E 181. President Pieck.

1960. German Railways. 125th Anniv.

E 536. **E 180.** 10 pf. black and green .. 5 5
E 537. – 20 pf. blk. & red .. 5 5
E 538. – 25 pf. blk. & bl. 2·10 2·25

DESIGNS—As Type **E 180:** 25 pf. Locomotive "Adler" of 1835 and modern diesel loco. No. V 180 with train. ($43 \times 25\frac{1}{2}$ mm.): 20 pf. Sassnitz Harbour station and train-ferry "Sassnitz".

1961. President Pieck. 85th Birth Anniv.

E 539. **E 181.** 20 pf. red & blk. 5 5

1961. More Concentration Camp Victims. As Type **E 118.** Portraits in black.

E 540. 5 pf. + 5 pf. emerald .. 5 5
E 541. 10 pf. + 5 pf. green .. 5 5
E 542. 15 pf. + 5 pf. mauve .. 60 75
E 543. 20 pf. + 10 pf. red .. 5 5
E 544. 25 pf. + 10 pf. blue .. 5 5

PORTRAITS: 5 pf. W. Kube. 10 pf. H. Gunther. 15 pf. Elvira Eisenschneider. 20 pf. Hertha Lindner. 25 pf. H. Tschape.

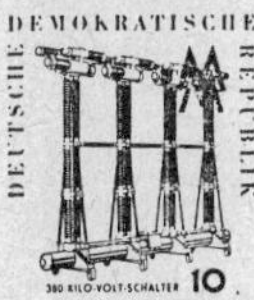

E 182. High-voltage Switchgear.

E 183. Lilienstein, Saxony.

1961. Leipzig Spring Fair. Inscr. as in Type **E 182.**

E 545. **E 182.** 10 pf. slate & emer. 5 5
E 546. – 25 pf. slate & blue 5 5

DESIGN: 25 pf. Fair Press Centre.

1961. Landscapes and Historical Buildings.

E 547. – 5 pf. grey .. 5 5
E 548. – 10 pf. green .. 5 5
E 549. **E 183.** 20 pf. red-brown 5 5
E 550. – 20 pf. brown-red 5 5
E 551. – 25 pf. blue .. 5 5

DESIGNS—VERT. 5 pf. Ruins of Rudelsburg. 10 pf. Wartburg. 20 pf. (No. E 550), Town Hall, Wernigerode. HORIZ. 25 pf. Brocken, Oberharz.

DESIGNS: 20 pf. Hauling nets. 25 pf. Trawler "Robert Koch". 40 pf. Fish-processing machine.

E 184. Trawler.

1961. Deep Sea Fishing Industry.

E 552. **E 184.** 10 pf. green .. 5 5
E 553. – 20 pf. maroon .. 5 5
E 554. – 25 pf. Slate-blue . 5 5
E 555. – 40 pf. Slate-violet 75 65

E 185. Marx, Engels, Lenin and demonstrators.

1961. German Socialist Unity Party ("S.E.D."). 15th Anniv.

E 556. **E 185.** 20 pf. red .. 5 5

DESIGNS: 10 pf. Space rocket across globe. 25 pf. Capsule's parachute descent.

E 186. Space-man in Capsule.

1961. World's 1st Manned Space Flight. Inscr. "12.4.1961".

E 557. – 10 pf. red & turq. 5 5
E 558. **E 186.** 20 pf. red .. 5 5
E 559. – 25 pf. blue .. 1·25 1·25

DESIGN: 20 pf. Gibbon apes.

E 187. Zebra.

1961. Dresden Zoo. Cent. Inscr. "1861–1961".

E 560. **E 187.** 10 pf. black & grn. 85 60
E 561. – 20 pf. black & mag. 5 5

DESIGNS: 10 pf. Type **E 188.** 20 pf. Folk-dancing. 25 pf. Model aeroplane construction.

E 188. Pioneers playing Volleyball.

1961. Young Pioneers Meeting, Erfurt. Inscr. as in Type **E 188.**

E 562. 10 pf. + 5 pf. grn., yell., black and magenta .. 5 5
E 563. 20 pf. + 10 pf. magenta, yellow, black & blue 5 5
E 564. 25 pf. + 10 pf. vio., yell., black and magenta .. 85 85

E 189. High Jump.

E 190. Salt Miners and Castle.

1961. 3rd European Women's Gymnastic Championships, Leipzig. Inscr. as in Type **E 189.**

E 565. **E 189.** 10 pf. green .. 5 5
E 566. – 20 pf. magenta .. 5 5
E 567. – 25 pf. blue .. 1·10 1·10

DESIGNS—VERT. 20 pf. Gymnast. HORIZ. 25 pf. Exercise on parallel bars.

1961. Halle (Saale) Millenary. Inscr. as in Type **E 190.**

E 568. 10 pf. black, yell. & grn. 30 20
E 569. 20 pf. black, yell. & red 5 5

DESIGNS: 10 pf. Type **E 190.** 20 pf. Scientist and Five Towers of Halle.

DESIGNS: 5 pf. Folding canoe. 20 pf. Canadian two-seater canoe.

E 191. Canadian Canoe.

1961. World Canoeing Championships.

E 570. – 5 pf. blue & grey 80 80
E 571. **E 191.** 10 pf. grn. & grey 5 5
E 572. – 20 pf. pur. & grey 5 5

E 192. Line-casting.

E 193. Old Weigh-house, Leipzig.

1961. World Angling Championships.

E 573. **E 192.** 10 pf. grn. & blue 90 90
E 574. – 20 pf. lake & blue 5 5

DESIGN: 20 pf. River-fishing.

1961. Leipzig Autumn Fair. Inscr. "LEIPZIGER HERBSMESSE 1961".

E 575. 10 pf. olive and green .. 5 5
E 576. 25 pf. blue and ultram. 12 5

DESIGNS: 10 pf. Type **E 193.** 25 pf. Old Stock Exchange, Leipzig.

See also Nos. E 612/14.

E 194. Walter Ulbricht.

E 195. Dahlia.

1961. Type E 194 or larger, 24 × 29 mm. (Dm. values).
E 577. 5 pf. grey-blue .. 5 5
E 578. 10 pf. green 5 5
E 579. 15 pf. purple 5 5
E 580. 20 pf. red 8 5
E 581. 25 pf. turquoise .. 10 5
E 582. 30 pf. red 10 5
E 582a. 35 pf green 15 5
E 583. 40 pf. violet 12 5
E 584. 50 pf. blue 20 5
E 584a. 60 pf. olive-green .. 20 5
E 585. 70 pf. brown 30 5
E 585a. 80 pf. blue 30 5
E 586. 1 DM. bronze-green .. 35 5
E 587. 2 DM. brown 65 5
See also Nos E 805/6, E 1197/8 and E 1255.

1961. Concentration Camps Memorials Fund. As Type E 118. Portraits in grey and black.
E 588. 5 pf. + 5 pf. emerald .. 5 5
E 589. 10 pf. + 5 pf. green .. 5 5
E 590. 20 pf. + 10 pf. mauve .. 5 5
E 591. 25 pf. + 10 pf. blue .. 5 5
E 592. 40 pf. + 20 pf. lake .. 70 90
PORTRAITS—As Type E 118. 5 pf. C. Schonhaar. 10 pf. H. Baum. 20 pf. Liselotte Herrmann. HORIZ. (41 × 32½ mm.): 25 pf. Sophie and Hans Scholl. 40 pf. Hilde and Hans Coppi.

1961. Int. Horticultural Exn.
E 593. 10 pf. red, yellow & grn. 5 5
E 594. 20 pf. red, yellow & brn. 5 5
E 595. 40 pf. red, yellow & blue 1·50 1·50
FLOWERS: 10 pf. Tulip. 20 pf. Type E 195. 40 pf. Rose.

E 196. Liszt and Berlioz (after Von Kaulbach and Prinzhofer).

E 197. TV Camera and Screen.

1961. Liszt (composer). 150th Birth Anniv.
E 596. 5 pf. black 5 5
E 597. 10 pf. green 30 30
E 598. 20 pf. red 5 5
E 599. 25 pf. blue 40 40
DESIGNS: 5 pf. Type E 196. 10 pf. Young hand of Liszt (from French sculpture, Liszt Museum, Budapest). 20 pf. Liszt (after Rietschel). 25 pf. Liszt and Chopin (after Bartolini and Bovy).

1961. Stamp Day.
E 600. 10 pf. black and green 25 25
E 601. 20 pf. black and red .. 5 5
DESIGNS: 10 pf. Type E 197. 20 pf. Studio microphone and radio tuning-scale.

E 198. H. S. Titov with Young Pioneers.

1961. 2nd Russian Manned Space Flight.
E 602. 5 pf. violet and red .. 5 5
E 603. 10 pf. green and red .. 5 5
E 604. 15 pf. mauve and blue 1·75 2·40
E 605. 20 pf. red and blue .. 5 5
E 606. 25 pf. blue and red .. 5 5
E 607. 40 pf. indigo and red .. 25 5
DESIGNS—HORIZ. 5 pf. Type E 198. 15 pf. Titov in space-suit. 20 pf. Titov receiving Karl Marx Order from Ulbricht. 25 pf. Vostok 2 rocket in flight. 40 pf. Titov and Ulbricht in Berlin. VERT. 10 pf. Titov in Leipzig.

E 199. Red Ants ("Formica rufa").

DESIGNS: 5 pf. Type E 199. 10 pf. Mouse-weasels ("Mustela nivalis"). 20 pf. Shrews ("Soricidae"). 40 pf. Bat ("Chiroptera").

1962. Fauna Protection Campaign. (1st series).
E 608. 5 pf. yellow, brn. & blk. 65 50
E 609. 10 pf. brown and green 5 5
E 610. 20 pf. brown and red . 5 5
E 611. 40 pf. yellow, blk. & vio. 15 10
See also Nos. E 699/703.

1962. Leipzig Spring Fair. As Type E 193.
E 612. 10 pf. sepia and green 5 5
E 613. 20 pf. black and red .. 5 5
E 614. 25 pf. maroon and blue 20 10
BUILDINGS: 10 pf. "Zum Kaffeebaum". 20 pf. "Gohliser Schlosschen". 25 pf. "Romanus-Haus".

E 200. Air Force Pilot.

E 201. Danielle Casanova.

1962. East German People's Army. 6th Anniv.
E 615. E 200. 5 pf. blue.. .. 5 5
E 616. – 10 pf. green .. 5 5
E 617. – 20 pf. red .. 5 5
E 618. – 25 pf. blue .. 5 5
E 619. – 40 pf. brown .. 50 60
DESIGNS: 10 pf. Soldier and armoured car. 20 pf. Factory-guard. 25 pf. Sailor and warship. 40 pf. Tank and driver.

1962. Concentration Camps Memorial Fund. Camp Victims.
E 620. 5 pf. + 5 pf. black .. 5 5
E 621. 10 pf. + 5 pf. green .. 5 5
E 622. 20 pf. + 10 pf. purple .. 5 5
E 623. 25 pf. + 10 pf. blue .. 10 5
E 624. 40 pf. + 20 pf. maroon 95 80
PORTRAITS: 5 pf. Type E 201. 10 pf. Julius Fucik. 20 pf. Johanna J. Schaft. 25 pf. Pawel Finder. 40 pf. Soja A. Kosmodemjanskaja.

E 202. Racing Cyclists and Prague Castle.

E 203. Johann Fichte.

1962. Int. Peace Cycle Race.
E 625. 10 pf. red, black, blue and green 5 5
E 626. 20 pf. + 10 pf. red, black, blue and yellow .. 5 5
E 627. 25 pf. yellow, black, red and blue 65 40
DESIGNS: 10 pf. Type E 202. 20 pf. Cyclists and Palace of Culture and Science, Warsaw 25 pf. Cyclist and Town Hall, East Berlin.

1962. Fichte (philosopher). Birth Bicent.
E 628. 10 pf. green and black.. 30 30
E 629. 20 pf. red and black .. 5 5
DESIGNS: 10 pf. Fichte's birthplace, Rammenau. 20 pf. Type E 203.

E 204. Cross of Lidice.

E 205. Dimitrov at Leipzig.

1962. Destruction of Lidice. 20th Anniv.
E 630. E 204. 20 pf. red & black 5 5
E 631. 25 pf. blue & black 40 40

1962. G. Dimitrov (Bulgarian statesman). 80th Birth Anniv.
E 632. E 205. 5 pf. black & green 25 20
E 633. – 20 pf. black & red 5 5
DESIGN: 20 pf. Dimitrov as Premier of Bulgaria.

E 206. Maize-planting machine.

E 207. M S. "Frieden".

1962. 10th D.D.R. Agricultural Exn., Markkleeberg. Multicoloured.
E 634. 10 pf. Type 206 .. 5 5
E 635. 20 pf. Milking shed .. 5 5
E 636. 40 pf. Combine-harvester 50 50

1962. 5th Baltic Sea Week, Rostock.
E 637. – 10 pf. turq. & blue 5 5
E 638. – 20 pf. red & yellow 5 5
E 639. E 207. 25 pf. bistre & blue 40 40
DESIGNS—HORIZ. 10 pf. Map of Baltic Sea inscr. "Meer des Friedens" ("Sea of Peace"). VERT. 20 pf. Railway-station hotel, Rostock.

E 212. Dove. E 213. National Theatre, Helsinki.

E 208. Brandenburg Gate, Berlin. E 209. Youth of Three Races.

E 210. Folk-dancers. E 211. Youth of Three Nations.

1962. World Youth Festival Games, Helsinki. Multicoloured.
E 640. E 208. 5 pf. 15 12
E 641. E 209. 5 pf. 15 12
E 642. E 210. 10 pf. + 5 pf. .. 5 5
E 643. E 211. 15 pf. + 5 pf. .. 5 5
E 644. E 212. 20 pf. 15 12
E 645. E 213. 20 pf. 15 12
The blocks of four and pairs forming complete designs are printed together in sheets of 60 (10 × 6) and 80 (8 × 10) respectively.

E 214. Free-style Swimming.

E 215. Municipal Store, Leipzig.

1962. 10th European Swimming Championships, Leipzig. Design in blue: value colours given.
E 646. E 214. 5 pf. orange .. 5 5
E 647. – 10 pf. blue .. 5 5
E 648. – 20 pf. + 10 pf. mag. 5 5
E 649. – 25 pf. ultram. .. 5 5
E 650. – 40 pf. violet .. 1·10 1·10
E 651. – 70 pf. brown .. 5 5
DESIGNS: 10 pf. Back stroke. 20 pf. High diving. 25 pf. Butterfly stroke. 40 pf. Breast stroke. 70 pf. Water-polo. On Nos. E 649/51 the value, etc., appears at the foot of the design.

1962. Leipzig Autumn Fair.
E 652. E 215. 10 pf. blk. & green 5 5
E 653. – 20 pf. black & red 5 5
E 654. – 25 pf. black & blue 15 8
DESIGNS: 20 pf. Madler Arcade, Leipzig. 25 pf. Leipzig Airport and aircraft.

E 216. "Transport and Communications".

E 217. Rene Blieck.

1962. "Friedrich List" Transport High School, Dresden. 10th Anniv.
E 655. E 216. 5 pf. black & blue 5 5

1962. Concentration Camp Victims. Memorials Fund.
E 656. E 217. 5 pf. + 5 pf. blue.. 5 5
E 657. – 10 pf. + 5 pf. green 5 5
E 658. – 15 pf. + 5 pf. violet 5 5
E 659. – 20 pf. + 10 pf. claret 5 5
E 660. – 70 pf. + 30 pf. choc. 1·00 1·00
PORTRAITS—As Type E 217: 10 pf. Dr. A. Klahr. 15 pf. J. Diaz. 20 pf. J. Alpari. HORIZ. (39 × 21 mm.): 70 pf. Seven Cervi brothers.

E 218. Television Screen and Call-sign.

E 219. G. Hauptmann.

1962. Stamp Day and 10th Anniv. of German Television.
E 661. E 218. 20 pf. slate-purple and green .. 5 5
E 662. – 40 pf. slate-purple and magenta .. 45 45
DESIGN: 40 pf. Children with stamp album (inscr. "TAG DER BRIEFMARKE 1962").

1962. Gerhart Hauptmann (author). Birth Cent.
E 663. E 219. 20 pf. black & red 5 5

In 1962 eight stamps (5, 10, 15, 20, 25, 30, 40, and 50 pf.) forming a complete design showing the Earth, Moon and astronauts, etc., were issued to commemorate the Soviet development of space flights in the last five years. Unlike Nos. E 640/5 these were only issued as a miniature sheet (price £2 un., £2·25 us.).

E 220. Pierre de Coubertin.

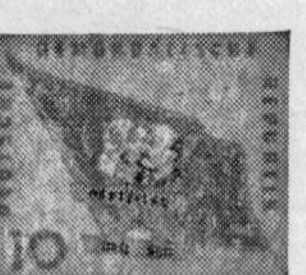

E 221. Party Flag.

1963. Pierre de Coubertin (reviver of Olympic Games). Birth Cent.
E 664. E 220. 20 pf. red & grey 5 5
E 665. – 25 pf. bl. & ochre 35 35
DESIGN: 25 pf. Stadium.

1963. 6th Socialists Unity Party Day.
E 666. E 221. 10 pf. red, black and yellow .. 5 5

E 222. Insecticide Sprayer.

DESIGNS: 20 pf. Type E 222. 25 pf. Rod of Aesculapius. 50 pf. Mosquito. Map is common to all values.

1963. Malaria Eradication.
E 667. 20 pf. black, red & orge. 5 5
E 668. 25 pf. black, red, vio. & bl. 5 5
E 669. 50 pf. black, yellow, olive and green .. 65 60

E 223. Silver Fox.

E 224. Barthels Hof, Leipzig. (1748-1872)

1963. Int. Fur Auctions, Leipzig.
E 670. E 223. 20 pf. indigo & red 5 5
E 671. – 25 pf. indigo & blue 30 25
DESIGN: 25 pf. Karakul lamb.

1963. Leipzig Spring Fair.
E 672. E 224. 10 pf. black and olive-yellow .. 5 5
E 673. – 20 pf. blk. & chest. 8 8
E 674. – 25 pf. black & blue 20 15
LEIPZIG BUILDINGS: 20 pf. New Town Hall. 25 pf. Clock-tower. Karl-Marx Square.

E 225. J. G. Seume (poet) and Scene from "Syracuse Walk" (Birth Bicent.).

1963. Cultural Anniversaries. Design and portrait in black.

E 675. E **225.** 5 pf. olive-yellow 5 5
E 676. – 10 pf. blue-green 5 5
E 677. – 20 pf. red-orange 5 5
E 678. – 25 pf. blue .. 55 35

DESIGNS: 10 pf. F. Hebbel (poet) and scene from "Mary Magdalene" (150th Birth Anniv.). 20 pf. G. Buchner (poet) and scene from "Woyzeck" (150th Birth Anniv.). 25 pf. R. Wagner (composer) and scene from "The Flying Dutchman" (150th Birth Anniv.).

E 226. Nurse bandaging Patient.

E 227. W. Bohne (runner).

1963. Red Cross Cent.

E 679. 10 pf. black, grn. & grey 40 40
E 680. 20 pf. black, grey & red 5 5

DESIGNS: 10 pf. Type E **226.** 20 pf. Barkas type" B 1000" ambulance.

1963. Concentration Camps Memorial Fund. Sportsmen Victims (1st series). Designs in black.

E 681. 5 pf.+5 pf. yellow .. 5 5
E 682. 10 pf.+5 pf. green .. 5 5
E 683. 15 pf.+5 pf. mauve .. 5 5
E 684. 20 pf.+10 pf. pink .. 5 5
E 685. 25 pf.+10 pf. blue .. 75 85

SPORTSMEN: 5 pf. Type E **227.** 10 pf. W. Seelenbinder (wrestler). 15 pf. A. Richter (cyclist). 20 pf. H. Steyer (footballer). 25 pf. K. Schlosser (mountaineer). Nos. E 681/5 were issued in sheets with se-tenant stamp-size labels depicting the various sports associated with the sportsmen.

See also Nos. E 704/8.

E 228. Gymnastics.

E 229. E. Pottier (lyricist) and Opening Bars of the "Internationale".

1963. 4th East German Gymnastics and Sports Festival, Leipzig. Inscr. in black.

E 686. 10 pf.+5 pf. olive-yellow and green .. 5 5
E 687. 20 pf.+10 pf. violet and red .. 5 5
E 688. 25 pf.+10 pf. green and blue 70 70

DESIGNS: 10 pf. Type E **228.** 20 pf. Dederon kerchief exercises. 25 pf. Relay-racing.

1963. "Internationale" (song). 75th Anniv.

E 689. E **229.** 20 pf. black & red 5 5
E 690. – 25 pf. blk. & blue 35 35

DESIGN: 25 pf. As 20 pf. but portrait of P.-C. Degeyter.

E 230. V. Tereshkova and "Vostok 6".

E 231. V. Bykovsky and "Vostok 5".

1963. 2nd "Team" Manned Space Flights.

E 691. E **230.** 20 pf. black, grey-blue and blue.. 10 5
E 692. E **231.** 20 pf. black, grey-blue and blue.. 10 5

Nos. E 691/2 are arranged together "se-tenant" in sheets each pair of stamps forming a whole design.

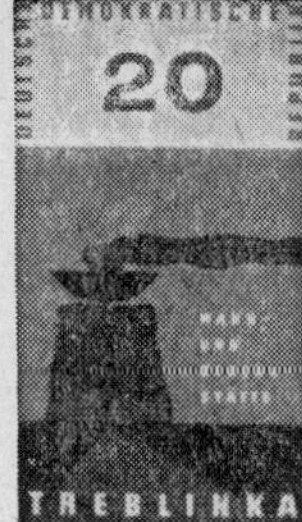

E 232. Motor-cyclist competing in "Motocross", Apolda.

E 233. Treblinka Memorial.

1963. World Motor-cycle Racing Championships.

E 693. E **232.** 10 pf. emer. & grn. 85 85
E 694. – 20 pf. red and pink 5 5
E 695. – 25 pf. bl. & lt.-blue 5 5

DESIGNS—HORIZ. (39×22 mm.); 20 pf. Motorcyclist. 25 pf. Two motor-cyclists cornering.

1963. Erection of Treblinka Memorial, Poland.

E 696. E **233.** 20 pf. blue & red.. 10 5

E 234. Transport. E 235.

1963. Leipzig Autumn Fair.

E 697. E **234.** 10 pf. myrtle, mag., yell. & ol. 5 5
E 698. E **235.** 10 pf. myrtle, mag., yell. & ol. 5 5

Nos. E 697/8 are arranged together "se-tenant" in sheets, each pair of stamps forming a whole design.

1963. Fauna Protection Campaign (2nd series). As Type E **199.** Fauna in natural colours, background colours given.

E 699. 10 pf. green 5 5
E 700. 20 pf. red 5 5
E 701. 30 pf. lake 5 5
E 702. 50 pf. blue .. .. 1·00 95
E 703. 70 pf. brown 8 5

DESIGNS: 10 pf. Stag-beetle. 20 pf. Salamander. 30 pf. Marsh turtle. 50 pf. Toad. 70 pf. Hedgehogs.

1963. Concentration Camps Memorial Fund. Sportsmen Victims (2nd series). As Type E **227.** Designs in black.

E 704. 5 pf.+5 pf. yellow .. 5 5
E 705. 10 pf.+5 pf. green .. 5 5
E 706. 15 pf.+5 pf. violet .. 5 5
E 707. 20 pf. 10 pf. red .. 5 5
E 708. 40 pf.+20 pf. blue .. 1·00 1·00

SPORTSMEN: 5 pf. H. Tops (Gymnast). 10 pf. Kate Tucholla (hockey-player). 15 pf. R. Seiffert (swimmer). 20 pf. E. Grube (athlete). 40 pf. K. Biedermann (canoeist). Nos. E 704/8 were issued in sheets with "se-tenant" stamp-size labels depicting the various sports.

E 236. N. von Gneisenau and G. L. von Blucher.

1963. German war of Liberation. 150th Anniv.

E 709. 5 pf. blk., buff & yell... 5 5
E 710. 10 pf. blk., buff & green 5 5
E 711. 20 pf. blk., buff & orge... 5 5
E 712. 25 pf. blk., buff & blue.. 5 5
E 713. 40 pf. blk., buff & red .. 55 55

DESIGNS: 5 pf. Type E **236.** 10 pf. "Cossacks and (German) Soldiers in Berlin." (after painting by Ludwig Wolf). 20 pf. E. M. Arndt and Baron vom Stein. 25 pf. Lutzow corps in battle order (detail from painting by Hans Kohlschein). 40 pf. G. von Scharnhorst and Prince Kutusov.

E 237. V. Tereshkova.

E 238. Synagogue aflame.

1963. Visit of Soviet Cosmonauts to East Berlin.

E 714. 10 pf. green and blue .. 5 5
E 715. 20 pf. black, red & buff 5 5
E 716. 20 pf. green, red & buff 5 5
E 717. 25 pf. orange and blue 55 55

DESIGNS—SQUARE: 10 pf. Type E **237.** 25 pf Tereshkova in capsule. VERT. (24×32 mm): No. E 715, Tereshkova with bouquet. No. E 716, Gagarin (visit to Berlin).

1963. "Kristallnacht" (Nazi pogrom). 25th anniv.

E 718. E **238.** 20 pf. mult. .. 5 5

E 239. Letter-sorting Machine.

1963. Stamp Day. Multicoloured.

E 719. 10 pf. Type E **239** .. 25 20
E 720. 20 pf. Railway fork-truck and trolley .. 5 5

E 240. Ski-jumper commencing Run.

E 241. "Vanessa atalanta L.".

1963. Winter Olympic Games, Innsbruck, 1964. Rings in different colours: skier in black.

E 721. E **240.** 5 pf. yellow .. 5 5
E 722. – 10 pf. green .. 5 5
E 723. – 20 pf.+10 pf. red 5 5
E 724. – 25 pf. blue .. 55 55

DESIGNS: Ski-jumper—10 pf. Taking-off. 20 pf. In mid-air. 25 pf. Landing.

1964. Butterflies. Butterflies in natural colours; inscr. in black.

E 725. E **241.** 10 pf. olive .. 5 5
E 726. – 15 pf. lilac .. 5 5
E 727. – 20 pf. salmon .. 5 5
E 728. – 25 pf. blue .. 5 5
E 729. – 40 pf. cobalt .. 70 60

BUTTERFLIES: 15 pf. "Parnassius phoebus L.". 20 pf. "Papilio machaon L.". 25 pf. "Colias croceus". 40 pf. "Nymphalis polychloros L.".

E 242. Shakespeare. (b. 1564).

E 243. "Elektrotecknik" Hall.

1964. Cultural Anniversaries.

E 730. 20 pf. indigo and pink 5 5
E 731. 25 pf. purple and blue.. 5 5
E 732. 40 pf. blue and lilac .. 50 35

DESIGNS: 20 pf. Quadriga, Brandenburg Gate (J. G. Schadow, sculptor, b. 1764). 25 pf. Portal keystone, German Historical Museum (A. Schluter, sculptor, b. 1664).

1964. Leipzig Spring Fair.

E 733. 10 pf. black and green.. 30 5
E 734. 20 pf. black & vermilion 55 5

DESIGNS: 10 pf. Type E **243.** 20 pf. Braunigkes Hof, c. 1700. These were issued together in sheets with "se-tenant" stamp-size labels depicting emblems of the Leipzig Fair and Municipality.

E 244. A. Saefkow.

1964. Concentration Camp Victims. Memorials Fund.

E 735. 5 pf.+5 pf. brown & blue 5 5
E 736. 10 pf.+5 pf. brown & ol. 5 5
E 737. 15 pf.+5 pf. brown & vio. 5 5
E 738. 20 pf.+5 pf. olive & red 8 5
E 739. 25 pf.+10 pf. blue & ol. 10 8
E 740. 40 pf.+10 pf. olive & brn. 95 70

PORTRAITS—As Type E **244:** 5 pf. Type E **244.** 10 pf. F. Jacob. 15 pf. B. Bastlein. 20 pf. H. Schulze-Boysen. 25 pf. Dr. A. Kuckhoff. (49×27½ mm.): 40 pf. Dr. A. and Mildred Harnack.

E 245. Mr. Kruschev with East German Officials.

E 246. Boys and Girls.

1964. Mr. Kruschev's 70th Birthday.

E 741. E **245.** 25 pf. blue .. 5 5
E 742. – 40 pf. black & pur. 1·10 60

DESIGN: 40 pf. Mr. Kruschev with cosmonauts Tereshkova and Gagarin.

1964. German Youth Meeting, Berlin. Black, magenta, green and blue.

E 743. 10 pf. Type E **246** .. 5 5
E 744. 20 pf. Young gymnasts.. 5 5
E 745. 25 pf. Youth with accordion and girl with flowers 50 30

The designs show characters from children's T.V. programmes.

E 247. Flax, Krumel and Struppi, the dog.

1964. Children's Day. Inscr. "TAG DES KINDES 1964". Multicoloured

E 746. 5 pf. Type E **247** .. 5 5
E 747. 10 pf. Master Nadelohr 5 5
E 748. 15 pf. Pittiplatsch .. 5 5
E 749. 20 pf. Sandmannschen (sandman) 5 5
E 750. 40 pf. Bummi (teddy bear) and Schnatterinchen (duckling) .. 1·00 65

E 248. Governess and Child (with portrait of Jenny Marx).

1964. East German Women's Congress Multicoloured.

E 751. 20 pf. Type E **248** .. 5 5
E 752. 25 pf. Switchboard technicians 90 60
E 753 70 pf. Farm girls .. 5 5

E 249. Cycling

E 250. Diving.

1964. Olympic Games, Tokyo. Inscr. "XVIII. OLYMPISCHE SPIELE TOKIO 1964". Multicoloured.

(a) 1st Series. As Type E **249.**

E 754. 5 pf. Type E **249** .. 5 5
E 755. 10 pf. Volleyball .. 5 5
E 756. 20 pf. Judo 5 5
E 757. 25 pf. Diving 5 5
E 758. 40 pf.+20 pf. Running 15 5
E 759. 70 pf. Horse-jumping .. 1·10 90

(b) 2nd Series. As Type E **250.**

E 760. 10 pf. Type E **250** .. 15 15
E 761. 10 pf.+5 pf. Horse-jumping 15 15
E 762. 10 pf. Volleyball .. 15 15
E 763. 10 pf. Cycling .. 15 15
E 764 10 pf.+5 pf. Running.. 15 15
E 765. 10 pf. Judo 15 15
Per block of 6 .. 1·50 1·50

Nos. E. 760/5 were printed together in se-tenant blocks of six (3×2) within sheets of 60 (6×10), and with an overall pattern of the five Olympic "rings" in each block.

E 251. Young Artists.

1964. 5th Young Pioneer's Meeting, East Berlin. Multicoloured.
E 766. 10 pf.+5 pf. Type E **251** 5 5
E 767. 20 pf.+10 pf. Planting tree 5 5
E 768. 25 pf.+10 pf. Playing with ball 65 45

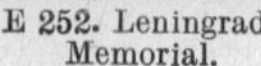

E 252. Leningrad Memorial. E 253. F. Joliot-Curie.

1964. Victims of Leningrad Siege Commem.
E 769. E **252.** 25 pf. black, yell. and blue 15 5

1964. "World Peace".
E 770. E **253.** 20 pf. sepia & red 5 5
E 771. – 25 pf. black & blue 5 5
E 772. – 50 pf. blk. & lilac 65 50
PORTRAITS: (Campaigners for "World Peace"): 25 pf. B. von Suttner. 50 pf. C. von Ossietzky.

E 254. Ancient Glazier's Shop. E 255. I.W.M.A. Cachet.

1964. Leipzig Autumn Fair. Multicoloured.
E 773. 10 pf. Type **254** 12 5
E 774. 15 pf. Jena glass factory 12 5

1964. "First International". Cent.
E 775. E **255.** 20 pf. black & red 5 5
E 776. 25 pf. black & blue 40 30

E 256. "Rostock Port" Stamp of 1958. E 257. Modern Buildings and Flag ("Reconstruction").

1964. National Stamp Exn., East Berlin.
E 777. 10 pf.+5 pf. grn. & orge. 5 5
E 778. 20 pf.+10 pf. blue & pur. 5 5
E 779. 50 pf. brown and grey 70 45
DESIGNS: 10 pf. Type E **256.** 20 pf., 12 pf. "Peace" stamp of 1950. 50 pf., 5 pf. "Dresden Paintings" stamp of 1955.

1964. German Democratic Republic. 15th Anniv. Multicoloured.
E 780. 10 pf. Type E **257** 8 5
E 781. 10 pf. Surveyor and conveyor ("Coal") 8 5
E 782. 10 pf. Scientist and chemical works ("Chemical Industry") 8 5
E 783. 10 pf. Guard and chemical works ("Chemical Industry") 8 5
E 784. 10 pf. Milkmaid and dairy pen ("Agriculture") 8 5
E 785. 10 pf. Furnaceman and mills ("Steel") 8 5
E 786. 10 pf. Student with microscope, and lecture hall ("Education") 8 5
E 787. 10 pf. Operator and lathe ("Engineering") 8 5
E 788. 10 pf. Scientist and planetarium" (Optics") 8 5
E 789. 10 pf. Girl with cloth, and loom ("Textiles") 8 5
E 790. 10 pf. Docker and ship at quayside ("Shipping") 8 5
E 791. 10 pf. Leipzig buildings and "businessmen" formed of Fair emblem ("Exports") 8 5
E 792. 10 pf. Building worker and flats ("New Construction") 8 5
E 793. 10 pf. Sculptor modelling and Dresden gateway ("Culture") 8 5
E 794. 10 pf. Girl skier and holiday resort ("Recreation") 8 5

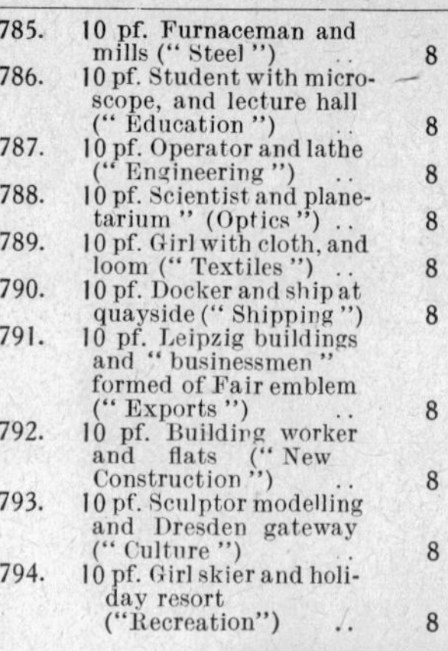

E 258. Monchgut (Rugen) Costume. E 259. Dr. Schweitzer and Lambarene River.

1964. Provincial costumes (1st series). Multicoloured.
E 795. 5 pf. Type E **258** 1·40 1·25
E 796. 5 pf. Type E **258** (male) 1·40 1·25
E 797. 10 pf. Spreewald (female) 5 5
E 798. 10 pf. Spreewald (male) 5 5
E 799. 20 pf. Thuringen (female) 8 5
E 800. 20 pf. Thuringen (male) 8 5
See Nos. E 932/7 and E 1073/6.

1965. Dr. Albert Schweitzer. 90th Birthday.
E 802. E **259.** 10 pf. yellow, black and green 5 5
E 803. – 20 pf. yellow, black and red 5 5
E 804. – 25 pf. yellow, black and blue 1·00 75
DESIGNS: 20 pf. Schweitzer and "nuclear disarmament" marchers. 25 pf. Schweitzer and part of a Bach organ prelude.

1965. As Nos. E 589/90 but values expressed in "MDN" (Deutschen Notenbank Marks) instead of "DM".
E 805. 1 MDN. bronze-green 65 5
E 806. 2 MDN. brown 65 5

E 260. A. Bebel. E 261. Fair Medal (obverse).

1965. August Bebel (founder of Social Democratic Party). 125th Birth Anniv.
E 807. E **260.** 20 pf. yellow, brn. and red 12 5
See also Nos. E 814/5, E 839, E 842 and E 871.

1965. Leipzig Spring Fair and 800th Anniv. of Leipzig Fair.
E 808. E **261.** 10 pf. gold & mag. 5 5
E 809. – 15 pf. gold & mag. 8 5
E 810. – 25 pf. mult. 15 10
DESIGNS: 15 pf. Fair medal (reverse). 25 pf. Chemical works.

E 262. Giraffe. E 263. Beliaiev and Leonov.

1965. East Berlin Zoo. 10th Anniv.
E 811. E **262.** 10 pf. grey & grn. 5 5
E 812. – 25 pf. grey & blue 5 5
E 813. – 30 pf. grey & sepia 50 45
ANIMALS—HORIZ. 25 pf. Iguana. 30 pf. White-tailed gnu.

1965. W. C. Rontgen (physicist). 120th Birth Anniv. As Type E **260** but portrait of Rontgen.
E 814. 10 pf. yellow, brn. & grn. 5 5

1965. Dante. 700th Birth Anniv. As Type E **260** but portrait of Dante.
E 815. 50 pf. yellow, brown and lemon 25 5

1965. Space Flight of "Voskhod 2". Inscr. "18. MARZ 1965".
E 816. E **263.** 10 pf. red 5 5
E 817. – 25 pf. blue 35 35
DESIGN: 25 pf. Leonov in space

E 264. Boxing Gloves. E 266. Transmitter Aerial and Globe.

E 265. Dimitrov denouncing Fascism.

1965. European Boxing Championships, Berlin.
E 818. E **264.** 10 pf.+5 pf. red, blue, blk. & gold 5 5
E 819. – 20 pf. gold, black and red 35 30
DESIGN: 20 pf. Boxing glove.

1965. Liberation. 20th Anniv. Multicoloured.
E 820. 5 pf.+5 pf. Type E **265** 5 5
E 821. 10 pf.+5 pf. Distributing "Communist Manifesto" 5 5
E 822. 15 pf.+5 pf. Soldiers of International Brigade fighting in Spain 5 5
E 823. 20 pf.+10 pf. "Freedom for Ernst Thalmann" demonstration 5 5
E 824. 25 pf.+10 pf. Founding of "Free Germany" National Committee (Moscow) 5 5
E 825. 40 pf. Ulbricht and Weinert distributing "Manifesto" on Eastern Front 5 5
E 826. 50 pf. Liberation of concentration camps 5 5
E 827. 60 pf. Hoisting Red Flag on Reichstag 2·10 1·90
E 828. 70 pf. Bilateral demonstration of Communist and Socialist parties 5 5

1965. East German Broadcasting Service. 20th Anniv.
E 829. E **266.** 20 pf. black, red and cerise 5 5
E 830. – 40 pf. black & blue 45 35
DESIGN: 40 pf. Radio workers.

E 267. I.T.U. Emblem and Radio Circuit Diagram. E 268. F.D.G.B. Emblem.

1965. I.T.U. Cent.
E 831. E **267.** 20 pf. blk., yellow and olive 5 5
E 832. – 25 pf. black, mauve and violet 35 25
DESIGN: 25 pf. I.T.U. emblem and switch diagram.

1965. Free German (F.D.G.B.) and World Trade Unions. 20th Anniv.
E 833. E **268.** 20 pf. gold and red 5 5
E 834. – 25 pf. black, blue and gold 35 25
DESIGN—HORIZ. (39×21½ mm.): 25 pf. Workers of "two hemispheres" (inscr. "20 JAHRE WELTGEWERKSCHAFTSBUND").

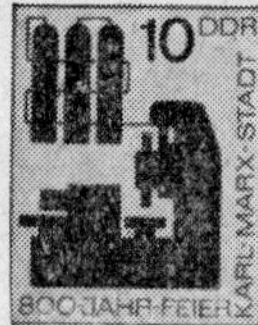

E 269. Industrial Machine. E 270. Marx and Lenin.

1965. Karl Marx City (Chemnitz). 800th Anniv.
E 835. E **269.** 10 pf. green & gold 5 5
E 836. – 20 pf. red and gold 5 5
E 837. – 25 pf. blue & gold 40 30
DESIGNS: 20 pf. Red Tower, Chemnitz. 25 pf. Town Hall, Chemnitz.

1965. Postal Ministers' Conf., Peking.
E 838. E **270.** 20 pf. black, yellow and red 10 5

1965. Dr. Wilhelm Kulz (politician). 90th Birth Anniv. As Type E **260** but portrait of Kulz.
E 839. 25 pf. yellow, brown & bl. 12 5

E 271. Congress Emblem.

1965. World Peace Congress, Helsinki.
E 840. E **271.** 10 pf.+5 pf. green and blue 5 5
E 841. 20 pf.+5 pf. blue and red 35 25

1965. Erich Weinert (poet). 75th Birth Anniv. As Type E **260**, but portrait of Weinert.
E 842. 40 pf. yell., brn. & cerise 25 5

1965. "Help for Vietnam". Surch. **Hilfe fur VIETNAM+10.**
E 843. E **257.** 10 pf.+10 pf. mult. 10 5

E 272. Rebuilt Weigh-house and Modern Buildings, Katharinenstrasse.

1965. Leipzig. 800th Anniv.
E 844. E **272.** 10 pf. maroon, blue and gold 5 5
E 845. – 25 pf. orange, sepia and gold 5 5
E 846. – 40 pf. orange, sepia, green and gold 5 5
E 847. – 70 pf. blue & gold 1·00 00
DESIGNS: 25 pf. Old Town Hall. 40 pf. Opera House and new G.P.O. 70 pf. "Stadt Leipzig" Hotel.

E 273. "Praktica" and "Praktisix" Cameras. E 274. Horse-jumping.

1965. Leipzig Autumn Fair. Inscr. "LEIPZIGER HERBSTMESSE 1965".
E 848. E **273.** 10 pf. black, gold and green 5 5
E 849. – 15 pf. black, yellow, gold and magenta 5 5
E 850. – 25 pf. black, gold and blue 20 10
DESIGNS: 15 pf. Clavichord and electric guitar. 25 pf. "Zeiss" microscope.

1965. World Modern Pentathlon Championships, Leipzig. Multicoloured.
E 852. 10 pf. Type E **274** 5 5
E 853. 10 pf. Swimming 5 5
E 854. 10 pf. Running 35 30
E 855. 10 pf.+5 pf. Fencing 5 5
E 856. 10 pf.+5 pf. Pistol-shooting 5 5

E 275. E. Leonov. E 276. Memorial at Putten, Netherlands.

1965. Soviet Cosmonauts Visit to East Germany.
E 857. E **275**. 20 pf. blue, silver and red .. 15 15
E 858. – 20 pf. blue, silver and red .. 15 15
E 859. – 25 pf. red, silver, drab and blue 25 25
DESIGNS—As Type E 275: No. E 858, Belailev. HORIZ. (48×29 mm.): E 859 "Voskhod 2" and Leonov in space.

1965. Putten War Victims Commem.
E 860. E **276**. 25 pf. black, yellow and blue .. 12 5

E 277. Stoking Furnace (from old engraving). E 278. Kite.

1965. Mining School, Freiberg. Bicent. Multicoloured.
E 861. 10 pf. Type E **277** .. 5 5
E 862. 15 pf. Mining ore (old engraving) 45 40
E 863. 20 pf. Ore 5 0
E 864. 25 pf. Sulphur 5 5

1965. Birds of Prey. Multicoloured.
E 865. 5 pf. Type E **278** .. 5 5
E 866. 10 pf. Bearded vulture (or lammergeyer) .. 5 5
E 867. 20 pf. Buzzard 5 5
E 868. 25 pf. Kestrel 5 5
E 869. 40 p.f Goshawk.. .. 5 5
E 870. 70 pf. Golden eagle .. 1·10 90

1965. A. von Menzel (painter). 150th Birth Anniv. As Type E **260** but portrait of Menzel.
E 871. 10 pf. yellow, brown and red 5 5

E 279. Otto Grotewohl. E 280. Ladies' Single-seater.

1965. Grotewohl Commem.
E 872. E **279**. 20 f. black .. 10 5

1966. World Tobogganing Championships, Friedrichroda.
E 874. E **280**. 10 pf. green & ol. 5 5
E 875. – 20 pf. blue & red 5 5
E 876. – 25 pf. indigo & blue 50 50
DESIGNS: 20 pf. Men's double-seater. 25 pf. Men's single seater.

E 281. Electronic Punch-card Computer.

1966. Leipzig Spring Fair.
E 877. E **281**. 10 pf. black, yellow, blue and magenta 5 5
E 878. – 15 pf. black, salmon, green and blue .. 10 5
DESIGN: 15 pf. Drilling and milling plant.

E 282. Soldier and National Gallery, Berlin. E 283. J. A. Smoler (Sorb patriot and savant).

1966. National People's Army. 10th Anniv.
E 879. E **282**. 5 pf. black, olive and yellow .. 5 5
E 880. – 10 pf. black, olive and yellow .. 5 5
E 881. – 20 pf. black, olive and yellow .. 5 5
E 882. – 25 pf. black, olive and yellow .. 40 40
DESIGNS: Soldier and—10 pf. Brandenburg Gate. 20 pf. Industrial plant. 25 pf. Combine-harvester.

1966. Jan Smoler. 150th Birth Anniv.
E 883. E **283**. 20 pf. black, red and blue .. 5 5
E 884. – 25 pf. black, red and blue .. 25 25
DESIGN: 25 pf. House of the Sorbs, Bautzen.

E 284. "Good Knowledge" Badge. E 285. "Luna 9" on Moon.

1966. "Freie Deutsche Jugend" (Socialist Youth Movement). 20th Anniv.
E 885. E **284**. 20 pf. blue, black, yellow and red 10 5

1966. Moon Landing of "Luna 9".
E 886. E **285**. 20 pf. mult. .. 20 5

E 286. Road Signs.

1966. Road Safety.
E 887. E **286**. 10 pf. red, blue and ultramarine .. 5 5
E 888. – 15 pf. black, yell. and green .. 5 5
E 889. – 25 pf. black, blue and bistre .. 5 5
E 890. – 50 pf. black, yellow, and red .. 80 65
DESIGNS: 15 pf. Child on scooter crossing in front of car. 25 pf. Cyclist and hand-signal. 50 pf. Motor-cyclist, glass of beer and ambulance.

E 287. Marx and Lenin Banner.

1966. Socialist Unity Party (S.E.D.). 20th Anniv.
E 891. – 5 pf. yellow, black, blue and red .. 5 5
E 892. E **287**. 10 pf. yellow, black and red .. 5 5
E 893. – 15 pf. blk. & green 5 5
E 894. – 20 pf. black & red 5 5
E 895. – 25 pf. black, yellow and red .. 35 35
DESIGNS—VERT. 5 pf. Party badge and demonstrators. 15 pf. Marx, Engels and manifesto. 20 pf. Pieck and Grotewohl. HORIZ. 25 pf. Workers greeting Ulbricht.

E 288. W.H.O. Building.

1966. W.H.O. Headquarters, Geneva. Inaug.
E 896. E **288**. 20 pf. mult. .. 10 5

E 289. Spreewald.

E 290. Lace "Flower". E 291. Lily of the Valley.

1966. National Parks. Multicoloured.
E 897. 10 pf. Type E **289** .. 5 5
E 898. 15 pf. Konigsstuhl (Isle of Rugen) .. 5 5
E 899. 20 pf. Sachsische Schweiz 5 5
E 900. 25 pf. Westdarss .. 5 5
E 901. 30 pf. Teufelsmauer .. 5 5
E 902. 50 pf. Feldberg Lakes.. 90 80

1966. Plauen Lace. Floral Patterns as Type E **290**.
E 903. E **290**. 10 pf. myrtle & grn. 5 5
E 904. – 20 pf. indigo & bl. 5 5
E 905. – 25 pf. red & rose 5 5
E 906. – 50 pf. violet & lilac 65 60

1966. Int. Horticultural Show, Erfurt. Multicoloured.
E 907. 20 pf. Type E **291** .. 5 5
E 908. 25 pf. Rhododendrons.. 5 5
E 909. 40 pf. Dahlias .. 5 5
E 910. 50 pf. Cyclamen .. 1·00 80

E 292. Parachutist on Target.

DESIGNS: 15 pf. Group descent. 20 pf. Free fall.

1966. 8th World Parachute Jumping Championships, Leipzig.
E 911. E **292**. 10 pf. bl., blk. & bis. 5 5
E 912. – 15 pf. magenta, black & blue .. 35 35
E 913. – 20 pf. blk., bis. & bl. 5 5

E 293. Hans Kahle and Music of German Battle Hymn.

1966. Int. Brigade in Spain. 30th Anniv. Multicoloured.
E 914. 5 pf. Type E **293** .. 5 5
E 915. 10 pf. + 5 pf. W. Bredel and open-air class .. 5 5
E 916. 15 pf. H. Beimler and Madrid street-fighting 5 5
E 917. 20 pf. + 10 pf. H. Rau and march-past after Battle of Brunete 5 5
E 918. 25 pf. + 10 pf. H. Marchwitza and soldiers .. 5 5
E 919. 40 pf. + 10 pf. A. Becker and Ebro battle .. 90 75

E 294. Canoeing.

1966. World Canoeing Championships, Berlin. Multicoloured.
E 920. 10 pf. + 5 pf. Type E **294** 5 5
E 921. 15 pf. Kayak doubles .. 20 20

E 295. Television Set. E 297. "Blood Donors". E 296. Oradour Memorial.

1966. Leipzig Autumn Fair. Multicoloured.
E 922. 10 pf. Type E **295** .. 5 5
E 923. 15 pf. Electric typewriter 5 5

1966. Oradour-sur-Glane War Victims. Commem.
E 924. E **296**. 25 pf. blk., bl. & red 15 5

1966. Int. Health Co-operation.
E 925. E **297**. 5 pf. red and green 5 5
E 926. – 20 pf. + 10 pf. red and violet .. 5 5
E 927. – 40 pf. red and blue 55 50
DESIGNS—HORIZ. 20 pf. I.C.Y. emblem. VERT. 40 pf. Health symbol.

E 298. Weightlifting ("snatch"). E 299. Congress Hall

1966. World and European Weightlifting Championships, Berlin.
E 928. E **298**. 15 pf. black & brn. 30 30
E 929. – 20 pf. + 5 pf. black and blue .. 5 5
DESIGN: 20 pf. Weightlifting ("jerk").

1966. 6th Int. Journalists' Congress, Berlin.
E 930. E **299**. 10 pf. blue, black, yellow and lake 20 15
E 931. – 20 pf. yellow & blue 5 5
DESIGN—VERT. 20 pf. Emblem of Int Organisation of journalists.

1966. Provincial Costumes (2nd series). As Type E **258**. Multicoloured.
E 932. 5 pf. Altenburg (female) 5 5
E 933. 10 pf. Altenburg (male) 5 5
E 934. 10 pf. Mecklenburg (female) 5 5
E 935. 15 pf. Mecklenburg (male) 5 5
E 936. 20 pf. Magdeburger Borde (female) .. 30 30
E 937. 30 pf. Magdeburger Borde (male).. .. 30 30

E 300. "Vietnam is Invincible".

1966. Aid for Vietnam.
E 938. E **300**. 20 pf. + 5 pf. black and pink .. 15

E 301. Oil Rigs and Pipeline Map.

1966. Int. "Friendship" Oil Pipeline. Inaug.
E 939. E **301**. 20 pf. black & red 5 5
E 940. – 25 pf. black & blue 35 35
DESIGN: 25 pf. "Walter Ulbricht" Oil Works, Leuna and pipeline map.

E 302. Black Phantom Tetra.

1966. Aquarium Fishes. Multicoloured.
E 941. 5 pf. Type E **302** .. 5 5
E 942. 10 pf. Cardinal tetra .. 5 5
E 943. 15 pf. Rio Grande perch 75 65
E 944. 20 pf. Blue gularis .. 5 5
E 945. 25 pf. Butterfly dwarf cichlid 5 5
E 946. 40 pf. Sunset gourami .. 8 5

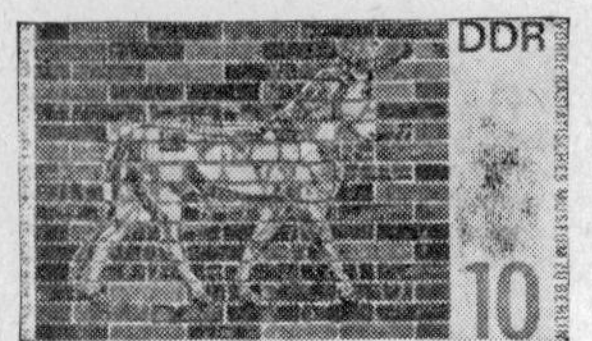

E **303.** "Horse" (detail from Ishtar Gate).

1966. Babylonian Art Treasures, Vorderasiatisches Museum, Berlin. Multicoloured.
E 947. 10 pf. Type E **303** .. 5 5
E 948. 20 pf. Mythological animal, Ishtar Gate 5 5
E 949. 25 pf. Lion facing right (vert.) .. 5 5
E 950. 50 pf. Lion facing left (vert.) 80 70

E **304.** The Wartburg from the East.

E **305.** "Gentiana pneumonanthe".

1966. Wartburg Castle. 900th Anniv.
E 951. E **304.** 10 pf. + 5 pf. slate 5 5
E 952. – 20 pf. green .. 5 5
E 953 – 25 pf. maroon .. 35 30
DESIGNS: 20 pf. Castle bailiwick. 25 pf. Residence.

1966. Protected Plants (1st Series). Multicoloured.
E 954. 10 pf. Type E **305** 5 5
E 955. 20 pf. "Cephalanthera rubra" 5 5
E 956. 25 pf. "Arnica montana" 35 30
See also Nos. E 1177/82 and E 1284/9.

E **306.** Son leaves Home.

E **307.** Worlitz Castle.

1966. Fairy Tales (1st Series). "The Wishing Table". Multicoloured.
E 957. 5 pf. Type E **306** .. 20 20
E 958. 10 pf. Setting the table 20 20
E 959. 20 pf. The thieving innkeeper 20 20
E 960. 25 pf. The magic donkey 20 20
E 961. 30 pf. The cudgel in the sack 20 20
E 962. 50 pf. Return of the son 20 20
See also Nos. E 1045/50, E 1147/52, E 1171/6, E 1266/71, E 1437/42, E 1525/30, E 1623/8 and E 1711/16.

1967. Principal East German Buildings. (1st Series). Multicoloured.
E 964. 5 pf. Type E **307** .. 5 5
E 965. 10 pf. Stralsund Town Hall 5 5
E 966. 15 pf. Chorin Monastery 5 5
E 967. 20 pf. Ribbeck House, Berlin 5 5
E 968. 25 pf. Moritzburg, Zeitz 5 5
E 969. 40 pf. Old Town Hall Potsdam 80 80
The 10 pf., 15 pf., 25 pf. and 40 pf. are vert. See also Nos E 1100/3 and E 1155/60.

E **308.** Rifle-shooting.

1967. World Biathlon Championships, Altenburg.
E 970. E **308.** 10 pf. blue, drab and magenta .. 5 5
E 971. – 20 pf. olive, blue and green .. 5 5
E 972. – 25 pf. green, blue and olive .. 35 30
DESIGNS: 20 pf. Shooting on skis. 25 pf. Riflemen racing on skis.

E **309.** "Multilock" Loom.

1967. Leipzig Spring Fair.
E 973. E **309.** 10 pf. green, grey and purple .. 5 5
E 974. – 15 pf. bistre & blue 10 5
DESIGN: 15 pf. Zeiss tracking telescope.

E **310.** Mother and Child.

E **312.** "Portrait of a Girl" (after F. Hodler).

E **311.** Industrial Control Desk.

1967. German Democratic Women's Federation. 20th Anniv.
E 975. E **310.** 20 pf. grey, red & maroon 5 5
E 976. – 25 pf. brown, turquoise & blue 30 30
DESIGN: 25 pf. Professional woman.

1967. Socialist Party Rally. Multicoloured.
(a) 1st Series.
E 977. 10 pf. Type E **311** .. 5 5
E 978. 20 pf. Ulbricht meeting workers 5 5
E 979. 25 pf. Servicemen guarding industrial plants.. 5 5
E 980. 40 pf. Agricultural workers and harvesters .. 55 55
Each with inset portraits of Marx, Engels and Lenin.

(b) 2nd Series. As Type E **311** but vert.
E 981. 5 pf. Agricultural worker 5 5
E 982. 10 pf. Teacher and pupil 5 5
E 983. 15 pf. Socialist family .. 25 25
E 984. 20 pf. Servicemen .. 5 5
Each with inset portraits as above.

1967. Dresden Gallery Paintings (1st Series). Multicoloured.
E 985. 20 pf. Type E **312** .. 5 5
E 986. 25 pf. "Peter at the Zoo" (H. Hakenbeck) .. 5 5
E 987. 30 pf. "Venetian Episode" (R. Bergander) .. 5 5
E 988. 40 pf. "Tahitian Women" (Gauguin) 8 8
E 989. 50 pf. "The Grandchild" (J. Scholtz) .. 1·60 1·60
E 990. 70 pf. "Cairn in the Snow" (C. D. Friedrich) 8 8
The 40 pf. and 70 pf. are horiz.
See also Nos. E 1114/19 and E 1249/54.

E **314.** Cycle Wheels.

E **313.** Barn Owl.

E **315.** "Tom Cat".

1967. Protected Birds. Multicoloured.
E 991. 5 pf. Type E **313** .. 5 5
E 992. 10 pf. Crane 5 5
E 993. 20 pf. Peregrine falcon 5 5
E 994. 25 pf. Bullfinches .. 5 5
E 995. 30 pf. Kingfisher .. 90 80
E 996. 40 pf. Roller 5 5

1967. 20th Warsaw-Berlin-Prague Cycle Race.
E 997. E **314.** 10 pf. violet, black and yellow .. 5 5
E 998. – 25 pf. red and blue 25 25
DESIGN: 25 pf. Racing cyclists.

1967. Int. Children's Day. Multicoloured.
E 999. 5 pf. Type E **315** .. 5 5
E 1000. 10 pf. "Snow White" 5 5
E 1001. 15 pf. "Fire Brigade" 5 5
E 1002. 20 pf. "Cockerel" .. 5 5
E 1003. 25 pf. "Vase of Flowers" 5 5
E 1004. 30 pf. "Children Playing with Ball" .. 65 65

E **316.** "Girl with Grapes" (Gerard Dou).

E **317.** Exhibition Emblem.

1967. Paintings Missing from German National Galleries (after World War II).
E 1005. 5 pf. blue 5 5
E 1006. 10 pf. chestnut .. 5 5
E 1007. 20 pf. green 5 5
E 1008. 25 pf. purple 5 5
E 1009. 40 pf. olive 5 5
E 1010. 50 pf sepia 90 90
DESIGNS—VERT 10 pf. Type E **316.** 25 pf. "Portrait of W Schroeder-Devrient" (after K. Begas). 40 pf. "Young Girl in Straw Hat" (after S. Bray). 50 pf. "The Four Evangelists" (after Jordaens). HORIZ. 5 pf. "Three Horsemen" (after Rubens) 20 pf. "Spring Idyl" (after H. Thoma).

1967. 15th Agricultural Exn., Markkleeberg.
E 1011. E **317.** 20 pf. red, green and yellow .. 10 5

E **318.** Marie Curie (Birth Cent.).

E **319.** Jack of Diamonds.

1967. Birth Annivs.
E 1012. – 5 pf. brown .. 5 5
E 1013. E **318.** 10 pf. blue .. 5 5
E 1014. – 20 pf. claret .. 5 5
E 1015 – 25 pf. sepia .. 5 5
E 1016. – 40 pf. green .. 50 45
PORTRAITS: 5 pf. G. Herwegh (poet—150th). 20 pf. Kathe Kollwitz (artist—Cent). 25 pf. J J. Winckelmann archaeologist—250th) 40 pf. T. Storm (poet—150th).

1967. German Playing-Cards Multicoloured.
E 1017. 5 pf. Type E **319** .. 5 5
E 1018. 10 pf. Jack of Hearts 5 5
E 1019. 20 pf. Jack of Spades 5 5
E 1020. 25 pf. Jack of Clubs .. 60 45

E **320.** Mare and Filly.

1971. Thoroughbred Horse Meeting, Berlin. Multicoloured.
1021. 5 pf. Type E **320** 5 5
1022. 10 pf. Stallion 5 5
1023. 20 pf. Horse-racing .. 5 5
1024. 50 pf. Two fillies (vert.) .. 70 70

321. Kitchen Equipment.

323. Kragujevac Memorial.

E **322.** Max Reichpietsch and Battleship of "Kaiser" Class.

1967. Leipzig Autumn Fair. Multicoloured.
E 1025. 10 pf. Type E **321** .. 5 5
E 1026. 15 pf. Fur coat and "Interpelz" brand-mark 5 5

1967. Revolutionary Sailors' Movement. 50th Anniv. Multicoloured.
E 1027. 10 pf. Type E **322** .. 5 5
E 1028. 15 pf. Albin Kobis and battleship "Prinzregent Luitpold" .. 25 25
E 1029. 20 pf. Sailors' demonstration with battlecruiser of "Seydlitz" class.. .. .. 5 5

1967. Victims of Kragujevac (Yugoslavia) Massacre.
E 1030. E **323.** 25 pf. black, yellow & lake 15 5

E **324.** Worker and Newspaper Headline: "Hands off Soviet Russia".

E **325.** Martin Luther (from engraving by Lucas Cranach the elder).

1967. October Revolution. 50th Anniv.
E 1031. 5 pf. black, orge. & red 5 5
E 1032. 10 pf. black, red & bistre 5 5
E 1033. 15 pf. black, red & grey 5 5
E 1034. 20 pf. black, red & orge. 5 5
E 1035. 40 pf. black, red & orge. 60 55
DESIGNS: 5 pf. Type E **324.** 10 pf. Worker and dam ("Soviet Electrification"). 15 pf. Treptow Memorial ("Victory over Fascism"). 20 pf. German and Soviet soldiers ("Friendship"). 40 pf. Lenin and cruiser "Aurora". Each with hammer and sickle.

1967. Reformation. 450th Anniv.
E 1037. E **325.** 20 pf. black & mve. 5 5
E 1038. – 25 pf. black & blue 5 5
E 1039. – 40 pf. blk. & bistre 60 55
DESIGNS—HORIZ. 25 pf. Luther's house, Wittenberg. VERT. 40 pf. Castle church, Wittenberg.

E **326.** Young Workers.

E **327.** Goethe's House Weimar.

1967. 10th "Masters of Tomorrow" Fair, Leipzig.
E 1040. 20 pf. black, gold & blue 20 15
E 1041. 20 pf. black gold & blue 20 15
E 1042. 25 pf. multicoloured .. 20 15
DESIGNS—VERT. No. E 1040, Type E **326.** E 1041, Young man and woman. HORIZ.—(51 × 29 mm.): E 1042, Presentation of awards.

1967. Cultural Places.
E 1043. E **327.** 20 pf. black, brn. and grey .. 5 5
E 1044. – 25 pf. olive, brn. & yellow-olive 25 25
DESIGN: 25 pf. Schiller's House, Weimar.

E 328. Queen and Courtiers.

E 330. Nutcracker and Two "Smokers".

E 329. Peasants and Modern Farm Buildings.

1967. Fairy Tales (2nd Series). "King Thrushbeard". Designs showing different scenes.

E 1045. E 328. 5 pf. mult. .. 15 15
E 1046. – 10 pf. mult. .. 15 15
E 1047. – 15 pf. mult. .. 20 20
E 1048. – 20 pf. mult. .. 20 20
E 1049. – 25 pf. mult. .. 15 15
E 1050. – 30 pf. mult. .. 15 15

1967. Agricultural Co-operatives. 15th Anniv.

E 1052. E 329. 10 pf. sepia, green and olive .. 5 5

1967. Popular Art of the Ore Mountains. Multicoloured.

E 1053. 10 pf. Type E 330 .. 12 5
E 1054. 20 pf. "Angel" and miner with candles (carved figures) 5 5

E 331. Ice-skating. E 332. Actinometer.

1968. Winter Olympic Games. Grenoble.

E 1055. 5 pf. blue, red & lt. blue 5 5
E 1056. 10 pf.+5 pf. ultram., red and turquoise .. 5 5
E 1057. 15 pf. ultram., red & yell. 5 5
E 1058. 20 pf. ultram., red & blue 5 5
E 1059. 25 pf. turquoise, red, black and blue .. 5 5
E 1060. 30 pf. ultramarine, red and turquoise .. 70 70

DESIGNS: 5 pf. Type E 331. 10 pf. Tobogganing. 15 pf. Slalom. 20 pf. Ice-hockey. 25 pf. Figure-skating (pairs). 30 pf. Cross-country skiing.

1968. Potsdam Meteorological Observatory. 75th Anniv. and World Meteorological Day (23rd March).

E 1061. 10 pf. black, red & pur. 20 20
E 1062. 20 pf. blk., ind., bl. & red 20 20
E 1063. 25 pf. black, yell. & olive 20 20

DESIGNS—VERT. 10 pf. Type E 332. 25 pf. Cornfield by day and night. HORIZ.—(50×28 mm.): 20 pf. Satellite picture of clouds.

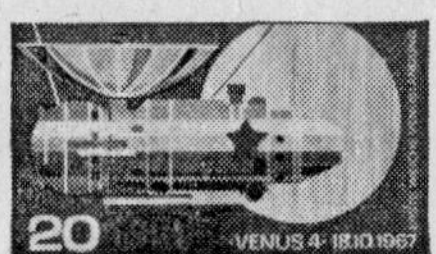

E 333. "Venus 4".

1968. Soviet Space Achievements.

E 1064. E 333. 20 pf. black, mag., blue & indigo 5 5
E 1065. – 25 pf. black, mag., blue & indigo 25 25

DESIGN: 25 pf. Coupled satellites "Cosmos 186" and "188".

E 334. "Illegal Struggle" (man, wife and child). E 336. Gorky.

E 335. Diesel Locomotive.

1968. Stained-glass Windows, Sachsenhausen National Memorial Museum. Multicoloured.

E 1066. 10 pf. Type E 334 .. 5 5
E 1067. 20 pf. "Liberation" .. 5 5
E 1068. 25 pf. "Partisans' Struggle" 35 35

1968. Leipzig Spring Fair. Multicoloured.

E 1069. 10 pf. Type E 335 .. 5 5
E 1070. 15 pf. Atlantic trawler 15 10

1968. Maxim Gorky (writer). Birth Cent.

E 1071. E 336. 20 pf. pur. & claret 5 5
E 1072. – 25 pf. pur. & claret 25 25

DESIGN: 25 pf. Symbolic bird (from "Song of the Stormy Petrel"—poem).

1968. Provincial Costumes (3rd series). As Type E 258. Multicoloured.

E 1073. 10 pf. Hoyerswerda (female) 5 5
E 1074. 20 pf. Schleife (female) 5 5
E 1075. 40 pf. Crostwitz (female) 5 5
E 1076. 50 pf. Spreewald (female) 95 95

E 337. Pheasants. E 338. Karl Marx.

1968. Small Game. Multicoloured.

E 1077. 10 pf. Type E 337 .. 5 5
E 1078. 15 pf. Partridges .. 5 5
E 1079. 20 pf. Mallards .. 5 5
E 1080. 25 pf. Greylag geese .. 5 5
E 1081. 30 pf. Ringdoves .. 5 5
E 1082. 40 pf. Hares 90 90

1968. Karl Marx. 150th Birth Anniv.

E 1083. – 10 pf. blk. & grn. 20 15
E 1084. E 338. 20 pf. black, yellow and red 20 15
E 1085. – 25 pf. black, brn. and yellow .. 20 15

DESIGNS: 10 pf. Title-page of "Communist Manifesto". 25 pf. Title-page of "Das Kapital".

E 339. "Fritz Heckert" (after E. Hering). E 340. Hammer and Anvil ("The right to work").

1968. 7th Confederation of Free German Trade Unions Congress. Multicoloured.

E 1087. 10 pf. Type E 339 .. 5 5
E 1088. 20 pf. Young workers and new tenements 12 10

1968. Human Rights Year.

E 1089. E 340. 5 pf. mag. & pur. 5 5
E 1090. – 10 pf. bistre & brn. 5 5
E 1091. – 25 pf. blue and turquoise-blue 25 25

DESIGNS: 10 pf. Tree and Globe ("The right to live"). 25 pf. Dove and Sun ("The right to peace").

E 341. Vietnamese Mother and Child.

1968. Aid for Vietnam.

E 1092. E 341. 10 pf.+5 pf. multicoloured .. 10 5

E 342. Angling (World Angling Championships, Gustrow).

1968. Sporting Events.

E 1093. E 342. 20 pf. blue, green and red .. 35 35
E 1094. – 20 pf. blue, turq.-blue & green .. 5 5
E 1095. – 20 pf. maroon, red and blue .. 5 5

DESIGNS: No. E 1094, Sculling (European Women's Rowing Championships, Berlin). No. E 1095, High-jumping (2nd European Youth Athletic Competitions).

E 343. Brandenburg Gate and Torch. E 344. Festival Emblem.

1968. German Youth Sports Day. Multicoloured.

E 1096. 10 pf. Type E 343 .. 5 5
E 1097. 25 pf. Stadium plan and torch 25 25

1968. Peace Festival, Sofia.

E 1098. E 344. 20 pf.+5 pf multicoloured 5 5
E 1099. 25 f. multicoloured 35 35

1968. Principal East German Buildings (2nd Series). As Type E 307. Multicoloured.

E 1100. 10 pf. Town Hall, Wernigerode .. 5 5
E 1101. 20 pf. Moritzburg Castle, Dresden 5 5
E 1102. 25 pf. Town Hall, Greifswald 5 5
E 1103. 30 pf. New Palace, Potsdam .. 55 55

DESIGN SIZES—VERT. 10 pf., 25 pf. (24×29 mm.). HORIZ: 20 pf., 30 pf. (51½×29½ mm.).

E 345. Walter Ulbricht.

E 346. Ancient Rostock. E 347. Dr. K. Landsteiner (physician and pathologist).

1968. Walter Ulbricht (Chairman of Council of State). 75th Birthday.

E 1104. E 345. 20 pf. black, red and orange .. 12 5

1968. Rostock. 750th Anniv. Multicoloured.

E 1105. 20 pf. Type E 346 .. 5 5
E 1106. 25 pf. Rostock, 1968 .. 30 30

1968. Celebrities' Annivs. (1st Series).

E 1107. E 347. 10 pf. grey .. 5 5
E 1108. – 15 pf. black .. 5 5
E 1109. – 20 pf. brown .. 5 5
E 1110. – 25 pf. blue .. 5 5
E 1111. – 40 pf. claret .. 60 60

DESIGNS: 15 pf. E. Lasker (chess master; birth cent.). 20 pf. H. Eisler (composer; 70th birth anniv.). 25 pf. I. Semmelweis (physician; 150th birth anniv.). 40 pf. M. von Pettenkofer (hygienist; 150th birth anniv.).

See also Nos. E 1161/4, E 1256/61, E 1367/72 and E 1427.

E 348. "Trener" Aircraft looping. E 349. "At the Seaside" (Wainacka).

1968. Aerobatics. World Championships, Magdeburg Multicoloured.

E 1112. 10 pf. Type E 348 .. 5 5
E 1113. 25 pf. Stunt flying .. 25 25

1968. Dresden Gallery Paintings (2nd Series). Multicoloured.

E 1114. 10 pf. Type E 349 .. 5 5
E 1115. 15 pf. "Highland Peasants Mowing Mountain Meadow" (Egger-Lienz) 5 5
E 1116. 20 pf. "Portrait of a Farmer's Wife" (Leibl) .. 5 5
E 1117. 40 pf. "Portrait of my Daughter" (Venturelli) 5 5
E 1118. 50 pf. "High-school Girl" (Michaelis) .. 10 10
E 1119. 70 pf. "Girl with Guitar" (Castelli) .. 1·10 1·10

The 20 pf. to 70 pf. are vert.

E 350. Model Trains.

1968. Leipzig Autumn Fair.

E 1120. E 350. 10 pf. mult. .. 5 5

E 351. Spremberg Dam.

1968. East German Post-War Dams. Multicoloured.

E 1121. 5 pf. Type E 351 .. 5 5
E 1122. 10 pf. Pohl Dam .. 5 5
E 1123. 15 pf. Ohra Valley Dam 30 30
E 1124. 20 pf. Rappbode Dam 5 5

The 10 pf. and 15 pf. are vert.

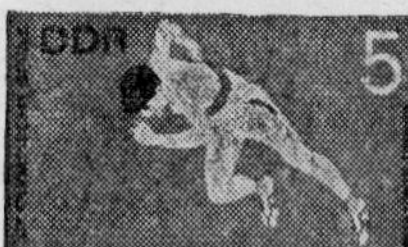

E 352. Sprinting.

1968. Olympic Games, Mexico. Multicoloured.

E 1125. 5 pf. Type E 352 .. 5 5
E 1126. 10 pf.+5 pf. Pole-vaulting 5 5
E 1127. 20 pf.+10 pf. Football 5 5
E 1128. 25 pf. Gymnastics .. 5 5
E 1129. 40 pf. Water-polo .. 5 5
E 1130. 70 pf. Sculling .. 1·10 1·10

The 10, 20, 25 and 40 pf. are vert.

E 353. Breendonk Memorial, Belgium. E 354. "Cicindela campestris".

1968. Breendonk War Victims. Commem.

E 1131. E 353. 25 pf. mult. .. 15 5

1968. "Useful Beetles". Multicoloured.

E 1132. 10 pf. Type E 354 .. 5 5
E 1133. 15 pf. "Cychrus caraboides" 5 5
E 1134. 20 pf. "Adalia bipunctata" .. 5 5
E 1135. 25 pf. "Carabus arcensis" .. .. 1·00 1·00
E 1136. 30 pf. "Hister bipustulatus" .. 8 5
E 1137. 40 pf. "Pseudoclerops mutillarius" .. 10 5

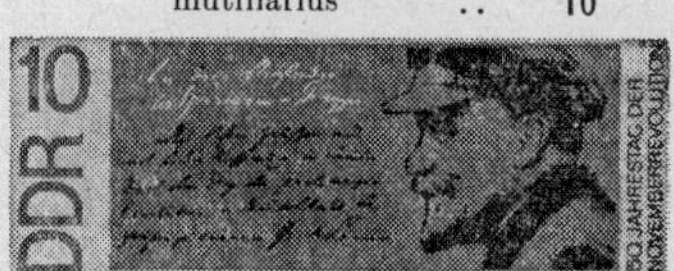

E 355. Lenin and Letter to Spartacus Group.

1968. German November Revolution. 50th Anniv.

E 1138. 10 pf. black, red and yellow 5 5
E 1139. 20 pf. black, red and yellow 5 5
E 1140. 25 pf. black, red and yellow 35 35

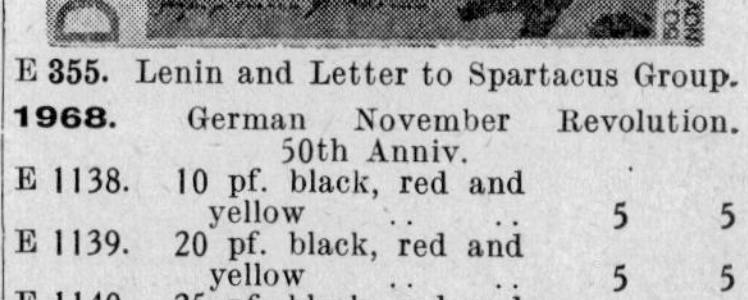

DESIGNS: 10 pf. Type E **355**. 20 pf. Revolutionaries and title of Spartacus newspaper "Die Rote Fahne". 25 pf. Karl Liebknecht and Rosa Luxemburg.

E **356**. "Laelo-cattleya" ("Maggie Raphaela").

1968. Orchids. Multicoloured.

E 1141. 5 pf. Type E **356** .. 5 5
E 1142. 10 pf. "Paphiopedilum albertianum" .. 5 5
E 1143. 15 pf. "Cattleya fabia" 5 5
E 1144. 20 pf. "Cattleya aclaniae" 5 5
E 1145. 40 pf. "Sobralia macrantha" 5 5
E 1146. 50 pf. "Dendrobium alpha" .. .. 1·10 1·10

E **357**. Trying on the Boots.

1968. Fairy Tales (3rd Series). "Puss in Boots". As Type E **357**. Designs showing different scenes.

E 1147. 5 pf. multicoloured .. 15 15
E 1148. 10 pf. multicoloured .. 15 15
E 1149. 15 pf. multicoloured .. 20 20
E 1150. 20 pf. multicoloured .. 20 20
E 1151. 25 pf. multicoloured .. 15 15
E 1152. 30 pf. multicoloured .. 15 15

E **358**. Young Pioneers.

1968. Ernst Thalmann's "Young Pioneers." 20th Anniv. Multicoloured.

E 1153. 10 pf. Type E **358** .. 5 5
E 1154. 15 pf. Young pioneers (diff.) 20 20

1969. Principal East German Buildings (3rd Series). As Type E **307**. Multicoloured.

E 1155. 5 pf. Town Hall, Tangermunde .. 5 5
E 1156. 10 pf. State Opera House, Berlin 5 5
E 1157. 20 pf. Rampart Pavilion, Dresden Castle .. 5 5
E 1158. 25 pf. Patrician's House, Luckau 75 75
E 1159. 30 pf. Dornburg Castle 5 5
E 1160. 40 pf. "Zum Stockfisch" Inn, Erfuet. . 10 10

The 5, 20, 25 and 40 pf. are vert.

1969. Celebrities' Annivs. (2nd Series). As Type E **347**.

E 1161. 10 pf. olive 5 5
E 1162. 20 pf. chocolate .. 5 5
E 1163. 25 pf. blue 55 55
E 1164. 40 pf. brown 5 5

DESIGNS: 10 pf. M. A. Nexo (Danish poet—birth cent.). 20 pf. O. Nagel (painter—75th birth anniv.) 25 pf. A von Humboldt (naturalist—bicent. of birth). 40 pf. T. Fontane writer—150th birth anniv.).

E **359**. Pedestrian Crossing.

E **360**. "E-512" Combine-harvester.

1969. Road Safety. Multicoloured.

E 1165. 5 pf. Type E **359** .. 5 5
E 1166. 10 pf. Traffic lights .. 5 5
E 1167. 20 pf. Level-crossing sign 5 5
E 1168. 25 pf. Motor-vehicle overtaking 35 35

1969. Leipzig Spring Fair. Multicoloured.

E 1169. 10 pf. Type E **360** .. 5 5
E 1170. 15 pf. "Planeta-variant" lithograph printing-press 12 5

E **361**. Jorinde and Joringel.

E **362**. "Leucojum vernum".

1969. Fairy Tales (4th Series). "Jorinde and Joringel". As Type E **361**, showing different scenes.

E 1171. 5 pf. multicoloured .. 15 15
E 1172. 10 pf. multicoloured .. 15 15
E 1173. 15 pf. multicoloured .. 15 15
E 1174. 20 pf. multicoloured .. 15 15
E 1175. 25 pf. multicoloured .. 15 15
E 1176. 30 pf. multicoloured .. 15 15

1969. Protected Plants (2nd Series). Multicoloured.

E 1177. 5 pf. Type E **362** .. 5 5
E 1178. 10 pf. "Adonis vernalis" 5 5
E 1179. 15 pf. "Trollius europaeus" 5 5
E 1180. 20 pf. "Lilium martagon" 5 5
E 1181. 25 pf. "Eryngium maritimum" 70 70
E 1182. 30 pf. "Dactylorchis latifolia" 5 5

See also Nos. E 1284/9.

E **363**. Plantation of Young Conifers.

E **364**. Symbols of the Societies.

1969. Forest Fires Prevention. Multicoloured.

E 1183. 5 pf. Type E **363** .. 5 5
E 1184. 10 pf. Lumber, and resin extraction .. 5 5
E 1185. 20 pf. Forest stream .. 5 5
E 1186. 25 pf. Woodland camp 35 35

1969. League of Red Cross Societies. 50th Anniv. Multicoloured.

E 1187. 10 pf. Type E **364** .. 5 5
E 1188. 15 pf. As Type E **364** (different) 20 20

E **365**. Erythrite (Schneeberg).

E **366**. Women and Symbols.

1969. East German Minerals. Multicoloured.

E 1189. 5 pf. Type E **365** .. 5 5
E 1190. 10 pf. Fluorite (Halsbrucke) 5 5
E 1191. 15 pf. Galena (Neudorf) 5 5
E 1192. 20 pf. Smoky Quartz (Lichtenberg) .. 5 5
E 1193. 25 pf. Calcite (Niederrabenstein) 75 75
E 1194. 50 pf. Silver (Freiberg) 12 5

1969. 2nd DDR Women's Congress.

E 1195. E **366**. 20 pf., red & blue 5 5
E 1196. – 25 pf. blue & red 30 30

DESIGN: 25 pf. Woman and Symbols (different).

INDEX

Countries can be quickly located by referring to the index at the end of this volume.

E **367**. Walter Ulbricht.

E **368**. Badge of DDR Philatelists' Association.

1969. As Nos. E 586/7 (Ulbricht), but with face values expressed in "M" (Mark).

E 1197. E **367**. 1 M green .. 35 30
E 1198. 2 M brown .. 60 60

1969. DDR Stamp Exn., Magdeburg. 20th Anniv. (1st Issue).

E 1199. E **368**. 10 pf. gold, blue and red .. 5

See also Nos. E 1233/4.

E **369**. Armed Volunteers.

E **370**. "Development of Youth".

1969. Aid for Vietnam.

E 1200. E **369**. 10 pf. + 5 pf. mult. 5 5

1969. Int. Peace Meeting, East Berlin. Multicoloured.

E 1201. 10 pf. Type E **370** .. 15 15
E 1202. 20 pf. + 5 pf. Berlin landmarks (50 × 28 mm.) 15 15
E 1203. 25 pf. "Workers of the World" 15 15

No. E 1202 is horiz.

E **371**. Inaugural Ceremony.

1969. Gymnastics and Sports Days, Leipzig. Multicoloured.

E 1204. 5 pf. Type E **371** .. 5 5
E 1205. 10 pf. + 5 pf. Gymnastics 5 5
E 1206. 15 pf. Athletes' parade 5 5
E 1207. 20 pf. + 5 pf. "Sport" Art Exhibition .. 5 5
E 1208. 25 pf. Athletic events.. 75 75
E 1209. 30 pf. Presentation of colours 5 5

E **372**. Pierre de Coubertin (from bust by W. Forster).

E **373**. Knight.

1969. Pierre de Coubertin's Revival of Olympic Games' Movement. 75th Anniv.

E 1210. E **372**. 10 pf. sepia, black and blue .. 5 5
E 1211. – 25 pf. sepia, black and red .. 25 25

DESIGN: 25 pf. Coubertin monument, Olympia.

1969. World Sports Championships. Multicoloured.

E 1212. E **373**. 20 pf. gold, red and maroon .. 10 5
E 1213. – 20 pf. gold, brn., red & green .. 10 5
E 1214. – 20 pf. gold, brn., black & green 10 5

DESIGNS AND EVENTS: No. E 1212, (16th World Students' Teams' Chess Tournament, Dresden). No. E 1213, Cycle Wheel (World Covered Court Cycling Championships, Erfurt). No. E 1214, Ball and net (2nd World Volleyball Cup-ties).

E **374**. Fair Display Samples.

1969. Leipzig Autumn Fair.

E 1215. E **374**. 10 pf. mult. .. 5 5

E **375**. Rostock.

E **376**. TV Tower, East Berlin.

1969. German Democratic Republic. 20th Anniv. Multicoloured.

(a) 1st Issue. As T E **375**.

E 1216. 10 pf. Type E **375** .. 8 5
E 1217. 10 pf. Neubrandenburg 8 5
E 1218. 10 pf. Potsdam .. 8 5
E 1219. 10 pf. Eisenhuttenstadt 8 5
E 1220. 10 pf. Hoyerswerda .. 8 5
E 1221. 10 pf. Magdeburg .. 8 5
E 1222. 10 pf. Halle-Neustadt 8 5
E 1223. 10 pf. Suhl 8 5
E 1224. 10 pf. Dresden .. 8 5
E 1225. 10 pf. Leipzig 8 5
E 1226. 10 pf. Karl-Marx Stadt 8 5
E 1227. 10 pf. East Berlin .. 8 5

(b) 2nd Issue. As T E **376**.

E 1230. 10 pf. Type E **376** .. 5 5
E 1231. 20 pf. "Globe" of Tower with TV Screen .. 12 5

E **377**. O. von Guericke Memorial, Cathedral and Hotel International, Magdeburg.

1969. D.D.R. Stamp Exn., Magdeburg. 20th Anniv. (2nd Issue). Multicoloured.

E 1233. 20 pf. Type E **377** .. 5 5
E 1234. 40 pf. + 10 pf. Von Guericke's vacuum experiment 50 50

E **378**. Ryvangen Memorial.

E **379**. U.F.I. Emblem.

1969. War Victims' Memorial, Ryvangen (Copenhagen).

E 1235. E **378**. 25 pf. mult. .. 15 5

1969. 36th Int. Fairs Union (U.F.I.) Congress, Leipzig.

E 1236. E **379**. 10 pf. mult. .. 5 5
E 1237. 15 pf. mult. .. 20 20

E **380**. I.L.O. Emblem.

E **381**. University Seal and Building.

1969. Int. Labour Organization. 50th Anniv.

E 1238. E **380**. 20 pf. silver & grn. 5 5
E 1239. 25 pf. silver & mag. 35 35

1969. Rostock University. 550th Anniv. Multicoloured.
E 1240. 10 pf. Type E 381 .. 5 5
E 1241. 15 pf. Steam-turbine rotor and curve (University emblem) 20 20

E 382. "Horseman" Pastry-mould. E 383. "An-24" Aircraft.

1969. Lausitz Folk Art.
E 1242. E 382. 10 pf. brown, black and flesh .. 12 12
E 1243. – 10 pf. + 5 pf. blue, grey, black and yellow .. 30 30
E 1244. – 50 pf. mult. .. 70 70
DESIGNS: 20 pf. Plate. 50 pf. Pastry in form of Negro couple.

1969. "Interflug" Aircraft. Multicoloured.
E 1245. 20 pf. Type E 383 .. 5 5
E 1246. 25 pf. Ilyushin "Il-18" 90 90
E 1247. 30 pf. Tupolev "Tu-134" 5 5
E 1248. 50 pf. "Mi-8" helicopter 12 5

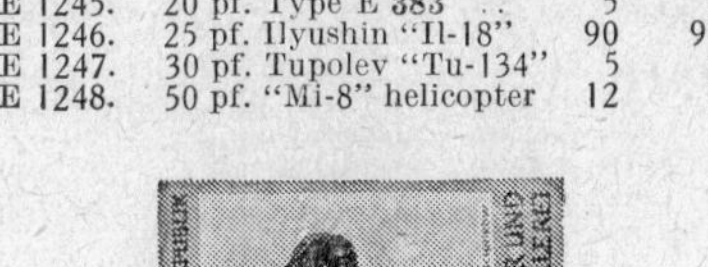

E 384. "Siberian Teacher" (Svechnikov).

1969. Dresden Gallery Paintings (3rd Series). Multicoloured.
E 1249. 5 pf. Type E 384 .. 5 5
E 1250. 10 pf. "Steel-worker" (Serov) 5 5
E 1251. 20 pf. "Still Life" (Aslamasjan) .. 5 5
E 1252. 25 pf. "A Warm Day" (Romas) .. .. 1·00 1·00
E 1253. 40 pf. "Springtime Again" (Kabatchek) 10 5
E 1254. 50 pf. "Man by the River" (Makovsky) 12 5

1970. Coil Stamp. As Nos. E 577 etc., but value expressed in "M".
E 1255. E 194. 1 M olive .. 45 5

1970. Celebrities Annivs. (3rd Series). As T 347.
E 1256. 5 pf. blue 5 5
E 1257. 10 pf. brown 5 5
E 1258. 15 pf. blue 5 5
E 1259. 20 pf. purple 5 5
E 1260. 25 pf. blue 75 75
E 1261. 40 pf. red 5 5
DESIGNS: 5 pf. E. Barlach (sculptor and playwright; birth cent.). 10 pf. J. Gutenberg (printer — 500th death anniv.) (1968). 15 pf. K. Tucholsky (author; 35th death anniv.). 20 pf. Beethoven (birth bicent.). 25 pf. F. Holderlin (poet—birth bicent.). 40 pf. G. W. F. Hegel (philosopher—birth bicent.).

E 385. Fox.

1970. Int. Fur Auction, Leipzig. Multicoloured.
E 1262. 10 pf. Rabbit 5 5
E 1263. 20 pf. Type 385 .. 5 5
E 1264. 25 pf. Mink 65 65
E 1265. 40 pf. Hamster .. 8 5

E 386. "Little Brother and Little Sister".

1970. Fairy Tales (5th Series). "Little Brother and Little Sister". As Type E 386, showing different scenes.
E 1266. 5 pf. multicoloured .. 12 12
E 1267. 10 pf. multicoloured .. 12 12
E 1268. 15 pf. multicoloured .. 20 20
E 1269. 20 pf. multicoloured .. 20 20
E 1270. 25 pf. multicoloured .. 12 12
E 1271. 30 pf. multicoloured .. 12 12

E 387. Telephone and Electrical Switchgear.

1970. Leipzig Spring Fair. Multicoloured.
E 1272. 10 pf. Type E 387 .. 5 5
E 1273. 15 pf. High-voltage transformer (vert.) 15 5

E 388. Horseman's Gravestone (A.D. 700).

1970. Archaeological Discoveries.
E 1274. E 388. 10 pf. ol., blk. & grn. 5 5
E 1275. – 20 pf. blk., yell. & red 5 5
E 1276. – 25 pf. green, black and yellow .. 65 65
E 1277. – 40 pf. chestnut, black & brown 5 5
DESIGNS: 20 pf. Helmet (A.D. 500). 25 pf. Bronze basin (1000 B.C.). 40 pf. Clay drum (2500 B.C.).

E 390. Lenin and "Iskra" (= the Spark) press.

1970. Lenin. Birth Cent. Multicoloured.
E 1278. 10 pf. Type E 390 .. 5 5
E 1279. 20 pf. Lenin and Clara Zetkin 5 5
E 1280. 25 pf. Lenin and "State & Revolution" (book) 1·10 1·10
E 1281. 40 pf. Lenin Monument, Eisleben 5 5
E 1282. 70 pf. Lenin Square, East Berlin .. 15 12

1970. Protected Plants (3rd Series). Vert. designs as Type E 362. Multicoloured.
E 1284. 10 pf. "Crambe maritima" 5 5
E 1285. 20 pf. "Pulsatilla vulgaris" 5 5
E 1286. 25 pf. "Gentiana ciliata" .. .. 1·40 1·40
E 1287. 30 pf. "Orchis militaris" 5 5
E 1288. 40 pf. "Ledum palustre" 5 5
E 1289. 70 pf. "Pyrola rotundifolia" 5 5

E 391. Capture of the Reichstag, 1945. E 392. Shortwave Aerial.

1970. "Liberation from Fascism". 25th Anniv. Multicoloured.
E 1290. 10 pf. Type E 391 .. 5 5
E 1291. 20 pf. Newspaper headline, Kremlin and State Building, East Berlin 5 5
E 1292. 25 pf. C.M.E.A. Building, Moscow, and flags 45 45

1970. D.D.R. Broadcasting Service. 25th Anniv. Multicoloured.
E 1294. 10 pf. Type E 392 .. 10 10
E 1295. 15 pf. Radio Station, East Berlin .. 15 15
No. E 1295 is a horiz. design, size 50 × 28 mm.

E 393. Globe and Ear of Corn. E 394. Fritz Heckert Medal.

1970. 5th World Corn and Bread Congress, Dresden. Multicoloured.
E 1296. 20 pf. Type E 393 .. 20 20
E 1297. 25 pf. Palace of Culture and ear of corn .. 25 25

1970. 25th Annivs. of German Confederation of Trade Unions and World Trade Union Federation ("Federation Syndicale Mondiale"). Multicoloured.
E 1298. 20 pf. Type E 394 .. 5 5
E 1299. 25 pf. F.S.M. Emblem .. 80 80

E 395. Gods Amon, Shu and Tefnut.

1970. Sudanese Archaeological Excavations by Humboldt University Expedition. Multicoloured.
E 1300. 10 pf. Type E 395 .. 5 5
E 1301. 15 pf. King Arnekhamani 5 5
E 1302. 20 pf. Cattle frieze .. 5 5
E 1303. 25 pf. Prince Arka .. 1·25 1·25
E 1304. 30 pf. God Arensnuphis (vert.) 5 5
E 1305. 40 pf. War elephants and prisoners .. 5 5
E 1306. 50 pf. God Apedemak .. 5 5
The above designs reproduce carvings unearthed at the Lions' Temple, Musawwarat, Sudan.

E 396. Road Patrol. E 397. D.K.B. Emblem.

1970. "Deutsche Volkspolizei" (East German Police). 25th Anniv. Multicoloured.
E 1307. 5 pf. Type E 396 .. 5 5
E 1308. 10 pf. Policewoman with children 5 5
E 1309. 15 pf. Radio patrol-car 5 5
E 1310. 20 pf. Railway policeman 5 5
E 1311. 25 pf. River police in patrol-boat 55 55

1970. "Deutscher Kulturbund" (German Cultural Assn.). 25th Anniv.
E 1312. E 397. 10 pf. chocolate, silver and blue 20 15
E 1313. – 25 pf. chocolate, gold and blue 20 15
DESIGN: 25 pf. Johannes Becher medal.

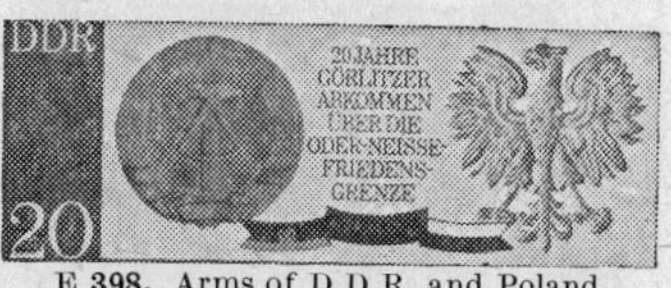

E 398. Arms of D.D.R. and Poland.

1970. Gorlitz Agreement on Oder-Neisse Border. 20th Anniv.
E 1314. E 398. 20 pf. multicoloured .. 12 5

E 399. Vaulting. E 401. Cecilienhof Castle.

E 400. Boy Pioneer with Neckerchief.

1970. Children and Youth Sports Days. Multicoloured.
E 1315. 10 pf. Type E 399 .. 5 5
E 1316. 20 pf. + 5 pf. Hurdling 20 10

1970. 6th Young Pioneers Meeting. Cottbus. Multicoloured.
E 1317. 10 pf. + 5 pf. Type E 400 20 20
E 1318. 25 pf. + 5 pf. Girl pioneer with neckerchief .. 20 20

1970. Potsdam Agreement. 25th Anniv.
E 1319. E 401. 10 pf. yellow, red and black .. 15 15
E 1320. 20 pf. black, red and yellow .. 15 15
E 1321. – 25 pf. black & red 15 15
DESIGNS—VERT. 20 pf. "Potsdam Agreement" in four languages. HORIZ. (77 × 28 mm.): 25 pf. Conference delegates around the table.

E 402. Pocket-watch and Wristwatch. E 403. T. Neubauer and M. Poser.

1970. Leipzig Autumn Fair.
E 1322. E 402. 10 pf. multicoloured .. 5 5

1970. "Anti-Fascist Resistance".
E 1323. E 403. 20 pf. maroon red and blue .. 10 10
E 1324. – 25 pf. olive and red .. 15 15
DESIGN—VERT. 25 pf. "Motherland"—detail from Soviet War Memorial, Treptow, Berlin.

E 404. Pres. Ho-Chi-Minh. E 405. Compass and Map.

1970. Aid for Vietnam and Ho-Chi-Minh. Commem.
E 1325. E 404. 20 pf. + 5 pf. blk., red and pink .. 15 5

1970. World "Orienteering" Championships. East Germany. Mult.
E 1326. 10 pf. Type E 405 .. 5 5
E 1327. 25 pf. Runner and three map sections .. 30 30

E 406. "Forester Scharf's Birthday" (Nagel).

1970. "The Art of Otto Nagel, Kathe Kollwitz and Ernst Barlach".

E 1328. **406.** 10 pf. multicoloured 5 5
E 1329. – 20 pf. multicoloured 5 5
E 1330. – 25 pf. brown & mauve 1·10 1·10
E 1331. – 30 pf. black & pink 5 5
E 1332. – 40 pf. black & yell. 5 5
E 1333. – 50 pf. black & yell. 5 5

DESIGNS: 20 pf. "Portrait of a Young Girl" (Nagel). 25 pf. "No More War" (Kollwitz). 30 pf. "Mother and Child" (Kollwitz). 40 pf. Sculptured head from Gustrow Cenotaph (Barlach). 50 pf. "The Flute-player" (Barlach).

E 407. "The Little Trumpeter" (Weineck Memorial, Halle). **E 409.** Musk-ox.

E 408. Flags Emblem.

1970. 2nd National Youth Stamp Exhibition, Karl-Marx-Stadt. Multicoloured.

E 1334. 10 pf. Type E **407** .. 5 5
E 1335. 15 pf.+5 pf. East German 25 pf. stamp of 1959 .. .. 12 5

1970. "Comrades-in-Arms". Warsaw Pact Military Manoeuvres.

E 1336. E **408.** 10 pf. multicoloured 5 5
E 1337. 20 pf. multicoloured 12 5

1970. Animals in East Berlin "Tierpark" (Zoo). Multicoloured.

E 1338. 10 pf. Type **409** .. 5 5
E 1339. 15 pf. Shoe-billed stork 5 5
E 1340. 20 pf. Mendes antelope 5 5
E 1341. 25 pf. Malayan bear .. 55 55

E 410. U.N. Emblem and Headquarters, New York. **E 411.** Engels.

1970. United Nations. 25th Anniv.

E 1342. E **410.** 20 pf. multicoloured 12 5

1970. Friedrich Engels. 150th Birth Anniv.

E 1343. E **411.** 10 pf. black, grey and orange .. 5 5
E 1344. – 20 pf. black, grn. and orange .. 5 5
E 1345. – 25 pf. black, red and orange .. 40 40

DESIGNS: 20 pf. Engels, Marx and Communist Manifesto. 25 pf. Engels and "Anti Duhring".

E 412. "Epiphyllum hybr.". **E 413.** Dancer's Mask, Bismarck Archipelago.

1970. Cacti Cultivation in D.D.R. Multicoloured.

E 1346. 5 pf. Type E **412** .. 5 5
E 1347. 10 pf. "Astrophytum myriostigma" .. 5 5
E 1348. 15 pf. "Echinocereus salm-dyckianus" .. 5 5
E 1349. 20 pf. "Selenicereus grandiflorus" .. 5 5
E 1350. 25 pf. "Hamatoc setispinus" .. 80 80
E 1351. 30 pf. "Mamillaria boolii" .. . 5 5

1971. Exhibits from the Ethnological Museum, Leipzig.

E 1353. E **413.** 10 pf. multicoloured 5 5
E 1354. – 20 pf. brn. & orge. 5 5
E 1355. – 25 pf. multicoloured 70 70
E 1356. – 40 pf. brown & red 5 5

DESIGNS: 20 pf. Bronze head, Benin. 25 pf. Tea-pot, Thailand. 40 pf. Zapotec earthenware Jaguar-god, Mexico.

E 414. "Venus 5". **E 415.** K. Liebknecht.

1971. Soviet Space Research. Multicoloured.

E 1357. 20 pf. Type E **414** .. 20 20
E 1358. 20 pf. Orbital Space station .. 20 20
E 1359. 20 pf. "Luna 10" and "Luna 16" 30 30
E 1360. 20 pf. Various "Soyuz" spacecraft 30 30
E 1361. 20 pf. "Proton 1" satellite and "Vostok" rocket 30 30
E 1362. 20 pf. "Molniya 1" communications satellite 30 30
E 1363. 20 pf. Gargarin and "Vostok 1" .. 30 30
E 1364. 20 pf. Leonov in Space 30 30

1971. Karl Liebknecht and Rosa Luxemburg (revolutionaries). Birth Cents.

E 1365. E **415.** 20 pf. magenta, black and gold 20 15
E 1366. – 25 pf. magenta, black and gold 20 15

DESIGN: 25 pf. Rosa Luxemburg.

E 416. J. R. Becher (poet).

1971. Celebrities' Birth Anniversaries.

E 1367. E **416.** 5 pf. brown .. 5 5
E 1368. – 10 pf. blue .. 5 5
E 1369. – 15 pf. black .. 5 5
E 1370. – 20 pf. purple .. 5 5
E 1371. – 25 pf. green .. 80 80
E 1372. – 50 pf. blue .. 5 5

DESIGNS: 5 pf. (80th Birth anniv.). 10 pf. H. Mann (writer—birth cent.). 15 pf. J. Heartfield (artist—80th birth anniv.). 20 pf. W. Brendel (70th birth anniv.). 25 pf. F. Mehring (politician—125th birth anniv.). 50 pf. J. Kepler (astronomer—400th birth anniv.).

See also Nos. E 1427 and E 1451/55.

E 417. Soldier and Army Badge.

1971. National People's Army. 15th Anniv.

E 1373. E **417.** 20 pf. multicoloured 12 5

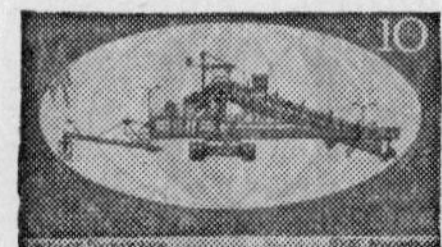

E 418. "Sket" Mobile Ore-crusher.

1971. Leipzig Spring Fair. Multicoloured.

E 1374. 10 pf. Type E **418** .. 5 5
E 1375. 15 pf. "Takraf" mobile dredger 8 5

E 419. Proclamation of the Commune. **E 421.** St. Mary's Church.

E 420. "Lunokhod 1" on Moon's Surface.

1971. Paris Commune. Cent.

E 1376. E **419.** 10 pf. black, brown and red .. 5 5
E 1377. – 20 pf. black, brown and red .. 5 5
E 1378. – 25 pf. black, brown and red .. 65 65
E 1379. – 30 pf. black, grey and red .. 5 5

DESIGNS: 20 pf. Women at the Place Blanche barricade. 25 pf. Cover of "L'Internationale". 30 pf. Title page of Karl Marx's "The Civil War in France".

1971. Moon Mission of "Lunokhod 1".

E 1380. E **420.** 20 pf. turquoise, blue and red .. 12 5

1971. Berlin Buildings. Multicoloured.

E 1381. 10 pf. Type E **421** .. 5 5
E 1382. 15 pf. Kopenick Castle (horiz.) 5 5
E 1383. 20 pf. Old Library (horiz.) 5 5
E 1384. 25 pf. Ermeler House .. 1·40 1·40
E 1385. 50 pf. New Guardhouse (horiz.) 5 5
E 1386. 70 pf. National Gallery (horiz.) 12 5

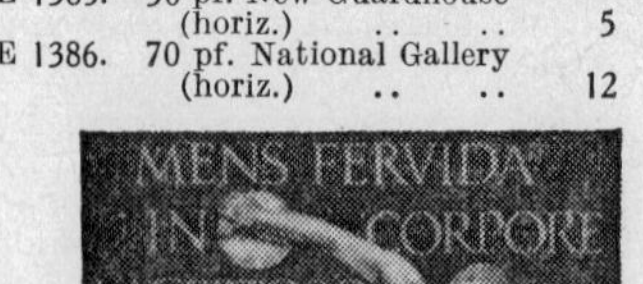

E 422. "The Discus-thrower".

1971. D.D.R. National Olympics Committee. 20th Anniv.

E 1387. E **422.** 20 pf. multicoloured .. 12 5

E 423. Handclasp and "XXV" Emblem. **E 424.** Schleife Costume.

1971. Labour Party Merger. 25th Anniv.

E 1388. E **423.** 20 pf. black, red and gold .. 12 5

1971. Sorbian Dance Costumes. Multicoloured.

E 1389. 10 pf. Type E **424** .. 5 5
E 1390. 20 pf. Hoyerswerda .. 5 5
E 1391. 25 pf. Cottbus 80 80
E 1392. 40 pf. Kamenz 5 5

For 10 pf. and 20 pf. in smaller size, see Nos. E 1443/4.

E 425. Self-portrait, c. 1500. **E 427.** "Internees".

E 426. Construction Worker **E 428.** Cherry stone with 180 Carved Heads.

1971. Albrecht Durer. 500th Birth Anniv. Paintings. Multicoloured.

E 1393. 10 pf. Type E **425** .. 5 5
E 1394. 40 pf. "The Three Peasants" 5 5
E 1395. 70 pf. "Philipp Melanchthon" .. 1·10 1·10

1971. 8th S.E.D. Party Conference.

E 1396. E **426.** 5 pf. multicoloured 5 5
E 1397. – 10 pf. multicoloured 5 5
E 1398. – 20 pf. multicoloured 5 5
E 1400. – 20 pf. gold, red & magenta .. 15 5
E 1399. – 25 pf. multicoloured 50 50

DESIGNS: 10 pf. Technician. 20 pf. (No. 1398) Farm girl. 20 pf. (No. 1400) Conference emblem (smaller, 23×29 mm.). 25 pf. Soldier.

1971. "Federation Internationale des Resistants", 20th Anniv. Lithographs from Fritz Cremer's "Buchenwaldzyklus".

E 1401. E **427.** 20 pf. blk. & yell. 25 25
E 1402. – 25 pf. blk. & blue 25 25

DESIGN: 25 pf. "Attack on Guard".

1971. Art Treasures of Dresden's Green Vaults. Multicoloured.

E 1403. 5 pf. Type E **428** .. 5 5
E 1404. 10 pf. Insignia of the Golden Fleece, c. 1730 5 5
E 1405. 15 pf. Nuremberg jug, c. 1530 .. .. 5 5
E 1406. 20 pf. Mounted Moorish drummer figurine, c. 1720 .. .. 5 5
E 1407. 25 pf. Writing-case, 1562 90 90
E 1408. 30 pf. St. George medallion, c. 1570 .. .. 5 5

E 429. Mongolian Arms. **E 430.** Child's Face.

1971. Mongolian People's Republic. 50th Anniv.

E 1409. E **429.** 20 pf. multicoloured 12 5

1971. U.N.I.C.E.F. 25th Anniv.

E 1410. E **430.** 20 pf. multicoloured 12 5

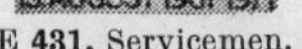

E 431. Servicemen. **E 433.** Vietnamese Woman and Child.

E 432. Cruise-liner "Ivan Franko".

1971. Berlin Wall. 10th Anniv. Multicoloured.

E 1411. 20 pf. Type E **431** .. 10 5
E 1412. 35 pf. Brandenburg Gate 20 12

1971. East German Shipbuilding Industry.

E 1413. E **432.** 10 pf. brown .. 5 5
E 1414. – 15 pf. bl. & brn. 5 5
E 1415. – 20 pf. green .. 5 5
E 1416. – 25 pf. blue .. 1·40 1·40
E 1417. – 40 pf. brown .. 5 5
E 1418. – 50 pf. blue .. 5 5

DESIGNS: 15 pf. "Type 17" freighter. 20 pf. M.V. "Rostock". 25 pf. Fish factory-ship "Junge Welt". 40 pf. "Type 451" container-ship. 50 pf. Research vessel "Akademik Kurtschatow".

1971. Aid for Vietnam.
E 1419. E **433.** 10 pf.+5 pf. mult. 10 5

E **434.** MAG-Butadien Plant. E **435.** Upraised Arms. (motif by J. Heartfield).

1971. Leipzig Autumn Fair.
E 1420. E **434.** 10 pf. violet, red and green .. 5 5
E 1421. – 25 pf. violet, grn. and blue .. 15 10
DESIGN: 25 pf. SKL reactor plant.

1971. Racial Equality Year.
E 1422. E **435.** 35 pf. black, silver and blue .. 20 5

E **436.** Mail-plane at Airport.

1971. Philatelists' Day.
E 1423. E **436.** 10 pf.+5 pf. blue, red and green 5 5
E 1424. – 25 pf. red, green and blue .. 35 35
DESIGN: 25 pf. Milestone and Zurner's measuring cart.

E **437.** Wiltz Memorial, Luxembourg. E **438.** German Violin.

1971. Monuments. Multicoloured.
E 1425. 25 pf. Type **437** .. 15 5
E 1426. 35 pf. Karl Marx monument, Karl-Marx-Stadt 20 5

1971. R. Virchow (physician). 150th Birth Anniv. As Type E **416.**
E 1427. 40 pf. plum 25 5

1971. Musical Instruments in Markneukirchen Museum. Multicoloured.
E 1428. 10 pf. North African "darbuka" 5 5
E 1429. 15 pf. Mongolian "morin chuur" 5 5
E 1430. 20 pf. Type E **438** .. 5 5
E 1431. 25 pf. Italian mandoline 5 5
E 1432. 40 pf. Bohemian bagpipes 5 5
E 1433. 50 pf. Sudanese "kasso" 1·40 1·40

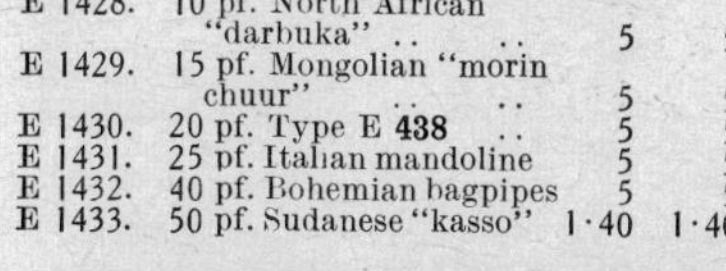

E **439.** "Dahlta 0 10 A" Theodolite. E **440.** Donkey and Windmill.

1971. Carl Zeiss Optical Works, Jena. 125th Anniv.
E 1434. E **439.** 10 pf. black, red and blue .. 25 25
E 1435. – 20 pf. black, red and blue .. 25 25
E 1436. – 25 pf. blue, yellow and ultram. .. 25 25
DESIGNS—VERT. 20 pf. "Ergaval" microscope. HORIZ. 25 pf. Planetarium.

1971. Fairy Tales (6th Series). As Type E **440.** "The Town Musicians of Bremen".
E 1437. 5 pf. multicoloured .. 15 15
E 1438. 10 pf. multicoloured .. 15 15
E 1439. 15 pf. multicoloured .. 25 25
E 1440. 20 pf. multicoloured .. 25 25
E 1441. 25 pf. multicoloured .. 15 15
E 1442. 30 pf. multicoloured .. 15 15

1972. Booklet Stamps. Sorbian Dance Costumes. As Nos. E 1389/90, but smaller, size 23×28 mm.
E 1443. E **424.** 10 pf. multicoloured 5 5
E 1444. – 20 pf. multicoloured 30 20

E **441.** Tobogganing.

1971. Winter Olympic Games, Sapporo, Japan (1972).
E 1445. E **441.** 5 pf. blk., grn. & red 5 5
E 1446. – 10 pf.+5 pf. blk., blue and red 5 5
E 1447. – 15 pf.+5 pf. blk., green & blue.. 5 5
E 1448. – 20 pf. blk., red & violet .. 5 5
E 1449. – 25 pf. blk., vio. and red .. 1·40 1·40
E 1450. – 70 pf. blk., blue and violet .. 12 12
DESIGNS: 10 pf. Figure skating. 15 pf. Speed-skating. 20 pf. Long distance skating. 25 pf. Biathalon. 70 pf. Ski-jumping.

1972. German Celebrities. As Type E **416.**
E 1451. 10 pf. green 5 5
E 1452. 20 pf. mauve 5 5
E 1453. 25 pf. blue 5 5
E 1454. 35 pf. brown 5 5
E 1455. 50 pf. lilac .. .. 1·25 1·25
CELEBRITIES: 10 pf. J. Tralow (writer). 20 pf. L. Frank (writer). 25 pf. K. A. Kocor (composer). 35 pf. H. Schliemann (archaeologist). 50 pf. Caroline Neuber (actress).

E **442.** Gypsum.

1972. Minerals. Multicoloured.
E 1456. 5 pf. Type E **442** .. 5 5
E 1457. 10 pf. Zinnwaldite .. 5 5
E 1458. 20 pf. Malachite .. 5 5
E 1459. 25 pf. Amethyst .. 5 5
E 1460. 35 pf. Halite 5 5
E 1461. 50 pf. Proustite .. 1·40 1·40

E **443.** Vietnamese Woman. E **444.** Soviet Exhibition Hall.

1972. Aid for Vietnam.
E 1462. E **443.** 10 pf.+5 pf. multicoloured .. 10 5

1972. Leipzig Spring Fair. Multicoloured.
E 1463. 10 pf. Type E **444** .. 5 5
E 1464. 25 pf. East German and Soviet flags .. 20 12

E **445.** W.H.O. Emblem.

1972. World Health Day.
E 1466. E **445.** 35 pf. ultram., silver & blue.. 25 5

E **446.** Kamov "K-26" Helicopter.

1972. East German Aircraft. Multicoloured.
E 1467. 5 pf. Type E **446** .. 5 5
E 1468. 10 pf. "Z-37" crop-spraying aircraft .. 5 5
E 1469. 35 pf. Ilyushin "Il-62" 5 5
E 1470. 1 m. Tailfin of Interflug airline .. .. 1·50 1·50

E **447.** Wrestling.

1972. Olympic Games, Munich. Mult.
E 1471. 5 pf. Type E **447** .. 5 5
E 1472. 10 pf.+5 pf. High-diving .. 5 5
E 1473. 20 pf. Pole-vaulting .. 5 5
E 1474. 25 pf.+10 pf. Rowing 5 5
E 1475. 35 pf. Handball 5 5
E 1476. 70 pf. Gymnastics .. 1·90 1·90

E **448.** Soviet and East German Flags.

1972. German-Soviet Friendship Society. 25th Anniv. Multicoloured.
E 1477. 10 pf. Type **448** .. 5 5
E 1478. 20 pf. Brezhnev (U.S.S.R.) meeting Honecker (D.D.R.) .. 15 15

E **449.** Steel Workers. E **450.** "Karneol" Rose.

1972. Trade Unions Federation Congress.
E 1479. E **449.** 10 pf. purple, orange & brown 20 20
E 1480. – 35 pf. blue & brn. 20 20
DESIGNS: 35 pf. Students.

1972. Int. Rose Exhib. German Species. Multicoloured.
E 1481. 5 pf. Type E **450** .. 5 5
E 1482. 10 pf. "Berger's Rose" 5 5
E 1497. 10 pf. "Berger's Rose" 5 5
E 1483. 15 pf. "Charme" .. 1·10 1·10
E 1484. 20 pf. "Izetka Spreeathen" .. 5 5
E 1485. 25 pf. "Kopenicker Sommer" 5 5
E 1498. 25 pf. "Kopenicker Sommer" 30 15
E 1486. 35 pf. "Professor Knoll" 5 5
E 1499. 35 pf. "Professor Knoll" 30 15
Nos. 1497/9 are smaller size 24×28 mm.

E **451.** "Nymph".

1972. Lucas Cranach the Elder. 500th Birth Anniv. Multicoloured.
E 1487. 5 pf. "Portrait of Young Man" (vert.) .. 5 5
E 1488. 20 pf. "Mother and Child" (vert.) .. 5 5
E 1489. 35 pf. "Margarete Luther" (vert.) .. 5 5
E 1490. 70 pf. Type E **451** .. 1·60 1·60

E **452.** Compass and Motor-cyclist.

1972. Sports and Technical Sciences Association. Multicoloured.
E 1491. 5 pf. Type **452** .. 5 5
E 1492. 10 pf. Light aircraft and parachute .. 5 5
E 1493. 20 pf. Target and obstacle race 5 5
E 1494. 25 pf. Radio set and Morse key .. .. 1·00 1·00
E 1495. 35 pf. Sailing ship and propeller 5 5

E **453.** "Young Worker Reading" (J. Damme).

1972. Int. Book Year.
E 1496. E **453.** 50 pf. mult. .. 40 15

E. **454.** Slide Projector.

1972. Leipzig Autumn Fair.
E 1500. – 10 pf. blk. & red 5 5
E 1501. E **454.** 25 pf. blk. & grn. 20 10
DESIGN—VERT. 10 pf. Daylight-writing projector.

E **455.** G. Dimitrov. E **456.** "Catching Birds" (Egyptian relief painting, c. 2400 B.C.).

1972. Georgi Dimitrov (Bulgarian statesman). 90th Birth Anniv.
E 1502. E **455.** 20 pf. blk. & red 15 8

1972. "Interartes" Stamp Exhib., East Berlin. Multicoloured.
E 1503. 10 pf. Type E **45** .. 5 5
E 1504. 15 pf. + 5 pf. Pesan Spearman (glazed tile, c. 500 – c.) .. 1·00 1·00
E 1505. 20 pf. Anatolian tapestry c. 1400 B.C... .. 5 5
E 1506. 35 pf.+5 pf. "The Grapesellers" (Max Lingner, 1949) (horiz.) 5 5

E **457.** Red Cross Team and Patient. E **458.** Terrestrial Globe (J. Praetorius, 1568).

1972. East German Red Cross.

E 1507. E **457.** 10 pf. ultram., blue and red .. 12 12
E 1508. – 15 pf. ultram., blue and red .. 20 20
E 1509. – 35 pf. red, blue and ultram. .. 45 45

DESIGNS—VERT. 15 pf. Sea-rescue launch. HORIZ. (50½ × 28 mm.). 35 pf. World map on cross, and transport.

1972. Terrestrial and Celestial Globes. Multicoloured.

E 1510. 5 pf. Arab celestial globe, 1279 .. 5 5
E 1511. 10 pf. Type E **458** .. 5 5
E 1512. 15 pf. Globe clock (J. Reinhold and G. Roll, 1586) .. .. 1·40 1·40
E 1513. 20 pf. Globe clock (J Burgi, 1590) 5 5
E 1514. 25 pf. Armillary sphere (J. Moeller, 1687) .. 5 5
E 1515. 35 pf. Heraldic celestial globe, 1690 .. .. 5 5

E **459.** Monument. E **461.** "Mauz and Hoppel" (Cat and Hare).

E **460.** Educating Juveniles.

1972. German-Polish Resistance Memorial, Berlin. Inaug.

E 1516. E **459.** 25 pf. mult. .. 20 10

1972. Juvenile Inventions Exhib. Mult.

E 1517. 10 pf. Type E **460** .. 20 20
E 1518. 25 pf. Juveniles with welding machine .. 20 20

1972. Children's T.V. Characters. Mult.

E 1519. 5 pf. Type E **461** .. 25 25
E 1520. 10 pf. "Fuchs and Elster" (Fox and Magpie) 25 25
E 1521. 15 pf. "Herr Uhu" (Eagle Owl) 30 30
E 1522. 20 pf. "Frau Igel and Borstel" (Hedgehogs) 30 30
E 1523. 25 pf. "Schauffel and Pieps" (Dog and Mouse) 25 25
E 1524. 35 pf. "Paulchen" (Paul from the children's library) 25 25

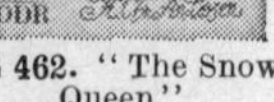

E **462.** "The Snow Queen". E **463.** Arms of U.S.S.R.

1972. Fairy Tales (7th Series). As Type E **462.** "The Snow Queen" (Hans Christian Andersen).

E 1525. 5 pf. multicoloured .. 25 25
E 1526. 10 pf. multicoloured .. 30 30
E 1527. 15 pf. multicoloured .. 25 25
E 1528. 20 pf. multicoloured .. 25 25
E 1529. 25 pf. multicoloured .. 30 30
E 1530. 35 pf. multicoloured .. 25 25

1972. U.S.S.R. 50th Anniv.

E 1532. E **463.** 20 pf. mult. .. 20 5

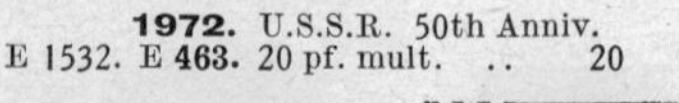

E **464.** Leninplatz, East Berlin. E **465.** M. da Caravaggio.

1973.

(a) Size 29 × 24 mm.

E 1533. – 5 pf. green .. 5 5
E 1534. – 10 pf. green .. 8 5
E 1535. – 15 pf. purple .. 10 5
E 1536. E **464.** 20 pf. mauve .. 15 5
E 1537. – 25 pf. green .. 15 5
E 1538. – 30 pf. orange .. 20 5
E 1539. – 35 pf. blue .. 25 5
E 1540. – 40 pf. violet .. 30 5
E 1541. – 50 pf. blue .. 30 5
E 1542. – 60 pf. lilac .. 35 5
E 1543. – 70 pf. brown .. 45 5
E 1544. – 80 pf. blue .. 55 5
E 1545. – 1 m. green .. 60 5
E 1546. – 2 m. red .. 1·25 5
E 1546a. – 3 m. violet .. 1·75 5

(b) Size 22 × 18 mm.

E 1547. – 5 pf. green .. 5 5
E 1548. – 10 pf. green .. 5 5
E 1549. E **464.** 20 pf. purple .. 15 5
E 1549a. – 25pf. green .. 15 15
E 1550. – 50 pf. blue .. 35 35
E 1550a. – 1 m. green .. 60 5

DESIGNS: 5 pf. (2) Pelican and Alfred Brehm House, Tierpark, Berlin. 10 pf. (2) Neptune Fountain and Rathausstrasse, Berlin. 15 pf. Apartment Blocks, Fishers' Island, Berlin. 25 pf. TV Tower, Alexander Square, Berlin. 30 pf. Workers' Memorial, Halle. 40 pf. Brandenburg Gate, Berlin. 50 pf. (2) New Guardhouse, Berlin. 60 pf. Crown Gate and Zwinger, Dresden. 70 pf. Old Town Hall, Leipzig. 80 pf. Rostock-Warnemunde. 1 m. (2) Soviet War Memorial, Treptow. 2 m., 3 m. Arms of East Germany.

1973. Cultural Anniversaries.

E 1551. E **465.** 5 pf. brown .. 90 90
E 1552. – 10 pf. green .. 5 5
E 1553. – 20 pf. purple .. 5 5
E 1554. – 25 pf. blue .. 5 5
E 1555. – 35 pf. red .. 5 5

PORTRAITS AND ANNIVERSARIES: 5 pf. (painter, 400th birth anniv.). 10 pf. Friedrich Wolf (dramatist, 85th birth anniv.). 20 pf. Max Reger (composer, birth cent.). 25 pf. Max Reinhardt (impresario, birth cent.). 35 pf. Johannes Diekmann (politician, 80th birth anniv.).

E **466.** "Lebachia speciosa".

1973. Fossils in Paleontological Collection, Berlin Nat. History Museum.

E 1556. E **466.** 10 pf. red, blk. and brown .. 5 5
E 1557. – 15 pf. blk., grey and blue .. 5 5
E 1558. – 20 pf. mult. .. 5 5
E 1559. – 25 pf. mult. .. 5 5
E 1560. – 35 pf. mult. .. 5 5
E 1561. – 70 pf. blue, black and yellow .. 1·90 1·90

DESIGNS: 15 pf. "Sphenopteris hollandica". 20 pf. "Pterodactylus kochi". 25 pf. "Botryopteris". 35 pf. "Archaeopteryx lithographica". 70 pf. "Odontopleura ovata".

E **467.** Copernicus.
(Illustration reduced. Actual size 77½ × 29mm.)

1973. Copernicus. 500th Birth Anniv.

E 1562. E **467.** 70 pf. mult. .. 60 30

E **468.** National Flags. E **469.** Bobsleigh Course.

1973. Tenth World Youth Festival, Berlin (1st issue). Multicoloured.

E 1563. 10 pf. + 5 pf. Type E **468** 12 5
E 1564. 25 pf. + 5 pf. Youths and peace dove .. 25 12

1973. 15th World Bobsleigh Championships, Oberhof.

E 1565. E **469.** 35 pf. orge., blue and black .. 30 20

E **470.** Combine Harvester.

1973. Leipzig Spring Fair. Multicoloured.

E 1566. 10 pf. Type E **470** .. 8 5
E 1567. 25 pf. Automatic lathe 20 12

E **471.** Firecrest.

1973. Songbirds. Multicoloured.

E 1568. 5 pf. Type **471** .. 5 5
E 1569. 10 pf. Two-barred crossbill 5 5
E 1570. 15 pf. Waxwing .. 5 5
E 1571. 20 pf. White-spotted and red-spotted blue-throats .. 5 5
E 1572. 25 pf. Goldfinch .. 5 5
E 1573. 35 pf. Golden oriole .. 5 5
E 1574. 40 pf. Grey wagtail .. 5 5
E 1575. 50 pf. Wall-creeper .. 2·25 2·25

E **472.** Electric Locomotive.

1973. Railway Rolling Stock.

E 1576. E **472.** 5 pf. mult. .. 5 5
E 1577. – 10 pf. blue, grey and black .. 5 5
E 1578. – 20 pf. mult. .. 5 5
E 1579. – 25 pf. mult. .. 5 5
E 1580. – 35 pf. mult. .. 5 5
E 1581. – 85 pf. mult. .. 2·00 2·00

DESIGNS: 10 pf. Refrigerator wagon. 20 pf. Long-distance coach. 25 pf. Tank wagon. 35 pf. Double-deck coach. 85 pf. Tourist coach.

E **473.** "King Lear" (directed by W. Langhoff). E **474.** H. Matern.

1973. Notable Theatrical Productions.

E 1582. E **473.** 10 pf. brn. & pur. 5 5
E 1583. – 25 pf. blue & red 5 5
E 1584. – 35 pf. green, dark green and blue 80 80

DESIGNS: 25 pf. "Midsummer Night's Dream" (Opera) (Benjamin Britten) (directed by W. Felenstein). 35 pf. "Mother Courage" (directed by Berthold Brecht).

1973. Hermann Matern (politician). 80th Birth Anniv.

E 1585. E **474.** 10 pf. red .. 30 5

E **475.** Goethe and House. E **476.** Firework Display.

1973. Cultural Celebrities and Houses in Weimar. Multicoloured.

E 1586. 10 pf. Type E **475** .. 5 5
E 1587. 15 pf. C. M. Wieland (writer) 5 5
E 1588. 20 pf. F. Schiller (writer) 5 5
E 1589. 25 pf. J. G. Herder (writer) 5 5
E 1590. 35 pf. Lucas Cranach the Elder (painter) .. 5 5
E 1591. 50 pf. Franz Liszt (composer) .. .. 1·50 1·50

1973. World Festival of Youth and Students, East Berlin. Multicoloured.

E 1592. 5 pf. Type E **476** .. 5 5
E 1593. 15 pf. Students ("Int. Solidarity") .. 5 5
E 1594. 20 pf. Young workers ("Economic Integration") 5 5
E 1595. 30 pf. Students ("Aid for Young Nations") 1·00 1·00
E 1596. 35 pf. Youth and Students' Emblems .. 8 5

E **477.** W. Ulbricht. E **478.** Power Network.

1973. Death of Walter Ulbricht.

E 1598. E **477.** 20 pf. black .. 15 8

1973. "Peace" United Energy Supply System. 10th Anniv.

E 1599. E **478.** 35 pf. orange, maroon & blue 30 15

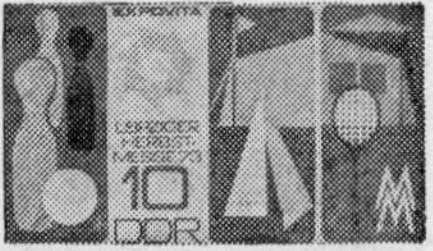

E **479.** "Leisure Activities".

1973. Leipzig Autumn Fair. Multicoloured.

E 1600. 10 pf. E **479** 5 5
E 1601. 25 pf. Yacht, guitar and power drill 20 12

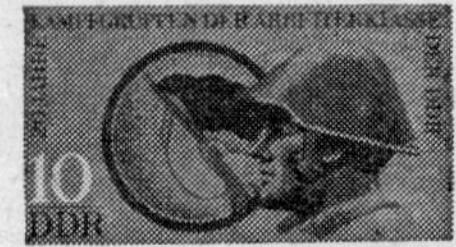

E **480.** Militiaman and Emblem.

1973. Workers Militia. 20th Anniv. Multicoloured.

E 1602. 10 pf. Type E **480** .. 5 5
E 1603. 20 pf. Militia guard .. 15 10

E **481.** Red Flag encircling Globe. E **482.** Langenstein-Zwieberge Memorial.

1973. "Problems of Peace and Socialism", 15th Anniv.

E 1605. E **481.** 20 pf. red & gold 15 8

1974. Langenstein-Zweiberge Monument.

E 1606. E **482.** 25 pf. mult. .. 25 10

E **483.** U.N. H.Q. and Emblems. E **484.** "Young Couple" (G. Glombitza).

1973. Admission of German Democratic Republic to United Nations Organization.

E 1607. E **483.** 35 pf. mult. .. 25 30

1973. Philatelists' Day and 3rd Young Philatelists' Stamp Exhibition, Halle.

E 1608.	E 484.	20 pf.+5 pf. mult.	20	8

E 485. Congress Emblem. E 486. Vietnamese Child.

1973. 8th World Trade Union Congress, Varna, Bulgaria.

E 1609.	E 485.	35 pf. mult. ..	25	15

1973. "Solidarity with Vietnam".

E 1610.	E 486.	10 pf.+5 pf. mult.	12	8

E 487. Soviet Map and Emblem.

1973. Soviet Science and Technology Days. Multicoloured.

E 1611.	10 pf. Launching rocket (vert.)	5	5
E 1612.	20 pf. Type E 487 ..	5	5
E 1613.	25 pf. Oil refinery (vert.)	65	65

E 488. L. Corvalan. E 489. "Child with Doll" (C. L. Vogel).

1973. Solidarity with the Chilean People. Multicoloured.

E 1614.	10 pf.+5 pf. Type E 488	20	15
E 1615.	25 pf.+5 pf. Pres. Allende	35	30

1973. Paintings by Old Masters. Mult.

E 1616.	10 pf. Type E 489 ..	5	5
E 1617.	15 pf. "Madonna with Rose" (Parmigianino)	5	5
E 1618.	20 pf. "Woman with Fair Hair" (Rubens)	5	5
E 1619.	25 pf. "Lady in White" (Titian) ..	5	5
E 1620.	35 pf. "Archimedes" (D. Fetti)	8	8
E 1621.	70 pf. "Flower Arrangement" (Jan D. de Heem)	1·75	1·75

E 490. Flame Emblem. E 491. "Catching the Pike".

1973. Declaration of Human Rights. 25th Anniv.

E 1622.	E 490.	35 pf. multicoloured	25	20

1973. Fairy Tales (8th series). As Type E 491. "At the Bidding of the Pike".

E 1623.	5 pf. multicoloured ..	30	30
E 1624.	10 pf. multicoloured ..	35	35
E 1625.	15 pf. multicoloured ..	30	30
E 1626.	20 pf. molticoloured ..	30	30
E 1627.	25 pf. multicoloured ..	35	35
E 1628.	35 pf. multicoloured ..	30	30

E 492. E. Hoernle. E 493. P. Neruda.

1974. Socialist Personalities.

E 1629.	E 492.	10 pf. grey ..	10	8
E 1630.	–	10 pf. lilac ..	10	8
E 1631.	–	10 pf. blue ..	10	8
E 1632.	–	10 pf. brown ..	10	8
E 1633.	–	10 pf. green ..	10	8
E 1634.	–	10 pf. brown ..	10	8
E 1635.	–	10 pf. blue ..	10	8
E 1636.	–	10 pf. brown ..	10	8

PERSONALITIES: No. 1630, Etkar Andre. No. 1631, Paul Merker. No. 1632, Hermann Duncker. No. 1633, Fritz Heckert. No. 1634, Otto Grotewohl. No. 1635, Wilhelm Florin. No. 1636, Georg Handke.

1974. Pablo Neruda (Chilean poet) Commemoration.

E 1637.	E 493.	20 pf. multicoloured	15	8

E 494. "Comecon" Emblem. E 495. "Echinopsis multiplex".

1974. Council for Mutual Economic Aid. 25th Anniv.

E 1638.	E 494.	20 pf. mult. ..	15	8

1974. Cacti. Multicoloured.

E 1639.	5 pf. Type E 495 ..	5	5
E 1640.	10 pf. "Lobivia haageana"	5	5
E 1641.	15 pf. "Parodia sanguinflora" ..	1·50	1·50
E 1642.	20 pf. "Gymocal monvillei" ..	12	8
E 1643.	25 pf. "Neoporteria rapifera" ..	15	10
E 1644.	35 pf. "Notocactus concinnus" ..	15	10

E 496. Handball Players. E 497. High-tension Testing Plant.

1974. Eighth Men's World Indoor Handball Championships.

E 1645.	E 496.	5 pf. multicoloured	8	8
E 1646.	–	10 pf. multicoloured	15	15
E 1647.	–	35 pf. multicoloured	60	60

Nos. 1645/7 form a composite design of a handball match.

1974. Leipzig Spring Fair. Multicoloured.

E 1648.	10 pf. Type E 497 ..	5	5
E 1649.	25 pf. "Robotron" computer (horiz.) ..	15	12

E 498. "Rhodophyllus sinuatus". E 499. Gustav Kirchhoff.

1974. Poisonous Toadstools. Multicoloured.

E 1650.	5 pf. Type E 498 ..	5	5
E 1651.	10 pf. "Boletus satanas"	5	5
E 1652.	15 pf. "Amanita pantherina"	8	5
E 1653.	20 pf. "Amanita muscaria"	8	5
E 1654.	25 pf. "Gyromitra esculenta"	12	10
E 1655.	30 pf. "Inocybe patouillardii"	15	10
E 1656.	35 pf. "Amanita phalloides"	15	10
E 1657.	40 pf. "Clitocybe dealbata"	1·75	1·75

1974. Celebrities. Birth Anniversaries.

E 1658.	E 499.	5 pf. blk., & grey	5	5
E 1659.	–	10 pf. ultram. & bl.	5	5
E 1660.	–	20 pf. red & pink	8	5
E 1661.	–	25 pf. grn. & turq.	15	10
E 1662.	–	35 pf. choc. & brn.	65	65

PORTRAITS AND ANNIVERSARIES: 5 pf. (physicist, 150th birth anniv.). 10 pf. Immanuel Kant (philosopher, 200th birth anniv.). 20 pf. Elm Welk (writer, 90th birth anniv.). 25 pf. Johann Herder (author, 230th birth anniv.). 35 pf. Lion Feuchtwanger (novelist, 90th birth anniv.).

E 500. Globe and "PEACE".

1974. 1st World Peace Congress. 25th Anniv.

E 1663.	E 500.	35 pf. multicoloured	25	15

E 501. Tractor Driver. E 502. Buk Lighthouse, 1878.

1974. German Democratic Republic. 25th Anniv. Multicoloured.

E 1664.	10 pf. Type 501 ..	5	5
E 1665.	20 pf. Students ..	8	5
E 1666.	25 pf. Woman worker	12	10
E 1667.	35 pf. East German family	95	95

1974. Lighthouses (1st series). Multicoloured.

E 1668.	10 pf. Type E 502 ..	5	5
E 1669.	15 pf. Warnemunde lighthouse, 1898 ..	5	5
E 1670.	20 pf. Darsser Ort lighthouse, 1848 ..	5	5
E 1671.	35 pf. Arkona lighthouse in 1827 and 1902 ..	12	8
E 1672.	40 pf. Greifswalder Oie lighthouse, 1855 ..	1·40	1·40

See also Nos. E 1760/4.

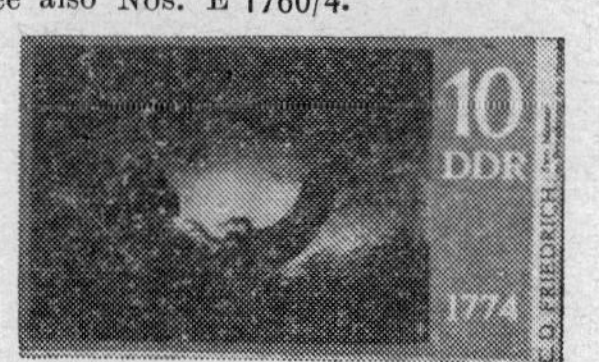

E 503. "Man and Woman watching the Moon" (Friedrich).

1974. Caspar Friedrich (painter). Birth Bicent. Multicoloured.

E 1673.	10 pf. Type E 503 ..	5	5
E 1674.	20 pf. "The Stages of Life" (seaside scene) ..	12	8
E 1675.	25 pf. "Heath near Dresden" ..	1·25	1·25
E 1676.	35 pf. "Trees in the Elbe Valley" ..	15	10

E 504. Lace Pattern. E 505. Horse-jumping.

1974. Plauen Lace.

E 1678.	E 504.	10 pf. vio. & blk.	5	5
E 1679.	–	20 pf. blk., brn. and bistre ..	10	5
E 1680.	–	25 pf. blue & blk.	1·10	1·10
E 1681.	–	35 pf. red & blk.	15	10

DESIGNS: Nos. 1679/81, Lace patterns similar to Type E 504.

1974. Socialist Personalities. As Type E 492.

E 1682.	10 pf. blue	10	10
E 1683.	10 pf. violet	10	10
E 1684.	10 pf. brown	10	10

DESIGNS: No. E 1682, R. Breitscheid. No. E 1683, K. Burger. No. E 1684, C. Moltmann.

1974. Int. Horse-breeders' Congress, Berlin. Multicoloured.

E 1685.	10 pf. Type E 505 ..	5	5
E 1686.	20 pf. horse & trap (horiz.)	5	5
E 1687.	25 pf. Three Haflinger draught horses (horiz.)	85	85
E 1688.	35 pf. Horse-racing—British thoroughbred (horiz.)	20	12

E 506. Mobile Railway Crane.

1974. Leipzig Autumn Fair. Multicoloured.

E 1689.	10 pf. Type E 506 ..	10	5
E 1690.	25 pf. Agricultural machine	20	12

E 507. "The Porcelain Shop". E 509. Old and New Ships.

E 508. Ardestine Caves Memorial, Rome.

1974. "Mon Plaisir". Exhibits in Dolls' Village, Castle Museum, Arnstadt. Multicoloured.

E 1691.	5 pf. Type E 507 ..	5	5
E 1692.	10 pf. "Fairground Crier"	5	5
E 1693.	15 pf. "Wine-tasting in Cellar" ..	5	5
E 1694.	20 pf. "Cooper and Apprentice" ..	5	5
E 1695.	25 pf. "Bagpiper playing for Dancing Bear"	1·40	1·40
E 1696.	35 pf. "Butcher's Wife and Crone" ..	20	15

1974. International War Memorials.

E 1697.	E 508.	35 pf. blk., grn. & red	30	30
E 1698.	–	35 pf. blk., bl. & red	30	30

DESIGN: No. E 1698, Resistance Memorial, Chateaubriant, France.

1974. Universal Postal Union. Cent. Multicoloured.

E 1700.	10 pf. Type E 509 ..	5	5
E 1701.	20 pf. Old and new locomotives ..	5	5
E 1702.	25 pf. Old and new aircraft	12	15
E 1703.	35 pf. Old and new road transport ..	90	90

E 510. "The Revolutionaries" (E. Rossdeutscher). E 511. "The Sun shines for all".

1974. "DDR 74" Stamp Exhibition. Sculptures in Karl-Marx-Stadt. Each black, bistre and green.

E 1704.	10 pf.+5 pf. Type E 510	20	20
E 1705.	20 pf. "The Dialectics"	25	25
E 1706.	25 pf. "The Party" ..	30	30

1974. Children's Paintings. Mult.

E 1707.	20 pf. Type E 511 ..	25	25
E 1708.	20 pf. "My Friend Sascha" ..	25	25
E 1709.	20 pf. "Carsten the Best Swimmer" ..	25	25
E 1710.	20 pf. "Me and the Blackboard" ..	25	25

E 512. "The Woodchopper". E 514. Banded Jasper.

1974. Fairy Tales (9th series). "Twittering To and Fro".

E 1711. E **512**. 10 pf. mult. .. 30 30
E 1712. – 15 pf. mult. .. 35 35
E 1713. – 20 pf. mult. .. 30 30
E 1714. – 30 pf. mult. .. 30 30
E 1715. – 35 pf. mult .. 35 35
E 1716. – 40 pf. mult. .. 30 30

DESIGNS: Nos. E 1712/6, Scenes from "Twittering To and Fro" fairy tale, similar to Type E **512**.

E **513**. "Still Life" (R. Paris).

1974. Paintings in Berlin Museums. Multicoloured.

E 1717. 10 pf. Type E **513** .. 5 5
E 1718. 15 pf. "Girl in Meditation" (W. Lachnit) (vert.) 8 5
E 1719. 20 pf. "Fisherman's House" (H. Hackenbeck) (vert.) 8 5
E 1720. 35 pf. "Girl in Red" (R. Bergander) .. 15 8
E 1721. 70 pf. "Parents" (W. Sitte) (vert.) .. 1·60 1·60

1974. Gem-stones in Freiberg Mining Academy Collection. Multicoloured.

E 1722. 10 pf. Type E **514** .. 5 5
E 1723. 15 pf. Smoky quartz .. 8 5
E 1724. 20 pf. Topaz 8 5
E 1725. 25 pf. Amethyst .. 12 5
E 1726. 35 pf. Aquamarine .. 15 5
E 1727. 70 pf. Agate .. .. 2·00 1·90

E **515**. M. Arendsee.

E **516**. "Forced Labour".

1975. Martha Arendsee (Socialist worker). 90th Birth Anniv.

E 1728. E **575**. 10 pf. red .. 5 5

1975. Peasant's War. 450th Anniv.

E 1729. E **516**. 5 pf. green, black and grey .. 5 5
E 1730. – 10 pf. brown, blk. and grey .. 12 12
E 1731. – 20 pf. blk. & grey 25 25
E 1732. – 25 pf. yellow, blk. and grey .. 30 30
E 1733. – 35 pf. brown, blk. and grey .. 40 40
E 1734. – 50 pf. blk. & grey 65 65

DESIGNS: 10 pf. "Paying Tithe". 20 pf. Thomas Muntzer (leader). 25 pf. "Armed Peasants". 35 pf. "Liberty" flag. 50 pf. Peasants on trial.

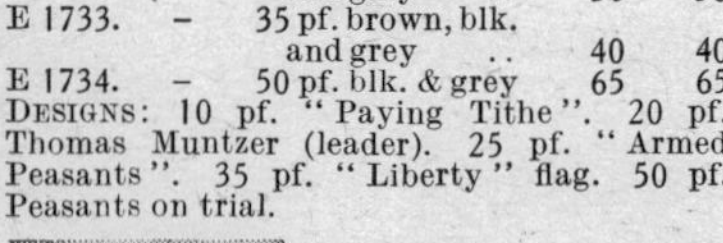

E **517**. "Women of Various Nations". E **518**. Pentakta "A-100" Microfilm Camera.

1975. International Women's Year.

E 1735. E **517**. 10 pf. mult. .. 25 25
E 1736. – 20 pf. mult. .. 25 25
E 1737. – 25 pf. mult. .. 30 30

DESIGNS: 20 pf., 25 pf. Similar to Type E **517**.

1975. Leipzig Spring Fair. Multicoloured.

E 1738. 10 pf. Type E **518** .. 5 5
E 1739. 25 pf. "Sket" Cement Factory 15 8

E **519**. Hans Otto (actor). E **520**. Parrots.

1975. Celebrities' Birth Anniversaries. Portraits.

E 1740. E **519**. 5 pf. blue .. 5 5
E 1741. – 10 pf. red .. 5 5
E 1742. – 20 pf. green .. 5 5
E 1743. – 25 pf. brown .. 10 5
E 1744. – 35 pf. blue .. 90 90

PORTRAITS AND ANNIVERSARIES: 5 pf. (75th birth anniv.). 10 pf. Thomas Mann, author (100th anniv.). 20 pf. Dr. A. Schweitzer (100th anniv.). 25 pf. Michelangelo (500th anniv.). 35 pf. Andre-Marie Ampere, scientist (200th anniv.).

1975. Zoo Animals. Multicoloured.

E 1745. 5 pf. Type E **520** .. 5 5
E 1746. 10 pf. Orang-utans .. 5 5
E 1747. 15 pf. Siberian Ibex .. 5 5
E 1748. 20 pf. Rhinoceros (horiz.) 5 5
E 1749. 25 pf. Dwarf hippopotamus (horiz.) .. 10 8
E 1750. 30 pf. Seal and pup (horiz.) 12 10
E 1751. 35 pf. Siberian tiger (horiz.) 15 12
E 1752. 50 pf. Boehm's zebra 1·75 1·75

E **521**. Serviceman, "Industry" and "Agriculture".

1975. Signing of Warsaw Treaty. 20th Anniv.

E 1753. E **521** 20 pf. multicoloured 12 5

E **522**. Soviet Memorial, Treptow. E **523**. Banners and Emblems.

1975. Liberation. 30th Anniv. Multicoloured.

E 1754. 10 pf. Type E **522** .. 5 5
E 1755. 20 pf. "Man" (Buchenwald) (detail) .. 8 5
E 1756. 25 pf. "Woman" (Buchenwald) (detail) 12 8
E 1757. 55 pf. "Economic Integration" (statues at Orenburg) .. 85 85

1975. 3rd Youth Friendship Festival, Halle.

E 1759. E **523** 10 pf. multicoloured 5 5

1975. Lighthouses (2nd series). As Type E **502**. Multicoloured.

E 1760. 5 pf. Timmendorf lighthouse, 1872 .. 5 5
E 1761. 10 pf. Gellenlighthouse, 1905 .. .. 5 5
E 1762. 20 pf. Sassnitz Pier lighthouse, 1904 .. 5 5
E 1763. 25 pf. Dornbusch lighthouse, 1888 .. 10 8
E 1764. 35 pf. Peenemunde lighthouse, 1954 .. 95 95

E **524**. W. Liebknecht and A. Bebel. E **525**. "Scientific Co-operation" (mosaic allegory by Womacka).

1975. Gotha Unity Congress. Cent. Mult.

E 1765. 10 pf. Type E **524** .. 12 12
E 1766. 20 pf. Tivoli building, Gotha, and title-page of Minutes 20 20
E 1767. 25 pf. Marx and Engels 30 30

1975. Eisenhuettenstadt. 25th Anniv.

E 1768. E **525**. 20 pf. multicoloured 12 5

E **526**. Construction Workers. E **527**. Paulus Schuster's Automatic Clock (1585).

1975. Free German Trade Unions Association. 30th Anniv.

E 1769. E **526**. 20 pf. multicoloured 15 5

1975. Ancient Clocks. Multicoloured.

E 1770. 5 pf. Type **527** .. 5 5
E 1771. 10 pf. Astronomical mantlepiece clock (Augsburg master, c. 1560) 5 5
E 1772. 15 pf. Hans Schlotteim's automatic clock (c. 1600) .. .. 1·60 1·60
E 1773. 20 pf. Johann H. Kohler's mantlepiece clock (c. 1720) 5 5
E 1774. 25 pf. Johann H. Kohler's mantlepiece clock (c. 1700) 10 5
E 1775. 35 pf. Johannes H. Klein's astronomical clock (1738) 15 12

E **528**. Jacob and Wilhelm Grimm's German Dictionary.

1975. Academy of Sciences. 275th Anniv.

E 1776. 10 pf. Type E **528** .. 5 5
E 1777. 20 pf. Karl Schwarzschildt Observatory, Tautenburg .. 5 5
E 1778. 25 pf. Electron microscope and chemical plant 12 5
E 1779. 35 pf. "Interkosmos 10" satellite .. 95 95

E **529**. Runner with Torch. E **530**. Map of Europe.

1975. 5th National Youth Sports Centre.

E 1780. E **529**. 10 pf. bld. & pink 5 5
E 1781. – 20 pf. blk. & yell. 5 5
E 1782. – 25 pf. blk. & blue 10 5
E 1783. – 35 pf. blk. & green 95 95

DESIGNS: 20 pf. Hurdling. 25 pf. Swimming. 35 pf. Gymnastics.

1975. Security and Co-operation Conference, Helsinki.

E 1784. E **530**. 20 pf. multicoloured 12 5

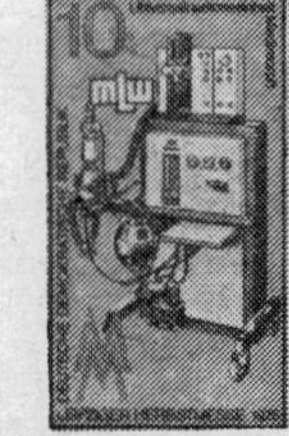

E **531**. Asters. E **532**. "Medimorph" Anaesthetizing Machine.

1975. German Flora. Multicoloured.

E 1785. 5 pf. Type E **531** .. 5 5
E 1786. 10 pf. Pelargoniums .. 5 5
E 1787. 20 pf. Gerberas .. 5 5
E 1788. 25 pf. Carnation .. 10 8
E 1789. 35 pf. Chrysanthemum 15 12
E 1790. 70 pf. Pansies .. 1·90 1·90

1975. Leipzig Autumn Fair. Multicoloured.

E 1791. 10 pf. E **532** 8 5
E 1792. 25 pf. Zschopau "TS-250" motor-cycle (horiz.) 20 12

E **533**. Children's Crossing.

1975. People's Police. Traffic Supervision. Multicoloured.

E 1793. 10 pf. Type E **533** .. 5 5
E 1794. 15 pf. Point-duty policewoman .. 1·25 1·25
E 1795. 20 pf. Policeman assisting motorist .. 5 5
E 1796. 25 pf. Checking motor vehicles 10 5
E 1797. 35 pf. Instruction in traffic code 15 12

E **534**. Launch of "Soyuz". E **535**. Solidarity Motif.

1975. "Apollo-Soyuz" Space Link. Multicoloured.

E 1798. 10 pf. Type E **534** .. 5 5
E 1799. 20 pf. Spacecraft manoeuvring 5 5
E 1800. 70 pf. Spacecraft docked (80 × 29 mm.) .. 1·40 1·40

1975. "International Solidarity".

E 1801. E **535**. 10 pf. + 5 pf. blk, olive and red 8 5

E **536**. Merian's View of Weimar, c. 1650.

1975. Weimar. Millenary. Multicoloured.

E 1802. 10 pf. Type E **536** .. 5 5
E 1803. 20 pf. Buchenwald Memorial (vert.) .. 5 5
E 1804. 35 pf. Ancient and modern Weimar .. 60 60

E **537**. Vienna Memorial. E **538**. Louis Braille.

1975. Patriots Monument, Vienna.

E 1805. E **537**. 35 pf. multicoloured 20 5

1975. International Braille Year. Multicoloured.

E 1806. 20 pf. Type E **538** .. 5 5
E 1807. 35 pf. Hands "reading" braille 15 10
E 1808. 50 pf. Eye diagram, eye shade and safety goggles. .. 1·10 1·10

E **539**. Post Office Gate, Wurzen.

1975. Philatelists' Day. Multicoloured.
E 1809. 10 pf.+5 pf. Type E **539** 30 30
E 1810. 20 pf. New Post Office, Barenfels 5 5

E **540.** Hans Christian Andersen and scene from " The Emperor's New Clothes ".

(Actual size 70×25 mm).

1975. Fairy Tales (10th series). " The Emperor's New Clothes ".
E 1811. E **540.** 20 pf. multicoloured 25 25
E 1812. – 35 pf. multicoloured 50 50
E 1813. – 50 pf. multicoloured 65 65
DESIGNS: 35, 50 pf. Different scenes.

E **541.** Mass Tobogganing.

1975. Winter Olympic Games, Innsbruck (1976). Multicoloured.
E 1814. 5 pf. Type E **541** .. 5 5
E 1815. 10 pf.+5 pf. Bobsleigh course 8 5
E 1816. 20 pf. Speed-skating rink 8 5
E 1817. 25 pf.+5 pf. Ski-jump 15 12
E 1818. 35 pf. Ice sports hall .. 15 12
E 1819. 70 pf. Mass skiing .. 1·90 1·90

E **542.** W. Pieck.

E **543.** Organ in Rotha, Leipzig.

1975. President Pieck. Birth Centenary.
E 1821. E **542.** 10 pf. black & blue 5 5

1976. Members of German Workers' Movement. As Type E **542.**
E 1822. 10 pf. black and red .. 8 8
E 1823. 10 pf. black and green 8 8
E 1824. 10 pf. black and brown 8 8
E 1825. 10 pf. black and lilac .. 8 8
PORTRAITS: No. E 1822, Ernst Thalmann. No. E 1823, George Schumann. No. E 1824, Wilhelm Koenen. No. E 1825, John Schehr.

1976. Organs by Gottfried Silbermann. Multicoloured.
E 1826. 10 pf. Type E **543** .. 5 5
E 1827. 20 pf. Freiberg .. 8 5
E 1828. 35 pf. Fraureuth .. 12 10
E 1829. 50 pf. Dresden .. 1·25 1·25

E **544.** Servicemen and Emblem.

1976. National People's Forces (NVA). 20th Anniv. Multicoloured.
E 1831. 10 pf. Type E **544** .. 8 5
E 1832. 20 pf. N.V.A. Equipment 15 10

E **545.** Telephone Hand-set.

E **546.** Tenement Building, Leipzig.

1976. First Telephone Transmission. Cent.
E 1833. E **545.** 20 pf. blue .. 12 5

1976. Leipzig Spring Fair. Multicoloured.
E 1834. 10 pf. Type E **546** .. 8 5
E 1835. 25 pf. Deep-sea " factory " trawler 20 12

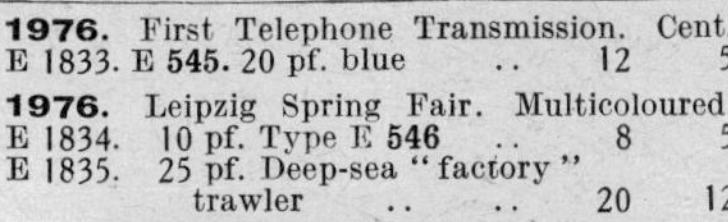

E **547.** Palace of the Republic, Berlin.

1976. Palace of the Republic, Berlin. Inauguration.
E 1836. E **547.** 10 pf. mult. .. 5 5

E **548.** Satellite Tracking Equipment.

E **549.** Marx, Engels, Lenin and Party Emblem.

1976. " Intersputnik ".
E 1837. E **548.** 20 pf. mult. .. 12 5

1976. 9th Party Day of Socialist Unity Party. Mult.
E 1838. 10 pf. Type E **549** .. 12 5
E 1839. 20 pf. Industrial plant, blocks of flats and party emblem (horiz.) 20 12

E **550.** Cycling.

1976. Olympic Games, Montreal. Mult.
E 1841. 5 pf. Type E **550** .. 5 5
E 1842. 10 pf.+5 pf. Swimming-pool, Leipzig .. 5 5
E 1843. 20 pf. Town Hall and Swimming-pool, Suhl 5 5
E 1844. 25 pf. Brandenburg Regatta course .. 10 5
E 1845. 35 pf.+10 pf. Rifle-range, Suhl 20 15
E 1846. 70 pf. Athletics .. 1·90 1·90

E **551.** Riband forming " X ".

1976. 10th Youth Parliament, East Berlin. Multicoloured.
E 1848. 10 pf. Type E **551** .. 10 5
E 1849. 20 pf. Youth members 25 12

E **552.** " Himantoglossum hircinum ".

E **554.** Marx, Engels and Lenin.

E **553.** " Shetland Pony " (H. Drake).

1976. East German Orchids. Multicoloured.
E 1850. 10 pf. Type E **552** .. 5 5
E 1851. 20 pf. " Dactylorhiza incarnata " 10 5
E 1852. 25 pf. " Anacamptis pyramidalis " .. 12 5
E 1853. 35 pf. " Dactylorhiza sambucina " .. 15 12
E 1854. 40 pf. " Orchis coriophora " 20 15
E 1855. 60 pf. " Cypripedium calceolus " .. .. 2·25 2·25

1976. Statuettes. East Berlin Museums.
E 1856. E **553.** 10 pf. blk. & blue 5 5
E 1857. – 20 pf. blk. & orge. 10 5
E 1858. – 25 pf. blk. & brn. 12 5
E 1859. – 35 pf. blk. & grn. 15 12
E 1860. – 50 pf. blk. & brn. 2·00 2·00
STATUETTES—VERT. 20 pf. " Tanzpause " (W. Arnold); 25 pf. " Am Strand " (L. Englehardt); 35 pf. " Herman Ducker " (W. Howard); 50 pf. " Das Gesprach " (G. Weidanz).

1976. Communist Parties' Congress.
E 1861. E **554.** 20 pf. mult. .. 25 5

E **555.** State Carriage, 1790.

1976. Historic Coaches. Multicoloured.
E 1862. 10 pf. Type E **555** .. 5 5
E 1863. 20 pf. Russian trap, 1800 8 5
E 1864. 25 pf. Court landau, 1840 10 5
E 1865. 35 pf. Court carriage, 1860 .. .. .. 15 12
E 1866. 40 pf. Stagecoach, circa 1850 .. .. .. 20 15
E 1867. 50 pf. Town carriage, 1889 .. .. .. 2·50 2·50

E **556.** View of Gera, circa 1652.

1976. National Philatelist's Day. Gera. Multicoloured.
E 1868. 10 pf.+5 pf. Type E **556** 25 25
E 1869. 20 pf. View of Gera, 1976 35 35

E **557.** Boxer.

1976. Domestic Dogs. Multicoloured.
E 1870. 5 pf. Type E **557** .. 5 5
E 1871. 10 pf. Airedale Terrier 5 5
E 1872. 20 pf. Alsatian .. 5 5
E 1873. 25 pf. Collie 12 10
E 1874. 35 pf. Schnauzer .. 15 12
E 1875. 70 pf. Great Dane .. 3·00 3·00

E **558.** Oil Refinery.

1976. Autumn Fair, Leipzig. Multicoloured.
E 1876. 10 pf. Type E **558** .. 10 5
E 1877. 25 pf. Library, Leipzig 25 15

E **559.** Templin Lake Bridge.

1976. East German Bridges. Multicoloured.
E 1878. 10 pf. Type E **559** .. 5 5
E 1879. 15 pf. Adlergestell Bridge, Berlin 5 5
E 1880. 20 pf. Elbe River Bridge, Rosslau 8 8
E 1881 25 pf. Goltzschtal Viaduct 12 12
E 1882. 35 pf. Elbe River Bridge, Magdeburg 15 15
E 1883. 50 pf. Grosser Dreesch Bridge, Scherwin .. 2·75 2·75

E **560.** Memorial Figures.

1976. Budapest Memorial.
E 1884. E **560.** 35 pf. mult. .. 30 15

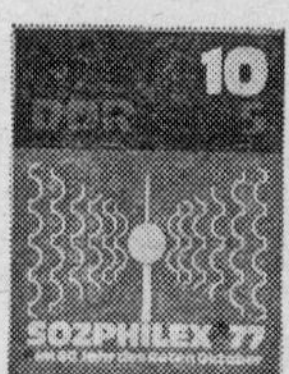

E **561.** Brass Jug.

E **562.** Berlin T.V. Tower.

1976. Historic Objects d'Art, Koepenic Castle Museum, Berlin. Multicoloured.
E 1885. 10 pf. Type E **561** .. 5 5
E 1886. 20 pf. Covered vase, circa 1710 .. .. 8 8
E 1887. 25 pf. Meisen porcelain fruit dish, circa 1768 12 12
E 1888. 35 pf. Basket-carrier silver statuette, circa 1700 15 15
E 1889. 70 pf. Art nouveau glass vase, circa 1900 .. 2·25 2·25

1976. " Sozphilex 77 " Stamp Exhibition, East Berlin.
E 1890. E **562.** 10 pf.+5 pf. blue and red .. 5 5

OFFICIAL STAMPS

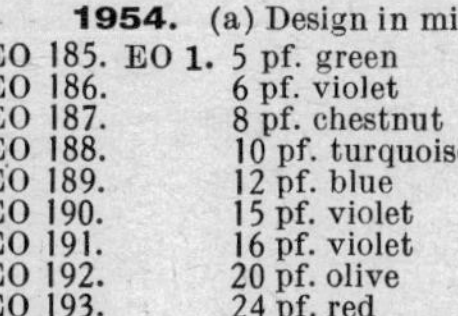

EO **1.** (Projects to left.)

EO **2.** (Projects to right.)

EO **3.**

1954. (a) Design in minute dots.
EO 185. EO **1.** 5 pf. green .. — 5
EO 186. 6 pf. violet .. — 35
EO 187. 8 pf. chestnut .. — 8
EO 188. 10 pf. turquoise .. — 5
EO 189. 12 pf. blue .. — 5
EO 190. 15 pf. violet .. — 5
EO 191. 16 pf. violet .. — 15
EO 192. 20 pf. olive .. — 5
EO 193. 24 pf. red .. — 8
EO 194. 25 pf. green .. — 10
EO 195. 30 pf. brown-red — 15
EO 196. 40 pf. red .. — 8
EO 197. 48 pf. lilac .. — 2·75
EO 198. 50 pf. lilac .. — 10
EO 199. 60 pf. blue .. — 25
EO 200. 70 pf. brown .. — 20
EO 201. 84 pf. brown .. — 7·00

(b) Design in lines.
EO 202. EO **2.** 5 pf. green .. — 5
EO 203. 10 pf. turquoise .. — 5
EO 204. 12 pf. blue .. — 5
EO 205. 15 pf. violet .. — 5
EO 206. 20 pf. olive .. — 5
EO 212. EO **1.** 20 pf. olive .. — 5
EO 207. EO **2.** 25 pf. green .. — 45
EO 208. 30 pf. brown-red — 1·50
EO 209. 40 pf. red .. — 5
EO 210. 50 pf. lilac .. — 8
EO 211. 70 pf. brown .. — 20

1956. For internal use.
EO 257. EO **3.** 5 pf. black .. — 1·00
EO 258. 10 pf. black .. — 15
EO 259. 20 pf. black .. — 8
EO 260. 40 pf. black .. — 60
EO 261. 70 pf. black .. — 32·00

Nos. EO 185/261 were not on sale to the public in unused condition, although specimens of all values are available on the market.

Used prices for Nos. EO 257/61 are for cancelled-to-order copies. Postally used stamps are in general worth much more.

REGISTRATION STAMPS

SELF-SERVICE POST OFFICE

These registration labels embody a face value to cover the registration fee and have franking value to this extent. They are issued in pairs from automatic machines together with a certificate of posting against a 50 pf. coin. The stamps are serially numbered in pairs and inscribed with the name of the town of issue.

The procedure is to affix one label to the letter (already franked with stamps for carriage of the letter) and complete page 1 of the certificate of posting which is then placed in the box provided together with the letter. The duplicate label is affixed to the second page of the certificate and retained for production as evidence in the event of a claim.

They are not obtainable over the post office counter.

ER 1.

1967.
ER 992. ER 1. 50 pf. red & black 1·25

ER 2.

1968.
ER 993. ER 2. 50 pf. red .. 55
Unused prices are for pairs.

ER 3.

1968. For Parcel Post.
ER 1089. ER 3. 50 pf. black .. 90

GHADAMES O3

A caravan halting place in the Libyan desert, under French administration from 1943 until 1951 when the area reverted to Libya.

1. Cross of Agadem.

ILLUSTRATIONS
British Commonwealth and all overprints and surcharges are FULL SIZE. Foreign Countries have been reduced to ¾-LINEAR.

1949.
1. 1. 4 f. brown and lilac (post.) 12 12
2. 5 f. green and blue .. 15 15
3. 8 f. brown and orange .. 55 35
4. 10 f. black and blue .. 60 50
5. 12 f. violet and mauve .. 1·60 1·10
6. 15 f. brown and orange .. 1·40 1·10
7. 20 f. brown and emerald 1·40 1·10
8. 25 f. brown and blue .. 1·40 1·10
9. 50 f. purple and red (air) 2·00 2·00
10. 100 f. brown .. .. 2·25 2·25

GHANA BC

Formerly the Br. Colony of Gold Coast. Attained Dominion status on 6 March, 1957, and became a republic within the Br. Commonwealth in 1960.

1965. 100 pesewas = 1 cedi.
1967. 100 new pesewas = 1 new cedi.
1972. 100 pesewas = 1 cedi = 0·8 (old) new cedi.

NOTE. CANCELLED REMAINDERS

In 1961 remainders of some issues of 1957 to 1960 were put on the market cancelled-to-order in such a way as to be indistinguishable from genuine postally used copies for all practical purposes. Our used quotations which are indicated by an asterisk are, therefore, for cancelled-to-order copies.

8. Dr. Kwame Nkrumah, Fish Eagle and Map of Africa.

1957. Independence Commem.
166. 8. 2d. red 5 5*
167. 2½d. green 5 5*
168. 4d. brown 5 5*
169. 1s. 3d. blue 15 5*

1957. Queen Elizabeth stamps of 1952 of Gold Coast optd. **GHANA INDEPENDENCE 6TH MARCH 1957.**
170. ½d. brown and red .. 5 5*
171. 1d. blue 5 5*
172. 1½d. green 10 5*
173. 2d. brown 12 10
174. 2½d. red 15 15
175. 3d. magenta 5 5*
176. 4d. blue 50 50
177. 6d. black and orange .. 8 5*
178. 1s. black and red .. 12 5*
179. 2s. olive and red .. 25 10*
180. 5s. purple and black .. 60 25*
181. 10s. black and olive .. 1·00 50*

9. Viking Ship.

1957. Black Star Shipping Line. Inaug.
182. 9. 2½d. green 10 10
183. – 1s. 3d. blue 25 30
184. – 5s. purple .. .. 1·10 1·25
DESIGNS—HORIZ. 1s. 3d. Galleon. 5s. M.V. "Volta River".

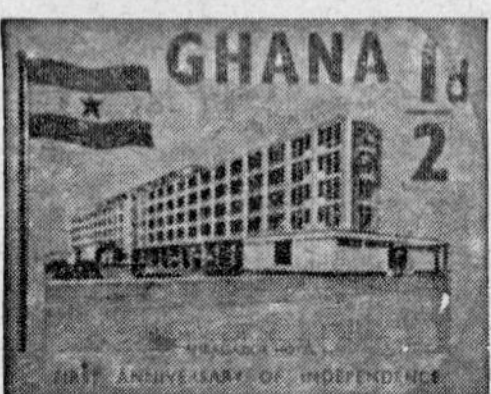

DESIGNS—HORIZ. 2½d. State Opening of Parliament. 1s. 3d. National Monument. VERT. 2s. Ghana Coat of Arms.

10. Ambassador Hotel, Accra.

1958. Independence. 1st Anniv. Flag and Coat of Arms in national colours.
185. 10. ½d. black and red .. 5 5
186. – 2½d. black, red & yellow 5 5
187. – 1s. 3d. black and blue .. 15 15
188. – 2s. yellow and black .. 25 40

11. Map showing the Independent African States.

12. Map of Africa and Flaming Torch.

1958. Independent African States, Accra. 1st Conf. Star in black and yellow.
189. 11. 2½d. red and yellow .. 5 5
190. 3d. green and brown .. 5 5
191. 12. 1s. blue, yellow & orge. 12 15
192. 2s. 6d. pur., yell. & orge. 30 40

13. Eagle over Globe.

DESIGNS — HORIZ. As T 14: 1s. 3d. "Britannia" airliner. As T 13: 2s. 6d. Fish Eagle and jet aircraft.

14. "Stratocruiser" and Albatross.

1958. Inaug. of Ghana Airways. Inscr. as in T 13/14.
193. 13. 2½d. black, bistre and red (postage) .. 5 5
194. – 1s. 3d. blue, black, red, yellow & green (air) .. 15 15
195. 14. 2s. black, blue, red, yell. and green .. 20 25
196. – 2s. 6d. black and bistre 25 30

1958. Prime Minister's Visit to United States and Canada. Optd. **PRIME MINISTER'S VISIT. U.S.A. AND CANADA.**
197. 8. 2d. red 5 5
198. 2½d. green 5 5
199. 4d. brown 5 8
200. 1s. 3d. blue 15 15

15. 16. Dr. Nkrumah and Lincoln Statue, Washington.

1958. United Nations Day.
201. 15. 2½d. choc., grn. & black 5 5
202. 1s. 3d. choc., bl. & blk. 12 12
203. 2s. 6d. choc., vio. & blk. 25 30

1959. Abraham Lincoln. 150th Birth Anniv.
204. 16. 2½d. pink and purple .. 5 5
205. 1s. 3d. light blue & blue 12 12
206. 2s. 6d. yellow and olive 30 30

17. Talking Drums and Elephant-horn Blower.

1959. Independence. Inscr. "SECOND ANNIVERSARY OF INDEPENDENCE".
207. – ½d. multicoloured .. 5 5
208. 17. 2½d. multicoloured .. 5 5
209. – 1s. 3d. multicoloured .. 12 12
210. – 2s. multicoloured .. 25 30

DESIGNS—HORIZ. ½d. Kente cloth and traditional symbols. 2s. Map of Africa, Ghana flag and palms. VERT. 1s. 3d. "Symbol of Greeting".

18. Globe and Flags.

1959. Africa Freedom Day.
211. 18. 2½d. multicoloured .. 5 5
212. 8½d. multicoloured .. 15 15

19. Nkrumah Statue, Accra.  20. Ghana Timber.

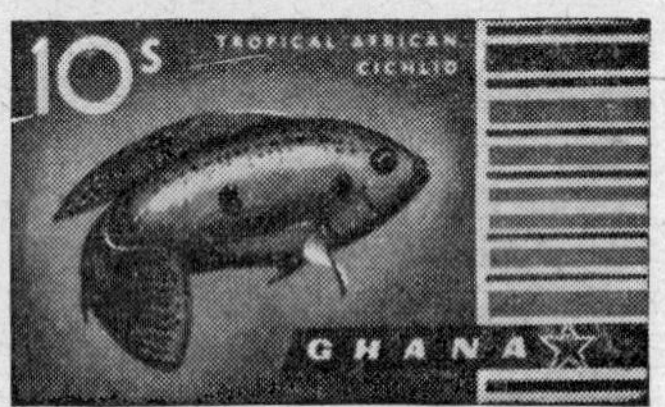

21. Tropical African Cichlid.

1959. Multicoloured.
213. ½d. "God's Omnipotence" (postage) 5 5
213a. ½d. "Gye Nayme" .. 5 5
214. 1d. T 19 .. .. .. 5 5
215. 1½d. T 20 .. .. 5 5
216. 2d. Volta River 5 5
217. 2½d. Cocoa bean .. 5 5
218. 3d. "God's Omnipotence" 5 5
218a. 3d. "Gye Nyame" .. 5 5
219. 4d. Diamond and mine .. 5 5
220. 6d. Fire-crowned Bishop (bird) 8 5
221. 11d. Golden spider lily .. 12 8
222. 1s. Shell ginger 12 5
223. 2s. 6d. Giant plantain eater 30 25
224. 5s. Tiger orchid 60 50
225. 10s. T 21 .. .. .. 1·50 80
225a. £1 Leaping antelope .. 3·50 3·25
226. 1s. 3d. Pennant-winged nightjar (air) 12 10
227. 2s. Crowned cranes .. 20 20
SIZES—HORIZ. As T 19 ½d. As T 20: 2d., 2½d., 3d., 4d., 6d., 1s. 3d., 2s. 6d. As T 21: £1. VERT. As T 20: 11d., 1s., 2s., 5s. The 3d. is a different symbolic design from the ½d.

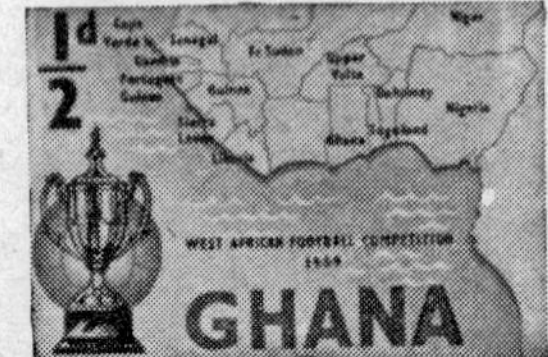

22. Gold Cup and West African Map.

1959. West African Football Competition, 1959. Multicoloured.
228. ½d. T 22 .. .. .. 5 5*
229. 1d. Footballers 5 5*
230. 3d. Goalkeeper saving ball 5 5*
231. 8d. Forward attacking goal 15 10
232. 2s. 6d. "Kwame Nkrumah" Gold Cup 35 30*
Nos. 229 and 232 are vert. and the rest horiz.

23. Duke of Edinburgh and Arms of Ghana.

1959. Visit of the Duke of Edinburgh.
233. 23. 3d. black and magenta 5 5*

24. Ghana Flag and Talking Drums.

1959. U.N. Trusteeship Council. Multicoloured.
234. 3d. Type 24 .. .. 5 5*
235. 6d. Ghana flag and U.N. emblem 8 8*
236. 1s. 3d. As 6d. but emblem above flag 15 12*
237. 2s. 6d. "Totem pole" .. 30 30
Nos. 235/7 are vert.

25. Eagles in Flight.

1960. Independence. 3rd Anniv. Multicoloured.
238. ½d. Type 25 .. .. 5 5*
239. 3d. Fireworks 5 5*
240. 1s. 3d. Figure "3" & dove 15 12*
241. 2s. "Ship of State" .. 25 25*

26. Flags and Map forming letter "A".

1960. African Freedom Day. Flags multicoloured.
242. 26. 3d. black, red and green 5 5*
243. – 6d. black and red .. 8 5*
244. – 1s. black, red and blue .. 12 10
DESIGNS: Flags forming letter "f" (6d.) and "d" (1s.).

27. Dr. Nkrumah.

1960. Republic Day. Inscr. "REPUBLIC DAY 1st JULY 1960". Multicoloured.
245. 3d. T 27 .. .. .. 5 5
246. 1s. 3d. Ghana Flag .. 12 12
247. 2s. Torch of Freedom .. 25 25
248. 10s. Ghana Arms .. .. 1·10 1·25
The 10s. is horiz. and the rest vert.

28. Athlete.

1960. Olympic Games.
249. – 3d. multicoloured .. 5 5
250. – 6d. multicoloured .. 5 5
251. 28. 1s. 3d. multicoloured .. 15 20
252. 2s. 6d. multicoloured .. 30 25
DESIGN—VERT. 3d., 6d. Olympic torch.

29. Pres. Nkrumah.

1960. Founder's Day. Inscr. as in T 29.
253. 29. 3d. multicoloured .. 5 5
254. – 6d. multicoloured .. 8 5
255. – 1s. 3d. multicoloured .. 20 15
DESIGNS—VERT. 6d. Pres. Nkrumah within star. 1s. 3d. Map of Africa and column.

30. U.N. Emblem and Ghana Flag.

1960. Human Rights Day.
256. 30. 3d. multicoloured .. 5 5
257. – 6d. yellow, black & blue 8 5
258. – 1s. 3d. multicoloured .. 30 15
DESIGNS U.N. Emblem with torch (6d.) or within laurel (1s. 3d.).

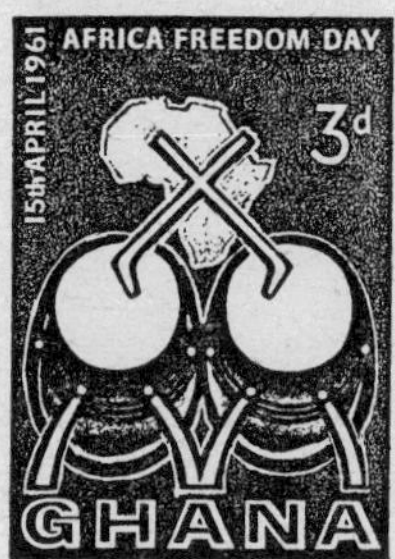

31. Talking Drums.

1961. Africa Freedom Day. Inscr. "15th APRIL 1961".
259. 31. 3d. multicoloured .. 5 5
260. – 6d. red, black and green 8 5
261. – 2s. multicoloured .. 30 25
DESIGNS—VERT. 6d. Map of Africa. HORIZ. 2s. Flags and map.

32. Eagle over Column.

1961. Republic. 1st Anniv. Inscr. "1st JULY 1961". Multicoloured.
262. 3d. T 32 .. .. .. 5 5
263. 1s. 3d. "Flower" .. 15 12
264. 2s. Ghana flags. 30 25

33. Dove with Olive Branch.

DESIGNS—HORIZ 1s. 3d. World map, chain and olive branch. 5s. Rostrum, Conference room.

1961. Belgrade Conf.
265. 33. 3d. green 8 8
266. – 1s. 3d. blue 20 20
267. – 5s. purple 70 85

34. Pres. Nkrumah and Globe.

1961. Founder's Day. Multicoloured.
268. 3d. Type 34 .. .. 5 5
269. 1s. 3d. Pres. in Kente cloth 20 20
270. 5s. Pres. in national costume 80 85
Nos. 269/70 are vert.

35. Queen Elizabeth II and African Map.

1961. Royal Visit.
271. 35. 3d. multicoloured .. 5 5
272. 1s. 3d. multicoloured .. 20 20
273. 5s. multicoloured .. 80 85

36. Ships in Tema Harbour.

1962. Opening of Tema Harbour.
274. 36. 3d. multicoloured (post) 5 5
275. – 1s. 3d. multicoloured (air) 15 15
276. – 2s. 6d. multicoloured .. 35 40
DESIGN 1s. 3d., 2s. 6d. Aircraft and ships at Tema.

37. Africa and Peace Dove.

1962. Casablanca Conf. 1st Anniv.
277. 37. 3d. multicoloured (post.) 5 5
278. 1s. 3d. multicoloured (air) 12 12
279. 2s. 6d. multicoloured .. 25 25

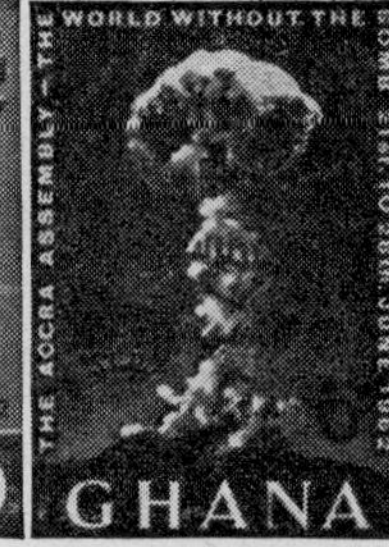

38. Compass over Africa.
39. Atomic Bomb-burst Skull.

1962. Africa Freedom Day.
280. 38. 3d. sepia, turq. & purple 5 5
281. 6d. sepia, turq. & chest. 8 5
282. 1s. 3d. sepia, turq. & red 20 20

1962. The Accra Assembly.
283. – 3d. black and lake .. 5 5
284. 39. 6d. black and red .. 10 10
285. – 1s. 3d. turquoise .. 25 25
DESIGNS: 3d. Ghana Star over "five continents". 1s. 3d. Dove of Peace.

40. Patrice Lumumba.

1962. Lumumba. 1st Death Anniv.
286. 40. 3d. black and yellow .. 5 5
287. 6d. black, green & lake 8 8
288. 1s. 3d. blk., pink & grn. 15 20

41. Star over Two Columns.

1962. Republic. 2nd Anniv. Inscr. "1st JULY 1962". Multicoloured.
289. 3d. T 41 .. .. .. 5 5
290. 6d. Flaming torch .. 8 8
291. 1s. 3d. Eagle trailing flag .. 25 20
The 1s. 3d. is horiz.

42. President Nkrumah.

DESIGNS: 3d. Nkrumah Medallion. 1s. 3d. President and Ghana Star. 2s. Laying "Ghana" brick.

1962. Founder's Day.
292. 42. 1d. blk., red, grn. & yell. 5 5
293. – 3d. orange, black, red, green, yellow & cream 5 5
294. – 1s. 3d. black and blue .. 15 15
295. – 2s. black, red, ol. & yell. 25 25

43. Campaign Emblem. **44.** Campaign Emblem.

1962. Malaria Eradication.

296. **43.** 1d. red 5 5
297. 4d. green 5 5
298. 6d. bistre 8 5
299. 1s. 3d. violet 20 15

1963. Freedom from Hunger.

300. **44.** 1d. yellow, red, green, black and blue .. 5 5
301. – 4d. sepia, yellow & orge. 5 5
302. – 1s. 3d. ochre, blk. & grn. 15 15

DESIGNS—HORIZ. 4d. Emblem in hands. 1s. 3d. World map and emblem.

45. Map of Africa. **46.** Red Cross.

1963. Africa Freedom Day.

303. **45.** 1d. gold and red .. 5 5
304. – 4d. red, black & yellow 5 5
305. – 1s. 3d. multicoloured .. 15 15
306. – 2s. 6d. multicoloured .. 35 35

DESIGNS—HORIZ. 4d. Carved stool. VERT. 1s. 3d. Map and bowl of fire. 2s. 6d. Antelope and flag.

1963. Red Cross Cent. Multicoloured.

307. 1d. T **46** 5 5
308. 1½d. Centenary emblem .. 5 5
309. 4d. Nurses and child .. 5 5
310. 1s. 3d. Emblem, Globe and laurel 15 15

The 1½d. and 4d. are horiz.

47. "3rd. Anniversary".

1963. Republic. 3rd Anniv.

311. **47.** 1d. red, yellow, green, black and sepia .. 5 5
312. – 4d. red, yellow, green, black and blue .. 5 5
313. – 1s. 3d. green, black, red and yellow 15 15
314. – 2s. 6d. red, yellow, green, black and blue .. 30 30

DESIGNS—HORIZ. 4d. Three Ghanaian flags. VERT. 1s. 3d. Map, flag and star. 2s. 6d. Flag and torch.

48. Pres. Nkrumah and Ghanaian Flag. **49.** Rameses II, Abu Simbel.

1963. Founder's Day.

315. **48.** 1d. blk., red, yell. & grn. 5 5
316. – 4d. red, yell., grn. & blk. 5 5
317. – 1s. 3d. red, yellow, green and brown .. 15 15
318. – 5s. yellow and magenta 65 75

DESIGNS—VERT. 4d. As T **48** but with larger flag behind Pres. Nkrumah. HORIZ. 1s. 3d. Pres. Nkrumah and fireworks. 5s. Native symbol of wisdom.

1963. Preservation of Nubian Monuments. Multicoloured.

319. 1d. Type **49** 5 5
320. 1½d. Rock paintings .. 5 5
321. 2d. Queen Nefertari .. 5 5
322. 4d. Sphinx, Sebua .. 5 5
323. 1s. 3d. Rock Temple, Abu Simbel 25 25

The 1d. and 4d. are vert., the rest horiz.

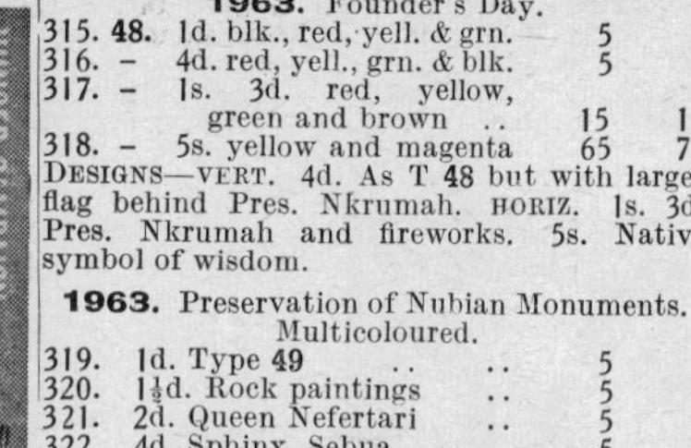

50. Steam and Diesel Locomotives.

1963. Ghana Railway. 60th Anniv.

324. **50.** 1d. multicoloured .. 5 5
325. 6d. multicoloured .. 8 8
326. 1s. 3d. multicoloured .. 20 20
327. 2s. 6d. multicoloured .. 40 40

51. Eleanor Roosevelt and "Flame of Freedom".

1963. Declaration of Human Rights. 15th Anniv.

328. **51.** 1d. red., bl., yell. & blk. 5 5
329. 4d. red, black, yell. & bl. 5 5
330. – 6d. blk., yell., grn. & red 8 8
331. – 1s. 3d. black, red, yellow and green .. 20 20

DESIGNS—VERT. 6d. Eleanor Roosevelt. HORIZ. 1s. 3d. Eleanor Roosevelt and emblems.

52. Sun and Globe Emblem.

1964. Int. Quiet Sun Years.

332. **52.** 3d. multicoloured .. 5 5
333. 6d. multicoloured .. 8 8
334. 1s. 3d. multicoloured .. 15 15

53. Harvesting Corn on State Farm.

1964. Republic. 4th Anniv.

335. **53.** 3d. olive, brown and yellow-olive .. 5 5
336. – 6d. grn., brn. & turquoise 8 5
337. – 1s. 3d. red, brn. & salmon 15 15
338. – 5s. red, grn., brn. & lav. 70 70

DESIGNS: 6d. Oil refinery, Tema. 1s. 3d. "Communal Labour". 5s. Procession headed by flag.

54. Globe and Dov

1964. African Unity Charter. 1st Anniv.

339. **54.** 3d. multicoloured .. 5 5
340. – 6d. bronze-green & red 8 5
341. – 1s. 3d. multicoloured .. 15 15
342. – 5s. multicoloured 60 60

DESIGNS—VERT. 6d. Map of Africa and quill pen. 5s. Planting flower. HORIZ. 1s. 3d. Hitched rope on map of Africa.

55. Pres Nkrumah and Hibiscus Flowers.

1964. Founder's Day.

343. **55.** 3d. multicoloured .. 5 5
344. 6d. multicoloured .. 8 8
345. 1s. 3d. multicoloured .. 15 15
346. 2s. 6d. multicoloured .. 35 35

56. Hurdling.

1964. Olympic Games, Tokyo. Multicoloured.

347. 1d. Type **56** 5 5
348. 2½d. Running 5 5
349. 3d. Boxing.. .. .. 5 5
350. 4d. Long-jumping .. 5 5
351. 6d. Football 8 8
352. 1s. 3d. Athlete holding Olympic Torch .. 15 15
353. 5s. Olympic "Rings" and Flags 75 75

Nos. 349/52 are vert.

57. G. Washington Carver (botanist) and Plant.

1964. UNESCO Week.

354. **57.** 6d. blue and green .. 5 5
355. – 1s. 3d. maroon and blue 15 15
356. **57.** 5s. sepia and vermilion 70 70

DESIGN: 1s. 3d. Albert Einstein (scientist) and Atomic symbol.

58. Secretary Bird.

1964. Multicoloured.

357. 1d. African Elephant .. 5 5
358. 1½d. Type **58** 8 10
359. 2½d. Purple Wreath (flower) 10 12
360. 3d. Grey Parrot 12 15
361. 4d. Mousebird 12 15
362. 6d. African Tulip Tree .. 15 12
363. 1s. 3d. Amethyst Starling 35 40
364. 2s. 6d. Hippopotamus .. 70 70

Nos. 357, 359/60 are vert.

59. I.C.Y. Emblem.

1965. Int. Co-operation Year.

365. **59.** 1d. multicoloured .. 5 5
366. 4d. multicoloured .. 5 5
367. 6d. multicoloured .. 10 10
368. 1s. 3d. multicoloured .. 20 20

60. I.T.U. Emblem and Symbols.

1965. I.T.U. Cent.

369. **60.** 1d. multicoloured .. 5 5
370. 6d. multicoloured .. 8 5
371. 1s. 3d. multicoloured .. 15 15
372. 5s. multicoloured .. 65 70

61. Lincoln's Home.

1965. Abraham Lincoln. Death Cent.

373. **61.** 6d. multicoloured .. 8 5
374. – 1s. 3d. black, red & blue 15 15
375. – 2s. black, brn. & yellow 30 30
376. – 5s. black and red .. 60 60

DESIGNS: 1s. 3d. Lincoln's Inaugural Address. 2s. Abraham Lincoln. 5s. Adaption of U.S. 90 c. Lincoln stamp of 1869.

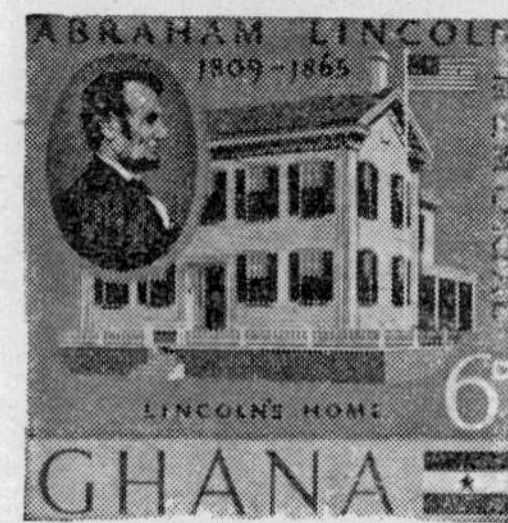

62. Obverse (Pres. Nkrumah) and Reverse of 5 p. Coin.

1965. Introduction of Decimal Currency. Multicoloured designs showing coins expressed in the same denominations as on the stamps.

377. 5 p. Type **62** 8 5
378. 10 p. As Type **62** 10 10
379. 25 p. Size 63 × 39 mm. .. 30 30
380. 50 p. Size 71 × 43½ mm. .. 60 65

1965. Nos. 214/27 surch. **Ghana New Currency 19th July, 1965,** and value. Multicoloured.

381. **19.** 1 p. on 1d. (postage .. 5 5
382. – 2 p. on 2d. 5 5
383. – 3 p. on 3d. (No. 218a) 20 25
384. – 4 p. on 4d. 8 5
385. – 6 p. on 6d. 8 5
386. – 11 p. on 11d. 12 20
387. – 12 p. on 1s. 12 20
388. – 30 p. on 2s. 6d. .. 30 40
389. – 60 p. on 5s. 60 80
390. **21.** ₵1.20 on 10s. .. 1·25 1·75
391. – ₵2.40 on £1 .. .. 2·50 3·50
392. – 15 p. on 1s. 3d. (air) .. 15 20
393. – 24 p. on 2s. 35 40

63. "OAU" and Flag (reduced size illustration. Actual size 60 × 30 mm.).

1965. O.A.U. Summit Conf., Accra. Multicoloured.

394. 1 p. Type **63** .. 5 5
395. 2 p. "OAU", Heads & Flag 5 5
396. 5 p. O.A.U. Emblem & Flag 5 5
397. 6 p. African Map and Flag 8 5
398. 15 p. "Sunburst" and Flag 15 15
399. 24 p. "OAU" on Map, and Flag 25 30

Nos. 397/9 are horiz., 37½ × 27½ mm.

64. Goalkeeper saving Ball.

1965. African Soccer Cup Competition. Multicoloured.

400. 6 p. Type **64**	8	8
401. 15 p. Player with ball (vert.)	20	20
402. 24 p. Player, ball and Soccer Cup	30	30

65. Pres. Kennedy and Grave Memorial.

1965. Pres. Kennedy's 2nd Death Anniv.

403. **65.** 6 p. multicoloured ..	8	5
404. – 15 p. violet, red & green	20	20
405. – 24 p. black and purple..	25	25
406. – 30 p. dull purple & black	35	35

DESIGNS: 15 p. Pres. Kennedy and Eternal Flame. 24 p. Pres. Kennedy and Memorial Inscription. 30 p. Pres. Kennedy.

66. Section of Dam and Generators.

1966. Volta River Project.

408. **66.** 6 p. multicoloured ..	8	5
409. – 15 p. multicoloured ..	20	20
410. – 24 p. multicoloured ..	25	25
411. – 30 p. black and blue ..	35	35

DESIGNS: 15 p. Dam and Lake Volta. 24 p. Word "GHANA" as Dam. 30 p. "Fertility".

1966. "Black Stars" Victory in African Soccer Cup Competition. Optd. **Black Stars Retain Africa Cup 21st Nov. 1965.**

412. **64.** 6 p. multicoloured ..	8	10
413. – 15 p. multicoloured ..	20	20
414. – 24 p. multicoloured ..	30	35

67. W.H.O. Building and Ghana Flag.

1966. W.H.O. Headquarters, Geneva. Inaug. Multicoloured.

415. 6 p. Type **67**	8	5
416. 15 p. Type **67**	15	15
417. 24 p. W.H.O. Building and Emblem	25	30
418. 30 p. W.H.O. Building and Emblem..	30	40

68. Tuna.

1966. Freedom from Hunger. Multicoloured.

420. 6 p. Herring	8	5
421. 15 p. Flat Fish	15	12
422. 24 p. Spade Fish	25	25
423. 30 p. Red Snapper ..	35	30
424. 60 p. Type **68** . ..	75	75

69. Flags as "Quill", and Diamond.

1966. African Charter. 3rd Anniv. Multicoloured.

426. 6 p. African "Links" and Ghana Flag	8	5
427. 15 p. Type **69**	15	15
428. 24 p. Ship's Wheel, Map and Cocoa Bean .. .	25	30

70. Player Heading Ball, and Jules Rimet Cup.

1966. World Cup Football Championships. Multicoloured.

429. 5 p. Type **70**	8	5
430. 15 p. Goalkeeper clearing ball	12	12
431. 24 p. Player and Jules Rimet Cup (Replica)	35	20
432. 30 p. Players and Jules Rimet Cup (Replica) ..	25	25
433. 60 p. Players with ball ..	65	50

71. U.N.E.S.C.O. Emblem.

1966. U.N.E.S.C.O. 20th Anniv.

435. **71.** 5 p. multicoloured ..	5	5
436. 15 p. multicoloured ..	15	15
437. 24 p. multicoloured ..	25	25
438. 30 p. multicoloured ..	35	35
439. 60 p. multicoloured ..	70	70

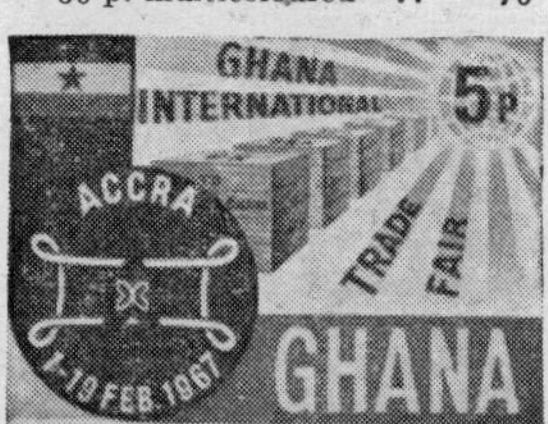

72. Fair Emblem and Crates.

1967. Ghana Trade Fair, Accra. Multicoloured.

441. 5 p. Type **72**	5	5
442. 15 p. Fair Emblem and World Map	15	15
443. 24 p. Shipping and flags ..	25	35
444. 36 p. Fair Emblem and hand-held hoist.. ..	35	45

1967. New Currency. Nos. 216/26 and 393 surch. with new value.

445. 1½ n.p. on 2d. (postage) ..	4·00	2·50
446. 3½ n.p. on 4d.	8	5
447. 5 n.p. on 6d.	8	5
448. 9 n.p. on 11d.	20	25
449. 10 n.p. on 1s.	20	25
450. 25 n.p. on 2s. 6d.. ..	1·00	1·25
451. 1 n.c. on 10s.	3·50	4·00
452. 2 n.c. on £1	7·00	8·00
453. 12½ n.p. on 1s. 3d. (air) ..	50	60
454. 20 n.p. on 24 p. on 2s. ..	1·00	1·25

73. Ghana Eagle and Flag.

1967. February 24th Revolution. 1st Anniv.

455. **73.** 1 n.p. multicoloured ..	5	5
456. 4 n.p. multicoloured ..	5	5
457. 12½ n.p. multicoloured	20	20
458. 25 n.p. multicoloured	35	40

74. Maize.

75. The Ghana Mace.

1967. Multicoloured.

460. 1 n.p. Type **74**	5	5
461. 1½ n.p. Forest Kingfisher..	5	5
462. 2 n.p. Type **75**	5	5
463. 2½ n.p. Commelina ..	5	5
464. 3 n.p. Mud-fish	5	5
465. 4 n.p. Rufous-crowned Roller	5	5
466. 6 n.p. Akosombo Dam ..	5	5
467. 8 n.p. Adomi Bridge ..	5	8
468. 9 n.p. Chameleon	5	8
469. 10 n.p. Tema Harbour ..	8	8
470. 20 n.p. Hare (blue) ..	15	15
471. 50 n.p. Black-winged Stilt	35	40
472. 1 n.c. Wooden Stool ..	75	85
473. 2 n.c. Frangipani	1·50	1·60
474. 2 n.c. 50 Seat of State ..	1·75	2·00

SIZES—(As T 74)—VERT. 4 n.p. HORIZ. 8 n.p. (As T 75). VERT. 1½ n.p., 2½ n.p., 20 n.p. 2 n.c. and 2 n.c. 50. HORIZ. 3 n.p., 6 n.p., 9 n.p., 10 n.p., 50 n.p. and 1 n.c.

6. Kumasi Fort.

1967. Castles and Forts.

475. **76.** 4 n.p. multicoloured ..	5	10
476. – 12½ n.p. multicoloured	20	30
477. – 20 n.p. multicoloured ..	30	50
478. – 25 n.p. multicoloured ..	40	70

DESIGNS: 12½ n.p. Christiansborg Castle and British Galleon. 20 n.p. Elimina Castle and Portuguese Galleon. 25 n.p. Cape Coast, Castle and Spanish Galleon.

77. "Luna 10".

1967. "Peaceful Use of Outer Space". Multicoloured.

479. 4 n.p. Type **77**	5	5
480. 10 n.p. "Orbiter 1" ..	12	12
481. 12½ n.p. Man in Space ..	20	20

78. Scouts and Camp-fire.

1967. Ghanaian Scout Movement. 50th Anniv. Multicoloured.

483. 4 n.p. Type **78**	5	5
484. 10 n.p. Scout on march ..	12	12
485. 12½ n.p. Lord Baden-Powell	20	20

79. U.N. Headquarters Building.

1967. U.N. Day (24th October).

487. **79.** 4 n.p. multicoloured ..	5	5
488. 10 n.p. multicoloured..	12	10
489. – 50 n.p. multicoloured ..	50	50
490. – 2 n.c. 50 multicoloured	2·50	2·50

DESIGN: 50 n.p., 2 n.c. 50, General View of U.N. H.Q., Manhattan.

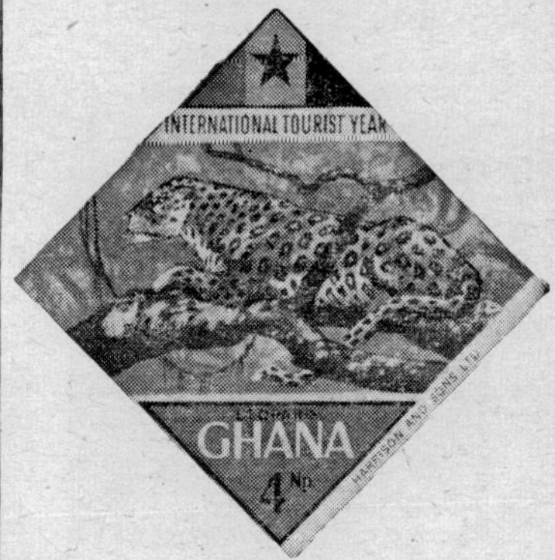

80. Leopard.

1967. Int. Tourist Year. Multicoloured.

492. 4 n.p. Type **80**	5	5
493. 12½ n.p. Christmas Butterfly	15	15
494. 20 n.p. Carmine-Bee-eater	25	25
495. 50 n.p. Water Buck ..	55	55

81. Revolutionaries entering Accra.

1968. February Revolution. 2nd Anniv. Multicoloured.

497. 4 n.p. Type **81**	5	5
498. 12½ n.p. Marching Troops	12	15
499. 20 n.p. Cheering People ..	20	25
500. 40 n.p. Victory Celebrations	45	50

82. Microscope and Cocoa Beans.

1968. Cocoa Research.
501. **82.** 2½ n.p. multicoloured .. 5 5
502. – 4 n.p. multicoloured .. 5 5
503. **82.** 10 n.p. multicoloured .. 12 12
504. – 25 n.p. multicoloured .. 30 40
DESIGNS: 4 n.p. and 25 n.p. Microscope and Cocoa Tree, Beans and Pods.

83. Lt.-Gen. E. K. Kotoka and Flowers.

1968. Lt.-Gen. E. K. Kotoka. 1st Death Anniv. Multicoloured.
506. 4 n.p. Type **83** 5 5
507. 12½ n.p. Kotoka & Wreath 15 15
508. 20 n.p. Kotoka in Civilian Clothes 25 30
509. 40 n.p. Lt.-Gen. Kotoka .. 50 60

84. Tobacco.

1968. Multicoloured.
510. 4 n.p. Type **84** 5 5
511. 5 n.p. Porcupine 5 5
512. 12½ n.p. Rubber 15 15
513. 20 n.p. "Cymothoe sangaris" (butterfly) .. 25 25
514. 40 n.p. "Charaxes ameliae" (butterfly) .. 45 45

85. Surgeons, Flag and W.H.O. Emblem.

1968. W.H.O. 20th Anniv.
516. **85.** 4 n.p. multicoloured .. 5 5
517. 12½ n.p. multicoloured 15 15
518. 20 n.p. multicoloured .. 25 25
519. 40 n.p. multicoloured .. 40 50

86. Hurdling.

1969. Olympic Games, Mexico (1968). Multicoloured.
521. 4 n.p. Type **86** 5 5
522. 12½ n.p. Boxing 15 15
523. 20 n.p. Torch, Olympic Rings and Flags .. 25 25
524. 40 n.p. Football 50 50

87. U.N. Building.

1969. U.N. Day. Multicoloured.
526. 4 n.p. Type **87** 5 5
527. 12½ n.p. Native school staff and U.N. Emblem 15 15
528. 20 n.p. U.N. Building and Emblem over Ghanaian Flag 25 25
529. 40 n.p. U.N. Emblem encircled by flags .. 50 50

88. Dr. J. B. Danquah.

1969. Human Rights Year. Multicoloured.
531. 4 n.p. Type **88** 5 5
532. 12½ n.p. Dr. Martin Luther King 15 15
533. 20 n.p. As 12½ n.p. .. 25 25
534. 40 n.p. Type **88** 50 55

89. Constituent Assembly Building.

1969. Revolution. 3rd Anniv. Multicoloured.
536. 4 n.p. Type **89** 5 5
537. 12½ n.p. Arms of Ghana .. 15 12
538. 20 n.p. As Type **89** .. 25 25
539. 40 n.p. As 12½ n.p. .. 45 45

1969. New Constitution. Nos. 460/74 optd. **NEW CONSTITUTION 1969.**
541. **74.** 1 n.p. multicoloured .. 5 5
542. – 1½ n.p. multicoloured .. 5 5
543. **75.** 2 n.p. multicoloured .. 5 5
544. – 2½ n.p. multicoloured .. 5 5
545. – 3 n.p. multicoloured .. 5 5
546. – 4 n.p. multicoloured .. 8 5
547. – 6 n.p. multicoloured .. 8 5
548. – 8 n.p. multicoloured .. 8 10
549. – 9 n.p. multicoloured .. 10 8
550. – 10 n.p. multicoloured .. 10 8
551. – 20 n.p. multicoloured .. 15 20
552. – 50 n.p. multicoloured .. 90 90
553. – 1 n.c. multicoloured .. 1·00 95
554. – 2 n.c. multicoloured .. 2·00 1·75
555. – 2 n.c. 50 multicoloured 2·75 2·50
On Nos. 541, 545, 547/50 and 552/3 the overprint is horiz. The rest are vert.

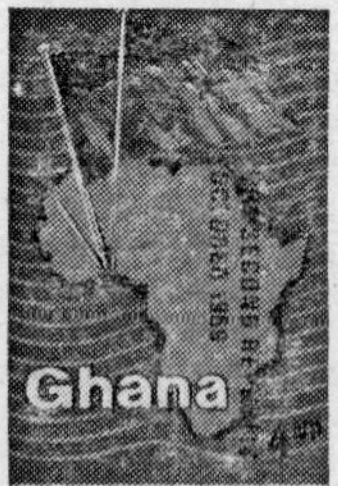

90. Map of Africa and Flags.

1969. 2nd Republic. Inaug. Multicoloured.
556. 4 n.p. Type **90** 5 5
557. 12½ n.p. Figure "2", Branch and Ghanaian Colours .. 15 15
558. 20 n.p. Hands receiving egg 25 25
559. 40 n.p. As T **90** 45 50

91. I.L.O. Emblem and Cog-wheels.

1970. I.L.O. 50th Anniv.
560. **91.** 4 np. multicoloured .. 5 5
561. 12½ n.p. multicoloured 15 15
562. 20 n.p. multicoloured .. 25 25

92. Red Cross and Globe.

1970. League of Red Cross Societies. 50th Anniv. Multicoloured.
564. 4 n.p. Type **92** 5 5
565. 12½ n.p. Henri Dunant and Red Cross emblem .. 15 12
566. 20 n.p. Patient receiving medicine 30 30
567. 40 n.p. Patient having arm bandaged 45 45
Nos. 565/7 are horiz.

93. General Kotoka, "VC-10" and Airport.

1970. Kotoka Airport Inaug. Multicoloured.
569. 4 n.p. Type **93** 5 5
570. 12½ n.p. Control Tower and tail of "VC-10" .. 15 15
571. 20 n.p. Aerial view of airport 25 25
572. 40 n.p. Airport and flags .. 45 45

94. Lunar Module landing on Moon.

1970. Moon Landing. Multicoloured.
573. 4 n.p. Type **94** 5 5
574. 12½ n.p. Astronaut's first step onto the Moon .. 25 25
575. 20 n.p. Astronaut with equipment on Moon .. 50 50
576. 40 n.p. Astronauts .. 1·00 1·00
Nos. 575/6 are horiz.

95. Adult Education.

1970. Int. Education Year. Multicoloured.
578. 4 n.p. Type **95** 5 5
579. 12½ n.p. International education 15 15
580. 20 n.p. "Ntesie" and I.E.Y. symbols .. 25 25
581. 40 n.p. Nursery School .. 41 45

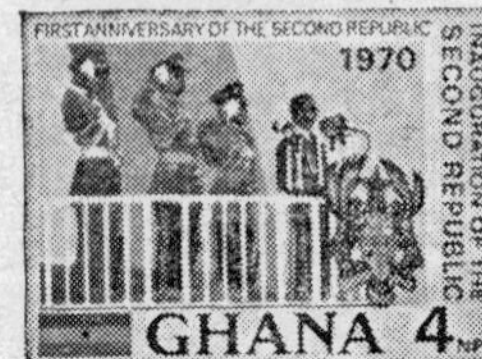

96. Saluting March-Past.

1970. Second Republic. 1st Anniv. Multicoloured.
582. 4 n.p. Type **96** 5 5
583. 12½ n.p. Busia Declaration 15 15
584. 20 n.p. Doves Symbol .. 25 25
585. 40 n.p. Opening of Parliament 50 50

97. "Crinum ornatum".

1970. Flora and Fauna. Multicoloured.
586. 4 n.p. Type **97** 5 5
587. 12½ n.p. Lioness .. 15 15
588. 20 n.p. "Ansellia africana" (flower) 25 25
589. 40 n.p. Elephant .. 50 50

98. Kuduo Brass Casket.

1970. Monuments and Archaeological Sites in Ghana. Multicoloured.
590. 4 n.p. Type **98** 5 5
591. 12½ n.p. Akan Traditional House 15 15
592. 20 n.p. Larabanga Mosque 25 25
593. 40 n.p. Funerary Clay Head 40 50

99. Trade Fair Building.

1971. Int. Trade Fair, Accra. Multicoloured.
595. 4 n.p. Type **99** 5 5
596. 12½ n.p. Cosmetics and pharmaceutical goods .. 15 15
597. 20 n.p. Vehicles 25 25
598. 40 n.p. Construction equipment 45 45
599. 50 n.p. Transport and packing case 60 60
The 50 n.p. is vert.

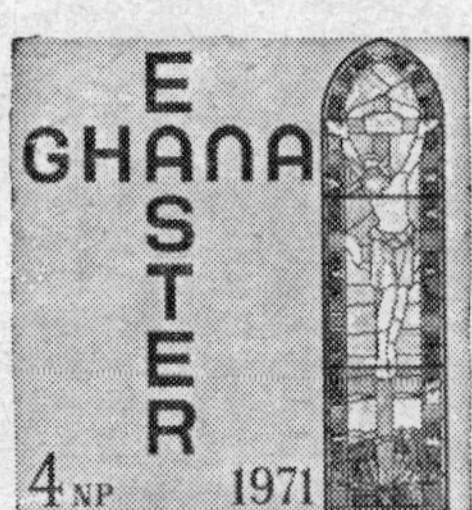

100. Christ on the Cross.

1971. Easter. Multicoloured.
600. 4 n.p. Type **100** .. 5 5
601. 12½ n.p. Christ & Disciples 15 15
602. 20 n.p. Christ blessing Disciples 30 30

101. Corn Cob.

1971. Freedom From Hunger Campaign.
603. **101.** 4 n.p. multicoloured .. 5 5
604. 12½ n.p. multicoloured 15 15
605. 20 n.p. multicoloured 25 25

Remainder stocks of the above stamps were overprinted on the occasion of the death of Lord Boyd Orr and further surcharged 12½, 20 and 60 n.p.

It is understood that 8070 sets from the agency were overprinted locally and returned to New York. Limited remainders of these stamps (only 330 of 60 n.p.) were sold at the G.P.O. We do not list these as they were not freely on sale in Ghana.

102. Guides Emblem and Ghana Flag.

1971. Ghana Girl Guides Golden Jubilee. Each design includes Guides emblem. Multicoloured.
606. 4 n.p. Type **102** 5 5
607. 12½ n.p. Mrs. E. Ofuatey-Kodjoe (founder) and guides with flags .. 15 15
608. 20 n.p. Guides laying stones 25 25
609. 40 n.p. Camp-fire and tent 45 45
610. 50 n.p. Signallers 60 60

103. Child-care Centre.

1971. Y.W.C.A. World Council Meeting, Accra. Multicoloured.
612. 4 n.p. Type **103** 5 5
613. 12½ n.p. Council Meeting 15 15
614. 20 n.p. School typing class 20 20
615. 40 n.p. Building Fund Day 40 45

104. Firework Display.

1971. Christmas. Multicoloured.
617. 1 n.p. Type **104** 5 5
618. 3 n.p. African Nativity 8 8
619. 6 n.p. The Flight into Egypt 10 10

105. Weighing Baby.

1971. U.N.I.C.E.F. 25th Anniv.
620. 5 n.p. Type **105** 5 5
621. 15 n.p. Mother and child (horiz.) 15 15
622. 30 n.p. Nurse 30 30
623. 50 n.p. Young boy (horiz.) 50 55

106. Unity Symbol on Map of Africa.

1972. All African Trade Fair. Multicoloured.
625. 5 np. Type **106** 5 5
626. 15 np. Horn of Plenty .. 15 15
627. 30 np. Fireworks on map of Africa 30 30
628. 60 np. "Participating Nations" 60 60
629. 1 nc. As No. 628 .. 1·00 1·00

On 24 June, 1972, on the occasion of the Belgian International Philatelic Exhibition, Nos. 625/9 were issued overprinted "**BELGICA 72**". Only very limited supplies were sent to Ghana (we understand not more than 900 sets), and for this reason we do not list them.

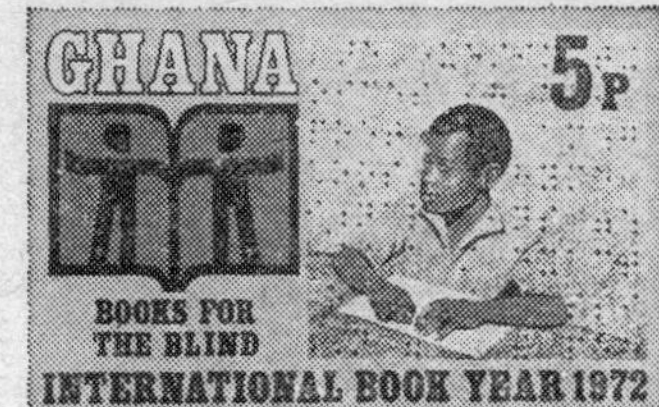

107. Books for the Blind.

1972. Int. Book Year. Multicoloured.
630. 5 p. Type **107** 5 5
631. 15 p. Children's books .. 15 20
632. 30 p. Books for recreation 30 35
633. 50 p. Books for students .. 50 60
634. 1 c. Book and flame of knowledge (vert.) .. 1·00 1·10

108. "Hypoxis urceolata".

1972. Flora and Fauna. Multicoloured.
636. 5 p. Type **108** 5 5
637. 15 p. "Cercopithecus mona" (monkey) .. 15 15
638. 30 p. "Crinum ornatum" 30 30
639. 1 c. "Funisciurus substriatus" (squirrel) 1·00 1·00

109. Football.

1972. Olympic Games, Munich. Mult.
640. 5 p. Type **109** 5 5
641. 15 p. Running 15 15
642. 30 p. Boxing 30 30
643. 50 p. Long-jumping .. 50 50
644. 1 c. High-jumping .. 1·00 1·00

110. Senior Scout and Cub.

1972. Boy Scouts. 65th Anniv. Mult.
646. 5 p. Type **110** 5 5
647. 15 p. Scout and tent .. 15 15
648. 30 p. Sea scouts 30 30
649. 50 p. Leader with cubs .. 50 50
650. 1 c. Training school .. 1·00 1·00

111. "The Holy Night" (Correggio).

1972. Christmas. Multicoloured.
652. 1 p. Type **111** 5 5
653. 3 p. Epiphany scene (Holbein) 5 5
654. 15 p. Madonna and Child (Andrea Rico) 15 15
655. 30 p. King Melchior .. 30 30
656. 60 p. King Gaspar, Mary and Jesus 60 60
657. 1 c. King Balthasar .. 1·25 1·25

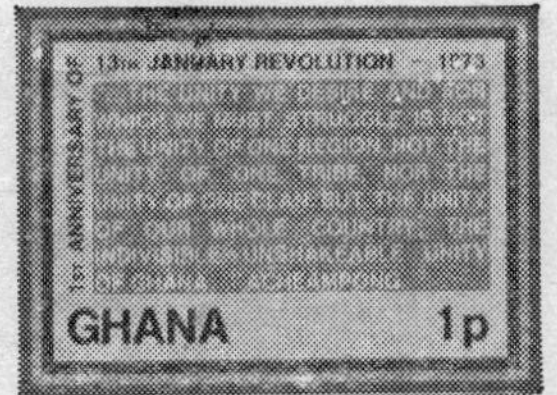

112. Extract from Speech.

1973. January 13th Revolution. 1st Anniv. Multicoloured.
659. 1 p. Type **112** 5 5
660. 3 p. Market scene .. 5 5
661. 5 p. Selling bananas (vert.) 5 5
662. 15 p. Farmer with hoe and produce (vert.) 15 15
663. 30 p. Market traders .. 30 30
664. 1 c. Farmer cutting palm-nuts 90 90

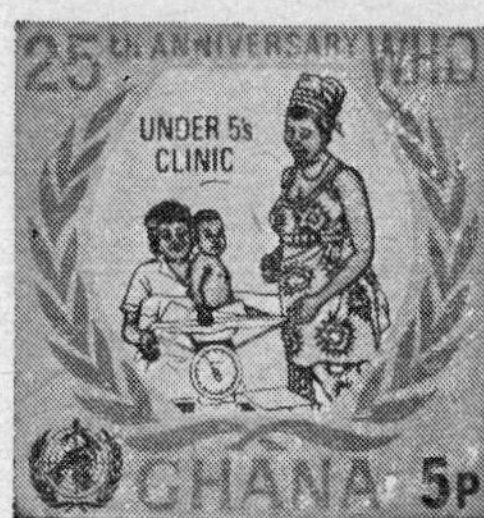

113. Under 5's Clinic.

1973. W.H.O. 25th Anniv. Multicoloured.
666. 5 p. Type **113** 5 5
667. 15 p. Radiography .. 15 15
668. 30 p. Immunisation .. 30 30
669. 50 p. Starving child .. 45 45
670. 1 c. W H.O. H.Q., Geneva 90 90

1973. World Scouting Conference, Nairobi/Addis Ababa. Nos. 646/50 optd. **1st WORLD SCOUTING CONFERENCE IN AFRICA.**
671. **110.** 5 p. multicoloured .. 5 5
672. – 15 p. multicoloured .. 15 15
673. – 30 p. multicoloured .. 30 30
674. – 50 p. multicoloured .. 45 45
675. – 1 c. multicoloured .. 85 85

114. Poultry Farming.

1973. World Food Programme. 10th Anniv. Multicoloured.
677. 5 p. Type **114** 5 5
678. 15 p. Mechanisation .. 15 15
679. 50 p. Cocoa harvest .. 45 45
680. 1 c. F.A.O. H.Q., Rome .. 90 90

115. "Green Alert".

1973. Interpol. 50th Anniv. Multicoloured.
682. 5 p. Type **115** 5 5
683. 30 p. "Red Alert" .. 30 30
684. 50 p. "Blue Alert" .. 50 50
685. 1 c. "Black Alert" .. 90 90

116. Handshake.

1973. O.A.U. 10th Anniv. Multicoloured.
686. 5 p. Type **116** 5 5
687. 30 p. Africa Hall, Addis Ababa 30 30
688. 50 p. O.A.U. emblem .. 50 50
689. 1 c. "X" in colours of Ghana flag 90 90

117. Weather Balloon.

1973. I.M.O./W.M.O. Cent. Multicoloured.
690. 5 p. Type **117** 5 5
691. 15 p. Satellite "Tiros" .. 15 15
692. 30 p. Computer weather map 30 30
693. 1 c. Radar screen .. 90 90

118. Epiphany Scene.

1973. Christmas. Multicoloured.
695. 1 p. Type **118** 5 5
696. 3 p. Madonna and Child .. 5 5
697. 30 p. "Madonna and Child" (Murillo) .. 30 30
698. 50 p. "Epiphany Scene" (Tiepolo) 50 50

119. "Carrying the Cross" (Thomas de Coloswar).

1974. Easter.
700. **119.** 5 p. multicoloured .. 5 5
701. – 30 p. bl., silver & brn. 30 30
702. – 50 p. red, silver & brn. 45 45
703. – 1 c. green, silver & brn. 90 90

DESIGNS (from 15th-century English carved alabaster)—30 p. "The Betrayal". 50 p. "The Deposition". 1 c. "The Risen Christ and Mary Magdalene".

120. Letters.

1974. U.P.U. Centenary. Multicoloured.
705. 5 p. Type **120** 5 5
706. 9 p. U.P.U. Monument and H.Q. 8 8
707. 50 p. Airmail letter .. 45 45
708. 1 c. U.P.U. Monument and Ghana stamp 90 90

1974. "Internaba 1974" Stamp Exn. As Nos. 705/8 additionally inscr. "INTERNABA 1974".
710. 5 p. multicoloured .. 5 5
711. 9 p. multicoloured .. 8 8
712. 50 p. multicoloured .. 45 45
713. 1 c. multicoloured .. 90 90

121. Footballers.

1974. World Cup Football Championships.
715. **121.** 5 p. multicoloured .. 5 5
716. – 30 p. multicoloured .. 30 30
717. – 50 p. multicoloured .. 45 45
718. – 1 c. multicoloured .. 90 90
DESIGNS: As Type **121** showing footballers in action.

122. Roundabout.

1974. Change to Driving on the Right.
720. **122.** 5 p. grn., red & blk. .. 8 8
721. – 15 p. pur., red & blk. 15 15
722. – 30 p. multicoloured .. 25 25
723. – 50 p. multicoloured .. 40 40
724. – 1 c. multicoloured .. 80 80
DESIGNS—HORIZ. 15 p. Warning triangle sign. VERT. 30 p. Highway arrow and slogan. 50 p. Warning hands. 1 c. Car on symbolic hands.

1974. West Germany's Victory in World Cup. Nos. 715/18 optd. **WEST GERMANY WINNERS.**
725. 5 p. multicoloured .. 5 5
726. 30 p. multicoloured .. 25 30
727. 50 p. multicoloured .. 40 40
728. 1 c. multicoloured .. 80 80

123. "Planned Family".

1974. World Population Year. Multicoloured.
730. 5 p. Type **123** 5 5
731. 30 p. Family planning clinic 25 25
732. 50 p. Immunization .. 40 40
733. 1 c. Population census enumeration 80 80

124. Angel.

1974. Christmas. Multicoloured.
734. 5 p. Type **124** 5 5
735. 7 p. The Magi (diamond 47 × 47 mm.) 8 8
736. 9 p. The Nativity .. 8 8
737. 1 c. The Annunciation .. 85 85

1975. "Apollo-Soyuz" Space Link. Nos. 715/18 optd. with **Apollo Soyuz July 15, 1975.**
739. **121.** 5 p. multicoloured .. 5 5
740. – 30 p. multicoloured .. 25 30
741. – 50 p. multicoloured .. 40 45
742. – 1 c. multicoloured .. 85 90

125. Tractor Driver.

1975. International Women's Year. Multicoloured.
744. 7 p. Type **125** 8 5
745. 30 p. Motor mechanic .. 35 30
746. 60 p. Factory workers .. 50 55
747. 1 c. Cocoa research .. 85 90

126. Angel.

1975. Christmas.
749. **125.** 2 p. multicoloured .. 5 5
750. – 5 p. yellow and green 5 5
751. – 7 p. yellow and green 5 5
752. – 30 p. yellow and green 25 30
753. – 1 c. yellow and green 85 90
DESIGNS: 5 p. Angel with harp. 7 p. Angel with lute. 30 p. Angel with viol. 1 c. Angel with trumpet.

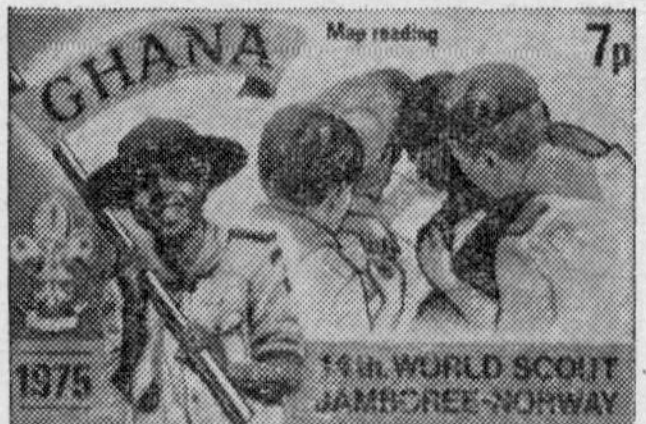

127. Map Reading.

1976. 14th World Scout Jamboree, Norway. Multicoloured.
755. 7 p. Type **127** 5 5
756. 30 p. Sailing 25 30
757. 60 p. Hiking 50 55
758. 1 c. Life-saving 85 90

128. Bottles (litre).

1975. Metrication Publicity. Mult.
760. 7 p. Type **128** 5 5
761. 30 p. Scales (kilogramme) 25 30
762. 60 p. Tape measure and bale of cloth (metre) .. 50 55
763. 1 c. Ice, thermometer and kettle (temperature) .. 85 90

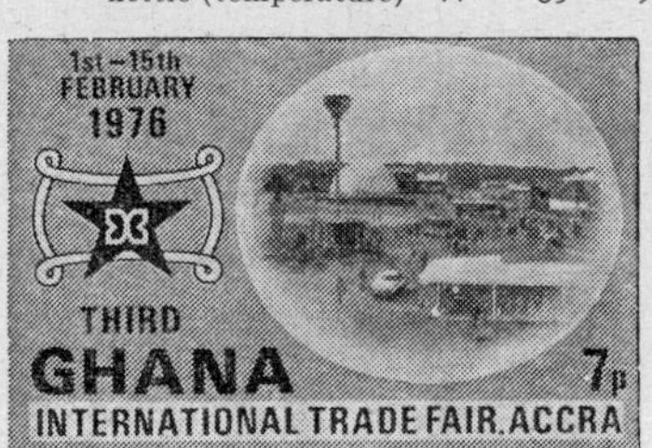

129. Fair Site.

1976. Int. Trade Fair, Accra.
764. **129.** 7 p. multicoloured .. 5 5
765. – 30 p. multicoloured .. 25 40
766. – 60 p. multicoloured .. 50 55
767. – 1 c. multicoloured .. 85 95
DESIGNS: As T **129**, showing different views of the Fair.

1976. Interphil Stamp Exn. Nos. 755/9 optd. **"INTERPHIL" 76 BICENTENNIAL EXHIBITION.**
768. **127.** 7 p. multicoloured .. 5 5
769. – 30 p. multicoloured .. 25 30
770. – 60 p. multicoloured .. 50 55
771. – 1 c. multicoloured .. 85 90

130. Shot-put.

1976. Olympic Games, Montreal. Mult.
773. 7 p. Type **130** 5 5
774. 30 p. Football 25 30
775. 60 p. Women's 1500 metres 50 55
776. 1 c. Boxing 85 95

131. Supreme Court.

1976. Supreme Court. Centenary.
778. **131.** 8 p. multicoloured .. 5 8
779. – 30 p. multicoloured .. 25 30
780. – 60 p. multicoloured .. 50 55
781. – 1 c. multicoloured .. 85 95
DESIGNS: As T **131** showing different views of the Court Buildings.

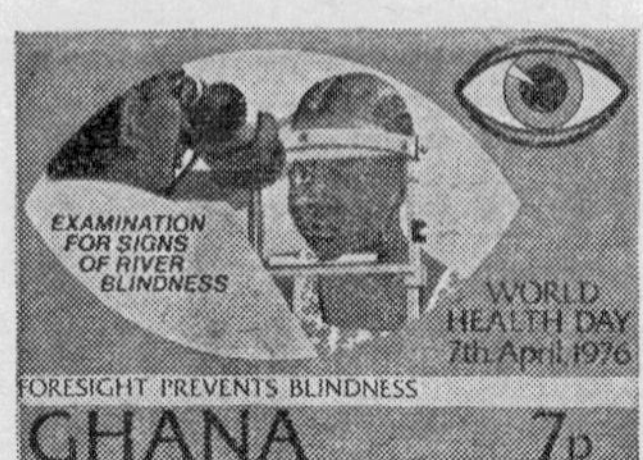

132. Examination for River Blindness.

1976. Prevention of Blindness. Mult.
782. 7 p. Type **132** 5 5
783. 30 p. Entomologist .. 25 30
784. 60 p. Checking effects of insecticide 50 55
785. 1 c. Normal eye's view .. 85 95

POSTAGE DUE STAMPS

1958. Postage Due stamps of Gold Coast optd. **GHANA** and bar.
D 9. **D 1.** 1d. black 5 5
D 10. 2d. black 5 5
D 11. 3d. black 5 8
D 12. 6d. black 12 15
D 13. 1s. black 20 25

D 2.

1958.
D 14. **D 2.** 1d. red 5 5
D 15. 2d. green 5 5
D 16. 3d. orange 5 8
D 17. 6d. blue 10 12
D 18. 1s. violet 15 25

1965. Surch. **Ghana New Currency 19th July, 1965,** and value.
D 19. **D 2.** 1 p. on 1d. 5 5
D 20. 2 p. on 2d. 5 5
D 21. 3 p. on 3d. 5 5
D 22. 6 p. on 6d. 8 8
D 23. 12 p. on 1s. 15 15

1968. Nos. D 20/2 additionally surch.
D 24. **D 2.** 1½ n.p. on 2 p. on 2d. 2·00 1·50
D 25. 2½ n.p. on 3 p. on 3d. 75
D 26. 5 n.p. on 6 p. on 6d.. . 75

1970. Inscr. in new currency.
D 27. **D 2.** 1 n.p. red 5 5
D 28. 1½ n.p. green 5 5
D 29. 2½ n.p. orange 5 5
D 30. 5 n.p. blue 5 5
D 31. 10 n.p. violet 8 10

GIBRALTAR BC

A Br. colony at the W. entrance to the Mediterranean.

1886. Stamps of Bermuda (Queen Victoria) optd. **GIBRALTAR**
1. **1.** ½d. green .. .. .. 3·00 3·00
2. 1d. red .. .. .. 8·00 4·50
3. 2d. purple .. .. .. 25·00 13·00
4. 2½d. blue .. .. .. 25·00 3·50
5. 4d. orange .. .. .. 32·00 32·00
6. 6d. lilac .. .. .. 70·00 70·00
7. 1s. brown £130 £140

1.

2.

1886. As T **1.** Various frames.
39. **1.** ½d. green 20 55
40. 1d. red 40 35
10. 2d. purple.. .. .. 11·00 11·00
42. 2½d. blue .. .. .. 2·50 85
12. 4d. brown .. .. .. 24·00 16·00
13. 6d. lilac .. .. .. 30·00 27·00
14. 1s. brown .. .. .. 70·00 60·00

1889. Surch. with new value in **CENTIMOS.**
15. **1.** 5 c. on ½d. green .. .. 2·75 2·75
16. 10 c. on 1d. red .. .. 2·75 2·75
17. 25 c. on 2d. purple .. 2 75 3·00
18. 25 c. on 2½d. blue .. 5·50 2·75
19. 40 c. on 4d. brown .. 11·00 12·00
20. 50 c. on 6d. lilac .. .. 12·00 14·00
21. 75 c. on 1s. brown .. 12·00 15·00

1889.
22. **2.** 5 c. green 30 35
23. 10 c. red 30 35
24. 20 c. olive .. .. .. 1·60 3·00
25. 20 c. green and brown .. 2·75 3·00
26. 25 c. blue .. .. .. 1·60 55
27. 40 c. brown .. .. 1·10 1·60
28. 50 c. lilac .. .. .. 1·40 2·25
29. 75 c. olive.. .. .. 11·00 12·00
30. 1 p. brown .. .. 12·00 13·00
31. 1 p. brown and blue .. 2·25 2·75
32. 2 p. black and red .. 4·00 4·50
33. 5 p. grey .. .. 17·00 18·00

1898. As 1886.
41. **1.** 2d. purple and blue .. 25 55
43. 4d. brown and green .. 25 35
44. 6d. violet and red .. 7·50 7·50
45. 1s. brown and red .. 7·00 9·00

3.

4.

1903.

66. 3. ½d. green 30 30
57. 1d. purple on red .. 40 40
58. 2d. green and red .. 1·60 1·60
49. 2½d. purple & blk. on blue 85 1·60
60. 6d. purple and violet .. 1·40 2·50
61. 1s. black and red .. .. 4·00 3·75
62. 4. 2s. green and blue .. 19·00 21·00
53. 4s. purple and green .. 23·00 30·00
54. 8s. purple & blk. on blue 30·00 35·00
55. £1 purple & black on red .. £250 £325

1907.

67. 3. 1d. red 30 25
68. 2d. grey .. .. .. 1·25 1·90
69. 2½d. blue .. .. .. 65 1·90
70. 6d. purple .. .. 35·00 50·00
71. 1s. black on green .. 4·00 6·00
72. 4. 2s. purple & blue on blue 19·00 23·00
73. 4s. black and red .. .. 28·00 32·00
74. 8s. purple and green .. £110 £120

1912. As T 3/4, but portrait of King George V. (3d. A. Inscr. "3 PENCE". B. Inscr. "THREE PENCE".)

89. ½d. green 10 15
90. 1d. red 20 20
91a. 1½d. brown 30 30
93. 2d. grey 55 60
79. 2½d. blue .. .. .. 1·60 50
95a. 3d. blue (A) .. .. 85 1·00
109. 3d. blue (B) .. .. 4·00 2·00
80. 6d. purple .. .. .. 2·50 1·60
81. 1s. black on green .. 1·60 1·60
102. 1s. olive and black .. 4·00 5·50
82. 2s. purple & blue on blue 6·00 4·50
103. 2s. brown and black .. 11·00 14·00
104. 2s. 6d. green and black .. 6·00 9·00
83. 4s. black and red .. .. 12·00 15·00
105. 5s. red and black .. .. 12·00 18·00
84. 8s. purple and green .. 23·00 16·00
106. 10s. blue and black .. 22·00 27·00
85. £1 purple & black on red .. 55·00 70·00
107. £1 orange and black .. 75·00 £110
108. £5 violet and black .. £900 £1100

1918. Optd. **WAR TAX.**

86. ½d. green (No. 89) .. 25 30

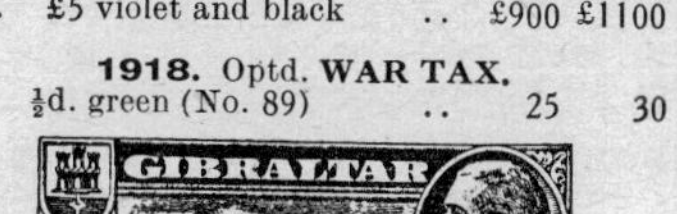

5. The Rock of Gibraltar.

1931.

110. 5. 1d. red 65 65
111. 1½d. brown 95 65
112. 2d. grey 85 65
113. 3d. blue .. .. .. 1·00 1·50

1935. Silver Jubilee. As T 11 of Antigua.

114. 2d. blue and black .. 95 95
115. 3d. brown and blue .. 80 1·40
116. 6d. green and blue .. 2·00 3·00
117. 1s. grey and purple .. 5·00 5·50

1937. Coronation. As T 2 of Aden.

118. ½d. green 25 20
119. 2d. grey 65 55
120. 3d. blue 85 65

7. King George VI.

DESIGNS—HORIZ. 2d. The Rock (North side). 3d., 5d. Europa Point. 6d. Moorish Castle. 1s. Southport Gate. 2s. Eliott Memorial. 5s. Govt. House. 10s. Catalan Bay.

8. Rock of Gibraltar.

1938. King George VI.

121. 7. ½d. green 8 10
122b. 8. 1d. brown 10 35
123. 1½d. red .. .. 1·90 45
123b. – 1½d. violet 12 30
124a. – 2d. grey 12 25
124c. – 2d. red 20 20
125b. – 3d. blue 15 20
125c. – 5d. orange 45 55
126b. – 6d. red and violet .. 25 65
127b. – 1s. black and green .. 55 55
128b. – 2s. black and brown .. 1·10 1·25
129b. – 5s. black and red .. 2·75 3·75
130a. – 10s. black and blue .. 6·00 7·50
131. 7. £1 orange .. .. 10·00 14·00

1946. Victory. As T 4 of Aden.

132. ½d. green 10 15
133. 3d. blue 20 25

1948. Silver Wedding. As T 5/6 of Aden.

134. ½d. green 10 10
135. £1 orange .. .. .. 17·00 20·00

1949. U.P.U. As T 14/17 of Antigua.

136. 2d. red 65 65
137. 3d. blue 70 70
138. 6d. purple .. .. 1·40 1·40
139. 1s. green .. .. .. 2·75 3·25

1950. Legislative Council Inaug. Optd. **NEW CONSTITUTION 1950.**

140. 2d. red (No. 124c) .. 25 35
141. 3d. blue (No. 125b) .. 30 50
142. 6d. red & vio. (No. 126b) .. 60 90
143. 1s. black & grn. (No. 127b) 95 1·75

1953. Coronation. As T 7 of Aden.

144. ½d. black and green .. 15 12

9. Cargo and Passenger Wharves.

1953.

145. 9. ½d. indigo and green .. 8 8
146. – 1d. green 10 8
147. – 1½d. black 12 12
148. – 2d. brown 20 15
149. – 2½d. red 35 30
150. – 3d. blue 20 10
151. – 4d. ultramarine .. 30 25
152. – 5d. maroon 30 25
153. – 6d. black and blue .. 35 35
154. – 1s. blue and brown .. 1·00 85
155. – 2s. orange and violet .. 3·50 1·50
156. – 5s. brown .. .. 6·50 4·50
157. – 10s. brown and ultram. 27·00 20·00
158. – £1 red and yellow .. 45·00 27·00

DESIGNS—HORIZ. 1d. South view from Straits. 1½d. Tunny-fish industry. 2d. Southport Gate. 2½d. Sailing in the Bay. 3d. Liner. 4d. Coaling wharf. 5d. Airport. 6d. Europa Point. 1s. Straits from Buena Vista. 2s. Rosia Bay and Straits. 5s. Main entrance, Govt. House. VERT. 10s. Tower of Homage, Moorish Castle. £1 Arms of Gibraltar.

1954. Royal Visit. As No. 150 but inscr. "ROYAL VISIT 1954".

159. 3d. blue 30 25

10. Gibraltar Candytuft.

DESIGNS—As T 10—HORIZ. 1d. Moorish Castle. 2d. St. George's Hall. 3d. The Rock by moonlight. 4d. Catalan Bay. 1s. Rock ape. 2s. Barbary partridge. 5s. Blue Rock thrush. VERT. 2½d. The keys. 6d. Map of Gibraltar. 7d. Air Terminal. 9d. American War Memorial. 10s. Rock lily.

11. Rock and Badge of Gibraltar Regiment.

1960.

160. 10. ½d. purple and green .. 5 5
161. – 1d. black & yellow-green 5 5
162. – 2d. indigo and chestnut 8 8
163. – 2½d. black and blue .. 10 10
164. – 3d. blue and orange .. 12 20
165. – 4d. brown and turquoise 25 20
166. – 6d. sepia and emerald 25 10
167. – 7d. indigo and red .. 35 20
168. – 9d. grey-blue & turquoise 40 35
169. – 1s. sepia and green .. 35 20
170. – 2s. chocolate and blue 70 70
171. – 5s. turquoise and olive 2·25 2·25
172. – 10s. yellow and blue .. 5·00 4·50
173. 11. £1 black and chestnut 10·00 8·00

1963. Freedom from Hunger. As T 10 of Aden.

174. 9d. sepia .. .. .. 6·50 6·00

1963. Red Cross Cent. As T 24 of Antigua.

175. 1d. red and black .. 20 20
176. 9d. red and blue .. .. 6·50 6·00

1964. Shakespeare. 400th Birth Anniv. As T 25 of Antigua.

177. 7d. bistre 30 30

1964. New Constitution. Nos. 164 and 166 optd. **NEW CONSTITUTION 1964.**

178. 3d. blue and orange .. 15 15
179. 6d. sepia and green .. 25 25

1965. I.T.U. Cent. As T 26 of Antigua.

180. 4d. emerald and yellow .. 30 25
181. 2s. green and blue .. 9·00 7·00

1965. I.C.Y. As T 27 of Antigua.

182. ½d. green and lavender .. 10 10
183. 4d. purple and turquoise .. 60 60

The value of the ½d. stamp is shown as "1/2".

1966. Churchill Commem. As T 28 of Antigua.

184. ½d. blue 5 5
185. 1d. green 8 8
186. 4d. brown 30 30
187. 9d. violet 70 70

1966. World Cup Football Championships. As T 30 of Antigua.

188. 2½d. vio., grn., lake & brn. 12 12
189. 6d. choc., turq., lake & brn. 40 35

12. Bream.

1966. European Sea Angling Championships, Gibraltar.

190. 12. 4d. red, blue and black 5 5
191. – 7d. red, green and black 20 20
192. – 1s. brown, emer. & black 25 25

DESIGNS: 7d. Scorpion Fish. 1s. Stone Bass.

1966. W.H.O. Headquarters, Geneva. Inaug. As T 31 of Antigua.

193. 6d. black, green and blue 40 40
194. 9d. black, purple & ochre 60 55

13. "Our Lady of Europa".

1966. Re-enthronement of "Our Lady of Europa". Cent.

195. 13. 2s. blue and black .. 1·00 95

1966. U.N.E.S.C.O. 20th Anniv. As T 33/5 of Antigua.

196. 2d. violet, red, yell. & orge. 5 5
197. 7d. yellow, violet & olive .. 15 15
198. 5s. black, purple & orange 90 90

14. H.M.S. "Victory".

1967. Multicoloured.

200. ½d. Type 14 .. .. 5 5
201. 1d. S.S. "Arab" 5 5
202. 2d. H.M.S. "Carmania" .. 8 8
203. 2½d. M.V. "Mons Calpe" 6 12
204. 3d. S.S. "Canberra" .. 10 10
205. 4d. H.M.S. "Hood" .. 10 10
205a. 5d. Cable Ship "Mirror" 15 12
206. 6d. Xebec (sailing vessel) 15 15
207. 7d. "Amerigo Vespucci" (training ship) 15 20
208. 9d. T. V. "Raffaello" .. 25 25
209. 1s. H.M.S. "Royal Katherine" 30 30
210. 2s. H.M.S. "Ark Royal" 50 50
211. 5s. H.M.S. "Dreadnought" 1·50 1·75
212. 10s. S.S. "Neuralia" .. 2·75 3·50
213. £1 "Mary Celeste" (sailing vessel) .. .. 7·00 7·50

15. Aerial Ropeway.

1967. Int. Tourist Year. Multicoloured.

214. 7d. Type 15 .. .. 12 12
215. 9d. Shark fishing (horiz.) 15 15
216. 1s. Skin-diving (horiz.) .. 25 25

16. Mary, Joseph and Child Jesus.

1967. Christmas. Multicoloured.

217. 2d. Type 16 .. .. 8 8
218. 6d. Church window (vert.) 15 15

17. Gen. Eliott and Route Map.

1967. General Eliott. 250th Birth Anniv. Multicoloured.

219. 4d. Type 17 .. .. 5 8
220. 9d. Heathfield Tower and Monument, Sussex .. 15 15
221. 1s. General Eliott (vert.) 20 20
222. 2s. Eliott directing Rescue Operations 35 35

No. 222 is 55×21 mm.

18. Lord Baden-Powell.

1968. Gibraltar Scout Assn. 60th Anniv.

223. 18. 4d. buff and violet .. 8 8
224. – 7d. ochre and green .. 12 12
225. – 9d. blue, orge. & black 15 15
226. – 1s. yellow and emerald 25 25

DESIGNS: 7d. Scout Flag over the Rock. 9d. Tent, Scouts and Salute. 1s. Scout Badges.

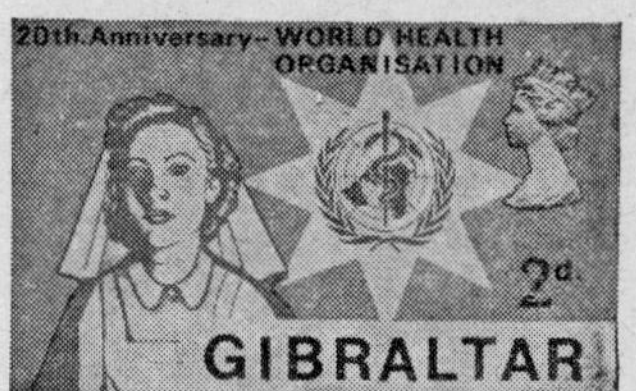

19. Nurse and W.H.O. Emblem.

1968. World Health Organization. 20th Anniv. Multicoloured.

227. 2d. Type 19 .. .. 10 10
228. 4d. Doctor and W.H.O. Emblem 20 20

20. King John signing Magna Carta.

21. Shepherd, Lamb and Star.

1968. Human Rights Year.

229. **20.** 1s. orange, brown & gold 20 20
230. – 2s. myrtle and gold .. 35 35

DESIGN: 2s. "Freedom" and Rock of Gibraltar.

1968. Christmas. Multicoloured.

231. 4d. Type **21** 12 12
232. 9d. Mary holding Holy Child 30 30

22. Parliament Houses.

1969. Commonwealth Parliamentary Assn., Conf.

233. **22.** 4d. green and gold .. 8 8
234. – 9d. violet and gold .. 15 15
235. – 2s. verm., gold & blue 30 30

DESIGNS—HORIZ. 9d. Parliamentary Emblem and outline of "The Rock". VERT. 2s. Clock Tower, Westminster, and Arms of Gibraltar.

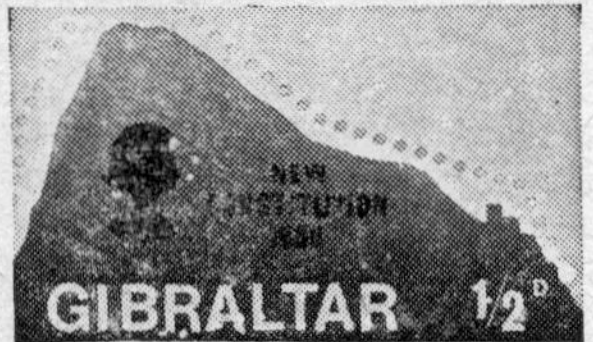

23. Silhouette of Rock, and Queen Elizabeth.

1969. New Constitution.

236. **23.** ½d. gold and orange .. 5 5
237. 5d. silver and green .. 8 8
238. 7d. silver and purple .. 20 30
239. 5s. silver & ultramarine 90 1·00

24. Soldier and Cap Badge, Royal Anglian Regiment, 1969.

1969. Military Uniforms (1st Series). Mult.

240. 1d. Royal Artillery Officer, 1758, and modern cap badge 5 5
241. 6d. Type **24** 30 30
242. 9d. Royal Engineers' Artificer, 1786, and modern cap badge 40 40
243. 2s. Private, Fox's Marines, 1704, and modern Royal Marines' cap badge .. 75 75

See also Nos. 248/51, 290/3, 300/303, 313/16, 331/4, 340/3 and 363/6.

25. "Madonna della Seggiola" (detail, Raphael).

1969. Christmas. Multicoloured.

244. 5d. Type **25** 10 10
245. 7d. "Virgin and Child" (detail, Morales) .. 15 15
246. 1s. "Madonna of the Rocks" (detail, Leonardo da Vinci) 30 30

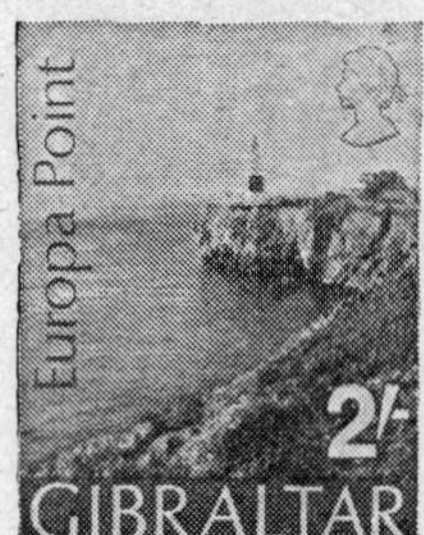

26. Europa Point.

1970. Europa Point.

247. **26.** 2s. multicoloured .. 25 30

1970. Military Uniforms (2nd Series). As T **24**. Multicoloured.

248. 2d. Royal Scots Officer (1839) and Cap Badge .. 8 8
249. 5d. South Wales Borderers Private (1763) and Cap Badge 20 20
250. 7d. Queen's Royal Regiment Private (1742) and Cap Badge 30 30
251. 2s. Royal Irish Rangers Piper (1969) and Cap Badge .. .. .. 1·00 1·00

27. Stamp and Rock of Gibraltar.

1970. "Philympia 70" Stamp Exhibition, London.

252. **27.** 1s. verm. and green .. 20 20
253. – 2s. blue and magenta .. 35 35

DESIGN: 2s. Stamp and Moorish Castle. The stamps shown in the designs are well known varieties with values omitted.

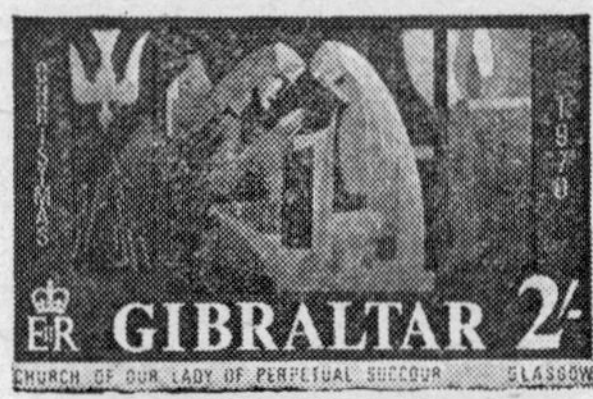

28. "The Virgin Mary".

1970. Christmas.

254. **28.** 2s. multicoloured .. 50 50

29. Saluting Battery, Rosia.

30. Saluting Battery, Rosia, Modern View.

1971. Decimal Currency. Each value printed se-tenant in two designs showing respectively old and new views.

255. ½p. Type **29** 5 5
256. ½p. Type **30** 5 5
257. 1p. } Prince George of 8 5
258. 1p. } Cambridge Quarters and Trinity Church 8 5
259. 1½p. } The Wellington Bust, 5 5
260. 1½p. } Almeda Gardens .. 5 5
261. 2p. } Gibraltar from the 8 5
262. 2p. } North Bastion .. 8 5
263. 2½p. } Catalan Bay .. 5 5
264. 2½p. } 5 5
265. 3p. } Covent Garden .. 5 8
266. 3p. } 5 8
319. 4p. } The Exchange and 8 8
320. 4p. } Spanish Chapel .. 8 8
269. 5p. } Commercial Square 10 10
270. 5p. } and Library .. 10 10
271. 7p. } South Barracks 15 15
272. 7p. } and Rosia Magazine 15 15
273. 8p. } Moorish Mosque 15 20
274. 8p. } and Castle 15 20
275. 9p. } Europa Pass Road.. 20 20
276. 9p. } 20 20
277. 10p. } South Barracks 20 25
278. 10p. } from Rosia Bay .. 20 25
279. 12½p. } Southport Gates.. 25 30
280. 12½p. } 25 30
281. 25p. } The Alameda, 50 55
282. 25p. } Trooping the Guards 50 55
283. 50p. } Europa Pass Gorge 95 1·10
284. 50p. } (vert.) .. .. 95 1·10
285. £1 } Prince Edward's 2·00 2·10
286. £1 } Gate (vert.) .. 2·00 2·10

31.

32. Regimental Arms.

1971. Coil Stamps.

287. **31.** ½p. orange 5 5
288. 1p. blue.. .. .. 5 5
289. 2p. green 5 5

Nos. 287/9 were issued se-tenant in coils giving two ½p., two 1p. and a 2p. stamp for a 5p. coin.

1971. Military Uniforms (Third Series). As T **24**. Multicoloured.

290. 1p. The Black Watch (1845) 12 12
291. 2p. Royal Regt. of Fusiliers (1971) 20 20
292. 4p. King's Own Royal Border Regt. (1704) .. 40 40
293. 10p. Devonshire and Dorset Regt. (1801) .. 1·00 1·00

1971. Presentation of Colours to the Gibraltar Regiment.

294. **32.** 3p. black, gold and red 20 20

33. Nativity Scene.

1971. Christmas. Multicoloured.

295. 3p. Type **33** 20 20
296. 5p. Mary and Joseph going to Bethlehem 30 30

34. Soldier Artificer, 1773.

1972. Royal Engineers in Gibraltar. Bicent. Multicoloured.

297. 1p. Type **34** 8 8
298. 3p. Modern Tunneller .. 20 20
299. 5p. Old and new uniforms and Badge (horiz.) .. 30 30

1972. Military Uniforms (4th Series). As T **24**. Multicoloured.

300. 1p. The Duke of Cornwall's Light Infantry, 1704 .. 5 5
301. 3p. King's Royal Rifle Corps, 1830 .. .. 20 20
302. 7p. 37th North Hampshire, Officer, 1825 .. .. 35 35
303. 10p. Royal Navy, 1972 .. 60 60

35. "Our Lady of Europa".

1972. Christmas.

304. **35.** 3p. multicoloured .. 12 12
305. 5p. multicoloured .. 25 25

1972. Royal Silver Wedding. As T **19** of Ascension, but with Keys of Gibraltar and "Narcissus niveus" in background.

306. 5p. red 20 20
307. 7p. green 25 30

36. Flags of Nine Member Nations and E.E.C. Symbol.

1973. Britain's Entry into the European Economic Community.

308. **36.** 5p. multicoloured .. 20 20
309. 10p. multicoloured .. 35 40

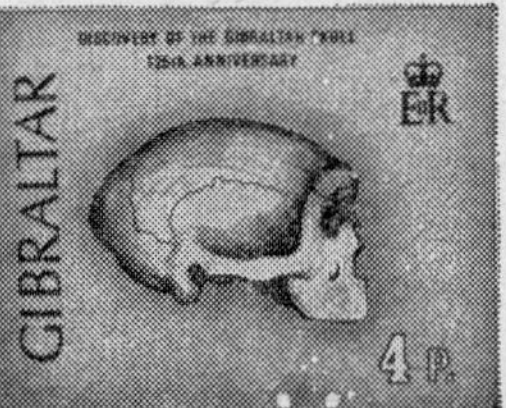

37. Skull.

1973. Gibraltar Skull Discovery. 125th Anniv. Multicoloured.

310. 4p. Type **37** 12 12
311. 6p Prehistoric man .. 20 20
312. 10p. Prehistoric family .. 35 35

No. 312 is size 40 × 26 mm.

1973. Military Uniforms (5th series). As T 24. Multicoloured.

313.	1p. King's Own Scottish Borderers, 1770	5	5
314.	4p. Royal Welsh Fusiliers, 1800	25	25
315.	6p. Royal Northumberland Fusiliers, 1736	35	35
316.	10p. Grenadier Guards, 1898	55	55

38. Nativity Scene (Danckerts).

1973. Christmas.

321. 38.	4p. violet and red	15	15
322. –	6p. mauve and blue	20	25

1973. Royal Wedding. As Type 16 of Anguilla. Background colours given. Multicoloured.

323.	6p. blue	25	15
324.	14p. green	35	35

39. Victorian Pillar-box.

1974. U.P.U. Centenary. Multicoloured.

325.	2p. Type 39	10	10
326.	6p. Pillar-box of George VI	20	20
327.	14p. Pillar-box of Elizabeth II	40	40

Nos. 325/7 also come self-adhesive from booklet panes.

1974. Military Uniforms (6th series). As T 24. Multicoloured.

331.	4p. East Lancashire Regt., 1742	15	15
332.	6p. Somerset Light Infantry, 1833	20	25
333.	10p. Royal Sussex Regt., 1790	30	30
334.	16p. R.A.F. Officer, 1974	45	50

40. "Virgin with the Green Cushion" (Solario).

1974. Christmas. Multicoloured.

335.	4p. Type 40	12	15
336.	6p. "Madonna of the Meadow" (Bellini)	20	25

41. Churchill and Houses of Parliament.

1974. Sir Winston Churchill. Birth Cent. Multicoloured.

337.	6p. Type 41	15	15
338.	20p. Churchill and battleship	45	45

1975. Military Uniforms (7th series). As Type 24. Multicoloured.

340.	4p. East Surrey Regt., 1846	10	10
341.	6p. Highland Light Infantry, 1777	15	15
342.	10p. Coldstream Guards, 1704	25	25
343.	20p. Gibraltar Regt., 1974	50	50

42. Girl Guides' Badge.

1975. Gibraltar Girl Guides 50th Anniv.

346. 42.	5p. gold, blue & violet	12	12
347.	7p. gold and brown	15	15
348. –	15p. silver, blk. & brn.	35	35

No. 348 is as T 42 but shows a different badge.

43. Child at Prayer.

1975. Christmas. Multicoloured.

349.	6p. Type 43	15	15
350.	6p. "Angel" with lute	15	15
351.	6p. Child singing with guitar	15	15
352.	6p. Child with toddlers	15	15
353.	6p. Young girl at prayer with candle	15	15
354.	6p. Boy with lamb	15	15

44. "Bruges Madonna".

1975. Michelangelo. 500th Birth Anniv. Multicoloured.

355.	6p. Type 44	12	15
356.	9p. "Taddei Madonna"	20	25
357.	15p. "Pieta"	30	35

Nos. 355/7 also come self-adhesive from booklet panes.

45. Bicentennial Emblem and Arms of Gibraltar.

1976. American Revolution. Bicent.

361. 45.	25p. multicoloured	50	60

1976. Military Uniforms (8th series). As T 24. Mult.

363.	1p. Suffolk Regt., 1795	5	5
364.	6p. Northamptonshire Regt., 1779	12	15
365.	12p. Lancashire Fusiliers, 1793	25	30
366.	25p. Ordnance Corps, 1896	50	50

46. The Holy Family.

1976. Christmas. Multicoloured.

367.	6p. Type 46	12	15
368.	9p. The Holy Family (different)	20	20
369.	12p. Angel with dove	25	30
370.	20p. Archangel Michael	40	45

Nos. 367/70 show different stained-glass windows from St. Joseph's Church, Gibraltar.

POSTAGE DUE STAMPS.

1956. As Type D 1 of Barbados.

D 1.	1d. green	8	10
D 2.	2d. brown	20	25
D 3.	4d. blue	50	55

1971. As Nos. D1/3, inscr. in decimal currency.

D 4.	½p. green	5	5
D 5.	1p. brown	5	5
D 6.	2p. blue	5	5

D 1.

1976.

D 7. D 1.	1p. orange	5	5
D 8.	3p. blue	5	5
D 9.	5p. red	8	10
D 10.	7p. violet	15	15
D 11.	10p. green	20	20
D 12.	20p. green	35	40

GILBERT AND ELLICE ISLANDS BC

A Br. colony in the S. Pacific.

1966. 100 cents = $1 Australian.

1911. Stamps of Fiji (King Edward VII) optd. GILBERT & ELLICE PROTECTORATE.

1. 9.	½d. green	3·75	12·00
2.	1d. red	20·00	22·00
3.	2d. grey	5·00	9·00
4.	2½d. blue	8·00	11·00
5.	5d. purple and green	18·00	17·00
6.	6d. purple	20·00	18·00
7.	1s. black on green	12·00	17·00

1. Pandanus pine.

2.

1911.

8. 1.	½d. green	80	2·75
9.	1d. red	95	2·75
10.	2d. grey	95	2·75
11.	2½d. blue	95	3·25

1912.

12. 2.	½d. green	35	55
13.	1d. red	55	80
28.	1d. violet	55	80
29.	1½d. red	95	1·10
30.	2d. grey	1·40	2·00
15.	2½d. blue	1·40	2·75
16.	3d. purple on yellow	55	1·60
17.	4d. black & red on yellow	65	1·75
18.	5d. purple and green	2·00	5·50
19.	6d. purple	80	4·00
20.	1s. black on green	2·75	5·50
21.	2s. purple & blue on blue	11·00	14·00
22.	2s. 6d. black & red on blue	12·00	15·00
23.	5s. green & red on yellow	15·00	20·00
35.	10s. green & red on green	60·00	70·00
24.	£1 purple and black on red	£225	£350

1918. Optd. WAR TAX.

26. 2.	1d. red	20	75

1935. Silver Jubilee. As T 11 of Antigua.

36.	1d. blue and black	65	1·75
37.	1½d. blue and red	65	1·35
38.	3d. brown and blue	2·50	3·50
39.	1s. grey and purple	7·50	9·00

1937. Coronation. As T 2 of Aden.

40.	1d. violet	8	12
41.	1½d. red	15	25
42.	3d. blue	25	30

3. Frigate Bird

4. Pandanus Pine.

1939.

43. 3.	½d. blue and green	12	25
44. 4.	1d. green and purple	12	25
45. –	1½d. black and red	25	25
46. –	2d. brown and black	15	40
47. –	2½d. black and olive	15	40
48. –	3d. black and blue	20	30
49. –	5d. blue and brown	65	50
50. –	6d. olive and violet	45	55
51. –	1s. black and blue	35	55
52. –	2s. blue and orange	2·00	2·75
53. –	2s. 6d. blue and green	2·50	3·50
54. –	5s. red and blue	4·50	5·50

DESIGNS: 1½d. Canoe crossing reef. 2d. Canoe and boat-house. 2½d. House. 3d. Seascape. 5d. Ellice Is. canoe. 6d. Coco-nut palms. 1s. Jetty, Ocean Is. 2s. H.M.C.S. "Nimanoa". 2s. 6d. Gilbert Is. canoe. 5s. Arms.

1946. Victory. As T 4 of Aden.

55.	1d. purple	10	12
56.	3d. blue	12	12

1949. Silver Wedding. As T 5/6 of Aden.

57.	1d. violet	10	15
58.	£1 red	9·50	14·00

1949. U.P.U. As T 14/17 of Antigua.

59.	1d. purple	20	30
60.	2d. black	25	40
61.	3d. blue	40	55
62.	1s. blue	45	1·40

1953. Coronation. As T 7 of Aden.

63.	2d. black and grey	35	40

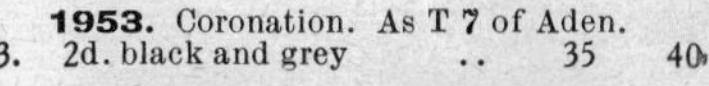

5. Frigate Bird.

1956. As 1939 issue but with portrait of Queen Elizabeth II as in T 5 and colours changed.

64. 5.	½d. black and blue	8	8
65. 4.	1d. olive and violet	8	8
66. –	2d. green and purple	10	12
67. –	2½d. black and green	10	12
68. –	3d. black and red	12	15
69. –	5d. blue and orange	20	25
70. –	6d. chestnut and black	25	30
71. –	1s. black and olive	45	60
72. –	2s. blue and sepia	1·50	2·00
73. –	2s. 6d. red and blue	1·50	2·00
74. –	5s. blue and green	4·00	4·50
75. –	10s. blk. & turq. (as 1½d.)	9·00	10·00

6. Loading Phosphate from Cantilever.

1960. Diamond Jubilee of Phosphate Discovery at Ocean Is. Inscr. "1900 1960".

76. 6.	2d. green and rose	30	30
77. –	2½d. black and olive	35	35
78. –	1s. black and turquoise	95	1·10

DESIGNS: 2½d. Phosphate rock. 1s. Phosphate mining.

1963. Freedom from Hunger. As T **10** of Aden.
79. 10d. blue .. .. .. 2·50 2·50

1963. Red Cross Cent. As T **24** of Antigua.
80. 2d. red and black 15 20
81. 10d. red and blue .. .. 2·00 2·00

7. Heron in Flight.

1964. First Air Service.
82. – 3d. blue, blk. & light blue 15 15
83. **7.** 1s. light blue, blk. & dp. bl. 30 30
84. – 3s. 7d. green, black & emer. 1·25 1·40
DESIGNS—VERT. 3d. D. H. "Heron" aircraft and route map. 3s. 7d. D. H. "Heron" aircraft over Tarawa Lagoon.

1965. I.T.U. Cent. As T **26** of Antigua.
87. 3d. orange and green .. 12 15
88. 2s. 6d. turquoise and purple 85 90

8. Gilbertese Women's Dance.

1965. Multicoloured.
89. ½d. Maneaba and Gilbertese Man blowing Bu Shell.. 5 5
90. 1d. Ellice Islanders Reef-fishing by Flare .. 5 5
91. 2d. Gilbertese Girl weaving Head-garland .. 5 5
92. 3d. Gilbertese Woman performing Ruoia .. 8 10
93. 4d. Gilbertese Man performing Kamel 10 12
94. 5d. Gilbertese Girl drawing water 12 15
95. 6d. Ellice Islander performing a Fatele .. 15 20
96. 7d. Ellice Youths performing Spear dance .. 20 25
97. 1s. Gilbertese Girl tending Ikaroa Babai plant .. 25 30
98. 1s. 6d. Ellice islanders dancing a Fatele .. 50 60
99. 2s. Ellice Islanders pounding Pulaka 75 90
100. 3s. 7d. Type **8** .. .. 1·10 1·25
101. 5s. Gilbertese Boys playing a Stick game .. 1·50 1·75
102. 10s. Ellice Youths beating the Box for the Fatele.. 3·50 4·00
103. £1 Coat of arms .. .. 7·00 8·00
Nos. 89/99 are vert

1965. I.C.Y. As T **27** of Antigua.
104. ½d. purple and turquoise.. 5 5
105. 3s. 7d. green and lavender 90 95

1966. Churchill Commem. As T **28** of Antigua.
106. ½d. blue 5 5
107. 3d. green 12 12
108. 3s. brown 85 90
109. 3s. 7d. violet .. .. .. 95 1·00

1966. Decimal Currency. Nos. 89/103 surch.
110. 1 c. on 1d. 5 5
111. 2 c. on 2d. 5 5
112. 3 c. on 3d. 5 5
113. 4 c. on ½d. 5 5
114. 5 c. on 6d. 8 10
115. 6 c. on 4d. 10 10
116. 8 c. on 5d. 12 12
117. 10 c. on 1s. 15 20
118. 15 c. on 7d. 20 25
119. 20 c. on 1s. 6d. 40 50
120. 25 c. on 2s. 65 75
121. 35 c. on 3s. 7d. 75 90
122. 50 c. on 5s. .. .. .. 1·00 1·10
123. $1 on 10s. .. .. .. 2·25 2·50
124. $2 on £1 .. .. .. 4·25 4·75

1966. World Cup Football Championships. As T **30** of Antigua.
125. 3 c. vio., grn., lake & brn. 10 10
126. 35 c. choc., turq., lake & brn. 80 85

1966. W.H.O. Headquarters, Geneva. Inaug. As T **31** of Antigua.
127. 3 c. black, green and blue.. 10 10
128. 12 c. black, purple & ochre 45 45

1966. U.N.E.S.C.O. 20th Anniv. As T **33/5** of Antigua.
129. 5 c. violet, red, yell. & orge. 10 12
130. 10 c. yellow, violet & olive 30 30
131. 20 c. black, purple & orge. 55 55

9. H.M.S. "Royalist".

1967. Protectorate. 75th Anniv.
132. **9.** 3 c. red, blue and green.. 8 8
133. – 10 c. multicoloured .. 25 25
134. – 35 c. sepia, yellow & grn. 75 80
DESIGNS: 10 c. Trading post. 35 c. Island family.

1968. Decimal Currency. As Nos. 89/103, but with values inscr. in decimal currency.
135. – 1 c. multicoloured .. 5 5
136. – 2 c. multicoloured .. 5 5
137. – 3 c. multicoloured .. 5 5
138. – 4 c. multicoloured .. 8 8
139. – 5 c. multicoloured .. 10 10
140. – 6 c. multicoloured .. 12 12
141. – 8 c. multicoloured .. 15 15
142. – 10 c. multicoloured .. 20 25
143. – 15 c. multicoloured .. 25 30
144. – 20 c. multicoloured .. 35 40
145. – 25 c. multicoloured .. 50 55
146. **8.** 35 c. multicoloured .. 70 90
147. – 50 c. multicoloured .. 1·10 1·25
148. – $1 multicoloured .. 2·25 2·50
149. – $2 multicoloured .. 4·25 4·75

10. Map of Tarawa Atoll.

1968. Battle of Tarawa. 25th Anniv. Multicoloured.
150. 3 c. Type **10** 10 10
151. 10 c. Marines landing .. 20 20
152. 15 c. Beach-head assault 30 30
153. 35 c. Raising U.S. and British Flags 80 80

11. Young Pupil against outline of Abemama Island.

1969. End of Inaugural Year of South Pacific University.
154. **11.** 3 c. multicoloured .. 12 12
155. – 10 c. multicoloured .. 20 20
156. – 35 c. black, brown & grn. 75 80
DESIGNS: 10 c. Boy and girl students and Tarawa atoll. 35 c. University graduate and South Pacific Islands.

12. "Virgin and Child" in Pacific setting.

1969. Christmas.
157. – 2 c. multicoloured .. 30 30
158. **12.** 10 c. multicoloured .. 80 80
DESIGN: 2 c. as T **12** but with grass foreground instead of sand.

13. "Kiss of Life".

1970. British Red Cross. Cent.
159. **13.** 10 c. multicoloured .. 25 25
160. – 15 c. multicoloured .. 35 35
161. – 35 c. multicoloured .. 70 75
Nos. 160/1 are as T **13**, but arranged differently.

14. Foetus and Patients.

1970. U.N. 25th Anniv.
162. **14.** 5 c. multicoloured .. 12 12
163. – 10 c. black, grey & red 25 25
164. – 15 c. multicoloured .. 30 30
165. – 35 c. blue, grn. & black 80 85
DESIGNS: 10 c. Nurse and Surgical Instruments. 15 c. X-ray Plate and Technician. 35 c. U.N. Emblem and Map.

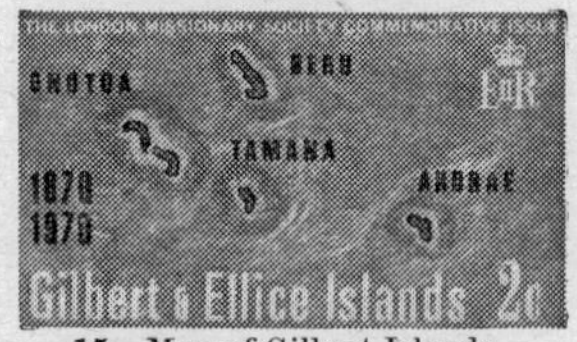

15. Map of Gilbert Islands.

1970. Landing in Gilbert Islands by London Missionary Society. Cent.
166. **15.** 2 c. multicoloured .. 10 10
167. – 10 c. black and green .. 25 25
168. – 25 c. brown and blue .. 45 50
169. – 35 c. blue, blk. & red 75 85
DESIGNS—VERT. 10 c. Sailing-Ship "John Williams III". 25 c. Rev. S. J. Whitmee. HORIZ. 35 c. M.V. "John Williams VII".

16. Child with Halo.

1970. Christmas. Multicoloured.
170. 2 c. Type **16** 5 5
171. 10 c. Sanctuary, Tarawa Cathedral 30 30
172. 35 c. Three Ships inside Star 85 90

17. Casting Nets.

1971. Multicoloured.
173. 1 c. Cutting toddy (vert.) 5 5
174. 2 c. Lagoon fishing .. 5 5
175. 3 c. Cleaning pandanus leaves 5 5
176. 4 c. Type **17** 5 5
177. 5 c. Gilbertese canoe .. 8 10
178. 6 c. De-husking coconuts (vert.) 10 10
179. 8 c. Weaving pandanus fronds (vert.) .. 12 15
180. 10 c. Weaving a basket (vert.) 15 20
211. 15 c. Tiger shark and fisherman (vert.) .. 15 15
212. 20 c. Beating rolled pandanus leaf 20 25
183. 25 c. Loading copra .. 40 45
184. 35 c. Fishing at night .. 55 65
185. 50 c. Local handicrafts (vert.) 85 1·00
186. $1 Weaving coconut screens (vert.) .. .. 1·75 2·00
187. $2 Coat of arms (vert.) .. 3·50 3·75

18. House of Representatives.

1971. New Constitution. Multicoloured.
188. 3 c. Type **18** 8 8
189. 10 c. Maneaba Betio (Assembly hut) .. 25 30

19. Pacific Nativity Scene.

1971. Christmas.
190. **19.** 3 c. blk., yell. & blue .. 10 10
191. – 10 c. black, gold & blue 30 30
192. – 35 c. black, gold & red.. 75 80
DESIGNS: 10 c. Star and palm leaves. 35 c. Outrigger canoe and star.

20. Emblem and Young Boys.

1971. U.N.I.C.E.F. 25th Anniv. Multicoloured.
193. 3 c. Type **20** 8 8
194. 10 c. Young boy .. 30 30
195. 35 c. Young boy's face .. 75 80
Nos. 193/5 include the Unicef Emblem within each design.

21. Flag and Map of South Pacific.

1972. South Pacific Commission. 25th Anniv. Multicoloured.
196. 3 c. Type **21** 8 8
197. 10 c. Flag and native boats 20 20
198. 35 c. Flags of member nations 75 75

22. "Alveopora".

1972. Coral. Multicoloured.
199. 3 c. Type **22** .. 5 8
200. 10 c. "Euphyllia" .. 25 25
201. 15 c. "Melithea" .. 30 30
202. 35 c. "Spongodes" .. 75 75

23. Star of Peace.

1972. Christmas. Multicoloured.

208. 3 c. Type 23 .. .. 5 5
209. 10 c. " The Nativity " .. 30 30
210. 35 c. Baby in " manger " (horiz.) 70 75

1972. Royal Silver Wedding. As T 19 of Ascension, but with Floral Head-dresses in background.

211. 3 c. brown 10 10
212. 35 c. brown 75 80

24. Funafuti (" Land of Bananas ").

1973. Legends of Island Names. (1st series). Multicoloured.

213. 3 c. Type 24 .. .. 5 5
214. 10 c. Butariti (" The Smell of the Sea ") 25 25
215. 25 c. Tarawa (" The Centre of the World ") .. 45 50
216. 33 c. Abemama (" The Land of the Moon ") .. 70 75

See also Nos. 262/5.

25. Ellice Dancer.

1973. Christmas. Multicoloured.

217. 3 c. Type 25 .. .. 5 5
218. 10 c. Canoe and lagoon .. 25 25
219. 35 c. Lagoon at evening .. 60 65
220. 50 c. Map of Christmas Island 80 90

1973. Royal Wedding. As Type 16 of Anguilla. Background colours given. Multicoloured.

221. 3 c. green 5 5
222. 35 c. blue 50 55

26. Meteorological Observation.

1973. I.M.O./W.M.O. Cent. Multicoloured.

223. 3 c. Type 26 .. .. 5 5
224. 10 c. Island observing-station 20 20
225. 35 c. Wind-finding radar .. 55 60
226. 50 c. World weather watch stations 90 95

27. Te Mataaua Crest.

1974. Canoe Crests. Multicoloured.

227. 3 c. Type 27 .. .. 5 5
228. 10 c. " Te-nimta-wawa " 20 25
229. 35 c. " Tara-tara-venei-na " 60 65
230. 50 c. " Te-bou-uoua " .. 85 90

28. £1 Stamp of 1924 and Te Koroba (canoe).

1974. U.P.U. Centenary.

232. 28. 4 c. multicoloured .. 5 8
233. – 10 c. multicoloured .. 20 25
234. – 25 c. multicoloured .. 45 50
235. – 35 c. multicoloured .. 60 65

DESIGNS: 10 c. 5 s. stamp of 1939 and sailing vessel "Kiakia". 25 c. $2 stamp of 1971 and B.A.C. "1–11". 35 c. U.P.U. Emblem.

29. Toy Canoe.

1974. Christmas. Multicoloured.

236. 4 c. Type 29 .. .. 5 5
237. 10 c. Toy windmill .. 20 25
238. 25 c. Coconut "ball" .. 45 50
239. 35 c. Canoes and constellation Pleiades 55 60

30. North Front Entrance, Blenheim Palace.

1974. Sir Winston Churchill. Birth Cent. Mult.

240. 4 c. Type 30 .. .. 5 5
241. 10 c. Churchill painting .. 20 25
242. 35 c. Churchill's statue, London 55 60

31. " Carpilius maculatus ".

1975. Crabs. Multicoloured.

243. 4 c. Type 31 .. .. 5 5
244. 10 c. " Ranina ranina " .. 20 25
245. 25 c. " Portunus pelagicus " 40 45
246. 35 c. " Ocypode ceratophthalma " .. 50 60

32. Eyed Cowrie.

1975. Cowrie Shells. Multicoloured.

247. 4 c. Type 32 .. .. 5 5
248. 10 c. Sieve Cowrie .. 15 15
249. 25 c. Mole Cowrie .. 40 40
250. 35 c. Map Cowrie .. 50 55

1975. Legends of Island Names (2nd series). As T 24. Multicoloured.

252. 4 c. Beru (" The Bud ") .. 5 5
253. 10 c. Onotoa (" Six Giants ") 15 15
254. 25 c. Abaiang (" Land to the North ") 40 40
255. 35 c. Marakei (" Fish-trap floating on eaves ") .. 50 55

33. " Christ is Born ".

1975. Christmas. Multicoloured.

256. 4 c. Type 33 .. .. 5 5
257. 10 c. Protestant Chapel, Tarawa 15 15
258. 25 c. Catholic Church, Ocean Island 40 40
259. 35 c. Fishermen and star 50 50

POSTAGE DUE STAMPS

D 1.

ILLUSTRATIONS British Commonwealth and all overprints and surcharges are FULL SIZE. Foreign Countries have been reduced to ¾-LINEAR.

1940.

D 1. D 1. 1d. emerald 15 50
D 2. 2d. red 20 50
D 3. 3d. brown 25 60
D 4. 4d. blue .. .. 30 1·00
D 5. 5d. olive .. .. 40 1·25
D 6. 6d. purple .. .. 50 1·75
D 7. 1s. violet .. .. 80 5·00
D 8. 1s. 6d. green .. .. 2·25 10·00

GILBERT ISLANDS BC

100 cents = $1.

On 1st January, 1976 the Gilbert Islands and Tuvalu (Ellice) Islands became separate Crown Colonies.

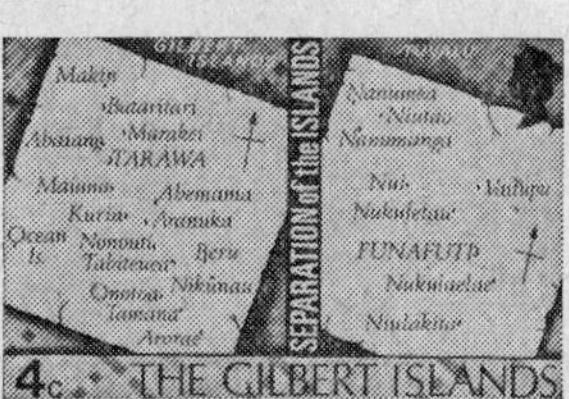

1. Charts of Gilbert Islands and Tuvalu (formerly Ellice) Islands.

1976. Separation of the Islands. Mult.

1. 4 c. Type 1 .. .. .. 8 8
2. 35 c. Maps of Tarawa and Funafuti 50 50

1976. Nos. 173/87 of Gilbert and Ellice Islands optd. **THE GILBERT ISLANDS.**

3. 1 c. Cutting toddy 5 5
4. 2 c. Lagoon fishing 12 12
6. 3 c. Cleaning pandanus leaves 5 8
7. 4 c. Casting nets 5 8
13. 5 c. Gilbertese canoe .. 8 10
14. 6 c. De-husking coconuts .. 10 12
15. 8 c. Weaving pandanus fronds 12 15
16. 10 c. Weaving a basket .. 15 20
17. 15 c. Tiger shark and fisherman 20 25
18. 20 c. Beating a rolled pandanus leaf 30 35
19. 25 c. Loading copra .. 35 40
20. 35 c. Fishing at night .. 50 60
21. 50 c. Local handicrafts .. 70 80
22. $1 Weaving coconut screens 1·40 1·60

2. M.V. " Teraaka ".

1976. Multicoloured.

23. 1 c. Type 2 .. .. .. 5 5
24. 3 c. N.V. " Tautuna " .. 5 5
25. 4 c. Moorish Idol 5 5
26. 5 c. Hibiscus 5 8
27. 6 c. Reef Egret 8 8
28. 7 c. Tarawa Cathedral .. 8 10
29. 8 c. Frangipani 10 10
30. 10 c. Maneaba building .. 12 12
31. 12 c. Betio Harbour .. 15 15
32. 15 c. Evening scene .. 20 20
33. 20 c. Marakei Atoll .. 25 25
34. 35 c. Tanginteebu Chapel .. 40 45
35. 40 c. Flamboyant tree .. 45 50
36. 50 c. " Hypolimnas bolina elliciana (butterfly) .. 60 65
37. $1 Ferry " Tabakea " .. 1·25 1·40
38. $2 National Flag .. .. 2·40 2·60

3. Church.

1976. Christmas. Multicoloured.

39. 5 c. Type 3 .. .. .. 8 10
40. 15 c. Feasting (vert.) .. 20 25
41. 20 c. Maneaba (vert.) .. 30 35
42. 35 c. Dancing 50 55

4. Porcupine Fish Helmet.

1976. Artefacts. Multicoloured.

43. 5 c. Type 4 .. .. .. 8 10
44. 15 c. Shark's Teeth Dagger 20 25
45. 20 c. Fighting Gauntlet .. 30 35
46. 35 c. Coconut Body Armour 50 55

GOLD COAST BC

A Br. colony on the W. coast of Africa. For later issues after independence in 1957 see under Ghana.

1.

2.

1875.

4. 1.	½d. yellow..	7·00	7·00
11.	½d. green ..	25	25
5.	1d. blue ..	6·00	3·50
12a.	1d. red	30	20
6.	2d. green ..	13·00	7·00
13b.	2d. grey ..	75	65
14.	2½d. blue and orange	50	50
15a.	3d. olive ..	1·25	2·00
16.	4d. mauve	85	85
17a.	6d. orange	2·00	1·00
18a.	1s. mauve	2·00	1·10
19a.	2s. brown ..	6·50	5·50

1889. Surch. **ONE PENNY** and bar.

20. 1.	1d. on 6d. orange	18·00	10·00

1889.

26. 2.	½d. mauve and green	15	15
27.	1d. mauve and red	20	20
27a.	2d. mauve and red	4·50	5·50
28.	2½d. mauve and blue	1·60	3·00
29.	3d. mauve and orange	1·50	1·10
30.	6d. mauve and violet	1·10	1·10
31.	1s. green and black	2·50	2·75
32.	2s. green and red..	6·50	5·50
22.	5s. mauve and blue	12·00	6·50
33.	5s. green and mauve	15·00	6·50
23.	10s. mauve and red	25·00	9·00
34.	10s. green and brown	30·00	9·50
24.	20s. green and red	£1400	
25.	20s. mauve & black on red	48·00	12·00

1901. Surch. **ONE PENNY** and bar.

35. 2.	1d. on 2½d. mauve & blue	45	1·60
36.	1d. on 6d. mauve & violet	45	1·60

1902. As T **2**, but with portrait of King Edward VII.

38.	½d. purple and green	35	40
39.	1d. purple and red	20	40
40.	2d. purple and orange	80	80
41.	2½d. purple and blue	2·75	2·75
42.	3d. purple and orange	1·40	55
43.	6d. purple and violet	1·50	1·25
44.	1s. green and black	1·60	2·00
45.	2s. green and red..	9·00	6·50
57.	2s. 6d. green and yellow..	17·00	20·00
46.	5s. green and mauve	12·00	8·00
47.	10s. green and brown	22·00	18·00
48.	20s. purple & black on red	55·00	42·00

1907. As last.

59.	½d. green ..	20	30
60.	1d. red	40	15
61.	2d. grey ..	1·00	45
62.	2½d. blue ..	1·10	45
63.	3d. purple on yellow	1·50	55
64a.	6d. purple	1·10	1·25
65.	1s. black and green	4·00	1·00
66.	2s. purple & blue on blue..	9·50	9·50
67.	2s. 6d. black & red on blue	14·00	13·00
68.	5s. green and red on yellow	24·00	26·00

3.

4. King George V and Christiansborg Castle.

1908.

69. 3.	1d. red	8	5

1913. As T **2** and **3** (1d.) but portraits of King George V.

86.	½d. green..	8	15
72.	1d. red	12	5
87.	1d. brown	8	8
88.	1½d. red	12	10
89.	2d. grey ..	20	10
76.	2½d. blue..	65	65
90.	2½d. orange	20	1·40
77.	3d. purple on yellow	65	25
91.	3d. blue ..	20	30
94.	6d. purple	50	95
79.	1s. black on green	70	60
80.	2s. purple & blue on blue	3·25	1·40
81.	2s. 6d. blk. & red on blue	6·00	2·00
98.	5s. green & red on yellow	5·50	5·50
83a.	10s. green and red on grn.	8·00	9·00
100a.	15s. purple and green ..	60·00	80·00
84.	20s. purple & black on red	45·00	40·00
102.	£2 green and orange ..	£150	£200

1918. Surch. **WAR TAX ONE PENNY.**

85.	1d. on 1d. red (No. 72) ..	5	12

1928.

103. 4.	½d. green..	8	12
104.	1d. brown	8	8
105.	1½d. red ..	45	50
106.	2d. grey ..	15	8
107.	2½d. orange	65	1·60
108.	3d. blue ..	65	30
109.	6d. black and purple	70	40
110.	1s. black and orange	1·75	1·25
111.	2s. black and violet	5·50	3·25
112.	5s. red and olive	10·00	11·00

1935. Silver Jubilee. As T **11** of Antigua.

113.	1d. blue and black	12	15
114.	3d. brown and blue	80	90
115.	6d. green and blue	2·00	2·25
116.	1s. grey and purple	2·25	2·75

1937. Coronation. As T **2** of Aden.

117.	1d. brown	12	12
118.	2d. grey	15	15
119.	3d. blue ..	25	25

5.

6. King George VI and Christiansborg Castle, Accra.

1938.

120. 5.	½d. green..	5	5
121.	1d. brown	5	5
122.	1½d. red	5	5
123.	2d. black..	8	8
124.	3d. blue ..	10	10
125.	4d. mauve	10	10
126.	6d. purple	10	10
127.	9d. orange	25	25
128. 6.	1s. black and olive	20	15
129.	1s. 3d. brown and blue ..	20	25
130.	2s. blue and violet	95	85
131.	5s. olive and red..	2·00	1·75
132.	10s. black and violet	3·00	3·25

1946. Victory. As T **4** of Aden.

133a.	2d. grey	8	8
134a.	4d. mauve	12	12

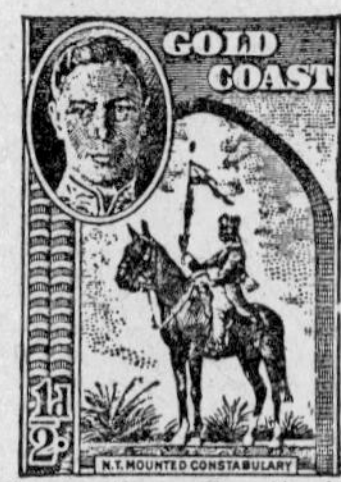

7. Northern Territories Mounted Constabulary.

DESIGNS—HORIZ. 1d. Christiansborg Castle. 1½d. Emblem of Joint Provincial Council. 2½d. Map showing position of Gold Coast. 3d. Manganese mine. 4d. Lake Bosumtwi. 1s. Breaking cocoa pods. 2s. Trooping the Colour. 5s. Surfboats. VERT. 2d. Talking drums. 6d. Cocoa farmer. 10s. Forest.

1948.

135. 7.	½d. green..	10	10
136. –	1d. blue ..	8	10
137. –	1½d. red ..	12	15
138. –	2d. brown	8	8
139. –	2½d. brown and red	15	20
140. –	3d. blue ..	12	12
141. –	4d. mauve	25	25
142. –	6d. black and orange	25	12
143. –	1s. black and red	25	8
144. –	2s. olive and red	55	45
145. –	5s. purple and black	2·00	1·10
146. –	10s. black and olive	3·00	2·25

1948. Silver Wedding. As T **5/6** of Aden.

147.	1½d. red ..	8	5
148.	10s. olive	3·00	4·50

1949. U.P.U. As T **14/17** of Antigua.

149.	2d. brown	12	25
150.	2½d. orange	20	55
151.	3d. blue ..	45	95
152.	1s. green..	1·00	1·50

1952. As 1948 but portrait of Queen Elizabeth II. Designs as for corresponding values except where stated.

153.	½d. brown & red (as 2½d.)	5	5
154.	1d. blue ..	5	5
155.	1½d. green	5	8
156.	2d. brown	5	5
157.	2½d. red (as ½d.)	5	8
158.	3d. magenta	5	5
159.	4d. blue ..	10	10
160.	6d. black and orange	10	8
161.	1s. black and red	20	8
162.	2s. olive and red	50	12
163.	5s. purple and black	2·00	80
164.	10s. black and olive	4·00	1·50

1953. Coronation. As T **7** of Aden.

165.	2d. black and brown	10	5

POSTAGE DUE STAMPS

D 1.

ILLUSTRATIONS British Commonwealth and all overprints and surcharges are FULL SIZE. Foreign Countries have been reduced to ¾-LINEAR.

1923.

D 1. D 1.	½d. black	5·00	4·50
D 2.	1d. black	10	20
D 5.	2d. black	5	15
D 6.	3d. black	10	30
D 7.	6d. black	20	25
D 8.	1s. black	40	50

For later issues see **GHANA**.

GREAT BRITAIN BC

Consisting of England, Wales Scotland and Northern Ireland, lying to the N.W. of the European continent.

12 pence = 1 shilling,
20 shillings = 1 pound sterling.

1971. 100 (new) pence = 1 pound sterling.

1.

2.

1840. Letters in lower corners Imperf.

2. 1.	1d. black ..	£550	35·00
5.	2d. blue ..	£2000	£100

1841. Imperf.

8. 1.	1d. brown	45·00	80
14. 2.	2d. blue ..	£350	13·00

In T **2** there are white lines below "POSTAGE" and above "TWO PENCE".

3. 4.

1847. Imperf.

59. 3.	6d. purple..	£900	75·00
57. 4.	10d. brown	£700	£110
54.	1s. green ..	£1000	65·00

1854. Perf.

29. 1.	1d. brown	40·00	45
41.	1d. red ..	25·00	30
34. 2.	2d. blue ..	£275	9·00

5.

6.

7.

1855. No letters in corners.

66a. 5.	4d. red ..	£170	10·00
70. 6.	6d. lilac ..	£150	12·00
73. 7.	1s. green	£200	20·00

8.

9.

10.

11.

1858. Letters in four corners.

48. 8.	½d. red ..	15·00	1·40
43. 9.	1d. red ..	4·50	35
51. 10.	1½d. red ..	55·00	5·00
45. 11.	2d. blue ..	45·00	1·25

12.

13.

14.

15.

16.

1862. Small white letters in corners.

76. 12.	3d. red ..	£190	30·00
82. 13.	4d. red ..	£140	10·00
84. 14.	6d. lilac ..	£150	11·00
87. 15.	9d. bistre	£300	35·00
90. 16.	1s. green	£200	16·00

21. 23.

1865. Designs as 1862 and T **21** and **23**, but large white letters in corners.

103. 12.	3d. red ..	80·00	5·00
94. 13.	4d. red ..	90·00	8·00
109. 14.	6d. lilac	£110	9·00
111. 15.	9d. straw	£200	28·00
112. 21.	10d. brown	£350	32·00
117. 16.	1s. green	£110	2·50
119. 23.	2s. blue ..	£400	22·00
121.	2s. brown	£1800	£300

24.

27. (Reduced size.)

1867.

126.	**24.**	5s. red	£550	45·00
128.	–	10s. green	£5000	£250
129.	–	£1 brown	£6000	£450
137.	**27.**	£5 orange	£1800	£500

The 10s. and £1 are as T 24, but have different frames.

28.

1872. Large white letters in corners.

123.	**28.**	6d. brown	£100	7·00
125.		6d. grey	£150	14·00

29.

33.

1873. Large coloured letters in c[illegible]

141.	**29.**	2½d. mauve	70·[illegible]	[illegible]
142.		2½d. blue	60[illegible]	[illegible]
158.	**2.**	3d. red	6[illegible]	[illegible]
152.	**13.**	4d. red	[illegible]	[illegible]
153.		4d. green	[illegible]	[illegible]
160.		4d. brown	[illegible]	[illegible]
161.	**28.**	6d. grey	[illegible]	[illegible]
156.	**33.**	8d. orange ..	[illegible]	[illegible]
150.	**16.**	1s. green ..	[illegible]	[illegible]
163.		1s. brown ..	[illegible]	[illegible]

The 3d., 4d. and 1s. are a[illegible] as T 28, but all with lar[illegible]

35.

1880. Various frames.

165.	**35.**	½d. green	6·00	1·00
187.		½d. blue	2·50	40
166.	**36.**	1d. brown	2·00	25
167.	–	1½d. brown	22·00	6·00
168.	–	2d. red	32·00	7·50
169.		5d. indigo	£140	14·00

40.

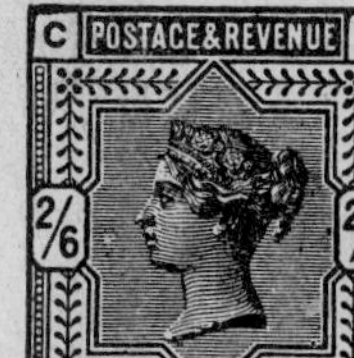

41.

44. (Reduced size.)

1881.

172.	**40.**	1d. lilac	40	15

1883. Types, as 1873, surch. **3d.** or **6d.**

159.	**12.**	3d. on 3d. lilac ..	60·00	18·00
162.	**28.**	6d. on 6d. lilac ..	60·00	18·00

1883.

178.	**41.**	2s. 6d. lilac	£125	18·00
181.	–	5s. red	£160	25·00
183.	–	10s. blue	£275	60·00
185.	**44.**	£1 brown	£2750	£250
212.		£1 green	£550	£110

The 5s. and 10s. are similar to T **41**, but have different frames.

45.

46.

1883. Various frames.

188.	**45.**	1½d. purple	18·00	4·00
189.	**46.**	2d. purple	20·00	5·50
190.		2½d. purple	15·00	1·50
191.	**45.**	3d. purple	35·00	9·00
192.		4d. green	45·00	18·00
193.		5d. green	40·00	18·00
194.	**46.**	6d. green	45·00	20·00
195.		9d. green	£175	65·00
196.	**45.**	1s. green	£125	40·00

54.

55.

56.

57.

58.

59.

60.

61.

62

63.

64.

65.

1887.

197.	**54.**	½d. red	30	15
213.		½d. green*	45	20
198.	**55.**	1½d. purple and green	5·00	40
200.	**56.**	2d. green and red ..	6·00	1·25
201.	**57.**	2½d. purple on blue ..	2·00	15
202.	**58.**	3d. purple on yellow ..	6·00	50
205.	**59.**	4d. green and brown ..	10·00	2·00
206.	**60.**	4½d. green and red ..	1·50	5·00
207a.	**61.**	5d. purple and blue ..	12·00	1·50
208a.	**62.**	6d. purple on red ..	5·00	1·50
209.	**63.**	9d. purple and blue ..	15·00	6·00
210.	**64.**	10d. purple and red ..	13·00	6·00
211.	**65.**	1s. green	70·00	10·00
214.		1s. green and red ..	18·00	15·00

* No. 213, in blue, has had the colour changed after issue.

66.

72.

1902. Designs not shown are as 1887 (2s. 6d. to £1 as 1883) but with portrait of King Edward VII.

215.	**66.**	½d. blue-green	40	25
217.		½d. yellow-green ..	30	15
219.		1d. red	20	10
288.	–	1½d. purple and green ..	5·00	1·00
290.	–	2d. green and red ..	5·00	1·00
230.	**66.**	2½d. blue	1·50	50
285.	–	3d. purple on yellow ..	5·00	50
235.	–	4d. green and brown ..	22·00	3·00
241.	–	4d. orange	5·00	2·00
294.	–	5d. purple and blue ..	7·00	2·00
246.	**66.**	6d. purple	8·00	1·00
249.	**72.**	7d. grey	1·00	2·00
307.	–	9d. purple and blue ..	14·00	7·00
311.	–	10d. purple and red ..	14·00	6·00
314.	·	1s. green and red ..	7·00	2·00
261.	–	2s. 6d. purple	80·00	18·00
263.	–	5s. red	£125	22·00
265.	–	10s. blue	£225	65·00
320.	–	£1 green	£425	£100

80. (Hair heavy).

81. (Lion unshaded).

1911.

325.	**80.**	½d. green	1·25	30
329.	**81.**	1d. red	80	25

82. (Hair light).

83. (Lion shaded).

1912.

339.	**82.**	½d. green	75	15
342.	**83.**	1d. red	35	15

84.

85.

86.

87.

88.

89.

1912. Lined background.

418.	**85.**	½d. green	10	10
419.	**84.**	1d. red	40	12
362.	**85.**	1½d. brown	10	10
368.	**86.**	2d. orange	35	12
371a.	**84.**	2½d. blue	2·00	40
375.	**86.**	3d. violet	1·50	30
379.		4d. grey-green	1·50	35
381.	**87.**	5d. brown	3·00	1·75
426a.		6d. purple	2·00	15
387.		7d. olive-green	7·00	2·25
390.		8d. black on yellow ..	16·00	4·50
393.	**88.**	9d. black	6·00	1·75
427.		9d. olive-green	8·00	75
428.		10d. blue	15·00	6·00
395.		1s. brown	5·00	50
413a.	**89.**	2s. 6d. brown	40·00	10·00
416.		5s. red	45·00	12·00
417.		10s. blue	90·00	28·00
404.		£1 green	£600	£250

90.

1924. British Empire Exn. Dated "1924".

430.	**90.**	1d. red	6·00	6·00
431.		1½d. brown	10·00	10·00

1925. Dated "1925".

432.	**90.**	1d. red	10·00	10·00
433.		1½d. brown	35·00	35·00

91.

92.

93.

94. St. George and the Dragon.

1929. 9th U.P.U. Congress, London.

No.	Type	Description	Unused	Used
434.	91.	½d. green	1·75	10
435.	92.	1d. red	1·25	50
436.		1½d. brown	75	10
437.	93.	2½d. blue	10·00	3·50
438.	94.	£1 black	£400	£275

95.  96.

97.  98.

99.

1934. Solid background.

No.	Type	Description	Unused	Used
439.	95.	½d. green	8	8
440.	96.	1d. red	20	10
441.	95.	1½d. brown	8	8
442.	97.	2d. orange	20	15
443.	96.	2½d. blue	2·00	35
444.	97.	3d. violet	1·50	30
445.		4d. green	1·50	30
446.	98.	5d. brown	3·50	40
447.	99.	9d. olive	10·00	40
448.		10d. blue	10·00	3·00
449.		1s. brown	18·00	40

100.

1935. Silver Jubilee.

No.	Type	Description	Unused	Used
453.	100.	½d. green	5	5
454.		1d. red	75	50
455.		1½d. brown	50	5
456.		2½d. blue	4·75	4·00

Emblems at right differ.

101. King Edward VIII.

ILLUSTRATIONS British Commonwealth and all overprints and surcharges are FULL SIZE. Foreign Countries have been reduced to ¾-LINEAR.

1936.

No.	Type	Description	Unused	Used
457.	101.	½d. green	8	5
458.		1d. red	8	5
459.		1½d. brown	10	5
460.		2½d. blue	20	30

102. King George VI and Queen Elizabeth.

1937. Coronation.

No.	Type	Description	Unused	Used
461.	102.	1½d. brown	8	5

103.

104.

105.

106.

1937.

No.	Type	Description	Unused	Used
462.	103.	½d. green	10	8
485.		½d. pale green	12	8
503.		½d. orange	10	5
463.		1d. red	10	8
486.		1d. pale red	15	8
504.		1d. blue	10	5
464.		1½d. brown	10	8
487.		1½d. pale brown	40	20
505.		1½d. green	40	15
465.		2d. orange	60	8
488.		2d. pale orange	30	8
506a.		2d. brown	50	50
466.		2½d. blue	20	10
489.		2½d. light blue	20	8
507.		2½d. red	25	5
467.		3d. violet	1·50	20
490.		3d. pale violet	75	15
468.	104.	4d. green	45	20
508.		4d. blue	70	20
469.		5d. brown	1·25	20
470.		6d. purple	1·50	15
471.	105.	7d. green	2·75	20
472.		8d. red	5·00	20
473.		9d. olive	3·50	20
474.		10d. blue	3·00	30
474a.		11d. plum	2·50	50
475.		1s. brown	4·00	10

1939.

No.	Type	Description	Unused	Used
476.	106.	2s. 6d. brown	22·00	4·00
476a.		2s. 6d. green	6·00	30
477.		5s. red	15·00	70
478.	–	10s. dark blue	£100	8·00
478a.	–	10s. bright blue	12·00	1·00
478b.	–	£1 brown	12·00	10·00

The 10s. and £1 values have the portrait in the centre in an ornamental frame.

108. Queen Victoria and King George VI.

1940. First Adhesive Postage Stamps. Cent.

No.	Type	Description	Unused	Used
479.	108.	½d. green	12	10
480.		1d. red	20	10
481.		1½d. brown	40	10
482.		2d. orange	20	20
483.		2½d. blue	50	10
484.		3d. violet	4·00	3·50

109. "Peace and Reconstruction at Home."

1946. Victory Commemoration.

No.	Type	Description	Unused	Used
491.	109.	2½d. blue	10	10
492.	–	3d. violet	10	10

DESIGN—HORIZ. 3d. "Peace and Rebuilding Abroad".

110.

111. King George VI and Queen Elizabeth.

1948. Royal Silver Wedding.

No.	Type	Description	Unused	Used
493.	110.	2½d. blue	10	10
494.	111	£1 blue	20·00	20·00

112. Globe and Laurel Wreath.

113. "Speed".

1948. Olympic Games. Inscr. "OLYMPIC GAMES 1948".

No.	Type	Description	Unused	Used
495.	112.	2½d. blue	5	5
496.	113.	3d. violet	20	20
497.	–	6d. purple	30	35
498.	–	1s. brown	45	50

DESIGNS: 6d. Olympic symbol. 1s. Winged Victory.

114. Two Hemispheres.

115. U.P.U. Monument, Berne.

1949. U.P.U. 75th Anniv. Inscr. as in T 114/5.

No.	Type	Description	Unused	Used
499.	114.	2½d. blue	5	5
500.	115.	3d. violet	15	30
501.	–	6d. purple	45	50
502.	–	1s. brown	80	1·00

DESIGNS: 6d. Goddess Concordia, globe and points of compass, 1s. Posthorn and globe.

116. H.M.S. "Victory".

1951.

No.	Type	Description	Unused	Used
509.	116.	2s. 6d. green	6·50	30
510.	–	5s. red	15·00	70
511.	–	10s. blue	8·00	4·00
512.	–	£1 brown	25·00	6·00

DESIGNS; 5s. Cliffs of Dover. 10s. St. George and dragon. £1 Royal Arms.

117. Festival Emblem.

1951. Festival of Britain.

No.	Type	Description	Unused	Used
513.	–	2½d. red	10	10
514.	117.	4d. blue	25	25

DESIGN; 2½d. Britannia, cornucopia and Mercury.

118.

119.

120.

121.

122.

Queen Elizabeth II and National Emblems.

1952.

No.	Type	Description	Unused	Used
515.	118.	½d. orange	8	8
571.		1d. blue	5	5
572.		1½d. green	5	5
518.		2d. brown	50	8
573.		2d. pale brown	5	5
574.	119.	2½d. red	5	5
575.		3d. lilac	8	5
616a.		4d. blue	15	5
577.		4½d. chestnut	10	8
578.	120.	5d. brown	45	8
617.		6d. purple	15	8
617a.		7d. green	25	10
617b.	121.	8d. magenta	25	10
617c.		9d. olive	25	10
617d.		10d. blue	25	10
553.		11d. plum	1·00	1·50
617e.	122.	1s. bistre	50	8
618.		1s. 3d. green	70	30
618a.		1s. 6d. indigo	90	40

The 4d., 4½d. and 1s. 3d. values are printed with colour tones reversed.

Stamps with either one or two vertical black lines on the back were issued in 1957 in connection with the Post Office automatic facing machine experiment in the Southampton area. Later the lines were replaced by almost invisible phosphor bands on the face, in the above and later issues. They are listed in the Stanley Gibbons British Commonwealth Catalogue.

123.

124.

1953. Coronation. Portraits of Queen Elizabeth II.

No.	Type	Description	Unused	Used
532.	123.	2½d. red	15	5
533.		4d. ultramarine	75	75
534.	124.	1s. 3d. green	2·50	3·50
535.	–	1s. 6d. blue	3·50	3·50

DESIGNS: 4d. Coronation and National Emblems. 1s. 6d. Crowns and Sceptres dated "2 JUNE 1953".

125. Carrickfergus Castle.

1955.

759. 125. 2s. 6d. brown .. 60 20
760. – 5s. red .. .. 1·40 40
761. – 10s. blue .. .. 5·00 1·25
762. – £1 black .. 6·00 2·50

CASTLES: 5s. Caernarvon. 10s. Edinburgh. £1 Windsor.

126. Scout Badge and "Rolling Hitch".

127. "Scouts coming to Britain".

1957. World Scout Jubilee Jamboree.

557. 126. 2½d. red 15 8
558. 127. 4d. blue .. .. 1·50 75
559. – 1s. 3d. green.. .. 5·50 7·50

DESIGN: 1s. 3d. Globe within a compass.

1957. 46th Inter-Parliamentary Union Conf. No. 616a, inscr. "46TH PARLIAMENTARY CONFERENCE".

560. 4d. blue .. .. 2·00 3·00

128. Welsh Dragon.

1958. 6th British Empire and Commonwealth Games, Cardiff. Inscr. as in T 128.

567. 128. 3d. lilac 15 8
568. – 6d. mauve 75 45
569. – 1s. 3d. green .. .. 2·50 2·00

DESIGNS: 6d. Flag and Games Emblem. 1s. 3d. Welsh Dragon.

129. Postboy of 1660.

130. Posthorn of 1660.

1960. "General Letter Office" Tercent.

619. 129. 3d. lilac 25 5
620. 130. 1s. 3d. green .. .. 6·50 6·00

131. Conference Emblem.

1960. European Postal and Telecommunications Conference. 1st Anniv.

621. 131. 6d. green and purple 1·00 1·00
622. 1s. 6d. brown and blue 6·00 6·00

132. "Growth of Savings".

1961. Post Office Savings Bank Cent. Inscr. "POST OFFICE SAVINGS BANK".

623. – 2½d. black and red .. 20 15
624. 132. 3d. chestnut and violet 30 10
625. – 1s. 6d. red and blue .. 2·50 2·50

DESIGNS—VERT. 2½d. Thrift plant. HORIZ. 1s. 6d. Thrift plant.

133. C.E.P.T. Emblem.

134. Doves.

1961. Europa.

626. 133. 2d. orge., pink & brown 8 8
627. 134. 4d. buff. mve. & ultram. 15 20
628. – 10d. turq., green & blue 60 60

DESIGN: 10d. As 4d. but arranged differently.

135. Hammer Beam Roof, Westminster Hall.

1961. 7th Commonwealth Parliamentary Conference.

629. 135. 6d. purple and gold .. 50 50
630. – 1s. 3d. green and blue 3·00 3·00

DESIGN—VERT. 1s. 3d. Palace of Westminster.

136. "Units of Productivity".

1962. National Productivity Year.

631. 136. 2½d. green and red .. 10 5
632. – 3d. blue and violet .. 25 10
633. – 1s. 3d. red, blue & grn. 2·25 2·25

DESIGN: 3d. Arrows over map. 1s. 3d. Arrows in formation.

137. Campaign Emblem and Family.

1963. Freedom from Hunger.

634. 137. 2½d. crimson and pink 25 10
635. – 1s. 3d. brown and yell. 2·25 1·75

DESIGN: 1s. 3d. Children of three races.

138. "Paris Conference".

1963. Paris Postal Conf. Cent.

636. 138. 6d. green and mauve .. 1·10 75

139. Posy of Flowers.

1963. National Nature Week. Multicoloured.

637. 3d. T 139 .. .. 8 5
638. 4½d. Woodland life .. 85 50

140. Rescue at Sea.

1963. 9th Int. Lifeboat Conference, Edinburgh. Multicoloured.

639. 2½d. T 140 .. .. 15 5
640. 4d. 19th-cent. lifeboat .. 75 1·00
641. 1s. 6d. Lifeboatmen .. 3·00 2·25

141. Red Cross.

1963. Red Cross Centenary Congress.

642. 141. 3d. red and lilac .. 8 5
643. – 1s. 3d. red, blue & grey 3·00 4·00
644. – 1s. 6d. red, bl. & bistre 4·00 3·00

DESIGNS: Nos. 643/4 are as T 141 but differently arranged.

142. "Commonwealth Cable".

1963. COMPAC (Trans-Pacific Telephone Cable). Opening.

645. 142. 1s. 6d. blue and black 2·25 1·75

143. Puck and Bottom. ("A Midsummer Night's Dream").

144. Hamlet contemplating Yorick's skull ("Hamlet") and Queen Elizabeth II.

1964. Shakespeare Festival.

646. 143. 3d. multicoloured .. 8 5
647. – 6d. multicoloured .. 35 30
648. – 1s. 3d. multicoloured 2·00 1·75
649. – 1s. 6d. multicoloured 2·00 2·00
650. 144. 2s. 6d. slate-purple .. 3·00 2·50

DESIGNS—As T 143: 6d. Feste ("Twelfth Night"). 1s. 3d. Balcony Scene ("Romeo and Juliet"). 1s. 6d. "Eve of Agincourt" ("Henry V").

145. Flats near Richmond Park.

1964. 20th Int. Geographical Congress, London. Multicoloured.

651. 2½d. Type 145 .. .. 8 5
652. 4d. Shipbuilding yards, Belfast 85 75
653. 8d. Beddgelert Forest Park, Snowdonia .. .. 1·75 1·25
654. 1s. 6d. Nuclear reactor, Dounreay .. .. 2·50 2·25

The designs represent "Urban development", "Industrial activity", "Forestry" and "Technological development" respectively.

146. Spring Gentian.

1964. 10th Int. Botanical Congress, Edinburgh. Multicoloured.

655. 3d. Type 146 .. .. 8 5
656. 6d. Dog Rose 35 50
657. 9d. Honeysuckle .. .. 2·00 1·75
658. 1s. 3d. Fringed Water Lily 2·00 1·75

147. Forth Road Bridge.

1964. Opening of Forth Road Bridge.

659. 147. 3d. black, blue & violet 10 5
660. – 6d. black, blue & red .. 80 60

DESIGN: 6d. Forth Road and Railway Bridges.

148. Sir Winston Churchill.

1965. Churchill Commem.

661. 148. 4d. black and drab .. 10 10
662. 1s. 3d. black and grey 80 80

The 1s. 3d. shows a closer view of Churchill's head.

149. Simon de Montfort's Seal.

1965. Simon de Montfort's Parliament. 700th Anniv.

663. 149. 6d. olive 25 25
664. – 2s. 6d. blk., grey & drab 1·50 1·75

DESIGN: (58½ × 21½ mm.): 2s. 6d. Parliament buildings (after engraving by Hollar, 1647).

150. Bandsmen and Banner.

1965. Salvation Army Cent. Multicoloured.

665. 3d. Type 150 .. .. 15 10
666. 1s. 6d. Three Salvationists 1·50 1·25

151. Lister's Carbolic Spray.

1965. Joseph Lister's Discovery of Antiseptic Surgery. Cent.

667. 151. 4d. indigo, chest. & grey 8 5
668. – 1s. black, purple & blue 1·00 85

DESIGN: 1s. Lister and chemical symbols.

152. Trinidad Carnival Dancers.

1965. Commonwealth Arts Festival.

No.	Type	Description	Unused	Used
669.	152.	6d. black and orange . .	50	35
670.	–	1s. 6d. black and violet	1·75	1·50

DESIGN: 1s. 6d. Canadian folk-dancers.

153. Flight of Spitfires.

154. Spitfires attacking Stuka Dive-bomber.

1965. Battle of Britain. 25th Anniv. Inscr. "Battle of Britain 1940".

No.	Type	Description	Unused	Used
671.	153.	4d. olive and black . .	25	20
672.	–	4d. olive and black . .	25	20
673.	–	4d. multicoloured . .	25	20
674.	–	4d. olive and black . .	25	20
675.	154.	4d. olive and black . .	25	20
676.	–	4d. grey, olive, bl. & blk.	25	20
677.	–	9d. violet, orange and maroon	3·00	3·00
678.	–	1s. 3d. grey, blk. & blue	3·00	3·00

DESIGNS: No. 672, Pilot in Hurricane. 673, Wing-tips of Spitfire and Messerschmitt "ME-109". 674, Spitfires attacking Heinkel "HE-111" bomber. 676, Hurricanes over wreck of Dornier "DO-17Z2" bomber. 9d. Anti-aircraft artillery in action. 1s. 3d. Air battle over St. Paul's Cathedral.

155. Tower and "Nash" Terrace, Regent's Park.

1965. Opening of Post Office Tower.

No.	Type	Description	Unused	Used
679.	–	3d. yellow, blue & grn.	8	5
680.	155.	1s. 3d. green and blue	80	80

DESIGN—VERT. 3d. Tower and Georgian Buildings.

156. U.N. Emblem.

1965. U.N.O. 20th Anniv. and Int. Co-operation Year.

No.	Type	Description	Unused	Used
681.	156.	3d. black, orge. & blue	12	8
682.	–	1s. 6d. blk., pur. & blue	1·50	1·25

DESIGN: 1s. 6d. I.C.Y. Emblem.

157. Telecommunications Network.

1965. I.T.U. Cent. Multicoloured.

No.	Description	Unused	Used
683.	9d. Type 157	65	50
684.	1s. 6d. Radio waves and switchboard	85	85

158. Robert Burns (after Skirving chalk drawing).

1966. Burns Commem.

No.	Type	Description	Unused	Used
685.	158.	4d. black, indigo & blue	10	5
686.	–	1s. 3d. blk., bl. & orge.	80	70

DESIGN: 1s. 3d. Robert Burns (after Nasmyth portrait).

159. Westminster Abbey.

1966. Westminster Abbey. 900th Anniv.

No.	Type	Description	Unused	Used
687.	159.	3d. black, brown & blue	8	5
688.	–	2s. 6d. black	1·25	1·00

DESIGN: 2s. 6d. Fan Vaulting, Henry VII Chapel.

160. View near Hassocks, Sussex.

1966. Landscapes.

No.	Type	Description	Unused	Used
689.	160.	4d. black, yellow-green and blue	8	5
690.	–	6d. black, green & blue	15	10
691.	–	1s. 3d. black, yell. & bl.	50	50
692.	–	1s. 6d. blk., orge. & bl.	50	50

VIEWS: 6d. Antrim, Northern Ireland. 1s. 3d. Harlech Castle, Wales. 1s. 6d. Cairngorm Mountains, Scotland.

161. Goalmouth Melee.

1966. World Cup Football Competition. Multicoloured.

No.	Description	Unused	Used
693.	4d. Players with ball (vert.)	8	5
694.	6d. Type 161	20	15
695.	1s. 3d. Goalkeeper saving goal	50	40

162. Black-headed Gull.

1966. British Birds. Multicoloured.

No.	Description	Unused	Used
696.	4d. Type 162	15	12
697.	4d. Blue Tit	15	12
698.	4d. Robin	15	12
699.	4d. Blackbird	15	12

1966. England's World Cup Football Victory. As No. 693 but inscr. "ENGLAND WINNERS".

No.	Type	Description	Unused	Used
700.	–	4d. multicoloured . .	12	25

163. Jodrell Bank Radio Telescope.

1966. British Technology.

No.	Type	Description	Unused	Used
701.	163.	4d black and lemon . .	8	5
702.	–	6d. red, blue & orange	15	15
703.	–	1s. 3d. multicoloured . .	40	40
704.	–	1s. 6d. multicoloured . .	40	40

DESIGNS: 6d. British Motor-Cars. 1s. 3d. SRN 6 Hovercraft. 1s. 6d. Windscale Reactor.

164.

165.

1966. Battle of Hastings. 900th Anniv. Multicoloured.

No.	Description	Unused	Used
705.	4d. Type 164	10	8
706.	4d. Type 165	10	8
707.	4d. "Yellow" horse . .	10	8
708.	4d. "Blue" horse . .	10	8
709.	4d. "Purple" horse . .	10	8
710.	4d. "Grey" horse . .	10	8
711.	6d. Norman ship . .	30	20
712.	1s. 3d. Norman horsemen attacking Harold's Troops (59 × 22½ mm). . .	60	50

166. King of the Orient.

1966. Christmas. Multicoloured.

No.	Description	Unused	Used
713.	3d. Type 166	8	12
714.	1s. 6d. Snowman . .	25	30

167. Sea Freight.

1967. European Free Trade Assn. (EFTA). Multicoloured.

No.	Description	Unused	Used
715.	9d. Type 167	20	20
716.	1s. 6d. Air Freight . .	25	25

168. Hawthorn and Bramble.

1967. British Wild Flowers. Multicoloured.

No.	Description	Unused	Used
717.	4d. Type 168	20	10
718.	4d. Large Bindweed and Viper's Bugloss . .	20	10
719.	4d. Ox-eye Daisy, Coltsfoot and Buttercup . .	20	10
720.	4d. Bluebell, Red Campion and Wood Anemone . .	20	10
721.	9d. Dog Violet	40	45
722.	1s. 9d. Primroses	40	40

169.

1967.

No.	Type	Description	Unused	Used
723.	169.	½d. chestnut	5	10
724.		1d. olive	8	5
727.		2d. brown	12	10
729.		3d. violet	10	5
731.		4d. sepia	12	5
733.		4d. vermilion	12	5
735.		5d. blue	12	5
736.		6d. purple	15	5
737.		7d. emerald	35	12
738.		8d. vermilion	20	30
739.		8d. turquoise-blue . .	75	20
740.		9d. green	40	15
741.		10d. drab	50	20
742.		1s. violet	40	8
743.		1s. 6d. blue and indigo	50	5
744.		1s. 9d. orange & black	75	25

For decimal issue, see Nos. 841/73.

170. "Mares and Foals in a Landscape" (after George Stubbs).

1967. British Paintings.

No.	Type	Description	Unused	Used
748.	–	4d. multicoloured . .	8	5
749.	170.	9d. multicoloured . .	20	20
750.	–	1s. 6d. multicoloured	30	30

PAINTINGS—VERT. 4d. "Master Lambton" (after Sir Thomas Lawrence). HORIZ. 1s. 6d. "Children Coming Out of School" (after L. S. Lowry).

171. Gipsy Moth IV.

1967. Sir Francis Chichester's World Voyage.

No.	Type	Description	Unused	Used
751.	171.	1s. 9d. multicoloured . .	30	30

172. Radar Screen.

1967. British Discovery and Invention. Multicoloured.

No.	Description	Unused	Used
752.	4d. Type 172	8	5
753.	1s. Penicillin Mould	20	20
754.	1s. 6d. "VC-10" Jet Engines	25	25
755.	1s. 9d. Television Equipment	25	25

173. "Madonna and Child" (Murillo).

1967. Christmas.

No.	Type	Description	Unused	Used
756.	–	3d. multicoloured . .	8	5
757.	173.	4d. multicoloured . .	8	5
758.	–	1s. 6d. multicoloured . .	25	25

PAINTINGS—VERT. 3d. "The Adoration of the Shepherds" (School of Seville). HORIZ. 1s. 6d. "The Adoration of the Shepherds" (Louis Le Nain).

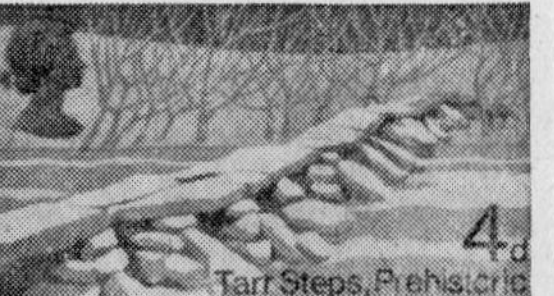

174. Tarr Steps, Exmoor.

1968. British Bridges. Multicoloured.

763.		4d. Type **174**	8	5
764.		9d. Aberfeldy Bridge	25	25
765.		1s. 6d. Menai Bridge	25	25
766.		1s. 9d. M4 Viaduct	40	50

175. " T U C " and Trades Unionists.

1968. British Annivs. Events described on stamps.

767.	**175.**	4d. green, ol., bl. & blk.	8	5
768.	–	9d. violet, grey & black	25	25
769.	–	1s. multicoloured	25	25
770.	–	1s. 9d. ochre & brown	40	35

DESIGNS: 9d. Mrs. Emmeline Pankhurst (statue). 1s. Sopwith " Camel " and Lightning Fighters. 1s. 9d. Captain Cook's " Endeavour " and Signature.

176. " Queen Elizabeth I " (Unknown Artist).

1968. British Paintings.

771.	**176.**	4d. multicoloured	8	5
772.	–	1s. multicoloured	15	15
773.	–	1s. 6d. multicoloured	30	30
774.	–	1s. 9d. multicoloured	45	45

PAINTINGS—VERT. 1s. " Pinkie " (Lawrence). 1s. 6d. " Ruins of St. Mary Le Port " (Piper). HORIZ. 1s. 9d. " The Hay Wain " (Constable).

177. Boy and Girl with Rocking Horse.

1968. Christmas. Multicoloured.

775.		4d. Type **177**	5	5
776.		9d. Girl with Doll's House	15	15
777.		1s. 6d. Boy with Train Set	25	25

Nos. 776/7 are vert.

178. Elizabethan Galleon.

1969. British Ships. Multicoloured.

778.		5d. R.M.S. " Queen Elizabeth 2 "	10	5
779.		9d. Type **178**	25	35
780.		9d. East Indiaman	25	35
781.		9d. " Cutty Sark "	25	35
782.		1s. S.S. " Great Britain "	30	40
783.		1s. R.M.S. " Mauretania "	30	40

Nos. 778 and 782/3 are 58 × 23 mm.

179. " Concorde " in Flight.

1969. 1st Flight of " Concorde ".

784.	**179.**	4d. multicoloured	8	5
785.	–	9d. multicoloured	20	20
786.	–	1s. 6d. indigo, grey and blue	25	30

DESIGNS: 9d. Plan and elevation views. 1s. 6d. " Concorde's " nose and tail.

180. Queen Elizabeth II.

1969.

787.	**180.**	2s. 6d. brown	1·00	15
788.		5s. lake	2·50	30
789.		10s. ultramarine	15·00	10·00
790.		£1 black	2·50	1·50

For decimal issue, see Nos. 829/31a.

No. 790 has an italic " £ ". For later version with roman " £ " see No. 831a.

181. Page from the Daily Mail, and Vickers " Vimy " Aircraft.

1969. Annivs. Events described on stamps.

791.	**181.**	5d. multicoloured	8	5
792.	–	9d. multicoloured	20	20
793.	–	1s. claret, red and blue	25	25
794.	–	1s. 6d. multicoloured	30	30
795.	–	1s. 9d. turquoise-green, yellow and sepia	30	30

DESIGNS: 9d. Europa and C.E.P.T. Emblems. 1s. I.L.O. Emblem. 1s. 6d. Flags of N.A.T.O. countries. 1s. 9d. Vickers " Vimy " Aircraft and globe showing Flight.

182. Durham Cathedral.

1969. British Architecture (Cathedrals). Multicoloured.

796.		5d. Canterbury Cathedral	8	8
797.		5d. York Minster	8	8
798.		5d. St. Giles' Cathedral, Edinburgh	8	8
799.		5d. Type **182**	8	8
800.		9d. St. Paul's Cathedral	25	25
801.		1s. 6d. Liverpool Metropolitan Cathedral	35	35

183. Queen Eleanor's Gate, Caernarvon Castle.

1969. Investiture of H.R.H. The Prince of Wales.

802.	–	5d. multicoloured	8	8
803.	–	5d. multicoloured	8	8
804.	**183.**	5d. multicoloured	8	8
805.	–	9d. multicoloured	30	30
806.	–	1s. black and gold	30	30

DESIGNS: No. 802, The King's Gate, Caernarvon Castle. 803, The Eagle Tower, Caernarvon Castle. 805, Celtic Cross, Margam Abbey. 806, H.R.H. The Prince of Wales.

184. Mahatma Gandhi.

1969. Gandhi Centenary Year.

807.	**184.**	1s. 6d. black, green, orange and grey	25	25

185. National Giro "G" Symbol.

1969. Post Office Technology Commem.

808.	**185.**	5d. blue, greenish blue, lilac and black	8	5
809.	–	9d. emerald, blue & blk.	20	20
810.	–	1s. emer., lav. & black	20	20
811.	–	1s. 6d. pur., blue & blk.	25	25

DESIGNS: 9d. International Subscriber dialling (Telecommunications). 1s. Pulse Code Modulations (Telecommunications). 1s. 6d. Automatic Sorting (Postal Mechanisation).

186. Herald Angel.

1969. Christmas. Multicoloured.

812.		4d. Type **186**	8	5
813.		5d. The Three Shepherds	10	8
814.		1s. 6d. The Three Kings	35	35

187. Fife Harling.

1970. British Rural Architecture. Multicoloured.

815.		5d. Type **187**	8	5
816.		9d. Cotswold Limestone	25	25
817.		1s. Welsh Stucco	30	30
818.		1s. 6d. Ulster Thatch	45	35

The 1s. and 1s. 6d. are larger (38 × 27 mm.).

188. Signing the Declaration of Arbroath.

1970. Anniversaries. Events described on stamps. Multicoloured.

819.		5d. Type **188**	8	5
820.		9d. Florence Nightingale attending patients	25	25
821.		1s. Signing of International Co-operative Alliance	25	25
822.		1s. 6d. Pilgrims and "Mayflower"	30	30
823.		1s. 9d. Sir William and Sir John Herschel, Francis Bailey and Telescope	35	35

189. Mr. Pickwick and Sam (" Pickwick Papers ").

190. Queen Elizabeth II.

1970. Literary Annivs. Charles Dickens (novelist) Death Cent. (5d. × 4). William Wordsworth (poet) Birth Bicent. (1s. 6d.) Multicoloured.

824.		5d. Type **189**	12	10
825.		5d. Mr. and Mrs. Micawber (" David Copperfield ")	12	10
826.		5d. David Copperfield and Betsy Trotwood (" David Copperfield ")	12	10
827.		5d. " Oliver asking for more " (" Oliver Twist ")	12	10
828.		1s. 6d. " Grasmere " (from engraving by J. Farrington, R.A.)	60	70

1970. Decimal Currency. Designs as T **180**, but inscr. in decimal currency as T **190**.

829.	**190.**	10p. cerise	1·75	20
830.		20p. green	30	15
831.		50p. ultramarine	75	35
831a.		£1 black	1·50	75

On No. 831a the " £ " is in roman type.

191. Cyclists.

1970. 9th British Commonwealth Games.

832.	–	5d. pink, emerald, yellow and green	10	5
833.	–	1s. 6d. greenish-blue, mauve, brown and blue	40	40
834.	**191.**	1s. 9d. orange, mauve, orange and brown	40	40

DESIGNS: 5d. Runners. 1s. 6d. Swimmers.

192. 1d. Black (1840).

1970. "Philympia 70" Stamp Exn. Multicoloured.

835.		5d. Type **192**	8	8
836.		9d. 1s. green (1847)	20	20
837.		1s. 6d. 4d. carmine (1855)	30	35

193. Shepherds and Apparition of the Angel.

1970. Christmas. Multicoloured.

838.		4d. Type **193**	8	5
839.		5d. Mary, Joseph, and Christ in the Manger	8	5
840.		1s. 6d. The Wise Men bearing Gifts	45	50

194.

1971. Decimal currency. As Nos. 723, etc., but new colours and with decimal figures of value, as in T **194**.

841.		$\frac{1}{2}$p. blue	5	5
843.		1p. crimson	5	5
844.		$1\frac{1}{2}$p. black	5	5
845.		2p. green	5	5
846.		$2\frac{1}{2}$p. magenta	5	5
849.		3p. blue	5	5
851.		$3\frac{1}{2}$p. grey	8	5

853. 4p. brown 8 8
854. 4½p. blue 35 10
855. 5p. violet 8 5
856. 5½p. violet 8 5
858. 6p. green 10 5
859. 6½p. blue 10 5
861. 7p. maroon 12 8
862. 7½p. brown 12 8
863. 8p. red 12 8
864. 8½p. green 12 5
866. 9p. yellow and black 20 8
867. 9p. violet 15 8
868. 9½p. purple 15 10
869. 10p. orange and brown 20 10
870. 10p. brown 15 10
871. 10½p. yellow 15 12
872. 11p. red 15 10
873. 20p. purple 30 12
874. 50p. brown 75 35

195. "A Mountain Road" (T. P. Flanagan).

1971. "Ulster '71" Festival. Paintings. Multicoloured.

881. 3p. Type **195** 10 5
882. 7½p. "Deer's Meadow" (Tom Carr) .. .. 1·00 1·00
883. 9p. "Slieve na brock" (Colin Middleton) 75 75

196. John Keats (150th Death Anniv.).

1971. Literary Annivs.

884. **196.** 3p. black, gold & blue 15 8
885. – 5p. black, gold & grn. 40 40
886. – 7½p. black, gold & brn. 1·00 1·00

DESIGNS AND ANNIVERSARIES: 5p. Thomas Gray (Death Bicent.). 7½p. Sir Walter Scott (Birth Bicent.).

197. Servicemen and Nurse of 1921.

1971. British Annivs. Events described on stamps. Multicoloured.

887. 3p. Type **197** 10 5
888. 7½p. Roman Centurion .. 85 85
889. 9p. Rugby Football, 1871 1·25 1·25

198. Physical Sciences Building, University College of Wales, Aberystwyth.

1971. British Architecture (Modern University Buildings).

890. **198.** 3p. multicoloured .. 15 8
891. – 5p. multicoloured .. 20 20
892. – 7½p. ochre, blk. & brn. 85 85
893. – 9p. multicoloured .. 1·25 1·25

DESIGNS: 5p. Faraday Building, Southampton University. 7½p. Engineering Department, Leicester University. 9p. Hexagon Restaurant, Essex University.

199. "Dream of the Wise Men".

1971. Christmas. Multicoloured.

894. 2½p. Type **199** .. 10 5
895. 3p. "Adoration of the Magi" 12 5
896. 7½p. "Ride of the Magi" 85 85

200. Sir James Clark Ross.

1972. British Polar Explorers. Multicoloured.

897. 3p. Type **200** 10 8
898. 5p. Sir Martin Frobisher 25 25
899. 7½p. Henry Hudson .. 85 85
900. 9p. Capt. Robert Scott.. 1·25 1·25

See also Nos. 923/7.

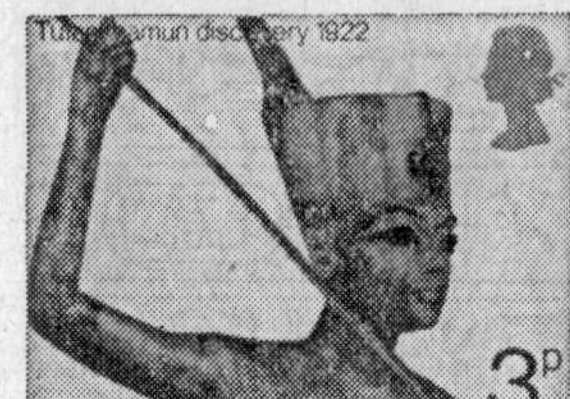

201. Statuette of Tutankhamun.

1972. General Anniversaries. Multicoloured.

901. 3p. Type **201** 10 5
902. 7½p. 19th-Century Coastguard 60 60
903. 9p. Ralph Vaughan Williams (composer) and Score 85 85

ANNIVERSARIES: 3p. Discovery of Tutankhamun's tomb. 50th Anniv. 7½p. Formation of H.M. Coastguard. 150th Anniv. 9p. Birth Cent.

202. St. Andrew's Church, Greensted-juxta-Ongar, Essex.

1972. British Architecture. Village Churches. Multicoloured.

904. 3p. Type **202** 10 8
905. 4p. All Saints, Earls Barton, Northants. 25 25
906. 5p. St. Andrew's, Letheringsett, Norfolk.. .. 50 30
907. 7½p. St. Andrew's, Helpringham, Lincs... .. 1·00 1·00
908. 9p. St. Mary the Virgin, Huish Episcopi, Somerset 1·00 1·00

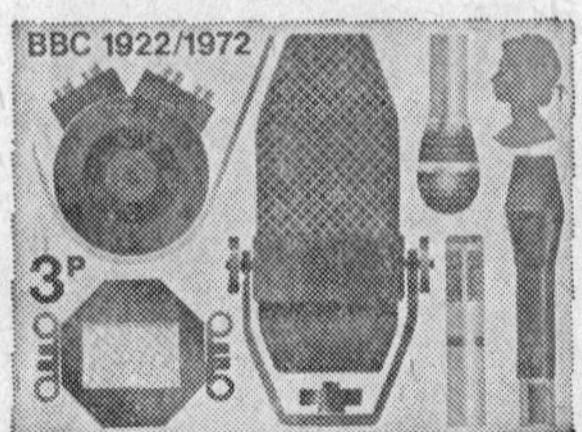

203. Microphones, 1924-69.

1972. Broadcasting Annivs. Multicoloured.

909. 3p. Type **203** 10 8
910. 5p. Horn Loudspeaker .. 30 30
911. 7½p. T.V. Camera, 1972 60 60
912. 9p. Oscillator and Spark Transmitter, 1897 85 85

ANNIVERSARIES: Nos. 909/11, Daily Broadcasting by the B.B.C. 50th Anniv. No. 912, Marconi and Kemp's Radio Experiments. 75th Anniv.

204. Angel holding Trumpet.

1972. Christmas. Multicoloured.

913. 2½p. Type **204** 8 5
914. 3p. Angel playing Lute .. 15 5
915. 7½p. Angel playing Harp 60 60

205. Queen Elizabeth and Duke of Edinburgh.

1972. Royal Silver Wedding.

916. **205.** 3p. blk., blue & silver 15 12
917. 20p. blk., purple & silver 1·00 1·00

206. "Europe".

1973. Britain's Entry into European Communities.

919. **206.** 3p multicoloured .. 15 5
920. 5p. mult. (blue jig-saw) 45 45
921. 5p. mult. (green jig-saw) 45 45

207. Oak Tree.

1973. Tree Planting Year. British Trees (1st issue).

922. **207.** 9 p. multicoloured .. 50 50

See also No. 949.

1973. British Explorers. As Type **200.** Multicoloured.

923. 3p. David Livingstone .. 15 12
924. 3p. H. M. Stanley .. 15 12
925. 5p. Sir Francis Drake .. 25 25
926. 7½p. Sir Walter Raleigh 45 45
927. 9p. Charles Sturt 65 65

208. W. G. Grace.

1973. County Cricket 1873-1973. Designs as T **208** showing caricatures of W. G. Grace by Harry Furniss.

928. **208.** 3p. blk., brn. & gold.. 10 10
929. – 7½p. blk., grn. & gold.. 40 35
930. 9p. blk., blue & gold 50 45

209. "Self-portrait" (Reynolds).

1973. British Paintings. Sir Joshua Reynolds. 250th Birth Anniv. and Sir Henry Raeburn. 150th Death Anniv. Multicoloured.

931. 3p. Type **209** 8 5
932. 5p. "Self-portrait" (Raeburn) 20 20
933. 7½p. "Nelly O' Brien" (Reynolds) 40 40
934. 9p. "Rev. R. Walker (The Skater)" (Raeburn) .. 45 45

210. Court Masque Costumes.

1973. Inigo Jones (architect and designer). 400th Birth Anniv. Multicoloured.

935. 3p. Type **210** 10 10
936. 3p. St. Paul's Church, Covent Garden 10 10
937. 5p. Prince's Lodging. Newmarket 35 35
938. 5p. Court Masque Stage Scene 35 35

211. Palace of Westminster, seen from Whitehall.

1973. 19th Commonwealth Parliamentary Conference.

939. **211.** 8p. stone, grey & black 40 40
940. – 10p. gold and black .. 45 45

DESIGN: 10p. Palace of Westminster, seen from Millbank.

212. Princess Anne and Capt. Mark Phillips.

1973. Royal Wedding.

941. **212.** 3½p. violet and silver.. 10 5
942. 20p. brown and silver 1·00 1·00

213. "Good King Wenceslas".

1973. Christmas. Designs as T **213** showing various scenes from the carol "Good King Wenceslas".

943. **213.** 3p multicoloured .. 20 12
944. – 3p. multicoloured .. 20 12
945. – 3p. multicoloured .. 20 12
946. – 3p. multicoloured .. 20 12
947. – 3p. multicoloured .. 20 12
948. – 3½p. multicoloured .. 20 12

214. Horse Chestnut.

1974. British Trees.

949. **214.** 10 p. multicoloured .. 45 45

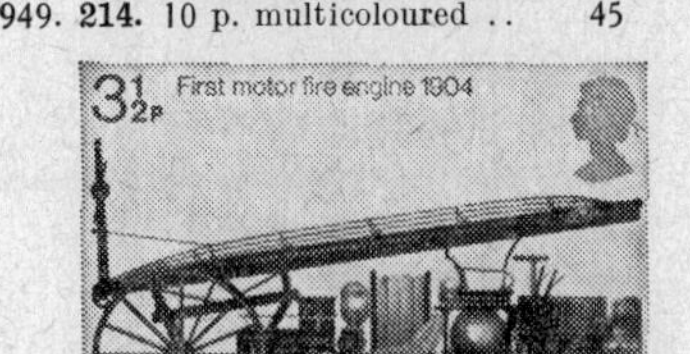

215. First Motor Fire-engine, 1904.

1974. Fire Prevention (Metropolis) Act. Bicent. Multicoloured.

950. 3½p. Type **215** 10 8
951. 5½p. Prize-winning fire-engine, 1863 .. .. 15 12
952. 8p. First steam fire-engine, 1830 .. .. 50 50
953. 10p. Fire-engine, 1766 .. .. 50 50

216. P. & O. Packet, "Peninsular", 1888.

1974. Universal Postal Union. Cent. Multicoloured.

954. 3½p. Type **216** 10 8
955. 5½p. Farman Biplane, 1911 15 12
956. 8p. Airmail-blue van and postbox, 1930 .. .. 50 50
957. 10p. Imperial Airways "C" Class Flying-boat, 1937 50 50

217. Robert the Bruce.

1974. Medieval Warriors. Multicoloured.

958. 4½p. Type **217** 10 10
959. 5½p. Owain Glydwr .. 12 12
960. 8p. Henry the Fifth .. 45 45
961. 10p. The Black Prince .. 45 45

218. Lord Warden of the Cinque Ports, 1942.

1974. Sir Winston Churchill. Birth Centenary.

962. **218.** 4½p. silver, bl. & grn. .. 10 10
963. – 5½p. silver, brn. & grey 60 60
964. – 8p. silver, red & pink . 45 45
965. – 10p. silver, brn. & stone 45 45

DESIGNS: 5½p. Prime Minister, 1940. 8p. Secretary for War and Air, 1919. 10p. War Correspondent, South Africa, 1899.

219. "Adoration of the Magi" (York Minster, c. 1355).

1974. Christmas. Church Roof Bosses. Multicoloured.

966. 3½p. Type **219** 8 8
967. 4½p. "The Nativity" (St. Helen's Church, Norwich, c. 1480) 10 10
968. 8p. "Virgin and Child" (Ottery St. Mary Church, c. 1350) 30 30
969. 10p. "Virgin and Child" (Worcester Cathedral, c. 1224) 30 30

220. Invalid in Wheelchair.

1975. Health and Handicap Funds.

970. **220.** 4½p.+1½p. blue & azure 20 20

221. "Peace—Burial at Sea".

1975. J. M. W. Turner (painter). Birth Bicentenary.

971. 4½p. Type **221** 12 12
972. 5½p. "Snowstorm—Steamer off a Harbour's Mouth" 15 15
973. 8p. "The Arsenal, Venice" 25 25
974. 10p. "St. Laurent" .. 40 40

222. Charlotte Square, Edinburgh.

1975. European Architectural Heritage Year. Multicoloured.

975. 7p. Type **222** 20 20
976. 7p. The Rows, Chester .. 20 20
977. 8p. Royal Observatory, Greenwich 20 20
978. 10p. St. George's Chapel, Windsor 30 30
979. 12p. National Theatre, London 35 35

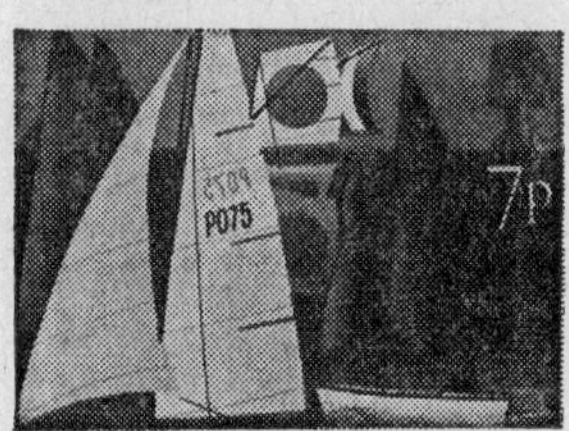

223. Sailing Dinghies.

1975. Sailing. Multicoloured.

980. 7p. Type **223** 15 15
981. 8p. Racing Keel Yachts .. 15 15
982. 10p. Cruising Yachts .. 30 35
983. 12p. Multihulls .. .. 1·00 1·25

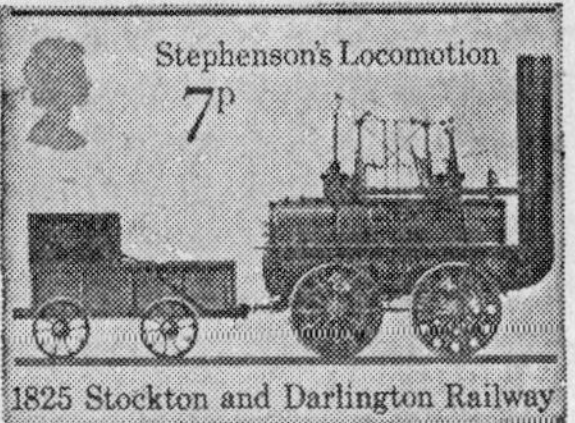

224. Stephenson's "Locomotion", 1825.

1975. Public Railways. 150th Anniversary. Multicoloured.

984. 7p. Type **224** 15 15
985. 8p. "Abbotsford", 1876 20 20
986. 10p. "Caerphilly Castle", 1923 .. .. .. 25 25
987. 12p. High Speed Train, 1975 .. .. .. 30 30

225. Palace of Westminster.

1975. 62nd Inter-Parliamentary Union Conference.

988. **225.** 12p. multicoloured .. 25 30

226. Emma and Mr. Woodhouse ("Emma").

1975. Jane Austen (novelist). Birth Bicentenary. Multicoloured.

989. 8½p. Type **226** 15 15
990. 10p. Catherine Morland ("Northanger Abbey") 25 25
991. 11p. Mr. Darcy ("Pride and Prejudice") .. 30 30
992. 13p. Mary and Henry Crawford ("Mansfield Park") 35 35

227. Angels with Harp and Lute.

1975. Christmas. Multicoloured.

993. 6½p. Type **227** .. 15 15
994. 8½p. Angel with Mandolin 20 20
995. 11p. Angel with Horn .. 25 25
996. 13p. Angel with Trumpet 30 30

228. Housewife.

1976. Telephone. Cent. Multicoloured.

997. 8½p. Type **228** 15 20
998. 10p. Policeman 20 20
999. 11p. District Nurse .. 20 25
1000. 13p. Industrialist .. 25 30

229. Hewing Coal (Thomas Hepburn).

1976. Industrial and Social Reformers. Mult.

1001. 8½p. Type **229** 15 20
1002. 10p. Machinery (Robert Owen) 20 20
1003. 11p. Chimney cleaning (Lord Shaftesbury) .. 20 25
1004. 13p. Hands clutching prison bars (Elizabeth Fry) .. 25 30

230. Benjamin Franklin (bust by Jean-Jacques Caffieri).

1976. American Revolution. Bicentenary.

1005. **230.** 11p. multicoloured .. 20 25

231. "Elizabeth of Glamis".

1976. Royal Nat. Rose Society. Cent. Multicoloured.

1006. 8½p. Type **231** 15 20
1007. 10p. "Grandpa Dickson" 20 20
1008. 11p. "Rosa Mundi" .. 20 25
1009. 13p. "Sweet Briar" .. 25 30

232. Archdruid.

1976. British Cultural Traditions. Mult.

1010. 8½p. Type **232** 15 20
1011. 10p. Morris dancing .. 20 20
1012. 11p. Scots piper 20 25
1013. 13p. Welsh harpist .. 25 30

The 8½p. and 13p. commemorate the 800th Anniv. of the Royal National Eisteddfod.

233. Woodcut from "The Canterbury Tales".

1976. British Printing. 500th Anniv. Multicoloured.

1014.	8½p. Type **233**	12	15
1015.	10p. Extract from "The Tretyse of Love" ..	15	20
1016.	11p. Woodcut from "The Game and Playe of Chesse"	15	20
1017.	13p. Early Printing Press	20	25

234. Virgin and Child.

1976. Christmas. English Medieval Embroidery. Mult.

1018.	6½p. Type **234**	10	12
1019.	8½p. Angel with crown ..	12	15
1020.	11p. Angel appearing to Shepherds	15	20
1021.	13p. The Three Kings ..	20	25

235. Lawn Tennis.

1976. Racket Sports. Multicoloured.

1022.	8½p. Type **235**	12	15
1023.	10p. Table tennis ..	15	20
1024.	11p. Squash	15	20
1025.	13p. Badminton	20	25

REGIONAL ISSUES.

I. NORTHERN IRELAND.

N 1.

N 2.

N 3.

N 4.

1958.

NI 1p.	N 1.	3d. lilac	15	8
NI 2.		4d. blue	15	10
NI 8.		4d. sepia	10	20
NI 9.		4d. vermilion ..	25	10
NI 10.		5d. blue	20	8
NI 3.	N 2.	6d. purple	20	10
NI 4.		9d. green	15	15
NI 5.	N 3.	1s. 3d. green ..	30	30
NI 6.		1s. 6d. blue	35	35

1971. Decimal Currency.

NI 12.	N 4.	2½p. red	20	15
NI 13.		3p. blue	25	15
NI 15.		3½p. green	15	12
NI 17.		4½p. blue	15	12
NI 18.		5p. violet	40	30
NI 19.		5½p. violet	10	10
NI 21.		6½p. blue	10	10
NI 22.		7½p. brown	60	60
NI 23.		8p. red	12	12
NI 24.		8½p. green	12	12
NI 25.		10p. brown	15	20
NI 26.		11p. red	15	20

II. SCOTLAND.

S 1. S 2.

S 3.

S 4.

1958.

S 7.	S 1.	3d. lilac	12	20
S 2.		4d. blue	12	15
S 9.		4d. sepia	12	8
S 10.		4d. vermilion ..	20	8
S 11.		5d. blue	25	12
S 3.	S 2.	6d. purple	12	5
S 4.		9d. green	15	30
S 5.	S 3.	1s. 3d. green ..	30	20
S 6.		1s. 6d. blue	30	45

1971. Decimal Currency.

S 14.	S 4.	2½d. red	20	15
S 15.		3p. blue	25	15
S 17.		3½p. green	15	12
S 19.		4½p. blue	15	12
S 20.		5p. violet	40	30
S 21.		5½p. violet	10	10
S 23.		6½p. blue	10	10
S 24.		7½p. brown	60	60
S 25.		8p. red	12	12
S 26.		8½p. green	12	12
S 27.		10p. brown	15	20
S 28.		11p. red	15	20

III. WALES AND MONMOUTHSHIRE.

W 1.

W 2.

W 3.

W 4.

1958.

W 1.	W 1.	3d. lilac	15	5
W 2.		4d. blue	15	5
W 9.		4d. sepia	12	5
W 10.		4d. vermilion	20	8
W 11.		5d. blue	25	12
W 3.	W 2.	6d. purple	30	15
W 4.		9d. green	15	30
W 5.	W 3.	1s. 3d. green ..	30	20
W 6.		1s. 6d. blue	30	20

1971. Decimal Currency.

W 13.	W 4.	2½p. red	20	15
W 14.		3p. blue	25	15
W 16.		3½p. green	15	12
W 18.		4½p. blue	15	12
W 19.		5p. violet	40	30
W 20.		5½p. violet	10	10
W 22.		6½p. blue	10	10
W 23.		7½p. brown	60	60
W 24.		8p. red	12	12
W 25.		8½p. green	12	12
W 26.		10p. brown	15	20
W 27.		11p. red	15	20

OFFICIAL STAMPS.

(for Government Departments)

ADMIRALTY

Overprinted **ADMIRALTY OFFICIAL**

1903. Stamps of King Edward VII.

O 107.	**66.**	½d. blue-green ..	3·50	1·50
O 102.	–	1d. red	2·00	1·00
O 103.		1½d. purple and green	22·00	12·00
O 104.	–	2d. green and red ..	28·00	15·00
O 105.	**66.**	2½d. blue	20·00	12·00
O 106.		3d. purple on yellow	32·00	12·00

ARMY

Overprinted **ARMY OFFICIAL.**

1896. Stamps of Queen Victoria.

O 41.	**54.**	½d. red	50	25
O 46.		½d. green	75	25
O 42.	**40.**	1d. lilac	50	25
O 43.	**57.**	2½d. purple on blue ..	1·50	65
O 47.	**62.**	6d. purple on red ..	6·00	4·00

1902. Stamps of King Edward VII.

O 48.	**66.**	½d. blue-green ..	75	30
O 49.		1d. red	50	25
O 50.		6d. purple	20·00	12·00

BOARD OF EDUCATION

Overprinted **BOARD OF EDUCATION.**

1902. Stamps of Queen Victoria.

O 81.	**61.**	5d. purple and blue ..	£120	30·00
O 82.	**65.**	1s. green and red ..	£275	£160

1902. Stamps of King Edward VII.

O 83.	**66.**	½d. blue-green ..	7·00	1·75
O 84.		1d. red	7·00	1·50
O 85.		2½d. blue	£110	22·00
O 86.		5d. purple and blue ..	£350	£140
O 87.		1s. green and red ..	£8000	£4250

GOVERNMENT PARCELS

Overprinted **GOVT. PARCELS.**

1883. Stamps of Queen Victoria.

O 69.	**40.**	1d. lilac	2·00	30
O 61.	**45.**	1½d. purple	26·00	7·00
O 62.	–	6d. green (No. 194) ..	£110	30·00
O 63.	–	9d. green (No. 195) ..	£118	75·00
O 64.	**16.**	1s. brown (No. 163) ..	£125	30·00

1887. Stamps of Queen Victoria.

O 65.	**55.**	1½d. purple and green	5·00	90
O 70.	**56.**	2d. green and red ..	15·00	2·00
O 71.	**60.**	4½d. green and red ..	18·00	25·00
O 66.	**62.**	6d. purple on red ..	10·00	4·00
O 67.	**63.**	9d. purple and blue ..	22·00	7·00
O 68.	**65.**	1s. green	38·00	30·00
O 72.		1s. green and red ..	55·00	20·00

1902. Stamps of King Edward VII.

O 74.	**66.**	1d. red	4·00	3·00
O 75.	–	2d. green and red ..	25·00	6·50
O 76.	**66.**	6d. purple	40·00	6·50
O 77.	–	9d. purple and blue ..	90·00	18·00
O 78.	–	1s. green and red ..	£160	35·00

INLAND REVENUE

Overprinted **I. R. OFFICIAL.**

Stamps of Queen Victoria.

1882.

O 1.	**35.**	½d. green	3·50	1·00
O 5.		½d. blue	5·50	1·00
O 3.	**40.**	1d. lilac	60	45
O 6.	–	2½d. purple (No. 190)	18·00	9·00
O 4.	**28.**	6d. grey (No. 161) ..	28·00	9·00
O 7.	–	1s. green (No. 196) ..	£900	£200
O 8.	–	5s. red (No. 181) ..	£500	£120
O 10.	–	10s. blue (No. 183) ..	£600	£140
O 12.	**44.**	£1 brown	£3000	£1400

1888.

O 13.	**54.**	½d. red	75	20
O 17.		½d. green	1·75	50
O 14.	**57.**	2½d. purple on blue ..	18·00	1·25
O 18.	**62.**	6d. purple on red ..	40·00	7·00
O 15.	**65.**	1s. green	50·00	9·00
O 19.		1s. green and red ..	£160	35·00
O 16.	**44.**	£1 green	£800	£160

1902. Stamps of King Edward VII.

O 20.	**66.**	½d. blue-green ..	2·00	50
O 21.		1d. red	1·00	25
O 22.		2½d. blue	£150	25·00
O 23.		6d. purple	£22000	£12000
O 24.	–	1s. green and red ..	£125	25·00
O 25.	–	5s. red	£1500	£550
O 26.	–	10s. blue	£7000	£4500
O 27.	–	£1 green	£4000	£1200

OFFICE OF WORKS

Overprinted **O.W. OFFICIAL.**

1896. Stamps of Queen Victoria.

O 31.	**54.**	½d. red	14·00	5·00
O 33.		½d. green	16·00	10·00
O 32.	**40.**	1d. lilac	11·00	4·00
O 34.	**61.**	5d. purple and blue ..	£150	55·00
O 35.	**64.**	10d. purple and red ..	£800	£110

1902. Stamps of King Edward VII.

O 36.	**66.**	½d. blue-green ..	20·00	3·00
O 37.	–	1d. red	20·00	2·50
O 38.	–	2d. green and red ..	80·00	15·00
O 39.	**66.**	2½d. blue	£180	18·00
O 40.	–	10d. purple and red ..	£350	£275

ROYAL HOUSEHOLD

Overprinted **R.H. OFFICIAL.**

1902. Stamps of King Edward VII.

O 91.	**66.**	½d. blue-green ..	40·00	30·00
O 92.		1d. red	35·00	25·00

POSTAGE DUE STAMPS.

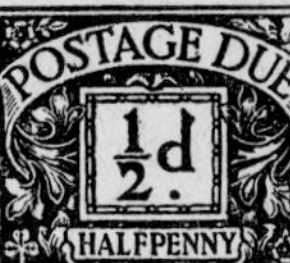

D 1.

D 2.

1914.

D 1.	D 1.	½d. green	40	20
D 56.		½d. orange	15	10
D 11.		1d. red	50	10
D 57.		1d. blue	15	8
D 3.		1½d. brown	15·00	6·00
D 37.		1½d. green	1·25	75
D 69.		2d. black	30	25
D 60.		3d. violet	40	10
D 15.		4d. grey-green ..	3·50	50
D 71.		4d. blue	60	25
D 72.		5d. brown	60	25
D 63.		6d. purple	40	12
D 76.		8d. red	75	40
D 17.		1s. blue	4·50	45
D 64.		1s. brown	60	15
D 65.		2s. 6d. purple on yell.	1·25	25
D 66.		5s. red on yellow ..	1·50	45
D 67.		10s. blue on yellow ..	4·00	2·00
D 68.		£1 black on yellow ..	25·00	2·50

On the 2s. 6d. to £1 the inscription reads "TO PAY".

1970. Decimal Currency.

D 77.		½p. blue	5	10
D 78.	–	1p. purple	5	5
D 79.	–	2p. green	5	5
D 80.	–	3p. blue	5	8
D 81.	–	4p. brown	8	10
D 82.	–	5p. violet	8	10
D 83.	–	7p. brown	12	15
D 84.	D 2.	10p. carmine ..	15	15
D 85.		11p. green	15	20
D 86.		20p. brown	30	20
D 87.		50p. ultramarine ..	75	30
D 88.		£1 black	1·50	50
D 89.		£5 yellow and black ..	7·50	3·50

DESIGN: ½p. to 7p. similar to Type D 2, but with "TO PAY" reading vertically upwards at the left.

CHANNEL ISLANDS

Islands in the English Channel off N.W. coast of France. Occupied by German Forces from June, 1940, to May, 1945, when separate issues for both islands were made. "Regional" issues were introduced from 1958, and the islands' Postal Services were organised as separate Postal Administrations in 1969.

A. GENERAL ISSUE.

C 1. Gathering Vraic (seaweed).

1948. Liberation. 3rd Anniv.

C 1.	C 1.	1d. red	10	10
C 2.	–	2½d. blue	15	15

DESIGN: 2½d. Islanders gathering vraic.

B. GUERNSEY.

(a) War Occupation Issues.

1.

ILLUSTRATIONS
British Commonwealth and all overprints and surcharges are FULL SIZE.
Foreign Countries have been reduced to ¾-LINEAR.

1941.

1.	1.	½d. green	2·50	1·00
2.		1d. red	1·50	30
3.		2½d. blue	3·00	2·75

(b) Regional Issues.

2.

3.

6.	2.	2½d. red	65	85
7p.	3.	3d. lilac	12	30
8p.		4d. blue	12	15
10.		4d. sepia	15	15
11.		4d. vermilion	40	35
12.		5d. blue	35	12

(c) Independent Postal Administration.

4. Castle Cornet and Edward the Confessor.

5. View of Sark.

1969.

13. **4.**	½d. magenta and black ..	8	8
14. –	1d. blue and black (I) ..	10	15
14b.–	1d. blue and black (II) ..	25	25
15. –	1½d. brown and black ..	10	10
16. –	2d. gold, red, blue & black	10	10
17. –	3d. gold, yell., red & black	10	10
18. –	4d. multicoloured ..	10	15
19. –	5d. gold, red, violet & blk.	25	25
20. –	6d. gold, yell., grn. & blk.	40	40
21. –	9d. gold, red, crimson & blk.	85	85
22. –	1s. gold, red, bistre & black	85	85
23. –	1s. 6d. green and black (I)	90	90
23b.–	1s. 6d. green & black (II)	4·00	2·00
24. –	1s. 9d. multicoloured ..	4·00	3·00
25. –	2s. 6d. violet and black ..	8·00	6·00
26. **5.**	5s. multicoloured	10·00	9·00
27. –	10s. multicoloured ..	40·00	30·00
28a.–	£1 multicoloured ..	3·00	3·00

DESIGNS—As T **4**: 1d. Map and William I. 1½d. Martello Tower and Henry II. 2d. Arms of Sark and King John. 3d. Arms of Alderney and Edward III. 4d. Guernsey Lily and Henry V. 5d. Arms of Guernsey and Elizabeth I. 6d. Arms of Alderney and Charles II. 9d. Arms of Sark and George III. 1s. Arms of Guernsey and Queen Victoria. 1s. 6d. as 1d. 1s. 9d. Guernsey Lily and Elizabeth I. 2s. 6d. Martello Tower and King John. As T **5**: 10s. View of Alderney. 20s. View of Guernsey.

In I the degree of latitude is inscr. (incorrectly) as 40° 30′ N. In II it has been corrected to 49° 30′.

6. Isaac Brock as Colonel.

1969. Sir Isaac Brock. Birth Bicent. Multicoloured.

29.	4d. As Type **6**	20	20
30.	5d. Sir Isaac Brock as Major-General	20	20
31.	1s. 9d. Isaac Brock as Ensign	3·00	3·00
32.	2s. 6d. Arms and flags ..	3·50	3·50

The 2s. 6d. is horiz.

7. Landing Craft entering St. Peter's Harbour.

1970. Liberation. 25th Anniv.

33. **7.**	4d. blue	30	30
34. –	5d. brown, lake and grey	30	30
35. –	1s. 6d. brn. & buff (vert.)	6·00	6·00

DESIGNS: 5d. British ships entering St. Peter's Port. 1s. 6d. Brigadier Snow reading Proclamation.

8. Guernsey "Toms".

1970. Agriculture and Horticulture. Multicoloured.

36.	4d. Type **8**	25	25
37.	5d. Guernsey cow	25	25
38.	9d. Guernsey bull	6·00	4·00
39.	1s. 6d. Freesias	7·50	6·00

9. St. Peter's Church, Sark.

1970. Christmas. Churches (1st Series). Multicoloured.

40.	4d. St. Anne's Church, Alderney (horiz.)	25	20
41.	5d. St. Peter's Church (horiz.)	25	25
42.	9d. Type **9**	2·50	2·00
43.	1s. 6d. St. Tugual Chapel, Herm	4·50	4·00

See also Nos. 63/6.

10. Martello Tower and King John.

1971. Decimal currency. Nos. 13, etc., but with new colours and decimal values as T **10**.

44.	½p. mve. & blk. (as No. 13)	15	15
45.	1p. blue & blk. (as No. 14)	10	8
46.	1½p. brn. & blk. (as No. 15)	12	12
47.	2p. mult. (as No. 18) ..	12	12
48.	2½p. mult. (as No. 19) ..	20	20
49.	3p. mult. (as No. 17) ..	20	20
50.	3½p. mult. (as No. 24) ..	20	20
51.	4p. mult. (as No. 16) ..	30	25
52.	5p. grn. & blk. (as No. 14)	25	25
53.	6p. mult. (as No. 20) ..	35	35
54.	7½p. mult. (as No. 22) ..	45	45
55.	9p. mult. (as No. 21) ..	2·50	2·50
56.	10p. violet & blk. (as No. 25)	2·50	2·50
57.	20p. mult. (as No. 26) ..	2·00	2·00
58.	50p. mult. (as No. 27) ..	2·50	2·00

11. Hong Kong 2 c. of 1862.

1971. Thomas De La Rue Commemoration.

59. **11.**	2p. purple	20	20
60. –	2½p. red	20	20
61. –	4p. green	3·50	3·00
62. –	7½p. blue	3·50	3·00

DESIGNS (Each showing portraits of Queen Elizabeth and Thomas De La Rue): 2½p. Great Britain 4d. of 1855–7. 4p. Italy. 5c. of 1862. 7½p. Confederate States 5c. of 1862.

1971. Christmas. Churches (2nd Series). As T **9**. Multicoloured.

63.	2p. Ebenezer Church, St. Peter Port (horiz.) ..	20	20
64.	2½p. Church of St. Pierre du Bois (horiz.)	20	20
65.	5p. St. Joseph's Church, St. Peter Port	3·00	2·50
66.	7½p. Church of St. Philippe de Torteval	4·00	3·50

12. "Earl of Chesterfield" (1794).

1972. Mail Packet Ships (1st Series). Mult.

67.	2p. Type **12**	20	20
68.	2½p. "Dasher" (1827) ..	20	20
69.	7½p. "Ibex" (1891) ..	2·75	3·00
70.	9p. "Alberta" (1900) ..	2·75	3·00

See also Nos. 80/3.

1972. World Conf. of Guernsey Breeders, Guernsey. As No. 38 but size 48×29 mm, and additional inscription with face value changed.

71.	5p. multicoloured	2·50	1·75

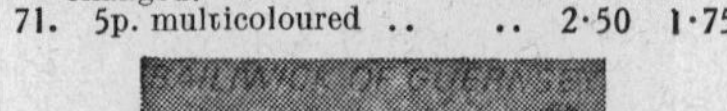

13. Bermuda Buttercup.

1972. Wild Flowers. Multicoloured.

72.	2p. Type **13**	15	15
73.	2½p. Heath Spotted Orchid (vert.)	15	15
74.	7½p. Kaffir Fig	1·25	1·25
75.	9p. Scarlet Pimpernel (vert.)	2·00	1·50

14. Angels adoring Christ.

1972. Royal Silver Wedding and Christmas. Stained-glass windows from Guernsey Churches. Multicoloured.

76.	2p. Type **14**	8	8
77.	2½p. The Epiphany ..	10	10
78.	7½p. The Virgin Mary ..	75	75
79.	9p. Christ	1·00	1·00

See also Nos. 89/92.

1973. Mail Packet Boats (2nd Series). As T **12**. Multicoloured.

80.	2½p. "St. Julien" (1925) ..	12	12
81.	3p. "Isle of Guernsey" (1930)	30	30
82.	7½p. "St. Patrick" (1947)	2·00	2·00
83.	9p. "Sarnia" (1961) ..	2·00	2·00

15. Supermarine "Sea Eagle".

1973. Air Service. 50th Anniv. Multicoloured.

84.	2½p. Type **15**	12	12
85.	3p. Westland "Wessex" ..	15	15
86.	5p. De Havilland "Rapide"	25	25
87.	7½p. Douglas "Dakota" ..	85	85
88.	9p. Vickers "Viscount" ..	85	85

16. "The Good Shepherd".

1973. Christmas. Stained-glass windows from Guernsey Churches. Multicoloured.

89.	2½p. Type **16**	10	10
90.	3p. Christ at the well of Samaria	15	15
91.	7½p. St. Dominic	25	25
92.	20p. Mary and the Child Jesus	50	50

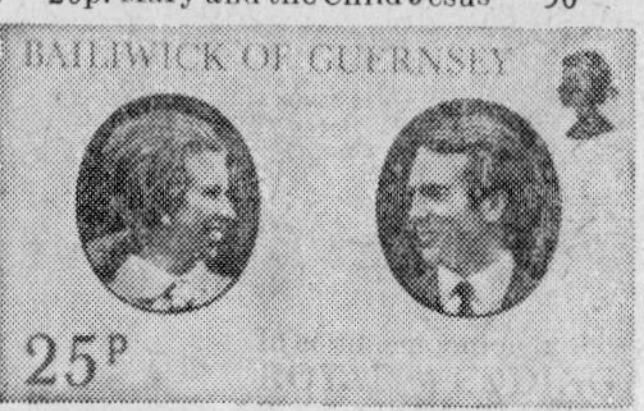

17. Princess Anne and Capt. Mark Phillips.

1973. Royal Wedding.

93. **17.**	25p. multicoloured ..	1·00	1·10

18. "John Lockett", 1875.

1974. Royal National Life-boat Institution. 150th Anniv. Multicoloured.

94.	2½p. Type **18**	10	10
95.	3p. "Arthur Lionel", 1912	15	15
96.	8p "Euphrosyne Kendal", 1954	50	50
97.	10p. "Arun", 1972 ..	50	50

19. Private, East Regt., 1815.

20. Driver, Field Battery Royal Guernsey Artillery, 1848.

1974. Guernsey Militia, Multicoloured. (a) As T **19**.

98.	½p. Type **19**	5	5
99.	1p. Officer, 2nd North Regt., 1825	5	5
100.	1½p. Gunner, Guernsey Artillery, 1787	5	5
101.	2p. Gunner, Guernsey Artillery, 1815	5	5
102.	2½p. Corporal, Royal Guernsey Artillery, 1868	5	5
103.	3p. Field Officer, Royal Guernsey Artillery, 1895	5	5
104.	3½p. Sergeant, 3rd Regt., 1867	5	8
105.	4p. Officer, East Regt., 1822	8	8
105a.	5p. Field Officer, Royal Guernsey Artillery ..	8	10
106.	5½p. Colour-Sergeant of Grenadiers, East Regt., 1833	10	10
107.	6p. Officer, North Regt., 1832	10	10
107a.	7p. Officer, East Regt., 1882	12	15
108.	8p. Field Officer, Rifle Company, 1868	15	15
109.	9p. Private, 4th West Regt., 1785	15	15
110.	10p. Field Officer, 4th West Regt., 1824	20	20

(b) As Type **20**.

111.	20p. Type **20**	35	35
112.	50p. Officer, Field Battery, Royal Guernsey Artillery, 1868	85	85
113.	£1 Cavalry Trooper, Light Dragoons, 1814 (horiz.)	1·75	1·75

21. Badge of Guernsey and U.P.U. Emblem.

1974. U.P.U. Centenary. Multicoloured

114.	2½p. Type **21**	5	5
115.	3p. Map of Guernsey ..	8	8
116.	8p. U.P.U. Building, Berne, and Guernsey flag ..	35	40
117.	10p. "Salle des Etats" ..	45	50

22. "Cradle Rock".

1974. Renoir Paintings. Multicoloured.

118.	3p. Type **22**	15	8
119.	5½p. "Moulin Huet Bay"..	25	12
120.	8p. "Au Bord de la Mer" (vert.)	50	50
121.	10p. Self-portrait (vert.)..	75	60

23. Guernsey Spleenwort.

1975. Guernsey Ferns. Multicoloured.

122.	3½p. Type **23**	8	8
123.	4p. Sand Quillwort ..	10	10
124.	8p. Guernsey Quillwort ..	20	20
125.	10p. Least Adder's Tongue	50	50

24. Victor Hugo House.

1975. Victor Hugo's Exile in Guernsey. Mult.

126.	3½p. Type **24**	8	8
127.	4p. Candie Gardens (vert.)	8	8
128.	8p. United Europe Oak, Hauteville (vert.) ..	20	20
129.	10p. Tapestry Room, Hauteville	30	30

25. Globe and Seal of Bailiwick.

1975. Christmas. Multicoloured.

131.	4p. Type **25**	8	10
132.	6p. Guernsey flag ..	12	15
133.	10p. Guernsey flag and Alderney shield (horiz.)	20	20
134.	12p. Guernsey flag and Sark shield (horiz.) ..	25	30

26. Les Hanois.

1976. Bailiwick Lighthouses. Mult.

135.	4p. Type **26**	8	10
136.	6p. Les Casquets	15	15
137.	11p. Quesnard	20	25
138.	13p. Point Robert ..	25	30

27. Milk Can.

1976. Europa.

139. **27.**	10p. brown and green..	30	30
140. –	25p. grey and blue ..	70	70

DESIGN. 25p. Christening Cup.

28. Pine Forest, Guernsey.

1976. Views. Multicoloured.

141.	5p. Type **28**	10	12
142.	7p. Herm and Jethou ..	15	15
143.	11p. Grand Greve Bay, Sark (vert.)	20	25
144.	13p. Trois Vaux Bay, Alderney (vert.) ..	25	30

29. Royal Court House, Guernsey.

1976. Buildings. Multicoloured.

145.	5p. Type **29**	10	12
146.	7p. Elizabeth College, Guernsey	15	15
147.	11p. La Seigneurie, Sark..	20	25
148.	13p. Island Hall, Alderney	25	30

30. Queen Elizabeth II (vert.).

1977. Silver Jubilee. Multicoloured.

149.	7p. Type **30**	15	15
150.	35p. Queen Elizabeth (half-length portrait) ..	70	80

POSTAGE DUE STAMPS

D 1. Castle Cornet.

1969.

D 1. D **1.**	1d. plum	1·00	1·00
D 2.	2d. green	1·50	1·00
D 3.	3d. red	3·00	2·00
D 4.	4d. blue	4·00	3·50
D 5.	5d. ochre	5·00	4·00
D 6.	6d. turquoise-blue ..	7·00	6·50
D 7.	1s. brown	17·00	16·00

1971. Decimal Currency.

D 8. D **1.**	½p. plum	5	5
D 9.	1p. green	5	5
D 10.	2p. red	5	5
D 11.	3p. blue	5	8
D 12.	4p. ochre	8	10
D 13.	5p. blue	8	10
D 14.	6p. violet	10	12
D 15.	8p. orange	15	15
D 16.	10p. brown	20	20
D 17.	15p. grey	25	30

C. JERSEY.

(a) War Occupation Issues.

1. **2.** Old Jersey Farm.

1941.

1. **1.**	½d. green	1·60	60
2.	1d. red	2·00	1·75

1943.

3. **2.**	½d. green	4·00	1·25
4. –	1d. red	40	15
5. –	1½d. brown..	1·00	1·50
6. –	2d. yellow	1·00	1·50
7a.–	2½d. blue	1·25	1·00
8. –	3d. violet	1·50	2·00

DESIGNS: 1d. Portelet Bay. 1½d. Corbiere Lighthouse. 2d. Elizabeth Castle. 2½d. Mont Orgueil Castle. 3d. Gathering vraic (seaweed).

(b) Regional Issues.

3. **4.**

1958.

9. **3.**	2½d. red	70	85
10p. **4.**	3d. lilac	12	15
11p.	4d. blue	15	20
12.	4d. sepia	20	20
13.	4d. vermilion	35	30
14.	5d. blue	35	15

(c) Independent Postal Administration.

5. Elizabeth Castle.

1969. Multicoloured.

15.	½d. Type **5**	30	35
16.	1d. La Haugue Bie (Prehistoric Tomb)	25	20
17.	2d. Portelet Bay ..	10	12
18.	3d. Corbiere Lighthouse ..	10	12
19.	4d. Mont Orgueil Castle by night	10	10
20.	5d. Arms and Royal Mace..	20	12
21.	6d. Jersey Cow	50	50
22.	9d. Chart of the English Channel	1·00	1·00
23.	1s. Mont Orgueil Castle by day	1·00	1·00
24.	1s. 6d. Chart of the English Channel	1·50	1·50
25.	1s. 9d. Queen Elizabeth II (after Cecil Beaton) ..	1·75	1·75
26.	2s. 6d. Jersey Airport ..	3·00	3·00
27.	5s. Legislative Chamber ..	20·00	14·00
28.	10s. The Royal Court ..	35·00	25·00
29.	£1 Queen Elizabeth II (after Cecil Beaton)	2·00	2·50

The 1s. 9d. and £1 are vert.

6. First Day Cover.

1969. Post Office Inaug.

30. **6.**	4d. multicoloured ..	25	20
31.	5d. multicoloured ..	50	30
32.	1s. 6d. multicoloured ..	3·25	3·00
33.	1s. 9d. multicoloured ..	3·25	3·00

7. Lord Coutanche, former Bailiff of Jersey.

1970. Liberation. 25th Anniv. Multicoloured.

34.	4d. Type **7**	20	20
35.	5d. Sir Winston Churchill..	25	25
36.	1s. 6d. "Liberation" (Edmund Blampied) ..	3·00	3·00
37.	1s. 9d. S.S. "Vega" ..	3·00	3·00

Nos. 36/7 are horiz.

8. "A Tribute to Enid Blyton".

1970. "Battle of Flowers" Parade. Mult.

38.	4d. Type **8**	20	20
39.	5d. "Rags to riches" (Cinderella and pumpkin)	30	20
40.	1s. 6d. "Gourmet's delight" (lobster and cornucopia)	9·00	5·00
41.	1s. 9d. "We're the greatest" (ostriches)..	9·00	5·00

9. Jersey Airport.

1970. Decimal currency. Nos. 15, etc., but with new colours, new design (6p.) and decimal values, as T **9**.

42.	½p. mult. (as No. 15) ..	5	5
43.	1p. mult. (as No. 18) ..	5	5
44.	1½p. mult. (as No. 21) ..	5	5
45.	2p. mult. (as No. 19) ..	5	5
46.	2½p. mult. (as No. 20) ..	8	8
47.	3p. mult. (as No. 16) ..	8	8
48.	3½p. mult. (as No. 17) ..	10	10
49.	4p. mult. (as No. 22) ..	10	10
49a.	4½p. mult. (as No. 20) ..	10	10
50.	5p. mult. (as No. 23) ..	15	12
50a.	5½p. mult. (as No. 21) ..	12	12
51.	6p. multicoloured (Martello Tower, Archirondel, 23×22 mm.) ..	15	15
52.	7½p. mult (as No. 24) ..	20	20
52a.	8p. mult. (as No. 19) ..	20	20
53.	9p. mult. (as No. 25) ..	25	25
54.	10p. mult. (as No. 26) ..	30	30
55.	20p. mult. (as No. 27) ..	50	50
56.	50p. mult. (as No. 28) ..	1·50	1·50

10. White-eared Pheasant.

1971. Wildlife Preservation Trust (1st series). Multicoloured.

57.	2p. Type **10**	20	20
58.	2½p. Thick-billed Parrot (vert.)	25	25
59.	7½p. Ursine Colobus Monkey (vert.)	8·00	5·00
60.	9p. Ring-tailed Lemur ..	8·00	5·00

See also Nos. 73/6.

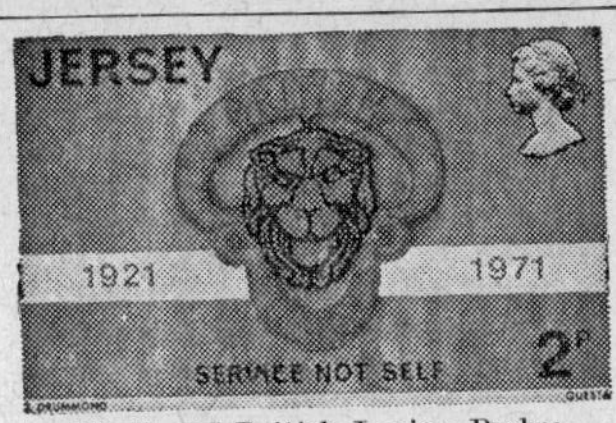

11. Royal British Legion Badge.

1971. Royal British Legion. 50th Anniv. Multicoloured.

61. 2p. Type **11** 15 15
62. 2½p. Poppy emblem and field 20 20
63. 7½p. Jack Counter and Victoria Cross .. .. 3·50 3·00
64. 9p. Crossed Tricolour and Union Jack .. .. 3·50 3·00

12. "Tante Elizabeth". (E. Blampied).

1971. Paintings (1st series). Multicoloured.

65. 2p. Type **12** 15 15
66. 2½p. "English Fleet in the Channel" (P. Monamy) (horiz.) 20 20
67. 7½p. "The Boyhood of Raleigh" (Millais) (horiz.) 5·00 4·00
68. 9p. "The Blind Beggar" (W. W. Ouless) .. .. 5·00 4·00

See also Nos. 115/118.

13. Jersey Fern.

14. Shako (Artillery).

1972. Wild Flowers of Jersey. Multicoloured.

69. 3p. Type **13** 15 15
70. 5p. Jersey Thrift 50 50
71. 7½p. Jersey Orchid .. 3·00 2·50
72. 9p. Jersey Viper's Bugloss 3·00 2·50

1972. Wildlife Preservation Trust (2nd series). As T **10**. Multicoloured.

73. 2½p. Cheetah 15 15
74. 3p. Rothschild's Mynah (vert.) 20 20
75. 7½p. Spectacled Bear .. 2·50 2·00
76. 9p. Tuatara.. .. .. 2·50 2·00

1972. Royal Jersey Militia. Multicoloured.

77. 2½p. Type **14** 15 15
78. 3p. Shako (2nd North Regt.) 20 20
79. 7½p. Shako (5th South-West Regt.) .. .. .. 2·00 1·50
80. 9p. Helmet (3rd Jersey Light Infantry).. .. .. 2·00 1·50

15. Princess Anne.

1972. Royal Silver Wedding. Multicoloured.

81. 2½p. Type **15** 5 5
82. 3p. Queen Elizabeth and Prince Philip (horiz.) .. 8 8
83. 7½p. Prince Charles .. 60 65
84. 20p. The Royal Family (horiz.) 60 75

16. Armorican Bronze Coins.

1973. La Societe Jersiase. Cent. Mult.

85. 2½p. Silver cups 15 15
86. 3p. Gold torque (vert.) .. 20 20
87. 7½p. Royal Seal of Charles II (vert.) .. .. .. 1·00 1·00
88. 9p. Type **16** .. .. 1·00 1·00

17. Balloon and Letter.

1973. Jersey Aviation History. Mult.

89. 3p. Type **17** 15 15
90. 5p. Seaplane "Astra" .. 20 20
91. 7½p. Supermarine "Sea Eagle" .. .. .. 1·00 1·00
92. 9p. De Havilland "Express" 1·00 1·00

18. "North Western".

1973. Jersey Eastern Railway. Centenary. Early Locomotives. Multicoloured.

93. 2½p. Type **18** 15 10
94. 3p. "Calvados" 20 25
95. 7½p. "Carteret" 85 85
96. 9p. "Caesarea" 85 85

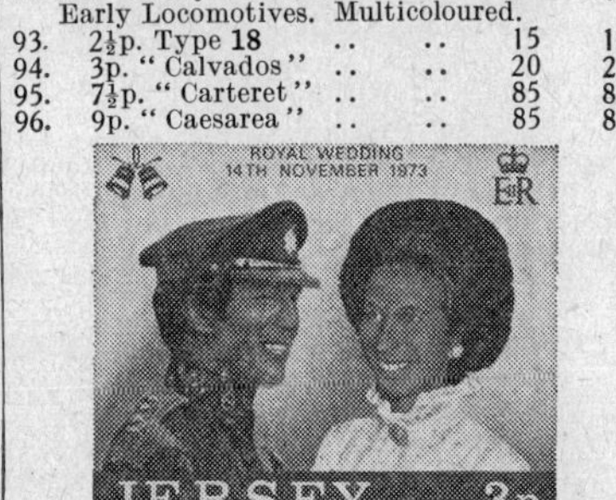

19. Princess Anne and Capt. Mark Phillips.

1973. Royal Wedding.

97. **19.** 3p. multicoloured .. 8 8
98. 20p. multicoloured .. 85 85

20. Spider Crab.

1973. Marine Life. Multicoloured.

99. 2½p. Type **20** 8 8
100. 3p. Conger-eel 8 8
101. 7½p. Lobster 35 45
102. 20p. Ormer 35 45

21. Freesias.

1974. Spring Flowers. Multicoloured.

103. 3p. Type **21** 8 8
104. 5½p. Anemones 12 12
105. 8p. Carnations and Gladioli 25 45
106. 10p. Daffodils and Iris .. 25 45

22. First Letter Box and Contemporary Cover.

1974. U.P.U. Centenary. Multicoloured.

107. 2½p. Type **22** 5 5
108. 3p. Postmen, 1862 and 1969 8 8
109. 5½p. Letter-box and letter, 1974 .. .. .. 20 20
110. 20p. R.M.S. "Aquila" (1874) and aeroplane (1974) 80 80

23. John Wesley.

1974. Anniversaries.

111. **23.** 3p. brown and black .. 5 8
112. – 3½p. blue and black .. 8 8
113. – 8p. mauve and blue .. 20 20
114. – 20p. stone and black .. 80 80

PORTRAITS AND EVENTS: 3p. (Methodism in Jersey. Bicent.). 3½p. Sir William Hillary, founder (R.N.L.I. 150th anniv.). 8p. Canon Wace, poet and historian (800th death anniv.). 20p. Sir Winston Churchill (birth cent.).

24. Royal Yacht.

1974. Paintings (2nd series). Works by Peter Monamy. Multicoloured.

115. 3½p. Type **24**. 8 8
116. 5½p. French two-decker .. 12 12
117. 8p. Dutch vessel (horiz.) .. 40 40
118. 25p. Battle of Cap La Hague (55×27 mm.) 80 80

25. Potato Digger.

1975. 19th Century Farming. Multicoloured.

119. 3p. Type **25** 5 5
120. 3½p. Cider Crusher .. 8 8
121. 8p. Six-horse plough .. 20 20
122. 10p. Hay cart 30 30

26. H.M. Queen Elizabeth, the Queen Mother (photograph by Cecil Beaton).

1975. Royal Visit.

123. **26.** 20p. multicoloured .. 40 45

27. Shell.

1975. Jersey Tourism. Multicoloured.

124. 5p. Type **27** 10 12
125. 8p. Parasol 15 20
126. 10p. Deckchair 20 20
127. 12p. Sandcastle with flags of Jersey and the U.K. 30 30

28. Common Tern.

1975. Sea Birds. Multicoloured.

129. 4p. Type **28** 8 10
130. 5p. Storm Petrel 10 12
131. 8p. Brent Geese 15 20
132. 25p. Shag 50 60

29. Siskin "3–A".

1975. Royal Air Force Association. Jersey Branch. 50th Anniv. Multicoloured.

133. 4p. Type **29** 8 10
134. 5p. "Southampton" flying-boat 10 10
135. 10. Mk. 1 "Spitfire" .. 20 20
136. 25p. Folland "Gnat" .. 50 50

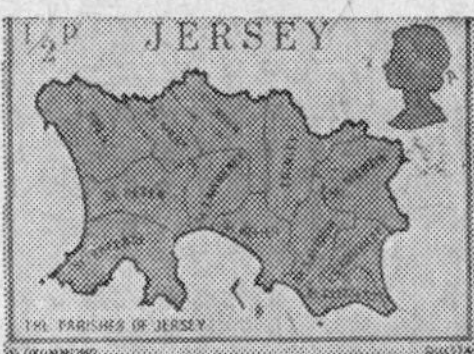

30. Map of Jersey Parishes.

31. Parish Arms and Island Scene.

1976. Multicoloured.

(a) Parish Arms and Views.

137. ½p. Type **30** 5 5
138. 1p. Zoological Park .. 5 5
139. 5p. St. Mary's Church .. 8 10
140. 6p. Seymour Tower .. 10 12
141. 7p. La Corbiere Lighthouse 12 15
142. 8p. St. Saviour's Church 15 15
143. 9p. Elizabeth Castle .. 15 20
144. 10p. Gorey Harbour .. 20 20
145. 11p. Jersey Airport .. 20 25
146. 12p. Grosnez Castle .. 20 25
147. 13p. Bonne Nuit Harbour 25 25
148. 14p. Le Hocq Tower .. 25 25
149. 15p. Morel Farm 25 30

(b) Emblems.

150.	20p. Type **31**	35	40
151.	30p. Flag and map ..	55	65
152.	40p. Postal H.Q. and badge	70	80
153.	50p. Parliament, Royal Court and arms ..	85	95
154.	£1 Lieutenant-Governor's flag and Government House	1·75	2·00

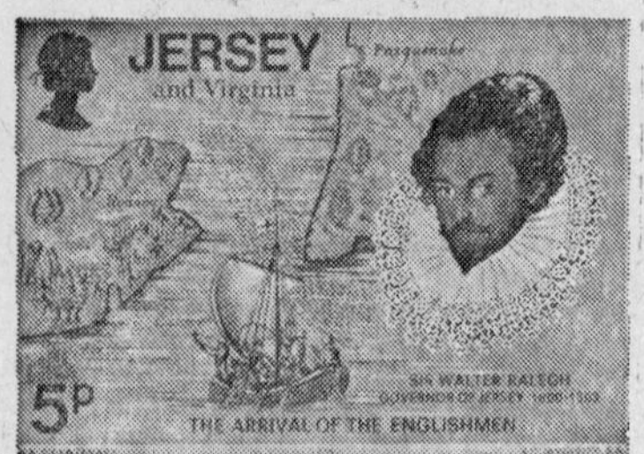

32. Sir Walter Raleigh and the Arrival of the English.

1976. American Independence. Bicentenary. Multicoloured.

160.	5p. Type **32**	10	12
161.	7p Sir George Carteret and map of New Jersey ..	12	15
162.	11p. Philippe Dauvergne and Long Island Landing	20	25
163.	13p. John Copley and sketch	25	30

33. Dr. Grandin and Map of China.

1976. Dr. Lilian Grandin (medical missionary). Birth Centenary.

164.	**33.**	5p. multicoloured	10	10
165.	–	7p. yell., brn. and blk.	15	15
166.	–	11p. multicoloured ..	20	25
167.	–	13p. multicoloured ..	25	30

DESIGNS: 7p. Sampan on the Yangtze. 11p. Overland trek. 13p. Dr. Grandin at work.

34. Coronation, 1953 (photograph by Cecil Beaton) (vert.).

1976. Silver Jubilee. Multicoloured.

168.	5p. Type **34**	10	12
169.	7p. Visit to Jersey, 1957..	15	15
170.	25p. Queen Elizabeth II (photo by Peter Grugeon)	50	60

POSTAGE DUE STAMPS

D 1.

1969.

D 1.	D **1.**	1d. violet	1·00	1·00
D 2.		2d. sepia	1·50	1·00
D 3.		3d. magenta	2·50	1·50
D 4.	–	1s. emerald	9·00	6·00
D 5.	–	2s. 6d. grey	22·00	14·00
D 6.	–	5s. vermilion	35·00	30·00

DESIGNS: 1s., 2s. 6d. and 5s. Map.

1971. Decimal Currency. Design as Nos. D 4/6, but values in new currency.

D 7.	½p. black..	5	5
D 8.	1p. blue	5	5
D 9.	2p. brown	5	5
D 10.	3p. purple	5	8
D 11.	4p. red	8	10
D 12.	5p. green..	8	10
D 13.	6p. orange	10	12
D 14.	7p. yellow	10	12
D 15.	8p. blue	15	20
D 16.	10p. green	20	25
D 17.	11p. brown	20	25
D 18.	14p. violet	25	30
D 19.	25p. green	45	50
D 20.	50p. purple	85	95

INDEX

Countries can be quickly located by referring to the index at the end of this volume.

ISLE OF MAN

An island in the Irish Sea to the north-west of England. Man became a possession of the English Crown during the Middle Ages, but retains its own Assembly.

(a) Regional Issues.

1.

2.

1958.

1.	**1.**	2½d. red	90	90
2.	**2.**	3d. lilac	20	8
3p.		4d. blue	15	12
5.		4d. sepia	40	30
6.		4d. vermilion ..	90	50
7.		5d. blue	1·50	20

3.

1971. Decimal Currency.

8.	**3.**	2½p. red	15	15
9.		3p. blue	25	25
10.		5p. violet	30	30
11.		7½p. brown	40	40

(b) Independent Postal Administration.

4. Castletown.

5. Manx Cat.

1973. Multicoloured.

12.	½p. Type **4**	5	5
13.	1p. Port Erin	5	5
14.	1½p. Snaefell	5	5
15.	2p. Laxey	5	5
16.	2½p. Tynwald Hill.. ..	5	5
17.	3p. Douglas Promenade ..	5	5
18.	3½p. Port St. Mary ..	5	5
19.	4p. Fairy Bridge	8	8
20.	4½p. As 2½p.	8	8
21.	5p. Peel	8	8
22.	5½p. As 3p..	10	10
23.	6p. Cregneish	10	10
24.	7p. As 2p.	12	12
25.	7½p. Ramsey Bay	12	12
26.	8p. As 7½p..	15	15
27.	9p. Douglas Bay	15	15
28.	10p. Type **5**	20	20
29.	11p. Monk's Bridge, Ballasalla	20	20
30.	13p. Derbyhaven	25	25
31.	20p. Manx Loaghtyn Ram	35	35
32.	50p. Manx Shearwater ..	85	85
33.	£1 Viking Longship ..	1·75	1·75

SIZES: Nos. 13/27 as Type **4**. Nos. 28/31 as Type **5**.

6. Viking landing on Man, A.D. 938.

1973. Postal Independence. Inaug.

34.	**6.**	15p. multicoloured ..	1·75	1·75

7. " Sutherland ".

1973. Steam Railway Cent. Multicoloured.

35.	2½p. Type **7**	10	10
36.	3p. " Caledonia " ..	10	10
37.	7½p. " Kissack " ..	1·75	1·75
38.	9p. " Pender "	1·75	1·75

8. Leslie Randles, First Winner, 1923.

1973. Manx Grand Prix. Golden Jubilee. Multicoloured.

39.	3p. Type **8**	30	30
40.	3½p. Alan Holmes, Double Winner, 1957	30	30

9. Princess Anne and Capt. Mark Phillips.

1973. Royal Wedding.

41.	**9.**	25p. multicoloured ..	2·00	1·75

10. Badge, Citation and Sir William Hillary (Founder).

1974. Royal National Lifeboat Institution. 150th Anniv. Multicoloured.

42.	3p. Type **10**	10	10
43.	3½p. Wreck of " St. George ", 1830	12	12
44.	8p. R.N.L.B. " Manchester and Salford ", 1868-87 ..	70	70
45.	10p. R.N.L.B. " Osman Gabriel"	70	70

11. Stanley Woods, 1935.

1974. Tourist Trophy Motor-cycle Races (1st issue). Multicoloured.

46.	3p. Type **11**	8	8
47.	3½p. Freddy Frith, 1937 ..	8	8
48.	8p. Max Deubel and Emil Horner, 1961	45	45
49.	10p. Mike Hailwood, 1961	45	45

See also Nos 63/6.

12. Rushen Abbey and Arms.

1974. Historical Anniversaries. Multicoloured.

50.	3½p. Type **12**	8	8
51.	4½p. Magnus Haraldson rows King Edgar on the Dee..	12	12
52.	8p. King Magnus and Norse fleet	35	35
53.	10p. Bridge at Avignon and bishop's mitre	35	35

COMMEMORATIONS: Nos. 50 and 53, William Russell, Bishop of Sodor and Man. 600th Death Anniv Nos. 51/2, Rule of King Magnus Haraldson. 1000th Anniv.

13. Churchill, and Bugler Dunne at Colenso, 1899.

1974. Sir Winston Churchill. Birth Cent. Multicoloured.

54.	3½p. Type **13**	8	8
55.	4½p. Churchill and Government Buildings, Douglas	10	10
56.	8p. Churchill and Manx ack-ack crew	50	50
57.	20p. Churchill as Freeman of Douglas	50	50

14. Cabin School and Names of Pioneers.

1975. Manx Pioneers in Cleveland, Ohio. Multicoloured.

59.	4½p. Type **14**	10	10
60.	5½p. Terminal Tower Building, J. Gill and R. Carran	12	12
61.	8p. Clague House Museum, & Robert & Margaret Clague	20	20
62.	10p. "S.S. William T. Graves" and Thomas Quayle ..	30	30

15. Tom Sheard, 1923.

1975. Tourist Trophy Motor-cycle Races (2nd issue). Multicoloured.

63. 5½p. Type **15** 10 12
64. 7p. Walter Handley, 1925 15 15
65. 10p. Geoff. Duke, 1955 20 25
66. 12p. Peter Williams, 1973 25 30

16. Sir George Goldie and Birthplace.

1975. Sir George Goldie. 50th Death Anniv. Multicoloured.

67. 5½p. Type **16** 10 12
68. 7p. Goldie and map of Africa (vert.) 15 15
69. 10p. Goldie as President of Geographical Society (vert.) 20 25
70. 12p. River scene on the Niger 25 30

17. Title Page of Manx Bible.

1975. Christmas. Manx Bible. Bicentenary. Multicoloured.

71. 5½p. Type **17** 10 12
72. 7p. Rev. Philip Moore and Ballaugh Old Church 15 15
73. 11p. Bishop Hildesley and Bishops Court 20 25
74. 13p. John Kelly saving Bible manuscript 25 30

18. William Christian listening to Patrick Henry.

1976. American Independence. Commemorating Col. William Christian. Mult.

75. 5½p. Type **18** 10 12
76. 7p. Conveying the Fincastle Resolutions 15 15
77. 13p. Patrick Henry and William Christian 25 30
78. 20p. Christian as an Indian fighter 40 45

19. First Horse Tram, 1876.

1976. Douglas Horse-Trams. Centenary. Multicoloured.

80. 5½p. Type **19** 10 12
81. 7p. "Toast-rack" tram, 1890 15 15
82. 11p. Horse-bus, 1895 20 25
83. 13p. Royal tram, 1972 25 30

20. Barrose Beaker **21.** Diocesan Banner.

1976. Europa. Ceramic Art. Multicoloured.

84. 5p. Type **20** 40 40
85. 5p. Souvenir teapot 40 40
86. 5p. Laxey jug 40 40
87. 10p. Cronk Aust food vessel (horiz.) 70 70
88. 10p. Sansbury bowl (horiz.) 70 70
89. 10p. Knox urn (horiz.) 70 70

1976. Christmas and Mothers' Union. Centenary. Mulitcoloured.

90. 6p. Type **21** 12 15
91. 7p. Onchan banner 15 15
92. 11p. Castletown banner 25 25
93. 13p. Ramsey banner 25 30

22. Queen Elizabeth II (horiz.).

1977. Silver Jubilee. Multicoloured.

94. 6p. Type **22** 12 15
95. 7p. Queen Elizabeth and Prince Philip (vert.) 15 15
96. 25p. Queen Elizabeth (different) 50 55

POSTAGE DUE STAMPS

D **1.** D **2.**

1973.

D 1. D **1.** ½p. red, black and yell. 15 20
D 2. 1p. red, black and cinn. 20 20
D 3. 2p. red, black and green 40 30
D 4. 3p. red, black and grey 60 45
D 5. 4p. red, black and pink 80 60
D 6. 5p. red, black and blue 1·00 75
D 7. 10p. red, black and vio. 2·00 1·50
D 8. 20p. red, black and grn. 4·00 3·00

1975.

D 9. D **2.** ½p. yellow, black & red 5 5
D 10. 1p. brown, black & red 5 5
D 11. 4p. lilac, black & red 8 8
D 12. 7p. blue, black & red 12 12
D 13. 9p. grey, black & red 15 15
D 14. 10p. mauve, blk. & red 20 20
D 15. 50p. orge., blk. & red 85 85
D 16. £1 grn., blk. & red 1·75 1·75

GREAT COMORO O1

A French island N.W. of Madagascar. It used the stamps of Madagascar for a period but now uses the stamps of Comoro Islands.

1897. "Tablet" key-type inscr. "GRANDE COMORE".

1. D. 1 c. black on blue 8 8
2. 2 c. brown on yellow 12 10
3. 4 c. lilac on grey 20 20
4. 5 c. green 20 20
5. 10 c. black on lilac 80 50
14. 10 c. red 1·60 1·60
6. 15 c. blue 1·75 1·20
15. 15 c. grey 1·60 1·10
7. 20 c. red on green 1·75 1·40
8. 25 c. black on red 2·25 1·40
16. 25 c. blue 2·75 1·60
9. 30 c. brown 2·75 1·60
17. 35 c. black on yellow 2·75 2·25
10. 40 c. red on yellow 2·75 2·25
18. 45 c. black on green 13·00 11·00
11. 50 c. red on rose 4·50 2·75
19. 50 c. brown on blue 5·50 4·50
12. 75 c. brown on orange 5·50 4·00
13. 1 f. olive 3·75 2·75

1912. Surch. in figures.

20. D. 05 on 2 c. brown on yell. 10 10
21. 05 on 4 c. lilac on grey 10 10
22. 05 on 15 c. blue 10 10
23. 05 on 20 c. red on green 10 10
24. 05 on 25 c. black on red 10 10
25. 05 on 30 c. brown 10 10
26. 10 on 40 c. red on yellow 10 10
27. 10 on 45 c. black on green 12 12
28. 10 on 50 c. red on rose 15 15
29. 10 on 75 c. brown on orge. 12 12

GREECE E2

A country in the S.E. of Europe, under Turkish rule till 1830, when it became a kingdom. A republic was established from 1924 to 1935 when the monarchy was restored. The country was under German occupation from April, 1941 to Oct. 1944.

The monarchy was once again abolished during 1973 and a republic set up.

100 lepta = 1 drachma.

1. Hermes or Mercury. **2.**

1861. Imperf. or perf.

45c. **1.** 1 l. brown 2·25 2·10
66. 2 l. buff 1·90 1·90
55. 5 l. green 1·75 90
19. 10 l. orange on blue 60·00 3·25
56. 10 l. orange 3·50 1·10
20. 20 l. blue 38·00 1·50
59a. 20 l. red 1·00 50
53b. 30 l. brown 18·00 2·75
60. 30 l. blue 25·00 3·50
28. 40 l. purple and blue 40·00 1·75
21b. 40 l. rose on lilac £225 6·00
37. 40 l. orange on green £160 35·00
43f. 40 l. green on blue 16·00 9·00
43d. 40 l. brown on blue 7·00 8·50
50. 40 l. buff 7·00 10·00
61. 40 l. purple 28·00 3·75
52. 60 l. green 7·00 42·00
22. 80 l. red 20·00 4·25

1886. Imperf.

85. **2.** 1 l. brown 30 15
86b. 2 l. buff 30 15
87. 5 l. green 1·00 12
88. 10 l. orange 3·00 15
89. 20 l. red 1·00 8
90d. 25 l. blue 14·00 50
91. 25 l. purple 75 20
79. 40 l. purple 30·00 10·00
93. 40 l. blue 2·75 1·10
80. 50 l. green 2·25 1·50
81. 1 d. grey 50·00 2·00

1886.

100. **2.** 1 l. brown 40 30
96. 2 l. buff 60 40
102. 5 l. green 2·00 35
103. 10 l. orange 5·00 75
104a. 20 l. red 2·10 45
105. 25 l. blue 17·00 55
106. 25 l. purple 1·50 40
107. 40 l. purple 32·00 10·00
108. 40 l. blue 3·75 1·10
83. 50 l. green 3·50 1·25
84. 1 d. grey 55·00 2·10

3. Wrestlers.

4. Discus thrower.

5. Pallas Athene.

6. Chariot driving.

1896. First Int. Olympic Games. Perf.

110. **3.** 1 l. yellow 30 20
111. 2 l. rose 40 20
112. **4.** 5 l. mauve 55 25
113. 10 l. grey 85 45
114. **5.** 20 l. brown 3·50 15
115. **6.** 25 l. red 7·00 55
116. **5.** 40 l. violet 5·00 1·60
117. **6.** 60 l. black 7·00 3·50
118. – 1 d. blue 28·00 4·25
119. – 2 d. olive 50·00 16·00
120. – 5 d. green £100 65·00
121. – 10 d. brown £130 90·00

DESIGNS—As T **6**—HORIZ. 1 d. Acropolis and Stadium. 10 d. Acropolis with Parthenon. VERT. 2 d. "Hermes". 5 d. "Victory".

1900. Surch. Imperf.

122. **2.** 20 l. on 25 l. blue 70 35
130. **1.** 30 l. on 40 l. purple 1·60 1·00
131. 40 l. on 2 l. buff 2·10 1·75
132. 50 l. on 40 l. buff 2·75 2·10
123. **2.** 1 d. on 40 l. purple 5·50 2·75
124. 2 d. on 40 l. purple £100 £100
133. **1.** 3 d. on 10 l. orange 7·00 5·50
134. 5 d. on 40 l. purple on blue 17·00 15·00

1900. Surch. Perf.

125. **2.** 20 l. on 25 l. blue 70 35
135. **1.** 30 l. on 40 l. purple 2·10 1·60
136. 40 l. on 2 l. buff 2·40 2·10
137. 50 l. on 40 l. buff 3·50 3·00
126. **2.** 1 d. on 40 l. purple 6·00 3·50
127a. 2 d. on 40 l. purple 3·50 3·50
138. **1.** 3 d. on 10 l. orange 8·00 6·00
139. 5 d. on 40 l. pur. on blue 32·00 28·00

1900. Surch. **AM** and value.

140. **2.** 25 l. on 40 l. pur. (No. 79) 2·10 1·75
142. 25 l. on 40 l. pur. (No. 107) 3·50 2·50
141. 50 l. on 25 l. blue (No. 90d) 5·50 5·00
143. 50 l. on 25 l. blue (No. 105) 8·00 7·00
144. **1.** 1 d. on 40 l. brown on blue (No. 43d) 28·00 23·00
146. 1 d. on 40 l. brown on blue (Perf.) 32·00 25·00
145. 2 d. on 5 l. green (No. 55) 6·50 6·50
147. 2 d. on 5 l. green (No. 102) 7·00 7·00

1900. Olympic Games stamps surch. **AM** and value.

148. – 5 l. on 1 d. blue 2·75 2·75
149. **5.** 25 l. on 40 l. violet 32·00 21·00
150. – 50 l. on 2 d. olive 25·00 22·00
151. – 1 d. on 5 d. green 90·00 70·00
152. – 2 d. on 10 d. brown 25·00 25·00

11. "Hermes". **12.** **13.**

1901.

153. **11.** 1 l. brown 8 5
154. 2 l. grey 8 5
155. 3 l. orange 12 5
170. **12.** 5 l. green 20 5
171. 10 l. red 30 5
172. **11.** 20 l. mauve 35 5
173. **12.** 25 l. blue 50 5
174. **11.** 30 l. purple 1·60 30
161a. 40 l. brown 1·60 30
176. 50 l. lake 1·60 20
163. **13.** 1 d. black 7·00 70
164. 2 d. bronze 3·50 2·10
165. 3 d. silver 4·25 3·25
166. 5 d. gold 6·50 6·00

14. Head of Hermes.

15. Discus-thrower.

16. Jumper.

18. Atlas and Hercules.

1902.

178. **14.** 5 l. orange 1·00 45
179. 25 l. green 4·25 1·10
180. 50 l. blue 7·00 2·00
181. 1 d. red 11·00 4·25
182. 2 d. brown 12·00 11·00

1906. Olympic Games. Dated "1906".

183. **15.** 1 l. brown 35 15
184. 2 l. black 50 15
185. **16.** 3 l. orange 55 20
186. 5 l. green 85 20
187. – 10 l. red 1·75 20
188. **18.** 20 l. claret 3·00 25
189. – 25 l. blue 6·50 60
190. – 30 l. purple 2·50 1·25
191. – 40 l. brown 2·50 1·10
192. **18.** 50 l. maroon 6·50 2·25
193. – 1 d. black 21·00 2·75
194. – 2 d. rose 32·00 8·50
195. – 3 d. yellow 50·00 32·00
196. – 5 d. blue 50·00 30·00

DESIGNS—As T **15**: 10 l. Victory. 30 l. Wrestlers. 40 l. Daemon of Games. As T **18**: 25 l. Hercules and Antaeus. 1 d., 2 d., 3 d. Race, Ancient Greeks. 5 d. Olympic Offerings.

24. Head of Hermes. 25. Iris. 26. Hermes.

27. Hermes and Arcass.

ΕΛΛΗΝΙΚΗ ΔΙΟΙΚΗΣΙΣ

(28.)

1911. Roul.

213. **24.** 1 l. green 5 5
214. **25.** 2 l. red 5 5
215. **24.** 3 l. red 5 5
216. **26.** 5 l. green 5 5
217. **24.** 10 l. red 5 5
218. **25.** 15 l. blue 5 5
219. 20 l. lilac 8 5
220. 25 l. blue 10 5
221. **26.** 30 l. red 12 5
222. **25.** 40 l. blue 25 5
223. **26.** 50 l. purple 85 5
224. 80 l. purple 55 5
225. **27.** 1 d. blue .. .. 1·50 10
226. 2 d. red .. .. 1·60 10
227. 3 d. red .. .. 1·40 10
210. 5 d. blue .. .. 8·00 90
228. 5 d. grey-blue .. 9·00 12
211b. 10 d. blue .. .. 7·00 2·10
229. 10 d. grey-blue .. 2·25 30
212. – 25 d. blue .. .. 11·00 11·00
230. – 25 d. slate .. .. 3·00 1·00

The 25 d. is as T **24** but larger (24×31 mm.).

1912. Optd. with T **28.**

248. **24.** 1 l. green 5 5
233. **25.** 2 l. red 5 5
234. **24.** 3 l. red 5 5
249. **26.** 5 l. green 12 8
250. **24.** 10 l. red 45 45
237. **25.** 20 l. lilac 60 50
231. **11.** 20 l. mauve 70 70
250. **25.** 25 l. blue 60 45
239. **26.** 30 l. red 90 80
240. **25.** 40 l. blue .. .. 1·00 70
241. **26.** 50 l. purple .. .. 2·10 1·60
242. **27.** 1 d. blue .. .. 3·50 2·50
243. 2 d. red .. .. 12·00 9·00
244. 3 d. red .. .. 8·00 6·50
245. 5 d. blue .. .. 10·00 7·50
246. 10 d. blue .. .. 10·00 7·50
247a. – 25 d. blue (No. 212) .. 11·00 11·00

29. Vision of Constantine. 30. Victorious Eagle over Mt. Olympus.

1913. Occupation of Macedonia, Epirus and the Aegean Is. Rouletted.

252. **29.** 1 l. brown 8 5
253. **30.** 2 l. red 8 5
254. 3 l. orange 8 5
255. **29.** 5 l. green 25 5
256. 10 l. red 40 5
257. 20 l. violet .. .. 1·25 40
258. **30.** 25 l. blue 80 25
259. **29.** 30 l. green .. .. 8·50 60
260. **30.** 40 l. blue .. .. 1·25 90
261. **29.** 50 l. blue .. .. 1·40 70
262. **30.** 1 d. purple .. .. 3·00 1·00
263. **29.** 2 d. brown .. .. 8·50 1·75
264. **30.** 3 d. blue .. .. 50·00 8·50
265. **29.** 5 d. grey .. .. 45·00 10·00
266. **30.** 10 d. red .. .. 38·00 38·00
267. **29.** 25 d. black .. .. 35·00 35·00

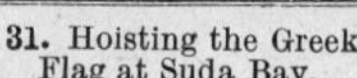

31. Hoisting the Greek Flag at Suda Bay. 32. Iris.

1913. Union of Crete with Greece.

268. **31.** 25 l. black and blue .. 2·00 1·10

1916. Perf. or imperf.

286. **32.** 1 l. green 12 5
287. 5 l. green 12 5
288. 10 l. rose 25 5
289. 25 l. blue 30 10
290. 50 l. purple 65 20
291. 1 d. blue 80 10
292. **32.** 2 d. red .. .. 1·10 15
293. 3 d. claret .. .. 6·00 1·10
294. 5 d. blue .. .. 1·50 35
295. 10 d. blue .. .. 16·00 5·00
296. 25 d. grey .. .. 18·00 16·00

ΕΠΑΝΑΣΤΑΣΙΣ 1922 ΛΕΠΤΑ 10

(33.) (38.)

1916. Stamps of 1911 optd. with T **33.**

269. **24.** 1 l. green 10 5
270. **25.** 2 l. red 10 5
271. **24.** 3 l. red 10 5
272. **26.** 5 l. green 15 5
273. **24.** 10 l. red 15 8
274. **25.** 20 l. lilac 25 8
275. 25 l. blue 35 8
276. **26.** 30 l. red 40 15
277. **25.** 40 l. blue .. .. 1·25 25
278. **26.** 50 l. purple .. .. 10·00 40
281. **27.** 1 d. blue .. .. 11·00 10
282. 2 d. red .. .. 5·00 45
283. 3 d. red .. .. 2·75 50
284. 5 d. blue .. .. 12·00 80
285. 10 d. blue .. .. 3·50 3·50

1923. Revolution of 1922. Stamps of 1913, surch. as T **38.**

340. **30.** 5 l. on 3 l. orange .. 8 8
341. **29.** 10 l. on 20 l. violet .. 15 15
342. **30.** 10 l. on 25 l. blue .. 15 15
343. **29.** 10 l. on 30 l. green .. 15 15
344. **30.** 10 l. on 40 l. blue .. 15 15
345. **29.** 50 l. on 50 l. blue .. 15 15
346. 2 d. on 2 d. brown .. 18·00 18·00
347. **30.** 3 d. on 3 d blue .. 70 70
348. **29.** 5 d. on 5 d. grey .. 85 85
349. **30.** 10 d. on 1 d. purple .. 85 85
350. 10 d. on 10 d. red .. £200

1923. Stamps of 1916 surch. as T **38.**

351. **32.** 5 l. on 10 l. rose .. 8 8
352. 50 l. on 50 l. purple .. 8 8
353. 1 d. on 1 d. blue .. 8 8
354. 2 d. on 2 d. red .. 15 15
355. 3 d. on 3 d. claret .. 40 40
356. 5 d. on 5 d. blue .. 30 30
357. 25 d. on 25 d. blue .. 4·50 4·50

1923. Cretan stamps of 1900 surch. as T **38.**

358. **1.** 5 l. on 1 l. brown .. 15·00
359. **3.** 10 l. on 10 l. red .. 20 20
361. 10 l. on 25 l. blue .. 20 20
362. **1.** 50 l. on 50 l. lilac .. 20 20
363. 50 l. on 50 l. blue .. 85 85
364. **4.** 50 l. on 1 d. violet .. 70 70
345. – 50 l. on 5 d. (No. 19) .. 8·50

1923. Cretan stamps of 1905 surch. as T **38.**

366. – 10 l. on 20 l. (No. 24) .. 25·00 25·00
367. – 10 l. on 25 l. (No. 25) .. 30 30
368. – 50 l. on 50 l. (No. 26) .. 35 35
369. **14.** 50 l. on 1 d. (No. 27) .. 1·60 1·60
370. – 3 d. on 3 d. (No. 28) .. 1·75 1·75
371. – 5 d. on 5 d. (No. 29) .. 2·40 2·40

1923. Cretan stamps of 1907/8 surch. as T **38.**

372. **23.** 10 l. on 10 l. red .. 12 12
373. **21.** 10 l. on 25 l. blk. & blue 50 50
374. 50 l. on 1 d. (No. 31) .. 1·10 1·10

No. 372 is as Crete No. 36 but without "HELLAS" optd. No. 377 is the optd. stamp.

1923. Optd. stamps of Crete surch. as T **38.**

375. **1.** 5 l. on 1 l. brn. (No. 32) 8 8
376. – 5 l. on 5 l. grn. (No. 34) 15 15
377. **22.** 10 l. on 10 l. red (No. 36) 20 20
378. – 10 l. on 20 l. (No. 37) .. 20 20
379. – 10 l. on 25 l. (No. 30) .. 25 25
381. – 50 l. on 50 l. (No. 39) .. 30 30
382. **14.** 50 l. on 1 d. (No. 40) .. 2·50 2·50
384. – 3 d. on 3 d. (No. 42) .. 3·25 3·25
385. – 5 d. on 5 d. (No. 43) .. 65·00 65·00

1923. Postage Due stamps of Crete of 1900 surch. as T **33.**

386. D **1.** 5 l. on 5 l. red .. 5 5
387. 5 l. on 10 l. red .. 5 5
388. 10 l. on 20 l. red .. 6·00 6·00
389. 10 l. on 40 l. red .. 12 12
390. 50 l. on 50 l. red .. 12 12
391. 50 l. on 1 d. red .. 25 25
392. 50 l. on 1 d. on 1 d. red 2·10 2·10
393. 2 d. on 2 d. red .. 30 25

1923. Postage Due stamps of Crete of 1908 with opt. surch. as T **38.**

397. D **1.** 5 l. on 5 l. red .. 15 15
398. 5 l. on 10 l. red .. 15 15
399. 10 l. on 20 l. red .. 15 15
400. 50 l. on 50 l. red .. 25 25
401. 50 l. on 1 d. red .. 45 45
402. 2 d. on 2 d red .. 1·75 1·75

39. Byron. 41. Grave of Marco Botzaris.

1924. Byron Cent. Inscr. "LORD BYRON 1824 1924".

403. **39.** 80 l. blue .. 55 12
404. – 2d. black and violet .. 1·60 70

DESIGN—HORIZ. (45×30 mm.): 2 d. Byron at Missolonghi.

1926. Fall of Missolonghi. Cent. Roul.

405. **41.** 25 l. mauve 30 15

42.

1926. Air. As T **42.**

406. 2 d. red, lilac, yell. & blue 35 30
407. 3 d. blue, red, lilac & grn. 7·00 4·00
408. 5 d. blue, lilac and red .. 70 50
409. 10 d. multicoloured .. 6·00 3·75

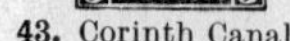

43. Corinth Canal. 44. Dodecanese Costume.

45. Temple of Theseus, Athens. 46. Acropolis.

1927.

410. **43.** 5 l. green 5 5
411. **44.** 10 l. red 8 5
412. – 20 l. violet 12 5
413. – 25 l. green 12 5
414. – 40 l. green 20 5
415. **43.** 50 l. violet .. .. 1·00 5
416. 80 l. black and indigo .. 25 5
417. **45.** 1 d. brown and blue .. 1·10 5
418b. – 2 d. black and green .. 2·00 5
419c. – 3 d. black and violet .. 2·40 5
419d. – 4 d. brown .. .. 6·00 20
420. – 5 d. black and orange .. 3·50 12
421. – 10 d. black and claret .. 12·00 30
422a. – 15 d. black and green .. 16·00 2·00
423a. **46.** 25 d. black and green .. 16·00 2·50

DESIGNS—As T **44**: 20 l. Macedonian costume. 25 l. Monastery of Simon Peter. 40 l. White Tower, Salonika. As T **45**: 2 d. Acropolis. 3 d. Cruiser "Averoff". 4 d. Mistra Cathedral. As T **46**: 5 d., 15 d. The Academy, Athens. 10 d. Temple of Theseus.

47. General Favier and Acropolis.

1927. Liberation of Athens. Cent.

424. **47.** 1 d. red 55 5
425. 3 d. blue .. .. 1·10 20
426. 6 d. green .. .. 7·50 3·25

48. Navarino Bay and Pylos. 50. Sir Edward Codrington.

1927. Battle of Navarino Cent.

427. **48.** 1 d. 50 green .. 1·00 5
428. – 4 d. blue .. .. 4·25 12
429. **50.** 5 d. black & brown (A) 7·00 1·10
430. – 5 d. black & brown (B) 15·00 4·25
431. – 5 d. black and blue .. 14·00 1·40
432. – 5 d. black and red .. 5·50 1·40

DESIGNS: 4 d. Battle of Navarino. 5 d. (No. 429) "Sir Codrington" (A). 5 d. (No. 430) "Sir Edward Codrington" (B). 5 d. (No. 431) De Rigny. 5 d. (No. 432) Van der Heyden.

51. R. Ferreo. 55. Monastery of Arkadi and Abbott Gabriel.

1930. Independence Cent.

433. **51.** 10 l. brown 5 5
434. – 20 l. black 5 5
435. – 40 l. green 8 8
436. – 50 l. red 10 10
437. – 50 l. blue 10 10
438. – 1 d. red 15 8
439. – 1 d. orange 15 10
440. – 1 d. 50 blue 20 8
441. – 1 d. 50 red 20 10
442. – 2 d. orange 25 15
443. – 3 d. brown 40 25
444. – 4 d. blue .. .. 1·00 45
445. – 5 d. purple .. .. 1·00 45
446. – 10 d. black .. .. 2·50 1·25
447. – 15 d. green .. .. 3·25 2·10
448. – 20 d. blue .. .. 5·50 3·00
449. – 25 d. black .. .. 7·00 4·25
450. – 50 d. brown .. .. 17·00 12·00

DESIGNS as T **51**: 20 l. Patriarch Gregory V. 40 l. A. Ypsilanti. 50 l. (No. 435) L. Bouboulina. 50 l. (437), Ath. Diakos. 1 d. (438), Th. Colocotroni. 1 d. (439), C. Kanaris. 1 d. 50, (440), Karaiskakes. 1 d. 50 (441), M. Botzaris, 2 d. A. Miaoulis. 3 d. L. Kondouriotis. 5 d. Capo d'Istria. 10 d. P. Mavromichalis. 15 d. Solomos. 20 d. Corais. (27½×40 mm.): 4 d. Map of Greece. (27×44 mm.): 50 d. Sortie from Missolonghi. (43×28½ mm.): 25 d. Declaration of Independence.

1930.

451. **55.** 8 d. violet .. .. 8·50 25

1932. Stamps of 1927 surch.

452. – 1 d. 50 l. on 5 d. black and blue (No. 431) .. 70 8
453. – 1 d. 50 l. on 5 d. black and red (No. 432) .. 70 8
454. **47.** 2 d. on 3 d. blue .. 1·75 8
455. **50.** 2 d. on 5 d. black and brown (No. 429) .. 1·75 8
456. – 2 d. on 5 d. black and brown (No. 430) .. 1·75 8
457. **47.** 4 d. on 6 d. green .. 2·00 40

56. Zeppelin over the Acropolis.

1933. Air.

458. **56.** 30 d. red .. .. 4·50 2·75
459. 100 d. blue .. .. 30·00 17·00
460. 120 d. brown .. .. 32·00 18·00

57. Swinging the Propeller. 58. "Flight".

1933. Air. Aero Espresso Company issue.

461. **57.** 50 l. orange and green .. 20 15
462. – 1 d. orange and blue .. 35 25
463. – 3 d. brown and purple .. 50 40
464. **58.** 5 d. blue and orange .. 4·25 2·75
465. – 10 d. black and red .. 1·00 60
466. – 20 d. green and black .. 2·25 1·40
467. – 50 d. blue and brown .. 32·00 23·00

DESIGNS—HORIZ. 1 d. Temple of Neptune, Corinth. 3 d. Aeroplane over Hermoupolis. 10 d. Map of air routes. VERT. 20 d. Hermes and seaplane. 50 d. Woman and aeroplane.

59. Aeroplane over Greece.

DESIGNS—VERT. 2 d., 10 d. Aeroplane over the Icarian Is. HORIZ. 5 d., 50 d. Aeroplane over the Acropolis.

1933. Air. Government issue.

468. **59.** 50 l. green 20 12
469. 1 d. claret 50 25
470. – 2 d. violet 70 40
471. – 5 d. blue .. .. 2·50 1·25
472. – 10 d. red .. .. 2·50 2·40
473. **59.** 25 d. blue .. .. 14·00 7·00
474. – 50 d. brown .. .. 21·00 17·00

61. Admiral Kondouriotis and Cruiser "Averoff". 62. "Greece".

1933.
475. 61. 50 d. blue and black .. 14·00 2·10
476. 62. 75 d. purple and black .. 55·00 42·00
477. – 100 d. green and brown £150 12·00
DESIGN—VERT. 100 d. Statue (Youth of Marathon).

65. Athens Stadium Entrance.

1934.
479. 65. 8 d. blue .. .. 28·00 35

66. Sun Chariot. 68. King Constantine.

1935. Air. Mythological designs.
488a. 66. 1 d. red 5 5
488b. – 2 d. blue 5 5
488c. – 5 d. mauve 5 5
488d. – 7 d. blue 5 5
484. – 10 d. brown .. .. 1·60 85
488e. – 10 d. orange 55 55
485. – 25 d. red .. .. 2·25 2·75
486. – 30 d. green 35 35
487. – 50 d. mauve .. .. 1·40 1·40
488. – 100 d. brown 70 70
DESIGNS—HORIZ. 2 d. Iris. 30 d. Triptolemus. 100 d. Phrixus and Helle. VERT. 5 d. Daedalus and Icarus. 7 d. Minerva. 10 d. Hermes. 25 d. Zeus and Ganymede. 50 d. Bellerophon on Pegasus.

1935. Restoration of Greek Monarchy. Surch. **3 November 1935** in Greek, with crown or arms, and value.
489. D 2. 50 l. on 40 l. blue .. 20 5
490. 3 d. on 3 d. red .. 40 12
492. – 5 d. on 100 d. green & brown (No. 477) .. 1·10 40
493. 62. 15 d. on 75 d. purple and black .. .. 5·00 1·40

1936. Re-burial of King and Queen.
494. 68. 3 d. brown and black .. 35 12
495. 8 d. blue and black .. 1·10 70

69. Bull-leaping.

72. King George II. 72a. Statue of King Constantine.

1937.
497. 69. 5 l. blue and brown .. 5 5
498. – 10 l. brown and blue .. 5 5
499. – 20 l. green and black 5 5
500. – 40 l. black and green 5 5
501. – 50 l. black and brown 5 5
502. – 80 l. brown and violet 5 5
503. 72. 1 d. green 12 8
515. 72a. 1 d. 50 green .. 20 8
504. – 2 d. blue 5 5
505. 72. 3 d. brown 5 5
506. – 5 d. red 5 5
507. – 6 d. olive 5 5
508. – 7 d. brown 15 12
509. 72. 8 d. blue 50 15
510. – 10 d. brown 5 5
511. – 15 d. green 8 5
512. – 25 d. blue 8 5
516. 72a. 30 d. red .. .. 1·75 1·40
513. 72. 100 d. red .. .. 5·00 4·25
DESIGNS—(Size as T 72a). VERT. 10 l. Court Lady of Tiryns. 20 l. Zeus and Thunderbolt. 80 l. Venus of Milo. 25 d. "Glory" of Psara. HORIZ. 40 l. Amphictyonic Coin. 50 l. Chairing Diagoras of Rhodes. 2 d. Battle of Salamis. 5 d. Panathenaic chariot. 6 d. Alexander the Great at Battle of Issus. 7 d. St. Paul on Mt. Areopagus. 10 d. Temple of St. Demetrius, Salonica. 15 d. Leo III (the Isaurian) destroying Saracens.

76. Pallas Athene. 77. Prince Paul and Princess Frederika Louise.

1937. Athens University Cent.
496. 76. 3 d. brown 35 12

1938. Royal Wedding.
517. 77. 1 d. green 12 5
518. 3 d. brown 40 8
519. 8 d. blue 80 55

78. Arms of Greece, Rumania, Turkey and Yugoslavia.

1938. Balkan Entente.
520. 78. 6 d. blue .. .. 5·00 90

1938. Air. Postage Due stamp optd. with an aeroplane.
521. D 2. 50 l. brown 5 5

79. Arms of Ionian Islands. 80. Corfu Bay and Citadel.

1939. Cession of Ionian Islands. 75th Anniv.
523. 79. 1 d. blue 45 12
524. 80. 4 d. green .. .. 1·50 50
525. – 20 d. orange .. .. 12·00 7·00
526. – 20 d. blue .. .. 12·00 7·00
527. – 20 d. red .. .. 12·00 7·00
DESIGN—HORIZ. 20 d. As T 1 of Ionian Is. but with portraits of George I of Greece and Queen Victoria.

81. Javelin Thrower. 82. Arms of Greece, Rumania, Turkey and Yugoslavia.

1939. 10th Pan-Balkan Games, Athens. Inscr. "I" BALKANIAS 1939."
528. – 50 l. green 15 15
529. 81. 3 d. red 65 20
530. – 6 d. red on brown .. 2·25 1·75
531. – 8 d. blue on grey .. 2·50 2·10
DESIGNS: 50 l. Runner. 6 d. Discus-thrower. 8 d. Jumper.

1940. Balkan Entente.
532. 82. 6 d. blue .. .. 1·75 40
533. 8 d. slate .. .. 1·75 40

83. Greek Youth Badge. 84. Meteora Monasteries.

1940. Greek Youth Organization. 4th Anniv. (a) Postage.
534. 83. 3 d. blue, red and silver 70 40
535. – 5 d. black and blue .. 2·00 1·40
536. – 10 d. black and orange 2·25 1·75
537. – 15 d. black and green .. 32·00 23·00
538. – 20 d. black and red .. 10·00 8·00
539. – 25 d. black and blue .. 11·00 8·00
540. – 30 d. black and purple .. 13·00 8·50
541. – 50 d. black and red .. 13·00 8·50
542. – 75 d. gold, brown & blue 17·00 12·00
543. 83. 100 d. blue, red & silver 19·00 13·00
DESIGNS—VERT. 5 d. Boy member. 10 d. Girl member. 15 d Javelin thrower. 20 d. Youths in column formation. 25 d. Standard bearer and buglers. 30 d. Three youths in uniform. 50 d. Youths on parade. 75 d. Coat of arms.

(b) Air.
544. 84. 2 d. black and orange .. 25 15
545. – 4 d. black and green .. 2·10 1·40
546. – 6 d. black and red .. 2·75 2·00
547. – 8 d. black and blue .. 4·00 2·10
548. – 16 d. black and violet .. 14·00 7·00
549. – 32 d. black and orange 15·00 10·00
550. – 45 d. black and green .. 15·00 10·00
551. – 55 d. black and red .. 15·00 10·00
552. – 65 d. black and blue .. 15·00 12·00
553. – 100 d. black and violet 18·00 14·00
DESIGNS—VERT. (views and aeroplanes): 4 d. Simon Peter Monastery, Mt. Athos 6d., 16 d. Isle of Santorin. 8 d. Church at Pantanassa. 32 d. Ponticonissi, Corfu. 45 d. Acropolis. 55 d. Erechtheum. 65 d. Temple of Nike. 100 d. Temple of Zeus.

1941. Air. Optd. with aeroplane or surch. **1 △ P** also.
554. D 2. 1 d. on 2 d. red .. 5 5
557. 5 d. blue 10 10
558. 10 d. green 15 15
559. 25 d. rose 25 25
560. 50 d. orange 90 90

85. "Boreas" (North Wind). 86. Windmills on Mykonos Is.

1942. Air. Designs symbolical of winds.
561. 85. 2 d. green 5 5
562. – 5 d. red 5 5
563. – 10 d. brown 10 10
567 – 10 d. red 5 5
564. – 20 d. blue 35 35
565. – 25 d. orange 5 5
568. – 25 d. green 5 5
566. – 50 d. black 70 70
569. – 50 d. blue 5 5
570. 85. 100 d. black 5 5
571. – 200 d. claret 5 5
572. – 400 d. grey 5 5
DESIGNS: 5 d. "Notos" (South). 10 d. "Apiliotis" (East). 20 d. "Lips" (South-west). 25 d. "Zephyr" (West). 50 d. "Kekias" (North-east). 200 d. "Evros" (South-east). 400 d. "Skiron" (North-west).

1942.
573. 86. 2 d. brown 5 5
574. – 5 d. green 5 5
575. – 10 d. blue 5 5
576. – 15 d. purple 5 5
577. – 25 d. orange 5 5
578. – 50 d. blue 5 5
579. – 75 d. red 5 5
580. – 100 d. black 5 5
581. – 200 d. blue 5 5
582. – 500 d. brown 5 5
583. – 1000 d. brown 5 5
584. – 2000 d. blue 5 5
585. – 5000 d. red 5 5
536. – 15,000 d. purple 5 5
587. – 25,000 d. green 5 5
588. – 500,000 d. blue 5 5
589. 86. 2,000,000 d. green .. 8 8
590. – 5,000,000 d. red .. 8 8
DESIGNS: 5 d., 5,000,000 d. Burzi Fortress. 10 d., 500,000 d. Katokhi on Aspropotamos River. 15 d. Heraklion, Crete. 25 d. Houses on Hydra Is. 50 d. Meteora Monastery. 75 d. Edessa. 100 d., 200 d. Monastery on Mt. Athos. 500 d., 5000 d. Konitza Bridge. 1000 d., 15,000 d. Ekatontapiliani Church. 2000 d., 25,000 d. Kerkyra Is., Corfu.

89. Child. 90. Madonna and Child.

1943. Children's Welfare Fund.
592. 89. 25 d. + 25 d. green .. 5 5
593. – 100 d. + 50 d. purple .. 10 10
594. 90. 200 d. + 100 d. brown .. 10 10
DESIGN: 100 d. Mother and child.

(91.)

1944. Children's Convalescent Camp Fund. Surch. as T 91. (a) Postage.
595. 85. 50,000 d. + 450,000 d. on 2 d. brown 15 15
596. – 50,000 d. + 450,000 d. on 5 d. green (No. 574) .. 15 15
597. – 50,000 d. + 450,000 d. on 10 d. blue (No. 575) .. 15 15
598. – 50,000 d. + 450,000 d. on 15 d. purple (No. 576) 15 15
599. – 50,000 d. + 450,000 d. on 25 d. orange (No. 577) 15 15

(b) Air.
600. – 50,000 d. + 450,000 d. on 10 d. red (No. 567) .. 15 15
601. – 50,000 d. + 450,000 d. on 25 d. green (No. 568) 15 15
602. – 50,000 d. + 450,000 d. on 50 d. blue (No. 569) 15 15
603. 88. 50,000 d. + 450,000 d. on 100 d. black .. 15 15
604. – 50,000 d. + 450,000 d. on 200 d. claret (No. 571) 15 15

1944. Optd. **△PAXMAI NEAI** ("New drachmas").
605. – 50 l. black and brown (No. 501) 5 5
606. – 2 d. blue (No. 504) .. 8 8
607. – 5 d. red (No. 506) .. 8 8
608. – 6 d. olive (No. 507) .. 8 8

92. "Glory" of Psara. 93. "OXI" = No.

1945.
609. 92. 1 d. purple 5 5
610. 3 d. claret 5 5
611. 5 d. blue 5 5
612. 10 d. brown 10 5
613. 20 d. violet 15 5
614. 50 d. green 30 20
615. 100 d. blue .. .. 2·10 1·40
616. 200 d. green .. .. 1·40 50
For 25 d. in T 92 but larger, see No. 512.

1945. Resistance to Italian Ultimatum.
617. 93. 20 d. orange 5 5
618. 40 d. blue 15 15

94. President Roosevelt. 95. E. Venizelos.

1945. Roosevelt Mourning Issue. Black borders.
619. 94. 30 d. purple 5 5
620. 60 d. grey 8 8
621. 200 d. violet 15 15

1946. Surch. **△ PX** and new value in ornamental rectangle.
622. – 10 d. on 10 d. (No. 567) 5 5
623. – 10 d. on 2000 d. (No. 584) 5 5
624. – 20 d. on 50 d. (No. 569) 5 5
625. – 20 d. on 500 d. (No. 582) 5 5
626. – 20 d. on 1000 d. (No. 583) 5 5
627. – 30 d. on 5 d. (No. 574) .. 8 5
628. – 50 d. on 50 d. (No. 578) 8 5
629. – 50 d. on 25,000 d. (No. 587) 8 5
630. – 100 d. on 10 d. (No. 575) 25 8
631. 85. 100 d. on 2,000,000 d. .. 20 8
632. – 130 d. on 20 l. (No. 499) 25 8
633. – 250 d. on 20 l. (No. 499) 30 8
634. – 300 d. on 80 l. (No. 502) 30 12
635. – 450 d. on 75 d. (No. 579) 35 12
636. – 500 d. on 5,000,000 d. (No. 590) 70 12
637. – 1000 d. on 500,000 d. (No. 588) .. .. 3·50 20
638. – 2000 d. on 5,000 d. (No. 585) .. .. .. 7·50 1·40
639. – 5000 d. on 15,000 d. (No. 586) .. .. 21·00 5·50

1946. Tenth Anniversary of Death of Venizelos (statesman).
640. 95. 130 d. green 5 5
641. 300 d. brown 25 25

1946. Restoration of Monarchy. Surch. with value in circle and date **1-9-1946.**
642. 72. 50 d. on 1 d. green .. 12 8
643. 250 d. on 3 d. brown .. 20 15
644. 600 d. on 8 d. blue .. 1·10 50
645. 3000 d. on 100 d. red .. 2·50 20

96. Panayiotis Tsaldaris. 97. Women carrying Munitions.

1946. P. Tsaldaris. 10th Death Anniv.
646. **96.** 250 d. brown and pink 40 8
647. 600 d. blue 85 55

1947. King George II Mourning issue. Surch. with value in circle in corner and black border.
648. **72.** 50 d. on 1 d. green .. 12 8
649. 250 d. on 3 d. brown .. 25 10
650. 600 d. on 8 d. blue .. 1·00 40

1948. Victory. War Scenes.
651. – 50 d. green 5 5
652. – 100 d. blue 8 5
653. **97.** 250 d. green 15 8
654. – 500 d. brown 25 10
655. – 600 d. brown 50 30
656. – 1000 d. violet 55 12
682. – 1000 d. green .. .. 1·10 12
657. – 2000 d. blue .. .. 2·25 1·00
658. – 5000 d. red .. .. 5·00 55

DESIGNS—HORIZ. 50 d. Convoy. 500 d. Infantry column. 1000 d. (No. 656) Aeroplane and pilot. 1000 d. (No. 682) Battle of Crete. 2000 d. Torpedo boat towing submarine. VERT. 100 d. Torpedoing of Cruiser "Helle". 600 d. Badge, Alpine troops and map of Italy. 5000 d. War Memorial at El Alamein.

98. Castelrosso Fortress.

99. Apollo.

1947. Restoration of Dodecanese Is. to Greece.
659. **98.** 20 d. blue 5 5
660. – 30 d. pink and black .. 5 5
661. – 50 d. blue 10 5
662. – 100 d. green and olive .. 12 5
663. – 200 d. orange 25 5
664. – 250 d. grey 35 5
665. – 300 d. orange 20 5
666. – 400 d. blue 35 5
667. **99.** 450 d. blue 50 5
668. – 450 d. blue 30 5
669. **99.** 500 d. red 30 5
670. – 600 d. purple 35 5
671. – 700 d. magenta .. 70 5
672. – 700 d. green .. .. 1·00 5
673. – 800 d. green and violet 35 5
674. – 1000 d. olive 35 5
675. **99.** 1300 d. red .. .. 1·60 5
676. **98.** 1500 d. brown .. .. 6·50 12
677. – 1600 d. blue .. .. 1·40 10
678. – 2000 d. red and brown 8·00 12
679. – 2600 d. green .. .. 2·10 35
680. – 5000 d. violet .. .. 4·25 12
681. – 10,000 d. blue .. .. 5·50 20

DESIGNS—HORIZ. 100 d., 400 d. St. John's Convent, Patmos. VERT. 30 d., 1600 d., 2000 d. Dodecanese vase. 50 d., 300 d. Woman in national costume. 200 d., 250 d. E. Xanthos. 450 d. (No. 668), 800 d. Casos Is. and frigate. 600 d., 700 d. (2), 5000 d. Statue of Hippocrates. 1000 d., 2600 d., 10000 d. Colossus of Rhodes.

100. Column of Women and Children.

DESIGNS — VERT. 1000 d. Captive children and map of Greece. 1800 d. Hand menacing children.

1949. Removal of Greek Children to other Countries.
683. **100.** 450 d. violet 45 45
684. – 1000 d. brown .. 1·00 15
685. – 1800 d. red .. .. 2·40 15

101. Maps and Flags.

1950. Battle of Crete.
686. **101.** 1000 d. blue .. .. 1·40 15

102. "Youth of Marathon".

1950. U.P.U. 75th Anniv. Inscr. "1874–1949" in white figures at top.
687. **102.** 1000 d. green on buff .. 35 15

103. St. Paul.

104.

1951. St. Paul's Travels in Greece. 19th Cent. Dated "51–1951".
688. – 700 d. purple 70 30
689. **103.** 1600 d. blue .. .. 2·75 1·00
690. **104.** 2600 d. brown .. 7·50 2·10
691. – 10,000 d. chestnut .. 25·00 14·00

DESIGNS—As T **104**: 700 d. Sword and altar (horiz.). 10,000 d. St. Paul preaching to Athenians (vert.).

105. "Industry".

106. Blessing before Battle.

1951. Reconstruction Issue.
692. **105.** 700 d. orange .. 85 8
693. – 800 d. green .. .. 2·40 20
694. – 1300 d. blue .. .. 3·00 10
695. – 1600 d. olive .. .. 7·50 10
696. – 2600 d. violet .. 22·00 85
697. – 5000 d. purple .. 22·00 20

DESIGNS—VERT. 800 d. Fish and trident. 1300 d. Workmen and column. 1600 d. Ceres and tractors. 2600 d. Women and loom. 5000 d. Map and stars ("Electrification").

1952. Air. Anti-Communist Campaign.
698. **106.** 1,000 d. blue 45 12
699. – 1,700 d. blue-green .. 90 70
700. – 2,700 d. brown .. 3·50 1·75
701. – 7,000 d. green .. 8·50 3·75

DESIGNS—VERT. 1,700 d. "Victory" over mountains. 2,700 d. Infantry attack. 7,000 d. "Victory" and soldiers.

107. King Paul.

108. "Spirit of Greece".

1952. 50th Birthday of King Paul.
702. **107.** 200 d. emerald .. 12 8
703. 1,000 d. red 50 8
704. **108.** 1,400 d. blue .. .. 2·10 25
705. **107.** 10,000 d. purple .. 14·00 5·00

109. "Oranges".

1953. National Products.
706. **109.** 500 d. orange and red 25 5
707. – 700 d. yellow and brown 40 5
708. – 1,000 d. green and blue 70 5
709. – 1,300 c. buff & purple 1·00 5
710. – 2,000 d. green & brown 1·60 5
711. – 2,600 d. bistre & violet 4·25 70
712. – 5,000 d. green & brown 8·50 20

DESIGNS—VERT. 700 d. "Tobacco" (tobacco plant). 1,300 d. "Wine" (wineglass and vase). 2,000 d. "Figs" (basket of figs). 2,600 d. "Dried Fruit" (grapes and currant bread). 5,000 d. "Grapes" (male figure holding grapes). HORIZ. 1,000 d. "Olive Oil" (Pallas Athene and olive branch).

110. Bust of Pericles.

111. Alexander the Great.

112. Athlete Bearing Torch.

1954. Ancient Greek Art. Sculptures, etc.
713. **110.** 100 d. brown 8 5
714. – 200 d. black 12 5
715. – 300 d. violet 20 5
716. – 500 d. green 25 5
717. – 600 d. red 55 5
718. **111.** 1,000 d. black & blue 70 5
719. – 1,200 d. olive 70 5
720. – 2,000 d. brown .. 2·10 5
721. – 2,400 d. blue .. .. 2·75 12
722. – 2,500 d. green .. 2·50 12
723. – 4,000 d. claret .. 4·00 15
724. – 20,000 d. purple .. 28·00 55

DESIGNS—As T **110**: VERT. 200 d. Mycenaean oxhead vase. 1,200 d. Head of charioteer of Delphi. 2,000 d. Vase of Dipylon. 2,500 d. Man carrying calf. 20,000 d. Two pitcher bearers. HORIZ. 2,400 d. Hunting wild boar. As T **111**: VERT. 300 d. Bust of Homer. 500 d. Zeus of Istiaca. 600 d. Youth's head. 4,000 d. Dish depicting voyage of Dionysus.
See also Nos. 733a/41.

1954. Air. 5th Anniv. of N.A.T.O. Inscr. "NATO".
725. **112.** 1,200 d. orange .. 2·75 15
726. – 2,400 d. green .. 8·50 1·10
727. – 4,000 d. blue .. 15·00 2·25

DESIGNS—VERT. 2,400 d. Amphictyonic coin. 4,000 d. Pallas Athene.

Currency revalued. 1000 old drachma = one new drachma.

113. Extracts from "Hansard" (Parliamentary Debates).

114. Samian Coin Depicting Pythagoras.

1954. "Enosis" (Union of Cyprus with Greece).
728. **113.** 1.20 d. black & yellow 40 12
729. 2 d. black and salmon 2·10 1·75
730. 2 d. black and blue .. 2·10 1·75
731. 2.40 d. blk. & lavender 2·10 45
732. 2.50 d. black and pink 2·40 45
733. 4 d. black and lemon .. 8·50 1·25

On No. 728 the text is in Greek, on Nos. 730/1 in French and on the remainder in English.

1955. As Nos. 713/24 but new colours and values.
733a. **110.** 10 l. green 5 5
734. – 20 l. myrtle (No. 714) 12 5
734a. – 20 l. purple (No. 714) 8 5
735. **110.** 30 l. brown 20 5
736. – 50 l. lake (No. 716) .. 50 5
736a. – 50 l. green (No. 716) 20 5
736b. – 70 l. orange (No. 719) 30 8
737. – 1 d. green (No. 717) 70 5
737a. – 1 d. brown (No. 717) 40 5
737b. – 1 d. 50 blue (No. 724) 1·60 10
738. **111.** 2 d. black and brown 1·25 5
738a. 2 d. 50 black & mag. 1·60 5
739. – 3 d. orange (No. 721) 2·75 12
739a. – 3 d. cobalt (No. 722) 85 8
740. – 3 d. 50 red (No. 715) 4·25 20
741. – 4 d. blue (No. 723) .. 9·00 15

1955. Pythagorean Congress.
742. **114.** 2 d. green 90 15
743. – 3 d. 50 black .. .. 3·00 90
744. **114.** 5 d. purple .. .. 6·50 35
745. – 6 d. blue .. .. 6·50 5·50

DESIGNS—VERT. 3 d. 50, Representation of Pythagoras theorem. HORIZ. 6 d. Map of Samos.

115. Rotary Emblem and Globe.

116. King George I.

1956. Rotary Int. 50th Anniv.
746. **115.** 2 d. blue .. .. 1·60 20

1956. Royal Family.
747. – 10 l. violet 8 5
748. – 20 l. purple 8 5
749. **116.** 30 l. sepia 10 5
750. – 50 l. brown 12 5
751. – 70 l. blue 20 8
752. – 1 d. turquoise 20 5
753. – 1 d. 50 slate 20 8
754. – 2 d. black 25 5
755. – 3 d. brown 70 8
756. – 3 d. 50 chestnut .. 1·00 20
757. – 4 d. green .. .. 1·60 10
758. – 5 d. red .. .. 1·00 10
759. – 7 d. 50 blue .. .. 1·40 55
760. – 10 d. blue .. .. 5·50 35

PORTRAITS—HORIZ. 10 l. King Alexander. 5 d. King Paul and Queen Frederica. 10 d. King and Queen and Crown Prince Constantine. VERT. 20 l. Crown Prince Constantine. 50 l. Queen Olga. 70 l. King Otto. 1 d. Queen Amalia. 1 d. 50, King Constantine. 2 d. King Paul. 3 d. King George II. 3d. 50, Queen Sophia. 4 d. Queen Frederica. 7 d. 50, King Paul.
See also Nos. 764/77.

117. Dionysios Solomos.

118. "Argo" (5th Century B.C.).

1957. D. Solomos (national poet). Death Cent.
761. – 2 d. yellow and brown 40 12
762. **117.** 3 d. 50 grey and blue 1·40 70
763. – 5 d. bistre and green 3·75 3·25

DESIGNS—HORIZ. 2 d. Solomos and K. Mantzaros (composer). 5 d. Zante landscape and Solomos.

1957. As Nos. 747/60. Colours changed.
764. – 10 l. claret 5 5
765. – 20 l. orange 8 5
766. **116.** 30 l. black 8 5
767. – 50 l. green 10 5
768. – 70 l. purple 25 20
769. – 1 d. red 20 5
770. – 1 d. 50 l. green .. 20 5
771. – 2 d. red 30 5
772. – 3 d. blue 70 8
773. – 3 d. 50 l. slate-purple 1·10 12
774. – 4 d. brown 70 8
775. – 5 d. blue .. .. 1·60 12
776. – 7 d. 50 l. yellow .. 2·10 60
777. 10 d. green .. .. 6·50 35

1958. Greek Merchant Marine Commemoration. Ship designs.
778. – 50 l. red, black, grey and blue .. 8 5
779. – 1 d. ochre, blk. & blue 10 5
780. – 1 d. 50 l. red, blk. & blue 12 10
781. – 2 d. brn., blk., vio. & bl. 15 8
782. – 3 d. 50 l. blk., red & bl. 55 30
783. **118.** 5 d. red, blk., grn. & bl. 3·25 3·25

SHIPS—HORIZ. 50 l. Tanker. 1 d. Liner. 1 d. 50 l. Sailing ship of 1821. 2 d. Byzantine galley. 3 d. 50 l. Vessel of 6th Century B.C.

119. The Piraeus (Port of Athens).

120. "Narcissus" and Flower.

1958. Air. Greek Ports.
784. **119.** 10 d. red, blue, black and grey .. .. 1·25 5
785. 15 d. red, slate, black and drab 70 15
786. – 20 d. blue, black, red and turquoise .. 1·40 10
787. – 25 d. red, black, blue and grey .. .. 1·00 45
788. – 30 d. red, black, slate and turquoise .. 1·10 45
789. – 50 d. blue, blk. & brn. 1·90 25
790. – 100 d. blue, blk. & brn. 3·75 2·10

PORTS: 15 d. Salonika. 20 d. Patras. 25 d. Hermoupolis (Syra). 30 d. Volos (Thessaly). 50 d. Cavalla. 100 d. Heraklion (Crete).

1958. Int. Congress for Protection of Nature, Athens. Mythological and Floral designs. Multicoloured.
791. 20 l. Type **120** 5 5
792. 30 l. "Daphne and Apollo" 5 5
793. 50 l. "Venus and Adonis" (Venus and rose) .. 5 5
794. 70 l. "Pan and the Nymph" (Pan and pine cones) .. 5 5
795. 1 d. Crocus 5 5
796. 2 d. Iris 12 5
797. 3 d. 50 Tulip 20 20
798. 5 d. Cyclamen .. .. 1·00 1·00

SIZES—As T **120**: 30 l. to 70 l. 21½ × 26 mm. 1 d.): 22 × 32 mm. (2 d., 3 d., 50 l. and 5 l.).

121. Jupiter's Head and Eagle (Olympia 4th-century B.C. coin).

1959. Ancient Greek Coins. Designs as T 121 showing both sides of each coin. Inscriptions in black.

799. **121.** 10 l. grey-grn. & brown 5 5
800. – 20 l. grey and blue .. 8 5
801. 50 l. grey and purple .. 12 10
802. – 70 l. grey and blue .. 20 12
803. – 1 d. drab and red .. 35 8
804. – 1 d. 50 grey and ochre 40 8
805. 2 d. 50 drab & magenta 70 5
806. 4 d. 50 grey and green 1·40 20
807. – 6 d. blue and olive .. 2·00 8
808. – 8 d. 50 drab and red .. 2·50 90

COINS—HORIZ. 20 l. Athene's head and owl (Athens 5th cent. B.C.). 50 l. Nymph Arethusa and chariot (Syracuse 5th cent. B.C.). 70 l. Hercules and jupiter (Alexander the Great 4th cent. B.C.). 1 d. 50, Griffin and squares (Abdera, Thrace 5th cent. B.C.). 2 d. 50, Apollo and lyre (Chalcidice, Macedonia 4th cent. B.C.). VERT. 1 d. Helios and rose (Rhodes 4th cent. B.C.). 4 d. 50, Apollo and labyrinth (Crete 3rd cent. B.C.). 6 d. Venus and Apollo (Paphos, Cyprus 4th cent. B.C.). 8 d. 50, Ram's heads and incised squares (Delphi 5th cent. B.C.).

See also Nos. 909/17.

122. Amphitheatre, Delphi.

123. "Victory" and Greek Soldiers through the Ages.

125. Imre Nagy (formerly Prime Minister of Hungary).

124. "The Good Samaritan".

1959. Ancient Greek Theatre.

809. – 20 l. chestnut, black, brown and blue .. 5 5
810. – 50 l. brown and olive .. 20 8
811. 1 d. brown, buff, grey and green .. 20 10
812. – 2 d. 50 brown and blue 30 5
813. **122.** 3 d. 50 brown, green, grey and red .. 2·10 2·10
814. – 4 d. 50 chestnut & blk. 60 40
815. – 6 d. chest., grey & blk. 70 20

DESIGNS—VERT. 20 l. Ancient theatre audience (after a Pharsala Thessaly, vase of 580 B.C.). 50 l. Clay mask of 3rd century B.C. 1 d. Flute, drum and lyre. 2 d. 50, Actor (3rd century statuette). 6 d. Performance of a satirical play (after a mixing-bowl of 410 B.C.). HORIZ. 4 d. 50, Performance of Euripides' "Andromeda" (after a vase of 4th century B.C.).

1959. Greek Anti-Communist Victory. 10th Anniv.

816. **123.** 2 d. 50 blue, black and brown 80 20

1959. Red Cross Commem. Cross in red

817. – 20 l. multicoloured .. 5 5
818. – 50 l. olive-grey, red and blue .. 8 5
819. – 70 l. black, red-brown, yell.-brown and blue 10 10
820. 2 d. 50 blk., orge-brn., grey-brn. & red-brn. 20 5
821. – 3 d. multicoloured .. 2·00 2·00
822. 4 d. 50 orange-brown and red-brown .. 30 30
823. **124.** 6 d. multicoloured .. 40 15

DESIGNS—HORIZ. 20 l. Hippocrates Tree, Cos. VERT. 50 l. Bust of Aesculapius. 70 l. St. Basil (after mosaic in Hosios Loukas Monastery, Boeotia). 2 d. 50, Achilles and Patroclus (from vase of 6th cent., B.C.). 3 d. (32×47½ mm.) Red Cross, globe, infirm people and nurses. 4 d. 50, J. H. Dunant.

1959. Hungarian Revolt (3rd Anniv.).

824. **125.** 4 d. 50 sepia, chestnut and brown-red .. 45 45
825. 6 d. blk., blue & ultram. 65 65

126. Kostes Palamas.

127. Ship in Storm.

129. Sprinting.

128. Scout emulating St. George.

1960. Palamas (poet). Birth Cent.

826. **126.** 2 d. 50 magenta, mauve, grey and maroon .. 85 20

1960. World Refugee Year. Multicoloured.

827. 2 d. 50 T **127** 20 8
828. 4 d. 50 Ship in calm waters 40 25

1960. Greek Boy Scout Movement. 50th Anniv. Multicoloured.

829. 20 l. T **128** 8 8
830. 30 l. Ephebi Oath and Scout Promise 10 10
831. 40 l. Fire rescue work .. 10 10
832. 50 l. Planting tree .. 15 5
833. 70 l. Map reading .. 20 15
834. 1 d. Scouts on beach .. 20 5
835. 2 d. 50 Crown Prince Constantine in uniform .. 50 12
836. 6 d. Greek Scout Flag and Medal .. .. .. 1·00 1·00

Nos. 829/30 and 835 are vert. and the rest horiz.

1960. Olympic Games.

837. – 20 l. brn., blk. & blue 5 5
838. – 50 l. brown and black 5 5
838. – 70 l. brn., blk. & green 10 10
840. – 80 l. brown, black, grey and drab 15 15
841. – 1 d. brown, black, buff and blue 12 8
842. – 1 d. 50 brown, black and orange-brown .. 15 10
843. – 2 d. 50 brn., blk. & blue 25 8
844. **129.** 4 d. 50 brown, black, blue and ochre .. 40 35
845. 5 d. brown, black, green and turquoise .. 1·00 75
846. – 6 d. brn., black & violet 70 45
847. 12 d. 50 black, buff grey, chest. & brown 3·50 3·50

DESIGNS—VERT. 20 l. "Armistice" (official holding plaque). 70 l. Athletic taking oath. 2 d. 50, Discus-throwing. 5 d. Javelin-throwing. HORIZ. 50 l. Olympic flame. 80 l. Cutting branches from crown-bearing olive tree. 1 d. Entrance of chief judges. 1 d. 50, Long. jumping. 6 d. Crowning the victor. 12 d. 50, Quadriga or chariot-driving (entrance of the victor).

1960. European Postal and Telecommunications Conference. 1st Anniv. As T 279 of Belgium.

848. 4 d. 50 blue .. .. 1·60 1·00

130. Crown Prince Constantine and Yachts.

1961. Victory of Crown Prince Constantine in Dragon-class Yacht Race, Olympic Games.

849. **130.** 2 d. 50 multicoloured .. 25 20

132. Lilies Vase of Knossos.

131. Kastoria.

133. Reactors Building.

1961. Tourist Publicity Issue.

850. **131.** 10 l. indigo 5 5
851. – 20 l. plum 5 5
852. – 50 l. blue 5 5
853. – 70 l. purple 12 8
854. – 80 l. blue 12 10
855. – 1 d. brown 8 5
856. – 1 d. 50 emerald .. 15 5
857. – 2 d. 50 red 40 5
858. – 3 d. 50 violet 30 30
859. – 4 d. green 20 5
860. – 4 d. 50 indigo 30 5
861. – 5 d. lake 55 5
862. – 6 d. myrtle 70 5
863. – 7 d. 50 black 45 15
864. – 8 d. blue 45 20
865. – 8 d. 50 orange .. 70 20
866. – 12 d. 50 sepia .. .. 1·00 35

DESIGNS—HORIZ. 20 l. The Meteora (Monasteries). 50 l. Hydra. 70 l. Parthenon, Athens. 80 l. Mykonos. 1 d. Salonika. 1 d. 50, Olympia. 2 d. 50 Knossos. 3 d. 50, Rhodes. 4 d. Epidavros. 4 d. 50, Sounion. 5 d. Temple of Zeus, Athens. 7 d. 50, Yannina. 12 d. 50, Delos. VERT. 6 d. Delphi. 8 d. Mount Athos. 8 d. 50, Santorini (Thira).

1961. Minoan Art.

867. **132.** 20 l. multicoloured .. 8 5
868. – 50 l. multicoloured .. 15 8
869. – 1 d. multicoloured .. 15 8
870. – 1 d. 50 multicoloured 20 12
871. – 2 d. 50 multicoloured 60 8
872. – 4 d. 50 multicoloured 90 90
873. – 6 d. multicoloured .. 1·00 30
874. – 10 d. multicoloured .. 3·25 3·25

DESIGNS—VERT. 1 d. 50, Knossos rhytonbearer. 4 d. 50, Part of Hagia trias sarcophagus. HORIZ. 50 l. Partridges and fig-pecker (Knossos frieze). 1 d. Kamares fruit dish. 2 d. 50, Ladies of Knossos Palace (painting). 6 d. Knossos dancer (painting). 10 d. Kamares prochus and pithos with spout.

1961. Inaug. of "Democritus" Nuclear Research Centre, Aghia Paraskevi.

875. **133.** 2 d. 50 magenta & mve. 20 8
876. – 4 d. 50 blue & grey-blue 40 35

DESIGN: 4 d. 50, Democritus and atomic symbol.

134. Doves.

135. Nicephorus Phocas.

1961. Europa.

877. **134.** 2 d. 50 red and pink .. 8 5
878. 4 d. 50 ultram. & blue 15 15

1961. Millenary of Liberation of Crete from the Saracens.

879. **135.** 2 d. 50 multicoloured .. 25 20

136. "Hermes" 1 l. Stamp of 1861.

137. Ptolemais Steam Plant.

1961. Greek Stamp Centenary. "Hermes" stamps of 1861. Multicoloured.

880. 20 l. Type **136** 5 5
881. 50 l. "2 l" 8 5
882. 1 d. 50 "5 l" 8 8
883. 2 d. 50 "10 l" 12 8
884. 4 d. 50 "20 l" 35 30
885. 6 d. "40 l" 45 20
886. 10 d. "80 l" .. .. 1·00 1·00

1962. Electrification Project. Multicoloured.

887. 20 l. Tauropos dam (vert.) 5 5
888. 50 l. Ladhon River hydro-electric plant (vert.) .. 5 5
889. 1 d. T **137** 8 5
890. 1 d. 50, Louros River dam 12 5
891. 2 d. 50, Aliverion steam plant 20 5
892. 4 d. 50, Salonika hydro-electric sub-station .. 40 25
893. 6 d. Agra River power station .. .. .. 1·10 1·00

138. Zappion Building.

139. Europa "Tree".

1962. N.A.T.O. Ministers' Conference, Athens.

894. **138.** 2 d. 50 sepia, green, red and blue 10 5
895. – 3 d. sepia, brown & buff 15 10
896. – 4 d. 50 black and blue 40 40
897. – 6 d. black & brown-red 30 25

Designs—VERT. 3 d. Ancient Greek warrior with shield. 4 d. 50, Soldier kneeling (after Marathon tomb). 6 d. (21×37 mm.), Soldier (statue in Temple of Aphea, Aegina).

1962. Europa.

898. **139.** 2 d. 50 red and black .. 15 5
899. 4 d. 50 blue and black 40 40

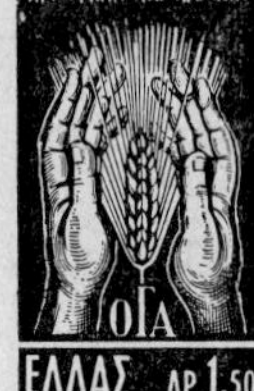

140. "Protection".

141. Demeter, Goddess of Corn.

1962. Greek Farmers' Social Insurance Scheme.

900. **140.** 1 d. 50 blk., brn. & red 15 5
901. 2 d. 50 blk., brn. & grn. 20 5

1963. Freedom from Hunger. Multicoloured.

902. 2 d. 50 T **141** 15 5
903. 4 d. Wheatears and Globe 35 35

142. Kings of the Greek Dynasty.

1963. Greek Royal Dynasty. Cent.

904. **142.** 50 l. red 12 8
905. 1 d. 50 green 15 10
906. 2 d. 50 brown 30 5
907. 4 d. 50 blue 70 40
908. 5 d. violet .. .. 1·10 20

1963. Ancient Greek Coins. As Nos. 799/808 but colours changed and some designs rearranged. Inscr. in black; coins in black and drab or grey; background colours given.

909. 50 l. vio.-blue (As No. 870l) 5 5
910. 80 l. purple (As 802) .. 10 8
911. 1 d. green (As 803) .. 10 5
912. 1 d. 50 cerise (As 804) .. 15 5
913. 3 d. olive (As 799) .. 20 5
914. 3 d. 50 red (As 800) .. 25 5
915. 4 d. 50 brown (As 806) .. 30 8
916. 6 d. blue-green (As 807) .. 40 8
917. 8 d. 50 blue (As 808) .. 85 35

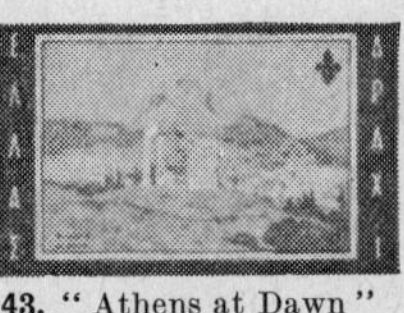

143. "Athens at Dawn" (after watercolour by Lord Baden-Powell).

144. Delphi.

1963. 11th World Scout Jamboree, Marathon.

918. 1 d. salmon, blue, olive & light brown 8 5
919. 1 d. 50 orge., black & blue 8 5
920. 2 d. 50 flesh, black, bistre, blue, lake and grey .. 20 5
921. 3 d. blk., cinnamon & grn. 30 15
922. 4 d. 50 buff, brown, black, blue and light blue .. 65 60

DESIGNS—HORIZ. 1 d. T **143**. 3 d. A. Lefkadites (founder of Greek Scout Movement) and Lord Baden-Powell. VERT. 1 d. 50, Jamboree Badge. 2 d. 50, Crown Prince Constantine, Chief Scout of Greece. 4 d. 50, Scout bugling with conch-shell.

1963. Red Cross Cent. Multicoloured.

923. 1 d. Type **144** 5 5
924. 2 d. Centenary emblem .. 12 5
925. 2 d. 50 Queen Olga .. 12 5
926. 4 d. 50 Henri Dunant .. 40 40

145. "Co-operation".

1963. Europa.
927. **145.** 2 d. 50 green 40 8
928. 4 d. 50 purple .. 1·00 85

146. Great Lavra Church. **147.** King Paul.

1963. Mt. Athos Monastic Community. Millenary. Multicoloured.
929. 30 l. Vatopediou Monastery 5 5
930. 80 l. Dionysion Monastery 10 8
931. 1 d. Protaton Church, Karyae 10 5
932. 2 d. Stavronikita Monastery 12 5
933. 2 d. 50 Cover of Nicephorus Phocas Gospel, Great Lavra Church .. 35 5
934. 3 d. 50 St. Athanasius the Anthonite (fresco) .. 55 50
935. 4 d. 50 11th-century papyrus, Iviron Monastery 55 40
936. 6 d. Type **146** 55 25
The 1 d. and 6 d. are horiz., the rest vert.

1964. Death of Paul I.
937. **147.** 30 l. brown 5 5
938. 50 l. violet 5 5
939. 1 d. bronze-green .. 8 5
940. 1 d. 50 orange .. 12 5
941. 2 d. blue 15 5
942. 2 d. 50 sepia 20 5
943. 3 d. 50 brown-purple 25 12
944. 4 d. ultramarine .. 35 8
945. 4 d. 50 indigo .. 55 30
946. 6 d. cerise 1 00 8

148. Gold Coin. **149.** Trident of Paxi.

150. Greek Child. **151.** Europa "Flower".

1964. Byzantine Art Exn., Athens. Multicoloured.
947. 1 d. Type **148** 5 5
948. 1 d. 50 "Two Saints" .. 10 10
949. 2 d. "Archangel Michael" 12 8
950. 2 d. 50 "Young Lady" .. 20 5
951. 4 d. 50 "Angel" 50 50
DESIGN origins: 1 d. reign of Emperor Basil II (976-1025). 1 d. 50, from Harbaville's 10th-cent. ivory triptych (Louvre). 2 d. 14th cent. Constantinople icon (Byzantine Museum, Athens). 2 d. 50, from 14th cent. fresco "The Birth of the Holy Virgin" by Panselinos (Protaton Church, Mt. Athos). 4 d. 50, from 11th cent. mosaic (Daphne Church, Athens).

1964. Union of Ionian Islands with Greece. Cent. Inscr. "1864–1964". Multicoloured.
952. 20 l. Type **149** 5 5
953. 30 l. Venus of Cythera .. 5 5
954. 1 d. Ulysses of Ithaca .. 5 5
955. 2 d. St. George of Leukas 8 5
956. 2 d. 50 Zakynthos of Zante 12 5
957. 4 d. 50 Cephalus of Cephalonia .. 35 35
958. 6 d. Trireme-emblem of Corfu 40 20

1964. National Institution of Social Welfare (P.I.K.P.A.). 50th Anniv.
959. **150.** 2 d. 50 multicoloured .. 15 8

1964. Europa.
960. **151.** 2 d. 50 red and green .. 20 5
961. 4 d. 50 brown & drab .. 40 40

152. King Constantine II and Queen Anne-Marie. **153.** Peleus and Atalanta (amphora).

1964. Royal Wedding.
962. **152.** 1 d. 50 green 10 5
963. 2 d. 50 red 12 5
964. 4 d. 50 blue 35 30

1964. Olympic Games, Tokyo. Multicoloured.
965. 10 l. Type **153** 5 5
966. 1 d. Running (bowl) .. 5 5
967. 2 d. Jumping (pot) .. 8 5
968. 2 d. 50 Throwing the discus 10 5
969. 4 d. 50 Chariot-racing (sculpture) 30 30
970. 6 d. Boxing (vase) 15 8
971. 10 d. Apollo (part of frieze, Zeus Temple, Olympia) 30 30
The 1 d., 2 d., 4 d. 50 and 6 d. are horiz.

154. "Christ stripping off His garments". **155.** Aesculapius Theatre, Epidauros.

1965. El Greco. 350th Death Anniv. Multicoloured.
972. 50 l. Type **154** 5 5
973. 1 d. "Angels' Concert" .. 5 5
974. 1 d. 50 El Greco's signature 10 5
975. 2 d. 50 Self-portrait .. 15 5
976. 4 d. 50 "Storm-lashed Toledo" 35 35
The 1 d. 50 is horiz.

1965. Greek Artistic Festivals. Multicoloured.
977. 1 d. 50 Type **155** 5 5
978. 4 d. 50 Herod Atticus Theatre, Athens .. 15 15

156. I.T.U. Emblem and Symbols.

1965. I.T.U. Cent.
979. **156.** 2 d. 50 red, blue & grey 12 5

157. "New member making affirmation" (after Tsokos).

1965. "Philiki Hetaeria" ("Friends Society"). 150th Anniv. Multicoloured.
980. 1 d. 50 Type **157** 5 5
981. 4 d. 50 Society flag .. 15 15

158. AHEPA Emblem. **159.** Venizelos as Revolutionary.

1965. American Hellenic Educational Progressive Assn. (AHEPA) Congress, Athens.
982. **158.** 6 d. blk., olive & blue 20 15

1965. E. Venizelos (statesman). Birth Cent.
983. **159.** 1 d. 50 green 5 5
984. – 2 d. blue 10 10
985. – 2 d. 50 brown 15 5
DESIGNS: 2 d. Venizelos signing Treaty of Sevres (1920). 2 d. 50, Venizelos.

160. Games' Flag. **161.** Symbols of the Planets.

1965. Balkan Games, Athens. Multicoloured.
986. 1 d. Type **160** 5 5
987. 2 d. Victor's medal (vert.) 8 5
988. 6 d. Karaiskakis Stadium, Athens 20 20

1965. Int. Astronautic Conf., Athens. Multicoloured.
989. 50 l. Type **161** 5 5
990. 2 d. 50 Astronaut in space 8 5
991. 6 d. Rocket and space-ship 25 20

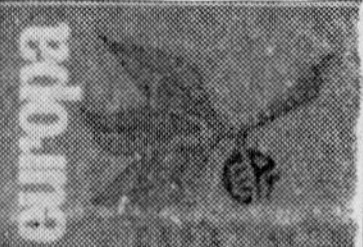

162. Europa "Sprig". **163.** Hipparchus (astronomer) and Astrolabe.

1965. Europa.
992. **162.** 2 d. 50 blue, blk. & grey 10 5
993. 4 d. 50 grn., blk. & ol. 30 30

1965. Opening of Evghenides Planetarium, Athens.
994. **163.** 2 d. 50 blk., red & grn. 10 5

164. Ants. **165.** St. Andrew's Church, Patrae.

1965. P.O. Savings Bank. 50th Anniv. Multicoloured.
995. 10 l. Type **164** 5 5
996. 2 d. 50 Savings Bank and book 12 5

1965. Restoration of St. Andrew's Head to Greece. Multicoloured.
997. 1 d. Type **165** 5 5
998. 5 d. St. Andrew, after 11th-cent. mosaic, Hosios Loukas Monastery, Boeotia .. 20 20

166. T. Brysakes. **168.** Geannares (revolutionary leader).

167. Greek 25 d. Banknote of 1867.

1966. Modern Greek Painters. Multicoloured.
999. 80 l. Type **166** 5 5
1000. 1 d. N. Lytras 5 5
1001. 2 d. 50 C. Volonakes .. 5 5
1002. 4 d. N. Gyses 12 10
1003. 5 d. G. Jacobides .. 20 12

1966. Greek National Bank. 125th Anniv.
1004. – 1 d. 50 green .. 8 5
1005. – 2 d. 50 brown .. 12 5
1006. – 4 d. blue 15 10
1007. **167.** 6 d. black 25 15
DESIGNS—VERT. (23 × 33½ mm.): 1 d. 50, J.-G. Eynard. 2 d. 50, G. Stavros (founders). HORIZ. (As T **167**): 4 d. National Bank Headquarters, Athens.

1966. Cretan Revolt. Cent. Multicoloured.
1008. 2 d. Type **168** 8 5
1009. 2 d. 50 Magazine explosion, Arkadi Monastery (vert.) 8 5
1010. 4 d. 50 Map of Crete (vert.) 20 20

169. "Movement of Water" (Decade of World Hydrology). **170.** Tragedian's Mask of 4th Century, B.C.

1966. U.N.O. Events.
1011. **169.** 1 d. brown, black & blue 5 5
1012. – 3 d. multicoloured .. 10 5
1013. – 5 d. black, red and blue 20 20
DESIGNS—VERT. 3 d. U.N.E.S.C.O. emblem (20th anniv.). 5 d. W.H.O. Building (inauguration of H.Q., Geneva).

1966. Greek Theatre. 2,500th Anniv.
1014. **170.** 1 d. grn., blk. bl. & grey 5 5
1015. – 1 d. 50 black, red & brn. 5 5
1016. – 2 d. 50 black, green and apple 8 5
1017. – 4 d. 50 red, flesh, black and lilac 20 20
DESIGNS—HORIZ. 1 d. 50, Dionysus in a Thespian ship-chariot (vase painting, 500-480 B.C.). 2 d. 50, Theatre of Dionysus, Athens. VERT. 4 d. 50, Dionysus dancing (after vase painting by Kleophrades, circa 500 B.C.).

171. Boeing "707" crossing Atlantic Ocean. **172.** Tending Plants

173. Europa "Ship". **174.** Horseman (embroidery).

1966. Greek Airways Transatlantic Flights. Inaug.
1018. **171.** 6 d. indigo and blue 25 15

1966. Greek Tobacco. Multicoloured.
1019. 1 d. Type **172** 5 5
1020. 5 d. Sorting leaf 20 15

1966. Europa.
1021. **173.** 1 d. 50 olive 8 5
1022. 4 d. 50 brown .. 30 20

1966. Greek "Popular" Art. Multicoloured.
1023. 10 l. Knitting-needle boxes 5 5
1024. 30 l. Type **174** 5 5
1025. 50 l. Cretan lyre 5 5
1026. 1 d. "Massa" (Musical instrument) 5 5
1027. 1 d. 50 "Cross and Angels" (bas-relief after Melios) 8 5
1028. 2 d. "Sts. Constantine and Helen" (icon) 10 5
1029. 2 d. 50 Carved altar screen, St. Nicholas' Church, Galaxidion 15 5
1030. 3 d. 19th-century ship of Skyros (embroidery) .. 15 8
1031. 4 d. "Psiki" (wedding procession) (embroidery) 20 8
1032. 4 d. 50 Distaff 25 10
1033. 5 d. Ear-rings and necklace 35 5
1034. 20 d. Detail of handwoven cloth .. .. .. 1·40 45
The 10 l., 50 l., 1 d., 1 d. 50, 2 d., 2 d. 50, 4 d. 50, and 5 d. designs are vert.

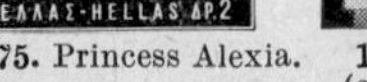

175. Princess Alexia. **176.** "Woodcutter" (after D. Filippotes).

1966. Princess Alexia's First Birthday.
1035. **175.** 2 d. green 10 5
1036. – 2 d. 50 chocolate .. 15 5
1037. – 3 d. 50 ultramarine.. 25 20
PORTRAITS: 2 d. 50, Royal Family. 3 d. 50, Queen Anne-Marie with Princess Alexia.

1967. Greek Sculpture. Multicoloured.
1038. 20 l. "Night" (I. Cossos) 5 5
1039. 50 l. "Penelope" (L. Drossos).. .. .. 5 5
1040. 80 l. "Shepherd" (G. Phitalis) 5 5
1041. 2 d. "Woman's Torso" (K. Demetriades) .. 5 5
1042. 2 d. 50 "Kolokotronis" (L. Sochos) 10 5
1043. 3 d. "Girl Sleeping" (I. Halepas) 25 25
1044. 10 d. Type **176** 30 20
Nos. 1038/42 are vert.

177. Olympic Rings ("Olympic Day"). **178.** Cogwheels.

1967. Sports Events. Multicoloured.
1045. 1 d. Type **177** 5 5
1046. 1 d. 50 Marathon Cup, first Olympics (1896).. 5 5
1047. 2 d. 50 Hurdling.. .. 10 5
1048. 5 d. "The Discus-thrower", after C. Demetriades .. 20 20
1049. 6 d. Ancient Olympic stadium 25 12
The 2 d. 50 commemorates the European Athletics Cup, 1967. 5 d. (vert.), The European Highest Award Championships, 1968. 6 d. The Inaug. of "International Academy" buildings, Olympia.

1967. Europa.
1050. **178.** 2 d. 50 multicoloured 20 5
1051. 4 d. 50 multicoloured 35 35

179. Destroyer and Sailor. **180.** The Plaka, Athens.

1967. Nautical Week.
1052. **179.** 20 l. multicoloured .. 5 5
1053. – 1 d. multicoloured .. 5 5
1054. – 2 d. 50 multicoloured 10 5
1055. – 3 d. multicoloured .. 15 15
1056. – 6 d. multicoloured .. 25 12
DESIGNS—VERT. 1 d. Training ship. HORIZ. 2 d. 50, Merchant Marine Academy, Aspropyrgos, Attica. 3 d. Cruiser "Averoff" and Naval School, Poros. 6 d. Merchant ship and figure-head.

1967. Int. Tourist Year.
1057. – 2 d. 50 multicoloured 8 5
1058. – 4 d. 50 multicoloured 20 20
1059. **180.** 6 d. multicoloured .. 35 12
DESIGNS—HORIZ. 2 d. 50, Island of Skopelos. 4 d. 50, Apollo's Temple, Bassai, Peleponnese.

181. Soldier and Phoenix. **182.** Industrial Skyline.

1967. National Revolution of April 21st (1967).
1060. **181.** 2 d. 50 multicoloured 15 5
1061. 3 d. multicoloured .. 25 12
1062. 4 d. 50 multicoloured 40 40

1967. 1st Convention of U.N. Industrial Development Organisation, Athens.
1063. **182.** 4 d. 50 ultramarine, black and blue .. 40 30

183. "Seaside Scene" (A. Pelaletos).

1967. Children's Drawings. Multicoloured.
1064. 20 l. Type **183** 5 5
1065. 1 d. 50 "Steamer and Island" (L. Tsirikas).. 12 5
1066. 3 d. 50 "Country Cottage" (K. Ambeliotis) .. 25 25
1067. 6 d. "The Church on the Hill" (N. Frangos) .. 30 12

184. Throwing the Javelin. **185.** F.I.A. and E.L.P.A. Emblems.

1968. Sports Events, 1968.
1068. **184.** 50 l. multicoloured .. 5 5
1069. – 1 d. multicoloured .. 5 5
1070. – 1 d. 50 multicoloured 8 5
1071. – 2 d. 50 multicoloured 12 5
1072. – 4 d. multicoloured .. 15 12
1073. – 4 d. 50 multicoloured 35 35
1074. – 6 d. multicoloured .. 35 8
DESIGNS—HORIZ. 1 d. Long-jumping. 4 d. Olympic rings (Olympic Day). VERT. 1 d. 50, "Apollo's Head", Temple of Zeus. 2d. 50, Olympic scene on Attic vase. 4 d. 50, "Throwing the Discus", sculpture by Demetriades (European Athletic Championships, 1969). 6 d. Long-distance running. The 50 l., 1 d. and 6 d. represent the Balkan Games, and the 1 d. 50, and 2 d. 50, the Olympic Academy Meeting.

1968. General Assembly of Int. Automobile Federation (F.I.A.), Athens.
1075. **185.** 5 d. blue and brown.. 40 25

186. Europa "Key".

1968. Europa.
1076. **186.** 2 d. 50 bistre, brown, black and red .. 20 8
1077. 4 d. 50 bistre, brown, black and violet .. 50 50

187. "Athene defeats Alkyoneus" (from frieze, Altar of Zeus, Permagos).

1968. "Hellenic Fight for Civilization" Exn., Athens.
1078. **187.** 10 l. multicoloured .. 5 5
1079. – 20 l. multicoloured .. 5 5
1080. – 50 l. multicoloured .. 5 5
1081. – 1 d. 50 multicoloured 5 5
1082. – 2 d. 50 multicoloured 12 5
1083. – 3 d. multicoloured .. 15 12
1084. – 4 d. 50 multicoloured 30 25
1085. – 6 d. multicoloured .. 40 40
DESIGNS—VERT. (24 × 37 mm.). 20 l. Athene attired for battle (bronze from Piraeus). 50 l. Alexander the Great (from sarcophagus of Alexander of Sidon.) 2 d. 50, Emperor Constantine Paleologos (lithograph by D. Tsokos). (28 × 40 mm.). 3 d. "Greece in Missolonghi" (painting by Delacroix). 4 d. 50, "Evzone" (Greek soldier, painting by G. B. Scott). 6 d. "Victory of Samothrace" (statue). HORIZ. (40 × 28 mm.). 1 d. 50, Emperors Constantine and Justinian making offerings to the Holy Mother (Byzantine mosaic).

INDEX

Countries can be quickly located by referring to the index at the end of this volume.

188. "The Unknown Priest and Teacher" (Rhodes monument). **189.** Congress Emblem.

1968. Dodecanese Union with Greece. 20th Anniv.
1086. **188.** 2 d. multicoloured .. 15 5
1087. – 5 d. multicoloured .. 40 40
DESIGN—VERT. 5 d. Greek flag on map.

1968. 19th Biennial Congress of Greek Orthodox Arch-diocese of North and South America.
1088. **189.** 6 d. multicoloured .. 50 35

190. GAPA Emblem. **191.** "Hand of Aesculapius" (fragment of bas-relief from Asclepios' Temple, Athens).

1968. Regional Congress of Greek-American Progressive Assn. (GAPA).
1089. **190.** 6 d. multicoloured .. 50 35

1968. 5th European Cardiological Congress, Athens.
1090. **191.** 4 d. 50 blk., yell. & lake 90 60

192. Panathenaic Stadium. **194.** Goddess "Hygeia".

193. Greek Fighter ramming Enemy Aircraft.

1968. Olympic Games, Mexico. Multicoloured.
1091. 2 d. 50 Type **192** .. 15 5
1092. 5 d. Ancient Olympia .. 30 12
1093. 10 d. One of Pindar's odes 50 50
The 10 d. is 28 × 40 mm.

1968. Royal Hellenic Air Force. Multicoloured.
1094. 2 d. 50 Type **193** .. 12 5
1095. 3 d. 50 Mediterranean Flight in Breguet "19", 1928 .. .. .. 15 10
1096. 8 d. Farman and Starfighter "F-104G" .. 65 65
The 8 d. is vert.

1968. World Health Organisation. 20th Anniv.
1097. **194.** 5 d. multicoloured .. 50 35

195. St. Zeno, the Letter-carrier. **196.** "Workers' Festival Parade" (detail from Minoan vase).

1969. Greek Post Office Festival.
1098. **195.** 2 d. 50 multicoloured 30 12

1969. Int. Labour Organisation. 50th Anniv.
1099. – 1 d. 50 multicoloured 10 10
1100. **196.** 10 d. multicoloured.. 55 30
DESIGN: 1 d. 50 "Hephaestus and Cyclops" (detail from ancient bas-relief).

197. Yacht Harbour, Vouliagmeni. **198.** Ancient Coin of Kamarina.

1969. Tourism. Multicoloured.
1101. 1 d. Type **197** 5 5
1102. 5 d. "Chorus of Elders" (Ancient drama) (vert.) 55 55
1103. 6 d. View of Astypalia .. 25 5

1969. N.A.T.O. 20th Anniv. Multicoloured.
1104. 2 d. 50 Type **198** .. 15 8
1105. 4 d. 50 "Going into Battle" (from Corinthian vase) 35 35
No. 1105 is horiz.

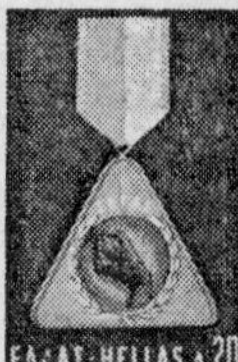

199. Colonnade. **200.** Gold Medal.

1969. Europa.
1106. **199.** 2 d. 50 multicoloured 20 8
1107. 4 d. 50 multicoloured 35 35

1969. 9th European Athletic Championships, Athens. Multicoloured.
1108. 20 l. Type **200** 5 5
1109. 3 d. Pole-vaulting, and ancient pentathlon contest.. .. .. 15 12
1110. 5 d. Relay-racing, and Olympic race c 525 B.C. (horiz.).. .. .. 30 8
1111. 8 d. Throwing the discus, modern and c 480 B.C... 55 50

201. "19th-century Brig and Steamship" (I. Poulakas). **202.** Raising the Flag on Mt. Grammos.

1969. Navy Week and Merchant Marine Year. Multicoloured.
1112. 80 l. Type **201** 12 10
1113. 2 d. Modern super-tanker 15 5
1114. 2 d. 50 "Naval and Merchant Ships. War of Independence, 1821" (Anon.) 15 5
1115. 4 d. 50 Modern Vessels of Greek Navy 40 40
1116. 6 d. "The Battle of Salamis" (C. Volonakis) 55 35

1969. Communists' Defeat on Mounts Grammos and Vitsi. 20th Anniv.
1117. **202.** 2 d. 50 multicoloured 25 12

203. Athena Promachos. **204.** Demetrius Karatasios (statue by G. Demetriades).

1969. Liberation. 25th Anniv. Multicoloured.
1118. 4 d. Type **203** 20 12
1119. 5 d. "Resistance" (21 × 37 mm) 45 40
1120. 6 d. Map of Eastern Mediterranean theatre .. 20 8

1969. Heroes of Macedonia's Fight for Freedom. Multicoloured.
1121. 1 d. 50 Type **204** 8 5
1122. 2 d. 50 Emmanuel Pappas (statue by N. Perantinos) 15 5
1123. 3 d. 50 Pavlos Melas (from painting by P. Mathiopoulos) .. 20 12
1124. 4 d. 50 Capetan Kotas .. 35 35

205. Dolphin Mosaic, Delos.

1970. Greek Mosaics. Multicoloured.
1125. 20 l. "Angel of the Annunciation", Daphne (11th-century) .. 8 5
1126. 1 d. Type **205** 10 5
1127. 1 d. 50 "The Holy Ghost", Hosios Loukas Monastery (11th-century) .. 12 8
1128. 2 d. "Hunter", Pella (4th-century B.C.) .. 20 5
1129. 5 d. "Bird", St. George's Church, Salonika (5th-century) 50 12
1130. 6 d. "Christ", Nea Moni Church, Khios (5th century) 55 55
SIZES—VERT. Nos. 1125, 1127/9, 23 × 34 mm. No. 1130 as Type **205**.

206. Overwhelming the Cretan Bull. **207.** "Flaming Sun".

1970. "The Labours of Hercules".
1131. 20 l. multicoloured .. 5 5
1132. 30 l. multicoloured .. 5 5
1133. 1 d. blk., blue & slate-bl. 5 5
1134. 1 d. 50 brn., green & ochre 5 5
1135. 2 d. multicoloured .. 8 5
1136. 2 d. 50 brn., red & buff 15 5
1137. 3 d. multicoloured .. 15 5
1138. 4 d. 50 multicoloured .. 25 12
1139. 5 d. multicoloured .. 30 5
1140. 6 d. multicoloured .. 35 5
1141. 20 d. multicoloured .. 90 50
DESIGNS—HORIZ. 30 l. Hercules and Cerberus (from decorated pitcher). 1 d. 50 The Lernean Hydra (from stamnos). 2 d. Hercules and Geryon (from amphora). 4 d. 50 Combat with the River-god Achelous (from pitcher). 5 d. Overwhelming the Nemean Lion (from amphora). 6 d. The Stymphalian Birds (from vase). 20 d. Wrestling with Antaeus (from bowl). VERT: 1 d. Golden Apples of the Hesperides (sculpture). 2 d. 50 The Erymanthine Boar (from amphora). 3 d. The Centaur Nessus (from vase).

1970. Europa.
1142. **207.** 2 d. 50 yellow & red 15 5
1143. – 3 d. blue & new blue 20 10
1144. **207.** 4 d. 50 yellow & blue 35 35
DESIGN—VERT. 3 d. "Owl" and CEPT emblem.

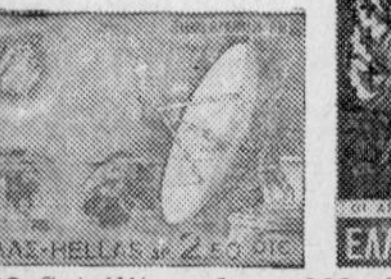

208. Satellite and Dish Aerial. **209.** Saints Cyril and Methodius with Emperor Michael III, (from 12th-cent. wall-painting).

1970. Satellite Earth Telecommunications Station, Thermopylae.
1145. **208.** 2 d. 50 multicoloured 15 8
1146. 4 d. 50 multicoloured 40 40

1970. Saints Cyril and Methodius Commemoration. Multicoloured.
1147. 50 l. Saints Demetrius, Cyril and Methodius (mosaic) 12 8
1148. 2 d. St. Cyril (Russian miniature) 35 30
1149. 5 d. Type **209** 30 15
1150. 10 d. St. Methodius (Russian miniature) .. 60 50
SIZES (all stamps are vert.): 50 l. 21 × 37 mm. 2 d. and 10 d. 26 × 37 mm. 5 d. $28\frac{1}{2}$ × 41 mm.
Nos. 1148 and 1150 were issued together se-tenant in the sheet forming a composite design.

210. Cephalonian Fir. **212.** New U.P.U. Headquarters Building, Berne (Opening).

211. "Cultural Links".

1970. Nature Conservation Year. Multicoloured.
1151. 80 l. Type **210** .. 8 8
1152. 2 d. 50 "Jankaea heldreichii" (plant) .. 8 5
1153. 6 d. Greek partridge (horiz.) 35 15
1154. 8 d. Cretan chamois .. 70 70
SIZES: 2 d. 50 is smaller, 23 × 34 mm.

1970. American-Hellenic Education Progressive Association Congress, Athens.
1155. **211.** 6 d. multicoloured .. 35 15

1970. Anniversaries. Multicoloured.
1156. 50 l. Type **212** 5 5
1157. 2 d. 50 Emblem (Int. Education Year) (vert.) .. 10 5
1158. 3 d. 50 Mahatma Gandhi (birth bicent.) (vert.) .. 15 5
1159. 4 d. "25" (25th Anniv. of United Nations) (vert.) 20 12
1160. 4 d. 50 Beethoven (birth bicent.) (vert.) .. 55 55
Nos. 1157 and 1160 are larger, $28\frac{1}{2}$ × 41 mm.

213. "The Nativity".

1970. Christmas. Scenes from "The Mosaic of the Nativity", Hosios Loukas Monastery. Multicoloured.
1161. 2 d. "The Shepherds" (vert.) 15 8
1162. 4 d. 50 "The Magi" (vert.) 40 35
1163. 6 d. Type **213** 70 55

214. "Death of Bishop of Salona in Battle, Alamana" (lithograph).

1971. War of Independence. 150th Anniv. (1st issue). The Church. Multicoloured.
1164. 50 l. Warriors taking the oath (medal) (vert.) .. 5 5
1165. 2 d. Patriarch Gregory V (statue by Phitalis) (vert.) 8 5
1166. 4 d. Type **214** 25 8
1167. 10 d. "Bishop Germanos blessing the Standard" (Vryzakis) 70 50
See also Nos. 1168/73, 1178/80, 1181/6 and 1187/89.

1971. War of Independence. 150th Anniv. (2nd issue). The War at Sea. Designs as T **214**. Multicoloured.
1168. 20 l. "Leonidas" .. 5 5
1169. 1 d. "Pericles" 5 5
1170. 1 d. 50 "Terpsichore" (from painting by Roux) 8 5
1171. 2 d. 50 "Karteria" (from painting by Hastings) 12 5
1172. 3 d. "Battle of Samos" (contemporary painting) 20 12
1173. 6 d. "Turkish Frigate ablaze, Battle of Yeronda" (Michalis) .. 55 40
SIZES: Nos. 1168/71, 37 × 24 mm. Nos. 1172/3, 40 × 28 mm.

215. Spyridon Louis winning 1896 Marathon, Athens Stadium.

1971. Olympic Games Revival. 75th Anniv. Multicoloured.
1174. 3 d. Type **215** 15 8
1175. 8 d. P. de Coubertin and Memorial, Olympia (vert.) 55 45

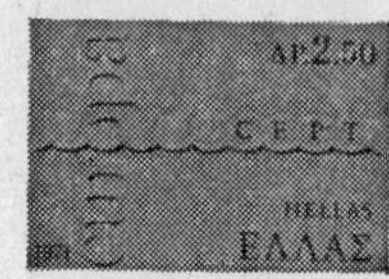

216. Europa Chain.

1971. Europa.
1176. **216.** 2 d. 50 yell., grn. & blk. 15 5
1177. 5 d. yell., orge. & blk. 40 40

1971. War of Independence. 150th Anniv. (3rd issue). "Teaching the People". Designs as T **214**. Multicoloured.
1178. 50 l. Eugenius Voulgaris (vert.) 5 5
1179. 2 d. 50 Adamantios Korais (vert.) 15 5
1180. 15 d. "The Secret School" (N. Ghyzis) (horiz.) .. 85 65
SIZES: 50 l., 2 d. 50 23 × 34 mm. 15 d. as T **214**.

1971. War of Independence. 150th Anniv. (4th issue). The War on Land. Designs as T **214**. Multicoloured.
1181. 50 l. "Battle of Corinth" (Krazeisen) (vert). .. 5 5
1182. 1 d. "Sacrifice of Kapsali" (Vryzakis) (vert.) .. 5 5
1183. 2 d. "Suliot Women in Battle" (Deneuville) (horiz.) 12 5
1184. 5 d. "Battle of Athens" (Zographos) (vert.) .. 25 15
1185. 6 d. 50 Battle of Maniaki" (lithograph) (horiz.) .. 35 12
1186. 9 d. "Death of Marcos Botsaris at Karpenisi" (Vryzakis) (horiz.) .. 50 50
SIZES: 50 l., 1 d., 5 d. 25 × 40 mm. 2 d. 40 × 25 mm. 6 d. 50, 9 d. as T **214**.

217. Kaltetsi Monastery and Sea of Peloponnesian Senate.

1971. War of Independence. 150th Anniv. (5th issue). Government.
1187. **217.** 2 d. blk., green & brn. 8 5
1188. – 2 d. 50 black, light bl. and blue .. 20 5
1189. – 20 d. blk., yell. & brn. 85 60
DESIGNS: 2 d. 50, National Assembly Memorial, Epidavros, and Seal of Provincial Administration. 20 d. Signature and seal of John Capodistria, first President of Greece.

218. Hosios Loukas Monastery, Boeotia.

1972. Greek Monasteries and Churches. Multicoloured.
1190. 50 l. Type **218** 5 5
1191. 1 d. Daphni Church, Attica 5 5
1192. 2 d. St. John the Divine Monastery, Patmos .. 5 5
1193. 2 d. 50 Panaghia Koumbelidiki Church, Castoria 12 5
1194. 4 d. 50 Panaghia ton Chalkeon, Thessaloniki 15 12
1195. 6 d. 50 Panaghia Paregoritissa Church, Arta 30 10
1196. 8 d. 50 St. Paul's Monastery, Mt. Athos 40 40

219. Cretan Costume. **220.** Flag and Map.

1972. Greek Costumes (1st series). Multicoloured.
1197. 50 l. Type **219** 5 5
1198. 1 d. Pindus bride .. 5 5
1199. 2 d. Warrior-chief Missolonghi 8 5
1200. 2 d. 50 Sarakatsana woman, Attica 5 5
1201. 3 d. Nisiros woman .. 15 5
1202. 4 d. 50 Megara woman .. 20 10
1203. 6 d. 50 Trikeri (rural) .. 25 8
1204. 10 d. Pylaia woman, Macedonia 40 40
See also Nos. 1233/48 and 1282/96.

1972. 1967 Revolution. 5th Anniv. Multicoloured.
1205. 2 d. 50 Commemorative medal (horiz.) 8 5
1206. 4 d. 50 Type **220** .. 20 20
1207. 5 d. Facets of modern development 20 15

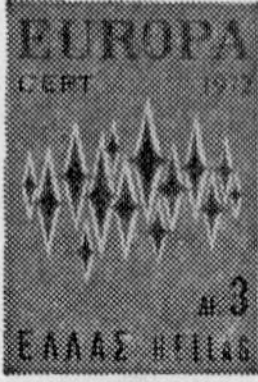

221. "Communications". **222.** Acropolis, Athens.

1972. Europa.
1208. **221.** 3 d. multicoloured .. 15 8
1209. 4 d. 50 multicoloured 25 25

1972. Acropolis Motor Rally. 20th Anniv. Multicoloured.
1210. 4 d. 50 Type **222** .. 25 25
1211. 5 d. Emblem and map .. 35 15

223. "Gaia delivering Erecthonius to Athene . . .".

1972. Greek Mythology. Museum Pieces (1st series).
1212. **223.** 1 d. 50 black and green 5 5
1213. – 2 d. black and blue .. 5 5
1214. – 2 d. 50 black & brn. 8 8
1215. – 5 d. black and brown 35 35
DESIGNS: 2 d. "Uranius" (altar-piece). 2 d. 50 "The Gods repulsing the Giants". 5 d. "Zeus".
See also Nos. 1252/5.

224. Runners (amphora).

1972. Olympic Games, Munich. Ancient Olympics. Multicoloured.
1216. – 50 l. grey, blk. & brn. 5 5
1217. – 1 d. 50 grey, blk. & brn. 5 5
1218. – 3 d. 50 grey, blk. & orge. 12 10
1219. – 4 d. 50 brn., grey & grn. 20 15
1220. **224.** 10 d. red, pink & brn. 40 40
DESIGNS—VERT. 50 l. "Young Athlete" (statue). 3 d. 50 "Female Athlete" (statuette). HORIZ. 1 d. 50 "Wrestlers" (bas-relief). 4 d. 50. "Ball game" (bas-relief).

225. "Young Stamp-collector". 226. "The Birth of Christ".

1972. Stamp Day.

1221. 225. 2 d. 50 multicoloured 15 12

1972. Christmas. Multicoloured.

1222. 2 d. 50 "Pilgrimage of the Magi" 15 5
1223. 4 d. 50 Type 226 .. 20 20

227. University Buildings.

1973. Nat. Polytechnic University, Athens. Cent.

1224. 227. 2 d. 50 multicoloured 20 12

228. "Spring" wall (fresco).

1973. Archaeological Discoveries, Island of Thera. Multicoloured.

1225. 10 l. Type 228 .. 5 5
1226. 20 l. "Barley" jug .. 5 5
1227. 30 l. "Blue Apes" fresco (horiz.) 5 5
1228. 1 d. 50 "Bird" (jug) .. 8 5
1229. 2 d. 50 "Swallows" (detail, "Spring" fresco) (horiz.) 12 5
1230. 5 d. "Wild Goats" fresco (horiz.) 20 15
1231. 6 d. 50 "Wrestlers" (detail, fresco) (horiz.) 45 45

1973. Greek Costumes (2nd series). As Type 219. Multicoloured.

1232. 10 l. Peloponneses .. 5 5
1233. 20 l. Central Greece .. 5 5
1234. 30 l. Skyros (Livantes) .. 5 5
1235. 50 l. Skyros (male) .. 5 5
1236. 1 d. Spetsai 5 5
1237. 1 d. 50 Almros 5 5
1238. 2 d. 50 Macedoni (Roumlouki) 8 5
1239. 3 d. 50 Salamis 10 8
1240. 4 d. 50 Epirus (Souli) .. 12 8
1241. 5 d. Lefkas (Santa Maura) 15 8
1242. 6 d. 50 Skyrus (female) .. 20 8
1243. 8 d. 50 Corinth 25 10
1244. 10 d. Corfu 30 10
1245. 15 d. Epirus 50 30
1246. 20 d. Thessaly (Karagouniko) 60 25
1247. 30 d. Macedonia (Episkopi) 90 30
1248. 50 d. Thrace (Makra Gefyra) .. .. 1·50 60

229. Europa "Posthorn".

1973. Europa.

1249. 229. 2 d. 50 blue & new blue 8 5
1250. 3 d. red, orge & lake 10 8
1251. 4 d. 50 brn., bronze-green and green .. 25 25

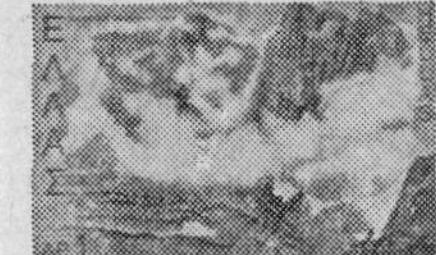

230. "Olympus" (from photograph by Boissonnas).

1973. Greek Mythology (2nd series).

1252. 230. 1 d. grey and black .. 5 5
1253. – 2 d. multicoloured .. 5 5
1254. – 2 d. 50 grey, yell. & blk. 10 5
1255. – 4 d. 50 multicoloured 20 20

DESIGNS: 2 d. "Zeus in combat with Typhoeus" (amphora). 2 d. 50 "Zeus at Battle of Giants" (alter relief). 4 d. 50 The "Punishment of Atlas and Prometheus" (vase).

231. Dr. G. Papanicolaou. 232. "Our Lady of the Annunciation".

1973. Honouring Dr. George Papanicolaou (cancer specialist).

1256. 231. 2 d. 50 multicoloured 12 5
1257. 6 d. 50 multicoloured 25 25

1973. Discovery of Miraculous Icon of Our Lady of the Annunciation, Tinos. 150th Anniv.

1258. 232. 2 d. 50 multicoloured 20 8

233. "Triptolemus in a Chariot" (vase). 235. G. Averof.

224. Child examining Stamp.

1973. European Transport Ministers Conf., Athens.

1259. 233. 4 d. 50 multicoloured 20 15

1973. Stamp Day.

1260. 234. 2 d. 50 multicoloured 15 10

1973. National Benefactors (1st series).

1261. 235. 1 d. 50 brown .. 5 5
1262. – 2 d. red .. 5 5
1263. – 2 d. 50 green .. 8 5
1264. – 4 d. lilac .. 12 5
1265. – 6 d. 50 black .. 20 20

DESIGNS: 2 d. A. Arsakis. 2 d. 50 C. Zappas. 4 d. A. Sygros. 6 d. 50 I. Varvakis.

See also Nos. 1315/18.

236. "Lord Byron taking the oath at Grave of Markos Botsaris" (lithograph). 237. "Harpist of Keros".

1974. Lord Byron. 150th Death Anniv. Multicoloured.

1266. 2 d. 50 "Lord Byron in Souliot costume" (anon.) 8 5
1267. 4 d. 50 Type 236 .. 25 25

1974. Europa. Ancient Greek Sculptures. Multicoloured.

1268. 3 d. Type 237 .. .. 8 5
1269. 4 d. 50 "Athenian Maiden" 15 8
1270. 6 d. 50 "Charioteer of Delphi" (bronze) .. 25 20

238. "Theocracy of Zeus" (vase). 239. U.P.U. Emblem within Mycenean motif.

1974. Greek Mythology (3rd series).

1271. 238. 1 d. 50 blk. & orange 5 5
1272. – 2 d. brn., red & orge. 5 5
1273. – 2 d. 50 blk., brn. & orge. 8 5
1274. – 10 d. brn., red & orge. 30 30

DESIGNS—HORIZ. 2 d. "Athena's Birth" (vase). 2 d. 50 "Artemis, Apollo and Lito" (vase). VERT. 10 d. "Hermes" (vase).

1974. Universal Postal Union. Cent. Each black, violet and blue.

1275. 2 d. Type 239 .. .. 5 5
1276. 4 d. 50 "Hermes" (horiz.) 12 8
1277. 6 d. 50 "Woman reading letter" 20 20

240. Crete 1 d. Stamp of 1905.

1974. Stamp Day.

1278. 240. 2 d. 50 blk. red & vio. 15 8

241. "Joseph". 242. Papaflessas.

1974. Christmas. "The Flight into Egypt" (from Codex No. 587, Dionysos Monastery, Mt. Athos). Multicoloured.

1279. 2 d. Type 241 .. .. 5 5
1280. 4 d. 50 "Virgin and Child on donkey" 15 15
1281. 8 d. 50 "Jacob leading donkey" 30 30

Nos. 1279/81 were issued together in the form of a triptych, making a composite design.

1974. Greek Costumes (3rd series). As T 219. Mult.

1282. 20 l. Megara 5 5
1283. 30 l. Salamis 5 5
1284. 50 l. Edipsos 5 5
1285. 1 d. Kymi 5 5
1286. 1 d. 50 Sterea Hellas .. 5 5
1287. 2 d. Desfina 8 5
1288. 3 d. Iaonnina (Epirus) .. 10 8
1289. 3 d. 50 Naousa 12 8
1290. 4 d. Hasia 15 10
1291. 4 d. 50 Thasos 15 12
1292. 5 d. Skopelos 20 15
1293. 6 d. 50 Grammenochoria (Epirus) 25 15
1294. 10 d. Pelion 35 25
1295. 25 d. Lefkimmi (Kerkyra) 85 60
1296. 30 d. Tanagra (Boeotia) 1·10 70

1975. Grigorios Dikeos Papaflessas (warrior). 150th Death Anniv. Multicoloured.

1297. 4 d. "Secret Assembly at Vostitsa" (horiz.) .. 12 10
1298. 7 d. Type 242 .. .. 25 20
1299. 11 d. Aghioi Apostoli (chapel), Kalamata (horiz.) 35 30

243. "Vase with Flowers". 245. Neolithic Goddess.

244. Papaterpou Mansion, Kastoria.

1975. Europa. Paintings by Theophilus Hatzimichael. Multicoloured.

1300. 4 d. Type 243 .. .. 12 10
1301. 7 d. "Erotokritos and Aretussa" .. 25 20
1302. 11 d. "Girl in Hat" .. 35 30

1975. Greek Folk Architecture.

1303. 244. 10 l. black and blue 5 5
1304. – 40 l. black and red .. 5 5
1305. – 4 d. black and brown 12 8
1306. – 6 d. black and blue .. 25 15
1307. – 11 d. black & orange 35 25

DESIGNS: 40 l. Mansion, Arnea, Halkidiki. 4 d. Sapountsoglou House, Veria. 6 d. Manousi Mansion, Siatista. 11 d. George Schwartz's House, Ampelakia, Thessaly.

1975. International Women's Year. Multicoloured.

1308. 1 d. 50 Type 245 .. 5 5
1309. 8 d. 50 Confrontation between Antigone and Creon 30 20
1310. 11 d. Modern women .. 35 25

246. Alex Papanastasiou (founder) and University Buildings.

1975. Thessaloniki University. 50th Anniv. Multicoloured.

1311. 1 d. 50 Type 246 .. 5 5
1312. 4 d. Original University Building 12 8
1313. 11 d. Plan of "University City" 35 25

247. Greek 100 d. Stamp of 1933.

1975. Stamp Day.

1314. 247. 11 d. green and brown 35 25

248. E. Zappas and Zappeion Building.

1975. National Benefactors (2nd series).

1315. 248. 1 d. blk., grey & grn. 5 5
1316. – 4 d. blk., grey & brn. 12 8
1317. – 6 d. blk., brn. & orge. 25 15
1318. – 11 d. blk., lilac & red 35 25

DESIGNS: 4 d. Georgios Rizaris and Rizarios Ecclesiastical School. 6 d. Michael Tositsas and Metsovion Technical University. 11 d. Nicolaos Zosimas and Zosimea Academy.

249. Pontos Lyre.

1975. Musical Instruments. Mult.
1319. 10 l. Type **249** 5 5
1320. 20 l. " Musicians " (Byzantine mural) 5 5
1321. 1 d. Cretan Lyre 5 5
1322. 1 d. 50 " Tambourine " .. 5 5
1323. 4 d. " Guitarist " (from amphora) (horiz.) .. 12 8
1324. 6 d. Bagpipes 20 15
1325. 7 d. Lute 25 20
1326. 10 d. Barrel-organ .. 35 25
1327. 11 d. Pipes and zournades 35 25
1328. 20 d. " Praise God " (Byzantine mural) (horiz) 70 50
1329. 25 d. Drums 90 60
1330. 30 d. Kanonaki (horiz.) .. 1·10 70

250. Early telephone.

1976. First Telephone Transmission. Cent. Multicoloured.
1331. 7 d. Type **250** 25 20
1332. 11 d. Modern Telephone .. 35 25

251. Battle of Missolonghi.

1976. Fall of Missolonghi. 150th Anniv.
1333. **251.** 4 d. multicoloured .. 12 8

252. Florina Jug. **253.** " Lion attacking Bull ".

1976. Europa. Multicoloured.
1334. 7 d. Type **252** .. 20 12
1335. 8 d. 50 Plate with birds .. 25 15
1336. 11 d. Egina pitcher .. 45 35
No. 1335 is larger, 24 × 28 mm.

1975. Ancient Sealing Stones. Multicoloured.
1337. 2 d. Type **253** 8 5
1338. 4 d. 50 " Water Birds " 15 10
1339. 7 d. " Wounded Bull " .. 20 12
1340. 8 d. 50 " Head of Silenus " 25 15
1341. 11 d. " Cow feeding Calf " 45 35
SIZES: 8 d. 50, 24 × 37 mm. 11 d. 37 × 24 mm. (horiz.).

254. Long-jumping.

1976. Olympic Games, Montreal. Multicoloured.
1342. 50 e. Type **254** 5 5
1343. 2 d. Handball 8 5
1344. 3 d. 50 Wrestling .. 12 8
1345. 4 d. Swimming 15 10
1346. 11 d. Athens and Montreal stadiums 45 35
1347. 25 d. " Lighting of Olympic Flame " and Olympic Torch, Montreal .. 85 75
No. 1346 is larger, 49 × 34 mm.

255. Lemnos.

1976. Tourism. Aegean Landscapes. Multicoloured.
1348. 30 d. Type **255** .. .. 1·00 90
1349. 50 d. Lesbos (horiz) .. 1·75 1·50
1350. 75 d. Chios (horiz.) .. 2·50 2·25
1351. 100 d. Samos (horiz.) .. 3·50 3·00

CHARITY TAX STAMPS

C **1.** Dying Soldier, Widow and Child. C **2.** Red Cross, Nurses, Wounded and Bearers.

1914. Roul.
C 269. C **1.** 2 l. rose 20 12
C 270. 5 l. blue 35 25

1915. Red Cross. Roul.
C 271. C **2.** (5 l.) red and blue 3·50 70

C **3.** Greek Women's Patriotic League.

1915. Greek Women's Patriotic League.
C 272. C **3.** (5 l.) red and blue 85 85

Κ. Π.
λεπτοῦ
1
(C **4.**)

C **5.**

Κ. Π.
λεπτοῦ
1
(C **6.**)

Κ.Π.
10 ΛΕΠΤΑ 10
(C **7.**)

1917. Surch. as Type C **4.**
C 297. **11.** 1 on 1 l. brown .. 70 70
C 303. 1 on 3 l. orange .. 15 15
C 299. 5 on 1 l. brown .. 80 80
C 300. 5 on 20 l. mauve .. 20 20
C 307. **30.** 5 on 25 l. blue .. 30 30
C 304. **11.** 5 on 40 l. brown .. 20 20
C 308. **30.** 5 on 40 l. blue .. 25 25
C 305. **11.** 5 on 50 l. lake .. 20 20
C 309. **29.** 5 on 50 l. blue .. 25 25
C 306. **13.** 5 on 1 d. black .. 55 50
C 301. **11.** 10 on 30 l. purple .. 50 50
C 302. 30 on 30 l. purple .. 85 85

1917. Fiscal stamps surch. as Type C **6.** Roul.
C 310. C **5.** 1 l. on 10 l. blue .. 1·00 70
C 328. 1 l on 50 l. purple .. 55 25
C 311. 1 l. on 80 l. blue .. 45 50
C 330. 5 l. on 10 l. purple .. 55 25
C 329. 5 l. on 10 l. blue .. 55 25
C 312. 5 l. on 60 l. blue .. 2·10 2·10
C 313. 5 l. on 80 l. blue .. 1·40 1·10
C 331. 10 l. on 50 l. purple 1·10 60
C 326. 10 l. on 70 l. blue .. 3·00 1·50
C 327. 10 l. on 90 l. blue .. 3·50 2·10
C 316. 20 l. on 20 l. blue .. £150 85·00
C 317. 20 l. on 30 l. blue .. 1·75 1·40
C 318. 20 l. on 40 l. blue .. 5·50 3·50
C 319. 20 l. on 50 l. blue .. 2·50 1·40
C 320. 20 l. on 60 l. blue .. 55·00 28·00
C 321. 20 l. on 80 l. blue .. 19·00 11·00
C 322. 20 l. on 90 l. blue .. 3·50 1·75
C 333. 20 l. on 2 d. blue .. 3·00 2·10

1917. Fiscal stamps surch. as Type C **7.** Roul.
C 334. C **5.** 1 l. on 10 l. blue .. 1·00 55
C 341. 5 l. on 10 l. pur. & red 1·40 1·00
C 335. 5 l. on 50 l blue .. 17·00 8·00
C 338. 10 l. on 50 l. blue .. 3·50 1·75
C 339. 20 l. on 50 l. blue .. 4·25 2·50
C 340. 30 l. on 50 l. blue .. 4·25 2·75

C **8.** Wounded Soldier. C **10.** St. Demetrius.

INDEX

Countries can be quickly located by referring to the index at the end of this volume.

C **9.**

1918. Red Cross. Roul.
C 342. C **8.** 5 l. red, blue & yellow 3·00 1·40

1918. Optd. Π. Ι. Π.
C 343. C **8.** 5 l. red, blue & yellow 3·00 1·40

1922. Greek Women's Patriotic League. Surch. as in Type C **9.**
C 344. C **9.** 5 l. on 10 l. red & blue — 1·40
C 345. 5 l. on 20 l. red & blue 8·50 7·00
C 346. 5 l. on 50 l. red & blue 32·00 17·00
C 347. 5 l. on 1 d. red & blue 2·10 2·10
Nos. C 344/7 were not issued without surcharge.

1924. Red Cross. As Type C **8** but wounded soldier and family.
C 405. 10 l. red, blue and yellow 25 12

1934. Salonika Int. Exn. Fund.
C 478. C **10.** 20 l. brown 8 8

C **11.** Allegory of Health.

ΠΡΟΝΟΙΑ
(C **12.**)

1934. Postal Staff. Anti-Tuberculosis Fund.
C 480. C **11.** 10 l. orange & green 12 8
C 481. 20 l. orange & blue 35 12
C 482. 50 l. orange & green 70 30

1935. As Type C **11** but inscr. "ΕΛΛΑΣ" at top.
C 494. 10 l. orange & green 8 5
C 495. 20 l. orange & blue 10 5
C 496. 50 l. orange & green 25 8
C 497. 50 l. orange & brown 20 10

1937. Nos. D 273 and 415 optd. with Type C **12.**
C 498. D **2.** 10 l. red 8 5
C 500. **43.** 50 l. violet 30 12

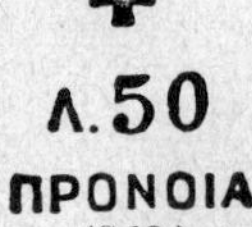
Λ.50
ΠΡΟΝΟΙΑ
(C **13.**)

C **14.** Queens Olga and Sophia.

1938. Surch. with Type C **13.**
C 521. D **2.** 50 l. on 5 l. green .. 20 8
C 522. 50 l. on 20 l. slate .. 40 12
C 523. **44.** 50 l. on 20 l. violet 20 8

1939.
C 524. C **14.** 10 l. red 5 5
C 525. 50 l. green 8 5
C 526. 1 d. blue 12 12

ΠΡΟΣΤΑΣΙΑ ΦΥΜΑΤΙΚΩΝ ΤΤΤ
(C **14a.**)

1940. Postal staff Anti-Tuberculosis Fund. Optd. with Type C **14a.**
C 554. C **14.** 50 l. green 8 8

Κ.Π.
λεπτῶν
50
(C **15.**)

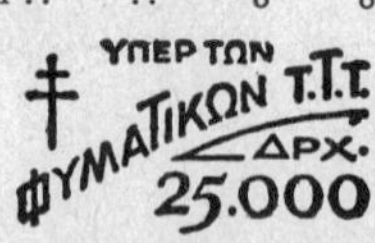

(C **16.**)

1941. Surch. with Type C **15.**
C 561. **43.** 50 l. on 5 l. green .. 12 5

1941. Postal Staff Anti-Tuberculosis Fund. Surch. **50** and bars.
C 562. C **11.** 50 l. on 10 l. .. 1·25 1·25
C 563. – 50 l. on 10 l. (No. C 494) 15 15

1942. Sample Fair, Salonika. Surch. △ **P. 1.**
C 565. C **10.** 1 d. on 20 l. brown .. 5 5

1942. Postal Staff Anti-Tuberculosis Fund. Surch. **ΦΥΜ. T.T.T. 10** △**P** and Cross of Lorraine.
C 591. **13.** 10 d. on 5 l. green .. 10 5
C 592. 10 l. on 25 l. green .. 10 5

1944. Postal Staff Anti-Tuberculosis Fund. Optd. **ΦΥΜ. T.T.T.** and Cross of Lorraine.
C 599. 100 d. black (No. 580) 5 5

1944. Postal Staff Anti-Tuberculosis Fund. Surch. **ΦΥΜ. T.T.T.** △**P.5000.**
C 600. 5000 d. on 75 d. (No. 579) 5 5

1944. Postal Staff Anti-Tuberculosis Fund. Surch. as Type C **16.**
C 619. – 1 d. on 40 l. (No. 500) 8 8
C 620. – 2 d. on 40 l. (No. 500) 5 5
C 605. **85.** 25,000 d. on 2 d. .. 8 8

ΠΡΟΝΟΙΑ
ΠΡΟΣΩΠΙΚΟΥ Τ.Τ.Τ.
ΔΡΑΧΜΑΙ 50
(C **17.**)

ΠΡΟΝΟΙΑ
ΤΑΧ. ΥΠΑΛΛΗΛΩΝ
ΔΡΑΧΜΑΙ 50
(C **18.**)

1946. Postal Staff Anti-Tuberculosis Fund. Surch. as Type C **17.**
C 640. **69.** 20 d. on 5 l. 20 12
C 641. 20 d. on 40 l. (No. 500) 15 5

1946. Red Cross. Surch as Type C **17.**
C 642. C **14.** 50 d. on 50 l. (No. C 525) 8 8

1946. Social Funds. Surch. as Type C **17.**
C 643. C **14.** 50 d. on 1 d. (No. C 526) 8 8

1947. Postal Staff Anti-Tuberculosis Fund. Surch.
C 659. C **14.** 50 d. on 50 l. (C 525) 10·00 11·00
C 660. 50 l. on 50 d. (C 554) 20 8

C **19.** St. Demetrius. C **20.** Argoston, Cephalonia.

1948. Church Restoration Fund.
C 682. C **19.** 50 d. brown .. 20 8

1950. Postal Staff Anti-Tuberculosis Fund. Surch. with Type C **17.**
C 686. 50 d. on 10 l. (No. 498) 12 8

1951. Postal Staff Welfare Fund. Surch. with Type C **18.**
C 698. **69.** 50 d. on 5 l. blue & brn. 20 8

1951. Postal Staff Anti-Tuberculosis Fund. Surch. with Cross of Lorraine and **50.**
C 699. **72.** 50 d. on 3 d. brown .. 10 10

1952. State Welfare Fund. Surch. *ΠΡΟΣΘΕΤΟΝ* and value.
C 706. **72.** 100 d. on 8 d. blue .. 10 10

1953. Ionian Is. Earthquake Fund.
C 713. – 300 d. slate 20 8
C 714. C **20.** 500 d. brown & yell. 60 12
DESIGN: 300 d. Church of Faneromeni, Zante.

C **21.** Zeus (Macedonian Coin of Philip II).

1956. Macedonian Cultural Fund.
C 761. C **21.** 50 l. red 35 10
C 762. – 1 d. blue (Aristotle) 1·00 55

POSTAGE DUE STAMPS

D **1.** D **2.**

1875.
D 73. D **1.** 1 l. green and black 35 20
D 74. 2 l. green and black 35 20
D 75. 5 l. green and black 35 20
D 88. 10 l. green and black 35 20
D 89. 20 l. green and black 35 20
D 78. 40 l. green and black 1·40 70
D 91a. 60 l. green and black 2·10 1·40
D 80. 70 l. green and black 2·10 1·40
D 81. 80 l. green and black 2·75 1·40
D 82. 90 l. green and black 2·75 1·40
D 95. 100 l. green and black 2·75 2·40
D 96. 200 l. green and black 4·25 2·75
D 83. 1 d. green and black 2·75 1·40
D 84. 2 d. green and black 3·50 1·40

1902.
D 183. D **2.** 1 l. brown 15 12
D 184. 2 l. grey 15 12
D 185. 3 l. orange .. 15 12
D 186. 5 l. green 8 8
D 273. 10 l. red 8 8
D 188. 20 l. mauve .. 25 15

D 275.		25 l. blue	8	8
D 190.		30 l. purple	20	12
D 191.		40 l. brown	25	15
D 451.		50 l. brown	8	8
D 193.		1 d. black	70	55
D 194.		2 d. bronze	1·00	70
D 195.		3 d. silver	2·00	1·75
D 196.		5 d. gold	4·25	3·25

1912. Optd. with T **28**.

D 252.	D 2.	1 l. brown	12	12
D 253.		2 l. grey	12	12
D 254.		3 l. orange	12	12
D 255.		5 l. green	20	20
D 256.		10 l. red	20	20
D 257.		20 l. mauve	35	35
D 258.		30 l. purple	85	85
D 259.		40 l. brown	90	90
D 260.		50 l. brown	35	35
D 261.		1 d. black	2·10	2·10
D 262.		2 d. bronze	3·50	3·50
D 263.		3 d. silver	11·00	11·00
D 264.		5 d. gold	20·00	20·00

1913. Perf. or roul.

D 269.	D 2.	1 l. green	8	8
D 270.		2 l. red	8	8
D 271.		3 l. red	8	8
D 274.		20 l. slate	8	8
D 276.		30 l. red	8	8
D 277.		40 l. blue	10	8
D 279.		80 l. purple	15	8
D 452.		1 d. blue	12	8
D 453.		2 d. red	8	8
D 282.		3 d. red	2·75	2·25
D 455.		5 d. blue	8	8
D 456.		10 d. green	8	8
D 595.		10 d. orange	8	8
D 457.		15 d. brown	8	8
D 458.		25 d. rose	20	20
D 596.		25 d. blue	5	5
D 480.		50 d. orange	20	20
D 481.		100 d. green	20	20
D 597.		100 d. brown	5	5
D 598.		200 d. violet	5	5

1942. Surch. **50.**

D 564.	D 2.	50 l. on 30 l. red	55	55

GREEK WAR ISSUES, 1912-1913

For provisional issues used in territories occupied by Greece during the Balkan War, 1911-13, see Stanley Gibbons' Europe Stamp Catalogue.

GREEK OCCUPATION OF ALBANIA E1

Stamps of Greece optd. with T **1.**

ΕΛΛΗΝΙΚΗ
ΔΙΟΙΚΗΣΙΣ
(1.)

1940. Stamps of 1927.

1.	69.	5 l. blue and brown	5	5
2.	–	10 l. brn. & blue (No. 498)	5	5
3.	–	20 l. grn. & blk. (No. 499)	5	5
4.	–	40 l. blk. & grn. (No. 500)	8	8
5.	–	50 l. blk. & brn. (No. 501)	10	10
6.	–	80 l. brn. & vio. (No. 502)	8	8
7.	72.	1 d. green	10	10
8.	–	2 d. blue (No. 504)	12	12
9.	72.	3 d. brown	10	12
10.	–	5 d. red (No. 506)	20	20
11.	–	6 d. olive (No. 507)	20	20
12.	–	7 d. brown (No. 508)	20	20
13.	72.	8 d. blue	20	20
14.	–	10 d. brown (No. 510)	25	25
15.	–	15 d. green (No. 511)	30	30
16.	–	25 d. blue (No. 512)	55	55
17.	72a.	30 d. red	1·00	1·00

1940. Charity Tax stamps of 1939.

18.	C 14.	10 l. red	8	8
19.		50 l. green	8	8
20.		1 d. blue	15	15

1940. Nos. 534/53 (Youth Organization).

26.	83.	3 d. bl., red & sil. (post.)	40	40
27.	–	5 d. black and blue	1·60	1·60
28.	–	10 d. black and orange	2·10	1·60
29.	–	15 d. black and green	10·00	9·00
30.	–	20 d. black and red	2·75	2·50
31.	–	25 d. black and blue	2·75	2·50
32.	–	30 d. black and violet	2·75	2·50
33.	–	50 d. black and red	3·50	2·75
34.	–	75 d. gold, blue & brown	4·25	3·50
35.	83.	100 d. blue, red and silver	5·00	4·25
36.	84.	2 d. black & orange (air)	30	30
37.	–	4 d. black and green	1·00	1·00
38.	–	6 d. black and red	1·40	1·40
39.	–	8d. black and blue	2·00	2·00
40.	–	16 d. black and violet	2·25	2·25
41.	–	32 d. black and orange	3·50	3·50
42.	–	45 d. black and green	4·25	3·50
43.	–	55 d. black and red	4·25	3·50
44.	–	65 d. black and blue	4·25	3·50
45.	–	100 d. black and violet	5·00	4·25

POSTAGE DUE STAMPS

1940. Postage Due stamps of 1913.

D 21.	D 2.	2 d. red	20	20
D 22.		5 d. blue	30	30
D 23.		10 d. green	35	35
D 24.		15 d. brown	50	50

1940. Postage Due stamp surch. also.

D 25.	D 2.	50 l. on 25 d. rose	10	10

GREEK OCCUPATION OF THE DODECANESE ISLANDS E1

The Dodecanese Islands, formerly Italian, were transferred to Greece in 1947. Now use Greek stamps.

1947. Stamps of Greece optd. Σ Δ Δ.

1.	–	10 d. on 2000 d. blue (No. 623)	10	10
3.	72.	50 d. on 1 d. grn. (No. 642)	20	20
4.		250 d. on 3 d. brn (No. 643)	20	20

Σ. Δ. Δ.
ΔΡΧ.
50
(1.)

1947. Stamps of Greece surch. as T **1.**

5.	–	20 d. on 500 d. brn. (No. 582)	10	10
6.	–	30 d. on 5 d. grn. (No. 574)	10	10
7.	85.	50 d. on 2 d. brown	20	20
8.	–	250 d. on 10 d. brown (No. 510)	60	60
9.	–	400 d. on 15 d. green (No. 511)	90	90
10.		1000 d. on 200 d. blue (No. 581)	90	90

GREENLAND E2

A Danish possession N.E. of Canada. On 5 June, 1963, Greenland became an integral part of the Danish Kingdom.

100 ore = 1 krone

1. Christian X.  **2.** Polar Bear.

1938.

1.	1.	1 ore green	8	8
2.		5 ore claret	45	20
3.		7 ore green	60	60
4.		10 ore violet	30	15
5.		15 ore red	30	15
5a.		20 ore red	40	15
6.	2.	30 ore blue	1·50	1·40
6a.		40 ore blue	4·75	1·75
7.		1 k. brown	2·00	2·00

3. Seal.  **4.** Christian X.

5. Eskimo Canoe.

DESIGNS—HORIZ. as T **5**: 30 ore Dog team. 1 k. Polar bear. 5 k. Eider duck.

1945.

8.	3.	1 ore violet and black	6·50	6·50
9.		5 ore buff and violet	6·50	6·50
10.		7 ore black and green	6·50	6·50
11.	4.	10 ore olive and purple	6·50	6·50
12.		15 ore blue and red	6·50	6·50
13.	–	30 ore brown and blue	6·50	6·50
14.	–	1 k. grey and brown	6·50	6·50
15.	5.	2 k. green and brown	6·50	6·50
16.	–	5 k. brown and purple	6·50	6·50

1945. Liberation of Denmark. Nos. 8/16 optd **DANMARK BEFRIET 5 MAJ 1945.**

17.	3.	1 ore violet and black	7·00	8·00
18.		5 ore buff and violet	7·00	8·00
19.		7 ore black and green	7·00	8·00
20.	4.	10 ore olive and purple	10·00	10·00
21.		15 ore blue and red	10·00	10·00
22.	–	30 ore brown and blue	10·00	10·00
23.	–	1 k. grey and brown	10·00	10·00
24.	5.	2 k. green and brown	10·00	10·00
25.	–	5 k. brown and purple	10·00	10·00

6. Frederick IX.  **7.** The "Gustav Holm".

1950.

26.	6.	1 ore green	5	5
27.		5 ore claret	8	8
28.		10 ore emerald	10	8
29a.		15 ore violet	15	15
30.		25 ore red	35	30
31.		30 ore blue	1·75	90
32.		30 ore red	15	10
33.	7.	50 ore blue	2·40	2·40
34.		1 k. brown	1·50	50
35.		2 k. red	1·00	60
36.		5 k. drab	60	50

1956. Surch.

37.	2.	60 ore on 40 ore blue	1·50	1·00
38.		60 ore on 1 k. brown	9·00	4·00

8. "Mother of the Sea".  **9.** Hans Egede.  **10.** Knud Rasmussen (founder of Thule).

1957. Greenland Legends.

39.	8.	60 ore blue	1·10	40

1958. Royal T.B. Relief Fund. Surch. with Cross of Lorraine and new value.

40.	7.	30+10 ore on 50 ore blue	60	60

1958. Hans Egede (missionary). Death Bicent.

41.	9.	30 ore red	1·75	60

1959. Greenland Fund. Surch. **Gronlands-fonden 30 + 10** and bars.

42.	6.	30 ore + 10 ore on 25 ore red	1·10	1·10

The note below No. 413 of Denmark also applies here.

1960. Thule Settlement. 50th Anniv.

43.	10.	30 ore red	40	25

11. Drum Dance.  **12.** Northern Lights.

13. Frederick IX.  **14.** Polar Bear.  **15.** S. Kleinschmidt.

1961. Greenland Legends.

44.	11.	35 ore bronze-green	35	10

1963.

45.	12.	1 ore bronze-green	5	5
46.		5 ore claret	5	5
47.		10 ore green	20	8
48.		12 ore yellow-green	12	12
49.		15 ore purple	20	20
50.	13.	20 ore blue	50	50
51.		25 ore brown	15	15
51a.		30 ore green	8	8
52.		35 ore red	5	5
53.		40 ore grey	20	20
54.		50 ore turquoise	70	70
54a.		50 ore red	8	8
54b.		60 ore claret	20	10
55.		80 ore orange	20	8
56.	14.	1 k. bistre	12	5
57.		2 k. red	40	10
58.		5 k. blue	60	25
59.		10 k. myrtle	1·40	25

1963. Bohr's Atomic Theory. 50th Anniv. As Nos. 455/6 of Denmark but inscr. "GRONLAND".

60.	93.	35 ore red	12	8
61.		60 ore blue	50	50

1964. S. Kleinschmidt. 150th Birth Anniv.

62.	15.	35 ore brown	15	10

16. "The Boy and the Fox".  **17.** "Great Northern Diver and Raven".

1966. Greenland Legends.

63.	16.	50 ore lake	25	25

1967. Royal Wedding. As No. 487 of Denmark, but inscr. "GRONLAND".

64.		50 ore red	75	75

1967. Greenland Legends.

65.	17.	90 ore blue	35	35

1968. Child Welfare. As No. 493 of Denmark, but inscr. "GRONLAND".

66.		60 ore + 10 ore red	35	35

18. King Frederick IX and Map of Greenland.  **19.** "The Girl and the Eagle".

1969. King Frederick's 70th Birthday.

67.	18.	60 ore red	40	40

1969. Greenland Legends.

68.	19.	80 ore brown	35	35

20. Musk Ox.  **21.** Celebrations at Jakobshavn.

1969.

69.	–	1 k. blue	12	12
69a.	–	2 k. green	25	25
69b.	–	5 k. blue	65	45
70.	–	10 k. brown	1·25	90
71.	20.	25 k. olive	3·00	1·25

DESIGN—HORIZ. 1 k. Whale and coastline. 2 k. Narwhal. 5 k. Polar bear. 10 k. Walruses.

1970. Denmark's Liberation. 25th Anniv.

72.	21.	60 ore red	35	35

22. Hans Egede and Gertrud Rask aboard the "Haabet".  **23.** Kayak Mail-Carriers.

1971. Hans Egede's Arrival in Greenland. 250th Anniv.

73.	22.	60 ore red	35	35
74.	–	60 ore + 10 ore red	35	35

DESIGN: No. 74, Hans Egede and Gertrud Rask meeting Greenlanders.

The premium on No. 74 was for the Greenland Church Building Fund.

1971. Greenland Mail Transport.

75.	2 .	50 ore green	8	8
76.	–	70 ore red	10	10
76a.	–	80 ore black	20	20
77.	–	90 ore blue	12	12
77a.	–	1 k. red	25	25
77b.	–	1 k. 30 blue	15	15
78.	–	1 k. 50 green	20	20

DESIGNS: 70 ore Umiak (women's boat). 80 ore Catalina aircraft. 90 ore Mail dog-sledge. 1 k. Coaster "Kununguak". 1 k. 30 Schooner "Sokongen". 1 k. 50 "Karen" Sailing long-boat.

24. King Frederick IX and Royal Yacht "Dannebrog".  **25.** Queen Margrethe of Denmark.

1972. King Frederick IX—In Memorial.

79.	24.	60+10 ore red	35	35

1973.

80.	25.	10 ore green	5	5
81.		60 ore brown	8	8
81a.		90 ore brown	12	12
81b.		1 k. 20 blue	15	15

1973. Aid for Victims of Heimaey (Iceland) Eruption. As T **169** of Denmark.

82.		70 ore + 20 ore blue and red	60	60

26. Trawler and Kayaks.  **27.** Falcon and Dish Aerial.

1974. Royal Greenland Trade Department. Bicent.

83.	26.	1 k. brown	12	12
84.	–	2 k. brown	25	25

DESIGN: 2 k. Trade Department Headquarters, Trangraven, Copenhagen.

1975. Greenlandic Telecommunications. 50th Anniv.

85.	27.	90 ore red	12	12

28. Sledge Patrol.

1975. Sirius Sledge Patrol. 25th Anniv.
86. **28.** 1 k. 20 brown 15 15

29. "Pull-arms" Contest.

1976. Greenland Sports.
87. **29.** 1 k.+20 ore brown and green on cream .. 30 30

PARCEL POST

P 1. Arms of Greenland.

1905.
P 4. **P 1.** 1 ore green .. .. 7·00 7·00
P 5. 2 ore yellow .. 20·00 15·00
P 6. 5 ore brown .. .. 18·00 18·00
P 7. 10 ore blue .. 7·00 7·00
P 8. 15 ore violet .. 35·00 25·00
P 9. 20 ore red .. .. 4·00 4·00
P 13. 70 ore violet .. 5·00 7·00
P 11. 1 k. yellow .. 4·00 6·00
P 12. 3 k. brown .. .. 15·00 15·00

Prices for used stamps are for rubber stamp cancellations applied in Copenhagen, the various Greenland cancellations being worth much more. Stamps with numeral cancellations have been used as saving stamps.

GRENADA BC

One of the Windward Is., Br. W. Indies. Ministerial Government was introduced on 1st January 1960. Achieved Associated Statehood on 3rd March 1967 and Independence during 1974.

1949. 100 cents = 1 West Indian dollar.

1. **2.**

1861.
4. **1.** 1d. green .. .. .. 25·00 13·00
6. 6d. rose .. .. £225 16·00
9. 6d. vermilion .. .. £225 16·00

1875. Surch. **POSTAGE** and value in words.
21. **2.** ½d. mauve.. .. .. 6·00 7·00
22. 2½d. lake .. .. 15·00 8·00
23. 4d. blue .. .. 40·00 11·00
13. 1s. mauve .. .. .. £200 12·00

1883. Revenue stamp surch. crown and value (in green) optd. **POSTAGE.**
27. **2.** 1d. orange.. .. .. 65·00 18·00

1883. Revenue stamp as last but optd. **POSTAGE** twice diagonally.
29. **2.** Half of 1d. orange .. 60·00 45·00

3. **4.**

1883.
30. **3.** ½d. green .. .. .. 1·00 1·00
31. 1d. red .. .. .. 10·00 3·00
32. 2½d. blue .. .. 4·80 1·20
33. 4d. grey .. .. 1·50 4·00
34. 6d. mauve .. .. 5·00 5·00
35. 8d. brown .. .. 10·00 10·00
36. 1s. violet .. .. 35·00 40·00

1886. Revenue stamps as No. 27 but surch **POSTAGE** and value in words or figures.
43. **2.** 1d. on 2s. orange .. .. 11·00 12·00
37. 1d. on 1½d. orange .. 13·00 13·00
39. 1d. on 4d. orange.. .. 45·00 32·00
38. 1d. on 1s. orange.. .. 13·00 13·00
41. 4d. on 2s. orange.. .. 11·00 11·00

1887. As Type **3**, but inscr. "GRENADA POSTAGE & REVENUE" at top.
40. **3.** 1d. red 25 25

1890. Revenue stamp as No. 27 but surch. **POSTAGE AND REVENUE 1d.**
44. **2.** 1d. on 2s. orange.. .. 18·00 18·00

1891. Surch **POSTAGE AND REVENUE 1d.**
46. **3.** 1d. on 8d. brown.. .. 11·00 11·00

1891. Surch. **2½d.**
47. **3.** 2½d. on 8d. brown .. 13·00 11·00

1895.
48. **4.** ½d. mauve and green .. 40 55
49. 1d. mauve and red .. 65 25
50. 2d. mauve and brown .. 9·50 12·00
51. 2½d. mauve and blue .. 2·75 95
52. 3d. mauve and orange .. 5·00 5·00
53. 6d. mauve and green .. 3·25 4·50
54. 8d. mauve and black .. 8·00 9·50
55. 1s. green and orange .. 9·50 11·00

5. Flagship of Columbus.

1898. Discovery of Grenada by Columbus.
56. **5.** 2½d. blue .. .. .. 6·00 6·00

1902. As T **4**, but portrait of King Edward VII.
57. ½d. purple and green .. 40 55
58. 1d. purple and red .. 45 30
59. 2d. purple and brown .. 2·00 2·75
60. 2½d. purple and blue .. 2·50 3·25
61. 3d. purple and orange .. 2·00 2·00
62. 6d. purple and green .. 3·75 5·00
63. 1s. green and orange .. 6·00 7·50
64. 2s. green and blue .. 12·00 17·00
65. 5s. green and red.. .. 20·00 25·00
66. 10s. green and purple .. 70·00 85·00

7. Badge of the Colony. **8.**

1906.
77. **7.** ½d. green 40 35
78. 1d. red 25 20
79. 2d. orange.. .. .. 1·75 2·25
80. 2½d. blue .. .. .. 3·00 2·75
84. 3d. purple on yellow .. 1·00 2·00
85. 6d. purple.. .. .. 5·00 6·00
86. 1s. black on green .. 2·50 4·00
87. 2s. blue & purple on blue 8·00 11·00
88. 5s. green & red on yellow 24·00 30·00
83. 10s. green & red on green 75·00 90·00

1913.
112. **8.** ½d. green.. .. .. 15 25
113. 1d. red 15 25
114. 1d. brown 20 20
115. 1½d. red 25 30
116. 2d. orange 30 45
117. 2d. grey 45 75
118. 2½d. blue.. .. .. 45 90
119. 2½d. grey.. .. .. 50 2·00
96. 2d. purple on yellow .. 45 95
121. 3d. blue .. .. .. 1·00 2·00
123. 4d. black & red on yellow 45 2·25
124. 5d. purple and olive .. 80 2·50
97. 6d. purple .. .. 1·10 1·75
126. 6d. black and red .. 1·10 2·50
127. 9d. purple and black .. 1·10 2·50
98. 1s. black on green .. 1·75 2·50
129. 1s. brown .. .. 5·00 6·50
99. 2s. purple & blue on blue 2·50 3·25
131. 2s. 6d. black & red on blue 7·00 10·00
132. 3s. green and violet .. 7·00 10·00
100. 5s. green & red on yellow 7·50 11·00
134. 10s. green & red on green 24·00 30·00

1916. Optd. **WAR TAX.**
111. **8.** 1d. red 20 25

9. Grand Anse Beach.

DESIGNS—VERT. 1½d. Grand Etang. 2½d. St. George's.

10. Badge of the Colony.

1934.
135. **9.** ½d. green 20 25
136. **10.** 1d. black and brown .. 20 20
137. – 1½d. black and red .. 45 45
138. **10.** 2d. black and orange .. 45 55
139. – 2½d. blue 25 50
140. **10.** 3d. black and olive-green 55 80
141. 6d. black and purple .. 90 1·25
142. 1s. black and brown .. 2·00 2·50
143. 2s. 6d. black and blue 7·00 10·00
144. 5s. black and violet .. 11·00 12·00

1935. Silver Jubilee. As T **11** of Antigua.
145. ½d. black and green .. 15 15
146. 1d. blue and grey .. 20 15
147. 1½d. blue and red .. 45 45
148. 1s. grey and purple .. 3·00 3·25

1937. Coronation. As T **2** of Aden.
149. 1d. violet 10 15
150. 1½d. red.. .. .. 10 15
151. 2½d. blue 12 30

13. King George VI. **16.** Badge of the Colony.

1937.
152. **13.** ¼d. brown 8 8

1938. As 1934, but with portrait of King George VI.
153b. ½d. green 10 10
154. 1d. black and brown .. 5 5
155. 1½d. black and red .. 8 5
156. 2d. black and orange .. 5 5
157. 2½ d. blue 10 8
158ab. 3d. black and olive .. 1·10 75
159. 6d. black and purple .. 15 15
160. 1s. black and brown .. 25 25
161. 2s. black and blue .. 80 80
162. 5s. black and violet .. 1·60 1·40
163b. **16.** 10s. blue and red .. 3·00 3·50

1946. Victory. As T **4** of Aden.
164. 1½d. red 8 8
165. 3½d. blue 12 10

1948. Silver Wedding. As T **5/6** of Aden.
166. 1½d. red 8 8
167. 10s. grey .. .. 3·50 5·50

1949. U.P.U. As T **14/7** of Antigua.
168. 5 c. blue 12 12
169. 6 c. olive 20 20
170. 12 c. magenta 40 40
171. 24 c. brown 65 65

17. King George VI. **18.** Badge of the Colony.

1951.
172. **17.** ½ c. black and brown .. 12 25
173. 1 c. black and green .. 12 12
174. 2 c. black and brown .. 12 12
175. 3 c. black and red .. 15 12
176. 4 c. black and orange .. 20 35
177. 5 c. black and violet .. 20 20
178. 6 c. black and olive .. 20 12
179. 7 c. black and blue .. 20 12
180. 12 c. black and purple 80 65
181. **18.** 25 c. black and brown.. 65 65
182. 50 c. black and blue .. 55 55
183. $1·50 black and orange 6·00 4·00
184. $2·50 slate and red .. 4·00 4·00
No. 184 is larger (24½ × 30½ mm.).

1951. B.W.I. University College. Inaug. As T **18/19** of Antigua.
185. **18.** 3 c. black and red .. 15 12
186. **19.** 6 c. black and olive .. 30 25

1951. New Constitution. Optd. **NEW CONSTITUTION 1951.**
187. **17.** 3 c. black and red .. 12 20
188. 4 c. black and orange.. 15 25
189. 5 c. black and violet .. 15 25
190. 12 c. black and purple.. 25 40

1953. Coronation. As T **7** of Aden.
191. 3 c. black and red .. 12 15

1953. As T **17**, but with portrait of Queen Elizabeth II, and T **18**, but Royal Cypher changed.
192. **17.** ½ c. black and brown .. 5 5
193. 1 c. black and green .. 5 5
212. 2 c. black and brown .. 5 5
213. 3 c. black and red .. 5 5
214. 4 c. black and orange.. 5 5
197. 5 c. black and violet .. 8 10
198. 6 c. black and olive .. 10 12
199. 7 c. black and blue .. 12 12
217. 12 c. black and purple.. 20 20
201. **18.** 25 c. black and brown.. 35 30
202. 50 c. black and blue .. 40 40
203. $1.50 black and orange 2·25 2·50
204. $2.50 slate and red .. 5·00 6·00
No. 204 is larger (24½ × 30½ mm.).

1958. British Caribbean Federation. As T **21** of Antigua.
205. 3 c. green 10 10
206. 6 c. blue 20 20
207. 12 c. red 30 30

19. Queen Victoria, Queen Elizabeth II and "La Concepcion".

1961. Stamp Cent.
208. – 3 c. crimson and black 15 15
209. **19.** 8 c. blue and orange .. 30 30
210. – 25 c. lake and blue .. 50 50

DESIGNS (incorporating Queen Victoria and Queen Elizabeth II): 3 c. Mail van and Post Office, St. George's. 25 c. R.M.S.P. "Solent" and Dakota aircraft.

1963. Freedom from Hunger. As T **10** of Aden.
211. 8 c. green 30 30

1963. Red Cross Cent. As T **24** of Antigua.
219. 3 c. red and black .. 10 12
220. 25 c. red and blue .. 50 50

1965. I.T.U. Cent. As T **26** of Antigua.
221. 2 c. orange and olive .. 8 8
222. 50 c. yellow and red .. 50 55

1965. I.C.Y. As T **27** of Antigua.
223. 1 c. purple and turquoise.. 8 8
224. 25 c. green and lavender.. 30 35

1966. Churchill Commem. As T **28** of Antigua.
225. 1 c. blue 5 5
226. 3 c. green 8 8
227. 25 c. brown 30 30
228. 35 c. violet.. .. .. 50 55

1966. Royal Visit. As T **29** of Antigua.
229. 3 c. black and blue .. 10 10
230. 35 c. black and magenta.. 40 40

20. Hillsborough, Carriacou.

1966. Multicoloured.
231. 1 c. Type **20** 5 5
232. 2 c. Bougainvillea .. 5 5
233. 3 c. Flamboyant Plant .. 5 5
234. 5 c. Levera Beach .. 5 5
235. 6 c. Careenage (inscr. "CARENAGE"), St. George's 5 5
236. 8 c. Annandale Falls .. 5 8
237. 10 c. Cocoa Pods .. 8 8
238. 12 c. Inner Harbour .. 10 12
239. 15 c. Nutmeg 12 15
240. 25 c. St. George's 15 25
241. 35 c. Grand Anse Beach .. 35 40
242. 50 c. Bananas .. 60 70
243. $1 Badge of the Colony .. 89 90
244. $2 Queen Elizabeth II .. 2·00 2·25
245. $3 Map of Grenada .. 3·00 3·50
Nos. 243/5 are vert. and larger, 25 × 39 mm.

1966. World Cup Football Championships. As T **30** of Antigua.
246. 5 c. vio., grn., lake & brn... 5 10
247. 50 c. choc., turq., lake & brn. 45 45

1966. W.H.O. Headquarters, Geneva. Inaug. As T **31** of Antigua.
248. 8 c. black, green and blue 10 10
249. 25 c. black, purple & ochre 30 35

1966. U.N.E.S.C.O. 20th Anniv. As T **33/5** of Antigua.
250. 2 c. vio., red, yell. & orge. 5 5
251. 15 c. yellow, violet & orge. 20 20
252. 50 c. black, purple & orge. 60 65

1967. Statehood. Nos. 232/3, 236 and 240 optd. **ASSOCIATED STATEHOOD 1967**

253. – 2 c. multicoloured .. 5 5
254. – 3 c. multicoloured .. 5 5
255. – 8 c. multicoloured .. 10 10
256. – 25 c. multicoloured .. 20 25

1967. World Fair, Montreal. Nos. 232, 237, 239 and 243/4 urch., or optd. **expo 67 MONTREAL · Canada** and emblem only.

257. 1 c. on 15 c. multicoloured 5 5
258. 2 c. multicoloured .. 5 5
259. 3 c. on 10 c. multicoloured 5 5
260. $1 multicoloured 50 55
261. $2 multicoloured .. 95 1·10

1967. Nos. 231/45 optd. **ASSOCIATED STATEHOOD.**

262. **20.** 1 c. multicoloured .. 5 5
263. – 2 c. multicoloured .. 5 5
264. – 3 c. multicoloured .. 5 5
265. – 5 c. multicoloured .. 5 5
266. – 6 c. multicoloured .. 5 5
267. – 8 c. multicoloured .. 5 5
268. – 10 c. multicoloured .. 8 8
269. – 12 c. multicoloured .. 6 12
270. – 15 c. multicoloured .. 12 12
271. – 25 c. multicoloured .. 20 20
272. – 35 c. multicoloured .. 30 35
273. – 50 c. multicoloured .. 50 60
274. – $1 multicoloured .. 75 85
275. – $2 multicoloured .. 1·75 2·00
276. – $3 multicoloured .. 2·50 3·00

21. Kennedy and Local Flower.

1968. Pres. Kennedy. 50th Birth Anniv. Multicoloured.

277. 1 c. Type **21** 5 5
278. 15 c. Type **21** 12 12
279. 25 c. Kennedy and Crane flower 20 20
280. 35 c. Kennedy and Roses 25 30
281. 50 c. As 25 c. 30 35
282. $1 As 35 c. 55 60

22. Scout Bugler.

1968. World Scout Jamboree, Idaho. Multicoloured.

283. 1 c. Type **22** 5 5
284. 2 c. Scouts camping .. 5 5
285. 3 c. Lord Baden Powell .. 5 5
286. 35 c. Type **22** 25 30
287. 50 c. As 2 c. 30 35
288. $1 As 3 c. 55 60

23. "Fishing Boat at Moorings".

1968. Paintings by Sir Winston Churchill. Multicoloured.

289. 10 c. Type **23** 10 10
290. 12 c. "View overlooking the Sea" 10 10
291. 15 c. "Waterfront Scene" 12 12
292. 25 c. Type **23** 20 20
293. 35 c. As No. 291 .. .. 30 30
294. 50 c. Sir Winston painting 35 40

1968. No. 275 surch.

295. $5 on $2 multicoloured .. 3·00 3·50

1968. "Children Need Milk". Surch. **CHILDREN NEED MILK** and value.

(a) Nos. 244/5.

296. 2 c.+3 c. on $2 multicoloured 15 20
297. 3 c.+3 c. on $3 multicoloured 15 25

(b) Nos. 243/4.

298. 1 c.+3 c. on $1 multicoloured .. .. 1·40 1·60
299. 2 c.+3 c. on $2 multicoloured .. .. 13·00 14·00

24. Edith McGuire (U.S.A.).

1968. Olympic Games, Mexico.

300. **24.** 1 c. brn., blk. & blue .. 5 5
301. – 2 c. orange, brown, blue and lilac 5 5
302. – 3 c. scarlet, brn. & grn. 5 5
303. **24.** 10 c. brown, black, blue and vermilion .. 10 10
304. – 50 c. orange. brown, blue & turquoise .. 30 35
305. – 60 c. scarlet, brn. & orge. 40 50

DESIGNS: 2 c., 50 c. Arthur Wint (Jamaica). 3 c., 60 c. Ferreira de Silva (Brazil).

25. Hibiscus.

26. Kidney Transplant.

1968. Multicoloured.

306. 1 c. Type **25** 5 5
307. 2 c. Strelitzia 5 5
308. 3 c. Bougainvillea 5 5
309. 5 c. Rock Hind 5 5
310. 6 c. Sailfish 5 5
311. 8 c. Snapper 5 8
312. 10 c. Giant Toad 8 10
313. 12 c. Turtle 10 12
314. 15 c. Tree Boa 20 20
314a. 15 c. Thunbergia 20 20
315. 25 c. Opossum 25 25
316. 35 c. Armadillo 25 25
317. 50 c. Mona Monkey .. 35 35
317a. 75 c. Yacht in St. Georges Harbour 45 50
318. $1 Bananaquit 65 70
319. $2 Pelican .. .. 1·25 1·40
320. $3 Frigate Bird .. 2·00 2·25
321. $5 Bare Eyed Thrush .. 3·25 3·50

Nos. 309, 311/12, 314, 316 and 317a are horiz. Nos. 318/21 are larger (25½ × 48 mm.).

1968. World Health Organisation. 20th Anniv. Multicoloured.

322. 5 c. Type **26** 5 5
323. 25 c. Heart Transplant 20 25
324. 35 c. Lung Transplant .. 25 30
325. 50 c. Eye Transplant .. 35 40

27. "The Adoration of the Magi" (Veronese).

1968. Christmas.

326. **27.** 5 c. multicoloured .. 5 5
327. – 15 c. multicoloured .. 15 15
328. – 35 c. multicoloured .. 30 30
329. – $1 multicoloured .. 65 80

DESIGNS: 15 c. "Madonna and Child with Saints John and Catherine" (Titian). 35 c. "The Adoration of the Magi" (Botticelli). $1, "A Knight adoring" (Catena).

1969. Caribbean Free Trade Area Exhibition. Nos. 300/5 surch. **VISIT CARIFTA EXPO '69 APRIL 5-30** and value.

330. **24.** 5 c. on 1 c. 5 5
331. – 8 c. on 2 c. 8 8
332. – 25 c. on 3 c. 20 20
333. **24.** 35 c. on 10 c. 25 25
334. – $1 on 50 c. 60 60
335. – $2 on 60 c. .. .. 1·25 1·25

28. Dame Hylda Bynoe and Island Scene.

1969. Carifta Expo '69. Multicoloured.

336. 5 c. Type **28** 5 5
337. 15 c. Premier E. M. Gairy and Island scene .. 12 15
338. 50 c. Type **28** 30 30
339. 60 c. Emblems of 1958 and 1967 World Fairs .. 35 40

29. Dame Hylda Bynoe.

1969. Human Rights Year. Multicoloured.

340. 5 c. Type **29** 5 5
341. 25 c. Dr. Martin Luther King 20 20
342. 35 c. As 5 c. 25 25
343. $1 "Balshazzar's Feast" (Rembrandt) 60 70

The $1 is horiz.

30. Batsman playing Off-Drive.

1969. Cricket.

344. **30.** 3 c. yell., brn. & ultram. 5 5
345. – 10 c. multicoloured .. 8 8
346. – 25 c. brn., ochre & grn. 20 25
347. – 35 c. multicoloured .. 25 30

DESIGNS: 10 c. Batsman playing defensive stroke. 25 c. Batsman sweeping ball. 35 c. Batsman playing off-drive.

31. Astronaut handling Moon Rock.

1969. 1st Man on the Moon. Multicoloured.

348. ½ c. Astronaut handling Moon Rock (different) .. 5 5
349. 1 c. Moon rocket en-route to the moon 5 5
350. 2 c. Space Module landing on moon 5 5
351. 3 c. Declaration left on the moon by astronauts .. 5 5
352. 8 c. Module separating from Space Ship 8 8
353. 25 c. Spacecraft after lift-off 15 15
354. 35 c. Spacecraft in orbit .. 25 25
355. 50 c. Final descent of Space Module 30 30
356. $1 Type **31** 70 70

The ½ c. is larger (56 × 36 mm.), and has a different frame design than T **31**.
The 25, 35 and 50 c. are vert.

32. Gandhi. (Reduced size illustration—actual size 54 × 30½ mm.).

1969. Mahatma Gandhi. Birth Cent. Multicoloured.

358. 6 c. Type **32** 5 5
359. 15 c. Gandhi (standing) .. 12 12
360. 25 c. Gandhi (walking) .. 20 20
361. $1 Head of Gandhi .. 60 65

1969. Christmas. Nos. 326/9 optd. **1969** and surch. (No. 363).

363. – 2 c. on 15 c. multicoloured 5 5
364. **27.** 5 c. multicoloured .. 5 5
365. – 35 c. multicoloured .. 30 35
366. – $1 multicoloured .. 75 80

33. "Blackbeard" (Edward Teach).

1970. Pirates.

367. **33.** 15 c. black 12 12
368. – 25 c. green 20 20
369. – 50 c. lilac 40 35
370. – $1 carmine 85 75

DESIGNS: 25 c. Anne Bonney. 50 c. Jean Lafitte. $1 Mary Read.

1970. No. 348 surch.

371. 5 c. on ½ c. multicoloured .. 8 8

34. "The Last Supper" (Del Sarto). **35.** (Illustration reduced. Actual size 64 × 45 mm.).

1970. Easter.

372. **34.** 5 c. multicoloured .. 5 5
373. **35.** 5 c. multicoloured .. 5 5
374. – 15 c. multicoloured .. 12 12
375. – 15 c. multicoloured .. 12 12
376. – 25 c. multicoloured .. 20 20
377. – 25 c. multicoloured .. 20 20
378. – 60 c. multicoloured .. 40 40
379. – 60 c. multicoloured .. 40 40

DESIGNS: 15 c. "Christ crowned with Thorns" (detail—Van Dyck). 25 c. "The Passion of Christ" (detail—Memling). 60 c. "Christ in the Tomb" (detail—Rubens).

Each value was issued in sheets containing the two stamps se-tenant. Each design is spread over two stamps as in T **34/5**.

36. Girl with Kittens in Pram. (Illustration reduced. Actual size 59 × 34 mm.)

1970. Wordsworth Birth Bicent. "Children and Pets". Multicoloured.

381. 5 c. Type **36** 5 5
382. 15 c. Girl with puppy and kitten 12 12
383. 30 c. Boy with fishing-rod and cat 20 20
384. 60 c. Boys and girls with cats and dogs 35 35

37. Parliament of India.

1970. Commonwealth Parliamentary Assn. 7th Regional Conf. Stamps showing Parliaments country given. Multicoloured.

386. 5 c. Type **37** 5 5
387. 25 c. Great Britain, Westminster 20 20
388. 50 c. Canada 30 35
389. 60 c. Grenada 35 40

38. Tower of the Sun.

1970. World Fair, Osaka. Multicoloured.

391. 1 c. Type **38** 5 5
392. 2 c. Livelihood and Industry Pavilion .. 5 5
393. 3 c. Flower Painting (1634) 5 5
394. 10 c. "Adam and Eve" (Titian) 8 8
395. 25 c. Organisation For Economic Co-operation and Development (O.E.C.D.) Pavilion 15 20
396. 50 c. San Francisco Pavilion 35 45

39. Roosevelt and "Raising U.S. Flag on Iwo Jima". (Illustration reduced. Actual size 60 × 35 mm.).

1970. Ending of World War Two. 25th Anniv. Multicoloured.

398. ½ c. Type **39** 5 5
399. 5 c. Zhukov and "Fall of Berlin" 5 5
400. 15 c. Churchill and "Evacuation at Dunkirk" .. 12 12
401. 25 c. De Gaulle and "Liberation of Paris" .. 20 20
402. 50 c. Eisenhower and "D-Day Landing" .. 40 40
403. 60 c. Montgomery and "Battle of Alamein" .. 50 50

1970. "Philympia 1970" Stamp Exhibition, London. Nos. 353/6 optd. **PHILYMPIA LONDON 1970.**

405. – 25 c. multicoloured .. 15 20
406. – 35 c. multicoloured .. 25 25
407. – 50 c. multicoloured .. 35 35
408. 31. $1 multicoloured .. 55 55

40. U.P.U. Emblem, Building and Transport.

1970. U.P.U. Headquarters Building. Multicoloured.

409. 15 c. Type **40** 12 12
410. 25 c. As Type **40**, but modern transport .. 20 20
411. 50 c. Sir Rowland Hill and U.P.U. Building .. 30 30
412. $1 Abraham Lincoln and U.P.U. Building .. 55 60

The 50 c. and $1 are both vert.

41. "The Madonna of the Goldfinch" (Tiepolo).

1970. Christmas. Multicoloured.

414. ½ c. Type **41** 5 5
415. ½ c. "The Virgin and Child with St. Peter and St. Paul" (Bouts) 5 5
416. ½ c. "The Virgin and the Child" (Bellini) 5 5
417. 2 c. "The Madonna of the Basket" (Correggio) .. 5 5
418. 3 c. Type **41** 5 5
419. 35 c. As No. 415 .. .. 30 30
420. 50 c. As 2 c. 40 40
421. $1 As No. 416 .. .. 65 65

42. 19th-Century Nursing.

1970. British Red Cross Cent. Multicoloured.

423. 5 c. Type **42** 5 5
424. 15 c. Military Ambulance, 1918 .. .. .. 12 12
425. 25 c. First-Aid Post, 1941 20 20
426. 60 c. Red Cross Transport, 1970 .. .. .. 40 40

43. John Dewey and Art Lesson.

1971. Int. Education Year. Multicoloured.

428. 5 c. Type **43** 5 5
429. 10 c. Jean-Jacques Rousseau and "Alphabetisation" .. 8 8
430. 50 c. Maimonides and laboratory 30 30
431. $1 Bertrand Russell and mathematics class .. 60 65

44. Jennifer Hosten and outline of Grenada.

1971. Winner of "Miss World" Competition (1970).

433. **44.** 5 c. multicoloured .. 5 5
434. 10 c. multicoloured .. 10 8
435. 15 c. multicoloured .. 12 10
436. 25 c. multicoloured .. 20 15
437. 35 c. multicoloured .. 30 25
438. 50 c. multicoloured .. 50 45

45. French and Canadian Scouts.

1971. 13th World Scout Jamboree, Asagiri, Japan. Multicoloured.

440. 5 c. Type **45** 5 5
441. 35 c. German and American scouts 20 20
442. 50 c. Australian and Japanese scouts 35 35
443. 75 c. Grenada and British scouts 45 50

46. "Napoleon reviewing Troops". (Edouard Detaille).

1971. Napoleon Bonaparte. 150th Death Anniv. Paintings. Multicoloured.

445. 5 c. Type **46** 5 5
446. 15 c. "Napoleon outside Madrid" (Vernet) .. 12 12
447. 35 c. "Napoleon crossing Alps" (David) 25 25
448. $2 "Napoleon Bonaparte" (David) .. .. .. 1·25 1·40

47. 1d. Stamp of 1861 and Badge of Grenada. (Illustration reduced, actual size 59 × 34 mm.)

1971. 110th Anniv. of the Postal Service. Multicoloured.

450. 5 c. Type **47** 5 5
451. 15 c. 5d. stamp of 1861 and Queen Elizabeth II .. 12 12
452. 35 c. 1d. and 6d. stamps of 1861 and badge of Grenada 25 25
453. 50 c. Scroll and 1d. stamps of 1861 .. .. .. 40 40

48. Apollo splashdown. (Illustration reduced. Actual size 58 × 35 mm.).

1971. Apollo Moon Exploration Series. Multicoloured.

455. 1 c. Type **48** 5 5
456. 2 c. Recovery of "Apollo 13" 5 5
457. 3 c. Separation of Lunar Module from "Apollo 14" 5 5
458. 10 c. Shepherd and Mitchell taking samples of moon rock 10 10
459. 25 c. Moon Buggy .. 25 25
460. $1 "Apollo 15" blast-off (vert.) 85 90

49. 67th Regt. of Foot, 1787.

1971. Military Uniforms. Multicoloured.

462. ½ c. Type **49** 5 5
463. 1 c. 45th Regt. of Foot, 1792 5 5
464. 2 c. 29th Regt. of Foot, 1794 5 5
465. 10 c. 9th Regt. of Foot, 1801 10 10
466. 25 c. 2nd Regt. of Foot, 1815 25 25
467. $1 70th Regt. of Foot, 1764 80 90

50. "The Adoration of the Magi". (Memling).

1972. Christmas (1971). Multicoloured.

469. 15 c. Type **50** 12 15
470. 25 c. "Madonna and Child" (Michelangelo) 20 20
471. 35 c. "Madonna and Child" (Murillo) 25 25
472. 50 c. "Virgin Mary with the Apple" (Memling) .. 35 40

1972. Winter Olympic Games, Sapporo, Japan. Nos. 462/4 surch. **WINTER OLYMPICS FEB. 3-13, 1972 SAPPORO, JAPAN.** Olympic rings and premium. Nos. 476/7 additionally surch. **AIR MAIL.**

474. $2 on 2 c. multicoloured (postage) .. .. 1·00 1·25
476. 35 c. on ½ c. multicoloured (air) 20 20
477. 50 c. on 1 c. multicoloured 30 35

1972. General Election. Nos. 307/8, 310 and 315 optd. **VOTE FEB. 28 1972.**

478. 2 c. multicoloured .. 5 5
479. 3 c. multicoloured .. 10 10
480. 6 c. multicoloured .. 12 15
481. 25 c. multicoloured .. 35 40

51. King Arthur.

1972. U.N.I.C.E.F. Multicoloured.

482. ½ c. Type **51** 5 5
483. 1 c. Robin Hood (horiz.) .. 5 5
484. 2 c. Robinson Crusoe (vert.) 5 5
485. 25 c. Type **51** 15 15
486. 50 c. As 1c. 30 30
487. 75 c. As 2c. 40 40
488. $1 Mary and her little lamb 55 55

1972. "Interpex" Stamp Exhib., New York. Nos. 433/8 optd. **INTERPEX 1972.**
490. **44.** 5 c. multicoloured .. 8 8
491. 10 c. multicoloured .. 10 10
492. 15 c. multicoloured .. 15 15
493. 25 c. multicoloured .. 25 25
494. 35 c. multicoloured .. 30 35
495. 50 c. multicoloured .. 50 60

1972. Nos. 306/8 and 433 surch.
497. – 12 c. on 1 c. multicoloured 15 15
498. – 12 c. on 2 c. multicoloured 15 15
499. – 12 c. on 3 c. multicoloured 15 15
500. **44.** 12 c. on 5 c. multicoloured 15 15

1972. Air. Optd. **AIR MAIL** or surch. in addition.
501. – 5 c. mult. (No. 309) .. 5 5
518. **45.** 5 c. multicoloured .. 5 5
502. – 8 c. mult. (No. 311) .. 5 5
503. – 10 c. mult. (No. 312) 8 8
504. – 15 c. mult. (No. 314a) 10 10
505. – 25 c. mult. (No. 315) .. 20 20
506. – 30 c. on 1 c. mult. (No. 306) 20 20
507. – 35 c. mult. (No. 316) 25 25
519. – 35 c. mult. (No. 441) .. 20 25
508. – 40 c. on 2 c. mult. (No. 307) 25 25
509. – 45 c. on 3 c. mult. (No. 308) 30 30
510. – 50 c. mult. (No. 317) .. 30 30
520. – 50 c. mult. (No. 442) .. 30 35
511. – 60 c. on 5 c. mult. (No. 309) 35 40
512. – 70 c. on 6 c. mult. (No. 310) 45 50
521. – 75 c. mult. (No. 443) .. 45 50
513. – $1 mult. (No. 318) .. 50 60
514. – $1·35 on 8 c. mult. (No. 311) 60 75
515. – $2 mult. (No. 319) .. 1·00 1·25
516. – $3 mult. (No. 320) .. 1·50 1·75
517. – $5 mult. (No. 321) .. 2·50 3·00

52. Yachting.

1972. Olympic Games, Munich. Multicoloured.
522. ½ c. Type **52** (postage) .. 5 5
523. 1 c. Show-jumping .. 5 5
524. 2 c. Running (vert.) .. 5 5
525. 35 c. As 2 c. 25 25
526. 50 c. As 1 c. 25 25
527. 25 c. Boxing (air) .. 20 20
528. **$1** as 25 c. 75 75

1972. Royal Silver Wedding. As T **19** of Ascension, but with Badge of Grenada and Nutmegs in background.
530. 8 c. brown 8 10
531. $1 blue 70 70

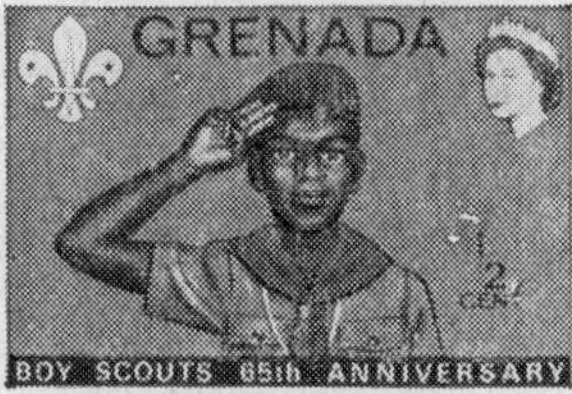

53. Boy Scout Saluting.

1972. Boy Scouts. 65th Anniv. Mult.
532. ½ c. Type **53** (postage) .. 5 5
533. 1 c. Scouts knotting ropes 5 5
534. 2 c. Scouts shaking hands 5 5
535. 3 c. Lord Baden Powell .. 5 5
536. 75 c. As 2 c. 40 40
537. **$1** As 3 c. 55 55
538. 25 c. Type **53** (air) .. 20 20
539. 25 c. As 1 c. 25 25

54. Madonna and Child.

1972. Christmas. Multicoloured.
541. 1 c. Type **54** 5 5
542. 3 c. The Three Kings .. 5 5
543. 5 c. The Nativity .. 5 5
544. 25 c. Type **54** 20 20
545. 35 c. As 3 c. 25 30
546. **$1** As 5 c. 75 85

55. Flamingoes.

1973. National Zoo. Multicoloured.
548. 25 c. Type **55** 15 15
549. 35 c. Tapir 20 25
550. 60 c. Macaws 30 35
551. 70 c. Leopard 35 35

56. Class II Racing Yacht.

1973. World Yachting Centre. Multicoloured.
552. 25 c. Type **56** 15 15
553. 35 c. Harbour, St. George's 20 20
554. 60 c. Yacht "Bloodhound" 30 30
555. 70 c. St. George's 35 35

57. Helios and Earth Orbiting the Sun.

1973. I.M.O./W.M.O. Cent. Greek Gods. Multicoloured.
556. ½ c. Type **57** 5 5
557. 1 c. Poseidon and "Normad" 5 5
558. 2 c. Zeus and radarscope .. 5 5
559. 3 c. Iris and weather balloon 5 5
560. 35 c. Hermes and "ATS-3" satellite 20 20
561. 50 c. Zephyrus and diagram of pressure zones .. 30 35
562. 75 c. Demeter and space photo 45 50
563. $1 Selene and rainfall diagram 50 55

58. Racing Class Yachts.

1973. Carriacou Regatta. Multicoloured.
565. ½ c. Type **58** 5 5
566. 1 c. Cruising Class Yacht .. 5 5
567. 2 c. Open-decked sloops .. 5 5
568. 35 c. "The Mermaid" (sloop) 20 20
569. 50 c. St. George's Harbour 25 30
570. 75 c. Map of Carriacou .. 40 55
571. $1 Boat-building 50 50

59. Ignatius Semmelweis (Obstetrician).

1973. W.H.O. 25th Anniv. Multicoloured.
573. ½ c. Type **59** 5 5
574. 1 c. Louis Pasteur .. 5 5
575. 2 c. Edward Jenner .. 5 5
576. 3 c. Sigmund Freud .. 5 5
577. 25 c. Emil Von Behring (bacteriologist) 15 20
578. 35 c. Carl Jung 20 20
579. 50 c. Charles Calmette (bacteriologist) 30 35
580. $1 William Harvey .. 50 50

60. Princess Anne and Capt. Mark Phillips.

1973. Royal Wedding.
582. **60.** 25 c. multicoloured .. 15 20
583. $2 multicoloured .. 1·25 1·25

61. "Virgin and Child" (Maratti).

1973. Christmas. Multicoloured.
585. ½ c. Type **61** 5 5
586. 1 c. "Virgin and Child" (Crivelli) 5 5
587. 2 c. "Virgin and Child" (Verrocchio) 5 5
588. 3 c. "Adoration of the Shepherds" (Roberti) .. 5 5
589. 25 c. "The Holy Family" (Baroccio) 15 15
590. 35 c. "The Holy Family" (Bronzino) 20 20
591. 77 c. "Mystic Nativity" (Botticelli) 40 40
592. $1 "Adoration of the Magi" (Geertgen) .. 50 55

1974. Independence. Nos. 306/21 optd. with **INDEPENDENCE 7TH FEB. 1974.**
594. **25.** 1 c. multicoloured .. 5 5
595. – 2 c. multicoloured .. 5 5
596. – 3 c. multicoloured .. 5 5
597. – 5 c. multicoloured .. 8 8
598. – 8 c. multicoloured .. 8 8
599. – 10 c. multicoloured .. 10 10
600. – 12 c. multicoloured .. 10 10
601. – 25 c. multicoloured .. 25 25
602. – 35 c. multicoloured .. 30 25
603. – 75 c. multicoloured .. 70 70
604. – $1 multicoloured .. 90 80
605. – $2 multicoloured .. 1·75 1·50
606. – $3 multicoloured .. 2·50 2·25
607. – $5 multicoloured .. 4·00 3·75

62. Creative Arts Theatre, Jamaica Campus.

1974. University of West Indies. 25th Anniv. Multicoloured.
608. 10 c. Type **62** 10 10
609. 25 c. Marryshow House .. 15 20
610. 50 c. Chapel, Jamaica Campus (vert.) 25 30
611. **$1** University arms (vert.) 55 55

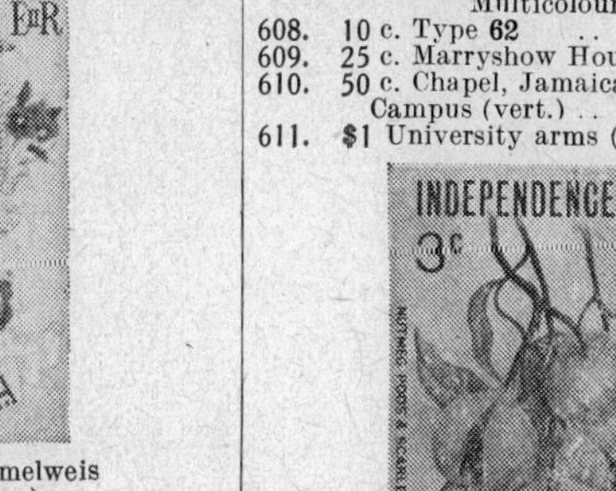

63. Nutmeg Pods and Scarlet Mace.

1974. Independence. Multicoloured.
613. 3 c. Type **63** 5 5
614. 8 c. Map of Grenada .. 5 5
615. 25 c. Prime Minister Eric Gairy 15 20
616. 35 c. Grand Anse beach and flag 25 25
617. $1 Coat of arms 50 60

64. Footballers (West Germany v. Chile).

1974. World Cup Football Championships. Multicoloured.
619. ½ c. Type **64** 5 5
620. 1 c. East Germany v. Australia 5 5
621. 2 c. Yugoslavia v. Brazil .. 5 5
622. 10 c. Scotland v. Zaire .. 5 5
623. 25 c. Netherlands v. Uruguay 15 20
624. 50 c. Sweden v. Bulgaria .. 30 35
625. 75 c. Italy v. Haiti .. 40 45
626. $1 Poland v. Argentina .. 50 55

65. Early Mail-trains and "Concorde".

1974. U.P.U. Centenary. Multicoloured.
628. ½ c. Type **65** 5 5
629. 1 c. Mailboat Caeser (1839) and helicopter 5 5
630. 2 c. Airmail transport .. 5 5
631. 8 c. Pigeon post (1480) and telephone dial 8 8
632. 15 c. 18th-century bellman and tracking antenna .. 12 12
633. 25 c. Messenger (1450) and satellite 15 20
634. 35 c. French pillar-box (1850) and mail-boat 25 25
635. $1 18th-century German postman and mail-train of the future 45 50

66. Sir Winston Churchill.

1974. Sir Winston Churchill. Birth Centenary.
637. **66.** 35 c. multicoloured .. 20 20
638. $2 multicoloured .. 90 95

67. " Madonna and Child " (Botticelli).

1974. Christmas. " Madonna and Child " paintings by named artists. Multicoloured.

640. ½ c. Type **67** 5 5
641. 1 c. Niccolo di Pietro 5 5
642. 2 c. Van der Weyden 5 5
643. 3 c. Bastiani 5 5
644. 10 c. Giovanni 8 8
645. 25 c. Van der Weyden .. 15 20
646. 50 c. Botticelli 30 35
647. $1 Mantegna 50 55

68. Yachts, Point Saline.

1975. Multicoloured.

649. ½ c. Type **68** 5 5
650. 1 c. Yacht Club race, St. George's 5 5
651. 2 c. Carenage taxi 5 5
652. 3 c. Large working boats .. 5 5
653. 5 c. Deep-water dock, St. George's 5 5
654. 6 c. Cocoa beans in drying tanks 5 5
655. 8 c. Nutmegs 5 5
656. 10 c. Rum distillery, River Antoine Estate 5 5
657. 12 c. Cocoa tree 5 5
658. 15 c. Fishermen at Fontenoy 5 5
659. 20 c. Parliament Building, St. George's 8 10
660. 25 c. Fort George cannons 10 12
661. 35 c. Pearls Airport .. 12 15
662. 50 c. General Post Office .. 20 25
663. 75 c. Caribs Leap, Sauteurs Bay 25 30
664. $1 Carenage, St. George's 35 40
665. $2 St. George's harbour by night 70 75
666. $3 Grand Anse beach .. 1·10 1·25
667. $5 Canoe Bay & Black Bay from Point Saline Lighthouse .. .. 1·75 2·00
668. $10 Sugar-loaf Island .. 3·50 4·00

Nos. 663/8 are size 45 × 28 mm.

69. Sail-fish.

1975. Big Game Fishing. Multicoloured.

669. ½ c. Type **69** 5 5
670. 1 c. Blue Marlin 5 5
671. 2 c. White Marlin 5 5
672. 10 c. Yellowfin Tuna .. 8 8
673. 25 c. Wahoo 15 20
674. 50 c. Dolphin 30 35
675. 70 c. Grouper 40 45
676. $1 Great Barracuda .. 50 55

70. Granadilla Barbadine.

1975. Flowers. Multicoloured.

678. ½ c. Type **70** 5 5
679. 1 c. Bleeding Heart (Easter Lily) 5 5
680. 2 c. Poinsettia 5 5
681. 3 c. Cocoa flower 5 5
682. 10 c. Gladioli 5 8
683. 25 c. Redhead/Yellowhead 15 15
684. 50 c. Plumbago 25 30
685. $1 Orange flower 45 50

71. Dove, Grenada Flag and U.N. Emblem.

1975. Grenada's Admission to the U.N. (1974). Multicoloured.

687. ½ c. Type **71** 5 5
688. 1 c. Grenada and U.N. flags 5 5
689. 2 c. Grenada coat of arms 5 5
690. 35 c. U.N. emblem over map of Grenada .. 20 20
691. 50 c. U.N. buildings and flags 25 30
692. $2 U.N. emblem and scroll 90 95

72. Paul Revere's Midnight Ride.

1975. American Revolution. Bicent. Multicoloured.

694. ½ c. Type **72** (postage) .. 5 5
695. 1 c. Crispus Attucks .. 5 5
696. 2 c. Patrick Henry .. 5 5
697. 3 c. Franklin visits Washington 5 5
698. 5 c. Rebel troops 5 5
699. 10 c. John Paul Jones .. 5 5
700. 40 c. John Hancock (air) 20 25
701. 50 c. Ben Franklin .. 25 30
702. 75 c. John Adams .. 35 40
703. $1 Lafayette 40 45

Nos. 700/3 are vert.

73. " The Holy Grail " (Bellini).

1975. Easter. Multicoloured.

705. ½ c. Type **73** 5 5
706. 1 c. " The Virgin Mary with Christ's Body " (Bellini) 5 5
707. 2 c. " The Entombment " (Van der Weyden) .. 5 5
708. 3 c. " Christ with the Virgin Mary " (Bellini) 5 5
709. 35 c. " Christ with the Apostles " (Bellini) .. 15 20
710. 75 c. " The Dead Christ " (Bellini) 35 40
711. $1 " The Deposition " (Procaccini) 40 45

HAVE YOU READ THE NOTES AT THE BEGINNING OF THIS CATALOGUE?

These often provide answers to the enquiries we receive.

74. Wildlife Study.

1975. 14th World Scout Jamboree, Norway. Multicoloured.

713. ½ c. Type **74** 5 5
714. 1 c. Sailing 5 5
715. 2 c. Map-reading 5 5
716. 35 c. First-aid 15 15
717. 40 c. Physical training .. 20 25
718. 75 c. Mountaineering .. 30 35
719. $2 Sing-song .. ..

75. Leafy Jewel Box.

1975. Seashells. Multicoloured.

721. ½ c. Type **75** 5 5
722. 1 c. Emerald Nerite .. 5 5
723. 2 c. Yellow Cockle .. 5 5
724. 25 c. Purple Sea Snail .. 12 12
725. 50 c. Turkey Wing .. 20 25
726. 75 c. West Indian Fighting Conch 30 35
727. $1 Noble Wentletrap .. 40 45

76. Lady or Large Tiger.

1975. Butterflies. Multicoloured.

729. ½ c. Type **76** 5 5
730. 1 c. Five Continent .. 5 5
731. 2 c. Large Striped Blue .. 5 5
732. 35 c. Gonatryx 15 15
733. 45 c. Spear-winged Cattle-heart 20 20
734. 75 c. Rusty Nymula .. 30 35
735. $2 Blue Night 80 90

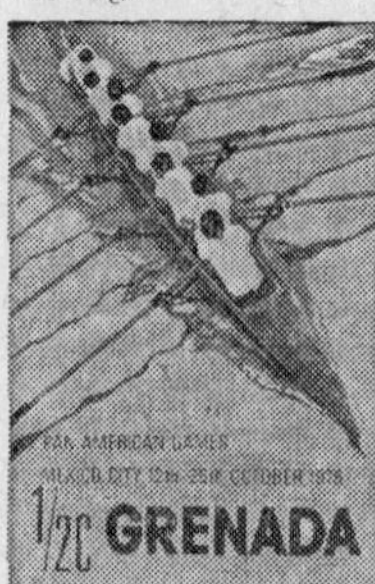

77. Rowing.

1975. Pan-American Games, Mexico City. Multicoloured.

737. ½ c. Type **77** 5 5
738. 1 c. Swimming 5 5
739. 2 c. Show-jumping .. 5 5
740. 35 c. Gymnastics 15 15
741. 45 c. Football 20 20
742. 75 c. Boxing 30 35
743. $2 Cycling 80 90

INDEX

Countries can be quickly located by referring to the index at the end of this volume.

78. " The Boy David " (Michelangelo).

1975. Michelangelo. 500th Birth Anniv.

745. **78.** ½ c. multicoloured .. 5 5
746. – 1 c. multicoloured .. 5 5
747. – 2 c. multicoloured .. 5 5
748. – 40 c. multicoloured .. 20 20
749. – 50 c. multicoloured .. 20 25
750. – 75 c. multicoloured .. 30 35
751. – $2 multicoloured .. 80 85

DESIGNS: 1 c. to $2 Paintings and sculptures by Michelangelo.

79. " Virgin and Child " (Filippino Lippi).

1975. Christmas. " Virgin and Child " paintings by Artists named. Multicoloured.

753. ½ c. Type **79** 5 5
754. 1 c. Mantegna 5 5
755. 2 c. Luis de Morales .. 5 5
756. 35 c. G. M. Morandi .. 15 20
757. 50 c. Antonello 20 25
758. 75 c. Durer 30 35
759. $1 Velasquez 40 45

80. Bananaquit.

1976. Flora and Fauna. Multicoloured.

761. ½ c. Type **80** 5 5
762. 1 c. Orange-rumped Agouti 5 5
763. 2 c. Hawksbill Turtle (horiz.) 5 5
764. 5 c. Dwarf Poinciana .. 5 5
765. 35 c. Albacore 15 15
766. 40 c. Cardinal's Guard .. 20 20
767. $2 Antillean Armadilla .. 75 85

81. Carnival Time.

1976. Tourism. Multicoloured.

769. ½ c. Type **81** 5 5
770. 1 c. Scuba diving 5 5
771. 2 c. Cruise Ship " Southward " at St. George's .. 5 5
772. 35 c. Game fishing .. 15 15
773. 50 c. St. George's Golf Course 20 20
774. 75 c. Tennis 30 30
775. $1 Ancient rock carvings at Mount Rich .. .. 95 1·10

82. " Pieta " (Master of Okoliesno).

1976. Easter. Paintings by Artists named. Multicoloured.

777.	½ c. Type **82**	5	5
778.	1 c. Correggio	5	5
779.	2 c. Van der Weyden ..	5	5
780.	3 c. Durer	5	5
781.	35 c. Unknown Master ..	15	15
782.	75 c. Raphael	30	35
783.	$1 Raphael	40	45

83. Sharpshooters.

1976. American Revolution. Bicent. Multicoloured.

785.	½ c. Type **83**	5	5
786.	1 c. Defending the Liberty Pole	5	5
787.	2 c. Loading muskets ..	5	5
788.	35 c. The fight for Liberty	15	15
789.	50 c. Peace Treaty, 1783..	20	25
790.	$1 Drummers	40	45
791.	$3 Gunboats	1·25	1·40

84. Nature Study.

1976. Girl Guides in Grenada. 50th Anniv. Mult.

793.	½ c. Type **84**	5	5
794.	1 c. Campfire cooking ..	5	5
795.	2 c. First Aid	5	5
796.	35 c. Camping	15	15
797.	45 c. Home economics ..	30	35
798.	$2 First Aid	80	90

85. Volleyball.

1976. Olympic Games, Montreal. Multicoloured.

800.	½ c. Type **85**	5	5
801.	1 c. Cycling	5	5
802.	2 c. Rowing	5	5
803.	35 c. Judo	15	15
804.	45 c. Hockey	20	20
805.	75 c. Gymnastics	30	35
806.	$1 High jump	40	45

86. " Cha-U-Kao at the Moulin Rouge.

1976. Toulouse-Lautrec. 75th Death Anniv. Mult.

808.	½ c. Type **86**	5	5
809.	1 c. " Quadrille Beginning "	5	5
810.	2 c. " Woman's Bust " ..	5	5
811.	3 c. " Hall at the Moulin Rouge "	5	5
812.	40 c. " Launderer Both Albi "	15	20
813.	50 c. " Bolero Dancer " ..	20	25
814.	$2 " Signor Boileau at Cafe "	80	90

1976. West Indian Victory in World Cricket Cup. Nos. 559/60 of Barbados.

816.	35 c. Map of the Caribbean	15	20
817.	$1 The Prudential Cup ..	40	45

87. Piper " Apache ".

1976. Aeroplanes. Multicoloured.

818.	½ c. Type **87**	5	5
819.	1 c. Beech " Twin Bonanza "	5	5
820.	2 c. D.H. " Twin Otter "	5	5
821.	40 c. Britten Norman " Islander "	15	20
822.	50 c. D.H. " Heron " ..	20	25
823.	$2 H.S. " 748 "	80	90

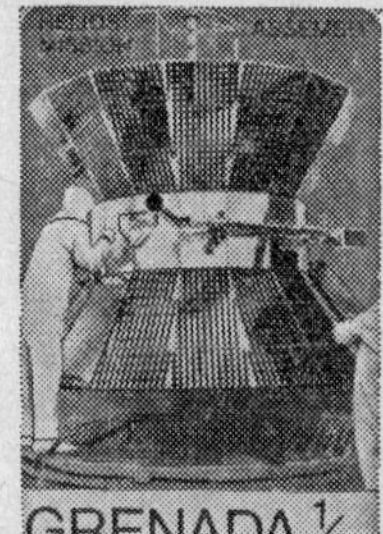

88. Satellite Assembly.

1976. Viking and Helios Space Missions. Multicoloured.

825.	½ c. Type **88**	5	5
826.	1 c. Helios satellite ..	5	5
827.	2 c. Helios encapsulation	5	5
828.	15 c. Systems test ..	5	8
829.	45 c. Viking lander (horiz.)	20	20
830.	75 c. Lander on Mars ..	30	35
831.	$2 Viking encapsulation ..	80	90

89. S.S. " Geestland ".

1976. Ships. Multicoloured.

833.	½ c. Type **89**	5	5
834.	1 c. M.V. " Federal Palm "	5	5
835.	2 c. H.M.S. " Blake " ..	5	5
836.	25 c. M.V. " Vistafjord "	10	12
837.	75 c. S.S. " Canberra " ..	30	35
838.	$1 S.S. " Regina " ..	40	45
839.	$5 S.S. " Arandora Star "	2·00	2·25

90. San Barnaba Altarpiece (Botticelli).

1976. Christmas. Multicoloured.

841.	½ c. Type **90**	5	5
842.	1 c. " Annunciation " (Botticelli)	5	5
843.	2 c. " Madonna with Chancellor Rolin " (Jan Van Eyck)	5	5
844.	50 c. " Madonna of the Magnificat " (Botticelli)	20	25
845.	75 c. " Madonna of the Pomegranate " (Botticelli)	30	35
846.	$3 " Madonna with St. Cosmas and other Saints " (Botticelli)	1·25	1·50

POSTAGE DUE STAMPS

D 1.

ILLUSTRATIONS
British Commonwealth and all overprints and surcharges are FULL SIZE. Foreign Countries have been reduced to ¾-LINEAR.

1892.

D 8. D **1.**	1d. black	25	35
D 9.	2d. black	40	40
D 10.	3d. black	65	90

1892. Surch. **SURCHARGE POSTAGE** and value.

D 4. **3.**	1d. on 6d. mauve ..	2·25	1·25
D 5.	1d. on 8d. brown ..	24·00	2·75
D 6.	2d. on 6d. mauve ..	6·50	2·00
D 7.	2d. on 8d. brown ..	50·00	6·50

1921. As Type D **1** but inscr. "POSTAGE DUE" instead of "SURCHARGE POSTAGE".

D 11. D **1.**	1d. black	25	30
D 12.	1½d. black	50	55
D 13.	2d. black	50	55
D 14.	3d. black	60	55

1952. As last but currency changed.

D 15. D **1.**	2 c. black	5	5
D 16.	4 c. black	8	8
D 17.	6 c. black	10	10
D 18.	8 c. black	12	12

GRENADINES OF GRENADA BC

The southern part of the group, attached to Grenada. Main islands Petit Martinique and Carriacou.

1973. Royal Wedding. Nos. 582/3 of Grenada optd. **GRENADINES.**

1. **60.**	25 c. multicoloured ..	20	25
2.	$2 multicoloured ..	1·25	1·25

1974. Stamps of Grenada optd. **GRENADINES.**

4.	1 c. multicoloured (No. 306)	5	5
5.	2 c. multicoloured (No. 307)	5	5
6.	3 c. multicoloured (No. 308)	5	5
7.	5 c. multicoloured (No. 309)	5	5
8.	8 c. multicoloured (No. 311)	5	5
9.	10 c. multicoloured (No. 312)	5	5
10.	12 c. multicoloured (No. 313)	8	8
11.	25 c. multicoloured (No. 315)	12	15
12.	$1 multicoloured (No. 318)..	40	45
13.	$2 multicoloured (No. 319)..	85	95
14.	$3 multicoloured (No. 320)..	1·25	1·40
15.	$5 multicoloured (No. 321)..	2·10	2·25

1974. World Cup Football Championships. As Nos. 619/26 of Grenada inscr. "GRENADA GRENADINES".

16.	½ c. multicoloured	5	5
17.	1 c. multicoloured	5	5
18.	2 c. multicoloured	5	5
19.	10 c. multicoloured	8	8
20.	25 c. multicoloured	15	20
21.	50 c. multicoloured	30	35
22.	75 c. multicoloured	40	45
23.	$1 multicoloured	50	55

1974. U.P.U. Cent. As Nos. 631 and 633/5 of Grenada inscr. "GRENADA GRENADINES".

25.	8 c. multicoloured	8	8
26.	25 c. multicoloured	15	20
27.	35 c. multicoloured	26	25
28.	$1 multicoloured	50	55

1974. Sir Winston Churchill. Birth Cent. As Nos. 637/8 of Grenada inscr. "GRENADA GRENADINES".

30.	35 c. multicoloured	15	15
31.	$2 multicoloured	85	90

1974. Christmas. As Nos. 640/7 of Grenada, but inscr. " GRENADA GRENADINES " and background colours changed.

33. **67.**	½ c. multicoloured ..	5	5
34. –	1 c. multicoloured ..	5	5
35. –	2 c. multicoloured ..	5	5
36. –	3 c. multicoloured ..	5	5
37. –	10 c. multicoloured ..	8	8
38.	25 c. multicoloured ..	15	20
39. –	50 c. multicoloured ..	30	35
40. –	$1 multicoloured ..	50	55

1975. Big Game Fishing. As Nos. 668/75 of Grenada inscr. " GRENADA GRENADINES " and background colours changed.

42. **69.**	½ c. multicoloured ..	5	5
43.	1 c. multicoloured ..	5	5
44.	2 c. multicoloured ..	5	5
45.	10 c. multicoloured ..	8	8
46.	25 c. multicoloured ..	15	20
47.	50 c. multicoloured ..	30	35
48.	70 c. multicoloured ..	40	40
49.	$1 multicoloured ..	50	55

1975. Flowers. As Nos. 678/85 of Grenada inscr. " GRENADINES ".

51.	½ c. multicoloured	5	5
52.	1 c. multicoloured	5	5
53.	2 c. multicoloured	5	5
54.	3 c. multicoloured	5	5
55.	10 c. multicoloured ..	8	8
56.	25 c. multicoloured ..	15	20
57.	50 c. multicoloured ..	30	35
58.	$1 multicoloured	50	55

CANCELLED REMAINDERS. Some of the following issues have been remaindered; cancelled-to-order at a fraction of their face value. For all practical purposes these are indistinguishable from genuine postally used copies. Our used quotations which are indicated by an asterisk are the same for cancelled-to-order or postally used copies.

1. " The Crucifixion " (Titian).

1975. Easter. Paintings showing Crucifixion and Deposition by artists listed. Multicoloured.

60.	½ c. Type **1**	5	5*
61.	1 c. Giotto	5	5*
62.	2 c. Tintoretto	5	5*
63.	3 c. Cranach	5	5*
64.	35 c. Caravaggio	15	8*
65.	75 c. Tiepolo	35	8*
66.	$2 Velasquez	80	8*

2. " Lorenzo de Medici ".

1975. Michelangelo. 500th Birth Anniv. Multicoloured.

68.	½ c. Type **2**	5	5*
69.	1 c. " Delphic Sybil " ..	5	5*
70.	2 c. " Giuliano de Medici "	5	5*
71.	40 c. " The Creation " (detail)	15	8*
72.	50 c. " Lorenzo de Medici " (different)	20	8*
73.	75 c. " Artist at work " ..	35	8*
74.	$2 " Head of Christ " ..	80	8*

1975. Butterflies. As T **76** of Grenada inscr. " GRENADINES ". Multicoloured.

76.	½ c. Emperor	5	5
77.	1 c. Queen	5	5
78.	2 c. Tiger Pierid	5	5
79.	35 c. Cracker	15	15
80.	45 c. Scarce Bamboo Page	20	20
81.	75 c. Apricot	30	35
82.	$2 Purple King Shoemaker	80	90

3. Progress " Standard " Badge.

1975. 14th World Scout Jamboree, Norway. Multicoloured.

84. ½ c. Type 3 .. .. .. 5 5
85. 1 c. Boatman's badge .. 5 5
86. 2 c. Coxswain's badge .. 5 5
87. 35 c. Interpreter's badge .. 15 15
88. 45 c. Ambulance badge .. 20 20
89. 75 c. Chief Scout's award .. 30 35
90. $2 Queen's Scout award .. 80 90

4. " The Surrender of Lord Cornwallis."

1976. American Revolution (1976) (1st issue). Bicent. Multicoloured.

92. ½ c. Type 4 .. .. 5 5*
93. 1 c. Minute-men 5 5*
94. 2 c. Paul Revere's ride .. 5 5*
95. 3 c. Battle of Bunker Hill 5 5*
96. 5 c. Fifer and drummer .. 5 5*
97. 45 c. Backwoodsman .. 20 8*
98. 75 c. Boston Tea Party .. 30 8*
99. $2 Naval engagement .. 80 8*
100. $2 George Washington .. 80 90
101. $2 White House and flags 80 90

Nos. 100/01 are larger, 35 × 60 mm.

5. Fencing.

1975. Pan-American Games, Mexico City. Multicoloured.

103. ½ c. Type 5 .. .. 5 5
104. 1 c. Hurdling 5 5
105. 2 c. Pole-vaulting .. 5 5
106. 35 c. Weightlifting .. 15 15
107. 45 c. Throwing the javelin 20 20
108. 75 c. Throwing the discus 30 35
109. $2 Diving 80 90

1975. Nos. 649/67 of Grenada additionally inscr. " GRENADINES ".

111. ½ c. Yachts, Port Saline .. 5 5
112. 1 c. Yacht Club race, St. George's 5 5
113. 2 c. Carneenage taxi .. 5 5
114. 3 c. Large working boats .. 5 5
115. 5 c. Deep-water dock, St. George's 5 5
116. 6 c. Cocoa beans in drying trays 5 5
117. 8 c. Nutmegs 5 5
118. 10 c. Rum distillery, River Antoine Estate, c. 1785 5 5
119. 12 c. Cocoa tree 5 5
120. 15 c. Fishermen at Fontenoy 5 5
121. 20 c. Parliament Building 8 8
122. 25 c. Fort George cannons 10 10
123. 35 c. Pearls Airport .. 12 15
124. 50 c. General Post Office .. 20 20
125. 75 c. Caribs Leap, Sauteurs Bay 20 25
126. $1 Careenage, St. George's 35 40
127. $2 St. George's Harbour by night 70 80
128. $3 Grand Anse beach .. 1·10 1·25
129. $5 Canoe Bay and Black Bay .. .. .. 1·75 2·00
130. $10 Sugar-loaf Island .. 3·50 4·00

6. " Virgin and Child " (Durer).

1975. Christmas. " Virgin and Child " paintings by Artists named. Mult.

131. ½ c. Type 6 .. .. .. 5 5
132. 1 c. Durer 5 5
133. 2 c. Correggio 5 5
134. 40 c. Botticelli 15 15
135. 50 c. Niccollo da Cremona 20 20
136. 75 c. Correggio 25 30
137. $2 Correggio 75 80

7. Bleeding Tooth.

1976. Shells. Multicoloured.

139. ½ c. Type 7 .. .. .. 5 5
140. 1 c. Wedge Cam 5 5
141. 2 c. Hawk Wing Conch .. 5 5
142. 3 c. " Distorsio clathrata " 5 5
143. 25 c. Scotch Bonnet .. 10 10
144. 50 c. King Helmet 20 20
145. 75 c. Queen Conch 20 25

8. Cocoa Thrush.

1976. Flora and Fauna. Multicoloured.

147. ½ c. " Lignum vitae " .. 5 5
148. 1 c. Type 8 .. .. .. 5 5
149. 2 c. Tarantula 5 5
150. 35 c. Hooded Tanager .. 15 15
151. 50 c. " Nyctaginsceae " .. 20 20
152. 75 c. Grenada Dove .. 30 30
153. $1 Marine Toad 35 40

9. Hooked Sailfish.

1976. Tourism. Multicoloured.

155. ½ c. Type 9 .. .. .. 5 5
156. 1 c. Careened schooner, Carriacou 5 5
157. 2 c. Carriacou Annual Regatta 5 5
158. 18 c. Boat building on Carriacou 5 8
159. 22 c. Workboat race, Carriacou Regatta .. 10 10
160. 75 c. Cruising off Petit Martinique 30 30
161. $1 Water skiing 35 40

10. Making a Camp Fire.

1976. Girl Guides in Grenada. 50th Anniv. Multicoloured.

163. ½ c. Type 10 .. .. 5 5
164. 1 c. First Aid 5 5
165. 2 c. Nature Study 5 5
166. 50 c. Cooking 20 25
167. $1 Sketching 40 45

11. " Christ Mocked " (Bosch).

1976. Easter. Multicoloured.

169. ½ c. Type 11 .. .. 5 5
170. 1 c. " Christ Crucified " (Antonello da Messina) 5 5
171. 2 c. " Adoration of the Trinity " (Durer) .. 5 5
172. 3 c. " Lamentation of Christ " (Durer) .. 5 5
173. 35 c. " The Entombment " (Van der Weyden) .. 15 15

12. Frigate " South Carolina ".

1976. American Revolution (2nd issue). Bicent. Multicoloured.

176. ½ c. Type 12 .. .. 5 5
177. 1 c. Schooner " Lee " .. 5 5
178. 2 c. H.M.S. " Roebuck " 5 5
179. 35 c. " Andrea Doria " .. 15 15
180. 50 c. Sloop " The Providence " 20 25
181. $1 American flagship " Alfred " 40 50
182. $2 Frigate " Confederacy " 80 90

13. Piper " Apache ".

1976. Aeroplanes. Multicoloured.

184. ½ c. Type 13 .. .. 5 5
185. 1 c. Beech " Twin Bonanza " 5 5
186. 2 c. D.H. " Twin Otter " 5 5
187. 40 c. Britten Morman " Islander " 15 20
188. 50 c. D.H. " Heron " .. 20 25
189. $2 H.S. " 748 " .. .. 90 1·00

14. Cycling.

1976. Olympic Games, Montreal. Multicoloured.

191. ½ c. Type 14 .. .. 5 5
192. 1 c. Pommel horse .. 5 5
193. 2 c. Hurdling 5 5
194. 35 c. Shot putting .. 15 20
195. 45 c. Diving 20 20
196. 75 c. Sprinting 30 35
197. $2 Rowing 80 90

15. " Virgin and Child " (Cima).

1976. Christmas. Multicoloured.

199. ½ c. Type 15 .. .. 5 5
200. 1 c. " The Nativity " (Romanio) 5 5
201. 2 c. " The Nativity " (Romanino) (different) 5 5
202. 35 c. " Adoration of the Kings " (Bruegal) .. 15 20
203. 50 c. " Madonna and Child " (Girolamo) 20 25
204. 75 c. " Adoration of the Magi " (Giorgione) (horiz.) 30 35
205. $2 " Adoration of the Kings " (Fra Angelico) (horiz.) .. 80 90

GRENADINES OF ST. VINCENT BC

Part of a group of islands south of St. Vincent which include Bequia, Mustique, Canouan and Union.

1973. Royal Wedding. As T 16 of Anguilla. Multicoloured. Background colours given.

1. 25 c. green 12 15
2. $1 brown 45 45

1974. Nos. 286/300 of St. Vincent optd. **GRENADINES OF.** Multicoloured.

3. 1 c. Green Heron 5 5
24. 2 c. Bullfinches 5 5
25. 3 c. St. Vincent Parrots .. 5 5
6. 4 c. Soufriere Bird (vert.) .. 5 5
7. 5 c. Ramier Pigeon (vert.) .. 5 5
8. 6 c. Bananaquits 8 8
9. 8 c. Hummingbird 8 8
10. 10 c. Mangrove Cuckoo (vert.) 8 8
11. 12 c. Black Hawk (vert.) .. 10 10
12. 20 c. Bare-eyed Thrush .. 15 15
13. 25 c. Prince 20 20
14. 50 c. Blue Hooded Euphonia 30 30
15. $1 Barn Owl (vert.) .. 55 60
16. $2·50 Crested Elaenia (vert.) 1·40 1·50
17. $5 Ruddy Quail Dove .. 2·75 3·00

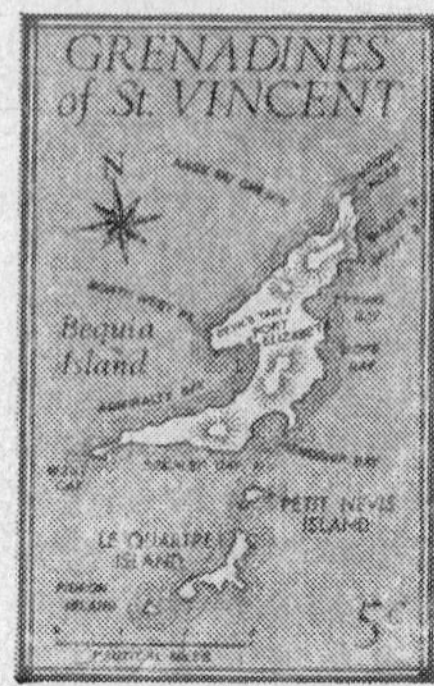

1. Map of Bequia.

1974. Maps (1st series).

18. 1. 5 c. black, grn. & deep grn. 5 5
19. – 15 c. multicoloured .. 8 10
20. – 20 c. multicoloured .. 12 12
21. – 30 c. black, pink & red .. 15 15
22. – 40 c. blk., violet & purple 20 20
23. – $1 black, ultram. & blue 45 50

MAPS: 15 c. Prune Island. 20 c. Mayreau Island and Tobago Cays. 30 c. Mustique Island. 40 c. Union Island. $1 Canouan Island.

See also Nos. 85/8.

1974. U.P.U. Cent. As Nos. 392/5 of St. Vincent.

26. 2 c. multicoloured 5 5
27. 15 c. multicoloured 10 12
28. 40 c. multicoloured 25 25
29. $1 multicoloured 50 55

2. Boat-building.

1974. Bequia Island. Multicoloured.

34. 5 c. Type 2 .. .. .. 5 5
31. 30 c. Careening at Port Elizabeth 20 25
32. 35 c. Admiralty Bay .. 25 25
33. $1 Fishing-boat race .. 50 55

3. Atlantic Thorny Oyster.

1975. Shells and molluscs. Multicoloured.

35. 1 c. Type 3 .. .. .. 5 5
36. 2 c. Zigzag Scallop 5 5
37. 3 c. Reticulated Helmet .. 5 5
38. 4 c. Music Volute 5 5
39. 5 c. Amber Pen Shell .. 5 5
40. 6 c. Angular Triton 5 5
41. 8 c. Flame Helmet 5 5
42. 10 c. Caribbean Olive .. 5 5
43. 12 c. Common Sundial .. 5 5
44. 15 c. Glory of the Atlantic Cone 5 5
45. 20 c. Flame Auger 8 8
46. 25 c. King Venus 10 10
47. 35 c. Long-spined Star-shell 12 15
48. 45 c. Speckled Tellin .. 15 20

No.	Description	Unused	Used
49.	50 c. Rooster Tail Conch	20	20
50.	$1 Green Star Shell	35	40
51.	$2·50 Incomparable Cone	90	1·00
52.	$5 Rough File Clam	1·75	2·00
52a.	$10 Measled Cowrie	3·50	4·00

Nos. 38/42, 45, 47 and 49/50 come with and without an imprint below the design.

1974. Sir Winston Churchill. Birth Centenary. As Nos. 403/6 of St. Vincent, but inscr. "GRENADINES OF ST. VINCENT", and values (Nos. 53/5) and colours changed.

No.	Description	Unused	Used
53. 45.	5 c. multicoloured	12	15
54. –	40 c. multicoloured	25	25
55. –	50 c. multicoloured	30	30
56. –	$1 multicoloured	50	55

4. Cotton House, Mustique.

1975. Mustique Island. Multicoloured.

No.	Description	Unused	Used
57.	5 c. Type 4	5	5
58.	35 c. "Blue Waters" Endeavour Bay	15	15
59.	45 c. Endeavour Bay	20	20
60.	$1 "Les Jolies Eaux", Gelliceaux Bay	45	45

5. Soldier Martinique.

1975. Butterflies. Multicoloured.

No.	Description	Unused	Used
61.	3 c. Type 5	5	5
62.	5 c. Silver-spotted Flambeau	5	5
63.	35 c. Gold Rim	15	20
64.	45 c. Bright Blue and Donkey's Eye	20	20
65.	$1 Biscuit	40	45

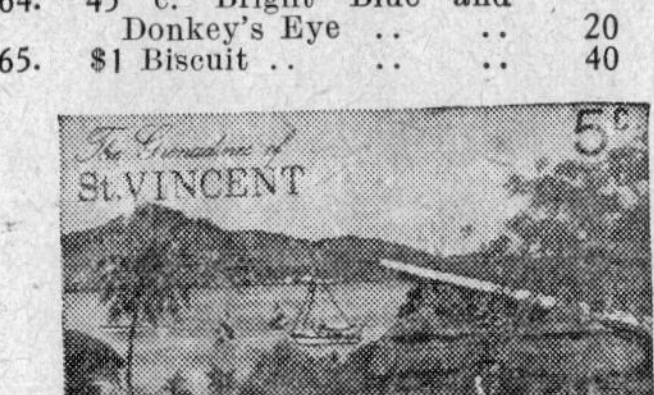

6. Resort Pavilion.

1975. Petit St. Vincent. Multicoloured.

No.	Description	Unused	Used
66.	5 c. Type 6	5	5
67.	35 c. The Harbour	15	20
68.	45 c. The Jetty	20	25
69.	$1 Sailing in coral lagoon	50	55

7. Ecumenical Church, Mustique.

1975. Christmas. Multicoloured.

No.	Description	Unused	Used
70.	5 c. Type 7	5	5
71.	25 c. Catholic Church, Union Island	12	15
72.	50 c. Catholic Church, Bequia	20	25
73.	$1 Anglican Church, Bequia	40	45

8. Sunset Scene.

1976. Union Island. Multicoloured.

No.	Description	Unused	Used
74.	5 c. Type 8	5	5
75.	35 c. Customs and Post Office, Clifton	15	20
76.	45 c. Anglican Church, Ashton	20	20
77.	$1 Mailboat, Clifton Harbour	40	45

9. Staghorn Coral.

1976. Corals. Multicoloured.

No.	Description	Unused	Used
78.	5 c. Type 9	5	5
79.	35 c. Elkhorn coral	15	15
80.	45 c. Pillar coral	20	20
81.	$1 Brain coral	40	45

10. 25 c. Bicentennial Coin.

1976. American Revolution. Bicent.

No.	Description	Unused	Used
82. 10.	25 c. silver, black and blue	12	15
83. –	50 c. 50 c. silver, blk. and red	20	25
84. –	$1 silver, blk. and mauve	40	45

DESIGNS: 50 c. Half-dollar coin. $1 One dollar coin.

1976. Maps (2nd series).

No.	Description	Unused	Used
85. –	5 c. blk., dark grn. & grn.	5	5
86. –	10 c. black, green & blue	5	5
87. –	35 c. black, brown & red	15	15
88. –	45 c. black, red & orange	20	20

Nos. 85/8 exist in 7 different designs to each value as follows: A. Bequia, B. Canouan, C. Mayreau, D. Mustique. E. Petit St. Vincent. F. Prune. G. Union. To indicate any particular design use the appropriate catalogue No. together with the prefix for the island concerned.

GRIQUALAND WEST BC

A Br. colony, later annexed to the Cape of Good Hope and now part of South Africa, whose stamps it uses.

1874. Stamp of Cape of Good Hope ("Hope" seated) with pen-and-ink surch.

No.	Description	Unused	Used
1. 3.	1d. on 4d. blue	£200	£275

1877. Stamps of Cape of Good Hope ("Hope" seated) optd. **G.W.**

No.	Description	Unused	Used
2. 4.	1d. red	£110	25·00
3.	4d. blue	75·00	18·00

1877. Stamps of Cape of Good Hope ("Hope" seated) optd. **G** in various types.

No.	Description	Unused	Used
92. 4.	½d grey	2·00	1·75
93.	1d. red	2·00	1·00
17. 3.	4d. blue	20·00	2·75
61. 4.	4d. blue	16·00	4·00
31. 3.	6d. violet	11·00	5·00
96.	1s. green	12·00	1·00
97. 4.	5s. orange	55·00	2·00

GUADELOUPE O2

An overseas department of France, formerly a Fr. colony in the W. Indies, consisting of a group of islands between Antigua and Dominica. Now uses the stamps of France.

1884. Fr. Colonies, "Peace and Commerce" type, surch. **G.P.E.** and figures of value in frame.

No.	Description	Unused	Used
6. 8.	20 on 30 c. brown	8·00	7·00
7.	25 on 35 c. blk. on orange	8·00	7·00

1889. Fr. Colonies, "Commerce" type, surch. **GUADELOUPE** and value in figures and words in plain frame.

No.	Description	Unused	Used
8. 9.	3 c. on 20 c. red on green	45	45
9.	15 c. on 20 c. red on green	4·50	4·00
10.	25 c. on 20 c. red on green	4·50	3·25

1889. Fr. Colonies, "Commerce" type, surch. **GUADELOUPE** and value in figures and words in ornamental frame.

No.	Description	Unused	Used
11. 9.	5 c. on 1 d. black on blue	1·75	1·75
12.	10 c. on 40 c. red on yellow	3·75	3·25
13.	15 c. on 20 c. red on green	3·50	2·75
14.	25 c. on 30 c. brown	5·50	4·50

1890. French Colonies, "Commerce" type surch. **5 c.** over **G.P.E.**

No.	Description	Unused	Used
15. 9.	5 c. on 10 c. black on lilac	1·75	1·40
16.	5 c. on 1 f. olive	1·75	1·40

1891. French Colonies, "Ceres" and "Commerce" types, optd. **GUADELOUPE.**

No.	Description	Unused	Used
21. 9.	1 c. black on blue	12	12
22.	2 c. brown on yellow	20	15
23.	4 c. claret on grey	55	55
24.	5 c. green	65	55
25.	10 c. black on lilac	2·00	1·60
26.	15 c. blue	5·00	45
27.	20 c. red on green	4·50	3·25
28.	25 c. black on red	4·50	45
19. 7.	30 c. brown	55·00	55·00
29. 9.	30 c. brown	4·50	8·50
30.	35 c. black on yellow	9·50	9·50
31.	40 c. red on yellow	7·00	6·00
32.	75 c. red	18·00	15·00
20. 7.	80 c. red	£170	£170
33. 9.	1 f. olive	11·00	11·00

1892. "Tablet" key-type inscr. "GUADELOUPE ET DEPENDANCES".

No.	Description	Unused	Used
34. D.	1 c. black on blue	15	10
35.	2 c. brown on yellow	12	10
37.	4 c. claret on grey	15	12
38.	5 c. green	40	8
39.	10 c. black on lilac	1·50	35
49.	10 c. red	70	15
40.	15 c. blue	1·10	8
50.	15 c. grey	1·25	8
41.	20 c. red on green	65	50
42.	25 c. black on red	85	20
51.	25 c. blue	15·00	14·00
43.	30 c. brown	2·25	1·75
44.	40 c. red on yellow	2·75	1·60
45.	50 c. red	4·50	3·50
52.	50 c. brown on blue	4·50	3·50
46.	75 c. brown on yellow	4·00	3·50
47.	1 f. olive	4·00	3·75

1903. "Tablet" key-type surch. **G & D** or **G et D** and value in figures

No.	Description	Unused	Used
53. D.	5 on 30 c. brown	50	50
54.	10 on 40 c. red on yellow	80	80
55.	15 on 50 c. red	1·50	1·40
56.	40 on 1 f. olive	1·40	1·40
57c.	1 f. on 75 c. brn. on yell.	5·50	5·50

1904. Same stamps optd. **1903** in frame.

No.	Description	Unused	Used
59d. D.	40 on 1 f. olive	6·00	7·50
60c.	1 f. on 75 c. brn. on yell.	11·00	11·00

1. Mount Houllemont, Basse-Terre.

2. La Soufriere.

3. Pointe-a-Pitre, Grande Terre.

1905.

No.	Description	Unused	Used
61. 1.	1 c. black on blue	5	5
62.	2 c. brown on yellow	5	5
63.	4 c. brown on grey	5	5
64.	5 c. green	10	8
83.	5 c. blue	5	5
65.	10 c. red	8	5
84.	10 c. green	5	5
85.	10 c. red on blue	5	5
66.	15 c. lilac	5	5
67. 2.	20 c. red on green	5	5
86.	20 c. green	5	5
68.	25 c. blue	5	5
87.	25 c. green	5	5
69.	30 c. black	40	20
88.	30 c. red	5	5
89.	30 c. olive on lilac	5	5
70.	35 c. black on yellow	5	5
71.	40 c. red on yellow	5	5
72.	45 c. brown on lilac	5	5
90.	45 c. red	5	5
73.	50 c. green on yellow	60	45
91.	50 c. blue	5	5
92.	50 c. mauve	5	5
93.	65 c. blue	5	5
74.	75 c. red on blue	8	5
75. 3.	1 f. black on green	10	8
94.	1 f. blue	5	5
76.	2 f. red on orange	15	15
77.	5 f. blue on orange	85	85

1912. "Tablet" key-type surch. in figures.

No.	Description	Unused	Used
78. D.	05 on 4 c. claret on grey	10	10
79.	05 on 30 c. brown	10	10
80.	10 on 40 c. red on yellow	15	15

1915. Surch. **5 c.** and red cross.

No.	Description	Unused	Used
81. 1.	10 c.+5 c. red	45	35
82.	15 c.+5 c. lilac	30	25

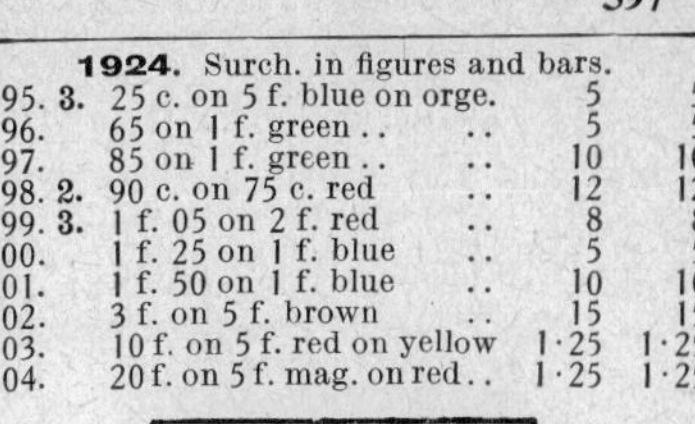

1924. Surch. in figures and bars.

No.	Description	Unused	Used
95. 3.	25 c. on 5 f. blue on orge.	5	5
96.	65 on 1 f. green	5	5
97.	85 on 1 f. green	10	10
98. 2.	90 c. on 75 c. red	12	12
99. 3.	1 f. 05 on 2 f. red	8	8
100.	1 f. 25 on 1 f. blue	5	5
101.	1 f. 50 on 1 f. blue	10	10
102.	3 f. on 5 f. brown	15	15
103.	10 f. on 5 f. red on yellow	1·25	1·25
104.	20 f. on 5 f. mag. on red	1·25	1·25

4. Sugar Refinery.

5. Saints Harbour.

6. Pointe-a-Pitre Harbour.

1928.

No.	Description	Unused	Used
105. 4.	1 c. mauve and yellow	5	5
106.	2 c. red and black	5	5
107.	3 c. mauve and yellow	5	5
108.	4 c. brown and olive	5	5
109.	5 c. green and red	5	5
110.	10 c. blue and brown	5	5
111.	15 c. black and red	5	5
112.	20 c. brown and mauve	5	5
113. 5.	25 c. olive and blue	5	5
114.	30 c. green	5	5
115.	35 c. green	5	5
116.	40 c. mauve and yellow	5	5
117.	45 c. blue and purple	5	5
118.	45 c. green	5	5
119.	50 c. red and green	5	5
120.	55 c. red and blue	5	5
121.	60 c. red and blue	5	5
122.	65 c. red and black	5	5
123.	70 c. red and black	5	5
124.	75 c. green and red	5	10
125.	80 c. brown and red	5	5
126.	90 c. red	30	25
127.	90 c. blue and red	8	8
128. 6.	1 f. blue and red	50	15
129.	1 f. orange and red	5	10
130.	1 f. brown and blue	5	5
131.	1 f. 05 red and blue	20	20
132.	1 f. 10 green and red	35	30
133.	1 f. 25 brown and blue	5	5
134.	1 f. 25 red	5	5
135.	1 f. 40 mauve and blue	8	8
136.	1 f. 50 blue	5	5
137.	1 f. 60 orange and mauve	5	5
138.	1 f. 75 brown and mauve	45	25
139.	1 f. 75 blue	55	50
140.	2 f. brown and green	5	5
141.	2 f. 25 blue	5	5
142.	2 f. 50 green and orange	5	5
143.	3 f. black and brown	5	5
144.	5 f. red and blue	5	5
145.	10 f. black and mauve	8	8
146.	20 f. red and green	12	12

1931. "Colonial Exhibition" key-types inscr. "GUADELOUPE".

No.	Description	Unused	Used
147. E.	40 c. black and green	45	45
148. F.	50 c. black and mauve	45	45
149. G.	90 c. black and red	65	65
150. H.	1 f. 50 black and blue	65	65

7. Richelieu founding W. India Co., 1635.

8. Victor Hugues and Corsairs 1793.

1935. West Indies Tercent.

No.	Description	Unused	Used
151. 7.	40 c. brown	1·50	1·25
152.	50 c. red	1·50	1·25
153.	1 f. 50 blue	1·50	1·25
154. 8.	1 f. 75 magenta	1·50	1·25
155.	5 f. brown	1·50	1·25
156.	10 f. green	1·50	1·25

1937. International Exhibition, Paris. As Nos. 110/15 of Cameroun.

No.	Description	Unused	Used
157.	20 c. violet	15	15
158.	30 c. green	15	15
159.	40 c. red	15	15
160.	50 c. brown	15	15
161.	90 c. red	15	15
162.	1 f. 50 blue	15	15

1938. Int. Anti-Cancer Fund. As T **10** of Cameroun.
163. 1 f. 75+50 c. blue .. 1·50 1·50

1939. New York World's Fair. As T **11** of Cameroun.
164. 1 f. 25 red 10 10
165. 2 f. 25 blue 10 10

1939. 150th Anniv. of French Revolution. As T **16** of Cameroun.
166. 45 c.+25 c. green & black 90 90
167. 70 c.+30 c. brown & black 90 90
168. 90 c.+35 c. orge. & black 90 90
169. 1 f. 25+1 f. red & black.. 90 90
170. 2 f. 25+2 f. blue & black 90 90

1944. Mutual Aid and Red Cross Funds. As T **19** of Cameroun.
180. 5 f.+20 f. blue 10 10

1944. Surch. in figures and bars or **UN FRANC** (No. 175).

(a) On Nos. 164/5.
178. 40 c. on 1 f. 25 red .. 12 12
179. 40 c. on 2 f. 25 blue .. 12 12

(b) On Issue of 1928.
172. **5.** 40 c. on 35 c. green .. 8 8
173. 50 c. on 25 c. olive & bl. 5 5
174. 50 c. on 65 c. red & blk.. 8 8
175. 1 f. on 65 c. red and black 5 5
176. 1 f. on 90 c. red .. 12 12
177. 1 f. on 90 c. blue and red 8 8
171. **6.** 4 f. on 1 f. 05 red & blue 20 20

1945. Eboue. As T **20** of Cameroun.
181. 2 f. black 5 5
182. 25 f. green 8 8

9.

1945.
183. **9.** 10 c. blue and orange .. 5 5
184. 30 c. green and orange.. 5 5
185. 40 c. blue and red .. 5 5
186. 50 c. orange and green.. 5 5
187. 60 c. grey and blue .. 5 5
188. 70 c. grey and green .. 5 5
189. 80 c. green and yellow.. 5 5
190. 1 f. purple and green .. 5 5
191. 1 f. 20 mauve and green 5 5
192. 1 f. 50 brown and red .. 5 5
193. 2 f. red and blue .. 5 5
194. 2 f. 40 red and green .. 10 10
195. 3 f. brown and blue .. 5 5
196. 4 f. blue and orange .. 5 5
197. 4 f. 50 orange and green 5 5
198. 5 f. violet and green .. 5 5
199. 10 f. green and mauve.. 8 8
200. 15 f. grey and orange .. 10 10
201. 20 f. grey and orange .. 12 12

1945. Air. As T **18** of Cameroun.
202. 50 f. green 15 15
203. 100 f. claret 20 20

1946. Air. Victory. As T **21** of Cameroun.
204. 8 f. brown 10 10

1946. Air. From Chad to the Rhine. As T **22** of Cameroun.
205. **9.** 5 f. olive 15 15
206. 10 f. blue 15 15
207. 15 f. purple 15 15
208. 20 f. claret 15 15
209. 25 f. black 15 15
210. 50 f. brown 20 20

10. Woman and Port Basse Terre.

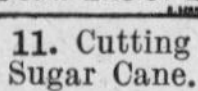

11. Cutting Sugar Cane.

12. Guadeloupe Woman.

13. Aeroplane, Woman and Boats.

1947.
211. **10.** 10 c. lake (postage) .. 5 5
212. 30 c. brown 5 5
213. 50 c. green 5 5
214. **11.** 60 c. brown 5 5
215. 1 f. red 5 5
216. 1 f. 50 blue 12 12
217. – 2 f. green 20 20
218. – 2 f. 50 red 8 8
219. – 3 f. blue 20 20
220. – 4 f. violet 12 12
221. – 5 f. green 12 12
222. – 6 f. red 12 12
223. – 10 f. blue 12 20
224. – 15 f. purple 20 20
225. 20 f. red 25 20
226. **12.** 25 f. green 40 40
227. 40 f. orange 45 45
228. – 50 f. purple (air) .. 95 85
229. 100 f. blue 95 85
230. **13.** 200 f. red .. .. 1·25 1·10

DESIGNS—As T **12**: 2 f. to 3 f. Woman carrying pineapples. 4 f. to 6 f. Guadeloupe woman facing left. 10 f. to 20 f. Picking coffee. As T **13**: 50 f. Aeroplane over village. 100 f. Flying-boat landing in bay.

POSTAGE DUE STAMPS.

D 1.

D 2.

1876.
D 1. **D 1.** 15 c. black on blue .. 6·50 4·50
D 2. 25 c. black on white .. £140 £120
D 3. 30 c. black on white .. 12·00 8·50
D 4. 40 c. black on blue .. — £4000
D 5. 40 c. black on white .. £170 £140

1884.
D 8. **D 2.** 5 c. black on white .. 2·75 2·25
D 9. 10 c. black on blue .. 8·50 5·50
D 10. 15 c. black on lilac .. 12·00 7·50
D 11. 20 c. black on red .. 20·00 14·00
D 12. 30 c. black on yellow 19·00 17·00
D 13. 35 c. black on grey .. 5·00 4·00
D 14. 50 c. black on green 2·50 2·50

1903. Postage Due stamps of French Colonies surch. **G & D 30** in frame,
D 59. **D 1.** 30 on 60 c. brown on yellow .. 42·00 42·00
D 61. 30 on 1 f. red on yell. 50·00 50·00

D 3. Gustavia Bay, Island of St. Bartholomew.

D 4. Alee Dumanoir, Capesterre.

D 5. Palms and Houses.

1905.
D 63. **D 3.** 5 c. blue 5 5
D 64. 10 c. brown 8 8
D 65. 15 c. green 8 8
D 66. 20 c. brown on yellow 8 8
D 67. 30 c. red 8 8
D 68. 50 c. black 25 25
D 69. 60 c. orange 10 10
D 70. 1 f. lilac 25 25

1926. Surch. in figures and words and **a percevoir.**
D 105. **D 3.** 2 f. on 1 f. grey .. 8 8
D 106. 3 f. on 1 f. blue .. 30 30

1928.
D 147. **D 4.** 2 c. mauve & brown 5 5
D 148. 4 c. brown and blue 5 5
D 149. 5 c. brown and green 5 5
D 150. 10 c. yellow & mauve 5 5
D 151. 15 c. olive and red.. 5 5
D 152. 20 c. olive and orange 5 5
D 153. 25 c. green and red.. 5 5
D 154. 30 c. yellow and blue 5 5
D 155. 50 c. red and brown 5 5
D 156. 60 c. black and blue 8 8
D 157. 1 f. red and green .. 25 25
D 158. 2 f. red and brown.. 10 10
D 159. 3 f. blue and mauve 12 12

1947.
D 231. **D 5.** 10 c. black 5 5
D 232. 30 c. green 5 5
D 233. 50 c. blue 5 5
D 234. 1 f. green 5 5
D 235. 2 f. blue 8 8
D 236. 3 f. brown 8 8
D 237. 4 f. purple 15 15
D 238. 5 f. violet 12 12
D 239. 10 f. red 12 12
D 240. 20 f. purple.. .. 20 20

INDEX

Countries can be quickly located by referring to the index at the end of this volume.

GUAM O3

An island in the Pacific Ocean belonging to the United States. Now uses U.S. stamps.

1899. Stamps of U.S.A. optd. **GUAM.**
1. 1 c. green (No. 283) .. 2·40 3·00
2. 2 c. red (No. 284C) .. 2·25 2·75
4. 3 c. violet (No. 271) .. 12·00 16·00
5. 4 c. brown (No. 285) .. 11·00 16·00
6. 5 c. blue (No. 286) .. 3·50 4·00
7. 6 c. brown (No. 287A) .. 11·00 4·00
8. 8 c. purple (No. 275) .. 8·00 12·00
9. 10 c. brown (No. 289) .. 5·00 6·00
11. 15 c. olive (No. 290) .. 12·00 16·00
12. 50 c. orange (No. 278A) .. 20·00 20·00
13. $1 black (No. 279) .. 32·00 32·00

SPECIAL DELIVERY STAMP

1899. Special Delivery stamp of U.S.A. optd. **GUAM.**
E 15. S **1.** 10 c. blue (No. E 5).. 20·00 20·00

GUANACASTE O1

A province of Costa Rica whose stamps it now uses.

Stamps of Costa Rica optd.

1885. Stamps of 1883 optd. **Guanacaste** or **GUANACASTE.**
G 1. **2.** 1 c. green 80 80
G 36. 2 c. red 55 55
G 3. 5 c. violet .. .. 3·75 80
G 4. 10 c. orange .. .. 2·50 2·50
G 5. 40 c. blue .. .. 5·00 5·00

1887. Stamps of 1887 optd. **Guanacaste.**
G 37. **3.** 5 c. violet .. .. 4·50 90
G 39. 10 c. orange 55 55

1887. Fiscal stamps optd. **Guanacaste** or **GUANACASTE.**
G 44. 1 c. red .. .. 35·00 35·00
G 41. 2 c. blue .. .. 7·00 7·00

1889. Stamps of 1889 optd. **GUANACASTE.**
G 62. **4.** 1 c. brown 30 30
G 63. 2 c. blue 30 30
G 64. 5 c. orange 30 30
G 65. 10 c. lake 30 30
G 56. 20 c. green 30 20
G 57. 50 c. red 80 80
G 59. 1 p. blue .. .. 1·50 1·50
G 60. 2 p. violet .. .. 1·50 1·50
G 61. 5 p. olive .. .. 8·00 7·00

GUATEMALA O2

A republic of Central America; independent since 1847.

1871. 100 centavos = 8 reales = 1 peso.
1927. 100 centavos de quetzal = 1 quetzal

1. Arms.

2.

3. Liberty.

1871.
1. **1.** 1 c. bistre .. .. 45 6·00
2. 5 c. brown .. .. 1·40 3·50
3. 10 c. blue .. .. 2·25 3·25
4. 20 c. red .. .. 2·00 4·75

1873.
5. **2.** 4 r. mauve .. .. £160 32·00
6. 1 p. yellow .. .. 65·00 48·00

1875. Various frames.
7. **3.** ¼ r. black .. .. 4·00 60
8. ½ r. green .. .. 4·00 60
9. 1 r. blue .. .. 4·00 60
10. 2 r. red .. .. 4·00 60

4. Native Indian.

5. Quetzal.

1878.
11. **4.** ½ r. green .. .. 60 1·75
12. 2 r. red .. .. 85 2·25
13. 4 r. mauve .. .. 85 2·75
14. 1 p. yellow .. .. 1·10 5·50

1879.
15. **5.** ¼ r. green and brown .. 1·40 1·75
16. 1 r. green and black .. 2·00 2·25

For similar stamps but inscr. differently see Nos. 549/j.

1881. Surch.
17. **5.** 1 c. on ¼ r. green & brown 3·75 4·25
18. **4.** 5 c. on ½ r. green .. 3·75 4·25
19. **5.** 10 c. on 1 r. green & black 5·00 7·50
20. **4.** 20 c. on 2 r. red .. 20·00 23·00

1881. As T **5** inscr. "UNION POSTAL UNIVERSAL—GUATEMALA". Centres in green.
21. **5.** 1 c. black 45 45
22. 2 c. brown.. .. 45 45
23. 5 c. red .. .. 1·00 60
24. 10 c. lilac 45 45
25. 20 c. yellow 45 50

7. President J. R. Barios.

Correos Nacionales
150 c. 150 c.
Guatemala.
150 c. 150 c.
150 Ctavos.
(8.)

1886. Railway stamp various surch. as T **8.**
26. **7.** 25 c. on 1 p. red 20 20
27. 50 c. on 1 p. red 20 20
28. 75 c. on 1 p. red 20 20
29. 100 c. on 1 p. red 35 50
30. 150 c. on 1 p. red 35 35

9. Arms of Guatemala.

10. Portrait on right Pres. J. M. R. Barrios.

1886.
43a. **9.** 1 c. blue 35 20
44. 2 c. brown 60 20
46. 5 c. violet 85 20
47. 6 c. mauve 85 20
48. 10 c. red 85 20
49. 20 c. green .. .. 1·75 45
50. 25 c. orange .. .. 3·00 60
37. 50 c. olive .. .. 6·00 2·25
38. 75 c. rose .. .. 6·50 1·75
39. 100 c. brown .. .. 6·50 1·10
40. 150 c. blue .. .. 8·00 1·75
41. 200 c. yellow .. .. 8·00 1·75

See also Nos. 101/9.

1886. Surch. **PROVISIONAL 1886 1 UN CENTAVO.**
42. **9.** 1 c. on 2 c. brown .. 1·40 1·75

1894. Surch. **1894** and bar and value.
55. **9.** 1 c. on 2 c. brown .. 45 45
51. 2 c. on 100 c. brown .. 2·50 2·50
57. 6 c. on 150 c. blue .. 2·50 2·50
53. 10 c. on 75 c. rose .. 2·75 2·75
54. 10 c. on 200 c. yellow .. 2·25 1·75

1895. Surch. **1895 1 CENTAVO** and bar.
59. **9.** 1 c. on 5 c. violet .. 30 25

1897. Central American Exhibition.
62. **10.** 1 c. black on grey .. 30 30
63. 2 c. black on green .. 30 30
64. 6 c. black on orange .. 30 30
65. 10 c. black on blue .. 30 30
66. 12 c. black on red .. 50 50
67. 18 c. black on white .. 5·50 5·50
68. 20 c. black on red .. 60 60
69. 25 c. black on brown .. 60 60
70. 50 c. black on brown .. 60 60
71. 75 c. black on blue .. 32·00 32·00
72. 100 c. black on green .. 60 60
73. 150 c. black on pink .. 55·00 55·00
74. 200 c. black on mauve .. 60 60
75. 500 c. black on green .. 60 60

1898. Surch. **1898** and value in words.
76. **10.** 1 c. on 12 c. black on red 50 50

1898. Surch. **1898** and bar and value.
77. **9.** 1 c. on 5 c. violet .. 55 55
78. 1 c. on 25 c. orange .. 1·75 1·75
79. 1 c. on 50 c. olive .. 1·10 1·10
80. 1 c. on 75 c. rose .. 1·10 1·10
81. 6 c. on 5 c. violet .. 1·75 30
82. 6 c. on 10 c. red .. 6·50 6·50
83. 6 c. on 20 c. green .. 2·50 2·50
84. 6 c. on 100 c. brown .. 2·50 2·50
85. 6 c. on 150 c. blue .. 2·50 2·50
86. 6 c. on 200 c. yellow .. 2·50 2·50
87. 10 c. on 20 c. green .. 2·50 2·50

11.

12.

1898. Fiscal stamps dated "1898" as T **11** surch. **CORREOS NACIONALES** and value.
90. **11.** 1 c. on 10 c. green .. 40 40
91. 2 c. on 1 c. rose .. .. 1·75 1·75
92. 2 c. on 5 c. violet .. 60 60
93. 2 c. on 10 c. green .. 3·25 3·25
94. 2 c. on 25 c. red .. .. 5·00 5·00
95. 2 c. on 50 c. blue .. 6·00 6·00
96. 6 c. on 1 p. violet .. 1·75 1·75
97. 6 c. on 5 p. blue .. 4·25 4·25
98. 6 c. on 10 p. green .. 4·25 4·25

1898. Fiscal stamps as T 12 optd. **CORREOS NACIONALES** or surch. **2 CENTAVOS** also.
88. **12.** 1 c. blue 60 60
89. 2 c. on 1 c. blue 85 85

1899. Surch. **Un 1 Centavo 1899.**
99. **9.** 1 c. on 5 c. violet .. 20 15

1900. Surch. **1900 1 CENTAVO.**
100. **9.** 1 c. on 10 c. red 25 25

1900.
101. **9.** 1 c. green 20 15
102. 2 c. red 20 15
103. 5 c. blue 85 30
104. 6 c. green 25 15
105. 10 c. brown .. .. 1·10 20
106. 20 c. mauve .. .. 2·25 2·25
107. 20 c. brown .. .. 3·00 3·00
108. 25 c. yellow .. .. 2·25 2·25
109. 25 c. green .. .. 3·25 3·25

1901. Surch. **1901** and value.
110. **9.** 1 c. on 20 c. green .. 60 60
111. 1 c. on 25 c. orange .. 45 45
112. 2 c. on 20 c. green .. 1·10 1·10

1902. Fiscal stamp surch. **CORREOS NACIONALES 1902** and value in figures and words.
113. **12.** 1 c. on 1 c. blue .. 85 85
114. 2 c. on 1 c. blue .. 85 85

1902. Fiscal stamp, dated "1898", surch. **CORREOS 1902 Seis 6 Cts.**
115. **11.** 6 c. on 25 c. red .. 1·10 1·10

13. Arms.  **14.** J. Rufino Barrios.

18. Signing the Declaration of Independence.  **25.** President M. E. Cabrera.

1902. Inscr. "U.P.U. 1902".
116. **13.** 1 c. purple and green .. 10 5
117. **14.** 2 c. black and red .. 10 5
118a. – 5 c. black and blue .. 10 5
119. – 6 c. green and yellow .. 12 5
120. 10 c. blue and orange .. 12 5
121. **18.** 12½ c. black and blue .. 15 10
122. 20 c. black and claret .. 25 12
141. – 25 c. black and blue .. 25 15
123. – 50 c. blue and brown .. 15 10
124. – 75 c. black and lilac .. 30 12
125. – 1 p. black and brown .. 35 12
126. – 2 p. black and orange .. 35 25
142. **25.** 5 p. black and red .. 55 55

DESIGNS—HORIZ. 5 c. Museum. 6 c. Temple of Minerva. 10 c. Lake Amatitlan. 20 c. Cathedral. 25 c. G.P.O. 50 c. Columbus Theatre. 75 c. Artillery Barracks. 1 p. Columbus Monument. 2 p. Native School.

1903. Surch. **1903. 25 CENTAVOS.**
127. **9.** 25 c. on 1 c. green .. 55 25
128. 25 c. on 2 c. red 80 25
129. 25 c. on 6 c. green .. 1·10 55
130. 25 c. on 10 c. brown .. 5·00 2·50
131. 25 c. on 75 c. rose .. 6·00 6·00
132. 25 c. on 150 c. blue .. 6·00 6·00
133. 25 c. on 200 c. yellow .. 8·00 8·00

1908. Surch. **1908** and value in figures and words.
134. – 1 c. on 10 c. blue and orange (No. 120) .. 30 30
135. **18.** 2 c. on 12½ c. blk. & blue 30 30
136. – 6 c. on 20 c. black and claret (No. 122) .. 25 25

1909. Surch **1909** and value in figures and words.
137. – 2 c. on 75 c. black and lilac (No. 124) .. 40 40
138. – 6 c. on 50 c. blue and brown (No. 123) .. 20 20
139. – 12½ c. on 2 p. black and orange (No. 126) .. 45 45

ILLUSTRATIONS
British Commonwealth and all overprints and surcharges are FULL SIZE. Foreign Countries have been reduced to ¾-LINEAR.

26. M. G. Granados.

1910. Granados Cent.
140. **26.** 6 c. black and bistre .. 30 25

1911. Surch. **Correos de Guatemala 1911** and value.
144. – 2 c. on 5 c. (No. 118a) .. 1·10 60
145. – 6 c. on 10 c. (No. 120) .. 80 80

1911. Surch. **1911 Un Centavo.**
143. **26.** 1 c. on 6 c. black & bis. 8·50 2·50

1912. Surch. **1912** and value.
146. – 1 c. on 20 c. (No. 121) .. 30 30
147. – 2 c. on 50 c. (No. 123) .. 30 30
148. – 5 c. on 75 c. (No. 124) .. 60 60

1913. Surch. **1913** and value.
149. – 1 c. on 50 c. (No. 123) .. 25 20
150. – 6 c. on 1 p. (No. 125) .. 35 30
151. 12½ c. on 2 p. (No. 126) 30 30

1916. Surch. with value only.
156 **13.** 2 c. on 1 c. pur. & grn. 25 15
152. 6 c. on 1 c. pur. & grn. 30 20
153. 12½ c. on 1 c. pur. & grn. 30 20
154. **14.** 25 c. on 2 c. blk. & red 20 15

27. Pres. M. E. Cabrera.  **27a.** Pres. M E. Cabrera.

1917. Re-election of President Cabrera.
155. **27.** 25 c. brown and blue .. 30 20

1918.
157. **27a.** 1 p. 50 c. blue .. 25 15

28. Arms.  **31.** Technical School.

1919. Obligatory Tax. G.P.O. Rebuilding Fund.
158. **28.** 12½ c. red 15 10
159. – 30 c. black & red (postage) 2·25 35
160. – 60 c. black and olive .. 45 30
161. **31.** 90 c. black and brown 45 35
169. – 1 p. 50 orange and blue 30 25
162. – 3 p. black and green .. 1·10 30
170. – 5 p. green and sepia .. 1·10 60
171. 15 p. red and black .. 4·25 2·25

DESIGNS—Dated 1918: 30 c. Radio station. 60 c. Maternity hospital. 3 p. Arms. Dated 1921: 1 p. 50, Monolith at Quirigua. 5 p. Garcia Granados Monument. 15 p. Railway bridge, Guatemala city.

1920. Nos. 159/60 surch. **1920 2 centavos.**
163. – 2 c. on 30 c. black and red 25 25
164. 2 c. on 60 c. black & olive 25 25

1920. No. 126 surch. **25 Centavos** and bars.
165. – 25 c. on 2 p. black & orange 25 20

36.

1920. Telegraph stamp as T **36** optd. **CORREOS.**
166. **36.** 25 c. green 25 20

1921. Optd. **1921. CORREOS.**
173. **36.** 25 c. green 25 15

1921. Surch. **1921. CORREOS** and value in words.
172. **36.** 12½ c. on 25 c. green .. 25 15

1921. Surch. **1921** and value in words.
167. – 12½ c. on 20 c. black and claret (No. 122) .. 25 15
168. – 50 c. on 75 c. black and lilac (No. 124) .. 45 20

1922. Surch. **1922** and values.
174. – 12½ c. on 20 c. (No. 122) 25 20
175. – 12½ c. on 60 c. (No. 160) 55 55
176. **31.** 12½ c. on 90 c. (No. 161) 55 55
179. – 12½ c. on 3 p. (No. 162) 20 15
180. – 12½ c. on 5 p. (No. 170) 45 45
181. – 12½ c. on 15 p. (No. 171) 45 45
185. – 25 c. on 30 c. (No. 159) 35 35
186. – 25 c. on 60 c. (No. 160) 80 80
187. – 25 c. on 75 c. (No. 124) 30 30
188. **31.** 25 c. on 90 c. (No. 161) 85 1·10
189. – 25 c. on 1 p. (No. 125) 20 20
190. – 25 c. on 1 p. 50 (No. 169) 25 25
191. – 25 c. on 2 p. (No. 126) 35 35
192. – 25 c. on 3 p. (No. 162) 25 25
193. – 25 c. on 5 p. (No. 170) 60 70
194. – 25 c. on 15 p. (No. 171) 70 1·00

37. Independence Centenary Palace.  **38.** National Palace, Antigua.

1922.
195. **37.** 12½ c. green 12 10
196. **38.** 25 c. brown 12 10

39. Columbus Theatre.  **40.** Quetzal.  **41.** Garcia Granados Monument.

1923.
197. **39.** 50 c. red 25 15
198. **40.** 1 p. green 25 15
199. **41.** 5 p. orange 85 35

1924. Surch. **1924** and value.
200. – 1 p. on 1 p. 50 (No. 169) 25 15
201. **41.** 1 p. 25 on 5 p. orange 35 30

42. J. R. Barrios. 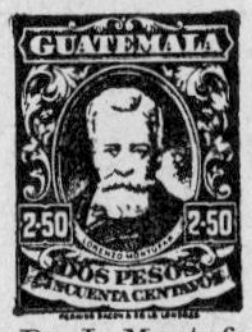 **43.** Dr. L. Montufar.

1924.
202. – 6 c. olive (as No. 119) .. 15 8
203. **38.** 25 c. brown 10 8
204. – 50 c. red (as No. 123) .. 10 8
205. – 1 p. brown (as No. 125) 10 8
206. **42.** 1 p. 25 blue 20 8
207. – 2 p. orange (as No. 126) 30 15
208. **43.** 2 p. 50 purple 30 12
209. – 3 p. green (as No. 162) .. 1·10 20
210. – 15 p. black (as No. 171) 1·60 50

These all have imprint "PERKINS BACON & CO. LD. LONDRES" at foot.

1925. No. 201 with two bars obliterating "25 cents" of surch. making it "UN PESO".
211. **41.** 1 p. on 5 p. orange .. 35 25

44. Aurora Park.  **45.** General Post Office.

46. National Observatory.  **47.** Proposed new G.P.O.

1926. Dated "1926".
212. – 6 c. bistre (as No. 119) 12 8
213. **44.** 12½ c. green 12 8
214. **38.** 25 c. brown 12 8
215. **45.** 50 c. red 12 8
216. – 1 p. brown (as No. 125) 15 12
217. **42.** 1 p. 50 blue 12 8
218. **46.** 2 p. orange .. .. 1·40 25
219. **43.** 2 p. 50 purple .. .. 1·40 45
220. – 3 p. green (as No. 162) 25 15
221. – 5 p. lilac (as No. 170) .. 60 25
222. – 15 p. black (as No. 171) 1·75 60

These all have imprint "WATERLOW & SONS LIMITED. LONDRES" at foot.

1927. Obligatory Tax. G.P.O. Rebuilding Fund.
223. **47.** 1 c. olive 10 5

1928. Surch. **1928** and value.
224. **46.** ½ c. de q. on 2 p. orange 55 35
225. – ½ c. de q. on 5 p. lilac (No. 221) 35 25
226. **43.** 1 c. de q. on 2 p. 50 purple (No. 219) .. 30 25

48. President Barrios.  **49.** Dr. L. Montufar.  **50.** Garcia Granados.

51. General Orellana.  **52.** City Arms, Guatemala.

1929.
227. **46.** ½ c. green 90 15
228. **38.** 1 c. sepia 10 8
229. **48.** 2 c. blue 10 8
230. **49.** 3 c. lilac 10 8
231. **50.** 4 c. yellow 20 8
232. **51.** 5 c. red 12 8
233. – 10 c. brown (as No. 119) 25 8
234. – 15 c. blue (as No. 125) 35 8
235. **14.** 25 c. brown 55 15
236. **44.** 30 c. green 85 35
237. – 50 c. red (as No. 120) .. 1·10 35
238. **52.** 1 q. black .. .. 2·25 35

These all have imprint "T. DE LA RUE & CO. Ld., LONDRES" at foot.

1929. Air. No. 222 surch. **SERVICIO POSTAL AEREO ANO DE 1928** and new value.
239. Q 0.03 on 15 p. black .. 40 40
240. Q 0.05 on 15 p. black .. 20 12
241. Q 0.15 on 15 p. black .. 60 20
242. Q 0.20 on 15 p. black .. 85 85

1929. Air. Surch. **SERVICIO POSTAL AEREO ANO DE 1929 Q0.03.**
243. **43.** Q 0.03 on 2 p. 50 c. purple (No. 208) .. 70 60

1929. Opening of Guatemala–Salvador Railway. No. 220 surch. **FERROCARRIL ORIENTAL 1929** and new value.
244. Q 0.03 on 3 p green .. 1·25 1·25
245. Q 0.05 on 3 p. green .. 1·00 1·00

1930. Opening of Los Altos Railway. No. 222 surch. **FERROCARRIL DE LOS ALTOS,** etc. and new value.
246. 1 c. on 15 p. black .. 50 50
247. 2 c. on 15 p. black .. 50 50
248. 3 c. on 15 p. black .. 50 50
249. 5 c. on 15 p. black .. 50 50
250. 15 c. on 15 p. black .. 50 50

53. Bridge and Permanent Way.

DESIGNS: 2 c. Embankment. 5 c. Station.

1930. Opening of Los Altos Railway.
251. – 2 c. black and purple .. 60 60
252. **53.** 3 c. black and red .. 1·25 1·25
253. – 5 c. blue and orange .. 1·50 1·50

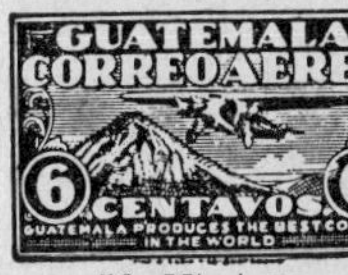

54. Mt. Agua.

1930. Air.
254. **54.** 6 c. red 85 40

1930. Air. Surch. **SERVICIO AEREO INTERIOR 1930** and value.
255. 1 c. on 3 p. grn. (No. 220) 40 40
256. 2 c. on 3 p. green .. 1·00 90
257. 3 c. on 3 p. green .. 1·00 1·00
258. 4 c. on 3 p. green .. 60 55
259. 10 c. on 15 p. blk. (No. 222) 1·40 1·40

1931. Air. Optd. **EXTERIOR—1931.**
260. **54.** 6 c. red .. .. 1·00 1·00

1931. Air. Optd. **AEREO EXTERIOR 1931.**
261. **50.** 4 c. yellow 45 20

1931. Air. Optd. **AEREO INTERNACIONAL 1931.**
262. – 15 c. blue (No. 234) .. 1·10 15
263. **44.** 30 c. green (No. 236) 2·50 25

1931. Air. Optd. **Primer Vuelo Posta BARRIOS—MIAMI 1931.**
264. **48.** 2 c. blue .. .. 2·50 2·50
265. **49.** 3 c. lilac .. .. 2·50 2·50
266. – 15 c. blue (No. 234) .. 2·50 2·50

1932. Air. Surch. **SERVICIO AEREO INTERIOR 1932** and value.
267. **42.** 2 c. on 1 p. 50 blue (217) 80 80
268. – 3 c. on 3 p. green (220) .. 35 20
270. – 10 c. on 15 p. blk. (222) 6·00 6·00
271. – 15 c. on 15 p. blk. (222) 8·50 8·50

55. Monolith of Quirigua. **56.** Flag of the Race.

1932.

272. **55.** 3 c. red 40 8
See also Nos. 272a/b (1942).

1933. Air. Optd. **AEREO INTERIOR 1933.**

273 **50.** 4 c. yellow 45 15

1933. Departure of Columbus from Palos. 441st Anniv.

274. **56.** ½ c. green 40 40
275. 1 c. chocolate 85 85
276. 2 c. blue 85 85
277. 3 c. mauve 55 55
278. 5 c. red 70 70

1934. Air. (a) Optd. **AERO EXTERIOR 1934.**

280. **51.** 5 c. red .. .. 1·10 12
281. – 15 c. blue (No. 234) .. 1·10 30

(b) Optd. **AEREO INTERIOR 1934.**

279. **49.** 2 c. blue 60 8

57. San Lorenzo.

58. Barrios and Decree.

59. Barrios and Port Barrios.

1935. J. R. Barrios. Birth Cent. Inscr. "19 DE JULIO 1835–1935".

282. – ½ c. purple & grn. (post.) 35 35
283. **57.** 1 c. blue and orange .. 35 35
284. **58.** 2 c. black and orange .. 35 35
285. – 3 c. blue and red .. 35 35
286. – 4 c. red and blue .. 3·25 3·00
287. – 5 c. brown and green .. 1·90 1·75
288. – 10 c. red and green .. 3·00 3·00
289. – 15 c. brown and green .. 3·00 3·00
290. – 25 c. black and red .. 3·25 3·00
291. **59.** 10 c. blue & brown (air) 2·00 1·75
292. – 15 c. brown and grey .. 2·00 1·75
293. – 30 c. violet and red .. 2·00 70

DESIGNS—POSTAGE—HORIZ. ½ c. Barrios' birthplace. 3 c. Arms and locomotive. 5 c. Telegraph office and Barrios. 10 c. Polytechnic School. 15 c. Police H.Q. 25 c. Pres. Ubico, arms and Barrios. VERT. 4 c. G.P.O. AIR—HORIZ. Barrios and (15 c.) tomb, (30 c.) statue.

60. Lake Atitlan. **61.** Quetzal.

62. Map of Guatemala.

1935.

293a. – ½ c. blue and green .. 8 5
294. **60.** 1 c. red and brown .. 15 8
295. **61.** 3 c. green and orange .. 35 8
296. 3 c. green and red .. 35 8
297. – 4 c. red and blue .. 25 10
297a. **62.** 5 c. brown and blue .. 35 15

DESIGNS—As T **60**: ½ c. Govt. Printing Works. 4 c. National Assembly.

63. Lake Amatitlan.

1935. Air.

(a) Inscr. 'INTERIOR' (37×17 mm.).

298. **63.** 2 c. brown 15 12
299. – 3 c. blue 50 35
300. – 4 c. black 25 5
300a. – 4 c. blue 15 5
301. **63.** 6 c. green 40 20
301a. 6 c. violet .. .. 1·50 10
302. – 10 c. claret .. .. 1·25 45
303. – 15 c. orange .. .. 1·90 60
303a. – 15 c. green .. .. 2·25 90
304. – 30 c. olive .. .. 5·50 5·50
304a. – 30 c. brown .. .. 1·25 1·25
305. – 50 c. purple .. .. 13·00 13·00
305a. – 50 c. blue .. .. 4·00 4·00
306. **63.** 1 q. orange .. .. 13·00 13·00
306a. 1 q. red .. .. 4·50 4·50

DESIGNS: 3 c. Puerto Barrios. 4 c. San Felipe. 10 c. Livingston. 15 c. San Jose. 30 c. Atitlan. 50 c. La Aurora Airport.

(b) Inscr. "EXTERIOR" (34 × 15 mm.) except Nos. 319/20 which are 46×20 mm.).

307. 1 c. brown 20 10
308. 2 c. red 25 10
309. 3 c. magenta 50 35
309a. 4 c. yellow .. .. 2·25 2·00
309b. 4 c. red .. .. 1·75 1·60
310. 5 c. blue 35 20
310a. 5 c. orange 20 10
311. 10 c. brown 70 40
311a. 10 c. green 50 40
312. 15 c. red 20 5
312a. 15 c. orange 20 5
313. 20 c. blue .. .. 2·10 2·00
313a. 20 c. claret 65 55
314. 25 c. black .. .. 2·75 2·75
314a. 25 c. green 65 65
315. 30 c. green .. .. 1·40 1·25
315a. 30 c. red 45 8
316. 50 c. red .. .. 7·50 7·00
316a. 50 c. violet .. .. 7·00 7·00
317. 1 q. blue .. .. 20·00 20·00
318. 1 q. green .. .. 6·00 6·00
319. 2 q. 50 olive and red .. 4·25 3·50
320. 5 q. blue and orange .. 7·00 5·50

DESIGNS: 1 c. Guatemala City. 2 c., 15 c. (No. 312) Views of Central Park. 3 c. Cerrito del Carmen. 4 c. Estuary of R. Dulce. 5 c. Plaza J. R. Barrios. 10 c. National Liberators' Monument. 15 c. (No. 312a) R. Dulce. 20 c. Quezaltenango. 25 c. Antigua. 30 c. Puerto Barrios. 50 c. San Jose. 1 q. La Aurora Airport. 2 q. 50, Islet. 5 q. Rocks on Atlantic Coast.

1936. Obligatory Tax. Liberal Revolution. 65th Anniv. Optd. **1871 30 DE JUNIO 1936.**

321. **47.** 1 c. olive 35 15

1936. Obligatory Tax. Independence. 115th Anniv. Optd. **1821. 15 de SEPTIEMBRE 1936.**

322. **47.** 1 c. olive 20 12

1936. Obligatory Tax. National Fair. Optd. **FERIA NACIONAL 1936.**

323. **47.** 1 c. olive 25 20

1937. Philatelic Exhibition Fund. Optd. **EXPOSICION FILATELICA 1937** or surch. also.

325. **60.** 1 c.+1 c. red & brown 30 30
326. **61.** 3 c.+1 c. green & orge. 30 30
327. 3 c.+1 c. green & red 30 30
329. – 4 c.+1 c. (No. 300a) .. 80 80
328. **62.** 5 c.+1 c. brown & blue 30 30
330. – 6 c.+1 c. (No. 301a) .. 80 80
331. – 10 c. +1 c. (No. 311a) 80 80
332. – 15 c.+1 c. (No. 312a).. 80 80
324. **47.** 1 c. olive 20 20

64. Quetzal. **65.** General Ubico.

66. Quezeltenango.

1937. Pres. Ubico. Second Term. Inscr. "1931-1937" (a) Postage.

333. **64.** ½ c. red and blue .. 20 20
334. 1 c. brown and grey .. 25 20
335. 2 c. red and violet .. 25 20
336. 3 c. blue and purple .. 25 15
337. 4 c. olive and yellow .. 1·25 1·10
338. – 5 c. purple and red .. 1·50 1·10
339. – 10 c. black and purple 1·10 1·10
340. – 15 c. red and blue .. 1·60 1·60
341. – 25 c. violet and orange 2·25 2·25
342. – 50 c. orange and green 3·25 3·25
343. **65.** 1 q. purple and brown.. 14·00 14·00
344. – 1 q. 50 brown and olive 14·00 14·00

DESIGNS: As T **64**—VERT. 1 c. Tower of the Reformer. 5 c. National Congress entrance. 10 c. Customs House. HORIZ. 2 c. Union Park, Quezaltenango. 3 c. G.P.O. 4 c. Government Building, Retalhuleu. 15 c. Aurora Airport. 25 c. National Fair. 50 c. Presidential Guards' Barracks. As T **65**: 1 q. 50, Gen. Ubico.

(b) Air. As T **66**, inscr. "INTERIOR" and optd. with aeroplane.

345. **66.** 2 c. black and red .. 25 12
346. – 3 c. black and blue .. 1·25 1·25
347. – 4 c. black and yellow .. 25 20
348. – 6 c. black and green .. 65 65
349. – 10 c. black, and purple 1·40 1·40
350. – 15 c. black and orange 1·90 1·90
351. – 30 c. black and olive .. 5·50 5·50
352. – 50 c. black and blue .. 5·50 5·50
353. – 75 c. black and violet .. 12·00 12·00
354. – 1 q. black and red .. 12·00 12·00

DESIGNS: 3 c. Lake Atitlan. 4 c. Progressive colony on Lake Amatitlan. 6 c. Carmen Hill. 10 c. Relief map. 15 c. National University. 30 c. Plaza Espana. 50 c. Aurora Police Station. 75 c. Aurora Amphitheatre. 1 q. Aurora Airport.

(c) Air. As T **66** inscr. "EXTERIOR" and optd. with aeroplane.

355. **66.** 1 c. blue and orange .. 20 15
356. – 2 c. violet and red .. 40 30
357. – 3 c. brown and purple 1·50 1·00
358. – 5 c. red and green .. 1·90 1·75
359. – 10 c. green and red .. 2·25 1·75
360. – 15 c. olive and pink .. 60 50
361. – 20 c. black and blue .. 2·40 2·00
362. – 25 c. red and grey .. 3·25 3·25
363. – 30 c. violet and green .. 2·50 2·50
364. – 50 c. blue and purple .. 10·00 10·00
365. – 1 q. purple and olive .. 10·00 10·00
366. – 1 q. 50 c. brown and red 10·00 10·00

DESIGNS: 1 c. Seventh Avenue. 2 c. Liberators' Monument. 3 c. National Printing Offices. 5 c. National Museum. 10 c. Central Park. 15 c. Escuintla Park. 20 c. Mobile Police. 25 c. Slaughter-house, Escuintla. 30 c. Campo de Marte Stadium. 50 c. Plaza Barrios. 1 q. Polytechnic. 1 q. 50 c. Aurora Airport.

1938. U.S. Constitution. 150th Anniv. Optd. **1787-1789 CL ANIVERSARIO DE LA CONSTITUCION,** etc.

367. **47.** 1 c. olive 12 8

1938. Obligatory Tax. Optd. **1938.**

368a. **47.** 1 c. olive 10 5

68.

1938. 1st Central American Philatelic Exn.

(a) Air. As T **68** inscr. "PRIMERA EXPOSICION FILATELICA CENTRO AMERICANA".

369. **68.** 1 c. brown and orange .. 40 40
370. – 2 c. brown and red .. 40 40
371. – 3 c. brown, buff & green 80 60
372. – 4 c. brown and purple .. 80 60
373. – 5 c. brown and grey .. 90 75
374. – 10 c. brown and blue .. 1·50 1·25

(b) Postage. Optd. **Primera Exposicion Filatelica Centroamericana 1938.**

375. **47.** 1 c. olive 12 5

69. La Merced Church.

1939. Optd. with flying quetzal.

(a) Inland Air Mail. As T **69** inscr. "CORREO AEREO INTERIOR".

376. **69.** 1 c. brown and olive .. 15 8
377. – 2 c. green and red .. 15 8
378. – 3 c. olive and blue .. 20 10
379. – 4 c. green and pink .. 15 8
380. – 5 c. blue and maroon .. 25 20
381. – 6 c. grey and orange .. 30 25
382. – 10 c. grey and brown .. 40 25
383. – 15 c. black and purple 50 25
384. – 30 c. red and blue .. 75 35
385. – 50 c. violet and orange 1·00 45
386. – 1 q. blue and green .. 1·60 1·10

DESIGNS: 2 c. Christ's Church Ruins, Antigua. 3 c. Aurora Airport. 4 c. Campo de Marte Stadium. 5 c. Cavalry Barracks. 6 c. Palace of Justice. 10 c. Customs House, San Jose. 15 c. Post Office, Retalhuleu. 30 c. Municipal Theatre, Quezaltenango. 50 c. Customs House, Retalhuleu. 1 q. Departmental Palace, Retalhuleu.

(b) Foreign Air Mail. As T **69** inscr. "AEREO EXTERIOR" (10 c. and 25 c.) or "AEREO INTERNACIONAL".

387. – 1 c. brown and green .. 15 8
388. – 2 c. black and green .. 20 10
389. – 3 c. green and blue .. 20 10
390. – 4 c. green and brown .. 20 10
391. – 5 c. red and green .. 25 10
392. – 10 c. slate and red .. 1·25 8
393. – 15 c. red and blue .. 1·25 8
394. – 20 c. yellow and green 35 20
395. – 25 c. olive and purple .. 40 15
396. – 30 c. grey and red .. 50 12
397. – 50 c. orange and red .. 95 20
398. – 1 q. green and orange .. 1·60 30

DESIGNS: 1 c. Mayan Altar, Aurora Park. 2 c. Ministry of Health. 3 c. Lake Amatitlan. 4 c. Lake Atitlan. 5 c. Bridge over Tamazulapa. 10 c. National Liberators' Monument. 15 c. Palace of the Captains General. 20 c. Carmen Hill. 25 c. Barrios Square. 30 c. Mayan Altar, Archaeological Museum. 50 c. Carlos III Fountain. 1 q. "Old Guatemala".

1939. Obligatory Tax. As No. 368a, but optd. **1939.**

399. **47.** 1 c. olive 12 5

74. National Flower (White Nun). **75.** Arms and Map of Guatemala.

1939.

400. – ½ c. brown and green .. 12 8
401. **74.** 2 c. black and blue .. 1·10 30
402. – 3 c. green and brown .. 40 15
403. – 3 c. green and red .. 40 15
404. **75.** 5 c. red and blue .. 1·25 55

DESIGNS—As T **74**: ½ c. Mayan Calendar. 3 c. Quetzal.

1939. No. 229 surch. **UN CENTAVO.**

405. **48.** 1 c. on 2 c. blue .. 20 12

1940. As No. 223, but optd. **1940.**

406. **47.** 1 c. olive 12 5

1940. 50th Anniv. of Pan-American Union.

(a) Optd. **Commemorative Union Panamericana 1890-1940.**

407. **47.** 1 c. olive 12 5

(b) Air. Optd. **UNION PANAMERICANA 1890-1940. CORREO AEREO.**

408. – 15 c. blue (No. 234) .. 40 15

1940. Surch. with new values.

409. **14.** 1 c. on 25 c brown .. 15 8
410. – 5 c. on 50 c. red (No. 237) 25 15

1941. Obligatory Tax. Optd. **1941.**

411. **47.** 1 c. olive 12 5

1941. Obligatory Tax. Surch. **CONSTRUCCION** (twice) and **UN CENTAVO.**

412. **48.** 1 c. on 2 c. blue .. 12 5

1941. Air. 2nd Pan-American Health Day. Optd. **DICIEMBRE 2 1941 SEGUNDO DIA PAN-AMERICANO,** etc.

414. – 2 c. blk. & grn. (No. 388) 35 20

1941. Surch. ½ **MEDIO CENTAVO** ½.

415. **14.** ½ c. on 25 c. brown .. 15 15

1942. Obligatory Tax. Surch. **CONSTRUCCION/1942/UN CENTAVO.**

416. **48.** 1 c. on 2 c. blue .. 12 5

1942. As T **55**, but tablet dated "1942".

416a. – 3 c. green 30 5
416b. – 3 c. blue 30 5

76. Archway at new G.P.O. **77.** Guastatoya Vase.

1942. Obligatory Tax.

417a. **76.** 1 c. brown 12 8

1942.

418. **77.** ½ c. brown 8 5
419. – 1 c. red 8 5

DESIGN—HORIZ. 1 c. Infirmary.

78. Ruins of Zakuleu. **78a.** National Printing Works.

79. National Police H.Q.

79a. San Carlos Borromeo University, Antigua.

1943.

420. 78. ½ c. brown (postage) .. 10 5
421. 78a. 2 c. red 15 8
422. 79. 10 c. mauve (air) .. 40 12
423. 79a. 15 c. brown 35 10

80. Don Pedro de Alvarado. 81. Archway, G.P.O.

1943. Air. Old Guatemala. 4th Cent.
424a. 80. 15 c. blue 35 12

1943.
425. 81. 1 c. orange 8 5

82. R. M. Landivar. 83. National Palace.

1943. Rafael Maria Landivar (poet). 150th Death Anniv.
426. 82. 5 c. blue 20 15

1944.
427. 83. 3 c. green (postage) .. 15 8
444. 5 c. red (air) 30 8
445. 10 c. lilac 30 10
446. 15 c. blue 50 20

1945. Optd. **25 de junio de 1944 PALACIO NACIONAL** and bar.
428. 83. 3 c. blue 20 12

1945. Air. Optd. **PALACIO NACIONAL** and bar.
429. 83. 5 c. red 20 15

1945. As T **81** but smaller (19×23 mm.).
430. 1 c. orange 10 5
479. 1 c. blue 8 5

84. Allegory of the Revolution of 20th Oct., 1944. 85. Jose Millan Vidaurre (author). 86. Archbishop P. E. de Rivera.

1945. Revolution of 20th October, 1944.
431. 84. 3 c. blue (postage) .. 12 8
432. 5 c. red (air) 35 20
433. 6 c. green 35 20
434. 10 c. violet 35 25
435. 15 c. blue 35 25

1945. Air. Book Fair. No. 389 surch. **1945 FERIA DEL LIBRO 2½ CENTAVOS.**
436. 2½ c. on 3 c. green and blue 2·10 2·10

1945.
437. 85. 1 c. green (postage) .. 8 5
438. 86. 2 c. violet 8 5
439. 86. 5 c. red (air) 25 15
678. 5 c. olive 12 8
679. 5 c. blue 12 8
680. 5 c. green 12 8
681. 5 c. orange 12 8
682. 5 c. violet 12 8
683. 5 c. grey 12 8
440. 85. 7½ c. purple 90 90
441. 7½ c. blue 60 60
For stamps as T **86** but dated "1660 1951" see Nos. 523/27.

87. 88. J. B. Montufar.

1945. Revolution of 20th October, 1944. 1st Anniv. Inscr. "1944–1945".
442. 87. 3 c. blue (postage) .. 15 8
443. 5 c. mauve (air) .. 35 20

1945.
447. 88. ½ c. brown (postage) .. 8 5
448. 3 c. blue 8 5
449. 3 c. green 12 5
450. – 10 c. green (air) .. 20 8
DESIGN—HORIZ. 10 c. Montufar.

89. Rowland Hill. 90. Signing the Declaration of Independence.

1946. Cent. of First Postage Stamps.
451. – 1 c. olive & violet (post.) 20 15
452. 89. 5 c. brown and grey (air) 50 15
453. – 15 c. blue, green and red 65 30
DESIGNS: 1 c. U.P.U. Monument, Berne. 15 c. Hemispheres and quetzal.

1946. Air. Independence. 125th Anniv.
454. 90. 5 c. red 10 5
455. 6 c. brown 20 8
456. 10 c. violet 20 8
457. 20 c. blue 70 20

1947. Air. 2nd Anniv. of Revolution of 20th October, 1944. As T **87** but inscr. "1946" instead of "1945" and "II" for "I".
458. 1 c. green 12 8
459. 2 c. red 15 8
460. 3 c. violet 15 8
461. 5 c. blue 20 8

91. President Roosevelt.

ILLUSTRATIONS
British Commonwealth and all overprints and surcharges are FULL SIZE. Foreign Countries have been reduced to ¾-LINEAR.

1947. Air.
462. 91. 5 c. red 12 8
463. 6 c. blue 15 8
464. 10 c. blue 20 12
465. 30 c. black .. .. 1·00 1·25
466. 50 c. violet .. .. 2·10 2·00
467. 1 q. green .. .. 3·00 3·00

92. "Labour". 93. Football Match.

1948. Labour Day and Adoption of Labour Code.
468. 92. 1 c. green 15 8
469. 2 c. purple 15 8
470. 3 c. blue 15 8
471. 5 c. red 20 12

1948. Air. Optd. **1948 AEREO.**
472. 75. 5 c. red and blue .. 15 12

1948. Optd. **1948.**
473. 75. 5 c. red and blue .. 15 8

1948. Air. 4th Central American and Caribbean Football Championship Games.
474. 93. 3 c. black and red .. 85 20
475. 5 c. black and green .. 1·00 20
476. 10 c. black and mauve 1·10 55
477. 30 c. black and blue .. 4·50 2·75
478. 50 c. black and yellow 4·75 2·75

94. Fray Bartolome de Las Casas and Indian. 95. Badge.

1949. Fray Bartolome de Las Casas ("Apostle of the Indians").
480. 94. ½ c. red 8 5
661. ½ c. blue 5 5
481. 1 c. brown 10 5
662. 1 c. violet 5 5
663. 2 c. green 10 5
664. 3 c. red 10 8
484. 4 c. blue 20 12
665. 4 c. brown 8 5

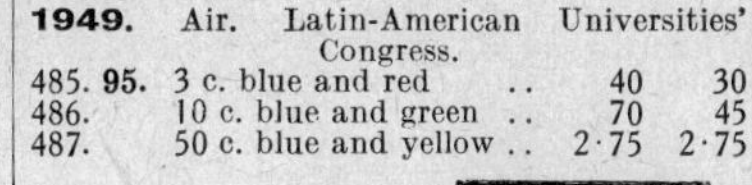

1949. Air. Latin-American Universities' Congress.
485. 95. 3 c. blue and red .. 40 30
486. 10 c. blue and green .. 70 45
487. 50 c. blue and yellow .. 2·75 2·75

96. Gathering Coffee. 97. Tecum Uman Monument.

1950. Tourist Propaganda. (a) Postage.
488. 96. ½ c. olive, blue and pink 15 8
489. – ½ c. blue and brown .. 15 8
490. – 1 c. olive, brn. & yellow 15 8
491. – 1 c. green and orange .. 15 8
492. – 2 c. blue, green and red 15 8
493. – 2 c. brown and red .. 15 8
494. – 3 c. brown, blue & violet 15 10
495. – 6 c. violet, orge. & green 35 15
DESIGNS—As T **96**: ½ c. (No. 489), 3 c. Cutting sugar canes. 1 c. (No. 490), 2 c. (No. 493), Agricultural colony. 1 c. (No. 491), 2 c. (No. 492), Banana trees. 6 c. International Bridge.

(b) Air. Multicoloured centres.
496. – 3 c. red 35 10
497. 97. 5 c. lake 35 12
498. – 8 c. black 40 15
499. – 13 c. brown 65 30
500. – 35 c. violet .. .. 2·50 2·25
DESIGNS—As T **97**—HORIZ. 3 c. Lake Atitlan. 8 c. San Cristobal Church. 35 c. Momostenango Cliffs. VERT. 13 c. Weaver.

98. Footballers.

DESIGNS—HORIZ. 4 c. Pole vaulting. 35 c. Diving. 65 c. Stadium. VERT. 3 c. Runners. 8 c. Tennis.

1950. Air. 6th Central American and Caribbean Games. Inscr. "VI JUEGOS DEPORTIVOS . . . 1950".
501. 98. 1 c. black and violet .. 70 35
502. – 3 c. black and red .. 75 35
503. – 4 c. black and brown .. 85 35
504. – 8 c. black and purple .. 95 45
505. – 35 c. black and blue .. 4·25 3·75
506. – 65 c. green .. .. 6·50 5·00

99. Health Badge. 100. Nursing School.

1950. National Hospitals Fund.
507. 99. 1 c. blue and red (post.) 15 12
508. – 3 c. red & green (Nurse) 30 20
509. – 5 c. brown & blue (Map) 45 30
511. – 5 c. red, grn. & vio. (air) 20 15
512. 100. 10 c. green and brown 45 25
513. – 50 c. purple, green & red 2·10 1·75
514. – 1 q. olive, grn. & yellow 2·25 2·10
DESIGNS—As T **100**: 5 c. Nurse. 70 c., 1 q. Zacapa and Roosevelt Hospitals.

1951. No. E 479 without surcharge for use as ordinary postage.
517. E 1. 4 c. black and green .. 35 20

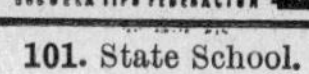

101. State School. 102. Ceremonial Axe-head.

1951. Aerial views of schools as T **101.**
519. ½ c. brown and violet 12 8
520. 1 c. green and lake 12 8
521. 2 c. brown and blue .. 12 8
522. 4 c. purple and black 12 8

1952. As No. 438 but dated "1660 1951" below portrait.
523. 87a. ½ c. violet 8 5
524. 1 c. red 8 5
525. 2 c. green 8 5
526. 4 c. orange 15 5
527. 4 c. blue 8 5

1953. Air.
528. 102. 3 c. drab and blue .. 15 8
529. 5 c. chestnut and slate 20 12
530. 10 c. slate and violet 35 25

103. Flag and Constitution. 104. R. A. Ovalle (music), J. J. Palma (words).

1953. Air. Presidential Election, 1951.
531. 103. 1 c. grn., brn., bl. & red 20 10
532. 2 c. green, brown, blue and blue-green .. 30 12
533. 4 c. grn., brn., bl. & sep. 35 15

1953. National Anthem.
534. 104. ½ c. grey and violet .. 20 12
535. 1 c. chestnut and grey 20 12
536 2 c. olive and chestnut 40 20
537. 3 c. olive and blue .. 45 20

105. "Work and Play". 106. Horse Racing.

1953. Air. National Fair. Inscr. "FERIA NACIONAL".
538. – 1 c. red and blue .. 15 8
539. – 4 c. green and orange .. 70 20
540. 105. 5 c. brown and green .. 40 25
541. 106. 15 c. lilac and brown .. 1·40 80
542. – 20 c. blue and red .. 1·70 80
543. – 30 c. blue and sepia .. 1·50 1·10
544. – 50 c. black and violet .. 2·75 2·25
545. – 65 c. green and blue .. 4·25 4·00
546. – 1 q. green and red .. 8·50 7·00
DESIGNS—VERT. 1 c. National dance. 4 c. National flower (White Nun). 30 c. Picture and corn cob. 1 q. Quetzal. HORIZ. 20 c. Ruins of Zakuleu. 50 c. Champion bull. 65 c. Cycle-racing.

107. Indian Warrior. 108. Flags of Guatemala and O.D.E.C.A.

1954. Air. National Revolutionary Army Commemoration.
547. 107. 1 c. red 12 8
548. 2 c. blue 20 10
549. 4 c. green 25 12
550. 5 c. turquoise .. 30 15
551. 6 c. orange 35 20
552. 10 c. violet 45 30
553. 20 c. sepia .. .. 2·00 1·75

1954. As T **5** but inscr. "UNION POSTAL UNIVERSAL" around oval.
554. 1 c. blue 8 5
555. 2 c. violet 5 5
556. 2 c. brown 5 5
557. 3 c. red 8 5
558. 3 c. blue 8 5
559. 4 c. orange 12 5
560. 4 c. violet 8 5
561. 5 c. brown 15 8
562. 5 c. red 15 8
563. 5 c. green 15 5
564. 5 c. slate-grey .. 25 8
565. 6 c. green 20 10

1954. Air. 3rd Anniv. of O.D.E.C.A.
566. 108. 1 c. multicoloured .. 12 8
567. 2 c. multicoloured .. 15 8
568. 4 c. multicoloured .. 20 12

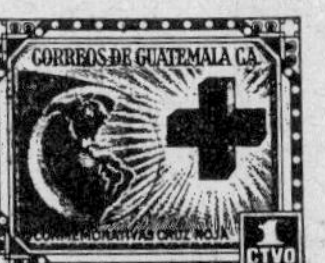

109. Goal-keeper. 110. Red Cross and Globe.

1955. Golden Jubilee of Football in Guatemala. Inscr. "1902—1952".
569. – 4 c. violet (Camposeco) 70 20
570. – 4 c. red (Camposeco) 70 20
571. – 4 c. green (Camposeco) 70 20
572. – 10 c. green (Matheu) .. 1·75 35
573. 109. 15 c. blue .. .. 2·10 1·75

1956. Red Cross. Inscr. "COMMEMORATIVAS CRUJ ROJA".
574. **110.** 1 c. red & brn. (post.) 15 12
575. – 3 c. red and green .. 15 12
576. – 4 c. red and black .. 20 15
577. – 5 c.+15 c. red & blue 60 60
578. – 15 c.+50 c. red & lilac 1·50 1·50
579. **110.** 25 c.+50 c. red and indigo .. .. 1·60 1·60

580. – 35 c.+1 q. green and red (air) .. .. 4·75 4·25
581. – 50 c.+1 q. red & blue 4·75 4·75
582. – 1 q.+1 q. red & green 4·75 4·50
DESIGNS: 3 c. 15 c. Telephone and red cross. 4 c., 5 c. Nurse, patient and red cross. 35 c. Red Cross ambulance. 1 q. Red Cross nurse.

111. Road Map of Guatemala.

112. Maya Warrior.

1956. Revolution of 1954-55. Inscr. "LIBERACION 1954-55".
583. – ½ c. violet (postage) .. 8 5
584. **111.** 1 c. green 8 5
585. – 3 c. sepia 12 8

586. **112.** 2 c. brown, red, blue and green (air) .. 15 8
587. – 4 c. black and red .. 15 10
588. – 5 c. chestnut and blue 20 15
589. – 6 c. blue and sepia .. 15 12
590. – 20 c. brn., blue & vio. 1·75 1·10
591. – 30 c. olive and blue .. 1·75 1·10
592. – 65 c. green and brown 3·50 3·00
593. – 1 q. multicoloured .. 4·25 3·75
594. – 5 q. brn., blue & green 9·00 8·50
DESIGNS: ½ c. Liberation dagger symbol. 3 c. Oil production. 4 c. Family. 5 c. Sword smashing Communist emblems. 6 c. Hands holding map and cogwheel. 20 c. Martyrs' Monument. 30 c. Champerico Port. 65 c. Telecommunications symbols. 1 q. Flags of ODECA countries. 5 q. Pres. Armas.

113. Rotary Emblem and Map.

114. Esquipulas Cathedral and Our Lord.

1956. Air. Rotary International 50th Anniv.
595. **113.** 4 c. bistre and blue .. 20 15
596. 6 c. bistre and green .. 20 20
597. 35 c. bistre and violet 1·40 1·40

1957. Air. Red Cross Fund. Nos. 577/9 optd. **AEREO-1957** and ornaments.
598. – 5 c.+15 c. red & blue 7·00 7·00
599. – 15 c.+20 c. red & lilac 8·50 8·50
600. **110.** 25 c.+50 c. red and indigo .. .. 8·50 8·50

1957. Esquipulas Highway Fund. Inscr. "PRO - CARRETERA ESQUIPULAS JUNIO 1957".
601. **114.** 1½ c.+½ c. slate-violet and brown (postage) 45 30

602. – 10 c.+1 q. brown and green (air) .. .. 6·50 6·50
603. – 15 c.+1 q. grn. & sepia 6·50 6·50
604. – 20 c.+1 q. slate & brn. 6·50 6·50
605. – 25 c.+1 q. red & lilac 6·50 6·50
DESIGNS—HORIZ. 10 c. Esquipulas Cathedral. VERT. 15 c. Cathedral and the Crucifixion. 20 c. Map of Guatemala and Our Lord. 25 c. Bishop of Esquipulas.

115. Red Cross, Map and Quetzal.

116. Caravel of 1532 and liner "Quetzaltenango".

1958. Air. Red Cross. Inscr. "CONMEMORATIVAS DE LA CRUZ ROJA".
606. **115.** 1 c. multicoloured .. 20 12
607. – 2 c. red, brown & blue 25 12
608. – 3 c. brown, red & blue 25 12
609. – 4 c. red, green & brown 30 12
DESIGNS—VERT. 2 c. J. R. Angulo; Mother and Child. HORIZ. 3 c. P. de Bethancourt and invalid. 4 c. R. Ayau and Red Cross.

1959. National Anthem Cent. Optd. **1858 1958 CENTENARIO.**
610. **104.** ½ c. grey and violet .. 15 15

1959. Air. Pres. Castillo Armas Commem. As No. 594 but inscr. "LIBERACION 3 DE Julio de 1954", etc. Centre in blue and yellow. Frame colours given.
615. 1 c. black 8 5
616. 2 c. red 10 5
617. 4 c. brown 12 8
618. 6 c. green 20 10
619. 10 c. violet 35 20
620. 20 c. green .. .. 1·10 65
621. 35 c. grey .. .. 1·40 90

1959. Air. United Nations. Optd. **HOMENAJE A LAS NACIONES UNIDAS.**
622. **86.** 7½ c. blue .. .. 1·25 1·25

1959. Air. Central American Merchant Marine Commem.
623. **116.** 6 c. blue and red .. 25 10

1959. Air. Guatemala's Claim to Belize (British Honduras). As No. 509 optd. **BELICE ES NUESTRO AEREO** ("Belize is Ours").
624. 5 c. brown and blue .. 25 15

1959. Air. Cent. of First Export of Coffee. No. 489 optd. **1859 CENTENARIO PRIMERA EXPORTACION DE CAFE 1939.**
625. 6 c. blue and sepia .. 45 15

117. Pres. Ramon V. Morales and his Wife.

1959. Air. Visit of President of Honduras.
626. **117.** 6 c. brown 15 12

118. Red Cross Shield.

119. Abraham Lincoln.

1960. Red Cross Commem. Cross in red.
627. **118.** 1 c.+1 c. blue and brown (postage) .. 15 15
628. – 3 c.+3 c. blue, pink and lilac 20 20
629. **118.** 4 c.+4 c. blue & black 20 20

630. – 5 c.+5 c. blue, pink and red (air) .. 2·75 2·50
631. – 6 c.+6 c. green and brown-red .. 2·75 2·50
632. – 10 c.+10 c. pink, blue and grey-blue .. 2·75 2·50
633. – 15 c.+15 c. red, blue and brown .. 2·75 2·50
634. – 20 c.+20 c. green, pink and purple .. 2·75 2·50
635. – 25 c.+25 c. pink, blue and grey .. 2·75 2·50
636. – 30 c.+30 c. red, blue, orange and green .. 2·75 2·50
DESIGNS—3 c., 5 c. Wounded soldier at Solferino. 6 c., 20 c. Houses and debris afloat on flood waters. 10 c., 25 c. Earth, Moon and planets. 15 c., 30 c. Red Cross H.Q., Guatemala City.

1960. Air. World Refugee Year. Nos. 606/9 optd. **ANO MUNDIAL DE REFUGIADOS** or **Ano Mundial de Refugiados** or surch. also.
637. 1 c. multicoloured .. 75 75
638. 2 c. red, brown and blue .. 75 75
639. 3 c. brown, red and blue .. 1·10 1·10
640. 4 c. red, green and brown 1·25 1·25
641. 6 c on 1 c. multicoloured 1·75 1·75
642. 7 c. on 2 c. red, brn. & blue 1·75 1·75
643. 10 c. on 3 c. brn., red & bl. 1·75 1·75
644. 20 c. on 4 c. red, grn. & brn. 2·40 2·40

1960. Air. Founding of City of Melchor de Mencos. No. 489 optd. **Fundacion de la ciudad de Melchor de Mencos 20-IV-1960.**
645. 6 c. blue and sepia .. 1·00 80

1960. Air. Abraham Lincoln. 150th Birth Anniv.
646. **119.** 5 c. blue 20 15
647. 30 c. violet .. .. 2·00 1·60
648. 50 c. slate .. .. 7·00 6·50

120. U.N.E.S.C.O. Headquarters, Paris.

1960. Air. Inaug. of U.N.E.S.C.O. Headquarters Building, Paris (1958).
649. **120.** 5 c. violet and magenta 12 10
650. 6 c. sepia and blue .. 15 10
651. 8 c. red and emerald .. 20 15
652. 20 c. blue and brown .. 1·10 70

1961. Air. Red Cross. Nos. 606/9 optd. **MAYO DE 1960.**
653. 1 c. multicoloured .. 20 10
654. 2 c. red, brown and blue .. 25 12
655. 3 c. brown, red and blue .. 25 15
656. 4 c. red, green and brown .. 25 15

121. Romulus and Remus Statue, Rome. **122.** Independence Ceremony.

1961. Plaza Italia Inauguration.
657. **121.** 3 c. blue 12 8

1962. Air. Independence. 140th Anniv.
658. **122.** 4 c. sepia 12 10
659. 5 c. blue 12 10
660. 15 c. violet 45 30

1962. Air. Malaria Eradication. Optd. **1962 EL MUNDO UNIDO CONTRA LA MALARIA.**
666. **120.** 6 c. sepia and blue .. 1·10 1·00

123. Dr. Jose Luna.

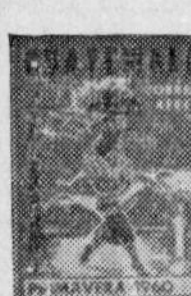
124. Girl with Basket of Fruit.

125. Arms. (As T 1).

1962. Air. Guatemalan Doctors.
667. **123.** 1 c. violet and olive .. 8 5
668. – 4 c. olive-grn. & yellow 12 8
669. – 5 c. brown and blue .. 25 10
670. – 6 c. black and salmon 25 10
671. – 10 c. brown and green 35 15
672. – 20 c. blue and mauve .. 60 35
DOCTORS: 4 c. R. Robles. 5 c. N. Esparragoza. 6 c. J. Ortega. 10 c. D. Gonsalez. 20 c. J. Flores.

1962. Air. Pres. Ydigoras's Tour of Central America. No. 489 optd. **PRESIDENTE YDIGORAS FUENTES RECORRE POR TIERRA CENTRO AMERICA 14 A 20 DIC. 1962.**
673. 6 c. blue and sepia .. 45 25

1963. Air. New ODECA Charter Commem. Optd. **CONMEMORACION FIRMA NUEVA CARTA ODECA.—1962.**
674. **120.** 6 c. sepia and blue .. 20 12
675. 8 c. red and emerald .. 30 12

1963. Air. National Fair, 1960.
676. **124.** 1 c. multicoloured .. 5 5

1963. Air. Presidents' Reunion. No. 489 with 11-line opt. starting **"REUNION PRESIDENTES KENNEDY, . . ."**
677. 6 c. blue and sepia .. 8·50 4·00

1963.
684. **125.** 10 c. red 20 10
685. 10 c. black 15 8
686. 10 c. brown 15 8
687. 20 c. violet 35 15
688. 20 c. blue 35 15

126. Harvester.

127. Ceiba (national tree).

1963. Air. Freedom from Hunger.
689. **126.** 5 c. blue-green .. 15 12
690. 10 c. blue 30 15

1963. Air.
691. **127.** 4 c. green and sepia .. 12 8

128. Pedro. Bethancourt tending sick man.

129. Patzun Palace.

1964. Campaign for Canonization of Pedro Bethancourt.
692. **128.** 2½ c. brown (postage) 8 5

693. **128.** 2½ c. blue (air) .. 8 5
694. 3 c. orange 8 5
695. 4 c. violet 8 5
696. 5 c. green 15 8

1964. Air. Guatemalan Palaces.
697. **129.** 1 c. brown and red .. 5 5
698. 3 c. green and magenta 8 5
699. – 4 c. lake and blue .. 8 5
700. 5 c. blue and brown .. 15 8
701. – 6 c. grey-blue & green 15 10
PALACES: 3 c. Coban. 4 c. Retalhuleu. 5 c. San Marcos. 6 c. Los Capitanes Generales.

130. Municipal Building.

131. Pres. Kennedy.

1964. Air. New Buildings. (a) As T **130.**
702. **130.** 3 c. brown and blue .. 5 5
703. – 4 c. blue and brown .. 8 5
DESIGN: 4 c. Social Security Building.

(b) Designs as Nos. 702/3 but different style frame and inscr., and new designs.
704. – 3 c. green (As No. 703) 8 5
705. 4 c. slate 8 5
706. **130.** 7 c. blue 15 10
707. – 7 c. bistre 15 10
DESIGNS: 4 c. University Rectory. 7 c. (No. 707), Engineering Faculty.

1964. Air. Olympic Games, Tokyo. Optd. with Olympic rings and **OLIMPIADAS TOKIO-1964.**
708. **115.** 1 c. 70 70
709. – 2 c. (No. 598) .. 70 70
710. – 3 c. (No. 599) .. 70 70
711. – 4 c. (No. 600) .. 70 70

1964. Air. New York World's Fair. Optd. **FERIA MUNDIAL DE NEW YORK.**
712. **115.** 1 c. 55 55
713. – 2 c. (No. 598) .. 55 55
714. – 3 c. (No. 599) .. 55 55
715. 4 c. (No. 600) .. 55 55

1964. Air. Surch. **HABILITADO-1964** and value.
716. **115.** 7 c. on 1 c. 15 15
717. – 9 c. on 2 c. (No. 598) 20 20
718. – 13 c. on 3 c. (No. 599) 25 25
719. – 21 c. on 4 c. (No. 600) 60 60

1964. Air. 8th Cycle Race. Optd. **VIII VUELTA CICLISTICA.**
720. **115.** 1 c. .. .. .. 1·10 1·10
721. – 2 c. (No. 598) .. 1·10 1·10
722. – 3 c. (No. 599) .. 1·10 1·10
723. – 4 c. (No. 600) .. 1·10 1·10

1964. Air. Pres. Kennedy Commem.
724. **131.** 1 c. violet 40 20
725. 2 c. green 40 20
726. 3 c. brown 50 25
727. 7 c. blue 55 35
728. 50 c. green .. .. 10·00 10·00

132. Centenary Emblem.

133. Bishop F. Marroquin.

1964. Air. Red Cross Cent. Emblem in silver and red.

730. **132.** 7 c. blue 40 25
731. 9 c. orange 40 25
732. 13 c. violet 55 55
733. 21 c. green 85 85
734. 35 c. brown 90 90
735. 1 q. bistre .. .. 4·25 4·25

1964. "International Collectors' Federation". 15th Anniv. (1963). No. 559 optd. **HOMENAJE A LA " I. S. G. C." 1948-1963.**

736. 4 c. orange 12 12

1965. Air. Bishop Marroquin Commem.

737. **133.** 4 c. brown and purple 10 5
738. 7 c. sepia and grey .. 15 10
739. 9 c. black and blue .. 20 12

1965. Air. Optd. **AYUDENOS MAYO 1965.** Emblem in silver and red.

740. **132.** 7 c. blue 20 20
741. 9 c. orange 30 25
742. 13 c. violet 35 25
743. 21 c. green 65 45
744. 35 c. brown 75 70

134. Scout Badge.

135. Flags.

1966. Air. Guatemalan Boy Scouts. Mult.

745. 5 c. Type **134** 15 10
746. 9 c. Scouts by campfire .. 30 20
747. 10 c. Scout carrying torch and flag 30 30
748. 15 c. Scout saluting .. 50 30
749. 20 c. Lord Baden-Powell.. 60 50

1966. Air. "Centro America".

750. **135.** 6 c. multicoloured .. 15 10

136. Nefertari's Temple, Abu Simbel.

137. Arms.

1966. Air. Nubian Monuments Preservation.

751. **136.** 21 c. violet and bistre 45 45

1966. Air.

752. **137.** 5 c. orange 10 5
753. 5 c. green 10 5
754. 5 c. grey 10 5
755. 5 c. violet 10 5
756. 5 c. blue 10 5
757. 5 c. deep blue.. .. 10 5
758. 5 c. violet 10 5
759. 5 c. yellow-grn. .. 8 5
760. 5 c. lake 8 5
761. 5 c. green on yellow .. 8 5

138. Mgr. M. R. Arellano.

139. Mario M. Montenegro (revolutionary)

1966. Air. Monseigneur Arellano Commem.

765. **138.** 1 c. violet 5 5
766. 2 c. green 5 5
767. 3 c. sepia 12 8
768. 7 c. blue 25 15
769. 50 c. slate .. .. 1·25 1·00

1966. Air. Montenegro. Commem.

770. **139.** 2 c. red 8 5
771. 3 c. orange 8 5
772. 4 c. claret 12 5
773. 5 c. grey 15 5
774. 5 c. blue 15 5
775. 5 c. green 15 5
776. 5 c. black 15 5

140. Morning Glory.

141. Institute Emblem.

1967. Air. Flowers. Multicoloured.

777. 4 c. Type **140** 20 10
778. 8 c. "Bird of Paradise" .. 25 12
779. 10 c. "White Nun" orchid (national flower) .. 30 25
780. 20 c. " Nymphs of Amatitlan " 55 35

Nos. 778/80 are horiz.

1967. Air. 8th General Assembly of Pan-American Geographical and Historical Institute (1965).

781. **141.** 4 c. purple, black & brn. 10 8
782. 5 c. blue, black & bistre 15 10
783. 7 c. blue, black & yellow 20 12

142. Map of Guatemala and British Honduras.

1967. Guatemala's Claim to British Honduras.

784. **142.** 4 c. blue, red & green 10 5
785. 5 c. blue, verm. & yell. 12 5
786. 6 c. blue, grey & orge. 15 8

1967. Air. Guatemalan Victory in "Norceca" Football Games. No. 704 optd. **GUATEMALA CAMPEON III Norcesa Foot-Ball** and football motif.

787. 3 c. green .. .. 1·25 1·25

1967. Air. American Heads of State Meeting, Punta del Este. No. 705 optd. **REUNION JEFES DE ESTADO AMERICANO, PUNTA DEL ESTE,** etc.

788. 4 c. slate 55 40

143. "Peace and Progress".

144. Yurrita Church.

1967. Air. Int. Co-operation.

789. **143.** 7 c. multicoloured .. 15 12
790. 21 c. multicoloured .. 45 25

1967. Air. Religion in Guatemala.

791. **144.** 1 c. brown, green & bl. 8 5
792. – 2 c. brn., pur. & salmon 10 5
793. – 3 c. indigo, cerise & blue 10 5
794. – 4 c. grn., mar. & salmon 12 5
795. – 5 c. brown, pur. & grn. 12 5
796. – 7 c. black, blue & mauve 20 10
797. – 10 c. indigo, violet & yell. 30 15

DESIGNS—HORIZ. 2 c. Santo Domingo Church. 3 c. San Francisco Church. 7 c. Mercy Church, Antigua. 10 c. Metropolitan Cathedral. VERT. 4 c. Antonio Jose de Irisarri. 5 c. Church of the Recollection.

145. Lincoln.

1967. Air. Death Centenary of Abraham Lincoln (1965).

798. **145.** 7 c. vermilion and blue 20 15
799. 9 c. black and green .. 20 15
800. 11 c. black & chestnut 25 15
801. 15 c. claret and blue.. 35 30
802. 30 c. green and purple 1·00 75

1967. Air. 8th Central American Scout Camporee. Nos. 745/9 optd. **VIII Camporee Scout Centroamericano Diciembre 1-8/1967.**

803. 5 c. Type **134** 25 25
804. 9 c. Scouts by campfire .. 45 45
805. 10 c. Scout carrying torch and flag.. .. 55 55
806. 15 c. Scout saluting .. 70 70
807. 20 c. Lord Baden Powell.. 85 85

1967. Air. Award of Nobel Prize for Literature to Miguel Angel Asturias (1st issue). Nos. 667/8 optd. **" Premio Nobel de Literatura – 10 diciembre 1967 – Miguel Angel Asturias ".**

808. **128.** 3 c. orange 20 20
809. – 4 c. violet 20 20

See also No. 838.

146. U.N.E.S.C.O. Emblem and Children.

147. Institute Emblem.

1967. Air. U.N.E.S.C.O. 20th Anniv. (in 1966).

810. **146.** 4 c. green 15 8
811. 5 c. blue 20 12
812. 7 c. grey 30 20
813. 21 c. purple 80 65

1967. Air. Inter-American Institute of Agricultural Sciences. 25th Anniv.

814. **147.** 9 c. black and green.. 20 12
815. 25 c. red and brown .. 60 50
816. 1 q. ultramarine & blue 2·25 2·00

1968. Air. 3rd Meeting of Central American Presidents. Optd. **III REUNION DE PRESIDENTES Nov. 15-18, 1967.**

817. **115.** 1 c. (No. 606).. .. 60 60
819. – 2 c. (No. 607).. .. 60 60
821. – 3 c. (No. 608).. .. 60 60
823. **132.** 7 c. (No. 730).. .. 60 60
824. 9 c. (No. 731).. .. 75 75
825. 13 c. (No. 732) .. 75 75
826. 21 c. (No. 733) .. 90 90
827. 35 c. (No. 734) .. 1·50 1·50

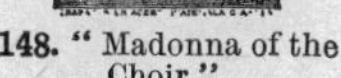

148. " Madonna of the Choir ".

149. Miguel Angel Asturias.

1968. Air. " Madonna of the Choir ". 400th Anniv. (in 1966).

828. **148.** 4 c. blue 25 10
829. 7 c. slate 20 10
830. 9 c. green 30 12
830a. 9 c. lilac 10 5
831. 10 c. red 30 10
832. 10 c. grey 20 10
832a. 10 c. blue 12 5
833. 1 q. maroon .. .. 1·90 1·10
834. 1 q. yellow .. .. 1·90 1·10

1968. Air. 11th Cycle Race. Nos. 784/6 optd. **AEREO XI VUELTA CICLISTICA 1967.**

835. **142.** 4 c. blue, red & green.. 35 35
836. 5 c. blue, verm. & yell. 35 35
837. 6 c. blue, grey & orge. 30 30

1968. Air. Award of Nobel Prize for Literature to Miguel Angel Asturias.

838. **149.** 20 c. ultramarine .. 35 30

1968. Air. Campaign for Conservation of the Forests". No. 789 optd. **AYUDA A CONSERVAR LOS BOSQUES.—1968.**

839. **143.** 7 c. multicoloured .. 20 12

1968. Air. Human Rights Year. No. 626 optd. **1968.—AÑO INTERNACIONAL DERECHOS HUMANOS.—ONU.**

840. **117.** 6 c. brown 40 20

1968. Air. Nahakin Scientific Expedition No. 589 optd. **Expedicion Cientifica etc.**

841. 6 c. blue and sepia .. 20 15

150. " Visit Guatemala".

151. Mexican Sculpture and Quetzal.

1968. Air. Tourism.

842. **140.** 10 c. claret and green 20 10
843. 20 c. vermilion & black 35 25
844. 50 c. ultramarine & red 85 80

1968. Olympic Games, Mexico. Quetzal in green and red.

845. **151.** 1 c. black 8 5
850. 1 c. slate 5 5
846. 5 c. yellow 10 5
851. 5 c. pink 8 5
852. 5 c. brown 8 5
853. 5 c. blue 8 5
847. 8 c. orange 15 5
848. 15 c. blue 30 12
849. 30 c. violet 60 50

1968. Air. Federation of Central American Universities. 20th Anniv. No. 705 optd. **CONFEDERACION DE UNIVERSIDADES CENTROAMERICANAS 1948 1968.**

854. 4 c. slate 25 12

152. Presidents Gustavos Diaz Ordaz and Julio Cesar Mendez Montenegro.

1968. Air. Exchange Visits of Mexican and Guatemalan Presidents.

855. **152.** 5 c. blue, ochre, green and vermilion .. 10 5
856. 10 c. blue and ochre .. 20 10
857. 25 c. blue and ochre .. 50 30

153. I.T.U. Emblem and Symbols.

154. Young Girl and Poinsettia.

1969. Air. Int. Telecommunications Union (1965). Cent.

858. **153.** 7 c. ultramarine .. 12 8
859. 15 c. black and emerald 25 10
859a. 15 c. brown and orange 30 12
860. 21 c. purple 35 25
861. 35 c. red and emerald 55 30
862. 75 c. emerald and red 1·40 1·25
863. 3 q. brown and red .. 4·50 4·25

1969. Help for Abandoned Children.

864. **154.** $2\frac{1}{2}$ c. ochre, red & green 8 5
865. $2\frac{1}{2}$ c. orge,. red & green 8 5
866. 5 c. black, red and grn. 15 8
867. 21 c. violet, red & green 45 40

1969. Air. Nos. 845/9 optd. **AEREO** and motif. Quetzal in green and red.

868. **151.** 1 c. black 40 20
869. 5 c. yellow 45 30
870. 8 c. orange 60 50
871. 15 c. blue 80 65
872. 30 c. violet 80 65

155. Dante.

157. "Apollo 11" and Module and Astronaut on Moon.

156. Map of Central and South America.

1969. Air. Dante. 700th Birth Anniv.
873. **155.** 7 c. blue and plum .. 12 5
874. 10 c. blue 20 5
875. 20 c. green 30 10
876. 21 c. slate and brown 45 20
877. 35 c. violet and green 75 30

1969. Air. Latin-American Universities Union. 20th Anniv.
878. **156.** 2 c. magenta and black 5 5
879. – 9 c. black and grey .. 20 10
DESIGN: (26×27 mm.). 9 c. University seal.

1969. Air. 1st Man on the Moon.
881. **157.** 50 c. black and purple 3·00 2·25
882. 1 q. black and blue .. 3·75 3·50

1970. Int. Labour Organization. 50th Anniv. Nos. 847/8 optd. **1968 Cincuentenario O. I. T.** in three lines.
884. **151.** 8 c. orge., grn. and red 12 8
886. 15 c. blue, green and red 20 15

158. Family of Grebes. **159.** Dr. V. M. Calderon.

1970. Air. Conservation of Giant Pied-billed Grebes, Lake Atitlan. Multicoloured.
888. 4 c. Lake Atitlan 5 5
889. 9 c. Type **158** 15 12
890. 20 c. Young grebe in nest (vert.) 35 20

1970. Air. Dr. Victor M. Calderon (medical scientist). Death Anniv.
892. **159.** 1 c. black and blue .. 5 5
893. 2 c. black and green .. 5 5
894. 9 c. black and yellow .. 12 8

160. Hand holding Bible.

1970. Air. 400th Anniv. of Spanish Bible.
895. **160.** 5 c. multicoloured .. 8 5

1971. Air. Surch **VALE QO. 50.**
896. **153.** 50 c. on 3 q. brn. & red 90 90

161. Arms and Newspaper.

1971. Air. First Postage Stamps and "Gaceta de Guatemala" Cent.
897. **161.** 2 c. blue and red .. 5 5
898. 5 c. brown and red .. 15 5
899. 25 c. blue and red .. 45 30

162. Maya Indians and C.A.R.E. Package.

163. Two Mayan Warriors and parcel.

1971. C.A.R.E. (Co-operative for American Relief Everywhere). 25th Anniv. Mult.
900. 1 c. Type **162** (black inscr.) (postage) 5 5
901. 1 c. Type **162** (brown inscr.) 5 5
902. 1 c. Type **162** (violet inscr.) 5 5
903. 2 c. Maya porter and C.A.R.E. parcel (air) .. 5 5
904. 5 c. Type **163** 10 5
905. 10 c. C.A.R.E. parcel within Maya border 15 12
SIZES: 2 c. (36×30 mm.). 10 c. (28×31 mm.).

164. J. Rufino Barrios, M. Garcia Granados and Emblems.

1971. Reforms. Cent.
909. **164.** 2 c. multicoloured .. 5 5
910. 10 c. multicoloured .. 15 10
911. 50 c. multicoloured .. 85 45
912. 1 q. multicoloured .. 1·40 85

165. J. A. Chavarry Arrue (stamp engraver) and Leon Bilak (philatelist).

1971. Air. "Homage to Philately".
913. **165.** 1 c. black and green .. 5 5
914. 2 c. black and brown 5 5
915. 5 c. black and orange 5 5

1971. Air. "INTERFER 71" Int. Fair, Guatemala. Optd. **FERIA INTERNACIONAL "INTERFER-71" 30 Oct. al 21 Nov.**
916. **116.** 6 c. blue and red .. 20 10

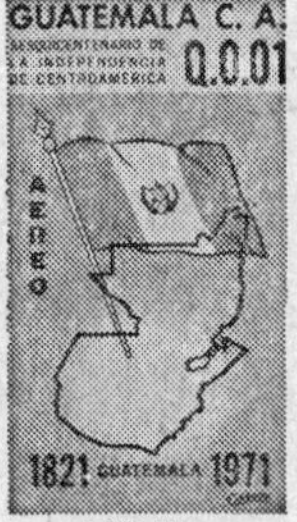

166. Flag and Map. **167.** Maya Statue and U.N.I.C.E.F. Emblem.

1971. Air. Central American Independence. 150th Anniv.
917. **166.** 1 c. blue, black & lilac 5 5
918. 3 c. bl., brown & pink 5 5
919. 5 c. bl., brown & orange 5 5
920. 9 c. bl., black & green 15 10

1971. Air. U.N.I.C.E.F. 25th Anniv.
921. **167.** 1 c. green 5 5
921a. 2 c. purple 5 5
922. 50 c. purple 70 50
923. 1 q. blue .. .. 1·50 1·00

168. Boeing "P-38" Fighter.

1972. Air. Guatemala Air Force. 50th Anniv.
924. **168.** 5 c. blue and brown .. 5 5
925. – 10 c. blue 12 10
DESIGN: (56×32 mm.). 10 c. Early "Bleriot XI" plane.

169. Ruins of Ancient Monastery. Antigua,

1972. Air. American Tourist Year. Ruins of Antigua.
927. **169.** 1 c. blue and light blue 5 5
928. A. 1 c. blue and light blue 5 5
929. B. 1 c. blue and light blue 5 5
930. C. 1 c. blue and light blue 5 5
931. D. 1 c. blue and light blue 5 5
932. E. 1 c. blue and light blue 5 5
933. **169.** 2 c. black and brown .. 5 5
934. A. 2 c. black and brown .. 5 5
935. B. 2 c. black and brown .. 5 5
936. C. 2 c. black and brown .. 5 5
937. D. 2 c. black and brown .. 5 5
938. E. 2 c. black and brown .. 5 5
939. **169.** 2½ c. blk., mve. & silver 5 5
940. A. 2½ c. blk., mve. & silver 5 5
941. B. 2½ c. blk., mve. & silver 5 5
942. C. 2½ c. blk., mve. & silver 5 5
943. D. 2½ c. blk., mve. & silver 5 5
944. E. 2½ c. blk., mve. & silver 5 5
945. **169.** 5 c. blk., blue & orange 5 5
946. A. 5 c. blk., blue & orange 5 5
947. B. 5 c. blk., blue & orange 5 5
948. C. 5 c. blk., blue & orange 5 5
949. D. 5 c. blk., blue & orange 5 5
950. E. 5 c. blk., blue & orange 5 5
951. **169.** 20 c. black and yellow 25 15
952. A. 20 c. black and yellow 25 15
953. B. 20 c. black and yellow 25 15
954. C. 20 c. black and yellow 25 15
955. D. 20 c. black and yellow 25 15
956. E. 20 c. black and yellow 25 15
957. **169.** 1 q. light bl., red & blue 1·10 80
958. A. 1 q. light bl., red & blue 1·10 80
959. B. 1 q. light bl., red & blue 1·10 80
960. C. 1 q. light bl., red & blue 1·10 80
961. D. 1 q. light bl., red & blue 1·10 80
962. E. 1 q. light bl., red & blue 1·10 80
DESIGNS: A. "La Recoleccion" archways. B. Cathedral ruins. C. Santa Clara courtyard. D. San Francisco gateway. E. Fountain, Central Park.

170. Pres. Carlos Arana Osorio.

1973. National Census.
963. **170.** 2 c. black and blue .. 5 5
964. – 3 c. brn., pink & orange 5 5
965. – 5 c. maroon, red & black 12 5
966. – 8 c. grn., blk. & emerald 20 5
DESIGNS—VERT. 3 c., 5 c. Pres. Osorio seated. 8 c. Pres. Osorio standing.

171. Francisco Ximenez.

1973. International Book Year (1972).
967. **171.** 2 c. black and green .. 5 5
968. 3 c. brown and orange 5 5
969. 6 c. black and blue .. 15 5

172. Simon Bolivar and Map. **173.** Eleanor Roosevelt.

1973. Air. Simon Bolivar "The Liberator".
970. **172.** 3 c. black and red .. 5 5
971. 3 c. blue and orange .. 5 5
972. 5 c. black and yellow .. 5 5
973. 5 c. black and green .. 5 5

1973. Air. Eleanor Roosevelt (sociologist). 90th Birth Anniv. (1974).
974. **173.** 7 c. blue 8 5

174. Star Emblem.

1973. Air. Polytechnic School. Centenary.
975. **174.** 5 c. yell., brn. & blue 5 5

1973. Air. Nos. 927/32 optd. **"II Feria Internacional" INTERFER/73 31 Octubre-Noviembre 18 1973 GUATEMALA.**
976. **169.** 1 c. blue and light blue 5 5
977. A. 1 c. blue and light blue 5 5
978. B. 1 c. blue and light blue 5 5
979. C. 1 c. blue and light blue 5 5
980. D. 1 c. blue and light blue 5 5
981. E. 1 c. blue and light blue 5 5

175. Guatamala 1 c. Stamp of 1871.

1973. Air. Stamp Centenary (1971).
988. **175.** 1 c. brown 5 5
988a. 6 c. orange 8 5
988b. 6 c. green 8 5
989. 1 q. red .. .. 1·10 80

176. School Building.

1973. Air. "Instituto Varones", Chiquimula Centenary.
990. **176.** 3 c. multicoloured .. 5 5
991. 5 c. red and black .. 5 5

1974. No. 863 surch. **Desvalorizadas, a** value and leaves.
992. **153.** 50 c. on 3 q. brn. & red 60 40

1974. Air. Universal Postal Union. Cent. Nos. 927/32 opt. **U P U HOMENAJE CENTENARIO 1874 1974** and U.P.U. emblem.
993. **169.** 1 c. blue and light blue 15 15
994. A. 1 c. blue and light blue 15 15
995. B. 1 c. blue and light blue 15 15
996. C. 1 c. blue and light blue 15 15
997. D. 1 c. blue and light blue 15 15
998. E. 1 c. blue and light blue 15 15

177. Barrios and Granados. **178.** Costume of San Martin Sacatepequez.

1974. Air. Polytechnic School. Centenary.
1000. **177.** 6 c. red, grey and blue 8 5
1001. – 25 c. multicoloured .. 30 12
DESIGN—VERT. 25 c. School building.

1974. Air. "Protection of the Quetzal" (Guatemala's national bird). No. 800 surch. **Preteccion del Ave Nacional el Quetzal,** bird and value.
1002. **145.** 10 c. on 11 c. black and chestnut 12 5

1974. Air. Guatemalan Costumes. Mult.
1003. 2 c. Solola costume .. 5 5
1004. 2½ c. Type **178** .. 5 5
1005. 9 c. Coban costume .. 12 5
1006. 20 c. Chichicastenango costume .. 25 15

179. Raza Maya Quekchi.

1975. Air. International Women's Year.
1007. **179.** 8 c. multicoloured .. 10 5
1008. 20 c. multicoloured .. 25 15

180. Rotary Emblem.

1975. Air. Guatemala City Rotary Club. 50th Anniv.
1009. **180.** 10 c. multicoloured .. 12 8

181. IWY Emblem and Orchid.

1975. Air. International Women's Year (2nd series).
1010. **181.** 1 c. multicoloured .. 5 5
1011. 8 c. multicoloured .. 10 5
1012. 26 c. multicoloured .. 35 25

182. Ruined Village.

1976. Air. Earthquake of 4 February 1976. Multicoloured.
1013. 1 c. Type **182** .. 5 5
1014. 3 c. Food queue .. 5 5
1015. 5 c. Jaguar Temple, Tikal 5 5
1016. 10 c. Broken bridge .. 12 8
1017. 15 c. Open-air casualty station .. 20 12
1018. 20 c. Harvesting sugar-cane .. 25 15
1019. 25 c. Ruined house .. 30 20
1020. 30 c. Reconstruction, Tecpan .. 40 30
1021. 50 c. Ruined church, Cerrodel Carmen .. 60 50
1022. 75 c. Clearing debris .. 90 80
1023. 1 q. Military aid .. 1·25 1·00
1024. 2 q. Lake Atitlan .. 2·50 2·00
Text in panels expresses gratitude for foreign aid.

183. Eagle and Quetzal Emblems.

1976. Air. American Revolution. Bicentary. Multicoloured.
1026. 1 c. Type **183** .. 5 5
1027. 2 c. Boston Tea Party .. 5 5
1028. 3 c. Thomas Jefferson (vert.) .. 5 5
1029. 4 c. Eagle and quetzal emblems .. 5 5
1030. 5 c. Warren's death at Bunker Hill .. 5 5
1031. 10 c. Washington's army at Valley Forge .. 12 8
1032. 15 c. Washington at Monmouth, N.J. .. 20 12
1033. 20 c. Eagle and quetzal emblems (different) .. 25 15
1034. 25 c. The Generals at Yorktown .. 30 20
1035. 30 c. Washington crossing the Delaware .. 40 30
1036. 35 c. Eagle and quetzal emblems (different) .. 45 35
1037. 40 c. Declaration of Independence .. 50 40
1038. 45 c. Patrick Henry (vert.) 55 45
1039. 50 c. Congress voting Independence .. 60 50
1040. 1 q. George Washington (vert.) .. 1·25 1·00
1041. 2 q. Abraham Lincoln (vert.) .. 2·50 2·00
1042. 3 q. Benjamin Franklin (vert.) .. 3·75 3·25
1043. 5 q. John F. Kennedy .. 6·25 5·75

EXPRESS LETTER STAMPS.

1940. No. 231 optd. **EXPRESO.**
E 411. **50.** 4 c. yellow 35 15

E 1. Motor cyclist.

1948. Surch.
E 479. **E 1.** 10 c. on 4 c. blk. & grn. 50 40

OFFICIAL STAMPS

O 1.

O 2.

1902.
O 127. **O 1.** 1 c. green .. 3·00 1·75
O 128. 2 c. red .. 3·00 1·75
O 129. 5 c. blue .. 2·75 1·40
O 130. 10 c. purple .. 4·00 1·40
O 131. 25 c. orange .. 4·00 1·40

1929.
O 239. **O 2.** 1 c. blue .. 10 10
O 240. 2 c. sepia .. 10 10
O 241. 3 c. green .. 10 10
O 242. 4 c. purple .. 15 15
O 243. 5 c. lake .. 15 15
O 244. 10 c. brown .. 30 20
O 245. 25 c. blue .. 60 30

1939. Air. Nos. 369/74 optd. **OFICIAL OFICIAL.**
O 400. **68.** 1 c. brown and orange 70 70
O 401. – 2 c. brown and red 70 70
O 402. – 3 c. brn., buff & green 70 70
O 403. – 4 c. brown and purple 70 70
O 404. – 5 c. brown and grey .. 80 80
O 405. – 10 c. brown and blue .. 80 80

GUINEA O2

The former French Colony on the W. coast of Africa which became fully independent in 1958.

1892. 100 centimes = 1 franc.
1973. 100 caury = 1 syli.

1959. Stamps of Fr. West Africa optd. **REPUBLIQUE DE GUINEA** or surch. also.
188. – 10 f. red, yellow, green & blue (No. 118) .. 1·00 1·10
189. **15.** 45 f. on 20 f. purple, bronze-green and olive 1·00 1·10

1. Pres. Sekou Toure.

1959. Proclamation of Independence.
190. **1.** 5 f. red 10 8
191. 10 f. blue 20 12
192. 20 f. orange 35 25
193. 65 f. green .. .. 1·00 75
194. 100 f. violet .. .. 2·00 1·50

2. Tamara Lighthouse and Fishing Boats. **3.** Flying Doves.

1959.
201. **2.** 1 f. red (postage) .. 5 5
202. 2 f. green 5 5
203. 3 f. brown 5 5
204. – 5 f. blue 5 5
205. – 10 f. purple 5 5
206. – 15 f. brown 25 12
207. – 20 f. purple 30 10
208. – 25 f. chestnut 40 15
209. **3.** 40 f. blue (air) 20 20
210. 50 f. green 40 30
211. 100 f. lake 65 55
212. 200 f. red .. .. 1·25 1·10
213. 500 f. orange-red .. 3·00 2·75
DESIGNS—VERT. 5 f. Palms and dhow. 20 f. Pres. Sekou Toure. HORIZ. 10 f. Pirogue being launched. 15 f. Elephant (front view). 25 f. Elephant (side view).

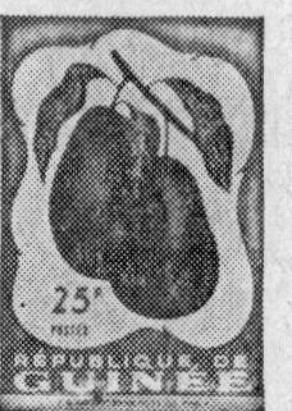
4. Mangoes.

6. "Raising the Flag".

5. Super Constellation Airliner.

1959. Fruits in natural colours. Frame colours given.
214. – 10 f. red (Bananas) .. 8 8
215. – 15 f. green (Grapefruit) 12 8
216. – 20 f. brown (Lemons) .. 15 12
217. **4.** 25 f. blue 20 15
218. – 50 f. violet (Pineapple) .. 45 20

1959. Air.
219. **5.** 100 f. blue, green & mag. 1·00 85
220. 200 f. mauve, brn. & grn. 1·25 1·10
221. – 500 f. black, green, blue, and orange .. .. 3·25 2·25
DESIGN: 500 f. Super Constellation airliner on ground.

1959. Independence. 1st Anniv.
222. **6.** 50 f. multicoloured .. 45 20
223. 100 f. multicoloured .. 90 55

7. Africans acclaiming U.N. Headquarters Building.

1959. U.N.O.
230. **7.** 1 f. blue and orange (post.) 5 5
231. 2 f. purple and green .. 5 5
232. 3 f. brown and red .. 5 5
233. 5 f. brown and turquoise .. 8 5
234. 50 f. green, blue and chocolate (air) 45 45
235. 100 f. green, red and blue 60 55
Nos. 234/5 are larger (45 × 26 mm.).

8. Eye-testing.

9. "Uprooted Tree".

1960. National Health. Inscr. "POUR NOTRE SANTE NATIONALE".
236. **8.** 20 f. + 10 f. red and blue 55 55
237. – 30 f. + 20 f. vio. and orge. 55 55
238. – 40 f. + 20 f. blue and red 60 60
239. – 50 f. + 50 f. brown & green 85 85
240. – 100 f. + 100 f. green & pur. 1·25 1·25
DESIGNS—HORIZ. 30 f. Laboratory assistant. 40 f. Spraying trees. VERT. (28½ × 40 mm.): 50 f. Research with microscope. 100 f. Operating theatre.

1960. World Refgugee Year.
241. **9.** 25 f. multicoloured .. 30 25
242. 50 f. multicoloured .. 45 30

10. U.P.U. Monument, Berne.

11. Flag and Map.

1960. Admission to U.P.U. 1st Anniv. Background differs for each value.
243. **10.** 10 f. black and chocolate 10 5
244. 15 f. lilac and mauve .. 12 8
245. 20 f. indigo and blue .. 15 10
246. – 25 f. myrtle and green .. 20 12
247. – 50 f. sepia and orange .. 40 20
DESIGN: 25 f, 50 f. As T **10** but vert.

1960. Olympic Games. Optd. **Jeux Olympiques Rome 1960** and Olympic rings.
248. **6.** 50 f. multicoloured (post.) 2·75 2·75
249. 100 f. multicoloured .. 4·00 4·00
250. **5.** 100 f. blue, green and magenta (air) .. 3·25 2·75
251. 200 f. mauve, brn. & grn. 6·50 4·50
252. – 500 f. black, green, blue and orange (No. 221) .. 15·00 15·00

1960. Independence. 2nd Anniv.
253. **11.** 25 f. multicoloured .. 20 20
254. 30 f. multicoloured .. 25 25

1960. U.N.O. 15th Anniv. Optd. **XVEME ANNIVERSAIRE DES NATIONS UNIES.** (a) Nos. 214/18 Fruits in natural colours.
255. – 10 f. red 20 20
256. – 15 f. green 20 20
257. – 20 f. brown 20 20
258. **4.** 25 f. blue 25 25
259. – 50 f. violet 55 50

(b) Nos. 230/35.
260. **7.** 1 f. blue & orange (post.) 8 8
261. 2 f. purple and green .. 8 8
262. 3 f. brown and red .. 8 8
263. 5 f. brown and turquoise 8 8
264. **7.** 50 f. green, blue and chocolate (air) .. 45 45
265. 100 f. green, red and blue 65 55

1961. World Refugee Year stamps surch. **1961 + 10 FRS.** (or **20 FRS.**).
266. **9.** 25 f. + 10 f. multicoloured 3·25 3·25
267. 50 f. + 20 f. multicoloured 3·25 3·25

12. Antelope.

1961. Centres in brown, green and blue. Inscriptions and value tablets in colours given.
268. **12.** 5 f. blue-green 5 5
269. 10 f. emerald 8 5
270. 25 f. violet 15 12
271. 40 f. orange 25 20
272. 50 f. red 40 25
273. 75 f. blue 55 30

13. Guinea Flag and Exhibition Hall, Conakry

1961. First Three-Year Plan. Flag in red, yellow and green.
274. **13.** 5 f. blue and red .. 5 5
275. 10 f. brown and red .. 8 8
276. 25 f. grey-green and red 15 15

14. Guinea-fowl.

1961. Guinea-fowl in purple and blue.
277. **14.** 5 f. mauve and blue .. 8 5
278. 10 f. red and blue .. 10 5
279. 25 f. rose and blue .. 12 8
280. 40 f. brown and blue .. 20 12
281. 50 f. bistre and blue .. 30 15
282. 75 f. olive and blue .. 55 30

1961. Protection of Animals. Surch. **POUR LA PROTECTION DE NOS ANIMAUX +5 FRS.**

283. 12. 5 f.+5 f. blue-green .. 8 8
284. 10 f.+5 f. emerald .. 12 8
285. 25 f.+5 f. violet .. 30 20
286. 40 f.+5 f. orange .. 45 25
287. 50 f.+5 f. red 55 40
288. 75 f.+5 f. blue.. .. 90 50

15. Patrice Lumumba.

1962. Lumumba (Congo leader). 1st Death Anniv.

289. 15. 10 f. multicoloured .. 40 25
290. 25 f. multicoloured .. 55 30
291. 50 f. multicoloured .. 90 55

1962. Malaria Eradication (1st issue). Nos. 236/40 opt. with Malaria Eradication emblem and **ERADICATION DE LA MALARIA.**

292. 8. 20 f.+10 f. red and blue 25 25
293. – 30 f.+20 f. violet & orge. 35 35
294. – 40 f.+20 f. blue and red 45 45
295. – 50 f.+50 f. brown & green 90 90
296. – 100 f.+100 f. grn. & pur. 1·75 1·75

16. King Mohamed V and Map. 17. Mosquito and Emblem.

1962. Casablanca Conf. 1st Anniv.

297. 16. 25 f. blk., yell., red & blue 70 25
298. 75 f. blk., yell., brn. & grn. 1·50 50

1962. Air. Malaria Eradication (2nd issue).

299. 17. 25 f. black and orange.. 25 15
300. 50 f. black and red .. 40 25
301. 100 f. black and green.. 65 50

1962. African Postal Union Commem. As T 172 of Egypt.

303. 25 f. green, brown & orge. 60 12
304. 100 f. orange and chocolate 1·50 40

1962. Guinea-fowl stamps surch. **POUR LA PROTECTION DE NOS OISEAUX +5 FRS.**

305. 14. 5 f.+5 f. 12 5
306. 10 f.+5 f. 12 8
307. 25 f.+5 f. 20 20
308. 40 f.+5 f. 35 30
309. 50 f.+5 f. 70 45
310. 75 f.+5 f. .. .. 1·40 90

18. Bote-player. 19. Hippopotamus.

1962. Native Musicians.

311. 18. 30 c. red, grn. & bl. (post.) 5 5
312. A. 50 c. grn., brn. & salmon 5 5
313. B. 1 f. purple and green .. 5 5
314. C. 1 f. 50 turq., red & yell. 5 5
315. D. 2 f. green, red and mauve 5 5
316. C. 3 f. violet, green & turq. 5 5
317. B. 10 f. blue, brn. & orge. 8 5
318. D. 20 f. red, sepia and olive 12 8
319. 18. 25 f. violet, sepia & olive 15 10
320. A. 40 f. magenta, grn. & bl. 25 15
321. 18. 50 f. blue, red and rose 35 20
322. A. 75 f. blue, brown & ochre 50 35
323. D. 100 f. bl., red & pink (air) 55 45
324. D. 200 f. red and blue .. 1·10 65
325. E. 500 f. blue, vio. & brown 3·25 2·25

DESIGNS—(Musicians playing). HORIZ. A, Bolon. C, Koni. D, Kora. E, Balafon. VERT. B, Flute.

1962. Wild Game.

326. 19. 10 f. sepia, grn. & orge. 12 5
327. – 25 f. brown, sepia & grn. 20 10
328. – 30 f. sepia, yell. & olive 25 12
329. 19. 50 f. sepia, green & blue 35 20
330. – 75 f. brown, pur. & lilac 45 35
331. – 100 f. sepia, yell. & turq. 60 45

DESIGNS: 25 f., 75 f. Lion. 30 f., 100 f. Panther.

20. Boy at Blackboard.

22. Crowned Crane. 21. Alfa Yaya.

1962. Campaign Against Illiteracy.

332. 20. 5 f. sepia, yellow & red 5 5
333. – 10 f. sepia, orge. & maroon 8 5
334. 20. 15 f. sepia, green & red 15 5
335. – 20 f. sepia, turq. & mar. 20 15

DESIGN: 10 f., 20 f. Teacher at blackboard.

1962. African Heroes and Martyrs.

336. 21. 25 f. sepia, turq. & gold 20 10
337. – 30 f. sepia, ochre & gold 35 15
338. – 50 f. sepia, pur. & gold 45 20
339. – 75 f. sepia, green & gold 1·00 40
340. – 100 f. sepia, red & gold 1·40 60

PORTRAITS: 30 f. King Behanzin. 50 f. King Ba Bemba of Sikasso. 75 f. Almamy Samory. 100 f. Chief Tierno Aliou of the Goumba.

1962. Algerian Refugees Fund. Surch. **Aide aux Refugies Algeriens** and premium.

341. 17. 25 f.+15 f. multicoloured 45 45
342. 75 f.+25 f. multicoloured 65 65

1962. Air. "The Conquest of Space". Optd. with capsule and **La Conquete De L'Espace.**

343. 3. 40 f. blue 40 25
344. 50 f. green 45 30
345. 100 f. lake 65 50
348. 200 f. red .. .. 1·40 95

1962. Birds. Multicoloured.

349. 30 c. T 22 (postage) .. 5 5
350. 50 c. African grey parrot 5 5
351. 1 f. Hornbill 5 5
352. 1 f. 50 spoonbill 5 5
353. 2 f. Bateleur eagle .. 5 5
354. 3 f. T 22 .. .. .. 5 5
355. 10 f. As 50 d. 8 5
356. 20 f. As 1 f. 12 8
357. 25 f. As 1 f. 50 .. .. 20 12
358. 40 f. As 2 f. 25 15
359. 50 f. T 22.. .. .. 30 20
360. 75 f. As 50 c. 45 35
361. 100 f. As 1 f. (air) .. 65 40
362. 200 f. As 1 f. 50 .. 1·25 70
363. 500 f. As 2 f. .. .. 3·25 2·00

All except T 22 are horiz.

23. Handball.

1963. Sports.

364. 23. 30 c. maroon, vermilion and green (postage).. 5 5
365. A. 50 c. violet, lilac & blue 5 5
366. B. 1 f. sepia, orange & green 5 5
367. C. 1 f. 50 ultramarine, orange and maroon.. 5 5
368. D. 2 f. blue, turq. & purple 5 5
369. 23. 3 f. mar., olive & indigo 5 5
370. A. 4 f. violet, magenta & bl. 5 5
371. B. 5 f. sepia, emerald & pur. 5 5
372. C. 10 f. ultramarine and bright purple .. 8 5
373. D. 20 f. blue, orge. & red.. 12 5
374. 23. 25 f. maroon, emerald and black 15 8
375. A. 30 f. violet, black & blue 20 15
376. B. 100 f. sepia, lake and green (air) 65 35
377. C. 200 f. ultramarine, olive-brown & maroon .. 1·50 65
378. D. 500 f. blue, brn. & purple 2·75 1·90

DESIGNS: A, Boxing. B, Running. C, Cycling. D, Canoeing.

24. Campaign Emblem. 26. "African Unity".

25. Butterfly (Papilionides family).

1963. Freedom from Hunger.

379. 24. 5 f. yellow and red .. 5 5
380. 10 f. yellow and green.. 5 5
381. 15 f. yellow and brown 8 8
382. 25 f. yellow and olive.. 15 12

1963. Butterflies. Multicoloured.

383. 10 c. Type 25 (postage) .. 5 5
384. 30 c. "Papilio demodocus" 5 5
385. 40 c. As 30 c. 5 5
386. 50 c. "Graphum policenes" 5 5
387. 1 f. "Papilio nireus" .. 5 5
388. 1 f. 50 Type 25 .. .. 5 5
389. 2 f. "Papilio menestheus" 5 5
390. 3 f. As 30 c. 5 5
391. 10 f. As 50 c. 8 5
392. 20 f. As 1 f. 12 5
393. 25 f. Type 25 .. .. 20 5
394. 40 f. As 2 f. 25 12
395. 50 f. As 30 c. 30 15
396. 75 f. As 1 f. 40 30
397. 100 f. Type 25 (air) .. 55 25
398. 200 f. As 50 c. .. .. 1·60 65
399. 500 f. As 2 f. .. .. 2·75 1·25

1963. Conference of African Heads of State, Addis Ababa.

400. 26. 5 f. sepia, black and turquoise on green .. 5 5
401. 10 f. sepia, black and yellow on yellow .. 5 5
402. 15 f. sepia, black and olive on olive .. 12 8
403. 25 f. sepia, black and brown on cinnamon.. 20 12

27. Capsule encircling Globe.

1963. Red Cross Centenary.

404. 27. 5 f. red & green (post.) 5 5
405. 10 f. red and blue .. 8 8
406. 15 f. red and yellow .. 12 8
407. 25 f. red & black (air).. 20 15

1963. Air. Conakry-New York Air Service. Optd. **PREMIER SERVICE DIRECT CONAKRY-NEW YORK PAN AMERICAN 30 JUILLET 1963.**

409. 5. 100 f. blue, green & mag. 1·10 80
410. 200 f. mauve, brn. & grn. 2·25 1·40

1963. Olympic Games Preparatory Commission, Conakry. Nos. 364/6 surch. **COMMISSION PREPARATOIRE AUX JEUX OLYMPIQUES A CONAKRY,** rings and new value.

411. 40 f. on 30 c. maroon, vermilion and green .. 75 75
412. 50 f. on 50 c. violet, lilac and blue.. .. 1·00 1·00
413. 75 f. on 1 f. sepia, orange and green .. .. 1·50 1·50

28. "Hemichromis bimaculatus".

1964. Guinea Fishes. Multicoloured.

414. 30 c. Type 28 (postage) .. 5 5
415. 40 c. "Golden Pheasant" carp 5 5
416. 50 c. "Aphyosemion coeruleum" 5 5
417. 1 f. Red cichlid and "Hemichromis fasciatus" 5 5
418. 1 f. 50 "Yellow Pride" carp 5 5
419. 2 f. Senegal herring .. 5 5
420. 5 f. Type 28 .. .. 5 5
421. 30 f. As 40 c. 15 12
422. 40 f. As 50 c. 30 15
423. 75 f. As 1 f. 45 35
424. 100 f. As 1 f. 50 (air) .. 55 45
425. 300 f. As 2 f. .. .. 1·50 1·10

29. President Kennedy. 30. Pipeline under Construction.

1964. Pres. Kennedy Memorial Issue. Flag in red and blue.

426. 29. 5 f. violet & black (post.) 5 5
427. 25 f. violet and green .. 15 12
428. 50 f. violet and brown.. 30 25
429. 100 f. blk. & violet (air) 65 65

1964. Inaug. of Piped Water Supply. Conakry.

430. – 5 f. red 5 5
431. – 10 f. violet 5 5
432. – 20 f. brown 12 8
433. – 30 f. blue 15 12
434. – 50 f. green 30 20

DESIGNS—HORIZ. 10 f. Reservoir. 20 f. Joining pipes. 30 f. Transporting pipes. 50 f. Laying pipes.

31. Ice hockey. 32. Eleanor Roosevelt with Children.

1964. Winter Olympic Games, Innsbruck. Rings, frame and tablet in gold.

435. 31. 10 f. olive green and emerald (postage) .. 12 8
436. – 25 f. slate violet & violet 25 12
437. – 50 f. black-green & blue 55 30
438. – 100 f. black & chest. (air) 55 45

DESIGNS: 25 f. Ski-jumping. 50 f. Skiing. 100 f. Figure-skating.

1964. Air. Olympic Games, Tokyo (1st issue). Nos. 376/8 optd. **JEUX OLYMPIQUES TOKYO 1964** and Olympic rings.

439. 100 f. sepia, lake & green 1·10 90
440. 200 f. ultram, olive-brown and maroon .. .. 1·60 1·25
441. 500 f. blue, brown & pur. 3·75 3·25

1964. Declaration of Human Rights. 15th Anniv.

442. 32. 5 f. green (postage) .. 5 5
443. 10 f. orange 8 5
444. 15 f. blue 12 8
445. 25 f. red 15 10
446. 32. 50 f. violet (air) .. 30 20

33. Hyena.

1964. Animals.

447. 33. 5 f. sepia and yellow .. 5 5
448. 30 f. sepia and blue .. 15 15
449. – 40 f. black and magenta 25 15
450. – 75 f. sepia and green .. 45 20
451. – 100 f. sepia and ochre.. 60 40
452. – 300 f. deep vio. & orge. 1·60 1·10

ANIMALS: 40 f., 300 f. Buffalo. 75 f., 100 f. Elephant.

34. Guinea Pavilion. 35. Nefertari, Isis and Hathor.

1964. New York World's Fair.

453. 34.	30 f. green and lilac ..	20	12
454.	40 f. green and purple..	30	15
455.	50 f. green and brown..	45	20
456.	75 f. blue and red ..	55	25

See also Nos. 484/87.

1964. Nubian Monuments Preservation. Multicoloured.

458.	10 f. Type **35** (postage) ..	8	5
459.	25 f. Pharaoh in battle ..	15	10
460.	50 f. The Nile—partly submerged sphinxes ..	25	20
461.	100 f. Rameses II, entrance hall of Great Temple, Abu Simbel ..	45	30
462.	200 f. Lower part of Colossi, Abu Simbel ..	1·00	70
463.	300 f. Nefertari (air) ..	1·75	1·40

36. Athlete with Torch. **37.** Doudou (Boke) Mask.

1965. Olympic Games, Tokyo (2nd issue). Multicoloured.

464.	5 f. Weightlifter and children (postage) ..	5	5
465.	10 f. Type **36**	5	5
466.	25 f. Pole-vaulting ..	12	10
467.	40 f. Running ..	20	15
468.	50 f. Judo	25	20
469.	75 f. Japanese hostess ..	45	30
470.	100 f. Air hostess and air liner (horiz.) (air) ..	65	35

1965. Native Masks and Dancers. Multicoloured.

472.	20 c. Type **37** (postage) ..	5	5
473.	40 c. Niamou (Nzerekore) mask ..	5	5
474.	60 c. "Yoki" (Boke) statuette ..	5	5
475.	80 c. Guekedou dancer ..	5	5
476.	1 f. Niamou (Nzerekore) mask ..	5	5
477.	2 f. Macenta dancer ..	8	5
478.	15 f. Niamou (Nzerekore) mask ..	10	8
479.	20 f. Tom-tom beater (forest region) ..	15	10
480.	60 f. Macenta "Bird-man" dancer ..	45	30
481.	80 f. Bassari (Koundara) dancer ..	50	40
482.	100 f. Karana sword dancer	55	55
483.	300 f. Niamou (Nzerekore) mask (air) ..	1·60	90

The 40 c., 1 f., 15 f. and 300 f. each show different masks.

1965. New York World's Fair. T **34** additionally inscr. "1965".

484. 34.	30 f. orange and green..	15	12
485.	40 f. green and red ..	20	15
486.	50 f. violet and blue ..	25	20
487.	75 f. violet and brown..	40	30

38. Metal-work.

1965. Native Handicrafts. Multicoloured.

489.	15 f. Type **38** (postage) ..	10	5
490.	20 f. Pottery ..	12	8
491.	60 f. Dyeing ..	30	25
492.	80 f. Basket-making ..	45	35
493.	100 f. Ebony-work (air) ..	55	40
494.	300 f. Ivory-work..	1·75	85

39. I.T.U. Emblem and Symbols.

1965. I.T.U. Cent.

495. 39.	25 f. mult. (postage) ..	12	12
496.	50 f. multicoloured ..	25	25
497. 39.	100 f. multicoloured (air)	55	30
498.	200 f. multicoloured ..	1·10	50

40. U.N. Headquarters and I.C.Y. Emblem.

1965. I.C.Y.

501. 40.	25 f. red and green (post.)	12	10
502.	45 f. red and violet ..	20	15
503.	75 f. red and brown ..	30	25
504. 40.	100 f. orange & blue (air)	55	35

41. Polytechnic Institute, Conakry.

1965. 7th Independence Anniv. Multicoloured.

505.	25 f. Type **41** (postage) ..	15	10
506.	30 f. Camayenne Hotel ..	20	15
507.	40 f. Gbessia Airport ..	35	25
508.	75 f. "28 Septembre" Stadium	45	30
509.	200 f. Polytechnic Institute, North facade (air) ..	1·10	80
510.	500 f. Ditto, West facade..	2·75	1·90

Nos. 505/10 are larger, 53 × 23 mm.

42. Moon, Globe and Satellite. **43.** Sabre Dance, Karana.

1965. "To the Moon". Multicoloured.

511.	5 f. Type **42** (postage) ..	5	5
512.	10 f. Trajectory of "Ranger 7"	5	5
513.	25 f. "Relay" satellite ..	12	10
514.	45 f. "Vostok 1, 2" and Globe	25	20
515.	100 f. "Ranger 7" approaching Moon (air) ..	45	30
516.	200 f. Launching of "Ranger 7"	90	55

Nos. 512/9 are larger, 36 × 25½ mm.; Nos. 515/6 are vert., 25 × 36 mm.

1966. Guinean Dances. Multicoloured.

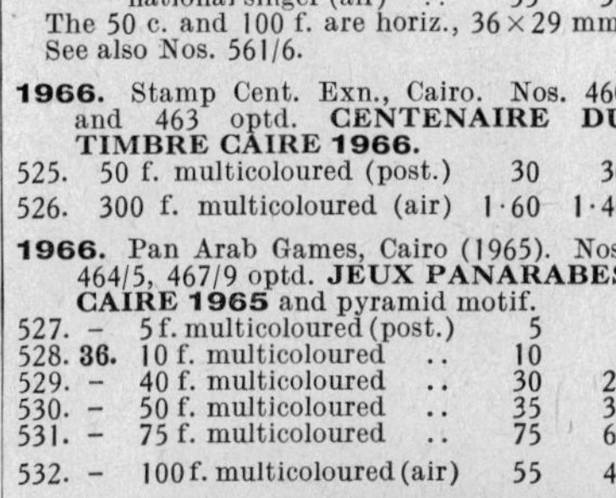

519.	10 c. Type **43** (postage) ..	5	5
520.	30 c. Young girls' dance, Lower Guinea ..	5	5
521.	50 c. Tiekere musicians, "Eyora" (bamboo) dance Bandjinguene ..	5	5
522.	5 f. Doundouba dance, Kouroussa ..	5	5
523.	40 f. Bird-man's dance, Macenta.. ..	30	15
524.	100 f. Kouyate Kandia, national singer (air) ..	55	35

The 50 c. and 100 f. are horiz., 36 × 29 mm. See also Nos. 561/6.

1966. Stamp Cent. Exn., Cairo. Nos. 460 and 463 optd. **CENTENAIRE DU TIMBRE CAIRE 1966.**

525.	50 f. multicoloured (post.)	30	30
526.	300 f. multicoloured (air)	1·60	1·40

1966. Pan Arab Games, Cairo (1965). Nos. 464/5, 467/9 optd. **JEUX PANARABES CAIRE 1965** and pyramid motif.

527. –	5 f. multicoloured (post.)	5	5
528. 36.	10 f. multicoloured ..	10	8
529. –	40 f. multicoloured ..	30	25
530. –	50 f. multicoloured ..	35	30
531. –	75 f. multicoloured ..	75	60
532. –	100 f. multicoloured (air)	55	40

44. Vonkou Rocks, Telimele. **45.** U.N.E.S.C.O. Emblem.

1966. Landscapes (1st series). Multicoloured.

534.	20 f. Type **44** (postage) ..	12	5
535.	25 f. Artificial lake, Coyah	15	5
536.	40 f. Waterfalls, Kate ..	20	10
537.	50 f. Bridge, Forecariah ..	25	12
538.	75 f. Liana bridge.. ..	40	25
539.	100 f. Lighthouse and bay, Boulbinet (air)	55	40

See also Nos. 603/608.

1966. U.N.E.S.C.O. 20th Anniv. (a) Postage.

540. 45.	25 f. multicoloured ..	15	10

(b) Air. Nos. 509/10 optd. **vingtans 1946-1966** and UNESCO Emblem.

541.	200 f. multicoloured ..	1·10	90
542.	500 f. multicoloured ..	2·75	2·25

46. **47.** Decade and U.N.E.S.C.O. Symbols.

1966. Guinean Flora and Female Head-dresses. Similar designs.

543. 46.	10 c. multicoloured (post.)	5	5
544. –	20 c. multicoloured ..	5	5
545. –	30 c. multicoloured ..	5	5
546. –	40 c. multicoloured ..	5	5
547. –	3 f. multicoloured ..	5	5
548. –	4 f. multicoloured ..	5	5
549. –	10 f. multicoloured ..	8	5
550. –	25 f. multicoloured ..	15	8
551. –	30 f. multicoloured ..	20	12
552. –	50 f. multicoloured ..	30	20
553. 46.	80 f. multicoloured ..	45	30
554. –	200 f. multicoloured (air)	1·10	65
555. –	300 f. multicoloured ..	1·60	1·10

Nos. 551/555 are 29 × 42 mm.

1966. Int. Hydrological Decade.

558. 47.	5 f. red and blue ..	5	5
559.	25 f. red and green ..	12	8
560.	100 f. red and purple ..	55	35

1966. Guinean National Ballet. Designs show various dances as T **43**.

561.	60 c. multicoloured ..	5	5
562.	1 f. multicoloured.. ..	5	5
563.	1 f. 50 multicoloured ..	5	5
564.	25 f. multicoloured ..	12	10
565.	50 f. multicoloured ..	25	15
566.	75 f. multicoloured ..	45	30

SIZES—VERT. (26 × 36 mm.): 60 c., 1 f., 1 f. 50, 50 f. HORIZ. (36 × 29 mm.): 25 f., 75 f.

48. "Village".

1966. U.N.I.C.E.F. 20th Anniv. Multicoloured designs showing children's drawings.

567.	2 f. "Elephant" ..	5	5
568.	3 f. "Doll" ..	5	5
569.	10 f. "Girl" ..	5	5
570.	20 f. Type **48** ..	10	5
571.	25 f. "Footballer" ..	12	8
572.	40 f. "Still Life" ..	15	12
573.	50 f. "Bird in Tree" ..	25	20

49. Dispensing Medicine.

1967. W.H.O. Headquarters, Geneva. Inaug. Multicoloured.

574.	30 f. Type **49**	15	10
575.	50 f. Doctor examining child	25	12
576.	75 f. Nurse weighing baby	30	20
577.	80 f. W.H.O. Building & flag	40	30

INDEX

Countries can be quickly located by referring to the index at the end of this volume.

50. Niamou Mask. **51.** Research Institute.

1967. Guinean Masks. Multicoloured.

578.	10 c. Banda-di (Kanfarade Boke region) ..	5	5
579.	30 c. Niamou (N'zerekore region) (different) ..	5	5
580.	50 c. Type **50**	5	5
581.	60 c. Yinadjinkele (Kankan region)	5	5
582.	1 f. As 10 c.	5	5
583.	1 f. 50, As 30 c.	5	5
584.	5 f. Type **50**	5	5
585.	25 f. As 60 c.	10	5
586.	30 f. As 10 c.	12	8
587.	50 f. As 30 c.	20	12
588.	75 f. As Type **50**	35	20
589.	100 f. As 60 c.	55	30

1967. Pastoria Research Institute. Multicoloured.

590.	20 c. Type **51** (postage) ..	5	5
591.	30 c. "Python regius" (snake) ..	5	5
592.	50 c. Extracting snake's venom	5	5
593.	1 f. "Python sebae" ..	5	5
594.	2 f. Attendants handling python ..	5	5
595.	5 f. "Bitis gabonica" (Gabon viper) ..	5	5
596.	20 f. "Dendroaspis viridis"	10	5
597.	30 f. As 5 f.	12	8
598.	50 f. As 1 f.	25	15
599.	75 f. As 50 c.	40	20
600.	200 f. As 20 c. (air) ..	1·00	55
601.	300 f. As 2 f.	1·75	85

Nos. 596/601 are 56 × 26 mm.

1967. Landscapes (2nd series). Multicoloured.

603.	5 f. Loos Islands (postage)	5	5
604.	30 f. Tinkisso waterfalls ..	12	5
605.	70 f. The "Elephant's Trunk", Kakoulima ..	35	8
606.	80 f. Seashore, Ratoma ..	40	12
607.	100 f. House of explorer Olivier de Sanderval (air)	45	35
608.	200 f. Aerial view of Conakry	90	65

52. People's Palace, Conakry.

1967. 20th Anniv. of Guinean Democratic Party and Inaug. of People's Palace. Multicoloured.

609.	5 f. Type **52** (postage) ..	5	5
610.	30 f. Elephant's head ..	15	5
611.	55 f. Type **52** ..	30	20
612.	200 f. As 30 f. (air) ..	1·00	65

1967. Lions Int. 50th Anniv. Landscape series optd. **AMITE DES PEUPLES GRACE AU TOURISME 1917-1967** and Lions Emblem.

613.	5 f. (No. 603) (postage) ..	8	5
614.	30 f. (No. 604)	20	15
615.	40 f. (No. 536)	25	15
616.	50 f. (No. 537)	30	20
617.	70 f. (No. 605)	40	25
618.	75 f. (No. 538)	55	40
619.	80 f. (No. 606)	65	40
620.	100 f. (No. 539) (air) ..	70	45
621.	100 f. (No. 607) ..	70	45
622.	200 f. (No. 608) ..	1·10	75

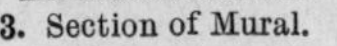

53. Section of Mural. **54.** W.H.O. Building, Brazzaville.

1967. Air. "World of Tomorrow". Jose Vanetti's Mural, Conf. Building, U.N. Headquarters. Designs showing various sections of mural.

623. 30 f. multicoloured .. 15 10
624. – 50 f. multicoloured .. 20 15
625. 53. 100 f. multicoloured .. 45 30
626. – 200 f. multicoloured .. 80 50

1967. W.H.O. Building, Brazzaville. Inaug.

628. 54. 30 f. olive, ochre & blue 15 10
629. 75 f. red, ochre and blue 40 25

55. Human Rights Emblem.

56. Coyah, Oubreka Region.

1968. Human Rights Year.

630. 55. 30 f. red, green & ochre 12 8
631. 40 f. red, blue & violet 15 10

1968. Regional Costumes and Habitations. Multicoloured.

632. 20 c. Type **56** (postage) .. 5 5
633. 30 c. Kankan Region .. 5 5
634. 40 c. Kankan, Upper Guinea 5 5
635. 50 c. Forest region .. 5 5
636. 60 c. Foulamory, Gaoual Region 5 5
637. 5 f. Cognagui, Koundara Region 5 5
638. 15 f. As 50 c. 8 5
639. 20 f. As 20 c. 12 8
640. 30 f. As 30 c. 12 10
641. 40 f. Fouta-Djallon, Middle Guinea 20 12
642. 100 f. Labe, Middle Guinea 55 20
643. 300 f. Bassari, Koundara Region (air) .. .. 1·40 75

The 60 c. to 300 f. are larger (60×39 mm.).

57. "The Village Story-teller."

1968. Paintings of African Legends (1st series.). Multicoloured.

644. 25 f. Type **57** (postage) .. 10 5
645. 30 f. "The Moon and the Stars" 12 8
646. 75 f. "Leuk the Hare sells his Sister" 30 20
647. 80 f. "The Hunter and the Female Antelope" .. 35 20
648. 100 f. "Old Faya's Inheritance" (air) 50 20
649. 200 f. "Soumangourou Kante killed by Djegue" .. 90 35

The 75 f. and 100 f. are vert. designs.

1968. Paintings of African Legends (2nd series). As T **57**. Multicoloured.

651. 15 f. "Little Demons of Mount Nimba" (postage) 5 5
652. 30 f. "Lan, the Baby Buffalo" 10 5
653. 40 f. "The Nianablas and the Crocodiles" 15 10
654. 50 f. "Leuk the Hare and the Drum" 20 12
655. 70 f. "Malissadio—the Young Girl and the Hippopotamus" (air) 30 12
656. 300 f. "Little Goune, Son of the Lion" .. .. 1·25 80

The 30, 50 and 300 f. are vert.

58. Baboon.

1968. African Fauna. Multicoloured.

658. 5 f. Type **58** (postage) .. 5 5
659. 10 f. Panthers 5 5
660. 15 f. Hippopotami .. 8 5
661. 20 f. Crocodile 10 5
662. 30 f. Warthog 12 8
663. 50 f. Antelope 20 12
664. 75 f. Buffalo 35 20
665. 100 f. Lions (air) 60 25
666. 200 f. Elephant .. .. 1·10 55

Nos. 665/6 are 50×35 mm.

59. Robert F. Kennedy.

1968. "Martyrs of Liberty". Multicoloured.

668. 30 f. Type **59** (postage) .. 12 5
669. 75 f. Martin Luther King .. 30 12
670. 100 f. John F. Kennedy .. 45 25
671. 50 f. Type **59** (air) .. 25 12
672. 100 f. Martin Luther King 55 20
673. 200 f. John F. Kennedy .. 1·10 50

60. Running.

1969. Olympic Games, Mexico (1968). Multicoloured.

674. 5 f. Type **60** (postage) .. 5 5
675. 10 f. Boxing 5 5
676. 15 f. Throwing the javelin 5 5
677. 25 f. Football 10 8
678. 30 f. Hurdling 12 8
679. 50 f. Throwing the hammer 25 15
680. 75 f. Cycling 40 20
681. 100 f. Gymnastics (air) .. 55 25
682. 200 f. Exercising on rings 1·10 45
683. 300 f. Pole-vaulting .. 1·60 65

The 25, 100, 200 and 300 f. are larger, 57×30 mm.

Each design also shows one of three different sculptured figures.

1969. Moon Flight of "Apollo 8". Nos. 514/16 optd. **APOLLO 8 DEC. 1968** and earth and moon motifs or surch.

684. 30 f. on 45 f. mult. (postage) 20 20
685. 45 f. multicoloured .. 25 25
686. 25 f. on 200 f. mult. (air) 12 12
687. 100 f. multicoloured .. 50 50
688. 200 f. multicoloured .. 90 90

61. "Tarzan".

63. "Apollo" Launch.

62. Pioneers lighting Fire.

1969. "Tarzan" (famous Guinea Chimpanzee). Multicoloured.

689. 25 f. Type **61** 12 8
690. 30 f. "Tarzan" in front of Pastoria Institute .. 20 10
691. 75 f. "Tarzan" and family 40 15
692. 100 f. "Tarzan" squatting on branch 55 30

1969. Guinean Pioneer Youth Organisation. Multicoloured.

693. 5 f. Type **62** 5 5
694. 25 f. Pioneer and village .. 10 5
695. 30 f. Pioneers squad .. 12 8
696. 40 f. Playing basketball .. 20 10
697. 45 f. Two pioneers .. 20 12
698. 50 f. Pioneers emblem .. 25 15

1969. 1st Man on the Moon. Multicoloured.

700. 25 f. Type **63** 12 5
701. 30 f. View of Earth .. 12 5
702. 50 f. Modules descent to the Moon 25 15
703. 60 f. Astronauts on Moon .. 30 15
704. 75 f. Landing module on Moon 40 25
705. 100 f. Take-off from Moon 50 25
706. 200 f. "Splashdown" .. 1·10 60

No. 705 is size 35×71 mm.

The above stamps were issued with English and French inscriptions.

64. Pylon and Heavy Industry.

1969. Int Labour Organization. 50th Anniv. Multicoloured.

707. 25 f. Type **64** 12 5
708. 30 f. Broadcasting studio .. 15 5
709. 75 f. Harvesting 35 15
710. 200 f. Making pottery .. 1·00 50

65. Dr. Edward Jenner (1749–1823).

66. O.E.R.S. Countries on Map of Africa.

1970. Campaign Against Measles and Smallpox. Multicoloured.

711. 25 f. Child suffering from smallpox 12 8
712. 30 f. Mother and child with measles 15 10
713. 40 f. Inoculating girl .. 20 12
714. 50 f. Inoculating boy .. 20 15
715. 60 f. Inoculating family .. 25 20
716. 200 f. Type **65** .. 1·00 70

1970. Meeting of Senegal River Riparian States Organization (Organisation des Etats Riverains du fleuve Senegal).

717. 66. 30 f. multicoloured .. 15 12
718. 200 f. multicoloured .. 90 70

NOTE: The Riparian States are Guinea, Mali, Mauritania and Senegal.

67. Dish Aerial and Open book.

1970. World Telecommunications Day.

719. 67. 5 f. black and blue .. 5 5
720. 10 f. black and red .. 5 5
721. 50 f. black and yellow .. 30 5
722. 200 f. black and lilac .. 1·10 75

68. Lenin.

1970. Lenin. Birth Cent. Multicoloured.

723. 5 f. Type **68** 5 5
724. 20 f. "Lenin in the Smolny" (Serov) .. 12 8
725. 30 f. "Lenin addressing Workers" (Serov) .. 15 10
726. 40 f. "Lenin speaking to Servicemen" (Vasiliev) 25 12
727. 100 f. "Lenin with Crowd" (Vasilev) 55 25
728. 200 f. Type **68** .. .. 1·10 65

69. Congo Tetra.

1971. Fishes. Multicoloured.

729. 5 f. Type **69** 5 5
730. 10 f. Blue gularis 5 5
731. 15 f. Fire mouth panchax 8 5
732. 20 f. Six-lined distichodus 10 8
733. 25 f. Jewel cichlid .. 12 10
734. 30 f. Dwarf rainbow cichlid 15 12
735. 40 f. Red lyretail 20 15
736. 45 f. Banded jewel fish .. 25 20
737. 50 f. Gunther's killy .. 25 20
738. 75 f. Butterfly fish .. 40 25
739. 100 f. Kingfish 50 30
740. 200 f. African mouth-breeder .. .. .. 1·00 65

70. Blue Touraco.

1971. Wild Birds. Multicoloured.

741. 5 f. Type **70** (postage) .. 5 5
742. 20 f. Golden oriole .. 10 8
743. 30 f. Coucal 15 10
744. 40 f. Great grey shrike .. 20 12
745. 75 f. Vulturine guineafowl 50 25
746. 100 f. Ground Hornbill 60 30
747. 50 f. Type **70** (air) .. 30 20
748. 100 f. As 20 f. 55 35
749. 200 f. As 75 f. .. .. 1·10 55

71. U.N.I.C.E.F. Emblem on Map of Africa.

1971. U.N.I.C.E.F. 25th Anniv.

750. 71. 25 f. multicoloured .. 12 5
751. 30 f. multicoloured .. 15 8
752. 50 f. multicoloured .. 25 12
753. 60 f. multicoloured .. 30 15
754. 100 f. multicoloured .. 55 30

72. J. F. & R. Kennedy and Martin Luther King.

1972. Air. Martyrs for Peace. Embossed on silver or gold foil.

755. 72. 300 f. silver .. .. 3·00
756. 1500 f. gold, cream and green .. .. .. 15·00

73. Jules Verne and Moon Rocket.

1972. Air. Moon Exploration. Embossed on silver or gold foil.

No.	Type	Description	Unused	Used
757.	73.	300 f. silver	3·00	
758.		1200 f. gold	12·00	

74. Pres. Richard Nixon.

1972. Air. Pres. Nixon's Visit to Peking. Embossed on gold or silver foil.

No.	Type	Description	Unused	Used
759.	74.	90 f. silver	70	
760.	–	90 f. silver	70	
761.	–	90 f. silver	70	
762.	–	90 f. silver	70	
763.	74.	290 f. gold	2·25	
764.	–	290 f. gold	2·25	
765.	–	290 f. gold	2·25	
766.	–	290 f. gold	2·25	
767.	–	1200 f. gold and red ..	12·00	

DESIGNS—VERT. Nos. 760, 764, Chinese ping-pong player. Nos. 761, 765, American ping-pong player. Nos. 762, 766, Mao Tse-tung. HORIZ. (45 × 35 mm.). No. 767, Pres. Nixon and Mao Tse-tung.

75. "Flying Flat fish".

1972. Imaginary Space Creatures. Mult.

No.	Description	Unused	Used
768.	5 f. Type 75	5	5
769.	20 f. "Radio active crab"	12	5
770.	30 f. "Space octopus" ..	15	8
771.	40 f. "Rocket-powered serpent"	20	12
772.	100 f. "Winged eel" ..	60	25
773.	200 f. "Flying dragon" ..	1·10	50

76. African Child.

1972. Racial Equality Year. Multicoloured.

No.	Description	Unused	Used
774.	15 f. Type 76 (postage) ..	8	5
775.	20 f. Asiatic child ..	10	8
776.	30 f. Indian youth ..	12	8
777.	50 f. European girl ..	25	12
778.	100 f. Heads of four races	50	30
779.	100 f. As No. 778 (air) ..	55	35

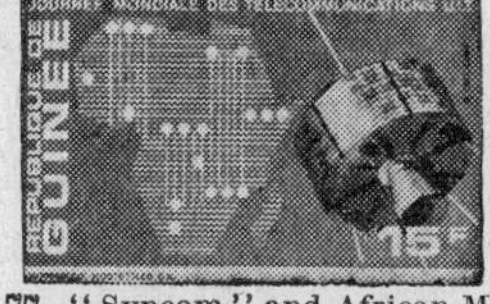

77. "Syncom" and African Map.

1972. World Telecommunications Day. Multicoloured.

No.	Description	Unused	Used
780.	15 f. Type 77 (postage) ..	5	5
781.	30 f. "Relay"	12	8
782.	75 f. "Early Bird" ..	30	20
783.	80 f. "Telstar"	40	30
784.	100 f. As 30 f. (air) ..	50	25
785.	200 f. As 75 f.	1·00	55

78. APU Emblem and Dove with Letter.

1972. African Postal Union. 10th Anniv.

No.	Type	Description	Unused	Used
786.	78.	15 f. mult. (postage) ..	8	5
787.		30 f. multicoloured ..	12	8
788.		75 f. multicoloured ..	30	20
789.		80 f. multicoloured ..	35	25
790.	–	100 f. multicoloured (air)	55	25
791.	–	200 f. multicoloured	1·10	55

DESIGNS: 100 f., 200 f. APU emblem airmail envelope.

79. Child reading Book. 80. Throwing the Javelin.

1972. Int. Book Year. Multicoloured.

No.	Description	Unused	Used
792.	5 f. Type 79	5	5
793.	15 f. Book with sails ..	8	5
794.	40 f. Girl with book and plant	20	12
795.	50 f. "Key of Knowledge" and open book ..	25	15
796.	75 f. "Man" reading book, and globe	40	25
797.	200 f. Open book and laurel sprigs	90	55

1972. Olympic Games, Munich. Mult.

No.	Description	Unused	Used
798.	5 f. Type 80 (postage) ..	5	5
799.	10 f. Pole-vaulting ..	5	5
800.	25 f. Hurdling	10	8
801.	30 f. Throwing the hammer	12	10
802.	40 f. Boxing	20	12
803.	50 f. Gymnastics (horse) ..	20	15
804.	75 f. Running	30	25
805.	100 f. Gymnastics (rings) (air)	55	25
806.	200 f. Cycling	1·10	55

1972. U.N. Environmental Conservation Conf., Stockholm. Nos. 750/4 optd. **UNE SEULE TERRE** and emblem.

No.	Type	Description	Unused	Used
808.	71.	25 f. multicoloured ..	12	8
809.		30 f. multicoloured ..	12	8
810.		50 f. multicoloured ..	20	12
811.		60 f. multicoloured ..	30	20
812.		100 f. multicoloured ..	45	30

81. Dimitrov addressing "Reichstag Fire" Court.

1972. George Dimitrov (Bulgarian statesman). 90th Birth Anniv.

No.	Type	Description	Unused	Used
813.	81.	5 f. blue, gold and green	5	5
814.	–	25 f. blue, gold and green	10	5
815.	–	40 f. blue, gold and green	20	12
816.	–	100 f. blue, gold & green	55	30

DESIGNS: 25 f. In Moabit Prison, Berlin, 1933. 40 f. Writing memoirs. 100 f. G. Dimitrov.

82. Emperor Haile Selassie. 83. "Syntomeida epilais".

1972. Emperor Haile Selassie of Ethiopia's 80th Birthday. Multicoloured.

No.	Description	Unused	Used
817.	40 f. Type 82	20	15
818.	200 f. Emperor Haile Selassie in military uniform ..	1·25	70

1973. Guinean Insects. Multicoloured.

No.	Description	Unused	Used
819.	5 f. Type 83	5	5
820.	15 f. "Hippodamia californica"	8	5
821.	30 f. "Tettigonia viridissima"	15	10
822.	40 f. "Apis mellifica" ..	20	12
823.	50 f. "Photinus pyralis" ..	25	15
824.	200 f. "Ancyluris formosissima"	1·10	70

84. Dr. Kwame Nkrumah.

1973. Organisation of African Unity. 10th Anniv.

No.	Type	Description	Unused	Used
825.	84.	1 s. 50 blk., gold & green	10	5
826.	–	2 s. 50 blk., gold & green	12	8
827.	–	5 s. blk., gold & green ..	30	25
828.	–	10 s. violet and gold ..	55	45

DESIGNS: Nos. 826/8, different portraits of Dr. Kwame Nkrumah similar to T **84**.

85. Institute of Applied Biology, Kindia.

1973. W.H.O. 25th Anniv. Multicoloured.

No.	Description	Unused	Used
829.	1 s. Type 85	5	5
830.	2 s. 50 Preparing vaccine from an egg ..	15	8
831.	3 s. Filling ampoules with vaccine	20	12
832.	4 s. Sterilization of vaccine	30	12
833.	5 s. Packing vaccines ..	30	15
834.	10 s. Preparation of vaccine base	60	30
835.	20 s. Inoculating patient ..	1·25	55

Nos. 833/35 are size 48 × 31 mm.

86. Volcanic Landscape.

1973. Copernicus. 500th Birth Anniv. Multicoloured.

No.	Description	Unused	Used
836.	50 c. Type 86	5	5
837.	2 s. Sun over desert ..	15	8
838.	4 s. Earth and Moon ..	30	10
839.	5 s. Lunar landscape ..	35	15
840.	10 s. Jupiter	60	30
841.	20 s. Saturn	1·25	60

87. Loading Bauxite at Quayside.

1974. Air. Bauxite Industry, Bok. Mult.

No.	Description	Unused	Used
843.	4 s. Type 87	30	10
844.	6 s. Bauxite train	40	20
845.	10 s. Bauxite mining ..	60	30

88. "Clappertonia ficifolia". 90. Pioneers testing Rope-bridge.

89. Drummers and Pigeon.

1974. Flowers of Guinea. Multicoloured.

No.	Description	Unused	Used
846.	50 c. Type 88 (postage) ..	5	5
847.	1 s. "Rothmannia longiflora"	5	5
848.	2 s. "Oncoba spinosa" ..	12	8
849.	3 s. "Venidium fastuosum"	20	12
850.	4 s. "Bombax costatum"	25	15
851.	5 s. "Clerodendrum splendens"	30	15
852.	7 s. 50 "Combretuni grandiflorum"	45	25
853.	10 s. "Mussaendra erythrophylla"	60	30
854.	12 s. "Argemone mexicana"	70	40
855.	20 s. "Thunbergia alata" (air)	1·25	60
856.	25 s. "Diascia barberae" ..	1·50	80
857.	50 s. "Kigelia africana" ..	3·00	1·60

SIZES—VERT. Nos. 847/9, As T **88**. Nos. 850/3, 36 × 47 mm. DIAMOND. Nos. 854/7, 61 × 61 mm.

No. 855 is wrongly inscribed "Thunbegia alata".

1974. Universal Postal Union. Cent. Mult.

No.	Description	Unused	Used
858.	5 s. Type 89	30	15
859.	6 s. Runner and pigeon ..	40	20
860.	7 s. 50 Monorail train, lorry and pigeon	45	25
861.	10 s. Airliner, ship & pigeon	60	30

1974. National Pioneers (Scouting) Movement. Multicoloured.

No.	Description	Unused	Used
863.	50 c. Type 90	5	5
864.	2 s. "On safari"	12	8
865.	4 s. Using field-telephone	25	15
866.	5 s. Cooking on camp-fire ..	30	15
867.	7 s. 50 Saluting	45	25
868.	10 s. Playing basketball ..	60	30

91. Chimpanzee.

1975. Wild Animals. Multicoloured.

No.	Description	Unused	Used
871.	1 s. Type 91	5	5
872.	2 s. Impala	12	5
873.	3 s. Warthog	20	8
874.	4 s. Defassa's buck ..	25	10
875.	5 s. Leopard	30	15
876.	6 s. Greater kudu ..	40	20
877.	6 s. 50 Zebra	40	25
878.	7 s. 50 Cape buffalo ..	45	30
879.	8 s. Hippopotamus ..	50	30
880.	10 s. Lion	60	30
881.	12 s. Rhinoceros	75	40
882.	15 s. Elephant	90	60

MORE DETAILED LISTS

are given in the Stanley Gibbons Catalogues referred to in the country headings:

BC	British Commonwealth
E1, E2, E3	Europe 1, 2, 3
O1, O2, O3, O4	Overseas 1, 2, 3, 4

92. Lion and Lioness beside Pipeline.

1975. African Development Bank. Tenth Anniv.

884.	5 s. Type **92**	35	15
885.	7 s. Elephants beside pipeline	50	30
886.	10 s. Lions beside pipeline (horiz.)	70	30
887.	20 s. Elephant and calf beside pipeline (horiz.)	1·40	60

93. Women playing Saxophones.

1976. Int. Women's Year (1975) Multicoloured.

888.	5 s. Type **93**	35	15
889.	7 s. Women playing guitars	50	30
890.	9 s. Woman railway shunter	60	35
891.	15 s. Woman doctor ..	90	60
892.	20 s. Genetics emblems ..	1·20	65

94. Gymnastics.

1976. Olympic Games, Montreal. Multicoloured.

894.	3 s. Type **94**	20	8
895.	4 s. Long jump	25	10
896.	5 s. Throwing the hammer	30	15
897.	6 s. Throwing the discus ..	40	20
898.	6 s. 50 Hurdling	40	25
899.	7 s. Throwing the javelin	50	30
900.	8 s. Running	50	30
901.	8 s. 50 Cycling	60	35
902.	10 s. High-jumping ..	60	35
903.	15 s. Putting the shot ..	90	60
904.	20 s. Pole vaulting ..	1·20	65
905.	25 s. Football	1·50	80

95. Bell and Early Telephone.

1976. Telephone Centenary. Multicoloured.

907.	5 s. Type **95**	30	15
908.	7 s. Bell and wall telephone	50	30
909.	12 s. Bell and satellite "Syncom"	80	45
910.	15 s. Bell and satellite "Telstar"	90	60

POSTAGE DUE STAMPS

D 1.

D 2.

1959.

D 195. D **1.**	1 f. green	5	5
D 196.	2 f. red	5	5
D 197.	3 f. brown	8	8
D 198.	5 f. blue	12	12
D 199.	10 f. orange	55	55
D 200.	20 f. mauve	1·10	1·10

1959.

D 224. D **2.**	1 f. red	10	10
D 225.	2 f. orange	10	10
D 226.	3 f. lake	15	15
D 227.	5 f. green	30	30
D 228.	10 f. sepia	55	55
D 229.	20 f. blue	1·25	1·10

GUINEA - BISSAU O2

Following an armed rebellion against Colonial rule, the independence of former Portuguese Guinea was recognised on September 10th 1974.

100 centavos = 1 escudo.
1976. 100 cents = 1 peso.

1975. No. 425 of Port. Guinea optd. **REP. DA BISSAU.**

426.	2 e. multicoloured ..	50	50

19. Cabral and Guineans.

1976. Amilcar Cabral Commemoration.

427. **19.**	3 p. multicoloured ..	20	20
428.	5 p. multicoloured ..	30	30
429.	6 p. multicoloured ..	35	35
430.	10 p. multicoloured ..	60	60

GUYANA BC

Formerly British Guiana, attained independence on 26th May, 1966, and changed its name to Guyana.

CANCELLED REMAINDERS. In 1969 remainders of some issues were put on the market cancelled-to-order in such a way as to be indistinguishable from genuine postally used copies for all practical purposes. Our quotations which are indicated by an asterisk are the same for cancelled-to-order or postally used copies.

1966. Nos. 331, etc., optd. **GUYANA INDEPENDENCE 1966.**

393. **21.**	1 c. black	5	5
379. –	2 c. myrtle	5	5
395. –	3 c. olive and brown ..	5	5
396. –	4 c. violet	5	5
397. –	5 c. red and black ..	5	5
383. –	6 c. green	5	5
399. –	8 c. blue	8	10
400. –	12 c. black and brown ..	10	15
401. –	24 c. black and orange ..	25	25
402. –	36 c. red and black ..	30	35
403. –	48 c. blue and brown ..	25	30
404. –	72 c. red and green ..	25	25
405. –	$1 pink, yellow, grn. & blk.	35	55
406. –	$2 mauve	45	70
407. –	$5 blue and black ..	1·10	1·25

1. Flag and Map.

1966. Independence. Multicoloured.

408.	5 c. Type **1**	5	5
409.	15 c. Type **1**	10	8
410.	25 c. Arms of Guyana ..	20	20
411.	$1 Arms of Guyana ..	60	60

2. Bank Building.

1966. Opening of Bank of Guyana.

412. **2.**	5 c. multicoloured ..	5	5
413.	25 c. multicoloured ..	15	15

3. British Guiana One Cent Stamp of 1856.

1967. World's Rarest Stamp Commem.

414. **3.**	5 c. multicoloured ..	5	*5
415.	25 c. multicoloured ..	15	*10

4. Chateau Margot.

1967. Independence. 1st Anniv. Multicoloured.

416.	6 c. Type **4**	5	*5
417.	15 c. Independence Arch ..	10	*5
418.	25 c. Fort Island ..	15	*5
419.	$1 National Assembly ..	60	65

Nos. 418/9 are horiz.

5. "Millie" (parrot).

6. Wicket-keeping.

1967. Christmas.

441. **5.**	5 c. yell., bl., blk. & green	8	*5
443.	5 c. yell., blue, black & red	5	*5
442.	25 c. yell., blue, blk. & vio.	20	*8
444.	25 c. yell., blue, blk. & grn.	20	*8

1968. M.C.C.'s. West Indies Tour. Multicoloured.

445.	5 c. Type **6**	5	*5
446.	6 c. Batting	5	*5
447.	25 c. Bowling	15	*8

Nos. 445/7 were only issued in sheets of 9 containing three se-tenant strips of each value.

7. Sunfish.

1968. Multicoloured.

448.	1 c. Type **7**	5	5
449.	2 c. Pirai	5	5
450.	3 c. Lukunani	5	5
451.	5 c. Hassar	5	5
452.	6 c. Patua	5	5
490a.	10 c. White-headed Piping Guan	5	5
491a.	15 c. Harpy Eagle	8	8
492.	20 c. Hoatzin, or Canje pheasant	12	10
493a.	25 c. Cock of the Rock ..	12	10
494.	40 c. Great Kiskadee ..	20	30
495.	50 c. Accouri	25	30
496.	60 c. Peccary	30	30
497.	$1 Labba	45	50
498.	$2 Armadillo	1·25	1·25
462.	$5 Ocelot	3·00	3·25

Nos. 490a/94 are vert.

8. "Christ of St. John of the Cross" (after Salvador Dali).

1968. Easter.

463. **8.**	5 c. multicoloured ..	5	*5
464.	25 c. multicoloured ..	20	*5

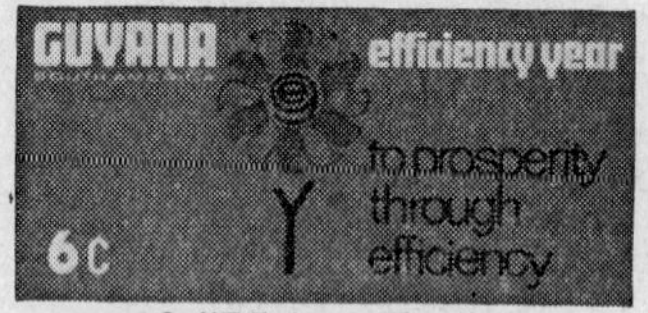

9. "Efficiency Year".

1968. "Savings Bonds and Efficiency". Multicoloured.

465.	6 c. Type **9**	5	*5
466.	25 c. Type **9**	12	*5
467.	30 c. "Savings Bonds" ..	15	*5
468.	40 c. "Savings Bonds" ..	20	*5

10. Open Book, Star and Crescent.

1968. Holy Quran. 1400th Anniv.

469. **10.**	6 c. black, gold & flesh	5	*5
470.	25 c. black, gold & lilac	12	*5
471.	30 c. black, gold & green	15	*5
472.	40 c. black, gold & cobalt	20	*5

11. Broadcasting Greetings.

1968. Christmas.

473. **11.**	6 c. brown, black & grn.	5	*5
474.	25 c. brown, violet & grn.	12	*5
475. –	30 c. green & turquoise	15	*5
476. –	40 c. red and turquoise	20	*5

DESIGNS: 30 c. and 40 c. Map showing Radio Link, Guyana – Trinidad.

12. Festival Ceremony.

1969. Hindu Festival of Phagwah. Multicoloured.

477.	6 c. Type **12**	5	5
478.	25 c. Ladies spraying Scent	12	12
479.	30 c. Type **12**	15	15
480.	40 c. As No. 478	20	25

13. "Sacrament of the Last Supper" (Dali).

1969. Easter Commemoration.

481. **13.**	6 c. multicoloured ..	5	5
482.	25 c. multicoloured ..	12	12
483.	30 c. multicoloured ..	15	15
484.	40 c. multicoloured ..	20	25

14. Map showing "CARIFTA" Countries. 15. First all-Aluminium Ship.

1969. "CARIFTA". 1st Anniv.

500. **14.**	6 c. red, blue & turquoise	5	5
501. –	25 c. lemon, brn. & red	15	15

DESIGN—HORIZ. 25 c. "Strength in Unity".

1969. Int. Labour Organisation. 50th Anniv.

502. **15.**	30 c. blue, black & silver	15	15
503. –	40 c. multicoloured ..	20	20

DESIGN—VERT. 40 c. Bauxite Processing plant.

16. Scouts raising Flag.

1969. 3rd Caribbean Scout Jamboree and Diamond Jubilee of Scouting in Guyana. Multicoloured.

504.	6 c. Type **16**	5	5
505.	8 c. Camp Fire cooking ..	5	5
506.	25 c. As T **16**	12	12
507.	30 c. As 8 c.	15	15
508.	50 c. As T **16**	30	35

17. Gandhi and Spinning Wheel.

1969. Mahatma Gandhi. Birth Cent.

509. **17.**	6 c. black, brn. & olive	5	5
510.	15 c. black, brown & lilac	12	12

18. "Mother Sally" Dance Troupe. 19. Forbes Burnham and Map.

1969. Christmas. Unissued stamps optd. as in T **18**. Multicoloured.

511.	5 c. Type **18**	5	5
512.	6 c. City Hall, Georgetown	5	5
513.	25 c. As T **18**	15	15
514.	60 c. As 6 c.	45	40

1970. Republic Day.

515. **19.**	5 c. sepia, ochre and blue	5	5
516. –	6 c. multicoloured ..	5	5
517. –	15 c. multicoloured ..	12	12
518. –	25 c. multicoloured ..	12	12

DESIGNS—VERT. 6 c. Rural self-help. HORIZ. 15 c. University of Guyana. 25 c. Guyana House.

20. "The Descent from the Cross" (Rubens).

1970. Easter. Multicoloured.

519.	5 c. Type **20**	5	5
520.	6 c. "Christ on the Cross" (Rubens)	5	5
521.	15 c. Type **20**	15	15
522.	25 c. As 6 c.	25	25

21. "Peace" and U.N. Emblem.

1970. United Nations. 25th Anniv. Multicoloured.

523.	5 c. Type **21**	5	5
524.	6 c. U.N. Emblem, Gold-panning and Drilling ..	5	5
525.	15 c. Type **21**	12	12
526.	25 c. As 6 c.	20	20

22. "Mother and Child" (Philip Moore).

1970. Christmas.

527. **22.**	5 c. multicoloured ..	5	5
528.	6 c. multicoloured ..	5	5
529.	15 c. multicoloured ..	12	12
530.	25 c. multicoloured ..	20	20

23. National Co-operative Bank.

1971. Republic Day.

531. **23.**	6 c. multicoloured ..	5	5
532.	15 c. multicoloured ..	10	10
533.	25 c. multicoloured ..	15	20

24. Racial Equality Symbol.

1971. Racial Equality Year.

534. **24.**	5 c. multicoloured ..	5	5
535.	6 c. multicoloured ..	5	5
536.	15 c. multicoloured ..	10	12
537.	25 c. multicoloured ..	15	20

25. Young Volunteer felling Tree.

1971. Self-help Road Project. 1st Anniv.

538. **25.**	5 c. multicoloured ..	5	5
539.	20 c. multicoloured ..	12	12
540.	25 c. multicoloured ..	15	15
541.	50 c. multicoloured ..	30	30

62. Yellow Allamanda.

1971. Flowering Plants. Multicoloured.

542.	1 c. Pitcher Plant of Mt. Roraima	5	5
543.	2 c. Type **26**	5	5
544.	3 c. Hanging Heliconia ..	5	5
545.	5 c. Annatto tree	5	5
546.	6 c. Cannon-ball tree ..	5	5
547.	10 c. Cattleya	5	8
548.	15 c. Christmas Orchid ..	8	8
549.	20 c. "Paphinia cristata"	8	10
550.	25 c. Marabunta	15	15
550a.	25 c. Marabunta	12	12
551.	40 c. Tiger Beard	15	20
552.	50 c. "Guzmania ligulata"	20	20
553.	60 c. Soldier's Cap ..	25	25
554.	$1 "Chelonanthus uliginoides"	40	45
555.	$2 "Norantea guianensis"	75	85
556.	$5 "Odontadenia grandiflora"	2·00	2·25

No. 550 shows the flowers facing upwards and has the value in the centre. No. 550a has the flowers facing downwards with the value to the right.

27. Child praying at Bedside.

1971. Christmas. Multicoloured.

557.	5 c. Type **27**	5	5
558.	20 c. Type **27**	15	15
559.	25 c. Carnival Masquerader (vert.)	15	15
560.	50 c. as 25 c.	30	30

28. Obverse and Reverse of Guyana $1 Coin.

1972. Republic Day.

561. **28.**	5 c. silver, black and red	5	5
562. –	20 c. silver, black and red	10	10
563. **28.**	25 c. silver, black & blue	15	15
564. –	50 c. silver, blk. & grn.	30	30

DESIGN: 20 c., 50 c. Reverse and obverse of Guyana $1 coin.

29. Hands and Irrigation Canal.

1972. Youman Nabi (Mohammed's Birthday)

565. **29.**	5 c. multicoloured ..	5	5
566.	25 c. multicoloured ..	12	12
567.	30 c. multicoloured ..	15	15
568.	60 c. multicoloured ..	35	35

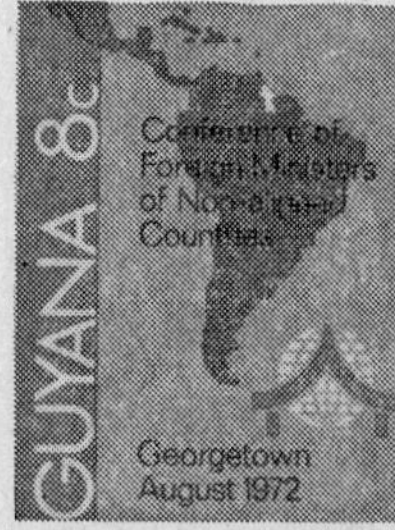

30. Map and Emblem.

1972. Conf. of Foreign Ministers of Non-aligned Countries.

569. **30.**	8 c. multicoloured ..	5	5
570.	25 c. multicoloured ..	12	12
571.	40 c. multicoloured ..	20	20
572.	50 c. multicoloured ..	30	30

31. Hand reaching for Sun.

1972. 1st Caribbean Festival of Arts.

573. **31.** 8 c. multicoloured .. 5 5
574. 25 c. multicoloured .. 12 12
575. 40 c. multicoloured .. 20 20
576. 50 c. multicoloured .. 30 30

32. Joseph, Mary and the Infant Jesus.

1972. Christmas.

577 **32.** 8 c. multicoloured .. 5 5
578. 25 c. multicoloured .. 12 12
579. 40 c. multicoloured .. 20 20
580. 50 c. multicoloured .. 30 30

33. Umana Yana (Meeting-house).

1973. Republic Day. Multicoloured.

581. 8 c. Type **33** 5 5
582. 25 c. Bethel Chapel .. 12 12
583. 40 c. As 25 c. 20 20
584. 50 c. Type **33** 25 25

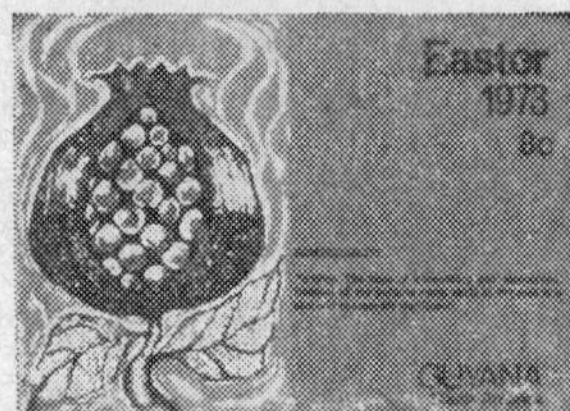

34. Pomegranate.

1973. Easter. Multicoloured.

585. 8 c. Type **34** 5 5
586. 25 c. Cross and map .. 12 12
587. 40 c. As 25 c. 20 20
588. 50 c. Type **34** 25 25

SIZES—VERT. 25 c., 40 c. 34 × 47 mm.

35. Stylized Blood Cell.

1973. Guyana Red Cross. 25th Anniv.

589. **35.** 8 c. red and black .. 5 5
590. 25 c. red and purple .. 12 12
591. 40 c. red and blue .. 20 20
592. 50 c. red and green .. 25 25

36. Steel-Band Players.

1973. Christmas. Multicoloured.

593. 8 c Type **36** 5 5
594. 25 c. Type **36** 12 12
595. 40 c. Stained-glass window 20 20
596. 50 c. As 40 c. 25 25

37. Symbol of Progress.

1974. Republic Day. Multicoloured.

597. 8 c. Type **37** 5 5
598. 25 c. Wai-Wai Indian .. 12 12
599. 40 c. Type **37** 20 20
600. 50 c. As 25 c. 25 25

1974. No. 546 surch.

601. 8 c. on 6 c. multicoloured .. 8 8

38. Kite with Crucifixion Motif.

1974. Easter.

602. **38.** 8 c. multicoloured .. 5 5
603. – 25 c. black and green 12 12
604. – 40 c. black and mauve 20 20
605. **38.** 50 c. multicoloured .. 25 25

DESIGN: Nos. 603/4, "Crucifixion" in pre-Columbian style.

39. British Guiana 24 c. Stamp of 1874.

1974. Universal Postal Union. Cent.

606. **39.** 8 c. multicoloured .. 5 5
607. – 25 c light grn., grn. & blk. 12 12
608. **39.** 40 c. multicoloured .. 20 20
609. – 50 c. grn., brn. & blk. .. 20 25

DESIGNS—VERT. (42 × 25 mm.). 25 c., 50 c. U.P.U. emblem and Guyana postman.

40. Guides with Banner.

1974. Girl Guides' Golden Jubilee. Multicoloured.

610. 8 c. Type **40** 5 5
611. 25 c. Guides in camp .. 12 12
612. 40 c. As 25 c. 20 20
613. 50 c. Type **40** 20 25

41. Buck Toyeau.

1974. Christmas. Multicoloured.

615. 8 c. Type **41** 5 5
616. 35 c. Five-fingers and awaras 15 15
617. 50 c. Pawpaw and tangerine 20 20
618. $1 Pineapple and sapodilla 40 45

1975. No. 544 surch.

620. 8 c. on 3 c. multicoloured 5 5

42. Golden Arrow of Courage. **43.** Old Sluice Gate.

1975. Republic Day. Guyana Orders and Decorations. Multicoloured.

621. 10 c. Type **42** 5 5
622. 35 c. Cacique's Crown of Honour 15 15
623. 50 c. Cacique's Crown of Valour 20 25
624. $1 Order of Excellence .. 40 45

1975. Silver Jubilee of International Commission on Irrigation and Drainage. Mult.

625. 10 c. Type **43** 5 5
626. 35 c. Modern sluice gate (horiz.) 12 15
627. 50 c. Type **43** 20 20
628. $1 As 35 c. 40 45

44. I.W.Y. Emblem and Rock Drawing.

1975. International Women's Year. Designs showing different rock drawings.

630. **44.** 10 c. green and yellow .. 5 5
631. – 35 c. violet and blue .. 12 15
632. – 50 c. blue and orange .. 20 20
633. – $1 brown and blue .. 40 45

45. Freedom Monument.

1975. Namibia Day. Multicoloured.

635. 10 c. Type **45** 5 5
636. 35 c. Unveiling of Monument 12 15
637. 50 c. Type **45** 20 20
638. $1 As 35 c. 40 45

46. G.N.S. Emblem.

1975. National Service. 1st Anniversary.

639. **46.** 10 c. yell., grn. & violet 5 5
640. – 35 c. oran., grn. & violet 12 15
641. – 50 c. blue, grn. & brown 20 20
642. – $1 mve., grn. & light grn. 40 45

Nos. 640/2 are as T **46** but have different symbols within the circle.

47. Court Building, 1875, and Forester's Badge.

1975. Guyanese Ancient Order of Foresters. Centenary. Multicoloured.

644. 10 c. Type **47** 5 5
645. 35 c. Rock drawing of hunter and quarry .. 12 15
646. 50 c. Crossed axes and bugle-horn 20 20
647. $1 Bow and arrow .. 40 45

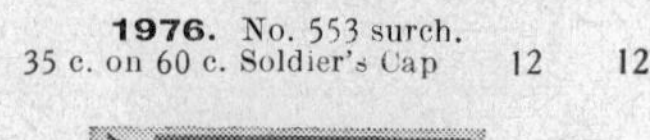

1976. No. 553 surch.

649. 35 c. on 60 c. Soldier's Cap 12 12

48. Shoulder Flash.

1976. St. John's Ambulance in Guyana. 50th Anniv.

650. **48.** 8 c. silver, blk. & mauve 5 5
651. – 15 c. silver, blk. & orge. 5 5
652. – 35 c. silver, blk. & grn. 12 12
653. – 40 c. silver, blk. & blue 12 15

Nos. 650/2 are as T **48** but show different shoulder flashes.

49. Triumphal Arch.

1976. Independence. 10th Anniv. Mult.
654. 8 c. Type **49** 5 5
655. 15 c. Stylised Victoria Regia lily 5 8
656. 35 c. "Onward to Socialism" 12 15
657. 40 c. Worker pointing the way 15 20

1976. West Indian Victory in World Cricket Cup. Nos. 559/60 of Barbados.
659. 15 c. Map of the Caribbean 8 8
660. 15 c. Prudential Cup 8 8

50. Flame in Archway.

1976. Deepavali Festival. Multicoloured.
661. 8 c. Type **50** 5 5
662. 15 c. Flame in hand 8 8
663. 35 c. Flame in bowl 15 20
664. 40 c. Goddess Latchmi 20 20

POSTAGE DUE STAMPS

D 1.

1967.
D 8. D 1. 1 c. green 5 5
D 9. 2 c. black 5 5
D 6. 4 c. blue 5 5
D 7. 12 c. violet 5 5
D 11. 12 c. red 5 5

GWALIOR BC

A "convention" state of Central India.

1885. Queen Victoria stamps of India optd. **GWALIOR** at foot and native opt. at top.
1. 14. ½ a. blue-green 4·00 4·00
2. – 1 a. purple 4·00 4·00
6. – 1½ a. brown 5·00
3. – 2 a. blue 5·00 4·00
8. – 4 a. green (No. 69) 5·00
9. – 6 a. brown (No. 80) 8·00
10. – 8 a. mauve 8·00
11. – 1 r. grey (No. 101) 8·00

Stamps of India overprinted **GWALIOR** over native overprint unless otherwise stated.

1885. Queen Victoria.
16. 14. ½ a. blue-green 5 5
17. – 9 p. red 5·00 4·50
19. – 1 a. purple 5 5
20. – 1½ a. brown 5 5
21. – 2 a. blue 15 5
23. – 2½ a. green 40 80
25. – 3 a. orange 10 8
14. – 4 a. green (No. 69) 3·00 3·50
27. – 4 a. green (No. 96) 30 12
29. – 6 a. brown (No. 80) 10 10
30. – 8 a. mauve 30 25
32. – 12 a. purple on red 30 10
33. – 1 r. grey (No. 101) 30 30
34. 26. 1 r. green and red 80 90
35. 27. 2 r. red and orange 4·50 4·00
36. 3 r. brown and green 8·00 5·00
37. 5 r. blue and violet 8·00 5·00

1899. Queen Victoria.
38. 25. 3 p. red 5 5
39. 3 p. grey 1·25
40. 14. ½ a. yellow-green 5 5
41. – 1 a. red 5 5
42. – 2 a. lilac 12 5
43. – 2½ a. blue 8 10

1903. King Edward VII.
46. 28. 3 p. grey 5 5
48. – ½ a. green (No. 122) 5 5
49. – 1 a. red (No. 123) 5 5
50a. – 2 a. lilac 5 5
52. – 2½ a. blue 12 25
53. – 3 a. orange 8 5
54. – 4 a. olive 5 5
56. – 6 a. yellow-brown 25 25
57a. – 8 a. mauve 35 35
59. – 12 a. purple on red 25 30
60. – 1 r. green and red 35 40
61. 39. 2 r. red and orange 3·50 3·50
62. 3 r. brown and green 6·50 6·50
63. 5 r. blue and violet 5·50 5·50

1907. King Edward VII inscr. "INDIA POSTAGE AND REVENUE".
65. ½ a. green (No. 149) 5 5
66. 1 a. red (No. 150) 5 5

1912. King George V.
67. 40. 3 p. grey 5 5
68. 41. ½ a. green 5 5
102. 62. ½ a. green 5 5
88. 63. 9 p. green 5 5
69. 42. 1 a. red 5 5
80. 1 a. chocolate 5 5
103. 64. 1 a. chocolate 5 5
90. 65. 1¼ a. mauve 5 5
81. 43. 1½ a. brown (No. 165) 10 12
82. 1½ a. red 5 5
70. 44. 2 a. lilac 5 5
91. 45. 2 a. lilac 5 5
104. 44. 2 a. orange-red 5 5
83. 47. 2½ a. blue 25 25
84. 2½ a. orange 8 5
71. 48. 3 a. orange 5 5
92. 3 a. blue 12 5
72. 49. 4 a. olive 5 5
93. 50. 4 a. green 25 5
73. 51. 6 a. yellow-brown 25 5
74. 52. 8 a. mauve 10 5
95. 53. 12 a. claret 30 25
76. 54. 1 r. brown and green 25 25
77. 2 r. red and orange 1·00 50
78. 5 r. blue and violet 2·00 2·00

1922. No. 192 (King George V) optd. **GWALIOR** only.
79. 42. 9 p. on 1 a. red 5 5

1928. King George V. Opt. in larger type (19 mm. long).
96. 54. 1 r. brown and green 65 65
97. 2 r. red and orange 1·25 1·25
98. 5 r. blue and violet 5·50 5·50
99. 10 r. green and red 11·00 11·00
100. 15 r. blue and olive 13·00 13·00
101. 25 r. orange and blue 21·00 21·00

1938. King George VI
105. 74. 3 p. slate 30 10
106. ½ a. brown 30 10
107. 9 p. green 8·00 6·00
108. 1 a. red 25 10
109. – 3 a. green (No. 253) 30 25
110. – 4 a. brown (No. 255) 3·00 3·00
111. – 6 a. green (No. 256) 40 40
112. 77. 1 r. slate and brown 65 80
113. 2 r. purple and brown 2·75 2·75
114. 5 r. green and blue 8·00 8·00
115. 10 r. purple and red 11·00 11·00
116. 15 r. brown and green 21·00 22·00
117. 25 r. slate and purple 26·00 28·00

1944. King George VI.
118. 78. 3 p. slate 8 8
119. ½ a. mauve 8 8
120. 9 p. green 8 8
121. 1 a. red 8 8
122. 79. 1½ a. violet 8 8
123. 2 a. red 8 8
124. 3 a. violet 20 15
125. 80. 4 a. brown 12 25
126. 6 a. green 1·50 1·50
127. 8 a. violet 1·50 1·50
128. 12 a. purple 1·50 1·50

OFFICIAL STAMPS

Stamps of India overprinted with native inscription at top and bottom, unless otherwise stated.

1895. Queen Victoria.
O 1. 14. ½ a. blue-green 5 5
O 3. – 1 a. purple 5 5
O 5. – 2 a. blue 5 5
O 7. – 4 a. green (No. 69) 15 12
O 9. – 8 a. mauve 35 20
O 10. 26. 1 r. green and red 55 60

1901. Queen Victoria.
O 23. 25. 3 p. red 5 5
O 24. 3 p. grey 10 8
O 25. 14. ½ a. yellow-green 5 5
O 27. – 1 a. red 15 5
O 28. – 2 a. lilac 10 15

1903. King Edward VII.
O 29. 28. 3 p. grey 5 5
O 31. – ½ a. green (No. 122) 5 5
O 32. – 1 a. red (No. 123) 5 5
O 33a. – 2 a. lilac 8 5
O 44. – 4 a. olive 50 30
O 36a. – 8 a. mauve 25 25
O 38. – 1 r. green and red 35 25

1907. King Edward VII inscr. "POSTAGE & REVENUE".
O 49. – ½ a. green (No. 149) 5 5
O 48. – 1 a. red (No. 150) 5 5

1913. King George V.
O 51. 40. 3 p. grey 5 5
O 52. 41. ½ a. green 5 5
O 73. 62. ½ a. green 5 5
O 63. 63. 9 p. green 5 5
O 53a. 42. 1 a. red 5 5
O 54. 1 a. chocolate 5 5
O 74. 64. 1 a. chocolate 5 5
O 65. 65. 1¼ a. mauve 5 5
O 55. 44. 2 a. lilac 5 5
O 66. 45. 2 a. lilac 5 5
O 75. 44. 2 a. orange-red 5 5
O 56. 49. 4 a. olive 5 5
O 67. 50. 4 a. green 5 5
O 68. 52. 8 a. mauve 15 5
O 58. 54. 1 r. brown and green 35 15

1922. No. O 97 (King George V. Official) optd. **GWALIOR** only.
O 59. 42. 9 p. on 1 a. red 5 5

1927. King George V. Optd. in larger type (21 mm. long).
O 69. 54. 1 r. brown and green 20 5
O 70. 2 r. red and orange 55 65
O 71. 5 r. blue and violet 3·00 3·00
O 72. 10 r. green and red 4·00 5·00

1938. King George VI.
O 78. 74. ½ a. brown 40 10
O 79. 1 a. red 40 10
O 91. 77. 1 r. slate and brown 25 35
O 92. 2 r. purple and brown 2·00 1·00
O 93. 5 r. green and blue 6·00 6·00
O 94. 10 r. purple and red 9·00 10·00

1940. King George VI. Optd at bottom only.
O 80. O 1. 3 p. slate 15 15
O 81. ½ a. brown 65 40
O 82. ½ a. purple 15 15
O 83. 9 p. green 15 15
O 84. 1 a. red 15 15
O 85. 1 a. 3 p. bistre 30 30
O 86. 1 a. 6 p. violet 20 15
O 87. 2 a. orange 20 20
O 88. 4 a. brown 15 30
O 89. 8 a. violet 40 45

1942. No. O 65 surch. **1 A** and bar.
O 90. 65. 1 a. on 1¼ a. mauve 1·25 40

HAITI O2

The W. portion of the island of San Domingo in the West Indies. A republic, independent from 1844.

100 centimes = 1 gourde or piastre.

1.

2. President Salomon.

1881. Imperf.
1. 1. 1 c. red 2·75 1·90
2. 2 c. purple 3·00 2·75
3a. 3 c. bistre 5·50 3·50
4. 5 c. green 11·00 6·00
5. 7 c. blue 6·00 1·75
6. 20 c. brown 30·00 11·00

1882. Perf.
7. 1. 1 c. red 2·00 65
9. 2 c. purple 3·25 1·00
12. 3 c. bistre 3·50 1·40
15. 5 c. green 3·00 60
17. 7 c. blue 2·75 90
20. 20 c. brown 2·50 65

1887.
24. 2. 1 c. lake 35 25
25. 2 c. mauve 40 30
26. 3 c. blue 40 30
27. 5 c. green 1·25 30

1890. Surch. **DEUX 2 CENT.**
28. 2. 2 c. on 3 c. blue 35 30

3. 4. 5.

1891. Tree with leaves upright.
29. 3. 1 c. mauve 20 20
30. 2 c. blue 30 25
31. 3 c. lilac 30 20
31a. 3 c. grey 40 25
32. 5 c. orange 1·50 20
33. 7 c. red 3·00 1·75

1892. Surch. **DEUX 2 CENT.**
34. 3. 2 c. on 3 c. lilac 60 60
34a. 2 c. on 3 c. grey 70 70

1893. Tree with leaves drooping.
35a. 4. 1 c. purple 8 5
41. 1 c. blue 10 10
36. 2 c. blue 10 5
42. 2 c. red 20 12
37. 3 c. lilac 30 20
43. 3 c. brown 10 8
38. 5 c. orange 1·10 12
44. 5 c. green 10 8
39. 7 c. red 20 20
45. 7 c. grey 12 10
40. 20 c. brown 45 35
46. 20 c. orange 20 20

1898. Surch. **DEUX 2 CENT.**
47. 4. 2 c. on 20 c. brown 45 25
48. 2 c. on 20 c. orange 30 25

1898.
49. 5. 2 c. red 10 10
50. 5 c. green 10 10

6. Pres. Simon Sam.

7.

1898.
51. 6. 1 c. blue 8 8
67. 7. 1 c. green 8 8
52. 6. 2 c. orange 8 8
68. 7. 2 c. red 8 8
53. 6. 3 c. green 8 8
54. 7. 4 c. red 8 8
55. 6. 5 c. brown 8 8
69. 7. 5 c. blue 8 5
56. 6. 7 c. grey 8 8
57. 7. 8 c. red 12 8
58. 10 c. orange 10 8
59. 15 c. olive 35 30
60. 6. 20 c. black 35 30
61. 50 c. lake 40 30
62. 1 g. mauve 1·25 1·25

1902. Optd. **MAI Gt. Pre 1902** in frame.
70. 6. 1 c. blue 30 30
71. 7. 1 c. green 25 15
72. 6. 2 c. orange 50 50
73. 7. 2 c. red 25 15
74. 6. 3 c. green 30 30
75. 7. 4 c. red 30 30
76. 6. 5 c. brown 90 90
77. 7. 5 c. blue 25 30
78. 6. 7 c. grey 40 40
79. 7. 8 c. red 40 40
80. 10 c. orange 40 40
81. 15 c. olive 2·00 1·50
82. 6. 20 c. black 2·25 2·25
83. 50 c. lake 4·50 3·00
84. 1 g. mauve 10·00 8·50

8. Arms. 9. Dessalines.

10. President Nord Alexis.

1904. Independence. Cent. Optd. **1804 POSTE PAYE 1904** in frame. T **8** and portraits as T **9.**
89. 8. 1 c. green 15 15
90. – 2 c. black and red 20 20
91. – 5 c. black and blue 20 20
92. 9. 7 c. black and claret 25 25
93. – 10 c. black and yellow 25 25
94. – 20 c. black and grey 25 25
95. – 50 c. black and olive 25 25
DESIGNS: 2 c., 5 c. Toussaint l'Ouverture. 20 c., 50 c. Petion.

1904. Nos. 89/95 but without opt.
96. 1 c. green 5 5
97. 2 c. black and red 8 8
98. 5 c. black and blue 10 10
99. 7 c. black and claret 15 15
100. 10 c. black and yellow 15 15
101. 20 c. black and grey 20 20
102. 50 c. black and olive 20 20

1904. External Mail. Optd. **1804 POSTE PAYE 1904** in frame.
103. 10. 1 c. green 20 20
104. 2 c. red 20 20
105. 5 c. blue 20 20
106. 10 c. brown 25 25
107. 20 c. orange 25 25
108. 50 c. plum 25 25

1904. Nos. 103/108, but without opt.
109. 10. 1 c. green 5 5
110. 2 c. red 5 5
111. 5 c. blue 5 5
112. 10 c. brown 5 5
113. 20 c. orange 5 5
114. 50 c. plum 10 10

1906. Optd. **SERVICE EXTERIEUR PROVISOIRE,** etc., in oval.
117. 6. 1 c. blue 45 45
118. 7. 1 c. green 35 35
119. 6. 2 c. orange 1·10 1·10
120. 7. 2 c. red 70 70
121. 6. 3 c. green 70 70
122. 7. 4 c. red 3·50 2·75
123. 6. 5 c. brown 3·00 2·50
124. 7. 5 c. blue 30 30
125. 6. 7 c. grey 2·25 2·25
126. 7. 8 c. red 45 45
127. 10 c. orange 60 60
128. 15 c. olive 75 75
129. 8. 20 c. black 3·00 2·75
130. 50 c. lake 2·75 2·10
131. 1 g. mauve 5·00 3·50

11. President Nord Alexis. 12. Arms.

1906.
132. 11. 1 c. de g. blue 15 8
133. 12. 2 c. de g. orange 20 10
134. 2 c. de g. yellow 25 10
135. 11. 3 c. de g. grey 20 10
136. 12. 7 c. de g. green 50 15

13. Iron Market, Port-au-Prince. 14. President A. T. Simon.

1906. Currency changed from "gourdes" to "piastres".
137. 12. 1 c. de p. green 12 10
138. 11. 2 c. de p. red 20 12
139. 13. 3 c. de p. sepia 35 15
140. 3 c. de p. orange 2·00 1·75
141. – 4 c. de p. red 35 20
167. – 4 c. de p. olive 3·50 2·75
142. 11. 5 c. de p. blue 90 10
143. – 7 c. de p. grey 75 45
168. – 7 c. de p. red 10·00 7·00
144. – 8 c. de p. rose 75 45
169. – 8 c. de p. olive 7·00 5·50
145. – 10 c. de p. orange 60 10
170. – 10 c. de p. brown 7·00 6·00
146. – 15 c. de p. olive 1·00 45
171. – 15 c. de p. yellow 2·25 2·00
147. 11. 20 c. de p. blue 75 40
148. 12. 50 c. de p. red 1·60 1·40
172. 50 c. de p. yellow 3·50 3·00
149. – 1 pi. claret 3·00 2·50
173. – 1 pi. red 3·50 3·50
DESIGNS—As T 13: 4 c. Palace of Sans Souci-Milot. 7 c. Independence Palace, Gonaives, 8 c. Entrance to Catholic College, Port-au-Prince. 10 c. Catholic Monastery and Church, Port-au-Prince. 15 c. Government Offices. Port-au-Prince. 1 p. President's Palace, Port-au-Prince.

1906. Surch. with value in double-lined frame Without opt.
154. 10. 1 c. on 5 c. blue 10 10
155. 1 c. on 10 c. brown 10 10
156. 1 c. on 20 c. orange 10 10
157. 2 c. on 10 c. brown 10 10
158. 2 c. on 20 c. orange 10 10
159. 2 c. on 50 c. plum 10 10

1910.
160. 14. 1 c. de g. black and lake 10 10
161. 2 c. de p. black and red 25 15
162. 5 c. de p. black & blue 4·75 35
163. 20 c. de p. blk. & green 4·25 4·00

15. President C. Leconte. 16.

1912. Various frames.
164. 15. 1 c. de g. lake 12 10
165. 2 c. de g. orange 15 12
166. 5 c. de p. blue 30 12

1914. Optd. **GL O.Z. 7 FEV. 1914** in frame. A. On 1898 issue.
174. 7. 8 c. red 6·00 5·50
B. On 1904 issue, without opt.
175. 10. 1 c. green (No. 109) 18·00 16·00
176. 2 c. red 18·00 16·00
177. 5 c. blue 15 12
178. 10 c. brown 25 15
179. 20 c. orange 45 25
180. 50 c. plum 70 35

C. On pictorial stamps of 1906.
181. 12. 2 c. de g. yellow 8 8
182. 11. 3 c. de g. grey 15 15
D. On pictorial stamps of 1906.
183. 11. 1 c. de p. green (No. 137) 20 20
184. 2 c. de p. red (No. 138) 25 25
185. 3 c. de p. sepia (No. 139) 45 35
186. 3 c. de p. orge. (No. 140) 20 15
187. 4 c. de p. red (No. 141) 45 45
198. 4 c. de p. olive (No. 147) 50 45
188. 7 c. de p. grey (No. 143) 1·75 1·75
200. 7 c. de p. red (No. 168) 1·75 1·75
189. 8 c. de p. rose (No. 144) 2·00 2·00
201. 8 c. de p. olive (No. 169) 2·25 2·25
190. 10 c. de p. orge. (No. 145) 45 35
202. 10 c. de p. brn. (No. 170) 75 75
191. 15 c. de p. ol. (No. 146) 1·75 1·75
203. 15 c. de p. yell. (No. 171) 40 40
192. 20 c. de p. bl. (No. 147) 1·10 1·10
194. 50 c. de p. red (No. 148) 3·00 3·00
204. 50 c. de p. yell. (No. 172) 3·00 3·00
195. 1 pi. claret (No. 149) 3·00 3·00
205. 1 pi. red (No. 173) 3·00 3·00
E. On pictorial stamp of 1910.
193. 14. 20 c. de p. black & grn. 2·00 2·00
F. On stamps of 1912.
196. 15. 1 c. de g. lake 15 10
197. 2 c. de g. orange 15 10
199. 5 c. de p. blue 45 12

1914. Stamps of 1904, without the opt., surch. **GL O.Z 7 FEV 1914 7 CENT** in diamond frame.
213. 10. 7 c. on 20 c. orange (No. 113) 20 15
214. 7 c. on 50 c. plum (No. 114) 15 15

1914. Pictorial stamps of 1906 (Nos. 148/73), surch. **GL OZ 1 CENT DE PIASTRE 7 FEV. 1914** in frame.
215. 12. 1 c. de p. on 50 c. red 15 15
216. 1 c. de p. on 50 c. yellow 15 15
217. – 1 c. de p. on 1 p. claret 20 15
218. – 1 c. de p. on 1 p. red 25 15

1915.
219. – 2 c. de g. black & yellow 30
220. 16. 5 c. de g. black & green 45
221. – 7 c. de g. black and rose 25
PORTRAIT: 2 c., 7 c. O. Zamor.

1915. As T 14, inscr. "EMISSION 1914".
222. 1 c. de p. black & green 55
223. 3 c. de p. black and olive 8
224. 5 c. de p. black and blue 8
225. 7 c. de p. black and orge. 35
226. 10 c. de p. black & brn. 12
227. 15 c. de p. blk. and olive 15
228. 20 c. de p. black & brn. 12
DESIGNS: 1 c., 5 c., 10 c., 15 c. O. Zamor. 3 c., 20 c. Arms. 7 c. T. Auguste.

1915. Surch. with figure in frame.
229. 1 on 5 c. blue (No. 111) 60 60
230. 1 on 7 c. grey (No. 143) 5 5
231. 1 on 10 c. brown (No. 112) 10 10
232. 1 on 20 c. orange (No. 107) 25 25
233. 1 on 20 c. orange (No. 113) 25 50
234. 1 on 50 c. plum (No. 108) 70 35
235. 1 on 50 c. plum (No. 114) 5 5
236. 2 on 1 pi. claret (No. 172) 12 8

1917. Surch. **GOURDE** and value in frame.
A. On provisional stamps of 1906.
237. 8. 1 c. on 50 c. lake (No. 130) 11·00 9·00
238. 1 c. on 1 g. mauve (No. 131) 13·00 12·00
B. On pictorial stamps of 1906.
239. – 1 c. on 4 c. de p. red (No. 141) 10 10
240. – 1 c. on 4 c. de p. olive (No. 167) 15 15
241. – 1 c. on 7 c. de p. red (No. 168) 15 15
242. – 1 c. on 10 c. de p. orange (No. 145) 5 5
243. – 1 c. on 15 c. de p. yellow (No. 171) 15 15
244. 11. 1 c. on 20 c. de p. blue (No. 147) 10 10
246. 14. 1 c. on 20 c. de p. black and green (No. 163) 2·00 2·00
247. 12. 1 c. on 50 c. de p. red (No. 148) 10 10
249. – 1 c. on 50 c. de p. yellow (No. 172) 75 75
250. – 1 c. on 1 p. red (No. 173) 75 75
251. 13. 2 c. on 3 c. de p. sepia (No. 139) 12 12
252. 2 c. on 3 c. de p. orange (No. 140) 20 20
253. – 2 c. on 8 c. de p. rose (No. 144) 10 10
255. – 2 c. on 8 c. de p. olive (No. 169) 20 20
256. – 2 c. de p. on 10 c. brown (No. 170) 20 12
257. – 2 c. on 15 c. de p. olive (No. 146) 8 8
258. – 2 c. on 15 c. de p. yellow (No. 171) 30 30
259. 11. 2 c. on 20 c. de p. blue (No. 147) 8 8
260. – 5 c. on 10 c. de p. brown (No. 170) 45 60
261. – 5 c. on 15 c. de p. yellow (No. 171) 2·25 2·40

1919. For inland use. Provisionals of 1914.
(a) Surch. with new value without frame.
262. 11. 1 c. on 15 c. de p. olive (No. 191) 12 12
263. 11. 1 c. on 20 c. de p. blue (No. 192) 12 12
264. 14. 1 c. on 20 c. de p. black and green (No. 193) 20 20
265. 11. 1 c. on 1 p. claret (No. 195) 20 20
267. 1 c. on 1 p. red (No. 205) 20 15
(b) Surch with new value in frame.
268. 11. 2 c. on 4 c. de p. red (No. 187) 20 20
269. 2 c. on 8 c. de p. rose (No. 189) 12 8
270. 2 c. on 8 c. de p. olive (No. 201) 10 10
271. 14. 2 c. on 20 c. de p. black and green 10 10
272. 11. 2 c. on 50 c. de p. red (No. 194) 5 5
274. 2 c. on 50 c. de p. yellow (No. 204) 12 12
275. 2 c. on 1 p. claret (No. 195) 1·25 1·25
276. 2 c. on 1 p. red (No. 205) 1·00 1·00
277. 3 c. on 3 c. de p. sepia (No. 185) 25 25
278. 3 c. on 7 c. de p. red (No. 200) 20 12
279. 5 c. on 3 c. de p. sepia (No. 185) 25 12
280. 5 c. on 3 c. de p. orange (No. 186) 85 85
281. 5 c. on 4 c. de p. red (No. 187) 30 30
282. 5 c. on 4 c. de p. olive (No. 198) 12 12
283. 5 c. on 7 c. de p. grey (No. 188) 15 15
284. 5 c. on 7 c. de p. red (No. 200) 25 25
285. 10. 5 c. on 7 c. on 20 c. orge. (No. 213) 25 25
286. 5 c. on 7 c. on 50 c. plum (No. 214) 1·75 1·75
287. 11. 5 c. on 10 c. de p. orange (No. 190) 15 15
289. 5 c. on 10 c. de p. orange (No. 190) 30 30
288. 5 c. on 15 c. de p. yellow (No. 203) 25 25
No. 289 has the word "PIASTRE" in the surcharge.

1919. Postage Due stamps surch. **POSTES** and new value in frame.
290. D 2. 5 c. de g. on 10 c. de p. purple (No. D 211) 25 25
291. 5 c. de g. on 50 c. de p. olive (No. D 153) 6·50 6·00
292. 5 c. de g. on 50 c. de p. olive (No. D 212) 30 30

20. Agriculture.

DESIGN: 10 c., 15 c., 25 c. Commerce.

1920.
294. 20. 3 c. de g. orange 15 12
295. 5 c. de g. green 20 12
296. – 10 c. de g. red 30 20
297. – 15 c. de g. violet 25 15
298. 25 c. de g. blue 30 15

22. Pres. L. J. Borno. 23. Christophe's Citadel.

25. Coffee.

DESIGNS—VERT. 20 c. Map of W. Indies. HORIZ. 1 g. National Palace.

1924.
299. 22. 5 c. green 12 8
300. 23. 10 c. red 20 8
301. – 20 c. blue 40 12
304. 25. 35 c. green 2·25 45
302. 22. 50 c. black and orange 40 12
303. – 1 g. olive 90 30

27. President Borno.

1929. Frontier Agreement between Haiti and Dominican Republic.
305. 27. 10 c. red 20 15

28. Port-au-Prince.

1929. Air.
306. 28. 25 c. green 25 15
307. 50 c. violet 30 15
308. 75 c. claret 1·00 85
309. 1 g. blue 1·25 95

29. Salomon and S. Vincent.

1931. U.P.U. Membership. 50th Anniv.
310. 29. 5 c. green 50 20
311. – 10 c. red (S. Vincent) 50 20

1933. Air. "Columbia" New York-Haiti Flight. Surch. **COLUMBIA VOL-DIRECT N.-Y.-P.AU-P. BOYD-LYON 60 CTS.**
311a. 60 c. on 20 c. blue (No. 301) 24·00 24·00

30. Pres. S. Vincent. 31. Prince's Aqueduct.

1933. T 30 and designs as T 31.
312. 30. 3 c. orange 8 5
313. 3 c. green 10 5
316. 31. 5 c. green 10 5
317. 5 c. olive 25 10
318. – 10 c. red 20 8
320. – 10 c. brown 15 8
321. – 25 c. blue 30 15
322. – 50 c. chocolate 1·40 40
323. – 1 g. green 1·25 40
324. – 2 g. 50 olive 1·60 55
DESIGNS: 10 c. Fort National. 25 c. Palace of Sans Souci. 50 c. Christophe's Chapel, Milot. 1 g. King's Gallery, Citadel. 2 g. 50 Vallieres Battery.

32. Aeroplane over Citadel Christophe.

1933. Air.
325. 32. 50 c. orange 3·25 45
326. 50 c. olive 1·75 45
327. 50 c. red 1·10 70
328. 50 c. black 75 45
329. 60 c. brown 45 8
330. 1 g. blue 85 25

33. Alexandre Dumas and his father and son.

1935. Visit of French Delegation to West Indies.
331. 33. 10 c. brown & red (post.) 45 15
332. 25 c. brown and blue 85 25
333. 60 c. brn. & violet (air) 2·25 1·75

34. Arms of Haiti, and George Washington.

1938. Air. U.S. Constitution. 150th Anniv.
334. 34. 60 c. blue 50 25

1939. Surch. **25 c** between bars.
335. 25. 25 c. on 35 c. green 45 20

35. Pierre de Coubertin. 36.

1939. Port-au-Prince Athletic Stadium Fund.
336. 35. 10 c.+10 c. red (postage) 22·00 22·00
337. 60 c.+40 c. violet (air) 20·00 20·00
338. 1 g. 25+60 c. black .. 20·00 20·00

1941. 3rd Caribbean Conf.
339. 36. 10 c. red (postage) .. 60 15
340. 25 c. blue 45 35
341. 60 c. olive (air) .. 3·50 85
342. 1 g. 25 violet .. .. 2·50 60

37. Our Lady of Perpetual Succour.

ILLUSTRATIONS
British Commonwealth and all overprints and surcharges are FULL SIZE. Foreign Countries have been reduced to ¾-LINEAR.

1942. Our Lady of Perpetual Succour (National Protectress).
343. 37. 3 c. purple (postage) .. 45 12
344. 5 c. green 50 12
345. 10 c. red 50 12
346. 15 c. orange 55 20
347. 20 c. brown 55 15
348. 25 c. blue 85 20
349. 50 c. red .. .. 1·75 45
350. 2 g. 50 brown .. 7·00 1·60
351. 5 g. violet .. .. 9·00 2·25
The 5 g. is larger (32½ × 47 mm.).
352. 37. 10 c. olive (air) .. 35 25
353. 25 c. blue 50 35
354. 50 c. green 65 30
355. 60 c. red 95 45
356. 1 g. 25 black .. .. 1·75 60

38. Admiral Killick and his Flagship.

1943. Admiral Killick. Death Anniv.
358. 38. 3 c. orange (postage) .. 25 8
359. 5 c. green 25 8
360. 10 c. red 30 8
361. 25 c. blue 40 15
362. 50 c. olive 85 30
363. 5 g. brown .. .. 4·25 1·40
364. 60 c. violet (air) .. 35 25
365. 1 g. 25 black .. .. 1·60 1·40

1944. Surch. (a) Postage.
366. 30. 0.02 on 3 c. green .. 10 10
367. 0.05 on 3 c. green .. 15 15
368. 37. 0.10 on 15 c. orange .. 30 20
369. 38. 0.10 on 25 c. blue .. 30 20
370. – 0.10 on 1 g. olive (No. 303) 25 12
371. – 0.20 on 2 g. 50 olive (No. 324) 30 20
(b) Air.
372. 32. 0.10 on 60 c. brown .. 40 25

39. 40. Nurse and Wounded Soldier.

1944. Obligatory Tax. United Nations Relief Fund.
373. 39. 5 c. blue .. .. 1·00 45
374. 5 c. black .. .. 1·00 45
375. 5 c. olive .. .. 1·00 45
376. 5 c. violet .. .. 1·00 45
377. 5 c. brown .. .. 1·00 45
378. 5 c. green .. .. 1·00 45
379. 5 c. red .. .. .. 1·00 45

1945. Red Cross stamps. Cross in red.
381. 40. 3 c. black (postage) .. 5 5
382. 5 c. green 12 5
383. 10 c. orange 20 5
384. 20 c. brown 15 8
385. 25 c. blue 20 10
386. 35 c. orange 15 12
387. 50 c. red 60 15
388. 1 g. olive 70 30
389. 2½ g. violet .. .. 2·25 60
390. 20 c. orange (air) .. 12 8
391. 25 c. blue 12 5
392. 50 c. brown 15 5
393. 60 c. purple 20 8
394. 1 g. yellow .. .. 1·00 15
395. 1 g. 25 c red 75 30
396. 1 g. 35 c. green .. 75 45
397. 5 g. black .. .. 3·50 2·50

41. Franklin D. Roosevelt. 42. Capois-la-Mort.

1946. Air.
398. 41. 20 c. black 15 12
399. 60 c. black 20 8

1946.
400. 42. 3 c. orange (postage) .. 8 5
401. 5 c. green 8 5
402. 10 c. red 8 5
403. 20 c. black 8 5
404. 25 c. blue 10 5
405. 35 c. orange 12 8
406. 50 c. brown 15 12
407. 1 g. olive 25 8
408. 2 g. 50 grey .. .. 1·10 30
409. 20 c. red (air) 5 5
410. 25 c. green 8 8
411. 50 c. orange 15 10
412. 60 c. purple 15 8
413. 1 g. slate 30 8
414. 1 g. 25 violet 60 35
415. 1 g. 35 black 70 60
416. 5 g. red .. .. 2·00 1·10

43. J. J. Dessalines.

1947. Emperor Jean-Jacques Dessalines, founder of National Independence. 141st Death Anniv.
417. 43. 3 c. orange (postage) .. 5 5
418. 5 c. green 5 5
419. 5 c. violet 35 5
420. 10 c. red 5 5
421. 25 c. blue 12 5
422. 20 c. brown (air) .. 15 5

1947. Surch.
423. 42. 10 c. on 35 c. orge. (post.) 15 8
424. 5 c. on 1 g. 35 black (air) 45 15
425. 30 c. on 50 c. orange .. 35 25
426. 30 c. on 1 g. 35 black .. 35 30

44. Sanatorium and Mosquito.

1949. Air. Anti-T.B. and Malaria Fund. Cross in red.
427. 44. 20 c.+20 c. sepia .. 7·00 4·25
428. 30 c.+30 c. green .. 7·00 4·25
429. 45 c.+45 c. brown .. 7·00 4·25
430. 89 c.+80 c. violet .. 7·00 4·25
431. 1 g. 25+1 g. 25 red .. 9·00 5·00
432. 1 g. 75+1 g. 75 blue .. 9·00 5·00

45. Washington, Dessalines and Bolivar.

1949. Obligatory Tax. Port-au-Prince Bicent.
434. 45. 5 c. red 20 12
435. 5 c. brown 20 12
436. 5 c. orange 20 12
437. 5 c. grey 20 12
438. 5 c. violet 20 12
439. 5 c. blue 20 12
440. 5 c. green 20 12
441. 5 c. black 20 12

46. Arms of Port-au-Prince.

47. Columbus and "Santa Maria". 48. Cocoa.

1950. Port-au-Prince Bicent. Exn.
(a) Postage. Multicoloured arms.
442. 46. 10 c. red 15 12
(b) Air.
443. 47. 30 c. blue and grey .. 50 25
444. – 1 g. black (Pres. D. Estime) 60 25

1950. U.P.U. 75th Anniv. Optd. **U P U 1874 1949** or surch. also.
445. 45. 3 on 5 c. grey (postage) 8 5
446. 5 c. green 20 15
447. 10 on 5 c. red 20 15
448. 20 on 5 c. blue 30 30
449. 42. 30 on 25 c. green (air) 30 30
450. 1 g. slate 60 55
451. 1.50 on 1 g. 35 black .. 95 75

1951. National Products.
456. 48. 5 c. green (postage) .. 20 10
457. – 30 c. orange (Bananas) (air) 45 20
458. – 80 c. pink and green (Coffee) .. .. 1·10 60
459. – 5 g. grey (Sisal) .. 4·00 2·25

49. Isabella the Catholic. 50. Pres. Magloire and Nursery, La Saline.

1951. Air. Isabella the Catholic. 5th Birth Cent.
460. 49. 15 c. brown 25 12
461. 30 c. blue 45 15

1953. Projects realized by Pres. Magloire. Designs with medallion of president.
462. 50. 5 c. green (postage) .. 8 5
463. – 10 c. red 10 5
464. – 20 c. blue (air) .. 15 10
465. – 30 c. brown 20 15
466. – 1.50 g. black 60 45
467. – 2.50 g. violet .. .. 1·40 85
DESIGNS—HORIZ. 10 c. Road-making. 20 c. Anchorage, Cap-Haitien. 30 c. Workers' estate, St. Martin. 1·50 g. Old Cathedral restoration. 2.50 g. School canteen.

1953. Toussaint l'Ouverture. 150th Death Anniv. No. 405 surch. **7 AVRIL 1803-1953 50.**
469. 42. 50 c. on 35 c. orange .. 30 15

1953. Air. 150th Anniv. of National Flag. Surch. **18 MAI 1803-1953 50.**
470. 42. 50 c. on 60 c. purple .. 35 12
471. 50 c. on 1 g. 35 black .. 35 15

51. J. J. Dessalines and Pres. Magloire. 52. Toussaint l'Ouverture.

53. Marie-Jeanne and Lamartiniere on La Crete-a-Pierrot. 54. Mme. Magloire.

1954. Independence. 150th Anniv.
(a) As T 51/2.
472. 51. 3 c. blk. & blue (post.) .. 5 5
473. 52. 5 c. black and green .. 15 5
474. – 5 c. black and green .. 12 5
475. – 5 c. black and green .. 15 5
476. – 5 c. black and green .. 12 5
477. 51. 10 c. black and red .. 12 5
478. – 15 c. black and lilac .. 15 8
479. 52. 50 c. black & green (air) 25 15
480. – 50 c. black and green .. 25 15
481. – 50 c. black and vermilion 25 15
482. – 50 c. black and brown 25 15
483. – 50 c. black and blue .. 25 15
484. – 1 g. black and grey .. 60 35
485. – 1 g. 50 black & magenta 1·10 85
486. 51. 7 g. 50 black and orange 4·00 4·00
PORTRAITS—As T 52: Nos. 474, 482, Lamartiniere; 475, 482, Boisrond-Tonnerre; 476, 483, 485, A. Petion; 478, Capois-La-Mort; 480, J. J. Dessalines; 481, H. Christophe.
For stamps as No. 480 without dates see Nos. 533/4.
(b) As T 53.
487. 53. 25 c. orange (postage) .. 15 8
488. – 25 c. slate 15 8
489. 53. 50 c. red (air) 20 10
490. 50 c. black 20 10
491. – 50 c. pink 20 12
492. – 50 c. blue 20 12
DESIGN—HORIZ. Nos. 488, 491, 492, Battle of Vertieres. Nos. 489/92 are larger (31½ × 26 mm.).

1954.
493. 54. 10 c. orange (postage) .. 12 8
494. 10 c. blue 12 5
495. 20 c. vermilion (air) .. 10 8
496. 50 c. brown 25 15
497. 1 g. green 40 35
498. 1 g. 50 red 60 50
499. 2 g. 50 emerald .. 1·00 75
500. 5 g. indigo .. .. 2·25 1·90

55. Tomb and Arms of King Henri Christophe. 56. Christophe, Citadel and Pres. Magloire.

1954. Restoration of Christophe's Citadel.
(a) T 55. Flag in black and red.
501. 55. 10 c. red (postage) .. 12 8
502. 50 c. orange (air) .. 25 15
503. 1 g. blue 55 50
504. 1 g. 50 green 85 75
505. 2 g. 50 grey .. .. 1·40 1·00
506. 5 g. vermilion .. .. 2·25 1·75
(b) T 56.
507. 56. 10 c. red (postage) .. 12 8
508. 50 c. black & orge. (air) 25 15
509. 1 g. black and blue .. 55 50
510. 1 g. 50 black and green 85 75
511. 2 g. 50 black and grey 1·40 1·00
512. 5 g. black and red .. 2·75 1·75

57. Columbus's Drawing of Nativity Fort.

ILLUSTRATIONS
British Commonwealth and all overprints and surcharges are FULL SIZE. Foreign Countries have been reduced to ¾-LINEAR.

1954. Air.
513. 57. 50 c. red 50 20
514. 50 c. slate 50 20

58. Helicopter over Ruins. 59. Helicopter.

1955. Obligatory Tax. Cyclone "Hazel" Relief Fund. (a) T **58.**
515. **58.** 10 c. blue (postage) .. 8 5
516. 10 c. emerald 8 5
517. 10 c. orange 8 5
519. 20 c. red 8 5
518. 10 c. black (air) .. 12 5
520. 20 c. green 12 5

(b) T **59.**
521. **59.** 10 c. slate (postage) .. 8 5
522. 20 c. blue 12 5
523. 10 c. brown (air) .. 12 5
524. 20 c. red 12 5

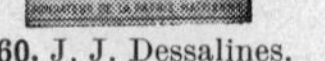
60. J. J. Dessalines. **61.** Pres. Magloire. and Monument.

1955. Dessalines Comm.
525. **60.** 3 c. black & brown (post.) 5 5
526. 5 c. black and lilac .. 5 5
527. 10 c. black and rose .. 10 5
528. 10 c. blk. & salmon-pink 8 5
529. 25 c. black and blue .. 15 5
530. 25 c. black and light blue 12 5
531. 20 c. black & green (air) 10 5
532. 20 c. black and orange .. 10 5

1955. Air. As No. 480 but without dates and colours changed.
533. 50 c. black and blue .. 25 8
534. 50 c. black and grey .. 25 8

1955. Haitian Army. 21st Anniv.
535. **61.** 10 c. blue & black (post.) 8 5
536. 10 c. red and black .. 8 5
537. 1 g. 50 grn. & blk. (air) 45 25
538. 1 g. 50 indigo & black 45 25

62. Wild Duck. **63.** 'Plane, Ship and Map

1955.
539. – 10 c. blue (postage) .. 20 10
540. **62.** 20 c. green & turquoise 60 20
541. **63.** 50 c. black & grey (air) 25 12
542. – 50 c. red and grey .. 20 12
543. **63.** 75 c. green & turquoise 45 40
544. – 1 g. olive and blue .. 50 30
545. – 2 g. 50 orange .. 2·25 1·10
546. **62.** 5 g. red and buff .. 3·50 2·10
DESIGNS—VERT. 10 c., 2 g. 50, Flamingo. HORIZ. 50 c. (No. 542), 1 g. Car on coast road.

64. Immanuel Kant. **65.** Zim Basin and Waterfall.

1956. 1st Int. Philosophical Congress. 10th Anniv.
547. **64.** 10 c. blue (postage) .. 10 8
548. 50 c. brown (air) .. 20 15
549. 75 c. green 35 25
550. 1 g. 50 magenta .. 1·00 45

1957.
552. **65.** 10 c. orge. & blue (post.) 12 5
553. 50 c. green & turq. (air) 15 10
554. 1 g. 50 olive and blue .. 45 40
555. 2 g. 50 blue & light blue 85 65
556. 5 g. slate-violet & blue 1·75 1·60

66. J.-J. Dessalines and Monument. **67.** The "Atomium".

1958. J. J. Dessalines. Birth Bicent.
557. **66.** 5 c. green & black (post.) 5 5
558. 10 c. red and black .. 5 5
559. 25 c. blue and black .. 10 5
560. 20 c. grey and black (air) 8 5
561. 50 c. orange and black .. 20 10

1958. Brussels Int. Exn.
562. **67.** 50 c. brown (postage) .. 25 15
563. – 75 c. green 25 20
564. **67.** 1 g. violet 70 25
565. – 1 g. 50 orange 50 25
566. **67.** 2 g. 50 red (air) .. 1·10 65
567. – 5 g. blue .. .. 1·40 85
DESIGN—HORIZ. 75 c., 1 g. 50, 5 g. Exhibition view.

68. Sylvio Cator making Long Jump. **69.** Head of U.S. Satellite.

1958. Sylvio Cator (athlete) Commem.
569. **68.** 5 c. grey-green (post.) .. 5 5
570. 10 c. brown 10 5
571. 20 c. purple and mauve 15 5
572. – 50 c. black (air) .. 15 8
573. – 50 c. green 15 8
574. – 1 g. chestnut 35 15
575. – 5 g. black and grey .. 2·00 1·00
DESIGN—HORIZ. Nos. 572/75; Sylvio Cator making long jump (head-on view).

1958. Red Cross. Nos. 564/66 surch. with red cross and +**50 CENTIMES.**
576. **67.** 1 g + 50 c. violet (post.) 2·25 2·25
577. – 1 g. 50+50 c. orange .. 2·25 2·25
578. **67.** 2 g. 50+50 c. red (air) 2·50 2·50

1958. I.G.Y. Inscr. as in T **69.**
579. **69.** 10 c. lake & turq. (post.) 15 5
580. – 20 c. black and orange .. 40 20
581. – 50 c. red and green .. 60 25
582. – 1 g. black and blue .. 70 20
583. **69.** 50 c. lake and blue (air) 40 20
584. – 1 g. 50 brown and red .. 1·40 40
585. – 2 g. red and blue .. 1·75 35
DESIGNS: 20 c., 1 g. 50, Antarctic penguins on ice-floe. 50 c., 2 g. Giant radio telescope. 1 g. Ocean-bed exploration.

70. Pres. F. Duvalier. **71.** Map of Haiti.

1958. Installation of President. 1st Anniv. Commem. inscr. in blue.
587. **70.** 10 c. blk. & pink (post.) 8 5
588. 50 c. black and green .. 30 10
589. 1 g. black and red .. 45 25
590. 5 g. black and salmon 2·25 1·75
591. – 50 c. black and red (air) 60 15
592. – 2 g. 50 black and orange 1·00 65
593. – 5 g. black and mauve .. 1·75 1·40
594. – 7 g. 50 black and green 2·75 2·10
DESIGN: Nos. 691/94 as T **70** but horiz.

1958. As T **70** but without commem. inscr. (a) Postage. Vert. portrait.
596. 5 c. black and blue .. 5 5
597. 10 c. black and pink .. 5 5
598. 20 c. black and yellow .. 8 5
599. 50 c. black and green .. 15 8
600. 1 g. black and red .. 30 15
601. 1 g. 50 c. black and pink .. 45 30
602. 2 g. 50 c. black & lavender 85 60
603. 5 g. black and salmon .. 1·75 1·10

(b) Air. Horiz. portrait.
604. 50 c. black and red .. 15 12
605. 1 g. black and violet .. 30 20
606. 1 g. 50 c. black and brown 45 35
607. 2 g. black and pink .. 60 45
608. 2 g. 50 c. black and orange 70 50
609. 5 g. black and mauve .. 1·50 1·25
610. 7 g. 50 c. black and green .. 2·25 1·75

1958. United Nations.
611. **71.** 10 c. red (postage) .. 8 5
612. 25 c. green 15 5
613. – 50 c. red and blue (air) 15 10
614. **71.** 75 c. blue 25 12
615. 1 g. brown 35 20
DESIGN: 50 c. Flags of Haiti and U.N.

1959. Declaration of Human Rights. 10th Anniv. Nos. 611/5 optd. **10TH ANNIVERSARY OF THE UNIVERSAL DECLARATION OF HUMAN RIGHTS.** (E), In English. (F), In French. (P), In Portuguese. (S), In Spanish. (a) Postage.

		E.		F.	
617. **71.**	10 c. red ..	10	8	10	8
618.	25 c. green	20	15	20	15
		P.		S.	
617. **71.**	10 c. red	10	8	10	8
618.	25 c. green	20	15	20	15

(b) Air.

		E.		F.	
619. –	50 c. red and blue	60	50	60	50
620. **71.**	75 c. blue	85	80	85	80
621.	1 g. brown	1·40	1·40	1·40	1·40
		P.		S.	
619. –	50 c. red & blue	60	50	60	60
620. **71.**	75 c. blue	85	80	85	80
621.	1 g. brown	1·40	1·40	1·40	1·40

Overprinted alternately in different languages throughout the sheet of 25.

72. Pope Pius XII with Children.

DESIGNS: 50 c. (No. 623), 1 g. 50, Pope at prayer. 2 g., 2 g. 50, Pope giving blessing.

1959. Pope Pius XII Commem. Inscr. "PIE XII PAPE DE LA PAIX".
622. **72.** 10 c. olive & blue (post.) 5 5
623. – 50 c. brown and green .. 20 12
624. – 2 g. sepia and lake .. 70 20
625. **72.** 50 c. violet & green (air) 15 8
626. – 1 g. 50 chestnut & olive 60 12
627. – 2 g. 50 blue and purple 85 20

1959. Red Cross. (a) United Nations stamps surch. with red cross and +**25 CENTIMES.**
628. **71.** 10 c.+25 c. (post) .. 20 15
629. 25 c.+25 c. 35 25
630. – 50 c.+25 c. (air) .. 35 35
631. **71.** 75 c.+25 c. 45 45
632. 1 g.+25 c. 70 70

(b) Pope Pius XII stamps surch. with red cross and +**50 CENTIMES.**
633. **72.** 10 c.+50 c. (postage) .. 65 65
634. – 50 c.+50 c. 65 50
635. – 2 g.+50 c. .. .. 1·00 90
636. **72.** 50 c.+50 c. (air) .. 70 70
637. – 1 g. 50+50 c. 90 90
638. – 2 g. 50+50 c. .. .. 1·10 1·10

73. Abraham Lincoln when a young man.

1959. Abraham Lincoln. 150th Birth Anniv.
639. **73.** 50 c. mar. & blue (post.) 20 15
640. – 1 g. brown & green (air) 30 20
641. – 2 g. myrtle & apple-grn. 60 25
642. – 2 g. 50 c. blue and buff .. 70 35
PORTRAITS of Lincoln (bearded); 1 g. Looking right. 2 g., 2 g. 50 Looking left. The designs include various buildings associated with Lincoln.

1959. World Refugee Year. (1st issue). Nos. 639/42 surch. **Nations Unies ANNEE DES REFUGIES 1959-1960 +20 Centimes.**
644. 50 c.+20 c. maroon & blue (postage) 70 70
645. 1 g.+20 c. brn. & grn. (air) 90 90
646. 2 g.+20 c. myrt. & app.-grn. 1·00 1·00
647. 2 g. 50+20 c. blue and buff 1·25 1·25

74. Chicago's First House and Modern Skyline.

DESIGNS—HORIZ. 50 c., 1 g. 50, Discus-thrower and Haitian flag. VERT 50 c. (air), 75 c. J. B. Paul Dessables (founder of Chicago) and map.

1959. 3rd Pan-American Games, Chicago.
649. **74.** 25 c. sepia & blue (post.) 30 15
650. – 50 c. maroon, red, blue and green 60 30
651. – 75 c. sepia and blue .. 70 35
652. – 50 c. chest. & turq. (air) 60 20
653. **74.** 1 g. turquoise & purple 70 35
654. – 1 g. 50 brown, red, blue and green .. .. 1·00 45

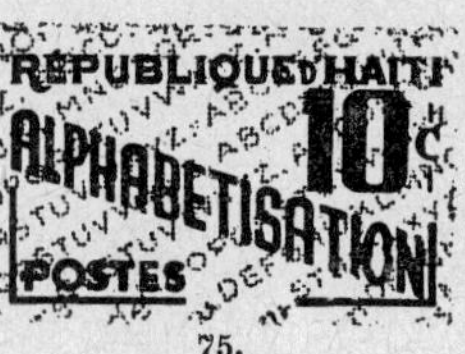

75. **76.** "Uprooted Tree".

1959. Obigatory Tax. Literacy Fund.
(a) Postage. (i) Size 40×23 mm.
655. **75.** 5 c. green 5 5
656. 5 c. black 5 5
657. 10 c. red 5 5

(ii) Size 29×17 mm.
658. **75.** 5 c. green 5 5
659. 5 c. red 5 5
660. 10 c. blue 5 5

(b) Air. Size 29×17 mm.
661. **75.** 5 c. yellow 5 5
662. 10 c. blue 5 5
663. 10 c. orange 5 5

1959. Sports Fund. Nos. 649/54 surch. **POUR LE SPORT +0.75 CENTIMES.**
664. 25 c.+75 c. sepia and blue (postage) 45 45
665. 50 c.+75 c. maroon, red, blue and green .. 60 60
666. 75 c.+75 c. sepia and blue 80 80
667. 50 c.+75 c. chestnut and turquoise (air) 60 60
668. 1 g.+75 c. turq. & purple 80 80
669. 1 g. 50+75 c. brown, red, blue and green .. 1·25 1·25

1960. UNICEF Commem. Nos. 600 and 607/8 surch. **Hommage a l'UNICEF +G.0.50.**
670. 1 g.+50 c. blk. & red (post.) 85 85
671. 2 g.+50 c. blk. & pink (air) 1·25 1·25
672. 2 g. 50+50 c. blk. & orge. 1·75 1·75

1960. Winter Olympic Games. Nos. 650 and 652/4 optd. with Olympic rings and **VIIIEME JEUX OLYMPIQUES D'HIVER CALIFORNIE USA 1960.**
673. 50 c. maroon, red, blue and green (postage) .. .. 1·40 1·10
674. 50 c. chest. & turq. (air) .. 1·75 70
675. 1 g. turquoise and purple .. 1·75 85
676. 1 g. 50 brn., red, bl. & grn. 1·75 1·40

1960. World Refugee Year (2nd issue).
677. **76.** 10 c. green & orge. (post.) 5 5
678. 50 c. purple and violet .. 25 12
679. 50 c. black and blue (air) 20 12
680. 1 g. red and green .. 45 30

1960. Surch. in figures.
682. **60.** 5 c. on 3 c. blk. & brown 5 5
683. 10 c. on 3 c. blk. & brn. 8 5

1960. Haitian Red Cross. 28th Anniv. 1945 Red Cross stamps optd. "**28 eme ANNIVERSAIRE**" or surch. also.
684. **40.** 1 g. on 2½ g. vio. (post.) 60 35
685. 2½ g. violet 85 85
686. 20 c. on 1 g. 35 grn. (air) 12 8
687. 50 c. on 60 c. purple .. 20 15
688. 50 c. on 1 g. 35 green .. 20 20
689. 50 c. on 2½ g. violet 20 20
690. 60 c. purple 30 25
691. 1 g. on 1 g. 35 green .. 40 35
692. 1 g. 35 green 50 45
693. 2 g. on 1 g. 35 green .. 85 80
No. 689 is also optd. **Avion.**

77. "Sugar Queen, 1960" and Beach.

1960. Election of Miss Claudinette Fouchard ("Miss Haiti") as World "Sugar Queen, 1960".
694. – 10 c. vio. & brn. (post.) 10 5
695. – 20 c. black and chestnut 12 5
696. **77.** 50 c. brown and blue .. 25 10
697. – 1 g. brown and green .. 50 20
698. – 50 c. brown & mag. (air) 35 12
699. **77.** 2 g. 50 brown and blue 1·40 40

DESIGNS: Sugar Queen and—10 c., 1 g. Plantation (different views); 20 c, 50 c. Harvesting.

1960. Education Campaign. Surch. **ALPHABETISATION** + and value.
700. **76.** 10 c.+20 c. green and orange (postage) .. 50 15
701. 10 c.+30 c. grn. & orge. 25 20
702. 50 c.+20 c. pur. & vio. 40 35
703. 50 c.+30 c. pur. & vio. 60 45
704. **76.** 50 c.+20 c. black and blue (air) 45 35
705. 50 c.+30 c. blk. & blue 65 50
706. 1 g.+20 c. red & green 85 60
707. 1 g.+30 c. red & green 85 70

78. Olympic Torch, Victory Parade at Athens, 1896, and Melbourne Stadium.

1960. Olympic Games, Rome.
708. **78.** 10 c. blk. & orge. (post) 5 5
709. – 20 c. blue and red .. 8 5
710. – 50 c. green and brown 20 10
711. – 1 g. blue and black .. 35 15
712. – 50 c. pur. & bis. (air) .. 15 10
713. – 1 g. 50 magenta & green 60 30
714. – 2 g. 50 slate, pur. & blk. 90 40
DESIGNS: 20 c. and 1 g. 50, "The Discus-thrower" and Rome Stadium. 50 c. (No. 710), Pierre de Coubertin (founder) and Athletes Parade, Melbourne. 50 c. (No. 712), As T **78** but P. de Coubertin inset. 1 g. Athens Stadium, 1896. 2 g. 50, Victory Parade, Athens, 1896, and Athletes Parade, Melbourne.

1960. Nos. 710/3 surch. **+25 CENTIMES.**
716. 50 c.+25 c. grn.& brn.(post.) 30 20
717. 1 g.+25 c. blue and black 35 30
718. 50 c.+25 c. pur. & bis. (air) 30 25
719. 1 g. 50+25 c. mag. & green 50 50

79. Occide Jeanty. **80.** U.N. Headquarters, New York.

1960. Occide Jeanty (composer). Birth Cent.
720. **79.** 10 c. pur. & orge. (post.) 10 5
721. – 20 c. purple and blue .. 25 10
722. **79.** 50 c. sepia and green .. 50 20
723. 50 c. blue & yellow (air) 45 10
724. – 1g. 50, slate and magenta 70 20
DESIGN: 20 c., 1 g. 50, Jeanty and Capitol. Port-au-Prince.

1960. U.N.O. 15th Anniv.
731. **80.** 1 g. black & grn. (post.) 35 20
732. **80.** 50 c. black and red (air) 20 8
733. 1 g. 50 black and blue.. 50 25

81. "Caravelle" Airliner.

1960. Air. Aviation Week.
735. **81.** 20 c. blue and red .. 8 5
736. – 50 c. brown and green 20 12
737. – 50 c. blue and green .. 20 12
738. – 50 c. black and green .. 20 12
739. **81.** 1 g. green and red .. 35 20
740. – 1 g. 50 pink and blue .. 50 35
DESIGNS: 50 c. (3) Boeing "707" jetliner and Wright biplane. 1 g. 50 Boeing "707" jetliner and 60 c. "Columbia" stamp of 1933.

1961. U.N.I.C.E.F. Child Welfare Fund. Surch. **UNICEF + 25 centimes.**
748. **80.** 1 g.+25 c. black and green (postage) .. 45 30
749. 50c.+25 c. blk.&red(air) 35 25
750. 1g. 50+25 c. blk. & blue 50 40

82. Alexandre Dumas (father and son).

1961. Alexandre Dumas Commem.
751. – 5 c. choc. & blue (post.) 5 5
752. – 10 c. black, pur. & red 8 5
753. **82.** 50 c. blue and red .. 25 15
754. – 50 c. black & blue (air) 25 12
755. – 1 g. red and black .. 50 25
756. – 1 g. 50 black and green 75 20
DESIGNS—HORIZ. 5 c. Dumas' House. 50 c. (No. 754), A. Dumas and "The Three Musketeers". VERT. 10 c. A. Dumas and horseman in "Twenty Years After". 1 g. A. Dumas (son) and "The Lady of the Camellias" (Marguerite Gauthier). 1 g. 50, A. Dumas, and "The Count of Monte Cristo".

83. Pirates.

1961. Tourist Publicity.
761. – 5 c. yell. & blue (post.) 5 5
762. **83.** 10 c. yellow and magenta 5 5
763. – 15 c. orange and green .. 10 5
764. – 20 c. orange & chocolate 12 8
765. – 50 c. yellow and blue .. 25 15
766. – 20 c. yell. & indigo (air) 12 5
767. – 50 c. orange and violet 25 15
768. – 1 g. yellow and green .. 50 25
DESIGNS: Nos. 761, 768, Map of Tortuga. 663, Two pirates on beach. 764, 766, Pirate ships. 765, 767, Pirate in rigging.

1961. Re-election of Pres. Duvalier. Optd. **Dr. F. Duvalier President 22 Mai 1961.**
769. **66.** 5 c. grn. & black (post.) 5 5
770. 10 c. red and black .. 5 5
771. 25 c. blue and black .. 15 10
772. **42.** 2 g. 50 grey 85 70
773. **66.** 20 c. grey & black (air) 8 5
774. 50 c. orange and black 15 12
775. **63.** 75 c. green & turquoise 30 20

1961. Air. 18th World Scout Conf., Lisbon. Nos. 735 and 739/40 surch. **18e CONFERENCE INTERNATIONALE DU SCOUTISME MONDIAL LISBONNE SEPTEMBRE 1961 +0,25** and scout emblem.
776. 20 c.+25 c. blue and red.. 30 20
777. 1 g.+25 c. green and red.. 45 40
778. 1 g. 50+25 c. pink & blue.. 60 55

1961. U.N. and Haitian Malaria Eradication Campaign. Surch. **OMS SNEM +20 CENTIMES.**
780. **80.** 1 g.+20 c. black and green (postage) .. 60 60
781. **80.** 50 c.+20 c. black & red (air) .. .. .. 1·25 1·25
782. 1 g. 50+20 c. blk. & bl. 1·75 1·75

1961. Duvalier-Ville Reconstruction Fund Nos. 598, 600, 602, 604/5 and 608/10 surch. with U.N.I.C.E.F. emblem, **Duvalier-Ville** and premium.
783. 20 c.+25 c. black & yellow (postage) 15 15
787. 1 g.+50 c. black and red.. 40 40
788. 2 g. 50+50 c. black & blue 90 90
784. 50 c.+25 c. blk. & red (air) 25 25
785. 1 g.+50 c. black and violet 50 50
789. 2 g. 50+50 c. blk. & orge. 75 75
786. 5 g.+50 c. black & mauve 1·40 1·40
790. 7 g. 50+50 c. blk. & green 2·25 2·25

1962. Colonel Glenn's Space Flight. Nos. 761, 768 optd. **EXPLORATION SPATIALE JOHN GLENN** and outline of capsule or surch. also.
795. 50 c. on 5 c. yell. & bl. (post.) 45 30
796. 1 g. 50 on 5 c. yell. & blue 1·10 1·00
797. 1 g. yellow and green (air) 75 65
798. 2 g. on 1 g. yellow & green 1·25 1·10

84. Campaign Emblem.

1962. Malaria Eradication.
799. **84.** 5 c. blue & red (postage) 5 5
800. – 10 c. green and brown.. 5 5
801. **84.** 50 c. red and blue .. 20 12
802. – 20 c. red and violet (air) 8 5
803 **84.** 50 c. red and green .. 20 12
804. – 1 g. violet-blue & orange 35 20
DESIGN: 10 c., 20 c., 1 g. As T **84** but with long side of triangle at top.

1962. World Refugee Year (3rd issue). As T **76** but additionally inscr. "1962" and colours changed.
806. **76.** 10 c. orange & bl. (post.) 5 5
807. 50 c. green and mauve 20 12
808. 50 c. brown & blue (air) 15 10
809. 1 g. black and buff .. 30 20

85. Scout Badge.

DESIGNS—VERT. 5 c., 20 c., 50 c. (post.) Scout and camp. HORIZ. 10 c., 1 g. 50, Lord and Lady Baden-Powell.

1962. Haitian Boy Scout Movement. 22nd Anniv.
811. **85.** 3 c. orange, black and violet (postage) .. 5 5
812. – 5 c. brown, olive & black 5 5
813. – 10 c. brown, black & grn. 5 5
814. **85.** 25 c. black, lake & olive 12 5
815. – 50 c. green, violet & red 20 12
816. – 20 c. slate, green and purple (air) 12 5
817. **85.** 50 c. brown, green & red 25 12
818. – 1 g. 50 turq., sepia & brn 45 35

1962. Surch. with premium.
(a) Nos. 799/804.
820. **84.** 5 c.+25 c. (postage) .. 15 10
821. – 10 c.+25 c. 15 12
822. **84.** 50 c.+25 c. 20 15
823. – 20 c.+25 c. (air) .. 20 20
824. **84.** 50 c.+25 c. 25 25
825. – 1 g. +25c. 35 35
(b) Nos. 806/9.
827. **76.** 10 c.+20 c. (postage).. 12 10
828. 50 c.+20 c. 20 15
829. 50 c.+20 c. (air) 20 15
830. 1 g.+20 c. 30 20

1962. Air. Port-au-Prince Airport Construction Fund. Optd. **AEROPORT INTERNATIONAL 1962** with No. 848 additionally optd. **Poste Aerienne.**
831. – 20 c. No. 816 .. .. 12 5
832. – 50 c. No. 815 .. .. 20 12
833. **85.** 50 c. No. 817 .. .. 20 12
834. – 1 g. 50 No. 818 .. 45 35

86. Tower, World's Fair.

1962. "Century 21" Exn. (World's Fair), Seattle.
835. **86.** 10 c. maroon & bl. (post.) 5 5
836. 20 c. blue and red .. 10 5
837. 50 c. green and yellow 35 8
838. 1 g. red and green .. 45 20
839. 50 c. black & lilac (air) 25 8
840. 1 g. red and grey .. 45 12
841. 1 g. 50 purple & orange 50 20

87. Town plan and 1904 10 c. stamp.

1963. Duvalierville Commem.
843. **87.** 5 c. black, yellow and violet (postage) 5 5
844. 10 c. black, yellow & red 5 5
845. 25 c. blk., yellow & grey 12 8
846. – 50 c. choc. & orge. (air) 20 12
847. – 1 g. chocolate and blue 30 20
848. – 1 g. 50 choc. and green.. 40 35
DESIGN: Nos. 846/8 Houses and 1881 2 c. stamp.

1963. "Peaceful Uses of Outer Space". Nos. 837/38 and 841/2 optd. **UTILISATIONS PACIFIQUES DE L'ESPACE** and space capsule.
853. **86.** 50 c. green and yellow (post.) 35 35
854. 1 g. red and green .. 60 50
855. **86.** 1 g. red and grey (air) 70 50
856. 1 g. 50 purple and orge. 1·00 1·00

1963. Literacy Campaign. Surch. **ALPHABETISATION + 0, 10.**
857. **87.** 25 c.+10 c. (postage).. 12 5
858. – 50 c.+10 c. (No. 846) (air) 25 15
859. – 1 g. 50+10 c. (No. 848) 45 40

88. Harvesting. **90.** Dessalines Statue.

89. Dag Hammarskjoeld and U.N. Emblem. **91.** "Alphabetisation".

1963. Freedom from Hunger.
860. **88.** 10 c. orge. & black (post.) 5 5
861. 20 c. turquoise & black 8 5
862. 50 c. magenta & blk. (air) 15 10
863. 1 g. green and black .. 30 20

1963. Air. Dag Hammarskjoeld Commemoration. Portrait in indigo.
864. **89.** 20 c. brown & yell.-brn. 8 5
865. 50 c. red and blue .. 15 10
866. 1 g. blue and mauve .. 30 20
867. 1 g. 50 green and grey.. 45 35
Nos. 864/67 were printed in sheets of 25 (5×5) with a map of Sweden in the background covering most stamps in the second and third vertical rows.

1963. Dessalines Commemoration.
869. **90.** 5 c. verm. & brn. (post.) 5 5
870. 10 c. blue grn. & ochre 5 5
871. 50 c. grn. & chestnut (air) 15 5
872. 50 c. pur., violet & blue 15 5

1963. Obligatory Tax. Education Fund.
873. **91.** 10 c. vermilion (postage) 5 5
874. 10 c. blue 5 5
875. 10 c. olive 5 5
876. 10 c. brown (air) .. 5 5
877. 10 c. violet 5 5
878. 10 c. slate-violet .. 5 5
See also Nos. 975/79 and 1157/63.

1964. Mothers' Festival. Optd. **FETE DES MERES 1964,** or surch. also.
879. **90.** 10 c. blue, green and ochre (postage) .. 5 5
880. 50 c. grn. & chest. (air) 20 12
881. 50 c. purple, vio. & blue 20 12
882. – 1 g. 50 on 80 c. pink and green (No. 458) 50 45

1964. Winter Olympic Games, Innsbruck. Surch. **JEUX OLYMPIQUES D'HIVER INNSBRUCK 1964 0.50+0.10,** Olympic rings and games emblem.
883. **85.** 50 c.+10 c. on 3 c. (post.) 45 40
884. 50 c+10 c. on 5 c. (No. 812) 45 40
885. – 50 c.+10 c. on 10 c. (No. 813) 45 40
886. **85.** 50 c.+10 c. on 25 c. .. 45 40
887. **65.** 50 c.+10 c. on 2 g. 50 (air) 70 60

1964. Air. Red Cross Cent. (1963). Optd. **1863, 1963** and Centenary Emblem, on surch. also. Portrait in indigo.
888. **89.** 20 c. brown & yell.-brn. 8 5
889. 50 c. red and blue .. 15 12
890. 1 g. blue and mauve .. 35 25
891. 1 g. 50 green and grey.. 45 40
892. 2 g. 50+1 g. 25 on 1 g. 50 green and grey .. 1·10 1·00

92. Weightlifting.

93. Our Lady of Perpetual Succour, and Airport.

1964. Olympic Games, Tokyo (1st issue).
893. **92.** 10 c. sepia and grey-blue (postage) 5 5
894. 25 c. sepia and salmon.. 10 8
895. – 50 c. sepia and mauve.. 15 12

896. **92.** 50 c. sep. & purple (air) 15 12
897. – 50 c. sepia and green .. 15 12
898. – 75 c. sepia and yellow.. 25 20
899. – 1 g. 50 sepia and grey .. 40 35
DESIGN: Nos. 895, 897/98, Hurdling.
Nos. 893/09 were printed in sheets of 50 (10×5) with a large map of Japan in the background.

1964. Int. Airport.
901. **93.** 10 c. blk. & ochre (post.) 5 5
902. 25 c. black & turquoise 8 5
903. 50 c. black and green .. 15 12
904. 1 g. black and red .. 30 20

905. **93.** 50 c. blk. & orange (air) 20 12
906. 1 g. 50 black & magenta 50 20
907. 2 g. 50 black and violet 85 45

1965. Int. Airport Opening. Optd. **1965.**
908. **93.** 10 c. blk. & ochre (post.) 5 5
909. 25 c. black & turquoise 10 8
910. 50 c. black and green .. 15 12
911. 1 g. black and red .. 30 20

912. **93.** 50 c. blk. & orge. (air) 20 8
913. 1 g. 50 black & magenta 60 35
914. 2 g. 50 black and violet 85 60

1965. Olympic Games. Tokyo (2nd issue). Nos. 893/9 surch. **+5 c.**
915. **92.** 10 c.+5 c. (postage) .. 5 5
916. – 25 c.+5 c. 12 12
917. – 50 c.+5 c. 20 20

918. **92.** 50 c.+5 c. (air) .. 20 20
919. – 50 c.+5 c. 20 20
920. – 75 c.+5 c. 35 35
921. – 1 g. 50+5 c. 70 70

94. Unisphere.

96. I.T.U. Emblem and Symbols.

95. Ships in Port.

1965. New York World's Fair.
923. **94.** 10 c. mult. (postage) .. 5 5
924. – 20 c. purple and yellow 8 5
925. **94.** 50 c. multicoloured .. 20 12

926. – 50 c. blue & yellow (air) 20 10
927. – 1 g. 50 black and yellow 45 25
928. **94.** 5 g. multicoloured .. 2·00 1·40
DESIGN: 20 c., 50 c. (No. 926), 1 g. 50, "Reaching for the Stars" (statue).

1965. Haitian Merchant Marine Commem.
929. **95.** 10 c. mult. (postage) .. 5 5
930. 50 c. multicoloured .. 20 12

931. **95.** 50 c. multicoloured (air) 12 8
932. 1 g. 50 multicoloured .. 35 25

1965. Air. U.N. 20th Anniv. Optd. **O.N.U. 1945-1965.** Portrait in indigo.
933. **89.** 20 c. brown & yell.-brn. 8 5
934. 50 c. red and blue .. 15 8
935. 1 g. blue and mauve .. 25 20
936. 1 g. 50 green and grey.. 40 30

1965. I.T.U. Cent.
937. **96.** 10 c. multicoloured (post.) 5 5
938. 25 c. multicoloured .. 10 5
939. 50 c. multicoloured .. 15 12

940. **96.** 50 c. multicoloured (air) 12 8
941. 1 g. multicoloured .. 25 20
942. 1 g. 50 multicoloured .. 35 30
943. 2 g. multicoloured .. 50 40

1965. U.N.E.S.C.O. 25th Anniv. Nos. 937/41 optd. **20e Anniversaire UNESCO.**
945. **96.** 10 c. multicoloured (post.) 15 15
946. 25 c. multicoloured .. 45 45
947. 50 c. multicoloured .. 85 85
948. **96.** 50 c. multicoloured (air) 90 35
949. 1 g. multicoloured .. 1·75 70

97. Cathedral Facade.

98. "Passiflora quadrangularis".

1965. Cathedral of Our Lady of the Assumption, Port-au-Prince. Bicent. Multicoloured.
951. 5 c. Type **97** (postage) .. 5 5
952. 10 c. High Altar (vert.) .. 5 5
953. 25 c. "Our Lady of the Assumption" (painting (vert.) 8 5

954. 50 c. Type **97** (air).. .. 15 10
955. 1 g. High Altar (vert.) .. 25 20
956. 7 g. 50, as 25 c., but larger, 38×51 mm. .. .. 1·75 1·40

1965. Haitian Flowers. Multicoloured.
957. 3 c. Type **98** (postage) .. 5 5
958. 5 c. "Sambucus canadensis" 5 5
959. 10 c. "Hibiscus esculentus" 5 5
960. 15 c. As 5 c. 8 5
961. 50 c. Type **98** 15 10

962. 50 c. Type **98** (air) .. 15 10
963. 50 c. As 5 c. 15 10
964. 50 c. As 10 c. 15 10
965. 1 g. 50, As 5 c. 35 25
966. 1 g. 50, As 10 c. 35 25
967. 5 g. Type **98** .. .. 1·25 80

90. Amulet.

100. Astronauts and "Gemini" Capsules.

1966. "Culture". Multicoloured.
968. 5 c. Type **99** (postage) .. 5 5
969. 10 c. Carved stool and Veve decoration (horiz.) .. 5 5
970. 50 c. Type **99** 15 12
971. 50 c. Carved stool and Veve decoration (horiz.) (air) 15 8
972. 1 g. 50 Type **99** 40 25
973. 2 g. 50 Modern abstract painting (52×37 mm.) 70 50

1966. Obligatory Tax. Education Fund. As T **91** but larger (17×25½ mm.).
974. **91.** 10 c. green (postage) .. 5 5
975. 10 c. violet 5 5
977. **91.** 10 c. orange (air) .. 5 5
978. 10 c. blue 5 5

1966. State Visit of Emperor Haile Selassie of Ethiopia. Nos. 969 and 971/3 optd. **Hommage Haile Selassie Ier 24-25 Avril 1966.**
979. – 10 c. multicoloured (post.) 12 10
980. – 50 c. multicoloured (air) 15 12
981. **99.** 1 g. 50 multicoloured.. 40 35
982. – 2 g. 50 multicoloured.. 70 60

1966. Space Rendezvous. Astronauts and capsules in brown.
983. **100.** 5 c. indigo & blue (post.) 5 5
984. 10 c. violet and blue.. 5 5
985. 25 c. green and blue.. 8 5
986. 50 c. red and blue .. 12 10
987. – 50 c. indigo & blue (air) 12 10
988. 1 g. green and blue .. 25 20
989. – 1 g. 50 red and blue .. 35 35
DESIGN: Nos. 987/9, Astronauts and "Gemini" capsules (different arrangement).

101. Football and Pres. Duvalier.

1966. Caribbean Football Championships. Portrait in black.

(i) Inscr. "CHAMPIONNAT DE FOOTBALL DES CARAIBES".
990. **101.** 5 c. grn. & flesh (post.) 5 5
991. – 10 c. green and cobalt 5 5
992. **101.** 15 c. green and apple 5 5
993. – 50 c. green and lilac.. 12 10

994. **101.** 50 c. maroon & sage (air) 12 12
995. – 1 g. 50 maroon & pink 35 30

(ii) As Nos. 990/5 but additionally inscr. "COUPE DR. FRANCOIS DUVALIER 22 JUIN".
996. **101.** 5 c. grn. & flesh (post.) 5 5
997. – 10 c. green and cobalt 5 5
998. **101.** 15 c. green and apple 5 5
999. – 50 c. green and lilac.. 12 10

1000. **101.** 50 c. mar. & sage (air) 12 12
1001. – 1 g. 50 maroon & pink 35 30
DESIGN: 10 c., 50 c. (Nos. 991, 993), 1 g. 50. Footballer and Pres. Duvalier.

102. Audio-visual Aids.

1966. National Education.
1002. – 5 c. maroon, green and pink (postage) .. 5 5
1003. – 10 c. sepia, lake & brn. 5 5
1004. **102.** 25 c. violet, blue & grn. 8 5
1005. – 50 c. maroon, green and yellow (air) .. 12 10
1006. – 1 g. sepia, brn. & orge. 25 20
1007. **102.** 1 g. 50 bl., turq. & grn. 35 35
DESIGNS—VERT. 5 c., 50 c. Young Haitians walking towards ABC "sun". 10 c., 1 g. Scouting—hat, knot and saluting hand.

103. Dr. Albert Schweitzer and Maps of Alsace and Gabon.

1967. Schweitzer Commem. Multicoloured.
1008. 5 c. Type **103** (postage).. 5 5
1009. 10 c. Dr. Schweitzer and organ pipes 5 5
1010. 20 c. Dr. Schweitzer and Hospital Deschapelles, Haiti 12 5
1011. 50 c. As 20 c. (air) .. 15 12
1012. 1 g. As 20 c. 30 20
1013. 1 g. 50 Type **103**.. .. 40 35
1014. 2 g. As 10 c. 50 45

104. J. J. Dessalines and Melon.

1967. Dessalines Commem. With portrait of Dessalines. Multicoloured.
1015. 5 c. Type **104** (postage).. 5 5
1016. 10 c. Chou (cabbage) .. 5 5
1017. 20 c. Mandarine (orange) 5 5
1018. 50 c. Mirliton (gourd) .. 15 12

1019. 50 c. Type **104** (air) .. 12 10
1020. 1 g. As 20 c. 25 20
1021. 1 g. 50 As 20 c. 35 30

1967. World Scout Jamboree, Idaho. Nos. 957/8, 960/1, 963 and 965 surch. **12e Jamboree Mondial 1967** or with additional premium only.
1022. 10 c.+10 c. on 5 c. (post.) 5 5
1023. 15 c.+10 c. 8 5
1024. 50 c. on 3 c. 15 12
1025. 50 c.+10 c. 15 12

1026. 50 c.+10 c. (air).. .. 15 12
1027. 1 g. 50+50 c. 45 30

1967. World Fair, Montreal. Nos. 968/70 and 972 optd. **EXPO CANADA 1967** and emblem, also surch. with new values (1 g. and 2 g.)
1028. **99.** 5 c. mult. (postage) .. 5 5
1029. – 10 c. multicoloured .. 5 5
1030. **99.** 50 c. multicoloured .. 15 12
1031. 1 g. on 5 c. mult. .. 30 20

1032. **99.** 1 g. 50 mult. (air) .. 45 35
1033. 2 g. on 1 g. 50 mult.. 60 45

105. Head of Duvalier and Guineafowl Emblem.

1967. Duvalierists Revolution. 10th Anniv.
1034. **105.** 5 c. gold & red (post.) 5 5
1035. 10 c. gold and blue .. 5 5
1036. 25 c. gold and brown 8 5
1037. 50 c. gold and purple 15 12

1038. **105.** 1 g. gold & green (air) 25 20
1039. 1 g. 50 gold and violet 40 35
1040. 2 g. gold and red .. 60 45

106. "Alphabetisation".

1967. National Education. Multicoloured.
1041. 5 c. Type **106** (postage).. 5 5
1042. 10 c. "Scouting" (Scout badge) (vert.) .. 5 5
1043. 25 c. "Visual Aids" (slide projection) 8 5

1044. 50 c. Type **106** (air) .. 12 10
1045. 1 g. As 10 c. (vert.) .. 25 20
1046. 1 g. 50 As 25 c. 40 30

1968. Olympic Games, Mexico. Nos. 990, 992 and 995 surch. **MEXICO 1968** with Olympic rings and value or optd. only (1 g. 50).
1047. **101.** 50 c. on 15 c. (post.).. 15 12
1048. 1 g. on 5 c. 30 20

1049. – 1 g. 50 (air) 40 35
1050. 2 g. 50+1 g. 25 on 1 g. 50 1·00 80

1968. Winter Olympic Games, Grenoble. Nos. 986/9 optd. **Xeme JEUX OLYMPIQUES D'HIVER-GRENOBLE 1968** and Games' emblem.
1051. **100.** 50 c. red & blue (post.) 55 55

1052. – 50 c. indigo & blue (air) 45 30
1053. 1 g. green and blue .. 90 60
1054. 1 g. 50 red and blue.. 1·50 75

107. "Bois Caiman" Ceremony.

108. "The Unknown Slave".

1968. Slaves' Revolt. Commem.
1055. **107.** 5 c. mult. (postage).. 5 5
1056. 10 c. multicoloured .. 5 5
1057. 25 c. multicoloured .. 8 5
1058. 50 c. multicoloured .. 15 12

1059. **107.** 50 c. multicoloured (air) 12 10
1060. 50 c. multicoloured .. 12 10
1061. 1 g. multicoloured .. 25 20
1062. 1 g. multicoloured .. 25 20
1063. 1 g. 50 multicoloured 35 35
1064. 2 g. multicoloured .. 50 45
1065. 5 g. multicoloured .. 1·25 1·00
Nos. 1060 and 1062/4 are in a larger size—49½×36 mm.

1968. Slavery Freedom Monument. Inaug.
1066. **108.** 5 c. black & blue (post.) 5 5
1067. 10 c. black and brown 5 5
1068. 20 c. black and violet 8 5
1069. 25 c. black and blue.. 10 8
1070. 50 c. black and green 20 12

1071. 50 c. black & ochre (air) 12 10
1072. 1 g. black and cerise.. 25 20
1073. 1 g. 50 black & orange 35 30

1968. Air. Nos. 1044/6 surch. **CULTURE +0.10.**
1074. **106.** 50 c.+10 c. mult. .. 15 15
1075. – 1 g.+10 c. mult. .. 30 30
1076. – 1 g. 50+10 c. mult. 40 40

109. Various Arms and Palm.

1968. Consecration of Haitian Bishopric.
1077. 109. 5 c. mult. (postage) .. 5 5
1078. – 10 c. multicoloured 8 5
1079. – 25 c. multicoloured .. 15 10
1080. 109. 50 c. mult. (air) .. 12 10
1081. – 1 g. multicoloured .. 20 15
1082. – 1 g. 50 multicoloured 35 30
1083. – 2 g. 50 multicoloured 60 50
DESIGNS—HORIZ. (50 × 30 mm.): 10 c., 1 g., 2 g. 50, Virgin Mary. 25 c., 1 g. 50, Cathedral, Port-au-Prince.

110. Jetliner over Control Tower.

1968. Duvalier Airport, Port-au-Prince. Inaug. Portrait in black.
1084. 110. 5 c. brown & blue (post.) 5 5
1085. – 10 c. brown and blue 5 5
1086. – 25 c. brown and lilac 10 8
1087. – 50 c. mar. & violet (air) 12 10
1088. – 1 g. 50 maroon & blue 35 30
1089. – 2 g. 50 mar. & turquoise 60 55
DESIGN: 50 c., 1 g. 50, 2 g. 50, Jetliner over airport entrance.

111. President Duvalier, Emblems and Map.

1968. Air. Francois Duvalier's "Life Presidency". 4th Anniv. Die-stamped in gold.
1090. 111. 30 g. gold, black & red 12·00

112. Slave breaking Chains.

1968. "Revolt of the Slaves" (1791).
1091. 112. 5 c. maroon, purple and blue (postage) 5 5
1092. 10 c. mar., pur. & orge. 5 5
1093. 25 c. mar., pur. & ochre 8 5
1094. 112. 50 c. maroon, purple and lilac (air) .. 12 8
1095. 1 g. mar., pur. & grn. 25 12
1096. 1 g. 50 mar., pur. & bl. 35 25
1097. 2 g. mar., pur. & turq. 45 35

113. "Learning the Alphabet".

1968. "National Education". Multicoloured.
1098. 5 c. Type 113 (postage) .. 5 5
1099. 10 c. Children watching TV screen ("Education by Audio-visual Methods") 5 5
1100. 50 c. Hands with ball ("Education Through Sport") 12 10
1101. 50 c. As No. 1099 (air) .. 12 8
1102. 1 g. As No. 1100 .. .. 20 12
1103. 1 g. 50 As No. 1099 .. 45 30

114. Boesman and Balloon. **115.** Airmail Cachet of 1925.

1968. Air. Boesman's Balloon Flight.
1104. 114. 70 c. chocolate & grn. 30 12
1105. 1 g. 75 chocolate & blue 70 40

1968. Air. Galiffet's Balloon Flight of 1784 Each black and purple on mauve.
1106. 70 c. Aircraft and "AVION" ("2 May 1925") .. 30 25
1107. 70 c. Type 115 .. .. 30 25
1108. 70 c. "AVION" and aircraft ("28 March 1927") .. 30 25
1109. 70 c. "HAITI POSTE AVION" and aircraft ("12 July 1927") 30 25
1110. 70 c. Aircraft and "AVION" within ring ("13 Sept. 1927") .. 30 25
1111. 70 c. "LINDBERGH" and aircraft ("6th February 1928") 30 25
Nos. 1106/11 were issued together se-tenant within a small sheet containing two blocks of six (3 × 2) with an overall background design representing Galiffet's balloon.

116. Churchill as Elder Brother of Trinity House. **117.** "Euphonia musica".

1968. Churchill Commem. Multicoloured.
1112. 3 c. Type 116 (postage) .. 5 5
1113. 5 c. Churchill painting .. 5 5
1114. 10 c. As Knight of the Garter 5 5
1115. 15 c. 79th birthday portrait and troops .. 8 5
1116. 20 c. Churchill & flying-boat 8 5
1117. 25 c. Karsh portrait and taking leave of the Queen 10 8
1118. 50 c. Giving "V"-sign and Houses of Parliament .. 15 10
1119. 50 c. As No. 1116 (air) .. 15 10
1120. 75 c. As No. 1115 .. 20 12
1121. 1 g. As No. 1117 .. .. 30 20
1122. 1 g. 50 As No. 1118 .. 45 25

1969. Nos. 1070/2 surch.
1124. 108. 70 c. on 50 c. (postage) 15 12
1125. 70 c. on 50 c. (air) .. 20 15
1126. 1 g. 75 on 1 g. .. 45 35

1969. Birds. Multicoloured.
1127. 5 c. Type 117 (postage) .. 5 5
1128. 10 c. "Temnotrogon roseigaster" 5 5
1129. 20 c. "Dulus dominicus" 8 5
1130. 25 c. "Spindalis dominicensis" 10 5
1131. 50 c. Type 117 .. .. 20 8
1132. 50 c. As 10 c. (air) .. 10 10
1133. 1 g. "Icterus dominicensis" .. 20 20
1134. 1 g. 50 As 25 c. 35 30
1135. 2 g. "Centurus striatus" 45 40

118. "Theato, Paris-1900".

1969. Winners of Olympic Marathon showing commemorative inscr. and stamp of "host" country. Multicoloured.
1136. 5 c. "Louis, Athens-1896" (postage) 8 8
1137. 10 c. Type 118 .. .. 12 12
1138. 15 c. "Hicks, St. Louis-1904" 15 15
1139. 20 c. "Hayes, London-1908" 25 25
1140. 20 c. "McArthur, Stockholm-1912" 25 25
1141. 25 c. Kolehmainen, Antwerp-1920" 40 40
1142. 25 c. "Steenroos, Paris-1924" 40 40
1143. 25 c. "El Quafi, Amsterdam-1928" .. 40 40
1144. 30 c. "Zabala, Los Angeles-1932" (air) 45 45
1145. 50 c. "Son, Berlin-1936" 70 70
1146. 60 c. "Cabrera, London-1948" 90 90
1148. 75 c. "Mimoun, Melbourne-1956" .. .. 1·10 1·10
1149. 90 c. "Bikila, Rome-1960" 1·25 1·25
1150. 1 g. "Bikila, Tokyo-1964" 1·40 1·40
1151. 1 g. 25 "Wolde, Mexico-1968" .. .. 1·60 1·60
Nos. 1136, 1139, 1142 and 1149 are larger, size 66 × 36 mm.

119. Pylons and Electric Light Bulb. **120.** Practising the Alphabet.

1969. Construction of Duvalier Hydro-electric Scheme.
1153. 119. 20 c. violet & blue (post.) 8 5
1154. 119. 20 c. blue and violet (air) 5 5
1155. 25 c. green and red .. 10 5
1156. 25 c. red and green .. 12 8

1969. Obligatory Tax. Education Fund. As Nos. 974/8.
1157. 91. 10 c. brown (postage) 5 5
1158. 10 c. ultramarine .. 5 5
1159. 91. 10 c. purple (air) .. 5 5
1160. 10 c. red 5 5
1161. 10 c. yellow 5 5
1162. 10 c. green 5 5
1163. 10 c. maroon 5 5

1969. League of Red Cross Societies. 50th Anniv. Various stamps surch. **50 eme. Anniversaire de la Ligue des Societes de la Croix Rouge.**
1164. 10 c. + 10 c. (No. 1099) (postage) 5 5
1165. 50 c. + 20 c. (No. 1100) .. 20 20
1166. 50 c. + 20 c. (No. 1101) (air) 20 20
1167. 1 g. 50 + 25 c. (No. 1103) 60 40

1969. "National Education". Multicoloured.
1168. 5 c. Type 120 (postage) .. 5 5
1169. 10 c. Children at play .. 5 5
1170. 50 c. Audio-visual education 12 8
1171. 50 c. As No. 1170 (air) .. 12 10
1172. 1 g. Type 120 .. .. 25 20
1173. 1 g. 50 As No. 1169 .. 45 30
Nos. 1169/71 and 1173 are vert.

121. I.L.O. Emblem. **122.** "Papilio zonaria"

1969. Int. Labour Organization. 50th Anniv.
1174. 121. 5 c. grn. & blk. (post.) 5 5
1175. 10 c. chestnut & black 5 5
1176. 20 c. ultramarine & blk. 8 8
1177. 121. 25 c. red and black (air) 12 8
1178. 70 c. orange and black 20 15
1179. 1 g. 75 violet & black 55 45

1970. Haitian Butterflies. Multicoloured.
1180. 10 c. Type 122 (postage) 5 5
1181. 20 c. "Zerene cesonia cynops" 5 5
1182. 25 c. "Papilio machaonides" 8 5
1183. 50 c. "Danaus eresimus kaempfferi" (air) .. 12 8
1184. 1 g. 50 "Anaea marthesia nemesis" 35 25
1185. 2 g. "Prepona antimache" 50 40

123. Dr. Martin Luther King.

1970. Dr. Martin Luther King (American Civil Rights leader). Commemoration.
1186. 123. 10 c. brown, red and ochre (postage) .. 5 5
1187. 20 c. blk., red & new bl. 5 5
1188. 25 c. blk., red & pink 8 5
1189. 123. 50 c. black, red and green (air) 15 8
1190. 1 g. blk., red & orange 30 15
1191. 1 g. 50 blk, red & blue 45 25

124. "Laeliopsis dominguensis". **125.** Stylised "Propeller".

1970. Haitian Orchids. Multicoloured.
1192. 10 c. Type 124 (postage) 5 5
1193. 20 c. "Oncidium haitiense" 8 5
1194. 25 c. "Oncidium calochilum" 10 8
1195. 50 c. "Tetramicra elegans" (air) .. 12 8
1196. 1 g. 50 "Epidendrum truncatum" 35 25
1197. 2 g. "Oncidium desertorum" 50 40

1970. 16th U.P.U. Congress, Tokyo.
1198. – 10 c. brown, black and green (postage) .. 5 5
1199. 125. 25 c. yellow, blk. & red 12 10
1200. – 50 c. grn., blk. & blue 20 20
1201. – 50 c. brown, black and violet (air) .. 15 10
1202. 125. 1 g. 50, yell., blk. & red 40 30
1203. – 2 g. brn., blk & green 60 40
DESIGNS—HORIZ. 10 c., 2 g. U.P.U. Monument, Berne and map of Haiti. 50 c. (both), Doves and globe.

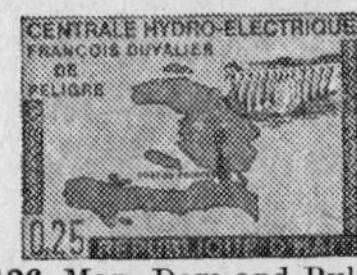

126. Map, Dam and Pylon.

1970. Construction of Duvalier Central. Hydro-electric Power Station. Multicoloured.
1205. 20 c. Map, dam and generator 12 5
1206. 25 c. Type 126 .. .. 15 8

1970. United Nations. 25th Anniv. Nos. 1200/203 optd. **XXVe ANNIVERSAIRE O.N.U.** and emblem
1207. – 50 c. grn., blk. & blue (postage) .. 15 12
1208. – 50 c. brn., blk & blue (air) .. 15 8
1209. 125. 1 g. 50 yell., blk. & red 45 25
1210. – 2 g. brn., blk. & grn. 60 40

127. Power Station and Pylon. **128.** Fort Nativity, 1492.

1970. Obligatory Tax. Duvalier Hydro-electric Project.
1212. 127. 20 c. brn. & lil. (post.) 8 5
1213. 127. 20 c. grey & brn. (air) 10 5
1214. 20 c violet and blue 8 5
See also Nos. 1268.

1970. Christmas.
1215. 128. 3 c. brn. & yell. (post.) 5 5
1216. 5 c. black and green .. 15 12
1217. – 1 g. 50 mult. (sepia panel) (air) .. 45 30
1218. – 1 g. 50 mult. (blue panel) 45 30
1219. – 2 g. multicoloured .. 70 40
DESIGN—SQUARE (33×33 mm.): Nos. 1217/19, 'Haitian Nativity' (Toussaint Auguste).

129. "The Oriental" (Rembrandt). **130.** Football.

1971. Paintings. Multicoloured.

1220. 5 c. Type **129** (postage).. 5 5
1221. 10 c. "The Ascension" (C. Bazile) 5 5
1222. 20 c "Irises in a vase" (Van Gogh) 5 5
1223. 50 c. "The Baptism of Christ" (C. Bazile) .. 15 10
1224. 50 c. "The Nativity" (R. Benoit) (air) 15 12
1225. 1 g. "Head of a Negro" (Rubens) 30 20
1226. 1 g. 50 As 10 c. 45 35

1971. World Cup Football Championships, Mexico (1970).

1228. **130.** 5 c. black & orange.. 5 5
1229. 50 c. black & brown.. 20 12
1230. – 50 c. blk., yell. & pink 20 12
1231. – 1 g. blk., yell & lilac 25 20
1232. **130.** 1 g. 50 black & drab.. 45 40
1233. – 5 g. blk., yell. & grey 1·50 1·25

DESIGNS: Nos. 1230/31, 1233, Jules Rimet Cup.

1971. Inauguration of Duvalier Central Power Station. Surch. **INAUGURATION 22-7-71** and premium.

1235. **127.** 20 c.+50 c. mult. .. 15 15
1236. – 25 c.+1 g. 50 mult. (No. 1206).. .. 40 30

131. Balloon and Airmail Stamp of 1929.

1971. Air. Airmail Service (1969). 40th Anniv.

1237. **131.** 20 c. black, red & bl. 10 5
1238. 50 c. black, red & bl. 20 8
1239. – 1 g. black and orange 35 15
1240. – 1 g. 50 black and mag. 60 25

DESIGNS: 1 g., 1 g. 50, "Concorde" and 1929 Air stamp.

1971. Obligatory Tax. Education Fund. Nos. 1205/6 surch. **ALPHABETISATION** and value.

1242. **126.** 20 c.+10 c. mult. .. 10 8
1243. – 25 c.+10 c. mult. .. 10 8

1972. Air. "INTERPEX" Int. Stamp Exhib., New York Nos. 1237/40 optd. **INTERPEX 72** and emblem.

1244. **131.** 20 c. black, red & blue 5 5
1245. 50 c. black, red & blue 12 12
1246. – 1 g. black and orange 25 25
1247. – 1 g. 50 black & mauve 40 45

132. J.-J. Dessalines and Emblem. **133.** "Sun" and "EXPO" Emblem.

1972. Jean-Jacques Dessalines ("founder of Haiti"). Commem.

1248. **132.** 5 c. black & grn. (post.) 5 5
1249. 10 c. black and blue.. 5 5
1250. 25 c. black and pink.. 8 5
1251. **132.** 50 c. blk. & grn. (air) 15 10
1252. 2 g. 50 black and lilac 75 45

1972. Air. Fifth "Haipex" Congress. Nos. 1237/40 optd. **HAIPEX 5eme. CONGRES** and emblem.

1253. **131.** 20 c. blk. red & blue 5 5
1254. – 50 c. blk., red and blue 12 8
1255. – 1 g black & orange.. 20 15
1256. – 1 g. 50 black & magenta 35 20

1972. Air. "Belgica 72" Stamp Exhibition, Brussels. Nos. 1238/40 optd. **BELGICA 72** and emblem.

1257. 50 c. blk., red and blue.. 12 8
1258. 1 g. black and orange .. 25 20
1259. 1 g. 50 black & magenta 40 30

1972. Obligatory Tax. As Nos. 974/8.

1260. **91.** 5 c. red 5 5
1261. 5 c. blue 5 5

1972. "EXPO 70" World Fair, Osaka, Japan (1970).

1262. **133.** 10 c. mult. (postage) 5 5
1263. 25 c. multicoloured.. 8 5
1264. – 50 c. multicoloured.. 12 8
1265. – 1 g. multicoloured .. 30 15
1266. – 1 g. 50 multicoloured 35 25
1267. – 2 g. 50 multicoloured 70 45

DESIGNS—HORIZ. Nos. 1264/7, Sun Tower and emblem.

1972. Obligatory Tax. Duvalier Hydro-electric Project. As Nos. 1212/14.

1268. **127.** 20 c. brown and blue 5 5

134. Basket Vendors. **135.** Headquarters and Map.

1973. Caribbean Travel Assn. 20th Anniv. Multicoloured.

1269. 50 c. Type **134** 12 8
1270. 80 c. Postal bus service .. 15 12
1271. 1 g. 50 Type **134** .. 35 25
1272. 2 g. 50 As 80 c. 60 40

1973. Air. Education Fund. As Nos. 973/8 but larger size 17 × 25 mm.

1273. **91.** 10 c. brown and blue .. 5 5
1274. 10 c. brown and green 5 5
1275. 10 c. brown and orange 5 5

1973. Air. Pan-American Health Organization. 70th Anniv. Multicoloured.

1276. **135.** 50 c. multicoloured .. 12 8
1277. 80 c. multicoloured .. 20 12
1278. 1 g. 50 multicoloured 40 25
1279. 2 g. multicoloured .. 50 35

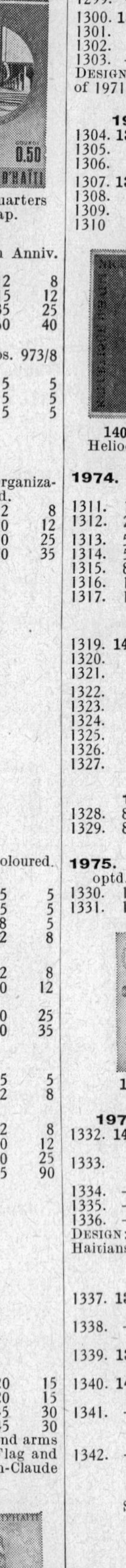

136. "Micromelo undata".

1973. Marine Life and Fishes. Multicoloured.

(i) Marine Life.

1280. 5 c. Type **136** (postage).. 5 5
1281. 10 c. "Nemaster rubiginosa" 5 5
1282. 25 c. "Cyerce cristallina" 8 5
1283. 50 c. "Desmophyllum riisei" 12 8
1284. 50 c. "Platypodia spectabilis" (air) 12 8
1285. 85 c. "Goniaster tessellatus" 20 12
1286. 1 g. 50 "Stephanocyathus diadema" 40 25
1287. 2 g. "Phyllangia americana" 50 35

(ii) Fishes.

1288. 10 c. "Gramma loreto" (postage) 5 5
1289. 50 c. "Acanthrus coeruleus" 12 8
1290. 50 c. "Gramma melacara" (air) 12 8
1291. 85 c. "Holacanthus tricolor" 20 12
1292. 1 g. 50 "Liopropoma rubre" 40 25
1293. 5 g. "Clepticus parrai" .. 1·25 90

137. Haitian Flag.

1973. Air.

1294. **137.** 80 c. black and red .. 20 15
1295. – 80 c. black and red .. 20 15
1296. – 1 g. 85 black and red 45 30
1297. – 1 g. 85 black and red 45 30

DESIGNS—As T **137**. No. 1295, Flag and arms (framed). (47 × 29 mm.). No. 1296, Flag and arms. No. 1297, Flag and Pres. Jean-Claude Duvalier.

138. Football Stadium. **139.** J. J. Dessalines.

1973. World Cup Football Championships. Preliminary Games between Caribbean Countries.

1298. **138.** 10 c. grn., blk. & brn. (postage) 5 5
1299. – 20 c. mve., blk. & brn. 5 5
1300. **138.** 50 c. grn., blk. & red (air) 12 8
1301. 80 c. grn., blk. & blue 20 12
1302. 1 g. 75 grn., blk. & brn. 45 30
1303. – 10 g. grn., blk. & brn. 2·50 1·75

DESIGNS: 20 c., 1 g. 75, 10 g. World Cup stamp of 1971.

1974. Dessalines Commemoration.

1304. **139.** 10 c. green & blue (post.) 5 5
1305. 20 c. black and red .. 5 5
1306. 25 c. violet & brown 8 5
1307. **139.** 50 c. bl. & brn. (air) .. 12 8
1308. 80 c. brn. & grey .. 20 12
1309. 1 g. purple & green .. 20 12
1310 1 g. 75 brn. & mauve 40 30

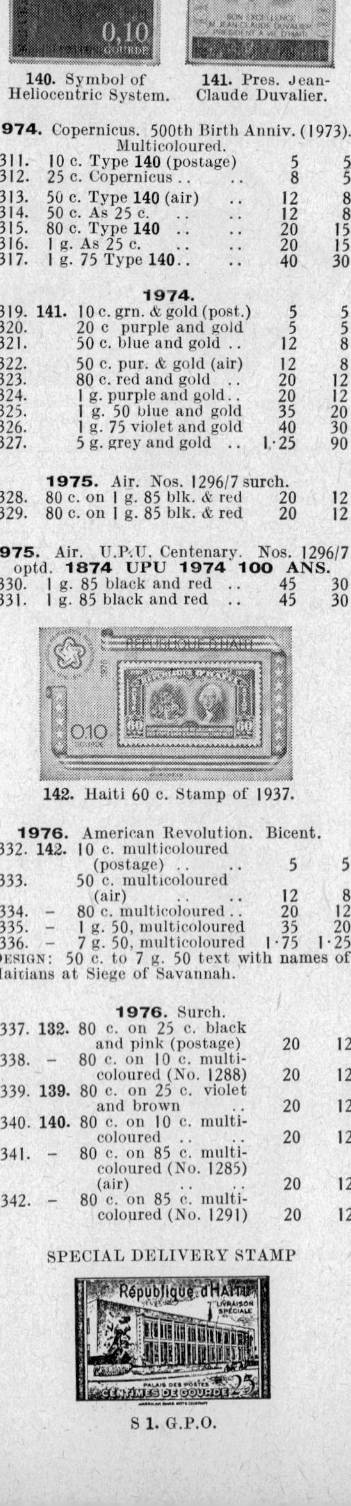

140. Symbol of Heliocentric System. **141.** Pres. Jean-Claude Duvalier.

1974. Copernicus. 500th Birth Anniv. (1973). Multicoloured.

1311. 10 c. Type **140** (postage) 5 5
1312. 25 c. Copernicus 8 5
1313. 50 c. Type **140** (air) .. 12 8
1314. 50 c. As 25 c. 12 8
1315. 80 c. Type **140** 20 15
1316. 1 g. As 25 c. 20 15
1317. 1 g. 75 Type **140**.. .. 40 30

1974.

1319. **141.** 10 c. grn. & gold (post.) 5 5
1320. 20 c purple and gold 5 5
1321. 50 c. blue and gold .. 12 8
1322. 50 c. pur. & gold (air) 12 8
1323. 80 c. red and gold .. 20 12
1324. 1 g. purple and gold .. 20 12
1325. 1 g. 50 blue and gold 35 20
1326. 1 g. 75 violet and gold 40 30
1327. 5 g. grey and gold .. 1·25 90

1975. Air. Nos. 1296/7 surch.

1328. 80 c. on 1 g. 85 blk. & red 20 12
1329. 80 c. on 1 g. 85 blk. & red 20 12

1975. Air. U.P.U. Centenary. Nos. 1296/7 optd. **1874 UPU 1974 100 ANS.**

1330. 1 g. 85 black and red .. 45 30
1331. 1 g. 85 black and red .. 45 30

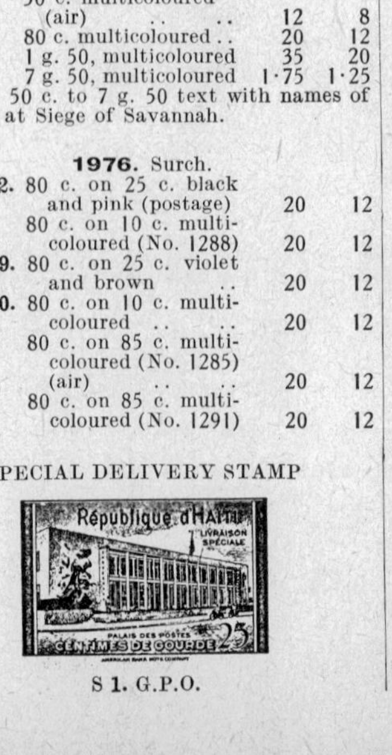

142. Haiti 60 c. Stamp of 1937.

1976. American Revolution. Bicent.

1332. **142.** 10 c. multicoloured (postage) 5 5
1333. 50 c. multicoloured (air) 12 8
1334. – 80 c. multicoloured .. 20 12
1335. – 1 g. 50, multicoloured 35 20
1336. – 7 g. 50, multicoloured 1·75 1·25

DESIGN: 50 c. to 7 g. 50 text with names of Haitians at Siege of Savannah.

1976. Surch.

1337. **132.** 80 c. on 25 c. black and pink (postage) 20 12
1338. – 80 c. on 10 c. multicoloured (No. 1288) 20 12
1339. **139.** 80 c. on 25 c. violet and brown .. 20 12
1340. **140.** 80 c. on 10 c. multicoloured 20 12
1341. – 80 c. on 85 c. multicoloured (No. 1285) (air) 20 12
1342. – 80 c. on 85 c. multicoloured (No. 1291) 20 12

SPECIAL DELIVERY STAMP

S 1. G.P.O.

1953.

E 468. **S 1.** 25 c. vermilion .. 20 15

PARCEL POST STAMPS

1960. Optd. **COLIS POSTAUX.**

P 725. **66.** 5 c. green & black (post.) 5 5
P 726. 10 c. red and black .. 5 5
P 727. 25 c. blue and black 8 8
P 728. **42.** 2 g. 50 grey 60 50
P 729. **66.** 50 c. orange & blk. (air) 20 15
P 730. **65.** 5 g. slate-violet & blue 1·75 1·40

P 1.

1961.

P 757. **P 1.** 50 c. violet and bistre (postage) 30 20
P 758. 1 g. blue and rose .. 45 25
P 759. 2 g. 50 lake & green (air) 85 60
P 760. 5 g. green and orange 1·75 1·10

OFFICIAL STAMPS

1960. Nos. 736/40 optd. **OFFICIEL.**

O 742. – 50 c. brown and green .. 20
O 743. – 50 c. blue and green .. 20
O 744. – 50 c. black and green .. 20
O 745. **81.** 1 g. green and red .. 35
O 746. – 1 g. 50 pink and blue .. 50

Set of 5 precancelled .. .. .. 1·25

The above were only issued precancelled.

O 1. Dessalines' Statue.

1962. Air (a) Size $20\frac{1}{2} \times 37\frac{1}{2}$ mm.

O 791. **O 1.** 50 c. sepia and blue 15 12
O 792. 1 g. red and blue .. 30 25
O 793. 1 g. 50 blue and bistre 45 35

(b) Size $30\frac{1}{2} \times 40$ mm.

O 794. **O 1.** 5 g. green and red.. 1·25 85

POSTAGE DUE STAMPS

D 1.

D 2.

1898.

D 63. **D 1.** 2 c. blue 12 12
D 64. 5 c. brown 20 20
D 65. 10 c. orange 30 25
D 66. 50 c. grey 35 30

1902. Optd. **MAI Gt Pre 1902** in frame.

D 85. **D 1.** 2 c. blue 40 35
D 86. 5 c. brown 60 35
D 87. 10 c. orange 75 60
D 88. 50 c. grey .. .. 3·00 2·25

1906.

D 150. **D 2.** 2 c. red 45 40
D 151. 5 c. blue .. .. 1·40 1·40
D 152. 10 c. purple .. 1·50 1·50
D 153. 50 c. olive .. .. 3·50 3·50

1914. Optd. **GL O.Z. 7 FEV. 1914** in frame.

D 206. **D 1.** 5 c. brown 35 35
D 207. 10 c. orange .. 35 35
D 208. 50 c. grey .. .. 1·90 1·90

1914. Optd. **GL O.Z. 7 FEV. 1914** in frame.

D 209. **D 2.** 2 c. red 20 20
D 210. 5 c. blue 35 35
D 211. 10 c. purple .. 2·75 2·75
D 212. 50 c. olive .. .. 3·00 3·00

D 3.

1951.
D 452. D **3.** 10 c. red 8 8
D 453. 20 c. brown .. 12 12
D 454. 40 c. green 20 20
D 455. 50 c. yellow .. 30 30

HAMBURG E2

A port in N.W. Germany, formerly a Free City, now forming part of West Germany.

16 schillinge = 1 mark.

1.

2.

3.

1859. Imperf.
1. **1.** ½ sch. black .. .. 50·00 £325
2. 1 sch. brown .. .. 45·00 40·00
3. 2 sch. red .. .. .. 45·00 50·00
4. 3 sch. blue .. .. 50·00 75·00
6. 4 sch. green .. .. 55·00 £500
7. 7 sch. orange .. .. 45·00 17·00
10. 9 sch. yellow £100 £900

1867. Perf.
46. **1.** 2½ sch. green .. .. 6·00 38·00

1864. Imperf.
13. **2.** 1¼ sch. lilac .. .. 75·00 55·00
15. 1¼ sch. grey .. .. 50·00 40·00
17. 1¼ sch. blue £225 £500
18. 2½ sch. green .. .. 85·00 75·00

1864. Perf.
19. **1.** ½ sch. black .. .. 4·00 6·00
20. 1 sch. brown .. .. 7·50 8·00
21. **2.** 1¼ sch. mauve .. .. 50·00 5·50
25. **1.** 2 sch. red .. .. 10·00 12·00
27. **2.** 2½ sch. green .. .. 80·00 17·00
30. **1.** 3 sch. blue .. .. 23·00 20·00
32. 4 sch. green .. .. 6·50 12·00
34. 7 sch. orange .. .. 95·00 70·00
37. 7 sch. mauve .. .. 6·50 12·00
38. 9 sch. yellow .. .. 17·00 £750

1866. Roul.
44. **3.** 1¼ sch. mauve .. .. 25·00 24·00
45. 1½ sch. rose .. .. 5·50 75·00

HANOVER E2

Until 1866 an independent kingdom of N.W. Germany, and then incorporated in Prussia. Now part of West Germany.

1850. 12 pfennige = gutegroschen.
24 gutengroschen = 1 thaler.
1858. 10 (new) pfennige = 1 (new) groschen.
30 (new) groschen = 1 thaler.

1.

2.

1851. Imperf.
18. **1.** 3 pf. rose .. .. 38·00 40·00
8. 3 pf. rose and black .. £180 £160
1. **2.** 1 ggr. black on blue .. £900 18·00
2. 1 ggr. black on green .. 17·00 2·10
3. 1 ggr. black and green .. 18·00 5·00
14. $\frac{1}{30}$ th. black on red .. 40·00 18·00
15. $\frac{1}{30}$ th. black and red .. 55·00 12·00
5. $\frac{1}{15}$ th. black on blue .. 55·00 23·00
16. $\frac{1}{15}$ th. black and blue .. 42·00 25·00
6. $\frac{1}{10}$ th. black on orange .. 70·00 25·00
10. $\frac{1}{10}$ th. black and orange .. £110 60·00

3. King George V.

4.

1859. Imperf. or roul.
23. **3.** 1 g. red .. .. .. 1·40 1·10
26. 2 g. blue .. .. 10·00 10·00
28. 3 g. yellow .. .. 75·00 22·00
29. 3 g. brown .. .. 13·00 15·00
31. 10 g. green £120 £375

1860. Imperf. or roul.
35. **1.** 3 pf. green .. .. 16·00 28·00
33. **4.** ½ g. black .. .. 40·00 60·00

HATAY O2

The territory of Alexandretta. Autonomous under French control from 1923 to Sept. 1938. Hatay was returned to Turkey in June 1939.

100 centiemes = 1 piastre.
1938. 100 santims = 40 paras = 1 kurus.

1938. Stamps of Syria of 1930 optd. **SANDJAK D'ALEXANDRETTE** or surch. also in figures.
1. 10 c. purple 5 5
2. 20 c. red 8 8
3. 50 c. violet 10 10
4. 75 c. red 10 10
5. 1 pi. brown 10 10
6. 2 pi. violet 20 20
7. 2 pi. 50 c. on 4 pi. orange .. 25 25
8. 3 pi. green 35 35
9. 4 pi. orange 45 45
10. 6 pi. green 40 40
11. 12 pi. 50 c. on 15 pi. red .. 65 65
12. 25 pi. claret .. .. 1·40 1·40

1938. Air. Stamps of Syria of 1937 (Nos. A 322, etc.) optd. **SANDJAK D'ALEXANDRETTE.**
13. ½ pi. violet 12 12
14. 1 pi. black 12 12
15. 2 pi. green 55 55
16. 3 pi. blue 60 60
17. 5 pi. mauve .. .. 1·60 1·60
18. 10 pi. brown .. .. 1·75 1·75
19. 15 pi. brown .. .. 2·00 2·00
20. 25 pi. blue .. .. 2·25 2·25

1938. Mourning for Kemal Ataturk. Nos. 45, 7, 9 and 11 optd. **Sandjak d'Alexandrette 10-11-1938** in frame.
27. 75 c. red .. .. 8·50 7·00
28. 1 pi. brown .. .. 5·00 4·50
29. 2 pi. 50 c. on 4 pi. orange 2·75 2·00
30. 4 pi. orange .. .. 4·50 3·50
31. 12 pi. 50 c. on 15 pi. red .. 12·00 11·00

1939. Stamps of Turkey surch. **HATAY DEVLETI** and value.
32. **84.** 10 s. on 20 p. orange .. 12 12
33. 25 s. on 1 k. green .. 12 12
34. 50 s. on 2 k. violet .. 12 12
35. 75 s. on 2½ k. green .. 12 12
36. 1 k. on 4 k. slate .. 15 15
37. 1 k. on 5 k. red .. 15 15
38. 1½ k. on 3 k. brown .. 20 20
39. 2½ k. on 3 k. slate .. 20 20
40. 5 k. on 8 k. blue .. 70 70
41. 12½ k. on 20 k. olive .. 1·00 1·00
42. 20 k. on 25 k. blue .. 1·25 1·25

1. Map of Hatay.

2. Flag of Hatay.

1939.
48. **1.** 10 pa. orange and blue .. 10 10
49. 30 pa. violet and blue .. 15 15
50. 1½ k. olive and blue .. 20 20
51. – 2½ k. green 20 20
52. – 3 k. blue 25 25
53. – 5 k. red 30 30
54. **2.** 6 k. red and blue .. 35 35
55. 7½ k. red and green .. 35 35
56. 12 k. red and violet .. 45 45
57. 12½ k. red and blue .. 45 45
58. – 17½ k. red 65 65
59. – 25 k. olive .. .. 1·00 1·00
60. – 50 k. blue .. .. 2·00 2·00

DESIGNS—HORIZ. 2½ k., 3 k., 5 k. Lions of Antioch. 17½ k., 25 k., 50 k. Parliament House, Antioch.

1939. Commemorating Turkish Annexation. Optd. **T.C. ilhak tarihi 30-6-1939.**
65. **1.** 10 pa. orange and blue .. 15 15
66. 30 pa. violet and blue .. 20 20
67. 1½ k. olive and blue .. 20 20
68. – 2½ k. green (No. 51) .. 25 25
69. – 3 k. blue (No. 52) .. 25 25
70. – 5 k. red (No. 53) .. 30 30
71. **2.** 6 k. red and blue .. 30 30
72. 7½ k. red and green .. 35 35
73. 12 k. red and violet .. 45 45
74. 12½ k. red and blue .. 45 45
75. – 17½ k. red (No. 58) .. 60 60
76. – 25 k. olive (No. 59) .. 1·00 1·00
77. – 50 k. blue (No. 60) .. 2·00 2·00

POSTAGE DUE STAMPS

1938. Postage Due stamps of Syria of 1925 optd. **SANDJAK D'ALEXANDRETTE.**
D 21. D **1.** 50 c. brown on yellow 35 35
D 22. – 1 pi. purple on red .. 60 60
D 23. – 2 pi. black on blue .. 75 75
D 24. – 3 pi. black on orange 1·25 1·25
D 25. – 5 pi. black on green .. 1·50 1·50
D 26. – 8 pi. black on blue (No. D 38) .. 1·50 1·50

1939. Postage Due stamps of Turkey, optd. **HATAY DEVLETI** or surch. also.
D 43. D **8.** 1 k. on 2 k. blue .. 20 20
D 44. 3 k. violet 25 25
D 45. 4 k. on 5 k. green .. 45 45
D 46. 5 k. on 12 k. red .. 85 85
D 47. 12 k. red .. .. 2·00 2·00

1939. As T **2**, but inscr. "POSTALARI TAKSE PULU" at foot.
D 61. 1 k. red 20 20
D 62. 3 k. brown 25 25
D 63. 4 k. green 30 30
D 64. 5 k. slate 40 40
DESIGN: Castle at Antioch.

1939. Nos. D 61/4 optd. **T.C. ilhak tarihi 30-6-1939.**
D 73. 1 k. red 15 15
D 74. 3 k. brown 20 20
D 75. 4 k. green 30 30
D 76. 5 k. slate 40 40

HAWAII O4

A group of islands in the central Pacific, an independent kingdom till 1893 when a provisional government was set up. Annexed in 1898 by the United States. Now a State of the U.S.A.

100 cents = 1 dollar.

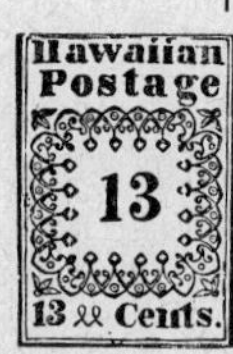

1.

2. Kamehameha III.

3. Kamehameha IV.

1851. Imperf.
1. **1.** 2 c. blue £40000 £20000
2. 5 c. blue £1500 £6500
3. 13 c. blue £6500 £4000
On Nos. 1/2 the value is expressed in words.

1853. Imperf.
9. **2.** 5 c. blue .. .. .. 40·00 40·00
6. 13 c. red £125 £150

1862. Imperf.
22. **3.** 2 c. red .. .. .. 15·00 30·00

4. Princess Victoria Kamamalu.

5. Princess Likelike.

6. Queen Liliuokalani.

1864. Perf.
31. **4.** 1 c. mauve .. .. 1·75 1·75
32. – 2 c. red .. .. 2·00 1·50
33. – 5 c. blue .. .. 2·25 75
34. – 6 c. green .. .. 3·00 1·50
35. – 18 c. red .. .. 3·50 1·50

DESIGNS: 2 c. Kamehameha IV. 5 c., 6 c. Portraits of Kamehameha V. 18 c. H.H. Mataio Kekuanaoa.

1875.
38. **5.** 1 c. blue .. .. 1·00 1·00
43a. 1 c. green 60 50
36. 2 c. brown .. .. 1·50 50
40a. 2 c. rose 75 40
41. 10 c. black .. .. 5·00 3·00
45. 10 c. red .. .. 4·00 2·50
46. 10 c. brown .. .. 3·00 1·50
37. 12 c. black .. .. 8·00 4·00
47. 12 c. claret .. .. 3·00 1·50
48. 15 c. brown .. .. 8·00 5·00
49. 25 c. purple .. .. 12·00 7·00
50. 50 c. red .. .. 25·00 15·00
51. $1 red .. .. 30·00 20·00

DESIGNS: 2 c. King Kalakaua. 10 c. Same in uniform. 12 c. Prince Lelejohoku. 15 c. Queen Kapiolani. 25 c. Statue of Kamehameha I. 50 c. King Lunalilo. $1 Queen Emma.

1889.
53. **6.** 2 c. violet 85 50

1893. Stamps of 1864, 1875 and 1890, optd. **Provisional GOVT. 1893.**
54. **4.** 1 c. mauve 75 75
55. **5.** 1 c. blue 75 75
56. 1 c. green 60 60
57. 2 c. brown .. .. 1·25 2·00
58. **6.** 2 c. violet 50 50
67. – 2 c. red .. .. 10·00 10·00
68. **5.** 2 c. rose 40 50
60. – 5 c. blue 85 75
61. – 6 c. green .. .. 2·00 2·50
62. **5.** 10 c. black .. .. 1·50 1·25
70. 10 c. red .. .. 2·00 5·00
71. 10 c. brown .. .. 1·25 1·75
64. 12 c. black .. .. 1·50 1·50
65. 12 c. claret .. .. 25·00 30·00
73. 15 c. brown .. .. 3·50 4·50
74. – 18 c. red .. .. 4·00 4·50
66. **5.** 25 c. purple .. .. 3·00 4·00
75. 30 c. red .. .. 8·00 10·00
76. $1 red .. .. 20·00 20·00

18. Arms.

20. Statue of Kamehameha I.

1894.
77. **18.** 1 c. orange 50 25
89. 1 c. green 50 50
78. – 2 c. brown 60 20
90. – 2 c. pink 50 25
79. **20.** 5 c. red .. .. 1·00 50
91. 5 c. blue .. .. 1·00 75
80. – 10 c. green .. .. 1·25 1·00
81. – 12 c. blue .. .. 2·00 1·75
82. – 25 c. blue .. .. 2·50 2·50

DESIGNS—HORIZ. 2 c. Honolulu. 12 c. S.S. "Arawa". VERT. 10 c. Star. 25 c. Pres. S. B. Dole.

INTER-ISLAND POSTAGE

For a list of stamps of the Inter-island Post, see Stanley Gibbons' Overseas Catalogue, Volume 4.

OFFICIAL STAMPS

O 1. Secretary L. A. Thurston.

1896.
O 1. O **1.** 2 c. green .. .. 4·00 4·00
O 2. 5 c. brown .. .. 4·00 4·00
O 3. 6 c. blue .. .. 4·00 4·00
O 4. 10 c. red .. .. 4·00 4·00
O 5. 12 c. orange .. .. 4·00 4·00
O 6. 25 c. violet .. .. 4·00 4·00

HELIGOLAND BC

An island off the N. coast of Germany, ceded to that country by Great Britain in 1890.

1867. 16 schillings = 1 mark.
1875. 100 pfennig = 1 mark.

Many of the Heligoland stamps found in old collections, and the majority of those offered at a small fraction of catalogue prices to-day, are reprints which have very little value.

1.

ILLUSTRATIONS
British Commonwealth and all overprints and surcharges are FULL SIZE. Foreign Countries have been reduced to ¾-LINEAR.

1867. Perf. (½, 1, 2 and 6 sch. also roul.).
10. **1.** ½ sch. green and red .. 14·00 £900
6. ½ sch. green and red .. 70·00 90·00
7. ½ sch. red and green .. 14·00 £750
8. 1 sch. red and green .. 65·00 80·00
13. 1½ sch. green and red .. 28·00 £150
4. 2 sch. red and green .. 5·50 35·00
5. 6 sch. green and red .. 7·50 £150

2.

3.

4.

5.

1875.

15. 2.	1 pf. (¼d.) green and red..	5·00	£300
16.	2 pf. (½d.) red and green..	5·00	£375
24. 3.	3 pf. (⅝d.) grn., red & yell.	85·00	£500
17. 2.	5 pf. (⅝d.) green and red..	5·00	10·00
20.	10 pf. (1¼d.) red and green	5·00	12·00
25. 3.	20 pf. (2½d.) green, red and yellow	8·00	14·00
22. 2.	25 pf. (3d.) green and red	6·00	15·00
23.	50 pf. (6d.) red and green	10·00	15·00
29. 4.	1 m. (1s.) grn., red & blk.	48·00	£100
31. 5.	5 m. (5s.) grn., red & blk.	65·00	£550

HOI-HAO (HOIHOW) O1

An Indo-Chinese post office in China, closed in 1922.

1901. 100 centimes = 1 franc.
1918. 100 cents = 1 piastre.

HOI HAO
州 瓊
(1.)

1902. Stamps of Indo-China "Tablet" key-type, optd. with T 1. Chinese characters read "HOI-HAO" and are the same on every value.

1. D.	1 c. black on blue ..	20	20
2.	2 c. brown on yellow ..	20	20
3.	4 c. claret on grey ..	20	20
4.	5 c. green	20	20
5.	10 c. black on lilac ..	20	20
6.	15 c. blue	£130	60·00
7.	15 c. grey	15	15
8.	20 c. red on green ..	1·25	1·25
9.	25 c. black on red ..	55	30
10.	30 c. brown	1·75	1·40
11.	40 c. red on yellow ..	2·50	2·00
12.	50 c. red on rose ..	3·25	2·50
13.	75 c. brown on orange ..	16·00	16·00
14.	1 f. olive	55·00	50·00
15.	5 f. mauve on lilac ..	50·00	48·00

1903. Stamps of Indo-China, "Tablet" key-type, surch. as T 1. Chinese characters indicate the value and differ for each denomination.

16. D.	1 c. black on blue ..	8	8
17.	2 c. brown on yellow ..	10	10
18.	4 c. claret on grey ..	15	15
19.	5 c. green	15	15
20.	10 c. red	15	15
21.	15 c. grey	15	15
22.	20 c. red on green ..	30	30
23.	25 c. blue	20	20
24.	25 c. black on red ..	20	20
25	30 c. brown	30	30
26.	40 c. red on yellow ..	2·10	2·10
27.	50 c. red on rose ..	2·50	2·50
28.	50 c. brown on blue ..	10·00	10·00
29.	75 c. brown on orange ..	3·50	3·50
30.	1 f. olive	4·00	4·00
31.	5 f. mauve on lilac ..	14·00	14·00

1906. Stamps of Indo-China surch. **HOI-HAO** and with value in Chinese.

32. 1.	1 c. olive	12	12
33.	2 c. claret on yellow ..	15	15
34.	4 c. mauve on blue ..	15	15
35.	5 c. green	25	25
36.	10 c red	25	25
37.	15 c. brown on blue ..	25	25
38.	20 c. red on green ..	40	40
39.	25 c. blue	40	40
40.	30 c. brown on cream ..	50	50
41.	35 c. black on yellow ..	55	55
42.	40 c. black on grey ..	55	55
43.	50 c. brown	1·10	1·10
44. D.	75 c. brown on orange ..	3·00	3·00
45. 1.	1 f. green	3·25	3·25
46.	2 f. brown on yellow ..	3·25	3·25
47. D.	5 f. mauve on lilac ..	12·00	12·00
48. 1.	10 f. red on green ..	13·00	13·00

1908. Stamps of Indo-China (native types) surch. **HOI HAO** or **HOI-HAO** and with value in Chinese.

49. 2.	1 c. black and olive ..	5	5
50.	2 c. black and brown ..	5	5
51.	4 c. black and blue ..	8	8
52.	5 c. black and green ..	15	15
53.	10 c. black and red ..	20	20
54.	15 c. black and violet ..	40	40
55. 3.	20 c. black and violet ..	50	50
56.	25 c. black and blue ..	50	50
57.	30 c. black & chocolate ..	50	50
58.	35 c. black and green ..	50	50
59.	40 c. black and brown ..	45	45
60	50 c. black and red ..	70	70
61. 4.	75 c. black and orange ..	60	60
62.	1 f. black and red ..	1·50	1·50
63.	2 f. black and green ..	3·25	3·25
64.	5 f. black and blue ..	8·00	8·00
65.	10 f black and violet ..	9·50	9·50

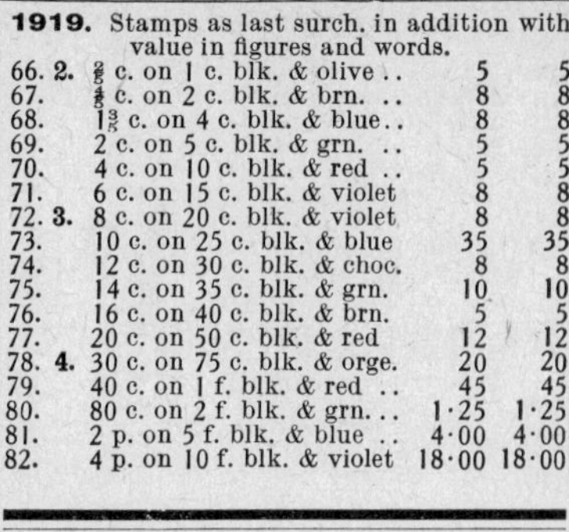

1919. Stamps as last surch. in addition with value in figures and words.

66. 2.	⅖ c. on 1 c. blk. & olive ..	5	5
67.	⅘ c. on 2 c. blk. & brn. ..	8	8
68.	1⅗ c. on 4 c. blk. & blue ..	8	8
69.	2 c. on 5 c. blk. & grn. ..	5	5
70.	4 c. on 10 c. blk. & red ..	5	5
71.	6 c. on 15 c. blk. & violet	8	8
72. 3.	8 c. on 20 c. blk. & violet	8	8
73.	10 c. on 25 c. blk. & blue	35	35
74.	12 c. on 30 c. blk. & choc.	8	8
75.	14 c. on 35 c. blk. & grn.	10	10
76.	16 c. on 40 c. blk. & brn.	5	5
77.	20 c. on 50 c. blk. & red	12	12
78. 4.	30 c. on 75 c. blk. & orge.	20	20
79.	40 c. on 1 f. blk. & red ..	45	45
80.	80 c. on 2 f. blk. & grn. ..	1·25	1·25
81.	2 p. on 5 f. blk. & blue ..	4·00	4·00
82.	4 p. on 10 f. blk. & violet	18·00	18·00

HONDURAS O2

A republic of C. America, independent since 1838.

1866. 8 reales = 1 peso.
1878. 100 centavos = 1 peso.
1933. 100 centavos = 1 lempira.

1.

2. Morazan.

3.

1866. Imperf.

1. 1.	2 r. black on green ..	15	
2.	2 r. black on rose ..	15	

1878. Perf.

31. 2.	1 c. violet	15	25
32.	2 c. brown	15	30
33.	½ r. black	15	25
34.	1 r. green	25	25
35.	2 r. blue	1·25	1·50
36.	4 r. red	1·00	1·25
37.	1 p. orange	1·60	2·00

1890.

45. 3.	1 c. green	8	10
46.	2 c. red	8	10
47.	5 c. blue	8	10
48.	10 c. orange	8	10
49.	20 c. bistre	8	10
50.	25 c. rose	8	12
51.	30 c. violet	8	25
52.	40 c. blue	10	50
53.	50 c. brown	10	50
54.	75 c. green	10	1·00
55.	1 p. lake	10	1·25

4. President Bogrand.

6.

1891.

56. 4.	1 c. blue	8	10
57.	2 c. brown	8	10
58.	5 c. green	8	10
59.	10 c. red	8	10
60.	20 c. lake	8	12
61.	25 c. claret	10	15
62.	30 c. grey	10	30
63.	40 c. green	8	30
64.	50 c. sepia	8	30
65.	75 c. violet	8	45
66.	1 p. brown	8	90
67. –	2 p. black and brown ..	15	2·75
68. –	5 p. black and violet ..	15	3·00
69. –	10 p. black and green ..	15	3·00

DESIGN (LARGER): 2, 5, 10 p. Pres. Bogrand facing left.

1892. Discovery of America. 4th Cent.

70. 6.	1 c. grey	8	12
71.	2 c. blue	8	12
72.	5 c. green	8	12
73.	10 c. green	8	15
74.	20 c. red	8	15
75.	25 c. brown	8	20
76.	30 c. blue	8	20
77.	40 c. orange	8	35
78.	50 c. brown	8	45
79.	75 c. lake	8	75
80.	1 p. violet	8	95

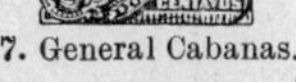

7. General Cabanas. 8.

1893.

81. 7.	1 c. green	8	12
82.	2 c. red	8	12
83.	5 c. blue	8	12
84.	10 c. brown	8	12
85.	20 c. brown	8	15
86.	25 c. blue	8	20
87.	30 c. orange	8	40
88. 7.	40 c. black	8	50
89.	50 c. sepia	8	70
90.	75 c. violet	8	1·00
91.	1 p. brown	8	1·25

1895.

92. 8.	1 c. red	8	8
93.	2 c. blue	8	8
94.	5 c. grey	8	12
95.	10 c. lake	8	12
96.	20 c. lilac	8	25
97.	30 c. lilac	8	55
98.	50 c. brown	8	85
99.	1 p. green	8	1·25

9. President Arias.

10.

1896.

100. 9.	1 c. blue	10	10
101.	2 c. brown	10	10
102.	5 c. purple	10	10
103.	10 c. red	12	12
104.	20 c. green	15	20
105.	30 c. blue	20	40
106.	50 c. lake	30	50
107.	1 p. sepia	35	1·00

1898.

108. 10.	1 c. brown	8	5
109.	2 c. red	10	5
110.	5 c. blue	10	5
111.	6 c. purple	15	12
112.	10 c. blue	15	12
113.	20 c. brown	35	30
114.	50 c. orange	50	85
115.	1 p. green	75	1·00

11. General Santos Guardiola.

12. President Medina.

1903.

118. 11.	1 c. green	8	8
119.	2 c. red	8	8
120.	5 c. blue	8	8
121.	6 c. lilac	10	10
122.	10 c. brown	15	15
123.	20 c. blue	20	20
124.	50 c. red	35	35
125.	1 p. orange	35	40

1907. Perf. or imperf.

127. 12.	1 c. green	8	8
136.	1 c. black	4·00	2·50
128a.	2 c. red	12	8
129.	5 c. blue	12	8
130.	6 c. violet	12	8
131.	10 c. sepia	20	20
132.	20 c. blue	20	20
133.	50 c. claret	20	20
134.	1 p. orange	35	35

1910. Surch. in figures.

137. 12.	1 on 20 c. blue	70	60
138.	5 on 20 c. blue	70	60
139.	10 on 20 c. blue ..	70	60

13.

14.

1911.

140. 13.	1 c. violet	8	8
141.	2 c. green	8	8
142.	5 c. red	12	8
143.	6 c. blue	12	8
144.	10 c. blue	5	5
145.	20 c. yellow	25	20
146.	50 c. brown	60	60
147.	1 p. olive	90	90

1911. Optd. **XC Aniversario de la Independencia.**

157. 13.	2 c. green	4·25	4·25

1912. Election of President Manual Bonilla.

158. 14.	1 c. red	4·50	4·50

1913. Independence. 90th Anniv. Surch. **2 CENTAVOS.**

159. 13.	2 c. on 1 c. violet ..	30	25

1913. Surch. in figures and cts.

161. 13.	2 c. on 1 c. violet ..	3·25	3·25
162.	2 c. on 10 c. blue ..	50	50
163.	2 c. on 20 c. yellow ..	2·40	2·40
164.	5 c. on 1 c. violet ..	60	30
165.	5 c. on 10 c. blue ..	70	45
166.	6 c. on 1 c. violet ..	70	40

15. Gen. T. Sierra.

16. Gen. M. Bonilla.

1913.

167. 15.	1 c. brown	10	10
168.	2 c. red	8	5
169. 16.	5 c. blue	8	5
170.	5 c. violet-blue ..	10	8
171.	6 c. violet	10	8
172.	6 c. mauve	10	5
173. 15.	10 c. blue	25	25
174.	10 c. brown	45	20
175.	20 c. brown	15	15
176. 16.	50 c. red	30	20
177.	1 p. green	70	60

1914. Surch.

178. 15.	1 c. on 2 c. red.. ..	15	15
179.	5 c. on 2 c. red	35	35
180. 16.	5 c. on 6 c. violet ..	90	90
181. 15.	5 c. on 10 c. brown ..	1·10	1·10
182.	10 c. on 2 c. red.. ..	1·25	1·25
184. 16.	10 c. on 6 c. violet ..	1·25	1·25
185.	10 c. on 50 c. red ..	2·75	2·10

17. Ulua Bridge.

19. Francisco Bertrand.

1915. Dated "1915".

186. 17.	1 c. brown	5	5
187.	2 c. red	8	8
188. –	5 c blue	10	5
189. –	6 c. violet	15	8
190. 17.	10 c. blue	15	8
191.	20 c. brown	40	40
192. –	50 c. red	35	35
193. –	1 p. green	75	70

DESIGN: 5 c., 6 c., 50 c., 1 p. Bonilla Theatre.

1916.

194. 19.	1 c. orange	70	70

1918. No. O 206 optd. **CORRIENTE** and bar.

195.	5 c. blue	75	45

20. Statue of Morazan.

21.

1919. Dated "1919" at top.

196. 20.	1 c. brown	5	5
197.	2 c. red	8	5
198.	5 c. red	8	5
199.	6 c. mauve	10	8
200.	10 c. blue	15	15
201	15 c. blue	30	15
202.	15 c. violet	25	15
203.	20 c. brown	20	20
204.	50 c. brown	50	50
205.	1 p green	75	75

1920. Assumption of Power by Gen. R. L. Gutierrez.

206. 21.	2 c. rose	1·10	1·10
207.	2 c. gold	3·25	3·25
208.	2 c. silver	3·25	3·25
209.	2 c red	3·75	3·75

Nos. 207/9 are larger (51 × 40 mm.).

1921. As T 20, but dated "1920" at top.

210. 20.	6 c. purple	1·60	1·25

1922. Surch. **VALE SEIS CTS.**

211. 20.	6 c. on 2 c. red ..	25	15

1923. Surch. **HABILITADO VALE** and value in words and figures.

212. 20.	$0.10 on 1 c. brown ..	10	10
213.	$0.50 on 2 c. red ..	25	25
214.	1 p. on 5 c. red ..	1·25	1·25

22. Dionisio de Herrera.

23. M. Paz Baraona.

1923.

215. 22.	1 c. olive	5	5
216.	2 c. red	5	5
217.	6 c. purple	8	5
218.	10 c. blue	10	10
219.	20 c. brown	20	12
220.	50 c. red	45	35
221.	1 p. green	80	45

1925. President Baraona. Inaug. Imperf. or perf.
222. 23. 1 c. blue .. .. 1·60 1·60
224. 1 c. red .. .. 2·75 2·75
225. 1 c. brown .. .. 8·00 8·00

1925. Air. Nos. 186/93 optd. **AERO. CORREO** or surch. also.
227. 5 c. blue .. .. 32·00 32·00
229. 10 c. blue .. .. 55·00 55·00
231. 20 c. brown .. .. 80·00 80·00
235. 25 c. on 1 c. brown .. 48·00 48·00
236. 25 c. on 5 c. blue .. £120 £120
236c. 25 c. on 10 c. blue .. £28000
237. 25 c. on 20 c. brown .. £120 £120
233. 50 c. red £140 £140
234. 1 p. green £550 £550

1926. Optd. **Acuerdo Mayo 3 de 1926 HABILITADO.**
238. 20. 6 c. mauve 35 35

1926. Optd. **HABILITADO 1926.**
242. 17. 2 c. red 8 8
243. 20. 2 c. red 8 8

1926. Optd. **1926.**
239. – 6 c. violet (No. 189) .. 85 85
240. 20. 6 c. violet .. .. 1·10 1·10

1926. Surch. **Vale 6 Cts. 1926** and bar.
243d. 20. 6 c. on 10 c. blue .. 15 12

1927. Surch. **vale 6 cts. 1927** and bar
244. 20. 6 c. on 15 c. violet .. 20 20
245. 17. 6 c. on 20 c. brown .. 20 20
246. 20. 6 c. on 20 c. brown .. 20 20

24.

26. President Colindres and Vice-President Chavez.

1927. Various designs as T 24.
247. – 1 c. blue (Road) .. 12 12
248. 24. 2 c. red (Ruins) .. 10 8
249. – 5 c. purple (Pine Tree) 12 10
250. – 5 c. blue (Pine Tree) .. 1·75 1·10
251. – 6 c. black (Palace) .. 35 35
252. – 6 c. blue (Palace) .. 20 15
253. – 10 c. blue (P. Leiva) .. 20 15
254. – 15 c. blue (Pres. Soto) 25 12
255. – 20 c. blue (Lempira) .. 30 20
256. – 30 c. brown (Map) .. 45 35
257. – 50 c. green (Pres. Lindo) 85 40
258. – 1 p. red (Columbus) .. 1·75 75

1929. Installation of President Colindres.
259. 26. 1 c. lake 90 90
260. – 2 c. green 90 90
DESIGN—VERT. 2 c. Pres. Colindres.

1929. Air. (a) Surch. **Servicio aereo Vale,** value and **1929.**
262. 22. 5 c. on 20 c. brown .. 40 40
263. 10 c. on 50 c. red .. 90 75
264. 15 c. on 1 p. green .. 1·75 1·75
261. 25 c. on 50 c. red .. 2·75 2·75

(b) Surch. **Servicio Aereo In-ternacional Vale,** value and **1929.**
265. 22. 5 c. on 10 c. blue .. 25 25
266. 20 c. on 50 c. red .. 45 45

1929. Herrera Monument type, dated 1924-1928. Surch. **Vale 1 cts. XI 1929.**
267. 1 c. on 6 c. mauve .. 12 12

1929. Nos. 247/58 optd. **1929 a 1930.**
268. – 1 c. blue 8 8
269. 24. 2 c. red 15 15
270. – 5 c. purple 20 20
271. – 5 c. blue 50 40
272. – 6 c. black .. .. 1·40 1·10
273. – 6 c. blue 15 12
274. – 10 c. blue 20 12
275. – 15 c. blue 20 15
276. – 20 c. blue 20 15
277. – 30 c. brown 35 25
278. – 50 c. green 45 40
279. – 1 p. red .. .. 1·25 1·00

1930. Air. No. O 264 optd. **HABILITADO Servicio Aereo Inter nacional 1930.**
281. – 50 c. green and yellow 85 85

1930. Air. Surch. **Servicio Aereo In-ternacional Vale,** value and **1930.**
282. 22. 5 c. on 10 c. blue .. 20 20
284. 5 c. on 20 c. brown .. 55·00 55·00
285. 10 c. on 20 c. brown .. 45 45
287. – 25 c. on 50 c. red (No. 192) 60 60

1930. Air. Surch. **Vale** and value in addition in large letters and figures.
290. 22. 10 c. on 5 c. on 20 c. brown (No. 284) .. 35 35
291. 10 c. on 10 c. on 20 c. brown (No. 285) .. 60·00 60·00
292. – 50 c. on 25 c. on 1 p. green (No. 193) .. 1·50 1·50

1930. Air. Surch. **Servicio aereo Vale,** value and **Marzo—1930.**
293. 22. 5 c. on 10 c. blue .. 20 20
294. 15 c. on 20 c. brown .. 35 35
295. – 20 c. on 50 c. red (No. 192) 50 50

1930. Surch. **Vale,** value and **1930.**
297. 22. 1 c. on 10 c. blue .. 12 12
298. 2 c. on 10 c. blue .. 15 12

1930. Nos. O 259/60 optd. **Habilitado para el servicio publi-co 1930.**
299. – 1 c. blue 15 15
300. O1. 2 c. red 45 45

1930. Air. Surch. **Servicio aereo Vale 5 centavos oro Mayo.**
301. 22. 5 c. on 20 c. brown .. 45 45

1930. Air. Nos. O 264/5 ptd. **HABILITADO Servicio Aereo MAYO, 1930.**
302. 20 c. blue 45 45
303. 50 c. green and yellow 60 60
304. 1 p. red 70 70

1930. Optd. **Habilitado julio—1930.**
305. 17. 1 c. brown 12 12
306. 20. 1 c. brown .. .. 1·60 1·60
309. 22. 1 c. olive 8 8
310. 2 c. red 10 10
307. 20. 20 c. brown .. .. 5·50 5·50
308. $0.50 on 2 c. red (No. 213) .. .. 50·00 50·00

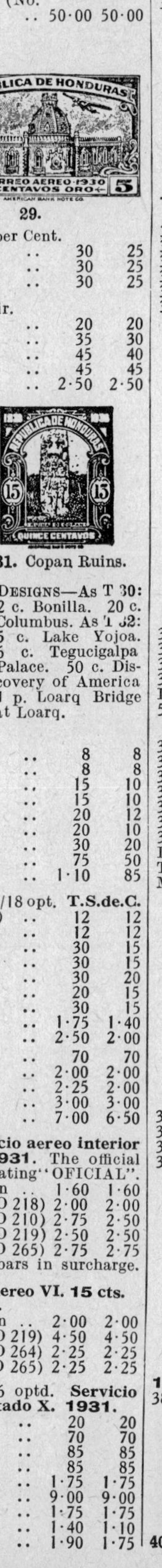

28. 29.

1930. Newspaper Cent.
311. 28. 2 c. blue 30 25
312. 2 c. orange 30 25
313. 2 c. red 30 25

1930. Air.
314. 29. 5 c. yellow 20 20
315. 10 c. red 35 30
316. 15 c. green 45 40
317. 20 c. violet 45 45
318. 1 p. brown .. .. 2·50 2·50

30. Baraona. 31. Copan Ruins.

32. Amapala.

DESIGNS—As T 30: 2 c. Bonilla. 20 c. Columbus. As T 32: 5 c. Lake Yojoa. 6 c. Tegucigalpa Palace. 50 c. Discovery of America 1 p. Loarq Bridge at Loarq.

1931.
319. 30. 1 c. sepia 8 8
320. – 2 c. red 8 8
321. – 5 c. violet 15 10
322. – 6 c. green 15 10
323. 32. 10 c. brown 20 12
324. 31. 15 c. blue 20 10
325. – 20 c. black 30 20
326. – 50 c. olive 75 50
327. – 1 p. slate .. .. 1·10 85

1931. Nos. 319/27 and 314/18 opt. **T.S.de.C.**
328. 30. 1 c. sepia (postage) .. 12 12
329. – 2 c. red 12 12
330. – 5 c. violet 30 15
331. – 6 c. green 30 15
332. 32. 10 c. brown 30 20
333. 31. 15 c. blue 20 15
334. – 20 c. black 30 15
335. – 50 c. olive .. .. 1·75 1·40
336. – 1 p. slate .. .. 2·50 2·00
337. 29. 5 c. yellow (air) .. 70 70
338. 10 c. red .. .. 2·00 2·00
339. 15 c. green .. .. 2·25 2·00
339a. 20 c. violet .. .. 3·00 3·00
339b. 1 p. brown .. .. 7·00 6·50

1931. Air. Surch. **Servicio aereo interior Vale 15 cts. Octubre 1931.** The official stamps with bars obliterating "OFICIAL".
340. 22. 15 c. on 20 c. brown .. 1·60 1·60
344. 20. 15 c. on 20 c. (No. O 218) 2·00 2·00
343. – 15 c. on 50 c. (No. O 210) 2·75 2·50
345. 20. 15 c. on 50 c. (No. O 219) 2·50 2·50
341. – 15 c. on 1 p. (No. O 265) 2·75 2·75
No. 345 exists without bars in surcharge.

1932. Air. Surch. **S.—Aereo VI. 15 cts. XI 1931.**
347. 22. 15 c. on 20 c. brown .. 2·00 2·00
348. 20. 15 c. on 50 c. (No. O 219) 4·50 4·50
349. – 15 c. on 50 c. (No. O 264) 2·25 2·25
350. – 15 c. on 1 p. (No. O 265) 2·25 2·25

1932. Air. Nos. O 328/36 optd. **Servicio Aereo Exterior. Habilitado X. 1931.**
350c. O 3. 1 c. blue 20 20
350d. 2 c. purple 70 70
350e. 5 c. olive 85 85
350f. 6 c. red 85 85
350g. 10 c. green .. .. 1·75 1·75
350h. 15 c. brown .. .. 9·00 9·00
350i. 20 c. brown .. .. 1·75 1·75
350j. 50 c. violet .. .. 1·40 1·10
350k. 1 p. orange .. .. 1·90 1·75

1932. Nos. O 223/25 surch. **Aereo interior VALE 15 Cts. 1932.**
351. 22. 15 c. on 2 c. red .. 30 30
352. 15 c. on 6 c. purple .. 25 25
353. 15 c. on 10 c. blue .. 30 25

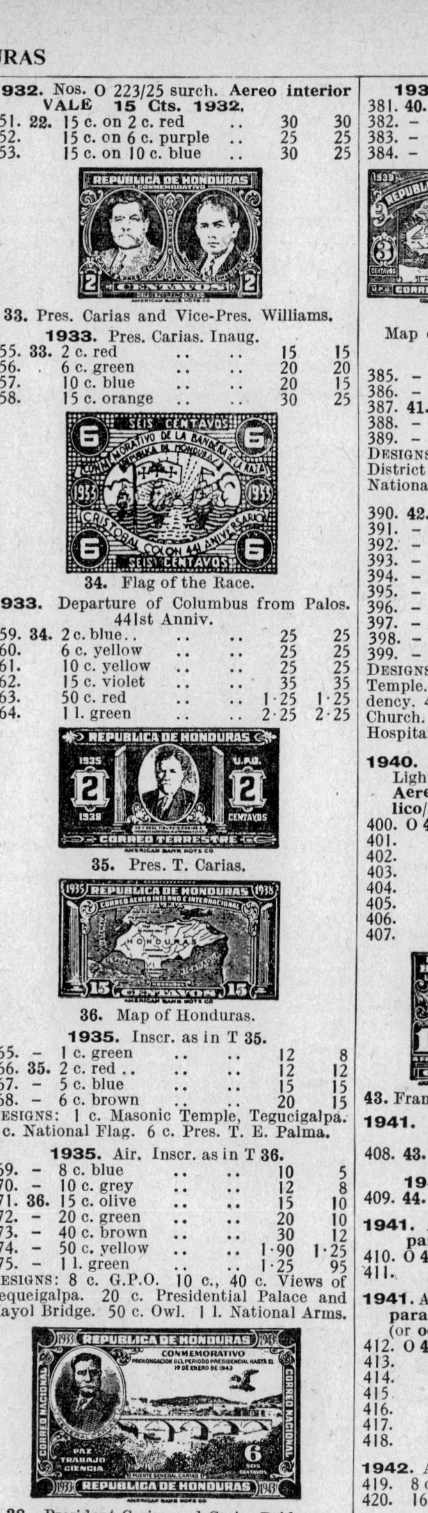

33. Pres. Carias and Vice-Pres. Williams.

1933. Pres. Carias. Inaug.
355. 33. 2 c. red 15 15
356. 6 c. green 20 20
357. 10 c. blue 20 15
358. 15 c. orange 30 25

34. Flag of the Race.

1933. Departure of Columbus from Palos. 441st Anniv.
359. 34. 2 c. blue 25 25
360. 6 c. yellow 25 25
361. 10 c. yellow 25 25
362. 15 c. violet 35 35
363. 50 c. red .. .. 1·25 1·25
364. 1 l. green .. .. 2·25 2·25

35. Pres. T. Carias.

36. Map of Honduras.

1935. Inscr. as in T 35.
365. – 1 c. green 12 8
366. 35. 2 c. red 12 12
367. – 5 c. blue 15 15
368. – 6 c. brown 20 15
DESIGNS: 1 c. Masonic Temple, Tegucigalpa. 5 c. National Flag. 6 c. Pres. T. E. Palma.

1935. Air. Inscr. as in T 36.
369. – 8 c. blue 10 5
370. – 10 c. grey 12 8
371. 36. 15 c. olive 15 10
372. – 20 c. green 20 10
373. – 40 c. brown 30 12
374. – 50 c. yellow .. .. 1·90 1·25
375. – 1 l. green .. .. 1·25 95
DESIGNS: 8 c. G.P.O. 10 c., 40 c. Views of Tequeigalpa. 20 c. Presidential Palace and Mayol Bridge. 50 c. Owl. 1 l. National Arms.

38. President Carias and Carias Bridge.

1937. Re-election of President Carias.
376. 38. 6 c. red and olive .. 25 20
377. 21 c. green and violet .. 30 25
378. 46 c. orange and brown 60 45
379. 55 c. blue and black .. 70 60

39. Book of the Constitution and Flags of U.S. and Honduras.

1937. Air. U.S. Constitution. 150th Anniv.
380. 39. 46 c. multicoloured .. 1·25 75

40. Comayagua Cathedral.

DESIGNS: 8 c. Founding of Comayagua City. 15 c. Miniature portraits of Caceres and Carias. 50 c. Inscribed lintel of Royal Palace.

1937. Air. Comayagua. 400th Anniv.
381. 40. 2 c. red 12 8
382. – 8 c. blue 15 5
383. – 15 c. black 30 25
384. – 50 c. brown 70 70

41. Map of Honduras. 42. Copan Ruins.

1939. Dated "1939 1942".
385. – 1 c. yellow (postage) .. 5 5
386. – 2 c. red 8 5
387. 41. 3 c. red 8 5
388. – 5 c. orange 12 5
389. – 8 c. blue 15 8
DESIGNS: 1 c. Arms of Honduras. 2 c. Central District Palace. 5 c. Choluteca Bridge. 8 c. National flag.

390. 42. 10 c. brown (air) .. 10 5
391. – 15 c. blue 12 5
392. – 21 c. slate 15 5
393. – 30 c. green 25 10
394. – 40 c. violet 35 12
395. – 46 c. brown 40 30
396. – 55 c. green 55 50
397. – 66 c. black 90 65
398. – 1 l. olive .. .. 1·25 60
399. – 2 l. red .. .. 2·40 1·75
DESIGNS: 15 c. Pres. Carias. 21 c. Mayan Temple. 30 c. J. C. del Valle. 40 c. The Presidency. 46 c. Statue of Lempira. 55 c. Suyapa Church. 66 c. J. T. Reyes. 1 l. Choluteca Hospital. 2 l. R. Rosa.

1940. Air. Dedication of Columbus Memorial Lighthouse. Type O 4 optd. **Correo Aereo/Habilitado para Servicio Publico/Pro-Faro Colon—1940.**
400. O 4. 2 c. blue and green .. 15 12
401. 5 c. blue and orange .. 10 15
402. 8 c. blue and brown .. 20 20
403. 15 c. blue and red .. 25 25
404. 46 c. blue and olive .. 60 60
405. 50 c. blue and violet .. 70 70
406. 1 l. blue and brown .. 2·00 2·00
407. 2 l. blue and red .. 4·50 4·50

43. Francisco Morazan. 44. Red Cross.

1941. Obligatory Tax. Gen. Morazan. Death Cent.
408. 43. 1 c. brown 8 5

1941. Obligatory Tax. Red Cross.
409. 44. 1 c. blue and red .. 8 5

1941. Air. Official stamps optd. **Habilitada para el Servicio Publico 1941.**
410. O 4. 5 c. blue and orange .. 1·75 15
411. 8 c. blue and brown .. 2·50 15

1941. Air. Official stamps surch. **Rehabilitada para/el Servicio Publico/1941/Vale tres (or ocho) cts.**
412. O 4. 3 c. on 2 c. blue & green 20 15
413. 8 c. on 2 c. blue & green 30 25
414. 8 c. on 15 c. blue & red 30 20
415. 8 c. on 46 c. blue & olive 40 30
416. 8 c. on 50 c. blue & violet 50 35
417. 8 c. on 1 l. blue & brown 70 45
418. 8 c. on 2 l. blue and red 85 60

1942. Air. Surch. **Correo Aereo** and value.
419. 8 c. on 15 c. blue (No. 391) 60 12
420. 16 c. on 46 c. brn. (No. 395) 60 20

45. Morazan's Birthplace. 46. Morazan.

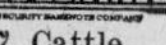

47. Cattle. 48. Banana Tree.

1942. Air. Gen. Morazan. Death Cent.
421. – 2 c. orange 8 5
422. – 5 c. blue 10 5

423. 45. 8 c. purple 12 5
424. – 14 c. black 25 20
425. – 16 c. olive 20 12
426. – 21 c. blue 65 50
427. – 1 l. blue.. .. .. 6·00 5·00
428. 46. 2 l. brown .. .. 8·50 7·00
DESIGNS—HORIZ. 2 c. Commemoration plate. 5 c. Battle of La Trinidad. 16 c. Morazan's monument (as in T 20). 21 c. Church where Morazan was baptised. 1 l. Arms of C. American Federation. VERT. 14 c. Morazan's tomb.

1943. Air.
429. – 1 c. green 50 5
430. – 2 c. blue 8 5
431. 47. 5 c. green 30 5
432. 48. 6 c. green 12 5
433. – 8 c. purple 15 5
434. – 10 c. brown 15 5
435. – 15 c. claret 25 8
436. – 16 c. red 30 10
437. – 21 c. blue 40 8
438. – 30 c. brown 40 8
439. – 40 c. red 40 8
440. – 55 c. black 70 35
441. – 1 l. green 90 75
442. – 2 l. lake.. .. .. 3·50 2·25
443. – 5 l. orange .. .. 9·00 7·50
DESIGNS—HORIZ. 1 c. Arms. 2 c. National flag. 8 c. Rosario. 15 c. Tobacco plant. 21 c. Orchid. 30 c. Oranges. 40 c. Wheat. 5 l. Map of Honduras. VERT. 10 c. Pine tree. 16 c. Sugar cane. 55 c. Coconut palms. 1 l. Maize. 2 l. Western hemisphere.

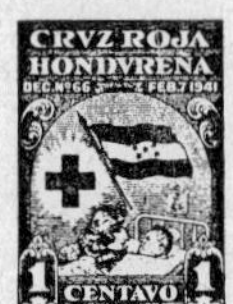

49. Agricultural College. 50. Red Cross, Flag, Mother and Child.

1944. Air. Pan-American Agricultural College. Inaug.
444. 49. 21 c. green 25 15

1944. Optd. **HABILITADO 1944-45.**
445. 41. 1 c. yellow 20 20
446. – 2 c. red (No. 386) .. 30 30

1945. Air. Surch. **Correo Aereo HABILITADO Acd. No. 798-1945** and value.
447. – 1 c on 50 c. (No. 384) 10 5
448. 40. 2 c. on 2 c. red 10 8
449. – 8 c. on 15 c. (No. 383) 15 12
450. 42. 10 c. on 10 c. brown .. 25 15
451. – 15 c. on 15 c. (No. 391) 20 15
452. – 30 c. on 21 c. (No. 392) 2·50 2·50
453. – 40 c. on 40 c. (No. 394) 1·25 95
454. – 1 l. on 46 c. (No. 395).. 1·10 1·00
455. – 2 l. on 66 c. (No. 397).. 2·40 2·40

1945. Obligatory Tax. Red Cross.
456. 50. 1 c. brown and red .. 8 5
456a.– 1 c. red and brown .. 8 5
DESIGN: No. 456a, Red Cross.

51. Arms of Honduras. 52. Franklin D. Roosevelt.

1946. Air. Coats of Arms.
457. 51. 1 c. red 5 5
458. – 2 c. orange 5 5
459. – 5 c. violet 10 5
461. – 15 c. purple 25 12
462. – 21 c. blue 20 12
463. – 1 l. green 90 60
464. – 2 l. grey .. .. 1·60 1·25
ARMS: 2 c. Von Gracias and Trujillo. 5 c. Comayagua and S. J. de Olancho. 15 c. Honduras Province and S. J. de Puerto Caballos. 21 c. Comayagua and Tencoa. 1 l. Jerez de la Frontera de Choluteca and San Pedro de Zula. 2 l. San Miguel de Heredia de Tegucigalpa.

1946. Air. Allied Victory over Japan and Death of Pres. Roosevelt.
(a) Inscribed "F.D.R."
460. 52. 8 c. brown 20 15
(b) "FRANKLIN D. ROOSEVELT".
465. 52. 8 c. brown 30 15

53. Honduras and Copan Antiquities.

1947. Air. 1st Int. Conference of Caribbean Archaeologists. Various frames.
466. 53. 16 c. green 20 12
467. 22 c. yellow 20 15
468. 40 c. orange 30 25
469. 1 l. blue.. .. .. 80 65
470. 2 l. mauve .. .. 2·40 2·10
471. 5 l. brown .. .. 5·50 5·00

54. Arms of Honduras. 55. Galvez, Carias and Lazano.

56. National Stadium. 57. President Galvez.

1949. Air. Inauguration of President Juan Manuel Galvez. Inscr. "CONMEMORATIVA DE LA SUCESION PRESIDENCIAL", etc.
472. 54. 1 c. blue 5 5
473. 57. 2 c. red 5 5
474. – 5 c. blue 5 5
475. – 9 c. brown 10 5
476. – 15 c. brown 12 8
477. 55. 21 c. black 15 10
478. 56. 30 c. olive .. .. 1·50 40
479. – 40 c. grey 45 15
480. – 1 l. brown 70 50
481. – 2 l. violet .. .. 1·75 1·25
482. 5 l. red .. .. .. 5·00 4·50
DESIGNS—HORIZ. 40 c. Toncontin Customs House. 5 l. Galvez and Lozano. VERT. 5 c., 15 c. Lazano (different frames). 9 c. Galvez. 1 l. Palace of Tegucigalpa. 2 l. Carias.

1951. Air. 75th Anniv. of U.P.U. Optd. **U.P.U. 75 Aniversario 1874-1949.**
483. 53. 16 c. green 40 40
484. – 22 c. yellow 40 40
485. – 40 c. orange 50 50
486. – 1 l. blue.. .. .. 1·40 1·40
487. – 2 l. mauve .. .. 2·25 2·25
488. – 5 l. brown .. .. 21·00 21·00

1951. Air. Founding of Central Bank. Nos. 472/81 optd. **Conmemorativa Fundacion Banco Central Administracion Galvez-Lozano Julio 1°. de 1950.**
489. 1 c. blue 5 5
490. 2 c. red 8 5
491. 5 c. blue 8 5
492. 9 c. brown 12 5
493. 15 c. brown 12 10
494. 21 c. black 20 15
495. 30 c. olive 35 25
496. 40 c. grey 65 50
497. 1 l. brown .. .. 1·25 1·00
498. 2 l. violet .. .. 3·50 3·25

58. Discovery of America. 59. Isabella the Catholic.

1952. Air. 500th Anniv. of Birth of Isabella the Catholic.
499. 58. 1 c. slate and orange .. 5 5
500. – 2 c. brown and blue .. 5 5
501. – 8 c. sepia and green .. 10 8
502. 59. 16 c. black and blue .. 15 12
503. – 30 c. green and violet.. 35 30
504. – 1 l. black and red .. 1·10 85
505. 58. 2 l. violet and brown .. 2·00 1·90
506. 59. 5 l. olive and purple .. 6·00 6·00
DESIGNS—HORIZ. 2 c. 1 l. King Ferdinand and Queen Isabella receive Columbus. 8 c. Surrender of Granada. 30 c. Queen Isabella pledging her jewels.

1953. Air. Surch. **HABILITADO 1953** and value.
507. 55. 5 c. on 21 c. black .. 8 5
508. 8 c. on 21 c. black .. 12 8
509. 16 c. on 21 c. black .. 15 8

1953. Air. Nos. O 507/509 and O 512/14 surch. **HABILITADO 1953** and value or optd. only.
510. 58. 10 c. on 1 c. olive & pur. 8 5
511. 12 c. on 1 c. olive & pur. 10 8
512. – 15 c. on 2 c. vio. & brn. 12 12
513. – 20 c. on 2 c. vio. & brn. 15 15
514. – 24 c. on 2 c. vio. & brn. 15 15
515. – 25 c. on 2 c. vio. & brn. 20 20
516. – 30 c. on 8 c. black & red 20 20
517. – 35 c. on 8 c. black & red 25 25

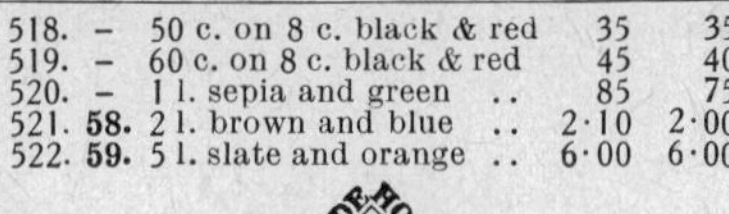
518. – 50 c. on 8 c. black & red 35 35
519. – 60 c. on 8 c. black & red 45 40
520. – 1 l. sepia and green .. 85 75
521. 58. 2 l. brown and blue .. 2·10 2·00
522. 59. 5 l. slate and orange .. 6·00 6·00

60. U.N. Emblem.

1953. Air. United Nations. Inscr. as in T 60.
523. – 1 c. blue and black .. 8 8
524. 60. 2 c. blue and black .. 15 10
525. – 3 c. violet and black .. 20 10
526. – 5 c. green and black .. 25 15
527. – 15 c. brown and black.. 40 30
528. – 30 c. brown and black.. 90 75
529. – 1 l. red and black .. 5·00 4·50
530. – 2 l. orange and black .. 6·00 5·00
531. – 5 l. green and black .. 16·00 15·00
DESIGNS: 1 c. U.N. and Honduras flags. 3 c. U.N. Building, New York. 5 c. Arms of U.S.A. 15 c. Pres. J. M. Galvez. 30 c. Indian girl (U.N.I.C.E.F.). 1 l. Refugee mother and child (U.N.R.R.A.). 2 l. Torch and open book (U.N.E.S.C.O.). 5 l. Cornucopia (F.A.O.).

1955. Air. Rotary International. 50th Anniv. Nos. O 532/38 optd. with rotary emblem, **1905 1955**, clasped hands and laurel sprigs or surch. also.
532. 1 c. blue and black .. 8 8
533. 2 c. green and black .. 8 8
534. 3 c. orange and black .. 10 10
535. 5 c. red and black .. 12 12
536. 8 c. on 1 c. blue and black 20 20
537. 10 c. on 2 c. green and black 25 25
538. 12 c. on 3 c. orange & black 30 30
539. 15 c. sepia and black .. 35 35
540. 30 c. purple and black .. 65 65
541. 1 l. olive and black .. 16·00 16·00

1956. Air. 10th Anniv. of U.N.O. Nos. O 523/5 and 527/31 optd. **O N U X ANIVERSARIO 1945-1955.**
542. 1 c. blue and black .. 12 12
543. 2 c. green and black .. 12 12
544. 3 c. orange and black .. 20 20
545. 5 c. red and black .. 20 20
546. 15 c. brown and black .. 30 30
547. 30 c. brown and black .. 60 60
548. 1 l. red and black .. 3·00 3·00
549. 2 l. orange and black .. 4·50 4·50
550. 5 l. green and black .. 11·00 11·00

61. J. L. Diaz. 62. Southern Highway.

1956. Air.
551. – 1 c. blue and black .. 5 5
552. 61. 2 c. indigo and black .. 8 5
553. 62. 3 c. sepia and black .. 5 5
554. – 4 c. purple and black 5 5
555. – 5 c. red and black 5 5
556. – 8 c. red, green, blue, yellow and brown .. 5 5
557. – 10 c. green and black .. 35 8
558. – 12 c. green and black .. 10 8
559. – 15 c. black and red 10 8
560. – 20 c. blue and black 15 12
561. 61. 24 c. purple and black.. 15 15
562. – 25 c. green and black .. 20 15
563. – 30 c. red and black .. 25 20
564. – 40 c. brown and black 30 20
565. – 50 c. turquoise & black 35 30
566. – 60 c. orange and black.. 45 35
567. – 1 l. purple and black 90 60
568. – 2 l. crimson and black.. 1·75 1·10
569. – 5 l. lake and black .. 4·25 3·00
DESIGNS—HORIZ. 1 c. Suyapa Basilica. 8 c. Landscape and cornucopia. 10 c. National Stadium. 12 c. United States School. 15 c. Projected Central Bank of Honduras. 20 c. Legislative Building. 25 c. Projected Development Bank 30 c. Toncontin Airport. 40 c. J. R. Molina Bridge. 60 c. Treasury Building. 1 l. Blood Bank. VERT. 4 c. Dona de Estrada Palma. 5 c. Dona de Morazan. 50 c. Peace Memori l. 2 l. Electrical Communications Building 5 l. Presidential Palace.

63. Revolutionary Flag. 64. Flags of Honduras and the U.S.A. and Book.

65. Abraham Lincoln. 66. Henri Dunant.

1957. Air. Revolution of October 21, 1956. Frames in black.
570. 63. 1 c. blue and yellow .. 5 5
571. – 2 c. purple green & orge. 8 5
572. 63. 5 c. blue and pink .. 10 5
573. – 8 c. violet, olive & orge. 12 8
574. – 10 c. brown and violet 12 10
575. 63. 12 c. blue and turquoise 20 12
576. – 15 c. brown and emerald 25 15
577. – 30 c. grey and pink .. 35 25
578. – 1 l. brown and blue .. 1·00 1·00
579. – 2 l. grey and green .. 1·90 1·90
DESIGNS: 2 c., 8 c. Obelisk and mountains. 10 c., 15 c., 1 l. Indian with bow and arrow. 30 c., 2 l. Arms of 1821.

NOTE. In July 1958 after stocks of current issues had been looted, eighteen different facsimile signatures validated the remaining stamps for use.

1958. Air. Bi-national Centre Commem (Institute of American Culture). Flags in national colours.
580. 64. 1 c. blue 5 5
581. 2 c. red 5 5
582. 5 c. green 8 8
583. 10 c. brown 10 8
584. 20 c. orange 20 15
585. 30 c. red 25 20
586. 50 c. grey 30 25
587. 1 l. yellow 70 70
588. 2 l. olive .. .. 1·75 1·25
589. 5 l. blue .. .. 4·25 4·25

1959. Air. Abraham Lincoln. 150th Birth Anniv. Inscr. "1809 1959". Flags in blue and red.
590. 65. 1 c. green 8 8
591. – 2 c. blue 8 8
592. – 3 c. violet 8 8
593. – 5 c. red 8 8
594. – 10 c. slate 10 8
595. – 12 c. sepia 12 10
596. 68. 15 c. orange 20 10
597. – 25 c. purple 25 20
598. – 50 c. blue 35 25
599. – 1 l. brown 70 60
600. – 2 l. olive .. .. 1·50 1·10
601. – 5 l. yellow .. .. 4·00 3·25
DESIGNS—HORIZ. 2 c., 25 c. Lincoln's birthplace. 3 c., 50 c. Gettysburg Address. 5 c., 1 l. Lincoln at conference to free slaves. 10 c., 2 l. Assassination of Lincoln. 12 c., 5 l. Lincoln Memorial, Washington.

1959. Obligatory Tax. Red Cross.
602. 66. 1 c. red and blue .. 5 5
647. 1 c. red and green .. 5 5
648. 1 c. red and brown .. 5 5
Nos. 647/8 have no frame around portrait and values are at left.

67. Constitution of December 21st, 1957. 68. King Alfonso XIII of Spain and Map.

1959. Air. 2nd Anniv. of New Constitution. Inscr. "21 DE DICIEMBRE DE 1857".
603. 67. 1 c. red, blue and brown 5 5
604. – 2 c. brown 5 5
605. – 3 c. blue 5 5
606. – 5 c. orange 8 8
607. 67. 10 c. red, blue and green 10 8
608. – 12 c. red 10 10
609. – 25 c. violet 25 20
610. – 50 c. grey blue.. .. 60 30
DESIGNS—HORIZ. 2 c., 12 c. Inaug. of Pres. R. V. Morales. VERT. 3 c., 25 c. Pres. R. V. Morales. 5 c., 50 c. Flaming torch.

1961. Air. Settlement of Boundary Dispute with Nicaragua.
611. 68. 1 c. blue 5 5
612. – 2 c. pink 5 5
613. – 5 c. green 5 5
614. – 10 c. orange-brown .. 10 8
615. – 20 c. red 20 12
616. – 50 c. brown 40 30
617. – 1 l. slate 75 60
DESIGNS: 2 c. 1906 award (document). 5 c. Arbitration commission, 1907. 10 c. International Court of Justice, The Hague. 20 c. 1960 award (document). 50 c Pres. Morales Foreign Minister Puerto and map. 1 l. Presidents Davila and Morales.

1964. Air. Freedom from Hunger. Flags in National colours. Optd. **F A O Luncha Contra el Hambre.**
621. **64.** 1 c. blue 12 12
622. 2 c. red 15 15
623. 5 c. green 20 20
624. 30 c. red 60 50
625. 2 l. olive .. .. 4·25 4·00

1964. Air. Olympic Games, Tokyo. Optd. with Olympic Rings and **1964.**
626. – 1 c. blue & black (No. 523) 8 8
627. **60.** 2 c. blue and black .. 10 10
628. – 3 c. violet & blk. (No. 525) 20 20
629. – 15 c. brn. & blk. (No. 527) 30 30
See also No. O 646.

69. Ancient Stadium.

1964. Air. "Homage to Sport" and Olympic Games, Tokyo.
630. **69.** 1 c. black and green .. 5 5
631. – 2 c. black and mauve .. 5 5
632. – 5 c. black and blue .. 8 8
633. – 8 c. black & grey green 15 15
634. **69.** 10 c. black & bistre .. 20 15
635. – 12 c. black and yellow 25 20
636. – 1 l. black and buff .. 70 70
637. – 2 l. black and olive .. 2·00 1·90
638. **69.** 3 l. black and red .. 2·50 2·50
DESIGNS: 2 c., 12 c. Boundary stones. 5 c., 1 l. Mayan ball player. 8 c., 2 l. Olympic Stadium, Tokyo.

1964. Air. Surch.
639. – 4 c. on 5 c. (No. 593) .. 5 5
618. **65.** 6 c. on 15 c. 8 8
619. – 8 c. on 25 c. (No. 597) 8 8
640. 10 c. on 15 c. (No. 476) 5 5
620. – 10 c. on 50 c. (No. 598) 12 12
641. – 12 c. on 16 c. (No. 425) 8 5
642. – 12 c. on 21 c. (No. 426) 8 5
643. **53.** 12 c. on 22 c. 8 5
644. 30 c. on 1 l. 20 12
645. – 40 c. on 1 l. (No. 480) .. 30 15
646. **53.** 40 c. on 2 l. 30 20
See also Nos. 716/8 and O 647/9.

1965. Air. Presidential Investiture of General Lopez. Optd. **Toma de Posesion General Oswaldo Lopez A. Junio 6, 1965.** Flags in blue and red.
649. **65.** 1 c. green 5 5
550. – 2 c. green 5 5
651. – 3 c. violet (No. 592) .. 8 8
652. – 5 c. red (No. 593) .. 8 8
653. **65.** 15 c. orange 12 10
654. 25 c. purple (No. 597) .. 20 15
655. – 50 c. red 40 30
656. – 2 l. olive (No. 600) .. 1·75 1·10
657. 5 l. yellow (No. 601) .. 4·50 3·50

70. Ambulance and Clinic.

1965. Air. Order of Malta Campaign Against Leprosy.
658. **70.** 1 c. blue 8 8
659. – 5 c. green 15 15
660. 12 c. black 20 15
661. 1 l. brown 90 80
DESIGNS: 5 c. Hospital. 12 c. Patients receiving treatment. 1 l. Map of Honduras.

71. Father Subirana.

72. Honduras 2 r. Stamp of 1866.

1965. Air. Father Manuel de Jesus Subirana. Death Cent. Centres in black and gold; inscr. in black.
662. 1 c. violet 5 5
663. 2 c. flesh 5 5
664. **71.** 8 c. pink 8 8
665. 10 c. purple 10 10
666. 12 c. brown 12 12
667. 20 c. green 20 20
668. 1 l. sage 70 55
669. – 2 l. blue .. .. 1·90 1·90
DESIGNS: 1 c. Abraham, Jicaque Indian. 2 c. Allegory of Catechism. 10 c. Msgr. Juan de Jesus Zepeda. 12 c. Pope Pius IX. 20 c. Subirana's Tomb, Yoro. 1 l. Hermitage. 2 l. Jicque Indian woman and child.

1965. Air. Churchill Commem. Nos. 499/500 and 470 optd. **IN MEMORIAM Sir Winston Churchill 1874-1965.**
671. **58.** 1 c. black and orange .. 30 30
672. – 2 c. brown and blue .. 60 60
673. – 2 l. mauve .. .. 4·25 4·25
See also No. O 674.

1966. Air. Pope Paul's Visit to U.N. Organisation. Nos. 662/68 optd. **CONMEMORATIVA Visita S. S. Pablo VI a la ONU. 4-X-1965.**
675. – 1 c. violet 5 5
676. – 2 c. flesh 5 5
677. **71.** 8 c. pink 10 8
678. – 10 c. purple 15 10
679. 12 c. brown 15 10
680. – 20 c. green 30 12
681. 1 l. sage .. .. .. 1·00 70

1966. Air. Stamp Cent. Inscriptions in black (1 c., 2 c.) or in gold (others).
682. **72.** 1 c. black, green & gold 5 5
683. – 2 c. blue, black & orge. 8 8
684. – 3 c. maroon and cerise 10 10
685. – 4 c. indigo and blue .. 10 10
686. – 5 c. purple and mauve 10 10
687. – 6 c. violet and lilac .. 10 10
688. 7 c. slate & turquoise .. 10 10
689. 8 c. indigo and blue .. 10 10
690. – 9 c. blue and cobalt .. 10 10
691. – 10 c. black and olive .. 12 12
692. – 12 c. yellow, blk. & grn. 12 12
693. – 15 c. purple and mauve 15 15
694. 20 c. black and orange 20 20
695. – 30 c. blue and yellow .. 25 25
696. – 40 c. multicoloured .. 30 30
697. – 1 l. green and emerald 70 60
698. – 2 l. black and grey .. 1·50 1·25
DESIGNS—VERT. 2 c. Honduras 5 c. air stamp, of 1925. 3 c. T. E. Palma, 1st Director of Posts. 8 c. Sir Rowland Hill. 10 c. Pres. Arellano. 12 c. Postal emblem. 15 c. H. von Stephan. 30 c. Honduras flag. 40 c. Honduras arms. 1 l. U.P.U. Monument, Berne. 2 l. J. M. Medina (statesman). HORIZ. 4 c. Post Office, Tegucigalpa. 5 c. Steam locomotive. 6 c. 19th-cent. mule transport. 7 c. 19th-cent. sorting office. 9 c. Mail-van. 20 c. Mail-plane.
See also No. E 700.

1966. Air. World Cup Football Championships, Final Match between England and Germany. Optd. **CAMPEONATO DE FOOTBALL Copa Mundial 1966 Inglaterra-Alemania Wembley, Julio 30.**
701. **58.** 2 c. violet and brown .. 15 15
702. **59.** 16 c. black and blue .. 30 30
703. **58.** 2 l. violet and brown .. 5·50 5·50

1967. Air. U.N.O. 20th Anniv. Nos. 662/4 and 666/9 optd. **CONMEMORATIVA del XX Aniversario ONU 1966.**
704. – 1 c. violet 12 12
705. – 2 c. flesh 15 15
706. **71.** 8 c. pink 30 30
707. – 12 c. brown 35 35
708. – 20 c. green 50 50
709. – 1 l. sage .. .. 1·25 1·25
710. – 2 l. blue .. .. 2·50 2·50

1967. Simeon Canas y Villacorta (slave liberator). Birth Bicent. Nos. 551, 553, 559, 552 and 568. Optd. **Simeon Canas y Villacorta Libertador de los esclavos en Centro America 1767-1967.**
711. 1 c. blue and black .. 12 12
712. 3 c. sepia and black .. 15 15
713. 15 c. black and red .. 30 30
714. 25 c. green and black .. 40 40
715. 2 l. crimson and black .. 1·75 1·75

1967. Air. Nos. E 570 and 480/1 surch.
716. E **1.** 10 c. on 20 c. grey, black and red 10 8
717. – 10 c. on 1 l. brown .. 10 8
718. – 10 c. on 2 l. violet .. 10 8

73. J. C. del Valle (Honduras).

1967. Air. Founding of Central-American Journalists' Federation.
719. **73.** 11 c. black, blue & gold 8 5
720. – 12 c. black, yellow & blue 8 5
721. 14 c. black, grn. & silver 10 8
722. – 20 c. black, grn. & mag. 15 10
723. 30 c. black, yell. & lilac 20 15
724. 40 c. gold, blue & violet 45 40
725. – 50 c. green, red & olive 60 60
DESIGNS: 12 c. Ruben Dario (Nicaragua). 14 c. J. B. Montufar (Guatemala). 20 c. F. Gavidia (El Salvador). 30 c. J. M. Fernandez (Costa Rica). 40 c. Federation emblem. 50 c. Central American map.

74. Olympic Rings and Flags of Mexico and Honduras.

1968. Air. Olympic Games, Mexico. Mult.
726. 1 c. Type **74** 5 5
727. 2 c. Type **74** 8 8
728. 5 c. Italian flag and boxing 10 10
729. 10 c. French flag and skiing 12 12
730. 12 c. West German flag and show-jumping 15 15
731. 50 c. British flag and athletics .. .. .. 1·75 1·75
732. 1 l. U.S. flag and running .. 3·50 3·50

75. Patient and Nurse.

1968. Obligatory Tax. Red Cross.
734. **75.** 1 c. red and blue .. 5 5

1970. No. E 700 optd. with **HABILITADO** for use as ordinary postage stamp.
735. 20 c. brn., orge.-brn. & gold 15 15

1970. Air. Various stamps surch. in figures.
736. **72.** 4 c. + 1 c. 5 5
737. 4 c. + 3 c. (No. 525) .. 5 5
738. 5 c. + 1 c. (No. 662) .. 5 5
739. 5 c. + 7 c. (No. 688) .. 8 8
740. 8 c. + 2 c. (No. 663) .. 8 8
741. 10 c. + 2 c. (No. 500) .. 8 8
742. 10 c. + 2 c. (No. 552) .. 8 8
743. 10 c. + 3 c. (No. 525) .. 8 8
744. 10 c. + 3 c. (No. 553) .. 8 8
745. **62.** 10 c. + 3 c. (No. 684) .. 8 8
746. 10 c. + 9 c. (No. 698) .. 8 8
747. 10 c. + 11 c. (No. 719) .. 8 8
748. 12 c. + 14 c. (No. 721) .. 12 12
749. 12 c. + 20 c. (No. E 570) 12 12
750. 12 c. + 1 l. (No. 480) .. 12 12
751. 15 c. + 12 c. (No. 757) .. 15 15
752. 30 c. + 12 c. (No. 757) .. 25 25
753. 40 c. + 24 c. (1969 Moon landing issue, see Appendix) 35 35
754. 40 c. + 50 c. (No. 731) .. 35 35

75. J. A. Sanhueza (Firefighter).

77. Hotel Honduras Maya.

1970. Air. Campaign Against Forest Fires. Multicoloured.
755. 5 c. Type **75** 5 5
756. 8 c. R. Ordonez Rodriguez (firefighter) 8 8
757. 12 c. Fire Brigade emblems (horiz.) 12 10
758. 20 c. Flag, map and emblems 20 15
759. 1 l. Emblems, and flags of Honduras, U N. and U.S.A. 65 60

1970. Air. Opening of Hotel Honduras Maya, Tegucigalpa.
761. **77.** 12 c. black and blue .. 15 12

Aniversario Gran Logia de Honduras 1922-1972
(78.)

1972. Air. Honduras Masonic Grand Lodge 50th Anniv. Various "Moon Landing" stamps (1969, Appendix) optd., or surch., also as T 78.
765. 5 c. multicoloured 20 20
766. 12 c. multicoloured .. 30 30
767. 1 l. on 20 c. multicoloured 70 60
768. 2 l. on 24 c. multicoloured 1·50 1·10

79. Soldiers' Bay, Guanaja.

1972. Air. Independence (1970). 150th Anniv. Multicoloured.
769. 4 c. Type **79** 5 5
770. 5 c. Bugler sounding "Last Post" (vert.) 5 5
771. 6 c. Lake Yojoa 5 5
772. 7 c. "The Banana Carrier" (R. Aguilar) (vert.) .. 5 5
773. 8 c. Soldiers marching and fly-past 5 5
774. 9 c. "Brassavola digbyana" (national flower) (vert.) .. 5 5
775. 10 c. As 9 c. 5 5
776. 12 c. Machine-gunner .. 5 5
777. 15 c. Tela beach at sunset 8 5
778. 20 c. Stretcher-bearers .. 10 8
779. 30 c. "San Antonio de Oriente" (A. Velasquez) 15 12
780. 40 c. Ruins of Copan .. 20 15
781. 50 c. "Woman from Hancal" (P. Zelaya Sierra) .. 25 20
782. 1 l. Trujilo Bay 55 45
783. 2 l. As 9 c. .. .. .. 1·10 90

80. Sister Maria Rosa and Child.

81. Map of Honduras.

1972. Air. "S.O.S." Children's Villages in Honduras, each brown, green and gold.
786. 10 c. Type **80** 5 5
787. 15 c. "S.O.S. Villages" emblem (horiz.) 5 5
788. 30 c. Father J. T. Reyes (educationalist) 15 12
789. 40 c. First Central American "S.O.S." village (horiz.) 20 15
790. 1 l. "Future Citizen" (boy) 50 40

1973. Air. Nat. Cartographic Service (10 c.) and Joint Cartographic Work (12 c.). 25th Annivs.
791. **81.** 10 c. multicoloured .. 10 8
792. – 12 c. multicoloured .. 15 12
DESIGN: 12 c. Similar to T **81**, but with two badges and inscr. "25 Anos de Labor Cartografica Conjunta".

82. U.N.E.S.C.O. Emblem.

1973. Air. U.N.E.S.C.O. 25th Anniv. and Juan Ramon Molina (poet). Commem. Multicoloured.
793. 8 c. Illustration from "Habitante de la Osa" .. 5 5
794. 20 c. Juan Ramon Molina 15 10
795. 1 l. Illustration from "Tierras Mares y Cielos" 60 40
796. 2 l. Type **82** .. .. 1·25 75

1973. Air. Census and World Population Year. Various stamps optd. **Censos de Poblacion y Vivienda, marzo 1974 1974 Ano Mundial de Poblacion.**
798. **80.** 10 c. brn., grn. & gold 5 5
802. **81.** 10 c. multicoloured .. 5 5
803. – 12 c. mult. (No. 792) .. 5 5
799. – 15 c. brn., grn. & gold (No. 787) 8 5
800. – 30 c. brn., grn. & gold (No. 788) 20 12
801. – 40 c. brn., grn. & gold (No. 789) 25 15

1974. Air. Various stamps surch.
804. – 2 c. on 1 c. bl. and blk. (No. 551) 5 5
805. **65.** 2 c. on 1 c. green .. 5 5
806. – 3 c. on 1 c. bl. & blk. (No. 551) 5 5
807. **65.** 3 c. on 1 c. green .. 5 5
808. **53.** 1 l. on 2 l. mauve .. 60 40
809. – 1 l. on 2 l. violet (No. 481) 60 40
810. – 1 l. on 50 c. blue .. 60 40

1974. Air. Honduras' Children's Villages. 25th Anniv. Nos. 786/9 optd. **1949-1974 SOS Kinderdorfer Internacional Honduras-Austria.**
813. **80.** 10 c. multicoloured .. 5 5
814. – 15 c. multicoloured .. 8 5
815. – 30 c. multicoloured .. 20 12
816. – 40 c. multicoloured .. 25 15

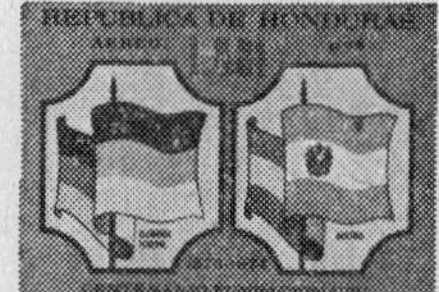

83. Flags of Germany and Austria.

1975. Air. Universal Postal Union. Cent. (1974). Multicoloured.
817. 1 c. Type **83** 5 5
818. 2 c. Belgium and Denmark 5 5
819. 3 c. Spain and France .. 5 5
820. 4 c. Hungary and Russia .. 5 5

821. 5 c. Great Britain and Italy 5 5
822. 10 c. Norway and Sweden 5 5
823. 12 c. Honduras 8 5
824. 15 c. United States and Switzerland 10 8
825. 20 c. Greece and Portugal 12 10
826. 30 c. Rumania and Yugoslavia 20 12
827. 1 l. Egypt and the Netherlands 60 35
828. 2 l. Luxembourg and Turkey .. .. .. 1·25 70

1975. Air. Various stamps surch.

830. – 2 c. on 1 c. bl. & blk.(551) 5 5
831. – 16 c. on 1 c. bl. & blk.(551) 10 8
832. 63. 16 c. on 1 c. bl., yell. & blk. 10 8
833. 65. 16 c. on 1 c. green 10 8
834. 66. 16 c. on 1 c. yellow .. 10 8
835. – 16 c. on 1 c. violet (662) 10 8
836. 81. 18 c. on 10 c. mult. .. 12 10
837. – 18 c. on 12 c. mult. (792) 12 10
838. – 18 c. on 8 c. mult. (793) 12 10
839. 80. 18 c. on 10 c. mult. .. 12 10
840. – 50 c. on 30 c. mult. (788) 30 20
841. – 1 l. on 30 c. mult. (788) 60 40

84. Humuya Youth Centre.

1976. Air. Int. Women's Year (1975). Multicoloured.

843. 8 c. Type **84** 5 5
844. 16 c. Jalteva Youth Centre 10 8
845. 18 c. Sra Arellano and I.W.Y. emblem .. 10 8
846. 30 c. El Carmen Youth Centre, San Pedro Sula 15 10
847. 55 c. Flag of National Social Welfare Organization .. 30 25
848. 1 l. Sports and recreation grounds, La Isla .. 55 50
849. 2 l. Women's Social Centre 1·10 90

85. " CARE " Package.

1976. Air. " CARE " (Co-operative for American Relief Everywhere). 20th Anniv. in Honduras.

850. **85.** 1 c. blue and black .. 5 5
851. – 5 c. mauve and black .. 5 5
852. **85.** 16 c. red and black .. 10 8
853. – 18 c. green and black .. 10 8
854. **85.** 30 c. blue and black .. 15 10
855. – 50 c. green and black .. 30 20
856. **85.** 55 c. brown and black .. 30 25
857. – 70 c. purple and black 45 35
858. **85.** 1 l. blue and black .. 55 50
859. – 2 l. orange and black .. 1·10 90

DESIGN—HORIZ. 5 c., 18 c., 50 c., 70 c., 2 l., " CARE " on globe.

Each of the above stamps has a different inscription detailing " CARE's " various field's of activities in Honduras.

86. Fawn in Burnt Forest.

1976. Air. Forest Protection. Multicoloured.

860. 10 c. Type **86** 5 8
861. 16 c. COHDEFOR emblem 10 8
862. 18 c. Forest stream (horiz.) 10 8
863. 30 c. Live and burning trees 15 10
864. 50 c. Type **86** 30 20
865. 60 c. Deer in forest .. 40 35
866. 70 c. Protection emblem .. 45 35
867. 1 l. Forest of young trees (horiz.) 55 50
868. 2 l. As 30 c. .. .. 1·10 90

COHDEFOR = Corporation Hondurena de Desarollo Forestal.

EXPRESS LETTER STAMPS

1953. No. O 507 surch. **ENTREGA INMEDIATA 1953 L O.20.**

E 1. **58.** 20 c. on 1 c. olive & pur. 25 20

E 1.

1956. Air. Optd. **ENTREGA INMEDIATA** as in Type E 1.

E 570. **E 1.** 20 c. grey and black 20 20

1966. Stamp Cent. Design similar to T **69.**

E 700. 20 c. brown, gold & chest. 20 20

DESIGN—HORIZ. 20 c. motor cyclist.

1972. As T **79**, but inscr. "ENTREGA INMEDIATA". Multicoloured.

E 785. 20 c. "Corsair" fighter aircraft 10 8

1975. No. E 785 surch.

E 842. 60 c. on 20 c. mult. .. 35 25

OFFICIAL STAMPS

Various stamps overprinted **OFICIAL.**

1890. Stamps of 1890.

O 56. **3.** 1 c. yellow 8
O 57. 2 c. yellow 8
O 58. 5 c. yellow 8
O 59. 10 c. yellow 8
O 60. 20 c. yellow 8
O 61. 25 c. yellow 8
O 62. 30 c. yellow 8
O 63. 40 c. yellow 8
O 64. 50 c. yellow 8
O 65. 75 c. yellow 8
O 66. 1 p. yellow 8

1891. Stamps of 1891.

O 70. **4.** 1 c. yellow 8
O 71. 2 c. yellow 8
O 72. 5 c. yellow 8
O 73. 10 c. yellow 8
O 74. 20 c. yellow 8
O 75. 25 c. yellow 8
O 76. 30 c. yellow 8
O 77. 40 c. yellow 8
O 78. 50 c. yellow 8
O 79. 75 c. yellow 8
O 80. 1 p. yellow 8

1898. Stamps of 1898.

O 116. **10.** 5 c. blue 10
O 117. 10 c. blue 10
O 118. 20 c. bistre 10
O 119. 50 c. orange 15
O 120. 1 p. green 30

1911. Stamps of 1911.

O 148. **13.** 1 c. violet 10 10
O 149. 2 c. green 15 15
O 150. 5 c. red 25 25
O 151. 6 c. blue .. .. 1·10 85
O 152. 10 c. blue 50 30
O 153. 20 c. yellow .. .. 1·25 1·25
O 154. 50 c. brown .. .. 2·75 2·75
O 155. 1 p. olive .. .. 6·00 4·25

1914. Nos. O 150 and O 148 surch.

O 186. **13.** 1 c. on 5 c. red .. 45 45
O 187. 2 c. on 5 c. red .. 45 45
O 188. 10 c. on 1 c. violet .. 60 55
O 190. 20 c. on 1 c. violet .. 70 60

1914. No. O 189 and O 150 surch. **OFICIAL —10 cts.**

O 191. **13.** 10 c. on 20 c. on 1 c. vio. 1·50 1·50
O 192. 10 c. on 5 c. red 5·50 5·50
O 193. 20 c. on 50 c. brown.. 1·75 1·75

1915. Stamps of 1913.

O 194. **15.** 1 c. brown 15 15
O 195. 2 c. red 15 15
O 197. **16.** 5 c. blue 20 20
O 198. 6 c. violet 50 50
O 199. **15.** 10 c. brown 45 45
O 200. 20 c. brown 90 90
O 202. **16.** 50 c. red .. .. 2·40 2·40

1915. No. 168 surch. **OFICIAL $001.**

O 203. **15.** 1 c. on 2 c. red .. 75 75

1915. Stamps of 1915.

O 204. **17.** 1 c. brown 5 5
O 205. 2 c. red 5 5
O 206. – 5 c. blue 5 5
O 207. – 6 c. violet 15 12
O 208. **17.** 10 c. blue 15 15
O 209. 20 c. brown 30 30
O 210. 50 c. red 70 70
O 211. – 1 p. green .. .. 1·10 1·10

1921. Stamps of 1919.

O 212. **20.** 1 c. brown 15 15
O 213. 2 c. red 15 15
O 214. 5 c. red 15 15
O 215. 6 c. mauve 20 20
O 216. 10 c. blue 30 30
O 217. 15 c. blue 30 30
O 218. 20 c. brown 50 50
O 219. 50 c. brown 65 65
O 220. 1 p. green .. .. 1·25 1·25

1925. Stamps of 1923.

O 222. **22.** 1 c. olive 5 5
O 223. 2 c. red 5 5
O 224. 6 c. purple 10 10
O 225. 10 c. blue 12 12
O 226. 20 c. brown 20 20
O 227. 50 c. red 40 50
O 228. 1 p. green .. .. 90 1·00

O 1. J. R. Molina.

DESIGNS: 1 c. J. C. de Valle. 5 c. Coffee Tree. 10 c. J. T. Reyes. 20 c. Tegucigalpa Cathedral 50 c. Lake Yojoa. 1 p. Wireless Station.

1929.

O 259. 1 c. blue 10 10
O 260. **O 1.** 2 c. red 15 15
O 261. – 5 c. violet 20 12
O 262. – 10 c. green 12 12
O 263. 20 c. blue 25 25
O 264. – 50 c. green & yellow 50 50
O 265. – 1 p. brown 75 75

1930. Air. Nos. O 224/8 surch. **Servicio aereo Vale 5 centavos VI—1930** or optd. **Servicio aereo Habilitado VI—1930.**

O 319. **22.** 5 c. on 6 c. purple .. 80 80
O 320. 6 c. purple .. 9·00 9·00
O 321. 10 c. blue 85 85
O 322. 20 c. brown 85 85
O 323. 50 c. red 85 85
O 324. 1 p. green 85 85

O 3. Tegucigalpa. O 4. Coat of Arms and National Flag.

1931.

O 328. **O 3.** 1 c. blue 12 12
O 329. 2 c. purple 12 12
O 330. 5 c. olive 15 15
O 331. 6 c. red 20 20
O 332. 10 c. green 25 25
O 333. 15 c. brown 25 25
O 334. 20 c. brown 30 30
O 335. 50 c. violet 45 45
O 336. 1 p. orange 75 35

1935. Stamps of 1931 optd. **HABILITADO 1935-1938.** between thick lines.

O 390. **O 3.** 1 c. blue 12 12
O 391. 2 c. purple 12 12
O 392. 5 c. olive 12 12
O 393. 6 c. red 20 20
O 394. 10 c. green 25 25
O 395. 15 c. brown 30 30
O 396. 20 c. brown 35 35
O 397. 50 c. violet 45 45

1939. Air.

O 400. **O 4.** 2 c. blue and green 8 8
O 401. 5 c. blue and orange 8 8
O 402. 8 c. blue and brown 12 12
O 403. 15 c. blue and red .. 30 25
O 404. 46 c. blue and olive 40 35
O 405. 50 c. blue and violet 50 45
O 406. 1 l. blue and brown 1·75 1·75
O 407. 2 l. blue and red .. 3·25 3·25

1952. Air. Isabella the Catholic. 500th Birth Anniv. As Nos. 499/506 but colours changed, optd. **OFICIAL.**

O 507. **58.** 1 c. olive and purple 5 5
O 508. – 2 c. violet and brown 8 8
O 509. – 8 c. black and red .. 12 12
O 510. **59.** 16 c. green and violet 20 20
O 511. – 30 c. black and blue 25 25
O 512. – 1 l. sepia and green.. 70 70
O 513. **58.** 2 l. brown and blue.. 1·60 1·60
O 514. **59.** 5 l. slate and orange 3·75 3·75

1953. Air. United Nations. As Nos. 523/31 but colours changed (except 1 c.), optd. **OFICIAL.**

O 532. – 1 c. blue and black .. 5 5
O 533. **60.** 2 c. green and black.. 10 10
O 534. – 3 c. orange and black 15 15
O 535. – 5 c. red and black .. 20 20
O 536. – 15 c. sepia and black 30 30
O 537. – 30 c. purple and black 60 45
O 538. – 1 l. olive and black .. 4·00 2·50
O 539. – 2 l. purple and black 5·00 3·50
O 540. – 5 l. blue and black .. 12·00 10·00

1956. Air. As Nos. 551/69 but colours changed. optd. **OFICIAL.**

O 570. 1 c. lake and black .. 5 5
O 571. 2 c. crimson and black 5 5
O 572. 3 c. purple and black .. 5 5
O 573. 4 c. orange and black .. 5 5
O 574. 5 c. turquoise and black 8 8
O 575. 8 c. red, green, blue, yellow and lilac .. 10 10
O 576. 10 c. brown and black.. 35 12
O 577. 12 c. red and black .. 12 10
O 578. 15 c. black and red .. 12 10
O 579. 20 c. olive and black .. 15 15
O 580. 24 c. blue and black .. 25 25
O 581. 25 c. purple and black.. 15 15
O 582. 30 c. green and black .. 20 20
O 583. 40 c. orange and black 30 30
O 584. 50 c. red and black .. 35 35
O 585. 60 c. purple and black.. 40 40
O 586. 1 l. sepia and black .. 1·25 1·00
O 587. 2 l. indigo and black .. 2·00 1·90
O 588. 5 f. blue and black .. 5·00 4·50

1957. Air. Revolution of October 21, 1956. Nos. 570/9 optd. **OFICIAL.** Frames in black.

O 589. 1 c. blue and yellow .. 5 5
O 590. 2 c. pur., green & orange 5 5
O 591. 5 c. blue and pink .. 8 8
O 592. 8 c. violet, olive & orange 8 8
O 593. 10 c. brown and violet 10 10
O 594. 12 c. blue and turquoise 12 12
O 595. 15 c. brown & emerald 15 15
O 596. 30 c. grey and pink .. 25 25
O 597. 1 l. brown and blue .. 1·00 1·00
O 598. 2 l. grey and green .. 2·25 2·25

1959. Air. Abraham Lincoln. 150th Birth Anniv. Nos. 590/601 but colours changed and optd. **OFICIAL.** Flags in blue and red.

O 602. 1 c. yellow 8 8
O 603. 2 c. olive 8 8
O 604. 3 c. brown 8 8
O 605. 5 c. blue.. .. .. 8 8
O 606. 10 c. maroon 10 10
O 607. 12 c. orange 12 12
O 608. 15 c. sepia 12 12
O 609. 25 c. slate 20 20
O 610. 50 c. red.. .. .. 40 40
O 611. 1 l. violet 90 90
O 612. 2 l. blue.. .. .. 1·90 1·90
O 613. 5 l. green .. .. 5·50 5·50

1964. Air. Pres. Kennedy Memorial Issue. Optd. **IN MEMORIAM JOHN F. KENNEDY 22 NOVIEMBRE 1963.**

O 626. 1 c. yellow (No. O 602) 10 10
O 627. 2 c. olive (No. O 603) .. 15 15
O 628. 3 c. brown (No. O 604) 20 20
O 629. 5 c. blue (No. O 605) .. 25 25
O 630. 15 c. sepia (No. O 608) 75 75
O 631. 50 c. red (No. O 610) .. 4·25 4·25

1964. Air. Nos. O 611/4 surch.

O 647. 10 c. on 50 c. red .. 5 5
O 648. 12 c. on 15 c. sepia .. 8 5
O 649. 12 c. on 25 c. slate .. 8 5
O 621. 20 c. on 25 c. slate .. 15 15

1964. Air. Olympic Games, Tokyo. Optd. with Olympic Rings and **1964.**

O 632. 2 l. purple and black (No. O 539) .. 3·50 3·50

1965. Air. Nos. 630/38 optd. **OFICIAL.**

O 650. **69.** 1 c. black and green 5 5
O 651. – 2 c. black and mauve 5 5
O 652. 5 c. black and blue .. 8 8
O 653. – 8 c. blk. & grey-green 10 10
O 654. **69.** 10 c. black and bistre 15 15
O 655. 12 c. black and yellow 25 25
O 656. 1 l. black and buff .. 2·50 2·50
O 657. – 2 l. black and olive .. 5·50 5·50
O 658. **69.** 3 l. black and red .. 7·00 7·00

1965. Air. Churchill Commem. Optd. **IN MEMORIAM Sir Winston Churchill 1874-1965.**

O 674. **59.** 16 c. green and violet 60 60

1970. Air. Various official stamps surch. in figures.

O 762. **62.** 10 c. on 3 c. (O 572) 8 8
O 763. 10 c. on 2 c. (O 603) 8 8
O 764. – 10 c. on 3 c. (O 604) 8 8

1974. Air. Nos. O 570 and O 602 surch.

O 811. 2 c. on 1 c. lake & black 5 5
O 812. 2 c. on 1 c. yellow .. 5 5

HONG KONG BC

A Br. colony at the mouth of the Canton R., consisting of the island of Hong Kong and peninsula of Kowloon. Under Japanese Occupation from 25th December, 1941, until liberated by British forces on 16th September, 1945.

100 cents = 1 Hong Kong dollar.

1.

ILLUSTRATIONS British Commonwealth and all overprints and surcharges are FULL SIZE. Foreign Countries have been reduced to ¾-LINEAR.

1862.

8a. **1.** 2 c. brown .. .. 17·00 1·00
51. 4 c. grey 25 12
10. 6 c. lilac .. .. 40·00 2·25
11a. 8 c. orange-yellow .. 25·00 3·00
12a. 12 c. blue .. .. 4·00 3·00
22. 16 c. yellow .. .. 70·00 10·00
4. 18 c. lilac .. .. 75·00 13·00
14. 24 c. green .. .. 25·00 3·00
15a. 30 c. red .. .. 55·00 4·50
16. 30 c. mauve .. .. 25·00 2·25
17. 48 c. red .. .. 40·00 9·00
19. 96 c. grey .. .. 40·00 6·50
18. 96 c. olive.. .. £1100 £110

1877. Surch. in figures and words, thus **5 cents.**

23. **1.** 5 c. on 8 c. orange-yellow 27·00 9·00
24. 5 c. on 18 c. lilac .. 25·00 8·00
25a. 10 c. on 12 c. blue .. 25·00 6·50
26. 10 c. on 16 c. yellow .. 48·00 22·00
27. 10 c. on 24 c. green .. 30·00 11·00
20. 16 c. on 18 c. lilac .. £100 20·00
21. 28 c. on 30 c. mauve .. 55·00 8·00

1880.

33. 1. 2 c. red .. .. .. 6·00 3·50
56. 2 c. green 40 15
57. 4 c. red 15 15
34a. 5 c. blue 75 12
58. 5 c. yellow 55 60
30. 10 c. mauve .. .. 11·00 2·25
36. 10 c. green .. .. 6·50 45
40. 10 c. purple on red .. 55 12
59. 10 c. blue 65 35
41a. 30 c. green .. .. 3·25 3·25
61. 30 c. brown .. .. 1·10 1·75
31. 48 c. brown .. .. 42·00 18·00

1885. Surch. in figures and words, thus **20 CENTS.**

54. 1. 10 c. on 30 c. green .. 22·00 70·00
37. 20 c. on 30 c. red .. .. 4·50 1·25
42a. 20 c. on 30 c. green .. 3·50 6·00
38. 50 c. on 48 c. brown .. 13·00 3·00
43. 50 c. on 48 c. purple .. 12·00 8·00
39. $1 on 96 c. olive .. .. 13·00 8·50
44. $1 on 96 c. purple on red 14·00 12·00
35. $1 on 96 c. black .. .. 42·00 2·25

弍 (2.) 五十 (3.) 壹員 (4.)

1891. T 1 surch. with figures and word and with Chinese surcharge also.

55. 2. 10 c. on 30 c. green .. 2·75 5·50
45a. 20 c. on 30 c. green .. 1·40 85
46. 3. 50 c. on 48 c. purple .. 3·50 1·50
47. 4. $1 on 96 c. purple on red 11·00 3·00
52. $1 on 96 c. black .. .. 7·00 6·00

The Chinese surch. on No. 55 is larger than T 2.

1891. 50th Anniv. of Colony. Optd. **1841 HONG KONG JUBILEE 1891.**

48. 1. 2 c. red .. .. .. 11·00 11·00

1891. Surch. in figures and words, thus **7 cents.**

49. 1. 7 c. on 10 c. green .. 7·50 7·00
50. 14 c. on 30 c. mauve .. 10·00 11·00

5. 6.

1903.

62. 5. 1 c. purple and brown .. 12 12
91. 1 c. brown 20 15
92a. 2 c. green 55 15
78. 4 c. purple on red .. 8 15
93. 4 c. red 40 12
79. 5 c. green and orange .. 30 30
94. 6 c. orange-brown & purple 85 40
66. 8 c. grey and violet .. 30 25
67. 10 c. purple & blue on blue 45 20
95. 10 c. blue 35 12
68. 12 c. green & purple on yell. 1·00 40
83. 20 c. grey and brown .. 45 30
96. 20 c. purple and green .. 3·25 1·60
84. 30 c. green and black .. 75 75
97. 30 c. purple and yellow .. 3·25 1·60
85. 50 c. green and purple .. 1·40 1·00
98. 50 c. black on green .. 2·00 1·40
72. $1 purple and olive .. 4·50 2·50
87. $2 grey and red .. .. 10·00 8·00
99. $2 red and black .. .. 14·00 16·00
74. $3 grey and blue .. .. 18·00 20·00
75. $5 purple and green .. 25·00 27·00
76. $10 grey & orange on blue £120 £140

1912.

117. 6. 1 c. brown 8 5
118. 2 c. green 8 10
118b. 2 c. grey 25 30
119. 3 c. grey 35 20
120a. 4 c. red 8 15
121. 5 c. violet 25 8
103a. 6 c. orange .. .. .. 1·10 50
122. 8 c. grey 25 60
123. 8 c. orange 30 25
124. 10 c. blue 12 12
124a. 12 c. purple on yellow .. 40 35
125. 20 c. purple and olive .. 80 15
126. 25 c. purple 45 30
127. 30 c. purple and orange .. 80 25
128. 50 c. black on green .. 60 25
129. $1 purple & blue on blue 2·00 50
130. $2 red and black .. .. 7·00 3·00
114. $3 green and purple .. 13·00 8·00
132. $5 green and red on green 20·00 6·00
116. $10 purple & black on red 30·00 16·00

1935. Silver Jubilee. As T 11 of Antigua.

133. 3 c. blue and black .. 15 20
134. 5 c. green and blue .. 40 25
135. 10 c. brown and blue .. 55 40
136. 20 c. grey and purple .. 1·25 1·25

1937. Coronation. As T 2 of Aden.

137. 4 c. green 20 20
138. 15 c. red 20 20
139. 25 c. blue 40 40

7. King George VI. 8. Street Scene.

1938.

140. 7. 1 c. brown 8 15
141. 2 c. grey 12 12
142a. 4 c. orange 12 12
143. 5 c. green 12 12
144. 8 c. brown 12 20
145a. 10 c. violet 15 10
146. 15 c. red 8 8
147. 20 c. black 8 10
148. 20 c. red 8 8
149. 25 c. blue 20 15
150. 25 c. olive 30 20
151a. 30 c. olive 40 65
152. 30 c. blue 8 8
153a. 50 c. lilac 10 8
154. 80 c. red 25 15
155. $1 purple and blue .. 60 90
156. $1 orange and green .. 25 35
157. $2 orange and green .. 8·00 4·00
158. $2 violet and red .. 80 25
159. $5 purple and red .. 3·25 2·00
160. $5 green and violet .. 2·00 1·60
161. $10 green and violet .. 15·00 5·50
162a. $10 violet and blue .. 7·00 2·00

1941. Cent. of British Occupation. Dated "1841 1941".

163. 8. 2 c. orange and chocolate 25 30
164. – 4 c. purple and mauve .. 50 90
165. – 5 c. black and green .. 12 12
166. – 15 c. black and red .. 45 60
167. – 25 c. chocolate and blue 1·00 1·10
168. – $1 blue and orange .. 4·00 2·00

DESIGNS—VERT. 25 c. Hong Kong Bank. HORIZ. 4 c. Liner and junk. 5 c. University. 15 c. Harbour. $1 China Clipper and seaplane.

For Japanese issues see "Japanese Occupation of Hong Kong".

9.

1946. Victory.

169. 9. 30 c. blue and red .. 25 25
170. $1 brown and red .. 70 55

1948. Silver Wedding. As T 5/6 of Aden.

171. 10 c. violet 15 15
172. $10 red .. .. .. 6·00 5·50

1949. U.P.U. As T 14/17 of Antigua.

173. 10 c. violet 15 15
174. 20 c. red 15 15
175. 30 c. blue 30 20
176. 80 c. mauve 70 70

1953. Coronation. As T 7 of Aden.

177. 10 c. black and purple .. 8 5

1954. As T 7 but portrait of Queen Elizabeth, facing left.

178. 5 c. orange 5 5
179. 10 c. lilac 5 5
180. 15 c. green 5 5
181. 20 c. brown 8 12
182. 25 c. red 8 10
183. 30 c. grey 12 8
184. 40 c. blue 15 12
185. 50 c. purple 25 10
186. 65 c. grey 40 45
187. $1 orange and green .. 30 12
188. $1.30 blue and red .. 80 30
189. $2 violet and red .. 1·10 30
190. $5 green and purple .. 3·50 60
191. $10 violet and blue .. 7·50 2·00

10. University Arms.

1961. Hong Kong University. Golden Jubilee.

192. 10. $1 multicoloured .. 1·00 75

11. Statue of Queen Victoria.

1962. Stamp Centenary.

193. 11. 10 c. black and magenta 10 10
194. 20 c. black and blue .. 15 15
195. 50 c. black and bistre .. 35 35

12. Queen Elizabeth II (after Annigoni).

1962.

196. 12. 5 c. orange 5 5
223. 10 c. violet 5 5
224. 15 c. emerald 8 8
225. 20 c. brown 10 8
226. 25 c. magenta 12 12
201. 30 c. grey-blue 8 5
228. 40 c. blue-green 12 10
229. 50 c. red 15 8
230. 65 c. ultramarine .. 35 25
205. $1 sepia 30 5
206. – $1.30 multicoloured .. 60 12
207. – $2 multicoloured .. 80 25
208. – $5 multicoloured .. 2·00 40
209. – $10 multicoloured .. 3·50 1·25
210. – $20 multicoloured .. 7·50 3·50

Nos. 206/10 are as T 12 but larger ($26 \times 40\frac{1}{2}$ mm).

1963. Freedom from Hunger. As T 10 of Aden.

211. $1·30 green .. .. 2·25 1·60

1963. Red Cross Cent. As T 24 of Antigua.

212. 10 c. red and black .. 15 15
213. $1·30 red and blue .. 1·50 1·25

1965. I.T.U. Cent. As T 26 of Antigua.

214. 10 c. purple and yellow .. 10 10
215. $1·30 olive and green .. 1·25 1·00

1965. I.C.Y. As T 27 of Antigua.

216. 10 c. purple and turquoise 10 10
217. $1·30 green and lavender 1·00 1·00

1966. Churchill Commem. As T 28 of Antigua.

218. 10 c. blue 8 8
219. 50 c. green 35 35
220. $1·30 brown .. .. 1·50 75
221. $2 violet .. .. .. 1·75 1·40

1966. W.H.O. Headquarters, Geneva. Inaug. As T 31 of Antigua.

237. 10 c. black, green and blue 5 5
238. 50 c. black, purple & ochre 35 35

1966. U.N.E.S.C.O. 20th Anniv. As T 33/5 of Antigua.

239. 10 c. vio., red, yell. & orge. 5 5
240. 50 c. yellow, violet & olive 35 35
241. $2 black, purple and orge. 1·40 1·25

13. Ram's Heads on Chinese Lanterns.

1967. Chinese New Year.

242. 13. 10 c. red, olive & yellow 8 8
243. – $1·30 green, red & yellow 85 80

DESIGN: $1·30, Three rams ("Year of the Ram").

14. Cable Route Map.

1967. Completion of Malaysia–Hong Kong Link of SEACOM Telephone Cable.

244. 14. $1·30 blue and red .. 75 75

15. Monkeys in Tree.

1968. Chinese New Year ("Year of the Monkey").

245. 15. 10 c. gold, black and red 5 5
246. – $1·30 gold, black & red 75 75

DESIGN: $1·30, Family of monkeys.

16. Liner at Sea Terminal.

1968. Sea Craft.

247. 16. 10 c. multicoloured .. 5 5
248. – 20 c. blue, black & brown 10 10
249. – 40 c. orge., blk. & mauve 25 25
250. – 50 c. red, black & green 30 25
251. – $1 yellow, black and red 1·00 1·00
252. – $1.30 blue, black & pink 1·50 1·50

DESIGNS: 20 c. Pleasure Launch. 40 c. Car Ferry. 50 c. Passenger Ferry. $1 Sampan. $1.30 Junk.

17. "Bauhinia blakeana".

1968. Multicoloured.

253. 65 c. Type 17 .. .. 35 35
254. $1 Arms of Hong Kong .. 50 50

18. "Aladdin's Lamp" and Human Rights Emblem.

1968. Human Rights Year.

255. 18. 10 c. orge., blk. & green 5 5
256. 50 c. yell., blk. & purple 30 30

19. Cockerel.

1969. Chinese New Year ("Year of the Cock"). Multicoloured.

257. 10 c. Type 19 .. .. 5 5
258. $1·30 Cockerel (different) (vert.) 85 85

20. Arms of Chinese University.

1969. Establishment of Chinese University of Hong Kong.

259. 20. 40 c. violet, gold & blue 25 25

21. Earth Station and Satellite.

1969. Opening of Communications Satellite Tracking Station.

260. 21. $1 multicoloured .. 50 50

22. Chow's Head. 23. Expo 70. Emblem.

1970. Chinese New Year ("Year of the Dog"). Multicoloured.

261. 10 c. Type 22 .. .. 10 10
262. $1.30 Chow standing (horiz.) 60 60

1970. Expo 70. Multicoloured.

263. 15 c. Type 23 .. .. 10 10
264. 25 c. Expo 70 emblem and junks (horiz.) 15 15

24. Plaque in Tung Wah Hospital.

1970. "Tung Wah Hospital". Cent.

265. 24. 10 c. multicoloured .. 5 5
266. 50 c. multicoloured .. 25 25

25. Symbol.

1970. Asian Productivity Year.

267. 25. 10 c. multicoloured .. 10 10

26. Pig.

1971. Chinese New Year ("Year of the Pig").

268. 26. 10 c. multicoloured .. 8 8
269. $1·30 multicoloured .. 55 55

27. "60" and Scout Badge.

1971. Scouting in Hong Kong. Diamond Jubilee.

270. 27. 10 c. blk., red & yellow 8 8
271. 50 c. blk., green & blue 20 20
272. $2 blk., mauve & violet 70 70

28. Festival Emblem.

1971. Hong Kong Festival.

273. 28. 10 c. orange & purple.. 8 8
274. – 50 c. multicoloured .. 15 15
275. – $1 multicoloured .. 35 35

DESIGNS—HORIZ. (39×23 mm.)—50 c. Coloured streamers. VERT. (23×39 mm.)—$1 "Orchid".

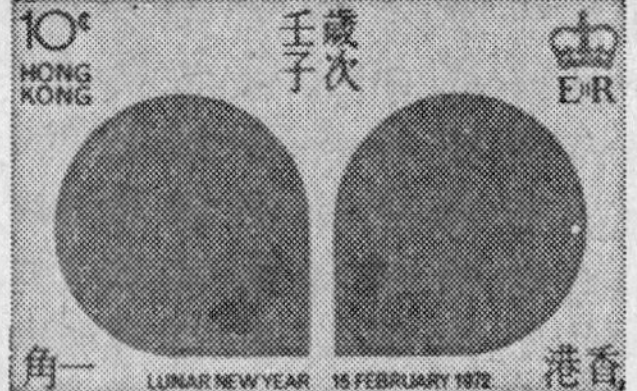

29. Stylised Rats.

1972. Chinese New Year. ("Year of the Rat").

276. 29. 10 c. red, black & gold.. 8 8
277. $1.30 red, blk. & gold 45 45

30. Tunnel Entrance.

1972. Opening of Cross Harbour Tunnel.

278. 30. $1 multicoloured .. 30 35

1972. Royal Silver Wedding. As T 19 of Ascension, but with Phoenix and Dragon in background.

279. 10 c. multicoloured .. 5 5
280. 50 c. multicoloured .. 25 25

31. Ox. 32. Queen Elizabeth II.

1973. Chinese New Year. ("Year of the Ox").

281. 31. 10 c. orge., brn. & black 5 5
282. – $1·30 yell., orge. & blk. 35 30

DESIGN—HORIZ. $1·30 Ox.

1973.

283. 32. 10 c. orange 5 5
284. 15 c. green 10 10
285. 20 c. violet 10 8
286. 25 c. brown 10 10
287. 30 c. blue 10 10
288. 40 c. blue 12 15
289. 50 c. red 12 15
290. 65 c. brown 20 20
291. $1 green 30 30
292. – $1·30 yellow and violet 35 35
293. – $2 green and brown .. 45 45
294. – $5 pink and blue .. 90 1·00
295. – $10 pink and green .. 1·90 2·10
296. – $20 pink and black .. 3·75 4·00

Nos. 292/6 are size 27×32 mm.

1973. Royal Wedding. As Type 26 of Anguilla. Multicoloured. Background colours given.

297. 50 c. brown 10 12
298. $2 mauve 45 45

33. Festival Symbols forming Chinese Character.

1973. Hong Kong Festival.

299. 33. 10 c. red and green .. 5 5
300. – 50 c. mauve & orange 15 15
301. – $1 green and mauve .. 35 35

DESIGNS—Festival symbols arranged to form a Chinese character: 10 c. "Hong". 50 c. "Kong". $1 "Festival".

34. Tiger.

1973. Chinese New Year ("Year of the Tiger").

302. 34. 10 c. multicoloured .. 5 5
303. – $1·30 multicoloured .. 30 30

DESIGN—VERT. $1·30 similar to T 34.

35. Chinese Mask.

1973. Arts Festival.

304. 35. 10 c. multicoloured .. 5 5
305. – $1 multicoloured .. 25 25
306. – $2 multicoloured .. 50 50

DESIGNS: $1, $2 Chinese masks similar to T 35.

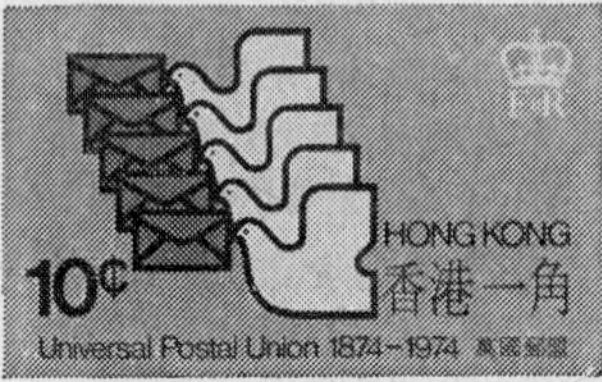

36. Pigeons with Letters.

1974. U.P.U. Centenary.

308. 36. 10 c. bl., grn. & blk. .. 5 5
309. – 50 c. mauve, orge., blk. 12 15
310. – $2 multicoloured .. 45 50

DESIGNS: 50 c. Globe within letters. $2 Hands holding letters.

37. Stylised Rabbit.

1975. Chinese New Year ("Year of the Rabbit").

325. 37. 10 c. silver and red .. 5 5
326. – $1·30 gold and green .. 35 40

DESIGN: $1·30 Pair of rabbits.

38. Queen Elizabeth II, the Duke of Edinburgh and Hong Kong Arms.

1975. Royal Visit.

329. 38. $1·30 multicoloured .. 30 35
330. $2 multicoloured .. 45 50

39. Mid-Autumn Festival.

1975. Chinese Festivals of 1975. Multicoloured.

331. 50 c. Type 39 .. .. 10 12
332. $1 Dragon-boat Festival 20 25
333. $2 Tin Hau Festival .. 40 45

40. Hwamei.

1975. Birds. Multicoloured.

335. 50 c. Type 40 .. .. 10 12
336. $1·30 Chinese Bulbul .. 25 30
337. $2 Black-capped Kingfisher 40 45

41. Dragon.

1976. Chinese New Year ("Year of the Dragon").

338. 41. 20 c. mauve, pur., & gold 5 8
339. – $1·30 green, red & gold 25 30

DESIGN: $1·30 As T 41 but dragon reversed.

42. "60" and Girl Guides Badge.

1976. Girl Guides Diamond Jubilee. Mult.

354. 20 c. Type 42 .. .. 5 8
355. $1·30 Badge, stylised diamond and "60" .. 25 30

43. "Postal Services" in Chinese Characters.

1976. Opening of New G.P.O.

356. 43. 20 c. green, grey & black 5 8
357. – $1·30 orge., grey & blk. 25 40
358. – $2 yellow, grey & black 40 45

DESIGNS: $1·30 Old G.P.O. $2 New G.P.O.

POSTAGE DUE STAMPS

D 1.

1923.

No.	Description	Unused	Used
D 1. D 1.	1 c. brown	15	25
D 2.	2 c. green	40	50
D 6.	2 c. grey	25	25
D 3.	4 c. red	50	70
D 13.	4 c. orange	5	5
D 14.	5 c. red (21 × 18 mm.)	5	5
D 4.	6 c. yellow	1·00	1·75
D 8.	6 c. red	35	15
D 9.	8 c. brown	35	40
D 5.	10 c. blue	1·00	1·25
D 15.	10 c. violet	8	8
D 16.	20 c. black	10	10
D 19.	50 c. blue	15	15

1976. As Type D 1 but smaller design (21 × 17 mm) with redrawn value.

No.	Description	Unused	Used
D 25. D 1.	10 c. violet	5	5
D 26.	20 c. grey	5	5
D 27.	50 c. blue	10	12
D 28.	$1 yellow	20	25

HORTA E1

A district of the Azores which used the stamps of the Azores from 1868.

1892. As T 9 of Portugal, but inscr. "HORTA".

No.	Description	Unused	Used
4.	5 r. yellow	1·00	60
5.	10 r. mauve	1·25	75
6.	15 r. brown	1·25	85
7.	20 r. lilac	1·60	1·25
2.	25 r. green	1·00	35
8a.	50 r. blue	1·50	1·10
9.	75 r. red	2·75	2·75
10.	80 r. green	3·50	3·00
23.	100 r. brown on yellow	2·50	2·25
24.	150 r. red on rose	12·00	9·50
13.	200 r. blue on blue	12·00	9·50
14.	300 r. blue on brown	14·00	12·00

1897. "King Carlos" key-type inscr. "HORTA".

No.	Description	Unused	Used
28. S.	2½ r. grey	30	20
29.	5 r. orange	30	20
30.	10 r. green	30	20
31.	15 r. brown	1·60	1·25
42.	15 r. green	50	40
32.	20 r. lilac	50	35
33.	25 r. green	1·00	30
43.	25 r. red	40	30
34.	50 r. blue	80	35
45.	65 r. blue	35	30
35.	75 r. red	80	60
46.	75 r. brown on yellow	3·00	2·40
36.	80 r. mauve	60	40
37.	100 r. blue on blue	60	60
47.	115 r. red on pink	50	40
48.	130 r. brown on yellow	50	40
38.	150 r. brown on yellow	50	40
49.	180 r. black on pink	60	50
39.	200 r. purple on pink	1·40	1·25
40.	300 r. blue on pink	2·00	1·60
41.	500 r. black on blue	2·50	2·25

HUNGARY E2

A Country in C. Europe. A Kingdom ruled by the Emperor of Austria until 1918. A Republic was then proclaimed, and later a Soviet style constitution was adopted. Parts of the country were occupied by France, Serbia and Rumania, including Budapest. Following the withdrawal of the Rumanians a National Republic was instituted, and in 1920, Hungary was declared a Monarchy, with Admiral Nicholas Horthy as Regent. Hungary became a Republic once more, and in 1949 a Peoples Republic.

1850. 60 krajczar (kreuzer) = 1 forint (gulden).
1858. 100 krajczar = 1 forint
1900. 100 filler (heller) = 1 korona (krone).
1926. 100 filler = 1 pengo.
1946. 100 filler = 1 forint.

1.

2.

1871.

No.	Description	Unused	Used
8. 1.	2 k. yellow	8·00	2·50
9.	3 k. green	9·00	5·00
10.	5 k. red	10·00	80
11.	10 k. blue	40·00	1·50
12.	15 k. brown	40·00	4·00
13.	25 k. lilac	35·00	15·00

1874.

No.	Description	Unused	Used
26. 2.	2 k. mauve	20	5
28.	3 k. green	20	5
17.	5 k. red	2·00	10
30a.	10 k. blue	2·00	5
32.	20 k. grey	1·00	5

1888. Numerals in black on the kreuzer values, in red on the forint values.

No.	Description	Unused	Used
38a 2.	1 k. black	10	5
39.	2 k. mauve	15	5
40.	3 k. green	20	5
41.	5 k. red	25	5
42.	8 k. orange	1·00	15
57.	10 k. blue	45	5
44.	12 k. brown	1·50	5
59.	15 k. claret	45	5
46.	20 k. grey	65	30
61.	24 k. purple	45	20
62.	30 k. olive	3·50	12
49.	50 k. red	5·00	15
50.	1 ft. blue-grey	15·00	12
51.	3 ft. brown	3·00	1·25

3. "Turul" or mythical bird of the Magyars.

4. King Francis Joseph wearing Hungarian Crown.

5.

1900. Figures of value in black.

No.	Description	Unused	Used
116. 3.	1 f. grey	5	5
100.	2 f. yellow	5	5
118.	3 f. orange	12	5
67.	4 f. mauve	5	5
102.	5 f. green	5	5
69.	6 f. maroon	15	5
120.	6 f. drab	5	5
104.	10 f. red	5	5
105.	12 f. lilac	15	5
122.	12 f. lilac on yellow	5	5
106.	16 f. green	5	5
124.	20 f. brown	5	5
125.	25 f. blue	5	5
126.	30 f. brown	5	5
127.	35 f. purple	5	5
111.	50 f. lake	15	5
128.	50 f. lake on blue	5	5
112.	60 f. green	1·00	5
130.	60 f. green on red	20	20
131.	70 f. brown on green	8	5
132.	80 f. violet	8	5
133. 4.	1 k. red	20	5
134.	2 k. blue	35	5
81.	3 k. blue	7·00	30
135.	5 k. claret	2·00	45

1913. Flood Charity stamps. As T 3/4, but with label as T 5.

No.	Description	Unused	Used
136. 5.	1 f.+2 f. grey	15	15
137.	2 f.+2 f. yellow	12	12
138.	3 f.+2 f. orange	12	12
139.	5 f.+2 f. green	12	12
140.	6 f.+2 f. drab	15	15
141.	10 f.+2 f. red	5	5
142.	12 f.+2 f. lilac on yellow	35	20
143.	16 f.+2 f. green	15	15
144.	20 f.+2 f. brown	75	25
145.	25 f.+2 f. blue	15	12
146.	30 f.+2 f. brown	35	20
147.	35 f.+2 f. purple	15	15
148.	50 f.+2 f. lake on blue	1·25	45
149.	60 f.+2 f. green on red	1·50	40
150. 4.	1 k.+2 f. red	6·50	3·50
151.	2 k.+2 f. blue	18·00	12·00
152.	5 k.+2 f. claret	5·50	4·50

1914. War Charity. Stamps with label surch. **Hadi segely Ozvegyeknek es arvaknak ket (2) filler** horiz.

No.	Description	Unused	Used
153. 5.	1 f.+2 f. grey	15	8
154.	2 f.+2 f. yellow	15	15
155.	3 f.+2 f. orange	15	15
156.	5 f.+2 f. green	12	5
157.	6 f.+2 f. drab	25	10
158.	10 f.+2 f. red	12	5
159.	12 f.+2 f. lilac on yellow	15	8
160.	16 f.+2 f. green	12	5
161.	20 f.+2 f. brown	15	10
162.	25 f.+2 f. blue	35	15
163.	30 f.+2 f. brown	30	15
164.	35 f.+2 f. purple	70	25
165.	50 f.+2 f. lake on blue	40	10
166.	60 f.+2 f. green on red	1·50	40
167. 4.	1 k.+2 f. red (No. 150)	18·00	10·00
168.	2 k.+2 f. blue (No. 151)	6·00	6·00
169.	5 k.+2 f. clar. (No. 153)	5·00	4·50

1915. War Charity. Stamps of 1900 without labels surch. as last round the stamp.

No.	Description	Unused	Used
170. 3.	1 f.+2 f. grey	5	5
171.	2 f.+2 f. yellow	5	5
172.	3 f.+2 f. orange	5	5
173.	5 f.+2 f. green	5	5
174.	6 f.+2 f. drab	5	5
175.	10 f.+2 f. red	5	5
176.	12 f.+2 f. lilac on yellow	5	5
177.	16 f.+2 f. green	5	5
178.	20 f.+2 f. brown	10	8
179.	25 f.+2 f. blue	5	5
180.	30 f.+2 f. brown	5	5
181.	35 f.+2 f. purple	5	5
182.	50 f.+2 f. lake on blue	5	5
184.	60 f.+2 f. green on red	5	5
185. 4.	1 k.+2 f. red (No. 133)	40	12
186.	2 k.+2 f. blue (No. 134)	70	50
187.	5 k.+2 f. claret (No. 135)	1·50	1·40

6. In Trenches.

8. "Turul" at bay.

9. Queen Zita.

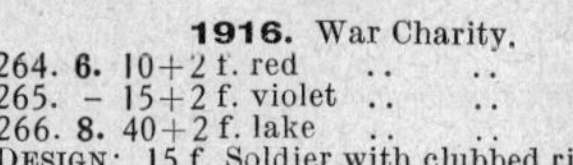

1916. War Charity.

No.	Description	Unused	Used
264. 6.	10+2 f. red	5	5
265. –	15+2 f. violet	5	5
266. 8.	40+2 f. lake	5	5

DESIGN: 15 f. Soldier with clubbed rifle.

1916. Coronation.

No.	Description	Unused	Used
267. 9.	10 f. mauve	10	5
268. –	15 f. red (Emperor Karl)	10	5

11. Harvester.

12. Parliament Buildings, Budapest.

1916. Inscr. "MAGYAR KIR POSTA".

No.	Description	Unused	Used
245. 11.	2 f. brown	5	5
246.	3 f. claret	5	5
247.	4 f. slate	5	5
248.	5 f. green	5	5
249.	6 f. blue	5	5
250.	10 f. red	5	5
251.	15 f. violet	5	5
252.	20 f. brown	5	5
253.	25 f. blue	5	5
254.	35 f. brown	5	5
255.	40 f. olive	5	5
256. 12.	50 f. purple	5	5
257.	75 f. blue	5	5
258.	80 f. green	5	5
259.	1 k. lake	5	5
260.	2 k. brown	5	5
261.	3 k. grey and violet	5	5
262.	5 k. brown	5	5
263.	10 k. lilac and brown	10	5

In T 12 the colours of the centres differ slightly from those of the frames.

For later issues in T 11 and 12, see Nos. 372 to 417.

1916. As T 11, but with white figures in top corners.

No.	Description	Unused	Used
243. 11.	10 f. red	5	5
244.	15 f. violet	5	5

1917. War Charity Exn. Surch. **Jozsef foherczeg vezerezredes hadi kiallitasa 1 korona.**

No.	Description	Unused	Used
269. 11.	10 f.+1 k. red (No. 250)	10	10
270.	15 f.+1 k. vio. (No. 251)	10	10

13. Karl.

14. Zita.

1918.

No.	Description	Unused	Used
273. 13.	10 f. red	5	5
274.	15 f. violet	8	8
275.	20 f. brown	5	5
276.	25 f. blue	5	5
277. 14.	40 f. olive	5	5
278.	50 f. purple	5	5

1918. Air. Surch. **REPULO POSTA** and value.

No.	Description	Unused	Used
271. 12.	1 k. 50 on 75 f. blue	3·00	3·00
272.	4 k. 50 on 2 k. brown	2·00	2·00

1918. War Charity stamps optd. **KOZTARSASAG.**

No.	Description	Unused	Used
279. 6.	10+2 f. red	5	5
280. –	15+2 f. violet	5	5
281. 8.	40+2 f. lake	10	10

1919. Stamps of 1916 optd. **KOZTARSASAG.**

No.	Description	Unused	Used
282. 11.	2 f. brown	5	5
283.	3 f. claret	5	5
284.	4 f. slate	5	5
285.	5 f. green	5	5
286.	6 f. blue	5	5
287.	10 f. red	5	5
288.	20 f. brown	5	5
289.	40 f. olive	5	5
290. 12.	1 k. lake	5	5
291. 12.	2 k. brown	5	5
292.	3 k. grey and violet	5	5
293.	5 k. brown	12	12
294.	10 k. lilac and brown	5	5

1919. Stamps of 1918 optd. **KOZTARSASAG.**

No.	Description	Unused	Used
295. 13.	10 f. red	5	5
296.	15 f. violet	5	5
297.	20 f. brown	5	5
298.	25 f. blue	5	5
299. 14.	40 f. olive	5	5
300.	50 f. purple	5	5

1919. As T 11/12, but inscr. "MAGYAR POSTA".

No.	Description	Unused	Used
301. 11.	2 f. brown	5	5
302.	4 f. slate	5	5
303.	5 f. green	5	5
304.	6 f. blue	5	5
305.	10 f. red	5	5
306.	15 f. violet	5	5
307.	20 f. brown	5	5
308.	20 f. green	5	5
309.	25 f. blue	5	5
310.	40 f. olive	5	5
311.	40 f. red	5	5
312.	45 f. orange	5	5
313. 12.	50 f. purple	5	5
314.	60 f. blue and brown	5	5
315.	95 f. blue	5	5
316.	1 k. lake	5	5
317.	1 k. blue	5	5
318.	1 k. 20 green	5	5
319.	1 k. 40 green	5	5
320.	2 k. brown	5	5
321.	3 k. grey and violet	5	5
322.	5 k. brown	5	5
323.	10 k. lilac and brown	10	5

15. Karl Marx.

PORTRAITS: 45 f. Petofi. 60 f. Martinovics. 75 f. Dozsa. 80 f. Engels.

1919.

No.	Description	Unused	Used
324. 15.	20 f. red and brown	15	15
325. –	45 f. green and orange	20	20
326. –	60 f. brown and grey	50	50
327. –	75 f. brown and claret	70	50
328. –	80 f. brown and olive	1·00	90

1919. Inscr. "MAGYAR POSTA" optd. **MAGYAR TANACS KOZTARSASAG** ("Hungarian Soviet Republic").

No.	Description	Unused	Used
329. 11.	2 f. brown	5	5
330.	3 f. claret	5	5
331.	4 f. slate	5	5
332.	5 f. green	5	5
333.	6 f. blue	5	5
334.	10 f. red	5	5
335.	15 f. violet	5	5
336.	20 f. brown	5	5
337.	25 f. blue	5	5
338.	40 f. olive	5	5
339.	45 f. orange	5	5
340. 12.	50 f. purple	5	5
341.	95 f. blue	5	5
342.	1 k. lake	5	5
343.	1 k. 20 green	5	5
344.	1 k. 40 green	5	5
345.	2 k. brown	15	15
346.	3 k. grey and violet	15	15
347.	5 k. brown	15	15
348.	10 k. lilac and brown	25	25

1919. Entry of National Army into Budapest. Inscr. "MAGYAR POSTA" and optd. **A nemzeti hadsereg bevonulasa 1919. XI/16.**

No.	Description	Unused	Used
348a. 11.	5 f. green	12	12
348b.	10 f. red	12	12
348c.	15 f. violet	12	12
348d.	20 f. brown	12	12
348e.	25 f. blue	12	12

(16.)

(17.)

1920. Nos. 329 to 348 optd. with T 16 or 17.

No.	Description	Unused	Used
349. 11.	2 f. brown	8	8
350.	3 f. claret	5	5
351.	4 f. slate	8	8
352.	5 f. green	5	5
353.	6 f. blue	5	5
354.	10 f. red	5	5
355.	15 f. violet	5	5
356.	20 f. brown	5	5
357.	25 f. blue	5	5
358.	40 f. olive	8	8
359.	45 f. orange	8	8
360. 12.	50 f. purple	10	10
361.	95 f. blue	10	10
362.	1 k. lake	10	10
363.	1 k. 20 green	10	10
364.	1 k. 40 green	12	12
365.	2 k. brown	75	75
366.	3 k. grey and violet	75	75
367.	5 k. brown	5	5
368.	10 k. lilac and brown	1·40	1·40

18. Returning P.O.W.

21. Madonna and Child.

1920. Returned Prisoners-of-War Charity. Inscr. "SEGITSUK HAZA VEREINKET".

369. 18. 40 f.+1 k. lake .. 15 15
370. – 60 f.+2 k. brown .. 12 12
371. – 1 k.+5 k. blue .. 12 12

DESIGNS—HORIZ. 60 f. Prisoners of War. VERT. 1 k. Homecoming of Soldier.

1920. Re-issue of T 11 inscr. "MAGYAR KIR POSTA".

372. 11. 5 f. brown 5 5
373. 10 f. purple 5 5
374. 40 f. red 5 5
375. 50 f. green 5 5
376. 50 f. blue 5 5
377. 60 f. black 5 5
378. 1 k. green 5 5
379. 1½ k. purple 5 5
380. 2 k. blue 5 5
381. 2½ k. green 5 5
382. 3 k. brown 5 5
383. 4 k. red 5 5
384. 4½ k. violet 5 5
385. 5 k. brown 5 5
386. 6 k. blue 5 5
387. 10 k. brown 5 5
388. 15 k. black 5 5
389. 20 k. claret 5 5
390. 25 k. orange 5 5
391. 40 k. green 5 5
392. 50 k. blue 5 5
393. 100 k. purple 5 5
394. 150 k. green 5 5
395. 200 k. green 5 5
396. 300 k. red 5 5
397. 350 k. violet 5 5
443. 400 k. blue 5 5
398. 500 k. black 8 5
399. 600 k. bistre 10 5
400. 800 k. yellow 10 5

1920. Re-issue of T 12 inscr. "MAGYAR KIR POSTA".

404. 12. 2 k. 50 blue 5 5
405. 3 k. 50 grey 5 5
406. 10 k. brown 5 5
407. 15 k. grey 5 5
408. 20 k. claret 5 5
409. 25 k. orange 5 5
410. 30 k. lake 5 5
411. 40 k. green 5 5
412. 50 k. blue 5 5
413. 100 k. brown 5 5
414. 400 k. green 5 5
415. 500 k. violet 8 5
416. 1000 k. claret 10 5
417. 2000 k. red 15 5

1920. Air. No. 263 surch. **LEGI POSTA** and value.

401. 12. 3 k. on 10 k. lilac & brn. 35 35
402. 8 k. on 10 k. lilac & brn. 35 35
403. 12 k. on 10 k. lilac & brn. 35 35

1921.

418. 21. 50 k. blue and brown .. 15 10
419. 100 k. brown and bistre 30 20
420. 200 k. blue 5 5
421. 500 k. mauve & purple 8 5
422. 1000 k. purple & mauve 10 5
423. 2000 k. mauve & green 12 5
424. 2500 k. brown and bistre 25 5
425. 3000 k. mauve and lake 15 5
426. 5000 k. green .. 20 5
427. 10,000 k. blue and violet 80 20

22. Statue of Petofi in National Dress.

23. John, the hero, on flying dragon.

25. Death of Petofi.

DESIGNS—VERT. As T 23: 25 k. Petofi. 50 k. Petofi addressing the people.

1923. Charity. Petofi (poet). Birth Cent.

428. 22. 10 k. (+10 k.) blue .. 10 10
429. 23. 15 k. (+15 k.) blue .. 45 45
430. – 25 k. (+25 k.) brown .. 10 10
431. 25. 40 k. (+40 k.) claret .. 45 45
432. – 50 k. (+50 k.) purple .. 50 50

27.

30. Icarus over Budapest.

1924. T.B. Relief Fund.

437. 27. 300 k. (+300 k.) blue 55 55
438. – 500 k. (+500 k.) brown 55 55
439. – 1000 k. (+1000 k.) grn. 55 55

DESIGNS: 500 k. Mother and child. 1000 k. Bowman.

1924. Air.

433. 30. 100 k. red and brown .. 20 20
434. 500 k. green 20 20
435. 1000 k. brown & bistre .. 20 20
436. 2000 k. blue 20 20
436a. 5000 k. mve. & purple 45 45
436b. 10,000 k. purple & red .. 35 35

31. M. Jokai.

32.

1925. Maurus Jokai (novelist). Birth Cent.

449. 31. 1000 k. brown and green 70 60
450. 2000 k. brown 30 25
451. 2500 k. brown and blue 55 55

1925. Charity. Sports Association.

452. – 100 k. (+100 k.) brown and green .. 45 45
453. – 200 k. (+200 k.) green and brown .. 55 55
454. – 300 k. (+300 k) blue 90 90
455. 32. 400 k. (+400 k.) green and blue .. 1·10 1·10
456. – 500 k. (+500 k.) pur. 1·90 1·60
457. – 1000 k. (+1000 k.) clar. 2·75 2·10
458. – 2000 k. (+2000 k.) pur. 2·75 2·10
459. – 2500 k. (+2500 k.) sep. 3·00 2·25

DESIGNS—HORIZ. 100 k. Athletes. 500 k. Fencing. 2000 k. Football. VERT. 200 k. Ski-ing. 300 k. Skating. 1000 k. Scouts. 2500 k. Hurdles.

34. Crown of St. Stephen.

35. St. Matthias Church and Fisher's Bastion.

38. Madonna and Child.

36 Royal Palace, Budapest 37.

1926. T 37 is without boat.

460. 34. 1 f. black 5 5
461. 2 f. blue 5 5
492. 3 f. orange 5 5
493. 4 f. mauve 5 5
464. 6 f. green 12 5
465. 8 f. red 15 5
496. 35. 10 f. blue 20 5
467. 16 f. violet 12 5
468. 20 f. red 12 5
469. 25 f. brown 12 5
470. 37. 30 f. green 15 5
471. 36. 32 f. violet 30 5
472. 40 f. blue 30 5
473. 37. 46 f. blue 25 5
474. 50 f. sepia 30 5
475. 70 f. red 35 5
476. 38. 1 p. violet .. .. 3·00 5
477. 2 p. red .. .. 2·10 5
478. 5 p. blue .. .. 5·50 5

39. The fabulous "Turul".

40. Mercury astride "Turul".

1927. Air.

478a. 39. 4 f. orange 20 10
479. 12 f. green 25 10
480. 16 f. brown 35 15
481. 20 f. red 35 20
482. 32 f. purple 90 75
483. 40 f. blue 80 15
484. 40. 50 f. claret 80 30
485. 72 f. olive 90 30
486. 40. 80 f. violet 90 20
487. 1 p. green 90 35
488. 2 p. red .. .. 1·40 95
489. 5 p. blue .. .. 5·00 4·00

41. St. Stephen.

42. Royal Palace, Budapest.

1928. St. Stephen of Hungary. 890th Death Anniv.

507. 41. 8 f. green 25 15
508. 16 f. red 25 15
509. 32 f. blue 60 50

1929. Re-issue of T 41.

510. 41. 8 f. red 8 5
511. 16 f. violet 12 10
512. 32 f. bistre 60 35

1928. T 42 is with boat.

502. 42. 30 f. green 30 5
503. 32 f. purple 30 5
504. 40 f. blue 40 5
505. 46 f. green 40 5
506. 50 f. brown 40 5

43. Admiral Horthy.

44. St. Emery.

1930. Regency. 10th Anniv.

513. 43. 8 f. green 50 10
514. 16 f. violet 50 10
515. 20 f. red .. .. 1·00 35
516. 32 f. brown 90 50
517. 40 f. blue .. .. 1·00 35

1930. St. Emery. 900th Death Anniv.

518. 44. 8 f.+2 f. green 20 20
519. – 16 f.+4 f. purple .. 30 30
520. – 20 f.+f. 4 red 55 55
521. – 32 f.+8 f. blue .. .. 1·00 1·00

DESIGNS—VERT. 16 f. Sts. Stephen and Gisela. 20 f. St. Launcelot. HORIZ. 32 f. Sts. Gerard and Emery.

1931. Surch. with value in circle over scroll.

526. 34. 2 on 3 f. orange .. 10 5
527. 6 on 8 f. red 20 5
528. 35. 10 on 16 f. violet .. 12 5
525. 20 on 25 f. brown .. 30 8

1931. Air. Optd. **Zeppelin 1931.**

529. 40. 1 p. orange .. .. 11·00 5·00
530. 2 p. purple .. .. 11·00 5·00

46. St. Elizabeth.

48. Madonna and Child.

49.

1932. St. Elizabeth of Hungary. 700th Death Anniv.

531. 46. 10 f. blue 15 5
532. 20 f. red 20 5
533. – 32 f. purple 55 45
534. – 40 f. blue 45 20

The design of the 32 f. and 40 f. is taller and shows St. Elizabeth helping children.

1932.

535. 48. 1 p. green .. .. 3·50 8
536. 2 p. red .. .. 3·75 15
537. 5 p. blue .. .. 11·00 1·25
538. 10 p. brown .. .. 32·00 11·00

1932. No. 527 surch. with large figure **2**.

540. 34. 2 on 6 on 8 f. red .. 5 5

1932. Famous Hungarians.

541. – 1 f. grey (I. Madach) .. 5 5
542. – 2 f. orange (J. Arany) .. 5 5
543. – 4 f. blue (I. Semmelweis) 5 5
543a. 49. 5 f. brown (F. Kolcsey) 5 5
544. – 6 f. green (L. Eotvos) . 5 5
545. – 10 f. green (I. Szechenyi) 5 5
546. – 16 f. violet (F. Deak) .. 5 5
547. – 20 f. red (F. Liszt) .. 8 5
547a. – 25 f. green (M. Vorosmarty) 10 5
548. – 30 f. brown (L. Kossuth) 8 5
549. – 32 f. claret (I. Tisza) 15 5
550. – 40 f. blue (M. Munkacsy) 25 5
551. – 50 f. green (S. Csoma) 25 5
552. – 70 f. lake (F. Bolyai) .. 35 5

1933. Surch.

553. 37. 10 on 70 f. red .. 15 5

50. Aeroplane over Danube.

51. Gift 'plane from Mussolini.

52. "The Stag of Hungary".

1933. Air.

554. 50. 10 f. green 55 8
555. 16 f. violet 55 12
556. 51. 20 f. red .. .. 1·25 20
557. 40 f. blue .. .. 1·00 35
558. – 48 f. black .. .. 1·75 50
559. – 72 f. brown .. .. 1·75 55
560. – 1 p. green .. .. 2·50 35
561. – 2 p. claret .. .. 4·25 2·00
562. – 5 p. grey .. .. 17·00 14·00

DESIGNS—VERT. as T 51: 48 f., 72 f. "Spirit of Flight" on aeroplane wing. 1 p., 2 p., 5 p. Mercury and propeller.

1933. Int. Scout Jamboree, Godollo.

563. 52. 10 f. green 25 15
564. 16 f. claret 90 35
565. 20 f. red 45 25
566. 32 f. yellow .. .. 1·40 1·00
567. 40 f. blue .. .. 1·40 70

1934. 2nd Hungarian Philatelic Exn., Budapest, and Jubilee of 1st Hungarian Philatelic Society. Miniature sheet inscr. "II ORSZAGOS BELYEGKIALLITAS/L.E.H.E. 1884-1934".

MS 568. 20 f. red (No. 547) .. 25·00 22·00

Sold at 90 f. (incl. 70 f. entrance charge).

53. Ferenc Rakoczi II.

54. Cardinal Pazmany.

1935. Rakoczi. 200th Death Anniv.

569. 53. 10 f. green 45 20
570. 16 f. violet .. .. 1·50 60
571. 20 f. red 45 20
572. 32 f. claret .. .. 3·50 1·60
573. 40 f. blue .. .. 2·75 1·50

1935. Budapest University Tercent. Dated "1635-1935".

574. 54. 6 f. green 60 45
575. – 10 f. green 15 10
576. 54. 16 f. violet 80 55
577. 20 f. magenta 15 12
578. – 32 f. claret .. .. 1·50 70
579. – 40 f. blue .. .. 1·50 75

DESIGN—HORIZ. (35×25 mm.): 10 f., 32 f., 40 f. Pazmany signing deed.

55. Tri-Motor Fokker.

DESIGNS: 40 f. to 80 f. Aeroplane over Parliament Buildings. 1 p. to 5 p. Aeroplane.

1936. Air.

580. 55. 10 f. green 10 5
581. 20 f. red 10 5
582. 36 f. brown 15 5
583. – 40 f. blue 20 5
584. – 52 f. orange 55 45
585. – 60 f. violet .. .. 2·50 12
586. – 80 f. green 55 35
587. – 1 p. green 80 15
588. – 2 p. lake .. .. 1·25 55
589. – 5 p. blue .. .. 4·25 3·50

58. Ancient Buda.

DESIGNS: 16 f. Angel of Peace over Buda. 20 f. Arms of Buda. 32 f. Colour bearer and bugler.

1936. Recapture of Buda from Turks. 250th Anniv. Inscr. "BUDAVAR 1686-1936".

590. 58. 10 f. green 20 8
591. – 16 f. mauve .. .. 1·25 90
592. – 20 f. red 20 8
593. – 32 f. brown .. .. 1·40 80
594 58. 40 f. blue .. .. 1·40 80

59. "Commerce", "May Fair, 1937" and R. Danube.

60. St. Stephen, the Church builder.

1937. Budapest Int. Fair.

595. **59.** 2 f. orange 5 5
596. 6 f. green 5 5
597. 10 f. green 5 5
598. 20 f. red 8 5
599. 32 f. violet 15 10
600. 40 f. blue 25 5

1938. St. Stephen. 900th Death Anniv. (1st issue).

601. – 1 f. violet 8 5
602. **60.** 2 f. sepia 8 5
603. – 4 f. blue 25 5
604. – 5 f. magenta 30 5
605. – 6 f. green 30 5
606. – 10 f. red 40 5
607. **60.** 16 f. violet 45 5
608. – 20 f. red 40 5
609. – 25 f. green 30 5
610. – 30 f. bistre 90 5
611. – 32 f. red 45 45
612. – 40 f. blue 60 5
613. – 50 f. purple 90 5
614. – 70 f. green .. .. 1·25 12

DESIGNS: 1 f., 10 f. Abbot Astrik receiving Crown from Pope. 4 f., 20 f. St. Stephen enthroned. 5 f., 25 f. St. Gellert, St. Emery and St. Stephen. 6 f., 30 f. St. Stephen offering Crown to Virgin Mary. 32 f., 50 f., St. Stephen. 40 f. Madonna and Child. 70 f. Crown of St. Stephen.

62. Admiral Horthy.

63. Eucharistic Symbols.

1938.

615. **62.** 1 p. green 15 5
616. 2 p. sepia 35 5
617. 5 p. blue .. .. 1·25 25

1938. 34th Int. Eucharistic Congress. Inscr. "XXXIV NEMZETKOZI EUCHARISZTIKUS KONGRESSZUS 1938".

618. – 16 f.+16 f. blue .. 1·00 1·00
619. **63.** 20 f.+20 f. red .. 1·00 1·00

DESIGN: 16 f. St. Ladislas.

64. St. Stephen the Victorious.

65. Debrecen College.

1938. St. Stephen. 900th Death Anniv. (2nd issue). Inscr. "PATRONA HUNGARIAE".

620. **64.** 10 f.+10 f. purple .. 1·00 1·00
621. – 20 f.+20 f. red .. 1·00 1·00

DESIGN: 20 f. St. Stephen offering crown to Virgin Mary.

1938. Debrecen College. 400th Anniv. Inscr. as in T **65**.

622. **65.** 6 f. green 5 5
623. – 10 f. brown 5 5
624. – 16 f. red 10 8
625. – 20 f. red 10 5
626. – 32 f. green 20 15
627. – 40 f. blue 25 12

DESIGNS—HORIZ. 10 f., 20 f. 18th and 19th-cent. views of College. VERT. 16 f. Ex-students in robes. 32 f. Prof. Marothi. 40 f. Dr. Hatvani.

1938. Acquisition of Czech Territory. As Nos. 608 and 614 optd. **HAZATERES 1938.**

628. 20 f. red 30 8
629. 70 f. brown 40 12

68. Statue "Northern Provinces".

69. Crown of St. Stephen.

1939. Patriotic Fund. Inscr. "MAGYAR A MAGYARERT".

630. **68.** 6 f.+3 f. green.. .. 25 15
631. – 10 f.+5 f. green .. 12 5
632. – 20 f.+10 f. red .. 20 10
633. – 30 f.+15 f. green .. 25 25
634. – 40 f.+20 f. blue .. 25 25

DESIGNS: 10 f. Fort at Munkacs. 20 f. Admiral Horthy leading troops into Komarom. 30 f. Cathedral of St. Elizabeth, Kassa. 40 f. Girls offering flowers to soldiers.

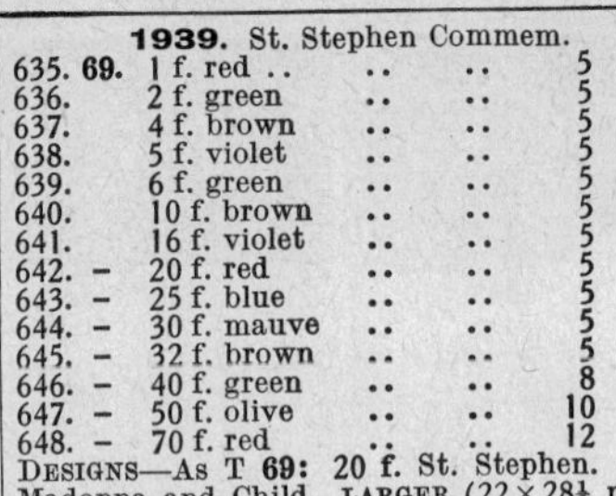

1939. St. Stephen Commem.

635. **69.** 1 f. red 5 5
636. 2 f. green 5 5
637. 4 f. brown 5 5
638. 5 f. violet 5 5
639. 6 f. green 5 5
640. 10 f. brown 5 5
641. 16 f. violet 5 5
642. – 20 f. red 5 5
643. – 25 f. blue 5 5
644. – 30 f. mauve 5 5
645. – 32 f. brown 8 5
646. – 40 f. green 8 5
647. – 50 f. olive 10 5
648. – 70 f. red 12 5

DESIGNS—As T **69**: 20 f. St. Stephen. 25 f. Madonna and Child. LARGER (22 × 28½ mm.): 30 f. Buda Cathedral. 32 f. Debrecen Reformed Church. 40 f. Esztergom Basilica. 50 f. Budapest Evangelical Church. 70 f. Kassa Cathedral.

For further issues in these designs, see Nos. 695/703 and 751/5.

71. Guides' Salute.

72. Memorial Tablets.

1939. Girl Guides' Rally, Godollo. Inscr. "I. PAX-TING".

649. **71.** 2 f. orange 5 5
650. – 6 f. green 12 8
651. – 10 f. brown 12 5
652. – 20 f. pink 25 15

DESIGNS: 6 f. Lily symbol and Hungarian arms. 10 f. Guide and girl in national costume. 20 f. Dove of peace.

1939. Hungarian Protestant Day and Int. Protestant Cultural Fund.

653. **72.** 6 f.+3 f. green.. .. 25 15
654. – 10 f.+5 f. purple .. 25 15
655. – 20 f.+10 f. red .. 30 15
656. – 32 f.+16 f. brown .. 35 25
657. – 40 f.+20 f. blue .. 35 15

DESIGNS—HORIZ. 10 f., 20 f. G. Karoli and A. Molnar di Szenci (translators of the Bible and the Psalms). VERT. 32 f. Prince Gabriel Bethlen. 40 f. Susanna Lorantffy.

74. Boy Scout with Kite.

75. Regent and Szeged Cathedral.

1940. Admiral Horthy Aviation Fund Inscr. "HORTHY-MIKLOS-NEMZETI-REPULO-ALAP".

658. **74.** 6 f.+6 f. green.. .. 8 8
659. – 10 f.+10 f. brown .. 20 20
660. – 20 f.+20 f. red .. 40 40

DESIGNS: 10 f. "Spirit of Flight". 20 f. St. Elizabeth carrying Crown and Cross.

1940. Regency. 20th Anniv.

661. **75.** 6 f. green 5 5
662. – 10 f. brown and olive .. 10 10
663. – 20 f. red 15 12

DESIGNS: 10 f. Admiral Horthy. 20 f. Kassa Cathedral and Angelic bellringer.

76. Stemming the Flood.

1940. Flood Relief Fund.

664. **76.** 10 f.+2 f. brown .. 5 5
665. 20 f.+4 f. orange .. 10 10
666. 20 f.+50 f. brown .. 30 25

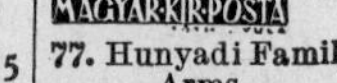
77. Hunyadi Family Arms.

78. Hunyadi Castle.

1940. King Matthias Hunyadi, 500th Birth Anniv. and Cultural Institutes Fund.

667. **77.** 6 f.+3 f. green.. .. 10 10
668. **78.** 10 f.+5 f. brown .. 10 10
669. – 16 f.+8 f. olive .. 10 10
670. – 20 f.+10 f. red .. 15 15
671. – 32 f.+16 f. grey .. 20 20

DESIGNS—VERT. 16 f. Bust of King Matthias 32 f. Rare manuscript dated "1473". HORIZ. 20 f. Equestrian Statue of King Matthias.

79. Crown of St. Stephen

80. Madonna and Martyr.

1940. Recovery from Rumania of North-Eastern Transylvania.

672. **79.** 10 f. green and yellow 5 5

1940. Transylvanian Relief Fund. Various designs dated "1940".

673. – 10 f.+50 f. green .. 25 20
674. **80.** 20 f.+50 f. red .. 25 20
675. – 32 f.+50 f. brown .. 25 20

DESIGNS: 10 f. Prince Csaba and soldier. 32 f. Mother offering child to Fatherland.

81. Spirit of Music.

DESIGNS—VERT. 10 f. Sculpture. 16 f. Painting. HORIZ. 20 f. Poetry (Pegasus).

1940. Artists' Relief Fund. Inscr. "MAGYAR MUVESZETERT".

676. **81.** 6 f.+6 f. green .. 35 35
677. – 10 f.+10 f. brown .. 35 35
678. – 16 f.+16 f. violet .. 35 35
679. – 20 f.+20 f. red .. 35 35

82. Pilot.

DESIGNS: 10 f. Youth releasing model aeroplane. 20 f. Glider. 32 f. Madonna.

1941. Air stamps. Horthy Aviation Fund. Various allegorical designs inscribed "HORTHY MIKLOS NEMZETI REPULO ALAP".

680. **82.** 6 f.+6 f. olive.. .. 10 10
681. – 10 f.+10 f. brown .. 15 15
682. – 20 f.+20 f. red .. 15 15
683. – 32 f.+32 f. blue .. 30 30

1941. Acquisition of Yugoslav Territory. Overprinted **DEL-UISSZATER** ("The South comes home").

684. **69.** 10 f. brown 5 5
685. – 20 f. red (No. 642) .. 8 5

83. Admiral Horthy.

84. Count Szechenyi.

85. Giant opening Straits of Kazan.

DESIGNS: 16 f. Count Szechenyi and Academy of Science. 32 f. Budapest Chain Bridge. 40 f. Mercury, Locomotive and Steamship.

1941.

686. **83.** 1 p. green and yellow .. 8 5
687. 2 p. brown and yellow 8 5
688 5 p. purple and yellow 30 5

1941. Count Szechenyi. 150th Birth Anniv.

689 **84.** 10 f. olive 5 5
690. – 16 f. brown 5 5
691. **85.** 20 f. red 8 5
692. – 32 f. orange 10 5
693. – 40 f. blue 12 5

1941. As Nos. 635/43, but new values and colours.

695. **69.** 3 f. brown 5 5
698. 8 f. green 5 5
700. 12 f. orange 5 5
702. – 24 f. purple 5 5
703. – 80 f. bistre 5 5

DESIGNS: 24 f. St. Stephen. 80 f. Madonna and Child.

86. Infantry in Action.

87. Pilot and Aeroplane.

88. Blood Transfusion.

89. Vice regent Stephen Horthy.

1941. Soldiers' Gifts Fund. Inscr. "HONVEDEINK KARACSONYARA 1941".

(a) First issue.

708. **86.** 8 f.+12 f. green .. 5 5
709. – 12 f.+18 f. brown .. 8 8
710. – 20 f.+30 f. blue .. 8 5
711. – 40 f.+60 f. brown .. 10 10

DESIGNS: 12 f. Artillery. 20 f. Tanks. 40 f. Cavalryman and cyclist.

(b) 2nd issue (for Christmas Gifts).

712. – 20 f.+40 f. red.. .. 60 45

DESIGN: Soldier in helmet, cross and sword.

1942. Air. Horthy Aviation Fund. Inscr. "HORTHY MIKLOS NEMZETI REPULO ALAP".

713. **87.** 8 f.+8 f. green .. 15 15
714. – 12 f.+12 f. blue .. 15 15
715. – 20 f.+20 f. brown .. 15 15
716. – 30 f.+30 f. red .. 15 15

DESIGNS—VERT. 30 f. Airmen and turul. HORIZ. 12 f. Aeroplanes and horsemen. 20 f. Aeroplane and archer.

1942. Red Cross Fund.

717. **88.** 3 f.+18 f. olive .. 35 35
718. – 8 f.+32 f. brown .. 35 35
719. – 12 f.+50 f. purple .. 35 35
720. – 20 f.+1 p. blue .. 35 35

DESIGNS: 8 f. First aid ("APOLAS"). 12 f. Wireless and Carrier Pigeon Service. ("GONDOZAS"). 20 f. Bereaved parents and orphans ("GYAMOLITAS").

1942. Air. Mourning for Stephen Horthy.

721. – 20 f. black 10 10
722. **89.** 30 f.+20 f. violet .. 8 8

No. 721 is squarer in shape than No. 722 and is dated "1904-1942".

90. Stephen Horthy's Widow.

91. King Ladislas.

1942. Red Cross Fund.

723. **90.** 6 f.+1 p. blue .. 80 80
724. – 8 f.+1 p. green .. 80 80
725. – 20 f.+1 p. brown .. 80 80

DESIGNS—HORIZ. 8 f. Nurse and wounded soldier. VERT. 20 f. Stephen Horthy's mother.

1942. Charity. Dated "1942".

726. **91.** 6 f.+6 f. brown .. 8 8
727. – 8 f.+8 f. green .. 8 8
728. – 12 f.+12 f. brown .. 8 8
729. – 20 f.+20 f. green .. 10 10
730. – 24 f.+24 f. brown .. 12 10
731. – 30 f.+30 f. red .. 15 10

DESIGNS—Statuettes: 8 f. Ladislas on horseback. 20 f. Royal architect. 30 f. King enthroned. King's heads: 12 f. Bela IV. 24 f. Lajos the Great.

92. Prince Arpad.

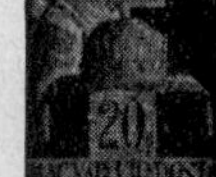
93. St. Stephen's Crown.

1943.

732. **92.** 1 f. grey 5 5
733. – 2 f. orange 5 5
734. – 3 f. blue 5 5
735. – 4 f. brown 5 5
736. – 5 f. red 5 5
737. – 6 f. blue 5 5
738. – 8 f. green 5 5
739. – 10 f. brown 5 5
740. – 12 f. green 5 5
741. – 18 f. black 5 5

742. 93. 20 f. brown 5 5
743. – 24 f. purple 5 5
744. – 30 f. red 5 5
745. 93. 30 f. red 5 5
746. – 50 f. blue 5 5
747. – 80 f. brown 5 5
748. – 1 p. green 5 5
749. – 2 p. brown 5 5
750. – 5 p. purple 5 5

DESIGNS: 2 f. King Ladislas. 3 f. Miklos Toldi. 4 f. Janos Hunyadi. 5 f. Pal Kiniszi. 6 f. Miklos Zrinyi. 8 f. Ferenc Rakoczi II. 10 f. Andre Hadik. 12 f. Artur Gorgey. 18 f. and 24 f. Madonna. 30 f. (No. 744), St. Margaret.

1943. As Nos. 644/8, but new colours and designs.

751. 30 f. red 5 5
752. 40 f. grey 5 5
753. 50 f. blue 5 5
754. 70 f. green 5 5
755. 80 f. brown 5 5

DESIGNS: 30 f. Kassa Cathedral. 40 f. Debreczin Reformed Church. 50 f. Esztergom Basilica. 70 f. Budapest Evangelical Church. 80 f. Buda Cathedral.

94. Mounted Archer. 95. Model Glider.

1943. Wounded Soldiers' Relief Fund. Inscr. as in T 94.

756. 94. 1 f.+1 f. grey .. 5 5
757. – 3 f.+1 f. lilac .. 5 5
758. – 4 f.+1 f. brown .. 5 5
759. – 8 f.+2 f. green .. 5 5
760. – 12 f.+2 f. brown .. 5 5
761. – 20 f.+2 f. brown .. 5 5
762. – 40 f.+4 f. grey .. 5 5
763. – 50 f.+6 f. brown .. 5 5
764. – 70 f.+8 f. blue .. 5 5

DESIGNS—VERT. 3 f., 4 f. Magyar soldier with battle-axe and buckler. 8 f. Warrior with shield and sword. 20 f. Musketeer. 50 f. Artilleryman. 70 f. Magyar Arms. HORIZ. 12 f. Lancer. 40 f. Hussar.

1943. Air. Horthy Aviation Fund. Inscr. "HORTHY MIKLOS NEMZETI REPULO ALAP".

765. 95. 8 f.+8 f. green .. 15 15
766. – 12 f.+12 f. blue .. 15 15
767. – 20 f.+20 f. brown .. 15 15
768. – 30 f.+30 f. red .. 15 15

DESIGNS: 12 f. Gliders in flight. 20 f. Eagle and aeroplanes. 30 f. Aeroplane and gliders.

96. Shepherds and Angels. 97. Nurse and Soldier.

1943. Christmas.

679. 96. 4 f. green 8 8
770. – 20 f. blue 8 8
771. – 30 f. red 8 8

DESIGNS: 20 f. Nativity. 30 f. Adoration of the Wise Men.

1944. Red Cross Funds.

772. 97. 20 f.+20 f. brown .. 5 5
773. – 30 f.+30 f. brown .. 5 5
774. – 50 f.+50 f. purple .. 5 5
775. – 70 f.+70 f. blue .. 5 5

DESIGNS: 30 f. Soldier, nurse, mother and child. 50 f. Nurse shielding a lamp over the Fallen. 70 f. Soldier with crutches, nurse and sapling.

98. Drummer and Flags. 99. St. Elizabeth

1944. Kossuth (statesman). 50th Death Anniv. Inscr. "KOSSUTH".

776. – 4 f. brown 5 5
777. 98. 20 f. green 5 5
778. – 30 f. red 5 5
779. – 50 f. blue 5 5

DESIGNS—VERT. 4 f. Kossuth and family group. 50 f. Portrait. HORIZ. 30 f. Kossuth speaking before an assembly.

1944. Famous Women.

780. 99. 20 f. brown 5 5
781. – 24 f. violet 5 5
782. – 30 f. red 5 5
783. – 50 f. blue 5 5
784. – 70 f. brown 5 5
785. – 80 f. brown 5 5

PORTRAITS: 24 f. St. Margaret. 30 f. Elizabeth Szilagyl. 50 f. Dorothy Kanizsai. 70 f. Susanna Lorantfy. 80 f. Ilona Zrinyi.

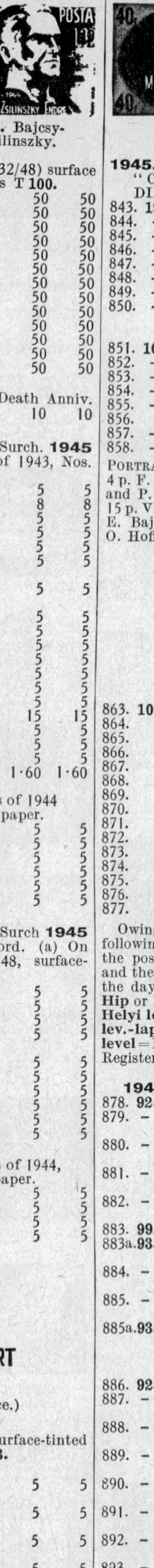

(100. "Felszabadulas" = Liberation.) 101. Bajcsy-Zsilinszky.

1945. Stamps of 1943 (Nos. 732/48) surface tinted papers and surch. as T 100.

786. 10 f. on 1 f. grey .. 50 50
787. 20 f. on 3 f. blue .. 50 50
788. 30 f. on 4 f. brown .. 50 50
789. 40 f. on 6 f. blue .. 50 50
790. 50 f. on 8 f. green .. 50 50
791. 1 p. on 10 f. brown .. 50 50
792. 150 f. on 12 f. green .. 50 50
793. 2 p. on 18 f. black .. 50 50
794. 3 p. on 20 f. brown .. 50 50
795. 5 p. on 24 f. purple .. 50 50
796. 6 p. on 50 f. blue 50 50
797. 10 p. on 80 f. brown .. 50 50
798. 20 p. on 1 p. green .. 50 50

1945. Bajcsy-Zsilinszky. 1st Death Anniv.

799. 101. 1 p.+1 p. purple .. 10 10

1945. Provisionals. 1st issue. Surch. **1945** and value. (a) On stamps of 1943, Nos. 732/50, surface tinted paper.

800. 10 f. on 4 f. brown on blue 5 5
801. 10 f. on 10 f. brown on blue 8 8
802. 10 f. on 12 f. green on yell. 5 5
803. 20 f. on 1 f. grey on yellow 5 5
804. 20 f. on 18 f. black on yell. 5 5
805. 28 f. on 5 f. red on blue .. 5 5
806. 30 f. on 30 f. red on blue (No. 745) 5 5
807. 30 f. on 30 f. red on blue (No. 744) 5 5
808. 40 f. on 24 f. purple on yell. 5 5
809. 42 f. on 20 f. brown on yell. 5 5
810. 50 f. on 50 f. blue on yell. 5 5
811. 60 f. on 8 f. green on yell. 5 5
812. 1 p. on 80 f. brown on blue 5 5
813. 1 p. on 1 p. green on yellow 5 5
814. 150 f. on 6 f. blue on yellow 15 15
815. 2 p. on 2 p. brown on blue 5 5
816. 3 p. on 3 f. blue on yellow 5 5
817. 5 p. on 5 p. purple on yellow 5 5
818. 10 p. on 2 f. orange on blue 1·60 1·60

(b) On Famous Women Series of 1944 (Nos. 780/5). surface-tinted paper.

819. 20 f. on 20 f. brown on blue 5 5
820. 30 f. on 30 f. red on blue .. 5 5
821. 40 f. on 24 f. violet on yell. 5 5
822. 50 f. on 50 f. blue on yellow 5 5
823. 80 f. on 80 f. brown on yell. 5 5
824. 1 p. on 70 f. brown on blue 5 5

1945. Provisionals. 2nd issue. Surch **1945** and value in figures and word. (a) On stamps of 1943, Nos. 732/48, surface-tinted paper.

825. 40 f. on 10 f. brown on blue 5 5
826. 1 p. on 20 f. brown on yell. 5 5
827. 1.60 p. on 12 f. grn. on yell. 5 5
828. 2 p. on 4 f. brown on blue 5 5
829. 4 p. on 30 f. red on blue (No. 745) 5 5
830. 5 p. on 8 f. green on yellow 5 5
831. 6 p. on 50 f. blue on yellow 5 5
832. 7 p. on 1 p. green on yellow 5 5
833. 9 p. on 1 f. grey on yellow 5 5
834. 10 p. on 80 f. brown on blue 5 5

(b) On Famous Women Series of 1944, (Nos. 780/3), surface-tinted paper.

835. 80 f. on 24 f. violet on yell. 5 5
836. 3 p. on 50 f. blue on yellow 5 5
837. 8 p. on 20 f. brown on blue 5 5
838. 20 p. on 30 f. red on blue .. 5 5

BÉKE
3P
A NÉPFŐISKOLÁKÉRT
+9P

(103. "Beke" = Peace.)

1945. Kossuth issue of 1944, surface-tinted paper, surch. as T 103.

839. 98. 3 p.+9 p. on 20 f. green on yellow 5 5
840. – 4 p.+12 p. on 4 f. brown on blue (No. 776) .. 5 5
841. – 8 p.+24 p. on 50 f. blue on yellow (No. 779).. 5 5
842. – 10 p.+30 p. on 30 f. red on blue (No. 778) .. 5 5

The premium was devoted to a National High School Fund.

1945. Provisionals. 3rd issue. Stamps of 1943, Nos. 738/44, surface-tinted paper, surch. **1945** and value in figures and word.

859. 40 p. on 8 f. green on yell. 5 5
860. 60 p. on 18 f. black on yell. 5 5
861. 100 p. on 12 f. green on yell. 5 5
862. 300 p. on 30 f. red on blue (No. 744) 5 5

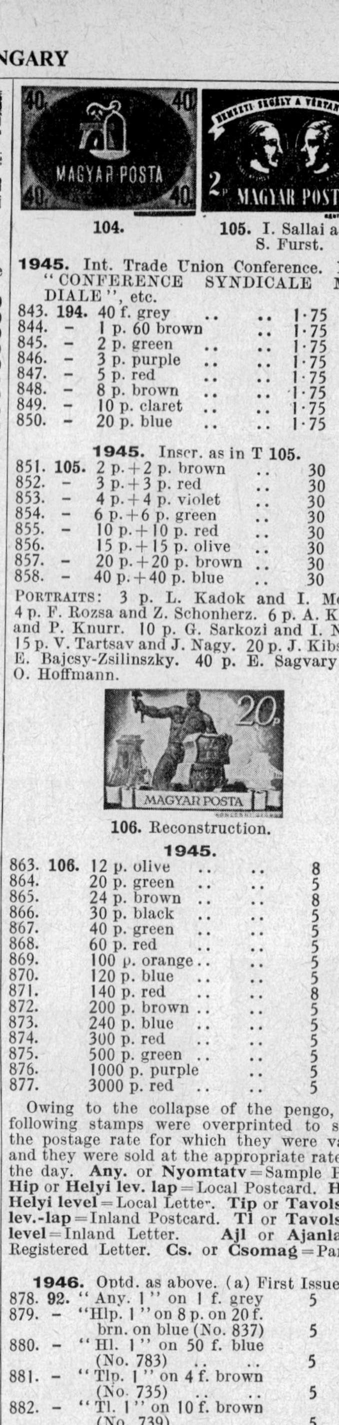

104. 105. I. Sallai and S. Furst.

1945. Int. Trade Union Conference. Inscr. "CONFERENCE SYNDICALE MONDIALE", etc.

843. 194. 40 f. grey .. .. 1·75 1·75
844. – 1 p. 60 brown .. 1·75 1·75
845. – 2 p. green .. .. 1·75 1·75
846. – 3 p. purple .. .. 1·75 1·75
847. – 5 p. red .. .. 1·75 1·75
848. – 8 p. brown .. .. 1·75 1·75
849. – 10 p. claret .. .. 1·75 1·75
850. – 20 p. blue .. .. 1·75 1·75

1945. Inscr. as in T 105.

851. 105. 2 p.+2 p. brown .. 30 30
852. – 3 p.+3 p. red .. 30 30
853. – 4 p.+4 p. violet .. 30 30
854. – 6 p.+6 p. green .. 30 30
855. – 10 p.+10 p. red .. 30 30
856. 15 p.+15 p. olive .. 30 30
857. – 20 p.+20 p. brown .. 30 30
858. – 40 p.+40 p. blue .. 30 30

PORTRAITS: 3 p. L. Kadok and I. Monus. 4 p. F. Rozsa and Z. Schonherz. 6 p. A. Koltoz and P. Knurr. 10 p. G. Sarkozi and I. Nagy. 15 p. V. Tartsav and J. Nagy. 20 p. J. Kibs and E. Bajcsy-Zsilinszky. 40 p. E. Sagvary and O. Hoffmann.

106. Reconstruction.

1945.

863. 106. 12 p. olive 8 8
864. 20 p. green 5 5
865. 24 p. brown 8 8
866. 30 p. black 5 5
867. 40 p. green 5 5
868. 60 p. red 5 5
869. 100 p. orange 5 5
870. 120 p. blue 5 5
871. 140 p. red 8 8
872. 200 p. brown 5 5
873. 240 p. blue 5 5
874. 300 p. red 5 5
875. 500 p. green 5 5
876. 1000 p. purple 5 5
877. 3000 p. red 5 5

Owing to the collapse of the pengo, the following stamps were overprinted to show the postage rate for which they were valid, and they were sold at the appropriate rate for the day. **Any.** or **Nyomtatv** = Sample Post. **Hip** or **Helyi lev. lap** = Local Postcard. **Hl** or **Helyi level** = Local Letter. **Tip** or **Tavolsagi lev.-lap** = Inland Postcard. **Tl** or **Tavolsagi level** = Inland Letter. **Ajl** or **Ajanlas** = Registered Letter. **Cs.** or **Csomag** = Parcel.

1946. Optd. as above. (a) First Issue.

878. 92. "Any. 1" on 1 f. grey 5 5
879. – "Hlp. 1" on 8 p. on 20 f. brn. on blue (No. 837) 5 5
880. – "Hl. 1" on 50 f. blue (No. 783) 5 5
881. – "Tlp. 1" on 4 f. brown (No. 735) 5 5
882. – "Tl. 1" on 10 f. brown (No. 739) 5 5
883. 99. "Ajl. 1" on 20 f. brown 5 5
883a. 93. "Cs. 5-1" on 30 f. red (No. 745) .. .. 1·75 1·75
884. – "Cs. 5-1" on 70 f. brown (No. 784) 5 5
885. – "Cs. 10-1" on 70 f. brn. (No. 784) 5 5
885a. 93. "Cs. 10-1" on 80 f. brn. (No. 747) .. .. 1·75 1·75

(b) Second Issue.

886. 92. "Any. 2" on 1 f. grey 5 5
887. – "Hlp. 2" on 8 p. on 20 f. brn. on blue (No. 837) 5 5
888. – "Hl. 2" on 40 f. on 10 f. brn. on blue (No. 825) 5 5
889. – "Tlp. 2" on 4 f. brown (No. 735) 5 5
890. – "Tl. 2" on 10 f. on 4 f. brn. on blue (No. 800) 5 5
891. – "Ajl. 2" on 12 f. green (No. 740) 5 5
892. – "Cs. 5-2" on 24 f. purple (No. 743) 5 5
893. – "Cs. 10-2" on 80 f. brn. (No. 785) 5 5

(c) Third Issue.

894. – "Nyomtatv 20 gr." on 60 f. on 8 f. green on yellow (No. 811) .. 5 5
895. – "Helyi lev.-lap" on 20 f. brn. on blue (as No. 780) 5 5
896. – "Helyi level" on 10 f. brown on blue (as No. 739) 5 5
897. – "Tavolsagilev.-lap" on 4 f. brown (No. 735) 5 5
898. – "Tavolsagi level" on 18 f. black (No. 741) 5 5
899. – "Ajanlas" on 24 f. violet (No. 781) .. 5 5
900. – "Csomag 5 kg" on 2 p. on 4 f. brn. on blue (No. 828) 5 5
901. – "Csomag 10 kg." on 30 f. red on bl. (as No. 782) 5 5

Abbreviations used in the following issues:
ez.p = thousand pengos.
m.p. = million pengos.
md. p. = thousand million pengos.
b.p. = million million pengos.
ez. ap = thousand "tax" pengos.
m. ap. = million "tax" pengos.

109.

110.

1946. Foundation of Republic.

902. 109. 3 ez. p. brown .. 5 5
903. 15 ez. p. blue 5 5

1946.

904. 110. 4 ez. p. brown .. 5 5
905. 10 ez. p. red 5 5
906. 15 ez. p. blue 5 5
907. 20 ez. p. brown .. 5 5
908. 30 ez. p. purple .. 5 5
909. 50 ez. p. grey .. 5 5
910. 80 ez. p. blue 5 5
911. 100 ez. p. red .. 5 5
912. 160 ez. p. green .. 5 5
913. 200 ez. p. green .. 5 5
914. 500 ez. p. red .. 5 5
915. 640 ez. p. olive .. 5 5
916. 800 ez. p. violet .. 5 5

111.

112.

1946. First Hungarian Stamps. 75th Anniv.

917. 111. 500 ez.p.+500 ez.p. grn. 35 35
918. 1 m.p.+1 m.p. brown 35 35
919. 1.5 m.p.+1.5 m.p. red 35 35
920. 2 m.p.+2 m.p. blue .. 35 35

1946.

921. 112. 1 m.p. red 5 5
922. 2 m.p. blue 5 5
923. 3 m.p. brown.. .. 5 5
924. 4 m.p. grey 5 5
925. 5 m.p. violet 5 5
926. 10 m.p. green 5 5
927. 20 m.p. red 5 5
928. 50 m.p. olive 5 5

113.

114.

115.

1946.

929. 113. 100 m.p. brown .. 5 5
930. 200 m.p. brown .. 5 5
931. 500 m.p. brown .. 5 5
932. 1000 m.p. brown .. 5 5
933. 2000 m.p. brown .. 5 5
934. 3000 m.p. brown .. 5 5
935. 5000 m.p. brown .. 5 5
936. 10,000 m.p. brown .. 5 5
937. 20,000 m.p. brown .. 5 5
938. 30,000 m.p. brown .. 5 5
939. 50,000 m.p. brown .. 5 5
940. 114. 100 md. p. olive & red 5 5
941. 200 md. p. olive & red 5 5
942. 500 md.p. olive & red 5 5
943. 115. 1 b.p. black and red .. 5 5
944. 2 b.p. black and red .. 5 5
945. 5 b.p. black and red .. 5 5
946. 10 b.p black and red .. 5 5
947. 20 b.p. black and red.. 5 5
948. 50 b.p. black and red .. 5 5
949. 100 b.p. black and red 5 5
950. 200 b.p. black and red 5 5
951. 500 b.p. black and red 5 5
952. 1000 b.p. black and red 5 5
953. 10,000 b.p. black & red 5 5
954. 50,000 b.p. black & red 5 5
955. 100,000 b.p. black & red 5 5
956. 500,000 b.p. black & red 5 5

116. "Heves" Locomotive. 117.

1946. Hungarian Railways Centenary.

No.	Type	Description	Unused	Used
957.	116.	10,000 ap. purple	60	60
958.	–	20,000 ap. blue	60	60
959.	–	30,000 ap. green	60	60
960.	–	40,000 ap. red	60	60

DESIGNS: 20,000 ap. 424 Class Steam locomotive. 30,000 ap. Electric locomotive. 40,000 ap. Arpad railcar.

1946.

No.	Type	Description	Unused	Used
961.	117.	5 ez. ap. green & black	5	5
962.		10 ez. ap. green & black	5	5
963.		20 ez. ap. green & black	5	5
964.		50 ez. ap. green & black	5	5
965.		80 ez. ap. green & black	5	5
966.		100 ez. ap. green & blk.	5	5
967.		200 ez. ap. green & blk.	5	5
968.		500 ez. ap. green & blk.	5	5
969.		1 m. ap. red and black	5	5
970.		5 m. ap. red and black	5	5

118. "Industry". 119. "Agriculture".

1946.

No.	Type	Description	Unused	Used
971.	118.	8 fi. brown	5	5
972.		10 fi. brown	5	5
973.		12 fi. brown	5	5
974.		20 fi. brown	5	5
975.		30 fi. brown	5	5
976.		40 fi. brown	5	5
977.		60 fi. brown	10	5
978.	119.	1 fo. green	20	5
979.		1 fo. 40 green	25	5
980.		2 fo. green	35	5
981.		3 fo. green	70	5
982.		5 fo. green	1·00	5
983.		10 fo. green	2·50	25

120. Ceres. 121. Liberty Bridge.

1946. Agricultural Fair.

No.	Type	Description	Unused	Used
984.	120.	30 fi.+60 fi. green	1·00	1·00
985.		60 fi.+1 fo. 20 red	1·00	1·00
986.		1 fo.+2 fo. blue	1·00	1·00

1947. Air. Views.

No.	Type	Description	Unused	Used
987.	–	10 fi. red	5	5
988.	–	20 fi. green	5	5
989.	121.	50 fi. brown	10	5
990.	–	70 fi. olive	15	5
991.	–	1 fo. blue	20	5
992.	–	1 fo. 40 brown	35	10
993.	–	3 fo. green	60	8
994.	–	5 fo. lilac	1·10	40

DESIGNS—VERT. 10 fi. Loyalty Tower, Sopron. 20 fi. Esztergom Cathedral. 70 fi. Palace Hotel, Lillafured. 1 fo. Vajdahunyad Castle, Budapest. 1 fo. 40, Visegrad Fortress. 3 fo. Yacht on Lake Balaton. 5 fo. Parliament Buildings and Kossuth Bridge.

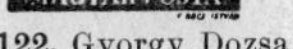

122. Gyorgy Dozsa. 123. Doctor Examining X-Ray Photograph.

1947. Liberty issue.

No.	Type	Description	Unused	Used
995.	122.	8 fi. red	5	5
996.	–	10 fi. blue	5	5
997.	–	12 fi. brown	5	5
998.	–	20 fi. green	5	5
999.	–	30 fi. brown	5	5
1000.	–	40 fi. maroon	5	5
1001.	–	60 fi. red	8	5
1002.	–	1 fo. blue	15	5
1003.	–	2 fo. violet	40	5
1004.	–	4 fo. green	80	12

PORTRAITS: 10 fi. A. Budai Nagy. 12 fi. T. Esze. 20 fi. I. Martinovics. 30 fi. J. Batsanyi. 40 fi. L. Kossuth. 60 fi. M. Tancsics. 1 fo. S. Petofi. 2 fo. E. Ady. 4 fo. A. Jozsef.

1947. Blood Donors' Fund. Inscr. "SIESS! ADJ! SEGITS!" (trans. "Come! Give! Help!").

No.	Type	Description	Unused	Used
1005.	–	8 fi.+50 fi. blue	80	80
1006.	123.	12 fi.+50 fi. brown	80	80
1007.	–	20 fi.+50 fi. green	80	80
1008.	–	60 fi.+50 fi. red	80	80

DESIGNS: 8 fi. Doctor testing syringe. 20 fi. Nurse and child. 60 fi. Released prisoner-of-war.

124. Emblem of Peace. 125. "Liberty".

1947. Peace Treaty.

No.	Type	Description	Unused	Used
1009.	124.	60 fi. red	15	10

1947. Soviet Union and Hungarian-Soviet Cultural Society Fund. 30th Anniv.

No.	Type	Description	Unused	Used
1010.	–	40 fi.+40 fi. brn. & grn.	1·75	1·75
1011.	125.	60 fi.+60 fi. grey & red	70	70
1012.	–	1 fo.+1 fo. blk. & blue	1·75	1·75

PORTRAITS: 40 fi. Lenin. 1 fo. Stalin.

126. Savings Bank. 127. XVIth Century Mail Coach.

1947. Savings Day. Type 126 and design inscr. "TAKAREKOS JELENBOLDOG JOVO".

No.	Type	Description	Unused	Used
1013.	–	40 fi. claret (beehive)	10	5
1014.	126.	60 fi. red	12	5

1947. Stamp Day.

No.	Type	Description	Unused	Used
1015.	127.	30 fi. (+50 fi.) brn.	3·00	3·00

128. Arms of Hungary. 129. John Gutenberg.

1948. Centenary of Insurrection.

No.	Type	Description	Unused	Used
1016.	–	8 fi. red	5	5
1017.	–	10 fi. blue	5	5
1018.	–	12 fi. brown	5	5
1019.	–	20 fi. green	15	5
1020.	–	30 fi. brown	5	5
1021.	–	40 fi. purple	8	5
1022.	–	60 fi. red	15	5
1023.	128.	1 fo. blue	15	5
1024.		2 fo. brown	35	5
1025.		3 fo. green	60	8
1026.		4 fo. red	75	12

DESIGNS—HORIZ. 8 fi., 40 fi. Hungarian flag. 10 fi. Printing press. 12 fi. Latticed window. 20 fi. Shako, trumpet and sword. 30 fi., 60 fi. Slogan.

1948. Air. Explorers and Inventors.

No.	Type	Description	Unused	Used
1027.	129.	1 fi. red	5	5
1028.	–	2 fi. mauve	5	5
1029.	–	4 fi. blue	5	5
1030.	–	5 fi. brown	8	8
1031.	–	6 fi. green	8	8
1032.	–	8 fi. purple	8	8
1033.	–	10 fi. brown	10	10
1034.	–	12 fi. green	25	25
1035.	–	30 fi. red	25	25
1036.	–	40 fi. violet	30	30

PORTRAITS: 2 fi. Christopher Columbus. 4 fi. Robert Fulton. 5 fi. George Stephenson. 6 fi. David Schwarz and Count Ferdinand von Zeppelin. 8 fi. Thomas Edison. 10 fi. Louis Bleriot. 12 fi. Ronald Amundsen. 30 fi. Kalman Kando. 40 fi. Alexander Popov.

130. Lorand Eotvos.

1948. L. Eotvos (physicist). Birth Cent.

No.	Type	Description	Unused	Used
1037.	130.	60 fi. red	10	8

131. William Shakespeare.

PORTRAITS: 2 fi. Voltaire. 4 fi. Goethe. 5 fi. Byron. 6 fi. Victor Hugo. 8 fi. Edgar Allan Poe. 10 fi. Petofi. 12 fi. Mark Twain. 30 fi. Tolstoy. 40 fi. Gorki.

1948. Air. Writers.

No.	Type	Description	Unused	Used
1038.	131.	1 fi. blue	5	5
1039.	–	2 fi. red	5	5
1040.	–	4 fi. green	5	5
1041.	–	5 fi. magenta	8	8
1042.	–	6 fi. blue	8	8
1043.	–	8 fi. brown	8	8
1044.	–	10 fi. red	10	10
1045.	–	12 fi. violet	20	20
1046.	–	30 fi. brown	25	25
1047.	–	40 fi. brown	35	35

132. Symbolizing the Post. 133. Symbolizing Industry, Agriculture and Art.

1948. 5th National Philatelic Exn.

No.	Type	Description	Unused	Used
1048.	132.	30 fi. blue	1·00	1·00

Sold at 1 fo. 30 (incl. 1 fo. entrance fee).

1948. 17th Trades' Union Congress.

No.	Type	Description	Unused	Used
1049.	133.	30 fi. red	10	10

134. Agricultural Worker. 135. Reproduction of T 15.

1949. Int. Women's Day.

No.	Type	Description	Unused	Used
1050.	134.	60 fi.+60 fi. mve.	30	25

1949. Bolshevist Regime. 30th Anniv.

No.	Type	Description	Unused	Used
1051.	135.	40 fi. brown and red	12	10
1052.	–	60 fi. olive and red	20	10

DESIGN: 60 fi. Reproduction of No. 325.

136. Pushkin holding Torch and Scroll. 137. Symbolising Workers of Five Continents.

1949. A. S. Pushkin (poet). 150th Birth Anniv.

No.	Type	Description	Unused	Used
1053.	136.	1 fo.+1 fo. red	90	90

1949. 2nd Trades' Union Congress. Flag in red.

No.	Type	Description	Unused	Used
1054.	137.	30 fi. brown	55	55
1055.		40 fi. purple	55	55
1056.		60 fi. red	55	55
1057.		1 fo. blue	55	55

138. Petofi. 139. Heads and Globe.

1949. Petofi. (poet). Death Cent.

No.	Type	Description	Unused	Used
1058.	138.	40 fi. purple	8	5
1096.		40 fi. brown	5	5
1059.		60 fi. red	10	5
1097.		60 fi. pink	10	5
1060.		1 fo. blue	15	8
1098.		1 fo. green	20	8

1949. World Youth Festival, Budapest.

No.	Type	Description	Unused	Used
1061.	139.	20 fi. brown	10	10
1062.	–	30 fi. green	10	10
1063.	–	40 fi. bistre	10	10
1064.	–	60 fi. red	10	10
1065.	–	1 fo. blue	20	20

DESIGNS: 30 fi. Three clenched fists. 40 fi. Man breaking chains. 60 fi. Young people and banner. 1 fo. Workers and tractor.

140. Hungarian Coat of Arms.

IMPERF. STAMPS. Many Hungarian stamps from No. 1069 onwards exist imperf. from limited printings.

1949. Ratification of Constitution. Arms in blue, brown, red and green.

No.	Type	Description	Unused	Used
1066.	140.	20 fi. green	20	20
1067.		60 fi. red	15	15
1068.		1 fo. blue	20	20

141. Globes & Posthorn. 142. Chain Bridge.

1949. U.P.U. 75th Anniv.

No.	Type	Description	Unused	Used
1069.	141.	60 fi. red (postage)	15	12
1070.		1 fo. blue	25	20
1071.	–	2 fo. brown (air)	35	30

DESIGN: 2 fo., Aeroplane.

1949. Re-opening of Budapest Chain Bridge.

No.	Type	Description	Unused	Used
1073.	142.	40 fi. green (postage)	8	5
1074.		60 fi. brown	10	8
1075.		1 fo. blue	12	10
1076.		1 fo. 60 red (air)	25	20
1077.		2 fo. olive	25	25

143. Joseph Stalin. 144. Postman and Mail Transport.

1949. Stalin's 70th Birthday.

No.	Type	Description	Unused	Used
1079.	143.	60 fi. red	12	10
1080.		1 fo. blue	20	15
1081.		2 fo. brown	40	35

1949. Air. Stamp Day.

No.	Type	Description	Unused	Used
1078.	144.	50 fi. grey	90	90

145. Miners.

1950. Five Year Plan. Inscr. "5 EVES TERV".

No.	Type	Description	Unused	Used
1082.	145.	8 fi. grey	5	5
1083.	–	10 fi. claret	5	5
1084.	–	12 fi. orange	5	5
1085.	–	20 fi. green	5	5
1086.	–	30 fi. magenta	5	5
1087.	–	40 fi. sepia	8	5
1088.	–	60 fi. red	12	5
1089.	–	1 fo. violet and yellow	15	5
1090.	–	1 fo. 70 green & yell.	35	5
1091.	–	2 fo. claret and yellow	45	5
1092.	–	3 fo. blue and yellow	50	5
1093.	–	4 fo. olive and pink	70	10
1094.	–	5 fo. purple and yellow	90	12
1095.	–	10 fo. brn. and yellow	1·40	25

DESIGNS—HORIZ. 10 fi. Iron foundry. 12 fi. Power station. 20 fi. Textiles. 30 fi. Factory workers' entertainment. 40 fi. Mechanical farming. 60 fi. Village co-operative office. 1 fo. Train on bridge. 1 fo. 70, Family at health resort. 2 fo. Soldier and tank. 3 fo. Steamer and aeroplane. 4 fo. Cattle. 5 fo. Draughtsman and factory. 10 fo. Sportsman, woman and football match.

146. Philatelic Museum.

DESIGN—HORIZ. 2 fo. Globe, mail-coach and stamps.

1950. P.O. Philatelic Museum. 20th Anniv. Inscr. "XX EVES A BELYEGMU. ZEUM". (a) Postage.

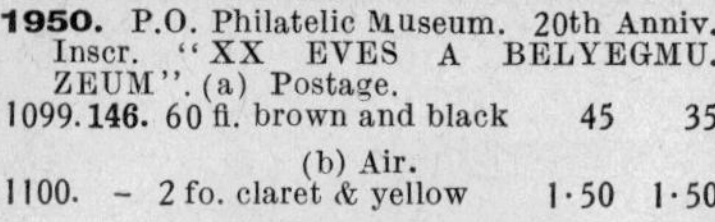

1099.	146.	60 fi. brown and black	45	35
		(b) Air.		
1100.	–	2 fo. claret & yellow	1·50	1·50

147. Greeting Soviet Troops.

1950. Liberation. 5th Anniv.

1101.	147.	40 fi. black	15	12
1102.		60 fi. lake	8	5
1103.		1 fo. blue	15	12
1104		2 fo. brown	30	20

148. Chess Match.

DESIGNS; 1 fo. Trade Union Building. 1 fo. 60, Map.

1950. World Chess Championship, Budapest. Designs incorporate castle and chessboard.

1105.	148.	60 fi. magenta (postage)	12	10
1106.	–	1 fo. blue	15	12
1107.	–	1 fo. 60 brn. (air) ..	35	35

149. Workers and Star.

DESIGN: 60 fi. Two workers.

1950. May Day. Inscr as in T 149.

1108.	149.	40 fi. brown	8	5
1109.	–	60 fi. red	5	5
1110.	149.	1 fo. blue	30	12

150. Workers and Flag.

DESIGNS: 40 fi. Statue, dove and globes. 1 fo. Globes, Chain Bridge and Parliament Bldgs.

1950. Federation of Trade Unions, Budapest.

1111.	–	40 fi. green (postage)	8	5
1112.	150.	60 fi. red	15	8
1113.	–	1 fo. brown (air) ..	20	8

151. Baby and Nursery.

DESIGNS: 30 fi. Baby boy and holiday scene. 40 fi. Schoolgirl and classroom. 60 fi. Pioneer boy and camp. 1 fo. 70, Pioneer boy and girl and model glider class.

1950. Children's Day.

1114.	151.	20 fi. grey and brown	15	12
1115.	–	30 fi. brown & purple	10	8
1116.	–	40 fi. blue and green ..	10	5
1117.	–	60 fi. brown and red	32·00	32·00
1117a.	–	60 fi. brown and red ..	8	5
1118.	–	1 fo. 70 green and blue	30	15

No. 1117 is inscr. "UTANPOTLASUNK A JOVO HARCAIHOZ" and No. 1117a is inscr. "SZABAD HAZABAN BOLDOG IFJUSAG".

152. Workers and Globe.

DESIGNS: — HORIZ. 30 fi. Foundry worker and cauldron. VERT. 40 fi. Man, woman and banner, 60 fi. Group at Liberty Statue. 1 fo. 70, Agricultural students.

1950. 1st Young Workers' Congress. Inscr. "BUDAPEST 1950. VI. 17–18".

1119.	152.	20 fi. green	12	12
1120.	–	30 fi. orange	5	5
1121.	–	40 fi. brown	5	5
1122.	–	60 fi. claret	8	5
1123.	–	1 fo. 70 black ..	20	8

153. Peonies.

154. Miner.

1950. Flowers.

1124.	153.	30 fi. purple and green	15	8
1125.	–	40 fi. grn., yell. & mve.	20	12
1126.	–	60 fi. brn., yell. & grn.	25	15
1127.	–	1 fo. vio. red & green	70	40
1128.	–	1 fo. 70 vio., mve., & grn.	75	50

DESIGNS: 40 fi. Anemones. 60 fi. "Adonis vernalis". 1 fo. Geranium. 1 fo. 70, Campanulas.

1950. 2nd National Industrial Exn. Inscr. "II ORSZAGOS UJITOKIALLITAS 1950".

1129.	154.	40 fi. brown	5	5
1130.	–	60 fi. red	8	8
1131.	–	1 fo. blue	25	15

DESIGNS: 60 fi. Turner and lathe. 1 fo. Factory construction.

155. Liberty Statue.

156. Tractor.

1950. Air.

1132.	155.	20 fi. claret	5	5
1133.	–	30 fi. violet	5	5
1134.	–	70 fi. purple	10	5
1135.	156.	1 fo. brown	12	5
1136.	–	1 fo. 60 blue	20	5
1137.	–	2 fo. red	25	5
1138.	–	3 fo. black	40	12
1139.	–	5 fo. blue	65	25
1140.	–	10 fo. chestnut ..	2·50	50
1140a.	–	20 fo. green	3·00	2·25

DESIGNS—VERT. 30 fi. Crane and buildings. 70 fi. Diosgyor steelworks. 1 fo. 60 Ship. 2 fo. Combine harvester. 3 fo. 303 Class steam loco. 5 fo. Matyas Rakosi works. 10 fo., 20 fo. Aeroplane at Budaors airport.

For No. 1139 but on silver paper see No. 1437.

157. Signing Peace Petition.

158. Swimmers.

1950. Peace Propaganda.

1141.	157.	40 fi. brown and blue	90	90
1142.	–	60 fi. green & orange	90	90
1143.	–	1 fo. brown and green	2·50	2·50

DESIGNS—VERT. 60 fi. Girl holding dove. HORIZ. 1 fo. Soldier, mother and children.

1950.

1144.	158.	10 fi. blue (postage) ..	5	5
1145.	–	20 fi. brown and orange	5	5
1146.	–	1 fo. green and olive ..	20	15
1147.	–	1 fo. 70 lake & orange	30	30
1148.	–	2 fo. violet and brown	55	55
1149.	–	30 fi. mauve & vio. (air)	5	5
1150.	–	40 fi. blue and olive ..	10	10
1151.	–	60 fi. orge., brn. & olive	12	12
1152.	–	70 fi. brown and grey	25	20
1153.	–	3 fo. brown	55	55

DESIGNS—POSTAGE: 20 fi. Vaulting. 1 fo. Mountaineering. 1 fo. 70, Basket-ball. 2 fo. Motorcycling. AIR: 30 fi. Volleyball. 40 fi. Throwing the javelin. 60 fi. Emblem of "Ready for work and action" movement. 70 fi. Football. 3 fo. Gliding.

159. Battle of Piski.

160. Partisans.

1950. Gen. Bem. Death Cent.

1154.	159.	40 fi. brown	5	5
1155.		60 fi. red	12	5
1156.		1 fo. blue	20	10

1951. 2nd Communist Party Conf.

1157.	160.	10 fi. green	5	5
1158.	–	30 fi. brown	5	5
1159.	–	60 fi. red	10	5
1160.	–	1 fo. blue	15	5

DESIGNS—HORIZ. 30 fi. Workers, soldier and banner. 60 fi. Portrait and four workers with flags. VERT. 1 fo. Procession with banner.

161. Flags.

162. Mare and Foal.

1951. Hungarian-Soviet Amity. Inscr. "MAGYAR SZOVJET BARATSAG HONAPJA 1951".

1161.	161.	60 fi. red	10	5
1162.	–	1 fo. violet	20	10

DESIGN: 1 fo. Hungarian and Russian workers.

1951. Livestock Expansion Plan. Dated "1952".

1163.	162.	10 fi. pur. & brn. (post.)	5	5
1164.	–	30 fi. brown and purple	12	12
1165.	–	40 fi. brown and green	15	15
1166.	–	60 fi. brown and orange	20	20
1167.	162.	20 fi. pur. & grn. (air)	8	8
1168.	–	70 fi. brn. & red-brn.	25	25
1169.	–	1 fo. brn. and blue ..	45	45
1170.	–	1 fo. 60 red-brn. & brn.	70	70

DESIGNS—HORIZ. 30 fi., 70 fi. Sow and litter. 40 fi., 1 fo. Ewe and lamb. 60 fi., 1 fo. 60 Cow and calf.

163. Worker.

DESIGNS — VERT. 60 fi. People with banners. HORIZ. 1 fo. Labour Day rally.

1951. May Day. Inscr. "1951 MAJUS".

1171.	163.	40 fi. brown	5	5
1172.	–	60 fi. red	10	5
1173.	–	1 fo. blue	20	8

164. Leo Frankel.

165. Street-fighting.

1951. Paris Commune. 80th Anniv.

1174.	164.	60 fi. brown	10	5
1175.	165.	1 fo. red and blue ..	20	5

166. Children's Heads.

167. Ganz Wagon Workshops.

1951. Int. Children's Day. Inscr. "NEMZETKOZI GYERMEKNAP 1951".

1176.	166.	30 fi. brown	5	5
1177.	–	40 fi. green	5	5
1178.	–	50 fi. brown	10	5
1179.	–	60 fi. magenta ..	12	5
1180.	–	1 fo. 70 fi. blue ..	25	20

DESIGNS: 40 fi. Flying model aeroplane. 50 fi. Crossing the road. 60 fi. Chemistry experiment. 1 fo. 70 fi. Boy bugler.

1951. Rebuilding Plan. (1st issue).

1180a.	–	8 fi. green	5	5
1180b.	–	10 fi. violet	5	5
1180c.	–	12 fi. red	5	5
1181.	167.	20 fi. green	5	5
1182.	–	30 fi. orange	5	5
1183.	–	40 fi. brown	10	5
1183a.	–	50 fi. blue	12	5
1184.	–	60 fi. red	15	5
1184a.	–	70 fi. brown	20	5
1184b.	–	80 fi. purple	25	5
1185.	–	1 fo. blue	25	5
1185a.	–	1 fo. 20 red	30	5
1185b.	–	1 fo. 70 blue ..	60	5
1185c.	–	2 fo. green	70	5
1186.	–	3 fo. purple	75	5
1186a.	–	4 fo. olive	1·10	5
1186b.	–	5 fo. black	1·25	5

BUILDINGS: 8 fi. Stalin School. 10 fi. Szekesfehervar terminus. 12 fi. Ujpest medical dispensary. 30 fi. Flats. 40 fi. Budapest terminus. 50 fi. Inota power station. 60 fi. Matyas Rakosi Cultural Institute. 70 fi. Hajdunanas elevator. 80 fi. Tiszalsk dam. 1 fo. Kilian Road School. 1 fo. 20, Mining Apprentices Institute, Ajkacsingervolgy. 1 fo. 70, Iron and Steel Apprentices Institute, Csepel. 2 fo. Cultural Centre, Hungarian Optical Works. 3 fo. Building Workers' Union Headquarters. 4 fo. Miners' Union Headquarters. 5 fo. Flats.

See also Nos. 1296/304.

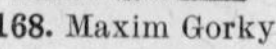

168. Maxim Gorky.

169. Engineers and Tractors.

1951. Gorky (author). 15th Death Anniv.

1187.	168.	60 fi. red	8	5
1188.		1 fo. blue	12	5
1189.		2 fo. purple	30	12

1951. Five Year Plan. 1st Anniv.

1190.	169.	20 fi. sepia (postage)	5	5
1191.	–	30 fi. blue	5	5
1192.	–	40 fi. red	8	5
1193.	–	60 fi. chestnut ..	10	5
1194.	–	70 fi. brown (air) ..	8	5
1195.	–	1 fo. green	25	12
1196.	–	2 fo. purple	65	25

DESIGNS: 30 fi. Patient being X-rayed. 40 fi. Workman instructing apprentices. 60 fi. Girl driving tractor. 70 fi. Electricians constructing pylon. 1 fo. Country recreation scene. 2 fo. Aeroplane over Stalin Bridge.

170. 1871 Stamp without portrait and Hungarian Arms.

171. Soldiers Parading.

173. Revolutionaries and Flags.

172. Lily of the Valley.

1951. 1st Hungarian Postage Stamp. 80th Anniv.

1197.	170.	60 fi. green	35	35
1198.		1 fo. + 1 fo. red ..	1·75	1·75
1199.		2 fo. + 2 fo. blue ..	3·00	3·00

1951. Army Day.

1200.	171.	1 fo. brown (postage)	20	8
1201.	–	60 fi. blue (air) ..	12	8

DESIGN—VERT. 60 fi. Tanks and Liberty Statue.

1951. Flowers.

1202.	–	30 fi. violet, bl. & grn.	8	5
1203.	172.	40 fi. myrtle & green	20	15
1204.	–	60 fi. clar., pink & grn.	15	10
1205.	–	1 fo. blue, red & green	30	12
1206.	–	1 fo. 70 brown, yellow and green	50	15

FLOWERS: 30 fi. Cornflowers. 60 fi. Tulips. 1 fo. Poppies. 1 fo. 70, Cowslips.

1951. Russian Revolution. 34th Anniv. Inscr. "A NAGY SZOCIALISTA" etc.

1207.	173.	40 fi. green	8	5
1208.	–	60 fi. blue	10	5
1209.	–	1 fo. claret	15	10

DESIGNS: 60 fi. Lenin addressing revolutionaries. 1 fo. Lenin, Stalin and Spasski Tower, Kremlin.

174. Stalin Statue, Budapest.

1951. Stalin's 72nd Birthday.

1210.	174.	60 fi. red	10	5
1211.		1 fo. blue	20	12

DESIGNS: 1 fo. Lenin Mausoleum. 1 fo. 60, Kremlin.

175. Bolshoi Theatre, Moscow.

1952. Views of Moscow.
1212. 175. 60 fl. lake and green .. 12 5
1213. – 1 fo. brown and claret 20 12
1214. – 1 fo. 60 olive and lake 30 15

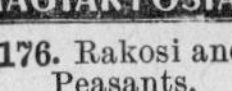

176. Rakosi and Peasants. 177. Rakosi.

1952. Rakosi. 60th Birth Anniv.
1215. 176. 60 fl. purple 8 5
1216. 177. 1 fo. brown 12 5
1217. – 2 fo. blue 30 20
DESIGN: 2 fo. Rakosi and foundry workers.

178. L. Kossuth.

1952. Heroes of 1848 Revolution.
1218. 178. 20 fl. green 5 5
1219. – 30 fl. purple (Petofi) .. 5 5
1220. – 50 fl. black (Bem) .. 8 5
1221. – 60 fl. lake (Tancsics) 10 5
1222. – 1 fo. bl. (Danyanich) 15 10
1223. – 1 fo. 50 brn. (Nagy) .. 25 15

179. Avocet.

1952. Air. Birds as T 179. Centres in black.
1224. 20 fl. emerald (T 179) .. 5 5
1225. 30 fl. green (Stork) .. 5 5
1226. 40 fl. yellow brown (Golden Oriole) .. 8 5
1227. 50 fl. orge. (Plover) .. 10 5
1228. 60 fl. red (Stilt) 15 8
1229. 70 fl. red orange (Lesser Grey Shrike) .. 15 8
1230. 80 fl. olive (Bustard) .. 20 8
1231. 1 fo. red & blue (Falcon) 20 12
1232. 1 fo. 40 brn., grn. & grey (Bee-eater) .. 25 15
1233. 1 fo. 60 grn. & brn. (Ibis) 30 20
1234. 2 fo. 50 purple (Heron) .. 60 35

1952. Budapest Philatelic Exn. and Int. Women's Day. No. 1050 with bars obliterating inscription and premium.
1235. 134. 60 fl. mauve .. .. 8·00 8·00

DESIGNS: 60 fl. Workers. 1 fo. Workman and globe.

180. Drummer and Flags.

1952. May Day. Inscr. "1952 MAJUS I".
1236. 180. 40 fl. red and green .. 5 5
1237. – 60 fl. red and brown 12 5
1238. – 1 fo. red and brown 15 12

181. Running.

1952. Olympic Games, Helsinki.
1239. 181. 30 fl. brown (postage) 10 5
1240. – 40 fl. green 12 5
1241. – 60 fl. red 15 5
1242. – 1 fo. blue 25 12
1243. – 1 fo. 70 orange (air) .. 35 20
1244. – 2 fo. bistre 50 25
DESIGNS: 40 fl. Swimming. 60 fl. Fencing. 1 fo. Gymnastics. 1 fo. 70, Throwing the hammer. 2 fo. Stadium.

182 Leonardo da Vinci. 183. Train and Railwayman.

184. Mechanical Coal-cutter. 185. L. Kossuth (Statesman).

1952. Air. Peace Propaganda.
1245. 182. 1 fo. 60 blue 20 10
1246. – 2 fo. pur. (Victor Hugo) 30 15

1952. Railway Day. Inscr. "1952 VIII 10".
1247. 183. 60 fl. brown 12 5
1248. – 1 fo. green 15 8
DESIGN: 1 fo. Railway tracks.

1952. Miners' Day. Inscr. as in T 184.
1249. 184. 60 fl. brown 12 5
1250. – 1 fo. green 15 8
DESIGN: 1 fo. Miners operating machinery.

1952. Kossuth. 150th Birth Anniv.
1251. 185. 40 fl. olive on pink .. 8 5
1252. – 60 fl. black on blue .. 8 5
1253. 185. 1 fo. lilac on yellow .. 15 10
DESIGN: 60 fl. Statue of Kossuth.

186. G. Dozsa. 187. Boy, Girl and Stamp Exhibition.

1952. Army Day. Inscr. as T 186.
1254. 20 fl. lilac (J. Hunyadi) .. 5 5
1255. 30 fl. green (T 186) .. 5 5
1256. 40 fl. blue (M. Zrinyi) .. 5 5
1257. 60 fl. purple (I. Zrinyi) .. 12 5
1258. 1 fo. blue-green (B. Vak) 20 8
1259. 1 fo. 50, brn. (A. Stromfeld) 30 15

1952. Air. Stamp Day. Inscr. "XXV. BELYEGNAP 1952".
1260. – 1 fo. + 1 fo. blue .. 60 60
1261. 187. 2 fo. + 2 fo. red .. 80 80
DESIGN: 1 fo. Children examining stamps.

188. Lenin and Revolutionary Council. 189. Harvester.

1952. Russian Revolution. 35th Anniv. Inscr. "A NAGY SZOCIALISTA".
1262. 188. 40 fl. olive and purple 5 5
1263. – 60 fl. olive and black 10 5
1264. – 1 fo. olive and red .. 15 10
DESIGNS: 60 fl. Stalin and Cossacks. 1 fo. Marx, Engels, Lenin, Stalin and Spasski Tower.

1952. 3rd Hungarian Peace Congress. Inscr. as in T 189.
1265. 189. 60 fl. red on yellow .. 12 5
1266. – 1 fo. brown on green 20 10
DESIGN—HORIZ. 1 fo. Workers' discussion group.

DESIGN — HORIZ. 1 fo. Underground map and station.

190. Tunnel Construction.

1953. Budapest Underground Railway. Inscr. "BUDAPESTI FOLDALATTI GYORSVASUT".
1267. 190. 60 fl. green 12 5
1268. – 1 fo. lake 25 10

191. Russian Flag and Tank. 192. Red Squirrel.

1953. Battle of Stalingrad. 10th Anniv. Inscr. "1943–1953".
1269. 191. 40 fl. red 8 5
1270. – 60 fl. brown 15 12
DESIGN: 60 fl. Soldier, map and flags.

1953. Air. Wild Animals.
1271. 192. 20 fl. brn. and olive .. 8 8
1272. – 30 fl. sepia & chest. .. 10 10
1273. – 40 fl. sepia & green .. 15 12
1274. – 50 fl. sepia & brown .. 15 12
1275. – 60 fl. brn. & blue-grn. 20 15
1276. – 70 fl. brn. and olive 25 20
1277. – 80 fl. brn. & green .. 35 30
1278. – 1 fo. brn. & green .. 45 40
1279. – 1 fo. 50, blk. & bistre 60 50
1280. – 2 fo. sepia & chest. .. 75 60
DESIGNS—HORIZ. 30 fl. Hedgehog. 40 fl. Hare. 60 fl. Otter. 70 fl. Fox. 1 fo. Roebuck. 1 fo. 50, Wild boar. VERT. 50 fl. Marten. 80 fl. Fallow deer. 2 fo. Red deer.

193. Stalin. 194. Rest Home, Galyateto.

1953. Death of Stalin.
1281. 193. 60 fl. black 15 12

1953. Workers' Rest Homes.
1282. 194. 30 fl. chestnut (post.) 5 5
1283. – 40 fl. blue 5 5
1284. – 50 fl. ochre 8 5
1285. – 60 fl. green 8 5
1286. – 70 fl. red 10 5
1287. – 1 fo. blue-green (air) .. 15 5
1288. – 1 fo. 50, purple .. 20 10
DESIGNS: 40 fl. Terrace, Mecsek. 50 fl. Parad Spa. 60 fl. Sports field, Kekes. 70 fl. Balatonfured Spa. 1 fo. Children paddling at Balaton. 1 fo. 50, Lillafured Rest Home.

195. Young People and Banner. 196. Karl Marx.

1953. May Day.
1289. 195. 60 fl. brn. & red on yell. 12 10

1953. Karl Marx. 70th Death Anniv.
1290. 196. 1 fo. black on flesh .. 15 10
See also No. 2354.

197. Peasants and Flag.

1953. Rakoczi Rebellion. 250th Anniv. Inscr. "1703".
1291. 197. 20 fl. orange & green on green 20 12
1292. – 30 fl. orange and lake 25 15
1293. – 40 fl. orange and blue on flesh .. 35 20
1294. – 60 fl. orange and olive on yellow .. 45 25
1295. – 1 fo. red and brown on yellow .. 65 40
DESIGNS: 30 fl. Drummer and insurgents. 40 fl. Battle scene. 60 fl. Cavalryman attacking soldier. 1 fo. Ferenc Rakoczi II.

1953. Rebuilding Plan. (2nd issue). As T 167.
1296. 8 fl. green 5 5
1297. 10 fl. lilac 5 5
1298. 12 fl. red 5 5
1299. 20 fl. green 5 5
1300. 30 fl. orange 8 5
1301. 40 fl. brown 10 5
1302. 50 fl. indigo 15 10
1303a. 60 fl. red 5 5
1304. 70 fl. brown 20 5
BUILDINGS: 8 fl. Day Nursery, Ozd. 10 fl. Nursing school, Szombathely. 12 fl. Workers' houses, Komlo. 20 fl. Department store, Ujpest. 30 fl. Factory, Maly. 40 fl. General Hospital, Fovaros. 50 fl. Gymnasium, Sztalinvaros. 60 fl. Post Office, Csepel. 70 fl. Blastfurnace, Diosgyor.

198. Cycling.

1953. Opening of People's Stadium. Budapest. Inscr. "1953 NEPSTADION".
1313. 198. 20 fl. brown & orange (postage) .. 5 5
1314. – 30 fl. brown & green 8 5
1315. – 40 fl. brown and blue 10 5
1316. – 50 fl. brown and olive 12 8
1317. – 60 fl. brown & yellow 15 10
1318. – 80 fl. brn. & turq. (air) 20 10
1319. – 1 fo. brn. & purple .. 25 12
1320. – 2 fo. brn. & green .. 55 30
1321. – 3 fo. brn. and red .. 75 45
1322. – 5 fo. turq. & brn. .. 1·25 70
DESIGNS: 30 fl. Swimming. 40 fl. Gymnastics 50 fl. Throwing the discus. 60 fl. Wrestling. 80 fl. Water polo. 1 fo. Boxing. 2 fo. Football. 3 fo. Running. 5 fo. Stadium.

199. Kazar. 200. Postwoman Delivering Letters.

1953. Girls wearing provincial costumes.
1323. 199. 20 fl. green 15 5
1324. – 30 fl. brown 25 10
1325. – 40 fl. blue 30 10
1326. – 60 fl. red 45 15
1327. – 1 fo. turquoise .. 90 35
1328. – 1 fo. 70 green .. 1·50 65
1329. – 2 fo. red .. .. 2·00 1·00
1330. – 2 fo. 50 purple .. 3·50 2·50
PROVINCES: 30 fl. Ersekcsanad. 40 fl. Kalocsa. 60 fl. Sioegard. 1 fo. Sarkoz. 1 fo. 70, Boldog. 2 fo. Orhalom. 2 fo. 50, Hosszuheteny.

1953. Stamp Day.
1331. 200. 1 fo. + 1 fo. turq. .. 50 50
1332. 2 fo. + 2 fo. lilac .. 55 55

1953. Air. Hungarian Football Team's Victory at Wembley. No. 1320 optd. **LONDON-WEMBLEY 1953. XI. 25 6 : 3.**
1333. 2 fo. brn. and green 3·50 3·50

201. Bihari.

202. Lenin.

203. Turnip Beetle.

204. Mother and Baby.

1953. Air. Hungarian Composers. Portraits in brown.

1334. **201.** 30 fl. slate 5 5
1335. – 40 fl. orge. (Erkel) .. 5 5
1336. – 60 fl. green (Liszt) .. 10 5
1337. – 70 fl. red (Mosonyi) .. 12 5
1338. – 80 fl. grey (Goldmark) 15 10
1339. – 1 fo. olive (Bartok) .. 20 12
1340. – 2 fo. lilac (Kodaly) .. 35 20

1954. Lenin. 30th Death Anniv. Inscr. as in T **202.**

1341. **302.** 40 fl. green 10 10
1342. – 60 fl. brown 15 5
1343. – 1 fo. lake 20 15

DESIGNS: 60 fl. Lenin addressing meeting. 1 fo. Profile of Lenin at a meeting.

1954. Air. Insects.

1344. **203.** 30 fl. sepia and orge. 12 10
1345. – 40 fl. sepia & green .. 15 10
1346. – 50 fl. black and red .. 20 12
1347. – 60 fl. sepia, yell. & lilac 25 12
1348. – 80 fl. clar., pur. & grn. 30 15
1349. – 1 fo. black and buff .. 45 25
1350. – 1 fo. 20 sepia & grn... 50 40
1351. – 1 fo. 50 brn. & olive .. 70 50
1352. – 2 fo. sepia & chest. .. 90 70
1353. – 3 fo. sepia & turq. .. 1·25 90

INSECTS—HORIZ. 40 fl. Crawling cockchafer. 50 fl. Greater Capricorn beetle. 60 fl. Hornet. 1 fo. 20, Black cricket. 1 fo. 50, Rhinoceros beetle. 2 fo. Stag beetle. VERT. 80 fl. Apple beetle. 1 fo. Corn beetle. 3 fo. Water beetle.

1954. Child Welfare.

1354. – 30 fl. blue (postage) .. 5 5
1355. **204.** 40 fl. bistre 8 5
1356. – 60 fl. lilac 10 5
1357. – 1 fo. green (air) .. 15 8
1358. – 1 fo. 50 claret .. 20 10
1359. – 2 fo. blue-green .. 25 12

DESIGNS: 30 fl. Woman having blood-test. 60 fl. Doctor examining child. 1 fo. Children in creche. 1 fo. 50, Doctor, mother and child. 2 fo. Children in nursery school.

205. Flag, and Worker.

206. Maypole.

1954. Bolshevist Regime. 35th Anniv. Inscr. as in T **205.**

1360. – 40 fl blue and red .. 15 10
1361. **205.** 60 fl. brown and red .. 55 40
1362. – 1 fo. black and red .. 60 45

DESIGNS—HORIZ. 40 fl. Worker reading book. 1 fo. Soldier with rifle.

1954. May Day. Inscr. "1954-MAJUS I.".

1363. **206.** 40 fl. olive 8 5
1364. – 60 fl. red 12 5

DESIGN: 60 fl. Worker and flag.

207. Agricultural Worker.

1954. 2rd Hungarian Communist Party Congress, Budapest.

1365. **207.** 60 fl. salmon 10 8

208. Boy Building Model Glider.

1954. Air. Inscr. "LEGIPOST".

1366. **208.** 40 fl. slate & olive .. 5 5
1367. – 50 fl. brn. and grey .. 5 5
1368. – 60 fl. slate & chest... 8 5
1369. – 80 fl. sepia & violet .. 8 5
1370. – 1 fo. slate & brown .. 10 8
1371. – 1 fo. 20 sep. & bronze 15 10
1372. – 1 fo. 50 slate & purple 40 15
1373. – 2 fo. brn. and blue .. 60 25

DESIGNS—As T **208:** 60 fl. Gliders. 1 fo. Parachutists. 1 fo. 50, Twin-engined monoplane. SQUARE: 50 fl. Boy flying model glider. 80 fl. Aeroplane and hanger. 1 fo. 20, Biplane. 2 fo. Jet fighters.

209. Hungarian National Museum.

210. Paprika.

1954. Constitution. 5th Anniv. Inscr. "OT EVES AZ ALKOTMANY".

1374. **209.** 40 fl. blue 5 5
1375. – 60 fl. chestnut .. 10 5
1376. – 1 fo. brown 15 8

DESIGNS: 60 fl. Hungarian Coat-of-Arms. 1 fo. Dome of Parliament Buildings, Budapest.

1954. Fruits.

1377. **210.** 40 fl. multicoloured .. 8 5
1378. – 50 fl. multicoloured 8 8
1379. – 60 fl. yellow, green & turquoise 12 8
1380. – 80 fl. multicoloured .. 15 10
1381. – 1 fo. multicoloured .. 20 12
1382. – 1 fo. 20 multicoloured 30 20
1383. – 1 fo. 50 red, green & purple 45 40
1384. – 2 fo. multicoloured .. 70 60

DESIGNS: 50 fl. Tomatoes. 60 fl. Grapes. 80 fl. Apricots. 1 fo. Apples. 1 fo. 20, Plums. 1 fo. 50, Cherries. 2 fo. Peaches.

211. M. Jokai.

212. C. J. Apacai.

1954. Jokai (novelist). 50th Death Anniv.

1385. **211.** 60 fl. olive 15 12
1386. 1 fo. lake 25 20

1954. Hungarian Scientists.

1387. **212.** 8 fl. black on yellow 5 5
1388. – 10 fl. lake on pink .. 5 5
1389. – 12 fl. black on blue .. 5 5
1390. – 20 fl. brown on yellow 5 5
1391. – 30 fl. blue on pink .. 5 5
1392. – 40 fl. green on yellow 8 5
1393. – 50 fl. choc. on green .. 8 5
1394. – 60 fl. blue on pink .. 10 5
1395. – 1 fo. olive 15 5
1396. – 1 fo. 70 red on yellow 25 10
1397. – 2 fo. turquoise .. 35 12

PORTRAITS: 10 fl. S. Korosi Csoma. 12 fl. A. Jedlic. 20 fl. I. Semmelweis. 30 fl. J. Irinyi. 40 fl. F. Koranyi. 50 fl. A. Vambery. 60 fl. K. Than. 1 fo. O. Herman. 1 fo. 70, T. Puskas. 2 fo. E. Hogyes.

213. Speed-skaters.

1955. Air. Winter Sports.

1398. – 40 fl. chestnut, turquoise and sepia .. 12 10
1399. – 50 fl. vermilion, grn. and chocolate .. 15 12
1400. – 60 fl. verm., bl. & sep. 20 15
1401. – 80 fl. grn., ochre & blk. 20 15
1402. – 1 fo. verm., bl. & brn. 25 20
1403. **213.** 1 fo. 20 red, grn. & black 35 30
1404. – 1 fo. 50 vermilion, green and brown .. 45 40
1405. – 2 fo. crim., grn. & brn. 65 55

DESIGNS—VERT. 40 fl. Boys on toboggan. 60 fl. Ice-yacht. 1 fo. Ski-jumper. 1 fo. 50, Skier turning. HORIZ. 50 fl. Skier walking. 80 fl. Ice-hockey players. 2 fo. Figure skaters.

214. Blast Furnace.

215. "1st May".

1955. Liberation. 10th Anniv. Inscr. "FELSZABADULASUNK" etc.

1406. – 40 fl. claret and lake 5 5
1407. **214.** 60 fl. red and green .. 8 5
1408. – 1 fo. green and brown 12 8
1409. – 2 fo. chocolate & grn. 25 15

DESIGNS—VERT. 40 fl. Reading room. 2 fo. Liberty statue. HORIZ. 1 fo. Combine harvester.

1955. May Day.

1410. **215.** 1 fo. red 20 10

216. State Printing Works.

1955. Hungarian State Printing Office. Cent.

1411. **216.** 60 fl. chestnut & grn. 10 8

217. Young Workers and Flag.

1955. 2nd Congress of Young Workers' Union.

1412. **217.** 1 fo. lake 20 10

218. Postilion.

219. Radio Mechanic.

1955. P.O. Museum. 25th Anniv.

1413. **218.** 1 fo. purple 20 10

1955. Workers.

1414. – 8 fl. brown 5 5
1415. – 10 fl. turquoise .. 5 5
1416. – 12 fl. orange 5 5
1417. **219.** 20 fl. olive 5 5
1418. – 30 fl. red 5 5
1419. – 40 fl. brown 5 5
1420. – 50 fl. blue 5 5
1421. – 60 fl. red 8 5
1422. – 70 fl. olive 10 5
1423. – 80 fl. purple 12 5
1424. – 1 fo. blue 15 5
1425. – 1 fo. 20 bistre .. 15 5
1426. – 1 fo. 40 green .. 20 5
1427. – 1 fo. 70 lilac 20 5
1428. – 2 fo. lake 25 5
1429. – 2 fo. 60 red 40 5
1430. – 3 fo. green 45 5
1431. – 4 fo. blue 55 8
1432. – 5 fo. chestnut .. 70 12
1433. – 10 fo. violet .. .. 1·50 20

DESIGNS: 8 fl. Market gardener. 10 fl. Fisherman. 12 fl. Bricklayer. 30 fl. Artist painting pottery. 40 fl. Railway guard. 50 fl. Shop assistant. 60 fl. Post Office worker. 70 fl. Herdsman. 80 fl. Mill-girl. 1 fo. Boat-builder. 1 fo. 20, Carpenter. 1 fo. 40, Bus conductor. 1 fo. 70, Swineherd. 2 fo. Welder. 2 fo. 60, Tractor-driver. 3 fo. Horse and groom. 4 fo. Bus driver. 5 fo. Telegraph lineman. 10 fo. Miner drilling.

220. M. Vitez Csokonai.

1955. Poets.

1434. **220.** 60 fl. black 10 5
1435. – 1 fo. blue 20 5
1436. – 2 fo. red 40 10

PORTRAITS: 1 fo. M. Vorosmarty. 2 fo. A. Jozsef.

1955. Air. Light Metal Industries Int. Congress, Budapest, As No. 1139.

1437. 5 fo. blue on silver .. 3·50 3·50

221. Bela Bartok (composer).

222. "Hargita" Diesel Multiple Unit.

1955. Bartok. 10th Death Anniv.

1438. **221.** 60 fl. brown (postage) 5 5
1439. 1 fo. green (air) .. 25 25
1440. 1 fo. chocolate .. 35 30

No. 1440 was also issued to commemorate Stamp Day with a 4 fo. ticket se-tenant which paid admission for any of 14 philatelic events.

1955. Transport.

1441. **222.** 40 fl. brown & green 8 5
1442. – 60 fl. bistre & turq... 12 5
1443. – 80 fl. brown and olive 12 8
1444. – 1 fo. green and ochre 15 10
1445. – 1 fo. 20 black & chest. 20 15
1446. – 1 fo. 50 brown & black 25 20
1447. – 2 fo. sepia and blue .. 35 25

DESIGNS: 60 fl. Motor coach. 80 fl. Motorcyclist. 1 fo. Lorry. 1 fo. 20 303 Class steam locomotive. 1 fo. 50, Tipper truck. 2 fo. Tanker.

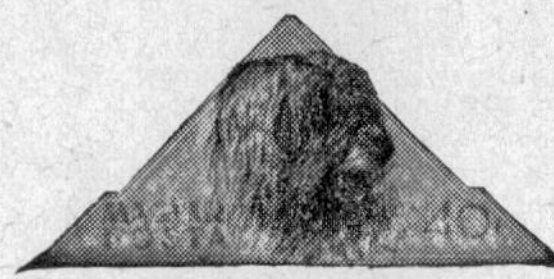

223. Puli Sheepdog.

1956. Hungarian Dogs.

1448. **223.** 40 fl. black, red & yell. 8 5
1449. – 50 fl. grey, buff, blue and black 8 5
1450. – 60 fl. blk., red & grn. 10 5
1451. – 80 fl. orange, black and slate 10 5
1452. – 1 fo. brn., blk. & blue 15 10
1453. – 1 fo. 20 black, brown and salmon .. 20 12
1454. – 1 fo. 50 black, buff and blue 40 20
1455. – 2 fo. black, brown & magenta 55 25

DESIGNS—RECTANGULAR (36×26 mm.): 50 fl. Puli and cattle. 1 fo. 50, Kuvasz sheepdog and cottage (27×35 mm.): 80 fl. Retriever (27×38 mm.): 1 fo. Retriever carrying duck. As T **223:** 60 fl. Pumi. 1 fo. 20, Kuvasz sheepdog. 2 fo. Komondor sheepdog.

224. Pioneers' Badge.

225. Hunyadi on Horseback.

1956. Pioneer Movement. 10th Anniv.
1456. 224. 1 fo. red 12 5
1457. 1 fo. grey 12 5

1956. Janos Hunyadi. 500th Death Anniv.
1458. 225. 1 fo. brown on yellow 20 10

226. Miner. 227. Horse-jumping,

1956. Miners' Day.
1459. 226. 1 fo. blue 20 10

1956. Olympic Games. Inscr. "1956". Centres in brown.
1460. – 20 fi. blue (Canoeing) 5 5
1461. 227. 30 fi. olive 5 5
1462. – 40 fi. chest. (Fencing) 5 5
1463. 60 fi. blue-green (Hurdling) .. 8 5
1464. – 1 fo. red (Football) .. 10 5
1465. – 1 fo. 50 violet (Weight-lifting) 15 8
1466. 2 fo. grn. (Gymnastics) 40 12
1467. 3 fo. magenta (Basket-ball) 55 15

228. Chopin. 229. Dr. L. Zamenhof.

1956. Hungarian-Polish Philatelic Exn. Budapest.
1468. – 1 fo. blue (Liszt) .. 45 45
1469. 228. 1 fo. magenta .. 45 45
Nos. 1468/9 were printed in sheets with the two designs se-tenant throughout.

1957. Hungarian Red Cross Rund. Nos. 1417 etc., surch. with shield, cross and premium.
1470. 219. 20 fi.+20 fi. olive .. 5 5
1471. – 30 fi.+30 fi. red .. 8 8
1472. – 40 fi.+40 fi. brown .. 10 10
1473. – 60 fi.+60 fi. red .. 15 15
1474. – 1 fo.+1 fo. blue .. 30 30
1475. – 2 fo.+2 fo. lake .. 65 65

1957. Air. Esperanto. 70th Anniv.
1476. – 60 fi. chestnut .. 10 5
1477. 229. 1 fo. green 15 5
DESIGN—HORIZ. 60 fi. "Conversing across the world".

230. Letters, Letter-box and Globe. 231. Janos Arany (poet).

1957. Air. Hungarian Red Cross Fund. Cross in red.
1478. 230. 60 fi.+30 fi. brown .. 12 5
1479. – 1 fo.+50 fi. lilac .. 35 8
1480. – 2 fo.+1 fo. verm. .. 45 12
1481. – 3 fo.+1 fo. 50 blue .. 60 20
1482. – 5 fo.+2 fo. 50 grey .. 1·10 70
1483. – 10 fo.+5 fo. green .. 2·00 1·00
DESIGNS: 1 fo. Postal coach. 2 fo. Top of telegraph pole. 3 fo. Radio mast. 5 fo. Desk telephone. 10 fo. (46×31 mm.) Posthorn.

1957. Janos Arany. 75 Death Anniv.
1484. 231. 2 fo. blue 30 10

232. Arms. 233. Congress Emblem.

1957. National Emblem Inaug.
1485. 232. 60 fi. red 5 5
1486. 1 fo. green 15 5

1957. 4th W.F.T.U. Congress, Leipzig.
1487. 233. 1 fo. red 15 10

DESIGN: No. 1489. Airliner over Budapest.

234. Courier.

1957. Air. Stamp Day.
1488. 234. 1 fo. (+ 4 fo.) brn. & bistre on cream 12 10
1489. – 1 fo. (+ 4 fo.) brn. & bistre on cream 12 10
Nos. 1488/9 were printed in strips of 3 separated by a rectangular green label. Price 45 p. un.

DESIGN: 1 fo. Lenin.

235. Dove of Peace and Flags.

1957. Russian Revolution. 40th Anniv. Inscr. "1917 1957". Flags multicoloured.
1490. 235. 60 fi. black and grey 8 5
1491. – 1 fo. indigo and drab 15 5

236. Komarom Tumbler Pigeons. 237. Television Building.

1957. Int. Pigeon-fanciers' Exn., Budapest
1492 236. 30 fi. brown, yellow and green (postage) 5 5
1493. – 40 fi. black and brown 5 5
1494. – 60 fi. grey and blue .. 8 5
1495. – 1 fo. brown and grey 15 5
1496. – 2 fo. grey & magenta 30 15
1497. – 3 fo. green, grey & red (air) 40 15
DESIGNS: 40 fi. Two short-beaked Budapest pigeons. 60 fi. Giant domestic pigeon. 1 fo. Three Szeged pigeons. 2 fo. Two Hungarian fantail pigeons. 3 fo. Two carrier pigeons.

IMPERF. STAMPS. Most modern Hungarian stamps also exist imperf.

1958. Hungarian Television Service Inaug.
1498. 237. 2 fo. purple 15 10

DESIGNS: 30 fi. Old man feeding pigeons. 40 fi. Schoolboys with savings stamps. 60 fi. "The Cricket and the Ant.". 1 fo. Bees on honeycomb. 2 fo. Hands holding banknotes.

238. Mother and Child.

1958. Savings Campaign. Inscr. "1958".
1404 238. 20 fi. olive-brn. & grn. 5 5
1503. – 30 fi. claret and olive 5 5
1502. – 40 fi. brown and bistre 5 5
1501. – 60 fi. myrtle and red 10 5
1500. – 1 fo. sepia and drab 12 8
1500. – 2 fo. green & orge. .. 30 12

239. Hungarian Pavilion.

1958. Air. Brussels Int. Exn. Inscr. "BRUXELLES 1958".
1505. 239. 20 fi. brown & red .. 5 5
1506. – 40 fi. sepia and blue .. 8 5
1507. – 60 fi. sepia and red .. 12 5
1508. – 1 fo. brn. and ochre .. 20 5
1509. – 1 fo. 40 red, grn., bl., yellow, blk. & violet 25 5
1510. – 2 fo. sepia and brown 35 8
1511. – 3 fo. sepia and green 65 12
1512. – 5 fo. blk., blue, red yellow and green .. 1·10 25

DESIGNS—HORIZ. 40 fi. Map of Hungary and exhibits. 60 fi. Parliament Buildings, Budapest. 1 fo. Chain Bridge, Budapest. 1 fo. 40, Arms of Belgium and Hungary. 5 fo. Exhibition emblem. VERT. 2 fo. "Mannekin Pis" statue, Brussels. 3 fo. Town Hall, Brussels.

240. Arms of Hungary. 241. Youth with Book.

1958. Amended Constitution. 1st Anniv. Arms multicoloured.
1513. 240. 60 fi. red 5 5
1514. 1 fo. green 8 5
1515. 2 fo. drab 20 10

1958. 5th Youth Festival, Keszthely.
1516. 241. 1 fo. brown 15 10
Issued alternately se-tenant with label inscr. "V IFJUSAGI TALALKOZO KESZTHELY 1958".

DESIGN: 1 fo. Prague Castle, telegraph pole and wires.
These stamps were issued together alternately se-tenant in sheets.

242. Town Hall, Prague, and Posthorn.

1958. Communist Postal Conf., Prague.
1517. 242. 60 fi. green (postage) 5 5
1518. – 1 fo. lake (air) .. 10 10

243. "Linum dolomiticum".

1958. Flowers.
1519. 243. 20 fi. yellow & purple 5 5
1520. – 30 fi. buff and blue .. 5 5
1521. – 40 fi. buff, yell. & sepia 10 5
1522. – 60 fi. mauve and green 12 5
1523. – 1 fo. green and red .. 20 5
1524. – 2 fo. yellow and green 40 8
1525. – 2 fo. 50, pink & blue 50 20
1526. – 3 fo. pink and green .. 65 25
FLOWERS—TRIANGULAR: 30 fi. "Kitaibelia vitifolia". 2 fo. 50. "Dianthus collinus". 3 fo. "Rosa sancti andreae". VERT. ($20\frac{1}{2}\times31$ mm.): 40 fi. "Doronicum hungaricum". 60 fi. "Colchicum arenarium". 1 fo. "Helleborus purpuracens". 2 fo. "Hemerocallis ilio-asphodelus".

DESIGNS—VERT. 30 fi. Table-tennis player. 40 fi. Wrestlers. 1 fo. Water-polo-player. 2 fo. 50, High-diver. HORIZ. 60 fi. Wrestlers. 3 fo. Swimmers.

244. Table-tennis Bat and Ball.

1958. European Table-tennis and Swimming Championships, and World Wrestling Championships, Budapest.
1527. 244. 20 fi. red on pink .. 5 5
1528. – 30 fi. olive on green 5 5
1529. – 40 fi. purple on yell. 5 5
1530. – 60 fi. brown on blue 8 5
1531. – 1 fo. blue on blue .. 15 5
1532. – 2 fo. 50, red on yellow 40 15
1533. – 3 fo. turquoise on grn. 50 20

245. 246. Airliner over Millennium Monument Budapest

1958. Air. Dated "1958". Centres in bistre.

(a) Int. Correspondence Week.
1534. 245. 60 fi. blk. and purple 8 5
1535. – 1 fo. blk. and blue .. 12 5

(b) National Stamp Exn., Budapest.
1536. – 1 fo. (+ 2 fo.) brn. and red .. 20 15
1537. 245. 1 fo. (+ 2 fo.) brn. & green .. 20 15
DESIGNS: No. 1535, Posthorn, envelope and transport. 1536, Stamp and magnifier.
Nos. 1536/7 were issued together in sheets separated by a buff label inscr. "MABEOSZ ORSZAGOS BELYEGKIALLITAS BUDAPEST 1958 OKTOBER HO—4—Ft.".

1958. Air. 1st Hungarian Air Mail Stamp. 40th Anniv.
1538. 246. 3 fo. mar., red & drab 45 20
1539. – 5 fo. blue, red & drab 75 30
DESIGN: 5 fo. Airliner over Sopron Tower.
For similar stamps but without commem. inscription see Nos. 1542/51.

DESIGN: 2 fo. Hand holding up the newspaper "VORUS UJSAG" (Red Journal).

247. Red Flag.

1958. Hungarian Communist Party and Founding of the "Red Journal". 40th Anniv.
1540. 247. 1 fo. red and brown .. 8 5
1541. – 2 fo. red and blue .. 15 8

1958. Air. As T 246 but with "LEGIPOSTA" at top in place of commem. inscription. On cream paper.
1542. – 20 fi. green and red .. 5 5
1543. – 30 fi. violet and red .. 5 5
1544. – 70 fi. maroon and green 5 5
1545. – 1 fo. blue and red .. 8 5
1546. – 1 fo. 60, pur. and red 10 5
1547. – 2 fo. green and red .. 12 5
1548. – 3 fo. brown and red (No. 1539) .. 15 8
1549. 246. 5 fo. green and red .. 35 12
1550. – 10 fo. blue and red .. 70 25
1551. – 20 fo. sepia and red 1·25 60
DESIGNS: Airliner over: 20 fi. Town Hall. Szeged. 30 fi. Sarospatak Castle. 70 fi. Town Hall, Gyor. 1 fo. Opera House, Budapest. 1 fo. 60, Old City of Veszprem. 2 fo. Chain Bridge, Budapest. 10 fo. Danube Embankment, Budapest. 20 fo. Budapest Cathedral.

248. Rocket approaching the Moon.

1959. I.G.Y. Achievements. Inscr. "GEOFIZIKAI EV 1957 1959".
1552. – 10 fi. brown and red 5 5
1553. – 20 fi. black and blue 5 5
1554. – 30 fi. buff and green 5 5
1555. – 40 fi. blue and slate 8 5
1556. 248. 60 fi. bistre and blue 20 5
1557. – 1 fo. ochre and red .. 25 12
1558. – 5 fo. red-brown and yellow-brown .. 90 35
DESIGNS—($31\frac{1}{2}\times21$ mm.): 10 fi. Eotvos torsion balance (gravimetry). 20 fi. Ship using echo-sounder (oceanography). 30 fi. "Northern Lights" and polar scene. ($35\frac{1}{2}\times26\frac{1}{2}$ mm.): 40 fi. Russian polar camp and Antarctic route map. 1 fo. Observatory and the sun. 5 fo. Russian "Sputnik" and American "Vanguard" (artificial satellites).
See also No. 1605.

249. Revolutionary. 251. Early Steam Locomotive 'Deru'.

MINIMUM PRICE

The minimum price quoted is 5p which represents a handling charge rather than a basis for valuing common stamps. For further notes about prices see introductory pages.

250. Rose.

1959. Proclamation of "Hungarian Soviet Republic". 40th Anniv.
1559. 249. 20 fi. red and purple 5 5
1560. 60 fi. red and blue .. 5 5
1561. 1 fo. red and brown .. 10 5

1959. May Day.
1562. 250. 60 fi. red, grn. & lilac 5 5
1563. 1 fo. red, grn. & brn. 12 5

1959. Transport Museum issue.
1564. 251. 20 fi. yell., grn., blk. and mauve (post.) 5 5
1565. – 30 fi. emer., blk. & buff 5 5
1566. – 40 fi. red, brown, black and blue .. 5 5
1567. – 60 fi. grn., red, blk. and yellow .. 10 5
1568. – 1 fo. blue, yellow, black and pink .. 15 5
1569. – 2 fo. orange, yellow, black and green .. 25 10
1570. – 2 fo. 50 yellow, red, green, black & blue 30 12
1571. – 3 fo. yellow, brown, black & lilac (air) .. 35 15

DESIGNS—HORIZ. 30 fi. Ganz diesel rail-car. 60 fi. Csonka motor car. 1 fo. Ikarusz rear-engine motor-coach. 2 fo. First Lake Balaton steamboat, "Kisfaludy". 2 fo. 50, Stage-coach. 3 fo. Zsilyi aeroplane. VERT. 40 fi. Early railway semaphore signal.

1959. Int. Philatelic Federation Congress, Hamburg. As No. 1570 but colours changed.
1572. 2 fo. 50, red, green, black, blue and yellow .. 60 60

No. 1572 was printed in sheets of four stamps with "se-tenant" red, black and blue labels bearing the Congress emblem (an envelope) and inscr. "HAMBURG 1959".

252. Posthorn.

253. Cormorant.

1959. Postal Ministers' Conf., Berlin.
1573. 252. 1 fo. red 10 8

No. 1573 was printed in sheets with "se-tenant" slate-coloured labels insc. "BERLIN 1959" and depicting the Berlin Opera House.

1959. Water Birds. Inscr. "1959".
1574. 253. 10 fi. blue-black & grn. 5 5
1575. – 20 fi. green and blue 5 5
1576. – 30 fi. violet, myrtle and orange .. 5 5
1577. – 40 fi. grey and green 5 5
1578. – 60 fi. cinnamon & pur. 8 5
1579. – 1 fo. black & turquoise 12 5
1580. – 2 fo. black and red .. 25 8
1581. – 3 fo. brown and bistre 55 30

DESIGNS: 20 fi. Little egret. 30 fi. Purple herons. 40 fi. Great egret. 60 fi. Spoonbill. 1 fo. Common herons. 2 fo. Crested heron. 3 fo. Curlews.

254. 10th-century Man-at-Arms.

255. Bathers at Lake Balaton.

1959. 24th World Fencing Championships, Budapest. Inscr. as in T 254.
1582. 254. 10 fi. black and blue 5 5
1583. – 20 fi. black and lemon 5 5
1584. – 30 fi. black and violet 5 5
1585. – 40 fi. black and red .. 5 5
1586. – 60 fi. black and purple 8 5
1587. – 1 fo. black and turq. 12 5
1588. – 1 fo. 40, black & orge. 25 5
1589. – 3 fo. black and green 55 20

DESIGNS (Evolution of Hungarian swordsmanship). 20 fi. 15th-century man-at-arms. 30 fi. 18th-century soldier. 40 fi. 19th-century soldier 60 fi. 19th-century cavalryman. Fencer: at the assault (1 fo.); on guard (1 fo. 40); saluting (3 fo.).

1959. Lake Balaton Summer Courses.
1590. – 30 fi. bl. on yell. (post.) 5 5
1591. – 40 fi. cerise on green 5 5
1592. 255. 60 fi. brown on pink 8 5
1593. – 1 fo. 20, violet on pink 15 8
1594. – 2 fo. verm. on yellow 30 12
1595. – 20 fi. green (air) .. 5 5
1596. – 70 fi. blue 10 5
1597. – 1 fo. red and blue .. 12 5
1598. – 1 fo. 70, brn. on yell. 15 10

DESIGNS—VERT. 20 fi. Tihany (view). 30 fi. Sailing boat. 70 fi. Water-bus. 1 fo. Water-lily and view of Heviz. 1 fo. 20, Anglers. 1 fo. 70, Sailing ship and statue of fishermen (Balaton pier). 2 fo. Holidaymakers and lake steamer. HORIZ. 40 fi. Vintner with grapes.

256.

257. Shepherd with Letter.

1959. Haydn (composer). 150th Death Anniv. Inscr. "JOS. HAYDN" etc.
1599. 256. 40 fi. yellow & maroon 10 5
1600. – 60 fi. buff and slate .. 12 5
1601. – 1 fo. orange & violet 20 10

DESIGNS—HORIZ. 60 fi. Fertod Chateau. VERT. 1 fo. Haydn.

1959. Schiller (poet) Birth Bicent. As T 256 but inscr. "F. SCHILLER", etc.
1602. 40 fi. yellow and olive .. 10 5
1603. 60 fi. pink and violet-blue 12 5
1604. 1 fo. yellow & brn.-purple 20 12

DESIGNS—VERT. 40 fi. Stylized initials. "F" and "Sch" and Schiller's birthplace. 1 fo. Schiller. HORIZ. 60 fi. Pegasus.

1959. Landing of Russian Rocket on the Moon. As T 243 with addition of Russian Flag and "22 h 02'34"" on Moon in red.
1605. 243. 60 fi. bistre and blue 20 10

1959. Stamp Day and National Stamp Exn.
1606. 257. 2 fo. maroon 55 55

No. 1606 is printed in sheets of 8 stamps with se-tenant maroon labels inscr. "BELEPODIJ 4 Ft" (Admission fee 4 fo.) depicting various stamps held by tweezers.

258. "Taking delivery".

259. Lenin and Szamuely.

1959. Int. Correspondence Week.
1607. 258. 60 fi. multicoloured .. 12 5

1959. Russian Stamp Exn., Budapest.
1608. 259. 20 fi. brn. & brn.-red 5 5
1609. – 40 fi. lake & brn. on bl. 10 5
1610. – 60 fi. buff & grey-blue 15 15
1611. – 1 fo. drab, yellow, red and blue 25 25

DESIGNS: 40 fi. Pushkin. 60 fi. Mayakovsky. 1 fo. Arms with hands clasping flag.

260. Swallow-tail Butterfly.

261.

1959. Hungarian Butterflies. Inscr. "1959". Butterflies in natural colours. Inscriptions in black. Background colours given.
1612. 260. 20 fi. green (postage) 10 5
1613. – 30 fi. blue 10 5
1614. – 40 fi. chestnut .. 12 5
1615. – 60 fi. bistre 12 10
1616. – 1 fo. turquoise (air) .. 20 12
1617. – 2 fo. lilac 50 20
1618. – 3 fo. emerald 90 45

DESIGNS—HORIZ. 30 fi. Tiger moth. 40 fi. Blue butterfly. 2 fo. Death's-head Hawk moth. VERT. 60 fi. Purple Emperor butterfly. 1 fo. Scarce copper butterfly. 3 fo. Red Admiral butterfly.

1959. 7th Socialist Workers' Congress. Flag in red and green.
1619. 261. 60 fi. orange-brown .. 5 5
1620. – 1 fo. brown-red .. 15 8

DESIGN: 1 fo. Flag inscr. "MSZMP VII. KONGRESSZUSA".

262. "Fairy Tales".

263. Sumeg Castle.

1959. Fairy Tales (1st series). Centres and inscr. in black.
1621. 262. 20 fi. multicoloured .. 5 5
1622. – 30 fi. pink 5 5
1623. – 40 fi. blue-green .. 5 5
1624. – 60 fi. blue 8 5
1625. – 1 fo. yellow 12 5
1626. – 2 fo. green 25 10
1627. – 2 fo. 50 salmon .. 30 12
1628. – 3 fo. red 40 15

FAIRY TALE SCENES: 30 fi. "The Sleeping Beauty". 40 fi. "Mat the Goose" 60 fi. 'The Cricket and the Ant". 1 fo. "Mashenka and the Bears". 2 fo. "The Babes in the Wood". 2 fo. 50, "The Pied Piper of Hamelin". 3 fo. "Little Red Riding Hood".

See also Nos. 1702/9 and 2133/41.

1960. Hungarian Castles. On white paper.
1629. 263. 8 fi. purple 5 5
1630. – 10 fi. chestnut .. 5 5
1631. – 12 fi. violet-blue .. 5 5
1632. – 20 fi. bronze-green .. 5 5
1633. – 30 fi. chestnut .. 5 5
1634. – 40 fi. turquoise .. 5 5
1635. – 50 fi. brown 5 5
1636. – 60 fi. red 8 5
1637. – 70 fi. emerald .. 8 5
1638. – 80 fi. maroon .. 8 5
1639. – 1 fo. blue 8 5
1640. – 1 fo. 20 purple .. 8 5
1641. – 1 fo. 40 blue .. 10 5
1642. – 1 fo. 70 lilac ("SOMLO") .. 12 5
1642a. – 1 fo. 70 lilac ("SOMLYO") .. 20 5
1643. – 2 fo. bistre 15 5
1644. – 2 fo. 60 blue .. 20 5
1645. – 3 fo. brown 20 5
1646. – 4 fo. violet 25 5
1647. – 5 fo. green 40 8
1648. – 10 fo. red 70 12

CASTLES—As T 263: 10 fi. Kisvarda. 12 fi. Szigliget. 20 fi. Tata. 30 fi. Diosgyor. 40 fi. Simon Tornya. 50 fi. Fuzer. 60 fi. Sarospatak. 70 fi. Nagyvazsony. 80 fi. Egervar. ($28\frac{1}{2}\times21\frac{1}{2}$ mm.): 1 fo. Vitany. 1 fo. 20, Sirok. 1 fo. 40, Siklos. 1 fo. 70, Somlyo. 2 fo. Boldocko. 2 fo. 60, Holloko. 4 fo. Eger: ($21\frac{1}{2}\times28\frac{1}{2}$ mm.): 3 fo. Csesnek. 5 fo. Koszeg. 10 fo. Sarvar.

See also Nos. 1694/700.

264. Halas Lace.

265. Ski-walking.

1960. Halas Lace (1st series). Designs showing lace as T 264. Inscriptions and values in orange.
1649. 20 fi. sepia 5 5
1650. 30 fi. violet 5 5
1651. 40 fi. turquoise 8 5
1652. 60 fi. brown 10 5
1653. 1 fo. bronze-green .. 15 5
1654. 1 fo. 50 olive-green .. 25 10
1655. 2 fo. blue 35 12
1656. 3 fo. red 55 15

Nos. 1650/1, 1654/5 are larger 38×44 mm.
See also Nos. 1971/8.

1960. Winter Olympic Games.
1657. 265. 30 fi. bistre and blue 5 5
1658. – 40 fi. bistre and green 5 5
1659. – 60 fi. bistre and red .. 8 5
1660. – 80 fi. bistre and violet 12 5
1661. – 1 fo. bistre & turquoise 20 5
1662. – 1 fo. 20 bistre & lake 35 10
1663. – 2 fo. + 1 fo. mult. .. 55 25

DESIGNS: 40 fi. Ice-hockey. 60 fi. Ski-jumping. 80 fi. Speed-skating. 1 fo. Ski-racing. 1 fo. 20, Free-skating. 2 fo. Games emblem.

266. Kato Haman.

267. "Adonis vernalis" and Quill.

1960. Celebrities and Anniversaries. Portrait as T 266.
1664. 60 fi. purple (T 266) .. 5 5
1665. 60 fi. brn. (Clara Zetkin) 5 5
1666. 60 fi. violet (Garibaldi) .. 5 5
1667. 60 fi. green (I. Turr) .. 5 5
1668. 60 fi. red (L. Tukory) .. 5 5
1669. 60 fi. blue (O. Herman) .. 5 5
1670. 60 fi. sepia (Beethoven) .. 5 5
1671. 60 fi. salmon (F. Mora) .. 5 5
1672. 60 fi. grey (B. I. Toth) .. 5 5
1673. 60 fi. purple (D. Banki) .. 20 15
1674. 60 fi. green. (A. G. Pattantyus) 5 5
1675. 60 fi. blue (I. P. Semmelweis) 5 5
1676. 60 fi. brown (Joliot-Curie) 10 8
1677. 60 fi. lake (F. Erkel) .. 5 5
1678. 60 fi. blue (J. Bolyai) .. 5 5
1679. 60 fi. red (V. I. Lenin) .. 50 25

COMMEMORATIVE EVENTS: Nos. 1664/5, Int. Women's Day; 1666, Sicilian Expedition Cent.; 1669, 125th Birth Anniv.; 1670, Martonvasar Beethoven Concerts; 1671, Szeged Festival; 1672, Miners' Day; 1677, 150th Birth Anniv.; 1678, Birth Cent.; 1679, 90th Birth Anniv.

1960. Stamp Exn., Budapest.
1680. 267. 2 fo. yell., grn. & brn. 65 65

No. 1680 was issued se-tenant with green label showing a building and inscr. "BELYEGBEMUTATO 4 Ft." etc., which also served as an entrance ticket to the Exhibition.

268. Soldier.

269. Rowing.

1960. Liberation. 15th Anniv.
1681. 268. 40 fi. brown and red 5 5
1682. – 60 fi. red, grn. & brn. 5 5

DESIGN—HORIZ. 60 fi. Student with flag (inscr. "1945 FELSZABADULASUNK ... 1960".).

1960. Summer Olympic Games. Centres and inscr. in black (3 fo. multicoloured). Circular frames in yellow-brown. Background colours given.
1683. 10 fi. blue (T 269) .. 5 5
1684. 20 fi. chestnut (Boxing) .. 5 5
1685. 30 fi. lilac (Archery) .. 5 5
1686. 40 fi. ochre (Discus) .. 8 5
1687. 50 fi. red (Ball game) .. 10 5
1688. 60 fi. green (Javelin) .. 10 5
1689. 1 fo. pur. (Horse-riding) 25 8
1690. 1 fo. 40 blue (Wrestling) 30 12
1691. 1 fo. 70 brown (Swordplay) 35 15
1692. 2 fo. + 1 fo. rose (Romulus, Remus and Wolf) .. 50 25
1693. 3 fo. grey (Olympic Rings and Arms of Hungary) 1·25 55

1960. Hungarian Castles. As Nos. 1629/42 but printed on coloured paper.
1694. 8 fi. purple on blue .. 5 5
1695. 20 fi. bronze-green on grn. 5 5
1696. 30 fi. chestnut on yellow 5 5
1697. 60 fi. red on pink .. 5 5
1698. 70 fi. emerald on blue .. 5 5
1699. 1 fo. 40 blue on blue .. 10 5
1700. 1 fo. 70 lilac on blue ("SOMLO") 10 5

INDEX

Countries can be quickly located by referring to the index at the end of this volume.

270. Girl in Mezokovesd Provincial Costume.

271. "The Turnip".

1960. Stamp Day.
1701. 270. 2 fo. multicoloured .. 60 60
No. 1701 was printed in sheets of 8 stamps with se-tenant yellow-brown labels inscr. "ORSZAGOS BELYEG KIALLITAS BUDAPEST" and "BELEPODIJ 4 FT" (admission fee 4 fo.) depicting a Mezokovesd apron bearing a postal emblem.

1960. Fairy Tales (2nd series). Multicoloured.
1702. 20 fi. Type 271 .. .. 5 5
1703. 30 fi. "Snow White and the Seven Dwarfs" .. 5 5
1704. 40 fi. "The Miller, Son and Donkey" 5 5
1705. 60 fi. "Puss in Boots" .. 8 5
1706. 80 fi. "The Fox and the Raven" 12 5
1707. 1 fo. "The Maple-wood Pipe" 25 5
1708. 1 fo. 70 "The Stork and the Fox" 40 15
1709. 2 fo. "Momotaro" (Japanese tale) .. 55 25

272. F.Rozsa.

273. Kangaroo with Young.

275. Launching of Rocket "Vostok".

274. Child chasing Butterfly.

1961. Celebrities and Anniversaries. Portraits as T 272.
1710. 1 fo. brown (T 272) .. 10 5
1711. 1 fo. turq. (G. Kilian) .. 10 5
1712. 1 fo. red (J. Rippi-Ronai) 10 5
1713. 1 fo. olive (S. Latinka) .. 10 5
1714. 1 fo. green (M. Zalka) .. 8 5
1715. 1 fo. lake (J. Katona) .. 8 5
COMMEMORATIVE EVENTS: No. 1710, Press Day; 1711, Gyorgy Kilian Sports Movement; 1712, Birth Cent.; 1713, 75th Birth Anniv.; 1714, 65th Birth Anniv.

1961. Budapest Zoo Animals. Inscr. "ZOO 1861".
1716. 273. 20 fi. black & orange 5 5
1717. – 30 fi. sepia and green 5 5
1718. – 40 fi. brown & chestnut 5 5
1719. – 60 fi. grey & magenta 5 5
1720. – 80 fi. yellow & black 10 5
1721. – 1 fo. brown & green 12 5
1722. – 1 fo. 40 sepia & turq. 15 5
1723. – 2 fo. black and red .. 20 8
1724. – 2 fo. 60 brown & violet 40 12
1725. – 3 fo. multicoloured .. 55 25
ANIMALS—HORIZ. 30 fi. Bison. 60 fi. Elephant and calf. 80 fi. Tiger and cubs. 1 fo. 40, Polar bear. 2 fo. Zebra and foal. 2 fo. 60, Bison cow with calf. VERT. 40 fi. Brown bear. 1 fo. Ibex. 3 fo. Main entrance, Budapest Zoo.

1961. Health. Inscr. "1961". Cross in red.
1726. 274. 30 fi. blk., pur. & brn. 5 5
1727. – 40 fi. sep., blue & turq. 5 5
1728. – 60 fi. yell., grey & vio. 5 5
1729. – 1 fo. yellow, red, black and green 12 5
1730. – 1 fo. 70 yellow, blue and grey-green .. 20 8
1731. – 4 fo. apple-grn. & grey 50 20
DESIGNS—As T 274.: 40 fi. Patient on operating table. LARGE (29½×35 mm.): 60 fi. Ambulance and stretcher. 1 fo. Traffic lights and scooter. 1 fo. 70, Syringe and jars. 4 fo. Torch and serpent emblem.

1961. World's First Manned Space Flight. Inscr. "1961.IV.12".
1732. 275. 1 fo. brown and blue 20 5
1733. – 2 fo. brown and blue 1·00 1·25
DESIGN: 2 fo. Gagarin, and "Vostok" in flight.

276. Roses.

277. "Venus" Rocket.

1961. May Day.
1734. 276. 1 fo. red and green .. 8 5
1735. – 2 fo. red and green .. 15 5
DESIGN: 2 fo. As T 276 but roses and inscr. reversed. Nos. 1734/5 were issued se-tenant together in sheets.

1961. Launching of Soviet "Venus" Rocket. Inscr. "VENUSZ-RAKETA 1961.11.12".
1736. 40 fi. black, bistre & blue 30 25
1737. 60 fi. black, bistre & blue 50 35
1738. 80 fi. black and blue .. 55 45
1739. 2 fo. bistre & violet-blue 1·25 70
DESIGNS: 40 fi. T 277. 60 fi. Separation of rocket capsule in flight. 80 fi. Capsule and orbit diagram. 2 fo. Allegory of flying woman and crescent moon.

278. Conference Emblem, Letter and Transport.

1961. Postal Ministers' Conference.
1740. 40 fi. blk. & orge. (T 278) 5 5
1741. 60 fi. black and mauve .. 5 5
1742. 1 fo. black and blue .. 12 5
DESIGNS: 60 fi. Television aerial. 1 fo. Radar-receiving equipment.

279. Hungarian Flag.

280. George Stephenson.

1961. Int. Stamp Exhibition, Budapest.
(a) 1st issue. Background in silver.
1743. 1 fo. red, green and black 20 20
1744. 1 fo. 70, purple, brown, yellow, green and red .. 35 35
1745. 2 fo. 60, orange, yellow blue, black and violet .. 50 50
1746. 3 fo. red, black, yellow, brown, green and blue 70 70

(b) 2nd issue. Background in gold. Inscriptions at left altered on 1 fo. and 3 fo.
1747. 1 fo. red, green and black 20 20
1748. 1 fo. 70, purple, brown, yellow green and red .. 30 30
1749. 2 fo. 60, orange, yellow, blue, black and violet .. 55 55
1750. 3 fo. red, black, yellow, brown, green and blue 65 65
DESIGNS: 1 fo. T 279. 1 fo. 70, Flowers ("Ophrys fuciflora"). 2 fo. 60, Butterfly ("Aglais urticae"). 3 fo. Goldfinch ("Carduelis carduelis").
See also Nos. 1765/8.

1961. Communications Ministers' Conference, Budapest. Insc. "KOZLEKEDESUGYI", etc.
1751. 280. 60 fi. olive 5 5
1752. – 1 fo. bis., blk. & blue 8 5
1753. – 2 fo. brown 15 8
DESIGNS: 1 fo. Communications emblems. 2 fo. J. Landler (Minister of Communications).

281. Football and Club Badge.

1961. 50th Anniv. of VASAS Sports Club. Badge in gold, red and blue.
1754. 40 fi. orange, black & gold 8 5
1755. 60 fi. green, black & gold 10 5
1756. 1 fo. bistre, black & gold 15 10
1757. 2 fo.+1 fo. bl., blk. & gold 45 25
DESIGNS: 40 fi. T. 281. 60 fi. Wrestling. 1 fo. Vaulting. 2 fo. Sailing.

282. Three Racehorses.

1961. Racehorses.
1758. 30 fi. multicoloured .. 5 5
1759. 40 fi. multicoloured .. 8 5
1760. 60 fi. multicoloured .. 10 5
1761. 1 fo. black, green & orge. 20 10
1762. 1 fo. 70, sepia, black and emerald 45 15
1763. 2 fo. black, blue and brown 50 20
1764. 3 fo. multicoloured .. 75 30
DESIGNS: 30 fi. T 282. 40 fi. Three hurdlers. 60 fi. Trotting race (two horses). 1 fo. Trotting race (three horses). 1 fo. 70, Two racehorses and two foals. 2 fo. Hungarian trotter "Baka". 3 fo. 19th century champion mare, "Kincsem".

283. Budapest.

1961. Stamp Day and Int. Stamp Exhibition, Budapest (3rd issue).
1765. 2 fo.+1 fo. bl., brn. & ol. 30 30
1766. 2 fo.+1 fo. bl., brn. & ol. 30 30
1767. 2 fo.+1 fo. bl., brn. & ol. 30 30
1768. 2 fo.+1 fo. bl., brn. & ol. 30 30
Nos. 1765/8 are printed together in sheets of 40 (4×10) with one vertical row of each design. Horizontal strips of four form a composite panorama of Budapest.

284. Music, Keyboard and Silhouette.

285. Lenin.

1961. Liszt (composer). 150th Birth and 75th Death Anniv.
1769. 284. 60 fi. black and gold 5 5
1770. – 1 fo. black .. 12 5
1771. – 2 fo. green and blue .. 25 15
DESIGNS—VERT. 1 fo. Statue. HORIZ. 2 fo. Music Academy.

1961. 22nd Communist Party Congress, Moscow.
1772. 285. 1 fo. brown 10 5

286. Monk's Hood.

237. Nightingale.

1961. Medicinal Plants. Multicoloured.
1773. 20 fi. T 286 .. .. 5 5
1774. 30 fi. Centaury 5 5
1775. 40 fi. Blue iris 5 5
1776. 60 fi. Thorn-apple .. 8 5
1777. 1 fo. Purple hollyhock .. 12 5
1778. 1 fo. 70, Hop 20 8
1779. 2 fo. Poppy 25 8
1780. 3 fo. Mullein 45 20

1961. Birds of Woods and Fields. Multicoloured. Inscr. "1961".
1781. 30 fi. Type 287 .. .. 5 5
1782. 40 fi. Great Tit 5 5
1783. 60 fi. Chaffinch (horiz.) .. 8 5
1784. 1 fo. Jay 12 5
1785. 1 fo. 2 Golden Oriole (horiz.) 15 5
1786. 1 fo. 50 Blackbird (horiz.) 20 8
1787. 2 fo. Yellow-hammer .. 30 10
1788. 3 fo. Lapwing (horiz.) .. 45 15

288. M. Karolyi.

289. Railway Signals.

1962. Celebrities and Anniversaries. Inscr. "1962".
1789. 288. 1 fo. sepia 8 5
1790. – 1 fo. chest. (F. Berkes) 8 5
1791. – 1 fo. blue (J. Pech) .. 10 5
1792. – 1 fo. violet (A. Chazar) 10 5
1793. – 1 fo. blue (Dr. F. Hutyra) 10 5
1794. – 1 fo. red (G. Egressy) 10 5
ANNIVERSARIES: No. 1790, 5th Co-operative Movement Congress. 1791, Hydrographic Institute, 75th Anniv. 1792, Sports Club for the deaf, 50th Anniv. 1793, Hungarian Veterinary Service, 175th Anniv. 1794, National Theatre, 125th Anniv.

1962. 14th Int. Railwaymen's Esperanto Congress.
1795. 289. 1 fo. green 8 5

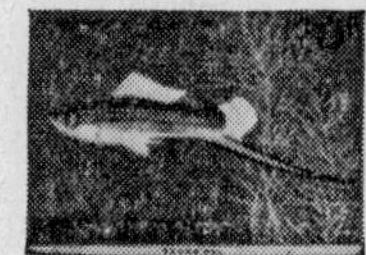
290. Swordtail.

1962. Ornamental Fishes. Inscr. "1962". Multicoloured.
1796. 20 fi. Type 290 .. .. 5 5
1797. 30 fi. Paradise fish .. 5 5
1798. 40 fi. Guppy 5 5
1799. 60 fi. Siamese Fighter .. 10 5
1800. 80 fi. Tiger Barb 12 5
1801. 1 fo. Angel fish 15 5
1802. 1 fo. 20 Sunfish 15 5
1803. 1 fo. 50 Lyretail .. 20 8
1804. 2 fo. Neon Tetra 25 10
1805. 3 fo. Pompadour 40 12

291. Flags of Argentina and Bulgaria.

1962. World Football Championships, 1962. Inscr. "CHILE 1962". Flags in national colours: ball, flagpole, value, etc., in bistre.
1806. – 30 fi. mauve 5 5
1807. – 40 fi. yellow-green .. 5 5
1808. – 60 fi. lilac 8 5
1809. – 1 fo. blue 12 5
1810. 291. 1 fo. 70 orange .. 20 5
1811. – 2 fo. turquoise .. 25 8
1812. – 3 fo. red 35 30
1813. – 4 fo.+1 fo. green .. 60 15
FLAGS: 30 fi. Colombia and Uruguay. 40 fi. U.S.S.R. and Yugoslavia. 60 fi. Switzerland and Chile. 1 fo. German Federal Republic and Italy. 2 fo. Hungary and Great Britain. 3 fo. Brazil and Mexico. 4 fo. Spain and Czechoslovakia. The two flags on each stamp represent the football teams playing against each other in the first round.

292. Gutenberg.

293. Campaign Emblem.

1962. Hungarian Printing Union Cent.
1814. 292. 1 fo. indigo 10 5
1815. – 1 fo. brown 10 5
PORTRAIT: No. 1815, Miklos Kis (first Hungarian printer).

1962. Malaria Eradication.
1816. 293. 2 fo. 50 bistre & black 50 20

294. "Beating Swords into Ploughshares".

295. Festival Emblem.

1962. World Peace Congress, Moscow.
1817. **294.** 1 fo. brown 10 5

1962. World Youth Festival, Helsinki.
1818. **295.** 3 fo. multicoloured.. 35 15

296. Icarus. **297.** Hybrid Tea.

1962. Air. Development of Flight.
1819. **296.** 30 fi. bistre and blue 5 5
1820. – 40 fi. blue and green 5 5
1821. – 60 fi. red and blue .. 5 5
1822. – 80 fi. silver, blue and turquoise 8 5
1823. – 1 fo. silver, bl. & pur. 10 5
1824. – 1 fo. 40 orge. & blue 15 5
1825. – 2 fo. brown and turq. 20 8
1826. – 3 fo. bl., silver & violet 35 12
1827. – 4 fo. silver, blk. & grn. 50 20
DESIGNS: 40 fi. Glider and Lilienthal's machine. 60 fi. Light monoplane and Rakos's machine. 80 fi. Airship and Montgolfier balloon. 1 fo. Russian IL-18 airliner and Wright Brothers' machine. 1 fo. 40, Inverted sports plane and Nyesterov's biplane. 2 fo. Modern helicopter and Asboth's helicopter. 3 fo. Jet liner and Zhukovsky's turbo-engine. 4 fo. Space rocket and Ziolkovsky's rocket.

1962. Rose Culture. Roses in natural colours. Background colours given.
1828. – 20 fi. brown 5 5
1829. **297.** 40 fi. myrtle 8 5
1830. – 60 fi. violet 10 5
1831. – 80 fi. red 12 5
1832. – 1 fo. myrtle 20 8
1833. – 1 fo. 20 orange .. 25 15
1834. – 2 fo. turquoise .. 40 15
ROSES: 20 fi. Floribunda. 60 fi. to 2 fo. Various hybrid teas.

298. Globe, "Vostok 3" and "Vostok 4".

1962. Air. 1st "Team" Manned Space Flight.
1835. **298.** 1 fo. chest. & blue .. 30 15
1836. – 2 fo. chest. & blue .. 60 35
DESIGN: 2 fo. Cosmonauts Nikolaev and Popovich. Nos. 1835/6 were issued together vertically se-tenant in sheets of 30 (3×10).

299. Weightlifting. **300.** Austrian 2 kr. stamp of 1850.

1962. European Weightlifting Championships, Budapest.
1837. **299.** 1 fo. chestnut .. 10 5

1962. 35th Stamp Day.
1838. **300.** 2 fo.+1 fo. brown and yellow .. 40 30
1839. – 2 fo.+1 fo. brown and pink 40 30
1840. – 2 fo.+1 fo. brown and blue 40 30
1841. – 2 fo.+1 fo. brown and green 40 30
DESIGNS: Hungarian stamps of: No. 1839, 1919 (75 fi. Dozsa); No. 1840, 1955 (1 fo. 50 Skiing); No. 1841, 1959 (3 fo. Butterfly). The four stamps are arranged together se-tenant in sheets.

301. Early and Modern Oilwells. **302.** Gagarin.

1962. Hungarian Oil Industry. 25th Anniv.
1842. **301.** 1 fo. green 10 5

1962. Air. Astronautical Congress, Paris.
1843. **302.** 40 fi. ochre & purple 8 5
1844. – 60 fi. ochre & green.. 10 5
1845. – 1 fo. ochre & turq. .. 15 5
1846. – 1 fo. 40 ochre & brown 25 8
1847. – 1 fo 70 ochre & blue.. 25 8
1848. – 2 fo. 60 ochre and violet 45 10
1849. – 3 fo. ochre and brown 50 20
ASTRONAUTS: 60 fi. Titov. 1 fo. Glenn. 1 fo. 40, Scott Carpenter. 1 fo. 70, Nikolaev. 2 fo. 60, Popovich. 3 fo. Schirra.

303. Cup and Football. **304.** Osprey.

1962. "Budapest Vasas" Football Team's Victory in Central European Cup Competition.
1850. **303.** 2 fo.+1 fo. mult. .. 15 10

1962. Air. Birds of Prey. Multicoloured.
1851. 30 fi. Eagle-owl 5 5
1852. 40 fi. T **304** 5 5
1853. 60 fi. Marsh harrier .. 5 5
1854. 80 fi. Dwarf eagle .. 8 5
1855. 1 fo. Bald eagle 10 5
1856. 2 fo. Vulture 20 5
1857. 3 fo. Golden eagle .. 35 12
1858. 4 fo. Kestrel 55 20

305. Racing Motor-cyclist.

1962. Motor-cycle and Car Sports. Multi-coloured.
1859. 20 fi. Type **305** 5 5
1860. 30 fi. Sidecar racing .. 5 5
1861. 40 fi. "Scrambling" (hill climb) 5 5
1862. 60 fi. Dirt-track racing .. 8 5
1863. 1 fo. Wearing "garland" 10 5
1864. 1 fo. 20 Speed trials .. 15 5
1865. 1 fo. 70 Sidecar trials .. 20 5
1866. 2 fo. "Go-kart" racing .. 25 8
1867. 3 fo. Car racing 40 20

306. Ice Skater. **308.** Bulgarian 2 l. Rocket Stamp of 1959.

307. J. Batsanyi.

1963. European Figure Skating and Ice Dancing Championships, Budapest.
1868. **306.** 20 fi. grn., brn. & lilac 5 5
1869. – 40 fi. blk., brn. & salmon 5 5
1870. – 60 fi. multicoloured.. 8 5
1871. – 1 fo. red, blk., brn. & bl. 15 5
1872. – 1 fo. 40 multicoloured 20 8
1873. – 2 fo. red, brn. & green 35 10
1874. – 3 fo. multicoloured.. 50 15
DESIGNS—VERT. 40 fi., 2 fo. Skater leaping. 60 fi., 1 fo. Pairs dancing. 1 fo. 40, Skater turning. HORIZ. 3 fo. Pair dancing.

1963. Celebrities and Anniversaries.
1875. 40 fi. lake (Type **307**) .. 5 5
1876. 40 fi. green (F. Entz) .. 5 5
1877. 40 fi. blue (I. Markovits) 5 5
1878. 40 fi. olive (L. Weiner) 5 5
1879. 60 fi. slate-purple (Dr. F. Koranyi) 5 5
1880. 60 fi bronze (G. Gardonyi) 5 5
1881. 60 fi. red-brown (P. de Coubertin) 8 5
1882. 60 fi. violet (J. Eotvos).. 5 5
ANNIVERSARIES: No. 1875, Revolutionary, Birth Bicent. 1876, Horticulture College founder, Horticulture Cent. 1877, Inventor, Hungarian Shorthand, Cent. 1878, Composer, Budapest Music Competitions. 1879, Tuberculosis researcher, 50th Death Anniv. 1880, Novelist, Birth Cent. 1881, Olympic Games reviver, Birth Cent. 1882, Author, 150th Birth Anniv.

1963. Postal Minister's Conference, Budapest.
1883 – 20 fi. red, yell. & grn. 5 5
1884. **308.** 30 fi. red, brn. & pur. 5 5
1885. – 40 fi. purple and blue 5 5
1886. – 50 fi. violet and blue 5 5
1887. – 60 fi. red, bl., yell. and brown .. 8 5
1888. – 80 fi. turq.-bl., black and blue 10 5
1889. – 1 fo. black, brown, blue and red .. 12 5
1890. – 1 fo. 20 yellow, violet and blue 15 5
1891. – 1 fo. 40 blue, red & brn. 20 5
1892. – 1 fo. 70 red-brn., grn. and brown .. 20 8
1893. – 2 fo. orange, blue and purple .. 25 10
1894. – 2 fo. 60 violet, red and green 35 12
DESIGNS: Various "space" stamps—HORIZ 20 fi. Albania 1 l. 50 (1962). 40 fi. Czechoslovakia 80 h. (1962). 50 fi. China 8 f. (1958). 60 fi. N. Korea 10 ch. (1961). 80 fi. Poland 40 g. (1959). 1 fo. Hungary 60 fi. (1961). 1 fo. 40 East Germany 25 pf. (1961). 1 fo. 70 Rumania 1 l. 20 (1957). 2 fo. 60 N. Vietnam 6 x. (1961). VERT. 1 fo. 20 Mongolia 30 m. (1959). 2 fo. Russia 6 k. (1961).

309. Fair Emblem.

1963. International Fair, Budapest.
1895. **309.** 1 fo. violet 8 5

310. Erkel (composer).

1963. Students' Erkel Memorial Festival, Gyula.
1896. **310.** 60 fi. brown 5 5

311. Roses.

1963. 5th National Rose Show, Budapest.
1897. **311.** 2 fo. red, green & brn. 20 5

312. Helicon Monument.

1963. 10th Youth Festival, Keszthely.
1898. **312.** 40 fi. blue 5 5

313. Chain Bridge and River Boat.

1963. Transport.
1899. **313.** 10 fi. blue 5 5
1900. – 20 fi. green 5 5
1901. – 30 fi. violet-blue .. 5 5
1902. – 40 fi. orange.. .. 5 5
1902a. – 40 fi. grey 5 5
1903. – 50 fi. brown 5 5
1904. – 60 fi. red 5 5
1905. – 70 fi. olive 5 5
1906. – 80 fi. brown 5 5
1906a. – 1 fo. brown 5 5
1907. – 1 fo. maroon.. .. 5 5
1908. – 1 fo. 20 brown .. 40 12
1909. – 1 fo. 20 violet .. 5 5
1910. – 1 fo. 40 bronze .. 8 5
1911. – 1 fo. 70 red-bronze .. 10 5
1912. – 2 fo. turquoise .. 12 5
1913. – 2 fo. 50 purple .. 12 5
1914. – 2 fo. 60 olive .. 12 5
1915. – 3 fo. ultramarine .. 15 5
1916. – 4 fo. blue 25 5
1917. – 5 fo. brown 30 5
1918. – 6 fo. ochre 35 5
1919. – 8 fo. mauve 55 12
1920. – 10 fo. green 60 25
DESIGNS—HORIZ. 20 fi. Tramcar. 30 fi. Open-deck bus. 40 fi. (No. 1902) Articulated bus. 40 fi. (No. 1902a) Budapest 100 Post Office. 50 fi. Railway truck and gas cylinders. 60 fi. Trolley bus. 70 fi. Railway T.P.O. coach. 80 fi. Motor-cyclist. LARGER ($28\frac{1}{2}\times21$ mm.): 1 fo. (No. 1907) Articulated trolley bus. 1 fo. 40 Postal coach. 1 fo. 70, Diesel multi-unit train. 2 fo. T.V. broadcast coach. 2 fo. 50, Tourist coach. 2 fo. 60, Signal, signalbox and train. 3 fo. Parcels conveyor. 5 fo. Railway fork-lift truck. 6 fo. Telex operator. 8 fo. Telephonist and map. 10 fo. Postwoman. VERT. 1 fo. (No. 1906a) Hotel Budapest. 1 fo. 20 (No. 1908), Mail 'plane and trolley on tarmac. 1 fo. 20 (No. 1909), Control tower, Miskolc. 4 fo. Pylon, Pecs.

314. Holiday-maker and lake Steamer.

1963. Siofok Resort, Lake Balaton. Cent.
1921. – 20 fi. blk., green & red 10 5
1922. **314.** 40 fi. orange, black, violet, red & turq. 10 5
1923. – 60 fi. orge., brown & bl. 15 5
DESIGNS—TRIANGULAR: 20 fi. Passenger launch. 60 fi. Sailing boat.

315. Mailcoach and Arc de Triomphe, Paris.

1963. Paris Postal Conf. Cent.
1924. **315.** 1 fo. red 12 5

316. Performance in front of Szeged Cathedral.

1963. Summer Drama Festival, Szeged.

1925. **316.**	40 fl. blue	5	5

317. Child with towel.

319. Karancssag.

318. Pylon and Map.

1963. Red Cross Cent. Inscr. "1863-1963". Multicoloured.

1926.	30 fl. Type **317**	5	5
1927.	40 fl. Girl with medicine bottle and tablets ..	8	5
1928.	60 fl. Girls of three races	10	5
1929.	1 fo. Girl and "heart" ..	12	8
1930.	1 fo. 40 Boys of three races	20	10
1931.	2 fo. Child being medically examined	30	12
1932.	3 fo. Hands tending plants	75	40

1963. Village Electrification.

1933. **318.**	1 fo. black and grey	8	5

1963. Provincial Costumes.

1934. **319.**	20 fl. lake	5	5
1935.	30 fl. green (Kapuvar)	5	5
1936. –	40 fl. brown (Debrecen)	5	5
1937.	60 fl. blue (Hortobagy)	5	5
1938. –	1 fo. red (Csokoly) ..	10	5
1939.	1 fo. 70 violet (Dunantul) ..	15	5
1940.	2 fo. bl.-green (Bujak)	20	8
1941.	2 fo. 50 red (Alfold) ..	25	10
1942. -	3 fo. ultramarine (Mezokovesd) ..	60	20

320. Hyacinth.

322. Calendar.

321. Ski-ing (slalom).

1963. Stamp Day. Flowers. Multicoloured.

1943.	2 fo.+1 fo. Type **320** ..	30	30
1944.	2 fo.+1 fo. Narcissus ..	30	30
1945.	2 fo.+1 fo. Chrysanthemum	30	30
1946.	2 fo.+1 fo. Tiger lily ..	30	30

Nos. 1943/6 were issued together in sheets of 20.

1963. Winter Olympic Games, Innsbruck, 1964. "MAGYAR" and emblems red and black; centres brown; background colours given.

1947. **321.**	40 fl. green	5	5
1948. –	60 fl. violet	5	5
1949.	70 fl. ultramarine ..	5	5
1950. –	80 fl. blue green ..	5	5
1951. –	1 fo. orange	8	5
1952. –	2 fo. blue	30	5
1953. –	2 fo. 60 claret ..	60	25
1954.	4 fo.+1 fo. turquoise	55	20

DESIGNS: 60 fl. Ski-ing (biathlon). 70 fl. Ski-jumping. 80 fl. Rifle-shooting on skis. 1 fo. Figure-skating (pairs). 2 fo. Ice-hockey. 2 f. 60, Speed-skating. 4 fo. Bob-sleighing.

1963. New Year Issue. Hungarian Postal and Philatelic Museum Fund. Mult.

1955.	20 fl. Type **322**	5	5
1956.	30 fl. Young chimney-sweep with glass of water ..	5	5
1957.	40 fl. Four-leafed clover ..	10	5
1958.	60 fl. Piglet in top-hat ..	5	5
1959.	1 fo. Young pierrot ..	10	5
1960.	2 fo. Chinese lanterns and mask	15	8
1961.	2 fo. 50+1 fo. 20 Holly, mistletoe, clover and horse-shoe	30	15
1962.	3 fo.+1 fo. 50 Piglets with balloon	45	20

SIZES: As T **322**—HORIZ. 20 fl., 1 fo., 3 fo. VERT. 40 fl. LARGER (28×38 mm.): 30 fl., 60 fl., 2 fo., 2 fo. 50.

323. Moon Rocket.

The 60 fl., 2 fo. and 3 fo. are horiz., the rest vert.

1964. Space Research. Multicoloured.

1963.	30 fl. Type **323**	5	5
1964.	40 fl. Venus rocket ..	5	5
1965.	60 fl. "Vostok 1" ..	5	5
1966.	1 fo. U.S. spaceship ..	12	5
1967.	1 fo. 70 Soviet team space flights	20	8
1968.	2 fo. "Telstar"	25	8
1969.	2 fo. 60 Mars rocket ..	35	12
1970.	3 fo. "Space Research" (Rockets and tracking equipment)	40	15

324. Swans.

1964. Halas Lace (2nd series). Lace patterns die-stamped in white on black; inscriptions black.

1971. **324.**	20 fl. emerald ..	5	5
1972.	30 fl. yellow ..	5	5
1973. –	40 fl. rose ..	5	5
1974.	60 fl. olive ..	8	5
1975.	1 fo. orange ..	15	5
1976. –	1 fo. 40 blue ..	20	5
1977. –	2 fo. turquoise	30	10
1978. –	2 fo. 60 violet	35	20

LACE PATTERNS—VERT. (38½×45 mm.): 30 fl. Peacocks. 40 fl. Pigeons. 60 fl. Peacock. 1 fo. Deer. 1 fo. 40, Fisherman. 2 fo. Pigeons. As T **324**.: 2 fo. 60, Butterfly.

325. Armour and Swords.

326. Basketball.

327. Dozsa and Kossuth.

328. Fair and Emblem.

329. "Breasting the Tape".

1964. Anniversaries and Events of 1964. Designs as T **325/9**, some showing portraits.

(a) As T **325.**

1979.	60 fl. purple (I. Madach)	5	5
1980.	60 fl. yell.-olive (E. Szabo)	5	5
1981.	60 fl. olive (A. Fay) ..	5	5
1982.	1 fo. red (Skittles) ..	8	5
1983.	2 fo. brown (T **325**) ..	15	5

ANNIV. OR EVENT: No. 1979, (author, death cent.). 1980, (founder of Municipal Libraries, 60th anniv.). 1981, (death cent.). 1982, (1st European Skittles Championships, Budapest). 1983, (50th anniv. of Hungarian Fencing Assn.).

No. 1982, was issued in sheets with marginal tabs bearing the Olympic "rings" and inscr. "'VERSO TOKIO' RIMINI 1964. VI.25-VII. 6" to commemorate the International Sports Stamp Exhibition at Rimini. (Price with tab, un. 15 p.).

(b) As T **326.**

1984.	60 fl. turquoise (Stalactites and stalagmites) ..	5	5
1985.	60 fl. blue (Bauxite excavator)	5	5
1986.	60 fl. red (K. Marx) ..	8	5
1987.	1 fo. green (Forest and waterfall) ..	15	5
1988.	2 fo. brown (Galileo) ..	20	5
1989.	2 fo. lake (Shakespeare)	15	5
1990.	2 fo. blue (T **326**) ..	5	5

ANNIV. OR EVENT—VERT. No. 1984, (Aggteleki Cave). 1985, (30th anniv. of Hungarian Aluminium Production). 1987, (National Forestry Federation Congress). 1988, (400th birth anniv.). 1989. (400th birth anniv.). 1990, (European Women's Basketball Championships). HORIZ. No. 1986, (cent. of "First International").

(c) As T **327.**

1991.	1 fo. blue (T **327**) ..	10	5
1992.	3 fo.+1 fo. 50, black, grey and orange (Sports Museum, Budapest)	45	15

ANNIV. OR EVENT: No. 1991, (60th Anniv. of City of Cegled). 1992, (Lawn Tennis Historical Exn., Budapest).

(d) T **328.**

1993.	1 fo. green (Budapest Int. Fair)	10	5

(e) As T **329.**

1994.	60 fl. slate ("Alba Regia" statue)	5	5
1995.	1 fo. chestnut (M. Ybl) ..	10	5
1996.	2 fo. brown (T **329**) ..	15	5
1997.	2 fo. dull purple (Michelangelo)	15	5

ANNIV. OR EVENT: No. 1994, (Szekesfehervar Days). 1995, (architect, 150th birth anniv.). 1996, (50th anniv. of Hungarian-Swedish Athletic Meeting). 1997, (400th death anniv.).

330. Eleanor Roosevelt.

332. Peaches ("Magyar Kajszi").

331. Fencing.

1964. Eleanor Roosevelt Commem.

1998. **330.**	2 fo. ochre & grey-brn.	10	5

1964. Olympic Games, Tokyo. Multicoloured.

1999.	30 fl. Type **331**	5	5
2000.	40 fl. Gymnastics ..	5	5
2001.	60 fl. Football	5	5
2002.	80 fl. Horse-jumping ..	8	5
2003.	1 fo. Running	10	5
2004.	1 fo. 40 Weightlifting ..	12	5
2005.	1 fo. 70 Gymnastics (trapeze)	15	5
2006.	2 fo. Throwing the hammer, and javelin ..	20	5
2007.	2 fo. 50 Boxing ..	45	10
2008.	3 fo.+1 fo. Water-polo ..	50	15

1964. National Peaches and Apricots, Exn. Budapest. Designs of peaches or apricots. Multicoloured.

2009.	40 fl. "J. H. Hale" ..	5	5
2010.	60 fl. Type **332** ..	5	5
2011.	1 fo. "Mandula Kajszi" ..	10	5
2012.	1 fo. 50 "Borsi Rozsa" ..	15	5
2013.	1 fo. 70 "Alexander" ..	15	5
2014.	2 fo. "Champion" ..	20	5
2015.	2 fo. 60 "Elberta" ..	25	12
2016.	3 fo. "Mayflower" ..	30	15

333. Lilac.

Nos. 2017/20 were issued together in sheets of 20 (4×5).

1964. Stamp Day. Multicoloured.

2017.	2 fo.+1 fo. Type **333** ..	30	30
2018.	2 fo.+1 fo. Wild duck ..	30	30
2019.	2 fo.+1 fo. Gymnast ..	30	30
2020.	2 fo.+1 fo. Rocket and Globe	30	30

334. Pedestrian Road Crossing.

1964. Road Safety. Multicoloured.

2021.	20 fl. Type **334**	5	5
2022.	60 fl. Child with ball running into road ..	5	5
2023.	1 fo. Woman and child waiting to cross road ..	8	5

335. Arpad Bridge, Budapest.

1964. Opening of Reconstructed Elisabeth Bridge, Budapest. Multicoloured.

2024.	20 fl. Type **335**	5	5
2025.	30 fl. Margaret	5	5
2026.	60 fl. Chain	5	5
2027.	1 fo. Elisabeth	10	5
2028.	1 fo. 50 Republic ..	15	5
2029.	2 fo. Petofi	20	10
2030.	2 fo. 50 Railway	45	25

336. Pheasant.

1964. "Hunting". Multicoloured.
2034. 20 fi. Type **336** 5 5
2035. 30 fi. Wild boar 5 5
2036. 40 fi. Partridges 5 5
2037. 60 fi. Hare 8 5
2038. 80 fi. Fallow deer .. 10 5
2039. 1 fo. Mouflon 12 5
2040. 1 fo. 70 Stag 20 5
2041. 2 fo. Great bustard .. 25 8
2042. 2 fo. 50 Roebuck .. 35 10
2043. 3 fo. Emblem of Hunters' Federation 40 15

337. Horse-riding and Medals.

1965. Olympic Games, Tokyo—Hungarian Winners' Medals. Medals: Gold and brown (G); Silver and black (S); Bronze and brown (B).
2044. 20 fi. brn. & yell.-ol. (G) 5 5
2045. 30 fi. brown and violet (S) 5 5
2046. 50 fi. brown and olive (G) 8 5
2047. 60 fi. brown & lt. blue (G) 8 5
2048. 70 fi. brn., slate & stone (B) 10 5
2049. 80 fi. brown & green (G) 12 5
2050. 1 fo. brn., vio. & mve. (S) 20 5
2051. 1 fo. 20 brown & blue (S) 20 8
2052. 1 fo. 40 brn. and grey (S) 25 8
2053. 1 fo. 50 brn. & yell.-brn. (G) 25 10
2054. 1 fo. 70 brown & rose (S) 30 12
2055. 3 fo. brown & turq. (G).. 50 25
DESIGNS: 20 fi. T **337**. 30 fi. Gymnastics. 50 fi. Rifle-shooting. 60 fi. Water-polo. 70 fi. Putting the shot. 80 fi. Football. 1 fo. Weight-lifting. 1 fo. 20, Canoeing. 1 fo. 40, Throwing the hammer. 1 fo. 50, Wrestling. 1 fo. 70, Throwing the javelin. 3 fo. Fencing.

338. Helicopter and Polar Station. **339.** Asters.

1965. Int. Quiet Sun Year.
2056. **338.** 20 fi. orge., blk. & blue 5 5
2057. – 30 fi. green, blk. & grey 5 5
2058. – 60 fi. yell., blk. & mve. 5 5
2059. – 80 fi. yell., blk. & grn. 8 5
2060. – 1 fo. 50 black, blue, green and yellow .. 15 5
2061. – 1 fo. 70 blk., mag. & bl. 15 5
2062. – 2 fo. salmon, blk. & bl. 20 5
2063. – 2 fo. 50 yellow, black and chestnut .. 35 10
2064. – 3 fo. blk., blue & yell. 50 25
DESIGNS: 30 fi. Rocket and radar aerials. 60 fi. Rocket and diagram. 80 fi. Radio telescope. 1 fo. 50, Compass needle on Globe. 1 fo. 70, Weather balloon. 2 fo. Northern Lights and penguins. 2 fo. 50, Space satellite. 3 fo. I.Q.S.Y. emblem and world map.

1965. Liberation. 20th Anniv. Multicoloured.
2066. 20 fi. Type **339** 5 5
2067. 30 fi. Peonies 5 5
2068. 50 fi. Carnations 5 5
2069. 60 fi. Roses 5 5
2070. 1 fo. 40 Lilies 10 5
2071. 1 fo. 70 Godetia 12 5
2072. 2 fo. Gladiolus 20 5
2073. 2 fo. 50 Parrot tulips .. 25 12
2074. 3 fo. Mixed bouquet .. 45 15

340. Leonov in Space. **341.** "Red Head" (after Leonardo da Vinci).

1965. Air. "Voskhod 2" Space Flight.
2075. **340.** 1 fo. grey and violet 20 10
2076. – 2 fo. brown & pur. .. 45 40
DESIGN: 2 fo. Beliaiev and Leonov.

1965. Int. Renaissance Conf., Budapest.
2077. **341.** 60 fi. chestnut & ochre 15 5

342. Nikolaev, Tereshkova and View of Budapest. **343.** I.T.U. Emblem and Symbols.

1965. Visit of Astronauts Nikolaev and Tereshkova.
2078. **342.** 1 fo. brown and blue 12 5

1965. I.T.U. Cent.
2079. **343.** 60 fi. violet 5 5

344. French 13th-cent. Tennis. **345.** Marx and Lenin.

1965. "History of Tennis".
2081. **344.** 30 fi.+10 fi. lake on buff 5 5
2082. – 40 fi.+10 fi. blk. on lilac 5 5
2083. – 60 fi.+10 fi. emerald on bistre .. 8 5
2084. – 70 fi.+30 fi. purple on turquoise .. 12 5
2085. – 80 fi.+40 fi. bl. on lavender 12 5
2086. – 1 fo.+50 fi. green on yellow .. 15 5
2087. – 1 fo. 50+50 fi. brn. on green 20 5
2088. – 1 fo. 70+50 fi. black on blue .. 25 10
2089. – 2 fo.+1 fo. red on green 30 15
DESIGNS: 40 fi. Hungarian 16th-cent. game. 60 fi. French 18th-cent. "long court". 70 fi. 16th-cent. "tennys courte". 80 fi. 16th-cent. court at Fontainebleau. 1 fo. 17th-cent. game. 1 fo. 50, W. C. Wingfield and Wimbledon Cup, 1877. 1 fo. 70, Davis Cup, 1900. 2 fo. Bela Kehrling in play.

1965. Postal Ministers' Congress, Peking.
2090. **345.** 60 fi. multicoloured .. 5 5

346. I.C.Y. Emblem and Pulleys. **347.** Equestrian Act.

1965. Int. Co-operation Year.
2091. **346.** 2 fo. red 15 5

1965. "Circus 1965". Multicoloured.
2093. 20 fi. Type **347** 5 5
2094. 30 fi. Musical clown .. 5 5
2095. 40 fi. Performing elephant 5 5
2096. 50 fi. Performing seal .. 5 5
2097. 60 fi. Lions 8 5
2098. 1 fo. Wild cat leaping through burning hoops 12 5
2099. 1 fo. 50 Black panthers .. 15 5
2100. 2 fo. 50 Acrobat with hoops 20 8
2101. 3 fo. Performing panther and dogs 30 10
2102. 4 fo. Bear on bicycle .. 50 20

348. Rescue Boat. **349.** Dr. I. Semmelweis.

1965. Danube Flood Relief.
2103. **348.** 1 fo.+50 fi. brn. & bl. 12 10

1965. Ignaz Semmelweis (physician). Death Cent.
2105. **349.** 60 fi. brown 5 5

350. Running.

1965. University Games, Budapest. Multicoloured.
2106. 20 fi. Type **350** 5 5
2107. 30 fi. Start of swimming race 5 5
2108. 50 fi. Diving 5 5
2109. 60 fi. Gymnastics 5 5
2110. 80 fi. Tennis 8 5
2111. 1 fo. 70 Fencing 15 5
2112. 2 fo. Handball 35 10
2113. 2 fo. 50 Basketball .. 55 20
2114. 4 fo. Water-polo .. 60 20

351. Congress Emblem. **352.** "Phyllocactus hybridum".

1965. 6th W.F.T.U. Congress, Warsaw.
2116. **351.** 60 fi. blue 5 5

1965. Cacti and Orchids. Multicoloured.
2117. 20 fi. Type **352** 5 5
2118. 30 fi. "Cattleya warszewiczii" 5 5
2119. 60 fi. "Rebutia calliantha" 5 5
2120. 70 fi. "Paphiopedilum hybridum" 8 5
2121. 80 fi. "Opuntia rhodantha" 8 5
2122. 1 fo. "Laelia elegans" .. 12 5
2123. 1 fo. 50 "Zygocactus truncatus" 15 5
2124. 2 fo. "Strelitzia reginae" 25 8
2125. 2 fo. 50 "Lithops weberi" 30 12
2126. 3 fo. "Victoria amazonica" 40 20

353. Reproduction of No. 1127. **354.** F.I.R. Emblem.

1965. Stamp Day. Designs show reproductions of Hungarian stamps. Multicoloured.
2127. 2 fo.+1 fo. Type **353** .. 30 30
2128. 2 fo.+1 fo. No. 1280 .. 30 30
2129. 2 fo.+1 fo. No. 1873 .. 30 30
2130. 2 fo.+1 fo. No. 1733 .. 30 30
Nos. 2127/30 were issued together in sheets of 32 (4×8) with the four stamps arranged in horiz. rows.

1965. 5th Int. Federation of Resistance Fighters Congress, Budapest.
2132. **354.** 2 fo. blue 15 5

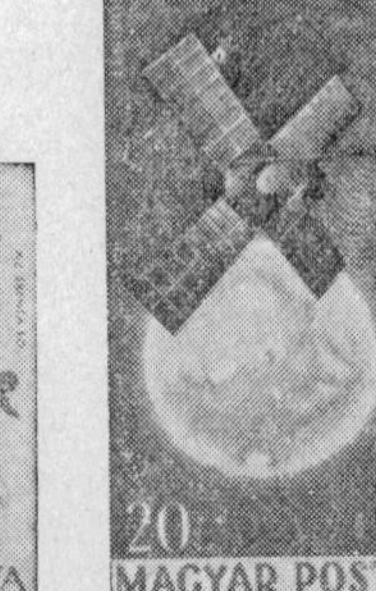

355. The Magic Horse. **356.** "Mariner 4".

1965. Fairy Tales (3rd series). Scenes from "The Arabian Nights Entertainments". Multicoloured.
2133. 20 fi. Type **355** 5 5
2134. 30 fi. Sultan Schahriah and Scheherazade 5 5
2135. 50 fi. Sinbad's 5th Voyage (ship) 5 5
2136. 60 fi. Aladdin and Genie of the Lamp 8 5
2137. 80 fi. Haroun al Rashid .. 10 5
2138. 1 fo. The Magic Carpet .. 12 5
2139. 1 fo. 70 The Fisherman and the Genie 25 5
2140. 2 fo. Ali Baba 25 8
2141. 3 fo. Sinbad's 2nd Voyage (roc—legendary bird) 55 15

1965. Air. Space Research.
2142. **356.** 20 fi. blk., yell. & blue 5 5
2143. – 30 fi. vio., yell. & brn. 5 5
2144. – 40 fi. brn., mve. & brn. 5 5
2145. – 60 fi. black, grey, yellow and violet .. 8 5
2146. – 1 fo. black, grey, brn. and violet 15 5
2147. – 2 fo. 50 blk., grey & pur. 45 20
2148. – 3 fo. blk., grn. & brn. 50 25
DESIGNS: 30 fi. "San Marco" (Italian satellite). 40 fi. "Molnyija 1" (Polish satellite). 60 fi. Moon rocket. 1 fo. "Shapir" rocket. 2 fo. 50 "Szonda 3" satellite. 3 fo. "Syncom 3" satellite.

357. "Callimorpha dominula". **358.** Bela Kun.

1966. Hungarian butterflies. Multicoloured.
2150. 20 fi. Type **357** 5 5
2151. 60 fi. "Anthocharis cardamines" 5 5
2152. 70 fi. "Meleageria daphnis" 8 5
2153. 80 fi. "Iphiclides podalirius" 8 5
2154. 1 fo. "Zygaena carniolica" 10 5
2155. 1 fo. 50 "Zerynthia hypermnestra" 15 5
2156. 2 fo. "Nymphalis antiopa" 20 5
2157. 2 fo. 50 "Libythea celtis" 25 8
2158. 3 fo. "Colias croceus" .. 45 20

1966. Anniversaries of 1966.
2159. 60 fi. black and red (T **358**) 5 5
2160. 60 fi. blk. & blue (T. Esze) 5 5
2161. 1 fo. violet (Shastri) .. 8 5
2162. 2 fo. brown and ochre (I. Szechenyi) .. 15 5
2163. 2 fo. sep. & bis. (M. Zrini) 8 5
2164. 2 fo. sepia and green (S. Koranyi) 15 5
EVENTS: No. 2159, 80th Birth Anniv. (workers' leader). 2160, (after statue by M. Nemth) 300th Birth Anniv. (war hero). 2161, Death commem. (Indian Prime Minister). 2162, 175th Birth Anniv. (statesman). 2163, 400th Death Anniv. (military commander). 2164, Birth Cent. (scientist).

359. "Luna 9" in Space. **360.** Crocus.

1966. Moon Landing of "Luna 9".
2165. **359.** 2 fo. blk. yell. & violet 20 8
2166. – 3 fo. blk., yellow & bl. 35 30
DESIGN—HORIZ. 3 fo. "Luna 9" on Moon.

1966. Flower Protection. Multicoloured.
2167. 20 fi. Type **360** 5 5
2168. 30 fi. European Cyclamen 5 5
2169. 60 fi. Ligularia 5 5
2170. 1 fo. 40 Orange Lily .. 15 5
2171. 1 fo. 50 Fritillary .. 15 10
2172. 3 fo. "Dracocephalum ruyschiana" 40 25

361. Order of Labour (bronze). **363.** Swallows.

362. Early Transport and Budapest Railway Station, 1846.

1966. Hungarian Medals and Orders. Mult.

2173.	361	20 fl. Type 361	5	5
2174.		30 fl. Order of Labour (silver)	5	5
2175.		50 fl. Banner Order of Republic, 2rd class ($21\frac{1}{2} \times 28\frac{1}{2}$ mm.)	5	5
2176.		60 fl. Order of Labour (gold)	5	5
2177.		70 fl. Banner Order of Republic, 2nd class ($25 \times 30\frac{1}{2}$ mm.)	5	5
2178.		1 fo. Red Banner Order of Labour	8	5
2179.		1 fo. 20 Banner Order of Republic, 1st class ($28\frac{1}{2} \times 38$ mm.)	10	5
2180.		2 fo. Order of Merit of Republic	20	10
2181.		2 fo. 50 Hero of Socialist Labour	25	12

1966. Re-opening of Transport Museum, Budapest.

2182.	362.	1 fo. brn., grn. & yell.	8	5
2183.	–	2 fo. blue, brn. & grn.	25	15

DESIGN: 2 fo. Modern transport and South Station, Budapest.

1966. Protection of Birds. Multicoloured.

2184.	20 fl. Type 363	5	5
2185.	30 fl. Long-tailed tits	5	5
2186.	60 fl. Crossbill	5	5
2187.	1 fo. 40 Middle spotted woodpecker	15	5
2188.	1 fo. 50 Hoopoe	20	10
2189.	3 fo. Forest and emblem of National Forestry Assn.	40	25

364. W.H.O. Building.

1966. W.H.O. Headquarters, Geneva. Inaug.

2190.	364.	2 fo. black and blue	15	5

365. Nuclear Research Institute.

1966. United Nuclear Research Institute, Dubna (U.S.S.R.). 10th Anniv.

2192.	365.	60 fl. black and green	5	5

366. Buda Fortress, after Schedel's "Chronicle" (1493).

1966. U.N.O. 20th Anniv. and 72nd Executive Board Session, Budapest.

2193.	366.	2 fo. violet and blue	15	5

367. Jules Rimet, Football and Cup.

1966. World Cup Football Championships. Multicoloured.

2194.	20 fl. Type 367	5	5
2195.	30 fl. Montevideo, 1930	5	5
2196.	60 fl. Rome, 1934	5	5
2197.	1 fo. Paris, 1938	8	5
2198.	1 fo. 40 Rio de Janeiro, 1950	10	5
2199.	1 fo. 70 Berne, 1954	12	5
2200.	2 fo. Stockholm, 1958	20	8
2201.	2 fo. 50 Santiago de Chile, 1962	45	12
2202.	3 fo. + 1 fo. World Cup emblem on Union Jack, and map of England	50	25

368. Girl Pioneer and Emblem.

1966. Hungarian Pioneers. 20th Anniv.

2203.	368.	60 fl. red and violet	5	5

369. Fire Engine.

1966. Voluntary Fire Brigades. Cent.

2204.	369.	2 fo. black and orange	15	5

370. Fox. **371.** Throwing the Discus.

1966. Hunting Trophies. Multicoloured.

2205.	20 fl. Type 370	5	5
2206.	60 fl. Wild boar	5	5
2207.	70 fl. Wild cat	8	5
2208.	80 fl. Roebuck	8	5
2209.	1 fo. 50 Stag	15	5
2210.	2 fo. 50 Fallow deer	30	10
2211.	3 fo. Moufflon	35	12

Nos. 2208/10 were issued alternately in sheets with se-tenant labels depicting trophies. Nos. 2208/9 were also issued in normal sheets without labels.

1966. 8th European Athletic Championships, Budapest. Multicoloured.

2212.	20 fl. Type 371	5	5
2213.	30 fl. High-jumping	5	5
2214.	40 fl. Throwing the javelin	5	5
2215.	50 fl. Throwing the hammer	5	5
2216.	60 fl. Long-jumping	10	5
2217.	1 fo. Putting the shot	15	8
2218.	2 fo. Pole-vaulting	30	12
2219.	3 fo. Running	40	20

372. Archery. **373.** Airliner over Helsinki.

1966. Stamp Day. Multicoloured.

2221.	2 fo. + 50 fl. Types 372	35	30
2222.	2 fo. + 50 fl. Grapes	35	30
2223.	2 fo. + 50 fl. Poppies	35	30
2224.	2 fo. + 50 fl. Space dogs	35	30

Nos. 2221/4 were issued together in sheets, the four stamps being arranged in horiz. rows.

1966. Air.

2226.	373.	20 fl. chestnut	5	5
2227.	–	50 fl. sepia	5	5
2228.	–	1 fo. blue	5	5
2229.	–	1 fo. 10 black	5	5
2230.	–	1 fo. 20 orange	8	5
2231.	–	1 fo. 50 turquoise	10	5
2232.	–	2 fo. blue	12	5
2233.	–	2 fo. 50 red	12	5
2234.	–	3 fo. green	15	5
2235.	–	4 fo. brown	20	8
2236.	–	5 fo. violet	25	8
2237.	–	10 fo. ultramarine	55	8
2238.	–	20 fo. green	1·00	15

DESIGNS (Airliner over): 50 fl. Athens. 1 fo. Beirut. 1 fo. 10, Frankfurt. 1 fo. 20, Cairo. 1 fo. 50, Copenhagen. 2 fo. London. 2 fo. 50, Moscow. 3 fo. Paris. 4 fo. Prague. 5 fo. Rome. 10 fo. Damascus. 20 fo. Budapest.

For 2 fo. 60 in similar design see No. 2369.

374. "Girl in the Woods" (after Barabos).

1966. Paintings from Hungarian National Gallery (1st series). Multicoloured.

2239.	60 fl. Type 374	10	5
2240.	1 fo. "Mrs. Istvan Bitto" (Barabas)	15	5
2241.	1 fo. 50 "Laszio Hunyadi" Farewell" (Benczur)	30	10
2242.	1 fo. 70 "Woman Reading" (Benczur)	40	12
2243.	2 fo. "The Faggot-carrier" (Munkacsy)	45	15
2244.	2 fo. 50 "The Yawning Apprentice" (Munkacsy)	55	20
2245.	3 fo. "Woman in Lilac" (Merse)	60	20

The 1 fo. 70 is horiz.

See also Nos. 2282/8, 2318/24, 2357/63, 2411/17, 2449/55, 2495/501, 2525/31, 2562/8 and 2595/602.

375. "Vostok 3" and "Vostok 4" (Nikolaev and Popovich).

1966. Twin Space Flights. Multicoloured.

2247.	20 fl. Type 375	5	5
2248.	60 fl. Borman and Lovell, Schirra and Stafford	8	5
2249.	80 fl. Bykovsky and Tereshkova	8	5
2250.	1 fo. Stafford and Cernan	12	5
2251.	1 fo. 50 Beliaiev and Leonov (Leonov in space)	15	5
2252.	2 fo. McDivitt and White (White in space)	20	8
2253.	2 fo. 50 Komarov, Feoktistov and Yegorov	40	10
2254.	3 fo. Conrad and Gordon	50	15

376. Kitaibel and "Vitifolia Kitaibelia". **377.** Militiaman.

1967. Pal Kitaibel (botanist). 150th Death Anniv. Carpathian Flowers. Multicoloured.

2255.	20 fl. Type 376	5	5
2256.	60 fl. "Dentaria glandulosa"	5	5
2257.	1 fo. "Edraianthus tenuifolius"	12	5
2258.	1 fo. 50 "Althaea pallida"	15	5
2259.	2 fo. "Centaurea mollis"	20	10
2260.	2 fo. 50 "Sternbergia colchiciflora"	35	12
2261.	3 fo. "Iris hungarica"	40	15

1967. Workers' Militia. 10th Anniv.

2262.	377.	2 fo. blue	15	8

378. Faustus Verancsics' Parachute Descent, 1617.

1967. Air. "Aerofila 67". Airmail Stamp Exn., Budapest.

2263.	2 fo. + 1 fo. sepia & yell.	30	30
2264.	2 fo. + 1 fo. sepia & bl.	30	30
2265.	2 fo. + 1 fo. sepia & grn.	30	30
2266.	2 fo. + 1 fo. sepia & pink	30	30
2268.	2 fo. + 1 fo. blue & grn.	30	30
2269.	2 fo. + 1 fo. blue & orge.	30	30
2270.	2 fo. + 1 fo. bl. & yell.	30	30
2271.	2 fo. + 1 fo. bl. & pink	30	30

DESIGNS: No. 2263, Type 378. 2264, David Schwarz's balloon, 1897. 2265, Erno Horvath's monoplane, 1911. 2266, "PKZ-2" helicopter, 1918. 2268, Parachutist. 2269, "Mi-1" helicopter. 2270, "TU-154" jetliner. 2271, "Luna 12".

Nos. 2263/6 and 2268/71 were issued se-tenant in horiz. strips of four.

379. I.T.Y. Emblem and Transport.

1967. Int. Tourist Year.

2273.	379.	1 fo. black and blue	8	5

380. S.S. "Ferenc Deak". Schonbuchel Castle and Austrian Flag.

1967. Danube Commission. 25th Session. Vessels of Mahart Shipping Company.

2275.	380.	30 fl. multicoloured	5	5
2276.	–	60 fl. multicoloured	8	5
2277.	–	1 fo. multicoloured	8	5
2278.	–	1 fo. 50 multicoloured	15	5
2279.	–	1 fo. 70 multicoloured	20	8
2280.	–	2 fo. multicoloured	25	10
2281.	–	2 fo. 50 multicoloured	30	15

DESIGNS (Vessels, backgrounds and flags): 60 fl. River-bus, Bratislava Castle, Czechoslovakia. 1 fo. Diesel passenger boat "Hunyadi", Buda Castle, Hungary. 1 fo. 50, Diesel tug "Szekszard", Golubac Castle, Yugoslavia. 1 fo. 70, Tug "Miscolc", Vidin Castle, Bulgaria. 2 fo. Motor-freighter "Tihany", Galati shipyard, Rumania. 2 fo. 50, Hydrofoil "Siraly I", port of Izmail, U.S.S.R.

381. "Szidonia Doak" (A. Gyorgyl).

1967. Paintings in National Gallery, Budapest (2nd series). Multicoloured.

2282.	60 fl. "Liszt" (M. Munkacsy)	8	5
2283.	1 fo. "Self-portrait" (S. Lanyl)	12	5
2284.	1 fo. 50 "Portrait of a Lady" (J. Borsos)	20	5
2285.	1 fo. 70 "The Lovers" (after P. Szinyei Merse)	20	5
2286.	2 fo. Type 381	25	8
2287.	2 fo. 50 "National Guardsman" (J. Borsos)	35	10
2288.	3 fo. "Louis XV and Madame Dubarry" (G. Benczur)	45	15

The 1 fo. 70 is horiz.

382. Poodle.

1967. Dogs. Multicoloured.

2289. 30 fi. Type 382 .. .. 5 5
2290. 60 fi. Collie 8 5
2291. 1 fo. Pointer 12 5
2292. 1 fo. 40 Fox terriers .. 15 5
2293. 2 fo. Pumi 25 5
2294. 3 fo. Alsatian 40 12
2295. 4 fo. Puli 55 15

The 60 fi., 1 fo. 40 and 3 fo. are vert., size $23\frac{1}{2} \times 35$ mm.

383. Sturgeon.

384. " Prince Igor " (Borodin).

385. " Teaching " (14th-cent. class).

1967. 14th Int. Anglers' Federation Congress, and World Angling Championships, Dunaujvaros. Multicoloured.

2296. 20 fi. Type 383 .. .. 5 5
2297. 60 fi. Pike perch 8 5
2298. 1 fo. Carp 12 5
2299. 1 fo. 70 European Wel .. 20 5
2300. 2 fo. Pike 25 5
2301. 2 fo. 50 Asp 30 8
2302. 3 fo.+1 fo. Anglers' and C.I.P.S. (Federation) emblem 50 15

1967. Popular Operas. Designs showing scenes from various operas. Multicoloured.

2303. 20 fi. Type 384 .. .. 5 5
2304. 30 fi. " Der Freischutz " (Weber) 5 5
2305. 40 fi. " The Magic Flute " (Mozart) 5 5
2306. 60 fi. " Bluebeard's Castle " (Bartok) 10 5
2307. 80 fi. " Carmen " (Bizet) 12 5
2308. 1 fo. "Don Carlos" (Verdi) 12 5
2309. 1 fo. 70 " Tannhauser " (Wagner) 25 10
2310. 3 fo. " Laszlo Hunyadi " (Erkel) 50 20

Nos. 2307/10 are vert.

1967. Higher Education in Hungary. 600th Anniv.

2311. 385. 2 fo. green and gold .. 25 8

386. Faculty Building.

1967. Political Law and Science Faculty, Lorand Eotvos University, Budapest. 300th Anniv.

2312. 386. 2 fo. green 25 8

387. " Lenin as Teacher ".

1967. October Revolution. 50th Anniv. Multicoloured.

2313. 60 fi. Type 387 .. .. 8 5
2314. 1 fo. " Lenin " 12 5
2315. 3 fo. " Lenin aboard the Aurora " 40 12

388. " Venus 4 ".

1967. Landing of " Venus 4 " on planet Venus.

2316. 388. 5 fo. multicoloured .. 70 40

388a. " Brother and Sister " (A. Fenyes).

1967. Paintings in National Gallery, Budapest (3rd series). As T 388a. Multicoloured.

2318. 60 fi. Type 388a .. 8 5
2319. 1 fo. " Boys Wrestling on Beach " (O. Glatz) .. 12 5
2320. 1 fo. 50 " October " (K. Ferenczy) 20 5
2321. 1 fo. 70 " Women by the River " (I. Szonyi) .. 20 5
2322. 2 fo. " Godfather's Breakfast " (I. Csok) 25 5
2323. 2 fo. 50 " The Eviction Order " (G. Derkovits) 25 8
2324. 3 fo. " Self-Portrait " (T. Csontvary) 35 15

The 1 fo. 70 is horiz.

" The Women by the River " (1 fo. 70) is in a private collection in Budapest.

389. Rifle-shooting on Skis.

1967. Winter Olympic Games, Grenoble. Multicoloured.

2326. 30 fi. Type 389 .. 5 5
2327. 60 fi. Figure-skating (pairs) 8 5
2328. 1 fo. Bob-sleighing .. 10 5
2329. 1 fo. 40 Downhill skiing .. 15 5
2330. 1 fo. 70 Figure-skating .. 20 5
2331. 2 fo. Speed-skating .. 20 5
2332. 3 fo. Ski-jumping .. 25 8
2333. 4 fo.+1 fo. Ice stadium, Grenoble 55 10

390. Kalman Kando, Class V43 Electric Locomotive and Map.

1968. Kando Commem.

2335. 390. 2 fo. blue 12 5

391. Cat.

1968. Cats. Multicoloured.

2336. 20 fi. Type 391 .. .. 5 5
2337. 60 fi. Cream angora .. 5 5
2338. 1 fo. Smoky angora .. 10 5
2339. 1 fo. 20 Domestic kitten 12 5
2340. 1 fo. 50 White angora .. 15 5
2341. 2 fo. Striped angora .. 20 5
2342. 2 fo. 50 Siamese 25 8
2343. 5 fo. Blue angora .. 55 12

392. Zoltan Kodaly (composer). 393. City Hall, Arms, Grapes and Apricot.

1968. Kodaly Commem.

2344. 392. 5 fo. multicoloured .. 60 40

1968. Kecskemet. 600th Anniv.

2345. 393. 2 fo. brown 12 5

394. White Stork. 395. Karl Marx.

1968. Int. Council for Bird Preservation Congress, Budapest. Protected Birds. Mult.

2346. 20 fi. Type 394 .. .. 5 5
2347. 50 fi. Golden orioles .. 8 5
2348. 60 fi. Imperial eagle .. 8 5
2349. 1 fo. Red-footed falcons 12 5
2350. 1 fo. 20 Scops owl .. 15 5
2351. 1 fo. 50 Great bustard .. 20 8
2352. 2 fo. Bee-eaters 25 10
2353. 2 fo. 50 Grey lag goose .. 40 12

1968. Karl Marx. 150th Birth Anniv.

2354. 395. 1 fo. maroon .. 8 5

396. Student.

1968. Mosonmagyarovar Agricultural College. 150th Anniv.

2356. 396. 2 fo. green 12 5

1968. Paintings in National Gallery, Budapest (4th series). As T 381. Multicoloured.

2357. 40 fi. " Girl with a Pitcher " (Goya) 5 5
2358. 60 fi. " Head of an Apostle " (El Greco) 5 5
2359. 1 fo. " Boy with Apples " (Nunez) 10 5
2360. 1 fo. 50 " The Repentant Magdalen " (El Greco) 12 5
2361. 2 fo. 50 " The Breakfast " (Velasquez) 20 8
2362. 4 fo. " St. Elizabeth " (detail from " The Holy Family "; El Greco) .. 40 12
2363. 5 fo. " The Knifegrinder " (Goya) 50 15

The 1 fo. and 2 fo. 50 are horiz.

397. Lake Steamer, Flags and Badacsony Hills. 398. Airliner over St. Stephen's Cathedral, Vienna.

1968. Lake Balaton Resorts. Multicoloured.

2365. 20 fi. Type 397 .. .. 5 5
2365a. 40 fi. Type 397 .. .. 5 5
2366. 60 fi. Tihany peninsula, tower and feather .. 8 5
2367. 1 fo. Sailing-boats and buoy, Balatonalmadi .. 8 5
2368. 2 fo. Szigliget bay, vineyard, wine and fish .. 20 8

1968. Air. Budapest-Vienna Airmail Service. 50th Anniv.

2369. 398. 2 fo. 60 violet .. 15 5

399. Steam Locomotive Type "424". 401. M. Tompa (poet).

400. Grazing Stud.

1968. Hungarian State Railways. Cent.

2370. 399. 2 fo. black, slate, blue and gold 15 8

1968. Horse-breeding on the Puszta (Hungarian steppe). Multicoloured.

2371. 30 fi. Type 400 .. .. 5 5
2372. 40 fi. Horses in storm .. 5 5
2373. 60 fi. Grooms horse-racing 8 5
2374. 80 fi. Horse-drawn sleigh 10 5
2375. 1 fo. Four-in-hand .. 12 5
2376. 1 fo. 40 Seven-in-hand .. 15 5
2377. 2 fo. Driving five horses .. 20 8
2378. 2 fo. 50 Groom preparing evening meal 25 15
2379. 4 fo. Five-in-hand .. 50 15

1968. Mihaly Tompa. Death Cent.

2380. 401. 60 fi. violet 5 5

402. Festival Emblem, Bulgarian and Hungarian Couples in National Costume.

1968. 9th World Youth Festival, Sofia.

2381. 402. 60 fi. multicoloured .. 5 5

403. Swimming.

1968. Air. Olympic Games, Mexico. Multicoloured.

2383. 20 fi. Type 403 .. 5 5
2384. 60 fi. Football 5 5
2385. 80 fi. Wrestling 5 5
2386. 1 fo. Canoeing 8 5
2387. 1 fo. 40 Gymnastics .. 15 5
2388. 2 fo.+1 fo. Horse-jumping 30 8
2389. 3 fo. Fencing 40 8
2390. 4 fo. Throwing the Javelin 50 12

404. Baja Plate, 1870. 405. Society Emblem.

1968. Stamp Day. Hungarian Ceramics. Multicoloured.

2391. 1 fo.+50 fi. Type **404** .. 15 8
2392. 1 fo.+50 fi. West Hungarian jug, 1618 .. 15 8
2393. 1 fo.+50 fi. Tiszafured flagon, 1874 .. .. 15 8
2394. 1 fo.+50 fi. Mezocsat flask, 1848 .. .. 15 8

1968. "Hungarian Society for Popularisation of Scientific Knowledge".

2396. **405.** 2 fo. black and blue 10 5

406. Rocket Hesperus. **407.** Two Girls Waving Flags.

1968. Garden Flowers. Multicoloured.

2397. 20 fi. Type **406** 5 5
2398. 60 fi. Pansy 8 5
2399. 80 fi. Zinnias 10 5
2400. 1 fo. Morning Glory .. 12 5
2401. 1 fo. 40 Petunia 15 5
2402. 1 fo. 50 Purslane .. 15 8
2403. 2 fo. Michaelmas daisies 25 8
2404. 2 fo. 50 Dahlia 30 12

1968. Children's Stamp Designs for 50th Anniv. of Hungarian Communist Party. Multicoloured.

2405. 40 fi. Type **407** 5 5
2406. 60 fi. Children with flags and banner 8 5
2407. 1 fo. Pioneer bugler in camp 25 8

408. "Workers of the World Unite" (Bertalan Por's 1918 poster). **409.** Human Rights Emblem.

1968. Hungarian Communist Party. 50th Anniv.

2408. **408.** 1 fo. blk., red & gold 8 5
2409. – 2 fo. multicoloured .. 12 5

DESIGN—HORIZ. 2 fo. "Martyrs" (statue by Zoltan Kiss).

1968. Human Rights Year.

2410. **409.** 1 fo. brown .. 5 5

1968. Paintings in National Gallery, Budapest (5th series). Italian Masters. Designs as T **381**. Multicoloured.

2411. 40 fi. "Esterhazy Madonna" (Raphael) 5 5
2412. 60 fi. "The Annunciation" (Strozzi) 5 5
2413. 1 fo. "Portrait of a Young Man" (Raphael) .. 8 5
2414. 1 fo. 50 "The Three Graces" (Naldini) 12 5
2415. 2 fo. 50 "Portrait of a Man" (Sebastian del Piombo) 25 10
2416. 4 fo. "The Doge Marcantonio Trevisani" (Titian) .. 40 15
2417. 5 fo. "Venus, Cupid and Jealousy" (Bronzino) 50 20

Nos. 2411/17 are vert.

410. Endre Ady. **411.** Press Emblem.

1969. Endre Ady. 50th Death Anniv.

2419. **410.** 1 fo. blk., pur. & gold 5 5

1969. Athenaeum Press. Cent.

2420. **411.** 2 fo. blk., slate & gold 12 5

412. Throwing the Javelin.

1969. Olympic Gold-medal Winners. Multicoloured.

2422. 40 fi. Type **412** 5 5
2423. 60 fi. Canoeing 5 5
2424. 1 fo. Football 5 5
2425. 1 fo. 20 Throwing the Hammer 8 5
2426. 2 fo. Fencing 15 5
2427. 3 fo. Wrestling 25 5
2428. 4 fo. Kayak-canoeing .. 40 10
2429. 5 fo. Horse-jumping .. 50 20

413. Poster by O. Danko. **414.** Space Link-up of "Soyuz 4" and "Soyuz 5".

1969. Hungarian Republic. 50th Anniv.

2431. **413.** 40 fi. blk., red & gold 5 5
2432. – 60 fi. black, red & gold 5 5
2433. – 1 fo. black, red & gold 8 5
2434. – 2 fo. multicoloured 20 5
2425. – 3 fo. multicoloured .. 25 8

DESIGNS: 60 fi. Poster of Lenin by unknown artist. 1 fo. Poster of young man breaking chains, by R. Steiner. 2 fo. Poster of engineer by I. Foldes and G. Vegh. 3 fo. Poster of Soldier by unknown artist.

A 60 fi. in black, magenta and gold, in same design as No. 2432, was issued for Presentation purposes, but was not valid for postage.

1969. Air. Space Flights of "Soyuz 4" and "Soyuz 5". Multicoloured.

2437. 2 fo. Type **414** .. 12 5
2438. 2 fo. Space link-up and astronauts "walking" in Space 12 5

415. Jersey Tiger.

1969. Butterflies and Moths. Multicoloured.

2439. 40 fi. Type **415** .. 5 5
2440. 60 fi. Eyed Hawk-moth 5 5
2441. 80 fi. Painted Lady .. 5 5
2442. 1 fo. Tiger Moth .. 8 5
2443. 1 fo. 20 Small Fire-moth 10 5
2444. 2 fo. Large Blue .. 20 8
2445. 3 fo. Belted Oak Eggar .. 30 10
2446. 4 fo. Peacock 45 15

417. I.L.O. Emblem.

1969. Int. Labour Organisation. 50th Anniv.

2447. **417.** 1 fo. brown and lake 8 5

418. Chain Bridge, Budapest.

1969. "Budapest 71" Stamp Exn.

2448. **418.** 5 fo. + 2 fo. black, yellow, brn. & blue 50 20

419. "Black Pigs" (Gauguin).

1969. Paintings in National Gallery, Budapest (6th series). French Masters. Multicoloured.

2449. 40 fi. Type **419** 5 5
2450. 60 fi. "The Ladies" (Toulouse-Lautrec) (horiz.) 5 5
2451. 1 fo. "Venus on Clouds" (Vouet) 8 5
2452. 2 fo. "Lady with Fan" (Manet) (horiz.) .. 15 5
2453. 3 fo. "Petra Camera" (Chasseriau) 30 8
2454. 4 fo. "The Cowherd" (Troyon) (horiz.) .. 45 12
2455. 5 fo. "The Wrestlers" (Courbet) 50 12

420. Vac. **421.** "PAX".

1969. Danube Towns. Multicoloured.

2457. 40 fi. Type **420** 5 5
2458. 1 fo. Szentendre 8 5
2459. 1 fo. 20 Visegrad .. 10 5
2460. 3 fo. Esztergom 25 5

1969. Int. Peace Movement. 20th Anniv.

2461. **421.** 1 fo. gold and blue .. 5 5

422. Zelkova Leaf (fossil). **423.** Okorag Stirrup-cup, 1880.

1969. Hungarian Geological Institute. Cent. Minerals and Fossils. Multicoloured.

2463. 40 fi. Type **422** 5 5
2464. 60 fi. Greenockite calcite sphalerite crystals .. 5 5
2465. 1 fo. "Clupea hungarica" (fossilized fish) .. 5 5
2466. 1 fo. 20 Quartz crystals .. 8 5
2467. 2 fo. Ammonite 10 5
2468. 3 fo. Copper ore 25 5
2469. 4 fo. "Placochelys placodonta" (fossilized turtle) 40 8
2470. 5 fo. Cuprite crystals .. 50 12

1969. Hungarian Folk Art. Wood-carvings. Multicoloured.

2471. 1 fo.+50 fi. Type **423** .. 15 8
2472. 1 fo.+50 fi. Felsotiszavidek jar, 1898 .. 15 8
2473. 1 fo.+50 fi. Somogyharsagy pot, 1935 .. 15 8
2474. 1 fo.+50 fi. Alfold smoking-pipe, 1740 .. 15 8

424. "The Scientist at his Table" (Rembrandt). **425.** Horse-jumping.

1969. Int. "History of Art" Congress, Budapest.

2476. **424.** 1 fo. sepia 8 5

1969. World Pentathlon Championships, Budapest. Multicoloured.

2477. 40 fi. Type **425** 5 5
2478. 60 fi. Fencing 5 5
2479. 1 fo. Pistol-shooting .. 8 5
2480. 2 fo. Swimming .. 15 5
2481. 3 fo. Running .. 35 8
2482. 5 fo. All five sports .. 50 12

426. Postcard and Letterbox. **427.** Mahatma Gandhi.

1969. 1st Hungarian Postcard. Cent.

2483. **426.** 60 fi. ochre and red .. 8 5

1969. Mahatma Gandhi. Birth Cent.

2484. **427.** 5 fo. multicoloured .. 50 20

428. Hemispheres. **429.** "Janos Nagy" (self-portrait).

1969. World Trade Unions Federations Congress, Budapest.

2485. **428.** 2 fo. blue and brown 12 5

1969. Janos Nagy (painter). 50th Death Anniv.

2486. **429.** 5 fo. multicoloured .. 50 20

430. "Flight to the Moon" (after Jules Verne).

1969. Air. 1st Man on the Moon. Multicoloured.

2487. 40 fi. Type **430** 5 5
2488. 60 fi. Tsiolkovsky's "space station" 5 5
2489. 1 fo. "Luna 1" 8 5
2490. 1 fo. 50 "Ranger 7" .. 12 5
2491. 2 fo. "Luna 9" 15 5
2492. 2 fo. 50 "Apollo 8" .. 20 10
2493. 3 fo. "Soyuz 4, 5" .. 25 12
2494. 4 fo. "Apollo 10" .. 40 20

431. "St. John the Evangelist" (Van Dyck). **432.** Kiskunfelegyhaza Pigeon.

1969. Dutch Paintings in Hungarian Museums. Multicoloured.

2495. 40 fi. Type **431** .. 5 5
2496. 60 fi. "Peasants" (P. de Molyn) 5 5
2497. 1 fo. "Boy lighting Pipe" (H. Terbruggen) .. 5 5
2498. 2 fo. "The Musicians" (detail, Jan Steen) .. 12 5
2499. 3 fo. "Woman reading Letter" (P. de Hooch) 30 10
2500. 4 fo. "The Fiddler" (Dirk Hals) 40 12
2501. 5 fo. "J. Asselyn" (Frans Hals) 55 20

1969. Int. Pigeon Exn., Budapest.
2503. **432.** 1 fo. multicoloured .. 5 5

433. Daimler (1886).

1970. Air. Old Motor-Cars. Multicoloured.
2504. 40 fl. Type **433** .. 5 5
2505. 60 fl. Peugeot (1894) .. 5 5
2506. 1 fo. Benz (1901) .. 5 5
2507. 1 fo. 50 Cudell (1902) .. 10 5
2508. 2 fo. Rolls-Royce (1908).. 15 5
2509. 2 fo. 50 Ford "T" (1908).. 20 5
2510. 3 fo. Vermorel (1912) .. 35 10
2511. 4 fo. Csonka (1912) .. 40 15

434. View of Budapest. **435.** "Soyuz 6, 7, 8".

1970. Budapest 71 Stamp Exn. and Hungarian Stamps Cent. (1st series). Multicoloured. Background colours given.
2512. **434.** 2 fo.+1 fo. brown .. 20 20
2513. – 2 fo.+1 fo. lilac .. 20 20
2514. – 2 fo.+1 fo. blue .. 20 20
DESIGNS: Nos. 2516/7 show different views of Budapest, in style as T **434**.

1970. Space Exploration. Multicoloured.
2515. 3 fo. (x 4) Type **435** .. 1·40 1·40
2516. 3 fo. (x 4) Astronauts on Moon (Apollo 12) 1·40 1·40
Nos. 2515/6 were only available each in small sheets of four, and are priced thus.

436. Metro Train at Station.

1970. Budapest Metro. Opening.
2517. **436.** 1 fo. blue, turq. & blk. 8 5

437. Cloud Formation, Satellite and Globe. **438.** Lenin.

1970. Hungarian Meteorological Service. Cent.
2519. **437.** 1 fo. multicoloured .. 8 5

1970. Lenin. Birth Cent. Multicoloured.
2520. 1 fo. Lenin Statue, Budapest 8 5
2521. 2 fo. Type **438** 12 10

439. Lehar and Music.

1970. Franz Lehar (composer). Birth Cent.
2522. **439.** 2 fo. multicoloured .. 20 10

440. Fujiyama and Hungarian Pavilion.

1970. Air. Expo 70. Multicoloured.
2523. 2 fo. Type **440** 35 25
2524. 3 fo. Tower of the sun and peace bell 55 40

441. "Samson and Delilah" (M. Rocca).

1970. Paintings in National Gallery, Budapest (7th series). Multicoloured.
2525. 40 fl. Type **441** 5 5
2526. 60 fl. "Joseph's Dream" (G. B. Langetti) .. 5 5
2527. 1 fo. "Clio" (P. Mignard) 8 5
2528. 1 fo. 50 "Venus and Satyr" (S. Ricci) (horiz.) 12 5
2529. 2 fo. 50 "Andromeda" (F. Furini) 20 8
2530. 4 fo. "Venus, Adonis and Cupid" (L. Giordano) 35 10
2531. 5 fo. "Allegory" (woman, C. Giaquinto) 55 20

442. Beethoven (statue at Martonvasar). **443.** Foundryman.

1970. Beethoven. Death Bicent.
2534. **442.** 1 fo. grn., lilac & yell. 10 5

1970. Diosgyor Foundry, Miskolc. Bicent.
2535. **443.** 1 fo. multicoloured .. 8 5

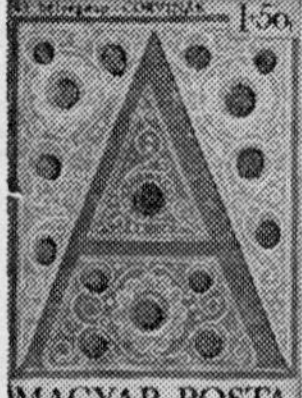

444. St. Stephen. **446.** Illuminated Initial.

445. Rowing Four.

1970. St. Stephen (King Stephen I of Hungary). 1,000th Birth Anniv.
2536. **444.** 3 fo. multicoloured 20 15

1970. 17th European Women's Rowing Championships, Lake Tata.
2537. **445.** 1 fo. multicoloured .. 10 5

1970. Stamp Day. Paintings and Illuminated Initials from Codices of King Matthias.
2538. 1 fo.+50 fl. Type **446** 25 5
2539. 1 fo. +50 fl. "N" and flowers .. 25 5
2540. 1 fo.+50 fl. "Ö" and ornamentation .. 25 5
2541. 1 fo.+50 fl. "King Matthias" 25 5

447. "Bread" (sculpture by I. Svabo) and F.A.O. Emblem.

1970. 7th F.A.O. European Regional Conference, Budapest.
2544. **447.** 1 fo. multicoloured.. 10 5

448. Boxing.

1970. Hungarian Olympic Committee. 75th Anniv. Multicoloured.
2545. 40 fl. Type **448** 5 5
2546. 60 fl. Canoeing 5 5
2547. 1 fo. Fencing 5 5
2548. 1 fo. 50 Water-polo .. 8 5
2549. 2 fo. Gymnastics .. 12 5
2550. 2 fo. 50 Throwing the Hammer 20 8
2551. 3 fo. Wrestling 20 8
2552. 5 fo. Swimming .. 40 15

449. Family and "Flame of Knowledge".

1970. 5th Education Congress, Budapest.
2553. **449.** 1 fo. red, blue & green 10 5

450. Chalice of Benedek Suky, c. 1400.

1970. Goldsmiths' Craft. Treasures from Budapest National Museum and Esztergom Treasury. Multicoloured.
2554. 40 fl. Type **450** .. 5 5
2555. 60 fl. Altar-cruet, c. 1500 5 5
2556. 1 fo. "Nadasdy" goblet, 16th-century 5 5
2557. 1 fo. 50 Coconut goblet with gold case, c. 1600 8 5
2558. 2 fo. Silver tankard of M. Toldalaghy, c. 1623 .. 12 5
2559. 2 fo. 50 Communion-cup of G.I. Rakoczi, c. 1670 20 5
2560. 3 fo. Tankard, c. 1690 .. 25 10
2561. 4 fo. "Bell-flower" cup, c. 1710 .. .. 40 15

451. "The Virgin and Child" ("Giampietrino", G. Pedrini).

1970. Paintings. Religious Art from Christian Museum, Esztergom. Multicoloured.
2562. 40 fl. Type **451**.. .. 5 5
2563. 60 fl. "Love" (G. Lazzarini) 5 5
2564. 1 fo. "Legend of St. Catherine of Alexandria" ("Master of Bat") .. 5 5
2565. 1 fo. 50 "Adoration of the Shepherds" (F. Fontebasso) (horiz.) .. 8 8
2566. 2 fo. 50 "Adoration of the Magi" ("Master of Aranyosmarot") .. 20 5
2567. 4 fo. "Temptation of St. Anthony the Hermit" (J. de Cock) 40 12
2568. 5 fo. "St. Sebastian" (Palmezzano) 50 15

452. Mauthausen Camp Memorial (A. Makrisz).

1970. Liberation of Concentration Camps. 25th Anniv.
2570. **452.** 1 fo. brown and blue 5 5

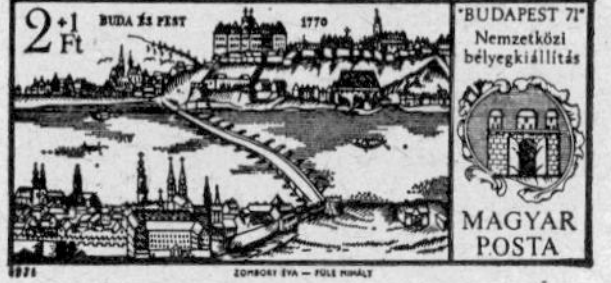

453. Budapest 1770.

1971. "Budapest 71" Stamp Exn., and Hungarian Stamp. Cent. (2nd series). "Budapest Through the Ages".
2572. – 2 fo.+1 fo. blk. & yell. 25 25
2573. – 2 fo.+1 fo. blk. & mve. 25 25
2574. – 2 fo.+1 fo. blk. & grn. 25 25
2575. **453.** 2 fo.+1 fo. blk. & orge. 25 25
DESIGNS: Budapest in: No. 2572, 1470. No. 2573, 1600. No. 2574, 1638.

454. "The Marseillaise" (sculpture by Rude). **455.** Bela Bartok.

1971. Paris Commune. Cent.
2578. **454.** 3 fo. brown & green 20 12

1971. Bela Bartok (composer). 90th Birth Anniv.
2579. **455.** 1 fo. black, grey & red 5 5

456. Gyor in 1594.

1971. Gyor. 700th Anniv.
2580. **456.** 2 fo. multicoloured .. 12 5

1971. Andras L. Achim (peasant leader). Birth Cent. Portrait in similar style to T **455.**
2582. 1 fo. black, grey & green 5 5

457. Hunting Bison.

1971. World Hunting Exhibition, Budapest. Multicoloured.

No.	Description	Unused	Used
2583.	40 fi. Type **457**	5	5
2584.	60 fi. Hunting wild boar	5	5
2585.	80 fi. Deer-stalking	5	5
2586.	1 fo. Falconry	5	5
2587.	1 fo. 20 Stag-hunting	8	5
2588.	2 fo. Bustards with young	12	8
2589.	3 fo. Netting fish	30	10
2590.	4 fo. Angling	45	15

458. Emblem on Flower.

1971. Hungarian Young Pioneers. 20th Anniv.

No.	Description	Unused	Used
2593.	**458.** 1 fo. multicoloured	5	5

459. F.I.R. Emblem.

1971. "Federation Internationale des Resistants". 20th Anniv.

No.	Description	Unused	Used
2594.	**459.** 1 fo. multicoloured	5	5

460. "Walking in the Garden" (Toyokuni School).

1971. Japanese Colour Prints from Ferenc Hopp Collection, Budapest. Multicoloured.

No.	Description	Unused	Used
2595.	40 fi. Type **460**	5	5
2596.	60 fi. "Geisha in boat" (Yeishi)	5	5
2597.	1 fo. "Woman with scroll-painting" (Yeishi)	5	5
2598.	1 fo. 50 "Oirans" (Kiyonaga)	8	5
2599.	2 fo. "Awabi Fishers" (Utamaro)	12	5
2600.	2 fo. 50 "Seated Oiran" (Harunobu)	20	5
2601.	3 fo. "Peasant Girl carrying Faggots" (Hokusai)	25	10
2602.	4 fo. "Women and Girls Walking" (Yeishi)	35	15

461. Locomotive "Bets" and Route Map (1846).

1971. Hungarian Railways. 125th Anniv.

No.	Description	Unused	Used
2603.	**461.** 1 fo. multicoloured	5	5

642. Hungarian Newspaper Stamp of 1871.

1971. "Budapest 71" Stamp Exhib. and Hungarian Stamp Cent. (3rd series). Multicoloured.

No.	Description	Unused	Used
2604.	2 fo.+1 fo. Type **462**	25	25
2605.	2 fo.+1 fo. 45 f. "Petofi" stamp of 1919	25	25
2606.	2 fo.+1 fo. 400 k. "Harvesters" stamp of 1920	25	25
2607.	2 fo.+1 fo. 16 f.+16 f. "Art" stamp of 1940	25	25

463. Griffin with Crucible.

1971. State Printing Office, Budapest. Cent.

No.	Description	Unused	Used
2609.	**463.** 1 fo. multicoloured	12	10

No. 2609 was issued with two flanking, stamp-size se-tenant labels showing stamp printing machines and Hungarian stamps.

464. O.I.J. Emblem and page of "Magyar Sajto".

1971. Int. Organisation of Journalists. 25th Anniv.

No.	Description	Unused	Used
2610.	**464.** 1 fo. gold and blue	5	5

465. J. Winterl (founder) and "Waldsteinia geoides".

1971. Botanical Gardens, Budapest. Bicent. Multicoloured.

No.	Description	Unused	Used
2612.	40 fi. Type **465**	5	5
2613.	60 fi. "Bromeliaceae"	5	5
2614.	80 fi. "Titanopsis calcarea"	5	5
2615.	1 fo. "Vinca herbacea"	8	5
2616.	1 fo. 20 "Gymnocalycium mihanovichii"	10	5
2617.	2 fo. "Nymphaea gigantea"	15	5
2618.	3 fo. "Iris arenaria"	25	8
2619.	5 fo. "Paeonia banatica"	40	15

466. Horse-racing.

1971. Equestrian Sport. Multicoloured.

No.	Description	Unused	Used
2620.	40 fi. Type **466**	5	5
2621.	60 fi. Trotting	5	5
2622.	80 fi. Cross-country riding	5	5
2623.	1 fo. Show-jumping	5	5
2624.	1 fo. 20 Start of race	5	5
2625.	2 fo. Polo	15	5
2626.	3 fo. Steeplechasing	25	10
2627.	5 fo. Dressage	55	15

467. "The Execution of Koppany".

1971. Miniatures from the "Illuminated Chronicle" of King Louis I of Hungary. Multicoloured.

No.	Description	Unused	Used
2628.	40 fi. Type **467**	5	5
2629.	60 fi. "The Pursuit of King Peter"	5	5
2630.	1 fo. "Basarad's Victory over King Charles Robert"	5	5
2631.	1 fo. 50 "The Strife between King Solomon and Prince Geza"	10	5
2632.	2 fo. 50 "The Founding of Obuda Church by King Stephen and Queen Gisela"	20	5
2633.	4 fo. "Reconciliation of King Coloman and his brother, Almos"	30	12
2634.	5 fo. "King Ladislas I supervising the construction of Nagyvarad Church"	40	15

468. Racial Equality Year Emblem.

1971. Racial Equality Year.

No.	Description	Unused	Used
2636.	**468.** 1 fo. multicoloured	5	5

469. Ice-hockey.

1971. Winter Olympic Games, Sapporo, Japan. Multicoloured.

No.	Description	Unused	Used
2637.	40 fi. Type **469**	5	5
2638.	60 fi. Downhill skiing	5	5
2639.	80 fi. Figure-skating (female)	5	5
2640.	1 fo. Ski-jumping	8	5
2641.	1 fo. 20 Cross-country skiing	10	5
2642.	2 fo. Figure-skating (male)	15	5
2643.	3 fo. Bob-sleighing	25	12
2644.	4 fo. Rifle-shooting (Biathlon)	35	15

470. Hungarian Class 303 (1950).

1972. Railway Steam Locomotives. Mult.

No.	Description	Unused	Used
2647.	40 fi. Type **470**	5	5
2648.	60 fi. Prussia Class P 6 (1902)	5	5
2649.	80 fi. Mediterranean Class 380 (Italy) (1894)	5	5
2650.	1 fo. Russia Class P 36 (1950)	5	5
2651.	1 fo. 20 Heisler locomotive (Japan)	8	5
2652.	2 fo. Caledonian 0-4-4T (1873)	15	5
2653.	4 fo. Austria Class 166 (1882)	30	12
2654.	5 fo. Crampton "Le Continent" (France) (1852)	40	15

471. J. Pannonius.

473. Doorway of Csempeszkopacs Church.

472. "Mariner 9".

1972. Janus Pannonius (poet). 500th Death Anniv.

No.	Description	Unused	Used
2655.	**471.** 1 fo. multicoloured	8	5

1972. Exploration of Mars. Multicoloured.

No.	Description	Unused	Used
2656.	2 fo. Type **472**	15	15
2657.	2 fo. "Mars 2 and 3"	15	15

1972. Protection of Monuments.

No.	Description	Unused	Used
2658.	**473.** 3 fo. green	20	12

474. Hungarian Greyhound.

1972. Hunting dogs. Multicoloured.

No.	Description	Unused	Used
2659.	40 fi. Type **474**	5	5
2660.	60 fi. Afghan hound (head)	5	5
2661.	80 fi. Irish wolfhound	5	5
2662.	1 fo. 20 Borzoi (head)	8	5
2663.	2 fo. Greyhound	15	10
2664.	4 fo. Whippet (head)	30	12
2665.	6 fo. Afghan hound	45	15

475. J. Imre, E. Grosz and L. Blaskovics.

1972. 1st. European Oculists' Congress, Budapest. Famous Oculists.

No.	Description	Unused	Used
2666.	**475.** 1 fo. brown and red	5	5
2667.	– 2 fo. brown and blue	15	10

DESIGN: 2 fo. A. Gullstrand, V. P. Filatov and J. Gonin.

476. Footballers and Flag of Hungary.

1972. Air. European Football Championships. Footballers and Flags of participating countries. Multicoloured.

No.	Description	Unused	Used
2668.	40 fi. Type **476**	5	5
2669.	60 fi. Rumania	5	5
2670.	80 fi. West Germany	5	5
2671.	1 fo. England	8	5
2672.	1 fo. 20 Yugoslavia	8	5
2673.	2 fo. Russia	15	10
2674.	4 fo. Italy	30	12
2675.	5 fo. Belgium	40	15

477. "V. Miskolcz" postmark, 1818-43.

1972. Stamp Day.

No.	Description	Unused	Used
2676.	**477.** 2 fo.+1 fo. black & bl.	30	30
2677.	– 2 fo.+1 fo. blk. & yell.	30	30
2678.	– 2 fo.+1 fo. blk. & grn.	30	30
2679.	– 2 fo.+1 fo. mult.	30	30

DESIGNS: No. 2677, "Szegedin" postmark, 1827-48. No. 2678, "Esztergom" postmark, 1848-51. No. 2679, "Budapest 71" stamp cent., cancellation, 1971.

478. Girl reading Book. **479.** Roses.

1972. Int. Book Year.
2681. **478.** 1 fo. multicoloured.. 8 5

1972. National Rose Exhib.
2682. **479.** 1 fo. multicoloured.. 8 5

480. G. Dimitrov. **481.** G. Dozsa.

1972. Georgi Dimitrov (Bulgarian leader). 90th Birth Anniv.
2684. **480.** 3 fo. multicoloured .. 20 12

1972. Georgi Dozsa (revolutionary). 500th Birth Anniv.
2686. **481.** 1 fo multicoloured.. 8 5

482. Football.

1972. Olympic Games, Munich. Mult.
2687. 40 fl. Type **482** 5 5
2688. 60 fl. Water-polo 5 5
2689. 80 fl. Javelin-throwing .. 5 5
2690. 1 fo. Kayak-canoeing .. 8 5
2691. 1 fo. 20 Boxing 8 5
2692. 2 fo. Gymnastics.. .. 15 10
2693. 3 fo.+1 fo. Wrestling .. 30 12
2694. 5 fo. Fencing 40 15

483. Prince Geza indicating site of Szekesfehervar.

1972. Szekesfehervar. Millennium and "Aranybulla" ("Golden Bull"). 750th Anniv. Multicoloured.
2696. 40 fl. Type **483** 5 5
2697. 60 fl. King Stephen and shield 5 5
2698. 80 fl. Soldiers and cavalry 5 5
2699. 1 fo. 20 King Stephen drawing up legislation 8 5
2700. 2 fo. Mason sculpting column 15 10
2701. 4 fo. Merchant displaying wares to King Stephen 30 12
2702. 6 fo. Views of Szekesfehervar and palace .. 45 15

484. Parliament Building, Budapest.

1972. Constitution Day. Multicoloured.
2704. 5 fo. Type **484** 35 8
2705. 6 fo. Parliament in session 40 12

485. Eger and "Bulls Blood".

1972. World Wines Competition, Budapest. Multicoloured.
2706. 1 fo. Type **485** 8 5
2707. 2 fo. Tokay and "Tokay Aszu" 15 10

486. Ear of Wheat and Emblems on Open Book.

1972. Georgikon Agricultural Academy, Keszthely. 175th Anniv.
2708. **486.** 1 fo. multicoloured.. 8 5

487. "Rothschild" Vase. **489.** Commemorative Emblem.

488. Diesel Train and U.I.C. Emblem.

1972. Herend Porcelain. Multicoloured.
2709. 40 fl. Type **487** 5 5
2710. 60 fl. "Poisson" bonbonniere 5 5
2711. 80 fl. "Victoria" case .. 5 5
2712. 1 fo. "Miramare" dish.. 8 5
2713. 1 fo. 20 "Godollo" pot.. 8 5
2714. 2 fo. "Empire" tea-set.. 15 10
2715. 4 fo. "Apponyi" dish .. 30 12
2716. 5 fo. "Baroque" vase .. 40 15
The 60 fl., 1 fo., 1 fo. 20, and 4 fo. are size 33×36 mm.

1972. Int. Railway Union. 50th Anniv.
2717. **488.** 1 fo. red 8 5

1972. National Economy Plan. 25th Anniv.
2718. **489.** 1 fo. yell., brn. & sepia 8 5

490. River Steamer and Old Obuda.

1972. Unification of Buda, Obuda and Pest as Budapest. Cent.
2719. **490.** 1 fo. red and blue .. 8 5
2720. – 1 fo. blue and red .. 8 5
2721. – 2 fo. green and brn... 15 5
2722. – 2 fo. brown and green 15 5
2723. – 3 fo. brn. and green 25 8
2724. – 3 fo. green and brown 25 8
DESIGNS: No. 2720, River hydrofoil and modern Budapest. No. 2721, View of Old Buda. No. 2722, View of Modern Budapest. No. 2723, View of Old Pest. No. 2724, Modern Budapest with Parliament Buildings.

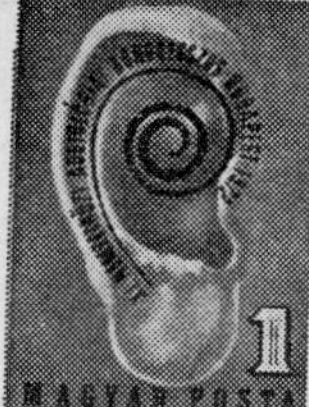

491. Congress Emblem within Ear. **493.** Miklos Radnoti (poet).

492. Postbox, Bell Telephone and Satellite "Molnya".

1972. Int. Audiological Congress, Budapest.
2725. **491.** 1 fo. blk., yellow-brn. and brown.. .. 8 5

1972. Reopening of Postal and Philatelic Museums, Budapest. Multicoloured.
2727. 4 fo.+2 fo. Type **492** .. 45 45
2728. 4 fo.+2 fo. Globe, post-horn and stamps .. 45 45

1972. Radnoti Commem.
2729. **493.** 1 fo. multicoloured.. 8 5

494. F. Martos. **495.** "The Muses" (J. Rippi-Ronai).

1972. Flora Martos (patriot). 75th Birth Anniv.
2730. **494.** 1 fo. multicoloured.. 8 5

1972. Stained-glass Windows. Mult.
2731. 40 fl. Type **495** 5 5
2732. 60 fl. "16th-century Scribe" (F. Sebestyen) 5 5
2733. 1 fo. "Exodus to Egypt" (K. Lotz) .. 8 5
2734. 1 fo. 50 "Prince Arpad's Messenger" (J. Percz) 10 5
2735. 2 fo. 50 "The Nativity" (L. Sztehlo) .. 20 8
2736. 4 fo. "Prince Arpad and Leaders" (K. Kernstok) 30 12
2737. 5 fo. "King Matthias reprimands the Rich Aristocrats" (J. Haranghy) .. 40 15

496. "Textiles".

1972. Opening of Textiles Technical Museum, Budapest.
2738. **496.** 1 fo. multicoloured.. 8 5

497. Main Square, Szarvas. **498.** S. Petofi.

1972.
2739. **497.** 40 fl. brown and pink 5 5
2740. – 1 fo. blue & light blue 8 5
2741. – 3 fo. green and blue.. 25 10
2742. – 4 fo. red and orange.. 30 12
2743. – 5 fo. deep blue & blue 40 20
2744. – 6 fo. brown and red.. 50 25

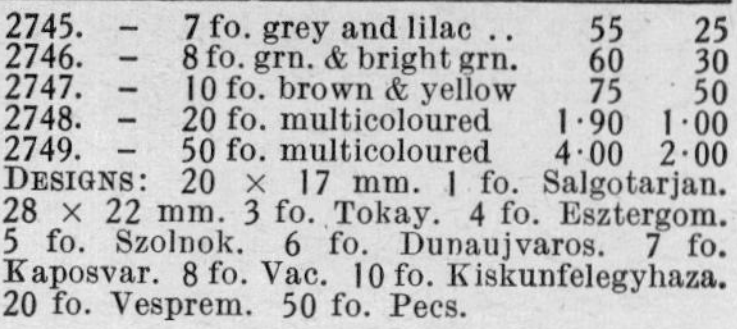
2745. – 7 fo. grey and lilac .. 55 25
2746. – 8 fo. grn. & bright grn. 60 30
2747. – 10 fo. brown & yellow 75 50
2748. – 20 fo. multicoloured 1·90 1·00
2749. – 50 fo. multicoloured 4·00 2·00
DESIGNS: 20 × 17 mm. 1 fo. Salgotarjan. 28 × 22 mm. 3 fo. Tokay. 4 fo. Esztergom. 5 fo. Szolnok. 6 fo. Dunaujvaros. 7 fo. Kaposvar. 8 fo. Vac. 10 fo. Kiskunfelegyhaza. 20 fo. Vesprem. 50 fo. Pecs.

1972. Sandor Petofi (poet and patriot). 150th Birth Anniv.
2762. – 1 fo. red 8 5
2763. **498.** 2 fo. lilac 15 5
2764. – 3 fo. green 25 8
DESIGNS: 1 fo. Petofi making speech in Cafe Pilvax. 3 fo. Petofi on horseback.

499. Arms of U.S.S.R.

1972. U.S.S.R. 50th Anniv.
2765. **499.** 1 fo. multicoloured .. 8 5

500. Code Map and Crow Symbol.

1973. Introduction of Postal Codes.
2766. **500.** 1 fo. black and red .. 8 5

1973. As Nos. 1912, 1915/16 and 1918 but smaller.
2767. 2 fo. blue 15 5
2768. 3 fo. blue 25 10
2769. 4 fo. green 30 12
2770. 6 fo. ochre 50 15
SIZES: 2767/8 and 2770, 22×19 mm. No. 2769, 19×22 mm.

501. Imre Madach. **502.** Carnival Mask.

1973. Imre Madach (writer). 150th Birth Anniv.
2772. **501.** 1 fo. multicoloured .. 8 5

1973. Busho-Walkinh Ceremony, Mohacs. Carnival Masks. As T **502**.
2773. **502.** 40 fl. multicoloured.. 5 5
2774. – 60 fl. multicoloured.. 5 5
2775. – 80 fl. multicoloured.. 5 5
2776. – 1 fo. 20 multicoloured 10 5
2777. – 2 fo. multicoloured.. 15 5
2778. – 4 fo. multicoloured .. 30 12
2779. – 6 fo. multicoloured 50 15

503. Copernicus. **504.** Horse-jumping and Gold Medal.

1973. Copernicus. 500th Birth Anniv.
2780. **503.** 3 fo. blue 25 25

1973. Air. Olympic Games, Munich. Hungarian Medal-winners. Mult.
2782. 40 fl. Type **504** .. 5 5
2783. 60 fl. Weightlifting .. 5 5
2784. 1 fo. Canoeing 8 5
2785. 1 fo. 20 Swimming .. 10 5
2786. 1 fo. 80 Boxing 15 5
2787. 4 fo. Wrestling 30 12
2788. 6 fo. Fencing 50 15

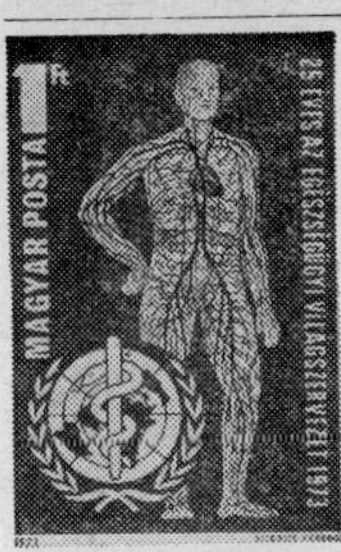
505. Biological Man.

506. Wrens.

1973. W.H.O. 25th Anniv.
2790. **505.** 1 fo. brown and green 8 5

1973. Hungarian Birds. Multicoloured.

2791.	40 fi. Type **506** ..	5	5
2792.	60 fi. Rock-thrush ..	5	5
2793.	80 fi. Robin	8	5
2794.	1 fo. Goldcrests	8	5
2795.	1 fo. 20 Linnets ..	10	5
2796.	2 fo. Blue tits	15	5
2797.	4 fo. Bluethroats ..	30	12
2798.	5 fo. Grey wagtails ..	40	15

507. Soldier and Weapon.

1973. Military Stamp Collectors' Exhibition, Budapest.
2799. **507.** 3 fo. multicoloured.. 25 25

508. " Budapest 61 " 1 fo. Stamp.

1973. "IBRA 73" Stamp Exn., Munich. Reproductions of Hungary Exhibition stamps.

2800.	40 fi. Type **508** ..	5	5
2801.	60 fi. " Budapest 61 " 1 fo. 70 stamp	5	5
2802.	80 fi. " Budapest 61 " 2 fo. 60 stamp	8	5
2803.	1 fo. " Budapest 61 " 3 fo. stamp	8	5
2804.	1 fo. 20 " Budapest 71 " 2 fo. stamp	10	5
2805.	2 fo. " Budapest 71 " 2 fo. stamp	15	5
2806.	4 fo. " Budapest 71 " 2 fo. stamp	30	12
2807.	5 fo. " Budapest 71 " 2 fo. stamp	40	15

Nos. 2800/7 depict miniature sheets.

509. Setting Type and Preparing Ink.

511. " Europa " Poster.

510. " Storm over Hortobagy Puszta ".

1973. Bookprinting in Hungary. 500th Anniv.
2809. **509.** 1 fo. black and gold 8 5
2810. – 3 fo. black and gold 25 8
DESIGN: 3 fo. Printer operating press.

1973. Paintings by Csontvary Kosztka. Multicoloured.

2811.	40 fi. Type **510**	5	5
2812.	60 fi. " Mary's Well, Nazareth "	5	5
2813.	1 fo. " Carriage drive by Moonlight "	8	5
2814.	1 fo. 50 " Pilgrimage to the Lebanese Cedars " ..	12	5
2815.	2 fo. 50 " The Lone Cedar "	20	8
2816.	4 fo. " Waterfall at Jajce "	30	12
2817.	5 fo. " Ruins of Greek Theatre at Taormina "	40	15

Nos. 2813/14 are vert.

1973. European Security and Co-operation Conference, Helsinki.
2819. **511.** 2 fo. 50 brown & blk. 20 8

512. " Rosa gallica ".

513. " Let's be friends . . . !".

1973. Wild Flowers. Multicoloured.

2820.	40 fi. Type **512** ..	5	5
2821.	60 fi. " Cyclamen europaeum "	5	5
2822.	80 fi. " Pulmonaria mollissima "	8	5
2823.	1 fo. 20 " Bellis perennis "	10	5
2824.	2 fo. " Adonis vernalis "	15	5
2825.	4 fo. " Viola cyanea " ..	30	12
2826.	6 fo. " Papaver rhoeas "	50	20

1973. Road Safety.

2827. **513.**	40 fi. green and red ..	5	5
2828. –	60 fi. orange and violet	5	5
2829. –	1 fo. blue and red ..	8	5

DESIGNS: 60 fi. " Not even a glass ! " (hand reaching for tumbler). 1 fo. " Cyclist – use a lamp " (car running down cyclist).

514. Silver "Eagle" Disc.

516. Csokonai's Statue, Debrecin.

515. " The Three Kings " (Master of the High Altar, Szmrecsany).

1973. Jewelled Treasures, National Museum.

2830. **513.**	2 fo. + 50 fi. silver, yell. and brown.. ..	25	10
2831. –	2 fo. + 50 fi. gold & pur.	25	10
2832. –	2 fo. + 50 fi. gold & bl.	25	10
2833. –	2 fo. + 50 fi. silver & green	25	10

DESIGNS: No. 2831, Serpent's head-ring. No. 2832. " Loving couple " buckle. 2833, Silver " floral " buckle.

1973. Esztergom Millenium. " Old Master " Paintings in the Christian Museum. Mult.

2836.	40 fi. Type **515**	5	5
2837.	60 fi. " Angels making Music " (Master " B.E.")	5	5
2838.	1 fo. " The Adoration of the Magi " (anon.) ..	8	5
2839.	1 fo. 50 " The Annunciation " (Szmrecsany Master)..	12	5
2840.	2 fo. 50 " Angels making Music " (different) (Master " B.E. ") ..	25	10
2841.	4 fo. " The Visitation of Mary Elizabeth " (Szmrecsany Master)..	35	12
2842.	5 fo. " The Legend of St. Catharine of Alexandria " (Master Bati) ..	45	15

1973. V. M. Csokonai (poet). 200th Birth Anniv.
2844. **516.** 2 fo. multicoloured.. 20 8

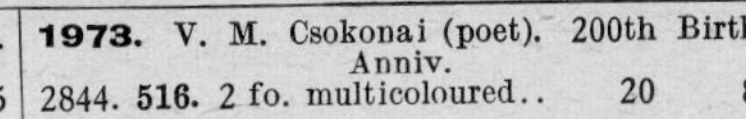

517. Jose Marti.

518. B. Pesti.

1973. Jose Marti (Cuban patriot). 120th Birth Anniv.
2845. **517.** 1 fo. brn., red & blue 8 5

1973. Barnabas Pesti (patriot). 30th Death Anniv.
2846. **518.** 1 fo. flesh, brn. & blue 8 5

519. Kayak-canoeing.

1973. World Aquatic Sports Championships, Belgrade and Tampere. Multicoloured.

2855.	40 fi. Type **519**	5	5
2856.	60 fi. Water polo.. ..	5	5
2857.	80 fi. Men's solo kayak ..	8	5
2858.	1 fo. 20 Swimming ..	10	5
2859.	2 fo. Men's kayak fours	20	8
2860.	4 fo. Men's solo canoe ..	35	12
2861.	6 fo. Men's double canoe..	55	20

520. Lenin.

1974. Lenin. 50th Death Anniv.
2863. **520.** 2 fo. brn., blue & gold 20 8

521. J. Boczor, I. Bekes and T. Elek.

1974. Hungarian Heroes of the French Resistance.
2864. **521.** 3 fo. multicoloured .. 25 10

522. " Comecon " H.Q., Moscow and Flags.

1974. Council for Mutual Economic Aid. 25th Anniv.
2865. **522.** 1 fo. multicoloured.. 10 5

523. Savings Bank Emblems.

525. Pres. Salvador Allende.

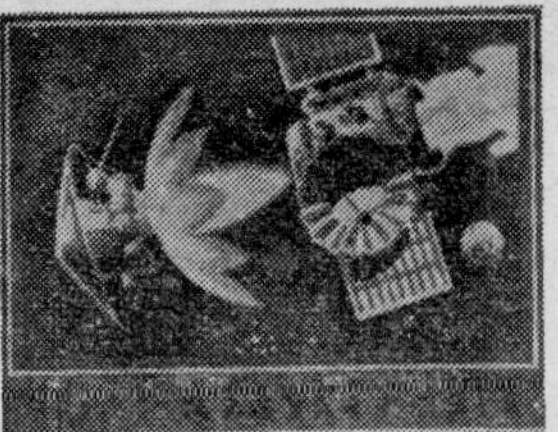
524. " Mariner 4 " on way to Mars.

1974. National Savings Bank. 25th Anniv.
2866. **523.** 1 fo. multicoloured .. 8 5

1974. Mars Research Projects. Mult.

2867.	40 fi. Type **524** (postage)	5	5
2868.	60 fi. "Mars 2" approaching Mars	5	5
2869.	80 fi. "Mariner 4" space probe	5	5
2870.	1 fo. Mt. Palomar telescope and Mars photo ..	8	5
2871.	1 fo. 20 "Mars 3" on planet's surface	10	5
2872.	5 fo. "Mariner 9" approaching Mars and satellites ..	50	20
2873.	6 fo. G. Schiaparelli and Martian "canals" map (air)	55	25

1974. Pres. Allende of Chile. Commem.
2875. **525.** 1 fo. multicoloured .. 8 5

526. "Mona Lisa" (Leonardo de Vinci).

1974. Exhibition of "Mona Lisa" in Japan.
2876. **526.** 4 fo. multicoloured .. 35 12

527. Dove with Letter.

1974. Universal Postal Union. Cent. Mult.

2878.	40 fi. Type **527**	5	5
2879.	60 fi. Mailcoach	5	5
2880.	80 fi. Early mail-van and postbox	8	5
2881.	1 fo. 20 Balloon-post ..	10	5
2882.	2 fo. Diesel mail-train ..	20	8
2883.	4 fo. Post-bus	35	12
2884.	6 fo. "TU 154" mail-plane	55	20

528. Swiss "Basle Dove" Stamp of 1845.

1974. "Internaba 1974" Stamp Exn., Basle.
2886. **528.** 3 fo. multicoloured .. 30 10

529. "The Chess Game" (13th-century miniature) and Pawn.

1974. International Chess Federation, and Chess Olympics, Nice. Multicoloured.

2887.	40 fi. Type **529**	5	5
2888.	60 fi. "The Chess Game" (woodcut by Caxton) and knight	5	5

2889. 80 fi. "Royal Chess Game" (15th-century Italian book) and pawn 8 5
2890. 1 fo. "The Chess Players" (engraving by Selenus) and castle 10 5
2891. 2 fo. Kempelen's chess-playing machine (1769) 20 8
2892. 4 fo. Hungarian Grand Master, Geza Maroczy, playing chess 35 12
2893. 6 fo. View of Nice, and Chess Olympics' emblem 55 20

530. Congress Emblem.

1974. World Economists' Congress, Budapest.
2895. 530. 2 fo. light blue, silver and dark blue .. 20 8

531. "Woman Bathing" (K. Lotz).

1974. "Nudes". Paintings. Multicoloured.
2896. 40 fi. Type 531 .. .. 5 5
2897. 60 fi. "Awakening" (K. Brocky) 5 5
2898. 1 fo. "Venus and Cupid" (K. Brocky) (horiz.) .. 10 5
2899. 1 fo. 50 "After Bathing" (K. Lotz) 15 5
2900. 2 fo. 50 "Honi soit qui mal y pense" (reclining nude) (horiz.) .. 25 10
2901. 4 fo. "After Bathing" (B. Szekely) 35 12
2902. 5 fo. "Devotion" (E. Korb) 45 20

532. "Mimi" (Czobel). 533. "Intersputnik" Earth Station.

1974. 91st Birth Anniv. of Bela Czobel (painter).
2904. 532. 1 fo. multicoloured .. 10 5

1974. Hungarian-Soviet Technical and Scientific Co-operation. 25th Anniv.
2905. 533. 1 fo. mauve and blue 10 5
2906. – 3 fo. purple and blue 30 10
DESIGN—HORIZ. 3 fo. Hungarian and Soviet power installations.

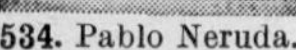

534. Pablo Neruda. 535. Swedish 3 s. Stamp of 1855 and Swedish "Lion".

1974. Neruda Commemoration.
2907. 534. 1 fo. pink, brown and blue 10 5

1974. "Stockholmia 74" International Stamp Exhibition.
2908. 535. 3 fo. green, gold and blue 30 10
No. 2908 was issued together se-tenant with a half stamp-size label, in small sheets of three stamps.

536. Tanks, and Soldier with Grenade-launcher.

1974. Military Day.
2909. 536. 1 fo. black, red and gold (postage) .. 10 5
2910. – 2 fo. blk., grn. & gold (air) 20 8
2911. – 3 fo. blk. bl. & gold .. 30 10
DESIGNS: 2 fo. Radar station and guided missile. 3 fo. Parachutist and helicopter.

537. Segner and Moon Crater.

1974. Janos Segner (scientist). 270th Birth Anniv.
2912. 537. 3 fo. multicoloured .. 30 10
No. 2912 was issued together se-tenant with a stamp-size label.

538. Mailplane of 1918.

1974. Air. "Aerofila 74" Stamp Exhibition, Budapest. Multicoloured.
2913. 2 fo. + 1 fo. Type 538 .. 30 10
2914. 2 fo. + 1 fo. "Graf Zeppelin" 30 10
2915. 2 fo. + 1 fo. Balloon post ("Aerofila 1967") .. 30 10
2916. 2 fo. + 1 fo. Mail helicopter 30 10
Nos. 2913/4 and 2915/6 were respectively issued together se-tenant within the sheet.

539. "Rhyparia purpurata".

1974. Butterflies. Multicoloured.
2918. 40 fi. Type 539 .. .. 5 5
2919. 60 fi. "Melanargia galathea" 5 5
2920. 80 fi. "Parnassius apollo" 8 5
2921. 1 fo. "Celerio euphorbia" 10 5
2922. 1 fo. 20 "Catocala fraxini" 10 5
2923. 5 fo. "Apatura iris" .. 45 20
2924. 6 fo. "Palaeochrysophanus hyppothoe" 55 20

540. Istvan Pataki. 541. Mother and Child.

1974. Hungarian Martyrs. Multicoloured.
2925. 1 fo. Type 540 .. .. 10 5
2926. 1 fo. Robert Kreutz .. 10 5

1974. "Motherhood".
2927. 541. 1 fo. blk., brn. and bl. 10 5

542. Puppy. 544. R. Bolyai.

543. Lambarene Hospital.

1974. Young Animals. Multicoloured.
2928. 40 fi. Type 542 .. .. 5 5
2929. 60 fi. Two kittens (horiz.) 5 5
2930. 80 fi. Rabbit 8 5
2931. 1 fo. 20 Foal (horiz.) .. 10 5
2932. 2 fo. Lamb 20 8
2933. 4 fo. Calf (horiz.) .. 35 12
2934. 6 fo. Piglet 55 20

1975. Dr. Albert Schweitzer. Birth Cent. Multicoloured.
2935. 40 fi. Type 543 .. .. 5 5
2936. 60 fi. Dr. Schweitzer treating patient .. 5 5
2937. 80 fi. Casualty arriving at Lambarene by canoe .. 8 5
2938. 1 fo. 20 Charitable stores arriving by ship .. 10 5
2939. 2 fo. View of Lambarene, doves, globe and Red Cross emblem 20 8
2940. 4 fo. Dr. Schweitzer's medal for Nobel Peace Prize (1953) .. 35 12
2941. 6 fo. Dr. Schweitzer and organ-pipes 55 20

1975. Farkas Bolyzi (mathematician). 200th Birth Anniv.
2942. 544. 1 fo. black and red .. 10 5

545. Carrier-pigeon. 546. Count M. Karolyi.

1975. Air. Carrier-pigeons' Olympiad, Budapest.
2943. 545. 3 fo. multicoloured .. 15 5

1975. Count Mihaly Karolyi (politician). Birth Centenary.
2944. 546. 1 fo. brown and blue 10 5

547. Woman's Head.

1975. International Woman's Year.
2945. 547. 1 fo. black and blue .. 10 5

548. "Rebuilding the Railways".

1975. Liberation. 30th Anniv. Multicoloured.
2946. 40 fi. Type 548 .. .. 5 5
2947. 60 fi. Hammer and sickle motif ("The bread starts here") 8 5
2948. 2 fo. Blacksmith's hammer ("The Party of action") 25 10
2949. 4 fo. Hammer as figure "3" ("Three-Year Plan for heavy industries") 50 20
2950. 5 fo. Apartment blocks ("A developed Socialist society") 60 25

549. Japanese "Arrow" (1915).

1975. Hungarian Automobile Club. 75th Anniv. Multicoloured.
2951. 40 fi. Type 549 .. .. 5 5
2952. 60 fi. British "Swift" (1911) 8 5
2953. 80 fi. American "Ford T" (1908) 10 5
2954. 1 fo. German "Mercedes" (1901) 12 5
2955. 1 fo. 20, French "Panhard-Levassor" (1912) 15 5
2956. 5 fo. Hungarian "Csonka" (1906) .. 60 25
2957. 6 fo. Club badge and emblems of international motoring organisations 70 30

550. Academy Building.

1975. Hungarian Academy of Sciences. 150th Anniv. Multicoloured.
2959. 1 fo. Type 550 .. .. 12 5
2960. 2 fo. Dates "1825" and "1975" in contrasting typography 25 10
2961. 3 fo. Count Szechenyi (pioneer of reforms) .. 35 15

551. Olympic Stadium, Moscow.

1975. "Socphilex V" Stamp Exhibition, Moscow.
2962. 551. 5 fo. multicoloured .. 60 25

552. French "Philatec" Stamp of 1964.

1975. "Arphila 75" International Stamp Exhibition, Paris.
2963. 552. 5 fo. multicoloured .. 60 25

553. Kando's Electric Locomotive and Transformer.

1975. Hungarian Electro-technical Assoc. 75th Anniv.
2964. 553. 1 fo. multicoloured .. 12 5

MINIMUM PRICE

The minimum price quoted is 5p which represents a handling charge rather than a basis for valuing common stamps. For further notes about prices see introductory pages.

554. " Sputnik ".

1975. Air. " Apollo-Soyuz " Space Link. Multicoloured.

2965. 40 fl. Type **554** 5 5
2966. 60 fl. " Mercury Atlas 5 " 8 5
2967. 80 fl. " Lunokhod 1 " Moon Vehicle 10 5
2968. 1 fo. 20 " Apollo 15 " Moon Vehicle 15 5
2969. 2 fo. Launch of " Soyuz " from Baikonur .. 25 10
2970. 4 fo. Launch of " Apollo " from Cape Canaveral .. 50 20
2971. 6 fo. " Apollo-Soyuz " Link-up 70 30

555. Sword, Epee and Rapier. **556.** Dr. A. Zimmermann.

1975. World Fencing Championships, Budapest.

2973. **555.** 1 fo. multicoloured .. 12 5

1975. Dr. Agoston Zimmermann (veterinary surgeon). Birth Cent.

2976. **556.** 1 fo. brown and blue 12 5

557. " Tree of 14 Languages ". **558.** Anjou Fountain.

1975. 4th International Finno-Ugrian Congress, Budapest.

2977. **557.** 1 fo. multicoloured .. 12 5

1975. Stamp Day. Protection of Historic Monuments. Visegrad Castle. Multicoloured.

2978. 2 fo. + 1 fo. Type **558** .. 35 15
2980. 2 fo. + 1 fo. Anjou canopied fountain 35 15
2981. 2 fo. + 1 fo. " Lions " fountain 35 15
2982. 2 fo. + 1 fo. Hercules fountain 35 15

559. Hungarian Arms and Map. **560.** Ocean Pollution.

1975. Hungarian Council System. 25th Anniv. Multicoloured.

2984. 1 fo. Type **559** 12 5
2985. 1 fo. Voters participating in council election .. 12 5

1975. Environmental Protection. Multicoloured.

2986. 40 fl. Type **560** 5 5
2987. 60 fl. Strangled rose (Water pollution) .. 8 5
2988. 80 fl. Dying fish (Pollution of precipitation) .. 10 5
2989. 1 fo. Dead carnation (Soil pollution) 12 5
2990. 1 fo. 20 Falling bird (Air pollution) 15 5
2991. 5 fo. Clean and infected lungs (Smoke pollution) 60 25
2992. 6 fo. Protective and skeletal hands (Global protection) 70 30

561. Imre Mezo.

1975. Hungarian Celebrities. Each black and red.

2993. 1 fo. Type **561** 12 5
2994. 1 fo. Mariska Gardos .. 12 5
2995. 1 fo. Imre Tarr 12 5

562. Organ, Orchestra and Treble Clef.

1975. Franz Liszt Music Academy. Centenary.

2996. **562.** 1 fo. multicoloured .. 12 5

563. Szigetcsepi Ikon.

1975. Regional Ikons showing Virgin and Child. Multicoloured.

2997. 40 fl. Type **563** 5 5
2998. 60 fl. Graboci ikon .. 8 5
2999. 1 fo. Esztergomi ikon .. 12 5
3000. 1 fo. 50 Vatopedi ikon .. 15 5
3001. 2 fo. 50, Tottosi ikon .. 30 12
3002. 4 fo. Gyori ikon 50 20
3003. 5 fo. Kazani ikon .. 60 25

564. Flags, Radar Equipment and Mother and Child.

1975. Warsaw Treaty. 20th Anniv.

3004. **564.** 1 fo. multicoloured .. 12 5

565. Ice-hockey.

1975. Winter Olympic Games, Innsbruck. Multicoloured.

3005. 40 fl. Type **565** 5 5
3006. 60 fl. Woman's slalom .. 8 5
3007. 80 fl. Men's slalom .. 10 5
3008. 1 fo. 20 Ski-jumping .. 15 5
3009. 2 fo. Women's speed-skating 25 10
3010. 4 fo. Cross-country skiing 50 20
3011. 6 fo. Bobsleighing .. 70 30

566. Engine-turned " P " and First and Latest Banknotes.

1976. State Banknote Printing Office, Budapest.

3013. **566.** 1 fo. multicoloured 12 5

567. Young Wild Hogs.

1976. Wild Animal Cubs. Multicoloured.

3014. 40 fl. Type **567** 5 5
3015. 60 fl. Squirrels (vert.) .. 8 5
3016. 80 fl. Lynxes 10 5
3017. 1 fo. 20 Wolves (vert.) .. 15 5
3018. 2 fo. Red foxes 25 10
3019. 4 fo. Brown bears (vert.) 50 20
3020. 6 fo. Lions 70 30

568. Bell and Modern Telecommunications.

1976. Telephone Centenary.

3021. **568.** 3 fo. multicoloured .. 45 20

569. " Clash between Rakoczi's Kuruts and Hapsburg Soldiers " (anon.).

1976. Prince Ferenc Rakoczi II. 300th Birth Anniv. Multicoloured.

3023. 40 fl. Type **569** 5 5
3024. 60 fl. " Meeting of Rakoczi and Tamas Esze " (E. Veszpremi) 10 5
3025. 1 fo. " The Parliament of Onod " (Mor Than) .. 15 5
3026. 2 fo. " Kuruts' Encampment " (anon.) .. 30 12
3027. 3 fo. " Ilona Zrinyi " (Rakoczi's mother) (anon.) (vert.) .. 45 20
3028. 4 fo. " Kurut Officers " (anon.) (vert.) .. 60 25
3029. 5 fo. " Prince Rakoczi II " (A. Manyoki) (vert.) .. 75 30

570. Metric System Act of 1876.

1976. Metric System in Hungary. Cent. Multicoloured.

3030. 1 fo. Type **570** 15 5
3031. 2 fo. Istvan Krusper and vacuum balance .. 30 12
3032. 3 fo. Interferometer and rocket 45 20

571. U.S. 6 c. Stamp of 1968.

1976. " Interphil '76 ". Int. Stamp Exn., Philadelphia.

3034. **571.** 5 fo. multicoloured .. 75 30

572. Pioneers within " 30 ".

1976. Hungarion Pioneer Organisation. 30th Anniv.

3035. **572.** 1 fo. multicoloured .. 15 5

573. Truck, Tractor and Safety Headgear.

1976. Industrial Safety.

3036. **573.** 1 fo. multicoloured .. 15 5

574. " Intelstar IV " (used for TV relays).

1976. Olympic Games, Montreal. Mult.

3037. 40 fl. Type **574** 5 5
3038. 60 fl. Horse-jumping .. 5 5
3039. 1 fo. Swimming 15 5
3040. 2 fo. Canoeing 30 12
3041. 3 fo. Fencing 45 20
3042. 4 fo. Javelin-throwing .. 60 25
3043. 5 fo. Gymnastics .. 75 30

575. " Little Mermaid " Statue, Copenhagen.

1976. " Hafnia '76 " International Stamp Exhibition, Copenhagen.

3045. **575.** 3 fo. multicoloured .. 45 20

576. " Flora " (Titian).

1976. Titian. 400th Death Anniv.
3046. 576. 4 fo. multicoloured .. 60 25

577. Knight.

578. Pal Gyulai (poet and historian).

1976. Stamp Day. Gothic Statues and Buda Castle.
3048. 2 fo. 50+1 fo. Type 577 55 25
3049. 2 fo. 50+1 fo. " Armour-bearer 55 25
3050. 2 fo. 50+1 fo. " Apostle " 55 25
3051. 2 fo. 50+1 fo. " Bishop " 55 25

1976. Cultural Anniversaries.
3052. 578. 2 fo. black and red .. 30 12
3053. – 2 fo. blk., grn. & gold 30 12
DESIGN: Daniel Berzsenyi (lyric poet) (birth bicent.).

579. " Hussar " (Z. Kisfaludy-Strobl).

1976. Herend China Factory. 150th Anniv.
3054. 579. 4 fo. multicoloured .. 60 25

580. Tuscany 1 q. Stamp of 1851 and Arms of Milan.

1976. "Italia '76" International Stamp Exhibition, Milan.
3055. 580. 5 fo. multicoloured .. 75 30

581. House of Culture and Soviet Dancer.

1976. House of Soviet Culture and Science, Budapest.
3056. 581. 1 fo. multicoloured .. 15 5

582. I. Bogar.

1976. Hungarian Labour Movement Celebrities.
3057. 582. 1 fo. brown and red .. 15 5
3058. – 1 fo. brown and red .. 15 5
3059. – 1 fo. brown and red .. 15 5
PORTRAITS: No. 3059 R. Golub. No. 3060 J. Madzar.

583. Dr. F. Koranyi and Dispensary.

1976. Koranyi T.B. Dispensary. 75th Anniv.
3060. 583. 2 fo. multicoloured .. 30 12

584. " Viking " Rocket.

1976. Air. " Viking " and " Venyera " Space Missions. Multicoloured.
3061. 40 fi. Type 584 .. .. 5 5
3062. 60 fi. " Viking " in flight 5 5
3063. 1 fo. " Viking " on Mars 15 5
3064. 2 fo. Launch of " Venyera " 30 12
3065. 3 fo. " Venyera 9 " in flight 45 20
3066. 4 fo. " Venyera 10 " in flight 60 25
3067. 5 fo. " Venyera " on Venus 75 30

EXPRESS LETTER STAMPS

E 1.

1916. Inscr. "MAGYAR KIR POSTA".
E 245. E 1. 2 f. olive and red .. 5 5

1918. Optd. **KOZTARSASAG.**
E 301. E 1. 2 f. olive and red .. 5 5

1919. Inscr. "MAGYAR POSTA".
E 349. E 1. 2 f. olive and red .. 5 5

JOURNAL TAX STAMPS

J 1.

1868. Imperf.
J 3. – 1 k. blue £3500 £2250
J 52. J 1. 1 k. blue 12 5
J 53. – 2 k. brown 75 75

Nos. J 3 and 53 show the crown at the bottom.

NEWSPAPER STAMPS

N 1.

N 2.

N 3.

1871. Posthorn turned to left. Imperf.
N 8. N 1. 1 k. red .. .. 15·00 6·00

1872. Posthorn turned to right. Imperf.
N 14. N 1. 1 k. red .. .. 2·50 75

1874. Imperf.
N 38. N 2. 1 k. orange 10 5

1900. Imperf.
N 136. N 3. (2 f.) orange .. 5 5
N 401. (10 f.) blue 5 5
N 402. (20 f.) purple .. 5 5

OFFICIAL STAMPS

O 1.

1921. Central inscr. "HIVATALOS" and figures in black.
O 428. O 1. 10 f. purple 5 5
O 429. 20 f. brown 5 5
O 430. 60 f. grey 5 5
O 431. 100 f. red 5 5
O 432. 250 f. blue 5 5
O 433. 350 f. blue 5 5
O 434. 500 f. brown .. 5 5
O 435. 1000 f. brown .. 5 5

1922. Surch.
O 436. O 1. 15 k. on 20 f. brown 5 5
O 437. 25 k. on 60 f. grey .. 5 5

1922. As 1921, but inscr. and value in colour of stamp or first colour.
O 441. O 1. 5 k. brown 5 5
O 442. 10 k. brown .. 5 5
O 443. 15 k. grey 5 5
O 444. 25 k. orange .. 5 5
O 445. 50 k. red and brown 5 5
O 446. 100 k. red and bistre 5 5
O 447. 150 k. red and green 5 5
O 448. 300 k. red 5 5
O 449. 350 k. red and violet 5 5
O 450. 500 k. red and orange 5 5
O 451. 600 k. red and bistre 5 5
O 452. 1000 k. red and blue 5 5
O 453. 3000 k. red and violet 8 5
O 454. 5000 k. red and blue 8 5

1922. Optd. **KORONA** or surch. also.
O 438. O 1. 150 k. on 1000 f. red 5 5
O 439. 350 f. blue 5 5
O 440. 2000 k. on 250 f. blue 5 5

PARCEL POST STAMPS

1954. No. 979 surch. in figures and **Ft.**
P 1398. 119. 1 fo. 70 on 1 fo. 40 grn. 15 5
P 1399. 2 fo. on 1 fo. 40 green .. 20 8
P 1400. 3 fo. on 1 fo. 40 green .. 40 12

POSTAGE DUE STAMPS

D 1.

ILLUSTRATIONS British Commonwealth and all overprints and surcharges are FULL SIZE. Foreign Countries have been reduced to ¾-LINEAR.

1903. Figures in centre in black.
D 170. D 1. 1 f. green 5 5
D 171. 2 f. green 5 5
D 172. 5 f. green 15 12
D 119. 6 f. green 8 8
D 120. 10 f. green 20 15
D 175. 12 f. green 5 5
D 176. 20 f. green 5 5
D 177. 50 f. green 10 10
D 91. 100 f. green .. 10 15

1915. Surch.
D 188. D 1. 20 on 100 f. blk. & grn. 12 12

1915. As Type D 1, but figures in red.
D 190. D 1. 1 f. green 5 5
D 191. 2 f. green 5 5
D 192. 5 f. green 12 8
D 193. 6 f. green 5 5
D 194. 10 f. green 5 5
D 195. 12 f. green 5 5
D 196. 15 f. green 5 5
D 197. 20 f. green 5 5
D 198. 30 f. green 5 5
D 349. 40 f. green 5 5
D 350. 50 f. green 5 5
D 351. 120 f. green 5 5
D 352. 200 f. green 5 5
D 430. 2 k. green 5 5
D 431. 5 k. green 5 5
D 432. 50 k. green 5 5

1919. Overprinted **KOSTARSASAG.**
D 325. D 1. 2 f. green (No. D 191) 5 5
D 326. 3 f. green 5 5
D 327. 10 f. green (No. D 194) 5 5
D 328. 20 f. green (No. D 197) 5 5
D 329. 40 f. green 5 5
D 324. 50 f. green (No. D 177) 25 25
D 340. 50 f. green (No. D 350) 5 5

1919. As Type D 1, but inscribed. "MAGYAR POSTA". Figures in Black.
D 375. D 1. 2 green 5 5
D 376. 3 f. green 5 5
D 377. 20 f. green 5 5
D 378. 40 f. green 5 5
D 379. 50 f. green 5 5

1919. As Type D 1, inscr. "MAGYAR POSTA" and optd. with T 17 and **MAGYAR TANACS KOZTARSASAG.**
D 369. D 1. 2 f. green 12 15
D 370. 3 f. green 12 15
D 371. 10 f. green 40 40
D 372. 20 f. green 12 15
D 373. 40 f. green 12 15
D 374. 50 f. green 12 15

1921. Surch. **PORTO** and value. Inscr. "MAGYAR KIR POSTA".
D 428. 11. 100 f. on 15 f. violet .. 5 5
D 429. 500 f. on 15 f. violet .. 5 5
D 433. 2½ k. on 10 f. purple .. 5 5
D 434. 3 k. on 15 f. violet .. 5 5
D 437. 6 k. on 1½ k. purple .. 5 5
D 435. 9 k. on 40 f. olive .. 5 5
D 438. 10 k. on 2½ k. green .. 5 5
D 436. 12 k. on 60 f. black .. 5 5
D 439. 15 k. on 1½ k. purple 5 5
D 440. 20 k. on 2½ k. green .. 5 5
D 441. 25 k. on 1½ k. purple 5 5
D 442. 30 k. on 1½ k. purple 5 5
D 443. 40 k. on 2½ k. green .. 5 5
D 444. 50 k. on 1½ k. purple 5 5
D 445. 100 k. on 4½ k. violet 5 5
D 446. 200 k. on 4½ k. violet 5 5
D 447. 300 k. on 4½ k. violet 5 5
D 448. 500 k. on 2 k. blue .. 5 5
D 449. 500 k. on 3 k. brown 5 5
D 450. 1000 k. on 2 k. blue .. 5 5
D 451. 1000 k. on 3 k. brown 10 5
D 452. 2000 k. on 2 k. blue .. 5 5
D 453. 2000 k. on 3 k. brown 15 5
D 454. 5000 k. on 5 k. brown 15 8

D 2.

D 3.

D 4.

1926.
D 479. 2. 1 f. red 5 5
D 480. 2 f. red 5 5
D 481. 3 f. red 5 5
D 482. 4 f. red 5 5
D 483. 5 f. red 8 8
D 484. 8 f. red 5 5
D 510. 10 f. red 5 5
D 486. 16 f. red 5 5
D 512. 20 f. red 5 5
D 487. 32 f. red 20 5
D 488. 40 f. red 25 5
D 489. 50 f. red 35 5
D 490. 80 f. red 55 5

1927. Nos. 434/66 surch. **PORTO** and value over moire pattern.
D 491. 30. 1 f. on 500 k. .. 5 5
D 492. 2 f. on 1000 k. .. 5 5
D 493. 3 f. on 2000 k. .. 5 5
D 494. 5 f. on 5000 k. .. 8 5
D 495. 10 f. on 10,000 k. .. 10 5

1931. Surch.
D 529. D 2. 4 f. on 5 red .. 5 5
D 534. 10 f. on 16 f. red .. 45 40
D 531. 10 f. on 80 f. red .. 5 5
D 532. 12 f. on 50 f. red .. 5 5
D 533. 20 f. on 32 f. red .. 10 5

1934.
D 569. D 3. 2 f. blue 5 5
D 570. 4 f. blue 5 5
D 571. 6 f. blue 5 5
D 572. 8 f. blue 5 5
D 573. 10 f. blue 5 5
D 574. 12 f. blue 5 5
D 575. 16 f. blue 5 5
D 576. 20 f. blue 5 5
D 577. 40 f. blue 5 5
D 578. 80 f. blue 15 5

1941.
D 684. D 4. 2 f. brown 5 5
D 685. 3 f. brown 5 5
D 686. 4 f. brown 5 5
D 687. 6 f. brown 5 5
D 688. 8 f. brown 5 5
D 689. 10 f. brown 5 5
D 690. 12 f. brown 5 5
D 691. 16 f. brown 5 5
D 692. 18 f. brown 5 5
D 693. 20 f. brown 5 5
D 694. 24 f. brown 5 5
D 695. 30 f. brown 5 5
D 696. 36 f. brown 5 5
D 697. 40 f. brown 5 5
D 698. 50 f. brown 5 5
D 699. 60 f. brown 5 5

1945. Surch. **1945** and value.
D 825. D 4. 10 f. on 2 f. brown .. 5 5
D 826. 10 f. on 3 f. brown .. 5 5
D 827. 20 f. on 4 f. brown .. 5 5
D 828. 20 f. on 6 f. brown .. 3·00 3·00

D 829. D 4. 20 f. on 8 f. brown .. 5 5
D 830. 40 f. on 12 f. brown 5 5
D 831. 40 f. on 16 f. brown 5 5
D 832. 40 f. on 18 f. brown 5 5
D 833. 60 f. on 24 f. brown 5 5
D 834. 80 f. on 30 f. brown 5 5
D 835. 90 f. on 36 f. brown 5 5
D 836. 1 p. on 10 f. brown .. 5 5
D 837. 1 p. on 40 f. brown .. 5 5
D 838. 2 p. on 20 f. brown .. 5 5
D 839. 2 p. on 50 f. brown .. 5 5
D 840. 2 p. on 60 f. brown .. 5 5
D 841. 10 p. on 3 f. brown .. 5 5
D 842. 12 p. on 8 f. brown .. 5 5
D 843. 20 p. on 24 f. brown 5 5

D 5. D 6. D 7.

1946.

D 984. D 5. 4 f. brown & purple 5 5
D 985. 10 f. brown & purple 5 5
D 986. 20 f. brown & purple 5 5
D 987. 30 f. brown & purple 8 5
D 988. 40 f. brown & purple 15 5
D 989. 50 f. brown & purple 20 5
D 990. 60 f. brown & purple 80 5
D 991. 1 fo. 20 brown & pur. 90 5
D 992. 2 fo. brn. & purple 1·00 5

1951. Fiscal stamps surch. with Arms. **MAGYAR POSTA PORTO** and value.
D 1157. D 6. 8 fi. brown 5 5
D 1158. 10 fi. brown .. 5 5
D 1159. 12 fi. brown .. 5 5

1951.

D 1210. D 7. 4 fi. brown 5 5
D 1211. 6 fi. brown .. 5 5
D 1212. 8 fi. brown .. 5 5
D 1213. 10 fi. brown .. 5 5
D 1214. 14 fi. brown .. 5 5
D 1215. 20 fi. brown .. 5 5
D 1216. 30 fi. brown .. 5 5
D 1217. 40 fi. brown .. 5 5
D 1218. 50 fi. brown .. 8 5
D 1219. 60 fi. brown .. 10 5
D 1220. 1 fo. 20 brown .. 15 5
D 1221. 2 fo. brown 25 10

D 8. D 9.

1953. First Hungarian Postage Due Stamps. 50th Anniv.
D 1305. D 8. 4 fi. black and green 5 5
D 1306. 6 fi. black and green 5 5
D 1307. 8 fi. black and green 5 5
D 1308. 10 fi. black & green 5 5
D 1309. 12 fi. black & green 5 5
D 1310. 14 fi. black & green 5 5
D 1311. 16 fi. black & green 5 5
D 1312. 20 fi. black & green 5 5
D 1313. 24 fi. black & green 5 5
D 1314. 30 fi. black & green 5 5
D 1315. 36 fi. black & green 5 5
D 1316. 40 fi. black & green 5 5
D 1317. 50 fi. black & green 8 5
D 1318. 60 fi. black & green 10 5
D 1319. 70 fi. black & green 10 5
D 1320. 80 fi. black & green 12 5
D 1321. 1 fo. 20 blk. & grn. 20 5
D 1322. 2 fo. black & green 35 5

1958. Forint values are larger (31 × 22 mm.).
D 1498. D 9. 4 fi. black and red 5 5
D 1499. 6 fi. black and red 5 5
D 1500. 8 fi. black and red 5 5
D 1501. 10 fi. black and red 5 5
D 1502. 12 fi. black and red 5 5
D 1503. 14 fi. black and red 5 5
D 1504. 16 fi. black and red 5 5
D 1505. 20 fi. black and red 5 5
D 1506. 24 fi. black and red 5 5
D 1507. 30 fi. black and red 5 5
D 1508. 36 fi. black and red 5 5
D 1509. 40 fi. black and red 5 5
D 1510. 50 fi. black and red 5 5
D 1511. 60 fi. black and red 8 5
D 1512. 70 fi. black and red 10 5
D 1513. 80 fi. black and red 10 5
D 1514 – 1 fo. red-brown .. 5 5
D 1515. – 1 fo. 20 brown .. 15 5
D 1516. – 2 fo. brown .. 30 8
D 1517. – 4 fo. brown 25 12

D 10. Money-order Cancelling Machine.

1973. Postal Operations.
D 2847. D 10. 20 fi. brown & red 5 5
D 2848. – 40 fi. blue & red .. 5 5
D 2849. – 80 fi. vio. & red .. 5 5
D 2850. – 1 fo. grn. & red .. 8 5
D 2851. – 1 fo. 20 grn & red 10 8
D 2852. – 2 fo. vio. & red .. 20 10
D 2853. – 3 fo. blue & red .. 25 15
D 2854. – 4 fo. brn. & red .. 35 25

DESIGNS—(21 × 18½ mm.). 40 fi. Parcel scales, self-service post office. 80 fi. Automatic parcels-registration machine. 1 fo. Data-recording machine. (28 × 22 mm.) 1 fo. 20 Mail-plane and van. 2 fo. Diesel mail-train. 3 fo. Postman on motor-cycle. 4 fo. Postmen at mail-boxes.

SAVINGS BANK STAMP

B 1.

ILLUSTRATIONS British Commonwealth and all overprints and surcharges are FULL SIZE. Foreign Countries have been reduced to ¾-LINEAR.

1916.
B 199. B 1. 10 f. purple 5 5

SZEGED

The following issues were made by the Hungarian National Government led by Admiral Horthy, which was set up in Szeged in 1919, then under French occupation, and which later replaced the Communist regime established by Bela Kun.

1919. Stamps of Hungary optd. **MAGYAR NEMZETI KORMANY Szeged, 1919.** or surch.

(a) War Charity stamps of 1916.
1. 6. 10 f. (+2 f.) red .. 8 8
2. – 15 f. (+2 f.) violet .. 12 12
3. 8. 40 f. (+2 f.) lake .. 25 25

(b) Harvesters and Parliament Types.
4. 11. 2 f. brown 8 8
5. 3 f. claret 5 5
6. 5 f. green 8 8
7. 6 f. blue .. .. 3·25 3·25
8. 15 f. violet 12 12
9. 20 f. brown (No. 307) .. 10·00 10·00
10. 25 f. blue (No. 309) .. 8 8
11. 12. 50 f. purple .. .. 1·25 1·25
12. 75 f. blue 10 10
13. 80 f. green 70 70
14. 1 k. lake 12 12
15. 2 k. brown 12 12
16. 3 k. grey and violet .. 20 20
17. 5 k. brown .. .. 10·00 10·00
18. 10 k. lilac and brown 10·00 10·00

(c) Nos. 5 and 14 further surch.
19. 11. 45 on 3 f. claret .. 8 8
20. 12. 10 on 1 k. lake .. 55 55

(d) Karl and Zita stamps.
21. 13. 10 f. red 10 10
22. 20 f. brown 10 10
23. 25 f. blue .. .. 3·25 3·25
24. 14. 40 f. olive 20 20

The following (Nos. 25/39) are also optd. **KOZTARSASAG.**

(e) War Charity stamp.
25. 8. 40 f. (+2 f.) lake .. 1·10 1·10

(f) Harvesters and Parliament Types.
26. 11. 3 f. claret .. .. 3·25 3·25
27. 4 f. slate 20 20
28. 5 f. green .. .. 2·10 2·10
29. 6 f. blue 45 45
30. 10 f. red .. .. 1·60 1·60
31. 20 f. brown .. .. 9·00 9·00
32. 20 (f) on 2 f. yellow-brn. 15 15
33. 40 f. olive 10 10
34. 12. 3 k. grey and violet .. 10·00 10·00

(g) Karl and Zita stamps.
35. 13. 10 f. red .. .. 1·10 1·10
36. 15 f. violet 20 20
37. 20 f. brown .. .. 9·00 9·00
38. 25 f. blue .. .. 1·60 1·60
39. 14. 50 f. purple 8 8

NEWSPAPER STAMP

1919. No. N 136 optd. **MAGYAR NEMZETI KORMANY Szeged, 1919.**
N 40. N 3. (2 f.) orange .. 15 15

EXPRESS LETTER STAMP

1919. No. E 245 optd. as above.
E 41. E 1. 2 f. olive and red .. 25 25

POSTAGE DUE STAMPS

1919. Nos. D 191, etc.

(a) Optd. as above, in red.
D 42. D 1. 2 f. red and green .. 20 20
D 43. 6 f. red and green .. 1·00 1·00
D 44. 10 f. red and green 20 20
D 45. 12 f. red and green .. 30 30
D 46. 20 f. red and green 35 35
D 47. 30 f. red and green 45 45

(b) No. E 41 surch. **PORTO** and new value in red.
D 48. E 1. 50 f. on 2 f. olive & red 25 25
D 49. 100 f. on 2 f. olive & red 25 25

HYDERABAD BC

A state in India. Now uses Indian stamps.

1.

1869.
1. 1. 1 a. green .. .. .. 5·00 4·00

2.

3.

1871.
2. 2. ½ a. brown .. .. .. 3·00 3·00
3. 2 a. green .. .. .. 12·00 9·00

1871.
13. 3. ½ a. brown 5 5
13b. ½ a. red 5 5
14. 1 a. purple 35 40
14b. 1 a. maroon 5 5
15. 2 a. green 8 5
16. 3 a. brown 15 10
17b. 4 a. grey 30 15
17c. 4 a. olive .. .. 1·10 1·00
18. 8 a. brown 70 45
19. 12 a. blue .. .. 1·25 1·00
19a. 12 a. green 90 70

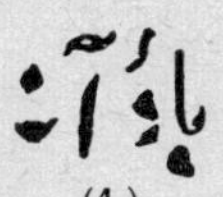

(4.)

1900. Surch. with T 4.
20. 3. ¼ a. on ½ a. brown .. 75 35

5.

6.

1902.
21. 5. ¼ a. blue .. .. 1·25 70

1905.
22. 6. ¼ a. blue 75 5
32. ¼ a grey 5 5
33. ¼ a. purple 5 5
23a. ½ a. orange .. .. 1·50 12
25. ½ a. green 25 5
26. 1 a. red 15 5
27. 2 a. lilac 12 5
28. 3 a. brown-orange .. 12 5
29. 4 a. olive-green .. 10 5
30. 8 a. purple 20 5
31. 12 a. green 35 12

7. 8.

1915.
35. 7. ½ a. green 25 5
58. ½ a claret 15 10
36. 1 a. red 25 5
37. 8. 1 r. yellow .. .. 2·50 5·00

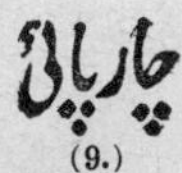

(9.)

1930. Surch as T 9.
38. 6. 4 p. on ¼ a. grey .. .. 12·00 3·00
39. 4 p. on ¼ a. purple 5 5
40. 7. 8 p. on ½ a. green 5 5

10. Symbols.

11. The Char Minar.

1931.
60. 10. 2 p. brown 60 10
41. 4 p. black 5 5
59. 6 p. claret 35 20
42. 8 p. green 5 5
43. 11. 1 a. brown 8 5
44. – 2 a. violet 15 5
45. – 4 a. blue 35 5
46. – 8 a. orange 75 15
47. – 12 a. red .. .. 1·25 2·00
48. – 1 r. yellow .. .. 1·75 1·75

In No. 59 "POSTAGE" is at foot.
DESIGNS—(Approx. 32½ × 21) HORIZ. 2 a. High Court of Justice. 4 a. Osman Sagar Reservoir. 12 a. Bidar College. VERT. 8 a. Entrance to Ajanta Caves. 1 r. Victory Tower, Daulatabad.

12. Unani General Hospital.

1937. Inscr. "H.E.H. THE NIZAM'S SILVER JUBILEE".
49. 12. 4 p. slate and violet .. 8 5
50. – 8 p. slate and brown .. 8 5
51. – 1 a. slate and yellow .. 10 5
52. – 2 a. slate and green .. 40 25

DESIGNS: 8 p. Osmania Hospital. 1 a. Osmania University. 2 a. Osmania Jubilee Hall.

13. Family Reunion.

1946. Victory Commemoration.
53. 13. 1 a. blue 5 5

14. Town Hall.

1947. Reformed Legislature.
54. 14. 1 a. black 5 5

15. Power House, Hyderabad.

1947. Inscr. as in T 15.
55. 15. 1 a. 4 p. green 25 5
56. – 3 a. blue 25 5
57. – 6 a. brown .. .. 1·25 75

DESIGNS—HORIZ. 3 a. Kaktyai Arch, Warangal Fort. 6 a. Golkunda Fort.

OFFICIAL STAMPS

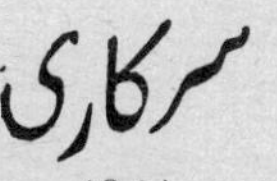

(O 1.)

1873. Optd. with Type O 1.
O 2. 2. ½ a. brown .. .. — 6·00
O 1. 1. 1 a. green .. .. — 6·00
O 3. 2. 2 a. olive .. .. — 7·00

1873. Optd. with Type O 1.
O 9. 3. ½ a. brown 60 30
O 11. 1 a. purple 1·50 1·25
O 12. 1 a. drab 30 30
O 13. 1 a. black 10 5
O 14. 2 a. green 30
O 16. 3 a. brown 30 25
O 17. 4 a. grey 75 60
O 19. 8 a. brown 3·00 1·75
O 20. 12 a. blue 2·00

1909. Optd. as Type O 1, or similar smaller opt.
O 30. 6. ¼ a. grey 5 5
O 31. ¼ a. lilac 10 15
O 21a. ½ a. orange 50 5
O 33. ½ a. green 5 5
O 40. 7. ½ a. green 12 5
O 54. ½ a. claret 75 20
O 34. 6. 1 a. red 5 5
O 41. 7. 1 a. red 12 5
O 35. 6. 2 a. lilac 8 5
O 36. 3 a. brown-orange 25 5
O 37. 4 a. olive-green 25 5
O 38. 8 a. purple 35 5
O 28. 12 a. green 50 12

1930. Official stamps surch. as T 9.
O 42. 6. 4 p. on ¼ a. grey 20·00 8·00
O 43. 4 p. on ¼ a. lilac 15 5
O 45. 8 p. on ½ a. green 45·00 20·00
O 44. 7. 8 p. on ½ a. green 20 5

1934. Optd. with Type O 1.
O 55. 10. 2 p. brown 75 20
O 46. 4 p. black 5 5
O 56. 6 p. claret 90 50
O 47. 8 p. green 5 5
O 48. 11. 1 a. brown 5 5
O 49. – 2 a. violet (No. 44) 10 5
O 50. – 4 a. blue (No. 45) 40 8
O 51. – 8 a. orange (No. 46) 1·25 25
O 52. – 12 a. red (No. 47) 1·00 30
O 53. – 1 r. yellow (No. 48) 1·50 70

ICELAND E2

An island lying S.E. of Greenland. An independent state formerly under the Danish sovereign, now a republic.

1873. 96 skilling = 1 riksdaler.
1876. 100 aurar = 1 krona.

þrír

1. (2.)

1873.
1. 1. 2 s. blue £150 £225
5. 3 s. grey 50·00 £180
2. 4 s. red 18·00 £120
3. 8 s. brown 38·00 £130
7. 16 s. yellow 17·00 70·00

1876.
26. 1. 3 a. yellow 7·00 1·10
27. 4 a. grey and rose 2·50 2·75
14. 5 a. blue 38·00 55·00
28. 5 a. green 70 35
29a. 6 a. grey 1·10 2·00
30. 10 a. red 70 30
31. 16 a. brown 7·00 7·00
18. 20 a. mauve £110 50·00
32a. 20 a. blue 2·50 2·50
33. 25 a. blue and brown 2·50 2·00
19. 40 a. green 14·00 16·00
23b. 40 a. mauve 4·25 6·50
24. 50 a. red and blue 10·00 6·00
25. 100 a. purple and brown 13·00 11·00

1897. Surch. as T 2.
40. 1. 3 on 5 a. green 85·00 70·00

1897. Surch. as T 2 with the figure 3 above or below.
38. 1. 3 on 5 a. green 80·00 60·00

1902. Optd. I GILDI '02-'03.
54. 1. 3 a. yellow 15 25
55. 4 a. grey and rose 3·00 6·00
56. 5 a. green 15 1·00
58. 6 a. grey 15 90
60. 10 a. red 15 1·10
61. 16 a. brown 2·00 4·50
62. 20 a. blue 15 80
64. 25 a. blue and brown 15 1·25
66. 40 a. mauve 15 6·00
67. 50 a. red and blue 60 7·50
52. 100 a. purple and brown 6·00 7·50

3. King Christian IX.  4. Kings. Christian IX and Frederick VIII.  5. Jon Sigurdsson.

1902.
68. 3. 3 a. orange 1·10 40
69. 4 a. rose and grey 50 10
70. 5 a. green 2·00 5
71. 6 a. brown 2·10 70
72. 10 a. red 1·10 5
73. 16 a. brown 70 55
74. 20 a. blue 35 30
75. 3. 25 a. green and brown 40 35
76. 40 a. mauve 45 30
77. 50 a. black and grey 55 2·75
78. 1 k. brown and blue 1·10 80
79. 2 k. blue and brown 3·00 8·00
80. 5 k. slate and brown 21·00 18·00

1907.
81. 4. 1 e. red and green 20 10
110. 3 a. brown 45 15
83. 4 a. red and grey 25 12
112. 5 a. green 8·00 5
85. 6 a. grey 3·00 35
114. 10 a. red 40 5
87. 15 a. green and red 90 5
88. 16 a. brown 80 3·50
89. 20 a. blue 1·25 25
90. 25 a. green and brown 60 1·00
91. 40 a. claret 60 1·60
92. 50 a. claret and grey 70 1·25
93. 1 k. brown and blue 3·50 6·00
94. 2 k. green and brown 3·00 6·00
95. 5 k. blue and brown 20·00 27·00

1911. Jon Sigurdsson. Birth Cent.
96. 5. 1 e. green 35 8
97. 3 a. brown 30 85
98. 4 a. blue 20 20
99. 6 a. grey 1·10 1·50
100. 15 a. violet 3·50 25
101. 25 a. orange 3·25 3·00

1912. As T 5, but portrait of King Frederick VIII and "JON SIGURDSSON" omitted.
102. 5 a. green 4·00 1·50
103. 10 a. red 4·00 1·50
104. 20 a. blue 7·00 2·00
105. 50 a. claret 2·50 3·50
106. 1 k. yellow 4·50 5·00
107. 2 k. red 4·00 6·00
108. 5 k. brown 25·00 28·00

6. King Christian X.  7. Landing Mails at Vik.

1920.
188. 6. 1 e. red and green 12 12
189. 3 a. brown 70 1·25
118. 4 a. red and grey 40 20
119. 5 a. green 30 25
191. 6 a. grey 30 50
192. 7 a. green 5 5
121. 8 a. brown 1·00 30
122. 10 a. red 15 70
133. 10 a. green 50 15
193. 10 a. brown 8·00 8
123. 15 a. violet 3·50 5
124. 20 a. blue 25 1·60
134. 20 a. brown 7·50 15
125. 25 a. green and brown 2·25 12
135. 25 a. red 1·00 2·50
195. 30 a. green and red 2·50 50
127. 40 a. claret 5·00 20
136. 40 a. blue 13·00 1·40
128. 50 a. claret and grey 18·00 1·25
129. 1 k. brown and blue 13·00 8
130. 2 k. green and brown 20·00 1·50
131. 5 k. blue and brown 10·00 2·10
199. 10 k. black and green 38·00 13·00

1921. Various types surch.
137. 3. 5 a. on 16 a. brown 40 4·00
138. 4. 5 a. on 16 a. brown 20 90
139. 6. 10 a. on 5 a. green 40 20
140. 3. 20 a. on 25 a. grn. & brn. 60 45
141. 4. 20 a. on 25 a. grn. & brn. 45 50
142. 3. 20 a. on 40 a. mauve 70 2·25
143. 4. 20 a. on 40 a. claret 1·00 2·00
144. 3. 30 a. on 50 a. grey 2·25 3·00
145. 50 a. on 5 k. slate & brown 8·00 3·00
146. 6. 1 k. on 40 a. blue 9·00 2·50
147. 5. 2 k. on 25 a. orange 11·00 10·00
148. – 10 k. on 50 a. claret (No. 105) 30·00 32·00
149. – 10 k. on 1 k. yell. (No. 106) 50·00 60·00
150. 3. 10 k. on 2 k. blue & brn. 8·00 2·25
150a. 4. 10 k. on 5 k. blue & brown 45·00 55·00

1925.
151. 7. 7 a. green 8·00 1·00
152. – 10 a. brown and blue 8·00 8
153. – 20 a. red 8·00 5
154. – 35 a. blue 10·00 1·25
155. 7. 50 a. brown and green 10·00 12

DESIGNS: 10 a., 35 a. Tjornin (Pond) and Cathedral, Reykjavik. 20 a. National Museum.

1928. Air. Optd. with aeroplane.
156. 6. 10 a. red 25 1·10
157. 4. 50 a. claret and grey 7·50 10·00

8. Discovery of Iceland.

9. Icelandic Falcon.

1930. Parliament Millenary Celebration.
158. – 3 a. violet (postage) 70 1·50
159. 8. 5 a. blue and grey 70 1·50
160. – 7 a. green 70 1·50
161. – 10 a. purple 1·75 1·75
162. – 15 a. blue 70 1·50
163. – 20 a. red 7·00 8·00
164. – 25 a. brown 1·75 1·60
165. – 30 a. grey-green 1·25 1·75
166. – 35 a. blue 1·50 1·75
167. – 40 a. red, blue and grey 1·25 1·75
168. – 50 a. brown 14·00 18·00
169. – 1 k. green 14·00 18·00
170. – 2 k. blue and green 15·00 18·00
171. – 5 k. orange and yellow 9·00 14·00
172. – 10 k. lake 10·00 14·00
173. 9. 10 a. blue (air) 5·00 8·00

DESIGNS—HORIZ. 3 a. Parliament House, Reykjavik. 7 a. Encampment at Thingvellir. 10 a. Arrival of Ingolf Arnarsson. 15 a. Naming the Island. 20 a. The Dash for "Althing" (Parliament). 25 a. Discovery of Arnarsson's pillar. 30 a. Lake Thingvellir. 35 a. Queen Aud. 40 a. National flag. 50 a. First "Althing" (Parliament), A.D. 930. 1 k. Map of Iceland. 2 k. Winter-bound farmstead. 5 k. Woman spinning. 10 k. Viking sacrifice to Thor.

10. Snaefellsjokull.

DESIGNS: 20 a. Old fishing boat. 35 a. Pony. 50 a. Gullfoss Falls. 1 k. Statue of Arnarsson, Reykjavik.

1930. Air. Parliamentary Millenary.
174. 10. 15 a. blue and brown 4·50 9·00
175. – 20 a. blue and brown 4·50 9·00
176. – 35 a. brown and olive 10·00 14·00
177. – 50 a. blue and green 10·00 14·00
178. – 1 k. red and olive 10·00 14·00

1931. Air. Optd. **Zeppelin 1931.**
179. 6. 30 a. green and red 7·50 15·00
180. 1 k. brown and blue 7·00 15·00
181. 2 k. green and brown 8·50 15·00

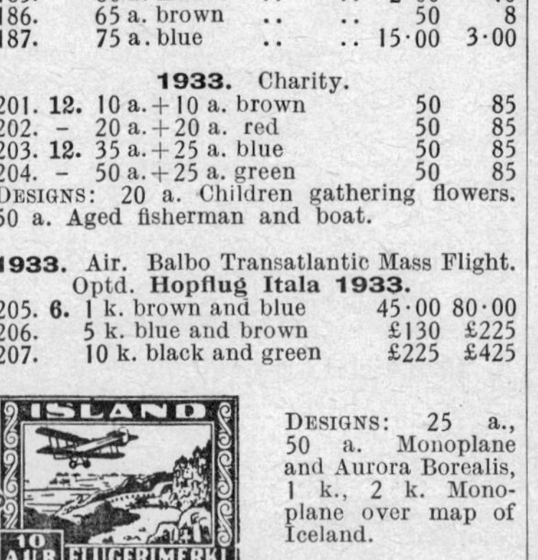

11. Gullfoss Falls. 12. Shipwreck and Rescue Work.

1931.
182. 11. 5 a. grey 2·50 10
183. 20 a. red 1·50 5
184. 35 a. blue 2·00 1·40
185. 60 a. mauve 2·00 10
186. 65 a. brown 50 8
187. 75 a. blue 15·00 3·00

1933. Charity.
201. 12. 10 a. + 10 a. brown 50 85
202. – 20 a. + 20 a. red 50 85
203. 12. 35 a. + 25 a. blue 50 85
204. – 50 a. + 25 a. green 50 85

DESIGNS: 20 a. Children gathering flowers. 50 a. Aged fisherman and boat.

1933. Air. Balbo Transatlantic Mass Flight. Optd. **Hopflug Itala 1933.**
205. 6. 1 k. brown and blue 45·00 80·00
206. 5 k. blue and brown £130 £225
207. 10 k. black and green £225 £425

13. Biplane over Thingvellir.

DESIGNS: 25 a., 50 a. Monoplane and Aurora Borealis, 1 k., 2 k. Monoplane over map of Iceland.

1934. Air.
208. 13. 10 a. blue 25 30
209. 20 a. green 60 50
210. – 25 a. violet 1·60 1·50
211. – 50 a. purple 90 40
212. – 1 k. brown 3·75 3·75
213. – 2 k. orange 1·50 1·10

14. Dynjandi falls. 16. Matthias Jochumsson. 17. King Christian X.

1935.
214. 14. 10 a. blue 2·50 5
215. – 1 k. olive 6·00 5

DESIGN—HORIZ. 1 k. Mt. Hekla.

1935. Matthias Jochumsson (poet). Birth Cent.
216. 16. 3 a. olive 8 60
217. 5 a. grey 2·00 5
218. 7 a. green 3·50 15
219. 35 a. blue 10 10

1937. Silver Jubilee of King Christian X.
220. 17. 10 a. green 60 2·50
221. 30 a. brown 60 1·25
222. 40 a. claret 60 1·25

1937. Miniature sheet of three stamps inscr. "CHRISTIAN X 1912–37".
MS 223. 17. 15 a. violet
23 a. red
50 a. blue
Per sheet 18·00 40·00

18. The Great Geyser. 19. Reykjavik University.

1938.
226. 18. 15 a. purple 80 1·00
227. 20 a. red 3·75 5
228. 35 a. blue 20 10
229. – 40 a. brown 1·75 1·60
230. – 45 a. blue 15 12
231. – 50 a. green 4·00 8
232a. – 60 a. blue 20 12
233. – 1 k. blue 30 5

The frames of the 40 a. to 1 k. differ from T 18.

1938. Independence. 20th Anniv.
234. 19. 25 a. green 2·25 2·50
235. 30 a. brown 2·25 2·50
236. 40 a. purple 2·25 2·50

1939. Surch. with bold figure **5**.
237. 16. 5 on 35 a. blue 20 20

20. Trylon and Perisphere. 21. Codfish. 22. Iceland Flag.

1939. New York World's Fair.
238. 20. 20 a. red 1·00 1·25
239. – 35 a. blue 1·10 1·50
240. – 45 a. green 1·25 1·60
241. – 2 k. black 14·00 20·00

DESIGNS: 35 a. Viking ship and route to America. 45 a., 2 k. Statue of Thorfinn Karlsefni, Reykjavik.

1939.
242. 21. 1 e. blue 5 50
243. – 3 a. violet 5 5
244. 21. 5 a. brown 5 5
245. – 7 a. green 70 90
246. 22. 10 a. red and blue 35 10
247. – 10 a. green 5·00 5
248. – 10 a. black 5 5
249. – 12 a. green 5 5
250. 21. 25 a. red 1·50 5
251. 25 a. brown 8 5
252. – 35 a. red 12 5
253. 21. 50 a. green 12 5

DESIGN: 3 a., 7 a., 10 a. (Nos. 247/8), 12 a., 35 a. Herring.

23. Statue of Thorfinn Karlsefni. 24. Statue of Snorre Sturlason.

1939.
254. 23. 2 k. grey 55 5
255. 5 k. brown 4·00 8
256. 10 k. brown 5·00 50

1940. New York World's Fair. Optd. **1940.**
257. 20. 20 a. red 4·00 6·00
258. – 35 a. blue (No. 239) 4·00 6·00
259. – 45 a green (No. 240) 4·00 6·00
260. – 2 k. black (No. 241) 28·00 38·00

1941. Surch. **25.**
261. 16. 25 a. on 3 a. olive 20 15

1941. Snorre Sturlason (historian). 700th Death Anniv.
262. 24. 25 a. red 40 35
263. 50 a. blue .. .. 1·00 1·10
264. 1 k. olive .. .. 1·00 90

25. Jon Sigurdsson. 26. Hvalfjorthur Thyrill.

1944. Proclamation of Republic.
265. 25. 10 a. grey 12 12
266. 25 a. brown 20 10
267. 50 a. green 20 10
268. 1 k. black 35 12
269. 5 k. brown .. .. 2·75 3·00
270. 10 k. brown .. .. 10·00 17·00

1947. Air.
271. – 15 a. orange 10 15
272. – 30 a. black 10 20
273. – 75 a. lake 12 12
274. – 1 k. blue 15 12
275. – 1 k. 80 blue .. .. 1·25 1·00
276. 26. 2 k. brown 40 45
277. – 2 k. 50 green .. 2·00 20
278. – 3 k. green 40 30
279. – 3 k. 30 blue .. 1·00 50
DESIGNS—HORIZ. 15 a. Catalina over Thingvellir. 30 a. Catalina over Isafjorthur. 75 a. Dakota over Akureyri. 1 k. 80 Dakota over Snaefellsjokull. 2 k. 50 Catalina over Eiriksjokull. 3 k. Skymaster over Reykjavik. 3 k. 30 Skymaster over Oraefajokull. VERT. 1 k. Catalina over Sethisfjorthur, Strandatindur.
For postage stamps in designs as T **26** without aeroplanes, see Nos. 346/8.

DESIGNS—VERT. 35 a., 60 a. Mt. Hekla in Eruption (different view). HORIZ. 25 a., 1 k., 10 k. Mt. Hekla.

27. Mt. Hekla in Eruption.

1948. Inscr. "HEKLA 1947".
280. 27. 12 a. purple 5 5
281. – 25 a. green 40 5
282. – 35 a. red 10 5
283. 27. 50 a. brown 60 5
284. – 60 a. blue .. .. 2·50 20
285. – 1 k. brown .. .. 5·00 8
286. – 10 k. violet .. .. 15·00 20

28. Hospital and Child. 29. Pony Pack-train.

1949. Red Cross Fund.
287. 28. 10 a.+10 a. green .. 12 20
288. – 35 a.+15 a. red .. 12 20
289. – 50 a.+25 a. brown .. 15 20
290. – 60 a.+25 a. blue .. 15 20
291. – 75 a.+25 a. slate .. 20 20
DESIGNS: 35 a. Nurse and patient. 50 a. Nurse arranging patient's bed. 60 a. Aged couple. 75 a. Ship and life-boat.

1949. U.P.U. 75th Anniv. Inscr. "1874 UPU 1949".
292. 29. 25 a. green 5 8
293. – 35 a. red 5 8
294. – 60 a. blue 15 25
295. – 2 k. orange 35 25
DESIGNS: 35 a. Reykjavik. 60 a. Map of Iceland. 2 k. Almannagja Gorge.

30. Trawler.

31. Bishop Arason.

1950.
296. – 5 a. sepia 5 5
297. 30. 10 a. slate 5 8
298. – 20 a. chestnut 5 5
299. 30. 25 a. red 5 5
300. – 60 a. green .. .. 1·25 3·50
301. – 75 a. orange 15 5
302. – 90 a. red 8 5
303. – 1 k. chocolate 60 5
304. 30. 1 k. 25 purple .. .. 1·25 5
305. 1 k. 50 blue .. .. 1·25 8
306. – 2 k. violet .. .. 2·00 5
307. – 5 k. green .. .. 4·00 12
308. – 25 k. black .. .. 45·00 2·25
DESIGNS: 5 a., 90 a., 2 k. Harbour. 20 a., 75 a., 1 k. Tractor. 60 a., 5 k. Sheep. 25 k. (29×33 mm.), Parliament Building, Reykjavik.

1950. Bishop Arason. 400th Death Anniv.
309. 31. 1 k. 80 red 60 50
310. 3 k. 30 green 15 55

32. Postman, 1776. 33. President Bjornsson.

1951. Icelandic Postal Service. 175th Anniv.
311. 32. 2 k. blue 45 12
312. – 3 k. purple 50 20
DESIGN: 3 k. as 2 k. but aeroplane replaces man.

1952. Death of S. Bjornsson (First President of Iceland).
313. 33. 1 k. 25 blue 40 8
314. 2 k. 20 green 12 50
315. 5 k. indigo 80 20
316. 10 k. brown .. .. 3·50 2·25

1953. Netherlands Flood Relief Fund. Surch. **Hollandshjalp 1953+25.**
317. – 75 a.+25 a. orange (No. 301) 12 40
318. 30. 1 k. 25+25 a. purple .. 30 40

34. "Reykjabok" (Saga of Burnt Njai). 35. Hannes Hafstein.

1953.
319. 34. 10 a. black 8 8
320. – 70 a. green 10 8
321. – 1 k. red 12 5
322. – 1 k. 75 blue .. .. 2·50 15
323. – 10 k. brown .. .. 1·75 12
DESIGNS: 70 a. Hand writing on manuscript. 1 k. "Stjorn" (15th century manuscript). 1 k. 75, "Reykjabok" and candle. 10 k. Page from "Skarosbok" (14th century law manuscript).

1954. No. 282 surch. **5 AURAR** and bars.
324. 5 a. on 35 a. red .. 8 8

1954. 50th Anniv. of Appointment of Hannes Hafstein as first native Minister of Iceland. Portraits of Hafstein.
325. 35. 1 k. 25 blue 60 8
326. – 2 k. 45 green .. .. 2·00 2·50
327. – 5 k. red .. .. 1·40 15

36. Icelandic Wrestling. 37. St. Thorlacus.

1955. Icelandic National Sports.
328. 36. 75 a. brown 8 8
329. – 1 k. 25 blue (Diving) .. 12 5
330. 36. 1 k. 50 red 25 5
331. – 1 k. 75 blue (Diving) .. 10 5

1956. 9th Cent. of Consecration of First Icelandic Bishop and Skaholt Rebuilding Fund. Inscr. as in T **37**.
332. 37. 75 a.+25 a. red .. 10 12
333. – 1 k. 25+75 a. brown .. 10 12
334. – 1 k. 75+1 k. 25 black .. 25 30
DESIGNS—HORIZ. 1 k. 25, Skaholt Cathedral, 1772. VERT. 1 k. 75, J. P. Vidalin, Bishop of Skaholt, 1698-1720.

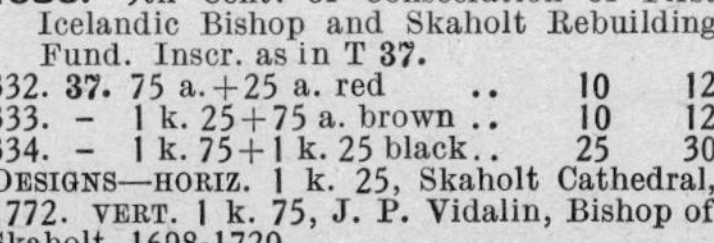

38. Skoga Waterfall. 39. Map of Iceland.

1956. Power Plants and Waterfalls.
335. 38. 15 a. blue 5 5
336. – 50 a. green 8 5
337. – 60 a. brown 40 30
338. – 1 k. 50 violet .. .. 1·25 8
339. – 2 k. sepia 35 8
340. – 2 k. 45 black .. .. 1·00 1·00
341. – 3 k. blue 60 12
342. – 5 k. green .. .. 1·25 30
DESIGNS—HORIZ. 50 a. Ellidaar power plant. 60 a. Goda waterfall. 1 k. 50, Sogs power plant. 2 k. Detti waterfall. 2 k. 45, Andakilsar power plant. 3 k. Laxar power plant. VERT. 5 k. Gull waterfall.

1956. Icelandic Telegraph System. 50th Anniv.
343. 39. 2 k. 30 blue 5 15

1956. Northern Countries' Day. As T **69** of Denmark.
344. 1 k. 50 red 15 15
345. 1 k. 75 blue .. .. 1·25 1·25

1957. Designs as T **26** but aeroplane omitted.
346. – 2 k. green 50 5
347. – 3 k. indigo 50 5
348. – 10 k. brown 70 12
DESIGNS—HORIZ. 2 k. Snaefellsjokull. 3 k. Eiriksjokull. 10 k. Oraefajokull.

40. Presidential Residence, Bessastadir. 41. Norwegian Spruce.

1957.
349. 40. 25 k. black .. . 3·00 60

1957. Reafforestation Campaign.
350. 41. 35 a. green 5 5
351. – 70 a. green 5 5
DESIGN: 70 a. Icelandic birch and saplings.

42. Jonas Hallgrimsson (poet). 43. "Epilobium latifolium" (willow-herb). 44. Icelandic Pony.

1957. Hallgrimsson. 150th Birth Anniv.
352. 42. 5 k. black and green .. 40 15

1958. Flowers.
353. 43. 1 k. red, green & blue .. 10 10
354. – 2 k. 50, violet, green, yellow and blue .. 20 15
DESIGN: 2 k. 50 "Viola tricolor" (viola).
See also Nos. 377/80, 412/5 and 446/7.

1958. Icelandic Pony Commem.
355. 44. 10 a. black 5 5
356. 1 k. red 10 5
357. 2 k. 25 brown 20 5

45. Icelandic Flag.

46. Old Government House.

1958. Icelandic Flag. 40th Anniv.
358. 45. 3 k. 50, red and blue .. 40 15
359. 50 k. red and blue .. 1·75 1·40
No. 359 is 23½×26½ mm.

1958.
360. 46. 1 k. 50 blue 15 5
361. 2 k. green 20 5
362. 3 k. lake 12 5
363. 4 k. brown 25 8

47. Jon Porkelsson with Children. 48. "Viscount" Airliner and Biplane of 1919.

1959. Jon Porkelsson (Johannes Tharkillius, Rector of Skalholt). Death Bicent.
364. 47. 2 k. turquoise 20 15
365. 3 k. purple 20 15

1959. Air. Iceland Civil Aviation. 40th Anniv.
366. 48. 3 k. 50 blue 20 15
367. – 4 k. 05 green 10 5
DESIGN: 4 k. 05, "Convair" airliner and 1919 biplane.

49. Salmon. 50. "The Outcast" (statue after Einar Jonsson).

1959.
368. 49. 25 a. blue 5 5
369. – 90 a. black and brown 5 5
370. – 2 k. black & olive-green 10 5
371. 49. 5 k. bronze-green .. 80 15
372. – 25 k. slate-violet & yell. 2·10 1·60
DESIGNS—VERT. 90 a., 2 k. Eider ducks. 25 k. Icelandic falcon.

1960. World Refugee Year.
373. 50. 2 k. 50 brown 10 5
374. 4 k. 50 blue 25 20

1960. Europa. As T **279** of Belgium, but size 33 × 22½ mm.
375. 3 k. green 50 15
376. 5 k. 50 blue 35 60

51. Dandelions. 52. Jon Sigurdsson.

1960. Wild Flowers (1st series).
377. – 50 a. vio., yell.-grn. & myrtle (Campanulas) 5 5
378. – 1 k. 20 violet, green and sepia (Geraniums) .. 5 5
379. 51. 2 k. 50 yell., grn. & brn. 10 5
380. – 3 k. 50 yellow, green and blue (Ranunculus) .. 15 8
See also Nos. 412/5 and 446/7.

1961. Jon Sigurdsson (statesman). 150th Birth Anniv.
381. 52. 50 a. red 5 5
382. 3 k. blue 15 5
383. 5 k. purple 25 15

53. Reykjavik Harbour. 54. Doves.

1961. 175th Anniv. of Reykjavik.
384. 53. 2 k. 50 blue and green .. 12 5
385. 4 k. 50 blue and violet .. 25 10

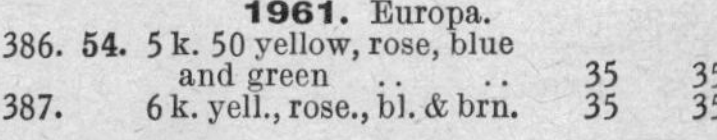

1961. Europa.
386. 54. 5 k. 50 yellow, rose, blue and green 35 35
387. 6 k. yell., rose., bl. & brn. 35 35

55. B. Sveinsson. 56. Productivity Institute.

1961. Iceland University. 50th Anniv.
388. 55. 1 k. brown 5 5
389. – 1 k. 40 blue 5 5
390. – 10 k. green 55 25
DESIGNS—VERT. 1 k. 40, B. M. Olsen. HORIZ. 10 k. University building.

1962. Buildings.
392. 56. 2 k. 50 blue 10 5
393. – 4 k. green 20 8
394. – 6 k. brown 25 10
DESIGNS: 4 k. Fishing Research Institute. 6 k. Agricultural Society's Headquarters.

57. Europa "Tree". 58. Cable Map.

1962. Europa.
395. 57. 5 k. 50 brn., emer. & yell. 8 8
396. 6 k. 50 brown, green and yellow-green .. 15 12

1962. Opening of North Atlantic Submarine Telephone Communications.
397. 58. 5 k. green, red and lavender 30 20
398. 7 k. green, red and blue 20 10

59. S. Gudmundsson (scholar and curator). 60. Herring Catch.

1963. National Museum Cent.
399. 59. 4 k. chocolate and bistre 20 8
400. – 5 k. 50 brown and olive 8 8
DESIGN: 5 k. 50, Detail from carving on church door, Valthjofsstad.

1963. Freedom from Hunger.
401. 60. 5 k. multicoloured .. 30 10
402. 7 k. 50 multicoloured 8 8

61. View of Akureyri. 62. "Co-operation".

1963.
403. 61. 3 k. myrtle 8 5

1963. Europa.
404. 62. 6 k. yell., ochre & chest. 15 10
405. 7 k. yell., green & blue 15 10

ILLUSTRATIONS
British Commonwealth and all overprints and surcharges are FULL SIZE. Foreign Countries have been reduced to ¾-LINEAR.

63. Ambulance.

1963. Red Cross Cent.
406. 63. 3 k.+50 a. mult. .. 5 5
407. 3 k. 50+50 a. mult. .. 10 5

64. M.S. "Gullfoss". 65. Scout Emblem.

1964. Iceland Steamship Co. 50th Anniv.
408. 64. 10 k. blk., purple & blue 45 30

1964. Icelandic Boy Scouts Commemoration.
409. 65. 3 k. 50 yell., rose & blue 20 8
410. 4 k. 50 yell., rose & green 20 8

66. Arms of Iceland. 67. Europa "Flower"

1964. Icelandic Republic. 20th Anniv.
411. 66. 25 k. multicoloured .. 1·00 70

1964. Wild Flowers (2nd series). As T 51. Multicoloured.
412. 50 a. "Dryas octopetala" 5 5
413. 1 k. "Ranunculus glacialis" 5 5
414. 1 k. 50 "Menyanthes trifoliata" 5 5
415. 2 k. "Trifolium repens" .. 8 5

1964. Europa.
416. 67. 4 k. 50 turquoise, cream and brown 20 10
417. 9 k. sepia, cream & blue 20 10

68. Running. 69. Ptarmigan (Summer Plumage).

1964. Olympic Games, Tokyo.
418. 68. 10 k. black and green .. 40 25

1965. Charity.
419. 69. 3 k. 50+50 a. mult. 15 15
420. – 4 k. 50+50 a. mult. 20 20
DESIGN: 4 k. 50, Ptarmigan in winter plumage.

70. "Sound Waves". 71. Eruption, November, 1963.

1965. I.T.U. Cent.
421. 70. 4 k. 50 green 35 10
422. 7 k. 50 blue 8 8

1965. Birth of Surtsey Island. Multicoloured.
423. 1 k. 50 Type 71 .. .. 25 15
424. 2 k. Surtsey in April 1964 .. 25 25
425. 3 k. 50 Surtsey in Sept. '64 35 25
Nos. 424/5 are horiz.

72. Europa "Sprig". 73. E. Benediktsson (poet).

1965. Europa.
426. 72. 5 k. grn, brown & ochre 25 12
427. 8 k. green, brown & turq. 25 12

1965. Einar Benediktsson. 25th Death Anniv.
428. 73. 10 k. brown. black & blue 70 50

74. Girl in National Costume. 75. White-tailed Eagle.

1965.
429. 74. 100 k. multicoloured .. 2·00 1·90

1966. Multicoloured.
430. 20 k. Great Northern Diver 80 70
431. 50 k. Type 75 .. .. 1·50 1·60

76. Londrangar. 77. Europa "Ship". 79. Cogwheels. 78. Society Emblem.

1966. Landscapes. Multicoloured.
432. 2 k. 50 Type 76 .. .. 10 5
433. 4 k. Myvatn 15 5
434. 5 k. Bulandstindur .. 20 8
435. 6 k. 50 Dyrholaey .. 20 8
See also Nos. 465/8.

1966. Europa.
436. 77. 7 k. turquoise, blue & red 15 8
437. 8 k brown. cream & red 15 8

1966. Icelandic Literary Society. 150th Anniv.
438. 78. 4 k. blue 15 5
439. 10 k. red 25 15

1967. Europa.
440. 79. 7 k. blue, brown & yellow 15 10
441. 8 k. blue, grey and green 15 10

80. Old and New Map of Iceland. 81. Trade Symbols.

1967. World Fair, Montreal.
442. 80. 10 k. multicoloured .. 15 15

1967. Icelandic Chamber of Commerce. 50th Anniv.
443. 81. 5 k. multicoloured .. 15 10

82. Nest and Eggs of Ringed Plover.

1967. Charity.
444. 4 k.+50 a. multicoloured 12 12
445. 5 k.+50 a. multicoloured 12 12
DESIGN: 5 k. Nest and eggs of ptarmigan.

1968. Wild Flower (3rd series). As T 43. Multicoloured.
446. 50 a. Saxifrage 5 5
447. 2 k. 50 Orchid 10 5

83. Europa "Key". 84. Right-hand Traffic.

1968. Europa.
448. 83. 9 k. 50 mag., black & yell. 15 8
449. 10 k. yell., sepia & green 15 10

1968. Adoption of Changed Rule of the Road.
450. 84. 4 k. brown and yellow 8 5
451. 5 k. brown 8 5

85. "Fridriksson and Boy" (statue by S. Olafsson). 86. Library Interior.

1968. Pastor Fridrik Fridriksson (founder of Icelandic Y.M.C.A. and Y.W.C.A.). Birth Cent.
452. 85. 10 k. black and blue .. 15 8

1968. National Library. 150th Anniv.
453. 86. 5 k. brown and buff .. 8 5
454. 20 k. ultram. and blue 35 20

87. Jon Magnusson (former Prime Minister). 88. Colonnade.

1968. Independence. 50th Anniv.
455. 87. 4 k. lake 10 5
456. 50 k. sepia .. .. 1·25 90

1969. Northern Countries' Union. 50th Anniv. Similar to T 125 of Denmark.
457. 6 k. 50 red 10 8
458. 10 k. blue 10 8

1969. Europa.
459. 88. 13 k. multicoloured .. 20 10
460. 14 k. 50 multicoloured 20 12

89. Republican Emblem (after S. Jonsson). 90. Boeing "727" Airliner.

1969. Republic. 25th Anniv.
461. 89. 25 k. red, ultram., gold & grey 30 20
462. 100 k. red, ultram., gold & bl. 1·50 1·25

1969. Icelandic Aviation. 50th Anniv.
463. 90. 9 k. 50 ultram. and blue 10 8
464. – 12 k. ultram. and blue .. 15 10
DESIGN: 12 k. Canadair "CL–44" (styled "Rolls-Royce 400").

91. Snaefellsjokull.

1970. Icelandic Views. Multicoloured.
465. 1 k. Type 91 .. .. 5 5
466. 4 k. Laxfoss og Baula .. 5 5
467. 5 k. Hattver 5 5
468. 20 k. Fjaroargil 30 15

92. First Court Session. 93. Part of "Skarosbok" (14th-cent. law manuscript).

1970. Icelandic Supreme Court. 50th Anniv.
469. 92. 6 k. 50 multicoloured 8 5

1970. Icelandic Manuscripts. Multicoloured.
470. 5 k. Type 93 .. .. 10 5
471. 15 k. Part of preface to "Flateyjarbok" (14th-cent.), the largest Icelandic manuscript .. 20 15
472. 30 k. Illuminated initial from "Flateyjarbok" .. 45 25

94. "Flaming Sun". 95. Nurse tending Patient.

1970. Europa.
473. 94. 9 k. lemon and brown .. 15 8
474. 25 k. ochre and green .. 35 25

1970. Icelandic Nurses Assn. 50th Anniv.
475. 95. 7 k. ultramarine and blue 12 5

96. G. Thomsen. **97.** "The Halt" (landscape by T. B. Thorlaksson).

1970. Grimur Thomsen (poet). 150th Birth Anniv.
476. **96.** 10 k. indigo and blue .. 15 8

1970. Int. Arts Festival, Reykjavik.
477. **97.** 50 k. multicoloured .. 90 70

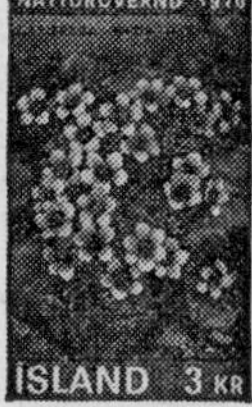

98. Saxifrage. **99.** U.N. Emblem and Map.

1970. Nature Conservation Year. Multicoloured.
478. 3 k. Type **98** 5 5
479. 15 k. Lakagigar (view) .. 15 12

1970. United Nations. 25th Anniv.
480. **99.** 12 k. multicoloured .. 20 12

100. "Flight" (A. Jonsson). **101.** Europa Chain.

1971. "Help for Refugees".
481. **100.** 10 k. multicoloured .. 15 8

1971. Europa.
482. **101.** 7 k. yell., red and black 10 5
483. 15 k. yellow, blue & blk. 20 12

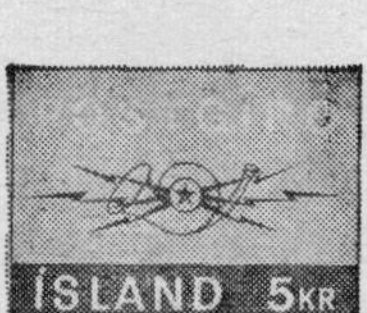

102. Postgiro Emblem. **103.** Society Emblem.

1971. Postal Giro Service. Inaug.
484. **102.** 5 k. blue & light blue 5 5
485. 7 k. green & light green 8 8

1971. Icelandic Patriotic Society. Cent.
486. **103.** 30 k. blue and colbalt 50 35
487. – 100 k. grey and black 1·50 1·25
DESIGN: 100 k. T. Gunnarsson (President and editor).

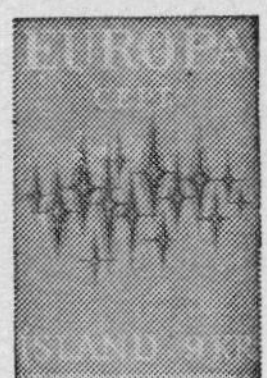

104. Freezing Plant and "Melanogrammus aeglefinus". **106.** "Communications".

105. Mt. Herdubreid.

1971. Icelandic Fishing Industry. Mult.
488. 5 k. Type **104** 5 5
489. 7 k. Landing catch and "Gadus morhua" 8 8
490. 20 k. Canning shrimps and "Pandalus borealis" .. 25 20

1972.
491. **105.** 250 k. multicoloured .. 2·00 1·75

1972. Europa.
492. **106.** 9 k. multicoloured .. 10 8
493. 13 k. multicoloured .. 20 15

107. "Municipalities".

1972. Icelandic Municipal Laws. Cent.
494. **107.** 16 k. multicoloured .. 20 20

108. World Map on Chessboard.

1972. World Chess Championships, Reykjavik.
495. **108.** 15 k. multicoloured .. 20 15

109. Tomatoes.

1972. Hot-house Plant Cultivation. Mult.
496. 8 k. Type **109** 10 8
497. 12 k. Steam source and valve 15 12
498 40 k. Rose cultivation .. 50 45

110. Contour Map and Continental Shelf.

1972. Iceland's Offshore Claims.
499. **110.** 9 k. multicoloured .. 12 10

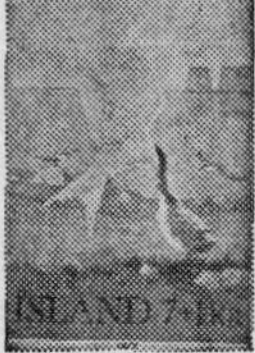

111. Tern feeding Young. **112.** Europa "Posthorn".

1972. Charity Stamps.
500. **111.** 7 k. + 1 k. multicoloured 10 10
501. 9 k. + 1 k. multicoloured 12 12

1973. Europa.
502. **112.** 13 k. multicoloured .. 20 15
503. 25 k. multicoloured .. 30 25

113. Postman and 2 s. stamp of 1873. **114.** Pres. Asgeirsson.

1973. Stamp Centenary.
504. **113.** 10 k. black and blue .. 12 12
505. – 15 k. blk., green & grey 20 15
506. – 20 k. blk., maroon & red 25 25
507. – 40 k. blk., brn. & pur. 50 45
508. – 80 k. blk., orge. & grn. 95 90
DESIGNS: 15 k. Pony train. 20 k. Mailboat "Esja". 40 k. Mail-van. 80 k. Beech "18" mail-plane.

1973. Nordic Countries' Postal Co-operation. As T **198** of Sweden.
509. 9 k. multicoloured .. 8 8
510. 10 k. multicoloured .. 15 10

1973. Asger Asgeirsson (politician). 5th Death Anniv.
511. **114.** 13 k. red 15 12
512. 15 k. blue 12 12

115. Exhibition Emblem. **116.** "The Elements".

1973. "Icelandia 73" Stamp Exhibition. Multicoloured.
513. 17 k. Type **115** 20 15
514. 20 k. Exhibition emblem (different) 20 15

1973. I.M.O. Centenary.
515. **116.** 50 k. multicoloured .. 45 45

117. "Ingolfur and High Seat Pillar" (tapestry). **118.** "Horseman" (17th-century wood-carving).

1974. Icelandic Settlement. 1100th Anniv. (1st issue). Multicoloured.
516. 10 k. Type **117** 8 8
517. 13 k. "Grimur Geitskor at Thingvellir" (painting) (horiz.) 12 12
518. 30 k. "Christ the King" (Mosaic alterpiece, Skahholt Cathedral) .. 25 25
519. 70 k. "Saemunder smiting the Devil" seal (bronze) 65 60
See also Nos. 522/4 and 525/8.

1974. Europa. Sculptures. Multicoloured.
520. 13 k. Type **118** 12 12
521. 20 k. "Through the Sound Barrier" (bronze, A. Sveinsson) 15 15

1974. Icelandic Settlement. 1100th Anniv. (2nd issue). As Type **117**.
522. 17 k. blk., brn. & silver .. 15 15
523. 25 k. multicoloured .. 20 20
524. 100 k. multicoloured .. 90 90
DESIGNS—VERT. "Snorri Sturluson slaying the King's messenger" (T. Skulason). 25 k. Illuminated "I" from "Flateyjarbok" (manuscript). HORIZ. 100 k. Altar-cloth, Church of Stafafell.

1974. Icelandic Settlement. 1100th Anniv. (3rd issue). As Type **117**.
525. 15 k. multicoloured .. 12 12
526. 20 k. multicoloured .. 15 15
527. 40 k. multicoloured .. 35 35
528. 60 k. brown, grey and black 55 50
DESIGNS: 15 k. Bishop Thorlaksson of Holar. 20 k. Stained-glass window, Hallgrimskirkja. 40 k. "Industrial Workers" (18th-century wood-carving). 60 k. "Curing the Catch" (concrete relief by S. Olafsson).

119. Purchasing Stamps. **120.** Skyline Ablaze.

1974. Universal Postal Union. Cent. Mult.
529. 17 k. Type **119** 12 12
530. 20 k. Postman delivering letter to "U.P.U." postbox 15 15

1975. Volcanic Eruption, Heimaey (1973).
531. **120.** 20 k. multicoloured .. 15 15
532. 25 k. multicoloured .. 20 20

121. "Haustfugl" (P. Skulason). **122.** S. G. Stephansson (settler poet).

1975. Europa. Paintings. Multicoloured.
533. 18 k. Type **121** 15 15
534. 23 k. "Regin Sund" (J. S. Kjarval) (vert.) 20 20

1975. Icelandic Settlement in North America. Centenary.
535. **122.** 27 k. brown and green 25 25

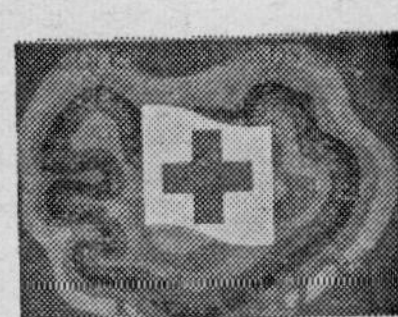

123. H. Petursson (religious poet). **124.** Red Cross Flag on Map.

1975. Icelandic Celebrities.
536. **123.** 18 k. black and green 15 15
537. – 23 k. blue 20 20
538. – 30 k. red 25 25
539. – 50 k. blue 45 45
PORTRAITS: 23 k. Arni Magnusson (historian). 30 k. Jon Eiriksson (statesman). 50 k. Einar Jonsson (painter and sculptor).

1975. Icelandic Red Cross. 50th Anniv.
540. **124.** 23 k. multicoloured .. 20 20

125. "Abstract" (Nina Tryggvadottir). **126.** Thorvaldsen's Statue.

1975. International Women's Year.
541. **125.** 100 k. multicoloured .. 90 90

1975. Thorvaldsen Society. Centenary.
542. **126.** 27 k. multicoloured .. 25 25

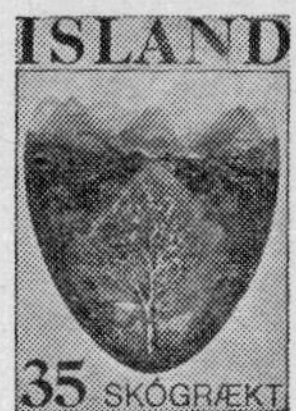

127. Forest Trees. **128.** "Landscape" (A. Jonsson).

1975. Reafforestation.
543. **127.** 35 k. multicoloured .. 30 30

1976. Icelandic Art.
544. **128.** 150 k. multicoloured .. 1·40 1·40

129. Wooden Bowl.

1976. Europa. Multicoloured.
545. 35 k. Type **129** 30 30
546. 45 k. Spinning-wheel (vert.) 35 35

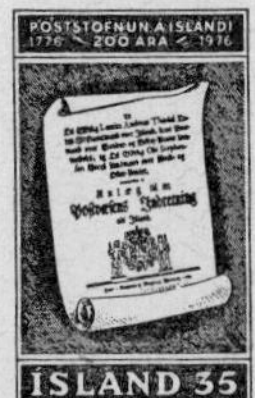

129. Postal Services' Order. Title-page.

1976. Icelandic Postal Services. Bicent.
547. **129.** 35 k. brown 30 30
548. – 45 k. blue 35 35
DESIGN: 45 k. Signature appended to Postal Services Order.

130. Block of 5 Aurar Stamps and "Reykjavik".

1976. Aurar-currency Stamps Centenary.

549. 131.	30 k. multicoloured ..	25	25

OFFICIAL STAMPS

1873. As T 1. but inscr. "PJON. FRIM". at foot.

O 8.	4 s. green	14·00	45·00
O 10.	8 s. mauve	70·00	70·00

O 1.

1876.

O 36. O 1.	3 a. yellow	1·40	3·00
O 37.	4 a. grey	4·00	4·00
O 21a.	5 a. brown	1·25	2·10
O 38.	10 a. blue	4·00	1·00
O 23a.	16 a. red	2·00	6·00
O 24a.	20 a. green	1·90	3·50
O 25.	50 a. mauve	10·00	10·00

1902. Optd. **1 GILDI '02-'03.**

O 87. O 1.	3 a. yellow	20	25
O 88.	4 a. grey	20	25
O 89.	5 a. brown	15	25
O 90.	10 a. blue	15	25
O 84.	16 a. red	1·40	7·00
O 91.	20 a. green	15	3·00
O 86.	50 a. mauve	80	7·00

1902. As T 3, but inscr. "PJONUSTA".

O 92.	3 a. sepia and yellow ..	45	25
O 93.	4 a. sepia and green ..	80	25
O 94.	5 a. sepia and brown ..	25	45
O 95.	10 a. sepia and blue ..	30	40
O 96.	16 a. sepia and red ..	35	1·50
O 97.	20 a. sepia and green ..	1·50	55
O 98.	50 a. sepia and mauve ..	65	1·10

1907. As T 4, but inscr. "PJONUSTU".

O 99.	3 a. grey and yellow ..	70	75
O 100.	4 a. grey and green ..	45	55
O 101.	5 a. grey and brown ..	1·25	55
O 102.	10 a. grey and blue ..	30	45
O 103.	15 a grey and blue ..	45	65
O 104.	16 a. grey and red ..	45	1·75
O 105.	20 a. grey and green ..	1·40	30
O 106.	50 a. grey and mauve..	70	65

1920. As T 6. but inscr. "PJONUSTU".

O 132.	3 a. black and yellow..	40	40
O 133.	4 a. black and green ..	15	30
O 134.	5 a. black and orange..	15	5
O 135.	10 a. black and blue ..	20	5
O 136.	15 a. black and blue ..	5	5
O 137.	20 a. black and green	3·00	40
O 138.	50 a. black and violet	3·50	20
O 139.	1 k. black and red	3·75	25
O 140.	2 k. black and blue	1·25	1·00
O 141.	5 k. black and brown	5·50	3·50

1922. Optd. **Pjonusta.**

O 153. 6.	20 a. on 10 a. red	2·00	25
O 151a. 5.	2 k. red (No. 107)	5·00	7·00
O 152.	5 k. brown (No. 108)..	35·00	23·00

1930. Parliamentary Commemoratives of 1930 optd. **Pjonustumerki.**

O 174. 8.	3 a. violet (postage) ..	3·00	6·00
O 175. –	5 a. blue and grey ..	3·00	6·00
O 176. –	7 a. green	3·00	6·00
O 177. –	10 a. purple	3·00	6·00
O 178. –	15 a. blue	3·00	6·00
O 179. –	20 a. red	3·00	6·00
O 180. –	25 a. brown	3·00	6·00
O 181 –	30 a. grey-green ..	3·00	6·00
O 182. –	35 a. blue	3·00	6·00
O 183. –	40 a. red, blue and grey	3·00	6·00
O 184. –	50 a. brown	28·00	30·00
O 185. –	1 k. green	28·00	30·00
O 186. –	2 k. blue and green ..	28·00	30·00
O 187. –	5 k. orange and yellow	28·00	30·00
O 188. –	10 k. lake	28·00	30·00
O 189. 9.	10 a. blue (air) ..	10·00	24·00

1936. Optd. **Pjonusta.**

O 220. 6.	7 a. green	40	3·00
O 221.	10 a. red	35	20
O 222. 4.	50 a. claret and grey..	3·50	3·00

IDAR BC

A State in Western India. Now uses Indian stamps.

1. Maharaja Shri Himatsinhji. 2.

1939.

1. 1.	½ a. green	1·50

1944.

3. 2.	½ a. green	25
4.	1 a. violet	12
5.	2 a. blue	30
6.	4 a. red	1·25

IFNI O3

Spanish enclave on the Atlantic coast of Northern Morocco ceded in 1860.

By an agreement, made effective on 30th June, 1969, Ifni was surrendered by Spain to Morocco.

1941. Stamps of Spain optd. **TERRITORIO DE IFNI.**

1. 122.	1 c. green (imperf.) ..	1·75	1·75
2. 123.	2 c. brown	1·75	1·75
3. 124.	5 c. brown	30	10
4.	10 c. red	1·25	50
5.	15 c. green	30	12
6. 133.	20 c. violet	30	12
7.	25 c. claret	30	15
8.	30 c. blue	40	15
9.	40 c. slate	50	8
10.	50 c. slate	1·00	30
11.	70 c. blue	1·25	80
12.	1 PTA. black	1·00	10
13.	2 PTAS. brown ..	11·00	2·00
14.	4 PTAS. red	48·00	7·50
15.	10 PTS. brown.. ..	85·00	22·00

1. Nomad Family. 2. El Santuario.

1943.

16. A.	1 c. magenta and brown..	5	5
17. B.	2 c. blue and green ..	5	5
18. C.	5 c. violet and claret ..	5	5
19. A.	15 c. green	8	8
20. B.	20 c. brown and violet ..	8	8
21. A.	40 c. violet and purple ..	12	12
22. B.	45 c. red and brown ..	20	20
35. 1.	50 c. black and brown ..	2·00	15
23. C.	75 c. blue..	20	20
24. A.	1 p. brown and red ..	50	50
25. B.	3 p. green and violet ..	75	75
26. C.	10 p. black and brown ..	8·00	8·00

DESIGNS: A. Nomadic shepherds. B. Arab rifleman. C. La Alcazaba.

1943. Air.

27. 2.	5 c. brown and claret ..	10	10
28. D.	25 c. brown and green ..	12	12
29. 2.	50 c. blue	15	15
30. D.	1 p. blue and violet ..	25	20
31. 3.	1 p. 40 blue and green ..	25	25
32. D.	2 p. brown and purple ..	50	50
33. 2.	5 p. violet and brown ..	70	70
34. D.	6 p. green and blue ..	9·00	9·00

DESIGN: D. Aeroplane over oasis.

1947. Air. Autogyro type of Spain optd. **IFNI.**

36. 132.	5 c. yellow	50	25
37.	10 c. green	70	30

1948. Stamps of Spain optd. **Territorio de Ifni** in Gothic letters.

45. 123.	2 c. brown (postage) ..	5	5
46. 124.	5 c. brown	5	5
47.	10 c. red	5	5
48.	15 c. green	5	5
39. 163.	15 c. green	25	15
49. 165.	25 c. orange	5	5
50. 133.	30 c. blue	5	5
51. 165.	40 c. brown	8	8
52.	45 c. red	8	8
53. 133.	50 c. slate	5	5
54. 165.	75 c. blue	10	10
55. 138.	90 c. green	15	15
41. 133.	1 PTA. black	30	30
56. 138.	1 p. 35 violet	70	50
57. 133.	2 PTAS. brown ..	50	40
58.	4 PTAS. rose	2·00	1·10
59.	10 PTAS. brown ..	4·50	3·00
60. 132.	25 c. red (air)	20	5
61.	50 c. brown	25	10
62.	1 p. blue	25	12
63.	2 p. green	80	25
64.	4 p. blue	2·40	1·10
65.	10 p. violet	3·00	2·00

1949. Stamp Day and 75th Anniv. of U.P.U. Spanish stamps optd. **Territorio de Ifni.**

42. 170.	50 c. brown (postage) ..	70	35
43.	75 c. blue	70	35
44.	4 p. olive (air)	70	35

3. General Franco. 4. Lope Sancho de Valenzuela.

1950. Child Welfare.

66. 3.	50 c.+10 c. sepia ..	30	20
67.	1 p.+25 c. blue	3·00	1·90
68.	6 p. 50+1 p. 65 green ..	1·50	90

1950. Air. Colonial Stamp Day.

69. 4.	5 p. black	70	20

5. Woman and Dove. 6. General Franco.

1951. Air. Isabella the Catholic. 500th Birth Anniv.

70. 5.	5 p. red	2·50	75

1951. Gen. Franco's Visit to Ifni.

71. 6.	50 c. orange	25	5
72.	1 p. brown	60	15
73.	5 p. green	5·00	2·00

7. Fennec. 8. Mother and Child. 9. Ferdinand the Catholic.

1951. Colonial Stamp Day.

74. 7.	5 c.+5 c. brown	5	5
75.	10 c.+5 c. orange ..	5	5
76.	60 c.+15 c. olive.. ..	10	8

1952. Child Welfare.

77. 8.	5 c.+5 c. brown	5	5
78.	50 c.+10 c. black ..	5	5
79.	2 p.+30 c. blue	35	25

1952. Air. Ferdinand the Catholic. 500th Birth Anniv.

80. 9.	5 p. brown	3·50	80

10. Cormorant. 11. 12. Gazelle and Aeroplane.

1952. Colonial Stamp Day.

81. 10.	5 c.+5 c. brown ..	8	5
82.	10 c.+5 c. claret ..	8	5
83.	60 c.+15 c. green ..	8	5

1952. Leo Africanus (geographer) 4th Death Cent.

84. 11.	5 c. vermilion	5	5
85.	35 c. green	5	5
86.	60 c. brown	10	5

1953. Air.

87. 12.	60 c. green	5	5
88.	1 p. 20 lake	15	5
89.	1 p. 60 brown	20	5
90.	2 p. blue	45	8
91.	4 p. myrtle	30	10
92.	10 p. purple	1·25	40

DESIGN: 10 c., 60 c. Two native musicians.

13. Native Musician.

1953. Child Welfare. Inscr. "PRO INFANCIA 1953".

93. 13.	5 c.+5 c. lake	5	5
94. –	10 c.+5 c. purple ..	5	5
95. 13.	15 c. olive	5	5
96. –	60 c. brown	5	5

DESIGN: 10 c. 60 c. Fish and seaweed.

14. Fish and Cuttlefish.

1953. Colonial Stamp Day. Inscr. "DIA DEL SELLO COLONIAL 1953".

97. 14.	5 c.+5 c. blue	5	5
98. –	10 c.+5 c. mauve ..	5	5
99. 14.	15 c. green	5	5
100. –	60 c. brown	10	5

15. Seagull.

16. Asclepiad.

17. Woman and child. 18. Lobster.

1954.

101. 15.	5 c. salmon	5	5
102. 16.	10 c. drab	5	5
103. –	25 c. claret	5	5
104. 15.	35 c. grey-green ..	5	5
105. 16.	40 c. violet	5	5
106. –	60 c. brown	5	5
107. 15.	1 p. brown	2·25	20
108. 16.	1 p. 25 rose	5	5
109. –	2 p. blue	5	5
110. 16.	4 p. 50 green	15	10
111. –	5 p. black	9·00	2·00

DESIGN—VERT. 25 c., 60 c., 2 p., 5 p. Another cactus.

1954. Child Welfare. Inscr. "PRO-INFANCIA 1954".

112. 17.	5 c.+5 c. orange ..	5	5
113. –	10 c.+5 c. mauve ..	5	5
114. 17.	15 c. green	5	5
115. –	60 c. brown	5	5

DESIGN: 10 c., 60 c. Woman and girl.

1954. Colonial Stamp Day. Inscr. "DIA DEL SELLO COLONIAL 1954".

116. 18.	5 c.+5 c. brown ..	5	5
117. –	10 c.+5 c. violet ..	5	5
118. 18.	15 c. green	5	5
119. –	60 c. lake	5	5

DESIGN: 10 c., 60 c. Hammer-headed shark.

DESIGN: 25 c. Camel caravan and "Spain".

19. Ploughman and "Justice".

1955. Native Welfare. Inscr. "PRO-INDIGENAS 1955".

120. **19.** 10 c.+5 c. purple .. 5 5
121. – 25 c.+10 c. lilac .. 5 5
122. **19.** 50 c. olive 5 5

20. Squirrel. **21.** " Senecio Antheuphorbium".

1955. Colonial Stamp Day. Inscr. "DIA DEL SELLO COLONIAL 1955".

123. **20.** 5 c.+5 c. lake 5 5
124. – 15 c.+5 c. brown .. 5 5
125. **20.** 70 c. green .. 5 5

DESIGN: 15 c. Squirrel holding nut.

1956. Child Welfare. Inscr. "PRO-INFANCIA 1956".

126. **21.** 5 c.+5 c. grey-green .. 5 5
127. – 15 c.+5 c. brown .. 5 5
128. **21.** 20 c. green 5 5
129. – 50 c. sepia 5 5

DESIGN: 15 c., 50 c. "Limoniastrum Ifniensis".

22. Arms of Sidi-Ifni and Drummer. **23.** Doves.

1956. Colonial Stamp Day. Inscr. "DIA DEL SELLO 1956".

130. – 5 c.+5 c. sepia .. 5 5
131. **22.** 15 c.+5 c. brown .. 5 5
132. – 70 c. green 5 5

DESIGNS—VERT. 5 c. Arms of Spain and gazelles. HORIZ. 70 c. Arms of Sidi-Ifni, shepherd and sheep.

1957. Child Welfare. Inscr. "PRO-INFANCIA 1957".

133. **23.** 5 c.+5 c. grn. & chest. 5 5
134. – 15 c.+5 c. pur. & bistre 5 5
135. **23.** 70 c. brown & green .. 5 5

DESIGN: 15 c. Doves in flight.

24. Jackal.

25. Swallows and Arms of Valencia and Sidi-Ifni. **26.** Basketball.

1957. Colonial Stamp Day. Inscr. "DIA DEL SELLO 1957".

136. **24.** 10 c.+5 c. brn. & pur. 5 5
137. – 15 c.+5 c. grn. & brn. 5 5
138. **24.** 20 c. brown & green .. 5 5
139. – 70 c. brown & green .. 10 8

DESIGN—VERT. 15 c., 70 c., Head of Jackal.

1958. "Aid for Valencia".

140. **25.** 10 c.+5 c. chestnut .. 5 5
141. 15 c.+10 c. ochre .. 5 5
142. 50 c.+10 c. olive-brn. 5 5

1958. Child Welfare. Inscr. "PRO-INFANCIA 1958".

143. **26.** 10 c.+5 c. chestnut .. 5 5
144. – 15 c.+5 c. ochre .. 5 5
145. – 20 c. blue-green .. 5 5
146. – 70 c. olive-green .. 8 5

DESIGNS: 15 c., 70 c. Cycling.

27.

DESIGNS—VERT. 25 c. Ray. HORIZ. 50 c. Fishing boats.

1958. Colonial Stamp Day. Inscr. "DIA DEL SELLO 1958".

147. **27.** 10 c.+5 c. red 5 5
148. – 25 c.+10 c. slate-pur.. 5 5
149. – 50 c.+10 c. olive .. 5 5

28. Ewe and Lamb.

29. Footballer.

30. Camels. **31.** Stork.

1959. Child Welfare. Inscr. "PRO-INFANCIA 1959".

150. **28.** 10 c.+5 c. brown .. 5 5
151. – 15 c.+5 c. brown .. 5 5
152. – 20 c. blue-green .. 5 5
153. **28.** 70 c. yellow-green .. 5 5

DESIGNS—VERT. 15 c. Native trader with mule. 20 c. Mountain goat.

1959. Colonial Stamp Day. Inscr. "DIA DEL SELLO 1959".

154. **29.** 10 c.+5 c. brown .. 5 5
155. – 20 c.+5 c. myrtle .. 5 5
156. – 50 c.+20 c. olive .. 8 5

DESIGNS: 20 c. Footballers. 50 c. Javelin-thrower.

1960. Child Welfare Inscr. "PRO-INFANCIA 1960".

157. **30.** 10 c.+5 c. claret .. 5 5
158. – 15 c.+5 c. brown .. 5 5
159. – 35 c. grey-green .. 5 5
160. **30.** 80 c. blue-green .. 5 5

DESIGNS: 15 c. Wild boar. 35 c. Birds.

1960. Birds.

161. **31.** 25 c. violet 5 5
162. – 50 c. olive-brown .. 5 5
163. – 75 c. purple 5 5
164. **31.** 1 p. vermilion.. .. 5 5
165. – 1 p. 50 turquoise .. 8 5
166. – 2 p. mauve 8 8
167. **31.** 3 p. grey-blue 20 8
168. – 5 p. brown 40 12
169. – 10 p. olive .. .. 1·10 25

BIRDS.—HORIZ. 50 c., 1 p. 50, 5 p. Four swallows. VERT. 75 c., 2 p., 10 p. Two finches.

32. Church of Santa Cruze del Mar. **33.** High Jump.

1960. Stamp Day. Inscr. "DIA DEL SELLO 1960".

170. **32.** 10 c.+5 c. chestnut .. 5 5
171. – 20 c.+5 c. grey-green.. 5 5
172. **32.** 30 c.+10 c. brown .. 5 5
173. – 50 c.+50 c. olive-brn. 5 5

DESIGN—HORIZ. 20 c., 50 c. School building.

1961. Child Welfare. Inscr. "PRO-INFANCIA 1961".

174. **33.** 10 c.+5 c. claret .. 5 5
175. – 25 c.+10 c. violet .. 5 5
176. **33.** 80 c.+20 c. blue-grn.. 5 5

DESIGN—VERT. 25 c. Football.

34.

DESIGNS—VERT. 25 c. Map. HORIZ. 70 c. Government Building.

1961. Gen. Franco as Head of State. 25th Anniv.

177. – 25 c. violet-grey .. 5 5
178. **34.** 50 c. olive-brown .. 5 5
179. – 70 c. green 5 5
180. **34.** 1 p. orange 5 5

35. Camel and Motor Lorry. **36.** Admiral Jofre Tenorio.

1961. Stamp Day. Inscr. "DIA DEL SELLO 1961".

181. **35.** 10 c.+5 c. lake .. 5 5
182. – 25 c.+10 c. plum .. 5 5
183. **35.** 30 c.+10 c. chocolate.. 5 5
184. – 1 p. +10c. orange .. 5 5

DESIGN: 25 c., 1 p. Ship in harbour.

1962. Child Welfare. Inscr. "PRO-INFANCIA 1962".

185. **36.** 25 c. violet 5 5
186. – 50 c. blue-green .. 5 5
187. **36.** 1 p. chestnut 5 5

DESIGN: 50 c. C. Fernandez-Duro (historian).

37. Desert Postman. **38.** "Golden Tower", Seville. **39.** Butterfly and Flower.

1962. Stamp Day. Inscr. "DIA DEL SELLO 1962".

188. **37.** 15 c. blue 5 5
189. – 35 c. magenta 5 5
190. **37.** 1 p. claret 5 5

DESIGN: 35 c. Winged letter on hands.

1963. Seville Flood Relief.

191. **38.** 50 c. green 5 5
192. 1 p. chestnut 5 5

1963. Child Welfare. Inscr. "PRO-INFANCIA 1963".

193. – 25 c. blue 5 5
194. **39.** 50 c. green 5 5
195. – 1 p. red 5 5

DESIGN: 25 c., 1 p. Two butterflies.

40. Child and Flowers. **41.** Beetle ("Steraspis speciosa").

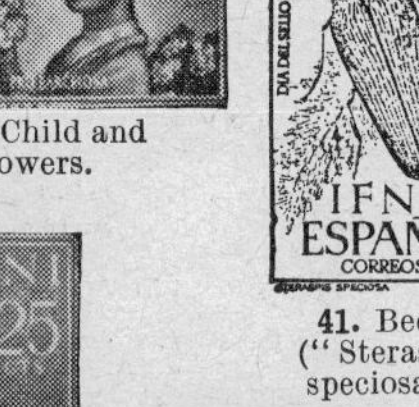

42. Antelope. **43.** Cycle-racing.

1963. "For Barcelona".

196. **40.** 50 c. olive-green .. 5 5
197. 1 p. chocolate .. 5 5

1964. Stamp Day. Inscr. "DIA DEL SELLO 1963".

198. **41.** 25 c. blue 5 5
199. – 50 c. olive 5 5
200. **41.** 1 p. brown 5 5

DESIGN: 50 c. Grasshopper ("Schistocerca gregaria").

1964. Child Welfare. Inscr. "PRO-INFANCIA 1964".

201. **42.** 25 c. violet 5 5
202. – 50 c. slate (Antelope head) 5 5
203. **42.** 1 p. orange 5 5

1964. Stamp Day. Inscr. "DIA DEL SELLO 1964".

204. **43.** 50 c. brown 5 5
205. – 1 p. orange 5 5
206. **43.** 1 p. 50 green 5 5

DESIGN: 1 p. Motor-cycle racing.

44. Port Installation, Sidi Ifni.

1965. End of Spanish Civil War. 25th Anniv. Inscr. "XXV ANOS DE PAZ".

207. – 50 c. green 5 5
208. – 1 p. red.. .. .. 5 5
209. **44.** 1 p. 50 blue 5 5

DESIGNS—VERT. 50 c. Ifnian. 1 p. "Education" (children in class).

45. " Eugaster fernandezi".

1965. Child Welfare.

210. **45.** 50 c. purple 5 5
211. – 1 p. red (" Halter halteratus") .. 5 5
212. **45.** 1 p. 50 ultramarine .. 5 5

46. Arms of Ifni.

1965. Stamp Day.

213. – 50 c. brown 5 5
214. **46.** 1 p. vermilion 5 5
215. – 1 p. 50 blue 5 5

DESIGN—VERT. 50 c., 1 p. 50, Eagle.

47. Antiguo Biplanes of 1934.

1966. Child Welfare.

216. – 1 p. brown 5 5
217. – 1 p. 50 blue 5 5
218. **47.** 2 p. 50 violet 55 55

DESIGN—VERT. 1 p., 1 p. 50, Jetliner over Sidi Ifni.

48. "Syntomis alicia" (butterfly).

49. Coconut Palm.

1966. Stamp Day.

219. **48.** 10 c. green and red .. 5 5
220. – 40 c. brown and sepia .. 5 5
221. **48.** 1 p. 50 violet & yellow.. 5 5
222. – 4 p. blue and maroon.. 8 8

DESIGN: 40 c., 4 p. " Danais chrysippus" (butterfly).

1967. Child Welfare.

223. **49.** 10 c. green and brown.. 5 5
224. – 40 c. green & orge.-brn. 5 5
225. **49.** 1 p. 50 turquoise & sepia 5 5
226. – 4 p. sepia and chestnut 8 8

DESIGN: 40 c., 4 p. Cactus.

50. Harbour Cranes.

1967. Port Ifni. Inaug.

227. **50.** 1 p. 50 chestnut and green 10 10

51. Saury Pike.

1967. Stamp Day.

228. **51.** 1 p. green and blue .. 5 5
229. – 1 p. 50 purple & yellow 5 5
230. – 3 p. 50 red and blue .. 8 8

FISH—VERT. 1 p. 50, John Dory. HORIZ. 3 p. 50, Gurnard.

52. Fishes (Pisces).

1968. Child Welfare. Signs of the Zodiac.

231. **52.** 1 p. magenta on yellow 5 5
232. – 1 p. 50 brown on pink 5 5
233. – 2 p. 50 violet on yellow 5 5

DESIGNS: 1 p. 50 Ram (Aries). 2 p. 50 Archer (Saggitarius).

53. Posting Letter.

1968. Stamp Day.

234. **53.** 1 p. black and yellow .. 5 5
235. – 1 p. 50 plum and blue .. 5 5
236. – 2 p. 50 black, blue & grn. 5 5

DESIGNS: 1 p. 50 Dove with letter. 2 p. 50 Magnifying-glass and stamp.

EXPRESS LETTER STAMPS

1943. As T **1**, but view of La Alcazaba inscr. "URGENTE".

E 35. 25 c. red and green .. 50 50

1949. Express Letter stamp of Spain optd. **TERRITORIO DE IFNI.**

E 66. E **11.** 25 c. red 8 8

INDIA BC

A peninsula in the S. of Asia. Formerly consisted of British India and numerous Native States, some of which issued stamps of their own. Divided in 1947 into the Dominion of India and the Dominion of Pakistan. Now a republic within the British Commonwealth.

12 pies = 1 anna; 16 annas = 1 rupee.
1957. 100 naye paise = 1 rupee.
1964. 100 paisa = 1 rupee.

1.

1852. Imperf.

S 1. **1.** $\frac{1}{2}$ a. white £1200 £400
S 2. $\frac{1}{2}$ a. blue £3000 £900
S 3. $\frac{1}{2}$ a. red .. .. .. — £2250

2.

3.

4.

5.

1854. Imperf.

1. **2.** $\frac{1}{2}$ a. red £160
2. $\frac{1}{2}$ a. blue .. .. 9·00 4·50
14. 1 a. red .. .. .. 12·00 12·00
31. **3.** 2 a. green .. .. 9·00 3·50
23. **4.** 4 a. blue and red .. £350 65·00

1855. Perf.

55. **5.** $\frac{1}{2}$ a. blue 60 8
59. 1 a. brown 65 8
41. 2 a. pink .. .. 12·00 3·50
63. 2 a. orange .. .. 2·75 1·25
46. 4 a. black .. .. 6·00 1·25
64. 4 a. green .. .. 18·00 7·00
73. 8 a. red .. .. 3·25 2·25

6.

ILLUSTRATIONS
British Commonwealth and all overprints and surcharges are FULL SIZE. Foreign Countries have been reduced to $\frac{3}{4}$-LINEAR.

1860. Inscr. "EAST INDIA POSTAGE". Various frames.

56. **6.** 8 p. mauve .. .. 2·75 2·00
77. – 9 p. lilac .. .. .. 2·50 2·75
69. – 4 a. green .. .. .. 4·00 20
80. – 6 a. brown .. .. 1·75 1·00
72. – 6 a. 8 p. grey .. .. 8·00 7·00
82. – 12 a. red-brown .. .. 2·00 2·75
79. – 1 r. grey .. .. .. 5·00 5·00

13.

14.

1866. Optd. **POSTAGE.**

66. **13.** 6 a. purple .. .. 50·00 25·00

1882. Inscr. "INDIA POSTAGE". Various frames.

84. **14.** $\frac{1}{2}$ a. blue-green 8 8
87. – 9 p. red 35 60
88. – 1 a. purple 20 8
90. – 1 a. 6 brown 45 25
91. – 2 a. blue 25 8
94. – 3 a. orange 90 8
96. – 4 a. green .. .. 1·10 10
97. – 4 a. 6 p. green .. .. 1·75 1·25
99. – 8 a. mauve .. .. 2·00 90
100. – 12 a. purple on red .. 2·00 1·00
101. – 1 r. grey .. .. 2·00 1·25

1891. No. 97 surch. **2$\frac{1}{2}$ As.**

102. 2$\frac{1}{2}$ a. on 4$\frac{1}{2}$ a. green .. 80 1·25

25.

26.

27.

1892. As 1882 and T **25/7.**

111. **25.** 3 p. red 8 8
112. 3 p grey 8 8
114. **14.** $\frac{1}{2}$ a. yellow-green .. 8 8
115. – 1 a. red 10 8
116. – 2 a. lilac .. .. .. 1·10 30
103. – 2$\frac{1}{2}$ a. green 25 25
118. – 2$\frac{1}{2}$ a. blue .. .. 2·00 2·00
106. **26.** 1 r. green and red .. 2·00 1·25
107. **27.** 2 r. red and orange .. 6·00 2·25
108. 3 r. brown and green .. 7·00 2·75
109. 5 r. blue and violet .. 7·00 6·50

1898. Surch. $\frac{1}{4}$.

110. **14.** "$\frac{1}{4}$" on $\frac{1}{2}$ a. blue-green .. 8 8

28.

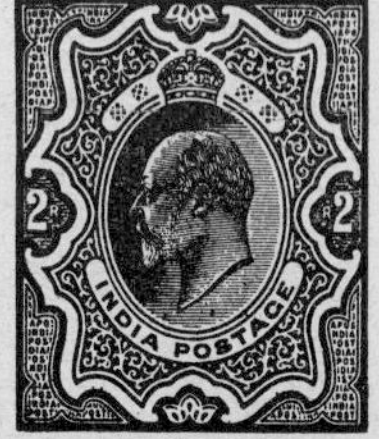

39.

1902. As 1882 and 1892, but portrait of King Edward VII (inscribed "INDIA POSTAGE").

119. **28.** 3 p. grey 12 12
122. – $\frac{1}{2}$ a. green 20 12
123. – 1 a. red 15 8
125. – 2 a. lilac 75 12
126. – 2$\frac{1}{2}$ a. blue .. .. 1·10 12
127. – 3 a. orange .. .. 1·00 15
129. – 4 a. olive .. .. .. 1·60 15
132. – 6 a. yellow-brown .. 3·50 2·00
133. – 8 a. mauve .. .. 2·75 80
135. – 12 a. purple on red .. 3·50 1·75
136. – 1 r. green and red .. 2·25 50
139. **39.** 2 r. red and orange .. 5·00 2·00
140. 3 r. brown and green .. 7·50 6·00
142. 5 r. blue and violet .. 18·00 18·00
144. 10 r. green and red .. 18·00 6·00
146. 15 r. blue and olive .. 50·00 17·00
147. 25 r. orange and blue .. £130 £120

1905. No. 122 surch. $\frac{1}{4}$.

148. "$\frac{1}{4}$" on $\frac{1}{2}$ a. green .. 12 12

1906. As Nos. 122 and 123, but inscr. "INDIA POSTAGE & REVENUE".

149. $\frac{1}{2}$ a. green 10 5
150. 1 a. red 10 5

40. **41.**

42. **43.**

44. **45.**

46. **47.**

48. **49.**

50. **51.**

52. **53.**

54.

1911.

* Two types of 1$\frac{1}{2}$ a. brown. Type A as illustrated. Type B inscr. "1$\frac{1}{2}$ As. ONE AND A HALF ANNAS".

152. **40.** 3 p. grey 5 5
155. **41.** $\frac{1}{2}$ a. green 12 10
160. **42.** 1 a. red 12 5
197. 1 a. chocolate 5 5
163. **43.** 1$\frac{1}{2}$ a. brown (A)* .. 40 5
165. 1$\frac{1}{2}$ a. brown (B)* .. 50 40
198. 1$\frac{1}{2}$ a. red (B)* 20 10
166. **44.** 2 a. lilac 35 5
206. **45.** 2 a. lilac 35 10
170. **46.** 2$\frac{1}{2}$ a. blue 90 85
171. **47.** 2$\frac{1}{2}$ a. blue 45 5
207. 2$\frac{1}{2}$ a. orange 25 5
172. **48.** 3 a. orange 75 10
209. 3 a. blue .. .. 1·25 15
210. **49.** 4 a. olive 40 5
211. **50.** 4 a. green .. .. 2·00 5
176. **51.** 6 a. yellow-brown .. 1·25 40
212. **52.** 8 a. mauve .. .. 1·25 5
213. **53.** 12 a. claret .. .. 2·50 10
214. **54.** 1 r. brown and green .. 1·25 5
215. 2 r. red and orange .. 2·50 45
216. 5 r. blue and violet .. 5·00 1·00
217. 10 r. green and red .. 15·00 2·00
218. 15 r. blue and olive .. 15·00 10·00
219. 25 r. orange and blue .. 18·00 12·00

See also Nos. 232, etc.

1921. Surch. **NINE PIES** and bar.

192. **42.** 9 p. on 1 a. red 10 5

1922. Surch. $\frac{1}{4}$.

195. **41.** "$\frac{1}{4}$" on $\frac{1}{2}$ a. green .. 10 10

55.

1929. Air.

220. **55.** 2 a. green 25 25
221. 3 a. blue .. .. 55 1·00
222. 4 a. olive .. .. 1·50 1·00
223. 6 a. yellow-brown .. 2·00 1·60
224. 8 a. purple .. .. 2·50 3·50
225. 12 a. red .. .. 4·50 7·00

56. Purana Qila.

1931. Inscr. as in T **56.**

226. **56.** $\frac{1}{4}$ a. green and orange .. 10 20
227. – $\frac{1}{2}$ a. violet and green .. 10 10
228. – 1 a. mauve and brown 10 5
229. – 2 a. green and blue .. 35 30
230. – 3 a. brown and red .. 75 90
231. – 1 r. violet and green .. 4·50 5·00

DESIGNS: $\frac{1}{2}$ a. War Memorial Arch. 1 a. Council House. 2 a. Viceroy's House. 3 a. Secretariat. 1 r. Dominion Columns and Secretariat.

62.

63.

64.

65.

66.

1932.

232. **62.** ½ a. green 5 5
233. **63.** 9 p. green 5 5
234. **64.** 1 a. chocolate 5 5
235. **65.** 1¼ a. mauve 5 5
236. **45.** 2 a. orange-red .. 6·00 3·00
236b. **44.** 2 a. orange-red .. 3·50 25
237. **48.** 3 a. red 40 10
238. **66.** 3½ a. blue 80 15

67. Gateway of India, Bombay.

1935. Silver Jubilee.

240. **67.** ½ a. black and green .. 12 5
241. – 9 p. black and green .. 10 5
242. – 1 a. black and brown .. 12 5
243. – 1¼ a. black and violet .. 10 10
244. – 2½ a. black and orange .. 25 12
245. – 3½ a. black and blue .. 40 45
246. 8 a. black and purple .. 1·25 80

DESIGNS: 9 p. Victoria Memorial, Calcutta. 1 a. Rameswaram Temple, Madras. 1¼ a. Jain Temple, Calcutta. 2½ a. Taj Mahal, Agra. 3½ a. Golden Temple, Amritsar. 8 a. Pagoda in Mandalay.

DESIGNS—As T 76: 2½ a. Bullock cart. 3 a. Tonga. 3½ a. Camel. 4 a. Mail train. 6 a. Mail steamer. 8 a. Mail lorry. 12 a. Mail 'plane.

74. King George VI.

76. Dak Runner (small head).

77. King George VI.

1937.

247. **74.** 3 p. slate 10 5
248. ½ a. brown 10 5
249. 9 p. green 20 12
250. 1 a. red 5 5
251. **76.** 2 a. red 25 5
252. – 2½ a. violet 20 5
253. – 3 a. green 30 5
254. – 3½ a. blue 30 25
255. – 4 a. brown 35 5
256. – 6 a. green 35 10
257. – 8 a. violet 80 5
258. – 12 a. red .. .. 1·60 30
259. **77.** 1 r. slate and brown .. 25 5
260. 2 r. purple and brown .. 85 5
261. 5 r. green and blue .. 2·25 10
262. 10 r. purple and red .. 3·75 35
263. 15 r. brown and green 6·50 4·50
264. 25 r. slate and purple .. 10·00 5·00

78. King George VI. **79.**

80. King George VI.

1940.

265. **78.** 3 p. slate 5 5
266. ½ a. mauve 5 5
267. 9 p. green 5 5
268. 1 a. red 5 5
269. **79.** 1 a. 3 p. bistre .. 30 10
269a. 1½ a. violet 12 5
270. 2 a. red 5 5
271. 3 a. violet 5 5
272. 3½ a. blue 10 5
273. **80.** 4 a. brown 10 5
274. 6 a. green 12 10
275. 8 a. violet 20 8
276. 12 a. purple 40 12
277. – 14 a. purple 40 12

No. 277 is as No. 258, but with large head.

81. "Victory" and King George VI.

1946. Victory Commem.

278. **81.** 9 p. green 10 5
279. 1½ a. purple 10 5
280. 3½ a. blue 10 10
281. 12 a. claret 20 20

1946. Surch. **3 PIES** and bars.

282. **79.** 3 p. on 1 a. 3 p. bistre .. 5 5

DOMINION OF INDIA

82. Douglas DC4.

1947. Indian Independence. Inscr. "15TH AUG 1947".

301. – 1½ a. green 5 5
302. – 3½ a. red, blue and green 10 5
303. **82.** 12 a. blue 25 5

DESIGNS—VERT. 1½ a. Asokan Capital. HORIZ. 3½ a. Indian National Flag.

1948. Air. Inauguration of India-Britain Service. As T 82, but showing Lockheed Constellation flying in opposite direction and inscr. "AIR INDIA INTERNATIONAL FIRST FLIGHT 8TH JUNE 1948".

304. **82.** 12 a. black and blue .. 30 25

The 10 r. depicts a profile portrait of Mahatma Gandhi and is larger (22½ × 37 mm.).

83. Mahatma Gandhi.

1948. Indian Independence. 1st Anniv.

305. **83.** 1½ a. brown 12 10
306. 3½ a. violet 20 10
307. 12 a. green 50 12
308. – 10 r. brown and red 20·00 20·00

84. Ajanta Panel.

85. Konarak Horse.

86. Bhuvanesvara.

87. Gol Gumbad, Bijapur.

88. Red Fort, Delhi.

89. Satrunjaya Temple, Palitana.

1949.

309. **84.** 3 p. violet 5 5
310. **85.** 6 p. brown 5 5
311. – 9 p. green 5 5
312. – 1 a. blue (A) 5 5
333. – 1 a. blue (B) 8 5
313. – 2 a. red 5 5
333a. – 2½ a. lake 8 5
314. – 3 a. salmon 5 5
315. – 3½ a. blue 60 50
316. **86.** 4 a. lake 40 5
333b. 4 a. blue 12 10
317. **87.** 6 a. violet 40 5
318. – 8 a. green 75 5
319. – 12 a. blue 45 12
320. – 1 r. violet and green .. 1·25 10
321. **88.** 2 r. claret and violet .. 1·60 15
322. – 5 r. green and brown .. 1·50 35
323. – 10 r. brown and blue .. 6·00 1·75
324. **89.** 15 r. brown and claret 8·00 2·50

1 anna: (A) Left arm of statue outstretched (B) Reversed—right arm outstretched.

DESIGNS—As T 84: 9 p. Trimurti. 1 a. Bodhisattva. 2 a. Nataraja. As T 86: 2½ a., 3½ a. Bodh Gaya Temple. 3 a. Sanchi Stupa, East Gate. As T 87: 8 a. Kandarya Mahadeva Temple. 12 a. Golden Temple, Amritsar. As T 88—VERT. 1 r. Victory Tower, Chittorgarh. 10 r. Qutb Minar, Delhi. HORIZ. 5 r. Taj Mahal, Agra.

90. Globe and Asokan Capital.

1949. U.P.U. 75th Anniv.

325. **90.** 9 p. green 15 12
326. 2 a. red 25 25
327. 3½ a. blue 25 30
328. 12 a. claret 40 45

REPUBLIC OF INDIA

91. Rejoicing Crowds.

1950. Republic. Inaug.

329. **91.** 2 a. red 15 10
330. – 3½ a. blue 25 10
331. – 4 a. violet 25 15
332. – 12 a. maroon 45 30

DESIGNS—VERT. 3½ a. Quill, ink-well and verse. HORIZ. 4 a. Ear of corn and plough. 12 a. Spinning-wheel and cloth.

92. Stegodon Ganesa.

1951. Geological Survey Cent.

334. **92.** 2 a. black and claret .. 30 30

93. Torch.

94. Kabir.

1951. 1st Asian Games, New Delhi.

335. **93.** 2 a purple and orange 15 15
336. 12 a. chocolate and blue 35 35

1952. Indian Saints and Poets.

337. **94.** 9 p. green 15 10
338. – 1 a. red (Tulsidas) .. 15 10
339. – 2 a. orange (Meera) .. 20 10
340. – 4 a. blue (Surdas) .. 20 10
341. – 4½ a. mauve (Ghalib) .. 30 15
342. – 12 a. brown (Tagore) .. 55 40

95. Locomotives in 1853 and 1953.

1953. Indian Railways Cent.

343. **95.** 2 a. black 8 8

96. Mount Everest.

1953. Conquest of Mount Everest.

344. **96.** 2 a. violet 10 10
345. 14 a. brown 40 40

97. Telegraph Poles of 1851 and 1951.

1953. Indian Telegraphs Cent.

346. **97.** 2 a. green 10 10
347. 12 a. blue 90 30

98. Postal Transport, 1854.

1954. Indian Stamp Cent.

348. **98.** 1 a. purple 10 10
349. – 2 a. magenta 10 10
350. – 4 a. brown 20 15
351. – 14 a. blue 50 25

DESIGNS: 2 a., 14 a. Dove and aeroplane. 4 a., Ship, cyclist, aeroplane and train.

99. U.N. Emblem and Lotus.

1954. U.N. Day.

352. **99.** 2 a. turquoise 12 10

100. Forest Research Institute.

1954. 4th World Forestry Congress, Dehra Dun.

353. **100.** 2 a. blue 10 10

101. Tractor. **102.** Woman Spinning.

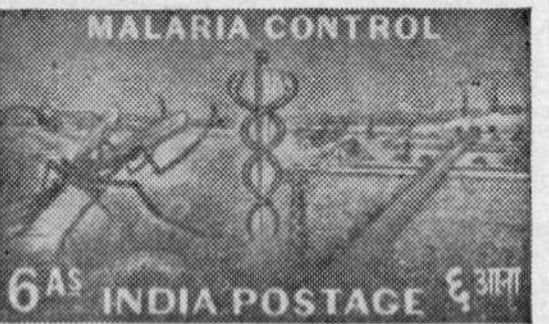

103. "Malaria Control" (Mosquito and Staff of Aesculapius).

1955. India's Five Year Plan.

354. **101.**	3 p. mauve	5	5
355. –	6 p. violet	5	5
356. –	9 p. chestnut	5	5
357. –	1 a. green	5	5
358. **102.**	2 a. blue	5	5
359. –	3 a. green	5	5
360. –	4 a. red	10	5
361. **103.**	6 a. brown	10	5
362. –	8 a. blue	12	5
363. –	10 a. turquoise ..	25	12
364. –	12 a. blue	25	5
365. –	14 a. emerald ..	20	12
413. –	1 r. myrtle	20	5
367. –	1 r. 2 a. grey	45	40
368. –	1 r. 8 a. purple ..	75	50
414. –	2 r. magenta	75	15
415. –	5 r. brown	1·50	40
416. –	10 r. orange	3·00	1·50

DESIGNS—As T **101**: 6 p. Power loom. 9 p. Bullock-driven well. 1 a. Damodar Valley Dam. 4 a. Bullocks. 8 a. Chittarajan Locomotive Works. 12 a. Hindustan Aircraft Factory, Bangalore. 1 r. Telephone engineer. 2 r. Rare Earth Factory, Alwaye. 5 r. Sindri Fertiliser Factory. 10 r. Steel plant. As T **102**: 3 a. Woman hand-weaving. As T **103**: 10 a. Aeroplane over Marine Drive, Bombay. 14 a. Aeroplane over Kashmir landscape. 1 r. 2 a. Aeroplane over Cape Comorin. 1 r. 8 a. Aeroplane over Mt. Kangchenjunga.

104. Bodhi Tree.

1956. Buddha Jayanti.

372. **104.** 2 a. sepia 10 10
373. – 14 a. vermilion .. 50 50

DESIGN—HORIZ. 14 a. Round parasol and Bodhi tree.

105. Lokmanya Bal Gangadhar Tilak. **106.** Map of India.

1956. Tilak (journalist). Birth Cent.

374. **105.** 2 a. chestnut 5 5

1957. Value in naye paise.

375. **106.**	1 n.p. green	5	5
376.	2 n.p. cinnamon ..	5	5
377.	3 n.p. brown	5	5
378.	5 n.p. emerald ..	5	5
403.	6 n.p. grey	5	5
404.	8 n.p. turquoise ..	5	5
405.	10 n.p. myrtle ..	5	5
381.	13 n.p. red	5	5
407.	15 n.p. violet ..	5	5
408.	20 n.p. blue	5	5
409.	25 n.p. ultramarine ..	8	5
410.	50 n.p. orange ..	8	5
411.	75 n.p. maroon ..	15	5
412.	90 n.p. purple ..	20	5

107. The Rani of Jhansi.

108. Shrine.

1957. Indian Mutiny Cent.

386. **107.** 15 n.p. brown .. 15 5
387. **108.** 90 n.p. purple .. 60 25

109. Henri Dunant and Conference Emblem.

1957. 19th Int. Red Cross Conf., New Delhi.

388. **109.** 15 n.p. grey and red .. 8 5

110. "Nutrition".

DESIGNS—HORIZ. 15 n.p. "Education". VERT. 90 n.p. "Recreation".

1957. National Children's Day. Inscr. "14.11.57".

389. **110.** 8 n.p. purple 8 5
390. – 15 n.p. turquoise .. 8 5
391. – 90 n.p. brown .. 25 15

111. Calcutta University.

DESIGNS—VERT. No. 392, Bombay University. As T **111**.—HORIZ. No. 394. Madras University.

1957. Indian Universities Cent.

392. – 10 n.p. violet ($21\frac{1}{2}\times$ 38 mm.) 8 8
393. **111.** 10 n.p. grey 8 8
394. – 10 n.p. brown.. .. 8 8

112. J. N. Tata (founder) and Steel Plant.

1958. Steel Industry. 50th Anniv.

395. **112.** 15 n.p. red 8 5

113. Dr. D. K. Karve.

1958. Karve (educationist). Birth Cent.

396. **113.** 15 n.p. chestnut .. 8 5

114. "Wapiti" and "Hunter" Aircraft.

1958. Silver Jubilee of Indian Air Force.

397. **114.** 15 n.p. blue 8 8
398. 90 n.p. ultramarine .. 40 25

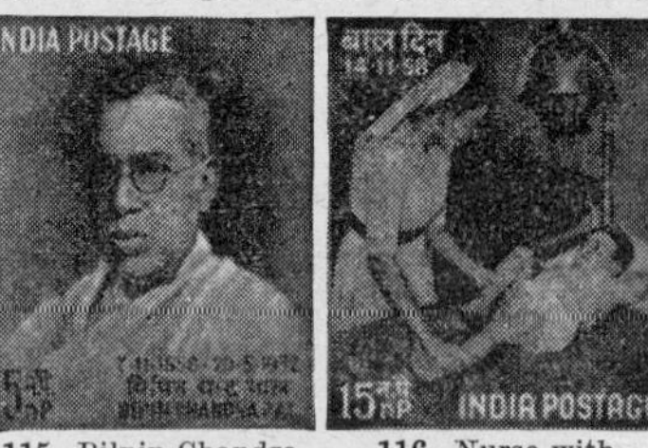

115. Bilpin Chandra Pal (patriot). **116.** Nurse with Child Patient.

1958. Pal. Birth Cent.

418. **115.** 15 n.p. green 5 5

1958. National Children's Day.

419. **116.** 15 n.p. violet .. 5 5

117. Jagadis Chandra Bose (botanist).

1958. Bose. Birth Cent.

420. **117.** 15 n.p. turquoise .. 5 5

118. Exhibition Gate.

1958. India 1958 Exn., New Delhi.

421. **118.** 15 n.p. purple .. 5 5

119. Sir Jamsetjee Jejeebhoy. **121.** Boys awaiting admission to Children's Home.

120. "The Triumph of Labour".

1959. Sir Jamsetjee Jejeebhoy (philanthropist). Death Cent.

422. **119.** 15 n.p. brown .. 5 5

1959. 40th Anniv. of I.L.O.

423. **120.** 5 n.p. green 5 5

1959. National Children's Day.

424. **121.** 15 n.p. green 5 5

122. "Agriculture".

1959. 1st World Agriculture Fair, New Delhi.

425. **122.** 15 n.p. grey 5 5

123. Thiruvalluvar (poet).

1960. Thiruvalluvar Commem.

426. **123.** 15 n.p. purple .. 5 5

124. Yaksha pleading with the Cloud (from the "Meghaduta").

125. Shakuntala writing a letter to Dushyanta (from the "Shakuntala").

1960. Kalidasa (poet) Commem.

427. **124.** 15 n.p. grey 8 8
428. **125.** 1 r. 3 n.p. yell. & brn. 25 25

126. S. Bharati (poet). **127.** Dr. M. Visvesvaraya (engineer).

1960. Subramania Bahrati Commem.
429. **126.** 15 n.p. blue 5 5

1960. Dr. M. Visvesvaraya. Birth Cent.
430. **127.** 15 n.p. brown and red 5 5

128. "Children's Health".

1960. Children's Day.
431. **128.** 15 n.p. green 5 5

129. Children greeting U.N. Emblem.

1960. U.N.I.C.E.F. Day.
432. **129.** 15 n.p. chest. & drab 5 5

130. Tyagaraja (Indian saint). **131.** "First Aerial Post" Cancellation.

132. "Air India" Boeing 707 Jetliner and Humber-Sommer 'Plane.

1961. Tyagaraja Commem.
433. **130.** 15 n.p. blue 5 5

1961. 1st Official Airmail Flight, Allahabad-Naini. 50th Anniv.
434. **131.** 5 n.p. olive 10 10
435. **132.** 15 n.p. green and grey 15 15
436. – 1 r. purple and grey .. 75 50

DESIGN—As T **132**: 1 r. H. Pecquet flying Humber-Sommer 'plane, and "Aerial Post" cancellation.

133. Shivaji on Horseback.

1961. Shivaji Commem.
437. **133.** 15 n.p. brown and green 5 5

134. Motilal Nehru (politician). **135.** R. Tagore (poet).

1961. Pandit Motilal Nehru. Birth Cent.
438. **134.** 15 n.p. ol.-brn. & orge. 5 5

1961. Rabindranath Tagore. Birth Cent.
439. **135.** 15 n.p. orge. & bl.-grn. 10 12

136. All India Radio Emblem and Transmitting Aerials.

1961. Silver Jubilee of All India Radio Broadcasting Service.
440. **136.** 15 n.p. blue 5 5

137. P. Chandra Ray. **138.** V. N. Bhatkande.

1961. Ray (scientist). Birth Cent.
441. **137.** 15 n.p. grey 5 5

1961. Bhatkande (musician). Birth Cent.
442. **138.** 15 n.p. drab 5 5

139. Child at Lathe. **140.** Fair Emblem and Main Gate.

1961. Children's Day.
443. **139.** 15 n.p. brown .. 5 5

1961. Indian Industries Fair, New Delhi.
444. **140.** 15 n.p. blue and red .. 5 5

141. Indian Forest. **142.** Pitalkhora, Yaksha.

1961. Scientific Forestry Cent.
445. **141.** 15 n.p. green and brown 5 5

1961. Indian Archaeological Survey Cent.
446. **142.** 15 n.p. chestnut .. 8 8
447. – 90 n.p. olive and brown 25 20

DESIGN—HORIZ. 90 n.p. Kalibangan seal.

143. M. M. Malaviya. **144.** Gauhati Refinery.

1961. Malaviya (President of National Congress). Birth Cent.
448. **143.** 15 n.p. slate 5 5

1962. Gauhati Oil Refinery Inaug.
449. **144.** 15 n.p. blue 5 5

145. Bhikaiji Cama. **146.** Panchayati at work and Parliament Building.

1962. Bhikaiji Cama (revolutionary). Birth Cent.
450. **145.** 15 n.p. purple .. 5 5

1962. Panchayati Raj Commem.
451. **146.** 15 n.p. magenta .. 5 5

147. D. Saraswati (religious educator). **148.** G. S. Vidhyarthi (patriot).

1962. Saraswati Commem.
452. **147.** 15 n.p. chestnut .. 5 5

1962. Vidhyarthi Commem.
453. **148.** 15 n.p. brown .. 5 8

149. Campaign Emblem. **150.** Dr. R. Prasad (former President of India).

1962. Malaria Eradication.
454. **149.** 15 n.p. yellow and lake 5 5

1962. Dr. Rajendra Prasad Commem.
455. **150.** 15 n.p. purple .. 5 5

151. Calcutta High Court.

1962. Indian High Courts. Cent.
456. **151.** 15 n.p. green 5 5
457. – 15 n.p. brown (Madras) 5 5
458. – 15 n.p. slate (Bombay) 5 5

152. Ramabai Ranade.

1962. Ramabai Ranade (social reformer). Birth Cent.
459. **152.** 15 n.p. orange 5 8

153. Indian One-horned Rhinoceros.

1962. Wild Life Week.
460. **153.** 15 n.p. brown and turq. 5 5
See also Nos. 472/6.

154. "Passing the Flag to Youth".

1962. Children's Day.
461. **154.** 15 n.p. red and green .. 5 5

155. Human Eye with Lotus Blossom.

1962. 19th Int. Ophthalmology Congress, New Delhi.
462. **155.** 15 n.p. olive-brown .. 5 5

156. S. Ramanujan.

1962. Ramanujan (mathematician). 75th Birth Anniv.
463. **156.** 15 n.p. olive-brown .. 5 5

157.
S. Vivekananda.

158. Hands reaching for F.A.O. Emblem.

1962. Vivekananda (philosopher). Birth Cent.
464. **157.** 15 n.p. brown and olive 5 5

1963. Surch.
465. **125.** 1 r. on 1 r. 3 n.p. yellow and brown .. 15 10

1963. Freedom from Hunger.
466. **158.** 15 n.p. grey-blue .. 5 5

159. Henri Dunant (founder) and Centenary Emblem.
161. D. Naoroji (patriot).

160. Artillery and Helicopter.

1963. Red Cross Cent.
467. **159.** 15 n.p. red and grey .. 8 5

1963. Defence Campaign.
468. **160.** 15 n.p. green .. 8 8
469. – 1 r. brown .. 25 20
DESIGN: 1 r. Sentry and parachutists.

1963. Dadabhoy Naoroji Commem.
470. **161.** 15 n.p. grey .. 5 5

162. Mrs. Annie Besant (patriot and theosophist, born 1847). (Stamp wrongly dated "1837").

1963. Mrs. Annie Besant Commem.
471. **162.** 15 n.p. turquoise .. 5 5

1963. Wild Life Preservation. Animal designs as T **153**.
472. 10 n.p. black and orange .. 10 15
473. 15 n.p. brown and green .. 10 10
474. 30 n.p. slate and ochre .. 20 10
475. 50 n.p. orge. and grey-green 30 10
476. 1 r. brown and blue .. 50 25
ANIMALS. As T **153**: 10 n.p. Gaur. LARGER ($25\frac{1}{2} \times 35\frac{1}{2}$ mm.): 15 n.p. Himalayan Panda. 30 n.p. Indian elephant. ($35\frac{1}{2} \times 25\frac{1}{2}$ mm.): 50 n.p. Tiger. 1 r. Indian lion.

163. " School Meals ".

1963. Children's Day.
477. **163.** 15 n.p. bistre 5 5

164. Eleanor Roosevelt at spinning-wheel.

1963. Declaration of Human Rights. 15th Anniv.
478. **164.** 15 n.p. purple .. 5 5

165. Dipalakshmi (bronze).

1964. 26th Int. Orientalists Congress, New Delhi.
479. **165.** 15 n.p. blue 5 5

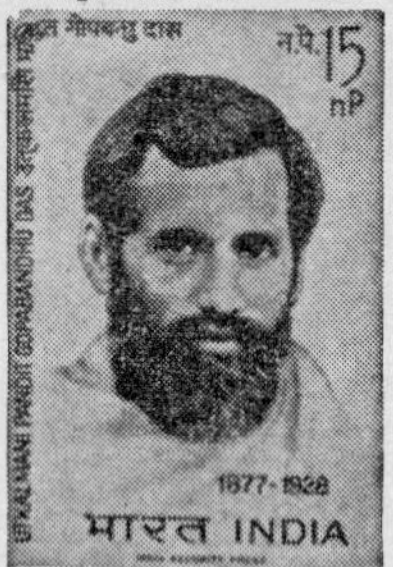

166. Gopabandhu Das (patriot and social reformer).

1964. Gopabandhu Das Commem.
480. **166.** 15 n.p. purple .. 5 5

167. Purandaradasa.

1964. Purandaradasa (musician). 400th Death Anniv.
481. **167.** 15 n.p. brown .. 5 5

168. S. C. Bose and I.N.A. Badge.

1964. Subhas Chandra Bose (nationalist). 67th Birth Anniv. Inscr. " I N A " on badge.
482. **168.** 15 n.p. olive .. 8 8
483. – 55 n.p. blk., orge & red 20 25
DESIGN: 55 n.p. Bose and Indian National Army.

169. Sarojini Naidu (patriot).

170. Kasturba Gandhi.

1964. Mrs. Sarojini Naidu. 85th Birth Anniv.
484. **169.** 15 n.p. grey-grn. & pur. 5 5

1964. Kasturba Gandhi. 20th Death Anniv.
485. **170.** 15 n.p. orange-brown 5 8

171. Dr. W. M. Haffkine (immunologist).

1964. Haffkine Commem.
486. **171.** 15 n.p. brown on buff 5 5

172. Jawaharlal Nehru (statesman).

1964. Nehru Mourning Issue.
487. **172.** 15 p. slate 5 5

173. Sir A. Mookerjee (education reformer).

1964. Sir Asutosh Mookerjee. Birth Cent.
488. **173.** 15 p. brown and olive 5 5

174. Sri Aurobindo (religious leader).

1964. Sri. Aurobindo. 92nd Birth Anniv.
489. **174.** 15 p. purple .. 5 8

175. Raja R. Roy (social reformer).

1964. Raja Rammohun Roy Commem.
490. **175.** 15 n.p. brown 5 8

HAVE YOU READ THE NOTES AT THE BEGINNING OF THIS CATALOGUE?

These often provide answers to the enquiries we receive.

176. I.S.O. Emblem and Globe.

1964. 6th Int. Organisation for Standardisation General Assembly, Bombay.
491. **176.** 15 p. red 5 8

177. Jawaharlal Nehru (medallion).
178. St. Thomas (after statue, Ortona Cathedral, Italy).

1964. Children's Day.
492. **177.** 15 p. slate 5 8

1964. St. Thomas Commem.
493. **178.** 15 p. purple 5 5
No. 493 was issued on the occasion of Pope Paul's visit to India.

179. Globe.

1964. 22nd Int. Geological Congress.
494. **179.** 15 p. green 5 5

180. J. Tata (industrialist).

1965. Jamsetji Tata Commem.
495. **180.** 15 p. dull purple & orge. 5 5

181. Lala Lajpat Rai (patriot).

1965. Lala Lajpat Rai. Birth Cent.
496. **181.** 15 p. brown 5 5

182. Globe and Congress Emblem.

1965. 20th Int. Chamber of Commerce Congress, New Delhi.
497. **182.** 15 p. green and red .. 5 5

183. Freighter "Jalausha" and Visakhapatnam.

1965. National Maritime Day.
498. **183.** 15 p. blue 5 5

184. Abraham Lincoln.

1965. Lincoln Death Cent.
499. **184.** 15 p. brown and ochre 5 8

185. I.T.U. Emblem and Symbols.

1965. I.T.U. Cent.
500. **185.** 15 p. purple .. 8 8

186. "Everlasting Flame".

1965. Nehru. 1st Death Anniv.
501. **186.** 15 p. red and blue .. 5 8

187. I.C.Y. Emblem.

1965. Int. Co-operation Year.
502. **187.** 15 p. green and brown 5 5

188. Climbers on Summit.  **189.** Plucking Tea.

190. Atomic Reactor, Trombay.

1965. Indian Mount Everest Expedition.
503. **188.** 15 p. purple .. 5 5

1965.

504.	–	2 p. brown	5	5
505.	–	3 p. olive	5	5
505a.	–	4 p. brown	5	5
506.	–	5 p. cerise	5	5
507.	–	6 p. black	5	5
508.	–	8 p. brown	5	5
509.	–	10 p. blue	5	5
510.	**189.**	15 p. green	5	5
511.	–	20 p. purple ..	5	5
512.	–	30 p. sepia	5	5
513.	–	40 p. maroon	5	5
514.	–	50 p. green	5	5
515.	–	60 p. grey	5	5
516.	–	70 p. blue	8	5
517.	–	1 r. brown and plum	10	5
518.	–	2 r. blue and violet ..	20	8
519.	–	5 r. violet and brown	50	15
520.	**190.**	10 r. black and green..	1·00	65

DESIGNS—As T **189**—VERT. 2 p. Bidr Vase. 3 p. Brass lamp. 4 p. Coffee Berries. 5 p. "Family Planning". 6 p. Konarak Elephant. 8 p. Chital (spotted deer). 30 p. Indian Dolls. 50 p. Mangoes. 60 p. Somnath Temple. HORIZ. 10 p. Electric Locomotive. 15 p. Plucking Tea. 20 p. Folland "Gnat" Fighter. 40 p. Calcutta G.P.O. 70 p. Hampi Chariot (sculpture). As T **190**—VERT. 1 r. Medieval Sculpture. HORIZ. 2 r. Dal Lake, Kashmir. 5 r. Bhakra Dam, Punjab.

191. G. B. Pant (statesman). **192.** V. Patel (statesman).

1965. Govind Ballabh Pant Commem.
522. **191.** 15 p. brown and green 5 5

1965. Vallabhbhai Patel. 90th Birth Anniv.
523. **192.** 15 p. brown 5 5

193. C. Das (lawyer and patriot). **194.** Vidyapati (poet).

1965. Chittaranjan Das. 95th Birth Anniv.
524. **193.** 15 p. brown .. 5 8

1965. Vidyapati Commem.
525. **194.** 15 p. brown 5 5

195. Sikandra, Agra.

1966 Pacific Area Travel Assn. Conf., New Delhi.
526. **195.** 15 p. slate 5 5

196. Soldier, Fighters and Warship.

1966. Indian Armed Forces.
527. **196.** 15 p. violet 5 8

197. Lal Bahadur Shastri (statesman). **198.** Kambar (poet).

1966. Shastri Mourning Issue.
528. **197.** 15 p. black 5 5

1966. Kambar Commem.
529. **198.** 15 p. green 5 8

199. B. R. Ambedkar. **200.** Kunwar Singh (patriot).

1966. Dr. B. R. Ambedkar (lawyer and reformer). 75th Birth Anniv.
530. **199.** 15 p. maroon .. 5 8

1966. Kunwar Singh Commem.
531. **200.** 15 p. chestnut .. 5 8

201. G. K. Gokhale (patriot).

1966. G. K. Gokhale. Birth Cent.
532. **201.** 15 p. maroon & yellow 5 5

202. Acharya Dvivedi (writer).

1966. Dvivedi Commem.
533. **202.** 15 p. drab 5 5

203. Maharaja Ranjit Singh (warrior).

1966. Maharaja Ranjit Singh Commem.
534. **203.** 15 p. purple .. 5 8

204. Homi Bhabha (scientist) and Nuclear Reactor.

1966. Homi Bhabha Commem.
535. **204.** 15 p. purple 8 8

205. A. K. Azad (scholar).

1966. Abul Kalam Azad Commem.
536. **205.** 15 p. blue 5 5

206. S. R. Tirtha (social reformer).

1966. Swami Rama Tirtha. 60th Death Anniv.
537. **206.** 15 p. blue 5 8

207. Infant and Dove Emblem.

1966. Children's Day.
538. **207.** 15 p. purple .. 8 8

208. Allahabad High Court.

1966. Allahabad High Court. Cent.
539. **208.** 15 p. purple .. 8 8

209. Indian Family.

1966. Family Planning.
540. **209.** 15 p. brown 5 8

210. Hockey Game.

1966. India's Hockey Victory in 5th Asian Games.
541. **210.** 15 p. blue 8 8

211. "Jai Kisan".

1967. Shastri's 1st Death Anniv.
542. **211.** 15 p. green 5 5

212. Voter and Polling Booth. 213. Guru Dwara Shrine, Patna.

1967. Indian General Election.
543. **212.** 15 p. brown 5 5

1967. Guru Gobind Singh (National leader). 300th Birth Anniv. (in 1966).
544. **213.** 15 p. violet 5 5

214. Taj Mahal.

1967. Int. Tourist Year.
545. **214.** 15 p. brown and orange 5 8

215. Nandalal Bose and "Garuda".

1967. Nandalal Bose (painter). 1st Death Anniv.
546. **215.** 15 p. brown 5 5

216. Survey Emblem and Activities.

1967. Survey of India Bicent.
547. **216.** 15 p. lilac .. 5 8

217. Basaveswara (reformer and statesman).

1967. Basaveswara. 800th Anniv.
548. **217.** 15 p. red 5 5

218. Narsinha Mehta (poet). **219.** Maharana Pratap (warrior).

1967. Narsinha Mehta Commem.
549. **218.** 15 p. sepia 5 8

1967. Maharana Pratap Commem.
550. **219.** 15 p. brown 5 8

INDEX

Countries can be quickly located by referring to the index at the end of this volume.

220. Narayana Guru. **221.** Pres. Radhakrishnan.

1967. Narayana (reformer) Commem.
551. **220.** 15 p. brown 5 8

1967. Radhakrishnan Commem.
552. **221.** 15 p. claret 5 8

222. Martyrs' Memorial, Patna.

1967. "Quit India" Movement. 25th Anniv.
553. **222.** 15 p. lake 8 8

223. Route Map.

1967. Indo-European Telegraph Service. Cent.
554. **223.** 15 p. black and blue 5 8

224. Wrestling.

1967. World Wrestling Championships.
555. **224.** 15 p. purple & chestnut 5 8

225. Nehru leading Naga Tribesmen. **226.** Rashbehari Basu (nationalist).

1967. "Nehru and Nagaland".
556. **225.** 15 p. ultramarine .. 5 8

1967. Rashbehari Basu Commem.
557. **226.** 15 p. maroon 5 8

227. Bugle, Badge and Scout Salute.

1967. Scout Movement. Diamond Jubilee.
558. **227.** 15 p. chestnut .. 5 5

228. Men Embracing Universe.

1968. Human Rights Year.
559. **228.** 15 p. green 5 5

229. Globe and Book of Tamil.

1968. Int. Conf.—Seminar of Tamil Studies, Madras.
560. **229.** 15 p. lilac 5 5

230. U.N. Emblem and Transport.

1968. United Nations Conf. on Trade and Development.
561. **230.** 15 p. blue 5 5

231. Quill and Bow Symbol.

1968. Amrita Bazar Patrika (newspaper). Cent.
562. **231.** 15 p. sepia and yellow 5 8

232. Maxim Gorky. **233.** Emblem and Medal.

1968. Maxim Gorky. Birth Cent.
563. **232.** 15 p. plum 5 8

1968. First Triennale, New Delhi.
564. **233.** 15 p. orange, blue and light blue .. 5 5

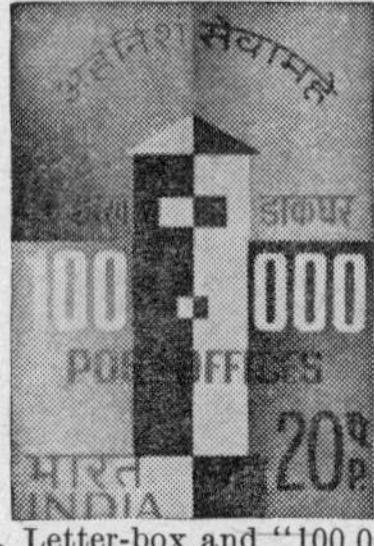

234. Letter-box and "100,000".

1968. Opening of 100,000th Indian Post Office.
565. **234.** 20 p. red, blue & black 5 8

235. Stalks of Wheat, Agricultural Institute and Production Graph.

1968. Wheat Revolution.
566. **235.** 20 p. green and brown 5 5

236. Gaganendranath Tagore.

1968. Gaganendranath Tagore. 30th Death Anniv.
567. **236.** 20 p. purple and ochre 5 8

237. Lakshminath Bezbaruah (writer).

1968. Lakshminath Bezbaruah. Birth Cent.
568. **237.** 20 p. brown 5 8

238. Athlete's Legs and Olympic Rings.

1968. Olympic Games, Mexico.
569. **238.** 20 p. brown and grey .. 8 5
570. 1 r. sepia and olive .. 25 20

239. Bhagat Singh and Followers.

1968. Bhagat Singh (revolutionary). 61st Birth Anniv.
571. **239.** 20 p. brown 5 8

240. Azad Hind Flag, Swords and Chandra Bose (founder). **241.** Sister Nivedita.

1968. Azad Hind Government. 25th Anniv.
572. **240.** 20 p. blue 5 8

1968. Sister Nivedita. Birth Cent.
573. **241.** 20 p. green 5 8

242. Marie Curie and Radium Treatment.

1968. Marie Curie. Birth Cent.
574. **242.** 20 p. lilac 5 8

243. Map of the World.

1968. 21st Int. Geographical Congress.
575. **243.** 20 p. blue 5 8

244. Cochin Synagogue.

1968. Cochin Synagogue. 400th Anniv.
576. **244.** 20 p. blue and red .. 5 8

245. I.N.S. "Nilgiri".

1968. Navy Day.
577. **245.** 20 p. grey-blue .. 5 8

246. Blue Magpie.

1968. Birds.
578. **246.** 20 p. multicoloured .. 8 8
579. – 50 p. red, black & green 10 10
580. – 1 r. blue and brown .. 20 15
581. – 2 r. multicoloured .. 40 40
DESIGNS—HORIZ. 50 p. Woodpecker. 2 r. Sunbird. VERT. 1 r. Babbler.

247. Bankim Chandra Chatterjee.
248. Dr. Bhagavan Das.

1969. Chatterjee (writer). 130th Birth Anniv.
582. **247.** 20 p. ultramarine .. 5 8

1969. Das (philosopher). Death Cent.
583. **248.** 20 p. chocolate .. 5 5

249. Dr. Martin Luther King.

1969. Martin Luther King Commem.
584. **249.** 20 p. brown 5 8

250. Mirza Ghalib (poet) and Letter Seal.

1969. Mirza Ghalib. Death Cent.
585. **250.** 20 p. sepia, red & flesh 5 5

251. Osmania University.

1969. Osmania University. 50th Anniv.
586. **251.** 20 p. green 5 8

252. Rafi Ahmed Kidwai.

1969. Rafi Ahmed Kidwai (Author of All-up Airmail Scheme).
587. **252.** 20 p. blue 5 8

253. ILO Badge and Emblem.

1969. Int. Labour Organisation. 50th Anniv.
588. **253.** 20 p. chestnut .. 5 8

254. Memorial and Hands dropping Flowers.

1969. Jallianwala Bagh Massacre. 50th Anniv.
589. **254.** 20 p. red 5 5

255. Shri Nageswara Rao (patriot).

1969. Kasinadhuni Nageswara Rao Pantulu Commem.
590. **255.** 20 p. brown 5 5

256. Ardaseer Cursetjee Wadia.

1969. Wadia (Ship-building Engineer).
591. **256.** 20 p. turquoise-green 5 5

257. Serampore College.

1969. Foundation of Serampore College. 150th Anniv.
592. **257.** 20 p. plum 5 8

258. Dr. Zakir Husain (patriot).

1969. Dr. Zakir Husain Commem.
593. **258.** 20 p. sepia 5 8

259. Laxmanrao Kirloskar.

1969. Laxmanrao Kirloskar (agriculturist.). Birth Cent.
594. **259.** 20 p. black .. 5 8

260. Gandhi and his wife.

1969. Mahatma Gandhi. Birth Cent.
595. **260.** 20 p. brown 8 8
596. – 75 p. flesh and drab .. 15 15
597. – 1 r. blue 25 25
598. – 5 r. brown and orange 1·00 85
DESIGNS AND SIZES—VERT. 75 p. Gandhi's head and shoulders (28 × 38 mm.). 1 r. Gandhi walking (woodcut) (20 × 38 mm.). HORIZ. 5 r. Gandhi with charkha (36 × 26 mm.).

261. Oil Tanker and I.M.C.O. Emblem.

1969. Inter-Governmental Maritime Consultative Organization. 10th Anniv.
599. **261.** 20 p. blue 5 8

262. Outline of Parliament Building and Globe.

1969. Inter-Parliamentary Conf., New Delhi.
600. **262.** 20 p. blue 5 8

263. Man walking beside Space Module on Moon.
264. "Shiri Nankana Sahib Gurudwara".

1969. 1st Man on the Moon.
601. **263.** 20 p. brown 5 8

1969. Guru Nanak. 500th Birth Anniv.
602. **264.** 20 p. violet 5 8

265. Tiger's Head and Hands holding Globe.

1969. Int. Union for the Conservation of Nature and Natural Resources Conf., New Delhi.
603. **265.** 20 p. brown and green 5 8

266. Sadhu Vaswani.
267. Thakkar Bapa.

1969. Sadhu Vaswani (educationist). 90th Birth Anniv.
604. **266.** 20 p. grey 5 5

1969. Thakkar Bapa (humanitarian). Birth Cent.
605. **267.** 20 p. chocolate .. 5 5

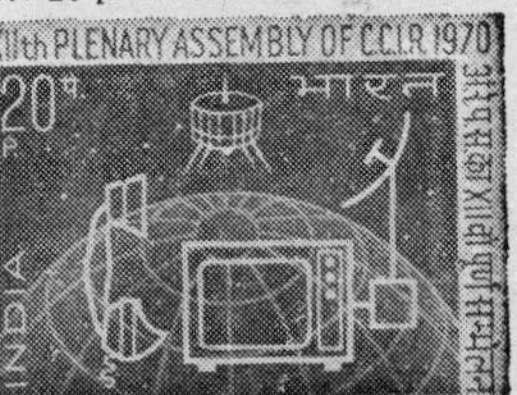

268. Satellite, Television, Telephone and Globe.

1970. 12th Plenary Assembly of Int. Radio Consultative Committee.
606. **268.** 20 p. blue 5 5

269. Thiru Annadurai (statesman).
270. M. N. Kishore (publisher), and Printing Press.

1970. Thiru Annadurai. 1st Death Anniv.
607. **269.** 20 p. purple and blue .. 5 8

1970. Kishore Commem.
608. **270.** 20 p. lake 5 8

271. Nalanda College.

1970. Nalanda College. Cent.
609. **271.** 20 p. brown 5 8

272. Swami Shraddhanand (social reformer).

1970. Swami Shraddhanand Commem.
610. **272.** 20 p. brown 5 5

273. Lenin.

1970. Lenin. Birth Cent.
611. **273.** 20 p. brown and sepia 5 5

274. New U.P.U. H.Q. Building.

1970. New U.P.U. Headquarters Building.
612. **274.** 20 p. emerald, grey & blk. 5 8

275. Sher Shah Suri (15th Century Ruler).

1970. Sher Shah Suri Commem.
613. **275.** 20 p. green 5 8

276. V. D. Savarkar (patriot) and Cellular Jail.

1970. V. D. Savarkar Commem.
614. **276.** 20 p. brown 5 8

277. "UN" and Globe.

1970. United Nations. 25th Anniv.
615. **277.** 20 p. blue 5 5

278. Factory and Agricultural Workers.

1970. Asian Productivity Year.
616. **278.** 20 p. violet 5 5

279. Dr. Montessori and I.E.Y. Emblem.

1970. Dr. Maria Montessori (educationist). Birth Cent.
617. **279.** 20 p. purple 5 5

280. J. N. Mukherjee (revolutionary) and Horse.

1970. Jatindra Nath Mukherjee Commem.
618. **280.** 20 p. brown 5 8

281. Srinivasa Sastri.

1970. Srinivasa Sastri (educationist).
619. **281.** 20 p. yellow and purple 5 5

282. I. C. Vidyasagar (educationist).

1970. I. C. Vidyasagar. 150th Birth Anniv.
620. **282.** 20 p. brown and purple 5 5

283. Maharishi Valmiki.

1970. Maharishi Valmiki (Holy poet).
621. **283.** 20 p. purple 5 8

284. Calcutta Port.

1970. Calcutta Port Trust Cent.
622. **284.** 20 p. blue 5 5

285. University Building.

1970. Jamia Millia Islamia University. 50th Anniv.
623. **285.** 20 p. green 5 5

286. Jamnalal Bajaj.

1970. Jamnalal Bajaj (patriot).
624. **286.** 20 p. grey 5 5

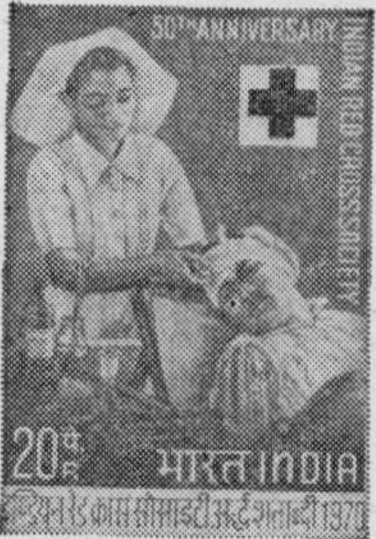

287. Nurse and Patient.

1970. Indian Red Cross. 50th Anniv.
625. **287.** 20 p. red and blue .. 5 5

288. Sant Namdeo.

1970. Sant (Saint) Namdeo. 700th Birth Anniv.
626. **288.** 20 p. orange 5 5

289. Beethoven.

1970. Beethoven. Birth Bicent.
627. **289.** 20 p. orange and black 5 5

290. Children examining Stamps.

1970. Indian National Philatelic Exhib.
628. **290.** 20 p. orange and green 5 5
629. – 1 r. brown and ochre .. 20 20
DESIGN: 1 r. Gandhi commemorative through magnifier.

291. Girl Guide.

1970. Girl Guide Movement. Diamond Jubilee.
630. **291.** 20 p. maroon .. 5 5

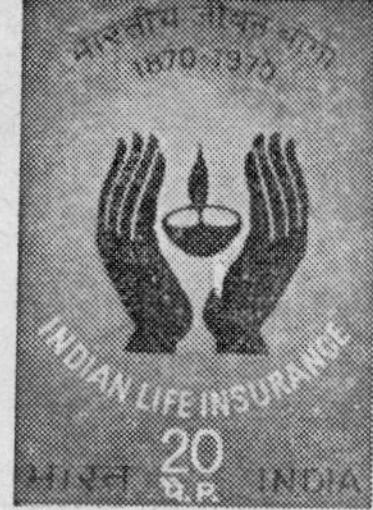

292. Hands and Lamp (emblem).

1971. Indian Life Insurance.
631. **292.** 20 p. brown and red .. 5 5

293. Vidyapith Building.

1971. Kashi Vidyapith. Golden Jubilee.
632. **293.** 20 p. brown 5 5

294. Saint Ravidas.

1971. Guru Ravidas (15th-cent. Saint).
633. **294.** 20 p. lake 5 5

295. C. F. Andrews.

1971. Deenabandhu C. F. Andrews (philosopher). Birth Cent.
634. **295.** 20 p. brown 5 5

296. Acharya Narendra Deo (reformer).

1971. Acharya Narendra Deo. 15th Death Anniv.
635. **296.** 20 p. green 5 5

297. Crowd and "100".

1971. Census Cent.
636. **297.** 20 p. brown and blue 5 5

298. Sri Ramana Maharshi (mystic).

1971. Ramana Maharshi. 21st Death Anniv.
637. **298.** 20 p. orange and brown 5 5

299. Raja Ravi Varma and "Damayanti and the Swan".

1971. Ravi Varma (artist). 65th Death Anniv.
638. **299.** 20 p. green 5 5

300. Dadasaheb Phalke and Camera (cinematographer).

1971. Dadasaheb Phalke. Birth Cent.
639. **300.** 20 p. maroon.. .. 5 5

301. "Abhisarika" (Abanindranath Tagore).
302. Swami Virjanand (Vedic scholar).

1971. Abanindranath Tagore Commemoration.
640. **301.** 20 p. grey, yellow & brn. 5 5

1971. Swami Virjanand Commemoration.
641. **302.** 20 p. brown 5 5

303. Cyrus the Great and Procession.

1971. Charter of Cyrus the Great. 2500th Anniv.
642. **303.** 20 p. brown 5 5

304. Globe and Money Box.

1971. World Thrift Day.
643. **304.** 20 p. grey 5 5

305. Ajanta Caves Painting.
306. Women at Work.

1971. UNESCO. 25th Anniv.
644. **305.** 20 p. brown 5 5

1971. Children's Day.
645. **306.** 20 p. red 5 5

307. Refugees.

1971. Obligatory Tax. Refugee Relief.

(a) Optd. **REFUGEE RELIEF** in English and Hindi.
646. – 5 p. red (No. 506) .. 5 5

(b) Optd. **Refugee Relief.**
647. – 5 p. red (No. 506) 15 15

(c) Optd. **REFUGEE RELIEF.**
649. – 5 p. red (No. 506) .. 50

(d) Type **307.**
651. **307.** 5 p. red 5 5

As from the 15th November 1971, the Indian Government levied a 5 p. surcharge on all mail, except postcards and newspapers, for the relief of refugees from the former East Pakistan.

No. 647 was issued in Maharashtra State and No. 649 in Rajastan.

308. C. V. Raman (scientist) and Jewel.

1971. Dr. C. V. Raman Commemoration.
652. **308.** 20 p. orange and brown 5 5

309. Visva Bharati Building and Rabindranath Tagore (pioneer).

1971. Visva Bharati. Golden Jubilee.
653. **309.** 20 p. sepia and brown 5 5

310. Cricketers.

1971. Indian Cricket Victories.
654. **310.** 20 p. green, myrtle & sage 5 5

311. Map and satellite.

1972. Arvi Satellite Earth Station.
655. **311.** 20 p. plum 5 5

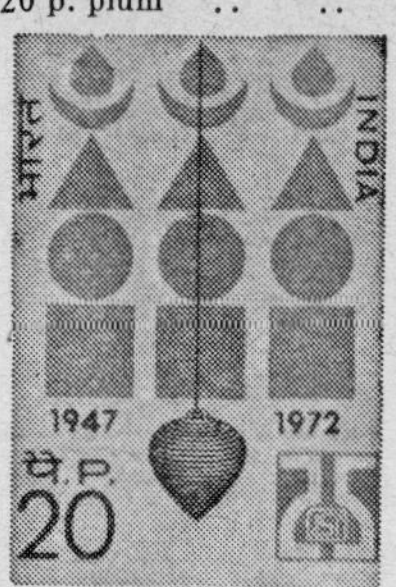

312. Elemental Symbols and plumbline.

1972. Indian Standards Institution. Silver Jubilee.
656. **312.** 20 p. grey and black.. 5 5

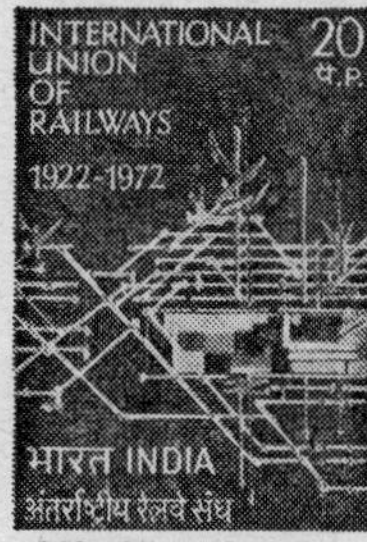

313. Signal-box Panel.

1972. Int. Railways Union. 50th Anniv.
657. **313.** 20 p. multicoloured .. 5 5

314. Hockey-player.

1972. Olympic Games, Munich.
658. **314.** 20 p. violet 5 5
659. – 1 r. 45 green and lake 20 20
DESIGN: 1 r. 45 Various sports.

315. Symbol of Sri Aurobindo.

1972. Sri Aurobindo. Birth Cent.
660. **315.** 20 p. yellow and blue 5 5

316. Celebrating Independence Day in front of Parliament.

1972. Independence. 25th Anniv. (1st issue).
661. **316.** 20 p. multicoloured .. 5 5
See also Nos. 673/4.

317. Inter-Services Crest.

1972. Defence Services Commem.
662. **317.** 20 p. multicoloured .. 5 5

318. V. O. Chidambaram Pillai (lawyer and politician) and Ship.

1972. V. O. Chidambaram Pillai. Birth Cent.
663. **318.** 20 p. blue and brown.. 5 5

319. Bhai Vir Singh.

1972. Bhai Vir Singh (poet and saint). Birth Cent.
664. **319.** 20 p. purple 5 5

320. T. Prakasam.

1972. T. Prakasam (lawyer). Birth Cent.
665. **320.** 20 p. brown 5 5

321. Vemana.

1972. Vemana (poet). 300th Birth Anniv.
666. **321.** 20 p. black 5 5

322. Bertrand Russell.

1972. Bertrand Russell (philosopher). Birth Cent.

667. **322.** 1 r. 45 black 20 20

323. Symbol of "Asia '72".

1972. "Asia '72" (Third Asian Int., Trade Fair).

668. **323.** 20 p. black & orange.. 5 5
669. – 1 r. 45 orange and blk. 20 20
DESIGN: 1 r. 45 Hand of Buddha.

324. V. A. Sarabhai and Rocket.

1972. Dr. Vikram A. Sarabhai (scientist). 1st Death Anniv.

670. **324.** 20 p. brown and green 5 5

325. Flag of U.S.S.R. and Kremlin Tower.

1972. U.S.S.R. 50th Anniv.

671. **325.** 20 p. red and yellow.. 5 5

326. Exhibition Symbol.

1973. "Interpex '73" Stamp Exhibition (1st issue).

672. **326.** 1 r. 45 mve., gold & blk. 25 25

327. "Democracy".

1973. Independence. 25th Anniv. (2nd issue). Multicoloured.

673. 20 p. Type **327** 5 5
674. 1 r. 45 "Gnat" fighters over India Gate.. .. 15 15
SIZE-HORIZ. 1 r. 45 38×20 mm.

328. Sri Ramakrishna Paramahamsa (religious leader).

1973. Sri Ramakrishna Paramahamsa Commemoration.

675. **328.** 20 p. brown 5 5

329. Postal Corps Emblem.

1973. Army Postal Corps. 1st Anniv.

676. **329.** 20 p. blue and red .. 5 5

330. Flag and Map of Bangladesh.

1973. "Jai Bangla" (1st Bangladesh Parliament. Inaug.).

677. **330.** 20 p. multicoloured .. 5 5

331. Kumaran Asan.

1973. Kumaran Asan (writer and poet). Birth Cent.

678. **331.** 20 p. brown 5 5

332. Flag and Flames.

1973. Homage to Martyrs for Independence.

679. **332.** 20 p. multicoloured .. 5 5

333. Dr. B. R. Ambedkar (social thinker and agitator).

1973. Ambedkar Commemoration.

680. **333.** 20 p. green and purple 5 5

334. "Radha-Kishangarh" (Nihal Chand).

1973. Indian Miniature Paintings. Mult.

681. 20 p. Type **334** 8 8
682. 50 p. "Dance Duet" (Aurangzeb's period) .. 10 10
683. 1 r. "Lovers on a Camel" (Nasir-ud-din) 20 20
684. 2 r. "Chained Elephant" (Zain-al-Abidin) .. 35 35

335. The Himalayas.

1973. Indian Mountaineering Foundation. 15th Anniv.

685. **335.** 20 p. blue 5 5

336. Tail-end of Boeing "747".

1973. Air-India's International Services. 25th Anniv.

686. **336.** 1 r. 45 blue and red .. 20 25

337. Cross, Church of St. Thomas' Mount, Madras.

1973. St. Thomas. 19th Death Cent.

687. **337.** 20 p. grey and brown.. 5 5

338. Michael Madhusudan Dutt (poet-Death Cent.).

1973. Centenaries.

688. **338.** 20 p. green and brown 5 5
689. – 30 p. brown 5 5
690. – 50 p. brown 5 8
691. – 1 r. violet and red .. 12 15
DESIGNS-HORIZ. 30 p. V. D. Paluskar (musician-birth cent.). 50 p. Dr. Hansen (Discovery of leprosy bacillus. Cent.). 1 r. Nicholas Copernicus (astronomer-5th birth cent.).

339. A. O. Hume.

1973. A. O. Hume Commemoration.

692. **339.** 20 p. grey 5 5

340. Gandhi and Nehru.

1973. Gandhi and Nehru Commemoration.

693. **340.** 20 p. multicoloured .. 5 5

341. R. C. Dutt.

1973. R. C. Dutt Commemoration.

694. **341.** 20 p. brown 5 5

342. K. S. Ranjitsinhji.

1973. K. S. Ranjitsinhji Commemoration.

695. **342.** 30 p. green 5 5

343. Vithalbhai Patel (nationalist).

1973. Vithalbhai Patel Commemoration.
696. **343.** 50 p. brown 5 8

344. President's Bodyguard.

1973. President's Bodyguard. 200th Anniv.
697. **344.** 20 p. multicoloured .. 5 5

345. Interpol Emblem.

1973. Interpol. 50th Anniv.
698. **345.** 20 p. brown 5 5

346. Syed Ahmad Khan (social reformer).

1973. Syed Ahmed Khan Commemoration.
699. **346.** 20 p. brown 5 5

347. " Children at Play " (detail, Bela Raval).

1973. Children's Day.
700. **347.** 20 p. multicoloured .. 5 5

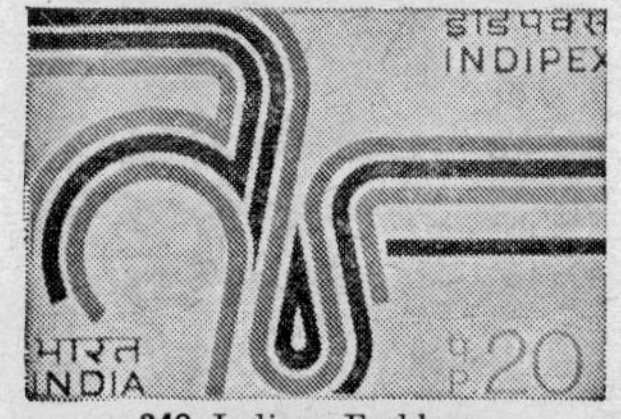

348. Indipex Emblem.
(Illustration reduced. Actual size 54 × 36 mm.)

1973. "Indipex '73" Philatelic Exhibition New Delhi. (2nd issue). Multicoloured.
701. 20 p. Type **348** 5 5
702. 1 r. Ceremonial elephant and 1½ a. stamp of 1947 (vert.) 12 15
703. 2 r. Peacock (vert.) .. 25 30

349. Emblem of National Cadet Corps.

1973. N.C.C. Silver Jubilee.
705. **349.** 20 p. multicoloured .. 5 5

350. Chakravarti Rajagopalachari (statesman).

1973. C. Rajagopalachari (statesman). Commemoration.
706. **350.** 20 p. brown 5 5

351. " Sun Mask".

1974. Indian Masks. Multicoloured.
707. 20 p. Type **351** 5 5
708. 50 p. " Moon " mask .. 5 8
709. 1 r. " Narasimha " .. 12 15
710. 2 r. " Ravana " (horiz.) .. 25 30

352. Chhatrapati.

1974. Coronation of Chhatrapati Shri Shivaji Maharaj (patriot and ruler). 300th Anniv.
712. **352.** 25 p. multicoloured .. 5 5

353. Maithili Sharan Gupta (poet).

1974. Indian Personalities (1st series).
713. **353.** 25 p. brown 5 5
714. – 25 p. deep brown .. 5 5
715. – 25 p. brown 5 5
PORTRAITS: No. 714, Jainarain Vyas (politician and journalist). No. 715, Utkal Gourab Madhusudan Das (social reformer).

354. Kandukuri Veeresalingam (reformer).

1974. Indian Personalities (2nd series).
716. **354.** 25 p. brown 5 5
717. – 50 p. purple 5 8
718. – 1 r. brown 12 15
PORTRAITS: 50 p. Tipu Sultan (portrait). 1 r. Max Mueller (Sanskrit scholar).

355. Kamala Nehru.

1974. Kamala Nehru Commemoration.
719. **355.** 25 p. multicoloured .. 5 5

356. W.P.Y. Emblem.

1974. World Population Year.
720. **356.** 25 p. maroon & brown 5 5

357. Chital.

358. Sitar.

1975.
(a) Values expressed with " p " or " Re ".
721. – 15 p. brown 5 5
722. **357.** 25 p. brown 5 5
723. **358.** 1 r. brown and black 12 15

(b) Values expressed as numerals only.
728. – 15 p. brown 5 5
729. – 20 p. green 5 5
730. – 50 p. violet 5 5
731. **358.** 1 r. brown and grey .. 10 12
732. – 2 r. violet and grey .. 20 25
DESIGNS:—As T **357.** VERT. 15 p. Tiger. HORIZ. 20 p. Handicrafts toy. 50 p. Crane in flight. As T **358.** 2 r. Himalayas.

359. President Giri.

1974. Giri Commemoration.
739. **359.** 25 p. multicoloured .. 5 5

360. U.P.U. Emblem.

1974. U.P.U. Centenary.
740. **360.** 25 p. vio., bl. & blk... 5 5
741. – 1 r. multicoloured .. 12 12
742. – 2 r. multicoloured .. 25 15
DESIGNS:—1 r. Birds and nest, "Madhubani" style. VERT. 2 r. Arrows around globe.

361. Lady Flute-player (sculpture).

1974. Mathura Museum.
744. **361.** 25 p. brown & black.. 5 5
745. – 25 p. brown & black.. 5 5
DESIGN: No. 745 Vidyadhara with garland.

362. Nicholas Roerich (medallion by H. Dropsy).

1974. Professor Roerich. Birth Centenary.
746. **362.** 1 r. green & yellow .. 12 15

363. Pavapuri Temple.

1974. Bhagwan Mahavira's 2,500th Nirvana Anniversary.
747. **363.** 25 p. black 5 5

364. " Cat " (Rajesh Bhatia).

1974. Children's Day.
748. **364.** 25 p. multicoloured . . 5 5

365. Indian Dancers.

1974. U.N.I.C.E.F. in India.
749. **365.** 25 p. multicoloured . . 5 5

366. Territorial Army Badge.

1974. Indian Territorial Army. 25th Anniv.
750. **366.** 25 p. blk., yell. & green 5 5

367. Krishna (as Gopal Bal) with Cows (Rajasthan painting on cloth).

1974. 19th International Dairy Congress, New Delhi.
751. **367.** 25 p. purple & brown 5 5

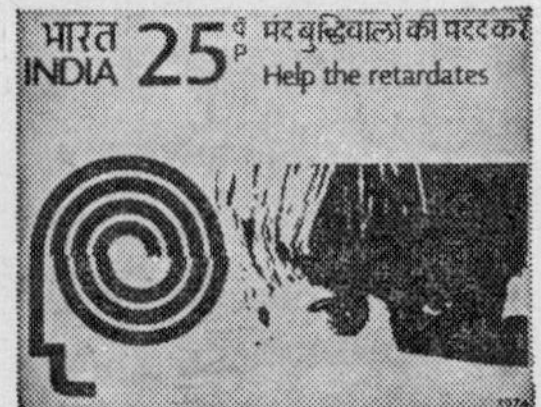

368. Symbol and Child's Face.

1974. Help for Retarded Children.
752. **368.** 25 p. red and black . . 5 5

HAVE YOU READ THE NOTES AT THE BEGINNING OF THIS CATALOGUE?

These often provide answers to the enquiries we receive.

369. Marconi.

1974. Guglielmo Marconi (radio pioneer). Birth Centenary.
753. **369.** 2 r. blue 5 5

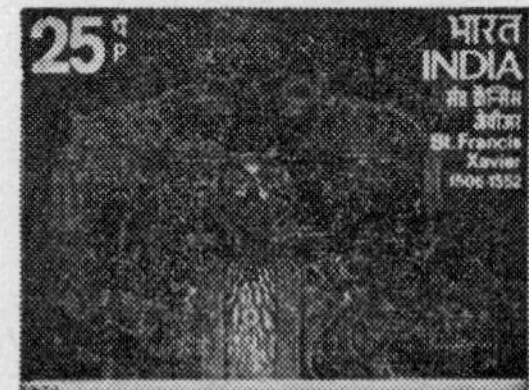

370. St. Francis Xavier's Shrine.

1974. St. Francis Xavier Celebrations.
754. **370.** 25 p. multicoloured . . 5 5

371. Saraswati (Deity of Language and Learning).

1975. World Hindi Convention, Nagpur.
755. **371.** 25 p. grey and red . . 5 5

372. Parliament House, New Delhi.

1975. Republic. 25th Anniv.
756. **372.** 25 p. blk., silver & blue 5 5

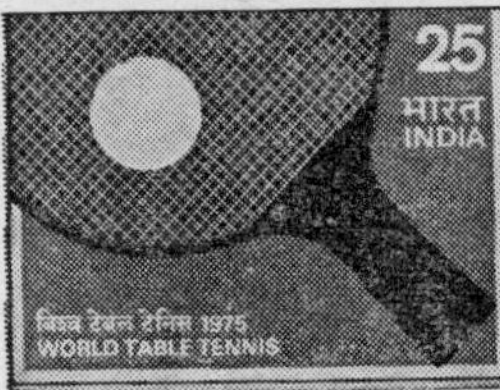

373. Table-tennis Bat.

1975. World Table-tennis Championships, Calcutta.
757. **373.** 25 p. blk., red & green 5 5

374. " Equality, Development and Peace ".

1975. International Women's Year.
758. **374.** 25 p. multicoloured . . 5 5

375. Stylised Cannon.

1975. Indian Army Ordnance Corps. Bicent.
759 **375.** 25 p. multicoloured . . 5 5

376. Arya Samaj Emblem.

1975. Arya Samaj Movement. Cent.
760. **376.** 25 p. red and brown . . 5 5

377. Saraswati (Chauhan sculpture).

1975. World Telugu Language Conf., Hyderabad.
761. **377.** 25 p. black & green . . 5 5

378. Satellite " Aryabhata ".

1975. First Indian Satellite Launch.
762. **378.** 25 p. light bl., bl. & pur. 5 5

379. Indian Pitta.

1975. Indian Birds. Multicoloured.
763. 25 p. Type **379** 5 5
764. 50 p. Black-headed Oriole 5 5
765. 1 r. Western Tragopan (vert.) 10 12
766. 2 r. Monal Pheasant (vert.) 20 25

380. " Ramcharitmanas " (poem by Goswami Tulsidas).

1975. Ramcharitmanas Commem.
767. **380.** 25 p. blk., yell. and red 5 5

381. Young Women within Y.W.C.A. Badge.

382. " The Creation " (Michelangelo).

1975. Indian Y.W.C.A. Centenary.
768. **381.** 25 p. multicoloured . . 5 5

1975. Michelangelo. 500th Birth Anniversary. Multicoloured.
769. **382.** 50 p. " Creation of the Sun, Moon and Planets " 5 5
770. – 50 p. " Creation of the Sun, Moon and Planets " 5 5
771. – 50 p. " Creation of Man " 5 5
772. – 50 p. " Creation of Man " 5 5

Nos. 770 and 772 are size 49 × 34 mm.
Nos. 769/70 and 771/2 form composite designs.

383. Commission Emblem.

1975. Int. Commission on Irrigation and Drainage. 25th Anniv.
773. **383.** 25 p. multicoloured . . 5 5

384. Stylised Ground Antenna.

1975. Satellite Instructional Television Experiment.
774. **384.** 25 p. multicoloured . . 5 5

385. St. Arunagirinathar.

1975. St. Arunagirinathar. 600th Birth Anniv.
775. **385.** 50 p. purple & black . . 5 5

386. Commemorative Text.

1975. Namibia Day.
776. **386.** 25 p. black and red . . 5 5

387. Mir Anees (poet). **388.** Memorial Temple to Ahilyabai Holkar (ruler).

1975. Indian Celebrities.

777. **387.** 25 p. green 5 5
778. **388.** 25 p. brown 5 5

389. Bharata Natyam Dance.

1975. Indian Dances. Multicoloured.

779. 25 p. Type **389** 5 5
780. 50 p. Orissi 5 5
781. 75 p. Kathak 8 10
782. 1 r. Kathakali 10 12
783. 1 r. 50 Kuchipudi .. 15 20
784. 2 r. Manipuri 20 25

390. Ameer Khusrau.

1975. Ameer Khusrau (poet). 650th Death Anniv.

785. **390.** 50 p. brown and bistre 5 5

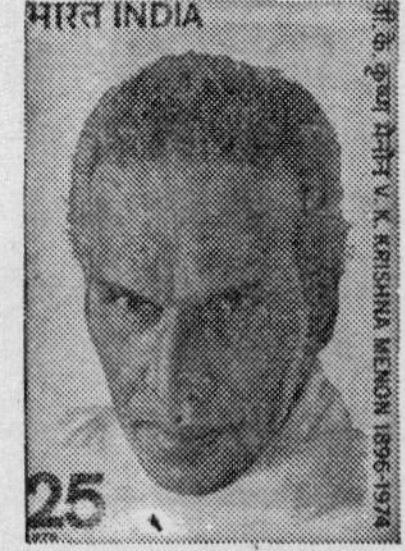

391. V. K. Krishna Menon.

1975. V. K. Krishna Menon (statesman). 1st Death Anniv.

786. **391.** 25 p. green 5 5

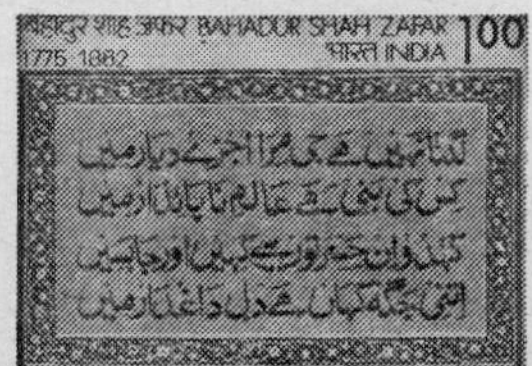

392. Text of Poem.

1975. Bahadur Shah Zafar. Birth Bicent.

787. **392.** 1 r. black, buff & brn. 10 12

393. Sansadiya Soudha, New Delhi.

1975. 21st Commonwealth Parliamentary Conference, New Delhi.

788. **393.** 2 r. green 20 25

394. V. Patel.

1975. Vallabhbhai Patel (statesman). Birth Centenary.

789. **394.** 25 p. green 5 5

395. N. C. Bardoloi.

1975. Nabin Chandra Bardoloi (politician). Birth Cent.

790. **395.** 25 p. brown 5 5

396. " Cow " (child's drawing).

1975. Children's Day.

791. **396.** 25 p. multicoloured .. 5 5

397. India Security Press Building.

1975. India Security Press. 50th Anniv.

792. **397.** 25 p. multicoloured .. 5 5

398. Gurdwara Sisganj (site of martyrdom).

1975. Martyrdom of Guru Tegh Bahadur. Tercentenary.

793. **398.** 25 p. multicoloured .. 5 5

399. Theosophical Society Emblem.

1975. Theosophical Society. Centenary.

794. **399.** 25 p. multicoloured .. 5 5

400. Weather Cock.

1975. Indian Meteorological Department. Centenary.

795. **400.** 25 p. multicoloured .. 5 5

401. Early Mail Cart.

1975. "Inpex 75" Nat. Philatelic Exn., Calcutta.

796. **401.** 25 p. black and brown 5 5
797. – 2 r. brn., pur. and blk. 20 20

DESIGN: 2 r. Indian Bishop Mark, 1775.

402. L. N. Mishra.

1976. L. N. Mishra (politician). 1st Death Anniversary.

798. **402.** 25 p. green 5 5

403. Tiger.

1976. Jim Corbett (naturalist). Birth Cent.

799. **403.** 25 p. multicoloured .. 5 5

404. Painted Storks.

1976. Keoladeo Ghana Bird Sanctuary, Bharatpur.

800. **404.** 25 p. multicoloured .. 5 5

405. Vijayanta Tank.

1976. 16th Light Cavalry Regiment. 200th Anniversary.

801. **405.** 25 p. green and brown 5 5

406. Alexander Graham Bell.

1976. Alexander Graham Bell. Commem.

802. **406.** 25 p. brown and black 5 5

407. Muthuswami Dikshitar.

1976. Muthuswami Dikshitar (composer). 200th Birth Anniv.

803. **407.** 25 p violet 5 5

408. Eye and Red Cross.

1976. World Health Day. Prevention of Blindness.

804. **408.** 25 p. brown and red .. 5 5

409. " Industries ".

1976. Industrial Development.

805. **409.** 25 p. multicoloured .. 5 5

410. Diesel Locomotive, 1963.

1976. Locomotives. Multicoloured.

806.	25 p. Type **410**	5	5
807.	50 p. Steam loco., 1895 ..	5	5
808.	1 r. Steam loco., 1963 ..	10	12
809.	2 r. Steam loco., 1853 ..	20	25

411. Nehru.

1976.

810.	**411.**	25 p. violet	5	5
811.	–	25 p. brown	5	5

DESIGN: No. 811, Gandhi.

412. " Spirit of 1776 " (Willard).

1976. American Revolution. Bicent.

812.	**412.**	2 r. 80 multicoloured ..	30	35

413. K. Kamaraj (politician).

1976. Kamaraj Commemoration.

813.	**413.**	25 p. brown	5	5

414. " Shooting ".

1976. Olympic Games, Montreal.

814.	**414.**	25 p. violet and red ..	5	5
815.	–	1 r. multicoloured ..	10	12
816.	–	1 r. 50 mauve & black	15	20
817.	–	2 r. 80 multicoloured ..	30	35

DESIGNS: 1 r. Shot-put. 1 r. 50 Hockey. 2 r. 80 Sprinting.

415. Subhadra Kumari Chauhan (poetess).

1976. S. K. Chauhan Commemoration.

818.	**415.**	25 p. blue	5	5

416. Param Vir Chakra Medal.

1976. Param Vir Chakra Commemoration.

819.	**416.**	25 p. multicoloured ..	5	5

417. University Building, Bombay.

1976. Shreemati Nathibai Damodar Thackersey Women's University. 50th Anniv.

820.	**417.**	25 p. violet	5	5

418. Bharatendu Harishchandra (poet).

1976. Harishchandra Commemoration.

821.	**418.**	25 p. brown	5	5

419. S. C. Chatterji (writer).

420. Planned Family.

1976. S. C. Chatterji. Birth Cent.

822.	**419.**	25 p. black	5	5

1976. Family Planning.

823.	**420.**	25 p. multicoloured ..	5	5

421. Maharaja Agrasen and Coins.

1976. Maharaja Agrasen.

824.	**421.**	25 p. brown	5	5

422. Swamp Deer.

1976. Indian Wildlife. Multicoloured.

825.	25 p. Type **422**	5	5
826.	50 p. Lion..	5	5
827.	1 r. Leopard	10	12
828.	2 r. Caracal	20	25

423. Hands holdin, Hearts.

1976. Voluntary Blood Donation.

829.	**423.**	25 p. yell., red & blk.	5	5

424. Suryakant Tripathi.

1976. Suryakant Tripathi " Nirala " (poet).

830.	**424.**	25 p. violet	5	5

OFFICIAL STAMPS

1866. Optd. **Service.**

O 21.	**5.**	$\frac{1}{2}$ a. blue	85	10
O 14.	**6.**	8 p. mauve	2·50	4·00
O 24.	**5.**	1 a. brown	1·10	8
O 27.		2 a. orange	40	8
O 12.		4 a. green	7·50	6·50
O 29.	–	4 a. green (No. 69) ..	15	8
O 30.	**5.**	8 a. red	25	8

1866. Fiscal stamp with head of Queen Victoria, surch. **SERVICE TWO ANNAS.**

O 15.		2 a. purple	£130	48·00

1866. Fiscal stamps optd. **SERVICE POSTAGE.**

O 19.		$\frac{1}{2}$ a. mauve on lilac ..	60·00	15·00
O 16.		2 a. purple	£130	50·00
O 17.		4 a. purple	£350	£225
O 18.		8 a. purple	£1100	£600

1874. Optd. **On H.M.S.** (Queen Victoria).

O 31.	**5.**	$\frac{1}{2}$ a. blue	35	8
O 32.		1 a. brown	35	8
O 33a.		2 a. orange	2·00	1·00
O 34.	–	4 a. green (No. 69) ..	70	20
O 35.	**5.**	8 a. red	75	75

1883. Queen Victoria stamps of 1882 and 1892 optd. **On H.M.S.**

O 37a.	**25.**	3 p. red	5	5
O 39.	**14.**	$\frac{1}{2}$ a. blue-green ..	5	5
O 49.		$\frac{1}{2}$ a. yellow-green ..	12	5
O 41.	–	1 a. purple	5	5
O 50.	–	1 a. red	5	5
O 43.	–	2 a. blue	5	5
O 51.	–	2 a. lilac	50	5
O 44.	–	4 a. green	12	5
O 46.	–	8 a. mauve	30	5
O 48.	**26.**	1 r. green and red ..	65	25

1902. King Edward VII stamps optd. **On H.M.S.**

O 55.	**28.**	3 p. grey	5	5
O 56.	–	$\frac{1}{2}$ a. green (No. 122) ..	20	5
O 66.	–	$\frac{1}{2}$ a. green (No. 149) ..	5	5
O 57.	–	1 a. red (No. 123) ..	5	5
O 67.	–	1 a. red (No. 150) ..	5	5
O 59.	–	2 a. lilac	5	5
O 61.	–	4 a. olive	15	5
O 62.	–	6 a. yellow-brown ..	15	5
O 63.	–	8 a. mauve	30	5
O 65.	–	1 r. green and red ..	30	5
O 68a.	**39.**	2 r. red and orange ..	70	20
O 69.		5 r. blue and violet ..	2·00	60
O 70.		10 r. green and red ..	3·00	1·10
O 71.		15 r. blue and olive ..	5·00	5·50
O 72.		25 r. orange and blue ..	8·00	9·00

1912. King George V stamps optd. **SERVICE.**

O 75.	**40.**	3 p. grey	5	5
O 76.	**41.**	$\frac{1}{2}$ a. green	5	5
O 80.	**42.**	1 a. red	5	5
O 98.		1 a. chocolate	5	5
O 83.	**44.**	2 a. lilac	5	5
O 112.	**45.**	2 a. lilac	5	5
O 129.		2 a. orange-red ..	30	5
O 86.	**49.**	4 a. olive	12	5
O 113.	**50.**	4 a. green	5	5
O 87.	**51.**	6 a. yellow-brown ..	45	20
O 115.	**52.**	8 a. mauve	20	5
O 116.	**53.**	12 a. claret	15	5
O 91.	**54.**	1 r. brown and green ..	40	5
O 92.		2 r. red and orange ..	70	35
O 93.		5 r. blue and violet ..	2·00	85
O 94.		10 r. green and red ..	5·00	3·50
O 95.		15 r. blue and olive ..	7·00	7·00
O 96.		25 r. orange and blue ..	11·00	12·00

1921. No. O 80 surch. in words.

O 97.	**42.**	9 p. on 1 a. red ..	5	5

1925. Nos. O 70/2 surch. in words.

O 99.	**33.**	1 r. on 15 r. blue & olive	70	40
O 100.		1 r. on 25 r. orge. & bl.	4·00	4·00
O 101.		2 r. on 10 r. grn. & red	80	70

1925. Nos. O 95/6 surch. in words.

O 102.	**54.**	1 r. on 15 r. blue & olive	3·00	3·00
O 103.		1 r. on 25 r. orge.& blue	95	50

1926. No. O 62 surch. in words.

O 105.		1 a. on 6 a. yell.-brown	12	12

1922. Surch. **SERVICE ONE ANNA** and two bars.

O 106.	**43.**	1 a. on $1\frac{1}{2}$ a. brown (A)	5	5
O 107.		1 a. on $1\frac{1}{2}$ a. brown (B)	12	5
O 108.	**47.**	1 a. on $2\frac{1}{2}$ a. blue ..	20	25

1932. Optd. **SERVICE.**

O 126.	**62.**	$\frac{1}{2}$ a. green	5	5
O 127.	**63.**	9 p. green	5	5
O 127a.	**64.**	1 a. brown	5	5
O 128.	**65.**	$1\frac{1}{4}$ a. mauve	5	5
O 130a.	**44.**	2 a. orange-red ..	12	5
O 131.	**47.**	$2\frac{1}{2}$ a. orange	5	5

1937. King George VI stamps optd. **SERVICE.**

O 135.	**74.**	$\frac{1}{2}$ a. brown	5	5
O 136.		9 p. green	35	5
O 137.		1 a. red	5	5
O 138.	**77.**	1 r. slate and brown ..	25	5
O 139.		2 r. purple and brown	60	25
O 140.		5 r. green and blue ..	1·25	60
O 141.		10 r. purple and red ..	2·00	1·10

1939. King George V stamp surch. **SERVICE 1A.**

O 142.	**65.**	1 a. on $1\frac{1}{4}$ a. mauve ..	5	5

O 1. King George VI.

O 2. Asokan Capital.

1939.

O 143. O 1. 3 p. slate 5 5
O 144. ½ a. brown 5 5
O 144a. ½ a purple 5 5
O 145. 9 p. green 5 5
O 146. 1 a. red 5 5
O 146a. 1 a. 3 bistre 5 5
O 146b. 1½ a. violet 5 5
O 147. 2 a. orange 5 5
O 148. 2½ a. violet 5 5
O 149. 4 a. brown 5 5
O 150. 8 a. violet 5 5

1948. Indian Independence. 1st Anniv. Optd. **SERVICE.**

O 150a. 83. 1½ a. brown 10·00 10·00
O 150b. 3½ a. violet 95·00 £100
O 150c. 12 a. green £225
O 150d. – 10 r. brown and red (No. 308) £750

1950.

O 151. O 2. 3 p. violet 5 5
O 152. 6 p. brown 5 5
O 153. 9 p. green 5 5
O 154. 1 a. blue 5 5
O 155. 2 a. red 5 5
O 156. 3 a. red 15 5
O 157. 4 a. purple 25 5
O 158. 4 a. blue 20 5
O 159. 6 a. violet 25 5
O 160. 8 a. brown 20 5
O 186. – 1 r. violet 10 5
O 187a. – 2 r. red 15 8
O 188a. – 5 r. green 50 20
O 189a. – 10 r. brown 85 40

The rupee values are larger and with a different frame.

1957. Value in naye paise.

O 175. O 2. 1 n.p. slate 5 5
O 176. 2 n.p. violet 5 5
O 177. 3 n.p. chocolate 5 5
O 178. 5 n.p. green 5 5
O 179. 6 n.p. turquoise 5 5
O 180a. 10 n.p. grey-green 8 5
O 181. 13 n.p. red 8 5
O 182a. 15 n.p. violet 8 5
O 183. 20 n.p. red 8 5
O 184. 25 n.p. blue 8 5
O 185a. 50 n.p. brown 8 5

O 3. O 4.

1976.

O 190. O 3. 1 r. purple 10 5

1968.

O 191. O 3. 2 p. violet 5 5
O 192. 3 p. chocolate 5 5
O 193. 5 p. green 5 5
O 194. 6 p. blue 5 5
O 195. 10 p. green 5 5
O 196. 15 p. plum 5 5
O 197. 20 p. red 5 5
O 198. 25 p. red 5 5
O 199. 30 p. ultramarine 5 5
O 200. 50 p. chestnut 5 8

1971. Obligatory Tax. Refugee Relief. Nos. O 201/2 are optd. **REFUGEE RELIEF** in English and Hindi (No. O 201 or in English only (No. O 202).

O 201. O 3. 5 p. green 5 5
O 202. 5 p. green 15 15
O 203. O 4. 5 p. green 5 5

See note below Nos. 646/8. No. O 202 was issued in Maharashtra State.

INDIAN CUSTODIAN FORCES IN KOREA BC

Stamps used by the Indian Forces on custodian duties in Korea in 1953.

भारतीय
संरक्षा कटक
कोरिया
(1.)

1953. Stamps of India (archaeological series), optd. with T **1**.

K 1. 84. 3 p. violet 5 5
K 2. 85. 6 p. brown 5 5
K 3. – 9 p. green 8 8
K 4. – 1 a. blue (B) 10 12
K 5. – 2 a. red 15 20
K 6. – 2½ a. lake 20 20
K 7. – 3 a. salmon 25 25
K 8. 86. 4 a. blue 25 50
K 9. 87. 6 a. violet 50 80
K 10. – 8 a. green 1·00 1·25
K 11. – 12 a. blue 1·00 1·75
K 12. – 1 r. violet and green 2·00 3·50

INDIAN EXPEDITIONARY FORCES BC

Stamps used by Indian Forces during, and after, the War of 1914-18.

1914. Stamps of India (King George V) optd. **I.E.F.**

E 1. 40. 3 p. grey 5 5
E 2. 41. ½ a. green 5 5
E 3. 42. 1 a. red 5 5
E 5. 44. 2 a. lilac 5 5
E 6. 47. 2½ a. blue 10 20
E 7. 48. 3 a. orange 10 12
E 8. 49. 4 a. olive 12 20
E 9. 52. 8 a. mauve 20 20
E 12. 53. 12 a. claret 75 2·50
E 13. 54. 1 r. brown and green 1·25 2·50

INDIAN FORCES IN INDO-CHINA BC

Stamps used by Indian Forces engaged in the International Commission in Indo-China.

अन्तर्राष्ट्रीय आयोग कम्बोज (1.) अन्तर्राष्ट्रीय आयोग लाओस (2.) अन्तर्राष्ट्रीय आयोग वियत नाम (3.)

1954. Stamps of India (archaeological series) overprinted.

(a) Optd. with T 1, for use in Cambodia.

N 1. 84. 3 p. violet 5 5
N 2. – 1 a. blue (B) 5 8
N 3. – 2 a. red 12 25
N 4. – 8 a. green 50 1·00
N 5. – 12 a. blue 75 1·50

(b) Optd. with T 2. for use in Laos.

N 6. 84. 3 p. violet 5 5
N 7. – 1 a. blue (B) 5 8
N 8. – 2 a. red 12 25
N 9. – 8 a. green 50 1·00
N 10. – 12 a. blue 75 1·50

(c) Optd. with T 3 for use in Viet-Nam.

N 11. 84. 3 p. violet 5 5
N 12. – 1 a. blue (B) 5 8
N 13. – 2 a. red 12 25
N 14. – 8 a. green 50 1·00
N 15. – 12 a. blue 75 1·50

1957. Map type of India overprinted.

(a) Optd. with T 1 for use in Cambodia.

N 16. 106. 2 n.p. cinnamon 5 5
N 17. 6 n.p. grey 5 10
N 18. 13 n.p. red 5 20
N 19. 50 n.p. orange 15 75
N 20. 75 n.p. maroon 25 1·25

(b) Optd. with T 2 for use in Laos.

N 21. 106. 2 n.p. cinnamon 5 5
N 39. 3 n.p. brown 15 30
N 40. 5 n.p. emerald 10 20
N 22. 6 n.p. grey 5 10
N 23. 13 n.p. red 5 20
N 24. 50 n.p. orange 15 75
N 25. 75 n.p. maroon 25 1·25

(c) Optd. with T 3 for use in Vietnam.

N 43. 106. 1 n.p. blue-green 20 40
N 26. 2 n.p. cinnamon 5 5
N 45. 3 n.p. brown 15 30
N 46. 5 n.p. emerald 10 20
N 27. 6 n.p. grey 5 10
N 28. 13 n.p. red 5 20
N 29. 50 n.p. orange 15 75
N 30. 75 n.p. maroon 25 1·25

1965. Children's Day stamp of India optd. **ICC** for use in Laos and Vietnam.

N 49. 177. 15 p. slate 20 35

1968. Nos. 504, etc., of India optd. **ICC** in English and Indian, for use in Laos and Vietnam.

N 50. – 2 p. brown 10 15
N 51. – 3 p. olive 10 15
N 52. – 5 p. cerise 10 15
N 53. – 10 p. blue 10 15
N 54. 189. 15 p. green 10 15
N 55. – 60 p. grey 15 30
N 56. – 1 r. brown and plum 25 50
N 57. – 2 r. blue and violet 50 1·00

INDIAN U.N. FORCE IN CONGO BC

Stamps used by Indian Forces attached to the United Nations Force in Congo.

1962. Map type of India optd. **U.N. FORCE (INDIA) CONGO.**

U 1. 106. 1 n.p. blue-green 5 5
U 2. 2 n.p. cinnamon 5 5
U 3. 5 n.p. emerald 8 8
U 4. 8 n.p. turquoise 10 12
U 5. 13 n.p. red 15 40
U 6. 50 n.p. orange 20 75

INDIAN U.N. FORCE IN GAZA (PALESTINE) BC

Stamps used by Indian Forces attached to the United Nations Force in Gaza.

1965. Children's Day stamp of India optd. **UNEF.**

Z 1. 177. 15 p. slate 10 10

INDIAN SETTLEMENTS O2

A group of five small French settlements in India. The inhabitants voted to join India in 1954.

1892. 100 centimes = 1 franc.
1923. 24 caches = 1 fanon. 8 fanons = 1 rupee.

1892. "Tablet" key-type inscr. "ETABLISSEMENTS DE L'INDE".

1. D. 1 c. black on blue 8 8
2. 2 c. brown on yellow 5 5
3. 4 c. claret on grey 10 8
4. 5 c. green 55 40
5. 10 c. black on lilac 1·10 30
14. 10 c. red 30 20
6. 15 c. blue 80 55
15. 15 c. grey 3·25 3·25
7. 20 c. red on green 45 35
8. 25 c. black on red 20 20
16. 25 c. blue 1·50 1·40
9. 30 c. brown 5·50 5·00
17. 35 c. black on yellow 1·60 65
10. 40 c. red on yellow 65 55
18. 45 c. black on green 30 25
11. D. 50 c. red 65 55
19. 50 c. brown on blue 1·10 95
12. 75 c. brown on yellow 80 80
13. 1 f. olive 1·10 1·00

1903. Surch. in figures.

20. D. 0.05 on 25 c. black on red 42·00 32·00
21. 0.10 on 25 c. black on red 45·00 35·00
22. 0.15 on 25 c. black on red 14·00 14·00
23. 0.40 on 50 c. red 75·00 60·00

1903. Fiscal stamp bisected and each half surch. **Inde Fcaise POSTES 0.05.**

24. 0.05 black and blue 2·75 2·50

1. Brahma.

2. Mosque near Pondicherry.

1914.

26. 1. 1 c. black and grey 5 5
52. 2 c. purple and green 5 5
30. 5 c. black and green 5 5
53. 5 c. black and purple 5 5
31. 10 c. black and red 5 5
54. 10 c. black and green 8 8
32. 15 c. black and violet 8 8
33. 20 c. black and red 15 15
34. 25 c. black and blue 15 15
55. 25 c. red and blue 10 10
35. 30 c. black and blue 12 12
56. 30 c. black and red 8 8
36. 2. 35 c. black and brown 15 15
37. 40 c. black and orange 15 15
38. 45 c. black and green 15 15
39. 50 c. black and red 12 12
57. 50 c. blue 12 10
40. 75 c. black and blue 25 25
41. 1 f. black and yellow 20 20
42. 2 f. black and violet 40 40
43. 5 f. black and blue 15 15
58. 5 f. black and red 40 40

1916. Surch. **5** and Maltese cross.

48. 1. 10 c. + 5 c. black and red 1·25 1·25

1916. Surch. with Maltese cross and **5 C.**

49. 1. 10 c. + 5 c. black and red 20 20

1916. Surch. with plain cross over **5 c.**

44. 1. 10 c. + 5 c. black and red 12 12

1916. Surch. with red cross and **5 c.**

50. 1. 10 c. + 5 c. black and red 8 8

1922. Surch. in figures and bars.

59. 1. 0.01 on 15 c. black & violet 5 5
60. 0.02 on 15 c. black & violet 5 5
61. 0.05 on 15 c. black & violet 5 5

1923. Surch. in new currency (caches, fanons and rupees) in figures and words.

62. 1. 1 c. on 1 c. black and grey 5 5
63. 2 c. on 5 c. black & purple 5 5
64. 3 c. on 3 c. black & brown 5 5
65. 4 c. on 4 c. black & orange 5 5
66. 6 c. on 10 c. black & green 10 8
67. 2. 6 c. on 45 c. black & green 5 5
68. 1. 10 c. on 20 c. green & red 25 25
69. 12 c. on 15 c. black & violet 10 8
70. 15 c. on 20 c. black & orge. 12 10
71. 2. 16 c. on 35 c. brn. & blue 20 20
72. 1. 18 c. on 30 c. black & red 10 10
73. 2. 20 c. on 45 c. red & green 10 10
74. 1. 1 f. on 25 c. red and green 35 35
75. 2. 1 f. 3 on 35 c. blk. & brn. 5 5
76. 1 f. 6 on 40 c. blk. & orge. 10 10
77. 1 f. 12 on 50 c. blue 8 8
78. 1 f. 12 on 75 c. blk. & bl. 8 5
79. 1 f. 16 on 75 c. grn. & red 30 25
80. 1. 2 f. 9 on 25 c. red & blue 12 12
81. 2. 2 f. 12 on 1 f. br. & mve. 20 20
82. 3 f. 3 on 1 f. blk. & yell. 15 15
83. 6 f. 6 on 2 f. blk. & violet 55 35
84. 1 r. on 1 f. blue and green 1·00 90
85. 2 r. on 5 f. black and red 85 80
86. 3 r. on 2 f. violet and grey 1·75 1·60
87. 5 r. on 5 f. black and red on green 1·90 1·90

1929. As T 1 and 2, but with value in caches, fanons or rupees.

88. 1. 1 c. black and grey 5 5
89. 2 c. black and purple 5 5
90. 3 c. black and brown 5 5
91. 4 c. black and orange 5 5
92. 6 c. green 5 5
93. 10 c. green and red 5 5
94. 2. 12 c. green 5 5
95. 1. 16 c. black and blue 8 8
96. 18 c. red 8 8
97. 20 c. green and blue 8 8
98. 2. 1 f. red and green 8 8
99. 1 f. 6 black and orange 8 8
100. 1 f. 12 blue 8 8
101. 1 f. 16 green and red 8 8
102. 2 f. 12 brown and mauve 8 8
103. 6 f. 6 black and violet 8 8
104. 1 r. blue and green 8 8
105. 2 r. black and red 12 12
106. 3 r. lilac and black 20 15
107. 5 r. black & red on green 30 25

1931. "Colonial Exhibition" key-types inscr. "ETS FRANCAIS DANS L'INDE".

108. E. 10 c. green 35 35
109. F. 12 c. mauve 35 35
110. G. 18 c. red 35 35
111. H. 1 f. 12 blue 35 35

1937. International Exn., Paris. As Nos. 110/15 of Cameroun.

112. 8 c. violet 15 15
113. 12 c. green 15 15
114. 16 c. red 15 15
115. 20 c. brown 15 15
116. 1 f. 12 red 15 15
117. 2 f. 12 blue 15 15

1938. Int. Anti-Cancer Fund. As T **10** of Cameroun.

118. 2 f. 12 + 20 c. blue 1·50 1·50

1939. New York World's Fair. As T **11** of Cameroun.

119. 1 f. 12 red 20 20
120. 2 f. 12 blue 20 20

1939. French Revolution. 150th Anniv. As T **16** of Cameroun.

121. 18 c. + 10 c. grn. & blk. 85 85
122. 1 f. 6 + 12 c. brn. & blk. 85 85
123. 1 f. 12 + 16 c. oran. & blk. 85 85
124. 1 f. 16 + 1 f. 16 red & blk. 85 85
125. 2 f. 12 + 3 f. blue & blk. 85 85

1941. Optd. **FRANCE LIBRE.**

(a) Stamps of 1923.

126. 1. 15 c. on 20 c. blk. & orge. 8·50 8·50
127. 18 c. on 30 c. black & red 25 25
128. 2. 1 f. 3 on 35 c. black and brown 11·00 11·00
131. 1. 2 f. 9 on 25 c. red & blue £180 £160

(b) Stamps of 1929.

133. 1. 2 c. black and purple 1·00 1·00
134. 3 c. black and brown 20 20
135. 4 c. black and orange 65 65
136. 6 c. green 15 15
137. 10 c. green and red 20 25
139. 2. 12 c. green 25 25
140. 1. 16 c. black and blue 15 15
141. 18 c. red £130 90·00
142. 20 c. green and blue 25 25
143. 2. 1 f. red and green 20 20
144. 1 f. 6 black and red 20 25
145. 1 f. 12 blue 40 40
146. 1 f. 16 green and red 20 25
147. 2 f. 12 brown & mauve 15 15
148. 6 f. 6 black and violet 15 15
149. 1 r. blue and green 20 20
150. 2 r. black and red 20 20
151. 3 r. lilac and black 25 25
152. 5 r. blk. and red on green 55 55

(c) Paris Exn. stamps of 1937.

154. 8 c. violet (No. 112) 90 90
157. 12 c. green 50 50
158. 16 c. red 50 50
159. 1 f. 12 red 50 50
160. 2 f. 12 blue 50 50

(d) New York Fair stamps of 1939.

161. 1 f. 12 red 20 20
162. 2 f. 12 blue 20 20

1942. Optd. **FRANCE LIBRE** and Cross of Lorraine or surch. also

(a) Stamps of 1929.

196. 1. 1 c. on 16 c. black & blue 10·00 6·00
203. 2. 1 c. on 6 f. 6 blk. & violet 1·60 1·10
204. 1 c. on 1 r. blue and green 25 20
165. 1. 2 c. black and purple 10 10
205. 2. 2 c. on 1 r. blue & green 10 10
166. 1. 3 c. black and brown 10 10
197. 4 c. on 16 c. black & blue 10·00 6·00
206. 2. 4 c. on 6 f. 6 blk. & violet 2·25 1·75
207. 4 c. on 1 r. blue and green 8 5
169. 1. 6 c. green 10 10
208. 2. 6 c. on 2 r. black and red 5 5
198. 1. 10 c. on 16 c. blk. & blue 5·50 1·25
209. 2. 10 c. on 6 f. 6 blk. & violet 35 12
210. 10 c. on 2 r. black and red 10 10
170. 12 c. green 25 20
211. 12 c. on 2 r. black & red 5 5
199. 1. 15 c. on 16 c. black & blue 4·25 1·10
212. 2. 15 c. on 6 f. 6 blk. & violet 55 20
213. 15 c. on 3 r. lilac & black 5 5
171. 1. 16 c. black and blue 12 12
214. 2. 16 c. on 3 r. lilac & black 5 5
172. 1. 18 c. red 15 15
173. 18 c. on 30 c. (No. 72) 30·00 28·00
174. 20 c. green and blue 15 15
176. 2. 1 f. red and green 8 8
200. 1. 1 f. 3 on 16 c. blk. & bl. 10·00 4·50
215. 2. 1 f. 3 on 6 f. 6 blk. & vio. 65 25
216. 1 f. 3 on 3 r. lilac & blk. 10 8

178. 2. 1 f. 6 black and orange .. 15 15
217. 1 f. 6 c. on 5 r. black and red on green .. 12 12
179. 1 f. 12 blue 12 12
218. 1 f. 12 c. on 5 r. black and red on green 12 12
180. 1 f. 16 green and red .. 12 12
219. 1 f. 16 c. on 5 r. black and red on green 12 12
201. 1. 2 f. 9 c. on 16 c. blk. & bl. 6·50 3·50
220. 2. 2 f. 9 c. on 6 f. 6 blk. & vio. 65 30
182. 2 f. 12 brown and mauve 12 12
202. 1. 3 f. 3 c. on 16 c. blk. & bl. 5·00 1·90
221. 2. 3 f. 3 c. on 6 f. 6 black and violet 65 35
183. 6 f. 6 black and violet .. 25 25
184. 1 r. blue and green .. 55 55
185. 2 r. black and red .. 45 45
187. 3 r. lilac and black .. 60 60
188. 5 r. black & red on green 60 60

(b) Paris Exn. stamps of 1937.
189. 8 c. violet 55 55
190. 12 c. green 45 45
191. 16 c. red £225 £170
192. 1 f. 12 red 10 10
193. 2 f. 12 blue 35 30

(c) New York Fair stamps of 1939.
194. 1 f. 12 red 15 12
195. 2 f. 12 blue 15 12

1943. No. 103 surch. but without "FRANCE LIBRE" and Cross of Lorraine.
222. 2. 1 c. on 6 f. 6 blk. & violet 3·25 2·75
223. 4 c. on 6 f. 6 blk. & violet 3·25 2·75
224. 10 c. on 6 f. 6 blk. & violet 80 65
225. 15 c. on 6 f. 6 blk. & violet 80 65
226. 1 f. 3 c. on 6 f. 6 blk. & vio. 2·75 2·75
227. 2 f. 9 c. on 6 f. 6 blk. & vio. 2·75 2·75
228. 3 f. 3 c. on 6 f. 6 blk. & vio. 2·75 2·75

3. Lotus Flowers. 4. Apsara.

6. Aeroplane and bas-relief.

1942. Free French issue. (a) Postage.
229. 3. 2 c. brown 5 5
230. 3 c. blue 5 5
231. 4 c. green 5 5
232. 6 c. orange 5 5
233. 12 c. green 5 5
234. 16 c. purple 5 5
235. 20c. maroon 5 5
236. 1 f. red 8 5
237. 1 f. 18 black 8 5
238. 6 f. 6 blue 8 5
239. 1 r. violet 10 8
240. 2 r. bistre 15 12
241. 3 r. brown 20 15
242. 5 r. green 25 20

(b) Air. As T 18 of Cameroun.
243. 18. 4 f. orange 8 8
244. 1 r. red 8 5
245. 2 r. maroon 15 15
246. 5 r. black 15 15
247. 8 r. blue 30 20
248. 10 r. green 30 25

1944. Mutual Aid and Red Cross Funds. As T 19 of Cameroun.
249. 3 f. + 1 r. 4 f. bistre .. 8 10

1945. Eboue. As T 20 of Cameroun.
250. 3 f. 8 black 5 5
251. 5 r. 1 f. 16 green 12 15

1946. Air. Victory. As T 21 of Cameroun.
252. 4 f. green 12 12

1946. Air. From Chad to the Rhine. As T 22 of Cameroun.
253. 2 f. 12 brown 15 15
254. 5 f. blue 15 15
255. 7 f. 12 violet 15 15
256. 1 r. 2 f. green 15 15
257. 1 r. 4 f. 12 red 15 15
258. 3 r. 1 f. maroon 15 15

1948.
259. 4. 1 c. olive (postage) .. 5 5
260. 2 c. brown 5 5
261. 4 c. violet on cream .. 5 5
262. A. 6 c. orange 5 8
263. 8 c. slate 12 12
264. 10 c. green on green .. 12 12
265. B. 12 c. purple 5 5
266. 15 c. blue 8 8
267. C. 18 c. lake 12 12
268. B. 1 f. violet on rose .. 12 10
269. D. 1 f. 6 red 8 8
270. C. 1 f. 15 violet 35 35
271. D. 2 f. green 10 8
272. 2 f. 2 blue on cream .. 20 12
273. E. 2 f. 12 brown 20 20
274. 3 f. red 30 25
275. C. 4 f. olive 35 35
276. E. 5 f. purple on rose .. 25 25
277. F. 7 f. 12 brown 25 25
278. 1 r. 2 f. black 60 60
279. 1 r. 4 f. 12 c. green .. 65 55
281. 6. 1 r. red and yellow (air). 70 55
282. – 2 r. green .. .. 1·40 1·10
283. – 5 r. purple and blue .. 3·75 3·50

DESIGNS—As T. 4: A. Dvarabalagar standing erect. B. Vishunu. C. Brahmin idol. D. Dvarabalagar with leg raised. E. Temple Guardian. F. One of the Tigoupalagar. As T. 5: 2 r. Wing and temple. 5 r. Bird and palm-trees.

1949. Air. U.P.U. As T 25 of Cameroun.
284. 6 f. red .. .. .. 1·00 1·00

1950. Colonial Welfare Fund. As T 26 of Cameroun.
285. 1 f. + 10 c. blue & slate .. 25 25

1952. Military Medal Cent. As T 27 of Cameroun.
286. 1 f. brown, yellow & green 30 30

1954. Air. Liberation. 10th Anniv. As T 29 of Cameroun.
287. 1 f. maroon and sepia .. 60 60

POSTAGE DUE STAMPS

1923. Postage Due stamps of France surch. in figures and letters.
D 88. D 2. 4 c. on 20 c. violet .. 8 8
D 89. 6 c. on 10 c. brown .. 10 10
D 90. 12 c. on 25 c. red .. 8 8
D 91. 15 c. on 20 c. olive .. 8 8
D 92. 1 f. on 30 c. orange .. 15 20
D 93. 1 f. 6 on 30 c. red .. 20 20
D 94. 1 f. 12 on 50 c. purple 20 20
D 95. 1 f. 15 on 5 c. blue .. 25 25
D 96. 1 f. 16 on 5 c. black .. 25 25
D 97. 3 f. on 1 f. green .. 40 40
D 98. 3 f. 3 on 1 f. brown on yellow 35 35

1929. Postage Due stamps as in France, but with currency altered and inscr. "INDE FRANCAISE".
D 108. D 2. 4 c. red 5 5
D 109. 6 c. blue 5 5
D 110. 12 c. green 5 5
D 111. 1 f. brown 5 5
D 112. 1 f. 12 violet 10 10
D 113. 1 f. 16 orange 12 12
D 114. 3 f. mauve 20 20

D 1.

1948.
D 280. D 1. 1 c. violet 5 5
D 281. 2 c. brown 5 5
D 282. 6 c. green 5 5
D 283. 12 c. red 5 5
D 284. 1 f. mauve 5 5
D 285. 1 f. 12 brown .. 8 8
D 286. 2 f. blue 10 10
D 287. 2 f. 12 lake 12 12
D 288. 5 f. green 20 20
D 289. 1 r. violet 25 25

INDO-CHINA O2

A French territory in S.E. Asia, which in 1949 was split up into the three states of Viet-Nam, Cambodia and Laos.

1889. 100 centimes = 1 franc.
1918. 100 cents = 1 piastre.

1889. Stamps of French Colonies, "Commerce" type, surch. **INDO-CHINE 89** (or **1889**) **5 R-D.**
3. 9. 5 on 35 c. black on orange .. 1·40 1·10

1892. "Tablet" key-type inscr. "INDO-CHINE".
6. D. 1 c. black on blue .. 5 5
7. 2 c. brown on yellow .. 10 8
8. 4 c. claret on grey .. 10 8
23. 5 c. green 5 5
10. 10 c. black on lilac .. 50 10
24. 10 c. red 25 12
11. 15 c. blue .. .. 3·75 5
25. 15 c. grey 85 5
12. 20 c. red on green .. 1·10 55
13. 25 c. black on red .. 2·00 10
26. 25 c. blue .. .. 2·50 25
14. 30 c. brown .. .. 2·75 1·60
15. 40 c. red on yellow .. 2·75 60
16. 50 c. red on rose .. 7·00 2·75
27. 50 c. brown on blue .. 3·00 1·25
17. 75 c. brown on orange .. 4·25 2·50
18. 1 f. olive .. .. 7·00 3·25
19. 5 f. mauve on lilac .. 17·00 16·00

1903. Surch.
28. D. 5 on 15 c. grey 12 12
29. 15 on 25 c. blue 20 15

1.

1904.
30. 1. 1 c. olive 5 5
31. 2 c. claret on yellow .. 5 5
32. 4 c. purple on grey .. 5 5
33. 5 c. green 5 5
34. 10 c. red 20 5
35. 15 c. brown on blue .. 10 5
36. 20 c. red on green .. 25 8
37. 25 c. blue .. .. 1·60 15
38. 30 c. brown on cream .. 55 35
39. 35 c. black on yellow .. 2·25 20
40. 40 c. black on grey .. 55 20
41. 50 c. olive on cream .. 90 30
42. 75 c. red on orange .. 7·00 4·50
43. 1 f. green .. .. 2·75 70
44. 2 f. brown on yellow .. 8·50 7·50
45. 5 f. violet .. .. .. 42·00 38·00
46. 10 f. red on green .. 35·00 30·00

2. Annamite. 3. Cambodian. 4. Cambodian.

1907.
51. 2. 1 c. black and sepia .. 5 5
52. 2 c. black and brown .. 5 5
53. 4 c. black and blue .. 10 10
54. 5 c. black and green .. 5 5
55. 10 c. black and red .. 5 5
56. 15 c. black and violet .. 15 8
57. 3. 20 c. black and violet .. 35 20
58. 25 c. black and blue .. 65 5
59. 30 c. black and brown .. 1·60 1·10
60. 35 c. black and green .. 12 5
61. 40 c. black and brown .. 40 25
62. 45 c. black and orange .. 1·75 1·10
63. 50 c. black and red .. 1·75 1·10
64. 4. 75 c. black and orange .. 1·50 1·40
65. – 1 f. black and red .. 7·50 2·25
66. – 2 f. black and green .. 2·75 2·25
67. – 5 f. black and blue .. 5·00 5·00
68. – 10 f. black and violet .. 20·00 17·00

DESIGNS—As T 4: 1 f. Annamites. 2 f. Muong. 5 f. Laotian. 10 f. Cambodian.

1912. Surch. in figures.
69. 1. 05 on 4 c. purple on blue .. 1·00 85
70. 05 on 15 c. brown on blue 5 5
71. 05 on 30 c. brown on cream 5 5
72. 10 on 40 c. black on grey .. 12 12
73. 10 on 50 c. olive on cream 8 8
74. 10 on 75 c. red on orange .. 75 65

1914. Surch. with red cross and **5** over **c.**
75. 2. 10 c. + 5 c. black on red .. 8 5

1915. Surch. **5 c.** and red cross.
76. 2. 5 c. + 5 c. black and green 5 5
77. 10 c. + 5 c. black and red 20 15
78. 15 c. + 5 c. black and violet 20 20

1918. Surch. **5 c** and red cross and value in centre and **INDOCHINE.**
79. 2. 4 c. on 5 c. + 5 c. blk. & grn. 40 30
80. 6 c. on 10 c. + 5 c. blk. & red 40 40
81. 8 c. on 15 c. + 5 c. blk. & vio. 1·60 1·50

1919. French stamps of "War Orphans" issue surch. **INDOCHINE** and value in figures and words.
82. 21. 10 c. on 15 c. + 10 c. grey 5 5
83. 16 c. on 25 c. + 15 c. blue 55 55
84. – 24 c. on 35 c. + 25 c. violet and grey 80 80
85. – 40 c. on 50 c. + 50 c. brn. 85 85
86. 24. 80 c. on 1 f. + 1 f. red .. 2·25 2·25
87. 4 p. on 5 f. + 5 f. bl. & blk. 25·00 25·00

1919. Surch in figures and words.
88. 2. ⅖ c. on 1 c. black and sepia 5 5
89. ⅘ c. on 2 c. black & brown 10 10
90. 1⅗ c. on 4 c. black and blue 15 10
91. 2 c. on 5 c. black & green 8 5
92. 4 c. on 10 c. black and red 5 5
93. 6 c. on 15 c. black & violet 20 5
94. 3. 8 c. on 20 c. black & violet 55 20
95. 10 c. on 24 c. black & blue 20 5
96. 12 c. on 30 c. black & brn. 75 10
97. 14 c. on 35 c. black & grn 8 5
98. 16 c. on 40 c. black & brn. 60 25
99. 18 c. on 45 c. black & orge. 80 35
100. 20 c. on 50 c. black & red 1·25 10
101. 4. 30 c. on 75 c. blk. & orge. 1·25 30
102. – 40 c. on 1 f. black and red 2·40 30
103. – 80 c. on 2 f. black & green 2·75 1·10
104. – 2 p. on 5 f. black and blue 15·00 14·00
105. – 4 p. on 10 f. black & violet 25·00 25·00

1922. As T 2 and 3 but value in cents or piastres.
115. 2. ⅒ c. red and grey .. 5 5
116. ⅕ c. black and blue .. 5 5
117. ⅖ c. black and olive .. 5 5
118. 2. ⅘ c. black and red .. 5 5
119. 1 c. black and brown .. 5 5
120. 2 c. black and green .. 5 5
121. 3 c. black and violet .. 5 5
122. 4 c. black and orange .. 5 5
123. 5 c. black and red .. 5 5
124. 3. 6 c. black and red .. 5 5
125. 7 c. black and olive .. 8 8
126. 8 c. black 12 10
127. 9 c. black and orange .. 12 10
128. 10 c. black and blue .. 5 5
129. 11 c. black and violet .. 5 5
130. 12 c. black and purple .. 5 5
131. 15 c. black and orange .. 8 5
132. 20 c. black and blue .. 12 8
133. 40 c. black and red .. 20 15
134. 1 p. black and green .. 65 60
135. 2 p. black and claret .. 90 75

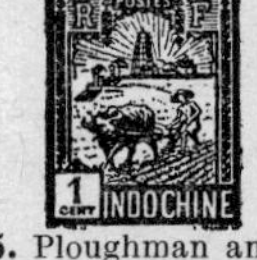

5. Ploughman and Tower of Confucius. 6. Bay of Along.

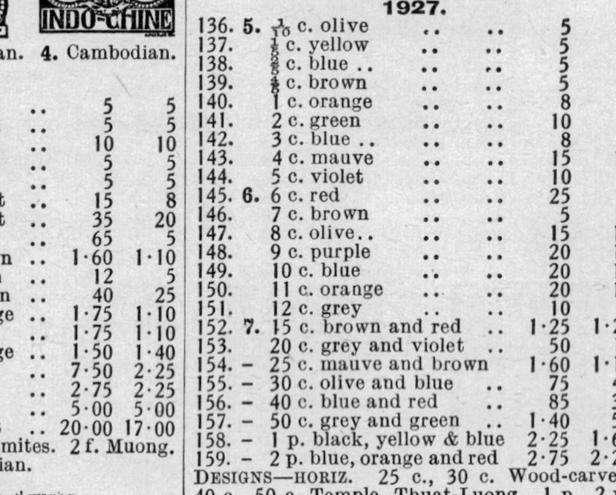

7. Ruins of Angkor.

1927.
136. 5. ⅒ c. olive 5 5
137. ⅕ c. yellow 5 5
138. ⅖ c. blue 5 5
139. ⅘ c. brown 5 5
140. 1 c. orange 8 5
141. 2 c. green 10 5
142. 3 c. blue 8 5
143. 4 c. mauve 15 12
144. 5 c. violet 10 5
145. 6. 6 c. red 25 5
146. 7 c. brown 5 5
147. 8 c. olive 15 15
148. 9 c. purple 20 15
149. 10 c. blue 20 10
150. 11 c. orange 20 10
151. 12 c. grey 10 8
152. 7. 15 c. brown and red .. 1·25 1·25
153. 20 c. grey and violet .. 50 12
154. – 25 c. mauve and brown 1·60 1·10
155. – 30 c. olive and blue .. 75 45
156. – 40 c. blue and red .. 85 30
157. – 50 c. grey and green .. 1·40 55
158. – 1 p. black, yellow & blue 2·25 1·60
159. – 2 p. blue, orange and red 2·75 2·25

DESIGNS—HORIZ. 25 c., 30 c. Wood-carver. 40 c., 50 c. Temple, Thuat-Luong. 1 p., 2 p. Founding of Saigon.

1931. "Colonial Exn." key-types inscr. "INDOCHINE" and surch. in figures and CTS.
160. F. 4 c. on 50 c. mauve .. 30 20
161. G. 6 c. on 90 c. red .. 55 55
162. H. 10 c. on 1 f. 50 blue .. 45 30

11. Junk. 14. "Apsara", or dancing Nymph.

1931.
163. 11. ⅒ c. blue 5 5
164. ⅕ c. lake 5 5
165. ⅖ c. red 5 5
166. ½ c. brown 5 5
167. ⅘ c. violet 5 5
168. 1 c. sepia 5 5
169. 2 c. green 5 5
170. – 3 c. brown 5 5
171. – 3 c. green 75 10
172. – 4 c. blue 8 5
173. – 4 c. green 10 10
174. – 4 c. yellow 5 5
175. – 5 c. purple 5 5
176. – 5 c. green 5 5
177. – 6 c. red 5 5
178. – 7 c. black 5 5
179. – 8 c. lake 5 5
180. – 9 c. black on yellow .. 5 5
181. – 10 c. blue 10 5
182. – 10 c. blue on pink .. 5 5
183. – 15 c. sepia 70 5
184. – 15 c. blue 5 5
185. – 18 c. blue 5 5
186. – 20 c. red 5 5
187. – 21 c. green 5 5
188. – 22 c. green 5 5
189. – 25 c. purple 40 25
190. – 25 c. blue 5 5
191. – 30 c. brown 5 5
192. 14. 50 c. sepia 5 5
193. 60 c. purple 5 5
194. 70 c. blue 5 5
195. 1 pi. green 10 5
196. 2 pi. red 15 5

DESIGNS—As T 11: 3 c. to 9 c. Ruins at Angkor. 10 c. to 30 c. Worker in rice field.

15. Airmail 'plane. 16. Emperor Bao-Dai, of Annam.

1933. Air

197. 15. 1 c. sepia 5 5
198. 2 c. green 5 5
199. 5 c. yellow-green 5 5
200. 10 c. claret 5 5
201. 11 c. red 5 5
202. 15 c. blue 5 5
203. 16 c. red 5 5
204. 20 c. grey 10 8
205. 30 c. brown 5 5
206. 36 c. rose 30 5
207. 37 c. olive 5 5
208. 39 c. olive 5 5
209. 60 c. purple 8 5
210. 66 c. olive 8 5
211. 67 c. blue 12 10
212. 69 c. blue 5 5
213. 1 p. black 5 5
214. 2 p. orange 12 5
215. 5 p. violet 30 5
216. 10 p. red 45 10
217. 20 p. green .. .. 2·25 80
218. 30 p. brown .. .. 2·40 85

1936. Issue for Annam.

219. 16. 1 c. brown 10 10
220. 2 c. green 10 10
221. 4 c. violet 20 12
222. 5 c. lake 15 12
223. 10 c. red 35 35
224. 15 c. blue 35 35
225. 20 c. red 40 35
226. 30 c. purple 55 45
227. 50 c. green 65 65
228. 1 p. mauve .. .. 80 1·00
229. 2 p. black .. .. 1·00 80

17. King Sisowath Monivong of Cambodia. 18. Railway and Pres. Doumer.

1936. Issue for Cambodia.

230. 17. 1 c. brown 10 10
231. 2 c. green 10 10
232. 4 c. violet 15 15
233. 5 c. lake 15 15
234. 10 c. red 50 45
235. 15 c. blue 65 55
236. 20 c. red 45 40
237. 30 c. purple 45 40
238. 50 c. green 45 40
239. 1 p. mauve 55 45
240. 2 p. black 65 55

1937. Int. Exn., Paris. As Nos. 110/5 of Cameroun.

241. 2 c. violet 15 12
242. 3 c. green 15 12
243. 4 c. red 10 10
244. 6 c. brown 10 10
245. 9 c. red 10 10
246. 15 c. blue 10 10

1938. Opening of Trans-Indo-China Railway.

247. 18. 5 c. red (postage) .. 15 5
248. 6 c. brown 12 5
249. 18 c. blue 12 8
250. 37 c. orange (air) .. 5 5

1938. Int. Anti-Cancer Fund. As T 10 of Cameroun.

251. 18 c.+5 c. blue .. .. 1·50 1·50

1939. New York World's Fair. As T 11 of Cameroun.

252. 13 c. red 5 5
253. 23 c. blue 5 5

19. Mot Cot Pagoda, Hanoi. 20. King Sihanouk of Cambodia.

1939. San Francisco Exn.

254. 19. 6 c. sepia 20 20
255. 9 c. red 10 10
256. 23 c. blue 10 10
257. 39 c. purple 20 20

1939. French Revolution. 150th Anniv. As T 16 of Cameroun.

258. 6 c.+2 c. green and black (postage) .. .. 1·00 1·00
259. 7 c.+3 c. brown and black 1·00 1·00
260. 9 c.+4 c. orange and black 1·00 1·00
261. 13 c.+10 c. red and black 1·00 1·00
262. 23 c.+20 c. blue and black 1·00 1·00
263. 39 c.+40 c. black and oran. (air) .. .. 3·50 3·50

1941. Coronation of King of Cambodia.

264. 20. 1 c. orange 10 10
265. 6 c. violet 20 20
266. 25 c. blue .. .. 3·75 3·25

21. Processional Elephant. 22. Hanoi University.

1942. Fetes of Nam-Giao.

267. 21. 3 c. brown 15 15
268. 6 c. red 15 15

1942. No. 189 surch. **10 cents** and bars.

269. 10 c. on 25 c. purple .. 5 5

1942.

270. 22. 6 c.+2 c. red 8 8
271. 15 c.+5 c. violet .. 10 10

Surch. **10 c.+2 c.** and bars.

272. 22. 10 c.+2 c. on 6 c.+2 c. red 5 5

23. Marshal Petain. 24. Shield and Sword.

1942.

273. 23. 1 c. brown 5 5
274. 3 c. brown 5 5
275. 6 c. red 5 5
276. 10 c. green 5 5
277. 40 c. blue 5 5
278. 40 c. grey 15 15

1942. National Relief Fund.

279. 24. 6 c.+2 c. red and blue 8 8
280. 15c.+5 c. blk., red & bl. 10 10

Surch. **10 c.+2 c.** and bars.

281. 24. 10 c.+2 c. on 6 c.+2 c. red and blue .. 5 5

25. Emperor Bao Dai of Annam. 26. King Sihanouk of Cambodia.

27. Empress Nam-Phaong of Annam. 28. King Sisavang-vong of Laos.

1942.

282. 25. ½ c. purple 5 5
283. 26. 1 c. purple 5 5
284. 28. 1 c. brown 5 5
285. 25. 6 c. red 8 5
286. 26. 6 c. red 5 5
287. 27. 6 c. red 12 10
288. 28. 6 c. red 5 5

29. Saigon Fair. 30. "Family, Homeland and Labour".

1942. Saigon Fair.

289. 29. 6 c. red 5 5

1943. National Revolution. 3rd Anniv.

312. 30. 6 c. red 5 5

31. Doudart de Lagree. 32. De Lanessan.

1943. (a) Vert. portraits.

300. 31. 1 c. brown 5 5
315. – 2 c. mauve (P. Doumer) 5 5
316. – 4 c. brown (P. Doumer) 5 5
318. – 5 c. purple (P. Pasquier) 5 5
306. – 6 c. red (Ch. Laubat) .. 5 5
290. – 6 c. red (Yersin) .. 12 12
322. – 10 c. green (P. Doumer) 5 5
321. – 10 c. green (P. Pasquier) 5 5
307. – 10 c. green (Charner) .. 5 5
291. – 15 c. purple (Yersin) .. 5 5
308. 31. 15 c. purple 5 5
293. – 20 c. red (Adran) .. 5 5
309. – 20 c. red (Charner) .. 5 5
310. 31. 40 c. blue 5 5
295. – $1 green (Yersin) .. 5 5
311. – $1 green (Charner) .. 8 8

(b) Horiz. portraits.

314. 32. 1 c. brown 5 5
313. – 1 c. brown (Vollenhoven) 5 5
302. – 1 c. brown (La Grandiere) 5 5
301. – 1 c. brown (F. Garnier) 8 8
317. – 4 c. yellow (A. Pavie) .. 5 5
303. – 5 c. brown (La Grandiere) 5 5
304. – 6 c. red (Courbet) .. 5 5
305. – 6 c. red (R. de Genouilly) 5 5
320. – 10 c. green (A. Pavie) .. 5 5
319. – 10 c. green (Vollenhoven) 5 5
323. 32. 15 c. purple 5 5
292. – 15 c. pur. (A. de Rhodes) 5 5
294. – 30 c. brn. (A. de Rhodes) 5 5

33. Do Hun-Vi.

1943. T 33 and similar vert. design inscr. "ROLAND GARROS".

296. 33. 6 c.+2 c. red 8 8
297. 6 c.+2 c. red 5 5

Surch. **10 c.+2 c.** and bars.

298. 33. 10 c.+2 c. on 6 c.+2 c. red 5 5
299. – 10 c.+2 c. on 6 c.+2 c. red (No. 297) .. 5 5

34. Athlete.

1944. Juvenile Sports.

324. 34. 10 c. purple and yellow 20 20
325. 50 c. red 20 20

35. Orleans Cathedral.

1944. Martyr Cities.

326. 35. 15 c.+60 c. purple .. 10 10
327. 40 c.+1 p. 10 blue .. 15 15

1945. As T. 134 of France surch. **INDOCHINE** and values.

328. 50 c.+50 c. on 2 f. olive .. 8 8
329. 1 p.+1 p. on 2 f. brown .. 8 8
330. 2 p.+2 p. on 2 f. grey .. 8 8

1946. Air. Victory. As T 21 of Cameroun.

331. 80 c. orange 5 5

1946. Air. From Chad to the Rhine. As T 22 of Cameroun.

332. 50 c. green 5 5
333. 1 p. mauve 5 5
334. 1 p. 50 red 5 5
335. 2 p. purple 10 10
336. 2 p. 50 blue 12 12
337. 5 p. red 20 20

1946. Unissued stamps similar to T 7 with portrait of Marshal Petain optd. with **R F** monogram.

338. 10 c. red 5 5
339. 25 c. blue 15 12

1949. Air. U.P.U. As T 25 of Cameroun.

340. 3 p. blue, violet, olive & red 40 40

OFFICIAL STAMPS

1933. Stamps of 1931 (Nos. 168, etc.) optd. **SERVICE.**

O 197. 1 c. sepia 10 5
O 198. 2 c. green 10 5
O 199. 3 c. brown 20 12
O 200. 4 c. blue 20 12
O 201. 5 c. purple 35 5
O 202. 6 c. red 35 5
O 203. 10 c. blue 10 5
O 204. 15 c. sepia 45 25
O 205. 20 c. red 30 5
O 206. 21 c. green 30 15
O 207. 25 c. purple 12 5
O 208. 30 c. brown 30 15
O 209. 50 c. sepia .. .. 2·25 65
O 210. 60 c. purple 25 25
O 211. 1 p. green .. .. 4·00 1·75
O 212. 2 p. red .. .. 1·75 1·60

1934. As T 3, but value in "CENTS" or "PIASTRES" and optd. **SERVICE.**

O 219. 1 c. olive 10 10
O 220. 2 c. brown 12 12
O 221. 3 c. green 10 8
O 222. 4 c. red 20 12
O 223. 5 c. orange 5 5
O 224. 6 c. red 65 40
O 225. 10 c. olive-green .. 55 45
O 226. 15 c. blue 30 15
O 227. 20 c. black 25 10
O 228. 21 c. violet .. .. 1·40 90
O 229. 25 c. claret .. .. 1·60 90
O 230. 30 c. grey 25 20
O 231. 50 c. mauve .. .. 1·50 1·10
O 232. 60 c. grey .. .. 1·75 1·25
O 233. 1 p. blue .. .. 5·00 3·25
O 234. 2 p. red .. .. 5·50 4·50

PARCEL POST STAMPS

1891. Stamp of French Colonies, "Commerce" type, optd. **INDO-CHINE TIMBRE COLIS POSTAUX.**

P 4. 9. 10 c. black on lilac .. 2·25 55

1898. "Tablet" key-type of Indo-China optd. **COLIS POSTAUX.**

P 20. D. 10 c. black on lilac .. 2·75 2·25

1899. "Tablet" key-type of Indio-China optd. **TIMBRE COLIS POSTAUX.**

P 21. D. 10 c. black on lilac .. 6·50 4·50
P 22. 10 c. red .. .. 5·50 2·75

POSTAGE DUE STAMPS.

1904. Postage Due stamps of French Colonies optd. with value in figures.

D 47. 5 on 60 c. brn. on yellow 1·10 90
D 48. D 1. 5 on 40 c. black .. 3·75 1·50
D 49. 10 on 60 c. black .. 4·50 2·75
D 50. 30 on 60 c. black .. 4·25 4·75

D 1. Annamite Dragon. D 2. Mot Cot Pagoda, Hanoi. D 3. Annamite Dragon.

1908.

D 69. D 1. 2 c. black 12 12
D 70. 4 c. blue 8 8
D 71. 5 c. green 8 8
F 72. 10 c. red 45 5
D 73. 15 c. violet 50 30
D 74. 20 c. brown 8 8
D 75. 30 c. olive 15 12
D 76. 40 c. maroon .. .. 1·50 1·40
D 77. 50 c. blue 65 8
D 78. 60 c. yellow .. .. 2·00 1·75
D 79. 1 f. grey .. .. 4·00 3·00
D 80. 2 f. brown .. .. 2·25 2·25
D 81. 5 f. red .. .. 3·75 3·25

1919. Surch. in figures and words.

D 106. D 1. ⅘ c. on 2 c. black .. 20 10
D 107. 1⅗ c. on 4 c. blue 20 10
D 108. 2 c. on 5 c. green .. 30 20
D 109. 4 c. on 10 c. red .. 20 5
D 110. 6 c. on 15 c. violet 60 45
D 111. 8 c. on 20 c. brown .. 75 15
D 112. 12 c. on 30 c. olive 75 20
D 113. 16 c. on 40 c. claret 75 10
D 114. 20 c. on 50 c. blue .. 1·10 70
D 115. 24 c. on 60 c. orange 40 30
D 116. 40 c. on 1 f. grey .. 35 10
D 117. 80 c. on 2 f. brown .. 4·00 3·25
D 118. 2 p. on 5 f. red .. 5·00 3·50

1922. Type D 1, but values in cents. or piastres.

D 136. D 1. ⅖ c. black 5 5
D 137. ⅘ c. black and red 5 5
D 138. 1 c. black and yellow 5 5
D 139. 2 c. black and green 10 5
D 140. 3 c. black and violet 10 5
D 141. 4 c. black and orange 5 5
D 142. 6 c. black and olive .. 12 8
D 143. 8 c. black on lilac .. 12 5
D 144. 10 c. black and blue 15 5
D 145. 12 c. black and orange on green 15 12
D 146. 20 c. blk. & bl. on yell. 15 5
D 147. 40 c. blk. & red on grey 12 8
D 148. 1 p. black and purple on pink 65 60

1927.

D 160. D 2. ⅖ c. orange & purple 5 5
D 161. ⅘ c. black and violet 5 5
D 162. 1 c. black and red .. 15 15
D 163. 2 c. brown & green 20 15
D 164. 3 c. blue and purple 12 12
D 165. 4 c. brown and blue 20 15
D 166. 6 c. red and brown 20 20
D 167. 8 c. violet and olive 20 20
D 168. D 3. 10 c. blue 20 12
D 169. 12 c. brown .. 55 50
D 170. 20 c. red 30 10
D 171. 40 c. green 40 30
D 172. 1 p. orange .. 2·75 2·25

D 4. D 5.

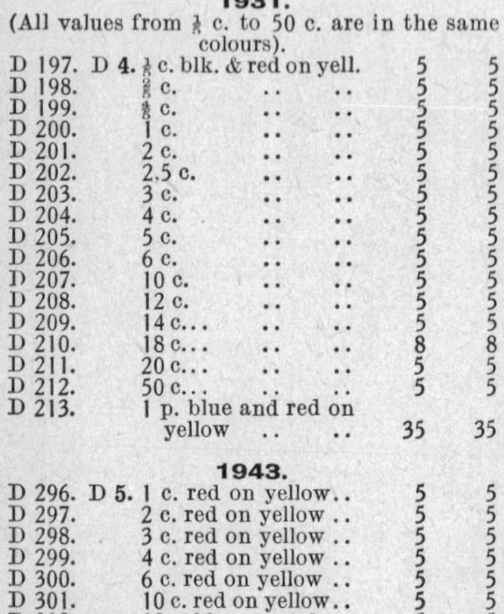

1931.

(All values from ⅕ c. to 50 c. are in the same colours).

D 197. D 4. ⅕ c. blk. & red on yell. 5 5
D 198. ⅖ c. 5 5
D 199. ⅘ c. 5 5
D 200. 1 c. 5 5
D 201. 2 c. 5 5
D 202. 2,5 c. 5 5
D 203. 3 c. 5 5
D 204. 4 c. 5 5
D 205. 5 c. 5 5
D 206. 6 c. 5 5
D 207. 10 c. 5 5
D 208. 12 c. 5 5
D 209. 14 c... .. 5 5
D 210. 18 c... .. 8 8
D 211. 20 c... .. 5 5
D 212. 50 c... .. 5 5
D 213. 1 p. blue and red on yellow 35 35

1943.

D 296. D 5. 1 c. red on yellow .. 5 5
D 297. 2 c. red on yellow .. 5 5
D 298. 3 c. red on yellow .. 5 5
D 299. 4 c. red on yellow .. 5 5
D 300. 6 c. red on yellow .. 5 5
D 301. 10 c. red on yellow .. 5 5
D 302. 12 c. blue on pink .. 5 5
D 303. 20 c. blue on pink .. 5 5
D 304. 30 c. blue on pink .. 5 5

INDONESIA O2

An independent republic was proclaimed in Java and Sumatra on 17 August 1945 and lasted until the end of 1948. During this period the Dutch controlled the rest of the Netherlands Indies, renamed " Indonesia " in September 1948. On 27 December 1949 all Indonesia except New Guinea became independent as the United States of Indonesia which, during 1950, amalgamated with the original Indonesian Republic (Java and Sumatra), a single state being proclaimed on 15 August 1950 as the Indonesian Republic. This was within the Netherlands-Indonesian Union which was abolished on 10 August 1954.

100 cents (or sen) = 1 gulden (or rupiah).

1948. Stamps of Netherlands Indies optd. **INDONESIA** and bar or bars.

541. 38. 15 c. orange 25 5
533. 20 c. blue 8 5
534. 25 c. green 5 5
535. 40 c. green 8 5
544. 45 c. mauve 30 25
545. 50 c. lake 12 5
536. 80 c. red 20 5
537. 1 g. violet 25 5
538. – 2½ g. orange (No. 479) .. 5·50 2·75
539. 38. 10 g. green .. .. 15·00 2·00
540. 25 g. orange .. .. 18·00 14·00

39.

40. Portal to Tjandi Poentadewa Temple.

41. Globe and Arms of Berne.

1949. New Currency.

548. 39. 1 s. grey 5 5
549. 2 s. purple 5 5
550. 2½ s. brown 5 5
551. 3 s. red 5 5
552. 4 s. green 12 12
553. 5 s. blue 5 5
554. 7½ s. green 10 5
555. 10 s. mauve 5 5
556. 12½ s. red 12 5
557. 40. 15 s. red 5 5
558. 20 s. black 5 5
559. 25 s. blue 5 5
560. – 30 s. red 5 5
561. – 40 s. green 8 5
562. – 45 s. purple 10 8
563. – 50 s. brown 8 5
564. – 60 s. brown 10 5
565. – 80 s. red 12 5
566. – 1 r. violet 10 5
567. – 2 r. green .. .. 1·00 5
568. – 3 r. purple .. .. 5·00 5
569. – 5 r. brown .. .. 5·00 5
570. – 10 r. black .. .. 8·00 12
571. – 25 r. brown 12 12

DESIGNS—As T 40: 30 s., 40 s. Sculpture from Temple at Bedjoening, Bali. 45 s. Detail of Temple of Bedjoening. 50 s., 60 s., 80 s., Minangkabaus house, Sumatra. LARGER: 1 r 2 r., 3 r. Toradja house. 5 r., 10 r., 25 r. Detail of Temple of Panahan.

1949. U.P.U. 75th Anniv.

572. 41. 15 s. red 20 15
573. 25 s. blue 25 12

A. REPUBLIC, 1945-48.

JAVA AND MADURA.

1945. Stamps of Netherlands Indies optd. **REPOEBLIK INDONESIA.**

J 1. 19. 1 c. violet 10 15
J 2. 2 c. purple 20 30
J 19. – 2 c. red (No. 462) .. 10 12
J 4. – 2½ c. claret (No. 462) .. 10 15
J 5. – 3 c. green (No. 463) 10 15
J 3. 19. 3½ c. grey 50 75
J 6. 33. 4 c. olive 10 15
J 7. 5 c. blue (No. 465) .. 1·25 1·75

1945. Stamps of Japanese Occupation of Netherlands Indies optd. as above.

J 8. – 3½ s. red (No. 2) .. 60 80
J 10. – 3½ c. red (No. 5) .. 50 70
J 9. – 5 s. green (No. 3) 20 40
J 11. 2. 5 s. green 8 10
J 12. – 10 c. blue (No. 7) .. 8 10
J 13. – 20 c. olive (No. 8) .. 12 15
J 14. – 40 c. purple (No. 9) .. 20 25
J 15. 3. 60 c. orange .. 20 25
J 16. – 80 s. brown (No. 11) .. 40 60

42. Bull.

DESIGN—VERT. 20 s. Bull and Indonesian flag.

1945. Declaration of Independence. Inscr. " 17 AGOESTOES 1945 ". Perf. or imperf.

J 23. 42. 10 s. (+10 s.) brown .. 40 50
J 24. 20 s. (+10 s.) brown & red 50 60

43. Boat in Storm.

44. Wayang Puppet.

1946.

J 49. – 5 s. blue 5 10
J 50. – 20 s. brown 5 8
J 51. 43. 30 s. red 5 12
J 52. 44. 50 s. blue 30 45
J 53. – 60 s. red 40 60
J 54. – 80 s. violet .. 2·00 3·00

DESIGNS—HORIZ. 5 s. Road and mountains. 20 s. Soldier on waterfront. VERT. 60 s. Kris and flag. 80 s. Temple.

45. Buffalo breaking Chains.

46. Bandung, March, 1946.

1946. Perf. or imperf.

J 55. 45. 3 s. red 5 8
J 56. 46. 5 s. blue 5 8
J 57. – 10 s. black 8 12
J 58. – 15 s. purple 5 8
J 59. – 30 s. green 5 8
J 60. – 40 s. blue 5 8
J 61. 45. 50 s. black 5 8
J 62. 46. 60 s. lilac 5 10
J 63. – 80 s. red 8 12
J 64. – 100 s. brown .. 10 15
J 65. – 200 s. lilac .. 10 15
J 66. – 500 s. red .. 30 40
J 67. – 1,000 s. green .. 40 50

DESIGNS—HORIZ. 10 s., 15 s. Soerabaya, Nov. 1945. 30 s. Anti-aircraft gunners. 100 s. Ambarawa, Nov. 1945. 200 s. Wonokromo Dam, Soerabaya. 1,000 s. Cavalryman. VERT. 40 s. Quay at Tandjong Priok. 80 s. Airman. 500 s. Mass meeting with flags, Djkurta.

1948. Postage Due Stamps of Netherlands Indies surch. **SEGEL 25 sen PORTO.**

J 68. D 2. 25 s. on 7½ c. red .. 1·50 2·00
J 69. 25 s. on 15 c. red .. 1·20 1·60

Although surcharged for use as postage due stamps the above were employed for ordinary postal use.

47. " Labour and Transport ".

48. Flag over Waves.

1948. Independence. 3rd Anniv. Imperf.

J 70. 47. 50 s. blue .. .. 1·00 1·25
J 71. 100 s. red .. .. 1·25 1·50

1949. Government's Return to Jogjakarta. Perf. or Imperf.

J 77. 48. 100 s. red 50 70
J 78. 150 s. red .. .. 70 1·00

SUMATRA

1946. Stamps of Netherlands Indies surch. **Repoeblik Indonesia** and value.

S 1. – 15 s. on 5 c. bl. (No. 465) 25 40
S 2. 19. 20 s. on 3½ c. grey .. 75 1·10
S 3. 30 s. on 1 c. violet .. 50 75
S 5. 40 s. on 2 c. purple .. 8 12
S 7. – 50 s. on 17½ c. orange (No. 431) .. 25 30
S 9. 19. 60 s. on 2½ c. bistre .. 50 70
S 10. 80 s. on 3 c. green .. 50 70
S 11. – 1 r. on 10 c. red (No. 429) 20 30

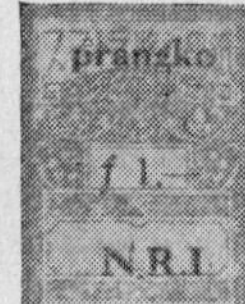

49. Ploughing. 50. Pres. Sukarno. 51.

1946. Liberation Fund.

S 17. 49. 5 s. (+25 s.) green .. 8 15
S 18. 5 s. (+25 s.) blue .. 8 12
S 19. – 15 s. (+35 s.) red .. 10 12
S 20. – 15 s. (+35 s.) blue .. 10 15
S 21. – 40 s. (+60 s.) orange 8 15
S 22. – 40 s. (+60 s.) red .. 8 15
S 23. – 40 s. (+60 s.) purple 10 15
S 24. – 40 s. (+60 s.) brown 8 15

DESIGNS—VERT. 15 s. Soldier and flag. 40 s. Oil well and factories, Palembang.

1946.

S 26. 50. 40 s. (+60 s.) red .. 8 8

1946. " FONDS KEMERDEKAAN " obliterated by one or two bars.

S 27. 49. 5 s. blue 50 75
S 28. – 40 s. red (No. S 22) .. 75 1·00

1946. As T 49 but without " FONDS KEMERDEKAAN ". Perf. or imperf.

S 29. 2 s. red 8 15
S 30. 2 s. brown 8 15
S 31. 3 s. olive 8 15
S 32. 3 s. red 5 10
S 33. 3 s. blue 50 75
S 34. 5 s. blue 5 10
S 35. 15 s. blue 8 15
S 36. 15 s. green 8 15
S 37. 40 s. purple 5 15
S 38. 40 s. blue 8 15

1947. Fiscal stamps of Japanese Occupation with blank panels optd. in black in Palembang with **prangko N.R.I.** and value as in T 51.

S 42. 51. 0 f. 50 salmon .. 75 1·25
S 43. 1 f. salmon .. 75 1·25
S 44. 2 f. salmon .. 75 1·25
S 45. 2 f. 50 salmon .. 75 1·25

1947. No. S 28 surch. with new value and bars.

S 46. 50 s. on 40 s. red .. 30 50
S 47. 1 f. on 40 s. red .. 30 50
S 48. 1 f. 50 on 40 s. red .. 30 50
S 49. 2 f. 50 on 40 s. red .. 25 35
S 50. 3 f. 50 on 40 s. red .. 25 35
S 51. 5 f. on 40 s. red .. 20 25

1947. Surch. with ornament and new value

S 63. 1 s. on 15 s. (No. S 35) .. 8 15
S 64. 5 s. on 3 s. (No. S 33) .. 5 10
S 65. 10 s. on 15 s. red (as Nos. S 35/6) 10 20
S 52. 30 s. on 40 s. (No. S 28) .. 8 12
S 66. 50 s. on 3 s. (No. S 32) .. 10 20
S 53. 50 s. on 5 s. (No. S 34) .. 25 40
S 59. 50 s. on 40 s. (No. S 28) 10 20
S 54. 1 f. on 5 s. (No. S 34) .. 15 25
S 60. 1 f. on 40 s. (No. S 28) .. 10 20
S 55. 1 f. 50 on 5 s. (No. S 34) .. 15 25
S 61. 1 f. 50 on 40 s. (No. S 28) 10 20
S 62. 2 f. 50 on 40 s. (No. S 28) 10 20
S 56. 1 r. on 40 s. (No. S 37) .. 8 12
S 57. 2 r. on 5 s. (No. S 34) .. 5 8

1947. No. S 56 surch. **50.**

S 58. 50 (r.) on 1 r. on 40 s. .. 10·00 15·00

1947. Stamps of 1946 (Nos. 69/70).

(a) Surch in large figures (5·7 mm. tall) and small square.

S 69. 10 s. on 15 s. blue .. 1·00 1·50
S 70. 20 s. on 15 s. blue .. 1·00 1·50
S 71. 30 s. on 15 s. blue .. 1·00 1·50
S 72. 1 r. on 2 s. red .. 3·00 4·50
S 88. 2 r. on 3 s. green .. 3·00 4·00
S 73. 2 f. 50 on 15 s. blue .. 2·00 3·00
S 74. 5 f. on 40 s. brown .. 3·00 4·50
S 89. 5 r. on 15 s. blue .. 2·00 3·00
S 90. 10 r. on 3 s. green .. 4·00 6·00
S 91. 20 r. on 2 s. red .. 5·00 7·50
S 92. 50 r. on 15 s. blue .. 8·00 12·00
S 93. 100 r. on 15 s. blue .. 12·00 15·00

(b) No. S 22 surch. and with penstroke through " FONDS KEMERDEKAAN ".

S 94. 150 r. on 40 s. red .. 10·00 12·00

(c) Surch in small figures (3-3½ mm. tall) and small square.

S 75. 50 s. on 5 s. blue .. 1·00 1·50
S 76. 50 s. on 15 s. blue .. 1·00 1·50
S 77. 0 f. 50 on 15 s. blue .. 1·00 1·50
S 78. 1 f. on 5 s. blue .. 80 1·25
S 79. 1 f. on 15 s. blue .. 1·00 1·50
S 80. 2 f. 50 on 5 s. blue .. 1·00 1·50
S 81. 2 f. 50 on 15 s. blue .. 1·00 1·50
S 82. 2 f. 50 on 40 s. brown .. 2·50 3·50
S 83. 5 f. on 15 s. blue .. 1·00 1·50
S 84. 5 f. on 40 s. brown .. 2·00 3·00
S 85. 2 r. 50 on 3 s. green .. 3·00 4·50
S 86. 5 r. on 15 s. blue .. 3·00 4·50
S 87. 10 r. on 3 s. green .. 4·00 6·00

1947. Air. Surch. **Pos Udara** with ornament and new value.

S 67. 10 r. on 40 s. (No. S 32) 40 60
S 68. 20 r. on 5 s. (No. S 34) .. 35 50

52. "O.R.I." = "Oeang Repoeblik Indonesia". (Indonesian Republican Money).)

1947. Change of Currency. Various stamps optd. with T 52.

(a) Stamps of Indonesia (Nos. S 96/100) and Sumatra.

S 99. D 2. 1 c. red (No. D 226) 2·00 2·75
S 101. – 1 c. green (No. 15) .. 25 40
S 149. – 1 s. on 15 s. blue (No. S 63) .. 15 25
S 102. – 2 c. green (No. 16) 25 40
S 136. – 2 s. red (No. S 29) .. 40 60
S 96. 19. 3 c. green (No. 399) 1·00 1·25
S 103. – 3 c. blue (No. 17) .. 25 40
S 137. – 3 s. green (No. S 31) 25 40
S 138. – 3 s. red (No. 32) .. 25 40
S 104. – 3½ c. red (No. 18) .. 40 60
S 97. 34. 4 c. olive (No. 464) 1·50 2·00
S 105. – 4 c. blue (No. 19) 70 1·00
S 98. – 5 c. blue (No. 465) 1·00 1·25
S 106. – 5 c. orange (No. 20) 40 60
S 132. 11. 5 s. green (No. S 17) 45 65
S 133. – 5 s. blue (No. S 18) 20 30
S 139. – 5 s. blue (No. S 34) .. 15 25
S 107. – 10 c. blue (No. 21) 1·00 1·25
S 111. – 10 c. red (No. 57) .. 20 30
S 150. – 10 s. on 15 s. red (No. S 65) .. 40 60
S 100. D 2. 15 c. red (No. D 448) 1·50 2·00
S 134. – 15 s. blue (No. S 20) 40 60
S 140. – 15 s. blue (No. S 35) 15 25
S 141. – 15 s. green (No. S 36) 25 40
S 108. – 20 c. brown (No. 22) 1·50 2·00
S 127. 19. 20 s. on 3½ c. grey (No. S 2) .. 80 1·25
S 113. – 25 c. green (No. 62) 2·00 3·00
S 109. 5. 30 c. purple (No. 23) 25 40
S 114. – 30 c. brown (No. 63) 2·00 3·00
S 128. 19. 30 s. on 1 c. violet (No. S 3) .. 1·25 2·00
S 146. – 30 s. on 40 s. red (No. S 52) .. 1·25 2·00
S 129. 19. 40 s. on 2 c. purple (No. S 4) .. 80 1·25
S 135. – 40 s. red (No. S 22) 50 75
S 142. – 40 s. brown (No. S 37) 15 25
S 110. – 50 c. brown (No. 25) 1·25 1·75
S 115. – 50 c. red (No. 66) .. 2·00 3·00

S 151. – 50 s. on 5 s. blue (No. S 53) .. 45 70
S 116. – 60 c. blue (No. 67) .. 1·25 1·75
S 117. – 80 c. red (No. 68) .. 1·50 2·25
S 118. – 1 g. violet (No. 69) 1·50 2·25
S 143. – 1 f. 50 on 40 s. red (No. S 48) .. 80 1·25
S 147. – 1 f. 50 on 40 s. red (No. S 61) .. 1·25 2·00
S 152. – 1 f. 50 on 5 s. blue (No. S 55) .. 75 1·25
S 153. – 2 r. on 5 s. blue (No. S 57) 45 70
S 144. – 2 f. 50 on 40 s. red (No. S 49) .. 80 1·25
S 148. – 2 f. 50 on 40 s. red (No. S 62) .. 1·25 2·00
S 145. – 3 f. 50 on 40 s. red (No. S 50) .. 80 1·25
S 154. – 10 r. on 40 s. red (No. S 67) .. 2·00 3·00

(b) Stamps of Japan.

S 119. – 1 s. brown (No. 317) 25 40
S 120. – 3 s. green (No. 319) 25 40
S 121. – 4 s. green (No. 320) 80 1·25
S 122. – 6 s. orange (No. 322) 40 60
S 123. – 25 s. brown (No. 329) 25 40
S 124. – 30 s. green (No. 330) 60 80
S 125. – 50 s. green and brown (No. 331) .. 25 40
S 126. 1 y. brown (No. 332) 60 80

B. UNITED STATES OF INDONESIA

53. Indonesian Flag.

ILLUSTRATIONS
British Commonwealth and all overprints and surcharges are FULL SIZE. Foreign Countries have been reduced to ¾-LINEAR.

1950. Inauguration of Republic.
554. 53. 15 s. red (20½ × 26 mm.) 15 5
555. 15 s. red (18 × 23 mm.) 1·10 15

1950. Stamps of 1949 optd. RIS.
579. 39. 1 s. grey 10 5
580. 2 s. purple 10 5
581. 2½ s. brown 20 10
582. 3 s. red 10 5
583. 4 s. green 20 8
584. 5 s. blue 10 5
585. 7½ s. green 10 5
586. 10 s. mauve 10 5
587. 12½ s. red 10 5
588. 40. 20 s. black .. .. 1·10 1·10
589. 25 s. blue 8 5
590. – 30 s. red 75 80
591. – 40 s. green 15 10
592. – 45 s. purple 25 15
593. – 50 s. brown 15 5
594. – 60 s. brown 80 80
595. – 80 s. red 50 12
596. – 1 r. violet 40 8
597. – 2 r. green .. .. 40·00 28·00
598. – 3 r. purple .. .. 38·00 13·00
599. – 5 r. chocolate .. .. 12·00 6·00
600. – 10 r. black .. .. 20·00 6·00
601. – 25 r. brown .. .. 18·00 3·75

C. INDONESIAN REPUBLIC

54. Indonesian Arms.

55. Map and Torch.

1950. Proclamation of Independence. 5th Anniv.
602. 54. 15 s. red 20 5
603. 25 s. green 40 15
604. 1 r. sepia .. .. 2·10 20

1951. Asiatic Olympic Games, New Delhi.
605. 55. 5 s. + 3 s. green .. 5 5
606. 10 s. + 5 s. blue .. 5 5
607. 20 s. + 5 s. red 5 5
608. 30 s. + 10 s. brown .. 8 8
609. 35 s. + 10 s. blue .. 60 45

56.

57. G.P.O., Bandung.

58. "Spirit of Indonesia".

59. President Sukarno.

1951.
610. 56. 1 s. grey 5 5
611. 2 s. magenta 10 10
612. 2½ s. brown .. .. 1·25 10
613. 5 s. red 5 5
614. 7½ s. green 5 5
615. 10 s. blue 12 5
616. 15 s. violet 10 5
618. 20 s. red 12 5
619. 25 s. green 12 5
620. 57. 30 s. red 5 5
621. 35 s. violet 5 5
622. 40 s. green 5 5
623. 45 s. purple 10 5
624. 50 s. brown .. .. 2·25 5
625. 58. 60 s. brown 5 5
626. 70 s. grey 5 5
627. 75 s. blue 5 5
628. 80 s. purple 5 5
629. 90 s. green 5 5
630. 59. 1 r. mauve 5 5
631. 1 r. 25 orange .. 5 5
632. 1 r. 50 brown 5 5
633. 2 r. green 5 5
634. 2 r. 50 lake 5 5
635. 3 r. blue 5 5
636. 4 r. olive 5 5
637. 5 r. brown 5 5
638. 6 r. purple 5 5
639. 10 r. slate 5 5
640. 15 r. yellow 5 5
641. 20 r. slate 5 5
642. 25 r. red 5 5
643. 40 r. green 8 5
644. 50 r. violet 12 5

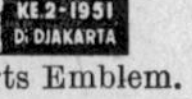
60. Sports Emblem.

61. Doves.

1951. National Sports Festival.
655. 60. 5 s. + 3 s. green .. 5 5
656. 10 s. + 5 s. blue .. 5 5
657. 20 s. + 5 s. orange .. 5 5
658. 30 s. + 10 s. sepia .. 5 5
659. 35 s. + 10 s. blue .. 10 5

1951. U.N. Day.
660. 61. 7½ s. green 85 15
661. 10 s. violet 20 20
662. 20 s. orange 75 40
663. 30 s. red 85 60
664. 35 s. blue 85 65
665. 1 r. sepia .. .. 5·50 90

1953. Natural Disasters Relief Fund. Surch. **1953 BENTJANA ALAM + 10 s.**
666. 57. 35 s. + 10 s. violet .. 5 5

62. Melati Flowers.

63. Merapi Volcano in Eruption.

1953. Mothers' Day and Indonesian Women's Congress. 25th Anniv.
667. 62. 50 s. green .. .. 1·75 10

1954. Natural Disasters Fund.
668. 63. 15 s. + 10 s. blue-green 5 5
669. 35 s. + 15 s. violet .. 5 5
670. 50 s. + 25 s. red .. 8 8
671. 75 s. + 25 s. blue .. 10 10
672. 1 r. + 25 s. red 15 20
673. 2 r. + 50 s. sepia .. 40 35
674. 3 r. + 1 r. bronze-green 3·75 3·00
675. 5 r. + 2 r. 50 brown .. 4·50 3·25

64. Girls with Musical Instruments.

65. Globe and Doves.

1954. Child Welfare.
676. 64. 10 s. + 10 s. purple .. 5 5
677. – 15 s. + 10 s. green .. 5 5
678. – 35 s. + 15 s. magenta .. 5 5
679. – 50 s. + 15 s. lake .. 5 5
680. – 75 s. + 25 s. blue .. 5 5
681. – 1 r. + 25 s. red 10 10
DESIGNS: 15 s. Menangkabau boy and girl performing Umbrella Dance. 35 s. Girls playing "Tjongkak". 50 s. Boy on bamboo stilts. 75 s. Ambonese boys playing flutes. 1 r. Srimpi dancing girl.

1955. Asian-African Conf., Bandung.
682. 65. 15 s. black 12 12
683. 35 s. brown 20 20
684. 50 s. red 70 12
685. 75 s. turquoise .. 1·25 50

66. Semaphore Signaller.

67. Proclamation of Independence.

1955. National Scout Jamboree.
686. – 15 s. + 10 s. green .. 5 5
687. 66. 35 s. + 15 s. blue .. 5 5
688. – 50 s. + 25 s. red .. 5 5
689. – 75 s. + 25 s. brown .. 5 5
690. – 1 r. + 50 s. violet .. 10 10
DESIGNS: 15 s. Indonesian scout badge. 50 s. Scouts round campfire. 75 s. Scout feeding baby deer. 1 r. Scout saluting.

1955. Independence. 10th Anniv.
691. 67. 15 s. green 15 12
692. 35 s. blue 20 20
693. 50 s. brown 50 8
694. 75 s. maroon 35 20

68. Postmaster Suparto.

69. Electors.

1955. Indonesian Post Office. 10th Anniv.
695. 68. 15 s. brown 10 10
696. 35 s. red 25 15
697. 50 s. blue .. .. 1·40 12
698. 75 s. green 75 20

1955. Indonesian Elections.
699. 69. 15 s. purple 20 12
700. 35 s. green 30 25
701. 50 s. red 80 10
702. 75 s. blue 30 15

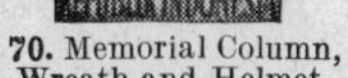
70. Memorial Column, Wreath and Helmet.

71. Weaving.

1955. Heroes' Day.
703. 70. 25 s. green 30 10
704. 50 s. blue 60 15
705. 1 r. red .. .. 1·60 5

1956. Blind Relief Fund.
706. 71. 15 s. + 10 s. green .. 5 5
707. – 35 s. + 15 s. brown .. 5 5
708. – 50 s. + 25 s. red .. 20 20
709. – 75 s. + 50 s. blue .. 15 15
DESIGNS—VERT. 35 s. Basketwork. 50 s. Map reading. 75 s. Reading.

72. Torch and Book.

73. Dwarf Deer.

1956. Asian and African Students' Conf., Bandung.
710. 72. 25 s. blue 40 8
711. 50 s. red .. .. 1·00 20
712. 1 r. green 80 15

1956.
713. 73. 5 s. grey-blue 5 5
714. 10 s. brown 5 5
715. 15 s. purple 5 5
716. – 20 s. green 5 5
717. – 25 s. maroon 5 5
718. – 30 s. orange 5 5
719. – 35 s. blue 5 5
720. – 40 s. green 5 5
721. – 45 s. purple 10 5
722. – 50 s. bistre 5 5
723. – 60 s. indigo 5 5
724. – 70 s. red 5 5
725. – 75 s. sepia 5 5
726. – 80 s. red 5 5
727. – 90 s. green 8 8
DESIGNS: 20 s. to 30 s. Otter. 35 s. to 45 s. Scaly ant-eater. 50 s. to 70 s. Buffalo. 75 s. to 90 s. Rhinoceros.

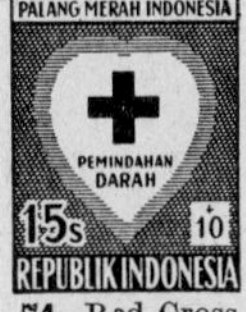
74. Red Cross.

75.

1956. Red Cross Fund.
728. 74. 10 s. + 10 s. red and blue 5 5
729. 15 s. + 10 s. red & carmine 5 5
730. – 35 s. + 15 s. red & brown 5 5
731. – 50 s. + 15 s. red & green 5 5
732. – 75 s. + 25 s. red & orge. 8 8
733. – 1 r. + 25 s. red & violet 10 10
DESIGNS: 35 s., 50 s. Blood transfusion bottle. 75 s., 1 r. Hands and drop of blood.

1956. Djakarta. 200th Anniv.
734. 75. 15 s. green 10 5
735. 35 s. purple 25 15
736. 50 s. slate 80 20
737. 75 s. claret .. .. 1·00 8

76. Crippled Child.

77. Telegraph Key and Tape.

78. Two men with Savings-box.

1957. Cripples' Rehabilitation Fund. Inscr. "UNTUK PENDERITA TJATJAT".
738. – 10 s. + 10 s. blue .. 5 5
739. – 15 s. + 10 s. brown .. 5 5
740. – 35 s. + 15 s. red .. 5 5
741. 76. 50 s. + 15 s. violet .. 5 5
742. – 75 s. + 25 s. green .. 8 5
743. – 1 r. + 25 s. crimson .. 12 10
DESIGNS: 10 s. One-legged woman painting cloth. 15 s. One-handed artist. 35 s. One-handed machinist. 75 s. Doctor tending cripple. 1 r. Man writing with artificial arm.

1957. Cent. of Telegraphs in Indonesia.
744. 77. 10 s. red 80 10
745. 15 s. blue 10 10
746. 25 s. black 15 10
747. 50 s. brown 20 12
748. 75 s. green 25 5

1957. Co-operation Day. Inscr. "HARI KOOPERASI".
749. 78. 10 s. blue 10 10
750. – 15 s. red 15 15
751. 78. 50 s. green 20 8
752. – 1 r. violet 55 5
DESIGN: 15 s., 1 r. "Co-operative Prosperity" (hands holding ear of rice and cotton).

79. Kembodja ("Plumeria acuminata").

80. Convair Airliner.

81. "Helping Hands".

82. Thomas Cup.

1957. Various Charity Funds. Floral designs Multicoloured.
753. 10 s. + 10 s. Type 79 .. 20 20
754. 15 s. + 10 s. Michelia .. 20 20
755. 35 s. + 15 s. Sunflower .. 5 5
756. 50 s. + 15 s. Jasmin .. 5 5
757. 75 s. + 50 s. Orchid .. 5 5
INSCRIPTIONS: 15 s. Tjempaka-kuning. 35 s. Matahari. 50 s. Melati. 75 s. Larat.

1958. National Aviation Day. Inscr. "HARI PENERBANGAN NASIONAL 9-4-1958".

758. **80.** 10 s. brown 5 5
759. – 15 s. blue 5 5
760. – 35 s. orange 5 5
761. **80.** 50 s. turquoise 10 8
762. – 75 s. slate 25 10

DESIGNS: 15 s. "Skeeter" Helicopter. 35s. Miles "Magister" training 'plane. 75 s. D. H. "Vampire" jet fighter.

1958. Indonesian Orphans Welfare Fund Inscr. "ANAK PIATU".

763. **81.** 10 s.+10 s. blue .. 5 5
764. – 15 s.+10 s. red .. 5 5
765. **81.** 35 s.+15 s. green .. 5 5
766. – 50 s.+25 s. drab .. 5 5
767. **81.** 75 s.+50 s. red-brown 8 5
768. – 1 r.+50 s. brown .. 8 5

DESIGN: 15 s., 50 s., 1 r. Girl and boy orphans.

1958. Indonesian Victory in Thomas Cup World Badminton Championships, Singapore.

769. **82.** 25 s. red 5 5
770. 50 s. orange 5 5
771. 1 r. brown 5 5

83. Satelite encircling Globe. **84.** Racing Cyclist.

1958. Int. Geophysical Year

785. **83.** 10 s. pink, green & blue 20 5
786. 15 s. drab, violet & grey 5 5
787. 35 s. blue, sepia & pink 5 8
788. 50 s. brn., blue & drab 10 10
789. 75 s. lilac, blk. & yellow 10 5

1958. Tour of Java Cycle Race.

790. **84.** 25 s. blue 5 5
791. 50 s. red 8 8
792. 1 r. grey 20 5

85. "Human Rights".

86. Wild Boar.

87. Indonesian Scout Badge.

1958. Declaration of Human Rights. 10th Anniv. Inscr. "10-XII 1948-'58".

793. **85.** 10 s. sepia 5 5
794. – 15 s. brown 5 5
795. – 35 s. blue 5 5
796. – 50 s. bistre 8 5
797. – 75 s. green 10 5

DESIGNS: 15 s. Hands grasping "Flame of Freedom". 35 s. Native holding candle. 50 s. Family acclaiming "Flame of Freedom". 75 s. "Flame" superimposed on figure "10".

1959. Animal Protection Campaign.

798. **86.** 10 s. sepia and olive .. 5 5
799. – 15 s. sepia and chestnut 5 5
800. – 20 s. sepia and green .. 5 5
801. – 50 s. sepia and brown .. 5 5
802. – 75 s. sepia and red .. 5 5
803. – 1 r. black and blue-green 10 5

ANIMALS: 15 s. Anoa (buffalo). 20 s. Orang-utan. 50 s. Rhinoceros. 75 s. Komodo lizard. 1 r. Tapir.

1959. 10th World Scout Jamboree, Manila. Inscr. as in T **48**. Badges in red.

804. **87.** 10 s.+5 s. bistre .. 5 5
805. – 15 s.+10 s. green .. 5 5
806. **87.** 20 s.+10 s. slate-violet 5 5
807. – 50 s.+25 s. olive .. 5 5
808. **87.** 75 s.+35 s. brown .. 10 8
809. – 1 r.+50 s. slate .. 12 12

DESIGN: 15 s., 50 s., 1 r. Scout badge within compass.

88.

89. Factory and Girder.

1959. Re-adoption of 1945 Constitution.

810. **88.** 20 s. red and blue .. 5 5
811. 50 s. black and red .. 5 5
812. 75 s. red and brown .. 5 5
813. 1 r. 50 black and green 12 5

1959. 11th Colombo Plan Conf., Djakarta.

814. **89.** 15 s. black and green .. 5 5
815. – 20 s. black and orange .. 5 5
816. **89.** 50 s. black and red .. 5 5
817. – 75 s. black and blue .. 5 5
818. – 1 r. 15 black and purple 5 5

DESIGNS: 20 s., 75 s. Cogwheel and diesel-train. 1 r. 15. Forms of transport and communications.

90.

91. Refugee Camp.

1960. Indonesian Youth Conf., Bandung Inscr. "1960".

819. **90.** 15 s.+5 s. sep. & bistre 5 5
820. – 20 s.+10 s. sep. & grn. 5 5
821. **90.** 50 s.+25 s. pur. & blue 5 5
822. – 75 s.+35 s. grn. & bis. 5 5
823. – 1 r. 15+50 s. blk. & red 5 5

DESIGNS: 20 s., 75 s. Test-tubes in frame. 1 r. 15, Youth wielding manifesto.

1960. World Refugee Year. Centres in black.

824. **91.** 10 s. purple 5 5
825. – 15 s. ochre 5 5
826. – 20 s. chestnut 5 5
827. **91.** 50 s. green 5 5
828. – 75 s. blue 5 5
829. – 1 r. 15 red 5 5

DESIGNS: 15 s., 75 s. Outcast family. 20 s., 1 r. 15, "Care of refugees" (refugee with protecting hands).

92. Tea plants.

93. Mosquito.

1960. Agricultural Products.

830. – 5 s. grey 5 5
831. – 10 s. brown 5 5
832. – 15 s. maroon 5 5
833. – 20 s. yellow-brown .. 5 5
834. **92.** 25 s. green 5 5
835. – 50 s. blue 5 5
836. – 75 s. red 5 5
837. – 1 r. 15 crimson 5 5

DESIGNS: 5 s. Oil palm. 10 s. Sugar cane. 15 s. Coffee plant. 20 s. Tobacco plant. 50 s. Coconut palm. 75 s. Rubber trees. 1 r. 15, Rice plants.

1960. World Health Day.

838. **93.** 25 s. red 5 5
839. 50 s. chestnut 5 5
840. 75 s. green 5 5
841. 3 r. orange 12 5

94. Socialist Emblem.

95. Pres. Sukarno and Workers Hoeing.

1960. 3rd Socialist Day. Inscr. as in T **94**.

842. **94.** 10 s.+10 s. brn. & black 5 5
843. – 15 s.+15 s. mar. & black 5 5
844. – 20 s.+20 s. blue & black 5 5
845. – 50 s.+25 s. black & brn. 5 5
846. – 75 s.+25 s. black & grn. 12 5
847. – 3 r.+50 s. black & red 20 5

DESIGNS: 15 s. Emblem similar to T **94** within plants. 20 s. Lotus flower. 50 s. Boy and girl. 75 s. Ceremonial watering of plant. 3 r. Mother with children.

1961. National Development Plan.

848. **95.** 75 s. black 8 5

1961. Flood Relief Fund. Surch. **BENTJANA ALAM 1961** and premium.

849. 15 s.+10 s. mar. (No. 832) 5 5
850. 20 s.+15 s. yell.-brn. (No. 833) 5 5
851. 75 s.+25 s. red (No. 836) 5 5

96. Bull Race.

1961. Tourist Publicity.

852. – 10 s. purple 5 5
853. – 15 s. olive-grey 5 5
854. **96.** 20 s. orange 5 5
855. – 25 s. red 5 5
856. – 50 s. lake 5 5
857. – 75 s. brown 8 5
858. – 1 r. green 10 8
859. – 1 r. 50 yellow-brown .. 20 10
860. – 2 r. blue 25 15
861. – 3 r. grey 35 25

DESIGNS: 10 s. Ambonese boat. 15 s. Tangkuban Perahu crater. 25 s. Daja dancer. 50 s. Toradja houses. 75 s. Balinese temple. 1 r. Lake Toba. 1 r. 50, Bali dancer. 2 r. "Buffalo Hole" (gorge). 3 r. Borobudur temple.

97. Stadium.

1961. Thomas Cup World Badminton Championships.

863. **97.** 75 s. lilac and blue .. 5 5
864. 1 r. olive and green .. 5 5
865. 3 r. salmon and blue 15 10

98. "United Efforts".

1961. Independence. 16th Anniv.

866. **98.** 75 s. violet and blue .. 5 5
867. 1 r. 50 green and cream 8 5
868. 3 r. red and salmon .. 20 12

99. Sultan Hasanuddin.

1961. National Independence Heroes. Portraits in sepia; inscriptions in black.

869. – 20 s. olive 5 5
870. **98.** 25 s. grey-olive .. 5 5
871. – 30 s. violet 5 5
872. – 40 s. orange-brown .. 5 5
873. – 50 s. myrtle 5 5
874. – 60 s. blue-green .. 5 5
875. – 75 s. brown 5 5
876. – 1 r. blue 5 5
877. – 1 r. 25 olive-green .. 5 5
878. – 1 r. 50 emerald .. 8 5
879. – 2 r. red 5 5
880. – 2 r. 50 claret 10 5
881. – 3 r. slate 12 5
882. – 4 r. olive-green .. 15 8
883. – 4 r. 50 purple 5 5
884. – 5 r. red 15 10
885. – 6 r. ochre 5 5
886. – 7 r. 50 violet-blue .. 5 5
887. – 10 r. green 8 8
888. – 15 r. orange 8 8

PORTRAITS: 20 s. Abdul Muis. 30 s. Surjopranoto. 40 s. Tengku Tjhik Di Tiro. 50 s. Teuku Umar. 60 s. K. H. Samanhudi. 75 s. Capt. Pattimura. 1 r. Raden Adjeng Kartini. 1 r. 25, K. H. Achmad Dahlan. 1 r. 50, Tuanku Imam Bondjol. 2 r. Si Singamangaradja XII. 2 r. 50, Mohammed Husni Thamriu. 3 r. Ki Hadjar Dewantoro. 4 r. Gen. Sudirman. 4 r. 50, Dr. G. S. S. J. Ratulangie. 5 r. Pangeran Diponegoro. 6 r. Dr. Setysbudi. 7 r. 50, H. O. S. Tjokroaminoto. 10 r. K. H. Agus Salim. 15 r. Dr. Soetomo.

100. Census Emblems.

101. Nenas (pineapples).

1961. 1st Indonesian Census.

889. **100.** 75 s. purple 15 5

1916. Charity Fruits.

890. **101.** 20 s.+10 s. yellow, red and blue 5 5
891. – 75 s. + 25 s. maroon, green and slate .. 8 5
892. – 3 r.+1 r. red, yell. & grn. 15 12

FRUITS: 75 s. Manggis. 3 r. Rambutan.

102. Djataju.

DANCERS: 40 s. Hanoman. 1 r. Dasamuka. 1 r. 50, Kidang Kentjana. 3 r. Dewi Sinta. 5 r. Rama.

1962. Ramayana Dancers.

893. **102.** 30 s. brown and ochre .. 5 5
894. – 40 s. violet and purple .. 5 5
895. – 1 r. maroon and green .. 5 5
896. – 1 r. 50 green and pink .. 5 5
897. – 3 r. blue and green .. 5 5
898. – 5 r. chocolate and buff .. 10 10

103. Aerial View of Mosque.

DESIGN: 40s., 3 r. Ground-level view of Mosque.

1962. Construction of Istiqlal Mosque.

899. **103.** 30 s.+20 s. blue & yell. 5 5
900. – 40 s.+20 s. red & yellow 5 5
901. **103.** 1 r. 50+50 s. brn. & yell. 8 5
902. – 3 r.+1 r. green & yellow 12 8

104. Games Emblem.

105. Campaign Emblem.

1962. 4th Asian Games. Djarkata. Inscr. as in T **104**.

903. – 10 s. green and yellow .. 5 5
904. – 15 s. olive and ochre .. 5 5
905. – 20 s. mauve & turquoise 5 5
906. – 25 s. brown & turquoise 5 5
907. – 30 s. blue-green and buff 5 5
908. – 40 s. blue and grey .. 5 5
909. – 50 s. chocolate and drab 5 5
910. – 60 s. purple & grey-blue 5 5
911. – 70 s. brn. & Venetian red 5 5
912. – 75 s. brown and orange 5 5
913. – 1 r. violet and blue .. 5 5
914. **104.** 1 r. 25 blue and magenta 5 5
915. – 1 r. 50 red and mauve .. 5 5
916. – 1 r. 75 red and rose .. 5 5
917. **104.** 2 r. sepia and green .. 5 5
918. – 2 r. 50 blue and green .. 5 5
919. **104.** 3 r. black and orange .. 5 5
920. – 4 r. 50 green and red .. 5 5
921. **104.** 5 r. bronze and bistre .. 5 5
922. – 6 r. chestnut and ochre 8 5
923. – 7 r. 50 brown and pink .. 8 5
924. – 10 r. ultramarine & blue 10 8
925. – 15 r. violet 15 10
926. – 20 r. myrtle and bistre .. 20 12

DESIGNS—VERT. 10 s. Basketball. 20 s. Weight-lifting. 40 s. Throwing the discus. 50 s. Diving. 60 s. Football. 70 s. Press building. 75 s. Boxing. 1 r. Volleyball. 1 r. 50, Badminton. 1 r. 75, Wrestling. 2 r. 50, Shooting. 4 r. 50, Hockey. 6 r. Water polo. 7 r. 50, Tennis. 10 r. Table-tennis. 15 r. Cycling. 20 r. "Welcome" monument. HORIZ. 15 s. Main stadium. 25 s. Hotel Indonesia. 30 s. Road improvement.

1962. Malaria Eradication.

927. **105.** 40 s. blue and violet .. 5 5
928. 1 r. 50 orange & choc. 5 5
929. 3 r. green and blue .. 5 5
930. 6 r. violet and black 8 5

On the 1 r. 50 and 6 r. the inscription is at top.

106. National Monument.

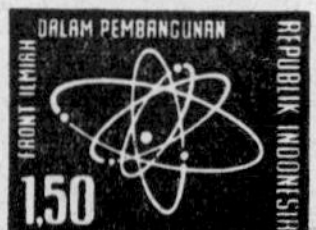

107. Atomic Symbol.

1962. National Monument.
931. 106. 1 r.+50 c. chest. & blk. 5 5
932. – 1 r. 50+50 c. grn. & blue 5 5
933. 106. 3 r.+1 r. magenta & grn. 5 5
934. – 6 r.+1 r. 50 blue & red 8 8
DESIGN: 1 r. 50, 6 r. Aerial view of Monument.

1962. "Science for Development".
935. 107. 1 r. 50 blue and yellow .. 5 5
936. 4 r. 50 red and yellow .. 8 5
937. 6 r. green and yellow .. 12 8

108. "Phalaenopis amabilis".

109. West Irian Monument, Djakarta.

1962. Charity. Orchids. Multicoloured.
938. 1 r.+50 s. "Vanda tricolor" 5 5
939. 1 r. 50+50 s. Type 108 .. 5 5
940. 3 r.+1 r. "Dendrobium phalaenopsis" .. 5 5
941. 6 r.+1 r. 50 "Paphiopedilum praestaus" 8 8
Nos. 938 and 941 are horiz.

1963. Construction of West Irian Monument.
942. 109. 1 r.+50 c. green & red .. 5 5
943. 1 r. 50+50 c. sepia, black and magenta .. 5 5
944. 3 r.+1 4. brown & blue 5 5
945. 6 r.+1 r. 50 bis. & grn. 5 5

110. Conference Emblem.

111. Rice Sheaves.

1963. 12th Pacific Area Travel Association Conference, Djakarta.
946. 110. 1 r. blue and green .. 5 5
947. – 1 r. 50 blue and olive .. 5 5
948. 110. 3 r. blue and brown .. 5 5
949. – 6 r. blue and red-orange 5 5
DESIGNS: 1 r. 50, Prambanan Temple and Mt. Merapi. 6 r. Balinese Meru in Pura Taman Ajun.

1963. Freedom from Hunger.
950. 111. 1 r. yellow and blue .. 5 5
951. – 1 r. 50 blue and green .. 5 5
952. 111. 3 r. yellow and red .. 5 5
953. – 6 r. orange and black .. 5 5
DESIGN—HORIZ. 1 r. 50, 6 r. Tractor. Nos. 950/1 are inscr. "CONTRE LA FAIM". Nos. 952/3, "FREEDOM FROM HUNGER".

112. Lobster.

1963. Marine Life. Multicoloured.
954. 1 r. T 112 .. .. .. 5 5
955. 1 r. 50 Little tuna .. 5 5
956. 3 r. Red snapper .. 5 5
957. 6 r. Chinese pomfret .. 5 5

113. Conference Emblem.

1963. Asian-African Journalists' Conference.
958. 113. 1 r. red and blue .. 5 5
959. – 1 r. 50 brown & lavender 5 5
960. – 3 r. blue, black & olive 5 5
961. – 6 r. salmon and black .. 5 5
DESIGNS—HORIZ. 1 r. 50, Pen, emblem and map. VERT. 3 r. Pen, Globe and broken chain. 6 r. Pen severing chain around Globe.

114. Indonesia, from Atjek to Merauke. 115. Centenary Emblem.

1963. Acquisition of West Irian (West New Guinea).
962. 114. 1 r. 50 orange-red, red and black 5 5
963. – 4 r. 50 blue, green and grey-purple 5 5
964. – 6 r. brown, yellow & grn. 5 5
DESIGNS: 4 r. 50, Parachutist. 6 r. Bird of Paradise.

1963. Red Cross Cent.
965. 115. 1 r. red and green .. 5 5
966. – 1 r. 50 red and blue .. 5 5
967. 115. 3 r. red and slate .. 5 5
968. – 6 r. red and bistre .. 5 5
DESIGN: 1 r. 50, 6 r. Red Cross (Inscr. "CENTENARY OF THE INTERNATIONAL RED CROSS".).

116. Volcano.

117. Bank of Indonesia, Djakarta.

1963. Bali Volcano Disaster Fund.
969. 116. 4 r. (+2 r.) red .. 5 5
970. 6 r. (+3 r.) green .. 5 5
Nos. 969/70 were issued in sheets with se-tenant (imperf. between) label attached inscr. "Bantulah" etc., and with premium.

1963. National Banking Day.
971. 117. 1 r. 75 purple and blue 5 5
972. – 4 r. green & olive-yell. 5 5
973. 117. 6 r. brown and green .. 5 5
974. – 12 r. purple and orange 5 5
DESIGN—VERT. 4 r., 12 r. Daneswara, God of Prosperity.

118. Athletes with Banners.

1963. Games of the New Emerging Forces, Djakarta.
975. 118. 1 r. 25 sepia and violet 5 5
976. – 1 r. 75 olive and buff .. 5 5
977. – 4 r. sepia and emerald 5 5
978. – 6 r. sepia and brown .. 5 5
979. – 10 r. sepia and green .. 5 5
980. – 12 r. olive and crimson 5 5
981. – 25 r. ultramarine & blue 5 5
982. – 50 r. sepia and red .. 5 5
DESIGNS: 1 r. 75, "Pendet" dance. 4 r. Conference Hall, Djakarta. 6 r. Archery. 10 r. Badminton. 12 r. Throwing the javelin. 25 r. Sailing. 50 r. "Ganefo" torch.

119. "Papilio blumei" (butterfly).

120. Pres. Sukarno.

1963. Social Day. Butterflies. Multicoloured.
983. 1 r. 75+50 s. Type 119 .. 5 5
984. 4 r.+1 r. "Charaxes dehaani" 5 5
985. 6 r.+1 r. 50 "Graphium" .. 5 5
986. 12 r.+3 r. "Troides amphrysus" 5 5

1964.
987. 120. 6 r. blue and brown .. 5 5
988. 12 r. purple and bistre 5 5
989. 20 r. orange and blue .. 5 5
990. 30 r. blue and orange .. 5 5
991. 40 r. brown and green 5 5
992. 50 r. green and red .. 5 5
993. 75 r. red and violet .. 5 5
994. 100 r. brown and grey 5 5
995. 250 r. grey and blue .. 5 5
996. 500 r. gold and red .. 10 5

121. Lorry and Trailer.

122. Rameses II, Abu Simbel.

1964.
997. – 1 r. purple 5 5
998. 121. 1 r. 25 brown .. 5 5
999. – 1 r. 75 turquoise-blue 5 5
1000. – 2 r. red 5 5
1001. – 2 r. 50 blue 5 5
1002. – 4 r. green 5 5
1003. – 5 r. drab 5 5
1004. – 7 r. 50 emerald .. 5 5
1005. – 10 r. orange 5 5
1006. – 15 r. indigo 5 5
1007. – 25 r. lavender .. 5 5
1008. – 35 r. chestnut .. 5 5
DESIGNS—HORIZ. 1 r. Ox-cart. 1 r. 75, Freighter. 2 r. "Electra" airliner. 4 r. Cycle-postman. 5 r. Dakota aircraft. 7 r. 50, Teletypist. 10 r. Diesel train. 15 r. Liner. 25 r. Convair "Coronado" airliner. 35 r. Telephone operator. VERT. 2 r. 50, Buginese sailing ship.

1964. Nubian Monuments Preservation. Monuments in olive-brown.
1009. 122. 4 r. drab 5 5
1010. – 6 r. blue 5 5
1011. 122. 12 r. pink 5 5
1012. – 18 r. green 5 5
DESIGN: 6 r., 18 r., Trajan' Kiosk, Philae.

123. Stamps of Netherlands Indies and Indonesia.

1964. Stamp Centenary.
1013. 123. 10 r. multicoloured .. 5 5

124. Indonesian Pavilion at Fair.

1964. New York World's Fair.
1014. 124. 25 r. red, blue & silver 5 5
1015. 50 r. red, turq. & gold 15 5

125. Thomas Cup.

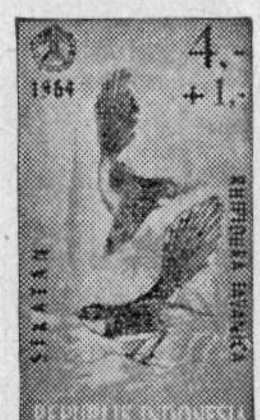

127. Java Fantail Flycatcher.

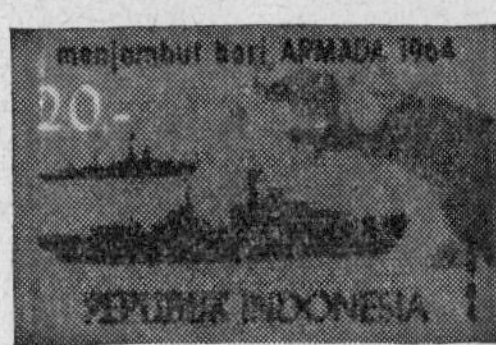

126. Destroyers.

1964. Thomas Cup World Badminton Championships.
1016. 125. 25 r. gold, red and grn. 5 5
1017. 50 r. gold, red and blue 5 5
1018. 75 r. gold, red & violet 10 10

1964. Indonesian Navy.
1019. 125. 20 r. brown & yellow 5 5
1020. – 30 r. black and red .. 5 5
1021. – 40 r. blue and green 10 10
DESIGNS: 30 r. Submarine. 40 r. Torpedo-boat.

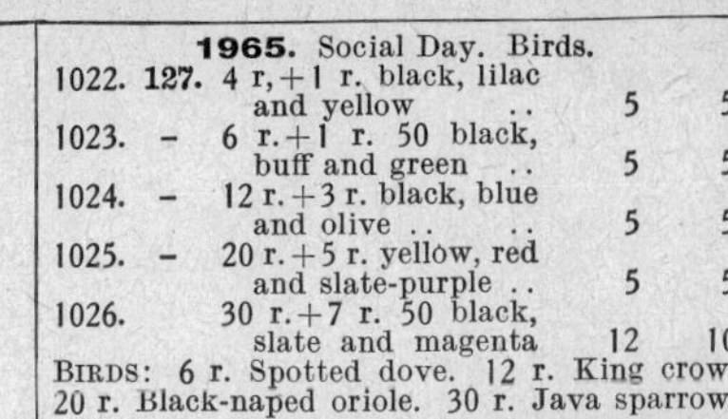

1965. Social Day. Birds.
1022. 127. 4 r.+1 r. black, lilac and yellow .. 5 5
1023. – 6 r.+1 r. 50 black, buff and green .. 5 5
1024. – 12 r.+3 r. black, blue and olive .. 5 5
1025. – 20 r.+5 r. yellow, red and slate-purple .. 5 5
1026. 30 r.+7 r. 50 black, slate and magenta 12 10
BIRDS: 6 r. Spotted dove. 12 r. King crow. 20 r. Black-naped oriole. 30 r. Java sparrow.

128. Map and Mosque.

129. Scroll in Hand.

1965. Afro-Asian Islamic Conf., Bandung.
1027. 128. 10 r. blue and violet .. 5 5
1028. – 15 r. chestnut & orange 5 5
1029. 128. 25 r. green and brown .. 5 5
1030. – 50 r. slate-purple & red 12 8
DESIGN: 15 r., 50 r. Mosque and handclasp.

1965. 1st Afro-Asian Conf., Bandung. 10th Anniv.
1031. 129. 15 r. red and silver .. 5 5
1032. – 25 r. gold, verm. & turq. 5 5
1033. 129. 50 r. ultramarine & gold 5 5
1034. – 75 r. gold, verm. & lilac 5 5
DESIGN: 25 r., 75 r. Conference 10th-anniv. emblem.

1965. Conf. of "New Emerging Forces", Djakarta. T 120additionally inscr. "Conefo". Value, "Conefo" and frame in red; portrait colour given.
1035. 1 r.+1 r. chestnut .. 5 5
1036. 1 r. 25+1 r. 25 red .. 5 5
1037. 1 r. 75+1 r. 75 slate-purple 5 5
1038. 2 r.+2 r. bronze .. 5 5
1039. 2 r. 50+2 r. 50 brown .. 5 5
1040. 4 r.+3 r. 50 blue 5 5
1041. 6 r.+4 r. green 5 5
1042. 10 r.+5 r. brown 5 5
1043. 12 r.+5 r. 50 orange .. 5 5
1044. 15 r.+7 r. 50 turquoise .. 5 5
1045. 20 r.+10 r. sepia 5 5
1046. 25 r.+10 r. violet 5 5
1047. 40 r.+15 r. purple .. 5 5
1048. 50 r.+15 r. violet 5 5
1049. 100 r.+25 r. brown .. 5 5

130. Makara Mask and Rays.

131. "Happy Family".

1965. Campaign against Cancer.
1050. 130. 20 r.+10 r. red and blue 5 5
1051. 30 r.+15 r. blue and red 5 5

1965. The State's Five Principles and Republic. 20th Anniv.
1052. 131. 10 r.+5 r. yellow, black and chestnut .. 5 5
1053. – 20 r.+10 r. red, black and yellow .. 5 5
1054. – 25 r.+10 r. green, black and red 5 5
1055. – 40 r.+15 r. black, red and blue 5 5
1056. – 50 r.+15 r. yellow, black and mauve .. 5 5
DESIGNS ("State's Principles"): 20 r. "Humanitarianism" (globe and clasped hands). 25 r. "Nationalism" (map and garland). 40 r. "Democracy" (council meeting). 50 r. "Belief in God" (churches and mosques).

132. Samudra Beach Hotel.

1965. Tourist Hotels.

1060. 132. 10 r.+5 r. blue & turq. 5 5
1061. – 25 r.+10 r. violet, black and green 5 5
1062. 132. 40 r.+15 r. chocolate, black and ultramarine 5 5
1063. – 80r.+20r. pur. & orge. 5 5

DESIGN: 25 r., 80 r. Ambarrukmo Palace Hotel.

133. "Gloriosa superb". 134. Pres. Sukarno.

1965. Flowers. Multicoloured. Inscr. "1965" and with commas and dashes after figures of value.

1064. 30 r.+10 r. Type **133** .. 5 5
1065. 40 r.+15 r. "Hibiscus tiliaceus" 5 5
1066. 80 r.+20 r. "Impatiens balsamina" 5 5
1067. 100 r.+25 r. "Lagerstroemia indica" 5 5

See also Nos. 1108/1116.

(Currency revalued. 100 (old) rupiahs = 1 (new) rupiah.)

1965. Revalued Currency. Optd **'65 Sen.**

(a) On Nos. 989/94.

1068. 120. (20) s. on 20 r... .. 5 5
1069. (30) s. on 30 r... .. 5 5
1070. (40) s. on 40r. .. 5 5
1071. (50) s. on 50 r... .. 5 5
1072. (75) s. on 75c. .. 5 5
1073. (100) s. on 100 r. .. 10 8

(b) On Nos. 1005/7.

1074. – (10) s. on 10 r. .. 5 5
1075. – (15) s. on 15 r... .. 5 5
1076. – (25) s. on 25 r... .. 5 5

1966. Revalued Currency. Inscr. "1967" (12 r.) or "1966" (others). Values and frames turquoise-green (12 r., 25 r.) or sepia (others); portrait and country name in colour given.

1077. 134. 1 s. blue 5 5
1078. 3 s. olive 5 5
1079. 5 s. red 5 5
1080. 8 s. turquoise 5 5
1081. 10 s. blue 5 5
1082. 15 s. black 5 5
1083. 20 s. green 5 5
1084. 25 s. brown 5 5
1085. 30 s. blue 5 5
1086. 40 s. chestnut 5 5
1087. 50 s. violet 5 5
1088. 80 s. orange 5 5
1089. 1 r. emerald 5 5
1090. 1 r. 25 brown 5 5
1091. 1 r. 50 green.. .. 5 5
1092. 2 r. purple 5 5
1093. 2 r. 50 slate 5 5
1094. 5 r. orange 8 5
1095. 10 r. olive 10 5
1096. 12 r. orange 20 5
1097. 25 r. violet 25 5

1966. Flowers. As T **133** but inscr. "1966" and additionally inscr. "sen" instead of commas and dashes. Multicoloured.

1108. 10 s.+5 s. "Cassia alata" 5 5
1109. 20 s.+5 s. "Barleria cristata" 5 5
1110. 30 s.+10 s. "Ixora coccinea" 5 5
1111. 40 s.+10 s. "Hibiscus rosa sinensis" 5 5

1966. National Disaster Fund. Floral designs as T **133** additionally inscr. "BENTJANA ALAM NASIONAL 1966". Multicoloured.

1113. 15 s.+5 s. "Gloriosa superba" 5 5
1114. 25 s.+5 s. "Hibiscus tiliaceus" 5 5
1115. 30 s.+10 s. "Impatiens balsimina" 5 5
1116. 80 s.+20 s. "Lagerstroemia indica" 5 5

135. Cleaning Ship's Rudder. **136.** Gen. A. Yani.

1966. Maritime Day.

1117. 135. 20 s. green and blue .. 5 5
1118. – 40 s. indigo and pink .. 5 5
1119. 50 s. brown and green.. 5 5
1120. – 1 r. gold, green, blue and salmon 5 5
1121. 1 r. 50 green and lilac.. 5 5
1122. – 2 r. red and grey .. 5 5
1123. – 2 r. 50 red and mauve.. 5 5
1124. – 3 r. black and emerald.. 8 5

DESIGNS: 40 s. Lighthouse. 50 s. Fisherman. 1 r. Maritime emblem. 1 r. 50, Sailing boat. 2 r. Quayside. 2 r. 50, Pearl-diving. 3 r. Ship in dry-dock.

1966. Victims of Attempted Communist Coup, 1965. Frames and date in blue.

1126. 136. 5 r. chestnut 8 5
1127. A. 5 r. green 8 5
1128. B. 5 r. purple 8 5
1129. C. 5 r. olive 8 5
1130. D. 5 r. grey 8 5
1131. E. 5 r. violet 8 5
1132. F. 5 r. purple 8 5
1133. G. 5 r. slate-green.. .. 8 5
1134. H. 5 r. purple 8 5
1135. I. 5 r. orange 8 5

PORTRAITS: A, Lt.-Gen. R. Soeprapto. B, Lt.-Gen. M. Harjono. C, Lt.-Gen. S. Parman. D, Maj.-Gen. D. Pandjaitan. E, Maj.-Gen. S. Siswomihardjo. F, Brig.-Gen. Katamso. G, Col. Soegijono. H, Capt. P. Tendean. I, Insp. K. S. Tubun.

137. Python. **138.** Tjlempung.

1966. Reptiles.

1136. 137. 2 r.+25 s. chocolate, green and flesh .. 5 5
1137. – 3 r.+50 s. green, brown and lilac .. 5 5
1138. – 4 r.+75 s. maroon, buff and emerald .. 8 8
1139. – 6 r.+1 r. black, brown and blue 12 12

REPTILES: 3 r. Chameleon. 4 r. Crocodile. 6 r. Green turtle.

1967. Musical Instruments.

1140. 138. 50 s. red and black .. 5 5
1141. – 1 r. sepia and vermilion 5 5
1142. – 1 r. 25 lake and blue .. 5 5
1143. – 1 r. 50 green and violet 5 5
1144. – 2 r. ultramarine & ochre 5 5
1145. – 2 r. 50 green and red .. 5 5
1146. – 3 r. green and maroon.. 5 5
1147. – 4 r. ultram. and orange 5 5
1148. – 5 r. red and blue .. 5 5
1149. – 6 r. blue and magenta.. 8 5
1150. – 8 r. lake and green .. 10 5
1151. – 10 r. violet and red .. 12 5
1152. – 12 r. green and violet .. 15 5
1153. – 15 r. violet and olive .. 20 8
1154. – 20 r. black and sepia .. 25 8
1155. – 25 r. black and green .. 30 12

INSTRUMENTS: 1 r Sasando. 1 r. 25, Foi doa. 1 r. 50, Kultjapi. 2 r. Arababu. 2 r. 50, Genderang. 3 r. Katjapi. 4 r. Hape. 5 r. Gangsa. 6 r. Serunai. 8 r. Rebab. 10 r. Trompet. 12 r. Totobuang. 15 r. Tamburu. 20 r. Kulintang. 25 r. Keledi.

139. Pilot and MiG-21 Fighter. **140.** Thomas Cup and Silhouettes.

1967. Aviation Day. Multicoloured.

1156. 2 r. 50 Type **139** 5 5
1157. 4 r. "Convair" 990A jetliner and control tower.. 5 5
1158. 5 r. "Hercules" transport aircraft on tarmac .. 8 5

1967. Thomas Cup World Badminton Championships. Multicoloured.

1159. 5 r. Type **140** 5 5
1160. 12 r. Thomas Cup on Globe 15 8

HAVE YOU READ THE NOTES AT THE BEGINNING OF THIS CATALOGUE?

These often provide answers to the enquiries we receive.

141. Balinese Girl. **142.** Heroes Monument.

1967. Int. Tourist Year.

1161. 141. 12 r. multicoloured .. 20 10

1967. "Heroes of the Revolution". Monument.

1163. 142. 2 r. 50, choc. & green.. 5 5
1164. – 5 r. purple and drab 5 5
1165. – 7 r. 50 green and pink 10 5

DESIGNS—HORIZ. 5 r. Monument and shrine. VERT. 7 r. 50, Shrine.

143. "Forest Fire".

1967. Paintings by Raden Saleh.

1175. 143. 25 r. red and green .. 30 20
1176. – 50 r. purple & vermilion 50 40

PAINTING: 50 r. "A Fight to the Death".

144. Flood Victims **145.** Human Rights Emblem.

1967. National Disaster Fund.

1178. 144. 1 r. 25+10 s. bl. & yell. 5 5
1179. – 2 r. 50+25 s. bl. & yell. 5 5
1180. – 4 r.+40 s. blk. & orge. 8 5
1181. – 5 r.+50 s. blk. & orge. 10 8

DESIGNS: 2 r. 50, Landslide. 4 r. Burning house. 5 r. Erupting volcano.

1968. Human Rights Year.

1183. 145. 5 r. red, green and blue 8 5
1184. 12 r. red, green & drab 12 10

146. Academy Badge. **150.** W.H.O. Emblem and "20".

147. 148. 149.
"Sudhana and Manohara at Court of Drama" (relief on wall of Borobudur).
(Reduced-size illustration. Actual size 69×29 mm.)

1968. Indonesian Military Academy.

1185. 146. 10 r. multicoloured.. 10 5

1968. "Save Borobudur Monument".

1186. 147. 2 r. 50+25 s. grey & grn. 12 8
1187. 148. 2 r. 50+25 s. grey & grn. 12 8
1188. 149. 2 r. 50+25 s. grey & grn. 12 8
1189. – 7 r. 50+75 s. grey & orge. 12 8

DESIGN—VERT. 7 r. 50, Buddhist and statue of Buddha.

1968. W.H.O. 20th Anniv.

1191. 150. 2 r. purple and yellow 5 5
1192. – 20 r. black and green.. 20 8

DESIGN: 20 r. W.H.O. emblem.

151. Trains of 1867 and 1967.

1968. Indonesian Railways. Cent. (1967).

1193. 151. 20 r. multicoloured .. 15 8
1194. 30 r. multicoloured .. 25 15

152. Scout with Pick. **153.** Butterfly Dancer.

1968. "Wirakarya" Scout Camp.

1195. 152. 5 r.+50 s. brn. & orge. 5 5
1196. – 10 r.+1 r. grey & chest. 10 8
1197. – 30 r.+3 r. brown & grn. 30 20

DESIGNS—VERT. 10 r. Bugler on hillside. HORIZ. (69 × 29 mm.): 30 r. Scouts in camp.

1968. Tourism.

1198. 153. 30 r. multicoloured .. 25 12

154. Observatory and Stars.

1968. Bosscha Observatory. 40th Anniv.

1207. 154. 15 r. blue, yell. & blk. 12 5
1208. – 30 r. violet & orange.. 25 15

DESIGN—VERT. 30 r. Observatory on Globe.

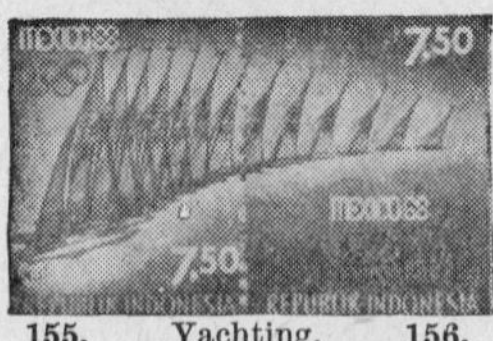

155. Yachting. **156.**

1968. Olympic Games, Mexico.

1209. – 5 r. green, blk. & chest. 5 5
1210. 155. 7 r. 50 blue, yell. & red 12 5
1211. 156. 7 r. 50 blue, yell. & red 12 5
1212. – 12 r. red, blue & yellow 10 5
1213. – 30 r. orge., brn. & turq. 20 15

DESIGNS—VERT. ($28\frac{1}{2} \times 44\frac{1}{2}$ mm.): 5 r. Weightlifting. 12 r. Basketball. HORIZ. ($44\frac{1}{2} \times 28\frac{1}{2}$ mm.): 30 r. Dove and Olympic flame.

Nos. 1210/11 were arranged together se-tenant in sheets, each pair forming a whole design.

157. "Eugenia aquea".

1968. Fruits. Multicoloured.
1215. 7 r. Type 157 .. .. 5 5
1216. 15 r. "Carica papaya" .. 10 5
1217. 30 r. "Durio zibethinus" (vert.) 20 15

158. I.L.O. Emblem and part of Globe.  159. R. Dewi Sartika.

1969. Int. Labour Organisation. 50th Anniv.
1219.158. 5 r. red and green .. 5 5
1220. – 7 r. 50 green & orange 5 5
1221.158. 15 r. red and violet .. 10 8
1222. – 25 r. red and turquoise 20 12
DESIGN: 7 r. 50, 25 r. I.L.O. emblem.

1969. National Independence Heroes.
1223.159. 15 r. green and violet 10 5
1224. – 15 r. purple and green 10 5
1225. – 15 r. ultram. and verm. 10 5
1226. – 15 r. ochre and red .. 10 5
1227. – 15 r. sepia and blue .. 10 5
1228. – 15 r. lilac and blue .. 10 5
PORTRAITS: No. 1224, Tjut Nja Din. 1225, Tjut Nja Meuthia. 1226 Sutan Sjahrir. 1227, Dr. F. L. Tobing. 1228 General G. Subroto.

160. Woman with Flower.  161. Red Cross "Mosaic".

1969. Women's Emancipation Campaign.
1229.160. 20 r. + 2 r. red, yellow and emerald .. 15 10

1969. League of Red Cross Societies. 50th Anniv.
1230.161. 15 r. red and green .. 10 5
1231. – 20 r. red and yellow .. 15 12
DESIGN: 20 r. Hands encircling Red Cross.

162. "Planned" Family and Factory.

1969. South-East Asia and Oceania Family Planning Conf.
1232.162. 10 r. orange and green 5 5
1233. – 20 r. magenta and green 12 10
DESIGN: 20 r. "Planned" family and "National Prosperity".

163. Balinese Mask.

1969. Tourism in Bali. Multicoloured.
1234. 12 r. Type 163 .. .. 8 5
1235. 15 r. Girl with offerings .. 10 8
1236. 30 r. Cremation rites .. 20 15

164. "Agriculture".  165. Dish Aerial.

1969. Five-year Development Plan.
1238. – 5 r. blue and green .. 5 5
1239. 164. 7 r. 50 yellow & pur. 5 5
1240. – 10 r. red and blue .. 5 5
1241. – 12 r. red and blue .. 8 5
1242. – 15 r. yellow & green 10 5
1243. – 20 r. yellow & violet 12 5
1244. – 25 r. red and black .. 15 5
1245. – 30 r. black and red .. 20 5
1246. – 40 r. orange & green 25 5
1247. – 50 r. brown & orange 30 10

DESIGNS: 5 r. Religious emblems ("Co-existence"). 10 r. Modern family ("Social Welfare"). 12 r. Crane and crate ("Overseas Trade"). 15 r. Bobbins ("Clothing Industry"). 20 r. Children in class ("Education"). 25 r. Research worker ("Scientific Research"). 30 r. Family and thermometer ("Health Care"). 40 r. Fish and net ("Fisheries"). 50 r. Graph ("Statistics").

1969. Satellite Communications and Djatiluhur Earth Station. Inaug. Mult.
1248. 15 r. Type 165 .. .. 10 5
1249. 30 r. Communications satellite 20 15

166. Vickers "Vimy" Aircraft over Borobudur Temple.  167. Noble Volute Shell.

1969. 1st England—Australia Flight. 50th Anniv.
1253.166. 75 r. purple and red .. 30 25
1254. – 100 r. green and yellow 40 25
DESIGN: 100 r. Vickers "Vimy" and map of Indonesia.

1969. Sea-shells. Multicoloured.
1255. 5 r. + 50 c. Type 167 .. 5 5
1256. 7 r. 50 + 50 c. Hairy triton 5 5
1257. 10 r. + 1 r. Spider conch .. 8 5
1258. 15 r. + 1 r. 50 Venus comb murex 12 10

168. Indonesian Pavilion"  169. Prisoner's Hands and Scales of Justice.

1970. "Expo 70" World Fair, Osaka, Japan.
1259. 168. 5 r. yell., grn. & brn. 5 5
1260. – 15 r. red, blue & green 15 8
1261. 168. 30 r. yell., blue & red 30 15
DESIGN: 15 r. Indonesian "Garuda" symbol.

1970. "Purification of Justice".
1262.169. 10 r. purple and red .. 10 5
1263. 15 r. purple and green 15 8

170. U.P.U. Monument, Berne.  171. Timor Dancers.

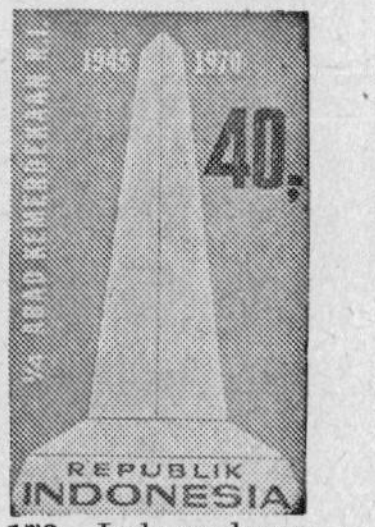

173. Independence Monument.  172. "Productivity" Symbol.

1970. New U.P.U. Headquarters Building, Berne. Inaug.
1264.170. 15 r. red & green 15 5
1265. – 30 r. blue and ochre .. 30 10
DESIGN: 30 r. New Headquarters building.

1970. "Visit Indonesia Year". Traditional Dancers. Multicoloured.
1266. 20 r. Type 171 .. .. 20 5
1267. 45 r. Bali dancers .. 40 15

1970. Asian Productivity Year.
1269. 172. 5 r. red, yell. & green 10 5
1270. 30 r. red, yell. & violet 25 15

1970. Independence. 25th Anniv.
1271. 173. 40 r. violet, purple & bl. 1·10 50

174. Emblems of Post and Giro, and of Telecommunications. 175. U.N. Emblem and Doves.

1970. Indonesian Post and Telecommunications Services. 25th Anniv.
1272.174. 10 r. brn., yell. & grn. 20 10
1273. – 25 r. blk., yell. & pink 60 15
DESIGN: 25 r. Telephone dial and P.T.T. worker.

1970. United Nations. 25th Anniv.
1274.175. 40 r. multicoloured 1·00 50

176. I.E.Y. Emblem on globe.  177. "Chrsocoris javanus".

1970. Int. Education Year.
1275.176. 25 r. brn., red & yellow 60 30
1276. – 50 r. red, blk. and blue 1·25 60
DESIGNS: 50 r. I.E.Y. emblem.

1970. Insects. Multicoloured.
1277. 7 r. 50 + 50 c. Type 177 .. 20 10
1278. 15 r. + 1 r. 50 "Orthetrum testaceum" 30 20
1279. 20 r. + 2 r. "Xylocopa flavonigrescens" 50 30

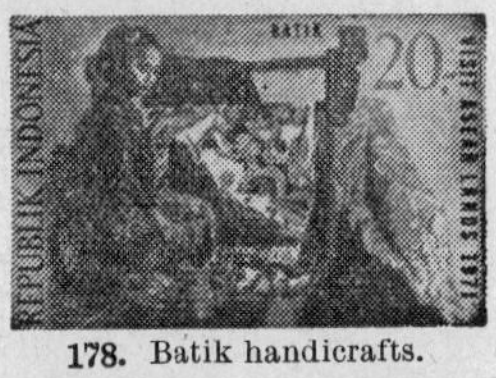

178. Batik handicrafts.

1971. "Visit ASEAN (South East Asian Nations Assn.) Year". Multicoloured.
1280. 20 r. Type 178 .. .. 15 10
1281. 50 r. Javanese girl playing angklung (musical instrument) (vert.) .. 30 20
1282. 75 r. Wedding group, Minangkabau 50 30

179. Restoration of Fatahillah Park.

1971. Djakarta. 444th Anniv. Multicoloured.
1284. 15 r. Type 179 .. .. 10 5
1285. 65 r. Performance at Lenong Theatre .. 35 20
1286. 80 r. Ismail Marzuki Cultural Centre 55 35

180. Sita and Rama.  181. Pigeon with Letter, and Workers.

1971. Int. Ramayana Festival.
1288. 180. 30 r. multicoloured .. 20 10
1289. – 100 r. black, blue & red 70 30
DESIGN: 100 r. Rama.

1971. 5th Asian Regional Telecommunications Conference.
1290. 181. 50 r. chocolate, yellow-brown and buff .. 30 15

182. U.P.U. Monument, Berne, and Hemispheres.

1971. U.P.U. Day.
1291.182. 40 r. purple, blk. & blue 35 12

183. Schoolgirl.

1971. U.N.I.C.E.F. 25th Anniv. Multicoloured.
1292. 20 r. Type 183 .. .. 15 8
1293. 40 r. Boy with rice-stalks 25 12

184. Lined Surgeon.  185. E.C.A.F.E. Emblem.

1971. Fishes (1st series). Multicoloured.
1294. 15 r. Type 184 .. .. 10 5
1295. 30 r. Moorish Idol .. 20 12
1296. 40 r. Emperor Angelfish 30 20
See also Nos. 1318/20, 1343/5, 1390/2 and 1423/5.

1972. E.C.A.F.E. 25th Anniv.
1297.185. 40 r. bl. & greenish bl. 25 10
1298. – 75 r. multicoloured .. 40 20
1299. – 100 r. multicoloured 50 30
DESIGNS—HORIZ. 75 r. Microwave tower. 100 r. Irrigation and highways.

186. Human Heart.  187. Ancient and Modern Textile Production.

1972. World Heart Month.
1300.186. 50 r. multicoloured .. 30 15

1972. Textile Technological Institute. 50th Anniv.
1301. 187. 35 r. pur., yell. & orge. 20 10

188. Children reading Books.  189. "Essa 8" Weather Satellite.

1972. Int. Book Year.
1302.188. 75 r. multicoloured .. 40 20

1972. Space Exploration.
1303. 189. 35 r. brn., violet & bl. 20 10
1304. – 50 r. bl., blk. & pink 30 15
1305. – 60 r. blk., grn. & brn. 35 20
DESIGNS: 50 r. Astronaut on Moon. 60 r. Indonesian "Kartika 1" rocket.

190. Hotel Indonesia.

1972. Hotel Indonesia. 10th Anniv.
1306.190. 50 r. grn., pale-grn. & red 35 15

191. "Silat" (unarmed combat).  192. Family and Religious Buildings.

1972. Olympic Games, Munich.
1307. 191. 20 r. blue, maroon and pale blue 10 5
1308. – 35 r. vio., brn. & mve. 15 8
1309. – 50 r. light grn., bl-grn. and olive 30 12
1310. – 75 r. maroon, brown-lilac and pink .. 40 20
1311. – 100 r. brn., bl. & grn. 60 30
DESIGNS: 35 r. Running. 50 r. Diving. 75 r. Badminton. 100 r. Olympic stadium.

1972. Family Planning Campaign. Mult.

1312. 30 r. Type **192** 15 10
1313. 75 r. " Healthy family " 40 20
1314. 80 r. " Family of workers " 45 20

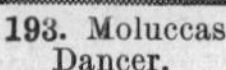

193. Moluccas Dancer.

194. Thomas Cup and Shuttlecock.

1972. Indonesian Art and Traditions. (1st series.).

1315. **193.** 30 r. grn., red & brn. 15 10
1316. – 60 r. multicoloured . . 30 15
1317. – 100 r. bl., brn. & red 50 25

DESIGNS—VERT. 60 r. Couple and Toraja traditional house. HORIZ. 100 r. West Irian traditional house.

See also 1336/8, 1373/5 and 1401/3.

1972. Fishes (2nd Series). As T **184**. Mult.

1318. 30 r. " Chaetodon triangulum " 15 10
1319. 50 r. " Pygoplites diacanthus " 30 15
1320. 100 r. " Balistoides conspicillum " 55 25

1972. Thomas Cup Badminton Championships, Djakarta.

1321 **194.** 30 r. blue and green 15 10
1322. – 75 r. red and green . . 35 20
1323. – 80 r. brown and red . . 40 20

DESIGNS: 75 r. Thomas Cup and Sports Centre. 80 r. Thomas Cup and player.

195. Emblem Anemometer and " Gatotkaca ".

1973. I.M.O. and W.M.O. Weather Organisation Centenary.

1324. **195.** 80 r. multicoloured . . 40 20

196. " Health begins at Home ".

197. Java Mask.

1973. W.H.O. 25th Anniv.

1325. **196.** 80 r. blue, pink & grn. 40 20

1973. Tourism. Indonesian Folk Masks. Multicoloured.

1326. 30 r. Type **197** 15 10
1327. 60 r. Kalimantan mask . . 30 15
1328. 100 r. Bali mask 50 25

198. Savings Bank and Thrift Plant.

199. Chess.

1973. Two-Year National Savings Drive.

1329. **198.** 25 r. blk., yell. & brn. 12 5
1330. – 30 r. grn., gold & yell. 15 8

DESIGN—HORIZ. 30 r. Hand and " City " savings bank.

1973. National Sports Week. Multicoloured.

1331. 30 r. Type **199** 15 5
1332. 60 r. Karate (vert.) . . 25 12
1333. 75 r. Hurdling (horiz.) . . 40 20

200. International Policemen.

1973. Interpol. 50th Anniv.

1334. **200.** 30 r. multicoloured . . 15 8
1335. – 50 r. yell., pur. & blk. 25 12

DESIGN—VERT. 50 r. Giant temple guard.

201. Weaving and Cloth.

1973. Indonesian Art and Traditions. (2nd series).

1336. **201.** 60 r. multicoloured . . 25 15
1337. – 80 r. multicoloured . . 35 20
1338. – 100 r. multicoloured 50 25

DESIGNS: 80 r., 100 r. Similar designs to T **201**.

202. " Food Cultivation ".

1973. World Food Programme. 10th Anniv.

1339. **202.** 30 r. multicoloured . . 15 8

203. "Religion".

205. Bengkulu Costume.

204. Admiral Sudarso and Naval Battle of Arafuru.

1973. Family Planning.

1340. **203.** 20 r. blue, light bl. & red 10 5
1341. – 30 r. blk., yell. & brn. 15 8
1342. – 60 r. blk., yell. & grn. 25 12

DESIGNS: 30 r. Teacher and class (" Population Education "), 60 r. Family and house (" Health ").

1973. Fishes (3rd series). As T **184**, dated " 1973 ". Multicoloured.

1343. 40 r. " Acanthrurus leucosternon " . . 20 10
1344. 65 r. " Chaetodon trifasciatus " 30 15
1345. 100 r. " Pomacanthus annularis " 45 25

1974. Naval Day.

1346. **204.** 40 r. multicoloured . . 20 10

1974. Pacific Area Travel Association Conference, Jakarta. Provincial Costumes. Multicoloured.

1347. 5 r. Type **205** 5 5
1348. 7 r. 50 Kalimantan (Timor) 5 5
1349. 10 r. Kalimantan (Tengah) 5 5
1350. 15 r. Jambi 5 5
1351. 20 r. Sulawesi (Tenggara) 5 5
1352. 25 r. Nusatenggara (Timor) 8 5
1353. 27 r. 50 Maluku . . 10 5
1354. 30 r. Lampung . . 12 5
1355. 35 r. Sumatera (Barat) . . 15 8
1356. 40 r. Aceh . . 20 10
1357. 45 r. Nusatenggara (Barat) 20 10
1358. 50 r. Riau . . 20 12
1359. 55 r. Kalimantan (Barat) 25 15
1360. 60 r. Sulawesi (Utara) . . 25 15
1361. 65 r. Sulawesi (Tengah) . . 30 20
1362. 70 r. Sumatera (Selatan) 30 20
1363. 75 r. Java (Barat) . . 30 20
1364. 80 r. Sumatera (Utara) . . 35 25
1365. 90 r. Yogyakarta . . 35 25
1366. 95 r. Kalimantan (Selatan) 40 30
1367. 100 r. Java (Timor) . . 40 35
1368. 120 r. Irian (Jaya) . . 50 40
1369. 130 r. Java (Tengah) . . 55 45
1370. 135 r. Sulawesi (Selatan) 55 50
1371. 150 r. Bali 60 50
1372. 160 r. Djakarta 65 60

206. Baladewa.

207. Pres. Sunarto.

1974. Indonesian Art and Traditions (3rd series). Shadow Plays. Multicoloured.

1373. 40 r. Type **206** 15 8
1374. 80 r. Kresna 35 15
1375. 100 r. Bima 40 20

1974.

1376. **207.** 40 r. brn., grn. & blk. 15 8
1377. 50 r. brn., blue & blk. 20 8
1378. 65 r. brn., pink & blk. 25 10
1379. 75 r. brn., yell. & blk. 30 12
1380. 100 r. brn., oran. & blk. 40 15
1381. 150 r. brn., grn. & blk. 60 20
1381a. 200 r. brn., blue & grn. 80 30
1381b. 300 r. brn., red & flesh 1·25 45
1381c. 400 r. brn., grn. & yell. 1·60 60
1381d. 500 r. brn., red & lilac 2·00 1·25

1974. World Population Year.

1382. **208.** 65 r. multicoloured . . 35 15

208. " Improvement of Living Standards ".

209. House (" Welfare ").

1974. Family Planning.

1383. **209.** 25 r. multicoloured . . 10 5
1384. – 40 r. blue, blk. & grn. 15 8
1385. – 65 r. ochre, brn. & yell. 25 12

DESIGNS: 40 r. Young couple (" Development "). 65 r. Arrows (" Religion ").

210. Bicycle Postmen.

1974. Universal Postal Union. Centenary.

1386. **210.** 20 r. brn., yell. & grn. 8 5
1387. – 40 r. brn., oran. & bl. 15 8
1388. – 65 r. brn., yell. & blk. 25 12
1389. – 100 r. blk., bl. & red 40 20

DESIGNS: 40 r. Mail-cart. 65 r. Mounted postman. 100 r. Ancient galley.

1974. Fishes (4th series). As Type **184**, but dated " 1974 ". Multicoloured.

1390. 40 r. " Zebrasoma veliferum " 15 8
1391. 80 r. " Euxiphipops navarchus " 35 15
1392. 100 r. " Synchiropus splendidus " 40 20

211. Drilling for Oil.

1975. " Pertamina " Oil Complex. 17th Anniv. Multicoloured.

1393. 40 r. Type **211** 15 5
1394. 75 r. Oil refinery 30 15
1395. 95 r. Control centre (vert.) 35 20
1396. 100 r. Road tanker (vert.) 40 20
1397. 120 r. Executive aircraft over storage tank farm (vert.) 45 20
1398. 130 r. Pipelines and tanker (vert.) 50 25
1399. 150 r. Petrol-chemical storage tanks 60 30
1400. 200 r. Offshore drilling rig 75 30

212. Sumatra Spittoon.

213. " Donorship ".

1975. Indonesian Art and Traditions. (4th series).

1401. **212.** 50 r. silver, red & blk. 20 10
1402. – 75 r. silver, grn. & blk. 30 15
1403. – 100 r. yell., bl. & blk. 40 20

DESIGNS: 75 r. Sumatran " sirih " dish. 100 r. Kalimantan " sirih " dish.

1975. Blood Donors' Campaign.

1404. **213.** 40 r. red, yell. & grn. 15 8

214. Measures and Globe.

216. " Dendrobium pakarena ".

215. Women in Public Service.

1975. Metre Convention. Cent.

1405. **214.** 65 r. blue, red & yell. 25 12

1975. International Women's Year. Multicoloured.

1406. 40 r. Type **215** 15 5
1407. 100 r. I.W.Y. emblem (21 × 29 mm.) . . 30 15

1975. Tourism. Indonesian Orchids (1st series). Multicoloured.

1408. 40 r. Type **216** 12 8
1409. 70 r. " Aeridchnis bogor " (var. Apple-blossom Pink) 25 12
1410. 85 r. " Vanda genta " (Bandung) 30 15

217. Stupas and Damaged Temple.

1975. U.N.E.S.C.O. " Save Borobudur Temple " Campaign. Multicoloured.

1411. 25 r. Type **217** 8 5
1412. 40 r. Buddhist shrines and broken wall 12 8
1413. 65 r. Stupas and damaged building (horiz.) . . 20 10
1414. 100 r. Buddha and stupas (horiz.) 30 15

218. Battle of Banjarmasin.

1975. Independence. 30th Anniv.
1415. **218.** 25 r. black and yell. 8 5
1416. – 40 r. black and red .. 12 8
1417. – 75 r. black and red .. 25 12
1418. – 100 r. black and orange 30 15
DESIGNS: 40, 75, 100r. Various battle scenes.

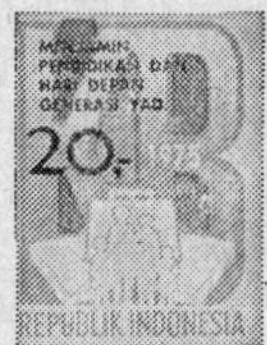

219. " Education ". **220.** Heroes' Monument, Surabaya.

1975. Family Planning. Multicoloured.
1419. 20 r. Type **219** .. 5 5
1420. 25 r. "Religion" .. 8 5
1421. 40 r. " Prosperity " .. 12 8

1975. Independence. War. 30th Anniv.
1422. **220.** 100 r. brown and grn. 30 15

1975. Fishes (5th series). As Type **184**, but dated " 1975 ". Multicoloured.
1423. 40 r. " Coris angulata " .. 12 8
1424. 75 r. " Chaetodon ephippium " .. 25 12
1425. 150 r. " Platex pinnatus " (vert.) 45 25

221. Thomas Cup.

1976. Indonesian Victory in World Badminton Championships. Multicoloured.
1426. 20 r. Type **221** 5 5
1427. 40 r. Uber cup 12 8
1428. 100 r. Thomas and Uber cups 30 15

222. Refugees and New Village.

1976. World Human Settlements Day. Multicoloured.
1429. 30 r. Type **222** .. 5 5
1430. 50 r. Old and restored villages .. 15 8
1431. 100 r. Derelict and rebuilt houses 30 15

223. Early and Modern Telephones. **224.** Human Eye.

1976. Telephone Centenary.
1432. **223.** 100 r. brn., red & yell. 30 15

1976. World Health Day. Multicoloured.
1433. 20 r. Type **224** .. 5 5
1434. 40 r. Blind man with stick 12 8

225. Main Stadium. Montreal.

1976. Olympic Games, Montreal.
1435. **225.** 100 r. blue 30 15

226. Lake Tondano, Sulawesi. **227.** " Light Traffic " Station.

1976. Tourism. Multicoloured.
1436. 35 r. Type **226** .. 10 8
1437. 40 r. Lake Kelimutu, Flores 12 8
1438. 75 r. Lake Maninjau, Sumatra .. 25 12

1976. Domestic Satellite System. Inauguration.
1439. 20 r. Type **227** 5 5
1440. 50 r. " Master Control " Station 15 8
1441. 100 r. " Palapa " Satellite 30 15

1976. Tourism. Indonesian Orchids (2nd series). As Type **216**, but dated " 1976 ". Multicoloured.
1412. 25 r. " Arachnis flos-aeris (var. insignis) " .. 8 5
1443. 40 r. " Vandra " ('Puti Serang') 12 8
1444. 100 r. " Coelogyne pandurata " 30 15

POSTAGE DUE STAMPS.

1950. Postage Due stamps of Netherlands Indies surch. **BAJAR PORTO** and new value.
D 576. 2½ s. on 50 c. (No. D 499) 25 25
D 577. 5 s. on 100 c. (No. D 501) 60 70
D 578. 10 s. on 75 c. (No. D 500) 90 60

D 1.

1951.
D 645. **D 1.** 2½ s. orange .. 5 5
D 646. 5 s. orange 5 5
D 647. 10 s. orange .. 5 5
D 648. 15 s. claret .. 5 5
D 773. 15 s. orange .. 5 5
D 649. 20 s. blue 5 5
D 774. 20 s. orange .. 5 5
D 650. 25 s. olive .. 15 15
D 775. 25 s. orange .. 5 5
D 651. 30 s. brown .. 8 8
D 776. 30 s. orange .. 5 5
D 652. 40 s. green 10 10
D 777. 50 s. orange .. 40 25
D 778. 50 s. green 5 5
D 779. 100 s. orange .. 15 10
D 780. 100 s. brown .. 5 5
D 781. 250 s. blue 5 5
D 782. 500 s. yellow .. 5 5
D 783. 750 s. lilac .. 5 5
D 784. 1000 s. salmon .. 8 8
D 654. 1 r. green .. .. 2·00 2·00

1966.
D 1058. **D 1.** 50 r. red 5 5
D 1059. 100 r. lake 5 5

1966. As Type **D 1**, but with coloured network background incorporating " 1966 ".
D 1098. 5 s. green and yellow .. 5 5
D 1099. 10 s. red and blue .. 5 5
D 1000. 20 s. blue and pink .. 5 5
D 1101. 30 s. sepia and red .. 5 5
D 1102. 40 s. violet and bistre 5 5
D 1103. 50 s. olive and mauve 5 5
D 1104. 100 s. lake and green 5 5
D 1105. 200 s. green and pink 5 5
D 1106. 500 s. yellow and blue 8 8
D 1107. 1000 s. claret and yellow 15 10

1967. As Nos. 1098/1107 but dated " 1967 ".
D 1168. 50 s. gfeen and lilac .. 5 5
D 1169. 100 s. red and green .. 5 5
D 1170. 200 s. green and pink 5 5
D 1171. 500 s. brown and blue 5 5
D 1172. 1000 s. mauve & yell. 5 5
D 1173. 15 r. orange & grey .. 15 8
D 1174. 25 r. violet and grey .. 25 15

1968. Design similar to Type **D 1**, but value circle within frame.
D 1200. 20 r. brown and yellow 8 5
D 1201. 30 r. lilac and green .. 12 8

1973. As Type **D 1**, but inscr. " BAYAR PORTO ", and dated " 1973 ".
D 1320a. 25 r. violet and grey .. 25 20
D 1320b. 65 r. green and yellow 20 25
D 1320.c 125 r. violet and rose .. 40 50

SPECIAL DELIVERY STAMPS.

E 1. " Garuda " Bird.

1967. Inser. " 1967 ".
E 1166. **E 1.** 10 r. pur. & cobalt 10 5
E 1167. 15 r. purple & orge. 20 15

1968. As Nos. E. 1166/7 but inscr. " 1968 ".
E 1202. **E 1.** 10 r. purple & cobalt 8 5
E 1203. 15 r. pur. & orange 12 5
E 1204. 20 r. pur. & yellow 15 5
E 1205. 30 r. purple & green 20 12
E 1206. 40 r. pur. & light pur 30 20

1969. As Nos. E 1166/7 but inscr. " 1969 ".
E 1250. **E 1.** 20 r. purple & yellow 15 12
E 1251. 30 r. purple & green 25 15
E 1252. 40 r. purple & light purple 30 20

INDORE (HOLKAR) BC

A state in C. India. Now uses Indian stamps.

1. Maharaja Tukoji Rao II Holkar XI.

1886.
2. **1.** ½ a. mauve 70 80

2.

1889. Imperf.
4. **2.** ½ a. black on pink 75 75

3. Maharaja Shivaji Rao Holkar XII. **4.** Maharaja Tukoji Rao III Holkar XIII.

1889.
5. **3.** ¼ a. orange 8 8
6a. ½ a. purple 10 8
7. 1 a. green 35 25
8. 1 a. red 75 40

1904.
9. **4.** ¼ a. orange 5 5
10. ½ a. red 75 5
11. 1 a. green .. .. 1·25 5
12. 2 a. brown .. .. 2·50 20
13. 3 a. violet .. .. 3·00 30
14. 4 a. blue .. .. 3·50 30
The ¼ a. is inscr. " HOLKAR ".

पाव आना.

(5.)

1905. No. 6a surch. as **T 5**.
15. **3.** ¼ a. on ½ a. purple .. 50 75

6. Maharaja Yeshwant Rao II Holkar XIV. **7.**

1928.
16. **6.** ¼ a. orange 10 5
17. ½ a. purple 10 5
18. 1 a. green 10 5
19. 1¼ a. green 15 5
20. 2 a. brown .. .. 1·25 50
21. 2 a. green 50 45
22. 3 a. violet .. .. 1·25 50
23. 3a blue .. .. 14·00
24. 3½ a. violet .. .. 1·75 1·50
25. 4 a. blue .. .. 1·75 1·00
26. 4 a. yellow .. .. 3·00 1·00
27. 8 a. grey .. .. 3·00 3·00
28. 8 a. orange .. .. 4·00 4·00
29. 12 a. red .. .. 7·00 7·00
30. – 1 r. black and blue .. 7·00 7·00
31. – 2 r. black and red .. 10·00 10·00
32. – 5 r. black and brown .. 12·00 14·00
The rupee values are larger (23 × 28 mm.).

1940. Surch. diagonally in words.
33. – ¼ a. on 5 r. (No. 32) .. 35 12
34. – ½ a. on 2 r. (No. 31) .. 60 15
35. **6.** 1 a. on 1¼ a. green (No. 19) 60 15

1941.
36. **7.** ¼ a. orange 15 5
37. ½ a. claret 20 5
38. 1 a. green 20 8
39. 1¼ a. green 30 20
40. 2 a. blue .. .. 6·00 2·50
41. 4 a. yellow .. .. 9·00 8·00
42. – 2 r. black and red .. 9·00 9·00
43. – 5 r. black and orange .. 10·00 11·00
The rupee values are larger (23 × 28 mm.).

OFFICIAL STAMPS

1904. Optd. **SERVICE.**
S 1. **4.** ¼ a. orange 5 5
S 2d. ½ a. red 5 5
S 3. 1 a. green 5 5
S 4. 2 a. brown 15 10
S 5. 3 a. violet .. .. 1·25 60
S 6. 4 a. blue .. .. 1·50 75

INHAMBANE O3

A district of Mozambique which used its own stamps from 1895 to 1920.

1895. St. Anthony Commem. Optd. **CENTENARIO DE S. ANTONIO Inhambane MDCCCXCV** on (a) " Embossed " key-type inscr. " PROVINCIA DE MOCAMBIQUE ".
1. **Q.** 5 r. black .. .. 8·00 7·00
2. 10 r. green .. .. 7·00 5·50
3. 20 r. red .. .. 13·00 11·00
5. 40 r. brown .. .. 15·00 10·00
6. 50 r. blue .. .. 15·00 10·00
7. 200 r. violet .. .. 20·00 19·00
8. 300 r. orange .. .. 20·00 19·00

(b) " Figures " key type inscr. " MOCAMBIQUE ".
12. **R.** 50 r. blue .. .. 13·00 9·50
16. 75 r. red .. .. 14·00 12·00
13. 80 r. green .. .. 32·00 30·00
14. 100 r. brown on yellow .. 22·00 16·00
17. 150 r. red on rose .. 17·00 14·00

1903. " King Carlos " key type inscr. " INHAMBANE ".
18. **S.** 2½ r. grey 15 12
19. 5 r. orange 15 12
20. 10 r. green 15 12
21. 15 r. green 40 30
22. 20 r. lilac 40 30
23. 25 r. red 40 30
24. 50 r. brown .. .. 1·00 80
25. 65 r. blue .. .. 2·50 2·25
26. 75 r. purple 80 70
27. 100 r. blue on blue .. 80 70
28. 115 r. brown on pink .. 1·50 1·25
29. 130 r. brown on yellow .. 1·50 1·25
30. 200 r. purple on pink .. 1·60 1·50
31. 400 r. blue on yellow .. 1·75 1·60
32. 500 r. black on blue .. 3·00 2·40
33. 700 r. grey on yellow .. 4·75 5·50

1905. No. 25 surch. **50 REIS** and bar.
34. **S.** 50 r. on 65 r. blue .. 75 60

1911. "King Carlos" key-type inscr. "INHAMBANE" and optd. **REPUBLICA.**

35. S. 2½ r. grey 15 12
36. 5 r. orange 15 12
37. 10 r. green 15 12
38. 15 r. green 15 12
39. 20 r. lilac 15 12
40. 25 r. red 20 15
41. 50 r. brown 12 8
42. 75 r. purple 15 15
43. 100 r. blue on blue .. 15 15
44. 115 r. brown on pink .. 20 20
45. 130 r. brown on yellow .. 20 20
46. 200 r. purple on pink .. 30 25
47. 400 r. blue on yellow .. 50 40
48. 500 r. black on blue .. 50 40
49. 700 r. black on yellow .. 60 50

1913. Surch. **REPUBLICA INHAMBANE** and value on "Vasco da Gama" stamps of

(a) **Portuguese Colonies.**

50. ¼ c. on 2½ r. green .. 35 30
51. ½ c. on 5 r. red .. 35 30
52. 1 c. on 10 r. purple .. 35 30
53. 2½ c. on 25 r. green .. 35 30
54. 5 c. on 50 r. blue .. 35 30
55. 7½ c. on 75 r. brown .. 60 45
56. 10 c. on 100 r. brown .. 40 30
57. 15 c. on 150 r. yell. brown 40 30

(b) **Macao.**

58. ¼ c. on ½ a. green .. 50 35
59. ½ c. on 1 a. red .. 50 35
60. 1 c. on 2 a. purple .. 50 35
61. 2½ c. on 4 a. green .. 50 35
62. 5 c. on 8 a. blue .. 50 35
63. 7½ c. on 12 a. brown .. 60 50
64. 10 c. on 16 a. brown .. 50 35
65. 15 c. on 24 a. yell brown 50 35

(c) **Timor.**

66. ¼ c. on ½ a. green .. 50 35
67. ½ c. on 1 a. red .. 50 35
68. 1 c. on 2 a. purple .. 50 35
69. 2½ c. on 4 a. green .. 50 35
70. 5 c. on 8 a. blue .. 50 35
71. 7½ c. on 12 a. brown .. 70 60
72. 10 c. on 16 a. brown .. 50 35
73. 15 c. on 24 a. yellow-brown 50 35

1914. No. 34 optd. **REPUBLICA.**

74. S. 50 r. on 65 r. blue .. 30 25

1914. "Ceres" key type inscr. "INHAMBANE".

75. U. ¼ c. olive 25 20
76a. ½ c. black 20 15
77. 1 c. green 25 20
78. 1½ c. brown 25 20
79. 2 c. red 25 20
80. 2½ c. violet 10 8
81. 5 c. blue 25 20
82. 7½ c. brown 40 35
83. 8 c. grey 40 35
84. 10 c. red 40 35
85. 15 c. claret 45 40
86. 20 c. green 45 40
87. 30 c. brown on green .. 65 55
88. 40 c. brown on red .. 65 55
89. 50 c. orange on pink .. 90 80
90. 1 e. green on blue .. 90 80

ININI O2

A territory in French Guiana, in the N.E. of S. America, separately administered from 1930 but reunited with Fr. Guiana in 1946.

1932. Stamps of French Guiana of 1929 optd. **TERRITOIRE DE L'ININI.**

1. 4. 1 c. green and lilac .. 5 5
2. 2 c. green and red .. 5 5
3. 3 c. green and violet .. 5 5
4. 4 c. mauve and brown .. 5 5
5. 5 c. red and blue .. 5 5
6. 10 c. brown and mauve .. 5 5
7. 15 c. red and yellow .. 5 5
8. 20 c. olive and blue .. 5 5
9. 25 c. brown and red .. 8 8
10. 5. 30 c. green 8 8
11. 30 c. brown and green .. 5 5
12. 35 c. green and blue .. 5 5
13. 40 c. olive and brown .. 5 5
14. 45 c. green and olive .. 5 5
15. 50 c. olive and blue .. 5 5
16. 55 c. red and blue .. 20 20
17. 60 c. green and red .. 5 5
18. 65 c. green and orange .. 8 8
19. 70 c. green and blue .. 8 8
20. 75 c. blue 25 25
21. 80 c. blue and black .. 8 8
22. 90 c. red 8 8
23. 90 c. brown and mauve .. 8 8
24. 1 f. brown and mauve .. 2·00 1·75
25. 1 f. red 8 8
26. 1 f. blue and black .. 5 5
27. 6. 1 f. 25 green and brown .. 5 5
28. 1 f. 25 red 8 8
29. 1 f. 40 mauve and brown .. 8 8
30. 1 f. 50 blue 5 5
31. 1 f. 60 green and brown .. 5 5
32. 1 f. 75 brown and red .. 3·00 2·25
33. 1 f. 75 blue 12 12
34. 2 f. red and green .. 5 5
35. 2 f. 25 blue 5 5
36. 2 f. 50 brown and red .. 5 5
37. 3 f. mauve and red .. 5 5
38. 5 f. green and violet .. 8 8
39. 10 f. blue and olive .. 8 8
40. 20 f. red and blue .. 10 10

1939. New York World's Fair. As T 11 of Cameroun.

51. 1 f. 25 red 45 45
52. 2 f. 25 blue 45 45

1939. 150th Anniv. of French Revolution. As T 16 of Cameroun.

53. 45 c.+25 c. green & black 1·60 1·60
54. 70 c.+30 c. brown & black 1·60 1·60
55. 90 c.+35 c. orange & black 1·60 1·60
56. 1 f. 25+1 f. red & black .. 1·60 1·60
57. 2 f. 25+2 f. blue & black .. 1·60 1·60

POSTAGE DUE STAMPS

1932. Postage Due stamps of Fr. Guiana of 1929 optd. **TERRITOIRE DE L'ININI.**

D 41. D 1. 5 c. blue 5 5
D 42. 10 c. blue and yellow 5 5
D 43. 20 c. red and grene .. 5 5
D 44. 30 c. red and brown .. 5 5
D 45. 50 c. brown & mauve 8 8
D 46. 60 c. brown and red .. 8 8
D 47. D 2. 1 f. brown and blue .. 10 10
D 48. 2 f. green and red .. 15 15
D 49. 3 f. grey and mauve .. 10 10

IONIAN ISLANDS BC; E2

A group of islands off the W. coast of Greece, placed under the protection of Gt. Britain in 1815 and ceded to Greece in 1864. Under Italian occupation in 1941 and occupied by Germany in 1943.

1.

ILLUSTRATIONS
British Commonwealth and all overprints and surcharges are FULL SIZE. Foreign Countries have been reduced to ¾-LINEAR.

1859. Imperf.

1. 1. (½d.) orange .. .. 24·00 £140
2. (1d.) blue .. .. .. 6·00 55·00
3. (2d.) red .. .. .. 5·50 55·00

ITALIAN OCCUPATION

For use in all islands except Kithyra.

1941. Stamps of Italy optd. **ISOLE JONIE**

(a) On postage stamps of 1929.

1. 69. 5 c. brown 5 5
2. 70. 10 c. brown 5 5
3. 20 c. red 5 5
4. 25 c. green 5 5
5. 74. 30 c. brown 5 5
6. 50 c. violet 5 5
7. 70. 75 c. red 5 5
8. 1 l. 25 blue 5 5

(b) On air stamp of 1930.

9. 81. 50 c. brown 5 5

(c) On Postage Due stamps of 1934.

D 10. D 6. 10 c. blue 5 5
D 11. 20 c. red 5 5
D 12. 30 c. orange 5 10
D 13. D 7. 1 l. orange 5 10

GERMAN OCCUPATION

For the island of Zante.
100 centesimi = 1 lira = 8 drachma.

(2.)

1943. Stamps a last further optd. with T 2.

1. 70. 25 c. green (postage) .. 1·00 2·50
2. 74. 50 c. violet .. .. 1·00 2·50
3. 81. 50 c. brown (air) .. 1·00 3·00

For separate issues for the Italian occupation of the islands of Corfu and Paxos and of Cephalonia and Ithaca see under these headings.

IRAN O2

A Kingdom of W. Asia.

1868. 20 shahis = 1 kran. 10 krans = 1 toman.
1881. 100 centimes = 1 franc.
1885. 20 chahis = 1 kran. 10 krans = 1 toman.
1932. 100 dinars = 1 rial.

NOTE.—The word "English" in the descriptive headings to various Persian issues is to be taken as referring to the lettering or figures and not to the language which is often French.

1.

2. Nasred-Din.

3. Nasred-Din.

1868. Imperf. or roul

1. 1. 1 (sh.) violet .. .. 15·00
1c. 1 (sh.) grey .. .. 12·00
15. 1 (sh.) black .. .. 1·50 1·50
2. 2 (sh.) green .. .. 10·00
16. 2 (sh.) blue .. .. 7·00 5·00
35. 2 (sh.) black .. .. 75·00
3d. 4 (sh.) green .. .. 12·00
17. 4 (sh.) red .. .. 8·00 5·00
4. 8 (sh.) red .. .. 15·00
8a. 8 (sh.) green .. .. 8·00 8·00
13. 1 (kr.) yellow .. .. 70·00 £200
18. 1 kr. red .. .. 15·00 5·00
38. 1 kr. red on yellow .. £170 12·00
19. 4 kr. yellow .. .. 30·00 5·00
36. 4 kr. blue .. .. 30·00 12·00
40. 5 kr. violet .. .. 55·00 30·00
41. 5 kr. gold .. .. £170 42·00
39. 1 to. bronze on blue .. £2000 £1000

1876. Perf.

20. 2. 1 (sh.) black and mauve .. 1·25 50
24. 2 (sh.) black and green .. 1·60 40
29. 5 (sh.) black and pink .. 1·25 35
22. 10 (sh.) black and blue .. 2·00 95

1879. Perf.

45. 3. 1 (sh.) black and red .. 4·00 75
46. 2 (sh.) black and yellow .. 6·00 2·50
47. 5 (sh.) black and green .. 3·75 35
48. 10 (sh.) black and mauve 18·00 1·75
49. 1 (kr.) black and brown .. 13·00 60
50. 5 (kr.) black and blue .. 3·50 35

4.

5.

1881.

56. 4. 5 c. mauve .. .. 2·50 1·25
57a. 10 c. red .. .. 2·25 90
61. 25 c. green .. .. 42·00 45
62. 5. 50 c. black, yell. & orge. 15·00 1·90
69. 50 c. black .. .. 3·00 1·60
63. 1 f. black and blue .. 3·75 45
64. 5 f. black and red .. 3·75 60
65. 10 f. black, yellow & red 4·25 2·25

The 10 f. is larger (30½ × 36 mm.).

1882. As T 4 and 5.

66. – 5 s. green 35 5
68. – 10 s. black, yell. & orange 2·25 30

8.

9.

10.

11. 12.

13.

1885.

70. 8. 1 c. green .. .. 1·25 15
71. 2 c. red .. .. 1·00 12
72. 5 c. blue .. .. 1·75 5
73. 9. 10 c. brown 60 8
74. 1 k. grey .. .. 1·25 15
75. 5 k. purple .. .. 9·00 55

1885. Surch. **OFFICIEL** and value in English and Persian.

81. – 3 on 5 s. green (No. 66) .. 3·25 1·50
77. – 6 on 5 s. green (No. 66) .. 10·00 3·74
83. – 6 on 10 s. (No. 68) .. 7·00 2·25
84. 5. 8 on 50 c. black .. .. 10·00 3·25
78. 12 on 50 c. black .. .. 12·00 1·75
79. – 18 on 10 s. (No. 68) .. 10·00 3·50
80. 5. 1 t. on 5 f. black and red 12·00 1·90

1889.

85. 10. 1 c. pink 10 5
86. 2 c. blue 5 5
87. 5 c. mauve 5 5
88. 7 c. brown 40 8
89. 11. 10 c. black 10 5
90. 1 k. orange 10 5
91. 2 k. rose 55 25
92. 5 k. green 25 15

1891.

93. 12. 1 c. black 10 5
94. 2 c. brown 15 5
95. 5 c. blue 5 5
96. 7 c. grey .. .. 6·50 75
97. 10 c. red 25 5
98. 14 c. orange 25 5
99. 13. 1 k. green .. .. 3·25 8
100. 2 k. orange .. .. 15·00 60
101. 5 k. orange 40 15

14.

15. 16. Muzaffer-ed-Din.

1894.

102. 14. 1 c. mauve 20 5
103. 2 c. green 20 5
104. 5 c. blue 20 5
105. 8 c. brown 20 5
106. 15. 10 c. orange 25 5
107. 16 c. rose .. .. 1·50 40
108. 1 k. rose and yellow .. 35 8
109. 2 k. brown and blue .. 35 10
110. 5 k. violet and silver .. 90 20
111. 10 k. rose and gold .. 4·00 1·25
112. 50 k. green and gold .. 3·50 1·00

1897. Surch. in English and Persian in frame.

113. 14. 5 c. on 8 c. brown .. 15 5
114. 15. 1 k. on 5 k. violet & silver 60 35
115. 2 k. on 5 k. violet & silver 75 35

1898. Chahi values on white or green paper.

116. 14. 1 c. grey 10 5
117. 2 c. brown 10 5
118. 3 c. purple 10 5
119. 4 c. red 15 5
120. 5 c. yellow 15 5
121. 8 c. orange 35 5
122. 10 c. blue 30 5
123. 12 c. red 30 5
124. 16 c. green 60 5
125. 16. 1 k. blue 60 5
157. 1 k. red .. .. 1·00 12
126. 2 k. pink 70 5
158. 2 k. green .. .. 2·25 35
127. 3 k. yellow 80 12
159. 3 k. brown .. .. 3·00 35
128. 4 k. grey 80 30
160. 4 k. red .. .. 3·00 35
129. 5 k. green 80 30
161. 5 k. brown .. .. 4·25 35
130. 10 k. orange .. .. 1·10 40
162. 10 k. blue .. .. 12·00 95
131. 50 k. mauve .. .. 2·25 1·25
163. 50 k. brown .. .. 7·50 1·00

(17.) (18.)

(19.)

1899. Optd. with control mark of various scroll devices as T 17.

132. 14. 1 c. grey 35 5
133. 2 c. brown 35 5
134. 3 c. purple 35 5
135. 4 c. red 35 5
136. 5 c. yellow 35 5
137. 8 c. orange 90 10
138. 10 c. blue 35 5
139. 12 c. red 70 5
140. 16 c. green 70 12
141. 16. 1 k. blue 85 10
142. 2 k. pink .. .. 1·75 45
143. 3 k. yellow .. .. 6·00 70
144. 4 k. grey .. .. 6·00 70
145. 5 k. green .. .. 2·75 70
146. 10 k. orange .. .. 8·00 70
147. 50 k. mauve .. .. 9·00 1·25

1900. Optd. with T 18 across two stamps.
164. 14. 1 c. grey .. .. 7·00 1·50
165. 2 c. brown .. .. 7·00 1·50
166. 3 c. purple .. .. 8·00 2·00
167. 4 c. red .. .. 16·00 2·50
168. 5 c. yellow .. .. 4·00 40
169. 10 c. blue .. .. 45·00 27·00
170. 12 c. red .. .. 9·00 1·40
Prices quoted in this issue are for pairs.

1900. Surch. in various ways in English and Persian.
176. 14. 5 on 8 c. brown 45 8
179. 16. 12 c. on 1 k. red .. 75 20
180. 5 k. on 50 k. brown .. 3·75 2·10

1902. Optd. **PROVISOIRE 1319** in ornamental frame.
181. 14. 1 c. grey 25 10
182. 2 c. brown 25 10
183. 3 c. purple 25 10
184. 4 c. red 30 15
185. 5 c. yellow 25 10
197. 5 on 8 c. brn (No. 176) 70 15
186. 8 c. orange 35 25
187. 10 c. blue 35 12
188. 12 c. red 35 15
198. 16. 12 c. on 1 k. (No. 179) .. 70 25
189. 14. 16 c. green 35 25
190. 16. 1 k. red .. 1·00 40
191. 2 k. green .. .. — 1·00
192. 3 k. brown .. .. — 3·00
193. 4 k. red .. .. — 4·00
194. 5 k. brown .. .. — 4·00
199. 5 k. on 50 k. (No. 180) .. 3·25 2·00
195. 10 k. blue .. .. — 7·50
196. 50 k. brown .. .. — 15·00

1902. Surch. with T 19.
177. 14. 5 c. on 10 c. blue .. 70 30
178. 16. 5 c. on 1 k. red .. 75 40

20. (21.)

1902. Words "CHAHIS", "KRANS", or "TOMANS" in capital or small letters. Optd. with T 21.
200. 20. 1 c. grey 30 8
201. 2 c. brown 70 8
202. 3 c. green 70 8
203. 5 c. red 35 5
204. 10 c. yellow 75 10
205. 12 c. blue .. .. 1·90 25
206. 1 k. mauve .. .. 1·90 10
207. 2 k. green .. .. 2·25 15
208. 10 k. blue .. .. 10·00 2·00
209. 50 k. red .. .. 70·00 10·00

1902. Surch. **5 KRANS** in English and Persian.
237. 20. 5 k. on 5 k. yellow .. 1·25 1·25

1902. Optd. **PROVISOIRE 1319** in ornamental frame.
211. 20. 1 c. grey .. .. 5·00 2·50
212. 2 c. brown .. .. 5·00 2·50
213. 3 c. green .. .. 5·00 2·50
214. 5 c. red .. .. 5·00 2·50
215. 12 c. blue .. .. 5·00 2·50

1903. Optd. **PROVISOIRE 1903** and lion in frame, but without Arms opt. (T 21).
239. 20. 1 c. grey .. .. — 70
240. 2 c. brown .. .. — 70
241. 5 c. red .. .. — 70
242. 10 c. yellow .. .. — 70
243. 12 c. blue .. .. — 70
244. 1 k. mauve .. .. — 70

22. 23.

1903.
246. 22. 1 c. lilac 5 5
247. 2 c. grey 8 5
248. 3 c. green 8 5
249. 5 c. red 15 5
250. 10 c. brown 15 5
251. 12 c. blue 15 5
252. 23. 1 k. purple 30 5
253. 2 k. blue 25 5
254. 5 k. brown 45 8
255. 10 k. red 60 15
256. 20 k. orange 75 40
257. 30 k. green .. .. 1·00 70
258. 50 k. green .. .. 7·50 4·00
See also Nos. 298/303.

1903. Surch. in both English and Persian except those marked * which are surch. in English only.
272. 22. "1 CHAHI" on 3 c. green 75 10
287. "1 CHAI" on 3 c. green 30 8
288. 23. 1 c. on 1 k. purple .. 1·75 75
273. 22. 2 c. on 3 c. green .. 1·75 75
289. 23. 2 c. on 5 k. brown .. 1·75 75
277. 22. 3 c. on 5 c. red .. 50 8
278. 6 c. on 10 c. brown .. 1·40 8
279. 23. 9 c. on 1 k. purple .. 1·40 8
274. 12 c. on 10 k. red .. 2·00 50
275. 2 t. on 50 k. green* .. 12·00 5·00
280. 2 t. on 50 k. green .. 10·00 3·00
276. 3 t. on 50 k. green* .. 12·00 5·00
281. 3 t. on 50 k. green .. 10·00 3·00

25. 26. Shah Muhammad Ali.

1906. Optd. **PROVISOIRE** and lion. Imperf. or perf.
292. 25. 1 c. violet 15 5
293. 2 c. grey 15 5
294. 3 c. green 15 5
295. 6 c. red 15 5
296. 10 c. brown 75 5
297. 13 c. blue 50 5

1907.
298. 22. 1 ch. violet on blue .. 8 5
299. 2 ch. grey on blue .. 8 5
300. 3 ch. green on blue .. 8 5
301. 6 ch. red on blue .. 8 5
302. 9 ch. yellow on blue .. 10 5
303. 10 ch. sepia on blue .. 12 5
305. 26. 13 c. blue 25 5
306. 26 c. brown 30 5
307. 1 k. red 35 5
308. 2 k. green 30 5
309. 3 k. blue 35 5
310. 4 k. yellow .. .. 8·00 65
312. 5 k. brown 50 12
313. 10 k. pink .. .. 1·50 12
314. 20 k. black .. .. 2·25 15
315. 30 k. purple .. .. 3·25 35
316. – 50 k. black, red & gold 6·00 1·10
The 50 k. is larger with the head facing the other way.

28. 29. Ahmed Mirza.

1909.
337. 28. 1 c. maroon and orange 5 5
338. 2 c. maroon and violet 5 5
339. 3 c. maroon and green 5 5
340. 6 c. maroon and red .. 8 5
341. 9 c. maroon and grey 8 5
342. 10 c. maroon and purple 10 5
343. 13 c. maroon and blue .. 10 5
344. 26 c. maroon and green 20 8
345. 1 k. olive, violet & silver 30 5
346. 2 k. olive, grn. & silver 50 5
347. 3 k. olive, grey & silver 5·00 5
348. 4 k. olive, blue & silver 5·50 15
349. 5 k. olive, brown & gold 10·00 15
350. 10 k. olive, orge. & gold 22·00 50
351. 20 k. olive, green & gold 22·00 50
352. 30 k. olive, red and gold 25·00 1·00
Stamps of this issue offered at very low prices are reprints.
For stamps as T 28 but with curved inscriptions, see Nos. O 836, etc.

(30.) (31.)

1909. Nos. 298/315 optd. as Type 30. Imperf.
320. 22. 1 ch. on 1 ch. violet on bl. 6·00 5·00
321. 1 ch. on 2 ch. grey on bl. 6·00 5·00
322. 1 ch. on 3 ch. grn. on bl. 6·00 5·00
323. 1 ch. on 6 ch. red on blue 6·00 5·00
324. 1 ch. on 9 ch. yell. on bl. 6·00 5·00
325. 1 ch. on 10 ch. brn. on bl. 6·00 5·00
326. 26. 2 ch. on 13 ch. blue .. 8·00 6·00
327. 2 ch. on 26 ch. brown .. 8·00 6·00
328. 2 ch. on 1 kr. red .. 8·00 6·00
329. 2 ch. on 2 kr. green .. 8·00 6·00
330. 2 ch. on 3 kr. blue .. 8·00 6·00
331. 2 ch. on 4 kr. yellow .. 8·00 6·00
333. 2 ch. on 5 kr. brown .. 8·00 6·00
334. 2 ch. on 10 kr. pink .. 12·00 10·00
335. 2 ch. on 20 kr. black .. 12·00 10·00
336. 2 ch. on 30 kr. purple .. 12·00 10·00

1911.
361. 29. 1 c. orange and green .. 10 5
362. 2 c. brown and red .. 10 5
363. 3 c. green and grey .. 10 5
365. 5 c. red and brown .. 10 5
366. 6 c. red and grey .. 10 5
367. 6 c. brown and green .. 10 5
368. 9 c. lilac and brown .. 10 5
369. 10 c. brown and red .. 10 5
370. 12 c. blue and green .. 10 5
371 13 c. blue and violet .. 10 5
372. 24 c. green and purple 10 5
373. 26 c. green and blue .. 10 5
374. 1 k. red and blue .. 10 5
375. 2 k. purple and green 10 5
376. 3 k. black and lilac .. 10 5
377. 4 k. black and blue .. 10 5
378. 5 k. blue and red .. 10 5
379. 10 k. rose and olive .. 10 5
380. 20 k. yellow & chocolate 10 5
381. 30 k. green and red .. 10 5

1911. Various stamps optd. **Relais** in English and Persian.
382. 28. 2 ch. maroon and violet 1·25 40
383. 3 ch. maroon and green 1·25 40
384. 6 ch. maroon and red .. 1·25 40
385. 13 ch. maroon and blue 1·25 40
386. 29. 2 ch. brown and red .. 1·25 70
387. 3 ch. green and grey .. 1·25 70
388. 6 ch. red and grey .. 1·25 90
388a. 13 ch. blue and violet .. 1·25 90

1912. Optd. **Officiel** in English and Persian.
389. 29. 1 c. orange and green .. 5 5
390. 2 c. brown and red .. 5 5
391. 3 c. green and grey .. 5 5
392. 6 c. red and grey .. 5 5
393. 9 c. lilac and brown .. 5 5
394. 10 c. brown and red .. 5 5
395. 13 c. blue and violet .. 70 10
396. 26 c. green and blue .. 2·75 20
397. 1 k. red and blue .. 2·75 10
398. 2 k. purple and green .. 3·00 15
399. 3 k. black and lilac .. 3·00 15
400. 5 k. blue and red .. 6·50 15
401. 10 k. rose and olive .. 12·00 70
402. 20 k. yellow & chocolate 12·00 70
403. 30 k. green and red .. 15·00 1·25

1914. Surch. with new value and **1914** in English and Persian.
412. 29. 1 c. on 13 c. bl. & violet 75 20
413. 3 c. on 26 c. grn. & blue 75 20

1915. Surch. with new value in frame and **1915** in English and Persian.
414. 29. 1 c. on 5 c. red & brown 60 10
415. 2 c. on 5 c. red & brown 7·00 60
416. 6 c. on 12 c. bl. & green 1·25 12

1915. Surch. with new value in English and Persian.
417. 28. 5 c. on 1 k. (No. 345) .. 1·40 5
418. 12 c. on 13 c. (No. 343) 1·40 5

1915. Optd. with T 31 ("1333").
419. 28. 1 c. maroon and orange 12 5
420. 2 c. maroon and violet .. 20 5
421. 3 c. maroon and green .. 30 5
422. 6 c. maroon and red .. 30 5
423. 9 c. maroon and grey .. 30 5
424. 10 c. maroon and purple 70 8
425. 1 k. olive, violet & silver 1·40 8

32. The Imperial Crown. 33. King Darius on his Throne.

1915. Coronation of Shah Ahmed.
426. 32. 1 c. blue and red .. 5 5
427. 2 c. red and blue .. 5 5
428. 3 c. green 5 5
429. 5 c. red 5 5
430. 6 c. red and green .. 5 5
431. 9 c. violet and brown .. 5 5
432. 10 c. brown and green 5 5
433. 12 c. blue .. 5 5
434. 24 c. chocolate & brown 5 5
435. 33. 1 k. black, brn. & silver 8 5
436. 2 k. red, blue and silver 8 5
437. 3 k. sepia, lilac & silver 8 5
438. 5 k. grey, sepia & silver 8 5
439. – 1 t. black, violet & gold 15 15
440. – 2 t. brown, green & gold 15 15
441. – 3 t. red and gold .. 20 20
442. – 5 t. grey, blue and gold 25 25
DESIGN: 1 t. to 5 t. Gateway of the Palace of Persepolis.

(34.) (35.)

1915. Optd. with T 34 ("1334").
477. 28. 1 k. blk., violet & silver 2·40 40
478. 10 k. blk., orge. & gold 3·50 75
479. 20 k. blk., grn. & gold 35·00 3·00
480. 30 k. black, red & gold 14·00 2·50

1917. Surch. with value in English only.
481. 29. 12 c. on 1 k. red & blue 55·00 32·00
482. 24 c. on 1 k. red & blue 14·00 14·00

1917. Optd. with T 35 ("1335") or surch. also with new value in English and Persian.
483. 28. 1 c. maroon and orange 15·00 2·00
484. 1 c. on 2 c. (No. 338) .. 80 5
485. 1 c. on 9 c. (No. 341) .. 80 8
486. 1 c. on 10 c. (No. 342) .. 80 8
490. 29. 1 c. on 10 c. brn. & red 80 5
487. 28. 3 c. on 9 c. mar. & grey 80 8
491. 29. 3 c. on 10 c. brn. & red 80 5
488. 28. 3 c. on 26 c. (No. 344) 1·25 8
489. 5 c. on 13 c. (No. 343) 1·25 8
492. 29. 5 c. on 1 k. red and blue 1·75 5
493. 6 c. on 10 c. brown & red 2·75 50
494. 6 c. on 12 c. blue & green 1·50 8

(36.) (37.)

1918. Optd. with T 36 ("1336").
507. 28. 2 k. olive, grn. & silver 3·00 30

1918. Surch. as T 36 and new value in English and Persian.
508. 28. 24 c. on 4 k. (No. 348) .. 3·00 30
509. 10 k. on 5 k. (No. 349) .. 7·00 45

1918. Coronation issue of 1915 optd. **Novembre Irrv-1918.**
510. 33. 2 k. red, blue and silver 2·50 2·00
511. 3 k. blk., lilac & silver 2·50 2·00
512. 5 k. grey, black & silver 4·00 2·00
513. – 1 t. black, violet & gold 3·25 2·00
514. – 2 t. brown, green & gold 4·00 2·40
515. – 3 t. red and gold .. 4·00 2·40
516. – 5 t. grey, blue and gold 4·00 3·25

1918. Surch. in English and Persian and with date in Persian only.
517. 29. 3 c. on 12 c. blue & green 2·75 5
518. 6 c. on 10 c. brown & red 2·00 5
519. 6 c. on 1 k. red and blue 2·00 5

1918. Optd. with T 37 ("1337").
520. 28. 2 k. olive, green & silver 2·25 20
521. 3 k. olive, grey & silver 3·50 20
522. 4 k. olive, blue & silver 3·75 60
523. 5 k. olive, brown & gold 3·75 40
524. 10 k. olive, orange & gold 3·75 50
525. 20 k. olive, green & gold 40·00 3·50
526. 30 k. olive, red and gold 22·00 1·40

1919. As T 26, but head of Sultan Ahmed Mirza, surch. **Provisoire 1919** and value in English and Persian.
527. 1 c. yellow 20 5
528. 3 c. green 25 8
529. 5 c. claret 30 8
530. 6 c. violet 60 8
531. 12 c. blue .. .. 1·25 12

1919. Surch. **1919** and value in English and Persian.
532. 10. 2 k. on 5 c. mauve .. 60 20
533. 3 k. on 5 c. mauve .. 35 20
534. 4 k. on 5 c. mauve .. 35 20
535. 5 k. on 5 c. mauve .. 35 20
536. 12. 10 k. on 10 c. red .. 35 20
537. 20 k. on 10 c. red .. 35 20
538. 30 k. on 10 c. red .. 35 35
539. 50 k. on 14 c. orange .. 65 30

1921. Surch. **6-CHAHIS** in English and Persian.
539a. 29. 6 c. on 12 c. blue & green 2·00 8

1921. Coup d'Etat of Raza Khan. Coronation issue of 1915 optd. **21. FEV. 1921** in English and Persian.
540. 32. 3 c. green .. .. 1·50
541. 5 c. red .. .. 1·50
542. 6 c. red and green .. 1·50
543. 10 c. brown and green 1·50
544. 12 c. blue .. .. 2·25
545. 33. 1 k. blk., brn. & silver 1·90
546. 2 k. red, blue & silver 2·25
547. 5 k. grey, brn. & silver 3·75
548. – 2 t. brown, grn. & gold 3·75
549. – 3 t. red and gold .. 3·75
550. – 5 t. grey, blue and gold 3·75

1922. Surch. with value in English only.
551. 29. 10 c. on 6 c. brn. & grn. 5·00 1·00
552. 1 k. on 12 c. blue & grn. 5·00 1·00

1922. Surcharged with value in English only over **BENADERS.**
553. 29. 10 c. on 6 c. brn. & grn. 6·00 1·00
554. 1 k. on 12 c. blue & grn. 6·00 2·50

1922. Optd. **CONTROLE 1922** in English and Persian.
555. 29. 1 c. orange and green .. 10 5
556. 2 c. brown and red .. 10 5
557. 3 c. green and grey .. 10 5
558. 3 c. green and brown .. 15 10
559. 3 c. red and brown .. 7·50 1·50
560. 6 c. brown and green .. 10 5
561. 9 c. lilac and brown .. 20 5
562. 10 c. brown and red .. 20 5

563. 29. 12 c. blue and green 30 5
564. 24 c. green and purple 1·00 5
565. 1 k. red and blue 2·00 5
566. 2 k. purple and green 3·25 5
567. 3 k. black and lilac 3·25 5
568. 4 k. blue and black 20·00 1·60
569. 5 k. blue and red 10·00 5
570. 10 k. rose and brown 20·00 5
571. 20 k. yellow & chocolate 20·00 8
572. 30 k. green and red 20·00 8

1922. Surch. in English and Persian.
573. 29. 3 c. on 12 c. (No. 543) 40 5
574. 6 c. on 24 c. (No. 564) 2·00 5
575. 10 c. on 20 k. (No. 571) 1·75 25
576. 1 k. on 30 k. (No. 572) 2·25 1·10

38. Ahmed Mirza.

1924.
577. 38. 1 c. orange 5 5
578. 2 c. claret 5 5
579. 3 c. brown 8 5
580. 6 c. sepia 8 5
581. 9 c. green 8 5
582. 10 c. violet 10 5
583. 12 c. red 8 10
584. 1 k. blue 15 10
585. 2 k. red and blue 25 10
586. 3 k. purple and violet 80 10
587. 5 k. sepia and red 2·50 30
588. 10 k. violet and sepia 2·50 70
589. 20 k. sepia and green 5·00 1·50
590. 30 k. black and orange 10·00 2·00

1924. Type as for 1919 (Nos. 527/31) but surch. **p.re** and value in English and Persian and date **1924** or **1925**.
591. 1 c. brown 5 5
592. 2 c. grey 5 5
595. 2 c. green 5 5
593. 3 c. red 5 5
594. 6 c. orange 35 5
597. 6 c. blue 30 5
598. 9 c. brown 50 5
599. 10 c. grey 2·00 8
600. 1 k. green 2·00 8
601. 2 k. mauve 4·00 15

39. (40. "Provisional Pahlavi Government, 31 Oct. 1925".)

1925. Deposition of Shah Ahmed and Provisional Government of Riza Kahn Pahlavi. Fiscal stamps as T 39 optd. with T 40.
602. 39. 1 c. red 40 15
603. 2 c. yellow 40 15
604. 3 c. green 30 15
605. 5 c. grey 1·00 50
606. 10 c. red 40 15
607. 1 k. blue 40 15

ILLUSTRATIONS British Commonwealth and all overprints and surcharges are FULL SIZE. Foreign Countries have been reduced to ¾-LINEAR.

(41.)

1926. Optd. with T 41.
608. 38. 1 c. orange 8 8
609. 2 c. claret 15 8
610. 3 c. brown 20 10
611. 6 c. sepia 2·00 1·25

1926. Optd. **Regne de Pahlavi 1926** in English and Persian.
612. 28. 1 c. maroon and orange 10 5
613. 2 c. maroon and violet 10 5
614. 3 c. maroon and green 10 5
615. 6 c. maroon and red 12 5
616. 9 c maroon and grey 20 5
617. 10 c. maroon and purple 20 5
618. 13 c. maroon and blue 1·25 5
619. 26 c. maroon and green 2·25 5
620. 1 k. olive, violet & silver 1·40 5
621. 2 k. olive, green & silver 2·10 5
622. 3 k. olive, grey & silver 2·10 5
623. 4 k. olive, blue & silver 28·00 12
624. 5 k. olive, brown & gold 18·00 12
625. 10 k. olive, oran. & gold 40·00 12
626. 20 k. olive, green & gold 55·00 30
627. 30 k. olive, red and gold 55·00 40

42. Riza Shah Pahlavi. 43.

1926.
628. 42. 1 c. green 10 5
639. 2 c. blue 20 5
630. 3 c. green 30 5
641. 6 c. claret 35 5
632. 9 c. red 1·50 5
633. 10 c. brown 2·75 5
634. 12 c. orange 2·75 5
635. 15 c. blue 3·00 5
636. 43. 1 k. blue 4·00 35
637. 2 k. mauve 8·00 2·00

1927. Air. Optd. with aeroplane and **POSTE AERIENNE** in English and Persian.
642. 28. 1 c. maroon and orange 10 5
643. 2 c. maroon and violet 10 8
644. 3 c. maroon and green 20 5
645. 6 c. maroon and red 20 5
646. 9 c. maroon and grey 20 5
647. 10 c. maroon and purple 20 5
648. 13 c. maroon and blue 20 5
649. 26 c. maroon and green 50 15
650. 1 k. olive, violet & silver 70 20
651. 2 k. olive, green & silver 1·50 45
652. 3 k. olive, grey & silver 1·50 50
653. 4 k. olive, blue & silver 3·75 1·00
654. 5 k. olive, brown & gold 3·75 1·25
655. 10 k. olive, oran. & gold 35·00 26·00
656. 20 k. olive, green & gold 32·00 25·00
657. 30 k. olive, red and gold 35·00 26·00

44. 45. Riza Shah Pahlavi.

1928. Air. Fiscal stamps surch. with aeroplane, **Poste aerienne** (or **Poste aerien** on 3 k. to 3 t. values) and new value in English and Persian.
658. 44. 1 c. green 8 5
659. 2 c. blue 8 5
660. 3 c. red 5 5
661. 5 c. brown 8 5
662. 10 c. green 8 5
663. 1 k. violet 8 5
664. 2 k. orange 15 8
657a. 39. 3 k. brown 22·00 12·00
657b. 5 k. chocolate 2·75 1·00
657c. 1 t. violet 4·00 3·25
657d. 2 t. olive 5·00 3·50
657e. 3 t. green 5·00 3·75

1929. Air. Fiscal stamps as Nos. 653/7 but surch. with aeroplane, **Poste aerienne** and value in English and Persian.
665. 39. 3 k. brown 10·00 3·75
666. 5 k. chocolate 2·10 75
667. 10 k. violet 4·00 2·50
668. 20 k. olive 4·75 2·10
669. 30 k. green 4·75 2·50

1929.
670. 45. 1 c. red and green 8 5
671. 2 c. blue and red 8 5
672. 3 c. green and claret 8 5
673. 6 c. green and brown 8 5
674. 9 c. red and blue 20 5
675. 10 c. brown and green 40 5
676. 12 c. violet and black 65 5
677. 15 c. blue and yellow 75 5
678. 24 c. lake and olive 1·60 5
679. 1 k. black and blue 2·75 5
680. 2 k. violet and orange 2·75 8
681. 3 k. red and green 4·00 10
682. 5 k. green and brown 4·25 20
683. 1 t. red and blue 4·75 30
684. 2 t. black and red 12·00 1·50
685. – 3 t. violet and gold 10·00 1·60
DESIGN: 3 t. Shah enthroned (28½ × 39 mm.).

47. Riza Shah Pahlavi and Elburz Mts.

1930. Air.
686. 47. 1 c. blue and yellow 8 5
687. 2 c. black and blue 8 5
688. 3 c. violet and olive 8 5
689. 4 c. blue and violet 8 5
690. 5 c. red and green 8 5
691. 6 c. green and claret 8 5
692. 8 c. violet and grey 8 5
693. 10 c. red and blue 8 5
694. 47. 12 c. orange and grey 15 8
695. 15 c. olive and brown 15 10
696. 1 k. red and blue 30 12
697. 2 k. blue and black 35 15
698. 3 k. green and brown 40 20
699. 5 k. black and red 1·00 60
700. 1 t. purple and orange 1·60 70
701. 2 t. brown and green 3·00 1·75
702. 3 t. green and purple 10·00 7·00

48. 49. Riza Shah Pahlavi. 50.

1931.
703. 48. 1 c. blue and brown 12 5
704. 2 c. black and claret 20 5
705. 3 c. brown and mauve 12 5
706. 6 c. violet and red 25 5
707. 9 c. red and blue 75 5
708. 10 c. grey and red 3·50 5
709. 11 c. red and blue 6·00 40
710. 12 c. mauve and blue 4·00 5
711. 16 c. red and black 3·25 5
712. 27 c. blue and black 3·50 5
713. 1 k. blue and red 3·50 8

1933. New Currency.
714. 49. 5 d. brown 8 5
715. 10 d. blue 8 5
716. 15 d. grey 12 5
717. 30 d. green 12 5
718. 45 d. blue 30 5
719. 50 d. mauve 35 5
720. 60 d. green 75 5
721. 75 d. brown 75 5
722. 90 d. red 75 5
723. 50. 1 r. black and red 75 5
724. 1 r. 20 red and black 3·50 5
725. 1 r. 50 blue and yellow 3·50 12
726. 2 r. brown and blue 2·50 8
727. 3 r. green and magenta 5·00 12
728. 5 r. red and brown 11·00 1·40

51. "Justice". 52. Cement works, Chah-Abdul-Azim.

1935. Riza Khan's Advent to Power. 10th Anniversary.
729. 51. 5 d. green and brown 10 5
730. – 10 d. grey and orange 10 5
731. – 15 d. blue and red 15 5
732. – 30 d. green and black 20 5
733. – 45 d. lake and olive 35 5
734. 52. 75 d. brown and green 1·25 12
735. – 90 d. red and blue 1·25 12
736. – 1 r. violet and brown 3·25 75
737. – 1 r. 50 blue and purple 2·50 1·10
DESIGNS: 10 d. Ruins of Persepolis. 15 d. "Education". 30 d. Aeroplanes over Teheran Aerodrome. 45 d. Sahktessar Sanatorium, Mazanderan. 90 d. Gunboat "Palang". 1 r. Railway bridge over R. Karoun. 1 r. 50, G.P.O. and Customs House, Teheran.

1935. Optd. **POSTES IRANIENNES.**
(a) Stamps of 1929.
738 45. 1 c. red and green 60·00 22·00
739. 2 c. blue and red 15·00 12·00
740. 3 c. green and red 8·00 4·00
741. 6 c. green and brown 8·00 4·00
742. 9 c. red and blue 5·00 4·00
743. 1 t. red and blue 5·00 60
744. 2 t. black and red 6·50 70
745. 3 t. violet and gold 8·00 1·50
(b) Stamps of 1931.
746. 48. 1 c. blue and brown 42·00 21·00
747. 2 c. black and red 4·00 2·00
748. 3 c. brown and mauve 2·50 2·00
749. 6 c. violet and red 12·00 7·00
750. 9 c. red and blue 12·00 7·00
751. 11 c. red and blue 35 8
752. 12 c. mauve and blue 40·00 20·00
753. 16 c. red and black 40 10
754. 27 c. blue and black 40 8
(c) Stamps of 1933.
755. 49. 5 c. brown 8 5
756. 10 d. blue 12 5
757. 15 d. grey 12 5
758. 30 d. green 70 5
759. 45 d. blue 35 15
760. 50 d. mauve 35 5
761. 60 d. green 35 5
762. 75 d. brown 2·00 20
763. 90 d. red 2·00 1·40
764. 50. 1 r. black and red 3·50 3·00
765. 1 r. 20 red and black 2·25 10
766. 1 r. 50 blue and green 2·00 10
767. 2 r. brown and blue 2·10 10
768. 3 r. green and mauve 3·50 15
769. 5 r. red and brown 22·00 14·00

1935. Air. Air stamps of 1930 optd. **IRAN.**
770. 47. 1 c. blue and yellow 8 5
771. 2 c. black and blue 8 5
772. 3 c. violet and olive 8 5
773. 4 c. blue and violet 8 5
774. 5 c. red and green 8 5
775. 6 c. green and claret 8 5
776. 8 c. violet and grey 8 5
777. 10 c. red and blue 10 5
778. 12 c. orange and blue 12 8
779. 15 c. olive and brown 12 8
780. 1 k. red and blue 2·75 50
781. 2 k. blue and black 1·50 70
782. 3 k. green and brown 1·60 1·00
783. 5 k. black and red 80 35
784. 1 t. purple and orange 9·00 6·50
785. 2 t. brown and green 2·50 75
786. 3 t. green and purple 2·75 1·10

53. 54. Riza Shah Pahlavi. 55.

1935. Rial values are larger.
787. 53. 5 d. violet 8 5
788. 10 d. purple 8 5
789. 15 d. blue 10 5
790. 30 d. green 20 5
791. 45 d. orange 35 5
792. 50 d. brown 35 5
793. 60 d. blue 3·00 5
794. 75 d. red 75 5
795. 90 d. red 75 5
796. – 1 r. purple 1·00 5
797. – 1 r. 50 blue 4·50 15
798. – 2 r. green 4·00 10
799. – 3 r. brown 4·00 15
800. – 5 r. grey 4·00 70

1936. Rial values are larger.
801. 54. 5 d. violet 5 5
802. 10 d. mauve 5 5
803. 15 d. blue 5 5
804. 30 d. green 8 5
805. 45 d. red 10 5
806. 50 d. brown 20 5
807. 60 d. brown 30 5
808. 75 d. claret 35 5
809. 90 d. red 40 5
810. – 1 r. green 70 5
811. – 1 r. 50 blue 1·75 5
812. – 2 r. blue 2·00 5
813. – 3 r. purple 2·00 8
814. – 5 r. green 10·00 25
815. – 10 r. blue and brown 14·00 1·00

1938. Rial values are larger.
816. 55. 5 d. violet 5 5
817. 10 d. mauve 5 5
818. 15 d. blue 5 5
819. 30 d. green 5 5
820. 45 d. red 10 5
821. 50 d. brown 20 5
822. 60 d. orange 30 5
823. 75 d. claret 30 5
824. 90 d. red 35 12
825. – 1 r. green 75 5
826. – 1 r. 50 blue 2·10 5
827. – 2 r. blue 2·50 5
828. – 3 r. purple 4·00 8
829. – 5 r. green 5·00 15
830. – 10 r. blue and brown 12·00 45

56. Princess Fawzieh and Crown Prince.

1939. Royal Wedding.
831. 56. 5 d. brown 12 8
832. 10 d. violet 20 8
833. 30 d. green 35 10
834. 90 d. red 60 40
835. 1 r. 50 blue 90 60

57. Bridge over Karun River. 58. Muhammed Riza Pahlavi.

1942.
850. 57. 5 d. violet 5 5
851. 5 d. orange 5 5
852. – 10 d. mauve 8 5
853. – 10 d. green 5 5
854. – 20 d. violet 15 5
855. – 20 d. magenta 8 5
856. – 25 d. red 45 5
857. – 25 d. violet 10 5
858. – 35 d. green 10 5
859. – 50 d. blue 45 5
860. – 50 d. green 45 5
861. – 70 d. brown 8 5
863. – 75 d. maroon 1·75 5

862. – 75 d. red .. .. 1·50 5
864. – 1 r. red .. .. .. 1·50 5
865. – 1 r. maroon .. .. 2·50 5
866. – 1 r. 50 red .. .. 1·25 5
867. – 2 r. blue .. .. 1·25 5
868. – 2 r. olive .. .. 2·50 5
869. – 2 r. 50 blue 80 5
870. – 3 r. green .. .. 12·00 5
871. – 3 r. purple .. .. 5·00 5
872. – 5 r. olive .. .. 15·00 8
873. – 5 r. blue .. .. 1·50 5
874. **58.** 10 r. black and orange 5·00 5
876. 20 r. violet and brown 60·00 1·75
877. 20 r. black and orange 2·00 5
878. 30 r. green and black .. £500 1·75
879. 30 r. black and green .. 2·50 15
880. 50 r. red and blue .. 12·00 3·00
881. 50 r. black and violet .. 3·00 75
882. 100 r. black and red .. 75·00 2·50
883. 200 r. black and blue .. 30·00 1·50

DESIGNS—HORIZ. 10 d. Beresk Bridge, N. Iran. 20 d. Granary, Ahwaz. 25 d. Train and bridge. 50 d. Ministry of Justice. 70 d. School building. VERT. 35 d. As 75 d. but different view of museum. 75 d. Side view of museum. 1 r. to 5 r. Full-face portrait of Mohammed Riza Pahlavi.

59. Lion and Bull, Persepolis.

DESIGNS—VERT. 1 r. Persian Warrior, Persepolis. HORIZ. $2\frac{1}{2}$ r. Palace of Darius, Persepolis. 5 r. Tomb of Cyrus, Pasargades. 10 r. King Darius enthroned.

1948. Fund to rebuild Avicenna's Tomb at Hamadan (1st issue).

899. **59.** 50 d.+25 d. green .. 12 12
900. – 1 r.+50 d. red 30 15
901. – $2\frac{1}{2}$ r.+$1\frac{1}{4}$ r. blue .. 55 30
902. – 5 r.+$2\frac{1}{2}$ r. violet .. 1·00 60
903. – 10 r.+5 r. purple .. 1·60 1·10

See also Nos. 909/13, 930/4, 939/43, and 1024/28.

60. National Flag.

DESIGNS—HORIZ. 50 d. Bandar Shahpur (port). 1 r. 50, Lorries on winding road. 2 r. 50, Mountain viaduct. 5 r. Muhammed Riza Pahlavi and map of Iran.

1949. Iran's War Effort.

904. **60.** 25 d. multicoloured .. 20 8
905. – 50 d. violet 30 8
906. – 1 r. 50 red 40 10
907. – 2 r. 50 blue .. .. 1·50 15
908. – 5 r. green .. .. 2·00 35

61. King Ardashir II.

62. King Ardashir I and Ahura Mazda.

1949. Fund to rebuild Avicenna's Tomb (2nd issue).

909. **61.** 50 d.+25 d. green .. 12 12
910. – 1 r.+50 d. red 15 12
911. – $2\frac{1}{2}$ r.+$1\frac{1}{4}$ r. blue .. 30 25
912. – 5 r.+$2\frac{1}{2}$ r. plum .. 80 70
913. **62.** 10 r.+5 r. green .. 1·25 1·10

DESIGNS—VERT. 1 r. King Narses. HORIZ. $2\frac{1}{2}$ r. King Shapur I and Emperor Valerian. 5 r. Arch of Ctesiphon.

63. Muhammed Riza Pahlavi and Parliament Building.

64. Old G.P.O., Teheran.

65. Mohammed Riza Pahlavi.

1949.

914. – 5 d. green and red .. 5 5
915. – 10 d. brown and blue .. 5 5
916. – 20 d. blue and violet .. 5 5
917. – 25 d. blue and brown .. 5 5
918. – 50 d. blue and green .. 5 5
919. – 75 d. red and brown .. 10 5
920. – 1 r. green and violet .. 15 5
921. – 1 r. 50 red and green .. 10 5
922. **63.** 2 r. brown and red .. 10 5
923. – 2 r. 50 blue 10 5
924. – 3 r. orange and blue .. 25 5
925. – 5 r. violet and red .. 25 5
926. **64.** 10 r. green and red .. 1·50 5
927. 20 r. red and black .. 20·00 2·50
928. **65.** 30 r. blue and brown .. 4·00 60
929. 50 r. blue and red .. 4·50 75

DESIGNS—HORIZ. All show buildings. In the dinar values, portrait is to right of stamp, and in rial values, to left. 5 d Ramsar Hotel, Darband, Caspian Sea. 10 d. Zayende River Bridge. 20 d. Foreign Office Building. 25 d. Old Royal Palace, Isfahan. 50 d. Qum Mosque. 75 d. Railway Square. 1 r. National Bank. 1 r. 50, Mosque of the Shah, Teheran. 2 r. Post and Customs Offices. 2 r. 50, Parliament Building. 3 r. The Great Gate, Isfahan. 5 r. Isfahan.

66. Tomb of Ali Abarquh.

67. Allegory.

1949. Fund to rebuild Avicenna's Tomb (3rd issue).

930. **66.** 50 d.+25 d. green .. 12 12
931. – 1 r.+50 d. brown .. 15 15
932. – $2\frac{1}{2}$ r.+$1\frac{1}{4}$ r. blue .. 30 30
933. – 5 r.+$2\frac{1}{2}$ r. red .. 60 60
934. – 10 r.+5 r. olive .. 1·25 1·25

DESIGNS—VERT. 1 r. Jami Mosque, Isfahan. HORIZ. $2\frac{1}{2}$ r. Tomb tower, Hamadan. 5 r. Jami Mosque, Ardistan. 10 r. Seljuk coin.

1950. U.P.U. 75th Anniv.

•935. – 50 d. lake .. .. 10·00 8·00
936. **67.** 2 r. 50 blue .. .. 20·00 12·00

DESIGN—HORIZ. 50 d. Hemispheres and doves.

68. Riza Shah Pahlavi and Mausoleum.

1950. Interment of Riza Shah Pahlavi at Shah Abdul Azim.

937. **68.** 50 d. brown .. .. 2·50 50
938. 2 r. black .. .. 2·75 80

69. Tomb of Baba Afzal, Kashan.

70. Flag and Book.

1950. Fund to rebuild Avicenna's Tomb (4th issue).

939. **69.** 50+25 d. green .. 10 10
940. – 1+$\frac{1}{2}$ r. blue .. 15 12
941. – $2\frac{1}{2}$+$1\frac{1}{4}$ r. purple .. 25 20
942. – 5+$2\frac{1}{2}$ r. red .. 60 50
943. – 10+5 r. grey .. 1·25 1·10

DESIGNS—VERT. Nos. 940, Gorgan vase. 941, Ghazan Tower, Bistam. HORIZ. Nos. 942, Masjid-i Gawhar Shad, Mosque, Meshed. 943, Niche in wall of mosque at Rezaieh.

1950. 2nd Islamic Economic Conf.

944. **70.** 1 r. 50+1 r. multicoloured 2·75 1·50

71. Muhammed Riza Pahlavi in Military School Uniform.

72. Memorial.

1950. Shah's 31st Birthday. Portraits of Shah at different ages, framed as T **71.**

945. **71.** 25 d. black and red .. 30 5
946. – 50 d. black and orange 35 5
947. – 75 d. black and brown 3·50 40
948. – 1 r. black and green .. 90 8
949. – 2 r. 50 black and blue .. 90 8
950. – 5 r. black and claret .. 5·00 50

PORTRAITS—Shah in uniform: 50 d. Nava cadet. 75 d. Boy scout. 1 r. Naval officer 2 r. 50, Army officer-cadet. 5 r. Army general

1950. Re-establishment of Control in Azerbaijan. 4th Anniv.

951. – 10+5 d. chocolate .. 50 15
952. **72.** 50+25 d. purple .. 60 20
953. – 1 r. +50 d. claret .. 1·10 35
954. – 1 r. 50+74 d. red & grn. 1·60 40
455. – 2 r.50+1 r. 25 blue .. 1·75 1·10
956. – 3+1 r. 50 blue .. .. 2·50 1·90

DESIGNS—VERT. Nos. 951, Shah and map, 954, Map and battle scene. 955, Shah and flags. HORIZ. 953, Troops marching. 956, Cavalry parade.

73. Shah and Queen Soraya.

74. Farabi.

1951. Royal Wedding. T **73** and similar portraits.

959. **73.** 5 d. purple 20 10
960. 25 d. orange 30 10
961. 50 d. green 40 15
962. – 1 r. brown 60 15
963. – 1.50 r. red 80 30
964. – 2.50 r. blue .. .. 1·25 50

1951. Farabi (philosopher). Death Millenary.

965. **74.** 50 d. red 50 15
966. 2 r. 50 blue .. .. 2·00 40

75. Mohammed Riza Pahlavi.

76.

1951.

967. **75.** 5 d. orange 5 5
968. 10 d. violet 5 5
969. 20 d. sepia 5 5
970. 25 d. blue 5 5
971. 50 d. green 5 5
972. 50 d. grey-green .. 80 8
973. 75 d. red 8 5
974. **76.** 1 r. grey-green .. 8 5
975. 1 r. emerald 5 5
976. 1 r. 50 rose 8 5
977. 2 r. chocolate .. 25 5
978. 2 r. 50 blue 25 5
979. 3 r. orange 45 5
980. 5 r. green .. .. 1·00 5
981. 10 r. olive .. .. 1·75 5
982. 20 r. brown .. .. 2·00 10
983. 30 r. blue .. .. 2·25 10
984. 50 r. black .. .. 2·50 40

1951. Saadi (poet). 660th Death Anniv. Horiz. pictorial designs and vert. portrait as T **74.**

985. 25 d.+25 d. green .. 15 12
986. 50 d.+50 d. olive .. 40 30
987. 1.50 r.+50 d. blue .. 90 60

DESIGNS—VERT. 1 r. 50 Saadi (Muslih-ud-Din). HORIZ. 25 d. Coran Gate, Shiruz (inscribed "DARVAZE-CORAN-CHIRAZ"). 50 d. Tomb of Saadi.

77. Shah and Aeroplane over Mosque.

78. Oil Well and Mosque.

1952. Air.

988. – 50 d. green 5 5
989. **77.** 1 r. red 8 5
990. 2 r. blue 12 5
991. 3 r. sepia 20 5
992. 5 r. lilac 35 8
993. 10 r. vermilion 50 12
994. 20 r. violet .. .. 1·10 30
995. 30 r. olive .. .. 1·75 60
996. 50 r. chestnut .. 3·50 1·50
997. 100 r. sepia .. .. 6·00 3·00
998. 200 r. green .. .. 9·00 4·00

DESIGN: 50 d. Shah and aeroplane over Mt. Demavend.

1953. Discovery of Oil at Qum. (a) Postage.

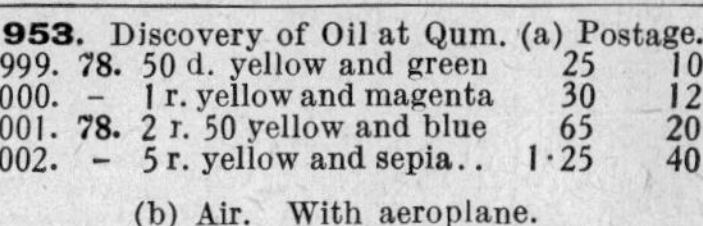

999. **78.** 50 d. yellow and green 25 10
1000. – 1 r. yellow and magenta 30 12
1001. **78.** 2 r. 50 yellow and blue 65 20
1002. – 5 r. yellow and sepia .. 1·25 40

(b) Air. With aeroplane.

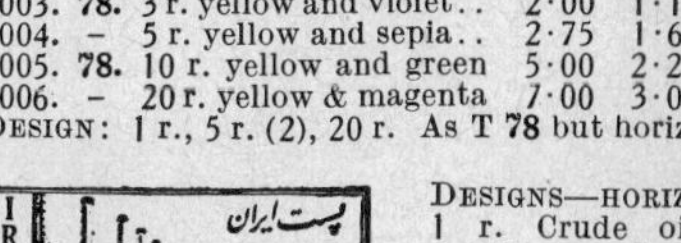

1003. **78.** 3 r. yellow and violet .. 2·00 1·10
1004. – 5 r. yellow and sepia .. 2·75 1·60
1005. **78.** 10 r. yellow and green 5·00 2·25
1006. – 20 r. yellow & magenta 7·00 3·00

DESIGN: 1 r., 5 r. (2), 20 r. As T **78** but horiz.

79. Power Station Boiler Plant.

DESIGNS—HORIZ. 1 r. Crude oil stabilizer. 5 r. Pipe-lines. 10 r. View of Abadan. VERT. 2.50 r. Super fractionaters.

1953. Nationalisation of Oil Industry. 2nd Anniv.

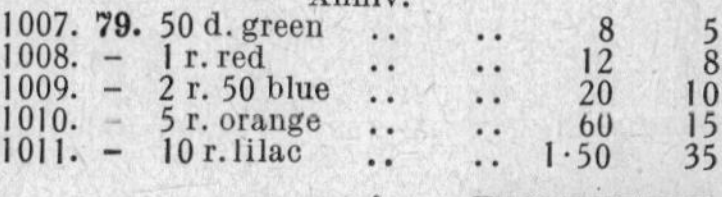

1007. **79.** 50 d. green 8 5
1008. – 1 r. red 12 8
1009. – 2 r. 50 blue 20 10
1010. – 5 r. orange 60 15
1011. – 10 r. lilac .. .. 1·50 35

80. Family and U.N. Emblem.

81. Gymnast.

1953. United Nations Day.

1012. **80** 1 r. green & blue-green 30 30
1013. 2 r. 50 blue & light blue 50 40

1953. Ancient Persian Sports.

1014. **81.** 1 r. green 80 25
1015. – 2 r. 50 blue .. .. 1·60 40
1016. – 3 r. grey .. .. 4·00 65
1017. – 5 r. ochre .. .. 4·00 1·50
1018. – 10 r. violet .. .. 6·50 2·10

DESIGNS—HORIZ. 2 r. 50 Archer. 3 r. Mountaineers. VERT. 5 r. Polo-player (Persian Sports Club Badge). 10 r. Lion-hunter.

82. Herring.

83. Machinery.

1954. Nationalization of Fishing Industry.

1019. **82.** 1 r. multicoloured .. 80 40
1020. – 2 r. 50 multicoloured .. 4·00 1·00
1021. – 3 r. vermilion .. .. 2·00 1·00
1022. **83.** 5 r. green .. .. 3·00 1·25
1023. – 10 r. multicoloured .. 2·25 1·25

DESIGNS—HORIZ. As T **82**: 2 r. 50 Sardines. 10 r. Sturgeon. As T **83**: 3 r. Refrigeration machinery.

84. Hamadan.

85. Avicenna.

1954. Fund to Rebuild Avicenna's Tomb (5th issue).

1024. **84.** 50 d.+25 d. green .. 8 8
1025. **85.** 1 r.+$\frac{1}{2}$ r. brown .. 15 12
1026. – $2\frac{1}{2}$ r.+$1\frac{1}{4}$ r. blue .. 35 15
1027. – 5 r.+$2\frac{1}{2}$ r. red .. 50 35
1028. – 10 r.+5 r. olive .. 1·00 85

DESIGNS—VERT. As T **85**: $2\frac{1}{2}$ r. Qabus tower, Gargan. HORIZ. As T **84**: 5 r. Old tomb of Avicenna. 10 r. New tomb of Avicenna.

86. Shah in Military uniform.

87. " Freedom ".

1954.

1029. **86.** 5 d. brown 5 5
1062. 5 d. violet 5 5
1030. 10 d. violet 5 5
1063. 10 d. red 5 5
1031. 25 d. red 5 5
1064. 25 d. brown 5 5
1032. 50 d. sepia 5 5
1065. 50 d. red 5 5
1033. – 1 r. yellow-green .. 8 5
1066. – 1 r. turquoise 5 5
1034. – 1 r. 50 carmine .. 12 5
1067. – 1 r. 50 brown 85 5
1035. – 2 r. ochre 15 5
1068. – 2 r. green 30 5
1069. – 2 r. 50 blue 10 5
1037. – 3 r. olive 25 5
1070. – 3 r. ochre 25 5
1038. – 5 r. slate 40 5
1071. – 5 r. magenta 40 5
1039. – 10 r. mauve 90 30
1072. – 10 r. blue 60 8
1040. – 20 r. indigo .. 1·75 50
1073. – 20 r. slate .. 1·25 10
1041. – 30 r. brown .. 6·00 1·60
1074. – 30 r. orange .. 2·50 1·00
1042. – 50 r. orange .. 1·90 80
1075. – 50 r. brown .. 2·75 1·00
1043. – 100 r. lavender 25·00 6·00
1044. – 200 r. yellow .. 10·00 2·25
DESIGN: 1 r. to 200 r. Shah in naval uniform.

1954. Return of Shah from Europe. 1st Anniv. Inscr. "FIDELITE AU ROI". Various sizes. Multicoloured.
1045. 2 r. Type **87** 40 15
1046. 3 r. Hand holding torch and Iranian flag .. 1·60 30
1047. 5 r. Man clasping Iranian flag .. 2·25 50
SIZES: 3 r. (19½ × 27½ mm.). 5 r. (20¼ × 28½ mm.).

88. Nurse and Child.

89. Felling Trees.

1954. U.N. Day.
1048. **88.** 2 r. orange and purple 80 40
1049. 3 r. orange and violet 1·25 60

1954. 4th World Forestry Congress. Inscr. "4eme congres mondial forestier".
1050. **89.** 1 r. green and brown .. 2·10 1·00
1051. – 2 r. 50 blue and green 4·00 1·75
1052. – 5 r. brown and lavender 7·50 2·50
1053. – 10 r. lake and blue .. 10·00 5·00
DESIGNS: 2 r. 50 Man carrying logs. 5 r. Man operating circular saw. 10 r. Ancient galley.

90.

91. Parliament Building.

1955. National Costumes.
1054. **90.** 1 r. multicoloured .. 50 20
1055. – 2 r. multicoloured .. 80 50
1056. – 2 r. 50 multicoloured 1·00 50
1057. – 3 r. multicoloured .. 1·10 90
1058. – 5 r. multicoloured .. 3·00 2·50
DESIGNS—2 r. Male costume. 2 r. 50, 3 r., 5 r. Female costumes.

1955. Constitution. 50th Anniv.
1059. – 2 r. green and purple .. 35 15
1060. – 3 r. blue 60 35
1061. **91.** 5 r. orange and green .. 1·25 60
DESIGNS—HORIZ. 2 r. Gateway of Parliament Building. VERT. (larger—27 × 36 mm.): 3 r. Winged Statue.

92. U.N. Emblem and Hemispheres.

93. Wrestlers.

1955. U.N. Day.
1077. **92.** 1 r. orange and red .. 45 30
1078. 2 r. 50 blue & deep blue 1·00 60

1955. Iranian Wrestlers. Int. Success.
1079. **93.** 2r. 50 multicoloured .. 90 50

94. Hospital Buildings.

95.

1956. Opening of Nemazi Hospital, Shiraz. Multicoloured. Various sizes.
1080. – 50 d. (24 × 3½ mm.) .. 30 20
1081. **94.** 1 r. (36 × 24½ mm.) .. 50 25
1082. – 2 r. 50 (24 × 33½ mm.) 1·60 50
1083. – 5 r. (36 × 23 mm.) .. 1·40 75
1084. – 10 r. (24 × 33½ mm.) .. 2·00 1·50
DESIGNS: 50 d. Hospital garden. 2 r. 50 Spear thrower. 5 r. Koran gate, Shiraz. 10 r. Poet Hafiz and his tomb.

1956. Nat. Olympic Committee. 10th Anniv.
1085. **95.** 5 r. purple .. .. 5·50 3·50

96. Tusi's Tomb, Maragheh.

97. Reveille.

1956. Nasir ed-Din Tusi, 1201–74 (astronomer and scientist). 7th Death Cent.
1086. **96.** 1 r. orange 35 10
1087. – 2 r. 50 blue (Astrolabe) 60 15
1088. – 5 r. lilac and sepia (Portrait) .. .. 1·10 40

1956. National Scout Jamboree.
1089. **97.** 2 r. 50 blue & ultram. 1·25 1·10
1090. – 5 r. mauve and lilac .. 2·00 1·40
DESIGN: 5 r. Shah in scout's uniform and badge.

98.

99. U.N. Emblem and Young People.

1956. World Health Organization.
1091. **98.** 6 r. magenta 80 45

1956. United Nations Day.
1092. **99.** 1 r. green 25 15
1093. – 2 r. 50 blue and green 35 30
DESIGN: 2 r. 50 U.N. emblem and scales of justice.

100. Telecommunications Centre, Teheran.

DESIGN: 6 r. Telegraph poles and mosque.

1956. Persian Telegraphs Cent.
1094. **100.** 2 r. 50 green and blue 70 30
1095. 6 r. mauve and pink .. 1·20 60

101. Shah and Pres. Mirza.

1956. Visit of President Mirza of Pakistan.
1096. **101.** 1 r. multicoloured .. 20 12

102. Mohammed Riza Pahlavi. **103.**

1956.
1122. **102.** 5 d. plum and violet .. 5 5
1123. 10 d. magenta & purple 5 5
1124. 25 d. orange and red 5 5
1125. 50 d. bronze-green and grey-green .. 5 5
1126. 1 r. blue-grn. & green 5 5
1127. 1 r. 50 pur. & mauve 5 5
1128. 2 r. turquoise and blue 8 5
1129. 2 r. 50 turq. and blue 8 5
1130. 3 r. vermilion and rose 10 5
1131. 5 r. vio.-blue & ultram. 12 5
1107. 6 r. mauve and lilac .. 20 5
1108. 10 r. green and blue .. 60 5
1109. 20 r. blue and green .. 1·25 10
1110. 30 r. orange and rose 2·40 1·60
1111. 50 r. sage and green .. 3·00 90
1112. 100 r. red and purple 25·00 10·00
1113. 200 r. violet & purple 11·00 5·00

1956.
1097. **103.** 5 d. vermilion & rose 5 5
1098. 10 d. violet and blue 5 5
1099. 25 d. brown and sepia 5 5
1100. 50 d. olive and sepia 5 5
1101. 1 r. green and brown 5 5
1102. 1 r. 50 choc. & mauve 5 5
1103. 2 r. red and magenta 5 5
1104. 2 r. 50 blue & ultram. 5 5
1105. 3 r. bistre and brown 10 5
1106. 5 r. claret & vermilion 15 5
1132. 6 r. blue and light blue 25 5
1133. 10 r. blue-grn. & green 50 5
1134. 20 r. olive and green 1·10 8
1135. 30 r. sepia and blue .. 4·00 1·00
1136. 50 r. brown and sepia 4·00 90
1137. 100 r. red & brt. purple 12·00 1·90
1138. 200 r. yell.-brn. & vio. 9·00 2·10

104. Lord Baden-Powell.

105. Express Train and Mosque.

1957. Lord Baden-Powell. Birth Cent.
1114. **104.** 10 r. brown and green 1·25 60

1957. Teheran-Meshed Railway. Inaug. Multicoloured.
1115. 2 r. 50 Track & signal .. 60 20
1116. 5 r. Diesel-electric train and map (horiz.) .. 1·20 30
1117. 10 r. Type **105** .. .. 1·90 70

106. President Gronchi and Shah.

1957. Visit of President of Italy.
1118. **106.** 2 r. slate, green & red 35 20
1119. – 6 r. black, green & red 55 30
DESIGN: 6 r. Plaque and flags between ruins of Persepolis and Colosseum.

107. Queen Soraya and Hospital.

1957. 6th Medical Congress, Ramsar.
1120. **107.** 2 r. green and blue .. 25 12

108. Shah and King Faisal II of Iraq.

1957. Visit of King of Iraq.
1121. **108.** 2 r. indigo, red & grn. 20 12

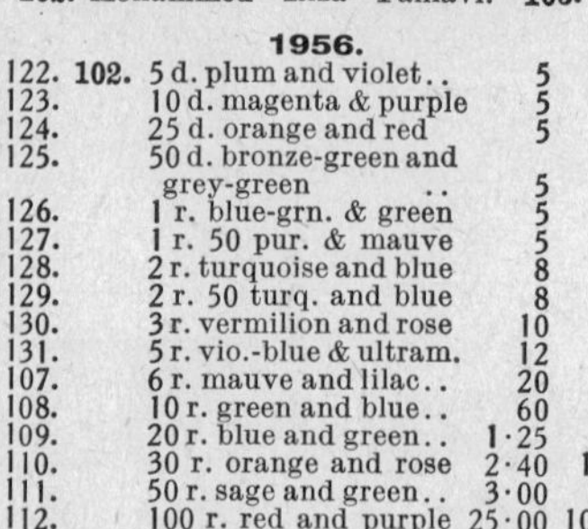
109. Globes with Laurel Sprays.

1957. Int. Cartographical Conf., Teheran.
1140. **109.** 10 r. multicoloured .. 1·25 50

110. "Flight".

111. "The Weight-lifter."

1957. Air. United Nations Day.
1141. **110.** 10 r. rose & magenta 90 60
1142. 20 r. purple and violet 1·40 1·10

1957. Int. Weightlifting Championships.
1143. **111.** 10 r. blue, green & red 90 35

112. Radio Mast and Buildings.

113. Oil Derrick and "Bowl of Flames".

1958. Iranian Broadcasting Service. 30th Anniv.
1144. **112.** 10 r. sepia, buff & blue 70 25

1958. Iranian Oil Industry. 50th Anniv.
1145. **113.** 2 r. chest., yell. & grey 25 5
1146. 10 r. chest., yell. & blue 70 25

114. Exhibition Emblem.

115. Train on Viaduct.

1958. Brussels Int. Exn.
1147. **114.** 2 r. 50 blue & light blue 20 10
1148. 6 r. carmine and red .. 30 25

1958. Inaug. of Teheran-Tabriz Railway.
1149. **115.** 6 r. purple 60 20
1150. – 8 r. green .. .. 1·25 30
DESIGN: 8 r. Express train and route map.

116. Mohammed Riza Pahlavi.

117. U.N. Emblem and Map of Persia.

1958.
1162. **116.** 5 d. violet 5 5
1163. 5 d. red-brown .. 5 5
1164. 10 d. red 5 5
1165. 10 d. myrtle 5 5
1166. 10 d. turquoise .. 5 5
1167. 25 d. red 5 5
1168. 25 d. orange 5 5
1169. 50 d. blue 5 5
1170. 50 d. red 5 5
1171. 1 r. myrtle 5 5
1172. 1 r. violet 10 5
1173. 2 r. sepia 40 5

1175. 116. 3 r. red-brown .. 35 5
1233. 3 r. olive-brown .. 12 5
1178. 6 r. cobalt 10 5
1179. 8 r. purple 20 5
1180. 8 r. bistre-brown .. 20 5
1181. 10 r. black 20 5
1182. 14 r. violet-blue .. 45 5
1183. 14 r. yellow-green .. 25 5
1184. 20 r. grey-green .. 75 5
1186. 30 r. red .. .. 1·00 8
1187. 30 r. chocolate .. 90 10
1188. 50 r. purple .. 2·00 35
1189. 50 r. blue .. .. 1·60 35
1190. 100 r. orange .. 3·50 60
1191. 100 r. green .. .. 4·50 1·00
1192. 200 r. slate-green .. 6·50 1·10
1193. 200 r. magenta .. 12·00 1·25

1958. United Nations Day.
1194. 117. 6 r. blue 50 25
1195. 10 r. violet and green 60 35

118. Clasped Hands.

119. Rudagi playing Lyre.

1958. Declaration of Human Rights. 10th Anniv.
1196. 118. 6 r. brown & chocolate 30 25
1197. 8 r. olive and green.. 60 35

1958. Rudagi (poet and musician). 1100th Birth Anniv.
1198. 119. 2 r. 50 indigo .. 25 15
1199. – 5 r. violet 35 30
1200. 119. 10 r. sepia 60 40
DESIGN: 5 r. Rudagi meditating.

120.

1959. Red Cross Commem.
1201. 120. 1 r. multicoloured .. 25 20
1202. 6 r. multicoloured .. 80 50

121. Wrestlers.

122. Torch of Freedom.

1959. World Wrestling Championships.
1203. 121. 6 r. multicoloured .. 90 45

1959. United Nations Day.
1204. 122. 6 r. red, choc. & bistre 40 25

123. Shah and President Khan.

1959. Visit of President of Pakistan.
1205. 123. 6 r. multicoloured .. 30 20

124. I.L.O. Emblem.

125. Pahlavi Foundation Bridge, Khorramshahr.

1959. I.L.O. 40th Anniv.
1206. 124. 1 r. blue 12 5
1207. 5 r. brown 30 15

1960. Opening of Pahlavi Foundation Bridge, Khorramshahr.
1208. 125. 1 r. blue and chocolate 25 5
1209. – 5 r. green and blue .. 75 10
DESIGN: 5 r. Close-up view of bridge.

126. "Uprooted Tree".

127. Insecticide Sprayer.

1960. World Refugee Year.
1210. – 1 r. blue 5 5
1211. 126. 6 r. green 30 15
DESIGN: 1 r. "Uprooted tree" and columns.

1960. Anti-Malaria Campaign.
1212. – 1 r. blk. & red on yell. 15 8
1213. 127. 2 r. blue, blk. & light-bl. 30 12
1214. – 3 r. blk. & red on green 60 30
DESIGNS (30×37 mm.): 1 r., 3 r. Different views of mosquito crossed out in red.

128. Polo-player.

130. Scout Emblem within Flower.

129. Shah and King Hussein.

1960. "Olympic Games Week". Inscr. "1960".
1215. 128. 1 r. chocolate .. 25 15
1216. – 6 r. violet and blue 65 35
DESIGN: 6 r. Archer.

1960. Visit of King of Jordan.
1217. 129. 6 r. multicoloured .. 20 12

1960. 3rd National Scout Jamboree.
1218. 130. 1 r. green 10 5
1219. – 6 r. ochre, sep. & blue 25 12
DESIGN: 6 r. Scout camp Persepolis.

131. Shah and Queen Farah.

1960. Royal Wedding.
1220. 131. 1 r. green 30 10
1221. 5 r. blue 35 20

132. U.N. Emblem.

133. Shah and Queen Elizabeth II.

1960. U.N.O. 15th Anniv.
1222. 132. 6 r. sepia, blue and yellow-brown .. 25 12

1961. Visit of Queen Elizabeth II.
1223. 133. 1 r. brown 10 5
1224. 6 r. blue 30 15

134. Girl playing Pan-pipes.

DESIGN — (24 × 39½ mm.): 6 r. Safiaddin Anmavi (musician).

1961. Int. Music Congress, Teheran.
1225. 134. 1 r. stone and brown 15 5
1226. – 6 r. slate 25 12

135. Royal Family.

1961. Birth of Crown Prince.
1227. 135. 1 r. purple 15 12
1228. 6 r. blue 75 40

136. U.N. Emblem. and Birds.

137. Tree-planting.

1961. United Nations Day.
1236. 136. 2 r. red and blue .. 8 5
1237. 6 r. violet and blue 20 12

1962. Afforestation Week.
1238. 137. 2 r. blue, cream and grey-green.. .. 20 5
1239. 6 r. grn. blue & ultram. 30 8

138. Worker.

139. Family on Map.

1962. Workers' Day.
1240. 138. 2 r. multicoloured .. 15 5
1241. 6 r. multicoloured .. 25 8

1962. Social Insurance.
1242. 139. 2 r. vio., black & yell. 12 5
1243. 6 r. blue, blk. & lt. blue 20 8

140. Sugar Plantation.

141. Karaj Dam.

1962. Sugar Cane Production.
1244. 140. 2 r. grn., bl. & ultram. 12 5
1245. 6 r. bl., cream & ultram. 20 8

1962. Karaj Dam Inaug.
1246. 141. 2 r. green & brown .. 15 5
1247. 6 r. bl. & ultramarine 35 8

142. Sefid Rud Dam.

143. U.N. Emblem.

1962. Sefid Rud Dam Inaug.
1248. 142. 2 r. buff, bl. & myrtle 15 5
1249. – 6 r. black, blue & brn. 40 8
DESIGN: 6 r. Distant view of dam.

1962. U.N.E.S.C.O. 15th Anniv.
1250. 143. 2 r. blk., green & red 12 5
1251. 6 r. blue, green & red 20 8

144. Arrow piercing mosquito.

145. Mohammed Riza Pahlavi.

146. Shah and Palace of Darius, Persepolis.

147. Oil Pipelines.

1962. Malaria Eradication.
1252. 144. 2 r. black and green 12 5
1253. – 6 r. blue and rose .. 20 5
1254. – 10 r. ultram. and blue 25 8
DESIGNS — VERT. (29½ × 34½ mm.) — 6 r. Mosquito and insecticide-sprayer. HORIZ. (As T 144)—10 r. Globe and campaign emblem.

1962.
1255. 145. 5 d. green 5 5
1256. 10 d. brown 5 5
1257. 25 d. violet-blue .. 5 5
1258. 50 d. turquoise .. 5 5
1259. 1 r. orange 5 5
1338. 2 r. blue-violet .. 5 5
1339. 5 r. sepia 10 5
1340. 146. 6 r. blue 25 5
1341. 8 r. yellow-green .. 25 5
1342. 10 r. turquoise .. 35 5
1343. 11 r. bronze 45 5
1344. 14 r. violet 60 5
1345. 20 r. red-brown .. 70 8
1346. 50 r. orange-red .. 1·50 35

1962. E.C.A.F.E. 2nd Petroleum Symposium.
1269. 147. 6 r. chocolate & blue 20 12
1270. 14 r. chocolate & grey 40 20

148. Hippocrates and Avicenna.

149. New Houses.

1962. W.H.O. Medical Congress, Teheran.
1271. 148. 3 r blue, brn. & cream 12 8
1272. 6 r. blue, sage & green 30 20

1962. United Nations Day.
1273. 149. 6 r. blue and indigo.. 20 10
1274. – 14 r. green and indigo 50 25
DESIGN—HORIZ. 14 r. Laying foundation stone.

150. "Bouquet for the Crown Prince".

1962. Crown Prince's Birthday.
1275. 150. 6 r. grey 30 10
1276. 14 r. green 50 20

151. Persian Gulf Map.

152. Hilton Hotel, Teheran.

1962. Persian Gulf Seminar.
1277. 151. 6 r. bl., pink & pale bl. 25 5
1278. 14 r. blue, flesh & pink 50 8

1963. Opening of Royal Teheran Hilton Hotel.
1279. 152. 6 r. blue 20 8
1280. 14 r chocolate .. 40 15

153. Refugees.

1963. Earthquake Relief Fund.
1281. 153. 14 r.+6 r. blue, brown and green 50 30

154. Mohammed Riza Shah Dam.
155. Worker with Pickaxe.

1963. Mohammed Riza Shah Dam Inaug.
1282. 154. 6 r. multicoloured .. 30 12
1283. 14 r. multicoloured.. 65 30

1963. Workers' Day.
1283a. 155. 2 r. black & yellow.. 10 5
1283b. 6 r. black and blue.. 20 10

156. Bird and Globe.

DESIGNS: 6 r. Globe and ears of wheat (stylized). 14 r. Globe encircled by scroll, and campaign emblem.

1963. Freedom from Hunger.
1284. 156. 2 r. ult., ochre & blue 10 5
1285. – 6 r. ochre, blk. & blue 30 15
1286. – 14 r. ochre & greenish blue 65 45

157. Shah and Scroll.

1963. Agrarian Reform Act.
1287. 157. 6 r. green and blue.. 45 10
1288. 14 r. green and yellow 65 25

158. Shah and King Frederick.

1963. Visit of King of Denmark.
1289. 158. 6 r. blue and indigo.. 20 8
1290. 14 r. brown and sepia 40 25

159. Flags of Iran and India; Ibn Sina Mosque, Teheran, and Taj Mahal, India.
160. Shahnaz Dam.

161. Centenary Emblem.
162. Shah and Queen Juliana.

1963. Visit of President Radhakrishnan of India.
1291. 159. 6 r. multicoloured .. 20 8
1292. 14 r. multicoloured .. 40 25

1963. Shahnaz Dam. Inaug.
1293. 160. 6 r. ultram., bl. & grn. 20 8
1294. 14 r. grey-green, blue and buff 40 25

1963. Red Cross Centenary.
1295. 161. 6 r. multicoloured .. 20 10
1296. 14 r. grey, red & buff 45 25

1963. Visit of Queen of the Netherlands.
1304. 162. 6 r. blue and ultram. 15 8
1305. 14 r. green & black-grn. 30 20

163. Students in Class.

1963. Formation of Literacy Teaching Corps.
1306. 163. 6 r. multicoloured .. 35 8
1307. 14 r. multicoloured .. 70 25

164. Pres. De Gaulle and View of Teheran.

1963. Visit of President of France.
1308. 164. 6 r. ultramarine & blue 25 10
1309. 14 r. brown and ochre 70 25

165. Plant, Route Map and Emblem.
166. Pres. Lubke and Mosque.

1963. Opening of Chemical Fertiliser Plant, Shiraz.
1310. 165. 6 r. black, yell. & red 25 10
1311. – 14 r. black, yell. & blue 55 25
DESIGN—HORIZ. 14 r. Fertiliser plant and emblem.

1963. Visit of President of German Federal Republic.
1312. 166. 6 r. blue & violet-blue 25 10
1313. 14 r. chocolate & grey 90 35

167. U.N. Emblem.

1963. United Nations Day.
1314. 167. 8 r. multicoloured .. 25 12

168. Aircraft crossing U.N. Emblem.
169. Crown Prince Riza.

1963. Iranian Air Force in Congo.
1315. 168. 6 r. multicoloured .. 25 12

1963. Children's Day.
1316. 169. 2 r. chocolate .. 15 5
1317. 6 r. blue 30 12

170. Chairman Brezhnev.
171. Ataturk's Mausoleum.

172. Scales of Justice and Globe.
173. Mother and Child.

1963. Visit of Chairman of Soviet Presidium.
1318. 170. 5 r. multicoloured .. 25 10
1319. 11 r. multicoloured .. 45 20

1963. Kemal Ataturk. 25th Death Anniv.
1320. 171. 4 r. brown, grey & grn. 25 10
1321. – 5 r. black, red & yell. 40 15
DESIGN: 5 r. Kemal Ataturk.

1963. Declaration of Human Rights. 15th Anniv.
1322. 172. 6 r. black, blue & green 20 8
1323. 14 r. blk., cream & brn. 40 20

1963. Mothers Day.
1324. 173. 2 r. multicoloured .. 8 5
1325. 4 r. multicoloured .. 15 8

174. Cogwheel and Map.
175. Hand with Document ("Profit-sharing").

1963. Industrial Development.
1326. 174. 8 r. bl., cream & turq. 40 15

1964. Six-Point Reform Law.
1327. 175. 2 r. brn., violet & indigo 8 5
1328. – 4 r. brown and grey.. 15 5
1329. – 6 r. multicoloured .. 20 10
1330. – 8 r. multicoloured .. 35 15
1331. – 10 r. red, grey-grn. & green 35 15
1332. – 12 r. brown and red.. 65 30
DESIGNS: 4 r. Factory and documents on scales ("Nationalization"). 6 r. Worker on Globe ("Education"). 8 r. Tractor ("Agriculture"). 10 r. Trees ("Forestry"). 12 r. Silhouettes within gateway ("Equal Rights for Women").

176. U.N. Emblem.
177. Blossom.

1964. 20th E.C.A.F.E. Session, Teheran.
1347. 176. 14 r. black and emerald 35 20

1964. New Year Greetings.
1348. 177. 50 d. orange, sepia and emerald .. 5 5
1349. 1 r. orge., black & blue 8 5

178. Weather Vane.
179. "Tourism".

1964. World Meteorological Day.
1350. 178. 6 r. violet and blue .. 20 12

1964. Iranian Tourist Organization (INTO). 1st Anniv.
1351. 179. 6 r. grn., vio. & black 12 8
1352. – 11 r. orge., brn. & blk. 35 15
DESIGN: 11 r. Winged beasts, column and INTO emblem.

180. Rudagi (blind poet).
181. Sculptured Head.

1964. Opening of Blind Institute.
1353. 180. 6 r. blue 15 8
1354. 8 r. brown 35 15

1964. "7000 Years of Persian Art" Exn.
1355. 181. 2 r. blue and grey .. 10 5
1356. – 4 r. ultramarine & blue 25 8
1357. – 6 r. yellow and brown 45 10
1358. – 10 r. green and yellow 90 30
DESIGNS—HORIZ. 4 r. Sumerian war chariot on map. VERT. 6 r. Golden cup with lion decorations. 10 r. Sculptured head of man.

182. Shah and Emperor Haile Selassie.

1964. Visit of Emperor of Ethiopia.
1359. 182. 6 r. ultramarine & blue 15 10

183. Congress Emblem.
184. Beetle under Lens.

1964. 2nd Iranian Dental Assn. Congress.
1360. 183. 2 r. red, deep blue and blue 10 5
1361. – 4 r. deep blue, blue, lt. blue and brown.. 20 12
DESIGN: 4 r. "2 IDA" in symbolic form.

1964. Plant Parasites and Diseases Research Institute. Inaug.
1362. – 2 r. brown, red & buff 8 5
1363. 184. 6 r. indigo, brn. & bl. 20 10
DESIGN: 2 r. Microscope, plants and research centre.

185. Plaque.
186. Eleanor Roosevelt.

1964. Mehregan Festival.
1364. 185. 8 r. chestnut & yellow 25 10

1964. Eleanor Roosevelt Commem.
1365. 186. 10 r. blue and violet.. 40 20

187. Clasped Hands and U.N. Emblem.
188. Gymnast.

1964. United Nations Day.
1366. 187. 6 r. multicoloured .. 12 10
1367. – 14 r. red, bl. & salmon 35 20
DESIGN: 14 r. U.N. and "Bird" emblems.

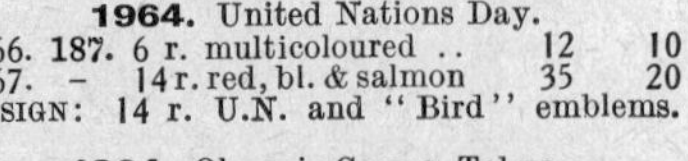

1964. Olympic Games, Tokyo.
1368. 188. 4 r. sepia, turquoise and pale drab .. 12 5
1369. – 6 r. red and blue .. 20 8
DESIGN—Diamond (39×39 mm.); 6 r. Polo.

189. Crown Prince Riza. **190.** Conference and U.N. Emblems.

1964. Children's Day.
1370. **189.** 1 r. green and brown 10 5
1371. 2 r. red and blue .. 15 8
1372. 6 r. blue and red .. 25 12

1964. Petro-Chemical Conf. and Gas Seminar.
1373. **190.** 6 r. multicoloured .. 15 8
1374. 8 r. multicoloured .. 20 10

191. Shah and King Baudouin.

1964. Visit of King of Belgium.
1375. **191.** 6 r. blk., orge. & yell. 15 8
1376. 8 r. blk., orge. & grn. 20 10

192. Rhazes.

1964. Birth of Rhazes (Zakariya Ar-Razi alchemist). 1100th Anniv.
1377. **192.** 2 r. multicoloured .. 8 5
1378. 6 r. multicoloured .. 25 12

193. Shah and King Olav.

1965. Visit of King of Norway.
1379. **193.** 2 r. purple and maroon 5 5
1380. 4 r. green and olive .. 12 5

194. Crown, Map and Star. **195.** Woman and U.N. Emblem.

1965. Six-Point Reform Law.
1381. **194.** 2 r. orge., blk. & blue 8 5

1965. Women's Rights and 18th Session of U.N. Commission, Teheran.
1382. **195.** 6 r. black and blue .. 12 8
1383. 8 r. blue and red .. 20 10

196. Festival Plant. **197.** Pres. Bourguiba and Minarets.

1965. New Year Festival.
1384. **196.** 50 d. multicoloured.. 5 5
1385. 1 r. multicoloured .. 5 5

1965. Visit of President of Tunisia.
1386. **197.** 4 r. multicoloured .. 10 5

198. Map of Oil Pipelines.

1965. Nationalisation of Oil Industry. 14th Anniv.
1387. **198.** 6 r. multicoloured .. 15 10
1388. 14 r. multicoloured .. 30 20

199. I.T.U. Emblem and Symbols.

1965. I.T.U. Cent.
1389. **199.** 14 r. red and grey .. 25 12

200. I.C.Y. Emblem.

1965. Int. Co-operation Year.
1390. **200.** 10 r. green and blue.. 15 12

201. Airline Emblem and Jetliner.

1965. Inaug. of Jet Services by Iranian National Airlines.
1391. **201.** 14 r. multicoloured.. 50 30

202. " Co-operation " (Hands holding Book).

1965. Regional Development Co-operation Plan. 1st Anniv. Inscr. " R C D ". Multicoloured.
1392. 2 r. Type **202** 5 5
1393. 4 r. Globe and flags of Turkey, Iran and Pakistan (40½ × 24½ mm.) .. 10 5

203. Moot Emblem and Arabesque Pattern.

1965. Middle East Rover (Scout) Moot.
1394. **203.** 2 r. multicoloured .. 12 5

204. Gateway of Parliament Building.

1965. Iranian Constitution. 60th Anniv.
1397. **204.** 2 r. brown & magenta 8 5

205. Congress Emblem. **206.** Teacher and Class.

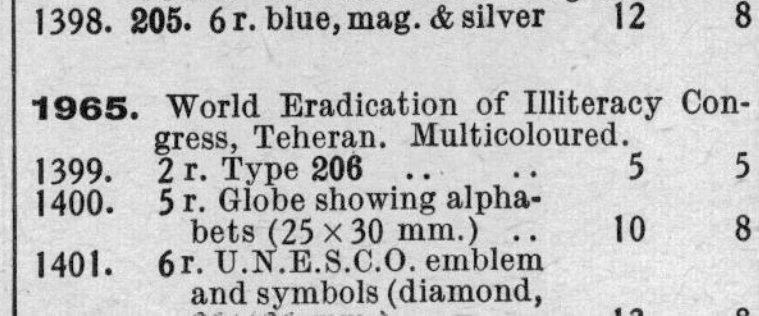

1965. Iranian Dental Congress.
1398. **205.** 6 r. blue, mag. & silver 12 8

1965. World Eradication of Illiteracy Congress, Teheran. Multicoloured.
1399. 2 r. Type **206** 5 5
1400. 5 r. Globe showing alphabets (25 × 30 mm.) .. 10 8
1401. 6 r. U.N.E.S.C.O. emblem and symbols (diamond, 36 × 36 mm.) .. 12 8
1402. 8 r. Various scripts (35 × 23 mm.) 15 10
1403. 14 r. Shah and multi-lingual inscriptions (41 × 52 mm.) 25 15

207. Shah Riza Pahlavi.

1965. Shah's Accession. 25th Anniversary (actually 24th).
1404. **207.** 1 r. red and grey .. 5 5
1405. 2 r. red and yellow .. 5 5

208. Congress Emblem.

1965. 14th Medical Congress.
1406. **208.** 5 r. ultram., bl. & gold 10 8

209. President Jonas.

1965. Visit of President of Austria.
1407. **209.** 6 r blue and drab .. 10 8

210. Plaque.

1965. Mehregan Festival.
1408. **210.** 4 r. brown, sepia, gold and green .. 8 5
See also No. 1464.

211. U.N. Emblem and " Flowers ". **212.** Emblem and " Arches ".

1965. United Nations Day.
1409. **211.** 5 r. multicoloured .. 10 8

1965. Iranian Industrial Exn., Teheran.
1410. **212.** 3 r. multicoloured .. 8 5

213. Crown Prince Riza. **214.** "Weightlifting".

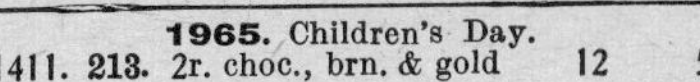

1965. Children's Day.
1411. **213.** 2r. choc., brn. & gold 12 5

1965. World Weightlifting Championships, Teheran.
1412. **214.** 10 r. mag., vio. & blue 20 12

215. Open Book **217.** Scales of Justice.

216. Shah and King Faisal.

1965. Book Week.
1416. **215.** 8 r. multicoloured .. 20 10

1965. Visit of King of Saudi Arabia.
1417. **216.** 4 r. chocolate & bistre 10 5

1965. Human Rights Day.
1418. **217.** 14 r. multicoloured .. 25 15

218. Tractor ("Agriculture").

1966. White Revolution. 3rd Anniv. (Shah's Reform Plan. Parliamentary Assent.).
1419. **218.** 1 r. chestnut & yellow 5 5
1420. – 2 r. green .. 5 5
1421. – 3 r. brown and silver 5 5
1422. – 4 r. violet 8 5
1423. – 5 r. lake and red .. 8 5
1424. – 6 r. brown and bistre 10 8
1425. – 7 r. ultramarine & blue 10 8
1426. – 8 r. ultramarine .. 12 10
1427. – 9 r. brown & chestnut 15 10
DESIGNS: 2 r. Trees ("Forestry"). 3 r. Cogwheel emblem ("Industry"). 4 r. Cylinders ("Printing"). 5 r. Gateway ("Architecture"). 6 r. Blackboard and pupils ("Education"). 7 r. Staff of Aesculapius ("Medical Services"). 8 r. Scales ("Justice"). 9 r. Girders ("Engineering").

219. Mohammed Riza Pahlavi. **220.** Shah and Ruins of Persepolis.

1966.
1428. **219.** 5 d. green 5 5
1429. 10 d. brown 5 5
1430. 25 d. blue 5 5
1431. 50 d. turquoise .. 5 5
1432. 1 r. orange 5 5
1433. 2 r. violet 5 5
1434. 4 r. brown 5 5
1435. 5 r. sepia 8 5
1436. **220.** 6 r. blue 10 5
1437. 8 r. green 12 5
1438. 10 r. blue 15 5
1439. 11 r. green 15 5
1440. 14 r. violet 25 5
1441. 20 r. brown .. 45 8
1442. 50 r. red .. .. 1·25 25
1443. 100 r. blue .. .. 2·00 60
1444. 200 r. brown .. 4·00 1·40

221. Nurse taking oath. **222.** Narcissus.

1966. Nurses' Day.
1445. **221.** 5 r. blue & ultram. .. 12 5
1446. 5 r. magenta and lake 12 5
Nos. 1445/6 were issued together se-tenant in the sheets.

1966. New Year Festival.
1447. **222.** 50 d. multicoloured .. 5 5
1448. 1 r. multicoloured .. 5 5
See also Nos. 1530/3.

223. Oil Rigs.

1966. Six New Oil Companies in Persian Gulf. Inaug.
1449. **223.** 14 r. black, pur. & blue 35 20

224. Radar Aerial.

1966. C.E.N.T.O. Telecommunications.
1450. **224.** 2 r. green 5 5
1451. – 4 r. orange and blue .. 5 5
1452. – 6 r. grey and purple .. 10 5
1453. – 8 r. indigo and blue .. 12 8
1454. – 10 r. brown and ochre 15 10
DESIGNS—VERT. 4 r. Aerial and radio "waves". 6 r. "CENTO" and emblem. 8 r. Emblem and "waves". 10 r. Bowl aerial and "waves".

225. W.H.O. Building.

1966. W.H.O. Headquarters, Geneva. Inaug.
1455. **225.** 10 r. black, blue & yell. 15 10

226. Globe Emblem and Motto.

1966. Int. Women's Council Conf. Teheran.
1456. **226.** 6 r. multicoloured .. 10 8
1457. 8 r. multicoloured .. 12 8

227. U.N.E.S.C.O. Emblem.

1966. Air. U.N.E.S.C.O. 20th Anniv.
1458. **227.** 14 r. multicoloured .. 40 25

228. Ruins of Persepolis, Map and Globe.

1966. Int. Iranology Congress, Teheran.
1459. **228.** 14 r. multicoloured .. 25 12

229. Medical Emblem.

1966. 15th Medical Congress, Teheran.
1460. **229.** 4 r. gold, blue & ultram. 8 5

230. Parliament Gateway.

1966. 55th Inter-Parliamentary Union Conf., Teheran.
1461. **230.** 6 r. grn., ultram. & red 10 5
1462. – 8 r. grn., ultram. & mve. 12 8
DESIGN: 8 r. Senate Building.

231. President Sunay.

1966. Turkish President's Visit.
1463. **231.** 6 r. brown and violet 10 5

1966. Mehregan Festival. Plaque design similar to T **210** but vert. (30×40 mm.).
1464. 6 r. brown and bistre .. 10 5

232. Farmers.

1966. Rural Courts of Justice.
1465. **232.** 5 r. brown and bistre 20 10

233. U.N. Emblem.

1966. U.N. Day and 21st Anniv. of U.N.O.
1466. **233.** 6 r. chestnut and black 10 5

234. Crown Prince. **235.** I.W.O. Emblem.

1966. Children's Day.
1467. **234.** 1 r. blue 5 5
1468. 2 r. violet 10 5
Nos. 1467/8 were issued together horiz. and vert. se-tenant.

1966. Iranian Women's Organisation.
1469. **235.** 5 r. blue, black & gold 8 5

236. Strip of Film.

1966. 1st Children's Film Festival, Teheran.
1470. **236.** 4 r. blk., pur. & violet 8 5

237. Counting on the Fingers. **238.** Cover of Book.

1966. National Census.
1471. **237.** 6 r. brown and grey 10 8

1966. Book Week.
1472. **238.** 8 r. brn., ochre & blue 12 10

239. Riza Shah Pahlavi.

Nos. 1475/6 show Riza Shah Pahlavi bare-headed. The two stamps in each denomination were respectively printed together se-tenant.

1966. Riza Shah Pahlavi. Commem.
1473. **239.** 1 r. brown 5 5
1474. 1 r. blue 5 5
1475. – 2 r. ultramarine .. 5 5
1476. – 2 r. green 5 5

240. E.R.O.P.A. Emblem and Map.

1966. 4th General Assembly of Public Administrators Organisation (E.R.O.P.A.).
1477. **240.** 8 r. brown and green 12 8

241. Shah with Farmers.

1967. Land Reform Laws. 5th Anniv.
1485. **241.** 6 r. chocolate, yellow and bistre 15 10

242. Torch and Stars.

1967. Shah's White Revolution. 4th Anniv.
1486. **242.** 2 r. multicoloured .. 5 5
1487. – 6 r. multicoloured .. 15 8
DESIGN: 6 r. Shah acknowledging greetings.

243. Golden "Bull".

1967. Museum Week. Multicoloured.
1488. 3 r. Type **243** 8 5
1489. 5 r. Golden "leopard" 12 8
1490. 8 r. Capital with rams' heads 20 10

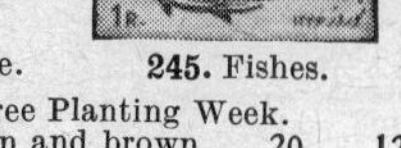

244. Planting a Tree. **245.** Fishes.

1967. Tree Planting Week.
1491. **244.** 8 r. green and brown 20 12

1967. New Year Festival.
1492. **245.** 1 r. red, brown & blue 5 5
1493. – 8 r. ult., red & blue .. 20 12
DESIGN (35×27 mm): 8 r. Swifts.

246. Microscope, Horses and Emblem.

1967. 2nd Veterinary Congress.
1494. **246.** 5 r. red, black & grey 12 5

247. Pres. Arif and Mosques.

1967. Visit of President of Iraq.
1495. **247.** 6 r. green and blue 15 10

248. U.N. Emblem and Fireworks.

1967. U.N. Stamp Day.
1496. **248.** 5 r. multicoloured .. 15 8

249. Map showing Pipeline Routes.

1967. Nationalisation of Oil Industry.
1497. **249.** 6 r. multicoloured .. 15 8

250. Fencing.

1967. Int. Youth Fencing Championships, Teheran.
1498. **250.** 5 r. yellow and violet 12 8

251. Shah and King Bhumibol.

1967. Visit of King of Thailand.
1499. **251.** 6 r. brown & chestnut 10 8

252. Emblem, Old and Young Couples.

1967. Social Insurance Scheme. 15th Anniv.
1500. **252.** 5 r. blue and bistre .. 8 5

253. Skiing.

1967. Olympic Committee Meeting, Teheran.
1501. **253.** 3 r. brown and black 5 5
1502. – 6 r. multicoloured .. 10 8
1503. – 8 r. brown and blue 15 10
DESIGNS: 6 r. Olympic " shield ". 8 r. Wrestling.

254. " LIONS " and Lion's Head.

1967. Lions Int. 50th Anniv.
1504. **254.** 3 r. multicoloured .. 5 5
1505. – 7 r. multicoloured .. 10 5
DESIGN—VERT. (36 × 42 mm.): 7 r. Lions emblem.

255. President Stoica.

1967. Visit of Pres. of Rumania.
1506. **255.** 6 r. blue and orange .. 10 5

256. I.T.U. Emblem. **257.** Persian Pavilion.

1967. Int. Tourist Year.
1507. **256.** 3 r. blue and red .. 5 5

1967. World Fair, Montreal.
1508. **257.** 4 r. red, gold & choc. 5 5
1509. 10 r. choc., gold & red 15 10

258. First Persian Stamp. **259.** Globe and Schoolchildren.

1967. Stamp Cent.
1510. **258.** 6 r. pur., blue & light bl. 12 10
1511. 8 r. purple, myrtle and green 15 12

1967. Campaign Against Illiteracy.
1512. **259.** 3 r. vio.-blue & blue 5 5
1513. 5 r. brown and yellow 8 5

260. " Musician ". **261.** " Helping Hand "

1967. Int. Musical Education in Oriental Countries Conf., Teheran.
1514. **260.** 14 r. maroon & chest. 20 15

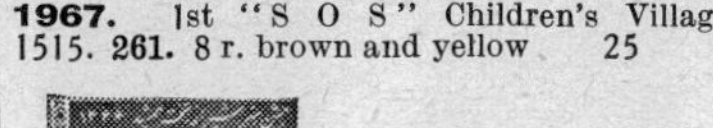

1967. 1st " S O S " Children's Village.
1515. **261.** 8 r. brown and yellow 25 15

262. Winged Ram. **263.** U.N. Emblem.

1967. Festival of Arts, Persepolis (Shiraz).
1516. **262.** 8 r. brown and bistre 15 12

1967. United Nations Day.
1517. **263.** 6 r. ultram. and bistre 12 8

264. Shah Mohammed Riza Pahlavi and Empress Farah. **265.** Crown Prince Riza.

1967. Coronation of Shah and Empress Farah.
1518. **264.** 2 r. brn., blue & silver 5 5
1519. 10 r. violet, bl. & silver 20 15
1520. 14 r. violet, gold & bl. 40 30

1967. Children's Day.
1521. **265.** 2 r. violet and silver 5 5
1522. 8 r. brown and silver 20 15

266. Pres. G. Traikov. **267.** Scout Emblem and Neckerchiefs.

1967. Visit of Pres. of Bulgaria.
1523. **266.** 10 r. maroon & violet 15 10

1967. Boy Scouts Co-operation Week.
1524. **267.** 8 r. brown and olive 12 10

268. " Co-operation " (linked hands). **269.** Shaikh Sabah

1967. Co-operation Year.
1525. **268.** 6 r. multicoloured .. 8 5

1968. Visit of Shaikh of Kuwait.
1526. **269.** 10 r. green and blue .. 15 10

270. Shah and Text of Reform Plan.

1968. Shah's White Revolution. 5th Anniv.
1527. **270.** 2 r. grn., sepia & flesh 5 5
1528. 8 r. violet, grn. & blue 12 8
1529. 14 r. choc., bl. & mve. 20 12

1968. New Year Festival. As T 222. Mult.
1530. 1 r. Almond blossom .. 5 5
1531. 2 r. Red tulips 5 5
1532. 2 r. Yellow tulips .. 5 5
1533. 6 r. Festival dancer .. 8 8

271. Oil Technician and Rig. **272.** W.H.O. Emblem.

1968. Nat. Oil Industry.
1534. **271.** 14 r. blk., yellow & grn. 20 12

1968. W.H.O. 20th Anniv.
1535. **272.** 14 r. orge., blue & pur. 20 12

273. Ancient Chariot (sculpture). **275.** Human Rights Emblem.

274. Shah and King Hassan.

1968. 5th World Congress of Persian Archaeology and Art, Teheran.
1536. **273.** 8 r multicoloured .. 12 8

1968. Visit of King of Morocco.
1537. **274.** 6 r. violet and flesh .. 8 5

1968. Human Rights Conference, Teheran.
1538. **275.** 8 r. red and green .. 10 8
1539. – 14 r. ultram and blue 15 12
DESIGN: 14 r. As T 275, but rearranged, and inscr. " INTERNATIONAL CONFERENCE ON HUMAN RIGHTS—TEHERAN 1968 ".

276. Footballer. **277.** Oil Refinery.

1968. Asian Football Cup Finals, Teheran.
1540. **276.** 8 r. multicoloured .. 10 8
1541. 10 r. multicoloured .. 12 10

1968. Inaug. of Teheran Oil Refinery.
1542. **277.** 14 r. multicoloured .. 20 12

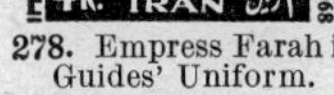

278. Empress Farah in Guides' Uniform. **279.** Mosquito Emblem.

1968. Iranian Girl Guides " Great Camp ".
1543. **278.** 4 r. blue and purple 8 5
1544. 14 r. brown and red .. 12 5

1968. 8th Int. Tropical Medicine and Malaria Congresses, Teheran.
1545. **279.** 6 r. purple and black 8 5
1546. 14 r. green and purple 20 12

280. Allegory of Literacy. **281.** " Horesman " and " Flower ".

1968. World Illiteracy Eradication Campaign Day.
1547. **280.** 6 r. blue, ochre & lav. 8 5
1548. 14 r. grn., brn. & yell. 20 12

1968. Festival of Arts (Shiraz) Persepolis.
1549. **281.** 14 r. multicoloured 20 12

282. Police Emblem on Map. **283.** Interpol Emblem.

1968. Police Day.
1550. **282.** 41 r. multicoloured .. 20 12

1968. 37th Interpol General Assembly.
1551. **283.** 10 r. maroon, blk. & bl. 12 8

284 U.N. Emblem and Dove.

1968. United Nations Day.
1552. **284.** 14 r. ultram. and blue 20 12

285. Empress Farah.

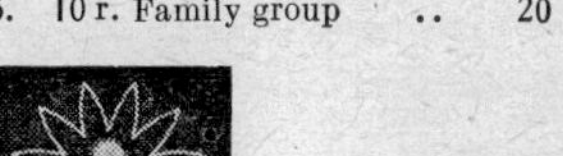

1968. Coronation. 1st Anniv. Multicoloured.
1553. 6 r. Type **285** 10 8
1554. 8 r. Shah Mohammed Riza Pahlavi 12 10
1555. 10 r. Family group .. 20 12

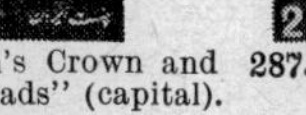

286. Shah's Crown and "Bulls' Heads" (capital). **287.** "Landscape".

1968. Education and Arts Festival.
1556. **286.** 14 r. multicoloured .. 20 12

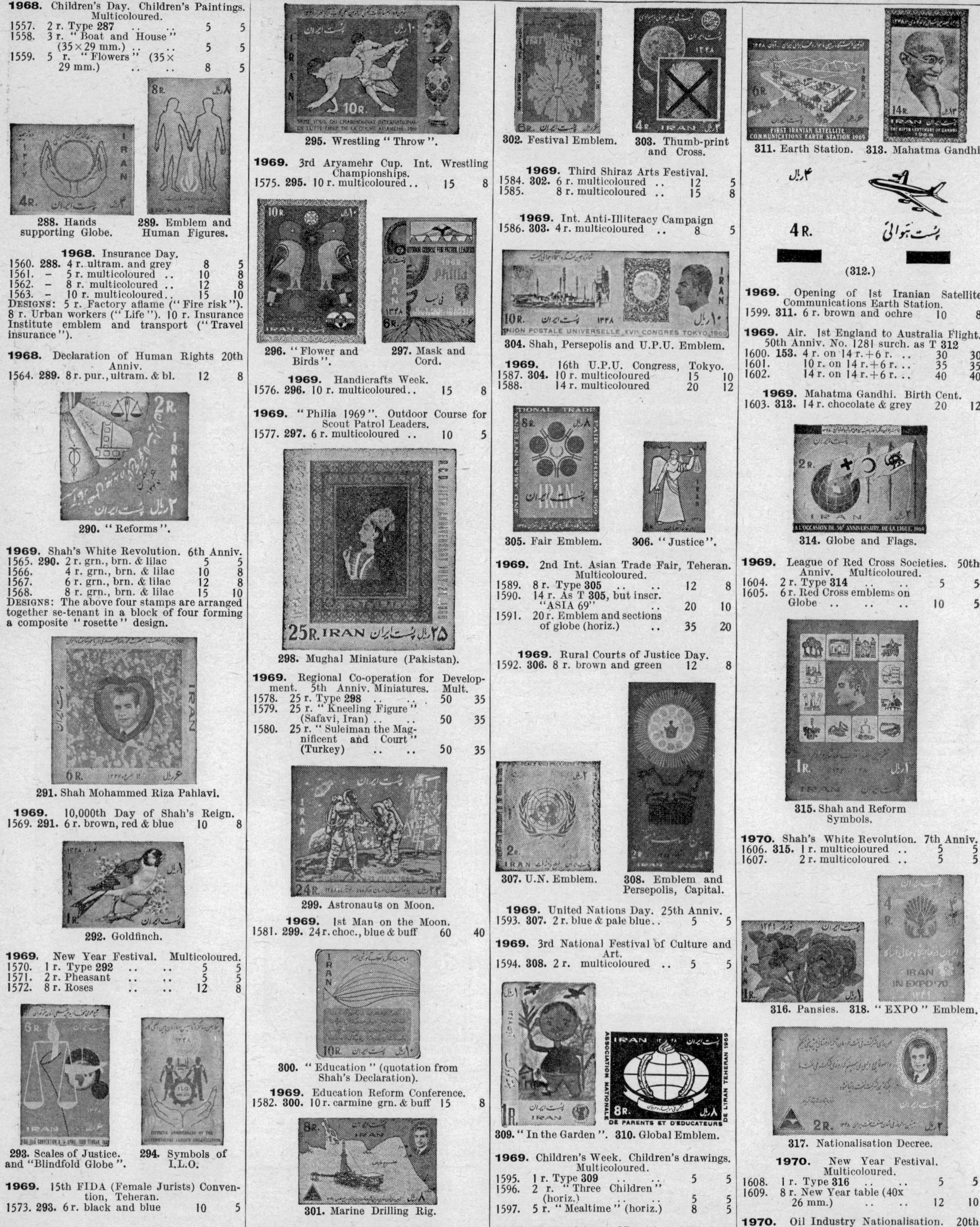

1968. Children's Day. Children's Paintings. Multicoloured.
1557. 2 r. Type **287** 5 5
1558. 3 r. "Boat and House" (35×29 mm.) 5 5
1559. 5 r. "Flowers" (35×29 mm.) 8 5

288. Hands supporting Globe. **289.** Emblem and Human Figures.

1968. Insurance Day.
1560. **288.** 4 r. ultram. and grey 8 5
1561. – 5 r. multicoloured .. 10 8
1562. – 8 r. multicoloured .. 12 8
1563. – 10 r. multicoloured .. 15 10
DESIGNS: 5 r. Factory aflame ("Fire risk"). 8 r. Urban workers ("Life"). 10 r. Insurance Institute emblem and transport ("Travel insurance").

1968. Declaration of Human Rights 20th Anniv.
1564. **289.** 8 r. pur., ultram. & bl. 12 8

290. "Reforms".

1969. Shah's White Revolution. 6th Anniv.
1565. **290.** 2 r. grn., brn. & lilac 5 5
1566. 4 r. grn., brn. & lilac 10 8
1567. 6 r. grn., brn. & lilac 12 8
1568. 8 r. grn., brn. & lilac 15 10
DESIGNS: The above four stamps are arranged together se-tenant in a block of four forming a composite "rosette" design.

291. Shah Mohammed Riza Pahlavi.

1969. 10,000th Day of Shah's Reign.
1569. **291.** 6 r. brown, red & blue 10 8

292. Goldfinch.

1969. New Year Festival. Multicoloured.
1570. 1 r. Type **292** 5 5
1571. 2 r. Pheasant 5 5
1572. 8 r. Roses 12 8

293. Scales of Justice and "Blindfold Globe". **294.** Symbols of I.L.O.

1969. 15th FIDA (Female Jurists) Convention, Teheran.
1573. **293.** 6 r. black and blue 10 5

1969. Int. Labour Organisation. 50th Anniv.
1574. **294.** 10 r. violet and blue 15 8

295. Wrestling "Throw".

1969. 3rd Aryamehr Cup. Int. Wrestling Championships.
1575. **295.** 10 r. multicoloured .. 15 8

296. "Flower and Birds". **297.** Mask and Cord.

1969. Handicrafts Week.
1576. **296.** 10 r. multicoloured .. 15 8

1969. "Philia 1969". Outdoor Course for Scout Patrol Leaders.
1577. **297.** 6 r. multicoloured .. 10 5

298. Mughal Miniature (Pakistan).

1969. Regional Co-operation for Development. 5th Anniv. Miniatures. Mult.
1578. 25 r. Type **298** 50 35
1579. 25 r. "Kneeling Figure" (Safavi, Iran) 50 35
1580. 25 r. "Suleiman the Magnificent and Court" (Turkey) 50 35

299. Astronauts on Moon.

1969. 1st Man on the Moon.
1581. **299.** 24 r. choc., blue & buff 60 40

300. "Education" (quotation from Shah's Declaration).

1969. Education Reform Conference.
1582. **300.** 10 r. carmine grn. & buff 15 8

301. Marine Drilling Rig.

1969. Iranian/Italian Marine Drilling Project. 10th Anniversary.
1583. **301.** 8 r. multicoloured .. 12 8

302. Festival Emblem. **303.** Thumb-print and Cross.

1969. Third Shiraz Arts Festival.
1584. **302.** 6 r. multicoloured .. 12 5
1585. 8 r. multicoloured .. 15 8

1969. Int. Anti-Illiteracy Campaign
1586. **303.** 4 r. multicoloured .. 8 5

304. Shah, Persepolis and U.P.U. Emblem.

1969. 16th U.P.U. Congress, Tokyo.
1587. **304.** 10 r. multicoloured 15 10
1588. 14 r. multicoloured 20 12

305. Fair Emblem. **306.** "Justice".

1969. 2nd Int. Asian Trade Fair, Teheran. Multicoloured.
1589. 8 r. Type **305** 12 8
1590. 14 r. As T **305**, but inscr. "ASIA 69" .. 20 10
1591. 20 r. Emblem and sections of globe (horiz.) .. 35 20

1969. Rural Courts of Justice Day.
1592. **306.** 8 r. brown and green 12 8

307. U.N. Emblem. **308.** Emblem and Persepolis, Capital.

1969. United Nations Day. 25th Anniv.
1593. **307.** 2 r. blue & pale blue .. 5 5

1969. 3rd National Festival of Culture and Art.
1594. **308.** 2 r. multicoloured .. 5 5

309. "In the Garden". **310.** Global Emblem.

1969. Children's Week. Children's drawings. Multicoloured.
1595. 1 r. Type **309** 5 5
1596. 2 r. "Three Children" (horiz.) 5 5
1597. 5 r. "Mealtime" (horiz.) 8 5

1969. National Assn. of Parents and Teachers Congress, Teheran.
1598. **310.** 8 r. brown and blue .. 12 8

311. Earth Station. **313.** Mahatma Gandhi.

(312.)

1969. Opening of 1st Iranian Satellite Communications Earth Station.
1599. **311.** 6 r. brown and ochre 10 8

1969. Air. 1st England to Australia Flight. 50th Anniv. No. 1281 surch. as T **312**
1600. **153.** 4 r. on 14 r.+6 r. .. 30 30
1601. 10 r. on 14 r.+6 r. .. 35 35
1602. 14 r. on 14 r.+6 r. .. 40 40

1969. Mahatma Gandhi. Birth Cent.
1603. **313.** 14 r. chocolate & grey 20 12

314. Globe and Flags.

1969. League of Red Cross Societies. 50th Anniv. Multicoloured.
1604. 2 r. Type **314** 5 5
1605. 6 r. Red Cross emblems on Globe 10 5

315. Shah and Reform Symbols.

1970. Shah's White Revolution. 7th Anniv.
1606. **315.** 1 r. multicoloured .. 5 5
1607. 2 r. multicoloured .. 5 5

316. Pansies. **318.** "EXPO" Emblem.

317. Nationalisation Decree.

1970. New Year Festival. Multicoloured.
1608. 1 r. Type **316** 5 5
1609. 8 r. New Year table (40x26 mm.) 12 10

1970. Oil Industry Nationalisation. 20th Anniv. Multicoloured.
1610. 2 r. Type **317** 8 5
1611. 4 r. Laying pipeline .. 8 5

1612. 6 r. Part of Kharg Island plant 10 5
1613. 8 r. Ocean terminal, Kharg Island (vert.) 20 8
1614. 10 r. Refinery, Teheran .. 35 12

1970. "EXPO 70" World Fair, Osaka Japan.
1615. **318.** 4 r. blue and mauve 5 5
1616. 10 r. violet and blue 15 12

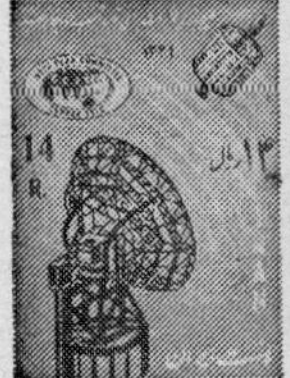

319. Dish Aerial and Satellite. **320.** New U.P.U. H.Q.

1970. Asian Plan Communications Committee Meeting, Teheran.
1617. **319.** 14 r. multicoloured .. 20 12

1970. New U.P.U. Headquarters Building, Berne.
1618. **320.** 2 r. sepia, mag. & grn. 5 5
1619. 4 r. sepia, mag. & lilac 5 5

321. A.P.Y. Emblem. **322.** Stork carrying baby.

1970. Asian Productivity Year.
1620. **321.** 8 r. multicoloured .. 12 8

1970. Midwifery School. 50th Anniv.
1621. **322.** 8 r. blue and brown .. 12 8

323. Columns, Palace of Apadama.

1970. Persian Empire. 2,500th Anniv. (1st Issue). Achaemenian Era.
1622. – 6 r. violet, red & grey 15 5
1623. **323.** 8 r. grn., blk. and pink 20 5
1624. – 10 r. choc., red & yell. 25 25
1625. – 14 r. brn., blk. & blue 40 50
DESIGNS-HORIZ. 6 r. Tomb of Cyrus the Great. 10 r. Religious ceremony (Median. bas-relief) 14 r. Achaemenian officers (bas-relief).
See also Nos. 1629/32, 1633/6, 1640/2, 1658/61, 1664/7, 1675/7 and 1679/82.

324. Saiful Malock Lake (Pakistan).

1970. Regional Co-operation for Development. 6th Anniv. Multicoloured.
1626. 2 r. Type **324** 5 5
1627. 2 r. Seeyo-Se-Pol Bridge, Isfahan (Iran) (62 × 46 mm.) 5 5
1628. 2 r. View from Fethiye (Turkey) 5 5

1970. Persian Empire 2,500th Anniv. (2nd issue). Achaemenian Era. Designs as T **323.**
1629. 2 r. gold and green 8 5
1630. 6 r. gold, violet & green 15 8
1631. 8 r. gold, blue and flesh .. 20 8
1632. 14 r. red, black and blue 40 15
DESIGNS—VERT. 2 r. Eagle amulet. 6 r. "Lion" goblet. 8 r. Winged ibex statue. HORIZ. 14 r. Tapestry.

1970. Persian Empire. 2500th Anniv. (3rd issue) Coins of Sassanid and Parthian Eras. Designs as T **332.** Multicoloured, frames in gold.
1633. 1 r. Queen Buran dirham 10 5
1634. 2 r. Mithridates I dirham 10 5
1635. 6 r. Shapur I dirham .. 15 8
1636. 8 r. Ardeshir I dirham .. 25 8

325. Candle and Globe Emblem.

1970. World Literacy Day.
1637. **325.** 1 r. multicoloured .. 5 5
1638. 2 r. multicoloured .. 5 5

326. Isfahan Tile. **327.** Councils Emblem.

1970. Int. Architects' Congress, Isfahan.
1639. **326.** 6 r. multicoloured .. 10 8

1970. Persian Empire. 2500th Anniv. (4th issue). Achaemenian and Sassanid Eras. Designs as T **323.**
1640. 2 r. multicoloured .. 5 5
1641. 6 r. brown, blue and grey 10 8
1642. 8 r. green, red and grey .. 12 8
DESIGNS—VERT. 2 r. Sassanid Arch and Art. HORIZ. 6 r. Achaemenian mounted courier. 8 r. Seal of Darius I.

1970. 1st Congress of Provincial Councils.
1643. **327.** 2 r. violet and blue .. 5 5

328. Dove and U.N. Emblem. **330.** Imperial Crown and Capital.

329. "1970" and I.A.T.A. Emblem.

1970. United Nations Day.
1644. **328.** 2 r. violet, pur. & blue 5 5

1970. Air. 26th Int. Air Transport Assn. General Meeting, Teheran.
1645. **329.** 14 r. multicoloured .. 50 15

1970. National Festival of Culture and Art.
1646. **330.** 2 r. multicoloured .. 5 5

331. "Goatherd and Goats".

1970. Children's Week. Children's Drawings. Multicoloured.
1647. 50 d. Type **331** .. 5 5
1648. 1 r. "Family picnic" .. 5 5
1649. 2 r. "Mosque" .. 5 5

332. Shah Mohammed Riza Pahlavi.

1971. Shah's White Revolution. 8th Anniv.
1650. **332.** 2 r. multicoloured .. 5 5

333. Common Shelduck.

1971. Int. Wetland and Waterfowl Conf., Ramsar. Multicoloured.
1651. 1 r. Type **333** .. 5 5
1652. 2 r. Ruddy shelduck .. 5 5
1653. 8 r. Flamingo (vert.) .. 10 8

334. Riza Shah Pahlavi. **335.** Cockerel.

1971. Rise of Pahlavi Dynasty. 50th Anniv.
1654. **334.** 6 r. multicoloured .. 8 5

1971. New Year Festival. Birds. Mult.
1655. 1 r. Type **335** 5 5
1656. 2 r. Swallow at nest .. 5 5
1657. 6 r. Hoopoe 8 5

336. Persian Archer (bas-relief).

1971. Persian Empire. 2,500th Anniv. (5th issue). Age of Cyrus the Great. Multicoloured.
1658. 4 r. Stone bull's head, Persepolis 5 5
1659. 5 r. Winged lion ornament 8 5
1660. 6 f. Type **336** 10 8
1661. 8 r. Imperial audience (bas-relief.) 25 20

337. Prisoners' Rehabilitation. **339.** "Shiraz Arts".

338. Selimiye Mosque Edirne (Turkey).

1971. Rehabilitation Week.
1662. **337.** 6 r. multicoloured .. 8 5
1663. 8 r. multicoloured .. 10 5

1971. Persian Empire 2500th Anniv. (6th issue). Art of Ancient Persia. As T **336.**
1664. 1 r. multicoloured .. 10 5
1665. 2 r. black and brown .. 10 5
1666. 2 r. brn. black and purple 10 5
1667. 10 r. black, blue & brown 30 10
DESIGNS—VERT. No. 1664, "Harpist" (mosaic). No. 1667, Bronze head of Parthian prince. HORIZ. No. 1665, "Shapur I hunting" (ornamental plate). No. 1666, "Investiture of Ardashir I" (bas-relief).

1971. Regional Co-operation for Development. 7th Anniv. Multicoloured.
1668. 2 r. Type **338** 5 5
1669. 2 r. Badshahi Mosque, Lahore (Pakistan) .. 5 5
1670. 2 r. Chaharbagh School, Ispahan (Iran) .. 5 5

1971. 5th Shiraz Arts Festival.
1671. **339.** 2 r. multicoloured .. 5 5

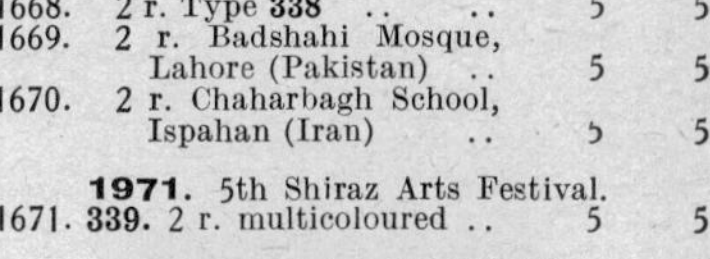

340. "Book-reading".

1971. Int. Literacy Day.
1672. **340.** 2 r. multicoloured .. 5 5

341. Kings Abdullah and Hussein II.

1971. Hashemite Kingdom of Jordan. 50th Anniv.
1673. **341.** 2 r. multicoloured .. 5 5

342. National Steel Foundry.

1971. Persian Empire. 2,500th Anniv. 7th issue). Modern Iran. Multicoloured.
1674. 1 r. Type **342** 10 5
1675. 2 r. Shayad Aryamehr Memorial 10 5
1676. 3 r. Senate Building, Teheran 10 5
1677. 11 r. Shah Abbas the Great Dam 30 10

343. Ghatour Rail Bridge.

1971. Iran-Turkey Railway Link. Inaug.
1678. **343.** 2 r. multicoloured .. 5 5

344. Shah Mohammed Riza Pahlavi.

1971. Persian Empire. 2,500th Anniv. (8th issue). Palavi Era. Multicoloured.
1679. 1 r. Type **344** 10 5
1680. 2 r. Riza Shah Pahlavi .. 10 5
1681. 5 r. Proclamation Tablet of Cyrus the Great (horiz.) 10 5
1682. 10 r. Pahlavi Crown .. 35 10

345. Racial Equality Year Emblem. **346.** Shah Mohammed Riza Pahlavi.

1971. Racial Equality Year.
1683. **345.** 2 r. multicoloured .. 5 5

1971.
1684. **346.** 5 d. purple 5 5
1685. 10 d. orange .. 5 5
1686. 50 d. green 5 5
1687. 1 r. green 5 5
1688. 2 r. brown 5 5
1689. – 6 r. green 12 5
1690. – 8 r. blue 15 5
1691. – 10 r. purple .. 25 5
1692. – 11 r. green 25 5
1693. – 14 r. blue 35 10
1694. – 20 r. red 50 12
1695. – 50 r. brown .. 1·50 30
Nos. 1689/95 as Type **346** but larger 27+37 mm.
See also Nos. 1715/26b and 1846/50.

347. " Waiters at a Banquet ".

1971. Children's Week. Children's Drawings. Multicoloured.
1696. 2 r. Type **347** 5 5
1697. 2 r. " Persepolis Ruins " (vert.) 5 5
1698. 2 r. " Persian Archer " (vert.) 5 5

348. U.N.E.S.C.O. Emblem.

1971. U.N.E.S.C.O. 25th Anniv.
1699. **348.** 6 r. blue and red .. 8 5

349. Congress Emblem and Livestock.

1971. 4th Iranian Veterinary Congress.
1700. **349.** 2 r. red, black & grey 5 5

350. I.L.O. Emblem and Globe.

1971. 7th Asian Regional I.L.O. Conference, Teheran.
1701. **350.** 2 r. orge., blue & blk. 5 5

351. Bird feeding Young. **352.** Shah Mohammed Riza Pahlavi.

1971. U.N.I.C.E.F. 25th Anniv.
1702. **351.** 2 r. multicoloured .. 5 5

1972. Shah's WhiteRevolution. 9th Anniv.
1703. **352.** 2 r. multicoloured .. 5 5

353. Rock Partridge. **354.** Human Heart.

1972. New Year Festival. Birds. Mult.
1705. 1 r. Type **353** 5 5
1706. 1 r. Printailed Sandgrouse 5 5
1707. 2 r. Yellow-bellied waxbill 5 5

1972. World Heart Day.
1708. **354.** 10 r. multicoloured .. 10 8

355. Winged Ibex Symbol. **356.** Scarlet Roses.

1972. Int. Film Festival, Teheran.
1709. **355.** 6 r. gold and blue .. 8 5
1710. – 8 r. multicoloured .. 10 5
DESIGN: 8 r. Symbolic spectrum.

1972. Persian Rose Cultivation. Mult.
1711. 1 r. Type **356** 5 5
1712. 2 r. Yellow roses 5 5
1713. 5 r. Red rose 8 5

357. " U.I.T. " Emblem.

1972. World Telecommunications Day.
1714. **357.** 14 r. multicoloured .. 15 12

1972. As Nos. 1684/95, but with bistre frames and inscriptions.
1715. **346.** 5 d. purple 5 5
1716. 10 d. brown 5 5
1717. 50 d. green 5 5
1718. 1 r. green 5 5
1719. 2 r. brown 5 5
1720. – 6 r. green 12 5
1721. – 8 r. violet 20 5
1722. – 10 r. purple 20 5
1723. – 11 r. blue 25 5
1724. – 14 r. blue 30 8
1725. – 20 r. red 40 8
1726. – 50 r. blue 60 10
1726a. – 100 r. violet 75 20
1726b. – 200 r. black .. .. 1·50 30
DESIGNS: 1720/26b, As T **346** but larger. size 27×37 mm.

358. " Fisherman " (Cevat Dereli, Turkey). **360.** Pens.

359. Floral Patterns.

1972. Regional Co-operation for Development. 8th Anniv. Paintings. Mult.
1727. 5 r. Type **358** 8 5
1728. 5 r. " Iranian Woman " (Behzad, Iran) .. 8 5
1729. 5 r. " Will and Power " (A. R. Chughtai, Pakistan) 8 5

1972. 6th Shiraz Arts Festival.
1730. **359.** 6 r. blk., grn. & red .. 8 5
1731. 8 r. black and purple 10 5

1972. World Literacy Day.
1732. **360.** 1 r. multicoloured .. 5 5
1733. 2 r. multicoloured .. 5 5

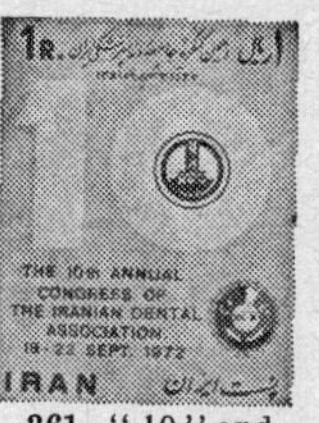

361. " 10 " and Dental Emblem. **362.** A.B.U. Emblem within " 9 ".

1972. 10th Annual Congress of Iranian Dental Association.
1734. **361.** 1 r. multicoloured .. 5 5
1735. 2 r multicoloured .. 5 5

1972. 9th General Assembly of Asian Broadcasting Union, Teheran.
1736. **362.** 6 r. multicoloured .. 8 5
1737. 8 r. multicoloured .. 10 5

363. 3ch. stamp of 1910 on Cover. **365.** Communications Emblem.

364. Chess.

1972. World Stamp Day.
1738. **363.** 10 r. multicoloured .. 10 8

1972. Olympic Games, Munich. Iranian Sports. Mult.
1739. 1 r. Type **364** 8 5
1740. 2 r. Hunting 8 5
1741. 3 r. Archery 10 5
1742. 5 r. Horse-racing .. 10 5
1743. 6 r. Polo 12 8
1744. 8 r. Wrestling 20 10

1972. United Nations Day.
1746. **365.** 10 r. multicoloured 10 8

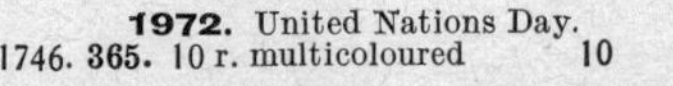

366. " Children at Play ".

367. Imperial Crown, Emblems and Capital.

369. Scouting Emblem. **368.** Family Planning Emblem.

1972 Children's Week. Children's Drawings. Multicoloured.
1747 2 r. " Children in garden " (vert.) 5 5
1748. 2 r. " At the Theatre " (vert.) 5 5
1749. 6 r. Type **366** 8 5

1972. National Festival of Art and Culture.
1750. **367.** 10 r. multicoloured .. 10 8

1972. Family Planning Campaign.
1751. **368.** 1 r. multicoloured .. 5 5
1752. 2 r. multicoloured .. 5 5

1972. Scouting in Iran. 20th Anniv.
1753. **369.** 2 r. multicoloured .. 5 5

370. Cuneiform Seal.

1973. "Origins of Writing" (1st issue). Impressions from ancient seals. Multicoloured. Background colours given.
1754. **370.** 1 r. blue 5 5
1755. – 1 r. mauve 5 5
1756. – 1 r. yellow 5 5
1757. – 1 r. green 5 5
1758. – 1 r. pink 5 5
1759. – 1 r. buff 5 5
See also Nos. 1774/9 and 1822/7.

371. Open Books in Space. **372** " Twelve Reforms ".

1973. Int. Book Year. Multicoloured.
1760. 2 r. Type **371** 5 5
1761. 6 r. Illuminated manuscript 8 5

1973. Shah's White Revolution. 10th Anniv. Multicoloured.
1762. 1 r. Type **372** 5 5
1763. 2 r. Pyramid of 12 balls .. 5 5
1764. 6 r. As Type **372** but size 71×92 mm. 25 25

373. "Sparus spinifer ". **375.** " Footballers ".

374. W.H.O. Emblem.

1973. New Year Festival. Fishes. Mult.
1766. 1 r. Type **373** 5 5
1767. 1 r. " Acanthurus " .. 5 5
1768. 2 r. " Anisotremus " .. 5 5
1769. 2 r. " Abdulef " 5 5
1770. 2 r. " Lutyanus fulniflamma " 5 5

1973. World Health Organization. 25th Anniv.
1771. **374.** 10 r. multicoloured .. 10 8

1973. 15th Asian Youth Football Tournament, Teheran.
1772. **375.** 14 r. multicoloured 15 12

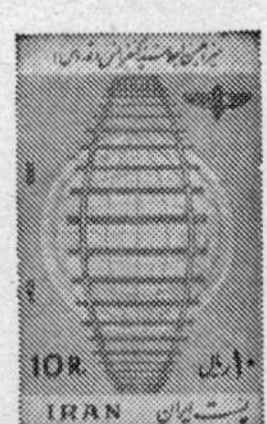

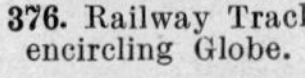

376. Railway Track encircling Globe. **377.** Ancient Aryan Script.

1973. International Railway Conference, Teheran
1773. **376.** 10 r. blue, blk. & mve. 25 10

1943. " Origins of Writing ". Multicoloured.
1774. 1 r. Type **377** 5 5
1775. 1 r. Kharochtahi tablet 5 5
1776. 1 r. Achaemenian priest and text 5 5
1777. 2 r. Parthian coin (Mianeh) 5 5
1778. 2 r. Parthian medallion (Arsacid) 5 5
1779. 2 r. Gachtak inscribed medallion (Dabireh) .. 5 5

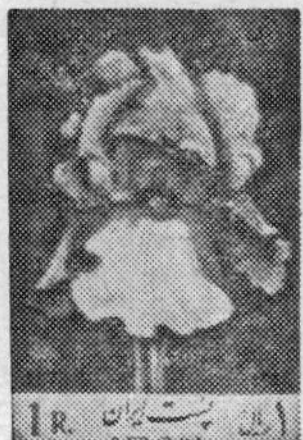
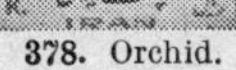
378. Orchid.

379. Carved Head, Tomb of Antiochus I (Turkey).

1973. Flowers. Multicoloured.
1780. 1 r. Type **378** 5 5
1781. 2 r. Hyacinth 5 5
1782. 6 r. Wild rose 8 5

1973. Regional Co-operation for Development. 9th Anniv. Multicoloured.
1783. 2 r. Type **379** 5 5
1784. 2 r. Statue, Lut excavations (Iran) 5 5
1785. 2 r. Street in Moenjodaro (Pakistan) 5 5

380. Shah and Oil Installations.

381. Soldiers and " Sun ".

1973. Full Independence for Iranian Oil Industry.
1786. **380.** 5 r. black and blue .. 5 5

1973. Defeat of Gen. Zahedi's Rebellion. 20th Anniv.
1787. **381.** 2 r. multicoloured .. 5 5

382. Sportswomen and Globe.

1973. 7th Int., Women's Congress on Physical Education and Sport, Teheran.
1788. **382.** 2 r. multicoloured (blue background) 5 5
1789. 2 r. multicoloured (green background) 5 5

383. Festival Poster.

385. Wrestling.

384. Riza Shah Memorial and Rainbow.

1973. 7th Shiraz Arts Festival.
1790. **382.** 1 r. multicoloured .. 5 5
1791. 5 r. multicoloured .. 5 5

1973. World Meteorological Organization. Cent.
1792. **384.** 5 r. multicoloured .. 8 5

1973. World Wrestling Championships, Teheran.
1793. **385.** 6 r. multicoloured .. 8 5

386. Alphabetic " Sun ". **387.** Globe wearing Earphones.

1973 World Literacy Day.
1794. **386.** 2 r. multicoloured .. 5 5

1973. Int., Audio-visual Exhibition, Teheran.
1795. **387.** 10 r. multicoloured.. 10 8

388. Al-Biruni. **390.** Crown Prince Cup.

389. C.I.S.M. Badge and Emblem.

1973. Abu al-Rayhan al-Biruni (mathematician and philosopher). Birth Millenary.
1796. **388.** 10 r. black and brown 10 8

1973. International Military Sports Council (C.I.S.M.). 25th Anniv.
1797. **389.** 8 r. multicoloured .. 10 5

1973. Crown Prince Cup Football Championship.
1798. **390.** 2 r. brown, black & lilac 5 5

391. Interpol Emblem.

393. U.P.U. Emblem, Post-horn and Letter.

392. Curves on Globe.

1973. Int., Criminal Police Organization (Interpol). 50th Anniv.
1799. **391.** 2 r. multicoloured .. 5 5

1973. World Mental Health Federation. 25th Anniv.
1800. **392.** 10 r. multicoloured .. 10 5

1973. World Post Day.
1801. **393.** 6 r. orange and blue.. 8 5

394. Emblems within Honeycomb. **395.** Imperial Crown, Emblem and " People ".

1973. United Nations Volunteers. 5th Anniv.
1802. **394.** 2 r. multicoloured (brown background) 5 5
1803. 2 r. multicoloured (green background) 5 5

1973. National Festival of Art and Culture.
1804. **395.** 2 r. multicoloured .. 5 5

396. Bosphorus Bridge.

1973. Turkish Republic. 50th Anniv. Mult.
1805. 2 r. Type **396** 5 5
1806. 8 r. Meeting of Kemal Ataturk and Riza Shah Pahlavi.. .. .. 10 5

397. "House and Garden".

399. Cylinder of Cyrus and Red Cross Emblems.

398. Ear of Grain and Cow.

1973. Children's Week. Children's Drawings. Multicoloured.
1807. 2 r. Type **397** 5 5
1808. 2 r. " Collecting Fruit " 5 5
1809. 2 r. " Caravan " (horiz.) 5 5

1973. World Food Programme. 10th Anniv.
1810. **398.** 10 r. multicoloured .. 10 8

1973. 22nd Int., Red Cross Conference, Teheran.
1811. **399.** 6 r. multicoloured .. 8 5

400. IATA Emblem.

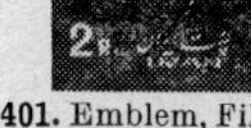
401. Emblem, Film and Flags.

1973. Tourist Managers Congress, Teheran.
1812. **400.** 10 r. multicoloured.. 10 8

1973. International Film Festival, Teheran.
1813. **401.** 2 r. multicoloured. .. 5 5

402. Flame Emblem. **403.** Harp Emblem.

1973. Declaration of Human Rights. 25th Anniv.
1814. **402.** 8 r. multicoloured .. 10 5

1973. " Art of Music " Frestival.
1815. **403.** 10 r. red, grn. & blk. 10 8
1816. – 10 r. ultramarine, blue and purple .. 10 8
DESIGN: No. 1816, Musical symbols.

404. Reform Symbols.

1974. 11th Anniv. of Shah's " White Revolution ".
1817. **404.** 1 r. multicoloured .. 5 5
1818. – 1 r. multicoloured .. 5 5
1819. – 2 r. multicoloured .. 5 5
1820. – 2 r. multicoloured .. 5 5
DESIGNS: Nos. 1818/20 show Reform symbols similar to Type **404**.
Nos. 1817/20 were issued in se-tenant blocks of four within the sheet.

405. Pir Amooz Ketabaty Script.

1974. " Origins of Writing " (3rd issue). Mult.
1822. 1 r. Type **405** 5 5
1823. 1 r. Mo Eghhely Ketabaty 5 5
1824. 1 r. Din Dabireh Avesta 5 5
1825 2 r. Pir Amooz, Maskh style 5 5
1826. 2 r. Pir Amooz, decorative 5 5
1827. 2 r. Pir Amooz, decorative and architectural .. 5 5

406. Chicken, Cow and Syringe.

1974 Fifth Iranian Veterinary Congress.
1828. **406.** 6 r. multicoloured .. 8 5

407. Butterfly.

408. Mevlana.

1974. Nawrooz and Spring Festivals. Butterflies.
1841. **407.** 1 r. multicoloured .. 5 5
1842. – 1 r. multicoloured .. 5 5
1843. – 2 r. multicoloured .. 5 5
1844. – 2 r. multicoloured .. 5 5
1845. – 2 r multicoloured .. 5 5
DESIGNS: Nos. 1841/5, show butterflies similar to T **407**.

1974. As Nos. 1684/95, but colours changed.
1846. **346.** 50 d. blue and orange 5 5
1847. 1 r. blue and green .. 5 5
1848. 2 r. blue and red .. 5 5
1849. – 10 r. blue and green .. 12 8
1850. – 20 r. blue and mauve 20 15
DESIGNS: Nos. 1849/50. As T **346**, but larger, size 27×37 mm.

1974. Jalal-udin Mevlana (poet). 700th Death Anniv.
1851. **408.** 2 r. multicoloured .. 5 5

409. Palace of Forty Columns, Isfahan.

1974. 9th Near and Middle East Medical Congress, Isfahan.
1852. **409.** 10 r. multicoloured .. 10 8

410. Onager (wild ass). **411.** Gymnastics.

1974. International Game and Wild Life Protection Congress, Teheran. Mult.
1853. 1 r. Type **410** 5 5
1854. 2 r. Bustard 5 5
1855. 6 r. Fawn and deer .. 8 5
1856. 8 r. Black grouse .. 10 5
Nos. 1853/6 were issued in se-tenant strips of four within the sheet.

1974. 7th Asian Games, Teheran (1st series). Multicoloured.
1857. **411.** 1 r. Type **411** .. 5 5
1858. – 1 r. Table-Tennis .. 5 5
1859. – 2 r. Boxing 5 5
1860. – 2 r. Hurdling .. 5 5
1861. – 6 r. Weightlifting .. 8 5
1862. – 8 r. Handball .. 10 5
See also Nos. 1874/9, 1890/3 and 1909.

412. Lion of St Mark's.

1974. U.N.E.S.C.O. "Save Venice" Campaign. Multicoloured.
1863. 6 r. Type **412** 8 5
1864. 8 r. Merchants at the Doge's court 10 5

413. Chain Link. **414.** Shah and Boeing 727 Jetliner.

1974. Farm Co-operatives' Day.
1865. **413.** 2 r. multicoloured .. 5 5

1974. Air.
1866. **414.** 4 r. black and orge... 5 5
1867. 10 r. black & blue .. 10 5
1868. 12 r. black & brown 12 5
1869. 14 r. black & green .. 15 5
1870. 20 r. black & mve. .. 20 5
1871. 50 r. black & blue 50 10

415. Fighter Aircraft 1924.

1974. Imperial Iranian Air Force. 50th Anniv. Multicoloured.
1872. 10 r. Type **415** 20 8
1873. 10 r. Fighter aircraft of 1974 .. .. .. 20 8

416. Tennis (men's doubles). **417.** Mazanderan Costume.

1974. Seventh Asian Games, Teheran (2nd series). Multicoloured.
1874. 1 r. Type **416** 5 5
1875. 1 r Swimming 5 5
1876. 2 r. Wrestling 5 5
1877. 2 r. Football 5 5
1878. 4 r. Handball 5 5
1879. 10 r Tennis (women's singles) 10 8
See also Nos. 1890/3 and 1895.

1974. Regional Costumes. Multicoloured.
1880. 2 r. Type **417** 5 5
1881. 2 r. Bakhtiari 5 5
1882. 2 r. Turkoman 5 5
1883. 2 r. Ghasgai 5 5
1884. 2 r. Kirmanshah (Kurdistan) 5 5
1885. 2 r. Sanandadj (Kurdistan) 5 5
Nos. 1880/5 were issued in se-tenant blocks of six within the sheet.

418. Gold Cup. **419.** Iranian Carpet.

1974. Iranian Football Championships.
1886. **418.** 2 r. yell., brn. and grn. 5 5

1974. Regional Co-operation for Development. Tenth Anniv. Carpets of Member Countries. Multicoloured.
1887. 2 r. Pakistani carpet ("diamond" centre) 5 5
1888. 2 r. Turkish carpet (striped) 5 5
1889 2 r. Type **419** 5 5
Nos. 1887/9 were issued in se-tenant strips of three within the sheet.

420. Rifle-shooting. **421.** Persian King.

1974. Seventh Asian Games, Teheran (3rd series). Multicoloured.
1890. 2 r. Type **420** 5 5
1891. 2 r. Fencing 5 5
1892. 2 r. Football 5 5
1893. 2 r. Cycling 5 5

1974. 8th Shiraz Arts Festival, Persepolis.
1894. **421.** 2 r. multicoloured .. 5 5

422. Shah and Petrochemical Works, Khark.

1974.

(a) As Type **422.**
1896. **422.** 5 d. green and brown 5 5
1897. – 10 d. orange & brown 5 5
1898. – 50 d. green and brown 5 5
1899. – 1 r. blue and brown.. 5 5
1900. – 2 r. purple and brown 5 5

(b) Size 37×27 mm.
1901. – 6 r. brown and blue.. 5 5
1902. – 8 r. turquoise & blue 8 5
1903. – 10 r. purple and blue 15 5
1904. – 14 r. green and blue.. 20 8
1905. – 20 r. mauve and blue 25 10
1906. – 50 r. violet and blue.. 55 15
DESIGN: 10 d. Railway bridge, Gatur. 50 d. Dam, Farahnaz. 1 r. Oil Refinery. 2 r. Radio telescope. 6 r. Steelworks, Aryamhr. 8 r. Tabriz University. 10 r. Shah Abbas Kabir Dam. 14 r. Teheran Opera House. 20 r. Shahyad Square. 50 r. Aryamehr Stadium.
See also Nos. 1974/8.

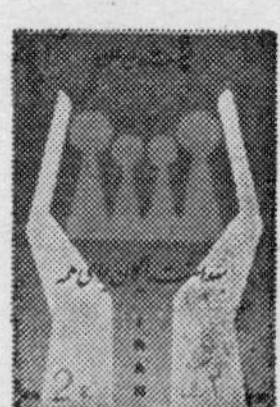

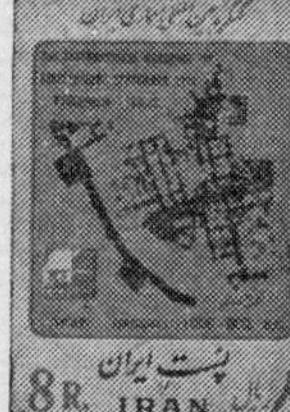

423. Family within Hands. **425.** Plan of Hasanlu.

424. Aryamethr Stadium, Teheran.

1974. State Education and Health Services. Multicoloured.
1907. 2 r. Type **423** 5 5
1908. 2 r. Children, pen and book within hands .. 5 5

1974. Seventh Asian Games, Teheran (4th series).
1909. **424.** 6 r. multicoloured .. 8 5

1974. 2nd International Architectural Congress, Shiraz.
1910. **425.** 8 r. multicoloured .. 10 5

426. Charioteer.

1974. Universal Postal Union. Cent. Mult.
1911. 6 r. Type **426** 12 5
1912. 14 r. U.P.U. emblem and letters 25 10

427. Road through Park.

1974. Opening of Farahabad Park, Teheran. Multicoloured.
1913 1 r. Type **427** 5 5
1914. 2 r. Recreation pavilion 5 5

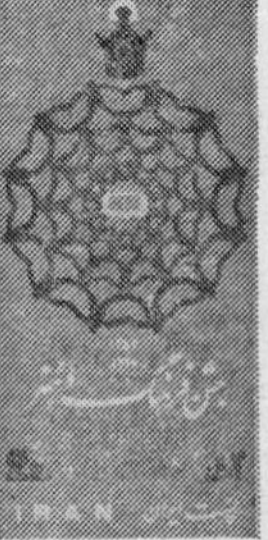

428. Festival Emblem.

1974. Festivals of Art and Culture.
1915. **428.** 2 r. multicoloured .. 5 5

429. Crown Prince in Aircraft Cockpit.

1974. Crown Prince's Birthday.
1916. **429.** 14 r. multicoloured .. 15 8

430. Destroyer "Palang".

1974. Navy Day.
1917. **430.** 10 r. multicoloured .. 10 8

431. Scarecrow. **432.** Winged Bull Emblem.

1974. Children's Week. Children's Drawings. Multicoloured.
1918. 2 r. Type **431** 5 5
1919. 2 r. Girl at spinning wheel 5 5
1920. 2 r. New Year picnic .. 5 5
Nos. 1919/20 are horiz.

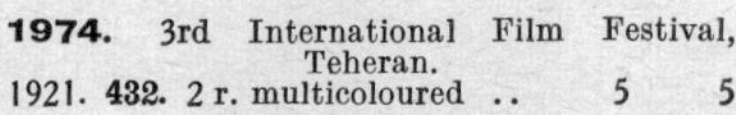

1974. 3rd International Film Festival, Teheran.
1921. **432.** 2 r. multicoloured .. 5 5

433. W.P.Y. Emblem.

1974. World Population Year.
1922. **433.** 8 r. multicoloured .. 10 5

434. Gold Butterfly Brooch.

1974. Shah and Empress Farah. 14th Wedding Anniversary. Multicoloured.
1923. 6 r. Type **434** 8 5
1924. 8 r. Gold diadem .. 10 5

435. Angel with Banner.

1975. International Women's Year.
1925. **435.** 2 r. oran., blue & red 5 5

436. Emblems of Agriculture, Industry and the Arts. **437.** Tourism Year Emblem.

1975. Shah's "White Revolution". 12th Anniv.
1926. **436.** 2 r. multicoloured .. 5 5

1975. South Asia Tourism Year.
1927. **437.** 6 r. multicoloured .. 8 5

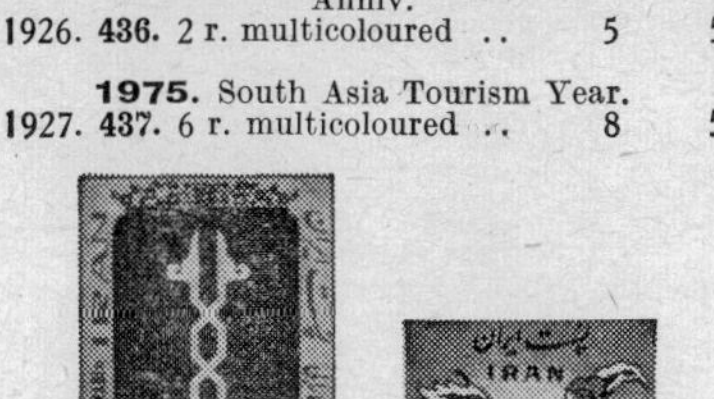
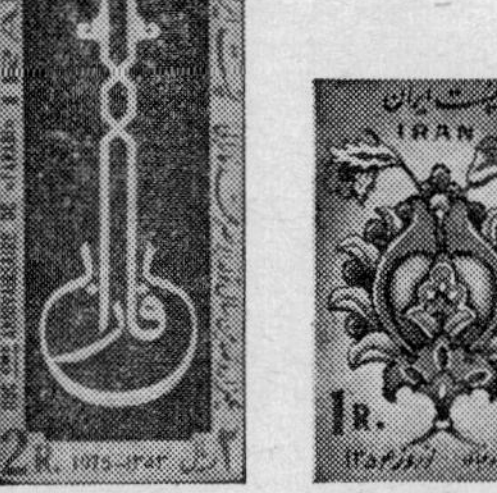

438. Faribi's Initial. **439.** Ornament.

1975. Abu-Nasr al-Faribi (philosopher). 1100th Birth Anniv.
1928. **438.** 2 r. multicoloured .. 5 5

1975. New Year Festival. Multicoloured.
1929. 1 r. Type **439** 5 5
1930. 1 r. Blossoms and tree .. 5 5
1931. 1 r. Arabesque and patterns 5 5

440. Nasser Khosrov. **441.** Persian Warriors.

1975. Nasser Khosrov (poet). Birth Millennary.
1932. **440.** 2 r. black, red & bistre 5 5

1975. Rotary International. 70th Anniv. Multicoloured.
1933. 2 r. Type **441** 5 5
1934. 10 r. Charioteer (horiz.) .. 10 8

442. Biochemical Emblem. **443.** "Co-operative Peoples".

1975. Fifth Biochemical Symposium.
1935. **442.** 2 r. multicoloured .. 5 5

1975. Co-operatives Day.
1936. **443.** 2 r. multicoloured .. 5 5

444. Ancient Signal Beacon.

1975. World Telecommunications Day. Multicoloured.
1937. 6 r. Type **444** 8 5
1938. 8 r. Telecommunications satellite 10 5

445. "Iran Air" Boeing "747".

1975. "Iran Air's" First Teheran–New York Flight.
1943. **445.** 10 r. multicoloured .. 10 8

446. Environmental Emblem. **448.** Party Emblem.

447. Dam and Reservoir.

1975. World Environment Day.
1944. **446.** 6 r. multicoloured .. 8 5

1975. 9th International Commission on Irrigation and Drainage.
1945. **447.** 10 r. multicoloured .. 10 8

1975. Formation of Revival Party.
1946. **448.** 2 r. multicoloured .. 5 5

449. Saluting Hand. **450.** Festival Motif.

1975. 2nd National Girl Scout Camp, Teheran.
1947. **449.** 2 r. multicoloured .. 5 5

1975. Festival of Tus (honouring poet Firdausi).
1948. **450.** 2 r. multicoloured .. 5 5

451. Iranian Tile.

1975. Regional Co-operation for Development. 11th Anniv. Multicoloured.
1949. 2 r. Type **451** 5 5
1950. 2 r. Pakistani camel-skin vase 5 5
1951. 2 r. Turkish porcelain vase 5 5

452. Parliament Gateway.

1975. Iranian Constitution. 70th Anniv.
1952. **452.** 10 r. multicoloured .. 10 8

453. Stylised Column. **454.** Flags over Globe.

1975. 9th Shiraz Arts Festival.
1953. **453.** 8 r. multicoloured .. 10 5

1975. International Literacy Symposium, Persepolis.
1954. **454.** 2 r. multicoloured .. 5 5

455. Stylised Globe. **457.** Crown and Column Capital.

456. Envelope on World Map.

1975. 3rd International Trade Fair, Teheran.
1955. **455.** 2 r. multicoloured .. 5 5

1975. World Post Day.
1956. **456.** 14 r. multicoloured .. 15 10

1975. Festivals of Art and Culture.
1957. **457.** 2 r. multicoloured .. 5 5

458. Face within Film. **459.** "Mother's Face".

1975. International Festival of Children's Films, Teheran.
1958. **458.** 6 r. multicoloured .. 8 5

1975. Children's Week. Multicoloured.
1959. 2 r. Type **459** 5 5
1960. 2 r. "Young Girl" .. 5 5
1961. 2 r. "Our House" (horiz.) 5 5

460. "Sound Film". **461.** Reform Symbols.

1975. 4th International Film Festival, Teheran.
1962. **460.** 8 r. multicoloured .. 10 5

1976. Shah's "White Revolution". 13th Anniversary. Multicoloured.
1963. 2 r. Type **461** 5 5
1964. 2 r. Symbols representing "People" 5 5
1965. 2 r. Five reform symbols 5 5

462. Motorcycle Patrol. **463.** Football Cup.

1976. Highway Police Day. Multicoloured.
1966. 2 r. Type **462** 5 5
1967. 6 r. Police helicopter (horiz.) 10 8

1976. Third Int. Football Cup.
1968. **463.** 2 r. multicoloured .. 5 5

464. Candlestick. **465.** Early and Modern Telephones.

1976. New Year. Multicoloured.
1969. 1 r. Type **464** 5 5
1970. 1 r. Incense burner .. 5 5
1971. 1 r. Rosewater jug .. 5 5

1976. Telephone Centenary.
1972. **465.** 10 r. multicoloured .. 15 12

466. Human Eye in Box.

1976. World Health Day.
1973. **466.** 6 r. multicoloured .. 10 8

1976. As Nos. 1896/1906, but colours changed.
(a) As Type **422.**
1974. **422.** 50 d. purple and green 5 5
1975. – 1 r. blue and green .. 5 5
1976. – 2 r. brown and green 5 5
(b) Size 37×27 mm.
1977. – 6 r. violet and brown 5 5
1978. – 14 r. purple and brown 20 8

467. Nurse holding Child.

1976. Social Services Organization. 30th Anniv. Multicoloured.
1979. 2 r. Type **467** 5 5
1980. 2 r. Workshop apprentices 5 5
1981. 2 r. Handclasp—care for the aged 5 5

468. Linked Men on on Map. **469.** Sound Waves and Headphones.

1976. Iranian Co-operative Movement. 10th Anniv.
1982. **468.** 2 r. multicoloured. .. 5 5

1976. World Telecommunications Day.
1983. **469.** 14 r. multicoloured .. 20 8

470. Patriotism. **471.** Nasser-Khosrowi, Oil-wells and Map.

1976. "Power of Stability".
1984. **470.** 2 r. multicoloured .. 5 5

1976. Tourism Day, and Nasser-Khosrow "the Great Iranian Tourist". Birth Anniv.
1985. **471.** 6 r. multicoloured .. 10 8

472. Riza Shah Pahlavi. **473.** Olympic Flame and Emblem.

1976. Regional Co-operation for Development. Multicoloured.

1986. 2 r. Type **472** 5 5
1987. 6 r. Mohamed Ali Jinnah (Pakistan) .. 10 8
1988. 8 r. Kemal Ataturk (Turkey) 12 8

1976. Olympic Games, Montreal.

1989. **473.** 14 r. multicoloured .. 20 8

474. Riza Shah Pahlavi and Shah Mohammed Riza Pahlavi (son).

1976. Pahlavi Dynasty. 50th Anniv. Multicoloured.

1990. 2 r. Type **474** 5 5
1991. 6 r. Riza Shah Pahlavi in Coronation dress (vert.) 10 8
1992. 14 r. Shah Mohammed Riza Pahlavi in Coronation dress (vert.) 20 8

475. Festival Emblem. **476.** Scout Emblem.

1976. 10th Shiraz Arts Festival.

1993. **475.** 10 r. multicoloured .. 15 12

1976. 10th Asia/Pacific Scout Conference, Teheran.

1994. **476.** 2 r. multicoloured .. 5 5

477. Radiation Treatment. **478.** Presentation to Policewoman.

1976. Campaign against Cancer.

1995. **477.** 2 r. multicoloured .. 5 5

1976. Police Day.

1996. **478.** 2 r. multicoloured .. 5 5

OFFICIAL STAMPS

1902. Stamp of 1898 surch. **Service** and value in English and Persian.

O 224. **16.** 5 c. on 1 k. red .. 45 12
O 225. 10 c. on 1 k. red .. 30 12
O 226. 12 c. on 1 k. red .. 60 35

1903. Stamps of 1903 optd. **Service.**

O 259. **22.** 1 c. lilac 5 5
O 260. 2 c. grey 5 5
O 261. 3 c. green 5 5
O 262. 5 c. red 5 5
O 263. 10 c. brown 5 5
O 264. 12 c. blue 10 5
O 265. **23.** 1 k. purple 10 5
O 266. 2 k. blue 20 5
O 267. 5 k. brown 30 12
O 268. 10 k. red 30 12
O 269. 20 k. orange 75 55
O 270. 30 k. green 95 60
O 271. 50 k. green .. .. 6·00 4·00

1905. Nos. 275/6 and 280/1 optd. **Service.**

O 283. **23.** 2 t. on 50 k. green .. 8·00 3·00
O 285. 2 t. on 50 k. green .. 8·00 3·00
O 284. 3 t. on 50 k. green .. 8·00 3·00
O 286. 3 t. on 50 k. green .. 8·00 3·00

(O 1.)

1911. Stamps of 1909 optd. **Service** and with Type **O 1.**

O 353. **28.** 1 c. maroon and orge. 10 5
O 354. 2 c. marron and violet 10 5
O 355. 3 c. maroon and green 10 5
O 356. 6 c. maroon and red .. 10 5
O 357. 9 c. maroon and grey 10 5
O 358. 10 c. maroon & purple 10 5
O 359. 1 k. olive, violet & silver 20 5
O 360. 2 k. olive, grn. & silver 50 25

1915. Coronation stamps of 1915 optd. **SERVICE** in English and Persian.

O 460. **31.** 1 c. blue and red .. 5 5
O 461 2 c. red and blue .. 5 5
O 462. 3 c. green 5 5
O 463. 5 c. red 5 5
O 464. 6 c. red and green .. 5 5
O 465. 9 c. violet and brown 5 5
O 466. 10 c. brown & green 5 5
O 467. 12 c. blue 5 5
O 468. 24 c. chocolate & brn. 5 5
O 469. **32.** 1 k. blck., brn. & silver 10 8
O 470. 2 k. red, blue & silver 10 8
O 471. 3 k. sepia, lilac & silver 10 8
O 472. 5 k. grey, sepia & silver 12 8
O 473. – 1 t. black, vio. & gold 12 10
O 474. – 2 t. brown, grn. & gold 25 12
O 475. – 3 t. red, crimson & gold 40 15
O 476. – 5 t. grey, blue & gold 50 20

1941. As T **28**, but with curved inscriptions.

O 836. 5 d. violet 15 5
O 837. 10 d. mauve 15 5
O 838. 25 d. red 15 5
O 839. 50 d. black 15 5
O 840. 75 d. claret 20 5
O 841. 1 r. green 35 5
O 842. 1 r. 50 blue .. .. 1·25 5
O 843. 2 r. blue .. .. 1·50 5
O 844. 3 r. purple .. .. 2·50 5
O 845. 5 r. green .. .. 3·50 5
O 846. 10 r. blue and brown .. 12·00 8
O 847. 20 r. mauve and blue .. 45·00 60
O 848. 30 r. green and violet .. 70·00 1·00
O 849. 50 r. brown and blue .. £100 7·00

The rial values are larger (23 × 30 mm.).

O 2. Red Lion and Sun Emblem.

1974.

O 1829. **O 2.** 5 d. violet & mauve 5 5
O 1830. 10 d. red & blue .. 5 5
O 1831. 50 d. orge.& grn. .. 5 5
O 1832. 1 r. grn. & gold .. 5 5
O 1833. 2 r. grn & orge. .. 5 5
O 1834. – 6 r. grn. & yell. .. 5 5
O 1835. – 8 r blue & yell. .. 8 5
O 1836. – 10 r. blue & pink .. 10 5
O 1837. – 11 r. maroon & blue 10 5
O 1838. – 14 r. red & blue .. 12 5
O 1839. – 20 r. blue & orge. 20 8
O 1840. – 50 r. brn. & grn. .. 45 10

DESIGNS: Nos. O 1854/60, As Type O 2, but size 23 × 37 mm.

PARCEL POST STAMPS

1915. Coronation stamps of 1915 optd. **COLIS POSTAUX** in English and Persian.

P 443. **31.** 1 c. blue and red .. 5 5
P 444. 2 c. red and blue .. 5 5
P 445. 3 c. green 5 5
P 446. 5 c. red 5 5
P 447. 6 c. red and green .. 5 5
P 448. 9 c. violet and brown 5 5
P 449. 10 d. brown and green 5 5
P 450. 12 c. blue 5 5
P 451. 24 c. choc. & brown .. 5 5
P 452. **32.** 1 k. black, brn. & silver 10 8
P 453. 2 k. red, blue & silver 10 8
P 454. 3 k. sepia, lilac & silver 10 8
P 455. 5 k. grey, sepia & silver 12 8
P 456. – 1 t. blk., violet & gold 20 10
P 457. – 2 t. brown, grn. & gold 20 10
P 458 – 3 t. red and gold .. 40 20
P 459. – 5 t. grey, blue & gold 50 20

P 1.

1958.

P 1151. **P 1.** 50 d. drab 5 5
P 1152. 1 r. red 5 5
P 1153. 2 r. blue 5 5
P 1154. 3 r. myrtle 5 5
P 1478. 5 r. violet 5 5
P 1479. 10 r. brown 10 8
P 1480. 20 r. orange 20 20
P 1481 30 r. mauve .. 50 40
P 1482. 50 r. lake .. 90 60
P 1483. 100 r. yellow .. 2·00 1·25
P 1484. 200 r. emerald .. 4·00 3·00

The word "IRAN" with a black frame is printed in reverse on the back of the above stamps and is intended to show through the stamps when attached to parcels.

POSTAL TAX STAMPS

T 1. Red Lion and Sun Emblem.

1950. Hospitals Fund.

T 1414. **T 1.** 50 d. red and green 5 5
T 1415. 2 r. red and lilac 5 5

IRAQ O2

A country W. of Persia, formerly under Turkish dominion, then under British mandate after the 1914-18 War. An independent kingdom since 1932 until 14 July, 1958, when the king was assassinated and a republic proclaimed.

1917. 16 annas = 1 rupee.
1931. 1,000 fils = 1 dinar.

1918. Stamps of Turkey (Pictorial issue, Nos. 501/514) surch. **IRAQ IN BRITISH OCCUPATION,** and value in Indian currency

1. ½ a. on 5 pa. purple 8 8
2. ½ a. on 10 pa. green 8 8
3. 1 a. on 20 pa. red 8 8
4. 1½ a. on 5 pa. purple .. 20 15
5. 2½ a. on 1 pi. blue 25 20
6. 3 a. on 1½ pi. grey and red .. 15 12
7. 4 a. on 1¾ pi. brown and grey 20 15
8. 6 a. on 2 pi. black and green 45 60
9. 8 a. on 2½ pi. green & orange 45 30
10. 12 a. on 5 pi. lilac .. 75 65
11. 1 r. on 10 pi. brown .. 1·00 75
12. 2 r. on 25 pi. green .. 2·00 1·75
13. 5 r. on 50 pi. red .. 7·00 3·50
14. 10 r. on 100 pi. blue .. 10·00 6·50

1. Sunni Mosque, Muadhdham.

3. Winged Cherub.

8. Allegory of Date Palm. 9. King Faisal I.

1923.

41. **1.** ½ a. green 5 5
42. – 1 a. brown 8 5
43. **3.** 1½ a. red 10 5
44. – 2 a. yellow-brown .. 15 10
45. – 3 a. blue 15 10
46. – 4 a. violet 25 15
47. – 6 a. blue 40 20
48. – 8 a. olive 45 25
49. **8.** 1 r. brown and green .. 75 50
50. **1.** 2 r. black .. .. 3·00 2·50
51. 2 r. olive .. .. 6·00 2·50
52. – 5 r. orange .. .. 9·00 5·00
53. – 10 r. red .. .. 11·00 7·00

DESIGNS—HORIZ. 1 a. Gufas on Tigris. 2 a. Bull from Babylonian wall-sculpture. 3 a. Arch of Ctesiphon. 6 a., 10 r. Shiah Mosque, Kadhimain. VERT. 4 a., 8 a., 5 r. Tribal Standard, Dulaim Camel Corps.

1927.

78. **9.** 1 r. brown .. .. .. 2·00 30

10. King Faisal I. 11. 10 Fils (12.)

1931.

80. **10.** ½ a. green 5 5
81. 1 a. brown 8 5
82. 1½ a. red 25 20
83. 2 a. orange 12 8
84. 3 a. blue 25 8
85. 4 a. purple 50 50
86. 6 a. blue 50 40
87. 8 a. green 60 60
88. **11.** 1 r. brown .. .. 1·75 70
89. 2 r. yellow-brown .. 2·50 1·50
90. 5 r. orange .. .. 5·00 5·00
91. 10 r. red .. .. 13·00 13·00
92. **9.** 25 r. violet £275 £275

1932. Surch. as T **12.**

106. **10.** 2 f. on ½ a green .. 5 5
107. 3 f. on ½ a. green .. 5 5
108. 4 f. on 1 a. brown .. 15 15
109. 5 f. on 1 a. brown .. 10 5
110. 8 f. on 1½ a. red .. 20 12
111. 10 f. on 2 a. orange .. 15 5
112. 15 f. on 3 a. blue .. 20 60
113. 20 f. on 4 a. purple .. 50 55
114. – 25 f. on 4 a. vio. (No. 46) 50 45
115. **10.** 30 f. on 6 a. blue .. 50 40
116. 40 f. on 8 a. green .. 75 1·00
117. **11.** 75 f. on 1 r. brown .. 1·00 1·00
118. 100 f. on 2 r. yellow-brn. 2·25 2·25
119. 200 f. on 5 r. orange .. 5·00 4·00
120. ½ d. on 10 r. red .. 12·00 10·00
121. **9.** 1 d. on 25 r. violet .. 35·00 32·00

1932. As Types **9/11** but value in FILS or DINAR.

138. **10.** 2 f. blue 5 5
139. 3 f. green 8 5
140. 4 f. purple 5 5
141. 5 f. green 5 5
142. 8 f. red 8 8
143. 10 f. yellow 8 5
144. 15 f. blue 15 5
145. 20 f. orange 15 15
146. 25 f. mauve 25 15
147. 30 f. olive 25 15
148. 40 f. violet 40 40
149. **11.** 50 f. brown 40 20
150. 75 f. blue .. .. 1·00 60
151. 100 f. green .. .. 1·25 50
152. 200 f. red .. .. 3·00 1·00
153. **9.** ½ d. blue .. .. 7·00 5·50
154. 1 d. purple .. .. 20·00 14·00

13. King Ghazi. 14.

1934.

172. **13.** 1 f. violet 5 5
173. 2 f. blue 5 5
174. 3 f. green 5 5
175. 4 f. purple 5 5
176. 5 f. green 5 5
177. 8 f. red 5 5
178. 10 f. yellow 5 5
179. 15 f. blue 8 5
180. 20 f. orange 15 8
181. 25 f. mauve 20 12
182. 30 f. green 25 12
183. 40 f. violet 25 15
184. **14.** 50 f. brown 40 15
185. 75 f. blue 60 20
186. 100 f. green 90 30
187. 200 f. red .. .. 2·00 40
188. – ½ d. blue .. .. 3·75 1·00
189. – 1 d. claret .. .. 8·00 2·50

The ½ d. and 1 d. are larger (23 × 27½ mm.).

15. Mausoleum of Sitt Zubaidah. 16. Lion of Babylon. 17. Spiral Tower of Samarra.

1941.

208. **15.** 1 f. purple 5 5
209. 2 f. brown 5 5
210. – 3 f. green 5 5
211. – 4 f. violet 5 5
212. – 5 f. red 5 5
213. **16.** 8 f. red 25 12
214. 8 f. yellow 10 25
215. 10 f. yellow .. .. 1·75 25
216. 10 f. red 10 5
217. 15 f. blue 35 12
218. 15 f. black 12 5
219. 20 f. black 50 25
220. 20 f. blue 20 8
221. **17.** 25 f. purple 25 8
222. 30 f. orange 25 15
223. 40 f. brown 65 20
224. – 50 f. blue 60 25
225. – 75 f. mauve .. .. 1·00 25
226. – 100 f. olive 60 20
227. – 200 f. orange .. .. 1·00 40
228. – ½ d. blue .. .. 2·00 1·00
229. – 1 d. green .. .. 6·00 2·00

DESIGNS—HORIZ. 3 f., 4 f., 5 f. King Faisal's Mausoleum (24 × 20 mm.). ½ d., 1 d. Mosque of the Golden Dome, Samarra (24 × 21 mm.). VERT. 50 f., 75 f. as T **17**, but larger (21 × 24 mm.). 100 f., 200 f. Oil Wells (20 × 22 mm.).

18. King Faisal II. 19.

1942.

255. 18. 1 f. brown and violet .. 5 5
256. 2 f. brown and blue .. 5 5
257. 3 f. brown and green .. 5 8
258. 4 f. brown 5 10
259. 5 f. brown and green .. 5 5
260. 6 f. brown and red .. 5 5
261. 10 f. brown and red .. 5 5
262. 12 f. brown and green 12 5

1948.

271. 19. 1 f. blue 5 5
272. 2 f. brown 5 5
273. 3 f. green 5 5
274. 3 f. claret 25 10
275. 4 f. violet 5 5
276. 5 f. claret 10 5
277. 5 f. green 25 10
278. 6 f. lilac 5 5
279. 8 f. yellow 5 5
280. 10 f. red 5 5
281. 12 f. olive 10 8
282. 14 f. olive 20 5
283. 15 f. black 12 5
284. 16 f. red 25 15
285. 20 f. blue 15 5
286. 25 f. mauve 15 5
287. 28 f. blue 50 20
288. 30 f. orange 30 5
289. 40 f. brown 25 8
290. 50 f. blue 40 12
291. 60 f. blue 30 12
292. 75 f. mauve 45 25
293. 100 f. olive 65 25
294. 200 f. orange .. .. 1·25 40
295. ½d. blue.. .. .. 2·50 1·25
296. 1 d. green .. .. 6·00 7·00
The 50 f. to 1 d. are larger (22½ × 27½ mm.).

20. Aeroplane over Basrah Aerodrome. 21. King Faisal I and Equestrian Statue.

1949. Air.

330. 20. 3 f. green 5 5
331. – 4 f. mauve 5 5
332. – 5 f. brown 5 5
333. 20. 10 f. red 12 5
334. – 20 f. blue 12 5
335. – 35 f. orange 15 10
336. – 50 f. olive 25 10
337. – 100 f. violet 40 20

DESIGNS—HORIZ. As T 20: 4 f., 20f. Aeroplane over Kut Barrage. 5 f., 35 f. Aeroplane over Faisal II Bridge. Larger (31×22½ mm.): 50 f., 100 f. Aeroplane over Dhiyala Bridge.

1949. U.P.U. 75th Anniv.

339. – 20 f. blue 15 10
340. 21. 40 f. orange 30 15
341. – 50 f. violet 40 25

DESIGNS: 20 f. King Ghazi and mounted postman. 50 f. King Faisal II, globe and wreath.

22. King Faisal II. 23. (24.)

1953. Coronation of King Faisal II.

342. 22. 3 f. red 12 10
343. 14 f. olive 20 15
344. 28 f. blue 40 25

1954.

346. 23. 1 f. blue 8 10
347. 2 f. brown 5 5
348. 3 f. lake.. .. .. 5 5
349. 4 f. violet 5 5
350. 5 f. green 5 5
351. 6 f. magenta 5 5
352. 8 f. chestnut 5 5
353. 10 f. blue 5 5
354. 15 f. black 20 5
355. 16 f. red 65 90
356. 20 f. olive 15 15
357. 25 f. purple 30 45
358. 30 f. red 30 30
359. 40 f. chestnut 40 60
360. – 50 f. blue 75 45
361. – 75 f. magenta .. .. 1·25 60
362. – 100 f. olive .. .. 1·10 50
363. – 200 f. salmon .. .. 2·50 90
The 50 f. to 200 f. are larger (22×28 mm.).

1955. Abrogation of Anglo-Iraqi Treaty. Optd. with T 24.

380. 23. 3 f. lake.. .. .. 5 10
381. 10 f. blue 15 12
382. 19. 28 f. blue 30 20

25. King Faisal II.

1955. 6th Arab Engineers' Conf.

383. 25. 3 f. lake 12 10
384. 10 f. blue 12 10
385. 28 f. blue 30 40

26. King Faisal II and Globe.

1956. 3rd Arab Postal Union Conf.

386. 26. 3 f. lake.. .. .. 10 5
387. 10 f. blue 15 12
388. 28 f. blue 40 40

27. King Faisal II and Power Loom. (29.) 28. King Faisal II and Exhibition Emblem.

1957. Development Week.

389. 27. 1 f. blue and buff .. 5 5
390. – 3 f. multicoloured .. 5 5
391. – 5 f. multicoloured .. 5 5
392. – 10 f. multicoloured .. 12 5
393. – 40 f. multicoloured .. 65 35

DESIGNS: 3 f. Irrigation dam. 5 f. Residential road, Baghdad. 10 f. Irrigation pipeline. 40 f. Tigris Bridge.

1957. Agricultural and Industrial Exn., Baghdad.

394. 28. 10 f. brown and cream.. 15 12

1957. Silver Jubilee of Iraqi Red Crescent Society. Optd. with T 29.

395. 26. 28 f. blue 45 25

30. King Faisal II. 31. King Faisal II and Tanks.

1957.

396. 30. 1 f. blue 15 15
397. 2 f. brown 10 15
398. 3 f. lake 10 15
399. 4 f. violet 10 15
400. 5 f. green 20 20
401. 6 f. magenta 10 25
402. 8 f. chestnut 15 50
403. 10 f. blue 15 15

1958. Army Day.

411. 31. 8 f. grey and green .. 15 25
412. – 10 f. black and brown.. 15 20
413. – 20 f. brown and blue .. 30 20
414. – 30 f. violet and red .. 45 15

DESIGNS—HORIZ. King Faisel II and: 10 f. platoon marching. 20 f. Mobile artillery unit and jet fighters. VERT. (22½×27½ mm.): 30 f. King Faisal II (full length portrait).

1958. Development Week. As T 27 inscr. "1958".

415. 3 f. green, drab and violet 8 10
416. 5 f. multicoloured.. .. 12 10
417. 10 f. multicoloured .. 20 10

DESIGNS—VERT. 3 f. Sugar beet and refining plant. HORIZ. 5 f. Building and pastoral scene. 10 f. Irrigation dam.

(32. "Iraqi Republic".) (33.)

1958. Optd. with T 32.

(a) On No. 189.

418. 1 d. claret .. .. .. 8·00 6·50

(b) On T 19.

419. 12 f. olive.. .. .. 12 8
420. 14 f. olive.. .. .. 12 8
421. 16 f. red .. .. .. 1·75 1·50
422. 28 f. blue 20 20
423. 60 f. blue 50 35
424. ½d. blue .. .. .. 3·00 2·00
425. 1 d. green.. .. .. 6·00 5·00

(c) On T 23.

426. 1 f. blue 8 5
427. 2 f. brown.. .. .. 5 5
428. 4 f. violet.. .. .. 12 15
429. 5 f. green 12 15
430. 6 f. magenta 10 5
431. 8 f. chestnut 15 10
432. 10 f. blue 15 8
433. 15 f. black 15 12
434. 16 f. red 30 20
435. 20 f. olive .. .. .. 1·10 75
436. 25 f. purple 20 12
437. 30 f. red 30 15
438. 40 f. chestnut 30 15
439. 50 f. blue .. .. .. 1·75 85
440. 75 f. magenta 95 50
441. 100 f. olive .. .. 1·50 85
442. 200 f. salmon .. .. 2·25 2·00

(d) On T 30.

443. 1 f. blue 5 5
444. 2 f. brown.. .. .. 5 5
445. 3 f. lake 10 5
446. 4 f. violet.. .. .. 8 5
447. 5 f. green 8 5
448. 6 f. magenta 8 5
449. 8 f. chestnut 8 5
450. 10 f. blue 12 5
451. 20 f. olive.. .. .. 15 5
452. 25 f. purple 50 30
453. 30 f. red 25 8
454. 40 f. chestnut 35 25
455. 50 f. purple 45 20
456. 75 f. olive.. .. .. 60 45
457. 100 f. orange 85 20
458. 200 f. blue .. .. 2·25 30
Nos. 455/458 are larger (22½×27½ mm.).

1958. Arab Lawyers Conf., Baghdad. Surch. with T 33.

506. 25. 10 f. on 28 f. blue .. 20 15

34. Republican Soldier and Flag. 35. Orange Tree.

1959. Army Day.

507. 34. 3 f. blue 8 10
508. 10 f. olive 8 10
509. 40 f. violet 25 20

1959. Afforestation Day.

510. 35. 10 f. orange and green.. 20 10

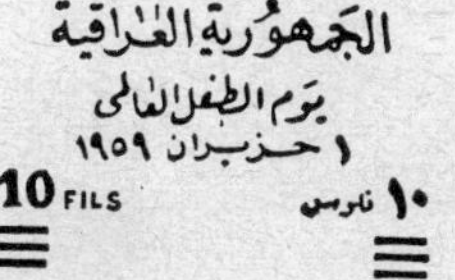

(36.)

1959. Int. Children's Day. Surch. with T 36.

511. 26. 10 f. on 28 f. blue .. 15 15

37. 38.

1959. Revolution. 1st Anniv. Inscr. "14TH JULY 1958".

512. 37. 10 f. blue and ochre .. 10 10
513. – 30 f. green and ochre .. 25 12

DESIGN—HORIZ. 30 f. Revolutionaries brandishing weapons.

1959. Agricultural Reform.

514. 38. 10 f. black and green .. 12 5

39. Republican Emblem. (40.)

1960.

515. 39. 1 f. multicoloured .. 5 5
516. 2 f. multicoloured .. 5 5
517. 3 f. multicoloured .. 5 5
518. 4 f. multicoloured .. 5 5
519. 5 f. multicoloured .. 5 5
520. 10 f. multicoloured .. 5 5
521. 15 f. multicoloured .. 8 5
522. 20 f. multicoloured .. 10 5
523. 30 f. multicoloured .. 12 8
524. 40 f. multicoloured .. 15 8
525. 50 f. multicoloured .. 20 10
526. 75 f. multicoloured .. 30 15
527. 100 f. multicoloured .. 40 20
528. 200 f. multicoloured .. 90 30
529. 500 f. multicoloured .. 2·00 1·10
530. 1 d. multicoloured .. 4·00 2·75

1959. "Health and Hygiene". Optd. with T 40.

531. 39. 10 f. multicoloured .. 15 10

41. Gen. Kassem and Military Parade. 42. Gen. Kassem.

1960. Army Day.

532. 41. 10 f. lake and green .. 5 5
533. – 16 f. red and blue .. 12 20
534. – 30 f. olive, brown & buff 20 10
535. – 40 f. violet and buff .. 25 15
536. – 60 f. buff, choc. & brown 35 20

DESIGNS—HORIZ. 16 f. Infantry on manoeuvres. 60 f. Partisans. VERT. 30 f. Anti-aircraft gun-crew. 40 f. Oilfield guards on parade.

1960. Gen. Kassem's Escape from Assassination.

537. 42. 10 f. violet 8 5
538. 30 f. green 20 10

43. Al Rasafi (poet). 44. Gen. Kassem at Tomb of Unknown soldier.

1960. Al Rasafi Commem. Optd. **1960** at top in English and Arabic, in black.

539. 43. 10 l. lake 8 5
See also No. 732.

1960. Revolution. 2nd Anniv.

540. – 6 f. gold, olive & orange 5 5
541. 44. 10 f. orge., grn. & blue 8 10
542. 16 f. orange, vio. & blue 12 20
543. – 18 f. gold, blue & orge. 20 25
544. – 30 f. gold, brown & orge. 20 15
545. 44. 60 f. orge., sep. & blue 30 35

DESIGN—VERT. 6 f., 18 f., 30 f. Symbol of Republic.

45. Gen. Kassem, Flag and Troops. 46. Gen. Kassem with Children.

1961. Army Day.

546. 45. 3 f. multicoloured .. 5 5
547. 6 f. multicoloured .. 5 5
548. 10 f. multicoloured .. 5 5
549. – 20 f. blk., yell. & emer. 12 8
550. – 30 f. blk., yell. & brown 15 12
551. – 40 f. black, yell. & blue 20 20

DESIGN: 20 f., 30 f., 40 f. Kassem and triumphal arch.

1961. World Children's Day. Main design brown; background colours given.

558. 46. 3 f. yellow 5 5
559. 6 f. blue 5 5
560. 10 f. pink 5 5
561. 30 f. lemon 15 12
562. 50 f. green 30 20

47. Gen. Kassem saluting on March. **48.** Gen. Kassem and Army Emblem.

1961. Revolution. 3rd Anniv.

No.	Type	Description		
563.	–	1 f. multicoloured ..	5	10
564.	–	3 f. multicoloured ..	5	5
565.	47.	5 f. multicoloured ..	5	30
566.	–	6 f. multicoloured ..	5	5
567.	–	10 f. multicoloured ..	8	5
568.	47.	30 f. multicoloured ..	15	15
569.		40 f. multicoloured ..	40	40
570.	–	50 f. multicoloured ..	25	50
571.	–	100 f. multicoloured ..	40	60

DESIGN: 1, 3, 6, 10, 50, 100 f. Gen. Kassem and Iraqi flag.

1962. Army Day.

No.	Type	Description		
572.	–	1 f. multicoloured ..	5	5
573.	–	3 f. multicoloured ..	5	5
574.	–	6 f. multicoloured ..	5	5
575.	48.	10 f. black, gold & lilac	5	5
576.		30 f. blk., gold & orange	15	15
577.		50 f. blk., gold & green	30	20

DESIGN—VERT. 1, 3, 6 f. Gen. Kassem and part of speech.

مؤتمر
العالم الاسلامي
بغداد
١٣٨١هـ-١٩٦٢م

(49.)

50. Gen. Kassem, Flag and Handclasp.

1962. 5th Islamic Congress. Optd. with T **49**.

No.	Type	Description		
578.	39.	3 f. lavendar	5	5
579.		10 f. mauve	10	8
580.		30 f. grey-brown ..	15	15

1962. Revolution. 4th Anniv. Flag in green and gold.

No.	Type	Description		
581.	50.	1 f. orange and sepia ..	5	5
582.		3 f. green and sepia ..	5	5
853.		6 f. brown and black ..	5	5
584.		10 f. lilac and sepia ..	5	5
585.		30 f. rose and sepia ..	15	30
586.		50 f. grey and sepia ..	30	20

51. Fanfare.

52. Republican Emblem.

1962. Baghdad Millenary. Multicoloured.

603.	3 f. Type **51**	5	5
604.	6 f. Al Kindi (philosopher)	5	5
605.	10 f. Map of old "Round City" of Baghdad ..	5	5
606.	40 f. Gen. Kassem and flag	30	50

1962. Aerogramme Stamps.

No.	Type	Description		
607.	52.	14 f. black and green ..	12	20
608.		35 f. black and red ..	20	15

Nos. 607/8 were originally issued only attached to aerogramme forms covering the old imprinted King Faisal II stamps, but later appeared in sheets.

53. Campaign Emblem. **54.** Gen. Kassem and Tanks.

1962. Malaria Eradication.

No.	Type	Description		
609.	53.	3 f. multicoloured ..	5	5
610.		10 f. multicoloured ..	8	5
611.		40 f. multicoloured ..	20	15

1963. Army Day.

No.	Type	Description		
612.	54.	3 f. black and yellow	5	5
613.		5 f. sepia and purple ..	5	5
614.		6 f. black and green ..	5	5
615.		10 f. black and blue ..	10	30
616.		10 f. black and pink ..	10	15
617		20 f. black and blue ..	12	15
618.		40 f. black and mauve	15	15
619.		50 f. sepia and blue ..	25	40

55. Gufas on the Tigris.

56. Shepherd with Sheep.

1963.

No.	Type	Description		
620.	55.	1 f. green	5	5
621.	–	2 f. violet	5	5
622.	55.	3 f. black	5	5
623.	–	4 f. black and lemon ..	5	5
624.	–	5 f. purple and green ..	5	5
625.	–	10 f. red	5	5
626.	–	15 f. brown and yellow	5	5
627.	–	20 f. violet-blue ..	10	5
628.	–	30 f. orange	12	5
629.	–	40 f. green	12	5
630.	–	50 f. sepia	15	8
631.	–	75 f. black and green ..	25	15
632.	–	100 f. purple	40	15
633.	–	200 f. brown	85	30
634.	–	500 f. blue	2·00	1·00
635.	–	1 d. maroon	3·50	2·50

DESIGNS: 2 f., 500 f. Spiral tower of Samarra. 4 f., 15 f. Harp. 5 f., 75 f. Republican emblem. 10 f., 50 f. Lion of Babylon. 20 f., 40 f. Mosque. 30 f., 200 f. Mosque and minarets. 100 f., 1 d. Winged bull of Kharsabad.

1963. Freedom from Hunger.

No.	Type	Description		
636.	56.	3 f. black and green ..	5	5
637.	–	10 f. magenta & chocolate	5	5
638.	–	20 f. brown and blue ..	10	10

DESIGNS: 10 f. Harvester. 20 f. Trees.

57. Centenary Emblem.

58. Helmet, Rifle and Flag.

1963. Red Cross Centenary.

No.	Type	Description		
640.	57.	3 f. violet and red ..	8	8
641.		10 f. slate-blue and red	8	8
642.	–	30 f. blue and red ..	10	10

DESIGN—HORIZ. 30 f. Hospital.

1964. Army Day.

No.	Type	Description		
643.	58.	3 f. sepia, green & blue	5	5
644.		10 f. sepia, green & pink	5	5
645.		30 f. sepia, green & yell.	10	10

59. Revolutionaries and Flag.

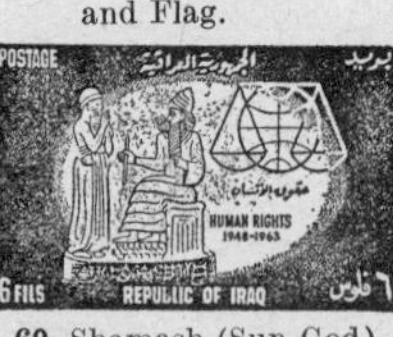

60. Shamash (Sun-God) and Hammurabi. **61.** Soldier raising flag.

1964. 14th Ramadan Revolution. 1st Anniv. Flag in red, green and black.

No.	Type	Description		
646.	59.	10 f. violet	5	8
647.		30 f. brown	10	10

1964. Declaration of Human Rights. 15th Anniv.

No.	Type	Description		
649.	60.	6 f. olive and purple ..	5	5
650.	–	10 f. violet and orange ..	8	8
651.	60.	30 f. green and blue ..	12	12

DESIGN: 10 f. U.N. Emblem and Scales of Justice.

1964. Revolution. 6th Anniv.

No.	Type	Description		
652.	–	3 f. orange, grey & black	5	5
653.	61.	10 f. red, black & green	5	5
654.		20 f. red, black & green	8	8
655.	–	30 f. orange, grey & black	12	12

DESIGNS—HORIZ. 3. f., 30 f. Soldier "protecting" people and factories with outstretched arm.

62. Soldier, Civilians and Star Emblem.

63. Musician.

1964. Nov. 18th Revolution. 1st Anniv.

No.	Type	Description		
656.	62.	5 f. orange and sepia ..	5	5
657.		10 f. orange and blue ..	5	5
658.		50 f. red and violet ..	15	15

1964. Int. Arab Music Conf., Baghdad.

No.	Type	Description		
659.	63.	3 f. multicoloured ..	5	8
660.		10 f. multicoloured ..	5	8
661.		30 f. multicoloured ..	12	12

64. Conference Emblem. and Map.

65. A.P.U. Emblem.

1964. 9th Arab Engineer's Conf., Baghdad.

No.	Type	Description		
662.	64.	10 f. green and mauve ..	5	5

1964. Arab Postal Union's Permanent Office. 10th Anniv.

No.	Type	Description		
663.	65.	3 f. blue and red ..	5	8
664.		10 f. slate-pur. & purple	5	8
665.		30 f. blue and orange ..	12	12

66. Soldier, Civilians and Flag.

67. Cogwheel and Factory.

1965. Army Day.

No.	Type	Description		
666.	66.	5 f. multicoloured ..	5	5
667.		15 f. multicoloured ..	5	5
668.		30 f. multicoloured ..	12	10

1965. 1st Arab Ministers of Labour Conf. Baghdad.

No.	Type	Description		
670.	67.	10 f. multicoloured ..	5	5

68. Armed Soldiers with Flag.

69. Oil Tanker.

1965. 14th Ramadan Revolution. 2nd Anniv.

No.	Type	Description		
671.	68.	10 f. multicoloured ..	5	5

1965. Deep Sea Terminal for Tankers. Inaug.

No.	Type	Description		
672.	69.	10 f. multicoloured ..	8	8

70. Tree.

71. Federation Emblem

1965. Tree Week.

No.	Type	Description		
673.	70.	6 f. multicoloured ..	5	5
674.		20 f. multicoloured ..	8	8

1965. Arab Insurance Federation. Sun in gold

No.	Type	Description		
675.	71.	3 f. ultram. and blne ..	5	5
676.		10 f. black and grey ..	5	5
677.		30 f. red and pink ..	12	12

72. Dagger of Deir Yasin, Paelstine.

73. "Threat of Disease".

1965. Deir Yasin Massacre.

No.	Type	Description		
678.	72.	10 f. drab and black ..	5	5
679.		20 f. brown and blue ..	8	8

1965. World Health Day.

No.	Type	Description		
680.	73.	3 f. multicoloured ..	5	5
681.		10 f. multicoloured ..	5	5
682.		20 f. multicoloured ..	8	8

74. I.T.U. Emblem and Symbols.

1965. I.T.U. Cent.

No.	Type	Description		
683.	74.	10 f. multicoloured ..	5	5
684.		20 f. multicoloured ..	10	10

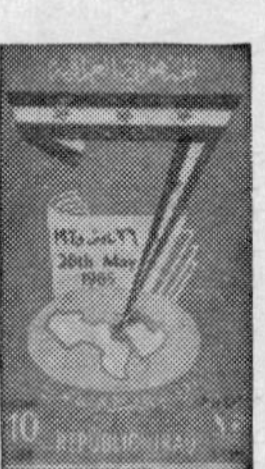

75. Flag and Map.

76. Revolutionary and Flames.

1965. Iraq U.A.R. Pact. 1st Anniv.

No.	Type	Description		
686.	75.	10 f. multicoloured ..	5	5

1965. Reconstitution of Algiers University Library. As T **232** of Egypt.

687.	5 f. red, green and black ..	5	
688.	10 f. green, red and black ..	5	5

1965. 1920 Rebellion. 45th Anniv.

No.	Type	Description		
689.	76.	5 f. multicoloured ..	5	5
690.		10 f. multicoloured ..	5	5

77. Mosque.

1965. Mohammed's Birthday.

No.	Type	Description		
691.	77.	10 f. multicoloured ..	5	5

78. Factory and Ear of Wheat.

80. Fair Emblem.

79. I.C.Y. Emblem.

1965. 14 July Revolution. 7th Anniv.
693. 78. 10 f. multicoloured .. 5 5

1965. Air. Int. Co-operation Year.
694. 79. 5 f. black and salmon .. 5 5
695. 10 f. brown and green .. 5 5
696. 30 f. black and blue .. 15 12

1965. Baghdad Fair.
697. 80. 10 f. multicoloured .. 5 5

81. Pres. Arif (photo. by Studio Jean).

1965. 18 November Revolution. 2nd Anniv.
698. 81. 5 f. blue and orange .. 5 8
699. 10 f. sepia and blue .. 5 10
700. 50 f. indigo and mauve 15 15

82. Census Graph.

1965. National Census.
701. 82. 3 f. black and purple .. 5 5
702. 5 f. chestnut and bistre 5 5
703. 15 f. bistre and blue .. 10 10

83. "Trident 1E" Aircraft.

1965. Air. Inaug. of "Trident" Aircraft by Iraqi Airways.
704. 83. 5 f. multicoloured .. 5 5
705. 10 f. multicoloured .. 5 5
706. 40 f. multicoloured .. 15 15

84. Date Palms. 85. Army Memorial.

1965. 2nd F.A.O. Dates Conf., Baghdad.
707. 84. 3 f. multicoloured .. 5 5
708. 10 f. multicoloured .. 5 5
709. 15 f. multicoloured .. 10 8

1966. Army Day. 45th Anniv.
710. 85. 2 f. multicoloured .. 5 5
711. 5 f. multicoloured .. 5 5
712. 40 f. multicoloured .. 15 8

86. "Eagle" and Flag. 87. Footballers.

1966. Ramadan Revolution. 3rd Anniv.
713. 86. 5 f. multicoloured .. 5 5
714. 10 f. multicoloured .. 5 5

1966. Arab Publicity Week. As T 247 of Egypt.
715. 5 f green, brown & orange 5 5
716. 15 f. blue, purple and olive 8 5

1966. Arab Football Cup, Baghdad. Mult.
717. 2 f. Type 87 .. .. 5 5
718. 5 f. Goalkeeper with ball .. 5 5
719. 15 f. Type 87 .. .. 8 8

88. Excavator. 89. Queen Nefertari.

1966. Labour Day.
721. 88. 15 f. multicoloured .. 5 5
722. 25 f. blk., silver & red .. 10 8

1966. Nubian Monuments Preservation.
723. 89. 5 f. yell., black & olive 5 5
724. 15 f. yellow, brn. & blue 5 8
725. – 40 f. brown, chest. & red 12 10
DESIGN—HORIZ. (41×32 mm.): 40 f. Rock temples, Abu Simbel.

90. President Arif.

1966. 14 July Revolution. 8th Anniv.
726. 90. 5 f. brn., red, grn. & blk. 5 5
727. 15 f. blue, red, grn. & blk. 5 5
728. 50 f. vio., red, grn. & blk. 20 15

91.

1966. Mohammed's Birthday.
729. 91. 5 f. multicoloured .. 5 5
730. 15 f. multicoloured .. 5 5
731. 30 f. multicoloured .. 12 10

1966. As No. 539 but without optd. "1960".
732. 43. 10 f. lake .. .. 3·00 3·00

92. Pool and Statue. 93. Revolutionaries.

1966. Iraqi Museum, Baghdad. Inaug. Multicoloured.
733. 15 f. Type 92 .. .. 5 5
734. 50 f. Gold head-dress .. 15 15
735. 80 f. Sumerian head (vert.) 30 30

1966. November 18 Revolution. 3rd Anniv.
736. 93. 15 f. multicoloured .. 5 5
737. 25 f. multicoloured .. 10 10

94. "Magic Carpet". 95. U.N.E.S.C.O. Emblem.

1966. Air. Meeting of Arab Int. Tourist Union, Baghdad. Multicoloured.
738. 2 f. Flying Crane emblem 5 8
739. 5 f. Type 94 .. .. 5 5
740. 15 f. As 2 f. 8 8
741. 50 f. Type 94 .. .. 20 20

1966. U.N.E.S.C.O. 20th Anniv.
742. 95. 5 f. cinnamon, blk. & bl. 5 5
743. 15 f. green, black & red 5 5

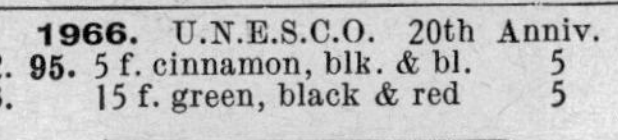

96. Soldier and Rocket-launchers.

1967. Army Day.
744. 96. 15 f. ochre, brn. & yell. 5 5
745. 20 f. ochre, brn. & lilac 10 8

97. Oil Refinery.

1967. 6th Arab Petroleum Congress, Baghdad. Multicoloured.
747. 5 f. Congress emblem (vert.) 5 5
748. 15 f. Type 97 .. .. 5 5
749. 40 f. Congress emblem (vert.) 12 12
750. 50 f. Type 97 .. .. 15 15

98. "Spider's Web" Emblem. 99. Worker holding Cogwheel.

1967. Hajeer Year (1967).
751. 98. 5 f. multicoloured .. 5 5
752. 15 f. multicoloured .. 5 5

1967. Labour Day.
753. 99. 10 f. multicoloured .. 5 5
754. 15 f. multicoloured .. 5 5

100.

1967. Mohammed's Birthday.
755. 100. 5 f. multicoloured .. 5 5
756. 15 f. multicoloured .. 5 5

101. Flags and Hands with Clubs.

1967. 1920 Rebellion. 47th Anniv.
757. 101. 5 f. multicoloured .. 5 5
758. 15 f. multicoloured .. 5 5

102. Um Qasr Port. 103. Costume.

1967. 9th Anniv. of 14 July Revolution and Inaug. of Um Qasr Port. Multicoloured.
759. 5 f. Type 102 .. .. 5 5
760. 10 f. Freighter at quayside 5 5
761. 15 f. As 10 f. 8 8
762. 40 f. Type 102 .. .. 15 12

1967. Iraqi Costumes. Designs showing different costumes.
765. 103. 2 f. mult. (postage) .. 5 5
766. – 5 f. multicoloured .. 5 5
767. – 10 f. multicoloured .. 5 5
768. – 15 f. multicoloured .. 5 5
769. – 20 f. multicoloured .. 8 5
770. – 25 f. multicoloured .. 10 8
771. – 30 f. multicoloured .. 12 10
772. – 40 f. multicoloured (air) 15 12
773. – 50 f. multicoloured .. 25 15
774. – 80 f. multicoloured .. 50 25

104. Pres. Arif and Map.

1967. November 18 Revolution. 4th Anniv. Multicoloured.
775. – 5 f. President Arif .. 10 10
776. 15 f. Type 104 .. .. 10 10

105. Ziggurat of Ur.

1967. Int. Tourist Year. Multicoloured.
777. 2 f. Type 105 (postage) .. 5 5
778. 5 f. Statues of Nimroud .. 5 5
779. 10 f. Babylon (arch) .. 5 5
780. 15 f. Minaret of Mosul .. 5 5
781. 25 f. Arch of Ctesiphon .. 10 8
782. 50 f. Statue, Temple of Hatra (air) 25 15
783. 80 f. Spiral Minaret of Samarra 30 25
784. 100 f. Adam's Tree .. 40 30
785. 200 f. Aladdin ("Aladdin's Cave") 75 65
786. 500 f. Golden Mosque of Kadhimain .. .. 2·00 1·75
Nos. 780 and 782/785 are vert.

106. Guide Emblem and Saluting Hand.

1967. Iraqi Scouts and Guides. Multicoloured.
787. 2 f. Type 106 .. .. 5 5
788. 5 f. Guides by camp-fire .. 5 5
789. 10 f. Scout emblem and saluting hand 5 5
790. 15 f. Scouts setting up camp 8 5

107. Soldiers Drilling.

1968. Army Day.
792. 107. 5 f. brown, grn. & blue 5 5
793. 15 f. indigo, olive & bl. 5 5

108. White-eared Bulbul.

1968. Iraqi Birds. Multicoloured.
794. 5 f. Type 108 .. .. 5 5
795. 10 f. Hoopoe 5 5
796. 15 f. Jay 5 5
797. 25 f. Peregrine falcon .. 10 10
798. 30 f. White stork .. 12 10
799. 40 f. Black partridge (or francolin) 15 8
800. 50 f. Marbled duck .. 20 15

109. Battle Scene.

1968. 14th Ramadan Revolution. 5th Anniv.
801. 109. 15 f. orange, blk. & blue 5 5

110. Symbols of "Labour".

1968. Labour Day.
802. 110. 15 f. multicoloured .. 5 5
803. 25 f. multicoloured .. 8 5

111. Football. 112. Soldier with Iraqi Flag.

1968. 23rd C.I.S.M. Football Championships. Multicoloured.
804. – 2 f. Type 111 .. 5 5
805. – 5 f. Goalkeeper in mid air 5 5
806. – 15 f. Type 111 .. .. 8 5
807. – 25 f. As 5 f. 10 10

1968. 14 July Revolution. 10th Anniv.
809. 112. 15 f. multicoloured .. 5 5

113. Anniversary and W.H.O. Emblems.

1968. W.H.O. 20th Anniv.
810. – 5 f. multicoloured .. 5 5
811. – 10 f. multicoloured .. 5 5
812. 113. 15 f. red, blue & black 5 5
813. 25 f. red, green and blk. 10 8
DESIGN—VERT. 5, 10 f. Combined anniversary and W.H.O. emblems.

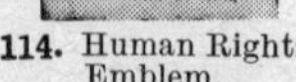

114. Human Rights Emblem. 115. Mother and children.

1968. Human Rights Year.
814. 114. 10 f. red, yellow and blue 5 5
815. 25 f. red, yellow & grn. 8 8

1968. U.N.I.C.E.F. Commem.
817. 115. 15 f. multicoloured .. 5 5
818. 25 f. multicoloured .. 8 8

116. Army Tanks.

1969. Army Day.
820. 116. 25 f. multicoloured .. 10 8

117. Agricultural Scene.

1969. 14th Ramadan Revolution. 6th Anniv.
821. 117. 15 f. multicoloured .. 5 5

118. Mosque and Worshippers.

1969. Hajeer Year.
822. 118. 15 f. multicoloured .. 8 8

119. Emblem of Iraqi Veterinary Medical Assn.

1969. 1st Arab Veterinary Union Conf. Baghdad.
823. 119. 10 f. multicoloured .. 5 5
824. 15 f. multicoloured .. 10 5

120. "Barbus grypus".

1969. Multicoloured.

(a) Fishes.
825. 2 f. Type 120 (postage) .. 5 5
826. 3 f. "Barbus puntius" .. 5 5
827. 10 f. "Pampus argenteus" 5 5
828. 100 f. "Barbus esocinus" 35 20

(b) Fauna.
829. 2 f. Hyena (air) .. 5 5
830. 3 f. Leopard 5 5
831. 5 f. Gazelle 5 5
832. 10 f. Head of Arab horse 5 5
833. 200 f. Arab horse .. 65 50

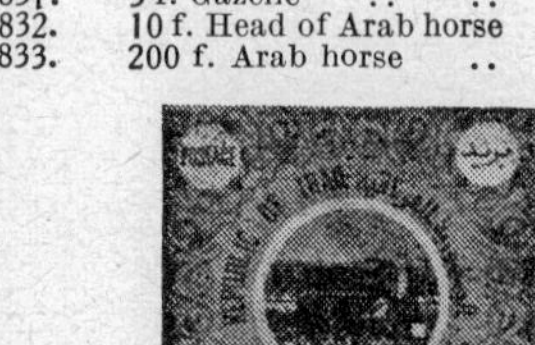

121. Kaaba, Mecca.

1969. Mohammed's Birthday.
834. 121. 15 f. multicoloured .. 5 5

122. I.L.O. Emblem. 123. Weightlifting.

1969. Int. Labour Organization. 50th Anniv.
835. 122. 5 f. yell., ultram. & blk. 5 5
836. 15 f. yellow, grn. & blk. 5 5
837. 50 f. yellow, red & black 15 12

1969. Olympic Games, Mexico (1968). Multicoloured.
839. 3 f. Type 123 .. .. 5 5
840. 5 f. High-jumping .. 5 5
841. 10 f. Type 123 .. .. 5 5
842. 35 f. As 5 f. 12 12

124. Arms of Iraq and "Industry". 125. Rebuilding Roads.

1969. 14 July Revolution, 11th Anniv.
844 124. 10 f. multicoloured 5 5
845. 15 f. multicoloured .. 5 5

1969. 17 July Revolution, Anniv., and Baghdad Int. Airport, Inaug. Multicoloured.
846. 10 f. Type 125 .. .. 5 5
847 15 f. Type 125 .. .. 5 5
848. 20 f. Airport building .. 8 8
849. 200 f. President Bakr (vert.) 70 60

126. Ear of Wheat and Fair Emblem. 128. Radio Beacon and Outline of Palestine.

127. Floating Crane "Antara".

1969. 6th Int. Baghdad Fair.
850. 126. 10 f. chest., gold & emer. 5 5
851. 15 f. red, gold & ultram. 5 5

1969. Port of Basra. 50th Anniv. Multicoloured.
852. 15 f. Type 127 .. .. 5 5
853. 20 f. MV "Al-Walid" .. 8 5
854. 30 f. Pilot-boat "Al-Rashid" 10 8
855. 35 f. Dredger "Hillah .. 12 12
856. 50 f. Survey-ship "Al-Faq" 20 15

1969. Iraqi News Agency. 10th Anniv.
857. 128. 15 f. multicoloured 5 5
858. 50 f. multicoloured 15 12

129. Emblem, Book and Hands. 130. Vickers "Vimy" Aircraft.

1969. Campaign Against Illiteracy.
859. 129. 15 f. multicoloured .. 5 5
860. 20 f. multicoloured .. 10 8

1969. Air. 1st England–Australia Flight. 50th Anniv.
861. 130. 15 f. multicoloured 5 5
862. 35 f. multicoloured 12 25

131. Newspaper Headline. 133. Iraqis supporting Wall.

132. Soldier and Map.

1969. Iraqi Press. Cent.
864. 131. 15 f. blk., orge. & yell. 5 5

1970. Army Day.
865. 132. 15 f. multicoloured .. 5 5
866. 20 f. multicolloured .. 10 8

1970. 14th Ramadan Revolution. 7th Anniv.
867. 133. 10 f. multicoloured .. 5 5
868. 15 f. multicoloured .. 5 5

عيدنوروز
1970
(134.)

مهرجان الربيع
الموصل
1970
(136.)

135. Map of Arab Countries, and Slogans.

1970. New Year ("Nawrooz"). Nos. 891/6 optd. with T 134.
869. 2 f. multicoloured 5 5
870. 3 f. multicoloured 5 5
871. 5 f. multicoloured 5 5
872. 10 f. multicoloured .. 5 5
873. 15 f. multicoloured .. 5 5
874. 50 f. multicoloured .. 20 20

1970. Al-Baath Party. 23rd Anniv. Multicoloured.
875. 15 f. Type 135 .. .. 5 5
876. 35 f. Type 135 .. .. 12 12
877. 50 f. Iraqis acclaiming Party 15 15

1970. Mosul Spring Festival. Nos. 891/6 optd. with T 136.
879. 2 f. multicoloured 5 5
880. 3 f. multicoloured 5 5
881. 5 f. multicoloured 5 5
882. 10 f. multicoloured .. 5 5
883. 15 f. multicoloured .. 5 5
884. 50 f. multicoloured .. 20 20

137. Iraqis celebrating Labour Day.

1970. Labour Day.
885. 137. 10 f. multicoloured .. 5 5
886. 15 f. multicoloured .. 5 5
887. 35 f. multicoloured .. 15 20

138. Kaaba, Mecca, Broken Statues and Koran.

1970. Mohammed's Birthday.
888. 138. 15 f. multicoloured .. 5 5
889. 20 f. multicoloured 10 8

139. Poppies.

1970 ١٩٧٠
عيد الصحافة
(140.)

1970. Spring Festival. Flowers. Multicoloured.
891. 2 f. Type 139 .. .. 5 5
892. 3 f. Narcissi 5 5
893. 5 f. Tulip 5 5
894. 10 f. Carnations ... 5 5
895. 15 f. Roses 5 5
896. 50 f. As 10 f. 20 20

1970. Press Day. No. 864 optd. with T 140.
896a. 131. 15 f. blk., oran. & yell. 5 5

141. Revolutionaries.

1970. Arab Revolt. 50th Anniv.
897. **141.** 10 f. black and green 5 5
898. 15 f. black and gold .. 5 5
899. 35 f. black and orange 12 15
DESIGN: 35 f. Revolutionary and sunrise.

142. Bomb-burst and Broken Chain.

1970. 14 July Revolution. 12th Anniv.
901. **142.** 15 f. multicoloured .. 5 5
902. 20 f. multicoloured .. 8 5

143. Hands and Arms with Weapons.

1970. 17 July Revolution. 2nd Anniv.
903. **143.** 15 f. multicoloured .. 5 5
904. 25 f. multicoloured .. 10 10

144. Pomegranates.

1970. Fruits. Multicoloured.
905. 3 f. Type **144** 5 5
906. 5 f. Grapefruit 5 5
907. 10 f. Grapes 5 5
908. 15 f. Oranges 5 5
909. 35 f. Dates 12 12
The Latin inscriptions on Nos. 906/7 are transposed.

145. Kaaba, Mecca.

1970. Hajeer Year.
910. **145.** 15 f. multicoloured .. 5 5
911. 25 f. multicoloured .. 10 8

الدورة السابعة

970 – ٩٧٠
(146.)

1971. 7th Int. Baghdad Fair (1970). Optd. with T **146.**
911. **126.** 10 f. brown, gold & grn. 5 5
912. 15 f. red, gold & blue .. 10 8

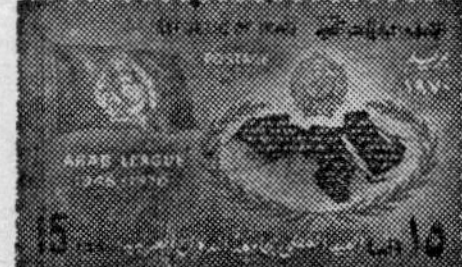
147. Arab League Flag and Map.

1970. Arab League. 25th Anniv.
914. **147.** 15 f. multicoloured .. 5 5
915. 35 f. multicoloured .. 12 12

148. Euphrates Bridge, Baghdad.

1970. Air. National Development Plan. Multicoloured.
916. 10 f. Type **148** 5 5
917. 15 f. Type **148** 8 8
918. 1 d. Pres. Bakr and bank-notes (37×27) .. 2·40 2·00

149. I.E.Y. Emblem.

1970. Int. Education Year.
919. **149.** 5 f. multicoloured .. 5 5
920. 15 f. multicoloured .. 12 5

150. Baghdad Hospital and Society Emblem.

1970. Iraq Medical Society. 50th Anniv.
922. **150.** 15 f. multicoloured .. 5 5
923. 40 f. multicoloured .. 15 12

151. Union Emblem. 152. Sugar Beet.

1970. Air. 10th Arab Telecommunications Union Conf., Baghdad.
924. **151.** 15 f. multicoloured .. 5 8
925. 25 f. multicoloured .. 10 10

1970. Mosul Sugar Factory. Multicoloured.
926. 5 f. Type **152** 5 5
927. 15 f. Factory (horiz.) .. 5 5
928. 30 f. Type **152** 12 10

153. O.P.E.C. Emblem.

1970. O.P.E.C. (Petroleum Exploitation Company). 10th Anniv.
929. **153.** 10 f. multicoloured .. 5 5
930. 40 f. multicoloured .. 8 12

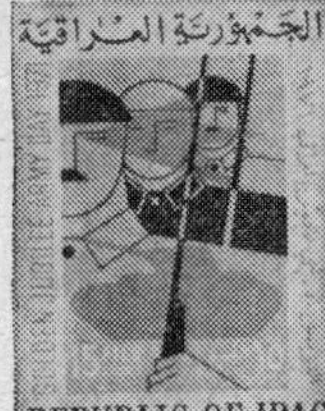
154. Soldiers.

1971. Army Day. Golden Jubilee. Multicoloured.
931. 15 f. Type **154** 5 5
932. 40 f. Soldiers, map and emblems (42 × 35 mm.) 12 12

155. Revolutionary Army.

1971. 14th Ramadan Revolution. 8th Anniv.
934. **155.** 15 f. multicoloured .. 5 5
935. 40 f. multicoloured 12 12

156. Pilgrims and Web.

1971. Hajeer Year.
936. **156.** 10 f. multicoloured .. 5 5
937. 15 f. multicoloured .. 5 5

157. Pres. Bakr with Torch.

1971. 11th March Manifesto. 1st Anniv.
938. **157.** 15 f. multicoloured .. 5 5
939. 100 f. multicoloured .. 40 25

158. Boatman in Marshland.

1971. Tourism Week. Multicoloured.
940. 5 f. Type **158** 5 5
941. 10 f. Stork over Baghdad 5 5
942. 15 f. Landscape ("Summer Resorts") 5 5
943. 100 f. "Return of Sinbad" 35 25

159. Blacksmith taming Serpent.

1971. Nawrooz Festival.
944. **159.** 15 f. multicoloured .. 5 5
945. 25 f. multicoloured .. 10 5

1971. World Meteorological Day. Nos. 780 and 788 optd. **W. M. DAY, 1971.** in English and Arabic.
946. 15 f. multicoloured (post.) 5 8
947. 80 f. multicoloured (air) .. 30 30

160. Emblem and Workers.

1971. Al-Baath Party. 24th Anniv.
948. **160.** 15 f. multicoloured .. 5 5
949. – 35 f. multicoloured .. 12 10
950. – 250 f. multicoloured .. 90 75
CIRCULAR (35 mm. diameter) 250 f. As Type **160**, but central portion of design only.
No. 950 was issued surrounded by a margin to give a square format within the sheet.

مهرجان الربيع
1971
(161.)

162. Worker and Farm-girl.

1971. Mosul Spring Festival. Nos. 765/6 and 770 optd. with T **161.**
951. **103.** 2 f. multicoloured 10 10
952. – 5 f. multicoloured .. 10 10
953. – 25 f. multicoloured .. 10 10

1971. Labour Day.
954. **162.** 15 f. multicoloured .. 5 5
955. 40 f. multicoloured .. 12 12

163. Mohammed at Prayer.

1971. Mohammed's Birthday.
956. **163.** 15 f. multicoloured .. 5 5
957. 100 f. multicoloured .. 35 30

164. Revolutionaries, and Hands with Broken Chains.

1971. 14 July Revolution. 13th Anniv.
958. **164.** 25 f. multicoloured .. 5 5
959. 50 f. multicoloured .. 15 12

165. Rising Sun and "Prosperity".

1971. 17 July Revolution. 3rd Anniv.
960. **165.** 25 f. multicoloured .. 8 8
961. 70 f. multicoloured .. 25 25

166. Bank Emblem.

1973. Rafidain Bank. 50th Anniv.
989. **166.** 10 f. multicoloured .. 5 5
990. 15 f. multicoloured .. 5 5
991. 25 f. multicoloured .. 10 8
992. – 65 f. multicoloured .. 25 30
993. – 250 f. multicoloured .. 1·25 1·00
DESIGNS: Nos. 992/3 As T **166** but larger, size 24×24 mm.

التعداد الزراعي العام

١٩٧١/١٠/١٥
(167.)

1971. Agricultural Census. Nos. 905, 908/9 optd. with T **167.**
994. 3 f. multicoloured 10 10
995. 15 f. multicoloured .. 10 10
996. 35 f. multicoloured .. 15 10

168. Football.

1971. 4th. Pan-Arab Schoolboy's Games, Baghdad. Multicoloured.

997.	15 f. Type 168	5	5
998.	25 f. Throwing the discus, and running	10	8
999.	35 f. Table-tennis	12	10
1000.	70 f. Gymnastics	25	25
1001.	95 f. Volleyball and basketball	40	35

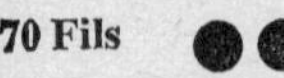

يوم الطالب
٢٣ تشرين الثاني
٩٦١ – ٩٧١
٧٠ فلسا

(169.)

170. Society Emblem.

1971. Students Day. Nos. 892/3 surch. and 895 optd. as T 169.

1003.	15 f. multicoloured ..	10	10
1004.	25 f. + 15 f. multicoloured	10	10
1005.	70 f. + 3 f. multicoloured	25	25

1971. Air. Iraqi Philatelic Society. 20th Anniv.

1006. 170.	25 f. multicoloured	12	8
1007.	70 f. multicoloured	25	20

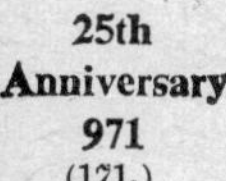

(171.)

172. Schoolchildren on Zebra Crossing.

1971. U.N.I.C.E.F. 25th Anniv. Nos. 817/18 optd. with T 171.

1008. 115.	15 f. multicoloured ..	10	10
1009.	25 f. multicoloured	10	10

1971. 2nd Traffic Week.

1010. 172.	15 f. multicoloured	5	5
1011.	25 f. multicoloured ..	10	10

173. A.P.U. Emblem. 174. Racial Equality Year Symbol.

1971. Founding of Arab Postal Union at Sofar Conf. 25th Anniversary.

1012. 173.	25 f. multicoloured ..	8	8
1013.	70 f. multicoloured ..	25	20

1971. Racial Equality Year.

1014. 174.	25 f. multicoloured	8	8
1015.	70 f. multicoloured	25	25

175. Soldiers with Flag and Torch. 176. Workers.

1972. Army Day.

1016. 175.	25 f. multicoloured ..	8	8
1017.	70 f. multicoloured ..	25	25

1972. 14th Ramadan Revolution. 9th Anniv.

1018. 176.	25 f. multicoloured ..	12	12
1019.	95 f. multicoloured ..	40	40

177. Mosque and Crescent.

1972. Hajeer Year.

1020. 177.	25 f. multicoloured	10	8
1021.	35 f. multicoloured	15	12

المؤتمر التاسع للاتحاد الوطني
لطلبة العراق
٢٥ شباط – ٢ آذار / ١٩٧٢

(178.)

1972. Air. 9th Iraqi Students' Union Congress. Nos. 916/17 optd. with T 178.

1022. 148.	10 f. multicoloured ..	10	10
1023.	15 f. multicoloured ..	10	10

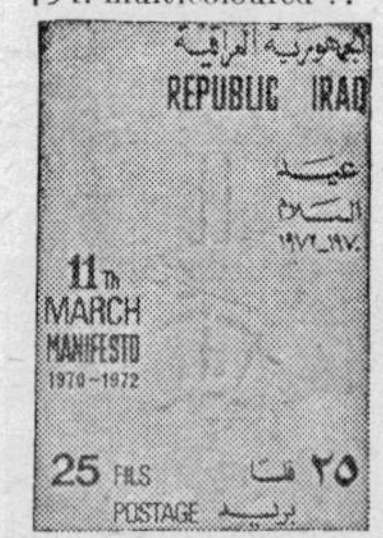

179. Dove, Olive Branch and Manifesto.

1972. 11 March Manifesto. 2nd Anniv.

1024. 179.	25 f. multicoloured ..	10	8
1025.	70 f. multicoloured ..	25	20

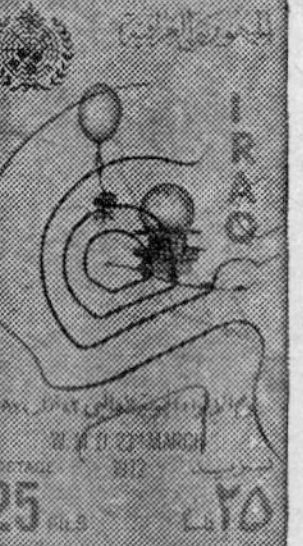

180. Observatory and Weather Balloon on Isobar Map. 181. Cogwheel Emblem.

1972. World Meteorological Day.

1026. 180.	25 f. multicoloured ..	10	8
1027.	35 f. multicoloured	12	12

1972. Iraqi Chamber of Commerce.

1028. 181.	25 f. multicoloured ..	10	8
1029.	35 f. multicoloured	12	12

182. Oil Rig and Flame.

1972. North Rumaila Oilfield. Inaug.

1030. 182.	25 f. multicoloured ..	12	8
1031.	35 f. multicoloured ..	15	12

183. Party Emblem.

1972. Al Baath Party. 25th Anniv. Mult.

1032.	10 f. Type 183	5	5
1033.	25 f. Emblem and inscription	8	8
1034.	35 f. Type 183	12	12
1035.	70 f. As 25 f.	25	25

SIZES—HORIZ. 25 f., 70 f. 51 × 27 mm.

184. Mountain Scene.

1972. New Year "Nawrooz".

1036. 184.	25 f. multicoloured ..	8	8
1037.	70 f. multicoloured	30	25

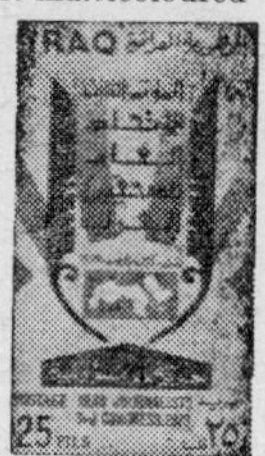

185. Congress "Quills" Emblem.

1972. 3rd Arab Journalists Congress.

1038. 185.	25 f. multicoloured ..	12	8
1039.	35 f. multicoloured	15	12

186. Federation Emblem. 187. Hand holding Spanner.

1972. Iraqi Women's Federation. 4th Anniv.

1040. 186.	25 f. multicoloured ..	10	8
1041.	35 f. multicoloured ..	12	12

1972. Labour Day.

1046. 187.	25 f. multicoloured ..	8	8
1047.	35 f. multicoloured ..	10	10

188. Kaaba, Mecca.

1972. Mohamed's Birthday.

1048. 188.	25 f. multicoloured ..	12	8
1049.	35 f. multicoloured ..	15	12

189. Shooting for Goal.

1972. Air. 25th Military Soccer Championships, Baghdad. Multicoloured.

1050.	10 f. Type 189	5	5
1051.	20 f. Players in goalmouth	8	5
1052.	25 f. Type 189	12	8
1053.	35 f. As 20 f.	15	12

190. Soldiers and Artillery.

1972. 14 July Revolution. 14th Anniv.

1055. 190.	35 f. multicoloured ..	15	12
1056. –	70 f. multicoloured ..	30	25

191. "Spirit of Revolution".

1972. 17 July Revolution. 4th Anniv.

1057. 191.	25 f. multicoloured ..	12	8
1058.	95 f. multicoloured ..	40	35

192. Scout Badge and Camp Scene.

1972. 10th Jamboree and Conference of Arab Scouts, Mosul.

1059. 192.	20 f. multicoloured ..	20	10
1060.	25 f. multicoloured ..	20	10

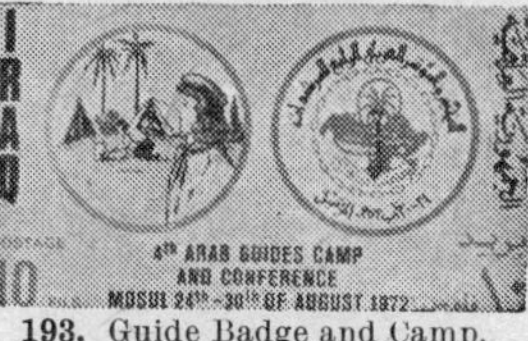

193. Guide Badge and Camp.

1972. 4th Conference and Camp of Arab Guides, Mosul.

1061. 193.	10 f. multicoloured ..	10	10
1062.	45 f. multicoloured ..	20	15

1972 ١٩٧٢

(194.)

1972. 3rd Traffic Week. Nos. 1010/11 surch. or optd. with T 195.

1063. 174.	25 f. multicoloured ..	25	25
1064.	70 f. on 15 f. mult. ..	70	70

مهرجان النخيل
وعيد التمور
١٩٧٢

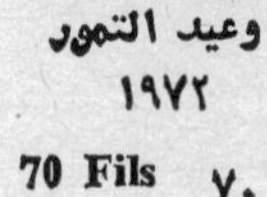

(195.)

196. "Strong Man" Statuette.

1972. Festival of Palm Trees and Feast of Dates. Nos. 707 and 709 surch. with T 195.

1065. 84.	25 f. on 3 f. mult. ..	30	30
1066.	70 f. on 15 f. mult. ..	70	70

1972. Air. World Body-building Championships and Asian Congress, Baghdad. Multicoloured.

1067.	25 f. Type 196	10	8
1068.	70 f. Ancient warriors and modern Strong Man ..	25	20

197. Bank Building.

1972. Central Bank of Iraq. 25th Anniv.

1069. 197.	25 f. multicoloured	10	8
1070.	70 f. multicoloured ..	25	20

198. International Railway Union Emblem.

1972. Int. Railway Union. 50th Anniv.
1073. **198.** 25 f. multicoloured .. 10 8
1074. 45 f. multicoloured .. 15 12

1973 Various stamps with portrait obliterated with 3 bars.

(a) 1954 issue.
1075. **23.** 10 f. blue 8 8
1076. 15 f. black 10 10
1077. 25 f. purple 15 15

(b) 1957 issue.
1078. **30.** 10 f. blue 20 25
1079. 15 f. black 20 25
1080. 25 f. purple 15 15

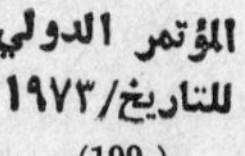

(199.)

1973. Int. History Congress. Nos. 780, 783 and 786 optd. with T **199.**
1094. 15 f. mult. (postage) .. 15 12
1095. 80 f. multicoloured (air) .. 80 80
1096. 500 f. multicoloured .. 4·50 5·00

200. Iraqi Oil Workers.

1973. Nationalisation of Iraqi Oil Industry. 1st Anniv.
1097. **200.** 25 f. multicoloured .. 10 5
1098. 70 f. multicoloured .. 25 20

201. Harp. **202.** Iraqis and Flags.

1973.
1099. **201.** 5 f. black and orange 5 5
1100. 10 f. black and brown 5 5
1101. 20 f. black and red .. 8 5
1102. – 25 f. black and blue .. 10 5
1103. – 35 f. black and green 12 20
1104. – 45 f. black and blue .. 15 20
1105. – 50 f. yellow and green 15 10
1106. – 70 f. yellow and violet 25 20
1107. – 95 f. yellow and brown 40 40

DESIGNS: 25, 35, 45 f. Minaret or Mosul. 50, 70, 95 f. Statue of a Goddess.

1973. July Festivals.
1122. **262.** 25 f. multicoloured .. 10 8
1123. 35 f. multicoloured .. 15 12

1973. Int. Journalists' Conference. Nos. 857/8 optd. **i.o.j. SEPTEMBER 26-29, 1973.**
1124. **128.** 15 f. multicoloured .. 10 10
1125. 50 f. multicoloured .. 30 40

203. Interpol H.Q., Paris. **204.** Flags and Fair Emblems.

1973. Int. Criminal Police Organization (Interpol). 50th Anniv.
1126. **203.** 25 f. multicoloured .. 10 5
1127. 70 f. multicoloured .. 25 20

1973. 10th Baghdad International Fair.
1128. **204.** 10 f. multicoloured .. 5 5
1129. 20 f. multicoloured .. 8 5
1130. 55 f. multicoloured .. 20 15

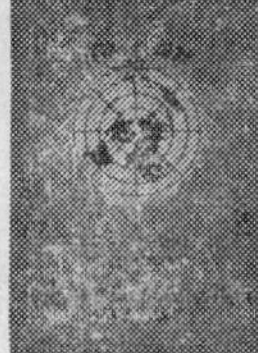

205. W.M.O. Emblem. **206.** Arab Flags and Map.

1973. World Meteorological Organization. Cent.
1148. **205.** 25 f. blk., grn. & orge. 10 8
1149. 35 f. blk., grn. & mve. 12 12

1973. Arab States' Civil Aviation Council, Baghdad. 11th Session.
1150. **206.** 20 f. multicoloured .. 10 5
1151. 35 f. multicoloured .. 12 12

دفاع
وطني

(207.)

208. Human Rights Emblem.

1973. Sixth Executive Council Meeting of Arab Postal Union, Baghdad. No. 665 optd. with Type **207.**
1153. **65.** 30 f. blue & orange .. 20 20

1973. Human Rights. 25th Anniv.
1154. **208.** 25 f. multicoloured .. 10 5
1155. 70 f. multicoloured .. 30 20

209. Shield and Military Activities.

1974. Military College. 50th Anniv.
1156. **209.** 25 f. multicoloured .. 10 5
1157. 35 f. multicoloured .. 12 10

210. U.P.U. Emblem.

1974. Universal Postal Union. Cent.
1159. **210.** 25 f. multicoloured .. 10 8
1160. 35 f. multicoloured .. 20 10
1161. 70 f. multicoloured .. 30 20

211. Allegory of Nationalisation.

1974. Nationalisation of Iraqi Oil Industry. 2nd Anniv.
1162. **211.** 10 f. multicoloured .. 5 5
1163. 25 f. multicoloured .. 10 5
1164. 70 f. multicoloured .. 25 25

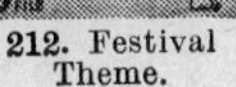

212. Festival Theme. **214.** Cement Plant.

213. National Front Emblem and Heads.

1975. "July Festivals".
1165. **212.** 20 f. multicoloured .. 10 8
1166. 35 f. multicoloured .. 15 15

1975. Progressive National Front. 1st. Anniv.
1167. **213.** 20 f. multicoloured .. 12 8
1168. 50 f. multicoloured .. 30 20

1975. Iraqi Cement. Industry. 25th Anniv.
1169. **214.** 20 f. multicoloured .. 10 5
1170. 25 f. multicoloured .. 12 8
1171. 70 f. multicoloured .. 30 20

1975. Surch.
1172. **144.** 10 f. on 3 f. mult. .. 10 8
1173. – 25 f. on 3 f. multicoloured (No. 892) .. 10 8

215. W.P.Y. Emblem.

1975. World Population Year (1974).
1174. **215.** 25 f. green and blue 12 8
1175. 35 f. blue & magenta 15 12
1176. 70 f. violet and olive 30 20

216. Festival Emblems.

1975. "July Festivals".
1177. **216.** 5 f. multicoloured .. 5 5
1178. 10 f. multicoloured .. 5 5
1179. 35 f. multicoloured .. 15 12

217. Map and Emblem. **218.** "Equality—Development—Peace".

1975. Arab Working Organization. 10th Anniv.
1180. **217.** 25 f. multicoloured .. 12 8
1181. 35 f. multicoloured .. 15 15
1182. 45 f. multicoloured .. 20 15

1975. International Women's Year.
1183. **218.** 10 f. multicoloured .. 5 5
1184. 35 f. multicoloured .. 15 12
1185. 70 f. multicoloured .. 30 25

219. Euphrates Dam.

1975. International Commission on Irrigation and Drainage.
1187. **219.** 3 f. multicoloured .. 5 5
1188. 25 f. multicoloured .. 10 5
1189. 70 f. multicoloured .. 30 25

220. Company Seal.

1975. National Insurance Company, Baghdad. 25th Amniv.
1190. **247.** 20 f. multicoloured .. 8 5
1191. 25 f. multicoloured .. 10 5

221. Court Musicians.

1975. Int. Music Conference, Baghdad.
1193. **221.** 25 f. multicoloured .. 10 10
1194. 45 f. multicoloured .. 20 20

222. Telecommunications Centre.

1975. Opening of Telecommunications Centre.
1203. **222.** 5 f. multicoloured .. 5 5
1204. 10 f. multicoloured .. 5 5
1205. 60 f. multicoloured .. 30 25

223. Diesel Train. **224.** Goddess (statue).

1975. 15th Taurus Railway Conf., Baghdad. Multicoloured.
1206. 25 f. Type **223** 10 10
1207. 30 f. Diesel-electric locomotive 15 12
1208. 35 f. Steam tank locomotive and train .. 20 20
1209. 50 f. German steam locomotive 30 15

1976.
1210. **224.** 5 f. multicoloured .. 5 5
1211. 10 f. multicoloured .. 5 5
1212. 15 f. multicoloured .. 8 5
1213. – 20 f. multicoloured .. 10 8
1214. – 25 f. multicoloured .. 10 5
1215. – 30 f. multicoloured .. 12 8
1216. – 35 f. multicoloured .. 15 10
1217. – 50 f. multicoloured .. 20 12
1218. – 75 f. multicoloured .. 30 15

DESIGNS: 20, 25, 30 f. Two females forming column. 35, 50, 75 f. Head of bearded man.

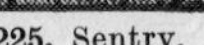

225. Sentry. **226.** Crossed-out Thumbprint.

1976. Arab Day.
1219. **225.** 5 f. multicoloured .. 5 5
1220. 25 f. multicoloured on silver 10 5
1221. 50 f. multicoloured on gold 20 10

1976. Arab Literacy Day.
1222. **226.** 5 f. multicoloured .. 5 5
1223. 15 f. multicoloured .. 5 5
1224. 35 f. multicoloured .. 15 12

227. Iraq Earth Station. **228.** Early and Modern Telephones.

1976. Revolution of 14th Ramadan. 13th Anniversary.
1225. **227.** 10 f. multicoloured .. 5 5
1226. 25 f. multicoloured on silver 10 5
1227. 75 f. multicoloured on gold 30 20

1976. Telephone Centenary.
1228. **228.** 35 f. multicoloured .. 15 12
1229. 50 f. multicoloured .. 20 10
1230. 75 f. multicoloured .. 30 20

229. Map and Emblem. **230.** Iraqi Family.

1976. 20th Int. Arab Trade Unions Conf.
1231. **229.** 5 f. multicoloured (postage) 5 5
1232. 10 f. multicoloured .. 5 5
1233. 75 f. multicoloured (air) 30 15

1976. Police Day.
1234. **230.** 5 f. multicoloured .. 5 5
1235. 15 f. multicoloured .. 8 5
1236. 35 f. multicoloured .. 15 12

231. Strategy Pipeline. **232.** Human Eye.

1976. Oil Nationalization. 4th Anniv.
1237. **231.** 25 f multicoloured .. 10 5
1238. 75 f. multicoloured .. 30 15

1976. World Health Day.
1240. **232.** 25 f. black and blue .. 10 5
1241. 35 f. black and green 15 12
1242. 50 f. brown and oran. 20 15

233. Festival's Allegory. **234.** Basketball.

1976. July Festivals.
1243. **233.** 15 f. multicoloured .. 8 5
1244. 35 f. multicoloured .. 15 12

1976. Olympic Games, Montreal. Mult.
1245. 25 f. Type **234** 10 5
1246. 35 f. Netball 15 12
1247. 50 f. Wrestling 20 15
1248. 75 f. Boxing 30 15

235. Bishop Kabotchi.

1976. Bishop Kabotchi's Detention in Israel. 2nd Anniv.
1250. **235.** 25 f. multicoloured .. 10 5
1251. 35 f. multicoloured .. 15 12
1252. 75 f. multicoloured .. 30 15

236. Kingfisher.

1976. Birds. Multicoloured.
1253. 5 f. Type **236** 5 5
1254. 10 f. Turtle dove 5 5
1256. 15 f. Pin-tailed sand grouse 8 5
1257. 25 f. Blue rock-thrush .. 10 5
1258. 50 f. Purple heron .. 20 15

OFFICIAL STAMPS

1920. Issue of 1918 (surch. Turkish stamps) optd. **ON STATE SERVICE** in wavy line.
O 33. ½ a. on 10 pa. green .. 5 5
O 34. 1 a. on 20 pa. red .. 8 8
O 35. 1½ a. on 5 pa. purple .. 15 15
O 22. 2½ a. on 1 pi. blue .. 40 40
O 23. 3 a. on 1½ pi. grey and red 40 25
O 36. 4 a. on 1¾ pi. brn. & grey 25 15
O 25. 6 a. on 2 pi. blk. & green 60 40
O 38. 8 a. on 2½ pi. green & orge. 60 60
O 27. 12 a. on 5 pi. lilac .. 75 65
O 28. 1 r. on 10 pi. brown .. 1·25 80
O 29. 2 r. on 25 pi. green .. 3·50 2·00
O 30. 5 r. on 50 pi. red .. 8·00 5·00
O 31. 10 r. on 100 pi. blue .. 16·00 11·00

1923. Nos. 41 to 53 optd. **ON STATE SERVICE** in English only.
O 54. ½ a. green 5 5
O 55. 1 a. brown 8 5
O 56. 1½ a. red 20 20
O 57. 2 a. yellow-brown .. 8 10
O 58. 3 a. blue 25 15
O 59. 4 a. violet 40 25
O 60. 6 a. blue 50 30
O 61. 8 a. olive 50 30
O 62. 1 r. brown and green .. 90 60
O 63. 2 r. black .. .. 4·00 1·25
O 64. 5 r. orange .. .. 10·00 5·00
O 65. 10 r. red .. .. 18·00 10·00

1924. Nos. 41 to 53 optd. **ON STATE SERVICE** in English and Arabic.
O 66. ½ a. green 5 5
O 67. 1 a. brown 5 5
O 68. 1½ a. red 8 5
O 69. 2 a. yellow-brown .. 10 8
O 70. 3 a. blue 10 8
O 71. 4 a. violet 20 10
O 72. 6 a. blue 40 20
O 73. 8 a. olive 50 25
O 74. 1 r. brown and green 1·50 50
O 75. 2 r. olive .. .. 2·50 1·00
O 76. 5 r. orange .. .. 6·00 7·00
O 77. 10 r. red .. .. 12·00 9·00

1927. Optd. **ON STATE SERVICE** in English and Arabic.
O 79. **9.** 1 r. brown .. .. 1·50 40

1931. Optd. **ON STATE SERVICE** in English and Arabic.
O 93. **10.** ½ a. green 5 20
O 94. 1 a. brown 8 8
O 95. 1½ a. red .. .. 1·25 1·25
O 96. 2 a. orange 20 8
O 97. 3 a. blue 30 30
O 98. 4 a. purple 35 20
O 99. 6 a. blue .. .. 70 1·00
O 100. 8 a. green .. .. 1·00 1·00
O 101. **11.** 1 r. brown .. .. 2·00 2·00
O 102. 2 r. yellow-brown .. 3·00 3·00
O 103. 5 r. orange .. .. 6·00 6·00
O 104. 10 r. red .. .. 12·00 12·00
O 105. **9.** 25 r. violet £300 £350

1932. Official stamps of 1924 and 1931 surch. with new values as T **12.**
O 122. **10.** 3 f. on ½ f. green .. 15 25
O 123. 4 f. on ½ f. green .. 8 8
O 124. 5 f. on 1 a. brown .. 8 8
O 125. **3.** 8 f. on 1½ a. red .. 20 15
O 126. **10.** 10 f. on 2 a. orange .. 20 8
O 127. 15 f. on 3 a. blue .. 35 25
O 128. 20 f. on 4 a. purple .. 35 20
O 129. 25 f. on 4 a. purple .. 45 25
O 130. – 30 f. on 6 a. blue (No. 47) 50 40
O 131. **10.** 40 f. on 8 a. green .. 70 45
O 132. **11.** 50 f. on 1 r. brown .. 90 80
O 133. 75 f. on 1 r. brown .. 1·75 1·75
O 134. **1.** 100 f. on 2 r. olive .. 1·50 1·00
O 135. – 200 f. on 5 r. orange (No. 52) .. .. 4·00 2·50
O 136. – ½ d. on 10 r. red (No. 53) .. .. .. 10·00 8·00
O 137. **9.** 1 d. on 25 r. violet .. 40·00 35·00

1932. Issue of 1932 optd. **ON STATE SERVICE** in English and Arabic.
O 155. **10.** 2 f. blue 15 5
O 156. 3 f. green 15 5
O 157. 4 f. purple 20 5
O 158. 5 f. green 20 5
O 159. 8 f. red 20 5
O 160. 10 f. yellow 25 8
O 161. 15 f. blue 25 8
O 162. 20 f. orange 25 10
O 163. 25 f. mauve 55 20
O 164. 30 f. olive 70 20
O 165. 40 f. violet 70 20
O 166. **11.** 50 f. brown 60 20
O 167. 75 f. blue 90 35
O 168. 100 f. green 90 35
O 169. 200 f. red .. .. 2·50 1·25
O 170. **9.** ½ d. blue .. .. 4·00 3·00
O 171. 1 d. purple .. .. 11·00 12·00

1934. Issue of 1934 optd. **ON STATE SERVICE** in English and Arabic.
O 190. **13.** 1 f. violet 10 5
O 191. 2 f. blue 10 5
O 192. 3 f. green 10 5
O 193. 4 f. purple 10 5
O 194. 5 f. green 10 5
O 195. 8 f. red 25 5
O 196. 10 f. yellow .. 10 5
O 197. 15 f. blue 40 15
O 198. 20 f. orange .. 20 8
O 199. 25 f. mauve .. 1·00 25
O 200. 30 f. green .. 40 10
O 201. 40 f. violet .. 60 20
O 202. **14.** 50 f. brown .. 30 15
O 203. 75 f. blue 45 40
O 204. 100 f. green .. 70 35
O 205. 200 f. red .. 1·50 75
O 206. – ½ d. blue (No. 188) 4·00 5·00
O 207. – 1 d. claret (No. 189) 6·00 8·00

1941. Issue of 1941 optd. **ON STATE SERVICE** in English and Arabic.
O 230. **15.** 1 f. purple 5 5
O 231. 2 f. brown 5 5
O 232. – 3 f. green (No. 210) 5 5
O 233. – 4 f. violet (No. 211) 5 5
O 234. – 5 f. red (No. 212b) 5 10
O 235. **16.** 8 f. red 30 5
O 236. 8 f. yellow 10 25
O 237. 10 f. yellow 70 15
O 238. 10 f. red 12 5
O 239. 15 f. blue .. .. 1·00 25
O 240. 15 f. black 15 15
O 241. 20 f. black 30 15
O 242. 20 f. blue 15 5
O 243. **17.** 25 f. purple 20 20
O 244. 30 f. orange 25 25
O 246. 40 f. brown 25 25
O 247. – 50 f. blue (No. 224b) 40 25
O 249 c. – 75 f. mauve (No. 225a) 50 20
O 250 c. – 100 f. olive (No. 226) 60 20
O 252. – 200 f. orge. (No. 227) 1·00 40
O 253. – ½ d. blue (No. 228) .. 2·00 1·00
O 254. – 1 d. green (No. 229) 6·00 2·00

1942. Issue of 1942 optd. **ON STATE SERVICE** in English and Arabic.
O 263. **18.** 1 f. brown and violet 5 5
O 264. 2 f. brown and blue .. 5 5
O 265. 3 f. brown and green 5 5
O 266. 4 f. brown 5 5
O 267. 5 f. brown and green 5 5
O 268. 6 f. brown and red .. 5 5
O 269. 10 f. brown and red .. 8 5
O 270. 12 f. brown and green 10 5

1948. Issue of 1948 optd. **ON STATE SERVICE** in English and Arabic.
O 298. **19.** 1 f. blue 5 5
O 299. 2 f. brown 5 5
O 300. 3 f. green 5 5
O 301. 3 f. claret 20 5
O 302. 4 f. violet 5 5
O 303. 5 f. purple 5 5
O 304. 5 f. green 20 5
O 305. 6 f. lilac 5 5
O 306. 8 f. yellow 5 5
O 307. 10 f. red 10 5
O 308. 12 f. olive 12 5
O 309. 14 f. olive 20 5
O 310. 15 f. black 15 75
O 311. 16 f. red 40 25
O 312. 20 f. blue 15 5
O 313. 25 f. purple 20 15
O 314. 28 f. blue 35 25
O 315. 30 f. orange 20 12
O 316. 40 f. brown 25 20
O 317. 50 f. blue 30 15
O 318. 60 f. blue 30 20
O 319. 75 f. mauve .. .. 50 1·00
O 320. 100 f. olive 60 40
O 321. 200 f. orange .. 1·25 80
O 322. ½ d. blue .. .. 3·00 5·00
O 323. 1 d. green .. .. 6·00 8·00

1955. Issue of 1954 optd. **ON STATE SERVICE** in English and Arabic.
O 364. **23.** 1 f. blue 10 10
O 365. 2 f. brown 5 5
O 366. 3 f. lake 5 5
O 367. 4 f. violet 5 5
O 368. 5 f. green 5 5
O 369. 6 f. magenta 20 5
O 370. 8 f. chestnut .. 5 5
O 371. 10 f. blue 5 5
O 372. 16 f. red .. .. 5·00 6·00
O 373. 20 f. olive 30 15
O 374. 25 f. purple 60 40
O 375. 30 f. red 45 15
O 376. 40 f. chestnut .. 55 20
O 377. – 50 f. blue 60 30
O 378. – 60 f. purple .. 6·00 6·00
O 379. – 100 f. olive .. 5·00 3·00
No. O 378 does not exist without opt.

1958. Issue of 1958 optd. **ON STATE SERVICE** in English and Arabic.
O 404. **30.** 1 f. blue 35 30
O 405. 2 f. brown .. .. 1·50 90
O 406. 3 f. lake .. .. 2·00 5·00
O 407. 4 f. violet .. .. 3·00 45
O 408. 5 f. green 50 45
O 409. 6 f. magenta .. 60 45
O 410. 10 f. blue 50 45

1958. Official stamps optd. with T **32.**
(a) No. 227.
O 459. – 200 f. orange .. 3·50 2·50
(b) Nos. O 298, etc.
O 460. **19.** 1 f. indigo .. .. 4·00
O 461. 2 f. brown .. .. 5·00
O 462. 3 f. green .. ..
O 463. 3 f. claret .. ..
O 464. 4 f. violet .. ..
O 465. 5 f. claret .. ..
O 466. 5 f. green .. ..
O 467. 6 f. mauve .. ..
O 468. 8 f. bistre .. ..
O 470. 12 f. olive 40 30
O 471. 14 f. olive 50 35
O 472. 15 f. black 20 20
O 473. 16 f. red .. .. 1·10 1·40
O 474. 25 f. mauve .. 90 1·10
O 475. 28 f. blue 65 45
O 476. 40 f. brown 45 45
O 477. 60 f. blue 75 75
O 478. – 75 f. mauve .. 80 80
O 479. – 200 f. orange .. 1·10 80
O 480. – ½ d. blue .. .. 2·50 2·50
O 481. – 1 d. green .. .. 5·00 5·00
(c) Nos. O 364, etc.
O 482. **23.** 1 f. blue 5 5
O 483. 2 f. brown 5 5
O 484. 3 f. lake 5 5
O 485. 4 f. violet 5 5
O 486. 5 f. green 12 5
O 487. 6 f. magenta 15 5
O 488. 8 f. chestnut .. 12 5
O 489. 10 f. blue 15 5
O 490. 16 f. red .. .. 2·10 1·00
O 491. 20 f. olive 20 15
O 492. 25 f. purple 25 15
O 493. 30 f. red 25 20
O 494. 40 f. chestnut .. 50 20
O 495. – 50 f. blue 40 30
O 496. – 60 f. purple .. 40 40
O 497. – 100 f. olive .. 80 45
(d) On Nos. O 404, etc.
O 498. **31.** 1 f. blue 5 5
O 499. 2 f. brown 5 5
O 500. 3 f. lake 5 5
O 501. 4 f. violet 5 5
O 502. 5 f. green 5 5
O 503. 6 f. magenta 8 5
O 504. 8 f. chestnut 8 8
O 505. 10 f. blue 12 5
No. O 504 does not exist without opt. T **32.**

1961. Nos. 515, etc., optd. **On State Service** in English and Arabic.
O 552. **39.** 1 f. multicoloured .. 5 5
O 553. 2 f. multicoloured .. 8 5
O 554. 4 f. multicoloured .. 10 5
O 555. 5 f. multicoloured .. 15 8
O 556. 10 f. multicoloured .. 20 15
O 557. 50 f. multicoloured .. 1·90 1·50

1962. Nos. 515, etc., optd. **ON STATE SERVICE** in English and Arabic.
O 587. **38.** 1 f. multicoloured .. 5 5
O 588. 2 f. multicoloured .. 5 5
O 589. 3 f. multicoloured .. 5 5
O 590. 4 f. multicoloured .. 5 5
O 591. 5 f. multicoloured .. 5 5
O 592. 10 f. multicoloured .. 5 5
O 593. 15 f. multicoloured .. 8 10
O 594. 20 f. multicoloured .. 8 5
O 595. 30 f. multicoloured .. 10 8
O 596. 40 f. multicoloured .. 12 8
O 597. 50 f. multicoloured .. 15 10
O 598. 75 f. multicoloured .. 30 15
O 599. 100 f. multicoloured .. 40 20
O 600. 200 f. multicoloured .. 75 50
O 601. 500 f. multicoloured .. 1·90 1·50
O 602. 1 d. multicoloured .. 4·00 3·00

1971. Various stamps optd. or surch. **Official** in English and Arabic.
(a) Costumes. Nos. 768 and 770/4.
O 962. 15 f. multicoloured (post.) 5 5
O 963. 25 f. multicoloured .. 10 8
O 964. 30 f. multicoloured .. 10 10
O 965. 40 f. multicoloured (air) 15 15
O 966. 50 f. multicoloured .. 20 20
O 967. 80 f. multicoloured .. 30 25

(b) Int., Tourist Year. Nos. 778 and 780/2.
O 969. 5 f. mult. (postage) .. 5 5
O 970. 15 f. multicoloured .. 5 5
O 971. 25 f. multicoloured .. 10 8
O 972. 50 f. multicoloured (air) 20 20

(c) W.H.O. 20th Anniv. Nos. 811/13.
O 973. – 10 f. multicoloured 5 5
O 974. 113. 15 f. red, green & blk. 5 5
O 975. 25 f. red, green & blk. 10 8

(d) Human Rights Year, Nos. 814/15.
O 976. 114. 15 f. red, yell. & blue 5 5
O 977. 25 f. red, yell. & grn. 12 12

(e) U.N.I.C.E.F. Nos. 817/18.
O 978. 115. 15 f. multicoloured 5 5
O 979. 25 f. multicoloured 12 12

(f) Army Day. No. 820.
O 980. 116. 25 f. multicoloured 10 8

(g) Fish and Fauna. Nos. 825/7, 829/30 and 832.
O 981. 10 f. mult. (postage) .. 5 5
O 982. 15 f. on 3 f. mult. .. 5 5
O 983. 25 f. on 2 f. mult. .. 10 8
O 984. 10 f. mult. (air) .. 5 5
O 985. 15 f. + 3 f. mult. .. 5 5
O 986. 25 f. + 2 f. mult. .. 10 8

(h) Fruits. Nos. 906/9.
O 987. 5 f. multicoloured .. 5 5
O 988. 10 f. multicoloured .. 5 5
O 989. 15 f. multicoloured .. 8 8
O 990. 35 f. multicoloured .. 15 10

(i) Arab Football Cup, Baghdad. No. 717.
O 991. 87. 2 f. multicoloured .. 5 5

(j) I.L.O. 50th Anniv. No. 836.
O 992. 122. 15 f. yell., grn. & blk. 5 5

1972. Nos. 625/8 optd. **Official** in English and Arabic.
O 1042. 10 f. red 5 5
O 1043. 15 f. brown and yellow 5 5
O 1044. 20 f. violet .. 10 5
O 1045. 30 f. orange 15 15

1973. Various stamps with portrait obliterated by 3 bars.

(i) 1948 issue.
O 1081. 19. 25 f. pur. (No. O 310) 15 15
O 1082. 50 f. blue (No. O 317) 30 30

(ii) 1955 issue.)
O 1083. 23. 25 f. pur. (No. O 374) 15 15
O 1084. – 50 f. blue (No. O 377) 30 30

(iii) As 1958 issue. Portrait 22½ × 27½ mm.
O 1085. – 50 f. purple .. 30 30

Official رسمي

(O 1.)

1973. Various stamps with portrait obliterated.

(a) Optd. with 3 bars and Type O 1.
O 1086. 23. 10 f. blue 12 12
O 1087. 30. 15 f. black 25 25

(b) Optd. with 3 bars and as Type O 1 but larger size 9 mm.
O 1088. 23. 10 f. blue .. .. 1·50 2·00
O 1089. 30. 15 f. black .. .. 1·50 1·75

(c) Optd. with Type O 1 only.
O 1090. 23. 15 f. black 25 12
O 1091. 30. 15 f. black 25 12
O 1092. 23. 25 f. purple 25 20
O 1093. 30. 25 f. purple 25 20

(d) Optd. as Type O 1 but larger size 9 mm. only.
O 1094. 23. 15 f. black 50 50
O 1095. 30. 15 f. black 40 40
O 1096. 19. 25 f. purple .. .. 2·00 1·00

See also Nos. O 1130a/47a.

1973. No. 1097 optd. **Official** in English and Arabic.
O 1099. 200. 25 f. multicoloured 10 5

1973. Nos. 1099/1107 optd. **OFFICIAL** in English and Arabic.
O 1108. 202. 5 f. black & orange 5 5
O 1109. 10 f. black & brown 5 5
O 1110. 20 f. black and red 8 5
O 1111. – 25 f. black and blue 10 5
O 1112. – 35 f. black and grn. 12 10
O 1113. – 45 f. black and blue 15 15
O 1114. – 50 f. yellow & green 15 15
O 1115. – 70 f. yellow & violet 25 30
O 1116. – 95 f. yellow & brn. 40 30

1973. Various "Faisal" Official stamps optd. ON STATE SERVICE in English and Arabic, with portrait obliterated by "leaf" motif similar to that used in Type O 1.

(a) 1948 issue.
O 1130a. 19. 12 f. olive .. 10 10
O 1131. 14 f. olive .. 25 20
O 1132. 15 f. black .. 15 12
O 1133. 16 f. red .. 60 60
O 1134. 28 f. blue .. 40 30
O 1134a. 30 f. orange .. 25 25
O 1134b. 40 f. brown .. 30 30
O 1135. – 60 f. blue .. 40 40
O 1136. – 100 f. green .. 2·00 1·50
O 1137. – ½ d. blue .. 4·00 4·00
O 1138. – 1 d. green .. 8·00 8·00

(b) 1955 issue.
O 1139. 23. 3 f. lake 5 5
O 1140. 6 f. magenta .. 50 35
O 1141. 8 f. brown 30 20
O 1142. 16 f. red 80 70
O 1142a. 20 f. green 15 10
O 1142b. 30 f. red 20 15
O 1142c. 40 f. chestnut .. 25 20
O 1143. – 60 f. purple 40 40
O 1144. – 100 f. green .. 1·00 75

(c) 1958 issue.
O 1145. 30. 3 f. lake 10 8
O 1146. 6 f. magenta .. 30 20
O 1147. 8 f. brown 15 10
O 1147a. 30 f. red 20 10

1975. Optd. **Official** in English and Arabic.
O 1177. 15 f. multicoloured (No. 780) 8 8
O 1178. 30 f. multicoloured (No. 798) 15 15

O 2. Eagle Emblem.

1975.
O 1195. O 2. 5 f. multicoloured 5 5
O 1196. 10 f. multicoloured 5 5
O 1197. 15 f. multicoloured 8 5
O 1198. 20 f. multicoloured 8 5
O 1199. 25 f. multicoloured 10 5
O 1200. 30 f. multicoloured 15 12
O 1201. 50 f. multicoloured 20 15
O 1202. 100 f. multicoloured 40 30

1976. Nos. 1253/7 additionally inscr. "OFFICIAL" in English and Arabic.
O 1258. 236. 5 f. multicoloured 5 5
O 1259. – 10 f. multicoloured 5 5
O 1260. – 15 f. multicoloured 8 8
O 1261. – 25 f. multicoloured 10 10
O 1262. – 50 f. multicoloured 20 20

OBLIGATORY TAX

مالية انقاذ فلسطين (T1.)

مالية ٥ فلوس انقاذ فلسطين (T2.)

1949. Nos. O 300 and 278 optd. as Type T 1, but with an additional line of overprint.
T 324. 19. 3 f. green .. .. 4·00 75
T 325. 6 f. lilac .. .. 4·00 90

1949.
(a) No. 324 optd. with Type T 1 and Nos. O 138 and O 141 with similar overprint but narrower.
T 326. 19. 2 f. brown .. .. 3·00 60
T 327. 5 f. purple .. .. 6·00 1·50
T 328. – 5 f. red .. .. 5·00 1·25

(b) Revenue stamps with portraits as T 18 (No. T 332) and T 19 surch. or optd. in Arabic similar to Type T 1.
T 329. 2 f. on 5 f. blue .. 50 15
T 330. 5 f. blue .. 50 20
T 331. 10 f. orange .. .. 1·50 40
T 332. 20 f. green .. .. 3·00 75

1949. No. 278 surch. with Type T 2.
T 333. 19. 5 f. on 6 f. lilac .. 4·50 5·00

NOTE: Nos. T324/32 were for compulsory use to aid the war in Palestine.

(T 3.)

دفاع وطني (T 4.)

1968. Flood Relief.
T 763. T 3. 5 f. brown 5 5

1968. Defence Fund. Optd. with Type T 4.
T 764. T 3. 5 f. brown 5 5

1970. Obligatory Tax. Defence Fund. Nos. 620 and 265/9 surch. with Type T 5.
T 931. 55. 5 f. on 1 f. green .. 45 45
T 932. – 5 f. on 10 f. red .. 45 45
T 933. – 5 f. on 15 f. brn. & yell. 45 45
T 934. – 5 f. on 20 f. violet .. 45 45
T 935. – 5 f. on 30 f. orange .. 45 45
T 936. – 5 f. on 40 f. green .. 45 45

دفاع وطني ٥ فلوس (T 5.)

دفاع وطني ٥ فلوس (T 6.)

1973. Obligatory Tax. Defence Fund. Nos. 607/8 surch. with Type T 6.
T 1071. 52. 5 f. on 14 f. blk. & grn. 15 15
T 1072. 5 f. on 35 f. blk. & red 15 15

دفاع وطني ٥ فلوس المجلس التنفيذي

(T 7.) بغداد/١٩٧٣ (T 8.)

1973. Nos. 738, 765, 777, 787 and 891 optd. similar to Type T 6 (No. 1119) or as Type T 7 others.
T 1117. – 5 f. on 2 f. mult. .. 20 20
T 1118. 103. 5 f. on 2 f. mult. .. 20 15
T 1119. 105. 5 f. on 2 f. mult. .. 20 15
T 1120. 106. 5 f. on 2 f. mult. .. 20 15
T 1121. 140. 5 f. on 2 f. mult. .. 20 15

1973. Obligatory Tax. No. 1099 optd. with Type T 8.
T 1152. 201. 5 f. black and orge. 10 8

T 9. Iraqi Soldier.

1974. Obligatory Tax. Defence Fund.
T 1158. T 9. 5 f. yell., blk. & brn. 10 8

IRELAND (REPUBLIC) BC

The Republic of Ireland (Eire) is an independent state comprising Ireland, except the six counties of N. Ireland. It was formerly part of the United Kingdom of Great Britain and Ireland.

Rialtap Sealatać na hÉipeann 1922 (1.)

Rialtap Sealadać na hÉipeann 1922. (2.)

"Provisional Government of Ireland, 1922".

King George V stamps of Gt. Britain overprinted.

1922. Optd. with T 1 (date in thin figures).
1. 85. ½d. green 12 10
2. 84. 1d. red 12 12
4. 2½d. blue 45 65
5. 86. 3d. violet .. .. 1·00 60
6. 4d. grey-green .. .. 1·00 1·50
7. 87. 5d. brown .. .. 1·75 2·25
8. 88. 9d. black .. .. 4·00 4·00
9. 10d. blue .. .. 3·00 4·50
17. 89. 2s. 6d. brown .. .. 12·00 15·00
19. 5s. red .. .. 16·00 22·00
21. 10s. blue .. ..

On Nos. 17/21 the opt. is in four lines instead of five.

1922. Optd. with T 2 (date in thick figures).
47. 85. ½d. green 20 20
31. 84. 1d. red 15 12
10. 86. 1½d. brown 35 35
34. 86. 2d. orange 40 12
35. 84. 2½d. blue .. .. 2·25 3·00
36. 86. 3d. violet 45 55
37. 4d. grey-green .. .. 1·25 1·25
38. 87. 5d. brown .. .. 1·50 2·75
39. 6d. purple .. .. 1·50 1·10
40. 88. 9d. black .. .. 2·25 3·00
41. 9d. olive-green .. .. 2·25 3·00
42. 10d. blue .. .. 4·50 5·50
51. 1s. brown .. .. 8·50 9·00

Saorstát Éireann 1922

(3. "Irish Free State, 1922".)

1922. Optd with T 3.
52. 85. ½d. green 10 10
53. 84. 1d. red 10 10
54. 85. 1½d. brown 40 65
55. 86. 2d orange 40 55
56 84. 2½d. blue 55 75
57. 86. 3d. violet .. .. 1·00 1·40
58. 4d. grey-green .. .. 80 1·00
59. 87. 5d. brown .. .. 1·00 1·40
60. 6d. purple 80 80
61. 88. 9d. olive-green .. .. 95 1·40
62. 10d. blue .. .. 5·50 7·00
63. 1s. brown .. .. 4·00 4·00
64. 89. 2s. 6d. brown .. .. 7·00 11·00
65. 5s red .. .. 13·00 20·00
66. 10s. blue .. .. 32·00 40·00

4. Sword of Light.

5. Map of Ireland.

6 Irish Arms.

7. Celtic Cross.

1922.
71. 4. ½d. green 20 8
112. 5. 1d. red 5 5
113. 1½d. purple .. .. 2·50 20
114. 2d. green 5 5
115. 6. 2½d. brown .. .. 1·75 20
116. 7. 3d. blue (18¾ × 22½ mm.) 25 12
227. 3d. blue (17 × 21 mm.) .. 40 30
117. 6. 4d. blue 12 5
118. 4. 5d. violet (18¾ × 22½ mm.) 20 8
228. 5d. violet (17 × 21 mm.) 45 35
119. 6d. purple 30 12
119a. 8d. red 30 30
120. 6. 9d. violet 30 30
121. 7. 10d. brown 35 30
121a. 11d. rose 40 50
82. 4. 1s. blue .. .. 15·00 2·75

8. Daniel O'Connell.

9. Shannon Bridge.

1929. Catholic Emancipation Cent.
89. 8. 2d. green 25 12
90. 3d. blue .. .. 1·50 1·10
91. 9d. violet .. .. 1·75 1·25

1930. Completion of Shannon Hydro-Electric Scheme.
92. 9. 2d. deep brown 40 25

10. Reaper.

11. Cross of Cong.

1931. Royal Dublin Society Bicent.
93. 10. 2d. blue 55 25

1932. Int. Eucharistic Congress.
94. 11. 2d. green 40 15
95. 3d. blue .. .. 1·75 2·00

12. Adoration of the Cross.

13. "Hurling" Player.

1933. Holy Year Issue.
96. 12. 2d. green 30 12
97. 3d. blue .. .. 1·50 1·10

1934. Gaelic Athletic Assn. 50th Anniv.
98. 13. 2d. green 60 20

14. St. Patrick.

15. Ireland and New Constitution.

1937.
123a. 14. 2s. 6d. green .. .. 1·25 60
124a. 5s. maroon .. .. 2·00 90
125a. 10s. blue .. .. 3·00 2·00

1937. Constitution Day.
105. 15. 2d. red 40 30
106. 3d. blue.. .. .. 1·10 1·25
For similar stamps see No. 176/7.

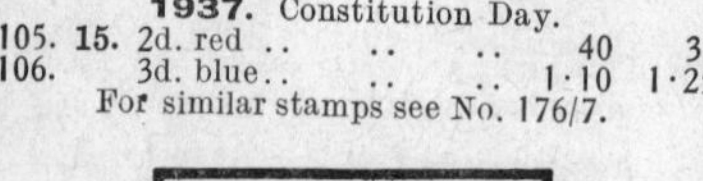

16. Father Mathew.

1938. Temperance Crusade Cent.
107. 16. 2d. black 45 35
108. 3d. blue.. .. .. 2·75 3·00

17. George Washington, American Eagle and Irish Harp.

1939. U.S. Constitution. 150th Anniv., and Installation of First U.S. President.
109. 17. 2d. red 40 50
110. 3d. blue.. .. 3·25 3·75

18. Volunteer and G.P.O., Dublin.

1941. Easter Rising (1916). 25th Anniv.
(a) Provisional issue. Optd. with two lines of Irish characters between the dates "1941" and "1916".
126. 5. 2d. orange 45 25
127. 7. 3d. blue .. .. .. 6·50 4·00

(b) Definitive Issue.
128. 18. 2½d. black 55 15

19. Dr. Douglas Hyde.

20. Sir William Rowan Hamilton.

1943. Gaelic League. 50th Anniv.
129. 19. ½d. green 25 20
130. 2½d. purple 50 35

1943. Announcement of Discovery of Quaternions. Cent.
131. 20. ½d. green .. .. 1·25 25
132. 2½d. brown .. .. 1·25 35

21. Michael O'Clery.

22. Edmund Ignatius Rice.

1944. O'Clery (Franciscan historian) Death Tercent.; commemorating the "Annals of the Four Masters".
133. 21. ½d. green 12 10
134. 1s. brown 30 12

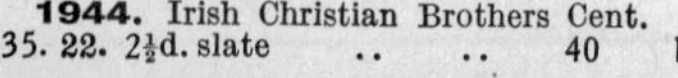

1944. Irish Christian Brothers Cent.
135. 22. 2½d. slate 40 15

23. Youth sowing Seeds of Freedom.

24. "Country and Homestead".

1945. Thomas Davis (Founder of Young Ireland Movement). Death Cent.
136. 23. 2½d. blue 35 20
137. 6d. purple .. .. 1·25 1·75

1946. Michael Davitt and Charles Parnell. Birth Cent.
138. 24. 2½d. red 35 20
139. 3d. blue.. .. .. 1·25 1·40

25. Angel Victor over Rock of Cashel.

DESIGNS: 3d., 8d. Angel Victor over Lough Derg. 6d. Over Croagh Patrick. 1s. Over Glendalough.

1948. Air. Inscr. "VOX HIBERNIÆ".
140. 25. 1d. brown 85 60
141. – 3d. blue .. .. 1·60 1·25
142. – 6d. purple 15 8
142a. – 8d. lake 15 25
143. – 1s. green 20 25
143a. 25. 1s 3d. orange 30 40
143b. 1s. 5d. ultramarine .. 20 35

26. Theobald Wolfe Tone.

1948. Insurrection. 150th Anniv.
144. 26. 2½d. purple 50 35
145. 3d. violet .. .. 2·00 2·25

INDEPENDENT REPUBLIC

27. Leinster House and Arms of Provinces.

28. J. C. Mangan (poet).

1949. Int. Recognition of Republic.
146. 27. 2½d. brown 25 20
147. 3d. blue.. .. .. 1·25 1·10

1949. J. C. Mangan. Death Cent.
148. 28. 1d. green .. .. 1·25 35

29. Statue of St. Peter.

30. Thomas Moore.

31. Irish Harp.

1950. Holy Year.
149. 29. 2½d. violet 30 35
150. 3d. blue.. .. .. 3·00 3·25
151. 9d. brown .. .. 3·25 3·50

1952. Thomas Moore (poet). Death Cent.
152. 30. 2½d. purple 15 20
153. 3½d. olive .. .. 1·50 1·50

1953. "An Tostal" (Ireland at Home) Festival.
154. 31. 2½d. green 30 35
155. 1s. 4d. blue .. .. 4·50 4·00

32. Robert Emmet.

33. Madonna and Child (Della Robbia).

1953. Emmet (patriot). 150th Death Anniv.
156. 32. 3d. green 50 50
157. 1s. 3d. red .. .. 6·00 5·00

1954. Marian Year.
158. 33. 3d. blue.. .. .. 65 15
159. 5d. green .. .. 3·50 4·00

34. Cardinal Newman.

35. Statue of Commodore Barry.

36. John Redmond.

1954. Founding of Catholic University of Ireland. Cent.
160. 34. 2d. purple 60 30
161. 1s. 3d. blue .. .. 4·50 3·50

1956. Barry Commem.
162. 35. 3d. lilac 20 20
163. 1s. 3d. blue .. .. 4·00 2·50

1957. John Redmond (politician). Birth Cent.
164. 36. 3d. blue.. .. .. 20 25
165. 1s. 3d. maroon .. .. 3·75 3·50

37. Thomas O'Crohan.

38. Admiral Brown.

39. Father Luke Wadding.

1957. Thomas O'Crohan (author). Birth Cent.
166. 37. 2d. maroon 65 20
167. 5d. violet .. .. 3·00 2·50

1957. Admiral Brown. Death Cent.
168. 38. 3d. blue.. .. .. 40 40
169. 1s. 3d. red .. .. 6·00 6·00

1957. Father Luke Wadding (theologian). Death Tercent.
170. 39. 3d. blue.. .. .. 30 25
171. 1s. 3d. lake .. .. 4·00 3·50

40. Tom Clarke (patriot).

41. Mother Mary Aikenhead.

1958. Thomas J. Clarke. Birth Cent.
172. 40. 3d. green 20 20
173. 1s. 3d. brown .. .. 3·50 3·25

1958. Mother Mary Aikenhead (foundress of Irish Sisters of Charity). Death Cent.
174. 41. 3d. blue.. .. .. 40 25
175. 1s. 3d. red .. .. 4·00 3·50

1958. Irish Constitution. 21st Anniv.
176. 15. 3d. brown 25 20
177. 5d. green .. .. 2·00 2·25

42. Arthur Guinness.

43. "The Flight of the Holy Family".

1959. Guinness Brewery. Bicent.
178. 42. 3d. purple 30 25
179. 1s. 3d. blue .. .. 3·50 3·75

1960. World Refugee Year.
180. 43. 3d. purple 10 8
181. 1s. 3d. sepia .. .. 1·10 1·25

1960. Europa. 1st Anniv. As T 279 of Belgium.
182. 6d. brown .. .. 1·25 1·50
183. 1s. 3d. violet .. .. 4·00 4·50

44. Dublin Airport, DH 84 "Dragon" and Boeing 720 Airliner.

45. St. Patrick.

1961. Aer Lingus Airlines. Silver Jubilee.
184. 44. 6d. blue.. .. .. 75 75
185. 1s. 3d. green .. .. 1·25 1·25

1961. St. Patrick. 15th Death Cent.
186. 45. 3d. blue.. .. .. 25 15
187. 8d. purple .. .. 80 1·00
188. 1s. 3d. green .. .. 90 1·10

46. J. O'Donovan and E. O'Curry.

1962. O'Donovan and O'Curry (scholars). Death Cent.
189. 46. 3d. red 25 20
190. 1s. 3d. purple .. .. 1·10 1·25

47. Europa "Tree".

1962. Europa.
191. 47. 6d. red 30 30
192. 1s. 3d. turquoise .. 60 65

48. Campaign Emblem.

1963. Freedom from Hunger.
193. 48. 4d. violet 12 12
194. 1s. 3d. red 65 75

49. "Co-operation".

1963. Europa.
195. 49. 6d. red 50 40
196. 1s. 3d. blue .. .. 1·40 1·50

50. Centenary Emblem.

1963. Red Cross Cent.
197. 50. 4d. red and grey .. 10 5
198. 1s. 3d. red, grey & green 45 45

51. Wolfe Tone.

1964. Wolfe Tone (patriot). Birth Bicent.
199. 51. 4d. black 40 20
200. 1s. 3d. blue .. .. 1·75 2·00

52. Irish Pavilion at Fair.

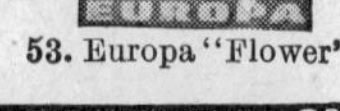

53. Europa "Flower"

55. W. B. Yeats (poet).

54. "Waves of Communications".

1964. New York World's Fair.
201. 52. 5d. multicoloured .. 40 20
202. 1s. 5d. multicoloured .. 1·75 2·00

1964. Europa.
203. 53. 8d. green and blue .. 40 35
204. 1s. 5d. brown and orge. 90 80

1965. I.T.U. Cent.
205. 54. 3d. blue and green .. 35 25
206. 8d. black and green .. 60 60

1965. Yeats' Birth Cent.
207. 55. 5d. black, chestnut and deep green 60 12
208. 1s. 5d. black, grey-green and brown 90 75

56. I.C.Y. Emblem.

1965. Int. Co-operation Year.
209. 56. 3d. blue.. .. .. 60 25
210. 10d. brown .. .. 1·50 2·00

57. Europa "Sprig".

1965. Europa.
211. 57. 8d. black and red .. 35 30
212. 1s. 5d. purple & turq... 90 85

58. James Connolly.  59. Roger Casement (patriot).

1966. Easter Rising. 50th Anniv.
213. 58. 3d. black and blue .. 25 20
214. – 3d. black and bronze .. 25 20
215. – 5d. black and olive .. 25 20
216. – 5d. black, orge. & grn. 25 20
217. – 7d. black and brown .. 55 55
218. – 7d. black and green .. 55 55
219. – 1s. 5d. black & turq. .. 55 50
220. – 1s. 5d. black and green 55 50
DESIGNS: No. 214, Thomas J. Clarke. 215, P. H. Pearse. 216, "Marching to Freedom". 217, Eamonn Ceannt. 218, Sean MacDiarmada. 219, Thomas MacDonagh. 220, Joseph Plunkett.
The two designs in each denomination were issued together in sheets with each pair of designs arranged in horiz. se-tenant rows.

1966. Roger Casement. 50th Death Anniv.
221. 59. 5d. black 20 8
222. 1s. brown 40 35

61. Interior of Abbey (from a lithograph).

60. Europa "Ship".

63. Maple Leaves.  62. Cogwheels.

1966. Europa.
223. 60. 7d. green and orange .. 25 25
224. 1s. 5d. green and grey.. 45 40

1966. Ballintubber Abbey. 750th Anniv.
225. 61. 5d. brown 12 10
226. 1s. black 40 40

1967. Europa.
229. 62. 7d. green, gold & cream 20 20
230. 1s. 5d. red, gold & cream 50 50

1967. Canadian Centennial.
231. 63. 5d. multicoloured .. 20 15
232. 1s. 5d. multicoloured .. 40 40

64. Rock of Cashel (from photo by Edwin Smith).

65. 1 c. Fenian Stamp Essay.

66. Jonathan Swift.  67. Europa Key.

1967. Int. Tourist Year.
233. 64. 7d. sepia 20 20
234. 10d. blue 35 40

1967. Fenian Rising. Cent.
235. 65. 5d. black and green .. 12 8
236. – 1s. black and pink .. 30 30
DESIGN: 1s. 24 c. Fenian Stamp Essay.

1967. Jonathan Swift. 300th Birth Anniv.
237. 66. 3d. black and grey .. 12 8
238. – 1s. 5d. brown and blue.. 30 30
DESIGN: 1s. 5d. Gulliver and Lilliputians.

1968. Europa.
239. 67. 7d. red, gold and brown 15 15
240. 1s. 5d. blue, gold & brn. 25 30

68. St. Mary's Cathedral, Limerick.

1968. St. Mary's Cathedral, Limerick. 800th Anniv.
241. 68. 5d. blue.. .. .. 12 8
242. 10d. green 25 25

69. Countess Markievicz (patriot).  70. James Connolly (patriot).

1968. Countess Markievicz. Birth Cent.
243. 69. 3d. black 10 8
244. 1s. 5d. indigo and blue 30 30

1968. James Connolly. Birth Cent.
245. 70. 6d. brown & chocolate 12 12
246. 1s. green, apple & myrtle 25 25

71. Stylised Dog (brooch).  72. Winged Ox (Symbol of St. Luke).

1968.
247. 71. ½d. orange 10 12
248. 1d. yellow-green .. 5 5
249. 2d. ochre 5 5
250. 3d. blue.. .. .. 12 5
251. 4d. red 12 10
252. 5d. green 20 25
253. 6d. brown 20 12
254. – 7d. brown and yellow 20 30
255. – 8d. chocolate & chestnut 20 30
256. – 9d. blue and green .. 30 45
257. – 10d. chocolate and violet 30 25
258. – 1s. chocolate and brown 30 35
259. – 1s. 9d. black & turquoise 55 60
260. 72. 2s. 6d. multicoloured .. 1·00 50
261. 5s. multicoloured .. 2·50 90
262. – 10s. multicoloured .. 5·00 2·00
DESIGNS—As T 71: 7d., 8d., 9d., 10d., 1s., 1s. 9d. Stag. As T 72: 10s. Eagle (Symbol of St. John The Evangelist).
See also Nos. 287/301.

73. Human Rights Emblem.  74. Dail Eireann Assembly.

1968. Human Rights Year.
263. 73. 5d. yell., gold & black.. 10 10
264. 7d. yellow, gold and red 25 25

1969. Dail Eireann (1st National Parliament). 50th Anniv.
265. 74. 6d. green 8 8
266. 9d. blue.. .. .. 25 25

75. Colonnade.  76. Quadruple I.L.O. Emblems

1969. Europa.
267. 75. 9d. grey, ochre and ultramarine 15 15
268. 1s. 9d. grey, gold and red 35 35

1969. I.L.O. 50th Anniv.
269. 76. 6d. black and grey .. 12 10
270. 9d. black and yellow .. 20 20

77. Evie Hone Window, Eton Chapel.

1969. Contemporary Irish Art (1st issue).
271. 77. 1s. multicoloured .. 30 35
See also Nos. 280, 306, 317, 329, 362, 375 and 398.

78. Mahatma Gandhi.

1969. Mahatma Gandhi. Birth Cent.
272. 78. 6d. black and green .. 12 10
273. 1s. 9d. black and yellow 40 40

79. Symbolic Bird in Tree.

1970. European Conservation Year.
274. 79. 6d. bistre and black .. 12 12
275. 9d. violet and black .. 30 25

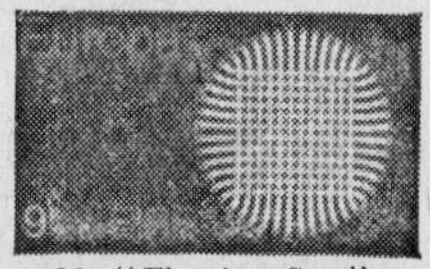

80. "Flaming Sun".

1970. Europa.
276. 80. 6d. violet and silver .. 12 10
277. 9d. brown and silver .. 20 20
278. 1s. 9d. olive-grey & silver 30 30

81. "Sailing Boats" (Peter Monamy).  82. "Madonna of Eire" (Mainie Jellett).

1970. Royal Cork Yacht Club. 250th Anniv.
279. 81. 4d. multicoloured .. 12 12

1970. Contemporary Irish Art (2nd issue).
280. 82. 1s. multicoloured .. 30 25

83. Thomas MacCurtain.  84. Kevin Barry.

1970. 50th Death Annivs. of Irish Patriots.
281. 83. 9d. black, violet & grey 35 35
282. – 9d. black, violet & grey 35 35
283. 83. 2s. 9d. black, blue & grey 1·00 1·00
284. – 2s. 9d. blk., blue & grey 1·00 1·00
DESIGN: Nos. 282 and 284, Terence MacSwiney.

1970. Kevin Barry (patriot). 50th Death Anniv.
285. 84. 6d. green 12 10
286. 1s. 2d. blue 30 30

1971. Decimal Currency. As Nos. 247/62, but with face values in new currency and some colours changed.
287. 71. ½p. green 5 5
288. 1p. blue.. .. .. 25 12
289. 1½p. brown 12 12
290. 2p. myrtle 12 8
291. 2½p. brown 12 8
292. 3p. brown 12 12
293. 3½p. brown 12 25
294. 4p. violet 12 12
295. – 5p. brown & olive .. 40 20
295a. 71. 5p. green .. 45 20
296. – 6p. grey and brown .. 85 25
296a. – 7p. blue and green .. 2·50 30
297. – 7½p. lilac and brown .. 25 20
298. – 9p. black and blue .. 40 25
299. 72. 10p. multicoloured .. 45 25
299a. 12p. multicoloured .. 25 30
300. 20p. multicoloured .. 1·25 45
301. – 50p. multicoloured .. 2·50 1·10
DESIGNS—As T 71: 5p., (No. 295), 6p., 7p, 7½p., 9p. Stag. A T 72: 50p. Eagle (symbol of St. John the Evangelist).

85. Europa Chain.  86. J. M. Synge.

1971. Europa.
302. 85. 4p. brown and yellow .. 12 15
303. 6p. black and blue .. 25 25

1971. J. M. Synge (playwright). Birth Cent.
304. 86. 4p. multicoloured .. 12 12
305. 10p. multicoloured .. 40 40

87. "An Island Man" (Jack B. Yeats). 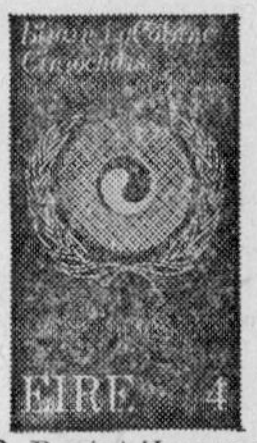 88. Racial Harmony Symbol.

1971. Contemporary Irish Art (3rd issue). J. B. Yeats (artist). Birth Cent.
306. 87. 6p. multicoloured .. 30 30

1971. Racial Equality Year.
307. 88. 4p. red 12 12
308. 10p. black 40 40

89. "Madonna and Child" (statue by J. Hughes). 90. Heart.

1971. Christmas.

309. **89.** 2½p. blk.,gold & green 12 12
310. 6p. blk.,gold and blue 40 40

1972. World Health Day.

311. **90.** 2½p. gold and brown .. 25 12
312. 12p. silver and grey .. 50 45

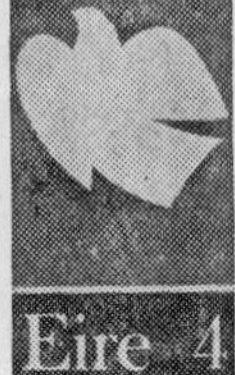

91. "Communications". 92. Dove and Moon.

313. **91.** 4p. orge., blk. & silver.. 25 12
314. 6p. blue, blk. & silver.. 50 45

1972. Patriot Dead 1922-23.

315. **92.** 4p. orge., grey bl. & blue 15 15
316. 6p. yell., grn. & dull grn. 30 30

93. "Black Lake" (Gerard Dillon). 94. "Horseman" (Carved Slab).

1972. Contemporary Irish Art (4th issue).

317. **93.** 3p. multicoloured .. 20 15

1972. Olympic Council of Ireland. 50th Anniv.

318. **94.** 3p. yell., black and gold 12 8
319. 6p. pink, blk. and gold 30 30

95. Madonna and Child (from Book of Kells). 96. 2d. Stamp of 1922.

1972. Christmas.

320. **95.** 2½p. multicoloured .. 12 8
321. 4p. multicoloured .. 30 25
322. 12p. multicoloured .. 50 50

1972. 1st Irish Postage Stamp. 50th Anniv.

323. **96.** 6p. grey and green .. 25 25

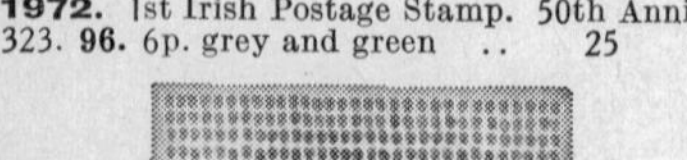

97. Celtic Head Motif.

1973. Entry into European Communities.

325. **97.** 6p. multicoloured .. 30 25
326. 12p. multicoloured .. 45 45

98. Europa "Posthorn".

1973. Europa.

327. **98.** 4p. blue.. .. .. 12 12
328. 6p. black 30 30

99. "Berlin Blues I" (W. Scott).

1973. Contemporary Irish Art (5th issue).

329. **99.** 5p. blue and black .. 25 25

100. Weather Map. 101. Tractor ploughing.

1973. I.M.O./W.M.O. Centenary.

330. **100.** 3½p. multicoloured .. 12 12
331. 12p. multicoloured .. 50 50

1973. World Ploughing Championships, Wellington Bridge.

332. **101.** 5p. multicoloured .. 15 15
333. 7p. multicoloured .. 20 20

102. "Flight into Egypt" (Jan de Cock). 103. Daunt Rock Lightship and Ballycotton Lifeboat, 1936.

1973. Christmas.

334. **102.** 3½p. multicoloured .. 12 12
335. 12p. multicoloured .. 40 40

1974. R.N.L.I. 150th Anniv.

336. **103.** 5p. multicoloured .. 15 15

104. "Edmund Burke" (Statue by J. H. Foley). 105. "Oliver Goldsmith" (Statue by J. H. Foley).

1974. Europa.

337. **104.** 5p. black and blue .. 15 15
338. 7p. black and green .. 20 20

1974. Oliver Goldsmith (writer). Birth Bicent.

360. **105.** 3½ p. black and yellow 12 12
361. 12p. black and green 35 30

106. "Kitchen Table" (Norah McGuiness). 107. Rugby Players.

1974. Contemporary Irish Art (6th issue).

362. **106.** 5p. multicoloured .. 15 15

1974. Irish Rugby Football. Centenary.

363. **107.** 3½p. green 12 12
364. 12p. multicoloured .. 30 35

108. U.P.U. "Postmark". 109. "Madonna and Child" (Bellini).

1974. Universal Postal Union. Cent.

365. **108.** 5p. green and black .. 12 15
366. 7p. blue and black .. 20 20

1974. Christmas.

367. **109.** 5p. multicoloured .. 10 12
368. 15p. multicoloured .. 35 40

110. "Peace".

1975. International Women's Year.

369. **110.** 8 p. purple and blue .. 25 25
370. 15 p. blue and green 40 40

111. "Castledown Hunt" (R. Healy).

1975. Europa.

371. **111.** 7 p. grey 20 20
372. 9 p. green 25 25

112. Putting.

1975. Ninth European Amateur Golf Team Championship, Killarney.

373. **112.** 6 p. multicoloured .. 15 15
374. – 9 p. multicoloured .. 25 25

No. 374 is similar to T **112** but shows a different view of the putting green.

113. "Bird of Prey" (sculpture by Oisin Kelly).

1975. Contemporary Irish Art (7th issue).

375. **113.** 15 p. brown 40 40

114. Nano Nagle (founder) and Waifs. 115. Tower of St. Annes Church, Shandon.

1975. Presentation Order of Nuns. Bicent.

376. **114.** 5 p. black and blue .. 12 12
377. 7 p. black and brown 20 20

1975. European Architectural Heritage Year.

378. **115.** 5 p. brown 12 12
379. 6 p. multicoloured .. 15 15
380. – 7 p. blue 20 20
381. – 9 p. multicoloured .. 25 25

DESIGN: Nos. 380/1, Interior of Holycross Abbey, Co. Tipperary.

116. St. Oliver Plunkett (commemorative medal by Imogen Stuart). 117. "Madonna and Child" (Fra Filippo Lippi).

1975. Oliver Plunkett. Canonisation.

382. **116.** 7 p. black 20 20
383. 15 p. brown 40 40

1975. Christmas.

384. **117.** 5 p. multicoloured .. 12 12
385. 7 p. multicoloured .. 20 20
386. 10 p. multicoloured .. 25 25

118. James Larkin (from a drawing by Sean O'Sullivan). 119. Alexander Graham Bell.

1975. James Larkin (Trade Union Leader). Birth Cent.

387. **118.** 7 p. green and grey .. 20 20
388. 11p. brown and yellow 25 25

1976. First Telephone Transmission. Cent.

389. **119.** 9p. multicoloured .. 20 20
390. 15 p. multicoloured .. 30 35

120. Thirteen Stars.

1976. American Revolution. Bicent.

391. **120.** 7d. blue, red and silver 15 15
392. – 8d. blue, red and silver 15 20
393. – 9p. blue, oran. & silver 20 20
394. – 15p. red, grey & silver 30 35

DESIGNS: 8p. Fifty stars. 9 and 15p. 1847 Benjamin Franklin Essay.

121. Spirit Barrel.

1976. Europa. Irish Delft. Multicoloured.

396. 9p. Type **121** 20 20
397. 11p. Dish 25 25

122. "The Lobster Pots, West of Ireland" (Paul Henry).

1976. Contemporary Irish Art (8th issue).

398. **122.** 15p. multicoloured .. 30 35

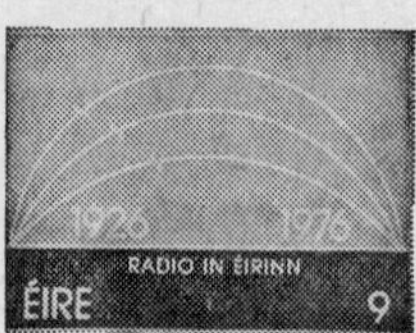

123. Radio Waves.

1976. Irish Broadcasting Service. 50th Anniv.

399. **123.** 9p. blue and green .. 20 20
400. – 11p. brn., red and blue 25 25

DESIGN: 11p. Transmitter, radio waves and globe.

124. "The Nativity" (Lorenzo Monaco).

1976. Christmas.

401. **124.** 7p. multicoloured .. 15 15
402. 9p. multicoloured .. 20 20
403. 15p. multicoloured .. 30 35

POSTAGE DUE STAMPS

D 1.

1925.

D 1.	D 1.	½d. green	4·00	5·00
D 6.		1d. red	40	50
D 7.		1½d. vermilion	50	90
D 8.		2d. green	40	50
D 9.		3d. blue	50	60
D 10.		5d. violet	50	60
D 11a.		6d. plum	55	70
D 12.		8d. orange	2·25	2·50
D 13.		10d. purple	2·00	3·00
D 14.		1s. green	5·00	5·00

1971. Decimal Currency. Colours changed.

D 15.	D 1.	1p. brown	5	5
D 16.		1½p. green	5	5
D 17.		3p. stone	10	12
D 18.		4p. orange	12	12
D 19.		5p. blue	12	12
D 20.		7p. yellow	20	20
D 21.		8p. red.	20	20

ISRAEL O2

The former British Mandate over Palestine was ended by the partition plan approved by the United Nations General Assembly on 29th November, 1947, and on 14th May, 1948, the new state of Israel was proclaimed.

1948, 1000 prutot (mils) = 1 Israeli pound.
1960, 1000 agorot = 1 Israeli pound.

"TABS". All Israeli stamps (except the Postage Dues) exist with descriptive sheet margin attached. These so-called "Tabs" are popular and in some cases scarce.
Prices to No. 97 are for stamps without "tab", but for nearly all stamps from No. 98 onwards our prices are for stamps with or without "tab". Separate prices for the earlier stamps with "tabs" are given in our Overseas Catalogue, Volume 2

1. Ancient Jewish Coins. 2.

1948. Ancient Jewish Coins. Perf. or roul.

1.	1.	3 m. orange	20	12
2.		5 m. green	20	5
3.		10 m. mauve	25	20
4.		15 m. red	30	8
5.		20 m. blue	80	8
6.		50 m. brown	6·00	15
7.	2.	250 m. green	18·00	15·00
8.		500 m. red on buff	£120	55·00
9.	–	1000 m. blue on blue	£225	£120

The 1000 m. is as T 2, but larger.
See also Nos. 21/6, 41/52 and 90/3.

3. "Flying Scroll" Emblem.

1948. Jewish New Year.

10.	3.	3 m. brown and blue	20	15
11.		5 m. green and blue	25	15
12.		10 m. claret and blue	35	20
13.		20 m. blue	75	35
14.		65 m. brown and red	9·00	3·50

4. Road to Jerusalem. 5. National Flag.

1949. Constituent Assembly. Inaug.

15.	4.	250 pr. brown and grey	80	60

1949. Adoption of New National Flag.

16.	5.	20 pr. blue	80	30

6. Petah-Tikva Well. 7. Air Force Badge.

1949. Founding of Petah-Tikva. 70th Anniv.

17.	6.	40 pr. brown and green	4·00	40

1949. Jewish New Year.

18.	7.	5 pr. blue	30	8
19.	–	10 pr. green	60	8
20.	–	35 pr. brown	5·00	1·25

BADGES: 10 pr. Navy. 35 pr. Army.

8. Ancient Jewish Coin. 9. Stag and Globe.

1949. Coin designs as T 3a.

(a) Inscr. as left is 9 mm. long.

21.	8.	3 pr. grey	20	15
22.		5 pr. violet	10	5
23.		10 pr. green	10	5
24.		15 pr. red	15	5
25.		30 pr. blue	15	10
26.		50 pr. brown	1·00	15

(b) Longer inscr. as left as in T 3a (11 mm.).

41.	8.	3 pr. grey	8	5
42.		5 pr. violet	5	5
43.		10 pr. green	5	5
44.		15 pr. red	5	5
45.		20 pr. orange	5	5
46.		30 pr. blue	5	5
47.		35 pr. olive	8	5
48.		40 pr. chestnut	8	5
49.		45 pr. purple	8	5
50.		50 pr. brown	8	5
51.		60 pr. red	8	5
90.		80 pr. bistre	8	5
52.		85 pr. blue	25	10
91.		95 pr. green	10	10
92.		100 pr. brown	8	5
93.		125 pr. blue	15	8

The 80, 95, 100 and 125 pr. have the value at foot on right.

1950. U.P.U. 75th Anniv.

27.	9.	40 pr. violet	60	45
28.		80 pr. red	1·00	70

10. Landing of Immigrants.

1950. Independence. 2nd Anniv.

29.	10.	20 pr. brown	1·00	60
30.	–	40 pr. green	4·00	2·00

DESIGN: 40 pr. Line of immigrant ships.

11. Library and Book. 12. Doves Pecking Grapes.

1950. Jerusalem University. 25th Anniv.

31.	11.	100 pr. green	35	15

1950. Air.

32.	12.	5 pr. blue	25	20
33.	–	30 pr. grey	12	12
34.	–	40 pr. green	20	12
35.	–	50 pr. brown	15	12
36.	–	100 pr. red	10·00	8·00
37.	–	250 pr. blue	1·10	60

DESIGNS—VERT. 30 pr. Eagle. 40 pr. Ostrich. 50 pr. Dove. HORIZ. 100 pr. Eagle. 250 pr. Dove with olive branch.

13. Star of David and Fruit. 14. Runner and Track.

1950. Jewish New Year.

38.	13.	5 pr. violet and orange	15	10
39.		15 pr. brown and green	60	30

1950. 3rd Maccabiah (sports meeting).

40.	14.	80 pr. black and olive	1·75	1·60

15. "The Negev" (after R. Rubin).

1950. Opening of Post Office at Elat.

53.	15.	500 pr. brown & orange	4·50	4·00

15a. Memorial Tablet.

1951. Tel Aviv. 40th Anniv.

54.	15a.	40 pr. brown	55	25

16. "Supporting Israel". 17. Metsudat Yesha.

1951. Independence Bonds Campaign.

55.	16.	80 pr. brown	20	15

1951. State of Israel. 3rd Anniv.

56.	17.	15 pr. brown	25	10
57.	–	40 pr. blue (Hakastel)	70	35

18. Tractor. 19. Ploughing and Savings Stamp.

1951. Jewish National Fund. 50th Anniv.

58.	18.	15 pr. brown	8	8
59.	–	25 pr. green	20	20
60.	19.	80 pr. blue	85	75

DESIGN—As T 18: 25 pr. Stylised tree.

20. Dr. T. Herzl. 21. Carrier Pigeons.

1951. 23rd Zionist Congress.

61.	20.	80 pr. green	15	15

1951. Jewish New Year. As T 21.

62.	21.	5 pr. blue	8	5
63.	–	15 pr. red	10	8
64.	–	40 pr. violet	20	15

DESIGNS: 15 pr. Woman and dove. 40 pr. Scroll of the Law.

21a. Menora and Emblems.

1952.

64a.	21a.	1000 pr. blk. and blue	7·50	3·50

21b. Haifa Bay, Mt. Carmel and City Seal.

1952. Air. National Stamp Exn. ("TABA").

64b.	–	100 pr. blue & blk.	40	40
64c.	21b.	120 pr. pur.& blk.	45	45

DESIGN: 100 pr. Haifa Bay and City Seal.

The above were sold at the Exhibition at 340 pr. incl. entrance fee.

22. Thistle and Yad Mordecai.

1952. Independence. 4th Anniv.

65.	22.	30 pr. brown & magenta	10	8
66.	–	60 pr. slate and blue	15	12
67.	–	110 pr. brown and red	45	35

DESIGNS: 60 pr. Cornflower and Degania. 110 pr. Anemone and Safed.

23. New York Skyline and Z.O.A. Building. 24. Figs.

1952. Opening of American Zionist Building, Tel Aviv.

68.	23.	220 pr. grey and blue	65	60

1952. Jewish New Year.

69.	24.	15 pr. yellow and green	10	8
70.	–	40 pr. yell., blue & violet	20	15
71.	–	110 pr. grey and red	40	30
72.	–	220 pr. grn., brn. & orge.	60	55

FLOWERS: 40 pr. Lily ("Rose of Sharon"). 110 pr. Dove. 220 pr Nuts.

25. Dr. F. Weizmann.

1952. Death of First President of Israel.

73.	25.	30 pr. indigo	8	8
74.		110 pr. black	40	40

26. 27. Aeroplane over Tel Aviv-Jaffa.

1952. 70th Anniv. of B.I.L.U. Immigration.

75.	26.	110 pr. buff, green & brn.	20	20

1953. Air.

76.	–	10 pr. olive	10	5
77.	–	70 pr. violet	12	12
78.	–	100 pr. green	10	5
79.	–	150 pr. brown	12	10
80.	–	350 pr. red	20	20
81.	–	500 pr. blue	30	20
81a.	–	750 pr. brown	35	20
82.	27.	1000 pr. blue-green	1·75	1·50
82a.	–	3000 pr. purple	90	45

DESIGNS—HORIZ. 10 pr. Olive tree. 70 pr. Sea of Galilee. 100 pr. Shaar Hogay on road to Jerusalem. 150 pr. Lion Rock, Negev. 350 pr. Bay of Elat. VERT. 500 pr. Tanour Falls, near Metoulla. 750 pr. Lake Hula. 3000 pr. Tomb of Meir Baal Haness.

28. Anemones and Arms. 29. Maimonides (philosopher).

1953. Independence. 5th Anniv.

83.	28.	110 pr. red and blue	25	25

1953. 7th Int. Congress of History of Science.

84.	29.	110 pr. brown	12	12

30. Holy Ark, Petah-Tikva. **31.**

1953. Jewish New Year.

85. – 20 pr. blue 5 5
86. **30.** 45 pr. red 10 5
87. – 200 pr. violet 20 15

DESIGNS: 20 pr. Holy Ark, Jerusalem. 200 pr. Holy Ark, Safed.

1953. 4th Maccabiah.

88. **31.** 110 pr. brown and blue.. 20 20

32. Exhibition Emblem. **33.** Gesher and Narcissus.

1953. "Conquest of the Desert" Exhibition.

89. **32.** 200 pr. multicoloured .. 25 25

1954. Independence. 6th Anniv.

94. – 60 pr. blue, red & grey .. 10 10
95. **33.** 350 pr. brown, yell. & grn. 25 25

DESIGN: 60 pr. Yehiam and helichrysum.

34. Dr. T. Z. Herzl.

1954. Herzl (founder of World Zionist Movement). 50th Death Anniv.

96. **34.** 160 pr. sepia, buff & blue 12 10

35.

1954. Jewish New Year.

97. **35.** 25 pr. sepia 8 8

DESIGN: 200 pr. Mail van and G.P.O., 1954.

36. 19th Century Mail-coach and P.O.

1954. National Stamp Exhibition.

98. **36.** 60 pr. black, yell. & blue 8 8
99. – 200 pr. grey, red & green 20 15

37. Baron Edmond de Rothschild (financier).

1954. De Rothschild. 20th Death Anniv.

100. **37.** 300 pr. turquoise .. 25 15

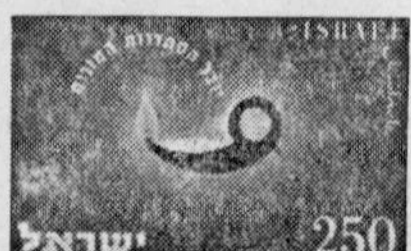

38. Lamp of Knowledge.

1955. Teachers' Association. 50th Anniv.

101. **38.** 250 pr. blue 15 12

39. Parachutist and Barbed Wire. **40.** Menora and Olive Branches.

1955. Jewish Mobilisation during 2nd World War.

102. **39.** 120 pr. black & turquoise 12 10

1955. Independence. 7th Anniv.

103. **40.** 150 pr. orge., blk. & grn. 12 10

41. Immigrants and Ship. **42.** Musicians playing Timbrel and Cymbals.

1955. Youth Immigration Scheme. 20th Anniv.

104. **41.** 5 pr. black and blue .. 5 5
105. – 10 pr. black and red .. 5 5
106. – 25 pr. black and green.. 5 5
107. – 30 pr. black and orange 5 5
108. – 60 pr. black and violet.. 10 10
109. – 750 pr. black and bistre 40 35

DESIGNS: 10 pr. Immigrants and aeroplane. 25 pr. Boy and calf. 30 pr. Girl watering flowers. 60 pr. Boy making pottery. 750 pr. Boy using theodolite.

1955. Jewish New Year.

110. **42.** 25 pr. green and orange 5 5
111. – 60 pr. grey and red .. 5 5
112. – 120 pr. blue and yellow 8 8
113. – 250 pr. chocolate and red 15 15

DESIGNS: Musicians playing: 60 pr. Ram's horn. 120 pr. Tuba. 250 pr. Harp.

43. Ambulance. **44.** "Reuben"

1955. Magen David Adom (Jewish Red Cross.) 25th Anniv.

114. **43.** 160 pr. green, black & red 10 10

1955. Emblems of the Twelve Tribes of Israel.

115. **44.** 10 pr. green 5 5
116. – 20 pr. mauve 5 5
117. – 30 pr. blue 5 5
118. – 40 pr. brown 5 5
119. – 50 pr. blue 5 5
120. – 60 pr. bistre 5 5
121. – 80 pr. violet 5 5
122. – 100 pr. red 5 5
123. – 120 pr. olive 5 5
124. – 180 pr. magenta .. 10 5
125. – 200 pr. green 12 5
126. – 250 pr. grey 15 5

EMBLEMS: 20 pr. "Simeon" (castle), 30 pr. "Levi" (studded plaque), 40 pr. "Judah" (lion), 50 pr. "Dan" (scales), 60 pr. "Naphtali" (gazelle), 80 pr. "Gad" (tents), 100 pr. "Asher" (tree), 120 pr. "Issachar" (sun and stars), 180 pr. "Zebulun" (ship), 200 pr. "Joseph" (sheaf of wheat), 250 pr. "Benjamin" (wolf).

45. Professor Einstein.

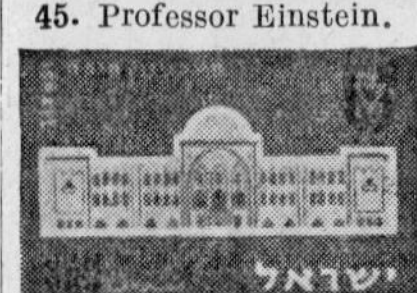

46. Technion. **47.** "Eight Years of Independence".

1956. Einstein Commem.

127. **45.** 350 pr. brown .. 30 25

1956. Israel Institute of Technology, Haifa. 30th Anniv.

128. **46.** 350 pr. green and black 25 15

1956. Independence. 8th Anniv.

129. **47.** 150 pr. brown, blue, yellow & green .. 8 8

48. Oranges. **49.** Musician playing Lyre. **50.** Insignia of "Hagana".

1956. 4th Int. Congress of Mediterranean Citrus Fruit Growers.

130. **48.** 300 pr. orange and green 15 12

1956. Jewish New Year. Musicians playing instruments.

131. **49.** 30 pr. brown and blue.. 5 5
132. – 50 pr. violet and orange 8 8
133. – 150 pr. turquoise & orge. 10 10

INSTRUMENTS—VERT. 50 pr. Sistrum. HORIZ. 150 pr. Double oboe.

1957. Defence Fund.

134. **50.** 80 pr.+20 pr. green .. 5 5
135. 150 pr.+50 pr. red .. 10 5
136. 350 pr.+50 pr. blue .. 15 12

51. 'Plane Sky-writing Figure "9". **52.** Bezalel Museum and Candelabrum.

1957. Independence. 9th Anniv.

137. **51.** 250 pr. black and blue.. 12 10

1957. Bezale Museum, Jerusalem. 50th Anniv.

138. **52.** 400 pr. red, lemon, black and grey 15 5

53. Horse and Seal of Tamach. **54.** Throwing the Hammer.

1957. Jewish New Year. Ancient Hebrew Seals.

139. **53.** 50 pr. blk. & brn. on blue 5 5
140. – 160 pr. blk. & grn. on buff 8 5
141. – 300 pr. blk. & red on pink 12 5

DESIGNS: 160 pr. Lion and seal of Shema. 300 pr. Gazelle and seal of Netanyahuv Ne'avadyahu.

1958. Maccabiah Games. 25th Anniv.

142. **54.** 500 pr. red and bistre.. 20 15

55. Ancient Ship.

57. Dancing Children forming "10". **56.** Menora and Olive-branch with ten Leaves.

1958. Israel Merchant Marine Commem.

143. **55.** 10 pr. red blue green and ochre 5 5
144. – 20 pr. brown & emerald 5 5
145. – 30 pr. turquoise & red.. 5 5
146. – 1000 pr. green and blue 40 30

DESIGNS: 20 pr. Immigration ship. 30 pr. Freighter "Shomron". 1000 pr. (57×22½ mm.): Liner "Zion".

1958. Independence. 10th Anniv.

147. **56.** 400 pr. grn. blk. & gold 15 12

1958. 1st World Conf. of Jewish Youth, Jerusalem.

148. **57.** 200 pr. myrtle and chest. 10 8

58. Convention Centre, Jerusalem, and Exhibition Emblem.

1958. 10th Anniv. (of Israel) Exn., Jerusalem.

149. **58.** 400 pr. orange and lilac on cream 15 12

59. Wheat. **60.** Ancient Stone.

61. Post Office Emblem. **62.** Sholem Aleichem (writer).

1958. Jewish New Year.

150. **59.** 50 pr. brown & ochre.. 5 5
151. – 60 pr. black and yellow 5 5
152. – 160 pr. purple & violet 8 5
153. – 300 pr. green and apple 12 10

DESIGNS: 60 pr. Barley. 160 pr. Grapes. 300 pr. Figs.

See also Nos. 166/8.

1958. Declaration of Human Rights. 10th Anniv.

154. **60.** 750 pr. blk., yell. & blue 40 35

1959. Israel Postal Services. 10th Anniv.

155. **61.** 60 pr. blk., red & olive 5 5
156. – 120 pr. blk., red & olive 8 8
157. – 250 pr. blk., red & olive 15 15
158. – 500 pr. blk., red & olive 30 25

DESIGNS—HORIZ. 120 pr. Mail van. VERT. 250 pr. Radio-telephone equipment. 500 pr. "Telex" dial and keyboard.

1959. Sholem Aleichem. Birth Cent.

159. **62.** 250 pr. brown and green 12 10

63. Tel Aviv. **64.** Anemone.

1959. Tel Aviv. 50th Anniv.

160. **63.** 120 pr. multicoloured.. 8 8

1959. Independence. 11th Anniv. Flowers.

161. **64.** 60 pr. red black yellow-green and green .. 5 5
162. – 120 pr. red, brown, green and purple .. 8 8
163. – 300 pr. yellow, green, drab and blue .. 25 15

FLOWERS: 120 pr. Cyclamen. 300 pr. Narcissus.

See also Nos. 188/9, 211/3 and 257/9.

65. C. N. Bialik. **66.** Israeli Airliner and Wind-sock.

1959. Chaim N. Bialik (poet). 25th Death Anniv.
164. **65.** 250 pr. olive and orange 15 12

1959. Civil Aviation in Israel. 10th Anniv.
165. **66.** 500 pr. blue, indigo, yellow and grey .. 25 15

1959. Jewish New Year. As T **59.**
166. 60 pr. red and chocolate.. 8 5
167. 200 pr. yellow and olive.. 12 8
168. 350 pr. orange and sepia.. 30 25
DESIGNS: 60 pr. Pomegranates. 200 pr. Olives. 350 pr. Dates.

67. E. Ben-Yehuda. **68.** Merhavya Settlement.

1959. Eliezer Ben-Yehuda (pioneer of Hebrew language). Birth Cent.
169. **67.** 250 pr. indigo and blue 20 15

1959. 50th Anniv. of Merhavya and Deganya Settlements and 75th Anniv. of Yesud Ha-maala Settlement.
170. **68.** 60 pr. green and olive.. 8 5
171. – 120 pr. brn. & yell.-brn. 12 8
172. – 180 pr. green and blue.. 20 15
DESIGNS: 120 pr. Yesud Ha-Maala, 180 pr. Deganya.

69. Ancient Jewish Coin. **70.** Tiberias.

1960. New currency. Values in black.
173. **69.** 1 a. bistre on pink .. 5 5
174. 3 a. red on pink .. 5 5
175. 5 a. slate on pink .. 5 5
176. 6 a. green on blue .. 5 5
176a. 7 a. grey on blue .. 5 5
177. 8 a. magenta on blue .. 5 5
178. 12 a. blue on blue .. 5 5
179. 18 a. orange 10 10
180. 25 a. blue 12 5
181. 30 a. red 15 5
182. 50 a. lilac 30 12

1960. Air.
183. – 15 a. black and lilac.. 10 5
184. – 20 a. black and green 12 5
184a. – 25 a. black and orange 15 10
184b. – 30 a. black & turquoise 25 20
184c. – 35 a. black and green 50 35
184d. – 40 a. black and lilac 40 45
184e. – 50 a. black and olive 35 25
185. **70.** 65 a. black and blue 45 30
185a. – I£1 black and pink .. 75 65
DESIGNS—VERT. 15 a. Old town, Zefat. 20 a. Tower, Ashqelon. 25 a. Akko Tower and boats. 30 a. View of Haifa from Mt. Carmel. HORIZ. 35 a. Ancient synagogue, Capernaum. 40 a. Kefar Hittim—Tomb of Jethro. 50 a. City walls, Jerusalem. I£1, Old city, Jaffa.

71. Operation "Magic Carpet".

1960. World Refugee Year.
186. **71.** 25 a. chestnut 12 10
187. – 50 a. green 25 20
DESIGN: 50 a. Resettled family.

1960. Independence. 12th Anniv. Flowers as T **64.**
188. 12 a. yell., grey, grn. & blue 10 5
189. 32 a. yell., grey, grn. & brown 25 12
FLOWERS: 12 a. "Pancratium maritimum". 32 a. "Oenothera drummondi".

72. Atomic Symbol and Reactor Building.

73. King Saul.

1960. Inaug. of Atomic Reactor.
190. **72.** 50 a. red, black and blue 25 25

1960. Jewish New Year. Centres multicoloured.
191. **73.** 7 a. green 5 5
192. – 25 a. brown 12 8
193. – 40 a. blue 45 35
DESIGNS: 25 a. King David. 40 a. King Solomon.

74. Dr. Theodor Herzl. **75.** Postal Courier, Prague, 1741.

1960. Dr. Theodor Herzl (founder of World Zionist Movement). Birth Cent.
194. **74.** 25 a. sepia and cream.. 15 15

1960. National Stamp Exhibition ("TAVIV"), Tel Aviv.
195. **75.** 25 a. blk. & olive-grey 40 35

76. Henrietta Szold.

1960. Henrietta Szold (founder of Youth Immigration Scheme). Birth Cent.
196. **76.** 25 a. violet and blue .. 15 12

77. Badges of First Zionist Congress, and Jerusalem. **78.** Ram (Aries).

79. The Twelve Signs.

DESIGNS—As T **78**: 2 a. Bull (Taurus). 6 a. Twins (Gemini). 7 a. Crab (Cancer). 8 a. Lion (Leo). 10 a. Virgin (Virgo). 12 a. Scales (Libra). 18 a. Scorpion (Scorpio). 20 a. Archer (Sagittarius). 25 a. Goat (Capricorn). 32 a. Water-man (Aquarius). 50 a. Fishes (Pisces).

1960. 25th Zionist Congress, Jerusalem.
197. **77.** 50 a. light and deep blue 30 20

1961. Signs of the Zodiac.
198. **78.** 1 a. emerald 5 5
199. – 2 a. red 5 5
200. – 6 a. blue 5 5
201. – 7 a. brown 5 5
202. – 8 a. myrtle 5 5
203. – 10 a. orange 5 5
204. – 12 a. violet 5 10
205. – 18 a. magenta 10 12
206. – 20 a. olive 12 5
207. – 25 a. purple 12 5
208. – 32 a. black 20 5
209. – 50 a. turquoise.. .. 60 5
210. **79.** I£1 blue, gold & indigo 1·25 40

1961. Independence. 13th Anniv. Flowers as T **64.**
211. 7 a. yellow, brown & green 5 5
212. 12 a. green, purple & mag. 8 5
213. 32 a. red, green and blue.. 35 25
FLOWERS: 7 a. Myrtle. 12 a. Squill. 32 a. Oleander.

80. Figure "7" and Javelin Thrower.

81. "A Decade of Israel Bonds".

82. Samson. **83.** Bet Hamidrash (synagogue), Medzibozh (Russia).

1961. 7th "Hapoel" Sports Association Int. Congress, Ramat Gan.
214. **80.** 25 a. multicoloured .. 25 20

1961. Israel Bond Issue. 10th Anniv.
215. **81.** 50 a. blue 25 20

1961. Jewish New Year. Heroes of Israel. Centres multicoloured.
216. **82.** 7 a. orange-red .. 5 5
217. – 25 a. slate-purple .. 15 10
218. – 40 a. mauve 40 35
HEROES: 25 a. Yehuda Maccabi. 40 a. Bar Kochba.

1961. Rabbi Baal Shem Tov (founder of Hassidism movement). Death Bicent.
219. **83.** 25 a. sepia and yellow.. 20 15

84. Fir Cone.

85. Musical Instruments.

1961. Afforestation.
220. **84.** 25 a. yellow, black & grn. 12 8
221. – 30 a. multicoloured .. 35 25
DESIGN: 30 a. Symbols of afforestation.

1961. Israel Philharmonic Orchestra. 25th Anniv.
222. **85.** 50 a. multicoloured .. 45 40
(Currency revaluation. I£3 new = I£1.80 old.)

86. Bay of Elat.

1962. Air.
A 223. **86.** I£3 multicoloured .. 3·00 2·00

1962. As Nos. 198, 201 and 208 but colours changed and surch.
224. **78.** 3 a. on 1 a. mauve .. 5 5
225. – 5 a. on 7 a. grey .. 5 5
226. – 30 a. on 32 a. green .. 15 10

87. Symbolic Flame ("Shema Yisrael").

88. Vautour Fighter-bomber.

1962. Heroes and Martyrs Day.
227. **87.** 12 a. yellow, red & black 10 8
228. – 55 a. yell., red, bl. & blk. 55 45
DESIGN: 55 a. Nazi "Yellow Star" (worn by Jews under German domination) and six candles ("Six million perished").

1962. Independence. 14th Anniv.
229. **88.** 12 a. blue 10 10
230. – 30 a. green 30 20
DESIGN: 30 a. Flight of Vautour fighter-bombers.

89. Mosquito and Malaria Graph.

90. Rosh Pinna.

1962. Malaria Eradication.
231. **89.** 25 a. bistre, red & black 15 12

1962. Rosh Pinna. 80th Anniv.
232. **90.** 20 a. green and yellow.. 15 12

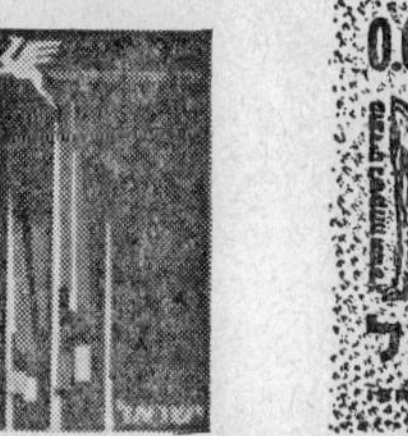
91. Fair Flags. **92.** "And the wolf shall dwell with the lamb . . .".

1962. Near East Int. Fair, Tel Aviv.
233. **91.** 55 a. multicoloured .. 30 30

1962 Jewish New Year. Illustrating quotations from the Book of Isaiah.
234. **92.** 8 a. black, red and olive 10 8
235. – 28 a. black, purple & olive 20 15
236. – 43 a. black, orge. & olive 50 30
DESIGNS: 28 a. "And the leopard shall lie down with the kid . . .". 43 a. "And the suckling child shall play on the hole of the asp . . .".

93. Boeing 707 Jetliner.

1962. El Al Airline Commem.
237. **93.** 55 a. indigo, lilac & blue 40 40

94. Pennant Coralfish.

1962. Red Sea Fish. (1st Series). Mult.
238. 3 a. Type **94** 5 5
239. 6 a. Butterfly Fish .. 8 5
240. 8 a. Scorpion Fish .. 10 8
241. 12 a. Imperial Angelfish .. 12 10
See also Nos. 265/8.

95. Symbolic Cogwheels.

1962. United Jewish Appeal. 25th Anniv.
242. **95.** 20 a. blue, silver and red 25 20

96. J. Korczak (child educator).

97. Houbara Bustard.

1962. Janusz Korczak Commem.
243. **96.** 30 a. sepia and olive .. 25 20

1963. Air Birds. Multicoloured.
244. 5 a. Sinai rosefinch .. 8 5
245. 20 a. White-throated kingfisher 12 10
246. 28 a. Pied wheatear .. 20 15
247. 30 a. Blue-cheeked bee-eater 15 10
248. 40 a. Graceful warbler .. 20 15
249. 45 a. Sunbird 25 20
250. 55 a. Type **97** 25 20
251. 70 a. Scops owl 30 25
252. I£1 Purple heron 45 30
253. I£3 White-tailed eagle .. 1·25 60
Nos. 244/6 are horiz.

98. Bird in the Hand.

1963. Freedom from Hunger.
254. 98. 55 a. grey and black .. 30 30

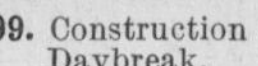
99. Construction at Daybreak.

100. Compositor.

1963. Stockade and Tower Settlements. 25th Anniv.
255. 99. 12 a. brown, blk. & yell. 10 8
256. – 30 a. purple, blk. & blue 30 25
DESIGN: 30 a. Settlement at night.

1963. Independence. 15th Anniv. As T 64.
257. 8 a. green, yell., brn. & slate 12 10
258. 30 a. yellow, rose and pink 45 20
259. 37 a. yellow, red, green and dull purple 70 30
FLOWERS: 8 a. White lily. 30 a. Bristly hollyhock. 37 a. Sharon tulip.

1963. Hebrew Press Cent.
260. 100. 12 a. maroon and buff 30 25
No. 260 comes in sheets of 16 (4×4) with overall background of replica of front page of first issue of Hebrew newspaper "Halbanon".

101. "And the sun beat upon the head of Jonah . . ."

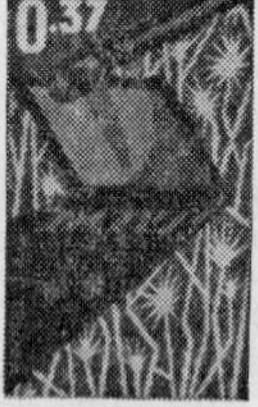
102. Hoe clearing Thistles.

1963. Jewish New Year. Illustrating quotations from the Book of Jonah. Multicoloured.
261. 8 a. Type 101 .. .. 10 10
262. 30 a. "And there was a mighty tempest in the sea" .. 30 25
263. 55 a. "And Jonah was in the belly of the fish" .. 50 45
Nos. 262/3 are horiz.

1963. Israeli Agricultural Settlements. 80th Anniv.
264. 102. 37 a. multicoloured .. 20 15

1963. Red Sea Fish (2nd Series). As T 94. Multicoloured.
265. 2 a. Undulate triggerfish 5 5
266. 6 a. Scorpion fish .. 5 5
267. 8 a. Scad 15 12
268. 12 a. Imperial angelfish .. 20 15

103. S.S. "Shalom".

1963. Maiden Voyage of S.S. "Shalom".
269. 103. I£1 blue, turq. & purple 1·75 1·50

104. "Old Age and Survivors . . ."

105. Pres. Ben-Zvi.

1964. National Insurance. 10th Anniv. Multicoloured.
270. 12 a. Type 104 .. .. 8 8
271. 25 a. Nurse and child within hands ("Maternity") 15 12
272. 37 a. Family within hand ("Large families") .. 30 25
273. 50 a. Hand with arm and crutch ("Employment injuries") 60 50

1964. President Ben-Zvi. 1st Death Anniv.
274. 105. 12 a. brown 15 12

106. "Terrestrial Spectroscopy".

107. Running.

1964. Independence. 16th Anniv. Israel's Contribution to Science. Multicoloured.
275. 8 a. Type 106 .. .. 10 8
276. 35 a. Macromolecules of living cell 20 15
277. 70 a. Electronic computer 30 25

1964. Olympic Games, Tokyo.
278. 107. 8 a. black and red .. 10 8
279. – 12 a. black and mauve 10 8
280. – 30 a. red, black & blue 20 15
281. – 50 a. red, maroon & grn. 30 20
DESIGNS: 12 a. Throwing the discus. 30 a. Basketball. 50 a. Football.

108. 3rd Century Glass Vessel.

109. Congress Emblem.

1964. Jewish New Year. Showing glass vessels in Haaretz Museum, Tel Aviv. Multicoloured.
282. 8 a. Type 108 .. .. 10 5
283. 35 a. 1st-2nd century vessel 20 15
284. 70 a. 1st century vessel .. 35 25

1964. 6th Israel Medical Assn's. World Congress.
285. 109. I£1 multicoloured .. 45 40

110. Immigrant Ship.

111. Eleanor Roosevelt.

1964. "Year of the Blockade-Runners".
286. 110. 25 a. blk., blue & turq. 15 12

1964. Eleanor Roosevelt Commem.
287. 111. 70 a. slate-purple .. 35 30

112. Olympics Symbols and Knight.

1964. 16th Chess Olympics.
288. 112. 12 a. brown 12 10
289. – 70 a. green 60 40
DESIGN: 70 a. Olympics symbol and rook.

113. African-Israeli Friendship".

114. Masada.

1964. "TABAI" National Stamp Exn., Haifa.
290. 113. 57 a. multicoloured .. 1·00 60

1965. Masada Commem.
291. 114. 25 a. green 20 15
292. – 36 a. blue 25 20
293. – I£1 brown 65 40
DESIGNS—HORIZ. 36 a. "Northern Palace", lower section. VERT. I£1, "Northern Palace" aerial view.

115. Ashdod.

116. Fair Emblem.

1965. Civic Arms. (1st series).
294. – 1 a. brown (Lod) .. 5 5
295. – 2 a. magenta (Qiryat Shmona) 5 5
296. – 5 a. black (Petah Tikva) 5 5
297. – 6 a. violet (Nazareth) .. 5 5
298. – 8 a. orange (Beersheba) 5 5
299. – 10 a. emer. (Beib Shean) 5 5
300. – 12 a. maroon (Tiberias) 5 5
301. 115. 15 a. green 10 5
302. – 20 a. red (Elat) .. 10 5
303. – 25 a. blue (Acre) .. 12 8
304. – 35 a. purple (Dimona) 15 8
305. – 37 a. olive (Zefat) .. 15 15
305a. 40 a. brown (Mizpe Ramon) 15 10
306. – 50 a. turquoise (Rishon Le Zion) 20 10
306a. – 55 a. crimson (Askelon) 20 20
307. – 70 a. brown (Jerusalem) 40 20
307a. – 80 a. red (Rosh Pinna) 25 20
308. – I£1 green (Tel Aviv—Yafo) 25 20
309. – I£3 magenta (Haifa) .. 60 50
Nos. 307, 308/9 are 22½+27mm. in size. See also Nos. 413/24.

1965. 2nd Int. Book Fair, Jerusalem.
310. 116. 70 a. black, blue and grey-green 30 25

117. Hands reaching for barbed wire.

118. "National Water Supply".

1965. Concentration Camps Liberation. 20th Anniv.
311. 117. 25 a. blk., yell. & grey 15 12

1965. Independence. 17th Anniv.
312. 118. 37 a. brown, drab, blue and light blue .. 20 15

119. Potash Works, Sedom.

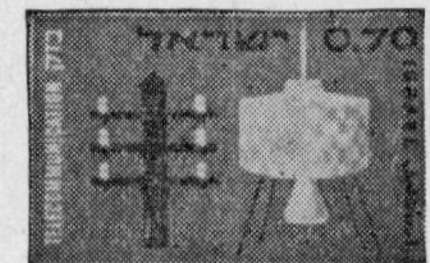

120. "Syncom" Satellite and Telegraph Pole.

1965. Dead Sea Industrial Development. Multicoloured.
313. 12 a. Potash Works, Sedom 8 8
314. 50 a. Type 119 .. .. 25 25
The two stamps form one composite design when placed side by side.

1965. I.T.U. Cent.
315. 120. 70 a. slate-purple, blue and violet 25 20

121. "Co-operation".

122. "Light".

1965. Int. Co-operation Year.
316. 121. 36 a. multicoloured .. 25 20

1965. Jewish New Year. "The Creation". Multicoloured.
317. 6 a. Type 122 .. .. 5 5
318. 8 a. "Heaven" 5 5
319. 12 a. "Earth" 5 5
320. 25 a. "Stars" 20 12
321. 35 a. "Birds and Beasts" 25 20
322. 70 a. "Man" 55 40

123. "Charaxes jasius".

124. War of Independence Memorial.

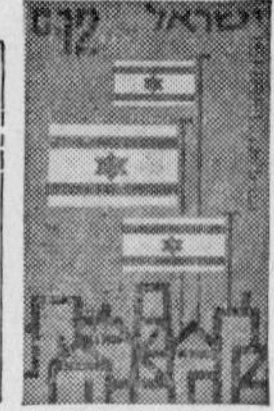
125. Flags.

1965. Israeli Butterflies. Multicoloured.
323. 2 a. Type 123 .. .. 5 5
324. 6 a. "Papilio alexanor" .. 5 5
325. 8 a. "Daphnis nerii" (moth) 8 8
326. 12 a. "Zegris eupheme" .. 10 10

1966. Memorial Day.
327. 124. 40 a. brown and black 20 20

1966. Independence. 18th Anniv. Multicoloured.
328. 12 a. Type 125 .. .. 5 5
329. 30 a. Fireworks 12 10
330. 80 a. Fighter aircraft and warships 35 30

126. Knesset Building.

1966. Knesset Building, Jerusalem. Inaug.
331. 126. I£1 blue 60 45

127. Scooter Rider.

129. Panther (bronze). 128. Spice Box.

1966. Road Safety. Multicoloured.
332. 2 a. Type 127 .. .. 5 5
333. 5 a. Cyclist 5 5
334. 10 a. Pedestrian on crossing 5 5
335. 12 a. Child with ball .. 5 5
336. 15 a. Motorist in car .. 10 10

1966. Jewish New Year. Religious Ceremonial Objects. Multicoloured.
337. 12 a. Type 128 .. .. 5 5
338. 15 a. Candlesticks .. 8 8
339. 35 a. Kiddush cup .. 10 8
340. 40 a. Torah pointer .. 12 10
341. 80 a. Hanging lamp .. 30 30

1966. Israel Museum Exhibits Multicoloured.
342. 15 a. Type 129 .. .. 10 8
343. 30 a. Synagogue menora (stone) 20 12
344. 40 a. Phoenician sphinx (ivory) .. 25 15
345. 55 a. Earring (gold) .. 40 20
346. 80 a. Miniature capital (gold) 55 30
347. I£1·15 Drinking horn (gold) 1·10 85
No. 347 is vert.

130. Levant Postman and Mail-coach.

131. "Fight Cancer and Save Life".

1966. Stamp Day.
348. 130. 12 a. green and brown 5 5
349. – 15 a. cerise, brn. & grn. 8 8
350. – 40 a. blue and magenta 20 10
351. – I£1 bistre & turquoise 35 30
DESIGNS: 15 a. Turkish postman and camels. 40 a. Palestine postman and locomotive. I£1, Israeli postman and jetliner.

1966. Cancer Research.
352. 131. 15 a. green and red .. 12 8

132. Akko (Acre). 133. Book and Crowns.

1967. Ancient Israeli Ports.
353. 132. 15 a. purple 8 8
354. – 40 a. green 20 15
355. – 80 a. blue 35 30
PORTS: 40 a. Caesarea 80 a. Yafo (Jaffa).

1967. Shulhan Arukh ("Book of Wisdom").
356. 133. 40 a. multicoloured .. 20 15

134. War of Independence Memorial.

1967. Memorial Day.
357. 134. 55 a. silver, blue & turq. 25 20

135. "Auster" Reconnaissance Aircraft.

136. Straits of Tiran. 137. Law Scroll.

1967. Independence Day. Military Aircraft.
358. 135. 15 a. blue and green .. 8 8
359. – 30 a. brown and orange 15 8
360. – 80 a. violet & turquoise 35 35
AIRCRAFT: 30 a. "Mystere IV jet fighter". 80 a. "Mirage" jet fighters.

1967. Victory in Arab-Israeli War.
361. – 15 a. black, yell. & red 8 8
362. 136. 40 a. green 15 12
363. – 80 a. violet 35 30
DESIGNS—VERT. 15 a. Sword emblem of "Zaha" (Israeli Defence Forces). HORIZ. 80 a. "Wailing Wall", Jerusalem.

1967. Jewish New Year. Scrolls of the Torah (Mosaic Law), and similar designs.
364. 137. 12 a. multicoloured .. 5 5
365. – 15 a. multicoloured .. 8 8
366. – 35 a. multicoloured .. 15 10
367. – 40 a. multicoloured .. 15 10
368. – 80 a. multicoloured .. 30 30

138. "Welcome to Israel". 139. Lord Balfour.

1967. Int. Tourist Year. Each with "Sun" emblem. Multicoloured.
369. 30 a. Type 138 .. .. 8 5
370. 40 a. "Air hostess" .. 12 10
371. 80 a. "Orange" child .. 40 35

1967. Balfour Declaration. 50th Anniv.
372. – 15 a. green 10 5
373. 139. 40 a. brown 20 20
DESIGN: 15 a. Dr. C. Weizmann.

140. Ibex. 141. Diamond.

1967. Israeli Nature Reserves. Multicoloured.
374. 12 a. Type 140 .. .. 5 5
375. 18 a. Lynx.. .. .. 8 8
376. 60 a. Gazelle 25 20

1968. Air. Israeli Exports.
377. – 10 a. multicoloured .. 5 5
378. – 30 a. multicoloured .. 8 5
379. – 40 a. multicoloured .. 10 5
380. – 50 a. multicoloured .. 12 8
381. – 55 a. multicoloured .. 15 12
382. – 60 a. multicoloured .. 15 15
383. – 80 a. multicoloured .. 20 15
384. – I£1 multicoloured .. 25 20
385. – I£1.50 multicoloured.. 35 30
386. 141. I£3 violet and green.. 75 50
DESIGNS: 10 a. Draped curtains ("Textiles"). 30 a. "Stamps". 40 a. Jar and necklace ("Arts and Crafts"). 50 a. Chick and egg ("Chicks"). 55 a. Melon, avocado and strawberries ("Fruits"). 60 a. Gladioli ("Flowers"). 80 a. Telecommunications equipment ("Electronics"). I£1, Atomic equipment ("Isotopes"). I£1.50, Models ("Fashion").

142. Beflagged Football. 143. "Immigration".

1968. Pre-Olympic Football Tournament.
387. 142. 80 a. multicoloured .. 30 25

1968. Independence Day. Multicoloured.
388. 15 a. Type 143 .. .. 5 5
389. 80 a. "Settlement" (drawing) 30 25

144. Rifles and Helmet. 145. Zahal Emblem.

1968. Memorial Day
390. 144. 55 a. multicoloured .. 15 15

1968. Independence Day (Zahal—Israel Defence Forces).
391. 145. 40 a. multicoloured .. 12 12

146. Resistance Fighter (detail from Warsaw Monument). 147. Moshe Sharett.

1968. Warsaw Ghetto Rising. 25th Anniv.
392. 146. 60 a. bistre 12 10

1968. 27th Zionist Congress, Jerusalem.
393. 147. I£1 sepia 25 25

148. Candle and Cell Bars. 149. Jerusalem.

1968. Fallen Freedom Fighters.
394. 148. 80 a. black, grey & brn. 25 20

1968. Jewish New Year.
395. 149. 12 a. multicoloured .. 5 5
396. – 15 a. multicoloured .. 5 5
397. – 35 a. multicoloured .. 10 10
398. – 40 a. multicoloured .. 15 15
399. – 60 a. multicoloured .. 20 20
DESIGNS: Jerusalem—views of the Old City (12, 15, 35 a.) and of the New City (40, 60 a.).

150. Scout Badge and Knot. 151. "Lions' Gate", Jerusalem (detail).

1968. Jewish Scout Movement. 50th Anniv.
400. 150. 30 a. multicoloured .. 12 12

1968. "Tabira" Stamp Exn., Jerusalem.
401. 151. I£1 chestnut 70 70

152. A. Mapu (writer). 153. Paralytics playing Basketball.

1968. Abraham Mapu. Death Cent.
403. 152. 30 a. olive 12 10

1968. Int. Games for the Paralysed.
404. 153. 40 a. green and apple 15 12

154. Elat.

1969. Israeli Ports.
405. 154. 30 a. magenta.. .. 12 12
406. – 60 a. brown (Ashdod) 20 20
407. I£1 green (Haifa) .. 35 35

155. "Worker" and ILO Emblem. 156. Israeli Flag at Half-mast.

1969. Int. Labour Organisation. 50th Anniv.
408. 155. 80 a. green and lilac .. 30 25

1969. Memorial Day.
409. 156. 55 a. gold, blue & violet 20 15

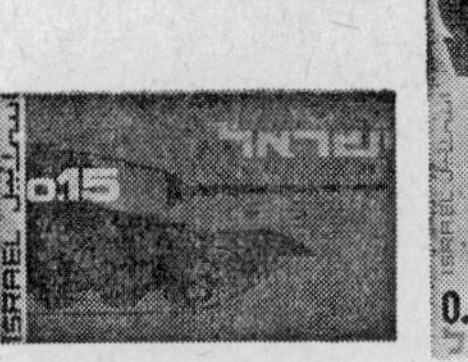

157. Army Tank. 158. Flaming Torch.

1969. Independence Day. Multicoloured.
410. 15 a. Type 157 .. .. 8 8
411. 80 a. Naval destroyer .. 25 25

1969. 8th Maccabiah.
412. 158. 60 a. multicoloured .. 25 20

159. Arms of Hadera. 160. Building the Ark.

1969. Civic Arms (2nd Series).
413. 2 a. green (Type 159) .. 5 5
414. 3 a. purple (Herzliyya) .. 8 5
415. 5 a. orange (Holon) 8 5
416. 15 a. carmine (Bat Yam) 20 5
417. 18 a. blue (Ramla) .. 5 5
418 20 a. brn. (Kefar Sava) .. 8 8
419. 25 a. blue (Giv'atayim) .. 12 8
420. 30 a. magenta (Rehovot) 10 5
421. 40 a. violet (Natanya) .. 50 10
422. 50 a. blue (Benei Beraq).. 15 10
423. 60 a. yellow (Nahariya) .. 25 12
424. 80 a. green (Ramat Gan) 50 15

1969. Jewish New Year, showing scenes from "The Flood". Multicoloured.
425. 12 a. Type 160 .. .. 5 5
426. 15 a. Animals going aboard 5 5
427. 35 a. Ark afloat 12 8
428. 40 a. Dove with olive branch 15 12
429. 60 a. Ark on Mt. Ararat .. 30 25

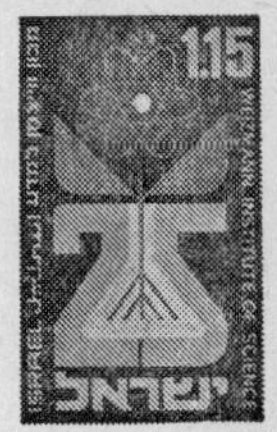

161. "King David" (Chagall). 162. Atomic "Plant".

1969. "King David".
430. 161. I£3 multicoloured .. 1·25 1·10

1969. Weizmann Institute of Science. 25th Anniv.
431. 162. I£1. 15 multicoloured 90 90

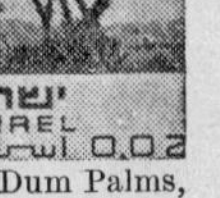

163. Dum Palms, Emeq Ha-Arava. 164. Immigrant "Aircraft".

1970. Nature Reserves.
432. 163. 2 a. yellow-olive .. 5 5
433. – 3 a. blue 5 5
434. – 5 a. red 5 5
435. – 6 a. green 5 5
436. – 30 a. violet 10 8
DESIGNS: 3 a. Tahana Waterfall, Nahal Iyon. 5 a. Nahal Baraq Canyon Negev. 6 a. Ha-Masreq, Judean Hills. 30 a. Soreq Cave, Judean Hills.

1970. Operation "Magic Carpet" (Immigration of Yemenite Jews). 20th Anniv.
437. 164. 30 a. multicoloured .. 15 10

165. Joseph Trumpeldor. 166. Prime-Minister Levi Eshkol.

1970. Defence of Tel Hay. 50th Anniv.
438. 165. I£1 violet 35 30

1970. Levi Eshkol Memorial.
439. 166. 15 a. multicoloured .. 10 10

167. Ze'ev Jabotinsky (Defence commander). 168. Camel and Diesel Train.

1970. Defence of Jerusalem. 50th Anniv.
440. 167. 80 a. green and cream 45 40

1970. Opening of Dimona-Oron Railway.
441. 168. 80 a. multicoloured .. 60 50

169. Mania Shochat (author). 171. Memorial Flame 172. "Orchis laxiflorus".

170. Scene from "The Dybbuk".

1970. 'Ha-Shomer'. 60th Anniv.
442. 169. 40 a. maroon and cream 20 20

1970. Habimah National Theatre. 50th Anniv.
443. 170. I£1 multicoloured .. 40 35

1970. Memorial Day.
444. 171. 55 a. blk., red & violet 20 20

1970. Independence Day. Israeli Wild Flowers. Multicoloured.
445. 12 a. Type 172 .. .. 5 5
446. 15 a. "Iris mariae" .. 8 8
447. 80 a. "Lupinus pilosus" 30 25

173. C. Netter (founder). 174. "Arava" Aircraft.

1970. Miqwe Yisrael Agricultural College. Cent. Multicoloured.
448. 40 a. Type 173 .. .. 15 10
449. 80a. College building and gate 30 30

1970. Israeli Aircraft Industries.
450. 174. I£1 silver, violet & blue 35 30

175. Yachts. 176. Keren Hayesod.

1970. World "420" Class Sailing Championships. Multicoloured.
451. 15 a. Type 175 .. .. 5 5
452. 30 a. Yacht with spinnaker 15 15
453. 80 a. Yachts turning around buoy 35 35

1970. Keren Hayesod. 50th Anniv.
454. 176. 40 a. multicoloured .. 20 15

177. Old Synagogue, Cracow. 179. Mother and Child.

178. Jewish "Bird" heading for Sun.

1970. Jewish New Year. Multicoloured.
455. 12 a. Type 177 .. .. 5 5
456. 15 a. Great Synagogue, Tunis 5 5
457. 35 a. Portuguese Synagogue, Amsterdam 12 10
458. 40 a. Great Synagogue, Moscow 15 12
459. 60 a. Shearith Israel Synagogue, New York 25 25

1970. Operation "Ezra and Nehemiah" (Exodus of Iraqi Jews to Israel).
460. 178. 80 a. multicoloured .. 30 25

1970. Women's International Zionist Organisation (W.I.Z.O.). 50th Anniv.
461. 179. 80 a. yell., grn. & silver 45 40

180. Tel Aviv Post Office, 1920. 181. Histadrut Emblem.

1970. "Tabit" Stamp Exhibition, Tel Aviv, and 50th Anniv. of Tel Aviv Post Office.
462. 180. I£1 multicoloured .. 30 30

1970. "Histadrut" (General Federation of Labour). 50th Anniv.
464. 181. 35 a. multicoloured .. 8 8

182 "Jewish Wedding" (J. Israels).

1970. Paintings in Tel Aviv Museum. Mult.
465. 85 a. Type 182 .. .. 25 20
466. I£1 "Landscape with Bridge" (C. Pissarro).. 35 30
467. I£2 "Flowers in a Vase" (F. Leger) 70 60

183. "Inn of the Ghosts" (Cameri Theatre).

1971. Israeli Theatre. Multicoloured.
468. 50 a. Type 183 .. .. 20 20
469. 50 a. "Samson and Delilah" (National Opera Company) 20 20
470. 50 a. "A Psalm of David" (I.N.B.A.L. Dance Theatre) 20 20

184. Mesopotamian Fallow Deer.

1971. Nature Reserves. Animals of Biblical Times. Multicoloured.
471. 2 a. Type 184 .. .. 5 5
472. 3 a. Wild ass 5 5
473. 5 a. White Oryx 8 8
474. 78 a. Cheetah 25 25

185. "Haganah" Emblem. 186. Jaffa Gate.

1971. Memorial Day.
475. 185. 78 a. multicoloured .. 30 30

1971. Independence Day. Gates of Jerusalem (1st series). Multicoloured.
476. 15 a. Type 186 .. .. 8 5
477. 18 a. New Gate .. 12 12
478. 35 a. Damascus Gate .. 25 20
479. 85 a. Herod's Gate .. 55 50
See also Nos. 527/30.

187. Gymnastics 188. "... and he wrote upon the tables ..."

1971. 9th "Hapoel" Games. Multicoloured.
481. 50 a. Type 187. .. .. 20 15
482. 50 a. Basketball 20 15
483. 50 a. Running 20 15

1971. Feast of Weeks ("Shavout"). Illuminated verses from the Bible. Multicoloured.
484. 50 a. Type 188 .. .. 20 15
485. 85 a. "The first of the firstfruits ..." 35 30
486. I£1. 50 "... and ye shall observe the feast .." .. 50 45
See also Nos. 488/92.

189. "Sun over the Emeq". 190. "You shall rejoice in your feast".

1971. Jubilee of Settlement in the "Emeq" (Yezreel Valley).
487. 189. 40 a. multicoloured .. 15 15

1971. Jewish New Year. Feast of the Tabernacles ("Sukko"). Illuminated Verses from the Bible. Multicoloured.
488. 15 a. Type 190 .. .. 5 5
489. 18 a. "You shall dwell in booths ..." 5 5
490. 20 a. "That I made the people ..." .. 8 8
491. 40 a. "... gathered in the produce" 12 10
492. 65 a. "... I will give you your rains ..." .. 30 25

191. Kinneret. 192. "Agricultural Research".

1971. Landscapes.
493. – 3 a. blue 5 5
494. – 5 a. green 5 5
495. – 15 a. pink 5 5
496. 191. 18 a. purple 12 5
497. – 20 a. green 8 5
498. – 22 a. blue 5 5
498a. – 25 a. red 8 5
499. – 30 a. mauve 8 5
500. – 35 a. purple 5 5
501. – 45 a. blue 12 8
502. – 50 a. green 12 8
503. – 55 a. green 12 8
504. – 65 a. brown 15 12
505. – 70 a. red 20 12
505a. – 80 a. blue 12 10
506. – 88 a. blue 40 20
507. – 95 a. brown 25 20
508. – I£1·10 brown.. .. 25 20
508a. – I£1·30 blue 25 15
508b. – I£1·70 brown.. .. 35 20
509. – I£2 brown 70 35
510. – I£3 violet 80 70
510a. – I£10 blue .. .. 3·00 2·00

DESIGNS: 3 a. Judean desert. 5 a. Gan Ha-Shelosha. 15 a. Negev desert. 20 a. Tel Dan. 22 a. Yafo. 25 a. Arava. 30 a. En Avedat. 35 a. Brekhat Ram. 45 a. Mt. Hermon. 50 a. Rosh Pinna. 55 a. Natanya. 65 a. Plain of Zebulun. 70 a. Engedi. 80 a. Beach at Elat. 88 a. Acre. 95 a. Hamifratz Hane' Elam. I£1·10 Aqueduct near Acre. I£1·30 Zefat. I£1·70 Nazerat Illit. I£2 Coral Island. I£3 Haifa. I£10 Elat.

1971. Volcani Institute of Agricultural Research. 50th Anniv.
511. 192. I£1 multicoloured .. 30 25

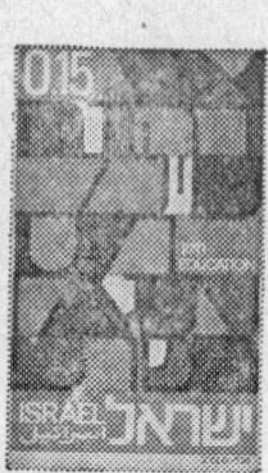

193. Hebrew Text. 194. "The Scribe" (sculpture, B. Schatz).

1971. Educational Development. Multicoloured.
512. 15 a. Type 193 .. .. 5 5
513. 18 a. Mathematical formulae 5 5
514. 20 a. Engineering symbols 15 12
515. 40 a. University degree abbreviations 20 20

1972. Jewish Art.
516. 194. 40 c. blackish brown, brown and black .. 10 10
517. – 55 a. multicoloured .. 20 15
518. – 70 a. multicoloured .. 25 20
519. – 85 a. black and yellow 35 30
520. – I£1 multicoloured 50 35

DESIGNS—VERT. 55 a. "Sarah" (A. Pann). 85 a. "Old Jerusalem" (woodcut J. Steinhardt). I£1 "Resurrection" (A. Kahana). HORIZ. 70 a. "Zefat" (M. Shemi).

195. The Flight from Egypt. 196. "Let My People Go".

1972. Passover Feast ("Pesah"). Mult.
521. 18 a. Type 195 .. .. 5 5
522. 45 a. Baking unleavened bread 25 20
523. 95 a. "Seder" table .. 40 35

1972. Campaign for Jewish Immigration.
524. 196. 55 a. multicoloured .. 90 75

197. Bouquet. 198. Jethro's Tomb.

1972. Memorial Day.
525. 197. 55 a. multicoloured .. 30 25

1972. "Nebi Shuaib" (Jethro's Tomb) (Druze shrine).
526. 198. 55 a. multicoloured .. 30 25

1972. Independence Day. Gates of Jerusalem (2nd series). Designs as T 186. Multicoloured.
527. 15 a. Lion's Gate 5 5
528. 18 a. Golden Gate .. 15 12
529. 45 a. Dung Gate .. 25 20
530. 55 a. Zion Gate 40 30

199. Ghetto Entrance. 200. Book Year Texts.

1972. Rabbi Yazhaq Luria ("Ari"). 400th Death Anniv.
532. 199. 70 a. multicoloured .. 45 40

1972. Int. Book Year.
533. 200. 95 a. blk., red and blue 30 30

201. Dish Aerial. 202. Ancona Ark.

1972. Opening of Satellite Earth Station.
534. 201. I£1 multicoloured .. 35 35

1972. Jewish New Year. Holy Arks from Italy.
535. 202. 15 a. brown & yellow .. 10 8
536. – 45 a. green, gold and yellow-green 25 15
537. – 70 a. red, blue & yellow 40 30
538. – 95 a. purple and gold .. 70 45
DESIGNS: 45a. Soragna Ark. 70a. Padua Ark. 95a. Reggio Emilia Ark.

203. Menora Emblem. 204. Hanukka Lamp (Morocco, 18th-19th century).

1972. State of Israel. 25th Anniv.
539. 203. I£1 blue & pur. and silver 35 30

1972. Festival of Lights ("Hanukka"). Ceremonial Lamps. Multicoloured.
540. 12 a. Type 204 .. .. 8 5
541. 25 a. 18th-century Polish lamp 12 10
542. 70 a. 17th-century German silver lamp 30 25

205. Pendant. 206. Head of Horse.

1973. Immigration of North African Jews.
543. 205. 18 a. multicoloured .. 12 12

1972. Children's Drawings. Multicoloured.
544. 2 a. Type 206 .. .. 5 5
545. 3 a. "Balloon ride" (17 × 48 mm.) 8 8
546. 55 a. "Partytime" 20 20

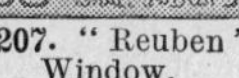

207. "Reuben" Window. 208. Flame of Remembrance.

1973. Chagall's Stained-glass Windows, Hadassah, Jerusalem. Multicoloured.
547. I£1 "Levi" 25 25
548. I£1 "Simeon" 25 25
549. I£1 Type 207 .. .. 25 25
550. I£1 "Issachar" 25 25
551. I£1 "Zebulun" 25 25
552. I£1 "Judah" 25 25
553. I£1 "Asher" 20 20
554. I£1 "Gad" 20 20
555. I£1 "Dan" 20 20
556. I£1 "Benjamin" 20 20
557. I£1 "Joseph" 20 20
558. I£1 "Naphtali" 20 20

1973. Memorial Day.
559. 208. 65 a. multicoloured .. 25 25

209. Skeletal Hand.

1973. Holocaust (Persecution of European Jews 1933-45) Memorial.
560. 209. 55 a. blue 15 15

210. Signatures of Declaration of Independence.

1973. Independence Day.
561. 210. I£1 multicoloured .. 30 25

211. Star of David and Runners. 212. Isaiah.

213. Jews in Boat, and Danish Flag. 214. Institute Emblem and Cogwheel.

1973. 9th Maccabiah.
563. 211. I£1.10 multicoloured 30 25

1973. Jewish New Year. Prophets of Israel.
564. 18 a. Type 212 .. .. 8 5
565. 65 a. Jeremiah 15 12
566. I£1.10 Ezekiel 30 20

1973. Rescue of Danish Jews. 30th Anniv.
567. 213. I£5 black, red & brn. 1·00 1·00

1973. "Technion" Israel Institute of Technology. 50th Anniv.
568. 214. I£1.25 multicoloured 30 30

215. Collectors within "Stamp". 216. Soldier with "Talith" (prayer shawl).

1973. "Jerusalem 74" International Stamp Exhibition. Multicoloured.
569. 20 a. Type 215 .. .. 8 8
570. I£1 Collectors within "Stamp" (different) .. 25 20

1974. Memorial Day.
572. 216. I£1 black and blue .. 30 25

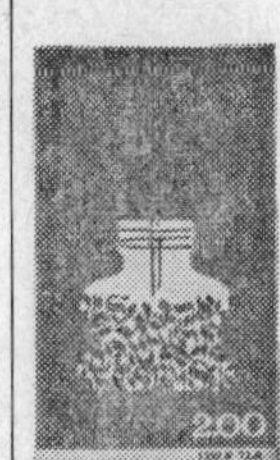

217. Quill Pen and Ink-bottle. 218. "Woman in Blue" (Moshe Kisling).

1974. Hebrew Writers' Association. 50th Anniv.
573. 217. I£2 black and gold .. 35 35

1974. Paintings and Sculpture. Multicoloured.
574. I£1.25 Type 218 .. .. 35 25
575. I£2 "Mother and Child" (bronze, Chana Orloff) .. 60 40
576. I£3 "Girl in Blue" (Chaim Soutine) 90 60
See also Nos. 604/6.

219. Spanner.

1974. Young Workers' Movement. 50th Anniv.
577. 219. 25 a. multicoloured .. 12 10

220. Lady Davis Technical Centre "Amal", Tel Aviv.

1974. "Architecture in Israel".
578. 220. 25 a. grey 5 5
579. – 60 a. blue 12 10
580. – I£1.45 brown 35 25
DESIGNS: 60 a. Elias Sourasky Library, Tel Aviv University. I£1.45 "Mivtahim" Rest-home, Zikhron Yaaqov.
See also Nos. 596/8.

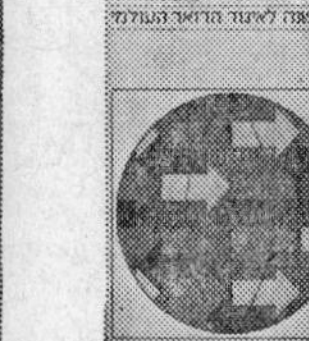

221. Istanbuli Synagogue. 222. Arrows on Globe.

1974. Jewish New Year. Rebuilt Synagogues in Jerusalem's Old City. Multicoloured.
581. 25 a. Type 221 .. .. 8 5
582. 70 a. Emtzai Synagogue .. 15 12
583. I£1 Yohanan Ben Zakai Synagogue 25 20

1974. Universal Postal Union. Cent. Mult.
584. 25 a. Type 222 .. .. 12 12
585. I£1.30 Dove as "postman" (27 × 27 mm.) 65 55

223. David Ben Gurion.

1974. Ben Gurion Memorial.
586. 223. 25 a. brown 12 12
587. I£1·30 green 65 55

224. Child with Plant, and Rainbow. 226. Welding.

225. Hebrew University, Jerusalem.

1975. Arbour Day. Multicoloured.
588. 1 a. Type 224 .. .. 5 5
589. 35 a. Bird in tree 8 5
590. I£2 Child with plant & sun 40 25

1975. Hebrew University, Jerusalem. 50th Anniv.
591. 225. I£2·50 multicoloured 45 40

1975. "Occupational Safety". Mult.
592. 30 a. Type 226 .. .. 5 5
593. 80 a. Tractor-driving .. 15 15
594. I£1·20 Telegraph-line maintenance 20 15

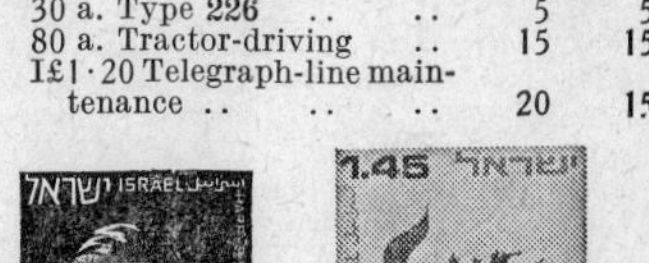

227. Harry S. Truman. 228. Memorial Flame.

1975. Truman Commemoration.
595. 227. I£5 brown 90 70

1975. "Architecture in Israel" (2nd series). As Type 220.
596. 80 a. brown 12 10
597. I£1·30 green 15 12
598. I£1·70 brown 25 20
DESIGNS: 80 a. Hebrew University Synagogue, Jerusalem. I£1·30 Museum, Yad Mordechai. I£1·70 Town Hall, Bat Yam.

1975. Memorial Day.
599. 228. I£1 red, blk. & mauve 25 20

229. Text and Poppy. 230. Obstacle Race.

1975. Fallen Soldiers' Memorial.
600. 229. I£1·45 black, red & grey 25 20

1975. Tenth Hapoel Games.
601. 230. 25 a. orange and purple 5 5
602. – I£1·70 red, grn. & blue 25 20
603. – I£3 blue and green .. 45 40
DESIGNS: I£1·70 Cycle race. I£3 Volleyball.

1975. Jewish Paintings. As T 218. Multicoloured.
604. I£1 "Hanukka" (M. D. Oppenheim) 15 12
605. I£1·40 "The Purim Players" (J. Adler) (horiz.) 25 20
606. I£4 "Yom Kippur" (M. Gottlieb) 60 50

231. Old People. 232. Gideon.

1975. Gerontology.
607. **231.** I£1·85 multicoloured 30 25

1975. Jewish New Year. Judges of Israel. Multicoloured.
608. 35 a. Type **232** 10 8
609. I£1 Deborah 15 12
610. I£1·40 Jephthah 25 20

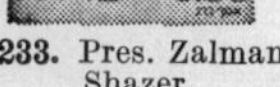
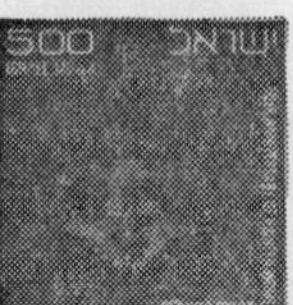

233. Pres. Zalman Shazer. **234.** Emblem of Pioneer Women.

1975. Zalman Shazar Memorial.
611. **233.** 35 a. black and silver 10 8

1975. Pioneer Women's Organization. 50th Anniv.
612. **234.** I£5 multicoloured .. 75 75

235. New Hospital Buildings.

1975. Return of Hadassah Hospital to Mt. Scopus.
613. **235.** I£4 multicoloured .. 60 50

236. Pratincole. **237.** "Air Pollution".

1975. Protected Wild Birds. Multicoloured.
614. I£1·10 Type **236** 20 15
615. I£1·70 Spur-winged plover 25 20
616. I£2 Blackwinged stilt .. 30 25

1975. "Environmental Quality". Multicoloured.
617. 50 a. Type **237** 10 8
618. 80 a. Ship spilling oil ("Water pollution") .. 12 10
619. I£1·70 Jet aircraft noise ("Noise pollution") .. 25 20

238. Star of David. **239.** Symbolic "Key".

1975. "Stand-by" Issue.
620. **238.** I£1·85 blue and brown 30 25
620a. I£2·45 blue and green 40 35

1976. Bezalel Academy of Arts and Design, Jerusalem. 70th Anniversary.
621. **239.** I£1·85 multicoloured 30 25

240. "Border Settlements". **241.** "In the days of Ahasuerus ..".

1976. Jewish Border Settlements.
622. **240.** I£1·50 multicoloured 25 20

1976. "Purim" Festival. Multicoloured.
623. 40 a. Type **241** 5 5
624. 80 a. "He set the royal crown ..." 12 10
625. I£1·60 "Thus shall it be done ..." 25 20

242. Monument to the Fallen. **243.** "Dancers of Meron" (R. Rubin).

1976. Memorial Day.
627. **242.** I£1·85 multicoloured 25 15

1976. Lag Ba-Omer Festival.
628. **243.** I£1·30 multicoloured 20 15

244. "200" Flag.

1976. American Revolution. Bicent.
629. **244.** I£4 multicoloured .. 55 45

245. High-jumping.

1976. Olympic Games, Montreal.
631. **245.** I£1·60, black and red .. 25 20
632. – I£2·40, black and blue 40 35
633. – I£4·40, black and purple 70 60
DESIGNS: I£2·40, Swimming, I£4·40, Gymnastics.

246. Multiple Tent Emblems. **247.** "Truth".

1976. Camping.
634. **246.** I£1·50, multicoloured 25 20

1976. Jewish New Year. Multicoloured.
635. 45 a. Type **247** 5 5
636. I£1·50, "Judgement" .. 25 20
637. I£1·90 "Peace" 30 25

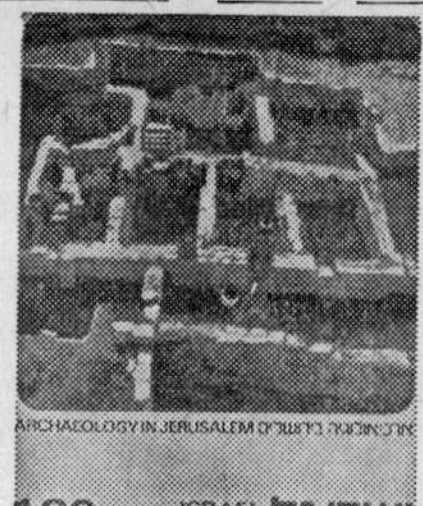

248. Ruins of Byzantine Building.

1976. Archaeological Discoveries. Mult.
638. 70 a. City wall, 1st period 10 8
639. I£1·30 Type **248** .. 20 15
640. I£2·40 Arch of 2nd Temple 40 35
641. I£2·80 Staircase of 2nd Temple 50 45
642. I£5·00 Omayyad Palace, 8th cent. 75 65

249. Chess Pawn.

1976. Chess Olympiad. Multicoloured.
643. I£1·30 Type **249** 20 15
644. I£1·60 Castle 25 20

250. Clearing Ground.

1976. Pioneers.
645. **250.** 5 a. brown and gold .. 5 5
646. – 10 a. plum and gold .. 5 5
647. – 60 a. red and gold .. 10 8
648. – I£1·40 indigo and gold 20 15
649. – I£1·80 green and gold 25 20
DESIGNS—HORIZ. 10 a. Building breakwater. I£1·40 Ploughing with horses. I£1·80 Tilling Land. VERT. 60 a. Road construction.

OFFICIAL STAMPS

בול שרות
(O 1.)

1951. Optd. with Type O **1**.
O 54. **8.** 5 pr. magenta 8 5
O 55. 15 pr. red 10 5
O 56. 30 pr. blue 15 10
O 57. 40 pr. brown 20 20

POSTAGE DUE STAMPS

דמי דאר
(D 1.)

1948. As T 1 optd. with Type D **1**.
D 10. **1.** 3 m. orange on yellow .. 2·25 1·10
D 11. 5 m. green on yellow .. 3·00 2·00
D 12. 10 m. mauve on yellow 6·00 2·50
D 13. 20 m. blue on yellow .. 15·00 7·50
D 14. 50 m. brown on yellow 60·00 48·00

D 2. D 3.

1949.
D 27. **D 2.** 2 pr. orange 5 5
D 28. 5 pr. violet 10 5
D 29. 10 pr. green 15 8
D 30. 20 pr. red 30 25
D 31. 30 pr. blue 50 35
D 32. 50 pr. brown .. 80 70

1952.
D 73. **D 3.** 5 pr. brown 5 5
D 74. 10 pr. blue 5 5
D 75. 20 pr. purple .. 5 5
D 76. 30 pr. black 5 5
D 77. 40 pr. green 5 5
D 78. 50 pr. sepia .. 8 8
D 79. 60 pr. violet .. 10 10
D 80. 100 pr. red 12 12
D 81. 250 pr. blue 20 20

ITALIAN AUSTRIA E1

Italian territory acquired from Austria at the close of the war of 1914-18, including Trentino and Trieste.

1918. 100 heller = 1 krone.
1918. 100 centesimi = 1 lira.
1919. 100 centesimi = 1 corona

TRENTINO

1918. Stamps of Austria overprinted **Regno d'Italia Trentino 3 nov 1918.**
1. **26.** 3 h. violet 75 75
2. 5 h. green 45 45
3. 6 h. orange .. .. 24·00 24·00
4. 10 h. claret 45 55
5. 12 h. blue .. .. 80·00 80·00
6. **30.** 15 h. brown .. .. 1·75 1·75
7. 20 h. green 15 20
8. 25 h. blue .. .. 11·00 11·00
9. 30 h. violet .. .. 2·75 2·75
10. **28.** 40 h. olive .. .. 22·00 22·00
11. 50 h. green .. .. 5·50 5·50
12. 60 h. blue .. .. 14·00 14·00
13. 80 h. red-brown .. 23·00 23·00
14. 90 h. purple £325 £325
15. 1 k. red and yellow .. 23·00 23·00
16. **29.** 2 k. blue £110 £110
17. 4 k. green £450 £450
18. 10 k. violet £1600

1918. Stamps of Italy optd. **Venezia Tridentina.**
19. **20.** 1 c. brown 5 5
20. **21.** 2 c. brown 5 5
21. **24.** 5 c. green 5 5
22. 10 c. red 5 5
23. **25.** 20 c. orange 5 8
24. **26.** 40 c. brown .. .. 3·25 3·50
25. **22.** 45 c. olive .. .. 2·10 2·50
26. **26.** 50 c. mauve .. .. 2·10 2·50
27. **23.** 1 l. brown and green .. 2·25 2·75

1919. Stamps of Italy surch. **Venezia Tridentina** and value.
28. **24.** 5 h. on 5 c. green .. 5 8
29. 10 h. on 10 c. red .. 5 8
30. **25.** 20 h. on 20 c. orange .. 5 8

VENEZIA GIULIA

TRIESTE

For use in Trieste and territory, Gorizia and province, and in Istria.

1918. Stamps of Austria optd. **Regno d'Italia Venezia Giulia 3.XI.18.**
31. **26.** 3 h. violet 8 8
32. 5 h. green 5 5
33. 6 h. orange 20 20
34. 10 h. claret 5 5
35. 12 h. blue 50 50
36. **30.** 15 h. brown 5 5
37. 20 h. green 5 5
38. 25 h. blue .. .. 1·50 1·50
39. 30 h. violet 20 20
40. **28.** 40 h. olive .. .. 18·00 18·00
41. 50 h. green 45 45
42. 60 h. blue 90 90
43. 80 h. red-brown .. 45 45
44. 1 k. red on yellow .. 45 45
45. **29.** 2 k. blue .. .. 32·00 30·00
46. 3 k. red .. .. 35·00 32·00
47. 4 k. green .. .. 55·00 55·00
48. 10 k. violet £5500 £5500

1918. Stamps of Italy optd. **Venezia Giulia.**
49. **20.** 1 c. brown 8 8
50. **21.** 2 c. brown 8 8
51. **24.** 5 c. green 5 5
52. 10 c. red 5 5
53. **25.** 20 c. orange 5 5
54. **26.** 25 c. blue 5 5
55. 40 c. brown 40 30
56. **22.** 45 c. green 5 5
57. **26.** 50 c. mauve 15 15
58. 60 c. red .. .. 2·75 1·90
59. **23.** 1 l. brown and green .. 70 50

1919. Stamps of Italy surch. **Venezia Giulia** and value.
60. **23.** 5 h. on 5 c. green .. 8 8
61. **25.** 20 h. on 20 c. orange .. 5 5

EXPRESS LETTER STAMPS

1919. Express Letter stamp of Italy optd. **Venezia Giulia.**
E 60. **E 1.** 25 c. red .. .. 2·00 2·00

POSTAGE DUE STAMPS

1918. Postage Due Stamps of Italy optd. **Venezia Giulia.**

D 60. D 3. 5 c. purple and orange 5 5
D 61. 10 c. purple & orange 5 5
D 62. 20 c. purple & orange 5 5
D 63. 30 c. purple & orange 8 8
D 64. 40 c. purple & orange 75 75
D 65. 50 c. purple & orange 4·50 4·50
D 66. 1 l. purple and blue.. 21·00 21·00

GENERAL ISSUE

For use throughout the liberated area of Trentino, Venezia Giulia or Dalmatia.

1919. Stamps of Italy surch. in new currency.

62. 20. 1 ce. di cor. on 1 c. brn. 5 5
63. 21. 2 ce. di cor. on 2 c. brown 5 5
65. 24. 5 ce. di cor. on 5 c. green 5 5
67. 10 ce. di cor. on 10 c. red 5 5
68. 25. 20 ce. di cor. on 20 c. orge. 5 5
70. 26. 25 ce. di cor. on 25 c. bl. 5 5
71. 40 ce di cor. on 40 c. brn. 5 5
72. 22. 45 ce. di cor. on 45 c. olive 5 5
73. 26. 50 ce. di cor. on 50 c. mve. 5 5
74. 60 ce. di cor. on 60 c. red 5 5
75. 23. 1 cor. on 1 l. brn. & grn. 5 5
82. 5 cor. on 5 l. blue & red.. 1·75 2·10
83. 10 cor. on 10 l. ol. & red 2·75 3·75

EXPRESS LETTER STAMPS

1919. Express Letter stamps of Italy surch. in new currency.

E 76. E 1. 25 ce. di cor. on 25 c. red 5 5
E 77. E 2. 30 ce. di cor. on 30 c. red and blue .. 8 8

POSTAGE DUE STAMPS

1919. Postage Due stamps of Italy surch. in new currency.

D 76. D 3. 5 ce. di cor. on 5 c. purple and orange 5 5
D 77. 10 ce. di cor. on 10 c. purple and orange 5 5
D 78. 20 ce. di cor. on 20 c. purple and orange 5 5
D 79. 30 ce. di cor. on 30 c. purple and orange 5 5
D 80. 40 ce. di cor. on 40 c. purple and orange 5 5
D 81. 50 ce. di cor. on 50 c. purple and orange 5 5
D 82. 1 cor. on 1 l. purple and blue 8 8
D 86. 2 cor. on 2 l. purple and blue .. .. 1·10 1·40
D 87. 5 cor. on 5 l. purple and blue .. .. 1·90 2·50

ITALIAN COLONIES O2

GENERAL ISSUES

1932. As Garibaldi stamps of Italy.

1. – 10 c. green (post.) .. 25 25
2. 99. 20 c. red 25 25
3. – 25 c. green 25 25
4. 99. 30 c. green 25 25
5. – 50 c. red 25 25
6. – 75 c. red 25 25
7. – 1 l. 25 c. blue 25 25
8. – 1 l. 75 c.+25 c. blue 1·50 1·75
9. – 2 l. 55 c.+50 c. sepia .. 1·50 1·75
10. – 5 l.+1 l. blue .. 1·50 1·75
11. 100. 50 c. red (air) .. 25 30
12. – 80 c. green 25 30
13. – 1 l.+25 c. sepia .. 1·10 1·40
14. – 2 l.+50 c. sepia .. 1·10 1·40
15. – 5 l.+1 l. sepia .. 1·10 1·40
16. 101. 2 l. 25 c.+1 l. black and violet (air express) .. 1·10 1·40
17. 4 l. 50 c.+1 l. 50 c. green and brown .. .. 1·10 1·40

1932. As Dante stamps of Italy optd. **COLONIE ITALIANE.**

18. – 10 c. slate (postage) .. 8 8
19. – 15 c. sepia 8 8
20. – 20 c. green 8 8
21. – 25 c. green 8 8
22. – 30 c. brown 8 8
23. – 50 c. blue 8 8
24. – 75 c. red 12 15
25. – 1 l. 25 c. blue 12 12
26. – 1 l. 75 c. violet .. 60 60
27. – 2 l. 75 c. orange.. .. 60 70
28. – 5 l.+2 l. olive 60 75
29. 96. 10 l.+2 l. 50 c. blue .. 60 80
30. 97. 50 c. slate (air) .. 20 20
31. – 1 l. blue 20 20
32. 3 l. green 60 70
33. – 5 l. sepia 60 70
34. 97. 7 l. 70 c.+2 l. red .. 60 80
35. – 10 l.+2 l. 50 c. orange.. 60 90
36. 98. 100 l. sepia and green .. 3·75 7·00

No. 36 is inscribed instead of optd.

1. Ploughing.

2. Savoia-Marchetti "SM 55".

1933. Eritrea. 50th Anniv.

37. 1. 10 c. brown (postage) .. 50 70
38. – 20 c. purple 50 70
39. – 25 c. green.. .. .. 50 70
40. – 65 c. violet 50 70
41. 1. 75 c. red 50 70
42. – 1 l. 25 blue 50 70
43. 1. 2 l. 75 orange .. .. 1·60 2·75
44. – 5 l.+2 l. green .. .. 7·00 10·00
45. – 10 l.+2 l. 50 brown .. 7·00 10·00
46. – 50 c. brown (air) .. .. 70 1·00
47. – 1 l. black .. .. .. 70 1·00
48. 2. 3 l. red .. .. .. 70 1·25
49. 5 l. brown .. .. .. 70 1·25
50. – 7 l. 70+2 l. green .. 6·00 8·00
51. 2. 10 l.+2 l. 50 blue.. .. 6·00 8·00
52. – 50 l. violet.. .. .. 6·00 8·00

DESIGNS—VERT. (Postage): 20 c., 75 c., 5 l. Camel transport. 25 c., 1 l. 25. 10 l. Lioness with star on left shoulder (Arms). HORIZ. (Air): 50 c., 1 l, 7 l. 70. Eagle. 50 l. Savoia-Marchetti "SM 55" aircraft over map of Eritrea.

4. Agricultural Implements.

DESIGNS—HORIZ. 50 c., 1 l. 75, 10 l. Tractor. VERT. 25 c., 1 l. 25, 5 l. Arab and camel. 25 l. Native soldier.

1933. Fascist March on Rome. 10th Anniv. Inscr. "DECENNALE". (a) Postage.

53. 4. 5 c. orange 35 55
54. – 25 c. green.. .. .. 35 55
55. – 50 c. violet 35 55
56. 4. 75 c. red 35 70
57. – 1 l. 25 blue 35 70
58. – 1 l. 75 red 35 80
59. 4. 2 l. 75 blue 35 80
60. – 5 l. black .. .. .. 2·25 3·50
61. – 10 l. blue .. .. 2·25 3·50
62. – 25 l. olive .. .. 8·00 10·00

6. Macchi "MC 72" Seaplane.

8.

(b) Air.

63. 6. 50 c. brown .. .. 65 1·00
64. – 75 c. purple .. .. 65 1·00
65. 6. 1 l. sepia .. .. 65 1·00
66. – 3 l. green .. .. 65 1·00
67. 6. 10 l. violet .. .. 65 1·00
68. – 12 l. blue .. .. 65 1·00
69. – 20 l. green .. .. 2·75 4·00
70. – 50 l. blue .. .. 8·50 11·00

DESIGNS—HORIZ. 75 c., 3 l., 12 l. S.A.N. tri-motor VERT. 20 l. Pilot swinging propeller. 50 l. Propeller.

1934. 15th Milan Fair.

71. 8. 20 c. red 20 30
72. 30 c. green.. .. .. 20 30
73. 50 c. black.. .. .. 20 30
74. 1 l. 25 blue 20 30

10. Scoring a Goal.

9. Hailing Airliner.

11. Seaplane over Stadium.

1934. Air. Duke of Abruzzi issue.

75. 9. 25 l. black .. .. 3·50 6·50

1934. World Football Championship.

76. 10. 10 c. green (postage) .. 1·25 1·75
77. 50 c. violet .. .. 1·25 1·75
78. 1 l. 25 blue .. .. 2·75 3·50
79. – 5 l. brown .. .. 7·00 12·00
80. – 10 l. blue .. .. 13·00 18·00

DESIGNS—VERT. 5 l., 10 l. Fascist salute.

81. 11. 50 c. brown (air).. .. 1·10 1·75
82. 75 c. purple .. .. 1·10 1·75
83. – 5 l. black.. .. .. 5·00 7·00
84. – 10 l. red .. .. .. 5·00 7·00
85. 11. 15 l. red .. .. .. 5·00 7·00
86. – 25 l. green .. .. 7·50 11·00
87. – 50 l. green .. .. 8·00 12·00

DESIGN—VERT. 5 l., 10 l., 25 l. "Saving a goal". HORIZ. 50 l. Giant Football and seaplane.

ITALIAN EAST AFRICA O2

Italian Empire in E. Africa comprising Eritrea, Ethiopia and It. Somaliland constituted by Royal Decree of 1st June, 1936. Occupied by British Forces 1942/3. See "Middle East Forces".

100 centesimi = 1 lira.

2. R. Nile, Statue and Lake Tsana.

1. Grant's Gazelle.

3. Mussolini Monument and Mt. Amba Aradam.

1938.

1. 1. 2 c. orange postage) .. 5 5
2. A. 5 c. brown.. .. .. 5 5
3. B. 7½ c. violet 5 8
4. 2. 10 c. brown 5 5
5. C. 15 c. green 5 5
6. B. 20 c. red 5 5
7. D. 25 c. green.. .. .. 5 5
8. 1. 30 c brown 5 5
9. A. 35 c. blue 5 5
10. B. 50 c. violet 5 5
11. C. 75 c. red 5 5
12. D. 1 l. olive 8 5
13. B. 1 l. 25 blue 5 5
14. 2. 1 l. 75 orange 90 5
15. A. 2 l. red 5 5
16. D. 2 l. 55 brown 30 30
17. 1. 3 l. 70 violet .. .. 2·75 1·60
18. C. 5 l. blue 20 8
19. A. 10 l. red 75 35
20. 2. 20 l. green.. .. .. 65 50
21. E. 25 c. green (air) 20 15
22. 3. 50 c. brown .. .. 2·50 5
23. F. 60 c. orange 8 15
24. E. 75 c. brown 45 8
25. G. 1 l. blue 5 5
26. 3. 1 l. 50 violet 5 5
27. F. 2 l. blue 5 5
28. E. 3 l. red 8 10
29. G. 5 l. brown 45 20
30. 3. 10 l. purple .. .. 1·00 35
31. E. 25 l. blue .. .. .. 1·60 80

DESIGNS—POSTAGE—VERT. A. Italian Eagle attacking Lion. B. Profile of King Victor Emmanuel III. C. Soldier implanting Fascist emblem. HORIZ. D. Road and banners. AIR—HORIZ. E. Aeroplane, Eagle and Mt. Amba Aradam. F. Aeroplane over Lake Tsana. VERT. G. Bateleur Eagle.

7. Statue of Augustus.

8. Eagle and Serpent.

1938. Augustus the Great. Birth Bimillenary.

36. 7. 5 c. brown (postage) .. 10 15
37. – 10 c. red 10 15
38. 7. 25 c. green.. .. .. 10 15
39. – 50 c. violet 10 15
40. 7. 75 c. red 15 20
41. – 1 l. 25 blue 15 20

DESIGN: 10 c., 50 c., 1 l. 25, Statue of Goddess of Abundance.

42. 8. 50 c. brown (air) 15 25
43. 1 l. violet 15 30

9. Native Boat.

1940. Naples Exn.

44. 9. 5 c. brown (postage) .. 8 10
45. – 10 c. orange 8 10
46. – 25 c. green.. .. .. 20 25
47. 9. 50 c. violet 20 25
48. – 75 c. red 20 25
49. – 1 l. 25 blue 20 25
50. – 2 l.+75 c. red 25 40

DESIGNS—VERT. 10 c., 75 c., 2 l. Soldier. 25 c., 1 l. 25 Allegory of Italian Conquest of Ethiopia.

51. 50 c. grey (air) 25 30
52. 1 l. violet 25 30
53. 2 l.+75 c. blue 30 40
54. 5 l.+2 l. brown 30 40

DESIGNS—VERT. 50 c., 2 l. Tractor. HORIZ. 1 l., 5 l. Aeroplane.

10. Hitler and Mussolini.

1941. Axis Commemoration.

55. 10. 5 c. yellow (postage) .. 8
56. 10 c. brown 8
57. 20 c. black 20
58. 25 c. green 20
59. 50 c. lilac 20
60. 75 c. red 20
61. 1 l. 25 blue 20
62. 10. 1 l. blue (air) .. .. 3·50
63. 1 l. blue 35

In No. 62 the "1 lira" tablet is in the centre: in No. 63 it is in the lower left corner.

EXPRESS LETTER STAMPS

1938. Air. As Nos. 1/31.

E 32. 2 l. blue 12 12
E 33. 2 l. 50 red 12 15

DESIGNS—VERT. 2 l., 2 l. 50., H. Plough and Native huts.

E 1. King Victor Emmanuel III.

1938.

E 34. E 1. 1 l. 25 green.. .. 10 10
E 35. 2 l. 50 red 20 25

POSTAGE DUE STAMPS

1941. Nos. D 395/407 of Italy optd. **A.O.I.**

D 64. D 6. 5 c. brown 10
D 65. 10 c. blue 10
D 66. 20 c. red 12
D 67. 25 c. green 12
D 68. 30 c. orange 20
D 69. 40 c. brown 20
D 70. 50 c. violet 25
D 71. 60 c. blue 30
D 72. D 7. 1 l. orange .. .. 5·00
D 73. 2 l. green .. .. 5·00
D 74. 5 l. violet .. .. 5·00
D 75. 10 l. blue .. .. 5·00
D 76. 20 l. red .. .. 5·00

ITALIAN POST OFFICES IN CHINA O1

Italian Military Posts in China, including Peking and Tientsin, now closed.

100 centesimi = 1 lira. 100 cents = 1 dollar.

Stamps of Italy overprinted or surcharged.

(a) Peking.

1917. Optd. **Pechino.**

9. 20. 1 c. brown 20 25
10. 21. 2 c. brown 20 25
11. 24. 5 c. green 5 5
12. 10 c. red 5 5
13. 25. 20 c. orange 35 35
14. 26. 25 c. blue 5 5
15. 22. 50 c. violet 5 5
16. 23. 1 l. brown and green .. 12 15
17. 5 l. blue and red .. 12 25
18. 10 l. olive and red .. 1·00 1·40

1917. Surch. **Pechino** and value.

19. 20. ½ c. on 1 c. brown .. 1·40 1·40
20. 21. 1 c. on 2 c. brown .. 5 5
21. 24. 2 c. on 5 c. green .. 5 5
22. 4 c. on 10 c. red .. 5 5
24. 25. 6 c. on 15 c. black .. 20·00 11·00
23. 8 c. on 20 c. orange .. 5 10
24. 26. 10 c. on 25 c. blue .. 5 10
25. 22. 20 c. on 50 c. violet .. 10 15
26. 23. 40 c. on 1 l. brown & grn. 1·25 1·75
27. 2 d. on 5 l. blue and red.. 13·00 15·00

EXPRESS LETTER STAMPS

1917. Express Letter stamp optd. **Pechino** or surch. **12 CENTS** also.
E 28. E 2. 12 c. on 30 c. bl. & red 1·50 1·75
E 19. 30 c. blue and red .. 20 25

POSTAGE DUE STAMPS

1917. Postage Due stamps optd. **Pechino** or surch. also.
D 28. D 3. 4 c. on 10 c. purple and orange .. £2,000 £1,600
D 29. 8 c. on 20 c. purple and orange 5 8
D 19. 10 c. purple & orange 5 5
D 30. 12 c. on 30 c. purple and orange .. 1·75 1·75
D 31. 16 c. on 40 c. purple and orange .. 4·50 4·50
D 20. 20 c. purple & orange 5 5
D 21. 30 c. purple & orange 5 5
D 22. 40 c. purple & orange 15 20

(b) Tientsin.

1917. Optd. **Tientsin.**
34. 20. 1 c. brown 15 25
35. 21. 2 c. brown 15 25
36. 24. 5 c. green 5 5
37. 10 c. red 5 5
38. 25. 20 c. orange 30 35
39. 26. 25 c. blue 5 5
40. 22. 50 c. violet 5 10
41. 23. 1 l. brown and green .. 12 15
42. 5 l. blue and red .. 12 25
43. 10 l. olive and red .. 1·00 1·40

1917. Surch. **Tientsin** and value.
44. 20. ½ c. on 1 c. brown .. 65 75
45. 21. 1 c. on 2 c. brown .. 5 5
46. 24. 2 c. on 5 c. green .. 5 5
47. 4 c. on 10 c. red .. 5 5
33. 25. 6 c. on 15 c. black .. 30·00 20·00
48. 8 c. on 20 c. orange .. 5 10
49. 26. 10 c. on 25 c. blue .. 5 10
50. 22. 20 c. on 50 c. violet 10 15
51. 23. 40 c. on 1 l. brn. & green 90 1·25
52. 2 d. on 5 l. blue and red .. 12·00 13·00

EXPRESS LETTER STAMPS

1917. Express Letter stamp optd. **Tientsin** or surch. **12 CENTS** also.
E 53. E 2. 12 c. on 30 c. blue & red 1·50 1·75
E 44. 30 c. blue and red .. 20 25

POSTAGE DUE STAMPS

1917. Postage Due stamps optd. **Tientsin** or surch. also.
D 53. D 3. 4 c. on 10 c. purple and orange .. £130 £140
D 54. 8 c. on 20 c. purple and orange 5 8
D 44. 10 c. purple & orange 5 5
D 55. 12 c. on 30 c. purple and orange .. 1·25 1·50
D 56. 16 c. on 40 c. purple and orange .. 3·75 4·25
D 45. 20 c. purple & orange 5 5
D 46. 30 c. purple & orange 5 5
D 47. 40 c. purple & orange 15 20

ITALIAN POST OFFICES IN CRETE E1

Italian P.O.s in Crete now closed.
Currency: Turkish or Italian.

Stamps of Italy surcharged or overprinted.

1900. Surch. **1 PIASTRA 1.**
1. 18. 1 pi. on 25 c. blue .. 35 30

1901. Surch. **LA CANEA 1 PIASTRA 1.**
2. 22. 1 pi. on 25 c. blue .. 35 30

1906. 1901 stamps optd. **LA CANEA.**
3. 20. 1 c. brown 8 10
4. 21. 2 c. brown 8 5
5. 5 c. green 10 8
6. 22. 10 c. red .. .. 28·00 17·00
7. 15 c. on 20 c. orange .. 12 12
8. 25 c. blue 55 50
9. 40 c. brown 40 40
10. 45 c. olive 35 35
11. 50 c. violet 40 50
12. 23. 1 l. brown and green .. 1·10 1·10
13. 5 l. blue and red .. 14·00 15·00

1907. 1906 stamps optd. **LA CANEA.**
14. 24. 5 c. green 8 12
15. 10 c. red 10 12
16. 25. 15 c. black 10 12
17. 26. 25 c. blue 20 20
18. 40 c. brown .. .. 1·00 1·25
19. 50 c. mauve 30 35

EXPRESS LETTER STAMP

1906. Express Letter stamp optd. **LA CANEA.**
E 1. E 1. 25 c. red 30 35

ITALIAN POST OFFICES IN THE LEVANT E3

Currency: Italian and Turkish.
Stamps of Italy overprinted and surcharged.

A. GENERAL ISSUES.

The following were in use in P.O.s in Alexandria, Assab, La Goletta, Massaouah, Susa, Tripoli and Tunis and also at Consular post offices at Buenos Aires and Montevideo.

1874. 1863 type, slightly altered, optd. **ESTERO.**
1a. 4. 1 c. green .. .. 15 2·50
2. 5. 2 c. brown .. .. 25 2·75
3. 6. 5 c. grey .. .. 25·00 1·90
4. 10 c. orange .. .. £100 6·50
10. 10 c. blue .. .. 20·00 1·00
5. 7. 20 c. blue .. .. 75·00 2·50
11. 20 c. orange .. .. £250 1·00
6. 6. 30 c. brown 30 40
7. 40 c. red 25 90
8. 60 c. mauve .. .. 50 9·50
9. 8. 2 l. red .. .. 10·00 50·00

1881. 1879 type, slightly altered, optd. **ESTERO.**
12. 9. 5 c. green .. .. 80 1·00
13. 10 c. red 30 40
14. 20 c. orange 30 40
15. 25 c. blue 30 50
16. 50 c. mauve .. .. 50 6·50

B. OFFICES IN TURKISH EMPIRE.

(a) Albania.

1902. Optd. **ALBANIA.**
18. 21. 10 pa. on 5 c. green .. 20 20
24. 24. 10 pa. on 5 c. green .. 4·50 4·50
25. 20 pa. on 10 c. red .. 70 70
19. 22. 35 pa. on 20 c. orange .. 85 70
20. 40 pa. on 25 c. blue .. 60 55
26. 80 pa. on 50 c. mauve .. 80 1·00

1902. Surch. with figures of value repeated twice and currency in words thus, **20 PARA 20.**
21. 21. 10 pa. on 5 c. green .. 15 15
27. 24. 10 pa. on 5 c. green .. 5 5
28. 20 pa. on 10 c. red .. 5 5
22. 22. 35 pa. on 20 c. orange .. 30 40
23. 40 pa. on 25 c. blue .. 2·75 80
29. 80 pa. on 50 c. mauve .. 2·75 2·40

(b) General Offices in Europe and Asia.

1908. Surch. with figures of value repeated twice and currency in words thus, **30 Para 30.**
32. 25. 30 pa. on 15 c. black .. 12 12
30. 26. 40 pa. on 25 c. blue .. 15 12
31. 80 pa. on 50 c. mauve .. 20 15

EXPRESS LETTER STAMPS

1908. Express Letter stamps surch. **LEVANTE** and new value.
E 33. E 1. 1 pi. on 25 c. red .. 12 12
E 34. E 2. 60 pa. on 30 c. bl. & red 15 15

C. INDIVIDUAL OFFICES IN EUROPE AND ASIA.

(a) Constantinople.

1908. Surch. in one line with figure of value and currency in words.
40. 24. 10 pa. on 5 c. green .. 20 20
41. 20 pa. on 10 c. red .. 20 20
47. 25. 30 pa. on 15 c. black .. 25 15
43. 26. 1 pi. on 25 c. blue .. 50 40
44. 2 pi. on 50 c. mauve .. 6·50 6·50
45. 23. 4 pi. on 1 l. brn. & green £110 70·00
46. 20 pi. on 5 l. blue and red £350 £190

1908. Surch. in two lines with figures of value repeated twice and currency in words.
50. 23. 4 pi. on 1 l. brown & green 3·00 2·10
51. 20 pi. on 5 l. blue and red 3·00 2·10

1909. Surch. **Costantinopoli** or **COSTANTINOPOLI** and value in figures twice repeated and currency in words.
52. 24. 10 pa. on 5 c. green .. 12 12
53. 20 pa. on 10 c. red .. 12 12
54. 25. 30 pa. on 15 c. black .. 12 12
55. 26. 1 pi. on 25 c. blue .. 12 12
56. 2 pi. on 50 c. mauve .. 15 15
57. 23. 4 pi. on 1 l. brown & grn. 15 15
58. 20 pi. on 5 l. blue and red 75 90
59. 40 pi. on 10 l. olive & red 50 75

1921. Surch. with value in figures and currency in words thus, **4 PIASTRE.**
60. 24. 1 pi. on 5 c. green .. 20·00 25·00
61. 2 pi. on 15 c. grey .. 12 20
62. 25. 4 pi. on 20 c. orange .. 70 80
63. 26. 5 pi. on 25 c. blue .. 75 80
64. 10 pi. on 60 c. red .. 8 8

1921. Surch. with value in figures and currency in words thus, **PARA 20.**
65. 20. 10 pa. on 1 c. brown .. 8 12
66. 21. 20 pa. on 2 c. brown .. 8 12
67. 24. 30 pa. on 5 c. green .. 12 15
68. 1 pi. 20 on 15 c. grey .. 20 12
69. 3 pi. on 20 c. orange .. 1·10 50
70. 26. 3 pi. 30 on 25 c. blue .. 25 25
71. 7 pi. 20 on 60 c. red .. 35 20
72. 23. 15 pi. on 1 l. brown & grn. 70 1·00

1922. Surch. **COSTANTINOPOLI** and value in figures once only after currency in words.
73. 24. 20 pa. on 5 c. green .. 75 1·00
74. 1 pi. 20 on 15 c. grey .. 8 8
75. 26. 3 pi. on 30 c. brown .. 12 15
76. 3 pi. 30 on 40 c. brown .. 12 15
77. 23. 7 pi. 20 on 1 l. brown and green 12 15

1922. Surch. **Piastre 3, 75** in two lines.
78. 26. 3.75 pi. on 25 c. blue .. 12 15

1922. Para values surch. in one line thus **30 PARA** and piastre values with **PIASTRE** over new value except Nos. 81, 86, 98 and 99 where the figures of value are above.
79. 21. 30 pa. on 2 c. brown .. 5 8
80. 24. 30 pa. on 5 c. green .. 30 40
81. 25. 1,50 pi. on 20 c. orange 8 12
82. 26. 1,50 pi. on 25 c. blue .. 15 25
83. 3,75 pi. on 40 c. brown 8 8
84. 4,50 pi. on 50 c. mauve 12 12
85. 7,50 pi. on 60 c. red 12 15
86. 15 pi. on 85 c. brown .. 30 50
87. 23. 18,75 pi. on 1 l. brown and green 15 30
98. 45 pi. on 5 l. blue and red 4·00 5·50
99. 90 pi. on 10 l. olive & red 4·00 5·50

1922. Para values surch. in two lines and piastre values with **PIASTRE** under new value.
90. 24. 30 pa. on 5 c. green .. 8 8
91. 1½ pi. on 10 c. red .. 8 8
92. 26. 3 pi. on 25 c. blue .. 12 12
93. 3¾ pi. on 40 c. brown .. 12 10
94. 4½ pi. on 50 c. mauve .. 2·00 2·00
95. 7½ pi. on 85 c. brown .. 40 50
96. 23. 7½ pi. on 1 l. brn. & green 65 80
97. 15 pi. on 1 l. brn. & green 9·00 10·00

1923. Surch. **COSTANTINOPOLI** and value in figures once only after currency in words.
100. 24. 30 pa. on 5 c. green .. 12 12
101. 26. 1 pi. 20 on 25 c. blue .. 12 12
102. 3 pi. 30 on 40 c. brown .. 12 12
103. 4 pi. 20 on 50 c. mauve 12 12
104. 7 pi. 20 on 60 c. red .. 12 12
105. 15 pi. on 85 c. brown .. 12 12
106. 23. 18 pi. 30 on 1 l. brown and green 20 30
107. 45 pi. on 5 l. blue & red 30 40
108. 90 pi. on 10 l. olive & red 40 55

EXPRESS LETTER STAMPS

1922. Express Letter stamps surch. with new value.
E 90. E 2. 15 pi. on 1 l. 20 on 30 c. blue and red .. 1·25 1·75
E 100. 15 pi. on 30 c. blue and red .. .. 25·00 29·00

1923. Express Letter stamp surch. **COSTANTINOPOLI** and new value.
E 109. E 2. 15 pi. on 1 l. 20 blue and red 30 40

POSTAGE DUE STAMPS

1922. Postage Due stamps optd. **CONSTANTINOPOLI.**
D 100. D 3. 10 c. purple and orge. 15 20
D 101. 30 c. purple and orge. 20 25
D 102. 60 c. purple and orge. 20 30
D 103. 1 l. purple and blue 25 40
D 104. 2 l. purple and blue £180 £180
D 105. 5 l. purple and blue 25·00 25·00

(b) Durazzo.

1909. Surch. **Durazzo** or **DURAZZO** and value.
109. 21. 10 pa. on 5 c. green .. 12 25
110. 24. 20 pa. on 10 c. red .. 12 15
111. 25. 30 pa. on 15 c. black .. 1·40 80
112. 26. 1 pi. on 25 c. blue .. 12 15
113. 2 pi. on 50 c. mauve .. 12 15
114. 23. 4 pi. on 1 l. brown & grn. 20 25
115. 20 pi. on 5 l. blue & red 9·00 10·00
116. 40 pi. on 10 l. olive & red 2·50 4·50

1915. Surch. **CENT. 20** and bars.
116a. 25. 20 c. on 30 pa. on 15 c. black (No. 111) .. 30 65

(c) Janina.

1909. Surch. **Janina** or **JANINA** and value.
117. 21. 10 pa. on 5 c. green .. 12 15
118. 24. 20 pa. on 10 c. red .. 12 15
119. 25. 30 pa. on 15 c. black .. 12 15
120. 26. 1 pi. on 25 c. blue .. 12 15
121. 2 pi. on 50 c. mauve .. 20 25
122. 23. 4 pi. on 1 l. brn. & green 30 35
123. 20 pi. on 5 l. blue & red 13·00 17·00
124. 40 pi. on 10 l. olive & red 2·75 5·00

(d) Jerusalem.

1909. Surch. **Gerusalemme** or **GERUSALEMME** and value.
125. 24. 10 pa. on 5 c. green .. 12 80
126. 20 pa. on 10 c. red .. 12 80
127. 25. 30 pa. on 15 c. black .. 12 80
128. 26. 1 pi. on 25 c. blue .. 12 80
129. 2 pi. on 50 c. mauve .. 20 2·10
130. 23. 4 pi. on 1 l. brown & grn. 25 4·00
131. 20 pi. on 5 l. blue & red 32·00 45·00
132. 40 pi. on 10 l. olive & red 3·25 15·00

(e) Salonica.

1909. Surch. **Salonicco** or **SALONICCO** and value.
133. 24. 10 pa. on 5 c. green .. 12 15
134. 20 pa. on 10 c. red .. 12 15
135. 25. 30 pa. on 15 c. black .. 12 15
136. 26. 1 pi. on 25 c. blue .. 12 15
137. 2 pi. on 50 c. mauve .. 20 25
138. 23. 4 pi. on 1 l. brown & grn. 30 40
139. 20 pi. on 5 l. blue & red 30·00 32·00
140. 40 pi. on 10 l. olive & red 2·75 4·50

(f) Scutari.

1909. Surch. **Scutari di Albania** or **SCUTARI DI ALBANIA** and value.
141. 21. 4 pa. on 2 c. brown .. 8 10
142. 10 pa. on 5 c. green .. 12 15
143. 24. 20 pa. on 10 c. red .. 12 15
144. 25. 30 pa. on 15 c. black .. 1·40 80
145. 26. 1 pi. on 25 c. blue .. 12 15
146. 2 pi. on 50 c. mauve .. 20 20
147. 23. 4 pi. on 1 l. brn. & green 25 30
148. 20 pi. on 5 l. blue and red 50 80
149. 40 pi. on 10 l. olive & grey 7·50 10·00

1916. Surch. **CENT 20** and bars.
150. 25. 20 c. on 30 pa. on 15 c. black (No. 144) .. 30 65

(g) Smyrna.

1909. Surch. **Smirne** or **SMIRNE** and value.
152. 24. 10 pa. on 5 c. green .. 10 10
153. 20 pa. on 10 c. red .. 10 10
153. 25. 30 pa. on 15 c. black .. 10 10
154. 26. 1 pi. on 25 c. blue .. 10 10
155. 2 pi. on 50 c. mauve .. 15 20
156. 23. 4 pi. on 1 l. brn. & grn. .. 25 30
157. 20 pi. on 5 l. blue & red 75 90
158. 40 pi. on 10 l. olive & red 2·50 4·50

(h) Valona.

1909. Surch. **Valona** or **VALONA** and value.
159 21. 10 pa. on 5 c. green .. 12 15
160. 24. 20 pa. on 10 c. red .. 12 15
161. 25. 30 pa. on 15 c. black† .. 1·40 80
167. 30 pa. on 15 c. black† .. 20 35
162. 26. 1 pi. on 25 c. blue .. 12 15
163. 2 pi. on 50 c. mauve .. 15 20
164. 23. 4 pi. on 1 l. brn. & green 20 25
165. 20 pi. on 5 l. blue and red 40 70
166. 40 pi. on 10 l. olive & red 8·50 11·00
On No. 161 the surcharge is **Para**, on No. 167, **PARA.**

1916. Surch. **CENT. 20** and bars.
168. 25. 20 c. on 30 pa. on 15 c. black (No. 161) .. 12 25

D. OFFICES IN AFRICA.

(a) Bengasi.

1901. Surch. **BENGASI I PIASTRA I.**
169. 22. 1 pi. on 25 c. blue .. 3·25 2·10
170. 26. 1 pi. on 25 c. blue .. 2·50 2·10

(b) Tripoli.

1909. Optd. **Tripoli di Barberia** or **TRIPOLI DI BARBERIA.**
171. 20. 1 c. brown 8 12
173. 21. 2 c. brown 12 15
174. 24. 5 c. green .. .. 3·25 80
175. 10 c. red 12 15
176. 25. 15 c. black 12 15
177. 26. 25 c. blue 12 15
178. 40 c. brown 15 20
179. 50 c. mauve 20 25
180. 23. 1 l. brown and green .. 21·00 8·00
181. 5 l. blue and red .. 7·50 10·00

EXPRESS LETTER STAMPS

1909. Express Letter stamps optd. **TRIPOLI DI BARBERIA.**
E 182. E 1. 25 c. red 20 25
E 183. E 2. 30 c. red and blue .. 65 75

ITALY E2

A Republic in S. Europe on the Mediterranean and Adriatic Seas. Originally a kingdom formed by the union of various smaller kingdoms and duchies which issued their own stamps.

100 centesimi = 1 lira.

1. King Victor Emmanuel II. 2. 3.

1862. Head embossed. Perf. (15 c. imperf.).
1. 1. 10 c. brown .. .. £2000 55·00
5. 15 c. blue .. .. 29·00 8·00
2a. 20 c. blue .. .. 3·25 5·50
3. 40 c. red .. .. 70·00 32·00
4. 80 c. yellow .. .. 11·00 £250
For stamps of this type imperf., see Sardinia, Nos. 27, etc.

1863. Imperf.
7. 2. 15 c. blue 15 35

1862. Newspaper stamp. Imperf.
N 5. 8. 2 c. yellow .. .. 12·00 14·00
For 1 c. and 2 c. stamps of similar type in black see Sardinia Nos. N 1/2.

4. 5. 6.

7. 8.

1863. Perf.

8.	4.	1 c. green..	60	10
9a.	5.	2 c. brown	3·00	5
10.	6.	5 c. grey	£250	10
11.		10 c. brown	£350	10
21.		10 c. blue..	£950	25
12.		15 c. blue..	£325	15
20a.	7.	20 c. blue..	£120	5
22.		20 c. orange	£650	5
13.	6.	30 c. brown	5·00	15
14.		40 c. red	£800	30
15.		60 c. mauve	6·00	2·50
16a.	8.	2 l. red	7·00	10·00

1865. Surch. **C 20 20 C** and curved bar.

17.	6.	20 c. on 15 c. blue ..	£110	12

1878. Official stamps surch. with value and wavy bars.

23.	O 1.	2 c. on 2 c. claret ..	17·00	2·00
24.		2 c. on 5 c. claret ..	21·00	2·75
25.		2 c. on 20 c. claret ..	£190	50
26.		2 c. on 30 c. claret ..	29·00	70
27.		2 c. on 1 l. claret ..	95·00	65
28.		2 c. on 2 l. claret ..	£100	75
29.		2 c. on 5 l. claret ..	£130	1·50
30.		2 c. on 10 l. claret ..	55·00	2·10

9. King Humbert I. 10. Arms of Savoy. 11.

1879.

31.	9.	5 c. green	6·00	8
32.		10 c. red	70·00	8
33.		20 c. orange	55·00	5
34.		25 c. blue	85·00	10
35.		30 c. brown	40·00	£325
36.		50 c. mauve	4·25	40
37.		2 l. orange	24·00	32·00

1889. Figures in four corners.

38.	10.	5 c. green	£140	25
39.	11.	40 c. brown	2·50	25
40.		45 c. grey-green ..	£550	40
41.		60 c. mauve	2·50	65
42.		1 l. brown and orange ..	4·00	35
43.		5 l. red and green ..	3·00	60·00

1890. Surch. thus **Cmi 2.**

44.	9.	2 c. on 5 c. green ..	6·00	7·50
45.		20 c. on 30 c. brown ..	65·00	60
46.		20 c. on 50 c. mauve ..	75·00	5·00

1890. Parcel Post stamps surch. **Valevole per le stampe** and value.

47.	P 1.	2 c. on 10 c. olive ..	60	40
48.		2 c. on 20 c. blue ..	1·00	65
49.		2 c. on 50 c. red ..	9·00	2·75
50.		2 c. on 75 c. green ..	80	40
51.		2 c. on 1 l. 25 orange ..	9·00	2·50
52.		2 c. on 1 l. 75 brown ..	4·00	8·00

12. 13. 14.

15. 16. 17.

18. 19.

1891.

53.	12.	1 c. brown	1·90	25
54.	13.	2 c. brown	2·25	5
55.	14.	5 c. green	£150	15
56.	15.	5 c. green	3·25	5
57.	16.	10 c. red	3·25	5
58.	17.	20 c. orange	3·25	5
59.	18.	25 c. blue	3·25	5
60.		45 c. olive	2·50	12
61.	19.	5 l. red and blue ..	21·00	21·00

20. 21.

King Victor Emmanuel III.
22. 23.

1901.

62.	20.	1 c. brown	5	5
63.	21.	2 c. brown	5	5
64.		5 c. green	23·00	5
65.	22.	10 c. red	27·00	5
66.		20 c. orange	2·00	5
67.		25 c. blue	18·00	5
68.		40 c. brown	£110	50
69.		45 c. olive	1·25	5
70.		50 c. violet	£110	1·40
71.	23.	1 l. brown and green ..	65	5
72.		5 l. blue and red ..	3·75	12

1905. Surch. **C. 15.**

73.	22.	15 c. on 20 c. orange ..	29·00	5

24. 25. 26.

1906.

75.	24.	5 c. green	5	5
76.		10 c. red	5	5
90.	25.	15 c. black	4·50	5
105.		20 c. orange	40	5
77.	26.	25 c. blue	12	5
78.		40 c. brown	25	5
79.		50 c. mauve	15	5
85.	23.	10 l. olive and red ..	18·00	1·50

27. Garibaldi. 28.

1910. Freedom of Sicily. 50th Anniv.

81.	27.	5 c. green	4·25	1·75
82.		15 c. red	17·00	10·00

1910. Southern Plebiscite of 1860.

83.	28.	5 c. red	40·00	13·00
84.		15 c. green	£100	21·00

29. 30. 33.

1911. Jubilee of Italian Kingdom.

86.	29.	2 c. (+3 c.) brown ..	85	40
87.	30.	5 c. (+5 c.) green ..	1·60	1·40
88.	–	10 c. (+5 c.) red ..	1·60	1·40
89.	–	15 c. (+5 c.) grey ..	2·10	1·25

DESIGNS: Symbolic of the Genius of Italy (10 c.) and the Glory of Rome (15 c.).

1912. Re-erection of Campanile of St. Mark, Venice.

91.	33.	5 c. black	1·25	2·00
92.		15 c. brown	4·50	3·25

1913. Surch. **22.**

93.	30.	2 on 5 c. green	35	35
94.	–	2 on 10 c. red (No. 88)..	55	45
95.	–	2 on 15 c. grey (No. 89)..	40	40

34. Banner of United Italy.

35. Italian Eagle and Arms of Savoy.

1915. Red Cross Society. No. 98 is surch. **20.**

96.	34.	10 c.+5 c. red ..	60	60
97.	35.	15 c.+5 c. grey ..	60	60
98.		"20" on 15 c.+5 c. grey..	3·50	7·00
99.		20 c.+5 c. orange ..	4·50	2·75

1916. Surch. **CENT 20** and bars.

100.	25.	20 c. on 15 c. black ..	2·75	5

1917. Air. Express Letter stamp, optd. **ESPERIMENTO POSTA AEREA MAGGIO 1917 TORINO-ROMA-ROMA-TONINO.**

102.	E 1.	25 c. red	5·00	4·00

1917. Air. Express Letter stamp surch. **IDROVOLANTE NAPOLI-PALERMO NAPOLI 25 CENT. 25.**

103.	E 1.	25 c. on 40 c. violet..	9·50	6·00

1917.

104.	24.	15 c. grey	20	5
178.	26.	20 c. orange	10	5
179.		20 c. green	10	5
180.		20 c. purple	15	5
181.	23.	25 c. green	10	5
182.	26.	25 c. green	1·10	35
106.		30 c. brown	20	5
183.		30 c. grey	40	5
107.		55 c. purple	1·40	65
108.		60 c. red	30	5
109.		60 c. blue	1·90	2·75
184.		60 c. orange	95	5
185.	23.	75 c. red	65	5
110.	26.	85 c. brown	90	20
186.	23.	1 l. 25 blue	75	5
111.		2 l. green and orange ..	3·25	20
187.		2 l. 50 green and orange	15·00	40

36. Ancient Seal of Republic of Trieste.

37.

41.

40. Victory.

1921. Reunion of Venezia Giulia with Italy.

112.	36.	15 c. red and black ..	55	1·60
113.		25 c. red and blue ..	55	1·60
114.		40 c. red and brown ..	55	1·60

1921. Dante. 600th Death Anniv.

115.	37.	15 c. claret	80	80
116.	–	25 c. green	80	80
117.	–	40 c. brown	80	80

DESIGNS: 25 c. Woman with book. 40 c. Dante.

1921. Victory of 1918.

118.	40.	5 c. green	20	25
119.		10 c. red	60	70
120.		15 c. grey	1·25	1·25
121.		25 c. blue	40	50

1922. 9th Italian Philatelic Congress. Optd. **IX CONGRESSO FILATELICO ITALIANO TRIESTE 1922.**

122.	24.	10 c. red	90·00	38·00
123.		15 c. grey	75·00	38·00
124.	26.	25 c. blue	75·00	38·00
125.		40 c. brown	£130	55·00

1922. Mazzini Commem. Inscr. "CINQUANTENARIO MAZZINIANO 1922".

126.	41.	25 c. claret	1·60	1·40
127.	–	40 c. purple	2·50	2·50
128.	–	80 c. blue	1·40	1·40

DESIGNS—VERT. 40 c. Mazzini. HORIZ. 80 c. Tomb of Mazzini.

44. Christ and His Disciples.

1923. Tercent of Propagation of the Faith.

129.	44.	20 c. orange and green	1·90	5·00
130.		30 c. orange and red ..	1·90	5·00
131.		50 c. orange and violet	1·50	5·00
132.		1 l. orange and blue ..	1·50	5·00

The portraits and arms in the corners at right vary for each value.

1923. Surch. in words and figures. (15 c. surch. **DIECI** only).

133.	26.	7½ c. on 85 c. brown ..	5	12
135.	20.	10 c. on 1 c. brown ..	10	5
136.	21.	10 c. on 2 c. brown ..	10	5
137.	24.	10 c. on 15 c. grey ..	8	5
138.	26.	20 c. on 25 c. blue ..	12	5
139.	22.	25 c. on 45 c. olive ..	12	30
140.	26.	25 c. on 60 c. blue ..	1·00	12
141.		30 c. on 50 c. mauve ..	8	5
142.		30 c. on 55 c. purple ..	20	5
143.		50 c. on 40 c. brown ..	20	5
144.		50 c. on 55 c. purple ..	10·00	1·00
145.	23.	1 l. 75 on 10 l. ol. & red	3·00	2·00

45.

46.

47.

1923. Fascisti Commemorative.

146.	45.	10 c. green	20	20
147.		30 c. violet	20	20
148.		50 c. red	40	40
149.	46.	1 l. blue	70	50
150.		2 l. brown	1·40	90
151.	47.	5 l. black and blue ..	4·50	3·25

48.

ILLUSTRATIONS British Commonwealth and all overprints and surcharges are FULL SIZE. Foreign Countries have been reduced to ¾-LINEAR.

1923. Charity. Fascist "Black Shirt".

152.	48.	30 c.+30 c. brown ..	10·00	13·00
153.		50 c.+50 c. mauve ..	10·00	13·00
154.		1 l. +1 l. grey ..	10·00	13·00

49.

DESIGNS: 10 c. to 50 c. Scenes from Manzoni's "I Promessi Sposi". 1 l. Manzoni's home, Milan. 5 l. Portrait of Manzoni.

1923. Manzoni.

155.	49.	10 c. black and red ..	30	80
156.	–	15 c. black and green ..	30	80
157.	–	30 c. black	30	80
158.	–	50 c. black and brown..	30	80
159.	–	1 l. black and blue ..	7·00	14·00
160.	–	5 l. black and purple ..	£200	£250

1924. Victory stamps surch. **LIRE UNA** between stars.

161.	40.	1 l. on 5 c. green ..	12·00	17·00
162.		1 l. on 10 c. red.. ..	6·50	8·50
163.		1 l. on 15 c. grey ..	10·00	13·00
164.		1 l. on 25 c. blue ..	4·25	4·25

1924. Optd. **CROCIERA ITALIANA 1924.**

165.	24.	10 c. red	30	70
166.	26.	30 c. brown	30	70
167.		50 c. mauve	30	70
168.		60 c. blue	5·50	6·50
169.		85 c. brown	2·00	3·75
170.	23.	1 l. brown and green ..	24·00	32·00
171.		2 l. green and orange ..	19·00	32·00

Used on an Italian cruiser which visited South America for trade propaganda.

51. Church of St. John Lateran.

1924. Holy Year.

172.	–	20 c.+10 c. brn. & grn...	35	45
173.	51.	30 c.+15 c. brn. & choc.	40	55
174.	–	50 c.+25 c. brn. & vio...	50	65
175.	–	60 c.+30 c. brn. & red..	60	85
176.	–	1 l.+50 c. pur. & blue..	1·50	1·90
177.	–	5 l.+2 l.50 pur. & red ..	3·25	5·50

DESIGNS: 20 c. Church of St. Maria Maggiore. 50 c. Church of St. Paul. 60 c. St. Peter's. 1 l. Pope opening Holy Door. 5 l. Pope shutting Holy Door.

53.

54. Vision of St. Francis.

1925. Royal Jubilee.

188.	53.	60 c. red..	10	5
189.		1 l. blue..	10	5
190.		1 l. 25 blue	1·90	30

1926. St. Francis of Assisi. Dated "1226 1926".

191.	54.	20 c. green	5	5
192.	–	30 c. grey	5	5
193.	–	40 c. violet	5	5
194.	–	60 c. red	5	5
195.	–	1 l. 25 blue	20	5
196.	–	5 l.+2 l. 50 brown	3·75	5·00

DESIGNS—HORIZ. 40 c. Church and Monastery of St. Damien. 60 c. Church and Monastery of Assisi. 1 l. 25, Death of St. Francis, from fresco in Church of The Holy Cross, Florence. VERT. 30 c., 5 l. St. Francis, after painting by Andrea della Robbia.

59.

1926. Air.

197.	59.	50 c. red	60	60
198.		60 c. grey	35	30
199.		80 c. brown and purple	1·90	2·25
200.		1 l. blue	50	50
201.		1 l. 20 brown	3·25	4·00
202.		1 l. 50 orange	2·10	2·10
203.		5 l. green	6·00	8·50

DESIGNS: 60 c. Aqueduct of Claudius. 1 l. 25, Capitol. 5 l. Porta del Popolo.

60. Castle of St. Angelo.

1926. 1st National Defence issue.

204.	60.	40 c.+20 c. blk. & brn.	25	40
205.	–	60 c.+30 c. brn. & red	25	60
206.	–	1 l. 25+60 c. blk. & grn.	30	80
207.	–	5 l.+2 l. 50 blk. & blue	4·25	7·50

See also Nos. 219/22 and 278/81.

61. Volta.

62.

63.

1927. Volta's Death. Cent.

208.	61.	20 c. red	12	10
209.		50 c. black	85	5
210.		60 c. brown	65	30
211.		1 l. 25 blue	95	30

1927. Air. Surch.

217.	59.	50 c. on 60 c. grey	1·25	1·25
218.		80 c. on 1 l. blue	2·50	3·25

1928. National Defence issue. As Nos. 204/7.

219.	60.	30 c.+10 c. black & vio.	40	80
220.		50 c.+20 c. blk. & olive	40	80
221.		1 l. 25+50 c. blk. & blue	1·25	2·10
222.		5 l.+2 l. blk. & red..	8·50	11·00

1927.

223.	62.	7½ c. brown	20	20
224.		15 c. orange	30	5
225.		35 c. grey	80	50
226.		50 c. mauve	60	5
216.	63.	50 c. grey and brown	35	5
212.		1 l. 75 brown	2·00	5
213.		1 l. 85 black	45	10
214.		2 l. 55 red	2·00	55
215.		2 l. 65 purple	2·50	3·00

No. 216 is smaller than T 63.

64. Emmanuel Philibert, Duke of Savoy.

65. Victories of Philibert and of 1918.

66. Philibert's Statue, Turin.

67. King Victor Emmanuel II.

1928. 4th Cent. of Emmanuel Philibert. 10th Anniv. of Victory and Turin Exhibition.

227a.	64.	20 c. blue and brown..	25	12
228a.		25 c. green and red	35	15
229a.		30 c. brown and green	50	20
230.	65.	50 c. brown and blue..	15	8
231.		75 c. red	25	12
232.	66.	1 l. 25 black and blue	50	20
233.	65.	1 l. 75 green	90	55
234.	64.	5 l. green and purple..	3·75	3·00
235.	65.	10 l. black and red	5·50	6·00
236.	66.	20 l. black and purple	8·00	11·00

1929. King Victor Emmanuel II. 50th Death Anniv. Veterans Fund.

237.	67.	50 c.+10 c. olive	85	85

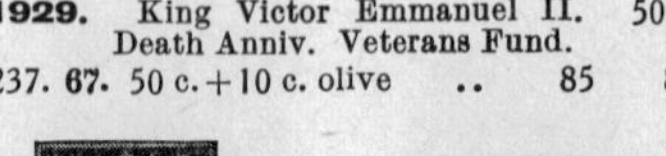

68. Fascist Arms of Italy.

69. Romulus, Remus and Wolf.

70. Julius Caesar.

74. King Victor Emmanuel III.

1929. Foundation of Rome and Labour Celebration.

238.	68.	2 c. orange	5	5
239.	69.	5 c. brown	5	5
240.	70.	7½ c. violet	5	5
241.	–	10 c. brown	5	5
242.	–	15 c. green	5	5
243.	70.	20 c. red	5	5
244.	–	25 c. green	5	5
245.	74.	30 c. brown	5	5
246.	–	35 c. blue	5	5
247.	74.	50 c. violet	5	5
248.	–	75 c red	5	5
249.	70.	1 l. violet	5	5
250.	–	1 l. 25 blue	5	5
251.	–	1 l. 75 orange	5	5
252.	–	2 l. claret	5	5
253.	69.	2 l. 55 green	5	5
254.		3 l. 70 violet	5	5
255.		5 l. red	5	5
256.	–	10 l. violet	12	5
257.	70.	20 l. green	60	30
258.	–	25 l. black	1·25	1·50
259.	–	50 l. violet	1·90	2·00

DESIGNS—As T 70: 10 c., 1 l. 75, 25 l. Augustus the Great. 15 c., 35 c., 2 l., 10 l. Italia (Woman with castle on her head). 25 c., 75 c., 1 l. 25, 50 l. Profile of King Victor Emmanuel III.

For stamps as above but without Fascist emblems, see Nos. 633, etc.

75. Bramante Courtyard.

1929. Abbey of Montecassino. 14th Cent. Inscr. "XIV CENTENARIO MONTE CASSINO".

260.	75.	20 c. orange	15	5
261.	–	25 c. green	15	5
262.	–	50 c.+10 c. brown	40	50
263.	–	75 c.+15 c. red	55	65
264.	75.	1 l. 25+25 c. blue	65	80
265.	–	5 l.+1 l. purple	1·75	2·50
266.	–	10 l.+2 l. grey..	2·50	3·75

DESIGNS—HORIZ. 25 c. "The Death of St. Benedict". 50 c. Monks laying corner stone. 75 c., 5 l. Abbey of Montecassino. VERT. 10 l. St. Benedict.

80.

1930. Marriage of Prince Humbert and Princess Marie Jose.

267.	80.	20 c. orange	10	8
268.		50 c.+10 c. brown	35	40
269.		1 l. 25+25 c. blue	1·40	1·60

81. Pegasus.

84.

1930. Air.

270.	–	25 c. green	5	5
271.	81.	50 c. brown	5	5
272.	–	75 c. brown	5	5
273.	–	80 c. orange	5	5
274.	–	1 l. violet	5	5
275.	84.	2 l. blue	5	5
276.	81.	5 l. green	5	5
277.	–	10 l. red	30	10

DESIGNS—As T 81: 25 c., 80 c. Wings. 75 c., 1 l. Angel.

1930. 3rd National Defence issue. Designs as Nos. 204/7.

278.	60.	30 c.+10 c. vio. & olive	30	50
279.	–	50 c.+10 c. bl. & olive..	40	40
280.	–	1 l. 25+30 c. grn. & bl...	50	75
281.	–	5 l.+1 l. 50 brown	5·00	8·00

85. Ferrucci on Horseback.

88. Francesco Ferrucci.

1930. Francesco Ferrucci. 400th Death Anniv. Inscr. "IV CENTENARIO FERRUCCI".

282.	85.	20 c. red (postage)	12	8
283.	–	25 c. green	15	10
284.	–	50 c. violet	8	5
285.	–	1 l. 25 blue	45	45
286.	–	5 l.+2 l. orange	3·50	5·50
287.	88.	50 c. violet (air)	30	50
288.		1 l. brown	30	50
289.		5 l.+2 l. purple	2·10	3·75

DESIGNS—HORIZ. 25 c., 50 c., 1 l. 25, Ferrucci's assassination. VERT. 5 l. Ferrucci in armour.

89. Jupiter and Eagle.

1930. Birth of Virgil. Bimillenary. Inscr. "SECONDO MILLENARIO VIRGILIANO".

290.	–	15 c. brown (postage)..	12	8
291.	–	20 c. orange	12	8
292.	–	25 c. green	25	8
293.	–	30 c. purple	25	8
294.	–	50 c. violet	15	5
295.	–	75 c. red	25	30
296.	–	1 l. 25 blue	40	20
297.	–	5 l.+1 l. 50 brown	9·50	13·00
298.	–	10 l.+2 l.50 olive	9·50	13·00
299.	89.	50 c. brown (air)	35	60
300.		1 l. orange	50	1·00
301.		7 l. 70+1 l. 30 purple	7·50	10·00
302.		9 l.+2 l. blue..	7·50	10·00

DESIGNS—As T 89—15 c. Helenus and Anchises. 20 c. The passing legions. 25 c. Landing of Aeneas. 30 c. Earth's bounties. 50 c. Harvesting. 75 c. Rural life. 1 l. 25 Aeneas sights Italy. 5 l. A shepherd's hut. 10 l. Turnus, King of the Rutuli.

91.

1930. Air. Transatlantic Mass Formation Flight.

303.	91.	7 l. 70 blue	£140	£140

92. St. Anthony's Installation as a Franciscan.

1931. St. Anthony of Padua. 700th Death Anniv.

304.		20 c. purple	25	5
305.		25 c. green	35	5
306.		30 c. brown	40	12
307.		50 c. violet	50	5
308.		75 c. lake	2·50	65
309.		1 l. 25 c. blue	1·10	25
310.		5 l.+2 l. 50 c. olive	9·00	14·00

DESIGNS—HORIZ. 25 c. Sermon to the fishes. 30 c. Hermitage of Olivares. 50 c. Basilica of the Saint at Padua. 75 c. Death of St. Anthony. 1 l. 25 c. St. Anthony liberating prisoners. VERT. 5 l. Vision of St. Anthony.

95. Training Ship, "Amerigo Vespucci".

DESIGNS—VERT. 20 c. Tower of the Marzocco. HORIZ. 1 l. 25 c. Cruiser "Trento".

1931. Naval Academy, Leghorn. 50th Anniv.

311.	–	20 c. red	15	5
312.	95.	50 c. violet	25	5
313.	–	1 l. 25 blue	1·25	35

96. Dante (1265–1321).

1932. Dante Alighieri Society. (a) Postage.

314.	–	10 c. brown	8	5
315.	–	15 c. green	8	5
316.	–	20 c. red	8	5
317.	–	25 c. green	15	8
318.	–	30 c. brown	20	8
319.	–	50 c. violet	8	5
320.	–	75 c. red	30	20
321.	–	1 l. 25 blue	30	15
322.	–	1 l. 75 orange	40	15
323.	–	2 l. 75 green	2·50	3·00
324.	–	5 l.+2 l. red	5·50	8·00
325.	96.	10 l.+2 l. 50 olive	7·00	9·00

DESIGNS: 10 c. Boccaccio. 15 c. Machiavelli. 20 c. Sarpi. 25 c. Alfieri. 30 c. Foscolo. 50 c. Leopardi. 75 c. Carducci. 1 l. 25 Botta. 1 l. 75 Tasso. 2 l. 75 Petrarch. 5 l. Ariosto.

97. Da Vinci's Flying Machine.

98. Leonardo da Vinci.

(b) Air.

326.	97.	50 c. brown	50	60
327.	–	1 l. violet	30	60
328.	–	3 l. red	1·00	1·40
329.	–	5 l. green	1·25	1·90
330.	97.	7 l. 70+2 l. blue	2·10	3·25
331.	–	10 l.+2 l. 50 purple	3·00	4·50
332.	98.	100 l. olive & blue	26·00	30·00

DESIGN—HORIZ. 1 l., 3 l., 5 l., 10 l. Leonardo da Vinci.

99. Garibaldi and Victor Emmanuel.

100. Caprera.

1932. Garibaldi. 50th Death Anniv. Inscr. as in **99/101.**
333. – 10 c. blue (postage) 15 5
334. **99.** 20 c. brown 15 5
335. – 25 c. green 50 10
336. **99.** 30 c. orange 40 10
337. – 50 c. violet 50 5
338. – 75 c. red .. .. 1·60 60
339. – 1 l. 25 blue .. .. 1·25 25
340. – 1 l. 75+25 c. blue .. 4·50 6·50
341. – 2 l. 55+50 c. brown .. 5·50 8·00
342. – 5 l.+1 l. lake .. .. 6·50 9·00
DESIGNS—HORIZ. 10 c. Garibaldi's birthplace at Nice. 25 c., 50 c. "Here we make Italy or die". 75 c. Anita's death. 1 l. 25, Garibaldi's tomb. 1 l. 75, Quarto Rock. VERT. 2 l. 55, Garibaldi's statue in Rome. 5 l. Garibaldi.

343. **100.** 50 c. lake (air) 40 50
344. – 80 c. green 60 80
345. – 1 l.+25 c. brown .. 1·25 1·75
346. – 2 l.+50 c. blue .. 2·00 3·00
347. – 5 l.+1 l. green .. 2·75 4·50
DESIGNS—VERT. 80 c. The Ravenna hut. 1 l. Caprera. 2 l. Anita. 5 l. Garibaldi.

102. Agriculture.

1932. March on Rome. 10th Anniv. Inscr. "X ANNUALE POSTE ITALIAEN".
350. **102.** 5 c. sepia 5 5
351. – 10 c. sepia 8 5
352. – 15 c. green 8 5
353. – 20 c. red 8 5
354. – 25 c. green 8 5
355. – 30 c. sepia 8 5
356. – 35 c. blue 90 75
357. – 50 c. violet 8 5
358. – 60 c. brown 90 60
359. – 75 c. red 40 25
360. – 1 l. violet 60 30
361. – 1 l. 25 blue 25 12
362. – 1 l. 75 orange 55 12
363. – 2 l. 55 green .. 6·00 7·50
364. – 2 l. 75 green .. 7·50 8·50
365. – 5 l.+2 l. 50 red .. 12·00 17·00
DESIGNS: 10 c. Fascist soldier. 15 c. Fascist coastguard. 20 c. Italian youth. 25 c. Tools forming a shadow of the Fasces. 30 c. Religion. 35 c. Imperial highways. 50 c. Equestrian statue of Mussolini. 60 c. Land reclamation. 75 c. Colonial expansion. 1 l. Marine development. 1 l. 25, Italians abroad. 1 l. 75, Sport, 2 l. 55, Child Welfare. 2 l. 75, "O.N.D." Recreation. 5 l. Caesar's statue.

DESIGN: 75 c. Italian buildings from the air.

105.

1932. Air. Fascist March on Rome. 10th Anniv. Inscr. "X ANNUALE ITALIA".
366. **105.** 50 c. brown .. .. 1·00 65
367. – 75 c. brown .. .. 1·90 2·25

108.

1933. Air. "Graf Zeppelin" issue.
372. **108.** 3 l. green and black .. 8·50 11·00
373. – 5 l. brown and green .. 3·50 11·00
374. – 10 l. blue and red .. 2·50 13·00
375. – 12 l. orange and blue .. 2·50 17·00
376. – 15 l. black and brown 2·50 19·00
377. – 20 l. blue and brown .. 2·25 23·00
DESIGNS (all with airship); 3 l. S. Paola Gate and tomb of Consul Caius Cestius. 5 l. Appian Way and tomb of Cecilia Metella. 10 l. Portion of Mussolini Stadium. 12 l. S. Angelo Castle. 15 l. Forum Romanum. 20 l. Empire Way, Colosseum and Terme Domizianc.

Italian Flag. King Victor Emmanuel III. "Flight".
109.

Italian Flag. King Victor Emmanuel III. Rome—Chicago.
110.
(Actual size 97 × 22 mm.)

1933. Air. Balbo Transatlantic Mass Formation Flight.

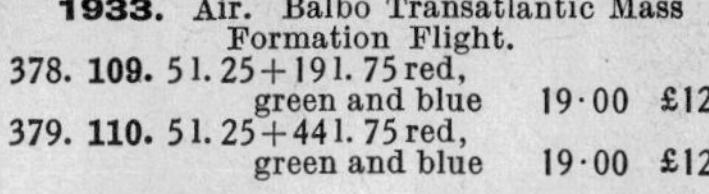

378. **109.** 5 l. 25+19 l. 75 red, green and blue 19·00 £120
379. **110.** 5 l. 25+44 l. 75 red, green and blue 19·00 £120

111. Athlete.

112. Dome of St. Peter's.

1933. Int. University Games, Turin.
380. **111.** 10 c. brown 12 5
381. 20 c. red 30 12
382. 50 c. violet 45 5
383. 1 l. 25 blue .. .. 1·75 80

1933. "Holy Year". Inscr. "ANNO SANTO".
384. **112.** 20 c. red 35 5
385. – 25 c. green 65 8
386. – 50 c. violet 55 5
387. **112.** 1 l. 25 blue .. .. 1·00 40
388. – 2 l. 55+2 l. 50 black .. 2·50 3·75
DESIGNS: 25 c., 50 c. Angel with Cross. 2 l. 55, Cross with Doves of Peace.

113. St. Peter's Cathedral and Church of the Holy Sepulchre. **114.** Anchor of the "Emmanuel Philibert".

1933. Air. "Holy Year".
389. **113.** 50 c.+25 c. brown .. 50 75
390. 75 c.+50 c. purple .. 75 1·25

1934. Air. Rome–Buenos Aires Flight. Surch. with aeroplane and **PRIMO VOLO DIRETTO ROMA=BUENOS-AYRES TRIMOTORE LOMBARDI MAZZOTTI** and value.
391. **84.** 2 l. on 2 l. yellow .. 4·50 10·00
392. 3 l. on 2 l. green .. 3·50 15·00
393. 5 l. on 2 l. red .. .. 3·50 17·00
394. 10 l. on 2 l. violet .. 3·50 21·00

1934. Annexation of Fiume. 10th Anniv. Inscr. as in T **114.**
395. **114.** 10 c. brown (postage) 45 10
396. 20 c. red 15 8
397. – 50 c. violet 30 5
398. – 1 l. 25 blue 50 30
399. – 1 l. 75+1 l. blue .. 80 1·25
400. – 2 l. 55+2 l. purple .. 1·00 1·75
401. – 2 l. 75+2 l. 50 olive .. 1·25 2·00
DESIGNS: 50 c. Gabriele d'Annunzio. 1 l. 25, St. Vito's Tower barricaded. 1 l. 75, Hands supporting crown of historical monuments. 2 l. 55, Emmanuel III's arrival in the "Brindisi". 2 l. 75, Galley, gondola and battleship.

402. 25 c. green (air) 12 15
403. 50 c. brown 12 15
404. 75 c. brown 15 20
405. 1 l.+50 c. purple .. 30 40
406. 2 l.+1 l. 50 blue .. 30 45
407. 3 l.+2 l. black 40 55
DESIGNS: 25 c., 75 c. Fiume Harbour. 50 c., 1 l. War Memorial. 2 l. Three Venetian lions. 3 l. Roman Wall.

117.

1934. World Football Championship. Inscr. as in T **117.**
411. – 20 c. red (postage) .. 80 60
412. **117.** 25 c. green 80 20
413. 50 c. violet 60 5
414. 1 l. 25 blue .. .. 1·40 1·25
415. – 5 l.+2 l. 50 brown .. 11·00 20·00
DESIGNS—VERT. 20 c. Goalkeeper. 5 l. Players heading the ball.

416. 50 c. red (air) .. .. 1·25 1·60
417. 75 c. blue .. .. 2·00 2·50
418. 5 l.+2 l. 50 olive .. 5·50 8·50
419. 10 l.+5 l. brown .. 5·50 9·50
DESIGNS—HORIZ. 50 c. Mussolini Stadium, Turin. 5 l. Flying-boat over the Stadium, Rome. VERT. 75 c. Footballer. 10 l. Flying-boat over Littoral Stadium, Bologna.

118. Antonio Pacinotti. **119.** Luigi Galvani. **120.** Military Symbol.

1934. Pacinotti's Dynamo. 75th Anniv.
420. **118.** 50 c. violet 80 5
421. 1 l. 25 blue 80 50

1934. 1st Int. Congress of Electro-Radio-Biology.
422. **119.** 30 c. brown on buff .. 1·60 15
423. 75 c. red on pink .. 1·60 65

1934. Military Medal Cent. Inscr. as in T **120.**
424. **120.** 10 c. brown (post.) .. 25 12
425. – 15 c. green 35 15
426. – 20 c. red 30 12
427. – 25 c. green 45 15
428. – 30 c. brown .. .. 1·10 25
429. – 50 c. violet 60 5
430. – 75 c. red .. .. 1·25 50
431. – 1 l. 25 blue .. .. 1·25 60
432. – 1 l. 75+1 l. orange .. 5·00 6·50
433. – 2 l. 55+2 l. claret .. 6·00 8·50
434. – 2 l. 75+2 l. purple .. 6·50 8·50
DESIGNS—VERT. 25 c. Mountaineers. 1 l. 75, Cavalry. HORIZ. 15 c., 50 c. Barbed-wire cutter. 20 c. Throwing hand-grenade. 30 c. Cripple wielding crutch. 75 c. Artillery 1 l. 25, Soldiers cheering. 2 l. 55, Sapper. 2 l. 75, First Aid.

435. 25 c. green (air) 20 30
436. 50 c. grey 20 30
437. 75 c. brown 20 30
438. 80 c. blue 65 85
439. 1 l.+50 c. brown .. 1·60 2·50
440. 2 l.+1 l. blue .. .. 1·60 2·50
441. 3 l.+2 l. black .. .. 2·10 3·25
DESIGNS—HORIZ. 25 c., 80 c. Airship under fire. 50 c., 75 c. Naval motor launch. 1 l. Aeroplane and troops in desert. 2 l. Biplane and troops. VERT. 3 l. Unknown soldier's tomb.

122. King Victor Emmanuel III.

1934. Air. Rome—Mogadiscio Flight and King's visit to Italian Somaliland.
444. **122.** 1 l. violet .. .. 15 4·25
445. 2 l. blue .. .. 25 4·25
446. 4 l. brown .. .. 40 6·00
447. 5 l. green .. .. 40 6·00
448. 8 l. red .. .. 11·00 29·00
449. 10 l. brown .. .. 12·00 32·00

123. Man with Fasces. **124.**

1935. University Contests. Inscr. "LITTORIALI".
450. **123.** 20 c. red 20 15
451. – 30 c. brown .. .. 1·00 75
452. – 50 c. violet 20 8
DESIGNS: 30 c. Eagle and soldier. 50 c. Standard-bearer and bayonet attack.

1935. National Militia. Inscr. "PRO OPERA PREVID. MILIZIA".
453. **124.** 20 c.+10 c. red (post.) 3·00 4·00
454. – 25 c.+15 c. green .. 2·50 3·25
455. – 50 c.+30 c. violet .. 2·50 3·25
456. – 1 l. 25+75 c. blue .. 2·50 4·00
457. – 50 c.+50 c. brown (air) 4·00 5·00
DESIGNS: 25 c. Roman standards. 50 c. Soldier and cross. 50 c.+50 c. Wing over Globe. 1 l., 25 Soldiers and arch.

125. Symbol of Flight.

126. Leonardo da Vinci.

127. Vincent Bellini. **128.** "Music".

1935. Int. Aeronautical Exn., Milan.
458. **125.** 20 c. red .. .. 1·60 15
459. 30 c. brown .. .. 9·00 35
460. **126.** 50 c. violet .. .. 15·00 8
461. 1 l. 25 blue .. .. 3·25 65

1935. Bellini (composer). Death Cent. Inscr. as in T **127/8.**
462. **127.** 20 c. red (postage) .. 40 12
463. 30 c. brown 60 15
464. 50 c. violet 50 8
465. 1 l. 25 blue .. .. 1·40 55
466. – 1 l. 75+1 l. orange .. 7·50 9·50
467. – 2 l. 75+2 l. olive .. 8·00 10·00
DESIGNS—VERT. 2 l. 75, Bellini's villa. HORIZ. 1 l. 75. Hands at piano.
468. **128.** 25 c. yellow (air) .. 25 15
469. 50 c. brown 30 25
470. 60 c. red 50 40
471. – 1 l.+1 l. violet .. 4·25 5·50
472. – 5 l.+2 l. green .. 5·00 6·00
DESIGNS: 1 l. Angelic musicians. 5 l. Mountain landscape (Bellini's birthplace).

DESIGN—HORIZ. 30 c., 50 c. Cogwheel and plough.

129. "Commerce" and Industrial Map of Italy.

1936. 17th Milan Fair. Inscr. as in T **129.**
473. **129.** 20 c. red 8 5
474. – 30 c. brown 15 5
475. – 50 c. violet 12 5
476. **129.** 1 l. 25 blue 65 20

130. "Fertility".

1936. Horace. Birth Bimillenary. Inscr. as in T **130.**
477. **130.** 10 c. green (postage) .. 40 5
478. – 20 c. red 20 5
479. – 30 c. brown 35 12
480. – 50 c. violet 60 5
481. – 75 c. red 60 25
482. – 1 l. 25+1 l. blue .. 5·50 8·50
483. – 1 l. 75+1 l. red .. 6·50 10·00
484. – 2 l. 55+1 l. blue .. 7·50 11·00
DESIGNS—HORIZ. 20 c., 1 l. 25, Landscape. 75 c. Capitol. 2 l. 55, Dying gladiator. VERT. 30 c. Ajax defying lightning. 50 c. Horace. 1 l. 75, Pan.
485. – 25 c. green (air) .. 25 30
486. – 50 c. brown 40 50
487. – 60 c. red .. .. 1·00 1·25
488. – 1 l.+1 l. violet .. 2·50 3·75
489. – 5 l.+2 l. green .. 4·00 6·50
DESIGNS—HORIZ. 25 c. Seaplane. 50 c. 1 l. Aeroplane over lake. 60 c. Eagle and oak tree. 5 l. Rome.

132.

133.

138. Augustus the Great.

136. Naval Memorial.

1937. Child Welfare. Inscr. as n T **132/3.**

490.	**132.**	10 c. brown (postage)	15	8
491.	**133.**	20 c. red	15	8
492.	**132.**	25 c. green	20	10
493.	–	30 c. sepia	40	15
494.	**133.**	50 c. violet	35	5
495.	–	75 c. red	1·40	35
496.	**133.**	1 l. 25 blue	1·50	50
497.	–	1 l. 75+75 c. orange	10·00	11·00
498.	–	2 l. 75+1 l. 25 green	7·50	11·00
499.	**133.**	5 l.+3 l. blue	7·50	11·00

DESIGNS—As T **132**: 30 c., 1 l. 75, Boy between Fasces. 75 c., 2 l. 75, "Bambino" (after della Robbia).

500.	–	25 c. green (air)	60	30
501.	–	50 c. brown	1·00	30
502.	–	1 l. violet	65	40
503.	–	2 l.+1 l. blue	7·00	9·50
504.	–	3 l.+2 l. orange	6·00	9·50
505.	–	5 l.+3 l. red	6·00	9·50

DESIGNS—As T **133**: 25 c., 1 l., 3 l. Little child with rifle. As T **132**: 50 c., 2 l., 5 l. Children's heads.

1937. Augustus the Great. Birth Bimillenary Inscr. "BIMILLENARIO AUGUSTEO".

506.	**136.**	10 c. green (postage)	20	5
507.	–	15 c. brown	20	5
508.	–	20 c. red	15	5
509.	–	25 c. green	30	5
510.	–	30 c. brown	30	5
511.	–	50 c. violet	30	5
512.	–	75 c. red	50	15
513.	–	1 l. 25 blue	55	20
514.	–	1 l. 75+1 l. purple	9·00	11·00
515.	–	2 l. 55+2 l. black	9·00	13·00

DESIGNS—VERT. 15 c. Military trophies. 20 c. Augustus offering sacrifice. 25 c. Symbols of Victory. 30 c. Statue of Julius Caesar. 50 c. Hands saluting Augustus. 75 c. Head of Augustus. 1 l. 25, Galleys symbolizing maritime glory. 1 l. 75, Sacrificial altar. 2 l. 55, The Capitol.

516.	–	25 c. purple (air)	60	60
517.	–	50 c. brown	60	60
518.	–	80 c. brown	1·25	1·40
519.	–	1 l.+1 l. blue	5·00	7·00
520.	**138.**	5 l.+1 l. violet	9·00	11·00

DESIGNS—HORIZ. 25 c. Prosperous Italy. 50 c. Prolific Italy. 80 c. Horses of the Sun Chariot. 1 l. Staff and map of ancient Roman Empire.

139. G. Spontini. **141.** Marconi.

1937. Famous Italians.

521.	**139.**	10 c. sepia	15	5
522.	–	20 c. red	15	5
523.	–	25 c. green	15	5
524.	–	30 c. brown	15	12
525.	–	50 c. violet	15	5
526.	–	75 c. red	60	50
527.	–	1 l. 25 blue	80	55
528.	**139.**	1 l. 75 orange	1·00	30
529.	–	2 l. 55+2 l. green	8·00	13·00
530.	–	2 l. 75+2 l. brown	9·00	14·00

DESIGNS: 20 c., 2 l. 55, Stradivarius. 25 c. 50 c. Leopardi. 30 c., 75 c. Pergolesi. 1 l. 25, 2 l. 75 Giotti di Bordoni.

1938. G. Marconi Commemoration.

531.	**141.**	20 c. red	40	12
532.		50 c. violet	20	5
533.		1 l. 25 blue	65	80

142. The Founding of Rome. **143.** Victor Emmanuel III.

1938. Proclamation of the Italian Empire. 2nd Anniv.

534.	**142.**	10 c. brown (postage)	12	5
535.	–	20 c. red	12	5
536.	–	25 c. green	12	5
537.	–	30 c. olive	12	5
538.	–	50 c. violet	12	5
539.	–	75 c. red	30	12
540.	–	1 l. 25 blue	30	12
541.	–	1 l. 75 violet	40	12
542.	–	2 l. 75 green	3·25	2·50
543.	–	5 l. red	4·50	3·25

DESIGNS—VERT. 20 c. Emperor Augustus. 25 c. Dante. 30 c. Columbus. 50 c. Leonardo da Vinci. 75 c. Garibaldi and Victor Emmanuel II. 1 l. 25, Italian Unknown Warrior's Tomb. 1 l. 75, "March on Rome". 2 l. 75, Wedding Ring on map of Ethiopia. 5 l. Victor Emmanuel III.

544.	**143.**	25 c. green (air)	12	15
545.	–	50 c. brown	12	15
546.	–	1 l. violet	15	15
547.	–	2 l. blue	35	55
548.	**143.**	3 l. lake	75	1·10
549.	–	5 l. green	1·40	2·10

DESIGNS—HORIZ. 50 c., 1 l. Dante 2 l., 5 l. Leonardo da Vinci.

144. Locomotives of 1839 and 1939. **145.** Hitler and Mussolini.

146. Hitler and Mussolini. **147.** Roman Cavalry.

1939. Italian Railways Cent.

550.	**144.**	20 c. red	12	8
551.		50 c. violet	15	5
552.		1 l. 25 blue	60	35

1941. Italo-German Friendship.

553.	**145.**	10 c. brown	5	5
554.		20 c. orange	5	5
555.		25 c. green	5	5
556.	**146.**	50 c. violet	20	5
557.		75 c. red	15	15
558.		1 l. 25 blue	25	20

1941. Livy (Latin historian). Birth Bimillenary.

559.	**147.**	20 c.+10 c. red	25	45
560.		30 c.+15 c. brown	30	45
561.		50 c.+25 c. violet	30	45
562.		1 l. 25+1 l. blue	65	80

DESIGN: 50 c., 1 l. 25, Roman Warriors.

148. Galileo teaching at Padua. **149.** Rossini.

1942. Galileo. Death Tercent.

575.	**148.**	10 c. red and orange	8	5
576.	–	25 c. green and orange	12	5
577.	–	50 c violet and purple	15	5
578.	–	1 l. 25 blue and grey	30	25

DESIGNS: Galileo at Venice (25 c.) and at Arcetri, near Florence (1 l. 25), 50 c. Portrait of Galileo.

1942. Rossini (composer). 150th Birth Anniv. Inscr. as in T **149**.

579.	–	25 c. green	5	5
580.	–	30 c. brown	5	8
581.	–	50 c. violet	8	5
582.		1 l. blue	15	15

DESIGN: 25 c., 30 c. Rossini Monument.

151.

ILLUSTRATIONS
British Commonwealth and all overprints and surcharges are FULL SIZE. Foreign Countries have been reduced to ¾-LINEAR.

1943. Allied Military Government issue.

583.	**151.**	15 c. orange	5	5
584.		25 c. bistre	5	5
585.		30 c. grey	5	5
586.		50 c. violet	5	5
587.		60 c. yellow	5	5
588.		1 l. green	5	5
589.		2 l. red	5	5
590.		5 l. blue	5	12
591.		10 l. brown	20	25

1943. Allied Military Government issue Stamps of 1929 optd. **GOVERNO MILITARE ALLEATO.**

592.	**70.**	20 c. red	12	15
593.		35 c. blue	1·00	1·00
594.	**74.**	50 c. violet	5	8

(152.)

(153.)

1944. (a) Optd. with T **152.**

595.	–	25 c. green (No. 244)	5	5
598.	–	75 c. red (No. 248)	5	5

(b) Optd. with T **153.**

596.	**74.**	30 c. brown	5	5
599.	–	1 l. 25 blue (No. 250)	5	5
600.	–	50 l. violet (No. 259)	80·00	£325

(c) Optd. **REPUBBLICA SOCIALE ITALIANA.**

597.	**74.**	50 c. violet	5	5

154. Loggia del Mercanti, Bologna. **155.**

156. Basilica de St. Lorenzo, Rome. **157.**

1944. Inscr. "REPUBBLICA SOCIALE ITALIANA".

605.	–	5 c. brown	5	5
606.	–	10 c. brown	5	5
601.	**154.**	20 c. red	5	5
607.	**155.**	20 c. red	5	5
602.	**156.**	25 c. green	5	5
608.	**157.**	25 c. green	5	5
603.	–	30 c. brown	5	5
610.	–	50 c. violet	5	5
611.	–	75 c. red	5	5
612.	–	1 l. violet	5	8
613.	–	1 l. 25 blue	5	10
614.	–	3 l. green	5	25

DESIGNS: 5 c. St. Ciriaco's Church, Ancona. 10 c., 1 l. Montecassino, Abbey. 30 c., 75 c. Drummer. 50 c. Fascist allegory. 1 l. 25, 3 l. St. Mary of Grace, Milan.

158. Bandiera Brothers. **159.** Romulus, Remus and Wolf.

1944. Bandiera Brothers. Death Cent.

615.	**158.**	25 c. green	5	15
616.		1 l. violet	5	25
617.		2 l. 50 red	5	80

1944.

618.	**159.**	50 c. violet	12	12

1945. Surch. in figures and bars or also with **POSTE ITALIANE** (Nos. 627/8).

627.	**154.**	1 l. 20 on 20 c. red	5	5
628.	**156.**	2 l. on 25 c. green	5	5
629.	**70.**	2 l. 50 on 1 l. 75 orge.	5	5

1945. As issue of 1929, but with Fascist emblems removed.

633.	**70.**	10 c. brown	5	5
640.		20 c. red	5	5
620.	**74.**	30 c. brown	5	5
635.	–	50 c. violet (Italia)	5	5
621.	**74.**	50 c. violet	5	5
636.	–	60 c. orange (Italia)	5	5
641.	**74.**	60 c. green	5	5
637.	**70.**	1 l. violet	5	5
643.	–	1 l. 20 brown (Itlaia)	5	5
644.	–	2 l. red (Italia)	5	5
645.	**69.**	5 l. red	10	5
646.	–	10 l. violet (Italia)	1·25	40

160. "Work, Justice and Family". **161.** Planting a Sapling.

162. "Peace". **163.** Clasped Hands and Aeroplane.

1945.

647.	–	10 c. brown	5	5
648.	**160.**	20 c. brown	5	5
649.	–	25 c. blue-green	5	5
650.	**161.**	40 c. grey	5	5
651.	–	50 c violet	5	5
652	–	60 c. green	5	5
653.	–	80 c. red	5	5
654.	**161.**	1 l. green	5	5
655.	–	1 l. 20 brown	5	5
656.	–	2 l. brown	5	5
657.	–	3 l. red	5	5
658.	–	4 l. red	15	5
659.	**160.**	5 l. blue	20	5
660.	**161.**	6 l. violet	80	5
661.	–	8 l. green	80	5
662.	–	10 l. grey	60	5
663.	**160.**	10 l. red	9·00	5
664.	**161.**	15 l. blue	3·25	5
665.	–	20 l. purple	1·00	5
666.	**162.**	25 l. green	5·00	5
667.	–	30 l. blue	38·00	5
668.	**162.**	50 l. purple	4·25	5

DESIGNS: 10 c., 50 c., 80 c., 8 l., 10 l. (No. 662), Hammer breaking chain. 60 c., 2 l. Gardener tying sapling to stake. 25 c., 1 l. 20, 3 l., 4 l., 20 l., 30 l. Flaming torch.

1945. Air.

670.	**163.**	1 l. slate	5	5
671.	–	2 l. blue	5	5
672.	**163.**	3 l. 20 orange	5	5
952.	–	5 l. green	5	5
674.	**163.**	10 l. red	5	5
675.	–	25 l. blue	4·25	1·25
676.	–	25 l. brown	5	5
677.	**163.**	50 l. green	6·50	3·00
953.	–	50 l. violet	5	5
911.	–	100 l. green	2·10	5
912.	–	300 l. mauve	1·40	10
913.	–	500 l. blue	1·50	20
914.	–	1000 l. claret	1·50	55

DESIGNS—HORIZ. 2 l., 5 l., 25 l. Swallows in flight. VERT. 100 l., 300 l., 500 l., 1000 l. Aeroplane over Rome.

For No. 911 in smaller format, size 20×36 mm. see No. 1297.

164. "Work, Justice and Family".

1946.

669.	**164.**	100 l. red	85·00	20

165. Venice.

166. Wireless Mast.

167. St. Catherine giving her Cloak to a Beggar. **168.** St. Catherine carrying the Cross.

1946. Mediaeval Italian Republics.

679.	–	1 l. sepia	5	5
680.	–	2 l. blue	5	5
681.	–	3 l. green	5	5
682.	–	4 l. orange	5	5
683.	–	5 l. violet	5	5
684.	–	10 l. red	10	5
685.	**165.**	15 l. blue	12	15
686.	–	20 l. brown	10	5

DESIGNS—VERT. 1 l. Amalfi. 2 l. Lucca. 3 l. Siena. 4 l. Florence. HORIZ. 5 l. Pisa. 10 l. Genoa. 20 l. "The Oath of Pontida".

1947. Air. Surch.

687.	**163.**	6 l. on 3 l. 20 orange	15	12

1947. Air. Radio. 50th Anniv. Inscr. as in T **166**.
688. **166.** 6 l. violet 5 5
689. – 10 l. claret 5 5
690. – 20 l. orange 40 15
691. **166.** 25 l. green 10 15
692. – 35 l. blue 15 30
693. – 50 l. purple 30 40
DESIGNS: 10 l., 35 l. Ship's aerial. 20 l., 50 l. Aeroplane equipped with wireless.

1948. St. Catherine of Siena. 6th Birth Cent. Inscr. "VI centenario dalla nascita di S. Caterina".
698. **167.** 3 l. blue & grn. (post.) 8 12
699. – 5 l. blue and violet .. 12 12
700. – 10 l. violet & brown .. 25 55
701. – 30 l. grey and brown .. 1·60 1·60

702. **168.** 100 l. vio. & brn. (air) 16·00 8·00
703. – 200 l. blue & brown .. 2·10 2·50
DESIGNS—VERT. All show St. Catherine. 5 l. Carrying the Cross. 10 l. Extending her arms to Italy. 30 l. Dictating "The Dialogue" to a Disciple. HORIZ. 200 l. Extending her arms to Italy.

169. "Proclamation of New Constitution".

1948. Proclamation of New Consititution.
704. **169.** 10 l. violet 30 35
705. 30 l. blue 60 30

170. Rising at Palermo.

1948. Revolution Cent. Inscr. "PRIMO CENTENARIO DEL RISORGIMENTO ITALIANO".
706. **170.** 3 l. brown 8 5
707. – 4 l. purple 10 5
708. – 5 l. blue 40 5
709. – 6 l. green 35 25
710. – 8 l. brown 25 25
711. – 10 l. red 40 8
712. – 12 l. green 55 40
713. – 15 l black .. .. 2·75 35
714. – 20 l. red .. .. 12·00 75
715. – 30 l. blue .. .. 3·00 8
716. – 50 l. violet .. .. 42·00 40
717. – 100 l. blue .. .. 65·00 4·25
DESIGNS: 4 l. Rising at Padua. 5 l. Concession of Statute, Turin. 6 l. Storming Porta Tosa, Milan. 8 l. Proclamation of Venetian Republic. 10 l. Defence of Vicenza. 12 l. Hero of Curtatone. 15 l. Hero of Goito. 20 l. Austrian retreat from Bologna. 30 l. Fighting at Brescia. 50 l. Garibaldi. 100 l. Promotion of a wounded officer.

171. Alpinist and Bassano Bridge.

172. Gaetano Donizetti (composer).

174.

173. Exhibition Grounds.

1948. Rebuilding of Bassano Bridge.
718. **171.** 15 l. green 45 30

1948. Donizetti. Death Cent.
719. **172.** 15 l. brown 50 30

1949. 27th Milan Fair.
720. **173.** 20 l. sepia .. .. 2·75 40

1949. 25th Biennial Art. Exn., Venice.
721. **174.** 5 l. lake and cream .. 5 5
722. – 15 l. green & cream .. 20 30
723. – 20 l. brown & cream .. 65 8
724. – 50 l. blue & cream .. 8·50 35
DESIGNS: 15 l. Bell-ringers, St. Mark's Column and Campanile. 20 l. Emblem of Venice and galley. 50 l. Winged lion.

175. Globes and Forms of Transport.

1949. U.P.U. 75th Anniv.
725. **175.** 50 l. blue .. .. 7·00 1·50

176. Vascello Castle.

1949. Roman Republic Cent.
726. **176.** 100 l. brown .. .. 75·00 18·00

177. Worker and Ship.

178. Statue of Mazzini.

180. San Giusto Cathedral.

179. Vittorio Alfieri.

1949. European Recovery Plan.
727. **177.** 5 l. green .. .. 6·00 2·75
728. 15 l. violet .. .. 6·00 2·00
729. 20 l. brown .. .. 32·00 5·00

1949. Honouring Giuseppe Mazzini (founder of "Young Italy").
730. **178.** 20 l. black .. .. 3·50 40

1949. Alfieri (poet). Birth Bicent.
731. **179.** 20 l. brown .. .. 4·50 40

1949. First Trieste Free Election.
732. **180.** 20 l. lake .. .. 5·00 2·75

181. Staff of Aesculapius and Globe.

182. A. Palladio and Vicenza Basilica.

1949. 2nd World Health Congress. Rome.
733. **181.** 20 l. violet .. .. 4·50 2·75

1949. Completion of Palladio's Basilica at Vicenza. 4th Cent.
734. **182.** 20 l. violet .. .. 2·40 1·75

183. Lorenzo de Medici.

184. Galleon and Exhibition Buildings.

1949. Lorenzo de Medici "The Magnificent". 5th Birth Cent.
735. **183.** 20 l. blue .. .. 2·50 30

1949. 13th Bari Fair.
736. **184.** 20 l. red .. .. 1·00 40

185. Voltaic Pile.

186. Count Alessandro Volta.

1949. Volta's Discovery of the Electric Cell. 150th Anniv.
737. **185.** 20 l. red .. .. 1·75 20
738. **186.** 50 l. blue .. .. 25·00 4·25

187. Holy Trinity Bridge, Florence.

188. Caius Valerius Catullus.

1949. Rebuilding of Holy Trinity Bridge, Florence.
739. **187.** 20 l. green .. .. 2·10 35

1949. Catullus (poet). Death Bimillenary.
740. **188.** 20 l. blue .. .. 2·75 30

189. Domenico Cimarosa.

190. Entrance to Exhibition.

1949. Cimarosa (composer). Birth Bicent.
741. **189.** 20 l. slate .. .. 1·75 35

1950. 28th Milan Fair.
742. **190.** 20 l. brown .. .. 1·90 30

191. Car and Flags.

1950. 32nd Int. Automobile Exn., Turin.
743. **191.** 20 l. violet .. .. 2·10 35

192. Pitti Palace, Florence.

193. St. Peter's Basilica.

1950. 5th General U.N.E.S.C.O. Conf.
744. **192.** 20 l. green .. .. 1·25 8
745. – 55 l. blue .. .. 11·00 1·25
DESIGN—VERT. 55 l. Statue of Perseus.

1950. Holy Year.
746. **193.** 20 l. violet .. .. 2·10 25
747. 55 l. blue .. .. 10·00 35

194. Gaudenzio Ferrari.

195. Wireless Mast.

196. L. Muratori.

1950. G. Ferrari (painter).
748. **194.** 20 l. grey .. .. 3·50 35

1950. Int. Radio Conf., Florence.
749. **195.** 20 l. violet .. .. 4·25 40
750. 55 l. blue .. .. 55·00 15·00

1950. Muratori (historian). Death Bicent.
751. **196.** 20 l. brown .. .. 3·75 30

MINIMUM PRICE

The minimum price quoted is 5p which represents a handling charge rather than a basis for valuing common stamps. For further notes about prices see introductory pages.

197. Guido D'Arezzo.

198. Galleon.

200. Tobacco Plant. **199.** Marzotto and Rossi.

1950. D'Arezzo (musician). 9th Death Cent.
752. **197.** 20 l. green .. .. 3·75 35

1950. 14th Bari Fair.
753. **198.** 20 l. brown .. .. 2·50 30

1950. Pioneers of Italian Wool Industry.
754. **199.** 20 l. blue 30 15

1950. European Tobacco Conf.
755. **200.** 5 l. green and claret .. 60 60
756. – 20 l. green and brown 1·90 20
757. – 55 l. brown and blue .. 22·00 4·00
DESIGNS: 20 l. Plant. 55 l. Girl and plant.

201. Seal of Academy.

202. A. Righi.

203. Blacksmith.

1950. Venice Fine Arts Academy Bicent.
758. **201.** 20 l. red and brown .. 1·75 30

1950. Righi (physicist). Birth Cent.
759. **202.** 20 l. black and buff .. 1·75 30

1950. Provincial Occupations. As T **203**.
760. 50 c. blue 5 5
881. 1 l. slate 5 5
882. 2 l. sepia 5 5
763. 5 l. black 30 5
764. 6 l. chocolate 5 5
765. 10 l. green .. .. .. 1·60 5
766. 12 l. green 40 5
883. 15 l slate 50 5
768. 20 l. violet .. .. .. 2·75 5
769. 25 l. orange .. .. .. 1·10 5
770. 30 l. purple 45 5
771. 35 l. red .. .. .. 1·00 5
772. 40 l. brown 15 5
773. 50 l. violet .. .. .. 1·60 5
774. 55 l. blue 15 5
775. 60 l. red .. .. .. 5·50 5
776. 65 l. green 20 5
777. 100 l. chestnut .. .. 16·00 5
778. 200 l. olive .. .. .. 3·00 8
DESIGNS: 1 l. Motor mechanic. 2 l. Stonemason. 5 l. Potter. 6 l. Girls embroidering and water-carrying. 10 l. Weaver. 12 l. Fisherman at tiller. 15 l. Boat builder. 20 l. Fisherman trawling. 25 l. Girl packing oranges. 30 l. Girl carrying grapes. 35 l. Gathering olives. 40 l. Carter and wagon. 50 l. Shepherd. 55 l. Ploughman. 60 l. Ox-cart. 65 l. Girl harvester. 100 l. Women handling maize. 200 l. Woodcutter.

204. First Tuscan Stamp.

205. Car and Flags.

1951. Tuscan Stamp Cent.
779. **204.** 20 l. red and purple .. 80 40
780. 55 l. blue .. .. 7·50 6·00

1951. 33rd Int. Motor Show. Turin.
781. **205.** 20 l. green .. .. 1·75 30

206. Peace Hall.

1951. Consecration of Hall of Peace, Rome.
782. **206.** 20 l. violet .. .. 2·10 40

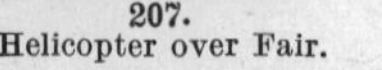

207. Helicopter over Fair. **208.** Fair Building.

1951. 29th Milan Fair.
783. **207.** 20 l. brown .. .. 1·60 40
784. **208.** 55 l. blue .. .. 15·00 6·00

209. Allegory. **210.** Columbus disembarking.

1951. 10th Int. Textiles Exn., Turin.
785. **209.** 20 l. violet .. .. 4·25 50

1951. Columbus. 5th Birth Cent.
786. **210.** 20 l. blue-green .. 2·10 55

210a. Gymnastics Symbols. **211.** Montecassino Abbey restored.

1951. Int. Gymnastic Festival Florence.
787. **210a.** 5 l. red and brown .. 7·00 30·00
788. 10 l. red and green .. 7·50 27·00
789. 15 l. red and blue .. 6·50 27·00

1951. Restoration of Montecassino Abbey.
790. **211.** 20 l. violet .. .. 1·75 30
791. – 55 l. blue .. .. 13·00 3·00
DESIGN: 55 l. Abbey in ruins, 1944.

212. Perugino. **213.** Modern Art.

214. Cyclist and Globe. **215.** Galleon and Hemispheres.

1951. Perugino (painter). 500th Birth Anniv.
792. **212.** 20 l. brown and sepia 2·40 1·00

1951. Triennial Art Exn., Milan.
793. **213.** 20 l. black and green .. 2·50 40
794. – 55 l. pink and blue .. 10·00 6·00
DESIGN—HORIZ. 55 l. Jug and symbols.

1951. World Cycling Championship.
795. **214.** 25 l. grey .. .. 1·90 60

1951. 15th Levant Fair, Bari.
796. **215.** 25 l. blue .. .. 1·50 35

216. "La di Jorio".

1951. F. P. Michetti (painter). Birth Cent.
797. **216.** 25 l. sepia .. .. 2·50 30

217. T 1 of Sardinia and Arms.

1951. Sardinian Postage Stamp Cent.
798. **217.** 10 l. black and sepia 65 65
799. – 25 l. green and red .. 1·00 45
800. – 60 l. red and blue .. 3·75 2·25
DESIGNS—As T **217** but with different arms: 25 l. shows 20 c. stamp. 60 l. shows 40 c. stamp.

218. "Industry and Commerce". **219.** Census in Ancient Rome.

220. Giuseppi Verdi and Roncole Church. **221.** Mountain Scenery.

1951. 3rd Industrial and Commercial Census.
801. **218.** 10 l. green 40 35

1951. 9th National Census.
802. **219.** 25 l. slate .. .. 1·25 50

1951. Verdi. 50th Death Anniv.
803. – 10 l. green and purple 60 55
804. **220.** 25 l. brown & choc. .. 2·50 70
805. – 60 l. blue and green .. 5·00 1·50
DESIGNS: 10 l. Verdi, Theatre Roya and Cathedral, Parma. 60 l. Verdi, La Scala Opera House and Cathedral, Milan.

1951. Forestry Festival. Inscr. "FESTA DEGLI ALBERI".
806. **221.** 10 l. green and olive.. 60 35
807. – 25 l. green .. .. 1·40 30
DESIGN—HORIZ. 25 l. Tree and wooded hills.

222. V. Bellini. **223.** Caserta Palace.

1952. Bellini (composer). 150th Birth Anniv.
808. **222.** 25 l. black .. .. 1·25 15

1952. Caserta Palace. Bicent.
809. **223.** 25 l. bistre and green .. 1·10 15

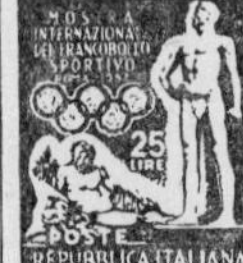

224. **225.** Motor-boat Pavilion.

1952. Int. Exn. of Sports Stamps. Rome.
810. **224.** 25 l. brown and grey 75 15

1952. 30th Milan Fair.
811. **225.** 60 l. blue .. .. 5·00 2·00

226. Leonardo da Vinci.

227. Campaniles and First Stamps.

XXVI BIENNALE D'ARTE DI VENEZIA

229. Lion of St. Mark. **228.** Hand, Torch and Globe.

1952. Leonardo da Vinci. 5th Birth Cent.
812. **226.** 25 l. orange 40 5
813. – 60 l. blue .. .. 1·25 1·00
814. **226.** 80 l red .. .. 4·50 5
DESIGN — (inscr. "LEONARDO DA VINCI 1452–1952"): 60 l. "The Virgin of the Rocks".

1952. Modena and Parma Stamp Cent.
815. **227.** 25 l. black & brown 20 15
816. 60 l. indigo and blue 3·50 2·25

1952. Overseas Fair, Naples.
817. **228.** 25 l. blue .. .. 1·60 15

1952. 26th Biennial Art Exn. Venice.
818. **229.** 25 l. black and cream 1·00 15

230. Emblem of Fair. **231.** San Giusto Cathedral and Flag.

232. Sailing Vessel and Fair Entrance. **233.** Girolamo Savonarola.

1952. 30th Padua Fair.
819. **230.** 25 l. red and blue .. 1·25 20

1952. 4th Trieste Fair.
820. **231.** 25 l. grn., red & brown 1·00 15

1952. 16th Levant Fair, Bari.
821. **232.** 25 l. green 90 15

1952. Savonarola (reformer). 5th Birth Cent.
822. **233.** 25 l. violet 80 15

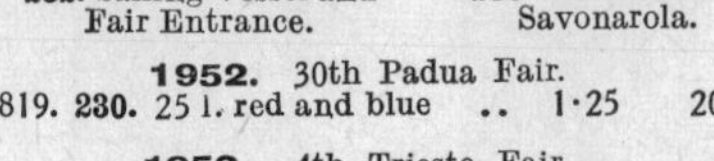

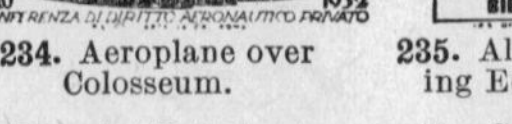

234. Aeroplane over Colosseum. **235.** Alpine Climbing Equipment.

1952. 1st Private Aeronautics Conf., Rome.
823. **234.** 60 l. bl. & ultramarine 2·50 2·00

1952. Alpine Troops National Exn.
824. **235.** 25 l. grey 55 15

236. Army, Navy and Air Force Symbols. **237.** Sailor, Soldier and Airman.

1952. Armed Forces Day. Inscr. as in T **237**.
825. **236.** 10 l. green 8 5
826. **237.** 25 l. sepia & brown .. 40 5
827. – 60 l. black and blue .. 1·50 25
DESIGN—as T **237**: 60 l. Aeroplane, torpedo-boat and tank.

238. Cardinal Massaia and Map. **239.** V. Gemito.

240. A. Mancini. **241.**

1952. Cent. of Mission to Ethiopia.
828. **238.** 25 l. deep brn. & brn. 80 20

1952. Gemito (sculptor). Birth Cent.
829. **239.** 25 l. brown 55 15

1952. Mancini (painter). Birth Cent.
830. **240.** 25 l. myrtle 55 20

1952. Martyrdom of Belfiore. Cent.
831. **241.** 25 l. blue and black .. 65 15

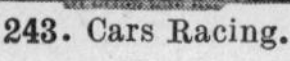

242. Antonello da Messina. **243.** Cars Racing.

1953. Antonello Exhibition, Messina.
832. **242.** 25 l. red .. .. 1·00 15

1953. 20th "Mille Miglia" Car Race.
833. **243.** 25 l. violet 45 15

244. Orders of Merit. **245.** Arcangelo Corelli. **246.** Coin of Syracuse.

1953. Labour Orders of Merit.
834. **244.** 25 l. violet 45 15

1953. Corelli (composer). Birth Tercent.
835. **245.** 25 l. brown 50 15

1953. (a) Size 17 × 21 mm.
887. **246.** 1 l. black 5 5
836. 5 l. slate 5 5
889. 6 l. brown 5 5
890. 10 l. vermilion .. 8 5
891. 12 l. green 12 5
892. 13 l. mauve 20 5
893. 15 l. violet-grey .. 12 5
894. 20 l. brown 15 5
895. 25 l. violet 50 5
896. 30 l. brown 12 5
897. 35 l. red 20 5
898. 40 l. magenta .. 60 5
899. 50 l. olive 80 5
900. 60 l. blue 15 5
901. 70 l. green 25 5
902. 80 l. chestnut .. 25 5
903. 90 l. brown .. .. 1·25 5
1008. 100 l. brown .. 1·90 5
905. 130 l. red and grey .. 30 5
1009. 200 l. blue .. .. 1·40 5

(b) Size $22\frac{1}{2}$ × 28 mm.
904. **246.** 100 l. brown .. 17·00 5
906. 200 l. blue .. .. 2·00 5
See also Nos. 1202/19.

247. St. Clare of Assisi. **248.** Mountains and Reservoirs. **249.** "Agriculture".

1953. St. Clare. 700th Death Anniv.
847. 247. 25 l. chestnut & brown 50 8

1953. Mountains Festival.
848. 248. 25 l. green .. .. 1·00 8

1953. Int. Agricultural Exn., Rome.
849. 249. 25 l. brown 50 8
850. 60 l. blue .. .. 2·00 30

250. Rainbow over Atlantic.

251. L. Signorelli.

252. A. Bassi.

253. Capri.

1953. Atlantic Pact. 4th Anniv.
851. 250. 25 l. slate & yellow .. 80 8
852. 60 l. blue & mauve .. 7·50 95

1953. Signorelli (painter). 500th Birth Anniv.
853. 251. 25 l. green & brown .. 55 8

1953. 6th Int. Microbiological Congress, Rome.
854. 252. 25 l. brown and slate 55 8

1953. Tourist Series.
855. – 10 l. brown and sepia 8 5
856. – 12 l. black and blue .. 12 5
857. – 20 l. brown and orange 20 5
858. – 25 l. blue-green .. 40 5
859. – 35 l. brown and buff .. 80 5
860. 253. 60 l. blue and turquoise 1·60 20
DESIGNS—VERT. 10 l. Siena. 25 l. Cortina d'Ampezzo. HORIZ. 12 l. Rapallo. 20 l. Gardone. 35 l. Taormina.

254. Lateran Palace.

255. Television Aerial and Screen.

257.

256. Inscription reads "Everyone Must Contribute to the Public Expense".

1954. Lateran Treaty. 25th Anniv.
861. 254. 25 l. brown and sepia 40 5
862. 60 l. blue and bright bl. 1·25 30

1954. Introduction of Television in Italy.
863. 255. 25 l. violet 40 5
864. 60 l. turquoise .. 1·60 35

1954. "Encouragement to Taxpayers".
865. 256. 25 l. violet 65 5

1954. 1st. Experimental Helicopter Mail Flight. Milan-Turin.
866. 257. 25 l. slate-green .. 40 10

258. Eagle and Campanile.

259. A. Catalani.

1954. Resistance Movement. 10th Anniv.
867. 258. 25 l. black & brown .. 35 5

1954. Catalani (composer). Birth Cent.
868. 259. 25 l. grey-green .. 40 5

260. Marco Polo, Lion of St. Mark, Venice, and Dragon Pillar, Peking.

1954. Marco Polo. 7th Birth Cent.
869. 260. 25 l. brown 50 5
870. 60 l. green .. .. 1·10 35

261. Cyclist, Car and Landscape.

1954. Italian Touring Club. 60th Anniv.
871. 261. 25 l. green and red .. 35 5

262. "St. Michael the Archangel" (after Guido Reni).

263. "Pinocchio".

264. Amerigo Vespucci (explorer).

1954. Int. Police Congress. Rome.
872. 262. 25 l. red 50 5
873. 60 l. blue .. .. 1·00 35

1954. Carlo Lorenzini (author).
874. 263. 25 l. red 35 5

1954. Vespucci. 500th Birth Anniv.
875. 264. 25 l. purple 20 5
876. 60 l. blue .. .. 1·00 35

265. "Madonna" (Perugino).

266. Silvio Pellico.

267.

1954. Termination of Marian Year.
877. 265. 25 l. brown and buff .. 25 5
878. – 60 l. black and cream 95 35
DESIGN: 60 l. Madonna's head (Michelangelo).

1955. Pellico (dramatist). Death Cent.
879. 266. 25 l. blue and violet .. 35 5

1955. "Encouragement to Taxpayers".
907. 267. 25 l. lilac .. .. 2·50 5
Inscription reads "The Nation Expects a Faithful Declaration of Your Income".

269. A. Rosmini.

268.

270. G. Fracastoro and Roman Arena, Verona.

1955. 4th World Petroleum Congress.
908. 268. 25 l. green .. .. 1·00 5
909. – 60 l. red 80 35
DESIGN: 60 l. Oil derricks and globe.

1955. Rosmini (theologian). Death Cent.
910. 269. 25 l. brown 30 5

1955. Int. Medical Conf., Verona.
915. 270. 25 l. brown and black 30 5

271. St. Francis Basilica.

272. Scholar and Drawing-board.

1955. Elevation of Basilica of St. Francis of Assisi to Papal Chapel. Bicent.
916. 271. 25 l. black & cream .. 30 5

1955. "Montani" Institute, Fermo. Cent.
917. 272. 25 l. green 30 5

273. "The Harvester".

274. F.A.O. Building, Rome.

1955. Int. Agricultural Institute. 50th Anniv.
918. 273. 25 l. brown and red .. 30 5

1955. F.A.O. 10th Anniv.
919. 274. 60 l. mauve & black.. 60 15

275. G. Matteotti.

276. B. Grassi (biologist).

1955. Matteotti Commem.
920. 275. 25 l. red 45 5

1955. Grassi. 30th Death Anniv.
921. 276. 25 l. green 45 5

277. "St. Stephen giving Alms to the Poor".

278. G. Pascoli.

280. "Italia" Ski-jump.

279. G. Mazzini.

1955. Fra Angelico (painter). 5th Death Cent. Inscr. as in T 277.
922. 277. 10 l. black and cream 8 5
923. – 25 l. blue 45 5
DESIGN—HORIZ. 25 l. "St. Lawrence giving goods of the Church to the poor".

1955. Pascoli (poet). Birth Cent.
924. 278. 25 l. black 30 5

1955. Air. Mazzini (revolutionary). 150th Birth Anniv.
925. 279. 100 l. green 90 50

1956. 7th Winter Olympic Games, Cortina d'Ampezzo. Inscr. as in T 280.
926. 280. 10 l. green and orange 5 5
927. – 12 l. black and yellow 5 5
928. – 25 l. red and slate .. 15 5
929. – 60 l. blue and orange 60 40
DESIGNS: 12 l. Snow Stadium. 25 l. Ice Stadium. 60 l. Skating Arena, Misurina.

1956. Air. Italian President's Visit to U.S.A and Canada. Surch. **1956 Visita del Presidente della Republica negli U.S.A. e nel Canada. L. 120.**
930. 163. 120 l. on 50 l. magenta 80 60

281. Coach and Train.

1956. Simplon Tunnel. 50th Anniv.
931. 281. 25 l. green 20 5

282.

1956. Republic. 10th Anniv.
932. 282. 10 l. grey 5 5
933. 25 l. red 12 5
934. 60 l. blue 45 30
935. 80 l. orange & brown.. 3·50 5

283. Count Avogadro.

1956. Avogadro (physicist). Death Cent.
936. 283. 25 l. grey 20 5

1956. Europa. As T 230 of Belgium.
937. 25 l. green 20 5
938. 60 l. blue .. .. 2·25 15

284.

286. Savings Bank, Books and Certificates.

285. The Globe.

1956. Int. Astronautical Congress, Rome.
939. 284. 25 l. blue 55 5

1956. Admission to U.N. 1st Anniv.
940. 285. 25 l. red & green on pink 10 5
941. 60 l. grn. & red on green 25 12

1956. Post Office Savings Bank. 80th Anniv.
942. 286. 25 l. blue and slate .. 15 5

287. Ovid.

288. St. George (after Donatello).

289. Antonio Canova.

1957. Ovid (poet). Birth Bimillenary.
943. 287. 25 l. black and olive.. 15 5

1957.
944. 288. 500 l. green .. .. 1·25 12
945. 1000 l. red .. .. 2·10 50

1957. Canova (sculptor). Birth Bicent.
946. 289. 25 l. brown 5 5
947. – 60 l. slate 30 30
948. – 80 l. blue 30 5
DESIGNS—VERT. 60 l. Hercules and Lica. HORIZ. 80 l. Pauline Borghese (bust).

290. Traffic Lights at Crossroads.

291. "Europa" Flags.

292. Giosue Carducci.

1957. Road Safety Campaign.
949. 290. 25 l. red, black & green 15 5

1957. Europa. Flags in National colours.
950. 291. 25 l. blue 8 5
951. 60 l. blue 55 12

1957. Carducci (poet). 50th Death Anniv.
954. 292. 25 l. sepia 8 5

293. Filippino Lippi (after self-portrait). 294. Cicero (bust).

1957. Filippino Lippi (painter). 500th Birth. Anniv.
955. 293. 25 l. brown 8 5

1957. Cicero(statesman). 2,000th Death Anniv.
956. 294. 25 l. red 8 5

295. Garibaldi (after M. Lorusso). 296. St. Domenico Savio and Youths.

1957. Garibaldi. 150th Birth Anniv. Inscr. " GIUSEPPE GARIBALDI 1807 1882 ".
957. 295. 15 l. grey 5 5
958. – 110 l. lilac 50 5
DESIGN—HORIZ. 110 l. Statue of Garibaldi on horseback (after Romanelli).

1957. St. Domenico Savio. Death Cent.
959. 296. 15 l. black and violet .. 8 5

297. St. Francis of Paola. 298. Dams, Peasant and Map of Sardinia.

1957. St. Francis of Paola. 450th Death Anniv.
960. 297. 25 l. black 15 5

1958. Inaug. of Flumendosa—Mulargia Irrigation Scheme, Sardinia.
961. 298. 25 l. turquoise .. 8 5

299. Statue of Immaculate Conception, Rome and Lourdes Sanctuary. 300. " The Constitution ".

302. Rodolfo's Attic (" La Boheme "). 301. Exhibition Emblem and Ancient Roman Road.

1958. Apparition at Lourdes. Cent.
962. 299. 15 l. red 5 5
963. 60 l. blue 12 8

1958. Constitution. 10th Anniv. Inscr. "X ANNUALE DELLA CONSTITUZIONE"
964. 300. 25 l. green & brown .. 8 5
965. – 60 l. sepia and blue .. 10 8
966. – 110 l. sepia & brown .. 25 5
DESIGNS:—VERT. 60 l. Oak tree with new growth. HORIZ. 110 l. Montecitorio Palace.

1958. Brussels Int. Exn.
967. 301. 60 l. yellow and blue .. 12 8

1958. Puccini (operatic composer). Birth Cent.
968. 302. 25 l. blue 8 5

303. The Prologue (" I Pagliacci "). 304. " Ave Maria " (after Segantini).

1958. Leoncavallo (operatic composer). Birth Cent.
969. 303. 25 l. red and indigo .. 8 5

1958. Giovanni Segantini (painter). Birth Cent.
970. 304. 110 l. grey on cream .. 35 5

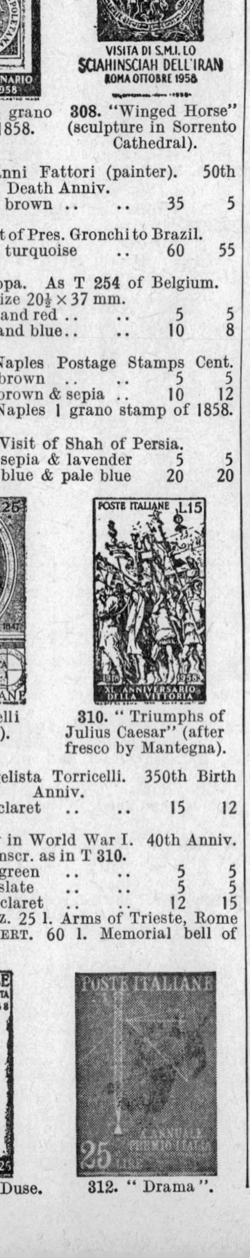

306. Federal Palace, Brasilia and Arch of Titus, Rome.

305. " Fattori in his study " (self-portrait.

307. Naples ½ grano stamp of 1858. 308. "Winged Horse" (sculpture in Sorrento Cathedral).

1958. Giovanni Fattori (painter). 50th Death Anniv.
971. 305. 110 l. brown 35 5

1958. Visit of Pres. Gronchi to Brazil.
972. 306. 175 l. turquoise .. 60 55

1958. Europa. As T 254 of Belgium. Size 20½ × 37 mm.
973. 25 l. blue and red 5 5
974. 60 l. red and blue 10 8

1958. 1st Naples Postage Stamps Cent.
975. 307. 25 l. brown 5 5
976. – 60 l. brown & sepia .. 10 12
DESIGN: 60 l. Naples 1 grano stamp of 1858.

1958. Visit of Shah of Persia.
977. 308. 25 l. sepia & lavender 5 5
978. 60 l. blue & pale blue 20 20

309. E. Torricelli (physicist). 310. " Triumphs of Julius Caesar" (after fresco by Mantegna).

1958. Evangelista Torricelli. 350th Birth Anniv.
979. 309. 25 l. claret 15 12

1958. Victory in World War I. 40th Anniv. Inscr. as in T 310.
980. 310. 15 l. green 5 5
981. – 25 l. slate 5 5
982. – 60 l. claret 12 15
DESIGNS—HORIZ. 25 l. Arms of Trieste, Rome and Trento. VERT. 60 l. Memorial bell of Rovereto.

311. Eleonora Duse. 312. " Drama ".

1958. Eleonora Duse (actress). Birth Cent.
983. 311. 25 l. blue 10 5

1958. " Premio Italia " (international contest for radio and television plays). 10th Anniv.
984. 312. 25 l. black, blue & red 5 5
985. – 60 l. black and blue .. 12 12
DESIGN: 60 l. " Music " (radio mast and grand piano).

313. Sicily 5 gr. stamp of 1859. 314. Capitol, Quirinal Square Obelisk and Dome of St. Peter's.

1959. 1st Sicilian Postage Stamps Cent.
986. – 25 l. turquoise .. 5 5
987. 313. 60 l. orange 12 10
DESIGN: 25 l. Sicily 2 gr. stamp of 1859.

1959. Lateran Treaty. 30th Anniv.
988. 314. 25 l. blue 12 5

315. N.A.T.O. Emblem and Map.

316. Arms of Paris and Rome. 317. Olive Branch growing from shattered Tree.

1959. N.A.T.O. 10th Anniv.
989. 315. 25 l. blue and yellow 5 5
990. 60 l. blue and green 12 12

1959. Rome–Paris Friendship.
991. 316. 15 l. red and blue .. 5 5
992. 25 l. red and blue .. 5 5

1959. Int. War Veterans' Assn. Convention, Rome.
993. 317. 25 l. green 8 5

318. Lord Byron Monument. 319. C. Prampolini (politician). 320. Quirinal Square Obelisk Rome.

1959. Unveiling of Lord Byron Monument, Rome.
994. 318. 15 l. grey-green .. 8 5

1959. Camillo Prampolini. Birth Cent.
995. 319. 15 l. red 15 5

1959. Olympic Games Propaganda. Roman Monuments and Ruins. Inscr. " ROMA MCMLX ".
996. 320. 15 l. sepia & orange 5 5
997. – 25 l. sepia & blue .. 5 5
998. – 35 l. sepia and buff 5 5
999. – 60 l. sepia & mauve 10 10
1000. – 110 l. sepia & yellow 20 5
DESIGNS—VERT. 25 l. Tower of City Hall, Quirinal Hill. HORIZ. 35 l. Baths of Caracalla. 60 l. Arch of Constantine (Colosseum). 110 l. Basilica of Massentius.

321. Victor Emmanuel II, Garibaldi, Cavour and Mazzini. 322. Workers' Monument and I.L.O. Building, Geneva.

1959. 2nd War of Independence. Cent. Inscr. " GUERRA DELL' INDIPENDENZA 1859 ".
1001. 321. 15 l. black 5 5
1002. – 25 l. red and brown .. 5 5
1003. – 35 l. violet 5 5
1004. – 60 l. blue 10 10
1005. – 110 l. lake 20 5
DESIGNS—VERT. 25 l. Italian camp after the Battle of Magenta (after painting by Fattori). 110 l. Battle of Magenta (after painting by Induno). HORIZ. 35 l. Battle of San Fermo (after painting by Trezzini). 60 l. Battle of Palestro.

The 25 l. is also a Red Cross commemorative.

1959. I.L.O. 40th Anniv.
1006. 322. 25 l. violet 5 5
1007. 60 l. brown 35 15

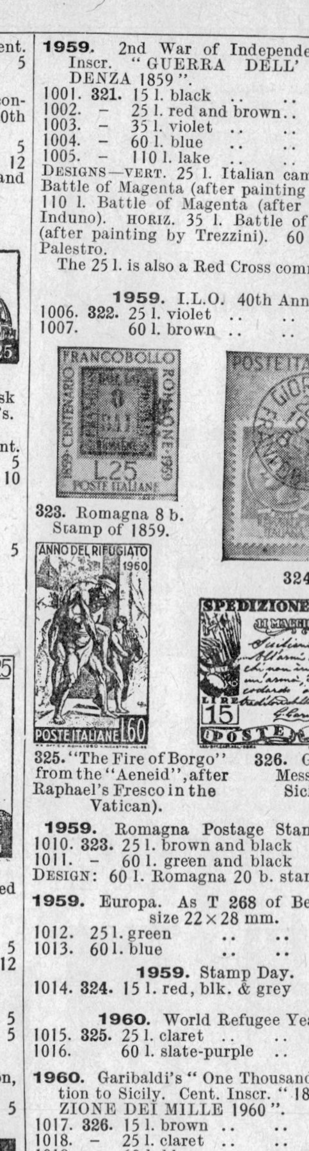

323. Romagna 8 b. Stamp of 1859. 324.

325. "The Fire of Borgo" from the "Aeneid", after Raphael's Fresco in the Vatican). 326. Garibaldi's Message to Sicilians.

1959. Romagna Postage Stamps Cent.
1010. 323. 25 l. brown and black 8 5
1011. – 60 l. green and black 8 8
DESIGN: 60 l. Romagna 20 b. stamp of 1859.

1959. Europa. As T 268 of Belgium, but size 22 × 28 mm.
1012. 25 l. green 8 5
1013. 60 l. blue 8 8

1959. Stamp Day.
1014. 324. 15 l. red, blk. & grey 5 5

1960. World Refugee Year.
1015. 325. 25 l. claret 5 5
1016. 60 l. slate-purple .. 12 12

1960. Garibaldi's " One Thousand " Expedition to Sicily. Cent. Inscr. " 1860 SPEDIZIONE DEI MILLE 1960 ".
1017. 326. 15 l. brown 5 5
1018. – 25 l. claret 5 5
1019. – 60 l. blue 12 12
DESIGNS—VERT. 25 l. Garibaldi's meeting King Victor Emmanuel II (after painting by Matania). HORIZ. 60 l. Embarkation of Volunteers at Quarto (after painting by T. van Elven).

327. " The Discus Thrower " (after Miron). 328. Vittorio Bottego (after statue by Ettore Ximenes at Parma).

1960. Olympic Games. Inscr. as in T 327.
1020. – 5 l. brown 5 5
1021. – 10 l. blue and orange 5 5
1022. – 15 l. blue 5 5
1023. – 25 l. sepia and lilac .. 5 5
1024. 327. 35 l. claret 5 5
1025. – 60 l. sepia and green 8 8
1026. – 110 l. purple 15 5
1027. – 150 l. brown and blue 40 40
1028. – 200 l. green 40 5
DESIGNS—VERT. 5 l. Games emblem (Romulus, Remus and Wolf, and Olympic rings). 15 l. " Starting the Race " (statue). 110 l. " Pugilist at rest " (after Apollonius). 200 l. " The Apoxiomenos " (athlete cleansing himself) (after Lisippos). HORIZ. 10 l. Olympic Stadium, Rome. 25 l. Cycling Stadium, Rome. 60 l. Sports Palace, Rome. 150 l. " Little Sports Palace " (Palazzetto dello Sport).

1960. Vittorio Bottego (explorer). Birth Cent.
1029. 328. 30 l. brown 8 5

1960. Europa. As T 279 of Belgium but size 36½ × 26 mm.
1030. 30 l. brown and green .. 5 5
1031. 70 l. salmon and blue .. 10 10

329. Caravaggio. **330.** Coach and Posthorn.

1960. Michaelangelo Merisi du Caravaggio (painter). 350th Death Anniv.

1032. **329.** 25 l. brown 8 5

1960. Stamp Day.

1033. **330.** 15 l. sepia and red .. 5 5

331. Michaelangelo. **332.** Douglas DC-8 Jetliner crossing Atalntic Ocean.

1961. Works of Michaelangelo. Frescoes on ceiling of Sistine Chapel. (a) Size 17×20½ mm.

1034. – 1 l. black 5 5
1035. – 5 l. chestnut 5 5
1036. – 10 l. red 8 5
1037. – 15 l. purple .. 8 5
1038. – 20 l. blue-green .. 10 5
1039. – 25 l. sepia .. 35 5
1040. – 30 l. plum .. 15 5
1041. – 40 l. red .. 10 5
1042. – 50 l. olive .. 60 5
1043. – 55 l. brown .. 20 5
1044. – 70 l. blue .. 15 5
1045. – 85 l. green .. 15 5
1046. – 90 l. magenta .. 40 5
1047. – 100 l. slate-violet .. 1·25 5
1048. – 115 l. blue .. 20 5
1049. – 150 l. brown .. .. 2·00 5
1050. **331.** 200 l. blue .. .. 3·75 5

(b) Size 22×26½ mm.

1051. – 500 l. turquoise .. 2·00 8
1052. – 1000 l. brown-red .. 2·40 50

DESIGNS: 1, 5, 10, 115, 150 l. Athlete (different versions). 15 l. Joel. 20 l. Lybian Sibyl. 25 l. Isaiah. 30 l. Eritrean Sibyl. 40 l. Daniel. 50 l. Delphic Sibyl. 55 l. Cumaean Sibyl. 70 l. Zachariah. 85 l. Jonah. 90 l. Jeremiah. 100 l. Ezekiel. 500 l. Adam. 1000 l. Eve.

1961. Visit of President Gronchi to S. America.

1053. **332.** 170 l. bl. (Argentina) 2·10 2·10
1054. 185 l. grn. (Uruguay) 3·25 3·25
1055. 205 l. violet (Peru) .. 7·00 7·00

The countries indicated are shown in deep colours on the map.

333. Pliny the Younger. **334.** Ippolito Nievo.

1961. Pliny the Younger. 19th Birth Cent.

1056. **333.** 30 l. brown and buff 15 8

1961. Ippolito Nievo (poet). Birth Cent.

1057. **334.** 30 l. blue and red .. 15 8

335. St. Paul in Ship (from 15th-century Bible of Borso d'Este).

1961. St. Paul's Arrival in Rome. 19th Cent.

1058. **335.** 30 l. multicoloured .. 8 5
1059. 70 l. multicoloured .. 40 35

336. Cannon and Gaeta Fortress.

1961. Italian Unification and Independence Cent. Inscr. " 1861 CENTENARIO UNITA D'ITALIA 1961 ".

1060. **336.** 15 l. chocolate & blue 5 5
1061. – 30 l. brown and blue 5 5
1062. – 40 l. brown and blue 20 25
1063. – 70 l. mauve and brown 35 5
1064. – 115 l. grey-bl. & chest. 2·50 5
1065. – 300 l. red, brn. & grn. 3·50 3·00

DESIGNS: 30 l. Carignano Palace, Turin. 40 l. Montecitorio Palace, Rome. 70 l. Vecchio Palace, Florence. 115 l. Madama Palace, Rome. 300 l. Capitals, " Palace of Work ", Int. Exn. of Work Turin.

337. Doves. **338.** G. Romagnosi.

1961. Europa.

1066. **337.** 30 l. rose 5 5
1067. 70 l. green 12 10

1961. Romagnosi (philosopher). Birth Bicent.

1068. **338.** 30 l. green 10 5

339. Imprint of 50 c. Provisional Postal Franked Paper of Sardinia, 1819.

1961. Stamp Day.

1069. **339.** 15 l. magenta & black 5 5

340. " The Sweet-burning Lamp " from Pascoli's " La Poesia " (after wood-eng. by P. Morbiducci).

1962. G. Pascoli (poet). 50th Death Anniv.

1070. **240.** 30 l. red 10 5
1071. 70 l. blue 30 25

341. Pacinotti's Dynamo (diagram). **342.** St. Catherine (after 15th-century woodcut.)

343. Camera Lens. **344.** Cyclist being paced.

1962. Antonio Pacinotti (physicist). 50th Death Anniv.

1072. **341.** 30 l. black and red .. 20 5
1073. 70 l. black and blue .. 20 25

1962. Canonization of St. Catherine of Siena. 5th Cent.

1074. – 30 l. slate-violet .. 20 5
1075. **342.** 70 l. black and red .. 30 25

DESIGN: 30 l. St. Catherine (after A. Vanni).

1962. Int. Cinematograph Art Fair. Venice. 30th Anniv.

1076. **343.** 30 l. black and blue .. 40 5
1077. – 70 l. black and red .. 35 35

DESIGN: 70 l. Lion of St. Mark.

1962. World Cycling Championships.

1078. **344.** 30 l. black and green 35 5
1079. – 70 l. blue and black .. 8 5
1080. – 300 l. black and red 1·75 1·75

DESIGNS: 70 l. Cyclists road-racing. 300 l. Cyclists on track.

345. Europa " Tree ".

1962. Europa.

1081. **345.** 30 l. red 8 5
1082. 70 l. blue 35 20

346. Balzan Medal. **347.** Campaign Emblem.

1962. Int. Balzan Foundation.

1083. **346.** 70 l. red and green .. 12 8

1962. Malaria Eradication.

1084. **347.** 30 l. violet 20 5
1085. 70 l. blue 35 30

348. 10 c. Stamp of 1862 and 30 l. Stamp of 1961. **349.** " The Pentecost" (from " Codex (Syriacus ").

1962. Stamp Day.

1086. **348.** 15 l. plum, bistre, violet and yellow .. 5 5

1962. Ecumenical Council. Vatican City.

1087. **349.** 30 l. orge & bl. on crm. 15 5
1088. 70 l. bl. & orge. on crm. 30 30

350. Statue of Cavour (statesman). **351.** Mirandola (scholar). **352.** D'Annunzio.

1962. Court of Accounts Cent.

1089. **350.** 30 l. green 15 5

1963. G. P. della Mirandola. 5th Birth Cent.

1090. **351.** 30 l. slate-violet .. 5 5

1963. Gabriele D'Annunzio (author and soldier). Birth Cent.

1091. **352.** 30 l. green 5 5

353. " Sowing " (bas-relief after G. and N. Pisano). **354.** Monviso, Italian Alps, Iceaxe and Rope.

1963. Freedom from Hunger.

1092. **353.** 30 l. sepia and rose .. 8 5
1093. – 70 l. sepia and blue .. 12 15

DESIGN: 70 l. "Harvesting" (bas-relief after G. and N. Pisano).

1963. Italian Alpine Club, Cent.

1094. **345.** 115 l. sepia and blue 35 5

355. " I.N.A. " Lighthouse. **356.** Posthorn and Globe.

1963. Italian National Insurance Corporation. 50th Anniv.

1095. **355.** 30 l. black and green 5 5

1963. Paris Postal Conference Cent.

1096. **356.** 70 l. blue and green 12 10

357. Three-dimensional Emblem. **358.** "World Tourism."

1963. Red Cross Cent.

1097. **357.** 30 l. red & slate-purple 8 5
1098. 70 l. red and blue .. 20 20

1963. U.N. Tourism Conf., Rome.

1099. **358.** 15 l. blue and olive 5 5
1100. 70 l. brown and blue 15 15

359. " Co-operation ". **360.** " Naples ".

1963. Europa.

1101. **359.** 30 l. brown and red .. 5 5
1102. 70 l. green and brown 12 12

1963. 4th Mediterranean Games, Naples. Inscr. "NAPOLI 1963 ".

1103. **360.** 15 l. ochre and blue 5 5
1104. – 70 l. orange & green .. 12 12

DESIGN: 70 l. Greek " Olympic " vase.

361. Verdi and La Scala Opera House. **362.** G. Belli.

1963. Composers, Verdi. 150th Birth Anniv. (No. 1105) and Mascagni. Birth Cent. (No. 1106).

1105. **361.** 30 l. brown and olive 5 5
1106. – 30 l. olive and brown 5 5

DESIGN: No. 1106, Mascagni and Costanzi Theatre.

1963. Giuseppi Belli (poet). Death Cent.

1107. **362.** 30 l. brown 5 5

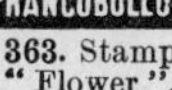

363. Stamp " Flower ". **364.** Galileo Galilei.

1963. Stamp Day.

1108. **363.** 15 l. red and blue .. 5 5

1964. Galileo Galilei. 400th Birth Anniv.

1109. **364.** 30 l. chestnut .. 5 5
1110. 70 l. black 12 12

ILLUSTRATIONS
British Commonwealth and all overprints and surcharges are FULL SIZE. Foreign Countries have been reduced to ¾-LINEAR.

365. Nicodemus (from Michelangelo's "Pieta").

1964. Michelangelo. 400th Death Anniv.

1111. **365.** 30 l. sepia (postage) .. 5 5
1112. – 185 l. black (air) .. 60 60

DESIGN: 185 l. Michelangelo's " Madonna of Bruges ".

DESIGN: 70 l. " The Charge of Pastrengo 1848 " after De Albertis.

366. Carabinieri on Parade.

1964. Carabinieri (military police). 150th Anniv.

1113. **366.** 30 l. red and blue .. 5 5

1114. – 70 l. brown 10 10

367. G. Bodoni. **368.** Europa "Flower".

1964. Giambattista Bodoni (type-designer and printer). 150th Death Anniv. (1963).

1115. **367.** 30 l. red 5 5

1964. Europa.

1116. **368.** 30 l. purple 5 5

1117. 70 l. turquoise blue.. 8 8

369. European Buildings. **370.** Victor Emmanuel Monument, Rome

1964. 7th European Municipalities' Assembly.

1118. **369.** 30 l. brown and green 5 5

1119. 70 l. brown and blue 8 5

1120. 500 l. red 60 60

1964. War Veteran's Pilgrimage to Rome.

1121. **370.** 30 l. brown 5 5

1122. 70 l. blue 8 8

371. G. da Verrazzano and Verrazano Bridge.

372. Italian Stamps.

373. Prisoners of War. **374.** I.T.U. Emblem, Meucci and Marconi.

1964. Opening of Verrazano Narrows Bridge, New York.

1123. **371.** 30 l. blk. & brn. (post.) 5 5

1124. 130 l. blk. & grn. (air) 12 12

This American bridge is designated "Verrazano" with one "z".

1964. Stamp Day.

1125. **372.** 15 l. brown & yell.-brn. 5 5

1965. Resistance. 20th Anniv.

1126. **373.** 10 l. black 5 5

1127. – 15 l. blk., red & grn. 5 5

1128. – 30 l. purple 5 5

1129. – 70 l. blue 8 12

1130. – 115 l. red 12 8

1131. – 130 l. brn., grn. & red 20 8

DESIGNS—VERT. 15 l. Servicemen and casualty ("Liberation Army"). 70 l. Alpine soldiers ("Resistance in the mountains"). HORIZ. 30 l. Gaunt hands and arms on swastika ("Political and Racial Persecution"). 115 l. Patriots with banners ("Resistance in the Towns"). 130 l. Ruined building and torn flags ("Martyred Cities").

1965. I.T.U. Cent.

1132. **374.** 70 l. red and green .. 8 5

375. Yachts of "Flying Dutchman" Class.

1965. World Sailing Championships, Alassio and Naples.

1133. **375.** 30 l. black and red .. 5 5

1134. – 70 l. black and blue.. 10 8

1135. – 500 l. black & grey-bl. 75 55

DESIGNS—VERT. 70 l. Yachts of "5.5 m. S.I" class. HORIZ. 500 l. Yachts of "Lightning" class.

376. Mont Blanc and Tunnel. **377.** A. Tassoni and Episode from his "Secchia Rapita".

1965. Opening of Mont Blanc Road Tunnel.

1136. **376.** 30 l. black 5 5

1965. Alessandro Tassoni (poet). 400th Birth Anniv.

1137. **377.** 40 l. multicoloured.. 5 5

378. Europa "Sprig". **379.** "Hell" (Codex, Vatican Library).

1965. Europa.

1138. **378.** 40 l. green and brown 5 5

1139. 90 l. green and blue.. 10 8

1965. Dante's 700th Birth Anniv.

1140. **379.** 40 l. multicoloured .. 5 5

1141. – 90 l. multicoloured .. 10 8

1142. – 130 l. multicoloured.. 15 5

1143. – 500 l. green 60 45

DESIGNS—VERT. 90 l. "Purgatory" (codex, Marciana Library, Venice). 500 l. Head of Dante (bronze, Naples Museum), HORIZ. 130 l. "Paradise" (codex, British Museum.)

380. House and Savings-bank. **381.** Aircraft passing Control-tower.

1965. Savings Day.

1144. **380.** 40 l. multicoloured.. 5 5

1965. Night Airmail Service.

1145. **381.** 40 l. red and blue .. 5 5

1146. 90 l. blue, cream, red and green 10 12

DESIGN: 90 l. Aircraft emblem within airmail envelope "border".

382. Map of "Highway to the Sun". **383.** Bob-sleigh at speed.

1965. Stamp Day.

1147. **382.** 20 l. multicoloured .. 5 5

1966. World Bob-sleigh Championships. Cortina d'Ampezzo.

1148. **383.** 40 l. red, blue & grey 5 5

1149. – 90 l. violet and blue.. 12 10

DESIGN: 90 l. Four-seater bob-sleigh at speed.

384. Skier carrying Torch. **385.** B. Croce.

1966. University Winter Games, Turin.

1150. **384.** 40 l. black and red 8 5

1151. – 90 l. violet and red 10 10

1152. – 500 l. brown & red 60 60

DESIGNS—VERT. 90 l. Ice-skating. 500 l. Ice-hockey.

1966. Benedetto Croce (philosopher). Birth Cent.

1153. **385.** 40 l. sepia 5 5

386. Arms of Cities of Venezia.

1966. Venezia and Italy. Cent. of Union.

1154. **386.** 40 l. multicoloured 5 5

387. Pine, Palatine Hill, Rome. **388.** "Visit Italy".

1966. "Trees and Flowers". Multicoloured.

1155. 20 l. Type **387** 5 5

1156. 25 l. Apples 12 5

1157. 40 l. Carnations 12 5

1158. 50 l. Irises 15 5

1241. 55 l. Cupressus 12 8

1159. 90 l. Anthemis (Golden Marguerite) 30 5

1160. 170 l. Olive tree, Villa Adriana, Tivoli .. 30 5

1242. 180 l. Broom 50 5

Nos. 1241 and 1242 are 26 × 35½ mm.

1966. Tourist Propaganda.

1161. **388.** 20 l. multicoloured 5 5

389. Capital "I". **390.** Battle Scene.

1966. Republic. 20th Anniv.

1162. **389.** 40 l. multicoloured 8 5

1163. 90 l. multicoloured 12 8

1966. Battle of Bezzecca. Cent.

1164. **390.** 90 l. olive .. 10 8

391. "Singing Angels" (from copper panel on altar of St. Anthony's Basilica, Padua). **392.** Europa "Ship".

1966. Donatello. 5th Death Cent.

1165. **391.** 40 l. multicoloured 8 5

1966. Europa.

1166. **392.** 40 l. violet 8 5

1167. 90 l. blue 12 8

393. "Madonna in Maesta" (after Giotto). **394.** Filzi, Battisti, Chiesa and Sauro.

1966. Giotto's 700th Birth Anniv.

1168. **393.** 40 l. multicoloured .. 5 5

1966. War Heroes. 50th Death Annivs.

1169. **394.** 40 l. green and slate.. 5 5

395. Postal Emblem. **396.** Compass and Globe.

1966. Stamp Day.

1170. **395.** 20 l. red, green, black and yellow .. 5 5

1967. Italian Geographical Society Cent.

1171. **396.** 40 l. blue and black.. 10 5

397. Toscanini (orchestral conductor).

1967. Arturo Toscanini Birth Cent.

1172. **397.** 40 l. buff and blue .. 10 5

398. Campidoglio, Rome.

1967. Rome Treaties. 10th Anniv.

1173. **398.** 40 l. brown & black.. 10 5

1174. 90 l. purple and black 15 8

399. Cogwheels. **400.** Brown Bear (Abruzzo Park).

1967. Europa.

1175. **399.** 40 l. purple and pink 10 5

1176. 90 l. blue and cream 15 5

1967. Italian National Parks. Multicoloured.

1177. 20 l. Ibex (Gran Paradiso Park) (vert.) 5 5

1178. 40 l. Type **400** 12 5

1179. 90 l. Stag (Stelvio Park).. 35 5

1180. 170 l. Tree (Circeo Park) (vert.) 45 10

401. Monteverdi (composer).

1967. Claudio Monteverdi. 400th Birth Anniv.

1181. **401.** 40 l. brown & chest. 10 5

402. Racing Cyclists.

1967. 50th Tour of Italy Cycle Race. Designs showing cyclists.

1182. **402.** 40 l. multicoloured 8 5

1183. – 90 l. multicoloured 15 5

1184. – 500 l. multicoloured 90 45

403. Pirandello (dramatist) and Stage.

1967. Luigi Pirandello. Birth Cent.
1185. 403. 40 l. multicoloured .. 8 5

404. Stylised Mask.

1967. Two Worlds Festival, Spoleto.
1186. 404. 20 l. black and green 5 5
1187. 40 l. black and red 10 5

405. Coded Addresses.

1967. Introduction of Postal Codes.
1188. 405. 20 l. black, blue & yell. 5 5
1189. 25 l. black, pur. & yell. 10 5
1190. 40 l. black, red & yell. 10 5
1191. 50 l. black, grn. & yell. 10 5

406. Pomilio "PC–1". Biplane, and Postmark.
407. St. Ivo's Church, Rome.

1967. 1st Airmail Stamp. 50th Anniv.
1192. 406. 40 l. black and blue .. 10 5

1967. Francesco Borromini (architect). 300th Death Anniv.
1193. 407. 90 l. multicoloured .. 20 5

408. U. Giordano and Music from "Andrea Chenier".
409. "The Oath of Pontida" (from painting by Adolfo Cao).

1967. Umberto Giordano (composer). Birth Cent.
1194. 408. 20 l. chestnut & black 5 5

1967. Oath of Pontida. 800th Anniv.
1195. 409. 20 l. brown .. 5 5

410. I.T.Y. Emblem.
411. Lions Emblem.

1967. Int. Tourist Year.
1196. 410. 20 l. blk., bl. & yell. 5 5
1197. 50 l. blk., bl. & orge. 12 5

1967. Lions Int. 50th Anniv.
1198. 411. 50 l. multicoloured 15 5

412. Sentry.
413. E. Fermi (scientist) and Reactor.

1967. Stand on the Piave. 50th Anniv.
1199. 412. 50 l. multicoloured 12 5

1967. 1st Nuclear Chain Reaction. 25th Anniv.
1200. 413. 50 l. black & chestnut 12 5

414. Stamp and Dove.

1967. Stamp Day.
1201. 414. 25 l. multicoloured 5 5

1968. As Nos. 887, etc. (1952) size 16 × 20 mm.
1202. 246. 1 l. black 5 5
1203. 5 l. slate 5 5
1204. 6 l. brown 5 5
1205. 10 l. red 5 5
1206. 15 l. violet 5 5
1207. 20 l. sepia 5 5
1208. 25 l. violet 5 5
1209. 30 l. brown 5 5
1210. 40 l. purple 5 5
1211. 50 l. olive 8 5
1212. 55 l. violet 8 5
1213. 60 l. blue 8 5
1214. 70 l. green 8 5
1215. 80 l. brown 10 5
1216. 90 l. brown 10 5
1217. 100 l. brown 15 5
1217a. 125 l. purple and brown 12 5
1218. 130 l. red and grey .. 15 5
1218a. 180 l. purple and grey 25 5
1218aa. 150 l. violet 25 5
1219. 200 l. blue 25 5
1219a. 300 l. green 40 5
1219b. 400 l. brown 60 15

415. Scouts around Camp-fire.
416. Europa "Key".

1968. Italian Boy Scouts.
1220. 415. 50 l. multicoloured 12 5

1968. Europa.
1221. 416. 50 l. green and pink 12 5
1222. 90 l. brown and blue 20 5

417. "Tending the Sick".
418. Boito and "Mephistopheles".

1968. Luigi Gonzaga (St. Aloysius). 400th Birth Anniv.
1223. 417. 25 l. violet and brown 8 5

1968. Arrigo Boito (composer and librettist). 50th Death Anniv.
1224. 418. 50 l. multicoloured 12 5

419. F. Baracca and "Aerial Combat" (abstract by G. Balla).
420. Giambattista Vico (300th Birth Anniv.).

1968. Francesco Baracca (airman of World War I). 50th Death Anniv.
1225. 419. 25 l. multicoloured 8 5

1968. Italian Philosophers' Birth Annivs.
1226. 420. 50 l. ultramarine .. 15 5
1227. – 50 l. black 15 5
DESIGN: No. 1227, Tommaso Campanella (400th birth anniv.).

421. Cycle Wheel and Stadium.
423. Rossini.

422. "St. Mark's Square, Venice" (Canaletto).

1968. World Road Cycling Championships.
1228. 421. 25 l. indigo, pink and brown 10 5
1229. – 90 l. indigo, red & bl. 30 5
DESIGN: 90 l. Cyclists and Imola Castle.

1968. Canaletto (painter). Death Bicent.
1230. 422. 50 l. multicoloured 15 5

1968. Gioacchino Rossini (composer). Death Cent.
1231. 423. 50 l. red 15 5

424. Mobilization.
425. "Conti Correnti Postali".

1968. Victory in World War I. 50th Anniv. Multicoloured.
1232. 20 l. Type 424 .. .. 10 5
1233. 25 l. Trench warfare .. 12 5
1234. 40 l. Naval forces .. 30 8
1235. 50 l. Air Force .. 30 5
1236. 90 l. Battle of Vittorio Veneto 40 8
1237. 180 l. Tomb of Unknown Soldier 40 10

1968. Postal Cheque Service. 50th Anniv.
1238. 425. 50 l. red, green, black and blue .. 15 5

426. Tracking Equipment and Buildings.
427. "Postal Development".

1968. Space Telecommunications Centre, Fucino.
1239. 426. 50 l. multicoloured 15 5

1968. Stamp Day.
1240. 427. 25 l. red & yellow .. 8 5

428. Commemorative Medal.
429. Colonnade.

1969. State Audit Department. Cent.
1243. 428. 50 l. black and pink 10 5

1969. Europa.
1244. 429. 50 l. multicoloured .. 15 5
1245. 90 l. multicoloured .. 20 5

430. Machiavelli.
431. I.L.O. Emblem.

1969. Niccolo Machiavelli (statesman). 500th Birth Anniv.
1246. 430. 50 l. multicoloured .. 12 5

1969. Int. Labour Organization. 50th Anniv.
1247. 431. 50 l. black and green 20 5
1248. 90 l. black and red .. 15 5

432. Postal Emblem.

1969. Italian Philatelic Federation. 50th Anniv.
1249. 432. 50 l. multicoloured .. 10 5

433. Sondrio-Tirano Mailcoach of 1903.

1969. Stamp Day.
1250. 433. 25 l. ultramarine .. 5 5

434. Skiing.
435. "Galatea" (detail of fresco).

1970. World Skiing Championships, Val Gardena. Multicoloured.
1251. 50 l. Type 434 .. .. 15 5
1252. 90 l. Dolomites 20 5

1970. Raphael. 450th Death Anniv. Multicoloured.
1253. 20 l. Type 435 .. .. 5 5
1254. 50 l. "Madonna of the Goldfinch" 12 5

436. Symbols of Flight.

1970. Rome–Tokyo Flight by A. Ferrarin. 50th Anniv.
1255. 436. 50 l. blue, red, emer. and black 12 5
1256. 90 l. blue, red, emer. and black 20 5

437. "Flaming Sun".
438. Erasmo da Narni (from statue by Donatello).

1970. Europa.
1257. 437. 50 l. yellow and verm. 15 5
1258. 90 l. yellow & green .. 25 5

1970. Erasmo da Narni "Il Gattamelata" (Condottiere). 600th Birth Anniv.
1259. 438. 50 l. green 12 5

439. Running.

1970. World University Games, Turin. Multicoloured.
1260. 20 l. Type **439** 5 5
1261. 180 l. Swimming .. 40 8

440. Dr. Montessori and children.

1970. Dr. Maria Montessori (educationist). Birth Cent.
1262. **440.** 50 l. multicoloured .. 12 5

441. Map and Cavour's Declaration.

1970. Rome-Italy Union. Cent.
1263. **441.** 50 l. brown, red, green and black 12 5

442. Loggetta of Campanile, St. Mark's Square, Venice.

1970. Iacopo Tatti ("Il Sansovino," architect). 400th Death Anniv.
1264. **442.** 50 l. chestnut .. 12 5

443. "Garibaldi at Digione" (engraving).

1970. Garibaldi's Participation in Franco-Prussian War. Cent.
1265. **443.** 20 l. grey and blue .. 8 5
1266. 50 l. purple and blue 15 5

444. U.N. Emblem within Tree. **445.** Rotary Emblem.

1970. United Nations. 25th Anniv.
1267. **444.** 25 l. grn., blk. & brn. 12 5
1268. 90 l. yell., black & blue 30 5

1970. Rotary International. 65th Anniv.
1269. **445.** 25 l. ultramarine, blue and yellow .. 15 5
1270. 90 l. ultramarine, blue and yellow .. 30 5

446. Telephone Dial and "Network". **447.** Urban Complex and Tree.

1970. Completion of Telephone Trunk-dialling System.
1271. **446.** 25 l. red and green .. 15 5
1272. 90 l. red and blue .. 30 5

1970. Nature Conservation Year.
1273. **447.** 20 l. red and green .. 8 5
1274. 25 l. grey and green 15 5

448. Electric Train. **449.** "The Adoration" (F. Lippi).

1970. Stamp Day.
1275 **448.** 25 l. black 5 5

1970. Christmas. Multicoloured.
1276. 25 l. Type **449** (postage) 5 5
1277. 150 l. "The Adoration of the Magi" (Gentile da Fabriano). (air) .. 30 12
No. 1277 is horiz., size 44 × 35 mm.

450. Saverio Mercadante.

1970. S. Mercadante (composer). Death Cent.
1278. **450.** 25 l. violet and grey .. 5 5

451. "Mercury" (part of Cellini's "Perseus with the Head of Medusa"). **452.** Bramante's "Little Temple", St. Peter's Montorio, Rome.

1971. Benvenuto Cellini (goldsmith and sculptor). 400th Death Anniv.
1279. **451.** 50 l. blue 12 5

1971.
1280. **452.** 50 l. black and brown 12 5

453. Adenauer, Schuman and De Gasperi.

1971. European Coal and Steel Community. 20th Anniv.
1281. **453.** 50 l. brn., blk. & grn. 12 5
1282. 90 l. brn., black & red 20 5

454. Europa Chain. **455.** Mazzini.

1971. Europa.
1283. **454.** 50 l. red 10 5
1284. 90 l. purple 30 5

1971. Republic. 25th Anniv.
1285. **455.** 50 l. multicoloured .. 12 5
1286. 90 l. multicoloured .. 25 5

456. Canoeist in Slalom.

1971. World Canoeing Slalom and Free Descent Championships. Merano. Multicoloured.
1287. 25 l. Type **456** 12 5
1288. 90 l. Canoeist making free descent 20 5

457. Various Sports.

1971. Youth Games.
1289. **457.** 20 l. blk., grn. & brn. 5 5
1290. – 50 l. blk., violet & orge. 12 5
DESIGN: 50 l. Four other sports.

458. Alitalia Emblem.

1971. Alitalia State Airline. 25th Anniv. Multicoloured.
1291. 50 l. Type **458** 20 5
1292. 90 l. Emblem and Globe 20 5
1293. 150 l. Tailplane of Boeing 747 .. .. .. 40 10

459. G. Deledda. **460.** Boy in "Savings" Barrel.

1971. Grazia Deledda (writer). Birth Cent.
1294. **459.** 50 l. black and brown 12 5

1971. Postal Savings Bank.
1295. **460.** 25 l. multicoloured .. 8 5
1296. 50 l. multicoloured .. 12 5

1971. Air. As No. 911 but smaller, 20 × 36 mm.
1297. 100 l. green 15 5

461. U.N.I.C.E.F. Emblem and Paper Dolls.

1971. U.N.I.C.E.F. 25th Anniv. Multicoloured.
1301. 25 l. Type **461** 12 5
1302. 90 l. Children acclaiming U.N.I.C.E.F. emblem 30 5

462. Mailboat "Tirrenia".

1971. Stamp Day.
1303. **462.** 25 l. green 8 5

463. "The Nativity".

1971. Christmas. Miniatures from "Matilda's Evangelarium", Nonantola Abbey, Modena. Multicoloured.
1304. 25 l. Type **463** 12 5
1305. 90 l. "The Adoration of the Magi" 15 5

464. G. Verga and Sicilian Cart.

1972. Giovanni Verga (writer). 50th Death Anniv.
1306. **464.** 25 l. multicoloured .. 5 5
1307. 50 l. multicoloured .. 10 5

465. G. Mazzini. **466.** Stylized Flags.

1972. Giuseppe Mazzini (statesman). Death Cent.
1308. **465.** 25 l. green & black .. 5 5
1309. 90 l. grey-black & blk. 15 5
1310. 150 l. red and black 35 8

1972. 50th Int. Fair, Milan.
1311. **466.** 25 l. green and black 5 5
1312. – 50 l. red and black .. 10 5
1313. – 90 l. blue and black 15 5
DESIGNS: 50 l. "Windows, stand and pavilions" (abstract). 90 l. Abstract general view of Fair.

467. "Communications". **468.** Alpine Soldier.

1972. Europa.
1314. **467.** 50 l. multicoloured 10 5
1315. 90 l. multicoloured .. 15 5

1972. Alpine Corps. Cent. Multicoloured.
1316. 25 l. Type **468** 5 5
1317. 50 l. Soldier's hat .. 10 5
1318. 90 l. Soldier and mountains 20 5

469. Brenta Mountains.

1972. Tridentine Alpinists Society. Cent. Multicoloured.
1319. 25 l. Type **469** 5 5
1320. 50 l. Alpinist 15 5
1321. 180 l. Mt. Crozzon .. 40 5

470. Diagram of Conference Hall.

1972. 60th Inter-Parliamentary Union Conference, Rome.
1322. **470.** 50 l. multicoloured .. 12 5
1323. 90 l. multicoloured .. 20 5

471. "St. Peter Damiani" (miniature, after G. di Paolo). **472.** "The Three Graces" (Canova).

1972. St. Peter Damiani. 900th Death Anniv.
1324. **471.** 50 l. multicoloured .. 10 5

1972. Antonio Canova. 150th Death Anniv.
1325. **472.** 50 l. green 10 5

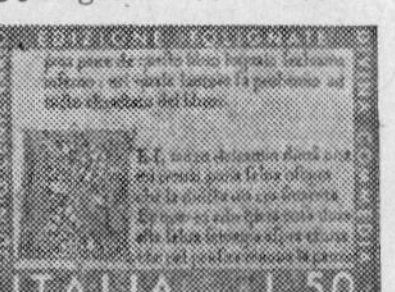

473. Initial and First Verse (Foligno edition).

1972. "The Divine Comedy". 500th Anniv. Multicoloured.

1326. 50 l. Type 473 .. .. 15 5
1327. 90 l. Initial and first verse (Mantua edition) (vert.) 20 5
1328. 180 l. Initial and first verse ("Jesino" edition) .. 35 5

474. "Holy Child in Crib".

1972. Christmas. Multicoloured.

1329. 20 l. "Angel" (looking to right) (vert.) .. 5 5
1330. 25 l. Type 474 .. .. 8 5
1331. 150 l. "Angel" (looking to left) (vert.) .. 25 5

475. Postal Coach.

1972. Stamp Day.

1332. **475.** 25 l. red 5 5

476. L. B. Alberti (from bronze by M. de Pasti. Louvre). 477. L. Perosi.

1972. Leon B. Alberti (writer and savant). 500th Death Anniv.

1333. **476.** 50 l. blue and yellow 10 5

1972. Lorenzo Perosi (composer and priest). Birth Cent.

1334. **477.** 50 l. brown & yellow 10 5
1335. 90 l. black and green 20 5

478. Don Orione. 479. Oceanic Survey.

1972. Don Orione (child-welfare pioneer). Birth Cent.

1336. **478.** 50 l. blue and turq... 10 5
1337. 90 l. green and yellow 20 5

1973. Military Marine Institute of Hydrography. Cent.

1338. **479.** 50 l. multicoloured.. 5 5

480. Grand Staircase, Royal Palace, Caserta.

1973 Luigi Vanvitelli (architect). 200th Death Anniv.

1339. **480.** 25 l. green 5 5

481. Schiavoni Shore.

1973. "Save Venice" Campaign. Mult.

1340. 20 l. Type 481 .. .. 5 5
1341. 25 l. "The Tetrarchs" (sculpture) (vert.) .. 5 5
1342. 50 l. "The Triumph of Venice" (V. Carpaccio) 5 5
1343. 90 l. Bronze horses, St. Mark's Basilica (vert.) 12 5
1344. 300 l. Piazetta S. Marco.. 40 20

482. Fair Theme. 483. Title-page of "Diverse Figure".

1973. 75th Int. Agricultural Fair, Verona.

1345. **482.** 50 l. multicoloured .. 5 5

1973. Salvator Rosa (painter and poet). Death Anniv.

1346. **483.** 25 l. black & orange 5 5

484. Formation of Fiat "G-91" Jet-fighters.

1973. Military Aviation. 50th Anniv. Mult.

1349. 20 l. Type 484 (postage).. 5 5
1350. 25 l. Formation of "S-55" flying-boats 5 5
1351. 50 l. Fiat "G-91Y" fighter-bombers on patrol .. 5 5
1352. 90 l. Fiat "CR-32" aircraft performing aerobatics 12 5
1353. 180 l. Italian built Campini-Caproni jet aircraft 25 5
1354. 150 l. "F-104S" Starfighter over Aeronautical Academy, Pozzuoli (air) 20 5

485. Ball and Pitch. 486. A. Manzoni (after F. Hayez).

1973. Italian Football Association. 75th Anniversary. Multicoloured.

1355. 25 l. Type 485 .. .. 5 5
1356. 90 l. Players in goal mouth 12 5

1973. Alessandro Manzoni (writer and politician). Death Cent.

1357. **486.** 25 l. brown & black.. 5 5

487. Palladio's "Rotunda" Vicenza. 488. Spring and Cogwheels.

1973. Andrea Palladio Commem.

1358. **487.** 90 l. multicoloured.. 12 5

1973. Italian State Supplies Office. 50th Anniversary.

1359. **488.** 50 l. multicoloured .. 5 5

489. Europa "Posthorn".

1973. Europa.

1360. **489.** 50 l. gold, lilac & yell. 5 5
1361. 90 l. gold, grn. & yell. 12 5

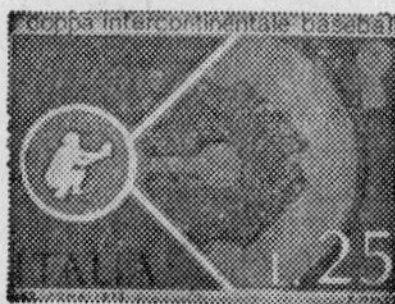

490. "Catcher" and Baseball Field.

1973. 1st Intercontinental Baseball Cup. Multicoloured.

1362. 25 l. Type 490 .. .. 5 5
1363. 90 l. As T 490, "Striker" and baseball field .. 12 5

491. Carnival Setting. 492. "Argenta Episode".

1973. Viareggio Carnival.

1364. **491.** 25 l. multicoloured.. 5 5

1973. Don Giovanni Minzoni (military chaplin). 50th Death Anniversary.

1365. **492.** 50 l. multicoloured .. 5 5

493. G. Salvamini. 494. Farnese Palace, Caprorola.

1973. Gaetano Salvamini (political historian) Birth Cent.

1366. **493.** 50 l. multicoloured .. 5 5

1973. "Vignola" (Jacopa Barozzi-architect). 400th Birth Anniv.

1367. **494.** 90 l. purple and yellow 12 5

495. "St. Giovanni Battista". 496. Leaning Tower of Pisa.

1973. Caravaggio (painter). 400th Birth Anniversary.

1368. **495.** 25 l. black & yellow.. 5 5

1973. Tourism.

1369. **496.** 50 l. multicoloured .. 5 5

497. Botticelli. 498. Immacolatella Fountain, Naples.

1973. Famous Italian Painters (1st series).

1370. **497.** 50 l. brown and red 8 5
1371. – 50 l. blue and brown 8 5
1372. – 50 l. green and emerald 8 5
1373. – 50 l. black and red .. 8 5
1374. – 50 l. brown and blue 8 5

PAINTERS: No. 1371, Piranesi. No. 1372, Veronese. No. 1373, Verrocchio. No. 1374, Tiepolo.

See also Nos. 1392/6.

1973. Italian Fountains. (1st series). Mult.

1375. 25 l. Type 498 .. .. 5 5
1376. 25 l. Trevi Fountain, Rome 5 5
1377. 25 l. Pretoria Fountain, Palermo 5 5

See also Nos. 1418/20, 1453/5 and 1503/5.

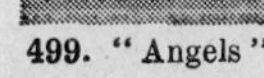

499. "Angels". 500. Map and Emblems.

1973. Christmas. Sculptures by A. di Duccio.

1378. **499.** 20 l. black and green 5 5
1379. – 25 l. black and blue.. 5 5
1380. – 150 l. black & yellow 20 12

DESIGNS: 25 l. "Virgin and Child". 150 l. "Angels" (different).

1973. Italian Rotary. 50th Anniv.

1381. **500.** 50 l. blue, green & red 5 5

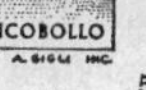

501. Alitalia "Caravelle". 502. Military Medal for Valour.

1973. Stamp Day.

1382. **501.** 25 l. blue 5 5

1973. Holders of the Gold Medal for Military Valour Organisation. 150th Anniv.

1383. **502.** 50 l. multicoloured.. 5 5

503. Caruso as Duke of Mantua (Verdi's "Rigoletto"). 504. "Christ crowning King Roger" (Martorana Church, Palermo).

1973. Enrico Caruso (operatic tenor). Birth Centenary.

1384. **503.** 50 l. red 5 5

1974. Norman Art in Sicily, Mosaics.

1385. **504.** 20 l. blue and yellow 5 5
1386. – 50 l. red and green .. 5 5

DESIGN: 50 l. "King William offering Church to the Virgin Mary" (Montreale Cathedral).

505. Pres. L. Einaudi. 506. G. Marconi in Headphones.

1974. Pres. Luigi Einaudi. Birth Cent.

1387. **505.** 50 l. green 5 5

1974. Guglielmo Marconi (radio pioneer). Birth Cent.

1388. **506.** 50 l. brn. & grn. .. 5 5
1389. – 90 l. multicoloured .. 12 5

DESIGN: 90 l. Marconi and world map.

507. "David" (Bernini). 508. Sardinian Chasseurs, 1774 and 1795, and Royal Fusilier of 1817.

1974. Europa. Sculptures. Multicoloured.

1390. 50 l. Type 507 .. .. 5 5
1391. 90 l. "Spirit of Victory" (Michelangelo).. .. 12 5

1974. Famous Italian Painters (2nd series). As Type 497.

1392. 50 l. blue and green .. 5 5
1393. 50 l. brown and blue .. 5 5
1394. 50 l. black and red .. 5 5
1395. 50 l. brown and yellow .. 5 5
1396. 50 l. blue and brown .. 5 5

PORTRAITS: No. 1392, Borromini. No. 1393, Carriera. No. 1394, Bellini. No. 1395, Mantegna. No. 1396, Raphael.

1974. Italian Excise Guards. Bicent. Uniforms. Multicoloured.

1397. 40 l. Type **508** .. 5 5

1398. 50 l. Guards from Lombardy-Venetia (1848), Sardinian Marines (1815) and Tebro Battalion (1849) .. 5 5

1399. 90 l. Lieutenant (1866), Sergeant-major of Marines (1892) and guard (1880) 12 5

1400. 180 l. Helicopter pilot, naval and alpine guards of 1974 25 5

509. Plumed Head-dress.

1974. Bersaglieri National Association. 50th Anniv. Multicoloured.

1401. 40 l. Type **509** 5 5

1402. 50 l. Bersaglieri emblem on rosette 5 5

510. "Start of Race". **512.** F. Petrarch.

511. Portofino.

1974. European Athletic Championships, Rome. Multicoloured.

1403. 40 l. Type **510** 5 5

1404. 50 l. "Pole-vaulting" .. 5 5

1974. Tourism (1st series). Multicoloured.

1405. 40 l. Type **511** 5 5

1406. 40 l. Gradara 5 5

See also Nos. 1442/4 and 1473/5.

1974. Francesco Petrarch (poet). 600th Death Anniv.

1407. **512.** 40 l. brn., red & yell. 5 5

1408. – 50 f. blue & yellow .. 5 5

DESIGN: 50 l. Petrarch at work in his study.

513. Tommaseo's Statue, Sebenico. **514.** G. Puccini.

1974. Niccolo Tommaseo (writer). Death Cent.

1409. **513.** 50 l. green and pink .. 5 5

1974. Giacomo Puccini (composer). 50th Death Anniv.

1410. **514.** 40 l. multicoloured .. 5 5

515. Frontispiece of Aristo's "Orlando Furioso". **516.** Commemoration Tablet (Quotation from Varrone's "Menippean Satire").

1974. Ludovico Aristo (poet). 500th Birth Anniv.

1411. **515.** 50 l. blue and red .. 5 5

1974. Marco Varrone ("Varrone Reatino") (author). 2,000th Death Anniv.

1412. **516.** 50 l. red and yellow .. 5 5

517. "The Month of October".

1974. 14th International Wine Congress.

1413. **517.** 50 l. multicoloured .. 5 5

518. "U.P.U." and Emblem.

1974. Universal Postal Union. Cent. Mult.

1414. 50 l. Type **518** 8 5

1415. 90 l. U.P.U. emblem and "letters" 15 5

519. "The Triumph of St. Thomas Aquinas" (detail—F. Traini). **520.** Detail of Bas-relief Ara Pacis.

1974. St. Thomas Aquinas. 700th Death Anniv.

1416. **519.** 50 l. multicoloured .. 5 5

1974. Italian Order of Advocates. Cent.

1417. **520.** 50 l. grn., blk. & brn. 5 5

1974. Italian Fountains (2nd series). As Type **498**. Multicoloured.

1418. 40 l. Oceanus Fountain, Florence 5 5

1419. 40 l. Neptune Fountain, Bologna 5 5

1420. 40 l. Fontana Maggiore, Perugia 5 5

521. "The Adoration" (Presepe di Greccio).

1974. Christmas.

1421. **521.** 40 l. multicoloured .. 5 5

522. Pulcinella. **523.** "God admonishing Adam" (detail—Quercia).

1974. Stamp Day. Characters in Italian Comedy. Multicoloured.

1422. 40 l. Type **522** 5 5

1423. 50 l. Masked dancers .. 8 5

1424. 90 l. Pantalon from Bisognosi 15 5

1974. Italian Cultural Anniversaries. (1st series).

1425. **523.** 90 l. violet 15 5

1426. – 90 l. multicoloured .. 15 5

DESIGNS AND ANNIVERSARIES: N9. 1425 (Jacopo della Quercia (sculptor). 600th birth anniv.). No. 1426. Uffizi Gallery, Florence (Giorgio Vasari (architect and painter). 400th death anniv.).

See also Nos. 1445/6.

524. "Angel with Tablet". **525.** "Madonna and Child, and St. John".

1975. Holy Year. Multicoloured.

1427. 40 l. Type **524** 5 5

1428. 50 l. Angel with column 8 5

1429. 90 l. Bridge of the Holy Angels, Rome (44×37mm.) 15 5

1430. 150 l. Angel with crown of thorns .. 25 5

1431. 180 l. Angel with cross .. 30 8

1975. Michelangelo. 500th Birth Anniv.

1432. **525.** 40 l. green 5 5

1433. – 50 l. brown 8 5

1434. – 90 l. red 15 5

DESIGNS: 50 l. Wall-sculpture, Vatican Palace. 90 l. Detail, fresco "Flood of the Universe".

526. "The Four Days of Naples". (M. Mazzacurati). **527.** "The Flagellation of Christ" (Caravaggio).

1975. Italian Resistance Movement. 30th Anniv. Resistance Monuments. Multicoloured.

1435. 70 l. Type **526** 10 5

1436. 100 l. "Martyrs of the Ardentine Caves" (F. Coccia) .. 15 5

1437. 150 l. "The Resistance Fighters of Cuneo" (U. Mastroianni) .. 25 5

1975. Europa. Multicoloured.

1438. 100 l. Type **527** 15 5

1439. 150 l. "The Appearance of the Angel to Agar and Ismael in the Desert" (Tiepolo) .. 25 5

528. Globe and Emblems.

1975. International Women's Year.

1440. **528.** 70 l. multicoloured .. 12 5

529. "San Marco" Satellite and "San Rita" Marine Launching Pad. **530.** "Palestrina" (from frontispiece of his "Primo Libro dells Messe").

1975. Italian Space Project.

1441. **529.** 70 l. multicoloured .. 12 5

1975. Tourism (2nd series). As T **511**. Mult.

1442. 150 l. Cefalu 25 5

1443. 150 l. Isola Bella .. 25 5

1444. 150 l. Montecatini Terme 25 5

1975. Italian Cultural Annivs. (2nd series). As T **523**. Multicoloured.

1445. 90 l. "Flora" (Guido Reni-400th birth anniv.) 15 5

1446. 90 l. "Artist and Model" (Armando Spadini-50th death anniv.) .. 15 5

1975. G. Pierluigi da Palestrina (composer). 450th Birth Anniv.

1447. **530.** 100 l. purple & grey 15 5

531. Ship at Quayside.

1975. Italian Emigration.

1448. **531.** 70 l. multicoloured .. 12 5

532. Emblem of Notoriat.

1975. Unification of Italian Laws. Centenary.

1449. **532.** 100 l. red, yell. & blue 15 5

533. Locomotive Driving-wheels.

1975. 21st International Railway Congress, Bologna.

1450. **533.** 70 l. multicoloured .. 12 5

534. "D'Acquisto's Sacrifice" (V. Pisani). **535.** Crowned "Italia".

1975. Salvo D'Acquisto Commem.

1451. **534.** 100 l. multicoloured 15 5

1975. State Archives Unification. Centenary.

1452. **535.** 100 l. multicoloured 15 5

1975. Italian Fountains (2nd series). As T **498**. Multicoloured.

1453. 70 l. Rosello Fountain, Sassari 12 5

1454. 70 l. Fountain of 99 Channels, L'Aquila .. 12 5

1455. 70 l. Piazza Fountain, Milan 12 5

536. Busoni. **537.** "Annunciation to the Shepherds".

1975. Famous Italian Composers.

1456. **536.** 100 l. blue and red .. 15 5

1457. – 100 l. violet and green 15 5

1458. – 100 l. blue and orange 15 5

1459. – 100 l. brown and red 15 5

1460. – 100 l. purple and grey 15 5

1461. – 100 l. blk., brn. & yell. 15 5

COMPOSERS: No. 1457, Scarlatti. No. 1458, Cilea. No. 1459, Vivaldi. No. 1460, Alfano. No. 1461, Spontini.

1975. Christmas. Alatri Cathedral Carvings. Multicoloured.

1462. 70 l. Type **537** 12 5

1463. 100 l. "The Nativity" .. 15 5

1464. 150 l. "Annunciation to the Kings" 25 5

538. "Children on Horseback". **539.** "Boccaccio" (from fresco by A. del Castagno.)

1975. Stamp Day. Children's Fables. Mult.

1465. 70 l. Type **538** 12 5

1466. 100 l. "The Magic Orchard" (vert.) .. 15 5

1467. 150 l. "Church Procession" 25 5

1975. Giovanni Boccaccio. 600th Death Anniv. Multicoloured.

1468. 100 l. Type **539** 15 5

1469. 150 l. Frontispiece from Boccaccio's "Fiammetta" 25 5

540. Entrance to State Advocate's Office. **541.** " 76 " Emblem.

1976. State Advocate's Office. Centenary.
1470. **540.** 150 l. multicoloured .. 25 5

1976. " Italia 76 " World Stamp Exn., Milan. Multicoloured.
1471. 150 l. Type **541** 25 5
1472. 180 l. Fair Hall, Milan .. 30 8

1976. Tourism (3rd series). As T **511.** Mult.
1473. 150 l. Fenis Castle, Aosta 30 10
1474. 150 l. Forio Ischia .. 30 10
1475. 150 l. Itria Valley .. 30 10

542. Majolica Plate. **543.** Proclamation Flags.

1976. Europa. Multicoloured.
1476. 150 l. Type **542** 30 10
1477. 180 l. Vase in form of woman's head .. 35 12

1976. Proclamation of Republic. 30th Anniv. Multicoloured.
1478. 100 l. Type **543** 20 5
1479. 150 l. Heads of State .. 30 10

544. " Fortitude " (G. Serpotta).

1976. Italian Art.
1480. **544.** 150 l. blue 30 10
1481. – 150 l. multicoloured 30 10
1482. – 150 l. black and red .. 30 10
DESIGNS: No. 1481, " Woman at Table " (U. Boccioni). No. 1482, " Gunner's Letter from the Front " (F. T. Marianetti).

545. " The Dragon ".

1976. Vittore Carpaccio (painter). 450th Death Anniv.
1483. **545.** 150 l. brown 30 10
1484. – 150 l. brown 30 10
DESIGN: No. 1484, " St. George ".
Nos. 1483/4 form Carpaccio's " St. George and the Dragon ".

546. " Flora " (Titian).

1976. Titian. 400th Death Anniv.
1485. **546.** 150 l. claret 30 10

547. St. Francis. **548.** Post Cart of Cursus Publicus.

1976. St. Francis of Assisi. 750th Death Anniv.
1486. **547.** 150 l. brown 30 10

1976. " Italia '76 " International Stamp Exhibition, Milan. Multicoloured.
1487. 70 l. Type **548** 15 5
1488. 100 l. Insignia of Royal Sardinian post .. 20 5
1489. 150 l. Lion's-head letter-box of 19th cent. .. 30 10
1490. 200 l. Early postmarking machine .. 40 15
1491. 400 l. Modern letter-coding machine 80 30

549. Protective Umbrella. **550.** C. Dolci (painter).

1976. Stamp Day. Nature Protection. Multicoloured.
1492. 40 l. Type **549** 5 5
1493. 100 l. Protective scarf .. 20 5
1494. 150 l. Doctor " sounding " bandaged tree .. 30 10

1976. Famous Italian Painters and Writers.
1495. **550.** 170 l. grn., oran. & red 35 12
1496. – 170 l. blk., blue & grn. 35 12
1497. – 170 l. black, purple and magenta .. 35 12
1498. – 170 l. brown, lavender and violet .. 35 12
1499. – 170 l. black and olive 35 12
DESIGNS: No. 1496, L. Ghiberti (historian and sculptor). No. 1497, D. Ghirlandaio (painter). No. 1498, G. B. Prazzetta (painter). No. 1499, " Sassoferrato ", G. B. Salvi (painter).

551. " The Visit " (S. Lega). **552.** " Adoration of the Magi " (Bartolo di Fredi).

1976. Silvestro Lega (painter). 150th Birth Anniv.
1500. **551.** 170 l. multicoloured 35 12

1976. Christmas. Multicoloured.
1501. 70 l. Type **552** .. 15 5
1502. 120 l. " The Nativity " (Taddeo Gaddi) 25 8

1976. Italian Fountains (4th series). As Type **498.** Multicoloured.
1503. 170 l. Antique Fountain, Gallipoli 35 12
1504. 170 l. Erbe Madonna Fountain, Verona .. 35 12
1505. 170 l. Fountain of Palazzo Doria, Gerona .. 35 12

EXPRESS LETTER STAMPS

E 1. King Victor Emmanuel III.

1903. For inland letters.
E 73. **E 1.** 25 c. red .. .. 5·50 5
E 113. 50 c. red 80 5
E 129. 60 c. red 12 5
E 178. 70 c. red 12 5
E 179. 1 l. 25 blue .. 15 5

E 2. King Victor Emmanuel III.

1908. For foreign letters.
E 80. **E 2.** 30 c. red and blue .. 35 15
E 130. 1 l. 20 red and blue .. 32·00
E 180. 2 l. red and blue .. 60 80
E 181. 2 l. 50 red and blue .. 90 30

1917. Surch. **25** and bars.
E 112. **E 1.** 25 c. on 40 c. violet 4·00 3·00

1922. Surch. in words and figures.
E 122. **E 1.** 60 c. on 50 c. red .. 5·50 8
E 172. "Cent 70" on 60 c. red 12 8

1921. Surch. in words, figures and bars.
E 118. **E 2.** L. 1.20 on 30 c. red and blue .. 75 1·00
E 173. L. 1.60 on 1 l. 20 red and blue .. 70 1·25

E 3.

1932. Air. Garibaldi. 50th Death Anniv.
E 348. **E 3.** 2 l. 25+1 l. violet & red .. 2·25 3·25
E 349. 4 l. 50+1 l. 50 brown & green .. 2·75 4·00

E 4. King Victor Emmanuel III.

1932.
E 350. **E 4.** 1 l. 25 green .. 5 5
E 351. 2 l. 50 orange .. 5 5

E 5.

1932. March on Rome. 10th Anniv.
(a) For inland letters.
E 368. **E 5.** 1 l. 25 green .. 20 20

E 6.

(b) For foreign letters.
E 369. **E 6.** 2 l. 50 orange .. 1·75 5·00

E 7.

1933. Air.
E 370. **E 7.** 2 l. black .. 5 5
E 371. 2 l. 25 black .. 3·00 2·10

1934. Air. Annexation of Fiume. 10th Anniv. Inscr. as in T **114.**
E 408. 2 l.+1 l. 25 blue .. 80 1·00
E 409. 2 l. 25+1 l. 25 green .. 40 70
E 410. 4 l. 50+2 l. red .. 60 80
DESIGN: Foundation of Fiume.

1934. Air. Military Medal Cent. Inscr. as in T **120.**
E 442. 2 l.+1 l. 25 brown .. 1·50 2·10
E 443. 4 l. 50+2 l. red .. 2·40 3·00
DESIGN—HORIZ. Aeroplane over triumphal arch.

REPUBBLICA SOCIALE ITALIANA

(E 8)

1944. Optd. with Type **E 8.**
E 600. **E 4.** 1 l. 25 green .. 5 5
E 601. 2 l. 50 orange .. 5 15

E 9. Palermo Cathedral.

1944.
E 615. **E 9.** 1 l. 25 green .. 5 8

E 10. Italia.

1945.
E 647 **E 10.** 5 l. red 5 5

E 11. Winged Foot of Mercury.

DESIGNS: 10, 15, 60 l. Horse and torchbearer. 75 l., 150 l. Etruscan horses (statue of Tarquinia).

1945.
E 679. **E 11.** 5 l. red 5 5
E 680. – 10 l. blue 8 5
E 681. – 15 l. lake .. .. 1·25 5
E 682. **E 11.** 25 l. orange .. 11·00 5
E 683. 30 l. violet .. 1·25 5
E 684. 50 l. purple .. 15·00 5
E 685. – 60 l. red .. 4·25 5
E 961. – 75 l. purple .. 20 5
E 962. – 150 l. green .. 1·00 5
E 1220. – 150 l. green .. 20 5
E 1221. – 250 l. blue .. 40 5
E 1221a. – 300 l. brown .. 60 15
Nos. E 1220/1a are size 36×20½ mm.

E 12. Rising at Naples.

1948. 1848 Revolution. Cent.
E 718. **E 12.** 35 l. violet .. .. 8·50 1·75

MILITARY POST STAMPS

1943. Stamps of Italy optd. **P.M.**
(a) Postage stamps of 1929 (Nos. 239/56).
M 583. 5 c. brown 5 5
M 584. 10 c. brown 5 5
M 585. 15 c. green 5 5
M 586. 20 c. red 5 5
M 587. 25 c. green 5 5
M 588. 30 c. brown 5 5
M 589. 50 c. violet 5 5
M 590. 1 l. violet 10 5
M 591. 1 l. 25 blue 5 5
M 592. 1 l. 75 orange 5 5
M 593. 2 l. claret 5 5
M 594. 5 l. red 5 5
M 595. 10 l. violet 5 5
(b) Air stamps of 1930 (Nos. 271/7).
M 596. 50 c. brown 5 5
M 597. 1 l. violet 5 5
M 598. 2 l. blue 5 5
M 599. 5 l. green 5 5
M 600. 10 l. red 5 10
(c) Air Express stamp of 1933 (No. E 370).
M 601. 2 l. black 5 5
(d) Express Letter stamp of 1932 (No. E 350).
M 602. 1 l. 25 green 5 5

OFFICIAL STAMPS

O 1.

1875.
O 21. **O 1.** 2 c. claret 20 10
O 22. 5 c. claret 20 12
O 23. 20 c. claret 5 5
O 24. 30 c. claret 5 8
O 25. 1 l. claret 50 50
O 26. 2 l. claret .. .. 4·25 2·10
O 27. 5 l. claret .. .. 25·00 20·00
O 28. 10 l. claret .. .. 45·00 18·00

PARCEL POST STAMPS

ILLUSTRATIONS British Commonwealth and all overprints and surcharges are FULL SIZE. Foreign Countries have been reduced to ¾-LINEAR.

P 1. King Humbert I.

1884.

P 38. P 1. 10 c. olive .. .. 21·00 1·60
P 39. 27 c. blue .. .. 40·00 3·75
P 40. 50 c. red .. .. 3·00 35
P 41. 75 c. green .. .. 3·00 35
P 42. 1 l. 25 orange .. 7·50 90
P 43. 1 l. 75 brown .. 7·50 6·00

P 2.

The left-hand portion of the following stamps is affixed to the packet-card, the right-hand portion to the receipt. The used prices are therefore for the half-stamp only. Unsevered stamps exist in used condition and are from cancelled to order material.

1914.

P 96. P 2. 5 c. brown .. 12 5
P 97. 10 c. blue 12 5
P 98. 20 c. black 12 5
P 99. 25 c. red 12 5
P 100. 50 c. orange .. 30 5
P 101. 1 l. violet 40 5
P 102. 2 l. green 85 5
P 103. 3 l. yellow .. .. 2·50 8
P 104. 4 l. grey .. .. 4·25 8
P 105. 10 l. purple.. .. 10·00 20
P 106. 12 l. brown.. .. 25·00 3·00
P 107. 15 l. olive .. 29·00 3·75
P 108. 20 l. purple.. .. 38·00 5·50

1923. Surch. with figures on left half and words and figures on right half.

P 146. P 2. 30 c. on 5 c. brown 15 5
P 147. 60 c. on 5 c. brown 70 5
P 148. 1 l. 50 on 5 c. brown 1·90 30
P 149. 3 l. on 10 l. purple 2·10 25

P 3.

1927.

P 217. P 3. 5 c. brown .. 5 5
P 218. 10 c. blue 5 5
P 219. 25 c. red 5 5
P 220. 30 c. blue 5 5
P 221. 50 c. orange .. 5 5
P 222. 60 c. red 5 5
P 223. 1 l. violet 5 5
P 224. 2 l. green 5 5
P 225. 3 l. yellow 5 5
P 226. 4 l. grey 5 5
P 227. 10 l. purple.. .. 15 5
P 228. 20 l. purple.. .. 30 5

1944. Optd. **REP. SOC. ITALIANA** on left-hand side and Fascist Emblem on right.

P 601. P 3. 5 c. brown 15 20
P 602. 10 c. blue 15 20
P 603. 25 c. red 15 20
P 604. 30 c. blue 15 20
P 605. 50 c. orange 15 20
P 606. 60 c. red 15 20
P 607. 1 l. violet 15 20
P 608. 2 l. green .. .. 21·00 20·00
P 609. 3 l. yellow .. .. 1·00 1·25
P 610. 4 l. grey .. .. 1·00 1·25
P 611. 10 l. purple.. .. 11·00 12·00
P 612. 20 l. purple.. .. 42·00 48·00

The used prices for Nos. P 601/12 are for unsevered stamps.

1945. Optd. with ornamental device obliterating Fascist Emblems in centre.

P 647. P 3. 5 c. brown 5 5
P 648. 10 c. blue 5 5
P 649. 25 c. red 5 5
P 650. 30 c. blue .. .. 1·25 20
P 651. 50 c. orange 5 5
P 652. 60 c. red 5 5
P 653. 1 l. violet 5 5
P 654. 2 l. green 5 5
P 655. 3 l. yellow 5 5
P 656. 4 l. grey 12 5
P 657. 10 l. purple.. .. 25 5
P 658. 20 l. purple.. .. 55 10

1946. As Type P 3, but without fasces between stamps.

P 679. P 3. 1 l. violet 50 5
P 680. 2 l. green 50 5
P 681. 3 l. yellow 65 5
P 682. 4 l. grey .. .. 1·25 5
P 683. 10 l. purple.. .. 6·00 25
P 684. 20 l. purple.. .. 12·00 40

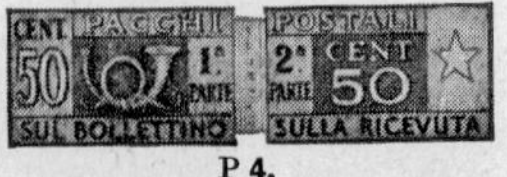
P 4.

1946.

P 687. P 4. 25 c. blue 8 5
P 688. 50 c. brown 12 5
P 689. 1 l. brown 5 5
P 690. 2 l. green 20 5
P 691. 3 l. orange 12 5
P 692. 4 l. grey .. .. 1·50 5
P 693. 5 l. mauve 12 5
P 911. 10 l. violet 15 5
P 912. 20 l. maroon.. .. 15 5
P 913. 30 l. purple 30 5
P 914. 40 l. slate 8 5
P 915. 50 l. red 8 5
P 916. 60 l. violet 8 5
P 917. 100 l. blue 15 5
P 918. 140 l. brown-red .. 25 5
P 919. 150 l. brown.. .. 25 5
P 920. 200 l. green 25 5
P 921. 280 l. yellow.. .. 35 12
P 922. 300 l. purple.. .. 40 5
P 923. 400 l. grey 55 5
P 924. 500 l. brown 65 5
P 925. 600 l. olive 80 30
P 926. 700 l. blue 95 20
P 927. 800 l. orange .. 1·10 20

P 5.

1954.

P 928. P 5. 1000 l. blue .. .. 1·25 30
P 929. 2000 l. red & brown 2·75 30

CONCESSIONAL PARCEL POST

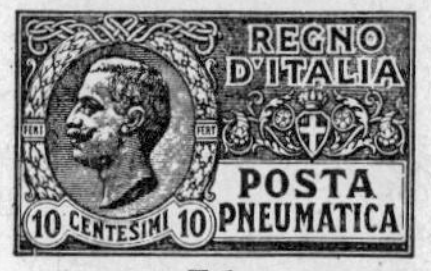
CP 1.

1953.

CP 918. CP 1. 40 l. orange .. 55 5
CP 919. 50 l. blue.. .. 1·40 5
CP 920. 60 l. violet .. 1·50 5
CP 921. 70 l. green .. 14·00 12
CP 922. 75 l. sepia .. 55·00 25
CP 923. 80 l. purple-brown 12 5
CP 924. 90 l. lilac.. .. 15 5
CP 851. 110 l. claret .. 55·00 25
CP 926. 110 l. yellow .. 15 5
CP 927. 120 l. green .. 20 5
CP 928. 140 l. black .. 20 5
CP 929. 150 l. red .. 20 5
CP 930. 180 l. vermilion .. 30 5
CP 931. 240 l. slate .. 35 5
CP 932. 500 l. brown .. 1·00 25

PNEUMATIC POST LETTERS

T 1.

1913.

PE 96. T 1. 10 c. brown .. 20 25
PE 97. 15 c. lilac .. 45 60
PE 192. 15 c. red .. 20 30
PE 193. 20 c. purple .. 60 1·00
PE 98. 30 c. blue .. 45 50
PE 194. 35 c. red .. 1·00 1·75
PE 195. 40 c. red .. 1·50 2·50

1924. Surch.

PE 165. T 1. 15 c. on 10 c. brown 35 50
PE 166. 15 c. on 20 c. purple 55 90
PE 167. 20 c. on 10 c. brown 60 90
PE 168. 20 c. on 15 c. lilac 40 70
PE 169. 35 c. on 40 c. red.. 85 1·40
PE 170. 40 c. on 30 c. blue 50 80

T 2. Galileo Galilei. T 3. Minerva.

1933.

PE 372. – 15 c. purple .. 8 8
PE 373. T 2. 35 c. red .. 8 8

DESIGN: 15 c. Dante Alighieri.

1945. As Type T 2, but inscr. "ITALIA" instead of "REGNO D'ITALIA".

PE 679. – 60 c. brown (Dante) 8 8
PE 680. T 2. 1 l. 40 blue.. .. 8 8

1947.

PE 694. T 3. 3 l. purple .. .. 2·50 2·25
PE 695. 5 l. blue 10 10
PE 961. 10 l. red 5 5
PE 962. 20 l. blue 5 5

POSTAGE DUE STAMPS

D 1. D 2.

1863. Imperf.

D 6. D 1. 10 c. orange .. .. 17·00 29·00

1869. Perf.

D 21. D 2. 10 c. orange .. .. £400 8·00

D 3. D 4. (D 5.)

1870.

D 22. D 3. 1 c. purple & orange 25 35
D 23. 2 c. purple & orange 2·10 2·10
D 24. 5 c. purple & orange 12 5
D 25. 10 c. purple & orange 15 5
D 26. 20 c. purple & orange 25 5
D 27. 30 c. purple & orange 25 5
D 28. 40 c. purple & orange 25 5
D 29. 50 c. purple & orange 30 5
D 30. 60 c. purple & orange 15·00 5
D 31. 60 c. brown & orange 1·50 20
D 32. 1 l. brown and blue .. £650 1·25
D 33. 1 l. purple and blue.. 20 5
D 34. 2 l. brown and blue .. £600 1·60
D 35. 2 l. purple and blue .. 4·50 5
D 36. 5 l. brown and blue .. 28·00 80
D 37. 5 l. purple and blue.. 14·00 25
D 38. 10 l. brown and blue £1000 2·75
D 39. 10 l. purple and blue 26·00 12

1884.

D 40. D 4. 50 l. green .. .. 5·00 1·60
D 73. 50 l. yellow .. .. 6·00 1·40
D 41. 100 l. red .. .. 5·00 1·60
D 74. 100 l. blue .. .. 4·50 60

1890. Surch. over numeral as Type D 5.

D 47. D 3. 10 (c.) on 2 c. (D 23) 25·00 3·00
D 48. 20 (c.) on 1 c. (D 22) 42·00 2·10
D 49. 30 (c.) on 2 c. (D 23) £200 1·00

D 6. D 7.

1934.

D 395. D 6. 5 c. brown 5 5
D 396. 10 c. blue 5 5
D 397. 20 c. red 5 5
D 398. 25 c. green 5 5
D 399. 30 c. orange 5 5
D 400. 40 c. brown 5 5
D 401. 50 c. violet 5 5
D 402. 60 c. blue 5 5
D 403. D 7. 1 l. orange 5 5
D 404. 2 l. green 8 5
D 405. 5 l. violet 20 5
D 406. 10 l. blue 40 15
D 407. 20 l. red 95 25

1944. Nos. D 395/407 overprinted with small Fascist Emblems.

D 601. D 6. 5 c. brown 5 5
D 602. 10 c. blue 5 5
D 603. 20 c. red 5 5
D 604. 25 c. green 5 5
D 605. 30 c. orange 5 5
D 606. 40 c. brown 5 5
D 607. 50 c. violet 5 5
D 608. 60 c. blue 40 50
D 609. D 7. 1 l. orange 12 5
D 610. 2 l. green .. .. 60 1·25
D 611. 5 l. violet .. .. 6·50 5·50
D 612. 10 l. blue .. .. 11·00 11·00
D 613. 20 l. red .. .. 11·00 11·00

D 8. D 9. D 10.

1945.

D 630. D 8. 5 c. brown 15 20
D 631. 10 c. blue 5 5
D 632. 20 c. red 20 20
D 633. 25 c. green 5 5
D 634. 30 c. orange 5 5
D 635. 40 c. black 5 5
D 636. 50 c. violet 5 5
D 637. 60 c. blue 5 5
D 638. 1 l. orange 45 5
D 639. 2 l. green 8 5
D 640. 5 l. violet 8 5
D 641. 10 l. blue 15 8
D 642. 20 l. red 20 12

1947.

D 690. D 10. 1 l. orange 5 5
D 691. 2 l. green 10 5
D 692. 3 l. red 40 15
D 693. 4 l. brown 25 8
D 924. 5 l. violet 15 5
D 695. 6 l. blue .. .. 1·25 5
D 696. 8 l. mauve .. .. 2·25 5
D 926. D 10. 10 l. blue 5 5
D 697. 12 l. brown .. 1·50 5
D 927. 20 l. purple.. .. 5 5
D 928. 25 l. red 5 5
D 929. 30 l. slate-purple .. 8 8
D 930. 40 l. brown .. 8 5
D 931. 50 l. green .. 10 5
D 932. 100 l. orange .. 20 5
D 933. 500 l. purple & blue 80 20

IVORY COAST

O2

A French colony in W. Africa on the Gulf of Guinea, incorporated in French West Africa in 1944. In 1958 it became an autonomous republic within the French Community, and in 1960 it became fully independent.

1892. "Tablet" key-type inscr. "COTE D'IVOIRE".

1. D. 1 c. black on blue .. 12 12
2. 2 c. brown on yellow .. 15 12
3. 4 c. claret on grey .. 30 25
4. 5 c. green .. .. 1·60 90
5. 10 c. black on lilac .. 2·50 1·10
14. 10 c. red .. .. 18·00 16·00
6. 15 c. blue .. .. 2·75 1·75
15. 15 c. grey .. .. 1·25 60
7. 20 c. red on green .. 2·25 1·25
8. 25 c. black on red .. 2·25 30
16. 25 c. blue .. .. 5·50 4·50
9. 30 c. brown .. .. 3·75 3·50
10. 40 c. red on yellow .. 3·00 2·50
11. 50 c. red .. .. 10·00 7·50
17. 50 c. brown on blue .. 3·25 1·75
12. 75 c. brown on orange .. 4·50 3·25
13. 1 f. olive .. .. 5·50 4·50

1904. Surch. in figures and bars.

18. D. 0.05 on 30 c. brown .. 13·00 13·00
19. 0.10 on 75 c. brn. on yell. 1·75 1·75
20. 0.15 on 1 f. olive .. 2·75 2·75

1906. "Faidherbe," "Palms," "Balay" key-types inscr. "COTE D'IVOIRE".

22. I. 1 c. blue 5 5
23. 2 c. brown 5 5
24. 4 c. brown on blue .. 12 12
25. 5 c. green 20 15
26. 10 c. red 35 15
27. J. 20 c. black on blue .. 1·00 85
28. 25 c. blue 55 40
29. 30 c. purple .. .. 1·25 1·10
30. 35 c. black on yellow .. 1·60 40
32. 45 c. purple .. .. 1·50 1·50
33. 50 c. violet .. .. 1·50 1·25
34. 75 c. blue on orange .. 1·60 1·50
35. K. 1 f. black on blue .. 6·00 6·00
36. 2 f. blue on pink .. 6·50 6·50
37. 5 f. red on yellow .. 15·00 15·00

1912. Surch. in figures.

38. D. 05 on 15 c. grey.. .. 8 8
39. 05 on 30 c. brown .. 12 12
40. 10 on 40 c. red on yellow 12 12
41. 10 on 50 c. brown on blue 20 20
42. 10 on 75 c. brn. on orge. 1·00 1·00

1. River Scene.

1913.

43. 1. 1 c. violet and purple .. 5 5
44. 2 c. black and brown .. 5 5
45. 4 c. purple and violet .. 5 5
46. 5 c. green 5 5
61. 5 c. brown and chocolate 5 5
47. 10 c. red and orange .. 12 12
62. 10 c. green 5 5
63. 10 c. red on blue .. 5 5
48. 15 c. red and yellow .. 5 5
49. 20 c. grey and black .. 5 5
50. 25 c. blue 70 45
64. 25 c. violet and black .. 5 5
51. 30 c. brown and chocolate 12 10
65. 30 c. red and orange .. 8 8
66. 30 c. red and blue .. 5 5
67. 30 c. green 5 5
52. 35 c. orange and violet .. 5 5
53. 40 c. green and grey .. 12 10
54. 45 c. brown and orange .. 8 5
68. 45 c. claret and red .. 55 55
55. 50 c. lilac and black .. 30 30
69. 50 c. blue 5 5
70. 50 c. blue and olive .. 5 5
71. 60 c. violet on red .. 5 5
72. 65 c. olive and red .. 12 12
56. 75 c. red and brown .. 5 5
73. 75 c. blue 35 35
74. 85 c. black and purple .. 10 10
75. 90 c. red .. .. 2·00 2·00
57. 1 f. black and orange .. 10 10
76. 1 f. 10 brown and green.. 70 70
77. 1 f. 50 blue .. .. 1·10 80
78. 1 f. 75 magenta and blue 1·40 80
58. 2 f. blue and brown .. 40 20
79. 3 f. purple on red .. 1·10 65
59. 5 f. brown and blue .. 85 50

1915. Surch. **5 c.** and red cross.

60. 1. 10 c.+5 c. red & orange.. 12 12

1934. Surch. in figures and bars.

80. 1. 50 on 45 c. claret & red 25 25
81. 50 on 75 c. blue 25 25
82. 50 on 90 c. red 25 25
83. 60 on 75 c. violet .. 5 5
84. 65 on 15 c. red and yellow 8 8
85. 85 on 75 c. red and brown 8 8

1922. Surch. in figures and bars.

86. 1. 25 c. on 2 f. blue & brown 10 10
87. 25 c. on 5 f. brown & blue 10 10
88. 90 c. on 75 c. red .. 8 8
89. 1 f. 25 on 1 f. blue .. 5 5
90. 1 f. 50 on 1 f. blue .. 12 12
91. 3 f. on 5 f. green and red .. 45 45
92. 10 f. on 5 f. mauve & red 2·25 2·25
93. 20 f. on 5 f. red and green 2·75 2·75

1931. "Colonial Exn." key-types inscr. "COTE D'IVOIRE".

94. E. 40 c. green 35 35
95. F. 50 c. mauve 95 95
96. G. 90 c. orange 20 20
97. H. 1 f. 50 blue 95 95

1933. Stamps of Upper Volta optd. **Cote d'Ivoire** or surch. also.

98. 1. 2 c. brown and lilac .. 5 5
99. 4 c. black and yellow .. 5 5
100. 5 c. blue 5 5
101. 10 c. blue and pink .. 5 5
102. 15 c. brown and blue .. 5 5
103. 20 c. brown and green .. 10 10
104. – 25 c. brown and yellow 30 25
105. – 30 c. green 30 25
106. – 45 c. brown and blue .. 90 80
107. – 65 c. blue 45 45
108. – 75 c. black and lilac .. 50 50
109. – 90 c. red 30 30
110. 3. 1 f. brown and green .. 30 30
111. – 1 f. 25 on 40 c. black and pink 20 15
112. 3. 1 f. 50 blue 30 30
113. – 1 f. 75 on 50 c. black and green 35 30

2. Baoule Woman. 3. General Binger.

1936.

114. 2. 1 c. red 5 5
115. 2 c. blue 5 5
116. 3 c. green 5 5
117. 4 c. brown 5 5
118. 5 c. violet 5 5
119. 10 c. blue 5 5
120. 15 c. red 5 5
121. – 20 c. blue 5 5
122. – 25 c. red 5 5
123. – 30 c. green 8 5
124. – 30 c. brown 5 5
125. 2. 35 c. green 5 5
126. – 40 c. red 5 5
127. – 45 c. brown 8 8
128. – 45 c. green 5 5
129. – 50 c. purple 5 5
130. – 55 c. violet 5 5
131. – 60 c. red 5 5
132. – 65 c. brown 5 5
133. – 70 c. brown 5 5
134. – 75 c. violet 5 5
135. – 80 c. brown 5 5
136. – 90 c. red 80 50
137. – 90 c. green 5 5
138. – 1 f. green 30 15
139. – 1 f. red 5 5
140. – 1 f. violet 5 5
141. – 1 f. 25 red 5 5
142. – 1 f. 40 blue 5 5
143. – 1 f. 50 blue 5 5
144. – 1 f. 50 grey 5 5
145. – 1 f. 60 brown 5 5
146. – 1 f. 75 red 5 5
147. – 1 f. 75 blue 5 5
148. – 2 f. blue 5 5
149. – 2 f. 50 blue 5 5
150. – 2 f. 50 red 5 5
151. – 3 f. green 8 5
152. – 5 f. brown 8 8
153. – 10 f. violet 10 10
154. – 20 f. red 20 15

DESIGNS—HORIZ. 20 c. to 30 c. and 40 c. to 55 c. Mosque at Bobo-Dioulasso. 60 c. to 1 f. 60 Coastal scene. VERT. 1 f. 75 to 20 f. Comoe Rapids.

1937. Int. Exn., Paris. As Nos. 110/15 of Cameroun.

155. 20 c. violet 15 15
156. 30 c. green 15 15
157. 40 c. red 15 15
158. 50 c. brown 15 15
159. 90 c. red 15 15
160. 1 f. 50 blue 20 20

1937. Gen. Binger's Exploration. 50th Anniv.

161. 3. 65 c. brown 5 5

1938. Int. Anti-Cancer Fund. As T **10** of Cameroun.

162. 1 f. 75+50 c. blue .. 1·25 1·25

1939. Caillie Cent. As T **2** of Dahomey.

163. 90 c. orange 10 10
164. 2 f. violet 12 12
165. 2 f. 25 blue 10 10

1939. New York World's Fair. As T **11** of Cameroun.

166. 1 f. 25 red 10 10
167. 2 f. 25 blue 10 10

1939. French Revolution. 150th Anniv. As T **16** of Cameroun.

168. 45 c.+25 c. green .. 1·00 1·00
169. 70 c.+30 c. brown .. 1·00 1·00
170. 90 c.+35 c. orange .. 1·00 1·00
171. 1 f. 25+1 f. red .. 1·00 1·00
172. 2 f. 25+2 f. blue .. 1·00 1·00

1940. Air. As T **3** of Dahomey.

173. 1 f. 90 blue 5 5
174. 2 f. 90 red 5 5
175. 4 f. 50 green 5 5
176. 4 f. 90 olive 5 5
177. 6 f. 90 orange 15 15

1941. National Defence Fund. Surch. **SECOURS NATIONAL** and value.

178. +1 f. on 50 c. (No. 129) .. 12 12
178a. +2 f. on 80 c. (No. 135) 2·00 2·00
178b. +2 f. on 1 f. 50 (No. 143) 2·00 2·00
178c. +3 f. on 2 f. (No. 148) .. 2·00 2·00

1942. Air. As T **4d** of Dahomey.

179. 50 f. brown and green .. 20 20

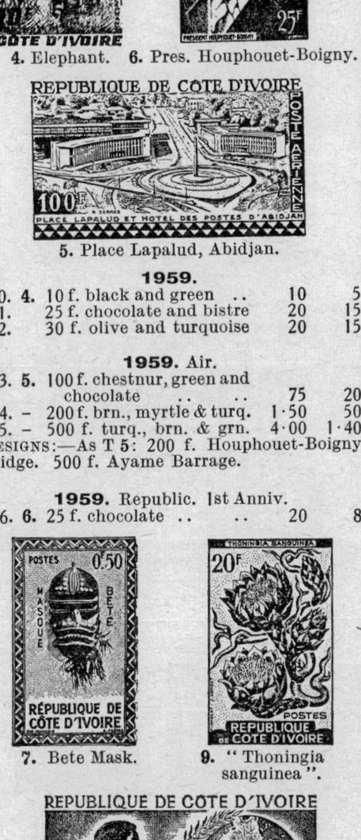

4. Elephant. 6. Pres. Houphouet-Boigny.

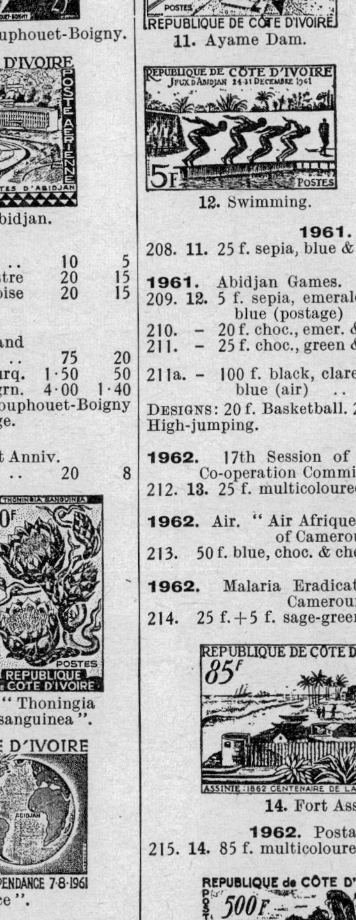

5. Place Lapalud, Abidjan.

1959.

180. 4. 10 f. black and green .. 10 5
181. 25 f. chocolate and bistre 20 15
182. 30 f. olive and turquoise 20 15

1959. Air.

183. 5. 100 f. chestnut, green and chocolate 75 20
184. – 200 f. brn., myrtle & turq. 1·50 50
185. – 500 f. turq., brn. & grn. 4·00 1·40

DESIGNS:—As T 5: 200 f. Houphouet-Boigny Bridge. 500 f. Ayame Barrage.

1959. Republic. 1st Anniv.

186. 6. 25 f. chocolate 20 8

7. Bete Mask. 9. "Thoningia sanguinea".

8. "World Peace".

1960. Native Masks.

187. 7. 50 c. chocolate & brown 5 5
188. – 1 f. violet and red .. 5 5
189. – 2 f. green and blue .. 5 5
190. – 4 f. red and green .. 5 5
191. – 5 f. brown and red .. 5 5
192. – 6 f. blue and maroon .. 5 5
193. – 45 f. maroon and green 35 12
194. – 50 f. blue and brown .. 45 10
195. – 85 f. green and red .. 65 30

DESIGNS—VERT. MASKS OF. 1 f. Guere. 2 f. Guere (different type). 45 f. Bete (different type). 50 f. Gouro. 85 f. Gouro (different type). HORIZ. 4 f. Baole. 5 f. Senoufo. 6 f. Senoufo (different type).

1960. African Technical Co-operation Commission. 10th Anniv. As T **39** of Cameroun.

196. 25 f. violet and turquoise .. 30 30

1960. Consell de l'Entente. 1st Anniv. As T **6** of Dahomey.

197. 25 f. multicoloured .. 35 35

1961. Independence. 1st Anniv.

198. 8. 25 f. black, green & brown 20 15

1961.

199. – 5 f. red, yellow and green 8 5
200. – 10 f. yellow, red and blue 8 5
201. – 15 f. pur., grn. & orange 10 5
202. 9. 20 f. yellow, red & brown 15 12
203. – 25 f. yellow, red & green 20 12
204. – 30 f. red, green & black .. 20 12
205. – 70 f. yellow red & green 55 25
206. – 85 f. multicoloured .. 65 45

FLOWERS: 5 f. "Plumeria rubra". 10 f. "Haemanthus cinnabarinus". 15 f. "Bougainvillea spectabilis". 25 f. "Eulophia cucullata". 30 f. "Newbouldia laevis". 70 f. "Mussaenda erythrophylla". 85 f. "Strophantus sarmentpsus".

10. Mail-carriers.

1961. Stamp Day.

207. 10. 25 f. choc., blue & green 20 15

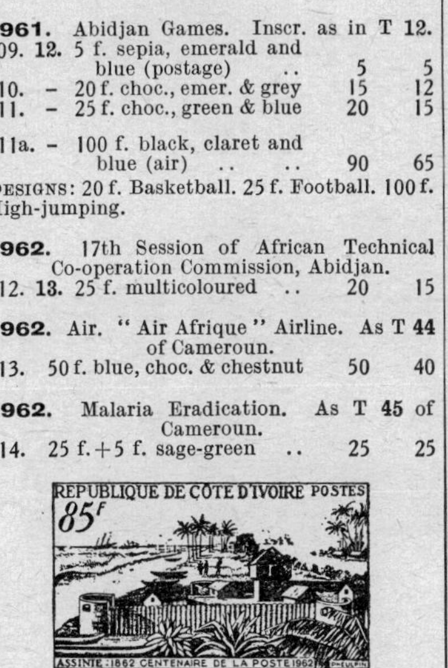

11. Ayame Dam.

12. Swimming. 13. Palms.

1961.

208. 11. 25 f. sepia, blue & green 20 12

1961. Abidjan Games. Inscr. as in T **12**.

209. 12. 5 f. sepia, emerald and blue (postage) .. 5 5
210. – 20 f. choc., emer. & grey 15 12
211. – 25 f. choc., green & blue 20 15
211a. – 100 f. black, claret and blue (air) 90 65

DESIGNS: 20 f. Basketball. 25 f. Football. 100 f. High-jumping.

1962. 17th Session of African Technical Co-operation Commission, Abidjan.

212. 13. 25 f. multicoloured .. 20 15

1962. Air. "Air Afrique" Airline. As T **44** of Cameroun.

213. 50 f. blue, choc. & chestnut 50 40

1962. Malaria Eradication. As T **45** of Cameroun.

214. 25 f.+5 f. sage-green .. 25 25

14. Fort Assinie.

1962. Postal Cent.

215. 14. 85 f. multicoloured .. 65 35

15. Village, Man Region.

1962. Air.

216. – 200 f. sepia, mar. & green 1·60 70
217. 15. 500 f. green, mar. & blk. 3·75 1·60

DESIGN—VERT. 200 f. Street Scene, Odienne.

1962. Union of African and Malagasy States, 1st Anniv. As No. 328 of Cameroun.

218. 47. 30 f. red 55 45

INDEX

Countries can be quickly located by referring to the index at the end of this volume.

16. U.N. Headquarters and Emblem.

1962. Air. Admission to U.N. 2nd Anniv.

219. 16. 100 f. multicoloured .. 75 55

17. Bouake Arms and Cotton Exhibit.

1963. Bourake Fair.

220. 17. 50 f. sepia, brown & grn. 40 25

1963. Freedom from Hunger. As T **51** of Cameroun.

221. 25 f.+5 f. vio., brn. & pur. 25 25

18. Map of Africa.

1963. Conf. of African Heads of State, Addis Ababa.

222. 18. 30 f. green and blue .. 30 25

19. Sassandra Bay.

1963. Air.

223. – 50 f. green, brown & blue 40 20
224. 19. 100 f. choc., bl. & myrtle 75 50
225. – 200 f. blue-green, yellow-green and brown .. 1·60 80

DESIGNS: 50 f. Moosou Bridge. 200 f. River Comoe.

1963. Air. African and Malagasian Posts and Telecommunications Union. As T **10** of Central African Republic.

226. 85 f. red, buff, pink & chest. 65 50

20. Hartebeest. 21. Scales of Justice, Globe and U.N.E.S.C.O. Emblem

1963. "Tourism and Hunting".

227. – 1 f. multicoloured .. 5 5
228. – 2 f. multicoloured .. 5 5
229. – 4 f. multicoloured .. 8 5
230. – 5 f. multicoloured .. 8 5
247. – 5 f. grn., yellow-green and brown 8 5
231. 20. 10 f. brn., green & grey 10 5
248. – 10 f. brn., green & pur. 10 8
232. – 15 f. black, grn. & brn. 15 8
249. – 15 f. brown, grn. & pur. 12 8
233. – 20 f. brn., green and red 20 10
234. – 25 f. brn., grn. & yell.-grn. 25 10
235. – 45 f. pur., grn. & bluish grn. 90 30
236. – 50 f. blk., grn. & brown 45 25

DESIGNS—HORIZ. 1 f. Yellow-backed duiker. 4 f. Tree hyrax. 5 f. (No. 247) Manatee. 10 f. (No. 248) Dwarf hippopotamus. 15 f. (No. 232) Wart-hog. 20 f. Wart-hog (different). 45 f. Wild African hunting dogs. VERT. 2 f. Potto. 5 f. (No. 230) African water chevrotain. 15 f. (No. 249) Royal antelope. 25 f. Bongo. 50 f. Colobus monkey.

1963. Air. "Air Afrique" 1st Anniv. and "DC-8" Service Inaug. As T **10** of Congo Republic.

237. 25 f. black, grn., grey & red 20 20

1963. Declaration of Human Rights. 15th Anniv.

238. 21. 85 f. black, blue & orge. 60 45

22. Rameses II and Nefertari, Abu Simbel. 23. Map of Africa.

1964. Air. Nubian Monuments Preservation.
239. **22.** 60 f. black, brown & red 60 40

1964. Inter-African National Education Ministers' Conference, Abidjan.
240. **23.** 30 f. red, grn. & vio.-blue 20 15

24. Weather Balloon. 25. Doctor tending Child.

1964. World Meteorological Day.
241. **24.** 25 f. multicoloured .. 20 12

1964. National Red Cross Society.
242. **25.** 50 f. multicoloured .. 40 25

26. Arms of the Ivory Coast.

1964. Air.
243. **26.** 200 f. gold, blue & green 1·50 75

27. Globe and Athletes. 28. Symbolic Tree.

1964. Olympic Games. Tokyo.
244. **27.** 35 f. brown, green & vio. 30 20
245. – 65 f. ochre, brown & blue 50 35
DESIGN—HORIZ. 65 f. Wrestling and Globe.

1964. European-African Convention. 1st Anniv.
246. **28.** 30 f. multicoloured .. 25 20

1964. French, African and Malagasy Co-operation. As T **500** of France.
250. 25 f. chocolate, red & green 20 15

29. Pres. Kennedy. 30. Korhogo Mail-carriers, 1914.

1964. Air. Pres. Kennedy Commem.
251. **29.** 100 f. brown and grey.. 80 65

1964. Stamp Day.
252. **30.** 85 f. sepia, chest. & blue 65 50

31. Pottery.

1965. Native Handicrafts.
253. **31.** 5 f. black, red & green.. 5 5
254. – 10 f. black, purple & grn. 8 5
255. – 20 f. blue, choc. & brown 15 8
256. – 25 f. choc., red & olive 20 12
DESIGNS: 10 f. Wood-carving. 20 f. Ivory-carving. 25 f. Weaving.

32. Mail coming ashore.

1965. Stamp Day.
257. **32.** 30 f. multicoloured .. 20 15

33. I.T.U. Emblem and Symbols.

1965. I.T.U. Cent.
258. **33.** 85 f. blue, red and green 65 45

34. Abidjan Railway Station.

1965.
259. **34.** 30 f. multicoloured .. 20 15

35. Pres. Houphouet-Boigny and Map. 36. Hammerhead.

1965. Independence. 5th Anniv.
260. **35.** 30 f. multicoloured .. 20 20

1965. Birds.
261. – 1 f. green, yell. & violet 5 5
262. – 2 f. grn., red, blk. & choc. 5 5
263. – 5 f. maroon, red & olive 8 8
264. **36.** 10 f. brn., black & pur. 10 8
265. – 15 f. red, grey and green 12 8
266. – 30 f. chest., green & lake 20 12
267. – 50 f. blue, black & brn. 40 20
268. – 75 f. claret, grn. & orge. 55 30
269. – 90 f. blk., brn. grn., & ol. 75 35
BIRDS—HORIZ. 1 f. Yellow-bellied fruit pigeon. 2 f. Spur-winged goose. 30 f. Namaqua (or masked) dove. 50 f. Lizard buzzard. VERT. 5 f. Stone partridge. 15 f. White-breasted guinea-fowl. 75 f. Wood ibis. 90 f. Latham's francolin.

37. Lieupleu Rope-bridge.

1965. Air.
270. **37.** 100 f. brn., grn. & apple 80 50
271. – 300 f. mar., flesh & blue 2·25 1·00
DESIGN: 300 f. Street in Kong.

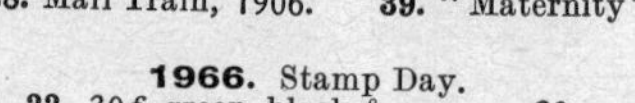

38. Mail Train, 1906. 39. "Maternity".

1966. Stamp Day.
272. **38.** 30 f. green, black & pur. 20 15

1966. World Festival of Negro Arts. Dakar.
273. **39.** 5 f. black and green .. 5 5
274. – 10 f. black and violet .. 8 5
275. – 20 f. black and orange 15 8
276. – 30 f. black and red .. 20 12
DESIGNS—CARVED WORK: 10 f. Pomade box. 20 f. Drums. 30 f. "Ancestor".

40. Ivory Hotel.

1966. Ivory Hotel, Inaug.
277. **40.** 15 f. multicoloured .. 12 8

41. Tractor Cultivation.

1966. 6th Independence Anniv.
278. **41.** 30 f. multicoloured .. 20 15

1966. Air. Inaug. of "DC-8" Air Services. As T **45** of Central African Republic.
279. 30 f. grey, black adn green 20 15

42. Open-air Class.

1966. National School of Administration.
280. **42.** 30 f. black, blue an dlake 20 15

43. Inoculating Cattle. 44. U.N.E.S.C.O. ("Waves" enveloping "Man").

1966. Campaign for Prevention of Cattle Plague.
281. **43.** 30 f. choc., green & blue 20 15

1966. U.N.E.S.C.O. 20th Anniv.
282. **44.** 30 f. violet and blue .. 20 15
283. – 30 f. blk., brown & blue 20 15
DESIGN: No. 283. Distributing food parcels to children.

45. Bouake Hospital. 46. "Air Afrique" Headquarters.

1966.
284. **45.** 30 f. multicoloured .. 20 15

1966. Air.
285. **46.** 500 f. ind., ochre & grn. 4·00 1·75

47. Sikorsky "S-43" Flying Boat (30th Anniv.).

1967. Stamp Day.
286. **47.** 30 f. blue, brown & turq. 25 20

48. Cutting Pineapples. 49. "African Mythology".

1967. Fruits.
287. **48.** 20 f. maroon, brn. & grn. 15 5
288. – 30 f. red, brown & green 20 10
289. – 100 f. brown, olive & bl. 75 45
DESIGNS: 30 f. Cutting palm-nuts. 100 f. Cutting bananas.

1967. 35th Pen Club Int. Congress, Abidjan.
290. **49.** 30 f. black, green & lake 20 10

50. "Improvement of Rural Housing".

1967. Independence. 7th Anniv.
291. **50.** 30 f. multicoloured .. 20 12

51. Lions Emblems. 52. African Man and Woman.

1967. Lions Int. 50th Anniv.
292. **51.** 30 f. multicoloured .. 20 10

1967. Air. U.A.M.P.T. 5th Anniv. As T **95** of Cameroun.
293. 100 f. red, blue and violet 80 45

1967. West African Monetary Union. 5th Anniv. As T **54** of Dahomey.
294. 30 f. black, green & mag. 20 15

1967. Recognition Days. 20th Anniv.
295. **52.** 90 f. multicoloured .. 70 50
See also No. 342.

53. Senoufo Village.

1968. Air.
296. **53.** 100 f. brn., yell. & grn. 70 40
297. – 500 f. brown, blue and green.. .. .. 3·50 1·75
DESIGN: 500 f. Tiegba lake village.

54. Tabou Radio Station, 1912. 55. Cotton Mill. 56. Canoeing.

1968. Stamp Day.
298. **54.** 30 f. grn., brn. & turq. 20 12

1968. Industries.
299. – 5 f. blk., red and green . . 5 5
300. **55.** 10 f. brown, grn. & slate 5 5
301. – 15 f. black, blue & red . . 10 5
302. – 20 f. blue and maroon . . 12 8
303. – 30 f. brown, green & bl. 20 12
304. – 50 f. black, green & mag. 30 15
305. – 70 f. choc., blue & brn. 45 25
306. – 90 f. black, maroon & bl. 65 30
DESIGNS—HORIZ. 5 f. Palm-oil works. 30 f. Flour mills. 50 f. Cocoa-butter extraction machine. 90 f. Timber sawmill and logs. VERT. 15 f. Oil refinery, Abidjan. 20 f. Raw cotton and reeling machine. 70 f. Soluble-coffee plant.
See also Nos. 335/7.

1968. Olympic Games, Mexico.
307. **56.** 30 f. brown, blue & grn. 20 12
308. – 100 f. purple, ult. & blue 70 45
DESIGN: 100 f. 100-metres sprint.

57. Sacrificial Offering.

1968. Independence. 8th Anniv.
309. **57.** 30 f. multicoloured . . 20 12

58. Doctor inoculating Patient. **59.** Deer in Forest.

1968. W.H.O. 20th Anniv.
310. **58.** 30 f. choc., brown & blue 20 12

1968. Fauna and Flora Protection.
311. **59.** 30 f. brn., grn. & blue . . 20 12

60. Museum and Carved Screen.

1968. Opening of Abidjan Museum.
312. **60.** 30 f. brown, red & blue 20 12

61. Human Rights Emblem and "Justice" Totems.

1968. Human Rights Year.
313. **61.** 30 f. orange, mar. & bl. 20 12

1969. Air. "Philexafrique" stamp Exn., Abidjan, Ivory Coast (1st issue). As T **109** of Cameroun. Multicoloured.
314. 100 f. "Grand Bassam" (Achalme) 80 80
Issued in sheets se-tenant with "PHILEXAFRIQUE" stamp-size label.

1969. Air. "Philexafrique" Stamp Exn., Abidjan, Ivory Coast (2nd issue). As T **110** of Cameroun.
315. 50 f. red, blue and green . . 40 40
316. 100 f. blue, brown & orge. 80 80
317. 200 f. slate, blue & brown 1·60 1·60
DESIGNS—HORIZ. 50 f. Aerial view of San Pedro village and stamp of 1936. 200 f. Chambers of Agriculture and Industry building, Abidjan, and 5 f. stamp of 1913. VERT. 100 f. Chief's costume and 5 f. stamp of 1936.

62. The "Villa de Maranhao" at Grand-Bassam.

1969. Stamp Day.
319. **62.** 30 f. maroon, blue & green 20 12

63. Ivory Hotel.

1969. Opening of Ivory Hotel.
320. **63.** 30 f. blue, verm. & emer. 20 12

64. "Man on Horse-back" (statuette). **65.** Hertzian-wave Radio Station, Man.

1969. Ivory Coast Art Exn., Vevey, Switzerland.
321. **64.** 30 f. blk., purple & verm. 20 12

1969. Independence. 9th Anniv.
322. **65.** 30 f. green, brn. & blue 20 12

1969. African Development Bank. 5th Anniv. As T **118** of Cameroun.
323. 30 f. brown, green and lake 20 12

66. Arms of Bouake. **67.** Game Fishing.

1969. Coats of Arms.
324. **66.** 10 f. multicoloured . . 5 5
325. – 15 f. multicoloured . . 12 5
326. – 30 f. blk., gold & green 20 10
ARMS: 15 f. Abidjan. 30 f. Ivory Coast Republic.
See also Nos. 402/3 and 432/3c.

1969. Int. SKAL Tourist Assn. Congress, Abidjan.
327. **67.** 30 f. blue, mar. & violet 20 12
328. – 100 f. multicoloured . . 65 35
DESIGN: 100 f. Assinie Holiday Village.

1969. Aerial Navigation Security Agency for Africa and Madagascar (A.S.E.C.N.A.) 10th Anniv. As T **121** of Cameroun.
329. 30 f. vermilion 20 12

68. Man Waterfall.

1970. Air.
330. **68.** 100 f. ultramarine, green and brown 70 40
331. – 200 f. red, green & emer. 1·40 55
DESIGN: 200 f. Mt. Niangbo.

69. University Hospital Centre, Abidjan.

1970. "10 Years of Higher Education"
332. **69.** 30 f. indigo, green & blue 20 12

70. Telegraphist and Gabriel Dadie. (Postal administrator.)

1970. Stamp Day.
333. **70.** 30 f. black, green & red 20 12

71. Abidjan University.

1970. 3rd A.U.P.E.L.F. (Association of French Speaking Universities). General Assembly, Abidjan.
334. **71.** 30 f. purple, green & blue 20 12

72. Manufacture of Safety-matches. **74.** Wild Life.

73. Dish Aerial and Television Class.

1970. Industrial Expansion.
335. **72.** 5 f. brn., blue & choc. 5 5
336. – 20 f. red, green & grey 12 8
337. – 50 f. brn., blue & green 30 15
DESIGNS: 20 f. Textile-printing. 50 f. Shipbuilding.

1970. World Telecommunications Day.
338. **73.** 40 f. green, drab and red 30 20

1970. New U.P.U. Headquarters Building Berne. As T **126** of Cameroun.
339. 30 f. brown, green & purple 20 12

1970. United Nations. 25th Anniv.
340. **74.** 30 f. choc., green & blue 20 12

76. Coffee Plant. **77.** Male and Female Africans.

1970. Independence. 10th Anniv. (1st issue).
341. **76.** 30 f. grn., brn. and orge. 20 12
See also Nos. 344/9.

1970. Fifth P.D.C.I. (Ivory Coast Democratic Party) Congress.
342. **77.** 40 f. multicoloured . . 25 15

78. Power Station, Vridi.

1970. Thermal Power Plant, Vridi.
343. **78.** 40 f. brn., blue and grn. 25 15

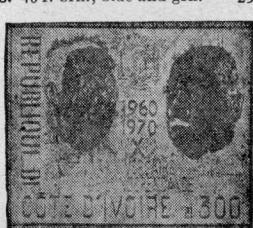

79. Pres. Houphouet-Boigny and De Gaulle.

1970. Independence. 10th Anniv. (2nd issue). Embossed on silver (300 f. values) or gold foil.
344. 300 f. Type **79** (postage) . . 2·25
345. 300 f. Ivory Coast Arms . . 2·25
346. 1000 f. Type **79** . . . . 7·00
347. 1000 f. As No. 345 . . 7·00
348. 300 f. Pres. Houphouet-Boigny and elephants (air) . . 2·00
349. 1200 f. As No. 348 . . 7·50
Nos. 345 and 348, and 347 and 349 were issued in joined pairs . . . .

80. Mail Bus, 1925.

1971. Stamp Day.
350. **80.** 40 f. mar., grn. & brn. 20 12

81. Port of San Pedro.

1971. Air.
351. **81.** 100 f. red, blue & green 60 30
352. – 500 f. grn., blue & brown 3·25 1·75
DESIGN: 500 f. African Riviera coastline.

82. "Marginella desjardini".

1971. Marine Life.
353. – 1 f. brn., bl. and green . . 5 5
354. – 5 f. red, lilac and blue . . 5 5
355. – 10 f. red, blue & green . . 8 5
356. **82.** 15 f. brn., maroon & blue 8 5
357. – 15 f. brn., violet & red 8 5
358. – 20 f. red and yellow . . 12 5
359. – 20 f. lake, maroon & red 10 5
360. – 25 f. brn., black & lake 12 8
361. – 35 f. red, yellow & green 15 8
362. – 40 f. brn., blue and green 20 12
363. – 40 f. red, blue-green and brown 15 10
364. – 45 f. brn., grn. & emerald 25 12
365. – 50 f. green, red & violet 25 12
366. – 65 f. blue, grn. and brn. 35 15
DESIGNS—HORIZ. 1 f. "Aporrhais pes gallinae". 5 f. "Neptunus validus". 20 f. (No. 359) "Xenophoradigitata". 25 f. "Conus prometheus". 40 f. (No. 362) "Conus genuanus", 45 f. "Strombus bubonius". 65 f. "Cypraea stercoraria". VERT. 10 f. "Hermodice carunculata". 15 f. (No. 357) "Natica fanel". 20 f. (No. 358) "Goniaster cuspidatus". 35 f. "Polycheles typhlops". 40 f. (No. 363) "Chlamys flabellum". 50 f. "Enoplometopus callistus".

83. Telegraph Station, Grand Bassam, 1891.

1971. World Telecommunications Day.
367. **83.** 100 f. brn., green and bl. 60 40

84. Treichville Swimming Pool.

1971. Air.
368. **84.** 100 f. multicoloured . . 60 30

85. Tool-making. **86.** African Telecommunications Map.

1971. Technical Training and Instruction.
369. **85.** 35 f. indigo, red & green 20 10

1971. Pan-African Telecommunications Network.
370. **86.** 45 f. yellow, red & pur. 25 12

88. Bondoukou Market.

1971. Independence. 11th Anniv.
371. **88.** 35 f. brn., bl. & grey (postage) 20 12
372. – 200 f. blk. & bl. on gold (air) 1·25 1·10
No. 372 has a similar design to T **88** but in smaller format, size 38×27 mm.

89. Children of Three Races.

1971. Racial Equality Year. Multicoloured.
373. 40 f. Type **89** 20 10
374. 45 f. Children around Globe 25 12

1971. U.A.M.P.T. 10th Anniv. As T **153** of Cameroun. Multicoloured.
375. 100 f. H.Q. and Ivory Coast Arms 65 40
U.A.M.P.T.=African and Malagasy Posts and Telecommunications Union.

90. Gaming Table.

1971. National Lottery.
376. **90.** 35 f. multicoloured .. 20 8

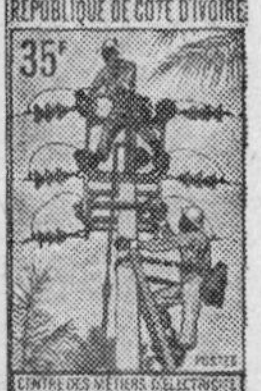

91. Technicians working on Power Cables. **93.** Cogwheel and Students.

92. Lion of St. Mark's.

1971. Electricity Works Centre, Akovai-Santai.
377. **91.** 35 f. multicoloured .. 20 10

1972. Air. U.N.E.S.C.O. "Save Venice" Campaign. Multicoloured.
378. 100 f. Type **92** 55 30
379. 200 f. St. Mark's Square 1·10 70

1972. Technical Instruction Week.
380. **93.** 35 f. blue, brn. and red 20 10

94. Heart Emblem. **95.** Child learning to write.

1972. World Heart Month.
381. **94.** 40 f. blue, red & green 20 12

1972. Int. Book Year.
382. – 35 f. brn,. orge. & grn. 20 10
383. **95.** 40 f. blk., orge. & grn. 20 12
DESIGN—HORIZ. 35 f. Students and open book.

96. Gouessesso Tourist Village.

1972. Air.
384. **96.** 100 f. brn., green & blue 55 30
385. – 200 f. grn., brown & blue 1·10 55
386. – 500 f. brn., yell.-brn. & bl. 2·75 1·60
DESIGNS: 200 f. Jacqueville Lake. 500 f. Mosque of Kawara.

97. Central Sorting Office, Abidjan. **98.** Aerial Mast, Abobo. Hertzian Centre.

1972. Stamp Day.
387. **97.** 40 f. bistre, grn. & pur. 20 10

1972. World Telecommunications Day.
388. **98.** 40 f. red, blue and green 20 10

100. Computer Operator.

1972. Development of Information Services.
393. **100.** 40 f. blue, brn. & green 20 12

101. Odienne.

1972. Independence. 12th Anniv.
394. **101.** 35 f. brn.,grn. and blue 20 10

1972. West African Monetary Union. 10th Anniv. As Type **109** of Dahomey.
395. 40 f. grey, pur. & brown .. 20 12

102. Diamond and Mine.

1972. Development of the Diamond Industry.
396. **102.** 40 f. blue, grey & brn. 20 12

103. Lake-dwellings Betankoro.

1972. Air.
397. **103.** 200 f. maroon, grn. & bl. 1·10 50
398. – 500 f. brn., green & blue 2·75 1·60
DESIGN: 500 f. Kossou Dam.

104. Institute and Louis Pasteur.

1972. Pasteur Institute, Abidjan. Inaug.
399. **104.** 35 f. blue, grn. & brown 20 10

105. Satellite Earth Station.

1972. Air. Opening of Satellite Earth Station Akakro.
400. **105.** 200 f. brn.,green & blue 1·10 55

106. Child pumping Water. **107.** Dr. A. G. Hansen.

1972. "Conserve Water" Campaign.
401. **106.** 35 f. blk., green & red 15 10
See also No. 414.

1973. Coats of Arms. As Type **66.** Mult.
402. 5 f. Arms of Daloa .. 5 5
403. 10 f. Arms of Gagnoa .. 5 5
See also Nos. 432/3c.

1973. Hansen's Identification of Leprosy Bacillus. Cent.
404. **107.** 35 f. brn., blue & purple 15 10

108. " Xyrichthys novacula ".

1973. Fishes.
405. **108.** 15 f. blue and green .. 8 5
406. – 20 f. red and brown .. 8 5
406a. – 25 f. red and green .. 10 5
406b. – 35 f. red and green .. 15 8
407. – 50 f. red, blue and black 25 12
FISHES: 15 f. " Balistes capriscus ". 20 f. " Pseudupeneus prayensis ". 25 f. " Cephalopholis taeniops ". 35 f. " Priacanthus arenatus "

109. Children and Emblem.

1973. Establishment of first S.O.S. Children's Village in Africa.
408. **109.** 40 f. blk., red & green 20 10

110. National Assembly Building.

1973. 112th Interparliamentary Council Session, Abidjan.
409. **110.** 100 f. multicoloured .. 45 30

111. Classroom and Shop. **112.** " Women's Work ".

1973. " Commercial Action " Programme.
410. **111.** 40 f. multicoloured .. 15 8

1973. Technical Institution for Women.
411. **112.** 35 f. multicoloured .. 15 8

113. Scouts helping with Food Cultivation.

1973. 24th World Scouting Congress, Nairobi, Kenya.
412. **113.** 40 f. multicoloured .. 15 8

114. Party Headquarters.

1973. New Party Headquarters Building, Yamoussokro.
413. **114.** 35 f. multicoloured .. 15 5

115. Children at Dry Pump.

1973. Pan-African Drought Relief.
414. **115.** 40 f. blackish brn., brn. and red 15 8

116. " The Judgement of Solomon " (Nandjui Legue).

1973. Air. 6th World Peace and Justic Conf.
415. **116.** 500 f. multicoloured.. 2·50 1·40

1973. U.A.M.P.T. As T **182** of Cameroun.
416. 100 f. black, red and violet 45 30

117. " Arrow-heads ". **119.** Motorway Junction.

118. Ivory Coast 1 c. Stamp of 1892.

1973. Abidjan Museum.
417. **117.** 5 f. black, red & brown 5 5

1973. Stamp and Post Day.
418. **118.** 40 f. blk., orge. & green 15 10

1973. Motorway Projects. Indenie Interchange, Abidjan.
419. **119.** 35 f. black, green & blue 15 8

120. Map of Africa and Emblem. **121.** " Elephants " Ticket.

1973. Int., Social Security Assn. 18th General Assembly.
420. **120.** 40 f. brown, ultramarine and blue 15 10

1973. Travel-Agents' Assns., 7th World Congress.
421. 121. 40 f. multicoloured .. 15 10

122. Kong Mosque.

1974.
426. 122. 35 f. brn., bl. & grn... 12 8

123. Grand-Lahou Post Office.

1974. Stamp Day.
427. 123. 35 f. brn., grn. & bl... 12 8

124. Converging Columns.

1974. "Formation Permanente".
428. 124. 35 f. multicoloured .. 12 8

125. Sassandra Bridge.

1974. Air.
429. 125. 100 f. brn. & green .. 45 30
430. 500 f. blk. & green .. 2·25 1·40

1974. Council of Accord. 15th Anniv. As T **131** of Dahomey.
431. 40 f. multicoloured .. 15 8

126. Arms of Ivory Coast. 128. Pres. Houphouet-Boigny.

127. View of Factory.

1974.
432. 126. 35 f. gold, grn. & brn. 12 5
433. 40 f. gold, grn. & blue 15 5
433a. 60 f. gold, grn. & red.. 20 12
433b. 65 f. gold, light grn. & green 25 15
433c. 70 f. gold, grn. & blue 25 15

1974. Air. Vridi Soap Factory, Abidjan.
434. 127. 200 f. multicoloured .. 90 60

1974.
435. 128. 25 f. brn., orge. & grn. 10 5

129. WPY Emblem.

130. Cotton-Picking.

1974. World Population Year.
436. 129. 40 f. blue and green .. 15 8

1974. "Cycle du Coton". (1st series).
437. 130. 50 f. multicoloured .. 20 10
See also Nos. 449/50.

131. U.P.U. Emblem. 132. Flag and U.P.U. Emblems.

1974. Universal Postal Union. Cent.
438. 131. 40 f. grn., bl. & brn. (post.) 15 10
439. 132. 200 f. multicoloured (air) 90 65
440. 300 f. multicoloured .. 1·25 90

133. Raoul Follereau (educator of the blind). 134. Civic Service Emblem.

1974. Follereau Commemoration.
441. 133. 35 f. red, yell. & green 12 8

1974. Independence. 14th Anniv.
442. 134. 35 f. multicoloured .. 12 8

135. Library Building and Students.

1975. Inauguration of National Library. 1st Anniv.
443. 135. 40 f. multicoloured .. 15 8

136. Congress Emblem. 137. Coffee-plant in Flower.

1975. 52nd International Seedcrushers Association Congress, Abidjan.
444. 136. 40 f. black and green.. 15 8

1975. "Cycle du Cafe" (Coffee Production). Multicoloured.
445. 5 f. Type **137** 5 5
446. 10 f. Coffee-berries .. 5 5

138. Sassandra Wharf.

1975.
447. 138. 100 f. brn., grn. & bl... 45 30

139. Postal Sorters.

1975. Stamp Day.
448. 139. 40 f. multicoloured .. 15 8

140. Cotton Flower.

1975. "Cycle du Coton" (2nd series). Mult.
449. 5 f. Type **140** 5 5
450. 10 f. Cotton bolls 5 5

141. Marie Kore and I.W.Y. Emblem.

1975. International Women's Year.
451. 141. 45 f. brn., bl. & grn... 20 10

142. Dabou Fort.

1975.
452. 142. 50 f. vio., bl. & grn. .. 20 10

145. Abidjan Harbour.

1975. Abidjan Port. 25th Anniv.
453. 143. 35 f. multicoloured .. 12 8

144. Cocoa Tree.

1975.
455. 144. 35 f. multicoloured .. 12 8

145. Rural Activities.

1975. Promotion of Rural Development.
456. 145. 50 f. mauve, vio. & black 20 10

146. Railway Bridge over the N'Zi, Dimbokro.

1975. Independence. 15th Anniv.
457. 146. 60 f. multicoloured .. 25 12

147. "Mother" (statue). 148. Baoule Mask.

1976. Mothers' Day.
458. 147. 65 f. multicoloured .. 25 12

1976. Ivory Coast Art. Multicoloured.
459. 20 f. Type **148** (postage).. 8 5
460. 25 f. Senoufo statuette .. 8 5
461. 150 f. Chief Abron's chair 70 60
462. 200 f. Akans royal symbols: fly swatter and panga (air) 90 75

149. Early and Modern Telephones. 150. Effigy, Map and Carrier Pigeon.

1976. Telephone Centenary.
463. 149. 70 f. blue, brn. & blk. 30 25

1976. Stamp Day and Ivory Coast Philatelic Club. 25th Anniversary.
464. 150. 65 f. multicoloured .. 30 25

151. "Smiling Trees" and Cat. 152. Children Reading.

1976. Nature Protection.
465. 151. 65 f. multicoloured .. 30 25

1976. Literature for Children.
466. 152. 65 f. multicoloured .. 30 25

153. Throwing the Javelin.

1976. Olympic Games, Montreal. Multicoloured.

467. 60 f. Type **153** 25 20
468. 65 f. Running 30 25

154. Cashew-nut.

1976.

469. **154.** 65 f. multicoloured .. 30 25

MILITARY FRANK STAMP

MF **1.**

1967. No value indicated.

MF 1. MF **1.** (–) brown, black, orange and green 30 30

OFFICIAL STAMPS

O 1. Arms of Ivory Coast.

1973. No value indicated. Multicoloured. Background colours given.

O 422. O **1.** (–) grn. & bluish grn. 15 12
O 423. (–) yellow & orange 35 20
O 424. (–) pink & magenta 45 30
O 425. (–) vio. & bluish vio. 1·10 75

Nos. O 422/25 represent the following face values. No. O 422, 35 f. No. O 423, 75 f. No. O 424, 100 f. No. O 425, 250 f.

PARCEL POST STAMPS

Stamps optd. **COTE D'IVOIRE COLIS POSTAUX** or **C.P.** are Parcel Post stamps. A full list will be found in Stanley Gibbons' Overseas Catalogue, Volume 2.

POSTAGE DUE STAMPS

1906. "Natives" key-type inscr. "COTE D'IVOIRE".

D 38. L. 5 c. green 45 45
D 39. 10 c. claret 35 35
D 40. 15 c. blue 65 65
D 41. 20 c. black on yellow .. 1·25 1·25
D 42. 30 c. red .. .. 1·40 1·40
D 43. 50 c. violet .. .. 1·00 1·00
D 44. 60 c. black on yellow .. 4·50 4·50
D 45. 1 f. black .. .. 4·50 4·50

1915. "Figure" key-type inscr. "COTE D'IVOIRE"

D 60. M. 5 c. green 5 5
D 61. 10 c. red 5 5
D 62. 15 c. grey 5 5
D 63. 20 c. brown 5 5
D 64. 30 c. blue 5 5
D 65. 50 c. black 8 8
D 66. 60 c. orange 8 8
D 67. 1 f. violet 8 8

1927. Surch. in figures.

D 94. M. "2 F." on 1 f. purple 12 12
D 95. "3 F." on 1 f. brown 12 12

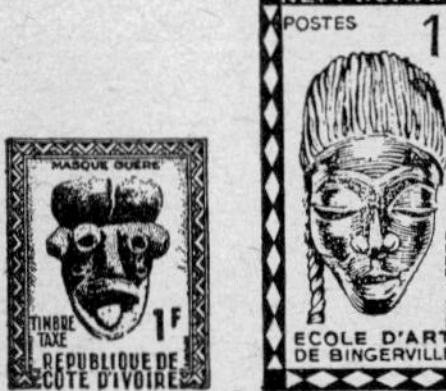

D 1. Guere Mask. D 2. Mask. D 3. Baoule Weight.

1960. Values in black.

D 196. D **1.** 1 f. violet 5 5
D 197. 2 f. green 5 5
D 198. 5 f. yellow 5 5
D 199. 10 f. blue 8 8
D 200. 20 f. magenta .. 12 12

1962.

D 220. D **2.** 1 f. blue and orange 5 5
D 221. – 2 f. red and black .. 5 5
D 222. – 5 f. green and red .. 5 5
D 223. – 10 f. purple and green 5 5
D 224. – 20 f. black and violet 8 8

DESIGNS: 2 f. to 20 f. Various native masks from Bingerville Art School.

1968. Designs showing different types of weights.

D 309. D **3.** 5 f. multicoloured .. 5 5
D 310. – 10 f. multicoloured .. 5 5
D 311. – 15 f. multicoloured .. 5 5
D 312. – 20 f. multicoloured .. 8 8
D 313. – 30 f. multicoloured .. 10 10

D 4. "Animal" Weight.

1972. Gold Weights and Measures.

D 389. D **4.** 20 f. brown and violet 12 10
D 390. – 40 f. brown and red 25 20
D 391. – 50 f. maroon & orange 30 25
D 392. – 100 f. brown and green 55 50

DESIGNS: 40 f. "Dagger". 50 f. "Bird". 100 f. "Triangle".

JAIPUR BC

A state of Rajasthan, India (q.v.). Now uses Indian stamps.

1. Chariot of the Sun-god, Surya. 2.

1904.

5. **1.** ½ a. blue .. .. .. 1·50 1·50
3. 1 a. red 60 65
4. 2 a. green .. .. .. 1·25 1·25

1904.

22. **2.** ¼ a. olive 5 5
25. ½ a. blue 5 5
26. 1 a. red 8 8
29. 2 a. green 40 15
13. 4 a. brown .. .. .. 1·40 1·40
14. 8 a. violet .. .. .. 1·75 1·75
15. 1 r. yellow .. .. .. 3·00 3·00

This set was issued engraved in 1904 and surface-printed in 1913.

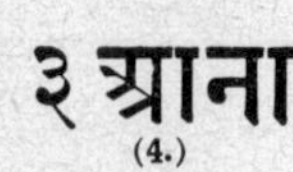

3. Chariot of the Sun-god, Surya. (4.)

1911.

17. **3.** ¼ a. olive 15 15
18. ¼ a. blue 15 15
20. 1 a. red 15 15
21. 2 a. green .. .. .. 3·00 2·50

1926. Surch. with T **4.**

32. **2.** 3 a. on 8 a. violet 50 80
33. 3 a. on 1 r. yellow 50 50

5. Chariot of the Sun.

6. Maharaja Sir Man Singh Bahadur.

1931. Investiture of H.H. the Maharaja. Centres in black.

40. **5.** ¼ a. brown-purple .. 5 5
58. **6.** ¼ a. red 5 5
41. ½ a. violet 10 5
59. ¾ a. orange 5 5
42. – 1 a. blue .. .. 1·00 30
60. **6.** 1 a. blue 8 8
43. – 2 a. orange .. .. 1·25 35
61. **6.** 2 a. orange 10 10
44. – 2½ a. red .. .. 7·00 4·00
62. **6.** 2½ a. red 10 10
45. – 3 a. green .. .. 7·00 4·00
63. **6.** 3 a. green 12 12
46. – 4 a. green .. .. 5·00 4·00
64. **6.** 4 a. green 20 20
47. – 6 a. blue .. .. 5·00 4·00
65. **6.** 6 a. blue 70 60
48. – 8 a. brown .. .. 7·00 6·00
66. **6.** 8 a. brown 75 75
49. – 1 r. olive .. .. 7·00 6·00
67. **6.** 1 r. bistre .. .. 4·00 3·00
50. – 2 r. green .. .. 8·00 10·00
51. – 5 r. purple .. .. 11·00 12·00

DESIGNS—VERT. 1 a. (No. 42), Elephant and banner. 2 a. (No. 43), Sowar in armour. 2½ a. (No. 44) Peacock. 8 a. (No. 48), Sireh-Deorhi Gate. HORIZ. 3 a. (No. 45), Bullock carriage. 4 a. (No. 46), Elephant carriage. 6 a. (No. 47), Albert Museum. 1 r. (No. 49), Chandra Mahal. 2 r. Amber Palace. 5 r. Maharajas Sawai Jai Singh and Sir Man Singh.

1932. As T **6**, but inscr. "POSTAGE & REVENUE". Portrait in black.

52. 1 a. blue 5 5
53. 2 a. brown 5 5
54. 4 a. green 10 10
55. 8 a. brown 35 40
56. 1 r. bistre .. .. .. 5·00 5·00
57. 2 r. green .. .. .. 18·00 18·00

1936. Nos. 57 and 51 surch. **One Rupee.**

68. 1 r. on 2 r. green .. .. 1·00 1·00
69. 1 r. on 5 r. purple .. .. 1·00 1·00

1938. No. 41 surch. in native characters.

70. **6.** ¼ a. on ½ a. violet .. .. 1·00 1·00

7. Maharaja and Amber Palace.

1947. Silver Jubilee of Reign of H.H. the Maharaja of Jaipur. Inscr. as in T **7.**

71. – ¼ a. brown and green .. 5 5
72. **7.** ½ a. green and violet .. 5 5
73. – ¾ a. black and red .. 5 5
74. – 1 a. brown and blue .. 15 15
75. – 2 a. violet and red .. 10 15
76. – 3 a. green and black .. 12 25
77. – 4 a. blue and brown .. 25 40
78. – 8 a. red and brown .. 35 65
79. – 1 r. purple and green .. 75 1·00

DESIGNS: ¼ a. Palace Gate. ¾ a. Map of Jaipur. 1 a. Observatory. 2 a. Wind Palace. 3 a. Coat of Arms. 4 a. Amber Fort Gate. 8 a. Chariot of the Sun. 1 r. Maharaja's portrait between State flags.

1947. No. 41 surch. **3 PIES** and bars.

80. **6.** 3 p. on ½ a. violet .. .. 3·00 3·00

OFFICIAL STAMPS

1929. Optd. **SERVICE.**

O 1. **2.** ¼ a. olive 5 5
O 2. ½ a. blue 5 5
O 4. 1 a. red 10 5
O 5. 2 a. green 20 20
O 6. 4 a. brown .. .. 1·00 1·25
O 7. 8 a. violet .. .. 10·00 10·00
O 8. 1 r. yellow .. .. 15·00 15·00

1932. No. O 5 surch.

O 13. **2.** ½ a. on 2 a. green .. 50·00 10

1931. Stamps of 1931-32 optd. **SERVICE.**

O 23. **6.** ¼ a. red 10 5
O 14. ½ a. violet 5 5
O 24. ¾ a. orange 10 5
O 25. 1 a. blue 20 20
O 15. – 1 a. blue (No. 42) .. 75·00 5
O 18. – 1 a. blue (No. 52) .. 5 5
O 16. – 2 a. orange (No. 43) .. 20 12
O 19. – 2 a. brown (No. 53) .. 15 5
O 26. **6.** 2 a. orange 25 25
O 27. 2½ a. red 35 40
O 17. – 4 a. green (No. 46) .. 40 15
O 20. – 4 a. green (No. 54) .. 1·75 1·00
O 28. **6.** 4 a. green 50 30
O 21. – 8 a. brown (No. 55) .. 45 50
O 29. **6.** 8 a. brown 75 75
O 22. 1 r. bistre (No. 56) .. 1·75 1·00

1947. Official stamps surch.

O 33. **6.** 3 p. on ½ a. violet .. 2·00 2·00
O 32. 9 p. on 1 a. blue .. 10 5

1949. No. O 14 surch. in native characters.

O 34. **6.** ¾ a. on ½ a. violet .. 1·50 1·50

For later issues see Rajasthan.

JAMAICA BC

An island in the Br. W. Indies. Part of the Br. Caribbean Federation from 3rd Jan. 1958, until 6th Aug. 1962 when Jamaica became an independent state within the Br. Commonwealth.

1969. 100 cents = 1 dollar.

1. 2.

1860. Portrait as T **1.** Various frames.

7a. **1.** ½d. claret .. .. 3·50 1·00
16a. ½d. green 20 10
8. 1d. blue .. .. 10·00 45
18a. 1d. red .. .. 4·00 40
9. 2d. red .. .. 12·00 15
20a. 2d. grey .. .. 8·00 15
10. 3d. green .. .. 35·00 1·40
46. 3d. olive .. .. 1·10 25
22a. 4d. orange .. .. 1·00 12
52a. 6d. lilac .. .. 4·00 4·50
23a. 6d. yellow .. .. 4·00 2·00
24. 1s. brown .. .. 4·00 2·50
25. 2s. brown .. .. 14·00 7·00
26. 5s. lilac .. .. 18·00 18·00

See also Nos. 47a, etc.

1889.

27. **2.** 1d. purple and mauve .. 60 10
28. 2d. green .. .. 4·00 1·25
29. 2½d. purple and blue .. 2·00 40

1890. No. 22a surch. **TWO PENCE HALF-PENNY.**

30. **1.** 2½d. on 4d. orange .. 5·00 3·50

3. Llandovery Falls, Jamaica.

1900.

31. **3.** 1d. red 35 15
32. 1d. black and red .. 1·00 15

10. Arms of Jamaica 11.

1903.

33. **10.** ½d. grey and green .. 65 15
34. 1d. grey and red .. 90 12
35. 2½d. grey and blue .. 1·10 55
42. 2½d. blue .. .. 1·60 70
36. 5d. grey and yellow .. 8·50 9·50
44. 6d. purple .. .. 4·00 5·00
45. 5s. grey and violet .. 16·00 15·00

1906.

38a. **11.** ½d. green 35 15
40. 1d. red 40 10

1905. Queen Victoria portraits as 1860.

47a. 3d. purple on yellow .. 80 55
48. 4d. brown .. .. 13·00 12·00
49. 4d. black on yellow .. 4·50 8·50
50. 4d. red on yellow .. 1·00 2·00
54. 1s. black on green .. 2·75 5·00
56. 2s. purple on blue .. 5·00 4·50

12.

ILLUSTRATIONS British Commonwealth and all overprints and surcharges are FULL SIZE. Foreign Countries have been reduced to ¾-LINEAR.

1911.

57. 2d. grey .. .. 1·10 2·75

1912. As T **12**, but King George V.

107. ½d. green 12 12
58. 1d. red 15 8
59. 1½d. orange 65 15
60a. 2d. grey 55 90
61. 2½d. blue 55 20

62.		3d. purple on yellow ..	55	40
63.		4d. black and red on yellow	95	55
64.		6d. purple	2·20	2·25
64b.		6d. purple and magenta ..	85	55
65.		1s. black on green ..	1·50	1·25
66.		2s. purple and blue on blue	4·00	5·00
67.		5s. green and red on yellow	14·00	17·00

WAR STAMP. (14.) WAR STAMP. (15.)

1916. Optd. with T 14.

68.	11.	½d. green..	10	20
69b.	–	3d. purple on yellow (62)	80	95

1916. Optd. with T 15.

70.	11.	½d. green	12	15
71.	–	1½d. orange (No. 59) ..	12	12
72.	–	3d. purple on yellow (62)	30	70

WAR STAMP. (16.) WAR STAMP (17.)

1917. Optd. with T 16.

73.	11.	½d. green..	12	15
74.	–	1½d. orange (No. 59) ..	8	8
75.	–	3d. purple on yellow (62)	20	25

1919. Optd. with T 17.

76.	11.	½d green	8	8
77a.	–	3d. purple on yellow (62)	15	45

18. Exhibition, 1891.  19. Arawak Woman preparing Cassava.

22. Return of War Contingent.

30.

1913.

78.	18.	½d. green and olive ..	15	15
79.	19.	1d. red and orange (A)*	80	25
92.		1d. red and orange (B)*	45	12
80.	–	1½d. green	20	12
94.	–	2d. blue and green ..	95	25
95.	22.	2½d. blue	1·50	25
96a.	–	3d. green and blue ..	25	12
97a.	–	4d. brown and green ..	25	12
98a.	–	6d. black and blue ..	8·00	1·25
99a.	–	1s. orange	1·40	40
100.	–	2s. blue and brown ..	1·40	75
101.	–	3s. violet and orange ..	7·00	7·50
102c.	–	5s. blue & yellow-brown	11·00	10·00
103.	30.	10s. green	18·00	22·00

* Two types of the 1d. (A) Without and (B) with "POSTAGE & REVENUE" at foot.

DESIGNS—41½ × 26 mm.: 1½d. War Contingent embarking. 6d. Port Royal, 1853. 27 × 22 mm.: 3d. Landing of Columbus. 22 × 29 mm.: 2d. King's House, Spanish Town. 22 × 28 mm.: 4d. Cathedral, Spanish Town. 25 × 30 mm.: 1s. Statue of Queen Victoria. 3s. Sir Charles Metcalfe Monument. 25 × 31 mm.: 2s Admiral Rodney Memorial. 5s. Jamaican scenery.

31.

1923. Child Welfare. Designs as T 31.

104.	31.	½d.+½d. black and green	80	1·10
105.	–	1d.+½d. black and red	5·00	6·00
106.	–	2½d.+½d. black and blue	11·00	12·00

34.  35. Coco palms at Columbus Cove.

1929. Various frames.

108a.	34.	1d. red	12	12
109.		1½d. brown	20	20
110.		9d. claret	3·00	2·25

1932.

111.	35.	2d. black and green ..	1·50	55
112.	–	2½d. green and blue ..	1·10	1·40
113.	–	6d. grey and purple ..	2·50	2·00

DESIGNS—VERT. 2½d. Wag Water River, St. Andrew. HORIZ. 6d. Priestman's River, Portland.

1935. Silver Jubilee. As T 11 of Antigua.

114.	1d. blue and red	12	12
115.	1½d. blue and black ..	15	20
116.	6d. green and blue ..	1·50	2·00
117.	1s. grey and purple ..	1·75	2·25

1937. Coronation. As T 2 of Aden.

118.	1d. red	12	12
119.	1½d. grey	20	15
120.	2½d. blue	45	25

38. King George VI.  39. Coco Palms at Columbus Cove.

41. Bananas.

40. Priestman's River, Portland.

46. Bamboo Walk.

DESIGNS—As T 39: 2½d. Wag Water River, St. Andrew. As T 41: 4d. Citrus Grove. 9d. Kingston Harbour. 1s. Sugar Industry. £1, Tobacco growing and cigar making. As No. 102c, but with King's portrait added, 5s. As T 30: 10s. King George VI.

1938.

121.	38.	½d. green	5	5
121b.		½d. orange	10	10
122.		1d. red	5	5
122a.		1d. green	20	12
123.		1½d. brown	5	5
124.	39.	2d. black and green ..	5	5
125.	–	2½d. green and blue ..	80	95
126.	41.	3d. blue and green ..	10	5
126a.		3d. green and blue ..	35	15
126b.		3d. green and red ..	20	12
127.	–	4d. brown and green ..	12	12
128a.	43.	6d. black and purple ..	12	12
129.	–	9d. claret	25	20
130.	–	1s. green and brown ..	30	20
131.	46.	2s. blue and brown ..	95	40
132ab.	–	5s. blue and brown ..	1·75	1·75
133aa.	–	10s. green	4·50	4·50
133a.	–	£1 brown and violet ..	12·00	12·00

47. Courthouse, Falmouth.

48. Institute of Jamaica.

DESIGNS—As T47—VERT. 2s. "Labour and Learning". HORIZ. 2d. Kings Charles II and George VI. As T48—HORIZ. 4½d. House of Assembly. 5s. Scroll, flag and King George VI.

1945. New Constitution. Inscr. "NEW CONSTITUTION 1944".

134.	47.	1½d. brown	12	12
135a.	–	2d. green	12	20
136.	48.	3d. blue..	12	12
137.	–	4½d. black	12	15
138.	–	2s. brown	70	70
139.	–	5s. blue	85	1·75
140.	18.	10s. green	2·25	4·00

1946. Victory. As T 4 of Aden.

141a.	1½d. brown	8	8
142.	3d. blue	15	20

1948. Silver Wedding. As T 5/6 of Aden.

143.	1½d. brown..	12	12
144.	£1 red	11·00	14·00

1949. U.P.U. As T 14/17 of Antigua.

145.	1½d. brown	12	12
146.	2d. green	15	25
147.	3d. blue	30	40
148.	6d. purple	45	45

1951. B.W.I. University College. Inaug. As T 18/19 of Antigua.

149.	2d. black and brown ..	12	12
150.	6d. black and purple ..	30	25

49. Scout Badge and Caribbean.

50. Scout Badge and Jamaica.

1952. 1st Caribbean Scout Jamboree.

151.	49.	2d. blue, green & black	12	12
152.	50.	6d. green, red and black	35	45

1953. Coronation. As T 7 of Aden.

153.	2d. black and green ..	8	5

1953. Royal Visit. As T 39 but with portrait of Queen Elizabeth II and inscr. "ROYAL VISIT 1953".

154.	2d. black and green ..	8	8

INDEX

Countries can be quickly located by referring to the index at the end of this volume.

51. Man-o'-War at Port Royal.

1955. Tercentenary Issue.

155.	51.	2d. black and green ..	8	8
156.	–	2½d. black and blue ..	20	25
157.	–	3d. black and claret ..	20	20
158.	–	6d. black and red ..	30	35

DESIGNS: 2½d. Old Montego Bay. 3d. Old Kingston. 6d. Proclamation of Abolition of Slavery, 1838.

52. Palms.  53. Mahoe.

54. Blue Mountain Peak.

55. Arms of Jamaica.

1956.

159.	52.	½d. black & vermilion..	5	5
160.	–	1d. black and emerald..	5	5
161.	–	2d. black and red ..	5	5
162.	–	2½d. black and blue ..	8	8
163.	53.	3d. emerald and brown	8	10
164.	–	4d. olive and blue ..	10	10
165.	–	5d. red and olive ..	12	12
166.	–	6d. black and red ..	12	10
167.	54.	8d. blue and orange ..	15	10
168.	–	1s. green and blue ..	20	10
169.	–	1s. 6d. blue and purple	40	15
170.	–	2s. blue and olive ..	1·10	65
171.	55.	3s. black and blue	90	50
172.		5s. black and red ..	1·50	75
173.	–	10s. black and green ..	3·00	4·00
174.	–	£1 black and purple ..	5·50	4·00

DESIGNS—As T 52: 1d. Sugar-cane. 2d. Pineapples. 2½d. Bananas. As T 53: 4d. Breadfruit. 5d. Ackee. 6d. Doctor Bird. As T 54: 1s. Royal Botanic Gardens, Hope. 1s. 6d. Rafting on the Rio Grande. 2s. Fort Charles. As T 55 but vert. 10s., £1, Arms without portrait.

1958. British Caribbean Federation. As T 21 of Antigua.

175.	2d. green	5	5
176.	5d. blue	15	15
177.	6d. red	20	20

56. "Britannia" flying over 1860 Packet steamer.

57. 1s. Stamps of 1860 and 1956.

1960. Jamaica Postage Stamps Cent.
178. **56.** 2d. blue and purple .. 10 5
179. – 6d. red and olive .. 25 25
180. **57.** 1s. brown, green & blue 35 35
DESIGN—As T **56**: 6d. Postal mule-cart and motor-van.

1962. Independence. (a) Nos. 159/74 optd. **INDEPENDENCE** and **1962**. (3d. to 2s.) or **1962 1962** (others).
181. **52.** ½d. black and vermilion 5 5
182. – 1d. black and emerald.. 5 5
183. – 2½d. black and blue .. 10 5
184. **53.** 3d. emerald and brown 10 10
185. – 5d. red and olive .. 12 12
186. – 6d. black and red .. 12 10
187. **54.** 8d. blue and orange .. 15 12
188. – 1s. green and blue .. 20 15
189. – 2s. blue and olive .. 55 45
190. **55.** 3s. black and blue .. 1·25 1·25
191. – 10s. black and green .. 3·50 3·50
192. – £1 black and purple .. 5·50 5·50

58. Military Bugler and Map.

(b) As T **58** inscr. " INDEPENDENCE ".
193. **58.** 2d. red, black, yellow and green 5 5
194. 4d. red, black, yellow and blue 8 5
195. – 1s. 6d. black and red .. 35 40
196. – 5s. indigo, yellow, green and blue .. .. 95 1·10
DESIGNS: 1s. 6d. Gordon House and banner. 5s. Map, factories and fruit.

59. Weightlifting, Boxing, Football and Cycling.

1962. 9th Central American and Caribbean Games, Kingston.
197. **59.** 1d. sepia and red .. 5 5
198. – 6d. sepia and blue .. 12 10
199. – 8d. sepia and bistre .. 20 20
200. – 2s. sepia, yellow, red and light blue 50 55
DESIGNS: 6d. Diver, sailing, swimming and water polo. 8d. Javelin, discus, pole-vault hurdles and relay-racing. 2s. Arms of Kingston and athlete.

60. Farmer and Crops.

1963. Freedom from Hunger.
201. **60.** 1d. multicoloured .. 8 8
202. 8d. multicoloured .. 35 35

1963. Red Cross Cent. As T **24** of Antigua
203. 2d. red and black 5 5
204. 1s. 6d. red and blue .. 30 30

61. Carole Joan Crawford.

1964. " Miss World 1963 " Commem.
214. **61.** 3d. multicoloured .. 8 5
215. 1s. multicoloured .. 15 15
216. 1s. 6d. multicoloured .. 30 30

62. Lignum Vitae.

63. Gypsum Industry.

1964.
217. **62.** 1d. blue, green & brown 5 5
218. – 1½d. multicoloured .. 5 5
219. – 2d. red, yell. & grey-grn. 5 5
220. – 2½d. multicoloured .. 5 5
221. – 3d. yellow, black & emer. 5 5
222. – 4d. ochre and violet .. 8 5
223. – 6d. multicoloured .. 8 8
224. – 8d. multicoloured .. 12 10
225. **63.** 9d. blue & yellow-bistre 20 10
226. – 1s. black and brown .. 20 12
227. – 1s. 6d. black, blue & buff 30 20
228. – 2s. brown, black & blue 40 25
229. – 3s. blue and green .. 60 55
230. – 5s. black, ochre & blue 90 55
231. – 10s. multicoloured .. 2·00 1·50
232. – £1 multicoloured .. 4·00 2·50
DESIGNS—As T **62**—HORIZ. 1½d. Ackee (fruit). 2½d. Land shells. 3d. National flag over Jamaica. 4d. " Murex Antillarum " (sea shell). 6d. " Papilio homerus " (butterfly). 8d. Doctor Bird. VERT. 2d. Blue Mahoe (tree). As T **63**—HORIZ. 1s. National Stadium. 1s 6d. Palisadoes International Airport. 2s. Bauxite mining. 3s. Blue Marlin (sport fishing). 5s. Exploration of Sunken City, Port Royal. £1 Queen Elizabeth II and National Flag. VERT. 10s. Arms of Jamaica.

64. Scout Badge and Alligator (reduced size Illustration. Actual size 61½×30½ mm.).

1964. 6th Inter-American Scout Conf., Kingston.
233. 3d. red, black and pink 5 5
234. 8d. blue, olive and black 20 20
235. **64.** 1s. gold, blue & lt. blue 30 35
DESIGNS—VERT (25½×30 mm.): 3d. Scout belt. 8d. Globe, scout hat and scarf.

65. Gordon House, Kingston.

1964. 10th Commonwealth Parliamentary Conf. Kingston.
236. **65.** 3d. black and green .. 5 5
237. – 6d. black and red .. 10 10
238. 1s. 6d. black and blue.. 30 30
DESIGNS: 6d. Headquarters House, Kingston. 1s. 6d. House of Assembly, Spanish Town.

66. Eleanor Roosevelt.

1964. Declaration of Human Rights. 16th Anniv.
239. **66.** 1s. black, red and green 20 20

67. Guides' Emblem on Map.

DESIGN — TRIANGULAR (61½ × 30½ mm.): 1s. Guide emblems.

1965. Golden Jubilee of Jamaica Girl Guides' Assn. Inscr. " 1915-1965 ".
240. **67.** 3d. yellow, green & black 5 5
241. – 1s. yellow, black & grn. 20 25

68. Uniform Cap.

1965. Salvation Army Cent. Multicoloured.
242. 3d. Type **68** 5 5
243. 1s. 6d. Flag-bearer and drummer.. .. .. 25 25

69. Paul Bogle, William Gordon and Morant Bay Court House.

1965. Morant Bay Rebellion. Cent.
244. **69.** 3d. brown, ultram & blk. 5 5
245. 1s. 6d. brn., grn. & blk. 25 25
246. 3s. brown, red & black.. 40 45

70. Abeng-blower " Telstar ", Morse Key and I.T.U. Emblem.

1965. I.T.U. Cent.
247. **70.** 1s. black, slate and red 15 15

1966. Royal Visit. Nos. 221, 223, 226/7 optd. **ROYAL VISIT MARCH 1966.**
248. 3d. yellow, black & emerald 5 5
249. 6d. multicoloured .. 8 8
250. 1s. black and brown .. 15 15
251. 1s. 6d. black, blue & buff.. 25 30

71. Sir Winston Churchill.

1966. Churchill Commem.
252. **71.** 6d. black and green .. 15 15
253. 1s. brown and blue .. 25 25

72. Statue of Athlete and Flags.

1965. 8th British Empire and Commonwealth Games.
254. **72.** 3d. multicoloured .. 5 5
255. – 6d. multicoloured .. 10 10
256. – 1s. multicoloured .. 25 25
257. – 3s. gold and blue .. 65 65
DESIGNS: 6d. Racing cyclists. 1s. Stadium, Kingston. 3s. Games Emblem.

73. Bolivar's Statue and Flags of Jamaica and Venezuela.

1966. "Jamaica Letter". 150th Anniv.
259. **73.** 8d. multicoloured .. 12 12

74. Jamaican Pavilion.

1967. World Fair, Montreal.
260. **74.** 6d. multicoloured .. 8 10
261. 1s. multicoloured .. 15 15

75. Sir Donald Sangster (Prime Minister).

1967. Sangster Memorial Issue.
262. **75.** 3d. multicoloured .. 5 5
263. 1s. 6d. multicoloured .. 25 25

76. Traffic Duty.

1967. Constabulary Force Cent.
264. **76.** 3d. multicoloured .. 10 10
265. – 1s. multicoloured .. 20 20
266. – 1s. 6d. multicoloured .. 25 25
DESIGNS: 1s. 6d. Badge and Constables of 1867 and 1967. (56½×20½ mm.): 1s. Personnel of the Force.

1968. M.C.C.'s West Indies Tour. As Nos. 445/7 of Guyana but inscr. JAMAICA.
267. 6d. multicoloured .. 12 15
268. 6d. multicoloured .. 12 15
269. 6d. multicoloured .. 12 15

77. Sir Alexander and Lady Bustamante.

1968. Labour Day.
270. **77.** 3d. rose and black .. 5 5
271. 1s. olive and black .. 15 15

78. Human Rights Emblem over Map of Jamaica.

1968. Human Rights Year. Multicoloured.
272. 3d. Type **78** 5 5
273. 1s. Hands cupping Human Rights Emblem .. 15 15
274. 3s. Jamaican holding "Human Rights" .. 40 40

Three designs, in similar values, showing 3d. Bowls of Grain, 1s. Abacus, 3s. Hands in Prayer, were prepared, but not issued.

79. I.L.O. Emblem.

1969. Int. Labour Organisation. 50th Anniv.
275. **79.** 6d. yellow and brown .. 10 10
276. 3s. green and brown .. 45 45

80. Nurse, and Children being weighed and measured.

1969. W.H.O. 20th Anniv. Multicoloured.
277. 6d. Type **80** 8 8
278. 1s. Malaria Eradication (horiz.) 15 15
279. 3s. Trainee nurse 50 50

1969. Decimal Currency. Nos. 217, 219, 221/3 and 225/32 surch. **C-DAY 8th September 1969** in three lines, and value.
280. **62.** 1 c. on 1d. bl., grn. & brn. 5 5
281. – 2 c. on 2d. red, yell. & grn. 5 5
282. – 3 c. on 3d. yell., blk. and emerald .. 5 5
283. – 4 c. on 4d. ochre & violet 5 5
284. – 5 c. on 6d. multicoloured 8 8
285. **63.** 8 c. on 9d. blue & bistre 12 12
286. – 10 c. on 1s. blk. & brn. 15 12
287. – 15 c. on 1s. 6d. black, blue and buff .. 20 20
288. – 20 c. on 2s. brn., blk. & bl. 30 25
289. – 30 c. on 3s. blue & green 40 35
290. – 50 c. on 5s. black, ochre and blue .. 75 70
291. – $1 on 10s. multicoloured 1·50 1·50
292. – $2 on £1 multicoloured 3·00 3·00

81. "The Adoration of the Kings" (detail) (Foppa).

1969. Christmas. Multicoloured.
293. 2 c. Type **81** 5 5
294. 5 c. "Madonna, Child and St. John" (Raphael) .. 8 8
295. 8 c. "The Adoration of the Kings" (detail) (Dosso Dossi) 15 15

82. Half Penny, 1869.

1969. 1st Jamaican Coins. Cent.
296. **82.** 3 c. silver, black & mve. 5 5
297. – 15 c. silver, blk. & emer. 20 20

DESIGN: 15 c. One Penny, 1869.

83. George William Gordon. **84.** "Christ Appearing to St. Peter" (Carracci).

1970. National Heroes. Multicoloured; background colours given.
298. **83.** 1 c. mauve 5 5
299. – 3 c. blue 5 5
300. – 5 c. grey 8 8
301. – 10 c. red 15 15
302. – 15 c. green 25 25

PORTRAITS: 3 c. Sir Alexander Bustamante. 5 c. Norman Manley. 10 c. Marcus Garvey. 15 c. Paul Bogle.

1970. Easter. Centres multicoloured; frame colours given.
303. **84.** 3 c. red 5 5
304. – 10 c. green 20 20
305. – 20 c. grey 30 30

DESIGNS: 10 c. "Christ Crucified" (Antonello). 20 c. Easter Lily.

1970. No. 219 surch.
306. 2 c. on 2d. red, yell. & grn. 8 8

85. Lignum Vitae.

1970. Decimal currency. Designs as Nos. 217, 219, 221/223, 225/232, but with values inscribed in decimal currency as T **85**.
307. **85.** 1 c. blue, grn. and brn. 5 5
308. – 2 c. red, yellow and green (as 2d.) .. 5 5
309. – 3 c. yellow, black and green (as 3d.) .. 5 5
310. – 4 c. ochre & violet (as 4d.) 5 5
311. – 5 c. multicoloured (as 6d.) 8 5
312. – 8 c. blue and yell. (as 9d.) 12 10
313. – 10 c. blk. & brn. (as 1s.) 15 12
314. – 15 c. black, blue and buff (as 1s. 6d.) .. 20 30
315. – 20 c. brown, black and blue (as 2s.) 30 25
316. – 30 c. blue & grn. (as 3s.) 40 35
317. – 50 c. black, ochre and blue (as 5s.) 75 70
318. – $1 multicoloured (as 10s.) 1·50 1·50
319. – $2 multicoloured (as £1) 3·00 3·00

86. Cable Ship "Dacia".

1970. Telegraph Service. Cent.
320. **86.** 3 c. yell., blk. and red 5 5
321. – 10 c. black and green .. 20 20
322. – 50 c. multicoloured .. 70 75

DESIGNS: 10 c. Bright's Cable Gear aboard "Dacia". 50 c. Morse key and chart.

87. Bananas, Citrus, Sugar-Cane and Tobacco.

1970. Jamaican Agricultural Society. 75th Anniv.
323. **87.** 2 c. multicoloured .. 5 5
324. 10 c. multicoloured .. 15 20

88. "The Projector" (1845).

1970. Jamaican Railways. 125th Anniv.
325. 3 c. Type **88** 10 10
326. 15 c. Engine "54" (1944) 30 30
327. 50 c. Engine "102" (1967) 70 70

89. Church of St. Jago de la Vega.

1971. Dis-establishment of Church of England in Jamaica. Cent.
328. **89.** 3 c. multicoloured .. 5 5
329. 10 c. multicoloured .. 12 12
330. 20 c. multicoloured .. 30 30
331. – 30 c. multicoloured .. 40 40

DESIGNS: 30 c. Emblem of Church of England in Jamaica.

90. Henry Morgan and Ships.

1971. Pirates and Buccaneers. Multicoloured.
332. 3 c. Type **90** 10 10
333. 15 c. Mary Read, Anne Bonny and trial pamphlet 25 25
334. 30 c. Pirate schooner attacking merchantman 50 50

91. 1s. Stamp of 1919 with Frame Inverted.

1971. Post Office. Tercent.
335. – 3 c. black and brown .. 8 8
336. – 5 c. black and green .. 8 10
337. – 8 c. black and violet .. 12 15
338. – 10 c. brn., black and blue 15 15
339. – 20 c. multicoloured .. 25 30
340. **91.** 50 c. brn., black and grey 70 70

DESIGNS—HORIZ. 3 c. Dummer packet letter, 1705. 5 c. Pre-stamp inland letter, 1793. 8 c. Harbour St. P.O., Kingston, 1820. 10 c. Modern stamp and cancellation. 20 c. British stamps used in Jamaica, 1859.

92. Satellite and Dish Aerial.

1972. Opening of Jamaican Earth Satellite Station.
341. **92.** 3 c. multicoloured .. 5 5
342. 15 c. multicoloured .. 20 20
343. 50 c. multicoloured .. 60 65

93. Causeway, Kingston Harbour.

1972. Multicoloured.
344. 1 c. Pimento 5 5
345. 2 c. Red Ginger 5 5
346. 3 c. Bauxite Industry .. 5 5
347. 4 c. Type **93** 5 5
348. 5 c. Oil Refinery 5 5
349. 6 c. Senate Building, University of the West Indies 5 8
350. 8 c. National Stadium .. 8 10
351. 9 c. Devon House .. 10 10
352. 10 c. Air Jamaica Hostess and aircraft 10 12
353. 15 c. Old Iron Bridge, Spanish Town 15 20
354. 20 c. College of Arts, Science and Technology .. 20 25
355. 30 c. Dunn's River Falls .. 30 35
356. 50 c. River rafting .. 55 65
357. $1 Jamaica House .. 1·10 1·25
358. $2 Kings House .. .. 2·10 2·25

The 1, 2, 15 and 30 c. are vert. designs, size 35×27 mm., and the remainder are horiz. as T **93**.

1972. Independence. 10th Anniv. Nos. 346, 352 and 356 optd. **TENTH ANNIVERSARY INDEPENDENCE 1962-1972.**
359. 3 c. multicoloured 5 5
360. 10 c. multicoloured .. 15 15
361. 50 c. multicoloured .. 60 60

94. Arms of Kingston.

1972. Kingston as Capital. Cent.
362. **94.** 5 c. multicoloured .. 8 8
363. 30 c. multicoloured .. 40 40
364. – 50 c. multicoloured .. 60 60

DESIGN—HORIZ. 50 c. design similar to T **94**.

95. Mongoose on Map.

1973. Introduction of the Mongoose. Cent.

No.	Type	Description	Unused	Used
365.	**95.**	8 c. green, yellow-green and black	12	12
366.	–	40 c. cobalt, bl. & black	50	50
367.	–	60 c. pink, salmon & blk.	80	80

DESIGNS: 40 c. Mongoose and rat. 60 c. Mongoose and chicken.

96. " Euphorbia punicea ".

1973. Flora. Multicoloured.

No.	Description	Unused	Used
369.	1 c. Type **96**	5	5
370.	6 c. " Hylocereus triangularis "	8	8
371.	9 c. " Columnea argentea "	10	10
372.	15 c. " Portlandia grandiflora "	20	20
373.	30 c. " Samyda pubescens "	35	35
374.	50 c. "Cordia sebestena "	60	60

97. " Broughtonia sanguinea ".

1973. Orchids. Multicoloured.

No.	Description	Unused	Used
375.	5 c. Type **97**	5	5
376.	10 c. " Arpophyllum jamaicense " (vert.) ..	12	12
377.	20 c. " Oncidium pulchellum " (vert.) ..	25	25
378.	$1 " Brassia maculata "..	1·10	1·10

98. " Mary ", 1808–15.

1974. Mail Packet Boats. Multicoloured.

No.	Description	Unused	Used
380.	5 c. Type **98**	5	8
381.	10 c. " Queensbury ", 1814-27	15	15
382.	15 c. " Sheldrake ", 1829-34	25	25
383.	50 c. " Thames ", 1842 ..	60	60

99. "Journeys".

1974. National Dance Theatre Company. Mult.

No.	Description	Unused	Used
385.	5 c. Type **99**	5	50
386.	10 c. "Jamaican Promenade"	12	12
387.	30 c. "Jamaican Promenade" (diff.)	30	35
388.	50 c. "Misa Criolla" ..	50	55

100. U.P.U. Emblem and Globe.

1974. U.P.U. Centenary.

No.	Type	Description	Unused	Used
390.	**100.**	5 c. multicoloured ..	5	5
391.		9 c. multicoloured ..	10	10
392.		50 c. multicoloured ..	50	55

101. Senate Building and Sir Hugh Wooding.

1975. University of West Indies. 25th Anniv. Multicoloured.

No.	Description	Unused	Used
393.	5 c. Type **101**	5	5
394.	10 c. University Chapel and Princess Alice	12	12
395.	30 c. Type **101**	30	35
396.	50 c. As 10 c.	50	55

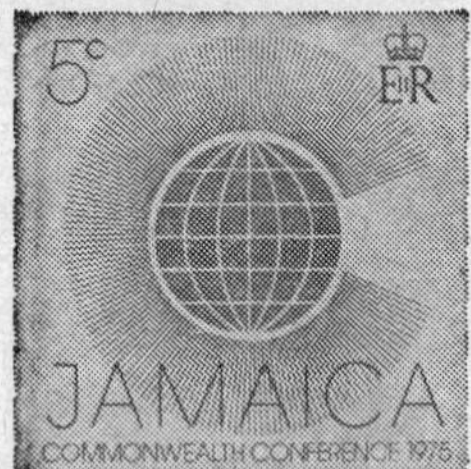

102. Commonwealth Symbol.

1975. Heads of Commonwealth Conf. Mult.

No.	Description	Unused	Used
397.	5 c. Type **102**	5	5
398.	10 c. Jamaican coat of arms	12	12
399.	30 c. Dove of Peace ..	30	35
400.	50 c. Jamaican flag ..	50	55

103. Jamaican Kite Swallowtail.

1975. Butterflies. Multicoloured.

No.	Description	Unused	Used
401.	10 c. Type **103**	12	12
402.	20 c. Jamaican Swallowtail	20	25
403.	25 c. Thersites Swallowtail	25	30
404.	30 c. Homerus Swallowtail	30	35

104. Koo Koo or Actor Boy

1975. Christmas. Belisario prints of " John Canoe " Festival (1st series). Multicoloured

No.	Description	Unused	Used
406.	8 c. Type **104**	8	10
407.	10 c. Red Set-girls ..	12	12
408.	20 c. French Set-girls ..	25	25
409.	50 c. Jaw-bone or House John Canoe	50	60

See also Nos. 421/3.

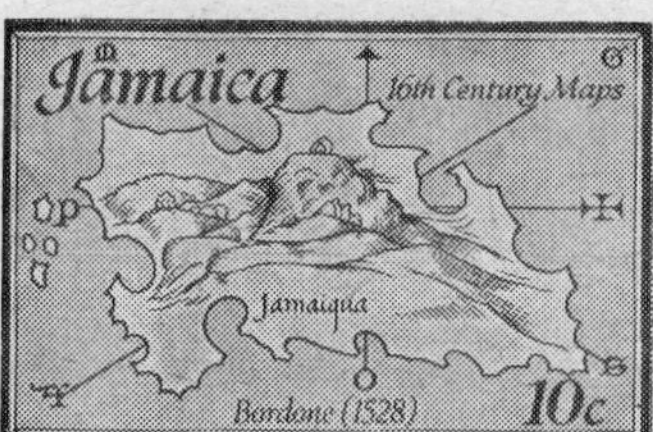

105. Bordone Map. 1528.

1976. 16th Century Maps of Jamaica.

No.	Type	Description	Unused	Used
411.	**105.**	10 c. brn., light brn. & red	10	10
412.	–	20 c. multicoloured ..	20	20
413.	–	30 c. multicoloured ..	30	35
414.	–	50 c. multicoloured ..	50	55

DESIGNS:. 20 c. Porcacchi map, 1576. 30 c. De Bry map, 1594. 50 c. Langenes map, 1598.

106. Olympic Rings.

1976. Olympic Games, Montreal.

No.	Type	Description	Unused	Used
415.	**106.**	10 c. multicoloured ..	12	15
416.		20 c. multicoloured ..	25	30
417.		25 c. multicoloured ..	30	35
418.		50 c. multicoloured ..	60	70

1976. West Indian Victory in World Cricket Cup. As Nos. 559/60 of Barbados.

No.	Description	Unused	Used
419.	15 c. Map of the Caribbean	20	25
420.	15 c. Prudential Cup ..	20	25

1976. Christmas. Belisario Prints (2nd series). As T **104**. Multicoloured.

No.	Description	Unused	Used
421.	10 c. Queen of the set-girls	12	15
422.	20 c. Band of the Jaw-bone John-Canoe	25	30
423.	50 c. Koo Koo (actor-boy)	60	70

OFFICIAL STAMPS

1890. Optd. **OFFICIAL**

No.	Type	Description	Unused	Used
O 3.	**1.**	½d. green..	25	12
O 4.	**2.**	1d. red	35	12
O 5.		2d. grey	50	20

JAMMU AND KASHMIR BC

A state in the extreme N. of India.

1.

1866. Imperf.

No.	Type	Description	Unused	Used
1.	**1.**	½ a. black	5·00	1·25
26.		½ a. red	1·25	1·75
44.		½ a. blue	50	
20.		½ a. green	1·25	
23a.		½ a. yellow	5·00	
15.		1 a. black	4·00	
9.		1 a. red	1·25	
5.		1 a. blue	15·00	8·00
21.		1 a. green	1·75	
24.		1 a. yellow	5·00	
3.		4 a. black	8·00	8·00
28.		4 a red	1·25	
34.		4 a. blue	45	
22.		4 a. green	2·00	
25.		4 a. yellow ..	5·00	

The above prices are for stamps cut round Stamps cut square are worth more.

½ a. ½ a.

1 a. **2.** ½ a.

1867.

No.	Type	Description	Unused	Used
69a.	**2.**	½ a. black	20·00	28·00
56.		½ a. blue	15·00	12·00
60.		½ a. red	1·50	1·50
64.		½ a. orange	22·00	20·00
68.		½ a. green	£175	£110
69b.		1 a. black	£110	£110
67.		1 a. blue	18·00	20·00
61.		1 a. red	3·00	3·00
63.		1 a. orange	18·00	6·00
69.		1 a. green	£175	£110

The characters denoting the value are in the upper part of the inner circle.

3.

4.

1867. Imperf.

No.	Type	Description	Unused	Used
90.	**3.**	¼ a. black	15	15
91.		½ a. blue	40	12
93.		1 a. blue	£1100	£450
95.		1 a. orange	1·50	1·25
97.		2 a. yellow	2·00	1·50
99.		4 a. green	4·00	3·50
101.		8 a. red	4·00	4·00

1878. Imperf. or perf.

No.	Type	Description	Unused	Used
139.	**4.**	⅛ a. yellow	5	5
125.		¼ a. red	25	25
131.		¼ a. orange	3·00	1·50
130a.		¼ a. blue	£110	70·00
142.		¼ a. brown	5	5
105.		½ a. violet	7·00	7·00
126.		½ a. red	20	20
132.		½ a. orange	8·00	6·00
143.		½ a. blue	1·75	
127.		1 a. red	25	30
107.		1 a. mauve	7·00	7·00
133.		1 a. orange	6·00	1·50
148.		1 a. grey	8	8
150.		1 a. green	8	8
108.		2 a. violet	8·00	8·00
110.		2 a. blue	8·00	8·00
128.		2 a. red	40	40
134.		2 a. orange	6·00	2·00
152.		2 a. red on yellow ..	15	10
153.		2 a. red on green ..	20	25
129.		4 a. red	50	60
135.		4 a. orange	8·00	
155.		4 a. green	70	70
130.		8 a. red	60	80
136.		8 a. orange	12·00	
159.		8 a. blue	2·00	2·00
161a.		8 a. lilac	5·00	5·00

OFFICIAL STAMPS

1878. Imperf. or perf.

No.	Type	Description	Unused	Used
O 6.	**4.**	¼ a. black	5	5
O 7.		½ a. black	5	5
O 8.		1 a. black	5	5
O 9.		2 a. black	8	5
O 10.		4 a. black	10	10
O 11.		8 a. black	12	12

JAPAN O2

An empire of E. Asia, consisting of numerous islands.

1871. 100 mon = 1 sen.
1872. 10 rin = 1 sen. 100 sen = 1 yen.

1.

1871. Imperf.

1. 1. 48 m. brown .. .. 45·00 50·00
3. 100 m. blue .. .. 40·00 40·00
5. 200 m. red .. .. 50·00 50·00
7b. 500 m. reen .. .. 48·00 48·00

1872. Perf.

17. 1. ½ s. brown .. .. 25·00 30·00
19. 1 s. blue .. .. 38·00 38·00
21. 2 s. red .. .. 75·00 70·00
22. 5 s. green .. .. 85·00 85·00

2. 3. 4. Wild Goose.

1872. Various sizes. Design details differ.

34. 2. ½ s. brown .. .. 5·00 3·75
66. ½ s. grey .. .. 4·00 3·50
41. 1 s. blue .. .. 10·00 6·00
67. 1 s. brown .. .. 12·00 3·75
42. 2 s. red .. .. 15·00 9·00
55. 2 s. yellow .. .. 38·00 7·00
46. 4 s. rose .. .. 14·00 8·00
68. 4 s. green .. .. 28·00 4·25
75. 3. 5 s. green .. .. 42·00 15·00
57. 6 s. brown .. .. 42·00 11·00
69. 6 s. orange .. .. 25·00 5·00
58. 2. 10 s. green .. .. 18·00 10·00
70. 10 s. blue .. .. 25·00 4·50
59. 20 s. violet .. .. 50·00 18·00
71. 20 s. red .. .. 15·00 3·25
60. 30 s. black .. .. 38·00 15·00
72. 30 s. violet .. .. 30·00 13·00

1875.

61. 4. 12 s. rose .. .. 45·00 30·00
62. – 15 s. lilac (Wagtail) .. 50·00 25·00
63. – 45 a. red (Hawk) .. .. 70·00 25·00

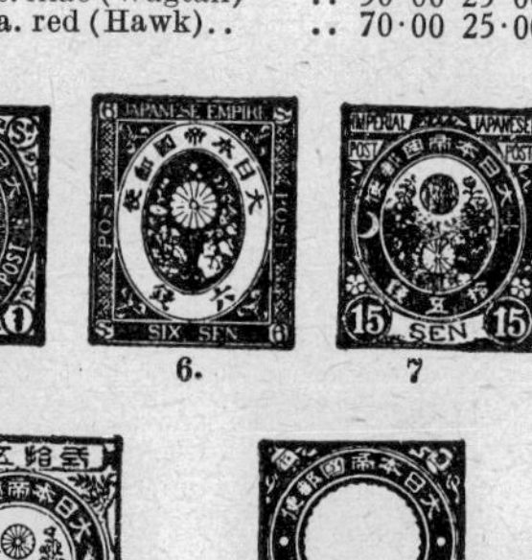

5. 6. 7

8. 9.

1876.

116. 5. 5 r. grey .. .. 1·25 8
77. 1 s. black .. .. 3·25 12
78. 1 s. brown .. .. 1·50 8
113. 1 s. green .. .. 1·50 10
79. 2 s. grey .. .. 4·50 10
80. 2 s. violet .. .. 3·75 8
114. 2 s. red .. .. 1·50 10
81. 3 s. orange .. .. 13·00 4·25
117. 3 s. claret .. .. 5·50 8
82a. 4 s. blue .. .. 5·00 45
103. 4 s. green .. .. 7·50 8
118. 4 s. bistre .. .. 4·75 8
83. 6. 5 s. brown .. .. 12·00 1·00
115. 5 s. blue .. .. 5·50 12
104. 6 s. orange .. .. 25·00 2·50
105. 8 s. brown .. .. 8·00 20
119. 8 s. violet .. .. 7·00 10
106. 10 s. blue .. .. 11·00 15
120. 10 s. brown .. .. 8·00 8
87. 12 s. rose .. .. 75·00 35·00
88. 7. 15 s. green .. .. 30·00 1·00
121. 15 s. violet .. .. 18·00 10
89. 20 s. blue .. .. 35·00 3·75
122. 20 s. orange .. .. 20·00 10
123. 8. 25 s. green .. .. 40·00 20
110. 7. 30 s. mauve .. .. 65·00 35·00
91. 45 s. red £120 £110
99. 50 s. red .. .. 26·00 60
124. 50 s. brown .. .. 35·00 1·60
125. 9. 1 y. red .. .. 55·00 1·75

10. Imperial Crest and Cranes.

1894. Emperor's Silver Wedding.

126. 10. 2 s. red .. .. 8·00 80
127. 5 a. blue .. .. 16·00 5·00

11. Prince Kitashirakawa.

12. Prince Arisugawa.

1896. China War.

128. 11. 2 s. red .. .. 8·00 1·10
129. 12. 2 s. red .. .. 8·00 1·10
130. 11. 5 s. blue .. .. 24·00 1·25
131. 12. 5 s. blue .. .. 24·00 1·25

Both 2 s. have an oval medallion, and both 5 s. a circular one.

13.

14.

15.

16.

17. Empress Jingu.

1899.

132. 13. 5 r. grey .. .. 1·40 15
133. ½ s. grey 60 8
134. 1 s. brown .. .. 1·00 8
135. 1½ s. blue .. .. 4·50 20
136. 1½ s. violet .. .. 3·00 8
137. 2 s. green .. .. 2·25 8
138. 3 s. claret .. .. 3·00 8
139. 3 s. red .. .. 1·75 8
140. 4 s. rose .. .. 1·60 25
141. 5 s. yellow .. .. 5·00 10
142. 14. 6 s. claret .. .. 9·00 70
143. 8 s. olive .. .. 13·00 90
144. 10 s. blue .. .. 3·50 8
145. 15 s. violet .. .. 10·00 15
146. 20 s. orange .. .. 11·00 10
147. 15. 25 s. green .. .. 25·00 30
148. 50 s. brown .. .. 23·00 40
149. 16. 1 y. red .. .. 30·00 50
183. 17. 5 y. green .. .. £160 1·75
184. 10 y. violet .. .. £275 2·50

18. Rice Cakes used at Japanese Weddings.

ILLUSTRATIONS
British Commonwealth and all overprints and surcharges are FULL SIZE. Foreign Countries have been reduced to ¾-LINEAR.

1900. Prince Imperial Wedding.

152. 18. 3 s. red .. .. .. 12·00 50

19. Symbols of Korea and Japan. 20. Gun and Japanese Flag.

1905. Amalgamation of Japanese and Korean Postal Services.

153. 19. 3 s. red .. .. .. 35·00 6·00

1906. Triumphal Military Review of Russo-Japanese War.

154. 20. 1½ s. blue .. .. 17·00 1·10
155. 3 s. red .. .. 30·00 5·00

21.

22.

23.

1913.

167. 21. ½ s. brown .. .. 1·00 8
231. 1 s. orange .. .. 1·25 30
232. 1½ s. blue 95 8
170. 2 s. green .. .. 1·25 8
171. 3 s. red 75 8
172. 22. 4 s. red .. .. 8·00 35
300. 5 s. violet .. .. 3·50 8
174. 6 s. brown .. .. 8·00 1·25
302. 7 s. orange .. .. 5·00 12
303. 8 s. grey .. .. 7·50 30
176. 10 s. blue .. .. 4·25 8
236. 13 s. brown .. .. 4·50 8
178. 22. 20 s. claret .. .. 22·00 40
179. 25 s. olive .. .. 6·50 50
180. 23. 30 s. chestnut .. .. 12·00 35
238. 30 s. orange and green 14·00 15
181. 50 s. chocolate .. .. 15·00 55
239. 50 s. chestnut and blue 9·00 20
309. 1 y. green and brown .. 32·00 25

24. Ceremonial Cap. 26. Hall of Ceremony.

1915. Emperor's Coronation.

185. 24. 1½ s. grey and red .. 2·25 45
186. – 3 s. violet and orange .. 2·50 60
187. 26. 4 s. red .. .. 9·50 5·00
188. 10 s. blue .. .. 17·00 8·50

DESIGN: 3 s. Imperial throne.

27. Mandarin Duck. 28. "Kammuri" (Ceremonial Cap).

1916. Proclamation of Prince Hirohito as Heir Apparent.

189. 27. 1½ s. green, red & yellow 2·50 70
190. 3 s. red and yellow .. 3·50 85
191. 28. 10 s. blue .. .. £250 95·00

29. Dove of Peace. 30. Dove of Peace.

1919. Restoration of Peace.

192. 29. 1½ s. brown .. .. 1·75 80
193. 30. 3 s. green .. .. 2·40 85
194. 29. 4 s. red .. .. 5·00 2·50
195. 30. 10 s. blue .. .. 14·00 5·50

1919. Air. 1st Tokyo-Osaka Airmail Service. Optd. with aeroplane.

196. 21. 1½ s. blue £120 35
197. 3 s. red £180 85

31. 7th Century Censor. 32. Meiji Shrine.

1920. First Census.

198. 31. 1½ s. purple .. .. 6·00 2·50
199. 3 s. red .. .. 6·00 2·50

1920. Dedication of Meiji Shrine.

200. 32. 1½ s. violet .. .. 2·40 80
201. 3 s. red .. .. 2·40 80

33. Postal and National Flags.

34. Dept. of Communications, Tokyo.

1921. 50th Anniv. Japanese Post

202. 33. 1½ s. red and green .. 2·25 90
203. 34. 3 s. brown .. .. 3·00 1·10
204. 33. 4 s. red .. .. 35·00 14·00
205. 34. 10 s. blue .. .. £150 55·00

35. Warships "Katori" and "Kashima".

36. Mt. Fuji and Deer.

1921. Return of Crown Prince from Europe.

206. 35. 1½ s. violet .. .. 2·10 85
207. 3 s. olive .. .. 2·40 85
208. 4 s. red .. .. 23·00 8·50
209. 10 s. blue .. .. 28·00 11·00

1922.

293. 36. 4 s. green .. .. 2·10 20
266. 4 s. orange .. .. 5·00 12
211. 8 s. red .. .. 11·00 4·00
267. 8 s. olive .. .. 8·00 12
305. 20 s. blue .. .. 8·50 20
268. 20 s. purple .. .. 28·00 20

37. Mt. Nitaka.

38.

39.

40. Empress Jingu.

1923. Crown Prince's visit to Formosa.

213. 37. 1½ s. yellow .. .. 8·00 4·75
214. 3 s. violet .. .. 10·00 3·75

1923. Imperf.

215. 38. ½ s. grey .. .. 1·75 1·40
216. 1½ s. blue .. .. 2·75 80
217. 2 s. brown .. .. 1·75 70
218. 3 s. red .. .. 1·50 60
219. 4 s. green .. .. 9·50 8·00
220. 5 s. violet .. .. 5·50 80
221. 8 s. red .. .. 16·00 12·00
222. 39. 10 s. brown .. .. 11·00 85
223. 20 s. blue .. .. 15·00 1·00

1924.

224a. 40. 5 y. green .. .. £100 1·40
225a. 10 y. violet .. .. £180 1·00

41. Cranes.

42. Phoenix.

1925. Imperial Silver Wedding.

226. 41. 1½ s. purple .. .. 1·50 70
227. 42. 3 s. brown and silver .. 2·75 1·40
228. 41. 8 s. red .. .. 10·00 5·50
229. 42. 20 s. green and silver .. 45·00 35·00

43. Yomei Gate, Nikko.

DESIGNS: 2 s. Mt. Fuji
10 s. Nagoya Castle

1926.

241. – 2 s. green .. .. 1·00 8
242. 43. 6 s. red .. .. 4·75 15
243. – 10 s. blue .. .. 4·00 8
304. – 10 s. red .. .. 4·50 15

44. Baron Maeshima.

45. Globe.

1927. Entry into U.P.U. 50th Anniv.

244.	44.	1½ s. purple	2·00	20
245.		3 s. olive	2·00	25
246.	45.	6 s. red	35·00	27·00
247.		10 s. blue	45·00	28·00

46. Phoenix.

47. Ceremonial Shrines.

1928. Emperor's Enthronement.

248.	46.	1½ s. green on yellow	1·00	40
249.	47.	3 s. purple on yellow	1·00	40
250.	46.	6 s. red on yellow	2·75	1·40
251.	47.	10 s. blue on yellow	3·25	1·75

48. Shrine of Ise.

49. Aeroplane over Lake Ashi, Hakone.

1929. 58th Vicennial Removal of Shrine.

255.	48.	1½ s. violet	1·40	70
256.		3 s. red	2·10	70

1929. Air.

257.	49.	8½ s. brown	16·00	11·00
258.		9½ s. red	4·50	2·40
259.		16½ s. green	5·00	3·75
260.		18 s. blue	7·50	2·75
261.		33 s. grey	16·00	2·40

50. Japan.

51. Meiji Shrine.

1930. 2nd Census.

262.	50.	1½ s. purple	2·10	85
263.		3 s. red	2·40	1·00

Although Type **50** is inscr. "Second Census", this was actually the third census.

1930. Meiji Shrine Dedication. 10th Anniv.

264.	51.	1½ s. green	1·50	80
265.		3 s. orange	2·10	1·00

52. Red Cross Society Insignia.

DESIGN—HORIZ. 3 s., 10 s. Red Cross Society Buildings, Tokyo.

1934. 15th Int. Red Cross Conf., Tokyo.

272.	52.	1½ s. green	2·00	80
273.	–	3 s. violet	2·25	1·00
274.	52.	6 s. red	8·50	3·50
275.	–	10 s. blue	11·00	5·00

54. Cruiser "Hiyei" and Pagoda, Liaoyang.

55. Akasaka Palace, Tokyo.

1935. Visit of Emperor of Manchukuo.

276.	54.	1½ s. olive-green	1·50	70
277.	55.	3 s. brown	2·10	85
278.	54.	6 s. red	7·00	3·00
279.	55.	10 s. blue	11·00	3·75

56. Mt. Fuji.

57. Mt. Fuji from Mishima.

1935. New Year's Greetings.

280.	56.	1½ s. red	6·50	15

1936. Fuji-Hakone National Park.

281.	–	1½ s. brown	3·25	2·00
282.	–	3 s. green	6·00	3·50
283.	–	6 s. red	12·00	7·00
284.	57.	10 s. blue	16·00	8·50

DESIGNS: Mt. Fuji (1½ s.), from Lake Ashi (3 s.), from Lake Kawaguchi (6 s.).

58. Dove of Peace.

59. Shinto Shrine Port Arthur.

1936. 30 years Occupation of Kwantung.

285.	58.	1½ s. violet	7·50	6·00
286.	59.	3 s. brown	8·00	7·00
287.	–	10 s. green	80·00	55·00

DESIGN—HORIZ. 10 s. Govt. House, Kwantung.

61. Imperial Diet.

DESIGN: 3 s., 6 s. Grand Staircase.

1936. Inauguration of New Houses of the Imperial Diet, Tokyo.

288.	61.	1½ s. green	2·00	85
289.	–	3 s. purple	2·10	1·00
290.	–	6 s. red	5·00	3·25
291.	61.	10 s. blue	8·50	4·25

63. "Wedded Rocks", Futamigaura.

64. Aeroplane.

1936. New Year's Greetings.

292.	63.	1½ s. red	2·75	15

1937. Aerodrome Fund

313.	64.	2 s.+2 s. red	1·60	60
314.		3 s.+2 s. violet	1·60	1·00
315.		4 s.+2 s. green	2·40	85

65. Goshuinbune (primitive merchant vessel).

66. General Nogi.

67. Lake Taisho, Kamikochi.

68. Aeroplane and Map.

69. Kamatari Fujiwara.

70. Plum Tree.

1937. Imperf. of perf.

316.	65.	½ s. violet	25	12
317.	–	1 s. brown	50	10
318.	66.	2 s. red	20	8
319.	–	3 s. green	15	8
394.	66.	3 s. brown	20	8
320.	–	4 s. green	20	8
321.	67.	5 s. blue	40	8
396.	–	5 s. claret	15	10
322.	–	6 s. orange	80	30
323.	–	7 s. green	20	8
398.	–	7 s. red	12	10
324.	–	8 s. violet	20	8
325.	–	10 s. red	1·40	8
326.	48.	12 s. slate	20	12
327.	–	14 s. lake and red	30	10
328.	–	20 s. blue	30	8
329.	–	25 s. brown	30	8
330.	–	30 s. blue	45	8
331.	–	50 s. olive and bistre	45	8
332.	–	1 y. brown	1·10	20
424.	69.	5 y. olive	1·60	25
334.	70.	10 y. purple	9·50	30

DESIGNS: 1 s. Rice Harvesting. 3 s. Hydro-Electric Power Station. 4 s., 5 s. (No. 296), 7 s. (No. 398), Admiral Togo. 6 s. Garambi Lighthouse, Taiwan. 7 s. (No. 323) Diamond Mts. Korea. 8 s. Meiji Shrine. 10 s. Yomei Gate, Nikko. 14 s. Kasuga Shrine. 20 s. Mt. Fuji and cherry blossom. 25 s. Horyu Temple. 30 s. Torii, Itsukushima Shrine at Miyajima. 50 s. Kinkaku Temple. 1 y. Great Buddha, Kamakura.

ILLUSTRATIONS
British Commonwealth and all overprints and surcharges are FULL SIZE. Foreign Countries have been reduced to ¾-LINEAR.

71. New Year's Emblem.

1937. New Year's Greetings.

339.	71.	2 s. red	3·75	15

73. Nantai Volcano.

75. Shinkyo Bridge.

76. Hiuchi Volcano.

74. Kegon Falls.

1938. National Parks. (a) Nikko Park.

340.	73.	2 s. brown	70	40
341.	74.	4 s. green	55	40
342.	75.	10 s. red	3·75	2·10
343.	76.	20 s. blue	3·50	2·10

Types **77** to **100**. Actual size, 39×22 mm.

77/80 (illustrations much reduced).

(b) Daisen and Setonaikai Parks.

345.	77.	2 s brown	45	40
346.	78.	4 s. green	75	55
347.	79.	10 s. red	5·00	2·25
348.	80.	20 s. blue	5·00	2·25

DESIGNS: 2 s. Daisen Volcano and meadow. 4 s. Yashima plateau and estuary. 10 s. Abuto Kwannon shrine. 20 s. Tomo Bay.

81/4 (illustrations much reduced).

(c) Aso Park.

350.	81.	2 s. brown	45	35
351.	82.	4 s. green	2·00	1·40
352.	83.	10 s. red	17·00	8·50
353.	84.	20 s. blue	22·00	9·50

DESIGNS: 2 s. Mt. Kuju and village. 4 s. Naka Volcano. 10 s. Naka crater. 20 s. Volcanic Cones of Mt. Aso.

85/8 (illustrations much reduced).

(d) Daisetsu-zan Park.

363.	85.	2 s. brown	45	35
364.	86.	4 s. green	1·40	1·00
365.	87.	10 s. red	4·25	2·25
366.	88.	20 s. blue	5·00	2·25

DESIGNS—HORIZ. 2 s. Mt. Hokuchin. 4 s. Mt. Asahi. 20 s. Tokachi Range. VERT. 10 s. So-unkyo Gorge, Kobako.

89/92 (illustrations much reduced).

(e) Kirishima Park. Kyushu.

368.	89.	2 s. brown	40	35
369.	90.	4 s. green	70	55
370.	91.	10 s. red	3·50	2·40
371.	92.	20 s. blue	4·00	2·75

DESIGNS: 2 s. Mt. Karakuni. 4 s. Takachiho Peak. 10 s. Kirishima Shrine. 20 s. Lake Roku-Kwannon.

93/6 (illustrations much reduced).

(f) Daiton and Niitaka-Arisan Parks.

375.	93.	2 s. brown	65	55
376.	94.	4 s. green	75	65
377.	95.	10 s. red	1·60	1·10
378.	96.	20 s. blue	1·75	1·10

DESIGNS: 2 s. Mt. Daiton. 4 s. Central Peak, Mt. Niitaka. 10 s. Buddhist Temple, Mt. Kwannon. 20 s. View from Mt. Niitaka.

97/100 (illustrations much reduced).

(g) Tsugitaka and Taroko Park.

380.	97.	2 s. brown	65	55
381.	98.	4 s. green	75	65
382.	99.	10 s. red	1·60	1·10
383.	100.	20 s. blue	1·75	1·10

DESIGNS—VERT. 2 s. Seisui Precipice, East Formosan coast. 10 s. Taroko Gorge. HORIZ. 4 s. Mt. Tsugitaka. 20 s. Upper reaches of R. Takkiri.

101. Globe.

DESIGN: 4 s., 20 s. Count Tsunetami Sano.

1939. International Red Cross Union. 75th Anniv. of Membership.

355.	101.	2 s. brown	1·10	70
356.	–	4 s. green	1·25	70
357.	101.	10 s. red	5·00	4·25
358.	–	20 s. blue	7·00	4·25

102. Golden Bird.

103. Mt. Takachiho.

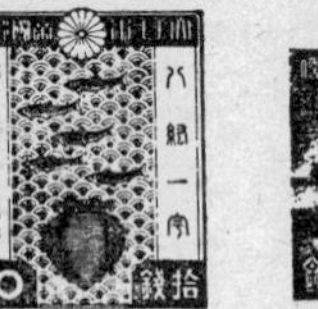

104. Sake Jar and Trout.

105. Kashiwara Shrine.

1940. Japanese Empire. 26th Cent.

359.	102.	2 s. brown	85	50
360.	103.	4 s. green	40	25
361.	104.	10 s. red	3·75	2·40
362.	105.	20 s. blue	85	70

106. Ceremonial Shrine (after Y. Ataka).

107. "Loyalty and Filial Piety".

1940. Imperial Rescript on Education 50th Anniv.
373. **106.** 2 s. violet 85 45
374. **107.** 4 s. green .. .. 1·10 45

シンガポール 陥落 +1
(108.)

109. Kenkoku Shrine.

110. Orchids and Crest of Manchukuo.

1942. Surrender of Singapore. With additional inscr. as T **108.**
385. **66.** 2 s.+1 s. red and blue 45 35
386. – 4 s.+2 s. green & red (No. 320) 45 35

1942. Establishment of Manchukuo. 10th Anniv.
387. **109.** 2 s. brown 35 25
388. – 5 s. olive 55 30
389. **109.** 10 s. red 80 55
390. **110.** 20 s. blue .. .. 2·00 1·40
DESIGN—VERT. 5 s. Boys of Japan and Manchukuo.

111. Girl War-worker.
112. "The Enemy will surrender".
113. Garambi Lighthouse.
114. Garambi Lighthouse. 

1942. Imperf. or perf.
391. **111.** 1 s. brown 8 8
393. – 2 s. green 10 8
395. – 4 s. green 10 8
397. – 6 s. blue 10 8
399. – 10 s. red and pink .. 20 10
400. **112.** 10 s. grey 55 15
417. – 10 s. blue .. .. 2·25 2·25
419. – 10 s. orange 5 5
401. – 15 s. blue 25 10
402. – 17 s. violet 20 8
420. – 20 s. blue 12 8
404. – 27 s. purple 50 20
405. – 30 s. green 60 20
421. – 30 s. blue 30 15
406. **113.** 40 s. purple 25 8
407. **114.** 40 s. purple 50 20
DESIGNS: 2 s. Shipbuilding. 4 s. Hyuga Monument and Mt. Fuji. 6 s. War-worker, 10 s. (No. 399) Palms and map of Greater East Asia. 10 s. (No. 419), 20 s. Mt. Fuji. 15 s. Airman. 17 s., 27 s. Yasukuni Shrine. 30 s. 2) Myajima Shrine.

115. Locomotive.
116. Tanks in action at Bataan.

1942. First National Railway. 70th Anniv.
408. **115.** 5 s. green .. .. 2·50 1·25

1942. Declaration of War. 1st Anniv.
409. **116.** 2 s.+1 s. brown .. 1·50 1·00
410. – 5 s.+2 s. blue .. 1·90 1·00
DESIGN: 5 s. Attack on Pearl Harbour.

117. Yasukuni Shrine.
118. Kwantung Shrine and Map of Kwantung Peninsula.

1944. Yasukuni Shrine. 75th Anniv.
411. **117.** 7 s. green 60 45

1944. Dedication of Kwantung Shrine.
412. **118.** 3 s. brown .. .. 2·00 2·00
413. 7 s. grey .. .. 2·25 2·25

119. Sun and Cherry Blossom.
120. Torii of Yasukuni Shrine.

1945. Imperf. or perf.
415. **119.** 3 s. claret 10 8
416. – 5 s. green 10 8
422. – 50 s. brown 15 8
423. **120.** 1 y. olive 60 50
DESIGNS: 5 s. Sunrise and Aeroplane. 50 s. Coal miners.

121. Pagoda of Horyu Temple, Nara.
122. Kiyomizu Temple, Kyoto.
123. Noh Mask.

1946. Imperf., perf. or roul.
426. – 15 s. green 15 12
427. **121.** 30 s. violet 20 8
428. – 1 y. blue 45 8
445. **121.** 1 y. 20 green 40 8
429. – 1 y. 30 brown 70 20
430. – 1 y. 50 grey 70 12
431. **122.** 2 y. red 70 8
446. – 4 y. blue .. .. 1·40 8
432. – 5 y. mauve .. .. 2·10 12
449. – 10 y. purple .. .. 13·00 25
433. **123.** 50 y. brown .. .. 18·00 30
434. – 100 y. claret .. .. 17·00 25
DESIGNS: 15 s. Baron H. Maeshima. 1 y. Mt. Fuji, after Hokusai. 1 y. 30, 4 y. Wild Geese, after Hokusai. 1 y. 50, Kintai Bridge, Iwakuni. 5 y. Goldfish. 10 y., 100 y. Plum tree.

124. Mediaeval Postman's Bell.
125. Baron Maeshima.

1946. Govt. Postal Service. 75th Anniv.
436. **124.** 15 s. orange .. .. 2·00 1·10
437. **125.** 30 s. green .. .. 2·40 2·40
438. – 50 s. red .. .. 1·90 1·10
439 – 1 y. blue .. .. 1·90 1·10
DESIGNS—As T **124**: 50 s. First Japanese Postage Stamp. 1 y. Symbols of communication.

126.
127. Baron Maeshima.
128. National Art.

1947.
442. **126.** 35 s. green 20 8
443. – 45 s. magenta 20 20
444. **127.** 1 y. brown 50 12
447. – 5 y. blue .. .. 1·50 8
448. **128.** 10 y. violet .. .. 6·00 8
DESIGNS—VERT. 45 s. Numeral type as T **126.** 5 y. Whaling.

For similar designs, but without the chrysanthemum emblem, see Nos. 467/70.

129. Mother and Child.
129a. Roses and Wistaria.

1947. New Constitution. Inaug.
451. **129.** 50 s. red 35 15
452. **129a.** 1 y. blue 45 15

130. National Products.
131. Lily of the Valley.

1947. Re-opening of Private Foreign Trade.
455. **130.** 1 y. 20 brown .. .. 2·00 55
456. 4 y. blue .. .. 3·75 70

1947. Relief of Ex-convicts Day.
458. **131.** 2 y. green .. .. 2·25 1·00

132. Hurdling.
133.

1947. 2nd National Athletic Meeting, Kanazawa.
460. **132.** 1 y. 20 magenta .. 3·50 1·75
461. – 1 y. 20 mag. (diving) 3·50 1·75
462. – 1 y. 20 magenta (discus throwing) .. .. 3·50 1·75
463. – 1 y. 30 magenta (volley-ball) .. .. 3·50 1·75

Issued in sheets containing the four designs in se-tenant blocks.

1947. Community Chest.
465. **133.** 1 y. 20+80 s. red .. 60 50

133a. Kiyomizu Temple, Kyoto.
133b. National Art.

1948. Designs without chrysanthemum.
467. – 1 y. 50 blue 40 8
468. **133a.** 2 y. red 90 8
469. – 3 y. 80 brown .. 1·50 1·00
470. **133b.** 10 y. violet .. .. 5·50 8
DESIGNS: 1 y. 50, 3 y. 80, Numeral types.

134. Stylised Tree.
135. Boy and Girl reading.

1948. Encouragement of Afforestation.
474. **134.** 1 y. 20 green 60 25

1948. Re-organisation of Educational System.
480. **135.** 1 y. 20 claret 70 25

136. Horse Race.
137. Swimmer.

1948. Japanese Horse Racing Laws. 25th Anniv.
481. **136.** 5 y. brown .. .. 1·50 50

1948. 3rd National Athletic Meeting, Yawata.
482. **137.** 5 y. blue .. .. 2·00 55

138. Distillery Towers.
139. Nurse.
140. Bird Feeding Young. 

1948. Govt. Alcohol Monopoly. 10th Anniv.
483. **138.** 5 y. olive .. .. 2·00 55

1948. Red Cross and Community Chest.
485. **139.** 5 y.+2 y. 50 red .. 3·50 1·60
486. **140.** 5 y.+2 y. 50 green 3·50 1·60

141. Farm Girl.
142. Harpooning.
143. Miner.
144. Girl plucking Tea. 
145. Girl Printer.
145a. Mill Girl.
145b Mt. Hodaka. 
145c. Tree Planting.
145d. Postman. 
145e. Blast-Furnace.
145f. Locomotive Construction.

1948.
488. **141.** 2 y. green 45 8
489. **142.** 3 y. turquoise .. 70 8
490. **143.** 5 y. olive-bistre .. 4·50 8
491. **144.** 5 y. green .. .. 6·50 1·10
492. **145.** 6 y. orange .. .. 1·25 8
493. **143.** 8 y. chestnut .. 2·00 8
494. **145a.** 15 y. blue 50 8
495. **145b.** 16 y. blue .. .. 2·00 1·25
496. **145c.** 20 y. green .. .. 5·50 8
497. **145d.** 30 y. blue .. .. 6·50 8
506. **145e.** 100 y. red .. .. 45·00 25
507. **145f.** 500 y. blue .. .. 40·00 30

146. Baseball.
146a. "Woman looking back" (after Moronobu).
147. Girl playing with Shuttlecock.

1948. 3rd National Athletic Meeting, Fukuoke.
509. **146.** 5 y. green .. .. 4·50 1·40
510. – 5 y. green (bicycle race) 4·50 1·40
511. – 5 y. green (sprinter) .. 4·50 1·40
512. – 5 y. green (high jumper) 4·50 1·40

Issued in sheets containing blocks of the four designs se-tenant.

1948. Philatelic Week.
514. **146a.** 5 y. brown .. .. 28·00 17·00

1948. New Year s Greetings.
516. **147.** 2 y. red .. .. 3·25 1·40

148. Skater.
149. Ski-jumper.

1949. 4th National Athletic Meeting.

(a) Suwa City.

517. **148.** 5 y. violet .. .. 1·60 70

(b) Sapporo, Hokkaido.

518. **149.** 5 y. blue .. .. 2·10 65

150. Beppu Harbour.  **151.** Exhibition Grounds.

1949.

519. **150.** 2 y. blue and red .. 80 35
520. 5 y. blue and green .. 2·40 55

1949. Foreign Trade Fair, Yokohama. Perf. or imperf.

521. **151.** 5 y. red .. .. 2·00 55

152. Seto Inland Sea.  **153.** Stylised Trees.

1949. Matsuyama, Okayama and Takamatsu Exhibitions.

522. **152.** 10 y. red (Matsuyama) 10·00 3·25
523. 10 y. pink (Okayama) 14·00 4·25
524. 10 y. clar. (Takamatsu) 20·00 6·50

1949. Encouragement of Afforestation.

525. **153.** 5 y. green .. .. 2·00 50

154/7 (illustrations much reduced).

1949. Yoshino-Kumano National Park.

526. **154.** 2 y. brown 70 20
527. **155.** 5 y. green .. .. 2·00 35
528. **156.** 10 y. red .. .. 7·00 2·00
529. **157.** 16 y. blue .. .. 2·10 85

DESIGNS: 2 y. Shishi-Iwa (Lion Rock). 5 y. Mt. Omine. 10 y. Ooro-Hatcho (river pool). 16 y. Hashikui-Iwa.

ILLUSTRATIONS
British Commonwealth and all overprints and surcharges are FULL SIZE. Foreign Countries have been reduced to ¾-LINEAR.

158. Japanese Boy.

1949. Children's Day.

531. **158.** 5 y. purple and buff .. 4·50 70

159. Observatory Tower.  **160.** Radio Mast, Pigeon and Globe.

1949. Central Meteorological Observatory. Tokyo. 75th Anniv.

534. **159.** 8 y. green .. .. 2·00 55

1949. Establishment of Joint Ministries of Postal and Electrical Communications.

535. **160.** 8 y. blue .. .. 2·00 75

161/4. Autumn, Spring, Summer, Winter. (illustrations much reduced).

1949. Fuji-Hakone National Park.

536. **161.** 2 y. brown .. .. 1·10 20
537. **162.** 8 y. green .. .. 1·25 35
538. **163.** 14 y. red .. .. 1·00 15
539. **164.** 24 y. blue .. .. 1·10 15

165. Woman holding Rose.

167. Swimmer.  **166.** Doves.

1949. Establishment of Memorial City at Hiroshima.

541. **165.** 8 y. brown .. .. 3·50 1·00

1949. Establishment of Int. Cultural City at Nagasaki.

542. **166.** 8 y. green .. .. 2·50 85

1949. 4th National Swimming Meeting.

543. **167.** 8 y. blue .. .. 2·00 1·00

168. Boy Scout.  **169.** Symbolical of Writing and Printing.

1949. 1st National Scout Jamboree, Tokyo.

544. **168.** 8 y. brown .. .. 4·50 1·00

1949. Press Week.

545. **169.** 8 y. blue .. .. 3·00 1·00

170. Map of Japan and Letters.  **171.** Globe and Forms of Transport.

1949. U.P.U. 75th Anniv.

546. **170.** 2 y. green .. .. 1·50 60
547. **171.** 8 y. claret .. .. 2·10 60
548. **170.** 14 y. red .. .. 5·50 2·00
549. **171.** 24 y. blue .. .. 7·00 2·50

172. Javelin Throwing.  **173.** Telescope.

1949. 4th National Athletic Meeting, Tokyo.

551. **172.** 8 y. brown .. .. 2·75 80
552. – 8 y. brown (yachting) 2·75 80
553. – 8 y. brn. (relay racing) 2·75 80
554. – 8 y. brown (tennis) .. 2·75 80

Issued in sheets containing the four designs in se-tenant blocks.

1949. Establishment of Latitude Observatory, Mizusawa. 50th Anniv.

555. **173.** 8 y. green .. .. 2·00 50

174. "Moon and Geese" (after Hiroshige).  **175.** Dr. H. Noguchi.

A B C D

E F G H I

J K L M N

O P Q R

1949. Postal Week.

556. **174.** 8 y. violet .. .. 50·00 18·00

1949. Various portraits as illustrated, in frame as T **175.**

557. A. 8 y. emerald .. .. 5·50 40
558. B. 8 y. grey-olive .. 2·00 40
559. C. 8 y. blue-green .. 2·00 40
560. D. 8 y. blue-green .. 2·00 40
561. E. 8 y. violet .. .. 4·50 1·00
562. F. 8 y brown-purple .. 2·00 40
563. G. 8 y. grey-green .. 2·75 70
564. H. 8 y. violet .. .. 2·75 55
565. I. 8 y. red .. .. 6·50 80
566. J. 8 y. brown-lake .. 8·50 80
567. K. 8 y. brown .. .. 6·00 80
568. L. 8 y. blue .. .. 3·25 80
569. M. 10 y. green .. .. 30·00 1·25
570. N. 10 y. maroon .. .. 4·50 45
571. O. 10 y. red .. .. 2·10 45
572. P. 10 y. slate .. .. 2·10 45
573. Q. 10 y. brown .. .. 2·40 45
574. R. 10 y. grey-blue .. 2·50 45

PORTRAITS: A, Hideyo Noguchi (bacteriologist). B, Y. Fukuzawa (educationist). C, Soseki Natsume (novelist). D, Shoyo Tsobouchi (dramatist). E, Danjuro Ichikawa (actor). F, Jo Niijima (religious leader). G, Hogai Kano (painter). H, Kanzo Uchimura (religious leader). I, Mme. Higuchi (author). J, Ogai Mori (doctor). K, S. Masaoka (poet). L, S. Hishida (painter). M, A. Nishi (scholar). N, K. Ume (lawyer) O, H. Kimura (astrophysicist). P, I. Nitobe (statesman). Q. T. Terada (physicist). R. T. Okakura (painter).

176. Pheasant and Pampas Grass.  **177.** Tiger (after Maruyama Okyo).

1950. Air.

575. **176.** 16 y. grey .. .. 7·00 2·40
576. 34 y. purple .. 14·00 3·00
577. 59 y. red .. .. 20·00 3·50
578. 103 y. orange .. 11·00 3·75
579. 144 y. olive .. 14·00 3·75

1950. New Year's Greetings.

580. **177.** 2 y. red .. .. 4·25 45

179. Microphones of 1925 and 1950.  **180.** Dove.

1950. Japanese Broadcasting System. 25th Anniv.

582. **179.** 8 y. blue .. .. 2·25 50

1950. Joint Ministries of Postal and Electrical Communications. 1st Anniv.

583. **180.** 8 y. green .. .. 2·00 50

181/4 (illustrations much reduced).

1950. Akan National Park.

584. **181.** 2 y. brown .. .. 1·00 20
585. **182.** 8 y. green .. .. 1·40 35
586. **183.** 14 y. red .. .. 5·50 1·00
587. **184.** 24 y. blue .. .. 6·50 1·40

DESIGNS: 2 y. Lake Akan and Mt. O.-Akani. 8 y. Lake Kutcharo. 14 y. Mt. Akan-Fuji. 24 y. Lake Mashu.

185. Gymnast on rings.

1950. 5th National Athletic Meeting.

589. **185.** 8 y. brown (Gymnast) 16·00 2·75
590. – 8 y. brown (Pole-vaulting) .. .. 16·00 2·75
591. – 8 y. brown (Football 16·00 2·75
592. – 8 y. brown (Horse-jumping) .. 16·00 2·75

Nos. 589/92 were issued in sheets, comprising horiz. rows of 4 designs se-tenant.

186. Tahoto Pagoda, Ishiyama Temple. **187.** Baron Maeshima. **188.** Long-tailed Cock.

189. Kanzeon Bosatsu.  **190.** Himeji Castle.

191. Phoenix Temple, Uji. **192.** Buddhisattva Statue, Chugu Temple.

1950. With or without noughts for sen after value.

593. **186.** 80 s. red 40 30
594. **187.** 1 y. brown 50 8
595. **188.** 5 y. green and brown 2·00 15
659. **189.** 10 y. lake and mauve 45 5
597. **190.** 14 y. brown .. .. 6·50 4·00
660. 14 y. olive .. .. 1·10 20
598. **191.** 24 y. blue .. .. 10·00 3·25
662. 24 y. violet .. .. 1·60 20
663. 30 y. purple .. .. 2·40 8
666. **192.** 50 y. brown .. .. 1·25 5

The 1 y., 10 y. and 50 y. exist both with and without noughts. Other values and colours are either with or without noughts. The 10 y. also exists with different inscriptions, from a booklet issued for 1954 Philatelic Week.

For designs additionally inscr. "NIPPON" see Nos. 1041/59.

193. Girl and Rabbit. **194.** Skier on Mt. Zao.

1951. New Year's Greetings.

604. **193.** 2 y. red .. .. 3·00 25

1951. Tourist Issue. Mt. Zao.

606. **194.** 8 y. olive .. .. 6·00 90
607. – 24 y. blue .. .. 6·00 1·60

DESIGN—HORIZ. 24 y. Two skiers on Mt. Zao.

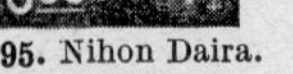

195. Nihon Daira. **196.** Mt. Fuji from Nihon Daira.

196a. Hot Springs, Owaki Valley. **196b.** Lake Ashi.

196c. Senju Waterfall. **196d.** Ninai Waterfall.

196e. Waka-no-Ura. **196f.** Tomo-ga-Shima.

196g. Uji River. **196h.** Uji Bridge.

196i. Oura Catholic Church, Nagasaki. **196j.** Sea-god Palace Gateway.

196k. Lake Marunuma. **196l.** Lake Sugenuma.

196m. Shosenkyo Valley. **196n.** Nagatoro Bridge.

1951. Tourist Issue.

608. **195.** 8 y. olive-green .. 6·00 1·00
609. **196.** 24 y. blue .. 28·00 5·50
612. **196a.** 8 y. red-brown .. 4·25 85
613. **196b.** 24 y. ultramarine .. 3·00 1·10
614. **196c.** 8 y. green .. 4·25 85
615. **196d.** 24 y. blue .. 3·00 1·10
616. **196e.** 8 y. yellow-brown .. 2·75 85
617. **196f.** 24 y. blue .. 2·40 1·10
623. **196g.** 8 y. brown .. 2·75 85
624. **196h.** 24 y. blue .. 2·50 1·10
639. **196i** 8 y. red .. 4·25 85
640. **196j.** 24 y. blue .. 2·75 1·10
641. **196k.** 8 y. purple .. 4·25 85
642. **196l.** 24 y. green .. 2·50 1·10
643. **196m.** 8 y. red .. 4·25 85
644. **196n.** 24 y. blue .. 3·00 1·10

197. Child's Head.

1951. Children's Charter.

611. **197.** 8 y. brown .. .. 12·00 1·10

198/201 (illustrations much reduced).

1951. Towada National Park.

618. **198.** 2 y. brown .. .. 1·10 20
619. **199.** 8 y. green .. .. 3·25 35
620. **200.** 14 y. red .. .. 2·75 90
621. **201.** 24 y. blue .. .. 3·75 1·40

DESIGNS: 2 y. Oirase River. 8 y. Lake Towada. 14 y. View from Kandodai. 24 y. Hakkoda Mts.

202. Aeroplane over Horyuji Pagoda. **202a.** Aeroplane and Mt. Tate.

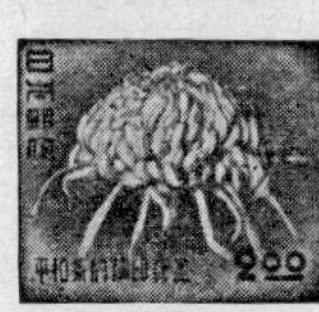

203. Chrysanthemum. **204.** Japanese Flag.

1951. Air. With or without noughts for sen after values.

671. **202.** 15 y. violet.. .. 50 15
626. 20 y. blue .. .. 10·00 45
673. 25 y. green .. 40 5
674. 30 y. red .. 1·25 5
675. 40 y. black .. 2·00 10
676. **202a.** 55 y. blue .. 20·00 1·60
631. 75 y. red .. 32·00 4·25
632. 80 y. magenta .. 7·50 2·25
679. 85 y. black .. 1·40 90
680. 125 y. brown .. 2·50 90
681. 160 y. green .. 5·00 90

1951. Peace Treaty.

636. **203.** 2 y. brown .. .. 1·10 35
637. **204.** 8 y. red and blue .. 4·25 1·00
638. **203.** 24 y. green .. .. 3·50 1·00

205. Putting the Shot. **206.** Noh Mask.

1951. 6th National Athletic Meeting.

645. **205.** 2 y. brown .. .. 1·50 45
646. – 2 y. blue (hockey) .. 1·50 45

Sheet contain alternate copies of each design.

1952. New Year's Greetings.

647. **206.** 5 y. red .. 4·50 25

207. Ship's Davit and Southern Cross. **208.** Red Cross and Lily.

1952. U.P.U. Membership. 75th Anniv.

649. **207.** 5 y. violet .. .. 3·75 45
650. – 10 y. green .. .. 6·50 85

DESIGN: 10 y. Earth and Ursa Major. Inscr. "1952".

1952. Japanese Red Cross. 75th Anniv.

651. **208.** 5 y. red .. .. 2·50 45
652. – 10 y. grn. & red (Nurse) 5·50 85

209. Akita Dog. **209a.** Cuckoo. **209b.** Tahoto Pagoda, Ishiyama Temple.

209c. Mandarin Ducks. **209d.** Serow (Goat-antelope). **209e.** Chuson Temple.

210. Goldfish. **210a.** Yomei Gate, Tosho Shrine. **210b.** "Marimo" (water plant) and Fish.

210c. Big Purple Butterfly. **210d.** Fishing with Cormorants. **211.** "Bridge and Irises" (from lacquered box).

1952.

654. **209.** 2 y. black 5 5
655. **209a.** 3 y. blue-green .. 5 5
656. **209b.** 4 y. purple and red .. 25 5
657. **209c.** 5 y. brown and blue .. 5 5
658. **209d.** 8 y. brn. and pale brn. 5 5
661. **209e.** 20 y. olive 20 5
664. **210.** 35 y. orange 55 5
665. **210a.** 45 y. blue 60 5
667. **210b.** 55 y. grn., blk. & blue 1·10 5
668. **210c.** 75 y. violet, yellow, black & vermilion 1·50 8
669. **210d.** 100 y. red .. .. 3·00 5
670. **211.** 500 y. purple .. .. 5·00 5

For 3 y., 55 y. and 75 y. in same designs, but inscr. "NIPPON", see Nos. 1042, 1060 and 1064.

212/5 (illustrations much reduced).

1952. Chubu-Sangaku National Park.

682. **212.** 5 y. brown .. .. 2·00 25
683. **213.** 10 y. green .. .. 6·00 85
684. **214.** 14 y. vermilion .. 2·10 1·00
685. **215.** 24 y. blue .. .. 4·25 1·25

DESIGNS—VERT. 5 y. Yarigatake. 10 y. Kurobe Valley. HORIZ. 14 y. Shirouma-dake. 24 y. Norikura-dake.

216. Central Hall. **217.** Wrestlers.

1952. Tokyo University. 75th Anniv.

687. **216.** 10 y. green .. .. 5·00 90

1952. 7th National Athletic Meeting.

688. – 5 y. blue (Mountaineer) 4·00 55
689. **217.** 5 y. brown .. .. 4·00 55

Sheets contain alternate copies of each design.

218/21. (illustrations much reduced).

1952. Bandai-Asahi National Park.

690. **218.** 5 y. brown .. .. 1·50 25
691. **219.** 10 y. olive .. .. 4·50 55
692. **220.** 14 y. red .. .. 1·75 80
693. **221.** 24 y. blue .. .. 3·75 1·40

DESIGNS: 5 y. Azuma-Fuji. 10 y. Mt. Asahi. 14 y. Mt. Bandai. 24 y. Mt. Gessan.

222. "Kirin" and Chrysanthemums. **223.** Flag of Crown Prince.

1952. Investiture of Crown Prince Akihito.

695. **222.** 5 y. orange and brown 1·25 25
696. 10 y. orange and green 1·50 40
697. **223.** 24 y. blue .. .. 3·50 1·10

224. Dancing Doll. **225.** First Japanese Electric Lamp.

1953. New Year's Greetings.

699. **224.** 5 y. red .. .. 3·50 20

1953. Electric Lamp in Japan. 75th Anniv.

701. **225.** 10 y. brown .. .. 3·75 85

226. Kintai Bridge. **228a.** Great Buddha, Kamakura.

227. Lake Shikotsu. **228.** Mt. Yotei. (Illustrations much reduced.)

1953. Tourist Issue. Kintai Bridge.

702. – 10 y. brown .. .. 3·50 1·00
703. **226.** 24 y. blue .. .. 3·00 1·00

DESIGN—VERT. 10 y. Kintai Bridge (after Hiroshige).

1953. Shikotsu-Toya National Park.

704. **227.** 5 y. blue .. .. 1·40 25
705. **228.** 10 y. green .. .. 2·75 40

1953. Air.

707. **228a.** 70 y. brown 70 5
708. 80 y. blue 95 5
709. 115 y. olive 85 12
710. 145 y. turquoise .. 1·40 30

229. Futamigaura Beach. **230.** Nakiri Coast. (Illustrations much reduced.)

1953. Iseshima National Park.

711. **229.** 5 y. red .. .. 1·25 20
712. **230.** 10 y. blue .. .. 2·40 35

231. "Ho-o" (Happy Phoenix).

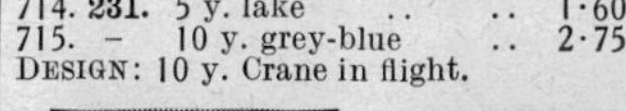

1953. Return of Crown Prince from Overseas Tour.

714. **231.** 5 y. lake .. .. 1·60 35
715. – 10 y. grey-blue .. 2·75 70

DESIGN: 10 y. Crane in flight.

232. Judo. **233.** Tokyo Observatory.

1953. 8th National Athletic Meeting.

716. **232.** 5 y. green .. .. 3·25 60
717. – 5 y. black .. .. 3·25 60

DESIGN: 5 y. Rugby footballers.

Nos. 716/17 were printed se-tenant alternately throughout the sheet.

1953. Tokyo Observatory. 75th Anniv.

718. **233.** 10 y. grey-blue .. 5·00 70

234. Mt. Unzen. 235.
(Illustrations much reduced.)

1953. Unzen National Park.
719. 234. 5 y. red .. .. 1·10 20
720. 235. 10 y. blue .. .. 2·40 35

236. Wooden Horse. 237. Ice skaters.

1953. New Year's Greetings.
722. 236. 5 y. red .. .. 3·00 20

1954. World Speed Skating Championships, Sapporo.
724. 237. 10 y. blue .. .. 2·50 55

238. 239. Wrestlers.

1954. Int. Trade Fair, Osaka.
725. 238. 10 y. red .. .. 2·25 55

1954. Int. Free-style Wrestling Championship.
726. 239. 10 y. green .. .. 2·25 55

240. Mt. Asama. 241. Tanigawadake.
(Illustrations much reduced).

1954. Jo-Shin-Etsu Kogen National Park.
727. 240. 5 y. sepia .. .. 1·25 20
728. 241. 10 y. turquoise .. .. 1·75 35

242. Archery. 243. Telegraph Table.

1954. 9th National Athletic Meeting.
730. 242. 5 y. green .. .. 1·75 40
731. – 5 y. sepia (Table-tennis) 1·75 40
Nos. 730/1 were printed se-tenant alternately throughout the sheet.

1954. I.T.U. Japan's Membership. 75th Anniv.
732. 243. 5 y. purple .. .. 1·25 25
733. – 10 y. blue .. .. 2·25 55
DESIGN—HORIZ. 10 y. I.T.U. Monument.

244. Tumbler. 245. Tama Gorge.

246. Chichibu Mountains.

1954. New Year's Greetings.
735. 244. 5 y. red and black .. 2·50 20

1955. Chichibu-Tama National Park.
737. 245. 5 y. blue .. .. 1·00 20
738. 246. 10 y. lake .. .. 1·25 25

248. Paper Carp.

250. Jodoga Beach. 249. Bentenzaki Peninsula.

1955. 15th Int. Chamber of Commerce Congress, Tokyo.
740. 248. 10 y. vermilion, yellow, black and blue .. 2·75 1·00

1955. Rikuchu-Kaigan National Park.
741. 249. 5 y. green .. .. 1·00 20
742. 250. 10 y. red .. .. 1·25 30

251. Gymnastics. 252. "Girl Playing Glass Flute" (Utamaro).

1955. 10th National Athletic Meeting.
744. 251. 5 y. red .. .. 1·50 35
745. – 5 y. blue (Running).. 1·50 35
Nos. 744/5 were printed se-tenant alternately throughout the sheet.

1955. Philatelic Week.
746. 252. 10 y. black, brown, red and green .. 10·00 4·25

253. "Kokeshi" Dolls. 254. Table-Tennis.

1955. New Year's Greetings.
747. 253. 5 y. green and red .. 1·60 8

1956. World Table-Tennis Championships.
749. 254. 10 y. brown .. .. 1·10 25

255. Judo. 256. Children and Paper Carps.

1956. World Judo Championships.
750. 255. 10 y. purple and green 1·40 35

1956. Int. Children's Day.
751. 256. 5 y. black and blue .. 85 25

257. Osezaki Lighthouse. 258. Kujuku Island.
(Illustrations much reduced.)

1956. 25th Anniv. of National Park Law. Saikai National Park.
752. 257. 5 y. brown 70 20
753. 258. 10 y. indigo and blue.. 70 30

INDEX

Countries can be quickly located by referring to the index at the end of this volume.

259. Imperial Palace, and Modern Buildings. 260. Sakuma Dam.

1956. 5th Cent. of Tokyo.
755. 259. 10 y. purple .. .. 1·50 35

1956. Completion of Sakuma Dam.
756. 260. 10 y. blue .. .. 1·25 30

261. Basketball. 262. Ebizo Ichikawa (actor), (after Sharaku).

1956. 11th National Athletic Meeting.
757. 261. 5 y. slate 85 20
758. – 5 y. purple (Long jumping) 85 20
Nos. 757/8 were printed se-tenant alternately throughout the sheet.

1956. Philatelic Week.
759. 262. 10 y. blk., orge. & grey 10·00 3·00

263. Mt. Manaslu and Mountaineer.

1956. Conquest of Mt. Manaslu.
760. 263. 10 y. pink, blue & brn. 2·50 85

264. Electric Train and View of Yui (after Hiroshige).

1956. Electrification of Tokaido Railway Line.
761. 264. 10 y. blk., grn. & brn. 4·25 85

265. Cogwheel, Valve and Ship. 266. Whale (float).

1956. Floating Machinery Fair.
762. 265. 10 y. blue 60 20

1956. New Year's Greetings.
763. 266. 5 y. multicoloured .. 1·10 8

267. U.N.O. Emblem. 268. I.G.Y. Emblem, Penguin, and Antarctic ship, "Soya".

1957. Japan's Admission into U.N. 1st Anniv.
765. 267. 10 y. red and blue .. 85 25

1957. Int. Geophysical Year.
766. 268. 10 y. blue, yell. & blk. 85 25

269. Atomic Reactor. 270. Gymnast.

1957. Completion of Atomic Reactor at Tokai-Mura.
767. 269. 10 y. violet 35 10

1957. 12th National Athletic Meeting.
768. 270. 5 y. blue 25 10
769. – 5 y. red (Boxing) .. 25 10
Sheets contain alternate copies of each design.

271. "Girl Bouncing Ball" (after Harunobu). 272. Ogochi Dam.

1957. Philatelic Week.
770. 271. 10 y red, blk., bl. & ochre 2·25 80

1957. Completion of Ogochi Dam.
771. 272. 10 y blue 25 8

273. Japan's First Blast Furnace and Modern Plant. 274. "Inu-hariko" (toy dog).

1957. Japanese Iron Industry. Cent.
772. 273. 10 y. purple & orange 25 5

1957. New Year's Greetings.
773. 274. 5 y. multicoloured .. 45 5

275. Kan-Mon Tunnel.

1958. Opening of Kan-Mon Undersea Tunnel.
775. 275. 10 y. black, pink, blue and drab 20 8

276. "Lady returning from bath-house" (after Kiyonaga).

1958. Philatelic Week.
776. 276. 10 y. pink, blk., grey-grn., buff, red and cream 1·00 12

277. Statue of Ii Naosuke and Ships. 278. National Stadium, Tokyo.

1958. Freedom of Ports. Cent.
777. 277. 10 y. red and turquoise 20 8

1958. 3rd Asian Games, Tokyo. Inscr. as in T 278.
778. **278.** 5 y. drab, black, rose and green 20 8
779. – 10 y. brown, red, blue and yellow 35 8
780. – 14 y. ochre, blue, black and red 55 10
781. – 24 y. pink, yell., black and blue 70 15
DESIGNS: 10 y. Flame and Games emblem. 14 y. Runner breasting tape. 24 y. High-diver.

279. Emigration Ship "Kasato Maru" and South American Map.

1958. Japanese Emigration to Brazil. 50th Anniv.
782. **279.** 10 y. sepia, red, yellow and green .. 15 8

280. Sado-Okesa Dancer on Sado Island. **280a.** Mt. Yahiko and Echigo Plain.

1958. Sado-Yahiko Quasi-National Park.
783. **280.** 10 y. multicoloured .. 75 8
784. **280a.** 10 y. multicoloured .. 60 8

281. Stethoscope.

1958. Int. Congresses of Chest Diseases and Bronchoesophagology, Tokyo.
785. **281.** 10 y. turquoise .. 25 8

282. "Old Kyoto Bridge" (after Hiroshige). **283.** Badminton Player.

1958. Int. Correspondence Week.
786. **282.** 24 y. multicoloured .. 1·50 15
The design is taken from the series of 53 woodcuts, showing stages of the Tokaido Road. Others from this series are shown on Nos. 810, 836, 878 and 908.

1958. 13th National Athletic Meeting. Inscr. "1958".
787. **283.** 5 y. purple 25 8
788. – 5 y. slate (Weight-lifting) 35 8
Sheets contain alternate copies of each design.

284. Yukichi Fukuzawa (founder) and Keio University. **285.** Children Skipping across Globe.

1958. Keio University Cent.
789. **284.** 10 y. claret 20 8

1958. Int. Child and Social Welfare Conferences, Tokyo.
790. **285.** 10 y. green 30 8

286. "Flame of Freedom". **287.** Ebisu with Bream (toy).

1958. Declaration of Human Rights. 10th Anniv.
791. **286.** 10 y. orange, blue, yellow and violet .. 35 8

1958. New Year's Greetings.
792. **287.** 5 y. red, yell., bl. & blk. 50 5

288. Map of Kojima Bay and Tractor.

1959. Completion of Kojima Bay Reclamation Project.
794. **288.** 10 y. purple and ochre 30 8

289. Karst Plateau. **289a.** Akiyoshi Cavern.

1959. Akiyoshidai Quasi-National Parks.
795. **289.** 10 y. multicoloured.. 1·00 8
796. **289a.** 10 y. multicoloured.. 1·40 8

290. Map of Asia. **291.** Crown Prince Akihito and Princess Michiko.

1959. Asian Cultural Congress in Commem. of 2,500th Anniv. of Buddha's Death.
797. **290.** 10 y. red 25 8

1958. Imperial Wedding.
798. – 5 y. violet and magenta 25 8
799. **291.** 10 y. maroon & brown 70 10
800. – 20 y. sepia & chestnut 85 12
801. **291.** 30 y. grn. & yell-grn... 1·50 15
DESIGN: 5 y., 20 y. Ceremonial fan.

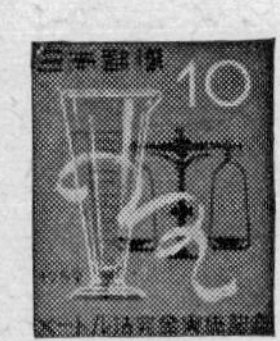
292. "Ladies reading poems" (from "Ukiyo Genji" after Eishi). **293.** Graduated Glass and Scales.

1959. Philatelic Week.
803. **292.** 10 y. multicoloured .. 2·00 1·10

1959. Ratification of Adoption of Metric System in Japan.
804. **293.** 10 y. sepia and blue .. 25 8

294. Stretcher-party with Casualty. **295.** Mt. Fuji from Lake Motosu.

1959. Red Cross.
805. **294.** 10 y. red and green .. 25 8

1959. National Parks Day.
806. **295.** 10 y. grn., mar. & blue 70 12

296. Ao Caves. Yabakei. **296a.** Cormorant with Hita and Mt. Hiko background.
(Illustrations much reduced.)

1958. Yaba-Hita-Hikosan Quasi-National Parks.
807. **296.** 10 y. multicoloured.. 1·25 8
808. **296a.** 10 y. multicoloured.. 1·25 8

297. Nagoya and Golden Dolphin. **298.** "Kuwana" (after Hiroshige).

1959. Founding of Nagoya. 350th Anniv.
809. **297.** 10 y. gold, blk. & blue 60 8

1959. Int. Correspondence Week.
810. **298.** 30 y. multicoloured .. 1·90 20

299. Flying Crane and I.A.T.A. Emblem. **300.** Throwing the Hammer.

1959. 15th Int. Air Transport Association Meeting.
811. **299.** 10 y. blue 40 8

1959. 14th National Athletic Meeting. Inscr. "1959".
812. **300.** 5 y. blue 50 8
813. – 5 y. brown (Fencer) .. 50 8
Sheets contain alternate copies of each design.

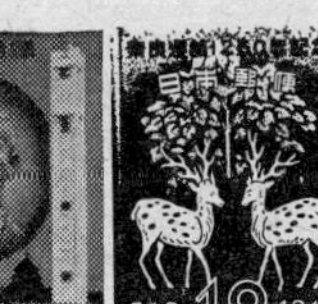
301. Open Book showing portrait of Shoin Yoshida. **302.** Halves of Globe.

1959. Shoin Yoshida (educator). Death Cent. and Nat. Parents/Teachers Assoc. Convention.
814. **301.** 10 y. brown 40 8

1959. 15th Session of Contracting Parties to G.A.T.T.
815. **302.** 10 y. red-brown .. 40 8

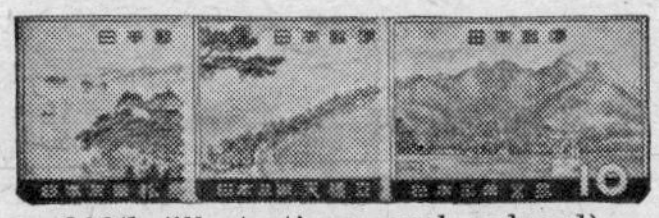
303. Rice-eating Rat of Kanazawa (toy). **304.** Yukio Ozaki and Clock Tower Memorial Hall. **305.** Deer.

1959. New Year's Greetings.
816. **303.** 5 y. red, black, green and gold 70 5

1960. Completion of Ozaki Memorial Hall, Tokyo.
818. **304.** 10 y. maroon & brown 25 8

1960. Transfer of Capital to Nara. 1250th Anniv.
819. **305.** 10 y. olive 35 8

306/b (illustrations much reduced).

1960. "Scenic Trio".
820. **306.** 10 y. turquoise & brn. 1·10 15
821. **306a.** 10 y. green and blue.. 1·50 15
822. **306b.** 10 y. grn. & blkish vio. 1·50 15
DESIGNS: No. 820, Godaido Temple, Matsushima. 821, Bridge of Heaven (sandbank), Miyazu Bay. 822, Miyajima from the sea.

307. Takeshima-Gamagori Pier.

1960. Mikawa Bay Quasi-National Park.
823. **307.** 10 y. multicoloured .. 1·10 8

308. "Ise" (Thirty-six Poets). (after Fujiwara's "Thirty-six Poets")

1960. Philatelic Week.
824. **308.** 10 y. multicoloured .. 3·25 1·10

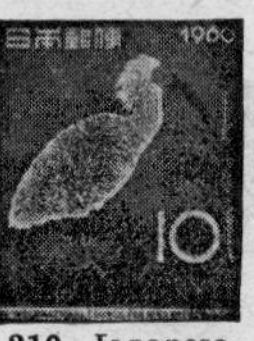
309. "Kanrin Maru" crossing the Pacific. **310.** Japanese Crested Ibis.

1960. Japanese-American Treaty Cent.
825. **309.** 10 y. sepia and green 70 10
826. – 30 y. blue-black & red 1·00 12
DESIGN: 30 y. Pres. Buchanan receiving Japanese mission.

1960. 12th Int. Bird Preservation Congress, Tokyo.
827. **310.** 10 y. verm., pink & grey 70 10

311. Radio Waves around Globe. **312.** Abashiri Flower Gardens.

1960. Japanese Overseas Broadcasting Service, "Radio Japan". 25th Anniv.
828. **311.** 10 y. red 25 8

1960. Abashiri Quasi-National Park.
829. **311.** 10 y. multicoloured .. 1·25 10

313. Cape Ashizuri. **314.** Rainbow linking Hawaii and Japan.

1960. Ashizuri Quasi-National Park.
830. **313.** 10 y. multicoloured .. 1·25 10

1960. Japanese Emigration to Hawaii. 75th Anniv.
831. **314.** 10 y. multicoloured .. 85 15

315. Farman Biplane and Jet Plane. **316.** Seat Plan of the Diet.

1960. Japanese Aviation. 50th Anniv.
832. **315.** 10 y. brown and grey.. 50 8

1960. 49th Inter-Parliamentary Union Conf. Inscr. "49TH INTER-PARLIAMENTARY CONFERENCE TOKYO 1960".
833. **316.** 5 y. orange and indigo 30 8
834. – 10 y. brown and blue 50 8
DESIGN: 10 y. "Aka Fuji" (after Hokusai) and Diet Building.

317. "Kambara" (after Hiroshige). **318.** Okayama Observatory.

1960. Int. Correspondence Week.
836. **317.** 30 y. black, blue, yellow and brown .. .. 12·00 1·60

1960. Opening of Okayama Astro-physical Observatory.
837. **318.** 10 y. violet 50 10

319. "Kendo" (Japanese fencing).

320. Lieut. Shirase and Map of Antarctica.

1960. 15th National Athletic Meeting Inscr. "1960".
838. **319.** 5 y. blue 50 8
839. – 5 y. maroon (Vaulting) 50 8
Nos. 838/9 were issued se-tenant alternately throughout the Sheet.

1960. 1st. Japanese Antarctic Expedition. 50th Anniv.
840. **320.** 10 y. black and brown 55 8

321. Red Beko and Golden Bekokko (Japanese toys).

322. Diet Building and Stars.

1960. New Year's Greetings.
841. **321.** 5 y. multicoloured .. 55 5

1960. Diet. 70th Anniv.
843. **322.** 5 y. violet and black .. 35 8
844. – 10 y. red 55 8
DESIGN: 10 y. Opening ceremony of first session of Diet.

323. Narcissus.

324. Pearl-divers at Shirahama.

1961. Japanese Flowers. Flowers in natural colours. Background colours given.
845. 10 y. purple (T **323**) .. 3·00 45
846. 10 y. brown (Plum blossom) 1·90 40
847 10 y. bistre (Camellia) .. 1·25 35
848. 10 y. grey (Cherry blossom) 1·40 35
849. 10 y. sepia (Peony) .. 1·25 35
850. 10 y. grey (Iris) .. 1·00 30
851. 10 y. turquoise (Lily) .. 55 15
852. 10 y. blue (Morning Glory) 55 15
853. 10 y. sage (Bellflower) .. 55 15
854. 10 y. orange (Gentjan) .. 55 15
855. 10 y. blue (Chrysanthemum) 80 15
856. 10 y. slate (Camellia) .. 55 15

1961. Minami-Boso Quasi-National Park.
857. **324.** 10 y. multicoloured .. 85 8

324a. Beniokinaebisu Shell.

324b. Nanten.

324c. Cherry Blossoms.

324d. Engaku Temple.

324e. Yomei Gate.

324f. Noh Mask.

324g. Long-tailed Pheasant.

324h. "The Wind God".

324i. Japanese Cranes.

324j. "Kalavinka" (legendary bird).

1961.
858. **324a.** 4 y. vermilion & brown 5 5
859. **324b.** 6 y. red and green .. 5 5
860. **324c.** 10 y. magenta & pur. 8 5
861. **324d.** 30 y. violet 40 5
862. **324e.** 40 y. red 45 5
863. **324f.** 70 y. black and ochre 50 5
864. **324g.** 80 y. brown and red .. 55 5
865. **324h.** 90 y. green .. .. 1·75 5
866. **324i.** 100 y. grey, blk. & pink 1·75 5
867. **324j.** 120 y. violet .. 1·40 5
For 70 y, 80 y, 90 y, 100 y. and 120 y. in different colours and additionally inscr. "NIPPON" see Nos. 1066 and 1232/5.

325. Baron Maeshima.

326. "Dancing Girl" (from 17th-century screen).

1961. Japanese Postal Service. 90th Anniv.
868. **325.** 10 y. green and black .. 1·10 8

1961. Philatelic Week.
869. **336.** 10 y. multicoloured .. 1·75 60

327. Lake Biwa.

328. Rotary Emblem and "Peoples of the World".

1961. Lake Biwa Quasi-National Park.
870. **327.** 10 y. multicoloured .. 70 8

1961. 52nd Rotary International Convention.
871. **328.** 10 y. orange and black 20 8

329. "Benefits of Irrigation".

330. Globe showing Longitude 135° E. and Sun.

1961. Aichi Irrigation Scheme Inaug.
872. **329.** 10 y. blue and purple .. 25 8

1961. Japanese Standard Time. 75th Anniv.
873. **330.** 10 y. red, blk. & ochre 30 8

331. Parasol Dancer, Tottori Beach.

332. Komagatake Volcano.

1961. San'in Kaigan Quasi-National Park.
874. **331.** 10 y. multicoloured .. 70 8

1961. Onuma Quasi-National Park.
875. **332.** 10 y. multicoloured .. 85 8

333. Athlete.

334. "Hakone" (after Hiroshige).

1961. 16th National Athletic Meeting. Inscr. "1961".
876. **333.** 5 y. green 50 8
877. – 5 y. blue (Rowing) .. 50 8
Nos. 876/7 were issued se-tenant alternately throughout the sheet.

1961. International Correspondence Week.
878. **334.** 30 y. multicoloured .. 6·00 1·25

335. Javelin-throwing.

336. Library and Book.

1961. Olympic Games, Tokyo, 1964. (1st issue).
879. **335.** 5 y. + 5 y. brown .. 75 30
880. – 5 y. + 5 y. green .. 75 30
881. – 5 y. + 5 y. red .. 75 30
DESIGNS: No. 880, Wrestling. No. 881, Gymnastics (Male).
See also Nos. 899/901, 909/11, 935/7, 949/52, 969/72, 981/5.

1961. Opening of National Diet Library.
882. **336.** 10 y. blue and gold .. 25 8

337. Tiger. (Izumo toy).

1961. New Year's Greetings.
883. **337.** 5 y. multicoloured .. 40 5

338/c (illustrations much reduced).

1962. Fuji-Hakone-Izu National Park.
885. **338.** 5 y. green 50 8
886. **338a.** 5 y. blue 50 8
887. **338b.** 10 y. brown .. .. 1·10 15
888. **338c.** 10 y. black .. .. 1·10 15
VIEWS: No. 885, Mt. Fuji from Lake Ashi Hakone. 886, Minokake-Iwa, Irozaki (rocks in sea). 887, Mt. Fuji from Mitsutoge. 888, Mt. Fuji from Osezaki.

339. Omishima Island.

340. Doll Festival.

1962. Kitanagato-Kaigan Quasi-National Park.
889. **339.** 10 y. multicoloured .. 55 8

1962. National Festivals.
890. **340.** 10 y. multicoloured .. 1·25 15
891. – 10 y. multicoloured .. 45 10
892. – 10 y. multicoloured .. 40 10
893. – 10 y. multicoloured .. 30 10
DESIGNS: No. 891, Boy, girl and decorated tree (Star Festival). 892, Three children ("Seven-Five-Three" Festival). 893, Child throwing beans (Spring Festival).

341. "Dancer" (after N. Kano).

342. Sakurajima Volcano.

343. Mount Kongo.

1962. Philatelic Week.
894. **341.** 10 y. multicoloured .. 1·75 80

1962. Kinkowan Quasi-National Park.
895. **342.** 10 y. multicoloured .. 50 8

1962. Kongo-Ikoma Quasi-National Park.
896. **343** 10 y. multicoloured .. 50 8

344. Suigo View.

345. Train emerging from tunnel.

1962. Suigo Quasi-National Park.
897. **344.** 10 y. multicoloured .. 60 8

1962. Opening of Hokuriku Railway Tunnel.
898. **345.** 10 y. olive 75 10

1962. Olympic Games, Tokyo, 1964 (2nd issue). Sports designs as T **335.**
899. – 5 y. + 5 y. red .. 35 25
900. – 5 y. + 5 y. green .. 35 25
901. – 5 y. + 5 y. purple .. 35 25
SPORTS: No. C 899 Judo. C 900, Water-polo. C 901, Gymnastics (female).

346. Scout's Hat on Map.

1962. Asian Scout Jamboree, Mt. Fuji.
902. **346.** 10 y. black, bistre & red 20 12

347/c (illustrations much reduced).

1962. Nikko National Park.
903. **347.** 5 y. turquoise .. 30 8
904. **347a.** 5 y. lake 30 8
905. **347b.** 10 y. purple .. 45 8
906. **347c.** 10 y. olive 45 8
DESIGNS: No. 903, Mt. Shibutsu and Ozegahara Swamp. 904, Smoking Summit of Mt. Chausu Nasu. 905, Lake Chuzenji and Mt. Nantai 906, Senryu-kyo Narrows, Shiobara.

348. Wakato Suspension Bridge.

349. "Nihonbashi" (after Hiroshige).

1962. Opening of Wakato Suspension Bridge.
907. **348.** 10 y. red 80 15

1962. Int. Correspondence Week.
908. **349.** 40 y. multicoloured .. 1·90 25

1962. Olympic Games, Tokyo, 1964 (3rd issue). Sports designs as T **335.**
909. – 5 y. + 5 y. slate-green .. 30 20
910. – 5 y. + 5 y. lilac 30 20
911. – 5 y. + 5 y. red 30 20
SPORTS: No. 909, Basketball. 910, Rowing. 911, Fencing.

350. Rifle-shooting.

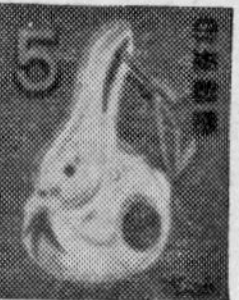
351. Hare-bell (Nogomi toy).

1962. 17th National Athletic Meeting.
912. **350.** 5 y. maroon 30 8
913. – 5 y. indigo 30 8
DESIGN: No. 913, Softball.
Nos. 912/13 were issued se-tenant alternately throughout the sheet.

1962. New Year's Greetings.
914. **351.** 5 y. orange, green black and violet .. 20 5

352. Mt. Ishizuchi and Kamega Forest.

353. "Five Towns".

1963. Ishizuchi Quasi-National Park.
916. **352.** 10 y. multicoloured .. 25 8

1963. Amalgamation of Five Towns as Kita-Kyushu.
917. **353.** 10 y. brown 20 8

354. Frosted Foliage, Fugen Peak. **354a.** Amakusa-Matsushima and view of Mt. Unzen.
(Illustrations much reduced.)

1963. Unzen-Amakusa National Park.
918. **354.** 5 y. grey-blue 25 5
919. **354a.** 10 y. red 25 5

355. Midorigaike (Green Pond). **355a.** Hakusan Mountains.
(Illustrations much reduced.)

1963. Hakusan National Park.
920. **355.** 5 y. chocolate .. 20 5
921. **355a.** 10 y. grey-green .. 25 5

356. Great Rocks, Keya. **357.** Globe and Emblem.

1963. Genkai Quasi-National Park.
922. **356.** 10 y. multicoloured .. 20 5

1963. Freedom from Hunger.
923. **357.** 10 y. grey-green .. 15 8

359. Centenary Emblem and World Map.

358. "Portrait of Helhachiro Honda" (anon.-Yedo period). **360.** Globe and Leaf.

1963. Philatelic Week
924. **358.** 10 y. multicoloured .. 1·00 40

1963. Red Cross Cent.
925. **359.** 10 y. multicoloured .. 15 8

1963. 5th Int. Irrigation and Drainage Commission Congress, Toyko.
926. **360.** 10 y. blue 15 8

361. Ito-dake, Asahi Range. **361a.** Mt. Bandai across Lake Hibara.
(Illustrations much reduced.)

1963. Bandai-Asahi National Park.
927. **361.** 5 y. green 20 5
928. **361a.** 10 y. brown 20 5

362. Japanese Jay.

1963. Japanese Birds. Multicoloured.
929. 10 y. Type **362** 90 20
930. 10 y. Ptarmigan 25 8
931. 10 y. Turtle dove 25 8
932. 10 y. White stork 25 8
933. 10 y. Bush warbler 25 8
934. 10 y. Meadow bunting .. 10 5

1963. Olympic Games, Tokyo, 1964 (4th issue). Sports designs as T **335.**
935. – 5 y.+5 y. blue 30 20
936. – 5 y.+5 y. chocolate .. 30 20
937. – 5 y.+5 y. brown .. 30 20
SPORTS: No. 935, Yachting. 936, Boxing. 937, Volleyball.

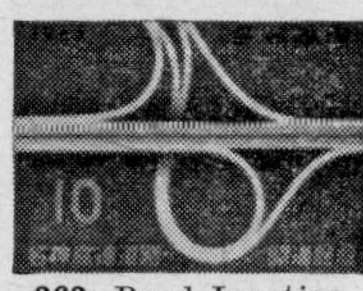

363. Road Junction, Ritto, Shiga. **364.** Girl Scout and Flag.

1963. Opening of Nagoya-Kobe Expressway.
938. **363.** 10 y. green, blk. & orge. 20 8

1963. Asian Girl Scout Camp, Nagano.
939. **364.** 10 y. multicoloured .. 15 8

365. Mt. Washiu. **365a.** Whirlpool at Naruto.
(Illustrations much reduced.)

1963. Seto Inland Sea National Park.
940. **365.** 5 y. brown 12 5
941. **365a.** 10 y. green 15 5

366. Lake Shikaribetsu. **366a.** Mt. Kurodake.
(Illustrations much reduced.)

1963. Daisetsuzan National Park.
942. **366.** 5 y. blue 12 5
943. **366a.** 10 y. purple 15 5

367. Antennae. **368.** Mt. Fuji and Waves (after woodcut by Hokusai).

1963. 14th Int. Scientific Radio Union Conference, Tokyo.
944. **367.** 10 y multicoloured .. 15 8

1963. Int. Correspondence Week.
945. **368.** 40 y. multicoloured .. 2·20 35
The design is taken from the series of 36 woodcuts showing Mt. Fuji. Others from this series are shown as Nos. 989, 1010, 1075, 1100, 1140 and 1185.

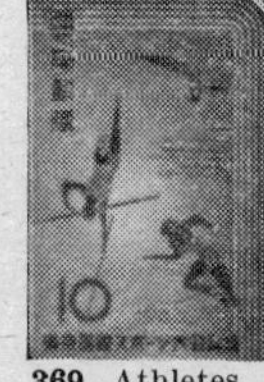

369. Athletes. **370.** Wrestling.

1963. "Pre-Olympic" Athletic Meeting, Tokyo.
946. **369.** 10 y. multicoloured .. 15 5

1963. 18th National Athletic Meeting. Inscr. "1963".
947. **370.** 5 y. brown 12 5
948. – 5 y. green 12 5
DESIGN: No. 948, Free-style gymnastics.
Sheets contain alternate copies of each design.

1963. Olympic Games, Tokyo, 1964 (5th issue). Sports designs as T **335.**
949. – 5 y.+5 y. blue .. 8 5
950. – 5 y.+5 y. olive .. 8 5
951. – 5 y.+5 y. black .. 8 5
952. – 5 y.+5 y. purple .. 8 5
SPORTS: No. 949, Cycling. 950, Horse-jumping. 951, Hockey. 952, Pistol-shooting.

371. Hachijo Island. **372.** Kai and Iwai Dragon Toys.

1963. Izu Islands Quasi-National Park.
953. **371.** 10 y. multicoloured .. 15 5

1963. New Year's Greetings.
954. **372.** 5 y. multicoloured .. 12 5

373. Wakasa Bay. **374.** View from Horikiri Pass and Agave Plant.

1964. Wakasa Bay Quasi-National Park.
956. **373.** 10 y. multicoloured .. 15 5

1964. Nichinan-Kaigan Quasi-National Park.
957. **374.** 10 y. multicoloured .. 15 5

375. Uji Bridge. **375a.** View of Toba.
(Illustrations much reduced.)

1964. Ise-Shima National Park.
958. **375.** 5 y. brown 12 5
959. **375a.** 10 y. purple .. 15 5

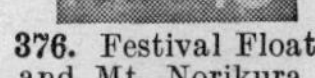

376. Festival Float and Mt. Norikura. **376a.** "Yamaboko" Shrine.

376. Warriors on Horseback.

376c. Festival Scene.

1964. Regional Festivals. Multicoloured.
960. **376.** 10 y. Tokayama Festival 12 5
961. **376a.** 10 y. Gion Festival .. 12 5
962. **376b.** 10 y. Soma Horse Festival 15 5
963. **376c.** 10 y. Chichibu Festival 15 5

377. "Yodorigi", from Genji-Mor ogatari Scroll.

1964. Philatelic Week.
964. **377.** 10 y. multicoloured .. 35 8

378. Himeji Castle. **379.** Handball.

1964. Rebuilding of Himeji Castle.
965. **378.** 10 y. chocolate .. 12 5

1964. 19th National Athletic Meeting. Inscr. "1964".
966. **379.** 5 y. green 5 5
967. – 5 y. red (Gymnastics) 5 5
Nos. 966/7 were issued se-tenant alternately throughout the sheet.

380. Cross-section of Cable.

1964. Opening of Japan–U.S. Submarine Telephone Cable.
968. **380.** 10 y. multicoloured .. 12 5

1964. Olympic Games, Tokyo (6th issue) Sports designs as T **335.**
969. 5 y.+5 y. violet 10 5
970. 5 y.+5 y. blue 10 5
971. 5 y.+5 y. lake 10 5
972. 5 y.+5 y. olive 10 5
SPORTS: No. 969, Modern, pentathlon. 970, Canoeing. 971, Football. 972, Weight-lifting.

382. Nihonbashi Bridge. **383.** "Coins".

1964. Opening of Tokyo Expressway.
973. **382.** 10 y. grn., silver & blk. 12 5

1964. Int. Monetary Fund Convention, Tokyo.
980. **383.** 10 y. gold and red .. 12 5

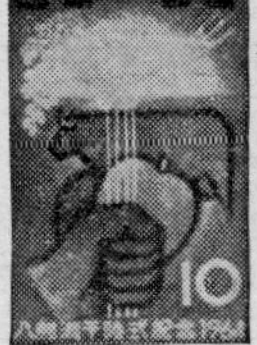

384. Olympic Flame. **385.** "Agriculture".

1964. Olympic Games, Tokyo (7th issue). Inscr. "1964". Multicoloured.
981. 5 y. Type **384** 5 5
982. 10 y. Main stadium .. 12 5
983. 30 y. Fencing hall .. 20 10
984. 40 y. Indoor stadium .. 30 10
985. 50 y. Komazawa hall .. 35 10
Nos. 982/5 are horiz.

1964. Reclamation of Hachirogata Lagoon.
987. **385.** 10 y. gold and maroon 12 5

386. Electric Express Train.

1964. Inaug. of Tokyo-Osaka Railway.
988. **386.** 10 y. blue and black .. 20 5

387. Mt. Fuji and Tokaido Highway (after woodcut by Hokusai). **388.** Straw Snake.

1964. Int. Correspondence Week.
989. **387.** 40 y. multicoloured .. 1·10 15

1964. New Year's Greetings.
990. **388.** 5 y. multicoloured .. 5 5

389. Mt. Daisen and Akamatsu Pond. **389a.** Jodo-ga-Ura (Paradise Islands) of Oki.
(Illustrations much reduced.)

1965. Daisen-Oki National Park.
992. **389.** 5 y. blue 12 5
993. **389a.** 10 y. chestnut .. 12 5

390. Niseko-Annupuri Mountains. **391.** Radar Station.

1965. Niseko Shakotan Otaru Quasi-National Park.
994. **390.** 10 y. multicoloured .. 12 5

1965. Completion of Meteorological Radar Station, Mt. Fuji.
995. **391.** 10 y. multicoloured .. 12 5

392. Kiyotsu Gorge. **392a.** Mt. Myoko across Lake Nojiri.

1965. Jo-Shin-Etsu Kogen National Park
996. **392.** 5 y. brown 12 5
997. **392a.** 10 y. purple 12 5

393. Postal Museum.

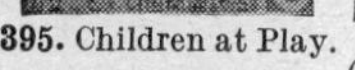

395. Children at Play. **394.** "The Prelude" (after Shoen Uyemura)

1965. Inaug. of Postal Museum, Ote-machi, Tokyo, and Stamp Exn.
998. **393.** 10 y. green 12 5

1965. Philatelic Week.
999. **394.** 10 y. multicoloured .. 30 8

1965. National Children's Gardens Inaug.
1000. **395.** 10 y. multicoloured .. 12 5

396. Tree within "Leaf". **397.** Globe and Symbols.

1965. Reafforestation.
1001. **396.** 10 y. multicoloured .. 12 5

1965. I.T.U. Cent.
1002. **397.** 10 y. multicoloured .. 12 5

398. Naka-Dake Crater. **398a.** Aso Peaks.
(Illustrations much reduced.)

1965. Aso National Park.
1003. **398.** 5 y. cerise 8 5
1004. **398a.** 10 y. green 12 5

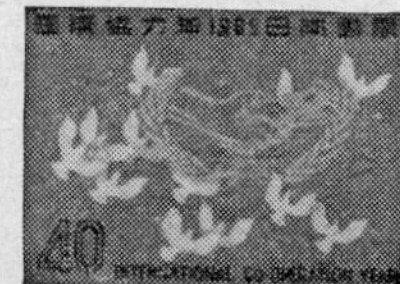

399. I.C.Y. Emblem and Doves.

1965. Int. Co-operation Year.
1005. **399.** 40 y. multicoloured .. 35 5

401. S.S. "Merji Maru" and Gulls. **402.** "Blood Donation".

1965. 25th Maritime Day.
1006. **401.** 10 y. multicoloured .. 12 5

1965. Campaign for Blood Donors.
1007. **402.** 10 y. multicoloured .. 12 5

403. Atomic Power Station, Tokyo. **404.** "Population".

1965. 9th I.A.E.A. Conf., Tokyo.
1008. **403.** 10 y. multicoloured .. 12 5

1965. 10th National Census.
1009. **404.** 10 y. multicoloured .. 12 5

405. Mt. Fuji from Misaka Pass (after Hokusai). **404.** Emblems and Plan of Diet.

1965. Int. Correspondence Week.
1010. **405.** 40 y. multicoloured .. 65 15

1965. National Suffrage. 75th Anniv.
1011. **406.** 10 y. multicoloured .. 12 5

407. Walking. **408.** Outline of Face, and Baby.

1965. 20th National Athletic Meeting. Inscr. "1965".
1012. **407.** 5 y. green 5 5
1013. – 5 y. brown (Gymnastics) 5 5
Sheets contain alternate copies of each design.

1965. Int. Conferences of Otology, Rhinology and Laryngology (ICORL) and Pediatrics (ICP), Tokyo.
1014. **408.** 30 y. multicoloured .. 25 8

408. Mt. Iwo. **409a.** Mt. Rausu.

410. Antarctic Map, Ship "Fuji" and Aurora Australis. **412.** Straw Horse".

1965. Shiretoko National Park.
1015. **409.** 5 y. turquoise .. 8 5
1016. **409a.** 10 y. blue 12 8

1965. Antarctic Expedition of 1965.
1017. **410.** 10 y. multicoloured .. 10 5

1965. New Year's Greetings.
1018. **412.** 5 y. multicoloured 5 5

413. Telephone Switchboard (1890) and Modern Dial. **414.** Spiny Lobster.

1965. Japanese Telephone Service. 75th Anniv.
1020. **413.** 10 y. multicoloured .. 12 5

NIPPON. From this point onwards all stamps are additionally inscribed "NIPPON".

1966. Fishery Products. Multicoloured.
1021. 10 y. Type **414** 12 5
1022. 10 y. Carp 12 5
1023. 10 y. Bream 12 5
1024. 10 y. Bonito 12 5
1025. 10 y. "Ayu" (trout) .. 12 5
1026. 15 y. Eel 15 5
1027. 15 y. Mackerel 15 5
1028. 15 y. Salmon 20 5
1029. 15 y. Buri 25 5
1030. 15 y. Globefish 25 5
1031. 15 y. Surume-ika (squid) 25 5
1032. 15 y. Sazae (shellfish) .. 35 5

415. Pleasure Garden, Mito. **416.** Crater of Mt. Zzo.

1966. Famous Japanese Gardens.
1033. **415.** 10 y. green, blk. & gold 15 5
1034. – 15 y. blk., red & blue 30 5
1035. – 15 y. choc., grn. & silver 30 5
DESIGNS: No. 1034, Pleasure garden and cranes, Okayama. 1035, Kenrokuen Garden, Kanazawa.

1966. Zao Quasi-National Park.
1036. **416.** 10 y. multicoloured .. 12 5

417. Muroto Cape. **417a.** Senba Cliffs, Anan.

1966. Muroto-Anan Kaigan Quasi-National Park.
1037. **417.** 10 y. multicoloured 12 5
1038. **417a.** 10 y. multicoloured 12 5

418. A.I.P.P.I. Emblem.

1966. General Assembly of Int. Assn. for Protection of Industrial Property (A.I.P.P.I.).
1039. **418.** 40 y. multicoloured .. 35 8

419. "Butterflies" (after T. Fujishima).

1966. Philatelic Week.
1040. **419.** 10 y. multicoloured .. 30 8

420. Goldfish. **420a.** Chrysanthemums. **420b.** Fuji (wisteria).

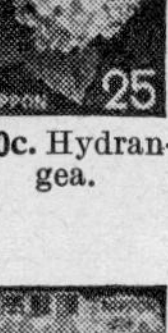

420c. Hydrangea. **420d.** Golden Hall, Chuson Temple. **420e.** Squid.

420f. Yomei Gate, Tosho Shrine. **420g.** Mizubasho. **420h.** Konponchudo Hall, Enryaku Temple.

420i. Ancient Clay Horse. **420j.** Garden of Katsura Palace.

421. Onjo Bosatsu (relief from bronze lantern, Todai Temple). **421a.** Kongo-Rikishi Statue, Todai Temple Nara.

1966. Inscr. "NIPPON".
1041. **187.** 1 y. brown 5 5
1046. **420.** 7 y. orange and green 8 5
1050. **420a.** 15 y. yellow and blue 8 5
1052. **420b.** 20 y. multicoloured 15 5
1053. **420c.** 25 y. blue & green .. 15 5
1054. **420d.** 30 y. gold and blue 15 5
1055. **420e.** 35 y. blk., brn. & bl. 20 5
1056. **420f.** 40 y. green & brown 20 5
1057 **420g.** 45 y. multicoloured 25 5
1058. **192.** 50 y. brown .. 80 8
1059. 50 y. red 25 5
1060. **210b.** 55 y. grn., blk. & bl. 25 5
1061. **420h.** 60 y. green 35 5
1062. **420i.** 65 y. brown .. 95 5
1063. 65 y. orange .. 35 5
1064. **210c.** 75 y. multicoloured 40 5
1065. **324h.** 90 y. brown & gold 55 5
1066. **324i.** 100 y. grey, blk. & red 55 5
1067. **420j.** 110 y. brown .. 60 5
1068. **324j.** 120 y. red 75 5
1069. **421.** 200 y. green .. 1·10 5
1070. **421a.** 500 y. plum .. 2·75 5
See also Nos. 1226/38.

422. U.N. and U.N.E.S.C.O. Emblems. **433.** Pacific Ocean.

1966. U.N.E.S.C.O. 20th Anniv.
1071. **422.** 15 y. multicoloured .. 12 5

1966. 11th Pacific Science Congress, Tokyo.
1072. **423.** 15 y. multicoloured .. 12 5

ILLUSTRATIONS
British Commonwealth and all overprints and surcharges are FULL SIZE. Foreign Countries have been reduced to ¾-LINEAR.

424. Amakusa Bridges.

1966. Completion of Amakusa Bridges.
1073. **424.** 15 y. multicoloured .. 12 5

425. Family and Emblem. **426.** " Sekiya on the Sumida " (after Hokusai).

1966. Post Office Life Insurance Office. 50th Anniv.
1074. **425.** 15 y. multicoloured.. 12 5

1966. Int. Correspondence Week.
1075. **426.** 50 y. multicoloured.. 1·25 20

427. Rotary Cobalt Radiator. **428.** " Hop, Step and Jump " Event.

1966. 9th. Int. Cancer Congress, Tokyo.
1076. **427.** 7 y.+3 y. blk. & orge. 8 5
1077. – 15 y.+5 y. mult. .. 15 5
DESIGN—VERT. 15 y. Detection by X-rays.

1966. 21st National Athletic Meeting. Inscr. " 1966. "
1078. **428.** 7 y. red 12 5
1079. – 7 y. blue (clay-pigeon shooting) 12 5
Sheets contain alternate copies of each design.

429. National Theatre. **430.** Rice Year Emblem.

1966. Japanese National Theatre. Inaug. Multicoloured.
1080. 15 y. Type **429** 15 5
1081. 25 y. "Kabuki" performance (48 × 33½ mm.) .. 30 12
1082. 50 y. "Bunraku" puppet act (33½ × 48 mm.) .. 50 20

1966. Int. Rice Year.
1083. **430.** 15 y. black, ochre & red 12 5

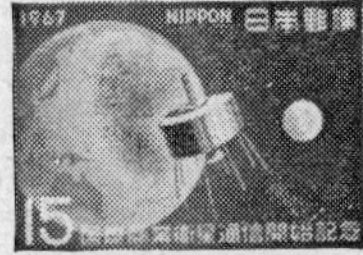

431. Ittobori Sheep (sculpture). **432.** Satellite "Intelsat 2" Earth and Moon.

1966. New Year's Greetings.
1084. **431.** 7 y. multicoloured .. 8 5

1967. Int. Commercial Satellite Communications in Japan. Inaug.
1086. **432.** 15 y. brown and blue 15 5

433. Jet Plane and Flight Route. **434.** Literature Museum.

1967. Round-the-World Air Service. Inaug.
1087. **433.** 15 y. multicoloured.. 12 5

1967. Opening of Japanese Modern Literature Museum, Meguro-ku, Tokyo.
1088. **434.** 15 y. multicoloured.. 12 5

435. " Lakeside " (after S. Kuroda).

1967. Philatelic Week.
1089. **435.** 15 y. multicoloured.. 50 15

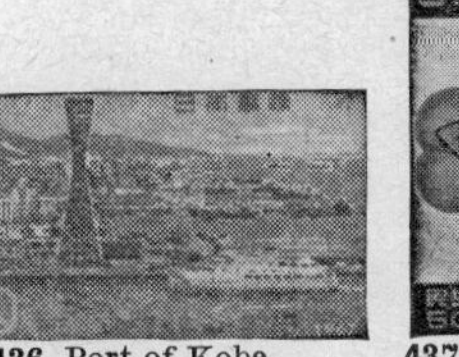

436. Port of Kobe. **437.** Emblem of Welfare Service.

1967. 5th Int. Assn. of Ports and Harbours Congress, Tokyo.
1090. **436.** 50 y. multicoloured.. 50 12

1967. Welfare Commissioner Service. 50th Anniv.
1091. **437.** 15 y. gold and agate.. 12 5

438. Pedestrian Road Crossing.

1967. Road Safety Campaign. 20th Anniv.
1092. **438.** 15 y. black, red, yellow and green 12 5

439. Kita-dake and Koma-ga-dake. **440.** Akashi-dake, Hijiri-dake and Higashi-dake.

(Illustrations much reduced).

1967. Southern Alps National Park.
1093. **439.** 7 y. blue 15 5
1094. **440.** 15 y. purple .. 20 5

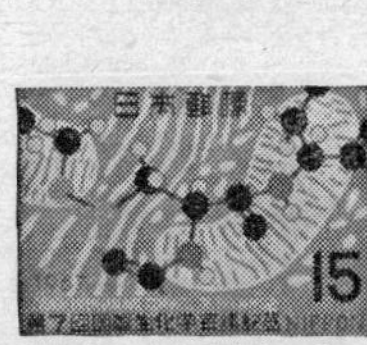

441. Protein Molecules. **442.** Gymnast.

1967. 7th Int. Biochemistry Congress, Tokyo.
1095. **441.** 15 y. multicoloured.. 12 5

1967. " Universiade 1967 " (Sports Meeting), Tokyo. Type **442** and similar multicoloured design.
1096. 15 y. Type **442** 15 5
1097. 50 y. Universiade " U " emblem (25 × 35½ mm.) 55 15

443. Paper Lantern.

444. Mt. Fuji (after T. Yokoyama).

1967. Int. Tourist Year.
1098. **443.** 15 y. multicoloured .. 12 5
1099. **444.** 50 y. multicoloured .. 2·00 85

445. " Kajikazaqa, Koshu ", (from woodcut by Hokusai). **446.** Athletic.

1967. Int. Correspondence Week.
1100. **445.** 50 y. multicoloured .. 2·00 20

1967. 22nd National Athletic Meeting.
1101. **446.** 15 y. multicoloured .. 40 5

447. Buddha Koryu Temple, Kyoto. **448.** Kudara Kannon (Budda), Horyu Temple, Nara.

449. Horyu Temple, Nara.

1967. National Treasures. Asuka Period.
1102. **447.** 15 y. multicoloured.. 35 15
1103. **448.** 15 y. multicoloured.. 45 15
1104. **449.** 50 y. multicoloured.. 1·75 35
See also Nos. 1113/15, 1120/2, 1134/6, 1152/4, 1170/2 and 1177/80.

450. Motor Expressway. **453.** "Noborizaru" (Miyazaki toy).

451. Mt. Kumotori. **452.** Lake Chichibu.

1967. 13th World Road Congress Tokyo.
1105. **450.** 50 y. multicoloured .. 50 8

1967. Chichibu-Tama National Park.
1106. **451.** 7 y. olive 15 5
1107. **452.** 15 y. violet 15 5

1967. New Year's Greetings.
1108. **453.** 7 y. multicoloured .. 12 5

454. Mt. Sobo. **455.** Takachiho Gorge.

1967. Sobo-Katamuki Quasi-National Park.
1110. **454.** 15 y. multicoloured .. 20 5
1111. **455.** 15 y. multicoloured .. 20 5

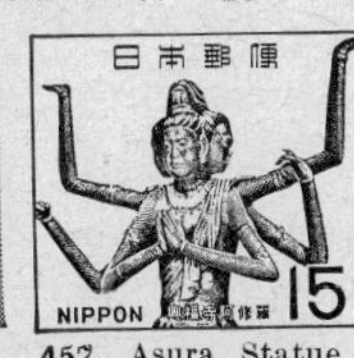

456. Boy and Girl, and Cruise Ship, "Sakura Maru". **457.** Asura Statue, Kofuku Temple, Nara.

458. Gakko Bosatsu, Todai Temple, Nara. **459.** Srimaha devi (painting), Yakushi Temple, Nara.

1968. Meiji Cent. Youth Goodwill Cruise.
1112. **456.** 15 y. violet, yell. & bl. 12 5

1968. National Treasures. Nara Period.
1113. **457.** 15 y. multicoloured.. 25 12
1114. **458.** 15 y. multicoloured.. 40 12
1115. **459.** 50 y. multicoloured.. 1·25 25

460. Mt. Yatsugatake and Cattle. **461.** Mt. Tateshina and Lake.

1968. Yatsugatake-Chushin Kogen Quasi-National Park.
1116. **460.** 15 y. multicoloured .. 15 5
1117. **461.** 15 y. multicoloured .. 15 5

462. " Dancer in a Garden " (after Bakusen Tsuchida). **463.** View of Rishiri Island from Rebun Island.

1968. Philatelic Week.
1118. **462.** 15 y. multicoloured .. 40 10

1968. Rishiri-Rebun Quasi-National Park.
1119. **463.** 15 y. multicoloured.. 12 5

464. Lacquer Casket. **466.** " Fugen Bosatsu " (painting of Bodishattra Samantabhadra).

465. " The Origin of Shigisan " (painting in Chogo-sonshi Temple).

1968. National Treasures. Heinan Period. Multicoloured.
1120. 15 y. Type **464** 20 12
1121. 15 y. Type **465** 20 12
1122. 50 y. Type **466** .. .. 2·25 40

467. Centenary Tower and Star. **468.** Biro Trees and Pacific Sunrise.

1968. Hokkaido Cent.
1123. **467.** 15 y. multicoloured .. 10 5

1968. Return of Ogasawara Islands to Japan.
1124. **468.** 15 y. multicoloured .. 12 5

469. " Map of Japan " in Figures.

1968. Postal Codes Campaign. (1st Issue).
1125. **469.** 7 y. red, brn. & grn. (I) 65 5
1126. – 7 y. red, brn. & grn. (II) 65 5
1127. **469.** 15 y. mag., vio. & bl. (I) 50 5
1128. – 15 y. mag., vio. & bl. (II) 50 5

(I) Inscr. as in Type **469** reading "Don't omit postal code on the address" measures 11 mm.

(II) Inscr. reading " Postal code also on your address " measures 12 mm.

Sheets of each denomination contain alternate copies of each inscr.

See also Nos. 1166/7, 1204/5, 1263/4 and 1296/7.

470. River Kiso. **471.** Inuyama Castle. and View.

1968. Hida-Kisogawa Quasi-National Park
1129. **470.** 15 y. multicoloured .. 12 5
1130. **471.** 15 y. multicoloured .. 12 5

472. Federation Emblem and " Sun ".

1968. Int. Youth Hostel Conf., Tokyo.
1131. **472.** 15 y. multicoloured .. 10 5

473. Humans forming Emblem. **474.** Baseball " Pitcher ".

1968. 50th All-Japan High School Baseball Championships, Koshi-en, Tokyo.
1132. **473.** 15 y. multicoloured .. 20 5
1133. **474.** 15 y. multicoloured .. 20 5

Sheets contain alternate copies of each design.

475. " Minamoto Yoritomo " (Jingo Temple Collection). **477.** Red-braided Armour (Kasuga Grand Shrine Collection).

476. " Heiji Monogatari " Scroll Painting.

1968. National Treasures. Kamakura Period. Multicoloured.
1134. 15 y. Type **475** 25 12
1135. 15 y. Type **476** 25 12
1136. 50 y. Type **477** .. .. 1·25 20

478. Mount Iwate. **479.** Lake Towada.

1968. Towada-Hachimantai National Park.
1137. **478.** 7 y. chestnut 12 5
1138. **479.** 15 y. green 12 5

480. Gymnastics. **481.** " Fujimihara, Bishu " (after Hokusai).

1968. 23rd National Athletic Meeting.
1139. **480.** 15 y. multicoloured .. 20 5

1968. Int. Correspondence Week.
1140. **481.** 50 y. multicoloured .. 90 20

482. Centenary Emblem and Japanese man-o'-war " Shohei Maru ". **483.** " Arrival of the Imperial Carriage in Tokyo " (after Tomone Kobori).

1968. Meiji Era. Cent.
1141. **482.** 15 y. multicoloured .. 10 5
1142. **483.** 15 y. multicoloured .. 15 5

484. Old and New Lighthouse.

1968. Japanese Lighthouses. Cent.
1143. **484.** 15 y. multicoloured .. 10 5

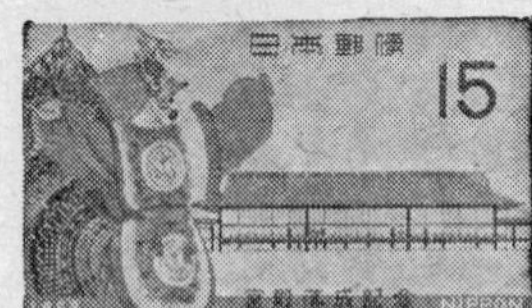

485. Ryo's Dancer and State Hall.

1968. Completion of Imperial Palace.
1144. **485.** 15 y. multicoloured .. 15 5

486. Mount Takachiho. **487.** Mount Motobu, Yaku Island.

1968. Kirishima-Yaku National Park.
1145. **486.** 7 y. violet 10 5
1146. **487.** 15 y. orange 12 5

488. " Niwatori " (Yamagata toy). **489.** Human Rights Emblem and Dancers.

1968. New Year's Greetings.
1147. **488.** 7 y. multicoloured .. 10 5

1968. Human Rights Year.
1149. **489.** 50 y. multicoloured .. 50 60

490. Squirrel with Nuts. **491.** Coastal Scenery.

1968. Savings Promotion.
1150. **490.** 15 y. sepia and green 20 5

1969. Echizen-Kaga-Kaigan Quasi-National Park.
1151. **491.** 15 y. multicoloured .. 12 5

492. Ginkaku, Jisho Temple, Kyoto. **493.** Pagoda, Anraku Temple, Nagano.

494. " Winter Landscape " (Sesshu).

1969. National Treasures. Muromachi Period. Multicoloured.
1152. 15 y. Type **492** 20 10
1153. 15 y. Type **493** 20 10
1154. 50 y. Type **494** .. .. 1·10 20

495. Mt. Chokai, from Tobishima.

1969. Chokai Quasi-National Park.
1155. **495.** 15 y. multicoloured 12 5

496. " Expo " Emblem and Globe.

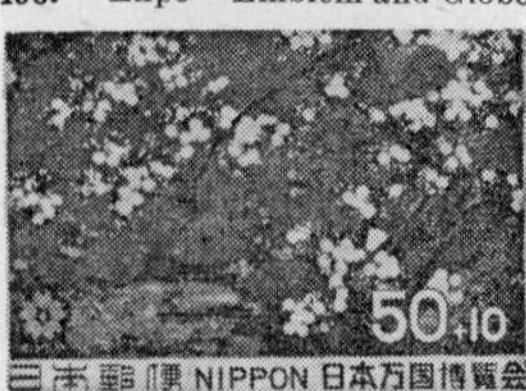

497. " Cherry Blossom " (from mural Chichakuin Temple, Kyoto).

1969. World Fair, Osaka (EXPO 70) (1st issue).
1156. **496.** 15 y. + 5 y. mult. 40 20
1157. **497.** 50 y. + 10 y. mult. 80 40

See also Nos. 1193/5 and 1200/2.

498. Koyasan, from Jinnogamine. **499.** Gomadanzan and Rhododendrons.

1969. Koya-Ryujin Quasi-National Park.
1158. **498.** 15 y. multicoloured .. 10 5
1159. **499.** 15 y. multicoloured .. 10 5

500. "Hair" (Kokei Kobayashi). **501.** Woman and Child crossing "Roads".

1969. Philatelic Week.
1160. **500.** 15 y. multicoloured .. 25 8

1969. Road Safety Campaign.
1161. **501.** 15 y. multicoloured .. 5 5

502. Sakawagawa Bridge.

1969. Completion of Tokyo-Nagoya Expressway.
1162. **502.** 15 y. multicoloured .. 12 5

503. Museum Building.

1969. Opening of National Museum of Modern Art, Tokyo.
1163. **503.** 15 y. multicoloured .. 12 5

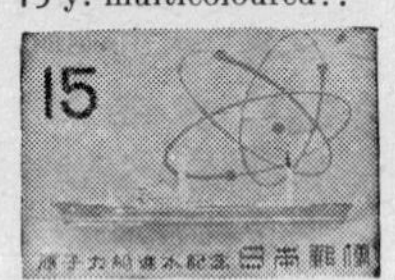

504. Nuclear Ship " Mutsu " and Atomic Symbol.

1969. Launching of Japan's 1st Nuclear Ship " Mutsu ".
1164. **504.** 15 y. multicoloured .. 10 5

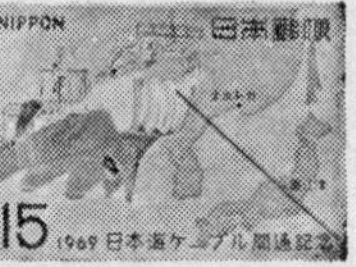

505. Cable Ship and Map. **506.** Symbol and Cards.

1969. Opening of Japanese Ocean Cable.
1165. **505.** 15 y. multicoloured .. 10 5

1969. Postal Codes Campaign (2nd issue).
1166. **506.** 7 y. red & yellow-grn. 12 5
1167. – 15 y. red and blue .. 20 5

DESIGN: 15 y. Symbol, postbox and code numbers.

507. Lions Emblem and Rose. **508.** Hotoke-ga-ura (coast).

1969. 52nd Lions Int. Convention, Tokyo.
1168. **507.** 15 y. multicoloured .. 10 5

1969. Shimokita-Hanto Quasi-National Park.
1169. **508.** 15 y. multicoloured .. 10 5

509. Himeji Castle, Hyogo Prefecture. **510.** " Pinewoods " (T. Hasegawa).

511. "The Japanese Cypress".

1969. National Treasures. Momoyama Period.
1170. **509.** 15 y. multicoloured .. 20 10
1171. **510.** 15 y. black and drab 20 10
1172. **511.** 50 y. multicoloured .. 60 25

512. Harano-fudo Waterfalls. **513.** Mount Nagisan.

1969. Hyonosen-Ushiroyama-Nagisan Quasi-National Park.
1173. **512.** 15 y. multicoloured .. 10 5
1174. **513.** 15 y. multicoloured .. 10 5

514. Mount O-akan. **515.** Mount Iwo.

1969. Akan National Park.
1175. **514.** 7 y. blue 10 5
1176. **515.** 15 y. sepia 10 5

516. "Choben" (T. Ikeno).

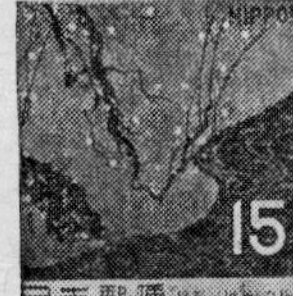

517. "The Red-plum Tree" (K. Ogata). **518.** "The White-plum Tree" (K. Ogata).

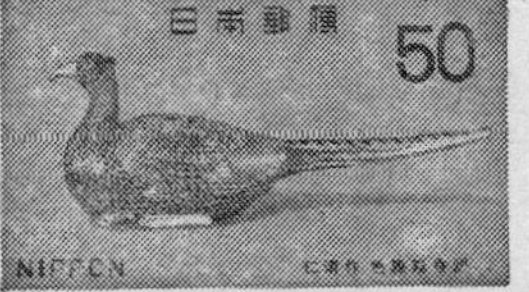

519. "Pheasant" Incense-burner, after Ninsei.

1969. National Treasures. Edo Period.
1177. **516.** 15 y. multicoloured .. 10 8
1178. **517.** 15 y. multicoloured .. 30 10
1179. **518.** 15 y. multicoloured .. 30 10
1180. **519.** 50 y. multicoloured .. 50 25

520. Globe and Doves.

521. "Woman Reading a Letter" (Utamaro).

522. "The Letter" (Harunobu).

523. "Portrait of Dennai" (Sharaku).

1969. 16th U.P.U. Congress, Tokyo.
1181. **520.** 15 y. multicoloured .. 10 5
1182. **521.** 30 y. multicoloured .. 40 15
1183. **522.** 50 y. multicoloured .. 50 25
1184. **523.** 60 y. multicoloured .. 50 25

524. "Mishimagoe" (Hokusai). **525.** Rugby Football.

1969. Int. Correspondence Week.
1185. **524.** 50 y. multicoloured .. 70 20

1969. 24th National Athletic Meeting.
1186. **525.** 15 y. multicoloured .. 15 5

526. Cape Kitayama. **527.** Goishi Coast.

1969. Rikuchu-Kaigan National Park.
1187. **526.** 7 y. blue 10 5
1188. **527.** 15 y. red and salmon 10 5

528. Worker in Safety Helmet. **529.** Guardian Dog, Hokkeji Temple.

1969. Int. Labour Organization. 50th Anniv.
1189. **528.** 15 y. black, yellow, brown and blue .. 10 5

1969. New Year's Greetings.
1190. **529.** 7 y. multicoloured .. 10 5

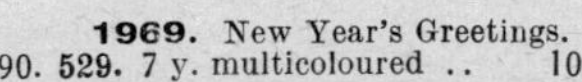

530. Peasants, Tsushima Island.

1970. Iki-Tsushima Quasi-National Park.
1192. **530.** 15 y. multicoloured .. 10 5

531. View of Exposition and Firework Display. **532.** "Woman with Drum" (Saburosuke Okada).

1970. World Fair, Osako. Expo 70 (2nd issue). Multicoloured.
1193. 7 y. Type 531 .. .. 10 5
1194. 15 y. Earth and Cherry Blossom Garland .. 10 5
1195. 50 y. "Irises" (Korin Ogata) 25 5
No. 1195 is horiz. size 48 × 33 mm.

1970. Philatelic Week.
1197. **532.** 15 y. multicoloured .. 25 8

533. Cherry-blossom, Yoshinoyama. **534.** Waterfall, Nachi.

1970. Yoshino-Kumano National Park.
1198. **533** 7 y. black and pink 10 5
1199. **534.** 15 y. green and blue 10 5

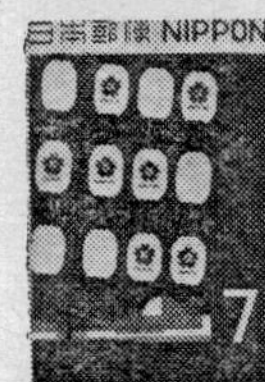

535. Kanto (lantern) Festival. **536.** Japanese Pavilions.

537. "Flowers of Autumn" (part of painting by Hoitsu Sakai).

1970. World Fair, Osako. Expo 70 (3rd issue).
1200. **535.** 7 y. multicoloured .. 10 5
1201. **536.** 15 y. multicoloured .. 10 5
1202. **537.** 50 y. multicoloured .. 25 5

538. Houses and Code Symbol. **539.** "Musume Dojoji".

540. "Sukeroku". **542.** Girl Scout saluting.

541. "Kanjincho".

1970. Postal Codes Campaign (3rd issue).
1204. **538.** 7 y. violet and green 12 5
1205. 15 y. maroon and blue 20 5

1970. Japanese Theatre "Kabuki".
1206. **539.** 15 y. multicoloured .. 12 5
1207. **540.** 15 y. multicoloured .. 12 5
1208. **541.** 50 y. multicoloured .. 35 10
See also Nos. 1250/2, 1284/6 and 1300/2.

1970. Japanese Girl Scouts. 50th Anniv.
1209. **542.** 15 y. multicoloured .. 10 5

543. Kinoura Coastline and Festival Drummer.

544. Mt. Tate-yama Range from Himi Shore.

1970. Noto-Hanto Quasi-National Park.
1210. **543.** 15 y. multicoloured .. 10 5
1211. **544.** 15 y. multicoloured .. 10 5

545. "Sunflower" and U.N. Emblem. **548.** "Post Office" (Tokyo) (from woodcut by Hiroshige).

546. Mt. Myogi **547.** Mt. Arafune.

1970. 4th U.N. Congress on Prevention of Crime and Treatment of Offenders, Kyoto.
1212. **545.** 15 y. multicoloured .. 10 5

1970. Myogi-Arafune-Sakukuogen Quasi-National Park.
1213. **546.** 15 y. multicoloured .. 10 5
1214. **547.** 15 y. multicoloured .. 10 5

1970. International Correspondence Week.
1215. **548.** 50 y. multicoloured .. 35 10

549. Show-jumping. **550.** "Hodogaya Stage" (from print by Hiroshige).

1970. 25th National Athletic Meeting.
1216. **549.** 15 y. multicoloured .. 15 5

1970. Telegraph Service Cent.
1217. **550.** 15 y. multicoloured .. 10 5

551. U.N. Emblem within "Tree". **552.** Competition Emblem.

1970. United Nations. 25th Anniv. Multicoloured.
1218. 15 y. Type **551** 10 5
1219. 50 y. U.N. emblem, New York H.Q. and flags .. 25 8

1970. 19th International Vocational Training Competition, Chiba City.
1220. **552.** 15 y. multicoloured .. 10 5

553. Diet Building and Doves. **554.** "Wild Boar" (folk-handicraft).

1970. Japanese Diet. 80th Anniv.
1221. **553.** 15 y. multicoloured .. 10 5

1970. New Year's Greetings.
1222. **554.** 7 y. multicoloured .. 10 5

555. Ski-jumping.

1971. Winter Olympic Games, Sapporo (1972) (1st issue). Multicoloured.
1224. 15 y. + 5 y. Type **555** 15 8
1225. 15 y. + 5 y. Ice-hockey (horiz.) 15 8

556. Mute Swan **557.** Japanese Deer. **558.** Beetle, "Allomyria dichotomus".

559. "Pine Tree" (T. Kano). **559a.** Golden Eagle. **560.** "Ho-o" Phoenix), Byodoin Temple, Uji.

1971. Inscr. "NIPPON".
1226. **209a.** 3 y. green 5 5
1227. **556..** 5 y. blue 5 5
1228. **557.** 10 y. brown & green 5 5
1229. **558.** 12 y. brown .. 5 5
1230. **559.** 20 y. brown & green 10 5
1231. **420c.** 25 y. blue and green 12 5
1231a. **192.** 50 y. green .. 25 5
1231b. – 60 y. green & yell. 30 5
1232. **324.** 70 y. black & orge. 30 5
1233. **324g.** 80 y. brown and red 35 5
1234. **324h.** 90 y. brown & orge. 40 5
1235. **559a.** 90 y. black & red .. 40 5
1236. **324j.** 120 y. brn. & grn. 55 5
1236a. – 140 y. mauve .. 60 5
1237. **560.** 150 y. green & blue 70 5
1237a. 150 y. brown & red 60 5
1238. **421.** 200 y. lake .. 85 5
1239. – 200 y. brown .. 80 5
1239a. – 200 y. red 80 5
1239b. – 250 y. blue .. 1·00 8
1240. – 300 y. blue .. 1·10 8
1240a. – 350 y. purple .. 1·50 8
1241. – 400 y. red .. .. 2·00 8
1242. – 500 y. green .. 2·00 15

DESIGNS: 60 y. Narcissus. 140 y. "Okina" Noh – mask. 250 y. Guard dog. 200 y. (Nos. 1239/a) "Warrior" (statuette): 300 y. Buddha, Kofukuji Temple. 350 y. Goddess of Mercy, Yak ushi-ji Temple, Nara. 400 y. Tenkoki (demon). 500 y. Buddhist deity.

No. 1231 is T **420c,** redrawn, the inscr. and face value are smaller, but the main difference is in the position of the leaves. On No. 1053 they touch the left edge of the design, but on No. 1231 they are completely clear of it.

No. 1237 is size 18 × 22 mm.

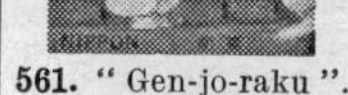
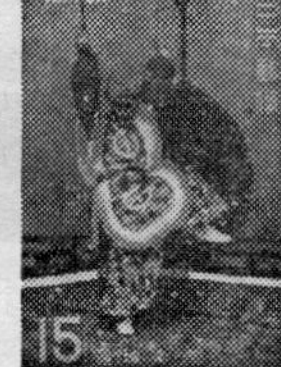

561. "Gen-jo-raku". **562.** "Kocho".

563. "Tai-hei-raku" (Four performers with staves).

1971. Japanese Theatre "Gagaku".
1250. **561.** 15 y. multicoloured .. 10 5
1251. **562.** 15 y. multicoloured .. 10 5
1252. **563.** 50 y. multicoloured .. 30 8

564. Voter and Diet Building. **565.** Pine Trees and Maple Leaves.

1971. Women's Suffrage. 25th Anniv.
1253. **564.** 15 y. multicoloured .. 10 5

1971. National Afforestation Campaign.
1254. **565.** 7 y. blk., violet & grn. 10 5

566. "Tsukiji-akashicho" (K. Kaburagi). **567.** "Posting a Letter" (K. Dogishi).

568. "Postman" (K. Kasai). **569.** "Railway Post Office". (S. Onozaki).

1971. Philatelic Week.
1255. **566.** 15 y. multicoloured .. 12 5

1971. Japanese Postal Services. Cent.
1256. **567.** 15 y. multicoloured .. 10 5
1257. **568.** 15 y. black & brown .. 10 5
1258. **569.** 15 y. multicoloured .. 10 5

570. Great Tit.

571. Penguins.

572. Goto-Wakamatsu-Seto. **573.** Kuzyuku-shima.

1971. 25th Bird Week.
1259. **570.** 15 y. multicoloured .. 5 5

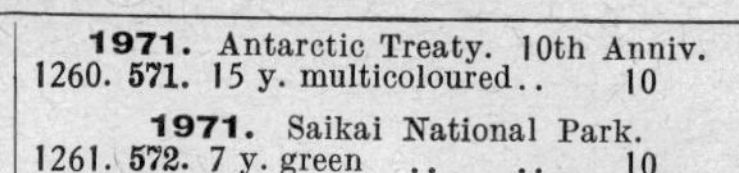

1971. Antarctic Treaty. 10th Anniv.
1260. **571.** 15 y. multicoloured .. 10 5

1971. Saikai National Park.
1261. **572.** 7 y. green 10 5
1262. **573.** 15 y. brown 10 5

574. Postal Code Numerals. **575.** Scout Bugler.

1971. Postal Code Campaign.
1263. **574.** 7 y. red and green .. 12 5
1264. 15 y. red and blue .. 20 5

1971. 13th World Scout Jamboree, Asagiri.
1265. **575.** 15 y. multicoloured .. 10 5

576. Rose Emblem. **577.** "Tokyo Horse-tram" (Yoshimura).

1971. Family Conciliation System. 50th Anniv.
1266. **576.** 15 y. multicoloured .. 10 5

1971. Int. Correspondence Week.
1267. **577.** 50 y. multicoloured .. 30 10

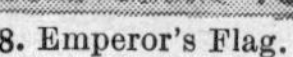

578. Emperor's Flag. **579.** Tennis.

1971. Emperor Hirohito and Empress Nagako's European Tour. Multicoloured.
1268. 15 y. Type **578** .. 10 5
1269. 15 y. "Beyond the Sea" (drawing by Empress Nagako) 10 5

Nos. 1268/69 were issued together horizontally and vertically se-tenant within the sheet of 20 stamps.

1971. 26th National Athletic Meeting.
1271. **579.** 15 y. multicoloured .. 12 5

580. Childs Face and "100". **581.** "Dragon" (G. Hashimoto.)

1971. National Family Registration System. Cent.
1272. **580.** 15 y. multicoloured .. 10 5

1971. Government Printing Works, Tokyo. Cent. Multicoloured.
1273. 15 y. Type **581** .. 15 5
1274. 15 y. "Tiger" (from same drawing as above) 15 5

582. Mt. Yotei from Lake Toya. **584.** Takarabune ("Treasure Ship").

583. Mt. Showa-Shinzan.

1971. Shikotsu-Toya National Park.
1275. **582.** 7 y. green and olive-grn. 10 5
1276. **583.** 15 y. blue and brown 10 5

1971. New Year.
1277. **584.** 7 y. multicoloured .. 10 5
1278. 10 y. multicoloured .. 10 5

585. Skiing.

1972. Winter Olympic Games, Sapporo. (2nd issue). Multicoloured.
1280. 20 y. Type **585** .. 10 5
1281. 20 y. Bobsleighing .. 10 5
1282. 50 y. Figure skating (pair) (horiz. 52 × 36 mm.) .. 25 10

586. "Kumagai-jinya". **587.** "Nozaki-mura".

588. "Awa-no-Natatu".

1972. Japanese Theatre "Banraku" Puppet Theatre.
1284. **586.** 20 y. multicoloured .. 10 5
1285. **587.** 20 y. multicoloured .. 10 5
1286. **588.** 50 y. multicoloured .. 20 8

589. High-speed Train on Sanyo Line. **590.** Fishing, Taishaku-kyo Valley.

591. Hiba Mountains.

1972. Japanese Railways Cent. (1st issue) and Opening of Sanyo Line.
1287. **589.** 20 y. multicoloured .. 12 5
See also Nos. 1305/6.

1972. Hiba-Dogo-Taishaku Quasi-National Park.
1288. **590.** 20 y. multicoloured .. 10 5
1289. **591.** 20 y. multicoloured .. 10 5

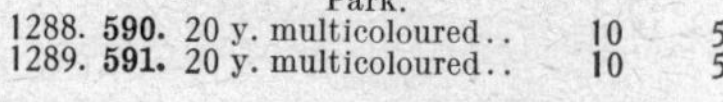

592. Adult with Human Heart. **593.** "Rising Balloon" (Gakuryo Nakamura).

1972. World Heart Month.
1290. **592.** 20 y. multicoloured .. 10 5

1972. Philatelic Week.
1291. **593.** 20 y. multicoloured .. 12 5

594. Shuri-mon Gate, Naha. **595.** Japanese Camellia.

1972. Return of Ryukyu Islands to Japan.
1292. **594.** 20 y. multicoloured . . 10 5

1972. National Afforrestation Campaign.
1293. **595.** 20 y. yell., bl. & grn. 10 5

596. Mt. Kurikoma and Kokeshi Doll. **597.** Naruko-kyo Gorge and Kokeshi Doll.

1972. Kurikoma Quasi-National Park.
1294. **596.** 20 y. multicoloured . . 10 5
1295. **597.** 20 y. multicoloured . . 10 5

598. Envelope and Code Symbol. **599.** Mt. Tate-yama

600. Mt. Hodaka.

1972. Postal Codes Campaign (5th issue).
1296. **598.** 10 y. blk., purple & blue 12 5
1297. – 20 y. red and green . . 15 5
DESIGN: 20 y. Mail-box and Code symbol.

1972. Chubu Sangaku National Park.
1298. **599.** 10 y. violet & mauve 10 5
1299. **600.** 20 y. blue & brown . . 10 5

601. Tamura. **602.** Aoi-no-ue.

603. "Hagoromo".

1972. Japanese Theatre "Noh".
1300. **601.** 20 y. multicoloured . . 10 5
1301. **602.** 20 y. multicoloured . . 10 5
1302. **603.** 50 y. multicoloured . . 30 8

604. "Schoolchildren". **605.** "Eitai Bridge" (Hiroshige).

1972. Japanese Educational System. Cent.
1303. **604.** 20 y. multicoloured . . 10 5

1972. Int. Correspondence Week.
1304. **605.** 50 y. multicoloured . . 25 10

606. "Inauguration of Railway Service" (Hiroshige). **607.** Kendo (Japanese fencing).

1972. Japanese Railways. Cent. (2nd issue). Multicoloured.
1305. 20 y. Type **606** . . 12 5
1306. 20 y. Steam locomotive, Class G-62 . . . . 15 5

1972. 27th National Athletic Meeting.
1307. **607.** 10 y. multicoloured . . 10 5

608. Scout and Cub. **609.** "Harbour and Bund, Yokohama" (Hiroshige).

1972. Japanese Boy Scouts. 50th Anniv.
1308. **608.** 20 y. multicoloured . . 10 5

1972. Japanese Customs Office. Cent.
1309. **609.** 20 y. multicoloured . . 10 5

610. "Plum Blossoms" Plate (K. Ogata). **611.** Mt. Tsurugi-san.

612. River Yoshino, Oboke Valley.

1972. New Year's Greetings.
1310. **610.** 10 y. multicoloured . . 10 5

1973. Tsurugi-San Quasi-National Park.
1312. **611.** 20 y. multicoloured . . 10 5
1313. **612.** 20 y. multicoloured . . 10 5

613. Mt. Takao. **614.** Minoo Falls.

1973. Meiji-no-mori Quasi National Park.
1314. **613.** 20 y. multicoloured . . 10 5
1315. **614.** 20 y. multicoloured . . 10 5

615. "Dragon" (East Wall).

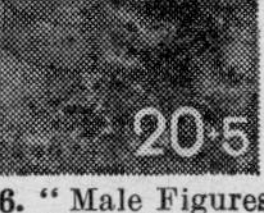

616. "Male Figures" (East Wall). **617.** "Female Figures" (West Wall).

1973. Asuka Archaelogical Conservation Fund. Takamatsuzuka Kofun Tomb Murals.
1316. **615.** 20 y. + 5 y. mult. . . 15 8
1317. **616.** 20 y. + 5 y. mult. . . 15 8
1318. **617.** 50 y. + 10 y. mult. . . 50 15

618. Phoenix Tree. **619.** "Sumiyoshi-mode" (R. Kishida).

1973. National Afforestation Campaign.
1319. **618.** 20 y. multicoloured . . 10 5

1973. Philatelic Week.
1320. **619.** 20 y. multicoloured . . 12 5

620. Mt. Kama-ga-take. **621.** Rock Outcrops, Mt. Haguro-san.

1973. Suzuka Quasi-National Park.
1321. **620.** 20 y. multicoloured . . 10 5
1322. **621.** 20 y. multicoloured . . 10 5

622. Chichi-jima Island Beach. **623.** Coral Reef, Minami-jimi Island.

1973. Ogasawara Islands National Park.
1323. **622.** 10 y. blue 10 5
1324. **623.** 20 y. maroon . . 10 5

624. Postal Code Symbol and Tree. **626.** Waterfall, Sanden-kyo Gorge.

625. Mt. Shinnyu.

1973. Postal Codes Campaign.
1325. **624.** 10 y. gold and green . . 10 5
1326. – 20 y. lilac, red & blue 12 5
DESIGN: 20 y. Postman and Symbol.

1973. Nishi-Chugoku-Sanchi Quasi-National Park.
1327. **625.** 20 y. multicoloured . . 10 5
1328. **626.** 20 y. multicoloured . . 10 5

627. Valley of River Tenryu. **628.** Woodland Path, Mt. Horaiji.

1973. Tenryu-Okumikowa Quasi-National Park.
1329. **627.** 20 y. multicoloured . . 10 5
1330. **628.** 20 y. blue, grn. & sil. 10 5

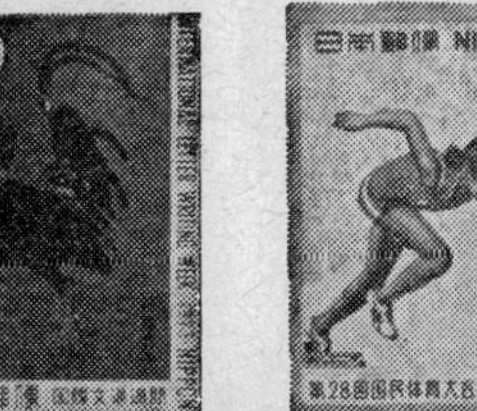

629. "Cock" (J. Ito). **630.** Sprinting.

1973. International Correspondence Week.
1331. **629.** 50 y. multicoloured . . 25 8

1973. 28th Nat. Athletic Meeting.
1332. **630.** 10 y. multicoloured . . 10 5

631. Kan-Mon Bridge.

1973. Kan-Mon Suspension Bridge. Opening.
1333. **631.** 20 y. multicoloured . . 10 5

632. Hanasaka-jijii and His Dog. **633.** Hanasaka-jijii finds the Gold.

634. Hanasaka-jijii and Tree in Blossom.

1973. Japanese Folk-tales (1st series). "Hanasaka-jijii".
1334. **632.** 20 y. multicoloured . . 15 5
1335. **633.** 20 y. multicoloured . . 15 5
1336. **634.** 20 y. multicoloured . . 15 5
See also Nos. 1342/4, 1352/4, 1358/60, 1362/4, 1378/80 and 1387/9.

635. Lantern. **636.** Niju-bashi Bridge.

1973. New Year.
1337. **635.** 10 y. multicoloured . . 10 5

1974. Imperial Golden Wedding. Mult.
1339. 20 y. Type **636** 10 5
1340. 20 y. Imperial Palace . . 10 5

637. "The Crane Damsel".

1974. Japanese Folk-tales (2nd series). "Tsuru-Nyobo". Multicoloured.
1342. 20 y. Type **637** . . 15 5
1343. 20 y. Crane "weaving" . . 15 5
1344. 20 y. Cranes in flight . . 15 5

638. "A Reefy Coast" (Hyakusui Hirafuku).

1974. International Ocean Exposition. Okinawa.
1345. **638.** 20 y. + 5 y. mult. . . 15 8

639. Marudu Falls. **640.** Seascape.

1974. Iriomote National Park.
1346. **639.** 20 y. multicoloured . . 10 5
1347. **640.** 20 y. multicoloured . . 10 5

641. Iromote Jungle Cat.

1974. Nature Conservation.
1348. **641.** 20 y. multicoloured . . 12 5
See also Nos. 1356, 1361, 1372, 1377, 1381, 1405, 1419, 1422, 1430 and 1433/4.

642. "Finger" (Shinsui Ito).

1974. Philatelic Week.
1349. **642.** 20 y. multicoloured . . 12 5

643. Nambu Red Pine.

644. Supreme Court Building.

1974. National Afforestation Campaign.
1350. **643.** 20 y. multicoloured . . 10 5

1974. Completion of Supreme Court Building, Tokyo.
1351. **644.** 20 y. brown 10 5

645. "Sailing in a Wooden Bowl".

646. "Conquering the Goblins".

647. "Wielding the little Magic Mallet".

1974. Japanese Folk-tales (3rd series). "The Dwarf".
1352. **645.** 20 y. multicoloured . . 12 5
1353. **646.** 20 y. multicoloured . . 12 5
1354. **647.** 20 y. multicoloured . . 12 5

648. "Uniform Rivalry" (detail after Kunimasa Baido).

649. World Blood Donation.

1974. Centenary of Japanese Police System.
1355. **648.** 20 y. multicoloured . . 12 5

1974. Nature Conservation. As Type **641.**
1356. 20 y. multicoloured . . 12 5
DESIGN: 20 y. Japanese otter.

1974. Int. Red Cross Day. World Blood Donation.
1357. **649.** 20 y. multicoloured . . 10 5

650. "Discovery of Kaguya Hime".

651. "Kaguya Hime as Young Woman".

652. "The Ascent to Heaven".

1974. Japanese Folk-tales (4th series). "Kaguya Hime".
1358. **650.** 20 y. multicoloured . . 12 5
1359. **651.** 20 y. multicoloured . . 12 5
1360. **652.** 20 y. multicoloured . . 12 5

1974. Nature Conservation. As Type **641.**
1361. 20 y. multicoloured . . 12 5
DESIGN: 20 y. Amami rabbit.

653. Old Men in front of Yahata Shrine.

654. Old Man dancing with Demons.

655. Old Man with Two Warts.

1974. Japanese Folk-tales (5th series). "Kobutori-Jiisan".
1362. **653.** 20 y. multicoloured . . 12 5
1363. **654.** 20 y. multicoloured . . 12 5
1364. **655.** 20 y. multicoloured . . 12 5

656. Map of World.

657. "Pine and Hawk" (detail—Sesson).

1974. 61st Inter-Parliamentary Union Congress, Tokyo. Multicoloured.
1365. 20 y. Type **656** 12 5
1366. 50 y. "Alzen"—Ducks in pond (Kawabata) (48 × 33 mm.) 25 8

1974. International Correspondence Week.
1367. **657.** 50 y. brown & purple 25 8

658. U.P.U. Emblem.

659. Footballers.

1974. Universal Postal Union. Cent. Mult.
1368. 20 y. Type **658** 10 5
1369. 50 y. "Tending a Cow" (fan-painting—Sotatsu Tawaraya) (50 × 29 mm.) 25 8

1974. 29th National Athletic Meeting.
1370. **659.** 10 y. multicoloured . . 10 5

660. Edible Fungi.

661. Class D-51 Locomotive.

662. Class C-57 Locomotive.

1974. Ninth International Scientific Congress on Cultivation of Edible Fungi.
1371. **660.** 20 y. multicoloured . . 10 5

1974. Nature Conservation. As Type **641.**
1372. 20 y. multicoloured . . 12 5
DESIGN: 20 y. Ogasawara flying fox.

1974. Railway Steam Locomotives (1st series).
1373. **661.** 20 y. multicoloured . . 15 5
1374. **662.** 20 y. multicoloured . . 15 5
See also Nos. 1382/3, 1385/6, 1395/6 and 1398/9.

663. "Daffodill" "Kugikakushi".

1974. New Year's Greetings.
1375. **663.** 10 y. multicoloured . . 10 5
A "kugikakushi" is an ornamental covering.

1975. Nature Conservation. As Type **641.**
1377. 20 y. multicoloured . . 12 5
DESIGN—VERT. 20 y. Albatrosses.

664. Taro releasing Tortoise.

665. Sea-God's Palace.

666. Taro and Pandora's Box.

1975. Japanese Folk-tales (6th series). "Urashima Taro".
1378. **664.** 20 y. multicoloured . . 12 5
1379. **665.** 20 y. multicoloured . . 12 5
1380. **666.** 20 y. multicoloured . . 12 5

1975. Nature Conservation. As Type **641.**
1381. 20 y. multicoloured . . 12 5
DESIGN—VERT. 20 y. Japanese cranes.

667. Class C-58 Locomotive.

668. Class D-52 Locomotive.

1975. Railway Steam Locomotives (2nd series).
1382. **667.** 20 y. multicoloured . . 12 5
1383. **668.** 20 y. multicoloured . . 12 5

669. "Kan-mon-sho" (Shiko Munakata).

1975. Japanese Broadcasting Corporation. 50th Anniv.
1384. **669.** 20 y. multicoloured . . 10 5

670. Class 8620 Locomotive.

671. Class C-11 Locomotive.

1975. Railway Steam Locomotives (3rd series).
1385. **670.** 20 y. multicoloured . . 12 5
1386. **671.** 20 y. multicoloured . . 12 5

672. Old Man feeding Mouse.

673. Old Man holding Mouse's Tail.

674. Mice giving Feast to Old Man.

1975. Japanese Folk-tales (7th series). "Nezumi No Jodo".
1387. **672.** 20 y. multicoloured . . 12 5
1388. **673.** 20 y. multicoloured . . 12 5
1389. **674.** 20 y. multicoloured . . 12 5

675. Matsuura Screen. **676.**

1975. Philatelic Week.
1390. **675.** 20 y. multicoloured . . 12 5
1391. **676.** 20 y. multicoloured . . 12 5

677. Statue of " Kisshoten ", Joruri-ji Temple. **678.** Drilling Rigs.

1975.
1392. **677.** 1000 y. multicoloured 4·00 60

1975. Ninth World Petroleum Congress, Tokyo.
1394. **678.** 20 y. multicoloured . . 10 5

679. Class 9600 Locomotive.

680. Class C-51 Locomotive. **681.** Plantation of Trees.

1975. Railway Steam Locomotives (4th series)
1395. **679.** 20 y. multicoloured . . 12 5
1396. **680.** 20 y. multicoloured . . 12 5

1975. National Land Afforestation Campaign.
1397. **681.** 20 y. multicoloured . . 10 5

682. Class 7100 Locomotive.

683. Class 150 Locomotive.

1975. Railway Steam Locomotives (5th series).
1398. **682.** 20 y. black & buff . . 12 5
1399. **683.** 20 y. black & yellow 12 5

684. Woman's Head and Emblem. **685.** Okinawa Dance.

1975. International Women's Year.
1400. **684.** 20 y. multicoloured . . 10 5

1975. International Exposition, Okinawa Multicoloured.
1401. 20 y. Type **685** 10 5
1402. 30 y. Bingata textile pattern 15 5
1403. 50 y. " Aquapolis and Globe " emblem (48 × 34 mm.) 20 8

1975. Nature Conservation. As T **641.** Multicoloured.
1405. 20 y. Bulbul (bird) . . 10 5

686. " Kentoshisen ".

687. " Kenminsen ".

1975. Japanese Ships (1st series).
1406. **686.** 20 y. red 10 5
1407. **687.** 20 y. brown 10 5
See also Nos. 1409/10, 1420/1, 1423/4, 1428/9 and 1431/2.

688. Apple. **691.** " Kujaka-kika-zu " (Y. Kikuchi).

689. " Goshuin-sen ".

690. " Tenchi-maru ".

1975. Apple Cultivation. Centenary.
1408. **688.** 20 y. multicoloured . . 10 5

1975. Japanese Ships (2nd series).
1409. **689.** 20 y. green 10 5
1410. **690.** 20 y. blue 10 5

1975. International Correspondence Week.
1411. **691.** 50 y. multicoloured . . 20 8

692. American Flag.

1975. American Tour by Emperor Hirohito and Empress Nagako. Multicoloured.
1412. 20 y. Type **692** 10 5
1413. 20 y. Japanese flag . . 10 5

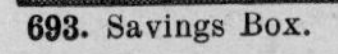

693. Savings Box. **694.** Weightlifting.

1975. Japanese Savings Bank. Centenary.
1415. **693.** 20 y. multicoloured . . 10 5

1975. 30th National Athletic Meeting.
1416. **694.** 10 y. multicoloured . . 5 5

695. " Tatsu-guruma " (toy). **696.** " Sengoku-bune ".

697. " Shohei-maru ".

1975. New Years' Greetings.
1417. **695.** 10 y. multicoloured . . 5 5

1976. Nature Conservation. As T **641.** Multicoloured.
1419. 50 y. Akahige (bird) . . 20 15

1976. Japanese Ships (3rd series).
1420. **696.** 50 y. blue 20 15
1421. **697.** 50 y. violet 20 15

1976. Nature Conservation. As T **641.** Multicoloured.
1422. 50 y. Tortoise 20 15

698. " Taisei-maru ".

699. " Tenyo-maru ".

1976. Japanese Ships (4th series).
1423. **698.** 50 y. black 20 15
1424. **699.** 50 y. brown 20 15

700. Section of Screen. **701.** Plum Blossom.

1976. Philatelic Week. Multicoloured.
1425. 50 y. Type **700** 20 15
1426 50 y. Similar to Type **700** 20 15
NOTE: The two stamps form a composite design of the " Hikone Folding Screen ".

1976. National Land Afforestation Campaign.
1427. **701.** 50 y. multicoloured . . 20 15

702. " Asama Maru ".

703. " Kinai Maru ".

1976. Japanese Ships (5th series).
1428. **702.** 50 y. brown 20 15
1429. **703.** 50 y. brown 20 15

1976. Nature Conservation. As T **641.** Multicoloured.
1430. 50 y. Arboreal green frog (vert.) . . 20 15

704. Container-ship " Kamakura Maru ".

705. Oil-tanker " Nissei Maru ".

1976. Japanese Ships (6th series).
1431. **704.** 50 y. blue 20 15
1432. **705.** 50 y. blue 20 15

1976. Nature Conservation. As T **641.** Multicoloured.
1433. 50 y. " Tanakia tanago " (carp) 20 15
1434. 50 y. " Gasterosteus aculeatus " (three-spined stickleback) 20 15

706. " Kite and Crows " (Yosa Buson).

1976. International Correspondence Week.
1435. **706.** 100 y. black, grey and cream 40 30

707. Gymnastics.

1976. 31st National Athletics Meeting.
1436. **707.** 20 y. multicoloured . . 10 8

MILITARY FRANK STAMPS

軍
事

(M 1.)

1910. No. 139 optd. with Type M **1.**
M 167. **13.** 3 s. red . . . . 80·00 32·00

1914. No. 171 optd. with Type M **1.**
M 185. **21.** 3 s. red . . . . 16·00 6·00

JAPANESE TAIWAN (FORMOSA) O1

From 1895 to 1945 Taiwan was part of the Japanese Empire, using stamps of Japan. During 1945 American naval and air forces disrupted communications between Taiwan and Japan. The following were issued when supplies of Japanese stamps ran short.

1. Numeral and Chrysanthemum.

1945. Imperf.

J 1.	1.	3 s. red	3·00	3·00
J 2.		5 s. green	2·50	2·50
J 3.		10 s. blue	4·75	5·00

JAPANESE OCCUPATION OF BRUNEI BC

These stamps were valid throughout British Borneo (i.e., in Brunei, Labuan, North Borneo and Sarawak).

(1. "Imperial Japanese Government").

1942. Stamps of Brunei optd. with T 1.

J 1.	1.	1 c. black	2·00	2·50
J 2.		2 c. green	15·00	20·00
J 3.		2 c. orange	1·00	1·25
J 4.		3 c. green	12·00	14·00
J 5.		4 c. orange	1·25	2·00
J 6.		5 c. brown	1·25	2·00
J 6a.	2.	6 c. grey	20·00	22·00
J 6b.		6 c. red	90·00	£110
J 7.	1.	8 c. black	70·00	75·00
J 8.	2.	8 c. red	1·00	1·00
J 9.	1.	10 c. purple on yellow	2·00	2·50
J 10.	2.	12 c. blue	2·00	2·50
J 11.		15 c. blue	2·00	2·50
J 12.	1.	25 c. lilac	5·00	6·00
J 13.		30 c. purple and orange	40·00	50·00
J 14.		50 c. black on green	8·00	8·00
J 15.		$1 black and red on blue	8·00	8·00
J 16.		$5 red on green	£100	
J 17.		$25 black on red	£200	

1944. Stamp of Brunei surch. with Japanese characters reading "Imperial Japanese Post $3".

J 18.	1.	$3 on 1 c. black	£300	£250

JAPANESE OCCUPATION OF BURMA BC

(1.)

(2.)

Note.—There are various types of the Peacock overprint. Our prices, as usual in this Catalogue, are for the cheapest type.

1942. Postage stamps of Burma of 1937 (India types) optd. as T 1.

J 22.	40.	3 p. grey	35	80
J 23.	63.	9 p. green	2·50	4·50
J 24.	44.	2 a. red	15·00	23·00
J 2.	66.	3½ a. blue	4·50	

1942. Official stamp of Burma of 1937 (India type) optd. as T 1.

J 3.	51.	6 a. yellow-brown	9·50	

1942. Postage stamps of Burma, 1938, optd. as T 1 or with T 2 (rupee values).

J 25.	1.	1 p. orange	16·00	25·00
J 12.		3 p. violet	1·60	6·00
J 27.		6 p. blue	2·50	8·00
J 14.		9 p. green	1·60	4·50
J 15.	2.	1 a. brown	80	2·00
J 30.		1½ a. green	2·00	4·50
J 16.		2 a. red	1·25	2·75
J 32.		4 a. blue	6·00	9·50
J 18.	7.	1 r. purple and blue	32·00	
J 19.		2 r. brown and purple	21·00	

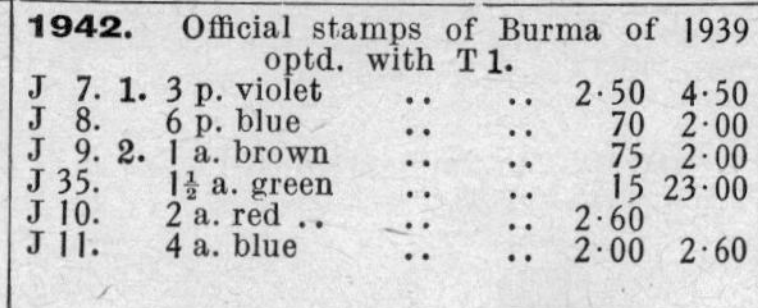

1942. Official stamps of Burma of 1939 optd. with T 1.

J 7.	1.	3 p. violet	2·50	4·50
J 8.		6 p. blue	70	2·00
J 9.	2.	1 a. brown	75	2·00
J 35.		1½ a. green	15	23·00
J 10.		2 a. red	2·60	
J 11.		4 a. blue	2·00	2·60

(3.) ("Yon Thon"="Official use").

1942. Official stamp of Burma of 1939 optd. with T 3.

J 44.	–	8. a green (No. O 23)	16·00	

4.

5. Farmer.

1942. Yano Seal.

J 45.	4.	(No value) red	9·00	14·00

1942.

J 46.	5.	1 a. red	5·50	6·00

1942. Stamps of Japan surch. in figures.

J 47.	–	¼ a. on 1 s. brn. (No. 317)	4·50	6·00
J 48.	66.	½ a. on 2 s. red	4·50	6·00
J 49.	–	¾ a. on 3 s. grn. (No. 319)	6·00	
J 50.	–	1 a. on 5 s. claret No. 396)	6·00	8·00
J 51.	–	3 a. on 7 s. grn. (No. 323)	7·50	8·50
J 52.	–	4 a. on 4 s. grn. (No. 320)	7·50	8·50
J 53.	–	8 a. on 8 s. vio. (No. 324)	25·00	32·00
J 54.	–	1 r. on 10 s. red (No. 325)	4·50	5·50
J 55.	–	2 r. on 20 s. blue (No. 328)	9·00	9·00
J 56.	–	5 r. on 30 s. bl. (No. 330)	3·00	3·50

1942. No. 386 of Japan commemorating the fall of Singapore, surch. in figures.

J 56g.	–	4 a. on 4 s. + 2 s. green and red	17·00	20·00

(New currency. 100 cents = 1 rupee.)

1942. Handstamped with new value.

J 57.	5.	5 c. on 1 a. red (No. J 46)	3·50	4·50

1942. Nos. J 47/53 with anna surcharges obliterated, and handstamped with new value in figures.

J 58.	–	1 c. on ¼ a. on 1 s. brown	9·00	9·00
J 59.	66.	2 c. on ½ a. on 2 s. red	9·00	9·00
J 60.	–	3 c. on ¾ a. on 3 s. green	9·00	9·00
J 61.	–	5 c. on 1 a. on 5 s. claret	9·00	
J 62.	–	10 c. on 3 a. on 7 s. green	13·00	13·00
J 63.	–	15 c. on 4 a. on 4 s. green	4·50	5·00
J 64.	–	20 c. on 8 a. on 8 s. violet	17·00	20·00

1942. Stamps of Japan surch. in cents only in figures.

J 65.	–	1 c. on 1 s. brn. (No. 317)	4·00	4·50
J 66.	66.	2 c. on 2 s. red	4·50	5·50
J 67.	–	3 c. on 3 s. grn. (No. 319)	7·00	8·00
J 68.	–	5 c. on 5 s. claret (No. 396)	7·50	9·00
J 69.	–	10 c. on 7 s. grn. (No. 323)	7·00	8·00
J 70.	–	15 c. on 4 s. grn. (No. 320)	4·50	6·00
J 71.	–	20 c. on 8 s. vio. (No. 324)	17·00	17·00

6. Burma State Crest.

7. Farmer.

1943. Perf. or Imperf.

J 72a.	6.	5 c. red	4·50	6·00

1943.

J 73.	7.	1 c. orange	30	50
J 74.		2 c. green	30	60
J 75.		3 c. blue	30	
J 77.		5 c. red	30	40
J 78.		10 c. brown	50	75
J 79.		15 c. mauve	12	45
J 80.		20 c. lilac	12	45
J 81.		30 c. green	12	50

8. "Independence".

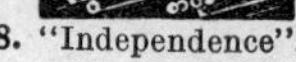

9. Rejoicing Peasant.

10. Boy with National Flag.

1943. Independence Day. Perf. or roul

J 82a.	8.	1 c. orange	45	70
J 83a.	9.	3 c. blue	45	70
J 84a.	10.	5 c. red	45	70

11. Burmese Girl.

12. Elephant carrying Log.

13. Watch Tower, Mandalay.

1943.

J 85.	11.	1 c. orange	1·25	1·40
J 86.		2 c. green	8	30
J 87.		3 c. violet	10	12
J 88.	12.	5 c. red	8	12
J 89.		10 c. blue	12	12
J 90.		15 c. orange	8	12
J 91.		20 c. green	8	30
J 92.		30 c. brown	8	30
J 93.	13.	1 r. orange	10	35
J 94.		2 r. violet	12	40

14. Bullock Cart.

15. Shan Woman.

(16. "Burma State").

1943. Shan States issue.

J 95.	14.	1 c. brown	6·00	
J 96.		2 c. green	6·00	
J 97.		3 c. violet	9·00	
J 98.		5 c. blue	80	
J 99.	15.	10 c. blue	6·00	
J 100.		20 c. red	6·00	
J 101.		30 c. brown	6·00	

1944. Optd. with T 16.

J 102.	14.	1 c. brown	60	70
J 103.		2 c. green	8	25
J 104.		3 c. violet	45	65
J 105.		5 c. blue	30	40
J 106.	15.	10 c. blue	45	70
J 107.		20 c. red	12	40
J 108.		30 c. brown	12	40

JAPANESE OCCUPATION OF CHINA O1

I. KWANGTUNG

Japanese troops occupied Canton in 1938 and by 1945 had overrun much of Kwangtung province. Unoverprinted stamps of China were used until the following stamps were issued.

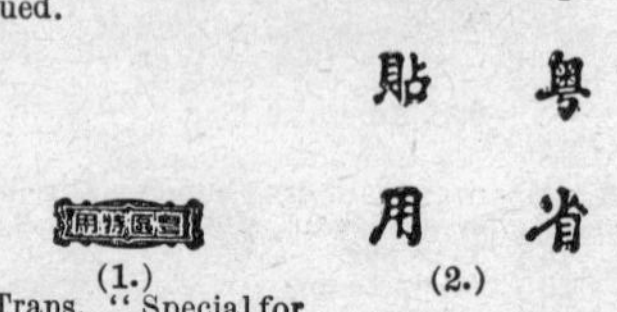

(1.) (Trans. "Special for Kwantung"). (2.)

1942. Stamps of China optd. with T 1.

1.	30.	1 c. orange	5	5
2.	41.	1 c. orange	5	5
3.	28.	2 c. olive	5	5
4.	38.	3 c. lake	5	5
5.	41.	5 c. green	5	5
6.	38.	8 c. olive	5	5
7.	41.	8 c. green	5	5
9.	38.	10 c. green	5	5
10.	41.	10 c. green	5	5
12.	38.	16 c. olive	12	12
13.	41.	17 c. olive	15	15
14.	30.	20 c. blue	12	12
15.	38.	30 c. red	10	10
16.	41.	30 c. red	12	12
17.	38.	50 c. blue	8	8
18.	41.	50 c. blue	12	12
19.	38.	$1 brown and red	15	15
20.		$2 brown and blue	15	15
21.		$5 green and red	20	20
22.		$10 violet and green	35	35
23.		$20 blue and purple	20	20

1942. Stamps of China optd. with T 2.

(a) On 1938 issue.

24.	38.	2 c. olive	5	5
25.		3 c. lake	5	5
26.		5 c. olive	5	5
28.		8 c. olive	5	5
29.		10 c. green	8	8
30.		16 c. olive	10	10
31.		25 c. blue	10	10
32.		30 c. red	5	5
33.		50 c. blue	5	5
34.		$1 brown and red	15	15
36.		$2 brown and blue	15	15
38.		$5 green and red	25	25
40.		$10 violet and green	40	40
42.		$20 blue and purple	45	45

(b) On 1941 issue.

44.	41.	2 c. blue	5	5
45.		5 c. green	5	5
46.		8 c. green	5	5
47.		8 c. orange	5	5
48.		10 c. green	10	10
49.		17 c. olive	12	12
50.		25 c. claret	12	12
51.		30 c. red	12	12
52.		50 c. blue	12	12
53.		$1 black and brown	15	15
54.		$2 black and blue	15	15
55.		$5 black and red	20	20
56.		$10 black and green	25	25
57.		$20 black and claret	40	40

(3.) (4.)

1945. Canton provisionals. Surch. as T 3.

58.	38.	$200 on 10 c. green (No. 29)	9·00	5·50
59.		$400 on 8 c. olive (No. 28)	9·00	5·50

1945. Swatow provisional. Stamp of China surch. with T 4.

60.	30.	$400 on 1 c. orange	65·00	38·00

POSTAGE DUE STAMP

(D 1.)

1945. Postage Due stamp of China surch. with Type D 1.

D 58.	D 4.	$100 on $2 orange	60·00	65·00

II. MENGKIANG (INNER MONGOLIA)

The autonomous area of Mengkiang ("the Mongolian Borderlands"), consisting of Suiyuan, South Chahar and North Shansi, was established by the Japanese in November, 1937.

For the first issue in 1941 see the note at the beginning of North China.

ILLUSTRATIONS British Commonwealth and all overprints and surcharges are FULL SIZE. Foreign Countries have been reduced to ½-LINEAR.

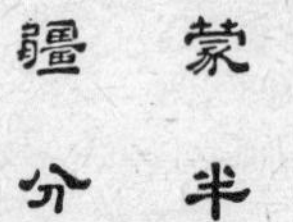

(1.)

1942. Stamps of China optd. "Mengkiang" and surch. half original value as T 1.

86.	30.	½ c. on 1 c. orange	5	5
66.	28.	1 c. on 2 c. olive	15	15
69.	38.	1 c. on 2 c. olive	10	5
67.	28.	2 c. on 4 c. green	10	10
87.	30.	2 c. on 4 c. lilac	5	5
72.	38.	4 c. on 8 c. green	5	5
99.	30.	5 c. on 10 c. purple	5	5
73.	38.	5 c. on 10 c. green	10	8
74.		8 c. on 16 c. olive	15	12
68.	28.	10 c. on 20 c. blue	1·00	1·00
100.	30.	10 c. on 20 c. lake	8	8

88. 30. 10 c. on 20 c. blue .. 5 5
101. 15 c. on 30 c. maroon.. 10 10
75. 38. 15 c. on 30 c. red .. 10 10
102. 30. 20 c. on 40 c. orange 15 15
103. 25 c. on 50 c. green .. 20 20
77. 38. 25 c. on 50 c. blue .. 25 20
80. 50 c. on $1 brown & red 30 25
82. $1 on $2 brown and blue 50 40
83. $5 on $10 violet & green 2·00 2·25
84. $10 on $20 blue & mar. 7·50 8·00

2. Dragon Pillar, Peking. 3. Miners.

1943. Establishment of Mengkiang Post and Telegraph Service. 5th Anniv.
104. 2. 4 c. orange 5 5
105. 8 c. blue 10 12

1943. War in East Asia. 2nd Anniv.
106. 3. 4 c. green 5 5
107. 8 c. red 10 10

4. Stylised Horse. 5. Prince Yun. 6. Blast Furnace.

1943. Federation of Autonomous Governments of Mongolian Provinces. 1st Anniv.
108. 4. 3 c. red 5 5
109. 5. 8 c. blue 10 10

1944. Productivity Campaign.
110. 6. 8 c. brown 5 5

1945. Stamps of China optd. "Mengkiang" as top characters in T 1.
117. 30. 1 c. orange 5 5
111. 28. 2 c. olive 5 5
112. 4 c. green 20 20
113. 5 c. green 5 5
118. 30. 8 c. orange 5 5
119. 10 c. purple 5 5
120. 20 c. lake 5 5
121. 30 c. claret 5 5
122. 40 c. orange 5 5
123. 50 c. green 15 15
114. 38. $1 brown and red .. 15 15
115. $2 brown and blue .. 55 55
116. $5 green and red .. 1·40 1·40

角伍
(7.)

1945. Stamps of China optd. "Mengkiang" (as T 1 of North China) and surch. as T 7.
124. 30. 10 c. on ½ c. sepia .. 5 5
126. 10 c. on 1 c. orange .. 8 8
130. 28. 50 c. on 2 c. olive .. 5 5
135. 38. 50 c. on 2 c. olive .. 5 5
136. 28. 50 c. on 4 c. green .. 40 40
131. 30. 50 c. on 4 c. lilac .. 8 8
137. 28. 50 c. on 5 c. green .. 5 5
132. 38. 50 c. on 5 c. olive .. 5 5
138. 30. $1 on 8 c. orange .. 10 10

The Japanese conquered North China in 1937 and formed a puppet Government in Peking.

III. NORTH CHINA.

蒙疆 (1. "Mengkiang.") 河南 (2. "Honan.")
河北 (3. "Hopei.") 山西 (4. "Shansi.")
山東 (5. "Shantung.") 蘇北 (6. "Supeh.")

T 1 to 6 are the six "district" overprints comprising North China (including Mengkiang) and a detailed list of the overprints on the stamps of China is given in the large Stanley Gibbons' Overseas Catalogue, Volume 1.

新嘉坡陷落紀念 (7.) 滿洲國建國十週年紀念 (8.)

In 1942 stamps of China overprinted with T 2 to 6 were further overprinted with T 7 (to commemorate the Fall of Singapore) or with T 8 (to commemorate the tenth Anniversary of Manchukuo). These stamps are also listed in the Stanley Gibbons' Overseas Catalogue. Volume 1.

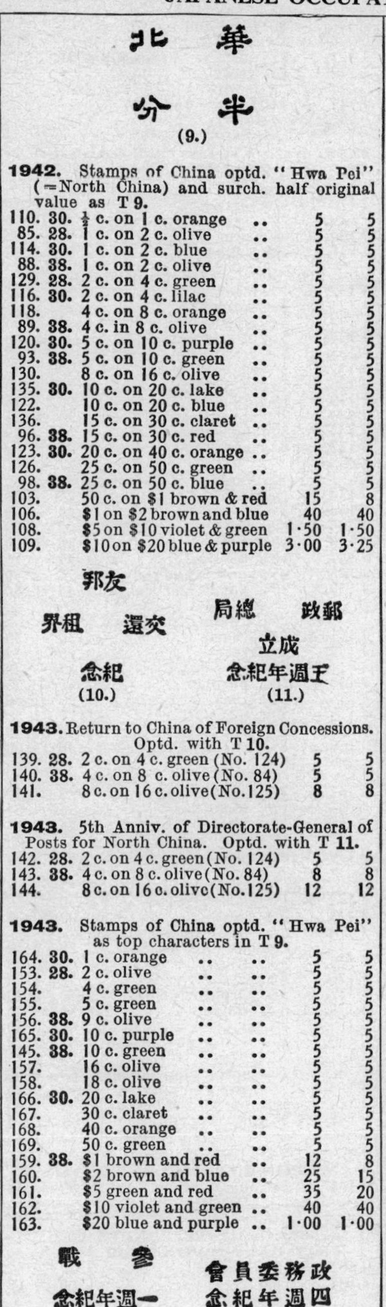

華北 半分
(9.)

1942. Stamps of China optd. "Hwa Pei" (=North China) and surch. half original value as T 9.
110. 30. ½ c. on 1 c. orange .. 5 5
85. 28. 1 c. on 2 c. olive .. 5 5
114. 30. 1 c. on 2 c. blue .. 5 5
88. 38. 1 c. on 2 c. olive .. 5 5
129. 28. 2 c. on 4 c. green .. 5 5
116. 30. 2 c. on 4 c. lilac .. 5 5
118. 4 c. on 8 c. orange .. 5 5
89. 38. 4 c. in 8 c. olive .. 5 5
120. 30. 5 c. on 10 c. purple .. 5 5
93. 38. 5 c. on 10 c. green .. 5 5
130. 8 c. on 16 c. olive .. 5 5
135. 30. 10 c. on 20 c. lake .. 5 5
122. 10 c. on 20 c. blue .. 5 5
136. 15 c. on 30 c. claret .. 5 5
96. 38. 15 c. on 30 c. red .. 5 5
123. 30. 20 c. on 40 c. orange .. 5 5
126. 25 c. on 50 c. green .. 5 5
98. 38. 25 c. on 50 c. blue .. 5 5
103. 50 c. on $1 brown & red 15 8
106. $1 on $2 brown and blue 40 40
108. $5 on $10 violet & green 1·50 1·50
109. $10 on $20 blue & purple 3·00 3·25

友邦租界交還紀念 (10.) 郵政總局成立五週年紀念 (11.)

1943. Return to China of Foreign Concessions. Optd. with T 10.
139. 28. 2 c. on 4 c. green (No. 124) 5 5
140. 38. 4 c. on 8 c. olive (No. 84) 5 5
141. 8 c. on 16 c. olive (No. 125) 8 8

1943. 5th Anniv. of Directorate-General of Posts for North China. Optd. with T 11.
142. 28. 2 c. on 4 c. green (No. 124) 5 5
143. 38. 4 c. on 8 c. olive (No. 84) 8 8
144. 8 c. on 16 c. olive (No. 125) 12 12

1943. Stamps of China optd. "Hwa Pei" as top characters in T 9.
164. 30. 1 c. orange 5 5
153. 28. 2 c. olive 5 5
154. 4 c. green 5 5
155. 5 c. green 5 5
156. 38. 9 c. olive 5 5
165. 30. 10 c. purple 5 5
145. 38. 10 c. green 5 5
157. 16 c. olive 5 5
158. 18 c. olive 5 5
166. 30. 20 c. lake 5 5
167. 30 c. claret 5 5
168. 40 c. orange 5 5
169. 50 c. green 5 5
159. 38. $1 brown and red .. 12 8
160. $2 brown and blue .. 25 15
161. $5 green and red .. 35 20
162. $10 violet and green .. 40 40
163. $20 blue and purple .. 1·00 1·00

參戰一週年紀念 (12.) 政務委員會四週年紀念 (13.)

1944. Declaration of War on Allies by Japanese-controlled Nanking Govt. 1st Anniv. Optd. with T 12.
170. 28. 4 c. green (No. 149) .. 5 5
171. 38. 10 c. green (No. 140) .. 5 5

1944. North China Political Council. 4th Anniv. Optd. with T 13.
172. 38. 9 c. olive (No. 151) .. 5 5
173. 18 c. olive (No. 153) .. 5 5
174. 30. 50 c. green (No. 164) .. 12 12
175. 38. $1 brown & red (No. 154) 20 20

華北玖分 (14.) 郵政總局成立六週年紀念 (15.)

1944. Stamps of Japanese Occupation of Shanghai and Nanking optd. "Hwa Pei" and surch. as T 14.
176. 5. 9 c. on 50 c. orange .. 5 5
177. 18 c. on $1 green .. 5 5
178. 6. 36 c. on $2 blue .. 8 8
179. 90 c. on $5 red .. 10 10

1944. 6th Anniv. of Directorate-General of Posts for North China. Optd. with T 15.
180. 38. 9 c. olive (No. 151) .. 5 5
181. 18 c. olive (No. 153) .. 5 5
182. 30. 50 c. green (No. 164) .. 8 8
183. 38. $1 brown & red (No. 154) 15 15

汪主席葬典紀念 (16.) 參戰二週年紀念 (17.) 華北壹圓 (18.)

1944. Death of Wang Ching-wei. Optd. with T 16.
184. 30. 20 c. lake (No. 161) .. 5 5
185. 50 c. green (No. 164) .. 5 5
186. 38. $1 brown & red (No. 154) 8 8
187. $2 brown & blue (No. 155) 8 8

1945. Declaration of War on Allies by Nanking Govt. 2nd Anniv. Optd. with T 17.
188. 30. 20 c. lake (No. 161) .. 5 5
189. 50 c. green (No. 164) .. 10 10
190. 38. $1 brown & red (No. 154) 10 10
191. $2 brown & blue (No. 155) 15 15

1945. Stamps of Japanese Occupation of Shanghai and Nanking surch. as T 18.
192. 7. 50 c. on $3 orange .. 5 5
193. $1 on $6 blue .. 5 5

19. Dragon Pillar. 20. Long Bridge.

21. Imperial City Tower. 22. Marble Boat, Summer Palace. 23.

1945. Establishment of North China Political Council. 5th Anniv. Views of Peking.
194. 19. $1 yellow 5 5
195. 20. $2 blue 5 5
196. 21. $5 red 8 8
197. 22. $10 green 8 8

1945. Optd. "Hwa Pei" as top characters in T 9.
198. 23. $1 brown 5 5
199. $2 blue 5 5
200. $5 red 10 5
201. $10 green 15 10
202. $20 purple 20 10
203. $50 brown .. .. 1·50 1·10

24. Wutai Mountain, Shansi. 25. Kaifeng Iron Pagoda, Honan. 26. Int. Bridge, Tientsin.

27. Taishan Mountain, Shantung. 28. G.P.O., Peking.

1945. Directorate General of Posts for North China. 7th Anniv.
204. 24. $5 green 5 5
205. 25. $10 brown 5 5
206. 26. $20 purple 5 5
207. 27. $30 grey 5 5
208. 28. $50 red 10 5

IV. NANKING AND SHANGHAI

The Japanese captured Shanghai and Nanking in 1937 and Hankow in 1938. During the same year Nanking was made the seat of Japanese-controlled administration for the Yangtse Basin. The stamps listed below were used in parts of Anhwei, Southern Kiangsu, Chekiang, Hupeh, Kiangsi, Hunan and Fukien.

N.B. With the exception of Nos. 114 to 119 the following are all surcharged on stamps of China.

20
國內信函之航空費已付
(1.)

1941. Air. Surch. as T 1.
1. 31. 10 s. on 50 c. chocolate .. 5 5
2. 18 s. on 90 c. olive .. 5 5
3. 20 s. on $1 green 5 5
5. 25 s. on 90 c. olive .. 5 5
6. 35 s. on $2 brown .. 5 5
7. 60 s. on 35 s. on $2 brown (No. 6) 5 5

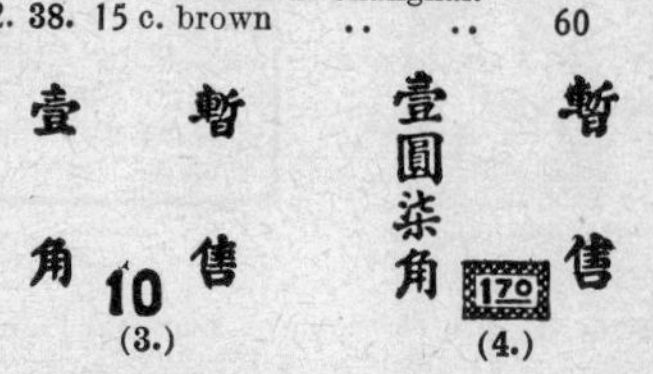

收回租界紀念 三十二年八月一日 伍角
(2.)

1943. Return to China of Shanghai Concessions. Surch. as T 2.
8. 38. 25 c. on 5 c. green .. 5 5
9. 41. 50 c. on 8 c. orange .. 5 5
10. 38. $1 on 16 c. olive .. 5 5
11. 41. $2 on 50 c. blue.. .. 5 5

1943. As No. 422 but colour changed. Issued at Shanghai.
12. 38. 15 c. brown 60 80

暫售 10 角 壹 (3.) 暫售 壹圓柒角 (4.)

1943. Stamps of China and No. 12 above surch. as T 3 (cent values) or T 4 (dollar values).

(a) On T 28.
13. 28. $6 on 5 c. green .. 5 5
14. $20 on 15 c. red .. 5 5
15. $500 on 15 c. green .. 5 5
17. $1000 on 20 c. blue .. 5 5
18. $1000 on 25 c. blue .. 5 5

(b) On Martyrs issue.
88. 30. $7.50 c. on ½ c. sepia .. 5 5
89. $15 on 1 c. orange .. 5 5
91. $30 on 2 c. blue .. 5 5
93. $200 on 1 c. orange .. 5 5
94. $200 on 8 c. orange .. 5 5

(c) On T 38.
19. 38. 25 c. on 5 c. olive .. 5 5
20. 30 c. on 2 c. olive .. 5 5
21. 50 c. on 3 c. lake .. 5 5
22. 50 c. on 5 c. olive .. 5 5
23. 50 c. on 8 c. olive .. 5 5
24. $1 on 8 c. olive .. 5 5
26. $1 on 15 c. brown .. 5 5
27. $1 30 c. on 16 c. olive .. 5 5
28. $1 50 c. on 3 c. lake .. 5 5
54. $1 70 c. on 30 c. red .. 5 5
29. $2 on 5 c. olive .. 5 5
30. $2 on 10 c. green .. 5 5
56. $2 on $1 brown and red .. 5 5
59. $3 on 8 c. olive .. 5 5
31. $3 on 15 c. brown .. 5 5
32. $4 on 16 c. olive .. 5 5
33. $5 on 15 c. brown .. 5 5
34. $6 on 5 c. green .. 5 5
35. $6 on 5 c. olive .. 5 5
36. $6 on 8 c. olive .. 5 5
38. $6 on 10 c. green .. 5 5
39. $10 on 10 c. green .. 5 5
40. $10 on 16 c. olive .. 5 5
41. $20 on 3 c. lake.. .. 5 5
42. $20 on 15 c. red .. 5 5
43. $20 on 15 c. brown .. 5 5
44. $20 on $2 brown & blue 20 20
65. $50 on 30 c. red .. 5 5
66. $50 on 50 c. blue .. 5 5
67. $50 on $5 green and red 5 5
68. $50 on $20 blue & clar. 25 20
45. $100 on 3 c. lake .. 5 5
46. $100 on $10 vio. & grn. 10 10
70. $200 on $20 bl. & clar. 5 5
72. $500 on 8 c. olive .. 5 5
47. $500 on 10 c. green .. 5 5
48. $500 on 15 c. red .. 5 5
49. $500 on 15 c. brown .. 5 5
50. $500 on 16 c. olive .. 5 5
51. $1000 on 25 c. blue .. 5 5
74. $1000 on 30 c. red .. 5 5
75. $1000 on 50 c. blue .. 5 5
76. $1000 on $2 brn. & blue 30 30
52. $2000 on $5 grn. & red 5 5
87a. $5000 on $10 vio. & grn. 75 75

(d) On T 41.
95. 41. 5 c. on ½ c. sepia .. 5 5
96. 10 c. on 1 c. orange .. 5 5
97. 20 c. on 1 c. orange .. 5 5
98. 40 c. on 5 c. green .. 5 5
99. $5 on 5 c. green .. 5 5
100. $10 on 10 c. green .. 5 5
101. $50 on ½ c. sepia .. 5 5
102. $50 on 1 c. orange .. 5 5
103. $50 on 17 c. olive .. 5 5
104. $200 on 5 c. green .. 5 5
105. $200 on 8 c. green .. 5 5
106. $200 on 8 c. orange .. 5 5
107. $500 on $5 black & red 5 5
108. $1000 on 1 c. orange .. 5 5
109. $1000 on 25 c. purple.. 8 8
110. $1000 on 30 c. red .. 8 8
111. $1000 on $2 blk. & blue 12 12
112. $1000 on $10 blk. & grn. 8 8
113. $2000 on $5 blk. & red 12 12

5. Wheat and Cotton Flower, 6. Purple Mountain, Nanking.

1944. Establishment of Chinese Puppet Government at Nanking. 4th Anniv.
114. 5. 50 c. orange 5 5
115. $1 green 5 5
116. 6. $2 blue 5 5
117. $5 red 5 5

ILLUSTRATIONS
British Commonwealth and all overprints and surcharges are FULL SIZE. Foreign Countries have been reduced to ¾-LINEAR.

7. Map of Shanghai and Foreign Concessions.

1944. Return to China of Shanghai Foreign Concessions. 1st Anniv.
118. 7. $3 orange 5 5
119. $6 blue 5 5

1945. Establishment of Chinese Puppet Government at Nanking. 5th Anniv. Surch. as T 4.
124. $15 on 50 c. orange 5 5
125. $30 on $1 green 5 5
126. 6. $60 on $2 blue 5 5
127. $200 on $5 red 5 5

防空
250

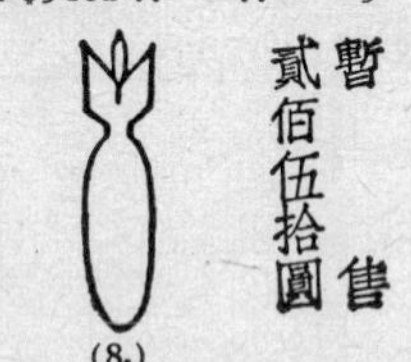

(8.)

1945. Air Raid Precautions Propaganda. Air stamps surch. as T 8.
128. 31. $150 on 15 c. green 5 5
129. $250 on 25 c. orange 5 5
130. $600 on 60 c. blue 5 8
131. $1000 on $1 green 5 10

POSTAGE DUE STAMPS

壹 改
圓 作
1^{00}
(D 1.)

1945. Postage Due stamps surch. as Type D 1.
D 120. D 4. $1 on 2 c. orange 5 5
D 121. $2 on 5 c. orange 5 5
D 122. $5 on 10 c. orange 5 5
D 123. $10 on 20 c. orange 5 5

JAPANESE OCCUPATION OF HONG KONG BC

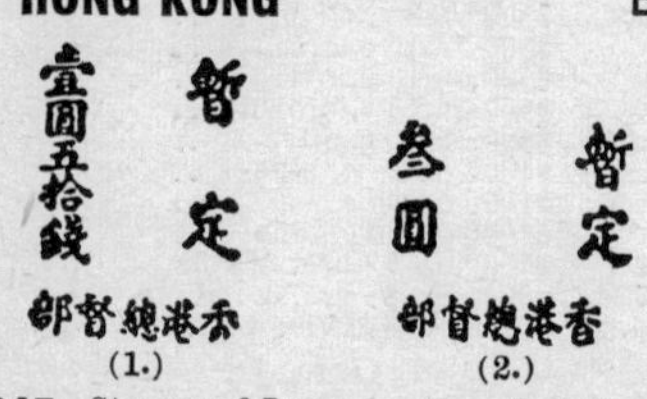

(1.) (2.)

1945. Stamps of Japan surch as T 1 (No. 1) or 2.
1. 108. 1.50 yen on 1 s. brown 60 1·75
2. 66. 3 yen on 2 s. red 60 1·75
3. – 5 yen on 5 s. claret (No. 396) 22·00 6·50

MINIMUM PRICE

The minimum price quoted is 5p which represents a handling charge rather than a basis for valuing common stamps. For further notes about prices see introductory pages.

JAPANESE OCCUPATION OF MALAYA BC

1

1942. Stamps of various states optd. with T 1.

(a) Straits Settlements.
J 6. 17. 1 c. black 75 75
J 7. 2 c. green £200 £200
J 8. 2 c. orange 80 80
J 9. 3 c. green 90 85
J 10. 5 c. brown 2·75 3·50
J 12. 8 c. grey 1·00 85
J 13. 10 c. purple 3·75 5·00
J 14. 12 c. blue 12·00 14·00
J 15. 15 c. blue 1·50 1·25
J 17. 30 c. purple and orange £140 £170
J 18. 40 c. red and purple 12·00 14·00
J 19. 50 c. black and green 8·00 8·50
J 20. $1 black and red on blue 12·00 13·00
J 21. $2 green and red 18·00 20·00
J 22. $5 green & red on green 23·00 26·00
There also exists a similar overprint with double-lined frame.

(b) Negri Sembilan.
J 23. 3. 1 c. black 5·50 6·50
J 24. 2 c. orange 3·00 4·00
J 25. 3 c. green 4·50 5·00
J 27b. 5 c. brown 2·50 3·00
J 29. 6 c. grey 20·00 22·00
J 31. 8 c. red 6·50 11·00
J 32a. 10 c. purple 8·50 9·00
J 32c. 12 c. blue 70·00 70·00
J 33. 15 c. blue 4·00 3·50
J 34. 25 c. purple and red 9·00 9·00
J 35. 30 c. purple and orange 23·00 27·00
J 36. 40 c. red and purple 60·00 65·00
J 37. 50 c. black on green 24·00 28·00
J 38. $1 black & red on blue 13·00 16·00
J 39. $5 green & red on green 55·00 65·00

(c) Pahang.
J 40. 3. 1 c. black 8·00 9·00
J 41. 3 c. green 12·00 16·00
J 42. 5 c. brown 2·75 2·40
J 44. 8 c. grey 20·00 20·00
J 45. 8 c. red 5·00 2·50
J 46. 10 c. purple 8·00 9·00
J 47. 12 c. blue £180 £180
J 48. 15 c. blue 13·00 13·00
J 49. 25 c. purple and red 8·00 9·00
J 50. 30 c. purple and orange 6·50 7·50
J 51. 40 c. red and purple 5·00 6·50
J 52. 50 c. black on green 35·00 45·00
J 53. $1 black and red on blue 18·00 18·00
J 54. $5 green & red on green 80·00 85·00

(d) Perak.
J 55. 5. 1 c. black 6·00 6·50
J 57. 2 c. orange 4·00 4·50
J 58. 3 c. green 7·00 8·00
J 59. 5 c. brown 2·00 2·00
J 61. 8 c. grey 8·00 8·50
J 62. 8 c. red 4·00 12·00
J 63. 10 c. purple 4·00 8·00
J 64. 12 c. blue 20·00 22·00
J 65. 15 c. blue 6·50 8·50
J 66. 25 c. purple and red 4·00 5·50
J 67. 30 c. purple and orange 7·50 9·50
J 68. 40 c. red and purple 42·00 45·00
J 69. 50 c. black on green 5·50 8·00
J 70. $1 black and red on blue 42·00 50·00
J 71. $2 green and red £150 £150
J 72. $5 green & red on green £120

(e) Selangor.
J 73. 4. 1 c. black 2·50 2·50
J 74. 2 c. green 75·00 75·00
J 75. 2 c. orange 8·00 9·00
J 77c. 3 c. green 2·50 2·50
J 78. 5 c. brown 1·75 1·60
J 79. 6 c. red 30·00 32·00
J 80. 8 c. grey 4·00 4·50
J 81. 10 c. purple 4·00 5·00
J 82. 12 c. blue 8·00 9·00
J 83. 15 c. blue 4·00 4·50
J 84a. 25 c. purple and red 17·00 18·00
J 85. 30 c. purple and orange 5·50 7·00
J 86. 40 c. red and purple 10·00 11·00
J 87. 50 c. black on green 10·00 11·00
J 88. 6. $1 black & red on blue 9·00 9·00
J 89. $2 green and red 10·00 11·00
J 91. $5 green and red on grn. 15·00 15·00

(f) Trengganu.
J 92. 3. 1 c. black 20·00 22·00
J 93. 2 c. green 30·00 35·00
J 94a. 2 c. on 5 c. purple on yellow (No. 59) 12·00 12·00
J 95. 3 c. brown 21·00 20·00
J 96. 4 c. red 38·00 30·00
J 97. 5 c. purple on yellow 3·50 4·00
J 98. 6 c. orange 4·00 6·00
J 99. 8 c. grey 4·50 4·50
J 100. 8 c. on 10 c. bl. (No. 60) 4·00 7·50
J 101. 10 c. blue 4·50 7·00
J 102. 12 c. blue 4·00 5·50
J 103. 20 c. purple and orange 4·50 6·00
J 104. 25 c. green and purple 4·50 6·00
J 105. 30 c. purple and black 4·50 6·00
J 106. 35 c. red on yellow 4·50 6·00
J 107. 50 c. green and red 14·00 16·00
J 108. $1 purple & blue on blue £225 £225
J 109. $3 green & red on green 13·00 14·00
J 110. – $5 green and red on yellow (No. 31) 30·00 32·00
J 111. – $25 pur. and bl. (No. 40) £110
J 112. $50 green and yellow (No. 41) £225
J 113. – $100 green and red (No. 42) £150

1942. Various stamps optd. DAI NIPPON 2602 MALAYA.

(a) Stamps of Straits Settlements.
J 128. 17. 2 c. orange 30 30
J 129. 3 c. green 12·00 15·00
J 130. 8 c. grey 90 90
J 131. 15 c. blue 2·50 2·25

(b) Stamps of Negri Sembilan.
J 132. 3. 1 c. black 25 25
J 133. 2 c. orange 25 25
J 134. 3 c. green 25 35
J 135. 5 c. brown 30 40
J 136. 6 c. grey 55 60
J 137. 8 c. red 90 80
J 138. 10 c. purple 2·25 2·00
J 139. 15 c. blue 2·00 2·25
J 140. 25 c. purple and red 90 2·25
J 141. 30 c. purple and orange 1·10 2·00
J 142. $1 black & red on blue 30·00 38·00

(c) Stamps of Pahang.
J 143. 3. 1 c. black 20 20
J 144. 5 c. brown 40 50
J 145. 8 c. red 7·00 20
J 146. 10 c. purple 4·50 2·50
J 147. 12 c. blue 45 75
J 148. 25 c. purple and red 1·75 2·50
J 149. 30 c. purple and orange 45 80

(d) Stamps of Perak.
J 151. 5. 2 c. orange 30 30
J 152. 3 c. green 25 30
J 154. 8 c. red 40 20
J 155. 10 c. purple 2·50 3·25
J 156. 15 c. blue 1·25 1·10
J 158. 50 c. black on green 1·10 1·50
J 159. $1 black & red on blue 50·00 60·00
J 160. $5 green & red on green 12·00 13·00

(e) Stamps of Selangor.
J 162. 4. 3 c. green 25 30
J 165. 12 c. blue 55 95
J 166. 15 c. blue 1·75 2·25
J 168. 40 c. red and purple 1·25 1·60
J 170. 6. $2 green and red 6·00 7·00

(f) Stamps of Trengganu.
J 172. 3. 1 c. black 2·50 2·50
J 173. 2 c. green 40·00 42·00
J 174. 2 c. on 5 c. purple on yellow (No. 65) 2·50 2·50
J 175. 3 c. brown 2·50 5·50
J 176. 4 c. red 2·50 3·50
J 177. 5 c. purple on yellow 2·50 2·50
J 178. 6 c. orange 2·50 3·50
J 179. 8 c. grey 12·00 7·50
J 180. 8 c. on 10 c. blue (No. 66) 2·00 2·50
J 181. 12 c. blue 1·90 3·25
J 182. 20 c. purple and orange 2·50 4·00
J 183. 25 c. green and purple 2·50 5·00
J 184. 30 c. purple and black 2·50 5·00
J 185. $3 green & red on green 12·00 17·00

1942. No. 104 of Perak surch. DAI NIPPON 2602 MALAYA 2 cents.
J 186. 5. 2 c. on 5 c. brown 80 30

1942. Agri-horticultural Exhibition. Stamps of Straits optd. SELANGOR EXHIBITION DAI NIPPON 2602 MALAYA.
J 187. 17. 2 c. orange 2·50 2·50
J 188. 8 c. grey 1·60 1·60

1942. Stamps of Kedah optd. DAI NIPPON 2602.
J 189. 1. 1 c. black 60 80
J 190. 2 c. green 4·50 5·50
J 191. 4 c. violet 45 50
J 192. 5 c. yellow 45 45
J 193. 6 c. red 45 80
J 194. 8 c. black 80 60
J 195. 4. 10 c. blue and brown 90 90
J 196. 12 c. black and violet 3·00 5·50
J 197. 25 c. blue and purple 1·60 1·60
J 198. 30 c. green and red 13·00 14·00
J 199. 40 c. black and purple 4·50 6·00
J 200. 50 c. brown and blue 5·00 7·50
J 201. $1 black and green 22·00 22·00
J 202. $2 green and brown 30·00 30·00
J 203. $5 black and red 12·00 12·00

1942. Stamps of Straits Settlements optd. DAI NIPPON 2602 PENANG.
J 204. 17. 1 c. black 40 45
J 205. 2 c. orange 60 70
J 206. 3 c. green 40 45
J 207. 5 c. brown 40 50
J 208 8 c. grey 90 80
J 209. 10 c. purple 90 90
J 210. 12 c. blue 90 95
J 211. 15 c. blue 90 90
J 212. 40 c. red and purple 1·10 1·25
J 213. 50 c. black and green 2·25 2·40
J 214. $1 black & red on blue 3·00 4·00
J 215. $2 green and red 7·50 8·50
J 216. $5 green & red on grn. 65·00 70·00

1942. Stamps of Perak optd. DAI NIPPON YUBIN ("Japanese Postal Service") or surch. also in figures and words.
J 217. 5. 1 c. black 70 1·10
J 218. 2 c. on 5 c. brown 80 65
J 219. 8 c. red 1·00 70

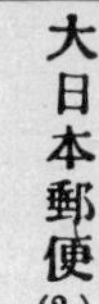

(2.)

1943. Various stamps optd. vert. or horiz. with T 2 or surch. also in figures and words.

(a) Stamps of Straits Settlements.
J 221. 17. 8 c. grey 20 20
J 222. 12 c. blue 30 80
J 223. 40 c. red and purple 40 65

(b) Stamps of Negri Sembilan.
J 224. 3. 1 c. black 12 25
J 225. 2 c. on 5 c. brown 15 15
J 226. 6 c. on 5 c. brown 20 20
J 227. 25 c. purple and red 60 70

(c) Stamp of Pahang.
J 228. 3. 6 c. on 5 c. brown 30 40

(d) Stamps of Perak.
J 230. 5. 1 c. black 20 25
J 232. 2 c. on 5 c. brown 30 30
J 235. 5 c. brown 30 30
J 237. 8 c. red 40 35
J 238. 10 c. purple 45 35
J 239. 30 c. purple and orange 90 1·10
J 240. 50 c. black on green 2·00 2·25
J 241. $5 grn. & red on green 16·00 18·00

(e) Stamps of Selangor.
J 249. 4. 1 c. black 15 20
J 250. 2 c. on 5 c. brown 12 30
J 243. 3 c. green 25 30
J 251. 3 c. on 5 c. brown 12 30
J 252. 5 c. brown 15 25
J 254. 6 c. on 5 c. brown 10 12
J 244 12 c. blue 30 65
J 245. 15 c. blue 1·60 1·60
J 246. 6. $1 black & red on blue 1·75 2·00
J 256. 4. $1 on 10 c. purple 12 60
J 257. $1.50 on 30 c. purple and orange 12 60
J 247. 6. $2 green and red 5·50 6·00
J 248. $5 green & red on green 8·00 7·50

(f) Stamps of Trengganu.
J 258. 3 1 c. black 2·00 6·00
J 259. 2 c. green 2·00 7·50
J 260. 2 c. on 5 c. purple on yellow (No. 59) 2·00 6·00
J 261. 5 c. purple on yellow 2·00 6·00
J 262. 6 c. orange 3·00 7·00
J 263. 8 c. grey 12·00 16·00
J 264. 8 c. on 10 c. bl. (No. 60) 6·00 11·00
J 265. 10 c. blue 22·00 38·00
J 266. 12 c. blue 4·00 9·00
J 267. 20 c. purple and orange 4·00 9·00
J 268. 25 c. green and purple 4·00 10·00
J 269. 30 c. purple and black 4·00 10·00
J 270. 35 c. red on yellow 4·00 10·00

3. Tapping Rubber. 4. Malay Mosque, Kuala Lumpur.

1943.
J 271. 3. 1 c. green 10 10
J 272. – 2 c. green 10 10
J 273. 3. 3 c. grey 10 10
J 274. – 4 c. red 10 10
J 275. – 8 c. blue 10 10
J 276. – 10 c. purple 10 10
J 277. – 15 c. violet 15 12
J 278. – 30 c. olive 15 15
J 279. – 50 c. blue 30 30
J 280. 4. 70 c. blue 3·00 2·50

DESIGNS—VERT. 2 c. Fruit. 4 c. Tin dredger. 8 c. War Memorial. 10 c. Huts. 30 c. Sago palms. 50 c. Straits of Johore. HORIZ. 15 c. Japanese Shrine, Singapore.

5. Ploughman. 6. Rice-planting.

1943. Savings Campaign.
J 281. 5. 8 c. violet 3·00 75
J 282. 15 c. red 1·75 80

1944. "Re-birth of Malaya".
J 283. 6. 8 c. red 1·40 1·00
J 284. 15 c. mauve 1·40 1·00

POSTAGE DUE STAMPS

1942. Postage Due stamps of Malayan Postal Union optd. with T 1.
JD 1. D 1. 1 c. violet 3·00 3·50
JD 2. 3 c. green 3·25 4·00
JD 3. 4 c. green 3·25 1·60
JD 4. 8 c. red 4·50 5·50
JD 5. 10 c. orange 4·50 5·50
JD 6. 12 c. blue 5·00 5·50
JD 7. 50 c. black 8·50 9·00

1942. Postage Due stamps of Trengganu optd. with **T 1**.

JD 13.	**D 1.**	1 c. red	10·00	13·00
JD 14.		4 c. green	12·00	10·00
JD 15.		8 c. yellow	6·50	10·00
JD 16.		10 c. brown ..	6·50	10·00

1942. Postage Due stamps of Malayan Postal Union optd. **DAI NIPPON 2620 MALAYA.**

JD 23.	**D 1.**	1 c. violet	40	45
JD 24.		3 c. green	1·00	1·10
JD 25.		4 c. green	1·25	1·10
JD 26.		8 c. scarlet	1·75	2·00
JD 27.		10 c. orange ..	1·00	1·10
JD 28.		12 c. blue	1·00	1·10

1943. Postage Due stamps of Malayan Postal Union optd. with **T 2**.

JD 29.	**D 1.**	1 c. violet	20	45
JD 30.		3 c. green	20	55
JD 31.		4 c. green ..	8·00	10·00
JD 32.		5 c. red	25	85
JD 33.		9 c. orange ..	40	90
JD 34.		10 c. orange ..	40	1·10
JD 35.		12 c. blue	40	1·25
JD 36.		15 c. blue	40	1·25

1943. Postage Due stamps of Johore optd. with **T 2**.

JD 37.	**D 1.**	1 c. red	40	1·40
JD 38.		4 c. green	40	1·40
JD 39.		8 c. orange	1·00	3·00
JD 40.		10 c. brown ..	85	3·50
JD 41.		12 c. purple ..	85	3·50

JAPANESE OCCUPATION OF NETHERLANDS INDIES O2

100 sen (cents) = 1 rupee (gulden).

I. JAVA

1. Eastern Asia.

DESIGNS: 3½ s. Farmer ploughing rice field. 5 s. Mt. Soemer. 10 s. Bantam Bay.

1943. Designs with vert. inscr. as in **T 1**.

1.	**1.**	2 s. brown	1·00	60
2.	–	3½ s. red	1·00	60
3.	–	5 s. green	1·50	60
4.	–	10 s. blue	3·00	1·00

2. Wayang puppet. 3. Bird of Vishnu. 4. Native Soldier.

1943. Designs with rectangular panel of characters as at foot of **T 2/3**.

5.	–	3½ c. red	40	15
6.	**2.**	5 c. green	40	20
7.	–	10 c. blue	40	15
8.	–	20 c. olive	60	25
9.	–	40 c. purple	80	25
10.	**3.**	60 c. orange	1·00	40
11.	–	80 s. brown	2·00	50
12.	–	1 r. violet	5·00	60

DESIGNS—As **T 2**: 3½ c. Native head. 10 c. Boroboudur Temple. 20 c. Map of Java. 40 c. Seated dancer and Temple. As **T 3**: 80 c. Ploughing with oxen. 1 r. Terraced rice-fields.

1943. Savings Campaign.

13.	**4.**	3½ c. red	7·00	1·75
14.		10 c. blue	8·00	1·10

II. SUMATRA

5. Lake Tobal

DESIGNS: 1 c. to 3 c. Batak house, 3½ c. to 5 c. Minangkabau house. 10 c., 20 c. Ploughing with oxen. 50 c., 1 r. Carabao Canyon (20 × 28 mm.).

1943. Designs with rectangular panel characters as at foot of **T 5**.

15.	–	1 c. olive	30	15
16.	–	2 c. green	30	15
17.	–	3 c. blue	30	15
18.	–	3½ c. red	30	15
19.	–	4 c. blue	30	15
20.	–	5 c. orange	30	15
21.	–	10 c. blue	40	30
22.	–	20 c. brown	60	40
23.	**5.**	30 c. purple	1·00	50
24.		40 c. brown	1·25	70
25.	–	50 c. bistre	3·50	1·25
26.	–	1 r. violet	5·00	1·40

便郵國帝本日大

スマトラ

6.

1944. Various stamps of Netherlands (Nos. 78/9) and Netherlands Indies optd. with **T 6**.

38.	**19.**	1 c. violet (No. 335) ..	15	20
39.		2 c. purple (No. 336) ..	15	20
40.		2½ c. brown (No. 337) ..	15	20
41.		3 c. green (No. 338) ..	2·75	3·25
74.	–	3 c. green (No. 463) ..	2·75	3·25
27.	**19.**	3½ c. grey (No. 339) ..	15	20
75.	**34.**	4 c. olive (No. 515) ..	12	20
76.	–	5 c. blue (No. 465) ..	12	20
78.	**78.**	5 c. green (No. 506) ..	4·00	5·00
77.	–	7½ c. violet (No. 466) ..	12	20
42.	**20.**	10 c. red (No. 344) ..	2·75	3·25
57.	–	10 c. red (No. 429) ..	1·00	1·50
29.	**20.**	12½ c. red (No. 345) ..	4·75	6·50
79.	**78.**	12½ c. blue (No. 509) ..	2·25	4·00
51.	**20.**	15 c. blue (No. 414) ..	70	2·10
59.	–	15 c. blue (No. 430) ..	25	30
60.	–	17½ c. orange (No. 431)	30	35
52.	**20.**	20 c. purple (No. 405)	25	30
61.	–	20 c. mauve (No. 432) ..	12	12
53.	**20.**	25 c. green (No. 348) ..	8·50	11·00
62.	–	25 c. green (No. 433) ..	60	70
46.	**20.**	30 c. blue (No. 349) ..	90	1·75
63.	–	30 c. brown (No. 434) ..	5·30	7·00
54.	**20.**	35 c. violet (No. 408) ..	30	45
64.	–	35 c. purple (No. 435) ..	60	70
55.	**20.**	40 c. green (No. 352) ..	6·00	7·00
65.	–	40 c. green (No. 436) ..	4·50	5·50
34.	**20.**	42½ c. yellow (No. 353)	30	50
35.		50 c. blue (No. 354) ..	17·00	21·00
66.	–	50 c. brown (No. 437) ..	7·00	8·00
67.	–	60 c. blue (No. 438) ..	60	60
68.	–	80 c. red (No. 439) ..	45	45
69.	–	1 g. violet (No. 440) ..	60	60
49.	**20.**	2 g. green (No. 414) ..	14·00	17·00
70.	–	2 g. green (No. 441) ..	1·10	1·50
36.	**20.**	2 g. 50 purple (No. 359)	21·00	28·00
56.		5 g. brown (No. 415) ..	4·50	5·50
71.	–	5 g. brown (No. 442) ..	22·00	30·00
72.	–	10 g. green (No. 443) ..	7·50	9·00
73.	–	25 g. orange (No. 444) ..	4·50	60·00

III JAPANESE NAVAL CONTROL AREA

大日本

(7.)

1942. Various stamps of Netherlands (Nos. 129/30) and Netherlands Indies optd. with **T 7**.

80.	**19.**	1 c. violet (No. 335) ..	20	65
90.		2 c. purple (No. 336)	20	40
91.		2½ c. brown (No. 337) ..	15	35
124.	–	2½ c. red (No. 462) ..	1·50	2·25
92.	**19.**	3 c. green (No. 338) ..	20	55
125.	–	3 c. green (No. 463) ..	70	1·00
82.	**19.**	3½ c. grey (No. 339) ..	2·00	3·50
83.		4 c. green (No. 340) ..	3·00	3·75
126.	**34.**	4 c. olive (No. 464) ..	25	70
84.	**19.**	5 c. blue (No. 401) ..	4·00	5·00
107.	**7.**	5 c. blue (No. 270) ..	20	35
127.	–	5 c. blue (No. 465) ..	1·00	1·90
129.	**78.**	5 c. green (No. 506) ..		
128.	–	7½ c. violet (No. 466) ..	20	70
95.	**20.**	10 c. red (No. 344) ..	9·00	12·00
108.	–	10 c. red (No. 429) ..	50	50
130.	**78.**	12½ c. blue (No. 509)		
96.	**20.**	15 c. blue (No. 404) ..	1·50	2·25
110.	–	15 c. blue (No. 430) ..	25	70
111.	–	17½ c. orange (No. 431)	30	70
97.	**20.**	20 c. purple (No. 405)	35	1·00
112.	–	30 c. mauve (No. 432)	7·00	10·00
98.	**20.**	25 c. green (No. 348)	1·00	1·75
113.	–	25 c. green (No. 433)	6·00	9·00
86.	**20.**	30 c. blue (No. 349) ..	4·50	6·00
106.	**21.**	30 c. blue (No. 360) ..	45·00	60·00
114.	–	30 c. brown (No. 434) ..	35	70
100.	**20.**	35 c. violet (No. 400) ..	35	1·00
115.	–	35 c. purple (No. 435)	15·00	18·00
101.	**20.**	40 c. green (No. 352) ..	35	1·00
116.	–	40 c. green (No. 436) ..	6·00	9·00
88.	**20.**	50 c. blue (No. 354) ..	11·00	15·00
117.	–	50 c. red (No. 437) ..	1·00	1·00
118.	–	60 c. blue (No. 438) ..	1·25	1·90
102.	**20.**	80 c. red (No. 356) ..	12·00	15·00
119.	–	80 c. red (No. 439) ..	1·25	1·90
103.	**20.**	1 g. violet (No. 357)		
120.	–	1 g. violet (No. 440) ..	1·00	1·50
104.	**20.**	2 g. green (No. 414) ..		
121.	–	2 g. green (No. 441) ..	7·50	10·00
105.	**20.**	5 g. brown (No. 415)		
122.	–	5 g. brown (No. 442)		
123.	**31.**	25 g. orange (No. 444)		

1943. Air. Nos. 335 and 337 of Netherlands Indies optd. with **T 7** and further surch.

148.	**19.**	"f. 2" on 1 c. violet ..	3·50	4·75
149.		"f. 8·50" on 2½ c. brn.	5·50	7·00

8. Japanese Flag and Palms. 9. Mt. Fuji, Flag and Bird.

1943.

152.	**8.**	2 c. orange	20	15
153.		3 c. green	20	15
154.		3½ c. orange ..	20	15
155.		5 c. blue	20	15
156.		10 c. red	20	15
157.	**8.**	15 c. blue	30	25
158.		20 c. violet	30	25
159.	**9.**	25 c. orange ..	75	50
160.		30 c. blue	90	70
161.		50 c. green	1·75	1·25
162.		1 g. lilac	6·00	5·00

POSTAGE DUE STAMPS

1942. Nos. D 226/31, D 233/6, D 448, D 452 and D 384 of Netherlands Indies optd. with **T 7**.

D 142.	**D 2.**	1 c. red	1·10	1·50
D 132.		2½ c. red ..	20	25
D 133.		3½ c. red ..	1·00	1·50
D 134.		5 c. red	40	50
D 135.		7½ c. red ..	40	50
D 136.		10 c. red ..	25	20
D 144.		15 c. red ..	40	50
D 137.		20 c. red ..	40	60
D 138.		20 c. on 37½ c. red	3·75	4·50
D 139.		25 c. red ..	40	60
D 140.		30 c. red ..	40	60
D 141.		40 c. red ..	40	60
D 147.		1 g. blue ..	1·50	2·25

JAPANESE OCCUPATION OF NORTH BORNEO BC

1942. Stamps of North Borneo optd. as **T 1** of Japanese Occupation of Brunei.

(a) Issue of 1939.

J 1.	**55.**	1 c. green and brown ..	24·00	35·00
J 2.	**56.**	2 c. purple and blue ..	18·00	30·00
J 3.	–	3 c. blue and green ..	18·00	30·00
J 4.	–	4 c. green and violet ..	11·00	21·00
J 5.	–	6 c. blue and claret ..	18·00	30·00
J 6.	–	8 c. red	18·00	30·00
J 7.	–	10 c. violet and green	18·00	30·00
J 8.	–	12 c. green and blue ..	27·00	55·00
J 9.	–	15 c. green and brown	27·00	55·00
J 10.	–	20 c. violet and blue ..	27·00	55·00
J 11.	–	25 c. green and brown	27·00	55·00
J 12.	–	50 c. brown and violet	30·00	60·00
J 13.	–	$1 brown and red ..	32·00	75·00
J 14.	–	$2 violet and olive ..	60·00	£110
J 15.	–	$5 blue	80·00	£150

(b) War Tax issue of 1941.

J 16.	**55.**	1 c. green and brown ..	27·00	18·00
J 17.	**56.**	2 c. purple and blue ..	22·00	18·00

1. Mt. Kinabalu. 2. Borneo Scene.

1943.

J 18.	**1.**	4 c. red	5·50	6·00
J 19.	**2.**	8 c. blue	5·50	6·00

本日大
便郵國帝
オネルボ北

(3.)

本日大
便郵國帝
貳
弗

(4.)

("Imperial Japanese Postal Service, North Borneo".)

1944. Stamps of North Borneo of 1939 optd. as **T 3**.

J 20.	**55.**	1 c. green and brown	50	75
J 21.	**56.**	2 c. purple and blue ..	50	75
J 22.	–	3 c. blue and green ..	50	80
J 23.	–	4 c. green and violet	60	80
J 24.	–	6 c. blue and claret ..	75	80
J 25.	–	8 c. red	1·25	1·00
J 26.	–	10 c. violet and green	80	1·00
J 27.	–	12 c. green and blue ..	60	1·00
J 28.	–	15 c. green and brown	1·00	1·25
J 29.	–	20 c. violet and blue	3·00	3·00
J 30.	–	25 c. green and brown	2·75	3·75
J 31.	–	50 c. brown and violet	6·00	7·50
J 32.	–	$1 brown and red ..	11·00	12·00

1944. No. J 7 optd. with **T 3**.

J 32a.	–	10 c. violet and green ..	25·00	

1945. No. J 1 surch. with **T 4**.

J 33.	**55.**	$2 on 1 c. green & brn.	£240	£300

本日大
五
弗
便郵國帝

(5.)

1945. No. 315 of North Borneo surch. with **T 5**.

J 34.		$5 on $1 brown and red	£375	£375

1945. Stamps of Japan optd. as bottom line in **T 3**.

J 35.	**108.**	1 s. brown	25	30
J 36.	**66.**	2 s. red	25	30
J 37.	–	3 s. green (No. 319) ..	30	30
J 38.	**110.**	4 s. green	30	30
J 39.	–	5 s. claret (No. 396)	45	50
J 40.	–	6 s. orange (No. 322)	50	75
J 41.	–	8 s. violet (No. 324) ..	50	75
J 42.	–	10 s. red (No. 399) ..	60	75
J 43.	–	15 s. blue (No. 401) ..	60	75
J 44.	–	20 s. blue (No. 328) ..	16·00	21·00
J 45.	–	25 s. brown (No. 329)	12·00	14·00
J 46.	–	30 s. blue (No. 330) ..	42·00	32·00
J 47.	–	50 s. olive and brown (No. 331)	11·00	15·00
J 48.	–	1 y. brown (No. 332)	11·00	15·00

JAPANESE OCCUPATION OF PHILIPPINE ISLANDS O4

100 centavos or sentimos = 1 peso.

1942. Stamps of Philippine Is. optd. with bars or surch. also.

J 1.	**23.**	2 c. green	5	5
J 4.	–	5 c. on 6 c. brn. (No. 526)	5	5
J 2.	–	12 c. black (No. 529) ..	5	5
J 3.	–	16 c. blue (No. 530) ..	1·10	95
J 5.	–	16 c. on 30 c. red (No. 505)	10	10
J 6.	–	50 c. on 1 p. black and orange (No. 543) ..	20	20
J 7.	–	1 p. on 4 p. black and blue (No. 508) ..	11·00	10·00

1942. No. 460 of Philippine Is. surch. **CONGRATULATIONS FALL OF BATAAN AND CORREGIDOR 2.**

J 8.		2 c. on 4 c. green ..	1·00	80

ILLUSTRATIONS British Commonwealth and all overprints and surcharges are FULL SIZE. Foreign Countries have been reduced to ¾-LINEAR.

1. Agricultural Produce.

1942. Red Cross Fund.

J 9.	**1.**	2 c. + 1 c. violet ..	5	5
J 10.		5 c. + 1 c. green ..	5	5
J 11.		16 c. + 2 c. orange ..	2·25	1·90

1942. "Greater East Asia War". 1st Anniv. No. 460 of Philippine Is. surch. with native characters **12-8-1942** and **5.**

J 12.		5 c. on 4 c. green ..	15	12

1943. Philippine Executive Commission. 1st Anniv. Nos. 566 and 569 of Philippine Is. surch. with native characters, **1-23-43** and values.

J 13.	**24.**	2 c. on 8 c. red ..	5	5
J 14.		5 c. on 1 p. sepia ..	12	12

2. Native Hut. 3. Mts. Mayou and Fuji.

1943.

J 15.	**2.**	1 c. orange	5	5
J 16.	–	2 c. green	5	5
J 17.	**2.**	4 c. green	5	5
J 18.	**3.**	5 c. brown	5	5
J 19.	–	6 c. red	5	5
J 20.	**3.**	10 c. blue	5	5
J 21.	–	12 c. blue	15	15
J 22.	–	16 c. brown	5	5
J 23.	**2.**	20 c. purple	25	25
J 24.	**3.**	21 c. violet	8	8
J 25.	–	25 c. brown	5	5
J 26.	**3.**	1 p. red	12	12
J 27.	–	2 p. purple	70	70
J 28.	–	5 p. olive	1·40	1·25

DESIGNS—VERT. 2 c., 6 c., 25 c. Rice planter. 12 c., 16 c., 2 p., 5 p. Sailing vessel.

4. Map of Manila Bay. 5. Philippine Girl.

1943. Fall of Bataan and Corregidor. 1st Anniv.

J 29.	**4.**	2 c. red	5	5
J 30.		5 c. green	8	8

1943. Printing in the Philippines. 350th Anniv. No. 531 of Philippine Is. surch. **Limbagan 1593-1943** and value.

J 31.		12 c. on 20 c. bistre ..	12	10

1943. Declaration of the Japanese "Independence of the Philippines". Imperf or perf.

J 32.	**5.**	5 c. blue	5	5
J 33.		12 c. orange	5	5
J 34.		17 c. red	8	8

1943. Luzon Flood Relief. Surch. **BAHA 1943** + and premium.

J 36.	–	12 c. + 21 c. blue (No. J 21)	8	8
J 37.	**2.**	20 c. + 36 c. purple ..	8	8
J 38.	**3.**	21 c. + 40 c. violet ..	8	8

6. Rev. Jose Burgos. 7. Jose P. Laurel.

1944. National Heroes. Imperf. or perf.
J 39. – 5 c. blue (Rizal) 8 8
J 40. **6.** 12 c. red 5 5
J 41. – 17 c. orange (Mabini) 8 8

1944. Fall of Bataan and Corregidor 2nd Anniv. Nos. 567/8 of Philippine Is surch. **REPUBLIKA NG PILIPINAS 5-7-44** and value
J 43. **24.** 5 c. on 20 c. blue 20 20
J 44. 12 c. on 60 c. green 35 35

1945. Republican Government. 1st Anniv. Imperf.
J 45. **7.** 5 s. brown 5 5
J 46. 7 s. green 5 5
J 47. 20 s. blue 8 5

POSTAGE DUE STAMP

1942. Postage Due stamp of Philippine Is. surch. **3 CVOS 3** and bar.
JD 9. **D 1.** 3 c. on 4 c. red 1·25 80

OFFICIAL STAMPS

1943. Stamps of Philippine Is. optd. variously with bars (**K.P.**) in Roman and Japanese characters or surch. also.
JO 29. **23.** 2 c. green (No. 526) 5 5
JO 30. – 5 c. on 6 c. brn. (No. 563) 8 8
JO 32. – 16 c. on 30 c. red (No. 505) 20 20

1944. No. 526 of Philippine Is. surch. **5 REPUBLIKA NG PILIPINAS (K.P.)** and four bars.
JO 45. – 5 c. on 6 c. brown 5 5

1944. Official stamp of Philippine Is. (No. 531 Optd. **O.B.**), optd. **Pilipinas REPUBLIKA K.P.** and bars.
JO 46. – 20 c. bistre 12 12

1944. Air stamp of Philippine Is. optd. **REPUBLIKA NG PILIPINAS (K.P.)** and two bars.
JO 47. **24.** 1 p. sepia 45 45

JAPANESE OCCUPATION OF SARAWAK BC

大日本帝國政府

(1. "Imperial Japanese Government".)

1942. Stamps of Sarawak optd. with T 1.
J 1. **7.** 1 c. purple 2·50 3·00
J 2. 2 c. green 7·50 9·00
J 3. 2 c. black 7·50 9·00
J 4. 3 c. black 14·00 16·00
J 5. 3 c. green 5·50 6·00
J 6. 4 c. purple 3·00 3·00
J 7. 5 c. violet 4·00 5·00
J 8. 6 c. red 6·00 6·00
J 9. 6 c. brown 4·50 6·00
J 10. 8 c. brown 14·00 16·00
J 11. 8 c. red 16·00 20·00
J 12. 10 c. red 4·00 4·50
J 13. 12 c. blue 8·00 9·00
J 14. 12 c. orange 16·00 20·00
J 15. 15 c. orange 14·00 16·00
J 16. 15 c. blue 7·50 9·00
J 17. 20 c. green and red 4·00 5·50
J 18. 25 c. violet and orange 4·00 5·50
J 19. 30 c. brown and violet 4·00 5·50
J 20. 50 c. violet and red 6·00 6·00
J 21. $1 red and brown 6·50 8·00
J 22. $2 purple and violet 16·00 20·00
J 23. $3 red and green 60·00 80·00
J 24. $4 blue and red 20·00 24·00
J 25. $5 red and brown 16·00 20·00
J 26. $10 black and yellow 23·00 27·00

JAPANESE POST OFFICES IN CHINA O1

Post Offices at Shanghai and other Treaty Ports operated between 1876 and 1922.

支那
(1.)

1900. Stamps of Japan, 1899, optd. with T 1.
1. **13.** 5 r. grey 1·75 1·10
2. ½ s. grey 1·10 30
3. 1 s. brown 1·10 30
4. 1½ s. blue 2·50 75
5. 1½ s. lilac 1·25 40
6. 2 s. green 1·50 25
7. 3 s. claret 1·60 40
8. 3 s. red 1·00 20
9. 4 s. rose 1·40 30
10. 5 s. yellow 4·50 50
11. **14.** 6 s. claret 7·00 6·00
12. 8 s. olive 4·00 4·00
13. 10 s. blue 3·25 55
14. 15 s. violet 7·00 60
15. 20 s. red 7·00 45
16. **15.** 25 s. green 14·00 1·50
17. 50 s. brown 18·00 1·10
18. **16.** 1 y. red 30·00 1·10
19. **17.** 5 y. green £200 20·00
20. 10 y. violet £325 45·00

1900. Imperial Wedding issue of Japan optd. with T 1.
21. **18.** 3 s. red 17·00 12·00

1913. Stamps of Japan, 1913, optd. with T 1.
33. **21.** ½ s. brown 40 25
34. 1 s. orange 60 25
35. 1½ s. blue 70 25
36. 2 s. green 80 30
37a. 3 s. red 50 25
38. **22.** 4 s. red 1·75 75
39. 5 s. violet 3·00 60
40. 6 s. brown 5·50 4·50
41. 8 s. grey 6·50 6·00
42. 10 s. blue 2·50 50
43. 20 s. claret 9·00 1·00
44. 25 s. olive 10·00 1·10
45. **23.** 30 s. chestnut 22·00 7·00
46. 50 s. chocolate 32·00 15·00
47. 1 y. green and brown 32·00 5·00
48. 5 y. green £400 £200
49. 10 y. violet £700 £325

JAPANESE POST OFFICES IN KOREA O3

朝鮮
(1.)

1900. Stamps of Japan, 1899, optd. with T 1.
1. **13.** 5 r. grey 8·00 5·00
2. 1 s. brown 10·00 4·00
3a. 1½ s. blue £110 75·00
4. 2 s. green 11·00 7·00
5. 3 s. claret 8·50 3·00
6. 4 s. rose 40·00 18·00
7. 5 s. yellow 35·00 15·00
8. **14.** 8 s. olive £100 85·00
9. 10 s. blue 20·00 2·50
10. 15 s. violet 45·00 4·00
11. 20 s. red 40·00 2·50
12. **15.** 25 s. green £100 30·00
13. 50 s. brown 85·00 10·00
14. **16.** 1 y. red £275 8·50

1900. Wedding of Prince Imperial. No. 152 of Japan. optd. with T 1.
15. **18.** 3 s. red 23·00 7·50

JASDAN BC

A State of India. Now uses Indian stamps.

1. Sun.

1942.
2. **1.** 1 a. green 30

JHALAWAR BC

A State of Rajasthan, India. Now uses Indian stamps.

4 paisa = 1 anna.

1. Apsara.

ILLUSTRATIONS
British Commonwealth and all overprints and surcharges are FULL SIZE. Foreign Countries have been reduced to ⅔-LINEAR.

1887. Imperf.
1. **1.** 1 paisa green 75 1·00
2. – ¼ a. green 35 50

The ¼ a. is larger and has a different frame.

JIND BC

A "convention" state of the Punjab, India. which now uses Indian stamps.

1.

2.

1874. Imperf.
J 8. **1.** ½ a. blue 12 60
J 9. 1 a. purple 25 80
J 10. 2 a. yellow-brown 30 1·50
J 11. 4 a. green 50 1·50
J 12. 8 a. purple 3·00 4·50

1882. Various designs and sizes. Imperf. or perf.
J 15. **2.** ½ a. yellow-brown 12 20
J 17. ½ a. yellow-brown 20 20
J 20. 1 a. brown 35 30
J 21. 2 a. blue 40 50
J 23. 4 a. green 40 50
J 25. 8 a. red 1·50 1·00

Stamps of India (Queen Victoria overprinted.

1885. Optd. **JHIND STATE** vert (curved).
1. **14.** ½ a. blue-green 25 20
2. – 1 a. purple 1·25 1·25
3. – 2 a. blue 1·00 1·00
4. – 4 a. green (No. 89) 3·50 3·50
5. – 8 a. mauve 18·00
6. – 1 r. grey (No. 101) 18·00

1885. Optd. **JEEND STATE.**
7. **14.** ½ a. blue-green 6·00
8. – 1 a. purple 6·00
9. – 2 a. blue 6·00
10. – 4 a. green (No. 89) 6·00
11. – 8 a. mauve 7·00
12. – 1 c. grey (No. 101) 8·00

1886. Optd. **JHIND STATE** horiz.
17. **14.** ½ a. blue-green 5 5
19. – 1 a. purple 10 10
20. – 1½ a. brown 15 15
21. – 2 a. blue 10 10
23. – 3 a. orange 8 12
15. – 4 a. green (No. 89) 4·00
24. – 4 a. green (No. 96) 15 15
27. – 6 a. brown 25 45
29. – 8 a. mauve 35 45
30. – 12 a purple on red 25 35
31. – 1 r. grey (No. 101) 1·50 1·50
32. **26.** 1 r. green and red 2·00 2·00
33. **27.** 2 r. red and orange 18·00
34. 3 r. brown and green 20·00
35. 5 r. blue and violet 25·00

1900. Optd. **JHIND STATE** horiz.
36. **25.** 3 p. red 5 5
37. 3 p. grey 5 5
38. **14.** ½ a. yellow-green 8 12
40. – 1 a. red 8 12

Stamps of India optd. **JHIND STATE.**

1903. King Edward VII.
42. **28.** 3 p. grey 5 5
43. ½ a. green (No. 122) 5 5
44. 1 a. red (No. 123) 5 5
46. 2 a. lilac 12 10
47. 2½ a. blue 8 12
48. 3 a. orange 5 5
49. 4 a. olive 12 15
51. 6 a. yellow-brown 15 20
52. 8 a. mauve 15 20
54. 12 a. purple on red 30 35
55. 1 r. green and red 30 40

1907. King Edward VII (inscr. "INDIA POSTAGE and REVENUE")
56. ½ a. green (No 149) 5 5
57. 1 a. red (No 150) 5 5

1913. King George V.
58. **40.** 3 p. grey 5 5
59. **41.** ½ a. green 5 5
60. **42.** 1 a. red 5 5
61. **44.** 2 a. lilac 10 15
62. **48.** 3 a. orange 40 60
63. **51.** 6 a. yellow-brown 75 1·00

1914. Stamps of India (King George V) optd. **JIND STATE** in two lines
64. **40.** 3 p. grey 5 5
65. **41.** ½ a. green 5 5
66. **42.** 1 a. red 5 5
80. 1 a. chocolate 5 5
67. **43.** 1½ a. brown (A. No. 163) 15 20
68. 1½ a. brown (B. No. 165) 15 20
81. 1½ a. red (B.) 5 10
69. **44.** 2 a. lilac 5 5
70. **47.** 2½ a. blue 15 30
82. 2½ a. orange 5 10
71. **48.** 3 a. orange 8 15
83. 3 a. blue 15 15
72. **49.** 4 a. olive 10 15
73. **51.** 6 a. yellow-brown 15 15
74. **52.** 8 a. mauve 15 20
75. **53.** 12 a. claret 15 20
76. **54.** 1 r. brown and green 40 50
77. 2 r. red and orange 1·75 2·25
78. 5 r. blue and violet 8·00 8·00

1922. No. 192 of India optd. **JIND.**
79. 42. 9 p. on 1 a. red 1·00 1·25

Stamps of India optd. **JIND STATE** in one line.

1927. King George V.
84. **40.** 3 p. grey 5 5
85. **41.** ½ a. green 5 5
86. **63.** 9 p. green 5 5
87. **42.** 1 a. chocolate 5 5
88. **65.** 1½ a. mauve 5 5
89. **43.** 1½ a. red 5 5
90. **45.** 2 a. lilac 5 5
91. **47.** 2½ a. orange 5 8
92. **48.** 3 a. blue 10 12
93. **66.** 3½ a. blue 5 8
94. **50.** 4 a. green 5 8
95. **51.** 6 a. yellow-brown 10 8
96. **52.** 8 a. mauve 20 20
97. **53.** 12 a. claret 35 40
98. **54.** 1 r. brown and green 35 50
99. 2 r. red and orange 1·75 2·75
100. 5 r. blue and violet 5·00 5·50
101. 10 r. green and red 9·00 10·00
102. 15 r. blue and olive 15·00 20·00
103. 25 r. orange and blue 22·00 25·00

1934. King George V.
104. **62.** ½ a. green 5 5
105. **64.** 1 a. chocolate 5 5
106. **44.** 2 a. orange-red 5 5
107. **48.** 3 a. red 5 5
108. **49.** 4 a. olive 5 5

1937. King George VI.
109. **74.** 3 p. slate 8 5
110. ½ a. brown 8 12
111. 9 p. green 10 12
112. 1 a. red 8 5
113. **76.** 2 a. red 8 10
114. – 2½ a. violet 8 12
115. – 3 a. green 8 12
116. – 3½ a. blue 10 15
117. – 4 a. brown 10 15
118. – 6 a. green 15 20
119. – 8 a. violet 15 20
120. – 12 a. red 40 70
121. **77.** 1 r. slate and brown 85 1·00
122. 2 r. purple and brown 1·25 1·75
123. 5 r. green and blue 5·00 5·00
124. 10 r. purple and red 9·00 10·00
125. 15 r. brown and green 30·00 32·00
126. 25 r. slate and purple 35·00 40·00

1942. Stamps of India (King George VI) optd. **JIND.**

(a) On issue of 1938.
127. **74.** 3 p. slate 80 80
128. ½ a. brown 70 70
129. 9 p. green 90 90
130. 1 a. red 80 80
131. **77.** 1 r. slate and brown 1·25 1·50
132. 2 r. purple and brown 2·00 3·00
133. 5 r. green and blue 5·00 7·00
134. 10 r. purple and red 11·00 12·00
135. 15 r. brown and green 16·00 18·00
136. 25 r. slate and purple 22·00 25·00

(b) On issue of 1940.
137. **78.** 3 p. slate 8 8
138. ½ a. mauve 8 8
139. 9 p. green 8 10
140. 1 a. red 8 10
141. **79.** 1 a. 3 bistre 8 15
142. 1½ a. violet 20 20
143. 2 a. red 8 8
144. 3 a. violet 15 15
145. 3½ a. blue 15 20
146. **80.** 4 a. brown 8 20
147. 6 a. green 10 30
148. 8 a. violet 35 40
149. 12 a. purple 50 60

OFFICIAL STAMPS

Postage stamps of Jind optd. **SERVICE.**

1885. Nos. 1/3 (Queen Victoria).
O 1. **14.** ½ a. blue-green 5 5
O 2. – 1 a. purple 5 5
O 3. – 2 a. blue 6·00 6·00

1886. Nos. 17/32 and No. 38 (Q.V.).
O 12. **14.** ½ a. blue-green 5 5
O 22. ½ a. yell.-grn. (No. 38) 5 5
O 14. 1 a. purple 8 5
O 16. 2 a. blue 8 5
O 17. 4 a. green (No. 24) 15 8
O 19. 8 a. mauve 45 60
O 21. **26.** 1 r. green and red 1·25 1·50

1903. Nos. 42/55 (King Edward VII).
O 24. **28.** 3 p. grey 5 5
O 25. ½ a. green (No. 43) 15 5
O 26. 1 a. red (No. 44) 20 5
O 28. 2 a. lilac 5 5
O 29. 4 a. olive 15 10
O 31. 8 a. mauve 1·25 75
O 32. 1 r. green and red 1·25 80

1907. Nos. 56/7 (King Edward VII).
O 33. ½ a. green 5 5
O 34. 1 a. red 5 5

1914. Official stamps of India, Nos. O 75/96 (King George V), optd. **JIND STATE.**
O 35. **40.** 3 p. grey 5 5
O 36. **41.** ½ a. green 5 5
O 37. **42.** 1 a. red 5 5
O 46. 1 a. chocolate 5 5
O 39. **44.** 2 a. lilac 5 5
O 40. **49.** 4 a. olive 5 5
O 41. **51.** 6 a. yellow-brown 12 15
O 42. **52.** 8 a. mauve 5 8
O 43. **54.** 1 r. brown and green 50 20
O 44. 2 r. red and orange 1·50 2·00
O 45. 5 r. blue and violet 6·00 7·00

Stamps of India optd. **JIND STATE SERVICE.**

1927. King George V.
O 47. **40.** 3 p. grey 5 5
O 48. **41.** ½ a. green 5 5
O 49. **63.** 9 p. green 5 5
O 50. **42.** 1 a. chocolate 5 5
O 51. **65.** 1½ a. mauve 5 5
O 52. **45.** 2 a. lilac 8 5
O 64. **44.** 2 a. orange-red 5 5
O 53. **47.** 2½ a. orange 5 5
O 54. **50.** 4 a. green 5 5
O 55. **51.** 6 a. yellow-brown 12 10
O 56. **52.** 8 a. mauve 10 15
O 57. **53.** 12 a. claret 15 25
O 58. **54.** 1 r. brown and green 30 50
O 59. 2 r. red and orange 75 1·00
O 60. 5 r. blue and purple 2·50 2·50
O 61. 10 r. green and red 4·50 5·00

1934. King George V.
O 62. **62.** ½ a. green 5 5
O 63. **64.** 1 a. chocolate 5 5
O 65. **49.** 4 a. olive 5 5

1937. King George VI.

O 66. **74.** ½ a. brown 50 8
O 57. 9 p. green 15 8
O 68. 1 a. red 12 8
O 69. **77.** 1 r. slate and brown.. 1·50 1·25
O 70. 2 r. purple and brown 2·00 3·00
O 71. 5 r. green and blue .. 7·00 7·00
O 72. 10 r. purple and red .. 9·00 9·00

1940. Official stamps of India optd. **JIND.**

O 73. O **1.** 3 p. slate 8 8
O 74. ½ a. brown .. .. 1·00 60
O 75. ½ a. purple 8 8
O 76. 9 p. green 8 8
O 77. 1 a. red 8 8
O 78. 1½ a. violet 20 15
O 79. 2 a. orange 8 8
O 80. 2½ a. violet 8 8
O 81. 4 a. brown 25 25
O 82. 8 a. violet 40 40

1943. Stamps of India (King George VI) optd. **JIND SERVICE.**

O 83. **77.** 1 r. slate and brown.. 1·25 1·25
O 84. 2 r. purple and brown 2·00 2·00
O 85. 5 r. green and blue .. 4·00 6·00
O 86. 10 r. purple and red.. 10·00 10·00

JOHORE BC

A State of the Federation of Malaya incorporated in Malaysia in 1963.

100 cents=1 dollar (Straits of Malayan).

Queen Victoria stamps of Straits Settlements overprinted.

1876. Optd. with Crescent and star.

1. 2 cents brown £700 £450

1884. Optd. **JOHORE.**

3. **1.** 2 c. rose .. .. .. 15·00 18·00

1884. Optd. **JOHOR.**

8. **1.** 2 c. rose .. .. .. 2·50 2·75

1891. Surch. **JOHOR Two CENTS.**

20. **1.** 2 c. on 24 c. green .. 6·00 6·50

1. Sultan Aboubakar. 2. Sultan Ibrahim.

1891.

21. **1.** 1 c. purple 20 25
22. 2 c. purple and yellow .. 25 50
23. 3 c. purple and red .. 40 25
24. 4 c. purple and black .. 1·50 75
25. 5 c. purple and green .. 3·00 3·00
26. 6 c. purple and blue .. 3·00 3·25
27. $1 green and red.. .. 6·00 7·50

1892. Surch. **3 CENTS** and bar.

28. **1.** 3 c. on 4 c. purple & black 40 25
29. 3 c. on 5 c. purple & green 45 65
30. 3 c. on 6 c. purple & blue 45 50
31. 3 c. on $1 green and red.. 3·00 3·50

1896. Sultan's Coronation. Optd. **KEMAHKOTAAN.**

32. **1.** 1 c. purple 30 45
33. 2 c. purple and yellow .. 20 35
34. 3 c. purple and red .. 45 60
35. 4 c. purple and black .. 60 70
36. 5 c. purple and green .. 1·50 1·75
37. 6 c. purple and blue .. 80 1·00
38a. $1 green and red.. .. 11·00 12·00

1896.

39. **2.** 1 c. green 45 12
40. 2 c. green and blue .. 20 12
41. 3 c. green and purple .. 50 12
42. 4 c. green and red .. 25 12
43. 4 c. yellow and red .. 40 20
44. 5 c. green and brown .. 45 35
45. 6 c. green and yellow .. 50 55
46. 10 c. green and black .. 3·50 4·50
47. 25 c. green and mauve .. 4·00 4·50
48. 50 c. green and red .. 6·00 5·50
49. $1 purple and green .. 5·50 5·50
50. $2 purple and red .. 7·00 7·00
51. $3 purple and blue .. 9·00 9·00
52. $4 purple and brown .. 10·00 11·00
53. $5 purple and yellow .. 17·00 15·00

1903. Surch. in figures and words.

54. **2.** 3 c. on 4 c. yellow and red 30 40
55. 10 c. on 4 c. grn. & red (A) 90 1·40
59. 10 c. on 4 c. grn. & red (B) 3·50 3·50
58. 10 c. on 4 c. yellow & red.. 9·00 8·00
56. 50 c. on $3 purple & blue 5·00 8·00
60. 50 c. on $5 purple & yellow 13·00 14·00
57. $1 on $2 purple and red.. 13·00 14·00

10 c. on 4 c. Type A, " cents " in small letters. Type B " CENTS " in capitals.

3. Sultan Sir Ibrahim.

1904.

78. **3.** 1 c. purple and green .. 12 10
90. 2 c. purple and orange .. 15 15
80. 3 c. purple and black .. 65 20
91. 4 c. purple and red .. 20 12
109. 5 c. purple and olive .. 15 10
66. 8 c. purple and blue .. 90 90
84. 10 c. purple and black .. 1·25 60
116. 25 c. purple and green .. 50 40
119. 50 c. purple and red .. 60 40
120. $1 green and mauve .. 1·25 50
121. $2 green and red .. 2·50 1·10
122. $3 green and blue .. 7·00 7·50
123. $4 green and brown .. 8·00 8·50
124. $5 green and orange .. 10·00 7·50
125. $10 green and black .. 30·00 24·00

1912. Surch. **3 CENTS** and bars.

88. **3.** 3 c. on 8 c. purple & blue 90 90

1918.

103. **3.** 1 c. purple and black .. 20 20
89. 2 c. purple and green .. 15 15
104. 2 c. purple and sepia .. 50 45
105. 2 c. green 15 15
106. 3 c. green 70 75
107. 3 c. purple and sepia .. 40 35
110. 6 c. purple and claret .. 15 12
93. 10 c. purple and blue .. 60 60
112. 10 c. purple and yellow 15 12
113. 12 c. purple and blue .. 90 35
114. 12 c. blue .. .. 4·00 3·50
94. 21 c. purple and orange 90 1·00
117. 30 c. purple and orange.. 50 50
118. 40 c. purple and brown.. 70 1·00

4. Sultan Sir Ibrahim and Sultana.

5. Sultan Sir Ibrahim.

1935.

129. **4.** 8 c. violet and grey .. 40 35

1940.

130. **5.** 8 c. black and blue .. 30 25

1948. Silver Wedding. As T 5/6 of Aden.

131. 10 c. violet 10 10
132. $5 green .. .. 5·50 6·50

6. Sultan Sir Ibrahim.

ILLUSTRATIONS
British Commonwealth and all overprints and surcharges are FULL SIZE.
Foreign Countries have been reduced to ¾-LINEAR.

1949.

133. **6.** 1 c. black 10 10
134. 2 c. orange 10 10
135. 3 c. green 15 12
136. 4 c. brown 10 10
136a. 5 c. purple 10 10
137. 6 c. grey 15 15
138. 8 c. red 25 35
138a. 8 c. green 15 20
139. 10 c. magenta 12 10
139a. 12 c. red 20 30
140. 15 c. blue 40 20
141. 20 c. black and green .. 30 15
141a. 20 c. blue 20 15
142. 25 c. purple and orange 20 15
142a. 30 c. red and purple .. 55 35
142b. 35 c. red and purple .. 50 45
143. 40 c. red and purple .. 60 70
144. 50 c. black and blue .. 40 12
145. $1 blue and purple .. 70 50
146. $2 green and red .. 2·25 1·10
147. $5 green and brown .. 3·50 2·50

1949. U.P.U. As T 14/7 of Antigua.

148. 10 c. purple 10 12
149. 15 c. blue 12 20
150. 25 c. orange 30 35
151. 50 c. black 50 55

1953. Coronation. As T 7 of Aden.

152. 10 c. black and purple.. 8 8

7. Sultan Sir Ibrahim.

1955. Diamond Jubilee of Sultan.

153. **7.** 10 c. red 8 8

8. Sultan Sir Ismail and Johore Coat-of-Arms.

1960. Coronation of Sultan.

154. **8.** 10 c. multicoloured .. 8 8

1960. As Nos. 92/102 of Kedah but with inset portrait of Sultan Sir Ismail.

155. 1 c. black 10 12
156. 2 c. red 10 10
157. 4 c. sepia 10 10
158. 5 c. lake 10 10
159. 8 c. green 10 12
160. 10 c. maroon 10 10
161. 20 c. blue 10 10
162. 50 c. black and blue .. 25 10
163. $1 blue and purple .. 45 35
164. $2 green and red 90 90
165. $5 brown and green .. 2·25 1·75

9. " Vanda hookeriana ".

1965. Inset portrait of Sultan Ismail. Multicoloured.

166. 1 c. Type **9** 5 5
167. 2 c. "Arundina graminifolia" 5 5
168. 5 c. "Paphiopedilum niveum" 5 5
169. 6 c. "Spathoglottis plicata" 5 5
170. 10 c. "Arachnis flos-aeris".. 5 5
171. 15 c. "Rhyncostylis retusa" 5 8
172. 20 c. "Phalaenopsis violacea" 8 8

The higher values used in Johore were Nos. 20/7 of Malaysia.

10. Malayan Jezebel.

1971. Butterflies. Inset portrait of Sultan Ismail. Multicoloured.

175. 1 c. Type **10** 5 5
176. 2 c. Black-veined Tiger .. 5 5
177. 5 c. Clipper Butterfly .. 5 5
178. 6 c. Lime Butterfly .. 5 5
179. 10 c. Great Orange Tip .. 5 5
180. 15 c. Blue Pansy Butterfly 5 5
181. 20 c. Wanderer 8 8

The higher values in use with this issue are Nos. 64/71 of Malaysia.

POSTAGE DUE STAMPS

D 1.

1938

D 1. **D 1.** 1 c. red 60 80
D 2. 4 c. green .. .. 1·00 1·25
D 3. 8 c. orange .. .. 1·50 1·75
D 4. 10 c. brown .. .. 1·75 2·00
D 5. 12 c. purple .. .. 3·00 4·50

JORDAN O2

A territory to the E. of Israel, formerly called Transjordan; under British mandate from 1918 to 1946. Independent kingdom since 1946.

1920. 1000 milliemes = 100 piastres = £1 Egyptian.
1927. 1000 milliemes = £1 Palestinian.
1950. 1000 fils = 1 Jordan dinar.

شرقي الاردن

(1. " East of Jordan ".)

1920. Stamps of Palestine optd. with T **1.**

1. **3.** 1 m. brown 10 15
10. 2 m. green 8 12
3. 3 m. brown 12 15
4. 4 m. red 12 15
13. 5 m. orange 15 15
14. 1 p. blue 20 25
15. 2 p. olive 25 35
16. 5 p. purple 45 85
17. 9 p. ochre .. .. 1·10 2·10
18. 10 p. blue .. .. 1·25 2·50
19. 20 p. grey .. .. 2·00 4·25

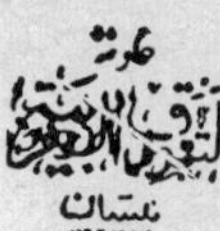

(2.) (3.)

1922. Stamps of Jordan handstamped with T 2 or 3 (piastre values).

28. **3.** 1/10 p. on 1 m. brown .. 2·50 2·50
29. 2/10 p. on 2 m. green .. 3·00 3·25
22. 3/10 p. on 3 m. brown .. 1·60 1·60
23. 4/10 p. on 4 m. red .. 11·00 11·00
30. 5/10 p. on 5 m. orange .. 15·00 7·00
31. 1 p. on 1 p. blue .. .. 15·00 7·00
25. 2 p. on 2 p. olive.. .. 25·00 9·00
26. 5 p. on 5 p. purple .. 10·00 12·00
27a. 9 p. on 9 p. ochre .. 24·00 15·00
33. 10 p. on 10 p. blue .. £160 £140
34. 20 p. on 20 p. grey .. £140 £120

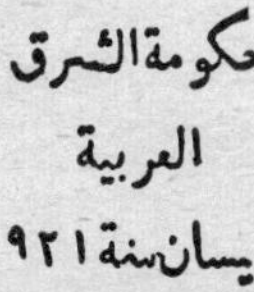

(4. "Arab Government of the East, April, 1921".)

1922. Stamps of Jordan handstamped with T 4.

45. **3.** 1 m. brown .. .. 2·00 2·00
46b. 2 m. green .. .. 1·50 1·50
39b. 3 m. brown 90 90
40b. 4 m. red .. .. 10·00 10·00
41a. 5 m. orange .. .. 4·50 1·25
48a. 1 p. blue .. .. 5·00 2·00
42b. 2 p. olive .. .. 2·00 1·50
43a. 5 p. purple .. .. 8·00 8·00
44b. 9 p. ochre .. .. 12·00 11·00
52a. 10 p. blue £160 £160
53a. 20 p. grey £170 £170

حكومة الشرق
العربية
يسان سنة ١٩٢١

(5. "Arab Government of the East, April, 1921".)

1923. Stamps of Jordan optd. with T **5.**

62. **3.** 1 m. brown .. .. 4·00 4·00
63. 2 m. green .. .. 3·00 3·00
56. 3 m. brown .. .. 3·00 3·00
57. 4 m. red .. .. 3·00 3·00
64. 5 m. orange .. .. 2·50 2·50
65. 1 p. blue .. .. 3·00 3·00
59. 2 p. olive .. .. 4·00 3·50
60. 5 p. purple .. .. 8·00 10·00
66. 9 p. ochre .. .. 12·00 12·00
67. 10 p. blue .. .. 14·00 14·00
68. 20 p. grey .. .. 15·00 15·00

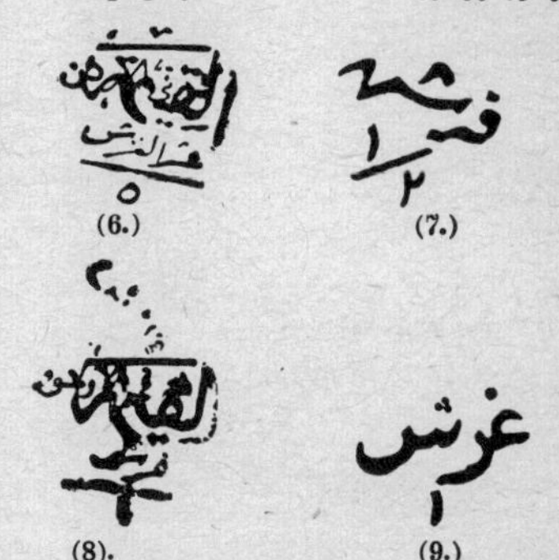

(6.) (7.)

(8). (9.)

1923. Stamps of the preceding four issues surch. with T **6/9.**

70b. – 2½/10th p. on 5 m. (No. 13) 25·00 25·00
71. **6.** 5/10 p. on 3 m. (3) .. £1700
72. 5/10 p. on 3 m. (22) .. 15·00 15·00
78a. 5/10 p. on 3 m. (39a) .. 16·00 16·00
84. 5/10 p. on 3 m. (56) .. 2·00 2·00
73. 5/10 p. on 5 p. (26) .. 15·00 15·00
79. 5/10 p. on 5 p. (43a) .. 70 1·00
73b. 5/10 p. on 9 p. (27a) .. 35·00
79d. 5/10 p. on 9 p. (44b) .. £140
80. **7.** ½ p. on 2 p. ol. (42b) .. 18·00 18·00
74. ½ p. on 5 p. pur. (26) .. 26·00 26·00
81. ½ p. on 5 p. pur. (43a) .. £250
75a. ½ p. on 9 p. ochre (27a).. 26·00 24·00
85. ½ p. on 9 p. ochre (66).. 20·00 20·00
77. **8.** 1 p. on 5 p. purple (26).. 17·00 18·00
83. 1 p. on 5 p. purple (43a).. £120
87. **9.** 1 p. on 10 p. blue (67) .. £140 £130
88. 2 p. on 20 p. grey (68) .. 15·00 15·00

حكومة

الشرق العربية

٩ شعبان ١٣٤١

(10. "Arab Government of the East, 9 Sha'ban, 1341".)

1923. Stamps of Saudi Arabia optd. with T 10.

No.	Type	Description	Unused	Used
89.	5.	⅛ p. brown	40	20
96.		⅛ on ½ p. brown	1·00	1·00
90.		¼ p. red	40	20
91.		1 p. blue	20	20
92.		1½ p. violet	25	30
93.		2 p. orange	35	40
94.		3 p. brown	60	80
95.		5 p. olive	1·00	1·00
97.		10 on 5 p. olive	2·50	2·50

حكومة الشرق العربي تذكار الاستقلال ٢٥ مايس ٩٢٣

(11. "Arab Government of the East, Commemoration of Independence, 25 May,(1)923".)

1923. Stamps of Palestine optd. with T 11.

No.	Type	Description	Unused	Used
98.	3.	1 m. brown	5·00	5·00
99.		2 m. green	8·00	8·00
100.		3 m. brown	3·00	3·00
101.		4 m. red	3·00	3·00
102.		5 m. orange	10·00	10·00
103.		1 p. blue	10·00	10·00
104.		2 p. olive	10·00	10·00
105.		5 p. purple	15·00	15·00
106.		9 p. ochre	12·00	12·00
107.		10 p. blue	15·00	15·00
108.		20 p. grey	15·00	15·00

1923. No. 107 surch. with T 9.

No.	Type	Description	Unused	Used
109.		1 p. on 10 p. blue	£1800	

نصف قرش

(12.)

1923. No. 92 surch. with T12.

No.	Type	Description	Unused	Used
110.		½ p. on 1½ p. violet	1·50	1·50

حكومة

الشرق العربية

٩ شعبان ١٣٤١

(12a. "Arab Government of the East, 9 Sha'ban, 1341".)

1923. Stamp of Saudi Arabia handstamped as T 12a.

No.	Type	Description	Unused	Used
112.	5.	¼ p. red	75	75

حكومة الشرق العربية

(13. "Arab Government of the East".)

1924. Stamps of Saudi Arabia optd. with T 13.

No.	Type	Description	Unused	Used
114.	5.	¼ p. red	1·50	1·75
115.		1 p. blue	40·00	40·00
116.		1½ p. violet	75·00	

ذ ٠ ق ٠ ج

ملك العرب

ا ج ٠ ث ٣٤٢

(14. "Commemorating the coming of His Majesty the King of the Arabs" and date.)

1942. Stamps of Saudi Arabia optd. with T 13 and 14.

No.	Type	Description	Unused	Used
117.	5.	⅛ p. red	20	20
118.		¼ p. blue	25	25
119.		1½ p. violet	30	30
120.		2 p. orange	40	40

حكومة الشرق

العربي

١٣٤٢

(15. "Government of the Arab East, 1342".)

1924. Stamps of Saudi Arabia optd. with T 14.

No.	Type	Description	Unused	Used
125.	5.	⅛ p. brown	8	8
126.		¼ p. green	8	8
127.		½ p. red	8	8
129.		1 p. blue	20	20
130.		1½ p. mauve	60	60
131.		2 p. orange	40	40
132.		3 p. brown	25	30
133.		5 p. olive	45	60
134.		10 p. brown and mauve	75	1·00

حكومة الشرق العربي

سنة ١٣٤٣

(16. "Government of the Arab East, 1343".)

1925. Stamps as T 14 of Saudi Arabia optd. with T 16.

No.	Type	Description	Unused	Used
135.		⅛ p. brown	5	5
136.		¼ p. blue	5	5
137.		½ p. red	8	8
138.		1 p. green	8	8
139.		1½ p. orange	15	30
140.		2 p. blue	15	45
141.		3 p. olive	25	50
142.		5 p. brown	40	65

شرق

الاردن

(17. "East of the Jordan".)

1925. Stamps of Palestine, 1922, optd. with T 17.

No.	Type	Description	Unused	Used
143.	3.	1 m. brown	5	5
144.		2 m. yellow	5	5
145.		3 m. blue	5	5
146.		4 m. red	5	5
147.		5 m. orange	5	5
148.		6 m. green	8	8
149.		7 m. brown	8	8
150.		8 m. red	10	10
151.		13 m. blue	20	20
152.		1 p. grey	20	10
153.		2 p. olive	30	30
154.		5 p. purple	50	50
155.		9 p. ochre	65	70
156.		10 p. blue	80	80
157.		20 p. violet	1·60	2·00

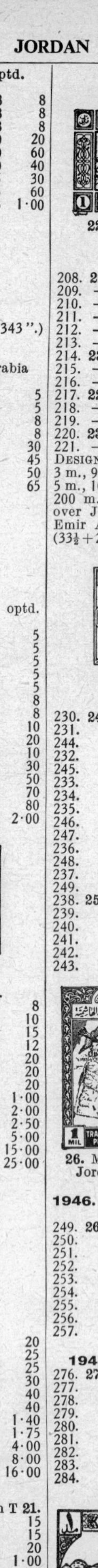

18. Emir Abdullah. 19.

1927. Figures at left and right.

No.	Type	Description	Unused	Used
159.	18.	2 m. blue	8	8
160.		3 m. red	10	10
161.		4 m. green	15	15
162.		5 m. orange	12	12
163.		10 m. red	20	20
164.		15 m. blue	20	20
165.		20 m. olive	20	20
166.	19.	50 m. purple	90	1·00
167.		90 m. brown	2·00	2·00
168.		100 m. blue	3·00	2·50
169.		200 m. violet	7·00	5·00
170.		500 m. brown	22·00	15·00
171.		1000 m. grey	35·00	25·00

دستور LOCUST CAMPAIGN

(20. "Constitution".) (21.)

1928. Optd. with T 20.

No.	Type	Description	Unused	Used
172.	18.	2 m. blue	20	20
173.		3 m. red	25	25
174.		4 m. green	25	25
175.		5 m. orange	30	30
176.		10 m. red	45	40
177.		15 m. blue	45	40
178.	18.	20 m. olive	1·40	1·40
179.	19.	50 m. purple	2·25	1·75
180.		90 m. brown	4·00	4·00
181.		100 m. blue	8·00	8·00
182.		200 m. violet	18·00	16·00

1930. "Locust campaign". Optd. with T 21.

No.	Type	Description	Unused	Used
183.	18.	2 m. blue	15	15
184.		3 m. red	15	15
185.		4 m. green	20	20
186.		5 m. orange	1·25	1·00
187.		10 m. red	15	15
188.		15 m. blue	30	30
189.		20 m. olive	35	35
190.	19.	50 m. purple	1·00	1·00
191.		90 m. brown	3·00	2·50
192.		100 m. blue	4·00	3·50
193.		200 m. violet	10·00	10·00
194.		500 m. brown	22·00	22·00

22. Mushetta. 23. The Khasneh at Petra.

1933.

No.	Type	Description	Unused	Used
208.	22.	1 m. black and maroon	15	15
209.	–	2 m. black and claret	15	15
210.	–	3 m. green	15	20
211.	–	4 m. black and brown	25	30
212.	–	5 m. black and orange	40	40
213.	–	10 m. red	40	50
214.	23.	15 m. blue	90	65
215.	–	20 m. black and olive	70	70
216.	–	50 m. black and purple	2·00	1·50
217.	22.	90 m. black and yellow	3·00	3·00
218.	–	100 m. black and blue	4·50	4·50
219.	–	200 m. black and violet	14·00	14·00
220.	23.	500 m. red and brown	48·00	40·00
221.	–	£P1 black and green	£120	£120

DESIGNS—HORIZ. 2 m. Nymphaeum, Jerash. 3 m., 90 m. Kasr Kharana. 4 m. Kerak Castle. 5 m., 100 m. Temple of Artemis, Jerash. 10 m., 200 m. Ajlun Castle. 20 m. Allenby Bridge over Jordan. 50 m. Threshing. VERT. £P1 Emir Abdullah. Nos. 216 to 221 are larger (33½+24 mm. or 24+33½ mm.).

24. 25.

1943. Figures at left only.

No.	Type	Description	Unused	Used
230.	24.	1 m. maroon	5	5
231.		2 m. green	5	5
244.		3 m. red	5	5
232.		3 m. green	5	5
245.		4 m. green	5	5
233.		4 m. red	5	5
234.		5 m. orange	5	5
235.		10 m. red	10	8
246.		10 m. violet	5	5
247.		12 m. red	8	10
236.		15 m. blue	15	12
248.		15 m. olive	12	12
237.		20 m. olive	15	12
249.		20 m. blue	12	15
238.	25.	50 m. purple	30	20
239.		90 m. brown	50	30
240.		100 m. blue	60	35
241.		200 m. violet	1·50	1·00
242.		500 m. brown	3·25	3·00
243.		£P 1 grey	9·00	5·00

26. Map of Jordan. 27. Parliament Building.

1946. Installation of King Abdullah and National Independence.

No.	Type	Description	Unused	Used
249.	26.	1 m. purple	5	5
250.		2 m. orange	5	5
251.		3 m. green	5	5
252.		4 m. violet	5	5
253.		10 m. brown	5	5
254.		12 m. red	8	5
255.		20 m. blue	10	8
256.		50 m. blue	20	15
257.		200 m. green	75	55

1947. 1st National Parliament Inaug.

No.	Type	Description	Unused	Used
276.	27.	1 m. violet	5	5
277.		3 m. red	5	5
278.		4 m. green	5	5
279.		10 m. purple	5	5
280.		12 m. red	8	5
281.		20 m. blue	8	5
282.		50 m. claret	20	15
283.		100 m. pink	30	30
284.		200 m. green	65	60

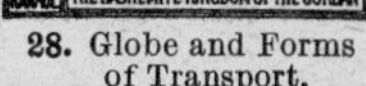

28. Globe and Forms of Transport. 29. Aeroplane and Globe.

1949. U.P.U. 75th Anniv. Inscr. "UNIVERSAL POSTAL UNION 1874-1949".

No.	Type	Description	Unused	Used
285.	28.	1 m. brown	5	5
286.		4 m. green	5	5
287.		10 m. red	8	5
288.		20 m. blue	15	12
289.		50 m. green	30	20

DESIGN: 50 m. King Abdullah.

1950. Air. Currency changed.

No.	Type	Description	Unused	Used
295.	29.	5 f. purple and yellow	8	8
296.		10 f. brown and violet	10	8
297.		15 f. red and olive	15	10
298.		20 f. black and blue	15	10
299.		50 f. green and magenta	30	15
300.		100 f. brown and blue	55	35
301.		150 f. orange and black	90	60

1952. Optd. FILS and bars or J.D. (on 1 d.).

No.	Type	Description	Unused	Used
313.	22.	1 f. on 1 m. maroon	5	5
314.		2 f. on 2 m. green	5	5
316.		3 f. on 3 m. red	5	5
318.		4 f. on 4 m. green	5	5
319.		5 f. on 5 m. orange	10	10
321.		10 f. on 10 m. violet	10	10
322.		12 f. on 12 m. red	12	10
325.		15 f. on 15 m. olive	15	12
327.		20 f. on 20 m. blue	25	20
328.	23.	50 f. on 50 m. purple	40	25
329.		90 f. on 90 m. brown	2·25	2·25
330.		100 f. on 100 m. blue	1·10	70
331.		200 f. on 200 m. violet	1·40	75
332.		500 f. on 500 m. brown	3·50	2·50
333.		1 d. on £P1 grey	8·00	5·00

30. Dome of the Rock and Khazneh at Petra. 31. King Abdullah.

1952. Unity of Jordan.

No.	Type	Description	Unused	Used
355.	30.	1 f. green and brown	5	5
356.		2 f. red and green	5	5
357.		3 f. black and red	5	5
358.		4 f. orange and green	5	5
359.		5 f. purple and chocolate	5	5
360.		10 f. brown and violet	5	5
361.		20 f. black and blue	10	8
362.		100 f. sepia and brown	60	50
363.		200 f. orange and violet	1·10	85

1952.

(a) Size 18×21½ mm.

No.	Type	Description	Unused	Used
364.	31.	5 f. orange	5	5
365.		10 f. lilac	5	5
366.		12 f. red	15	10
367.		15 f. olive	8	5
368.		20 f. blue	10	5

(b) Size 20×24½ mm.

No.	Type	Description	Unused	Used
369.	31.	50 f. purple	25	12
370.		90 f. brown	40	30
371.		100 f. blue	50	35

1953. Optd. with two horiz. bars across Arabic commemorative inscription.

No.	Type	Description	Unused	Used
378.	30.	1 f. green and brown	5	5
379.		2 f. red and green	5	5
380.		3 f. black and red	5	5
381.		4 f. orange and green	5	5
382.		5 f. purple and chocolate	8	5
383.		10 f. brown and violet	8	5
384.		20 f. black and blue	20	15
385		100 f. sepia and brown	80	40
386.		200 f. orange and violet	1·50	1·00

32. Omar Mosque, Jerusalem. 33. King Hussein.

1953. Obligatory Tax stamps optd. for postal use as in T 32. (a) Inscr. "MILS".

No.	Type	Description	Unused	Used
387.	–	1 m. blue	5	5
388.	–	3 m. green	5	5
389.	–	5 m. claret	12·00	5
390.	32.	10 m. red	3·50	3·00
391.		15 m. black	25	25
392.		20 m. brown	12·00	8·00
393.		50 m. purple	30	25
394.	–	100 m. orange	1·00	1·00

(b) Inscr. "MILS" and optd. with Type P 1.

No.	Type	Description	Unused	Used
395.	–	1 m. ultramarine	8·00	8·00
396.	–	3 m. green	8·00	8·00
397.	–	5 m. claret	8·00	8·00
398.	32.	10 m. red	8·00	8·00
399.		15 m. black	8·00	8·00
400.		20 m. brown	8·00	8·00
401.	–	100 m. orange	6·00	5·00

(c) Inscr. "FILS".

No.	Type	Description	Unused	Used
408.	–	5 f. claret	10	10
409.	32.	10 f. red	10	10
410.		15 f. black	20	12
411.		20 f. brown	25	25
412.	–	100 f. orange	75	35

DESIGNS: 1 m., 3 m., 5 m., 5 f., Hebron Mosque. 100 m., 100 f. Mosque, Acre.

1953. Enthronement of King Hussein.

413.	33.	1 f. black and green ..	5	5
414.		4 f. black and claret ..	5	5
415.		15 f. black and blue ..	10	5
416.		20 f. black and lilac ..	12	8
417.		50 f. black and green ..	35	20
418.		100 f. black and blue ..	65	40

34. The Deir, Petra. **35.** Temple of Artemis Jerash.

1954.

445.	34.	1 f. brn. & grn. (postage)	5	5
446.	–	2 f. black and red ..	5	5
447.	34.	3 f. violet and purple ..	5	5
448.	–	4 f. green and brown ..	5	5
449.	34.	5 f. green and violet ..	5	5
450.	–	10 f. green and purple ..	5	5
451.	–	12 f. sepia and red ..	5	5
452.	–	15 f. red and brown ..	5	5
453.	–	20 f. grey-green & blue	8	5
454.	–	50 f. red and blue ..	12	8
455.	–	100 f. blue and green ..	30	20
456.	–	200 f. blue and lake ..	1·00	50
457.	–	500 f. purple and brown	4·00	2·00
458.	–	1 d. lake and olive ..	10·00	4·50
432.	35.	5 f. orge. & indigo (air)	5	5
433.		10 f. vermilion & choc.	5	5
434.		25 f. blue and green ..	12	5
435.		35 f. blue and mauve	20	12
436.		40 f. slate and red ..	25	20
437.		50 f. orange and blue	30	25
438.		100 f. chocolate & blue	70	50
439.		150 f. lake & turquoise	90	65

DESIGNS—VERT. 2 f., 4 f., 500 f., 1 d. King Hussein. HORIZ. 10 f., 15 f., 20 f. Dome of the Rock, Jerusalem. 12 f., 50 f., 100 f., 200 f. Facade of Mosque of El Aqsa.

1955. Arab Postal Union. As T **37** of Egypt but inscr. "H. K. JORDAN" at top and "ARAB POSTAL UNION" at foot.

440.	15 f. green	5	5
441.	20 f. violet	10	10
442.	25 f. brown	15	12

36. King Hussein and Queen Dina.

1955. Royal Wedding.

443.	36.	15 f. blue	15	15
444.		100 f. lake	70	50

37. **38.** "Flame of Freedom".

1956. 1st Arab Postal Congress, Amman.

459.	37.	1 f. black and brown ..	5	5
460.		4 f. black and red ..	5	5
461.		15 f. black and blue ..	8	5
462.		20 f. black and olive ..	10	5
463		50 f. black and indigo ..	25	15
464.		100 f. black and orange	45	30

1958. Declaration of Human Rights. 10th Anniv.

476.	38.	5 f. red and blue ..	5	5
477.		15 f. black and brown ..	10	10
478.		35 f. purple and green ..	20	20
479.		45 f. black and red ..	25	20

39. King Hussein.

1959. Centres in black.

480.	39.	1 f. green	5	5
481.		2 f. violet	5	5
482.		3 f. red	5	5
483.		4 f. chocolate	5	5
484.		7 f. green	5	5
485.		12 f. red	8	5
486.		15 f. vermilion ..	8	5
487.		21 f. green	10	5
488.		25 f. brown	10	5
489.		35 f. blue	15	5
490.		40 f. green	20	5
491.		50 f. red	25	10
492.		100 f. blue-green ..	50	40
493.		200 f. maroon ..	90	50
494.		500 f. blue	2·50	1·25
495.		1 d. purple	5·00	3·00

1960. Inaug. of Arab League Centre, Cairo. As T **144** of Egypt but with portrait of King Hussein instead of Arms and inscr. "JORDAN".

496.	15 f. black and green ..	10	5

40. "Care of Refugees".

1960. World Refugee Year.

497.	40.	15 f. red and blue ..	10	5
498.		35 f. blue and bistre ..	20	15

41. Shah of Iran and King Hussein.

1960. Visit of Shah of Iran.

499.	41.	15 f. multicoloured ..	10	12
500.		35 f. multicoloured ..	20	25
501.		50 f. multicoloured ..	25	30

42. Petroleum Refinery.

1961. Jordanian Petroleum Refinery Inaug.

502.	42.	15 f. blue & slate-violet	12	5
503.		35 f. chestnut and violet	20	12

43. Jordanian Families and Graph.

45. Telephone Exchange, Amman. **44.** Campaign Emblem.

1961. 1st Jordanian Census Commem.

504.	43.	15 f. chestnut	12	5

1961. Dag Hammarskjoeld Memorial Issue. Optd. **IN MEMORIAL OF DAG HAMMARSKJOELD 1904-1961** in English and Arabic and laurel leaves at top and bottom.

505.	40.	15 f. red and blue ..	2·40	2·10
506.		35 f. blue and bistre ..	2·40	2·10

1962. Malaria Eradication.

507.	44.	15 f. magenta	8	5
508.		35 f. blue	15	15

1962. Amman's Automatic Telephone Exchange. Inaug.

510.	45.	15 f. blue and purple ..	8	5
511.		35 f. purple and green ..	20	15

46. Aqaba Port and King Hussein.

1962. Opening of Aqaba Port.

512.	46.	15 f. black and purple	5	8
513.		35 f. black and blue ..	15	15

47. Dag Hammarskjoeld and U.N. Headquarters.

1963. U.N.O. 17th Anniv.

515.	47.	15 f. red, olive & blue ..	15	15
516.		35 f. blue, red & olive ..	40	30
517.		50 f. olive, blue & red ..	70	50

48. Church of St. Virgin's Tomb, Jerusalem.

DESIGNS: No. 520, Basilica of the Agony, Gethsemane. 521, Holy Sepulchre, Jerusalem. 522, Nativity Church, Bethlehem. 523, Haram of Ibrahim, Hebron. 524, Dome of the Rock, Jerusalem. 525, Omar el-Khatab Mosque, Jerusalem. 526, Al-Aksa Mosque, Jerusalem.

1963. "Holy Places". Vignettes multicoloured. Frame colours given.

519.	48.	50 f. light blue ..	30	30
520.	–	50 f. carmine-red ..	30	30
521.	–	50 f. blue ..	30	30
522.	–	50 f. yellow-olive ..	30	30
523.	–	50 f. grey	30	30
524.	–	50 f. violet	30	30
525.	–	50 f. rose-red ..	30	30
526.	–	50 f. deep lilac ..	30	30

1963. Arab League. As T **170** of Egypt but inscr. "HASHEMITE KINGDOM OF JORDAN" and with inset portrait of King Hussein.

527.	15 f. blue	8	5
528.	35 f. red	20	12

49. Wheat and F.A.O. Emblem. **50.** Canal and Symbols.

1963. Freedom from Hunger.

529.	49.	15 f. green, black & blue	8	5
530.		35 f. green, black & apple	15	10

1963. East Ghor Canal Project.

532.	50.	1 f. black and bistre ..	5	5
533.		4 f. black and blue ..	5	5
534.		5 f. black and purple ..	5	5
535.		10 f. black and green ..	5	5
536.		35 f. black and orange ..	20	15

51. Scales of Justice and Globe.

1963. Declaration of Human Rights. 15th Anniv.

537.	51.	50 f. red and blue ..	30	25
538.		50 f. blue and red ..	30	25

1963. Surch. in English and Arabic.

539.	39.	1 f. on 21 f. blk. & green	10	5
540.		2 f. on 21 f. blk. & green	10	5
541.		4 f. on 12 f. black & red	3·50	3·50
542.	–	4 f. on 12 f. sepia and red (No. 451)	12	5
543.	39.	5 f. on 21 f. blk. & green	12	5
544.		25 f. on 35 f. blk. & blue	30	20

52. King Hussein and Red Crescent.

1963. Red Crescent Commemoration.

545.	52.	1 f. purple and red ..	5	5
546.		2 f. turquoise and red ..	5	5
547.		3 f. indigo and red ..	5	5
548.		4 f. blue-green and red	5	5
549.		5 f. sepia and red ..	5	5
550.		85 f. green and red ..	1·00	1·00

53. Red Cross Emblem.

1963. Red Cross Centenary.

552	53.	1 f. purple and red ..	5	5
553.		2 f. turquoise and red ..	5	5
554.		3 f. indigo and red ..	5	5
555.		4 f. blue-green and red	5	5
556.		5 f. sepia and red ..	5	5
557.		85 f. green and red ..	3·50	3·50

54. Kings Hussein of Hejaz and Hussein of Jordan.

1963. Arab Renaissance Day.

559.	54.	15 f. multicoloured ..	15	15
560.		25 f. multicoloured ..	20	20
561.		35 f. multicoloured ..	40	40
562.		50 f. multicoloured ..	55	50

55. El Aqsa Mosque, Pope Paul and King Hussein.

1964. Pope Paul's Visit to the Holy Land.

564.	55.	15 f. green and sepia ..	15	15
565.	–	35 f. red and sepia ..	30	25
566.	–	50 f. brown and sepia ..	45	40
567.		80 f. blue and sepia ..	75	70

DESIGNS: 35 f. Dome of the Rock (Mosque of Omar), Jerusalem. 50 f. Church of the Holy Sepulchre, Jerusalem. 80 f. Church of the Nativity, Bethlehem.

56. Crown Prince Abdullah.

1964. 2nd Birthday of Crown Prince Abdullah. Multicoloured.

568.	5 f. Prince standing by wall	5	5
569.	10 f. Head of Prince and roses	8	5
570.	35 f. Type **56**	25	25

SIZES: 5 f. as T **56** but vert. 10 f. diamond (63 × 63 mm.).

NOTE.—A set of ten triangular 20 f. stamps showing astronauts and rockets was issued, but very few were put on sale at the Post Office and we are not listing them unless we receive satisfactory evidence as to their status.

56a. Basketball.

57. Woman and Child.

1964. Olympic Games, Tokyo (1st Issue).

571. 56a. 1 f. red 8 8
572. – 2 f. blue 8 8
573. – 3 f. green 8 8
574. – 4 f. buff 8 8
575. – 5 f. violet 8 8
576. – 35 f. vermilion .. 50 50
577. – 50 f. green 60 60
578. – 100 f. chocolate .. 1·00 1·00

DESIGNS—VERT. 2 f. Volley-ball. 3 f. Football. 5 f. Running. HORIZ. 4 f. Table-tennis. 35 f. Cycling. 50 f. Fencing. 100 f. Pole-vaulting.
See also Nos. 610/17 and 641/6.

1964. Social Studies Seminar, Amman. 4th Session.

580. 57. 5 f. multicoloured .. 5 5
581. 10 f. multicoloured .. 8 5
582. 25 f. multicoloured .. 15 10

59. President Kennedy.

58. Stadium.

61. King Hussein and Map of Jordan.

60. Statues at Abu Simbel.

1964. Air. "Hussein Sports City". Inaug.

583. 58. 1 f. multicoloured .. 5 5
584. 4 f. multicoloured .. 5 5
585. 10 f. multicoloured 5 5
586. 35 f. multicoloured .. 20 20

1964. Pres. Kennedy Memorial Issue.

588. 59. 1 f. violet 12 12
589. 2 f. carmine 12 12
590. 3 f. blue 12 12
591. 4 f. brown 12 12
592. 5 f. green 12 12
593. 85 f. red .. .. 3·00 3·00

1964. Nubian Monuments Preservation.

595. 60. 4 f. black and blue .. 5 5
596. 15 f. violet and yellow .. 8 5
597. 25 f. red and green .. 12 10

1964. Arab Summit Conf.

598. 61. 10 f. multicoloured .. 5 5
599. 15 f. multicoloured .. 5 5
600. 25 f. multicoloured .. 10 5
601. 50 f. multicoloured .. 25 15
602. 80 f. multicoloured .. 30 25

62. Pope Paul VI, King Hussein and Ecumenical Patriarch.

1964. Meeting of Pope, King and Patriarch, Jerusalem. Inscr. at top in black; portraits in sepia, gold and black; background colours given.

604. 62. 10 f. green 5 5
605. 15 f. purple 10 10
606. 25 f. chocolate .. 15 12
607. 50 f. blue 40 35
608. 80 f. emerald 75 70

63. Olympic Flame.

1964. Olympic Games, Tokyo. (2nd issue).

610. 63. 1 f. red 5 5
611. 2 f. violet 5 5
612. 3 f. green 5 5
613. 4 f. brown 5 5
614. 5 f. red 5 5
615. 35 f. indigo 35 35
616. 50 f. olive 60 60
617. 100 f. blue .. .. 1·25 1·25

64. Scouts crossing River.

1964. Jordanian Scouts.

619. 64. 1 f. brown 5 5
620. – 2 f. violet 5 5
621. – 3 f. ochre 5 5
622. – 4 f. lake 5 5
623. – 5 f. green 5 5
624. – 35 f. blue 40 35
625. – 50 f. grey-green .. 70 50

DESIGNS: 2 f. First Aid. 3 f. Exercising. 4 f. Practising knots. 5 f. Cooking meal. 35 f. Sailing. 50 f. Around camp-fire.

65. Gorgeous Bush-shrike.

1964. Air. Birds. Multicoloured.

627. 150 f. Type 65 .. .. 80 40
628. 500 f. Ornate hawk eagle .. 4·00 2·25
629. 1000 f. Grey-hooded kingfisher .. .. 7·00 4·50

Nos. 628/9 are vert.

66. Bykovsky.

1965. Russian Astronauts.

630. 40 f. brown and green (Type 66) 70 70
631. 40 f. violet and brown (Gagarin) 70 70
632. 40 f. maroon and blue (Nikolaev) 70 70
633. 40 f. lilac and bistre (Popovich) 70 70
634. 40 f. sepia and blue (Tereshkova) 70 70
635. 40 f. green & pink (Titov) 70 70

67. U.N. Headquarters and Emblem.

1965. U.N. 19th Anniv. (1964).

638. 67. 30 f. violet, turquoise and brown 30 20
639. 70 f. brown, blue & vio. 70 50

68. Olympic Flame.

1965. Air. Olympic Games, Tokyo. (3rd issue).

641. 68. 10 f. red 8 5
642. 15 f. violet 8 5
643. 20 f. blue 20 10
644. 30 f. green 30 20
645. 40 f. brown 40 40
646. 60 f. magenta 60 60

1965. Deir Yasin Massacre. As T 230 of Egypt, but inscr. "THE HASHEMITE KINGDOM OF JORDAN" in English and Arabic.

648. 25 f. red and olive .. 10 8

69. Horse-jumping.

70. Volleyball Player and Cup.

1965. Army Day.

649. 69. 5 f. green 5 5
650. – 10 f. ultramarine .. 10 8
651. – 35 f. lake 20 15

DESIGNS: 10 f. Tank. 35 f. King Hussein making inspection in army car.

1965. Arab Volleyball Championships.

652. 70. 15 f. olive 10 8
653. 35 f. lake 20 20
654. 50 f. blue 30 30

71. President Kennedy.

1965. Pres. Kennedy's 1st Death Anniv.

656. 71. 10 f. black and green .. 10 8
657. 15 f. violet and orange .. 20 15
658. 25 f. brown and blue .. 25 20
659. 50 f. maroon and green 50 35

72. Pope Paul, King Hussein and Dome of the Rock.

1965. Pope Paul's Visit to the Holy Land. 1st Anniv.

661. 72. 5 f. brown and mauve .. 10 10
662. 10 f. lake and green .. 15 15
663. 15 f. blue and flesh .. 20 20
664. 50 f. grey and pink .. 60 60

73. Cathedral Steps.

75. I.T.U. Emblem and Symbols.

74. Jordan Pavilion at Fair.

1965. Air. Jerash Antiquities. Multicoloured.

666. 55 f. Type 73 .. .. 35 35
667. 55 f. Artemis Temple Gate 35 35
668. 55 f. Street of Columns .. 35 35
669. 55 f. Columns of South Theatre 35 35
670. 55 f. Forum 35 35
671. 55 f. South Theatre .. 35 35
672. 55 f. Triumphal Arch .. 35 35
673. 55 f. Temple of Artemis .. 35 35

Nos. 670/3 are horiz.

1965. New York World's Fair.

674. 74. 15 f. multicoloured .. 8 5
675. 25 f. multicoloured .. 12 10
676. 50 f. multicoloured .. 25 20

1965. Burning of Algiers Library. As T 232 of Egypt, but inscr. "THE HASHEMITE KINGDOM OF JORDAN" in English and Arabic.

678. 25 f. green, red and black .. 12 10

1965. I.T.U. Cent.

679. 75. 25 f. indigo and blue .. 12 10
680. 45 f. black and green .. 20 20

76. "Syncom" Satellite and Pagoda.

1965. Space Achievements. Multicoloured.

682. 5 f. Type 76 .. .. 5 5
683. 10 f. Spaceship 8 8
684. 15 f. Astronauts .. 15 12
685. 20 f. Spaceship 15 12
686. 50 f. Type 76 .. .. 35 30

77. Dead Sea.

1965. Dead Sea. Multicoloured.

688. 35 f. Type 77 .. .. 25 25
689. 35 f. Boats and palms .. 12 12
690. 35 f. Qumran Caves .. 12 12
691. 35 f. Dead Sea Scrolls .. 12 12

1965. Air. Space Flight of McDivitt and White. Nos. 641/6 optd. **James McDivitt Edward White 2-6-1965** in English and Arabic and Rocket.

692. 63. 10 f. red 20 20
693. 15 f. violet 20 20
694. 20 f. blue 30 30
695. 30 f. green 40 35
696. 40 f. brown 60 55
697. 60 f. magenta .. .. 1·00 80

78. King Hussein, U.N. Emblem and Headquarters.

1965. King Hussein's Visit to France and the U.S.A.

699. **78.** 5 f. sepia, blue and pink 5 5
700. – 10 f. sepia, green & grey 8 5
701. – 20 f. agate, brown & blue 20 15
702. **78.** 50 f. lilac, brown & blue 45 40

DESIGNS: 10 f. King Hussein, Pres. de Gaulle. 20 f. King Hussein, Pres. Johnson and Statue of Liberty.

79. I.C.Y. Emblem. **80.** A.P.U. Emblem.

1965. Int. Co-operation Year.

704. **79.** 5 f. red and orange .. 5 5
705. 10 f. violet and blue .. 5 5
706. 45 f. purple and green 25 15

1965. Arab Postal Union. 10th Anniv.

707. **80.** 15 f. black and blue .. 8 5
708. 25 f. black and green .. 12 5

81. Dome of the Rock.

1965. "Dome of the Rock". Inaug.

709. **81.** 15 f. multicoloured .. 8 5
710. 25 f. multicoloured .. 15 10

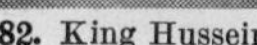

82. King Hussein. **83.** First Station of the Cross.

82a.

1966.

(a) Postage. Portraits in blue (1 f. to 15 f.) or maroon (21 f. to 150 f.); background colours given.

711. **82.** 1 f. orange 5 5
712. 2 f. ultramarine .. 5 5
713. 3 f. violet 5 5
714. 4 f. purple 5 5
715. 7 f. chestnut 5 5
716. 12 f. magenta 5 5
717. 15 f. bistre 5 5
718. 21 f. green 8 5
719. 25 f. blue 8 5
720. 35 f. ochre 12 5
721. 40 f. yellow 15 10
722. 50 f. olive 20 12
723. 100 f. green 50 30
724. 150 f. violet 75 25

(b) **Air.** Portraits in bistre; background colours given.

725. **82.** 200 f. turquoise .. 1·00 50
726. 500 f. green .. .. 2·50 1·75
727. 1 d. blue .. .. 5·00 2·75

1966. Space Flights of Beliaiev and Leonov. Nos. 630/35 optd. **Alexei Leonov Pavel Belyaev 18.3.65** in English and Arabic and spacecraft motif.

728. 40 f. brown and green .. 1·00 1·00
729. 40 f. violet and brown .. 1·00 1·00
730. 40 f. maroon and blue .. 1·00 1·00
731. 40 f. lilac and bistre .. 1·00 1·00
732. 40 f. sepia and blue .. 1·00 1·00
733. 40 f. green and pink .. 1·00 1·00

1966. Pope Paul's Visit to U.N. (1965). Nos. 604/8 optd. **PAPA PAULUS VI WORLD PEACE VISIT TO UNITED NATIONS 1965** in English and Arabic.

736. **62.** 10 f. green 8 10
737. 15 f. purple 12 15
738. 25 f. chocolate 15 30
739. 50 f. blue 30 30
740. 80 f. emerald 40 40

1966. Anti-T.B. Campaign. (a) Unissued "Freedom from Hunger" stamps optd. as in T **82a**

741. **82a.** 15 f. multicoloured .. 12 12
742. 35 f. multicoloured .. 25 25
743. 50 f. multicoloured .. 35 35

(b) As Nos. 741/3 but with additional premium obliterated by bars.

745. – 15 f. multicoloured .. 12 12
746. – 35 f. multicoloured .. 25 25
747. – 50 f. multicoloured .. 35 35

1966. Christ's Passion. The Stations of the Cross.

749. **83.** 1 f. multicoloured .. 20 10
750. – 2 f. multicoloured .. 20 10
751. – 3 f. multicoloured .. 20 10
752. – 4 f. multicoloured .. 20 10
753. – 5 f. multicoloured .. 20 10
754. – 6 f. multicoloured .. 20 10
755. – 7 f. multicoloured .. 20 10
756. – 8 f. multicoloured .. 20 10
757. – 9 f. multicoloured .. 20 10
758. – 10 f. multicoloured .. 20 10
759. – 11 f. multicoloured .. 20 10
760. – 12 f. multicoloured .. 20 10
761. – 13 f. multicoloured .. 20 10
762. – 14 f. multicoloured .. 20 10

DESIGNS: The 14 Stations. The denominations, expressed in Roman numerals, correspond to the numbers of the Stations.

84. Schirra and "Gemini 6". **86.** Dag Hammarskjoeld.

85. The Three Kings.

1966. Space Achievements.

764. **84.** 1 f. blue, violet & green 5 5
765. – 2 f. green, violet & blue 5 5
766. – 3 f. violet, blue & green 5 5
767. – 4 f. violet, green & ochre 5 5
768. – 30 f. turq., chest. & vio. 20 10
769. – 60 f. chest., turq. & vio. 40 15

DESIGNS: 2 f. Stafford and "Gemini 6". 3 f. Bormrn and "Gemini 7". 4 f. Lovell and "Gemini 7". 30 f. Armstrong and "Gemini 8". 60 f. Scott and "Gemini 8".

1966. Christmas. Multicoloured.

771. 5 f. Type **85** 5 5
772. 10 f. The Magi presenting gifts to the infant Christ 12 12
773. 35 f. The flight to Egypt (vert.) 30 25

1967. "Builders of World Peace". Multicoloured.

775. 5 f. Type **86** .. 5 5
781. 5 f. U Thant .. 5 5
776. 10 f. Pandit Nehru .. 5 5
782. 10 f. Pres. De Gaulle .. 5 5
777. 35 f. Pres. Kennedy .. 25 20
783. 35 f. Pres. Johnson .. 25 30
778. 50 f. Pope John XXIII .. 35 35
784. 50 f. Pope Paul VI .. 35 35
779. 100 f. King Abdullah (of Jordan) 70 65
785. 100 f. King Hussein .. 70 65

87. King Hussein.

1967. "Gold Coins". Circular designs, centre and rim embossed on gold foil. Imperf.

(a) As T **87**. (i) Diameter 1⅝ in.

787. **87.** 5 f. salmon and ultram. 5 5
788. 10 f. salmon and violet 8 8

(ii) Diameter 1⅞ in.

789. **87.** 50 f. lavender and brown 35 35
790. 100 f. pink and green .. 70 70

(iii) Diameter 2⅛ in.

791. **87.** 200 f. blue and indigo .. 1·40 1·40

(b) Crown Prince Hassan of Jordan. (i) Diam. 1⅝ in.

792. – 5 f. black and green .. 5 5
793. – 10 f. black and lilac .. 8 8

(ii) Diameter 1⅞ in.

794. – 50 f. black and blue .. 35 35
795. – 100 f. pink and green .. 70 70

(iii) Diameter 2⅛ in.

796. – 200 f. black and magenta 1·40 1·40

A similar set was also issued in the same values and sizes but different colours with portrait of John F. Kennedy.

88. University City, Statue and Olympic Torch.

1967. Preparation for Olympic Games in Mexico (1968).

797. **88.** 1 f. red, black and violet 5 5
798. – 2 f. black, violet and red 5 5
799. – 3 f. violet, red & black 5 5
800. – 4 f. ultram., brn. & grn. 5 5
801. – 30 f. grn., ultram. & brn. 20 20
802. – 60 f. brn., grn. & ultram. 40 30

DESIGNS (each with Olympic torch): 2 f. Fisherman on Lake Patzcuaro. 3 f. University City and sky scraper, Mexico City. 4 f. Avenida de la Reforma, Mexico City. 30 f. Guadalajara Cathedral. 60 f. Fine Arts Theatre, Mexico City.

89. Decade Emblem.

1967. Int. Hydrological Decade.

804. **89.** 10 f. black and red .. 5 5
805. 15 f. black & turquoise 8 8
806. 25 f. black and purple .. 15 15

90. U.N.E.S.C.O. Emblem.

1967. U.N.E.S.C.O. 20th Anniv.

807. **90.** 100 f. multicoloured .. 50 50

91. Dromedary.

1967. Animals. Multicoloured.

808. 1 f. Type **91** (postage) .. 5 5
809. 2 f. Karakul sheep .. 5 5
810. 3 f. Angora goat .. 5 5
811. 4 f. Hyena (air) .. 5 5
812. 30 f. Arab horses .. 20 20
813. 60 f. Oryx 40 35

92. W.H.O. Building. **93.** Arab League Emblem, Open Book and Reaching Hands.

1967. W.H.O. Headquarters, Geneva. Inaug.

815. **92.** 5 f. black and green .. 5 5
816. 45 f. black and orange .. 25 25

1968. Literacy Campaign.

817. **93.** 20 f. green & orange .. 12 12
818. 20 f. blue & magenta .. 12 12

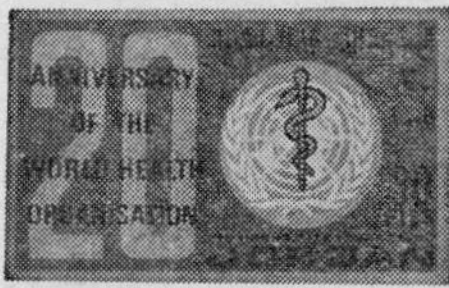

94. W.H.O. Emblem and "20".

1968. World Health Organisation. 20th Anniv.

819. **94.** 30 f. multicoloured 15 15
820. 100 f. multicoloured 50 50

95. Goldfinch. **96.** Human Rights Emblem.

1968. Game Protection. Multicoloured.

821. 5 f. Type **95** (postage) .. 5 5
822. 10 f. Rock partridge .. 5 5
823. 15 f. Ostriches .. 8 8
824. 20 f. Sand partridge .. 10 10
825. 30 f. Gazelle .. 15 15
826. 40 f. Oryx 20 20
827. 50 f. Bustard .. 25 25
828. 60 f. Ibex (air) .. 35 35
829. 100 f. Flock of mallard 60 60

The 10, 15 and 60 f. are vert.

1968. Human Rights Year.

830. **96.** 20 f. blk., buff & chest. 10 10
831. 60 f. black, bl. & grn. .. 35 35

97. I.L.O. Emblem.

1969. Int. Labour Organization. 50th Anniv.

832. **97.** 10 f. black and blue .. 5 5
833. 20 f. black and brown 10 10
834. 25 f. black and green .. 12 12
835. 45 f. black and magenta 25 25
836. 60 f. black and orange .. 35 35

98. Horses in Pasture.

1969. Arab Horses. Multicoloured.

837. 10 f. Type **98** .. 5 5
838. 20 f. White horse .. 10 10
839. 45 f. Black mare and foal 20 20

INDEX

Countries can be quickly located by referring to the index at the end of this volume.

99. Al-Aqsa Mosque.

100. Oranges.

1969. Al-Aqsa Mosque. Multicoloured.

840. 5 f. Kaaba, Mecca, and El-Aqsa Mosque, Jerusalem 5 5
841. 10 f. Type **99** 5 5
842. 20 f. Type **99** 10 10
843. 45 f. As 5 f. 20 20

Nos. 840 and 843 are larger, size 56 × 26 mm.

1969. Fruits. Multicoloured.

844. 10 f. Type **100** 5 5
845. 20 f. Gooseberry 10 10
846. 30 f. Lemons 15 15
847. 40 f. Grapes 20 20
848. 50 f. Olives 30 30
849. 100 f. Apples 60 60

101. Prince Hassan and Bride.

1969. Wedding of Prince Hassan (1968).

850. – 20 f. multicoloured .. 10 10
851. – 60 f. multicoloured .. 30 30
852. **101.** 100 f. multicoloured .. 60 60

Nos. 850/1 show a similar design to T **101**.

102. Wrecked Houses.

1970. "Tragedy of the Refugees". Various vert. designs as T **102**. Multicoloured.

853/82. 1 f. to 30 f. inclusive Set of 30 .. .. 3·00 3·00

103. Bombed Mosque.

104. Pomegranate.

1970. "Tragedy in the Holy Lands". Various vert. designs as T **103**. Multicoloured.

883/912 1 f. to 30 f. inclusive Set of 30 .. .. 3·00 3·00

1970. Flowers. Multicoloured.

913. 5 f. Type **104** 5 5
914. 15 f. Wattle 8 8
915. 25 f. Caper 12 12
916. 35 f. Convolvulus 15 15
917. 45 f. Desert Scabious .. 25 25
918. 75 f. Black Iris 40 40

Nos. 913/5 and 917 are wrongly inscribed on the stamps.

105. Football.

1970. Sports. Multicoloured.

919. 5 f. Type **105** 5 5
920. 10 f. Diving 5 5
921. 15 f. Boxing 8 8
922. 50 f. Running 25 20
923. 100 f. Cycling (vert.) .. 60 50
924. 150 f. Basketball (vert.) 80 70

106. Arab Children.

107. Black Chat.

1970. Children's Day. Multicoloured.

925. 5 f. Type **106** 5 5
926. 10 f. Refugee boy with kettle 5 5
927. 15 f. Refugee girl in camp 8 8
928. 20 f. Refugee child in tent 10 8

Nos. 926/8 are vert.

1970. Birds. Multicoloured.

929. 120 f. Type **107** 70 50
930. 180 f. Masked shrike .. 90 80
931. 200 f. Palestine sunbird .. 1·00 90

108. Grotto of the Nativity, Bethlehem.

1970. Christmas. Church of the Nativity. Bethlehem. Multicoloured.

932. 5 f. Type **108** 5 5
933. 10 f. Christmas crib .. 5 5
934. 20 f. Crypt Altar 10 8
935. 25 f. Nave, Church of the Nativity 12 10

109. Arab League Flag, Emblem and Map.

1971. Silver Jubilee of Arab League (1970).

936. **109.** 10 f. grn., violet & orge. 5 5
937. 20 f. grn., brn. & blue 10 8
938. 30 f. grn., blue & brn. 15 12

110. "Doves" and Emblem.

1971. Racial Equality Year. Multicoloured.

939. 5 f. Heads of Four Races and Emblem (vert.) .. 5 5
940. 10 f. "Plant" and emblem (vert.) 5 5
941. 15 f. Type **110** 10 8

No. 939 is inscribed "KINIGDOM" in error.

111. Shore of the Dead Sea.

112. Ibn Sinai.

1971. Tourism. Multicoloured.

942. 5 f. Type **111** 5 5
943. 30 f. Ed Deir, Petra .. 15 12
944. 45 f. Via Dolorosa, Jerusalem (vert.) .. 20 15
945. 60 f. River Jordan 30 25
946. 100 f. Christmas Bell, Bethlehem (vert.) .. 60 50

1971. Famous Arab Scholars. Multicoloured.

947. 5 f. Type **112** 5 5
948. 10 f. Ibn Rusho 5 5
949. 20 f. Ibn Khaldun 10 8
950. 25 f. Ibn Tufail 12 10
951. 30 f. Ibn El Haytham .. 15 12

113. New U.P.U. HQ. Building.

1971. New U.P.U. Headquarters Building, Berne, Inaug.

952. **113.** 10 f. multicoloured 5 5
953. 20 f. multicoloured .. 10 8

114. Young Pupil.

115. Arab Mothers and Children.

1972. Int. Education Year.

954. **114.** 5 f. multicoloured .. 5 5
955. 15 f. multicoloured .. 8 8
956. 20 f. multicoloured .. 10 8
957. 30 f. multicoloured .. 15 12

1972. Mothers' Day. Multicoloured.

958. 10 f. Type **115** 5 5
959. 20 f. Mother and child (vert.) 10 8
960. 30 f. Bedouin mother and child (vert.) 15 12

116. Pope Paul leaving Holy Sepulchre, Jerusalem.

117. Child with Toy Bricks.

1972. Easter Festivals. Multicoloured.

961. 30 f. Type **117** (postage) .. 15 15
962. 60 f. The Calvary, Church of the Holy Sepulchre (air) 30 30
963. 100 f. "Washing of the Feet", Jerusalem .. 60 50

1972. U.N.I.C.E.F. 25th Anniv. Mult.

964. 10 f. Children and U.N.I.C.E.F. emblem .. 5 5
965. 20 f. Type **117** 8 5
966. 30 f. Nurse holding baby .. 15 12

118. Dove of Peace.

119. Al Aqsa Mosque.

120. Arab holding Kestrel.

1972. United Nations. 25th Anniv.

967. **118.** 5 f. multicoloured .. 5 5
968. 10 f. multicoloured .. 5 5
969. 15 f. multicoloured .. 8 5
970. 20 f. multicoloured .. 10 8
971. 30 f. multicoloured .. 15 12

1972. Burning of Al Aqsa Mosque. Mult.

972. 30 f. Type **119** 12 12
973. 60 f. Mosque in flames .. 25 20
974. 100 f. Mosque Interior .. 50 40

1972. Jordanian Desert Life. Multicoloured.

975. 5 f. Type **120** 5 5
976. 10 f. Desert bungalow .. 5 5
977. 15 f. Camel trooper, Arab Legion 8 5
978. 20 f. Boring operations .. 10 8
979. 25 f. Shepherd 10 8
980. 30 f. Camels at water-trough 12 10
981. 35 f. Chicken farm .. 15 12
982. 45 f. Irrigation scheme .. 25 20

Nos. 976/82 are horizontal designs.

121. Wasfi el Tell and Dome of the Rock, Jerusalem.

1972. Wasfi el Tell (assassinated statesman) Memorial Issue, Multicoloured.

983. 5 f. Type **121** 5 5
984. 10 f. Wasfi el Tell, map and flag 5 5
985. 20 f. Type **121** 10 8
986. 30 f. As 10 f. 12 12

122. Clay-pigeon shooting.

123. Commemorative Emblem.

1972. World Clay-shooting Championships. Multicoloured.

987. 25 f. Type **122** 10 8
988. 75 f. Marksman (shooting to right) (horiz.) .. 35 30
989. 120 f. Marksman (shooting to left) (horiz.) 60 50

1973. Royal Jordanian Club.

990. **123.** 5 f. blk., bl. & yell. (post.) 5 5
991. – 10 f. blk., blue & yellow 5 5
992. – 15 f. multicoloured (air) 5 5
993. – 20 f. multicoloured .. 8 5
994. – 40 f. multicoloured .. 20 15

DESIGNS: 15 f., Two Piper "140" aircraft 20 f. "Beechcraft aeroplane". 40 f. Winged horse emblem.

124. Dove and Map.

1973. Hashemite Kingdom of Jordan. 50th Anniv. Multicoloured.

995. 5 f. Type **124** 5 5
996. 10 f. Anniversary emblem 5 5
997. 15 f. King Hussein .. 8 5
998. 30 f. Map and emblems .. 12 10

125. Map of Jordanian Advance.

1973. Battle of Karama. 5th Anniv. Mult.

999. 5 f. Type **125** 5 5
1000. 10 f. Jordanian attack, and map 5 5
1001. 15 f. Map, and King Hussein on tank 8 5

126. Father and Son.

127. Phosphate Mines.

1973. Fathers' Day. Multicoloured.

1002. 10 f. Type **126** 5 5
1003. 20 f. Father and daughter 10 8
1004. 30 f. Family group .. 15 12

1973. Development Projects. Multicoloured.

1005. 5 f. Type **127** 5 5
1006. 10 f. Cement factories .. 5 5
1007. 15 f. Sharmabil Dam .. 8 5
1008. 20 f. Kafrein Dam .. 12 10

128. Racing Camel.

1973. Camel Racing. Multicoloured.
1009. 5 f. Type **128** 5 5
1010. 10 f. Camels in "paddock" 5 5
1011. 15 f. Start of race .. 8 5
1012. 20 f. Camel racing .. 12 10

129. Book Year Emblem.

1973. International Book Year (1972).
1013. **129.** 30 f. multicoloured 15 12
1014. 60 f. multicoloured .. 30 25

130. Family Group.

1973. Family Day.
1015. **130.** 20 f. multicoloured .. 12 12
1016. 30 f. multicoloured .. 15 15
1017. 60 f. multicoloured .. 30 25

131. Shah of Iran, King Hussein, Cyrus's Tomb of Mosque of Omar.

1973. Iranian Monarchy. 2500th Anniv.
1018. **131.** 5 f. multicoloured 5 5
1019. 10 f. multicoloured .. 5 5
1020. 15 f. multicoloured .. 8 8
1021. 30 f. multicoloured .. 15 15

132. Emblem of Palestine Week.

1973. Palestine Week. Multicoloured.
1022. 5 f. Type **132** 5 5
1023. 10 f. Torch and emblem 5 5
1024. 15 f. Refugees (26 × 47mm.) 8 8
1025. 30 f. Children and map on Globe 15 15

133. Traditional Harvesting.

1973. Ancient and Modern Agriculture. Multicoloured.
1026. 5 f. Type **133** (postage) .. 5 5
1027. 10 f. Modern harvesting 5 5
1028. 15 f. Traditional seeding 8 8
1029. 20 f. Modern seeding .. 10 10
1030. 30 f. Traditional ploughing 15 15
1031. 35 f. Modern ploughing 20 20
1032. 45 f. Pest Control .. 25 30
1033. 60 f. Horticulture .. 35 30
1034. 100 f. Tree-planting and soil conservation (air) .. 55 45

134. Red Sea Fish.

136. "The Club-footed Boy" (Murillo).

135. Battle of Muta.

1974. Red Sea Fishes.
1035. **134.** 5 f. multicoloured .. 5 5
1036. – 10 f. multicoloured .. 5 5
1037. – 15 f. multicoloured .. 8 8
1038. – 20 f. multicoloured .. 10 10
1039. – 25 f. multicoloured .. 12 12
1040. – 30 f. multicoloured .. 15 15
1041. – 35 f. multicoloured .. 20 20
1042. – 40 f. multicoloured .. 25 20
1043. – 45 f. multicoloured .. 25 20
1044. **134.** 50 f. multicoloured .. 30 25
1045. – 60 f. multicoloured .. 35 30
DESIGNS: Nos. 1036/43 and 1045, Various fish designs as T **134.**

1974. Islamic battles against the Crusaders. Multicoloured.
1046. 10 f. Type **135** 5 5
1047. 20 f. Battle of Yarmouk 10 10
1048. 30 f. Hitteen Battle .. 15 15

1974. Famous Paintings. Multicoloured.
1049. 5 f. Type **136** 5 5
1050. 10 f. "Praying Hands" (Durer) 5 5
1051. 15 f. "St. George and the Dragon" (Uccello) .. 8 8
1052. 20 f. "The Mona Lisa" (L. da Vinci) 10 10
1053. 30 f. "Hope" (F. Watts) 15 15
1054. 40 f. "The Angelus" (Jean Millet) (horiz.) .. 25 20
1055. 50 f. "The Artist and her Daughter" (Angelica Kauffmann) 30 25
1056. 60 f. "Whistler's Mother" (J. Whistler) (horiz.) .. 35 30
1057. 100 f. "Master Hare" (Sir J. Reynolds) 55 45

المؤتمر الدولي لتاريخ بلاد الشام

٢٠ – ١٩٧٤/٤/٢٥

الجامعة الاردنية

(137.)

1974. International Conference for Damascus History. Nos. 1013/4 optd. with Type **137.**
1058. **129.** 30 f. multicoloured .. 15 15
1059. 60 f. multicoloured .. 35 30

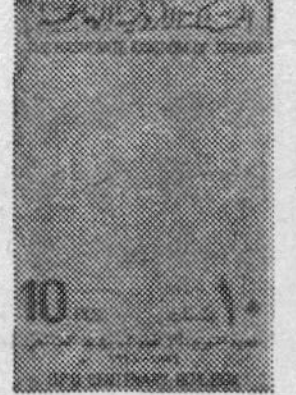
138. U.P.U. Emblem.

139. Camel Caravan.

1974. Universal Postal Union. Cent.
1060. **138.** 10 f. multicoloured .. 5 5
1061. 30 f. multicoloured .. 15 15
1062. 60 f. multicoloured .. 35 30

1974. The Dead Sea. Multicoloured.
1063. 2 f. Type **139** 5 5
1064. 3 f. Palm and shore .. 5 5
1065. 4 f. Hotel on coast .. 5 5
1066. 5 f. Jars from Qumram Caves 5 5
1067. 6 f. Copper scrolls (vert.) 5 5
1068. 10 f. Cistern steps, Qumram (vert.) 5 5
1069. 20 f. Type **139** 10 8
1070. 30 f. As 3 f. 15 12
1071. 40 f. As 4 f. 20 15
1072. 50 f. As 5 f. 25 20
1073. 60 f. As 6 f. 30 25
1074. 100 f. As 10 f. 55 45

140. WPY Emblem.

141. Water-skier.

1974. World Population Year.
1075. **140.** 5 f. purple, grn. & blk. 5 5
1076. 10 f red grn. & blk.. 5 5
1077. 20 f. orange, grn. & blk. 10 10

1974. Water-skiing. Multicoloured.
1078. 5 f. Type **141** 5 5
1079. 10 f. Water-skier (side view) (horiz.) 5 5
1080. 20 f. Skier turning (horiz.) 10 8
1081. 50 f. Type **141** 30 25
1082. 100 f. As 10 f. 55 45
1083. 200 f. As 20 f. .. .. 1·10 90

142. Ka'aba, Mecca, and Pilgrims.

1974. "Pilgrimage Season".
1084. **142.** 10 f. multicoloured .. 5 5
1085. 20 f. multicoloured .. 10 10

143. Amrah Palace.

144. King Hussein at Wheel of Car.

1974. Desert Ruins. Multicoloured.
1086. 10 f. Type **143** 5 5
1087. 20 f. Hisham Palace .. 10 10
1088. 30 f. Kharraneh Castle .. 15 12

1975. Air. Royal (Jordanian) Automobile Club.
1089. **144.** 30 f. multicoloured .. 15 15
1090. 60 f. multicoloured .. 35 30

145. Woman in Costume.

146. Treasury, Petra.

1975. Jordanian Women's Costumes.
1091. **145.** 5 f. multicoloured .. 5 5
1092. – 10 f. multicoloured .. 5 5
1093. – 15 f. multicoloured .. 8 8
1094. – 20 f. multicoloured .. 10 8
1095. – 25 f. multicoloured .. 12 10
DESIGNS: 10 f. to 25 f. Various costumes as T **145.**

1975. Tourism. Multicoloured.
1096. 15 f. Type **146** 8 8
1097. 20 f. Ommayyad Palace, Amman (horiz.) .. 10 8
1098. 30 f. Dome of the Rock, Jerusalem (horiz.) .. 15 12
1099. 40 f. Forum columns, Jerash (horiz.) 25 20
1100. 50 f. Palms, Aqaba .. 30 25
1101. 60 f. Obelisj Tomb, Petra (horiz.) 35 30
1102. 80 f. Fort of Wadi Rum (horiz.) 40 35

147. King Hussein.

148. Globe and "Desert".

1975.
1103. **147.** 5 f. black & green .. 5 5
1104. 10 f. black & violet .. 5 5
1105. 15 f. black & rose .. 8 5
1106. 20 f. black & brown 10 8
1107. 25 f. black & blue .. 12 8
1108. 30 f. black & brown 15 10
1109. **147.** 35 f. blue and violet .. 15 10
1110. 40 f. blue and red .. 20 15
1111. 45 f. blue and mauve 20 15
1112. 50 f. blue and green .. 25 20
1113. 60 f. brown and green 30 25
1114. 100 f. brn. & orange 50 40
1115. 120 f. brown & blue 60 50
1116. 180 f. brown & purple 90 80
1117. 200 f. brown and blue 1·00 90
1118. 400 f. brown and pur. 2·00 1·75
1119. 500 f. brn. & red .. 2·25 2·00
Nos. 1113/9 are larger, 22 × 27 mm.

1975. ALIA (Royal Jordanian Airlines). Tenth Anniv. Multicoloured.
1120. 10 f. Type **148** 5 5
1121. 30 f. Boeing "727" linking Globe and map of Jordan (horiz.) 12 8
1122. 60 f. Globe and "ALIA" logo 30 25

149. Satellite and Earth Station.

1975. Satellite Earth Station Opening.
1123. **149.** 20 f. multicoloured .. 10 8
1124. 30 f. multicoloured .. 12 10

150. Emblem of Chamber of Commerce.

1975. Amman Chamber of Commerce. 70th Anniversary.
1125. **150.** 10 f. multicoloured .. 5 5
1126. 15 f. multicoloured .. 8 5
1127. 20 f. multicoloured .. 10 8

151. Emblem and Hand with Spanner.

1975. Completion of Three Year Development Plan.
1128. **151.** 5 f. blk., red & green 5 5
1129. 10 f. blk., red & grn. 5 5
1130. 20 f. blk., red & grn. 10 8

152. Jordanian Family.

153. A.L.O. Emblem and Salt Mine.

1976. Int. Women's Year (1975). Mult.
1131. 5 f. Type **152** 5 5
1132. 25 f. Woman scientist .. 10 8
1133. 60 f. Woman graduate .. 20 15

1976. Arab Labour Organization. Mult.
1134. 10 f. Type **153** 5 5
1135. 30 f. Welding 10 8
1136. 60 f. Quayside, Aqaba .. 20 15

1976. Nos. 853/82, surch. in English and Arabic.
1137/46. 25 f. on 1 f. to 10 f...
1147/51. 40 f. on 11 f. to 15 f...
1152/56. 50 f. on 16 f. to 20 f...
1157/61. 75 f. on 21 f. to 25 f...
1162/66. 125 f. on 26 f. to 30 f.
Set of 30 .. .. 8·00 8·00

1976. Nos. 883/912, surch. in English and Arabic.
1167/76. 25 f. on 1 f. to 10 f...
1178/82. 40 f. on 11 f. to 15 f...
1183/87. 50 f. on 16 f. to 20 f...
1188/92. 75 f. on 21 f. to 25 f...
1192/96. 125 f. 26 f. to 30 f. ..
Set of 30 .. .. 8·00 8·00

POSTAGE DUE STAMPS

مستحق
(D 1. "Due".)

1923. Stamps of Saudi Arabia optd. with T 10 and Type D 1 in addition.
D 112. 5. ½ p. on 3 p. brown 3·25 4·00
D 113. 1 p. blue .. .. 2·50 2·50
D 114. 1½ p. violet .. .. 2·50 2·50
D 115. 2 p. orange .. .. 2·50 2·50

(D 2.) (D 3.)

1923. Optd. with Type D 2 and surch. as before.
D 116. 5. ½ p. on 3 p. brown .. 6·50

1923. Stamps of Saudi Arabia hand-stamped with Type D 3.
D 117. 5. ½ p. red 15
D 118. 1 p. blue 20
D 119. 1½ p. violet 25
D 120. 2 p. orange 35
D 121. 3 p. brown 65
D 122. 5 p. olive .. .. 1·00

(D 4. "Due East of the Jordan".) (D 5.)

1925. Stamps of Palestine, 1922, optd. with Type D 4.
D 159. 3. 1 m. brown 5 8
D 160. 2 m. yellow 8 10
D 161. 4 m. red 10 12
D 162. 8 m. red 20 25
D 163. 13 m. blue 25 30
D 164. 5 p. purple 70 75

1926. Stamps of Palestine as last surch. as Type D 5 ("DUE" and new value in Arabic).
D 165. 3. 1 m. on 1 m. brown .. 40 40
D 166. 2 m. on 1 m. brown .. 40 40
D 167. 4 m. on 3 m. blue .. 40 40
D 168. 8 m. on 3 m. blue .. 50 50
D 169. 13 m. on 13 m. blue .. 70 70
D 170. 5 p. on 13 m. blue .. 70 70
The lower line of the surcharge differs for each value.

(D 6.) D 7 D 8.

1928. Surch. as Type D 6 or optd. only.
D 183. 18. 1 m. on 3 m. red .. 10 10
D 184. 2 m. blue 10 10
D 185. 4 m. on 15 m. blue .. 20 20
D 186. 10 m. red 25 30
D 187. 19. 20 m. on 100 m. blue 65 65
D 188. 50 m. purple .. 1·00 1·00

1929.
D 244. D 7. 1 m. brown .. 5 5
D 245. 2 m. yellow .. 5 5
D 246. 4 m. green .. 8 5
D 247. 10 m. red .. 20 15
D 248. 20 m. olive .. 25 20
D 194. 50 m. blue .. 50 50

1952. Optd. FILS and bars.
D 350. D 7. 1 f. on 1 m. brown 10·00 10·00
D 351. 2f. on 2 m. yellow 12 10
D 352. 4 f. on 4 m. green 20 12
D 353. 10 f. on 10 m. red 40 25
D 354 20 f. on 20 m. olive 70 35
D 346. 50 f. on 50 m. blue 1·00 50

1952.
D 372. D 8. 1 f. brown 5 5
D 373. 2 f. yellow 5 5
D 374. 4 f. green 5 5
D 375. 10 f. red 8 8
D 376. 20 f. brown 15 10
D 377. 50 f. blue 25 15

1957. As Type D 8 but inscr. "THE HASHEMITE KINGDOM OF JORDAN".
D 465. 1 f. brown 5 5
D 466. 2 f. yellow 5 5
D 467. 4 f. green 5 5
D 468. 10 f. red 5 5
D 469. 20 f. brown 15 10

OFFICIAL STAMPS

(O 1. "Arab Government of the East" = 1924.)

1924. Type 5 of Saudi Arabia, optd. with Type O 1.
O 117. ½ p. red .. .. 4·00 30·00

OBLIGATORY TAX

T 1. Mosque in Hebron. T 2. Ruins at Palmyra, Syria.

1947.
T 264. T 1. 1 m. blue 12 5
T 265. 2 m. red 12 8
T 266. 3 m. green 20 12
T 267. 5 m. red 20 12
T 268. – 10 m. red 25 20
T 269. – 15 m. grey 35 20
T 270. – 20 m. brown .. 50 25
T 271. – 50 m. violet .. 80 50
T 272. – 100 m. red .. .. 2·50 2·00
T 273. – 200 m. blue .. 7·00 4·50
T 274. – 500 m. green .. 12·00 9·00
T 275. – £1P1 brown .. 24·00 18·00
DESIGNS: Nos. T 268/71, Dome of the Rock. Nos. T 272/75, Acre.

1950. Optd. with Aid in English and Arabic.
T 290. 24. 5 m. orange (234) .. 3·00
T 291. 10 m. violet (277) .. 4·00
T 292. 15 m. green (279) .. 5·00

1950. Revenue stamps optd. with Aid in English and Arabic.
T 293. T 2. 5 m. orange .. 3·00
T 294. 10 m. violet .. 4·00

1951.
T 302. T 1. 5 f. red 8 8
T 303. – 10 f. red 15 15
T 304. – 15 f. black .. 20 20
T 305. – 20 f. brown 20 20
T 306. – 100 f. orange .. 1·00 1·00
DESIGNS: Nos. T 303/305, Dome of the Rock. No. T 306, Acre.

1952. Nos. T 264/75 surch. in FILS.
T 334. T 1. 1 f. on 1 m. blue 8 5
T 335. 2 f. on 2 m. red .. 24·00
T 336. 3 f. on 3 m. green 12 8
T 337. – 10 f. on 10 m. red .. 15 12
T 338. – 15 f. on 15 m. grey .. 25 20
T 339. – 20 f. on 20 m. brown 35 30
T 340. – 50 f. on 50 m. violet 60 50
T 341. – 100 f. on 100 m. orange 3·00 2·00
T 342. – 200 f. on 200 m. blue 8·00 7·00
T 343. – 500 f. on 500 m. grn. 18·00 15·00
T 344. – 1 d. on £P1 brown .. 30·00 28·00

JORDANIAN OCCUPATION OF PALESTINE

فلسطين
PALESTINE
(P 1.)

1948. Stamps of Jordan optd. with Type P 1.
P 1. 22. 1 m. maroon 5 5
P 2. 2 m. green 5 5
P 3. 3 m. green 5 5
P 4. 3 m. red 5 5
P 5. 4 m. green 5 5
P 6. 5 m. orange 5 5
P 7. 10 m. violet 10 10
P 8. 12 m. red 12 10
P 9. 15 m. olive 15 12
P 10. 20 m. blue 20 12
P 11. 23. 50 m. purple 40 35
P 12. 90 m. brown .. .. 1·00 75
P 13. 100 m. blue .. .. 1·25 1·00
P 14. 200 m. violet .. 3·00 2·00
P 15. 500 m. brown .. 6·00 3·00
P 16. £P1 grey .. .. 15·00 6·00

1949. U.P.U. 75th Anniv. Stamps of Jordan optd. PALESTINE in English and Arabic.
P 30. 28. 1 m. brown 10 10
P 31. 4 m. green 12 12
P 32. 10 m. red 15 15
P 33. 20 m. blue 20 20
P 34. – 50 m. green (No. 289) 55 55

POSTAGE DUE STAMPS

1948. Postage Due stamps of Jordan optd. as Type P 1, but with 10½ mm. space between lines of opt.
PD 25. D 7. 1 m. brown 12 12
PD 26. 2 m. yellow 12 12
PD 18. 4 m. green 20 20
PD 28. 10 m. red 25 25
PD 20. 20 m. olive 10 10
PD 21. 50 m. blue 25 20
After a time the stamps of Jordan were used in the occupied areas.

OBLIGATORY TAX

1973. Nos. T 264/75 of Jordan optd. with PALESTINE in English and Arabic.
PT 35. T 1. 1 m. blue 5 5
PT 36. 2 m. red 5 5
PT 37. 3 m. green .. 10 10
PT 38. 5 m. red .. 15 10
PT 39. – 10 m. red .. 15 12
PT 40. – 15 m. grey .. 25 20
PT 41. – 20 m. brown .. 50 35
PT 42. – 50 m. violet .. 65 60
PT 43. – 100 m. orange .. 90 55
PT 44. – 200 m. blue .. 2·75 1·40
PT 45. – 500 m. green .. 11·00 5·00
PT 46. – £P1 brown .. .. 20·00 9·00

JUBALAND O4

A district in E. Africa, formerly part of Kenya, ceded by Gt. Britain to Italy in 1925, and incorporated in Italian Somaliland.

1925. Stamps of Italy optd. OLTRE GIUBA.
1. 20. 1 c. brown 20 30
2. 21. 2 c. brown 20 30
3. 24. 5 c. green 8 15
4. 10 c. red 8 15
5. 15 c. grey 8 15
6. 25. 20 c. orange 8 15
39. 26. 20 c. green 12 20
7. 25 c. blue 10 15
8. 30 c. brown 10 15
40. 30 c. grey 12 20
9. 40 c. brown 15 25
10. 50 c. mauve 20 35
11. 60 c. red 30 45
41. 23. 75 c. red .. .. 1·25 1·75
12. 1 l. brown and green .. 30 45
42. 1 l. 25 c. blue .. .. 1·90 2·50
13. 2 l. green and orange .. 3·00 3·25
43. 2 l. 50 c. green & orange 2·25 3·25
14. 5 l. blue and red .. 5·00 5·50
15. 10 l. olive and red .. 60 1·25

1925. Royal Jubilee stamps of Italy optd. OLTRE GIUBA.
44. 53. 60 c. red 15 30
45. 1 l. blue 15 30
46. 1 l. 25 blue .. .. 55 1·10

1926. St. Francis of Assisi stamps of Italy, as Nos. 191/6, optd. OLTRE GIUBA.
47. 20 c. green 25 40
48. 40 c. violet 25 40
49. 60 c. red 25 40
50. 1 l. 25 blue 25 40
51. 5 l. × 2 l. 50 olive .. 1·00 1·75

ILLUSTRATIONS British Commonwealth and all overprints and surcharges are FULL SIZE. Foreign Countries have been reduced to ¾-LINEAR.

1.

1926. Acquisition of Jubaland. First Anniv.
54. 1. 5 c. orange 8 20
55. 20 c. green 8 20
56. 25 c. brown 8 20
57. 40 c. red 8 20
58. 60 c. purple 8 20
59. 1 l. blue 8 20
60. 2 l. grey 8 20

1926. As Colonial Propaganda T 1 of Cyrenaica, but inscr. "OLTRE GIUBA".
61. 5 c.+5c. brown .. 12 25
62. 10 c.+5 c. olive .. 12 25
63. 20 c.+5 c. green .. 12 25
64. 40 c.+5 c. red .. 12 25
65. 60 c.+ 5 c. orange .. 12 25
66. 1 l.+5 c. blue 12 25

EXPRESS LETTER STAMPS

1926. Express Letter stamps of Italy optd. OLTRE GIUBA.
E 52. E 1. 70 c. red .. .. 1·00 1·40
E 53. E 2. 2 l. 50 red and blue .. 2·25 3·00

PARCEL POST STAMPS

1925. Parcel Post stamps of Italy optd. OLTRE GIUBA.
P 16. P 2. 5 c. brown .. .. 3·25 20
P 17. 10 c. blue 12 5
P 18. 20 c. black 12 5
P 19. 25 c. red 12 5
P 20. 50 c. orange 40 8
P 21. 1 l. violet 12 5
P 22. 2 l. green 30 8
P 23. 3 l. yellow 35 8
P 24. 4 l. grey 80 12
P 25. 10 l. purple .. .. 2·10 20
P 26. 12 l. brown .. .. 12·00 75
P 27. 15 l. olive .. .. 4·25 50
P 28. 20 l. purple .. .. 5·00 70
Unused prices are for complete stamps.

POSTAGE DUE STAMPS

1925. Postage Due stamps of Italy optd. OLTRE GIUBA.
D 29. D 3. 5 c. purple and orange 2·50 3·00
D 30. 10 c. purple & orange 15 35
D 31. 20 c. purple & orange 15 35
D 32. 30 c. purple & orange 15 35
D 33. 40 c. purple & orange 25 50
D 34. 50 c. purple & orange 35 65
D 35. 60 c. brown & orange 40 80
D 36. 1 l. purple and blue 60 1·25
D 37. 2 l. purple and blue 3·25 5·00
D 38. 5 l. purple and blue 4·50 7·00

KATANGA O4

The following stamps were issued by Mr. Tshombe's Government for independent Katanga. In 1963 Katanga was reunited with the Central Government of Congo.

1960. Various stamps of Belgian Congo optd. KATANGA and bar or surch. also.

(a) Masks issue of 1948.
1. 1 f. 50 on 1 f. 25 mauve & blue 25 15
2. 3 f. 50 on 2 f. 50 green & brn. 25 20
3. 20 f. purple and red .. 75 65
4. 50 f. black and brown .. 2·75 2·25
5. 100 f. black and red .. 21·00 16·00

(b) Flowers issue of 1952. Flowers in natural colours; colours given are of backgrounds and inscriptions.
6. 10 c. yellow and purple .. 5 5
7. 15 c. green and red .. 5 5
8. 20 c. grey and green .. 8 8
9. 25 c. orange and green .. 10 10
10. 40 c. salmon and green .. 8 8
11. 50 c. turquoise and red .. 12 12
12. 60 c. purple and green .. 10 10
13. 75 c. grey and lake .. 12 12
14. 1 f. lemon and red .. 15 15
15. 2 f. buff and olive .. 15 15
16. 3 f. pink and green .. 20 20
17. 4 f. lavender and sepia .. 35 30
18. 5 f. green and purple .. 35 30
19. 6 f. 50 lilac and red .. 35 20
20. 7 f. brown and green .. 45 35
21. 8 f. yellow and green .. 40 35
22. 10 f. olive and purple .. 4·50 4·00

(c) Wild animals issue of 1959.
23. 10 c. brown, sepia and blue 5 5
24. 20 c. grey-blue & vermilion 5 5
25. 40 c. brown and blue .. 5 5
26. 50 c. red, olive, black & blue 5 5
27. 1 f. black, green & brown .. 2·00 1·90
28. 1 f. 50 black and yellow .. 3·50 3·50
29. 2 f. black, brown and red .. 12 8
30. 3 f. black, purple and slate 1·60 1·60
31. 5 f. brown, green and sepia 30 20
32. 6 f. 50 brown, yellow & blue 40 20
33. 8 f. bistre, violet & chestnut 55 25
34. 10 f. brn., blk., orge. & yell. 70 35

(d) Madonna.
35. 56. 50 c. brn., ochre & chest. 10 10
36. 1 f. brown, violet & blue 10 10
37. 2 f. brown, blue and slate 12 12

(e) African Technical Co-operation Commission. Inscr. in French or Flemish.
38. 57. 3 f. salmon and slate .. 4·50 4·50
39. 3 f. 50 on 3 f. sal. & slate 1·60 1·60

1960. Independence. Independence issue of Congo optd. 11 JUILLET DE L'ETAT DU KATANGA:
40. 59. 20 c. bistre-brown .. 5 5
41. 50 c. red 5 5
42. 1 f. green 5 5
43. 1 f. 50 red-brown .. 5 5
44. 2 f. magenta 5 5
45. 3 f. 50 violet 5 5
46. 5 f. blue 8 5
47. 6 f. 50 black 10 5
48. 10 f. orange 15 12
49. 20 f. ultramarin .. 30 20

1. 2. Pres. Tshombe.

1961. Katanga Art.
50. 1. 10 c. green 5 5
51. 20 c. violet 5 5
52. 50 c. blue 5 5
53. 1 f. 50 green 5 5
54. 2 f. brown.. .. .. 5 5
55. – 3 f. 50 blue 5 5
56. – 5 f. blue-green 5 5
57. – 6 f. brown.. .. .. 5 5
58. – 6 f. 50 blue 5 5
59. – 8 f. maroon 8 5
60. – 10 f. chocolate 10 8
61. – 20 f. myrtle 15 12
62. – 50 f. brown 30 25
63. – 100 f. turquoise 65 50
DESIGNS: 3 f. 50 to 8 f. "Preparing food". 10 f. to 100 f. "Family circle".

1961. Independence. 1st Anniv. Portrait in brown.
64. 2. 6 f. 50 red, green and gold 75 75
65. 8 f. red, green and gold .. 75 75
66. 10 f. red, green and gold 75 75

3. "Tree". 4. Early Aircraft, Train and Safari.

1961. Katanga International Fair. Vert. symbolic designs as T 3.
67. 3. 50 c. red, green and black 5 5
68. – 1 f. black and blue .. 5 5
69. – 2 f. 50 black and yellow.. 8 8
70. 3. 3 f. red, brown and black 10 10
71. – 5 f. black and violet .. 15 15
72. – 6 f. 50 black and orange.. 20 20

1961. Air.
73. 4. 3 f. 50 multicoloured .. 70 70
74. – 6 f. 50 multicoloured .. 70 70
75. 4. 8 f. multicoloured .. 70 70
76. – 10 f. multicoloured .. 70 70
DESIGN: 6 f. 50, 10 f. Tail of aeroplane.

5. Gendarme in armoured Vehicle.

1962. Katanga Gendarmerie.
77. 5. 6 f. multicoloured .. 1·60 1·60
78. 8 f. multicoloured .. 25 25
79. 10 f. multicoloured .. 30 30

POSTAGE DUE STAMPS

1960. Postage Due stamps of Belgian Congo handstamped **KATANGA.**

(a) On Nos. D 270/4.
D 50. D 2. 10 c. olive 30 30
D 51. 20 c. blue 30 30
D 52. 50 c. green 45 45
D 53. 1 f. brown .. ..
D 54. 2 f. orange .. ..

(b) On Nos. D 330/6.
D 55. D 3. 10 c. brown .. ..
D 56. 20 c. maroon ..
D 57. 50 c. green .. .. 1·50 1·50
D 58. 1 f. blue 45 45
D 59. 2 f. red 50 50
D 60. 4 f. violet 85 85
D 61. 6 f. blue 85 85

KEDAH BC

A state of the Federation of Malaya, incorporated in Malaysia in 1963.

100 cents = 1 dollar (Straits or Malayan).

1. Sheaf of Rice. 2. Malay ploughing.

1912.
1. 1. 1 c. black and green .. 12 12
26. 1 c. brown 15 12
52. 1 c. black 10 10
27. 2 c. green 10 20
2. 3 c. black and red .. 30 20
28. 3 c. purple 50 50
53. 3 c. green 30 25
3. 4 c. red and grey .. 1·00 15
29. 4 c. red 55 10
54. 4 c. violet 45 12
4. 5 c. green and brown .. 80 80
55. 5 c. yellow 25 12
56. 6 c. red 12 25
5. 8 c. black and blue .. 35 65
57. 8 c. black .. .. .. 2·50 12
6. 2. 10 c. blue and sepia .. 65 40
58. 12 c. black and blue .. 1·25 2·25
31. 20 c. black and green .. 80 90
22. 21 c. purple .. .. 2·50 3·00
33. 25 c. blue and purple .. 90 1·00
34. 30 c. black and red .. 1·25 80
59. 35 c. purple .. .. 3·25 6·00
35. 40 c. black and purple .. 1·25 1·40
36. 50 c. brown and blue .. 70 80
37. – $1 black & red on yellow 2·50 2·00
38. – $2 green and brown .. 7·00 8·00
39. – $3 black and blue on blue 11·00 13·00
40. – $5 black and red .. 20·00 20·00
DESIGN—As T 2: $1 to $5 Council Chamber.

1919. Surch. in words.
24. 50 c. on $2 green and brown 15·00 16·00
25. $1 on $3 blk. & blue on blue 9·00 11·00

1922. Optd. **MALAYA-BORNEO EXHIBITION.**
45. 1. 1 c. brown .. .. 90 1·25
41. 2 c. green .. .. .. 1·25 1·75
46. 3 c. purple .. .. 1·00 1·75
47. 4 c. red .. .. .. 1·25 2·75
48. 2. 10 c. blue and sepia .. 2·00 3·00
42. 21 c. purple .. .. 4·50 6·00
43. 25 c. blue and purple .. 6·50 7·50
44. 50 c. brown and blue .. 6·00 9·50

4. Sultan Abdul Hamid Halimshah.

1937.
60. 4. 10 c. blue and brown .. 30 10
61. 12 c. black and violet .. 2·50 2·50
62. 25 c. blue and purple .. 75 75
63. 30 c. green and red .. 95 1·10
64. 40 c. black and purple .. 30 1·25
65. 50 c. brown and blue .. 30 1·00
66. $1 black and green .. 80 1·00
67. $2 green and brown .. 13·00 9·00
68. $5 black and red .. 3·50 5·50

1948. Silver Wedding. As T 5/6 of Aden.
70. 10 c. violet 12 15
71. $5 red .. .. .. 6·00 8·00

1949. U.P.U. As T 14/17 of Antigua.
72. 10 c. purple 10 12
73. 15 c. blue 12 15
74. 25 c. orange 30 40
75. 50 c. black 55 70

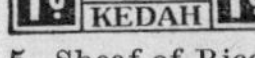

5. Sheaf of Rice. 6. Sultan Tengku Badlishah.

1950.
76. 5. 1 c. black 5 5
77. 2 c. orange 5 5
78. 3 c. green 15 15
79. 4 c. brown 5 5
79a. 5 c. purple 5 5
80. 6 c. grey 10 10
81. 8 c. red 20 35
81a. 8 c. green 25 15
82. 10 c. magenta 20 15
82a. 12 c. red 12 12
83. 15 c. blue 30 20
84. 20 c. black and green .. 30 35
84a. 20 c. blue 30 25
85. 6. 25 c. purple and orange .. 20 10
85a. 30 c. red and purple .. 30 25
85b. 35 c. red and purple .. 35 40
86. 40 c. red and purple .. 30 85
87. 50 c. black and blue .. 30 12
88. $1 blue and purple .. 60 40
89. $2 green and red .. .. 2·25 2·75
90. $5 green and brown .. 3·75 5·00

1953. Coronation. As T 7 of Aden.
91. 10 c. black and purple .. 5 5

7. Fishing Craft. 8. Sultan Tengku Abdul.

1957. Inset portrait of Sultan Tengku Badlishah.
92. – 1 c. black 5 10
93. – 2 c. red 5 10
94. – 4 c. sepia 5 12
95. – 5 c. lake 5 12
96. – 8 c. green 10 25
97. – 10 c. sepia 10 12
98. 7. 20 c. blue 12 12
99. – 50 c. black and blue .. 30 25
100. – $1 blue and purple .. 60 1·25
101. – $2 green and red .. 1·75 1·75
102. – $5 brown and green .. 2·75 3·75
DESIGNS—HORIZ. 1 c. Copra. 2 c. Pineapples. 4 c. Ricefield. 5 c. Masjid Alwi Mosque, Kangar. 8 c. East Coast Railway. $1 Govt. Offices. $2 Bersilat (form of wrestling). $5 Weaving. VERT. 10 c. Tiger. 50 c. Aborigines with blowpipes.

1959. Installation of Sultan.
103. 8. 10 c. yellow, brown & blue 5 5

9. Sultan Tengku Abdul.

1959. As Nos. 92/102 but with inset portrait of Sultan Tengku Abdul as in T 9.
104. 1 c. black 5 5
105. 2 c. red 5 5
106. 4 c. sepia 5 5
107. 5 c. lake 5 5
108. 8 c. green 5 8
109 10 c. sepia 5 5
109a. 10 c. maroon 5 5
110. 20 c. blue 8 5
111. 50 c. black and blue .. 30 20
112. $1 blue and purple .. 40 35
113. $2 green and red .. .. 80 1·75
114a. $5 brown and green .. 2·00 1·75

10. "Vanda hookeriana".

1965. As Nos. 166/72 of Johore but with inset portrait of Sultan Tengku Abdul as in T 10.
115. 10. 1 c. multicoloured .. 5 5
116. – 2 c. multicoloured .. 5 5
117. – 5 c. multicoloured .. 5 5
118. – 6 c. multicoloured .. 5 5
119. – 10 c. multicoloured .. 5 5
120. – 15 c. multicoloured .. 8 5
121. – 20 c. multicoloured .. 8 8
The higher values used in Kedah were Nos. 20/7 of Malaysia.

11. Black-veined Tiger.

1971. Butterflies. As Nos. 175/81 of Johore, but with portrait of Sultan Tengku Abdul as in T 11.
124. – 1 c. multicoloured .. 5 5
125. 11. 2 c. multicoloured .. 5 5
126. – 5 c. multicoloured .. 5 5
127. – 6 c. multicoloured .. 5 5
128. – 10 c. multicoloured .. 5 5
129. – 15 c. multicoloured .. 5 5
130. – 20 c. multicoloured .. 8 8
The higher values in use with this issue are Nos. 64/71 of Malaysia.

KELANTAN BC

A state in the Federation of Malaya, incorporated in Malaysia in 1963.

100 cents = 1 dollar (Straits or Malayan).

1. Emblem of State. 2. Sultan Ismail.

1911.
1a. 1. 1 c. green 20 12
15. 1 c. black 30 25
16. 2 c. brown .. .. 90 1·00
16a. 2 c. green 30 25
2. 3 c. red 20 8
16b. 3 c. brown 40 65
17. 4 c. black and red .. 12 15
18. 5 c. green & red on yellow 20 12
19. 6 c. claret 75 90
19a. 6 c. red .. .. .. 1·50 1·75
5. 8 c. blue 90 45
20. 10 c. black and mauve .. 60 20
7. 30 c. purple and red .. 1·25 10
8. 50 c. black and orange.. 1·25 1·10
9. $1 green .. .. .. 6·50 7·00
13. $1 green and brown .. 6·00 1·50
10. $2 green and red .. .. 75 2·00
11. $5 green and blue .. 3·75 4·00
12. $25 green and orange .. 15·00 17·00

1922. Optd. **MALAYA BORNEO EXHIBITION.**
37. 1. 1 c. green .. .. .. 90 2·00
30. 4 c. black and red .. 1·00 2·50
31. 5 c. green & red on yellow 1·25 2·50
38. 10 c. black and mauve .. 1·75 4·00
32. 30 c. purple and red .. 1·50 3·75
33. 50 c. black and orange .. 2·50 4·75
34. $1 green and brown .. 6·00 8·00
35. $2 green and red.. .. 10·00 15·00
36. $5 green and blue .. 35·00 40·00

1928.
40. 2. 1 c. olive and yellow .. 15 15
41. 2 c. green 15 8
42. 4 c. red 40 20
43. 5 c. brown 45 12
44. 6 c. red .. .. .. 1·00 30
45. 8 c. olive 55 20
46. 10 c. purple .. .. 1·00 50
47. 12 c. blue 50 80
48. 25 c. red and purple .. 1·10 1·00
49. 30 c. violet and red .. 3·00 3·00
50. 40 c. orange and green .. 2·00 2·00
51. 50 c. olive and orange .. 3·50 3·50
39. $1 blue .. .. .. 3·50 6·50
52. $1 violet and green .. 1·75 2·50
53. $2 red .. .. .. 30·00 30·00
54. $5 red .. .. .. 45·00 48·00
All except No. 39 are larger than T 2.

1948. Silver Wedding. As T 5/6 of Aden.
55. 10 c. violet 10 12
56. $5 red .. .. .. 4·50 7·50

1949. U.P.U. As T 14/17 of Antigua.
57. 10 c. purple 15 25
58. 15 c. blue 25 40
59. 25 c. orange 40 60
60. 50 c. black .. .. 60 1·00

3. Sultan Tengu Ibrahim.

1951.
61. 3. 1 c. black 5 8
62. 2 c. orange 5 5
63. 3 c. green 15 20
64. 4 c. brown.. .. .. 5 5
65. 5 c. purple 5 5
66. 6 c. grey 8 10
67. 8 c. red 20 25
68. 8 c. green 15 15
69. 10 c. magenta 10 5
70. 12 c. red 15 20
71. 15 c. blue 20 25
72. 20 c. black and green .. 40 35
73. 20 c. blue 30 25
74. 25 c. purple and orange .. 30 25
75. 30 c. red and purple .. 40 50
76. 35 c. red and purple .. 50 70
77. 40 c. red and purple .. 60 1·10
78. 50 c. black and blue .. 35 40
79. $1 blue and purple .. 75 75
80. $2 green and red.. .. 1·50 3·25
81. $5 green and brown .. 4·00 7·50

1953. Coronation. As T **7** of Aden.

82.	10 c. black and purple	5	5

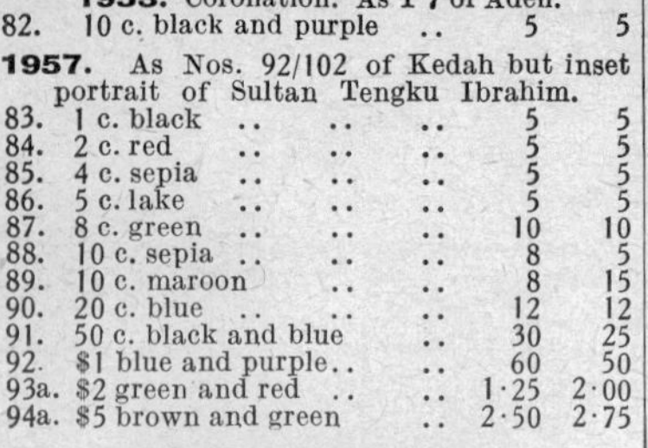

1957. As Nos. 92/102 of Kedah but inset portrait of Sultan Tengku Ibrahim.

83.	1 c. black	5	5
84.	2 c. red	5	5
85.	4 c. sepia	5	5
86.	5 c. lake	5	5
87.	8 c. green	10	10
88.	10 c. sepia	8	5
89.	10 c. maroon	8	15
90.	20 c. blue	12	12
91.	50 c. black and blue	30	25
92.	$1 blue and purple	60	50
93a.	$2 green and red	1·25	2·00
94a.	$5 brown and green	2·50	2·75

4. Sultan Yahya Petra and Crest of Kelantan.

1961. Installation of the Sultan.

95. **4.**	10 c. multicoloured	8	8

5. Sultan Yahya Petra.

1961. As Nos. 77, etc., but with inset portrait of Sultan Yahya Petra as in T **5**.

96.	1 c. black	5	5
97.	2 c. red	5	5
98.	4 c. sepia	5	5
99.	5 c. lake	5	5
100.	8 c. green	5	8
101.	10 c. maroon	5	5
102.	20 c. blue	10	10

6. "Vanda hookeriana".

1965. As Nos. 166/72 of Johore but with inset portrait of Sultan Yahya Petra as in T **6**.

103. **6.**	1 c. multicoloured	5	5
104. –	2 c. multicoloured	5	5
105. –	5 c. multicoloured	5	5
106. –	6 c. multicoloured	5	5
107. –	10 c. multicoloured	8	5
108. –	15 c. multicoloured	5	5
109. –	20 c. multicoloured	8	8

The higher values used in Kelantan were Nos. 20/7 of Malaysia.

7. Clipper Butterfly.

1971. Butterflies. As Nos. 175/81 of Johore, but with portrait of Sultan Yahya Petra as in T **7**.

112. –	1 c. multicoloured	5	5
113. –	2 c. multicoloured	5	5
114. **7.**	5 c. multicoloured	5	5
115. –	6 c. multicoloured	5	5
116. –	10 c. multicoloured	5	5
117. –	15 c. multicoloured	5	5
118. –	20 c. multicoloured	8	8

The higher values in use with this series are Nos. 64/71 of Malaysia.

KENYA BC

Formerly part of Kenya, Uganda and Tanganyika (q.v.). Became Independent in 1963 and a Republic in 1964.

For commemorative issues from 1964 to 1976, inscribed "UGANDA KENYA TANGANYIKA & ZANZIBAR" or "TANZANIA UGANDA KENYA", see under East Africa.

100 cents = 1 shilling.

25. Cattle Ranching.

26. National Assembly.

1963. Independence

207. **25.**	5 c. brn., bl., grn. & buff	5	5
208. –	10 c. brown	5	5
209. –	15 c. magenta	5	5
210. –	20 c. black and green	5	5
211. –	30 c. black and yellow	5	5
212. –	40 c. brown and blue	5	8
213. –	50 c. red, black & green	8	8
214. –	65 c. turq.-green & yell.	10	10
215. **26.**	1s. multicoloured	12	10
216. –	1s. 30 brown, blk. & grn.	25	10
217. –	2s. multicoloured	40	20
218. –	5s. brown, blue & green	1·00	40
219. –	10s. brown and blue	2·50	1·25
220. –	20s. black and rose	5·00	3·75

DESIGNS—As T. **25**: 10 c. Wood-carving. 15 c. Heavy industry. 20 c. Timber industry. 30 c. Jomo Kenyatta facing Mt. Kenya. 40 c. Fishing industry. 50 c. Kenya flag. 65 c. Pyrethrum industry. As T **26**: 1s. 30, Tourism (Treetops hotel). 2s. Coffee industry. 5s. Tea industry. 10s. Mombasa Port. 20s. Education Royal College, Nairobi).

27. Cockerel.

1964. Republic. Inaug. Multicoloured.

221.	15 c. Type **27**	5	5
222.	30 c. Pres. Kenyatta	10	8
223.	50 c. African Lion	15	20
224.	1 s. 30 Hartlaub's Touraco	45	75
225.	2 s. 50 Nandi Flame	1·10	1·75

ILLUSTRATIONS British Commonwealth and all overprints and surcharges are FULL SIZE. Foreign Countries have been reduced to ¾-LINEAR.

28. Thomson's Gazelle.

29. Greater Kudu.

1966.

226. **28.**	5 c. orange, black & sepia	5	5
227. –	10 c. black and green	5	5
228. –	15 c. black and orange	5	5
229. –	20 c. ochre, black & blue	5	5
230. –	30 c. indigo, blue & blk.	5	5
231. –	40 c. black and brown	5	5
232. –	50 c. black and orange	8	5
233. –	65 c. black and green	12	10
233a. –	70 c. black and claret	12	12
234. **29.**	1s. brown, black & blue	15	8
235. –	1s. 30 indigo, grn. & blk.	20	12
235a. –	1s. 50 black, brn. & grn.	20	35
236. –	2s. 50 yellow, blk. & brn.	35	35
237. –	5s. yellow, blk. & emer.	85	60
238. –	10s. ochre, black & brn.	1·75	1·50
239. –	20s. ochre, orange, black and gold	3·50	2·75

DESIGNS—As T **28**: 10 c. Sable Antelope. 15 c. Ant Bear. 20 c. Bush Baby. 30 c. Wart-hog. 40 c. Zebra. 50 c. Buffalo. 65 c. Rhinoceros. 70 c. Ostrich. As T **29**. 1s. 30, Elephant. 1s. 50, Bat-eared Fox. 2s. 50, Cheetah. 5s. Vervet Monkey. 10 s. Pangolin. 20s. Lion.

30. Rose Dawn. **31.** Rock Shell.

1971. Seashells. Multicoloured.

240.	5 c. Type **30**	5	5
241.	10 c. Bishop's Cap	5	5
242.	15 c. Strawberry Shell	5	5
243.	20 c. Black Prince	5	5
244.	30 c. Mermaid's Ear	5	5
245.	40 c. Top Shell	5	5
246.	50 c. Violet Shell	5	5
247.	50 c. Violet Shell	5	8
248.	60 c. Cameo	5	8
249.	70 c. Pearly Nautilus	8	8
250.	70 c. Pearly Nautilus	8	10
251.	1 s. Type **31**	10	12
252.	1 s. 50 Triton	15	20
253.	2 s. 50 "Fascivlaria trapezium"	25	30
254.	5 s. Turban Shell	50	60
255.	10 s. Cloth of Gold	1·00	1·10
256.	20 s. Spider Shell	2·10	2·25

INSCRIPTIONS: No. 246, "Janthina globosa". No. 247, "Janthina janthina". No. 249, "Nautilus pompileus". No. 250, "Nautilus pompilius".

Nos. 251/56 are larger as T **31**.

1975. Nos. 252/3 and 256 surch.

257.	2 s. on 1 s. 50 Triton	25	30
258.	3 s. on 2 s. 50 Neptune's Trumpet	10·00	10·00
259.	40 s. on 20 s. Spider Shell	5·00	5·25

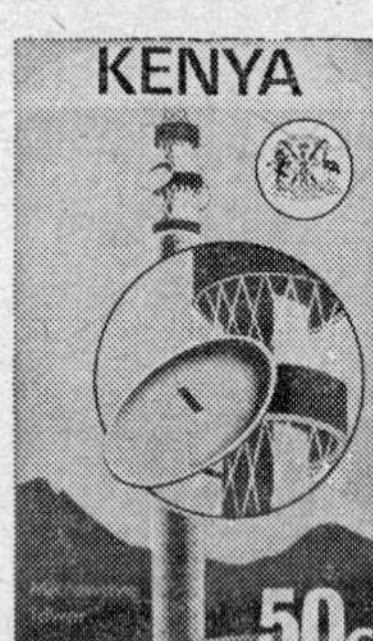

32. Microwave Tower.

1976. Telecommunications Development. Multicoloured.

260.	50 c. Type **32**	5	8
261.	1 s. Cordless switchboard (horiz.)	12	15
262.	2 s. Telephones	25	30
263.	3 s. Message Switching Centre (horiz.)	35	40

33. Akii Bua, Ugandan Hurdler.

1976. Olympic Games, Montreal. Mult.

265.	50 c. Type **33**	5	8
266.	1 s. Filbert Bayi, Tanzanian runner	12	15
267.	2 s. Steve Muchoki, Kenyan boxer	25	30
268.	3 s. Olympic flame and East African flags	35	40

34. Tanzania-Zambia Railway.

1976. Railway Transport. Multicoloured.

270.	50 c. Type **34**	5	8
271.	1 s. Nile Bridge, Uganda	12	15
272.	2 s. Nakuru Station, Kenya	25	30
273.	3 s. Class A locomotive, 1896	35	40

POSTAGE DUE STAMPS

D **3**.

1967.

D 13. D **3**.	5 c. red	5	5
D 14.	10 c. green	5	5
D 15.	20 c. blue	5	5
D 16.	30 c. brown	5	5
D 27.	40 c. purple	12	12
D 34.	1 s. orange	10	12

OFFICIAL STAMPS

Intended for use on official correspondence of the Kenya Government only, but there is no evidence that they were so used.

1964. Stamps of 1963 optd. **OFFICIAL.**

O 21. **25.**	5 c. brn., bl., grn. & buff	5
O 22. –	10 c. brown	5
O 23. –	15 c. magenta	8
O 24. –	20 c. black and green	10
O 25. –	30 c. black and yellow	15
O 26. –	50 c. red, black & grn.	20

KENYA, UGANDA AND TANGANYIKA BC

Kenya, a Br. Crown colony and Protectorate including British East Africa. From 1935 it had a common postal service with Tanganyika and Uganda. Tanganyika became independent and had its own stamps in 1961, Uganda in 1962 and Kenya in December 1963, when the stamps of Kenya, Tanganyika and Uganda (except for the Postage Due Stamps) were withdrawn. For earlier issues see under Br. East Africa, Tanganyika and Uganda.

1903–19. 16 annas = 100 cents = 1 rupee.
1922. 100 cents = 1s sterling.

1.

2.

1903.

17. **1.**	½ a. green	30	30
18.	1 a. grey and red	50	40
19.	2 a. purple	1·90	1·90
21.	2½ a. blue	3·00	3·50
22.	3 a. purple and green	2·25	3·00
23.	4 a. green and black	3·00	3·75
24.	5 a. grey and brown	4·00	4·50
25.	8 a. grey and blue	4·50	5·00
9. **2.**	1 r. green	6·50	7·50
27.	2 r. purple	12·00	11·00
28.	3 r. green and black	15·00	15·00
29.	4 r. grey and green	15·00	20·00
30.	5 r. grey and red	19·00	20·00
14.	10 r. grey and blue	60·00	50·00
32.	20 r. grey and stone	£160	£190
16.	50 r. grey and brown	£450	£450

1907.

34. **1.**	1 c. brown	20	30
35.	3 c. green	20	30
36.	6 c. red	70	25
37.	10 c. lilac and olive	2·50	2·50
38.	12 c. purple	2·50	2·50
39.	15 c. blue	2·50	2·50
40.	25 c. green and black	3·00	4·00
41.	50 c. green and brown	3·75	4·50
42.	75 c. grey and blue	5·00	7·00

1912. As T 1/2, but portraits of King George V.
44. 1 c. black 25 20
45. 3 c. green 50 20
46. 6 c. red 25 25
68. 10 c. orange 85 25
48. 12 c. grey .. .. .. 1·00 90
49. 15 c. blue .. .. .. 1·00 60
50. 25 c. blk. & red on yellow 80 55
51. 50 c. black and lilac .. 1·50 1·10
52. 75 c. black on green .. 2·00 2·50
53. 1 r. black on green .. 3·00 2·75
54. 2 r. red & black on blue .. 8·00 8·00
55. 3 r. violet and green .. 8·00 9·00
56. 4 r. red & green on yellow 14·00 14·00
57. 5 r. blue and purple .. 15·00 15·00
58. 10 r. red & green on green .. 20·00 25·00
59. 20 r. black & purple on red £100 90·00
60. 20 r. purple & blue on blue £100 90·00
61. 50 r. red and green .. £350 £350

1919. No. 46 surch **4 cents.**
64. 4 c. on 6 c. red 12 20

5. 6.

1922.
76 5. 1 c. brown 20 25
77. 5 c. violet 45 20
78. 5 c. green 45 12
79. 10 c. green 45 20
80. 10 c. black 20 12
81a. 12 c. black .. .. 95 2·25
82. 15 c. red 40 20
83. 20 c. orange .. .. 1·10 20
84. 30 c. blue 45 20
85. 50 c. grey 80 20
86. 75 c. olive .. .. 1·75 2·75
87. 6. 1s. green .. .. 2·00 85
88. 2s. purple .. .. 2·75 2·00
89. 2s. 50 brown .. .. 10·00 20·00
90. 3s. grey .. .. 6·00 5·00
91. 4s. grey .. .. 14·00 20·00
92. 5s. red .. .. 11·00 11·00
93. 7s. 50 orange .. .. 20·00 35·00
94. 10s. blue .. .. 23·00 23·00
95. £1 black and orange .. 75·00 75·00
96. £2 green and purple .. £350
97. £3 purple and yellow .. £500
98. £4 black and magenta .. £850
99. £5 black and blue .. £900
100. £10 black and green .. £2500
101. £20 red and green .. £4500
102. £25 black and red .. £4500

7. Kavirondo Cranes.

DESIGNS—VERT. 10 c. £1 Lion. 30 c., 5s. Jinja Bridge, Ripon Falls. HORIZ. 15 c., 2s. Mt. Kilimanjaro. 65 c. Mt. Kenya. 1s., 3s. Lake Naivasha.

8. Dhow on Lake Victoria.

1935. King George V.
110. 7. 1 c. black and brown .. 10 10
111. 8. 5 c. black and green .. 10 10
112. – 10 c. black and yellow .. 55 10
113. – 15 c. black and red .. 40 10
114. 7. 20 c. black and orange .. 12 10
115. – 30 c. black and blue .. 25 50
116. 8. 50 c. purple and black .. 55 45
117. – 65 c. black and brown .. 65 70
118. – 1s. black and green .. 70 55
119. – 2s. red and purple .. 3·00 4·00
120. – 3s. blue and black .. 4·00 5·00
121. – 5s. black and red .. 8·00 8·00
122. 7. 10s. purple and blue .. 18·00 17·00
123. – £1 black and red .. 38·00 35·00

1935. Silver Jubilee. As T 11 of Antigua.
124. 20 c. blue and olive .. 10 8
125. 30 c. brown and blue .. 55 40
126. 65 c. green and blue .. 1·40 1·40
127. 1s. grey and purple .. 1·50 1·50

1937. Coronation. As T 2 of Aden.
128. 5 c. green 8 8
129. 20 c. orange 8 8
130. 30 c. blue 15 25

14. Dhow on Lake Victoria.

1938. As 1935 (except 10 c.), but with portrait of King George VI as in T 14.
131. 7. 1 c. black and brown 10 20
132. 14. 5 c. black and green 8 10
133a. 5 c. brown and orange 10 25
134. – 10 c. brown and orange 8 10
135. – 10 c. black and green 8 12
136. – 10 c. brown and grey 8 12
137. – 15 c. black and red .. 15 10
138. – 15 c. black and green 10 25
139b. 7. 20 c. black and orange 10 10
140. 14. 25 c. black and red .. 30 65
141b. – 30 c. black and blue .. 10 10
142. – 30 c. purple and brown 8 8
143. 7. 40 c. black and blue .. 10 10
144b. 14. 50 c. purple and black 15 15
145a. – 1s. black and brown 10 10
146b. – 2s. red and purple 40 20
147a. – 3s. blue and black .. 1·25 1·25
148b. – 5s. black and red 85 40
149b. 7. 10s. purple and blue .. 2·00 1·25
150a. – £1 black and red .. 4·50 4·00
DESIGN—HORIZ. 10 c. Lake Naivasha.

1941. Stamps of South Africa surch. **KENYA TANGANYIKA UGANDA** and value. Alternate stamps inscr. in English or Afrikaans (same price for either language).
151. 5. 5 c. on 1d. blk. and red 30 40
152. 33. 10 c. on 3d. blue 30 40
153. 10. 20 c. on 6d. grn. & red 25 40
154. – 70 c. on 1s. (No. 120) .. 25 40

1946. Victory. As T 4 of Aden.
155. 20 c. orange 15 10
156. 30 c. blue 8 8

1948. Silver Wedding. As T 5/6 of Aden.
157. 20 c. orange 12 12
158. £1 red .. .. .. 9·50 12·00

1949. U.P.U. As T 14/17 of Antigua.
159. 20 c. orange 12 12
160. 30 c. blue 12 20
161. 50 c. grey 20 15
162. 1s. brown 40 45

1952. Visit of Queen Elizabeth II (as Princess and Duke of Edinburgh). As Nos. 135 and 145a, but inscr. "ROYAL VISIT 1952".
163. 10 c. black and green .. 8 12
164. 1s. black and brown .. 55 80

1953. Coronation. As T 7 of Aden.
165. 20 c. black and orange .. 8 8

1954. Royal Visit. As No. 171 but inscr. "ROYAL VISIT 1954".
166. 15. 30 c. black and blue .. 8 8

15. Owen Falls Dam. 17. Queen Elizabeth II.

16. Kilimanjaro.

DESIGNS (Size as T 15)—VERT. 10 c., 50 c. Giraffe. 20 c., 40 c., 1s. Lion. HORIZ. 15 c., 1s. 30, 5s. Elephants. 10s. Royal Lodge, Sagana.

1954.
167. 15. 5 c. black and brown .. 5 8
168. – 10 c. red .. 5 5
169. – 15 c. black and blue .. 10 5
170. – 20 c. black and orange 5 5
171. 15. 30 c. black and blue .. 5 5
172. – 40 c. brown 8 8
173. – 50 c. purple 10 5
174. 16. 65 c. green and lake .. 30 25
175. – 1s. black and claret 15 5
176. – 1s. 30 orange and lilac 20 5
177. 16. 2s. black and green .. 40 12
178. – 5s. black and orange .. 1·00 40
179. – 10s. black and blue .. 2·75 95
180. 17. £1 red and black .. 5·00 3·50

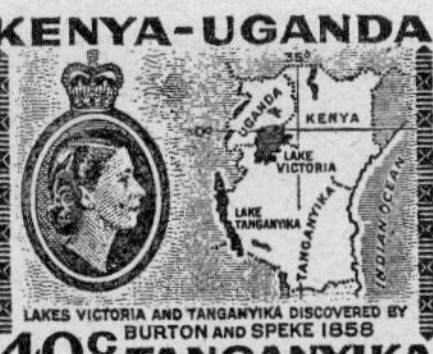

18. Map of E. Africa showing Lakes.

1958. Cent. of Discovery of Lakes Tanganyika and Victoria by Burton and Speke.
181. 18. 40 c. blue and green .. 15 20
182. 1 s. 30c. green & purple 30 55

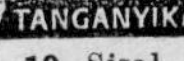

19. Sisal.

21. Queen Elizabeth II.

20. Mt. Kenya and Giant Plants.

1960.
183. 19. 5 c. blue .. 5 5
184. – 10 c. yellow-green .. 5 5
185. – 15 c. purple .. 5 5
186. – 20 c. magenta .. 5 5
187. – 25 c. bronze-green .. 8 5
188. – 30 c. vermilion .. 8 5
189. – 40 c. blue .. 8 5
190. – 50 c. violet .. 10 5
191. – 65 c. yellow-olive .. 25 25
192. 20. 1s. violet and purple .. 20 5
193. – 1s. 30 chocolate and red 25 8
194. – 2s. indigo and blue .. 30 10
195. – 2s. 50 olive & blue-green 45 45
196. – 5s. red and purple .. 80 35
197. – 10s. myrtle & olive-grn. 2·00 1·00
198. 21. 20s. violet-blue and lake 5·00 3·25
DESIGNS—As T 19: 10 c. Cotton. 15 c. Coffee. 20 c. Wildebeest. 25 c. Ostrich. 30 c. Thomson's gazelle. 40 c. Manta ray. 50 c. Zebra. 65 c. Cheetah. As T 20: 1s. 30, Murchison Falls and hippopotamus. 2s. Mt. Kilimanjaro and giraffe. 2s. 50, Candelabra tree and rhinoceros. 5s. Crater Lake and Mountains of the Moon. 10s. Ngorongoro Crater and buffalo.

22. Land Tillage.

1963. Freedom from Hunger.
199. 22. 15 c. blue and olive .. 5 5
200. – 30 c. brown and yellow 12 10
201. 22. 50 c. blue & orge.-grown 15 12
202. – 1s. 30 brown and blue 30 30
DESIGN: 30 c., 1 s. 30. African with corncob.

23. Scholars and Open Book.

1963. Founding of East African University.
203. 23. 30 c. lake, vio., blk. & bl. 8 8
204. 1s. 30 lake, bl., red & brn. 20 20

24. Red Cross Emblem.

1963. Red Cross Cent.
205. 24. 30 c. red and blue .. 5 8
206. 50 c. red and brown .. 15 15

POSTAGE DUE STAMPS

D 1.

D 2.

1923.
D 1. D 1. 5 c. violet 15 30
D 2. 10 c. red 20 35
D 3. 20 c. green 25 45
D 4. 30 c. brown 60 85
D 5. 40 c. blue .. .. 1·10 1·75
D 6. 1s. green .. .. 4·00 5·50

1935.
D 7. D 2. 5 c. violet 8 10
D 8. 10 c. red 8 10
D 9 20 c. green 12 10
D 10a. 30 c. brown 25 10
D 11. 40 c. blue 25 12
D 12. 1s. grey 40 20

OFFICIAL STAMPS

For use on official correspondence of the Tanganyika Government only.

1959. Stamps of 1954 optd. **OFFICIAL.**
O 1. 15. 5 c. black and brown 5 5
O 2. – 10 c. red .. 5 5
O 3. – 15 c. black and blue 5 5
O 4. – 20 c. black and orange 5 5
O 5. 15. 30 c. black and blue .. 5 5
O 6. – 50 c. purple .. 8 5
O 7. – 1s black and claret .. 12 10
O 8. – 1s. 30 orange and lilac 25 30
O 9. 16. 2s. black and green .. 30 40
O 10. – 5s. black and orange .. 80 80
O 11. – 10s. black and blue .. 2·00 2·25
O 12. 17. £1 red and black .. 4·50 4·50

1960. Stamps of 1960 optd. **OFFICIAL.**
O 13. 19. 5 c. blue .. 5 5
O 14. – 10 c. yellow-green .. 5 5
O 15. – 15 c. purple .. 5 5
O 16. – 20 c. magenta .. 5 5
O 17. – 30 c. vermilion .. 5 5
O 18. – 50 c. violet .. 8 8
O 19. 20. 1s. violet and purple 15 25
O 20. – 5s. red and purple .. 75 1·00

KHMER REPUBLIC O3

Cambodia was renamed Khmer Republic on 9th October 1970.

100 cents = 1 riel.

65. "Attack".

1971. Defence of Khmer Territory.
285. 65. 1 r. multicoloured .. 5 5
286. 3 r. multicoloured .. 8 5
287. 10 r. multicoloured .. 20 12

66. "World Races" and U.N. Emblem.

1971. Racial Equality Year.
288. 66. 3 r. multicoloured .. 8 5
289. 7 r. multicoloured .. 15 10
290. 8 r. multicoloured .. 20 15

67. General Post Office, Phnom Penh.

1971.
291. 67. 3 r. multicoloured .. 5 5
292. 9 r. multicoloured .. 20 12
293. 10 r. multicoloured .. 20 12

68. Global Emblem.

1971. World Telecommunications Day. Multicoloured.
294. 3 r. Type **68** 5 5
295. 4 r. Type **68** 8 5
296. 7 r. I.T.U. emblem .. 15 10
297. 8 r. I.T.U. emblem .. 20 12

69. "Erythrina indica".

1971. Wild Flowers. Multicoloured.
298. 2 r. Type **69** 5 5
299. 3 r. "Bauhinia variegata" 8 5
300. 6 r. "Butea frondosa" .. 15 8
301. 10 r. "Lagerstroemia floribunda" (vert.) .. 20 12

70. Arms of the Republic.

71. Monument and Flag.

1971. Republican Regime. 1st Anniv.
302. 70. 3 r. brown and green .. 8 5
303. 71. 3 r. multicoloured .. 8 5
304. 4 r. multicoloured .. 12 8
305. 70. 8 r. brown & orange .. 25 12
306. 10 r. brown and red .. 30 15
307. 71. 10 r. multicoloured .. 30 15

72. U.N.I.C.E.F. Emblem.

73. Book Year Emblem.

1971. U.N.I.C.E.F. 25th Anniv.
309. 72. 3 r. maroon 8 5
310. 5 r. blue 15 10
311. 9 r. red and violet .. 25 20

1972. Int. Book Year.
312. 73. 3 r. grn., pur. & blue .. 8 5
313. 8 r. bl., grn. & purple .. 20 12
314. 9 r. bistre, bl. & grn. .. 25 20

74. Lion of St. Mark's.

1972. U.N.E.S.C.O. "Save Venice" Campaign.
316. 74. 3 r. brn., buff & pur. .. 8 5
317. – 5 r. brn., buff & grn. .. 12 8
318. – 10 r. brn., bl. & grn. .. 25 15
DESIGNS—HORIZ. 5 r. St. Mark's Basilica. VERT. 10 r. Bridge of Sighs.

75. U.N. Emblem.

76. Dancing Apsaras (relief), Angkor.

1972. Economic Commission for Asia and the Far East (C.E.A.E.O.). 25th Anniv.
320. 75. 3 r. red 8 5
321. 6 r. blue 15 12
322. 9 r. red 25 15

1972.
324. 76. 1 r. brown 5 5
325. 3 r. violet 8 5
326. 7 r. red 20 12
327. 8 r. brown 25 15
328. 9 r. green 25 15
329. 10 r. blue 30 20
330. 12 r. purple 35 20
331. 14 r. blue 40 25

77. "UIT" on TV Screen.

78. Conference Emblem.

1972. World Telecommunications Day.
332. 77. 3 r. blk., grn. & yellow 10 8
333. 9 r. blk., blue and red .. 25 15
334. 14 r. blk., blue & brown 45 25

1972. U.N. Environmental Conservation Conference, Stockholm.
335. 78. 3 r. grn., brown & violet 8 5
336. 12 r. violet and green .. 30 20
337. 15 r. green and violet .. 45 35

79. Java Rhinoceros.

80. Hoisting Flag.

1972. Wild Animals.
339. 79. 3 r. blk., red and violet 8 5
340. – 4 r. violet, brn. & purple 10 5
341. – 6 r. brn., green & blue .. 15 10
342. – 7 r. brn., green & bistre 20 12
343. – 8 r. blk., green and blue 20 12
344. – 10 r. black, blue & green 30 20
DESIGNS: 4 r. Sumatran serow. 6 r. Eld deer. 7 r. Banteng. 8 r. Water buffalo. 10 r. Gaur.

1972. Olympic Games, Munich. Nos. 302, 304, 164 and 336/7 optd. **XXE JEUX OLYMPIQUES MUNICH 1972** and emblem.
345. 70. 3 r. brown and green .. 8 5
346. 10 r. brown and red .. 25 20
347. – 12 r. turquoise & maroon 25 20
348. 78. 12 r. violet and green .. 25 20
349. 15 r. green and violet .. 40 30

1972. 2nd Anniv. of Republic.
350. 80. 3 r. multicoloured .. 8 5
351. 5 r. multicoloured .. 12 8
352. 9 r. multicoloured .. 25 20

1972. Red Cross Aid for War Victims. Various stamps surch. **SECOURS AUX VICTIMES DE GUERRE**, red cross and value.
353. 70. 3 r.+2 r. (No. 304) .. 15 15
354. 10 r.+6 r. (No. 304) .. 35 35
355. – 12 r.+7 r. (No. 164) .. 45 45
356. 78. 12 r.+7 r. (No. 336) .. 45 45
357. 15 r.+8 r. (No. 337) .. 85 85

81. Garuda.

82. Crest and Temple.

1973. Air.
358. 81. 3 r. red 8 5
359. 30 r. blue 75 50
360. 50 r. lilac .. .. 1·40 85
361. 100 r. green .. .. 2·25 1·40

1973. New Constitution.
362. 82. 3 r. multicoloured .. 5 5
363. 12 r. multicoloured .. 20 15
364. 14 r. multicoloured .. 25 15

83. Apsara.

84. Interpol Emblem.

1973. Angkor Sculptures.
366. 83. 3 r. black 5 5
367. – 8 r. blue 12 8
368. – 10 r. brown 15 10
DESIGNS: 8 r. Devata (12th century). 10 r. Devata (10th century).

1973. International Criminal Police Organization (Interpol). 50th Anniv.
370. 84. 3 r. green & blue-green 5 5
371. 7 r. green and brown .. 10 8
372. 10 r. green and brown 15 12

85. President Lon Nol.

1973. Honouring Marshal Lon Nol, 1st President of Republic.
374. 85. 3 r. blk., brn. & grn. .. 5 5
375. 8 r. brn., blk. and green 12 10
376. 14 r. brown and black .. 20 15

POSTAGE DUE STAMPS

D 1. Frieze, Angkor Vat.

1974.
D 378. D 1. 2 r. brown 5 5
D 379. 6 r. green 8 5
D 380. 8 r. mauve 10 8
D 381. 10 r. blue 12 12

KHOR FAKKAN

From 1965 various issues were produced for this dependency, some being overprinted on, or in the same designs as, issues for Sharjah. These stamps are recorded in the Appendix at the end of this catalogue.

KIAUTSCHOU (KIAOCHOW) O1

A port in Shantung, China, leased by Germany from China in 1898. It was occupied by Japan in 1914, but reverted to China in 1922.

1900. 100 pfennige = 1 mark.
1905. 100 cents = 1 dollar (Chinese).

1901. No. 9 of German P.Os in China surch. **5 Pfg.**
3. 7. 5 pf. on 10 pf. red .. 12 12

1901. "Yacht" key-types inscr. "KIAUTSCHOU".
11. N. 3 pf. brown 35 30
12. 5 pf. green 25 25
13. 10 pf. red 55 45
14. 20 pf. blue .. .. 1·75 2·00
15. 25 pf. black & red on yell. 4·00 4·50
16. 30 pf. blk. & oran. on buff 4·00 4·50
17. 40 pf. black and red .. 4·75 5·50
18. 50 pf. blk. & pur. on buff 4·75 6·50
19. 80 pf. blk. & red on rose .. 8·00 17·00
20. O. 1 m. red .. .. 12·00 18·00
21. 2 m. blue .. .. 22·00 25·00
22. 3 m. black .. .. 22·00 55·00
23. 5 m. red and black .. 45·00 £150

1905. "Yacht" key-types inscr. "KIAUTSCHOU".
34. N. 1 c. brown 15 35
35. 2 c. green 15 25
36. 4 c. red 20 25
37. 10 c. blue 25 80
38. 20 c. black and red .. 60 7·00
39. 40 c. black and red on rose 80 16·00
40. O. ½ dol. red .. .. 1·60 18·00
41. 1 dol. blue .. .. 2·10 12·00
42. 1½ dol. black .. .. 4·00 48·00
43. 2½ dol. red and black .. 12·00 £140

KING EDWARD VII LAND BC

Stamp issued in connection with the Shackleton Antarctic Expedition in 1908.

1908. Stamp of New Zealand optd. **KING EDWARD VII LAND.**
A 1. 35. 1d. red .. .. £180 15·00

KIONGA O3

Part of German E. Africa, occupied by the Portuguese during the 1914/18 war, and now incorporated in Mozambique.

1916. "King Carlos" key-type of Lourenzo Marques optd. **REPUBLICA** and surch. **KIONGA** and new value.
1. S. ½ c. on 100 r. blue on blue 2·25 2·00
2. 1 c. on 100 r. blue on blue 2·25 2·00
3. 2½ c. on 100 r. blue on blue 2·25 2·00
4. 5 c. on 100 r. blue on blue 2·25 2·00

KISHANGARH BC

A state of Rajasthan, India. Now uses Indian stamps.

1. State Arms.

1899. Imperf. or perf.
1. 1. 1 a. green .. .. .. 9·00 12·00
3. 1 a. blue .. .. .. 80·00

2.

3. Maharaja Sardul.

1899. Various arms designs. Perf. or imperf.
21. 2. ¼ a. green .. .. .. 3·00 7·00
22. ¼ a. red 10 20
22a. ¼ a. pink 15
24. ½ a. green .. .. .. 5·00 5·00
8. ½ a. red .. .. .. 7·00 4·00
26a. ½ a. blue 20 20
7. ½ a. lilac .. .. .. 7·00 7·00

29.	2.	1 a. purple	40	20
28.		1 a. grey	40	40
12.		1 a. pink	30·00	30·00
15.	3.	2 a. orange	2·50	2·50
31.	2.	4 a. chocolate	60	40
32.		1 r. green	8·00	10·00
17.		1 r. lilac	13·00	
34.		2 r. red	18·00	
35.		5 r. mauve	12·00	

4.

5. Maharaja Sardul Singh.

1903. Imperf. or perf.

39.	4.	½ a. pink	3·00	3·00
40.	5.	2 a. orange	2·25	2·50
41.	2.	8 a. grey	3·00	

6. Maharaja Madan Singh.

7. Maharaja Madan Singh.

1904.

42.	6.	¼ a. red	15	15
43.		½ a. chestnut	15	15
44.		1 a. blue	25	15
45.		2 a. orange	3·50	2·50
46.		4 a. brown	3·00	2·00
47.		8 a. violet	3·00	3·00
48.		1 r. green	4·00	4·00
49.		2 r. yellow	5·00	7·00
50.		5 r. chocolate	9·00	12·00

1912.

63.	7.	¼ a. blue	10	10
64.		½ a. green	10	10
65.		1 a. red	60	50
66.		2 a. purple	2·50	2·50
67.		4 a. blue	4·00	4·00
68.		8 a. brown	4·00	5·00
69.		1 r. mauve	7·00	8·00
70.		2 r. green	10·00	12·00
71.		5 r. brown	14·00	16·00

8.

9. Maharaja Yagyanarain Singhiji.

1913.

59.	8.	¼ a. blue	10	12
60.		2 a. purple	6·00	6·00

1928.

72.	9.	¼ a. blue	20	25
73.		½ a. green	20	25
74.	–	1 a. red	40	40
75.	–	2 a. purple	1·75	2·00
76.	9.	4 a. brown	70	80
77.		8 a. violet	2·50	2·50
78.		1 r. green	5·00	6·00
79.		2 r yellow	10·00	11·00
80.		5 r. claret	14·00	15·00

Nos. 74/5 are larger.

OFFICIAL STAMPS

1918. Optd. **ON K S D.**

O 2b.	2.	¼ a. green		
O 3.		¼ a. pink	10	12
O 4.		½ a. blue		
O 1.		1 a. grey	—	35
O 5.		1 a. lilac	60	
O 8.	3.	2 a. orange		
O 9.	2.	4 a. chocolate	8·00	8·00
O 13a.		8 a. grey	10·00	10·00
O 10.		1 r. green	18·00	18·00
O 11.		2 r. brown	28·00	28·00
O 12.		5 r. mauve	40·00	40·00

1918. Optd. **ON K S D.**

O 13.	5.	2 a. orange	9·00	9·00

1918. Optd. **ON K S D.**

O 14.	6.	¼ a. red	7·00	7·00
O 15.		½ a. chestnut	30	10
O 16.		1 a. blue	4·00	3·00
O 17.		2 a. orange		
O 18.		4 a. brown	7·00	7·00
O 19.		8 a. violet	18·00	18·00
O 20.		1 r. green	60·00	60·00
O 21.		5 r. chocolate		

1918. Optd. **ON K S D.**

O 22.	7.	¼ a. blue	30	30
O 23.		½ a. green	45	50
O 24.		1 a. red	45	50
O 25.		2 a. purple	1·00	1·00
O 26.		4 a. blue	9·00	9·00
O 27.		8 a. brown	12·00	12·00
O 28.		1 r. mauve	20·00	20·00
O 29.		2 r. green		
O 30.		5 r. brown		

1918. Optd. **ON K S D.**

O 31.	8.	¼ a. blue	3·50	
O 32.		2 a. purple	6·00	

For later issues see **RAJASTHAN.**

KOREA O3

A peninsula to the S. of Manchuria in E. Asia. Formerly an empire under Chinese suzerainty, it was annexed by Japan in 1910 and used Japanese stamps. After the defeat of Japan in 1945, Russian and United States Military administrations were set up in Korea to the north and south of the 38th Parallel respectively; in 1948 South Korea and North Korea became independent republics.

10 mons = 1 poon.
1000 re = 100 cheun = 1 won.

In S. Korea (1953) 1 hwan = 100 old won.
(1962) 100 chon = 1 won = 10 old hwan.
In N. Korea (1959) 1 old won = 1 chon.
100 chon = 1 new won.

EMPIRE OF KOREA.

1.

2. Korean flag.

(3.)

1884.

1.	1.	5 m. red	2·50	£400
2.		10 m. blue	2·00	£400

1895.

7.	2.	5 p. green	1·75	1·75
8.		10 p. blue	2·50	2·50
9.		25 p. lake	2·00	2·50
10a.		50 p. violet	2·00	1·50

1897. Optd. with T 3.

12.	2.	5 p. green	4·00	4·00
13.		10 p. blue	7·00	4·00
14.		25 p. lake	5·00	5·00
16.		50 p. violet	4·00	4·00

1899. Surch. in Korean characters.

19.	2.	1 (ch.) on 5 p. green	40·00	25·00
21.		1 (ch.) on 25 p. lake	7·00	2·50

4. 5. 6.
National Imperial Emblems.

1900. T 4, 5 (2 ch.), 6 (2 ch.) and similar designs.

22.	2 r. grey	50	1·25
23.	1 ch. green	50	75
24.	2 ch. blue (T 5)	12·00	20·00
25.	2 ch. blue (T 6)	90	1·25
26.	3 ch. orange	75	75
27.	4 ch. red	1·50	1·75
28.	5 ch. pink	1·50	1·75
29.	6 ch. blue	1·75	1·50
30.	10 ch. purple	1·50	2·00
31.	15 ch. purple	2·50	3·00
32.	20 ch. brown	3·00	5·00
33.	50 ch. olive and pink	15·00	15·00
34.	1 wn. blue, slate and red	20·00	25·00
35.	2 wn. green and purple	25·00	30·00

7. Imperial Crown.

10. Eagle, Baton and Sphere.

1902. 40th Year of Emperor's Reign.

36.	7.	3 ch. orange	1·40	1·00

(8.)

(9.)

(9a.) (9b.)

Types 8 to 9a are in two parts, the horizontal strokes (one, two or three) representing the value figures and the bottom part being the character for "cheun".

Some variation can be found in these woodblock overprints.

1902.

(a) Surch. as Types 8 to 9a.

37.	2.	1 ch. on 25 p. lake	1·50	1·10
39.		2 ch. on 25 p. lake	1·50	1·10
42.		2 ch. on 50 p. violet	—	£200
43.		3 ch. on 25 p. lake	17·00	35·00
46.		3 ch. on 50 p. violet	1·50	3·00

(b) Surch. as T 9b (Japanese "sen" character) and strokes.

49a.	2.	3 ch. on 50 p. violet	90·00	60·00

1903.

50.	10.	2 r. grey	20	15
51.		1 ch. purple	25	20
52.		2 ch. green	35	30
53.		3 ch. orange	50	40
54.		4 ch. red	75	75
55.		5 ch. brown	1·00	1·25
56.		6 ch. lilac	1·25	1·50
57.		10 ch. blue	1·50	2·00
58.		15 ch. red on yellow	3·00	3·50
59.		20 ch. purple on yellow	3·50	4·50
60.		50 ch. red on green	6·00	10·00
61.		1 wn. lilac on lilac	12·00	20·00
62.		2 wn. purple on orange	25·00	35·00

SOUTH KOREA.

(a) United States Military Government.

(11.) 12. Family and Flag. 13. National Emblem.

1946. Stamps of Japan surch. as T 11.

69.	5 ch. on 5 s. clar. (No. 396)	2·00	2·00
70.	5 ch. on 14 s. mauve (No. 327)	20	20
71.	10 ch. on 40 s. pur. (No. 406)	15	15
72.	20 ch. on 6 s. blue (No. 397)	15	15
73.	30 ch. on 27 s. red (No. 404)	15	20
74.	5 wn. on 17 s. violet (No. 402)	1·50	1·50

1946. Liberation from Japanese Rule.

75.	12.	3 ch. yellow	8	20
76.		5 ch. green	10	15
77.		10 ch. red	10	15
78.		20 ch. blue	15	15
79.	13.	50 ch. purple	25	30
80.		1 wn. brown	45	45

14. Dove of Peace and Map of Korea.

1946. Liberation. 1st Anniv.

81.	14.	50 ch. violet	50	50

15. U.S.A. and Korean Flags.

16. Observatory, Kyongju.

17. Golden Crown of Silla.

18. Admiral Li Sun Sin.

1946. Resumption of Postal Service between Korea and U.S.A.

82.	15.	10 wn. red	1·75	1·50

1946.

83.	16.	50 ch. blue	40	12
84.	–	1 wn. brown	15	12
85.	–	2 wn. blue	30	12
86.	17.	5 wn. magenta	1·90	1·25
87.	18.	10 wn. green	1·90	1·25

DESIGNS—As T 16: 1 wn. Hibiscus. 2 wn. Map of Korea.

19. Korean Alphabet.

20. Li Jun, patriot.

21. "Turtle Ship".

21a. Letters Surrounding Globe.

1946. Creation of Korean Alphabet. 500th Anniv.

88.	19.	50 ch. blue	70	60

1947.

89.	20.	5 w. green	2·10	1·40
90.	–	10 w. blue	2·10	1·40
91.	–	20 w. red	1·25	60
92.	21.	50 w. brown	4·00	2·50

1947. Resumption of Int. Postal Service.

93.	21a.	10 w. blue	2·00	1·75

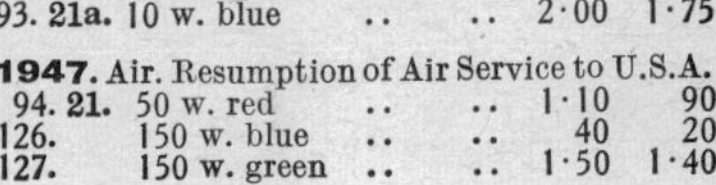

1947. Air. Resumption of Air Service to U.S.A.

94.	21.	50 w. red	1·10	90
126.		150 w. blue	40	20
127.		150 w. green	1·50	1·40

23. Hand and Ballot Slip.

24. Casting Votes.

1948. South Korea Election.

95.	23.	2 w. orange	55	25
96.		5 w. mauve	1·00	70
97.		10 w. violet	2·25	1·60
98.	24.	20 w. red	4·25	3·25
99.		50 w. blue	6·00	4·00

25. Korean Flag and Laurel Wreath.

1948. Olympic Games.

100.	25.	5 w. green	35·00	25·00
101.	–	10 w. violet	8·00	5·50

DESIGN—VERT. 10 w. Runner with torch.

26. Capitol and Ears of Rice. 27. Korean Family.

1948. Meeting of First National Assembly.

102.	26.	4 w. brown	3·00	3·00

(b) Republic of Korea.

1948. Promulgation of Constitution.

103.	27.	4 w. green	4·00	3·25
104.	–	10 w. brown	4·00	3·75

DESIGN—HORIZ. 10 w. Flag of Korea.

28. Dr. Syngman Rhee.

29. Hibiscus.

1948. Election of First President.

105.	28.	5 w. blue	3·00	2·00

1948. Proclamation of Republic.

106.	–	4 w. blue	9·50	8·50
107.	29.	5 w. mauve	8·50	7·00

DESIGN: 4 w. Dove and olive branch.

29a. Li Jun. 29b. Kyongju Observatory.

1948.

108.	29a.	4 w. red	10	12
109.	29b.	14 w. blue	30	15

30. Doves, Globe and Laurel Wreath.

31. Citizen and Date.

1949. Arrival of U.N. Commission.

110.	30.	10 w. blue	8·50	6·00

1949. National Census.

111.	31.	15 w. violet	5·00	4·00

32. Children and Plant.

1949. Children's Day. 20th Anniv.

112.	32.	15 w. violet	4·00	3·00

33. Hibiscus.

34. Map of Korea and Magpies.

34a. Dove and Globe.

34b. Admiral Li Sun Sin.

1949.

113.	–	1 w. red	70	40
114.	–	2 w. grey	12	10
115.	–	5 w. green	60	55
116.	–	10 w. green	12	8
117.	33.	15 w. red	15	8
118.	–	20 w. brown	8	8
119.	–	30 w. green	30	12
120.	–	50 w. blue	15	12
121.	34.	65 w. blue	15	12
122.	–	100 w. olive	15	15
123.	34a.	200 w. green	15	12
124.	–	400 w. brown	20	15
125.	34b.	500 w. blue	20	15

DESIGNS—VERT. As T 33: 1 w. Postman. 2 w. Worker and factory. 5 w. Harvesting rice. 10 w. Cranes. 20 w. Diamond Mountains. 30 w. Ginseng plant. 50 w. South Gate, Seoul. 100 w. Tabo Pagoda, Kyongju. HORIZ. As T 34a: 400 w. Diamond Mountains.

35. Symbol and Phoenix.

36. Railway Train.

1949. Independence. 1st Anniv.

128.	35.	15 w. blue	4·00	2·50

1949. Korean Railways. 50th Anniv.

129.	36.	15 w. blue	8·00	9·00

37. Korean Flag. 38. Post-horse Warrant.

1949. U.P.U. 75th Anniv.

130.	37.	15 w. multicoloured ..	2·50	2·50

1950. Membership of U.P.U. 50th Anniv.

131.	38.	15 w. green	3·50	2·00
132.		65 w. brown	2·50	2·00

39. Aeroplane and Globe.

40. Demonstrators. 41. Capitol, Seoul.

1950. Air. Opening of Internal Air Mail Service.

133.	39.	60 w. blue	2·00	1·75

1950. Abortive Proclamation of Independence. 31st Anniv.

134.	41.	15 w. olive	2·50	1·60
135.		65 w. violet	1·35	85

1950. 2nd South Korean Election.

136.	41.	30 w. multicoloured ..	2·25	1·75

42. Dr. Syngman Rhee.

43. Flag and Mountains.

1950. Unification of Korea.

137.	42.	100 w. blue	50	40
138.	43.	100 w. green	70	50
139.	–	200 w. green	70	60

DESIGN—HORIZ. 200 w. Map of Korea and flags of U.N. and Korea (35 × 24 mm.).

44. Crane. 45. Post-horse Warrant. 46. Fairy (8th Cent. painting).

1951. Perf. or roul.

140.	44.	5 w. brown	35	45
141.	–	20 w. violet	25	25
142.	–	50 w. green	35	25
183.	45.	100 w. blue	50	20
193.	46.	1,000 w. green	90	30

DESIGNS—HORIZ. 20 w. Astrological Tiger (ancient painting). 50 w. Dove and Korean flag.

≈100원≈

(47.)

200원

(48.)

1951. No. 145 surch. with T 47, the rest as T 48.

145.	29a.	100 w. on 4 w. red ..	25	20
146.	33.	200 w. on 15 w. red ..	35	25
147.	29a.	300 w. on 4 w. red ..	45	25
148.	–	300 w. on 10 w. (116)	1·00	75
149.	29b.	300 w. on 14 w. blue ..	65	45
150.	33.	300 w. on 15 w. red ..	45	35
151.	–	300 w. on 20 w. (118)	75	60
152.	–	300 w. on 30 w. (119)	70	50
153.	–	300 w. on 50 w. (120)	45	25
154.	34.	300 w. on 65 w. blue ..	45	35
155.	–	300 w. on 100 w. (122)		

49. Statue of Liberty and Flags.

1951. Participation in Korean War. Flags in national colours. A. As Type 49 in green. B. As Type 49 but showing U.N. Emblem and doves in blue.

			A	B
158.	500 w. Australia		1·50	1·50
159.	500 w. Belgium		1·50	1·50
160.	500 w. Britain		1·50	1·50
161.	500 w. Canada		1·50	1·50
162.	500 w. Colombia		1·50	1·50
163.	500 w. Denmark		2·00	3·50
164.	500 w. Ethiopia		1·50	1·50
165.	500 w. France		1·50	1·50
166.	500 w. Greece		1·50	1·50
167.	500 w. India		1·50	1·50
168.	500 w. Italy (with crown)		1·50	1·50
169.	500 w. Italy (without crown)		3·00	3·00
170.	500 w. Luxembourg ..		1·50	1·50
171.	500 w. Netherland ..		1·50	1·50
172.	500 w. New Zealand ..		1·50	1·50
173.	500 w. Norway		1·50	1·50
174.	500 w. Philippines ..		1·50	1·50
175.	500 w. Sweden		1·50	1·50
176.	500 w. Thailand		1·50	1·50
177.	500 w. Turkey		1·50	1·50
178.	500 w. Union of S. Africa		1·50	1·50
179.	500 w. U.S.A.		2·00	2·00

The prices are the same for unused or used.

500 WON

(50.)

1951. Air. No. 126 surch with T 50.

180.	21.	500 w. on 150 w. blue	70	60

51. Buddha of Sokkuram. 52. Pulguksa Temple, Kyongju.

53. Monument to King Muryol, Kyongju.

54. Shrine of Admiral Li Sun Sin, Tongyong.

1952. Inscr. "KOREA".

189.	51.	200 w. red	20	12
190.	52.	300 w. green	20	12
191.	53.	500 w. red	30	25
192.		500 w. blue	3·00	2·00
194.	54.	2,000 w. blue	30	8

55. President Syngman Rhee.

1952. President's Election to 2nd Term of Office.

195.	55.	1,000 w. green	25	15

56. Aeroplane over Ship.

1952. Air.

196.	56.	1,2000 w. brown ..	15	8
197.		1,800 w. blue	25	8
198.		4,200 w. violet	50	15

For stamps in new currency, see Nos. 210/12.

57. Tree-planting.

58. Monument to King Muryol. Kyongju.

59. "Rebirth of Industry."

60. Hibiscus.

61. King Sejong.

62. Pagoda Park, Seoul.

63. Kyongju Observatory.

64. Deer.

65. Deer.

1953. New Currency.

199.	57.	1 h. blue	8	5
200.	53.	2 h. blue	8	5
308.	57.	2 h. blue	5	5
274.	58.	4 h. blue	5	5
201.	53.	5 h. myrtle	15	8
202.	58.	5 h. green	8	5
203.	57.	10 h. green	30	8
204.	–	10 h. brown	20	8
229.	59.	10 h. brown	30	12
247.	60.	10 h. magenta ..	25	12
276.	–	10 h. green	25	10
277.	–	10 h. green	40	15
328.	59.	15 h. violet	8	5
205.	54.	20 h. brown	70	15
235.	59.	20 h. blue	15	5
248.	61.	20 h. purple	20	5
279.	60.	20 h. magenta ..	5	5
206.	62.	30 h. indigo	40	8
280.	–	30 h. violet	15	5
281.	61.	40 h. purple	20	5
232.	59.	50 h. mauve	60	10
269.	–	50 h. claret	30	8
282.	63.	50 h. violet	30	8
315.	–	55 h. brown-purple ..	65	15
250.	64.	100 h. brown-purple	70	20
316.	63.	100 h. slate-violet ..	65	15
243.	62.	200 h. violet	1·50	20
285.	64.	200 h. brown-purple ..	2·10	30
286.	62.	400 h. violet	2·10	30
319.	65.	500 h. yellow-brown ..	2·50	60
320.		1,000 h. bistre-brown ..	40	30

DESIGNS—HORIZ. 10 h. (No. 204) Moth and Korean flag. 10 h. (No. 277) South Gate, Seoul. 30 h. (No. 280) Tiger. VERT. 55 h. Haegumgang.

1953. Air. New Currency.
210. **56.** 12 h. blue 20 8
211. 18 h. violet 40 15
212. 42 h. green 80 20

DESIGN — VERT. No. 214, Nurses supporting wounded soldier.

66. Field Hospital.

1953. Red Cross Fund. Crosses in red.
213. **66.** 10 h.+5 h. green .. 80 50
214. – 10 h.+5 h. blue .. 80 50

67. Y.M.C.A. Badge and Map. **68.** Aeroplane over East Gate, Seoul.

1953. Korean Y.M.C.A. 50th Anniv.
215. **67.** 10 h. red and indigo .. 50 40

1954. Air.
216. **68.** 25 h. brown 15 10
217. 35 h. bright purple .. 25 12
218. 38 h. green 30 12
219. 58 h. blue 35 15
296. 70 h. turquoise.. .. 25 12
220. 71 h. deep blue .. 40 25
297. 110 h. brown 35 15
298. 205 h. magenta .. 35 12

69. Tokto Island. **70.**

1954.
221. – 2 h. purple 5 5
222. – 5 h. blue 5 5
223. **69.** 10 h. green 15 8
DESIGN: 2 h., 5 h. Rocks off Tokto Is.

1954. 4th World Forestry Congress.
224. **70.** 10 h. green 8 5
225. 19 h. green 15 8

71. Presidents Syngman Rhee and Eisenhower.

1954. Korea–United States Mutual Defence Treaty.
226. **71.** 10 h. blue 25 10
227. 19 h. brown 35 10
228. 71 h. green 80 40

72. Rotary Emblem. **73.** Pres. Syngman Rhee.

1955. Rotary International. 50th Anniv.
236. **72.** 20 h. violet 25 20
237. 25 h. green 35 25
238. 71 h. purple 60 45

1955. 80th Birthday of President.
239. **73.** 20 b. blue 30 12

74. Independence Arch, Seoul. **75.** Runner and Torch.

1955. Liberation. 10th Anniv.
240. **74.** 40 h. green 30 15
241. 100 h. brown 50 25

1955. 36th National Athletic Meeting.
252. **75.** 20 h. purple 20 10
253. 55 h. green 35 20

75a. U.N. Emblem. **76.** Admiral Li Sun Sin and "Turtle Ship".

1955. U.N. 10th Anniv.
254. **75a.** 20 h. green 40 25
255. 55 h. blue 65 40

1955. Korean Navy. 10th Anniv.
256. **76.** 20 h. blue 50 30

77. Admiration Pagoda. **78.** Pres. Syngman Rhee.

1956. 81st Birthday of President.
257. **77.** 20 h. green 40 25

1956. President's Election to Third Term of Office.
261. **78.** 20 h. brown 40 20
262. 55 h. blue 70 40

79. Torch and Olympic Rings. **80.** Central P.O., Seoul.

1956. Olympic Games.
263. **79.** 20 h. brown 60 40
264. 55 h. green .. .. 1·25 90

1956. Stamp Day. Inscr. "4289.12.4".
265. **80.** 20 h. turquoise.. .. 25 20
266. – 50 h. red 40 30
267. – 55 h. green 35 25
DESIGNS—VERT. 50 h. Stamp of 1884. HORIZ. 55 h. Man leading post-pony.

81. I.T.U. Emblem and Radio Mast. **82.** Korean Scout and Badge.

1957. Korea's Admission to Int. Telecommunications Union. 5th Anniv.
290. **81.** 40 h. blue 30 15
291. 55 h. green 45 30

1957. Boy Scout Movement. 50th Anniv.
293. **82.** 40 h. purple 30 15
294. 55 h. purple 60 25

1957. Flood Relief Fund. As No. 281 but Korean inscr. and premium added and colour changed.
299. 40 h.+10 h. green .. 25 12

83. Mercury, Flags and Ships.

84. Star of Bethlehem and Pine Cone.

1957. Korean-American Friendship Treaty.
301. **83.** 40 h. orange 30 8
302. 205 h. emerald.. .. 80 15

1957. Christmas and New Year Issue.
304. **84.** 15 h. brown, grn. & orge. 45 25
305. – 25 h. green, red & yellow 65 40
306. – 30 h. blue, green & yell. 90 60
DESIGNS: 25 h. Christmas tree and tassels. 30 h. Christmas tree and dog by window.

85. Winged Letter. **86.** Korean Children regarding future.

1958. Postal Week.
321. **85.** 40 h. blue and red .. 30 10

1958. Republic of Korea. 10th Anniv.
323. **86.** 20 h. grey 20 8
324. – 40 h. red 35 15
DESIGN—HORIZ. 40 h. Hibiscus flowers forming figure "10".

87. U.N.E.S.C.O. Headquarters, Paris. **88.** Children flying Kites.

1958. U.N.E.S.C.O. Building, Paris. Inaug.
326. **87.** 40 h. orange and green 30 20

1958. Christmas and New Year.
330. **88.** 15 h. green 40 30
331. – 25 h. red, yellow & blue 40 30
332. – 30 h. red, blue & yellow 60 45
DESIGNS—VERT. 25 h. Christmas tree, tassels and wicker basket (cooking sieve). 30 h. Children in traditional festive costume.

89. Rejoicing Crowds in Pagoda Park, Flag and Torch.

1958. Abortive Proclamation of Independence. 40th Anniv.
334. **89.** 40 h. purple and brown 20 15

90. Marines going Ashore from Landing craft.

1959. Korean Marine Corps. 10th Anniv.
336. **90.** 40 h. green 20 15

91.

1959. Korea's Admission to W.H.O. 10th Anniv.
339. **91.** 40 h. purple and pink 30 15

92. Diesel Train.

1959. Korean Railways. 60th Anniv.
341. **92.** 40 h. sepia and brown.. 30 15

93. Runners in Relay Race.

1959. 40th Korean National Games.
343. **93.** 40 h. brown and blue .. 30 20

94. Red Cross and Korea.

1959. Red Cross. Inscr. "1959 4292".
345. **94.** 40 h. red and green .. 20 12
346. – 55 h. red and mauve .. 25 15
DESIGN: 55 h. Red Cross on Globe.

95. Korean Postal Flags Old and New. **96.** Mice in Korean Costume and New Year Emblem.

1959. Korean Postal Service. 75th Anniv.
348. **95.** 40 h. red and blue .. 30 15

1959. Christmas and New Year.
350. **96.** 15 h. pink, blue and grey 25 15
351. – 25 h. red, green and blue 30 15
352. – 30 h. red, black & mauve 35 20
DESIGNS: 25 h. Carol singers. 30 h. Crane.

97. U.P.U. Monument. **98.** Bee and Clover.

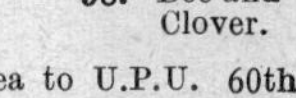

1960. Admission of Korea to U.P.U. 60th Anniv.

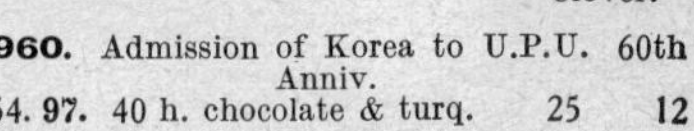

354. **97.** 40 h. chocolate & turq. 25 12

1960. Children's Savings Campaign.
356. **98.** 10 h. yell., sepia & green 10 5
357. – 20 h. brn., blue & pink.. 20 10
DESIGN: 20 h. Snail and Korean money-bag.
For these stamps in new currency, see Nos. 569/70.

99. "Uprooted Tree". **100.** Pres. Eisenhower.

1960. World Refugee Year.
358. **99.** 40 h. red, blue & green 25 10

1960. Visit of President Eisenhower.
360. **100.** 40 h. blue, red & turq. 40 15

101. Schoolchildren.

1960. Educational System. 75th Anniv.
362. **101.** 40 h. pur., chest. & ol. 20 10

102. Assembly.  **103.** "Liberation".

105. Swallow and Insulats.

104. Weightlifting.

1960. Inauguration of House of Councillors.
364. 102. 40 h. blue 20 10

1960. Liberation. 15th Anniv.
365. 103. 40 h. lake, blue & ochre 10 5

1960. Olympic Games.
368. 104. 20 h. brn., flesh & turq. 15 8
369. – 40 h. brn., blue & turq. 30 12
DESIGN: 40 h. South Gate, Seoul.

1960. Korean Telegraph Service. 75th Anniv.
371. 105. 40 h. vio., grey & blue 25 10

106. " Rebirth of Republic".

107. " Torch of Culture".

1960. Establishment of New Government
373. 106. 40 h. yell., blue & orge. 20 10

1960. Cultural Month.
376. 107. 40 h. yellow, pale blue and blue 20 10

108. U.N. Flag.

109. U.N. Emblem and Gravestones.

1960. U.N. 15th Anniv.
378. 108. 40 h. blue, brn. & mve. 25 10

1960. Establishment of U.N. Memorial Cemetery.
380. 109. 40 h. brown & orange 25 10

110. " National Stocktaking".

111. Festival Stocking.

1960. Census of Population and Resources.
382. 110. 40 h. red, drab & blue 25 10

1960. Christmas and New Year Issue.
384. – 15 h. brn., yell. & grey 25 10
385. 111. 25 h. red, grn. & blue 30 10
386. – 30 h. red, yell. & blue 35 15
DESIGNS: 15 h. Ox's head. 30 h. Girl bowing in New Year's greeting.

112. W.M.O. Emblem, Wind-sock and Ancient Rain-gauge.

1961. World Meteorological Day.
388. 112. 40 h. ultram. and blue 25 15

113. W.H.O. Emblem, Family, Sun and Globe.

1961. World Health Day.
390. 113. 40 h. brown & salmon 25 15

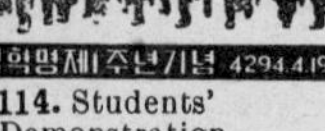
114. Students' Demonstration.

115. Woodchoppers

117. Soldier's Grave.

116. Girl Guide, Camp and Badge.

1961. April Revolution (Overthrow of Pres. Syngman Rhee). 1st Anniv.
392. 114. 40 h. green, red & blue 25 15

1961. Int. Community Development Conf. Seoul.
394. 115. 40 h. blue-green .. 25 15

1961. Korean Girl Guide Movement. 15th Anniv.
296. 116. 40 h. blue-green .. 30 15

1961. Memorial Day.
398. 117. 40 h. black and drab.. 25 15

118. Soldier with Torch.

119. " Three Liberations".

1961. Revolution of 16 May (Seizure of Power by Gen. Pak Chung Hi).
400. 118. 40 h. brown and yellow 20 10

1961. Liberation Day.
402. 119. 40 h. multicoloured .. 25 10

120. Korean Forces, Flag and Battleship.

121. "Korean Art" (Kyongbok Palace Art Gallery).

1961. Armed Forces Day.
404. 120. 40 h. multicoloured .. 25 10

1961. 10th Korean Art Exhibition.
406. 121. 40 h. chocolate & brown 25 10

121a. Birthday Candle.

1961. U.N.E.S.C.O. 15th Anniv.
408. 121a. 40 h. blue and green 25 15

122. Mobile X-Ray Unit.

1961. T.B.-Vaccination Week.
410. 122. 40 h. brown & choc... 25 15

122a. Ginseng.

123. King Sejong.

123a. Woodpecker.

123b. Rice Harvester.

123c. Korean Drum.

124. 'Plane over Pagoda.

1961.
412. 122a. 20 h. red 30 8
413. 123. 30 h. lilac 40 8
414. 123a. 40 h. blue and red .. 45 8
415. 123b. 40 h. green 80 8
416. 123c 100 h. brown .. 70 20
See also Nos. 467, etc., and for stamps inscribed "REPUBLIC OF KOREA", see Nos. 641, etc. and 785/95.

1961. Air.
417. 124. 50 h. violet and blue.. 15 8
418. – 100 h. brown & blue.. 30 12
419. – 200 h. brown & blue.. 60 20
420. – 400 h. green & blue .. 80 40
DESIGNS—Plane over: 100 h. West Gate, Suwon. 200 h. Gateway and wall of Toksu Palace, Seoul. 400 h. Pavilion, Kyongbok Palace, Seoul.
See also Nos. 454 etc.

125. I.T.U. Emblem as Satellite.

1962. Admission into I.T.U. 10th Anniv.
421. 125. 40 h. red and blue .. 20 15

126. Triga Mark II Reactor.

1962. 1st Korean Atomic Reactor.
423. 126. 40h. green, drab & blue 15 10

127. Mosquito and Emblem.

1962. Malaria Eradication.
424. 127. 40 h. red and green .. 25 8

128. Girl and Y.W.C.A. Emblem.

1962. Korean Y.W.C.A. 40th Anniv.
426. 128. 40 h. blue and orange 25 10

129. Emblem of Asian Film Producers' Federation.

130. Soldiers crossing Han River Bridge.

1962. 9th Asian Film Festival, Seoul.
427. 129. 40 h. violet, red & turq. 25 10

1962. 16th May Revolution. 1st Anniv. Inscr. " 1962.5.16".
428. – 30 h. sage and brown 30 15
429. 130. 40 h. brn., grn. & turq. 30 15
430. – 200 h. red, yell. & blue 90 30
DESIGNS—HORIZ. 30 h. " Industrial Progress" (men moving cogwheel up slope). 200 h. " Egg" containing Korean badge and industrial skyline.

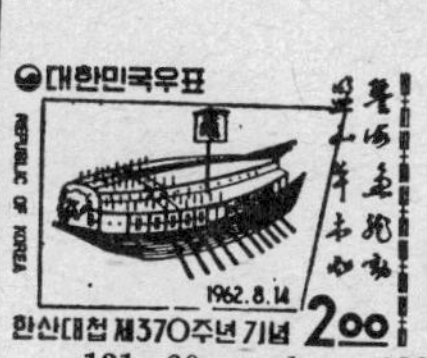
131. 20-oared " Turtle Ship".

132. Scout Badge and Korean Flag.

1962. Hansan Naval Victory over Japanese. 370th Anniv.
433. 131. 2 w. blue and light blue 35 20
434. – 4 w. black, vio. & turq. 50 35
DESIGN: 4 w. 16-oared " Turtle Ship".

1962. Korean Scout Movement. 40th Anniv.
446. 132. 4 w. choc., red and blue 25 15
447. 4 w. green, red & blue 25 15

133. Mackerel, Trawler and Nets.

1962. 10th Indo-Pacific Fishery Council Meeting, Seoul.
449. 133. 4 w. blue & turquoise 15 8

133a. Chindo Dog.

134. "Hanabusaya asiatica".

134a. Statue of Goddess Mikuk Bearak.

134b. Stag Beetle.

134c. Farmers' Dance.

134d. 12th-century Wine-jug.

134e. Factory, Fishes and Corn.

134f. Mison.

134g. 13th-century Printing-block and Impression used for "Tripitaka Koreana".

134h. Deer (Swinhoe's Manchurian Sika).

134i. Bell of King Kyongbok. 134j. Boddhisatva Sokkuram Shrine.

134k. Tile, Silla Dynasty. 134l. "Azure Dragon", Koguryo period.

1962. New Currency.

467.	133a.	20 ch. brown ..	8	5
468.	134.	40 ch. blue	12	5
469.	134a.	50 ch. maroon ..	8	5
540.	134b.	60 ch. brown ..	12	5
470.	134c.	1 wn. blue	8	5
542.	134a.	1 wn. 50 grey ..	20	10
471.	122a.	2 wn. red	8	5
472.	123.	3 wn. lilac	15	5
473.	123b.	4 wn. green	20	5
442.	134d.	5 wn. blue	8	5
547.	134e.	7 wn. mauve ..	45	20
474.	123c.	10 wn. brown ..	45	12
549.	134f.	20 wn. mauve ..	55	25
709.		20 wn. green.. ..	20	10
550.	134g.	40 wn. maroon ..	1·50	45
710.		40 wn. green & olive	40	15
551.	134h.	50 wn. brown ..	1·50	40
711.		50 wn. brown & bistre	50	25
552.	134i	100 wn. green ..	40	15
553.	134j.	200 wn. bronze & grn.	3·00	50
554.	134k.	300 wn. bronze & yell.	4·00	1·25
555.	134l.	500 wn. indigo & blue	5·00	2·00

See also Nos. 641/9, 709/11 and 785/95.

1962. Air. New Currency.

454.	124.	5 w. violet & blue	20	5
455.	–	10 w. sepia & turquoise (As No.418) ..	30	10
456.	–	20 w. sepia & turquoise (As No. 419) ..	60	30
563.	124.	39 w. violet and blue..	40	15
457.	–	40 w. green & turquoise (As No. 420) ..	90	50
564.	–	64 w. sepia & turquoise (As No. 418) ..	50	25
565.	–	78 w. sepia & turquoise (As No. 419) ..	70	30
566.	–	112 w. green & turq. (As No. 420) ..	1·10	40

135. I.C.A.O. Emblem.

1962. Korea's Entry into International Civil Aviation Organization. 10th Anniv.

450.	135.	4 w. blue and brown..	20	12

136. Electric Power Plant.

DESIGN: No. 459, Irrigation Dam.

1962. 1st Korean Economic Five Year Plan. Inaug.

458.	136.	4 w. violet and orange	30	15
459.	–	4 w. ultram. and blue	30	15

See also Nos. 482/3, 593/4 and 634/5.

1963. Juvenile Savings Campaign. New Currency. As Nos. 356/7.

569.	98.	1 w. yell., sep. & grn.	25	15
570.	–	2 w. brn., blue & pink	12	5

137. Campaign Emblem.

1963. Freedom from Hunger.

460.	137.	4 w. green, buff & blue	25	15

138. Globe and Letters.

1963. Asian—Oceanic Postal Union. 1st Anniv.

462.	138.	4 w. mauve, olive & bl.	20	15

139. Centenary Emblem and Map.

1963. Red Cross Cent.

464.	139.	4 w. red, grey and blue	30	15
465.		4 w. red, grey & salmon	30	15

1963. Flood Relief. As No. 473 but new colour and inscr. with premium.

479.		4 w.+1 w. blue	10	8

140. "15" and Hibiscus.

1963. Republic. 15th Anniv.

480.	140.	4 w. red, violet & blue	25	20

141. Nurse and Emblem.

1963. Korean Army Nursing Corps. 15th Anniv.

481.	141.	4 w. black, blue-green and yellow-green ..	20	15

1963. Five Year Plan. Dated "1963". As T 136.

482.		4 w. violet and blue	20	15
483.		4 w. chocolate and brown	20	15

DESIGNS: No. 482, Cement Factory, Mun'gyong, and bag of cement. No. 483, Miner and coal train Samch'ok region.

142. Rock Temples of Abu Simbe . 143.

1963. Nubian Monuments Preservation.

484.	142.	3 w. olive and green ..	30	20
485.	143.	4 w. olive and green ..	40	30

Nos. 484/5 are arranged together se-tenant in sheets, the two stamps forming one composite design.

144. Rugby Football and Athlete. 145. Nurse and Motor Clinic.

1963. 44th National Games.

487.	144.	4 w. green, brown & blue	25	15

1963. Korean T.B. Prevention Society 10th Anniv.

488.	145.	4 w indigo and red ..	25	15

146. Eleanor Roosevelt. 147. U.N. Headquarters.

1963. Declaration of Human Rights. 15th Anniv. Inscr. "1963.12.10".

489.	146.	3 w. chestnut & indigo	20	10
490.	–	4 w. indigo, olive & buff	30	15

DESIGN: 4 w. Freedom torch and globe.

1963. U.N. Recognition of Korea. 15th Anniv.

492.	147.	4 w. olive, blue & black	30	15

148. Pres. Pak Chong Hi and Capitol.

149. "Tai-Keum" (Bamboo Flute).

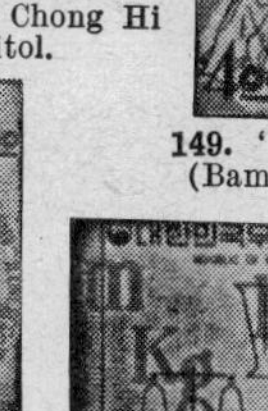

151. "U.N.E.S.C.O.".

150. Symbols of Metric System.

1963. President Pak Chong Hi Inauguration.

494.	148.	4 w. bl.-grn., turq. & blk.	35	15

1963. Musical Instruments and Players. As T 149.

495.		4 w. olive, brown and drab	25	15
496.		4 w. black, blue & light bl.	25	15
497.		4 w. olive, magenta & pink	25	15
498.		4 w. sepia, violet & grey..	25	15
499.		4 w. blue, brown and pink	25	15
500.		4 w. turq., black and blue	25	15
501.		4 w. violet, bistre & yellow	25	15
502.		4 w. blue, brown & mauve	25	15
503.		4 w. black, blue and purple	25	15
504.		4 w. black, brown and pink	25	15

MUSICAL INSTRUMENTS (and players): VERT. No. 495, T 149. 496, "Wul-keum" (banjo). 497, "Tang-piri" (flageolet). 498, "Na-bal" (trumpet). 499, "Hyang-pipa" (lute). 500, "Pyen-kyeng" (jade chimes). 501, "Taip-yeng-so" (clarinet). 502, "Chang-ko" (double-ended drum). HORIZ. No. 503, "Wa-kong-hu" (harp). 504, "Kaya-ko" (zither).

1964. Introduction of Metric System in Korea.

505.	150.	4 w. multicoloured ..	25	15

1964. Korean U.N.E.S.C.O. Committee. 10th Anniv.

506.	151.	4 w. ultram., red & blue	25	15

152. Symbols of Industry and Census.

1964. National Industrial Census (1963).

597.	152.	4 w. brown, black & grey	25	15

153. Y.M.C.A. Emblem and Profile of Young Man.

1964. Korean Y.M.C.A. 50th Anniv.

508.	153.	5 w. red, blue & green	25	15

154. Fair Emblem, Ginseng Root and Freighter.

1964. New York World's Fair.

509.	154.	40 w. brown, green and buff	75	30
510.	–	100 w. blue, chocolate and pale blue ..	1·60	80

DESIGN: 100 w. Korean pavilion at Fair.

155. Secret Garden.

1964. Background in pale blue.

517.	155.	1 w. green	8	5
518.	–	2 w. olive	10	5
519.	–	3 w. blue-green ..	12	5
520.	–	4 w. yellow-green ..	15	8
521.	–	5 w. violet ..	20	8
522.	–	6 w. ultramarine ..	25	10
523.	–	7 w. chocolate ..	30	10
524.	–	8 w. brown	35	12
525.	–	9 w. violet	40	15
526.	–	10 w. green	50	20

DESIGNS: 2 w. Whahong Gate. 3 w. Uisang Pavilion. 4 w. Mt. Songni. 5 w. Paekma River. 6 w. Anab Pond. 7 w. Choksok Pavilion. 8 w. Kwanghan Pavilion. 9 w. Whaom Temple. 10 w. Chonjeyon Falls.

1964. Five Year Plan. Dated "1964". As T 136.

528.		4 w. black and turquoise..	20	10
529.		4 w. blue and yellow ..	20	10

DESIGNS: No. 528, Trawlers and fish. No. 529, Oil refinery and barrels.

156. Wheel and Globe.

1964. Colombo Plan Day.

530.	156.	4 w. brn., sep. & grn.	25	15

157. "Helping Hand".

1964. Korea's Admission to W.H.O. 15th Anniv.

532.	157.	4 w. blk., olive & green	25	15

158. Running. 160. Federation Emblem.

161. Olympic "V" Emblem. 159. U.P.U. Monument, Berne, and Ribbons.

1964. 45th National Games, Inchon.

534.	158.	4 w. pink, green & pur.	25	15

1964. U.P.U. 90th Anniv.

535.	159.	4 w. brown, blue & pink	50	35

1964. 5th Meeting of Int. Federation of Asian and Western Pacific Contractors' Assns.

556.	160.	4 w. green, light green and brown ..	5	5

1964. Olympic Games, Tokyo.

No.	Type	Description	Unused	Used
557.	161.	4 w. ind., turq. & brn.	15	5
558.	–	4 w. mag., blue & grn.	15	5
559.	–	4 w. brn., ult. & blue	15	5
560.	–	4 w. mar., brn. & blue	15	5
561.	–	4 w. brn., pur. & blue	15	5

DESIGNS—HORIZ. No. 558, Running. 559, Rowing. 560, Horse-jumping. 561, Gymnastics.

162. 1st Korean Stamp. **163.** Pine Cone.

1964. Korean Postal Services. 80th Anniv

No.	Type	Description	Unused	Used
567.	162.	3 w. blue, vio. & mauve	20	10
568.	–	4 w. blk., violet & olive	25	15

DESIGN: 4 w. Hong Yong Sik, 1st Korean Post-master-general (inscr. "1964.12.4").

1965. Korean Plants. Plants multicoloured background colours given.

No.	Type	Description	Unused	Used
571.	163.	4 w. turquoise	10	8
572.	–	4 w. grey (Plum blossom)	15	8
573.	–	4 w. blue (Forsythia)	10	8
574.	–	4 w. green (Azalea)	25	8
575.	–	4 w. pink (Lilac)	15	8
576.	–	4 w. bl.-grey (Wild rose)	10	8
577.	–	4 w. apple (Balsam)	10	8
578.	–	4 w. grey (Hibiscus)	10	8
579.	–	4 w. flesh (Crepe myrtle)	15	8
580.	–	4 w. turquoise-blue (Ullung chrysanthemum)	15	8
581.	–	4 w. buff (Paulownia, tree)	15	8
582.	–	4 w. ultram. (Bamboo)	15	8

164. Folk-dancing.

1965. Pacific Area Travel Assn. Conf., Seoul.

No.	Type	Description	Unused	Used
584.	164.	4 w. violet, brn. & turq.	25	15

165. Flag and Doves.

1965. Military Aid for Vietnam.

No.	Type	Description	Unused	Used
586.	165.	4 w. brn., grn. & turq.	25	15

166. "Food Production". **167.** "Family Scales"

1965. Agricultural Seven-Year Plan.

No.	Type	Description	Unused	Used
588.	166.	4 w. brn., blk. & green	25	15

1965. Family-Planning Month.

No.	Type	Description	Unused	Used
589.	167.	4 w. green and drab	25	15

168. I.T.U. Emblem and Symbols.

1965. I.T.U. Cent.

No.	Type	Description	Unused	Used
591.	168.	4 w. black, red & blue	25	15

1965. Five-Year Plan. Dated "1965". As T **136.**

No.	Type	Description	Unused	Used
593.		4 w. ultramarine and pink	15	10
594.		4 w. sepia and brown	15	10

DESIGNS: No. 593, Ship at quayside and crates. 594, Fertiliser plant and wheat.

169. Flags of Australia, Belgium, Great Britain, Canada and Colombia.

1965. Outbreak of Korean War. 15th Anniv.

No.	Type	Description	Unused	Used
595.	169.	4 w. multicoloured	20	10
596.	–	4 w. multicoloured	20	10
597.	–	4 w. multicoloured	20	10
598.	–	4 w. multicoloured	20	10
599.	–	10 w. multicoloured	50	30

DESIGNS (U.N. Emblem and flags of): No. 596, Denmark, Ethiopia, France, Greece and India. 597, Italy, Luxemburg, Netherlands, New Zealand and Norway. 598, Philippines, Sweden, Thailand, Turkey and South Africa. 599, General MacArthur and flags of Korea, U.N. and U.S.A.

170. Flag and Sky-writing ("20"). **171.** Ants and Leaf.

1965. Liberation. 20th Anniv.

No.	Type	Description	Unused	Used
601.	170.	4 w. red, violet-blue and blue	15	8
602.	–	10 w. red, blue and violet-blue	40	15

DESIGN: 10 w. South Gate and fireworks.

1965. Savings Campaign.

No.	Type	Description	Unused	Used
603.	171.	4 w. sepia, ochre & grn.	15	5

172. Hoisting Flag. **173.** Radio Aerial.

1965. Recapture of Seoul. 15th Anniv.

No.	Type	Description	Unused	Used
604.	172.	3 w. olive, bl. & salmon	20	8

1965. Korean Telecommunications. 80th Anniv. Inscr. "1865–1965".

No.	Type	Description	Unused	Used
605.	173.	3 w. green, black & blue	10	8
606.	–	10 w. blk., blue & yell.	25	20

DESIGN: 10 w. Telegraphist of 1885.

1965. Flood Relief. As No. 545, but colour changed and inscr. with premium.

No.	Type	Description	Unused	Used
706.		4 w.+2 w. blue	30	15

174. Pole-vaulting.

1965. National Athletic Meeting, Kwangju.

No.	Type	Description	Unused	Used
608.	174.	3 w. multicoloured	20	8

1965. Aid for Children. As No. 545, but colour changed and inscr. with premium.

No.	Type	Description	Unused	Used
699.		4 w.+2 w. purple	35	15

175. I.C.Y. Emblem.

1965. Int. Co-operation Year and 20th Anniv. of U.N. Inscr. "1955.10.24".

No.	Type	Description	Unused	Used
610.	175.	3 w. red, apple & green	20	8
611.	–	10 w. ultram., grn. & bl.	30	8

DESIGN—VERT. 10 w. U.N. Flag and Head-quarters.

176. Child posting Letter. **177.** Children with Toboggan.

1965. 10th Communications Day.

No.	Type	Description	Unused	Used
613.	176.	3 w. multicoloured	15	10
614.	–	10 w. red, blue & green	30	15

DESIGN: 10 w. Airmail envelope and telephone receiver.

1965. New Year.

No.	Type	Description	Unused	Used
615.	177.	3 w. ultram., red & grn.	25	15
616.	–	4 w. ult., red & turq.	12	5

DESIGN: 4 w. Boy and girl in traditional costume.

178. Freedom House. **179.** Mandarin Duck.

1966. Opening of Freedom House, Panmunjom.

No.	Type	Description	Unused	Used
618.	178.	7 w. black, emer. & grn.	20	15
619.		39 w. black, lilac & grn.	60	30

1966. Korean Birds. Multicoloured.

No.	Type	Description	Unused	Used
621.		3 w. Type **179**	20	12
622.		5 w. Manchurian crane	25	15
623.		7 w. Mongolian ring-necked pheasant	30	20

180. Pine Forest. **181.** Printing Press and Pen.

1966. Reafforestation Campaign.

No.	Type	Description	Unused	Used
625.	180.	7 w. brown and green	20	12

1966. 10th Newspaper Day.

No.	Type	Description	Unused	Used
626.	181.	7 w. maroon, yellow and turquoise	20	12

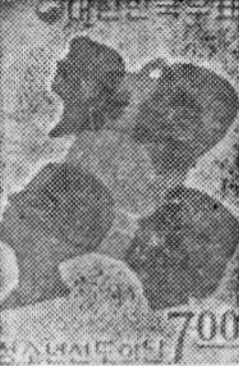

182. Curfew Bell and Young Koreans. **183.** W.H.O. Building.

1966. Youth Guidance Month.

No.	Type	Description	Unused	Used
627.	182.	7 w. orge., grn. & blue	20	10

1966. W.H.O. Headquarters, Geneva. Inaug.

No.	Type	Description	Unused	Used
628.	183.	7 w. blk., yell. & blue	12	8
629.		39 w. red, yellow & lav.	40	25

184. Pres. Pak, Handclasp and Flags.

1966. Pres. Pak Chung Hi's State Tour of South-East Asia.

No.	Type	Description	Unused	Used
631.	184.	7 w. blk., bl., red & yell.	20	10

185. Girl Scout and Flag.

1966. Korean Girl Scouts. 20th Anniv.

No.	Type	Description	Unused	Used
632.	185.	7 w. blk., grn. & yellow	25	15

186. Student and Ewha Women's University. **187.** Alaska Pollack.

1966. Korean Women's Education. 80th Anniv.

No.	Type	Description	Unused	Used
633.	186.	7 w. multicoloured	20	10

1966. 5-Year Plan. Dated "1966". As T **136.**

No.	Type	Description	Unused	Used
634.		7 w. ultramarine and blue	15	10
635.		7 w. black and yellow	15	10

DESIGNS: No. 634, Map and transport. 635, Radar aerials and telephone.

1966. Korean Fishes. Multicoloured.

No.	Type	Description	Unused	Used
637.		3 w. Type **187**	15	10
638.		5 w. Manchurian trout	15	10
639.		7 w. Yellow corvina	20	15

188. Incense-burner. **188a.** Buddha, Kwanchok Temple.

1966. Inscr. "REPUBLIC OF KOREA".

No.	Type	Description	Unused	Used
641.	134b.	60 ch. green	8	5
642.	134c.	1 wn. green	8	8
643.	122a.	2 wn. green	8	8
644.	123.	3 wn. brown	8	8
645.	134d.	5 wn. blue	10	5
646.	134e.	7 wn. blue	15	5
647.	188.	13 wn. blue	20	8
709.	134f.	20 wn. grn., & lt. grn.	20	10
710.	134g.	40 wn. grn. & olive	40	15
711.	134h.	50 wn. brn. & bistre	50	25
648.	–	60 wn. green	60	20
649.	188a.	80 wn. green	90	30

DESIGN—As T **188.** 60 wn. 12th-century Porcelain vessel.

189. Children and Hemispheres.

1966. 15th Assembly of World Conf. of Teaching Profession (WCOTP), Seoul.

No.	Type	Description	Unused	Used
650.	189.	7 w. violet, chest. & blue	50	50

190. Factory within Pouch.

1966. Savings Campaign.

No.	Type	Description	Unused	Used
652.	190.	7 w. multicoloured	20	10

191. People on Map of Korea.

1966. National Census.

No.	Type	Description	Unused	Used
653.	191.	7 w. multicoloured	20	10

192. Beetle.

1966. Insects. Multicoloured.

No.	Type	Description	Unused	Used
654.		3 w. Type **192**	15	10
655.		5 w. Grasshopper	15	12
656.		7 w. Butterfly	20	15

193. C.I.S.M. Emblem and "Round Table" Meeting. **194.** Soldiers and Flags.

1966. Int. Military Sports Council (C.I.S.M.) 21st General Assembly, Seoul.
658. **193.** 7 w. multicoloured .. 20 10

1966. Korean Troops in Vietnam. 1st Anniv.
660. **194.** 7 w. multicoloured .. 25 15

195. Wrestling. **196.** Lions Emblem and Map.

1966. 47th Athletic Meeting, Seoul.
661. **195.** 7 w. multicoloured .. 25 10

1966. 5th Orient and South-East Asian Lions Convention, Seoul.
662. **196.** 7 w. multicoloured .. 20 10

197. University Emblem " 20 " and Shields.

1966. Seoul University. 20th Anniv.
664. **197.** 7 w. multicoloured .. 25 10

198. A.P.A.C.L. Emblem.

1966. Asian People's Anti-Communist League (A.P.A.C.L.), Seoul. 12th Conf.
665. **198.** 7 w. multicoloured .. 20 10

199. Presidents Pak and Johnson. **200.** U.N.E.S.C.O. Symbols and Emblem.

1966. President Johnson's Visit to Korea.
667. **199.** 7 w. multicoloured .. 25 10
668. 83 w. multicoloured .. 75 50

1966. U.N.E.S.C.O. 20th Anniv.
670. **200.** 7 w. multicoloured .. 15 10

1966. Hurricane Relief. As No. 646 but colour changed and premium added.
672. 7 w.+2 w. red 30 20

201. " Lucky Bag ". **202.** Badger.

1969. Christmas and New Year. Multicoloured.
673. 5 w. Type **201** 15 8
674. 7 w. Sheep (vert.) 25 10

1966. Korean Fauna. Multicoloured.
676. 3 w. Type **202** 15 10
677. 5 w. Bear 15 10
678. 7 w. Tiger 25 15

203. " Syncom " Satellite. **204.** Presidents Pak and Lubke.

1967. Korea's Admission to I.T.U. 15th Anniv.
680. **203.** 7 w. multicoloured .. 25 10

1967. Visit of Pres. Lubke of West Germany to Korea.
683. **204.** 7 w. multicoloured .. 5 5

205. Coin, Factories and Houses. **206.** Okwangdae Mask.

1967. Korean Revenue Office. 1st Anniv.
684. **205.** 7 w. sepia and green .. 20 10

1967. Folklore. Multicoloured.
685. 4 w. Type **206** 12 8
686. 5 w. Sandi mask 15 8
687. 7 w. Mafoe mask 20 15
The 5 w. is horiz.

207. J.C.I. Emblem and Pavilion. **208.** Map Emblem.

1967. Int. Junior Chamber of Commerce Conf., Seoul.
689. **207.** 7 w. blue, green, red and brown 15 10

1967. 5th Asian Pacific Dental Congress, Seoul.
691. **208.** 7 w. multicoloured .. 15 10

209. Korean Pavilion. **210** Worker and Soldier.

1967. World Fair, Montreal.
693. **209.** 7 w. black, red & yellow 20 15
694. 83 w. black, red & blue 80 50

1967. Veterans' Day.
696. **210.** 7 w. multicoloured .. 15 10

211. Wheel and Rail. **212.** Sword Dance.

1967. 2nd Five Year Plan.
697. **211.** 7 w. black, yell. & chest 15 10
698. – 7 w. orge., brown & blk. 15 10
DESIGN: No. 698, Nut and bolt.
See also 773/4, 833/4, 895/6 and 981/2.

1967. Folklore. Multicoloured.
699. 4 w. Type **212** 12 8
700. 5 w. Peace dance (vert.) .. 15 8
701. 7 w. Buddhist dance (vert.) 8 5

213. Soldier and Family. **214.** President Pak and Phoenix.

1967. Korean Troops Serving in Vietnam Fund.
703. **213.** 7 w.+3 w. black & pur. 10 10

1967. Inaug. of President Pak for 2nd Term.
704. **214.** 7 w. multicoloured .. 5 5

215. Scout, Badge and Camp.

1967. 3rd Korean Scout Jamboree. Multicoloured.
706. 7 w. Type **215** 5 5
707. 20 w. Scout badge, bridge and tent 12 5

216. Girls on Swing.

1967. Folklore. Multicoloured.
712. 4 w. Type **216** 12 8
713. 5 w. Girls on seesaw (vert.) 15 8
714. 7 w. Girls dancing (vert.) .. 20 15

217. Freedom Centre. **218.** Boxing.

1967. 1st World Anti-Communist League Conf., Taipei. Multicoloured.
716. 5 w. Type **217** 12 8
717. 7 w. Hand grasping chain (vert.) 15 10

1967. National Athletic Meeting, Seoul. Mult.
719. 5 w. Type **218** 15 8
720. 7 w. Basketball 20 10

219. Student's Memorial, Kwangjoo. **220.** Decade Emblem.

1967. Student's Day.
721. **219.** 7 w. multicoloured .. 20 10

1967. Int. Hydrological Decade.
722. **220.** 7 w. multicoloured .. 20 10

221. Children spinning Top. **222.** Playing Shuttlecock.

1967. Christmas and New Year.
723. 5 w. blue, verm. & pink .. 15 8
724. 7 w. brn., blue & bistre .. 20 10
DESIGNS: 5 w. Type **221.** 7 w. Monkey and Signs of the Zodiac.

1967. Folklore. Multicoloured.
726. 4 w. Type **222** 10 5
727. 5 w. "Dalmaji" (horiz.) .. 15 5
728. 7 w. Archery 20 10

223. Micro-wave Transmitter.

1967. Micro-wave Telecommunications Service. Inaug.
730. **223.** 7 w. black, yellow, green and blue 20 10

224. Carving, King Songdok's Bell. **224a.** 5th-6th century Earrings. **224b.** Korean Flag.

1968.
732. **224.** 1 w. brown & yellow 5 5
733. **224a.** 5 w. yellow & green .. 8 5
734. **224b.** 7 w. red and blue .. 10 8
For designs similar to T **224b** see Nos. 771, 780, 787/8 and 827.

225. W.H.O. Emblem **226.** E.A.T.A. Emblem and Korean Motif.

1968. W.H.O. 20th Anniv.
735. **225.** 7 w. multicoloured .. 20 10

1968. East Asia Travel Association (E.A.T.A.) 2nd Conf., Seoul.
737. **226.** 7 w. multicoloured .. 20 10

227. C.A.C.C.I. Emblem, Korean Door-knocker and factories. **228.** Pres. Pak and Emperor Haile Selassie.

1968. 2nd Conference of Confederation of Asian Chambers of Commerce and Industry (C.A.C.C.I.), Seoul.
739. **227.** 7 w. multicoloured .. 20 10

1968. Visit of Emperor of Ethiopia.
741. **228.** 7 w. multicoloured .. 25 10

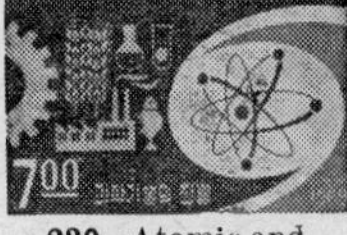

229. Post-bag. **230.** Atomic and Development Symbols.

1968. Postman's Day. Multicoloured.
743. 5 w. Type **229** 10 8
744. 7 w. Postman 15 10

1968. Promotion of Science and Technology.
745. **230.** 7 w. bl., green & red 20 10

231. Kyung Hi University and Conference Emblem. **232.** "Liberation".

1968. 2nd Conf. of Int. Assn. of University Presidents.
746. **231.** 7 w. multicoloured .. 15 10

1968. Liberation of Suppressed People's Campaign.
748. **232.** 7 w. multicoloured .. 15 10

233. Reservist. **234.** Stylised Peacock.

1968. Army Reservists' Fund.
749. **233.** 7 w.+3 w. black & grn. 50 30

1968. Republic. 20th Anniv.
750. **234.** 7 w. multicoloured .. 15 10

235. Fair Entrance. **236.** Assembly Emblem.

1968. 1st Korean Trade Fair, Seoul.
751. **235.** 7 w. multicoloured .. 20 12

1968. 3rd General Assembly of Asian Pharmaceutical Assn. Federation.
752. **236.** 7 w. multicoloured .. 15 10

237. Scout Badge.

238. Soldier and Battle Scene.

1968. 6th Far East Scout Conf., Seoul.
753. **237.** 7 w. multicoloured .. 20 10

1968. Korean Armed Forces. 20th Anniv. Multicoloured.
754. 7 w. Type **238** .. 15 12
755. 7 w. Sailor & naval guns 15 12
756. 7 w. Servicemen and flags 15 12
757. 7 w. Airman and fighters 15 12
758. 7 w. Marine and landings 15 12
Nos. 754/8 were issued together vertically se-tenant in strips of five within the sheet.

239. Colombo Plan Emblem and Globe.

1968. 19th Meeting of Colombo Plan Consultative Committee, Seoul.
759. **239.** 7 w. multicoloured .. 20 15

240. (I). Olympic Emblems. **241.** (II).

1968. Olympic Games, Mexico. Multicoloured.
760. 7 w. Type **240** 15 8
761. 7 w. Type **241** 15 8
762. 7 w. Cycling (I) 15 8
763. 7 w. Cycling (II) 15 8
764. 7 w. Boxing (I) 15 8
765. 7 w. Boxing (II) 15 8
766. 7 w. Wrestling (I) .. 15 8
767. 7 w. Wrestling (II) .. 15 8
The two types of each design may be identified by the position of the country name at the foot of the design—ranged right in types I, and left in types II. On three of the designs (excluding "Cycling") the figures of value are on left and right respectively. Types I and II of each design were issued together horizontally se-tenant within the sheets of 50 stamps.

242. Statue of Woman.

243. Coin and Symbols.

1968. Women's Secondary Education. 60th Anniv.
769. **242.** 7 w. multicoloured .. 15 8

1968. National Wealth Survey.
770. **243.** 7 w. multicoloured .. 15 8

244. Korean Flag.

245. Shin Eui Ju Memorial.

1968. Disaster Relief Fund.
771. **244.** 7 w. + 3 w. red and blue .. .. .. 1·25 1·00

1968. Anniv. of Student Uprising, Shin Eui Ju (1945).
772. **245.** 7 w. multicoloured .. 15 10

1968. 2nd Five Year Plan. As T **211.** Dated "1968". Multicoloured.
773. 7 w. Express motorway .. 20 10
774. 7 w. "Clover-leaf" road junction 20 10

247. Demonstrators.

248. Christmas Lanterns.

1968. Human Rights Year.
775. **247.** 7 w. multicoloured .. 5 5

1968. Christmas and New Year. Multicoloured.
776. 5 w. Type **248** 15 10
777. 7 w. Cockerel 20 15

249. Korean House and UN Emblems.

250. Korean Flag.

1968. South Korea's Admission to U.N. 20th Anniv.
779. **249.** 7 w. multicoloured .. 15 10

1969. Military Helicopter Fund.
780. **250.** 7 w.+3 w. red, bl. & grn. 35 25

251. Torch and Monument, Pagoda Park, Seoul.

252. Hyun Choong Sa and Turtle Ship.

1969. Samil (Independence) Movement. 50th Anniv.
781. **251.** 7 w. multicoloured .. 20 8

1969. Dedication of Rebuilt Hyun Choong Sa (Shrine of Admiral Li Sun Sin).
782. **252.** 7 w. multicoloured .. 20 8

253. President Pak and Yang di-Pertuan Agong.

254. Stone Temple Lamp.

1969. Visit of Yang di-Pertuan Agong (Malaysian Head-of-State).
783. **253.** 7 w. multicoloured .. 25 15

1969.
785. **134.** 40 ch. green (18×22 mm.) 5 5
786. **254.** 5 wn. purple 5 5
787. **224b.** 7 wn. blue 8 5
788. 7 wn. blue* 8 5
789. **123c.** 10 wn. blue (22×18 mm.) 10 8
790. **224b.** 10 wn. blue 10 8
791. – 20 wn. green 20 10
792. – 30 wn. green 25 12
793. **134g.** 40 wn. blue and pink (18×22 mm.) .. 40 15
794. – 40 wn. mauve & blue 40 12
795. – 100 wn. brn. & purple 1·00 60
DESIGNS—As T **254.** VERT. 20 wn. Wine jug. 40 wn. (No. 794), Porcelain Jar, Yi Dynasty. 100 wn. Seated Buddha (bronze). HORIZ. 30 wn. "Duck" Vase.
*No. 788 has the face value shown as "7" only, omitting the noughts shown on No. 787.

MINIMUM PRICE

The minimum price quoted is 5p which represents a handling charge rather than a basis for valuing common stamps. For further notes about prices see introductory pages.

255. "Red Cross" between Faces.

256. "Building the Nation's Economy".

1969. League of Red Cross Societies. 50th Anniv.
796. **255.** 7 w. multicoloured .. 15 8

1969. "Second Economy Drive".
798. **256.** 7 w. multicoloured .. 15 8

257. Presidents Pak and Nguyen van Thieu.

1969. Visit of President Nguyen van Thieu of South Vietnam.
799. **257.** 7 w. multicoloured .. 20 15

259. Reafforestation and Flooded Fields.

260. Ignition of Second-stage Rocket.

1969. Flood and Drought Damage Prevention Campaign. Multicoloured.
801. 7 w. Type **259** 20 8
802. 7 w. Withered and flourishing plants 20 8

1969. First Man on the Moon.
803. **260.** 10 w. bl., red & blk. .. 12 8
804. – 10 w. bl., red & blk. .. 12 8
805. – 20 w. multicoloured .. 25 10
806. – 20 w. multicoloured .. 25 10
807. – 40 w. bl., red & blk. .. 40 20
DESIGNS: No. 804, Separation of modules from rocket. No. 805, Diagram of lunar orbit. No. 806, Astronauts on Moon. No. 807, Splash-down of "Apollo 11".
Nos. 803/7 were issued together in se-tenant strips of five within the sheet.

261. Stepmother admonishing Kongji. **262.** Steam Locomotive of 1899.

1969. Korean Fairy Tales (1st Series). "Kongji and Patji". Multicoloured.
809. 5 w. Type **261** 8 5
810. 7 w. Kongji and Sparrows 10 8
811. 10 w. Kongji and Ox .. 15 10
812. 20 w. Kongji in Sedan-chair 30 15
See also Nos. 828/32, 839/43, 844/8 and 853/7.

1969. Korean Railways. 70th Anniv. Multicoloured.
814. 7 w. Type **262** 15 8
815. 7 w. Early steam and modern diesel locomotives .. 15 8

263. "F-5A" Fighters.

264. Game of Cha-jun.

1969. Korean Air Force. 20th Anniv. Multicoloured.
816. 10 w. Type **263** 15 8
817. 10 w. "F-4D Phantom" fighter 15 8

1969. 10th Korean Traditional Arts Contest, Taegu.
818. **264.** 7 w. multicoloured .. 15 8

265. Molecule and Institute Building.

266. Presidents Pak and Hamani.

1969. Completion of Korean Institute of Science and Technology.
819. **265.** 7 w. multicoloured .. 15 8

1969. Visit of President Hamani of Niger Republic.
820. **266.** 7 w. multicoloured .. 20 15

267. Football.

269. Students ringing "Education".

1969. National Athletic Meeting. 50th Anniv. Multicoloured.
822. 10 w. Type **267** 15 8
823. 10 w. Volleyball .. 15 8
824. 10 w. Korean wrestling .. 15 8
825. 10 w. Fencing 15 8
826. 10 w. Korean karate .. 15 8
Nos. 824/6 are horiz.

1969. Searchlight Fund. As Type **250**, but inscr. "7+3" only.
827. 7 w.+3 w. blue and red .. 25 15

1969. Korean Fairy Tales. (2nd Series). "The Hare's Liver". As T **261.** Mult.
828. 5 w. Princess and Doctors 8 5
829. 7 w. Hare arriving at Palace 10 8
830. 10 w. Preparing to remove the Hare's liver 15 10
831. 20 w. Escape of the Hare 55 30

1969. Second Five-year Plan. As T **211.** Dated "1969". Multicoloured.
833. 7 w. "Agriculture and Fisheries" 15 8
834. 7 w. Emblems of Industry 15 8

1969. National Education Charter. 1st Anniv.
835. **269.** 7 w. multicoloured .. 15 8

270. Toy Dogs.

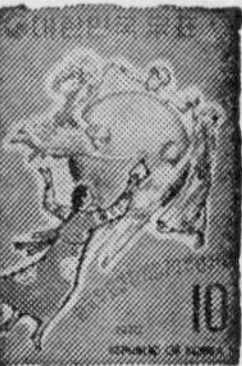

271. Woman with Letter and U.P.U. Monument, Berne.

1969. Lunar New Year ("Year of the Dog"). Multicoloured.
836. 5 w. Type **270** 15 8
837. 7 w. Candle and lattice doorway 20 10

1970. Korea's Admission to U.P.U. 70th Anniv.
838. **271.** 10 w. multicoloured .. 15 8

1970. Korean Fairy Tales. (3rd Series). "The Sun and the Moon". As T **261.** Mult.
839. 5 w. Mother meets the tiger 8 5
840. 7 w. Tiger in disguise .. 10 8
841. 10 w. Children chased up a tree 15 10
842. 20 w. Children escape to Heaven 30 15

1970. Korean Fairy Tales. (4th Series). "The Woodcutter and the Fairy". As T **261.** Mult.
844. 10 w. Woodcutter hiding Fairy's dress 15 10
845. 10 w. Fairy as Woodcutter's Wife 15 10
846. 10 w. Fairy and children fly to Heaven 15 10
847. 10 w. Happy reunion .. 15 10

272. I.E.Y. Emblem and Open Book. 273. Seated Buddha and Korean Pavilion.

1970. Int. Education Year.
849. 272. 10 w. multicoloured .. 15 8

1970. "EXPO 70" World Fair, Osaka, Japan.
850. 273. 10 w. multicoloured .. 15 10

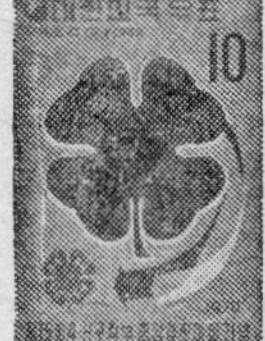

274. "4-H" Club Emblem. 275. Bank Emblem and Cash.

1970. 15th "4-H" Club (young farmers' organization) Central Contest, Suwon.
851. 274. 10 w. multicoloured .. 15 8

1970. 3rd General Meeting of Asian Development Bank, Seoul.
852. 275. 10 w. multicoloured .. 15 8

1970. Korean Fairy Tales (5th Series). "Heungbu and Nolbu". As T 261. Mult.
853. 10 w. Heungbu tending swallow 15 8
854. 10 w. Heungbu finds treasure in pumpkin 15 8
855. 10 w. Nolbu with pumpkin 15 8
856. 10 w. Nolbu chased by devil 15 8

276. Royal Palanquin (Yi dynasty). 277. New Headquarters Building.

1970. Early Korean Transport. Mult.
858. 10 w. Type 276 .. .. 15 8
859. 10 w. Tramcar, 1899 .. 15 8
860. 10 w. Emperor Sunjong's Cadillac, 1903 .. .. 15 8
861. 10 w. An Chang Nam's Nieuport aircraft, 1922 15 8
Nos. 859/61 are horiz.

1970. Opening of New U.P.U. Headquarters Building.
862. 277. 10 w. multicoloured .. 15 12

278. Dish Aerial and Hemispheres.

1970. Satellite Communications Station, Kum San, Inaug.
863. 278. 10 w. multicoloured .. 15 10

279. "PEN" and Quill Pen. 281. Postal Code Symbol.

280. Section of Motorway.

1970. 37th Int. P.E.N. (literary organization) Congress, Seoul.
864. 279. 10 w. multicoloured .. 15 10

1970. Opening of Seoul-Pusan Motorway.
865. 280. 10 w. multicoloured .. 15 10

1970. Introduction of Postal Codes.
866. 281. 10 w. multicoloured .. 15 10

282. Parcel Sorting Area. 283. Children's Hall and Boy.

1970. Postal Mechanisation. Inaug.
867. 282. 10 w. multicoloured .. 15 10

1970. Opening of Children's Hall, Seoul.
869. 283. 10 w. multicoloured .. 15 10

284. "Mountain and River" (Yi In Moon).

1970. Korean Paintings of Yi Dynasty (1st Series). Multicoloured.
870. 10 w. Type 284 .. .. 15 10
871. 10 w. "Jongyangsa Temple" (Chong Son) .. 15 10
872. 10 w. "Mountain and River by Moonlight" (Kim Doo Ryang) (vert.) 15 10
See also Nos. 887/90, 897/900, 947/53, 956/9 and 961/6.

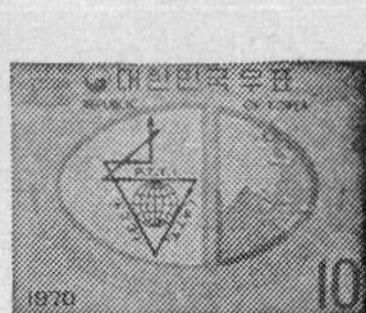

285. P.T.T.I. Emblem. 286. WAC and Corps Badge.

1970. Councillors' Meeting, Asian Chapter of Postal, Telegraph and Telephone International (Post Office Trade Union Federation).
874. 285. 10 w. multicoloured .. 15 10

1970. Korean Women's Army Corps. 20th Anniv.
875. 286. 10 w. multicoloured .. 15 10

286a. Pres. Pak and Flag.

1970.
876. 286a. 10 w. multicoloured 20 15
877. – 10 w. blk., grn. & blue 20 15
DESIGN—VERT. No. 877, Pres. Pak and industrial complex.

287. Presidents Pak and Sanchez Hernandez.

1970. Visit of Pres. Hernandez of El Salvador.
878. 287. 10 w. multicoloured .. 15 10

288. "People and Houses".

1970. National Census.
880. 288. 10 w. multicoloured .. 8 5

289. Diving.

1970. 51st National Athletic Games, Seoul. Multicoloured.
881. 10 w. Type 289 .. .. 15 12
882. 10 w. Hockey 15 12
883. 10 w. Baseball 15 12

289a. Police Badge and Activities. 290. Bell and Globe.

1970. National Police Day.
885. 289a. 10 w. multicoloured 15 10

1970. United Nations. 25th Anniv.
886. 290. 10 w. multicoloured .. 15 10

1970. Korean Paintings of the Yi Dynasty. (2nd Series). Vert. designs as T 284, showing animals. Multicoloured.
887. 30 w. "Fierce Tiger" (Shim Sa Yung) 30 15
888. 30 w. "Cats and Sparrows" (Pyun Sang Byuk) .. 30 15
889. 30 w. "Dogs" (Yi Am) .. 30 15

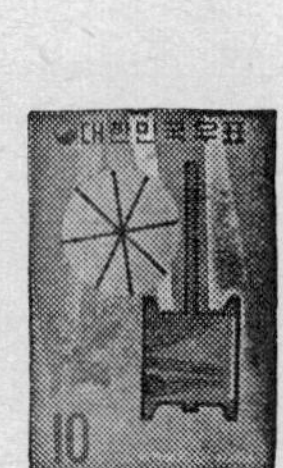

291. Kite and Parasol. 294. Fields "Food Production".

292. Quotation and Emblems on Globe.

1970. Lunar New Year ("Year of the Pig"). Multicoloured.
891. 10 w. Type 291 .. .. 10 8
892. 10 w. Toy pig 10 8

1970. 15th Communications Day.
894. 292. 10 w. multicoloured .. 15 8

1970. 2nd Five Year Plan. As T 211. Dated "1970". Multicoloured.
895. 10 w. "Port Development" 15 8
896. 10 w. "House Construction" 15 8

1970. Korean Paintings of the Yi Dynasty (3rd Series). Vert. designs as T 284. Mult.
897. 10 w. "Chokpyokdo" (river cliff) (Kim Hong Do) .. 15 10
898. 10 w. "Hen and Chicks" ("Hwajae"—Pyon Sang-Byok) 15 10
899. 10 w. "The Flute-player" (Shin Yun Bok) .. 15 10

1971. Economic Development. (1st Series.) Multicoloured.
901. 10 w. Type 294 .. .. 15 8
902. 10 w. Dam ("Electric Power") (horiz.) .. 15 8
903. 10 w. Map on crate ("Exports") (horiz.) .. 15 8
See also Nos. 905/8 and 910/13.

295. Coal-mining. 296 Globe, Torch and Spider.

1971. Economic Development (2nd series) Multicoloured.
905. 10 w. Type 295 .. .. 15 8
906. 10 w. Cement works (vert.) 15 8
907. 10 w. Fertilizer plant .. 15 8

1971. Anti-Espionage Month.
909. 296. 10 w. multicoloured .. 15 8

297. Motorway Junction. 298. Reservist and Badge.

1971. Economic Development (3rd series). Multicoloured.
910. 10 w. Type 297 .. .. 12 8
911. 10 w. Scales ("Gross National Income") (horiz.) .. 12 8
912. 10 w. Bee and coins ("Increased Savings") (horiz.) 12 8

1971. Homeland Reserve Forces Day.
914. 298. 10 w. multicoloured .. 15 8

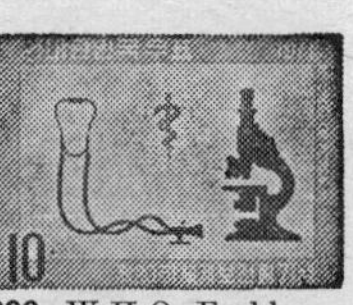

299. W.H.O. Emblem, Stethoscope and Microscope. 300. Underground Train.

1971. 20th World Health Day.
915. 299. 10 w. multicoloured .. 15 8

1971. Construction of Seoul Underground Railway System.
916. 300. 10 w. multicoloured .. 15 8

301. Footballer. 302. Veteran and Association Flag.

1971. First Asian Soccer Games, Seoul.
917. 301. 10 w. multicoloured .. 20 10

1971. 20th Korean Veterans' Day.
918. 302. 10 w. multicoloured .. 15 8

303. Girl Scouts. 304. Torch and Symbols.

1971. Korean Girl Scouts Federation. 25th Anniv.
919. 303. 10 w. multicoloured .. 20 10

1971. May 16th Revolution. 10th Anniv.
920. 304. 10 w. multicoloured .. 15 8

305. "Telecommunications". 306. I.L.O. Emblem.

1971. 3rd World Telecommunications Day.
921. **305.** 10 w. multicoloured .. 8 5

1971. "The Work of the United Nations Organization".

922. **306.**	10 w. mauve, blk. & grn.	10	8
923. –	10 w. bl., blk. & mauve	10	8
924. –	10 w. multicoloured ..	10	8
925. –	10 w. bl., blk. & mauve	10	8
926. –	10 w. mauve, blk. & grn.	10	8
927. –	10 w. bl., blk. & mauve	10	8
928. –	10 w. mauve, blk. & bl.	10	8
929. –	10 w. blk., grn. & mauve	10	8
930. –	10 w. mauve, blk. & bl.	10	8
931. –	10 w. bl., blk. & mauve	10	8
932. –	10 w. mauve, blk. & bl.	10	8
933. –	10 w. blk., mauve & grn.	10	8
934. –	10 w. mauve, bl. & blk.	10	8
935. –	10 w. blk., mauve & grn.	10	8
936. –	10 w. mauve, blk. & blue	10	8
937. –	10 w bl., blk. & mauve	10	8
938. –	10 w. mauve, blk. & blue	10	8
939. –	10 w. blk. mauve & grn.	10	8
940. –	10 w. mauve, blk. & blue	10	8
941. –	10 w. blue, blk. & mauve	10	8
942. –	10 w. mauve, blk. & grn.	10	8
943. –	10 w. blk., blue & mauve	10	8
944. –	10 w. multicoloured ..	10	8
945. –	10 w. blk., blue & mauve	10	8
946. –	10 w. blk., mauve & grn.	10	8

EMBLEMS: No. 923, Food and Agriculture Organization. No. 924, General Assembly and New York Headquarters. No. 925, U.N.E.S.C.O. No. 926, W.H.O. No. 927, World Bank. No. 928, International Development Association. No. 929, Security Council. No. 930, International Finance Corporation. No. 931, International Monetary Fund. No. 932, International Aviation Organization. No. 933, Economic and Social Council. No. 934, South Korean Flag. No. 935, Trusteeship Council. No. 936, U.P.U. No. 937, I.T.U. No. 938, World Meteorological Organization. No. 939, Int. Court of Justice. No. 940, I.M.C.O. No. 941, U.N.I.C.E.F. No. 942, International Atomic Energy Agency. No. 943, United Nations Industrial Development Organization. No. 944, United Nations Commission for the Unification and Rehabilitation of Korea. No. 945, United Nations Development Programme. No. 946, United Nations Conference on Trade and Development.

Nos. 922/46 were issued se-tenant within the sheet.

307. "Boating" (Shin Yun Bok).

1971. Korean Paintings of the Yi Dynasty (4th series). Multicoloured.

947.	10 w. Type **307**	15	10
948.	10 w. "Greeting Travellers"	15	10
949.	10 w. "Tea Ceremony" ..	15	10
950.	10 w. "Lady and Servants on Country Road" ..	15	10
951.	10 w. "Couple Walking" ..	15	10
952.	10 w. "Fairy and Boy beneath Pine Tree" (Lee Chae Kwan) (vert.) ..	15	10

Nos. 947/51, representing a selection of Shin Yun-bok's "Folk Customs" paintings, were issued together, vertically se-tenant within the sheet.

308. Pres. Pak, Emblem and Motorway.

309. "Chasing the Cat" (Kim Deuk Shin).

1971. Re-election of Pres. Pak for 3rd Term.
954. **308.** 10 w. multicoloured .. 60 60

1971. Korean Paintings of the Yi Dynasty (5th series). Multicoloured.

956.	10 w. Type **309**	15	10
957.	10 w. "Valley Family" (Lee Chae Kwan) (vert.)	15	10
958.	10 w. "Man Reading" (Lee Chae Kwan) (vert.) ..	15	10

1971. 13th World Scout Jamboree, Asagiri, Japan.
960. **310.** 10 w. multicoloured .. 20 10

310. Camp Fire and Badge.

311. Classroom.

1971. Korean Painting of the Yi Dynasty (6th series). Multicoloured.

961.	10 w. Type **311**	15	10
962.	10 w. "Wrestling Match"	15	10
963.	10 w. "Dancer with Musicians"	15	10
964.	10 w. "Weavers"	15	10
965.	10 w. "Drawing Water at the Well"	15	10

Nos. 961/5, representing a selection of Kim Hong-do's genre paintings, were issued horizontally se-tenant within the sheet.

312. Cogwheel and Asian Map.

1971. Asian Labour Ministers' Conference, Seoul.
967. **312.** 10 w. multicoloured .. 20 10

313. Judo.

1971. 52nd National Athletic Meeting, Seoul. Multicoloured.

969. **313.**	10 w. bl., blk. & flesh	15	8
970. –	10 w. multicoloured ..	15	8

DESIGN: No. 970, Archery.

314. Korean symbol on Palette.

1971. 20th National Fine Art Exhib.
972. **314.** 10 w. multicoloured .. 15 8

315. Doctor and Globe.

316. Emblems and "Vocational Skills".

1971. 7th Congress of Medical Associations from Asia and Oceania.
973. **315.** 10 w. multicoloured .. 15 8

1971. 2nd National Vocational Skill Contest for High School Students.
976. **316.** 10 w. multicoloured .. 12 8

317. Callipers and "K" Emblem.

1971. Industrial Standardisation. 10th Anniv.
976. **317.** 10 w. multicoloured .. 12 8

318. Fairy Tale Rats.

319. Emblem and Hangul Alphabet.

1971. Lunar New Year ("Year of the Rat"). Multicoloured.

977.	10 w. Type **318**	12	8
978.	10 w. Flying Crane ..	12	8

1971. Hangul Hakhoe (Korean Language Research Society). 50th Anniv.
980. **319.** 10 w. multicoloured .. 12 8

1971. 2nd Five-Year Plan. As T **211**. Dated "1971". Multicoloured.

981.	10 w. Atomic power plant	12	8
982.	10 w. Hydro-electric power project	12	8

320. Korean Red Cross Building on Map.

321. Globe and Open Book.

1971. South-North Korean Red Cross Conference, Panmunjom.
983. **320.** 10 w. multicoloured .. 12 8

1971. Int. Book Year.
985. **321.** 10 w. multicoloured .. 20 10

322. "Intelsat 4" and Korean Earth Station.

323. Speed-skating.

1971. Korean's Membership of I.T.U. 20th Anniv.
987. **322.** 10 w. multicoloured .. 15 10

1972. Winter Olympic Games, Sapporo, Japan. Multicoloured.

988.	10 w. Type **323** ..	15	10
989.	10 w. Figure-skating ..	15	10

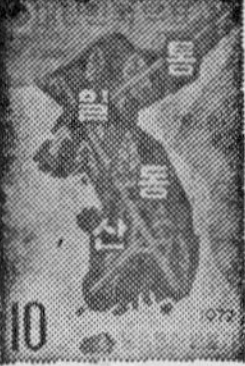

324. Forestry Map.

326. E.C.A.F.E. Emblem and Industrial Symbols.

325. Beetles and J.C.I. Emblem.

1972. "Trees for Unity" Campaign.
991. **324.** 10 w. multicoloured .. 12 8

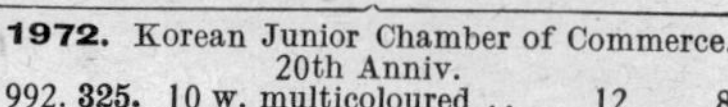

1972. Korean Junior Chamber of Commerce. 20th Anniv.
992. **325.** 10 w. multicoloured .. 12 8

1972. Economic Commission for Asia and the Far East. 25th Anniv.
993. **326.** 10 w. multicoloured .. 12 8

327. Flags of Member Countries.

328. Reserve Forces' Flag.

1972. Asian and Oceanic Postal Union. 10th Anniv.
994. **327.** 10 w. multicoloured .. 12 8

1972. Homeland Reserve Forces Day.
995. **328.** 10 w. multicoloured 12 8

329. Y.W.C.A. Emblem and Butterflies.

330. Rural Activities.

1972. Korean Young Women's Christian Association. 50th Anniv.
996. **329.** 10 w. multicoloured .. 15 10

1972. "New Community" (rural development) Movement.
997. **330.** 10 w. multicoloured .. 12 8

331. "Anti-Espionage" and Korean Flag.

332. Children with Balloons.

1972. Anti-Espionage Month.
998. **331.** 10 w. multicoloured .. 12 8

1972. 50th Children's Day.
999. **332.** 10 w. multicoloured .. 12 8

333. Leaf Ornament from Gold Crown.

335. Kalkot, Koje Island, Hanryo Straits Park.

334. Lake Paengnekdam, Mt. Halla Park.

1972. Treasures from King Munyong's Tomb. Multicoloured.

1000.	10 w. Type **333**	12	8
1001.	10 w. Gold earrings (horiz.)	12	8

1972. National Parks (1st series).

1002. **334.**	10 w. multicoloured	12	8
1003. **335.**	10 w. multicoloured	12	8

See also Nos. 1018/19 and 1026/7.

336. Marguerite and Conference Emblem.

337. Gwanghwa Gate and National Flags.

1972. U.N. Environmental Conservation Conference, Stockholm.

1004. 336. 10 w. multicoloured 15 8

1972. 7th Asian and Pacific Council (ASPAC) Ministerial Meeting, Seoul.

1006. 337. 10 w. multicoloured 12 8

338. Pasture ("Development of Rural Economy"). 339. "Love Pin".

1972. 3rd Five-Year Plan. Dated "1972". Multicoloured.

1007. 10 w. Type 338 .. .. 12 8

1008. 10 w. Foundry ladle ("Heavy Industries") 12 8

1009. 10 w. Crate and Globe ("Increased Exports") 12 8

1972. Disaster Relief Fund.

1010. 339. 10 w.+5 w. mult. .. 25 20

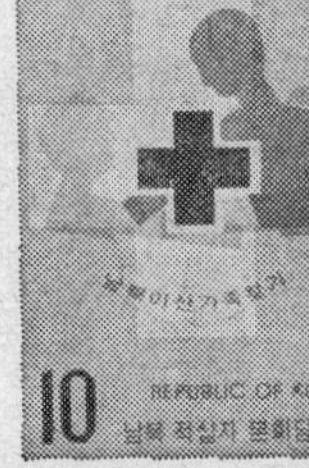

340. Judo. 341. Family Reunion through Red Cross.

1972. Olympic Games, Munich. Multicoloured.

1011. 20 w. Type 340 .. .. 25 15

1012. 20 w. Weightlifting .. 25 15

1013. 20 w. Wrestling 25 15

1014. 20 w. Boxing 25 15

1972. 1st Plenary Meeting of South-North Korean Red Cross Conference, Pyongyang.

1016. 341. 10 w. multicoloured 10 5

342. Bulkuk-sa Temple, Kyongju Park. 344. Conference Emblem within "5".

343. Statue and Bopju-sa Temple, Mt. Sokri Park.

1972. National Park (2nd series).

1018. 342. 10 w. multicoloured 10 5

1019. 343. 10 w. multicoloured 10 5

1972. 5th Asian Judicial Conf., Seoul.

1020. 344. 10 w. multicoloured 10 5

345. Lions Badge between Korean Emblem.

1972. 11th Orient and South-East Asian Lions Convention, Seoul.

1021. 345. 10 w. multicoloured 10 5

346. Scout taking Oath. 347. Dolls and Ox's Head.

1972. Korean Boy Scouts Movement. 50th Anniv.

1022. 346. 10 w. multicoloured 8 10

1972. Lunar New Year ("Year of the Ox"). Multicoloured.

1023. 10 w. Type 347 .. .. 10 8

1024. 10 w. Revellers in balloon 10 8

348. Temple, Mt. Naejang Park. 349. Madeungryong Palace, Mt. Sorak Park.

1972. National Parks. (3rd series).

1026. 348. 10 w. multicoloured 10 8

1027. 349. 10 w. multicoloured 10 8

350. President Pak, Flag and "Development".

1972. Re-election of President Pak.

1028. 350. 10 w. multicoloured 10 8

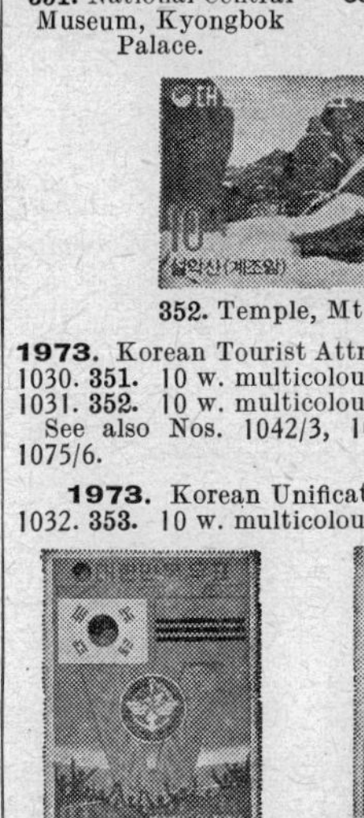

351. National Central Museum, Kyongbok Palace. 353. Korean Family.

352. Temple, Mt. Sorak.

1973. Korean Tourist Attractions (1st series).

1030. 351. 10 w. multicoloured 10 8

1031. 352. 10 w. multicoloured 10 8

See also Nos. 1042/3, 1048/9, 1057/8 and 1075/6.

1973. Korean Unification Campaign.

1032. 353. 10 w. multicoloured 10 8

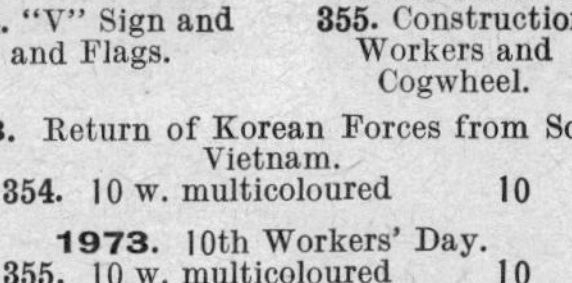

354. "V" Sign and Flags. 355. Construction Workers and Cogwheel.

1973. Return of Korean Forces from South Vietnam.

1033. 354. 10 w. multicoloured 10 8

1973. 10th Workers' Day.

1034. 355. 10 w. multicoloured 10 8

356. W.M.O. Emblem and Satellite. 357. Kujangbok (King's) Costume.

1973. World Meteorological Organization. Centenary.

1035. 356. 10 w. multicoloured .. 10 8

1973. Korean Court Costumes of the Yi Dynasty (1st series). Multicoloured. Background colours given.

1037. 357. 10 w. orange.. .. 8 5

1038. – 10 w. orange.. .. 8 5

DESIGN: No. 1038, Wonsam (queen's) costume.

See also Nos. 1045/6, 1053/4, 1060/2 and 1078/9.

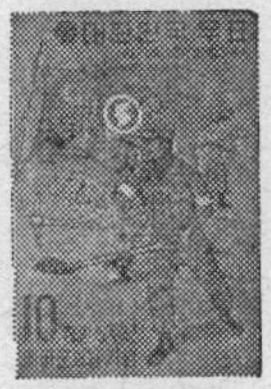

358. Nurse with Lamp. 359. Reservists and Flag.

1973. Korean Nurses' Association. 50th Anniv.

1040. 358. 10 w. multicoloured 8 5

1973. Home Reserve Forces Day.

1041. 359. 10 w. multicoloured 8 5

360. Palmi Island. 361. Sain-am Rock, Mt. Dokjol.

1973. Korean Tourist Attractions (2nd series).

1042. 360. 10 w. multicoloured 8 5

1043. 361. 10 w. multicoloured 8 5

362. Table-tennis Player.

1973. Victory of Korean Women's Team in World Table-tennis Championships, Sarajevo.

1044. 362. 10 w. multicoloured 5 5

1973. Korean Court Costumes of the Yi Dynasty (2nd series). As T 357. Multicoloured. Background colours given.

1045. 10 w. purple 8 5

1046. 10 w. green 8 5

DESIGNS: No. 1045, Konryongpo (king's) costume. No. 1046, Jokui (queen's) costume.

363. Admiral Li Sun Sin's Shrine, Asan. 364. Limestone Cavern, Kusan-ni.

1973. Korean Tourist Attractions (3rd series).

1048. 363. 10 w. multicoloured 5 5

1049. 364. 10 w. multicoloured 5 5

365. Children's Choir.

1973. World Vision Int. 25th Anniv.

1050. 365. 10 w. multicoloured 8 5

366. Love Pin and "Disasters".

1973. Disaster Relief Fund.

1051. 366. 10 w.+5 w. mult. .. 12 10

366a. Steel Converter. 367. Table-tennis Bat and Ball.

1973. Pohang Steel Works. Inaug.

1052. 366a. 10 w. multcoloured 8 5

1973. Korean Court Costumes of the Yi Dynasty. (3rd series). As T 357. Multicoloured. Background colours given.

1053. 10 w. blue 8 5

1054. 10 w. pink 8 5

DESIGNS: No. 1053, Kangsapo (crown prince's) costume. No. 1054, Tangui (princess's) costume.

1973. Table-tennis Gymnasium Construction Fund.

1056. 367. 10 w.+5 w. grn. & red 20 15

368. Namhae Suspension Bridge. 369. Hongdo Island.

1973. Korean Tourist Attractions (4th series).

1057. 368. 10 w. multicoloured 8 5

1058. 369. 10 w. multicoloured 8 5

370. Interpol and Korean Police Emblems.

1973. International Criminal Police Organisation (Interpol). 50th Anniv.

1059. 370. 10 w. multicoloured 8 5

1973. Korean Court Costumes of the Yi Dynasty (4th series). As Type 357. Multicoloured. Background colours given.

1060. 10 w. yellow 8 5

1061. 10 w. blue 8 5

DESIGNS: No. 1060, Kumkwanchobok (court official's) costume. No. 1061, Hwalot (queen's wedding) costume.

371. Japanese Cranes. 372. Sommal Lily. 373. Motorway and Farm.

1973.

1063. 1 w. brown 5 5

1064. – 5 w. brown 5 5

1064a. – 6 w. turq. and green .. 5 5

1065. 371. 10 w. ultram. & blue 8 5

1066. 372. 10 w. red, blk. & grn. 8 5

1067. 373. 10 w. green and red .. 8 5

1068. – 30 w. brown & yellow 25 12

1068a. – 50 w. green & brown 40 20

1068b. – 60 w. brown & yellow 50 25

1069. – 100 w. yellow & brown 80 40

1069a. – 100 w. red 25 12

DESIGNS: 1 w Mask of old man. 5 w. Striped squirrel. 6 w. Lily. 30 w. Bee. 50 w. Korean pot with lid. 60 w. Korean jar. 100 w. (No. 1069) Gold Crown, Silla dynasty. 100 w. (No. 1069a) Admiral Yi Soon Shin.

374. Tennis.

1973. 54th National Athletic Meeting, Pusan. Multicoloured.

1070. 10 w. Type 374.. .. 8 5

1071. 10 w. Hurdling 8 5

375. Children with Stamp Albums.

1973. Philatelic Week.

1072. 375. 10 w. multicoloured 25 25

376. Soyang River Dam.

1973. Soyang River Dam. Inauguration.
1074. 376. 10 w. multicoloured 8 5

377. Mt. Mai, Chinan. 378. Tangerine Grove, Cheju Island.

1973. Korean Tourist Attraction (5th series).
1075. 377. 10 w. multicoloured 8 5
1076. 378. 10 w. multicoloured 8 5

379. Match, Cigarette and Flames. 380. Tiger and Candles.

1973. 10th Fire Prevention Day.
1077. 379. 10 w. multicoloured 8 5

1973. Korean Court Costumes of the Yi Dynasty (5th series). As Type 357. Multicoloured. Background colours given.
1078. 10 w. orange 5 5
1079. 10 w. pink 5 5
DESIGNS: No. 1078, Pyongsangbok (official's wife) costume. No. 1079, Kokunbok (military officer's) costume.

1973. Lunar New Year ("Year of the Tiger"). Multicoloured.
1081. 10 w. Type 380 .. .. 8 5
1082. 10 w. Decorated top .. 8 5

381. Korean Girl and Flame Emblem.

1973. Declaration of Human Rights. 25th Anniv.
1084. 381. 10 w. multicoloured 8 5

382. Jetliner and Polar Zone.

1973. Air.
1085. 382. 110 w. blue and pink 50 25
1086. – 135 w. red and green 60 30
1087. – 145 w. red and blue 65 35
1088. – 180 w. yellow and lilac 80 40
DESIGNS—Jetliner and Postal Zones on Map. 135 w. South-east Asia. 145 w. India, Australasia and North America. 180 w. Europe, Africa and South America.

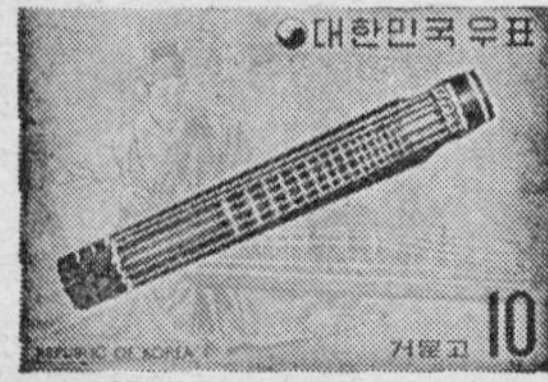

383. "Komunko" (zither).

1974. Traditional Musical Instruments (1st series). Mult. Background colours given.
1089. 383. 10 w. blue 8 5
1090. – 30 w. orange 20 10
DESIGN: 30 w. "Nagak" (conch trumpet).
See also Nos. 1098/9, 1108/9 and 1117/8.

384. Apricots. 385. Reservist and Factory.

1974. Fruits (1st series). Multicoloured.
1092. 10 w. Type 384 .. .. 8 5
1093. 30 w. Strawberries .. 20 10
See also Nos. 1104/5, 1111/2 and 1120/1.

1974. Home Reserve Forces Day.
1095. 385. 10 w. multicoloured 8 5

386. W.P.Y. Emblem. 387. Mail-train and Communications Emblem.

1974. World Population Year.
1096. 386. 10 w. multicoloured 8 5

1974. Traditional Musical Instruments (2nd series). As T 383. Multicoloured. Background colours given.
1098. 10 w. blue 8 5
1099. 30 w. green 20 10
CEREMONIAL INSTRUMENTS: 10 w. "Tchouk". 30 w. "Eu".

1974. Communications Day.
1101. 387. 10 w. multicoloured 5 5

388. C.A.F.E.A.-I.C.C. Emblem on Globe. 389. Port Installations.

1974. 22nd Session of Int., Chamber of Commerce's Commission on Asian and Far Eastern Affairs, Seoul.
1102. 388. 10 w. multicoloured 8 5

1974. New Port Facilities, Inchon. Inaug.
1103. 389. 10 w. multicoloured 8 5

1974. Fruits (2nd series). As T 384. Mult.
1104. 10 w. Peaches 8 5
1105. 30 w. Grapes 20 10

390. U.N.E.S.C.O. Emblem and Extended Fan. 391. Cross and Emblems.

1974. South Korean U.N.E.S.C.O. Commission. 20th Anniv.
1107. 390. 10 w. multicoloured 8 5

1974. Traditional Musical Instruments (3rd series). As T 383. Multicoloured. Background colours given.
1108. 10 w. orange 5 5
1109. 30 w. pink 12 8
DESIGNS: 10 w. "A-chaing" (stringed instrument). 30 w. "Kyobang-ko" (drum).

1974. Fruits (3rd series). As T 384. Mult.
1111. 10 w. Pears 8 5
1112. 30 w. Apples 20 10

1974. "Explo 74"—2nd International Training Congress on Evangelism. Mult.
1114. 10 w. Type 391 .. .. 8 5
1115. 10 w. Emblem and Korean map on Globe 8 5

392. Underground Train.

1974. Opening of Seoul Underground Railway.
1116. 392. 10 w. multicoloured 8 5

1974. Traditional Musical Instruments (4th series). As T 383. Multicoloured. Background colours given.
1117. 10 w. blue 8 5
1118. 30 w. pink 20 10
DESIGNS: No. 1117, So ("Pan pipes"). No. 1118, Haiken (Two-stringed fiddle).

1974. Fruits (4th series). As T 384. Mult.
1120. 10 w. Cherries 8 5
1121. 30 w. Persimmons .. 20 10

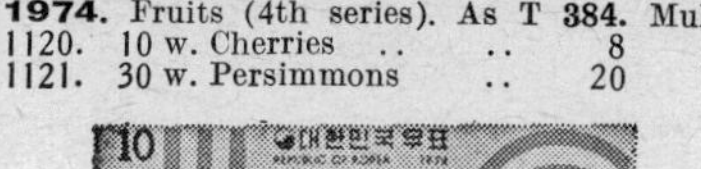

393. Rifle-shooting.

1974. 55th National Athletic Meeting, Seoul. Multicoloured.
1123. 10 w. Type 393 .. .. 8 5
1124. 30 w. Rowing 20 12

394. U.P.U. Emblem. 395. Symbols of Member Countries.

1974. Universal Postal Union. Centenary.
1125. 394. 10 w. mult. (postage) 8 5
1126. 394. 110 w. mult. (air) .. 70 30

1974. First World Conference of People-to-people International.
1128. 395. 10 w. multicoloured 8 5

396. Korean Stamps of 1884.

1974. Philatelic Week and 90th Anniv. of First Korean Stamps.
1129. 396. 10 w. multicoloured 8 5

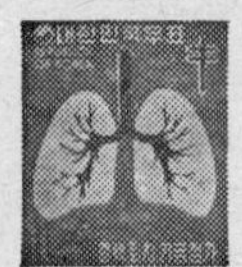

397. Taikwondo Contestants. 398. Pair of Lungs.

1974. First Asian Taikwondo Championships, Seoul.
1131. 397. 10 w. multicoloured 8 5

1974. Traditional Musical Instruments (5th series). As Type 383. Multicoloured. Background colours given.
1132. 10 w. pink 8 5
1133. 30 w. ochre 20 10
DESIGNS: 10 w. Pak (clappers). 30 w. Pyenchong (chimes).

1974. Tuberculosis Control Fund.
1135. 398. 10 w. + 5 w. red & grn. 15 12

399. Presidents Pak and Ford. 400. Yook Young Soo (wife of Pres. Pak).

1974. President Ford's State Visit to Korea.
1136. 399. 10 w. multicoloured 8 5

1974. Yook Young Soo Memorial Issue.
1138. 400. 10 w. green 8 5
1139. 10 w. orange 8 5
1140. 10 w. violet 8 5
1141. 10 w. blue 8 5

1974. Fruits (5th series). As T 384. Mult.
1143. 10 w. Tangerines .. 8 5
1144. 30 w. Chestnuts 20 10

401. " Good Luck " Purse. 402. U.P.U. Emblem and " 75 ".

1974. Lunar New Year ("Year of the Rabbit"). Multicoloured.
1146. 10 w. Type 401 .. .. 8 5
1147. 10 w. Toy rabbits .. 8 5

1975. Korea's Entry into U.P.U. 75th Anniv.
1149. 10 w. Type 402 .. .. 8 5
1150. 10 w. U.P.U. emblem and paper dart 8 5

403. Dove with " Good Luck " Card.

1975. National Welfare Insurance System. Inauguration.
1151. 403. 10 w. multicoloured 8 5

404. Dr. Schweitzer, Map and Syringe. 405. Salpuli Dancer.

1975. Dr. Albert Schweitzer. Birth Cent.
1152. 404. 10 w. bistre 8 5
1153. 10 w. magenta .. 8 5
1154. 10 w. orange 8 5
1155. 10 w. green 8 5

1975. Korean Folk Dances (1st series). Mult.
1156. 10 w. Type 405 .. .. 8 5
1157. 10 w. Mudang-chum dancer with fan and bell .. 8 5
See also Nos. 1168/9, 1175/6, 1193/4 and 1208/9.

406. Globe and Rotary Emblem. 407. Women and Emblem.

1975. Rotary International. 70th Anniv.
1159. 406. 10 w. multicoloured 8 5

1975. International Women's Year.
1160. 407. 10 w. multicoloured 8 5

408. Violets. 409. Saemaeul Township.

1975. Korean Flowers (1st series). Mult.
1161. 10 w. Type 408 .. .. 8 5
1162. 10 w. Anemones 8 5
See also Nos. 1171/2, 1184/5 and 1199/200.

1975. National Tree-planting Campaign. Multicoloured.
1163. 10 w. Type 409 .. .. 8 5
1164. 10 w. Lake and trees .. 8 5
1165. 10 w. " Green " forest .. 8 5
1166. 10 w. Felling timber .. 8 5

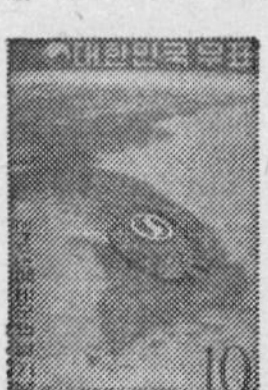

410. H.R.F. Emblem. 411. Butterfly Dance.

1975. Homeland Reserve Forces Day.
1167. 410. 10 w. multicoloured 5 5

1975. Korean Folk Dances (2nd series). Multicoloured.
1168. 10 w. Type 411 .. .. 5 5
1169. 10 w. Victory dance .. 5 5

412. Rhododendron.

413. Metric Symbols.

1975. Korean Flowers (2nd series). Mult.
1171. 10 w. Type **412** 8 5
1172. 10 w. Clematis 8 5

1975. Metric Convention. Centenary.
1173. **413.** 10 w. multicoloured 8 5

414. Soldier and Incense Pot.

415. Mokjoong (Pongsan Mask Dance)

1975. 20th Memorial Day.
1174. **414.** 10 w. multicoloured 8 5

1975. Korean Folk Dances (3rd series). Mult.
1175. 10 w. Type **415** 8 5
1176. 10 w. Malttugi (Tongnae Yaryoo) 8 5

416. Korean, U.N. and U.S. Flags.

1975. Korean War. 25th Anniv. Mult.
1178. 10 w. Type **416** 8 5
1179. 10 w. Flags of Ethiopia, France, Greece, Canada and South Africa .. 8 5
1180. 10 w. Flags of Luxembourg, Australia, U.K., Colombia and Turkey .. 8 5
1181. 10 w. Flags of Netherlands, Belgium, Philippines, New Zealand and Thailand 8 5

417. Presidents Pak and Bongo.

418. Iris.

1975. State Visit of President Bongo of Gabon.
1182. **417.** 10 w. multicoloured 8 5

1975. Korean Flowers (3rd series). Mult.
1184. 10 w. Type **418** 8 5
1185. 10 w. Thistle 8 5

419. Scout Scarf.

420. Freedom Flame.

1975. "Nordjamb 75" World Scout Jamboree, Norway. Multicoloured.
1186. 10 w. Type **419** 5 5
1187. 10 w. Scout oath .. 5 5
1188. 10 w. Scout camp .. 5 5
1189. 10 w. Axe and rope .. 5 5
1190. 10 w. Camp fire 5 5

1975. Liberation. 30th Anniv. Mult.
1191. 20 w. Type **420** 8 5
1192. 20 w. Balloon emblems .. 8 5

421. Drum Dance.

422. Taikwondo Contestanto.

1975. Korean Folk Dances (4th series). Mult.
1193. 20 w. Type **421** 8 5
1194. 20 w. Bara dance (monk with cymbal) 8 5

1975. Second World Taikwondo Championships, Seoul.
1196. **422.** 20 w. multicoloured 8 5

423. Assembly Hall.

1975. Completion of National Assembly Hall.
1197. **423.** 20 w. multicoloured 8 5

424. Dumper Truck and Emblem.

425. Broad-bell Flower.

1975. Contractors' Association Convention, Seoul.
1198. **424.** 20 w. multicoloured 8 5

1975. Korean Flowers (4th series). Mult.
1199. 20 w. Type **425** 8 5
1200. 20 w. Bush clover .. 8 5

426. Morse Key and Antenna.

1975. Korean Telecommunications. 90th Anniv.
1201. **426.** 20 w. blk., orge. & pur. 8 5

427. Stalactites, Yeongweol.

428. Flag and Missiles.

1975. International Tourism Day. Mult.
1202. 20 w. Type **427** 8 5
1203. 20 w. Mount Sorak .. 8 5

1975. Korean Armed Forces Day.
1204. **428.** 20 w. multicoloured 8 5

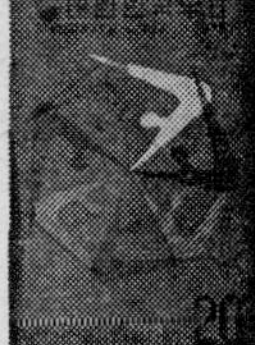
429. "Gymnastics".

430. "Kangaroo" Collector.

1975. 56th National Athletic Meeting. Mult.
1205. 20 w. Type **429** 8 5
1206. 20 w. "Handball" .. 8 5

1975. Philatelic Week.
1207. **430.** 20 w. multicoloured 8 5

431. Sogo Dance.

432. U.N. Emblem and Handclasps.

1975. Korean Folk Dances (5th series). Mult.
1208. 20 w. Type **431** 8 5
1209. 20 w. Bupo Nori dance .. 8 5

1975. United Nations. 30th Anniv.
1211. **432.** 20 w. multicoloured 8 5

433. Red Cross and Emblems.

434. Camellia.

1975. Korean Red Cross. 70th Anniv.
1212. **433.** 20 w. multicoloured 8 5

1975. Flowers (5th series). Multicoloured.
1213. 20 w. Type **434** 8 5
1214. 20 w. Gentian 8 5

435. A.P.U. Emblem.

436. Children at Play.

1975. Asian Parliamentary Union. 10th Anniv.
1215. **435.** 20 w. multicoloured 8 5

1975. New Year's Greetings. Multicoloured.
1216. 20 w. Type **436** 8 5
1217. 20 w. Dragon ("Year of the Dragon") 8 5

437. Electric Train.

1975. Opening of Cross-country Electric Railway.
1219. **437.** 20 w. multicoloured 8 5

438. "Dilipa fenestra".

1976. Korean Butterflies (1st series). Mult.
1220. 20 w. Type **438** 8 5
1221. 20 w. "Luehdorfia puziloi E" 8 5
See also Nos. 1226/7, 1246/7, 1254/5 and 1264/5.

439. K.I.S.T. and Science Emblems.

440. White-naped Crane.

1976. Korean Institute of Science and Technology (K.I.S.T.). 10th Anniversary.
1222. **439.** 20 w. multicoloured .. 8 5

1976. Korean Birds (1st series). Multicoloured
1223. 20 w. Type **440** 8 5
1224. 20 w. Siberian bustard .. 8 5
See also Nos. 1243/4, 1251/2, 1257/8 and 1266/7.

441. Globe and Telephones.

1976. Telephone Centenary.
1225. **441.** 20 w. multicoloured .. 8 5

442. "Papilio xuthus".

1976. Korean Butterflies (2nd series). Multicoloured.
1226. 20 w. Type **442** 8 5
1227. 20 w. "Parnassius bremeri" 8 5

443. "National Development".

444. "Eye" and People.

1976. Homeland Reserve Forces Day.
1228. **443.** 20 w. multicoloured 8 5

1976. World Health Day.
1229. **444.** 20 w. multicoloured 8 5

445. Pres. Pak and Flag.

446. Ruins of Moenjodaro (Pakistan).

1976. Saemaul Undong (New Village Movement). Sixth Anniversary. Multicoloured.
1230. 20 w. Type **445** 8 5
1231. 20 w. "People" ("Intellectual edification") .. 8 5
1232. 20 w. "Village" ("Welfare") 8 5
1233. 20 w. "Growth" ("Production") 8 5
1234. 20 w. "Produce" ("Increase of Income") .. 8 5

1976. Moenjodaro Preservation Campaign.
1235. **446.** 20 w. multicoloured .. 8 5

447. U.S. Flags of 1776 and 1976. **448.** Camp Scene on Emblem.

1976. American Revolution. Bicentenary.
1236. **447.** 20 w. red, blue & blk. 40 25
1237. – 20 w. red, blue & blk. 40 25
1238. – 20 w. red, blue & blk. 40 25
1239. – 20 w. red, blue & blk. 40 25
1240. – 20 w. red, blue & blk. 40 25

DESIGNS: No. 1237, Statue of Liberty. No. 1238, Map of United States. 1239, Liberty Bell. 1240, First astronaut on Moon.

1976. Korean Girl Scouts Federation. 30th Anniv.
1242. **448.** 20 w. multicoloured .. 8 5

449. Fairy Pitta. **450.** Buddha and Temple.

1976. Korean Birds (2nd series). Mult.
1243. 20 w. Type **449** 8 5
1244. 20 w. Tristram's woodpecker 8 5

1976. UNESCO. Presentation of Borobudur Temple.
1245. **450.** 20 w. multicoloured .. 8 5

451. " Colias eraste E ".

1976. Korean Butterflies (3rd series). Multicoloured.
1246. 20 w. Type **451** 8 5
1247. 20 w. " Byasa alcinous K " 8 5

452. The Protected Family. **453.** Volleyball.

1976. National Life Insurance.
1248. **452.** 20 w. multicoloured .. 8 5

1976. Olympic Games, Montreal. Mult.
1249. 20 w. Type **453** 8 5
1250. 20 w. Boxing 8 5

454. Wood Pigeon.

1976. Korean Birds (3rd series). Mult.
1251. 20 w. Type **454** 8 5
1252. 20 w. Oystercatcher .. 8 5

455. Children and Books.

1976. Books for Children.
1253. **455.** 20 w. multicoloured .. 8 5

456. " Hestina assimilis L ".

1976. Korean Butterflies (4th series). Mult.
1254. 20 w. Type **456** 8 5
1255. 20 w. " Graphium sarpedon " 8 5

457. Corps Members and Flag. **458.** Black-faced Spoonbill.

1976. Korean Civil Defence Corps. 1st Anniv.
1256. **457.** 20 w. multicoloured .. 8 5

1976. Korean Birds (4th series). Mult.
1257. 20 w. Type **458** .. 8 5
1258. 20 w. Black stork .. 8 5

459. Chamsungdan, Mani Mountain.

1976. International Tourism Day. Mult.
1259. 20 w. Type **459** 8 5
1260. 20 w. Ilchumun Gate, Tongdosa 8 5

460. Cadet and Parade. **461.** " Musa basjoo " (flower arrangement).

1976. Korean Military Academy. 30th Anniv.
1261. **460.** 20 w. multicoloured .. 8 5

1976. Philatelic Week.
1262. **461.** 20 w. blk., red & drab 8 5

462. " Nymphalis xanthomlas ".

1976. Korean Butterflies (5th series). Mult.
1264. 20 w. Type **462** 8 5
1265. 20 w. " Fabriciana nerippe " 8 5

463. Black Vulture (Vert).

1976. Korean Birds (5th series). Mult.
1266. 20 w. Type **463** 8 5
1267. 20 w. Whooper swan .. 8 5

MINIMUM PRICE

The minimum price quoted is 5p which represents a handling charge rather than a basis for valuing common stamps. For further notes about prices see introductory pages.

464. Zodiac Dragon.

1976 New Year's Greetings. Multicoloured.
1268. 20 w. Type **464** 8 5
1269. 20 w. Door-knocker and crane emblem .. 8 5

(c) North Korean Occupation.

(1. "Democratic People's Republic of Korea".)

1950. Nos. 116 and 118/9, optd. with Type **1**.
1. 10 w. green 70
2. 20 w. brown 70
3. 30 w. green 70

NORTH KOREA

GUM. All stamps of North Korea are without gum, except where otherwise stated.

(a) Russian Occupation.

1. Hibiscus. **2.** Diamond Mountains.

1946. Perf., roul. or imp.
N 1. **1.** 20 ch. green .. .. 4·50 6·00
N 2. **2.** 50 ch. green .. .. 3·00 4·00
N 4. 50 ch. red .. .. 4·50 6·00
N 5b. 50 ch. violet .. .. 3·00 4·00

3. Gen. Kim Il Sung and Flag. **4.** Peasants.

1946. Liberation from Japan. 1st Anniv. Perf. or imperf.
N 6. **3.** 50 ch. brown .. .. 18·00 22·00

1947. Perf., roul or imp..
N 7. **4.** 1 wn. green .. .. 1·40 1·40
N 8. 1 wn. violet .. .. 3·50 3·00
N 9. 1 wn. blue on buff .. 90 90
N 10. 1 wn. blue 75 75

5. **6.** **7.**

1948. Labour Law. 2nd Anniv.
N 11. **5.** 50 ch. blue .. .. 42·00 42·00

1948. Liberation from Japan. 3rd Anniv.
N 12. **6.** 50 ch. red .. .. 40·00

1948. Promulgation of Constitution.
N 13. **7.** 50 ch. blue and red .. 35·00 14·00

(b) Korean People's Democratic Republic.

8. North Korean Flag. **9.**

1948. Establishment of People's Republic. Roul.
N 16. **8.** 25 ch. violet 85 85
N 17. 50 ch. blue .. .. 2·00 2·00

1949. Roul.
N 18. **9.** 6 wn. red and blue .. 50 65

10. Kim Il Sung University, Pyongyang. **11.** North Korean Flags.

10a. Kim Il Sung University, Pyongyang.

1949. Roul.
N 19. **10.** 1 wn. violet .. .. 10·00 4·00
N 20. **10a.** 1 wn. blue .. .. 10·00 3·00

1949. Liberation from Japan. 4th Anniv. Roul or perf.
N 22. **11.** 1 wn. red, grn. & blue 8·00 3·00

12. Order of the National Flag. **13.** Liberation Pagoda, Pyongyang.

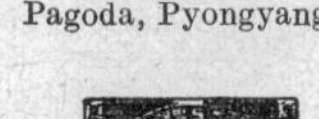

14. Soldier and Flags. **15.** Peasant and Worker.

16. Tractor. **17.** Capitol, Seoul.

1950. Perf., roul or imp. Various sizes.
N 24. **12.** 1 wn. green (A) .. 40 40
N 25. 1 wn. brown-orange (A) 15·00
N 26. 1 wn. red-orange (B) .. 3·50 5·00
N 27. 1 wn. green (C) .. 50 35
N 28. 1 wn. olive (D) .. 1·50 1·50

SIZES: (A) $23\frac{1}{2} \times 37\frac{1}{2}$ mm. (B) $20 \times 32\frac{1}{2}$ mm. (C) $22 \times 35\frac{1}{2}$ mm. (D) $22\frac{1}{2} \times 36\frac{1}{2}$ mm.

1950. Liberation from Japan. 5th Anniv. Roul., perf. or imperf. Various sizes.
N 29. **13.** 1 wn. red, ind. & blue 15 20
N 30. 1 wn. orange .. .. 1·40 1·75
N 31. **14.** 2 wn. blk., bl. & red .. 20 25
N 32. **15.** 6 wn. green (A) .. 25 30
N 34. 6 wn. red (B) .. .. 1·40 1·75
N 33. **16.** 10 wn. brown (C) .. 25 30
N 35. 10 wn. brown (D) .. 2·10 2·75

SIZES: (A) 20×30 mm. (B) 22×33 mm. (C) 20×28 mm. D) 22×30 mm.

1950. Capture of Seoul by North Korean Forces. Roul.
N 38. **17.** 1 wn. red, bl. & green 8·00 10·00

18.

19. Kim Ki Ok and Aeroplane.

1951. Order of Admiral Li Sun Sin. Imperf.
N 39. **18.** 6 wn. orange 75 90

1951. Air Force Hero Kim Ki Ok. Imperf.
N 40. **19.** 1 wn. blue 40 40

20. Russian and North Korean Flags.

21. Kim Ki U (hero).

22. N. Korean and Chinese Soldiers.

1951. Liberation from Japan. 6th Anniv. Roul. or perf.
N 41. **20.** 1 wn. blue 60 60
N 42. 1 wn. red 60 60
N 43. **21.** 1 wn. blue 60 60
N 44. 1 wn. red 75 75
N 45. **22.** 1 wn. blue 60 60
N 46. 1 wn. red 75 75
All values exist on buff and on white paper.

23. Order of Honour.

24.

25. Woman Partisan, Li Su Dok.

1951. Imperf. or perf.
N 47. **23.** 40 wn. red 75 60

1951. Co-operation of Chinese People's Volunteers. Imperf. or perf.
N 49. **24.** 10 wn. blue .. .. 1·00 1·00

1952. Partisan Heroes. Imperf. or perf.
N 50. **25.** 70 wn. brown.. .. 60 30

26.

27. Gen. P'eng Teh-huai.

28. Munition Worker.

1952. Peace Propaganda. Imperf. or perf.
N 51. **26.** 20 wn. bl., grn. & red 70 30

1952. Honouring Commander of Chinese People's Volunteers. Imperf.
N 52. **27.** 10 wn. purple.. .. 1·50 60

1952. Labour Day. Imperf. or perf.
N 53. **28.** 10 wn. red .. .. 3·00 4·00

29.

30.

31.

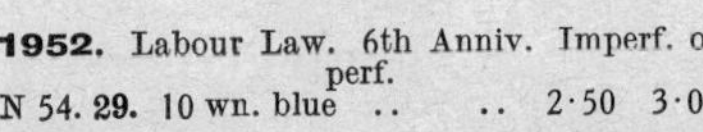

1952. Labour Law. 6th Anniv. Imperf. or perf.
N 54. **29.** 10 wn. blue .. .. 2·50 3·00

1952. Imperialism Day. Imperf.
N 55. **30.** 10 wn. red .. .. 3·00 3·50

1952. North Korean and Chinese Friendship. Imperf. or perf.
N 56. **31.** 20 wn. dp. blue .. 2·50 3·00

32.

33.

1952. Liberation from Japan. 7th Anniv. Imperf. or perf.
N 57. **32.** 10 wn. carmine .. 3·50 4·00
N 58. **33.** 10 wn. red .. .. 3·50 4·00

34. 35. 36.

1952. Int. Youth Day. With gum. Imperf. or perf.
N 59. **34.** 10 wn. green .. .. 2·50 3·00

1953. People's Army. 5th Anniv. Imperf. or perf.
N 60. **35.** 10 wn. red .. .. 3·50 3·75
N 61. **36.** 40 wn. purple.. .. 3·50 3·75

37.

38.

1953. Int. Women's Day. With gum. Imperf. or perf.
N 62. **37.** 40 wn. carmine .. 3·00 3·50
N 63. **38.** 40 wn. yell.-grn. .. 3·00 3·50

39.

40.

1953. Labour Day. Imperf. or perf.
N 64. **39.** 10 wn. yell.-grn. .. 3·00 3·50
N 65. **40.** 40 wn. brn.-orange .. 3·00 3·50

41.

42.

1953. Anti-U.S. Imperialism Day. With gum. Imperf. or perf.
N 66. **41.** 10 wn. greenish blue.. 3·50 3·75
N 67. **42.** 40 wn. red .. .. 3·25 3·50

43.

44.

1953. 4th World Youth Festival, Bucharest. With gum. Imperf. or perf.
N 68. **43.** 10 wn. blue and green 1·25 1·00
N 69. **44.** 20 wn. green and pink 1·25 1·00

45.

46.

1953. Armistice and Victory Issue. With gum. Imperf. or perf.
N 70a. **45.** 10 wn. brn. & yellow 17·00 14·00

1953. Liberation from Japan. 8th Anniv. Imperf.
N 71. **46.** 10 wn. red .. .. 35·00 40·00

47.

48. Liberation Pagoda, Pyongyang.

1953. People's Republic. 5th Anniv. Imperf. or perf.
N 72. **47.** 10 wn. blue and red .. 5·00 6·50

1953. With gum. Imperf. or perf.
N 73. **48.** 10 wn. slate .. .. 1·25 1·25

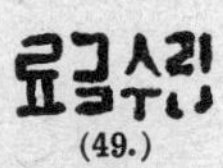
(49.)

(50.)

1954. Optd. with Type **49.**
N 74. **9.** 6 wn. red & blue .. 40·00 50·00

1954. Surch. as Type **50.**
N 75. **9.** 5 wn. on 6 wn. red & bl. 3·00 2·00
N 76. **18.** 5 wn. on 6 wn. orange 15·00 15·00

51.

52.

1954. Post-War Economic Reconstruction. With gum. Imperf. or perf.
N 77. **51.** 10 wn. blue .. .. 1·75 2·00

1954. 6th Anniv. of People's Army. With gum. Imperf. or perf.
N 78. **52.** 10 wn. red .. .. 3·00 3·50

53.

54.

1954 Int. Women's Day. With gum. Imperf. or perf.
N 79. **53.** 10 wn. carm.-red .. 2·00 2·50

1954. Labour Day. With gum. Imperf. or perf.
N 80. **54.** 10 wn. scarlet.. .. 1·75 2·00

55.

56. Taedong Gate, Pyongyang.

1954. Anti-U.S. Imperialism Day. 4th Anniv. With gum. Imperf.
N 81. **55.** 10 wn. red .. .. 3·25 4·00

1954. Imperf. or perf.
N 82. **56.** 5 wn. lake .. .. 1·25 40
N 83. 5 wn. brown .. .. 1·25 35

57.

58. Soldier.

1954. National Young Activists' Conf. With gum. Imperf. or perf.
N 84. **57.** 10 wn. red, bl. & slate 1·50 2·00

1954. Liberation. 9th Anniv. With gum. Imperf. or perf.
N 85. **58.** 10 wn. red .. .. 1·75 2·00

59. North Korean Flag.

60. Hwanghae Metal Works.

61. Hwanghae Metal Works and Workers.

1954. People's Republic. 6th Anniv. With gum. Imperf or perf.
N 86. **59.** 10 wn. bl. & red .. 2·00 2·50

1954. Economic Reconstruction. Imperf. or perf.
N 87. **60.** 10 wn. blue .. .. 1·75 20
N 88. **61.** 10 wn. chocolate .. 1·75 20

62.

63.

1955. People's Army. 7th Anniv. With gum. Imperf. or perf.
N 89. **62.** 10 wn. red .. .. 1·50 2·00

1955. Int. Women's Day. With gum. Imperf. or perf.
N 90. **63.** 10 wn. deep blue .. 1·75 2·00

64.

65.

1955. Labour Day. With gum. Imperf. or perf.
N 91. **64.** 10 wn. green .. .. 1·75 2·00
N 92. **65.** 10 wn. red .. .. 1·75 2·00

66. Admiral Li Sun Sin.

67.

1955. Imperf. or perf.
N 93. **66.** 1 wn. blue on grn. .. 90 20
N 94. 2 wn. rose on buff .. 90 20
N 95. 2 wn. red .. .. 1·10 30

1955. 9th Anniv. of Labour Law. With gum. Imperf. or perf.
N 96. **67.** 10 wn. rose .. .. 2·00 2·50

68. 69. 70.

1955. Soviet Union Friendship Month. Imperf. or perf.
N 97. **68.** 10 wn. red 60 60
N 98. 10 wn. red & blue .. 60 60
N 99. **69.** 20 wn. red & slate .. 1·50 1·50
N 100. 20 wn. red & blue .. 60 60
SIZES: No. N 97, 22×32½ mm. No. N 98, 29½×32 mm. No. N 99, 19¾×32 mm. No. N 100, 29×43 mm.

1955. Liberation. 10th Anniv. Various sizes. Imperf. or perf.
N 101. **70.** 10 wn. green.. .. 60 60
N 102. 10 wn. red, blue and brown (29½×42½ mm.) 60 60

71. 72. 73.

1956. Haegumgang Maritime Park. Imperf. or perf.
N 103. **71.** 10 wn. blue on blue 75 60

1956. People's Army. 8th Anniv. Imperf. or perf.
N 104. **72.** 10 wn. red on green.. 3·00 3·50

1956. Labour Day. Imperf. or perf.
N 105. **73.** 10 wn. blue .. .. 1·75 1·75

74. Machinist.

75. Taedong Gate, Pyongyang.

76. Woman Harvester.

77. Moranbong Theatre, Pyongyang.

1956. Imperf. or perf.
N 106. **74.** 1 wn. brown.. .. 30 30
N 107. **75.** 2 wn. blue 40 40
N 108. **76.** 10 wn. red 40 40
N 109. **77.** 40 wn. green.. .. 1·25 1·25

78. Miner.

79. Boy Bugler and Girl Drummer.

1956. Labour Law. 10th Anniv. Imperf. or perf.
N 110. **78.** 10 wn. brown .. 40 40

1956. Young Pioneers. 10th Anniv. Imperf. or perf.
N 111. **79.** 10 wn. brown .. 85 85

80. Workers.

81. Industrial Plant.

1956. Sex Equality Law. 10th Anniv. Imperf. or perf.
N 112. **80.** 10 wn. brown .. 85 85

1956. Nationalization of Industry. 10th Anniv. Imperf. or perf.
N 113. **81.** 10 wn. brown .. 85 85

82. Liberation Tower.

83. Kim Il Sung University.

1956. Liberation from Japan. 11th Anniv. Imperf. or perf.
N 114. **82.** 10 wn. red .. .. 1·00 1·00

1956. Kim Il Sung University. 10th Anniv. Imperf. or perf.
N 115. **83.** 10 wn. brown .. 75 75

84. Boy and Girl.

85. Pak Chi-won.

1956. 4th Democratic Youth Congress. Imperf. or perf.
N 116. **84.** 10 wn. brown .. 75 75

1957. Pak Chi Won ("Yonam"), statesman. 220th Birth Anniv. Imperf. or perf.
N 117. **85.** 10 wn. blue 75 75

86. Tabo Pagoda, Pulguksa.

87. Moranbong Pavilion Pyongyang.

89. Furnaceman.

1957. Imperf., perf. or roul.
N 118. **86.** 5 wn. blue 30 25
N 119. **87.** 40 wn. green.. .. 1·25 1·00

1957. Production and Economy Campaign. With or without gum. Imperf. or perf.
N 121. **89.** 10 wn. blue 85 85

90. Furnaceman.

91. Voters and Polling Booth.

1957. 2nd General Election. Imperf. or perf.
N 122. **90.** 1 wn. orange .. 20 20
N 123. 2 wn. brown.. .. 20 20
N 124. **91.** 10 wn. red 40 40

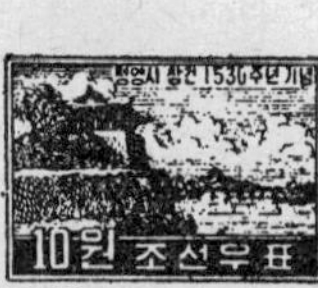

92. Ryongwangjong, Pyongyang.

93. Lenin and Flags.

94. Kim Il Sung at Pochonbo.

95. Lenin.

96. Pouring Steel.

1957. Pyongyang. 1530th Anniv. Imperf. or perf.
N 125. **92.** 10 wn. green.. .. 30 20

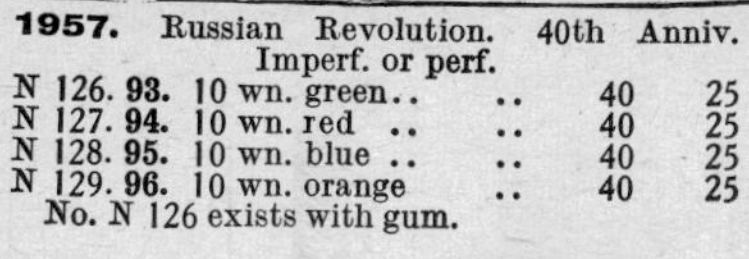

1957. Russian Revolution. 40th Anniv. Imperf. or perf.
N 126. **93.** 10 wn. green.. .. 40 25
N 127. **94.** 10 wn. red 40 25
N 128. **95.** 10 wn. blue 40 25
N 129. **96.** 10 wn. orange .. 40 25
No. N 126 exists with gum.

97. Congress Emblem.

98. Liberation Pagoda, Spassky Tower and Flags.

1957. 4th World T.U.C. Leipzig. Imperf. (with or without gum) or perf.
N 130. **97.** 10 wn. bl. & grn. .. 75 25

1957. Russian Friendship Month. Imperf. or perf.
N 131. **98.** 10 wn. green.. .. 50 25

99. Weighing a Baby.

100. Bandaging a Hand.

1957. Red Cross. Imperf., perf. or roul.
N 132. **99.** 1 wn. red 35 25
N 133. 2 wn. red 35 25
N 134. **100** 10 wn. red 45 45
No. N 133 exists with or without gum.

101. Koryo Celadon Jug (12th cent.).

102. Koryo Incense-burner (12th cent.).

1958. Korean Antiquities. Imperf. (with or without gum) or perf.
N 135. **101.** 10 wn. blue.. .. 60 25
N 136. **102.** 10 wn. grey-green .. 60 25

103. Woljongsa Pagoda.

104. Soldier.

1958. With gum (5 wn.), without gum (10 wn.). Imperf. or perf.
N 137. **103.** 5 wn. green.. .. 40 25
N 138. 10 wn. blue.. .. 60 25

1958. People's Army. 10th Anniv. No gum (No. N 139) with or without gum (No. N 140). Imperf. or perf.
N 139. **104.** 10 wn. blue.. .. 35 35
N 140. – 10 wn. red 35 35
DESIGN—HORIZ. (37½×26 mm.): No. N 140, Soldier, flag and Hwanghae Metal Works.

105. Airliner over Pyongyang.

1958. Air. Imperf. or perf.
N 141. **105.** 20 wn. blue.. .. 70 55

106. Sputniks.

107. Sputnik encircling Globe.

1958. I.G.Y. Inscr. "1957–1958". Imperf. or perf.
N 142. **106.** 10 wn. slate .. 1·50 1·25
N 143. **107.** 20 wn. slate .. 1·50 1·25
N 144. – 40 wn. slate .. 1·50 1·25
N 145. **106.** 70 wn. slate .. 3·00 2·25
DESIGN—HORIZ. 40 wn. Sputnik over Pyongyang Observatory.
Nos. N 142/4 exist with or without gum.

108. Furnaceman.

109. Hwanghae Metal Works.

1958. Socialist Constructors' Congress, Pyongyang. Imperf. or perf.
N 146. **108.** 10 wn. blue.. .. 50 20

1958. Opening of Hwanghae Metal Works. Imperf. or perf.
N 147. **109.** 10 wn. blue.. .. 35 20

110. Commemorative Badge.

111. Federation Emblem.

1958. Farewell to Chinese People's Volunteers (1st issue). Imperf. or perf.
N 148. **110.** 10 wn. claret, pur. & blue 35 20

1958. 4th Int. Women's Federation Congress Imperf. or perf.
N 149. **111.** 10 wn. blue.. .. 35 20

112. Conference Emblem.

1958. 1st World T.U. Young Worker's Conference, Prague. Imperf. or perf.
N 150. **112.** 10 wn. brown & grn. 40 20

113. Flats, East Ward, Pyongyang.

114. Workers' Flats, Pyongyang.

1958. Rehousing Progress. Imperf. or perf.
N 151. **113.** 10 wn. blue.. .. 35 20
N 152. **114.** 10 wn. blue-grey .. 35 20

115. Pyongyang Railway Station.

116. Textile Worker.

1958. Korean People's Republic. 10th Anniv. Inscr. "1948 1958". Imperf. or perf.
N 153. – 10 wn. green .. 40 35
N 154. **115.** 10 wn. slate .. 40 35
N 155. – 10 wn. yellow & buff 40 35
N 156. **116.** 10 wn. sepia .. 40 35
N 157. – 10 wn. sepia .. 40 35
DESIGNS—HORIZ. No. N 153, Hungnam Fertiliser Plant. No. N 157, Yongp'ung Dam, Pyongyang. VERT. No. N 155, Arms of People's Republic.

117. Volunteer and Troop Train.

118. Farm Girl and Cattle.

1958. Farewell to Chinese People's Volunteers (2nd issue). Imperf. or perf.
N 158. **117.** 10 wn. sepia .. 35 20

1958. Imperf. or perf.
N 159. **118.** 10 wn. sepia .. 35 20

118a. Winged Horse.

119. N. Korean and Chinese Flags.

1958. National Production Executives' Meeting, Pyongyang. With or without gum. Imperf. or perf.
N 160. **118a.** 10 wn. red .. 50 20

1958. N. Korean-Chinese Friendship Month. With or without gum. Imperf. or perf.
N 161. **119.** 10 wn. red and blue 40 20

120. Farm Workers.

121. Gen. Eul Che Mun Dok.

1959. National Co-operative Farming Congress, Pyongyang. With or without gum. Imperf. or perf.
N 162. **120.** 10 wn. blue.. .. 40 25

1959. With gum. Imperf. or perf.
N 163. **121.** 10 wn. brn. on cream 60 40

1959. New currency. Portraits as Type **121.** Imperf. (with or without gum) or perf. (with gum).
N 164. 2 ch. blue on green .. 20 5
N 165. 5 ch. purple on buff .. 30 15
N 166. 10 ch. lake on cream .. 40 25
PORTRAITS: 2 ch. Gen. Kong Kam Chan. 5 ch. Gen. Chou Pong Jun. 10 ch. Type **121.**

122. Women with Banner.

123. Rocket and Moon.

1959. National Conference of Women Socialist Constructors, Pyongyang. With or without gum. Imperf. or perf.
N 167. **122.** 10 ch. choc. & red.. 40 20

1959. First Cosmic Rocket. With or without gum. Imperf. or perf.
N 168. **123.** 2 ch. purple on buff 4·00 2·50
N 169. 10 ch. blue on green 5·00 3·00

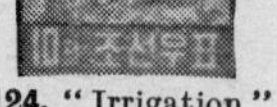
124. "Irrigation".

125. Inscribed Tree at Partisan H.Q. Chongbong.

126. Kim Il Sung Statue.

127. Mt. Paekdu-san.

1959. Land Irrigation Project. Imperf. or perf.
N 170. **124.** 10 ch. mult. .. 50 25

1959. Partisan Successes against Japanese 1937-39. With gum (No. N 172) or no gum (others). Perf. (N 172) or imperf. or perf. (others).
N 171. **125.** 5 ch. mult... .. 35 12
N 172. **126.** 10 ch. blue and turq. 60 20
N 173. **127.** 10 ch. violet .. 60 20

128. "Flying Horse" Tractor.

1959. "Great Perspectives" (1st issue: Development of Industrial Mechanisation). As Type **128.** With or without gum.
N 174. 1 ch. red, olive & green 15 8
N 175. 2 ch. blue, green & buff 15 8
N 176. 2 ch. red, pink & violet 15 8
N 177. 5 ch. orge., brn. & ochre 25 10
N 178. 10 ch. blue, grn. & brn. 40 12
N 179. 10 ch. green, pale green and purple 40 12
DESIGNS: No. N 175, Electric shunting loco. N 176, "Red Star" bulldozer. N 177, "Flying Horse" excavator. N 178, "SU-50" universal lathe. N 179, "Victory 58" lorry.
See also Nos. N 189/99a and N 272/6.

129. Armistice Building, Panmunjom.

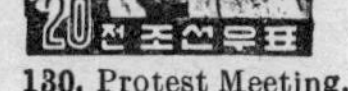
130. Protest Meeting.

131. "Hoisting the link between N. and S. Korea".

1959. Campaign for Withdrawal of U.S. Forces from S. Korea. With gum. Perf. (20 ch.) or imperf. or perf. (others).
N 180. **129.** 10 ch. blue 35 25
N 181. **130.** 20 ch. blue 65 35
N 182. **131.** 70 ch. brown .. 2·10 80

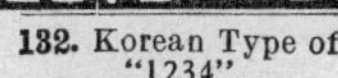
132. Korean Type of "1234".

133. Books breaking Chains.

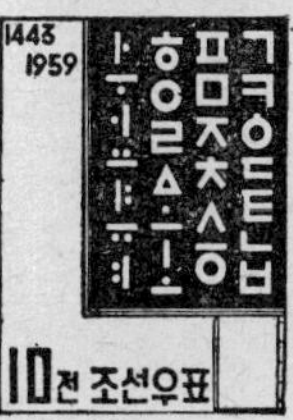
135. Korean Alphabet, 1443.

134. Emblems of Peace, Labour and Letters.

1959. Int. Book Exn., Leipzig. With gum (No. N 183) or no gum (others).
N 183. **132.** 5 ch. sepia 25 12
N 184. **133.** 5 ch. red & grn. .. 25 12
N 185. **134.** 10 ch. blue 60 30
N 186. **135.** 10 ch. vio-blue & blue 60 30

136. Pig Farm.

137. Rotary Cement Kiln.

1959. Animal Husbandry. With gum (5 ch.) or no gum (2 ch.).
N 187. – 2 ch. brn., grn. & buff 40 15
N 188. **136.** 5 ch. cream, bl. & brn. 60 25
DESIGN—HORIZ. 2 ch. Cow-girl with cattle.

1959. "Great Perspectives" (2nd issue: Production Targets). As Type **137.** With gum (Nos. N 190 and N 191) or no gum (others). Perf., or imperf. (all except N 197/8 and N 199a.).
N 189. **137.** 1 ch. brn., choc. & blue 12 8
N 190. – 2 ch. multicoloured 20 12
N 191. – 5 ch. slate, yell. & grey 25 15
N 192. – 10 ch. ultram., bl. & orge. 40 20
N 193. – 10 ch. purple, yell. & bl. 40 20
N 194. – 10 ch. red, grn. & yell. 40 20
N 195. – 10 ch. multicoloured 40 20
N 196. – 10 ch. bl., lt. bl. & turq. 40 20
N 197. – 10 ch. multicoloured 40 20
N 198. – 10 ch. grn., buff & brn. 40 20
N 199. – 10 ch. brn. & orange 40 20
N 199a. – 10 ch. multicoloured 40 20
DESIGNS—VERT. No. N 190, Electric power lines and dam. No. N 191, Loading fertilizers into truck. HORIZ. No. N 192, Factory, electric power lines and dam. No. N 193, Harvesting. No. N 194, Sugar-beet, factory and pieces of sugar. No. N 195, Steel furnace. No. N 196, Trawlers. No. N 197, Pig-iron workers. No. N 198, Coal miners. No. N 199, Girl picking apples. No. N 199a, Textile worker.

138. Emigration "Pickets".

139. Freighter.

1959. Campaign Against Emigration of South Koreans. With gum.
N 200. **138.** 20 ch. brn. & sepia 55 30

1959. Transport. With gum.
N 201. – 5 ch. purple .. 40 20
N 202. **139.** 10 ch. green .. 80 40
DESIGN: 5 ch. Electric train.

140. Deer.

141. Congress Emblem.

1959. Game Preservation. No gum (5 ch.) with gum (10 ch.).
N 203. – 5 ch. multicoloured 25 12
N 204. – 5 ch. yell., brn. & blue 20 8
N 205. – 5 ch. sepia, grn. & brn. 20 8
N 206. – 5 ch. brn., blk. & blue 20 8
N 207. **140.** 10 ch. multicoloured 40 20
N 208. – 10 ch. red, brn. and cream on cream .. 40 20
DESIGNS—HORIZ. No. N 203, Water deer. No. N 204, Sable. No. N 205, Marten. No. N 206, Otter. No. N 208, Pheasant.

1960. 3rd Workers' Union Congress. With gum.
N 209. **141.** 5 ch. multicoloured 35 15

142. Soldier, tractor and Plough.

143. Knife Dance.

1960. Korean People's Army. 12th Anniv. With gum.
N 210. **142.** 5 ch. vio. & blue .. 20·00 25·00

1960. Korean National Dancers. Mult.
N 211. 5 ch. Type **142**.. .. 30 8
N 212. 5 ch. Drum dance .. 30 8
N 213. 10 ch. Farmers' dance.. 45 20

143a. Women of Three Races.

144. Kim Chong Ho (geographer).

1960. Int. Women's Day. 50th Anniv. With gum.
N 214. **143a.** 5 ch. mauve and blue 25 10
N 215. — 10 ch. grn. & orange 30 25
DESIGN—VERT. 10 ch. Woman operating lathe.

1960. Korean Celebrities. With gum.
N 216. **144.** 1 ch. grey on green 10 5
N 217. – 2 ch. blue on cream 10 5
N 218. – 5 ch. blue on yellow 20 10
N 219. – 10 ch. brn., on buff 30 12
PORTRAITS: 2 ch. Kim Hong Do (painter). 5 ch. Pak Yon (musician). 10 ch. Chong Tasan (scholar).

145. Grapes.

146. Lenin.

1960. Wild Fruits. As Type **145.** Fruits in natural colours. With gum.
N 220. 5 ch. olive & turquoise 15 12
N 221. 5 ch. drab and blue .. 15 12
N 222. 5 ch. olive and blue .. 15 12
N 223. 10 ch. olive & orange .. 30 20
N 224. 10 ch. grey-grn. & pink 30 20
FRUITS: No. N 220, Type **145.** 221, Fruit of "Actinidia arguta planch". 222, Pine-cone. 223, May pear. 224, Horse-chestnut.

1960. Lenin. 90th Birth Anniv. With gum.
N 225. **146.** 10 ch. purple .. 30 15

147. Koreans and American Soldier (caricature).

148. Mao Tse-tung Square, Pyongyang.

1960. Campaign Day for Withdrawal of U.S. Forces from South Korea. With gum.
N 226. **147.** 10 ch. blue 30 10

1960. Views of Pyongyang.
N 227. **148.** 10 ch. green .. 25 5
N 228. – 20 ch. slate.. .. 40 10
N 229. – 40 ch. green .. 85 25
N 230. – 70 ch. emerald .. 1·25 45
N 231. – 1 wn. blue .. .. 1·75 75
VIEWS: 20 ch. River Taedong promenade. 40 ch. Youth Street. 70 ch. People's Army Street. 1 wn. Stalin Street.

149. Russian Flag on Moon (14.9.59).

150. "Mirror Rock".

1960. Russian Cosmic Rocket Flights. With gum (5 ch.) or no gum (10 ch.).
N 232. – 5 ch. turquoise .. 2·50 2·50
N 233. **149.** 10 ch. mult. .. 4·00 1·00
DESIGN: 5 ch. "Lunik 3" approaching Moon (4.10.59).

1960. Diamond Mountains Scenery (1st issue). Multicoloured.
N 234. 5 ch. Type **150**.. .. 10 5
N 235. 5 ch. Devil-faced Rock 10 5
N 236. 10 ch. Dancing Dragon Bridge (horiz.) .. 25 12
N 237. 10 ch. Nine Dragon Falls 25 12
N 238. 10 ch. Mt. Diamond on the Sea (horiz.) .. 25 12
See also Nos. N 569/72, N 599/601 and N 1176/80.

151. Lily.

152. Guerrillas in the Snow.

1960. Flowers. Multicoloured. With gum.
N 239. 5 ch. Type **151** 15 8
N 240. 5 ch. Rhododendron . . 15 8
N 241. 10 ch. Hibiscus 40 12
N 242. 10 ch. Blue campanula 40 12
N 243. 10 ch. Mauve campanula 40 12

1960. Revolutionary Leadership of Kim Il Sung.
N 244. **152.** 5 ch. red 12 8
N 245. – 10 ch. blue 30 20
N 246. – 10 ch. red 30 20
N 247. – 10 ch. blue 30 20
N 248. – 10 ch. red 30 20
DESIGNS: No. N 245, Kim Il Sung talks to guerrillas. No. N 246, Kim Il Sung at Pochonbo. No. N 247, Kim Il Sung leaves to fight in China. No. N 248, Kim Il Sung returns to Pyongyang.

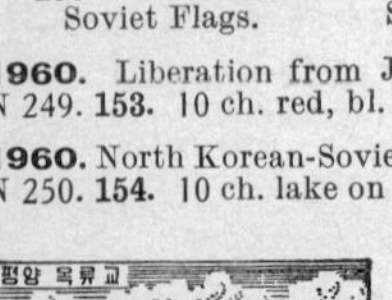
153. Korean and Soviet Flags.

154. "North Korean-Soviet Friendship".

1960. Liberation from Japan. 15th Anniv.
N 249. **153.** 10 ch. red, bl. & brn. 30 12

1960. North Korean-Soviet Friendship Month.
N 250. **154.** 10 ch. lake on cream 30 12

155. Ongnyu Bridge, Pyongyang.

156.

1960. Liberation Anniv. Construction.
N 251. **155.** 10 ch. blue 30 12
N 252. – 10 ch. violet . . 30 12
N 253. – 10 ch. green . . 30 12
DESIGNS: No. N 252, Grand Theatre, Pyongyang. N 253, Ongnyu-gwan Restaurant.

1960. World Trade Union Federation. 15th Anniv.
N 254. **156.** 10 ch. pale & deep blue 30 12

157. Tokro-gang Dam.

158. Quay-side Welcome.

1960. Inaug. of Tokro-gang Hydro-Electric Power Station. With gum.
N 255. **157.** 5 ch. blue 25 8

1960. Repatriation of Korean Nationals from Japan.
N 256. **158.** 10 ch. maroon . . 30 12

159. Lenin and Workers.

160. Football.

1960. Russian October Revolution. 43rd Anniv. With gum.
N 257. **159.** 10 ch. brn. & flesh . . 30 12

1960. Liberation Day Sports Meeting, Pyongyang. Multicoloured.
N 258. 5 ch. Running (vert.) . . 25 8
N 259. 5 ch. Weightlifting (vert.) 25 8
N 260. 5 ch. Cycling (vert.) . . 25 8
N 261. 5 ch. Gymnastics (vert.) 25 8
N 262. 5 ch. Type **160** 25 8
N 263. 10 ch. Swimming . . 40 20
N 264. 10 ch. Moranbong Stadium, Pyongyang 40 20

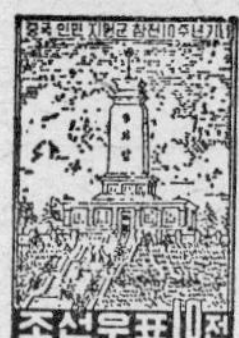
161. Friendship Monument, Pyongyang.

162. Federation Emblem.

1960. Entry of Chinese Volunteers into Korean War. 10th Anniv. With gum.
N 265. – 5 ch. magenta . . 20 12
N 266. **161.** 10 ch. blue 30 15
DESIGN—HORIZ. 5 ch. Chinese and Korean soldiers celebrating.

1960. World Democratic Youth Federation. 15th Anniv.
N 267. **162.** 10 ch. yell., blk. & bl. 30 12

163. Woodpecker.

164. Korean Wrestling.

1960. Birds.
N 268. **163.** 2 ch. multicoloured 8 5
N 268a. – 5 ch. multicoloured 25 12
N 269. – 5 ch. brn., yell & bl. 15 8
N 270. – 10 ch. yell., brn. & grn. 25 10
DESIGNS—HORIZ. 5 ch. (N 268a), Mandarin ducks. 10 ch. Golden oriole. VERT. 5 ch. (N 269), Owl.

1960. Sports and Games. Multicoloured.
N 271. 5 ch. Type **164** 20 8
N 272. 5 ch. Riding on swing (vert.) 20 8
N 273. 5 ch. Archery 20 8
N 274. 10 ch. Jumping on see-saw (vert.) 30 15

165. Cogwheel and Corn. ("Mechanization of Rural Economy").

166. Cultivated Ginseng.

1961. "Great Perspectives" (3rd issue: Targets of Seven-Year Plan, 1961-67. Inscr. "1961"). Multicoloured.
N 275. 5 ch. Type **165** 10 5
N 276. 5 ch. Cogwheel and textiles 10 5
N 277. 10 ch. Hammer, sickle and torch on flag (vert.) . . 20 10
N 278. 10 ch. Cogwheels around power station . . 20 10
N 279. 10 ch. Cogwheel and molten steel 20 10

1961. Multicoloured.
N 280. 5 ch. Type **166** 20 8
N 281. 10 ch. Wild ginseng (perennial herb) . . 35 12

167. Aldehyde Shop.

1961. Construction of Vinalon Factory. With gum.
N 282. **167.** 5 ch. red on yellow 8 5
N 283. – 10 ch. blue on yellow 20 10
N 284. – 10 ch. blue on yellow 20 10
N 285. – 20 ch. purple on yellow 30 20
DESIGNS: No. N 283, Glacial acetic acid shop. No. N 284, Polymerization and saponification shop. No. N 285, Spinning shop.
See also Nos. N 338/41.

168. Construction Work.

169. Museum Building.

1961. Construction of Children's Cultural Centre, Pyongyang. With gum.
N 286. **168.** 2 ch. red on yellow . . 15 5

1961. Completion of Museum of Revolution, Pyongyang. With gum.
N 287. **169.** 10 ch. red 20 8

170. Cosmic Rocket.

171. Wheat Harvester.

1961. Launching of Second Soviet Cosmic Rocket.
N 288. **170.** 10 ch. red, yell.& bl. 1·75 50

1961. Agricultural Mechanisation. With gum.
N 289. – 5 ch. violet 10 5
N 290. – 5 ch. green 10 5
N 291. **171.** 5 ch. green 10 5
N 292. – 10 ch. blue 25 10
N 293. – 10 ch. purple . . 25 10
DESIGNS: No. N 289, Tractor-plough. No. N 290, Disc-harrow. No. N 292, Maize-harvester. No. N 293, Tractors.

172.

173. Agriculture.

1961. Opening of Communist Institute.
N 294. **172.** 10 ch. brn. on buff 25 10

1961. Land Reform Law. 15th Anniv. With gum.
N 295. **173.** 10 ch. grn. on yell. 25 10

174.

175. Mackerel.

1961. National Programme. 15th Anniv. With gum.
N 296. **174.** 10 ch. pur. & yell. . . 20 10

1961. Fish.
N 297. **175.** 5 ch. multicoloured 15 5
N 298. – 5 ch. blk. & blue . . 15 5
N 299. – 10 ch. bl., blk. & lt. bl. 20 10
N 300. – 10 ch. multicoloured 20 10
N 301. – 10 ch. brn., yell. & grn. 20 10
DESIGNS: No. N 298, Dolphin. No. N 299, Whale. No. N 300, Tunny. No. N 301. Pollock.

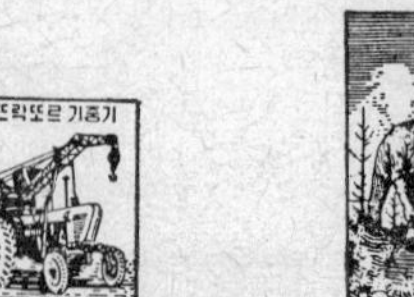
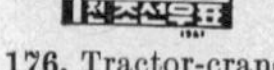
176. Tractor-crane.

177. Tree-planting.

1961. With gum.
N 302. **176.** 1 ch. purple . . 5 5
N 303. – 2 ch. brown . . 8 5
N 304. – 5 ch. green 10 5
N 305. – 10 ch. violet . . 15 8
DESIGNS—HORIZ. 2 ch. Heavy-duty lorry. 5 ch. Eight-metres turning lathe. VERT. 10 ch. 3000-ton press.
See also Nos. N 378/9c, N 415122, N 513/5 and N 573.

1961. Re-afforestation Campaign. With gum.
N 306. **177.** 10 ch. green . . 20 15

178. "Peaceful Unification" Banner.

179. Pioneers visiting Battlefield.

1961. Propaganda for Peaceful Reunification of Korea.
N 307. **178.** 10 ch. multicoloured 20 10

1961. Young Pioneers. 15th Anniv. Mult.
N 308. 5 ch. Pioneers bathing 10 8
N 309. 10 ch. Pioneer bugler . . 20 10
N 310. 10 ch. Type **179** . . 20 10

180. "Labour Law".

181. Apples.

1961. Labour Law. 15th Anniv. With gum.
N 311. **180.** 10 ch. blue on yellow 20 10

1961. Fruit. Multicoloured.
N 312. 5 ch. Peaches 8 5
N 313. 5 ch. Plums 8 5
N 314. 5 ch. Type **181** 8 5
N 315. 10 ch. Persimmons . . 25 8
N 316. 10 ch. Pears 25 8

182. Yuri Gagarin and "Vostok-I".

1961. World's First Manned Space Flight.
N 317. **182.** 10 ch. ultram. & blue 75 25
N 318. 10 ch. violet & blue 75 25

183. Power Station.

1961. Nationalisation of Industries Law. 15th Anniv. With gum.
N 319. **183.** 10 ch. brown . . 25 5

184. Women at Work.

185. Children planting Tree.

1961. Sex Equality Law. 15th Anniv. With gum.
N 320. **184.** 10 ch. red 25 5

1961. Children. Multicoloured.
N 321. 5 ch. Type **185** 8 5
N 322. 5 ch. Reading book . . 8 5
N 323. 10 ch. Playing with ball 20 12
N 324. 10 ch. Building a house 20 12
N 325. 10 ch. Waving flag . . 20 12

186. Poultry and Stock-breeding.

187. Party Emblem and Members.

1961. Improvement in Living Standards. Mult.
N 326. 5 ch. Type **186** 8 5
N 327. 10 ch. Fabrics and textile factory 15 10
N 328. 10 ch. Trawler and fish (horiz.) 15 10
N 329. 10 ch. Grain-harvesting (horiz.) 15 10

1961. Fourth Korean Workers' Party Congress, Pyongyang. With gum.
N 330. **187.** 10 ch. green . . 15 10
N 331. – 10 ch. purple . . 15 10
N 332. – 10 ch. red 15 10
DESIGNS—VERT. No. N 331, "Flying Horse" statue, Pyongyang. HORIZ. No. N 332, Marshal Kim Il Sung.

188. Soldiers on March (statue). 189. Miner.

1961. Fatherland Restoration Association. 25th Anniv. With gum.

N 333. – 10 ch. violet .. 15 10
N 334. – 10 ch. violet .. 15 10
N 335. 188. 10 ch. blue & buff .. 15 10

DESIGNS—Marshal Kim Il Sung. No. N 333, Seated under tree. No. N 334, Working at desk.

1961. Miners' Day. With gum.

N 336. 189. 10 ch. brown .. 15 10

190. Pak in Ro. 191. Aldehyde Shop.

1961. Pak in Ro (poet). 400th Birth Anniv.

N 337. 190. 10 ch. indigo on blue 15 10

1961. Completion of Vinalon Factory. With gum.

N 338. 191. 5 ch. red on cream 8 5
N 339. – 10 ch. brn. on cream 20 10
N 340. – 10 ch. blue on cream 20 10
N 341. – 20 ch. purple on cream 30 12

DESIGNS: No. N 339, Glacial-acetic shop. No. N 340, Polymerization and saponification shop. No. N 341, Spinning shop.

192. Korean and Chinese Flags. 193. Basketball.

1961. North Korean Friendship Treaties with China and the U.S.S.R.

N 342. – 10 ch. multicoloured 20 8
N 343. 192. 10 ch. red, bl. & yell. 20 8

DESIGN: No. N 342, Korean and Soviet flags.

1961. Physical Culture Day. With gum.

N 344. – 2 ch. grey 8 8
N 345. – 5 ch. blue 12 8
N 346. 193. 10 ch. blue 20 12
N 347. – 10 ch. blue 20 12
N 348. – 10 ch. purple .. 20 12
N 349. – 20 ch. red 35 20

DESIGNS: 2 ch. Table-tennis. 5 ch. Model aircraft flying. 10 ch. (No. N 347), Rowing. 10 ch. (No. N 348), High-jumping. 20 ch. Sports emblem.

(194.) 195. General Rock.

1961. Publication of Map "Taidong Yu Jido" by Kim Jung Ho. Cent. No. N 216 surch. with T 194.

N 350. 144. 5 ch. on 1 ch. grey on green .. .. 18·00 18·00

1961. Mt. Chil-bo Scenery. With gum.

N 351. 195. 5 ch. blue 8 5
N 352. – 5 ch. brown 8 5
N 353. – 10 ch. violet .. 20 10
N 354. – 10 ch. blue 20 10
N 355. – 10 ch. blue 20 10

DESIGNS—HORIZ. No. N 352, Chonbul Peak. No. N 354, Tiled House Rock. No. N 355, Rainbow Rock. VERT. No. N 353, Mansa Peak.

196. "Agriculture and Industry". 197. Winged Horse and Congress Emblem.

1961. With gum.

N 356. 196. 10 ch. green .. 20 10

1961. Fifth World Federation of Trade Unions Congress, Moscow. With gum.

N 357. 197. 10 ch. bl., pur. & vio. 20 8

198. Electric Locomotive ("Red Banner" class). 199. Ice-hockey.

1961. Railway Electrification. With gum.

N 358. 198. 10 ch. vio. & yellow 20 8

1961. Winter Sports. With gum.

N 359. – 10 ch. brown & grey 20 10
N 360. – 10 ch. brown & green 20 10
N 361. 199. 10 ch. brown and violet 20 10
N 362. – 10 ch. brown & blue 20 10

DESIGNS: No. N 359, Figure-skating. No. N 360, Speed-skating. No. 362, Skiing.

200. Grain-harvest. 201. Tiger.

1962. "Six Heights" of Production Targets (1st series.) Inscr. "1962". With gum.

N 363. – 5 ch. red, vio. & grey 12 8
N 364. – 5 ch. brown & grey 12 8
N 365. 200. 10 ch. yell., blk. & bl. 20 10
N 366. – 10 ch. red, yell. & bl. 20 10
N 367. – 10 ch. black & blue 20 10
N 368. – 10 ch. yell., brn. & bl. 20 10

DESIGNS: No. N 363, Ladle and molten ore. No. N 364, Coal-trucks. No. N 366, Fabrics and mill. No. N 367, Trawler and catch. No. N 368, Construction of flats.

See also Nos. N 440/5.

1962. Animals.

N 369. 201. 2 ch. multicoloured 8 5
N 370. – 2 ch. brown & green 8 5
N 371. – 5 ch. brown & green 15 8
N 372. – 10 ch. brown & green 30 12

ANIMALS—HORIZ. 2 ch. (No. N 370), Racoon. 5 ch. Badger. 10 ch. Bear.

202. Kayakeum Player. 203. "Luedorfia pusiloi Erschoff".

1962. Musical Instruments and Players (1st series). Multicoloured.

N 373. 10 ch. Type 202 .. 25 12
N 374. 10 ch. Man playing haekeum (two-stringed bowed instrument) .. 25 12
N 375. 10 ch. Woman playing wolkeum ("Banjo") .. 25 12
N 376. 10 ch. Man playing jutte ("flute") 25 12
N 377. 10 ch. Woman playing wakonghoo ("harp") 25 12

See also Nos N 473/7.

1962. As T 176. Inscr. "1962". With gum (Nos. N 379 and 379b), no gum (others).

N 378. 5 ch. green 10 5
N 379. 10 ch. blue 20 10
N 379a. 10 ch. brown .. .. 2·75
N 379b. 5 wn. brown .. .. 4·50 2·25
N 379c. 10 wn. purple .. .. 8·50 4·50

DESIGNS—VERT. 5 ch. Hydraulic press. 10 ch. (2), Three-ton hammer. 10 wn. Tunnel drill. HORIZ. 5 wn. Hobbing machine.

See also Nos. N 415/225, N 513/5 and 573.

1962. Butterflies. Multicoloured.

N 380. 5 ch. Type 203 .. .. 12 8
N 381. 10 ch. "Sericinus telamon Donovan" 25 12
N 382. 10 ch. "Parnassius memion Fischer" 25 12
N 383. 10 ch. "Neptis io Lanne" 25 12

204. G. S. Titov and Vostok-2.

1962. Second Soviet Manned Space Flight.

N 384. 204. 10 ch. multicoloured 75 25

205. Marshal Kim Il Sung and (inset) addressing workers. 206. Kim Chaek.

1962. Marshal Kim Il Sung's 50th Birthday. With gum.

N 385. 205. 10 ch. red 25 12
N 386. 10 ch. green .. 25 12
N 387. – 10 ch. blue 25 12

DESIGN: No. 387, Kim Il Sung in fur hat and (inset) inspecting battle-front.

1962. Korean Revolutionaries. (1st issue). With gum.

N 388. 206. 10 ch. sepia .. 20 10
N 389. – 10 ch. blue 20 10
N 390. – 10 ch. red 20 10
N 391. – 10 ch. purple .. 20 10
N 392. – 10 ch. green .. 20 10
N 393. – 10 ch. indigo .. 20 10
N 394. – 10 ch. chocolate .. 20 10

PORTRAITS: No. N 389, Kang Yon. N 390, An Kil. N 391. Yu Kyong-Su. N 392/3, Kim Chong Suk. N 394, Choe Chun-Guk.

See also Nos. N 478/82 and 733/5.

207. Mother with Children. 208. Blackfaced Spoonbill.

1962. National Mothers' Meeting, Pyongyang.

N 395. 207. 10 ch. multicoloured 25 8

1962. Birds. Inscr. "1962". Multicoloured.

N 396. 5 ch. Type 208 .. .. 12 5
N 397. 5 ch. Korean Wood-owl 12 5
N 398. 10 ch. Himalayan Broad-billed Roller 25 8
N 399. 10 ch. Japanese Paradise Fly-catcher 25 8
N 400. 20 ch. Eastern Berwick's Swan .. 40 20

209. Victory Flame. 210. Gilthead.

1962. Battle of Pochonbo. 25th Anniv.

N 401. 209. 10 ch. multicoloured 15 5

1962. Fish. Inscr. "1962". Multicoloured.

N 402. 5 ch. Type 210 .. .. 8 5
N 403. 5 ch. Hairtail 8 5
N 404. 10 ch. Shad 12 5
N 405. 10 ch. Sea bass 12 5
N 406. 10 ch. Stonehead .. 12 5

211. Waterdropper. 212. Radial Drill 213. Chong Ta San.

1962. Antiques. With gum.

N 407. – 4 ch. black & blue .. 8 5
N 408. 211. 5 ch. black & ochre 8 5
N 409. A. 10 ch. black & green 15 5
N 410. B. 10 ch. black & orange 15 5
N 411. C. 10 ch. black & purple 15 5
N 412. D. 10 ch. black & brown 15 5
N 413. E. 10 ch. black & yellow 15 5
N 414. – 40 ch. black & grey 50 25

DESIGNS—VERT. 4 ch. Brush pot. 40 ch. Porcelain decanter. HORIZ. A, Inkstand. B, Brushstand. C, Turtle paperweight. D, Inkstone. E, Document case.

1962. Double frame-line. With gum.

N 415. – 2 ch. green 5 5
N 416. – 4 ch. blue 5 5
N 417. 212. 5 ch. blue 8 5
N 418. – 5 ch. purple .. 8 5
N 419. – 10 ch. purple .. 15 5
N 420. – 40 ch. blue 40 12
N 421. – 90 ch. blue 90 30
N 422. – 1 wn. brown .. 1·25 40

DESIGNS—VERT. 2 ch. Vertical milling machine. 5 ch. (No. N 418), Hydraulic hammer. 1 w. Spindle drill. HORIZ. 4 ch. "Victory April 15" motor-car. 10 ch. All-purpose excavator. 40 ch. Trolley-bus. 90 ch. Planing machine.

See also No. N 513/5 and N 573.

1962. Chong Ta San. (philosopher). 200th Birth Anniv.

N 423. 213. 10 ch. slate-purple .. 20 8

214. Voter. 216. Globe and "Vostoks 3 and 4".

215. Pyongyang.

1962. Election of Deputies to National Assembly. Multicoloured.

N 424. 10 ch. Type 214 .. 20 5
N 425. 10 ch. Family going to poll. 20 5

1962. Pyongyang. 1535th Anniv. With gum.

N 426. 215. 10 ch. black and blue 20 8

1962. 1st "Team" Manned Space Flight.

N 427. 216. 10 ch. ind., bl. & red 1·25 75

217. Spiraea. 218. "Uibang Yuch'wi".

1962. Korean Plants. Plants in natural colours; frame and inscr. colours given.

N 428. 217. 5 ch. grn. & grey-grn. 10 5
N 429. – 10 ch. bl. & red .. 15 5
N 430. – 10 ch. bl. & pur. .. 15 5
N 431. – 10 ch. grn. & ol. .. 15 5

PLANTS: Nos. N 429, Ginseng. N 430, Campanula. N 431, "Rheumcoreanum Makai (Polyonaceae)".

1962. 485th Anniv. of Publication of "Uibang Yuch'wi" (medical encyclopaedia).

N 432. 218. 10 ch. yell., blk., bl. and lavender .. 20 8

219. Science Academy.

220. Fisherwomen.

1962. Korean Science Academy. 10th Anniv.
N 433. **219.** 10 ch. bl. & turq. .. 20 8

1962.
N 434. **220.** 10 ch. blue 20 8

221. Weasel.

1962. Korean Animals.
N 435 **221.** 4 ch. brown & apple 5 5
N 436. – 5 ch. bl., drab & grn. 5 5
N 437. – 10 ch. grey-bl. & yell. 15 5
N 438. – 10 ch. sepia & turq. 15 5
N 439. – 20 ch. brn. & blue .. 30 15
ANIMALS—HORIZ. 5 ch. Hare. VERT. No. N 437, Flying squirrel. No. N 438, Goat. 20 ch. Red squirrel.

222. Miner.

1963. "Six Heights" of Production Targets (2nd issue). Inscr. "1963". Multicoloured.
N 440. 5 ch. Type **222** 10 5
N 441. 10 ch. Harvest-girl and tractor 15 5
N 442. 10 ch. Furnaceman .. 15 5
N 443. 10 ch. Construction worker 15 5
N 444. 10 ch. Textiles loom operator 15 5
N 445. 40 ch. Fisherman and boat 60 25

223. Soldier.

224. Peony.

1963. Korean People's Army. 15th Anniv. With gum.
N 446. – 5 ch. brown .. 8 5
N 447. **223.** 10 ch. red 15 5
N 448. – 10 ch. blue 15 8
DESIGNS: 5 ch. Airman. 10 ch. blue, Sailor.

1963. Korean Flowers. Multicoloured.
N 449. 5 ch. Type **224** 8 5
N 450. 10 ch. Rugosa rose .. 20 5
N 451. 10 ch. Azalea 20 5
N 452. 10 ch. Campion 20 5
N 453. 40 ch. Orchid 60 25

225. Revolutionaries.

226. "Sadang-ch'um" (Korean folk dance).

1963. South Korean Rising of April, 1960. 3rd Anniv.
N 454. **225.** 10 ch. mult. .. 20 8

1963. Int. Music and Dancing Contest, Pyongyang. Multicoloured.
N 455. 10 ch Type **226** .. 20 8
N 456. 10 ch. Dancer with fan 20 8

227. Karl Marx.

228. Children in Chemistry Class.

1963. Karl Marx. 145th Birth Anniv. With gum.
N 457. **227.** 10 ch. blue 15 8

1963. Child Care and Amenities. Mult.
N 458. 2 ch. Type **228** 5 5
N 459. 5 ch. Children running 8 5
N 460. 10 ch. Boy conducting choir 15 8
N 461. 10 ch. Girl chasing butterfly 15 8

229. Armed Koreans and American Soldier (caricature).

1963. Campaign Month for Withdrawal of U.S. Forces from South Korea.
N 462. **229.** 10 ch. multicoloured 15 8

230. "Cyprotoclytus capra" (beetle).

ILLUSTRATIONS British Commonwealth and all overprints and surcharges are FULL SIZE. Foreign Countries have been reduced to ¾-LINEAR.

1963. Korean Beetles. Multicoloured designs. Colours of beetles given.
N 463. 5 ch. Type **230** 10 8
N 464. 10 ch. bl., red, yell. & grn. 20 10
N 465. 10 ch. red and blue .. 20 10
N 466. 10 ch. ind., bl. & pur. .. 20 10
BEETLES: No. N 464, "Cicindela chinenis". N 465, "Purpuricenus lituratus". N 466, "Agapantnia pilicoris".

231. Soldier with Flag.

232. North Korean Flag.

1963. Victory in Korean War. 10th Anniv.
N 467. **231.** 10 ch. mult. .. 15 8

1963. People's Republic. 15th Anniv. Mult.
N 468. 10 ch. Type **232** .. 15 8
N 469. 10 ch. N. Korean Badge 15 8

233. Namdaemun, Kaesong.

234. Ajaeng (bowed zither).

1963. Ancient Korean Buildings (1st series). With gum.
N 470. **233.** 5 ch. black 8 5
N 471. – 10 ch. blue 15 5
N 472. – 10 ch. choc. .. 15 5
BUILDINGS: No. N 471, Pot'ong-mun, Pyongyang. No. N 472, Taedong-mun, Pyongyang. See also Nos. N 537/8.

1963. Musical Instruments and Players (2nd series). Multicoloured. Nos. N 473 and 476 with gum.
N 473. 5 ch. Type **234** 10 5
N 474. 5 ch. Pyon-gyong (jade chimes) 10 5
N 475. 10 ch. Saenap (brass bowl) 20 5
N 476. 10 ch. Rogo (drums in frame) 20 5
N 477. 10 ch. Piri ("wooden pipe") 20 5

1963. Korean Revolutionaries (2nd issue). As Type **206.** With gum.
N 478. 5 ch. brown 15 8
N 479. 5 ch. brown-purple .. 15 8
N 480. 10 ch. rose 20 8
N 481. 10 ch. slate-blue .. 20 8
N 482. 10 ch. dull purple .. 20 8
PORTRAITS: No. N 478 Kwon Yung Byuk. N 479, Ma Dong Hi. N 480, Li Je Sun. N 481, Pak Dal. N 482, Kim Yong Bum.

235. Nurse with Children.

236. Mt. Myohyang.

1963. Child Welfare. Multicoloured.
N 483. 10 ch. Type **235** .. 20 8
N 484. 10 ch. Children in play ground 20 8

1963. Mount Myohyang Resort. Mult.
N 485. 5 ch. Type **236** 8 5
N 486. 10 ch. Mountain stream and chalet 20 5
N 487. 10 ch. House and tower 20 5
N 488. 10 ch. Rope bridge across river 20 5
Nos. N 487/8 are horiz.

237. Furnaceman.

238. Children hoeing.

1963. Seven Year Plan. With gum.
N 489. **237.** 5 ch. red 8 5
N 490. – 10 ch. slate 15 8
N 491. – 10 ch. brown .. 15 8
N 492. – 10 ch. violet .. 15 8
DESIGNS—VERT. No. N 490, Construction workers. HORIZ. 491, Power technicians. 492, Miners.

1963. Heungbo Fairy Tale. Multicoloured.
N 493. 5 ch. Type **238** 8 5
N 494. 10 ch. "Treasure chest" 15 5
N 495. 10 ch. Family group .. 15 5
N 496. 10 ch. "Giant fruit" .. 15 5
N 497. 10 ch. "Bird messenger" 15 5

239. Marksman.

1963 Marksmanship. Multicoloured.
N 498. 5 ch. Type **239** 8 5
N 499. 10 ch. Marksman with small-bore rifle .. 15 5
N 500. 10 ch. Marksman with standard rifle .. 15 5

240. Sinuiju Chemical Fibre Factory.

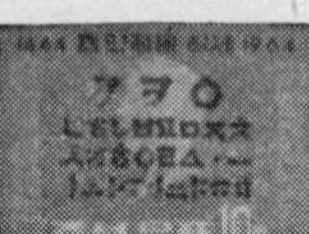
242. Korean Alphabet.

241. Strikers.

243. Lenin.

1964. Chemical Fibres Factories. With gum.
N 501. **240.** 10 ch. slate 10 5
N 502. – 10 ch. slate-purple 10 5
DESIGN: No. N 502, Chungjin Chemical Fibre Factory.

1964. Wonsan General Strike. 35th Anniv. With gum.
N 503. **241.** 10 ch. brown .. 15 8

1964. Korean Alphabet. 520th Anniv.
N 504. **242.** 10 ch. grn., buff & brn. 15 8

1964. Lenin. 40th Death Anniv. With gum.
N 505. **243.** 10 ch. red 15 8

DESIGNS: Nos. N 507/9, Fishing vessels.

244. Whaler.

1964. Fishing Industry.
N 506. **244.** 5 ch. ind., bl., blk., red and yellow .. 8 5
N 507. – 5 ch. grey, blk., red, blue and pale blue 8 5
N 508. – 10 ch. bl., blk. & turq. 20 8
N 509. – 10 ch. ind., bl., olive and pale blue .. 20 8

245. Insurgents.

246. Warring Peasants.

1964. Rising of 1st March. 45th Anniv. With gum.
N 510. **245.** 10 ch. slate-purple 15 8

1964. Kabo Peasant's War. 70th Anniv. With gum.
N 511. **246.** 10 ch. slate-purple .. 15 8

247. Students' Palace, Pyongyang.

248. "Horning-500" Machine.

1964. With gum.
N 512. **247.** 10 ch. bronze-green 15 8

1964. Single frame-line. Dated "1964" or "1965" (No. N 569). With gum.
N 513. A. 5 ch. slate-violet .. 8 5
N 514. B. 10 ch. grey-green .. 12 5
N 515. C. 10 ch. slate-blue .. 12 5
N 573. **248.** 10 ch. slate-violet .. 15 5
DESIGNS—VERT. A. 200-Metre drill. B. "Chang baek" excavator. HORIZ. C, 400 h.p. Diesel engine.

249. "On the March".

1964. 5th Korean Youth League Congress, Pyongyang.
N 516. **249.** 10 ch. multicoloured 15 8

250. Electric Train.

1964. Pyongyang-Sinuiju Electric Railway. Inaug.
N 517. **250.** 10 ch. multicoloured 15 8

CATALOGUE NUMBERS WITH ASTERISKS. Certain issues have been reported in *Korean Stamps*, the journal of the Philatelists' Union of North Korea, but at the time of going to press have not been distributed outside North Korea. The issues in question are Nos. N517*a*, N733/5, N753, N839/MSN849, N885/7, N918, N1035, N1045/6, N1048/50, N1113/4 and N1189. They are indicated by asterisks after the catalogue numbers and are not priced.

251. Rejoicing in Chungsan-ri Village.

1964. Popular movement at Chungsan-ri. With gum.

N 517a.* **251.** 5 ch. brown ..

252. Drum Dance. **253.** Li Su Bok in battle.

1964. Korean Dances.

N 518. **252.** 2 ch. mag., buff & blk. 5 5
N 519. – 5 ch. red, blk. & yell. 8 5
N 520. – 10 ch. multicoloured 15 8
DANCES: 5 ch. "Ecstasy" (solo). 10 ch. Tabor.

1964. Li Su Bok Commem. With gum.

N 521. **253.** 5 ch. red 8 5

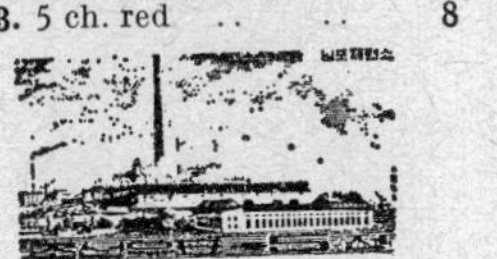

254. Nampo Smelting Works.

1964. With gum.

N 522. **254.** 5 ch. green 8 5
N 523. – 10 ch. slate.. .. 15 8
DESIGNS: 10 ch. Hwanghae iron works.

255. Torch, statue and Cogwheel.

1964. Asian Economic Seminar, Pyongyang. Multicoloured.

N 524. 5 ch. Type **255** .. 8 5
N 525. 10 ch. Flags, statue and cogwheel 15 8

256. Korean People and Statue of Kang Ho Yong (war hero).

1964. Struggle for Reunification of Korea.

N 526. **256.** 10 ch. multcoloured 15 8

257. Mae-dak (Hawk fowl).

1964. Domestic Poultry. Multicoloured.

N 527. 2 ch. Type **257** 5 5
N 528. 4 ch. Hin-dak (white fowl) 5 5
N 529. 5 ch. Pyongyun-dak (fowl of Pyongyun) .. 8 5
N 530. 5 ch. Komun-dak (black fowl) 8 5
N 531. 40 ch. Chinju-dak (pearl fowl) 50 25

258. Skiing.

DESIGNS: No. N 533, Ice-skating. N 534, Skiing (slalom).

1964. Winter Olympic Games, Innsbruck.

N 532. **258.** 5 ch. red, bl. & buff 8 5
N 533. – 10 ch. bl., grn. & buff 15 8
N 534. – 10 ch. bl., red & buff 15 8

259. Ship and Flags. **260.** Tonggun Pavilion Uiju.

1964. Agreement for Repatriation of Koreans in Japan.

N 535. **259.** 10 ch. red, bl. & lt. bl. 20 8
N 536. – 30 ch. multicoloured 50 20
DESIGN: 30 ch. Return of repatriates.

1964. Ancient Korean Buildings (2nd series). With gum.

N 537. **260.** 5 ch. purple .. 8 5
N 538. – 10 ch. green .. 20 5
DESIGN: 10 ch. Inp'ang Pavilion, Kanggye City.

261. Cycling. **262.** Burning of the U.S.S. "General Sherman".

1964. Olympic Games, Tokyo.

N 539. – 2 ch. chestnut and slate 5 5
N 540. **261.** 5 ch. brown & green 8 5
N 541. – 10 ch. orge. & blue 15 5
N 542. – 10 ch. orge. & bl.-grn. 15 5
N 543. – 40 ch. brn. & ultram. 60 20
DESIGNS—HORIZ. 2 ch. Rifle-shooting. 10 ch. blue Running. VERT. 10 ch. green, Wrestling. 40 ch. Volleyball.

1964. The "General Sherman" Incident, 1866. With gum.

N 544. **262.** 30 ch. brown .. 50 15

DESIGNS: 5 ch. Kim Il Sung addressing guerrillas. 10 ch. Battle scene at Sowangchun.

263. Organising Guerrillas.

1964. Guerrilla Operations in the 1930's against the Japanese. With gum.

N 545. **263.** 2 ch. violet 5 5
N 546. – 5 ch. blue 12 5
N 547. – 10 ch. black .. 15 8

264. Students attacking. **265.** Weightlifting.

1964. Kwangju Students Rising, 1929. With gum.

N 548. **264.** 10 ch. slate-violet 20 8

1964. "GANEFO" Athletic Games, Jakarta (1963). Multicoloured.

N 549. 2 ch. Type **265** .. 5 5
N 550. 5 ch. Athlete breasting tape 8 5
N 551. 5 ch. Boxing 8 5
N 552. 10 ch. Football 20 8
N 553. 10 ch. Globe emblem .. 20 8
Nos. N 251/3 are horiz.

266. Lynx. **267.** Vietnamese Attack.

1964. Animals. With gum.

N 554. 2 ch. sepia (Type **266**) .. 5 5
N 555. 5 ch. sepia (Wild cat) .. 10 5
N 556. 10 ch. brown (Leopard) 20 8
N 557. 10 ch. sepia (Weasel) .. 20 8

1964. Support for People of Vietnam.

N 558. **267.** 10 ch. multicoloured 20 8

268. Prof. Bong Kim Han and Emblems.

1964. Kyungrak Biological System.

N 559. **268.** 2 ch. maroon & olive 5 5
N 560. – 5 ch. grn., orge. & bl. 8 5
N 561. – 10 ch. red, yell. & bl. 20 8
DESIGNS (33×23½ mm.): 5 ch. "Bonghan" duct. 10 ch. "Bonghan" corpuscle. Each include emblems as in Type **268.**

269. Farmers, Tractor and Lorry.

1964. Agrarian Programme. Multicoloured.

N 562. 5 ch. Type **269** 5 5
N 563. 10 ch. Peasants with scroll and book .. 15 8
N 564. 10 ch. Peasants—one writing in book .. 15 8

270. Chung Jin gets a Pistol. **271.** Girl with Korean Products.

1964. The Struggle to capture Japanese Arms. With gum.

N 565. **270.** 4 ch. brown .. 8 5

1964. Economic 7-Year Plan. Multicoloured. With gum (5 ch.) or no gum (others).

N 566. 5 ch. Type **271** 5 5
N 567. 10 ch. Farm girl .. 15 8
N 568. 10 ch. Couple on winged horse (23½×23½ mm.) 15 8

272. Three Fairies Rock. **273.** Soldiers Advancing, Fusung.

1964. Diamond Mountains Scenery (2nd issue). Inscr. "1964". Multicoloured. Without gum (2, 4 ch.) or with gum (others).

N 569. 2 ch. Type **272** 5 5
N 570. 4 ch. Ryunjoo Falls .. 5 5
N 571. 10 ch. The Ten Thousand Rocks, Manmoolsang 15 8
N 572. 10 ch. Jinjoo Falls .. 15 8

1965. Guerrilla Operations against the Japanese, 1934-40. With gum.

N 574. **273.** 10 ch. violet .. 15 8
N 575. – 10 ch. slate-violet .. 15 8
N 576. – 10 ch. green .. 15 8
DESIGNS: No. N 575, Soldiers descending hill, Hungchiho. N 576, Soldiers attacking hill post, Lotzukou.

274. Tumen River. **275.** Union Badge.

1965. Korean Rivers. Multicoloured.

N 577. 2 ch. Type **274** 5 5
N 578. 5 ch. Daidong (vert.) .. 5 5
N 579. 10 ch. Amnok 15 8

1965. First Congress of Landworkers' Union, Pyongyang. With gum.

N 580. **275.** 10 ch. multicoloured 15 8

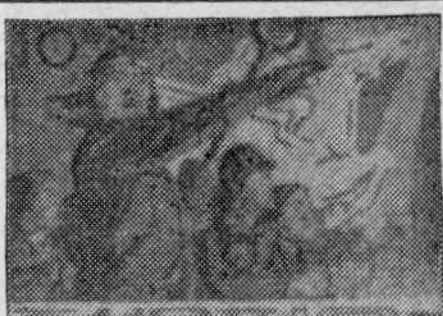

276. Furnacemen and Workers.

1965. 10 Major Tasks of 7-Year Plan.

N 581. **276.** 10 ch. multicoloured 15 8

277. Colliery Scene (Miners' Strike, Sinhung Colliery).

1965. Strikes and Peasants' Revolt. 35th Annivs. With gum.

N 582. **277.** 10 ch. olive.. .. 15 8
N 583. – 10 ch. brown .. 15 8
N 584. – 40 ch. maroon .. 60 30
DESIGNS: 10 ch. Strikers at Pyongyang Rubber Factory. 40 ch. Revolt of Tanch'on peasants.

278. Embankment Construction. **279.** Hand holding Torch.

1965. Sunhwa River Works. With gum.

N 585. **278.** 10 ch. multicoloured 15 8

1965. South Korean Rising of April 19th. 5th Anniv. Inscr. "4,19". Mult. With gum.

N 586. 10 ch. Type **279** .. 15 8
N 587. 40 ch. Student-hero, Kim Chio 60 25

280. Power Station under Construction.

1965. Construction of Thermal Power Station, Pyongyang.

N 588. **280.** 5 ch. brown & blue 8 5

281. African and Asian.

1965. 1st Afro-Asian Conf., Bandung. 10th Anniv. With gum.

N 589. **281.** 10 ch. multicoloured 15 8

282. Rejoicing Koreans.

1965. General Assn. of Koreans in Japan. 10th Anniv. Inscr. "1955-1965". With gum.

N 590. **282.** 10 ch. bl. & red .. 15 8
N 591. – 40 ch. ind., blue & red 65 25
DESIGN: 40 ch. Patriot and flag.

MINIMUM PRICE

The minimum price quoted is 5p which represents a handling charge rather than a basis for valuing common stamps. For further notes about prices see introductory pages.

283. Workers in Battle.

284. "Victory 64" 10-ton Lorry.

1965. 2nd Afro-Asian Conf., Algiers. With gum.

N 592. **283.** 10 ch. black, yell. & red 15 8
N 593. – 40 ch. black, yell. & red 60 25

DESIGN: 40 ch. Korean and African soldiers. The Algiers Conf. did not take place.

1965. With gum.

N 594. **284.** 10 ch. green .. 15 5

285. Kim Chang Gul.

1965. War Heroes (1st series). With gum

N 595. **285.** 10 ch. green .. 15 8
N 596. – 10 ch. brown .. 15 8
N 597. – 40 ch. purple .. 70 25

PORTRAITS: No. N 596, Cho Kun Sil and machine-gun. No. N 597, An Hag Yong and machine-gun.

See also Nos. N 781/3 and N 850/1.

286. Marx and Lenin.

1965. Postal Ministers' Congress, Peking. With gum.

N 598. **286.** 10 ch. blk., yell & red 15 8

287. Lake Samilpo.

1965. Diamond Mountains Scenery (3rd issue). Multicoloured. With gum.

N 599. 2 ch. Type **287** 5 5
N 600. 5 ch. Chipsunbong Rocks 8 5
N 601. 10 ch. Kwanum Falls .. 15 8

288. Amnok River, Kusimultong.

289. Footballer and Games' Emblem.

1965. Scenes of Japanese War.

N 602. **288.** 5 ch. green & blue.. 8 5
N 603. – 10 ch. turq. & blue.. 15 8

DESIGN: 10 ch. Lake Samjiyun.

1965. "GANEFO" Football Games, Pyongyang. Multicoloured. With gum, perf. or without gum, imperf.

N 604. 10 ch. Type **289** .. 20 8
N 605. 10 ch. Games emblem and Moranbong Stadium 20 8

290. Workers and Map.

291. Engels.

1965. Liberation from Japan. 20th Anniv. With gum.

N 606. **290.** 10 ch. multicoloured 15 8

1965. Engels' 145th Birth Anniv. With gum.

N 607. **291.** 10 ch. brown .. 15 8

292. Pole-vaulting.

294. Kim Ch'aek Iron Works.

293. Korean Fighters.

1965. Sports. Multicoloured.

N 608. 2 ch. Type **292** 5 5
N 609. 4 ch. Throwing the javelin 8 5
N 610. 10 ch. Throwing the discus 20 8
N 611. 10 ch. High-jumping .. 20 8
N 612. 10 ch. Putting the shot 20 8

Nos. N 611/2 are horiz.

1965. Korean Workers' Party. 20th Anniv. Each black, yellow and red. With gum.

N 613. 10 ch. Type **293** .. 15 8
N 614. 10 ch. Party emblem .. 15 8
N 615. 10 ch. Lenin and Marx 15 8
N 616. 10 ch. Workers marching 15 8
N 617. 10 ch. Fighters 15 8
N 618. 40 ch. Workers 50 20

Nos. N 613/8 each have a red banner in the background and were issued together in blocks of 6 (3×2), forming a composite design, within the sheet.

1965. With gum.

N 620. **294.** 10 ch. maroon .. 15 8
N 621. – 10 ch. brown .. 15 8

DESIGN: 10 ch. Chungjin Steel Works.

295. Cho (grass) Fish.

296. Family at Home.

1965. Freshwater Fish. Multicoloured. With gum.

N 622. 2 ch. Rainbow trout .. 5 5
N 623. 4 ch. Sanchun fish .. 8 5
N 624. 10 ch. Yulmook fish (surfacing water) .. 15 8
N 625. 10 ch. Carp diving (date at left) 15 8
N 626. 10 ch. Type **295** .. 15 8
N 627. 40 ch. Crucian carp .. 60 25

1965. Kim Hong Do's Drawings. With gum.

N 628. 2 ch. green (Type **296**) 5 5
N 629. 4 ch. maroon (Weaving) 5 5
N 630. 10 ch. brown (Wrestling) 20 8
N 631. 10 ch. blue (School class) 20 8
N 632. 10 ch. crimson (Dancing) 20 8
N 633. 10 ch. violet (Preparing out-door meal) .. 20 8

297. Children in Workshop.

298. Whale-catcher.

1965. Life at Pyongyang Children's and Students' Palace. Multicoloured.

N 634. 2 ch. Type **297** 5 5
N 635. 4 ch. Boxing 8 5
N 636. 10 ch. Chemistry .. 15 8
N 637. 10 ch. Music-making .. 15 8

1965. Korean Fishing Boats. With gum.

N 638. **298.** 10 ch. indigo .. 20 8
N 639. – 10 ch. green .. 20 8

DESIGN: 10 ch. Fishing Fleet Service Vessel.

299. Manchurian Great Tit.

300. Moth ("Bombyx mori") and Cocoon.

1965. Korean Birds. Inscr. "1965". Multicoloured. With gum.

N 640. 4 ch. Black-capped Kingfisher (vert.) .. 10 5
N 641. 10 ch. Type **299** .. 20 8
N 642. 10 ch. Korean pied wagtail (facing left) .. 20 8
N 643. 10 ch. Azure-winged magpie (facing right) 20 8
N 644. 40 ch. Korean grosbeak 60 25

1965. Korean Sericulture. With gum.

N 645. **300.** 2 ch. green 5 5
N 646. – 10 ch. brown .. 20 8
N 647. – 10 ch. purple .. 20 8

MOTHS AND COCOONS: No. N 646, "Philosomia cynthia". N 647, "Antheraea pernyi".

301. Hooded Crane.

302. Squid.

1965. Wading Birds.

N 648. **301.** 2 ch. brown .. 5 5
N 649. – 10 ch. violet .. 20 8
N 650. – 10 ch. purple .. 20 8
N 651. – 40 ch. green .. 60 25

BIRDS: No. N 649, White-necked crane. N 650, Manchurian crane. N 651, Jouy's grey heron.

1965. Korean Molluscs. Mult. With gum.

N 652. 5 ch. Type **302** .. 8 5
N 653. 10 ch. Octopus 20 8

303. Spotted-bill Duck.

304. Circus Theatre, Pyongyang.

1965. Korean Ducks. Mult. With gum.

N 654. 2 ch. Type **303** 5 5
N 655. 4 ch. Ruddy Shelduck.. 8 5
N 656. 10 ch. Mallard 20 8
N 657. 40 ch. Baikal teal .. 65 35

1965. Korean Circus. With gum except No. N 661.

N 658. **304.** 2 ch. bl., blk. & chestnut 5 5
N 659. – 10 ch. bl., verm. & blk. 20 8
N 660. – 10 ch. verm., blk. & grn. 20 8
N 661. – 10 ch. orge., sepia & grn. 20 8
N 662. – 10 ch. red, yell & turq. 20 8

DESIGNS—VERT. No. N 659, Trapeze artistes. N 660, Performer with hoops on seesaw. N 661, Tightrope dancers. N 662, Performer with revolving cap on stick.

305. "Marvel of Peru" ("Mirabelis jalopa").

306. Finn-class Yacht.

1965. Korean Flowers. Multicoloured. With gum except No. N 663.

N 663. 4 ch. Type **305**. .. 8 5
N 664. 10 ch. Peony 20 8
N 665. 10 ch. Moss rose .. 20 8
N 666. 10 ch. Magnolia .. 20 8

1965. Yachts. Multicoloured. With gum.

N 667. 2 ch. Type **306** 5 5
N 668. 10 ch. "5.5" 20 8
N 669. 10 ch. "Dragon" .. 20 8
N 670. 40 ch. "Star" 65 20

307. Cuban, Korean and African.

308. Hosta.

1966. Afro-Asian and Latin American Friendship Conf., Havana. With gum.

N 671. **307.** 10 ch. multicoloured 15 8

1966. Wild Flowers. Mult. With gum.

(a) 1st series.

N 672. 2 ch. Type **308** 5 5
N 673. 4 ch. Dandelion .. 8 5
N 674. 10 ch. Pink convolvulus 20 8
N 675. 10 ch. Lily-of-the-Valley 20 8
N 676. 40 ch. Catalpa blossom 65 25

(b) 2nd Series.

N 677. 2 ch. Polyanthus .. 5 5
N 678. 4 ch. Lychnis 8 5
N 679. 10 ch. Adonis 20 8
N 680. 10 ch. Orange lily .. 20 8
N 681. 90 ch. Rhododendron .. 1·25 60

309. Farmer and Wife.

1966. Land Reform Law. 20th Anniv. With gum.

N 682. **309.** 10 ch. multicoloured 15 8

310. Troops advancing, Tashaho.

311. Silla Bowl.

1966. Paintings of Guerrilla Battles, 1937-39. With gum.

N 683. **310.** 10 ch. red 20 8
N 684. – 10 ch. turquoise .. 20 8
N 685. – 10 ch. maroon .. 20 8

DESIGNS AND BATTLES: No. N 684, Troops firing from trees. Dalhongdan. N 685, Troops on hillside, Kansambong.

1966. Art Treasures of Silla Dynasty. With gum.

N 686. **311.** 2 ch. ochre 5 5
N 687. – 5 ch. black 8 5
N 688. – 10 ch. violet .. 20 8

DESIGNS: 5 ch. Earthenware jar. 10 ch. Censer.

312. Hands holding Torch, Rifle and Hammer.

313. Torch and Patriots.

1966. Labour Day. 80th Anniv. With gum.

N 689. **312.** 10 ch. multicoloured 20 8

1966. Restoration of Fatherland Assn. 30th Anniv.

N 690. **313.** 10 ch. red & yellow 20 8

314. Harvester.

1966. Aid for Agriculture. Multicoloured.
N 691. 5 ch. Type **314** 8 5
N 692. 10 ch. Labourer 20 8

315. Young Pioneers.

1966. Korean Young Pioneers. 20th Anniv. Without gum.
N 693. **315.** 10 ch. multicoloured 20 8

316. Kangson Steel Works.

1966. Korean Industries. With gum.
N 694. **316.** 10 ch. grey 20 8
N 695. 10 ch. red (Bongung Chemical Works) 20 8

317. Saury.

1966. Korean Fishes. With gum except Nos. 699/700.
N 696. **317.** 2 ch. bl., grn. & pur. 5 5
N 697. – 5 ch. mar., grn. & cinn. 8 5
N 698. – 10 ch. bl., buff & grn. 20 8
N 699. – 10 ch. mar. & green 20 8
N 700. – 40 ch. grn., buff & blue 65 20
FISHES: 5 ch. Cod. 10 ch. (No. N 698), Salmon, (No. N 699), "Pleurogrammus azonus". 40 ch. "Pink" salmon.

318. Professor Kim Bong Han.

1966. Kyungrak Biological System. With gum.
N 701. **318.** 2 ch. multicoloured 5 5
N 702. – 4 ch. multicoloured 5 5
N 703. – 5 ch. multicoloured 8 5
N 704. – 10 ch. multicoloured 15 8
N 705. – 10 ch. multicoloured 15 8
N 706. – 10 ch. multicoloured 15 8
N 707. – 15 ch. multicoloured 20 10
N 708. – 40 ch. multicoloured 65 25
DESIGNS: Nos. N 701/8 were issued together in the form of a block of 8 (2×4) within the sheet, forming a composite design of the Kyungrak biological system.

319. Leonov in Space ("Voskhod 2").

1966. Cosmonauts Day. Multicoloured.
N 710. 5 ch. Type **319** 8 5
N 711. 10 ch. "Luna 9" .. 25 5
N 712. 10 ch. "Luna 10" .. 75 30

320. Footballers.

1966. World Cup Football Championships. Multicoloured.
N 713. 10 ch. Type **320.** .. 20 8
N 714. 10 ch. Jules Rimet Cup, football and boots .. 20 8
N 715. 10 ch. Goalkeeper saving goal (vert.) 20 8

321. Defence of Seoul.

1966. Korean War of 1950-53.
N 716. **321.** 10 ch. green .. 15 8
N 717. – 10 ch. purple .. 15 8
N 718. – 10 ch. purple .. 15 8
DESIGNS: No. N 714, Battle on Mt. Napal. N 718, Battle for Height 1211.

322. Women in Industry.

1966. Sex Equality Law. 20th Anniv.
N 719. **322.** 10 ch. multicoloured 20 8

323. Industrial Workers. **324.** Water-jar Dance.

1966. Industrial Nationalisation. 20th Anniv.
N 720. **323.** 10 ch. multicoloured 20 8

1966. Korean Dances. Multicoloured. 5 ch., 40 ch. with or without gum; others without.
N 721. 5 ch. Type **324** 8 5
N 722. 10 ch. Bell dance .. 20 8
N 723. 10 ch. "Dancer in a Mural Painting" 20 8
N 724. 15 ch. Sword dance .. 25 8
N 725. 40 ch. Gold Cymbal dance 50 30

325. Korean attacking U.S. Soldier. **326.** Crop-spraying.

1966. Korean Reunification Campaign. With gum.
N 726. **325.** 10 ch. green .. 20 8
N 727. – 10 ch. purple .. 20 8
N 728. – 10 ch. lilac 20 8
DESIGNS: No. N 727, Korean with young child. N 728, Korean with shovel.

1966. Industrial Uses of Aircraft. With gum except 2 ch. and 5 ch.
N 729. **326.** 2 ch. green & maroon 5 5
N 730. – 5 ch. brn. & green .. 8 5
N 731. – 10 ch. sepia and blue 20 8
N 732. – 40 ch. brn. & blue .. 60 30
DESIGNS (each with aircraft): 5 ch. Forest-fire observation. 10 ch. Geological survey. 40 ch. Detection of fish shoals.

1966. Korean Revolutionaries (3rd issue). As T **206.** With gum.
N 733.* 10 ch. violet (Oh Joong Heup) .. ..
N 734.* 10 ch. green (Kim Kyung Suk) .. ..
N 735.* 10 ch. blue (Li Dong Kul)

327. Kim Il Sung University.

1966. Kim Il Sung University. 20th Anniv. With gum.
N 736. **327.** 10 ch. violet .. 15 8

INDEX

Countries can be quickly located by referring to the index at the end of this volume.

328. Wrestling. **329.** Hoopoe.

1966. Ganefo Games, Phnom-Penh.
N 737. **328.** 5 ch. blk., grn. & bl. 8 5
N 738. – 10 ch. black, myrtle and green .. 20 8
N 739. – 10 ch. black and red 20 8
DESIGNS: No. N 738, Basketball. N 739, Table-tennis.
Nos. N 737/9 were issued together se-tenant vert. within the sheet.

1966. Korean Birds. Mult. Inscr. "1966".
N 740. 2 ch. Grebnitzky's sparrow 5 5
N 741. 5 ch. Type **329** 8 5
N 742. 10 ch. Korean thrush (blue background) .. 20 8
N 743. 10 ch. Crested lark (green background .. 20 8
N 744. 40 ch. Korean wood-pecker 60 25
The 2 ch. and 10 ch. (both) are horiz.

330. Building Construction.

1966. "Increased Production with Economy". Multicoloured. Without gum (40 ch.) or with gum (others).
N 745. 5 ch. Type **330** 8 5
N 746. 10 ch. Furnaceman and graph 15 8
N 747. 10 ch. Machine-tool production 15 8
N 748. 40 ch. Miners and pithead 50 25

331. Parachuting.

1966. National Defence Sports. With gum
N 749. **331.** 2 ch. maroon .. 5 5
N 750. – 5 ch. red 8 5
N 751. – 10 ch. blue 20 8
N 752. – 40 ch. green .. 60 25
DESIGNS: 5 ch. Horse-jumping. 10 ch. Motor-cycle racing. 40 ch. Radio receiving and transmitting competition.

332. "Samil Wolgan" (Assn. Magazine). **333.** Red Deer.

1966. "Samil Wolgan" Magazine. 30th Anniv.
N 753.* **332.** 10 ch. multicoloured

1966. Korean Deer. Multicoloured.
N 754. 2 ch. Type **333** 5 5
N 755. 5 ch. Fallow deer .. 8 5
N 756. 10 ch. Sambur (erect) .. 20 8
N 757. 10 ch. Jawan Sambur (grazing) 20 8
N 758. 70 ch. Reindeer .. 1·00 40

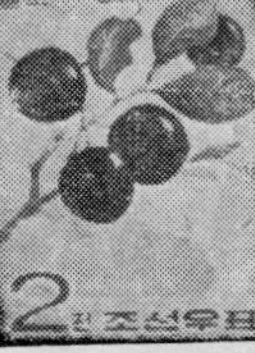

334. Blueberries. **335.** Ju-ul Rest Home.

1966. Wild Fruit. Multicoloured.
N 759. 2 ch. Type **334** 5 5
N 760. 5 ch. Wild pears .. 8 5
N 761. 10 ch. Wild raspberries 20 8
N 762. 10 ch. Schizandra .. 20 8
N 763. 10 ch. Wild apples .. 20 8
N 764. 40 ch. Jujube 60 25

1966. Korean Rest Homes. With gum.
N 765. **335.** 2 ch. violet 5 5
N 766. – 5 ch. turquoise .. 8 5
N 767. – 10 ch. green .. 20 8
N 768. – 40 ch. black .. 55 25
REST HOMES: 5 ch. Mt. Myohyang. 10 ch. Songdowon. 40 ch. Hongwon.

336. Soldier.

1967. Army Day. 19th Anniv. Without gum.
N 769. **336.** 10 ch. grn., yell. & red 15 8

337. Sow.

1967. Domestic Animals. Multicoloured. Without gum. 40 ch. also with gum.
N 770. 5 ch. Type **337** 8 5
N 771. 10 ch. Goat 20 8
N 772. 40 ch. Bull 60 25

338. Battle Scene.

1967. Battle of Bochonbo. 30th Anniv.
N 773. **338.** 10 ch. orange red & grn. 15 8

339. Students.

1967. Compulsory Technical Education for Nine Years.
N 774. **339.** 10 ch. multicoloured 15 8

340. Table-Tennis Player.

1967. 29th Int. Table-Tennis Championships, Pyongyang. Designs showing players in action.
N 775. **340.** 5 ch. multicoloured 8 5
N 776. – 10 ch. multicoloured 20 8
N 777. – 40 ch. multicoloured 60 25

341. Anti-aircraft Defences.

1967. Paintings of Guerrilla War against the Japanese. With gum.
N 778. **341.** 10 ch. blue 15 8
N 779. – 10 ch. purple .. 15 8
N 780. – 10 ch. violet .. 15 8
PAINTINGS: No. N 779, Blowing-up railway bridge. N 780, People helping guerrillas in Wangwikou.

1967. War Heroes (2nd series). As T **285.** Designs showing portraits and combat scenes. With gum.
N 781. 10 ch. slate 15 8
N 782. 10 ch. violet 15 8
N 783. 10 ch. blue 15 8
PORTRAITS: No. N 781, Li Dae Hun and grenade-throwing. No. N 782, Choe Jong Un and soldiers charging. No. N 783, Kim Hwa Ryong and air dog-fight.

342. Workers.

1967. Labour Day.
N 784. **342.** 10 ch. multicoloured 15 8

343. Card Game.

1967. Korean Children. Multicoloured.
N 785. 5 ch. Type **343** 8 5
N 786. 10 ch. Children modelling tractor 20 8
N 787. 40 ch. Children playing with ball 60 25

344. Victory Monument.

1967. Unveiling of Battle of Ponchonbo Monument.
N 788. **344.** 10 ch. multicoloured 20 8

345. Attacking Tank.

346. "Polygonatum japonicum".

1967. Monuments to War of 1950–53. 2 ch. with or without gum.
N 789. **345.** 2 ch. green & turquoise 5 5
N 790. – 5 ch. sepia and green 8 5
N 791. – 10 ch. brown and buff 15 8
N 792. – 40 ch. brown and blue 55 25
MONUMENTS: 5 ch. Soldier-musicians. 10 ch. Soldier. 40 ch. Soldier with children.

1967. Medicinal Plants. Multicoloured; background colour of 10 ch. values given to aid identification. Nos. 793/5, 797 with or without gum.
N 793. 2 ch. Type **346** 5 5
N 794. 5 ch. "Hibiscus manihot" 8 5
N 795. 10 ch. "Scutellaria baicalensis" (turq.) .. 20 8
N 796. 10 ch. "Pursatilla koreana" (blue) .. 20 8
N 797. 10 ch. "Rehmannian glutinosa" (yellow) .. 20 8
N 798. 40 ch. "Tanacetum boreale" 65 25

347. Servicemen.

1967. People's Army. Multicoloured. 5 ch. with or without gum.
N 799. 5 ch. Type **347** .. 8 5
N 800. 10 ch. Soldier & Farmer 15 8
N 801. 10 ch. Officer decorating soldier 15 8

348. Freighter " Chollima ".

1967. With gum.
N 802. **348.** 10 ch. green .. 20 8

349. "Farming".

1967. " Heroic Struggle of the Chollima Riders". Paintings. Without gum (5 ch.) or with gum (others).
N 803. – 5 ch. agate 8 5
N 804. **349.** 10 ch. slate 15 8
N 805. – 10 ch. green .. 15 8
DESIGNS—VERT. 5 ch. "Drilling Rock Precipice". 10 ch. (N 805), "Felling Trees".

350. Crab.

1967. Crabs. Designs showing crabs.
N 806. **350.** 2 ch. multicoloured 5 5
N 807. – 5 ch. multicoloured 8 5
N 808. – 10 ch. multicoloured 20 8
N 809. – 40 ch. multicoloured 60 25

351. Electric Train and Hand switching points.

1967. Propaganda for Reunification of Korea.
N 810. **351.** 10 ch. multicoloured 20 8

352.

353. Chollima Flying Horse and Banners.

1967. Korean Waterfalls. Designs showing waterfalls. 2 ch. with or without gum.
N 811. **352.** 2 ch. multicoloured 5 5
N 812. – 10 ch. multicoloured 20 8
N 813. – 40 ch. multicoloured 60 25

1967. "The Revolutionary Surge Upwards". Various designs incorporating the Chollima Flying Horse.
N 814. – 5 ch. blue 8 5
N 815. – 10 ch. red 15 8
N 816. – 10 ch. green .. 15 8
N 817. – 10 ch. lilac 15 8
N 818. **353.** 10 ch. red 15 8
DESIGNS—HORIZ. 5 ch. Ship, train and lorry (Transport). No. 815, Bulldozers (Building construction). No. 816, Tractors (Rural development). No. N 817, Heavy presses (Machine-building industry).

354. Lenin.

1967. Russian October Revolution. 50th Anniv.
N 819. **354.** 10 ch. brn., yell. & red 15 8

355. Voters and Banner.

1967. Korean Elections. Multicoloured.
N 820. 10 ch. Type **355** .. 15 8
N 821. 10 ch. Woman casting vote (vert.) 15 8

356.

1967. Eagles.
N 822. **356.** 2 ch. mult. 5 5
N 823. – 10 ch. mult. (vert.) 20 8
N 824. – 40 ch. mult. .. 60 30
Nos. N 823/4 show similar designs as Type **356.**

357. Chongjin.

1967. North Korean Cities. With gum.
N 825. **357.** 5 ch. green 8 5
N 826. – 10 ch. lilac 15 8
N 827. – 10 ch. violet .. 15 8
DESIGNS: No. N 826, Humhung. No. 827, Sinuiju.

358. Kim Il Sung at Head of Columns.

1967. Battle of Pochonbo Monument. Detail of Monument. Multicoloured.
N 828. 10 ch. Type **358** .. 15 10
N 829. 10 ch. Head of right-hand column .. 15 10
N 830. 10 ch. Tail of right-hand column .. 15 10
N 831. 10 ch. Head of left-hand column .. 15 10
N 832. 10 ch. Tail of left-hand column .. 15 10
N 833. 10 ch. Centre of right-hand column .. 15 10
N 834. 10 ch. Centre of left-hand column .. 15 10
SIZES—HORIZ. Nos. N 829/32, 43 × 28 mm. Nos. 833/34, 56 × 28 mm.
The centrepiece of the Monument is flanked by two columns of soldiers, headed by Kim Il Sung.

359. Soldier brandishing Red Book.

1967. "Let us carry out the Decisions of the Workers' Party Conference!". Mult.
N 835. 10 ch. Type **359** .. 15 10
N 836. 10 ch. Militiaman holding bayonet 15 10
N 837. 10 ch. Foundryman and bayonet 15 10

360. Whaler firing Harpoon.

1967. With gum.
N 838. **360.** 10 ch. blue 15 10

361. Airman, Soldier and Sailor.

1968. People's Army. 20th Anniv. Inscr. "1948 1968". Multicoloured. With gum.
N 839.* 10 ch. Type **361** ..
N 840.* 10 ch. Soldier below attack in snow ..
N 841.* 10 ch. Soldier below massed ranks ..
N 842.* 10 ch. Soldier holding flag
N 843.* 10 ch. Soldier holding book
N 844.* 10 ch. Soldiers and armed workers with flag ..
N 845.* 10 ch. Furnaceman and soldier .. ..
N 846.* 10 ch. Soldier saluting
N 847.* 10 ch. Charging soldiers
N 848.* 10 ch. Soldier, sailor and airman below flag ..

1968. War Heroes (3rd series). As T **285** With gum.
N 850. 10 ch. violet 15 8
N 851. 10 ch. purple 15 8
PORTRAITS: No. N 850, Han Gye Ryol firing Bren gun. No. N 851, Li Su Bok charging up hill.

362. Dredger "September 2".

363. Ten-storey Flats, East Pyongyang.

364. Palace of Students and Children, Kaesong.

1968. With gum.
N 852. **362.** 5 ch. green 8 5
N 853. **363.** 10 ch. blue 15 8
N 854. **364.** 10 ch. blue 15 8

365. Marshal Kim Il Sung.

1968. Marshal Kim Il Sung's 56th Birthday. With gum.
N 855. **365.** 40 ch. multicoloured 50 30

366. Kim Il Sung with Mother.

1968. Childhood of Kim Il Sung. Mult.
N 856. 10 ch. Type **366** .. 12 8
N 857. 10 ch. Kim Il Sung with his father 12 8
N 858. 10 ch. Setting out from home, aged 14 .. 12 8
N 859. 10 ch. Birthplace at Manyongdae 12 8
N 860. 10 ch. Hilltop pagoda, where he studied .. 12 8

367. Mushroom.

1968. Mushrooms. With gum.
N 861. **367.** 5 ch. brown & green 8 5
N 862. – 10 ch. ochre, brown and green .. 15 8
N 863. – 10 ch. brown & green 15 8
DESIGNS: Nos. N 862/3, Mushrooms similar to T **367.**

368. Leaping Horseman.

1968. Korean People's Democratic Republic. 20th Anniv. Inscr. "1948 1968". Mult. With gum.
N 864. 10 ch. Type **368** .. 12 8
N 865. 10 ch. Four servicemen 12 8
N 866. 10 ch. Soldier with bayonet 12 8
N 867. 10 ch. Advancing with banners 12 8
N 868. 10 ch. Statue 12 8
N 869. 10 ch. Korean flag .. 12 8
N 870. 10 ch. Soldier and peasant with flag 12 8
N 871. 10 ch. Machine-gunner with flag 12 8

369. Domestic Products. 370. Proclaiming the Ten Points.

1968. Development of Light Industries. Multicoloured. With gum.
N 872. 2 ch. Type **369** 5 5
N 873. 5 ch. Textiles 8 5
N 874. 10 ch. Tinned produce .. 12 8

1968. Kim Il Sung's Ten Point Political Programme. Multicoloured.
N 875. 2 ch. Type **370** 5 5
N 876. 5 ch. Soldier and artisan (horiz.) 12 8

371. Livestock.

1968. Development of Agriculture. Mult. With gum.
N 877. 5 ch. Type **371** 8 5
N 878. 10 ch. Fruit-growing .. 12 8
N 879. 10 ch. Wheat-harvesting 12 8

374. Pecten yessoensis.

1968. Shellfish. Multicoloured. With gum.
N 880. 5 ch. "Meretrix chione" 8 5
N 881. 5 ch. Type **372** 8 5
N 882. 10 ch. Mussel 12 8

373. Museum of the Revolution, Pochonbo.

374. Grand Theatre, Pyongyang.

1968.
N 883. **373.** 2 ch. green 5 5
N 884. **374.** 10 ch. brown .. 12 8

375. "The Commander is also a Son of the People".

1969. Paintings of Kim Il Sung among the Guerrillas.
N 885.* 2 ch. Type **375** ..
N 886.* 5 ch. "A Bowl of parched Rice Powder" ..
N 887.* 10 ch. "A Sentinel for the Campfire" ..

376. Armed Workers

1969. Struggle for the Reunification of Korea. Multicoloured.
N 888. 10 ch. Workers stabbing U.S. soldier 12 8
N 889. 10 ch. Kim Il Sung and crowd with flags .. 12 8
N 890. 50 ch. Type **376** .. 50 40
Nos. N 888/9 are vert.

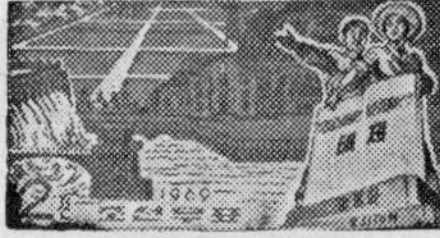
377. Irrigation.

1969. Rural Development. Multicoloured.
N 891. 3 ch. Type **377** .. 5 5
N 892. 5 ch. Agricultural mechanisation 8 5
N 893. 10 ch. Electrification .. 12 8
N 894. 40 ch. Applying fertilisers and spraying trees .. 40 30

378. Rabbits.

1969. Rabbits. Mult. With or without gum.
N 895. 2 ch. Type **378** 5 5
N 896. 10 ch. Black rabbits .. 15 8
N 897. 10 ch. Brown rabbits .. 15 8
N 898. 10 ch. White rabbits .. 15 8
N 899. 40 ch. Doe and young .. 40 30

379. "Age and Youth".

1969. Public Health Service.
N 900. **379.** 2 ch. brown and blue 5 5
N 901. – 10 ch. blue and red 12 8
N 902. – 40 ch. green & yellow 35 30
DESIGNS: 10 ch. Nurse with syringe. 40 ch. Auscultation by woman doctor.

380. Sowing Seed.

1969. Agricultural Mechanisation.
N 903. **380.** 10 ch. green .. 12 8
N 904. – 10 ch. pink 12 8
N 905. – 10 ch. black .. 12 8
N 906. – 10 ch. brown .. 12 8
DESIGNS: No. N 904, Harvester. No. N 905, Weed-spraying machine. No. 906, Threshing machine.

381. Mangyongdae, birthplace of Kim Il Sung.

1969. "Ponghwari—Cradle of Revolution". Multicoloured.
N 907. 10 ch. Ponghwari .. 12 8
N 908. 10 ch. Type **381** .. 12 8

382. Teaching at Myongsin School.

1969. Kim Hyong Jik, father of Kim Il Sung. Commem. Multicoloured.
N 909. 10 ch. Type **382** .. 12 8
N 910. 10 ch. Secret meeting with Korean National Association members 12 8

383. Birthplace at Chilgol.

1969. Mrs. Kang Ban Sok, mother of Kim Il Sung. Commem. Multicoloured.
N 911. 10 ch. Type **383** .. 12 8
N 912. 10 ch. With members of Women's Association 12 8
N 913. 10 ch. Resisting Japanese police 12 8

384. Begaebong Camp.

1969. Bivouac Sites in the Guerrilla War against the Japanese. Multicoloured.
N 914. 5 ch. Type **384** 8 5
N 915. 10 ch. Mupo site (horiz.) 12 8
N 916. 10 ch. Chongbong site .. 12 8
N 917. 40 ch. Konchang site (horiz.) 40 30

385. Kim Il Sung addressing Guerrillas.

1969. Founding of Anti-Japanese Guerrilla Army. 37th Anniv.
N 918.* **385.** 10 ch. multicoloured

386. Chollima Statue.

387. Museum of the Revolution, Pyongyang.

1969.
N 919. **386.** 10 ch. blue 12 8
N 920. **387.** 10 ch. green .. 12 8

388. Mangyong Chickens.

390. Statue of Marshal Kim Il Sung.

389. Marshal Kim Il Sung and Children.

1969. Korean Poultry.
N 921. **388.** 10 ch. blue 12 8
N 922. – 10 ch. violet .. 12 8
DESIGN: No. N 922, Kwangpo ducks.

1969. Kim Il Sung's Educational System. Multicoloured.
N 923. 2 ch. Type **389** 5 5
N 924. 10 ch. Worker with books 12 8
N 925. 40 ch. Students with books 40 30

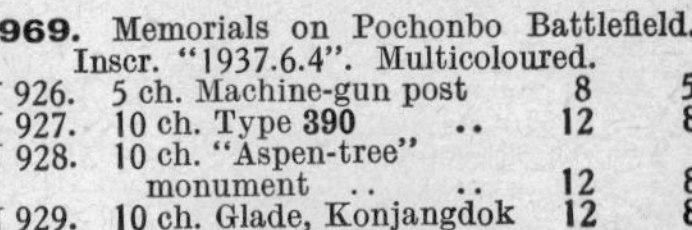

1969. Memorials on Pochonbo Battlefield. Inscr. "1937.6.4". Multicoloured.
N 926. 5 ch. Machine-gun post 8 5
N 927. 10 ch. Type **390** .. 12 8
N 928. 10 ch. "Aspen-tree" monument 12 8
N 929. 10 ch. Glade, Konjangdok 12 8

391. Relay Runner.

1969. Sports Day. 20th Anniv.
N 930. **391.** 10 ch. multicoloured 15 10

392. President Nixon attacked by Pens.

1969. Anti-U.S. Imperialism Journalists' Conference, Pyongyang.
N 931. **392.** 10 ch. multicoloured 15 10

393. Fighters and Battle.

1969. Implementation of Ten-point Programme of Kim Il Sung. Multicoloured.
N 932. 10 ch. Type **393** .. 12 8
N 933. 10 ch. Workers upholding slogan (vert.) .. 12 8

394. Bayonet Attack over U.S. Flag.

1969. Anti-American Campaign.
N 934. **394.** 10 ch. multicoloured 12 8

395. Yellowtail.

1969. Korean Fishes. Multicoloured.
N 935. 5 ch. Type **395** .. 5 8
N 936. 10 ch. "Leucissus Brandti" Mullet .. 15 8
N 937. 40 ch. Mullet .. 50 40

396. Freighter "Taesungsan".

1969.
N 938. **396.** 10 ch. purple .. 15 10

397. Kim crosses into Manchuria, 1926, aged 13.

1969. Kim Il Sung in Manchuria. Mult. No. N 943 with gum.
N 939. 10 ch. Type **397** .. 15 10
N 940. 10 ch. Leading strike of Yuwen Middle School boys, 1927 .. .. 15 10
N 941. 10 ch. Leading anti-Japanese demonstration in Kirin, 1928 .. .. .. 15 10
N 942. 10 ch. Presiding at meeting of Young Communist League, 1930.. .. 15 10
N 943. 10 ch. Meeting of young revolutionaries .. 15 10

398. Tchongwae (1935).

1970. Guerrilla Conference Places.
N 944. **398.** 2 ch. blue & green.. 5 5
N 945. – 5 ch. brown & green 8 5
N 946. – 10 ch. light grn. & grn. 12 8
DESIGNS: 5 ch. Yoyonggu (barn) (1935). 10 ch. Cholbaryong (tent) (1940).

399. Lake Chonji.

400. Vietnamese Soldier and Furnaceman.

1970. Mt. Paekdu-san, Home of Revolution (1st issue). Inscr. "1970".
N 947. **399.** 10 ch. blk., brn. & grn. 12 8
N 948. – 10 ch. blk., grn. & yell. 12 8
N 949. – 10 ch. pur., bl. & yell. 12 8
N 950. – 10 ch. blk., bl. & pink 12 8
DESIGNS: No. N 948, Piryu-bong Peak. No. N 949, Pyongsa-bong. (Soldier) Peak. No. N 950, Changgun-bong (General) Peak.
See also Nos. 998/1000.

1970. Help for the Vietnamese People.
N 951. **400.** 10 ch. grn., brn. & red 8 5

401. Lenin.

402. March of Koreans.

401a. Receiving his Father's Revolvers from his Mother.

1970. Lenin. Birth Centenary.
N 952. **401.** 10 ch. brn. & cinn... 12 8
N 953. – 10 ch. brown & green 12 8
DESIGN: No. N 953, Lenin making a speech.

1970. Revolutionary Career of Kim Il Sung. Multicoloured.
N 953a. 10 ch. Type **401a** .. 12 8
N 953b. 10 ch. Receiving smuggled weapons from his mother 12 8
N 953c. 10 ch. Talking to farm workers 12 8
N 953d. 10 ch. At Chialun meeting, 1930 .. 12 8

1970. Association of Koreans in Japan. 15th Anniv.
N 954. **402.** 10 ch. red 12 8
N 955. 10 ch. maroon .. 12 8

403. Uniformed Factory Worker.

404. Students and Newspapers.

1970. Workers' Militia.
N 956. **403.** 10 ch. grn., brn. & mve. 12 8
N 957. – 10 ch. grn., brn. & bl. 12 8
DESIGN—HORIZ. No. N 957, Militiaman saluting.

1970. Peasant Education. Multicoloured.
N 958. 2 ch. Type **404** .. 5 5
N 959. 5 ch. Peasant with book 8 5
N 960. 10 ch. Students in class 12 8

405. "Electricity Flows".

1970. Army Electrical Engineers. Commem.
N 961. **405.** 10 ch. brown .. 12 8

406. Soldier with Rifle.

1970. Campaign Month for Withdrawal of U.S. Troops from South Korea.
N 962. **406.** 5 ch. violet 8 5
N 963. – 10 ch. purple .. 12 8
DESIGN: 10 ch. Soldier and partisan.

407. Rebel wielding Weapons.

1970. Struggle in South Korea against U.S. Imperialism.
N 964. **407.** 10 ch. violet .. 12 8

408. Labourer ("Fertilisers").

1970. Encouragement of Increased Productivity.
N 965. **408.** 10 ch. grn., pink & brn. 12 8
N 966. – 10 ch. grn., red & brn. 12 8
N 967. – 10 ch. bl., grn. & brn. 12 8
N 968. – 10 ch. bistre, brn. & grn. 12 8
N 969. – 10 ch. vio., grn. & brn. 12 8
DESIGNS: No. N 966, Furnaceman ("Steel"). No. N 967, Operative ("Machines"). No. 968, Labourer ("Building Construction"). No. N 969, Miner ("Mining").

409. Railway Guard.

1970. "Speed the Transport System",
N 970. **409.** 10 ch. bl., orge. & grn. 12 8

410. Agricultural.

1970. Executive Decisions of the Workers' Party Congress. Designs embodying book.
N 971. **410.** 5 ch. red 8 5
N 972. – 10 ch. green .. 12 8
N 973. – 40 ch. green .. 50 30
DESIGNS: 10 ch. Industry. 40 ch. The Armed Forces.

411. Chollima Statue and Workers' Party Banner.

412. League Emblem.

1970. Korean Workers' Party. 25th Anniv.
N 974. **411.** 10 ch. red, brn. & buff 12 8

1971. League of Socialist Working Youth. 25th Anniv.
N 976. **412.** 10 ch. red, brn. & bl. 12 8

413. Log Cabin, Namhodu.

1971. Namhodu Guerrilla Conference. 35th Anniv.
N 977. **413.** 10 ch. multicoloured 12 8

414. Tractor Driver.

1971. Land Reform Law. 25th Anniv.
N 978. **414.** 2 ch. red, grn. & blk. 5 5

415. Popyong Museum.

1971. Museums of the Revolution.
N 979. **415.** 10 ch. brn. & yellow 10 5
N 980. – 10 ch. bl. & orge. .. 10 5
N 981. – 10 ch. grn. & orge... 10 5
DESIGNS: No. N 980, Mangyongdae Museum. No. N 981, Chunggang Museum.

416. Miner.

417. Hands holding Hammer and Rifle.

1971. Six Year Plan for Coal Industry.
N 982. **416.** 10 ch. multicoloured 12 8

1971. Labour Day. 85th Anniv.
N 983. **417.** 1 w. red, brn. & buff 1·00 60

418. Soldiers and Map.

419. Monument.

1971. Association for Restoration of Fatherland. 35th Anniv.
N 984. **418.** 10 ch. red, buff & blk. 12 8

1971. Battlefields in Musan Area, May 1939. Multicoloured.
N 985. 5 ch. Type **419** 8 5
N 986. 10 ch. Machine guns in perspex cases (horiz.) 12 8
N 987. 40 ch. Huts among birch trees (horiz.) 40 30

420. Koreans Marching.

421. Flame Emblem.

1971. Solidarity of Koreans in Japan.
N 988. **420.** 10 ch. brown .. 12 8

1971. Korean Young Pioneers. 25th Anniv.
N 989. **421.** 10 ch. red, yell. & bl. 12 8

422. Marchers and Banners.

423. Foundryman.

1971. League of Socialist Working Youth. Sixth Congress.
N 990. **422.** 5 ch. red, buff & blk. 8 5
N 991. – 10 ch. red, grn. & blk. 12 8
DESIGN: 10 ch. Marchers and banner under globe.

1971. Labour Law. 25th Anniv.
N 992. **423.** 5 ch. blk., pur. & buff 8 5

424. Young Women.

1971. Sex Equality Law. 25th Anniv.
N 993. **424.** 5 ch. multicoloured 8 5

425. Schoolchildren.

1971. Compulsory Primary Education. 15th Anniv.
N 994. **425.** 10 ch. multicoloured 12 8

426. Choe Yong Do and Combat Scene.

1971. Heroes of the Revolutionary Struggle in South Korea.

N 995. 426. 5 ch. black & green 5 5
N 996. – 10 ch. red & brown 12 8
N 997. – 10 ch. black & red .. 12 8

DESIGNS: No. N 996, Revolutionary with book. No. N 997, Kim Jong Tae and scene of triumph.

1971. Mt. Paekdu-san, Home of Revolution (2nd issue). As T 399 but inscr. "1971".

N 998. 2 ch. blk., olive & grn. 5 5
N 999. 5 ch. pink, blk. & slate 8 5
N 1000. 10 ch. blk. red & grey 12 8

DESIGNS—HORIZ. 2 ch. General view. 10 ch. Western peak. VERT. 5 ch. Waterfall.

427. Two Foundrymen.

1971. Nationalisation of Industry Law. 25th Anniv.

N 1001. 427. 5 ch. blk. grn. & brn. 8 5

428. Struggle in Korea.

1971. The Anti-Imperialist and Anti-U.S. Imperialism Struggles.

N 1002. 428. 10 ch. red, blk. & brn. 12 8
N 1003. – 10 ch. brn., blk. & bl. 12 8
N 1004. – 10 ch. red, blk. & pink 12 8
N 1005. – 10 ch. blk., olive & grn. 12 8
N 1006. – 10 ch. orge., blk. & red 12 8
N 1007. – 40 ch. green, blk & pink 40 30

DESIGNS: No. N 1003, Struggle in Vietnam. No. N 1004, Soldier with rifle and 'plane marked "EC". No. N 1005, Struggle in Africa. No. N 1006, Cuban soldier and Central America. No. N 1007, Bayonetting U.S. soldier.

429. Kim Il Sung University. 430. Kim Il Sung.

431. Kim Il Sung founding Anti-Japanese Guerrilla Army.

1971. Kim Il Sung University. 25th Anniv.

N 1008. 429. 10 ch. grey, red & yell. 12 8

1971. Founding of Anti-Japanese Guerrilla Army. Multicoloured.

N 1009. 10 ch. Type 430 .. 12 8
N 1010. 10 ch. Type 431 . 12 8
N 1011. 10 ch. Kim Il Sung addressing the people 12 8
N 1012. 10 ch. Kim Il Sung and members of Children's Corps 12 8

432. Iron-ore Ladle (Mining).

1971. Tasks of Six-Year Plan. Inscr. "1971-1976". Multicoloured.

N 1013. 10 ch. Type 432 .. 10 5
N 1014. 10 ch. Workers and text 10 5
N 1015. 10 ch. Railway track (Transport) 10 5
N 1016. 10 ch. Hand and wrench (Industry) 10 5
N 1017. 10 ch. Mechanical scoop (Construction) .. 10 5
N 1018. 10 ch. Manufactured goods (Trade) 10 5
N 1019. 10 ch. Crate on hoists (Exports) 10 5
N 1020. 10 ch. Lathe (Heavy Industries) 10 5
N 1021. 10 ch. Freighter (Shipping) 10 5
N 1022. 10 ch. Household equipment (Light Industries) .. 10 5
N 1023. 10 ch. Corncob and wheat (Agriculture) .. 10 5

433. Technicians.

1971. Cultural Revolution. Multicoloured.

N 1024. 2 ch. Type 433 .. 5 5
N 1025. 5 ch. Mechanic .. 8 5
N 1026. 10 ch. Schoolchildren 10 5
N 1027. 10 ch. Chemist .. 10 5
N 1028. 10 ch. Composer at piano 10 5

434. Workers with Red Books.

1971. Ideological Revolution. Mult.

N 1029. 10 ch. Type 434 .. 10 5
N 1030. 10 ch. Workers reading book 10 5
N 1031. 10 ch. Workers' lecture 10 5
N 1032. 10 ch. Worker and pneumatic drill .. 10 5

435. Korean Family.

1971. Improvement in Living Standards.

N 1033. 435. 10 ch. multicoloured 10 5

436. Furnaceman.

1971. Implementation of Decisions of Fifth Workers' Party Conference. Multicoloured.

N 1034. 10 ch. Type 436 .. 10 5
N 1035.* 10 ch. Worker and Red Book .. ..

437. 438. 6000-ton Press.

1971. Solidarity with South Korean Revolutionaries.

N 1036. 437. 10 ch. brn., bl. & blk. 10 5
N 1037. – 10 ch. brn., red & blk. 10 5
N 1038. – 10 ch. multicoloured 10 5
N 1039. – 10 ch. multicoloured 10 5

DESIGNS—VERT. No. N 1037, U.S. soldier attacked by poster boards. No. N 1038, Hands holding rifles aloft. HORIZ. No. N 1039, Men advancing with rifles.

1971.

N 1040. 438. 2 ch. brown .. 5 5
N 1041. – 5 ch. blue 8 5
N 1042. – 10 ch. green .. 10 5
N 1043. – 10 ch. green .. 10 5

DESIGNS: No. N 1041, Freighter. No. N 1042, 300 h.p. bulldozer. No. N 1043, "Sungrisan" lorry.

439. Title-page and Militants.

1971. "Samil Wolgan" Magazine. 35th Anniv.

N 1044. 439. 10 ch. red, grn. & blk. 10 5

440. "The People Advance".

1971. "Forward with Socialism". Mult.

N 1045.* 10 ch. Type 440 ..
N 1046.* 10 ch. Industry and transport .. ..

441. Chollima Street, Pyongyang.

1971. Chollima Street, Pyongyang. Mult.

N 1048.* 5 ch. Bridge and sky-scraper blocks ..
N 1049.* 10 ch. Type 441 ..
N 1050.* 10 ch. Another view of street .. ..

442. Poultry Chicks.

1972. Poultry Breeding.

N 1051. 442. 5 ch. yell., bl. & brn. 5 5
N 1052. – 10 ch. orge-brn., bistre and brown .. 10 8
N 1053. – 40 ch. bl., orge. and deep blue .. 40 30

DESIGNS: 10 ch. Chickens and battery egg house. 40 ch. Eggs and fowls suspended from hooks.

442a. Soldier with Shell.

1972. North Korean Armed Forces. Mult.

N 1053a. 10 ch. Type 442a .. 10 5
N 1053b. 10 ch. Marine .. 10 5
N 1053c. 10 ch. Air Force pilot 10 5

443. Scene from "Village Shrine".

1972. Films of Guerrilla War.

N 1054. 443. 10 ch. grey & green 10 5
N 1055. – 10 ch. bl., mar. & orge. 10 5
N 1056. – 10 ch. pur., bl. & yell. 10 5

DESIGNS: No. N 1055, Patriot with pistol ("A Sea of Blood"). No. N 1056, Guerrilla using bayonet ("The Lot of a Self-defence Corps member").

444. Kim Il Sung acknowledging Greetings.

1972. Kim Il Sung's 60th Birthday. Scenes in the life of Kim Il Sung, dated "1912-1972". Multicoloured.

N 1057. 5 ch. Type 444 .. 5 5
N 1058. 5 ch. In campaign H.Q. 5 5
N 1059. 5 ch. Military conference (horiz.) 5 5
N 1060. 10 ch. In wheatfield .. (horiz.) 10 5
N 1061. 10 ch. Directing construction (horiz.) 10 5
N 1062. 10 ch. Talking to foundry workers (horiz.) .. 10 5
N 1063. 10 ch. Aboard whaler (horiz.) 10 5
N 1064. 10 ch. Visiting a hospital (horiz.) 10 5
N 1065. 10 ch. Viewing garden (horiz.) 10 5
N 1066. 10 ch. With survey party (horiz.) 10 5
N 1067. 10 ch. Meeting female workers (horiz.) .. 10 5
N 1068. 10 ch. Village conference (horiz.) 10 5
N 1069. 10 ch. Touring factory (horiz.) 10 5
N 1070. 40 ch. Relaxing with children (horiz.) .. 40 25
N 1071. 1 wn. Giant portrait and marchers .. .. 1·10 50

445. Bugler sounding "Charge".

1972. Guerrilla Army. 40th Anniv.

N 1073. 445. 10 ch. muticoloured 10 5

446. Pavilion of Ryongpo.

1972. Historic Sites of the 1950-53 War. Multicoloured.

N 1074. 2 ch. Type 446 .. 5 5
N 1075. 5 ch. Houses at Onjong 5 5
N 1076. 10 ch. Headquarters, Kosanjin 10 5
N 1077. 40 ch. Victory Museum, Chonsung-dong .. 40 25

447. Volley-ball. 448. Revolutionaries.

1972. Olympic Games, Munich. Multicoloured.

N 1078. 2 ch. Type 447 .. 5 5
N 1079. 5 ch. Boxing (horiz.) .. 8 5
N 1080. 10 ch. Judo .. 15 12
N 1081. 10 ch. Wrestling (horiz.) 15 12
N 1082. 40 ch. Rifle-shooting .. 60 40

1972. The Struggle for Reunification of Korea. Multicoloured.

N 1083. 10 ch. Type **448** .. 10 5
N 1084. 10 ch. Marchers with banner 10 5
N 1085. 10 ch. Insurgents with red banner 10 5
N 1086. 10 ch. Attacking U.S. and South Korean soldiers 10 5
N 1087. 10 ch. Workers with posters 10 5
N 1088. 10 ch. Workers acclaiming revolution 10 5
N 1089. 10 ch. Workers and manifesto 10 5

449. Electronic and Automation Industry.

1972. Tasks of the Six-Year Plan. The Engineering Industry. Inscr. "1971-1976". Multicoloured.

N 1090. 10 ch. Type **449** .. 10 5
N 1091. 10 ch. Single-purpose machines 10 5
N 1092. 10 ch. Machine tools .. 10 5

450. Clearing Virgin Soil.

1972. Tasks of the Six-Year Plan. Agriculture. Inscr. "1971-76". Mult.

N 1093. 10 ch. Type **450** .. 10 5
N 1094. 10 ch. Irrigation .. 10 5
N 1095. 10 ch. Harvesting .. 10 5

451. Automation.

1972. Tasks of the Six-Year Plan. Inscr. "1971-1976". Multicoloured.

N 1096. 10 ch. Type **451** .. 10 5
N 1097. 10 ch. Agricultural mechanisation .. 10 5
N 1098. 10 ch. Lightening household chores 10 5

452. Ferrous Industry.

1972. Tasks of the Six-Year Plan. The Metallurgical Industry. Inscr. "1971-1976". Multicoloured.

N 1099. 10 ch. Type **452** .. 10 5
N 1100. 10 ch. Non-ferrous Industry 10 5

453. Iron Ore Industry.

1972. Tasks of the Six-Year Plan. The Mining Industry. Inscr. "1971-1976". Multicoloured.

N 1101. 10 ch. Type **453** .. 10 5
N 1102. 10 ch. Coal mining industry 10 5

454. Chemical Fibres and Materials.

1972. Tasks of the Six-Year Plan. The Chemical Industry. Inscr. "1971-1976". Multicoloured.

N 1103. 10 ch. Type **454** .. 10 5
N 1104. 10 ch. Fertilisers, insecticides and weed killers 10 5

455. Textiles.

1972. Tasks of the Six-Year Plan. Consumer Goods Inscr. "1971-1976". Multicoloured.

N 1105. 10 ch. Type **455** .. 10 5
N 1106. 10 ch. Kitchen ware and overalls 10 5
N 1107. 10 ch. Household goods 10 5

456. Casting Vote.

1972. National Elections. Multicoloured.

N 1108. 10 ch. Type **456** .. 10 5
N 1109. 10 ch. Election campaigner 10 5

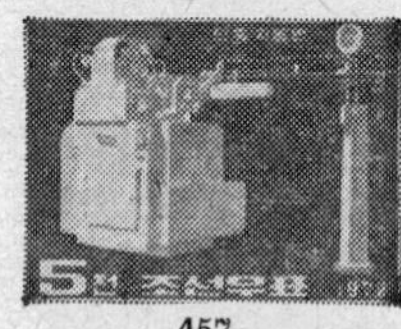

457.

1972. Technical Achievements.

N 1110. **457.** 5 ch. grn. & mar... 5 5
N 1111. – 10 ch. bl. & green.. 10 5
N 1112. – 40 ch. grn. & brn... 35 30

DESIGNS—HORIZ. 10 ch. Lathe. VERT. 40 ch. Computer.

458. Improvements for Urban Population.

1972. Improvement of Living Standards. Multicoloured.

N 1113.* 10 ch. Type **458** .. 8 5
N 1114.* 10 ch. Rural improvement (domestic water supply) 8 5

459. Dredger.

1972. Development of Natural Resources. Multicoloured.

N 1115. 5 ch. Type **459** .. 5 5
N 1116. 10 ch. Forestry .. 10 5
N 1117. 40 ch. Reclaiming land from the sea .. 40 30

460. Fish, Fruit and Vegetables.

1972. Tasks of the Six-Year Plan. The Food Industry. Inscr. "1971-1976". Mult.

N 1118. 10 ch. Type **460** .. 10 5
N 1119. 10 ch. Tinned foods .. 10 5
N 1120. 10 ch. Food packaging 10 5

461. Electrifying Railway Lines.

1972. Tasks of the Six-Year Plan. Transport. Inscr. "1971-1976". Multicoloured.

N 1121. 10 ch. Type **461** .. 10 5
N 1122. 10 ch. Laying new railway track 10 5
N 1123. 10 ch Freighters .. 10 5

464. Soldier.

1973. Founding of Korean People's Army. 25th Anniv. Multicoloured.

N 1130. 5 ch. Type **464** .. 5 5
N 1131. 10 ch. Soldier 10 5
N 1132. 40 ch. Airman.. .. 40 30

465. Wrestling Site.

1973. Scenes of Kim Il Sung's Childhood, Mangyongdae. Multicoloured.

N 1133. 2 ch. Type **465** .. 5 5
N 1134. 5 ch. Warship rock .. 5 5
N 1135. 10 ch. Swinging site (vert.) 10 5
N 1136. 10 ch. Sliding rock .. 10 5
N 1137. 40 ch. Fishing site .. 40 30

465a. Monument to Anti-Japanese Guerrillas, Mansudae Hill.

1973. Museum of the Korean Revolution.

N 1137a. **465a.** 10 ch. multicoloured.. .. 10 5
N 1137b. – 10 ch. multicoloured.. .. 10 5
N 1137c. – 40 ch. multicoloured.. .. 40 30
N 1137d. – 3 w. yell. & pale yellow .. 3·00 1·50

DESIGNS—As T **465a**: 10 ch. (No. 1137b) Similar monument but men in civilian clothes. 40 ch. Statue of Kim Il Sung. HORIZ. (60×29 mm.): 3 w. Museum building.

466.

1973. Menace of Japanese Influence in South Korea.

N 1138. **466.** 10 ch. multicoloured 10 5

467. Lorries.

468. Volleyball.

1973. Lorries and Tractors. Multicoloured.

N 1139. 10 ch. Type **467** .. 10 5
N 1140. 10 ch. Tractors and earth-moving machine .. 10 5

1973. Socialist Countries' Junior Women's Volleyball Games, Pyongyang.

N 1141. **468.** 10 ch. multicoloured 15 8

469. Battlefield.

1973. Victory in Korean War. 20th Anniv.

N 1142. **469.** 10 ch. grn., red & blk. 15 8
N 1143. – 10 ch. brn., bl. & blk. 15 8

DESIGN: 10 ch. Urban fighting.

470. "The Snow Falls".

1973. Mansudae Art Troupe. Dances. Mult.

N 1144. 10 ch. Type **470** .. 10 5
N 1145. 25 ch. "A Bumper Harvest of Apples" 30 25
N 1146. 40 ch. "Azalea of the Fatherland" .. 40 30

471. Schoolchildren.

1973. Ten Years Compulsory Secondary Education.

N 1147. **471.** 10 ch. multicoloured 10 5

472. "Fervour in the Revolution".

1973. The Works of Kim Il Sung. (1st series).

N 1148. **472.** 10 ch. brn., red & yell. 10 5
N 1149. – 10 ch. brn., grn. & yell. 10 5
N 1150. – 10 ch. lake, brn. & yell. 10 5

DESIGNS: No. N 1149, Selected works. No. N 1150 "Strengthen the Socialist System". See also Nos. N 1217/8.

473. Celebrating Republic.

1973. People's Republic. 25th Anniv. Mult.

N 1151. 5 ch. Type **473** .. 5 5
N 1152. 10 ch. Fighting in Korean War 10 5
N 1153. 40 ch. Peace and reconstruction .. 40 30

474. Party Memorial Building.

1973. Party Memorial Building.

N 1154.	474.	1 wn. brn., grey and buff	1·00	60

475. Handball.

1973. National People's Athletic Meeting. Multicoloured.

N 1155.	2 ch. Type **475** ..	5	5
N 1156.	5 ch. High jumper and woman sprinter ..	5	5
N 1157.	10 ch. Skaters	10	5
N 1158.	10 ch. Wrestling ..	10	5
N 1159.	40 ch. Parachutist ..	35	30

476. Weightlifting. 477. Chongryubyok.

1973. Junior Weightlifting Championships of Socialist Countries.

N 1160.	**476.**	10 ch. bl., brn. & grn.	10	5

1973. Scenery of Moran-bong Hill, Pyongyang. Multicoloured.

N 1161.	2 ch. Type **477** ..	5	5
N 1162.	5 ch. Moran Waterfall	5	5
N 1163.	10 ch. Pubyokryu ..	10	5
N 1164.	40 ch. Ulmildae Pavilion	35	30

477a. Magnolia Flower.

1973.

N 1164a.	**477a.**	10 ch. mult. ..	10	5

478. Cock perceiving Butterflies.

1973. Scenes from "Cock Chasing Butterflies" Fairy Tale. Multicoloured.

N 1165.	2 ch. Type **478** ..	5	5
N 1166.	5 ch. Cock preparing to catch butterflies ..	5	5
N 1167.	10 ch. Cock chasing butterflies with basket ..	10	5
N 1168.	10 ch. Cock chasing butterfly up cliff	10	5
N 1169.	40 ch. Cock chasing butterflies over cliff	35	30
N 1170.	90 ch. Cock falls into sea and butterflies escape	1·00	45

479. Wrecked U.S. Tanks. 480. Stone Bridge.

1973. Five-point Programme for Reunification of Korea. Multicoloured.

N 1171.	2 ch. Type **479** ..	5	5
N 1172.	5 ch. Train and crane lifting tractor ..	8	5
N 1173.	10 ch. Leaflets falling on crowd	10	5
N 1174.	10 ch. Hand holding leaflet and map of Korea ..	10	5
N 1175.	40 ch. Banner and globe	35	30

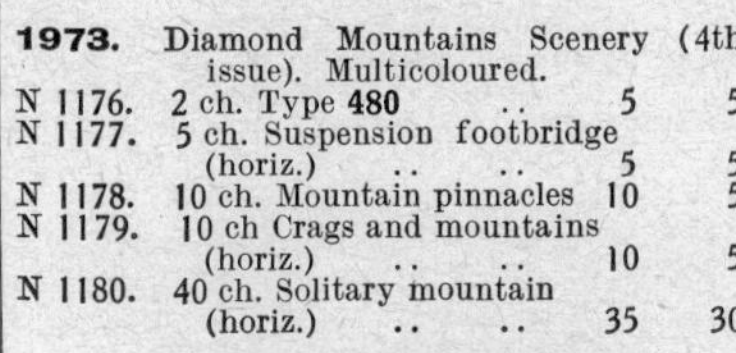

1973. Diamond Mountains Scenery (4th issue). Multicoloured.

N 1176.	2 ch. Type **480** ..	5	5
N 1177.	5 ch. Suspension footbridge (horiz.) ..	5	5
N 1178.	10 ch. Mountain pinnacles	10	5
N 1179.	10 ch Crags and mountains (horiz.)	10	5
N 1180.	40 ch. Solitary mountain (horiz.)	35	30

481. Popwang-gong Peak.

1973. Hills and Waterfalls. Multicoloured.

N 1181.	2 ch. Type **481.** ..	5	5
N 1182.	5 ch. Inhodae Pavilion	5	5
N 1183.	10 ch. Taeha Falls (vert.)	10	5
N 1184.	40 ch. Rongyon Falls (vert.)	35	30

482. S. Korean Revolutionaries.

1973. South Korean Revolution. Mult.

N 1186.	10 ch. Type **482** ..	10	5
N 1187.	10 ch. Marching revolutionaries ..	10	5

483. Heroine with Guerrillas.

1973. "Flower Girl" Feature Film.

N 1189. ***483.** 10 ch. multicoloured

486. Yonpung.

1973. Historical Sites of War and Revolution. Multicoloured.

N 1196.	2 ch. Type **486** ..	5	5
N 1197.	5 ch. Hyangha ..	5	5
N 1198.	10 ch. Changgol ..	10	5
N 1199.	40 ch. Paeksong ..	35	30

487. Gymnasium.

1973. New Building in Pyongyang.

N 1200.	–	2 ch. violet ..	5	5
N 1201.	–	5 ch. green ..	5	5
N 1202.	–	10 ch. brown ..	10	5
N 1203.	–	40 ch. brown & buff	35	30
N 1204.	**487.**	90 ch. buff ..	85	45

DESIGNS—HORIZ. 2 ch. Science Library, Kim Il Sung University. 10 ch. Victory Museum. 40 ch. People's Palace of Culture. VERT. 50 ch. Building No. 2, Kim Il Sung University.

488. Eastern Great Reed-Warbler.

1973. Korean Songbirds. Multicoloured.

N 1205.	5 ch. Type **488** ..	5	5
N 1206.	10 ch. Grey Starling ..	10	5
N 1207.	10 ch. Red-cheeked Myna	10	5

489. Karajibol Camp.

1973. Secret Camps by Tuman-Gang in Guerrilla War. Multicoloured.

N 1208.	10 ch. Type **489** ..	10	5
N 1209.	10 ch. Soksaegol Camp	10	5

490. Red Book.

1973. Socialist Constitution of North Korea. Multicoloured.

N 1210.	10 ch. Type **490** ..	10	5
N 1211.	10 ch. Marchers with red book & banners	10	5
N 1212.	10 ch. Marchers with red book & emblem	10	5

491.

1974. Historic Sites of the Revolution.

N 1212a.	–	5 ch. multicoloured	5	5
N 1212b.	**491.**	10 ch. multicoloured	10	5

DESIGN: 5 ch. Similar building.

492.

1974. Oil-producing Plants.

N 1213.	**492.**	2 ch. multicoloured	5	5
N 1214.	–	5 ch. multicoloured	5	5
N 1215.	–	10 ch. multicoloured	10	5
N 1216.	–	40 ch. multicoloured	35	30

DESIGNS: 5 ch. to 40 ch. Various plants.

493. Chollima Statue.

1974. The Works of Kim Il Sung (2nd series). Multicoloured.

N 1217.	10 ch. Type **493** ..	10	5
N 1218.	10 ch. Bayonets threatening U.S. soldier ..	10	5

494. Train in Station.

1974. Opening of Pyongyang Metro. Mult.

N 1219.	10 ch. Type **494** ..	10	5
N 1220.	10 ch. Escalators ..	10	5
N 1221.	10 ch. Station Hall ..	10	5

495. Capital Construction Front.

1974. Five Fronts of Socialist Construction. Multicoloured.

N 1222.	10 ch. Type **495** ..	10	5
N 1223.	10 ch. Agricultural front	10	5
N 1224.	10 ch. Transport front	10	5
N 1225.	10 ch. Fisheries front ..	10	5
N 1226.	10 ch. Industrial front	10	5

496. Marchers with Banners.

1974. 10th Anniv. of Publication of "Theses on the Socialist Rural Question in Our Country". Multicoloured.

N 1227.	10 ch. Type **496** ..	10	5
N 1228.	10 ch. Book and rejoicing crowd	10	5
N 1229.	10 ch. Tractor & banners	10	5

497. Manure Spreader.

1974. Farm Machinery.

N 1230.	**497.**	2 ch. grn., blk. & red	5	5
N 1231.	–	5 ch. red, blk. & bl.	5	5
N 1232.	–	10 ch. red, blk. & grn.	10	5

DESIGNS: 5 ch. "Progress" tractor. 10 ch. "Mount Taedoksan" tractor.

498. Archery (Grenoble).

1974. North Korean Victories at International Sports Meetings. Multicoloured.

N 1233.	2 ch. Type **498** ..	5	5
N 1234.	5 ch. Gymnastics (Varna)	5	5
N 1235.	10 ch. Boxing (Bucharest)	10	5
N 1236.	20 ch. Volleyball (Pyongyang) ..	20	15
N 1237.	30 ch. Rifle shooting (Sofia)	30	20
N 1238.	40 ch. Judo (Tbilisi) ..	35	25
N 1239.	60 ch. Model aircraft flying (Vienna) (horiz.)	60	45
N 1240.	1 w. 50, Table-tennis (Peking) (horiz.) ..	1·50	80

499. Book and rejoicing Crowd.

1974. First Country with No Taxes.

N 1241. **499.** 10 ch. multicoloured 10 5

500. Drawing up Programme in Woods.

1974. Kim Il Sung during the Anti-Japanese Struggle. Multicoloured.

N 1242. 10 ch. Type **500** .. 10 5
N 1243. 10 ch. Giving directions to Pak Dal 10 5
N 1244. 10 ch. Presiding over Nanhutan Conference 10 5
N 1245. 10 ch. Supervising construction of strongpoint 10 5

501. Sun Hui loses her Sight.

1974. Revolutionary Opera "The Flower Girl". Multicoloured.

N 1246. 2 ch. Type **501** .. 5 5
N 1247. 5 ch. Death of Ggot Bun's mother 5 5
N 1248. 10 ch. Ggot Bun throws boiling water at landlord 10 5
N 1249. 40 ch. Ggot Bun joins revolutionaries .. 35 30

502. Wildcat.

1974. Pyongyang Zoo. 15th Anniv. Mult.

N 1251. 2 ch. Type **502** 5 5
N 1252. 5 ch. Lynx 5 5
N 1253. 10 ch. Fox 10 5
N 1254. 10 ch. Wild boar 10 5
N 1255. 20 ch. Wolf 20 12
N 1256. 40 ch. Bear 35 25
N 1257. 60 ch. Leopard .. 60 45
N 1258. 70 ch. Tiger 75 50
N 1259. 90 ch. Lion .. .. 1·00 75

503. "Rosa acucularis lindly".

1974. Roses. Multicoloured.

N 1261. 2 ch. Type **503** .. 5 5
N 1262. 5 ch. Yellow sweet brier 5 5
N 1263. 10 ch. Pink aromatic rose 10 5
N 1264. 10 ch. Aronia sweet brier (yellow centres) .. 10 5
N 1265. 40 ch. Multi-petal sweet brier 35 25

504. Frog.

1975. Frogs and Toad. Mult.

N 1267. 2 ch. Type **504** .. 5 5
N 1268. 5 ch. Silk frog .. 5 5
N 1269. 10 ch. Bullfrog .. 8 5
N 1270. 40 ch. Toad 35 25

505. Weigela.

1974. Flowering Plants of Mt. Paekdu-san. Multicoloured.

N 1271. 2 ch. Type **505** .. 5 5
N 1272. 5 ch. Amaryllis .. 5 5
N 1273. 10 ch. Red lily .. 8 5
N 1274. 20 ch. Orange lily .. 20 12
N 1275. 40 ch. Azalea 35 25
N 1276. 60 ch. Yellow lily .. 60 45

506. Postwoman and Construction Site.

1974. U.P.U. Centenary. Multicoloured.

N 1277. 10 ch. Type **506** .. 8 5
N 1278. 25 ch. Chollima monument 25 15
N 1279. 40 ch. Globe and airliners 35 25

507. "Women of Namgang Village".

1974. Korean Paintings. Multicoloured.

N 1281. 2 ch. Type **507** .. 5 5
N 1282. 5 ch. "An Old Man on the Rakdong-gang River" (60 × 49 mm.) 5 5
N 1283. 10 ch. "Morning in the Nae-kumgang" (bridge) 8 5
N 1284. 20 ch. "Mt. Kaumgang-san" (60 × 49 mm.) 20 12

508. "Elektron 1" and "Elektron 2", 1964.

1974. Cosmonauts Day. Multicoloured.

N 1286. 10 ch. Type **508** .. 10 5
N 1287. 20 ch. "Proton 1", 1965 20 12
N 1288. 30 ch. "Elektron 3", 1966.. .. .. 30 20
N 1289. 40 ch. "Elektron 5" and "Elektron 6", 1969 35 25

509.

1974. Civil Aviation.

N 1292. **509.** 2 ch. multicoloured 5 5
N 1293. – 5 ch. multicoloured 5 5
N 1294. – 10 ch. multicoloured 10 5
N 1295. – 40 ch. multicoloured 40 25
N 1296. – 60 ch. multicoloured 60 45

DESIGNS: 5 ch. to 60 ch. Various aircraft.

510. "Rhododendron redowskianum".

1974. Alpine Plants. Multicoloured.

N 1298. 2 ch. Type **510** .. 5 5
N 1299. 5 ch. "Dryas octopetala" 5 5
N 1300. 10 ch. "Potentilla fructiersa" 8 5
N 1301. 20 ch. "Papaver radicatum" 20 10
N 1302. 40 ch. "Phyllodoce caerulea" 35 20
N 1303. 60 ch. "Oxytropis anertii" 60 40

511. "A Mountain Stream".

1974. Modern Korean Paintings. (1st series). Multicoloured.

N 1304. 10 ch. Type **511** .. 8 5
N 1305. 20 ch. "Army Musicians" (60 × 40 mm.) .. 20 10
N 1306. 30 ch. "Spring in the Fields" 25 12
N 1307. 40 ch. "Flight of Geese" 35 20
N 1308. 60 ch. "Peasant Family" (60 × 54 mm.) .. 60 40

512. Kim Il Sung as Guerrilla Leader.

1974. Kim Il Sung. Multicoloured.

N 1310. 10 ch. Type **512** .. 8 5
N 1311. 10 ch. Commander of the People's Army (52 × 35 mm.) .. 8 5
N 1312. 10 ch. "The commander is also a son of the people" (52 × 35 mm.) 8 5
N 1313. 10 ch. "Negotiating with the Chinese anti-Japanese unit" (52 × 35 mm.) 8 5

513.

1974. Grand Monument on Mansudae Hill. Multicoloured.

N 1314. 10 ch. Type **513** .. 8 5
N 1315. 10 ch. As T **513** but men in civilian clothes .. 8 5
N 1316. 10 ch. As T **513** but men facing left 8 5
N 1317. 10 ch. As No. N 1316 but men in civilian clothes 8 5

514. Factory Mother-ship.

1974. Deep-sea Fishing. Multicoloured.

N 1318. 2 ch. Type **514** .. 5 5
N 1319. 5 ch. Mother-ship and trawler 5 5
N 1320. 10 ch. Transport ship 8 5
N 1321. 20 ch. General purpose ship 20 10
N 1322. 30 ch. Trawler .. 25 12
N 1323. 40 ch. Stern trawler .. 35 20

515.

1975. Flowers.

N 1350. **515.** 10 ch. multicoloured 8 5
N 1351. – 15 ch. multicoloured 12 8
N 1352. – 20 ch. multicoloured 20 10
N 1353. – 25 ch. multicoloured 25 12
N 1354. – 30 ch. multicoloured 25 12

DESIGNS: 15 ch. to 30 ch. Various flowers.

516.

1975. Flower Paintings.

N 1355. **516.** 5 ch. multicoloured 5 5
N 1356. – 10 ch. multicoloured 8 5
N 1357. – 15 ch. multicoloured 12 5
N 1358. – 25 ch. multicoloured 25 12
N 1359. – 30 ch. multicoloured 30 12

DESIGNS: 10 ch. to 30 ch. Various paintings.

517.

519. Cosmonaut.

518. Gliders.

1975. Landscapes in the Diamond Mountains.
N 1360. **517.** 5 ch. multicoloured 5 5
N 1361. – 10 ch. multicoloured 8 5
N 1362. – 15 ch. multicoloured 12 5
N 1363. – 25 ch. multicoloured 25 12
N 1364. – 30 ch. multicoloured 30 12
DESIGNS: 10 ch. to 30 ch. Various landscapes.

1975. The Air Corps. Multicoloured.
N 1365. 5 ch. Type **518** .. 5 5
N 1366. 5 ch. Radio-controlled model aircraft .. 5 5
N 1367. 10 ch. "Free fall parachutist" (horiz.) .. 8 5
N 1368. 10 ch. Parachutist landing on target (horiz.) 8 5
N 1369. 20 ch. Parachutist with bouquet of flowers (horiz.) 20 8

1975. Space Achievements. Multicoloured.
N 1370. 10 ch. Type **519** .. 8 5
N 1371. 30 ch. "Lunokhod" moon vehicle 30 12
N 1372. 40 ch. "Soyuz" spacecraft and "Salyut" space laboratory .. 40 15

520. Pak Tong Sun.

1975. "World Table Tennis Queen".
N 1373. **520.** 10 ch. multicoloured 10 5

521. "Spring in the Guerrilla Base" (1968)

1975. Modern Korean Paintings (2nd series). Multicoloured.
N 1376. 5 ch. "On the Advance Southward" (1966) (vert.) .. 5 5
N 1377. 10 ch. "A Green Lamp" (1960) (vert.) 8 5
N 1378. 10 ch. "Pine Teee" (1966) (vert.) .. 8 5
N 1379. 10 ch. "Girl Sentry" (1968) (vert.) .. 8 5
N 1380. 10 ch. Type **521** .. 8 5
N 1381. 10 ch. "The Guerrilla Charge" (1969) .. 8 5
N 1382. 15 ch. "Guerrilla Women" (1961) .. 12 5
N 1383. 15 ch. "A Night of Snowfall" (1963) .. 12 5
N 1384. 15 ch. "The Heroism of Li Su Bok" (1965) 12 5
N 1385. 20 ch. "Stoking the Furnace" (1968) .. 20 8
N 1386. 20 ch. "Girl Watering Horse" (1969) .. 20 8
N 1387. 25 ch. "Tideland Reclamation" (1961) 25 10
N 1388. 25 ch. "Woman Machine-gunner" (1970) .. 25 10
N 1389. 30 ch. "Mountainous Country" (1966) .. 30 12
N 1390. 30 ch. "Soldiers and Civilians" (1970) .. 30 12
N 1391. 30 ch. "Schoolchildren in the Country" (1970) 30 12

522. Zebra.

1975. Pyongyang Zoo. Multicoloured.
N 1392. 10 ch. Type **522** .. 8 5
N 1393. 10 ch. Buffalo .. 8 5
N 1394. 20 ch. Giant Panda (horiz.) 20 8
N 1395. 25 ch. Camel 25 10
N 1396. 30 ch. Elephant .. 30 12

523. "Blue Dragon".

1975. 7th-century Mural Paintings. Mult.
N 1397. 10 ch. Type **523** .. 8 5
N 1398. 15 ch. "White Tiger" 12 5
N 1399. 25 ch. "Red Phoenix" (vert.) 25 10
N 1400. 40 ch. "Snake-turtle" 40 15

524. The Beacon lit at Pochonbo, 1937.

1975. Kim Il Sung during the Guerrilla War against the Japanese. Multicoloured.
N 1401. 10 ch. Type **524** .. 8 5
N 1402. 10 ch. "A Bowl of Parched-rice Powder", 1938 .. .. .. 8 5
N 1403. 10 ch. Guiding the Naipatzu meeting, November, 1938 .. 8 5
N 1404. 10 ch. Welcoming helpers 8 5
N 1405. 10 ch. Lecturing the guerrillas 8 5
N 1406. 15 ch. Advancing into the homeland, May 1939 .. .. .. 12 5
N 1407. 25 ch. By Lake Samjiyon, May 1939 .. 25 10
N 1408. 30 ch. At Sinsadong, May 1939 .. .. 30 12
N 1409. 40 ch. Hsiaohierpaling meeting, 1940 .. 40 15

525. South Korean Insurgent.

1975. South Korean Rising.
N 1410. **525.** 10 ch. multicoloured 8 5

526. Flag and Building. **527.** "Feet first" entry (man).

1975. "Chongryon" Assn. 20th Anniv.
N 1411. **526.** 10 ch. multicoloured 8 5

1975. Diving. Multicoloured.
N 1413. 10 ch. Type **527** .. 8 5
N 1414. 25 ch. Piked somersault (man) .. 25 10
N 1415. 40 ch. "Head first" entry (woman) .. 40 15

528.

1975. Campaign against U.S. Imperialism.
N 1416. **528.** 10 ch. multicoloured 8 5

529. Memorial Fish.

1975. Fishes. Multicoloured.
N 1417. 10 ch. Type **529** .. 8 5
N 1418. 10 ch. "Ilisha elongata" (fish swimming to right) 8 5
N 1419. 15 ch. "Opsariichthys bidens G" 12 5
N 1420. 25 ch. Naere 25 10
N 1421. 30 ch. Sheat-fish (fish swimming to right) 30 12
N 1422. 30 ch. Snakehead (fish swimming to left) .. 30 12

530.

1975. 10th Socialist Countries' Football Tournament.
N 1423. **530.** 5 ch. multicoloured 5 5
N 1424. – 10 ch. multicoloured 8 5
N 1425. – 15 ch. multicoloured 12 5
N 1426. – 20 ch. multicoloured 20 8
N 1427. – 50 ch. multicoloured 50 20
DESIGNS: 10 ch. to 50 ch. Various footballers.

531. White Peach Blossom.

1975. Blossoms of Flowering Trees. Mult.
N 1429. 10 ch. Type **531** .. 8 5
N 1430. 15 ch. Red peach blossom 12 5
N 1431. 20 ch. Red plum blossom 20 8
N 1432. 25 ch. Apricot blossom 25 10
N 1433. 30 ch. Cherry blossom 30 12

532. Azalea.

1975. Flowers of the Azalea Family. Mult.
N 1434. 5 ch. Type **532** .. 5 5
N 1435. 10 ch. White Azalea .. 8 5
N 1436. 15 ch. "Rhododendron yedoense" 12 5
N 1437. 20 ch. White Rhododendron 20 8
N 1438. 25 ch. Rhododendron 25 10
N 1439. 30 ch. Yellow Rhododendron 30 12

533. Torch of Juche.

1975. Korean Workers' Party. 30th Anniv. Multicoloured.
N 1440. 5 ch. Type **533** .. 5 5
N 1441. 5 ch. Chollima Statue and sunset over Pyongyang 5 5
N 1442. 10 ch. Korean with Red Book 8 5
N 1443. 10 ch. Chollima Statue 8 5
N 1444. 25 ch. Crowds and burning building .. 25 10
N 1445. 70 ch. Flowers and map of Korea 70 30
N 1446. 2 w. "Victory" and American graves .. 1·75 1·00
N 1447. 2 w. Sunrise over Mt. Paekdu-san .. .. 1·75 1·00

534. Welcoming Crowd.

1975. Kim Il Sung's Return to Pyongyang. 30th Anniv.
N 1449. **534.** 20 ch. multicoloured 20 8

535. Workers holding "Juche" Torch.

1975. "Rodong Simmun". 30th Anniv.
N 1450. **535.** 10 ch. multicoloured 8 5

536.

1975. Ancient Wall-Gates.
N 1452. **536.** 10 ch. multicoloured 8 5
N 1453. – 10 ch. multicoloured 8 5
N 1454. – 15 ch. multicoloured 12 5
N 1455. – 20 ch. multicoloured 20 8
N 1456. – 30 ch. multicoloured 30 12
DESIGNS: Various Gates (30 ch. vert., others horiz.).

537.

1975. Mt. Chilbo-san.
N 1457. **537.** 10 ch. multicoloured 8 5
N 1458. – 10 ch. multicoloured 8 5
N 1459. – 15 ch. multicoloured 12 5
N 1460. – 20 ch. multicoloured 20 8
N 1461. – 30 ch. multicoloured 30 12
DESIGNS: Nos. N 1458/61, Various views.

538.

1975. Birds.

N 1462.	538.	10 ch. multicoloured	8	5
N 1463.	–	15 ch. multicoloured	12	5
N 1464.	–	20 ch. multicoloured	20	8
N 1465.	–	25 ch. multicoloured	25	10
N 1466.	–	30 ch. multicoloured	30	12

DESIGNS: 15 ch. to 30 ch. Various birds.

539.

1976. Flowers.

N 1491.	539.	5 ch. multicoloured	5	5
N 1492.	–	10 ch. multicoloured	8	5
N 1493.	–	20 ch. multicoloured	20	8
N 1494.	–	40 ch. multicoloured	40	15

DESIGNS: 10 ch. to 40 ch. Various flowers.

540. Bat and Ribbon.

1976. Table-tennis. Mult.

N 1495.	5 ch. Type **540** ..	5	5
N 1496.	10 ch. Three women players with flowers	8	5
N 1497.	20 ch. Player defending	20	8
N 1498.	25 ch. Player making attacking shot ..	25	10

541. Electric Locomotive.

1976. Railway Locomotives. Mult.

N 1500.	5 ch. Type **541** ..	5	5
N 1501.	10 ch. Diesel multiple unit ..	8	5
N 1502.	15 ch. Diesel locomotive	12	5

542.

1976. Ducks and Geese.

N 1503.	542.	10 ch. multicoloured	8	5
N 1504.	–	20 ch. multicoloured	20	8
N 1505.	–	40 ch. multicoloured	40	15

543. " Going to School " (1965).

1976. Social Welfare. Modern Korean Paintings. Multicoloured.

N 1506.	10 ch. Type **543** ..	8	5
N 1507.	15 ch. " Learning at Work " (1970) ..	12	5
N 1508.	25 ch. " Teaching Child " (1965) ..	25	10
N 1509.	30 ch. " Medical Examination at School " (1970) (horiz.) ..	30	12
N 1510.	40 ch. " Nurse with Child " (1970) (horiz.)	40	15

544. Marchers with Flags.

1976. Korean League of Socialist Working Youth. 30th Anniv. Multicoloured.

N 1511.	70 ch. Type **544** ..	70	30
N 1512.	2 w. Flags and Emblem	1·75	1·00

KOUANG TCHEOU (KWANGCHOW) O1

An area and port of S. China, leased by France from China in April 1898. It was returned to China in February 1943.

1906. 100 centimes = 1 franc.
1919. 100 cents = 1 piastre.

Unless otherwise stated the following are optd. or surch. on stamps of Indo-China.

1906. Surch. **Kouang Tcheou-Wan** and value in Chinese.

1.	1.	1 c. olive	30	30
2.		2 c. claret on yellow ..	30	30
3.		4 c. purple on grey ..	30	30
4.		5 c. green	55	55
5.		10 c. red	40	40
6.		15 c. brown on blue ..	55	55
7.		20 c. red on green ..	35	35
8.		25 c. blue	35	35
9.		30 c. brown on cream ..	35	35
10.		35 c. black on yellow ..	35	35
11.		40 c. black on grey ..	50	50
12.		50 c. brown on cream ..	1·60	1·60
13.	D.	75 c. brown on orange ..	2·50	2·50
14.	1.	1 f. green	2·75	2·75
15.		2 f. brown on yellow ..	2·75	2·75
16.	D.	5 f. mauve on lilac ..	25·00	25·00
17.	1.	10 f. red on green ..	28·00	28·00

1908. Native types surch. **KOUANG-TCHEOU** and value in Chinese.

18.	2.	1 c. black and olive ..	5	5
19.		2 c. black and brown ..	5	5
20.		4 c. black and blue ..	8	8
21.		5 c. black and green ..	10	10
22.		10 c. black and red ..	5	5
23.		15 c. black and violet ..	30	30
24.	3.	20 c. black and violet ..	55	55
25.		25 c. black and blue ..	55	55
26.		30 c. black and purple ..	65	65
27.		35 c. black and green ..	1·10	1·10
28.		40 c. black and brown ..	1·40	1·40
29.		50 c. black and red ..	1·25	1·25
30.	4.	75 c. black and orange ..	1·10	1·10
31.		1 f. black and red ..	1·75	1·75
32.		2 f. black and green ..	5·50	5·50
33.		5 f. black and blue ..	9·50	9·50
34.		10 f. black and violet ..	11·00	11·00

1919. Nos. 18/34 surch. in figures and words.

35.	2.	⅖ on 1 c. black & olive ..	5	5
36.		⅘ c. on 2 c. blk. & brn. ..	8	8
37.		1⅗ c. on 4 c. blk. & blue ..	12	8
38.		2 c. on 5 c. blk. & green ..	12	8
39.		4 c. on 10 c. black & red ..	25	10
40.		6 c. on 15 c. blk. & violet	10	8
41.	3.	8 c. on 20 c. blk. & violet	65	40
42.		10 c. on 25 c. blk. & blue	1·40	1·25
43.		12 c. on 30 c. blk. & purple	12	12
44.		14 c. on 35 c. blk. & green	30	30
45.		16 c. on 40 c. blk. & brown	12	10
46.		20 c. on 50 c. black & red	15	15
47.	4.	30 c. on 75 c. blk. & orange	70	45
48.		40 c. on 1 f. black & red ..	70	45
49.		80 c. on 2 f. blk. & green ..	1·10	45
50.		2 p. on 5 f. black & blue ..	25·00	25·00
51.		4 p. on 10 f. blk. & violet	2·25	2·25

1923. Native types optd. **KOUANG-TCHEOU** only. (Value in cents and piastres).

52.	2.	⅒ c. red and grey ..	5	5
53.		⅕ c. black and blue ..	5	5
54.		⅖ c. black and olive ..	5	5
55.		⅘ c. black and red ..	5	5
56.		1 c. black and brown ..	8	8
57.		2 c. black and green ..	10	10
58.		3 c. black and violet ..	10	10
59.		4 c. black and orange ..	10	10
60.		5 c. black and red ..	12	12
61	3.	6 c. black and red ..	12	12
62.		7 c. black and olive ..	12	12
63.		8 c. black	20	20
64.		9 c. black and orange ..	15	15
65.		10 c. black and blue ..	15	15
66.		11 c. black and violet ..	15	15
67.		12 c. black and purple ..	20	20
68.		15 c. black and orange ..	25	25
69.		20 c. black and blue ..	20	20
70.		40 c. black and red ..	40	40
71.		1 p. black and green ..	85	85
72.		2 p. black and claret ..	1·50	1·50

1927. Pictorial types optd. **KOUANG-TCHEOU.**

73.	5.	⅒ c. olive	5	5
74.		⅕ c. yellow	5	5
75.		⅖ c. blue	5	5
76.		⅘ c. brown	8	8
77.		1 c. orange	5	5
78.		2 c. green	10	10
79.		3 c. blue	10	10
80.		4 c. mauve	12	12
81.		5 c. violet	10	10
82.	6.	6 c. red	12	12
83.		7 c. brown	12	12
84.		8 c. olive	12	12
85.		9 c. purple	15	15
86.		10 c. blue	15	15
87.		11 c. orange	15	15
88.		12 c. green	15	15
89.	7.	15 c. brown and red ..	40	40
90.		20 c. grey and violet ..	40	40
91.	–	25 c. mauve and brown ..	40	40
92.	–	30 c. olive and blue ..	25	25
93.	–	40 c. blue and red ..	12	12
94.	–	50 c. grey and green ..	25	25
95.	–	1 p. blk., yellow & blue ..	60	60
96.	–	2 p. blue, orange & red ..	45	45

1937. 1931 issue optd. **KOUANG-TCHEOU.**

98.	11.	⅒ c. blue	5	5
99.		⅕ c. lake	5	5
100.		⅖ c. red	5	5
101.		½ c. brown	5	5
102.		⅘ c. violet	5	5
103.		1 c. brown	5	5
104.		2 c. green	5	5
126.	–	3 c. brown	5	5
105.	–	3 c. green	8	8
106.	–	4 c. blue	10	10
127.	–	4 c. green	5	5
128.	–	4 c. yellow	20	20
107.	–	5 c. purple	8	8
129.	–	5 c. green	5	5
108.	–	6 c. red	5	5
130.	–	7 c. black	5	5
131.	–	8 c. lake	5	5
132.	–	9 c. black on yellow ..	5	5
109.	–	10 c. blue	12	12
133.	–	10 c. blue on pink ..	5	5
110.	–	15 c. blue	8	8
134.	–	18 c. blue	5	5
111.	–	20 c. red	8	8
112.	–	21 c. green	8	8
135.	–	22 c. green	5	5
113.	–	25 c. purple	35	35
136.	–	25 c. blue	5	5
114.	–	30 c. brown	8	8
115.	14.	50 c. brown	8	8
116.		60 c. purple	12	12
137.		70 c. blue	5	5
117.		1 p. green	20	20
118.		2 p. red	25	25

1939. New York World's Fair. As T **11** of Cameroun.

119.	13 c. red	8	8
120.	23 c. blue	8	8

1939. French Revolution. 150th Anniv. As T **16** of Cameroun.

121.	6 c.+2 c. green ..	80	80
122.	7 c.+3 c. brown ..	80	80
123.	9 c.+4 c. orange ..	80	80
124.	13 c.+10 c. red ..	80	80
125.	23 c.+20 c. blue ..	3·50	3·50

KUWAIT BC; O3

An independent Arab Shaikhdom on the N.W. coast of the Persian Gulf with Indian and later British postal administration. On 1st February, 1959, the Kuwait Government assumed responsibility for running its own postal service. In special treaty relations with Great Britain until June 19th, 1961, when Kuwait became completely independent.

Currency. 1923. As India.
1961. 1,000 fils = 1 dinar.

Stamps of India optd. **KUWAIT.**

1923. King George V.

16.	41.	½ a. green	12	30
16a.	62.	½ a. green	1·10	30
2.	42.	1 a. chocolate	25	40
17a.	64.	1 a. chocolate	80	30
3.	43.	1½ a. brown (No. 163) ..	25	45
4.	44.	2 a. lilac	25	30
19b.		2 a. orange-red	35	30
18.	45.	2 a. lilac	25	30
19.		2 a. orange-red	7·50	7·00
5.	47.	2½ a. blue	65	1·75
6.	48.	3 a. orange	1·25	3·00
20.		3 a. blue	2·25	50
21.		3 a. red	2·25	2·25
22a.	49.	4 a. olive	1·50	1·50
22.	50.	4 a. green	7·50	7·50
22b.	51.	6 a. yellow-brown ..	1·50	2·00
23.	52.	8 a. mauve	3·00	3·00
11.	53.	12 a. claret	4·00	4·00
12.	54.	1 r. brown and green ..	4·50	2·00
26.		2 r. red and orange ..	5·50	5·50
27.		5 r. blue and violet ..	15·00	16·00
28.		10 r. green and red ..	28·00	30·00
29.		15 r. blue and olive ..	48·00	50·00

1933. Air.

31.	55.	2 a. green	1·60	2·25
32.		3 a. blue	50	40
33.		4 a. olive	35·00	40·00
34.		6 a. yellow-brown ..	1·60	1·75

1939. King George VI.

36.	74.	½ a. brown	25	25
38.		1 a. red	25	25
39.	76.	2 a. red	35	35
41.	–	3 a. green	50	55
43.	–	4 a. brown	65	1·40
44.	–	6 a. green	75	1·75
45.	–	8 a. violet	1·40	2·00
46.	–	12 a. red	1·75	2·75
47.	77.	1 r. slate and brown ..	75	75
48.		2 r. purple and brown ..	1·50	1·75
49.		5 r. green and blue ..	4·50	4·00
50.		10 r. purple and red ..	11·00	11·00
51.		15 r. brown and green ..	15·00	17·00

1942. King George VI stamps of 1940.

52.	78.	3 p. slate	15	20
53.		1 a. mauve	15	20
54.		9 p. green	15	30
55.		1 a. red	15	25
56.	79.	1½ a. violet	15	25
57.		2 a. red	15	25
58.		3 a. violet	15	25
59.		3½ a. blue	15	25
60.	80.	4 a. brown	15	50
60a.		6 a. green	2·25	2·50
61.		8 a. violet	30	40
62.		12 a. purple	35	75
63.	–	14 a. purple (No. 277) ..	2·00	3·00

From 1948 onwards, for stamps with similar surcharges, but without name of country, see Muscat.

Stamps of Great Britain surch. **KUWAIT** and new values in Indian currency.

1948. King George VI.

64.	103.	½ a. on ½d. pale green ..	8	12
84.		½ a. on ½d. orange ..	5	10
65.		1 a. on 1d. pale red ..	8	12
85.		1 a. on 1d. blue ..	5	10
66.		1½ a. on 1½d. pale brown	8	12
86.		1½ a. on 1½d. green ..	8	10
67.		2 a. on 2d. pale orange	8	15
87.		2 a. on 2d. brown ..	8	10
68.	103.	2½ a. on 2½d. light blue	8	25
88.		2½ a. on 2½d. red ..	15	10
69.		3 a. on 3d. pale violet ..	8	15
89.	104.	4 a. on 4d. blue	10	10
70.		6 a. on 6d. purple ..	12	12
71.	105.	1 r. on 1s. brown ..	25	25
72.	106.	2 r. on 2s. 6d. green ..	80	1·00
73.		5 r. on 5s. red	1·75	2·00
73a.	–	10 r. on 10s. bright blue (No. 478a)	8·50	6·50

1948. Silver Wedding.

74.	110.	2½ a. on 2½d. blue ..	10	10
75.	111.	15 r. on £1 blue ..	6·50	9·00

1948. Olympic Games.

76.	112.	2½ a. on 2½d. blue ..	12	15
77.	113.	3 a. on 2d. violet ..	15	25
78.	–	6 a. on 5d. Kpurple ..	25	40
79.	–	1 r. on 1s. brown ..	50	60

1949. U.P.U.

80.	114.	2½ a. on 2½d. blue ..	15	25
81.	115.	3 a. on 3d. violet ..	25	35
82.	–	6 a. on 6d. purple ..	35	55
83.	–	1 r. on 1s. brown ..	60	65

1951. Pictorial high values.
90. 116. 2 r. on 2s. 6d. green .. 1·25 1·00
91. – 5 r. on 5s. red (No. 510) 1·75 2·25
92. – 10 r. on 10s. blue No. 511) .. .. .. 3·00 2·50

1952. Queen Elizabeth II.
93. 118. ½ a. on ½d. orange .. 5 5
94. 1 a. on 1d. blue .. 5 5
95. 1½ a. on 1½d. green .. 5 5
96. 2 a. on 2d. brown .. 5 5
97. 119. 2½ a. on 2½d. red .. 5 5
98. 3 a. on 3d. lilac .. 5 5
99. 4 a. on 4d. blue .. 8 10
100. 120. 6 a. on 6d. purple .. 10 8
101. 122. 12 a. on 1s. 3d. green.. 25 25
102. 1 r. on 1s. 6d. indigo.. 25 25

1953. Coronation.
103. 123. 2½ a. on 2½d. red 25 25
104. – 4 a. on 4d. ultramarine 35 35
105. 124. 12 a. on 1s. 3d. green.. 85 85
106. – 1 r. on 1s. 6d. blue .. 95 95

1955. Pictorials.
107. 125. 2 r. on 2s. 6d. brown.. 55 90
108. – 5 r. on 5s. red.. .. 1·25 1·75
109. – 10 r. on 10s. blue .. 2·50 2·50

1957. Queen Elizabeth II.
120. 120. 1 n.p. on 5d. brown .. 5 5
121. 118. 3 n.p. on ½d. orange .. 5 5
122. 6 n.p. on 1d. blue .. 5 5
123. 9 n.p. on 1½d. green .. 5 5
124. 12 n.p. on 2d. pale brn. 5 5
125. 119. 15 n.p. on 2½d. red .. 12 12
126. 20 n.p. on 3d. lilac .. 12 5
127. 25 n.p. on 4d. blue .. 12 30
128. 120. 40 n.p. on 6d. purple.. 20 15
129. 121. 50 n.p. on 9d. olive .. 35 60
130. 122. 75 n.p. on 1s. 3d. green 35 50

1. Shaikh Abdullah as-Salum as-Sabah.

2. Dhow.

3. Single-masted Dhow.

1959.
131. 1. 5 n.p. green 8 5
132. 10 n.p. red 8 5
133. 15 n.p. brown 8 5
134. 20 n.p. slate-violet .. 8 5
135. 25 n.p. salmon 8 5
136. 40 n.p. maroon 50 30
137. 2. 40 n.p. blue 10 5
138. – 50 n.p. red 10 5
139. – 75 n.p. bronze-green .. 20 12
140. – 1 r. purple 20 12
141. 3. 2 r. blue and brown .. 50 35
142. – 5 r. blue-green .. .. 1·00 75
143. – 10 r. lilac .. .. 5·00 3·00
DESIGNS—HORIZ. As T 2: 50 n.p. Oil pipelines. 75 n.p. Power station. As T 3: 1 r. Oil-drilling rig (without portrait). 5 r. Kuwait Mosque. 10 r. Main Square, Kuwait Town.

4. Shaikh Abdullah and Flag.

1960. Shaik's Accession. 10th Anniv.
144. 4. 40 n.p. red and olive .. 20 20
145. 60 n.p. red and blue .. 25 25

1961. As 1959 issue but currency changed and new designs as T 3.
146. 1. 1 f. green 5 5
147. 2 f. red 5 5
148. 4 f. brown 5 5
149. 5 f. slate-violet 5 5
150. 8 f. salmon 5 5
151. 15 f. maroon 5 5
152. – 20 f. blue-green (as 5 r.).. 5 5
153. – 25 f. blue 8 5
154. 3. 30 f. blue and brown .. 8 8
155. – 35 f. black and red .. 8 8
156. 2. 40 f. blue 10 8
157. – 45 f. chocolate 15 8
158. 3. 75 f. sepia and emerald.. 25 20

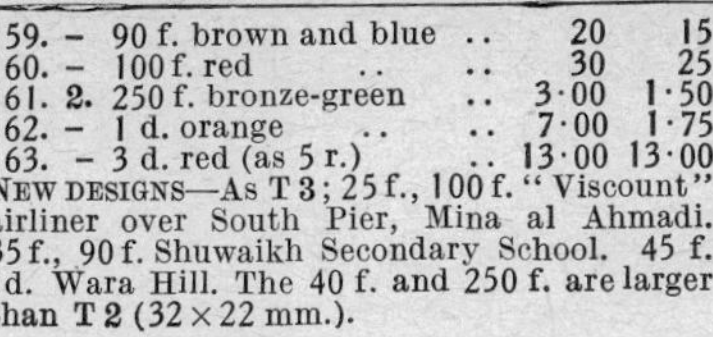

159. – 90 f. brown and blue .. 20 15
160. – 100 f. red 30 25
161. 2. 250 f. bronze-green .. 3·00 1·50
162. – 1 d. orange .. .. 7·00 1·75
163. – 3 d. red (as 5 r.) .. 13·00 13·00
NEW DESIGNS—As T 3; 25 f., 100 f. "Viscount" airliner over South Pier, Mina al Ahmadi. 35 f., 90 f. Shuwaikh Secondary School. 45 f. 1d. Wara Hill. The 40 f. and 250 f. are larger than T 2 (32 × 22 mm.).

INDEPENDENT STATE

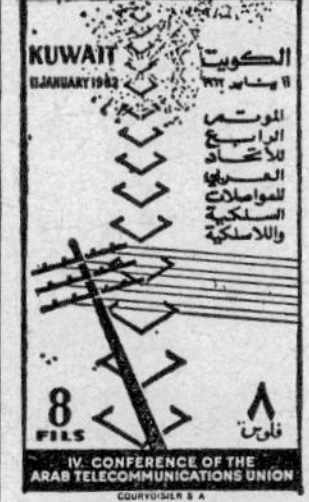

5. Telegraph Pole.

ILLUSTRATIONS British Commonwealth and all overprints and surcharges are FULL SIZE. Foreign Countries have been reduced to ¾-LINEAR.

1962. 4th Arab Telecommunications Union Conf.
164. 5. 8 f. blue and black .. 10 10
165. 20 f. red and black .. 30 30

1962. Arab League Week. As T 170 of Egypt
166. 20 f. purple 12 12
167. 45 f. brown 45 45

6. Mubarakiya School, Shaikh Sir Abdullah and Shaikh Mubarak.

1962. Golden Jubilee on Mubarakiya School.
168. 6 8 f. blk., gold, red & brn. 8 8
169. 20 f. blk., gold, red & bl. 25 25

7. National Flag and Crest.

1962. National Day.
170. 7. 8 f. multicoloured .. 15 15
171. 20 f. multicoloured .. 25 30
172. 45 f. multicoloured .. 80 60
173. 90 f. multicoloured .. 1·50 1·25

1962. Malaria Eradication. As T 174 of Egypt.
174. 4 f. green and blue-green 10 10
175. 25 f. grey and green .. 40 40

8. " Industry and Progress ".

1962. Sabah Dynasty. Bicent.
176. 8. 8 f. black, yell., red & bl. 10 10
177. 20 f. blk., bl., red & yell. 20 20
178. 45 f. blk., yell., grn. & red 35 35
179. 75 f. blk., yell., red & grn. 85 70

9. Mother and Child.

11. " Education from Oil ".

10. Campaign Emblem, Palm and Domestic Animals.

1963. Mothers' Day. Centres black and green; value black; country name red.
180. 9. 8 f. yellow 8 8
181. 20 f. blue 20 20
182. 45 f. olive 50 50
183. 75 f. grey 70 70

1963. Freedom from Hunger. Design in brown and green. Background colours given.
184. 10. 4 f. blue 8 8
185. 8 f. yellow 25 25
186. 20 f. lilac 40 40
187. 45 f. pink 85 85

1963. Education Day.
188. 11. 4 f. brown, blue & yellow 8 8
189. 20 f. green, blue & yellow 15 15
190. 45 f. purple, blue & yell. 35 35

12. Shaikh Sir Abdullah and Flags.

1963. National Day. 2nd Anniv. Flags in green, black and red; values in black.
191. 12. 4 f. blue 35 35
192. 5 f. ochre 60 60
193. 20 f. violet .. .. 1·75 1·75
194. 50 f. olive .. .. 3·00 3·00

13. Human Lungs, W.H.O. Emblem and Kuwait Arms.

1963. W.H.O. "Tuberculosis Control" Campaign. Emblem yellow: Arms black, green and red.
195. 13. 2 f. black and ochre .. 5 5
196. 4 f. black and green .. 8 5
197. 8 f. black and blue .. 10 8
198. 20 f. black and lake .. 20 12

14. Municipal Hall and Scroll.

1963. New Constitution. Centres dull purple; Amir brown-red.
199. 14. 4 f. red 5 5
200. 8 f. green 8 8
201. 20 f. brown-purple .. 15 15
202. 45 f. chestnut 30 30
203. 75 f. violet 50 50
204. 90 f. blue 70 70

15. Football.

16. Scales of Justice and Globe.

1963. Arab Schools Games. Multicoloured.
205. 1 f. Type 15 .. .. 5 5
206. 4 f. Basketball 5 5
207. 5 f. Swimming 8 8
208. 8 f. Running 8 8
209. 15 f. Throwing the javelin 15 15
210. 20 f. Pole-vaulting .. 20 20
211. 35 f. Gymnastics 40 30
212. 45 f. Gymnastics 80 50
Nos. 207, 209/11 are horiz.

1963. Declaration of Human Rights. 15th Anniv.
213. 16. 8 f. black, turq. & violet 8 8
214. 20 f. black, yellow & grey 20 20
215. 25 f. black, buff & blue 30 30

17. Shaikh Sir Abdullah.

18. Rameses II in War Chariot.

1964. Multicoloured.
216. 17. 1 f. 5 5
217. 2 f. 5 5
218. 4 f. 5 5
219. 5 f. 5 5
220. 8 f. 5 5
221. 10 f. 5 5
222. 15 f. 8 5
223. 20 f. 10 8
224. 25 f. 15 10
225. 30 f. 20 12
226. 40 f. 25 15
227. 45 f. 30 20
228. 50 f. 35 25
229. 70 f. 40 30
230. 75 f. 45 30
231. 90 f. 50 45
232. 100 f. 55 50
233. – 250 f. .. .. .. 1·50 1·25
234. – 1 d. .. .. .. 6·50 5·50
Nos. 233/4 are larger (25 × 30 mm.).

1964. Nubian Monuments Preservation.
235. 18. 8 f. purple, blue & buff 10 10
236. 20 f. vio., blue & lt. blue 30 25
237. 30 f. violet, blue & turq. 30 25

19. Mother and Child.

1964. Mothers' Day.
238. 19. 8 f. indigo, green & grey 8 8
239. 20 f. indigo, green & red 15 15
240. 30 f. indigo, grn. & bistre 25 20
241. 45 f. indigo, green & blue 30 30

20. Nurse giving B.C.G. Vaccine to Patient and Bones of Chest.

21. Dhow and Microscope.

1964. World Health Day.
242. 20. 8 f. green and brown.. 10 8
243. 20 f. red and green .. 20 15

1964. Education Day.
244. 21. 8 f. multicoloured .. 10 8
245. 15 f. multicoloured .. 15 15
246. 20 f. multicoloured .. 20 15
247. 30 f. multicoloured .. 25 25

22. Arab Dhow and Doves.

1964. National Day. 3rd Anniv. Badge in blue, brown, black, red and green.
248. 22. 8 f. black and bistre .. 15 15
249. 20 f. black and green .. 25 25
250. 30 f. black and grey .. 30 30
251. 45 f. black and blue .. 45 45

23. A.P.U. Emblem. 24. Comet and Dakota Airliners.

1964. Arab Postal Union's Permanent Office, Cairo. 10th Anniv.
252. 23. 8 f. brown and blue .. 10 10
253. 20 f. ultram. and yellow 20 20
254. 45 f. brown and olive .. 40 40

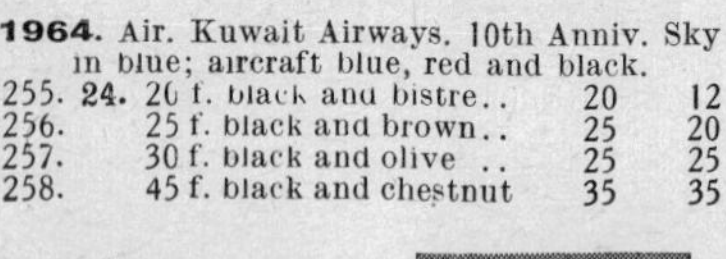

1964. Air. Kuwait Airways. 10th Anniv. Sky in blue; aircraft blue, red and black.
255. 24. 20 f. black and bistre.. 20 12
256. 25 f. black and brown.. 25 20
257. 30 f. black and olive .. 25 25
258. 45 f. black and chestnut 35 35

25. Conference Emblem. 26. Dhow, Doves and Oil-drilling Rig.

1965. 1st Arab Journalists' Conf., Kuwait.
259. 25. 8 f. red, yellow, black and chestnut .. 8 5
260. 20 f. red, yellow, black and green 15 10

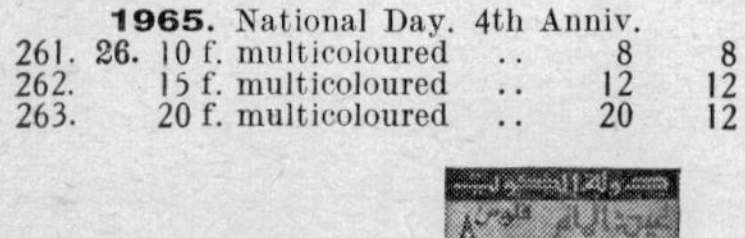

1965. National Day. 4th Anniv.
261. 26. 10 f. multicoloured .. 8 8
262. 15 f. multicoloured .. 12 12
263. 20 f. multicoloured .. 20 12

27. I.C.Y. Emblem. 28. Mother and Children.

1965. Int. Co-operation Year.
264. 27. 8 f. black and green .. 8 5
265. 20 f. black and blue .. 15 10
266. 30 f. black and green .. 25 12
The stamps are inscribed "CO-OPERATIVE".

1965. Mothers' Day.
267. 28. 8 f. multicoloured .. 8 5
268. 15 f. multicoloured .. 12 10
269. 20 f. multicoloured .. 15 12

29. Weather Kite.

1965. World Meteorological Day.
270. 29. 4 f. ultramarine & yellow 8 5
271. 5 f. blue and orange .. 8 5
272. 20 f. blue and green .. 20 15

30. Census Graph.

1965. Population Census.
273. 30. 8 f. black, chest. & turq. 8 5
274. 20 f. black, pink & green 20 12
275. 50 f. black, green & red 40 25

1965. Deir Yasin Massacre. As T 230 of Egypt.
276. 4 f. red and blue 5 5
277. 45 f. red and green .. 30 25

31. Atomic Symbol and Tower of Shuwaikh Secondary School.

1965. Education Day.
278. 31. 4 f. multicoloured .. 8 5
279. 20 f. multicoloured .. 15 12
280. 45 f. multicoloured .. 25 20

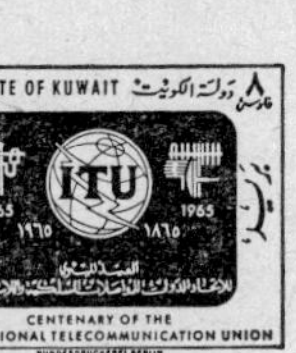

32. I.T.U. Emblem and Symbols. 33. Peregrine.

1965. I.T.U. Cent.
281. 32. 8 f. red and blue .. 8 5
282. 20 f. red and green .. 20 12
283. 45 f. blue and red .. 30 25

1965. Reconstruction of Burnt Algiers Library. As T 232 of Egypt.
284. 8 f. green, red and black.. 8 5
285. 15 f. red, green and black.. 12 8

1965. Centre in sepia.
286. 33. 8 f. purple 8 5
287. 15 f. olive 10 8
288. 20 f. indigo 15 10
289. 25 f. vermilion 20 15
290. 30 f. green 25 20
291. 45 f. blue 35 25
292. 50 f. purple 40 30
293. 90 f. red 60 50

34. Open Book. 35. Shaikh Sabah.

1966. Education Day.
294. 34. 8 f. multicoloured .. 8 5
295. 20 f. multicoloured .. 15 12
296. 30 f. multicoloured .. 20 15

1966.
297. 35. 4 f. multicoloured .. 5 5
298. 5 f. multicoloured .. 5 5
299. 20 f. multicoloured .. 10 8
300. 30 f. multicoloured .. 15 12
301. 40 f. multicoloured .. 20 15
302. 45 f. multicoloured .. 25 20
303. 70 f. multicoloured .. 35 30
304. 90 f. multicoloured .. 60 50

36. Fishes and Ears of Wheat.

1966. Freedom from Hunger.
305. 36. 20 f. multicoloured .. 25 15
306. 45 f. multicoloured .. 40 30

37. Eagle and Scales of Justice.

1966. National Day. 5th Anniv.
307. 37. 20 f. multicoloured .. 15 12
308. 25 f. multicoloured .. 20 15
309. 45 f. multicoloured .. 40 30

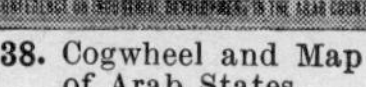

38. Cogwheel and Map of Arab States. 39. Mother and Children.

1966. Arab Countries Industrial Development Conf. Kuwait.
310. 38. 20 f. grn. black & blue 20 12
311. 50 f. grn., black & brown 40 30

1966. Mothers' Day.
312. 39. 20 f. multicoloured .. 20 12
313. 40 f. multicoloured .. 40 30

40. Red Crescent Emblem of Medicine. 41. "Man and his Cities".

1966. 5th Arab Medical Conf., Kuwait.
314. 40. 15 f. red and blue .. 12 8
315. 30 f. red, blue and pink 25 15

1966. World Health Day.
316. 41. 8 f. multicoloured .. 10 8
317. 10 f. multicoloured .. 10 8

42. W.H.O. Building. 43. Symbol of Blood Donation.

1966. W.H.O. Headquarters, Geneva. Inaug.
318. 42. 5 f. green, blue and red 8 5
319. 10 f. green, blue & turq. 10 8

1966. Traffic Day. As T 250 of Egypt.
320. 10 f. red, emerald & green 5 5
321. 20 f. emerald, red & green 12 10

1966. Blood Bank Day.
322. 43. 4 f. multicoloured .. 5 5
323. 8 f. multicoloured .. 30 25

44. Shaikh Ahmad and "British Fusilier".

1966. 1st Crude Oil Shipment. 20th Anniv.
324. 44. 20 f. multicoloured .. 20 15
325. 45 f. multicoloured .. 40 30

45. Ministry Building.

1966. Ministry of Guidance and Information Building. Inaug.
326. 45. 4 f. red and brown .. 5 5
327. 5 f. chestnut and green 5 5
328. 8 f. green and violet .. 8 5
329. 20 f. orange and blue .. 20 12

46. Dhow, Lobster, Fish and Crab. 47. U.N. Flag.

1966. F.A.O. Near East Countries Fisheries Conf., Kuwait.
330. 46. 4 f. multicoloured .. 8 5
331. 20 f. multicoloured .. 20 15

1966. U.N. Day.
332. 47. 20 f. multicoloured .. 20 15
333. 45 f. multicoloured .. 40 30

48. U.N.E.S.C.O. Emblem. 49. Ruler and University Shield.

1966. U.N.E.S.C.O. 20th Anniv.
334. 48. 20 f. multicoloured .. 20 15
335. 45 f. multicoloured .. 40 30

1966. Opening of Kuwait University.
336. 49. 8 f. multicoloured .. 8 5
337. 10 f. multicoloured .. 10 8
338. 20 f. multicoloured .. 20 15
339. 45 f. multicoloured .. 40 30

50. Ruler and Heir-Apparent.

1966. Appointment of Heir-Apparent.
340. 50. 8 f. multicoloured .. 8 5
341. 20 f. multicoloured .. 20 15
342. 45 f. multicoloured .. 40 40

51. Scout Badge. 52. Symbol of Learning.

1966. Kuwait Scouts. 30th Anniv.
343. 51. 4 f. chestnut and green 8 8
344. 20 f. green and brown 20 15

1967. Education Day.
345. 52. 10 f. multicoloured .. 8 5
346. 45 f. multicoloured .. 40 30

53. Fertiliser Plant.

1967. Chemical Fertiliser Plant. Inaug.
347. 53. 8 f. purple, green & blue 8 5
348. 20 f. blue, green & buff 25 12

54. Ruler, Dove and Olive-Branch.

1967. National Day. 6th Anniv.
349. 54. 8 f. multicoloured .. 8 5
350. 20 f. multicoloured .. 20 15

55. Map and Municipality Building. 56. Arab Family.

1967. 1st Arab Cities Organization Conf., Kuwait.
351. 55. 20 f. multicoloured .. 20 15
352. 30 f. multicoloured .. 30 20

1967. Family's Day.
353. 56. 20 f. multicoloured .. 20 12
354. 45 f. multicoloured .. 30 25

57. Arab League Emblem. 58. Sabah Hospital.

1967. Arab Cause Week.
355. 57. 8 f. blue and grey .. 8 5
356. 10 f. green and yellow 8 5

1967. World Health Day.
357. 58. 8 f. multicoloured .. 8 5
358. 20 f. multicoloured .. 20 15

59. Nubian Statues.

1967. Arab Week for Nubian Monuments Preservation.
359. 59. 15 f. green, brown & yell. 15 10
360. 20 f. green, purple & blue 25 20

60. Traffic Policeman.

61. I.T.Y. Emblem. 62. "Reaching for Knowledge".

1967. Traffic Day.
361. 60. 8 f. multicoloured .. 8 5
362. 20 f. multicoloured .. 20 15

1967. Int. Tourist Year.
363. 61. 20 f. black, blue & turq. 20 12
364. 45 f. black, blue & mve. 35 25

1967. "Eliminate Illiteracy" Campaign.
365. 62. 8 f. multicoloured .. 8 8
366. 20 f. multicoloured .. 25 20

63. Map of Palestine. 64. Factory and Cogwheels.

1967. U.N. Day.
367. 63. 20 f. red and blue .. 20 12
368. 45 f. red and orange .. 35 25

1967. 3rd Arab Labour Ministers' Conf.
369. 64. 20 f. yellow and red .. 20 12
370. 45 f. yellow and slate .. 35 25

65. Open Book and Kuwaiti Flag. 66. Oil Rig and Map.

1968. Education Day.
371. 65. 20 f. multicoloured .. 12 12
372. 45 f. multicoloured .. 35 25

1968. Oil Discovery in Greater Burgan Field. 30th Anniv.
373. 66. 10 f. multicoloured .. 15 8
374. 20 f. multicoloured .. 30 25

67. Ruler and Sun Rays. 68. Book, Eagle and Sun.

1968. National Day. 7th Anniv.
375. 67. 8 f. multicoloured .. 5 5
376. 10 f. multicoloured .. 8 5
377. 15 f. multicoloured .. 10 8
378. 20 f. multicoloured .. 20 15

1968. Teachers' Day.
379. 68. 8 f. multicoloured .. 8 5
380. 20 f. multicoloured .. 20 8
381. 45 f. multicoloured .. 30 25

69. Family Picnicking.

1968. Family's Day.
382. 69. 8 f. multicoloured .. 5 5
383. 10 f. multicoloured .. 8 5
384. 15 f. multicoloured .. 10 8
385. 20 f. multicoloured .. 15 10

70. Ruler, W.H.O. and State Emblems.

1968. World Health Day and W.H.O. 20th Anniv.
386. 70. 20 f. multicoloured .. 15 15
387. 45 f. multicoloured .. 30 25

71. Dagger on Deir Yasin and Scroll.

1968. Deir Yasin Massacre. 20th Anniv.
388. 71. 20 f. red and blue .. 15 10
389. 45 f. red and violet .. 30 25

72. Pedestrians on Road Crossing.

1968. Traffic Day.
390. 72. 10 f. multicoloured .. 8 5
391. 15 f. multicoloured .. 10 8
392. 20 f. multicoloured .. 15 10

73. Torch and Map. 74. Palestine Refugees.

1968. Palestine Day.
393. 73. 10 f. multicoloured .. 8 5
394. 20 f. multicoloured .. 20 15
395. 45 f. multicoloured .. 30 25

1968. Human Rights Year.
396. 74. 20 f. multicoloured .. 20 15
397. 30 f. multicoloured .. 25 20
398. 45 f. multicoloured .. 35 25
399. 90 f. multicoloured .. 80 60

75. National Museum. 76. Man reading Book.

1968.
400. 75. 1 f. green and sepia .. 5 5
401. 2 f. green and plum .. 5 5
402. 5 f. vermilion and black 5 5
403. 8 f. green and brown .. 5 5
404. 10 f. maroon and blue.. 5 5
405. 20 f. blue and chestnut 12 8
406. 25 f. orange & ultram. 15 12
407. 30 f. green and blue .. 20 15
408. 45 f. slate-purple & pur. 30 25
409. 50 f. red and green .. 40 35

1968. Int. Literacy Day.
410. 76. 15 f. multicoloured .. 10 8
411. 20 f. multicoloured .. 15 10

77. Refugee Children and U.N. Headquarters.

1968. United Nations Day.
412. 77. 20 f. multicoloured .. 15 10
413. 30 f. multicoloured .. 25 15
414. 45 f. multicoloured .. 30 25

78. Chamber of Commerce Building.

1968. Kuwait Chamber of Commerce and Industry Building. Inaug.
415. 78. 10 f. maroon and orange 5 5
416. 15 f. blue and magenta 8 5
417. 20 f. green and chestnut 12 8

79. Conference Emblem.

1968. 14th Arab Chambers of Commerce Conf.
418. 79. 10 f. multicoloured .. 5 5
419. 15 f. multicoloured .. 8 8
420. 20 f. multicoloured .. 12 12
421. 30 f. multicoloured .. 20 20

80. Refinery Plant. 81. Holy Quran, Scales and People.

1968. Shuaiba Refinery. Inaug.
422. 80. 10 f. multicoloured .. 8 5
423. 20 f. multicoloured .. 12 10
424. 30 f. multicoloured .. 15 15
425. 45 f. multicoloured .. 25 20

1968. 1,400th Anniv. of the Holy Quran.
426. 81. 8 f. multicoloured .. 5 5
427. 20 f. multicoloured .. 12 12
428. 30 f. multicoloured .. 15 15
429. 45 f. multicoloured .. 25 20

82. Boeing "707" Jetliner.

1969. Inaug. of Boeing "707" Aircraft by Kuwait Airways.
430. 82. 10 f. multicoloured .. 8 8
431. 20 f. multicoloured .. 12 12
432. 25 f. multicoloured .. 20 20
433. 45 f. multicoloured .. 30 30

83. Globe and Symbols of Engineering and Science.

1969. Education Day.
434. 83. 15 f. multicoloured .. 8 5
435. 20 f. multicoloured .. 12 8

84. Hilton Hotel. 85. Family and Teachers Society Emblem.

1969. Kuwait Hilton Hotel. Inaug.
436. 84. 10 f. multicoloured .. 8 5
437. 20 f. multicoloured .. 12 8

1969. Education Week.
438. 85. 10 f. multicoloured .. 8 5
439. 20 f. multicoloured .. 12 8

86. Flags and Laurel. 87. Emblem, Teacher and Class.

1969. National Day. 8th Anniv.
440. 86. 15 f. multicoloured .. 8 5
441. 20 f. multicoloured .. 12 8
442. 30 f. multicoloured .. 20 15

1969. Teachers' Day.
443. 87. 10 f. multicoloured .. 8 8
444. 20 f. multicoloured .. 12 12

88. Kuwaiti Family.

1969. Family Day.
445. 88. 10 f. multicoloured .. 8 8
446. 20 f. multicoloured .. 12 12

89. Ibn Sina, Nurse with Patient and W.H.O. Emblem. 90. Motor-cycle Police.

1969. World Health Day.
447. 89. 15 f. multicoloured .. 8 8
448. 20 f. multicoloured .. 12 12

1969. Traffic Day.
449. 90. 10 f. multicoloured .. 8 8
450. 20 f. multicoloured .. 12 12

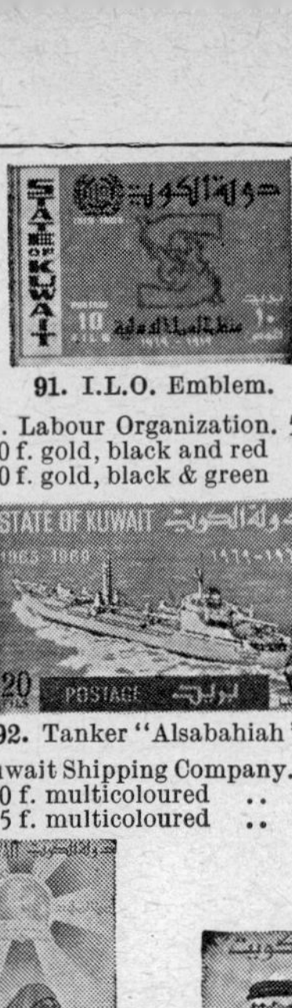

91. I.L.O. Emblem.

1969. Int. Labour Organization. 50th Anniv.

451.	91.	10 f. gold, black and red	8	8
452.		20 f. gold, black & green	12	12

92. Tanker "Alsabahiah".

1969. Kuwait Shipping Company. 4th Anniv.

453.	92.	20 f. multicoloured ..	15	15
454.		45 f. multicoloured ..	30	30

93. Woman writing Letter. 94. Amir Shaikh Sabah.

1969. Int. Literacy Day.

455.	93.	10 f. multicoloured ..	5	5
456.		20 f. multicoloured ..	8	8

1969. Portraits multicoloured; background colours given.

457.	94.	8 f. blue	5	5
458.		10 f. red	5	5
459.		15 f. grey	8	8
460.		20 f. yellow	10	10
461.		25 f. lilac	12	12
462.		30 f. orange	15	15
463.		45 f. drab	20	20
464.		50 f. green	25	25
465.		70 f. blue	30	30
466.		75 f. blue	35	35
467.		90 f. brown	40	40
468.		250 f. purple	1·25	1·25
469.		500 f. green	3·00	3·00
470.		1 d. purple	6·00	6·00

95. "Appeal to World Conscience". 96. Earth Station.

1969. United Nations Day.

471.	95.	10 f. blue, black & green	8	8
472.		20 f. blue, black & ochre	10	12
473.		45 f. blue, black & red	25	20

1969. Kuwait Satellite Communications Station. Inaug. Multicoloured.

474.	20 Type **96**	12	10
475.	45 f. Dish aerial on Globe (vert.)	25	25

97. Refugee Family. 98. Globe, Symbols and I.E.Y. Emblem.

1969. Palestinian Refugee Week.

476.	97.	20 f. multicoloured ..	12	12
477.		45 f. multicoloured ..	25	25

1970. Int. Education Year.

478.	98.	20 f. multicoloured ..	12	12
479.		45 f. multicoloured ..	25	25

99. Shoue.

1970. Kuwait Sailing Dhows. Multicoloured.

480.	8 f. Type **99**	5	5
481.	10 f. Sambook	5	5
482.	15 f. Baghla	8	5
483.	20 f. Batteel	10	8
484.	25 f. Boom	15	12
485.	45 f. Bakkara	25	20
486.	50 f. Dhow-building ..	30	20

100. Kuwaiti Flag.

1970. National Day. 9th Anniv.

487.	100.	15 f. multicoloured ..	8	5
488.		20 f. multicoloured ..	12	8

101. Young Commando and Dome of the Rock, Jerusalem.

1970. Support for Palestine Commandos. Multicoloured.

489.	10 f. Type **101**	5	5
490.	20 f. Commando in battle-dress	12	8
491.	45 f. Woman commando..	25	25

102. Parents with "Children".

1970. Family Day.

492.	102.	20 f. multicoloured ..	12	8
493.		30 f. multicoloured ..	20	15

103. Arab League Flag, Emblem and Map.

1970. Arab League. 25th Anniv.

494.	103.	20 f. ochre, emer. & blue	12	8
495.		45 f. violet, emer. & pink	25	20

104. Census Emblem and Graph.

1970. Population Census.

496.	104.	15 f. multicoloured ..	8	5
497.		20 f. multicoloured ..	12	8
498.		30 f. multicoloured ..	20	12

105. Cancer the Crab in "Pincers". 106. Traffic Lights and Road Signs.

1970. World Health Day.

499.	105.	20 f. multicoloured ..	12	8
500.		30 f. multicoloured ..	20	12

1970. Traffic Day.

501.	106.	20 f. multicoloured ..	12	8
502.		30 f. multicoloured ..	20	12

107. Red Crescent.

1970. Int. Red Cross and Crescent Day.

503.	107.	10 f. multicoloured ..	5	5
504.		15 f. multicoloured ..	8	5
505.		30 f. multicoloured ..	20	12

108. New Headquarters Building.

1970. New U.P.U. Headquarters Building, Berne.

506.	108.	20 f. multicoloured ..	10	8
507.		30 f. multicoloured ..	20	15

109. Amir Shaikh Sabah. 110. U.N. Symbols.

1970.

508.	109.	20 f. multicoloured ..	10	8
509.		45 f. multicoloured ..	25	20

1970. United Nations. 25th Anniv.

511.	110.	20 f. multicoloured ..	12	8
512.		45 f. multicoloured ..	25	20

111. Sea Island Jetty.

1970. Oil Shipment Facilities, Kuwait.

513.	111.	20 f. multicoloured ..	12	8
514.		45 f. multicoloured ..	30	25

112. Kuwait and U.N. Emblems and Hand writing.

1970. International Literacy Day.

515.	112.	10 f. multicoloured ..	5	5
516.		15 f. multicoloured ..	8	8

113. Guards and Badge.

1970. First Graduation of National Guards.

517.	113.	10 f. multicoloured ..	5	5
518.		20 f. multicoloured ..	10	8

114. Symbols and Flag. 116. Map of Palestine on Globe.

115. Dr. C. H. Best, Sir F. G. Banting (discoverers of insulin) and Syringe.

1971. National Day. 10th Anniv.

519.	114.	20 f. multicoloured ..	10	8
520.		30 f. multicoloured ..	20	15

1971. World Health Day.

521.	115.	20 f. multicoloured ..	12	8
522.		45 f. multicoloured ..	25	20

1971. Palestine Week.

523.	116.	20 f. multicoloured ..	12	8
524.		45 f. multicoloured ..	25	20

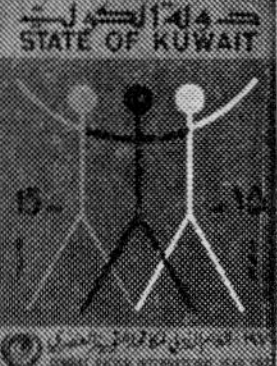

117. I.T.U. Emblem. 118. "Three Races".

1971. World Telecommunications Day.

525.	117.	20 f. blk., brn. & silver	12	8
526.		45 f. blk., brn. & gold..	25	20

1971. Racial Equality Year.

527.	118.	15 f. multicoloured ..	8	5
528.		30 f. multicoloured ..	20	12

119. A.P.U. Emblem.

1971. Founding of Arab Postal Union at Sofar Conference. 25th Anniv.

529.	119.	20 f. multicoloured ..	12	8
530.		45 f. multicoloured ..	25	20

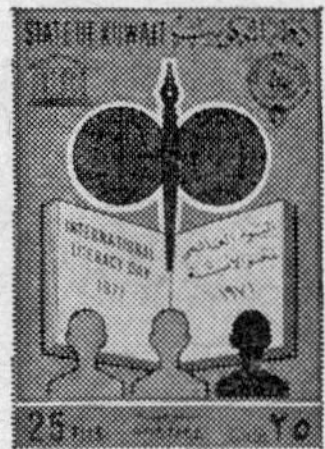

120. Book, Pupils, Globes and Pen.

1971. Int. Literacy Day.

531.	120.	25 f. multicoloured ..	12	8
532.		60 f. multicoloured ..	35	25

121. Footballers.

1971. Regional Sports Tournament, Kuwait. Multicoloured.

533.	20 f. Type **121**	12	8
534.	30 f. Footballer blocking attack	20	12

Stanley Gibbons the complete philatelists

Gibbons stay-at-home services

The collector can make use of virtually all the Stanley Gibbons facilities without ever coming to London! Apart from the catalogues, albums and accessories which he can get from us by mail-order, the stay-at-home collector can use Stanley Gibbons Approval and New Issue services to build up his collection.

The Approvals Service offers the collector the opportunity to browse at leisure through a specially chosen selection of Great Britain or British Commonwealth stamps in the quiet of his own home with his album close at hand.

The New Issues Service provides the collector with a sure and comprehensive service designed to keep his stamp collection right up-to-date.

We also buy stamps

Our buyers search the world for stamps to maintain our stocks against the enormous demands of collectors. Every day individuals walk in casually to offer us their stamps, and collections are posted to us for sale, or for valuation for insurance or probate. If we do buy, immediate cash payment is given no matter what the figure. Please write in the first instance, giving general particulars, before sending stamps or asking our valuer to make a visit.

Rare stamps

We retain a large 'bank' of rare and elusive philatelic material at Romano House. Serious collectors have their wants recorded on our Specialist Register, or send us lists of their 'rare stamp' wants. Investment advice and assistance in building up valuable collections is given here, and collectors appreciate the luxurious, quiet atmosphere of the viewing rooms.

Auctions

The auction is the culmination of many weeks of expert cataloguing and organisation, and of the dissemination well in advance to enquirers throughout the world of fine, illustrated catalogues. Thanks to these catalogues, much of the bidding is by post, but the auction itself is always an occasion of excitement for collectors present.

'The Shop' itself

If you do come to London, 'the Shop' at 391 Strand is the Philatelist's Mecca, with the latest and most complete range of albums, catalogues and accessories; the sales counters for new issues and for a wide selection of stamps of most countries. There's always an interesting window display on some topical aspect of philately. And there's always a welcome for stamp collectors, new and old.

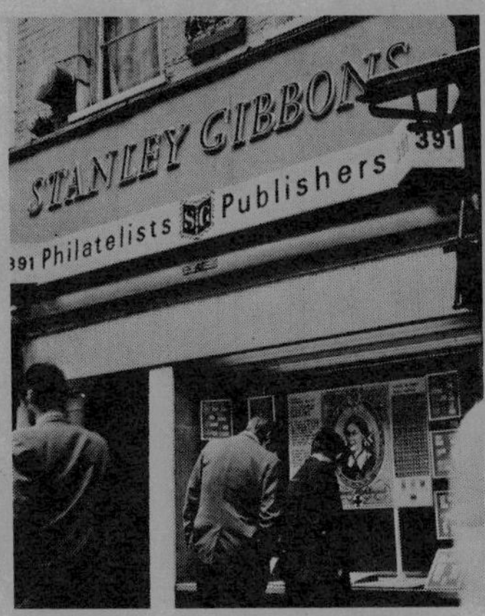

Stamp Publications

Stanley Gibbons Stamp Catalogues (the first was in 1865) are the world's most authoritative and best-known reference guides. They are supported by *Stamp Monthly* the popular Gibbons magazine with its record circulation, fully detailed Catalogue Supplement, regular Stamp Market, Great Britain and Through the Magnifying Glass features and articles on all stamp topics. And there are Gibbons albums and accessories which cater for all the needs of the enthusiast no matter how long he collects. Some of these are shown on the following pages.

Want to know more?

This is only an introduction to the complete service offered by Stanley Gibbons to the collector. If you'd like detailed information about any of the services mentioned here just fill in the coupon and send it off today.

Keep your Catalogue up-to-date!

with a regular subscription to Gibbons STAMP MONTHLY. 8-page Supplements to the Gibbons Catalogues, Crown Agents Gazette, Stamp Market, fine articles and features – plus a wide range of advertisements. Tick coupon for full details.

One-Country and G.B. albums

The Popular albums of the Stanley Gibbons One-Country range contain fully illustrated pages, finely printed in black on pure white cartridge size 276 x 222 mm. ($10\frac{7}{8}$ x $8\frac{3}{4}$ in.).

Each album is loose-leaf enabling easy insertion of the supplements which are normally issued annually.

3140 The G.B. One-Country Album is ideal for a straightforward collection and is complete from 1840 to the end of 1976. The G.B. is bound in a luxury padded four-ring maroon P.V.C. binder with Great Britain blocked in gold on the spine. **£6·42**

3264 The Channel Islands One-Country Album is housed in an elegant gold blocked padded 22-ring maroon P.V.C. binder. The pages have spaces for all Jersey and Guernsey issues from 1941 to the end of 1976. **£6·36**

3276 The Isle of Man One-Country Album is designed to house the 1958–1971 Regionals and the issues of the Independent Postal Administration from 1973 to the end of 1976. The Coat of Arms of the Isle of Man is gold blocked on the front of the padded 22-ring maroon P.V.C. binder. **£4·56**

313 Australia One-Country Album £6·19
316 Canada One-Country Album £6·55
3114 New Zealand One-Country Album £6·55

These One-Country Albums are ideal for forming a straightforward and attractive collection. Each album is bound in a luxury padded four-ring maroon P.V.C. binder with the respective national emblem gold blocked on the front cover. Each complete to the end of 1976.

The Windsor G.B. Album is a printed loose-leaf album for the postage, postage due and official stamps of Great Britain from 1840 to the end of 1976. There is also a section for the Channel Islands excluding the independent issues. Each page is printed on quality cartridge paper, size 283 x 248 mm. ($11\frac{1}{8}$ x $9\frac{3}{4}$ in.), and has spaces for stamps on one side only, the other, showing a detailed illustrated catalogue. Includes separate spaces for the plate numbers of the Victorian issues.

This album is supplied complete in a spring-back binder in a choice of two styles.

323 Popular Edition in a choice of red or green. **£7·02**

325 De luxe Presentation Edition in black-padded binder with slip-in box. **£10·80**

The 'Windsor' keeps up-to-date by means of supplements which are normally issued annually.

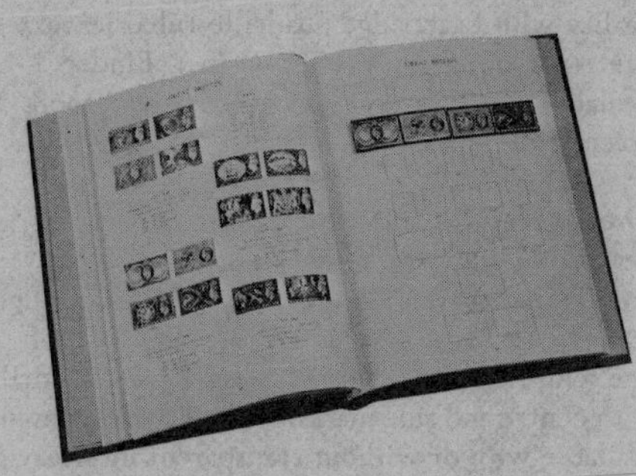

Stanley Gibbons Publications
the right way for stamp collectors

Blank Loose-leaf Albums

**Our Blank Loose-Leaf Album range provides a choice of spring-back, ring-fitting or peg-fitting albums.
Extra binders and packets of extra leaves for loose-leaf albums are available.**

386 The Senator Standard spring-back album is bound in a choice of three colours, red, green or black, and is complete with 100 white leaves finely printed in feint grey quadrille, size 282 x 251 mm. ($11\frac{1}{8}$ x $9\frac{7}{8}$ in.). **£5·65**

3834 The Devon has a strong, elegant, large capacity peg-fitting binder and contains 250 fine quality white cartridge quadrille-ruled leaves, size 264 x 248 mm. ($10\frac{3}{8}$ x $9\frac{3}{4}$ in.). Binder available in a choice of four colours – maroon, green, black or blue. **£7·56**

The Exeter has a handsome, fine quality, peg-fitting binder in a choice of red, blue or green. The album includes 40 double linen-hinged leaves, size 264 x 248 mm. ($10\frac{3}{8}$ x $9\frac{3}{4}$ in.), of fine white cartridge, ruled in feint grey quadrille with centre and side markings to aid arrangement, available with or without transparent interleaving attached.
3830 Album complete with 40 double linen-hinged leaves. **£9·42**
3832 Album complete with 40 double linen-hinged transparent faced leaves. **£9·99**

331 The Tower is a modern style spring-back album. The binder is available in a choice of red, green or black, is blocked in gold and contains 100 feint grey quadrille-ruled leaves of white cartridge, size 282 x 251 mm. ($11\frac{1}{8}$ x $9\frac{7}{8}$ in.). **£5·49**

The Ring 22 is Gibbons quality loose-leaf multi-ring fitting album. The padded P.V.C. binder, available in a choice of three colours, olive-green, maroon or dark blue, contains 50 feint quadrille-ruled leaves of black or white cartridge, size 276 x 216 mm. ($10\frac{7}{8}$ x $8\frac{1}{2}$ in.), available with or without transparent inter-leaving attached. The 22-ring proved patent fitting opens at a touch and enables leaves to lie absolutely flat.

3842 Album complete with 50 white transparent faced leaves. **£5·93**
3845 Album complete with 50 black transparent faced leaves. **£5·93**

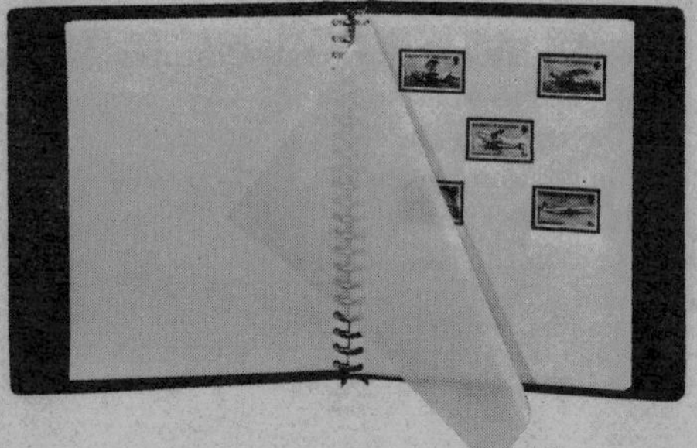

Stanley Gibbons Publications

122. Emblems of U.N.I.C.E.F. and Kuwait.

1971. U.N.I.C.E.F. 25th Anniv.

535. **122.** 25 f. multicoloured .. 15 10
536. 60 f. multicoloured .. 35 25

123. Book Year Emblem.

1972. Int. Book Year.

537. **123.** 20 f. black and brown 12 8
538. 45 f. black and green.. 25 20

124. Crest and Laurel.

1972. National Day. 11th Anniv.

539. **124.** 20 f. multicoloured .. 12 8
540. 45 f. multicoloured .. 25 20

125. Telecommunications Centre.

1972. Telecommunications Centre, Kuwait. Inaug.

541. **125.** 20 f. multicoloured .. 12 8
542. 45 f. multicoloured .. 25 20

126. Human Heart. **127.** Nurse and Child.

1972. World Health Day and World Heart Month.

543. **126.** 20 f. multicoloured .. 12 8
544. 45 f. multicoloured .. 25 20

1972. Int. Red Cross and Crescent Day.

545. **127.** 8 f. multicoloured .. 5 5
546. 40 f. multicoloured .. 25 20

128. Football.

1972. Olympic Games, Munich. Mult.

547. 2 f. Type **128** 5 5
548. 4 f. Running 5 5
549. 5 f. Swimming 5 5
550. 8 f. Gymnastics 5 5
551. 10 f. Throwing the discus 8 5
552. 15 f. Show jumping .. 10 8
553. 20 f. Basketball 12 10
554. 25 f. Volleyball 15 12

129. Produce and Ship. **131.** Ancient Capitals.

130. Bank Emblem.

1972. 11th F.A.O. Regional Conf., for the Near East, Kuwait.

555. **129.** 5 f. multicoloured .. 5 5
556. 10 f. multicoloured .. 8 5
557. 20 f. multicoloured .. 15 8

1972. National Bank of Kuwait. 20th Anniv.

558. **130.** 10 f. multicoloured .. 5 5
559. 35 f. multicoloured .. 20 15

1972. Archaelogical Excavations on Failaka Island. Multicoloured.

560. 2 f. Type **131** 5 5
561. 5 f. View of excavations .. 5 5
562. 10 f. "Leaf" capital 5 5
563. 15 f. Excavated building.. 8 5

132. Floral Emblem. **133.** Interpol Emblem.

1973. National Day. 12th Anniv.

564. **132.** 10 f. multicoloured .. 5 5
565. 20 f. multicoloured .. 12 8
566. 30 f. multicoloured .. 20 12

1973. Int. Criminal Police Organization (Interpol). 50th Anniv.

567. **133.** 10 f. multicoloured .. 5 5
568. 15 f. multicoloured .. 8 5
569. 20 f. multicoloured .. 12 8

134. C.I.S.M. Emblem and Flags. **135.** Airways Building.

1973. Int. Military Sports Council (C.I.S.M.) 25th Anniv.

570. **134.** 30 f. multicoloured .. 20 12
571. 40 f. multicoloured .. 25 20

1973. Opening of Kuwait Airways H.Q. Building.

572. **135.** 10 f. multicoloured .. 5 5
573. 15 f. multicoloured .. 8 5
574. 20 f. multicoloured .. 12 8

136. Weather Map of Middle East.

1973. Int. World Meteorological Organization. Cent.

575. **136.** 5 f. multicoloured .. 5 5
576. 10 f. multicoloured .. 5 5
577. 15 f. multicoloured .. 8 5

137. Shaikhs Ahmed and Sabah.

1973. 1st Kuwait Stamp Issue (overprints on India of 1923). 50th Anniv.

578. **137.** 10 f. multicoloured .. 5 5
579. 20 f. multicoloured .. 12 8
580. 70 f. multicoloured .. 40 35

138. " Zenaidura macroura ".

1973. Birds and Hunting Equipment. Multicoloured.

581. 5 f. Type **138** 5 5
582. 5 f. " Upupa epops " .. 5 5
583. 5 f. " Columba livia " .. 5 5
584. 5 f. " Burhinus oedicnemus " 5 5
585. 8 f. " Lanius excubitor ".. 5 5
586. 8 f. " Lanius collurio " .. 5 5
587. 8 f. " Lanius Schach " .. 5 5
588. 8 f. " Oriolus chinensis ".. 5 5
589. 10 f. " Phylloscopus trochilus " 5 5
590. 10 f. " Acroeephalus arundinaceus " .. 5 5
591. 10 f. " Sylvia atrcapilla " 5 5
592. 10 f. " Hirundo rustica " 5 5
593. 15 f. " Monticola solitarius " 8 5
594. 15 f. " Phoenicurus phoenicurus " 8 5
595. 15 f. " Oenanthe oenanthe " 8 5
596. 15 f. " Luscinia svecica " 8 5
597. 20 f. " Chlamydotis undulata " .. 10 8
598. 20 f. " Pterocles alchata " 10 8
599. 20 f. " Aramides ypecaha " 10 8
600. 20 f. " Porzana " 10 8
601. 25 f. " Falco sparverius " 15 10
602. 25 f. " Larus marinus " .. 15 10
603. 25 f. " Ardea purpurea ".. 15 10
604. 25 f. " Jynx torquilla " .. 15 10
605. 30 f. " Merops apiaster ".. 20 12
606. 30 f. " Accipiter " .. 20 12
607. 30 f. " Motacilla cinerea " 20 12
608. 30 f. " Motacilla alba " .. 20 12
609. 45 f. Bird snares .. 25 20
610. 45 f. Driving birds into net 25 20
611. 45 f. Stalking bird with hand net 25 20
612. 45 f. Disguised lure .. 25 20

Nos. 602/12 are size 38 × 38 mm.

139. Flame Emblem. **140.** Congress Emblem.

1973. Declaration of Human Rights. 25th Anniv.

613. **139.** 10 f. multicoloured .. 8 5
614. 40 f. multicoloured .. 25 20
615. 75 f. multicoloured .. 40 35

1974. 4th Arab Veterinary Union Congress.

616. **140.** 30 f. multicoloured .. 20 12
617. 40 f. multicoloured .. 25 20

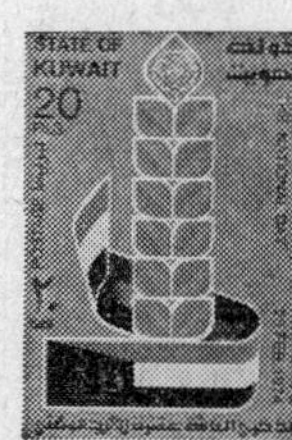

141. Flag and Wheat Ear Symbol. **143.** Tournament Emblem.

142. A.M.U. Emblem.

1974. National Day. 13th Anniv.

618. **141.** 20 f. multicoloured .. 12 8
619. 30 f. multicoloured .. 20 12
620. 70 f. multicoloured .. 40 35

1974. 12th Conference of Arab Medical Union and 1st Conference of Kuwait Medical Society.

621. **142.** 30 f. multicoloured .. 20 12
622. 40 f. multicoloured .. 25 20

1974. 3rd Arabian Gulf Trophy Football Tournament, Kuwait.

623. **143.** 25 f. multicoloured .. 15 8
624. 45 f. multicoloured .. 25 20

144. Institute Buildings.

1974. Kuwait Institute for Scientific Research. Inauguration.

625. **144.** 15 f. multicoloured .. 8 5
626. 20 f. multicoloured .. 12 8

145. Emblems of Kuwait, Arab Postal Union and U.P.U. **147.** Council Emblem and Flags of Member States.

146. Symbolic Telephone Dial.

1974. Universal Postal Union. Centenary.

627. **145.** 20 f. multicoloured .. 12 8
628. 30 f. multicoloured .. 20 12
629. 60 f. multicoloured .. 40 25

1974. World Telecommunications Day.

630. **146.** 10 f. multicoloured .. 5 5
631. 30 f. multicoloured .. 20 12
632. 40 f. multicoloured .. 25 20

1974. Signing Arab Economic Unity Agreement. 17th Anniv.

633. **147.** 20 f. grn., blk. and red 12 8
634. 30 f. red, blk. & green 25 12

148. "Population Growth".

1974. World Population Year.

635. **148.** 30 f. multicoloured .. 25 12
636. 70 f. multicoloured .. 60 40

149. Fund Building.

1974. Kuwait Fund for Arab Economic Development.

637. **149.** 10 f. multicoloured .. 5 5
638. 20 f. multicoloured .. 12 8

150. Shuaiba Emblem.

1974. Shuaiba Industrial Area. Tenth Anniv.

639. **150.** 10 f. multicoloured .. 5 5
640. 20 f. multicoloured .. 12 8
641. 30 f. multicoloured .. 25 12

151. Arms of Kuwait and " 14 ".

1975. National Day. 14th Anniv.

642. **151.** 20 f. multicoloured .. 12 8
643. 70 f. multicoloured .. 50 30
644. 75 f. multicoloured .. 55 40

152. Census Symbols.

1975. Population Census.

645. **152.** 8 f. multicoloured .. 5 5
646. 20 f. multicoloured .. 12 8
647. 30 f. multicoloured .. 25 12
648. 70 f. multicoloured .. 50 30
649. 100 f. multicoloured .. 75 45

153. I.W.Y. and Kuwaiti Women's Union Emblems.

1975. International Women's Year.

650. **153.** 15 f. multicoloured .. 5 5
651. 20 f. multicoloured .. 8 8
652. 30 f. multicoloured .. 20 15

154. Classroom within Open Book.

1975. International Literacy Day.

653. **154.** 20 f. multicoloured .. 10 8
654. 30 f. multicoloured .. 20 15

155. I.S.O. Emblem. 156. U.N. Flag, Rifle and Olive-branch.

1975. World Standards Day.

655. **155.** 10 f. multicoloured .. 5 5
656. 20 f. multicoloured .. 10 8

1975. United Nations Organization. 30th Anniv.

657. **156.** 20 f. multicoloured .. 10 8
658. 45 f. multicoloured .. 30 20

157. Shaikh Sabah.

1975.

659. **157.** 8 f. multicoloured .. 5 5
660. 20 f. multicoloured .. 10 8
661. 30 f. multicoloured .. 20 15
662. 50 f. multicoloured .. 30 20
663. 90 f. multicoloured .. 60 35
664. 100 f. multicoloured .. 70 45

158. Kuwait " Skyline ".

1976. National Day. 15th Anniversary.

665. **158.** 10 f. multicoloured .. 5 5
666. 20 f. multicoloured .. 10 8

159. Emblem, Electronic Microscope and Surgery. 160. Early and Modern Telephones.

1976. Kuwait Medical Association. 2nd Annual Conference.

667. **159.** 5 f. multicoloured .. 5 5
668. 10 f. multicoloured .. 5 5
669. 30 f. multicoloured .. 20 15

1976. Telephone Centenary.

670. **160.** 5 f. black and orange .. 5 5
671. 15 f. black and blue .. 10 8

161. Human Eye.

1976. World Health Day.

672. **161.** 10 f. multicoloured .. 5 5
673. 20 f. multicoloured .. 10 8
674. 30 f. multicoloured .. 20 15

162. Red Crescent Emblem.

1976. Kuwait Red Crescent Society. 10th Anniv.

675. **162.** 20 f. multicoloured .. 10 8
676. 30 f. multicoloured .. 20 15
677. 45 f. multicoloured .. 30 20
678. 75 f. multicoloured .. 50 30

163. Kuwait Suburb.

1976. U.N. Human Settlements Conference.

679. **163.** 10 f. multicoloured .. 5 5
680. 20 f. multicoloured .. 10 8

164. Basketball.

1976. Olympic Games, Montreal. Mult.

681. 4 f. Type **164** 5 5
682. 8 f. Running 5 5
683. 10 f. Judo 5 5
684. 15 f. Handball 8 5
685. 20 f. Figure-skating .. 10 8
686. 30 f. Volleyball 20 15
687. 45 f. Football 30 20
688. 70 f. Swimming 50 30

OFFICIAL STAMPS

1923. Stamps of India (King George V) optd. **KUWAIT SERVICE.**

O 1. **41.** ½ a. green 10 40
O 16. **42.** 1 a. chocolate 12 35
O 3. **43.** 1½ a. brown (No. 163) 30 80
O 4. **44.** 2 a. lilac 30 80
O 17. **45.** 2 a. lilac .. .. 2·25 2·25
O 5. **47.** 2½ a. blue .. .. 60 1·00
O 6. **48.** 3 a. orange .. .. 80 2·00
O 19. 3 a. blue 25 35
O 8. **49.** 4 a. olive .. .. 60 2·00
O 20. **50.** 4 a. green .. .. 90 1·00
O 21. **52.** 8 a. mauve .. .. 55 1·25
O 22. **53.** 12 a. claret .. .. 1·50 2·25
O 23. **54.** 1 r. brown and green 1·25 5·00
O 24. 2 r. red and orange .. 1·75 11·00
O 25. 5 r. blue and violet .. 3·50 17·00
O 26. 10 r. green and red .. 7·00 35·00
O 14. 15 r. blue and olive .. 15·00 35·00

POSTAGE DUE STAMPS

D 1.

D 2.

1963.

D 199. **D 1.** 1 f. brown and black 5 5
D 200. 2 f. violet and black 5 5
D 201. 5 f. blue and black 8 8
D 202. 8 f. green and black 8 8
D 203. 10 f. yellow and black 10 10
D 204. 25 f. red and black 25 25

The above stamps were not sold to the public unused until 1st July, 1964.

1965.

D 276. **D 2.** 4 f. red and yellow 8 8
D 277. 15 f. red and blue .. 12 12
D 278. 40 f. blue and green 25 25
D 279. 50 f. green & magenta 35 35
D 280. 100 f. blue and yellow 70 70

MORE DETAILED LISTS
are given in the Stanley Gibbons Catalogues referred to in the country headings:

BC	British Commonwealth
E1, E2, E3	Europe 1, 2, 3
O1, O2, O3, O4	Overseas 1, 2, 3, 4

LA AGUERA O4

An administrative district of Spanish Sahara whose stamps it now uses.

1920. Rio de Oro stamps optd. **LA AGUERA.**

1. **6.** 1 c. green 60 60
2. 2 c. brown 60 60
3. 5 c. green 60 60
4. 10 c. red 60 60
5. 15 c. yellow 60 60
6. 20 c. violet 60 60
7. 25 c. blue 60 60
8. 30 c. brown 60 60
9. 40 c. pink 60 60
10. 50 c. blue .. .. .. 1·10 1·10
11. 1 p. red .. .. .. 2·10 2·10
12. 4 p. purple .. .. .. 6·50 6·50
13. 10 p. orange .. .. .. 11·00 11·00

1.

ILLUSTRATIONS
British Commonwealth and all overprints and surcharges are FULL SIZE. Foreign Countries have been reduced to ¾-LINEAR.

1923.

14. **1.** 1 c. blue 20 20
15. 2 c. green 20 20
16. 5 c. green 25 25
17. 10 c. red 25 25
18. 15 c. claret 25 25
19. 20 c. yellow 25 25
20. 25 c. blue 25 25
21. 30 c. brown 25 25
22. 40 c. red 30 30
23. 50 c. purple 70 70
24. 1 p. red .. .. .. 1·25 1·25
25. 4 p. violet .. .. .. 3·25 3·25
26. 10 p. orange .. .. .. 5·50 5·50

LABUAN BC

An island off the N. coast of Borneo, ceded to Great Britain in 1846, and a Crown Colony from 1902. Incorporated with Straits Settlements in 1906, it used Straits stamps till it became part of N. Borneo in 1946.

100 Cents = 1 Dollar.

1.

6 Cents (2.)

Two CENTS (3.)

1879.

17. **1.** 2 c. green .. .. .. 2·25 2·50
51. 2 c. red 50 50
6. 6 c. orange .. .. .. 11·00 11·00
52. 6 c. green .. .. .. 1·10 80
7. 8 c. red .. .. .. 11·00 11·00
41. 8 c. violet 65 70
43a. 10 c. brown 50 70
9. 12 c. red .. .. .. 25·00 25·00
45. 12 c. blue 65 70
4. 16 c. blue .. .. .. 10·00 10·00
46. 16 c. grey .. .. .. 80·00 70·00
57. 40 c. orange .. .. .. 4·00 2·50

1880. Surch. in figures.

12. **1.** 6 on 16 c. blue £130 £120
13. 8 on 12 c. red £120 £110

1881. Surch. **EIGHT CENTS.**

14. **1.** 8 c. on 12 c. red .. .. 28·00 28·00

1881. Surch. **Eight Cents.**

15. **1.** 8 c. on 12 c. red .. .. 10·00 10·00

1883. Manuscript surch. **one Dollar A.S.H.**

22. **1.** $1 on 16 c. blue £225

1885. Surch. **2 CENTS** horiz.

23. **1.** 2 c. on 8 c. red .. .. 7·00
24. 2 c. on 16 c. blue .. .. 85·00 75·00

1885. Surch. **2 Cents** horiz.

25. **1.** 2 c. on 16 c. blue .. .. 10·00 11·00

1885. Surch. with large **2 Cents** diag.

26. **1.** 2 c. on 8 c. red .. .. 4·00 4·75

1891. Surch. as T 2.

35. **1.** 6 c. on 8 c. violet .. 60 65
37. 6 c. on 16 c. blue £170 £140
38. 6 c. on 40 c. orange .. £190 £170

1892. Surch. as T 3.

49. **1.** 2 c. on 40 c. orange .. 8·00 7·00
50. 6 c. on 16 c. grey .. .. 11·00 10·00

Most issues from 1894 exist cancelled-to-order with black bars. Our prices are for stamps postally used, cancelled-to-order examples being worth considerably less.

1894. Types of North Borneo (different colours) optd. **LABUAN.**

62. **12.** 1 c. black and mauve .. 40 50
63. **13.** 2 c. black and blue .. 50 50
64a.**14.** 3 c. black and yellow .. 50 60
65a.**15.** 5 c. black and green .. 70 65
67. **16.** 6 c. black and red .. 75 65
69. **17.** 8 c. black and pink .. 55 1·25
70. **18.** 12 c. black and orange .. 2·00 2·50
71. **19.** 18 c. black and olive .. 2·00 2·50
73. **20.** 24 c. blue and mauve .. 2·00 2·50
80. **5.** 25 c. green .. .. 4·00 4·00
81. – 50 c. mauve (as No. 82) 5·00 5·00
82. – $1 blue (as No. 83) .. 5·50 4·00

1895. No. 83 of North Borneo surch. **LABUAN** and value in cents.

75. 4 c. on $1 red 40 50
76. 10 c. on $1 red .. 50 65
77. 20 c. on $1 red .. 1·25 90
78. 30 c. on $1 red .. 1·00 1·00
79. 40 c. on $1 red .. .. 1·40 1·50

1896. Jubilee of Cession of Labuan to Gt. Britain. Nos. 62 to 68 optd. **1846 JUBILEE 1896.**

83e.**12.** 1 c. black and mauve .. 1·25 3·25
84. **13.** 2 c. black and blue .. 1·50 1·75
85. **14.** 3 c. black and yellow .. 2·00 2·50
86. **15.** 5 c. black and green .. 2·50 2·50
87. **16.** 6 c. black and red .. 2·25 2·25
88. **17.** 8 c. black and pink .. 2·50 2·50

1897. Stamps of North Borneo. Nos. 92 to 106 (different colours) optd. **LABUAN.**

Opt. at top of stamp.

89b. 1 c. black and brown .. 85 85
90. 2 c. black and blue .. 1·25 1·25
91. 3 c. black and yellow .. 1·10 1·25
92. 5 c. black and green .. 1·60 2·00
93b. 6 c. black and red .. 85 2·00
94a. 8 c. black and pink .. 1·25 80
95. 12 c. black and orange .. 2·75 3·00

Overprint at foot of stamp.

98a.– 12 c. black and orange (as No. 106) .. 2·75 2·75

Opt. at foot. Inscr. "POSTAL REVENUE".

96. – 18 c. black and olive (as No. 108) .. 1·40 1·75

Opt. at foot. Inscr. "POSTAGE AND REVENUE".

99a.– 18 c. black and olive (as No. 110) .. 6·50 6·50

Opt. at top. Inscr. "POSTAGE AND REVENUE".

101b.– 18 c. black and olive (as No. 110) .. 1·40 1·40

Opt. at top. "POSTAGE AND REVENUE" omitted.

97. – 24 c. blue and lilac (as No. 109) .. 1·60 2·00

Opt. at top. Inscr. "POSTAGE AND REVENUE".

100. – 24 c. blue and mauve (No. 111) .. .. 2·50 3·75

1899. Stamps of North Borneo (different colours) surch. **4 CENTS.**

102. 4 c. on 5 c. black & grn. (100) 2·25 4·00
103. 4 c. on 6 c. blk. & red (101a) 2·25 4·00
104a. 4 c. on 8 c. blk. & pink (102b) 2·25 4·00
105. 4 c. on 12 c. black and orange (106) .. 2·25 4·00
106. 4 c. on 18 c. blk. & ol. (108) 2·25 4·00
107. 4 c. on 24 c. bl. & mve. (109) 2·25 4·00
108. 4 c. on 25 c. green (47) .. 2·25 2·95
109. 4 c. on 50 c. maroon (48) .. 2·25 3·25
110. 4 c. on $1 blue (49) .. 2·25 3·25

1900. Stamps of North Borneo, as Nos. 95 to 107, optd. **LABUAN.**

111. 2 c. black and green .. 80 1·40
112. 4 c. black and brown .. 1·25
113. 4 c. black and red .. .. 1·10 55
114. 5 c. black and blue .. 1·75 2·25
115. 10 c. brown and grey .. 1·25
116a. 16 c. green and brown .. 2·75 2·75

4.

1902.

116c. **4.** 1 c. black and purple .. 40 40
117. 2 c. black and green .. 40 25
117a. 3 c. black and brown .. 40 30
118. 4 c. black and red .. 35 25
119. 8 c. black and orange .. 25 35
120. 10 c. brown and blue .. 35 45
121. 12 c. black and yellow .. 50 50
122. 16 c. green and brown .. 35 40
123. 18 c. black and brown .. 35 75
124. 25 c. green and blue .. 35 80
125. 50 c. purple and lilac .. 1·00 1·75
126. $1 claret and orange .. 60 3·00

1904. Surch. **4 cents.**

127. – 4 c. on 5 c. blk. & grn. (92) 2·00
128. – 4 c. on 6 c. blk. & red (93) 2·00
129. – 4 c. on 8 c. blk. & pink (94) 2·00
130. – 4 c. on 12 c. black and orange (98) .. .. 2·00
131. – 4 c. on 18 c. blk. & ol. (101) 2·00 2·50
132. – 4 c. on 24 c. bl. & mve. (100) 2·00
133. **5.** 4 c. on 25 c. green (80) .. 2·00
134. 4 c. on 50 c. maroon (81) 2·00
135. 4 c. on $1 blue (82) .. 2·00

POSTAGE DUE STAMPS

1901. Optd. **POSTAGE DUE.**

D 1. 2 c. black and green (111) 1·25 30
D 2. 3 c. black & yellow (91) .. 1·00
D 3. 4 c. black and red (113) .. 1·25
D 4. 5 c. black and blue (114) .. 1·10
D 5. 6 c. black and red (93) .. 1·40
D 6. 8 c. black and pink (94) .. 2·00
D 7. 12 c. black & orange (98) 4·00 6·00
D 8. 18 c. black & olive (101) 1·10
D 9. 24 c. blue & mauve (100) 2·00

LAGOS BC

A Br. Colony on the S. coast of Nigeria, united with Southern Nigeria in 1906 to form the Colony and Protectorate of Southern Nigeria. Now uses stamps of Nigeria.

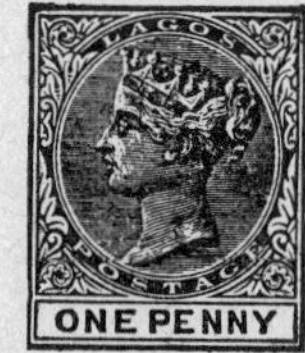

1.

2.

1874.

21. **1.** ½d. green 15 15
17. 1d. mauve .. .. .. 5·00 3·50
22. 1d. red 25 20
11. 2d. blue .. .. .. 12·00 4·25
23. 2d. grey .. .. .. 7·00 2·75
19. 3d. brown .. .. .. 4·00 3·00
5. 4d. red .. .. .. 20·00 12·00
24. 4d. lilac .. .. .. 11·00 4·00
25. 6d. green .. .. .. 3·00 4·00
26. 1s. orange .. .. .. 3·00 4·50
27. 2s. 6d. black £140 £120
28. 5s. blue £300 £140
29. 10s. brown £650 £400

1887.

30. **1.** 2d. mauve and blue .. 50 45
31. 2½d. blue 45 50
32. 3d. mauve and brown .. 1·10 1·40
33. 4d. mauve and black .. 1·00 1·25
34. 5d. mauve and green .. 1·10 4·50
35. 6d. mauve .. .. 3·00 3·00
35a. 6d. mauve and red .. 2·75 3·50
36. 7½d. mauve and red .. 1·40 4·50
37. 10d. mauve and yellow .. 1·75 4·50
38. 1s. green and black .. 2·00 4·50
39. 2s. 6d. green and red .. 8·00 9·00
40. 5s. green and blue .. 10·00 15·00
41. 10s. green and brown .. 16·00 20·00

1893. Surch. **HALF PENNY** and bars.

42. **1.** ½d. on 4d. mauve & black 1·00 1·10

1904.

54. **2.** ½d. green 20 35
55. 1d. purple & black on red 12 15
56. 2d. purple and blue .. 55 65
57. 2½d. purple & blue on blue 1·00 1·60
58. 3d. purple and brown .. 60 85
59. 6d. purple and mauve .. 1·10 1·10
60. 1s. green and black .. 1·75 1·50
61. 2s. 6d. green and red .. 6·00 7·00
62. 5s. green and blue .. 7·00 8·00
63. 30s. green and brown .. 18·00 20·00

MINIMUM PRICE

The minimum price quoted is 5p which represents a handling charge rather than a basis for valuing common stamps. For further notes about prices see introductory pages.

LAOS O3

Laos (previously part of Fr. Indo-China) became independent in 1951.

1951. 100 cents = 1 piastre.
1955. 100 cents = 1 kip.

1. River Mekong.

2. King Sisavang Vong.

1951.

1. **1.** 10 c. green and blue-green 5 5
2. 20 c. red and claret .. 8 8
3. 30 c. blue and indigo .. 45 35
4. – 50 c. brown 15 10
5. – 60 c. orange and red .. 15 10
6. – 70 c. blue-green and blue 15 10
7. – 1 p. violet and purple .. 20 15
8. **2.** 1 p. 50 purple and brown 35 25
9. – 2 p. green and grey .. 7·00 1·00
10. – 3 p. red and claret .. 35 30
11. – 5 p. blue and indigo .. 50 45
12. – 10 p. purple and brown .. 90 65

DESIGNS—HORIZ. As T **1**: 50 c. to 70 c. Luang Prabang. 1 p. and 2 p. to 10 p. Vientiane.

3. Laotian Woman.

4. Laotian Woman Weaving.

1952.

13. **3.** 30 c. violet & indigo (post.) 15 10
14. 80 c. blue-green & emerald 12 10
15. 1 p. 10 vermilion and red 15 15
16. 1 p. 90 blue and indigo .. 45 45
17. 3 p. sepia and purple .. 50 40
18. – 3 p. 30 pur. & violet (air) 45 30
19. **4.** 10 p. green and blue .. 1·00 70
20. 20 p. vermilion and red .. 1·50 1·00
21. 30 p. purple and sepia .. 2·10 1·75

DESIGN—As T **4**: 3 p. 30, Vat Pra Keo shrine.

5. King Sisavang Vong and U.P.U. Monument, Berne.

1952. Admission to U.P.U. 1st Anniv.

22. **5.** 80 c. vio., bl. & ind. (post.) 30 30
23. 1 p. chestnut, red and lake 30 30
24. 1 p. 20 blue and violet .. 30 30
25. 1 p. 50 brn., emer. & grn. 30 30
26. 1 p. 90 blue-green & sepia 30 30
27. 25 p. indigo & blue (air) .. 2·00 2·00
28. 50 p. sepia, maroon & brn. 2·00 2·00

6. Mother and Child.

7. Native Musicians.

1953. Red Cross Fund. Cross in red.

29. **6.** 1 p. 50 + 1 p. brn. & indigo 1·00 1·00
30. 3 p. + 1 p. 50 red & green 1·00 1·00
31. 3 p. 90 + 2 p. 50 brn. & sep. 1·00 1·00

1953.

32. **7.** 4 p. 50 turquoise & indigo 40 40
33. 6 p. brown and slate .. 50 50

8. Buddha.

1953. Air. Statues of Buddha.

34. – 4 p. green 60 30
35. – 6 p. 50 green .. 50 50
36. – 9 p. green 55 55
37. **8.** 11 p. 50 orge., brn. & red 80 80
38. – 40 p. purple .. .. 1·50 1·50
39. – 100 p. bistre .. .. 4·50 4·00

Nos. 34 and 37 are horiz. and the rest vert.

9. Vientiane.

1954. Jubilee of King Sisavang Vong.

40. **9.** 2 p. violet & indigo (post.) 25·00 10·00
41. 3 p. red and brown .. 25·00 15·00
42. 50 p. turq. & indigo (air) .. 70·00 70·00

10. Ravana.

1955. Air. "Ramayana" (dramatic poem).

43. **10.** 2 k. indigo and green .. 35 35
44. – 4 k. red and brown .. 50 50
45. – 5 k. olive, brown and red 70 70
46. – 10 k. black, orge. & brn. 1·50 1·50
47. – 20 k. olive, grn. & violet 1·75 1·75
48. – 30 k. black, brown & blue 2·25 2·25

DESIGNS—HORIZ. 4 k. Harruman, the white monkey. 5 k. Ninh Laphath, the black monkey. VERT. 10 k. Sita and Rama. 20 k. Luci and Ravana's friend. 30 k. Rama.

11. Buddha and Worshippers.

1956. Birth of Buddha. 2500th Anniv.

49. **11.** 2 k. brown (postage) .. 2·00 1·50
50. 3 k. black .. .. 2·00 1·50
51. 5 k. sepia .. .. 2·50 2·00
52. 20 k. red (air) .. .. 15·00 15·00
53. 30 k. olive & sage-green 15·00 15·00

12. U.N. Emblem. **13.**

1956. Admission to U.N. 1st Anniv.

54. **12.** 1 k. black (postage) .. 35 35
55. 2 k. blue 45 45
56. 4 k. red 55 55
57. 6 k. violet 70 70
58. **13.** 15 k. blue (air) .. .. 3·00 3·00
59. 30 k. lake .. .. 4·50 4·50

14. Flute-player.

1957. Native Musical Instruments.

60. 14. 2 k. green, red, chestnut and blue (postage) .. 60 60
61. – 4 k. brn., blue, red & slate 60 60
62. – 8 k. blue, chest. & orge. 70 70
63. 12 k. ol., vio. & red (air) 90 90
64. – 14 k. brn., indigo & red 90 90
65. – 20 k. blue-green, yellow-green and violet .. 1·25 1·25

DESIGNS: Natives playing instruments—VERT. 4 k. Pipes. 14 k. Violin. 20 k. Drum. HORIZ. 8 k. Xylophone. 12 k. Bells.

DESIGNS—VERT. 5 k. Drying rice. 16 k. Winnowing rice. HORIZ. 26 k. Polishing rice.

15. Harvesting Rice.

1957. Rice Cultivation.

66. 15. 3 k. chocolate, chestnut, green and blue .. 40 40
67. – 5 k. brown, red and green 40 40
68. – 16 k. violet, olive and blue 70 70
69. – 26 k. choc., brn. & green 1·10 1·10

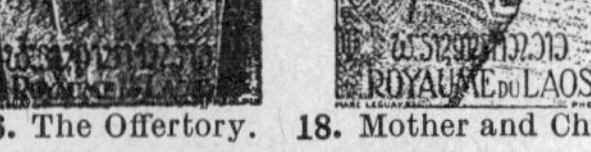

16. The Offertory. 18. Mother and Child.

17. Carrier Elephants.

1957. Air. Buddhism Commem.

70. 16. 10 k. indigo, brn. & violet 40 40
71. – 15 k. chest., yell. & choc. 55 55
72. – 18 k. bistre and green .. 70 70
73. – 24 k. lake, black & yellow 65 65

DESIGNS—HORIZ. 15 k. "Meditation" (children on river craft). 24 k. (48×36½ mm.) "The Cup of Hair" (natives with horse). VERT. 18 k. "Serenity" (head of Buddhist).

1958. Laotian Elephants. Multicoloured.

74. 10 c. Type 17 .. .. 8 8
75. 20 c. Elephant's head with head-dress 8 8
76. 30 c. Elephant with howdah (vert.) 8 8
77. 2 k. Elephant hauling log .. 15 15
78. 5 k. Elephant walking with calf (vert.) 60 60
79. 10 k. Caparisoned elephant (vert.) 60 60
80. 13 k. Elephant bearing throne (vert.) .. .. 1·00 1·00

1958. Air. Laotian Red Cross. 3rd Anniv. Cross in red.

81. 18. 8 k. black & slate-violet 60 60
82. 12 k. olive-brn. & brown 60 60
83. 15 k. blue-green and bronze-green .. 60 60
84. 20 k. violet and bistre .. 70 70

19.

1958. Inaug. of U.N.E.S.C.O. Headquarters Building, Paris.

85. 19. 50 c. multicoloured .. 8 8
86. – 60 c. multicoloured .. 8 8
87. – 70 c. multicoloured .. 8 8
88. – 1 k. multicoloured .. 8 8

DESIGNS—VERT. 60 c. Woman, children and part of exterior of U.N.E.S.C.O. building. 70 c. Woman and children hailing U.N.E.S.C.O. building superimposed on globe. HORIZ. 1 k. General view of U.N.E.S.C.O. building and Eiffel Tower.

20. King Sisavang Vong.

1959.

89. 20. 4 k. lake 25 25
90. 6 k. 50 chestnut 25 25
91. 9 k. magenta 25 25
92. 13 k. green 35 35

21. Stage Performance. 22. Portal of Vat Phou Temple, Pakse.

1959. Education and Fine Arts.

93. 21. 1 k. bis., vio., bl. & black 8 8
94. – 2 k. lake, violet & black 10 10
95. – 3 k. black, green & purple 15 15
96. – 5 k. green, yellow & violet 20 20

DESIGNS—VERT. 2 k. Student and "Lamp of Learning". 5 k. Stage performers and Buddhist temple. HORIZ. 3 k. Teacher and children with "Key to Education".

1959. Laotian Monuments. Multicoloured.

97. 50 c. T 22 .. .. .. 8 8
98. 1 k. 50 That Ing Hang, Savannakhet 10 10
99. 2 k. 50 Vat Phou Temple, Pakse 15 15
100. 7 k. That Luang, Vientiane 20 20
101. 11 k. As 7 k., different view 30 30
102. 12 k. 50 Phou-si Temple, Luang-Prabang 30 30

The 1 k. 50, 2 k. 50 and 11 k. are horiz. and the rest vert.

1960. World Refugee Year. Nos. 89 and 79 surch. **ANNEE MONDIALE DU REFUGIE 1959-1960** and premium.

103. 4 k. + 1 k. lake .. .. 1·00 1·00
104. 10 k. + 1 k. violet, orge., red, green, yellow, blue & blk. 1·00 1·00

23. Plain of Stones Xieng Khouang. 24. Funeral Urn.

1960. Air. Tourist Propaganda. Multicoloured.

105. 9 k. 50 T 23 .. .. 40 40
106. 12 k. Papheng Falls, Champassak 40 40
107. 15 k. Pair of bullocks with cart 65 65
108. 19 k. Buddhist monk and village 65 65

The 12 k. and 15 k. are horiz. and the rest vert.

1961. Funeral of King Sisavang Vong.

109. 24. 4 k. bistre, black and red 50 50
110. – 6 k. 50 brown and black 50 50
111. – 9 k. brown and black .. 50 50
112. – 25 k. black .. .. 1·25 1·25

DESIGNS: 6 k. 50, Urn under canopy. 9 k. Catafalque on dragon carriage. 25 k. King Sisavang Vong.

25. Temples and Statues. ("Pougney Nhagneu"). 26. King Savang Vatthana.

1962. Air. Festival of Makha Bousa.

113. 25. 11 k. green, red & yellow 40 40
114. – 14 k. blue and orange .. 50 50
115. – 20 k. multicoloured .. 70 60
116. – 25 k. multicoloured .. 70 60

DESIGNS: 14 k. Bird ("Garuda"). 20 k. Flying deities ("Hanuman"). LARGER (36×48 mm.): 25 k. Warriors ("Nang Teng One").

1962.

117. 26. 1 k. maroon, red & blue 8 8
118. 2 k. maroon, red & mve. 10 10
119. 5 k. maroon, red & turq. 15 15
120. 10 k. mar., red & bistre 40 40

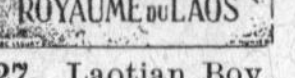

27. Laotian Boy. 28. Royal Courier.

1962. Malaria Eradication.

121. 27. 4 k. olive, black & green 15 15
122. – 9 k. brown, blk. & turq. 25 25
123. – 10 k. red, yellow & olive 35 35

DESIGNS: 9 k. Laotian girl. 10 k. Campaign emblem.

1962. Philatelic Exn., Vientiane and Stamp Day. Multicoloured.

124. 50 c. Modern mail transport (horiz.) 30 30
125. 70 c. Dancer and globe (horiz.) 30 30
126. 1 k. Royal courier on elephant 40 40
127. 1 k. 50 Type 28 .. .. 40 40

29. Fisherman.

1963. Freedom from Hunger. Multicoloured.

128. 1 k. Type 29 .. .. 10 10
129. 4 k. Threshing rice (horiz.) 15 15
130. 5 k. Planting rice and oxen in paddy field 20 20
131. 9 k. Harvesting rice (horiz.) 30 30

30. Queen of Laos. 31. Laotian supporting U.N. Emblem.

1963. Red Cross Centenary.

132. 30. 4 k. multicoloured .. 25 25
133. 6 k. multicoloured .. 35 35
134. 10 k. multicoloured .. 50 50

1963. Declaration of Human Rights. 15th Anniv. Imperf. or perf.

135. 31. 4 k. purple, blue and red 50 50

32. Temple, Map and Rameses II.

1964. Nubian Monuments Preservation.

136. 32. 4 k. multicoloured .. 25 25
137. 6 k. multicoloured .. 40 40
138. 10 k. multicoloured .. 50 50

33. Offertory Vase and Horn.

1964. "Constitutional Monarchy". Multicoloured.

139. 10 k. Type 33 .. .. 20 20
140. 15 k. Seated Buddha of Vat Pra Keo 15 15
141. 20 k. Laotians walking across map 25 25
142. 40 k. Royal Palace, Luang Prabang 40 40

34. Phra Vet and wife. 35. Meo Warrior.

1964. Folklore. Phra Vet Legend. Multicoloured.

143. 10 k. Type 34 .. .. 15 15
144. 32 k. "Benediction" .. 30 30
145. 45 k. Phame and wife .. 35 35
146. 55 k. Arrest of Phame .. 45 45

1964. "People of Laos".

147. – 25 k. black, brown and green (post.) 25 25
148. 35. 5 k. slate, brown, red and green (air) .. 10 8
149. – 10 k. flesh, slate & pur. 15 15
150. – 50 k. chest., drab & lilac 55 55

DESIGNS: 10 k. Kha hunter. 25 k. Girls of three races. 50 k. Thai woman.

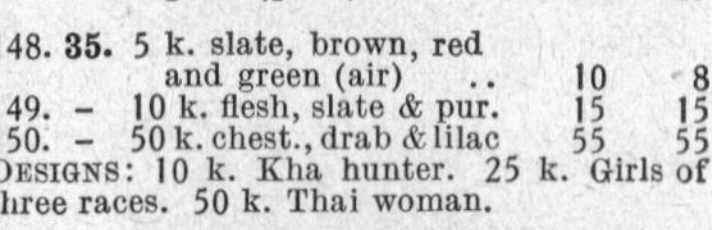

36. "Cothosia biblis".

1965. Laotian Butterflies.

151. 36. 10 k. chest., sepia, green and black (postage) .. 25 25
152. – 25 k. violet, black & yell. 35 35
153. – 40 k. yellow, choc. & grn. 55 55
154. – 20 k. chest. & ochre (air) 35 35

BUTTERFLIES—As T 36: 25 k. "Precis cebrene". HORIZ. (48×27 mm.): 20 k. "Attacus atlas". 40 k. "Dysphanis militaris".

37. Wattay Airport ("French Aid").

1965. Foreign Aid.

155. 37. 25 k. mag., brn. & turq. 25 25
156. – 45 k. brown and green .. 40 35
157. – 55 k. brown and blue .. 50 40
158. – 75 k. drab, violet, brown, red and green .. 70 60

DESIGNS—VERT. 45 k. Mother bathing child (water resources: "Japanese Aid"). 75 k. School and plants (education and cultivation: "American Aid"). HORIZ. 55 k. Studio of radio station ("British Aid").

38. Hophabang.

1965.

159. **38.** 10 k. multicoloured .. 15 15

39. Teleprinter operator, Globe and Map.

1965. I.T.U. Cent.

160. **39.**	5 k. brown, violet & pur.	8	8
161. –	30 k. chest., blue & grn.	30	30
162. –	50 k. multicoloured ..	45	45

DESIGNS: 30 k. Globe, map, telephonist and radio operator. 50 k. Globe, radio receiver and mast.

1965. Surch.

163. **20.**	1 k. on 4 k. lake ..	8	8
164.	5 k. on 6 k. 50 chestnut	12	8

40. Mother and Baby. **41.** Leopard-cat.

1965. U.N. "Protection of Mother and Child". 6th Anniv.

165. **40.** 35 k. ultramarine & red 35 30

1965. Air. Laotian Fauna.

166. **41.**	25 k. yell., brn. & grn.	25	20
167. –	55 k. brown, sepia & blue	50	45
168. –	75 k. brown and green..	55	50
169. –	100 k. brown, blk. & yell.	85	75
170. –	200 k. black and red ..	1·50	1·25

DESIGNS: 55 k. Flying squirrel. 75 k. Ichneumon (mongoose). 100 k. Porcupine. 200 k. Civet-cat.

42. U.N. Emblem on Map. **43.** Bulls in Combat.

1965. U.N. 20th Anniv.

171. **42.**	5 k. ultram, drab & grn.	12	12
172.	25 k. ultram., drab & pur.	25	25
173.	40 k. ultram., drab & bl.	35	30

1965. Laotian Folklore. Multicoloured.

174.	10 k. Type **43**	12	8
175.	20 k. Tikhy (form of hockey)	25	15
176.	25 k. Pirogue race ..	30	20
177.	50 k. Rocket festival ..	40	35

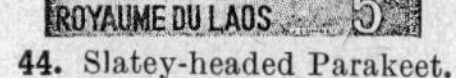

44. Slatey-headed Parakeet.

1966. Laotian Birds.

178. **44.**	5 k. green, brown & red	12	12
179. –	15 k. brown, black & turq.	15	15
180. –	20 k. sepia, ochre & blue	20	20
181. –	45 k. blue, sepia & violet	40	30

BIRDS: 15 k. White-crested laughing thrush (babbler). 20 k. Osprey. 45 k. Indian roller (or "blue jay").

45. W.H.O. Building.

1966. W.H.O. Headquarters, Geneva. Inaug.

182. **45.**	10 k. indigo & turquoise	12	8
183.	25 k. green and red ..	25	20
184.	50 k. black and blue ..	45	40

46. Ordination of Priests.

1966. Laotian Folklore. Multicoloured.

186.	10 k. Type **46**	10	8
187.	25 k. Sand-hills ceremony	20	10
188.	30 k. "Wax pagoda" procession (vert.)	30	20
189.	40 k. "Sou-Khouan" ceremony (vert.)	35	35

47. U.N.E.S.C.O. Emblem.

1966. U.N.E.S.C.O. 20th Anniv.

190. **47.**	20 k. orange and black	20	15
191.	30 k. blue and black ..	30	25
192.	40 k. green and black..	35	30
193.	60 k. red and black ..	50	40

48. Letter, Carrier Pigeon and Emblem.

1966. Int. Correspondence Week.

195. **48.**	5 k. blue, brown and red	10	10
196.	20 k. purple, black & grn.	15	15
197.	40 k. brown, red & blue	30	30
198.	45 k. black, green & pur.	35	30

49. Flooded Village. **50.** Carving, Siprapouthbat Pagoda.

1967. Mekong Delta Flood Relief. Multicoloured.

200.	20 k. + 5 k. Type **49** ..	25	25
201.	40 k. + 10 k. Flooded market-place	50	50
202.	60 k. + 15 k. Flooded airport	70	70

1967. Buddhist Art.

204. **50.**	5 k. green and brown ..	8	8
205. –	20 k. blue and sepia ..	15	15
206. –	50 k. maroon and sepia	45	40
207. –	70 k. drab and maroon	60	50

DESIGNS (carvings in temple pagodas, Luang Prabang): 30 k. Visoun. 50 k. Xiengthong. 70 k. Visoun (different).

51. General Post Office.

1967. Opening of New G.P.O. Building. Vientiane.

208. **51.**	25 k. brown, grn. & mar.	20	15
209.	50 k. blue, green & slate	35	30
210.	70 k. red, green & brown	60	50

52. "Ophicephaius micropeltes". **53.** "Cassia fistula".

1967. Fishes.

211. **52.**	20 k. black, bistre & blue	15	10
212. –	35 k. slate, bistre & turq.	30	25
213. –	45 k. sepia, ochre & grn.	40	30
214. –	60 k. black, bistre & grn.	50	40

DESIGNS: 35 k. "Oangasianodon gigas". 45 k. "Mastocembelus armatus". 60 k. "Notopterus".

1967. Flowers. Multicoloured.

215.	30 k. Type **53**	25	15
216.	55 k. "Curcuma singularia"	40	30
217.	75 k. "Poinciana regia" ..	60	50
218.	80 k. "Plumeria acutifolia"	70	50

54. Harvesting.

1967. Laotian Red Cross. 10th Anniv.

219. **54.**	20 k. + 5 k. multicoloured	25	25
220.	50 k. + 10 k. mult. ..	50	50
221.	60 k. + 15 k. mult. ..	65	65

55. Banded Krait.

1967. Reptiles. Multicoloured.

223.	5 k. Type **55**	8	8
224.	40 k. Marsh crocodile ..	35	35
225.	100 k. Pit viper	1·00	1·00
226.	200 k. Water moniter (lizard)	2·00	2·00

56. Human Rights Emblem.

1968. Human Rights Year. Emblem in red and green.

227. **56.**	20 k. emerald	15	15
228.	30 k. brown	25	25
229.	50 k. blue	40	40

57. W.H.O. Emblem. **58.** Military Parade.

1968. World Health Organization. 20th Anniv.

231. **57.**	15 k. brown, red & pur.	8	8
232.	30 k. brown, green & bl.	15	10
233.	70 k. brown, pur. & red	40	20
234.	110 k. brown and purple	70	50
235.	250 k. brown, blue & grn.	1·00	60

1968. Army Day. Multicoloured.

237.	15 k. Type **58** (postage) ..	8	8
238.	20 k. Soldiers and tank in battle	10	10
239.	60 k. Soldiers and Laotian flag	30	30
240.	200 k. Parade of colours before National Assembly building (air)	85	55
241.	300 k. As 200 k.	1·25	80

59. "Chrysochroa mnizechi". **60.** "Mangifera indica".

1968. Insects.

243. **59.**	30 k. ultram., yellow and green (postage) ..	15	15
244. –	50 k. black, orge. & pur.	20	20
245. –	90 k. indigo, orge. & ochre	35	35
246. –	120 k. blk. & orge. (air)	55	45
247. –	160 k. multicoloured ..	70	65

INSECTS—VERT. 50 k. "Aristobia approximator". 90 k. "Eutaenia corbetti". HORIZ. 120 k. "Dorysthenes walker". 160 k. "Megaloxantha bicolor".

1968. Laotian Fruits.

248. **60.**	20 k. green, blue & blk.	8	8
249. –	50 k. green, red & blue	30	30
250. –	180 k. grn., brn. & orge.	80	80
251. –	250 k. grn., brn. & yell.	1·25	1·25

DESIGNS—VERT. 50 k. "Tamarindus indica". HORIZ. 180 k. "Artocarpus intregrifolia". 250 k. "Citrullus vulgaris".

61. Hurdling.

1968. Olympic Games, Mexico.

252. **61.**	15 k. emer., ind. & brn.	8	8
253. –	80 k. brn., turq. & indigo	35	30
254. –	100 k. indigo, brn. & grn.	45	40
255. –	110 k. brn., red & indigo	50	45

DESIGNS: 80 k. Tennis. 100 k. Football. 110 k. High-jumping.

62. Oriental Door, Wat Ongtu (detail).

1969. Wat Ongtu Temple.

256. **62.**	150 k. gold, blk. & red	90	50
257. –	200 k. gold, black & red	1·25	60

DESIGN: 200 k. Central door, Wat Ongtu.

63. "Pharak praying to the Gods".

1969. Laotian "Ballet Royal". Designs showing dance characters. Multicoloured.

258.	10 k. Type **63** (postage) ..	15	10
259.	15 k. "Soukhib ordered to attack"	15	15
260.	20 k. "Thotsakan reviewing troops"	20	15
261.	30 k. "Nang Sida awaiting punishment"	25	15
262.	40 k. "Pharam inspecting his troops"	30	20
263.	60 k. "Hanuman about to rescue Nang Sida" ..	50	25
264.	110 k. "Soudagnou battling with Thotsakan" (air) ..	70	55
265.	300 k. "Pharam dancing with Thotsakan" ..	1·50	1·25

64. Handicrafts Workshop, Vientiane.

1969. Int. Labour Organisation. 50th Anniv.

267. **64.**	30 k. vio. & claret (post.)	15	15
268.	60 k. maroon and green	30	30
269. –	300 k. black & brown (air)	1·50	1·25

DESIGN: 300 k. Elephants moving logs.

65. Pangolin.

1969. "Wild Animals" (1st series). Multicoloured.
270. 15 k. Type **65** (postage) 10 8
271. 30 k. Type **65** 20 15

272. 70 k. Malayan bear (air) .. 35 25
273. 120 k. Gibbon (vert.) .. 60 45
274. 150 k. Tiger 75 55
See also Nos. 300/3 and 331/5.

66. Royal Mausoleum, Luang Prabang.

1969. King Sisavang Vong. 10th Death Anniv.
275. **66.** 50 k. ochre, blue & grn. 25 15
276. – 70 k. ochre and lake .. 35 30
DESIGN: 70 k. King Sisavang Vong (medallion).

67. "Lao Woman being Groomed" (Leguay).

1969. Air. Paintings by Marc Leguay (1st series). Multicoloured.
277. 120 k. Type **67** 60 45
278. 150 k. "Village Market" (horiz.) 75 50
See also Nos. 285, 307/9 and 357/61.

68. Carved Capital, Wat Xiengthong.

1970. Laotian Pagodas. Multicoloured.
279. 70 k. Type **68** (postage) .. 35 30
280. 100 k. Library, Wat Sisaket (air) 50 40
281. 120 k. Wat Xiengthong (horiz.) 60 45

69. "Noon" Drum.

1970. Laotian Drums.
282. **69.** 30 k. mult. (post.) .. 15 12
283. – 55 k. black, grn. & brn. 30 25
284. – 125 k. brown, yellow and flesh (air) 70 60
DESIGNS—HORIZ. 55 k. Bronze drum. VERT. 125 k. Wooden drum.

70. "Banks of the Mekong" (M. Leguay).

1970. Air. Paintings by Marc Lequay (2nd series).
285. **70.** 150 k. multicoloured .. 75 60

71. Franklin D. Roosevelt.

1970. Air. Franklin D. Roosevelt (American statesman). 25th Death Anniv.
286. **71.** 120 k. slate and green 70 60

72. "Lenin explaining Electrification Plan" (after L. Shmatko).

1970. Lenin. Birth Cent.
287. **72.** 30 k. multicoloured .. 15 12
288. 70 k. multicoloured .. 40 30

1970. "Support for War Victims". Nos. 258/65 ("Ballet Royal") surch. **Soutien aux Victimes de la Guerre** and value.
289. 10 k. + 5 k. mult. (post.) .. 15 10
290. 15 k. + 5 k. multicoloured 15 10
291. 20 k. + 5 k. multicoloured 20 15
292. 30 k. + 5 k. multicoloured 25 25
293. 40 k. + 5 k. multicoloured 30 30
294. 60 k. + 5 k. multicoloured 35 35

295. 110 k. + 5 k. mult. (air) .. 70 70
296. 300 k. + 5 k. multicoloured 1·50 1·50

73. Weaving Silk.

1970. "EXPO 70" World Fair, Osaka, Japan. Laotian Silk Industry.
297. **73.** 30 k. bl., brn. & red (post.) 15 12
298. – 70 k. multicoloured .. 35 25
299. – 125 k. mult. (air) .. 70 60
DESIGNS: 70 k. Silk-spinning. 125 k. Winding skeins.

74. Wild Boar.

75. Buddha, U.N. Emblem and New York H.Q.

1970. Wild Animals (2nd series).
300. **74.** 20 k. brn. & grn. (postage) 15 10
301. 60 k. brn. and olive .. 35 25
302. – 210 k. black, red and yellow (air) .. .. 1·00 85
303. – 500 k. green, brn. & orge. 2·50 2·00
ANIMALS: 210 k. Leopard. 500 k. Gaur.

1970. United Nations. 25th Anniv. Mult.
304. 30 k. Type **75** (postage) .. 15 10
305. 70 k. Type **75** 40 30
306. 125 k. Nang Thorani ("Goddess of the Earth") (air) 70 60

76. "Village Track".

1970. Air. Paintings by Marc Leguay (3rd series). Multicoloured.
307. 100 k. Type **76** 50 45
308. 120 k. "Paddy-field in Rainy Season" (horiz.) .. 60 50
309. 150 k. "Village Elder" .. 70 60

77. "Nakhanet".

1971. Laotian Mythology (1st series). Frescoes from Triumphal Arch, Vientiane. Mult.
310. **77.** 70 k. orge., brn. & red (postage) 40 35
311. – 85 k. green, yell. & blue 45 40
312. – 125 k. mult. (air) .. 60 50
DESIGNS—DIAMOND. 85 k. "Rahu". HORIZ. 49 × 36 mm. 125 k. "Underwater dual between Nang Matsa and Hanuman".
See also Nos. 352/4 and 385/7.

78. Silversmiths.

1971. Laotian Traditional Crafts. Mult.
313. 30 k. Type **78** 15 10
314. 50 k. Potters 20 15
315. 70 k. Pirogue-builder (horiz. 49 × 36 mm.) .. 30 25

79. Lao and African Children.

1971. Racial Equality Year.
316. **79.** 30 k. blue, red and green 15 10
317. – 60 k. vio., red & yellow 30 20
DESIGN: 60 k. Laotian dancers and musicians.

80. Buddhist Monk at That Luang.

1971. Vientiane Rotary Club. 50th Anniv.
318. **80.** 30 k. violet, brn. & blue 15 10
319. – 70 k. grey, red & blue .. 30 25
DESIGN—VERT. 70 k. Laotian girl on "Dragon" staircase.

81. "Ascocentrum miniatur".

1971. Laotian Orchids. Multicoloured.
320. 30 k. "Dendrobium agregagatum" (vert.) (postage) 10 8
321. 40 k. "Rynchostylis giganterum" (vert.) .. 8 5
322. 50 k. Type **81** 15 12
323. 60 k. "Paphiopedilum exul" (vert.) 15 8
324. 70 k. "Trichoglottis fasciata" 30 25
325. 80 k. Cattleya 25 15

326. 125 k. Brasilian cattleya (air) 70 50
327. 150 k. "Vanda teres" .. 70 50
Nos. 321, 323 and 325 are smaller 22 × 36 or, 36 × 22 mm. Nos. 326/7 are larger, 48 × 27 mm.
The orchid on No. 320 is depicted in its normal (inverted) position.

82. Dancers from France and Laos.

1971. Air. "Twin Cities" of St. Astier (France) and Keng-Kok (Laos).
328. **82.** 30 k. lake and brown .. 15 10
329. 70 k. purple and plum .. 30 15
330. 100 k. grn. & blackish grn. 40 25

1971. Wild Animals (3rd series). As T **74** but with square format (36 × 36 mm).
331. 25 k. blk., vio. & blue (post.) 15 12
332. 40 k. blk., green & olive .. 20 15
333. 50 k. orange and green .. 25 20
334. 85 k. brn., green & emerald 45 35

335. 300 k. brn. and green (air) 1·50 1·00
DESIGNS: 25 k., 40 k. Civet-cat. 50 k. Kanchil (chevrotain). 85 k. Sambar. 300 k. Sumatran rhinoceros.

83. Laotian Woman. (As T **3**.)

1971. Laotian Stamps. 20th Anniv. Inscr. "Vingtieme Anniversaire de la Philatelie LAO".
336. **83.** 30 k. chocolate, brown & violet (postage) .. 15 10
337. – 40 k. multicoloured .. 20 15
338. – 50 k. blk., flesh and blue 25 15

339. – 125 k. vio., brn. & grn. (air) 65 50
DESIGNS—VERT. (36 × 48 mm.). 40 k. Violinist (As No. 64). 50 k. Rama (As No. 48). 125 k. "The Offertory" (As T **16**).

84. "Sunset on the Mekong" (Prisayane).

1971. Air. Paintings by Chamnane Prisayane Multicoloured.
341. 125 k. Type **84** 60 40
342. 150 k. "Quiet Morning at Ban Tane Pieo" .. 70 50

85. Children reading Book.

1972. Int. Book Year.
343. **85.** 30 k. green (postage) .. 15 10
344. – 70 k. brown 15 10
345. – 125 k. violet (air) .. 50 35
DESIGNS: 70 k. Laotian illustrating manuscript. (48×27 mm.) 125 k. Father showing manuscripts to children.

86. Nam Ngum Dam and Obelisk.

1972. E.C.A.F.E. (Economic Commission for Asia and the Far East). 25th Anniv. Multicoloured.
346. 40 k. Type **86** (postage) .. 15 12
347. 80 k. Type **86** 30 20
348. 145 k. Lake and Spill-way, Nam Ngum Dam (air) .. 60 60

87. "The Water-carrier".

1972. U.N.I.C.E.F. 25th Anniv. Drawings by Lao Schoolchildren. Multicoloured.
349. 50 k. Type **87** 25 25
350. 80 k. "Teaching Bamboo-weaving" 30 30
351. 120 k. "Riding a Water-buffalo" 60 50

88. "Nakharath".

1972. Laotian Mythology (2nd series).
352. **88.** 100 k. green 45 40
353. – 120 k. lilac 50 40
354. – 150 k. brown 65 50
DESIGNS: 120 k. "Nang Kinnali". 150 k. "Norasing".

89. Festival Offerings.

1972. Air. That Luang Religious Festival.
355. **89.** 110 k. brown 45 40
356. – 125 k. purple 50 40
DESIGN: 125 k. Festival procession.

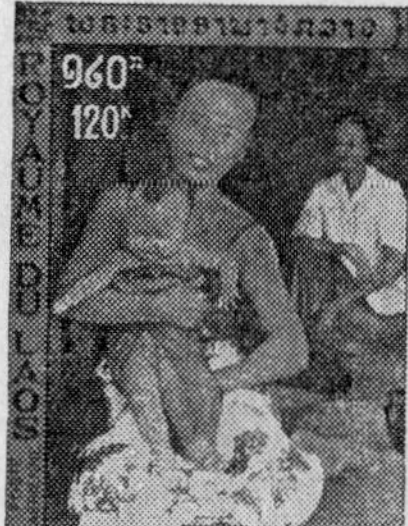

90. Laotian Mother. **91.** Attopeu Religious Costume.

1972. Air. Paintings by Marc Leguay (4th series). Multicoloured.
357. 50 k. "In the Paddy Field" (detail) 20 15
358. 50 k. "In the Paddy Field" (different detail) .. 20 15
359. 70 k. "Village in the Rainy Season" (detail) .. 25 20
360. 70 k. "Village in the Rainy Season" (different detail) 25 20
361. 120 k. Type **90** 45 35
Nos. 357/8 and 359/60 when placed together form the complete painting in each case.

1973. Regional Costumes.
362. **91.** 40 k. yell., mve. & brn. (postage) 15 10
363. – 90 k. blk., lake & brn... 40 25
364. – 120 k. brn., sepia & mve. (air) 40 35
365. – 150 k. ochre, lake & brn. 50 35
DESIGNS: 90 k. Phongsaly festival costume. 120 k. Luang Prabang wedding costume. 150 k. Vientiane evening dress.

92. "Lion" Guarding Vat That-Luang.

1973. Lions International. 55th Anniv.
366. **92.** 40 k. red, purple & blue 15 8
367. 80 k. red, yellow & blue 30 20
368. – 150 k. mult. (air) .. 50 40
DESIGN: 150 k. Lions emblems and statue of King Saysetthathirath, Vientiane.

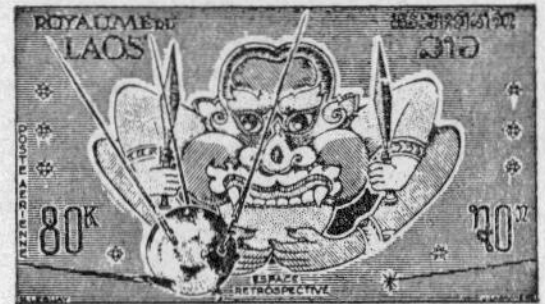

93. Satelite passing Rahou.

1973. Space in Retrospect. Multicoloured.
369. 80 k. Type **93** 25 20
370. 150 k. Landing module and Laotian festival rocket .. 40 30

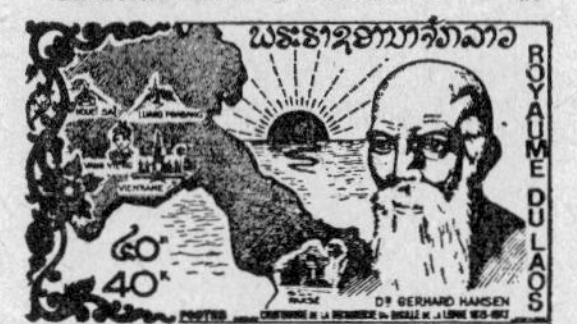

94. Dr. Gerhard Hansen and Map of Laos.

1973. Identification of Leprosy Bacillus by Hansen. Cent.
371. **94.** 40 k. pur., dull pur. & orge 15 8
372. 80 k. red, brn. & yellow 30 20

95. "Benediction". **96.** Nang Mekhal (Goddess of the Sea).

1973. Laotian Boy Scouts Association. 25th Anniv.
373. **95.** 70 k. yell. & brn. (post.) 25 20
374. – 110 k. vio. & orge. (air) 30 25
375. – 150 k. bl., drab & brn... 35 25
DESIGNS—HORIZ. 110 k. Camp-fire entertainment. 150 k. Scouts helping flood victims, Vientiane, 1966.

1973. Air. I.M.O. Cent.
376. **96.** 90 k. brn., red & mauve 25 20
377. – 150 k. brn., red & light-brn. 40 30
DESIGN: 150 k. "Chariot of the Sun".

97. Interpol H.Q., Paris.

1973. Int. Criminal Police Organization (Interpol). 50th Anniv.
382. **97.** 40 k. blue (postage) .. 15 8
383. 80 k. brn. & yell.-brown 30 20
384. – 150 k. violet, red and green (air) 40 40
DESIGN: (48×27 mm.). 150 k. Laotian woman tending poppies.

98. "Phra Sratsvady".

1974. Air. Laotian Mythology (3rd series).
385. **98.** 100 k. red, brn. & lilac .. 30 25
386. – 110 k. brn., lilac & red .. 35 25
387. – 150 k. vio., brn. & orge-brn. 40 30
DESIGNS: 110 k. "Phra Indra". 150 k. "Phra Phrom".

99. Boy and Postbox. **100.** "Eranthemum nervosum".

1974. Universal Postal Union. Cent.
388. **99.** 70 k. brn., grn. & bl. (post.) 25 20
389. 80 k. brn., bl. & grn. .. 30 20
390. – 200 k. brn. & red (air) .. 60 50
DESIGN—HORIZ. (48×36 mm.). 200 k. Laotian girls with letters, and U.P.U. Monument, Berne.

1974. Laotian Flora.
391. **100.** 30 k. vio. & grn. (post.) 15 10
392. – 50 k. multicoloured .. 20 15
393. – 80 k. red, grn. & brn. 30 20
394. – 500 k. grn. & brn. (air) 1·40 1·00
DESIGNS—HORIZ. (36×26 mm.). 50 k. "Nenuphar nymphea lotus". 80 k. "Kapokier des falaises Schefflera". SQUARE. (36×36 mm.). 500 k. "Nepenthes phillamphora".

101. Mekong Ferry carrying Bus.

1974. Loatian Transport.
395. **101.** 25 k. brn. & orge. (post.) 10 8
396. – 90 k. brn. and bistre .. 30 20
397. – 250 k. brn. & grn. (air) 60 50
DESIGNS—VERT. 90 k. Bicycle rickshaw. HORIZ. 250 k. Mekong river-boat.

102. Marconi, and Laotian with Transistor Radio Set.

1974. Guglielmo Marconi (radio pioneer). Birth Cent.
398. **102.** 60 k. grey, grn. & brn. (postage) 25 20
399. 90 k. gry, brn. & grn. 30 25
400. – 200 k. bl. & brn. (air) .. 50 40
DESIGN: 200 k. Communications methods.

103. U.P.U. Monument and Laotian Girls.

1974. Air. Universal Postal Union. Centenary.
401. **103.** 500 k. lilac and red .. 1·00 80

104. "Diastocera wallichi tonkinensis".

1974. Insects. Beetles.
403. **104.** 50 k. brn., blk. & grn. (postage) 20 15
404. – 90 k. blk., bluish grn. and green 30 25
405. – 100 k. blk., orge. & brn. 35 30
406. – 110 k. vio., brn. & grn. (air) 35 30
DESIGNS: 90 k. "Macrochenus isabellunis". 100 k. "Purpuricenus malaccensis". 110 k. "Sternocera multipunctata".

105. Pagoda and Sapphire.

1974. "Mineral Riches".
407. **105.** 100 k. brn., green & blue 30 20
408. – 110 k. brn., blue & yell. 30 20
DESIGN: 110 k. Gold-panning at Attopeu.

106. King Savang Vatthana and Princes Souvanna Phouma and Soupha Nouvong.

1975. Laotian Peace Treaty. 1st Anniv.
409. **106.** 80 k. brn., ochre & grn. 25 20
410. 300 k. brn., ochre & pur. 80 60
411. 420 k. brn., ochre & turq. 1·00 80

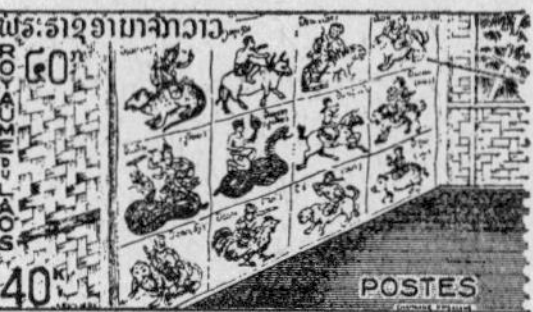

107. Fortune-teller's Chart.

1975. Chinese New Year "Year of the Rabbit". Multicoloured.
413. 40 k. Type **107** 10 8
414. 200 k. Fortune-teller .. 35 30
415. 350 k. Lao woman riding Rabbit (vert.) 70 60

108. U.N. Emblem and Frieze. **109.** Laotian Legend.

1975. International Women's Year.
416. **108.** 100 k. blue and green .. 20 15
417. – 200 k. orange and blue 35 25

1975. "Pravet Sandone" Religious Festival. Laotian Legends.
420. **109.** 80 k. multicoloured .. 20 15
421. – 110 k. multicoloured .. 25 20
422. – 120 k. multicoloured .. 30 25
423. – 130 k. multicoloured .. 35 30
DESIGNS: 110 k. to 130 k. various legends.

110. Buddha and Stupas.

1975. U.N.E.S.C.O. Campaign to Save the Temple of Borobudur.
424. **110.** 110 k. grn., blue & brn. 20 15
425. – 200 k. brn., grn. & bist. 35 30
DESIGN: 200 k. Temple sculptures.

POSTAGE DUE STAMPS.

D 1. Vat Sisaket Shrine. D 2. Sampans. D 3. Serpent.

1952.

D 22. D 1. 10 c. chocolate .. 10 10
D 23. 20 c. violet 10 10
D 24. 50 c. red 8 8
D 25. 1 p. green 10 10
D 26. 2 p. blue 10 10
D 27. 5 p. purple 40 35
D 28. D 2. 10 p. indigo 50 50

1973.

D 378. D 3. 10 k. blk., brn. & yell. 5 5
D 379. 15 k. blk., yell. & grn. 5 5
D 380. 20 k. blk., grn. & bl. 8 8
D 381. 50 k. blk., bl. & red 15 12

LAS BELA BC

A state of Baluchistan. Now part of Pakistan.

1.

The 1 a. has the English inscriptions in a circle with the native inscription across the centre.

1897.

1. 1. ½ a. black on white .. 3·00 2·50
2 ½ a. black on blue .. 2·00 2·00
3. ½ a. black on grey .. 2·00 2·00
12. ½ a. black on green .. 3·50 4·00
8. – 1 a. black on orange .. 4·00 5·00

LATAKIA O4

Formerly known as Alaouites, this Syrian state changed its name to Latakia in 1930. Now uses Syrian stamps.

100 centiemes = 1 piastre.

1931. As 1930 stamps of Syria (T 6/7) optd. **LATTAQUIE** and in Arabic.

65. 10 c. purple 8 8
66. 20 c. blue 5 5
67. 20 c. red 10 10
68. 25 c. green 5 5
69. 25 c. blue 12 12
70. 50 c. violet 10 10
71. 75 c. red 10 10
72. 1 p. green 20 20
73. 1 p. 50 brown 30 30
74. 1 p. 50 green 45 45
75. 2 p. violet 30 30
76. 3 p. green 40 40
77. 4 p. orange 50 50
78. 4 p. 50 red 55 55
79. 6 p. green 55 55
80. 7 p. 50 blue 60 60
81. 10 p. brown 60 60
82. 15 p. green 80 80
83. 25 p. claret .. .. .. 1·75 1·75
84. 50 p. sepia .. .. .. 1·75 1·75
85. 100 p. red .. .. .. 6·50 6·50

1931. Air. As 1931 air stamps of Syria optd. **LATTAQUIE** and in Arabic.

86. 50 c. brown 10 10
87. 50 c. sepia 10 10
88. 1 p. brown 20 20
89. 2 p. blue 45 45
90. 3 p. green 55 55
91. 5 p. purple .. .. .. 1·10 1·10
92. 10 p. blue .. .. .. 1·40 1·40
93. 15 p. red .. .. .. 1·50 1·50
94. 25 p. brown .. .. .. 2·00 2·00
95. 50 p. black .. .. .. 4·00 4·00
96. 100 p. mauve .. .. .. 5·00 5·00

POSTAGE DUE STAMPS

1931. Nos. D 197/8 of Syria optd. **LATTAQUIE** and in Arabic.

D 86. 8 p. black on blue .. 2·75 2·75
D 87. 15 p. black on red .. 2·25 2·25

LATVIA E2

A country on the Baltic Sea, formerly under Russian rule, which became independent in 1918. Now part of Soviet Russia.

100 kapeikas = 1 rouble.
1923. 100 santimi (centimes) = 1 lat.

1.

2.

3.

1918. Printed on back of German war maps.

1. 1. 5 k. red (Imperf.) .. 5 12
2. 5 k. red (Perf.) 5 12

1919. On plain or ruled paper. Imperf. or perf.

15. 1. 3 k. lilac 5 5
16. 5 k. red 5 5
17. 10 k. blue 5 5
18. 15 k. green 5 5
19. 20 k. orange 5 5
20. 25 k. grey 12 12
21. 35 k. brown 5 5
42. 40 k. purple 8 8
22. 50 k. violet 5 5
23. 75 k. green 5 5
29. 3 r. red and blue .. 25 20
30. 5 r. red and brown .. 20 15

1919. Liberation of Riga. Imperf.

24. 2. 5 k. red 8 5
25. 15 k. green 8 5
26. 35 k. brown 12 8

For stamps of T 1/2 optd. with a cross, with or without Russian letters "Z A" see under North-West Russia Nos. 21/42.

1919. Imperf. or perf.

27. 3. 10 k. blue 10 10

4.

ILLUSTRATIONS British Commonwealth and all overprints and surcharges are FULL SIZE. Foreign Countries have been reduced to ¾-LINEAR.

1919. Independence. 1st Anniv. Perf.
(a) Size 29 × 38 mm.

33. 4. 10 k. red and brown .. 8 8
34. 35 k. green and blue .. 10 10
35. 1 r. red and green .. 15 15
(b) Size 33 × 45 mm.
31. 4. 10 k. red and brown .. 10 12

5.

6.

1919. Liberation of Courland.

36. 5. 10 k. red and brown .. 5 5
37. 25 k. green and blue .. 8 8
38. 35 k. blue and black .. 10 10
39. 1 r. brown and green .. 25 25

1920. Red Cross stamps.
A. On backs of blue Bolshevist notes. Perf.

46. 6. 20–30 k. red and brown .. 12 15
47. 40–55 k. red and blue .. 12 15
48. 50–70 k. red and green .. 12 15
49. 1 r.–1 r. 30 red and black .. 25 30

B. On backs of green notes. Perf.

50. 6. 20–30 k. red and brown .. 12 12
51. 40–55 k. red and blue .. 12 15
52. 50–70 k. red and green .. 15 15
53. 1 r.–1 r. 30 red and black .. 15 15

C. On backs of red, green and brown Bolshevist notes. Imperf.

54. 6. 20–30 k. red and brown .. 12 12
55. 40–55 k. red and blue .. 12 12
56. 50–70 k. red and green .. 15 15
57. 1 r.–1 r. 30 red and black .. 20 20

CHARITY PREMIUMS. In the above and later issues where two values are expressed, the lower value represents the franking value and the higher the price charged, the difference being the charity premium.

7.

8.

1920. Freeing of Latgale.

58. 7. 50 k. pink and green .. 12 12
59. 1 r. brown and green .. 15 15

1920. 1st Constituent Assembly.

60. 8. 50 k. red 8 8
61. 1 r. blue 5 5
62. 3 r. green and brown .. 20 20
63. 5 r. purple and grey .. 25 25

1920. Surch. in white figures on black oval.

64. 4. 10 r. on 1 r. red and green 45 45
65. 20 r. on 1 r. red and green 90 90
66. 30 r. on 1 r. red and green 1·00 1·00

1920. Surch. **2 DIWI RUBLI.** Perf.

67. 1. 2 r. on 10 k. blue .. 25 25
68. 2. 2 r. on 35 k. brown .. 15 15

1920. Surch. **WEENS** or **DIVI**, value and **RUBLIS.**

69. 5. 1 (WEENS) r. on 35 k. blue and black 8 8
70. 2 (DIVI) r. on 10 k. red and brown 15 15
71. 2 (DIVI) r. on 25 k. green and blue 8 8
Surch. **DIWI RUBLI 2.**
72. 4. 2 r. on 35 k. green and blue 12 12
Surch. **DIVI 2 RUB. 2.**
73. 8. 2 r. on 50 k. red 8 8
Surch. **Desmit rubli.**
74 4. 10 r. on 10 r. on 1 r. red and green (No. 64) .. 25 25

1921. Red Cross. Surch. **RUB 2 RUB.**

75. 8. 2 r. on 20+10 k. red and brown (No. 56) .. 45 65
76. 2 r. on 40+15 k. red and blue (No. 57) .. 45 65
77. 2 r. on 50+20 k. red and green (No. 58) .. 45 65
78. 2 r. on 1 r.+30 k. red and black (No. 59) .. 45 65

1921. Surch. in figures and words over thick bar of crossed lines.

79. 6. 10 r. on 50 k. pink & green 45 25
80. 20 r. on 50 k. pink & green 1·25 90
81. 30 r. on 50 k. pink & green 1·10 90
82. 50 r. on 50 k. pink & green 1·75 1·60
83. 100 r. on 50 k. pink & grn. 4·50 5·50

9.

1921. Air. Imperf. or perf.

84. 9. 10 r. green 55 50
85. 20 r. blue 55 40

10.

11.

1921. Value in "Kopecks" or "Roubles".

86. 10. 50 k. violet 8 5
87. 1 r. yellow 8 10
88. 2 r. green 5 5
89. 3 r. green 10 10
90. 5 r. red 20 25
91. 6 r. claret 30 20
92. 9 r. orange 15 5
93. 10 r. blue 20 5
94. 15 r. blue 60 30
95. 20 r. lilac .. .. 2·25 70
96. 11. 50 r. brown .. .. 5·50 1·75
97. 100 r. blue .. .. 6·00 1·40

1923. Value in "Santimi" or "Lats".

98. 10. 1 s. mauve 5 5
99. 2 s. yellow 10 5
130. 3 s. red 5 5
100. 4 s. green 10 5
132. 5 s. green 10 5
133. 6 s. green on yellow .. 5 5
134. 7 s. blue 8 5
103. 10 s. red 20 5
136. 10 s. green on yellow .. 80 5
104. 12 s. claret 5 5
105a. 15 s. chocolate on brown 25 5
107. 20 s. blue 25 5
139. 20 s. pink 35 5
108. 25 s. blue 5 5
109. 30 s. pink 55 5
140. 30 s. blue 35 5
141. 35 s. blue 25 5
142. 40 s. purple 45 5
143. 50 s. grey 70 5
144. 11. 1 l. brown .. .. 1·25 8
145. 2 l. blue .. .. 3·00 12
146. 5 l. green .. .. 16·00 2·50
118. 10 l. red .. .. 55 1·00

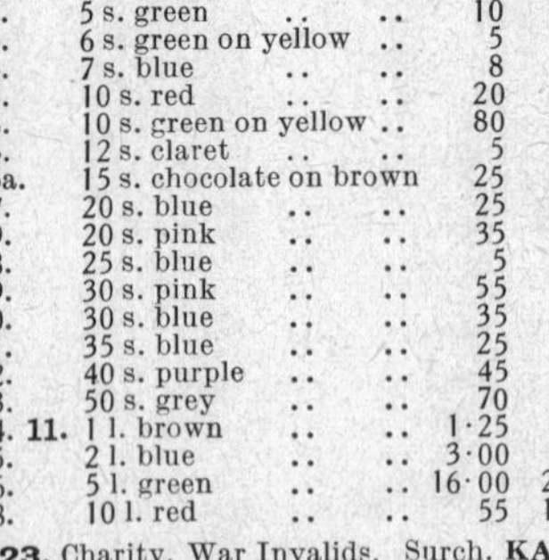

1923. Charity. War Invalids. Surch. **KARA INVALIDIEM S.10.S.** and cross.

112. 10. 1 s.+10 s. mauve .. 8 15
113. 2 s.+10 s. yellow .. 8 15
114. 4 s.+10 s. green .. 8 15

12. Town Hall.

14. Pres. J. Cakste.

1925. Libau Tercent. Inscr. "PARDOSANAS CENA".

119. – 6–12 s. blue and claret .. 20 45
120. 12. 15–25 s. brown and blue 20 35
121. – 25–35 s. green and violet 30 35
122. – 30–40 s. lake and blue .. 35 1·50
123. – 50–60 s. violet and green 1·10 1·75

DESIGNS—HORIZ. 6–12 s. Harbour and Lighthouse. VERT. 25–35 s. Bathing Pavilion. 30–40 s. Gertrude Church. 50–60 s. Arms of Libau.

1927. Surch.

124. 1. 15 s. on 40 k. purple .. 15 8
125. 15 s. on 50 k. violet .. 30 15
126. 8. 1 l. on 3 r. green & brown 1·10 2·25

1928. Death of Pres. Cakste.

150. 14. 2–12 s. orange 35 45
151. 6–16 s. green 35 45
152. 15–25 s. lake 35 54
153. 25–35 s. blue 35 45
154. 30–40 s. claret 35 45

15. Ruins at Rezekne.

16. Venta.

1928. Independence. 10th Anniv. Views.

158. 15. 6 s. violet and green .. 10 5
159. – 15 d. olive and brown .. 10 5
160. – 20 s. green and red .. 12 8
161. – 30 s. purple and blue .. 20 8
162. – 50 s. lake and grey .. 30 20
163. – 1 l. brown and sepia .. 90 50

DESIGNS: 15 s. Jelgava. 20 s. Cesis (Wenden). 30 s. Liepaja (Libau). 50 s. Riga. 1 l. National Theatre, Riga.

1928. Liberty Memorial Fund. Imperf. or perf.

164. 16. 6–16 s. green 60 60
165. – 10–20 s. red 60 60
166. – 15–25 s. chocolate .. 60 60
167. – 30–40 s. blue 60 60
168. – 50–60 s. black 60 60
169. – 1 l.–1 l. 10 s. purple .. 60 60

DESIGNS: 10–20 s. "Latvia" (Woman). 15–25 s. Mitau. 30–40 s. National Theatre, Riga. 50–60 s. Wenden. 1 l.–1 l. 10 s. Trenches, Riga Bridge.

19. Z. A. Meicrovics.

20. J. Rainis.

1929. Meierovics (Foreign Minister). 3rd Death Anniv. Imperf. or perf.

170. 19. 2–4 s. yellow 60 60
171. 6–12 s. green 60 60
172. 15–25 s. maroon 60 60
173. 25–35 s. green 60 60
174. 30–40 s. blue 60 60

1930. Designs as T 20 containing portrait of Rainis. Imperf. or perf.

175. 20. 1–2 s. violet 20 35
176. 2–4 s. orange 20 35
177. 4–8 s. green 20 35
178. 6–12 s. brown and green 20 35
179. 10–20 s. red .. .. 2·25 4·50
180. 15–30 s. green & brown 2·25 4·50

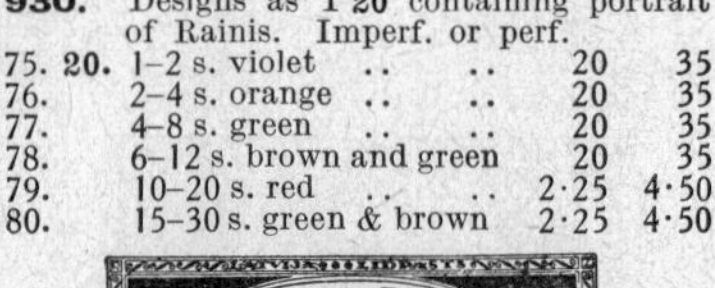

21, Durben Castle.

1930. Air. Imperf. or perf.

181. 21. 10–20 s. green and red .. 1·50 1·75
182. 15–30 s. red and green 1·50 1·75

22.

23.

1930. Anti-T.B. Fund.

183. – 1–2 s. red and violet .. 15 15
184. – 2–4 s. red and orange .. 15 15
185. 22. 4–8 s. red and green .. 20 20
186. – 5–10 s. sepia and green 20 20
187. – 6–12 s. yellow and green 25 25
188. – 10–20 s. black and red .. 25 25
189. – 15–30 s. green and claret 35 35
190. – 20–40 s. blue and red .. 35 35
191. – 25–50 s. pur., blue & red 65 65
192. 23. 30–60 s. pur., grn. & bl. 80 80

DESIGNS—VERT. As T 22: 1–2 s., 2–4 s. The Crusaders' Cross. 5–10 s. G Zemgalis. 6–12 s. Tower. 10–20 s. J. Cakste. 15–30 s. Floral design. 20–40 s. A. Kuiesis. HORIZ. As T 23: 25–50 s. Sanatorium.

1931-32. Air. As T 9 but value in "Santimi". Perf.
193. **9.** 10 s. green 30 15
194. 15 s. red 50 25
195. 25 s. blue 80 45

1931. Nos. 183/92 surch.
196. 9 on 6–12 s. yellow & green 35 40
197. 16 on 1–2 s. red and violet 2·00 3·00
198. 17 on 2–4 s. red and orange 65 75
199. 19 on 4–8 s. red and green 1·25 2·50
200. 20 on 5–10 s. sepia & green 75 3·00
201. 23 on 15–30 s. green & clar. 25 35
202. 25 on 10–20 s. black and red 75 1·25
203. 35 on 20–40 s. blue and red 1·25 1·50
204. 45 on 25–50 s. pur., bl. & red 2·50 5·00
205. 55 on 30–60 s. purple, green and blue .. .. 4·00 4·75

1931. Air. Charity. Nos. 193/5 surch. **LATVIJAS AIZSARGI** and value. Imperf. or perf.
206. **9.** 50 on 10 s. green .. 1·75 2·25
207. 1 l. on 15 s. red .. 1·75 2·25
208. 1 l. 50 on 25 s. blue .. 1·75 2·25

24. Foreign Invasion.

1932. Militia Maintenance Fund. Imperf. or perf.
209. – 1–11 s. blue and purple 80 80
210. **24.** 2–17 s. orange and olive 80 80
211. – 3–23 s. red and brown 80 80
213. – 4–34 s. green 80 80
212. – 5–45 s. green 80 80
DESIGNS: 1–11 s. The Holy Oak and Kriva telling stories. 3–23 s. Lacplesis, the deliverer. 4–34 s. The Black Knight (enemy) slaughtered. 5 45 s. Laimdota, the spirit of Latvia, freed.

25. Infantry Manoeuvres.

1932. Militia Maintenance Fund. Imperf. or perf.
214. – 6–25 s. purple & brown 90 90
215. **25.** 7–35 s. blue and green .. 90 90
216. – 10–45 s. sepia and green 90 90
217. – 12–55 s. green & claret 90 90
218. – 15–75 s. violet and red 90 90
DESIGNS—HORIZ. 6–25 s. Troops on march. VERT. 10–45 s. First aid to soldier. 12–55 s. Army kitchen. 15–75 s. Gen. J. Balodis.

27.

1932. Air. Charity. Imperf. or perf.
219. **27.** 10–20 s. black and green 2·25 3·50
220. 15–30 s. red and grey .. 2·25 3·50
221. 25–50 s. blue and grey .. 2·25 3·50

1932. Riga Exn. of Lettish Products. Optd. **Latvijas razojumu izstade Riga. 1932.g.10.-18.IX.**
222. **10.** 3 s. red 15 10
223. 10 s. green on yellow .. 25 12
224. 20 s. pink 45 15
225. 35 s. blue 90 30

29. Wright's Biplane. **29a.** "Mourning Mother" Memorial, Riga.

1932. Air. Pioneers of Aviation. Imperf. or perf.
226. – 5–25 s. green & brown 3·00 3·50
227. – 10–50 s. green & brown 3·00 3·50
228. – 15–75 s. green & choc. 3·00 3·50
229. **29.** 20–100 s. mauve & green 3·00 3·50
230. – 25–125 s. blue & brown 3·00 3·50
DESIGNS—VERT. 5–25 s. Icarus. 10–50 s. Leonardo da Vinci. 15–75 s. Charhere's balloon. HORIZ. 20–100 s. Wright's biplane. 25–125s. Bleriot's monoplane.

1933. Air. Wounded Latvian Airmen Fund.
231. – 2–52 s. brown and black 1·75 2·50
232. **29a.** 3–53 s. red and black .. 1·75 2·50
233. – 10–60 s. green and black 1·75 2·50
234. – 20–70 s. red and black .. 1·75 2·50
DESIGNS: 2 s. Fall of Icarus. 10 s., 20 s. Proposed tombs for airmen.

1933. Air Charity. Riga-Bathurst Flight As Type **9** optd. **LATVIJA-AFRIKA. 1933** on surch. also.
235. 10 s. green .. .. 2·75 7·00
236. 15 s. red .. .. .. 2·75 7·00
237. 25 s. blue .. .. .. 2·75 7·00
238. 50 s. on 15 s. red .. .. 22·00 50·00
239. 100 s. on 25 s. blue .. 22·00 50·00
In the event the aircraft crashed at Neustettin, Germany and the mail was forwarded by ordinary post.

29b. Biplane under fire at Riga.

1933. Air Charity. Wounded Latvian Airmen Fund.
240. – 3–53 s. blue and orange 2·75 3·50
241. **29b.** 7–57 s. brown and blue 2·75 3·50
242. – 35–135 s. black and blue 2·75 3·50
DESIGNS: 3 s. Monoplane taking off. 35 s. Map and planes.

29c. American "Gee-Bee" Plane.

1933. Air Charity. Wounded Latvian Airmen Fund.
243. **29c.** 8–68 s. grey and brown 3·50 4·50
244. – 12–112 s. green & purple 3·50 4·50
245. – 30–130 s. grey and blue 3·50 4·50
246. – 40–190 s. blue & maroon 3·50 4·50
DESIGNS: 12 s. British "S6S" plane. 30 s. "Graf Zeppelin" over Riga. 40 s. Dornier "Do X".

30. President's Palace. **34.** A. Kronvalds. **35.**

1934. New Constitution. 15th Anniv.
247. **30.** 3 s. red 5 5
248. – 5 s. green 5 5
249. – 10 s. green 25 5
250. – 20 s. red 40 5
251. – 35 s. blue 5 5
252. **30.** 40 s. brown 5 5
DESIGNS: 5 s., 10 s. Arms and sword. 20 s. Latvia (woman), with soldiers in side panels. 35 s. Govt. Building.

1936. Lettish Intellectuals.
253. **34.** 3 s. red 45 45
254. – 10 s. green 45 45
255. – 20 s. magenta 45 45
256. – 35 s. blue 45 45
PORTRAITS: 10 s. A. Pumpurs. 20 s. J. Maters. 35 s. Auseklis (Mikus Krogsemis).

1936. White Cross Fund. Designs incorporating Cross and Stars device as in T **35**.
257. **35.** 3 s. red 45 60
258. – 10 s. green 45 60
259. – 20 s. pink 45 60
260. – 35 s. blue 45 60
DESIGNS: 10 s. Device and foliage. 20 s. Doctor and man. 35 s. Woman holding shield.

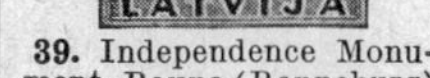

39. Independence Monument, Rauna (Ronneburg). **41.** President Ulmanis.

1937.
261. **39.** 3 s. red 5 5
262. – 5 s. green 5 5
263. – 10 s. green 8 8
264. – 20 s. red 12 20
265. – 30 s. blue 25 25
266. – 35 s. blue 30 30
267. – 40 s. brown 35 35
DESIGNS—VERT. 10, 30, 35 s. Independence Monuments of Jelgava, Iecava and Riga. 20 s. War Memorial, Valka. 40 s. Col. Kalpak's Grave. HORIZ. 5 s. Cemetery Gate, Riga.

1937. President Ulmanis' 60th Birthday.
268. **41.** 3 s. red 5 5
269. 5 s. green 5 5
270. 10 s. green 8 5
271. 20 s. red 12 8
272. 25 s. blue 15 20
273. 30 s. blue 15 20
274. 35 s. blue 15 20
275. 40 s. brown 30 20
276. 50 s. black 35 35

42. Galzinkalns, Livonia. **43.** General J. Balodis.

1938. Independence. 20th Anniv. Dated "1918 1938".
278. **42.** 3 s. red 5 5
279. – 5 s. green 5 5
280. **43.** 10 s. green 5 5
281. – 20 s. mauve 8 5
282. – 30 s. blue 25 8
283. – 35 s. slate 25 5
284. – 40 s. mauve 35 5
DESIGNS—As T **42**: 5 s. Latgale landscape. 30 s. Riga. 35 s. Rumba waterfall, Courland. 40 s. Zemgale landscape. As T **43**: 20 s. Pres. Ulmanis.

DESIGNS: 5 s. Jelgava Castle. 10 s. Riga Castle. 20 s. Independence Memorial. 30 s. Eagle and National Flag. 35 s. Town Hall, Daugavpils. 40 s. War Museum and Powder-magazine, Riga 50 s. Pres. Ulmanis.
44. Elementary School, Riga.

1939. Rebirth of Authoritarian Govt. 5th Anniv. Inscr. "1934 1939".
285. **44.** 3 s. brown 5 5
286. – 5 s. green 5 5
287. – 10 s. green 5 5
288. – 20 s. red 10 5
289. – 30 s. blue 15 10
290. – 35 s. blue 20 10
291. – 40 s. purple 25 15
292. – 50 s. black 40 25

45. Reaping. **46.** Arms of Courland, Livonia and Latgale. **47.** Arms of Latvian S.S.R.

1939. Harvest Festival. Dated "8 X 1939".
294. **45.** 10 s. green 8 5
295. – 20 s. red (Apples) .. 15 8

1940.
296. **46.** 1 s. violet 5 5
297. 2 s. yellow 5 5
298. 3 s. red 5 5
299. 5 s. brown 5 5
300. 7 s. green 5 5
301. 10 s. green 15 5
302. 20 s. red 15 5
303. 30 s. brown 20 10
304. 35 s. blue 20 15
305. 50 s. green 25 12
306. 1 l. olive 30 15

1940. Incorporation of Latvia in U.S.S.R.
307. **47.** 1 s. violet 5 5
308. 2 s. yellow 5 5
309. 3 s. red 5 5
310. 5 s. olive 5 5
311. 7 s. green 5 20
312. 10 s. green 8 5
313. 20 s. red 35 5
314. 30 s. blue 45 15
315. 35 s. blue 5 25
316. 40 s. brown 25 10
317. 50 s. grey 35 10
318. 1 l. brown 75 15
319. 5 l. green .. .. 2·75 1·90

LEBANON O3

A territory N. of Israel, formerly Turkish. Great Lebanon, the Christian area of Syria, was given a separate status under French Mandate in 1920. Until September, 1923, the French occupation stamps of Syria were used and these were followed by the joint issue of 1923, Nos. 97 etc., of Syria. Independence was proclaimed in 1941, but the country was not evacuated by foreign troops until 1947.

100 centiemes = 1 piastre.

1924. Stamps of France surch. **GRAND LIBAN** and value.
1. **11.** 10 c. on 2 c. claret .. 12 10
2. **17.** 25 c. on 5 c. orange .. 10 10
3. 50 c. on 10 c. green .. 10 8
4. **15.** 75 c. on 15 c. green .. 20 20
5. **17.** 1 p. on 20 c. chocolate .. 20 5
6. 1 p. 25 on 25 c. blue .. 30 25
7. 1 p. 50 on 30 c. orange .. 20 20
8. 1 p. 50 on 30 c. red .. 20 15
9. **15.** 2 p. 50 on 50 c. blue .. 20 10
10. **13.** 2 p. on 40 c. red & blue .. 40 25
11. 3 p. on 60 c. vio. & blue .. 1·00 80
12. 5 p. on 1 f. red & green .. 1·10 1·00
13. 10 p. on 2 f. orge. & grn. 1·50 1·25
14. 25 p. on 5 f. blue & yell. 2·40 2·00

1924. Air. Nos. 10/13 optd. **Poste par Avion.**
22. **13.** 2 p. on 40 c. red & blue .. 1·00 1·10
23. 3 p. on 60 c. vio. & bl. .. 1·00 1·10
24. 5 p. on 1 f. red & green .. 1·00 1·10
25. 10 p. on 2 f. orge. & grn. 1·00 1·10

1924. "Pasteur" issue of France surch. **GRAND LIBAN** and value.
15. **26.** 50 c. on 10 c. green .. 10 8
16. 1 p. 50 on 30 c. red .. 20 15
17. 2 p. 50 on 50 c. blue .. 15 8

1924. "Olympic Games" issue of France surch. **GRAND LIBAN** and value.
18. **27.** 50 c. on 10 c. green .. 2·50 2·50
19. – 1 p. 25 on 25 c. red .. 2·50 2·50
20. – 1 p. 50 on 30 c. red & blk. 2·50 2·50
21. – 2 p. 50 on 50 c. blue .. 2·50 2·50

1924. Stamps of France surch. **Gd Liban** and value in English and Arabic.
26. **11.** 10 c. on 2 c. claret .. 5 5
27. **17.** 25 c. on 5 c. orange .. 10 10
28. 50 c. on 10 c. green .. 15 15
29. **15.** 75 c. on 15 c. green .. 12 12
30. **17.** 1 p. on 20 c. chocolate 10 10
31. 1 p. 25 on 25 c. blue .. 20 20
32. 1 p. 50 on 30 c. red .. 15 15
33. 1 p. 50 on 30 c. orange 6·00 6·00
34. 2 p. on 35 c. violet .. 12 12
35. **13.** 2 p. on 40 c. red & blue 10 10
36. 2 p. on 45 c. grn. & bl. 2·10 2·10
37. 3 p. on 60 c. violet & bl. 25 25
38. **15.** 3 p. on 60 c. violet .. 25 25
39. 4 p. on 85 c. red .. 20 15
40. **13.** 5 p. on 1 f. red & green 55 50
41. 10 p. on 2 f. orge. & grn. 70 70
42. 25 p. on 5 f. blue & yell. 1·00 1·00

1924. "Pasteur" issue of France surch. **Gd Liban** and value in English and Arabic.
43. **26.** 50 c. on 10 c. green .. 5 5
44. 75 c. on 15 c. green .. 15 15
45. 1 p. 50 on 30 c. red .. 15 15
46. 2 p. on 45 c. red .. 25 25
47. 2 p. 50 on 50 c. blue .. 5 5
48. 4 p. on 75 c. blue .. 30 30

1924. Nos. 401/4 (Olympic Games) and Ronsard stamps of France surch. **Gd Liban** and value in English and Arabic.
49. **27.** 50 c. on 10 c. green .. 2·75 2·75
50. – 1 p. 25 on 25 c. red .. 2·75 2·75
51. – 1 p. 50 on 30 c. red & blk. 2·75 2·75
52. – 2 p. 50 on 50 c. blue .. 2·75 2·75
53. **31.** 4 p. on 75 c. blue .. 15 15

1924. Air. Stamps of France surch. **Gd Liban Avion** and value in English and Arabic.
54. **13.** 2 p. on 40 c. red & blue .. 1·00 1·00
55. 3 p. on 60 c. vio. & bl. .. 1·00 1·00
56. 5 p. on 1 f. red & green .. 1·00 1·00
57. 10 p. on 2 f. red & grn. .. 1·00 1·00

1. Cedar of Lebanon. **2.** Beirut.

3. Tripoli.

ILLUSTRATIONS
British Commonwealth and all overprints and surcharges are FULL SIZE. Foreign Countries have been reduced to ¾-LINEAR.

1925. Views.
58. **1.** 10 c. violet 5 5
59. **2.** 25 c. black 8 5
60. 50 c. green (Tripoli) .. 5 5
61. 75 c. red (Beiteddin) .. 8 5
62. 1 p. claret (Baalbek) .. 25 20
63. 1 p. 25 c. grn. (Mouktara) 25 25
64. 1 p. 50 c. red (Tyre) .. 5 5
65. 2 p. sepia (Zahle) .. 15 5
66. 2 p. 50 c. blue (Baalbek) 20 10
67. 3 p. brn. (Deir-el-Kamar) 20 10
68. 5 p. violet (Saida) .. 25 25
69. **3.** 10 p. plum 35 30
70. **2.** 25 p. blue (Beirut) .. 1·10 80

1925. Air. Stamps as last optd. **AVION** in English and Arabic.
71. **2.** 2 p. sepia 30 25
72. 3 p. brown 30 25
73. 5 p. violet 30 25
74. **3.** 10 p. plum 30 25

1926. Air. Same stamps but optd. with aeroplane instead.
75. **2.** 2 p. sepia 40 40
76. 3 p. brown 40 40
77. 5 p. violet 40 40
78. **3.** 10 p. plum 40 40

1926. War Refugee Charity. As 1925 but surch. **Secours aux Refugies Afft.** and premium in English and Arabic.
79. **2.** 25 c.+25 c. black .. 55 55
80. 50 c.+25 c. green .. 55 55
81. 75 c.+25 c. red .. 55 55
82. 1 p.+50 c. claret .. 55 55
83. 1 p. 25+50 c. green .. 55 55
84. 1 p. 50+50 c. red .. 55 55
85. 2 p.+75 c. sepia .. 55 55
86. 2 p. 50+75 c. blue .. 55 55
87. 3 p.+1 p. brown .. 55 55
88. 5 p.+1 p. violet .. 55 55
89. **3.** 10 p.+2 p. plum .. 55 55
90. **2.** 25 p.+5 p. blue .. 55 55

1926. Air. Nos. 75/78 surch. **Secours aux Refugies Afft.** and premium in English and Arabic.
91. **2.** 2 p.+1 p. sepia .. .. 1·00 1·00
92. 3 p.+2 p. brown .. .. 1·00 1·00
93. 5 p.+3 p. violet .. .. 1·00 1·00
94. **3.** 10 p.+5 p. plum .. .. 1·00 1·00

1926. As 1925 surch. in English and Arabic figures and bars.
95. **2.** 3 p. 50 c. on 75 c. red .. 8 5
96a. 4 p. on 25 c. black .. 20 15
98. 4 p. 50 on 75 c. red .. 15 15
99. 6 p. on 2 p. 50 blue .. 8 8
100. 7 p. 50 on 2 p. 50 blue .. 20 20
101. 12 p. on 1 p. 25 green .. 10 10
102. 15 p. on 25 p. blue .. 8 8
103. 20 p. on 1 p. 25 green 60 60

1927. Pictorial and provisional stamps of Lebanon optd. **Republique Libanaise.**
104. **1.** 10 c. violet 5 5
105. **2.** 50 c. green 5 5
106. 1 p. claret 5 5
107. 1 p. 50 red 10 10
108. 2 p. sepia 20 10
109. 3 p. brown 12 8
110. 4 p. on 25 c. blk. (No. 96a) 10 5
111. 4 p. 50 on 75 c. red .. 10 10
112. 5 p. violet 30 20
113. 7 p. 50 on 2 p. 50 blue (No. 100) 10 8
114. **3.** 10 p. plum 35 15
115. **2.** 15 p. on 25 p. blue (No. 102) 75 60
117. 25 p. blue .. .. 1·00 80

1927. Air. Nos. 75/78 optd. **Republique Libanaise** in one or two lines and bar.
118. **2.** 2 p. sepia 45 45
119. 3 p. brown 45 45
120. 5 p. violet 45 45
121. **3.** 10 p. plum 45 45

الجمهورية اللبنانية

(4.)

1928. Nos. 104/117 optd. with T 4 and in some cases surch. also.
145. **1.** 5 c. on 10 c. violet .. 5 5
124. 10 c. violet 5 5
125. **2.** 50 c. green 12 10
146. 50 c. on 75 c. red .. 10 10
126. 1 p. claret 8 5
127. 1 p. 50 red 15 12
128. 2 p. sepia 30 25
147. 2 p. on 1 p. 25 green .. 10 10
129. 3 p. brown 12 8
148. 4 p. on 25 c. black .. 15 15
131. 4 p. 50 on 75 c. red .. 15 12
132. 5 p. violet 25 25
149. 7 p. 50 on 2 p. 50 blue 15 5
134. **3.** 10 p. plum 35 20
135. **2.** 15 p. on 25 p. blue .. 90 90
136. 25 p. blue .. .. 1·25 1·25

1928. Air. Optd. **Republique Libanaise** in English and Arabic (latter as T 4) and aeroplane.
151. **2.** 50 c. green 5 5
15[illegible] 50 c. on 75 c. (No. 146) 10 10
153. 1 p. claret 12 12
141. 2 p. sepia 30 30
154. 2 p. on 1 p. 25 (No. 147) 25 25
142. 3 p. brown 20 20
143. 5 p. violet 20 20
144. **3.** 10 p. plum 30 50
155. **2.** 15 p. on 25 p. (No. 135) 32·00 32·00
156. 25 p. blue .. .. 20·00 20·00

5. Silk-worm, Larva, Cocoon and Moth.

1930. Silk Congress.
157. **5.** 4 pi. sepia .. .. 1·60 1·40
158. 4½ pi. red .. .. 1·60 1·40
159. 7½ pi. blue .. .. 1·60 1·40
160. 10 pi. violet .. .. 1·60 1·40
161. 15 pi. green .. .. 1·60 1·40
162. 25 pi. claret .. .. 1·60 1·40

6. Cedars of Lebanon. **7.** Baalbek.

1930. Views.
163. **6.** 10 c. orange (Beirut) .. 5 5
164. 20 c. brown 5 5
165. 25 c. blue (Baalbek) .. 5 5
166. **7.** 50 c. brown (Bickfaya) .. 15 12
166b. 75 c. brown (Baalbek) .. 5 5
167. 1 p. green (Saida) .. 12 8
167a. 1 p. plum (Saida) .. 12 5
168. 1 p. 50 plum (Beiteddin) 25 20
168a. 1 p. 50 green (Beiteddin) 12 5
169. 2 p. blue (Tripoli) .. 30 15
170. 3 p. sepia (Baalbek) .. 30 10
171. 4 p. brown (Nahr-el-Kelb) 30 5
172. 4 p. 50 red (Beaufort) .. 30 15
173. 5 p. black (Beiteddin) .. 15 10
251. 5 p. blue (Nahr-el-Kelb) 5 5
174. 6 p. purple (Tyre) .. 30 20
175. 7 p. 50 blue 30 10
176. 10 p. green (Hasbaya) .. 45 10
177. 15 p. purple (Afka Falls) 60 15
178. 25 p. green (Beirut) .. 1·00 20
179. 50 p. grn. (Deir-el-Kamar) 3·75 1·10
180. 100 p. black (Baalbek) .. 2·75 1·40

8.

1930. Air. Aeroplane and views as T **8.**
181. 50 c. purple (Rachaya) .. 5 5
182. 1 p. green (Broumana) .. 10 5
183. 2 p. orange (Baalbek) .. 15 12
184. 3 p. red (Hasroun) .. 20 15
185. 5 p. green (Byblos) .. 10 8
186. 10 p. red (Kadisha) .. 30 15
187. 15 p. brown (Beirut) .. 20 12
188. 25 p. violet (Tripoli) .. 25 15
189. 50 p. lake (Kabelais) .. 1·10 80
190. 100 p. brown (Zahle) .. 1·25 90

9. Skiing.

1936. Air. Tourist Propaganda.
191. **9.** 50 c. green 25 25
192. – 1 p. orange 25 25
193. **9.** 2 p. violet 35 35
194. – 3 p. green 40 40
195. **9.** 5 p. red 60 60
196. – 10 p. brown 75 75
197. – 15 p. red .. .. 1·40 1·40
198. **9.** 25 p. green .. .. 17·00 17·00
DESIGN: 1, 3, 10, 15 p. Djouni Bay.

11. Cedar of Lebanon.

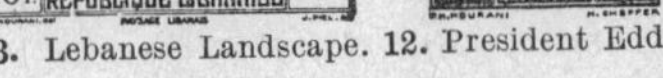

13. Lebanese Landscape. **12.** President Edde.

1937.
199. **11.** 10 c. red 5 5
200. 20 c. blue 5 5
201. 25 c. lilac 5 5
202. 50 c. red 5 5
203. 75 c. brown 5 5
207. **12.** 3 p. violet 15 10
208. 4 p. brown 5 5
209. 4 p. 50 red 8 5
211. **13.** 10 p. red 8 5
212. 12½ p. blue 10 5
213. 15 p. green 12 5
214. 20 p. brown 10 8
215. 25 p. red 15 15
216. 50 p. violet 30 30
217. 100 p. sepia 40 70

14. Exhibition Pavilion, Paris.

1937. Air. Paris Int. Exn.
218. **14.** 50 c. black 20 20
219. 1 p. green 15 15
220. 2 p. brown 15 15
221. 3 p. green 15 15
222. 5 p. green 20 20
223. 10 p. red .. .. 1·00 1·00
224. 15 p. claret .. .. 1·00 1·00
225. 25 p. brown .. .. 1·00 1·00

15. Ruins of Baalbek.

1937. Air.
226. – 50 c. blue 5 5
227. – 1 p. brown 5 5
228. – 2 p. sepia 8 10
229. – 3 p. red 15 15
230. – 5 p. green 10 10
231. **15.** 10 p. violet 10 5
232. 15 p. blue 25 20
233. 25 p. violet 40 30
234. 50 p. green 60 30
235. 100 p. brown 35 35
DESIGN: 50 c. to 5 p. Beit ed-Din.

1938. Surch. in English and Arabic figures.
236. **12.** 2 p. on 3 p. violet .. 12 5
237. 2½ p. on 4 p. brown .. 12 5

16. Medical College, Beirut.

1938. Air. Medical Congress.
238. **16.** 2 p. green 30 30
239. 3 p. orange 30 30
240. 5 p. violet 30 30
241. 10 p. red 30 30

17. M. Nogues and Aeroplane over Beirut. **18.** Emir Bechir Chehab.

1938. Air. 1st France-Lebanon Air Service 10th Anniv.
242. **17.** 10 p. maroon 50 50

1938. Surch.
243. – 6 p. on 7 p. 50 (No. 175) 50 20
244. – 7 p. 50 on 50 p. (No. 179) 35 25
245. – 7 p. 50 on 100 p. (180) 35 30
246. **13.** 12 p. 50 on 7 p. 50 blue 35 10
247. 12½ on 7 p. 50 blue 15 8

1939. As T 7 but with differing figures and Arabic inscriptions in side panels, and imprint at foot "IMP. CATHOLIQUE-BEYROUTH-LIBAN" instead of "HELIO VAUGIRARD".
248. 1 p. grey 5 5
249. 1 p. 50 purple 12 12
250. 7 p. 50 red 20 20
DESIGN: Beit ed-Din.

1942. Independence. 1st Anniv.
252. **18.** 50 c. green (postage) .. 50 50
253. 1 p. 50 purple .. 50 50
254. 6 p. red 50 50
255. 15 p. blue 50 50
256. – 10 p. purple (air) .. 90 90
257. – 50 p. green 90 90
DESIGN: 10 p., 50 p. (air), Aeroplane over mountains.

1943. Surch. in English and Arabic and with old values cancelled with ornaments.
258. 2 p. on 4 p. brown (208) .. 60 40
259. 6 p. on 7 p. 50 red (250) .. 15 15
260. 10 p. on 12½ p. blue (212) .. 10 10

19. Parliament House.

20. Bchamoun.

1944. Proclamation of Independence. 2nd Anniv.
265. **19.** 25 p. red (postage) .. 80 80
266. – 50 p. blue 80 80
267. **19.** 150 p. blue 80 80
268. – 200 p. purple 80 80
DESIGN: 50 p. 200 p. Government House.
269. **20.** 25 p. green (air) .. 80 70
270. 50 p. orange 90 70
271. – 100 p. brown 80 80
272. – 200 p. violet 90 80
273. – 300 p. green .. .. 3·00 3·00
274. – 500 p. brown .. .. 6·00 5·00
DESIGNS: 100 p., 200 p. Rachaya Citadel. 300 p., 500 p. Beirut.

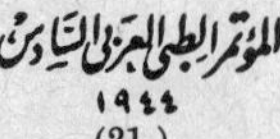

(21.)

1944. 10th Medical Congress. Horiz. designs inscr. "CONGRES MEDICAL BEYROUTH 1943" and optd. with T **21.**
275. – 10 p. red (postage) .. 60 60
276. – 20 p. blue 60 60
277. – 20 p. orange (air) .. 65 65
278. – 50 p. blue 65 65
279. – 100 p. purple .. .. 1·10 1·10
DESIGNS: Nos. 275/6, Beirut Isolation Hospital. Nos. 277/9, Bhannes Sanatorium.

٢٣ تشرين ثاني ١٩٤٣

22. (Translation "Nov. 23, 1943").

1944. President's Return to Office. 1st Anniv. Nos. 265/74 optd. with T **22.**
280. **19.** 25 p. red (postage) .. 2·00 1·60
281. – 50 p. blue .. .. 2·00 1·60
282. **19.** 150 p. blue .. .. 2·00 1·60
283. – 200 p. purple .. .. 2·00 1·60
284. **20.** 25 p. green (air) .. 1·50 1·50
285. 50 p. orange .. .. 1·50 1·50
286. – 100 p. brown .. .. 2·25 2·00
287. – 200 p. violet .. .. 4·50 2·50
288. – 300 p. green .. .. 7·00 5·50
289. – 500 p. brown .. .. 10·00 9·00

1945. Surch. in English and Arabic figures and ornaments.
261. – 2 p. on 5 p. blue (251) 10 10
262. – 3 p. on 5 p. blue (251) 10 10
263. **13.** 6 p. on 12½ pi. blue .. 10 10
264. 7½ pi. on 12½ pi. blue .. 15 15

23. Crusader Castle, Byblos. **24.** Falls of R. Litani.

1945.
397. **23.** 7 p. 50 red (postage) .. 25 5
398. 10 p. purple 60 8
399. 12 p. 50 blue .. .. 1·60 8
290. 15 p. brown 30 30
291. 20 p. green 50 30
292. – 25 p. blue 60 30
400. **23.** 25 p. violet .. .. 3·00 12
293. – 50 p. red .. .. 1·00 30
401. **23.** 50 p. green .. .. 4·50 1·50
294. **24.** 25 p. brown (air) .. 40 12
295. 50 p. purple 80 20
296. – 200 p. violet .. .. 2·75 55
297. – 300 p. black .. .. 3·50 1·25
DESIGNS—HORIZ. Nos. 292, 293, Crusader Castle, Tripoli. Nos. 296/7, Cedar of Lebanon and skier.

25. V(ictory) and National Flag.

26. V(ictory) and Lebanese Soldiers at Bir-Hakeim.

1946. Victory. "V" in design. (a) Postage.

298. **25.** 7 p. 50 brown and red .. 12 8
299. 10 p. violet and red .. 15 8
300. 12 p. 50 claret and red .. 25 8
301. 15 p. green and red .. 30 8
302. 20 p. green and red .. 30 8
303. 25 p. blue and red .. 50 15
304. 50 p. blue and red .. 60 20
305. 100 p. black and red .. 1·00 95

(b) Air.

306. **26.** 15 p. green, yell. & red 20 12
307. 20 p. red and blue .. 25 12
308. 25 p. blue, yell. & red .. 25 12
309. 50 p. grey, vio. & red .. 35 15
310. 100 p. violet and red .. 90 25
311. 150 p. brown and red .. 1·10 60

1946. As T **25** but without "V" sign.

312. 7 p. 50 lake and red .. 30 8
313. 10 p. violet and red .. 40 8
314. 12 p. 50 brown, green & red 50 8
315. 15 p. brown and red .. 50 8
316. 20 p. blue and red 70 8
317. 25 p. green and red .. 1·00 15
318. 50 p. blue and red .. .. 2·00 90
319. 100 p. black and red .. 3·00 1·60

27. Night Herons.

1946.

320. **27.** 12 p. 50 c. red (postage) 1·10 5
321. 10 p. orange(air) .. 80 30
322. 25 p. blue .. .. 1·10 15
323. 50 p. green .. .. 4·00 20
324. 100 p. purple .. .. 2·00 1·60

28 Cedar of Lebanon. **29.**

1946.

325. **28.** 50 c. brown 5 5
326. 1 p. purple 5 5
327. 2 p. 50 violet 10 5
328. 5 p. red 12 5
329. 6 p. grey 15 5

1946. Air. Arab Postal Congress.

330. **29.** 25 p. blue 20 15
331. 50 p. green 25 25
332. 75 p. red 60 40
333. 150 p. violet 90 60

29a. Cedar of Lebanon. **30.** President, Bridge and Tablet.

1947.

333a. **29a.** 50 c. brown 20 5
333b. 2p. 50 green 30 5
333c. 5 p. red 40 5

1947. Air. Evacuation of Foreign Troops from Lebanon.

334. **30.** 25 p. blue 30 25
335. 50 p. red 50 40
336. 75 p. black 60 50
337. 150 p. green .. .. 1·00 1·00

31. Crusader Castle, Tripoli.

32. Djounie Bay.

DESIGN: 150 p. to 300 p. Grand Serail Palace.

1947.

338. **31.** 12 p. 50 red (postage) 1·10 5
339. 25 p. blue .. .. 1·40 8
340. 50 p. green .. .. 3·50 20
341. 100 p. violet .. .. 6·00 1·40
342. **32.** 5 p. green (air) 8 5
343. 10 p. mauve 15 5
344. 15 p. red 25 5
344a. 15 p. green .. .. 1·60 25
345. 20 p. orange 25 5
345a. 20 p. red 40 8
346. 25 p. blue 40 5
347. 50 p. red 80 12
348. 100 p. purple .. .. 1·60 20
349. – 150 p. purple .. .. 2·75 25
350. – 200 p. slate .. .. 4·00 1·40
351. – 300 p. black .. .. 5·50 3·00

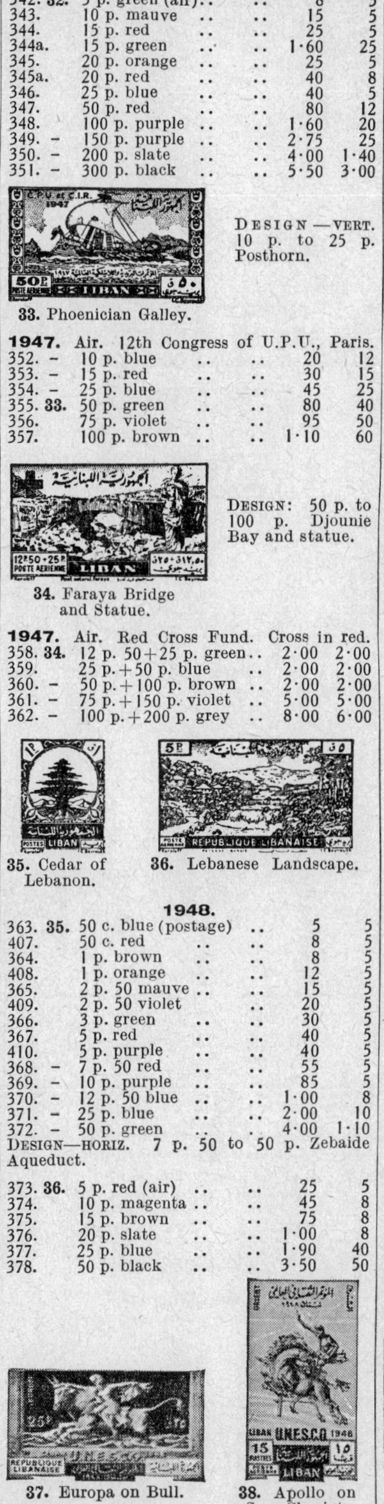

33. Phoenician Galley.

DESIGN—VERT. 10 p. to 25 p. Posthorn.

1947. Air. 12th Congress of U.P.U., Paris.

352. – 10 p. blue 20 12
353. – 15 p. red 30 15
354. – 25 p. blue 45 25
355. **33.** 50 p. green 80 40
356. 75 p. violet 95 50
357. 100 p. brown .. .. 1·10 60

34. Faraya Bridge and Statue.

DESIGN: 50 p. to 100 p. Djounie Bay and statue.

1947. Air. Red Cross Fund. Cross in red.

358. **34.** 12 p. 50+25 p. green .. 2·00 2·00
359. 25 p.+50 p. blue .. 2·00 2·00
360. – 50 p.+100 p. brown .. 2·00 2·00
361. – 75 p.+150 p. violet .. 5·00 5·00
362. – 100 p.+200 p. grey .. 8·00 6·00

35. Cedar of Lebanon. **36.** Lebanese Landscape.

1948.

363. **35.** 50 c. blue (postage) .. 5 5
407. 50 c. red 8 5
364. 1 p. brown 8 5
408. 1 p. orange 12 5
365. 2 p. 50 mauve 15 5
409. 2 p. 50 violet 20 5
366. 3 p. green 30 5
367. 5 p. red 40 5
410. 5 p. purple 40 5
368. – 7 p. 50 red 55 5
369. – 10 p. purple 85 5
370. – 12 p. 50 blue .. .. 1·00 8
371. – 25 p. blue .. .. 2·00 10
372. – 50 p. green .. .. 4·00 1·10

DESIGN—HORIZ. 7 p. 50 to 50 p. Zebaide Aqueduct.

373. **36.** 5 p. red (air) 25 5
374. 10 p. magenta 45 8
375. 15 p. brown 75 8
376. 20 p. slate .. .. 1·00 8
377. 25 p. blue .. .. 1·90 40
378. 50 p. black .. .. 3·50 50

37. Europa on Bull. **38.** Apollo on Sun Chariot.

1948. 3rd Meeting of U.N.E.S.C.O., Beirut.

379. **37.** 10 p. red (postage) .. 60 60
380. 12 p. 50 violet .. 70 70
381. 25 p. olive 70 70
382. – 30 p. brown 80 80
383. – 40 p. green .. .. 1·00 80

DESIGN—VERT. 30 p. 40 p. Avicenna (philosopher and scientist).

384. **38.** 7 p. 50 blue (air) .. 60 60
385. 15 p. black 60 60
386. 20 p. brown 60 60
387. – 35 p. red .. .. 1·25 1·00
388. – 75 p. green .. .. 2·00 1·60

DESIGN—HORIZ. 35 p. 75 p. Symbolical figure.

39. Camel.

40. Helicopter. **41.** Nahr-el-Kalb Bridge.

1949. U.P.U. 75th Anniv.

389. **39.** 5 p. violet (postage) .. 20 15
390. 7 p. 50, red 30 20
391. 12 p. 50 blue 40 30
392. **40.** 25 p. blue (air) 80 30
393. 50 p. green .. .. 1·10 50

1950.

411. **41.** 7 p. 50 rose 40 5
412. 10 p. lilac 60 5
413. 12 p. 50 pale blue .. 80 8
414. 25 p. deep blue .. 1·75 10
415. 50 p. emerald .. .. 3·25 75

See also Nos. 433/7.

42. Congressional Flags.

DESIGNS—HORIZ. 5 p., 15 p. Swallows. 25 p., 35 p. Pres. Bishara al-Khoury and bldg.

1950. Lebanese Emigrants' Congress. Inscr. "MOIS DES EMIGRES—ETE 1950".

416. **42.** 7 p. 50 green (postage) 15 5
417. 12 p. 50 magenta .. 15 8

A 418. – 5 p. blue (air) .. 25 12
A 419. – 15 p. violet 30 25
A 420. – 25 p. brown.. .. 35 30
A 421. – 35 p. green 60 45

43. Crusader Castle, Sidon.

1950. Air.

422. **43.** 10 p. brown 15 12
423. 15 p. green 30 8
424. 20 p. red 65 12
425. 25 p. blue .. .. 1·25 40
426. 50 p. grey .. .. 1·75 1·00

1950. Surch. with figures and bars.

427. **35.** 1 p. on 3 p. green .. 10 10
428. **28.** 2 p. on 50 6 p. grey .. 10 10

44. Cedar of Lebanon. **45.** Nahr el-Kalb Bridge.

46. Crusader Castle, Sidon.

T **45** is similar to T **41** but left value tablets differ.

1951.

429. **44.** 50 c. red (postage) .. 8 5
430. 1 p. brown 10 5
431. 2 p. 50 grey 12 5
432. 5 p. claret 40 5
433. **45.** 7 p. 50 vermilion .. 50 8
434. 10 p. purple 80 5
435. 12 p. 50 turquoise-blue 1·40 12
436. 25 p. blue .. .. 2·00 20
437. 50 p. green .. .. 3·50 1·75
438. **46.** 10 p. blue-green (air) .. 15 5
439. 15 p. brown 30 5
440. 20 p. red 35 8
441. 25 p. blue 70 8
442. 35 p. magenta 90 85
443. 50 p. violet .. .. 2·00 65

For other values as T **45** see Nos. 561/3.

47. Cedar. **48.** Baalbek.

1952.

444. **47.** 50 c. green (postage) .. 15 5
445. 1 p. chestnut 15 5
446. 2 p. 50 blue 20 5
447. 5 p. red 35 8
448. **48.** 7 p. 50 red 40 8
449. 10 p. violet 80 12
450. 12 p. 50 blue 85 12
451. 25 p. ultramarine .. 1·40 20
452. – 50 p. green .. .. 2·50 40
453. – 100 p. brown .. .. 3·00 1·90
454. – 5 p. red (air) 5 5
455. – 10 p. grey 8 5
456. – 15 p. magenta 15 5
457. – 20 p. orange 25 10
458. – 25 p. blue 25 12
459. – 35 p. ultramarine .. 40 12
460. – 50 p. emerald .. .. 1·10 20
461. – 100 p. blue .. .. 10·00 50
462. – 200 p. green .. .. 5·00 1·10
463. – 300 p. sepia .. .. 8·00 2·40

DESIGNS—HORIZ. s T **48**. Postage: 50 p., 100 p. Beaufort Castle. Air: 5 p. to 35 p. Beirut Airport. 50 p. to 300 p. Amphitheatre, Byblos.

49. Cedar of Lebanon. **50.** G.P.O. **51.** Mail-plane.

1953.

464. **49.** 50 c. blue (postage) .. 15 5
465. 1 p. crimson 15 5
466. 2 p. 50 lilac 20 5
560. 2 p. 50 claret 5 5
467. 5 p. emerald 40 5
468. **50.** 7 p. 50 red 60 8
469. 10 p. green 80 15
470. 12 p. 50 turquoise .. 1·10 12
471. 25 p. blue .. .. 1·60 20
472. 50 p. chocolate .. .. 2·75 50
473. **51.** 5 p. green (air) 5 5
474. 10 p. crimson 12 5
475. 15 p. vermilion 15 5
476. 20 p. turquoise 25 8
477. 25 p. blue 60 8
478. 35 p. chestnut 80 10
479. 50 p. blue .. .. 1·60 10
480. 100 p. sepia .. .. 2·75 1·25

For 20 p. green as T **50** see No. 636.

52. Khalde Airport, Beirut.

1954. Air. Opening of Beirut Int. Airport.

501. **52.** 10 p. red and pink .. 12 8
502. 25 p. blue and ultram. 25 20
503. 35 p. brown and sepia 40 25
504. 65 p. green & grey-green 1·10 65

53. Cedar. **54.** Beiteddin.

55. Baalbek.

DESIGN — HORIZ. 50 p. to 300 p. Litani Irrigation Canal.

1954.

481. **53.** 50 c. blue (postage) .. 5 5
482. 1 p. orange 10 5
483. 2½ p. violet 20 8
484. 5 p. emerald 30 8
485. **54.** 7 p. 50 red 85 12
486. 10 p. green .. .. 1·00 15
487. 12 p. 50 blue .. .. 1·60 25
488. 25 p. deep blue .. 2·50 40
489. 50 p. turquoise .. 4·00 1·00
490. 100 p. sepia .. .. 8·00 2·10
491. **55.** 5 p. green (air).. .. 8 5
492. 10 p. violet 10 5
493. 15 p. red 20 5
494. 20 p. brown 25 5
495. 25 p. blue 30 8
496. 35 p. sepia 40 12
497. – 50 p. bronze-green .. 1·60 15

498. – 100 p. rose .. .. 3·25 25
499. – 200 p. sepia .. .. 5·00 60
500. – 300 p. grey-blue .. 9·50 1·10
For other values in this design see Nos. 564/7.

1955. Arab Postal Union. As T **87** of Egypt but smaller, 27×37 mm. Inscr. "LIBAN" at top.
505. 12 p. 50 green (postage) .. 15 10
506. 25 p. violet 20 10
507. 2 p. 50 brown (air) .. 8 8

56. Rotary Emblem.

57. Cedar of Lebanon.

58. Jeita Grotto.

59. Skiers.

1955. Air. Rotary Int. 50th Anniv.
508. **56.** 35 p. green 45 25
509. 65 p. blue 65 40

1955.
510. **57.** 50 c. blue (postage) .. 5 5
511. 1 p. red 8 5
512. 2 p. 50 red-violet .. 10 5
552. 2 p. 50 violet-blue .. 15 5
513. 5 p. emerald 25 5
514. **58.** 7 p. 50 red 45 5
515. 10 p. green 30 5
516. 12 p. 50 blue 55 5
517. 25 p. blue .. .. 1·10 5
518. 50 p. grey-green .. 1·60 15
519. **59.** 5 p. blue-green (air) .. 20 5
520. 15 p. red 30 5
521. 20 p. violet 55 8
522. 25 p. blue 80 8
523. 35 p. brown .. .. 1·25 20
524. 50 p. chocolate .. .. 2·55 20
525. 65 p. blue .. .. 3·75 65
For other colours and new value as T **59** see Nos. 568/70 and for redrawn T **57** see Nos. 582/5, 686 and 695/7.

60. Visitor from Abroad.

61. Cedar of Lebanon. **62.** Globe and Columns.

63. Oranges.

1955. Air. Tourist Propaganda.
526. **60.** 2 p. 50 slate & maroon 5 5
527. 12 p. 50 blue & ultram. 20 8
528. 25 p. blue and indigo .. 30 12
529. 35 p. blue and green .. 50 20

1955.
530. **61.** 50 c. blue (postage) .. 5 5
531. 1 p. orange 5 5
532. 2 p. 50 violet 8 5
533. 5 p. green 10 5
534. **62.** 7 p. 50 red and yellow .. 15 5
535. 10 p. green and brown 20 5
536. 12 p. 50 blue and green 25 5
537. 25 p. blue and magenta 45 8
538. 50 p. myrtle and blue .. 75 15
539. 100 p. sepia and pink .. 1·25 35
540. **63.** 5 p. yellow & green (air) 8 5
541. 10 p. orange & green .. 10 5
542. 15 p. red and green .. 12 5
543. 20 p. orange & brown .. 20 5
544. – 25 p. violet and blue .. 30 5
545. – 35 p. lake and green .. 50 8
546. – 50 p. yellow and black 60 10
547. – 65 p. yellow and green 1·25 12
548. – 100 p. orge. and green 2·10 35
549. – 200 p. red and green .. 2·75 1·50
DESIGNS—VERT. 25 p. to 50 p. Grapes. HORIZ. 4p. to 200 p. Quinces.

64. U.N. Emblem. **65.** Masks, Columns and Gargoyle.

1956. Air. U.N. 10th Anniv.
550. **64.** 35 p. blue .. .. 1·60 1·40
551. 65 p. green .. .. 2·10 1·90

1956. Air. Baalbek Int. Drama Festival. Inscr. "FESTIVAL INTERNATIONAL DE BAALBECK".
553. **65.** 2 p. 50 sepia 10 5
554. 10 p. green 12 8
555. – 12 p. 50 blue 15 10
556. – 25 p. violet 30 15
557. – 35 p. purple 55 25
558. – 65 p. slate 90 60
DESIGNS—HORIZ. 12 p. 50, 25 p. Temple ruins at Baalbek. VERT. 35 p., 65 p. Double bass, masks and columns.

1957. As T **45** but inscr. "LIBAN".
561. 7 p. 50 red 25 5
562. 10 p. chestnut 40 5
563. 12 p. 50 blue 45 5

1957. Air. Arabic inscription changed. New values and colours.
564. – 10 p. violet 8 5
565. – 15 p. orange 10 5
566. – 20 p. green 12 5
567. – 25 p. blue 20 5
568. **59.** 35 p. green 65 8
569. 65 p. purple .. .. 1·25 20
570. 100 p. brown .. .. 1·75 45
DESIGN: 10 p. to 25 p. As Nos. 497/500.

66. Pres. Chamoun and King Faisal II of Iraq.

67. Runner.

1957. Air. Arab Leaders' Conf., Beirut.
571. **66.** 15 p. orange 20 10
572. – 15 p. blue 20 10
573. – 15 p. purple 20 10
574. – 15 p. mauve 20 10
575. – 15 p. green 20 10
576. – 25 p. turquoise 25 15
577. – 100 p. brown .. .. 1·60 1·00
DESIGNS—HORIZ. 15 p. values as T **66** show Pres. Chamoun and King Hussein of Jordan (572), Abdallah Khalil of Sudan (573), Pres. Shukri Bey of al-Quwatli of Syria (574) and King Saud of Saudi Arabia (575). 25 p. Map and Pres. Chamoun. 100 p. (44×44 mm. Diamond shape), The six Arab Leaders.

1957. 2nd Pan-Arabian Games. Inscr. as in T **67**.
578. **67.** 2 p. 50 c. sepia (post.) 15 8
579. – 12½ p. indigo 20 12
580. – 35 p. maroon (air) .. 65 45
581. – 50 p. green .. .. 1·00 55
DESIGNS—VERT. 12½ p. Footballers. HORIZ. 35 p. Fencers. 50 p. Stadium.

68. Miners.

DESIGNS—POSTAGE—As T **57**: 50 c., 2 p. 50 c. Figures in uniform size. 1 p., 5 p. Short dash under "P". As T **68**—VERT. 25 p. to 100 p. Potter. AIR — As T **68** — HORIZ. 5 p. to 25 p. Cedar of Lebanon with signs of the Zodiac, bird and ship. 25 p. to 100 p. Chamoun Electric Power Station.

1957.
582. **57.** 50 c. blue (postage) .. 5 5
582a. 50 c. violet 5 5
583. 1 p. brown 5 5
583a. 1 p. claret 5 5
584. 2 p. 50 c. violet 8 5
584a. 2 p. 50 c. blue 8 5
584b. 2 p. 50 c. myrtle .. 8 5
585. 5 p. green 10 5
586. **68.** 7½ p. pink 20 5
587. 10 p. brown 30 5
588. 12½ p. blue 35 5
589. – 25 p. blue 55 8
590. – 50 p. green 70 12
591. – 100 p. sepia .. .. 1·40 25
592. 5 p. emerald (air) 5 5
593. 10 p. orange 10 5
594. 15 p. brown 15 5
595. 20 p. claret 15 5
596. 25 p. blue 20 5
597. 35 p. maroon 30 8
598. 50 p. green 50 10
599. 65 p. sepia 75 12
600. 100 p. grey .. .. 1·00 45

70. Cedar of Lebanon.

71. Soldier and Flag.

72. Airliner at Khalde Airport.

1959.
601. **70.** 50 c. blue (postage) .. 5 5
602. 1 p. orange 8 5
603. 2 p. 50 c. violet .. 10 5
604. 5 p. green 12 5
605. **71.** 12 p. 50 c. blue .. 20 5
606. 25 p. indigo 25 5
607. 50 p. brown 55 10
608. 100 p. sepia .. .. 1·10 20
609. **72.** 5 p. green (air) .. 8 5
610. 10 p. maroon 8 5
611. 15 p. violet 12 5
612. 20 p. red 20 8
613. 25 p. violet-blue .. 25 10
614. – 35 p. myrtle 40 12
615. – 50 p. turquoise 45 12
616. – 65 p. sepia 90 15
617. – 100 p. ultramarine .. 1·10 30
DESIGN—HORIZ. Nos. 614/7, Factory cog-wheel and telegraph pylons.

مؤتمر المحامين العرب
من ١ الى ٥ ايلول ١٩٥٩

30P ق٣٠
= =
(**73.**)

1959. Lawyers' Conf. Nos. 538 and 546 (air) surch. as T **73**.
618. 30 p. on 50 p. myrtle and blue (postage) .. 25 15
619. 40 p. on 50 p. yellow and black (air) 35 20

ق٣٠
مؤتمر المهندسة العربي السابع
من ١٨ الى ٢٢ آب ١٩٥٩
30P
(**74.**)

1959. Air. Engineers' Conf. Nos. 614 and 616 surch. as T **74**.
620. 30 p. on 35 p. myrtle .. 20 15
621. 40 p. on 65 p. sepia .. 30 20

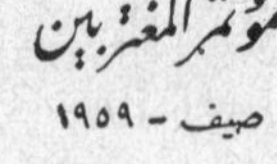

(**75.**)

76. Discus Thrower.

1959. Emigrants' Conf. No. 590 surch. as T **75**.
622. 30 p. on 50 p. green .. 20 8
623. 40 p. on 50 p. green .. 25 10

1959. Air. 3rd Mediterranean Games, Beirut.
624. **76.** 15 p. slate-green .. 15 10
625. – 30 p. chocolate 25 15
626. – 40 p. blue 50 20
DESIGNS—VERT. 30 p. Weight-lifting. HORIZ. 40 p. Games emblem.

77. Soldiers with Standard.

78. Planting Tree.

1959. Air. Independence. 16th Anniv.
627. **77.** 40 p. red and black .. 30 15
628. 60 p. red and green .. 35 20

1959. Surch.
629. **71.** 7 p. 50 on 12 p. 50 blue 5 5
630. 10 p. on 12 p. 50 blue .. 8 5
631. 15 p. on 25 p. indigo .. 10 5
632. – 40 p. on 50 p. green (No. 590) 25 10
633. **59.** 40 p. on 65 p. pur. (air) 70 20

1960. Air. Friends of the Tree Society. 25th Anniv.
634. **78.** 20 p. purple and green 20 10
635. 40 p. sepia and green .. 30 20

1960. Air. As T **50** but colours of name and value tablets reversed.
636. **50.** 20 p. green 15 10

79. Pres. Chehab.

80. Arab League Centre Cairo.

1960. Air.
637. **79.** 5 p. green 5 5
638. 10 p. blue 5 5
639. 15 p. chestnut 8 5
640. 20 p. sepia 10 5
641. 30 p. olive 12 5
642. 40 p. red 15 8
643. 50 p. blue 20 10
644. 70 p. purple 35 12
645. 100 p. green 45 25

1960. Arab League Centre, Cairo. Inaug.
646. **80.** 15 p. turquoise .. 15 10

81. "Uprooted Tree".

ILLUSTRATIONS British Commonwealth and all overprints and surcharges are FULL SIZE. Foreign Countries have been reduced to ¾-LINEAR.

1960. Air. World Refugee Year.
(a) Size 20½×36½ mm.
647. **81.** 25 p. brown 20 15
648. 40 p. green 30 20
(b) Size 19½×35½ mm.
648b. **81.** 25 p. brown 45 45
648c. 40 p. green 70 70

82. Martyrs' Monument.

1960. Air. Martyrs' Commem.
649. **82.** 20 p. purple and green 15 8
650. 40 p. blue and green .. 25 12
651. – 70 p. olive and black .. 45 25
DESIGN—VERT. 70 p. Detail of statues on monument.

83. Pres. Chehab and King Mohamed V. **84.** Pres. Chehab.

1960. Air. Visit of King Mohamed V of Morocco.
652. **83.** 30 p. chocolate & brown 25 12
653. 70 p. chestnut and black 50 25

1960.
654. **84.** 50 c. green 5 5
655. 2 p. 50 olive 5 5
656. 5 p. green 5 5
657. 7 p. 50 chestnut .. 8 5
658. 15 p. blue 12 8
659. 50 p. purple 35 8
660. 100 p. brown 65 15

84a. Child. **85.** Dove, Map and Flags.

1960. Air. Mother and Child Days.
661. **84a.** 20 p. red and yellow.. 15 10
662. 20 p.+10 p. red & yell. 20 12
663. – 60 p. blue & pale blue 40 20
664. – 60 p.+15 p. blue and pale blue 55 25
DESIGN: Nos. 663/4, Mother and child.

1960. Air. World Lebanese Union Meeting, Beirut.
665. **85.** 20 p. red, ulrtamarine, yellow and blue .. 12 5
666. – 40 p. green, black, vio. and blue 25 10
667. – 70 p. orange, green, blue and indigo 40 15
DESIGNS—VERT. 40 p. Cedar of Lebanon and homing pigeons. HORIZ. 70 p. Globes and Cedar of Lebanon.

(86.) **87.** Boxing.

1960. Arabian Oil Congress, Beirut. Optd. with T **86.**
668. **57.** 5 p. green (No. 585) .. 5 5
669. **80.** 15 p. turquoise .. 15 8

1960. Air. World Refugee Year. Nos. 647/8 surch. in English and Arabic.
669a. **81.** 20 p.+10 p. on 20 p. grn. 2·75 2·75
669b. 30 p.+15 p. on 25 p. brn. 3·25 3·25

1961. Olympic Games.
670. **87.** 2 p. 50+2 p. 50 brn. and blue (postage) .. 5 5
671. – 5 p.+5 p. brown and orge. 8 5
672. – 7 p. 50+7 p. 50 brn. & vio. 12 10
673. – 15 p.+15 p. brn. & red (air) 75 65
674. – 25 p.+25 p. brn. & grn. 75 65
675. – 35 p.+35 p. brn. & blue 75 65
DESIGNS: 5 p. Wrestling. 7 p. 50, Putting the shot. 15 p. Fencing. 25 p. Cycling. 35 p. Swimming.

88. Pres. Chehab. **89.** Pres. Chehab and Map of Lebanon. **90.** U.N. Emblem and Map.

1961.
676. **88.** 2 p. 50 ultram. & bl. (post). 5 5
677. 7 p. 50 pur. & indigo .. 5 5
678. 10 p. brown & yellow.. 10 5
679. **89.** 5 p. grn. & apple (air).. 5 5
680. 10 p. brown & ochre .. 10 5
681. 70 p. violet & mauve .. 45 25
682. – 200 p. blue and bistre.. 1·10 80
DESIGN—HORIZ. 200 p. Casino, Maameltein.

1961. Air. U.N.O. 15th Anniv.
683. **90.** 20 p. maroon & blue 12 8
684. – 30 p. green and brown 15 8
685. – 50 p. light blue & ult... 30 20
DESIGNS—VERT. 40 p. U.N. emblem and Baalbek ruins. HORIZ. 50 p. View of U.N. Headquarters and Manhattan.

91. Cedar. **92.** Bay of Maameltein.

1961. Redrawn version of T **57** (different arrangement at foot).
(a) Shaded background.
686. **91.** 2 p. 50 myrtle 10 5
(b) As T **91** but plain background.
695. 2 p. 50 yellow .. 8 5
696. 5 p. lake 10 5
697. 10 p. black 10 5

1961. Air.
687. **92.** 15 p. lake 10 5
688. 30 p. blue 15 8
689. 40 p. sepia 20 12

93. Weaving. DESIGN: 30 p. Pottery.

1961. Air. Labour Day.
690. – 30 p. claret 25 12
691. **93.** 70 p. blue 70 30

94. Water-skiers. DESIGNS — VERT. 15 p. Firework display. HORIZ. 70 p. Tourists in punt.

1961. Air. Tourist Month.
692. – 15 p. violet and blue .. 12 8
693. **94.** 40 p. blue and flesh .. 30 15
694. – 70 p. olive & flesh .. 35 30

95. G.P.O., Beirut.

1961.
698. **95.** 2 p. 50 magenta (post.) 8 5
699. 5 p. emerald 8 5
700. 15 p. blue 15 8
701. – 35 p. olive-green (air).. 25 12
702. – 50 p. brown 30 15
703. – 100 p. black 50 30
DESIGN: 35 p. to 100 p. Motor highway, Dora.

96. Cedars of Lebanon. **97.** Tyre Waterfront.

1961.
704. **96.** 50 c. green 5 5
705. 1 p. brown 5 5
706. 2 p. 50 blue 5 5
707. 5 p. red 5 5
708. 7 p. 50 violet 8 5
709. – 10 p. purple 15 5
710. – 15 p. grey-blue 20 5
711. – 50 p. green 35 10
712. – 100 p. black 65 25
713. **97.** 5 p. red (air) 5 5
714. 10 p. violet 8 5
715. 15 p. blue 10 5
716. 20 p. orange 12 5
717. 30 p. emerald 20 8
718. – 40 p. maroon 20 10
719. – 50 p. blue 25 12
720. – 70 p. green 35 15
721. – 100 p. sepia 60 25
DESIGNS—HORIZ. Nos. 718/21, Zahle. VERT. Nos. 709/12, Afka Falls.
See also Nos. 729/34.

98. U.N.E.S.C.O. Building, Beirut.

1961. Air. U.N.E.S.C.O. 15th Anniv. Mult.
722. 20 p. T **98** 12 8
723. 30 p. U.N.E.S.C.O. emblem and cedar (vert.) .. 15 12
724. 50 p. U.N.E.S.C.O. Building, Paris 35 20

99. Columns. **100.** Scout Bugler.

1961. Independence and Evacuation of Foreign Troops Commem. Multicoloured.
725. 10 p. T **99** (postage) .. 8 5
726. 15 p. Soldier and flag .. 10 5
727. 25 p. Cedar emblem (air) 15 10
728. 50 p. Emirs Bashir and Fakhreddin .. 30 20
The 25 p. and 50 p. are horiz.

1962. As Nos. 704/21 but with larger figures of value.
729. **97.** 50 c. green (postage) .. 8 5
730. 1 p. brown 8 5
731. 2 p. 50 blue 10 5
732. – 15 p. grey-blue.. .. 90 10
733. **96.** 5 p. red (air) 5 5
734. – 40 p. maroon .. .. 2·00 20

1962. Lebanese Scout Movement Commem.
735. ½ p.blk., yell. & grn. (post.) 5 5
736. 1 p. grn., apple, red & blk. 5 5
737. 2½ p. green, black & red .. 5 5
738. 6 p. multicoloured .. 5 5
739. 10 p. yellow, black & blue 5 5
740. 15 p. red, green, yellow and black (air) 10 8
741. 20 p. yell., blk. & violet .. 15 10
742. 25 p. grn., ochre, red & blk. 25 12
DESIGNS—VERT. ½ p. T **100.** 6 p. Lord Baden-Powell. 20 p. Saluting hand. HORIZ. 1 p. Scout with flag, cedar and badge. 2½ p. Stretcher party, badge and laurel. 10 p. Scouts and camp fire. 15 p. Cedar and Guide badge. 25 p. Cedar and Scout badge.

101. Arab League Centre, Cairo, and Emblem. **102.** Blacksmith.

1962. Air. Arab League Week.
743. **101.** 20 p. blue & turq. .. 12 10
744. 30 p. lake and pink .. 15 12
745. 50 p. green & turq. .. 25 20
See also Nos. 792/5.

1962. Air. Labour Day.
746. **102.** 5 p. green and blue .. 8 5
747. 10 p. blue and pink .. 8 5
748. – 25 p. violet and pink 20 8
749. – 35 p. magenta & blue 25 12
DESIGN—HORIZ. 25 p., 35 p. Tractor.

1962. European Shooting Championships Nos. 670/5 optd. **CHAMPIONNAT D'EUROPE DE TIR/2 JUIN 1962** in English and Arabic.
750. **87.** 2 p. 50+2 p. 50 (post.) 8 5
751. – 5 p.+5 p. 10 8
752. – 7 p. 50+7 p. 50 .. 12 12
753. – 15 p.+15 p. (air) .. 25 25
754. – 25 p.+25 p. 45 45
755. – 35 p.+35 p. 80 80

103. Hand grasping Emblem. **104.** Rock Temples of Abu Simbel.

1962. Air. Malaria Eradication.
756. **103.** 30 p. brown and pale chocolate 20 12
757. – 70 p. violet and lilac.. 40 30
DESIGN: 70 p. Campaign emblem.

1962. Nubian Monuments.
758. **104.** 5 p. bl. & ultram. (post.) 12 5
759. 15 p. lake and brown 15 8
760. – 30 p. yell.-grn. & grn. air 35 15
761. – 50 p. olive-grey & grey 70 30
DESIGNS: 30 p., 50 p. Bas-relief.

105. Playing-card Symbols. **106.** Schoolboy.

1962. Air. European Bridge Championships.
762. **105.** 25 p. blk., red, mag. & pink.. .. 50 40
763. 40 p. blk., red, brn. & yellow 60 40

1962. Scholars' Day.
764. **106.** 30 p. mult. (postage).. 20 8
765. – 45 p. mult. (air) .. 25 15
DESIGN: 45 p. Teacher.

107. **108.** Cherries.

1962. Air. Independence. 19th Anniv.
766. **107.** 25 p. grn., red & turq. 15 12
767. 25 p. vio., red & turq. 15 12
768. 25 p. bl., red & turq. 15 12

1962. Fruits. Multicoloured.
769. 50 c. T **108** (postage) .. 5 5
770. 1 p. Figs 5 5
771. 2 p. 50 T **108** 5 5
772. 5 p. Figs 5 5
773. 7 p. 50 T **108** 5 5
774. 10 p. Grapes 8 5
775. 17 p. 50 Grapes .. 15 5
776. 30 p. Grapes 30 8
777. 50 p. Oranges 50 20
778. 100 p. Pomegranates .. 90 50
779. 5 p. Apricots (air).. .. 5 5
780. 10 p. Plums 8 5
781. 20 p. Apples 15 8
782. 30 p. Plums 20 10
783. 40 p. Apples 25 15
784. 50 p. Pears 40 20
785. 70 p. Medlars 50 20
786. 100 p. Lemons 75 35

109. Reaping. **110.** Nurse tending Baby.

1963. Air. Freedom from Hunger.
787. **109.** 2 p. 50 yellow & blue 5 5
788. 5 p. yellow and green 5 5
789. 7 p. 50 yellow & pur. 8 5
790. – 15 p. yellow-green & brown-red 15 8
791. – 20 p. yell.-grn. & red 20 10
DESIGN—HORIZ. 15 p., 20 p. Three ears of wheat within hand.

1963. Air. Arab League Week. As T **101** but inscr. "1963".
792. 5 p. violet and blue .. 5 5
793. 10 p. green and blue .. 8 8
794. 15 p. chocolate and blue.. 12 12
795. 20 p. grey and blue .. 20 15

1963. Air. Red Cross Cent.
796. – 5 p. green and red .. 5 5
797. – 20 p. blue and red .. 10 8
798. **110.** 35 p. red and black .. 20 12
799. 40 p. violet and red .. 25 15
DESIGN—HORIZ. 5 p., 20 p. Blood transfusion.

111. Allegory of Music. **112.** Flag and rising Sun.

1963. Air. Baalbek Festival.
800. **111.** 35 p. orange and blue 25 15

1963. Air. Independence. 20th Anniv. Flag and Sun in red and yellow.
801. **112.** 5 p. turquoise 8 5
802. 10 p. yellow-green .. 12 10
803. 25 p. blue 20 20
804. 40 p. drab 30 30

113. Cycling. **114.** Hyacinth.

1964. 4th Mediterranean Games, Naples (1963).
805. **113.** 2 p. 50 chestnut and purple (postage) .. 5 5
806. – 5 p. orange and blue .. 5 5
807. – 10 p. brown & violet .. 8 5
808. – 15 p. orge. & grn. (air) 8 8
809. – 17 p. 50 chest. & blue 10 8
810. – 30 p. chest. & turq. .. 15 10
DESIGNS—VERT. 5 p. Basketball. 10 p. Running. 15 p. Tennis. HORIZ. 17 p. 50. Swimming. 30 p. Skiing.

1964. Flowers. Multicoloured.
811. 50 c. Type **114** (postage) .. 5 5
812. 1 p. Type **114** 5 5
813. 2 p. 50 Type **114** 5 5
814. 5 p. Cyclamen 5 5
815. 7 p. 50 Cyclamen 5 5
816. 10 p. Poinsettia 8 5
817. 17 p. 50 Anemone .. 12 5
818. 30 p. Iris 25 10
819. 50 p. Poppy 50 15
820. 5 p. Lily (air) 5 5
821. 10 p. Ranunculus 5 5
822. 20 p. Anemone 10 8
823. 40 p. Tuberose 25 12
824. 45 p. Rhododendron .. 25 15
825. 50 p. Jasmine 25 15
826. 70 p. Yellow broom .. 40 20
Nos. 816/26 are vert., size 26½ × 37 mm.

115. Cedar of Lebanon. **116.**

1964.
827. **115.** 50 c. green 5 5
828. **116.** 50 c. green 5 5
829. 2 p. 50 blue 5 5
830. 5 p. magenta 5 5
831. 7 p. 50 orange 5 5
832. 17 p. 50 purple .. 15 8

117. Boy on Rocking-horse. **119.** "Flame of Freedom".

118. League Session.

1964. Air. Children's Day.
833. – 5 p. multicoloured .. 5 5
834. – 10 p. multicoloured .. 8 8
835. **117.** 20 p. multicoloured .. 12 10
836. 40 p. multicoloured .. 20 15
DESIGN—HORIZ. 5 p., 10 p. Girls skipping.

1964. Air. Arab League Meeting.
837. **118.** 5 p. buff, brn. & blk. 12 8
838. 10 p. black 12 10
839. 15 p. blue-green .. 15 10
840. 20 p. mauve, brown and sepia 20 12

1964. Air. Declaration of Human Rights. 15th Anniv.
841. **119.** 20 p. red, salmon & brn. 10 8
842. – 40 p. orge., grey-bl. & bl. 15 12
DESIGN: 40 p. Flame on pedestal bearing U.N. emblem.

120. Sick Child. **121.** Clasped Wrists.

1964. Air. "Bal des Petits Lits Blancs" (Ball for children's charity).
843. **120.** 2 p. 50 multicoloured 5 5
844. 5 p. multicoloured .. 5 5
845. 15 p. multicoloured .. 8 5
846. – 17 p. 50 multicoloured 12 8
847. – 20 p. multicoloured .. 15 8
848. – 40 p. multicoloured .. 20 15
DESIGN—HORIZ. (55×25½ mm.): 17 p. 50 to 40 p. Children in front of palace (venue of ball).

1964. Air. World Lebanese Union Congress, Beirut.
849. **121.** 20 p. blk., yell. & grn. 15 10
850. 40 p. blk., yell. & pur. 25 20

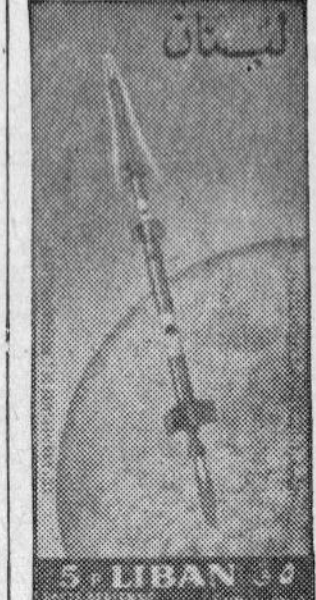

123. Temple Columns.

122. Rocket in Flight. **124.** Swimming.

1964. Air. Independence. 21st Anniv.
851. **122.** 5 p. multicoloured .. 10 10
852. 10 p. multicoloured .. 10 10
853. – 40 p. slate-blue & black 25 20
854. – 70 p. maroon & black 40 30
DESIGNS—HORIZ. 40 p., 70 p. "Struggle for Independence" (battle scene).

1965. Baalbek Festival.
855. **123.** 2 p. 50 blk. & orge. (post.) 5 5
856. – 7 p. 50 black & blue .. 12 10
857. – 10 p. mult. (air) .. 5 5
858. – 15 p. multicoloured .. 8 5
859. – 25 p. multicoloured .. 12 10
860. – 40 p. multicoloured .. 30 20
DESIGNS—VERT. (28×55 mm.): 10 p., 15 p. Man in costume. 25 p., 40 p. Woman in costume.

1965. Olympic Games, Tokyo.
861. **124.** 2 p. 50 blk., turquoise & magenta (post.) .. 5 5
862. – 7 p. 50 maroon, grey-green and sepia .. 15 15
863. – 10 p. slate, brn. & grn. 20 20
864. 15 p. blk. & grn. (air) 8 5
865. – 25 p. green & purple .. 10 10
866. – 40 p. brn. & indigo .. 20 12
DESIGNS—HORIZ. 7 p. 50, Fencing. 15 p. Horse-jumping. 40 p. Gymnastics. VERT. 10 p. Basket-ball. 25 p. Rifle-shooting.

125. "Vulcain".

1965. (a) Postage. Birds.
867. – 5 p. multicoloured .. 5 5
868. – 10 p. multicoloured .. 5 5
869. – 15 p. choc., orge. & brn. 8 5
870. – 17 p. 50 mar., red & bl. 10 5
871. – 20 p. blk., yell. & grn. 12 8
872. – 32 p. 50 yell., brn. & grn. 20 10

(b) Air. Butterflies.
873. – 30 p. yell., choc. & verm. 15 8
874. – 35 p. bl., red & bistre 15 10
875. **125.** 40 p. brn., red & grn. 20 12
876. – 45 p. brn., yell. & bl. 25 15
877. – 70 p. multicoloured .. 30 20
878. – 85 p. blk., orge. & grn. 35 25
879. – 100 p. blue & plum .. 50 30
880. – 200 p. brn., bl. & pur. 1·00 45
881. – 300 p. sepia, yellow & green .. .. 1·25 65
882. – 500 p. brown & blue .. 2·50 1·40
DESIGNS—BIRDS: 5 p. Bullfinch. 10 p. Goldfinch. 15 p. Hoopoe. 17 p. 50, Partridge. 20 p. Golden oriole. 32 p. 50, Bee-eater. BUTTERFLIES: 30 p. "Pericallia matronula". 35 p. "Heliconius cyrbia". 45 p. "Satyrus semele". 70 p. "Machaon". 85 p. "Aurore". 100 p. "Morpho cypris". 200 p. "Erasmia sanguiflua". 300 p. "Papilio crassus". LARGER (35½×25 mm.): 500 p. "Charaxes ameliae".

126. Pope Paul and Pres. Helou.

1965. Air. Pope Paul's Visit to Lebanon.
883. **126.** 45 p. violet and gold .. 65 35

127. Sheep.

1965.
884. – 50 c. brown, chestnut, red and lemon 5 5
885. – 1 p. grey, black & mve. 5 5
886. **127.** 2 p. 50 yell., sep. & grn. 5 5
DESIGNS: 50 c. Cow and calf. 1 p. Rabbit.

128. "Cedars of Friendship". **129.** "Silk Manufacture".

1965. Air.
887. **128.** 40 p. multicoloured .. 20 10

1965. Air. World Silk Congress, Beirut. Multicoloured.
888. 2 p. 50 Type **129** 5 5
889. 5 p. Type **129** 5 5
890. 7 p. 50 Type **129** 5 5
891. 15 p. Weaver and loom .. 8 5
892. 30 p. As 15 p. 15 12
893. 40 p. As 15 p. 20 12
894. 50 p. As 15 p. 30 15

130. Parliament Building.

1965. Air. Lebanese Parliament. Cent.
895. **130.** 35 p. brn., ochre & red 15 10
896. 40 p. brn., ochre & grn. 20 12

131. U.N. Emblem and Headquarters. **132.** Playing-card "King".

1965. Air. U.N. 20th Anniv.
897. **131.** 2 p. 50 blue 5 5
898. 10 p. red 5 5
899. 17 p. 50 violet .. 8 5
900. 30 p. green 12 10
901. 40 p. brown 20 12

1965. Air. World Bridge Championships, Beirut.
902. **143.** 2 p. 50 multicoloured 5 5
903. 15 p. multicoloured .. 10 5
904. 17 p. 50 multicoloured 12 5
905. 40 p. multicoloured .. 20 12

133. Dagger on Deir Yasin, Palestine. **134.** I.T.U. Emblem and Symbols.

1965. Air. Deir Yasin Massacre.
906. **133.** 50 p. red, bl., grey & blk. 30 20

1966. Air. I.T.U. Cent.
907. **134.** 2 p. 50 multicoloured 5 5
908. 15 p. multicoloured .. 8 5
909. 17 p. 50 multicoloured 10 8
910. 25 p. multicoloured .. 15 10
911. 40 p. multicoloured .. 20 15

135. Stage Performance.

1966. Air. Baalbek Festival. Multicoloured.
912. 2 p. 50 Type **135** 5 5
913. 5 p. Type **135** 5 5
914. 7 p. 50 Ballet performance 5 5
915. 15 p. Ballet performance .. 8 5
916. 30 p. Concert 12 10
917. 40 p. Concert 20 15
The 7 p. 50 and 15 p. are vert.

136. Tabarja. **137.** W.H.O. Building.

1966. Tourism Multicoloured.
918. 50 c. Hippodrome, Beirut (postage) 5 5
919. 1 p. Pigeons' Grotto .. 5 5
920. 2 p. 50 Type **136** 5 5
921. 5 p. Ruins, Beit-Mery .. 5 5
922. 7 p. 50 Ruins, Anfar .. 5 5
923. 10 p. Djezzine Falls (air) .. 5 5
924. 15 p. Saida Castle 8 5
925. 20 p. Amphitheatre, Byblos 8 5
926. 30 p. Sun Temple, Baalbek 12 5
927. 50 p. Palace, Beit ed-Din 20 8
928. 60 p. Nahr-el-Kalb .. 25 10
929. 75 p. Tripoli 40 12

1966. Air. W.H.O. Headquarters, Geneva. Inaug.
930. **137.** 7 p. 50 green 5 5
931. 17 p. 50 red 8 8
932. 25 p. blue 12 10

138. Skiing. **140.** Child in Bath.

139. Inscribed Sarcophagus.

1966. Air. Int. Cedars Festival.

933.	138.	2 p. 50 brn., red & grn.	5	5
934.	–	5 p. multicoloured ..	5	5
935.	–	17 p. 50 multicoloured	8	5
936.	–	25 p. red, brn. & grn.	15	10

DESIGNS: 5 p. Toboganning. 17 p. 50, Cedar in snow. 25 p. Ski-lift.

1966. Air. Phoenician Invention of the Alphabet.

937.	139.	10 p. brn., blk. & grn.	5	5
938.	–	15 p. brn., ochre & mve.	8	5
939.	–	20 p. sep., bl. & ochre	10	8
940.	–	30 p. brn., orge. & yell.	20	15

DESIGNS: 15 p. Phoenician ship. 20 p. Mediterranean route map showing spread of Phoenician alphabet. 30 p. Kadmos with alphabet tablet.

1966. Air. Int. Children's Day. Multicoloured.

941.	2 p. 50 Type **140** ..	5	5
942.	5 p. Boy and doll in rowing-boat	5	5
943.	7 p. 50 Girl skiing	8	5
944.	15 p. Girl giving food to bird	10	8
945.	20 p. Boy doing homework	15	10

141. Decade Emblem. 142. Rev. Daniel Bliss (founder).

1966. Air. Int. Hydrological Decade.

947.	141.	5 p. ultram., bl. & orge.	5	5
948.		10 p. red, bl. & orge...	5	5
949.	–	15 p. sep., grn. & orge.	8	5
950.	–	20 p. bl., grn. & orge.	10	8

DESIGN: 15 p., 20 p. Similar "wave" pattern.

1966. Air. American University, Beirut. Cent.

951.	142.	20 p. brn., yell. & grn.	12	5
952.	–	30 p. grn., chest. & bl.	15	10

DESIGN: 30 p. University Chapel.

Nos. 951/2 were each issued with se-tenant labels showing the University emblem.

143. I.T.Y. Emblem.

144. Beit-ed-Din Palace.

1967. Int. Tourist Year (1st issue).

(a) Postage.

954.	143.	50 c. multicoloured ..	5	5
955.		1 p. multicoloured ..	5	5
956.		2 p. 50 multicoloured	5	5
957.		5 p. multicoloured ..	5	5
958.		7 p. 50 multicoloured	5	5

(b) Air. Multicoloured.

959.	10 p. Tabarja	5	5
960.	15 p. Pigeon Rock, Beirut	5	5
961.	17 p. 50 Type **144**	5	5
962.	20 p. Sidon	8	5
963.	25 p. Tripoli	10	5
964.	30 p. Byblos	10	5
965.	35 p. Ruins, Tyre.. ..	15	5
966.	40 p. Temple, Baalbek ..	20	8

Nos. 959/66 were also used as definitives. See also Nos. 977/80.

145. Signing Pact, and Flags.

1967. Air. Arab League Pact. 22nd Anniv.

967.	145.	5 p. multicoloured ..	5	5
968.		10 p. multicoloured ..	5	5
969.		15 p. multicoloured ..	8	8
970.		20 p. multicoloured ..	10	10

146. Veterans War Memorial Building, San Francisco.

1967. Air. San Francisco Pact of 1945. Mult.

971.	2 p. 50 Type **146**	5	5
972.	5 p. Type **146**	5	5
973.	7 p. 50 Type **146**	5	5
974.	10 p. Scroll and flags of U.N. and Lebanon	5	5
975.	20 p. As 10 p.	8	5
976.	30 p. As 10 p.	12	10

147. Temple Ruins, Baalbek.

1967. Air. Int. Tourist Year (2nd issue) Multicoloured.

977.	5 p. Type **147**	5	5
978.	10 p. Ruins, Anjar ..	8	5
979.	15 p. Ancient bridge, Nahr-Ibrahim	10	5
980.	20 p. Grotto, Jeita ..	12	5

148.

1967. Air. India Day.

981.	148.	2 p. 50 vermilion ..	5	5
982.		5 p. claret	5	5
983.		7 p. 50 brown.. ..	5	5
984.		10 p. blue	5	5
985.		15 p. green	10	5

149.

1967. Air. Lebanon's Admission to U.N. 22nd Anniv.

986.	149.	2 p. 50 red	5	5
987.		5 p. blue	5	5
988.		7 p. 50 green	5	5
989.	–	10 p. red	8	5
990.	–	20 p. ultramarine ..	10	5
991.	–	30 p. green	12	8

DESIGN: 10, 20, 30 p. U.N. Emblem.

150. Goat and Kid.

1967. Animals and Fishes. Multicoloured.

992.	50 c. Type **150** (postage)	5	5
993.	1 p. Cattle	5	5
994.	2 p. 50 Sheep	5	5
995.	5 p. Dromedaries ..	5	5
996.	10 p. Donkey	5	5
997.	15 p. Horses	8	5
998.	20 p. Shark (air).. ..	8	5
999.	30 p. Needle-fish.. ..	10	5
1000.	40 p. Pollock	12	8
1001.	50 p. Wrasse	20	10
1002.	70 p. Red mullet ..	30	15
1003.	100 p. Salmon	45	20

151. Ski-jumping.

1968. Air. Int. Ski Congress. Beirut.

1004.	151.	2 p. 50 multicoloured	5	5
1005.	–	5 p. multicoloured ..	5	5
1006.	–	7 p. 50 multicoloured	5	5
1007.		10 p. multicoloured..	5	5
1008.		25 p. multicoloured..	12	8

DESIGNS: 5 p. to 10 p. Skiing (all different). 25 p. Congress emblem of Cedar and skis.

152. Princess Khaskiah.

1968. Air. Emir Fakhreddine II Commem. Multicoloured.

1009.	2 p. 50 Type **152** ..	5	5
1010.	5 p. Emir Fakhreddine II	5	5
1011.	10 p. Saida Citadel ..	5	5
1012.	15 p. Chekif Citadel ..	8	5
1013.	17 p. 50 Beirut Citadel ..	10	5

The 10 p., 15 p. and 17 p. 50 are horiz. designs.

153. Colonnade.

1968. Air. Tyre Antiquities.

1014.	–	2 p. 50 brn., cream & pink	5	5
1015.	153.	5 p. brn., bl. & yell...	5	5
1016.	–	7 p. 50 brn., buff & grn.	5	5
1017.	–	10 p. brn., bl. & orge.	5	5

DESIGNS—VERT. 2 p. 50, Roman Bust. 10 p. Bas-relief. HORIZ. 7 p. 50, Arch.

154. Justinian and Mediterranean Map.

1968. Air. Faculty of Law, Beirut. 1st Anniv. Multicoloured.

1019.	5 p. Justinian (vert.) ..	5	5
1020.	10 p. Justinian (vert.) ..	5	5
1021.	15 p. Type **154**	8	5
1022.	20 p. Type **154**	10	5

155. Arab League Emblem. 157. Jupiter's Temple Ruins, Baalbeck.

156. Cedar on Globe.

1968. Air. Arab Appeal Week.

1023.	155.	5 p. multicoloured ..	5	5
1024.		10 p. multicoloured..	5	5
1025.		15 p. multicoloured..	8	5
1026.		20 p. multicoloured..	10	5

1968. Air. 3rd World Lebanese Union Congress.

1027.	156.	2 p. 50 multicoloured	5	5
1028.		5 p. multicoloured ..	5	5
1029.		7 p. 50 multicoloured	5	5
1030.		10 p. multicoloured..	5	5

1968. Air. Baalbek Festival. Multicoloured.

1031.	5 p. Type **157**	5	5
1032.	10 p. Bacchus' Temple ..	5	5
1033.	15 p. Corniche, Jupiter's Temple..	8	5
1034.	20 p. Portal, Bacchus' Temple..	10	8
1035.	25 p. Columns, Bacchus' Temple..	12	10

158. Long-jumping and Atlantes.

1968. Air. Olympic Games, Mexico.

1036.	158.	5 p. blk., yell. & bl...	5	5
1037.	–	10 p. blk., bl. & pur...	5	5
1038.	–	15 p. sepia, drab, yell. and olive ..	5	5
1039.	–	20 p. sepia, drab, yell. and orange ..	8	5
1040.	–	25 p. brown	12	8

DESIGNS (each incorporating Aztec relic): 10 p. High-jumping. 15 p. Fencing. 20 p. Weightlifting. 25 p. "Sailing boat" with oars.

159. Lebanese driving Tractor ("Work protection"). 160. Minshiya Stairs.

1968. Air. Human Rights Year. Mult.

1041.	10 p. Type **159**	5	5
1042.	15 p. Citizens ("Social Security")	5	5
1043.	25 p. Young men of three races ("Unity") ..	10	8

1968. Air. 1st Municipal Council (Deir el Kamar) Cent. Multicoloured.

1044.	10 p. Type **160**	5	5
1045.	15 p. Seral kiosk.. ..	5	5
1046.	25 p. Ancient highway ..	10	8

161. Nurse and Child.

1969. Air. U.N.I.C.E.F. Commem. Mult.

1047.	161.	5 p. blk., brn. & bl...	5	5
1048.	–	10 p. blk., grn. & yell.	5	5
1049.	–	15 p. black, vermilion and purple ..	5	5
1050.	–	20 p. blk., bl. & yell.	8	5
1051.	–	25 p. black, ochre and magenta	10	8

DESIGNS: 10 p. Produce. 15 p. Mother and child. 20 p. Child with book. 25 p. Children with flowers.

162. Ancient Coin.

1969. Air. Int. Museums Council (I.C.O.M.) 20th Anniv. Exhibits in National Museum Beirut. Multicoloured.

1052.	2 p 50 Type **162** ..	5	5
1053.	5 p. Gold dagger, Byblos	5	5
1054.	7 p. 50 Detail of Ahiram's Sarcophagus ..	5	5
1055.	30 p. Jewelled pectoral ..	10	8
1056.	40 p. Khalde "bird" vase	12	10

163. Water-skiing.

1969. Air. Water-Sports. Multicoloured.

1057.	2 p. 50 Type **163** ..	5	5
1058.	5 p. Water-skiing (group)	5	5
1059.	7 p. 50 Water-skiing with parachute	5	5
1060.	30 p. Sailing	10	5
1061.	40 p. Yacht-racing ..	15	12

The 7 p. 50 and 30 p. are vert.

164. Frontier Guard.

1969. Air. Independence. 25th Anniv. The Lebanese Army.

1062.	2 p. Type **164**	5	5
1063.	5 p. Unknown Soldier's Tomb	5	5
1064.	7 p. 50 Army Foresters ..	5	5
1065.	15 p. Road-making ..	5	5
1066.	30 p. Military Ambulance and Helicopter ..	10	5
1067.	40 p. Skiing Patrol ..	15	8

165. Concentric Red Crosses.

1971. Air. Lebanese Red Cross. 25th Anniv.

1068.	165.	15 p. verm. & black.	8	5
1069.	–	85 p. verm. & black.	40	30

DESIGN: 85 p. Red Cross in shape of cedar of Lebanon.

166. Flags of Arab States and Foil.

1971. Air. 10th Int. Fencing Championships. Multicoloured.

1070.	10 p. Type **166**	5	5
1071.	15 p. Foil and flags of foreign nations ..	5	5
1072.	35 p. Contest with foils ..	12	10
1073.	40 p. Epee contest	15	12
1074.	50 p. Contest with sabres	20	15

167. 12th-Century Arab Painting.

1971. Air. Int. Labour Organization. 50th Anniv. (1969).

1075.	167	10 p. multicoloured..	5	5
1076.		40 p. multicoloured..	15	12

168. U.P.U. Monument and New H.Q. Building, Berne.

1971. Air. New U.P.U. Headquarters Building, Berne.

1077.	168.	15 p. red, blk. & yell.	5	5
1078.		35 p. yell., blk. & pink	15	12

169. "Ravens setting fire to Owls" (14th-century painting).

1971. Air. Children's Day. Multicoloured.

1079.	15 p. Type **169**	5	5
1080.	85 p. "The Lion and the Jackal" (13th-century painting (horiz. 39 × 29 mm.)	35	25

170. Arab League Flag and Map.

1971. Air. Arab League. 25th Anniv.

1081.	170.	30 p. multicoloured..	10	8
1082.		70 p. multicoloured..	30	20

171. Interior of T.V. Set (" Industry ").

1971. Air. Multicoloured.

1083.	5 p. Jamhour Electricity Sub-station ..	5	5
1084.	10 p. Maameltein Bridge	5	5
1085.	15 p. Hoteliers' School ..	5	5
1086.	20 p. Litani Dam ..	8	5
1087.	25 p. Type **171** ..	10	5
1088.	35 p. Bziza Temple ..	15	5
1089.	40 p. Jounieh Harbour ..	15	5
1090.	45 p. Radar scanner, Beirut Airport	20	8
1091.	50 p. Hibiscus	20	10
1092.	70 p. School of Sciences Building	30	10
1093.	85 p. Oranges ..	35	12
1094.	100 p. Satellite Communications Station, Arbanieh	40	20

172. Insignia of Iman al Ouzai (theologian).

1971. Air. Lebanese Celebrities.

1095.	172.	25 p. brn. gold & grn.	10	8
1096.	–	25 p. brn., gold & yell.	10	8
1097.	–	25 p. brn., gold & yell.	10	8
1098.	–	25 p. brn., gold & grn.	10	8

PORTRAITS: No. 1096, Bechara el Khoury (poet and writer). No. 1097, Hassan Kamel el Sabbah (scientist). No. 1098, Gibran Khalil Gibran (writer).

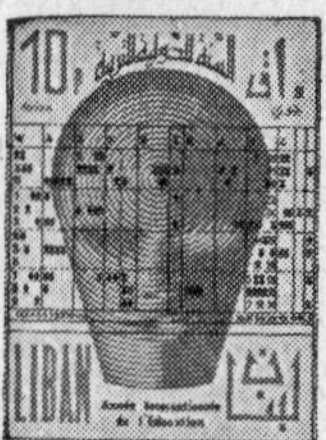

173. I.E.Y. Emblem.

1971. Air. Int. Education Year.

1099.	173.	10 p. multicoloured..	5	5
1100.		40 p. multicoloured..	15	12

174. Dahr-el-Basheq Sanatorium.

176. Field-gun.

1971. Air. Tuberculosis Relief Campaign.

1101.	174.	50 p. multicoloured..	25	15
1102.	–	100 p. multicoloured	40	25

DESIGN: 100 p. Different view of Sanatorium.

175. Wheel Emblem.

1971. Air. 16th Baalbek Festival.

1103.	175.	15 p. orge. & blue ..	5	5
1104.	–	85 p. blk , bl. & orge.	35	25

DESIGN: 85 p. Corinthian capital.

1971. Air. Army Day. Multicoloured.

1105.	15 p. Type **176**	5	5
1106.	25 p. "Mirage" jet fighters	10	8
1107.	40 p. Army Command H.Q.	15	12
1108.	70 p. Patrol-boat ..	30	20

177. Interior Decoration. 179. U.N. Emblem.

178. Lenin.

1971. Air. Burning of Al-Aqsa Mosque, Jerusalem. 2nd Anniv.

1109.	177.	15 p. yell.-brn. & brn.	5	5
1110.		35 p. yell.-brn. & brn.	15	12

1971. Air. Lenin Birth Cent. Multicoloured.

1111.	30 p. Type **178**	12	8
1112.	70 p. Lenin in profile ..	30	20

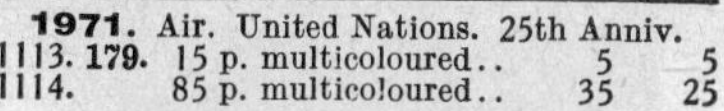

1971. Air. United Nations. 25th Anniv.

1113.	179.	15 p. multicoloured..	5	5
1114.		85 p. multicoloured..	35	25

180. "Europa" Mosaic, Byblos.

1971. Air. World Lebanese Union.

1115.	180.	10 p. multicoloured..	5	5
1116.		40 p. multicoloured..	15	10

1972. Various stamps surch.

1117.	5 p. on 7 p. 50 (No. 922) (postage)	5	5
1118.	5 p. on 7 p. 50 (No. 958)..	5	5
1119.	25 p. on 32 p. 50 (No. 872)	10	8
1120.	5 p. on 7 p. 50 (No. 1016) (air)	5	5
1121.	100 p. on 300 p. (No. 881)	40	30
1122.	100 p. on 500 p. (No. 882)	40	30
1123.	200 p. on 300 p. (No. 881)	80	60

181. Roses.

182. Arches.

1973. Air. Multicoloured.

1124.	2 p. 50 Morning glory ..	5	5
1125.	5 p. Type **181**	5	5
1126.	15 p. Tulips	5	5
1127.	25 p. Lilies	10	5
1128.	40 p. Carnations	15	5
1129.	50 p. Iris	20	5
1130.	70 p. Apples	30	5
1131.	75 p. Grapes	30	5
1132.	100 p. Peaches	40	8
1133.	200 p. Pears	80	15
1134.	300 p. Cherries	1·25	25
1135.	500 p. Oranges	2·00	50

1973. Air. Lebanese Domestic Architecture.

1136.	–	35 p. multicoloured..	15	12
1137.	182.	50 p. multicoloured..	20	15
1138.	–	85 p. multicoloured..	35	30
1139.	–	100 p. multicoloured	40	35

DESIGNS: Nos. 1136 and 1138/39, Various Lebanese dwellings.

183. Girl with Lute.

1973. Air. Ancient Costumes. Multicoloured.

1140.	5 p. Woman with rose ..	5	5
1141.	10 p. Seated man ..	5	5
1142.	20 p. Horseman	8	5
1143.	25 p. Type **183**	10	8

184. Swimming.

1973. Air 5th Pan-Arab Schools' Games, Beirut. Multicoloured.

1144.	5 p. Type **184**	5	5
1145.	10 p. Running	5	5
1146.	15 p. Gymnastics ..	5	5
1147.	20 p. Volleyball	8	5
1148.	25 p. Basketball	10	8
1149.	50 p. Table-tennis ..	20	15
1150.	75 p. Handball	30	25
1151.	100 p. Football	40	35

185. Brasilia.

1973. Air. Brazil's Independence. 150th Anniv. Multicoloured.

1153. 5 p. Type **185** 5 5
1154. 20 p. Salvador (Bahia) in 1823 .. .. .. 8 5
1155. 25 p. Map and ancient galley 10 8
1156. 50 p. Emperor Pedro I and Emir Fakhreddine II .. 20 15

186. Marquetry.

187. Cedar of Lebanon.

1973. Air. Lebanese Handicrafts. Mult.

1157. 10 p. Type **186** 5 5
1158. 20 p. Weaving 8 5
1159. 35 p. Glass-blowing .. 15 12
1160. 40 p. Pottery 15 12
1161. 50 p. Metal-working .. 20 15
1162. 70 p. Cutlery-making .. 30 25
1163. 85 p. Lace-making .. 35 30
1164. 100 p. Handicrafts Museum 40 35

1974.

1165. **187.** 50 c. grn., brn. & oran. 5 5

188. Camp Site and Emblems.

1974. Air. Arab Scout Jamboree, Smar-Jubeil, Lebanon. Multicoloured.

1166. 2 p. Type **188** 5 5
1167. 5 p. Scout badge and map 5 5
1168. 7 p. 50 Map of Arab countries 5 5
1169. 10 p. Lord Baden-Powell and Baalbek 5 5
1170. 15 p. Guide and camp .. 8 5
1171. 20 p. Lebanese Guide and Scout badge 8 5
1172. 25 p. Scouts around camp-fire 12 10
1173. 30 p. Globe and Scout badge 12 10
1174. 35 p. Flags of participating countries 15 12
1175. 50 p. Scout chopping wood for old man 20 15

189. Mail Train.

1974. Universal Postal Union. Cent. Multicoloured.

1176. 5 p. Type **189** 5 5
1177. 20 p. Container ship .. 8 5
1178. 25 p. Congress building, Lausanne, and U.P.U. H.Q., Berne 8 5
1179. 50 p. Mail-plane 20 15

190. Congress Building, Sofar.

192. Hunter killing Lion.

191. " Mountain Road " (O. Onsi) (vert.)

1974. Air. Arab Postal Union. 25th Anniv. Multicoloured.

1180. 5 p. Type **190** 5 5
1181. 20 p. View of Sofar .. 8 5
1182. 25 p. A.P.U. H.Q., Cairo 8 5
1183. 50 p. Ministry of Posts, Beirut 20 15

1974. Air. Lebanese Paintings. Mult.

1184. 50 p. Type **191** 20 15
1185. 50 p. " Clouds " (M. Farroukh) .. 20 15
1186. 50 p. " Woman " (G. K. Gebran) .. 20 15
1187. 50 p. " Embrace " (C. Gemayel) 20 15
1188. 50 p. " Self-portrait " (H. Serour) 20 15
1189. 50 p. " Portrait " (D. Corm) 20 15

1974. Air. Hermel Excavations. Mult.

1190. 5 p. Type **192** 5 5
1191. 10 p. Astarte 5 5
1192. 25 p. Dogs hunting boar .. 8 5
1193. 35 p. Greco-Roman tomb 15 12

193. Book Year Emblem.

1974. Air. International Book Year (1972).

1194. **193.** 5 p. multicoloured .. 5 5
1195. 10 p. multicoloured .. 5 5
1196. 25 p. multicoloured .. 8 5
1197. 35 p. multicoloured .. 15 12

194. Magnifying Glass.

1974. Air. Stamp Day. Multicoloured.

1198. 5 p. Type **194** 5 5
1199. 10 p. Linked posthorns .. 5 5
1200. 15 p. Stamp-printing .. 8 5
1201. 20 p. " Stamp " in mount 8 5

195. Georgina Rizk in Lebanese Costume (vert.).

1974. Air. Miss Universe 1971 (Georgina Rizk). Multicoloured.

1202. 5 p. Type **195** 5 5
1203. 20p. Head-and-shoulders portrait 8 5
1204. 25 p. Type **195** 8 5
1205. 50 p. As 20 p. 20 15

196. U.N.I.C.E.F. Emblem and Helicopter.

1974. Air. U.N.I.C.E.F. 25th Anniv. Mult.

1207. 20 p. Type **196** 8 5
1208. 25 p. Emblem and child welfare clinic 8 5
1209. 35 p. Emblem and kindergarten class 15 12
1210. 70 p. Emblem and schoolgirls in laboratory .. 30 25

199. Symbols of Archaeology.

1975. Air. " Beirut—University City ". Multicoloured.

1212. 20 p. Type **199** 8 5
1213. 25 p. Science and medicine 8 5
1214. 35 p. Law and commerce 15 12
1215. 70 p. Industry & commerce 30 25

POSTAGE DUE STAMPS

1924. Postage Due stamps of France surch. **GRAND LIBAN** and value in "CENTIEMES" or "PIASTRES".

D 26. D 2. 50 c. on 10 c. brown 50 45
D 27. 1 p. on 20 c. olive .. 50 45
D 28. 2 p. on 30 c. red .. 50 45
D 29. 3 p. on 50 c. purple .. 50 45
D 30. 5 p. on 1 f. claret on yellow 50 45

1924. Postage Due stamps of France surch. **GdLiban** and value in English and Arabic.

D 58. D 2. 50 c. on 10 c. brown .. 45 30
D 59. 1 p. on 20 c. olive .. 45 30
D 60. 2 p. on 30 c. red .. 45 30
D 61. 3 p. on 50 c. purple .. 45 30
D 62. 5 p. on 1 f. claret on yellow 45 30

D 1. Nahr-el-Kelb.

DESIGNS — HORIZ. 1 p. Pine Forest, Beirut. 2 p. Pigeon Grotto, Beirut. 3 p. Beaufort Castle. 5 p. Baalbek.

1925.

D 75. D 1. 50 c. brown on yellow 5 5
D 76. – 1 p. black on red .. 10 10
D 77. – 2 p. black on blue .. 15 15
D 78. – 3 p. brown on orange 45 45
D 79. – 5 p. black on green .. 1·00 70

1927. Optd. **Republique Libanaise** and bars.

D 122. D 1. 50 c. brown on yellow 8 8
D 123. – 1 p. black on red .. 12 12
D 124. – 2 p. black on blue .. 25 25
D 125. – 5 p. brown on orange 50 50
D 126. – 5 p. black on green 65 65

1928. Nos. D 16/20 optd. with T **4.**

D 145. D 1. 50 .c brown on yellow 15 5
D 146. – 1 p. black on red .. 25 12
D 147. – 2 p. black on blue .. 80 40
D 148. – 3 p. brown on orange 90 40
D 149. – 5 p. black on green 1·50 80

D 2.

D 3. Bas-relief from Sarcophagus of King Ahiram at Byblos.

D 4.

DESIGNS: 1 p. Bas-relief of a ship. 2 p. Arabesque. 3 p. Garland. 15 p. Statuettes.

1931.

D 191. D 2. 50 c. black on red .. 5 5
D 192. – 1 p. black on blue .. 12 12
D 193. – 2 p. black on yellow 8 8
D 194. – 3 p. black on green .. 15 15
D 195. D 4. 5 p. black on orange 65 65
D 196. D 3. 8 p. black on red .. 30 30
D 252. D 4. 10 p. green .. .. 1·50 60
D 197. – 15 p. black 40 40

D 5. National Museum.

1945.

D 298. D 5. 2 p. black on lemon 40 20
D 299. 5 p. blue on red .. 40 20
D 300. 25 p. blue on green 80 25
D 301. 50 p. purple on blue 1·00 40

D 6.

1947.

D 352. D 6. 5 p. black on green 60 8
D 353. 25 p. black on yellow 6·50 25
D 354. 50 p. black on blue 2·50 50

D 7. Monument at Hermel.

1948.

D 379. D 7. 2 p. black on yellow 40 8
D 380. 3 p. black on red .. 1·10 20
D 381. 10 p. black on blue 2·75 55

D 8.

1950.

D 416. D 8. 1 p. red 20 5
D 417. 5 p. blue 60 12
D 418. 10 p. green .. .. 1·10 25

D 9.

1952.

D 464. D 9. 1 p. magenta .. 5 5
D 465. 2 p. violet 8 5
D 466. 3 p. green 12 5
D 467. 5 p. blue 15 5
D 468. 10 p. brown .. 20 5
D 469. 25 p. black .. .. 1·50 15

D 10.

D 11.

1953.

D 481. D 10. 1 p. red 5 5
D 482. 2 p. green 5 5
D 483. 3 p. orange .. 5 5
D 484. 5 p. purple .. 5 5
D 485. 10 p. brown .. 10 5
D 486. 15 p. blue 25 8

1955.

D 550. D 11. 1 p. brown .. 5 5
D 551. 2 p. green 5 5
D 552. 3 p. turquoise .. 5 5
D 553. 5 p. red 5 5
D 554. 10 p. myrtle .. 5 5
D 555. 15 p. blue 8 5
D 556. 25 p. purple .. 15 8

D 12.

D 13. Emir Fakhreddine II.

1967.

D 967. D 12. 1 p. green 5 5
D 968. 5 p. mauve 5 5
D 969. 15 p. blue 5 5

1968.

D 1004. D 13. p. slate and grey 5 5
D 1005. 2 p. bluish grn. & grn. 5 5
D 1006. 3 p. orge. & yell.-orge. 5 5
D 1007. 5 p. purple and reddish purple 5 5
D 1008. 10 p. olive & yell.-ol. 5 5
D 1009. 15 p. violet-blue and pale violet-blue 5 5
D 1010. 25 p. bl. & pale blue 10 8

POSTAL TAX STAMPS

These were issued between 1946 and 1962 for compulsory use on inland mail (and sometimes on mail to Arab countries) to provide funds for various purposes.

(T 1.) (T 2.)

1946. Lebanese Army. Fiscal stamp as Type T 1 surch. with Type T 2.

T 334. T 1. 5 p. on 30 p. brown 5·00 30

طابع فلسطين

ضريبة فلسطين

(T 3.) (T 4.)

1948. Lebanese Army. Type T 1 surch. with T **3.**

T 363. T 1. 5 p. on 30 c. brown .. 5·00 50

1948. Aid to War in Palestine. Surch. as Type T 2 but with top line as Type **4.**

T 369. T 1. 5 p. on 10 p. red .. 24·00 1·00
T 364. 5 p. on 25 c. green 5·00 50
T 365. 5 p. on 30 c. brown 7·00 50
T 366. 5 p. on 60 c. blue .. 11·00 50
T 367. 5 p. on 3 p. pink .. 5·00 50
T 368. 5 p. on 15 p. blue .. 5·50 50

The top line of the overprint on No. T 369 differs from Type T **4,** and No. T367 comes both as Type T **4** and also with a similar inscription.

1948. Aid to War in Palestine. As No. T 367 but with figure "5" at left instead of "0" and without inscr. between figures.

T 371. T 1. 5 p. on 3 p. pink .. £160 6·00

T 5. Family and Ruined House.

1956. Earthquake Victims.
T 559. T 5. 2 p. 50 brown .. 45 5

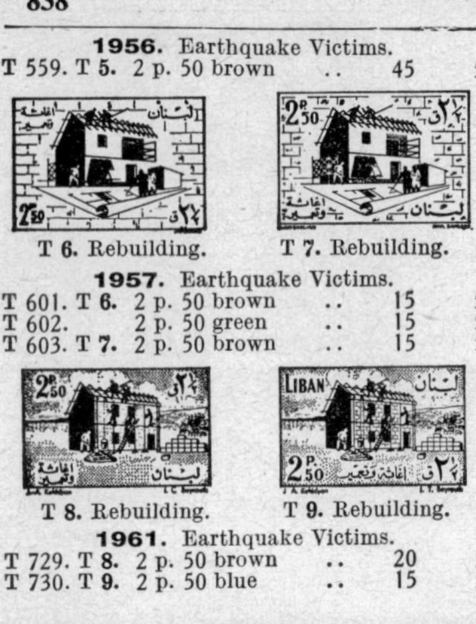

T 6. Rebuilding. T 7. Rebuilding.

1957. Earthquake Victims.
T 601. T 6. 2 p. 50 brown .. 15 5
T 602. 2 p. 50 green .. 15 5
T 603. T 7. 2 p. 50 brown .. 15 5

T 8. Rebuilding. T 9. Rebuilding.

1961. Earthquake Victims.
T 729. T 8. 2 p. 50 brown .. 20 5
T 730. T 9. 2 p. 50 blue .. 15 5

LEEWARD ISLANDS BC

A group of islands in the Br. W. Indies, including Antigua, Barbuda, Dominica (till end of 1939), Montserrat, Nevis, St. Christopher (St. Kitts) and Virgin Islands. Stamps of Leeward Islands were used concurrently with the issues for the respective islands until they were withdrawn on the 1st July, 1956.

1951. 100 cents = 1 West Indian dollar.

1.

(2.)

1890.
1. 1. ½d. mauve and green .. 25 15
2. 1d. mauve and red .. 45 15
3. 2½d. mauve and blue .. 1·25 35
4. 4d. mauve and orange .. 2·50 2·50
5. 6d. mauve and brown .. 2·50 2·75
6. 7d. mauve and grey .. 1·75 2·50
7. 1s. green and red .. .. 10·00 10·00
8. 5s. green and blue .. 50·00 60·00

1897. Diamond Jubilee. Optd. with T 2.
9. 1. ½d. mauve and green .. 3·00 4·00
10. 1d. mauve and red .. 3·00 4·50
11. 2½d. mauve and blue .. 4·00 4·50
12. 4d. mauve and orange .. 10·00 12·00
13. 6d. mauve and brown .. 18·00 20·00
14. 7d. mauve and grey .. 18·00 20·00
15. 1s. green and red .. 70·00 85·00
16. 5s. green and blue .. £350 £350

1902. Surch. in words.
17. 1. 1d. on 4d. mauve & orange 85 2·00
18. 1d. on 6d. mauve & brown 55 2·00
19. 1d. on 7d. mauve and grey 85 2·00

1902. As T 1, but portrait of King Edward VII.
29. ½d. purple and green .. 20 25
21. 1d. purple and red 55 20
22. 2d. purple and brown .. 1·25 1·25
23. 2½d. purple and blue .. 1·40 1·40
24. 3d. purple and black .. 1·25 1·75
25. 6d. purple and brown .. 1·40 4·00
26. 1s. green and red .. 4·50 4·50
27. 2s. 6d. green and black .. 11·00 11·00
28. 5s. green and blue .. .. 18·00 23·00

1907. As last. Colours changed.
36. ½d. brown 12 30
37. ½d. green 25 15
38. 1d. red 40 15
39. 2d. grey .. .. .. 65 2·00
40. 2½d. blue .. .. .. 75 1·60
41. 3d. purple and yellow .. 95 1·90
42. 6d. purple .. .. .. 1·00 2·00
43. 1s. black on green .. .. 3·50 5·50
44. 2s. 6d. black & red on blue 11·00 15·00
45. 5s. green and red on yellow 24·00 26·00

4. King George V

6. King George VI.

1912.
46a.4. ¼d. brown 20 20
59. ½d. green 12 20
62. 1d. red 10 10
61. 1d. violet 15 15
63. 1½d. red 15 40
64. 1½d. brown 12 10
65. 2d. grey 25 40
67. 2½d. blue 40 40
66. 2½d. yellow .. .. 4·00 8·00
51. 3d. purple on yellow .. 40 1·10
68. 3d. blue .. .. .. 3·50 4·00
70. 4. 4d. black & red on yellow 50 1·75
71. 5d. purple and green .. 40 1·95
53. 6d. purple .. .. .. 65 1·50
54. 1s. black on green .. 2·75 2·25
55. 2s. purple & blue on blue 2·75 4·00
56. 2s. 6d. black & red on blue 9·00 8·50
76. 3s. green and violet .. 7·00 10·00
77. 4s. black and red .. .. 8·00 12·00
57. 5s. green & red on yellow 10·00 11·00
Larger type, as T 7 of Bermuda.
79. 10s. green and red on green 30·00 35·00
80. £1 purple and black on red 60·00 80·00

1935. Silver Jubilee. As T 11 of Antigua.
88. 1d. blue and red .. 15 15
89. 1½d. blue and grey .. 25 45
90. 2½d. brown and blue .. 95 1·25
91. 1s. grey and purple .. 2·00 2·75

1937. Coronation. As T 2 of Aden.
92. 1d. red 15 15
93. 1½d. brown 15 15
94. 2½d. blue 25 25

1938.
95. 6. ¼d. brown 15 15
96. ½d. green 15 15
97. ½d. grey 15 15
99. 1d. red 15 15
100. 1d. green 15 15
101. 1½d. brown 15 15
102. 1½d. orange and black .. 15 15
103. 2d. grey 15 15
104. 2d. red 40 40
105. 2½d. blue 15 15
106. 2½d. black and purple .. 30 25
107a. 3d. orange 30 30
108. 3d. blue 25 15
109. 6d. purple 15 15
110. 1s. black on green .. 55 55
111. 2s. purple & blue on blue 1·25 1·00
112. 5s. green & red on yellow 1·75 2·00
113. 10s. green & red on green 4·50 5·00
114b. £1 purple and black on red 5·30 9·00
Nos. 113/4b are as T 7 of Bermuda but with portrait of King George VI.

1946. Victory. As T 4 of Aden.
115. 1½d. brown 8 8
116. 3d. orange 8 8

1949. Silver Wedding. As T 5/6 of Aden.
117. 2½d. blue 8 8
118. 5s. green .. .. 2·75 3·50

1949. U.P.U. As T 14/17 of Antigua.
119. 2½d. black 12 12
120. 3d. blue 20 25
121. 6d. magenta 40 40
122. 1s. green 55 55

1951. Inaug. of B.W.I. University College. As T 18/19 of Antigua.
123. 18. 3 c. orange and black .. 10 10
124. 19. 12 c. red and violet .. 25 25

1953. Coronation. As T 7 of Aden.
125. 3 c. black and green .. 20 30

1954. As T 6 but portrait of Queen Elizabeth II facing left.
126. ½ c. brown 5 5
127. 1 c. grey 5 5
128. 2 c. green 5 5
129. 3 c. yellow and black .. 5 5
130. 4 c. red 5 5
131. 5 c. black and purple .. 5 5
132. 6 c. yellow 5 5
133. 8 c. blue 8 8
134. 12 c. purple 12 12
135. 24 c. black and green .. 25 30
136. 48 c. purple and blue .. 60 60
137. 60 c. brown and green .. 70 80
138. $1.20 green and red .. 1·00 1·10
Larger type as T 7 of Bermuda.
139. $2.40 green and red .. 2·00 2·50
140. $4.80 purple and black 3·50 4·00

LESOTHO BC

Formerly Basutoland, attained independence on 4th October, 1966, and changed its name to Lesotho.

1. Moshoeshoe I and Moshoeshoe II.

1966. Independence.
106. 1. 2½ c. brown, black & red 5 5
107. 5 c. brown, black & blue 8 8
108. 10 c. brown, black & grn. 20 20
109. 20 c. brown, black & pur. 30 35

1966. Nos. 69 etc. of Basutoland optd. LESOTHO.
110. 3. ½ c. black and sepia .. 5 5
111. – 1 c. black and green .. 5 5
112. – 2 c. blue and orange .. 5 5
113. 6. 2½ c. sage and red .. 8 8
114. – 3½ c. indigo and blue .. 5 5
115. – 5 c. chestnut and green .. 12 12
116. – 10 c. bronze and purple .. 20 25
117. – 12½ c. brown & turquoise 45 45
118. – 25 c. blue and crimson .. 40 45
119. – 50 c. black and red 80 1·25
120. 4. 1 r. black and maroon .. 1·50 2·50

2. "Education, Culture and Science".

1966. U.N.E.S.C.O. 20th Anniv.
121. 2. 2½ c. yellow and green .. 5 5
122. 5 c. green and olive .. 8 8
123. 12½ c. blue and red 15 20
124. 25 c. orange and blue .. 35 45

3. Maize.

1967.
147. 3. ½ c. green and violet .. 5 5
148. – 1 c. sepia and red .. 5 5
149. – 2 c. yellow and green .. 5 5
150. – 2½ c. black and ochre .. 8 8
151. – 3 c. choc., green & brown 10 10
152. – 3½ c. blue and yellow .. 10 12
153. – 5 c. bistre and blue .. 12 15
154. – 10 c. brown and grey .. 20 25
155. – 12½ c. black and orange 25 25
156. – 25 c. black and blue .. 50 60
157. – 50 c. black, blue & turq. 1·00 1·25
158. – 1 r. multicoloured .. 2·00 2·25
159. – 2 r. black, gold & mag. 4·00 4·50
DESIGNS—HORIZ. 1 c. Cattle. 2 c. Aloes. 2½ c. Basotho Hat. 3 c. Sorghum. 3½ c. Merino Sheep ("Wool"). 5 c. Basotho Pony. 10 c. Wheat. 12½ c. Angora Goat ("Mohair"). 25 c. Maletsunyane Falls. 50 c. Diamonds. 1 r. Arms of Lesotho. VERT. 2 r. Moshoeshoe II.
See also Nos. 191/203.

4. Students and University.

1967. 1st Conferment of University Degrees.
137. 4. 1 c. sepia, ultram. & orge. 5 5
138. 2½ c. sepia, ultram. & blue 5 5
139. 12½ c. sepia, ultram. & red 15 20
140. 25 c. sepia, ultram. & vio. 30 35

5. Statue of Moshoeshoe I.

1967. Independence. 1st Anniv.
141. 5. 2½ c. black and green .. 5 5
142. – 12½ c. multicoloured .. 20 20
143. – 25 c. black, green & ochre 30 30
DESIGNS: 12½ c. National Flag. 25 c. Crocodile (national emblem).

6. Lord Baden-Powell and Scout Saluting.

1967. Scout Movement. 60th Anniv.
144. 6. 15 c. multicoloured .. 20 25

7. W.H.O. Emblem and World Map.

1968. World Health Organization. 20th Anniv.
145. 7. 2½ c. blue, gold and red .. 5 5
146. – 25 c. multicoloured .. 30 35
DESIGN: 25 c. Nurse and Child.

8. Running Hunters.

1968. Rock Paintings.
160. 8. 3 c. brn., bl.-grn. & grn. 5 8
161. – 3½ c. yellow, olive & sep. 8 8
162. – 5 c. red, ochre & brown 10 10
163. – 10 c. yellow, red & maroon 15 15
164. – 15 c. buff, yellow & brn. 25 25
165. – 20 c. green, yellow & brn. 35 35
166. – 25 c. yellow, chest. & blk. 40 40
DESIGNS—HORIZ. 3½ c. Baboons. 10 c. Archers. 20 c. Eland. 25 c. Hunting Scene. VERT. 5 c. Javelin thrower. 15 c. Blue Cranes.

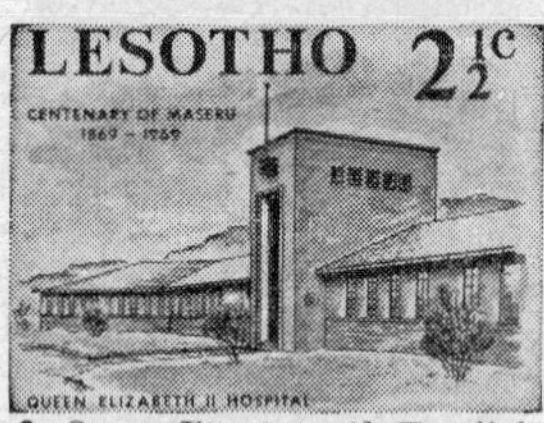

9. Queen Elizabeth II Hospital.

1969. Maseru (capital). Cent. Multicoloured.
167. 2½ c. Type 9 .. .. 5 5
168. 10 c. Lesotho Radio Station 15 15
169. 12½ c. Leabua Jonathan Airport 20 25
170. 25 c. Royal Palace .. 35 35

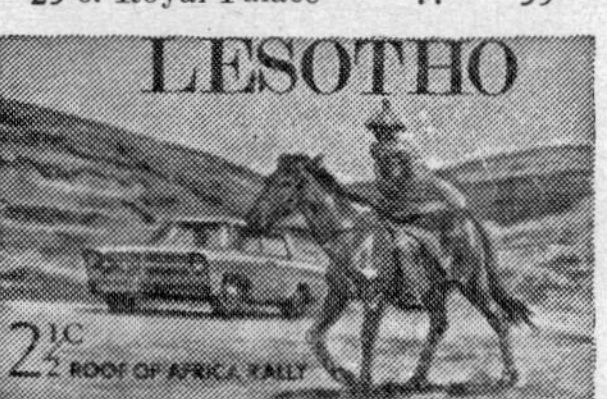

10. Rally Car passing Basuto Tribesman.

1969. "Roof of Africa" Car Rally.
171. 10. 2½ c. yell., mve. & plum 5 5
172. – 12½ c. blue, yell. & grey 20 20
173. – 15 c. blue, blk. & mauve 20 25
174. – 20 c. blk., red & yellow 30 35
DESIGNS: 12½ c. Rally car on mountain road. 15 c. Chequered flags and "Roof of Africa" Plateau. 20 c. Map of rally route and Independence Trophy.

11. Gryponyx and Footprints.

1970. Prehistoric Reptiles' Footprints.
175. – 3 c. brown and sepia .. 5 5
176. 11. 5 c. purple, pink & sepia 10 10
177. – 10 c. yell., blk. & sepia 20 20
178. – 15 c. yell, black & sepia 30 30
179. – 25 c. blue and black .. 50 50
DESIGNS: 3 c. Dinosaur footprints at Moyeni. 10 c. Plateosauravus and footprints. 15 c. Tritylodon and footprints. 25 c. Massospondylus and footprints.
No. 175 is larger, 60 × 23 mm.

12. Moshoeshoe I, as a Young Man.

1970. Chief Moshoeshoe I. Death Cent.

180. **12.** 2½ c. green and magenta .. 5 5
181. – 25 c. blue and chestnut .. 40 40

DESIGN: 25 c. Moshoeshoe I, as an old man.

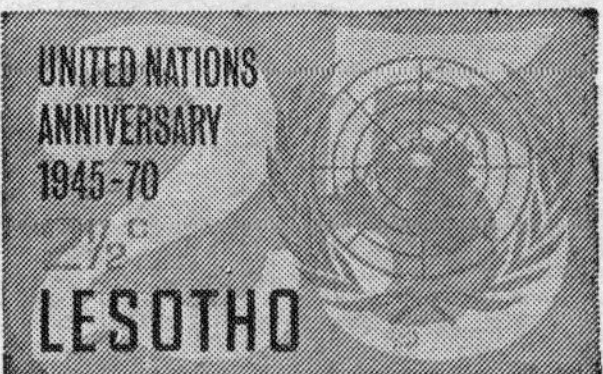

13. U.N. Emblem and "25".

1970. U.N. 25th Anniv.

182. **13.** 2½ c. pink, blue & maroon 5 5
183. – 10 c. multicoloured .. 15 15
184. – 12½ c. red, blue & drab 20 20
185. – 25 c. multicoloured .. 40 40

DESIGNS: 10 c. U.N. Building. 12½ c. "People of the World". 25 c. Symbolic Dove.

14. Gift Shop, Maseru.

1970. Tourism. Multicoloured.

186. 2½ c. Type **14** 8 8
187. 5 c. Trout Fishing .. 10 10
188. 10 c. Pony Trekking .. 20 20
189. 12½ c. Skiing, Maluti Mountains 25 25
190. 20 c. Holiday Inn, Maseru 40 40

15. Maize.

1971. As Nos. 147/58 but in new format omitting portrait, as in T **15**. New designs for 4 c., 2 r.

191. **15.** ½ c. green and violet .. 5 5
192. – 1 c. brown and red .. 5 5
193. – 2 c. yellow and green .. 5 5
194. – 2½ c. blk., grn. & yell. 5 5
195. – 3 c. brn., grn. & yellow 5 5
196. – 3½ c. blue and yellow .. 5 5
196a. – 4 c. multicoloured .. 8 8
197. – 5 c. brown and blue .. 8 8
198. – 10 c. brown and blue .. 12 15
199. – 12½ c. brown and orange 15 20
200. – 25 c. slate and blue .. 30 35
201. – 50 c. black, blue & green 60 70
202. – 1 r. multicoloured .. 1·25 1·40
203. – 2 r. brown and blue .. 2·25 2·50

DESIGNS—HORIZ. 4 c. National flag. VERT. 2 r. Statue of Moshoeshoe I.

16. Lammergeier.

1971. Birds. Multicoloured.

204. 2½ c. Type **16** 10 10
205. 5 c. Bald Ibis 10 10
206. 10 c. Orange-breasted Rock Jumper .. 20 20
207. 12½ c. Blue Korhaan .. 25 25
208. 15 c. Painted Snipe .. 30 30
209. 20 c. Golden-breasted Bunting 40 40
210. 25 c. Ground Woodpecker 40 55

17. Lionel Collett Dam.

1971. Soil Conservation. Multicoloured.

211. 4 c. Type **17** 8 8
212. 10 c. Contour ridges .. 15 15
213. 15 c. Earth dams .. 25 25
214. 25 c. Beaver dams .. 40 40

18. Diamond Mining.

1971. Development. Multicoloured.

215. 4 c. Type **18** 8 8
216. 10 c. Pottery 20 20
217. 15 c. Weaving 30 30
218. 20 c. Construction .. 40 40

19. Mail Cart.

1972. Post Office. Cent

219. **19.** 5 c. brown and pink .. 10 10
220. – 10 c. multicoloured .. 25 25
221. – 15 c. blue, black and brown (vert.) 35 35
222. – 20 c. multicoloured .. 45 45

DESIGNS: 10 c. Postal Bus. 15 c. 4 d. Cape of Good Hope stamp of 1876. 20 c. Maseru Post Office.

20. Sprinting.

1972. Olympic Games, Munich. Mult.

223. 4 c. Type **20** 5 5
224. 10 c. Shot putting .. 20 20
225. 15 c. Hurdling 30 30
226. 25 c. Long-jumping .. 50 50

21. "Adoration of the Shepherds" (Matthias Stomer).

1972. Christmas.

227. **21.** 4 c. multicoloured .. 8 8
228. 10 c. multicoloured .. 20 20
229. 25 c. multicoloured .. 50 50

22. W.H.O. Emblem.

1973. W.H.O. 25th Anniv.

230. **22.** 20 c. yellow and blue.. 35 35

1973. O.A.U. 10th Anniv. Nos. 194 and 196a/8 optd **O.A.U. 10th Anniversary Freedom in Unity.**

231. 2½ c. black, green & brown 5 5
232. 4 c. multicoloured .. 5 5
233. 5 c. brown and blue .. 10 10
234. 10 c. brown and blue .. 20 20

23. Basuto Hat and W.F.P. Emblem.

1973. World Food Programme. 10th Anniv. Multicoloured.

235. 4 c. Type **23** 10 10
236. 15 c. School feeding .. 25 25
237. 20 c. Infant feeding .. 30 30
238. 25 c. "Food for work" .. 40 40

24. Mountain Beauty.

1973. Butterflies. Multicoloured.

239. 4 c. Type **24** 8 8
240. 5 c. Christmas Butterfly .. 8 8
241. 10 c. Painted Lady .. 15 15
242. 15 c. Yellow Pansy .. 25 25
243. 20 c. Blue Pansy .. 25 30
244. 25 c. African Monarch .. 35 35
245. 30 c. Orange Tip .. 45 50

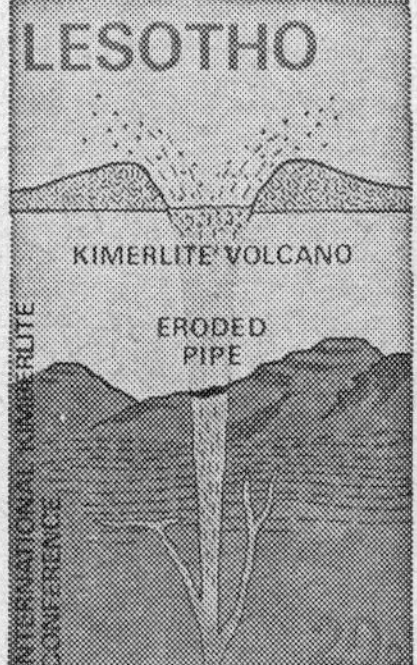

25. Kimberlite Volcano.

1973. Int., Kimberlite Conference. Mult.

246. 10 c. Map of diamond-mines (horiz.) 15 15
247. 15 c. Kimberlite-diamond rock (horiz.) 20 20
248. 20 c. Type **25** 25 30
249. 30 c. Diamond prospecting 40 45

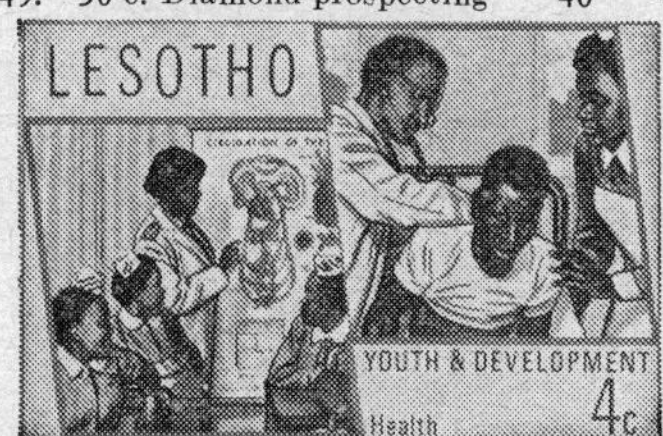

26. "Health".

1974. Youth and Development. Mult.

250. 4 c. Type **26** 8 8
251. 10 c. "Education" .. 12 15
252. 20 c. "Agriculture" .. 25 30
253. 25 c. "Industry".. .. 30 35
254. 30 c. "Service" 40 45

27. Open Book and Wreath.

1974. U.B.L.S. 10th Anniv. Multicoloured.

255. 10 c. Type **27** 12 15
256. 15 c. Flags, mortar-board and scroll 20 25
257. 20 c. Map of Africa .. 25 30
258. 25 c. King Moshoeshoe II capping a graduate .. 30 35

28. Senqunyane River Bridge, Marakabei.

1974. Rivers and Bridges. Multicoloured.

259. 4 c. Type **28** 8 8
260. 5 c. Tsoelike River and bridge 8 8
261. 10 c. Makhaleng River Bridge 12 15
262. 15 c. Seaka Bridge, Orange/Senqu River 20 20
263. 20 c. Masianokeng Bridge, Phuthiatsana River .. 25 30
264. 25 c. Mahobong Bridge, Hlotse River 30 35

29. U.P.U. Emblem.

1974. U.P.U. Centenary.

265. **29.** 4 c. green and black .. 8 8
266. – 10 c. orge., yell. & blk. 12 15
267. – 15 c. multicoloured .. 20 20
268. – 20 c. multicoloured .. 25 30

DESIGNS: 10 c. Map of air-mail routes. 15 c. Post Office H.Q., Maseru. 20 c. Horseman taking rural mail.

30. Siege of Thaba-Bosiu.

1974. Siege of Thaba-Bosiu. 150th Anniv. Multicoloured.

269. 4 c. Type **30** 8 8
270. 5 c. The wreath-laying .. 8 8
271. 10 c. Moshoeshoe I (vert.) 12 15
272. 20 c. Makoanyane, the warrior (vert.) 25 30

31. Mamokhorong.

1974. Basotho Musical Instruments. Mult.

273. 4 c. Type **31** 8 8
274. 10 c. Lesiba 12 15
275. 15 c. Setolotolo 20 20
276. 20 c. Meropa (drums) .. 25 30

32. Horseman in Rock Archway.

1975. Sehlabathebe National Park. Mult.
278. 4 c. Type **32** 8 8
279. 5 c. Mountain view through arch 8 8
280. 15 c. Antelope by stream .. 20 20
281. 20 c. Mountains and lake .. 25 30
282. 25 c. Tourists by waterfall 30 35

33. Morena Moshoeshoe I.

1975. Leaders of Lesotho.
283. **33.** 3 c. black and blue .. 5 5
284. – 4 c. black and mauve .. 8 8
285. – 5 c. black and pink .. 8 8
286. – 6 c. black and brown .. 8 8
287. – 10 c. black and red .. 12 15
288. – 15 c. black and red .. 20 20
289. – 20 c. black and green .. 25 25
290. – 25 c. black and blue .. 30 30

DESIGNS: 4 c. King Moshoeshoe II. 5 c. Morena Letsie I. 6 c. Morena Lerotholi. 10 c. Morena Letsie II. 15 c. Morena Griffith. 20 c. Morena Seeiso Griffith Lerotholi. 25 c. Mofumahali Mantsebo Seeiso, O.B.E.

The 25 c. also commemorates International Women's Year.

34. Mokhibo Dance.

1975. Traditional Dances. Multicoloured.
291. 4 c. Type **34** 5 5
292. 10 c. Ndlamo 12 75
293. 15 c. Baleseli 20 25
294. 20 c. Mohobelo 25 25

35. Enrolment.

1976. Lesotho Red Cross. 25th Anniv. Multicoloured.
296. 4 c. Type **35** 5 5
297. 10 c. Medical aid 12 15
298. 15 c. Rural service .. 20 25
299. 25 c. Relief supplies .. 30 30

36. Tapestry.

1976. Multicoloured.
300. 2 c. Type **36** 5 5
301. 3 c. Mosotho horseman .. 5 5
302. 4 c. Map of Lesotho .. 5 5
303. 5 c. Lesotho brown diamond 5 5
304. 10 c. Lesotho Bank .. 12 12
305. 15 c. Lesotho and O.A.U. flags 20 20
306. 25 c. Sehlabathebe National Park 30 35
307. 40 c. Pottery 50 55
308. 50 c. Pre-historic Rock art 60 70
309. 1 r. King Moshoeshoe II (vert.) .. .. .. 1·25 1·40

37. Football.

1976. Olympic Games, Montreal. Multicoloured.
310. 4 c. Type **37** 5 5
311. 10 c. Weightlifting .. 12 15
312. 15 c. Boxing 20 20
313. 25 c. Throwing the discus 30 35

38. "Rising Sun".

1976. Independence. 10th Anniv. Multicoloured.
314. 4 c. Type **38** 5 5
315. 10 c. Open gates 12 15
316. 15 c. Broken chains .. 20 20
317. 25 c. Aeroplane over hotel 30 35

39. Telephones, 1876 and 1976.

1976. Telephone Centenary. Multicoloured.
318. 4 c. Type **39** 5 5
319. 10 c. Early handset and telephone-user, 1976 .. 12 15
320. 15 c. Wall telephone and telephone exchange .. 20 25
321. 25 c. Stick telephone and Alexander Graham Bell 35 40

40. "Aloe striatula".

1977. Aloes and Succulents. Multicoloured.
322. 3 c. Type **40** 5 5
323. 4 c. "Aloe aristata" .. 5 5
324. 5 c. "Kniphotia caulescens" 5 5
325. 10 c. "Euphorbia pulvinata" 12 15
326. 15 c. "Aloe saponaria" .. 20 25
327. 20 c. "Caralluma lutea" 25 30
328. 25 c. "Aloe polyphylla" 35 40

POSTAGE DUE STAMPS

1966. Nos. D 9/10 of Basutoland optd. **LESOTHO.**
D 11. **D 1.** 1 c. red 15 25
D 12. 5 c. violet 25 35

D 1.

1967.
D 13. **D 1.** 1 c. blue 5 5
D 14. 2 c. red 5 5
D 15. 5 c. green 5 8

LIBERIA

O3

A republic on the W. coast of Africa, founded as a home for freed slaves.

100 cents = 1 dollar.

1.

2.

1860.
7 **1.** 6 c. red .. .. .. 12·00 20·00
8. 12 c. blue .. .. 10·00 20·00
9. 24 c. green .. .. .. 10·00 20·00

1880.
13. **1.** 1 c. blue .. .. .. 1·25 2·00
14. 2 c. rose .. .. .. 1·25 2·00
15. 6 c. mauve .. .. 1·00 2·00
16. 12 c. yellow .. .. 1·40 2·00
17. 24 c. red .. .. .. 1·75 3·50

1881.
18. **2.** 3 c. black .. .. .. 2·25 2·25

3.

4.

6.

1882.
19. **3.** 8 c. blue .. .. .. 4·00 3·00
20. 16 c. rose .. .. .. 3·00 2·50

1886.
43. **3.** 1 c. red 45 50
44. 2 c. green 45 50
23. 3 c. mauve 50 50
46. 4 c. brown 50 50
47. 6 c. grey 60 60
48. **4.** 8 c. grey 80 90
28. 16 c. yellow .. .. 2·00 2·00
29. **6.** 32 c. blue .. .. 4·00 4·00

7.

8.

9.

10. Pres H. R. W. Johnson.

11.

12.

13.

14.

15. President Johnson.

1892.
73. **7.** 1 c. red 25 25
74. 2 c. blue 30 30
75. **8.** 4 c. black and green .. 1·00 60
76. **9.** 6 c. green 35 45
77. **10.** 8 c. black and brown .. 50 60
78. **11.** 12 c. rose 50 50
79. **12.** 16 c. lilac 50 50
81. **13.** 24 c. green on yellow .. 80 80
83. **12.** 32 c. blue .. .. 2·00 2·00
85. **14.** $1 black and blue .. 4·00 3·00
87. **13.** $2 brown on buff .. 2·25 3·00
88. **15.** $5 black and red .. 4·00 5·00

1893. Surch. **55 Five Cents.**
89. **5.** 5 c. on 6 c. green 75 75

16.

1894. Imperf. or roul.
90. **16.** 5 c. black and red .. 1·25 1·25

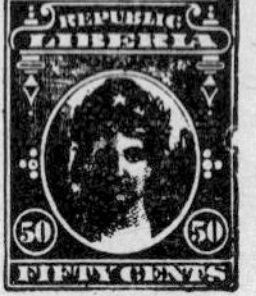

17.

18.

1897.
92. **9.** 1 c. purple 40 30
93. 1 c. green 50 30
94. **14.** 2 c. black and bistre .. 1·00 60
95. 2 c. black and red .. 1·25 60
96. **8.** 5 c. black and lake .. 1·00 60
97a. **8.** 5 c. black and blue .. 1·40 1·00
98. **10.** 10 c. blue and yellow .. 50 50
99. **11.** 15 c. black 50 50
100. **12.** 20 c red 60 80
101. **13.** 25 c. green .. .. 1·00 85
102. **12.** 30 c. blue .. .. 1·00 1·25
103. **17.** 50 c. black and brown 1·25 1·25

†1897.
104. **18.** 3 c. red and green .. 15 8

The prices in the "used" column of sets marked with a dagger (†) against the date of issue are for stamps "cancelled to order" from remainder stocks. Postally used specimens are worth appreciably more.

1901. Official stamps of 1892 optd. **ORDINARY**
108. **9.** 1 c. green (No. O 24) .. 15·00 15·00
109. **7.** 2 c. blue (O 103) .. 35·00 35·00
110. **14.** 2 c black & red (O 126) 15·00 15·00
113. **8.** 5 c. blk. & bl. (O 128) .. 14·00 14·00
111. **16.** 5 c. grn. & lilac (O 113) £100 £100
112. **8.** 5 c. blk. & lake (O 127) 50·00 50·00
114. **10.** 10 c. bl. & yell. (O 129) 17·00 17·00
115. **11.** 15 c black (O 130) .. 17·00 17·00
116. **12.** 16 c. lilac (O 107) .. 90·00 90·00
117. 20 c. red (O 131) .. 20·00 20·00
118. **13.** 24 c grn. on yell. (O 108) 20·00 20·00
119. 25 c. green (O 132) .. 20·00 20·00
120. **12.** 30 c. blue (O 133) .. 17·00 17·00
121. **17.** 50 c. blk. & brn (O 134) 25·00 25·00
122. **14.** $1 blk. & bl. (O 98) .. £150 £150
106. $1 blk. & bl. (O 100) .. £250 £250
123. **13.** $2 brn. on buff (O 111) £500 £500
124. **15.** $5 blk. & red (O 112) .. £1200 £1200

1902. Surch. **75 c.** and bar.
134. **14.** 75 c. on $1 blk. & blue 2·25 2·25

19. Liberty.

ILLUSTRATIONS
British Commonwealth and all overprints and surcharges are FULL SIZE. Foreign Countries have been reduced to ¾-LINEAR.

1903.
138. **19.** 3 c. black 20 25

1903. Surch. in words.
139. **12.** 10 c. on 16 c. lilac .. 60 50
140. **18.** 15 c. on 24 c. grn. on yell. 1·50 1·00
141. **12.** 20 c. on 32 c. blue .. 2·00 1·50

1904. Surch.
142. **9.** 1 c. on 5 c. on 6 c. green (No. 89) 35 20
143. **8.** 2 c. on 4 c. black and green (No. O 91) .. 75 1·00
144. **12.** 2 c. on 30 c. blue (No. 102) 2·75 2·50

20. African Elephant.

21. Head of Mercury.

27. Mandingos.

30. Pres. Barclay and Executive Mansions.

†1906.
145. **20.** 1 c. black and green .. 60 30
146. **21.** 2 c. black and red .. 12 12
147. – 5 c. black and blue .. 1·25 45
148. – 10 c. black and claret .. 2·00 50
149. – 15 c. green and violet .. 4·50 1·25
150. – 20 c. black & orange .. 3·75 70
151. – 25 c. grey and blue .. 45 15
152. 30 c. violet 50 15
153. – 50 c. black and green .. 50 15
154. – 75 c. black & brown .. 5·00 1·25
155. – $1 black and pink .. 1·25 20
156. **27.** $2 black and green .. 2·00 25
157. **30** $5 grey and claret .. 4·00 30
DESIGNS—As T **20:** 5 c. Chimpanzee. 15 c. Agama lizard. 75 c. Liberian hippopotamus. As T **21:** 10 c. Plantain eater (bird). 20 c. Great Egret. 25 c. Head of Liberty on coin. 30 c. Figures "30". 50 c. Liberian flag. As T **30:** $1 Head of Liberty.

33. Coffee Plantation.

35. Gunboat "Lark".

36. Commerce.

†1909. The 10 c. is perf. or roul.
158. **33.** 1 c. black and green .. 20 15
159. – 2 c. black and red .. 20 15
160. **35.** 5 c. black and blue .. 25 20
162. **36.** 10 c. black and purple 15 15
163. – 15 c. black and blue .. 35 25
164. – 20 c. green and rose .. 1·50 40
165. – 25 c. black and brown 50 20
166. – 30 c. brown .. .. 1·00 25
167. – 50 c. black and green .. 1·25 25
168. – 75 c. black and brown 1·00 30
DESIGNS—As T **33:** 2 c. Pres. Barclay. 15 c. Vai woman spinning cotton. 20 c. Pepper plant. 25 c. Village hut. 30 c. Pres. Barclay (in picture frame). As T **35:** 50 c. Canoeing. 75 c. Village (design shaped like a book).

1909. No. 148 surch. **Inland 3 Cents**
169. – 3 c. on 10 c. blk. & claret 1·25 1·25

†1910. Surcharged **3 CENTS INLAND POSTAGE.** Perf. or rouletted.
172. **36.** 3 c. on 10 c. blk. & pur. 25 20

1913. Various types surch. with new value and bars or ornaments.
209. – 1 c. on 2 c. blk. & red (No. 159) 60 60
182. **36.** + 2 c. on 3 c. on 10 c. blk. and purple 35 35
210. **35.** 2 c. on 5 c. blk. & blue 60 60
183. – 2 c. on 15 c. black and blue (No. 163) .. 60 60
175. – 2 c. on 25 c. grey & blue (A) (No. 151) .. 6·00 3·50
177. – 2 c. on 25 c. black and brown (A) (No. 165) 6·00 3·50
186. – 2 c. on 25 c. black and brown (B) (No. 165) 2·50 2·50
187. – 5 c. on 20 c. grn. & rose (No. 164) 75 75
176. – 5 c. on 30 c. violet (C) (No. 152) .. .. 6·00 3·50
178. – 5 c. on 30 c. brown (C) (No. 166) .. .. 6·00 3·50
188. – 5 c. on 30 c. brown (D) (No. 166) .. .. 1·40 1·40
174. **18.** 8 c. on 3 c. red & green 12 12
179. – 10 c. on 50 c. black and green (E) (No. 167) .. 6·00 3·50
190. – 10 c. on 50 c. black and green (F) (No. 167) .. 4·00 4·00
191b. – 10 c. on 50 c. black and green (F) (No. 153) .. 5·00 5·00
192. – 20 c. on 75 c. black and brown (No. 168) .. 3·00 3·00
193. **30.** 25 c. on $1 blk. & pink 11·00 11·00
194. – 50 c. on $2 black and green (No. 156) .. 4·50 4·50
196. – $1 on $5 green and claret (No. 157) .. .. 10·00 10·00
Descriptions of surcharges. (A) **1914 2 CENTS.** (B) **2** over ornaments. (C) **1914 5 CENTS.** (D) **5** over ornaments. (E) **1914 10 CENTS.** (F) **10** and ornaments.

43.

44.

†1915.
180. **43.** 2 c. red 12 5
181. **44.** 3 c. violet 12 5

1916. Surch. **1916** over new value.
217. **1.** 3 c. on 6 c. mauve .. 3·00 1·50
218. 5 c. on 12 c. yellow .. 1·25 1·00
219. 10 c. on 24 c. red .. 1·25 1·00

1917. Surch. **1917** and value in words.
220. **13.** 4 c. on 25 c. green .. 2·50 2·50
221. **27.** 5 c. on 30 c. violet .. 20·00 20·00

1918. Surch. **3 CENTS.**
223. **36.** 3 c. on 10 c. black & pur. 75 75

45. Bongo Antelope.

48.

46. Palm Civet.

51. Traveller's Tree.

†1918.
225. **45.** 1 c. black and green .. 40 12
226. **46.** 2 c. black and rose .. 40 12
227. – 5 c. black and blue .. 10 5
228. **48.** 10 c. green 12 5
229. – 15 c. green and black .. 1·50 15
230. – 20 c. black and claret .. 20 5
231. **51.** 25 c. green .. .. 2·00 15
232. – 30 c. black and mauve .. 3·00 50
233. – 50 c. black and blue .. 5·00 40
234. – 75 c. black and olive .. 60 8
235. – $1 blue and brown .. 2·50 10
236. – $2 black and violet .. 3·00 10
237. – $5 brown .. .. 2·00 15
DESIGNS—As T **45:** 5 c. Coat of Arms. 15 c. Oil palm. 20 c. Statue of Mercury. 75 c. Heads of Mandingos. $5 "Liberia" seated. As T **46:** 50 c. Lungfish (or Mudskipper). $1 Coast view. $2 Liberia College. As T **48:** 30 c. Eagle owl.

1918. Geneva Red Cross Fund. Surch. **TWO CENTS** and red cross.
238. **45.** 2 c. on 1 c. black & green 30 30
239. **46.** 2 c. on 2 c. black & rose 30 30
240. – 2 c. on 5 c. black & blue 12 8
241. **48.** 2 c. on 10 c. green .. 12 8
242. – 2 c. on 15 c. green & blk. 12 8
243. – 2 c. on 20 c. black & clar. 25 12
244. **51.** 2 c. on 25 c. green .. 50 50
245. – 2 c. on 30 c. blk. & mve. 30 30
246. – 2 c. on 50 c. blk. & blue 50 50
247. – 2 c. on 75 c. blk. & olive 1·00 75
248. – 2 c. on $1 blue & brown 1·50 1·00
249. – 2 c. on $2 black & violet 2·00 1·25
250. – 2 c. on $5 brown .. 6·00 5·00

1920. Surch. **1920** and value and two bars.
251. **45.** 3 c. on 1 c. black & green 60 60
252. **46.** 4 c. on 2 c. black & rose 75 75
253. R **2.** 5 c. on 10 c. blue .. 2·00 2·00
254. 5 c. on 10 c. red .. 2·00 1·10
255. 5 c. on 10 c. green .. 2·00 1·10
256. 5 c. on 10 c. violet .. 2·00 1·50
257. 5 c. on 10 c. red .. 1·25 1·00

58. Coast Scene.

59. Pres. D. E. Howard.

†1921.
259. **58.** 1 c. green 8 5
260. **59.** 5 c. black and blue .. 8 5
261. – 10 c. blue and red .. 12 8
262. – 15 c. green and purple .. 2·50 35
263. – 20 c. green and red .. 2·50 25
264. – 25 c. black and yellow .. 2·75 35
265. – 30 c. purple and green .. 15 8
266. – 50 c. blue and yellow .. 25 8
267. – 75 c. sepia and red .. 30 10
268. – $1 black and red .. 12·00 75
269. – $2 violet and yellow .. 5·50 75
270. – $5 red and purple .. 14·00 1·00
DESIGNS—VERT. 10 c. Arms. HORIZ. 15 c. Crocodile. 20 c. Pepper plant. 25 c. Leopard. 30 c. Village. 50 c. Canoe. 75 c. St. Paul's R. $1 Bongo (antelope). $2 Hornbill. $5 Elephant.

†1921. Optd. **1921.**
271. **58.** 1 c. green 50 10
272. **43.** 2 c. red 50 10
273. **44.** 3 c. violet .. .. 1·00 10
274. **59.** 5 c. black and blue .. 1·00 10
275. – 10 c. blue and red .. 3·00 10
276. – 15 c. green and purple 1·50 40
277. – 20 c. green and red .. 2·50 30
278. – 25 c. black and yellow 1·50 40
279. – 30 c. purple and green .. 60 10
280. – 50 c. blue and yellow .. 1·00 10
281. – 75 c. sepia and red .. 2·50 10
282. – $1 black and red .. 10·00 60
283. – $2 violet and yellow .. 5·00 60
284. – $5 red and purple .. 12·00 75

70. Arrival of First Settlers.

†1923. Centennial issue.
285. **70.** 1 c. black and blue .. 2·50 20
286. 2 c. brown and claret .. 2·50 20
287. 5 c. blue and olive .. 2·50 20
288. 10 c. mauve and green 35 20
289. $1 brown and rose .. 1·10 35

71. J. J. Roberts Memorial.

72. Monrovia College.

82. Rubber Forester's Hut.

†1923.
290. **71.** 1 c. green 8 5
291. **72.** 2 c. brown and claret .. 8 5
292. – 3 c. black and lilac .. 8 5
293. – 5 c. black and blue .. 30 8
294. – 10 c. brown and grey .. 10 8
295. – 15 c. blue and bistre .. 2·00 25
296. – 20 c. mauve and green 2·00 25
297. – 25 c. brown and red .. 4·00 40
298. – 30 c. mauve and brown 15 8
299. – 50 c. orange and purple 1·25 25
300. – 75 c. blue and grey .. 30 15
301. **82.** $1 violet and red .. 2·00 50
302. – $2 blue and orange .. 50 15
303. – $5 brown and green .. 1·50 20
DESIGNS—As T **71:** 3 c. Star. 5 c., 10 c. Pres. King. 50 c. Pineapple. As T **72:** 15 c. Hippopotamus. 20 c. W. African Kob (antelope). 25 c. Buffalo. 30 c. Natives making palm oil. 75 c. Carrying elephant tusk. As T **82:** $2 Stockton lagoon. $5 Styles of huts.

1926. Surch. **Two Cents** and thick bar or wavy lines or ornamental scroll.
304. **45.** 2 c. on 1 c. black & green 2·00 2·00

85. Palm Trees.

86. Map of Africa.

87. President King.

1928.
306. **85.** 1 c. green 12 12
307. 2 c. violet 20 20
308. 3 c. brown 20 20
309. **86.** 5 c. blue 50 40
310. **87.** 10 c. grey 60 40
311. **86.** 15 c. purple .. .. 2·50 1·25
312. $1 brown .. .. 17·00 9·00

1928. Nos. O 313 and 307/8 surch. **AIR MAIL SIX CENTS.**
313. **85.** 6 c. on 1 c. green .. 90·00 60·00
314. 6 c. on 2 c. violet .. 60·00 40·00
315. 6 c. on 3 c. brown .. 60·00 40·00

88. Ford Trimotor.

1936. Air. First Air Mail Service of 28th February.
318. **88.** 1 c. black and green .. 20 5
319. 2 c. black and red .. 20 5
320. 3 c. black and violet .. 20 5
321. 4 c. black and orange 20 5
322. 5 c. black and blue .. 20 5
323. 6 c. black and green .. 20 5

1936. Nos. 226/37 surch. **1936** and new values in figures.
324. 1 c. on 2 c. black and rose 20 10
325. 3 c. on 5 c. black and blue 10 8
326. 4 c. on 10 c. green .. 10 8
327. 6 c. on 15 c. green and black 20 30
328. 8 c. on 20 c. black & claret 12 12
329. 12 c. on 30 c. black & mauve 35 15
330. 14 c. on 50 c. black & blue 45 25
331. 16 c. on 75 c. black & olive 20 20
332. 18 c. on $1 blue and brown 20 20
333. 22 c. on $2 black & violet 30 30
334. 24 c. on $5 brown .. 40 40

1936. Nos. O 239/50 optd. with Star and **1936** or surch. also in figures and words.
335. 1 c. on 2 c. black and red .. 15 12
336. 3 c. on 5 c. black and blue 8 8
337. 4 c. on 10 c. green 8 8
338. 6 c. on 15 c. green & brown 15 10
339. 8 c. on 20 c. black and lilac 12 12
340. 12 c. on 30 c. black & violet 30 20
341. 14 c. on 50 c. black & brown 40 25
342. 16 c. on 75 c. black & brown 20 20
343. 18 c. on $1 blue and olive .. 20 20
344. 22 c. on $2 black and olive 25 25
345. 24 c. on $5 green .. 30 20
346. 25 c. green and brown .. 40 30

89. Hippopotamus.

1937.

347. – 1 c. black and green .. 60 30
348. – 2 c. black and red .. 60 30
349. – 3 c. black and purple .. 60 30
350. **89.** 4 c. black and orange .. 1·00 50
351. – 5 c. black and blue .. 1·00 50
352. – 6 c. black and green .. 45 15

DESIGNS: 1 c. Allied hornbill. 2 c. Harnessed antelope. 3 c. W. African buffalo. 5 c. Great white egret. 6 c. Pres. Barclay.

90. Eagle in Flight. **91.** Sikorsky Flying-boat.

92. Great Egrets.

1938. Air.

353. **90.** 1 c. green 8 8
354. **91.** 2 c. red 10 8
355. – 3 c. olive 10 8
356. **92.** 4 c. orange 12 8
357. 5 c. green 20 8
358. **91.** 10 c. violet 20 10
359. – 20 c. mauve 25 10
360. – 30 c. grey 40 10
361. **90.** 50 c. brown 50 10
362. – $1 blue 60 15

DESIGNS—VERT. 20 c., $1 Bimotor flying-boat. HORIZ. 3 c., 30 c. Tern in flight.

93. Ships nearing Liberian Coast.

1940. Founding of Liberian Commonwealth. Cent.

363. **93.** 3 c. blue 8 5
364. – 5 c. brown 10 10
365. – 10 c. green 15 12

DESIGNS: 5 c. Seal of Liberia and Flags of original Settlements. 10 c. Thos. Buchanan's house and portrait.

1941. First Postage Stamps. Cent. Nos. 363/5 optd. **POSTAGE STAMP CENTENNIAL 1840-1940** and portrait of Rowland Hill.

366. **93.** 3 c. blue (postage) .. 1·25 1·25
367. – 5 c. brown .. .. 1·25 1·25
368. – 10 c. green .. .. 1·25 1·25
369. **93.** 3 c. blue (air) .. .. 1·40 1·40
370. – 5 c. brown .. .. 1·40 1·40
371. – 10 c. green .. .. 1·40 1·40

Nos. 369/71 are additionally optd. **AIR MAIL** and aeroplane.

1941. Red Cross Fund. Nos. 363/5 surch. **RED CROSS** plus Red Cross and **TWO CENTS.**

372. **93.** +2c. on 3 c. blue (post.) 1·25 1·25
373. – +2 c. on 5 c. brown .. 1·25 1·25
374. – +2 c. on 10 c. green .. 1·25 1·25
375. **93.** +2 c. on 3 c. blue (air) 1·25 1·25
376. – +2 c. on 5 c. brown .. 1·25 1·25
377. – +2 c. on 10 c. green .. 1·25 1·25

Nos. 375/7 are additionally optd. **AIR MAIL** and aeroplane.

1941. Air. 1st Flight to U.S.A. Nos. 353/62 surch. **First Flight LIBERIA-U.S. 1941. 50 c.** and bar.

382. **90.** 50 c. on 1 c. £1200 £150
383. **91.** 50 c. on 2 c. .. .. £100 50·00
384. – 50 c. on 3 c. .. .. £100 50·00
385. **92.** 50 c. on 4 c. .. .. 40·00 25·00
386. 50 c. on 5 c. .. .. 40·00 25·00
387. **91.** 50 c. on 10 c. .. .. 40·00 25·00
388. – 50 c. on 20 c. .. .. £1200 40·00
389. – 50 c. on 30 c. .. .. 35·00 20·00
390. **90.** 50 c. brown .. .. 35·00 20·00
391. – $1 blue .. .. .. 40·00 20·00

The first flight was cancelled and covers were sent by ordinary mail. The flight took place in 1942 and the stamps were reissued but with the date obliterated.

1942. As Nos. 382/91 but with date "1941" obliterated by two bars.

392. **90.** 50 c. on 1 c. green .. 5·50 5·50
393. **91.** 50 c. on 2 c. red .. 5·50 5·00
394. – 50 c. on 3 c. green .. 5·00 5·00
395. **92.** 50 c. on 4 c. orange .. 4·50 5·00
396. 50 c. on 5 c. green .. 2·50 2·50
397. **91.** 50 c. on 10 c. violet .. 3·00 3·00
398. – 50 c. on 20 c. mauve .. 3·00 3·00
399. – 50 c. on 30 c. grey .. 4·00 4·00
400. **90.** 50 c. brown .. .. 4·00 4·00
401. – $1 blue .. .. .. 3·00 3·00

94. Miami-Monrovia Air Route. **95.** Harnessed Antelope.

1942. Air.

402. **94.** 10 c. red 15 10
403. – 12 c. blue 15 10
404. – 24 c. green 15 10
405. **94.** 30 c. green 15 10
406. 35 c. lilac 15 10
407. 50 c. purple 20 12
408. 70 c. olive 30 20
409. $1·40 red 40 30

DESIGN: 12 c., 24 c. Aeroplane over Liberian Agricultural and Industrial Fair.

1942.

410. – 1 c. brown and violet .. 30 15
411. – 2 c. brown and blue .. 30 15
412. – 3 c. brown and green .. 60 30
413. **95.** 4 c. red and black .. 75 50
414. – 5 c. brown and olive .. 1·00 60
415. – 10 c. black and red .. 1·50 75

DESIGNS—HORIZ. 1 c. Royal antelope. 2 c. Water chevrotain. 3 c. White-shouldered duiker. 5 c. Zebra antelope. VERT. 10 c. Diana monkey.

1944. Stamps of 1928 and 1937 surch.

416. **85.** 1 c. on 2 c. violet .. 6·00 6·00
417. **89.** 1 c. on 4 c. blk. & oran. 40·00 30·00
418. **87.** 1 c. on 10 c. grey .. 6·00 5·00
419. – 2 c. on 3 c. black and purple (No. 349) .. 35·00 6·00
420. **86.** 2 c. on 5 c. blue .. 2·00 2·00
421. **85.** 3 c. on 2 c. violet .. 20·00
422. – 4 c. on 5 c. black and blue (No. 351) .. 7·00 5·00
423. **87.** 4 c. on 10 c. grey .. 2·50 2·50
424. – 5 c. on 1 c. black and green (No. 347) .. 35·00 30·00
425. – 6 c. on 2 c. black and red (No. 348) .. 8·00 6·00
426. – 10 c. on 6 c. black and green (No. 352) .. 8·00 6·00

1944. Air stamps of 1936 and 1938 surch.

428. **91.** 10 c. on 2 c. red .. 25·00 5·00
429. **92.** 10 c. on 5 c. green .. 12·00 11·00
430. **88.** 30 c. on 1 c. blk. and grn. 40·00 25·00
431. 30 c. on 3 c. olive (No. 355) .. .. 80·00 80·00
432. **92.** 30 c. on 4 c. orange .. 10·00 10·00
433. **88.** 50 c. on 3 c. blk. and vio. 18·00 18·00
434. 70 c. on 2 c. black & red 35·00 35·00
435. – $1 on 3 c. olive (No. 355) 40·00 40·00
436. **90.** $1 on 50 c. brown .. 25·00 15·00

96. Pres. Roosevelt reviewing Troops.

1945. Pres. Roosevelt Memorial.

437. **96.** 3 c. black & pur. (post.) 12 12
438. 5 c. black and blue .. 25 25
439. 70 c. black & brown (air) 1·10 1·10

97. Opening of Monrovia Harbour Project.

1946. Opening of Monrovia Harbour Project by Pres. Tubman.

440. **97.** 5 c. blue (postage)) .. 12 12
441. 42 c. green (air) .. 1·10 1·10

1947. As T **97**, but without inscr. at top.

442. 5 c. violet (postage) .. 15 12
443. 25 c. red (air) 30 25

98. 1st Postage Stamps of U.S.A. and Liberia.

1947. U.S. Postage Stamps Cent. and 87th Anniv. of Liberian Postal Issues.

444. **98.** 5 c. red (postage) .. 12 12
445. 12 c. green (air) .. 12 12
446. 25 c. violet 15 15
447. 50 c. blue 20 20

99. Matilda Newport Firing Cannon. **100.** Liberty.

1947. Defence of Monrovia. 125th Anniv.

449. **99.** 1 c. black & grn. (post.) 5 5
450. 3 c. black and violet .. 8 8
451. 5 c. black and blue .. 12 12
452. 10 c. black and yellow 35 35
453. 25 c. black and red (air) 50 35

1947. National Independence Cent.

454. – 1 c. green (postage) .. 5 5
455. **100.** 2 c. purple 5 5
456. – 3 c. purple 8 8
457. – 5 c. blue 12 10
458. – 12 c. orange (air) .. 12 10
459. – 25 c. red 35 25
460. – 50 c. brown 70 40

DESIGNS—VERT. 1 c. Liberian star. 3 c. Arms of Liberia. 4 c. Map of Liberia. 12 c. J. J. Roberts Monument. 25 c. Liberian Flag 50 c. (26½ × 33 mm.) Centenary Monument.

101. Aeroplane.

1948. Air. First Liberian Int. Airways Flight (Monrovia-Dakar).

461. **101.** 25 c. red .. .. 1·25 50
462. 50 c. blue 60 50

102. J. J. Roberts.

103. Colonists and Map. **104.** Hand Holding Book.

1949. Liberian Presidents. Portrait and name in black. (a) Postage.

463. – 1 c. green (Roberts) .. 1·50 1·50
463a. **102.** 1 c. green (Roberts) .. 5 5
464. – 1 c. pink (Roberts) .. 20 10
465. – 2 c. pink (Benson) .. 35 35
466. – 2 c. yellow (Benson) .. 20 10
467. – 3 c. mauve (Warner) .. 35 35
468. – 4 c. olive (Payne) .. 35 35
469. – 5 c. blue (Mansion) .. 40 35
470. – 6 c. orange (Roye) .. 50 60
471. – 7 c. green (Gardner and Russell) .. 60 60
472. – 8 c. red (Johnson) .. 60 60
473. – 9 c. pur. (Cheeseman) 1·00 1·00
474. – 10 c. yell. (Coleman) .. 60 30
475. – 10 c. grey (Coleman) .. 30 20
476. – 15 c. orange (Gibson) .. 75 40
477. – 15 c. blue (Gibson) .. 25 15
478. – 20 c. grey (A. Barclay) 1·25 60
479. – 20 c. red (A. Barclay) 40 30
480. – 25 c. red (Howard) .. 1·40 80
481. – 25 c. blue (Howard) .. 40 30
482. – 50 c. turquoise (King) 2·75 1·50
483. – 50 c. purple (King) .. 60 50
484. – $1 mag. (E. Barclay) 5·00 4·00
485. – $1 brown (E. Barclay) 1·50 75

(b) Air.

486. – 25 c. blue (Tubman) .. 1·00 50
486a. – 25 c. green (Tubman) 40 30

Nos. 463 and 464 have a different portrait of Roberts wearing a moustache.

1949. Multicoloured.

487. 1 c. Settlers approaching village (postage) .. 50 50
488. 2 c. Rubber tapping and planting 50 50
489. 3 c. Landing of first colonists in 1822 .. .. 50 50
490. 5 c. Jehudi Ashman and Matilda Newport defending stockage 50 50
491. 25 c. Type **103** (air) .. 1·25 1·25
492. 50 c. Africans and coat of arms .. .. 1·50 1·50

1950. National Literacy Campaign

493. **104.** 5 c. blue (postage) .. 15 12
494. – 25 c. red (air) .. 60 60

DESIGN—VERT. 25 c. Open book and rising sun.

105. U.P.U. Monument, Berne. **106.** Carey, Ashmun and Careysburg.

1950. U.P.U. 75th Anniv. Inscr. "1874 1949".

496. **105.** 5 c. black & grn. (post.) 15 12
497. – 10 c. black & magenta 25 25
498. – 25 c. mag. & orge. (air) 2·50 2·50

DESIGNS—HORIZ. 10 c. Standehaus, Berne. VERT. 25 c. U.P.U. Monument, Berne.

1952. Designs all show portrait of Ashmun

500. – 1 c. green (postage) .. 5 5
501. **106.** 2 c. indigo and red .. 5 5
502. – 3 c. green and purple .. 5 5
503. – 4 c. green and brown 8 8
504. – 5 c. red and blue .. 12 10
505. 10 c. blue and red .. 15 12
506. – 25 c. black & pur. (air) 35 25
507. – 50 c. red and blue .. 60 35

DESIGNS—VERT. 1 c. Seal of Liberia. 3 c. Harper and Harper City. 5 c. Buchanan and Upper Buchanan. HORIZ. 4 c. Marshall and Marshall City. 10 c. Roberts and Robertsport. 25 c. Monroe and Monrovia. 50 c. Tubman and map.

107. U.N. Headquarters. **108.** Flags and U.N. Emblem.

1952. U.N. Commem.

509. **107.** 1 c. blue (postage) .. 5 5
510. – 4 c. blue and pink .. 12 10
511. – 10 c. brown and yellow 20 15
512. **108.** 25 c. red and blue (air) 50 40

DESIGNS—HORIZ. 4 c. Liberian and U.N. flags and scroll. 10 c. Liberian and U.N. emblems.

DESIGNS: 25 c. Ships in Monrovia Harbour. 35 c. Diesel loco. 50 c. Free Port of Monrovia. 70 c. Robertsfield Airport. $1 Tubman Bridge.

109. Modern Road-building.

1953. Air. Transport.

514. **109.** 12 c. brown 10 10
515. – 25 c. purple 25 20
516. – 35 c. violet 30 25
517. – 50 c. orange 45 30
518. – 70 c. green 75 35
519. – $1 blue .. .. 1·00 50

110. Pepper Bird.

111. Roller.

1953. Imperf. or perf.

520. **110.** 1 c. red and blue .. 5 5
521. **111.** 3 c. blue and salmon .. 5 5
522. – 4 c. brown and yellow 8 5
523. – 5 c. turquoise & mauve 12 5
524. – 10 c. magenta & green 25 8
525. – 12 c. orange and brown 40 10

BIRDS—As T **110**: 4 c. Hornbill. 5 c. Kingfisher. As T **111**: 10 c. Jacana. 12 c. Weaver.

DESIGNS—As T **112**: 5 c. Medical research workers. 10 c. Nurses. Larger (46 × 35 mm.): 25 c. Doctor examining patient.

112. Hospital.

1954. Liberian Govt. Hospital Fund.
526. – 5 c. + 5 c. black and purple (postage) 15 12
527. – 10 c. + 5 c. black and carmine (air) .. 25 15
528. **112.** 20 c. + 5 c. black & grn. 35 20
529. – 25 c. + 5 c. black, red and blue 45 25

113. Children of the World.

1954. Air. U.N.I.C.E.F.
530. **113.** $5 ultram., red & blue 50·00 50·00

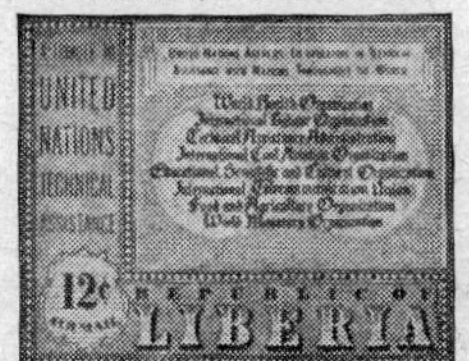

114. U.N. Organizations.

1954. Air. U.N. Technical Assistance.
531. **114.** 12 c. black and blue .. 20 10
532. – 15 c. chocolate & yellow 25 12
533. – 20 c. black and green .. 30 15
534. – 25 c. ultram. and red 1·00 45
DESIGNS: 15 c. Printers. 20 c. Mechanic. 25 c. Teachers and students.

1954. Air. Visit of Pres. Tubman to U.S.A. As Nos. 514/9 but colours changed and inscr. "COMMEMORATING PRESIDENTIAL VISIT U.S.A.".
535. 12 c. orange 15 8
536. 25 c. blue 30 12
537. 35 c. carmine 50 12
538. 50 c. mauve 60 25
539. 70 c. brown 75 40
540. $1 green .. .. .. 1·25 50

115. Football.

116. "Callichilia Stenosepala".

1955. Sports.
541. – 3 c. red & grn. (postage) 5 5
542. **115.** 5 c. black and orange 5 5
543. – 25 c. violet and yellow 35 25
544. – 10 c. ultramarine and magenta (air) .. 15 10
545. – 12 c. chocolate & blue 20 12
546. – 25 c. magenta & green 35 15
DESIGNS—VERT. 3 c. Tennis. 25 c. Boxing (No. 543). HORIZ. 10 c. Baseball. 12 c. Swimming. 25 c. Running (No. 546).

1955. Flowers.
548. **116.** 6 c. yellow, salmon & green (postage) .. 8 5
549. – 7 c. red, yell. & green 10 5
550. – 8 c. buff, blue & green 12 8
551. – 9 c. green and orange 15 10
552. – 20 c. yellow, green and violet (air) .. 30 12
553. – 25 c. yell., green & red 35 15
FLOWERS—VERT. 7 c. "Gomphia subcordata". 8 c. "Listristachys caudata". 9 c. "Mussaenda isertiana". HORIZ. 20 s. "Costus". 25 c. "Barteria nigritiana".

117. U.N. General Assembly.

118. Tapping Rubber and Rotary Emblem.

1955. Air. U.N. 10th Anniv.
554. – 10 c. blue and red .. 15 5
555. **117.** 15 c. black and violet 20 10
556. – 25 c. brown and green 35 10
557. – 50 c. green and red .. 75 15
DESIGNS—VERT. 10 c. U.N. emblem. 25 c. Liberian Secretary of State signing U.N. Charter. HORIZ. 50 c. Page from U.N. Charter.

1955. Rotary International. 50th Anniv. Inscr. "1905–1955".
558. **118.** 5 c. grn. & yell. (post.) 20 12
559. – 10 c. blue and red (air) 25 20
560. – 15 c. brown, yell. & red 35 30
DESIGNS: 10 c. Rotary Int. H.Q., Evanston. 15 c. View of Monrovia.

DESIGNS—VERT 3 c., 15c. Statue of Liberty. HORIZ. 6 c., 12 c. Globe.

119. Coliseum, New York.

1956. 5th Int. Philatelic Exn., New York.
562. – 3 c. brown & emerald (postage) 5 5
563. **119.** 4 c. chestnut & green 5 5
564. – 6 c. purple and black 8 8
565. **119.** 10 c. blue and red (air) 15 10
566. – 12 c. violet and orange 20 12
567. – 15 c. purple & turquoise 30 12

DESIGNS—HORIZ. 4 c. Olympic rings, kangaroo and emu. 8 c. Goddess of Victory. 12 c., 20 c. Olympic Stadium, Melbourne. VERT. 6 c. Discus thrower.

120. Chariot Race.

1956. Olympic Games.
569. – 4 c. brn. & olive (post.) 5 5
570. – 6 c. black and green .. 8 5
571. – 8 c. brown and blue .. 12 5
572. **120.** 10 c. black and red .. 20 8
573. – 12 c. pur. & grn. (air) 25 10
574. – 20 c. black, lilac, blue and rose 35 15

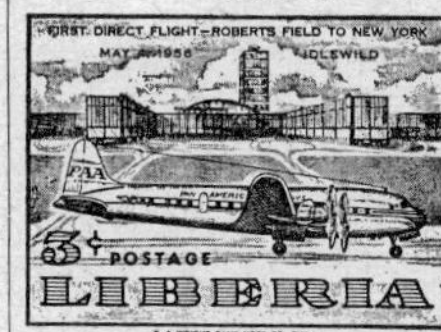

DESIGN: 5 c. 15 c., 50 c. President Tubman and clipper "John Alden" at Roberts Field, Liberia.

121. Clipper "John Alden" at Idlewild Airport.

1957. 1st Anniv. of Inauguration of Liberia-U.S. Direct Air Service.
576. **121.** 3 c. blue & orge. (post.) 5 5
577. – 5 c. black and mauve 8 5
578. **121.** 12 c. blue & green (air) 15 5
579. – 15 c. black and chestnut 20 8
580. **121.** 25 c. blue and red .. 35 8
581. – 50 c. black and blue .. 50 10

DESIGNS: 5 c. Teacher with pupil. 6 c. National anthem with Choristers. 10 c. Children viewing welfare home. 15 c. Nurse inoculating youth. 35 c. Kamara triplets.

122. Children's Playground.

1957. Inaug. of Antionette Tubman Child Welfare Foundation. Inscr. as in T 122.
582. **122.** 4 c. green & red (post.) 5 5
583. – 5 c. brown & turquoise 5 5
584. – 6 c. violet and bistre.. 8 5
585. – 10 c. blue and red .. 15 8
586. – 15 c. brn. & blue (air) 20 10
587. – 35 c. purple and grey 40 20

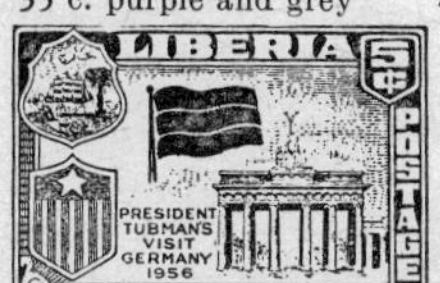

123. German Flag and Brandenburg Gate.

1958. Pres. Tubman's European Tour. Flags in national colours.
589. **123.** 5 c. blue (postage) .. 5 5
590. – 5 c. brown 5 5
591. – 5 c. red 5 5
592. – 10 c. black (air) .. 12 5
593. – 15 c. green 20 8
594. – 15 c. blue 20 8
595. – 15 c. violet 20 8
DESIGNS: Flags of: Netherlands and windmill (590); Sweden and Royal Palace, Stockholm (591); Italy and Colosseum (592); France and Arc de Triomphe (593); Switzerland and Alpine chalet (594); Vatican City and St. Peter's Basilica (595).

124. Map of the World.

125. Africans and Map.

1958. Declaration of Human Rights. 10th Anniv. Inscr. "1948–1958",
596. **124.** 3 c. blue and black .. 5 5
597. – 5 c. brown and blue .. 12 5
598. – 10 c. orange and black 20 12
599. – 12 c. black and red .. 30 15
DESIGNS: 5 c. U.N. Emblem and H.Q. building. 10 c. U.N. Emblem. 12 c. U.N. Emblem and initials of U.N. Agencies.

1959. Africa Freedom Day.
601. **125.** 20 c. orge. & brn. (post.) 25 20
602. – 25 c. brn. & blue (air) 30 20
DESIGN: 25 c. Two Africans looking at Pres. Tubman's declaration of Africa Freedom Day.

126.

127. Abraham Lincoln.

1959. U.N.E.S.C.O. Building. Inaug.
603. **126.** 25 c. pur. & grn. (post.) 30 25
604. – 25 c. red & blue (air).. 30 25
DESIGN—HORIZ. No. 526, U.N.E.S.C.O. Headquarters, Paris.

1959. Abraham Lincoln. 150th Birth Anniv.
606. **127.** 10 c. blk. & blue (post.) 20 15
607. 15 c. black and orange 25 15
608. 25 c. black & grn. (air) 45 30

128. Presidents Toure, Tubman and Nkrumah.

129. "Care of Refugees".

1960. "Big Three" Conf., Saniquellie, Liberia.
610. **128.** 25 c. black & red (post.) 30 20
611. – 25 c. blk., bl. & buff (air) 30 20
DESIGN: No. 611, Medallion portraits of Presidents Toure (Guinea), Tubman (Liberia) and Nkrumah (Ghana).

1960. World Refugee Year.
612. **129.** 25 c. grn. & blk. (post.) 30 20
613. 25 c. blue & black (air) 50 30

130.

131. Weightlifting.

1960. African Technical Co-operation Commission (C.C.T.A.). 10th Anniv.
615. **130.** 25 c. grn. & blk. (post.) 30 20
616. – 25 c. choc. & blue (air) 40 30
DESIGN: No. 616, Map of Africa with symbols showing fields of assistance.

1960. Olympic Games, Rome.
617. **131.** 5 c. choc. & grn. (post.) 10 8
618. – 10 c. chocolate & purple 15 10
619. – 15 c. chocolate & orange 30 20
620. – 25 c. choc. & blue (air) 60 35
DESIGNS—HORIZ. 10 c. Rowing. 25 c. Javelin-throwing. VERT. 15 c. Walking.

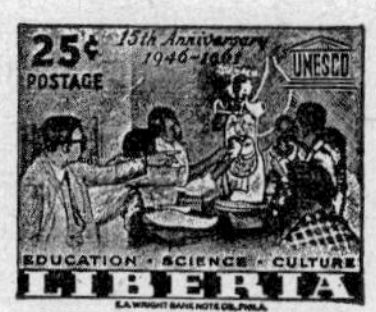

132. Stamps of 1860 and Map.

133. "Guardians of Peace".

1960. Liberian Stamp Cent. Stamps, etc., in green, red and blue. Colours of map and inscriptions given.
622. **132.** 5 c. black (postage) .. 8 5
623. 20 c. brown 25 20
624. 25 c. ultramarine (air) 30 25

1961. Membership of U.N. Security Council.
626. **133.** 25 c. blue & red (post.) 30 20
627. – 25 c. indigo & red (air) 30 20
DESIGN—HORIZ. No. 627, Dove of Peace, Globe and U.N. Emblem.

134. Anatomy Class, University of Liberia.

135. President Roberts.

1961. U.N.E.S.C.O. 15th Anniv.
630. **134.** 25 c. brn. & grn. (post.) 25 20
631. – 25 c. brn. & violet (air) 30 20
DESIGN: No. 631, Science class, University of Liberia.

1961. Joseph J. Roberts (first President of Liberia). 150th Birth Anniv.
633. **135.** 5 c. sepia & orge. (post.) 8 5
634. – 10 c. sepia and blue .. 12 8
635. 25 c. sepia & emer. (air) 35 20
DESIGNS—HORIZ. 10 c. Pres. Roberts and old and new presidential mansions. 25 c. Pres. Roberts and Providence Is.

DESIGNS—HORIZ. 10 c. Scout badge and scouts in camp. VERT. 25 c. Scout and badge.

136. Scout and Sports.

1961. Liberian Boy Scout Movement.
637. **136.** 5 c. sepia & vio. (post.) 8 5
638. – 10 c. ochre and blue.. 15 10
639. – 25 c. sepia & emer. (air) 35 20

137. Dag Hammarskjoeld.

138. Campaign Emblem.

1962. Dag Hammarskjoeld Commem.
641. **137.** 20 c. blk. & blue (post.) 20 15
642. 25 c. black & pur. (air) 25 20

1962. Malaria Eradication.
644. **138.** 25 c. grn. & red (post.) 25 20
645. – 25 c. orge. & violet (air) 25 20
DESIGN—HORIZ. No. 645, Campaign emblem and slogan.

139. Pres. Tubman and New York Skyline.

140. "un" and Emblem.

1962. Air. President's Visit to U.S.A.
647. **139.** 12 c. sep., red, bl. & grn. 15 10
648. 25 c. sep., red, bl. & blk. 30 25
649. 50 c. sep., red, bl. & orge. 60 45

1962. U.N. Day.
650. **140.** 20 c. bistre & grn. (post.) 30 20
651. – 25 c. blue & cobalt (air) 1·00 1·00
DESIGN: 25 c. U.N. emblem and flags.

141. Treasury Building.

142. F.A.O. Emblem, Bowl and Spoon.

1962. Liberian Government Buildings.
653. 1 c. orge. & blue (post.) 5 5
654. **141.** 5 c. violet and blue .. 5 5
655. – 10 c. brown and buff.. 12 10
656. – 15 c. blue and salmon 20 15
657. – 80 c. yellow and brown 1·00 50
658. – 12 c. lake & green (air) 15 10
659. – 50 c. ultram. & orange 60 50
660. – 70 c. indigo & magenta 1·00 60
661. **141.** $1 black and orange.. 1·25 70
BUILDINGS: 1 c., 80 c. Executive. 10 c., 50 c. Information. 12 c., 15 c., 70 c. Capitol.

1963. Freedom from Hunger.
662. **142.** 5 c. mar. & turq. (post.) 5 5
663. – 25 c. yellow & green (air) 30 25
DESIGN: 25 c. F.A.O. emblem and Globe.

DESIGNS — HORIZ. 15 c. Space capsule. VERT. 25 c. "Telstar". TV satellite.

143. Rocket.

1963. Space Exploration.
665. **143.** 10 c. yell. & ult. (post.) 10 8
666. – 15 c. chestnut and blue 15 12
667. – 25 c. grn. & orge. (air) 25 25

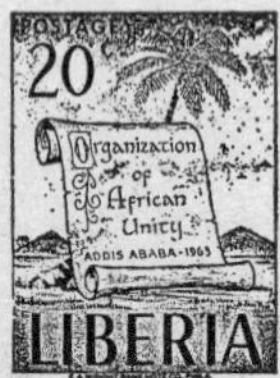

144. Red Cross. **145.** "Unity" Scroll.

1963. Red Cross Centenary.
669. **144.** 5 c. green & red (post.) 8 5
670. – 10 c. grey and red .. 10 8
671. – 25 c. violet & red (air) 25 20
672. – 50 c. blue and red .. 55 45
DESIGNS—VERT. 10 c. Emblem and torch. HORIZ 25 c. Red Cross and Globe. 50 c. Emblem and Globe.

1963. Conference of African Heads of State, Addis Ababa.
673. **145.** 20 c. brn. & grn. (post.) 20 15
674. – 25 c. red and green (air) 25 20
DESIGN: 25 c. Map of Africa (insc. "AFRICAN SUMMIT CONFERENCE").

146. Ski-jumping. **147.** President Kennedy.

1963. Winter Olympic Games, Innsbruck. (1964).
675. **146.** 5 c. blue and red (post.) 8 5
676. – 10 c. red and blue (air) 12 8
677. – 25 c. orange and green 25 20
DESIGNS—VERT. 10 c. Olympic flame. HORIZ. 25 c. Olympic rings. All have mountain scenery as backgrounds.

1964. President Kennedy Memorial Issue.
679. **147.** 20 c. blk. & blue (post.) 20 15
680. – 25 c. black & pur. (air) 25 20
DESIGN—VERT. 25 c. Pres. Kennedy, full face portrait.

148. "Relay I" Satellite. **149.** Mt. Fuji.

1964. Space Communications.
682. – 10 c. orange and green 10 5
683. **148.** 15 c. ultram. & magenta 15 12
684. – 25 c. yell., blk. & blue 25 15
SATELLITES—HORIZ. 10 c. "Syncom". 25 c. "Mariner II".

1964. Olympic Games, Tokyo.
686. **149.** 10 c. green and yellow 10 5
687. – 15 c. purple and red .. 15 10
688. – 25 c. red and buff .. 25 15
DESIGNS: 15 c. Japanese arch and Olympic Flame. 25 c. Cherry blossom and stadium.

150. Scout Bugle. **151.** "The Great Emancipator" (statue).

1965. Liberian Boy Scouts.
690. – 5 c. brown and blue (postage) 5 5
691. **150.** 10 c. ochre and green.. 10 8
692. – 25 c. blue & red (air).. 25 20
DESIGNS—VERT. 5 c. Scout badge and saluting hand. 25 c. Liberian flag within scout badge.

1965. Abraham Lincoln. Death Cent.
694. **151.** 5 c. chestnut and sepia 5 5
695. – 20 c. green & pale brown 20 15
696. – 25 c. blue and maroon 25 20
DESIGNS—HORIZ. 20 c. Bust of Lincoln, and Pres. Kennedy. VERT. 25 c. Lincoln statue Chicago (after St. Gaudens).

152. I.C.Y. Emblem.

1965. Int. Co-operation Year.
698 **152.** 12 c. brown and orange 12 8
699. 25 c. brown and blue.. 25 15
700. 50 c. brown and green 40 30

153. I.T.U. Emblem and Symbols.

1965. I.T.U. Cent.
702. **153.** 25 c. brn. & grn. (post.) 30 20
703. 35 c. magenta & black 40 25
704. 50 c. blue & verm. (air) 70 60

154. Pres. Tubman and Flag. **155.** Sir Winston Churchill.

1965. Pres. Tubman's 70th Birthday.
706. **154.** 25 c. brown, red, ultram. and blue (postage).. 30 15
707. – 25 c. brown, red, ultram. and pink (air) .. 30 15
DESIGN: 25 c. President and Liberian arms.

1966. Churchill Commem.
709. **155.** 15 c. black & orge. (post.) 20 12
710. – 20 c. black and green.. 25 15
711. – 25 c. black and blue (air) 30 25
DESIGNS—HORIZ. 20 c. Churchill in Admiral's full dress uniform. 25 c. Churchill and Houses of Parliament.

156. Pres. Roberts. **157.** Footballers and Hemispheres.

1966. Liberian Presidents.
713. **156.** 1 c. black and pink .. 5 5
714. – 2 c. black and yellow.. 5 5
715. – 3 c. black and violet.. 5 5
716. – 4 c. black and yellow.. 5 5
717. – 5 c. black and orange 8 5
718. – 10 c. black and green.. 12 5
719. – 25 c. black and blue .. 35 15
720. – 50 c. black and mauve 60 40
721. – 80 c. black and cerise 1·00 75
722. – $1 black and chestnut 1·25 80
723. – $2 black and purple.. 2·50 2·00
724. – 25 c. blk. & emerald (air) 25 20
PRESIDENTS: 2 c. Benson. 3 c. Warner. 4 c. Payne. 5 c. Roye. 10 c. Coleman. 25 c. (postage), Howard. 25 c. (air), Tubman. 50 c. King. 80 c. Johnson. $1 Barclay. $2 Cheesman

1966. World Cup Football Championships.
725. **157.** 10 c. brown & turquoise 12 8
726. – 25 c. brown and magenta 30 20
727. – 35 c. brown & orange 40 25
DESIGNS—VERT. 25 c. Presentation cup football and boots. 35 c. Footballer.

158. Pres. Kennedy Taking Oath. **159.** Children on See-saw.

1966. Pres. Kennedy. 3rd Death Anniv. (Nov. 22nd).
729. **158.** 15 c. black & red (post.) 20 5
730. – 20 c. purple and blue.. 30 8
731. – 25 c. ultram., black and ochre (air) .. 40 20
732. – 35 c. blue and pink .. 50 30
DESIGNS: 20 c. Kennedy stamps of 1964. 25 c. U.N. General Assembly and Pres. Kennedy. 35 c. Pres. Kennedy and rocket on launching pad.

1966. U.N.I.C.E.F. 20th Anniv.
734. **159.** 5 c. blue and red .. 5 5
735. – 80 c. brown and green 90 50
DESIGN: 80 c. Child playing "Doctors".

160. Giraffe. **161.** Scout Emblem and Various Sports.

1966. Wild Animals. Multicoloured.
736. 2 c. Type **160** 5 5
737. 3 c. Lion 5 5
738. 5 c. Crocodile (horiz.) .. 5 5
739. 10 c. Chimpanzees .. 10 8
740. 15 c. Leopard (horiz.) .. 15 10
741. 20 c. Rhinoceros (horiz.).. 20 15
742. 25 c. Elephant .. 25 20

1967. World Scout Jamboree, Idaho.
743. – 10 c. purple and green 10 8
744. **161.** 25 c. red and blue .. 25 15
745. – 40 c. chestnut & green 40 35
DESIGNS—VERT. 10 c. Jamboree emblem. HORIZ. 40 c. Scout by campfire, and Moon landing.

162. Pre-Hispanic Sculpture. **163.** W.H.O. Building, Brazzaville.

1967. Publicity for Olympic Games, Mexico (1968).
747. **162.** 10 c. violet & orange.. 10 8
748. – 25 c. orge., black & blue 25 20
749. – 40 c. red and green .. 40 35
DESIGNS—VERT. 25 c. Aztec calendar. HORIZ. 40 c. Mexican sombrero, guitar and ceramics.

1967. W.H.O.'s Regional Office, Brazzaville. Inaug.
751. **163.** 5 c. yellow and blue.. 8 5
752. – 80 c. green and yellow 1·00 80
DESIGN—VERT. 80 c. As T **163** but in vertical format.

164. Boy with Rattle. **165.** Ice-hockey.

1967. Musicians and Instruments. Multicoloured.
753. 2 c. Type **164** 5 5
754. 3 c. Tomtom and soko violin 5 5
755. 5 c. Mang harp 8 5
756. 10 c. Alimilim 12 8
757. 15 c. Xylophone drums .. 20 12
758. 25 c. Tomtoms 30 20
759. 35 c. Oral harp 45 25
The 3 c. and 5 c. are horiz. designs.

1967. Publicity for Winter Olympic Games, Grenoble (1968).
760. **165.** 10 c. blue and green.. 12 10
761. – 25 c. violet and blue.. 30 25
762. – 40 c. brown and orange 60 30
DESIGNS: 25 c. Ski-jumping. 40 c. Tobogganing.

166. Pres. Tubman. **167.** Human Rights Emblem.

1967. Re-election of Pres. Tubman for 6th Term.
764. **166.** 25 c. brown and blue 25 20

1968. Human Rights Year.
766. **167.** 3 c. blue and vermilion 5 5
767. 80 c. green and brown 70 50

168. Dr. King and Hearse. **169.** Throwing the Javelin and Statue of Diana.

1968. Martin Luther King Commem.
769. **168.** 15 c. brown and blue 20 15
770. – 25 c. brown and blue 30 25
771. – 35 c. black and olive 40 30
DESIGNS—VERT. 25 c. Dr. Martin Luther King. HORIZ. 35 c. Dr. King and Lincoln Monument.

1968. Olympic Games, Mexico.
773. **169.** 15 c. violet and chestnut 20 8
774. – 25 c. blue & vermilion 30 10
775. – 35 c. brown and green 40 15
DESIGNS: 25 c. Throwing the discus and Quetzalcoatl sculpture. 35 c. High-diving and Xochilcalco bas-relief.

170. President Tubman. **171.** I.L.O. Symbol.

1968. Pres. Tubman's Administration. 25th Anniv.
777. **170.** 25 c. blk., brn. & silver 35 30

1969. Int. Labour Organization. 50th Anniv.
779. **171.** 25 c. blue & gold (post.) 35 30
780. – 80 c. green & gold (air) 65 65
DESIGN: 80 c. As Type **171**, but vertical.

172. "Prince Balthasar Carlos" (Velasquez). **173.** Bank Emblem on "Tree".

1969. Paintings (1st Series.) Multicoloured.
781. 3 c. Type **172** 5 5
782. 5 c. "Red Roofs" (Pissarro) 8 5
783. 10 c. "David and Goliath" (Caravaggio) 12 5
784. 12 c. "Still Life" (Chardin) 15 5
785. 15 c. "The Last Supper" (Leonardo da Vinci) .. 20 8
786. 20c. "Regatta at Argenteul" (Monet) 25 12
787. 25 c. "Judgement of Solomon" (Giogione) .. 30 15
788. 35 c. "The Sistine Madonna" (Raphael) 45 20
Nos. 782/6 are horiz.
See also Nos. 795/802.

1969. African Development Bank. 5th Anniv.
789. **173.** 25 c. brown and blue 30 20
790. 80 c. red and green .. 90 60

174. Memorial Plaque. **175.** Peace Dove and Emblems.

1969. 1st Man on the Moon.
791. **174.** 15 c. blue and ochre .. 20 5
792. – 25 c. blue and orange .. 30 12
793. – 35 c. vermilion & slate 45 15
DESIGNS—VERT. 25 c. Moon landing and Liberian 35 c. "Kennedy" stamp of 1966. 35 c. Module lifting off from Moon.

1969. Paintings (2nd Series). As T **172**. Multicoloured.
795. 3 c. "The Gleaners" (Millet) 5 5
796. 5 c. "View of Toledo" (El Greco) 5 5
797. 10 c. "Heads of Negroes" (Rubens) 10 5
798. 12 c. "The Last Supper" (El Greco) 12 8
799. 15 c. "Peasants Dancing" (Bruegel) 15 10
800. 20c. "Hunters in the Snow" (Bruegel) 20 15
801. 25 c. "Descent from the Cross" (detail, Weyden) 25 20
802. 35 c. "The Conception" (Murillo) 35 30
Nos. 795, 797/800 are horiz.

1970. United Nations. 25th Anniv.
803. **175.** 5 c. grn. & silver (postage) 5 5
804. – $1 ultramarine and silver (air) .. .. 1·00 70
DESIGN: $1, U.N. emblem and olive branch.

176. World Cup "Football" Emblem.

1970. World Cup Football Championships, Mexico.
805. **176.** 5 c. brown and blue .. 8 5
806. – 10 c. brown and green 15 10
807. – 25 c. gold and purple 30 20
808. – 35 c. red and blue .. 45 30
DESIGNS—VERT. 10 c. Tlaloc, Mexican Rain God. 25 c. Jules Rimet Cup. HORIZ. 35 c. Football in sombrero.

177. Pop Singer and Festival Plaza.

1970. Expo 70. Multicoloured.
810. 2 c. Type **177** 5 5
811. 3 c. Japanese singer and Expo hall 5 5
812. 5 c. Aerial view of "EXPO 70" 5 5
813. 7 c. "Tanabata" Festival .. 8 5
814. 8 c. "Awa" Dance Festival 12 8
815. 25 c. "Sado-Okesa" Dance Festival 30 20

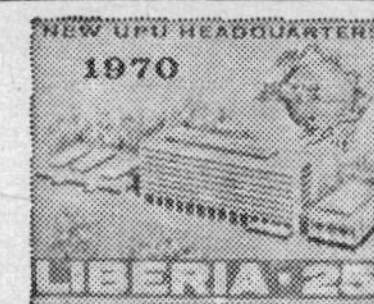

178. New H.Q. Building.

1970. New U.P.U. Headquarters Building, Berne. Inaug.
817. **178.** 25 c. brown and blue 25 15
818. – 80 c. brown and chestnut 85 55
DESIGN—VERT. 80 c. Similar to T **178** but with larger U.P.U. monument.

179. "The First Consul" (J. M. Vien).

1970. Napoleon Bonaparte. Birth Bicent. Multicoloured.
819. 3 c. Type **179** 5 5
820. 5 c. "Napoleon visiting School" (unknown artist) 5 5
821. 10 c. "Napoleon Bonaparte" (detail, Isabey) 12 10
822. 12 c. "The French Campaign" (Meissonier) .. 15 12
823. 20 c. "The Abdication" (Bouchot) 25 20
824. 25 c. "Meeting of Napoleon and Pope Pius VII" (Demarne) 30 20

180. Pres. Tubman.

1970. Pres. Tubman's 75th Birthday.
826. **180.** 25 c. multicoloured .. 30 20

181. "The Adoration of the Magi" (R. van der Weyden).

1970. Christmas. "The Adoration of the Magi" by artists as below. Multicoloured.
828. 3 c. Type **181** 5 5
829. 5 c. H. Memling 5 5
830. 10 c. S. Lochner 12 5
831. 12 c. A. Altdorfer (vert.) .. 15 8
832. 20 c. H. van der Goes .. 25 12
833. 25 c. H. Bosch (vert.) .. 30 20

182. Bapende Mask.

184. Pres. Tubman and Women at Ballot Box.

183. Astronauts on Moon.

1971. African Ceremonial Masks. Mask from different tribes. Multicoloured.
835. 2 c. Type **182** 5 5
836. 3 c. Dogon 5 5
837. 5 c. Baoule 5 5
838. 6 c. Dedougou 5 5
839. 9 c. Dan 10 5
840. 15 c. Bamileke 20 10
841. 20 c. Bapende (different) .. 25 12
842. 25 c. Bamileke costume .. 30 20

1971. "Apollo 14". Moon Mission. Mult.
843. 3 c. Type **183** 5 5
844. 5 c. Astronaut and Moon vehicle 5 5
845. 10 c. Erecting U.S. flag on Moon 12 8
846. 12 c. Splashdown 15 8
847. 20 c. Astronauts leaving capsule 25 12
848. 25 c. "Apollo 14" crew .. 30 15

1971. Liberian Women's Suffrage. 25th Anniv.
850. **184.** 3 c. blue and brown .. 5 5
851. – 80 c. brown and green 1·00 55
DESIGN—HORIZ. 80 c. Pres. Tubman, women and map.

185. Hall of Honour, Munich.

1971. Olympic Games, Munich (1972) (1st issue). Views of Munich. Multicoloured.
852. 3 c. Type **185** 5 5
853. 5 c. View of central Munich 5 5
854. 10 c. National Museum .. 12 8
855. 12 c. Max Joseph's Square 15 8
856. 20 c. Propylaen, King's Square 25 12
857. 25 c. Liesel-Karlstadt Fountain 30 15

186. American Scout. **187.** Pres. Tubman.

1971. World Scout Jamboree, Asagiri, Japan. Scouts in national uniforms. Multicoloured.
859. 3 c. Type **186** 5 5
860. 5 c. West Germany .. 5 5
861. 10 c. Australia 12 8
862. 12 c. Great Britain .. 15 8
863. 20 c. Japan 25 12
864. 25 c. Liberia 30 15

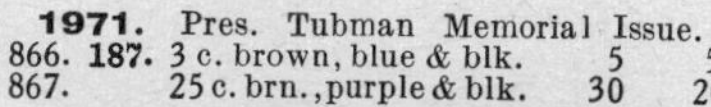
1971. Pres. Tubman Memorial Issue.
866. **187.** 3 c. brown, blue & blk. 5 5
867. 25 c. brn., purple & blk. 30 20

188. Zebra and Foal.

1971. U.N.I.C.E.F. 25th Anniv. Animals with young. Multicoloured.
868. 5 c. Type **188** 5 5
869. 7 c. Koala bears 8 5
870. 8 c. Llamas 10 5
871. 10 c. Fox and cubs .. 12 8
872. 20 c. Monkeys 25 12
873. 25 c. Brown bears .. 30 15

189. Cross-country Skiing and Japanese Deer.

1971. Winter Olympic Games, Sapporo, Japan. Sports and Hokkaido Animals. Multicoloured.
875. 2 c. Type **189** 5 5
876. 3 c. Tobogganing and Black woodpecker 5 5
877. 5 c. Ski-jumping and Brown bear 5 5
878. 10 c. Bob-sleighing and guillemots 12 8
879. 15 c. Figure-skating and chipmunks 15 10
880. 25 c. Slalom-skiing and Japanese cranes .. 30 15

190. A.P.U. Emblem, Dove and Letter. **191.** The "Elizabeth" at Providence Island.

1971. African Postal Union. 10th Anniv.
882. **190.** 25 c. orge. & blue .. 30 15
883. 80 c. brown and grey .. 85 50

1972. Liberia. 150th Anniv.
884. **191.** 3 c. green and blue .. 5 5
885. – 20 c. blue and orge. .. 20 12
886. **191.** 25 c. purple and orge. 30 15
887. – 35 c. purple and grn. 40 20
DESIGNS—VERT. 20 c., 35 c. Arms and Founding Fathers Monument, Monrovia.

192. Pres. Tolbert and Map.

1972. Pres. Wm. R. Tolbert Jnr. Inaug.
889. **192.** 25 c. brown & green 30 15
890. – 80 c. brown and blue 85 50
DESIGN—VERT. 80 c. Pres. Tolbert standing by desk.

193. Football.

1972. Olympic Games, Munich. (2nd issue). Multicoloured.
891. 3 c. Type **193** 5 5
892. 5 c. Swimming 5 5
893. 10 c. Show-jumping .. 12 8
894. 12 c. Cycling 12 8
895. 20 c. Long-jumping .. 20 15
896. 25 c. Running 25 20

194. Globe and Emblem.

196. Emperor Haile Selassie.

195. Astronaut and Moon Rover.

1972. Int. Y's Men's Clubs. 50th Anniv.
898. **194.** 15 c. violet and gold .. 15 10
899. – 90 c. green and blue .. 1·00 55
DESIGN: 90 c. Club emblem on World Map.

1972. Moon Mission of "Apollo 16". Mult.
900. 3 c. Type **195** 5 5
901. 5 c. Reflection on visor .. 5 5
902. 10 c. Astronauts with cameras 10 5
903. 12 c. Setting up equipment 12 10
904. 20 c. "Apollo 16" emblem 20 15
905. 25 c. Astronatus in Moon Rover 25 20

1972. Emperor Haile Selassie of Ethiopia's 80th Birthday.
907. **196.** 20 c. green and yellow 20 15
908. 25 c. purple & yellow 25 20
909. 35 c. brown & yellow 40 25

197. H.M.S. "Ajax" (battleship), 1809.

1972. Famous Ships of the British Royal Navy. Multicoloured.
910. 3 c. Type **197** 5 5
911. 5 c. H.M.S. "Hogue" (battleship), 1811 .. 5 5
912. 7 c. H.M.S. "Ariadne" (frigate), 1816 .. 8 5
913. 15 c. H.M.S. "Royal Adelaide" (battleship), 1828 .. 15 12
914. 20 c. H.M.S. "Rinaldo" (screw sloop), 1860 .. 20 15
915. 25 c. H.M.S. "Nymphe" (steam frigate), 1888 .. 25 20

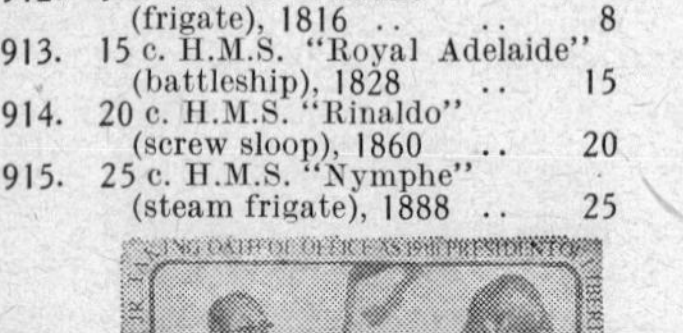

198. Pres. Tolbert taking Oath.

1972. First Year President Tolbert Presidency.
917. **198.** 15 c. multicoloured .. 12 10
918. 25 c. multicoloured .. 20 15

199. Klaus Dibasi and Italian Flag.

1973. Olympic Games, Munich. Gold-medal Winners. Multicoloured.
920. 5 c. Type **199** 5 5
921. 8 c. Borzov and Soviet flag 8 5
922. 10 c. Yanagida and Japanese flag 10 8
923. 12 c. Spitz and U.S. flag .. 12 10
924. 15 c. Keino and Kenyan flag 15 12
925. 25 c. Meade and Union Jack 25 20

200. Astronaut on Moon.

1973. Moon Flight of "Apollo 17". Mult.
927. 2 c. Type **200** 5 5
928. 3 c. Testing lunar rover at Cape Kennedy 5 5
929. 10 c. Collecting Moon rocks 10 8
930. 15 c. Lunar rover on Moon 15 12
931. 20 c. "Apollo 17" crew at Cape Kennedy 20 15
932. 25 c. Astronatus on Moon 25 20

201. British G.N.R. Locomotive.

1973. Historical Railways. Steam locomotives of 1895-1905. Multicoloured.
934. 2 c. Type **201** 5 5
935. 3 c. Holland 5 5
936. 10 c. France 10 8
937. 15 c. U.S.A. 15 12
938. 20 c. Japan 20 15
939. 25 c. Germany 25 20

202. O.A.U. Emblem.

1973. Organization of African Unity. 10th Anniv.
941. **202.** 3 c. multicoloured .. 5 5
942. 5 c. multicoloured .. 5 5
943. 10 c. multicoloured .. 10 8
944. 15 c. multicoloured .. 15 12
945. 25 c. multicoloured .. 25 20
946. 50 c. multicoloured .. 50 40

203. Edward Jenner and Roses.

1973. W.H.O. 25th Anniv. Multicoloured.
947. 1 c. Type **203** 5 5
948. 4 c. Sigmund Freud and violets 5 5
949. 10 c. Jonas Salk and chrysanthemums 10 8
950. 15 c. Louis Pasteur and scabious 15 12
951. 20 c. Emil von Behring and mallow 20 15
952. 25 c. Sir Alexander Fleming and rhododendrons .. 25 20

204. Stanley Steamer, 1910.

1973. Vintage Cars. Multicoloured.
954. 2 c. Type **204** 5 5
955. 3 c. Cadillac Model A, 1903 5 5
956. 10 c. Clement-Baynard, 1904 10 8
957. 15 c. Rolls-Royce Silver Ghost tourer, 1907 .. 15 12
958. 20 c. Maxwell gentlemen's speedster, 1905 .. .. 20 15
959. 25 c. Chadwick, 1907 .. 25 20

205. Copernicus, Armillary Sphere and Tracking System.

1973. Copernicus. 500th Birth Anniv. Mult.
961. 1 c. Type **205** 5 5
962. 4 c. Eudoxus solar system 5 5
963. 10 c. Aristotle, Ptolemy and Copernicus 10 8
964. 15 c. "Saturn" and "Apollo" spacecraft 15 12
965. 20 c. Astronomical observatory satellite 20 15
966. 25 c. Satellite tracking-station 25 20

206. Radio Mast and Map of Africa.

1974. "Eternal Love Winning Africa" Radio Station. 20th Anniv. Multicoloured.
968. 13 c. Type **206** 12 10
969. 15 c. Radio Mast and map of Liberia 15 12
970. 17 c. Type **206** 20 15
971. 25 c. As 15 c. 25 20

207. Sailing-ship "Thomas Coutts" (1817) and Liner "Aureol" (1974).

1974. Universal Postal Union. Cent. Mult.
972. 2 c. Type **207** 5 5
973. 3 c. Mail-plane and ship, satellite and Morovia Post Office 5 5
974. 10 c. U.S. and Soviet Telecommunications satellites 10 8
975. 15 c. Postal runner and aircraft 15 12
976. 20 c. British Rail High-speed Train and Liberian mail-van 20 15
977. 25 c. American Pony Express rider 25 20

208. Fox Terrier.

1974. Dogs. Multicoloured.
979. 5 c. Type **208** 5 5
980. 10 c. Boxer 10 8
981. 16 c. Chihuahua 15 12
982. 19 c. Beagle 20 15
983. 25 c. Golden retriever .. 25 20
984. 50 c. Collie 50 40

209. West Germany v. Chile Match.

1974. World Cup Football Championships, West Germany. Scenes from semi-final matches. Multicoloured.
986. 1 c. Type **209** 5 5
987. 2 c. Australia v. East Germany 5 5
988. 5 c. Brazil v. Yugoslavia .. 5 5
989. 10 c. Zaire v. Scotland .. 10 8
990. 12 c. Netherlands v. Uruguay 12 10
991. 15 c. Sweden v. Bulgaria 15 12
992. 20 c. Italy v. Haiti .. 20 15
993. 25 c. Poland v. Argentina 25 20

210. "Chrysiridia Madagascariensis".

1974. Tropical Butterflies. Multicoloured.
995. 1 c. Type **210** 5 5
996. 2 c. "Catagramma sorana" 5 5
997. 5 c. "Erasmia pulchella" 8 5
998. 17 c. "Morpho cypris" .. 20 12
999. 25 c. "Agrias amydon" .. 30 20
1000. 40 c. "Vanessa cardui" .. 45 30

MINIMUM PRICE

The minimum price quoted is 5p which represents a handling charge rather than a basis for valuing common stamps. For further notes about prices see introductory pages.

211. Pres. Tolbert and Gold Medallion.

1974. "Family of Man" Award to President Tolbert. Mult.
1002. 3 c. Type **211** 5 5
1003. $1 Pres. Tolbert, medallion and flag .. .. 1·10 50

212. Churchill with Troops.

1975. Sir Winston Churchill. Birth Cent. Multicoloured.
1004. 3 c. Type **212** 5 5
1005. 10 c. Churchill and aerial combat 10 8
1006. 15 c. Churchill aboard ship in Channel 15 12
1007. 17 c. Churchill reviewing troops in desert .. 20 15
1008. 20 c. Churchill crossing Rhine 30 15
1009. 25 c. Churchill with Roosevelt 30 20

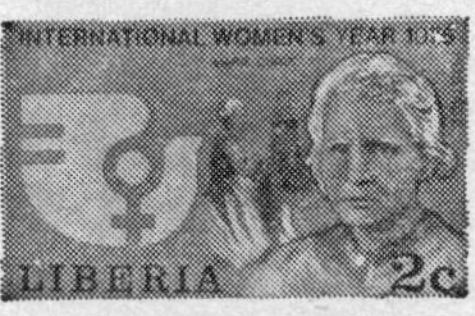

213. Marie Curie.

1975. International Women's Year. Mult.
1011. 2 c. Type **213** 5 5
1012. 3 c. Mahalia Jackson .. 5 5
1013. 5 c. Joan of Arc 5 5
1014. 10 c. Eleanor Roosevelt 10 8
1015. 25 c. Matilda Newport .. 25 20
1016. 50 c. Valentina Tereshkova 50 40

214. Old State House, Boston, and U.S. 2 c. "Liberty Bell" Stamp of 1926.

1975. American Independence. Bicentenary.
1018. 5 c. Type **214** 5 5
1019. 10 c. George Washington & 1928 "Valley Forge" stamp 10 8
1020. 15 c. Philadelphia, & 1937 "Constitution" stamp 15 12
1021. 20 c. Benjamin Franklin & 1938 "Ratification" stamp 20 15
1022. 25 c. Paul Revere's Ride & 1925 "Lexington-Concord" stamp .. 25 20
1023. 50 c. "Santa Maria" and 1893 "Columbus' Landing" stamp .. 45 40

215. Dr. Schweitzer, Baboon and Lambarene Hospital.

1975. Dr. Albert Schweitzer. Birth Cent. Multicoloured.
1025. 1 c. Type **215** 5 5
1026. 3 c. Schweitzer, elephant and canoe 5 5
1027. 5 c. Schweitzer, buffalo & canoe 5 5
1028. 6 c. Schweitzer, antelope and dancer 5 5
1029. 25 c. Schweitzer, lioness and village woman .. 25 20
1030. 50 c. Schweitzer, zebras & clinic scene 50 40

216. " Apollo " Spacecraft.

1975. " Apollo-Soyuz " Space Link. Mult.
1032. 5 c Type **216** 5 5
1033. 10 c. " Soyuz " spacecraft 10 8
1034. 15 c. American-Russian hand-clasp 15 12
1035. 20 c. Flags and maps of America and Russia .. 20 15
1036. 25 c. Leonov and Kubasov 25 20
1037. 50 c. Slayton, Brand and Stafford 50 40

217. Presidents Tolbert and Stevens, and Signing Ceremony.

1975. Liberia-Sierra Leone Mano River Union Agreement.
1039. **217.** 2 c. multicoloured .. 5 5
1040. 3 c. multicoloured .. 5 5
1041. 5 c. multicoloured .. 5 5
1042. 10 c. multicoloured.. 10 8
1043. 25 c. multicoloured.. 25 20
1044. 50 c. multicoloured.. 50 40

218. Figure-skating.

1976. Winter Olympic Games, Innsbruck. Multicoloured.
1045. 1 c. Type **218** (postage).. 5 5
1046. 4 c. Ski-jumping 5 5
1047. 10 c. Skiing (slalom) .. 10 8
1048. 25 c. Ice-hockey.. .. 25 20
1049. 35 c. Speed-skating .. 35 30
1050. 50 c. Two-man bobsledding 45 40

219. Pres. Tolbert taking Oath

1976. President William R. Tolbert, Jnr. Inauguration. Multicoloured.
1052. 3 c. Type **219** 5 5
1053. 25 c. Pres. Tolbert taking office (vert.) 25 20
1054. $1 Liberian crest, flag & commemorative gold coin .. .. .. 1·10 60

220. Weightlifting.

1976. Olympic Games, Montreal. Multicoloured.
1055. 2 c. Type **220** 5 5
1056. 3 c. Pole-vaulting .. 5 5
1057. 10 c. Hammer and shot-put 10 8
1058. 25 c. Sailing 25 20
1059. 35 c. Gymnastics .. 35 25
1060. 50 c. Hurdling 50 40

221. Bell's First Telephone and Receiver of 1876.

1976. Telephone Centenary. Multicoloured.
1062. 1 c. Type **221** 5 5
1063. 4 c. Mail-coach 5 5
1064. 5 c. " Intelsat 4 " satellite 5 5
1065. 25 c. Cable-ship " Dominia ", 1926 .. 25 20
1066. 40 c. Futuristic train .. 40 30
1067. 50 c. Wright brothers plane, " Graf Zeppelin " and " Concorde " .. 1·10 90

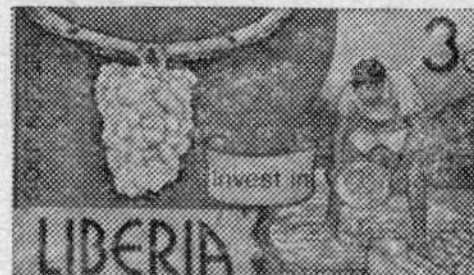

222. Gold Nugget Pendant.

1976. Liberian Gold Products. Multicoloured.
1069. 3 c. Type **222** 5 5
1070. 5 c. " V " ring 5 5

223. Rhinoceros.

1976. Animals. Multicoloured.
1071. 2 c. Type **223** 5 5
1072. 3 c. Striped antelope .. 5 5
1073. 5 c. Chimpanzee (vert.).. 5 5
1074. 15 c. Pygmy hippopotamus 15 12
1075. 25 c. Leopard 25 20
1076. $1 Gorilla .. .. 1·10 60

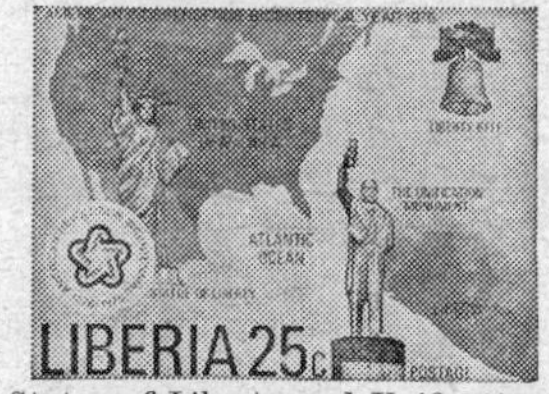

224. Statue of Liberty and Unification Monument on Maps of U.S.A. and Liberia.

1976. American Revolution Bicentenary. Multicoloured.
1078. 25 c. Type **224** 25 20
1079. $1 Presidents Washington & Ford (U.S.A.), Roberts and Tolbert (Liberia) 1·10 60

MILITARY FIELD POST.

1916. Liberian Frontier Force. Surch. **LFF 1 c.**
M 213. **9.** 1 c. on 1 c. green .. 20·00 20·00
M 214. **20.** 1 c. on 1 c. blk. & grn. £100 £100
M 215. **33.** 1 c. on 1 c. blk. & grn. 40 40
M 216. – 1 c. on 2 c. blk. & red (No. 159) 40 40

OFFICIAL STAMPS

1892. 1892 stamps optd. **OFFICIAL.**
O 89. **7.** 1 c. red 30 30
O 90. 2 c. blue 30 30
O 91. **8.** 4 c. black and green 40 30
O 101. **9.** 5 c. on 6 c. grn. (No. 89) 20 25
O 92. 6 c. green 40 30
O 93. **10.** 8 c. black and brown 40 40
O 94. **11.** 12 c. rose 50 50
O 95. **12.** 16 c. lilac 75 60
O 96. **13.** 24 c. green on yellow 75 60
O 97. **12.** 32 c. blue 80 80
O 98. **14.** $1 black and blue .. 4·50 2·00
O 99. **13.** $2 brown on buff .. 6·00 2·50
O 100. **15.** $5 black and red .. 8·00 3·00

1894. 1892 stamps optd. **O S.**
O 102. **7.** 1 c. red 25 25
O 103. 2 c. blue 40 30
O 104. **8.** 4 c. black and green 50 40
O 105. **10.** 8 c. black and brown 50 40
O 106. **11.** 12 c. rose 60 50
O 107. **12.** 16 c. lilac 60 50
O 108. **13.** 24 c. green on yellow 60 50
O 109. **12.** 32 c. blue .. .. 1·00 60
O 110. **14.** $1 black and blue .. 3·50 3·50
O 111. **13.** $2 brown on buff .. 3·50 3·50
O 112. **15.** $5 black and red .. 9·00 7·00

1894. 1894 stamp in different colours optd. **O S** Imperf. or roul.
O 113. **16.** 5 c. green and lilac .. 1·50 1·75

1898. 1897 stamps optd. **O S.**
O 123. **9.** 1 c. purple 35 35
O 124. 1 c. green 35 35
O 125. **14.** 2 c. black and bistre 60 60
O 126. 2 c. black and red .. 80 80
O 127. **8.** 5 c. black and lake .. 75 75
O 128. 5 c. black and blue .. 1·00 1·00
O 129. **10.** 10 c. blue and yellow 60 60
O 130. **11.** 15 c. black 60 60
O 131. **12.** 20 c. red 80 80
O 132. **13.** 25 c. green 60 60
O 133. **12.** 30 c. blue .. .. 1·10 1·10
O 134. **17.** 50 c. black and brown 1·10 1·10

†1903. Stamp of 1903, but different colour, optd. **O S**
O 139. **19.** 3 c. green 15 15

1904. Nos. O 101 and 102 surch. **ONE O S.** and bars or **O S 2** and bars.
O 145. **9.** 1 c. on 5 c. on 6 c. green 90 90
O 146. **12.** 2 c. on 30 c. blue .. 2·50 2·50

†1906. Stamps of 1906, but different colours, optd. **O S**
O 158. **20.** 1 c. black and green 40 40
O 159. **21.** 2 c. black and red .. 12 8
O 160. – 5 c. black and blue .. 40 25
O 161. – 10 c. black and violet 50 40
O 162. – 15 c. black and brown 1·90 40
O 163. – 20 c. black and green 50 40
O 164. – 25 c. grey and purple 30 8
O 165. – 30 c. brown 30 15
O 166. – 50 c. green and brown 50 15
O 167. – 75 c. black and blue 1·00 60
O 168. – $1 black and green .. 60 12
O 169. **27.** $2 black and purple 1·00 12
O 170. **30.** $5 black and orange 2·25 15

†1909. Stamps of 1909, but different colours, optd. **O S.**
O 171. **33.** 1 c. black and green 10 8
O 172. – 2 c. brown and red .. 10 8
O 173. **35.** 5 c. black and blue .. 15 8
O 175. **36.** 10 c. blue and black 35 15
O 176. – 15 c. black and purple 20 15
O 177. – 20 c. green and bistre 20 15
O 178. – 25 c. green and blue 35 25
O 179. – 30 c. blue 50 25
O 180. 50 c. green and brown 75 25
O 181. – 75 c. black and violet 1·00 25

1910. As No. 172, colours changed, optd. **O S.** Perf. or roul.
O 182. **36.** 3 c. on 10 c. blue & blk. 40 20

1914. Official stamps surch.: (A) **1914 2 CENTS.** (B) **+2 c.** (C) **5.** (D) **CENTS 20 OFFICIAL.**
O 188. **36.** +2 c. on 3 c. on 10 c. blue and black (B) (No. O 182) .. 20 20
O 184. 2 c. on 25 c. grey and pur. (A) (No. O 164) 5·00 3·50
O 185. – 5 c. on 30 c. blue (C) (No. O 179) .. 5·00 3·50
O 186. – 20 c. on 75 c black & violet (D) (No. O 181) 5·00 3·50

1914. No. 154 surch. **CENTS 20 OFFICIAL**
O 187. 20 c. on 75 c. black and brown .. .. 5·00 3·50

1915. Official stamps of 1906 and 1909 surch. in different ways.
O 209. – 1 c. on 2 c. brown and red (No. O 172) .. 1·50 1·50
O 210. **35.** 2 c. on 5 c. black and blue (No. O 173) .. 1·50 1·50
O 198. – 2 c. on 15 c. black and purple (No. O 176) 60 50
O 199. 2 c. on 25 c. green and blue (No. O 178) .. 65 50
O 200. – 5 c. on 20 c. green and bistre (No. O 177) 60 50
O 201. – 5 c. on 30 c. blue (No. O 179) .. 80 40
O 202. – 10 c. on 50 c. green & brown (No. O 180) 1·50 1·50
O 203. – 20 c. on 75 c. black & violet (No. O 181) 2·00 2·00
O 204. – 25 c. on $1 black and green (No. O 168) 8·00 7·00
O 205. **27.** 50 c. on $2 black and purple (No. O 169) 10·00 10·00
O 207. **30.** $1 on $5 black and orange (No. O 170) 12·00 12·00

1915. No. O 134 surch. **10 10** and ornaments and bars.
O 208. **17.** 10 c. on 50 c. blk. & brn. 6·00 5·50

1915. Military Field Post. Official stamps surch. **L F F 1 c.**
OM 214. **20.** 1 c. on 1 c. black and green (No. O 158) £150 £150
OM 215. **33.** 1 c. on 1 c. black and green (No. O 171) 60 60
OM 216. – 1 c. on 2 c. black and red (No. O 172).. 60 60

1917. No. O 165 surch. **FIVE CENTS 1917** and bars.
O 221. – 5 c. on 30 c. brown.. 3·00 2·00

1918. No. O 175 surch. **3 CENTS.**
O 224. **36.** 3 c. on 10 c. blue & blk. 40 40

†1918. Stamps of 1918, but in different colours, optd. **O S.**
O 238. **45.** 1 c. brown and green 30 12
O 239. **46.** 2 c. black and red .. 30 12
O 240. – 5 c. black and blue .. 60 5
O 241. **48.** 10 c. blue 30 5
O 242. – 15 c. green and brown 50 15
O 243. – 20 c. black and lilac 50 5
O 244. **51.** 25 c. green and brown 2·50 30
O 245. – 30 c. black and violet 3·00 30
O 246. – 50 c. black and brown 4·00 30
O 247. – 75 c. black and brown 1·50 12
O 248. – $1 blue and olive .. 3·00 12
O 249. – $2 black and olive .. 6·00 12
O 250. – $5 green .. .. 6·00 15

1920. Nos. O 238/9 surch. **1920** and value and two bars.
O 258. **45.** 3 c. on 1 c. brn. & grn. 70 40
O 259. **46.** 4 c. on 2 c. blk. & red 50 50

†1921. Stamps of 1915 and 1921, in different colours, optd. **O S** or **OFFICIAL.**
O 285. **58.** 1 c. green 25 5
O 286. **43.** 2 c. red 40 8
O 287. **44.** 3 c. brown 25 8
O 288. **59.** 5 c. brown and blue.. 40 8
O 289. – 10 c. black and purple 20 8
O 290. – 15 c. green and black 2·00 30
O 291. – 20 c. blue and brown 75 25
O 292. – 25 c. green and orange 2·50 30
O 293. – 30 c. red and brown.. 60 8
O 294. – 50 c. green and black 60 8
O 295. – 75 c. purple and blue 1·25 8
O 296. – $1 black and blue .. 7·00 50
O 297. – $2 green and orange 7·00 75
O 298. – $5 blue and green .. 7·00 1·25

†1921. Nos. O 258/98 optd. **1921.**
O 299. **58.** 1 c. green 20 8
O 300. **43.** 2 c. red 25 8
O 301. **44.** 3 c. brown 25 10
O 302. **59.** 5 c. brown and blue.. 25 10
O 303. – 10 c. black and purple 25 10
O 304. – 15 c. green and black 2·00 10
O 305. – 20 c. blue and brown 2·10 25
O 306. – 25 c. green and orange 3·00 50
O 307. – 30 c. red and brown.. 1·25 10
O 308. – 50 c. green and black 2·50 10
O 309. – 75 c. purple and blue 1·00 10
O 310. – $1 black and blue .. 6·00 1·00
O 311. – $2 green and orange 5·00 1·50
O 312. – $5 blue and green .. 6·00 2·50

†1923. Stamps of 1923, but different colours, optd **O S.**
O 313. **71.** 1 c. black and green 8 5
O 314. **72.** 2 c. brown and red .. 8 5
O 315. – 3 c. black and blue .. 20 8
O 316. – 5 c. green and orange 20 8
O 317. – 10 c. purple and olive 20 10
O 318. – 15 c. blue and green.. 60 20
O 319. – 20 c. blue and lilac .. 60 25
O 320. – 25 c. brown .. 1·50 25
O 321. – 30 c. brown and blue 1·00 10
O 322. – 50 c. brown and bistre 1·00 25
O 323. – 75 c. green and grey.. 1·10 12
O 324. **82.** $1 green and red .. 1·25 40
O 325. – $2 red and purple .. 2·50 20
O 326. – $5 brown and blue.. 3·50 35

1926. No. O 238 surch. **Two Cents** and thick bar of wavy lines or ornamental scroll or two bars.
O 327. **45.** 2 c. on 1 c. brn. & grn. 1·00 1·00

1928. Stamps of 1928 optd. **OFFICIAL SERVICE.**
O 333. **85.** 1 c. green 8 8
O 334. 2 c. violet 12 10
O 335. 3 c. brown 15 10
O 336. **86.** 5 c. blue 25 15
O 337. **87.** 10 c. grey 50 35
O 338. **86.** 15 c. lilac .. 1·00 35
O 339. $1 brown .. .. 10·00 4·00

1944. No. O 317. surch.
O 427. 4 c. on 10 c. grey .. 3·25 3·25

POSTAGE DUE STAMPS

1892. Stamps of 1886 surch. **POSTAGE DUE** and value in frame.
D 89. **4.** 3 c. on 3 c. mauve .. 40 40
D 90. 6 c. on 6 c. grey .. 2·00 2·00

ILLUSTRATIONS British Commonwealth and all overprints and surcharges are FULL SIZE. Foreign Countries have been reduced to ¾-LINEAR.

D 1.

1894.
D 93. D **1.** 2 c. black and orange on yellow 50 30
D 94. 4 c. black & red on rose 50 40
D 95. 6 c. blk. & brn. on buff 50 50
D 96. 8 c. blk. & blue on blue 50 50
D 97. 10 c. black and green on mauve .. 60 60
D 98. 20 c. black and violet on grey 60 60
D 99. 40 c. black and brown on green .. .. 1·10 90

REGISTRATION STAMPS

R 1.

1893.

R 90. R 1. (10 c.) blk. (Buchanan) 80·00 80·00
R 91. (10 c.) blk. ("Grenville") £350 £350
R 92. (10 c.) black (Harper) £475 £475
R 93. (10 c.) blk. (Monrovia) 15·00 15·00
R 94. (10 c.) black (Robertsport) £130 £130

1894. Surch. **10 CENTS 10**, twice.

R 95. R 1. 10 c. blue on rose .. 80 80
R 96. 10 c. green on buff .. 80 80
R 97. 10 c. red on yellow .. 80 80
R 98. 10 c. red on blue .. 80 80

Each stamp in the above and succeeding issues of Registration stamps bears the name of a different town.

R 2. President Gibson. R 3.

†1903.

R 139. R 2. 10 c. black and blue 1·00 20
R 140. 10 c. black and red .. 1·00 20
R 141. 10 c. black and green 1·00 20
R 142. 10 c. black and violet 1·00 20
R 143. 10 c. black and claret 1·00 20

1919. Roul. or perf.

R 250. R 3. 10 c. blue and black 20 15
R 251. 10 c. black and bistre 30 25
R 252. 10 c. black and green 30 25
R 253. 10 c. blue and violet 30 25
R 254. 10 c. black and lake 30 25

R 4. Gabon Viper.

†1921.

R 285. R 4. 10 c. black and lake 8·00 1·50
R 286. 10 c. black and red 8·00 1·50
R 287. 10 c. black and blue 8·00 1·50
R 288. 10 c. black and orange 8·00 1·50
R 289. 10 c. black and green 8·00 1·50

†1921. Optd. **1921.**

R 290. R 4. 10 c. black and lake 7·00 2·50
R 291. 10 c. black and red 7·00 2·50
R 292. 10 c. black and blue 7·00 2·50
R 293. 10 c. black and orange 7·00 2·50
R 294. 10 c. black and green 7·00 2·50

R 5. Landing Ship's Passengers.

DESIGNS: No. R 37, Tug and ship. No. R 38, Sailing ship. No. R 39, Liner. No. R 40, Canoe.

†1923. Various sea views.

R 304. R 5. 10 c. red and black 3·50 35
R 305. – 10 c. green and black 3·50 35
R 306. – 10 c. orge. & black 3·50 35
R 307. – 10 c. blue & black .. 3·50 35
R 308. – 10 c. violet & black 3·50 35

1941. No. 364 surch. **REGISTERED** and **10 CENTS 10.**

R 380. 10 c. on 5 c. brown (post.) 1·10 1·10
R 381. 10 c. on 5 c. brown (air) 1·10 1·10

No. R 381 additionally optd. **AIR MAIL** and aeroplane.

SPECIAL DELIVERY STAMPS

1941. No. 364 surch. **SPECIAL DELIVERY** and **10 CENTS 10.**

S 378. 10 c. on 5 c. brown (post.) 1·10 1·10
S 379. 10 c. on 5 c. brown (air) 1·10 1·10

No. S 379 additionally optd. **AIR MAIL**, aeroplane and postman.

LIBYA O3

A former Italian colony in N. Africa, comprising the governorates of Cyrenaica and Tripolitania. From the end of 1951 an independent kingdom including the Fezzan also. Following a revolution in 1969 the country is now known as the Libyan Arab Republic.

A. ITALIAN COLONY.

1912. Stamps of Italy optd. **Libia.**

1. 20. 1 c. brown 5 5
2. 21. 2 c. brown 5 5
3. 24. 5 c. green 5 5
4. 10 c. red 5 5
5. 25. 15 c. black .. .. 1·75 8
6. 15 c. grey 8 8
7. 22. 20 c. orange 5 5
8. 25. 20 c. orange 8 8
9. 26. 25 c. blue 5 5
10. 40 c. brown 8 5
11. 22. 45 c. olive 10 12
12. 26. 50 c. mauve 30 10
13. 60 c. red 15 15
14. 23. 1 l. brown and green .. 2·10 15
15. 5 l. blue and red .. 12·00 12·00
16. 10 l. olive and red .. 1·00 1·75

1915. Red Cross stamps of Italy. optd. **LIBIA.**

17. 34. 10 c. + 5 c. red 20 20
18. 35. 15 c. + 5 c. grey .. .. 1·00 1·00
19. 20 c. on 15 c. + 5 c. grey 25 25
20. 20 c. + 5 c. orange .. 1·10 1·10

1916. No. 100 of Italy Optd. **LIBIA.**

21. 22. 20 c. on 15 c. grey .. 2·10 30

1. Roman Legionary.

2. Goddess of Plenty.

3. Libyan Sibyl.

4. Galley leaving Tripoli.

5. Victory.

6. Bedouin Woman.

1921.

22. 1. 1 c. brown and black .. 5 5
23. 2 c. brown and black .. 5 5
24. 5 c. green and black .. 5 5
50. 7½ c. brown and black .. 5 8
25. 2. 10 c. red and black .. 5 5
26. 15 c. orange and brown .. 8 5
41. 3. 20 c. green 5 5
27. 2. 25 c. blue 8 5
54. 4. 30 c. brown and black .. 5 5
42. 3. 40 c. brown 8 5
55. 4. 50 c. olive and black .. 5 5
30. 55 c. violet and black .. 15 12
43. 3. 60 c. blue 10 5
57. 5. 75 c. red and violet .. 5 5
31. 1 l. brown 25 5
59. 4. 1 l. 25 blue 5 5
44. 3. 1 l. 75 orange 10 5
45. 2 l. red 20 8
46. 3. 2 l. 55 violet 30 25
32. 5. 5 l. blue and black .. 70 25
33. 10 l. olive and blue .. 2·25 1·90

1922. Victory stamps of Italy optd. **LIBIA.**

34. 40. 5 c. green 12 12
35. 10 c. red 10 10
36. 15 c. grey 15 15
37. 25 c. blue 25 25

1922. Stamps of Italy surch. **Libia** and new value.

38. 26. 40 c. on 50 c. mauve .. 15 5
39. 80 c. on 25 c. blue .. 15 15

1928. Types of Italy optd. **Libia** or **LIBIA.**

65. 61. 7½ c. brown 55 70
66. 23. 1 l. 25 blue .. .. 1·40 35
67. 62. 1 l. 75 brown 60 8

1928. Air. Air stamps of Italy optd. **Libia.**

63. 60. 50 c. red 15 12
64. 80 c. brown and purple 25 30

1936. 10th Tripoli Exn.

68. 6. 50 c. violet 15 15
69. 1 l. 25 blue 35 35

1936. Air. Nos. 96 and 99 of Cyrenaica optd. **LIBIA.**

70. – 50 c. violet 12 5
71. 5. 1 l. black 35 70

1937. Air. Stamps of Tripolitania optd. **LIBIA.**

72. 5. 50 c. red 8 5
73. 60 c. orange 8 5
74. 75 c. blue 8 5
75. 80 c. purple 8 5
76. 6. 1 l. blue 15 8
77. 1 l. 20 brown 8 5
78. 1 l. 50 orange 10 8
79. 5 l. green 25 12

7. Triumphal Arch.

8. Roman Theatre, Sabrata.

1937. Inaug. of Coastal Highway.

80. 7. 50 c. red (postage) .. 25 25
81. 1 l. 25 blue 25 40
82. 8. 50 c. purple (air) .. 25 25
83. 1 l. black 25 40

1937. 11th Tripoli Exn. Optd. **XI FIERA DI TRIPOLI.**

84. 7. 50 c. red (postage) .. 70 1·25
85. 1 l. 25 blue .. .. 70 1·25
86. 8. 50 c. purple (air) .. 70 1·25
87. 1 l. black .. .. .. 70 1·25

9. Benghazi Waterfront.

1938. 12th Tripoli Exn. Inscr. "XII FIERA CAMPIONARIA TRIPOLI".

88. 9. 5 c. brown (postage) .. 8 8
89. – 10 c. sepia 8 8
90. 9. 25 c. green 8 8
91. – 50 c. violet 15 8
92. 9. 75 c. red 20 25
93. – 1 l. 25 blue 30 40

DESIGN: 10 c., 50 c., 1 l. 25 Fair Buildings.

94. 50 c. olive (air) 15 20
95. 1 l. blue 20 30

DESIGN—VERT. View of Benghazi.

1938. Bimillenary of Augustus. As Nos. 21/6 and A 14/15 of Italian East Africa.

96. 7. 5 c. olive 8 8
97. – 10 c. red 8 8
98. 7. 25 c. green 10 10
99. – 50 c. mauve 10 10
100. 7. 75 c. red 12 12
101. – 1 l. 25 blue 12 12
102. 8. 50 c. olive (air) 20 20
103. 1 l. mauve 20 20

10. Agricultural Landscape.

1939. 13th Tripoli Trade Fair. Inscr. "XIII FIERA CAMPIONARIA DE TRIPOLI" etc.

104. 10. 5 c. olive (postage) .. 8 8
105. – 20 c. brown 8 8
106. 10. 50 c. mauve 10 5
107. – 75 c. red 12 15
108. 10. 1 l. 25 blue 12 15
109. – 25 c. green (air) 10 10
110. – 50 c. green 10 10
111. – 1 l. mauve 15 15

DESIGNS: 20 c., 75 c. Ghadames. 25 c., 1 l. Airliner over desert. 50 c. Airliner over Exhibition entrance.

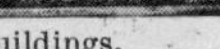

11. Buildings.

12. Mosque.

1940. Naples Exn.

112. 11. 5 c. brown (postage) .. 5 8
113. – 10 c. orange 5 8
114. 12. 25 c. green 8 10
115. 11. 50 c. violet 10 10
116. – 75 c. red 10 10
117. 12. 1 l. 25 blue 10 10
118. – 2 l. + 75 c. lake .. 20 25
119. – 50 c. black (air) .. 10 10
120. – 1 l. violet 10 15
121. – 2 l. + 75 c. blue .. 10 15
122. – 5 l. + 2 l. 50 brown .. 10 25

DESIGNS—HORIZ. 10 c., 75 c., 2 l. Oxen and plough. 50 c., 2 l. Aeroplane over city. 1 l., 5 l. Aeroplane over oasis.

1941. As T 10 of Italian East Africa, but inscr. "LIBIA".

123. 5 c. orange (postage) .. 5 35
124. 10 c. brown 5 35
125. 20 c. purple 8 35
126. 25 c. green 8 35
127. 50 c. violet 10 35
128. 75 c. red .. .. 12 1·50
129. 1 l. 25 blue .. .. 15 1·50
130. 50 c. green (air) .. .. 15 2·50

B. INDEPENDENT

ليبيا (13.) LIBYA
– ليبيا – ٤ ليرة ع. 4 MAL. LIBYA (14.)
– ليبيا – ٨ فرنك 8 FRANCS LIBYA (15.)

1951. Stamps of Cyrenaica optd.

(a) For use in Cyrenaica. Optd. as T 13.

131. 9. 1 m. brown 8 8
132. 2 m. red 8 8
133. 3 m. yellow 12 8
134. 4 m. green .. .. 7·50 3·50
135. 5 m. brown 15 15
136. 8 m. orange 20 20
137. 10 m. violet 30 30
138. 12 m. red 40 40
139. 20 m. blue 70 90
140. 10. 50 m. blue and brown 3·25 3·00
141. 100 m. red and black .. 5·00 5·00
142. 200 m. violet and blue 18·00 14·00
143. 500 m. yellow & green 70·00 65·00

(b) For use in Tripolitania. Surch. as T 14 in Military Authority lire.

151. 9. 1 mal. on 2 m. red .. 5 5
152. 2 mal. on 4 m. green .. 8 8
153. 4 mal. on 8 m. orange .. 8 8
154. 5 mal. on 10 m. violet 12 12
155. 6 mal. on 12 m. red .. 15 15
156. 10 mal. on 20 m. blue .. 30 30
157. 10. 24 mal. on 50 m. blue and brown .. 70 70
158. 48 mal. on 100 m. red and black .. 2·10 2·10
159. 96 mal. on 200 m. violet and blue .. 9·00 9·00
160. 240 mal. on 500 m. yellow and green .. 20·00 20·00

(c) For use in the Fezzan Surch. as T 15.

166. 9. 2 f. on 2 m. red .. 8 5
167. 4 f. on 4 m. green .. 8 10
168. 8 f. on 8 m. orange .. 8 10
169. 10 f. on 10 m. violet .. 10 10
170. 12 f. on 12 m. red .. 12 15
171. 20 f. on 20 m. blue .. 15 20
172. 10. 48 f. on 50 m. bl. & brn. 14·00 14·00
173. 96 f. on 100 m. red and black .. 14·00 14·00
174. 192 f. on 200 m. violet and blue .. 32·00 32·00
175. 480 f. on 500 m. yellow and green .. 60·00 60·00

(1000 mills = 1 Libyan pound.)

16. King Idris I.

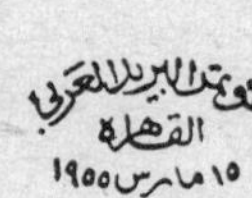

(17.)

18.

1952.

176. 16. 2 m. brown 5 5
177. 4 m. grey 5 5
178. 5 m. emerald .. .. 4·25 12
179. 8 m. vermilion 8 5
180. 10 m. violet .. .. 4·00 5
181. 12 m. red 12 8
182. 20 m. blue .. .. 5·00 15
183. 25 m. brown .. .. 5·50 20
184. – 50 m. blue and brown 45 20
185. – 100 m. red and black .. 70 35
186. – 200 m. violet and blue 1·40 1·00
187. – 500 m. orange & green 4·75 3·00

Nos. 184/7 are larger.

1955. Arab Postal Union. As T **87** of Egypt but inscr. "LIBYE" at top.

200.	5 m. brown	35	25
201.	10 m. green	50	40
202.	30 m. violet	90	70

1955. 2nd Arab Postal Congress, Cairo. Nos. 200/2 optd. with T **17**.

203.	5 m. brown	20	15
204.	10 m. green	25	20
205.	30 m. violet	50	35

1955. No. 177 surch.

206 **16.**	5 m. on 4 m. grey ..	25	15

1955.

207. **18.**	1 m. black on yellow ..	5	5
208.	2 m. bistre	40	15
209.	2 m. brown	5	5
210.	3 m. indigo	5	5
211.	4 m. black	40	15
212.	4 m. lake	8	5
213.	5 m. green	20	5
214.	10 m. lilac	35	5
215.	18 m. red	10	8
216.	20 m. orange	15	8
217.	30 m. blue	35	8
218.	35 m. brown	20	8
219.	40 m. lake	40	10
220.	50 m. olive	35	10
221. –	100 m. purple and slate	50	20
222. –	200 m. lake and blue ..	90	35
223. –	500 m. orange & green	3·75	1·60
224. –	£L1 grn. & brn. on yell.	6·00	4·25

Nos. 221/4 are larger (27×32 mm.).
See also Nos. 245/60.

19. Senussi's Tomb at Djaghboub.

20. Map of Libya.

21.

22.

1956. Imam Essayed Mohamed Aly el Senussi. Death Cent.

225. **19.**	5 m. green	8	8
226.	10 m. lilac	12	10
227.	15 m. red	20	20
228.	30 m. blue	45	30

1956. Admission to U.N. 1st Anniv.

229. **20.**	15 m. buff and blue ..	12	5
230.	35 m. buff, purple & blue	30	15

1957. Arab Postal Congress, Tripoli.

231. **21.**	15 m. blue	15	10
232.	500 m. brown	3·25	2·10

1958. Declaration of Human Rights. 10th Anniv.

233. **22.**	10 m. violet	8	5
234.	15 m. green	10	8
235.	30 m. blue	25	15

23. F.A.O. Emblem and Date Palms.

24.

1959. 1st Int. Dates Conf., Tripoli.

236. **23.**	10 m. black and violet	8	8
237.	15 m. black and green	10	10
238.	45 m. black and blue ..	25	25

1960. Arab League Centre, Cairo. Inaug. As T **144** of Egypt but with Arms of Libya and inscr. "LIBYA".

239.	10 m. black and green ..	8	5

1960. World Refugee Year.

240. **24.**	10 m. black and violet	10	8
241.	45 m. black and blue ..	25	15

25. Palm Tree and Radio Mast.

26. Military Watch-tower (medallion).

1960. 3rd Arab Telecommunications Conf. Tripoli.

242. **25.**	10 m. violet	8	5
243.	25 m. blue-green ..	10	5
244.	45 m. lake	35	12

1960. As Nos. 207, etc. On coloured paper.

245. **18.**	1 m. black on grey ..	5	5
246.	2 m. brown on buff ..	5	5
247.	3 m. indigo on blue ..	5	5
248.	4 m. lake on rose ..	5	5
249.	5 m. green on green ..	5	5
250.	10 m. lilac on violet ..	5	5
251.	15 m. sepia on buff ..	5	5
252.	20 m. orange on orange	5	5
253.	30 m. red on pink ..	8	5
254.	40 m. lake on rose ..	10	8
255.	45 m. blue on blue ..	10	10
256.	50 m. olive on bistre ..	12	10
257. –	100 m. purple & slate on blue	20	15
258. –	200 m. lake & blue on blue	45	35
259. –	500 m. orange & green on green ..	2·50	1·60
260. –	£L1 grn. & brn. on brn.	4·75	3·00

1961. Army Day.

261. **26.**	5 m. brown and green ..	5	5
262.	15 m. brown and blue ..	8	12

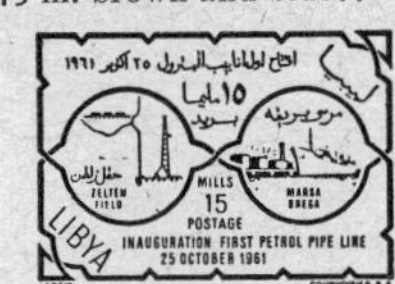

27. Zelten Field and Marsa Brega Port.

1961. First Libyan Petrol Pipeline Inaug.

263. **27.**	15 m. green and buff ..	5	5
264.	50 m. brown & lavender	20	10
265.	100 m. blue & pale blue	45	20

28. Broken Chain and Agricultural Scenes.

1961. Independence. 10th Anniv.

266. **28.**	15 m. sepia, blue-green and green	8	5
267. –	50 m. sep., brn. & buff	15	12
268. –	100 m. sep., bl. & salmon	45	20

DESIGNS (embodying broken chain): 50 m. Modern highway and buildings. 100 m. Industrial machinery.

29. Tuareg Horsemen.

1962. Int. Fair, Tripoli.

269. **29.**	10 m. chestnut & brown	5	5
270. –	15 m. green and maroon	8	5
271. –	50 m. blue and green ..	20	12

DESIGNS: 15 m. Well. 50 m. Oil derrick.

30. Campaign Emblem.

31. Ahmed Rafik.

1962. Malaria Eradication.

273. **30.**	15 m. multicoloured ..	8	5
274.	50 m. multicoloured ..	25	10

1962. Ahmed Rafik el Mehdawi (poet). 1st Death Anniv.

276. **31.**	15 m. green	5	5
277.	20 m. brown	10	8

32. Scout Badge and Handclasp.

33. City within Oildrop.

1962. 3rd Philia ("Friendship") Camp, Tripoli.

278. **32.**	5 m. sepia, red & yellow	5	5
279. –	10 m. sepia, yell. & blue	5	5
280. –	15 m. sep., yell. & grey	10	8

DESIGNS: 10 m. Scouts and badge. 15 m. Badge and camp.

1962. Essider Terminal, Sidrah Oil Pipeline. Inaug.

282. **33.**	15 m. maroon and green	10	5
283.	50 m. olive and brown ..	30	20

ILLUSTRATIONS
British Commonwealth and all overprints and surcharges are FULL SIZE. Foreign Countries have been reduced to ¾-LINEAR.

34. Red Crescent encircling Globe.

1963. Int. Red Cross Cent.

284. **34.**	10 m. red, blue, grey and pink	10	5
285.	15 m. red, blue, grey and olive	12	10
286.	20 m. red, blue, grey and pale grey	20	15

35. Rainbow over Map of Tripoli.

1963. International Fair. Tripoli.

287. **35.**	15 m. multicoloured ..	12	8
288.	30 m. multicoloured ..	15	10
289.	50 m. multicoloured ..	35	15

Nos. 287/9 are arranged together in sheets with alternate horiz. rows inverted.

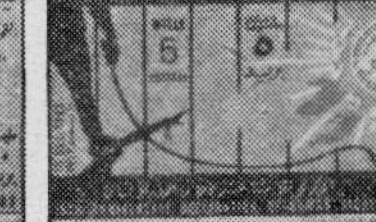

36. Palm and Well.

37. "Emancipation".

1963. Freedom from Hunger.

290. **36**	10 m. green, brown & bl.	8	5
291. –	15 m. ochre, mar. & grn.	8	5
292. –	45 m. sep., bl. & salmon	20	15

DESIGNS: 15 m. Camel and sheep. 45 m. Farmer sowing and tractor.

1963. Declaration of Human Rights. 15th Anniv.

293. **37.**	5 m. brown and blue ..	5	5
294.	15 m. purple and blue ..	8	5
295.	50 m. green and blue ..	12	8

39. Child playing in Sun.

38. Map and Fair Entrance.

40. Lungs and Stethoscope.

1964. International Fair, Tripoli.

300. **38.**	10 m. green, brown and red-brown	10	5
301.	15 m. grn., brn. & purple	12	8
302.	30 m. green, brown & bl.	30	20

1964. Children's Day. Sun gold.

303. **39.**	5 m. violet, red and pink	5	5
304. –	15 m. brown, brown-yellow and buff ..	8	8
305. **39.**	45 m. vio., blue & lt. blue	25	15

DESIGN: 15 m. Child in bird's nest.

1964. "Fight against T.B.".

307. **40.**	20 m. violet	20	10

41. Crown and Map.

42. Libyan Woman, Silk Moth and Cocoon.

1964. Libyan Union. 1st Anniv.

308. **41.**	5 m. orange and green ..	5	5
309.	50 m. yellow and blue ..	25	15

1964. Emancipation of Libyan Women.

310. **42.**	10 m. blue and green ..	5	5
311.	20 m. blue and yellow ..	8	5
312.	35 m. blue and pink ..	12	8

43. Flags and Scout Salute.

44. Bayonet.

1964. Libya Scouts "Promise" Camp. Multicoloured.

314.	10 m. Type **43** ..	15	8
315.	20 m. Scout badge and saluting hand	30	15

1964. Foundation of the Senoussi Army.

317. **44.**	10 m. brown and green	5	5
318.	20 m. black and orange	12	8

45. El-Sharef (poet).

46. Football.

1964. Ahmed Bahloul El-Sharef Commem.

319. **45.**	15 m. purple	8	5
320.	20 m. blue	12	8

1964. Olympic Games, Tokyo. Rings in Gold.

321.	5 m. black & blue (Type **46**	10	8
322.	10 m. blk. & pur. (Cycling)	10	8
323.	20 m. blk. & red (Boxing)	10	8
324.	30 m. blk. & buff (Runner)	10	8
325.	35 m. blk. & olive (High-diving)	10	8
326.	50 m. blk. & grn. (Hurdling)	10	8

Nos. 321/6 were arranged together se-tenant in the sheets, each block of six being superimposed with the Olympic "rings" symbol.

47. A.P.U. Emblem.

48. I.C.Y. Emblem.

1964. Arab Postal Union. 10th Anniv.

328. **47.**	10 m. blue and yellow ..	5	5
329.	15 m. chestnut and lilac	10	5
330.	30 m. brown and green	25	15

1965. Int. Co-operation Year.
331. 48. 5 m. gold & blue (post.) 5 5
332. 15 m. gold and red .. 8 5
333. 50 m. gold & violet (air) 20 15

49. Bee-eater.

1965. Birds. Multicoloured.
335. 5 m. Long-legged buzzard 5 5
336. 10 m. Type 49 .. 5 5
337. 15 m. Pin-tailed sandgrouse 8 5
338. 20 m. Houbara bustard .. 10 5
339. 30 m. Spotted sandgrouse 15 8
340. 40 m. Red-legged partridge 20 8
The 5 m. and 40 m. are vert.

50. Fair Emblem.

1965. Int. Trade Fair, Tripoli.
341. 50. 50 m. brown, gold, blue and grey-blue .. 15 8

51. Compass, Rocket and Balloons.

1965. World Meteorological Day.
342. 51. 10 m. multicoloured .. 5 5
343. 15 m. multicoloured .. 8 8
344. 50 m. multicoloured .. 25 20

52. I.T.U. Emblem and Symbols.

1965. I.T.U. Cent.
345. 52. 10 m. brown 5 5
346. 20 m. purple 8 5
347. 50 m. magenta 20 10

53. Lamp and Burning Library. 54. Rose.

1965. Burning of Algiers Library.
348. 53. 15 m. multicoloured .. 5 5
349. 50 m. multicoloured .. 15 10

1965. Flowers. Multicoloured.
351. 1 m. Type 54 .. .. 5 5
352. 2 m. Iris 5 5
353. 3 m. Cactus flower .. 5 5
354. 4 m. Sunflower 5 5

55. Airliner over Globe. 56. Forum, Cyrene.

1965. Kingdom of Libya Airlines. Inaug.
355. 55. 5 m. multicoloured .. 5 5
356. 10 m. multicoloured .. 8 5
357. 15 m. multicoloured .. 12 5

1965.
358. 56. 50 m. olive and blue .. 12 8
359. – 100 m. chestnut and blue 25 10
360. – 200 m. blue and purple 50 20
361. – 500 m. green and red .. 1·25 55
362. – £L1 brown and green .. 2·50 1·00
DESIGNS—VERT. 100 m. Trajan's Arch, Leptis Magna. 200 m. Apollo's Temple, Cyrene. HORIZ. 500 m. Antonine Temple, Sabratha. £L1, Theatre, Sabratha.

57. "Helping Hands".

1966. Air. Nubian Monuments Preservation.
363. 57. 10 m. brown and bistre 5 5
364. 15 m. brown and green 8 5
365. 40 m. brown & chestnut 20 10

Nos. 367 and E 368 have the Libyan crest printed in green on the back.

58. Germa Mausoleum.

1966.
367. 58. 70 m. violet & chestnut 30 15
See also No. E 368.

59. Globe and Satellites.

1966. Int. Trade Fair, Tripoli.
369. 59. 15 m. blk., gold & grn. 8 5
370. 45 m. black, gold & blue 20 10
371. 55 m. black,gold & mar. 25 12

1966. Arab League Week. As T 170 of Egypt, but smaller, 20½ × 35½ mm.
372. 20 m. red, green and black 5 5
373. 55 m. blue, red and black 20 12

60. W.H.O. Building.

1966. Air. W.H.O. Headquarters, Geneva. Inaug.
374. 60. 20 m. blk., yellow & blue 5 5
375. 50 m. black, green & red 15 12
376. 65 m. blk., salmon & ake 20 20

61. Tuareg with Camel. 62. Leaping Deer.

1966. Tuaregs.
378. 61. 10 m. red 5 5
379. – 20 m. blue 8 5
380. – 50 m. multicoloured .. 15 12
DESIGNS—VERT. 20 m. As T 61 but positions of Tuareg and camel reversed. HORIZ. (62×39 mm.). 50 m. Tuareg with camel (different).

1966. 1st Arab Girl Scouts Camp (5 m.) and 7th Arab Boy Scouts Camp (25 and 65 m.). Multicoloured.
382. 5 m. Type 62 .. .. 5 5
383. 25 m. } Boy Scouts 8 5
384. 65 m. } Camp Emblem (vert.) 25 15

63. Airline Emblem. 64. U.N.E.S.C.O. Emblem.

1966. Air. Kingdom of Libya Airlines. 1st Anniv.
385. 63. 25 m. multicoloured .. 10 8
386. 60 m. multicoloured .. 25 20
387. 85 m. multicoloured .. 35 30

1967. U.N.E.S.C.O. 20th Anniv.
388. 64. 15 m. multicoloured .. 8 5
389. 25 m. multicoloured .. 15 5

65. Castle of Columns, Tolemaide. 67. Fair Emblem.

66. Tankers at Oil Terminal.

1967. Tourism.
390. 65. 25 m. blk., brn. & violet 8 5
391. – 55 m. brn., violet & blk. 15 12
DESIGN—HORIZ. 55 m. Sebha Fort.

1967. Marsa al Hariga Oil Terminal Inaug.
392. 66. 60 m. multicoloured .. 25 12

1967. Int. Fair. Tripoli.
393. 67. 15 m. multicoloured .. 8 5
394. 55 m. multicoloured .. 20 12

68. I.T.Y. Emblem. 69. Running.

1967. Int. Tourist Year.
395. 68. 5 m. black and blue .. 5 5
396. 10 m. black and blue .. 5 5
397. 45 m. black, blue & pink 20 10

1967. Mediterranean Games, Tunisia. Designs showing action "close-ups".
398. 5 m. black, orange and blue 5 5
399. 10 m. black, chocolate & blue 5 5
400. 15 m. black, violet & blue 5 5
401. 45 m. black, cerise & blue 15 12
402. 75 m. black, green and blue 25 15
DESIGNS: 5 m. T 69. 10 m. Throwing the javelin. 15 m. Cycling. 45 m. Football. 75 m. Boxing.

70. Open Book and Arab League Emblem. 71. Human Rights Emblem.

1967. Literacy Campaign.
403. 70. 5 m. orange and violet .. 5 5
404. 10 m. green and violet 8 5
405. 15 m. purple and violet 8 5
406. 25 m. blue and violet .. 8 8

1968. Human Rights Year.
407. 71. 15 m. red and green .. 5 5
408. 60 m. blue and orange .. 20 12

72. Cameleers, Aircraft, Oil Rig and Map.

1968. Int. Fair, Tripoli.
409. 72. 55 m. brown, yellow, black and red .. 20 12

73. Arab League Emblem.

1968. Arab League Week.
410. 73. 10 m. red and blue .. 8 5
411. 45 m. green and orange 15 12

74. Children "Wrestling" (statue). 75. W.H.O. Emblem and Reaching Hands.

1968. Children's Day. Multicoloured.
412. 25 m. Type 74 .. .. 8 5
413. 55 m. Libyan mother and children 15 12

1968. W.H.O. 20th Anniv.
414. 75. 25 m. blue and purple .. 10 8
415. 55 m. brown and blue .. 20 12

76. Oil Pipeline Map.

1968. Zueitina Oil Terminal. Inaug.
416. 76. 10 m. multicoloured .. 5 5
417. 60 m. multicoloured .. 20 15

77. "Teaching the People".

1968. "Eliminate Illiteracy".
418. 77. 5 m. magenta 5 5
419. 10 m. orange 5 5
420. 15 m. blue 5 5
421. 20 m. green 8 8

78. Conference Emblem.

1968. 4th Session of Arab Labour Ministries Conf., Tripoli.
422. 78. 10 m. multicoloured 5 5
423. 15 m. multicoloured .. 5 5

79. Treble Clef, Eye and T.V. Screen.

1968. Libyan Television Service. Inaug.
424. 79. 10 m. multicoloured 5 5
425. 30 m. multicoloured .. 10 8

80. Bridge, Callipers and Road Sign.

1968. Opening of Wadi El Kuf Bridge.
426. **80.** 25 m. blk., yell., red & ult. 8 5
427. 60 m. blk., yell., red & grn. 15 12

81. Melons. **82.** Fair Emblem.

1969. Fruits. Multicoloured.
428. 5 m. Type **81** 5 5
429. 10 m. Dates 5 5
430. 15 m. Lemons 5 5
431. 20 m. Oranges 8 5
432. 25 m. Peaches 8 5
433. 35 m. Pears 15 10

1969. 8th Int. Trade Fair, Tripoli.
434. **82.** 25 m. muticoloured .. 8 5
435. 35 m. multicoloured .. 10 8
436. 40 m. multicoloured .. 12 10

83. Hoisting Weather Balloon.

1969. World Meteorological Day.
437. **83.** 60 m. multicoloured 20 15

84. Family on Staircase within Cogwheel. **85.** I.L.O. Emblem.

1969. Libyan Social Insurance. 10th Anniv.
438. **84.** 15 m. multicoloured .. 5 5
439. 55 m. multicoloured .. 15 15

1969. Int. Labour Organization. 50th Anniv.
440. **85.** 10 m. grn., blk. & turq. 5 5
441. 60 m. green, black & red 20 15

86. Emblem and Desert Scene.

1969. African Tourist Year.
442. **86.** 15 m. multicoloured .. 5 5
443. 30 m. multicoloured .. 15 15

87. Members of Armed Forces and Olive Branch. **88.** Communications Satellite and Flags.

1969. Revolution of 1st September.
444. **87.** 5 m. multicoloured .. 5 5
445. 10 m. multicoloured .. 5 5
446. 15 m. multicoloured .. 8 8
447. 25 m. multicoloured .. 12 12
448. 45 m. multicoloured .. 20 20
449. 60 m. multicoloured .. 25 25

On Nos. 404/9 the value is in white and the designers name appears at the foot of design.

1970. Arab Satellite Communications Co-operation Agreement. 5th Anniv.
450. **88.** 15 m. multicoloured .. 8 8
451. 20 m. multicoloured .. 10 10
452. 25 m. multicoloured .. 12 12
453. 40 m. multicoloured .. 20 20

89. Arab League Flag, Arms and Map.

1970. Arab League. Silver Jubilee.
454. **99.** 10 m. sepia, grn. & blue 5 5
455. 15 m. brn., grn., orge. 8 8
456. 20 m. pur., grn. & olive 12 12

1970. Revolution of 1st September. Designs as T **87**, but without imprint "M. A. Siala" at foot, and figures of value differently inscr.
457. **87.** 5 m. multicoloured .. 5 5
458. 10 m. multicoloured .. 5 5
459. 15 m. multicoloured .. 8 8
460. 25 m. multicoloured .. 10 10
461. 45 m. multicoloured .. 15 15
462. 60 m. multicoloured .. 25 25

90. New U.P.U. Headquarters Building. **91.** Eagle and Shield.

1970. New U.P.U. Headquarters Building, Berne.
463. **90.** 10 m. multicoloured .. 5 5
464. 25 m. multicoloured .. 10 10
465. 60 m. multicoloured .. 20 20

1970. Nos. 360/2 with "KINGDOM OF LIBYA" inscriptions obliterated.
466. 200 m. blue and purple ..
467. 500 m. green and pink ..
468. £L1 brown and green ..

These stamps were sold only for use on parcel post items. Other values may exist so overprinted, but were unauthorised.

See also Nos. 518/23.

1970. Evacuation of Foreign Military bases in Libya.
469. **91.** 15 m. black and red .. 8 8
470. 25 m. yell., bl. & red .. 10 10
471. 45 m. yell., red & grn... 20 20

92. Soldiers and Libyan Flag. **93.** U.N. Emblem, Dove and Scales.

1970. Libyan Arab Republic. 1st Anniv.
472. **92.** 20 m. multicoloured .. 8 8
473. 25 m. multicoloured .. 10 10
474. 30 m. multicoloured .. 15 15

1970. United Nations. 25th Anniv.
475. **93.** 5 m. brn., red & grn. .. 5 5
476. 10 m. grn., red & emerald 5 5
477. 60 m. grn., red & blue 25 25

94. Map and Flags. **95.** U.N. Emblem Dove and Globe.

1970. Signing of Tripoli Charter of Co-operation.
478. **94.** 15 m. grn., blk. & red.. 8 8

1971. U.N. De-colonisation Declaration. 10th Anniv.
479. **95.** 15 m. multicoloured .. 8 8
480. 20 m. multicoloured .. 8 8
481. 60 m. multicoloured .. 25 25

MINIMUM PRICE

The minimum price quoted is 5p which represents a handling charge rather than a basis for valuing common stamps. For further notes about prices see introductory pages.

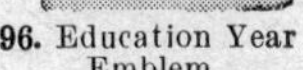

96. Education Year Emblem. **97.** Palestinian Guerrilla.

1971. Int. Education Year.
482. **96.** 5 m. brn., red & blk. .. 5 5
483. 10 m. grn., red & blk... 5 5
484. 20 m. bl., red & blk. .. 10 10

1971. "Al-Fatah" Movement for the Liberation of Palestine.
485. **97.** 5 m. multicoloured .. 5 5
486. 10 m. multicoloured .. 5 5
487. 100 m. multicoloured .. 35 35

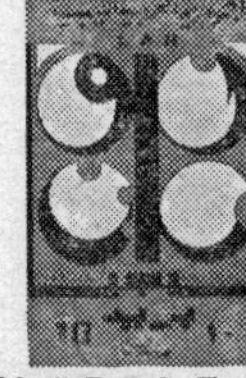

98. Fair Emblem. **99.** O.P.E.C. Emblem.

1971. 9th Int. Trade Fair, Tripoli.
488. **98.** 15 m. multicoloured .. 8 8
489. 30 m. multicoloured .. 10 10

1971. Organization of Petroleum Exporting Countries (O.P.E.C.).
490. **99.** 10 m. brown and yellow 5 5
491. 70 m. violet and pink.. 25 25

100. Global Symbol. **101.** Soldier, Torch and Flag.

1971. World Telecommunications Day (Nos. 494/5) and Pan-African Telecommunications Network.
492. – 5 m. multicoloured .. 5 5
493. – 15 m. multicoloured .. 5 5
494. **100.** 25 m. multicoloured .. 10 10
495. 35 m. multicoloured .. 15 15

1971. Evacuation of Foreign Troops. 1st Anniv.
496. **101.** 5 m. multicoloured .. 5 5
497. 10 m. multicoloured .. 5 5
498. 15 m. multicoloured .. 8 5

102. Ramadan Suehli. **103.** Palm and Dates.

1971. Ramadan Suehli (patriot). Commem.
499. **102.** 15 m. multicoloured .. 8 8
500. 55 m. multicoloured .. 20 20

For similar portraits see Nos. 503/4, 507/8, 526/7 and 553/4.

1971. 1st September Revolution. 2nd Anniv.
501. **103.** 5 m. multicoloured .. 5 5
502. 15 m. multicoloured .. 5 5

1971. Omar el Mukhtar (patriot). 40th Death Anniv. As T **102**.
503. 5 m. multicoloured .. 5 5
504. 100 m. multicoloured .. 35 35

HAVE YOU READ THE NOTES AT THE BEGINNING OF THIS CATALOGUE?

These often provide answers to the enquiries we receive.

104. Pres. Nasser. **105.** Emblem of Racial Equality Year.

1971. Pres. Nasser of Egypt. 1st Death Anniv.
505. **104.** 5 m. blk., grn. and pur. 5 5
506. 15 m. blk., pur. and grn. 8 8

1971. Ibrahim Usta Omar (poet). 21st Death Anniv. As T **102**.
507. 25 m. multicoloured .. 10 10
508. 30 m. multicoloured .. 12 12

1971. Racial Equality Year.
509. **105.** 25 m. multicoloured .. 10 10
510. 35 m. multicoloured .. 12 12

106. A.P.U. Emblem. **107.** Arab Postal Union. Emblem and Envelope.

1971. Founding of Arab Postal Union at Sofar Conf. 25th Anniv.
511. **106.** 5 m. multicoloured .. 5 5
512. 10 m. multicoloured .. 5 5
513. 15 m. multicoloured .. 8 5

1971. African Postal Union. 10th Anniv. Multicoloured.
514. 10 m. Type **107** 5 5
515. 15 m. Type **107** 8 5
516. 25 m. A.P.U. Emblem and dove with letter .. 10 8
517. 55 m. As 25 m. 20 15

1971. Nos. 428/33 with "KINGDOM OF LIBYA" inscriptions obliterated.
518. 5 m. Type **81** .. ..
519. 10 m. Dates .. ..
520. 15 m. Lemons .. ..
521. 20 m. Oranges .. ..
522. 25 m. Peaches .. ..
523. 35 m. Pears .. ..

108. Book Year Emblem. **109.** Libyan Arms.

1972. Int. Book Year.
524. **108.** 15 m. multicoloured .. 5 5
525. 20 m. multicoloured .. 8 8

1972. Ahmed Gnaba (poet). Commem. As T **102**.
526. 20 m. multicoloured .. 8 5
527. 35 m. multicoloured .. 12 10

1972. Values in Milliemes.
528. **109.** 5 m. multicoloured .. 5 5
529. 10 m. multicoloured .. 5 5
530. 25 m. multicoloured .. 10 5
531. 30 m. multicoloured .. 12 8
532. 35 m. multicoloured .. 12 8
533. 40 m. multicoloured .. 15 10
534. 45 m. multicoloured .. 15 10
535. 55 m. multicoloured .. 20 12
536. 60 m. multicoloured .. 25 15
537. 90 m. multicoloured .. 35 25

110. Cufic Inscription, Ajdabiya.

1972. Libyan Antiquities. Multicoloured.
538. 5 m. Tombs, Ghirza (vert.) 5 5
539. 10 m. Type **110** 5 5
540. 15 m. Marcus Aurelius' Arch, Tripoli (vert.) .. 8 8
541. 25 m. Exchanging Weapons (cave painting, Wadi Zigza) (vert.) 10 10
542. 55 m. Garamantian chariot (wall drawing, Wadi Zigza) (vert.) 20 20
543. 70 m. "Libya crowning Cyrene" (Roman relief, Cyrene) (vert.) 30 30

111. Fair Emblem.

1972. 10th Int. Trade Fair, Tripoli.
544. **111.** 25 m. multicoloured .. 10 8
545. 35 m. multicoloured .. 12 10
546. 50 m. multicoloured .. 20 15
547. 70 m. multicoloured .. 30 25

112. Heart and Skeletal Arm. **113.** "Unity" Emblem on Map.

1972. World Health Day.
548. **112.** 15 m. multicoloured .. 8 8
549. 25 m. multicoloured .. 10 8

1972. Libyan-Egyptian Federation Agreement. 1st Anniv.
550. **113.** 15 m. yell., blue & blk. 8 5
551. 20 m. yell., grn. & emerald 8 5
552. 25 m. yell., red & black 10 8

1972. Suleiman el Baruni (writer). Birth Cent. (1970). As T **102.**
553. 10 m. multicoloured .. 5 5
554. 70 m. multicoloured .. 30 25

1972. New Currency. As Type **109.**
(a) Size 19 × 24 mm.
555. **109.** 15 dh. multicoloured .. 8 5
556. 65 dh. multicoloured .. 25 15
557. 70 dh. multicoloured .. 25 15
558. 80 dh. multicoloured .. 30 25
(b) Size 27 × 32 mm.
559. **109.** 100 dh. multicoloured 35 30
560. 200 dh. multicoloured 70 60
561. 500 dh. multicoloured 1·75 1·50
562. 1 D. multicoloured .. 3·50 3·00

114.

1972.
563. **114.** 5 m. multicoloured .. 5 5
564. 20 m. multicoloured .. 10 8
565. 50 m. multicoloured .. 30 5
Nos. 563/5 were also issued with the Arabic face values expressed in the new currency.
See also Nos. 657/9.

115. Environment Emblem. **116.** Olympic Emblems.

1972. U.N. Environmental Conservation Conf., Stockholm.
566. **115.** 15 dh. multicoloured .. 8 5
567. 55 dh. multicoloured .. 25 20

1972. Olympic Games, Munich.
568. **116.** 25 dh. multicoloured .. 10 8
569. 35 dh. multicoloured .. 15 12

117. Symbolic Tree and "Fruit". **118.** Dome of the Rock.

1972. 1st September Revolution. 3rd Anniv.
570. **117.** 15 dh. multicoloured .. 8 5
571. 25 dh. multicoloured .. 10 8

1973. Dome of the Rock, Jerusalem.
572. **118.** 10 dh. multicoloured .. 5 5
573. 25 dh. multicoloured .. 10 8

119. Copernicus. **120.** Libyan Eagle and Fair.

1973. Copernicus. 500th Birth Anniv. Multicoloured.
574. 15 dh. Type **119** 8 5
575. 25 dh. "Copernicus in his Observatory" (horiz.) .. 12 10

1973. 11th Int. Trade Fair, Tripoli.
576. **120.** 5 dh. multicoloured .. 5 5
577. 10 dh. multicoloured .. 5 5
578. 15 dh. multicoloured .. 8 5

121. Blind Persons and Occupations. **122.** Map and Laurel.

1973. Role of the Blind in Society.
579. **121.** 20 dh. multicoloured .. 10 8
580. 25 dh. multicoloured .. 10 8

1973. Organization of African Unity. 10th Anniv.
584. **122.** 15 dh. multicoloured .. 8 5
585. 25 dh. multicoloured .. 10 8

123. Interpol H.Q., Paris.

1973. Int. Criminal Police Organization (Interpol). 50th Anniv.
586. **123.** 10 dh. multicoloured .. 5 5
587. 15 dh. multicoloured .. 8 5
588. 25 dh. multicoloured .. 10 8

124. Map and Emblems. **125.** W.M.O. Emblem.

1973. Census.
589. **124.** 10 dh. bl., blk. & red 5 5
590. 25 dh. grn., blk. & bl. 10 8
591. 35 dh. orge., blk. & grn. 15 12

1973. W.M.O. Centenary.
592. **125.** 5 d. blue, black & red 5 5
593. 10 d. blue, blk. & grn. 5 5

126. Footballers.

1973. 2nd Palestinian Cup Football Championships.
594. **126.** 5 dh. brown & green .. 5 5
595. 25 dh. brown and red 10 8

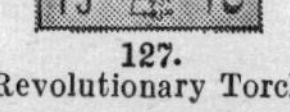

127. Revolutionary Torch. **128.** "Writing Ability".

1973. September 1st Revolution. 4th Anniv.
596. **127.** 15 dh. multicoloured .. 8 5
597. 25 dh. multicoloured .. 10 8

1973. Literacy Campaign.
598. **128.** 25 dh. multicoloured .. 10 8

129. Doorway of Old City Hall. **130.** Militiamen and Flag.

1973. Tripoli Municipality. Centenary. Multicoloured.
599. 10 dh. Type **129** 5 5
600. 25 dh. Khondok fountain 10 8
601. 35 dh. Clock tower .. 15 12

1973. Libyan Militia.
602. **130.** 15 dh. multicoloured .. 8 5
603. 25 dh. multicoloured .. 10 8

131. Arabic Quotation from Speech of 15 April 1973.

1973. Declaration of Cultural Revolution by Col. Gadhafi. Multicoloured.
604. 25 dh. Type **131** 10 8
605. 70 dh. As Type **131** but text in English 30 25

132. Ploughing with Camel. **133.** Human Rights Emblem.

1973. World Food Programme. 10th Anniv.
606. **132.** 10 dh. multicoloured .. 5 5
607. 25 dh. multicoloured .. 10 8
608. 35 dh. multicoloured .. 15 12

1973. Declaration of Human Rights. 25th Anniv.
609. **133.** 25 dh. red, pur. & bl... 10 8
610. 70 dh. red, grn. & bl... 30 25

134. Mullet. **136.** Emblem formed with National Flags.

135. Lookout Post and Scout Salute.

1973. Fishes. Multicoloured.
611. 5 dh. Type **134** 5 5
612. 10 dh. Sea-bream 5 5
613. 15 dh. Perch 8 5
614. 20 dh. Sea-perch 10 8
615. 25 dh. Tunny 10 8

1974. Scouting in Libya. 20th Anniv.
616. **135.** 5 dh. multicoloured .. 5 5
617. 20 dh. multicoloured .. 10 8
618. 25 dh. multicoloured .. 10 8

1974. 12th Int. Trade Fair, Tripoli.
619. **136.** 10 dh. multicoloured .. 5 5
620. 25 dh. multicoloured .. 10 8
621. 35 dh. multicoloured .. 15 12

137. Family within Protective Hands. **138.** Minaret within Star.

1974. World Health Day.
622. **137.** 5 dh. multicoloured .. 5 5
623. 25 dh. multicoloured .. 10 8

1974. Inauguration of Benghazi University.
624. **138.** 10 dh. multicoloured .. 5 5
625. 25 dh. multicoloured .. 10 8
626. 35 dh. multicoloured .. 15 12

139. U.P.U. Emblem within Star. **140.** Traffic Lights and Signs.

1974. Universal Postal Union. Centenary.
627. **139.** 25 dh. multicoloured .. 10 8
628. 70 dh. multicoloured .. 30 25

1974. Motoring and Touring Club of Libya.
629. **140.** 5 dh. multicoloured .. 5 5
630. 10 dh. multicoloured .. 5 5
631. 25 dh. multicoloured .. 10 8

141. Tank, Oil Refinery and Pipeline. **142.** W.P.Y. Emblem and People.

1974. 1st September Revolution. Fifth Anniv.
632. **141.** 5 dh. multicoloured .. 5 5
633. 20 dh multicoloured .. 10 8
634. 25 dh multicoloured .. 10 8
635. 35 dh multicoloured .. 15 12

1974. World Population Year.
637. **142.** 25 dh. multicoloured .. 10 8
638. 35 dh. multicoloured .. 15 12

143. Woman's Costume. **144.** Congress Emblem.

1975. Libyan Costumes.
639. **143.** 5 dh. multicoloured .. 5 5
640. – 10 dh. multicoloured .. 5 5
641. – 15 dh. multicoloured .. 5 5
642. – 20 dh. multicoloured .. 8 5
643. – 25 dh. multicoloured .. 10 8
644. – 50 dh. multicoloured .. 20 15
DESIGNS: 10 dh. to 50 dh. Various costumes.

1975. Arab Workers' Congress.
645. **144.** 10 dh. multicoloured .. 5 5
646. 25 dh. multicoloured .. 10 8
647. 35 dh. multicoloured .. 15 12

145. Teacher at Blackboard. 146. Human Figures, Text and Globe.

1975. Teachers' Day.

648. 145. 10 dh. multicoloured .. 5 5
649. 25 dh. multicoloured .. 10 8

1975. World Health Day.

650. 146. 20 dh. multicoloured .. 8 5
651. 25 dh. multicoloured .. 10 8

147. Library Visitors 148. Festival Emblem.

1975. Arab Book Exhibition.

652. 147. 10 dh. multicoloured .. 5 5
653. 20 dh. multicoloured .. 8 5
654. 25 dh. multicoloured .. 10 8

1975. 2nd Arab Youth Festival.

655. 148. 20 dh. multicoloured .. 8 5
656. 25 dh. multicoloured .. 10 8

1975. Coil Stamps. As Nos. 563/5 but without "L.A.R.".

657. 114. 5 dh. blk., oran. & blue 5 5
658. 20 dh. blk., yell. & blue 8 5
659. 50 dh. blk., grn. & blue 20 15

149. Games Emblem. 150. Peace Dove.

1975. 7th Mediterranean Games, Algiers.

660. 149. 10 dh. multicoloured .. 5 5
661. 25 dh. multicoloured .. 10 8
662. 50 dh. multicoloured .. 20 15

1975. September 1st Revolution. Sixth Anniversary. Multicoloured.

663. 25 dh. Type 150 .. .. 10 8
664. 70 dh. Peace dove with different background .. 30 25

151. Khalil Basha Mosque. 152. Arms and Populace.

1975. Mohamed's 1405th Birthday. Mosques. Multicoloured.

666. 5 dh. Type 151 .. .. 5 5
667. 10 dh. Sidi Abdulla El Shaab 5 5
668. 15 dh. Sisi Ali El Fergani 5 5
669. 20 dh. Al Kharruba (vert.) 8 5
670. 25 dh. Katikhtha (vert.) 10 5
671. 30 dh. Murad Agha (vert.) 12 10
672. 35 dh. Maulai Mohamed (vert.) 15 12

1976. National People's Congress.

673. 152. 35 dh. multicoloured 15 12
674. 40 dh. multicoloured. 15 12

153. Dialogue Emblem. 154. Woman blowing Bugle.

1976. Islamic-Christian Dialogue Seminar

675. 153. 40 dh. multicoloured .. 20 15
676. 115 dh. multicoloured 60 55

1976. Int. Trade Fair, Tripoli. Multicoloured

677. 10 dh. Type 154 .. .. 5 5
678. 20 dh. Lancer 10 8
679. 30 dh. Drummer 15 12
680. 40 dh. Bagpiper 20 15
681. 100 dh. Woman with jug on head 50 45

155. Early and Modern Telephones.

1976. Telephone Centenary. Multicoloured.

682. 40 dh. Type 155 .. .. 20 15
683. 70 dh. Bell with satellite and telephone 35 30

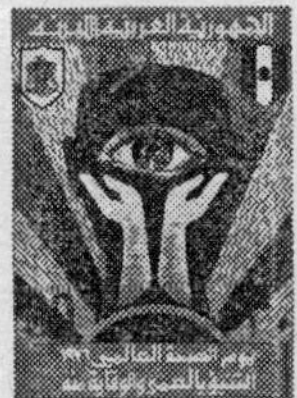

156. Mother and Child. 157. Hands supporting Human Eye.

1976. International Children's Day.

685. 156. 85 dh. multicoloured .. 45 40
686. 110 dh. multicoloured 55 50

1976. World Health Day.

687. 157. 30 dh. multicoloured .. 15 12
688. 35 dh. multicoloured .. 20 15
689. 40 dh. multicoloured .. 20 15

158. Bittern.

1976. Libyan Birds. Multicoloured.

690. 5 dh. Type 158 .. .. 5 5
691. 10 dh. Shrike 5 5
692. 15 dh. Warbler 8 5
693. 20 dh. Bee-eater (vert.) .. 10 8
694. 25 dh. Hoopoe 12 10

159. Barabekh Plant.

1976. Natural History Museum. Multicoloured.

695. 10 dh. Type 159 .. .. 5 5
696. 15 dh. Whale 8 5
697. 30 dh. Lizard 15 12
698. 40 dh. Elephant's skull .. 20 15
699. 70 dh. Eagle (vert.) .. 35 30
700. 115 dh. Mountain goat (vert.) 60 55

160. Cycling.

1976. Olympic Games, Montreal. Multicoloured.

701. 15 dh. Type 160 .. .. 8 5
702. 25 dh. Boxing 12 10
703. 70 dh. Football 35 30

EXPRESS LETTER STAMPS

A. ITALIAN ISSUES.

1915. Express Letter stamps of Italy optd. **Libia.**

E 17. E 1. 25 c. red 70 60
E 18. E 2. 30 c. red and blue .. 35 40

1921. As Type E 1 of Eritrea, but inscr. "LIBIA".

E 34. E 1. 30 c. red and blue .. 15 15
E 35. 50 c. brown and red 25 25
E 42. 60 c. brown and red 35 35
E 43. 2 l. red and blue .. 1·10 1·25

Nos. E 34 and E 43 are inscr. "EXPRES".

1922. Express Letter stamps of Italy surch. **Libia** and new value.

E 40. E 1. 60 c. on 25 c. red .. 40 35
E 41. E 2. 1 l. 60 on 30 c. red & bl. 90 90

1926. Nos. E 42/3 surch.

E 62. E 1. 70 c. on 60 c. brn. & red 40 40
E 64. 1 l. 25 on 60 c. brown and red 35 5
E 63. 2 l. 50 on 2 l. red & blue 90 1·00

B. INDEPENDENT ISSUE.

1966. Design similar to T **58** inscr. "EXPRES".

E 368. 90 m. red and green .. 30 25

DESIGN—HORIZ. 90 m. Saracen Castle, Zuela.

OFFICIAL STAMPS

1952. Optd. **Official** in English and Arabic.

O 192. 16. 2 m. brown 15 15
O 193. 4 m. grey 20 20
O 194. 5 m. emerald .. 1·00 75
O 195. 8 m. vermilion .. 55 35
O 196. 10 m. violet 90 70
O 197. 12 m. red .. .. 1·50 1·50
O 198. 20 m. blue .. .. 2·75 2·50
O 199. 25 m. brown .. .. 3·50 2·75

PARCEL POST STAMPS

1915. Parcel Post stamps of Italy optd. **LIBIA** on each half of the stamp.

P 17. P 2. 5 c. brown 8 5
P 18. 10 c. blue 8 5
P 19. 20 c. black 8 5
P 20. 25 c. red 15 5
P 21. 50 c. orange 25 5
P 22. 1 l. violet 15 5
P 23. 2 l. green 25 5
P 24. 3 l. yellow 25 10
P 25. 4 l. grey 30 12
P 26. 10 l. purple .. .. 5·50 35
P 27. 12 l. brown .. .. 6·50 80
P 28. 15 l. olive .. .. 9·00 1·10
P 29. 20 l. purple .. .. 10·00 1·75

1927. Parcel Post stamps of Italy optd. **LIBIA** on each half of the stamp.

P 62. P 3. 5 c. brown .. ..
P 63. 10 c. blue 15 5
P 64. 25 c. red 10 5
P 65. 30 c. blue 10 5
P 66. 50 c. orange .. .. 17·00 90
P 67. 60 c. red 15 5
P 68. 1 l. violet .. .. 2·75 5
P 69. 2 l. green .. .. 3·50 50
P 70. 3 l. yellow 20 15
P 71. 4 l. grey 25 15
P 72. 10 l. mauve .. .. 20·00 2·40
P 73. 20 l. purple .. .. 26·00 3·00

Unused prices are for complete stamps.

POSTAGE DUE STAMPS

A. ITALIAN ISSUES.

Postage Due stamps of Italy optd. **Libia.**

1915.

D 17. D 3. 5 c. purple & orange .. 8 10
D 18. 10 c. purple & orange 8 12
D 19 20 c. purple & orange 10 15
D 20. 30 c. purple & orange 10 15
D 21. 40 c. purple & orange 10 15
D 22. 50 c. purple & orange 10 15
D 23. 60 c. purple & orange 15 20
D 24. 60 c. brown & orange 2·75 3·50
D 25. 1 l. purple and blue .. 20 15
D 26. 2 l. purple and blue .. 2·00 2·50
D 27. 5 l. purple and blue .. 2·50 3·25

1934.

D 68. D 6. 5 c. brown 5 5
D 69. 10 c. blue 5 5
D 70. 20 c. red 5 5
D 71. 25 c. green 8 5
D 72. 30 c. orange 5 8
D 73. 40 c. brown 8 10
D 74. 50 c. violet 10 8
D 75. 60 c. blue 15 20
D 76. D 7. 1 l. orange 15 8
D 77. 2 l. green .. .. 2·50 35
D 78. 5 l. violet .. .. 7·00 1·60
D 79. 10 l. blue .. .. 90 1·10
D 80. 20 l. red .. .. 1·25 2·00

B. INDEPENDENT ISSUES.

1951. Postage Due stamps of Cyrenaica optd.

(a) For use in Cyrenaica. Optd. as T **13**.

D 144. D 1. 2 m. brown .. .. 1·75 2·10
D 145. 4 m. green .. .. 1·75 2·10
D 146. 8 m. red .. .. 2·50 3·00
D 147. 10 m. orange .. 3·00 4·25
D 148. 20 m. yellow .. 5·00 6·50
D 149. 40 m. blue .. .. 10·00 9·50
D 150. 100 m. black .. 14·00 12·00

(b) For use in Tripolitania. Surch. as T **14**.

D 161. D 1. 1 mal. on 2 m. brown 60 70
D 162. 2 mal. on 4 m. green 1·25 1·40
D 163. 4 mal. on 8 m. red .. 3·50 4·50
D 164. 10 mal. on 20 m. yell. 7·00 8·00
D 165. 20 mal. on 40 m. blue 14·00 16·00

D 1. D 2. Libyan Building.

1952.

D 188. D 1. 2 m. brown 5 5
D 189. 5 m. emerald .. 8 8
D 190. 10 m. red 12 10
D 191. 50 m. blue 65 50

1964.

D 296. D 2. 2 m. brown 5 5
D 297. 6 m. green 5 5
D 298. 10 m. red 5 5
D 299. 50 m. blue 12 12

LIECHTENSTEIN E2

A small independent principality lying between Austria and Switzerland.

1912. 100 heller = 1 krone.
1921. 100 rappen = 1 franc. (Swiss).

1. Prince John II. 2. 3.

1912.

1. 1. 5 h. green .. .. 2·50 1·90
5. 10 h. red .. .. 15·00 1·90
3. 25 h. blue .. .. 20·00 8·50

1917.

7. 2. 3 h. violet 25 45
8. 5 h. green 25 45
9. 3. 10 h. claret 25 45
10. 15 h. brown 25 45
11. 20 h. green 25 45
12. 25 h. blue 25 45

1918. Prince John's Accession. 60th Anniv. As T 3, but dated "1858-1918".

13. 3. 20 h. green 35 35

1920. Optd. with a scroll pattern.

14. 2. 5 h. green .. .. 85 2·10
15. 3. 10 h. claret .. .. 85 2·10
16. 25 h. blue .. .. 85 2·10

1920. Surch.

17. 2. 40 h. on 3 h. violet .. 85 2·10
18. 3. 1 k. on 15 h. brown .. 85 2·10
19. 2½ k. on 30 h. green .. 85 2·10

4.

5. Castle of Vaduz.

1920. Imperf.

20. **4.** 5 h. bistre .. .. 8 1·40
21. 10 h. orange .. .. 8 1·40
22. 15 h. blue .. .. 8 1·40
23. 20 h. brown .. .. 8 1·40
24. 25 h. green .. .. 8 1·40
25. 30 h. grey .. .. 8 1·40
26. 40 h. red .. .. .. 8 1·40
27. **5.** 1 k. blue .. .. .. 8 1·40

6. Prince John I.

7. Arms.

1920. Perf.

28. **4.** 5 h. bistre 8 15
29. 10 h. orange 8 15
30. 15 h. blue 8 15
31. 20 h. brown 8 15
32. – 25 h. olive 8 15
33. **4.** 30 h. grey 8 15
34. – 40 h. claret 8 15
35. – 50 h. green 8 15
36. – 60 h. brown 8 15
37. – 80 h. red 8 15
38. **5.** 1 k. lilac 8 15
39. – 2 k. blue 12 20
40. **6.** 5 k. grey 12 25
41. – 7½ k. slate 15 20
42. **7.** 10 k. yellow 15 20

DESIGNS—VERT. As T **5**. 25 h. St. Mamertus Chapel. 40 h. Gutenberg Castle. 50 h. Courtyard. Vaduz Castle. 60 h. Red House, Vaduz. 80 h. Church Tower, Schaan. 2 k. Bendern. As T **6**: 7½ k. Prince John II.

8.

10. Chapel of St. Mamertus.

9. Arms.

12. Vaduz.

1920. 80th Birthday of Prince. Imperf. or perf.

43. **8.** 50 h. olive 12 35
44. 80 h. red 25 40
45. 2 k. blue 20 35

1921. Surch. **2 Rp.** and bars.

47. **4.** 2 r. on 10 h. orge. (No. 21) 8 6·50

1921.

47a. **9.** 2 r. yellow .. .. 35 1·90
48. 2½ r. brown .. .. 35 2·50
49. 3 r. orange .. .. 60 2·50
50. 5 r. olive .. .. 1·50 25
51. 7½ r. blue .. .. 1·50 6·00
65. 10 r. green .. .. 2·50 35
53. 13 r. brown .. .. 2·50 20·00
54. 15 r. violet .. .. 3·00 1·25
55. **10.** 20 r. black and violet .. 19·00 60
56. – 25 r. black and red .. 50 60
57. – 30 r. black and green .. 25·00 5·00
66. – 30 r. black and blue .. 3·00 50
58. – 35 r. black and brown .. 1·25 2·50
59. – 40 r. black and blue .. 50 60
60. – 50 r. black and olive .. 50 60
61. – 80 r. black and grey .. 3·00 17·00
62. **12.** 1 f. black and lake .. 2·50 10·00

DESIGNS—As T **10**: 25 r. Vaduz Castle. 30 r. Bendern. 35 r. Prince John II. 40 r. Church Tower at Schaan. 50 r. Gutenberg Castle. 80 r. Red House, Vaduz.

1924. Surch.

63. **9.** 5 on 7½ r. blue 60 60
64. 10 on 13 r. brown .. 25 50

13. Vine-dresser.

15. Government Bldg. and Church, Vaduz.

1924.

67. **13.** 2½ r. mauve and olive .. 60 1·75
68. 5 r. blue and brown .. 50 25
69. 7½ r. brown and green .. 60 1·75
70. – 10 r. green 60 25
71. **13.** 15 r. green and chocolate 2·50 8·50
72. – 20 r. red .. .. .. 7·50 35
73. **15.** 1½ f. blue .. .. 22·00 35·00

DESIGN—As T **13**: 10 r., 20 r. Castle of Vaduz.

16. Prince John II.

17.

1925. Charity. 85th Birthday of Prince.

74. **16.** 10+5 r. green .. .. 12·00 2·50
75. 20+5 r. red .. .. 12·00 2·50
76. 30+5 r. blue .. .. 1·25 1·25

1927. Charity. 87th Birthday of Prince.

77. **17.** 10+5 r. green .. .. 5·00 7·50
78. 20+5 r. lake .. .. 5·00 7·50
79. 30+5 r. blue .. .. 3·00 7·50

18. Salvage work by Austrian soldiers.

DESIGNS — HORIZ. 5 r. Railway bridge. 10 r. Ruggell. 30 r. Salvage by Swiss soldiers.

1928. Flood Relief.

80. – 5 r.+5 r. brn. & claret .. 5·50 9·50
81. – 10 r.+10 r. brn. & grn... 5·50 9·50
82. **18.** 20 r.+10 r. brn. & red .. 5·50 9·50
83. – 30 r.+10 r. brn. & blue .. 5·50 9·50

20. Prince John II, 1858-1928.

DESIGN — VERT. 10 r. to 60 r. Prince John II.

1928. Accession of John II. 70th Anniv.

84. – 10 r. olive and brown .. 75 1·25
85. – 20 r. olive and red .. 1·25 2·50
86. – 30 r. olive and blue .. 12·00 7·50
87. – 60 r. olive and mauve .. 19·00 19·00
88. **20.** 1 f. 20 r. blue .. .. 20·00 25·00
89. 1 f. 50 r. sepia .. .. 22·00 45·00
90. 2 f. lake .. .. .. 22·00 38·00
91. 5 f. green .. .. .. 22·00 50·00

22. Prince Francis I.

25. Girl Vintager.

27. Prince Francis I and Princess Elsa.

28. Monoplane over Vaduz Castle and Rhine Valley.

1929. Accession of Prince Francis I.

92. – 10 r. green 35 75
93. **22.** 20 r. red .. .. .. 35 1·75
94. – 30 r. blue .. .. .. 75 2·50
95. – 70 r. brown .. .. 4·50 32·00

PORTRAITS: 10 r. Prince Francis I when a boy. 30 r. Princess Elsa. 70 r. Prince Francis I and Princess Elsa.

1930.

96. **25.** 3 r. lake 25 35
97. – 5 r. green 35 25
98. – 10 r. purple 35 12
99. – 20 r. red .. .. .. 6·50 25
100. – 25 r. black .. .. 2·50 9·00
101. – 30 r. blue .. .. 1·75 50
102. – 35 r. green .. .. 1·75 2·50
103. – 40 r. brown .. .. 1·00 1·00
104. – 50 r. sepia .. .. 20·00 6·00
105. – 60 r. olive .. .. 20·00 5·00
106. – 90 r. plum .. .. 24·00 32·00
107. – 1 f. 20 r. brown .. .. 24·00 45·00
108. – 1 f. 50 r. violet .. .. 12·00 19·00
109. **27.** 2 f. brown and green .. 13·00 32·00

DESIGNS—VERT. 5 r. Mt. Three Sisters—Edelweiss. 10 r. Alpine cattle—Alpine roses. 20 r. Courtyard of Vaduz Castle. 25 r. Mt. Naafkopf. 30 r. Valley of Samina. 35 r. Rofenberg Chapel. 40 r. St. Mamertus' Chapel. 50 r. Kurhaus at Malbun. 60 r. Gutenberg Castle. 90 r. Schellenberg Monastery. 1 f. 20 r. Vaduz Castle. 1 f. 50 r. Pfaelzer Club Hut.

1930. Air.

110. – 15 r. sepia .. .. 1·50 2·50
111. – 20 r. green .. .. 5·00 5·00
112. – 25 r. brown .. .. 5·00 3·75
113. – 35 r. blue .. .. 5·00 3·75
114. **28.** 45 r. green .. .. 11·00 20·00
115. 1 f. claret .. .. 22·00 15·00

DESIGNS—VERT. 15 r., 20 r. Biplane over mountains. HORIZ. 25 r., 35 r. Biplane over Vaduz Castle.

29. Zeppelin over Alps.

The 2 f. shows a different view.

1931. Air.

116. **29.** 1 f. green .. .. 20·00 32·00
117. – 2 f. blue .. .. 70·00 £120

30.

31. Mt. Naafkopf.

32. Prince Francis I.

1932. Charity. T **30** and medallion portraits.

118. – 10 r.+5 r. green .. 6·50 12·00
119. **30.** 20 r.+5 r. red .. 6·50 12·00
120. – 30 r.+10 r. blue .. 7·50 12·00

DESIGNS—VERT. (Smaller: 22 x 29 mm.) 10 r. Arms of Liechtenstein. (As T **30**). 30 r. Prince Francis.

1933.

121. **31.** 25 r. orange .. .. 55·00 19·00
122. – 90 r. green .. .. 3·75 19·00
123. – 1 f. 20 brown .. .. 55·00 75·00

DESIGNS: 90 r. Gutenberg Castle. 1 f. 20, Vaduz Castle.

1933. Prince Francis' 80th Birthday.

124. **32.** 10 r. violet .. .. 8·50 10·00
125. 20 r. red .. .. 7·50 10·00
126. 30 r. blue .. .. 7·50 10·00

33.

34. "Three Sisters".

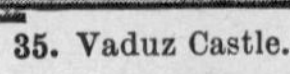

35. Vaduz Castle.

36.

37. Arms of Liechtenstein.

38. Eagle.

1933.

127. **33.** 3 r. red 5 12
128. **34.** 5 r. green 25 12
129. – 10 r. violet 12 12
130. – 15 r. red 12 40
131. – 20 r. red 20 12
132. – 25 r. brown .. .. 5·50 8·50
133. – 30 r. blue 20 25
134. – 35 r. green 25 75
135. – 40 r. brown 20 50
136. **35.** 50 r. chocolate .. .. 5·00 2·50
137. – 60 r. claret 35 85
138. – 90 r. green .. .. 1·25 3·75
139. – 1 f. 20 blue .. .. 50 2·50
140. – 1 f. 50 lake .. .. 55 3·00
141. – 2 f. brown .. .. 38·00 45·00
142. **36.** 3 f. blue .. .. 75·00 80·00
143. **35.** 5 f. purple £250 £300

DESIGNS—VERT.—As T **34**: 10 r. Schaan Church. 15 r. Bendern am Rhein. 20 r. Town Hall, Vaduz. 25 r. Samina Valley. As T **36**: 2 f. Princess Elsa. HORIZ. As T **35**: 30 r. Saminatal. 35 r. Schellenberg ruins. 40 r. Government Building, Vaduz. 60 r. Vaduz Castle. 90 r. Gutenberg Castle. 1 f. 20 Pfalzer Hut, Betterjoch. 1 f. 50 Valuna.

See also Nos. 174, 225/6 and 258.

1934. Agricultural Exn., Vaduz.

MS 144. **37.** 5 f. brown .. £800 £800

1934. Air. Eagle design as T **38.**

145. **38.** 10 r. violet .. .. 3·00 6·00
146. – 15 r. orange .. .. 7·50 12·00
147. – 20 r. red .. .. 8·50 12·00
148. – 30 r. blue .. .. 8·50 12·00
149. – 50 r. green .. .. 5·00 7·50

DESIGNS: 10 r. to 20 r. Birds in flight. 30 r. Birds in nest. 50 r. Eagle on rock.

1935. Air. No. 115 surch. **60 Rp.**

150. 60 r. on 1 f. claret 13·00 18·00

40. "Hindenburg" and Schaan Church.

DESIGN: 2 fr. "Graf Zeppelin" over Schaan Airport.

1936. Air.

151. **40.** 1 fr. red .. .. 18·00 32·00
152. – 2 fr. violet .. .. 11·00 24·00

41. Roadmakers at Triesenberg.

DESIGNS: 10 r. Bridge at Malbun. 30 r. Binnen Canal Junction. 50 r. Francis Bridge, near Planken.

1937. Workers' Issue.

155. – 10 r. mauve 25 35
156. **41.** 20 r. red 30 35
157. – 30 r. blue 35 50
158. – 50 r. brown 30 50

42. Knight and Vaduz Castle.

44. Schellenberg Castle.

1937.

159. – 3 r. brown 8 12
160. – 5 r. green 8 5
161. **42.** 10 r. violet 8 5
162. – 15 r. black 15 25
163. – 20 r. red 15 12
164. – 25 r. brown 35 50
165. – 30 r. blue 30 25
167. **44.** 40 r. green 30 60
168. – 50 r. brown 35 75
169. – 60 r. red 50 85
170. – 90 r. violet .. .. 3·00 2·50
171. – 1 f. red .. .. .. 1·00 1·50
172. – 1 f. 20 r. brown .. .. 4·00 7·50
173. – 1 f. 50 r. slate .. .. 75 5·00

DESIGNS—VERT. As T **42**: 3 r. Schalun ruins. 5 r. Masescha am Triesenberg. 15 r. Upper Saminatal. 20 r. Church and Bridge at Bendern. 25 r. Steg Chapel and girl. HORIZ. As T **44**: 30 r. Farmer and orchard, Triesenberg. 50 r. Knight and Gutenberg Castle. 60 r. Baron von Brandis and Vaduz Castle. 90 r. "Three Sisters" mountain. 1 fr. Boundary-stone on Luziensteig. 1 f. 20 r. Minstrel and Gutenberg Castle. 1 f. 50 r. Lawena Schwarzhorn).

1938. Death of Prince Francis I.

174. **33.** 3 fr. black on yellow .. 5·50 32·00

45. Joseph Rheinberger

46. Flying Mews.

1939. Rheinberger (composer). Birth Cent.
175. 45 50 r. green .. .. 30 1·25

1939. Air.
176. – 10 r. violet (Swallows) .. 12 12
177. 46. 15 r. orange 30 85
178. – 20 r. red (Mews) .. 50 25
179. – 30 r. blue (Buzzard) .. 50 35
180. – 50 r. green (Goshawk) .. 75 85
181. – 1 f. red (Eagle) .. .. 1·25 3·75
182. – 2 f. violet (Bearded Vulture) .. .. 1·25 4·50

47. Offering Homage to First Prince.

1939. Homage to Francis Joseph II
183. 47. 20 r. red 45 75
184. 30 r. blue 50 75
185. 50 r. green 45 75

48. Francis Joseph II.

DESIGNS: 2 f. Cantonal Arms. 3 f. Arms of Principality.

1939.
186. – 2 f. green on yellow .. 4·50 11·00
187. – 3 f. violet on yellow .. 4·25 11·00
188. 48. 5 f. brown on yellow .. 8·00 11·00

49. Prince John when a child.

1940. Prince John II. Birth Cent.
189. 49. 20 r. red .. .. 25 1·00
190. – 30 r. blue .. .. 25 2·00
191. – 50 r. green .. .. 50 2·00
192. – 1 f. violet .. .. 3·75 18·00
193. – 1 f. 50 black .. .. 3·25 12·00
194. – 3 f. brown .. .. 2·50 9·50
DESIGNS: HORIZ.—As T 49: Portraits of Prince John in early manhood (30 r.), in middle age (50 r.) and in later life (1 f.), and Memorial tablet (1 f. 50). VERT.—As T 33: 3 f. framed portrait of Prince John II.

49a. Wine Press.

1941. Agricultural Propaganda.
195. – 10 r. brown 12 12
196. 49a. 20 r. claret 25 35
197. – 30 r. blue 35 75
198. – 50 r. green .. .. 1·40 3·75
199. – 90 r. violet .. .. 95 6·00
DESIGNS: 10 r. Harvesting maize. 30 r. Sharpening scythe. 50 r. Milkmaid and cow. 90 r. Girl wearing traditional head-dress.

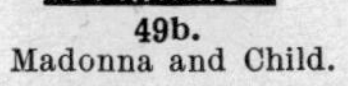
49b. Madonna and Child.

50. Prince Hans Adam.

1941.
200. 49b. 10 f. red on buff .. 45·00 60·00

1941. Princes. 1st Issue.
201. 50. 20 r. red 30 25
202. – 30 r. blue (Pr. Wenzel) 30 85
203. – 1 f. grey (Pr. A. Florian) 75 4·50
204. – 1 f. 50 r. green (Prince Joseph) .. .. 75 4·50

51. St. Lucius preaching.

1942. Separation from Estate of Montfort. 600th Anniv.
205. 51. 20 r. red 25 25
206. – 30 r. blue 40 75
207. – 50 r. green .. .. 1·60 2·00
208. – 1 f. violet .. .. 1·60 5·00
209. – 2 f. blue .. .. 1·25 5·00
DESIGNS: 30 r. Count of Montfort replanning Vaduz. 50 r. Counts of Montfort-Werdenberg and Sargans signing treaty. 1 f. Battle of Gutenberg. 2 f. Homage to Prince of Liechtenstein.

51a. Prince John Charles.

51b. Princess Georgina.

1941. Princes. 2nd Issue.
210. 51a. 20 r. red 12 25
211. – 30 r. blue (Francis) Joseph I) 40 75
212. – 1 f. purple (Alois I) .. 75 3·25
213. – 1 f. 50 r. brn. (John I) 95 3·25

1943. Marriage of Prince Francis Joseph II and Countess Georgina von Wildczek.
214. – 10 r. purple 45 65
215. 51b. 20 r. red 45 65
216. – 30 r. blue 40 65
PORTRAITS—VERT. 10 r. Prince Francis Joseph II. HORIZ. 30 r. Prince and Princess.

52. Alois II.

53. Marsh Land.

1943. Various Princes. 3rd Issue.
217. 52. 20 r. brown 12 25
218. – 30 r. blue 40 65
219. – 1 f. brown .. .. 75 3·00
220. – 1 f. 50 green .. .. 65 3·00
PORTRAITS—HORIZ. 30 r. John II. 1 f. Francis I. 1 f. 50, Francis Joseph II.

1943. Completion of Irrigation Canal.
221. 53. 10 r. violet 12 12
222. – 30 r. blue .. .. 40 1·90
223. – 50 r. green .. .. 75 1·75
224. – 2 f. brown .. .. 75 3·75
DESIGNS: 30 r. Draining the canal. 50 r. Ploughing reclaimed land. 2 f. Harvesting.

1943. Castles as T 34.
225. 10 r. grey (Vaduz) .. 12 12
226. 20 r. brown (Gutenberg) .. 40 50

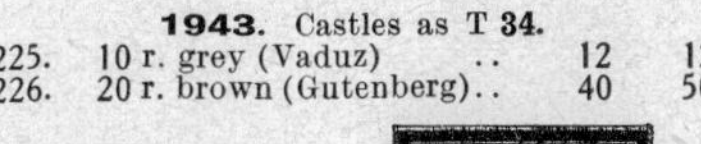

54. Planken.

54a. Prince Francis Joseph II.

1944. Various designs. Buff backgrounds.
227. 54. 3 r brown 8 12
228. – 5 r. green (Bendern) .. 8 5
228a. – 5 r. brown (Bendern) .. 1·25 25
229. – 10 r. violet (Triesen) .. 8 5
230. – 15 r. blue (Ruggell) .. 15 25
231. – 20 r. red (Vaduz) .. 15 12
232. – 25 r. pur. (Triesenberg) 15 50
233. – 30 r. blue (Schaan) .. 20 12
234. – 40 r. brown (Balzers) .. 40 50
235. – 50 r. grey (Mauren) .. 40 65
236. – 60 r. green (Schellenberg) 1·10 1·40
237. – 90 r. olive (Eschen) .. 90 1·10
238. – 1 f. claret (Vaduz Castle) 1·00 1·00
239. – 1 f. 20 brown (Valunatal) .. .. 1·10 1·40
240. – 1 f. 50 r. blue (Lawena) 75 1·50

1944.
241. 54a. 2 f. brown on buff .. 2·50 4·50
302. 2 f. blue .. .. 5·00 12·00
242. – 3 f. green on buff .. 2·00 3·75
303. – 3 f. brown .. .. 32·00 35·00
304. – 5 f. green .. .. 50·00 50·00
DESIGNS: 3 f. Princess Georgina (different portraits). 5 f. (25×34 mm.), Vaduz Castle.

55.

56.

1945. Birth of Crown Prince.
243. 55. 20 r. brn., yellow & gold 40 25
244. 30 r. blue, yellow & gold 40 75
245. 100 r. grey, yell. & gold 70 2·75

1945.
246. 56. 5 f. blue on buff .. 5·50 8·50
247. 5 f. brown on buff .. 5·00 10·00

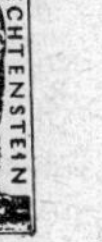
57. First Aid.

58. St. Lucius.

1945. Red Cross. Cross in red.
248. – 10 r. + 10 r. vio. on buff 30 65
249. 57. 20 r. + 20 r. red on buff 45 1·25
250. – 1 f. + 1 f. 40 r. grey on buff .. .. 2·40 9·00
DESIGNS: 10 r. Mother and children. 1 f. Nurse and invalid.

1946.
251. 58. 10 f. grey on buff .. 14·00 15·00

59. Stag.

60. Wilbur Wright.

1946. Wild Life.
252. 59. 20 r. red 75 90
255. – 20 r. red (Chamois) .. 90 2·00
283. – 20 r. red (Roebuck) .. 1·90 1·25
253. – 30 r. bl. (Mountain Hare) 75 90
256. – 30 r. blue (Marmot) .. 1·10 1·75
284. – 30 r. green (Game-cock) 1·90 1·50
285. – 80 r. brown (Badger) .. 9·00 15·00
254. – 1 f. 50 r. olive (Heath-cock) .. .. 1·60 5·50
257. – 1 f. 50 r. brown (Eagle) 1·75 3·75

1947. Death of Princess Elsa. As No. 141.
258. – 2 f. black on yellow .. 1·25 6·50

1948. Air. Pioneers of Flight.
259. – 10 r. green 40 20
260. – 15 r. violet 40 60
261. – 20 r. brown 40 20
262. – 25 r. red .. .. 50 1·00
263. – 40 r. blue 75 75
264. – 50 r. green .. .. 1·25 1·25
265. – 1 f. purple .. .. 1·25 1·50
266. – 2 f. claret .. .. 1·90 2·00
267. 60. 5 f. olive .. .. 2·25 4·50
268. – 10 f. black .. .. 15·00 11·00
PORTRAITS: 10 r. Leonardo da Vinci. 15 r. Joseph Montgolfier. 20 r. J. Degen. 25 r. Wilhelm Kress. 40 r. E. G. R. Robertson. 50 r. W. S. Henson. 1 f. O. Lilienthal. 2 f. S. A. Andree. 10 f. Icarus.

61. Ginevra de Benci (Da Vinci).

62. Posthorn and Map of World.

1949. Paintings. Size 27 x 31 mm.
269. 61. 10 r. green 25 20
270. – 20 r. red 25 20
271. – 30 r. black 75 75
272. – 40 r. blue .. .. 1·25 50
273. – 50 r. violet .. .. 2·50 3·25
274. – 60 r. grey .. .. 2·50 3·25
275. – 80 r. brown .. .. 1·10 1·90
276. – 90 r. olive .. .. 1·50 2·10
277. – 120 r. mauve .. .. 1·10 1·90
DESIGNS: 20 r. Young girl (Rubens). 30 r. Self-portrait, Rembrandt in plumed hat. 40 r. Chorister (Massys). 50 r. Blessed Virgin and Child (Memling). 60 r. Franz Meister in 1456 (Fouquet). 80 r. Girl with lute (Gentileschi). 90 r. Portrait of man (Strigel). 120 r. Portrait of man (Raphael).

1949. No. 227 surch. **5 Rp.** and bars.
278. 54. 5 r. on 3 r. brown .. 20 20

1949. U.P.U. 75th Anniv.
279. 62. 40 r. blue .. .. 1·50 3·00

63. Rossauer Castle.

64. Johann Adam Andreas.

1949. Acquisition of Domain of Schellenberg. 250th Anniv.
280. 63. 20 r. purple 65 75
281. – 40 r. blue .. .. 2·00 2·50
282. 64. 1 f. 50 r. red .. .. 2·40 3·00
DESIGN—HORIZ. 40 r. Bendern Church.

1950. Surch. with figures and bars.
286. 62. 100 r. on 40 r. blue .. 8·00 21·00
308. – 1 f. 20 on 40 r. blue (No. 281) .. .. 10·00 18·00

65. Boy cutting Loaf.

66. Canal (A. Cuyp).

67. Burgomaster (Frans Hals).

68. Lord Baden-Powell.

1951. Agricultural scenes.
287. 65. 5 r. claret 12 5
288. – 10 r. green 12 5
289. – 15 r. brown .. .. 65 1·25
290. – 20 r. sepia 25 12
291. – 25 r. red .. .. 65 1·25
292. – 30 r. green 50 12
293. – 40 r. blue .. .. 90 1·75
294. – 50 r. chocolate .. 65 1·50
295. – 60 r. brown .. .. 1·00 1·50
296. – 80 r. chestnut .. .. 1·00 1·25
297. – 90 r. olive .. .. 1·00 1·25
298. – 1 f. violet .. .. 11·00 2·50
DESIGNS: 10 r. Man whetting scythe. 15 r. Man scything. 20 r. Girl and sweet corn. 25 r. Hay cart. 30 r. Gathering grapes. 40 r. Man with scythe. 50 r. Herdsman and cows. 60 r. Two oxen drawing plough. 80 r. Woman and basket of fruit. 90 r. Woman gleaning. 1 f. Tractor and load of corn.

1951. Charity. Paintings.
299. 66. 10 r. + 10 r. olive .. 2·40 2·50
300. 67. 20 r. + 10 r. sepia .. 2·40 3·75
301. – 40 r. + 10 r. blue .. 1·90 2·50
DESIGN—As T 66: 40 r. Landscape (J. van Ruysdael).

1952. Paintings from Prince's Collection.
(a) As T 61 but size 25 × 30 mm.
309. 10 r. bronze-green .. 75 50
305. 20 r. plum .. .. 3·75 1·10
307. 40 r. deep blue .. 4·25 2·00
312. 40 r. Prussian blue .. 6·50 12·00
PAINTINGS: 10 r. Portrait of a Young Man (A.G.). 20 r. Portrait (Salvoldo). No. 307, St. John (Del Sarto). No. 312, Leonhard, Duke of Hag (Kulmbach).

(b) As T 67 (22½ × 24 mm.)
310. 20 r. bistre .. .. .. 2·50 1·90
306. 30 r. olive .. .. .. 5·00 2·25
311. 30 r. chocolate .. .. 4·50 3·00
PAINTINGS: 20 r. St. Nicholas (Zeitblom). No. 306, Madonna and Child (Botticelli). No. 311, St. Christopher (Cranach).

1953. 14th Int. Scout Conf.
313. 68. 10 r. green 50 50
314. 20 r. brown .. .. 3·75 1·25
315. 25 r. red .. .. 4·50 7·50
316. 40 r. blue .. .. 2·00 2·00

69. Alemannic Ornamental Disc, (about A.D. 600).

70. Prehistoric Walled Settlement, Borscht.

1953. Opening of National Museum, Vaduz.
317. **69.** 10 r. brown .. .. 3·75 9·00
318. **70.** 20 r. green .. .. 3·75 9·00
319. – 1 f. 20 r. indigo .. 13·00 7·50
DESIGN—VERT. 1 f. 20 r. Roessen jug (about 3000 B.C.).

71. Footballers. **72.** Madonna and Child.

1954. Football.
320. **71.** 10 r. brown and rose .. 80 50
321. – 20 r. green 90 50
322. – 25 r. brown .. .. 4·00 8·00
323. – 40 r. grey-violet .. 2·25 2·40
DESIGNS—HORIZ. 20 r. Footballer kicking ball. 25 r. Goal-keeper. 40 r. Two footballers.
For stamps in similar designs see Nos. 332/5, 340/3, 351/4, 363/6.

1954. Nos 299/301 surch. in figures.
324. **66.** 35 r. on 10 r.+10 r. olive .. .. 1·25 1·90
325. **67.** 60 r. on 20 r.+10 r. sepia .. .. 3·25 5·00
326. – 65 r. on 40 r.+10 r. bl. 1·90 1·90

1954. Termination of Marian Year.
327. **72.** 20 r. chestnut .. 1·10 75
328. 40 r. grey-green .. 4·00 9·00
329. 1 f. sepia .. .. 4·00 5·50

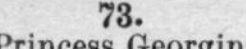

73. Princess Georgina.

74. Crown Prince John Adam Pius.

1955.
330. – 2 f. brown .. .. 11·00 11·00
331. **73.** 3 f. green .. .. 11·00 11·00
PORTRAIT: 2 f. Prince Francis Joseph II.

1955. Mountain Sports designs as T **71.**
332. 10 r. plum and turquoise.. 50 35
333. 20 r. myrtle and bistre .. 90 65
334. 25 r. sepia and cobalt .. 3·25 6·00
335. 40 r. olive and red .. 2·10 1·60
DESIGNS: 10 r. Slalom racer. 20 r. Mountaineer hammering in piton. 25 r. Skier. 40 r. Mountaineer resting on summit.

1955. Liechtenstein Red Cross. 10th Anniv. Cross in red.
336. **74.** 10 r. indigo 35 25
337. – 20 r. green .. .. 1·50 1·90
338. – 40 r. bistre .. .. 1·50 2·50
339. – 60 r. lake .. .. 1·40 1·60
PORTRAITS—VERT. 20 r. Prince Phillip. 40 r. Prince Nicholas. 60 r. Princess Nora.

1956. Athletic designs as T **71.**
340. 10 r. green and chestnut .. 45 25
341. 20 r. purple and green .. 1·00 50
342. 40 r. chocolate and blue .. 1·60 2·25
343. 1 f. brown and red .. 2·75 5·00
DESIGNS: 10 r. Throwing the javelin. 20 r. Hurdling. 40 r. Pole-vaulting. 1 f. Running.

75. **76.** Prince Francis Joseph II.

1956. Sovereignty of Liechtenstein. 150th Anniv.
344. **75.** 10 r. purple and gold .. 50 40
345. 1 f. 20 indigo and gold 90 1·60

1956. 50th Birthday of Prince Francis Joseph II.
346. **76.** 10 r. green 65 25
347. 15 r. blue .. .. 65 1·25
348. 25 r. purple .. .. 80 1·25
349. 60 r. brown .. .. 1·10 1·00

1956. 6th Philatelic Exn., Vaduz. As T **74** but inscr. "6 BRIEFMARKEN-AUSSTELLUNG".
350. 20 r. olive 50 40

1957. Gymnastic designs as T **71.**
351. 10 r. olive and pink .. 50 50
352. 15 r. maroon and green .. 1·50 3·00
353. 25 r. green and drab .. 1·50 3·00
354. 1 f. 50 r. sepia and yellow 3·00 3·50
DESIGNS: 10 r. Somersaulting around bar. 15 r. Vaulting. 25 r. Exercising with rings. 1 f. 50 r. Somersaulting on parallel bars.

77. Pine Trees.

78. Lord Baden-Powell.

1957. Liechtenstein Trees and Bushes.
355. **77.** 10 r. purple .. .. 1·10 1·10
356. – 20 r. lake .. .. 1·50 40
357. – 1 f. green .. .. 1·50 1·50
DESIGNS: 20 r. Wild rose bush. 1 f. Birch tree.
See also Nos. 369/71, 375/7 and 401/3.

1957. Boy Scout Movement. 50th Anniv. and Lord Baden-Powell. Birth Cent.
358. – 10 r. indigo .. .. 65 1·00
359. **78.** 20 r. brown .. .. 65 1·10
DESIGN: 10 r. Torchlight procession. Nos. 358/9 are arranged se-tenant in the sheets.

79. St. Mamertus Chapel.

80. Relief Map of Liechtenstein.

1957. Christmas.
360. **79.** 10 r. sepia 25 15
361. – 40 r. blue .. .. 1·60 2·50
362. – 1 f. 50 brown .. .. 4·50 3·75
DESIGNS: (from St. Mamertus Chapel). 40 r. Altar shrine. 1 f. 50 r. Statue "Piety".
See also Nos. 372/4 and 392/4.

1958. Sports designs as T **71.**
363. 15 r. purple and blue .. 55 75
364. 30 r. olive and purple .. 1·75 2·75
365. 40 r. slate and salmon .. 1·50 3·00
366. 90 r. sepia and apple .. 80 1·00
DESIGNS: 15 r. Swimmer. 30 r. Fencers. 40 r. Tennis-player. 90 r. Racing cyclists.

1958. Brussels Int. Exn.
367. **80.** 25 r. vio., ochre & red 25 50
368. 40 r. violet, blue and red 40 40

1958. Liechtenstein Trees and Bushes. As T **77.**
369. 20 r. sepia (Maples) .. 80 50
370. 50 r. olive (Holly) .. 1·90 1·10
371. 90 r. slate-violet (Yew) .. 1·00 1·00

1958. Christmas. As T **79.**
372. 20 r. myrtle 90 90
373. 35 r. slate-violet .. .. 1·00 90
374. 80 r. sepia .. .. 1·40 75
DESIGNS: 20 r. "St. Maurice and St. Agatha". 35 r. "St. Peter". 80 r. Chapel of St. Peter Mals-Balzers.

1959. Liechtenstein Trees and Bushes. As T **77.**
375. 20 r. lilac (Larch) .. .. 1·25 1·00
376. 50 r. brown-red (Elder) .. 1·10 75
377. 90 r. myrtle (Linden) .. 1·10 75

81.

83. Harvester.

82. Flags of Vaduz Castle, and Rhine Valley.

1959. Pope Pius XII Mourning Stamp.
378. **81.** 30 r. purple and gold .. 40 65

1959. Views.
379. – 5 r. olive-brown .. 5 5
380. **82.** 10 r. slate-purple .. 5 5
381. – 20 r. magenta 8 5
382. – 30 r. chestnut .. 10 8
383. – 40 r. bronze-green .. 30 25
384. – 50 r. blue .. 20 20
385. – 60 r. turquoise.. .. 25 25
386. **83.** 75 r. yellow-brown .. 30 40
387. – 80 r. olive-green .. 25 30
388. – 90 r. purple .. 30 35
389. – 1 f. brown .. 35 40
390. – 1 f. 20 salmon .. 40 45
390a. – 1 f. 30 green .. 40 50
391. – 1 f. 50 blue .. 50 55
DESIGNS—HORIZ. 5 r. Bendern Church. 20 r. Rhine Dam. 30 r. Gutenberg Castle. 40 r. View of Schellenberg. 50 r. Vaduz Castle. 60 r. Naafkopf-Falknis Mountains (view from the Bettlerjoch). 1 f. 20 Harvesting apples. 1 f. 30 Farmer and wife. 1 f. 50 Saying grace at table. VERT. 80 r. Alpine haymaker. 90 r. Girl in vineyard. 1 f. Mother in kitchen.

1959. Christmas. As T **79.**
392. 5 r. myrtle 15 12
393. 60 r. olive .. .. .. 2·50 1·40
394. 1 f. purple .. .. 1·50 1·10
DESIGNS: 5 r. Bendern Church belfry. 60 r. Sculpture on bell of St. Theodul's Church. 1 f. Sculpture on tower of St. Lucius' Church.

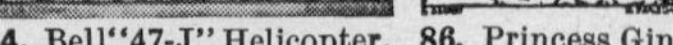

84. Bell "47-J" Helicopter. **86.** Princess Gina.

87. Heinrich von Frauenberg.

85. Europa "Honeycomb".

1960. Air. 1st Liechtenstein Air Stamps. 30th Anniv.
395. **84.** 30 r. orange .. .. 75 1·10
396. – 40 r. blue .. .. 1·25 1·00
397. – 50 r. maroon .. .. 1·25 2·25
398. – 75 r. olive-green .. 55 75
DESIGNS (Airliners in flight): 40 r. Boeing "707". 50 r. Convair "600". 75 r. Douglas "DC-8".

1960. World Refugee Year. Surch. with uprooted tree symbol and value.
399. **80.** 30+10 r. on 40 r. violet, blue and red .. 40 40
400. 50+10 r. on 25 r. violet, ochre and red.. .. 50 90

1960. Liechtenstein Trees and Bushes. As T **77.**
401. 20 r. brown (Beech) .. 75 75
402. 30 r. purple (Juniper) .. 1·25 1·00
403. 50 r. blue-green (Pines) .. 1·90 1·00

1960. United Europe.
404. **85.** 50 r. multicoloured .. 25·00 20·00

1960.
404a. – 1 f. 70 violet .. 65 55
405. **86.** 2 f. blue 75 65
406. – 3 f. brown .. .. 1·00 90
PORTRAITS: 1 f. 70, Crown Prince Hans Adam. 3 f. Prince Francis Joseph II.

1961. Minnesingers (1st issue). Multicoloured. Reproductions from the Manessian Manuscript of Songs.
407. 15 r. T **87** 25 35
408. 25 r. Ulrich von Liechtenstein 30 75
409. 35 r. Ulrich von Gutenberg 55 65
410. 1 f. Konrad von Altstatten 1·50 3·25
411. 1 f. 50 Walther von der Vogelweide .. .. 3·25 10·00
See also Nos. 415/8 and 428/31.

88. "Power Transmission".

89. Clasped Hands.

1961. Europa.
412. **88.** 50 r. multicoloured .. 15 20

1962. Europa.
413. **89.** 50 r. red and indigo .. 40 65

90. Campaign Emblem.

91. Pieta.

1962. Malaria Eradication.
414. **90.** 50 r. turquoise .. 20 40

1962. Minnesingers (2nd issue). As T **87** Multicoloured.
415. 20 r. King Konradin .. 20 25
416. 30 r. Kraft von Toggenburg 25 40
417. 40 r. Heinrich von Veldig.. 40 65
418. 2 f. Tannhauser 90 90

1962. Christmas.
419. **91.** 30 r. magenta 30 50
420. – 50 r. orange 40 50
421. – 1 f. 20 blue 70 60
DESIGNS: 50 r. Fresco with Angel. 1 f. 20, View of Mauren.
See also Nos. 438/40.

92. Prince Francis Joseph II.

93. Milk and Bread.

1963. Prince Francis Joseph II. 25th Anniv. of Reign.
422. **92.** 5 f. grey-green .. 1·50 1·60

1963. Freedom from Hunger.
423. **93.** 50 r. brown, pur. & red 65 50

94. "Angel of Annunciation".

95. "Europa".

96. Olympic Rings and Flags.

97. Arms of Counts of Werdenberg, Vaduz.

1963. Red Cross Cent. Cross in red; background grey.
424. **94.** 20 r. olive and emerald 25 25
425. – 80 r. violet and mauve 30 50
426. – 1 f. grey-blue & ultram. 35 50
DESIGNS: 80 r. "The Epiphany." 1 f. "Family".

1963. Europa.
427. **95.** 50 r. multicoloured .. 65 50

1963. Minnesingers (3rd issue). As T **87.** Multicoloured.
428. 25 r. Heinrich von Sax .. 25 25
429. 30 r. Kristan von Hamle.. 40 40
430. 75 r. Werner von Teufen.. 50 50
431. 1 f. 70 Hartmann von Aue 1·00 75

1964. Olympic Games, Tokyo.
432. **96.** 50 r. red, black & blue.. 30 30

1964. Arms (1st issue). Multicoloured.
433. 20 r. Type **97** .. 20 20
434. 30 r. Barons of Brandis .. 25 20
435. 80 r. Counts of Suiz .. 45 40
436. 1 f. 50 Counts of Hohenems 50 65
See also Nos. 443/6 and 458/61.

98. Roman Castle, Schaan. **99.** P. Kaiser (historian).

1964. Europa.
437. **98.** 50 f. multicoloured .. 65 45

1964. Christmas. As T **91.**
438. 10 r. slate-purple 5 5
439. 40 r. blue 40 30
440. 1 f. 30 purple 55 65
DESIGNS: 10 r. Masescha Chapel. 40 r. St. Magdalene (altar picture). 1 f 30, Madonna (altar picture, St. Sebastien).

1964. Peter Kaiser. Death Cent.
441. **99.** 1 f. green on cream .. 45 45

100. "Madonna" (wood sculpture, c. 1700). **101.** Europa "Links" (ancient belt-buckle).

1965.
442. **100.** 10 f. red .. .. 3·75 2·50

1965. Arms (2nd issue). As T **97.** Multicoloured.
443. 20 r. Von Schellenberg .. 12 12
444. 30 r. Von Gutenberg .. 20 12
445. 80 r. Von Frauenberg .. 40 40
446. 1 f. Von Ramschwag .. 30 40

1965. Europa.
447. **101.** 50 r. brown, grey & blue 40 30

102. "Jesus in the Temple". **103.** Princess Gina and Prince Franz.

1965. Ferdinand Nigg (painter). Birth Cent.
448. – 10 r. bronze and green .. 5 5
449. – 30 r. brown and orange 20 12
450. **102.** 1 f. 20 green and blue .. 40 45
DESIGNS—VERT. 10 r. "The Annunciation". 30 r. "The Magi".

1965. Special Issue.
451. **103.** 75 r. black, flesh, gold and grey 30 30

104. Telecommunication Symbols. **105.** Tree ("Wholesome Earth").

1965. I.T.U. Cent.
452. **104.** 25 r. multicoloured .. 10 10

1966. Nature Protection.
453. **105.** 10 r. green and yellow 5 5
454. – 20 r. indigo and blue .. 10 8
455. – 30 r. ultram. and green 15 15
456. – 1 f. 50 red and yellow 40 45
DESIGNS: 20 r. Bird ("Pure Air"). 30 r. Fish "Clean Water"). 1 f. 50, Sun ("Protection of Nature").

1966. Prince Franz Joseph II's 60th Birthday. As T **103**, but with portrait of Prince Franz and inscr. "1906–1966".
457. – 1 f. agate, brown, gold and grey 40 40

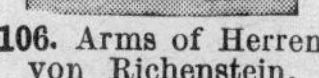

106. Arms of Herren von Richenstein. **107.** Europa "Ship".

1966. Arms of Triesen Families. Multicoloured.
458. 20 r. Type **106** 10 8
459. 30 r. Junker Vaistli .. 15 12
460. 60 r. Edle von Trisun .. 25 25
461. 1 f. 20 Die von Schiel .. 30 40

1966. Europa.
462. **107.** 50 r. multicoloured .. 40 25

108. Vaduz Parish Church. **109.** Cogwheels.

1966. Restoration of Vaduz Parish Church.
463. **108.** 5 r. green and red .. 5 5
464. – 20 r. purple and bistre 10 8
465. – 30 r. blue & brown-red 15 20
466. – 1 f. 70 lake and grey .. 50 50
DESIGNS: 20 r. St. Florin. 30 r. Madonna. 1 f. 70, God the Father.

1967. Europa.
467. **109.** 50 r. multicoloured .. 25 25

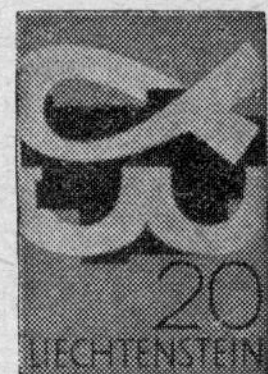

110. "The Manfrom Malanser". **111.** "Alpha and Omega".

1967. Liechtenstein Sagas. (1st Series). Multicoloured.
468. 20 r. Type **110** 12 12
469. 30 r. "The Treasure of Gutenberg" 20 20
470. 1 f. 20 "The Giant of Guflina" 55 45
See also Nos. 492/4 and 516/18.

1967. Christian Symbols. Multicoloured.
472. 20 r. Type **111** 10 10
473. 30 r. "Tropaion" (Cross as victory symbol) .. 15 15
474. 70 r. Christ's monogram .. 35 25

112. Father J. B. Buchel (educator, historian and poet). **113.** "E F T A".

1967. Buchel Commem.
475. **112.** 1 f. lake and green .. 45 40

1967. European Free Trade Assn.
476. **113** 50 r. multicoloured .. 40 25

114. "Peter and Paul", Mauren. **115.** Campaign Emblem.

1967. "Patrons of the Church". Multicoloured.
477. 5 r. "St. Joseph", Planken 5 5
478. 10 r. "St. Lawrence", Schaan 5 5
479. 20 r. Type **114** 8 5
480. 30 r. "St. Nicholas", Balzers 12 8
480a. 40 r. "St. Sebastian", Nendeln 25 25
481. 50 r. "St. George", Schellenberg 20 12
482. 60 r. "St. Martin", Eschen 25 15
483. 70 r. "St. Fridolin", Ruggell 30 20
484. 80 r. "St. Gallus", Triesen 30 25
485. 1 f. "St. Theodolus", Triesenberg 40 30
486. 1 f. 20 "St. Anna", Vaduz Castle 45 35
487. 1 f. 50 "St. Marie", Bendern-Camprin .. 55 45
488. 2 f. "St. Lucius", (patron saint of Liechtenstein) .. 75 65

1967. "Technical Assistance".
489. **115.** 50 r. + 20 r. mult. .. 65 50

116. Europa "Key".

1968. Europa.
490. **116.** 50 r. gold, blk., bl. & red 25 25

117. Arms of Liechtenstein and Wilczek. **118.** Sir Rowland Hill.

1968. Silver Wedding Anniv. of Prince Francis Joseph II and Princess Gina.
491. **117.** 75 r. multicoloured .. 65 50

1968. Liechtenstein Sagas (2nd Series). As T **110.** Multicoloured.
492. 30 r. "The Treasure of St. Mamerten" 20 20
493. 50 r. "The Hobgoblin in the Bergerwald" .. 25 25
494. 80 r. "The Three Sisters" 45 45

1968. "Pioneers of Philately". (1st Series)
495. **118.** 20 r. green 10 10
496. – 30 r. brown 15 15
497. – 1 f. black 50 50
PORTRAITS: 30 r. Philippe de Ferrary. 1 f. Maurice Burrus.
See also Nos. 504/5 and 554/6.

119. Arms of Liechtenstein. **120.** Colonnade.

1969.
498. **119.** 3 f. 50 brown .. 1·25 1·25

1969. Europa.
499. **120.** 50 r. multicoloured .. 50 40

121. "Biology".

1969. Liechtenstein. 250th Anniv. Multicoloured.
500. 10 r. Type **121** 5 5
501. 30 r. "Physics" 15 15
502. 50 r. "Astronomy" .. 25 25
503. 80 r. "Art" 40 40

1969. "Pioneers of Philately" (2nd Series). As T **118.**
504. 80 r. brown 40 40
505. 1 f. 20 blue 60 65
PORTRAITS: 80 r. Carl Lindenberg. 1 f. 20 Theodore Champion.

122. St. Luzi Monastery (arms). **123.** Symbolic "T".

1969. Arms of Church Patrons. Multicoloured.
506. 20 r. St. Johann's Abbey .. 10 10
507. 30 r. Type **122** 15 15
508. 30 r. Ladies' Priory, Schanis 15 15
509. 30 r. Knights Hospitalers, Feldkirch 20 15
510. 50 r. Pfafers Abbey .. 25 25
511. 50 r. Weingarten Abbey .. 30 25
512. 75 r. St. Gallen Abbey .. 40 40
513. 1 f. 20 Ottobeuren Abbey 80 60
514. 1 f. 50 Chur Episcopate .. 75 75

1969. Liechtenstein Telegraph System. Cent.
515. **123.** 30 r. multicoloured .. 15 15

1969. Liechtenstein Sagas (3rd Series). As T **110.** Multicoloured.
516. 20 r. "The Cheated Devil" 10 10
517. 50 r. "The Fiery Red Goat" 25 25
518. 60 r. "The Grafenberg Treasure" 30 30

124. Orange Lily. **125.** "Flaming Sun".

1970. Nature Conservation Year. Multicoloured.
519. 20 r. Type **124** 10 10
520. 30 r. Wild orchid 15 15
521. 50 r. Ranunculus 45 25
522. 1 f. 20 Bog bean 80 65
See also Nos. 532/5 and 548/51.

1970. Europa.
523. **125.** 50 r. yellow, blue & grn. 25 25

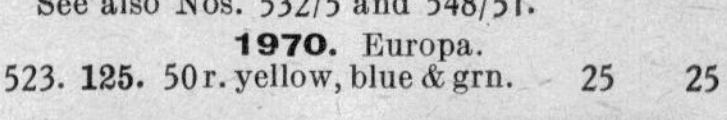

126. Prince Wenzel. **127.** Prince Francis Joseph II.

1970. Liechtenstein Red Cross. 25th Anniv.
524. **126.** 1 f. multicoloured .. 50 50

1970.
525a. – 1 f. 70 green 65 65
526. – 2 f. 50 blue 75 75
527. **127.** 3 f. black .. .. 1·00 1·00
DESIGNS: 1 f. 70 Prince Hans Adam. 2 f. 50 Princess Gina.

128. "Mother and Child" (R. Schaedler). **129.** Bronze Boar.

1970. Christmas.
528. **128.** 30 r. multicoloured .. 25 25

1971. Nat. Museum Inaug.
529. **129.** 25 r. blk., blue & ultram. 12 12
530. – 30 r. brown and green 15 15
531. – 75 r. multicoloured .. 40 35
DESIGNS: 30 r. Ornamental peacock (Roman, 2nd-century). 75 r. Engraved bowl (13th-century).

130. Cyclamen. **131.** Europa Chain.

1971. Liechtenstein Flowers (2nd Series). Multicoloured.
532. 10 r. Type **130** 5 5
533. 20 r. Moonwort 10 10
534. 50 r. Superb pink 25 25
535. 1 f. 50 Alpine columbine .. 75 75
See also 548/51.

1971. Europa.
536. **131.** 50 r. yellow, bl. & black 50 40

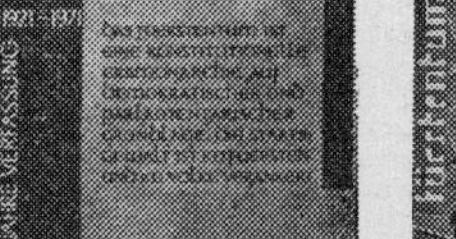

132. Part of Text. **133.** Cross-country Skiing.

1971. 1921 Constitution. 50th Anniv. Multicoloured.
537. 70 r. Type **132** 40 40
538. 80 r. Princely crown .. 40 40

1971. Winter Olympic Games, Sapporo, Japan (1972). Multicoloured.
539. 15 r. Type **133** 8 8
540. 40 r. Ice-hockey 20 20
541. 65 r. Downhill-skiing .. 30 30
542. 1 f. 50 Figure-skating .. 75 75

134. "Madonna and Child" (sculpture, Andrea della Robbia). 135. Gymnastics.

1971. Christmas.
543. 134. 30 r. multicoloured .. 15 15

1972. Olympic Games, Munich. Multicoloured.
544. 10 r. Type 135 .. .. 5 5
545. 20 r. High-jumping .. 10 10
546. 40 r. Running 40 20
547. 60 r. Throwing the discus 45 30

1972. Liechtenstein Flowers (3rd Series). As T 130. Multicoloured.
548. 20 r. Sulphur anemone .. 10 10
549. 30 r. Turk's-cap lily .. 15 15
550. 60 r. Alpine centaury .. 30 30
551. 1 f. 20 Reed-mace .. 55 55

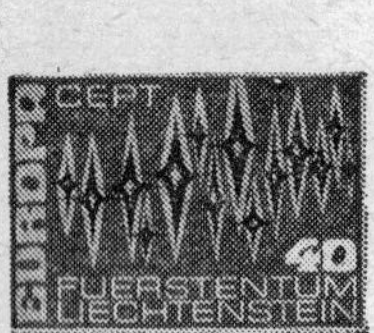

136. "Communications". 137. "Faun".

1972. Europa.
552. 136. 40 r. multicoloured .. 40 20

1972. "Pioneers of Philately" (3rd Series). As T 118.
554. 30 r. green 15 15
555. 40 r. maroon 30 20
556. 1 f. 30 blue 80 65
PORTRAITS: 30 r. Emilio Diena. 40 r. Andre de Cock. 1 f. 30 Theodore E. Steinway.

1972. "Natural Art". Motifs fashioned from roots and branches. Multicoloured.
557. 20 r. Type 137 .. .. 10 10
558. 30 r. "Dancer" 15 15
559. 1 f. 10 "Owl" 75 50

138. "Madonna with Angels" (F. Nigg). 139. Lawena Springs.

1972. Christmas.
560. 138. 30 r. multicoloured .. 20 15

1972. Landscapes.
561. – 5 r. purple & yellow .. 5 5
562. 139. 10 r. grn., blue & black 5 5
563. – 15 r. red and yellow 5 5
564. – 25 r. purple and blue 10 10
565. – 30 r. lilac and cream .. 12 12
566. – 40 r. mve., orge. & mar. 15 15
567. – 50 r. purple 20 20
568. – 60 r. green 25 25
569. – 70 r. blue 25 25
570. – 80 r. green and sage 30 30
571. – 1 f. red and green .. 40 40
572. – 1 f. 30 blue and green 50 50
573. – 1 f. 50 brown and blue 55 55
574. – 1 f. 80 brn. & cream .. 70 70
575. – 2 f. brown., blue & sepia 75 75
DESIGNS: 5 r. Silum. 15 r. Ruggeller Reed. 25 r. Steg, Kirchlispitz. 30 r. Feld Schellenberg. 40 r. Rennhof Mauren. 50 r. Tidruffe. 60 r. Eschner. 70 r. Mittagspitz. 80 r. Schaan Forest. 1 f. St. Peter at Mals. 1 f. 30 Frommenhaus. 1 f. 50 Ochsenkhopf. 1 f. 80 Hehlawangspitz. 2 f. Samina Gorge.

140. Europa "Posthorn".

1973. Europa.
576. 140. 30 r. multicoloured .. 20 20
577. 40 r. multicoloured .. 25 25

141. Nautilus Goblet. 142. Arms of Liechtenstein.

1973. Treasures from Prince's Collection (1st issue). Drinking Vessels. Mult.
578. 30 r. Type 141 .. .. 15 15
579. 70 r. Ivory tankard .. 40 40
580. 1 f. 10 Silver cup 65 65
See also Nos. 590/2.

1973.
581. 142. 5 f. multicoloured .. 1·90 1·90

143. "False Ringlet" Butterfly. 144. "Madonna" (Bartolomeio di Tommaso da Foligno).

1973. "Small Fauna of Liechtenstein". (1st series). Multicoloured.
582. 30 r. Type 143 .. .. 15 15
583. 40 r. Common curlew .. 20 20
584. 60 r. Edible frog 30 30
585. 80 r. Grass snake 40 40
See also Nos. 596/9.

1973. Christmas.
586. 144. 30 r. multicoloured .. 20 20

145. "Shouting Horseman" (sculpture-A. Riccio). 146. Footballers.

1974. Europa. Multicoloured.
587. 30 r. Type 145 .. .. 20 20
588. 40 r. "Squatting Aphrodite" (sculpture–A. Susini) 25 25

1974. Treasures from Prince's Collection (2nd issue). Porcelain. As T 141. Mult.
589. 30 r. Chinese vase, 19th century 15 15
590. 50 r. Chinese vase, 1740 .. 25 25
591. 60 r. Chinese vase, 1830 .. 30 30
592. 1 f. Chinese vase, c. 1700 50 50

1974. World Cup Football Championships, West Germany.
593. 146. 80 r. multicoloured .. 45 45

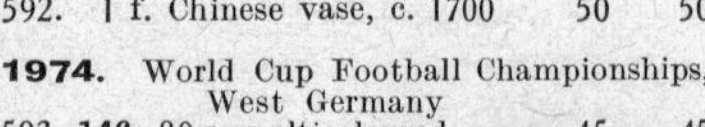

147. Posthorn and U.P.U. Emblem. 148. Bishop Marxer.

1974. Universal Postal Union Cent.
594. 147. 40 r. blk. grn. & gold .. 25 25
595. 60 r. blk, red & gold .. 40 40

1974. Small Fauna of Liechtenstein (2nd series). As Type 143. Multicoloured.
596. 15 r. Mountain newt .. 8 8
597. 25 r. Adder 12 12
598. 70 r. Dappled butterfly .. 35 35
599. 1 f. 10 Three-toed woodpecker 55 55

1974. Bishop Franz Marxer. Death Cent.
600. 148. 1 f. multicoloured .. 45 45

149. Prince Francis Joseph II and Princess Gina.

1974.
601. 149. 10 f. brown and gold .. 3·75 3·75

150. "St. Florian". 151. Prince Constantin.

1974. Christmas. Local Art. Glass Paintings. Multicoloured.
602. 30 r. Type 150 .. .. 20 20
603. 50 r. "St. Wendelin" .. 25 25
604. 60 r. "St. Mary, Anna and Joachim" 30 30
605. 70 r. "Jesus in Manger" .. 35 35

1975. Royal Princes.
606. 151. 70 r. green and gold .. 25 25
607. – 80 r. purple and gold .. 30 30
608. – 1 f. 20 blue and gold .. 45 45
PORTRAITS—80 r. Prince Maximilian. 1 f. 20 Prince Alois.

152. "Cold Sun" (M. Frommelt). 153. Imperial Cross.

1975. Europa. Multicoloured.
609. 30 r. Type 152 .. .. 15 15
610. 60 r. "Village" (L. Jager) 30 30

1975. Imperial Insignia. Multicoloured.
611. 30 r. Type 153 .. .. 12 12
612. 60 r. Imperial sword .. 25 20
613. 1 f. Imperial orb 40 40
614. 1 f. 30 Coronation robe (22 × 13 mm.) 50 50
615. 2 f. Imperial crown .. 75 75

154. "Red Cross Activities". 155. St. Mamerten, Triesen.

1975. Liechenstein Red Cross. 30th Anniv.
616. 154. 60 r. multicoloured .. 25 25

1975. European Architectural Heritage Year. Multicoloured.
617. 40 r. Type 155 .. .. 15 15
618. 50 r. Red House, Vaduz .. 20 20
619. 70 r. Prebendary buildings, Eschen 25 25
620. 1 f. Gutenberg Castle, Balzers 40 40

156. Speed Skating. 157. "Daniel in the Lions' Den".

1975. Winter Olympic Games, Innsbruck (1976). Multicoloured.
621. 20 r. Type 156 .. .. 8 8
622. 25 r. Ice hockey 12 12
623. 70 r. Downhill skiing .. 30 30
624. 1 f. 20 Slalom 45 45

1975. Christmas and Holy Year. Romanesque Sculptures from Chur Cathedral.
625. 157. 30 r. violet and gold .. 12 12
626. – 60 r. green and gold .. 25 25
627. – 90 r. lake and gold .. 40 40
DESIGNS: 60, 90 r. Different sculptures as T 157.

158. "Mouflon" (ceramic). 159. River Crayfish.

1976. Europa. Multicoloured.
628. 40 r. Type 153 .. .. 15 15
629. 80 r. "Pheasant and Brood" (ceramic) .. 30 30

1976. World Wildlife Fund. Multicoloured.
630. 25 r. Type 159 .. .. 10 10
631. 40 r. European pond turtle 15 15
632. 70 r. Old world otter .. 30 30
633. 80 r. Lapwing 30 30

160. Roman Fibula.

1976. Liechtenstein Historical Society. 75th Anniv.
634. 160. 90 r. multicoloured .. 35 35

161. Judo.

1976. Olympic Games, Montreal. Multicoloured.
636. 35 r. Type 161 .. .. 15 15
637. 50 r. Volleyball 20 20
638. 80 r. Relay-racing .. 30 30
639. 1 f. 10 Long-jumping .. 45 45

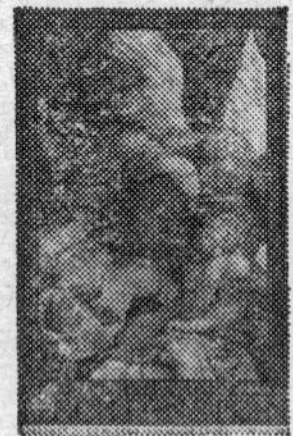

162. "Singing Angels" (Rubens).

1976. Rubens Commemoration. Paintings from Prince's Collection. Multicoloured.
640. 50 r. Type 162 .. .. 20 20
641. 70 r. "Sons of Rubens" .. 30 30
642. 1 f. "Daughters of Cecrops" (50 × 39 mm.) 40 40

163. "Pisces".

1976. Signs of the Zodiac. Multicoloured.
643. 20 r. Type 163 .. .. 8 8
644. 40 r. "Aries" 15 15
645. 80 r. "Taurus" 30 30
646. 90 r. "Gemini" 35 35

164. "Child Jesus of Prague."

1976. Christmas. Monastic Works in Wax. Multicoloured.
647. 20 r. Type 164 .. .. 8 8
648. 50 r. "The Flight into Egypt" (vert.) .. 20 20
649. 80 r. "Holy Trinity" (vert.) 30 30
650. 1 f. 50 "Holy Family" .. 60 60

165. Von Brandis' Sarcophagus.

1976. Bishop Orthlieb von Brandis Commemoration.
651. 165. 1 f. 10 multicoloured .. 45 45

OFFICIAL STAMPS

1932. Stamps of 1930 optd. **REGIERUNGS DIENSTSACHE** under crown.
O 118. 5 r. green (No. 97) .. 5·00 3·25
O 119. 10 r. purple .. .. 13·00 3·25
O 120. 20 r. red .. .. 10·00 3·25
O 121. 30 r. blue .. .. 6·50 3·25
O 122. 35 r. green .. .. 3·75 2·50
O 123. 50 r. sepia .. .. 19·00 5·50
O 124. 60 r. olive .. .. 3·75 6·00
O 125. 1 f. 20 brown .. .. 80·00 £120

1933. Stamps of 1933 optd. **REGIERUNGS DIENSTSACHE** round crown.
O 126. 31. 25 r. orange .. 19·00 23·00
O 127. – 1 f. 20 brown .. 19·00 70·00

1934. Stamps of 1934 optd. **REGIERUNGS DIENSTSACHE** in circle round crown.
O 150. 37. 5 r. green 12 40
O 151. – 10 r. violet 12 40
O 152. – 15 r. red 20 50
O 153. – 20 r. red 20 40
O 155. – 25 r. brown .. .. 1·10 3·00

1934. Landscape pictorial stamps of 1934 optd. **REGIERUNGS DIENSTSACHE** in circle round crown.
O 156. – 30 r. blue .. .. 75 1·50
O 157. 34. 50 r. chocolate .. 1·00 1·25
O 158. – 90 r. green .. 1·40 3·75
O 159. – 1 f. 50 lake .. 10·00 23·00

1937. Stamps of 1937 optd. **REGIERUNGS DIENSTSACHE** in circle round crown.
O 174. – 5 r. green 8 12
O 175. 42. 10 r. violet 8 12
O 176. – 20 r. red 50 50
O 177. – 25 r. brown 20 65
O 178. – 30 r. blue 25 25
O 179. – 50 r. brown 25 40
O 180. – 1 f. red .. .. 40 1·60
O 181. – 1 f. 50 slate .. .. 65 1·90

1947. Stamps of 1944 optd. **DIENSTMARKE** and crown.
O 255. 5 r. green 12 25
O 256. 10 r. violet 12 25
O 257. 20 r. red 25 25
O 258. 30 r. blue 30 40
O 259. 50 r. grey 50 65
O 260. 1 f. claret .. .. 1·25 3·50
O 261. 1 f. 50 blue .. .. 1·25 3·50

O 1.

1950. Buff paper.
O 287. O 1. 5 r. purple and grey .. 10 8
O 288. 10 r. olive and red .. 15 10
O 289. 20 r. brown and blue 15 12
O 290. 30 r. claret and red .. 30 25
O 291. 40 r. blue and brown 20 25
O 292. 55 r. green and red .. 65 50
O 293. 60 r. grey and red .. 65 80
O 294. 80 r. orange and grey 40 60
O 295. 90 r. sepia and blue .. 45 60
O 296. 1 f. 20 green & orange 75 75

1968. White paper.
O 495. O 1. 5 r. brown and orange 5 5
O 496. 10 r. violet and red .. 5 5
O 497. 20 r. red and green .. 8 8
O 498. 30 r. green and red .. 10 10
O 499. 50 r. blue and red 20 20
O 500. 60 r. orange and blue 25 25
O 501. 70 r. claret and green 25 25
O 502. 80 r. green and red .. 30 30
O 503. 95 r. green and red .. 35 35
O 504. 1 f. purple & turquoise 40 40
O 505. 1 f. 20 chestnut & turq. 45 45
O 506. 2 f. brown and orange 75 75

POSTAGE DUE STAMPS

D 1. D 2. D 3.

1920.
D 43. D 1. 5 h. red 5 5
D 44. 10 h. red 5 5
D 45. 15 h. red 5 5
D 46. 20 h. red 5 5
D 47. 25 h. red 5 5
D 48. 30 h. red 5 5
D 49. 40 h. red 5 5
D 50. 50 h. red 5 5
D 51. 80 h. red 5 5
D 52. 1 k. blue 8 20
D 53. 2 k. blue 8 20
D 54. 5 k. blue 10 20

1928.
D 84. D 2. 5 r. orange & violet .. 35 65
D 85. 10 r. orange & violet 35 50
D 86. 15 r. orange & violet 1·25 2·50
D 87. 20 r. orange & violet 50 50
D 88. 25 r. orange & violet 1·25 2·50
D 89. 30 r. orange & violet 1·25 2·50
D 90. 40 r. orange & violet 1·25 3·75
D 91. 50 r. orange & violet 1·50 5·00

1940.
D 189. D 3. 5 r. red and blue .. 1·25 1·90
D 190. 10 r. red and blue .. 30 25
D 191. 15 r. red and blue .. 40 35
D 192. 20 r. red and blue .. 40 25
D 193. 25 r. red and blue .. 70 1·25
D 194. 30 r. red and blue .. 90 2·50
D 195. 40 r. red and blue .. 1·10 2·50
D 196. 50 r. red and blue .. 1·10 3·75

LITHUANIA E2

A country on the Baltic Sea formerly under Russian rule. Later independent, and then under German control (see German Eastern Command). Now part of Soviet Russia.

1918. 100 skatiku = 1 auksinas.
1922. 100 centu = 1 litas.

ILLUSTRATIONS British Commonwealth and all overprints and surcharges are FULL SIZE. Foreign Countries have been reduced to ¾-LINEAR.

Lietuvos paštas sk. 10 sk.

(1.)

1918. Type-set stamps, inscr. "Lietuvos skatiku pasta" (or "pastas") or "Lietuvos pastas" and value, in border or circles, as T 1.
20. 1. 10 s. black 40 20
21. 15 s. black 40 20
22. 20 s. black 40 20
23. 30 s. black 40 20
24. 40 s. black 40 20
25. 50 s. black 40 20
26. 60 s. black 40 20

2. 3. 4.

1919.
40. 2. 10 s. red 5 5
50. 10 s. orange 5 5
41. 15 s. violet 5 5
42. 20 s. blue 5 5
43. 30 s. orange 5 5
44. 40 s. brown 5 5
45. 3. 50 s. green 5 5
56. 60 s. red and violet .. 5 5
46. 75 s. red and yellow .. 5 5
47. 4. 1 a. red and grey .. 10 8
48. 3 a. red and brown .. 12 10
49. 5 a. red and green .. 12 12

1921. As T 4, but "AUKSINAS" or "AUKSINAI" in capital letters.
58. 4. 1 a. red and grey .. 5 5
59. 3 a. red and brown .. 10 8
60. 5 a. red and green .. 12 10

5. "Lithuania" receiving Independence. 6. "Lithuania" arises.

1920. Independence. Dated "1918-11-16".
65. 5. 10 s. lake 60 60
66. 15 s. lilac 60 60
67. 20 s. blue 60 60
68. 6. 30 s. brown 60 60
69. – 40 s. green and brown .. 60 60
70. 6. 50 s. red 60 60
71. 60 s. lilac 60 60
72. – 80 s. red and violet .. 60 60
73. – 1 a. red and green .. 60 60
74. – 3 a. red and brown .. 60 60
75. – 5 a. red and green .. 60 60
DESIGNS—VERT. 40 s., 80 s., 1 a. "Lithuania" with chains broken. 3 a., 5 a. (25×25 mm.) Vytis".

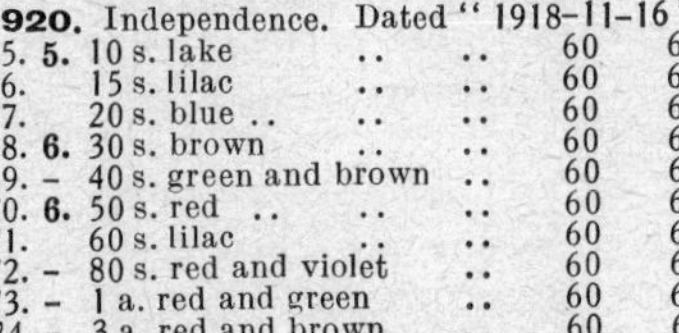

9. Arms. 10. Vytautas.

1920. National Assembly.
76. 9. 10 s. red 15 15
77. 15 s. violet 20 20
78. 10. 20 s. green 20 20
79. 9. 30 s. brown 20 20
80. – 40 s. violet and green .. 20 20
81. 10. 50 s. brown and orange .. 25 25
82. 60 s. red and orange .. 25 25
83. – 80 s. red, grey and black 25 25
84. – 1 a. yellow and black .. 25 25
85. – 3 a. green and black .. 30 30
86. – 5 a. violet and black .. 60 60
DESIGNS—As T 10: 40 s., 80 s. Gediminas. As T 9: 1 a. to 5 a. Sacred Oak and Altar.

13. Sower. 14. Kestutis. 15. Reaper.

16. 19. Allegory of Flight.

17. Flying Posthorn. 18. Junkers "F-130" over R. Niemen.

1921.
87. 13. 10 s. red 5 5
88. 15 s. mauve 5 5
89. 20 s. blue 5 5
90. 15. 30 s. brown 15 15
91. 14. 40 s. red 5 5
92. 15. 50 s. olive 5 5
93. 60 s. mauve and green .. 5 5
94. 14. 80 s. red and orange .. 5 5
95. 1 a. green and brown .. 5 5
96. 2 a. red and blue .. 5 5
97. 16. 3 a. blue and brown .. 25 25
124. 13. 4 a. blue and yellow .. 5 5
98. 16. 5 a. rose and grey .. 12 12
125. 13. 8 a. black and green .. 8 5
99. 16. 10 a. mauve and red .. 20 20
100. 25 a. green and brown .. 30 30
101. 100 a. grey and red .. 2·00 2·00

1921. Air. Kaunas-Konigsberg Air Service. Inaug.
102. 17. 20 s. blue 20 20
103. 40 s. orange 20 20
104. 60 s. green 20 20
105. 80 s. rose 25 20
106. 18. 1 a. green and red .. 40 40
107. – 2 a. brown and blue .. 60 60
108. – 5 a. grey and yellow .. 60 60
DESIGNS—As T 18: 2 a. Three aeroplanes in flight. As T 19: 5 a. Aeroplane over Gediminberg castle).

1921. Air Mail Service. Inaug.
109. 19. 20 s. lilac and orange .. 25 35
110. 40 s. red and blue .. 25 35
111. 60 s. olive and blue .. 25 35
112. 80 s. green and yellow .. 25 35
113. 1 a. blue and green .. 25 35
114. 2 a. red and grey .. 25 35
115. 5 a. green and purple .. 60 60

1922. Surch. **4 AUKSINAI** with or without frame.
116. 3. 4 a. on 75 s. red & yellow 12 12

22.

1922. Air.
118. 22. 1 a. red and brown .. 40 1·25
119. 3 a. green and violet .. 40 1·25
120. 5 a. yellow and blue .. 50 1·25

23. Gediminberg.

1922. Air.
121. 23. 2 a. rose and blue .. 20 20
122. 4 a. rose and brown .. 20 20
123. 10 a. blue and black .. 45 45

24. Pte. Luksis.

ILLUSTRATIONS British Commonwealth and all overprints and surcharges are FULL SIZE. Foreign Countries have been reduced to ¾-LINEAR.

1922. "De jure" recognition of Lithuania by League of Nations. Inscr. "LIETUVA DE JURE".
126. 24. 20 s. red and black .. 5 8
127. – 40 s. violet and green .. 5 8
128. – 50 s. blue and purple .. 5 8
129. – 60 s. orange and violet .. 5 8
130. – 1 a. blue and red .. 5 10
131. – 2 a. brown and blue .. 5 10
132. – 3 a. blue and brown .. 10 10
133. – 4 a. purple and green .. 10 10
134. – 5 a. red and brown .. 12 12
135. – 6 a. blue 12 12
136. – 8 a. yellow and blue .. 15 15
137. – 10 a. green and violet .. 25 30
DESIGNS—VERT. 40 s. Lt. Jouzapavicius. 50 s. Dr. Basanavicius. 60 s. Mrs. Petrivicvite. 1 a. Prof. Voldemaras. 2 a. Dovidaitis. 3 a. Dr. Slezevicius. 4 a. Dr. Galvanauskas. 5 a. Dr. Grinius. 6 a. Dr. Stulginskis. 8 a. Pres. Smetona. HORIZ. (39 x 27 mm.): 10 a. Stauguittis, Pres. Smetona and Sillingas.

1922. Surch.
138. 2. 1 c. on 10 s. red (post.) 10 50
139. 1 c. on 15 s. violet .. 10 50
141. 1 c. on 20 s. blue .. 10 50
145. 1 c. on 30 s. orange .. 5 20
146. 1 c. on 40 s. brown .. 15 20
148. 15. 1 c. on 50 s. olive .. 5 5
149. 3. 2 c. on 50 s. green .. 10 60
150. 2 c. on 60 s. red & violet 5 5
151. 2 c. on 75 s. red & yellow 10 70
152. 13. 3 c. on 10 s. red .. .. 40 1·00
153. 3 c. on 15 s. mauve .. 5 5
154. 3 c. on 20 s. blue .. 5 12
155. 15. 3 c. on 30 s. brown .. 30 1·00
156. 14. 3 c. on 40 s. red .. 5 8
157. 4. 3 c. on 1 a. (No. 47) 18·00 20·00
158. 3 c. on 1 a. (No. 58) 10 20
159. 3 c. on 3 a. (No. 48) 16·00 18·00
160. 3 c. on 3 a. (No. 59) 5 8
161. 3 c. on 5 a. (No. 49) 6·00 8·00
162. 3 c. on 5 a. (No. 60) 5 8
163. 15. 5 c. on 50 s. olive .. 5 5
164. 5 c. on 60 s. mve. & grn. 25 90
165. 14. 5 c. on 80 s. red & orge. 5 15
166. 3. 5 c. on 4 a. on 75 s. red and yellow .. 12 1·75
168. 14. 10 c. on 1 a. grn. & brn. 10 5
169. 10 c. on 2 a. red & blue 5 5
170. 13. 15 c. on 4 a. blue & yell. 5 5
171. 16. 25 c. on 3 a. blue & grn. 60 4·00
172. 25 c. on 5 a. rose & grey 45 1·25
173. 25 c. on 10 a. mve. & red 25 40
174. 13. 30 c. on 8 a. blk. & grn. 10 10
175. 16. 50 c. on 25 a. grn. & brn. 40 50
176. 1 l. on 100 a. grey & red 70 50
177. 18. 10 c. on 20 s. blue (air) 25 1·10
178. 10 c. on 40 s. orange .. 25 1·10
179. 10 c. on 60 s. green .. 25 1·10
180. 10 c. on 80 s. red .. 25 1·10
181. 19. 20 c. on 1 a. grn. & red 1·00 2·25
182. – 20 c. on 2 a. (No. 107) .. 1·60 3·25
183. 22. 25 c. on 2 a. rose & blue 20 20
184. 30 c. on 4 a. rose and brn. 20 20
185. – 50 c. on 5 a. (No. 108) .. 20 20
186. 22. 50 c. on 10 a. blue & blk. 20 20
187. 23. 1 l. on 5 a. yell. & blue 1·25 6·00

26. Arms of Memel. **27.** Ruins of Trakai.

1923. Union of Memel with Lithuania.

188.	**26.**	1 c. rose and green ..	30	30
189.	–	2 c. mauve	30	30
190.	–	3 c. yellow	30	30
191.	**26.**	5 c. buff and blue	35	35
192.	–	10 c. red	45	45
193.	–	15 c. green	45	45
194.	**27.**	25 c. violet	50	50
195.	–	30 c. claret	65	65
196.	–	60 c. green	65	65
197.	–	1 l. green	85	85
198.	–	2 l. red	1·25	1·25
199.	**27.**	3 l. blue	2·00	2·00
200.	–	5 l. blue	2·75	2·75

DESIGNS—As T **26**: 3 c., 2 l. Chapel of Biruta. 10 c., 15 c. War Memorial, Kovno. As T **27**: 2 c. 30 c. Arms of Lithuania. 60 c., 5 l. Memel Lighthouse. 1 l. Memel Harbour.

28. Wayside Cross. **29.** **30.** St. Nicholas Cathedral, Vilna.

1923.

214.	**28.**	2 c. brown	10	5
215.		3 c. olive	15	5
216.		5 c. green	20	5
201.		10 c. violet	5	5
212.		15 c. red	20	5
203.		20 c. olive	15	5
204.		25 c. blue	8	5
219.		36 c. brown	1·10	30
205.	**29.**	50 c. green	8	5
206.		60 c. red	20	8
207.	**30.**	1 l. orange and green ..	55	8
208.		3 l. claret and grey ..	2·10	25
209.		5 l. brown and blue ..	3·50	35

31.

32.

1924. Air.

223.	**31.**	20 c. yellow	15	12
224.		40 c. green	25	15
225.		60 c. red	30	20
226.	**32.**	1 l. brown	65	25

1924. Charity. War Orphans Fund. Nos. 214/226 surch. **KARO NASLAICIAMS** and premium.

227.	**28.**	2 c.+2 c. brn. (postage)	30	30
228.		3 c.+3 c. olive.. ..	30	30
229.		5 c.+5 c. green ..	30	30
231.		10 c.+10 c. violet ..	30	30
232.		15 c.+15 c. red ..	30	30
233.		20 c.+20 c. olive ..	60	60
235.		25 c.+25 c. blue ..	75	75
236.		36 c.+34 c. brown ..	1·50	1·50
237.	**29.**	50 c.+50 c. green ..	1·50	1·50
238.		60 c.+60 c. red ..	1·60	1·60
239.	**30.**	1 l.+1 l. orange & green	1·60	1·60
240.		3 l.+2 l. claret and grey	5·00	5·00
241.		5 l.+3 l. brown and blue	7·00	7·00
242.	**31.**	20 c.+20 c. yellow (air)	2·00	2·00
243.		40 c.+40 c. green ..	2·00	2·00
244.		60 c.+60 c. red.. ..	2·00	2·00
245.	**32.**	1 l.+1 l. brown.. ..	2·00	2·00

33. **34.** **35.**

1926. Air.

246.	**33.**	20 c. red	45	40
247.		40 c. orange and mauve	45	40
248.		60 c. black and blue ..	90	40

1926. Charity. War Invalids. Nos. 227/39 surch. with new values and small ornaments.

249.	**28.**	1 c.+1 c. on 2 c.+2 c.	30	30
250.		2 c.+2 c. on 3 c.+3 c.	30	30
251.		2 c.+2 c. on 5 c.+5 c.	30	30
253.		5 c.+5 c. on 10 c.+10 c.	40	40
254.		5 c.+5 c. on 15 c.+15 c.	30	30
255.		10 c.+10 c. on 20 c.+20 c.	40	40
257.		10 c.+10 c. on 25 c.+25 c.	50	50
258.		14 c.+14 c. on 36 c.+34 c.	65	65
259.	**29.**	20 c.+20 c. on 50 c.+50 c.	90	90
260.		25 c.+25 c. on 60 c.+60 c.	1·10	1·10
261.	**30.**	30 c.+30 c. on 1 l.+1 l.	1·60	1·60

1926. Charity. War Orphans. Nos. 227/39 surch. **V.P.** and new values in circular ornament.

262.	**28.**	1 c.+1 c. on 2 c.+2 c.	20	20
263.		2 c.+2 c. on 3 c.+3 c.	20	20
264.		2 c.+2 c. on 5 c.+5 c.	20	20
266.		5 c.+5 c. on 10 c.+10 c.	30	30
267.		10 c.+10 c. on 15c.+15 c.	30	30
268.		15 c.+15 c. on 20 c.+20 c.	30	30
270.		15 c.+15 c. on 25 c.+25 c.	75	75
271.		19 c.+19 c. on 36 c.+34 c.	75	75
272.	**29.**	25 c.+25 c. on 50 c.+50 c.	75	75
273.		30 c.+30 c. on 60 c.+60 c.	95	95
274.	**30.**	50 c.+50 c. on 1 l.+1 l.	1·60	1·60

1927.

275.	**34.**	2. c. orange	5	5
276.		3 c. brown	8	5
277.		5 c. green	5	5
278.		10 c. violet	10	5
279.		15 c. red	20	5
280.		25 c. blue	25	5
280b.		30 c. blue	15	5

1927. Dr. Basanavicius mourning issue.

285.	**35.**	15 c. claret	25	20
286.		25 c. blue	25	20
287.		50 c. green	35	25
288.		60 c. violet	70	50

36. "Vytautas".

1927.

289.	**36.**	1 l. green and grey ..	55	15
290.		3 l. violet and green ..	1·40	20
291.		5 l. brown and grey ..	1·60	60

37. President Antanas Smetona. **38.** Lithuania liberated.

1928. Independence. 10th Anniv.

292.	**37.**	5 c. green and brown ..	5	5
293.		10 c. black and violet ..	8	5
294.		15 c. brown and orange	10	5
295.		25 c. slate and blue ..	12	5
296.	**38.**	50 c. purple and blue ..	20	5
297.		60 c. black and red ..	40	15
298.	–	1 l. brown	65	15

DESIGN—HORIZ. 1 l. Lithuania's resurrection (angel and soldiers). Dated 1918-1928.

40. Grand Duke Vytautas. **41.**

42. J. Tubelis. **44.** Govt. Bldgs., Kaunas.

1930. Vytautas. 500th Death Anniv.

(a) Postage.

299.	**40.**	2 c. brown	5	5
300.		3 c. violet and brown	5	5
301.		5 c. red and green ..	5	5
302.		10 c. green and violet..	5	5
303.		15 c. violet and red ..	5	5
304.		30 c. purple and blue ..	5	5
305.		36 c. olive and purple..	8	5
306.		50 c. blue and green ..	12	12
307.		60 c. red and blue ..	15	12
308.	**41.**	1 l. maroon, grey & grn.	35	20
309.		3 l. violet, pink & mauve	65	40
310.		5 l. red, grey and brown	1·10	55
311.		10 l. black and blue ..	3·75	2·10
312.		25 l. green and brown..	10·00	8·00

(b) Air.

313.	**42.**	5 c. brown, yellow & grn.	15	15
314.		10 c. black and blue ..	15	15
315.		15 c. blue, grey & mar.	15	15
316.	–	20 c. red, orange & brn.	25	25
317.	–	40 c. lilac and blue ..	30	30
318.	–	60 c. black, lilac & green	45	45
319.	–	1 l. black, lilac and lake	60	60

DESIGNS—HORIZ. 20 c., 40 c. Vytautas and Kovno. 60 c., 1 l. Vytautas and Smetona.

1932. Orphans' Fund. Imperf. or perf.

320.	**44.**	5 c. blue and brown ..	10	10
321.		10 c. maroon and brown	10	10
322.	–	15 c. brown and green..	15	15
323.	–	25 c. blue and green ..	20	20
324.	–	50 c. grey and olive ..	30	30
325.	–	60 c. grey and mauve..	30	30
326.	–	1 l. blue and grey ..	55	55
327.	–	3 l. maroon and green..	1·50	1·50

DESIGNS—As T **44**: 15 c., 25 c. Lake. 50 c. G.P.O. VERT. 60 c., 1 l., 3 l. Vilna.

46. Map of Lithuania, Memel and Vilna.

1932. Air. Orphans' Fund. Imperf. or perf.

328.	**46.**	5 c. red and green ..	5	5
329.		10 c. maroon and brown	5	5
330.	–	15 c. blue and buff ..	8	8
331.	–	20 c. black and brown	12	12
332.	–	40 c. maroon and yellow	20	20
333.	–	60 c. blue and buff ..	30	30
334.	–	1 l. maroon and green	45	45
335.	–	2 l. blue and green ..	90	90

DESIGNS: 15 c., 20 c. Aeroplane over R. Niemen. 40 c., 60 c. Church. 1 l., 2 l. Building.

47. Vytautas escapes from prison.

48. Coronation of Mindaugas.

1932. Independence. 15th Anniv. Imperf. or perf.

336.	**47.**	5 c. purple & red (post.)	15	15
337.		10 c. brown and grey ..	15	15
338.	–	15 c. green and claret ..	15	15
339.	–	25 c. brown and purple	15	15
340.	–	50 c. brown and green..	35	35
341.	–	60 c. claret and green..	35	35
342.	–	1 l. black and blue ..	60	60
343.	–	3 l. green and purple ..	1·00	1·00
344.	–	5 c. lilac and green (air)	5	5
345.	–	10 c. red and green ..	5	5
346.	**48.**	15 c. brown and violet..	8	8
347.		20 c. black and red ..	12	12
348.	–	40 c. black and purple..	15	15
349.	–	60 c. black and orange..	30	30
350.	–	1 l. green and violet ..	45	45
351.	–	2 l. brown and blue ..	90	90

DESIGNS—POSTAGE. As T **47**: 15 c., 25 c. Vytautas and Jagello preaching. 50 c., 60 c. Battle of Grunewald. 1 l., 3 l. Proclamation of Independence. AIR. As T **48**: 5 c., 10 c. Battle of Saules. 40 c. Gediminas in Council. 60 c. Founding of Vilna. 1 l. Russians surrendering to Gediminas. 2 l. Algirdas before Moscow.

49. A. Visteliauskas.

PORTRAITS: 15 c., 25 c. P. Vileisis. 50 c., 60 c. J. Sliupas. 1 l., 3 l. J. Basanavicius.

1933. Publication of "Ausra". 50th Anniv. Inscr. "AUSRA 1883–1933".

352.	**49.**	5 c. red and green ..	10	10
353.		10 c. red and blue ..	10	10
354.	–	15 c. red and orange ..	10	10
355.	–	25 c. brown and blue ..	10	10
356.	–	50 c. blue and green ..	10	10
357.	–	60 c. chocolate & brown	30	30
358.	–	1 l. purple and red ..	55	55
359.	–	3 l. purple and blue ..	1·25	1·25

50. Trakai Castle.

1933. Air. Grand Duke Kestutis. 500th Death Anniv. Triangular designs inscr. "1382–1932".

360.	**50.**	5 c. blue and green ..	5	5
361.		10 c. brown and violet	5	5
362.	–	15 c. violet and blue ..	8	8
363.	–	20 c. purple and brown	12	12
364.	–	40 c. purple and blue ..	20	20
365.	–	60 c. blue and claret ..	45	45
366.	–	1 l. blue and green ..	60	60
367.	–	2 l. green and violet ..	1·10	1·10

DESIGNS: 15 c., 20 c. Kestutis encounters Birute. 40 c., 60 c. Birute. 1 l. 2 l. Kestutis Algirdas.

51. Mother and Child. **52.** J. Tumas Vaizgantas.

1933. Child Welfare. (a) Postage.

368.	**51.**	5 c. brown and green ..	8	8
369.		10 c. blue and claret ..	8	8
370.	–	15 c. purple and green	10	10
371.	–	25 c. black and orange	10	10
372.	–	50 c. red and green ..	30	30
373.	–	60 c. orange and black	50	50
374.	–	1 l. blue and brown ..	55	55
375.	–	3 l. green and purple ..	1·00	1·00

DESIGNS—VERT. 15 c., 25 c. Boy reading. 50 c., 60 c. Boy building bricks. 1 l., 3 l. Mother and child weaving.

(b) Air. Various medallion portraits in triangular frames.

376.	–	5 c. blue and red ..	5	5
377.	–	10 c. green and violet ..	5	5
378.	**52.**	15 c. brown and green..	5	5
379.		20 c. blue and black ..	5	5
380.	–	40 c. green and lake ..	25	25
381.	–	60 c. brown and blue ..	45	45
382.	–	1 l. blue and yellow ..	55	55
383.	–	2 l. lake and green ..	1·50	1·50

DESIGNS: 5 c., 10 c. Maironis. 40 c., 60 c. V. Kudirka. 1 l., 2 l. Zemaite.

53. Captains S. Darius and S. Girenas.

55. "Flight" mourning over Wreckage. **58.** President Antanas Smetona.

1934. Air. Death of Darius and Girenas (trans-Atlantic airmen).

389.	**53.**	20 c. red and black ..	5	5
390.	–	40 c. blue and red ..	5	5
391.	**53.**	60 c. violet and black ..	5	5
392.	**55.**	1 l. black and red ..	12	5
393.	–	3 l. orange and green ..	25	20
394.	–	5 l. blue and brown ..	80	55

DESIGNS—HORIZ. 40 c. Aeroplane "Lituanica" over Atlantic. 3 l. "Lituanica" and globe. 5 l. "Lituanica" and Vytautas.

1934. President's 60th Birthday.

395.	**58.**	15 c. red	20	5
396.		30 c. green	30	5
397.		60 c. blue	35	5

59. **60.** Gleaner. **61.**

62.

1934.
398. 59. 2 c. red and orange .. 10 5
399. 5 c. green 10 5
400. 61. 10 c. brown 20 5
401. 60. 25 c. brown and green 30 5
402. 61. 35 c. red 30 5
403. 60. 50 c. blue 55 5
404. 62. 1 l. purple and red .. 1·00 5
405. 3 l. green 10 5
406. – 5 l. purple and blue .. 12 10
407. – 10 l. brown and yellow 40 25
DESIGN—HORIZ. as T **62**: 5 l., 10 l. Knight.

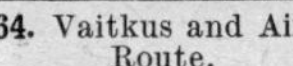
64. Vaitkus and Air Route.

65. President Antanas Smetona.

1936. Air. Vaitkus' New York–Ireland Flight.
408. 64. 15 c. maroon 30 15
409. 30 c. green 30 15
410. 60 c. blue .. .. 1·00 30

1936. As T **59** but smaller (18×23 mm.).
411. 59. 2 c. orange 5 5
412. 5 c. green 5 5

1936.
413. 65. 15 c. red 30 5
414. 30 c. green 40 5
415. 60 c. blue 55 8

66.

67. Archer.

69. Scoring a Goal.

68. President Smetona.

1937.
416. 66. 10 c. green 5 5
417. 25 c. mauve 5 5
418. 35 c. red 8 5
419. 50 c. brown 10 5
419a. 1 l. blue 5 5

1938. 1st National Olympiad Fund.
420. 67. 5 c.+5 c. green .. 2·10 1·60
421. – 15 c.+5 c. red .. 3·25 2·25
422. – 30 c.+10 c. blue .. 4·25 3·25
423. – 60 c.+15 c. brown .. 6·50 6·50
DESIGNS: 15 c. Javelin throwing. 30 c. Diving. 60 c. Relay runner at tape.

1938. Scouts' and Guides' National Camp Fund. Nos. 420/3 optd. **TAUTINE SKAUCIU** (or **SKAUTU**) **STOVYKLA** and badge.
424. 67. 5 c.+ 5 c. green .. 3·25 3·25
425. – 15 c.+5 c. red .. 4·25 4·25
426. – 30 c.+10 c. blue .. 5·50 5·50
427. – 60 c.+15 c. brown .. 6·50 6·50

1939. Independence. 20th Anniv.
428. – 15 c. red 8 5
429. 68. 30 c. green 12 5
430. – 35 c. mauve 15 5
431. 68. 60 c. blue 25 12
DESIGN: 15 c., 35 c. Dr. Basanavicius proclaiming independence.

1939. 3rd European Basket-ball Championship and Physical Culture Fund.
432. – 15 c. +10 c. brown .. 3·00 3·00
433. 69. 30 c.+15 c. green .. 3·00 3·00
434. – 60 c.+40 c. violet .. 6·50 6·50
DESIGNS—VERT. 15 c. Scoring a goal. HORIZ. (40½×36 mm.): 60 c. Flags and ball.

1939. Recovery of Vilna. Nos. 428/31 optd. **VILNIUS 1939-X-10** and trident.
435. – 15 c. red 25 10
436. 68. 30 c. green 25 15
437. – 35 c. mauve 40 20
438. 68. 60 c. blue 45 40

70. Vytautas.

71. Vilna.

1940. "Liberty" Issue.
439. 70. 5 c. brown 5 5
440. – 10 c. green 5 5
441. – 15 c. orange 5 5
442. – 25 c. brown 5 5
443. – 30 c. green 5 5
444. – 35 c. orange 10 10
DESIGNS: 10 c. Angel. 15 c. Woman releasing a dove. 25 c. Mother and children. 30 c. "Liberty Bell". 35 c. Mythical animal.

1940. Recovery of Vilna.
445. 71. 15 c. brown 12 8
446. – 30 c. green 25 10
447. – 60 c. blue 55 35
DESIGNS—VERT. 30 c. Portrait of Gediminas. HORIZ. 60 c. Ruins of Trakai Castle.

1940. Incorporation of Lithuania in U.S.S.R. Optd. **LTSR 1940 VII 21.**
448. 59. 2 c. red and orange .. 5 5
449. 70. 5 c. brown 5 5
450. – 10 c. green (No. 440) .. 75 95
451. – 15 c. orange (No. 441) 8 12
452. – 25 c. brown (No. 442).. 15 15
453. – 30 c. green (No. 443) 20 20
454. – 35 c. orange (No. 444) 15 30
455. 66. 50 c. brown 20 30

LOMBARDY AND VENETIA E1

Formerly known as Austrian Italy. Although these Provinces used a different currency the following issues were valid throughout Austria. Lombardy was annexed by Sardinia in 1859 and Venetia by Italy in 1866.

1850. 100 centesimi = 1 lira.
1858. 100 soldi = 1 florin.
100 kreuzer = 1 gulden.

1850. As T **1** of Austria, but value in "CENTES." Imperf.
1. 1. 5 c. orange .. .. £700 55·00
2. 10 c. black .. .. £700 50·00
7. 15 c. red .. .. £180 1·40
4. 30 c. brown .. .. £1100 3·50
9. 45 c. blue .. .. £2250 5·50

1859. As T **2** and **3** of Austria, but value in soldi. Perf.
16. 3. 2 s. yellow .. .. £190 29·00
17. 2. 3 s. black .. .. £425 95·00
18. 3 s. green .. .. £150 32·00
19. 3. 5 s. red .. .. 70·00 1·60
20. 10 s. brown .. .. £140 19·00
21. 15 s. blue .. .. £325 8·00

1. Emperor Francis Joseph I.

2. Arms of Austria.

1861.
25. 1. 5 s. red .. .. £600 1·00
26. 10 s. brown .. .. £500 10·00

1863.
27. 2. 2 s. yellow .. .. 50·00 38·00
33. 3 s. green .. .. 6·50 4·75
34. 5 s. red 1 25 75
35. 10 s. blue .. .. 6·50 2·50
36. 15 s. brown .. .. 12·00 16·00

JOURNAL STAMPS

1858. As Type J **1** of Austria. Imperf.
J 22. J 1. 1 k. black £650 £1800
J 23. 2 k. red .. .. 90·00 30·00
J 24. 4 k. red £20000 £1600

LOURENCO MARQUES O3

A Portuguese colony in E. Africa, now part of Mozambique, whose stamps it uses.

1895. "Figures" key-type inscr. "LOURENCO MARQUES"
1. R. 5 r. yellow 12 8
2. 10 r. mauve 15 12
3. 15 r. brown 25 25
4. 20 r. lilac 25 25
10. 25 r. green 20 5
12. 50 r. blue 25 12
6. 75 r. red 50 35
14. 80 r. green .. .. 1·10 90
7. 100 r. brown on yellow 60 35
16. 150 r. red on rose .. 1·00 80
8. 200 r. blue on blue .. 1·00 70
9. 300 r. blue on brown .. 1·00 70

1895. St. Anthony. 700th Death Anniv. optd. **L. MARQUES CENTENARIO DE S. ANTONIO MDCCCXCV** on (a) "Embossed" key-type inscr. "PROVINCIA DE MOCAMBIQUE".
19. Q. 5 r. black .. .. 3·25 2·75
20. 10 r. green .. .. 5·00 3·50
21. 20 r. red .. .. 6·50 4·00
22. 25 r. purple .. .. 8·00 6·00
23. 40 r. brown .. .. 6·00 5·00
27a. 50 r. blue .. .. 4·00 3·00
25. 100 r. brown .. .. 11·00 8·00
26. 200 r. violet .. .. 7·00 8·00
27. 300 r. orange .. .. 14·00 11·00

(b) "Figures" key-type inscr. "MOCAMBIQUE"
28. R. 5 r. orange .. .. 3·75 2·75
29. 10 r. mauve .. .. 5·50 5·00
30. 50 r. blue .. .. 10·00 6·00
35. 75 r. red.. .. 10·00 6·00
32. 80 r. green .. .. 15·00 12·00
33. 100 r. brown on yellow.. 17·00 15·00
35a. 150 r. red on rose .. 12·00 10·00

1897. "Figures" key-type inscr. "LOURENCO MARQUES", surch. **50 reis.**
36. R. 50 r. on 300 r. blue on brn. 50·00 30·00

1898. "King Carlos" key-type inscr. "LOURENCO MARQUES".
37. S. 2½ r. grey 12 10
38. 5 r. orange.. .. 12 10
39. 10 r. green.. .. 12 10
40. 15 r. brown 35 30
83. 15 r. green.. .. 20 15
41. 20 r. lilac 15 10
42. 25 r. green.. .. 25 10
84. 25 r. red 15 12
43. 50 r. blue.. .. 30 15
85. 50 r. brown 30 25
86. 65 r. blue .. .. 1·25 1·25
44. 75 r. red 65 50
87. 75 r. purple 50 40
45. 80 r. mauve 60 40
46. 100 r. blue on blue .. 30 15
88. 115 r. brown on pink .. 1·40 1·25
89. 130 r. brown on yellow .. 1·40 1·25
47. 150 r. brown on yellow .. 50 45
48. 200 r. purple on pink .. 1·00 45
49. 300 r. blue on pink .. 65 50
90. 400 r. blue on yellow .. 1·40 1·25
50. 500 r. black on blue .. 1·25 80
51. 700 r. mauve on yellow .. 2·25 1·60

1899. Green and brown fiscal stamps of Mozambique, as T **2** of Macao, bisected and each half surch. **Correio de Lourenco Marques** and value. Imperf.
55. – 5 r. on half of 10 r. .. 40 15
56. – 25 r. on half of 10 r. .. 40 15
57. – 50 r. on half of 30 r. .. 35 15
58. – 50 r. on half of 800 r. .. 70 30

1899. "King Carlos" key-type inscr. "LOURENCO MARQUES" surch **50 Reis.**
91. S. 50 r. on 65 r. blue .. 70 60
59. 50 r. on 75 r. red.. .. 60 40

1902. "Figures" and "Newspaper" key-types surch.
60. V. 65 r. on 2½ r. brown .. 80 70
62. R. 65 r. on 5 r. yellow .. 80 70
63. 65 r. on 15 r. brown .. 80 70
64. 65 r. on 20 r. lilac .. 80 70
66. 115 r. on 10 r. mauve .. 80 70
67. 115 r. on 200 r. bl. on bl. 80 70
68. 115 r. on 300 r. bl. on brn. 80 70
70. 130 r. on 25 r. green .. 80 70
72. 130 r. on 80 r. green .. 80 80
73. 130 r. on 150 r. red on rose 80 70
74. 400 r. on 50 r. blue .. 2·25 1·50
76. 400 r. on 75 r. red .. 2·25 1·50
78. 400 r. on 100 r. brown on yellow.. .. 1·60 1·40

1902. "King Carlos" key-type inscr. "LOURENCO MARQUES" optd. **PROVISORIO**
79. S. 15 r. brown 45 30
80. 25 r. green 40 25
81. 50 r. blue.. .. 45 30
82. 75 r. red 80 50

1911. "King Carlos" key-type inscr. "LOURENCO MARQUES" optd. **REPUBLICA.**
92. S. 2½ r. grey.. .. 12 10
93. 5 r. orange 12 10
94. 10 r. green 15 10
95. 15 r. green 15 10
96. 20 r. lilac.. .. 35 20
97. 25 r. red 15 12
98. 50 r. brown 25 15
99. 75 r. purple 25 15
100. 100 r. blue on blue .. 20 15
178. 115 r. brown on pink .. 25 25
102. 130 r. brown on yellow.. 20 15
103. 200 r. purple on pink .. 20 15
104. 400 r. blue on yellow .. 25 20
105. 500 r. black on blue .. 30 20
106. 700 r. mauve on yellow.. 50 30

1913. Surch. **REPUBLICA LOURENCO MARQUES** and value on "Vasco da Gama" issues of

(a) **Portuguese Colonies.**
107. ¼ c. on 2½ r. green .. 40 35
108. ½ c. on 5 r. red 40 35
109. 1 c. on 10 r. purple .. 40 35
110. 2½ c. on 25 r. green .. 40 35
111. 5 c. on 50 r. blue.. .. 40 35
112. 7½ c. on 75 r. brown .. 70 60
113. 10 c. on 100 r. brown .. 40 35
114. 15 c. on 150 r. yell.-brn... 40 35

(b) **Macao.**
115. ¼ c. on ½ a. green 45 35
116. ½ c. on 1 a. red 45 35
117. 1 c. on 2 a. purple .. 45 35
118. 2½ c. on 4 a. green .. 45 35
119. 5 c. on 8 a. blue 45 35
120. 7½ c. on 12 a. brown .. 70 60
121. 10 c. on 16 a. brown .. 45 35
122. 15 c. on 24 a. yell.-brn... 45 35

(c) **Timor.**
123. ¼ c. on ½ a. green.. .. 45 35
124. ½ c. on 1 a. red 45 35
125. 1 c. on 2 a. purple .. 45 35
126. 2½ c. on 4 a. green .. 45 35
127. 5 c. on 8 a. blue 45 35
128. 7½ c. on 12 a. brown .. 70 60
129. 10 c. on 16 a. brown .. 45 35
130. 15 c. on 24 a. yell.-brown 45 35

1914. "Ceres" key-type inscr. "LOURENCO MARQUES".
147. U. ¼ c. olive 5 5
148. ½ c. black 5 5
149. 1 c. green 5 5
150. 1½ c. brown 5 5
151. 2 c. red 5 5
152. 2½ c. violet 5 5
153. 5 c. blue.. .. 5 5
154. 7½ c. brown 5 5
155. 8 c. grey 5 5
140. 10 c. brown 35 25
157. 15 c. claret 5 5
142. 20 c. green 25 20
143. 30 c. brown on green .. 35 30
144. 40 c. brown on rose .. 1·25 1·25
145. 50 c. orange on pink .. 60 50
146. 1 e. green on blue .. 65 50

1914. Provisionals of 1902 overprinted **REPUBLICA.**
166. R. 115 r. on 10 r. mauve .. 20 12
167. 115 r. on 200 r. bl. on bl. 20 12
168. 115 r. on 300 r. blue on brown 20 12
161. 130 r. on 25 r. green .. 30 15
164. 130 r. on 80 r. green .. 30 15
165. 130 r. on 150 r. red on rose 30 15
184. 400 r. on 50 r. blue .. 30 15
186. 400 r. on 75 r. red .. 70 60

1915. Nos. 93 and 148 perf. diagonally and each half surch. ¼.
170. S. ¼ on half of 5 r. orange.. 80 70
171. U. ¼ on half of ½ c. black .. 80 70

1915. "King Carlos" key-type stamps of Lourenzo Marques, with or without "REPUBLICA" optd., surch. **Dois centavos.**
172. S. 2 c. on 15 r. (No. 83) .. 20 20
173. 2 c. on 15 r. (No. 95) .. 20 20

1918. Red Cross Fund. "Ceres" key-type inscr. "LOURENCO MARQUES", optd. **9-3-18** and Red Cross or surch. with value in figures and bars also.
188. U. ¼ c. olive 40 35
189. ½ c. black 40 35
190. 1 c. green 40 35
191. 2½ c. violet 50 40
192. 5 c. blue.. .. 40 35
193. 10 c. red 60 55
194. 20 c. on 1½ c. brown .. 60 55
195. 30 c. brown on green .. 60 55
196. 40 c. on 2 c. red.. .. 70 55
197. 50 c. on 7½ c. brown .. 60 55
198. 70 c. on 8 c. grey .. 60 55
199. 1 e. on 15 c. claret .. 60 55

1920. No. 166 surch. **Um quarto de centavo.**
200. R. ¼ c. on 115 r. on 10 r. mauve 15 12

1920. No. 152 surch. in figures or words.
201. U. 1 c. on 2½ c. violet .. 8 5
202. 1½ c. on 2½ c. violet .. 8 5
203. 4 c. on 2½ c. violet .. 8 8
For other surcharges on "Ceres" key-type of Lourenzo Marques, see Mozambique Nos. 309/10 and Nos. D 44 and 46.

NEWSPAPER STAMPS

1893. "Newspaper" key-type inscr. "LOURENCO MARQUES".
N 1. V. 2½ r. brown 10 8

1895. St. Anthony. 700th Death Anniv. "Newspaper" key-type inscr. "MOCAMBIQUE" and optd. **L. MARQUES CENTENARIO DE S. ANTONIO MDCCCXCV.**
N 3. V. 2½ r. brown .. .. 1·90 1·25

LUBECK E2

16 schillinge = 1 mark.

Formerly one of the free cities of the Hanseatic League, this Baltic port and district is now a part of West Germany.

1. 2.

1859. Imperf.

9.	1.	½ s. lilac	8·50	£800
10.		1 s. orange	18·00	£800
3.		2 s. brown	8·50	£150
2.		2½ s. red	25·00	£475
6.		4 s. green	8·50	£250

1863. Rouletted.

11.	2.	½ s. green	25·00	50·00
13.		1 s. orange	75·00	80·00
14.		2 s. red	14·00	38·00
16.		2½ s. blue	30·00	£190
17.		4 s. bistre	25·00	70·00

3. 4.

1864. Imperf.

18.	3.	1¼ s. brown	12·00	27·00

1865. Roul.

21.	4.	1½ s. mauve	11·00	40·00

LUXEMBOURG E2

An independent Grand Duchy lying between Belgium and the Saar District. Under German Occupation from 1940 to 1944.

1852. 12½ centimes = 1 silver groschen.
100 centimes = 1 franc.
1940. 100 pfennig = 1 reichsmark.
1944. 100 centimes = 1 franc (Belgian).

1. Grand Duke William III. 2. 3.

1852. Imperf.

2.	1.	10 c. black	£750	25·00
3a.		1 s. red	£500	45·00

1859. Imperf. or roul.

23.	2.	1 c. brown	6·00	1·10
21.		1 c. orange	6·00	1·25
17.		2 c. black	6·50	4·50
8.		4 c. yellow	95·00	85·00
20.		4 c. green	20·00	17·00
10.	3.	10 c. blue	55·00	5·00
25.		10 c. lilac	50·00	1·00
28.		12½ c. red	70·00	3·25
29.		20 c. brown	40·00	1·90
12.		25 c. brown	£130	£110
32.		25 c. blue	£110	9·00
34.		30 c. claret	£140	25·00
14.		37½ c. green	£120	95·00
35.		37½ c. bistre	£225	£110
39.		40 c. orange	15·00	17·00

1872. Surch. **UN FRANC.** Roul.

37.	3.	1 f. on 37½ c. bistre	£225	40·00

1874. Perf.

64.	2.	1 c. brown	3·50	2·25
65.		2 c. black	3·75	60
42.		4 c. green	50	1·25
43.		5 c. yellow	50·00	8·50
67.	3.	10 c. lilac	60·00	50
49.		12½ c. red	£130	11·00
69.		20 c. brown	28·00	10·00
70.		25 c. blue	80·00	1·50
71.		30 c. rose	1·25	3·25
55.		40 c. orange	35	85

1879. Surch. **Un Franc.** Perf.

56.	3.	1 f. on 37½ c. bistre	2·50	4·50

4. Agriculture and Trade. 5. Grand Duke Adolf. 6.

1882.

116.	4.	1 c. grey	12	10
117.		2 c. brown	8	5
118.		4 c. olive	30	30
119.		5 c. green	30	10
120.		10 c. red	8·50	10
98.		12½ c. blue	1·75	2·25
122.		20 c. orange	3·00	75
88.		25 c. blue	£120	90
101.	4.	30 c. olive	18·00	6·00
124.		50 c. brown	60	75
103.		1 f. lilac	90	1·50
92.		5 f. orange	15·00	18·00

1891.

144.	5.	10 c. red	20	12
128.		12½ c. green	45	15
146.		20 c. orange	9·50	20
147.		25 c. blue	45	15
148.		30 c. green	60	30
149.		37½ c. green	85	75
150.		50 c. brown	6·00	85
143a.		1 f. purple	9·00	1·50
135.		2½ f. black	90	1·50
136.		5 f. lake	27·00	26·00

1895.

152.	6.	1 c. grey	1·25	10
153.		2 c. brown	8	5
154.		4 c. bistre	12	12
155.		5 c. green	1·00	8
156.		10 c. red	7·50	8

7. 8. Grand Duke William IV. 9. Grand Duchess Adelaide.

1906.

157.	7.	1 c. grey	5	5
153.		2 c. brown	5	5
159.		4 c. bistre	12	5
160.		5 c. green	12	5
231.		5 c. mauve	5	5
161.		6 c. lilac	20	5
161a.		7½ c. orange	10	8
162.	8.	10 c. red	1·60	5
163.		12½ slate	1·75	10
164.		15 c. brown	1·25	25
165.		20 c. orange	2·75	12
166.		25 c. blue	38·00	8
166a.		30 c. olive	65	12
167.		37½ c. green	75	20
168.		50 c. brown	3·25	25
169.		87½ c. blue	1·90	1·60
170.		1 f. purple	3·25	50
171.		2½ f. red	25·00	25·00
172.		5 f. maroon	5·00	6·50

1912. Surch. **62½ cts.**

173.	8.	62½ c. on 87½ c. blue	1·50	75
173a.		62½ c. on 2½ f red	1·50	1·25
173b.		62½ c. on 5 f. maroon	30	30

1914.

174.	9.	10 c. claret	5	5
175.		12½ c. green	5	5
176.		15 c. black	5	5
176a.		17½ c. brown	15	8
177.		25 c. blue	12	5
178.		30 c. bistre	20	10
179.		35 c. blue	12	8
180.		37½ c. sepia	12	8
181.		40 c. orange	20	8
182.		50 c. grey	20	10
183.		62½ c. green	30	30
183a.		87½ c. orange	25	25
184.		1 f. brown	50	15
185.		2½ f. red	25	20
186.		5 f. violet	2·25	2·25

1916. Surch. in figures and bars.

187.	7.	2½ on 5 c. green	5	5
188.		3 on 2 c. brown	5	5
212.		5 on 1 c. grey	5	5
213.		5 on 4 c. bistre	5	5
214.		5 on 7½ c. orange	5	5
215.		6 on 2 c. brown	5	5
189.	9.	7½ on 10 c. claret	5	5
190.		17½ on 30 c. bistre	10	10
191.		20 on 17½ c. brown	5	5
216.		25 on 37½ c. sepia	5	5
217.		75 on 62½ c. green	5	5
218.		80 on 87½ c. orange	5	5
192.		87½ on 1 f. brown	30	40

10. Grand Duchess Charlotte. 11. Vianden Castle.

1921.

194.	10.	2 c. brown	5	5
195.		3 c. olive	5	5
196.		6 c. purple	5	5
197.		10 c. green	5	5
232.		10 c. olive	5	5
193a.		15 c. red*	5	5
198.		15 c. olive	5	5
233.		15 c. green	5	5
234.		15 c. orange	5	5
199.		20 c. orange	5	5
235.		20 c. green	5	5
200.		25 c. green	5	5
201.		30 c. red	5	5
202.		40 c. orange	5	5
203.		50 c. blue	20	8
236.		50 c. red	10	5
204.		75 c. red	12	10
237.		75 c. blue	10	5
205.		80 c. black	20	10
206.	11.	1 f. red	10	5
238.		1 f. blue	20	10
207.	–	2 f. blue	20	15
239.	–	2 f. brown	1·00	35
208a.	–	5 f. violet	6·50	70

DESIGNS—As T 11: 2 f. Factories at Esch. 5 f. Bridge over Alzette.

*No. 193a was originally issued on the occasion of the birth of Crown Prince Jean.

1922. Philatelic Exn. Imperf.

219.	10.	25 c. green	1·25	1·00
220.		30 c. red	1·25	1·00

12. Monastery at Clervaux.

DESIGNS—HORIZ. 15 c. Pfaffenthal. 25 c. as T 13.

1921. War Monument Fund.

209.	12.	10 c.+5 c. green	12	15
210.	–	15 c.+10 c. orange	12	15
211.	–	25 c.+10 c. green	12	15

13. Luxembourg. 14. Echternach.

1923.

MS 221.	13.	10 f. green (sheet)	£475	£550
222a.		10 f. black	1·90	1·90

1923. Unveiling of War Memorial by Prince Leopold of Belgium. Nos. 209/11 surch. **27 mai 1923** and additional values.

223.	12.	10+5+25 c. green	1·40	1·40
224.	–	15+10+25 c. orange	1·40	1·40
225.	–	25+10+25 c. green	1·40	1·40

1923.

226a.	14.	3 f. blue	45	12

1924. Charity. Death of Grand Duchess Marie Adelaide. Surch. **CARITAS** and new value.

227.	9.	12½ c.+7½ c. green	5	5
228.		35 c.+10 c. blue	5	5
229.		2½ f.+1 f. red	70	80
230.		5 f.+2 f. violet	60	65

1925. Surch. with new value and bars.

240.	10.	5 on 10 c. green	5	5
270a.	16.	10 on 30 c. green	15	10
271.	10.	15 on 20 c. green	5	5
272.	16.	15 on 25 c. green	10	8
273.	10.	35 on 40 c. orange	5	5
274.	16.	60 on 65 c. brown	10	10
275.	10.	60 on 75 c. blue	5	5
276.	16.	60 on 75 c. red	12	5
277.	10.	60 on 80 c. black	15	12
278.	16.	60 on 80 c. brown	12	5
278a.		70 on 75 c. brown	2·50	5
278b.		75 on 90 c. red	65	5
278c.		1¾ on 1½ f. blue	1·00	15

15. 16. Grand Duchess Charlotte.

1925. Anti-T.B. Fund.

241.	15.	5 c.+5 c. violet	5	5
242.		30 c.+5 c. orange	10	10
243.		50 c.+5 c. brown	12	12
244.		1 f.+10 c. blue	30	40

1926.

245.	16.	5 c. mauve	5	5
246.		10 c. olive	5	5
246a.		15 c. black	5	5
247.		20 c. orange	5	5
248.		25 c. green	8	5
248a.		25 c. brown	8	5
248b.		30 c. green	10	8
248c.		30 c. violet	30	8
248d.		35 c. violet	30	5
248e.		35 c. green	5	5
249.		40 c. brown	5	5
250.		50 c. brown	5	5
250a.		60 c. green	50	5
251.		65 c. brown	10	8
251a.		70 c. violet	5	5
252.		75 c. red	10	5
252a.		75 c. brown	5	5
253.		80 c. brown	20	12
253a.		90 c. red	20	20
254.		1 f. black	20	12
254a.		1 f. red	15	8
255.		1¼ f. blue	10	10
255a.		1¼ f. yellow	2·75	30
255b.		1¼ f. green	20	5
255c.		1¼ f. red	15·00	50
255d.		1½ f. blue	55	20
255e.		1¾ f. blue	40	20

17. Prince Jean. 18. Grand Duchess and Prince Felix.

1926. Child Welfare.

256.	17.	5 c.+5 c. blk. and mauve	5	5
257.		40 c.+10 c. black & grn.	8	8
258.		50 c.+15 c. black & yell.	8	10
259.		75 c.+20 c. black & red	20	25
260.		1 f. 50 c.+30 c. black and blue	20	25

1927. Int. Philatelic Exn.

261.	18.	25 c. purple	65	65
262.		50 c. green	95	95
263.		75 c. claret	65	65
264.		1 f. black	65	65
265.		1½ f. blue	65	65

19. Princess Elizabeth. 20. Clervaux.

1927. Child Welfare.

266.	19.	10 c.+5 c. blk. & blue	8	8
267.		50 c.+10 c. blk. & brn.	8	8
268.		75 c.+20 c. blk. & orge.	8	8
269.		1 f.+30 c. blk. & red	15	15
270.		1½ f.+50 c. blk. & bl.	12	12

1928.

279a.	20.	2 f. black	55	5

See also No. 339.

21. Princess Marie Adelaide. 22. Princess Marie Gabrielle.

1928. Child Welfare.

280.	21.	10 c.+5 c. pur. & green	10	10
281.		60 c.+10 c. olive & brn.	15	15
282.		75 c.+15 c. grn. & red	35	35
283.		1 f.+25 c. brn. & grn.	35	35
284.		1½ f.+50 c. blue & yell.	45	45

1929. Child Welfare.

285.	22.	10 c.+10 c. grn. & brn.	20	20
286.		35 c.+15 c. brn. & grn.	45	45
287.		75 c.+30 c. blk. & red	65	65
288.		1¼ f.+50 c. grn. & red	95	95
289.		1¾ f.+75 c. blk. & blue	1·60	1·60

23. Prince Charles. 24. Arms of Luxembourg.

1930. Child Welfare.

290.	23.	10 c.+5 c. brn. & grn.	12	12
291.		75 c.+10 c. grn. & brn.	25	25
292.		1 f.+25 c. violet & red	1·10	1·10
293.		1¼ f.+75 c. brn. & yell.	3·00	3·00
294.		1¾ f.+1 f. 50 brn. & bl.	3·00	3·00

1930.

295.	24.	5 c. claret	50	8
296.		10 c. green	65	5

25. Aeroplane over the Alzette. 26. Luxembourg (Lower Town).

1931. Air.

296a.	25.	50 c. green	50	40
297.		75 c. brown	40	40
298.		1 f. red	40	40
299.		1¼ f. purple	40	40
300.		1¾ f. blue	40	40
300a.		3 f. black	65	65

1931.
301. 26. 20 f. green .. .. 1·90 2·25

27. Princess Alix. 28. Countess Ermesinde. 29. Count Henry VII.

1931. Child Welfare.
302. 27. 10 c.+5 c. grey & brn. 20 20
303. 75 c.+10 c. grn. & clar. 45 45
304. 1 f.+25 c. grey & grn. 3·25 3·75
305. 1½ f.+75 c. grn. & vio. 3·75 3·75
306. 1¾ f.+1 f. 50 grey & bl. 5·50 5·50

1932. Child Welfare.
307. 28. 10 c.+5 c. brown .. 25 25
308. 75 c.+10 c. violet .. 1·00 1·00
309. 1 f.+25 c. red .. .. 5·50 5·50
310. 1½ f.+75 c. lake .. 6·50 6·50
311. 1¾ f.+1 f. 50 blue .. 6·50 6·50

1933. Child Welfare.
312. 29. 10 c.+5 c. brown .. 15 15
313. 75 c.+10 c. purple .. 1·75 1·75
314. 1 f.+25 c. red .. .. 6·50 6·50
315. 1½ f.+75 c. chestnut .. 8·50 8·50
316. 1¾ f.+1 f. 50 blue .. 8·00 8·00

30. Gateway of the Three Towers. 31. Arms of "John the Blind".

1934.
317. 30. 5 f. green 85 85
340. – 10 f. green .. .. 1·25 1·25
DESIGN—HORIZ. 10 f. Vianden.

1934. Charity.
318. 31. 10 c.+5 c. violet .. 15 12
319. 35 c.+10 c. green .. 1·10 1·10
320. 75 c.+15 c. red.. .. 1·90 1·90
321. 1 f.+25 c. red.. .. 8·50 8·50
322. 1¼ f.+75 c. orange .. 10·00 10·00
323. 1¾ f+1½ f. blue.. .. 9·50 9·50

33. Surgeon. 34. Charles I.

1935. Int. Relief Fund for Intellectuals.
324. – 5 c. violet 12 12
325. – 10 c. red 20 20
326. – 15 c. olive 25 25
327. – 20 c. orange 35 40
328. – 35 c. green 40 45
329. – 50 c. black 75 75
330. – 70 c. green .. .. 1·10 1·10
331. 33. 1 f. red .. .. 1·90 2·40
332. – 1 f. 25 greenish blue .. 4·50 5·00
333. – 1 f. 75 blue .. .. 6·50 7·50
334. – 2 f. brown .. .. 19·00 22·00
335. – 3 f. brown .. .. 25·00 29·00
336. – 5 f. blue .. .. 40·00 50 00
337. – 10 f. purple .. .. 90·00 95·00
338. 33. 20 f. green .. .. 95·00 £100
DESIGNS—HORIZ. 5 c., 10 f. School teacher. 15 c., 3 f. Journalist. 20 c., 1 f. 75, Engineer.
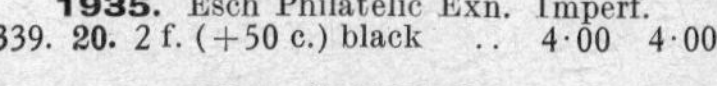
35 c., 1 f. 25, Chemist. VERT. 10 c., 2 f. "The Arts". 50 c., 5 f. Barrister. 70 c. University.
This set was sold at the P.O. at double face value.

1935. Esch Philatelic Exn. Imperf.
339. 20. 2 f. (+50 c.) black .. 4·00 4·00

1935. Child Welfare.
341. 34. 10 c.+5 c. violet .. 12 12
342. 35 c.+10 c. green .. 40 40
343. 70 c.+20 c. brown .. 75 75
344. 1 f.+25 c. claret .. 7·50 7·50
345. 1 f. 25+75 c. brown .. 5·00 5·00
346. 1 f. 75+1 f. 50 blue .. 5·00 5·00

35. Town Hall. 36. Wenceslas I. 37. Wenceslas II.

1936. XI Int. Philatelic Federation Congress.
347. 35. 10 c. brown 12 12
348. 35 c. green 20 20
349. 70 c. orange 25 25
350. 1 f. red 65 65
351. 1 f. 25 violet .. 1·90 1·90
352. 1 f. 75 blue 65 65

1936. Child Welfare.
353. 36. 10 c.+5 c. brown .. 5 5
354. 35 c.+10 c. green .. 12 12
355. 70 c.+20 c. slate .. 20 20
356. 1 f.+25 c. red 90 90
357. 1 f. 25+75 c. violet .. 2·75 2·75
358. 1 f. 75+1 f. 50 blue .. 2·50 2·50

1937. Dudelange Philatelic Exn. As No. 207 in pairs in miniature sheets inscr. "EXPOSITION NATIONALE DE TIMBRES-POSTE DUDELANGE 1937".
MS. 359. 11. 2 f. red (Sheet) .. 80 1·25

1937. Child Welfare.
360. 37. 10 c.+5 c. blk. & red.. 5 5
361. 35 c.+10 c. grn. & pur. 10 10
362. 70 c.+20 c. clar. & bl.. 15 15
363. 1 f.+25 c. red & green.. 65 65
364. 1 f. 25+75 c. purple.. and brown .. 1·25 1·25
365. 1 f. 75+1 f. 50 blue .. and black 2·25 2·25

38. St. Willibrord. 42. Sigismond of Luxembourg.

1938. Charity. Echternach Abbey Restoration Fund. St. Willibrord. 12th Death Cent. Inscr. as in T 38.
366. 38. 35 c.+10 c. green .. 20 15
367. – 70 c.+10 c. black .. 60 15
368. – 1 f. 25+25 c. red .. 1·10 1·10
369. – 1 f. 75+50 c. blue .. 1·50 50
370. – 3 f.+2 f. claret .. 6·50 2·25
371. – 5 f.+5 f. violet .. 8·00 2·25
DESIGNS—As T 38: 70 c. Town Hall, Echternach. 1 f. 25 c. Pavilion, Echternach Municipal Park. LARGE VERT. 1 f. 75 c. St. Willibrord. LARGE HORIZ. 3 f. Echternach Basilica. 5 f. Whitsuntide dancing procession.

1938. Child Welfare.
372. 42. 10 c.+5 c. blk. & mve. 10 10
373. 35 c.+10 c. blk. & grn. 15 15
374. 70 c.+20 c. blk. & brn. 40 40
375. 1 f.+25 c. blk. & red 1·60 1·60
376. 1 f. 25+75 c. blk. & grey 1·60 1·60
377. 1 f. 75+1 f. 50 black and blue .. 1·90 1·90

43. Arms of Luxembourg 44. William I.

1939. Independence Cent.
378. 43. 35 c. green 15 5
379. 44. 50 c. orange 20 12
380. – 70 c. green 5 5
381. – 75 c. olive 20 20
382. – 1 f. red 65 50
383. – 1 f. 25 violet 5 5
384. – 1 f. 75 blue 12 12
385. – 3 f. brown 20 20
386. – 5 f. black 30 25
387. – 10 f. red 50 50
PORTRAITS as T 44. 70 c. William II. 75 c. William III. 1 f. Prince Henry. 1 f. 25 Grand Duke Adolphe. 1 f. 75 William IV. 3 f. Marie-Anne. 5 f. Grand Duchess Marie Adelaide. 10 f. Grand Duchess Charlotte.

1939. Surch. in figures.
338. 16. 30 c. on 60 c. green .. 5 5

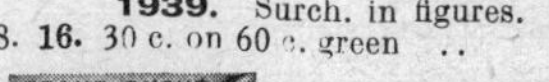

45. Allegory of Medicinal Spring. 46. Prince Jean.

1939. Mondorf-les-Bains Philatelic Propaganda.
389. 45. 2 f. red 30 30

1939. Charity. 20th Anniv. of Reign and of Royal Wedding.
390. 46. 10 c.+5 c. brn. on yell. 5 5
391. – 35 c.+10 c. grn. on yell. 20 20
392. – 70 c.+20 c. blk. on yell. 45 45
393. 46. 1 f.+25 c. red on yell. 2·25 2·25
394. – 1 f. 25+75 c. violet on yellow .. .. 2·50 2·50
395. – 1 f. 75+1 f. 50 blue on yellow .. .. 4·25 4·25
PORTRAITS: 35 c., 1 f. 25 Prince Felix. 70 c., 1 f. 75 Grand Duchess Charlotte.

1940. Anti-T.B. Fund. Surch. with cross and premium.
396. 45. 2 f.+50 c. grey.. .. 95 1·25

1940-44. GERMAN OCCUPATION.

1940. T 53 of Germany optd. **Luxemburg.**
397. 53. 3 pf. brown 5 5
398. 4 pf. slate 5 5
399. 5 pf. emerald 5 5
400. 6 pf. green 5 5
401. 8 pf. orange 5 5
402. 10 pf. chocolate 5 5
403. 12 pf. red 5 5
404. 15 pf. claret 10 8
405. 20 pf. blue 10 12
406. 25 pf. blue 10 12
407. 30 pf. olive 10 12
408. 40 pf. mauve 20 15
409. 50 pf. black and green.. 20 15
410. 60 pf. black and claret.. 25 20
411. 80 pf. black and blue .. 95 1·75
412. 100 pf. black and yellow 30 30

1940. Types of Luxembourg surch.
413. 16. 3 Rpf. on 15 c. black .. 5 5
414. 4 Rpf. on 20 c. orange.. 5 8
415. 5 Rpf. on 35 c. green .. 5 8
416. 6 Rpf. on 10 c. olive .. 5 8
417. 8 Rpf. on 25 c. brown.. 5 8
418. 10 Rpf. on 40 c. brown 5 8
419. 12 Rpf. on 50 c. green.. 8 8
420. 15 Rpf. on 1 f. red .. 10 25
421. 20 Rpf. on 50 c. brown 5 15
422. 25 Rpf. on 5 c. mauve.. 20 40
423. 30 Rpf. on 70 c. violet.. 5 20
424. 40 Rpf. on 75 c. brown 10 20
425. 50 Rfp. on 1½ f. green.. 10 20
426. 45. 60 Rpf. on 2 f. red .. 25 65
427. 30. 80 Rpf. on 5 f. green .. 10 20
428. – 100 Rpf. on 10 f. green (No. 340) 10 20

1941. Nos. 739/47 of Germany optd. **Luxemburg.**
429. 3 pf.+2 pf. brown .. 5 5
430. 4 pf.+3 pf. grey .. 5 5
431. 5 pf.+3 pf. emerald .. 5 5
432. 6 pf.+4 pf. green .. 5 5
433. 8 pf.+4 pf. orange .. 5 5
434. 12 pf.+6 pf. red .. 5 5
435. 15 pf.+10 pf. purple .. 25 25
436. 25 pf.+15 pf. blue .. 30 65
437. 40 pf.+35 pf. claret .. 30 65

1944. INDEPENDENCE REGAINED

47. Grand Duchess Charlotte. 48. "Britannia".

1944.
438. 47. 5 c. brown 5 5
439. 10 c. slate 5 5
440. 20 c. orange 5 5
441. 25 c. brown 5 5
442. 30 c. red 5 5
443. 35 c. green 5 5
444. 40 c. blue 5 5
445. 50 c. violet 5 5
445a. 60 c. orange 65 5
446. 70 c. red 5 5
447. 70 c. green 12 12
448. 75 c. brown 12 5
449. 1 f. olive 5 5
450. 1¼ f. orange 5 5
451. 1½ f. orange 12 5
452. 1¾ f. blue 5 5
453. 2 f. red 45 5
454. 2½ f. mauve 95 95
455. 3 f. green 20 12
456. 3½ f. blue 25 12
457. 5 f. green 12 5
458. 10 f. red 15 15
459. 20 f. blue 30 35

1945. Liberation.
460. – 60 c.+1 f. 40 green .. 12 8
461. – 1 f. 20+1 f. 80 red .. 12 10
462. 48. 2 f. 50+3 f. 50 blue .. 12 10
463. – 4 f. 20+4 f. 80 violet.. 12 10
DESIGNS. 60 c. Ship symbol of Paris, Cross of Lorraine and Arms of Luxembourg. 1 f. 20 c. Man killing a snake, Arms of Russia and Luxembourg. 4 f. 20 c. Eagle, Arms of U.S.A. and Luxembourg.

DESIGNS—VERT. As T 49: 1 f. 20, The Madonna. 2 f. 50, The Madonna and Luxembourg. 5 f. 50, Portal of Notre Dame Cathedral.

49. Statue of the Madonna in Procession.

50. Altar and Shrine of the Madonna.

1945. Charity. Our Lady of Luxembourg.
464. 49. 60 c.+40 c. green .. 5 5
465. – 1 f. 20+80 c. red .. 5 5
466. – 2 f. 50+2 f. 50 blue .. 12 15
467. – 5 f. 50+6 f. 50 violet .. 50 55
468. 50. 20 f.+20 f. brown .. 50 55

51. Lion of Luxembourg. 52. Members of the Maquis.

1945.
469. 51. 20 c. black 5 5
470. 30 c. green 5 5
470a. 60 c. violet 5 5
471. 75 c. brown 5 5
472. 1 f. 20 red 5 5
473. 1 f. 50 violet 5 5
474. 2 f. 50 blue 8 5

1945. National War Victims Fund.
475. 52. 20 c.+30 c. green .. 5 5
476. – 1 f. 50+1 f. red .. 5 5
477. – 3 f. 50+3 f. 50 blue .. 30 50
478. – 5 f.+10 f. brown .. 30 95
DESIGNS: 1 f. 50, Mother and children. 3 f. 50, Political prisoner. 5 f. Executed civilian.

53. 54. King "John the Blind" of Bohemia.

1946. Air.
479. – 1 f. olive 12 5
480. 53. 2 f. brown 12 5
481. – 3 f. brown 25 5
482. – 4 f. violet 15 8
483. 53. 5 f. claret 15 5
484. – 6 f. purple 15 10
485. – 10 f. brown 60 10
486. 53. 20 f. blue 65 35
487. – 50 f. green .. .. 1·25 50
DESIGNS: 1 f., 4 f., 10 f. Aeroplane wheel. 3 f., 6 f., 50 f. Aeroplane engine and castle.

1946. "John the Blind". 6th Death Cent.
488. 54. 60 c.+40 c. green .. 10 12
489. 1 f. 50+50 c. lake .. 20 25
490. 3 f. 50+3 f. 50 blue .. 65 75
491. 5 f.+10 f. brown .. 30 50

55. Exterior Ruins of St. Willibrord Basilica. 56. St Willibrord.

1947. Echternach Abbey Restoration (2nd issue). Inscr. "ECHTERNACH".

492. 55. 20 c.+10 c. black .. 12 12
493. – 60 c.+10 c. green .. 25 20
494. – 75 c.+25 c. red .. 40 30
495. – 1 f. 50 c.+50 c. brown 50 40
496. – 3 f. 50 c.+2 f. 50 blue 1·90 1·75
497. 56. 25 f.+25 f. purple .. 13·00 12·00

DESIGNS—As T 55: 60 c. Statue of Abbot Bertels. 75. c. Echternach Abbey. 1 f. 50 c. Ruined interior of Basilica. 3 f. 50 c. St. Irmine and Pepin II carrying model of Echternach Abbey.

57. U.S. Military Cemetery, Hamm. 58. Michel Lentz (national poet).

1947. In honour of Gen. George S. Patton.

498. 57. 1 f. 50 lake 5 5
499. – 3 f. 50 blue 95 95
500. 57. 5 f. green 95 95
501. – 10 f. purple .. .. 3·00 3·50

PORTRAIT: 3 f. 50, 10 f. Gen. G. S. Patton.

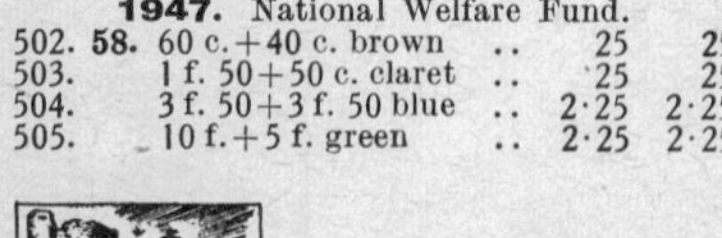

1947. National Welfare Fund.

502. 58. 60 c.+40 c. brown .. 25 25
503. 1 f. 50+50 c. claret .. 25 25
504. 3 f. 50+3 f. 50 blue .. 2·25 2·25
505. 10 f.+5 f. green .. 2·25 2·25

59. L'Oesling. 60. "Dicks" (Edmond de la Fontaine). 61. Grand Duchess Charlotte.

1948. Tourist Propaganda.

505a. – 2 f. 50 chocolate .. 40 12
505b. – 3 f. violet .. .. 2·50 75
505c. – 4 f. blue .. .. 1·25 75
506. 59. 7 f. brown .. .. 5·50 20
507. – 10 f. green 45 5
508. – 15 f. red 50 20
509. – 20 f. blue 55 20

DESIGNS—HORIZ. 2 f. 50, Television transmitter, Dudelange. 3 f. Radio Luxembourg. 4 f. Victor Hugo's house, Vianden. 10 f. River Moselle. 15 f. Mining district. VERT. 20 f. Luxembourg.

1948. National Welfare Fund.

510. 60. 60 c.+40 c. brown .. 30 30
511. 1 f. 50+50 c. red .. 30 30
512. 3 f. 50+3 f. 50 blue .. 3·25 3·25
513. 10 f.+5 f. green .. 3·75 3·75

1948.

513a. 61. 5 c. orange 5 5
513b. 10 c. blue 5 5
514. 15 c. olive 5 5
514a. 20 c. maroon 5 5
515. 25 c. grey 5 5
515a. 30 c. olive 8 5
515b. 40 c. red 5 5
515c. 50 c. orange 8 5
516. 60 c. brown 10 5
517. 80 c. green 10 5
518. 1 f. claret 15 5
518a. 1 f. 20 black 15 5
518b. 1 f. 25 brown 12 8
519. 1 f. 50 blue 12 5
520. 1 f. 60 grey 20 20
521. 2 f. purple 15 12
521a. 2 f. 50 red 12 5
521b. 3 f. blue 45 5
521c. 3 f. 50 claret 45 5
522. 4 f. blue 25 5
522a. 5 f. violet .. .. 1·10 8
523. 6 f. purple 50 8
524. 8 f. green 50 12

62. Date-stamp and Map.

1949. U.P.U. 75th Anniv.

525. 62. 80 c. green and black .. 30 30
526. 2 f. 50 red and black .. 75 75
527. 4 f. blue and black .. 3·00 3·00
528. 8 f. brown and black .. 10·00 10·00

63. Michel Rodange. 64. Young Girl.

1949. National Welfare Fund.

529. 63. 60 c.+40 c. olive .. 30 30
530. 2 f.+1 f. purple .. 1·90 1·90
531. 4 f.+2 f. blue .. 2·75 2·75
532. 10 f.+5 f. brown .. 3·75 3·75

1950. War Orphans' Fund.

533. – 60 c.+15 c. green .. 20 20
534. 64. 1 f.+20 c. red .. 40 40
535. – 2 f.+30 c. brown .. 40 40
536. 64. 4 f.+75 c. blue .. 2·75 2·75
537. – 8 f.+3 f. black .. 19·00 19·00
538. 64. 10 f.+5 f. purple .. 19·00 19·00

DESIGN: 60 c., 2 f., 8 f. Mother and boy.

65. J. A. Zinnen. 66. Ploughman and Factories.

1950. National Welfare Fund.

539. 65. 60 c.+10 c. vio. & grey 20 20
540. 2 f.+15 c. red & buff 25 25
541. 4 f.+15 c. blue & grey 1·25 1·25
542. 8 f.+5 f. brown & buff 7·00 7·00

1951. To Promote United Europe.

543. 66. 80 c. green .. .. 5·00 1·90
544. – 1 f. violet .. .. 1·90 30
545. – 2 f. grey .. .. 11·00 30
546. 66. 2 f. 50 red .. .. 16·00 9·00
547. – 3 f. brown .. .. 23·00 13·00
548. – 4 f. blue .. .. 45·00 20·00

DESIGNS: 1 f., 3 f. Map, people and "Rights of Man" Charter. 2 f., 4 f. Scales balancing "United Europe" and "Peace".

67. L. Menager (composer). 68. Hurdling.

1951. National Welfare Fund.

549. 67. 60 c.+10 c. black .. 12 12
550. 2 f.+15 c. green .. 20 20
551. 4 f.+15 c. blue .. 80 80
552. 8 f.+5 f. purple .. 9·00 9·00

1952. 15th Olympic Games. Black on coloured backgrounds.

553. 68. 1 f. green 40 12
554. – 2 f. brown (Football) .. 90 15
555. – 2 f. 50 pink (Boxing) .. 1·25 35
556. – 3 f. drab (Water polo) 2·50 45
557. – 4 f. blue (Cycling) .. 10·00 2·25
558. – 8 f. lilac (Fencing) .. 5·00 1·10

68a. Types 1 and 61.

68b. Type 1.

1952. Air. National Philatelic Exn. ("CENTILUX") and Stamp Cent.

552a. 68a. 80 c. blk., pur. & grn. 30 30
552f. 68b. 2 f. black and green .. 20·00 25·00
552b. 68a. 2 f. 50 blk., pur. & red 65 65
552c. 4 f. blk., pur. and blue 95 95
552g. 68b. 4 f. red and green .. 20·00 25·00
552d. 68a. 8 f. blk., pur. and clar. 15·00 28·00
552e. 10 f. blk., pur. & brn. 22·00 25·00

Nos. 552f and 552g were printed together in sheets of 32 (two panes of 16) arranged tete-beche separated by a gutter. The stamps therefore exist se-tenant horiz. or vert. as well in vert. tete-beche pairs with gutter.

Nos. 552a/e sold at face value plus 20 f. entrance fee to Exhibition.

69. J. B. Fresez (painter). 70. Prince Jean and Princess Josephine Charlotte.

1952. National Welfare Fund.

559. 69. 60 c.+15 c. blue-green .. 12 12
560. 2 f.+25 c. red-brown .. 12 12
561. 4 f.+25 c. violet .. 1·25 1·25
562. 8 f.+4 f. 75 purple .. 7·50 7·50

1953. Royal Wedding.

563. 70. 80 c. violet 20 10
564. 1 f. 20 brown 20 10
565. 2 f. green 50 5
566. 3 f. purple 50 20
567. 4 f. blue .. .. 2·75 40
568. 9 f. red .. .. .. 2·75 45

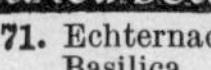

71. Echternach. Basilica. 72. Pierre D'Aspelt.

1953. Echternach Abbey Restoration (3rd issue).

569. 71. 2 f. red .. .. .. 1·60 20
570. – 2 f. 50 olive .. .. 2·25 1·50

DESIGN: 2 f. 50 Interior of Basilica.

1953. Pierre D'Aspelt. 7th Birth Cent.

571. 72. 4 f. black .. .. 2·25 1·25

73. "Candlemas Singing".

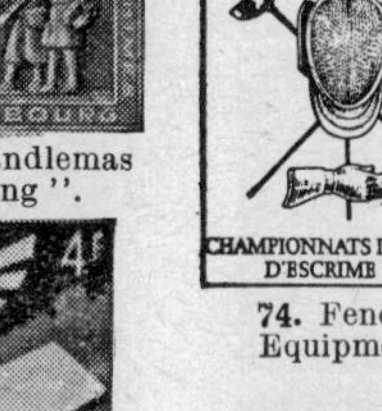

74. Fencing Equipment.

75. Emblem and Map.

76. Earthenware Whistle.

1953. National Welfare Fund. Allegorical designs inscr. "CARITAS 1953".

572. 73. 25 c.+15 c. red & verm. 12 12
573. – 80 c.+20 c. ind. & brn. 12 12
574. – 1 f. 20+30 c. ol. & grn. 20 20
575. 73. 2 f.+25 c. brn. & lake 15 15
576. – 4 f.+50 c. bl. & turq. 1·90 1·90
577. – 7 f.+3 f. 35 lilac & vio. 5·00 5·00

DESIGNS: 80 c., 4 f. "The Rattles". 1 f. 20, 7 f. "The Easter-eggs".

1954. 1954 World Fencing Championships, Luxembourg.

578. 74. 2 f. sepia and red-brown 2·75 20

1954. Luxembourg Fair.

579. 75. 4 f. yell., red, grn. & blue 4·00 75

1954. National Welfare Fund. Inscr. "CARITAS 1954".

580. 76. 25 c.+5 c. red & orge. .. 10 10
581. – 80 c.+20 c. black .. 10 10
582. – 1 f. 20+30 c. green .. 20 20
583. 76. 2 f.+25 c. brn. & buff. .. 20 20
584. – 4 f.+50 c. blue .. 1·25 1·25
585. – 7 f.+3 f. 45 violet .. 5·00 5·00

DESIGNS: 80 c., 4 f. Sheep and drum. 1 f. 20, 7 f. Merry-go-round horses.

77. Tulips. 78.

1955. Mondorf-les-Bains Flower Show.

586. 77. 80 c. red, green & brown 20 15
587. – 2 f. yellow, green & red 20 10
588. – 3 f. mag., green & emer. 1·25 1·25
589. – 4 f. orange, green & blue 1·25 1·25

FLOWERS: 2 f. Daffodils. 3 f. Hyacinths. 4 f. Parrot tulips.

1955. 1st National Crafts Exn.

590. 78. 2 f. brown and grey .. 40 5

79. "Charter". 80. "Christmas Day".

1955. U.N. 10th Anniv.

591. 79. 80 c. blue and black .. 40 20
592. – 2 f. brown and red .. 3·25 12
593. – 4 f. red and blue .. 1·90 1·50
594. – 9 f. green and brown 65 50

SYMBOLIC DESIGNS: 2 f. "Security". 4 f. "Justice". 9 f. "Assistance".

1955. National Welfare Fund. Inscr. "CARITAS 1955".

595. – 25 c.+5 c. red .. 12 12
596. 80. 80 c.+20 c. grey .. 12 12
597. – 1 f. 20+30 c. green .. 25 25
598. – 2 f.+25 c. brown .. 20 20
599. 80. 4 f.+50 c. blue .. 1·25 1·25
600. – 7 f.+3 f. 45 mauve .. 5·00 5·00

ALLEGORICAL DESIGNS: 25 c., 2 f. "St. Nicholas' Day". 1 f. 20 c., 7 f. "Twelfth Night".

1956. Mondorf-les-Bains Flower Show. As T 77 but inscr. at top in one line.

601. 2 f. red, green and grey 25 10
602. 3 f. purple, blue, green, yellow and brown .. 40 30

FLOWERS: 2 f. Anemones. 3 f. Crocuses.

1956. Roses. As T 77 but inscr. at top "LUXEMBOURG—VILLE DES ROSES".

603. 2 f. 50 yellow, grn. & bl. 2·75 1·90
604. 4 f. orge, red, grn. & pur. 95 50

DESIGNS: 2 f. 50, Yellow roses. 4 f. Red roses.

82. Blast Furnaces and Map.

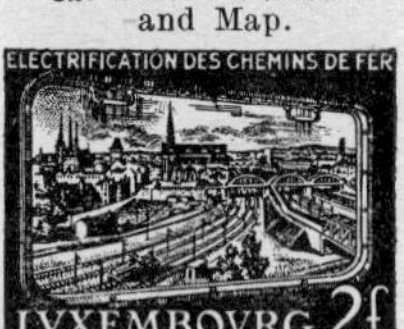

81. Steel Plant and Girder. 83. Luxembourg Central Station.

1956. Esch-sur-Alzette. 50th Anniv.

605. 81. 2 f. red, black and blue 65 12

1956. European Coal and Steel Community. Inscr. as in T 82.

606. 82. 2 f. red .. .. 7·00 20
607. – 3 f. blue .. .. 8·00 7·00
608. – 4 f. green .. .. 1·25 1·25

DESIGNS—VERT. 3 f. Girder supporting City of Luxemburg. HORIZ. 4 f. Chain and miner's lamp.

1956. Europa. As T 230 of Belgium.

609. 2 f. black and brown .. 48·00 65
610. 3 f. red and salmon .. 16·00 10·00
611. 4 f. indigo and blue .. 6·50 1·90

1956. Electrification of Luxembourg Railways.

612. 83. 2 f. sepia and black .. 50 12

84. I. de la Fontaine. 85. Arms of Echternach.

1956. Council of State Cent. Inscr. as in T 84.
613. 84. 2 f. sepia .. .. 1·00 12
614. – 7 f. purple .. .. 1·60 30
DESIGN: 7 f. Grand Duchess Charlotte.

1956. National Welfare Fund. Inscr. "CARITAS 1956". Arms. Multicoloured.
615. 25 c.+5 c. Type 85 .. 10 10
616. 80 c.+20 c. Esch-sur-Alzette 10 10
617. 1 f. 20+30 c. Grevenmacher 25 25
618. 2f.+25 c. Type 85 .. 12 12
619. 4f.+50 c. Esch-sur-Alzette .. .. 1·25 1·25
620. 7f.+3f. 45 Grevenmacher 2·25 2·25

86. Lord Baden-Powell and Scout Emblems.

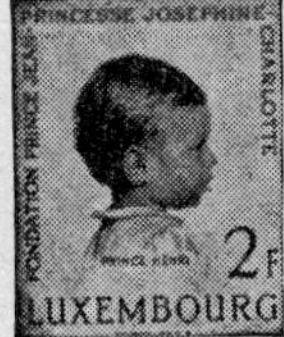

87. Prince Henri.

1957. Lord Baden-Powell. Birth Cent. and Scouting Movement. 50th Anniv.
621. 86. 2 f. chestnut and olive.. 30 5
622. – 2 f. 50 claret and violet 80 75
DESIGN: 2 f. 50. As T 86 but showing Girl Guide emblems.

1957. "Prince Jean and Princess Josephine-Charlotte Foundation" Child Welfare Clinic. Insc. as in T 87.
623. 87. 2 f. brown 12 5
624. – 3 f. green 95 80
625. – 4 f. blue 95 80
DESIGNS—HORIZ.: Children's Clinic Project. VERT. 4 f. Princess Marie-Astrid.

88. "Peace".

89. Fair Entrance and Flags.

1957. Europa.
626. 88. 2 f. brown 95 15
627. 3 f. red .. .. .. 7·50 4·50
628. 4 f. purple .. .. 4·50 3·75

1957. National Welfare Fund. Arms as T 85 inscr. "CARITAS 1957". Multicoloured.
629. 25 c.+5 c. Luxembourg .. 12 12
630. 80 c.+20 c. Mersch .. 12 12
631. 1 f. 20+30 c. Vianden .. 25 25
632. 2 f.+25 c. Luxembourg .. 12 12
633. 4 f.+50 c. Mersch .. 65 65
634. 7 f.+3 f. 45 Vianden .. 1·90 1·90

1958. Luxembourg Int. Fair. 10th Anniv. Flags in national colours.
635. 89. 2 f. blue 10 5

90. Luxembourg Pavilion.

91. St. Willibrord holding Child (after Puseel).

1958. Brussels Int. Exn.
636. 90. 2 f. 50 c. lilac and blue 12 5

1958. St. Willibrord. 1300th Birth Anniv.
637. – 1 f. red 15 15
638. 91. 2 f. 50 sepia .. 20 5
639. – 5 f. blue 40 35
DESIGNS: 1 f. St. Willibrord and St. Irmina holding inscribed plaque. 5 f. St. Willibrord and Suppliant. (Miracle of the wine-cask).

1958. Europa. As T 254 of Belgium. Size 21×35 mm.
640. 2 l. 50 blue and red .. 20 12
641. 3 f. 50 ochre and green .. 25 25
642. 5 f. red and blue .. 50 50

92. Open-air Theatre at Wiltz.

93. Vineyard.

94. Grand Duchess Charlotte.

1958. Wiltz Open-air Theatre Commem.
643. 92. 2 l. 50 sepia and grey 10 5

1958. Moselle Wine Industry. Bimillenary.
644. 93. 2 f. 50 brown and green 10 5

1958. National Welfare Fund. Arms as T 85 inscr. "CARITAS 1958". Multicoloured.
645. 30 c.+10 c. Capellen .. 5 5
646. 1 f.+25 c. Diekirch .. 5 5
647. 1 f. 50+25 c. Redange .. 15 15
648. 2 f. 50+50 c. Capellen .. 8 8
649. 5 f.+50 c. Diekirch .. 35 35
650. 8 f. 50+4 f. 60 Redange 1·75 1·75

1959. Accession of Grand Duchess Charlotte. 40th Anniv.
651. 94. 1 f. 50 grey-grn. & green 12 5
652. 2 f. 50 sepia and pink.. 12 5
653. 5 f. blue & ultramarine 20 20

95. N.A.T.O. Emblem.

96. Early Locomotive and First Bars of Hymn "De Feierwon".

1959. N.A.T.O. 10th Anniv.
654. 95. 2 f. 50 blue and olive .. 20 5
655. 8 f. 50 blue and chest. 25 12

1959. Mondorf-les-Bains Flower Show. As T 77 but inscr. "1959".
656. 1 f. violet, yellow and green 15 10
657. 2 f. 50 rose, green and blue 25 10
658. 3 f. blue, green and purple 30 25
FLOWERS: 1 f. Iris. 2 f. 50, Peony. 3 f. Hortensia.

1959. Europa. As T 268 of Belgium but size 22×33 mm.
659. 2 f. 50 olive 30 12
660. 5 f. indigo 50 30

1959. Luxembourg Railways Cent.
661. 96. 2 f. 50 blue and red .. 25 8

1959. National Welfare Fund. Arms as T 85 inscr. "CARITAS 1959". Multicoloured.
662. 30 c.+10 c. Clervaux .. 5 5
663. 1 f.+25 c. Remich .. 5 5
664. 1 f. 50+25 c. Wiltz .. 12 12
665 2f. 50+50 c. Clervaux .. 10 10
666. 5 f.+50 c. Remich .. 30 30
667. 8 f. 50+4 f. 60 Wiltz 1·60 1·60

97. Refugees seeking Shelter.

98. Steel Worker.

1960. World Refugee Year.
668. 97. 2 f. 50 indigo & salmon 12 5
669. – 5 f. indigo and violet .. 20 15
DESIGN—HORIZ. 5 f. "The Flight into Egypt" (Biblical scene).

1960. Schuman Plan. 10th Anniv.
670. 98. 2 f. 50 lake 20 12

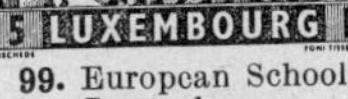

99. European School, Luxembourg.

100. Grand Duchess Charlotte.

1960. European School Commem.
671. 99. 5 f. black and blue .. 50 50

1960.
672. 100. 10 c. claret 5 5
673. 20 c. red 5 5
673a. 25 c. orange 5 5
674. 30 c. drab 5 5
675. 50 c. green 5 5
676. 1 f. violet 5 5
677. 1 f. 50 mauve.. .. 12 5
678. 2 f. blue 12 5
679. 2 f. 50 purple .. 12 5
680. 3 f. dull purple .. 30 5
680a. 3 f. 50 turquoise .. 45 45
681. 5 f. chestnut 25 5
681a. 6 f. grey-green .. 40 12

101. Heraldic Lion, and Tools.

102. Princess Marie-Astrid.

1960. 2nd National Crafts Exn.
682. 101. 2 f. 50 red, blue, black and grey 30 8

1960. Europa. As T 279 of Belgium but size 37×22 mm.
683. 2 f. 50 green and black .. 25 10
684. 5 f. black and lake .. 25 25

1960. National Welfare Fund. Inscr. "CARITAS 1960". Centres and inscr. in sepia.
685. 102. 30 c.+10 c. blue .. 5 5
686. – 1 f.+25 c. pink .. 5 5
687. – 1 f. 50+25 c. turquoise 12 12
688. 102. 2 f. 50+50 c. yellow.. 8 8
689. – 5 f. +50 c. lilac .. 45 45
690. – 8 f. 50+4 f. 60 sage .. 1·10 1·10
DESIGNS: Princess Marie-Astrid—standing (1 f., 5 f.), sitting with book on lap (1 f. 50, 8 f. 50).

103. Great Spotted Woodpecker.

104. Patton Monument, Ettelbruck.

1961. Animal Protection Campaign. Insc. "PROTECTION DES ANIMAUX".
691. 1 f. indigo, red, green, oran. and black (T 103) .. 5 5
692. 1 f. 50 buff, blue and black 5 5
693. 3 f. brown, buff and violet 25 20
694. 8 f. 50 ochre, brown, green and black.. .. .. 40 20
DESIGNS—VERT. 8 f. 50, Dachsund. HORIZ. 1 f. 50, Cat. 3 f. Horse.

1961. Tourist Publicity.
695. 104. 2 f. 50 blue and black.. 8 5
696. 2 f. 50 green .. 8 5
DESIGN—VERT. No. 696, Clervaux.

105. Doves.

106. Prince Henri.

1961. Europa.
697. 105. 2 f. 50 red 12 5
698. 5 f. blue 25 20

1961. National Welfare Fund. Inscr. "CARITAS 1961". Centres and inscr. in sepia.
699. 106. 30 c.+10 c. magenta 10 10
700. – 1 f.+25 c. lavender .. 10 10
701. – 1 f. 50+25 c. salmon 12 12
702. 106. 2 f. 50+50 c. grey-grn. 20 20
703. – 5 f.+50 c. yellow .. 30 30
704. – 8 f. 50+4 f. 60 grey.. 85 85
DESIGNS: Prince Henri when—young boy (1 f., 5 f.); youth in formal dress (1 f. 50, 8 f. 50).

107. Cyclist Carrying Cycle.

108. Europa "Tree".

110. Prince Jean and Princess Margaretha when Babies.

109. St. Laurent's Church, Diekirch.

1962. World Cross-country Cycling Championships, Esch-sur-Alzette.
705. 107. 2 f. 50 red, brown, blk. and blue 20 5
706. – 5 f. mult. (Emblem) 20 12

1962. Europa.
707. 108. 2 f. 50 chocolate, apple-green and bistre .. 12 5
708. 5 f. choc., grn. & bistre 20 12

1962.
709. 109. 2 f. 50 black and brown 8 5

1962. National Welfare Fund. Inscr. "CARITAS 1962". Centres and inscr. in sepia.
710. 110. 30 c.+10 c. buff .. 5 5
711. – 1 f.+25 c. blue .. 5 5
712. – 1 f. 50+25 c. olive .. 10 10
713. – 2 f. 50+50 c. pink .. 12 12
714. – 5 f.+50 c. apple .. 35 35
715. – 8 f. 50+4 f. 60 sl.-violet 85 85
PORTRAITS—VERT. 1 f., 2 f. 50, Prince Jean and: 2 f. 50, 5 f., Princess Margaretha, at various stages of childhood. HORIZ. 8 f. 50, The Royal Children.

111. Blackboard.

112. Benedictine Abbey, Munster.

113. Colpach Castle. 114. "Human Rights".

1963. European Schools. 10th Anniv.
716. 111. 2 f. 50 green, red & grey 8 5

1963. City of Luxembourg Millenary.
(a) Horiz. views.
717. – 1 f. slate-blue.. .. 30 30
718. 112. 1 f. 50 brown-red .. 30 30
719. – 2 f. 50 green 30 30
720. – 3f. red-brown.. .. 30 30
721. – 5 f. violet 40 40
722. – 11 f. blue 75 75
VIEWS: 1 f. Bock Rock. 2 f. 50, Rham Towers. 3 f. Grand Ducal Palace. 5 f. Castle Bridge. 11 f. Millenary Buildings.

(b) Vert. multicoloured designs.
723. 1 f. "Three Towers" Gate 5 5
724. 1 f. 50 Great Seal of Luxemburg .. 10 10
725. 2f. 50 "The Black Virgin" (statue), St. John's Church 15 15
726. 3 f. Citadel 12 12
727. 5 f. Town Hall 40 40

1963. Red Cross Cent.
728. 113. 2 f. 50 brown-red & slate 12 5

1963. European "Human Rights" Convention. 10th Anniv.
729. 114. 2 f. 50 blue on gold .. 12 5

115. "Co-operation". 116. Trout snapping bait.

1963. Europa.
730. **115.** 3 f. grn., orge. & bl.-grn. 12 5
731. 6 f. orge., red & red-brn. 20 12

1963. World Fishing Championships.
732. **116.** 3 f. slate 12 5

117. Telephone Dial. **118.** St. Roch (patron saint of bakers).

1963. Automatic Telephone System. Inaug.
733. **117.** 3 f. green, blk. & ultram. 10 5

1963. National Welfare Fund. Patron Saints of Crafts and Guilds. Inscr. "CARITAS 1963". Multicoloured.
734. 50 c.+10 c. Type **118** .. 5 5
735. 1 f.+25 c. St. Anne (tailors) 5 5
736. 2 f.+25 c. St. Eloi (smiths) 10 10
737. 3 f.+50 c. St. Michel (haberdashers) 12 12
738. 6 f.+50 c. St. Barthelemy (butchers) 30 30
739. 10 f.+5 f. 90 St. Thibaut (seven crafts) 65 65

119. Power House. **120.** Barge entering Canal.

122. Students thronging "New Athenaeum". **121.** Europa "Flower".

1964. Vianden Reservoir Inaug.
740. **119.** 2 f. sl.-bl., chest. & red 10 10
741. – 3 f. blue, myrtle & red 12 5
742. – 6 f. choc., blue & green 15 12
DESIGNS—HORIZ. 3 f. Upper reservoir. VERT. 6 f. Lohmuhle Dam.

1964. Moselle Canal Inaug.
743. **120.** 3 f. indigo and blue .. 12 5

1964. Europa.
744. **121.** 3 f. blue, chest. & cream 12 5
745. 6 f. sepia, green & yell. 20 10

1964. Opening of "New Athenaeum" (education centre).
746. **122.** 3 f. black and green .. 8 5

1964. "BENELUX". 20th Anniv. As T **332** of Belgium.
747. 3 f. sepia, yellow and blue 8 5

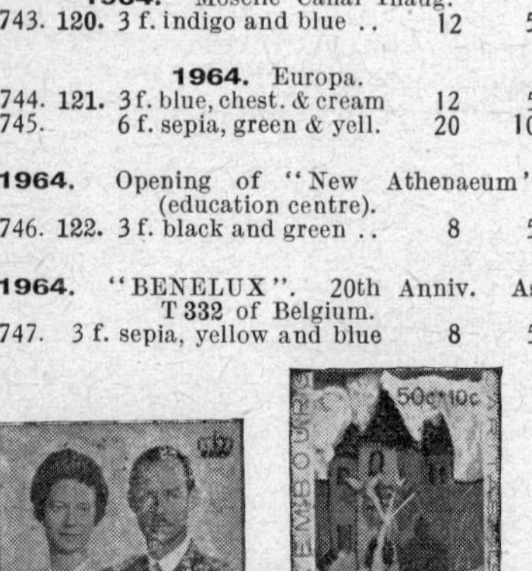

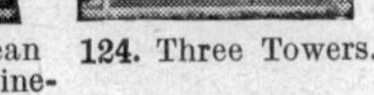

123. Grand Duke Jean and Princess Josephine-Charlotte. **124.** Three Towers.

1964. Accession of Grand Duke Jean.
748. **123.** 3 f. indigo and pale blue 10 5
749. 6 f. sepia & pale brown 12 8

1964. National Welfare Fund. Inscr. "CARITAS 1964". Multicoloured.
750. 50 c.+10 c. Type **124** .. 5 5
751. 1 f.+25 c. Grand Duke Adolphe Bridge 5 5
752. 2 f.+25 c. Lower Town .. 8 8
753. 3 f.+50 c. Type **124** .. 12 12
754. 6 f.+50 c. Grand Duke Adolphe Bridge 30 30
755. 10 f.+5 f. 90 Lower Town 50 50

125. Rotary Emblem and Cogwheels. **126.** Grand Duke Jean.

1965. Rotary Int. 60th Anniv.
756. **125.** 3 f. gold, blue, grey and red .. 8 5

1965.
757. **126.** 25 c. brown 5 5
758. 50 c. red 5 5
759. 1 f. blue 5 5
760. 1 f. purple 5 5
761. 2 f. purple 5 5
762. 2 f. 50 orange 8 5
763. 3 f. green 8 5
764. 3 f. 50 brown 10 5
765. 4 f. purple 12 5
766. 5 f. green 15 10
767. 6 f. violet 15 5
767a. 8 f. blue 25 15
767b. 9 f. green 25 15
767c. 10 f. olive 40 20
767d. 12 f. red 30 15
767e. 20 f. blue 55 20

127. I.T.U. Emblem and Symbols.

1965. I.T.U. Cent.
768. **127.** 3 f. blue, lake & violet 10 5

128. Europa "Sprig". **129.** "The Roman Lady of the Titelberg".

1965. Europa.
769. **128.** 3 f. green, red and black 15 5
770. 6 f. brown, blue & green 20 12

1965. National Welfare Fund. Fairy Tales. Inscr. "CARITAS 1965". Multicoloured.
771. 50 c.+10 c. Type **129** .. 5 5
772. 1 f.+25 c. "Schappchen, the Huntsman" .. 5 5
773. 2 f.+25 c. "The Witch of Koerich" 10 10
774. 3 f.+50 c. "The Goblins of Schoenfels" .. 12 12
775. 6 f.+50 c. "Tollchen, Watchman of Hesperange" 30 30
776. 10 f.+5 f. 90 "The Old Spinster of Heispelt" 65 65

130. "Flag" and Torch. **131.** W.H.O. Building.

1966. Luxembourg Workers' Union. 50th Anniv.
777. **130.** 3 f. red and grey .. 10 5

1966. W.H.O. Headquarters, Geneva. Inaug.
778. **131.** 3 f. green 10 5

132. Golden Key. **133.** Europa "Ship".

1966. Solemn Promise to Our Lady of Luxembourg. Tercent.
779. **132.** 1 f. 50 green 5 5
780. – 2 f. red 5 5
781. – 3 f. blue 12 5
782. – 6 f. brown 20 15
DESIGNS: 2 f. Interior of Luxembourg Cathedral (after painting by J. Martin). 3 f. Our Lady of Luxembourg (after engraving by R. Collin). 6 f. Gallery pillar, Luxembourg Cathedral (after sculpture by D. Muller).

1966. Europa.
783. **133.** 3 f. blue and grey .. 12 5
784. 6 f. green and brown .. 20 10

134. Diesel Locomotive.

1966. Luxembourg Railwaymen's Philatelic Exn. Multicoloured.
785. 1 f. 50 Type **134** 10 5
786. 3 f. Electric locomotive .. 12 5

135. Grand Duchess Charlotte Bridge. **136.** Kirchberg Building.

1966. Tourism.
787. **135.** 3 f. lake 8 5
See also Nos. 807/8.

1966. "Luxembourg-European Centre".
788. **136.** 1 f. 50 green 10 8
789. – 13 f. blue (Robert Schuman monuments) 35 12

137. "Mary, Veiled Matron of Wormeldange". **138.** City of Luxembourg, 1850 (after engraving by N. Liez).

1966. National Welfare Fund. Depicting Luxembourg Fairy Tales. Multicoloured.
790. 50 c.+10 c. Type **137** .. 5 5
791. 1 f. 50+25 c. "Jekel Warden of the Wark" 5 5
792. 2 f.+25 c. "The Black Gentlemen of Vianden" 8 8
793. 3 f.+50 c. "The Gracious Fairy of Rosport" .. 10 5
794. 6 f.+1 f. "The Friendly Shepherd of Donkolz" 25 30
795. 13 f.+6 f. 90 "The Little Sisters of Trois-Vierges" 55 50

1967. Treaty of London. Cent.
796. **138.** 3 f. choc., blue & green 10 5
797. – 6 f. red, brown & blue 15 10
DESIGN—VERT. 6 f. Plan of Luxembourg fortress c. 1850 (after T. de Cederstolpe).

139. Cogwheels. **140.** Lion on Globe.

1967. Europa.
798. **139.** 3 f. maroon, grey & buff 10 5
799. 6 f. sepia, purple & blue 20 12

1967. Lions Int. 50th Anniv.
800. **140.** 3 f. yellow, pur. & black 10 5

141. European Institutions Building, Luxembourg. **142.** Hikers and Hostel.

1967. NATO Council Meeting, Luxembourg.
801. **141.** 3 f. blue and green .. 12 5
802. 6 f. red and pink .. 25 20

1967. Luxembourg Youth Hostels.
803. **142.** 1 f. 50 multicoloured 5 5

143. Shaving-dish (after Degrotte). **144.** "Gardener".

1967. "200 Years of Luxembourg Pottery".
804. **143.** 1 f. 50 multicoloured 5 5
805. – 3 f. multicoloured .. 12 5
DESIGN—VERT. 3 f. Vase, circa 1820.

1967. "Family Gardens" Congress, Luxembourg.
806. **144.** 1 f. 50 orange and green 5 5

1967. Tourism. As T **135**.
807. 3 f. indigo and ultramarine 8 5
808. 3 f. maroon, olive and blue 8 5
DESIGNS—HORIZ. No. 807, Moselle River and quayside, Mertert. VERT. No. 808, Moselle, Church and vines, Wormeldange.

145. Prince Guillaume. **146.** Football.

1967. National Welfare Fund. Royal Children and Residence.
809. 50 c.+10 c. brn. & buff .. 5 5
810. 1 f. 50+25 c. brn. & blue 5 5
811. 2 f.+25 c. brown and red 10 10
812. 3 f.+50 c. brn. & yellow .. 12 12
813. 6 f.+1 f. brown & lavender 30 25
814. 13 f.+6 f. 90 brown, green and blue 70 65
DESIGNS: 50 c. T **145**. 1 f. 50, Princess Margaretha. 2 f. Prince Jean. 3 f. Prince Henri. 6 f. Princes Marie-Astrid. 13 f. Berg Castle.

1968. Olympic Games, Mexico.
815. – 50 c. blue 5 5
816. **146.** 1 f. 50 green & emerald 5 5
817. – 2 f. yellow and green .. 8 5
818. – 3 f. orange 12 5
819. – 6 f. green and blue .. 20 8
820. – 13 f. red and crimson .. 40 20
DESIGNS: 50 c. Diving. 2 f. Cycling. 3 f. Running. 6 f. Walking. 13 f. Fencing.

147. Europa "Key". **148.** Thermal Bath Pavilion, Mondorf-les-Bains.

1968. Europa.
821. **147.** 3 f. brown, black & grn. 8 5
822. 6 f. green, black & orge. 20 10

1968. Mondorf-les-Bains Thermal Baths.
823. **148.** 3 f. blue, black, orange and green 8 5

149. Fair Emblem. **151.** "Blood Transfusion".

150. Village Project.

1968. Luxembourg Int. Fair. 20th Anniv.
824. **149.** 3 f. multicoloured .. 8 5

1968. Luxembourg SOS Children's Village.
825. **150.** 3 f. maroon and green 10 5
826. – 6 f. black, blue & pur. 15 8
DESIGN—VERT. 6 f. Orphan with foster-mother.

1968. Blood Donors of Luxembourg Red Cross.
827. **151.** 3 f. red and blue .. 10 5

152. "Luxair" Airliner over Luxembourg.
153. Cap Institute.

1968. Tourism.
828. **152.** 50 f. indigo, brn. & blue 1·25 65

1968. National Welfare Fund. Luxembourg Handicapped Children.
829. **153.** 50 c.+10 c. brown and cobalt .. 5 5
830. – 1 f. 50+25 c. brown and green .. 5 5
831. – 2 f.+25 c. brn. & yell. 8 8
832. – 3 f.+50 c. brn. & bl. 10 10
833. – 6 f.+1 f. brn. & buff 25 30
834. – 13 f.+6 f. 90 brown and pink .. 55 50
DESIGNS: 1 f. 50, Deaf and dumb child. 2 f. Blind child. 3 f. Nurse supporting handicapped child. 6 f. and 13 f. Mentally handicapped children (different).

154. Colonnade.

1969. Europa.
836. **154.** 3 f. multicoloured .. 10 5
837. 6 f. multicoloured .. 20 10

155. "The Wooden Horse" (Kutter).

1969. Joseph Kutter (painter). 75th Birth Anniv. Multicoloured.
838. 3 f. Type **155** 20 5
839. 6 f. "Luxembourg" (Kutter) 20 15

156. ILO Emblem.

1969. Int. Labour Organisation 50th Anniv.
840. **156.** 3 f. gold, violet & green 10 5

1969. "BENELUX" Customs Union. 25th Anniv. As T **250** of Belgium.
841. 3 f. red, blue, yellow & black 10 5

157. N.A.T.O. Emblem. **158.** Ear of Wheat and Agrocenter, Mersch.

1969. N.A.T.O. 20th Anniv.
842. **157.** 3 f. brown and red .. 10 5

1969. "Modern Agriculture".
843. **158.** 3 f. grey and green .. 10 5

159. Echternach. **160.** Vianden Castle.

1969. Tourism.
844. **159.** 3 f. indigo and blue .. 10 5
845. – 3 f. blue and green .. 10 5
DESIGNS: No. 845, Wiltz.

1969. National Welfare Fund. Castles (1st Series). Multicoloured.
846. 50 c.+10 c. Type **160** .. 5 5
847. 1 f. 50+25 c. Lucilinburhuc 5 5
848. 2 f.+25 c. Bourglinster 8 8
849. 3 f.+50 c. Hollenfels .. 10 10
850. 6 f.+1 f. Ansembourg .. 20 25
851. 13 f.+6 f. 90 Beaufort .. 55 55
See also Nos. 862/7.

161. Pasque-Flower. **162.** Wren.

1970. Nature Conservation Year. Multicoloured.
852. 3 f. Type **161** 12 5
853. 6 f. Hedgehogs 15 10

1970. 50 Years of Bird Protection.
854. **162.** 1 f. 50 grn., blk. & orge. 5 5

163. "Flaming Sun".

1970. Europa.
855. **163.** 3 f. multicoloured .. 10 5
856. 6 f. multicoloured .. 20 12

164. Road Safety Assn. Emblem and Traffic.

1970. Road Safety.
857. **164.** 3 f. black, red and lake 20 5

165. "Empress Kunegonde and Emperor Henry II" (stained-glass windows, Luxembourg Cathedral).

1970. Luxembourg Diocese. Cent.
858. **165.** 3 f. multicoloured .. 12 5

166. Population Pictograph. **167.** Facade of Town Hall, Luxembourg.

1970. Population Census.
859. **166.** 3 f. red, blue & green 10 5

1970. Union of Four Suburbs with Luxembourg City. 50th Anniv.
860. **167.** 3 f. brown, ochre & blue 10 5

168. U.N. Emblem. **169.** Monks in the Scriptium.

1970. United Nations. 25th Anniv.
861. **168.** 1 f. 50 violet and blue 5 5

1970. National Welfare Fund. Castles (2nd Series). Designs as T **160**.
862. 50 c.+10 c. Clervaux .. 5 5
863. 1 f. 50+25 c. Septfontaines 5 5
864. 2 f.+25 c. Bourscheid .. 8 8
865. 3 f.+50 c. Esch-sur-Sure 10 8
866. 6 f.+1 f. Larochette .. 25 25
867. 13 f.+6 f. 90 Brandenbourg 55 55

1971. Medieval Miniatures produced at Echternach. Multicoloured.
868. 1 f. 50 Type **169** 5 5
869. 3 f. Vine-growers going to work 10 8
870. 6 f. Vine-growers at work and returning home .. 15 15
871. 13 f. Workers with spades and hoe 35 25

170. Europa Chain.

1971.
872. **170.** 3 f. blk., brn. & red .. 10 5
873. 6 f. black, brn. & green 20 12

171. Olympic Rings and Arms of Luxembourg. **172.** '50' and L.C.G.B. Emblem.

1971. Int. Olympic Committee Meeting, Luxembourg.
874. **171.** 3 f. red, gold and blue 15 5

1971. Luxembourg's Christian Workers' Union (L.C.G.B.). 50th Anniv.
875. **172.** 3 f. mar., orge. & yell. 10 5

173. Artificial Lake, Upper Sure. **174.** Child with Coin.

1971. Man-made Landscapes.
876. **173.** 3 f. blue, grey & brn. 10 5
877. – 3 f. brn., green & blue 10 5
878. – 15 f. blk., blue & brn. 45 25
DESIGNS: No. 877, Water-processing plant, Esch-sur-Sure. No. 878, ARBED (United Steelworks) Headquarters Building, Luxembourg.

1971. Schoolchildren's Saving Campaign.
879. **174.** 3 f. multicoloured .. 10 5

175. "Children of Bethlehem". **176.** Coins of Belgium and Luxembourg.

1971. National Welfare Fund. "The Nativity"—wood-carvings in Beaufort Church. Multicoloured.
880. 1 f.+25 c. Type **175** .. 5 5
881. 1 f. 50+25 c. "Shepherds" 5 5
882. 3 f.+50 c. "Virgin, Child Jesus and St. Joseph" 10 10
883. 8 f.+1 f. "Herdsmen" .. 30 25
884. 18 f.+6 f. 50 "One of the Magi" 75 70

1972. Belgium-Luxembourg Economic Union. 50th Anniv.
885. **176.** 1 f. 50 silver, blk. & grn. 8 5

INDEX

Countries can be quickly located by referring to the index at the end of this volume.

177. Bronze Mask (1st. cent.). **178.** "Communications".

1972. Gollo-Roman Exhibits from Luxembourg State Museum. Multicoloured.
886. 1 f. Samian bowl (horiz.) .. 12 5
887. 3 f. Type **177** 12 5
888. 8 f. Limestone head 45 35
889. 15 f. Glass "head" flagon 45 35

1972. Europa.
890. **178.** 3 f. multicoloured .. 10 5
891. 8 f. multicoloured .. 20 20

179. Archer. **180.** R. Schuman (after bronze by R. Zilli.)

1972. 3rd European Archery Championships, Luxembourg.
892. **179.** 3 f. multicoloured .. 10 5

1972. Establishment of European Coal and Steel Community in Luxembourg. 20th Anniv.
893. **180.** 3 f. green and grey .. 12 5

181. National Monument. **182.** "Renert".

1972. Monuments and Buildings.
894. **181.** 3 f. brn., grn. & violet 12 5
895. – 3 f. brn., green & blue 10 5
DESIGN: No. 895, European Communities' Court of Justice.

1972. Publication of Michel Rodange's "Renert" (satirical poem). Cent.
896. **182.** 3 f. multicoloured .. 10 5

183. "Angel". **184.** "Epona on Horseback".

1972. Nat. Welfare Fund. Stained-glass Windows in Luxembourg Cathedral. Mult.
897. 1 f.+25 c. Type **183** .. 5 5
898. 1 f. 50+25 c. "St. Joseph" 5 5
899. 3 f.+50 c. "Holy Virgin with Child Jesus" .. 10 10
900. 8 f.+1 f. "People of Bethlehem" 30 30
901. 18 f.+6 f. 50 "Angel" (facing left) 75 75

1973. Archaeological Relics. Multicoloured.
902. 1 f. Type **184** 5 5
903. 4 f. "Panther attacking swan" (horiz.) 15 8
904. 8 f. Celtic gold coin .. 25 25
905. 15 f. Bronze boar (horiz.) .. 45 30

185. Europa "Posthorn".

186. Bee on Honeycomb.

1973. Europa.
906. **185.** 4 f. red, blue and light blue 12 5
907. 8 f. grn, blk. and yell. 25 15

1973. Bee-keeping.
908. **186.** 4 f. multicoloured .. 12 8

187. Nurse and Child. 188. Capital, Vianden Castle.

1973. Day Nurseries in Luxembourg.
909. **187.** 4 f. multicoloured .. 12 5

1973. Romanesque Architecture in Luxembourg.
910. **188.** 4 f. maroon and green 12 5
911. – 8 f. blue and brown .. 25 20
DESIGN: 8 f. Detail of altar, St. Irminas' Chapel, Rosport (now Luxembourg State Museum).

189. Labour Emblem. 190. J. de Busleyden.

1973. Luxembourg Board of Labour. 50th Anniv.
912. **189.** 3 f. multicoloured .. 10 5

1973. Great Council of Malines. 500th Anniv.
913. **190.** 4 f. multicoloured .. 12 5

191. Monument, Wiltz. 192. Joachim and St. Anne.

1973. National Strike Monument.
914. **191.** 4 f. grn., bl. and brown 12 5

1973. National Welfare Fund. "The Nativity". Details from 16th century reredos, Hachiville hermitage. Mult.
915. 1 f. + 25 c. Type **192** 5 5
916. 3 f. + 25 c. "Mary meets Elizabeth" .. 10 10
917. 4 f. + 50 c. "Magus presenting gift" .. 12 12
918. 8 f. + 1 f. "Shepherds at the manger" 25 25
919. 15 f. + 7 f. "St. Joseph with Candle" 65 55

193. Princess Marie-Astrid, Association President. 194. Flame Emblem.

1974. Luxembourg Red Cross Youth Association.
920. **193.** 4 f. multicoloured .. 12 5

1974. Luxembourg Mutual Insurance Federation. 50th Anniv.
921. **194.** 4 f. multicoloured .. 12 5

195. Seal of Henry VII, King of the Romans. 196. "Hind" (A. Tremont).

1974. Seals in Luxembourg State Archives.
922. **195.** 1 f. brn., yell. & purple 5 5
923. – 3 f. brn., yell. & green 12 10
924. – 4 f. dark brn., yell. & brn. 15 8
925. – 19 f. brn., yell. & blue 65 45
DESIGNS: 3 f. Equestrian seal of John the blind, King of Bohemia. 4 f. Municipal seal of Diekirch. 19 f. Seal of Marienthal Convent.

1974. Europa. Sculptures. Multicoloured.
926. 4 f. Type **196** 12 5
927. 8 f. "Abstract" (L. Wercollier) 25 20

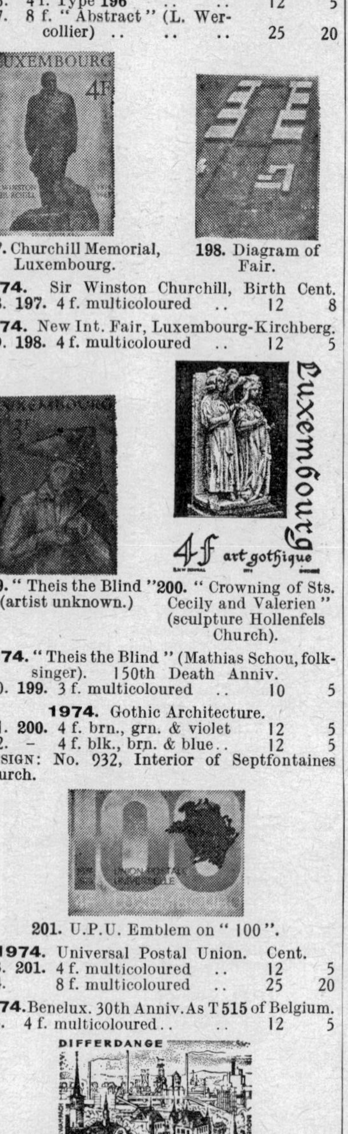

197. Churchill Memorial, Luxembourg. 198. Diagram of Fair.

1974. Sir Winston Churchill, Birth Cent.
928. **197.** 4 f. multicoloured .. 12 8

1974. New Int. Fair, Luxembourg-Kirchberg.
929. **198.** 4 f. multicoloured .. 12 5

199. "Theis the Blind" (artist unknown.) 200. "Crowning of Sts. Cecily and Valerien" (sculpture Hollenfels Church).

1974. "Theis the Blind" (Mathias Schou, folk-singer). 150th Death Anniv.
930. **199.** 3 f. multicoloured .. 10 5

1974. Gothic Architecture.
931. **200.** 4 f. brn., grn. & violet 12 5
932. – 4 f. blk., brn. & blue .. 12 5
DESIGN: No. 932, Interior of Septfontaines Church.

201. U.P.U. Emblem on "100".

1974. Universal Postal Union. Cent.
933. **201.** 4 f. multicoloured .. 12 5
934. 8 f. multicoloured .. 25 20

1974. Benelux. 30th Anniv. As T **515** of Belgium.
935. 4 f. multicoloured 12 5

202. Differdange.

1974. Tourism.
936. **202.** 4 f. red 12 5

203. "The Annunciation" 204. Old Luxembourg.

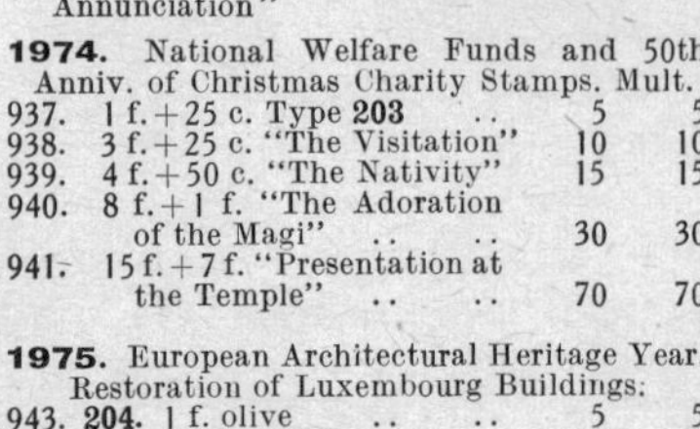

1974. National Welfare Funds and 50th Anniv. of Christmas Charity Stamps. Mult.
937. 1 f. + 25 c. Type **203** .. 5 5
938. 3 f. + 25 c. "The Visitation" 10 10
939. 4 f. + 50 c. "The Nativity" 15 15
940. 8 f. + 1 f. "The Adoration of the Magi" .. 30 30
941. 15 f. + 7 f. "Presentation at the Temple" .. 70 70

1975. European Architectural Heritage Year. Restoration of Luxembourg Buildings.
943. **204.** 1 f. olive 5 5
944. – 3 f. brown 10 5
945. – 4 f. violet 12 8
946. – 19 f. red 55 40
DESIGNS—HORIZ.: 3 f. Castle, Bourglinster. 4 f. Market Square, Echternach. VERT.: 19 f. St. Michael's Square, Mersch.

205. "Self-Portrait" (J. Kutter). 206. Dr. Schweitzer.

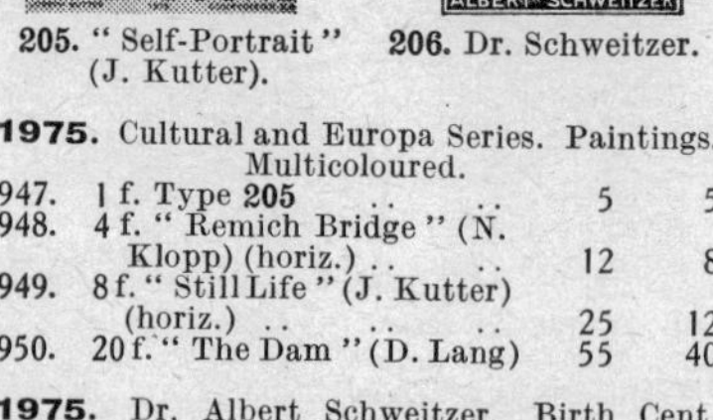

1975. Cultural and Europa Series. Paintings. Multicoloured.
947. 1 f. Type **205** 5 5
948. 4 f. "Remich Bridge" (N. Klopp) (horiz.) .. 12 8
949. 8 f. "Still Life" (J. Kutter) (horiz.) 25 12
950. 20 f. "The Dam" (D. Lang) 55 40

1975. Dr. Albert Schweitzer. Birth Cent.
951. **206.** 4 f. blue 12 8

207. Schuman, Martino and Spaak. 208. Civil Defence Emblem.

1975. Robert Schuman Declaration. 25th Anniv.
952. **207.** 4 f. brn., gold and yell. 12 8

1975. Civil Defence Reorganisation. 15th Anniv.
953. **208.** 4 f. multicoloured .. 12 8

209. Skating. 210. Fly Orchid.

1975. Sports. Multicoloured.
954. **209.** 3 f. violet, blue & green 8 5
955. – 4 f. brown and green .. 12 8
956. – 15 f. blue, brown & grn. 45 30
DESIGNS—HORIZ.: 4 f. Water-skiing. VERT. 15 f. Rock-climbing.

1975. National Welfare Fund. Protected Plants. Multicoloured.
957. 1 f. + 25 c. Type **210** .. 5 5
958. 3 f. + 25 c. Pyramid orchid 8 8
959. 4 f. + 50 c. Marsh helleborine 12 12
960. 8 f. + 1 f. Pasque flower .. 25 25
961. 15 f. + 7 f. Bee orchid .. 65 65

211. Grand Duchess Charlotte. 212. Circular Brooch.

1976. Royal Birthdays. Multicoloured.
962. 6 f. Type **211** (80th Birthday) 20 12
963. 6 f. Prince Henri (21st Birthday) 20 12

1976. Cultural Series. Museum Treasures. Multicoloured.
964. 2 f. Type **212** 5 5
965. 5 f. Glass beaker (horiz.) .. 15 10
966. 6 f. Bronze urn (horiz.) .. 20 12
967. 12 f. Merovingian "tremissis" (gold coin) 40 30

213. Soup Tureen.

1976. Europa. Multicoloured.
968. 6 f. Type **213** 20 12
969. 12 f. Deep bowl 40 30

214. Independence Hall, Philadelphia. 215. "Strength and Impetus".

1976. American Revolution. Bicent.
970. **214.** 6 f. multicoloured .. 20 12

1976. Olympic Games, Montreal.
971. **215.** 6 f. gold and purple .. 20 12

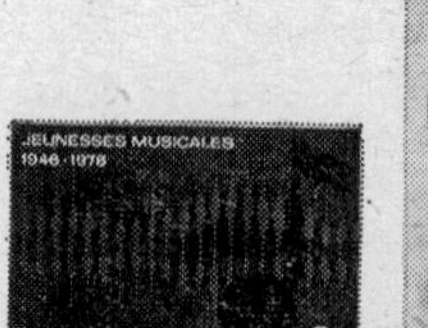

216. Emblem and Sound "Vibrations". 217. St. Anne, the Virgin and Child.

1976. "Jeunesses Musicales" Association in Luxembourg. 30th Anniversary.
972. **216.** 6 f. multicoloured .. 20 12

1976. Renaissance Art. Multicoloured.
973. 6 f. Type **217** 20 12
974. 12 f. Bernard de Velbruck, Lord of Beaufort (funeral monument) 40 30

218. Alexander Graham Bell. 219. Gentian.

1976. Telephone Centenary.
975. **218.** 6 f. green 20 12

1976. National Welfare Fund. Multicoloured.
976. 2 f. + 25 c. Type **219** .. 5 5
977. 5 f. + 25 c. Wild daffodil .. 20 20
978. 6 f. + 50 c. Red helleborine (orchid) 20 20
979. 12 f. + 1 f. Late spider orchid 45 45
980. 20 f. + 8 f. Twinleaved squill 95 95

OFFICIAL STAMPS

Overprinted **OFFICIEL**

1875. Stamps of 1859–72. Roul.
O 79. **2.** 1 c. brown .. .. 4·50 4·50
O 80. 2 c. black .. .. 8·00 8·00
O 81. **3.** 10 c. lilac £325 £325
O 82. 12½ c. red .. .. 55·00 55·00
O 83. 20 c. brown .. .. 9·00 9·00
O 84. 25 c. blue .. .. 90·00 70·00
O 85. 30 c. claret .. .. 16·00 16·00
O 105. 40 c. orange .. .. 22·00 22·00
O 87. 1 f. on 37½ c. bistre .. 45·00 13·00

1875. Stamps of 1874–79. Perf.
O 89. **2.** 1 c. brown .. .. 1·90 1·90
O 90. 2 c. black .. .. 3·75 3·75
O 91. 4 c. green .. .. 18·00 18·00
O 92. 5 c. yellow .. .. 15·00 15·00
O 93a. **3.** 10 c. lilac .. .. 17·00 17·00
O 94a. 12½ c. red .. .. 19·00 19·00
O 98. 20 c. brown .. .. 45·00 45·00
O 99. 25 c. blue .. .. 4·50 4·50
O 96. 1 f. on 37½ c. bistre .. 12·00 12·00

Overprinted **S.P.**

1881. Stamp of 1859. Roul.
O 116. **3.** 40 c. orange .. 11·00

1881. Stamps of 1874–79. Perf.
O 121. **2.** 1 c. brown .. .. 1·90 1·90
O 122. 2 c. black .. .. 1·90 1·90
O 118. 4 c. green .. .. 16·00 16·00
O 123. 5 c. yellow .. .. 25·00 25·00
O 124. **3.** 10 c. lilac .. .. 25·00 25·00
O 125. 12½ c. red .. .. 50·00 50·00
O 132. 20 c. brown .. .. 10·00 10·00
O 133. 25 c. blue .. .. 11·00 11·00
O 134. 30 c. rose .. .. 22·00 22·00
O 120. 1 f. on 37½ c. bistre .. 8·00 8·00

1882. Stamps of 1882.

O 141. **4.** 1 c. grey 25 20
O 142. 2 c. brown 25 20
O 143. 4 c. olive 25 20
O 144. 5 c. green 35 25
O 181. 10 c. red .. .. 5·50 3·00
O 158. 12½ c. blue .. .. 1·25 75
O 159. 20 c. orange .. .. 1·25 75
O 183. 25 c. blue .. .. 13·00 6·50
O 149. 30 c. olive .. .. 6·50 3·50
O 150. 50 c. brown .. .. 1·00 70
O 151. 3 f. lilac .. .. 1·00 70
O 152. 5 f. orange .. .. 7·50 5·50

1891. Stamps of 1891.

O 188. **5.** 10 c. red 25 12
O 191. 12½ c. green .. .. 5·00 1·50
O 192. 20 c. orange .. .. 4·50 75
O 189. 25 c. blue 35 12
O 194. 30 c. green .. .. 4·50 1·90
O 204. 37½ c. green .. .. 5·50 2·50
O 205. 50 c. brown .. .. 5·00 3·25
O 212. 1 f. purple .. .. 6·50 3·25
O 198. 2½ f. black .. .. 25·00 11·00
O 199. 5 f. lake .. .. 25·00 11·00

1898. Stamps of 1895.

O 213. **6.** 1 c. grey .. .. 1·60 75
O 214. 2 c. brown .. .. 1·60 75
O 215. 4 c. bistre .. .. 1·60 75
O 216. 5 c. green .. .. 2·75 1·25
O 217. 10 c. red .. .. 14·00 4·50

Overprinted **Officiel** in fancy letters.

1908. Stamps of 1906.

O 218. **7.** 1 c. grey 5 5
O 219. 2 c. brown 5 5
O 220. 4 c. bistre 5 5
O 221. 5 c. green 5 5
O 271. 5 c. mauve 5 5
O 222. 6 c. lilac 5 5
O 223. 7½ c. yellow 5 5
O 224. 10 c. red 20 12
O 225. 12½ c. slate 25 20
O 226. 15 c. brown 30 25
O 227. 20 c. orange 35 30
O 228. 25 c. blue 30 20
O 229. 30 c. olive .. .. 2·25 1·25
O 230. **8.** 37½ c. green 50 30
O 231. 50 c. brown 75 55
O 232. 87½ c. blue .. .. 2·25 1·10
O 233. 1 f. purple .. .. 2·50 1·00
O 234. 2½ f. red .. .. 42·00 19·00
O 235. 5 f. maroon .. .. 38·00 22·00

1915. Stamps of 1914.

O 236. **9.** 10 c. claret 20 20
O 237. 12½ c. green 20 20
O 238. 15 c. black 20 20
O 239. 17½ c. brown 20 20
O 240. 25 c. blue 20 20
O 241. 30 c. bistre 65 65
O 242. 35 c. blue 15 15
O 243. 37½ c. sepia 15 15
O 244. 40 c. orange 20 20
O 245. 50 c. grey 20 20
O 246. 62½ c. green 30 30
O 247. 87½ c. orange 30 30
O 248. 1 f. brown 30 30
O 249. 2½ f. red 25 25
O 250. 5 f. violet 30 30

1922. Stamps of 1921.

O 251. **10.** 2 c. brown 5 5
O 252. 3 c. olive 5 5
O 253. 6 c. purple 5 5
O 254. 10 c. green 5 5
O 272. 10 c. olive 5 5
O 255. 15 c. olive 5 5
O 273. 15 c. green 5 5
O 274. 15 c. orange 5 5
O 256. 20 c. orange 5 5
O 275. 20 c. green 5 5
O 257. 25 c. green 5 5
O 258. 30 c. red 5 5
O 259. 40 c. orange 5 5
O 260. 50 c. blue 5 5
O 276. 50 c. red 5 5
O 261. 75 c. red 5 5
O 277. 75 c. blue 5 5
O 266. 80 c. black 5 5
O 263. **11.** 1 f. red 12 12
O 278. 1 f. blue 20 20
O 267. 2 f. blue 30 30
O 279. 2 f. brown 95 95
O 269. 5 f. violet .. .. 2·50 2·50

1922. Stamps of 1923.

O 268. **14.** 3 f. blue 30 30
O 270. **13.** 10 f. black .. .. 7·50 7·50

1926. Stamps of 1926.

O 280. **16.** 5 c. violet 5 5
O 281. 10 c. olive 5 5
O 298. 15 c. black 25 25
O 282. 20 c. orange 5 5
O 283. 25 c. green 5 5
O 300. 25 c. brown 20 20
O 301. 30 c. green 20 20
O 302. 30 c. violet 25 25
O 303. 35 c. violet 30 30
O 304. 35 c. green 25 25
O 286. 40 c. grey 5 5
O 287. 50 c. brown 5 5
O 307. 60 c. green 25 25
O 288. 65 c. brown 5 5
O 308. 70 c. violet .. .. 1·60 1·60
O 289. 75 c. red 5 5
O 309. 75 c. brown 20 20
O 291. 80 c. brown 5 5
O 292. 90 c. red 12 12
O 293. 1 f. black 5 5
O 312. 1 f. red 25 25
O 294. 1¼ f. blue 5 5
O 313. 1¼ f. yellow 95 95
O 314. 1¼ f. green 95 95
O 315. **16.** 1½ f. blue 25 25
O 316. 1¾ f. blue 25 25

1928. Stamp of 1928.

O 317. **20.** 2 f. black 30 30

1931. Stamp of 1931.

O 318. **26.** 20 f. green .. .. 1·25 1·25

1934. Stamp of 1934.

O 319. **30.** 5 f. green 95 95

1935. No. 340 optd. **Officiel.**

O 341. – 10 f. green 95 95

POSTAGE DUE STAMPS.

D 1. Arms of Luxembourg. D 2.

1907.

D 173. **D 1.** 5 c. black and green 12 5
D 174. 10 c. black and green 1·25 10
D 175. 12½ c. black & green 40 20
D 176. 20 c. black and green 40 25
D 177. 25 c. black and green 7·50 40
D 178. 50 c. black and green 40 40
D 179. 1 f. black and green 12 25

1920. Surch.

D 193. **D 1.** 15 on 12½ c. blk. & grn. 75 50
D 194. 30 on 25 c. blk. & grn. 95 75

1922.

D 221. **D 1.** 5 c. red and green .. 10 8
D 222. 10 c. red and green .. 10 8
D 223. 20 c. red and green .. 10 8
D 224. 25 c. red and green .. 10 10
D 225. 30 c. red and green .. 15 10
D 226. 35 c. red and green .. 65 5
D 227. 50 c. red and green .. 12 10
D 228. 60 c. red and green .. 25 8
D 229. 70 c. red and green .. 65 8
D 230. 75 c. red and green .. 50 12
D 231. 1 f. red and green .. 20 10
D 232. 2 f. red and green .. 65 50
D 233. 3 f. red and green .. 1·10 1·10

1946.

D 488. **D 2.** 5 c. green 5 5
D 489. 10 c. green 5 5
D 490. 20 c. green 5 5
D 491. 30 c. green 5 5
D 492. 50 c. green 5 5
D 493. 70 c. green 5 5
D 494. 75 c. green 5 5
D 495. 1 f. red 5 5
D 496. 1 f. 50 red 5 5
D 497. 2 f. red 5 5
D 498. 3 f. red 10 5
D 499. 5 f. red 15 8
D 500. 10 f. red 25 15
D 501. 20 f. red 55 70

MACAO O3

A Portuguese territory in China at the mouth of the Canton River.

1884. 1,000 reis = 1 milreis.
1894. 78 avos = 1 rupee.
1913. 100 avos = 1 pataca.

1884. "Crown" key-type insc. "MACAU".

1. **P.** 5 r. black .. .. 1·25 1·00
2. 10 r. orange .. .. 2·00 1·75
21. 10 r. green .. .. 1·60 1·25
3. 20 r. olive .. .. 3·00 2·25
27. 20 r. red .. .. 1·75 1·25
4. 25 r. red .. .. 1·10 1·00
22. 25 r. lilac .. .. 1·00 85
14. 40 r. blue .. .. 3·75 3·25
23. 40 r. yellow .. .. 2·10 1·60
15. 50 r. green .. .. 5·50 3·00
24. 50 r. blue .. .. 1·10 85
31. 80 r. grey .. .. 3·00 2·25
7. 100 r. lilac .. .. 1·75 1·10
17. 200 r. orange .. .. 3·00 1·75
9. 300 r. brown .. .. 2·10 1·75

1884. "Crown" key-type of Macao surch. **80 reis** in a circle.

19. **P.** 80 r. on 100 r. lilac .. 1·75 1·60

1885. "Crown" key type of Macao surch. thus **5 Reis** diagonally and with bar.

32. **P.** 5 r. on 25 r. red 85 75
33. 10 r. on 25 r. red .. .. 2·00 1·50
34. 10 r. on 50 r. green .. 9·00 7·50
35. 20 r. on 50 r. green .. 1·40 75
36. 40 r. on 50 r. green .. 6·00 4·75

1885. "Crown" key-type of Macao surch. with figure of value only and bar.

41. **P.** 5 on 25 r. red 90 80
42a. 10 on 50 r. green .. .. 1·00 85

1887. "Crown" key-type of Macao surch. horizontally with new value and bar.

43. **P.** 5 r. on 80 r. grey 90 80
46. 5 r. on 100 r. lilac .. 4·50 3·75
44. 10 r. on 80 r. grey .. 1·40 1·25
47. 10 r. on 200 r. orange .. 4·50 3·75
45. 20 r. on 80 r. grey .. 1·75 1·60

1887. Long vertical fiscal stamps surch. **CORREIO** and new value.

50. 5 r. on 10 r. green & brn. 5·00 3·75
51. 5 r. on 20 r. green & brn. 5·00 3·75
52. 5 r. on 60 r. green & brn. 5·00 3·50
53. 10 r. on 10 r. green & brn. 5·00 3·50
54. 10 r. on 60 r. green & brn. 5·00 3·50
55. 40 r. on 20 r. green & brn. 5·00 3·75

1888. "Embossed" key-type inscr. "PROVINCIA DE MACAU"

56. **Q.** 5 r. black .. .. 1·00 70
57. 10 r. green .. .. 1·00 70
58. 20 r. red .. .. 1·10 80
59a. 25 r. mauve .. .. 1·50 95
60. 40 r. brown .. .. 1·50 95
61. 50 r. blue .. .. 1·50 95
62. 80 r. grey .. .. 1·75 1·25
63. 100 r. brown .. .. 1·75 1·40
64. 200 r. lilac .. .. 2·75 1·75
65. 300 r. orange .. .. 3·00 2·00

1892. No. 64 surch. **30 30.**

73. **Q.** 30 on 200 r. lilac .. 2·00 1·75

1894. "Embossed" key-type of Macao surch. **PROVISORIO** and value in Chinese characters.

75. **Q.** 1 a. on 5 r. black .. 40 35
76. 3 a. on 20 r. red 90 40
77. 4 a. on 25 r. mauve .. 95 55
89. 5 a. on 30 on 200 r. lilac (No. 73) .. .. 2·25 2·10
78. 6 a. on 40 r. brown .. 80 55
79. 8 a. on 50 r. blue .. 1·75 1·00
80. 13 a. on 80 r. grey .. 1·60 1·10
81. 16 a. on 100 r. brown .. 1·60 1·10
82. 31 a. on 200 r. lilac .. 3·25 3·75
84. 47 a. on 300 r. orange .. 3·00 2·50

1894. "Figures" key-type inscr. "MACAU".

91. **R.** 5 r. yellow 60 40
92. 10 r. mauve 60 40
93. 15 r. brown 85 70
94. 20 r. lilac 85 70
95. 25 r. green .. .. 2·10 80
96. 50 r. blue .. .. 1·60 95
97. 75 r. red .. .. 1·60 95
98. 80 r. green .. .. 2·00 1·60
99. 100 r. brown on buff .. 1·60 1·00
100. 150 r. red on rose .. 2·25 1·75
101. 200 r. blue on blue .. 3·00 2·25
102. 300 r. blue on brown .. 3·50 3·00

1898. As Vasco da Gama types of Portugal but inscr. "MACAU".

104. ½ a. green 35 25
105. 1 a. red 35 25
106. 2 a. purple 50 35
107. 4 a. green 50 35
108. 8 a. blue 75 60
109. 12 a. brown .. .. 1·50 1·25
110. 16 a. brown .. .. 1·10 75
111. 24 a. yellow-brown .. 1·50 1·10

1898. "King Carlos" key-type inscr. "MACAU".

112. **S.** ½ a. grey 15 12
113. 1 a. yellow 15 12
114. 2 a. green 15 12
115. 2½ a. brown 35 30
116. 3 a. lilac 35 30
174. 3 a. grey 35 30
117. 4 a. green 30 25
175. 4 a. red 35 30
176. 5 a. brown 30 25
177. 6 a. brown 40 25
119. 8 a. blue 45 35
178. 8 a. brown 60 30
120. 10 a. blue 55 45
121. 12 a. red 85 75
179. 12 a. purple .. .. 2·50 1·75
122. 13 a. mauve 85 75
123. 15 a. green .. .. 3·00 2·50
124. 16 a. blue on blue .. 85 75
181. 18 a. brown on pink .. 1·75 1·50
125. 20 a. brown on yellow .. 1·00 80
126. 24 a. brown on yellow .. 1·00 85
127. 31 a. purple on pink .. 1·25 95
128. 47 a. blue on pink .. 1·75 1·60
183. 47 a. blue on yellow .. 2·10 1·75
129. 78 a. black on blue .. 2·10 1·75

1900. "King Carlos" key-type of Macao surch. **PROVISORIO** and new value.

132. **S.** 5 on 13 a. mauve .. 60 45
133. 10 on 16 a. blue on blue .. 70 50
134. 15 on 24 a. brown on yell. 70 50
135. 20 on 31 a. purple on pink 80 70

1902. Various types of Macao surch.

138. **Q.** 6 a. on 5 r. black .. 40 30
142. **R.** 6 a. on 5 r. yellow .. 40 30
136. **P.** 6 a. on 10 r. orange .. 1·00 80
137. 6 a. on 10 r. green .. 50 35
139. **Q.** 6 a. on 10 r. green .. 40 35
143. **R.** 6 a. on 10 r. mauve .. 60 35
144. 6 a. on 15 r. brown .. 40 30
145. 6 a. on 25 r. green .. 40 30
140. **Q.** 6 a. on 40 r. brown .. 60 45
146. **R.** 6 a. on 80 r. green .. 40 30
148. 6 a. on 100 r. brown on buff 40 30
149. 6 a. on 200 r. blue on blue 80 45
151. **V.** 18 a. on 2½ r. brown .. 95 70
153. **Q.** 18 a. on 20 r. red .. 95 70
162. **R.** 18 a. on 25 r. lilac .. 90 60
154a. **Q.** 18 a. on 25 r. mauve .. 5·00 3·00
163. **R.** 18 a. on 50 r. blue .. 90 60
165. 18 a. on 75 r. red .. 90 70
155. **Q.** 18 a. on 80 r. grey .. 6·50 5·50
156. 18 a. on 100 r. brown .. 95 75
166. **R.** 18 a. on 150 r. red on rose 90 70
158. **Q.** 18 a. on 200 r. lilac .. 5·50 5·00
160. 18 a. on 300 r. orange .. 1·60 1·10
167. **R.** 18 a. on 300 r. bl. on brn. 90 80

1902. "King Carlos" type of Macao optd. **PROVISORIO.**

168. **S.** 2 a. green 75 50
169. 4 a. green 85 55
170. 8 a. blue 85 55
171. 10 a. blue 85 55
172. 12 a. red .. .. 1·50 1·00

1905. No. 179 surch. **10 AVOS** and bar.

184. **S.** 10 a. on 12 a. purple .. 85 60

1910. "Due" key-type of Macao, but with words "PORTEADO" and "RECEBER" cancelled.

185. **W.** ½ a. green 45 35
186. 1 a. green 45 35
187. 2 a. grey 45 35

2. 3.

1911. Fiscal stamp surch. **POSTAL 1 AVO** and bar.

188. **2.** 1 a. on 5 r. brown yellow and black 35 30

1911. Stamps bisected and surch.

189. **S.** 2 a. on half of 4 a. red (No. 175) 60 50
190. 5 a. on half of 10 a. blue (No. 120) .. .. 1·75 1·60
191. 5 a. on half of 10 a. blue (No. 171) .. .. 1·75 1·60

1911.

192. **3.** 1 a. black .. .. 17·00 15·00
193. 2 a. black .. .. 22·00 20·00

1911. "King Carlos" key-type of Macao optd. **REPUBLICA.**

196. **S.** ½ a. grey 15 12
197. 1 a. orange 15 12
198. 2 a. green 15 12
199. 3 a. lilac 15 12
200. 4 a. red 30 25
201. 5 a. brown 35 25
202. 6 a. brown 35 25
203. 8 a. brown 35 25
204. 10 a. blue 35 25
205. 13 a. lilac 40 30
206. 16 a. blue on blue .. 40 30
207. 18 a. brown on pink .. 70 45
208. 20 a. brown on yellow .. 70 45
209. 31 a. purple on pink .. 70 45
210. 47 a. blue on yellow .. 85 55
211 78 a. black on blue .. 1·75 1·25

1913. Provisionals of 1902 surch. in addition with new value and bars over old value and optd. **REPUBLICA.**

212. **R.** 2 a. on 18 a. on 20 r. lilac (No. 162) 30 25
213. 2 a. on 18 a. on 50 r. blue (No. 163) 30 25
215. **R.** 2 a. on 18 a. on 75 r. red (No. 165) 30 25
216. 2 a. on 18 a. on 150 r. red on rose (No. 166) .. 30 25

1913. Provisionals of 1902 optd. **REPUBLICA.**

218. **Q.** 6 a. on 5 r. (No. 138) .. 60 40
284. **R.** 6 a. on 5 r. (No. 142) .. 35 30
217. **P.** 6 a. on 10 r. (No. 137) .. 1·75 1·25
285. **Q.** 6 a. on 10 r. (No. 139) .. 50 30
286. **R.** 6 a. on 10 r. (No. 143) .. 35 30
287. 6 a. on 15 r. (No. 144) .. 30 20
288. 6 a. on 25 r. (No. 145) .. 30 20
220. **Q.** 6 a. on 40 r. (No. 140) .. 75 55
289. **R.** 6 a. on 80 r. (No. 146) .. 30 20
291. 6 a. on 100 r. (No. 148) 25 15
292. 6 a. on 200 r. (No. 149) 25 20
283. **S.** 10 a. on 12 a. (No. 184) 25 15
293. **V.** 18 a. on 2½ r. (No. 151) 50 25
229. **Q.** 18 a. on 20 r. (No. 153) 1·00 80
295. **R.** 18 a. on 20 r. (No. 162) 70 45
296. 18 a. on 50 r. (No. 163) 70 45
298. 18 a. on 75 r. (No. 165) 80 45
230. **Q.** 18 a. on 100 r. (No. 156) 3·00 1·50
299. **R.** 18 a. on 150 r. (No. 166) 80 45
233. **Q.** 18 a. on 300 r. (No. 160) 1·25 85
300. **R.** 18 a. on 300 r. (No. 167) 80 45

1913. Stamps of 1911 issue surch.

252. **S.** ½ a. on 5 a. brown .. 35 25
255. 1 a. on 13 a. lilac .. 45 40
253. 4 a. on 8 a. brown .. 30 25

1913. Vasco da Gama stamps of Macao optd. **REPUBLICA,** and the 12 a. surch. **10 A.**

256. ½ a. green 35 25
257. 1 a. red 35 25
258. 2 a. purple 40 30
259. 4 a. green 35 25
260. 8 a. blue 40 30
261. 10 a. on 12 a. brown .. 85 75
262. 16 a. brown 50 45
263. 24 a. yellow-brown .. 75 55

1913. "Ceres" key-type inscr. "MACAU".

309. **U.** ½ a. olive 10 5
310. 1 a. black 15 10
311. 1½ green 10 5
307. 2 a. green 10 5
313. 3 a. orange 40 35
308. 4 a. red 25 20
315. 4 a. yellow 40 35
268. 5 a. brown 50 35
269. 6 a. violet 45 25
270. 8 a. brown 45 25
271. 10 a. blue 45 25
272. 12 a. brown 55 30
320. 14 a. mauve 85 70
273. 16 a. grey 85 50
274 20 a. brown .. .. 1·00 50

322. U. 24 a. green 85 75
323. 32 a. brown .. .. 1·10 95
275. 40 a. purple .. .. 1·00 50
324. 56 a. red .. .. 1·60 1·10
276. 58 a. brown on green .. 1·25 1·00
325. 72 a. brown .. .. 1·75 1·25
277. 76 a. brown on red .. 1·60 1·10
278. 1 p. orange on pink .. 2·25 1·50
326. 1 p. orange .. .. 2·00 1·60
279. 3 p. green on blue .. 5·50 2·75
327. 3 p. blue .. .. 5·50 4·50
328. 5 p. red .. .. 8·50 4·50

1915. Nos. 170/1 optd. **REPUBLICA.**
281. S. 8 a. blue 25 15
282. 10 a. blue 25 15

1919. Surch.
301. U. ½ a. on 5 a. brn. (No. 268) 1·00 85
330. 1 a. on 24 a. grn. (No. 322) 30 25
302. R. 2 a. on 6 a. on 25 r. green (No. 288) .. 2·25 2·00
303. 2 a. on 6 a. on 80 r. green (No. 289) .. 1·75 1·50
304. S. "2 avos" on 6 a. (No. 202) 1·75 1·60
331. U. 2 a. on 32 a. (No. 323).. 30 25
332. 4 a. on 12 a. (No. 272).. 30 25
333. 5 a. on 6 a. vio. (No. 269) 85 70
334. 7 a. on 8 a. brn. (No. 270) 35 25
335. 12 a. on 14 a. (No. 320) 35 25
336. 15 a. on 16 a. (No. 273) 35 25
338. 20 a. on 56 a. red (No. 324) 60 35

1934. As T 6 of Portuguese India ("Portugal" and San Gabriel).
338. 6. ½ a. sepia 5 5
339. 1 a. sepia 5 5
340. 2 a. green 5 5
341. 3 a. mauve 8 5
342. 4 a. black 20 12
343. 5 a. grey 20 12
344. 6 a. brown 20 12
345. 7 a. red 20 12
346. 8 a. blue.. .. 20 12
347. 10 a. red.. .. 30 20
348. 12 a. blue 30 20
349. 14 a. olive 30 20
350. 15 a. red 30 20
351. 20 a. orange 30 20
352. 30 a. green 70 40
353. 40 a. violet 70 40
354. 50 a. brown 70 40
355. 1 p. blue .. .. 1·50 85
356. 2 p. brown .. .. 2·25 1·60
357. 3 p. green .. .. 3·75 2·25
358. 5 p. mauve .. .. 6·50 4·25

1936. Air. Stamps of 1934 optd. **Aviao** and with Greek characters or surch. also.
359. 6. 2 a. green 55 45
360. 3 a. mauve 55 45
361. 5 a. on 6 a. brown .. 55 45
362. 7 a. red 55 45
363. 8 a. blue 55 45
364. 15 a. red .. .. 2·25 1·60

1938. As 1938 issue of Angola.
365. 3. 1 a. olive (postage) .. 5 5
366. 2 a. brown 5 5
367. 3 a. violet 12 10
368. 4 a. green 12 10
369. – 5 a. red 12 10
370. – 6 a. slate 12 12
371. – 8 a. purple 15 15
372. – 10 a. mauve 15 15
373. – 12 a. red 15 15
374. – 15 a. orange 15 15
375. – 20 a. blue 25 15
376. – 40 a. black 50 30
377. – 50 a. brown 50 30
378. – 1 p. red .. .. 1·25 85
379. – 2 p. olive .. .. 2·25 1·00
380. – 3 p. blue .. .. 3·00 1·75
381. – 5 p. brown .. .. 5·50 3·25
382. 8. 1 a. red (air) 15 12
383. 2 a. violet 15 12
384. 3 a. orange 20 12
385. 5 a. blue 30 25
386. 10 a. red 30 20
387. 20 a. green 50 30
388. 50 a. brown .. .. 1·00 60
389. 70 a. red .. .. 1·10 75
390. 1 p. mauve .. .. 1·75 85

1940. Surch.
391. 6. 1 a. on 6 a brn. (No. 344) 35 30
394. 2 a. on 6 a. brn. (No. 344) 30 25
395. 3 a. on 6 a. brn. (No. 344) 30 25
401. 4. 3 a. on 6 a. slate (No. 370) 5·00 4·50
396. 6. 5 a. on 7 a. red (No. 345) 30 25
397. 5 a. on 8 a. blue (No. 346) 30 25
398. 8 a. on 30 a. (No. 352) .. 55 50
399. 8 a. on 40 a. (No. 353) .. 55 50
400. 8 a. on 50 a. (No. 354) .. 55 50

5. A Residency, Uma. **6.** Mountain Fort.

1948.
410. 5. 1 a. brown 15 5
427. 1 a. violet 10 10
411. 6. 2 a. claret 8 8
428 2 a. yellow 10 5
412. – 3 a. purple 25 12
429. – 3 a. orange 15 10
413. – 8 a. red 15 8
430. – 8 a. grey 12 8
414. – 10 a. mauve 15 12
431. – 10 a. brown 15 5
415. – 20 a. blue 30 15
416. – 30 a. grey 60 20
432. – 30 a. blue 35 12
417. – 50 a. brown 85 20
433. – 50 a. olive 45 12
418. – 1 p. green .. .. 6·50 2·25
419. – 1 p. blue .. .. 2·10
434. – 1 p. brown 55 20
420. – 2 p. red .. .. 5·50 1·75
421. – 3 p. green .. .. 6·50 2·00
422. – 5 p. violet .. .. 8·50 3·75
DESIGNS—HORIZ. 3 a. Macao. 8 a. Praia Grande Bay. 10 a. Leal Senado Sq. 20 a. St Jerome Hill. 30 a. Street scene. 50 a. Goddess Ma. 5 p. Forest road. VERT. 1 p. Cerco Gateway. 2 p. Barra Pagoda. 3 p. Post Office.

1948. Honouring the Statue of Our Lady of Fatima. As T 13 of Angola.
423. 8 a. red .. .. .. 2·50 2·00

7. Globe and Letter. **8.** Arms and Dragon.

1949. U.P.U. 75th Anniv.
424. 7. 32 a. purple .. .. 21·00 5·00

1950. Holy Year. As Angola T 20/1.
425. 32 a. black 50 30
426. 50 a. red 60 35

1950.
435. 8. 1 a. yellow 15 15
436. 2 a. green 15 15
437. 10 a. maroon 15 15
438. 10 a. pink 15 15

9. F. Mendes Pinto. **10.** Junk.

1951.
439. 9. 1 a. blue 5 5
440. – 2 a. olive-brown .. 5 5
441. – 3 a. green 5 5
442. – 6 a. violet 12 5
443. – 10 a. brown 15 10
444. 9. 20 a. claret 25 5
445. – 30 a. purple-brown .. 25 5
446. – 50 a. orange-red .. 35 15
447. – 1 p. blue .. .. 1·25 15
448. – 3 p. black and blue .. 3·75 60
449. 10. 5 p. brown .. .. 7·00 2·00
DESIGNS—As T 9: 2 a., 10 a., St. Francis Xavier. 3 a., 50 a. J. Alvares. 6 a., 30 a. L. de Camoens. As T 10—HORIZ. 1 p. Native boat. VERT. 3 p. Junk.

1951. Holy Year. As Angola T 23.
450. 60 a. magenta 85 45

11. St. Raphael Hospital. **12.** St. Francis Xavier Statue.

1952. 1st Tropical Medicine Congress, Lisbon.
451. 11. 6 a. mauve and black .. 20 10

1952. St. Francis Xavier. 400 h Death Anniv.
452. 12. 3 a. black on cream .. 10 5
453. – 16 a. brown on buff .. 20 15
454. – 40 a. black on blue .. 70 50
DESIGNS: 16 a. Miraculous Arm of St. Francis. 40 a. Tomb of St. Francis.

13. Virgin. **14.** Honeysuckle.

1953. Missionary Art Exn.
455. 13. 8 a. brown and drab .. 5 5
456. 10 a. blue and brown .. 10 5
457. 50 a. green and drab .. 20 15

1953. Flowers.
458. 14. 1 a. yellow, green & red 5 5
459. – 3 a. purple and green .. 5 5
460. – 5 a. red, green & brown 12 10
461. – 10 a. purple, grn. & blue 15 10
462. – 16 a. yellow, grn. & brn. 12 5
463. – 30 a. pink, brown & grn. 15 5
464. – 39 a. grey, green & blue 15 5
465. – 1 p. yell., grn. & purple 1·50 50
466. – 3 p. red, sepia and grey 2·50 1·25
467. – 5 p. yellow, green & red 5·00 1·75
FLOWERS: 3 a. Myosotis. 5 a. Dragon Claw. 10 a. Nunflower. 16 a. Narcissus. 30 a. Peach blossom. 39 a. Lotus blossom. 1 p. Chrysanthemum. 3 p. Cherry blossom. 5 p. Tangerine blossom.

1954. Portuguese Postage Stamp Cent. As T 27 of Angola.
468. 10 a. brown, olive & green 30 25

1954. Sao Paulo. 4th Cent. As T 28 of Angola.
469. 39 a. black, yell. & orge. 12 5

15. Map. **16.** Exhibition and Atomic Emblems.

1956. Map multicoloured. Values in red, inscr. in brown. Colours given are of the backgrounds.
470. 15. 1 a. drab 5 5
471. 3 a. slate 5 5
472. 5 a. chocolate 5 5
473. 10 a. buff 5 5
474. 30 a. blue 12 5
475. 40 a. green 12 5
476. 90 a. grey 30 10
477. 1 p. 50 pink 55 25

1958. Brussels Int. Exn.
478. 16. 70 a. multicoloured .. 20 15

1958. 6th Int. Congress of Tropical Medicine. As T 35 of Angola.
479. 20 a. grn., brn., red & pink 70 5
DESIGN: 20 a. "Cinnamomum camphora" (plant).

17. Globe girdled by Signs of the Zodiac. **18.** Airliner over Ermida da Penha.

1960. Prince Henry the Navigator. 500th Death Anniv.
480. 17. 2 p. multicoloured .. 30 20

1960. Air. Centres multicoloured. Frame colours given.
481. – 50 a. on brown.. .. 25 12
482. 18. 76 a. blue on pink .. 55 20
483. – 3 p. black and blue .. 95 40
484. – 5 p. on lavender .. 1·50 75
485. – 10 p. red on yellow .. 3·00 1·50
VIEWS—Airliner over: 50 a. Praia Grande Bay. 3 p. Macao. 5 p. Mong Ha. 10 p. Praia Grande Bay (shore).

1962. Sport. As T 41 of Angola. Multicoloured.
486. 10 a. Hockey 5 5
487. 16 a. Wrestling 20 12
488. 20 a. Table-tennis .. 5 5
489. 50 a. Motor-cycling .. 15 10
490. 1 p. 20 Relay-racing .. 35 20
491. 2 p. 50 Badminton .. 80 70

1962. Malaria Eradication. Mosquito design as T 42 of Angola. Multicoloured.
492. 40 a. "A. hyrcanus sinensis" 25 15

1964. National Overseas Bank Cent. As Angola T 50 but view of Bank building, Macao.
493. 20 a. multicoloured .. 15 10

1965. I.T.U. Cent. As T 52 of Angola.
494. 10 a. multicoloured .. 30 15

1966. National Revolution. 40th Anniv. As T 56 of Angola, but showing different buildings.
495. 10 a. Infante D. Henrique Academy and Count of S. Januario Hospital .. 8 5

19. Drummer, 1548.

1966. Portuguese Military Uniforms. Mult.
496. 10 a. Type **19** 10 10
497. 15 a. Soldier, 1548 .. 20 10
498. 20 a. Arquebusier, 1649 .. 15 12
499. 40 a. Infantry officer, 1783 35 12
500. 50 a. Infantryman, 1783.. 35 12
501. 60 a. Infantryman, 1902.. 35 15
502. 1 p. Infantryman, 1903 .. 35 25
503. 3 p. Infantryman, 1904 .. 1·25 1·00

1967. Military Naval Assn. Cent. As T 53 of Angola, but different designs.
504. 10 a. O. E. Carmo and patrol-boat "Vega" .. 5 5
505. 20 a. Silva Junior and frigate "Don Fernando" 5 5

1967. Fatima Apparitions. 50th Anniv. As T 59 of Angola.
506. 50 a. multicoloured .. 20 15
DESIGN: 50 a. Arms of Pope Paul VI, and "Golden Rose".

1968. Pedro Cabral (explorer). 500th Birth Anniv. As T 63 of Angola. Multicoloured.
507. 20 a. Cabral's monument, Lisbon 15 10
508. 70 a. Cabral's statue, Belmonte 45 15
Both values are vert.

1969. Admiral Gago Coutinho. Birth Cent. Multicoloured. As T 65 of Angola.
509. 20 a. Admiral Coutinho with sextant 5 5

1969. Vasco da Gama (explorer). 500th Birth Anniv. As T 66 of Angola. Multicoloured.
510. 1 p. Church and Convent of Our Lady of the Reliquary, Vidigueira (vert.) .. 30 15

1969. Overseas Administrative Reforms. Cent. As T 67 of Angola.
511. 90 a. multicoloured .. 25 12

20. Bishop D. Belchoir Carneiro. **21.** Dragon Mask.

1969. Misericordia Monastery, Macao. 400th Anniv.
512. 20. 50 a. multicoloured .. 15 5

1969. Manoel I. 500th Birth Anniv. As T 68 of Angola.
513. 30 a. multicoloured .. 8 5
DESIGN: 30 a Facade of Mother Church, Golega.

1970. Marshal Carmona. Birth Cent. As T 70 of Angola. Multicoloured.
514. 5 a. Portrait wearing cap.. 5 5

1971. Chinese Carnival Masks. Multicoloured.
515. 5 a. Type 21 .. .. 5 5
516. 10 a. Lion mask 5 5

22. Portugese Traders at the Chinese Imperial Court. **24.** Seaplane "Santa Cruz" arriving at Rio de Janeiro.

23. Hockey. **25.** Lyre Emblem and Facade.

1972. Camoens' "Lusiads". 400th Anniv.
517. 22. 20 a. multicoloured .. 5 5

1972. Olympic Games, Munich.
518. 23. 50 a. multicoloured .. 15 10

1972. First Flight. Lisbon-Rio de Janeiro. 50th Anniv.
519. 24. 5 p. multicoloured .. 1·25 75

1972. Dom Pedro V Theatre, Macao. Cent.
520. 25. 2 p. multicoloured .. 50 25

1973. W.M.O. Centenary. As Type 77 of Angola.
521. 20 a. multicoloured .. 5 5

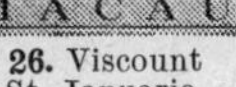

26. Viscount St. Januario.
27. " Chinnery and Painting " (self portrait).

1974. Viscount St. Januario Hospital. Cent. Multicoloured.
522. 15 a. Type 26 .. .. 5 5
523. 60 a. Hospital buildings of 1874 and 1974 .. .. 20 12

1974. George Chinnery (painter). Birth Bicent.
524. 27. 30 a. multicoloured .. 10 8

28. Macao-Taipa Bridge.

1975. Macao-Taipa Bridge. Inauguration. Multicoloured.
525. 20 a. Type 28 .. .. 5 5
526. 2 p. 20 View of Bridge from below 55 50

29. Rebel with Banner.

1975. 25th April 1974 Revolution. 1st Anniversary.
527. 29. 10 a. multicoloured .. 5 5
528. 1 p. multicoloured .. 35 35

CHARITY TAX STAMPS

The notes under this heading in Portugal, also apply here.

1919. Fiscal stamp optd. **TAXA DE GUERRA.**
C 305. 2 a. green 15 15
C 306. 11 a. green 40 35
The above was for use in Timor as well as Macao.

1925. Marquis de Pombal issue of Portugal but inscr. " MACAU ".
C 329. C 4. 2 a. red 12 10
C 330. – 2 a. red 12 10
C 331. C 5. 2 a. red 12 10

C 1. Mercy.

1930.
C 332. C 1. 5 a. purple on buff .. 5·50 5·50

1945. As Type C 1 but values in Arabic and Chinese numerals left and right, at bottom of design.
C 486. 1a. olive-green on green. 5 5
C 487. 2 a. purple on grey .. 5 5
C 410. 5 a. purple on buff .. 6·00 5·00
C 415. 5 a. brown on buff .. 5·50 5·00
C 416. 5 a. blue on blue.. .. 5·50 5·00
C 417. 10 a. green on green .. 3·00 1·00
C 470, 10 a. blue on green .. 20 12
C 418. 15 a. orange on buff .. 2·75 1·10
C 419. 20 a. red on cream .. 5·00 2·75
C 489. 20 a. chocolate on yellow 15 10
C 420. 50 a. lilac on lilac .. 5·00 2·75
C 472. 50 a. red on rose.. .. 2·75 1·75

NEWSPAPER STAMPS

1892. " Embossed " key-type of Macao surch. **JORNAES** and value in figures.
N 73. Q. 2½ r. on 10 r. green .. 15 15
N 74. 2½ r. on 40 r. brown .. 15 15
N 75. 2½ r. on 80 r. grey .. 15 15

1893. "Newspaper" key-type inscr. "Macau".
N 79. V. 2½ r. brown 20 15

1894. "Newspaper" key-type of Macao surch. ½ avo **PROVISORIO** and Chinese characters.
N 82. V. ½ a. on 2½ r. brown .. 35 30

POSTAGE DUE STAMPS

1904. " Due " key-type inscr. " MACAU ."
D 184. W. ½ a. green 15 5
D 185. 1 a. green 12 5
D 186. 2 a. grey 12 5
D 187. 4 a. brown 12 5
D 188. 5 a. orange 30 20
D 189. 8 a. brown 30 20
D 190. 12 a. brown 35 30
D 191. 20 a. blue 60 50
D 192. 40 a. red .. .. 1·25 1·10
D 193. 50 a. orange.. .. 2·00 1·75
D 194. 1 p. lilac .. .. 3·25 2·00

1911. " Due " key-type of Macao optd. **REPUBLICA.**
D 212. W. ½ a. green 10 8
D 213. 1 a. green 10 8
D 214. 2 a. grey 10 8
D 215. 4 a. brown 12 12
D 216. 5 a. orange 12 12
D 217. 8 a. brown 12 12
D 218. 12 a. brown 20 15
D 219. 20 a. blue 45 35
D 220. 40 a. red 75 65
D 290. 50 a. orange.. .. 1·25 1·10
D 291. 1 p. lilac .. .. 1·60 1·25

1925. Marquis de Pombal issue, as Nos. C 329/31 optd. **MULTA.**
D 329. C 4. 4 a. red 15 12
D 330. – 4 a. red 15 12
D 331. C 5. 4 a. red 15 12

1947. As Type D 1 of Portuguese Africa, but inscr. " MACAU ".
D 410. D 1. 1 a. purple 60 50
D 411. 2 a. violet 60 50
D 412. 4 a. blue 60 50
D 413. 5 a. brown 60 50
D 414. 8 a. purple.. .. 60 50
D 415. 12 a. brown.. .. 60 50
D 416. 20 a. green 85 75
D 417. 40 a. red .. .. 1·00 85
D 418. 50 a. yellow.. .. 1·75 1·50
D 419. 1 p. blue .. .. 1·75 1·50

1949. Postage stamps of 1934 surch. **PORTEADO** and new value.
D 424. 6. 1 a. on 4 a. black .. 60 50
D 425. 2 a. on 6 a. brown .. 60 50
D 426. 4 a. on 8 a. blue .. 60 50
D 427. 5 a. on 10 a. red .. 60 50
D 428. 8 a. on 12 a. blue .. 85 60
D 429. 12 a. on 30 a. green .. 1·10 85
D 430. 20 a. on 40 a. violet .. 1·10 85

1951. Optd. **PORTEADO** or surch. also.
D 439. 8. 1 a. yellow 15 12
D 440. 2 a. green 15 12
D 441. 7 a. on 10 a. pink .. 15 12

D 1.

1952. Numerals in red. Name in black.
D 451. D 1. 1 a. blue & grey-green 5 5
D 452. 3 a. brown & salmon 5 5
D 453. 5 a. slate and blue.. 5 5
D 454. 10 a. crim. & grey-bl. 5 5
D 455. 30 a. indigo & brown 8 5
D 456. 1 p. brn. & grey-brn. 25 5

MACEDONIA E3

GERMAN OCCUPATION.

Bulgarian Currency.

Македония

8. IX. 1944

1 лв.

(1.)

1944. Stamps of Bulgaria, 1940-44.
(a) Surch as T 1.
1. 1 l. on 10 st. orange.. .. 55 90
2. 3 l. on 15 st. blue 55 90
(b) Surch similar to T 1 but larger.
3. 6 l. on 10 st. blue .. .. 90 1·10
4. 9 l. on 15 st. green .. .. 90 1·40
5. 9 l. on 15 st. green .. .. 90 1·40
6. 15 l. on 4 l. black .. .. 2·00 2·75
7. 20 l. on 7 l. blue .. .. 2·40 3·00
8. 30 l. on 14 l. brown .. .. 3·25 4·00

MADAGASCAR AND DEPENDENCIES O3

A large island in the Indian Ocean off the E. Coast of S. Africa. The colony included Diego Suarez, Nossi Be, and St. Marie de Madagascar. On 14 Oct., 1958, the Malagasy Republic was founded and later issues are listed under that heading.

1889. Stamps of French Colonies " Commerce " type surch. with value in figures.
1. 9. 05 on 10 c. black on lilac.. £100 38·00
2. 05 on 25 c. black on red .. 90·00 32·00
4. 05 on 40 c. red on yellow .. 25·00 11·00
5. 5 on 10 c. black on lilac .. 32·00 15·00
6. 5 on 25 c. black on red .. 32·00 15·00
7. 15 on 25 c. black on red .. 25·00 14·00
3. 25 on 40 c. red on yellow .. 90·00 19·00

1891. Type-set design inscr. " POSTES FRANCAISES MADAGASCAR " and value in ornamental frame.
9. 5 c. black on green.. .. 11·00 3·75
10. 10 c. black on blue.. .. 13·00 4·25
11. 15 c. blue on grey.. .. 13·00 4·25
12. 25 c. brown on buff .. 1·60 1·10
13. 1 f. black on yellow .. £160 55·00
14. 5 f. black & lilac on grey .. £325 £160

1895. Stamps of France optd. **POSTE FRANCAISE Madagascar.**
15. 10. 5 c. green.. .. .. 1·10 30
16. 10 c. black on lilac .. 4·25 3·25
17. 15 c. blue.. .. .. 7·00 1·75
18. 25 c. black on red .. 9·50 1·75
19. 40 c. red on yellow .. 7·00 3·25
20. 50 c. red .. .. .. 9·50 5·00
21. 75 c. brown on orange .. 8·00 3·25
22. 1 f. olive .. .. .. 11·00 5·00
23. 5 f. mauve on lilac .. 16·00 6·50

1896. Stamps as above surch. with value in figures in oval.
24. 10. 5 c. on 1 c. black on blue £650 £325
25. 15 c. on 2 c. brn. on yell. £350 £160
26. 25 c. on 3 c. grey.. .. £450 £200
27. 25 c. on 4 c. clar. on grey £700 £300
28. 25 c. on 40 c. red on yell. £160 £120

1896. " Tablet " key-type inscr. " MADAGASCAR ET DEPENDANCES ".
1. D. 1 c. black on blue .. 5 5
2. 2 c. brown on yellow .. 5 5
3. 4 c. claret on grey .. 10 10
17. 5 c. green 10 12
6. 10 c. black on lilac .. 1·10 30
18. 10 c. red 15 8
7. 15 c. blue.. .. .. 2·00 5
19. 15 c. grey.. .. .. 15 8
8. 20 c. red on green .. 75 12
9. 25 c. black on red .. 1·10 60
20. 25 c. blue .. .. 3·25 2·75
10. 30 c. brown .. .. 1·00 50
21. 35 c. black on yellow .. 6·00 85
11. 40 c. red on yellow .. 1·00 20
12. 50 c. red on rose .. 1·60 20
22. 50 c. brown on blue .. 4·00 3·25
13. 75 c. brown on orange .. 30 25
14. 1 f. olive .. .. .. 1·40 35
16. 5 f. mauve on lilac .. 3·75 3·00

1902. " Tablet " key-type stamps as above surch. in figures and bar.
26. D. 0,01 on 2 c. brn. on yell. 85 85
28. 0,05 on 30 c. brown .. 1·10 1·10
23. 05 on 50 c. red on rose .. 35 35
30. 0,10 on 50 c. red on rose 1·10 1·10
24. 10 on 5 fr. mauve on lilac 3·25 2·25
32. 0,15 on 75 c. brn. on orge. 80 80
33. 0,15 on 1 fr. olive .. 1·40 1·40
25. 15 on 1 fr. olive 65 65

1902. Stamps of Diego-Suarez (" Tablet " type) surch. in figures and bar.
34. D. 0,05 on 30 c. (No. 46) .. 22·00 22·00
36. 0,10 on 50 c. (No. 48) .. £550 £550

1. Zebu and Lemur.
2. Transport in Madagascar.

1903.
38. 1. 1 c. purple 8 8
39. 2 c. grey 8 8
40. 4 c. brown 10 8
41. 5 c. green 85 20
42. 10 c. red.. .. .. 85 10
43. 15 c. red.. .. .. 2·10 10
44. 20 c. orange 65 20
45. 25 c. blue .. .. 5·00 60
46. 30 c. red .. .. 5·50 2·10
47. 40 c. lilac .. .. 5·00 65
48. 50 c. orange .. .. 8·50 3·75
49. 75 c. yellow .. .. 8·00 3·25
50. 1 f. green .. .. 8·50 5·00
51. 2 f. blue .. .. 10·00 5·00
52. 5 f. black .. .. 9·50 5·50

1908.
53. 2. 1 c. olive and violet .. 5 5
54. 2 c. olive and red .. 5 5
55. 4 c. brown and olive .. 5 5
56. 5 c. green and olive .. 5 5
90. 5 c. red and black .. 5 5
57. 10 c. brown and red .. 5 5
91. 10 c. olive and green .. 5 5
92. 10 c. purple and brown .. 5 5
93. 15 c. green and olive .. 5 5
58. 15 c. red and lilac .. 5 5
94. 15 c. red and blue .. 15 15
59. 20 c. brown and orange .. 5 5
60. 25 c. black and blue .. 20 8
95. 25 c. black and violet .. 5 5
61. 30 c. black and brown .. 30 15
96. 30 c. brown and red .. 5 5
97. 30 c. purple and green .. 5 5
98. 30 c. olive and green .. 5 5
62. 35 c. black and red .. 5 5
63. 40 c. black and brown .. 8 5
64. 45 c. black and green .. 5 5
99. 45 c. red 5 5
100. 45 c. claret and lilac .. 8 8
65. 50 c. black and violet .. 5 5
101. 50 c. black and blue .. 5 5
102. 50 c. yellow and black .. 5 5
103. 60 c violet on red .. 5 5
104. 2. 65 c. blue and black .. 8 8
66. 75 c. black and red .. 5 5
105. 85 c. red and green .. 5 5
67. 1 f. olive and brown .. 5 5
106. 1 f. blue 5 5
107. 1 f. green and mauve .. 90 90
108. 1 f. 10 green and brown 15 15
68. 2 f. olive and blue .. 65 10
69. 5 f. brown and violet .. 1·40 60

1912. " Tablet " key-type surch.
70. D. 05 on 15 c. grey.. .. 8 8
71. 05 on 20 c. red on green 8 8
72. 05 on 30 c. brown .. 8 8
73. 10 on 75 c. brn. on orge. 1·40 1·40
81. 0.60 on 75 c. brn. on orge. 1·00 1·00
82. 1 f. on 5 f. mauve on lilac 10 10

1912. Surch.
74. 1. 05 on 2 c. grey 5 5
75. 05 on 20 c. orange .. 5 5
76. 05 on 30 c. red 8 8
77. 10 on 40 c. lilac .. 10 10
78. 10 on 50 c. orange .. 40 40
79. 10 on 75 c. yellow .. 1·00 1·00
83. 1 f. on 5 f. black .. 11·00 11·00

1915. Surch. **5 c** and red cross.
80. 2. 10 c.+5 c. brown and red 8 8

1921. Surch. in figures.
81. 2. 0.30 on 40 c. black & brn. 5 5
82. 0.60 on 75 c. black & red 12 5

1921. Surch. **1 cent.**
84. 2. 1 c. on 15 c. red and lilac 5 5

1921. Surch. in figures and bars.
109. 2. 25 c. on 15 c. red & lilac 5 5
85. 25 on 35 c. black and red 50 40
86. 25 on 40 c. black & brown 50 30
87. 25 on 45 c. black & green 35 25
111. 25 c. on 2 f. olive & blue 5 5
112. 25 c. on 5 f. brown & vio. 5 5
113. 50 c. on 1 f. olive & brown 5 5
114. 60 on 75 c. violet on red 5 5
115. 65 c. on 75 c. black & red 5 5
116. 85 c. on 45 c. black & grn. 5 5
117. 90 c. on 75 c. red .. 5 5
118. 1 f. 25 on 1 f. blue .. 5 5
119. 1 f. 50 on 1 f. blue .. 5 5
120. 3 f. on 5 f. violet & green 15 15
121. 10 f. on 5 f. mauve & red 1·00 75
122. 20 f. on 5 f. blue & purple 1·25 1·00

3. Sakalava Chief.

4. Zebus.

15
MADAGASCAR

6. Betsileo Woman.
7. General Gallieni.

1930.
123. 7. 1 c. blue 5 5
124. 4. 1 c. green and blue .. 5 5
125. 3. 2 c. brown and red .. 5 5
177. 7. 3 c. blue 5 5
126. 3. 4 c. mauve and brown .. 5 5
127. 4. 5 c. red and green .. 5 5
128. – 10 c. green and red .. 5 5
129. 6. 15 c. red 5 5
130. 4. 20 c. blue and brown .. 5 5
131. – 25 c. brown and lilac .. 5 5
132. 6. 30 c. green 5 5
133. 3. 40 c. red and green .. 5 5
134. 6. 45 c. lilac 8 8
178. 7. 45 c. green 5 5
179. 50 c. brown 5 5
180. 60 c. mauve 5 5
136. 4. 65 c. mauve and brown 8 5
181. 7. 70 c. red.. .. .. 5 5
137. 6. 75 c. brown 10 5
138. 4. 90 c. red 12 8
182. 7. 90 c. brown 5 5
139. – 1 f. blue and brown .. 25 8
140. – 1 f. red 5 5
140a.– 1 f. 25 sepia and blue .. 20 8
183. 7. 1 f. 40 orange 5 5
141. 3. 1 f. 50 blue .. .. 1·00 12
142. 1 f. 50 red and brown .. 5 5
278. 1 f. 50 brown and red .. 5 5
184. 7. 1 f. 60 violet 5 5
143. 3. 1 f. 75 red and sepia .. 60 8
185. 7. 2 f. red 5 5
145. 3 f. green 70 25
186a. 3 f. grey 5 5
146. 3. 5 f. brown and mauve .. 8 8
147. 7. 10 f. orange 60 25
148. 3. 20 f. blue and brown .. 20 20
DESIGN—VERT. 10 c., 25 c., 1 f., 1 f. 25, Hova girl.

1931. "Colonial Exn." key-types, inscr. "MADAGASCAR".
149. E. 40 c. green 15 5
150. F. 50 c. mauve 40 8
151. G. 90 c. red.. .. .. 15 5
152. H. 1 f. 50 blue 35 5

8. Madagascar.

9. J. Laborde and Antananarivo Palace.

1935. Air.
153. 8. 50 c. red and green 10 10
154. 90 c. red and green 5
155. 1 f. 25 red and lake 5 5
156. 1 f. 50 red and blue 5 5
157. 1 f. 60 red and blue 5 5
158. 1 f. 75 red and orange 1·75 80
159. 2 f. red and blue 8 5
160. 3 f. red and orange 5 5
161. 3 f. 65 red and black 5 5
162. 3 f. 90 red and green 5 5
163. 4 f. red 7·50 30
164. 4 f. 50 red and black 4·50 25
165. 5 f. 50 red and olive 5 5
166. 6 f. red 5 5
167. 6 f. 90 red and purple 5 5
168. 8 f. red and purple 15 10
169. 8 f. 50 red and green 20 20
170. 9 f. red and olive 5 5
171. 12 f. red and brown 8 5
172. 12 f. 50 red and lilac 25 25
173. 15 f. red and orange 15 12
174. 16 f. red and olive-green 35 35
175. 20 f. red and brown 30 30
176. 50 f. red and blue 1·00 1·00

1937. Int. Exn. Paris. As Nos. 110/15 of Cameroun.
187. 20 c. violet 12 12
188. 30 c. green 12 12
189. 40 c. red 12 12
190. 50 c. brown 8 8
191. 90 c. red 25 20
192. 1 f. 50 blue 25 20

1938. Jean Laborde (explorer). 60th Death Anniv.
193. 9. 35 c. green 8 5
194. 55 c. violet 8 5
195. 65 c. red 8 5
196. 80 c. purple 8 5
197. 1 f. red 8 5
198. 1 f. 25 red 5 5
199. 1 f. 75 blue 15 5
200. 2 f. 15 brown 55 20
201. 2 f. 25 blue 5 5
202. 2 f. 50 brown 5 5
203. 10 f. green 12 8

1938. Int. Anti-Cancer Fund. As Type 10 of Cameroun.
204. 1 f. 75+50 c. blue 1·50 1·50

1939. New York World's Fair. As T 11 of Cameroun.
205. 1 f. 25 red 20 20
206. 2 f. 25 blue 20 20

1939. French Revolution. 150th Anniv. As T 16 of Cameroun.
207. 45 c.+25 c. green (post) 1·25 1·25
208. 70 c.+30 c. brown 1·25 1·25
209. 90 c.+35 c. orange 1·25 1·25
210. 1 f. 25+1 f. red 1·25 1·25
211. 2 f. 25+2 f. blue 1·25 1·25
212. 4 f. 50+4 f. black (air) 2·75 2·75

1942. Surch. **50** and bars.
213. 4. 50 on 65 c. mve. & brown 15 5

1942. Free French Administration. Optd. **FRANCE LIBRE** or surch. also.
214. 3. 2 c. brown & red (postage) 12 12
215. 7. 3 c. blue 11·00 11·00
216. 4. 5 c. on 1 c. green and blue 5 5
217. 9. 10 c. on 55 c. violet 15 15
218. 6. 15 c. red 1·40 1·10
219. 9. 30 c. on 65 c. red 8 8
220. 4. 50 c. on 5 c. on 1 c. green and blue 5 5
221. 50 c. on 65 c. mve. & brn. 5 5
222. 7. 50 c. on 90 c. brown 5 5
223. 4. 65 c. mauve and brown 8 8
224. 7. 70 c. red 5 5
225. 9. 80 c. purple 20 20
226. – 1 f. on 1 f. 25 sepia and blue (No. 140a) 30 30
227. 9. 1 f. on 1 f. 25 red 75 75
228. 7. 1 f. 40 orange 8 8
229. 2. 1 f. 50 on 1 f. blue 15 15
230. 3. 1 f. 50 blue 15 15
231. 1 f. 50 red and brown 15 15
232. 7. 1 f. 50 on 1 f. 60 violet 5 5
233. 3. 1 f. 50 on 1 f. 75 red & sep. 5 5
234. 9. 1 f. 50 on 1 f. 75 blue 5 5
235. 7. 1 f. 60 violet 8 8
236. 9. 2 f. on 2 f. 15 brown 12 10
237. 2 f. 25 blue 5 5
238. – 2 f. 25 blue (No. 206) 5 5
239. 9. 2 f. 50 brown 45 45
240. 2. 10 f. on 5 f. mauve and red 65 65
241. 9. 10 f. green 65 65
242. 2. 20 f. on 5 f. blue & purple 1·00 1·00
243. 3. 20 f. blue and brown £150 £130
244. 8. 1 f. on 1 f. 25 red & lake (air) 55 55
245. 1 f. 50 red and blue 70 70
246. 1 f. 75 red and orange 11·00 11·00
247. 8. 3 f. on 3 f. 65 red & black 12 12
248. 8 f. red and purple 20 20
249. 8 f. on 8 f. 50 red & green 12 12
250. 12 f. red and brown 40 40
251. 12 f. 50 red and lilac 25 25
252. 16 f. red and olive-green 55 55
253. 50 f. red and blue 45 45

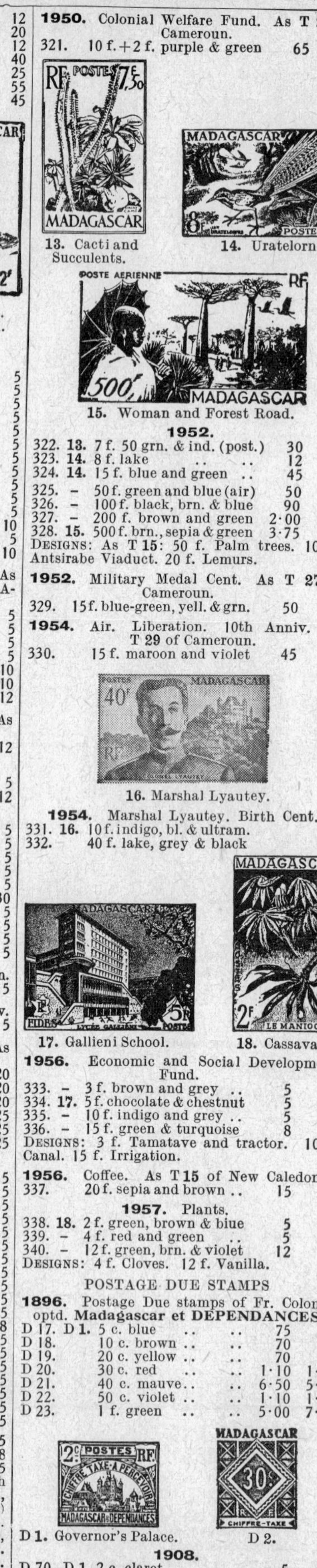

10. Traveller's Tree. 11. Gen. Gallieni and Typical View. 12. Gen. Gallieni.

1943. Free French Issue.
254. 10. 5 c. brown 5 5
255. 10 c. mauve 5 5
256. 25 c. green 5 5
257. 30 c. orange 5 5
258. 40 c. blue 5 5
259. 80 c. maroon 5 5
260. 1 f. blue 5 5
261. 1 f. 50 c. red 5 5
262. 2 f. yellow 5 5
263. 2 f. 50 c. blue 5 5
264. 4 f. blue and red 5 5
265. 5 f. green and black 10 10
266. 10 f. red and blue 10 5
267. 20 f. violet and brown 10 10

1943. Free French Administration. Air. As T 18 of Cameroun, but inscr. "MADAGASCAR".
268. 18. 1 f. orange 5 5
269. 1 f. 50 c. red 5 5
270. 5 f. maroon 5 5
271. 10 f. black 5 5
272. 25 f. blue 8 10
273. 50 f. green 20 10
274. 100 f. red 40 12

1944. Mutual Aid and Red Cross Funds. As T 19 of Cameroun.
275. 5 f.+20 f. green 10 12

1945. Eboue. As T 20 of Cameroun.
279. 2 f. black 5 5
280. 25 f. green 12 12

1945. Surch. with new value below bars.
282. 10. 50 c. on 5 c. brown 5 5
283. 60 c. on 5 c. brown 5 5
284. 70 c. on 5 c. brown 5 5
285. 1 f. 20 c. on 5 c. brown 5 5
276. 1 f. 50 c. on 5 c. brown 5 5
277. 1 f. 50 c. on 10 c. mauve 30 30
286. 2 f. 40 c. on 25 c. green 5 5
287. 3 f. on 25 c. green 5 5
288. 4 f. 50 c. on 25 c. green 5 5
289. 15 f. on 2 f. 50 c. blue 5 5

1946. Air. Victory. As T 21 of Cameroun.
281. 8 f. red 8 5

1946. French Protectorate. 50th Anniv.
318. 11. 10 f.+5 f. purple 5 5

1946. Air. From Chad to the Rhine. As T 23 of Cameroun.
290. 5 f. blue 20 20
291. 10 f. claret 20 20
292. 15 f. green 20 20
293. 20 f. brown 25 25
294. 25 f. violet 25 25
295. 50 f. red 25 25

1946.
296. – 10 c. green (postage) 5 5
297. – 30 c. orange 5 5
298. – 40 c. olive 5 5
299. – 50 c. purple 5 5
300. – 60 c. blue 5 5
301. – 80 c. green 5 5
302. – 1 f. sepia 5 5
303. – 1 f. 20 green 5 5
304. 12. 1 f. 50 red 5 5
305. 2 f. black 5 5
306. 3 f. purple 5 5
307. – 3 f. 60 red 8 8
308. – 4 f. blue 5 5
309. – 5 f. orange 5 5
310. – 6 f. blue 5 5
311. – 10 f. lake 8 5
312. – 15 f. brown 15 5
313. – 20 f. blue 20 5
314. – 25 f. brown 25 5
315. – 50 f. blue and red (air) 30 5
316. – 100 f. brown and red 65 8
317. – 200 f. brown and green 1·40 25

DESIGNS—VERT. 10 c. to 50 c. Native with spear. 6 f., 10 f. Gen. Duchesne. 15 f., 20 f., 25 f. Lt.-Col. Joffre. 100 f. (28×51 mm.) Allegory of flight. HORIZ. 60 c., 80 c. Zebus. 1 f., 1 f. 20 Sakalava man and woman. 3 f. 60, 4 f., 5 f. Betsimisaraka mother and child. 50 f. (49×28 mm.) Aerial view of Port of Tamatare. 200 f. (51×28 mm.) Aeroplane and map.

1948. Air. Discovery of Adelie Land, Antarctic. No. 316 optd. **TERRE ADELIE DUMONT D'URVILLE 1840.**
319. – 100 f. brown and red 8·50 7·00

1949. Air. U.P.U. As T 25 of Cameroun.
320. 25 f. red, pur., grn. & blue 80 65

1950. Colonial Welfare Fund. As T 26 Cameroun.
321. 10 f.+2 f. purple & green 65 65

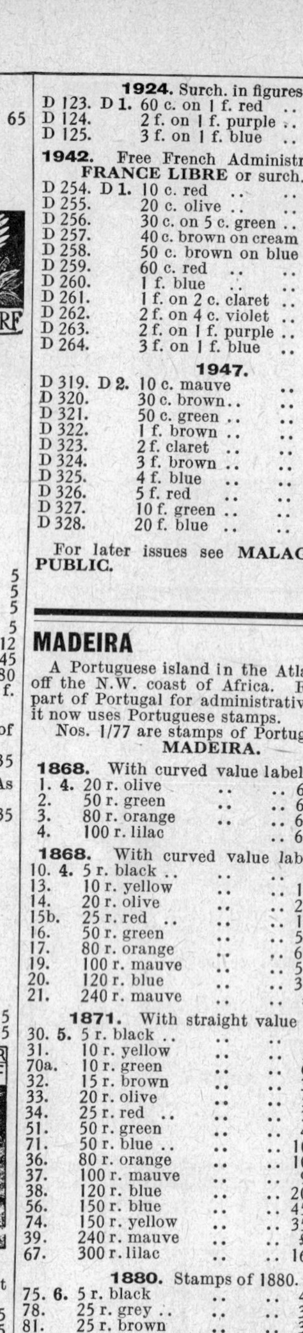

13. Cacti and Succulents. 14. Uratelornis.

15. Woman and Forest Road.

1952.
322. 13. 7 f. 50 grn. & ind. (post.) 30 5
323. 14. 8 f. lake 12 5
324. 14. 15 f. blue and green 45 5
325. – 50 f. green and blue (air) 50 5
326. – 100 f. black, brn. & blue 90 12
327. – 200 f. brown and green 2·00 45
328. 15. 500 f. brn., sepia & green 3·75 80

DESIGNS: As T 15: 50 f. Palm trees. 100 f. Antsirabe Viaduct. 200 f. Lemurs.

1952. Military Medal Cent. As T 27 of Cameroun.
329. 15 f. blue-green, yell. & grn. 50 35

1954. Air. Liberation. 10th Anniv. As T 29 of Cameroun.
330. 15 f. maroon and violet 45 35

16. Marshal Lyautey.

1954. Marshal Lyautey. Birth Cent.
331. 16. 10 f. indigo, bl. & ultram. 5
332. 40 f. lake, grey & black 5

17. Gallieni School. 18. Cassava.

1956. Economic and Social Development Fund.
333. – 3 f. brown and grey 5 5
334. 17. 5 f. chocolate & chestnut 5 5
335. – 10 f. indigo and grey 5 5
336. – 15 f. green & turquoise 8 5

DESIGNS: 3 f. Tamatave and tractor. 10 f. Canal. 15 f. Irrigation.

1956. Coffee. As T 15 of New Caledonia.
337. 20 f. sepia and brown 15 5

1957. Plants.
338. 18. 2 f. green, brown & blue 5 5
339. – 4 f. red and green 5 5
340. – 12 f. green, brn. & violet 12 5

DESIGNS: 4 f. Cloves. 12 f. Vanilla.

POSTAGE DUE STAMPS

1896. Postage Due stamps of Fr. Colonies optd. **Madagascar et DEPENDANCES.**
D 17. D 1. 5 c. blue 75 75
D 18. 10 c. brown 70 70
D 19. 20 c. yellow 70 70
D 20. 30 c. red 1·10 1·10
D 21. 40 c. mauve 6·50 5·50
D 22. 50 c. violet 1·10 1·10
D 23. 1 f. green 5·00 7·50

D 1. Governor's Palace. D 2.

1908.
D 70. D 1. 2 c. claret 5 5
D 71. 4 c. violet 5 5
D 72. 5 c. green 5 5
D 73. 10 c. red 5 5
D 74. 20 c. olive 5 5
D 75. 40 c. brown on cream 5 5
D 76. 50 c. brown on blue 5 5
D 77. 60 c. red 5 5
D 78. 1 f. blue 8 8

1924. Surch. in figures.
D 123. D 1. 60 c. on 1 f. red 30 30
D 124. 2 f. on 1 f. purple 8 8
D 125. 3 f. on 1 f. blue 8 8

1942. Free French Administration. Optd. **FRANCE LIBRE** or surch. also.
D 254. D 1. 10 c. red 10 10
D 255. 20 c. olive 10 10
D 256. 30 c. on 5 c. green 12 12
D 257. 40 c. brown on cream 10 10
D 258. 50 c. brown on blue 10 10
D 259. 60 c. red 10 10
D 260. 1 f. blue 10 10
D 261. 1 f. on 2 c. claret 55 55
D 262. 2 f. on 4 c. violet 20 20
D 263. 2 f. on 1 f. purple 10 10
D 264. 3 f. on 1 f. blue 10 10

1947.
D 319. D 2. 10 c. mauve 5 5
D 320. 30 c. brown 5 5
D 321. 50 c. green 5 5
D 322. 1 f. brown 5 5
D 323. 2 f. claret 5 5
D 324. 3 f. brown 5 5
D 325. 4 f. blue 5 5
D 326. 5 f. red 5 5
D 327. 10 f. green 8 8
D 328. 20 f. blue 15 15

For later issues see **MALAGASY REPUBLIC.**

MADEIRA E2

A Portuguese island in the Atlantic Ocean off the N.W. coast of Africa. Regarded as part of Portugal for administrative purposes, it now uses Portuguese stamps.

Nos. 1/77 are stamps of Portugal optd. **MADEIRA.**

1868. With curved value label. Imperf.
1. 4. 20 r. olive 60·00 45·00
2. 50 r. green 60·00 45·00
3. 80 r. orange 65·00 45·00
4. 100 r. lilac 65·00 45·00

1868. With curved value label. Perf.
10. 4. 5 r. black 3·00 3·00
13. 10 r. yellow 18·00 15·00
14. 20 r. olive 27·00 19·00
15b. 25 r. red 10·00 1·75
16. 50 r. green 50·00 42·00
17. 80 r. orange 65·00 25·00
19. 100 r. mauve 55·00 48·00
20. 120 r. blue 30·00 24·00
21. 240 r. mauve £100 65·00

1871. With straight value label.
30. 5. 5 r. black 1·60 95
31. 10 r. yellow 5·00 4·00
70a. 10 r. green 6·50 6·00
32. 15 r. brown 3·25 2·50
33. 20 r. olive 5·00 4·25
34. 25 r. red 2·25 1·00
51. 50 r. green 4·50 3·50
71. 50 r. blue 10·00 6·50
36. 80 r. orange 10·00 6·50
37. 100 r. mauve 9·00 6·00
38. 120 r. blue 20·00 9·00
56. 150 r. blue 45·00 35·00
74. 150 r. yellow 35·00 50·00
39. 240 r. mauve £160 80·00
67. 300 r. lilac 16·00 13·00

1880. Stamps of 1880.
75. 6. 5 r. black 4·00 2·75
78. 25 r. grey 3·75 1·10
81. 25 r. brown 3·75 1·10
77. 7. 25 r. grey 4·50 2·25

1898. Vasco da Gama. As Nos. 378/85 of Portugal.
134. 2½ r. green 40 25
135. 5 r. red 45 25
136. 10 r. purple 85 45
137. 25 r. green 60 30
138. 50 r. blue 75 60
139. 75 r. brown 1·75 1·50
140. 100 r. brown 1·00 85
141. 150 r. brown 1·50 1·25

For Nos. 134/41 with **REPUBLICA** opt., see Nos. 455/62 of Portugal.

1. Ceres.

ILLUSTRATIONS
British Commonwealth and all overprints and surcharges are FULL SIZE. Foreign Countries have been reduced to ¾-LINEAR.

1929. Funchal Museum Fund.
148. 1. 3 c. violet 5 5
149. 4 c. yellow 5 5
150. 5 c. blue 5 5
151. 6 c. brown 5 5
152. 10 c. red 5 5
153. 15 c. green 5 5
154. 16 c. brown 5 5
155. 25 c. claret 5 5
156. 32 c. green 5 5
157. 40 c. brown 5 5
158. 50 c. black 5 5
159. 64 c. blue-green 8 5
160. 80 c. brown 8 5
161. 96 c. red 8 5
162. 1 e. black 10 8

163. 1. 1 e. 20 red 12 12
164. 1 e. 60 blue 15 15
165. 2 e. 40 yellow 15 15
166. 3 e. 36 olive 25 25
167. 4 e. 50 red 35 35
168. 7 e. blue 60 60

CHARITY TAX STAMPS

The note under this heading in Portugal also applies here.

1925. Marquis de Pombal stamps of Portugal inscr. "MADEIRA".
C 142. C 4. 15 c. grey 20 15
C 143. – 15 c. grey 20 15
C 144. C 5. 15 c. grey 20 15

NEWSPAPER STAMP

1876. Newspaper stamp of Portugal optd. **MADEIRA.**
N 68. N 2. 2½ r. olive 60 40

POSTAGE DUE STAMPS

1925. Marquis de Pombal stamps as Nos. C 1/3 optd. **MULTA.**
D 145. C 4. 30 c. grey 20 15
D 146. – 30 c. grey 20 15
D 147. C 5. 30 c. grey 20 15

MAFEKING BC

A town in Bechuanaland. Special stamps issued by British garrison during Boer War.

1900. Stamps of Cape of Good Hope surch. **MAFEKING BESIEGED** and value.
1. 4. 1d. on ½d. green 35·00 14·00
2. 5. 1d. on ½d. green 40·00 15·00
3. 3d. on 1d. red 35·00 14·00
4. 4. 6d. on 3d. magenta £900 90·00
5. 1s. on 4d. olive £800 90·00

1900. Stamps of Bechuanaland Prot. (Queen Victoria) surch. **MAFEKING BESIEGED** and value.
6. 54. 1d. on ½d. red (No. 59) 25·00 14·00
12. 40. 3d. on 1d. lilac (No. 61) £250 18·00
13. 56. 6d. on 2d. green and red (No. 62) £325 20·00
9. 58. 6d. on 3d. purple on yell. (No. 63) £750 75·00
14. 62. 1s. on 6d. purple on red (No. 65) £500 28·00

1900. Stamps of Br. Bechuanaland surch **MAFEKING BESIEGED** and value.
10. 3. 6d. on 3d. lilac and black (No. 12) £120 20·00
11. 59. 1s. on 4d. green & brown (No. 35) £400 22·00
15 62. 1s. on 6d. purple on red (No. 36) £1000 £225
16. 65. 2s. on 1s. green (No. 37) £900 £100

1. Cadet Sergt.-Major Goodyear.

2. General Baden-Powell.

1900.
17. 1. 1d. blue on blue £300 £100
19. 2. 3d. blue on blue £450 £160

MALACCA BC

A British Settlement on the Malay Peninsula which became a state of the Federation of Malaya, incorporated in Malaysia in 1963.

100 cents = 1 dollar (Malayan).

1948. Silver Wedding. As T 5/6 of Aden.
1. 10 c. violet 10 12
2. $5 brown 7·50 8·50

1949. As T 17 of Straits Settlements.
3. 1 c. black 10 20
4. 2 c. orange 10 20
5. 3 c. green 12 35
6. 4 c. brown 10 15
6a. 5 c. purple 10 30
7. 6 c. grey 10 30
8. 8 c. red 25 35
8a. 8 c. green 15 40
9. 10 c. magenta 12 25
9a. 12 c. red 20 50
10. 15 c. blue 30 30
11. 20 c. black and green 25 50
11a. 20 c. blue 40 45
12. 25 c. purple and orange 20 35
12a. 35 c. red and purple 20 60
13. 40 c. red and purple 55 1·10
14. 50 c. black and blue 40 45
15. $1 blue and purple 90 1·10
16. $2 green and red 1·50 2·00
17. $5 green and brown 2·50 3·50

1949. U.P.U. As T 14/17 of Antigua.
18. 10 c. purple 10 15
19. 15 c. blue 10 15
20. 25 c. orange 30 40
21. 50 c. black 40 55

1953. Coronation. As T 7 of Aden.
22. 10 c. black and purple 10 10

1. Queen Elizabeth II.

1954.
23. 1. 1 c. black 5 10
24. 2 c. orange 5 10
25. 4 c. brown 8 10
26. 5 c. mauve 8 10
27. 6 c. grey 10 12
28. 8 c. green 15 15
29. 10 c. purple 12 5
30. 12 c. red 15 20
31. 20 c. blue 25 30
32. 25 c. purple and orange 30 15
33. 30 c. red and purple 40 35
34. 35 c. red and purple 50 30
35. 50 c. black and blue 50 35
36. $1 blue and purple 90 90
37. $2 green and red 2·25 3·50
38. $5 green and brown 6·50 6·50

1957. As Nos. 92/102 of Kedah but inset portrait of Queen Elizabeth II.
39. 1 c. black 5 5
40. 2 c. red 5 5
41. 4 c. sepia 5 5
42. 5 c. lake 5 5
43. 8 c. green 10 15
44. 10 c. sepia 10 5
45. 20 c. lake 20 10
46. 50 c. black and blue 30 15
47. $1 blue and purple 60 1·40
48. $2 green and red 1·50 2·50
49. $5 brown and green 3·00 5·00

2. Copra.

1960. As Nos. 39/49 but with inset picture of Melaka tree and Pelandok (mouse-deer) as in T 2.
50. 1 c. black 5 5
51. 2 c. red 5 5
52. 4 c. sepia 5 5
53. 5 c. lake 5 5
54. 8 c. green 8 10
55. 10 c. maroon 5 5
56. 20 c. blue 8 8
57. 50 c. black and blue 20 15
58. $1 blue and purple 40 40
59. $2 green and red 1·00 85
60. $5 brown and green 2·00 1·40

3. "Vanda hookeriana".

1965. As Nos. 166/72 of Johore but with Arms of Malacca inset and inscr. "MELAKA" as in T 3.
61. 3. 1 c. multicoloured 5 5
62. – 2 c. multicoloured 5 5
63. – 5 c. multicoloured 5 5
64. – 6 c. multicoloured 5 5
65. – 10 c. multicoloured 5 5
66. – 15 c. multicoloured 8 8
67. – 20 c. multicoloured 10 8

The higher values used in Malacca were Nos. 20/7 of Malaysia.

4. Lime Butterfly.

1971. Butterflies. As Nos. 175/81 of Johore, but with Arms of Malacca as in T 4. Inscr. "melaka".
70. – 1 c. multicoloured 5 5
71. – 2 c. multicoloured 5 5
72. – 5 c. multicoloured 5 5
73. 4. 6 c. multicoloured 5 5
74. – 10 c. multicoloured 5 5
75. – 15 c. multicoloured 5 5
76. – 20 c. multicoloured 8 8

The higher values in use with this issue are Malaysia Nos. 64/71.

MALAGASY REPUBLIC O3

The former areas covered by Madagascar and Dependencies were renamed the Malagasy Republic within the French Community on 14 Oct., 1958.

1958. Declaration of Human Rights. 10th Anniv. As T 5 of Comoro Islands.
1. 10 f. brown and blue 20 12

1959. Tropical Flora. As T 21 of French Equatorial Africa.
2. 6 f. green, brown and yellow 5 5
3. 25 f. red, green, yell. & blue 25 8

DESIGNS—HORIZ. 6 f. "Datura". 25 f. "Pointetia".

1. Malagasy Flag and Assembly Hall.

DESIGNS — VERT. 25 f. Malagasy flag on map of Madagascar. 60 f. Natives holding French and Malagasy flags.

1959. Proclamation of Malagasy Republic and "French Community" Commem. (60 f.).
4. 1. 20 f. red, green and purple 15 8
5. – 25 f. red, green and grey 20 8
6. – 60 f. red, blue, green & mar. 50 20

2. "Chionaema pauliani" (butterfly).

3. Reafforestation.

1960.
7. – 30 c. crimson, violet, yellow and blue (postage) 5 5
8. – 40 c. brown, choc. & green 5 5
9. – 50 c. turquoise and purple 5 5
10. 2. 1 f. red, purple and black 5 5
11. – 3 f. black, red and olive 5 5
12. – 5 f. emer., brown and red 5 5
13. – 6 f. yellow and green 5 5
14. – 8 f. black, emerald and red 8 5
15. – 10 f. yell.-grn., brown and blue-green 8 5
16. – 15 f. green and brown 12 5
17. – 30 f. multicoloured (air) 20 5
18. – 40 f. olive-brn. & blue-grn. 30 12
19. – 50 f. chocolate, yellow, chestnut and magenta 40 12
20. – 100 f. emerald, black, orange and grey-green 80 15
21. – 200 f. yellow and violet 1·50 40
22. – 500 f. brown, blue & green 4·00 95

BUTTERFLIES—HORIZ. As T 2: 30 c. "Colotis zoe". 40 c. "Acraea hova". 50 c. "Salamis duprei". 3 f. "Hypolimnas dexithea". LARGER. (48 × 27 mm.): 50 f. "Charaxes antamboulou". 100 f. "Chrysiridia madagascariensis". (27 × 48 mm.): 200 f. "Argema mittrei".

OTHER DESIGNS—As T 2—HORIZ. 5 f. Sisal. 8 f. Pepper. 15 f. Cotton. VERT. 6 f. Ylang ylang (vegetable). 10 f. Rice. LARGER (48 × 27 mm.): 30 f. Sugar-cane trucks. 40 f. Tobacco plantation. 500 f. Mandrare Bridge.

1960. Trees Festival.
23. 3. 20 f. brown, green & ochre 15 8

4.

5. Pres. Philibert Tsiranana.

1960. African Technical Co-operation Commission. 10th Anniv.
24. 4. 25 f. lake and green 25 20

1960.
25. 5. 20 f. chocolate and green 15 5

6. Young Athletes.

7. Pres. Tsiranana.

1960. 1st Youth Games, Tananarive.
26. 6. 25 f. choc., chest. & blue 30 15

1960.
27. 7. 20 f. black, red and green 15 5

1960. Independence. Surch. **+10 F FETES DE L'INDEPENDANCE.**
28. 7. 20 f. + 10 f. blk., red & grn. 30 20

8. Ruffed Lemur.

LEMURS:—POSTAGE—Vert. as T 8: 2 f. Gentle lemur. 12 f. Mongoose lemur. AIR (48 × 27 mm.); 65 f. Diademed sifaka. 85 f. Indris. 250 f. Coquerel's sifaka.

1961. Lemurs.
29. – 2 f. mar. & turq. (post.) 5 5
30. 8. 4 f. black, brown & myrtle 5 5
31. 12 f. brown and green 10 5
32. – 65 f. chestnut, sepia and myrtle (air) 55 20
33. – 85 f. black, sepia and green 65 25
34. – 250 f. mar., blk. & bl.-grn. 1·90 1·00

9. Diesel Train.

11. Ranomafana.

10. U.N. and Malagasy Flags, and Govt. Building. Tananarive.

1962.
35. 9. 20 f. myrtle 15 5
36. – 25 f. blue 20 5

DESIGN: 25 f. President Tsirianana Bridge.

1962. Admission into U.N.O.
37. 10. 25 f. bl. grn., mar. & red 20 15
38. 85 f. bl., red, mar. & grn. 65 45

1962. Malaria Eradication. As T 45 of Cameroun.
39. 25 f. + 5 f. green 25 20

1962. Tourist Publicity.
40. 11. 10 f. maroon, myrtle and blue (postage) 5 5
41. – 30 f. mar., blue & myrtle 15 8
42. – 50 f. ultram., myrtle & mar. 30 12
43. – 60 f. myrtle, mar. & blue 40 20
44. – 100 f. chestnut, myrtle and blue (air) 65 35

DESIGNS—As T 11: 30 f. Tritriva Lake. 50 f. Foulpointe. 60 f. Fort Dauphin. VERT. (27 × 47½ mm.): 100 f. Boeing airliner over Nossi-Be.

12. G.P.O., Tamatave.

1962. Stamp Day.
45. 12. 25 f. + 5 f. brown, myrtle and blue 25 20

13. Malagasy and U.N.E.S.C.O. Emblems.

14. Hydro-electric Station.

1962. U.N.E.S.C.O. Conf. on Higher Education in Africa, Tananarive.
46. 13. 20 f. black, green and red 15 8

1962. Union of African and Malagasy States. 1st Anniv. As No. 328 of Cameroun.
47. 47. 30 f. bronze-green .. 25 20

1962. Malagasy Industrialisation.
48. 14. 5 f. yell., blk., blue & red 5 5
49. – 8 f. blue, blk., yell. & red 5 5
50. – 10 f. blk., chest., buff & bl. 8 5
51. – 15 f. chestnut, black & blue 10 5
52. – 20 f. red, chestnut, brown, black and blue .. 15 8
DESIGNS—HORIZ. 8 f. Atomic plant. 15 f. Tanker "Gasikara". 20 f. Hertzian aerials at Tananarive-Fianarantsoa. VERT. 10 f. Oilwell.

15. Globe and Factory.

1963. Int. Fair, Tamatave.
53. 15. 25 f. orange and black .. 20 5

1963. Freedom from Hunger. As T 51 of Cameroun.
54. 25 f.+5 f. lake, brown & red 25 25

16. Boeing Airliner.

1963. Air. Malagasy Commercial Aviation.
55. 16. 500 f. blue, red and green 3·25 1·00

17. Central Post Office, Tananarive. 18. "Alectroenas madagascariensis".

1963. Stamp Day.
56. 17. 20 f.+5 f. brown-red and turquoise 20 20

1963. Malagasy Birds and Orchids (8 f. to 12 f.). Multicoloured. (a) Postage as T 18.
57. 1 f. Type 18 .. .. 5 5
58. 2 f. "Coua caerulea" 5 5
59. 3 f. "Foudia madagascariensis" .. 5 5
60. 6 f. "Ispidina madagascariensis" .. 5 5
61. 8 f. "Gastrorchis humblotii" .. 5 5
62. 10 f. "Eulophiella roempleriana" 5 5
63. 12 f. "Angraecum sesquipedale" 8 8
(b) Air. Horiz. (49½ × 28 mm.).
64. 40 f. "Euryceros prevostii" 20 12
65. 100 f. "Atelornis pittoides" 55 30
66. 200 f. "Lophotibis cristata" .. .. 1·25 50

19. Centenary Emblem and Map. 20. U.P.U. Monument, Berne and Malagasy Map.

1963. Red Cross Cent.
67. 19. 30 f. red, grey, violet-blue and black 30 25

1963. Air. African and Malagasy Posts and Telecommunications Union. As T 10 of Central African Republic.
68. 85 f. red, buff, bl.-grn. & grn. 60 50

1963. Air. Malagasy's admission to U.P.U. 2nd Anniv.
69. 20. 45 f. blue, red & turquoise 30 15
70. 85 f. blue, red and violet 55 30

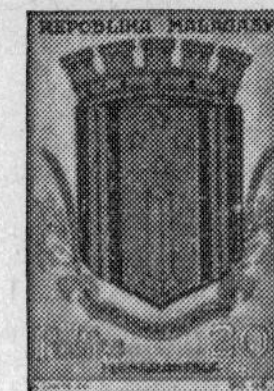

21. Arms of Fianarantsoa. 22. Flame, Globe and Hands.

1963. Town Arms (1st series). Multicoloured.
71. 1 f. 50 Antsirabe 5 5
72. 5 f. Antalaha 5 5
73. 10 f. Tulear 5 5
74. 15 f. Majunga 10 8
75. 20 f. Type 21 .. .. 12 8
75a. 20 f. Manajary 8 5
76. 25 f. Tananarive 15 8
76a. 30 f. Nossi Be 12 8
77. 50 f. Diego-Suarez 30 25
77a. 90 f. Antsohihy 35 25
See also Nos. 174/7 and 208/9.

1963. Declaration of Human Rights. 15th Anniv.
78. 22. 60 f. ochre, bronze & mag. 40 25

23. Met. Station, Tananarive.

1964. Air. World Meteorological Day.
79. 23. 90 f. chestnut, blue & grey 80 65

24. Postal Cheques and Savings Bank, Tananarive. 25. Scouts beside Camp-fire.

26. Symbolic Bird and Globe within "Egg". 27. Statuette of Woman.

1964. Stamp Day.
80. 24. 25 f.+5 f. brn., bl. & grn. 20 20

1964. Malagasy Scout Movement. 40th Anniv.
81. 25. 20 f. yell., carm., red & blk. 12 8

1964. "Europafrique".
82. 26. 45 f. brown and green 30 20

1964. Malagasy Art.
83. 27. 6 f. brown, blue & indigo (postage) 5 5
84. – 30 f. choc., bistre & grn. 20 8
85. – 100 f. choc., red & vio. (air) 70 40
DESIGNS: 30 f. Statuette of squatting vendor. (27 × 48½): 100 f. Statuary of peasant family, ox and calf.

1964. French, African and Malagasy Co-operation. As T 500 of France.
86. 25 f. choc., chestnut & black 15 8

28. Tree on Globe. 29. Cithern.

1964. University of Malagasy Republic.
87. 28. 65 f. black, red & green .. 40 25

1965. Malagasy Musical Instruments.
88. – 3 f. chocolate, blue and magenta (postage) .. 5 5
89. 29. 6 f. sepia, purple & green 5 5
90. – 8 f. brown, black & green 5 5
91. – 25 f. multicoloured .. 20 15
92. – 200 f. chocolate, orange and green (air) .. 1·25 70
DESIGNS—As T 29: 3 f. Kabosa (lute). 8 f. Hazolahy (sacred drum). LARGER—VERT. (35½ × 48 mm.): 25 f. "Valiha Player" (after E. Ralambo). (27 × 48 mm.): 200 f. Bara violin.

30. Foulpointe Post Office.

1965. Stamp Day.
93. 30. 20 f. chest., green & orge. 15 8

31. I.T.U. Emblem and Symbols. 32. J.-J. Rabearivelo (poet).

1965. I.T.U. Cent.
94. 31. 50 f. green, blue and red 55 25

1965. Rabearivelo Commem.
95. 32. 40 f. brown and orange 25 15

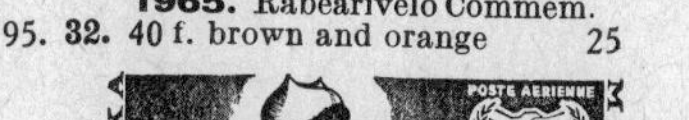

33. Nurse weighing Baby.

1965. Air. Int. Co-operation Year.
96. 33. 50 f. black, bistre & blue 35 20
97. – 100 f. purple, choc. & blue 70
DESIGN: 100 f. Boy and girl.

34. Pres. Tsiranana. 35. Bearer.

1965. Pres. Tsiranana's 55th Birthday.
98. 34. 20 f. multicoloured .. 12 5
99. 25 f. multicoloured .. 15 8

1965. Postal Transport.
102. – 3 f. violet, blue & brown 5 5
103. – 4 f. blue, brown & green 5 5
104. 35. 10 f. multicoloured .. 8 5
105. – 12 f. multicoloured .. 10 5
106. – 20 f. multicoloured .. 15 8
107. – 25 f. multicoloured .. 20 8
108. – 30 f. red, brown & blue 20 12
109. – 65 f. brn., blue & violet 40 25
DESIGNS—HORIZ. 3 f. Early car. 4 f. Filanzane (litter). 12 f. Pirogue. 20 f. Horse-drawn mail-cart. 25 f. Bullock cart. 30 f. Early railway postal carriage. 65 f. Hydrofoil, Betsiboka.

36. Diseased Hands.

1966. World Leprosy Day.
110. 36. 20 f. maroon, red & grn. 12 8

37. Planting Trees.

1966. Reafforestation Campaign.
111. 37. 20 f. violet, brn. & turq. 15 8

38. "Cicindelidae chaetodera andriana."

1966. Malagasy Insects. Multicoloured.
112. 1 f. Type 38 .. .. 5 5
113. 6 f. "Mantodea tisma freiji" 5 5
114. 12 f. "Cerambycini mastododera nodicollis" .. 8 5
115. 45 f. "Trachelophorus giraffa" 20 12

40. Madagascar 1 c. Stamp of 1903. 41. Betsileo Dance.

1966. Stamp Day.
116. 40. 25 f. bistre and red .. 15 12

1966. Folk Dances. Multicoloured.
117. 2 f. Bilo Sakalava dance (vert.) (postage) .. 5 5
118. 5 f. Type 41 .. .. 5 5
119. 30 f. Antandroy dance (vert.) 20 10
120. 200 f. Southern Malagasy dancer (air) .. .. 1·10 50
121. 250 f. Sakalava Net Dance 1·50 70
Nos. 120/1 are size 27 × 48 mm.

42. "Tree" of Emblems.

1966. O.C.A.M. Conf., Tananarive.
122. 42. 25 f. multicoloured .. 15 5
The above was issued with "Janvier 1966" obliterated by bars, and optd. **"JUIN 1966"**.

43. Singing Anthem. 44. U.N.E.S.C.O. Emblem.

46. Harvesting Rice. 45. Lions Emblem.

1966. National Anthem.
123. 43. 20 f. brown, mag. & grn. 8 5

1966. U.N.E.S.C.O. 20th Anniv.
124. 44. 30 f. indigo, bistre & red 20 10

1967. Lions Int. 50th Anniv.
125. 45. 30 f. multicoloured .. 20 8

1967. Int. Rice Year.
126. 46. 20 f. multicoloured .. 12 5

47. Adventist Temple, Tanambao-Tamatave.

1967. Religious Buildings. (1st series).
127. 47. 3 f. ochre, blue and green 5 5
128. – 5 f. lilac, purple & green 5 5
129. – 10 f. maroon, blue & grn. 5 5
BUILDINGS.—VERT. 5 f. Catholic Cathedral, Tananarive. HORIZ. 10 f. Mosque, Tamatave.
See also Nos. 148/50.

48. Raharisoa at Piano.

1967. Norbert Raharisoa (composer). 4th Death Anniv.
130. 48. 40 f. multicoloured .. 25 8

49. Jean Raoult's Flight of 1911.

1967. "History of Malagasy Aviation".
131. 49. 5 f. brown, blue and green (postage) .. 5 5
132. – 45 f. black, blue & brn. 25 12
133. – 500 f. black, blue and ochre (air) .. .. 2·75 1·10
DESIGNS: 45 f. Bernard Bougault and flying-boat, 1926. (48 × 27 mm.): 500 f. Dagnaux-Dufert and biplane, 1927.

50. Ministry of Communications, Tananarive.

51. Church, Torch and Map.

1967. Stamp Day.
134. 50. 20 f. green, blue & orge. 10 5

1967. Air. U.A.M.P.T. 5th Anniv. As T 55 of Central African Republic.
135. 100 f. magenta, bistre & red 55 30

1967. Malagasy Lutheran Church. Cent.
136. 51. 20 f. multicoloured .. 12 5

52. Map and Decade Emblem.

53. Woman's Face and Scales of Justice.

1967. Int. Hydrological Decade.
137. 52. 90 f. brown, red & blue 50 25

1967. Women's Rights Commission.
138. 53. 50 f. blue, ochre & green 25 15

54. Human Rights Emblem.

55. Congress and W.H.O. Emblems.

1968. Human Rights Year.
139. 54. 50 f. vermilion, green and black 25 15

1968. Air. 20th Anniv. of W.H.O. and Int. Medical Sciences Congress, Tananarive.
140. 55. 200 f. red, blue & ochre 1·00 55

56. International Airport, Tananarive-Ivato.

1968. Air. Stamp Day.
141. 56. 500 f. blue, green & brn. 2·50 1·25

1968. Nos. 33 and 38 surch.
142. 10. 20 f. on 85 f. (postage) 10 5
143. – 20 f. on 85 f. (No. 33)(air) 10 5

57. "Industry and Construction".

59. Isotry Protestant Church, Fitiavana, Tananarive.

58. Church and Open Bible.

1968. Five-Year Plan. (1st issue).
144. 57. 10 f. plum, red & green 5 5
145. – 20 f. black, red & green 12 8
146. – 40 f. ind., choc. & ultram. 25 10
DESIGNS—VERT. 20 f. "Agriculture". HORIZ. 40 f. "Transport".
See also Nos. 156/7.

1968. Christianity in Madagascar. 150th Anniv.
147. 58. 20 f. multicoloured .. 12 5

1968. Religious Buildings.
148. 59. 4 f. chocolate, grn. & red 5 5
149. – 12 f. brown, blue & violet 5 5
150. – 50 f. indigo, blue & grn. 20 15
DESIGNS: 12 f. Catholic Cathedral, Fianarantsoa. 50 f. Aga Khan Mosque, Tananarive.

60. President Tsiranana and Wife.

61. Cornucopia, Coins and Map.

1968. Republic. 10th Anniv.
151. 60. 20 f. brown, red & yell. 12 5
152. 30 f. brown, red and blue 15 8

1968. Malagasy Savings Bank. 50th Anniv.
154. 61. 20 f. multicoloured .. 12 5

62. "Dance of the Whirlwind".

1968. Air.
155. 62. 100 f. multicoloured .. 45 25

63. Malagasy Family.

1968. Five Year Plan. (2nd issue).
156. 63. 15 f. red, yellow & blue 8 5
157. – 45 f. multicoloured .. 20 12
DESIGN—VERT. 45 f. Allegory of "Achievement".

1968. Air. "Philexafrique" Stamp Exn., Abidjan (1969) (1st issue), as Type 109 of Cameroun.
158. 100 f. multicoloured .. 75 75
DESIGN: 100 f. "Young Woman sealing a Letter". (J. B. Santerre.)

1969. Air. "Philexafrique" Stamp Exn., Abidjan, Ivory Coast (2nd issue). As Type 110 of Cameroun.
159. 50 f. red, green and drab 45 35
DESIGN: 50 f. Malagasy Arms, map and Madagascar stamp of 1946.

64. "Queen Adelaide receiving Malagasy Mission, London" (1836–37).

1969.
160. 64. 250 f. multicoloured .. 1·10 60

65. Hand with Spanner, Cogwheels and I.L.O. Emblem.

1969. Int. Labour Organization. 50th Anniv.
161. 65. 20 f. multicoloured .. 10 5

66. Post and Telecommunications Building, Tananarive.

1969. Stamp Day.
162. 66. 30 f. multicoloured .. 15 8

67. Map, Steering Wheel and Vehicles.

68. President Tsiranana making Speech.

1969. Malagasy Motor Club. 20th Anniv.
163. 67. 65 f. multicoloured .. 30 20

1969. President Tsiranana's Assumption of Office. 10th Anniv.
164. 68. 20 f. multicoloured .. 10 5

69. Bananas.

70. Start of Race and Olympic Flame.

1969. Fruits.
165. 69. 5 f. green, brown & blue 5 5
166. – 15 f. vermilion, myrtle and green 8 5
DESIGN: 15 f. Lychees.

1969. Olympic Games, Mexico (1968).
167. 70. 15 f. brown, red & green 8 5

71. "Malagasy Seashore, East Coast" (A. Razafinjohany).

1969. Air. Paintings by Malagasy Artists. Multicoloured.
168. 100 f. Type 71 .. .. 45 35
169. 150 f. "Sunset on the High Plateaux (H. Ratovo) .. 70 35

72. Betsimisaraka Dwellings, East Coast.

1969. Malagasy Traditional Dwellings (1st series).
170. – 20 f. red, blue and grn. 8 5
171. – 20 f. brn., red and blue 8 5
172. – 40 f. red, blue & indigo 20 8
173. 72. 60 f. mar., grn. & blue .. 30 12
HOUSES—HORIZ. 20 f. (No. 170), Tsimihety hut, East Coast. VERT. 20 f. (No. 171), Betsileo house, High Plateaux. 40 f. Imerina House, High Plateaux.
See also Nos. 205/6.

73. Ambalavao Arms.

1970. Town Arms (2nd series). Multicoloured.
174. 10 f. Type 73 .. .. 5 5
175. 25 f. Morondava 10 5
176. 25 f. Ambatondrazaka .. 10 5
177. 80 f. Tamatave 45 20

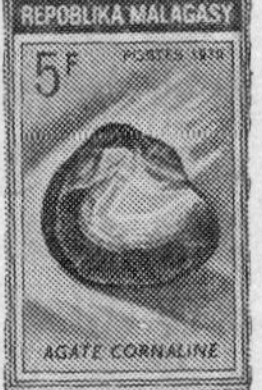

74. Agate.

75. U.N. Emblem and Symbols.

1970. Semi-precious Stones. Multicoloured.
178. 5 f. Type 74 .. .. 5 5
179. 20 f. Ammonite 10 5

1970. New U.P.U. Headquarters Building, Berne. As T 127 of Cameroun.
180. 20 f. ultram., brn. & mve. 10 5

1970. United Nations. 25th Anniv.
181. 75. 50 f. black, blue & orge 20 15

76. Astronaut and Module on Moon.

1970. Air. "Apollo II" Moon-landing 1st Anniv.
182. 76. 75 f. green, slate and blue. 35 25

77. Malagasy Fruits.

1970.
183. **77.** 20 f. multicoloured .. 10 5

78. "Volute delessertiana".

1970. Sea-shells (1st series). Multicoloured.
184. 5 f. Type **78** 5 5
185. 10 f. "Murex tribulus".. 5 5
186. 20 f. "Spondylus" .. 5 5

79. Aye-aye

1970. Int. Nature Conservation Conference, Tananarive.
187. **79.** 20 f. multicoloured .. 10 5

80. Boeing "737" in Flight.

1970. Air.
188. **80.** 200 f. red, green & blue 90 50

81. Pres. Tsiranana. **81a.** Calcite.

1970. Pres. Tsiranana's 60th Birthday.
189. **81.** 30 f. brown and green.. 15 5

1971. Minerals Multicoloured.
190. 12 f. Type **81a** 5 5
191. 15 f. Quartz 8 8

82. Soap Works, Tananarive.

1971. Malagasy Industries.
192. **82.** 5 f. multicoloured .. 5 5
193. – 15 f. black, brown & blue 5 5
194. – 50 f. multicoloured .. 25 12
DESIGNS: 15 f. Chrome works, Comina-Andriamena. 50 f. Textile complex, Sotema-Majunga.

83. Globe and Emblems.

1971. Council Meeting of Common Market Countries with African and Malagasy Associated States, Tananarive.
195. **83.** 5 f. multicoloured .. 5 5

MINIMUM PRICE

The minimum price quoted is 5p which represents a handling charge rather than a basis for valuing common stamps. For further notes about prices see introductory pages.

84. Rural Mobile Post Office. **85.** Gen. De Gaulle.

1971. Stamp Day.
196. **84.** 25 f. multicoloured .. 12 8

1971. Death of Gen. Charles De Gaulle (1970).
197. **85.** 30 f. blk., red and blue.. 15 8

86. Palm Beach Hotel, Nossi-Be. **87.** Forestry Emblem.

1971. Malagasy Hotels.
198. **86.** 25 f. multicoloured .. 12 5
199. – 65 f. brn., blue & green 30 15
DESIGN: 65 f. Hilton Hotel, Tananarive.

1971. Forest Preservation Campaign.
200. **87.** 3 f. multicoloured .. 5 5

88. Jean Ralaimongo. **89.** Vezo Dwellings.

1971. Air. Malagasy Celebrities.
201. **88.** 25 f. brn., red & orange 12 8
202. – 65 f. brn., myrtle-green and green 30 15
203. – 100 f. brown, ultram. and blue 45 30
CELEBRITIES: 65 f. Albert Sylla. 100 f. Joseph Ravoahangy Andrianavalona.

1971. Air. African and Malagasy Posts and Telecommunications Union. 10th Anniv. As T **153** of Cameroun. Multicoloured.
204. 100 f. U.A.M.P.T. H.Q. Brazzaville, and painting "Mpisikidy" (G. Rakotovao) 45 30

1971. Malagasy Traditional Dwellings (2nd series). Multicoloured.
205. 5 f. Type **89** 5 5
206. 10 f. Antandroy hut, South coast 5 5

90. "Children and Cattle in Meadow" (G. Rasoaharijaona).

1971. U.N.I.C.E.F. 25th Anniv.
207. **90.** 50 f. multicoloured .. 25 15

1972. Town Arms (3rd series). As T **73.** Multicoloured.
208. 1 f. Maintirano Arms .. 5 5
209. 25 f. Fenerive-Est.. .. 12 8

91. Cable-laying train.

1972. Co-axial Cable Link, Tananarive-Tamatave.
210. **91.** 45 f. brn., grn. and red 20 12

92. Telecommunications Station.

1972. Philibert Tsiranana Satellite Communications Station. Inaug.
211. **92.** 85. f. multicoloured .. 40 25

93. Pres. Tsiranana and Voters. **94.** "Moped" Postman.

1972. Presidential Elections.
212. **93.** 25 f. multicoloured .. 12 8

1972. Stamp Day.
213. **94.** 10 f. multicoloured .. 5 5

1972. De Gaulle Memorial. No. 197 surch. **MEMORIAL + 20F.**
214. **85.** 30 f. + 20 f. blk., red & bl. 25 15

95. Exhibition. Emblem and Stamps. **96.** Road and Monument.

1972. 2nd Nat. Stamp Exhib., Antanarive.
215. **95.** 25 f. multicoloured .. 12 8
216. 40 f. multicoloured .. 20 12
217. 100 f. multicoloured .. 45 30

1972. Opening of Andapa-Sambava Highway.
219. **96.** 50 f. multicoloured .. 25 15

97. Petroleum Refinery, Tamatave. **98.** R. Rakotobe.

1972. Malagasy Economic Development.
220. **97.** 2 f. blue, grn. & yell.. 5 5
221. – 100 f. multicoloured .. 45 35
DESIGN: 100 f. "3600 **CV**" railway locomotive.

1972. Air. Rene Rakotobe (poet). 1st Death Anniv.
222. **98.** 40 f. brn., purple & orge. 20 12

99. College Buildings.

1972. Razafindrahety College, Tanarive. 150th Anniv.
223. **99.** 10 f. purple-brn., brown and blue 5 5

100. Volleyball.

1972. African Volleyball Championships.
224. **100.** 12 f. blk., orge. & brn. 5 5

101. Runners breasting Tape.

1972. Air. Olympic Games, Munich. Mult.
225. 100 f. Type **101** 45 35
226. 200 f. Judo 90 60

103. Hospital Complex.

1972. Ravoahangy Andrianavalona Hospital. Inaug.
227. **103.** 6 f. multicoloured .. 5 5

104. Mohair Goat.

1972. Air. Malagasy Wool Production.
228. **104.** 250 f. multicoloured .. 1·10 70

105. Ploughing with Oxen.

1972. Agricultural Expansion.
229. **105.** 25 f. multicoloured .. 12 8

106. "Virgin and Child" (15th-cent. Florentine School).

1972. Air. Christmas Religious Paintings. Multicoloured.
230. 85 f. Type **106** 40 35
231. 150 f. "Adoration of the Magi" (A. Mantegna) (horiz.) 90 55

107. Betsimisarka Women.

1972. Traditional Costumes. Multicoloured.
232. 10 f. Type **107** 5 5
233. 15 f. Merina mother and child 5 5

108. Astronauts on Moon. **109.** "Natural Produce".

1973. Air. Moon Flight of "Apollo 17".

234. **108.** 300 f. pur., brn. & grey 1·25 80

1973. Malagasy Freedom from Hunger Campaign Committee. 10th Anniv.

235. **109.** 25 f. multicoloured .. 10 8

110. "The Entombment" (Grunewald).

1973. Air. Easter. Multicoloured.

236. 100 f. Type **110** 40 30

237. 200 f. "The Resurrection" (Grunewald) (vert.) .. 80 60

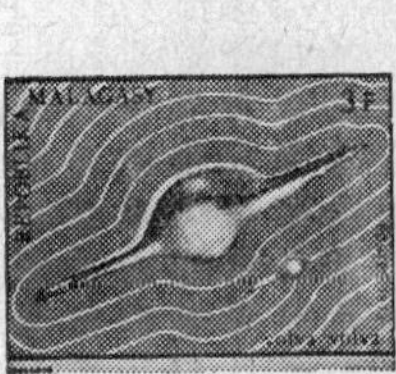

111. "Volva volva" Shell. **112.** Postal Courier, Tsimandoa.

1973. Sea-shells (2nd series). Multicoloured.

238. 3 f. Type **111** 5 5

239. 10 f. "Lambis chiragra" .. 5 5

240. 15 f. "Harpa major" .. 5 5

241. 25 f. Type **111** 10 8

242. 40 f. As 15 f. 15 10

243. 50 f. As 10 f. 20 12

1973. Stamp Day.

244. **112.** 50 f. blue, grn. & brn. 20 12

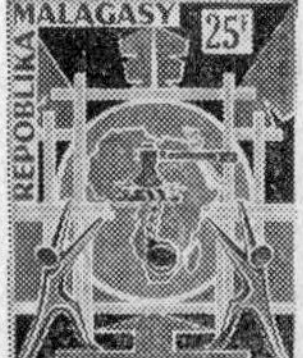

113. "Africa" within Scaffolding. **114.** "Cameleon campani".

1973. Organization of African Unity. 10th Anniv.

245. **113.** 25 f. multicoloured .. 10 8

1973. Malagasy Cameleons. Multicoloured.

246. 1 f. Type **114** 5 5

247. 5 f. "Cameleon nasutus" (male) 5 5

248. 10 f. "Cameleon nasutus" (female) 5 5

249. 40 f. As 5 f. 15 10

250. 60 f. Type **114** 25 15

251. 85 f. As 10 f. 35 25

115. Excursion Carriage.

1973. Air. Early Malagasy Railways. Mult.

252. 100 f. Type **115** 40 30

253. 150 f. Steam locomotive .. 60 45

116. "Cypripedium".

1973. Orchids. Multicoloured.

254. 10 f. Type **116** 5 5

255. 25 f. "Nepenthes pervillei" 10 8

256. 40 f. As 25 f. 15 10

257. 100 f. Type **116** 40 30

1973. Pan African Drought Relief. No. 235 surch. **SECHERESSE SOLIDARITE AFRICAINE** and value.

258. **109.** 100 f. on 25 f. mult. .. 40 30

117. Dish Aerial and Met. Station. **118.** "Cheirogaleus major".

1973. Air. W.M.O. Cent.

259. **117.** 100 f. orge., blue & blk. 40 30

1973. African and Malagasy Posts and Telecommunications. 12th Anniv. As Type **182** of Cameroun.

260. 100 f. red, violet and green 40 30

1973. Malagasy Lemurs.

261. **118.** 5 f. brn., grn. & purple (postage) 5 5

262. – 25 f. brn., sepia & grn. 10 8

263. – 150 f. brn., grn. & sepia (air) 60 45

264. **118.** 200 f. brn., tur. & blue 80 60

DESIGN—VERT. 25 f., 150 f. "Lepilemur mustelinus".

119. Pres. Kennedy.

1973. Air. Pres. John Kennedy. 10th Death Anniv.

265. **119.** 300 f. multicoloured .. 1·25 90

120. Footballers.

1973. Air. World Cup Football Championships. West Germany.

266. **120.** 500 f. mauve, brown and light brown .. 2·00 1·75

CURRENCY. Issues from No. 267 onwards have face values shown as "Fmg". This abbreviation denotes the Malagasy Franc which was introduced in 1966. The currency continues to be linked with that of France.

121. Copernicus, Satellite and Diagram.

1974. Air. Copernicus. 500th Birth Anniv.

267. **121.** 250 f. bl., brn. & green 1·00 80

1974. No. 76a surch.

268. 25 f. on 30 f. multicoloured 10 8

122. Agricultural Training. **124.** Family and House.

123. Male Player, and Hummingbird on Hibiscus.

1974. 25th World Scouting Conference, Nairobi, Kenya.

269. **122.** 4 f. grey, blue & green (postage) 5 5

270. – 15 f. pur., grn. & blue 5 5

271. – 100 f. ochre, red & blue (air) 40 30

272. – 300 f. brn., bl. & blk.. 1·25 90

DESIGNS—VERT. 15 f. Building construction. HORIZ. 100 f. First Aid training. 300 f. Fishing.

1974. Air. Asia, Africa and Latin America Table-Tennis Championships, Peking.

273. **123.** 50 f. red, blue & brown 20 15

274. – 100 f. r d, blue & vio. 40 30

DESIGN: 100 f. Female player, and stylised bird.

1974. World Population Year.

275. **124.** 25 f. red, orange-red & blue 10 8

125. Micheline Rail Car.

1974. Air. Malagasy Railway Locomotive.

276. **125.** 50 f. grn., red & brn... 20 15

277. – 85 f. red, blue & green 35 25

278. – 200 f. bl., light bl. & brown 80 60

DESIGNS: 85 f. Track-inspection trolly. 200 f. Garratt steam locomotive.

126. U.P.U. Emblem and Letters.

1974. Air. U.P.U. Centenary.

279. **126.** 250 f. red, bl. & violet 1·00 80

127. Rainibetsimisaraka.

1974. Rainibetsimisaraka Commemoration.

280. **127.** 25 f. multicoloured .. 10 8

1974. Air. West Germany's Victory in World Cup Football Championships. No. 266 optd. **R.F.A. 2 HOLLANDE 1.**

281. **120.** 500 f. mauve, brown & light brown.. .. 2·00 1·75

128. Satellite Link-up.

1974. Air. Soviet-U.S. Space Co-operation.

282. **128.** 150 f. orge., grn. & blue 60 45

283. – 250 f. grn., bl. & brown 1·00 80

DESIGN: No. 283, As Type **128** but different view.

129. Marble Slabs. **130.** African and European Faces.

1974. Marble Industry. Multicoloured.

284. 4. f. Type **129** 5 5

285. 25 f. Quarrying 10 8

1974. Air. Universal Postal Union. Cent. (2nd issue). No. 279 optd. **100 ANS COLLABORATION INTERNATIONALE.**

286. **126.** 250 f. red, blue & violet 1·00 80

1974. Europafrique.

287. **130.** 150 f. brn., red & orge. 60 45

131. "Food in Hand".

1974. "Freedom from Hunger".

288. **131.** 80 f. bl., brn. & grey.. 35 25

132. "Coton" of Tulear. **133.** Malagasy People.

1974. Malagasy Dogs. Multicoloured.

289. 50 f. Type **132** 20 15

290. 100 f. Hunting Dog .. 40 30

1974. Founding of "Fokonolona" Commem.

291. **133.** 5 f. multicoloured .. 5 5

292. 10 f. multicoloured .. 5 5

293. 20 f. multicoloured .. 8 5

294. 60 f. multicoloured .. 20 15

134. "Discovering Talents".

1974. National Development Council (CNPD).

295. **134.** 25 f. multicoloured .. 10 8

296. 35 f. multicoloured .. 15 10

CNPD = Conseil National Populaire pour le Developpement.

135. "Adoration of the Magi" (David). **136.** Malagasy Girl and Rose.

1974. Air. Christmas. Multicoloured.

297. 200 f. Type **135** 80 60
298. 300 f. "Virgin of the Cherries and Child" (Metzys) .. .. .. 1·25 90

1975. International Women's Year.

299. **136.** 100 f. brn., orge. & grn. 40 30

137. Colonel Richard Ratsimandrava (Chief of Government).

1975.

300. **137.** 15 f. brn., blk. & yell. 8 5
301. 25 f. brn., blk. & blue 10 8
302. 100 f. brn., blk. & grn. 40 30

138. Sofia Bridge.

1975.

303. **138.** 45 f. multicoloured .. 20 15

139. U.N. Emblem and Part of Globe.

1975. Air. U.N. Charter. 30th Anniv.

304. **139.** 300 f. multicoloured .. 1·25 1·10

140. De Grasse and "Randolph".

1975. American Revolution. Bicentenary. (1st issue). Multicoloured.

305. 40 f. Type **140** (postage) 15 12
306. 50 f. Lafayette, "Lexington" and H.M.S. "Edward" .. 20 15
307. 100 f. D'Estaing and "Languedoc" (air) .. 40 30
308. 200 f. Paul Jones, "Bonhomme Richard" and H.M.S. "Serapis" .. 85 80
309. 300 f. Benjamin Franklin, "Millern" and "Montgomery" .. .. 1·25 1·10

1975. Air. "Apollo-Soyus" Space Link Nos. 282/3 optd. **JONCTION 17 JUILLET 1975.**

311. **128.** 150 f. oran., grn. & blue 60 55
312. – 250f. grn., blue & brn. 1·10 1·00

141. "Euphoria viguieri".

1975. Malagasy Flora. Multicoloured.

313. 15 f. Type **141** (postage) .. 8 5
314. 25 f. "Hibiscus rosesinensis" 10 8
315. 30 f. "Plumieria rubra acutitolia" 12 10
316. 40 f. "Pachypodium rosulatum" 15 12
317. 85 f. "Turraea sericea" (air) 35 30

142. Temple Frieze.

1975. Air. "Save Borobudur Temple" Campaign.

318. **142.** 50 f. red, orange & blue 20 15

143. "Racial Unity". **144.** Lily Waterfall.

1975. Namibia Day.

319. **143.** 50 f. multicoloured .. 20 15

1975. Lily Waterfall. Multicoloured.

320. 25 f. Type **143** 10 8
321. 40 f. Lily Waterfall (distant view) 15 12

145. "Saphopipo noguchi" (woodpecker).

1975. International Exposition, Okinawa. Fauna. Multicoloured.

322. 25 f. Type **145** (postage) .. 10 8
323. 40 f. "Pentalagus furnessi" (hare) .. 15 12
324. 50 f. "Rana (babina) subaspera" (toad) .. 20 15
325. 75 f. "Cyclemys aavomarginata" (tortoise) .. 30 25
326. 125 f. "Cervus var Karama" (deer) (air) 50 45

146. Hurdling.

1975. Air. "Pre-Olympic Year". Olympic Games, Montreal (1976). Multicoloured.

328. 75 f. Type **146** 30 25
329 200 f. Weightlifting (vert.) 85 80

147. Bobsleigh "Fours".

1975. Winter Olympic Games, Innsbruck. Multicoloured.

330. 75 f. Type **147** (postage) .. 30 25
331. 100 f. Ski-jumping .. 40 35
332. 140 f. Speed-skating .. 55 50
333. 200 f. Cross-country skiing (air) 80 75
334. 245 f. Downhill skiing .. 95 90

148. Pirogue.

1975. Malagasy Sailing-vessels. Multicoloured.

336. 8 f. Type **148** 5 5
337. 45 f. "Boutre" 20 15

149. Canadian and Kayak Canoeing.

1976. Olympic Games, Montreal. Mult.

338. 40 f. Type **149** (postage) .. 15 12
339. 50 f. Sprinting and hurdling 20 15
340. 100 f. Putting the shot, and long-jumping (air) .. 40 35
341. 200 f. Gymnastics-horse and parallel bars 80 75
342. 300 f. Trampoline-jumping and high-diving .. .. 1·25 1·10

150. "Apollo 14" and Badge.

1976. Air. "Apollo 14" Mission. 5th Anniv.

344. **150.** 150 f. blue, red & grn. 60 55

1976. Air. "Apollo 14" Mission. 5th Anniversary. No. 344 optd. **5e Anniversaire de la mission APOLLO XIV.**

345. **150.** 150 f. blue, red & grn. 70 65

151. "Graf Zeppelin" over Fujiyama.

1976. Zeppelin Airships. 75th Anniversary. Multicoloured.

346. 40 f. Type **151** (postage) .. 15 12
347. 50 f. Zeppelin over Rio de Janeiro 25 20
348. 75 f. Zeppelin over New York 35 30
349. 100 f. Zeppelin over Sphinx and Pyramids 45 40
350. 200 f. Zeppelin over Berlin (air) 90 85
351. 300 f. Zeppelin over London 1·40 1·25

152. "Prevention of Blindness".

1976. World Health Day.

353. **152.** 100 f. multicoloured .. 45 40

153. Aragonite.

1976. Minerals and Fossils. Multicoloured.

354. 25 f. Type **153** 12 10
355. 50 f. Fossilised wood .. 25 20
356. 150 f. Celestyte 70 65

154. Bell and Early Telephone.

1976. Telephone Centenary. Multicoloured.

357. 25 f. Type **154** 12 10
358. 50 f. Cable maintenance, 1911 .. .. .. 25 20
359. 100 f. Telephone operator and switchboard, 1895 45 40
360. 200 f. Cable-laying ship, 1925 .. .. .. 90 85
361. 300 f. Man with "walkie-talkie" radio telephone 1·40 1·75

155. Children reading Book.

1976. Children's Books Promotion. Multicoloured.

363. 10 f. Type **155** 5 5
364. 25 f. Children reading book (vert.) 12 10

1976. Medal winners, Winter Olympic Games, Innsbruck. Nos. 330/4 optd. **VAINQUEUR** and medal winner.

365. 75 f. Type **147** (postage) .. 35 30
366. 100 f. Ski-jumping .. 45 40
367. 140 f. Skating 60 55
368. 200 f. Cross-country skiing (air) 90 85
369. 245 f. Downhill skiing .. 1·10 1·00

OPTS: 75 f. **ALLEMAGNE FEDERALE.** 100 f. **KARL SCHNABL, AUTRICHE.** 140 f. **SHEILA YOUNG, ETATS-UNIS.** 200 f. **IVAR FORMO, NORVEGE.** 245 f. **ROSI MITTERMAIR, ALLEMAGNE DE L'OUEST.**

The subject depicted on No. 367 is speed-skating, an event in which the gold medal was won by J. E. Storholt, Norway.

1976. American Revolution. Bicent. (2nd issue). Nos. 305/9 optd. **"4 JUILLET 1776-1976".**

371. **140.** 40 f. multicoloured (postage) 15 12
372. – 50 f. multicoloured .. 25 20
373. – 100 f. multicoloured (air) 45 40
374. – 200 f. multicoloured .. 90 85
375. – 300 f. multicoloured .. 1·40 1·25

156. Landing Trajectory.

1976. "Viking" Landing on Mars. Multicoloured.

377.	75 f. Type **156**	35	30
378.	100 f. "Viking" making descent	45	40
379.	200 f. "Viking" on Mars	90	85
380.	300 f. "Viking" making approach	1·40	1·25

POSTAGE DUE STAMPS

D 1. Independence Obelisk.

1962.

D 45.	D 1.	1 f. emerald	5	5
D 46.		2 f. chestnut	5	5
D 47.		3 f. violet	5	5
D 48.		4 f. slate	5	5
D 49.		5 f. red	5	5
D 50.		10 f. green	5	5
D 51.		20 f. maroon ..	8	8
D 52.		40 f. blue	15	12
D 53.		50 f. rose	20	20
D 54.		100 f. black ..	45	40

MALAWI BC

Formerly Nyasaland, became an independent Republic within the Commonwealth on the 6th July, 1966.

1970 100 tambalas = 1 kwacha.

1. Independence Monument.

1964. Independence.

211.	**1.**	3d. olive and sepia ..	5	5
212.	–	6d. multicoloured ..	10	10
213.	–	1s. 3d. red, grn., blk. & vio.	20	20
214.	–	2s. 6d. multicoloured ..	35	40

DESIGNS (each with Dr. Hastings Banda, Prime Minister): 6d. Rising Sun. 1s. 3d. National Flag. 2s. 6d. Arms.

2. Tung.

1964. As Nos. 199/210 of Nyasaland but inscr. "MALAWI" as in T **2**. The 9d., 1s. 6d. and £2 are new values and designs.

215.	½d. violet	5	5
216.	1d. black and green ..	5	5
217.	2d. brown	5	5
218.	3d. brown, green & bistre	8	8
219.	4d. blue and yellow ..	10	10
220.	6d. purple, green and blue	15	15
221.	9d. brown, green & yellow	25	25
222.	1s. brown, blue & yellow ..	30	30
223.	1s. 3d. bronze and chestnut	40	45
259.	1s. 6d. brown and green ..	25	25
224.	2s. 6d. brown and blue ..	6·00	1·00
225.	5s. blue, green, yellow and sepia (I)	1·25	1·50
225a.	5s. blue, green, yellow and sepia (II)	95	1·00
226.	10s. green, salmon & black	1·75	2·00
227.	£1 chocolate and yellow ..	3·50	4·00
262.	£2 blk., orge., yell. & violet	7·00	8·00

DESIGNS (New): 1s. 6d. Burley tobacco £2 "Cyrestis camillus sublineatus" (butterfly). Two types of 5s. I, inscr. "LAKE NYASA". II, inscr. "LAKE MALAWI".

3. Christmas Star and Globe.

1964. Christmas.

228.	**3.**	3d. green and gold ..	5	5
229.		6d. magenta and gold ..	12	12
230.		1s. 3d. violet and gold ..	25	25
231.		2s. 6d. blue and gold ..	45	45

4. Coins

1964. Malawi's 1st Coinage. Coins in black and silver.

232.	**4.**	3d. green	5	5
233.		9d. magenta	12	12
234.		1s. 6d. purple	20	20
235.		3s. blue	40	40

1965. Nos. 223/4 surch.

236.	1s. 6d. on 1s. 3d. bronze & chestnut	20	25
237.	3s. on 2s. 6d. brown & blue	35	40

5. Chilembwe leading Rebels.

1965. 1915 Rising. 50th Anniv.

238.	**5.**	3d. violet and green ..	5	5
239.		9d. olive and orange ..	12	12
240.		1s. 6d. chestnut and indigo	25	25
241.		3s. turquoise and blue ..	40	40

6. "Learning and Scholarship".

1965. Opening of Malawi University.

242.	**6.**	3d. black and green ..	5	5
243.		9d. black and magenta ..	12	15
244.		1s. 6d. black and violet ..	25	25
245.		3s. black and blue ..	40	40

7. "Papilio ophidicephalus mkuwadzi".

1966. Malawi Butterflies. Multicoloured

247.	4d. Type **7**	5	5
248.	9d. "Papilio magdae" ..	12	12
249.	1s. 6d. "Epamera handmani" ..	25	25
250.	3s. "Amauris crawshayi" ..	40	45

8. British Central Africa 6d. Stamp of 1891.

1966. Postal Services. 75th Anniv.

263.	**8.**	4d. grey-blue and green ..	5	5
264.		9d. grey-blue and claret	12	12
265.		1s. 6d. grey-blue & lilac ..	25	25
266.		3 s. grey-blue and blue ..	45	45

9. President Banda.

1966. Republic Day.

268.	**9.**	4d. brown, silver & emer.	5	5
269.		9d. brown, silver & mag.	12	12
270.		1s. 6d. brown, silver & vio.	20	20
271.		3s. brown, silver and blue	40	40

10. Bethlehem.

1966. Christmas.

273.	**10.**	4d. green and gold ..	8	8
274.		9d. purple and gold ..	20	20
275.		1s. 6d. red and gold ..	30	25
276.		3s. blue and gold ..	60	55

11. "Ilala I".

1967. Lake Malawi Steamers.

277.	**11.**	4d. black, yellow & grn.	8	8
278.	–	9d. black, yellow & mag.	12	12
279.	–	1s. 6d. black, red & violet	25	25
280.	–	3s. black, red and blue ..	45	45

DESIGNS: 9d. "Dove". 1s. 6d. "Chauncy Maples" (wrongly inscr. "Chauncey"). 3s. "Guendolen".

12. "Turquoise-gold Chichlid.

1967. Lake Malawi Chichlids. Multicoloured.

281.	4d. Type **12**	8	8
282.	9d. "Red Finned Chichlid"	15	15
283.	1s. 6d. "Zebra Chichlid"	25	25
284.	3s. "Golden Chichlid" ..	50	50

13. Rising Sun and Gearwheel.

1967. Industrial Development.

285.	**13.**	4d. black and green ..	5	5
286.		9d. black and red ..	10	10
287.		1s. 6d. black and violet	20	20
288.		3s. black and blue ..	35	35

14. Mary and Joseph Beside Crib.

1967. Christmas.

290.	**14.**	4d. blue and green ..	8	8
291.		9d. blue and red ..	15	15
292.		1s. 6d. blue and yellow	25	25
293.		3s. blue	50	50

15. "Calotropis procera".

1968. Wild Flowers. Multicoloured.

295.	4d. Type **15**	5	5
296.	9d. "Borreria dibrachiata"	15	15
297.	1s. 6d "Hibiscus rhodanthus"	25	25
298.	3s. "Bidens pinnatipartita"	50	50

16. Saddleback Steam Engine, "Thistle No. 1".

1968. Malawi Locomotives.

300.	**16.**	4d. green, blue and red	8	8
301.	–	9d. red, blue and green	20	20
302.	–	1s. 6d. multicoloured ..	30	30
303.	–	3s. multicoloured	60	60

DESIGNS: 9d. "G" Class Steam Engine. 1s. 6d. Diesel Electric Locomotive "Zambesi". 3s. Diesel Rail Car.

17. "The Nativity" (Piero della Francesca).

1968. Christmas. Multicoloured.

305.	4d. Type **17**	8	8
306.	9d. "The Adoration of the Shepherds" (Murillo) ..	15	15
307.	1s. 6d. "The Adoration of the Shepherds" (Reni) ..	25	25
308.	3s. "Nativity, with God the Father and Holy Ghost" (Pittoni) ..	50	50

18. Lilian's Lovebird. **19.** Paradise Flycatcher.

1968. Birds. (1st series). Multicoloured.

310.	1d. Scarlet-chested Sunbird	5	5
311.	2d. Violet-backed Starling	5	5
312.	3d. White-browed Robin ..	5	5
313.	4d. Red-billed Firefinch ..	8	8
314.	6d. Type **18**	8	10
315.	9d. Yellow Bishop (vert.) ..	10	12
316.	1s. Type **19**	15	20
317.	1s. 6d. Grey-headed Bush Shrike	35	35
318.	2s. Paradise Whydah ..	40	40
319.	3s. Paradise Flycatcher (vert.)	75	75
320.	5s. Bateleur (vert.) ..	75	75
321.	10s. Saddlebill (vert.) ..	1·60	2·25
322.	£1 Purple Heron (vert.) ..	2·75	3·00
323.	£2 Livingstone's Loerie ..	7·00	10·00

SIZES: 1d. to 9d. as T **18**. 1s. 6d. to £2 as T **19**.

See also Nos. 473/85.

20. I.L.O. Emblem.

1969. Int. Labour Organization. 50th Anniv.

324. 20. 4d. gold and green .. 5 5
325. 9d. gold and chocolate 12 12
326. 1s. 6d. gold and brown 20 20
327. 3s. gold and indigo .. 35 35

21. White-fringed Ground Orchid.

1969. Orchids of Malawi. Multicoloured

329. 4d. Type **21** 5 5
330. 9d. Red Ground Orchid .. 15 15
331. 1s. 6d. Leopard Tree Orchid 25 25
332. 3s. Blue Ground Orchid .. 50 50

22. African Development Bank Emblem.

1969. African Development Bank. 5th Anniv.

334. 22. 4d. yellow, brn. & ochre 5 5
335. 9d. yellow, ochre & green 10 10
336. 1s. 6d. yell., ochre & brn. 20 20
337. 3s. yellow, ochre & indigo 40 40

23. Dove over Bethlehem.

1969. Christmas.

339. 23. 2d. black and yellow .. 5 5
340. 4d. black and turquoise 8 8
341. 9d. black and red .. 15 15
342. 1s. 6d. black and violet 25 25
343. 3s. black and ultramarine 50 50

24. Elegant Grasshopper.

1970. Insects of Malawi. Multicoloured.

345. 4d. Type **24** 5 5
346. 9d. Bean Blister Beetle .. 15 15
347. 1s. 6d. Pumpkin Ladybird 25 25
348. 3s. Praying Mantis .. 50 50

1970. Rand Easter Show. No. 317 optd. **Rand Easter Show 1970.**

350. 1s. 6d. multicoloured .. 25 30

25. Runner.

1970. 9th Commonwealth Games.

351. 25. 4d. blue and green .. 5 5
352. 9d. blue and carmine .. 15 15
353. 1s. 6d. blue and yellow 25 25
354. 3s. blue 50 50

1970. Decimal Currency. Nos. 316 and 318 surch.

356. – 10 t. on 1 s. multicoloured 12 12
357. – 20 t. on 2s. multicoloured 25 25

26. " Aegocera trimenii ".

1970. Moths. Multicoloured.

358. 4d. Type **26** 5 5
359. 9d. " Epiphora bauhiniae " 15 15
360. 1s. 6d. " Parasa karschi ". 25 25
361. 3s. " Teracotona euprepia " 50 50

27. Mother and Child.

1970. Christmas.

363. 27. 2d. black and yellow .. 5 5
364. 4d. black and green .. 8 8
365. 9d. black and red .. 15 15
366. 1s. 6d. black and purple 25 25
367. 3s. black and blue .. 50 50

1971. No. 319 surch. **30 t Special United Kingdom Delivery Service.**

369. 19. 30 t. on 3s. multicoloured 50 50

No. 369 was issued for use on letters carried by an emergency airmail service from Malawi to Great Britain during the British postal strike. The fee of 30 t. was to cover the charge for delivery by a private service, and ordinary stamps to pay the normal airmail postage had to be affixed as well. These stamps were in use from 8th Feb. to 8th March.

28. Decimal Coinage and Cockerel.

1971. Decimal Coinage.

370. 28. 3 t. multicoloured .. 5 5
371. 8 t. multicoloured .. 10 10
372. 15 t. multicoloured .. 20 20
373. 30 t. multicoloured .. 35 35

29. Greater Kudu. 30. " Christ on the Cross " (Durer).

1971. Decimal Currency. Antelopes. Multicoloured.

375. 1 t. Type **29** 5 5
376. 2 t. Nyala 5 5
377. 3 t. Reedbuck 5 5
378. 5 t. Puku 8 8
379. 8 t. Impala 10 12
380. 10 t. Eland 15 12
381. 15 t. Klipspringer .. 25 20
382. 20 t. Livingstone's Suni 20 25
383. 30 t. Roan Antelope .. 35 40
384. 50 t. Waterbuck 60 65
385. 1 k. Bushbuck .. .. 1·10 1·25
386. 2 k. Red Duiker .. 2·25 2·40
387. 4 k. Grey Duiker .. 4·50 4·50

Nos. 380/7 are larger, size 25 × 42 mm.

No. 387 is incorrectly inscr. " Gray Duiker ".

1971. Easter. Multicoloured.

388. 30. 3 t. black and green .. 5 5
389. – 3 t. black and green .. 5 5
390. 30. 8 t. black and red .. 12 12
391. – 8 t. black and red .. 12 12
392. 30. 15 t. black and violet .. 25 25
393. – 15 t. black and violet .. 25 25
394. 30. 30 t. black and blue .. 45 45
395. – 30 t. black and blue .. 45 45

DESIGN: Nos. 389, 391, 393, 395, " The Resurrection ".

Both designs from " The Small Passion " (Durer). The two designs of each value were issued se-tenant within the sheet.

31. " Holarrhena febrifuga ".

1971. Flowering Shrubs and Trees. Multicoloured.

397. 3 t. Type **31** 5 5
398. 8 t. " Brachystegia spiciformis " 12 12
399. 15 t. " Securidaca longepedunculata " 25 25
400. 30 t. " Pterocarpus rotundifolius " 45 45

32. Drum Major. 33. " Madonna and Child " (William Dyce).

1971. Malawi Police Force. 50th Anniv.

402. 32. 30 t. multicoloured .. 40 45

1971. Christmas. Multicoloured.

403. 3 t. Type **33** 8 8
404. 8 t. " The Holy Family " (M. Shongauer) 12 12
405. 15 t. " The Holy Family with St. John " (Raphael) 25 25
406. 30 t. " The Holy Family " (Bronzino) 45 45

34. Vickers " Viscount ".

1972. Air. Malawi Aircraft. Multicoloured.

408. 3 t. Type **34** 5 5
409. 8 t. Hawker Siddeley " 748 " 12 12
410. 15 t. Britten-Norman " Islander " 25 25
411. 30 t. B.A.C. " One-Eleven " 45 50

35. Figures (Chencherere Hill).

1972. Rock Paintings.

413. 35. 3 t. green and black .. 5 5
414. – 8 t. red, grey and black 12 12
415. – 15 t. multicoloured .. 25 25
416. – 30 t. multicoloured .. 45 45

DESIGNS: 8 t. Lizard and Cat (Chencherere Hill). 15 t. Schematics (Diwa Hill). 30 t. Sun Through Rain (Mikolongwe Hill).

36. Boxing.

1972. Olympic Games, Munich.

418. 36. 3 t. multicoloured .. 5 5
419. 8 t. multicoloured .. 12 12
420. 15 t. multicoloured .. 25 25
421. 30 t. multicoloured .. 45 45

37. Arms of Malawi.

1972. Parliamentary Conf.

423. 37. 15 t. multicoloured .. 20 20

38. " Adoration of the Kings " (Orcagna).

1972. Christmas. Multicoloured.

No.	Description	Unused	Used
424.	3 t. Type **38**	5	5
425.	8 t. " Madonna and Child Enthroned " (Florentine School)	12	12
426.	15 t. " Virgin and Child " (Crivelli)	25	25
427.	30 t. " St. Anne with the Virgin and Child " (Bruges)	45	45

39. " Charaxes bohemani ".

1973. Butterflies. Multicoloured.

No.	Description	Unused	Used
429.	3 t. Type **39**	5	5
430.	8 t. " Uranothauma crawshayi "	12	12
431.	15 t. " Charaxes acuminatus"	25	25
432.	30 t. Inscr. " EUPHAEDRA ZADDACHI "	45	45
433.	30 t. Corrected to " AMAURIS ANSORGEI "	45	45

40. Livingstone and Map.

1973. David Livingstone. Death Cent. (1st issue).

No.	Description	Unused	Used
435. **40.**	3 t multicoloured	5	5
436.	8 t. multicoloured	12	12
437.	15 t. multicoloured	25	25
438.	30 t. multicoloured	45	45

See also No. 450.

41. Thumb Dulcitone.

1973. Musical Instruments. Multicoloured.

No.	Description	Unused	Used
440.	3 t. Type **41**	5	5
441.	8 t. Hand zither (vert.)	12	12
442.	15 t. Hand drum (vert.)	25	25
443.	30 t. One-stringed fiddle	45	45

42. The Magi.

1973. Christmas.

No.	Description	Unused	Used
445. **42.**	3 t. blue, lilac & ultram.	5	5
446.	8 t. red, lilac and brown	12	12
447.	15 t. mve., blue & deep mve.	25	25
448.	30 t. yell., lilac & brown	45	45

43. Stained-glass Window, Livingstone Mission.

1973. David Livingstone. Death Cent. (2nd issue.).

No.	Description	Unused	Used
450. **43.**	50 t. multicoloured	75	75

44. Largemouth Black Bass.

1973. Malawi Angling Society. 35th Anniv. Multicoloured.

No.	Description	Unused	Used
452.	3 t. Type **44**	5	5
453.	8 t. Rainbow trout	12	12
454.	15 t. Lake salmon	25	25
455.	30 t Tiger fish	45	45

45. U.P.U. Monument and Map of Africa.

1974. U.P.U. Centenary.

No.	Description	Unused	Used
457. **45.**	3 t. green and brown	5	5
458.	8 t. red and brown	12	12
459.	15 t. violet and brown	25	25
460.	30 t. blue and brown	45	45

46. Capital Hill, Lilogwe.

1974. Independence. 10th Anniv.

No.	Description	Unused	Used
462. **46.**	3 t. multicoloured	5	5
463.	8 t. multicoloured	10	12
464.	15 t. multicoloured	20	20
465.	30 t. multicoloured	35	35

47. " Madonna of the Meadow " (Bellini).

1974. Christmas. Multicoloured.

No.	Description	Unused	Used
467.	3 t. Type **47**	5	5
468.	8 t. " The Holy Family with Sts. John and Elizabeth " (Jordaens)	10	12
469.	15 t. " The Nativity " (Peter de Grebber)	20	20
470.	30 t. " Adoration of the Shepherds " (Lorenzo di Credi)	35	40

48. Arms of Malawi. **49.** African Snipe.

50. Spurwing Goose.

1975.

No.	Description	Unused	Used
472. **48.**	1 t. blue	5	5

1975. Birds (2nd series). Multicoloured.

(a) As Type **49**.

No.	Description	Unused	Used
473.	1 t. Type **49**	5	5
474.	2 t. Double-banded Sand-grouse (horiz.)	5	5
475.	3 t. Blue Quail (horiz.)	5	5
476.	5 t. Red-necked Francolin	5	5
477.	8 t. Harlequin Quail (horiz.)	10	12

(b) As Type **50**.

No.	Description	Unused	Used
478.	10 t. Type **50**	12	15
479.	15 t. Stanley Bustard	20	25
480.	20 t. Knob-billed Duck	20	25
481.	30 t. Crowned Guineafowl	30	35
482.	50 t. Pigmy Goose (horiz.)	55	65
483.	1 k. Garganey	1·00	1·10
484.	2 k. White-faced Tree Duck	2·50	2·75
485.	4 k. Green Pigeon	4·25	4·50

51. M.V. "Mpasa".

1975. Ships of Lake Malawi. Multicoloured.

No.	Description	Unused	Used
486.	3 t. Type **51**	5	5
487.	8 t. M.V. "Ilala II"	10	12
488.	15 t. M.V. "Chauncy Maples"	20	20
489.	30 t. M.V. "Nkwazi"	35	40

52. " Habenaria splendens ".

1975. Malawi Orchids. Multicoloured.

No.	Description	Unused	Used
491.	3 t. Type **52**	5	5
492.	10 t. " Eulophia cucullata "	12	15
493.	20 t. " Disa welwitschii "	20	25
494.	40 t. " Angraecum conchiferum "	40	45

53. Bush Baby.

1975. Malawi Animals. Multicoloured.

No.	Description	Unused	Used
496.	3 t. Type **53**	5	5
497.	10 t. Leopard	12	15
498.	20 t. Roan Antelope	25	30
499.	40 t. Burchell's Zebra	45	50

1975. 10th African, Caribbean and Pacific Ministerial Conference. No. 482 optd. **10th ACP Ministerial Conference 1975.**

No.	Description	Unused	Used
514.	50 t. Pigmy Goose	55	65

54. " Adoration of the Magi ".

1975. Christmas. Religious Medallions. Multicoloured.

No.	Description	Unused	Used
515.	3 t. Type **54**	5	5
516.	10 t. " The Nativity "	10	12
517.	20 t. " Adoration of the Magi (different)	25	30
518.	40 t. " Angel appearing to Shepherds "	45	50

55. Alexander Graham Bell.

1976. Telephone. Cent.

No.	Description	Unused	Used
520. **55.**	3 t. green and black	5	5
521.	10 t. purple and black	10	12
522.	20 t. violet and black	20	25
523.	40 t. blue and black	45	50

56. President Banda.

1976. Republic. 10th Anniv. Multicoloured.

No.	Description	Unused	Used
525. **56.**	3 t. green	5	5
526.	10 t. purple	12	15
527.	20 t. blue	25	30
528.	40 t. blue	50	55

57. Bagnall Shunter.

1976. Malawi Locomotives. Multicoloured.

No.	Description	Unused	Used
530.	3 t. Type **57**	5	5
531.	10 t. Shire Class loco	12	15
532.	20 t. Nippon Sharyo loco	25	30
533.	40 t. Hunslet shunter	50	55

1976. Blantyre Mission. Centenary. Nos. 479 and 481 optd. **Blantyre Mission Centenary 1876-1976.**

No.	Description	Unused	Used
535.	15 t. Stanley Bustard	20	25
536.	30 t. Crowned Guinea Fowl	35	40

58. Child on Bed of Straw.

1976. Christmas.

No.	Description	Unused	Used
537. **58.**	3 t. multicoloured	5	5
538.	10 t. multicoloured	12	15
539.	20 t. multicoloured	25	30
540.	40 t. multicoloured	50	55

POSTAGE DUE STAMPS

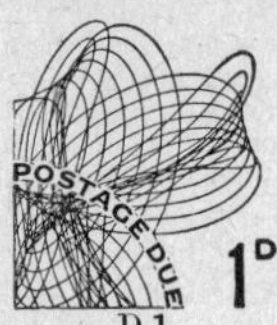

D 1.

1967.

No.	Type			
D 6.	D 1.	1d. red	5	8
D 7.		2d. sepia	5	8
D 8.		4d. violet	8	12
D 9.		6d. blue	10	15
D 10.		8d. green	12	20
D 11.		1s. black	20	30

1971. Values in tambalas.

No.	Type			
D 12.	D 1.	2 t. brown	5	5
D 13.		4 t. mauve	5	5
D 14.		6 t. blue	8	8
D 15.		8 t. green	8	10
D 16.		10 t. brown	10	12

MALAYA BC

BRITISH MILITARY ADMINISTRATION

The following stamps were for use throughout the Malayan States and in Singapore during the period of the British Military Administration and were gradually replaced by individual issues for each state.

100 cents = 1 dollar.

1945. Straits Settlements stamps optd. **BMA MALAYA.**

No.	Type			
1.	17.	1 c. black	8	5
2.		2 c. orange	8	5
4a.		3 c. green	12	5
5.		5 c. brown	8	5
6.		6 c. grey	8	5
7.		8 c. red	8	5
9.		10 c. purple	8	5
10.		12 c. blue	25	50
12.		15 c. blue	8	10
13.		25 c. purple and red	8	5
14.		50 c. black on green	10	10
15.		$1 black and red	30	8
16.		$2 green and red	55	20
17.		$5 green and red on grn.	12·00	15·00
18.		$5 purple and orange	1·75	45

For stamps inscribed "MALAYA" at top and with Arabic characters at foot see under Kelantan, Negri Sembilan, Pahang, Perak, Selangor or Trengganu.

For Japanese issues see "Japanese Occupation of Malaya", and for Siamese issue see "Thai Occupation of Malaya".

MALAYAN FEDERATION BC

An independent country within the British Commonwealth, comprising all the Malay States (except Singapore) and the Settlements of Malacca and Penang. The component units still retain their individual stamps. In 1963 the Federation became part of Malaysia (q.v.).

100 cents (sen) = 1 Malayan dollar.

1. Tapping Rubber.

1957.

No.	Type			
1.	1.	6 c. blue, red and yellow	5	5
2.	–	12 c. red, yell., blue & black	5	5
3.	–	25 c. mar., red, yell. & blue	12	5
4a.	–	30 c. red and lake	25	15

DESIGNS—HORIZ. 12 c. Federation coat of arms 25 c. Tin dredge. VERT. 30 c. Map of the Federation.

2. Chief Minister Tengku Abdul Rahman and Populace greeting Independence.

1957. Independence Day.

No.	Type			
5.	2.	10 c. brown	8	8

3. United Nations Emblem.

DESIGN: 30 c. as T 6 but vert.

1958. U.N. Economic Commission for Asia and Far East Conference, Kuala Lumpur.

No.	Type			
6.	3.	12 c. red	12	12
7.	–	30 c. maroon	15	12

4. Merdeka Stadium, Kuala Lumpur.

DESIGN— VERT. 30 c. Portrait of the Yang di-Pertuan Agong (Abdul Rahman).

1958. Independence. 1st Anniv.

No.	Type			
8.	4.	10 c. grn., yell., red & blue	5	5
9.	–	30 c. red, yell., vio. & grn.	12	10

5. Malayan with "Torch of Freedom".

DESIGN— VERT. 10 c. "Torch of Freedom".

1958. Declaration of Human Rights. 10th Anniv.

No.	Type			
10.	–	10 c. blue, blk., red & orge.	5	5
11.	5.	30 c. green	15	12

6. Mace and Malayan Peoples.

7.

1959. Parliament. Inaug.

No.	Type			
12.	6.	4 c. red	5	5
13.		10 c. violet	5	5
14.		25 c. green	10	8

1960. World Refugee Year.

No.	Type			
15.	–	12 c. purple	15	20
16.	7.	30 c. green	15	15

DESIGN: 12 c. As T 7 but horiz.

8. Seedling Rubber Tree and Map.

9. The Yang di-Pertuan Agong (Syed Putra).

1960. Natural Rubber Research Conf. and 15th Int. Rubber Study Group Meeting, Kuala Lumpur.

No.	Type			
17.	8.	6 c. grn., blk., orge. & brn.	5	5
18.		30 c. grn., blk., orge. & bl.	12	12

No. 18 is inscr. "INTERNATIONAL RUBBER STUDY GROUP 15TH MEETING KUALA LUMPUR" at foot.

1961. Installation of Yang di-Pertuan Agong, Tuanku Syed Putra.

No.	Type			
19.	9.	10 c. black and blue	5	5

INDEX

Countries can be quickly located by referring to the index at the end of this volume.

10. Colombo Plan Emblem.

11. Campaign Emblem.

1961. Colombo Plan Conf., Kuala Lumpur.

No.	Type			
20.	10.	12 c. black and magenta	5	8
21.		25 c. black and apple	10	8
22.		30 c. black and blue	15	10

1962. Malaria Eradication.

No.	Type			
23.	11.	25 c. chestnut	8	5
24.		30 c. lilac	10	10
25.		50 c. blue	20	25

12. Palmyra Palm Leaf.

1962. National Language Month.

No.	Type			
26.	12.	10 c. brown and violet	5	5
27.		20 c. brown and green	8	5
28.		50 c. brown and magenta	25	25

13. "Shadows of the Future".

ILLUSTRATIONS British Commonwealth and all overprints and surcharges are FULL SIZE. Foreign Countries have been reduced to ¾-LINEAR.

1962. Introduction of Free Primary Education.

No.	Type			
29.	13.	10 c. purple	5	5
30.		25 c. ochre	10	10
31.		30 c. green	20	20

14. Harvester and Fisherman.

1963. Freedom from Hunger.

No.	Type			
32.	14.	25 c. pink and green	10	8
33.		30 c. pink and lake	12	10
34.		50 c. pink and blue	20	20

15. Dam and Pylon.

1963. Cameron Highlands Hydro-Electric Scheme.

No.	Type			
35.	15.	20 c. green and violet	8	8
36.		30 c. blue-green and blue	12	12

MALAYAN POSTAL UNION BC

In 1936 postage due stamps were issued in Type D 1 for use in Negri Sembilan, Pahang, Perak, Selangor and Straits Settlements but later their use was extended to the whole of the Federation and in Singapore, and from 1963 throughout Malaysia.

POSTAGE DUE STAMPS

D 1.

1936.

No.	Type			
D 1.	D 1.	1 c. purple	15	30
D 14.		1 c. violet	8	10
D 23a.		2 c. slate	5	12
D 16.		3 c. green	40	50
D 2.		4 c. green	35	30
D 24a.		4 c. sepia	5	15
D 18.		5 c. red	50	75
D 3.		8 c. red	65	80
D 25.		8 c. orange	15	30
D 11.		9 c. orange	6·00	6·00
D 4.		10 c. orange	40	12
D 5.		12 c. blue	70	1·25
D 20a.		12 c. magenta	20	25
D 12.		15 c. blue	9·00	8·00
D 21a.		20 c. blue	25	40
D 6.		50 c. black	1·00	1·25

1965. Surch. **10 cents.**

No.	Type			
D 29.	D 1.	10 c. on 8 c. orange	12	20

MALAYSIA BC

General issues for use throughout the new Federation comprising the old Malayan Federation (Johore ("JOHOR"), Kedah, Kelantan, Malacca ("MELAKA"), Negri Sembilan ("NEGERI SEMBILAN"), Pahang, Penang ("PULAU PINANG"), Perak, Perlis, Selangor and Trengganu), Sabah (North Borneo), Sarawak and Singapore, until the latter became an independent state on 9th August, 1965.

Stamps inscr. "MALAYSIA" and state name are listed under the various states, as above.

100 cents (sen) = 1 Malaysian dollar.

1. Federation Map.

1963. Inauguration of Federation.

No.	Type			
1.	1.	10 c. yellow and violet	8	8
2.		12 c. yellow and green	12	12
3.		50 c. yellow and chocolate	25	25

2. Bouquet of Orchids.

1963. 4th World Orchid Congress, Singapore.

No.	Type			
4.	2.	6 c. multicoloured	8	8
5.		25 c. multicoloured	25	20

4. Parliament House, Kuala Lumpur.

1963. 9th Commonwealth Parliamentary Conference, Kuala Lumpur.

No.	Type			
7.	4.	20 c. magenta and gold	8	8
8.		30 c. green and gold	12	10

5. "Flame of Freedom" and Emblems of Goodwill, Health and Charity.

1964. Eleanor Roosevelt Commem.
9. 5. 25 c. blk., red & turq.-blue 10 8
10. 30 c. black, red and lilac 15 15
11. 50 c. black, red & yellow 25 25

6. Microwave Tower and I.T.U. Emblem.

1965. I.T.U. Cent.
12. 6. 2 c. multicoloured .. 5 5
13. 25 c. multicoloured .. 12 12
14. 50 c. multicoloured .. 25 25

7. National Mosque.

1965. Opening of National Mosque, Kuala Lumpur.
15. 7. 6 c. red 5 5
16. 15 c. brown 8 8
17. 20 c. green 10 10

8. Air Terminal.

1965. Opening of Int. Airport, Kuala Lumpur.
18. 8. 15 c. black, green and blue 5 5
19. 30 c. black, green & mag. 15 20

9. Crested Green Wood Partridge. 10. Sepak Raga (ball-game) and Football.

1965. Birds. Multicoloured.
20. 25 c. Type 9 .. .. 8 5
21. 30 c. Blue-backed Fairy Bluebird 12 10
22. 50 c. Black-naped Oriole .. 25 12
23. 75 c. Rhinoceros Hornbill .. 30 15
24. $1 Barred Ground Dove .. 50 20
25. $2 Great Argus Pheasant .. 1·00 25
26. $5 Paradise Flycatcher .. 2·50 75
27. $10 Banded Pitta .. .. 4·00 2·00

For the lower values see the individual sets listed under each of the states which form Malaysia.

1965. 3rd South East Asian Peninsular Games.
28. 10. 25 c. black and green .. 10 8
29. – 30 c. black and purple .. 12 12
30. – 50 c. black and blue .. 30 25

DESIGNS: 30 c. Running. 50 c. Diving.

11. National Monument.

1966. National Monument, Kuala Lumpur.
31. 11. 10 c. multicoloured .. 5 5
32. 20 c. multicoloured .. 12 12

12. The Yang di-Pertuan Agong (Ismail Nasiruddin Shah).

1966. Installation of Yang di-Pertuan Agang, Tuanku Ismail Nasiruddin Shah.
33. 12. 15 c. black and yellow .. 5 5
34. 50 c. black and blue .. 25 25

13. School Building.

1966. Penang Free School. 150th Anniv.
35. 13. 20 c. multicoloured .. 8 8
36. 50 c. multicoloured .. 30 25

14. "Agriculture".

1966. 1st Malaysia Plan. Multicoloured.
37. 15 c. Type 14 .. .. 10 8
38. 15 c. "Rural Health" .. 10 8
39. 15 c. "Communications" .. 10 8
40. 15 c. "Education" .. 10 8
41. 15 c. "Irrigation" 10 8

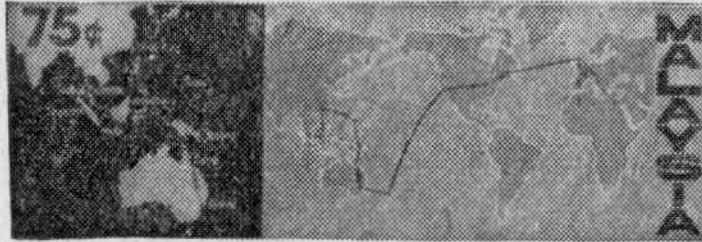

15. Cable Route Maps. (Reduced size illustration. Actual size 68 × 22 mm.).

1967. Completion of Malaysia-Hong Kong Link of SEACOM Telephone Cable.
42. 15. 30 c. multicoloured .. 10 10
43. 75 c. multicoloured .. 40 40

16. Hibiscus and Rulers.

1967. Independence. 10th Anniv.
44. 16. 15 c. multicoloured .. 5 5
45. 50 c. multicoloured .. 25 20

17. Mace and Shield.

1967. Sarawak Council. Cent.
46. 17. 15 c. multicoloured .. 5 5
47. 50 c. multicoloured .. 25 25

18. Straits Settlements 8 c. Stamp of 1867 and Malaysian 25 c. Stamp.

1967. Stamp Cent.
48. 18. 25 c. multicoloured .. 10 8
49. – 30 c. multicoloured .. 12 12
50. – 50 c. multicoloured .. 25 25

DESIGN: 30 c. Straits Settlements 24 c. Stamp of 1867 and Malaysian 30 c. Stamp. 50 c. Straits Settlements 32 c. Stamp of 1867 and Malaysian 50 c. Stamp.

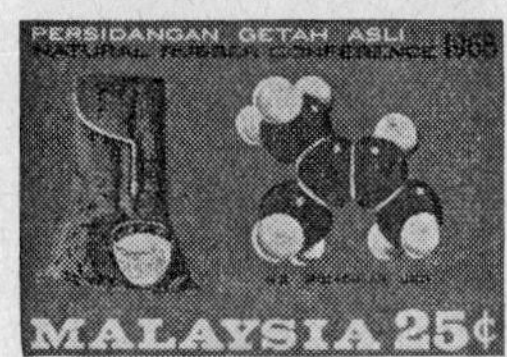

19. Tapping Rubber, and Molecular Unit.

1968. Natural Rubber Conf., Kuala Lumpur. Multicoloured.
51. 25 c. Type 19 .. .. 8 8
52. 30 c. Tapping Rubber, and Export Consignment .. 15 15
53. 50 c. Tapping Rubber, and Aircraft Tyres 30 30

20. Mexican Sombrero and Blanket with Olympic Rings. Multicoloured.

21. Tunku Abdul Rahman against background of Pandanus Weave.

1968. Olympic Games, Mexico.
54. 30 c. Type 20 .. .. 15 15
55. 75 c. Olympic Rings and Mexican Embroidery .. 45 45

1969. Solidarity Week.
56. 21. 15 c. multicoloured .. 5 5
57. – 20 c. multicoloured .. 15 15
58. – 50 c. multicoloured .. 35 35

DESIGNS—VERT. 20 c. As T 21 (different). HORIZ. 50 c. Tunku Rahman with Pandanus Pattern.

22. Peasant Girl with sheaves of Paddy.

1969. National Rice Year.
59. 22. 15 c. multicoloured .. 5 5
60. 75 c. multicoloured .. 40 40

23. Dish Aerial.

1970. Satellite Earth Station.
61. 23. 15 c. drab, black and blue 5 5
62. – 30 c. multicoloured .. 25 20
63. – 30 c. multicoloured .. 25 20

DESIGN—HORIZ. (40 × 27 mm.): Nos. 62/3, Satellite and earth.

No. 62 has inscription and value in white and No. 63 has them in gold.

24. Blue-branded King Crow Butterfly. 25. Emblem.

1970. Butterflies. Multicoloured.
64. 25 c. Type 24 .. .. 10 5
65. 30 c. Saturn 12 5
66. 50 c. Common Nawab .. 20 5
67. 75 c. Great Mormon .. 30 10
68. $1 Orange Albatross .. 40 12
69. $2 Raja Brooke's Birdwing 75 25
70. $5 Centaur Oak Bird .. 2·00 65
71. $10 Royal Assyrian .. 3·75 2·00

Lower values were issued for use in the individual States.

1970. Int. Labour Organisation. 50th Anniv.
72. 25. 30 c. grey and blue .. 12 10
73. 75 c. pink and blue .. 40 40

26. U.N. Emblem encircled by Doves.

1970. United Nations. 25th Anniv.
74. 26. 25 c. gold, black & brown 10 10
75. – 30 c. multicoloured .. 15 15
76. – 50 c. black and yellow .. 30 30

DESIGNS: 30 c. Line of Doves and U.N. Emblem. 50 c. Doves looping U.N. Emblem.

27. Yang di-Pertuan Agong.

1971. Installation of Yang di-Pertuan Agong. (Paramount Ruler of Malaysia).
77. 27. 10 c. blk., gold & yellow 5 5
78. 15 c. blk., gold & mauve 10 10
79. 50 c. blk., gold and blue 25 20

28. Bank Negara Complex.

1971. Opening of Bank Negara Building.
80. 28. 25 c. black and silver .. 10 10
81. 50 c. black and gold .. 30 30

29. Aerial view of Parliament Buildings. (Illustration reduced. Actual size 59 × 33 mm.)

1971. 17th Commonwealth Parliamentary Association Conference, Kuala Lumpur. Multicoloured.
82. 25 c. Type 29 .. .. 15 15
83. 75 c. Ground view of Parliament Buildings (horiz. 73 × 23½ mm) 40 40

30. 31. 32.
(Illustration reduced. Actual size 63½ × 32 mm.)

1971. Visit ASEAN Year.
84. 30. 30 c. multicoloured .. 20 20
85. 31. 30 c. multicoloured .. 20 20
86. 32. 30 c. multicoloured .. 20 20
ASEAN = Association of South East Asian Nations.
Nos. 84/6 form a composite design of a Malaysian Carnival, as Types 30/2.

33. Trees, Elephant and Tiger.

1971. U.N.I.C.E.F. 25th Anniv. Multicoloured.
87. 15 c. Type 33 .. .. 10 8
88. 15 c. Cat and kittens .. 10 8
89. 15 c. Sun, flower and bird (vert. 22 × 29 mm.) .. 10 8
90. 15 c. Monkey, elephant and lion in jungle .. 10 8
91. 15 c. Spider and butterflies 10 8

34. Athletics.

1971. 6th S.E.A.P. Games, Kuala Lumpur. Multicoloured.
92. 25 c. Type 34 .. .. 10 12
93. 30 c. Sepak Raga players 12 12
94. 50 c. Hockey 40 40
S.E.A.P. = South East Asian Peninsular.

35. 36. 37.
(Illustration reduced. Actual size 66 × 37 mm.).

1971. Pacific Area Tourist Association Conference.
95. 35. 30 c. multicoloured .. 20 15
96. 36. 30 c. multicoloured .. 20 15
97. 37. 30 c. multicoloured .. 20 15
Nos. 95/7 form a composite design of a map showing tourist attractions, as T 35/7.

38. Kuala Lumpur City Hall.
(Illustration reduced. Actual size 54 × 33 mm.).

1972. City Status for Kuala Lumpur. Multicoloured.
98. 25 c. Type 38 .. .. 10 12
99. 50 c. City Hall in Floodlights 30 30

39. SOCSO Emblem.

41. Fireworks, National Flag and Flower.

40. W.H.O. Emblem.

1973. Social Security Organization.
100. 39. 10 c. multicoloured .. 5 5
101. 15 c. multicoloured .. 5 5
102. 50 c. multicoloured .. 20 20

1973. W.H.O. 25th Anniv.
103. 40. 30 c. multicoloured .. 15 15
104. – 75 c. multicoloured .. 35 35
The 75 c. is similar to T 40, but vertical.

1973. Malaysia. 10th Anniv.
105. 41. 10 c. multicoloured .. 5 5
106. 15 c. multicoloured .. 5 5
107. 50 c. multicoloured .. 20 20

42. Emblems of Interpol and Royal Malaysian Police.

1973. Interpol. 50th Anniv. Multicoloured.
108. 25 c. Type 42 .. .. 12 12
109. 75 c. Emblems within "50" 35 35

43. Aeroplane and M.A.S. Emblem.

1973. Malaysian Airline System. Foundation.
110. 43. 15 c. multicoloured .. 5 5
111. 30 c. multicoloured .. 15 15
112. 50 c. multicoloured .. 25 25

44. Kuala Lumpur.

1974. Establishment of Kuala Lumpur as Federal Territory.
113. 44. 25 c. multicoloured .. 12 12
114. 50 c. multicoloured .. 25 25

45. Development Projects.

1974. Asian Development Bank's Board of Governors, Kuala Lumpur. 7th Annual Meeting.
115. 45. 30 c. multicoloured .. 15 15
116. 75 c. multicoloured .. 35 35

46. Scout Badge and Map.

1974. Malaysian Scout Jamboree. Mult.
117. 10 c. Type 46 .. .. 5 5
118. 15 c. Scouts saluting and flags (46 × 24 mm.) .. 5 5
119. 50 c. Scout Badge 25 25

47. Coat of Arms and Power Installations.

1974. National Electricity Board. 25th Anniv. Multicoloured.
120. 30 c. Type 47 .. .. 15 15
121. 75 c. National Electricity Board Building (37 × 27 mm.) 35 35

48. U.P.U. and Post Office Emblems within "100".

1974. U.P.U. Centenary.
122. 48. 27 c. green, yell. & red 12 12
123. 30 c. blue, yell. and red 15 15
124. 75 c. orange, yell. & red 35 35

49. Gravel Pump in Tin Mine.

1974. Fourth World Tin Conf., Kuala Lumpur. Multicoloured.
125. 15 c. Type 49 .. .. 5 5
126. 20 c. Open-cast mine .. 10 10
127. 50 c. Dredge within "ingot" 25 25

50. Hockey-players, World Cup and Federation Emblem.

1975. Third World Cup Hockey Championships.
128. 50. 30 c. multicoloured .. 12 12
129. 75 c. multicoloured .. 30 30

51. Congress Emblem.

1975. Malaysian Trade Union Congress. 25th Anniv.
130. 51. 20 c. multicoloured .. 8 8
131. 25 c. multicoloured .. 10 10
132. 30 c. multicoloured .. 12 12

52. Emblem of M.K.P.W. (Malayan Women's Organization).

1975. International Women's Year.
133. 52. 10 c. multicoloured .. 5 5
134. 15 c. multicoloured .. 8 5
135 50 c. multicoloured .. 20 20

53. Ubudiah Mosque, Kuala Kangsar.

1975. Koran Reading Competition. Multicoloured.
136. 15 c. Type 53 .. .. 8 5
137. 15 c. Zahir Mosque, Alor Star 8 5
138. 15 c. National Mosque, Kuala Lumpur .. 8 5
139. 15 c. Sultan Abu Bakar Mosque, Johore Bahru 8 5
140. 15 c. Kuching State Mosque, Sarawak .. 8 5

54. Plantation and Emblem.

1975. Malaysian Rubber Research Institute. 50th Anniv. Multicoloured.
141. 10 c. Type 54 .. .. 5 5
142. 30 c. Latex cup and emblem 12 12
143. 75 c. Natural rubber in test-tubes 30 30

55. Scrub Typhus.

56. Yang Di-Pertuan Agong.

1976. Institute of Medical Research. 75th Anniv. Multicoloured.
144. 20 c. Type 55 .. .. 8 8
145. 25 c. Malaria diagnosis .. 8 10
146. $1 Beri-beri 25 40

1976. H.M. The Yang di-Pertuan Agong. Installation.
147. 56. 10 c. blk., brn. & yell. 5 5
148. 15 c. blk., brn. & mauve 5 5
149. 50 c. blk., brn. & blue 15 20

57. State Council Complex.

1976. State Council Complex and Administrative Building, Sarawak. Opening.
150. 57. 15 c. green and yellow .. 8 8
151. 20 c. green and mauve .. 8 10
152. 50 c. green and blue .. 20 25

58. E.P.F. Building.

1976. Employees' Provident Fund. 25th Anniv. Mult.
153. 10 c. Type **58** 5 8
154. 25 c. E.P.F. emblems (27×27 mm.) 12 12
155. 50 c. E.P.F. Building at night 20 25

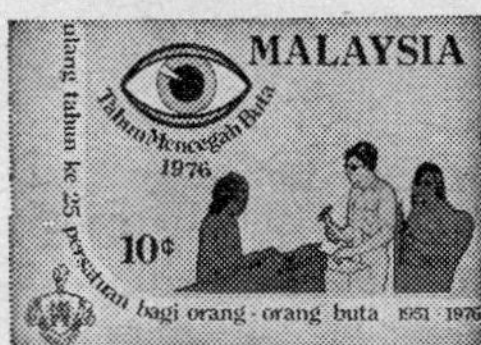

59. Blind People at Work.

1976. Malayan Assn. for the Blind. 25th Anniv. Mult.
156. 10 c. Type **59** 5 8
157. 75 c. Blind man and shadow 35 40

60. Independence Celebrations, 1957.

1977. Tun Abdul Razak (Prime Minister). 1st Death Anniv.
158. 15 c. Type **60** 8 8
159. 15 c. "Education" 8 8
160. 15 c. Tun Razak and map (Redevelopment) .. 8 8
161. 15 c. "Rukunegara" (National Philosophy) .. 8 8
162. 15 c. ASEAN meeting .. 8 8

POSTAGE DUE STAMPS

Until 15th August, 1966, the postage due stamps of Malayan Postal Union were in use throughout Malaysia.

D 1.

1966.
D 1. D 1. 1 c. red 5 5
D 2. 2 c. indigo 5 5
D 3. 4 c. apple 5 5
D 4. 8 c. green 8 8
D 5. 10 c. blue 8 5
D 6. 12 c. violet 10 8
D 15. 20 c. brown 8 5
D 8. 50 c. bistre 40 50

MALDIVE ISLANDS BC; O3

A group of islands W. of Ceylon. A republic from 1 Jan., 1953, but reverted to a sultanate in 1954. Became independent on 26 July, 1965, and left the British Commonwealth.

1906. 100 cents = 1 rupee.
1951. 100 larees = 1 rupee.

1906. Stamps of Ceylon optd. **MALDIVES**
1. 20. 2 c. brown .. .. 6·00 8·00
2. 21. 3 c. green .. .. 8·00 10·00
3. 4 c. orange and blue .. 20·00 35·00
4. – 5 c. purple (No. 268) .. 3·50 4·00
5. 21. 15 c. blue .. .. 30·00 38·00
6. 25 c. brown .. .. 32·00 38·00

1. Minaret, Juma Mosque, Male.

2. Palm Tree and Boat.

1909.
7. 1. 2 c. brown 75 25
11. 2 c. grey 40 35
8. 3 c. green 25 25
12. 3 c. brown 25 30
9. 5 c. purple 25 20
15. 6 c. red 60 60
10. 10 c. red 45 35
16. 10 c. green 30 30
17. 15 c. black 55 60
18. 25 c. brown 75 75
19. 50 c. purple 80 80
20. 1 r. blue .. .. 1·40 1·25

1950.
21. 2. 2 l. olive 35 35
22. 3 l. blue 80 70
23. 5 l. green 90 80
24. 6 l. brown 25 25
25. 10 l. red 25 25
26. 15 l. orange 30 35
27. 25 l. purple 35 40
28. 50 l. violet 50 50
29. 1 r. chocolate .. .. 2·50 2·75

3. Native Products.

1952.
30. – 3 l. blue (Fish) 25 30
31. 3. 5 l. emerald 12 20

4. Male Harbour.

5. Fort and Building.

1956.
32. 4. 2 l. purple 5 5
33. 3 l. slate 5 5
34. 5 l. brown 5 5
35. 6. l. violet 5 5
36. 10 l. emerald 5 5
37. 15 l. chocolate 5 5
38. 25 l. red 5 8
39. 50 l. orange 10 15
40. 5. 1 r. green 25 25
41. 5 r. blue 80 90
42. 10 r. magenta .. .. 1·75 2·00

6. Cycling.

1960. Olympic Games.
43. 6. 2 l. purple and green .. 5 5
44. 3 l. slate and purple .. 5 5
45. 5 l. brown and blue .. 5 5
46. 10 l. green and brown .. 5 5
47. 15 l. sepia and blue .. 5 8
48. – 25 l. red and olive .. 10 10
49. – 50 l. orange and violet .. 20 20
50. – 1 r. green and purple .. 30 35
DESIGN—VERT. 25 l. to 1 r. Basketball.

8. Tomb of Sultan.

1960.
51. 8. 2 l. purple 5 5
52. – 3 l. green 5 5
53. – 5 l. chestnut 5 5
54. – 6 l. blue 5 5
55. – 10 l. red 5 5
56. – 15 l. sepia 5 5
57. – 25 l. violet 5 5
58. – 50 l. grey 8 8
59. – 1 r. orange 15 15
60. – 5 r. blue 75 85
61. – 10 r. grey-green .. .. 1·50 1·75
DESIGNS: 3 l. Custom House. 5 l. Cowry shells. 6 l. Old Royal Palace. 10 l. Road to Juma Mosque, Male. 15 l. Council House. 25 l. New Government Secretariat. 50 l. Prime Minister's Office. 1 r. Old Ruler's Tomb. 5 r. Old Ruler's Tomb (distant view). 10 r. Maldivian Port.

Higher values were also issued, intended mainly for fiscal use.

9. "Care of Refugees".

1960. World Refugee Year.
62. 9. 2 l. violet, orange & green 5 5
63. 3 l. brown, green and red 5 5
64. 5 l. green, sepia and red .. 5 5
65. 10 l. green, violet and red 5 5
66. 15 l. violet, grey-grn. & red 5 5
67. 25 l. bl., brn. & bronze-grn. 8 8
68. 50 l. olive, red and blue .. 10 10
69. 1 r. red, slate and violet .. 20 45

10. Coconuts.

11. Map of Male.

1961.
70. 10. 2 l. brown and green .. 5 5
71. 3 l. brown and blue .. 5 5
72. 5 l. brown and magenta 5 5
73. 10 l. brown and orange .. 5 5
74. 15 l. brown and black .. 5 5
75. 11. 25 l. multicoloured .. 8 8
76. 50 l. multicoloured .. 10 10
77. 1 r. multicoloured .. 20 15

12. 5 c. Stamp of 1906.

1961. 1st Maldivian Stamp. 55th Anniv.
78. 12. 2 l. brn.-pur., bl. & grn. 5 5
79. 3 l. brn.-pur., bl. & grn. 5 5
80. 5 l. brn.-pur., bl. & grn. 5 5
81. 6 l. brn.-pur., bl. & grn. 5 5
82. – 10 l. grn., claret & mar. 5 5
83. – 15 l. grn., claret & mar. 5 5
84. – 20 l. grn., claret & mar. 8 8
85. – 25 l. claret, grn. & blk. 8 8
86. – 50 l. claret, green & blk. 15 20
87. – 1 r. claret, green & blk. 30 35
DESIGNS: 10 l. to 20 l. Posthorn and 3 c. stamp of 1906. 25 l. to 1 r. 2 c. stamp of 1906.

13. Campaign Emblem.

1962. Malaria Eradication.
88. 13. 2 l. chestnut 5 5
89. 3 l. emerald 5 5
90. 5 l. turquoise 5 5
91. 10 l. red 5 5
92. 15 l. sepia 5 5
93. 25 l. blue 8 10
94. 50 l. myrtle 12 15
95. 1 r. purple 25 35

14. Children of Europe and America.

1962. U.N.I.C.E.F. 15th Anniv.
96. 14. 2 l. multicoloured .. 5 5
97. 6 l. multicoloured .. 5 5
98. 10 l. multicoloured .. 5 5
99. 15 l. multicoloured .. 5 5
100. – 25 l. multicoloured .. 5 5
101. – 50 l. multicoloured .. 10 10
102. – 1 r. multicoloured .. 20 20
103. – 5 r. multicoloured .. 70 70
DESIGN: Nos. 100/3, Children of Middle and Far East.

15. Sultan Mohamed Farid Didi.

1962. Enthronement of Sultan. 9th Anniv.
104. 15. 3 l. brown and green .. 5 5
105. 5 l. brown and indigo .. 5 5
106. 10 l. brown and blue .. 5 5
107. 20 l. brown and olive .. 8 10
108. 50 l. brown and magenta 10 15
109. 1 r. brown & slate-violet 20 30

16. Angel Fish.

1963. Tropical Fish. Multicoloured.
110. 2 l. T **16** 5 5
111. 3 l. T **16** 5 5
112. 5 l. T **16** 5 5
113. 10 l. Moorish Idol 5 5
114. 25 l. Moorish Idol 8 8
115. 50 l. Soldier Fish 10 10
116. 1 r. Surgeon Fish 20 20
117. 5 r. Butterfly Fish .. 75 75

17. Fishes in Net.

1963. Freedom from Hunger.

118. 17. 2 l. brown and green .. 5 5
119. – 5 l. brown and red .. 5 5
120. 17. 7 l. brown & turquoise .. 5 5
121. – 10 l. brown and blue .. 5 5
122. 17. 25 l. brown & brn.-red .. 8 8
123. – 50 l. brown and violet .. 15 15
124. 17. 1 r. brown and magenta 25 30

DESIGNS—VERT. 5 l., 10 l., 50 l. Handful of grain.

18. Centenary Emblem.

1963. Red Cross Cent.

125. 18. 2 l. red and maroon .. 5 5
126. 15 l. red and green .. 5 5
127. 50 l. red and brown .. 8 8
128. 1 r. red and indigo .. 15 15
129. 4 r. red and olive .. 45 45

19. Maldivian Scout Badge.

1964. World Scout Jamboree, Marathon (1963).

130. 19. 2 l. green and violet .. 5 5
131. 3 l. green and brown .. 5 5
132. 25 l. green and blue .. 8 10
133. 1 r. green and red .. 25 40

20. Mosque, Male.

1964. "Maldive Embrace Islam".

134. 20. 2 l. purple 5 5
135. 3 l. green 5 5
136. 10 l. red 5 5
137. 40 l. dull purple .. 8 8
138. 60 l. blue 15 15
139. 85 l. chestnut 15 15

21. Putting the Shot.

1964. Olympic Games, Tokyo

140. 21. 2 l. maroon and blue .. 5 5
141. 3 l. red and chestnut .. 5 5
142. 5 l. bronze and green .. 5 5
143. 10 l. violet and purple .. 5 5
144. – 15 l. sepia and brown .. 5 5
145. – 25 l. indigo and blue .. 8 10
146. – 50 l. bronze and olive .. 15 20
147. – 1 r. maroon and grey .. 30 35

DESIGNS: 15 l. to 1 r. Running.

22. Telecommunications Satellite.

1965. Int. Quiet Sun Years.

148. 22. 5 l. blue 5 5
149. 10 l. brown 5 5
150. 25 l. green 10 10
151. 1 r. magenta 35 35

INDEPENDENT

NOTE.—Illustrations from this point are reduced to ¾ actual size.

23. Isis (wall carving, Abu Simbel). 24. Pres. Kennedy and Doves.

1965. Nubian Monuments Preservation.

152. 23. 2 l. green and maroon .. 5 5
153. – 3 l. lake and green .. 5 5
154. 23. 5 l. green and maroon .. 5 5
155. – 10 l. blue and orange .. 5 5
156. 23. 15 l. chestnut and violet 5 5
157. – 25 l. purple and blue .. 8 8
158. 23. 50 l. green and sepia .. 10 10
159. – 1 r. ochre and green .. 20 20

DESIGNS: 3, 10, 25 l., 1 r. Rameses II on throne (wall carving, Abu Simbel).

1965. Pres Kennedy's 2nd Death Anniv.

160. 24. 2 l. black and mauve .. 5 5
161. 5 l. brown and mauve .. 5 5
162. 25 l. indigo and mauve 8 8
163. – 1 r. pur., yellow & green 20 20
164. – 2 r. bronze, yellow & grn. 40 40

DESIGN: 1 r., 2 r. Pres. Kennedy and hands holding olive-branch.

25. "XX" and U.N. Flag. 26. I.C.Y. Emblem.

1965. U.N. 20th Anniv.

165. 25. 3 l. blue and brown .. 5 5
166. 10 l. blue and violet .. 5 5
167. 1 r. blue and green .. 25 20

1965. Int. Co-operation Year.

168. 26. 5 l. brown and bistre .. 5 5
169. 15 l. brown and lilac .. 5 5
170. 50 l. brown and olive .. 12 10
171. 1 r. brown and red .. 25 20
172. 2 r. brown and blue .. 45 40

27. Seashells.

1966. Multicoloured.

174. 2 l. Type **27** 5 5
175. 3 l. Yellow flowers .. 5 5
176. 5 l. Seashells (different) .. 5 5
177. 7 l. Camellias 5 5
178. 10 l. Type **27** 5 5
179. 15 l. Wader and seagull .. 5 5
180. 20 l. Yellow flowers .. 5 5
181. 30 l. Type **27** 8 8
182. 50 l. Wader and seagull .. 15 15
183. 1 r. Type **27** 25 25
184. 1 r. Camellias 25 25
185. 1 r. 50 Yellow flowers .. 35 35
186. 2 r. Camellias 45 45
187. 5 r. Wader and seagull .. 1·10 1·10
188. 10 r. Seashells (different) .. 2·25 2·25

The 3 l., 7 l., 20 l., 1 r. (No. 181), 1 r. 50 and 2 r. are DIAMOND (43½ × 43½ mm.).

28. Maldivian Flag. 30. U.N.E.S.C.O. Emblem and Owl on Book.

29. "Luna IX" on Moon.

1966. Independence. 1st Anniv.

189. 28. 10 l. green, red & turq. 5 5
190. 1 r. grn., red, brn. & yell. 25 25

1966. Space Rendezvous and Moon Landing.

191. 29. 10 l. brown, indigo & bl. 5 5
192. – 25 l. green and red .. 8 8
193. 29. 50 l. chestnut and green 10 10
194. – 1 r. turquoise & chestnut 25 25
195. – 2 r. green and violet .. 45 45
196. – 5 r. pink and turquoise 1·10 1·10

DESIGNS: 25 l., 1 r., 5 r. "Gemini VI" and "VII" rendezvous in space. 2 r. "Gemini" spaceship as seen from the other spaceship.

1966. U.N.E.S.C.O. 20th Anniv. Multi-coloured.

198. 2 l. Type **30** 5 5
199. 3 l. U.N.E.S.C.O. emblem and globe and microscope 5 5
200. 5 l. U.N.E.S.C.O emblem and mask, violin and palette 5 5
201. 50 l. Type **30** 15 15
202. 1 r. Design as 3 l. .. 25 25
203. 5 r. Design as 5 l. .. 1·10 1·10

31. Sir Winston Churchill and Cortege.

1966. Churchill Commem. Flag in red and blue.

204. 31. 2 l. brown 5 5
205. – 10 l. turquoise .. 5 5
206. 31. 15 l. green 5 5
207. – 25 l. violet 8 8
208. – 1 r. brown 25 25
209. 31. 2 r. 50 red 55 55

DESIGN: 10 l., 25 l., 1 r. Churchill and catafalque.

32. Footballers and Jules Rimet Cup.

1967. England's Victory in World Cup Football Championships.

210. 32. 2 l. blue, black and red 5 5
211. – 3 l. red, black and olive 5 5
212. – 5 l. yellow, black & violet 5 5
213. – 25 l. orange, blk. & grn. 8 8
214. – 50 l. green, blk. & orge. 12 12
215. 32. 1 r. orange, blk. & blue 25 25
216. – 2 r. brn., red, blue & blk. 45 45

DESIGNS: 3 l. to 50 l. Various football scenes. 2 r. Emblem on Union Jack, and Clock Tower, Westminster.

33. Clown Butterfly Fish.

1967. Tropical Fishes. Multicoloured.

218. 2 l. Type **33** 5 5
219. 3 l. Striped Puffer .. 5 5
220. 5 l. Blue Spotted Boxfish 5 5
221. 6 l. Picasso Fish 5 5
222. 50 l. Blue Angelfish .. 12 12
223. 1 r. Blue Spotted Boxfish 25 25
224. 2 r. Blue Angelfish .. 45 45

34. Aircraft over Airport Building.

1967. Hulule Airport. Inaug.

225. 34. 2 l. violet and olive .. 5 5
226. – 5 l. green and lavender 5 5
227. 34. 10 l. violet and green .. 5 5
228. – 15 l. green and ochre .. 5 5
229. 34. 30 l. ultramarine & blue 10 10
230. – 50 l. brown and magenta 12 12
231. 34. 5 r. ultram. & orange .. 1·10 1·10
232. – 10 r. brown and blue .. 2·25 2·25

DESIGN: 5 l., 15 l., 50 l. and 10 r. Airport building and aircraft.

35. "Man and Music" Pavilion.

1967. World Fair, Montreal. Multicoloured.

233. 2 l. Type **35** 5 5
234. 5 l. "Man and His Community" Pavilion .. 5 5
235. 10 l. Type **35** 5 5
236. 50 l. As 5 l. 15 15
237. 1 r. Type **35** 25 25
238. 2 r. As 5 l. 45 45

1968. Int. Tourist Year (1967). Nos. 225/32 optd. **International Tourist Year 1967.**

240. 34. 2 l. violet and olive .. 5 5
241. – 5 l. green and lavender 5 5
242. 34. 10 l. violet and green .. 5 5
243. – 15 l. green and ochre .. 8 8
244. 34. 30 l. ultramarine & blue 8 8
245. – 50 l. brown and magenta 10 10
246. 34. 5 r. ultram. and orange 1·10 1·10
247. – 10 r. brown and blue .. 2·25 2·25

36. Cub signalling and Lord Baden-Powell. 38. Putting the Shot.

37. French Satellite "A 1".

1968. Maldivian Scouts and Cubs.

248. 36. 2 l. brown, green & yell. 5 5
249. – 3 l. red and blue .. 5 5
250. 36. 25 l. violet, lake & red .. 8 8
251. – 1 r. bronze, chestnut and green 25 25

DESIGN: 3 l. and 1 r. Scouts and Lord Baden-Powell.

1968. Space Martyrs.

252. 37. 2 l. magenta & ultram. 5 5
253. – 3 l. violet and brown .. 5 5
254. – 7 l. brown and lake .. 5 5
255. – 10 l. blue, drab and black 5 5
256. – 25 l. emerald and violet 8 8
257. 37. 50 l. blue and brown .. 12 12
258. – 1 r. maroon and green .. 25 25
259. – 2 r. brown, blue & black 45 45
260. – 5 r. magenta, drab & blk. 1·00 1·00

DESIGNS: 3 l., 25 l. "Luna 10". 7 l., 1 r. "Orbiter" and "Mariner". 10 l., 2 r. Astronauts White, Grissom and Chaffee. 5 r. Cosmonaut V. M. Komarov.

1968. Olympic Games, Mexico. Multi-coloured.

262. 2 l. Type **38** 5 5
263. 6 l. Throwing the discus .. 5 5
264. 10 l. Type **38** 5 5
265. 25 l. As 6 l. 5 5
266. 1 r. Type **38** 25 25
267. 2 r. 50 As 6 l. 60 60

39. "Adriatic Seascape" (Bonington).

1968. Paintings. Multicoloured.
268. 50 l. Type **39** 12 12
269. 1 r. "Ulysses deriding Polyphemus" (Turner) 25 25
270. 2 r. "Sailing Boat at Argenteuil" (Monet) .. 45 45
271. 5 r. "Fishing Boat at Saintes-Maires" (Van Gogh) .. .. .. 1·10 1·10

40. "Graf Zeppelin" and Montgolfier's Balloon.

1968. Development of Civil Aviation.
272. **40.** 2 l. chest., grn. & ultram 5 5
273. – 3 l. blue, violet & chest. 5 5
274. – 5 l. green, red and blue 5 5
275. – 7 l. blue, purple & orge. 5 5
276. **40.** 10 l. brown, blue & pur 5 5
277. – 50 l. red, green & olive 12 12
278. – 1 r. green, blue & verm 25 25
279. – 2 r. maroon, bistre & blue 45 45
DESIGNS: 3 l., 1 r. Boeing "707" and Douglas "DC-3". 5 l., 50 l. Wright Brothers' aircraft and Lilienthal's glider. 7 l., 2 r. Boeing Supersonic "733" and "Concorde".

41. W.H.O. Building, Geneva.

1968. World Health Organisation. 20th Anniv.
280. **41.** 10 l. violet, turq. & blue 5 5
281. 25 l. green, brn. & yellow 8 8
282. 1 r. brown, emer. & grn. 25 25
283. 2 r. violet, mag. & mve. 45 45

1968. Scout Jamboree, Idaho. 1st Anniv. Nos. 248/51 optd. **International Boy Scout Jamboree, Farragut Park Idaho, U.S.A. August 1–9, 1967.**
284. **36.** 2 l. brown, grn. & yellow 5 5
285. – 3 l. red and blue .. 5 5
286. **36.** 25 l. violet, lake and red 8 8
287. – 1 r. bronze, chest. & grn. 25 25

42. Wading Birds.

1968. Multicoloured.
288. 2 l. Type **42** 5 5
289. 10 l. Conches 5 5
290. 25 l. Shells 8 8
291. 50 l. Type **42** 12 12
292. 1 r. Conches 25 25
293. 2 r. Shells 45 45

43. Throwing the Discus.

1968. Olympic Games, Mexico. Multicoloured.
294. 10 l. Type **43** 5 5
295. 50 l. Running 12 12
296. 1 r. Cycling 25 25
297. 2 r. Basketball 45 45

44. Fishing Boat. 45. "The Thinker" (Rodin).

1968. Republic Day.
298. **44.** 10 l. brown, blue & grn. 5 5
299. – 1 r. green, red and blue 25 25
DESIGN: 1 r. National flag, crest and map.

1969. U.N.E.S.C.O. "Human Rights". Designs showing sculptures by Rodin. Multicoloured.
300. 6 l. Type **45** 5 5
301. 10 l. "Hands" 5 5
302. 1 r. 50 "Eve" 40 40
303. 2 r. 50 "Adam" 60 60

46. Module nearing Moon's Surface.

1969. 1st Man on the Moon. Multicoloured.
305. 6 l. Type **46** 5 5
306. 10 l. Astronaut with hatchet 5 5
307. 1 r. 50 Astronaut and module 40 40
308. 2 r. 50 Astronaut using camera 60 60

1969. Gold Medal Winners, Olympic Games, Mexico (1968). Nos. 295/6 optd. **Gold Medal Winner Mohamed Gammaudi 5000m. run Tunisia REPUBLIC OF MALDIVES** and similar optd.
310. 50 l. multicoloured .. 15 15
311. 1 r. multicoloured .. 30 30
The inscription on No. 310 honours P. Trentin (cycling, France).

47. Red striped Butterfly Fish.

1970. Fishes. Multicoloured.
312. 2 l. Type **47** .. 5 5
313. 5 l. Spotted triggerfish .. 5 5
314. 25 l. Scorpion fish .. 8 8
315. 50 l. Forceps fish .. 15 15
316. 1 r. Imperial angelfish .. 30 30
317. 2 r. Regal angelfish .. 60 60

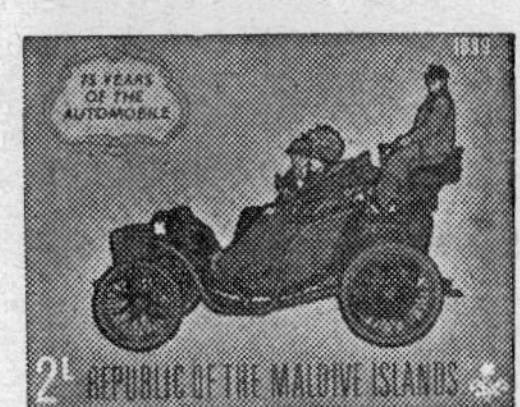

48. Columbia Dauman Victoria, 1899.

1970. "75 Years of the Automobile". Multicoloured.
318. 2 l. Type **48** 5 5
319. 5 l. Duryea phaeton, 1902 5 5
320. 7 l. Packard S-24, 1906 .. 5 5
321. 10 l. Autocar "runabout" 5 5
322. 25 l. Type **48** 8 8
323. 50 l. As 5 l. 15 15
324. 1 r. As 7 l. 30 30
325. 2 r. As 10 l. 60 60

49. U.N. Headquarters, New York.

1970. United Nations. 25th Anniv. Multicoloured.
327. 2 l. Type **49** 5 5
328. 10 l. Surgical operation (W.H.O.) 5 5
329. 25 l. Student, actress and musician (U.N.E.S.C.O.) 8 8
330. 50 l. Children at work and play (U.N.I.C.E.F.) .. 15 15
331. 1 r. Fish, corn and farm animals (F.A.O.) .. 30 30
332. 2 r. Miner hewing coal (I.L.O.) 60 60

50. Ship and Light Buoy.

1970. I.M.C.O. 10th Anniv. Multicoloured.
333. 50 l. Type **50** 15 15
334. 1 r. Ship and lighthouse .. 30 30

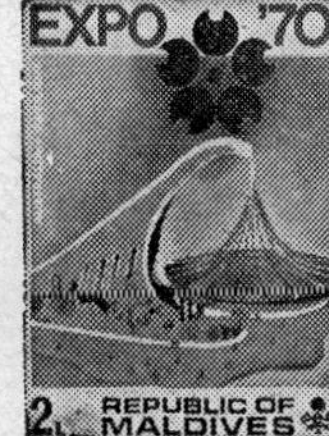

51. "Player and Masqueraders" (Watteau). 52. Australian Pavilion.

1970. Famous Paintings showing the Guitar. Multicoloured.
335. 3 l. Type **51** 5 5
336. 7 l. "Spanish Guitarist" (Manet) 5 5
337. 50 l. "Costumed Player" (Watteau) 15 15
338. 1 r. "Mandoline-player" (Roberti) 30 30
339. 2 r. 50 "The Guitar-player and Lady" (Watteau) 75 75
340. 5 r. "Mandoline-player" (Frans Hals) .. .. 1·40 1·40

1970. "EXPO 70" World Fair, Osaka, Japan. Multicoloured.
342. 2 l. Type **52** 5 5
343. 3 l. West German Pavilion 5 5
344. 10 l. U.S. Pavilion .. 5 5
345. 25 l. British Pavilion .. 8 8
346. 50 l. Soviet Pavilion .. 15 15
347. 1 r. Japanese Pavilion .. 30 30

53. Learning the Alphabet.

1970. Int. Education Year. Multicoloured.
348. 5 l. Type **53** 5 5
349. 10 l. Training teachers .. 5 5
350. 25 l. Geography lesson .. 8 8
351. 50 l. School inspector .. 15 15
352. 1 r. Education by television 30 30

1970. "Philympia 1970" Stamp Exn., London. Nos. 306/8 optd. "**Philympia London 1970**".
353. 10 l. multicoloured .. 5 5
354. 1 r. 50 multicoloured .. 45 45
355. 2 r. 50 multicoloured .. 75 75

54. Footballers. 55. Little Boy and U.N.I.C.E.F. "Flag".

1970. World Cup Football Championships, Mexico.
357. **54.** 3 l. multicoloured .. 5 5
358. – 6 l. multicoloured .. 5 5
359. – 7 l. multicoloured .. 5 5
360. – 25 l. multicoloured .. 8 8
361. – 1 r. multicoloured .. 30 30
DESIGNS: 6 l. to 1 r. Different designs showing footballers in action.

1970. U.N.I.C.E.F. 25th Anniv. Multicoloured.
362. 5 l. Type **55** 5 5
363. 10 l. Little girl with U.N.I.C.E.F. "balloon" 5 5
364. 1 r. Type **55** 30 30
365. 2 r. As 10 l. 60 60

56. Astronauts Lovell, Haise and Swigert. 57. "Multiracial Flower".

1971. Safe return of "Appollo 13". Multicoloured.
366. 5 l. Type **56** 5 5
367. 20 l. "Explosion in Space" 5 5
368. 1 r. Splashdown 30 30

1971. Racial Equality Year.
369. **57.** 10 l. multicoloured .. 5 5
370. 25 l. multicoloured .. 8 8

58. "Mme. Charpentier and her Children" (Renoir).

1971. Famous Paintings showing "Mother and Child". Multicoloured.
371. 5 l. Type **58** 5 5
372. 7 l. "Susanna van Collen and her Daughter" (Rembrandt) 5 5
373. 10 l. "Madonna nursing the Child" (Titian) .. 5 5
374. 20 l. "Baroness Belleli and her Children" (Degas) .. 5 5
375. 25 l. "The Cradle" (Morisot) 8 8
376. 1 r. "Helena Fourment and her Children" (Reubens) 30 30
377. 3 r. "On the Terrace" (Renoir) 90 90

59. Alan Shepard.

1971. Moon Flight of "Apollo 14". Mult.
378. 6 l. Type **59** 5 5
379. 10 l. Stuart Roosa 5 5
380. 1 r. 50 Edgar Mitchell .. 45 45
381. 5 r. Crew's insignia .. 1·40 1·40

60. " Ballerina " (Degas).

1971. Famous Paintings showing " Dancers ". Multicoloured.

382. 5 l. Type 60 .. .. 5 5
383. 10 l. " Dancing Couple " (Renoir) 5 5
384. 2 r. " Spanish Dancer " (Monet) 60 60
385. 5 r. " Ballerinas " (Degas) 1·40 1·40
386. 10 r. " La Goulue at the Moulin Rouge " (Toulouse-Lautrec) .. .. 2·75 2·75

1972. Visit of Queen Elizabeth II and Prince Philip. Nos. 381/5 optd. **ROYAL VISIT 1972.**

387. 60. 5 l. multicoloured .. 5 5
388. – 10 l. multicoloured .. 5 5
389. – 2 r. multicoloured .. 60 60
390. – 5 r. multicoloured .. 1·40 1·40
391. – 10 r. multicoloured .. 2·75 2·75

61. Book Year Emblem.

1972. Int. Book Year.

392. 61. 25 l. multicoloured .. 8 8
393. 5 r. multicoloured .. 1·40 1·40

62. Scottish Costume.

1972. National Costumes of the World. Mult.

394. 10 l. Type 62 .. .. 5 5
395. 15 l. Netherlands 5 5
396. 25 l. Norway 8 8
397. 50 l. Hungary 15 15
398. 1 r. Austria 30 30
399. 2 r. Spain 60 60

63. Stegosaurus.

1972. Prehistoric Animals. Multicoloured.

400. 2 l. Type 63 .. .. 5 5
401. 7 l. Edaphosaurus 5 5
402. 25 l. Diplodocus 8 8
403. 50 l. Triceratops 12 12
404. 2 r. Pteranodon 45 45
405. 5 r. Tyrannosaurus .. 1·25 1·25

64. Cross-country Skiing.

65. Scout Saluting.

1972. Winter Olympic Games, Sapporo, Japan. Multicoloured.

406. 3 l. Type 64 .. .. 5 5
407. 6 l. Bob-sleighing 5 5
408. 15 l. Speed-skating .. 5 5
409. 50 l. Ski-jumping 12 12
410. 1 r. Pairs-skating 25 25
411. 2 r. 50 Ice-hockey 60 60

1972. 13th Boy Scout Jamboree Asagiri, Japan (1971). Multicoloured.

412. 10 l. Type 65 .. .. 5 5
413. 15 l. Scout signalling .. 5 5
414. 50 l. Scout blowing bugle .. 12 12
415. 1 r. Scout playing drum .. 25 25

66. Cycling.

67. Globe and Conference Emblem.

1972. Olympic Games, Munich. Mult.

416. 5 l. Type 66 .. .. 5 5
417. 10 l. Running 5 5
418. 25 l. Wrestling 8 8
419. 50 l. Hurdling 12 12
420. 2 r. Boxing 45 45
421. 5 r. Volleyball .. .. 1·25 1·25

1972. U.N. Environmental Conservation Conf., Stockholm.

423. 67. 2 l. multicoloured .. 5 5
424. 3 l. multicoloured .. 5 5
425. 15 l. multicoloured .. 5 5
426. 50 l. multicoloured .. 12 12
427. 2 r. 50 multicoloured .. 60 60

68. " Flowers " (Van Gogh).

1973. Floral Paintings. Multicoloured.

428. 1 l. Type 68 .. .. 5 5
429. 2 l. " Flowers in Jug " (Renoir) 5 5
430. 3 l. " Chrysanthemums " (Renoir) 5 5
431. 50 l. " Mixed Bouquet " (Bosschaert) 12 12
432. 1 r. As 3 l. 25 25
433. 5 r. As 2 l. .. .. 1·25 1·25

1973. Gold-Medal Winners, Munich Olympic Games. Nos. 420/1 optd. as listed below.

435. 2 r. multicoloured 45 45
436. 5 r. multicoloured .. .. 1·25 1·25

OVERPRINTS: 2 r. **LEMECHEV MIDDLE-WEIGHT GOLD MEDALLIST.** 5 r. **JAPAN GOLD MEDAL WINNER.**

69. Animal Care.

1973. Int. Scouting Conf. Nairobi/Addis Ababa. Multicoloured.

438. 1 l. Type 69 .. .. 5 5
439. 2 l. Lifesaving 5 5
440. 3 l. Agricultural training .. 5 5
441. 4 l. Carpentry 5 5
442. 5 l. Playing leap-frog .. 5 5
443. 1 r. As 2 l. 25 25
444. 2 r. As 4 l. 45 45
445. 3 r. Type 69 .. .. 70 70

70. " Makaira herscheli ".

1973. Fishes. Multicoloured.

447. 1 l. Type 70 .. .. 5 5
448. 2 l. " Katsuwonus pelamys " 5 5
449. 3 l. " Thunnus thynnus " .. 5 5
450. 5 l. " Coryphaena hippurus " 5 5
451. 60 l. " Lutjanus gibbus " .. 12 12
452. 75 l. " Lutjanus gibbus " 15 15
453. 1 r. 50 " Variola louti " .. 35 35
454. 2 r. 50 " Coryphaena hippurus " 45 45
455. 3 r. " Plectropoma maculatum " 70 70
456. 10 r. " Scomberomorus commerson " .. .. 2·40 2·40

Nos. 451/2 are smaller, size 29 × 22 mm.

71. Golden-fronted Leafbird.

1973. Fauna. Multicoloured.

458. 1 l. Type 71 .. .. 5 5
459. 2 l. Fruit bat 5 5
460. 3 l. Land tortoise .. 5 5
461. 4 l. Butterfly (" Kallima inachus ") 5 5
462. 50 l. As 3 l. 12 12
463. 2 r. Type 71 .. .. 45 45
464. 3 r. As 2 l. 70 70

72. " Lantana camera ".

1973. Flowers of the Maldive Islands. Mult.

466. 1 l. Type 72 .. .. 5 5
467. 2 l. " Nerium oleander " .. 5 5
468. 3 l. " Rosa polyantha " .. 5 5
469. 4 l. " Hibiscus manihot " .. 5 5
470. 5 l. " Bougainvillea glabra " 5 5
471. 10 l. " Plumera alba " .. 5 5
472. 50 l. " Poinsettia pulcherrima " 12 12
473. 5 r. " Ononis natrix " .. 1·25 1·25

73. " Tiros " Weather Satellite.

1974. World Meteorological Organization. Multicoloured.

475. 1 l. Type 73 .. .. 5 5
476. 2 l. " Nimbus " satellite .. 5 5
477. 3 l. " Nomad " maritime weather station 5 5
478. 4 l. Scanner, A.P.T. Instant Weather Picture equipment 5 5
479. 5 l. Richard's wind-speed recorder 5 5
480. 2 r. Type 73 .. .. 45 45
481. 3 r. As 3 l. 70 70

74. " Apollo " Spacecraft and Pres. Kennedy.

1974. American and Russian Space Exploration Projects. Multicoloured.

483. 1 l. Type 74 .. .. 5 5
484. 2 l. " Mercury " capsule and John Glenn 5 5
485. 3 l. " Vostok 1 " and Yuri Gargarin 5 5
486. 4 l. " Vostok 6 " and Valentina Tereshkova 5 5
487. 5 l. " Soyuz 11 " and " Salyut " space-station 5 5
488. 2 r. " Skylab " space laboratory 45 45
489. 3 r. As 2 l. 70 70

75. Copernicus and " Skylab " Space Laboratory.

76. " Maternity " (Picasso).

1974. Nicholas Copernicus (astronomer). 500th Birth Anniv. Multicoloured.

491. 1 l. Type 75 .. .. 5 5
492. 2 l. Orbital space-station of the future 5 5
493. 3 l. Proposed " Space-shuttle " craft 5 5
494. 4 l. " Mariner 2 " Venus probe 5 5
495. 5 l. " Mariner 4 " Mars probe 5 5
496. 25 l. Type 75 .. .. 8 8
497. 1 r. 50 As 2 l. 35 35
498. 5 r. As 3 l. .. .. 1·25 1·25

1974. Paintings by Picasso. Multicoloured.

500. 1 l. Type 76 .. .. 5 5
501. 2 l. " Harlequin and Friend " 5 5
502. 3 l. " Pierrot Sitting " .. 5 5
503. 20 l. " Three Musicians " .. 5 5
504. 75 l. " L'Aficionado " .. 15 15
505. 5 r. " Still Life " .. .. 1·25 1·25

77. U.P.U. Emblem, Steam and Diesel Locomotives.

78. Footballers.

1974. Universal Postal Union. Cent. Mult.

507. 1 l. Type 77 .. .. 5 5
508. 2 l. Paddle-steamer and modern mailboat .. 5 5
509. 3 l. Airship and Boeing " 747 " airliner 5 5
510. 1 r. 50 Mailcoach and motor van 35 35
511. 2 r. 50 As 2 l. 70 70
512. 5 r. Type 77 .. .. 1·25 1·25

1974. World Cup Football Championships, West Germany.

514. 78. 1 l. multicoloured .. 5 5
515. – 2 l. multicoloured .. 5 5
516. – 3 l. multicoloured .. 5 5
517. – 4 l. multicoloured .. 5 5
518. – 75 l. multicoloured .. 35 35
519. – 4 r. multicoloured .. 90 90
520. – 5 r. multicoloured .. 1·25 1·25

DESIGNS: Nos. 515/20, show football scene similar to Type 78.

79. " Capricorn ".

1974. Signs of the Zodiac. Multicoloured.

522. 1 l. Type 79 .. .. 5 5
523. 2 l. " Aquarius " 5 5
524. 3 l. " Pisces " 5 5
525. 4 l. " Aries " 5 5
526. 5 l. " Taurus " 5 5
527. 6 l. " Gemini " 5 5
528. 7 l. " Cancer " 5 5
529. 10 l. " Leo " 5 5
530. 15 l. " Virgo " 5 5
531. 20 l. " Libra " 5 5
532. 25 l. " Scorpio " 8 8
533. 5 r. " Sagittarius " .. 1·25 1·25

80. Churchill and Bomber Aircraft.

1974. Sir Winston Churchill. Birth Cent. Multicoloured.

535.	1 l. Type **80**	5	5
536.	2 l. Churchill as pilot	5	5
537.	3 l. Churchill as First Lord of the Admiralty	5	5
538.	4 l. Churchill and aircraft carrier	5	5
539.	5 l. Churchill with fighter aircraft	5	5
540.	60 l. Churchill with anti-aircraft battery	12	12
541.	75 l. Churchill with tank in desert	35	35
542.	5 r. Churchill with flying boat	1·25	1·25

81. " Cassis nana ". **82.** Royal Throne.

1975. Seashells and Cowries. Multicoloured.

544.	1 l. Type **81**	5	5
545.	2 l. " Murex triremus "	5	5
546.	3 l. " Harpa major "	5	5
547.	4 l. " Lambis chiragra "	5	5
548.	5 l. " Conus pennaceus "	5	5
549.	60 l. " Cypraea diliculum " (22 × 30 mm.)	15	15
550.	75 l. "Clanculus pharaonis" (22 × 30 mm.)	20	20
551.	5 r. " Chicoreus ramosus "	1·25	1·25

1975. Historical Relics and Monuments. Multicoloured.

553.	1 l. Type **82**	5	5
554.	10 l. " Dullisa " (candlesticks)	5	5
555.	25 l. Lamp-tree	5	5
556.	60 l. Royal umbrellas	15	15
557.	75 l. Eid-Miskith Mosque (horiz.)	20	20
558.	3 r. Tomb of Al-Hafiz Abu-al Barakath-al Barubari (horiz.)	75	75

83. Guava.

85. Clock Tower and Customs Buildings.

84. " Phyllangia ".

1975. Exotic Fruits. Multicoloured.

559.	2 l. Type **83**	5	5
560.	4 l. Maldive mulberry	5	5
561.	5 l. Mountain apples	5	5
562.	10 l. Bananas	5	5
563.	20 l. Mangoes	5	5
564.	50 l. Papaya	12	12
565.	1 r. Pomegranates	25	25
566.	5 r. Coconut	1·25	1·25

1975. Marine Life. Corals, Urchins and Sea Stars. Multicoloured.

568.	1 l. Type **84**	5	5
569.	2 l. " Madrepora oculata "	5	5
570.	3 l. " Acropora gravida "	5	5
571.	4 l. " Stylotella "	5	5
572.	5 l. " Aeropora cervicornis "	5	5
573.	60 l. " Strongylocentrotus purpuratus "	15	15
574.	75 l. " Pisaster ochraceus "	20	20
575.	5 r. " Marthasterias glacialis "	1·25	1·25

1975. Independence. Tenth Anniv. Multicoloured.

577.	4 l. Type **85**	5	5
578.	5 l. Government offices	5	5
579.	7 l. N.E. Waterfront, Male	5	5
580.	15 l. Mosque and Minaret	5	5
581.	10 r. Sultan Park and Museum	2·50	2·50

1975. " Nordjamb 75 " World Scout Jamboree, Norway. Nos. 443/5 optd. **14th Boy Scout Jamboree July 29—August 7,1975.**

582. –	1 r. multicoloured	25	25
583. –	2 r. multicoloured	50	50
584. **69.**	3 r. multicoloured	75	75

86. Madura-Prau Bedang.

1975. Maldive Ships. Multicoloured.

586.	1 l. Type **86**	5	5
587.	2 l. Ganges patile	5	5
588.	3 l. Indian palla (vert.)	5	5
589.	4 l. " Odhi " (vert.)	5	5
590.	5 l. Maldivian schooner	5	5
591.	25 l. " Cutty Sark " (British tea clipper)	5	5
592.	1 r. Maldivian baggala (vert.)	25	25
593.	5 r. " Maldive Courage " (freighter)	1·25	1·25

87. " Brahmaea wallichii ". **88.** " The Rebellious Slave " (Michelangelo).

1975. Butterflies. Multicoloured.

595.	1 l. Type **87**	5	5
596.	2 l. " Teinopalpus imperialis "	5	5
597.	3 l. " Cethosia biblis "	5	5
598.	4 l. " Hestia jasonia "	5	5
599.	5 l. " Apartura ilia "	5	5
600.	25 l. " Kallima horsfieldi "	5	5
601.	1 r. 50 " Hebomoia leucippe "	35	35
602.	5 r. " Papilio memnon "	1·25	1·25

1975. Michelangelo. 500th Birth Anniv. Multicoloured.

604.	1 l. Type **88**	5	5
605.	2 l. Painting from Sistine Chapel	5	5
606.	3 l. " Apollo "	5	5
607.	4 l. Painting from Sistine Chapel	5	5
608.	5 l. " Bacchus "	5	5
609.	1 r. Painting from Sistine Chapel	25	25
610.	2 r. " David "	50	50
611.	5 r. Painting from Sistine Chapel	1·25	1·25

89. Beaker and Vase.

1975. Maldivian Lacquerware. Multicoloured.

613.	2 l. Type **89**	5	5
614.	4 l. Boxes	5	5
615.	50 l. Jar with lid	12	12
616.	75 l. Bowls with covers	20	20
617.	1 r. Craftsman at work	25	25

90. Map of Maldives.

1975. Tourism. Multicoloured.

618.	4 l. Type **90**	5	5
619.	5 l. Motor launch and small craft	5	5
620.	7 l. Sailing-boats	5	5
621.	15 l. Underwater diving	5	5
622.	3 r. Hulule Airport	75	75
623.	10 r. Motor cruisers	2·50	2·50

91. Cross-country. Skiing. **92.** " General Burgoyne " (Reynolds).

1976. Winter Olympic Games, Innsbruck. Multicoloured.

624.	1 l. Type **91**	5	5
625.	2 l. Speed-skating (pairs)	5	5
626.	3 l. Figure-skating (pairs)	5	5
627.	4 l. Two-man bobsleighing	5	5
628.	5 l. Ski-jumping	5	5
629.	25 l. Figure-skating (women's)	5	5
630.	1 r. 15 Skiing (slalom)	25	25
631.	4 r. Ice-hockey	1·00	1·00

1976. American Revolution. Bicent. Multicoloured.

633.	1 l. Type **92**	5	5
634.	2 l. " John Hancock " (Copley)	5	5
635.	3 l. " Death of Gen. Montgomery " (Trumbull) (horiz.)	5	5
636.	4 l. " Paul Revere " (Copley)	5	5
637.	5 l. " Battle of Bunker Hill " (Trumbull) (horiz.)	5	5
638.	2 r. " The Crossing of the Delaware " (Sully)(horiz.)	65	65
639.	3 r. " Samuel Adams " (Copley)	1·00	1·00
640.	5 r. " Surrender of Cornwallis " (Trumbull) (horiz.)	1·60	1·60

93. Thomas Edison.

1976. Telephone Centenary. Multicoloured.

642.	1 l. Type **93**	5	5
643.	2 l. Alexander Graham Bell	5	5
644.	3 l. Telephones of 1919, 1937 and 1972	5	5
645.	10 l. Cable entrance into station	5	5
646.	20 l. Equaliser circuit assembly	5	5
647.	1 r. Cable-ship laying cable	35	35
648.	10 r. " Intelsat IV-A "	3·25	3·25

94. Wrestling.

1976. Olympic Games, Montreal. Multicoloured.

650.	1 l. Type **94**	5	5
651.	2 l. Shot-putting	5	5
652.	3 l. Hurdling	5	5
653.	4 l. Hockey	5	5
654.	5 l. Running	5	5
655.	6 l. Javelin-throwing	5	5
656.	1 r. 50 Discus-throwing	50	50
657.	5 r. Volleyball	1·60	1·60

1976. " Interphil 76 " International Stamp Exhibition, Philadelphia. Nos. 638/40, optd. **" INTERPHIL "** and dates.

659.	2 r. multicoloured	65	65
660.	3 r. multicoloured	1·00	1·00
661.	5 r. multicoloured	1·60	1·60

95. " Dolichos lablab ".

1976. Maldive Vegetables. Multicoloured.

663.	2 l. Type **95**	5	5
664.	4 l. " Moringa pterygosperma "	5	5
665.	10 l. " Solanum melongena "	5	5
666.	50 l. " Cucumis sativus "	15	15
667.	75 l. " Trichosanthes anguina "	25	25
668.	1 r. " Momordica charantia "	35	35

MALI O3

Federation of French Sudan and Senegal, formed in 1959 as an autonomous republic within the French Community. In August 1960 the Federation was split up and the French Sudan part became the independent Mali Republic.

A. FEDERATION.

1. Map, Flag, Mali and Torch.

1959. Establishment of Mali Federation.

1. **1.**	25 f. red, buff, green & pur.	30	30

2.

1959. Air. St. Louis of Senegal. 300th Anniv.

2. **2.**	85 f. brn., blue, chest. & pur.	85	75

3. Parrot Fish. **4.** Amethyst Starling.

1960. (a) Postage. Fish as T **3.**

3. **3.**	5 f. orange, blue & bronze	8	5
4. –	10 f. black, brown & turq.	10	8
5. –	15 f. brown, slate and blue	15	10
6. –	20 f. black, bistre & ol.-grn.	20	15
7. –	25 f. yellow, sepia & green	25	20
8. –	30 f. red, maroon and blue	35	20
9. –	85 f. red, blue and green	1·00	75

(b) Air. Birds as T **4.**

10. **4.**	100 f. multicoloured	90	65
11. –	200 f. multicoloured	1·60	1·00
12. –	500 f. multicoloured	5·00	3·75

DESIGNS—HORIZ. 10 f. Trigger fish. 15 f. Batfish. 20 f. Thread fish. 25 f. Butterfly. 30 f. Surgeon. 85 f. Sea bream. 200 f. Bateleur eagle. VERT. 500 f. Gonolek.

1960. African Technical Co-operation Commission. 10th Anniv. As T **39** of Cameroun.

13.	25 f. purple and violet	55	40

B. REPUBLIC.

1960. Nos. 6, 7, 9 and 10/12 optd. **REPUBLIQUE DU MALI** and bar or bars or surch. also.

14.	20 f. black, bistre and olive-green (postage)	40	30
15.	25 f. red, maroon and blue	45	35
16.	85 f. red, blue and green	1·00	85
17.	100 f. multicoloured (air)	1·25	1·00
18.	200 f. multicoloured	2·00	1·75
19.	300 f. on 500 f. multicoloured	3·50	3·00
20.	500 f. multicoloured	5·50	4·00

DESIGN: 25 f., 300 f. President Keita. Nos. 23/4 are larger (27×38 mm.).

5. Pres. Mamadou Konate.

1961.
21. 5. 20 f. sepia & green (post.) 12 8
22. – 25 f. black and maroon .. 15 8
23. 5. 200 f. sepia & claret (air) 1·40 65
24. – 300 f. black and green .. 1·90 85

6. U.N. Emblem, Flag and Map.

1961. Air. Proclamation of Independence and Admission into U.N.O.
25. 6. 100 f. blue, red, yell. & grn. 70 60

7. Sankore Mosque, Timbuctu.

1961. Air.
26. 7. 100 f. chest., blue & sepia 70 25
27. – 200 f. brown, red & green 1·40 60
28. – 500 f. green, brown & blue 3·25 1·40
DESIGN: 200 f. View of Timbuctu. 500 f. Arms and view of Bamako.

8. Africans learning Vowels.

1961. Independence. 1st Anniv.
29. 8. 25 f. maroon, red, yellow and green 25 20

9. Sheep at Pool.

10. African Map and King Mohamed V of Morocco.

1961.
30. 9. 50 c. sepia, myrtle & red 5 5
31. A. 1 f. bistre, green and blue 5 5
32. B. 2 f. red, green and blue .. 5 5
33. C. 3 f. brown, green and blue 5 5
34. D. 4 f. blue, green and bistre 5 5
35. 9. 5 f. maroon, green and blue 5 5
36. A. 10 f. brown, myrtle & blue 8 5
37. B. 15 f. brown, green & blue 8 5
38. C. 20 f. red, green and blue 12 5
39. D. 25 f. brown and blue .. 12 5
40. 9. 30 f. choc., green & violet 20 10
41. A. 40 f. chest., green & blue 25 10
42. B. 50 f. lake, green and blue 30 10
43. C. 60 f. brown, green and blue 35 12
44. D. 85 f. choc., bistre and blue 45 15
DESIGNS: A, Oxen at pool. B, House of Arts, Mali. C, Land tillage. D, Combine-harvester in rice field.

1962. African Conf. Casablanca. 1st Anniv.
45. 10. 25 f. yell., brn., pink & bl. 20 10
46. 50 f. yellow, brown, pink and green 40 15

11. Patrice Lumumba.

12. Pegasus and U.P.U. Emblem.

13. Sansanding Dam.

1962. Patrice Lumumba (Congo leader). 1st Death Anniv.
47. 11. 25 f. brown & yell.-brn. 15 12
48. 100 f. brown and green .. 60 40

1962. Malaria Eradication. As T 45 of Cameroun.
49. 25 f. + 5 f. violet-blue .. 25 25

1962. Admission into U.P.U. 1st Anniv.
50. 12. 85 f. green, black, brown and yellow 55 45

1962. African Postal Union Commem. As T 172 of Egypt.
51. 25 f. green and chocolate .. 15 12
52. 85 f. orange and green .. 55 40

1962.
53. 13. 25 f. black, green & blue 15 8
54. – 45 f. multicoloured .. 35 20
DESIGN—HORIZ. 45 f. Cotton plant.

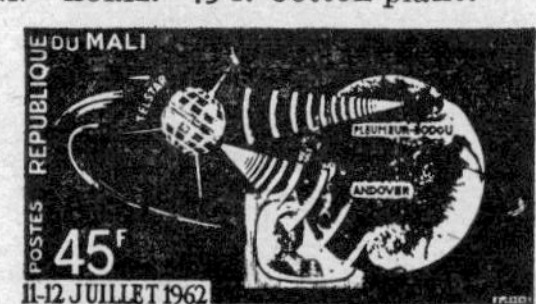

14. "Telstar" Satellite, Globe and Television Receiver.

1962. 1st Trans-Atlantic Telecommunications Satellite Link.
55. 14. 45 f. choc., violet & lake 35 25
56. 55 f. violet, olive & green 50 40

15. Soldier and Family.

16. Bull's Head, Laboratory Equipment and Chicks.

1962. Mali-Algerian Solidarity.
57. 15. 25 f. + 5 f. multicoloured 15 15

1963. Zoological Research Centre, Sotuba.
58. 16. 25 f. turq. & brn. (post.) 20 12
59. – 200 f. turquoise, maroon and bistre (air) .. 1·25 65
DESIGN: 200 f. As T 16 but horiz. (48×27 mm.).

17. Tractor and Campaign Emblem.

1963. Freedom from Hunger.
60. 17. 25 f. mar., black and blue 15 12
61. 45 f. chest., green & turq. 35 25

18. Balloon and W.M.O. Emblem.

1963. Atmospheric Research.
62. 18. 25 f. buff, grn., blk. & bl. 15 12
63. 45 f. buff, grn., blk & cerise 30 25
64. 60 f. buff, green, black and chestnut 40 35

19. Race Winners.

20. Centenary Emblem and Globe.

1963. Youth Week. Multicoloured.
65. 5 f. Type 19 .. .. 5 5
66. 10 f. Type 19 .. .. 8 5
67. 20 f. Acrobatic dance .. 15 8
68. 85 f. Football 50 35
Nos. 67/8 are horiz.

1963. Red Cross Cent. Inscr. in black
69. 20. 5 f. red, yell., grey & grn. 8 8
70. 10 f. red, yellow and grey 12 10
71. 85 f. red, yellow and grey 55 45

21. Stretcher case entering Ambulance 'Plane "Aero 145".

1963. Air.
72. 21. 25 f. brown, blue & emer. 15 12
73. – 55 f. blue, ochre & choc. 40 30
74. – 100 f. blue, brown & green 65 45
DESIGNS: 55 f. Airliner on tarmac. 100 f. Airliner taking off.

22. Crowned Crane standing on Giant Tortoise.

24. "Kaempferia aethiopica".

23. U.N. Emblem, Doves and Banner.

1963. Air. Fauna Protection.
75. 22. 25 f. choc., red & orange 25 20
76. 200 f. chocolate, red, orange and brown .. 1·50 1·10

1963. Air. Declaration of Human Rights 15th Anniv.
77. 23. 50 f. yellow, red & green 35 25

1963. Tropical Flora. Multicoloured.
78. 30 f. Type 24 .. .. 15 12
79. 70 f. "Bombax costatum" 35 25
80. 100 f. "Adenium honghel" 50 30

25. Pharaoh and Cleopatra, Philae.

26. Locust on Map of Africa.

1964. Air. Nubian Monuments Preservation.
81. 25. 25 f. brown and maroon 20 15
82. 55 f. olive and maroon .. 45 30

1964. Anti-Locust Campaign.
83. 26. 5 f. brown, green & maroon 5 5
84. – 10 f. brown, green & olive 8 5
85. – 20 f. brown, green & bistre 15 10
DESIGNS—VERT. 10 f. Locust and map. HORIZ. 20 f. Air-spraying, locust and village.

27. Football.

1964. Olympic Games, Tokyo.
86. 27. 5 f. purple, emer. & verm. 5 5
87. – 10 f. brown, blue & sepia 8 5
88. – 15 f. red and violet .. 12 10
89. – 85 f. green, choc. & violet 65 55
DESIGNS—VERT. 10 f. Boxing. 15 f. Running and Olympic Flame. HORIZ. 85 f. Hurdling. Each design has a stadium in the background.

28. Solar Flares.

30. Map of Vietnam.

29. Pres. Kennedy.

1964. Int. Quiet Sun Years.
90. 28. 45 f. olive, red and blue .. 30 20

1964. Air. Pres. Kennedy. 1st Death Anniv.
91. 29. 100 f. black, sepia, chest. and salmon 75 65

1964. Mali—South Vietnam Workers' Solidarity Campaign.
92. 30. 30 f. brown, yellow, black and blue 20 12

31. Touracos.

1965. Air. Birds.
93. 31. 100 f. green, blue and red 45 30
94. – 200 f. black, red and blue 80 60
95. – 300 f. black, ochre & grn. 1·25 90
96. – 500 f. red, choc. & green 2·25 1·50
BIRDS—VERT. 200 f. Hornbills. 300 f. Egyptian vultures. HORIZ. 500 f. Goliath herons.

32. I.C.Y. Emblem and U.N. Headquarters.

34. Abraham Lincoln.

33. Buffalo.

1965. Air. Int. Co-operation Year.
97. 32. 55 f. ochre, maroon & blue 40 30

1965. Animals.
98. – 1 f. choc., blue & green 5 5
99. 33. 5 f. choc., orge. & green 5 5
100. – 10 f. brn., mag. & green 5 5
101. – 30 f. choc., green & red 15 10
102. – 90 f. brown, grey & grn. 50 30
ANIMALS—VERT. 1 f. Defassa's waterbuck. 10 f. White oryx. 90 f. Giraffe. HORIZ. 30 f. Leopard.

1965. Abraham Lincoln. Death Cent.
103. 34. 45 f. blk., brn., grey & red 30 25
104. 55 f. blk., brn., grey & grn. 40 35

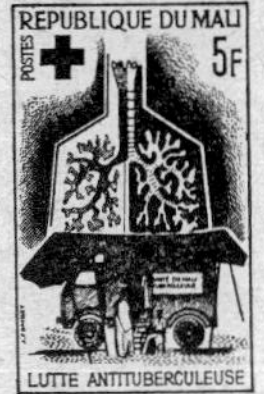

35. Hughes' Telegraph. 36. "Lungs" and Mobile X-Ray Unit (Anti-T.B.).

1965. I.T.U. Cent.
105. – 20 f. black, blue & orge. 20 15
106. 35. 30 f. green, brn. & orge. 25 20
107. – 50 f. grn., choc. & orge. 35 25
DESIGNS—VERT. 20 f. Denis's Pneumatic tube. 50 f. Lescurre's heliograph.

1965. Mali Health Service.
108. 36. 5 f. violet, red & crimson 5 5
109. – 10 f. green, bistre & red 8 5
110. – 25 f. emerald and brown 15 12
111. – 45 f. green and brown .. 30 20
DESIGNS: 10 f. Mother and children (Maternal and Child Care). 25 f. Examining patient (Marchoux Institute). 45 f. Nurse (Biological Laboratory).

37. Diving.

1965. 1st African Games, Brazzaville, Congo.
112. 37. 5 f. red, brown and blue 5 5
113. – 15 f. turquoise, chocolate and red (Judo) .. 12 10

38. Pope John XXIII. 39. Sir Winston Churchill.

1965. Air. Pope John Commem.
114. 38. 100 f. multicoloured .. 70 45

1965. Air. Churchill Commem.
115. 39. 100 f. indigo and brown 70 45

40. Dr. Schweitzer and Young African.

1965, Air. Dr. Albert Schweitzer Commem.
116. 40. 100 f. multicoloured .. 55 40

41. Leonov.

1966. Int. Astronautic Conf., Athens (1965). Multicoloured
117. 100 f. Type 41 .. .. 65 40
118. 100 f. White 65 40
119. 300 f. Cooper, Conrad, Leonov and Beliaiev (vert.) 2·00 1·25

42. Vase, Quill and Cornet.

1966. World Festival of Negro Arts, Dakar, Cameroun.
120. 42. 30 f. black, red & ochre 15 12
121. – 55 f. red, black and green 30 20
122. – 90 f. choc., orge. & blue 55 30
DESIGNS: 55 f. Mask, brushes and palette, microphones. 90 f. Dancers, mask, patterned cloth.

43. W.H.O. Building.

1966. W.H.O. Headquarters, Geneva. Inaug.
123. 43. 30 f. grn., blue & yellow 20 12
124. 45 f. red, blue & yellow 25 20

44. Fisherman with Net.

1966. River Fishing.
125. 44. 3 f. brown and blue .. 5 5
126. – 4 f. maroon, blue & chest. 5 5
127. – 20 f. maroon, grn. & blue 8 8
128. 44. 25 f. maroon, blue & grn. 15 8
129. – 60 f. maroon, lake & grn. 25 12
130. – 85 f. plum, grn. & blue 35 15
DESIGNS: 4 f., 60 f. Collective shore fishing. 20 f., 85 f. Fishing pirogue.

45. Papal Arms, U.N. and Peace Emblems.

1966. Air. Pope Paul's Visit to U.N.
131. 45. 200 f. blue, green & turq. 1·10 40

46. Initiation Ceremony. 47. People and U.N.E.S.C.O. Emblem.

1966. Mali Pioneers. Multicoloured.
132. 5 f. Type 46 .. .. 5 5
133. 25 f. Pioneers dancing .. 12 8

1966. Air. U.N.E.S.C.O. 20th Anniv.
134. 47. 100 f. red, green & blue 30 25

48. Footballers, Globe, Cup and Football.

1966. Air. World Cup Football Championships, England.
135. 48. 100 f. multicoloured .. 60 25

49. Cancer ("The Crab"). 50. U.N.I.C.E.F. Emblem and Children.

1966. Air. 9th Int. Cancer Congress, Tokyo.
136. 49. 100 f. multicoloured .. 60 25

1966. Air. U.N.I.C.E.F. 20th Anniv.
137. 50. 45 f. blue, purple & brn. 30 15

51. Inoculating Cattle.

1967. Campaign for Preventing Cattle Plague.
138. 51. 10 f. multicoloured .. 5 5
139. 30 f. multicoloured 15 12

52. Desert Vehicles in Pass.

1967. Air. Crossing of the Hoggar.
140. 52. 200 f. green, choc. & vio. 1·10 45

53. "Diamant" Rocket and Lana's "Aerial Ship". 54. Ancient City.

1967. Air. French Space Rockets and Satellites.
141. 53. 50 f. blue, turq. & pur. 20 10
142. – 100 f. lake, pur. & turq. 40 20
143. – 200 f. pur., olive & ind 75 45
DESIGNS: 100 f. Satellite "A 1" and Jules Verne's "rocket". 200 f. Satellite "D 1" and Da Vinci's "bird-powered" flying machine.

1967. Int. Tourist Year.
144. 54. 25 f. orge., blue & violet 12 5

55. Amelia Earhart and Mail Route-map.

1967. Air. Amelia Earhart's Flight, via Gao. 30th Anniv.
145. 55. 500 f. multicoloured .. 1·75 65

56. "The Bird Cage". 57. Scout Emblems and Rope Knots.

1967. Air. Picasso Commem. Designs showing paintings. Multicoloured.
146. 50 f. Type 56 .. .. 20 8
147. 100 f. "Paul as Harlequin" 40 20
148. 250 f. "The Pipes of Pan" 95 50
See also Nos. 164/7.

1967. Air. World Scout Jamboree, Idaho.
149. 57. 70 f. red and green .. 25 10
150. – 100 f. black, lake & grn. 40 15
DESIGN: 100 f. Scout with "walkie-talkie" radio.

58. "Chelorrhina polyphemus". 59. School Class.

60. "Europafrique". 61. Lions Emblem and Crocodile.

1967. Insects.
151. 58. 5 f. green, brown & blue 5 5
152. – 15 f. maroon, brn. & grn. 5 5
153. – 50 f. red, choc. & green 15 8
INSECTS—HORIZ. 15 f. "Ugada grandicollis". 50 f. "Phymateus cinctus".

1967. Int. Literary Day.
154. 59. 50 f. black, red & green 25 5

1967. Europafrique.
155. 60. 45 f. multicoloured .. 20 5

1967. Lions Int. 50th Anniv.
156. 61. 90 f. multicoloured .. 35 12

62. "Water Resources". 63. Block of Flats, Grenoble.

1967. Int. Hydrological Decade.
157. 62. 25 f. black, blue & bistre 10 5

1967. Air. Toulouse-Lautrec Commem. Paintings as T 56. Multicoloured.
158. 100 f. "Gazelle" (horse's head (horiz.) 35 20
159. 300 f. "Gig drawn by Cob" (vert.) .. .. .. 1·10 55

1968. Air. Winter Olympic Games, Grenoble.
160. 63. 50 f. brown, green & blue 20 8
161. – 150 f. chocolate, blue and ultramarine .. 55 25
DESIGN: 150 f. Bob-sleigh course, Huez mountain.

64. W.H.O. Emblem.

1968. W.H.O. 20th Anniv.
162. 64. 90 f. blue, lake & green 30 10

65. Human Figures and Entwined Hearts.

1968. World "Twin Towns" Day.
163. 65. 50 f. red, violet & green 20 8

1968. Air. Flower Paintings. As T 56. Multicoloured.
164. 50 f. "Roses and Anemones" (Van Gogh) 15 10
165. 150 f. "Vase of Flowers" (Manet) 50 30
166. 300 f. "Bouquet of Flowers" (Delacroix) .. .. 1·00 65
167. 500 f. "Marguerites" (Millet) .. .. 1·60 90
SIZES: 50 f., 300 f. 40 × $41\frac{1}{2}$ mm. 150 f. 36 × $47\frac{1}{2}$ mm. 500 f. 50 × 36 mm.

66. Dr. Martin Luther King. 67. "Draisienne" Bicycle, 1809.

1968. Air. Martin Luther King Commem.
168. **66.** 100 f. black, pink & pur. 30 20

1968. Veteran Bicycles and Motor Cars.
169. **67.** 2 f. brown, magenta and green (post.) .. 5 5
170. – 5 f. red, blue and bistre 5 5
171. – 10 f. blue, brown & grn. 5 5
172. – 45 f. black, grn. & chest. 15 10
173. – 50 f. red, grn. & brn. (air) 20 10
174. – 100 f. blue, mag. & bistre 40 20
DESIGNS—HORIZ. 5 f. De Dion-Bouton, 1894. 45 f. Panhard-Levassor, 1914. 100 f. Mercedes-Benz, 1927. VERT. 10 f. Michaux Bicycle, 1861. 50 f. "Bicylette, 1918".

68. Books, Graph and A.D.B.A. Emblem.

1968. Int. African Libraries and Archives Development Assn. 10th Anniv.
175. **68.** 100 f. cerise, black & brn. 35 20

69. Football.

1968. Air. Olympic Games, Mexico. Multicoloured.
176. 100 f. Type **69** 35 20
177. 150 f. Long-jumping (vert.) 55 25

1968. Air. "Philexafrique" Stamp Exn., Abidjan, Ivory Coast, 1969 (1st Issue). As T **109** of Cameroun. Multicoloured.
178. 200 f. "The Editors" (F. M. Granet) 75 75

1969. Air. "Philexafrique" Stamp Exn. Abidjan, Ivory Coast (2nd Issue). As T **110** of Cameroun.
179. 100 f. maroon, cerise & violet 35 35
DESIGN: 100 f. Carved animal and French Sudan stamp of 1931.

1969. Air. Napoleon Bonaparte. Birth Bicent. Multicoloured. As T **69** of Dahomey.
180. 150 f. "Napoleon Bonaparte, First Consul" (Gros) .. 50 30
181. 200 f. "The Bivouac—Battle of Austerlitz" (Lejeune) (horiz.) .. 50 45

70. Montgolfier's Balloon.

1969. Air. Aviation History. Multicoloured.
182. 50 f. Type **70** 12 8
183. 150 f. Ferber's "No. 5" Biplane 30 20
184. 300 f. "Concorde" .. 65 45
See also Nos. 202/4

71. African Tourist Emblem.

1969. African Touris Year.
185. **71.** 50 f. red, green & blue.. 15 8

72. "O.I.T." and I.L.O. Emblem.

1969. Int. Labour Organisation. 50th Anniv.
186. **72.** 50 f. violet, blue & green 15 8
187. 60 f. slate, red & brown 15 8

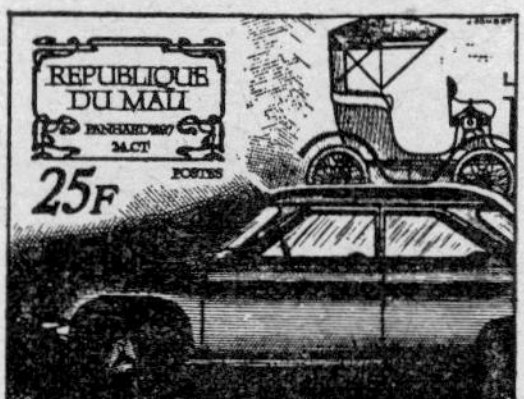

73. Panhard of 1897 and Model "24-CT".

1969. French Motor Industry.
188. **73.** 25 f. lake, black and bistre (postage) .. 8 5
189. – 30 f. green and black .. 10 5
190. – 55 f. red, black and purple (air) .. 20 20
191. – 90 f. indigo, blk. & red 30 30
DESIGNS: 30 f. Citroen of 1923 and Model "DS-21". 55 f. Renault of 1898 and Model "16". 90 f. Peugeot of 1893 and Model "404".

74. Clarke (Australia), 10,000 metres (1965).

1969. Air. World Athletics Records.
192. **74.** 60 f. brown and blue .. 20 12
193. – 90 f. brown and carmine 30 15
194. – 120 f. brown and green 35 15
195. – 140 f. brown and slate.. 40 25
196. – 150 f. black and red .. 40 25
DESIGNS: 90 f. Lusis (Russia), Javelin (1968). 120 f. Miyake (Japan), Weightlifting (1968). 140 f. Matson (U.S.A.), Shot-putting (1967). 150 f. Keino (Kenya), 3,000 metres (1965).

75. Hollow Blocks.

1969. Int. Toy Fair, Nuremberg.
197. **75.** 5 f. red, yellow and grey 5 5
198. – 10 f. green, lemon, yellow and red 5 5
199. – 15 f. green, red and pink 5 5
200. – 20 f. orge., blue and red 8 5
DESIGNS: 10 f. Toy donkey on wheels. 15 f. "Ducks" 20 f. Model car and race-track.

1969. Air. 1st Man on the Moon. Nos. 182/4 optd. **L'HOMME SUR LA LUNE JUILLET 1969** and **Apollo 11**.
201. 50 f. multicoloured .. 30 30
202. 150 f. multicoloured .. 30 30
203. 300 f. multicoloured .. 30 30

76. "Apollo 8", Earth and Moon.

1969. Air. Moon Flight of "Apollo 8".
204. **76.** 2,000 f. gold .. .. 5·50
This stamp is embossed on gold foil.

77. Sheep.

1969. Domestic Animals.
205. **77.** 1 f. olive, brown & green 5 5
206. – 2 f. brown, grey and red 5 5
207. – 10 f. olive, brown & blue 5 5
208. – 35 f. slate and red .. 8 5
209. – 90 f. brown and blue .. 25 15
ANIMALS: 2 f. Goat. 10 f. Donkey. 35 f. Horse. 90 f. Dromedary.

1969. African Development Bank. 5th Anniv. As T **118** of Cameroun.
210. 50 f. brown, green & purple 15 8
211. 90 f. orange, green & brown 25 15

78. "Mona Lisa" (Leonardo da Vinci).

1969. Air. Leonardo da Vinci. 450th Death Anniv.
212. **78.** 500 f. multicoloured 1·75 75

79. Vaccination. 80. Mahatma Gandhi.

1969. Campaign against Smallpox and Measles
213. **79.** 50 f. slate, brn. & emer. 15 5

1969. Air. Mahatma Gandhi. Birth Cent.
214. **80.** 150 f. brown and green 45 30

1969. Aerial Navigation Security Agency for Africa and Madagascar (A.S.E.C.N.A.). 10th Anniv. As T **121** of Cameroun.
215. 100 f. green 25 20

81. West African Map and Posthorns.

1970. Air. West African Postal Union (C.A.P.T.E.A.O.). 11th Anniv.
216. **31.** 100 f. multicoloured .. 25 30

1970. Air. Religious Paintings. As T **78**. Multicoloured.
217. 100 f. "The Virgin and Child" (Van der Weyden School) 30 20
218. 150 f. "The Nativity" (The Master of Flamalle) .. 45 25
219. 250 f. "Virgin, Child and St. John the Baptist" (Low Countries School).. 75 40

82. Franklin D. Roosevelt. 84. Lenin.

83. Women of Mali and Japan.

1970. Air. Franklin D. Roosevelt. 25th Death Anniv.
220. **82.** 500 f. black, red and blue 1·40 70

1970. "EXPO 70" World Fair, Osaka, Japan.
221. **83.** 100 f. orge., choc. & blue 25 12
222. – 150 f. red, emer. & yell. 40 20
DESIGN: 150 f. Flags and maps of Mali and Japan.

1970. Air. Lenin. Birth Cent.
223. **84.** 300 f. black, green & flesh 85 45

85. Verne and Moon Rockets.

1970. Air. Jules Verne, "Prophet of Space Travel". Multicoloured.
224. 50 f. Type **85** 15 8
225. 150 f. Moon orbit 45 25
226. 300 f. Splashdown .. .. 1·00 50

86. I.T.U. Emblem and Map.

1970. World Telecommunications Day.
227. **86.** 90 f. cerise, brown & sepia 25 12

1970. New U.P.U. Headquarters Building, Berne. As Type **126** of Cameroun.
228. 50 f. brown, green & crimson 15 8
229. 60 f. brown, blue & mauve 20 12

1970. Air. Space Flight of "Apollo 13". Nos. 224/6 optd. **APOLLO XIII EPOPEE SPATIALE 11-17 AVRIL 1970** in three lines.
230. 50 f. multicoloured .. 20 12
231. 150 f. multicoloured .. 45 30
232. 300 f. multicoloured .. 90 50

87. "Intelsat 3" Satellite.

1970. Air. Space Telecommunications.
233. **87.** 100 f. indigo, blue & orge. 25 12
234. – 200 f. purple, grey & blue 45 25
235. – 300 f. brn., orge & slate 70 70
236. – 500 f. brn., blue & indigo 1·25 60
DESIGNS: 200 f. "Molnya I" satellite. 300 f. Dish aerial, Type PB 2. 500 f. "Symphony Project" satellite.

88. Auguste and Louis Lumiere, Jean Harlow and Marilyn Monroe.

1970. Air. Lumiere Brothers (inventors of the cine camera). Commem.
237. **88.** 250 f. multicoloured .. 70 35

89. Footballers.

1970. Air. World Cup Football Championships, Mexico.
238. **89.** 80 f. grn., brn. and red 20 12
239. 200 f. red, brown and blue 50 30

INDEX

Countries can be quickly located by referring to the index at the end of this volume.

90. Rotary Emblem, Map and Antelope. **91.** "Supporting United Nations".

1970. Air. Rotary International.
240. **90.** 200 f. multicoloured .. 50 30

1970. Air. United Nations. 25th Anniv.
241. **91.** 100 f. blue, brn. & violet 30 20

92. Page from 11th century Baghdad Koran

1970. Air. Ancient Muslim Art. Mult.
242. 50 f. Type **92** 15 8
243. 200 f. "Tree and wild Animals" (Jordanian mosaic) 50 25
244. 250 f. "The Scribe" (Baghdad miniature, 1287) 65 30

1970. Air. Moon Landing of "Luna 16". Nos. 234/5 surch. **LUNA 16 PREMIERS PRELEVEMENTS AUTOMATIQUES SUR LA LUNE SEPTEMBRE 1970** and new values.
245. 150 f. on 200 f. purple, grey and blue .. 45 25
246. 250 f. on 300 f. brown, orange and grey .. 75 35

93. G.P.O., Bamako.

1970. Public Buildings.
247. **93.** 30 f. olive, grn. & brn. 5 5
248. – 40 f. purple, brn. & grn. 8 5
249. – 60 f. grey, green and red 15 8
250. – 80 f. brn., green and grey 20 12
BUILDINGS: 40 f. Chamber of Commerce, Bamako. 60 f. Ministry of Public Works, Bamako. 80 f. Town Hall, Segou.

94. President Nasser. **96.** Gallet "030T" Locomotive.

95. "The Nativity" (Antwerp School 1530).

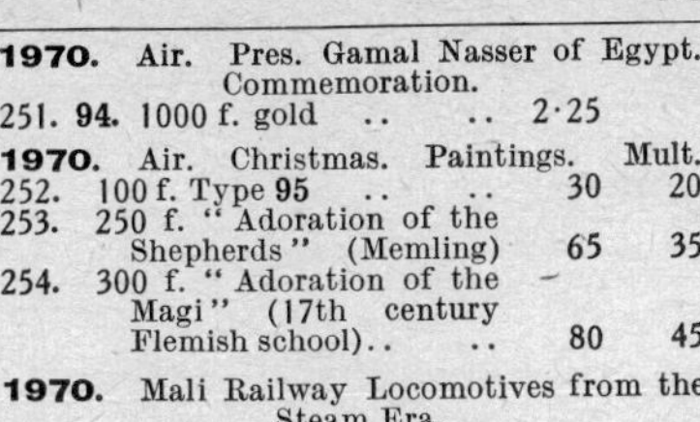

1970. Air. Pres. Gamal Nasser of Egypt. Commemoration.
251. **94.** 1000 f. gold .. .. 2·25

1970. Air. Christmas. Paintings. Mult.
252. 100 f. Type **95** 30 20
253. 250 f. "Adoration of the Shepherds" (Memling) 65 35
254. 300 f. "Adoration of the Magi" (17th century Flemish school) 80 45

1970. Mali Railway Locomotives from the Steam Era.
255. **96.** 20 f. black, red and green 5 5
256. – 40 f. black, green & brn. 10 5
257. – 50 f. black, green & brn. 15 8
258. – 80 f. black, red & green 20 12
259. – 100 f. black, grn. & brn. 25 15
LOCOMOTIVES: 40 f. Felou "030T". 50 f. Bechevel "230T". 80 f. "231". 100 f. Type "141".

97. Scouts crossing Log-bridge.

1970. Scouting in Mali. Multicoloured.
260. 5 f. Type **97** 5 5
261. 30 f. Bugler and scout camp (vert.) 8 5
262. 100 f. Scouts canoeing .. 25 12

98. Bambara de San Mask. **99.** General De Gaulle.

1971. Mali Masks and Ideograms. Multicoloured.
263. 20 f. Type **98** 5 5
264. 25 f. Dogon de Bandiagara mask 5 5
265. 50 f. Kanaga ideogram .. 12 5
266. 80 f. Bambara ideogram .. 20 8

1971. Air. Charles De Gaulle Commem. Die-stamped on gold foil.
267. **99.** 2000 f. gold, red & blue 5·50

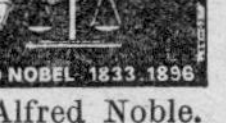

100. Alfred Noble. **102.** Youth, Sun and Microscope.

101. "Derby at Epsom".

1971. Air Alfred Nobel (philanthropist). 75th Death Anniv.
268. **100.** 300 f. lake, brn & grn. 80 45

1971. Air. World Sporting Events.
269. – 100 f. slate, pur. & blue 25 15
270. **101.** 150 f. olive, brn. & grn. 35 20
271. – 200 f. brn., olive & blue 45 30
DESIGNS—VERT. 100 f. Tennis-player (Davis Cup). 200 f. Yacht (America Cup).
NOTE: T **101** is inscr. "Derby d'Epsom". but shows a steeplechase, probably the Grand National.

1971. 1st B.C.G. Vaccine Inoculation. 50th Anniv.
272. **102.** 100 f. brn., grn. & red 35 25

103. "The Thousand and One Nights".

1971. Air. "Tales of the Arabian Nights". Multicoloured.
273. 120 f. Type **103** 30 20
274. 180 f. "Ali Baba and the Forty Thieves" .. 40 25
275. 200 f. "Aladdin's Lamp" .. 45 30

104. Scouts, Japanese Horseman and Mt. Fuji.

1971. World Scout Jamboree, Asagiri, Japan. (August 1971).
276. **104.** 80 f. plum, grn. & blue 20 10

105. Rose between Hands. **106.** Peasant Costume.

1971. U.N.I.C.E.F. 25th Anniv.
277. **105.** 50 f. brn., red & orge. 12 8
278. – 60 f. blue, green & brn. 15 8
DESIGN—VERT. 60 f. Nurses and children.

1971. National Costumes. Multicoloured.
279. 5 f. Type **106** 5 5
280. 10 f. Rural costume (female) 5 5
281. 15 f. Touareg 5 5
282. 60 f. Embroidered "boubou" 15 8
283. 80 f. Women's ceremonial costume 20 10

107. Olympic Rings and Events.

1971. Air. Olympic Games Publicity.
284. **107.** 80 f. blue, pur. & grn. 20 12

108. Telecommunications Map.

1971. Pan-African Telecommunications Network Year.
285. **108.** 50 f. multicoloured .. 12 8

109. "Mariner 4" and Mars.

1971. Air. Exploration of Outer Space.
286. **109.** 200 f. green, bl. & brn. 45 30
287. – 300 f. blue, plum & pur. 70 40
DESIGN: 300 f. "Venera 5" and Venus.

110. "Santa Maria" (1492).

1971. Air. Famous Ships.
288. **110.** 100 f. brn., violet & blue 25 15
289. – 150 f. vio., brn. & grn. 35 20
290. – 200 f. grn., blue & red 45 30
291. – 250 f. red, blue & blk. 60 40
DESIGNS: 150 f. "Mayflower" (1620). 200 f. Battleship "Potemkin" (1905). 250 f. Liner "Normandie" (1935).

111. "Hibiscus rose-sinensis".

1971. Flowers. Multicoloured.
292. 20 f. Type **111** 5 5
293. 50 f. "Euphorbia pulcherrima" 12 5
294. 60 f. "Adenium obesum" 15 5
295. 80 f. "Allamanda cathartica" 20 8
296. 100 f. "Satanocrater berhautii" 25 15

112. Allegory of Justice.

1971. Int. Court of Justice, The Hague. 25th Anniv.
297. **112.** 160 f. choc., red & brn. 40 20

113. Nat King Cole. **115.** "Family Life" (carving).

114. Temple of Artemis, Ephesus.

1971. Air. Famous Negro Musicians. Multicoloured.
298. 130 f. Type **113** 30 15
299. 150 f. Erroll Garner .. 35 20
300. 270 f. Louis Armstrong .. 60 25

1971. Air. "The Seven Wonders of the Ancient World".
301. – 70 f. blue, brn. & pur. 15 8
302. – 80 f. blk., brn. & blue 20 8
303. **114.** 100 f. blue, red & violet 25 12
304. – 130 f. blk., pur. & blue 30 15
305. – 150 f. brn., grn. & blue 35 20
306. – 270 f. blue, brn. & pur. 60 25
307. – 280 f. blue, pur. & brn. 65 30
DESIGNS—VERT. 70 f. Statue of Olympic Zeus Phidias. 80 f. Pyramid of Cheops, Egypt. 130 f. Pharos of Alexandria. 270 f. Mausoleum of Halicarnassos. 280 f. Colossus of Rhodes. HORIZ. 150 f. Hanging Gardens of Babylon.

1971. Social Security Service. 15th Anniv.
308. **115.** 70 f. brn., green & red 15 8

116. Slalom-skiing and Japanese Girl. **118.** Hands clasping Flagpole.

117. " Santa Maria della Salute " (Coffi).

1972. Air. Winter Olympic Games, Sapporo, Japan.
309. **116.** 150 f. brn., grn. & orge. 35 20
310. – 200 f. grn., brn. & red 45 25
DESIGN: 200 f. Ice-hockey and Japanese actor.

1972. Air. U.N.E.S.C.O. " Save Venice " Campaign. Multicoloured.
312. 130 f. Type **117** 30 15
313. 270 f. " Rialto Bridge " 60 25
314. 280 f. " St. Mark's Square " (vert.) 65 30

1972. Air. Int. Scout Seminar, Cotonou, Dahomey.
315. **118.** 200 f. grn., orge. & brn. 45 25

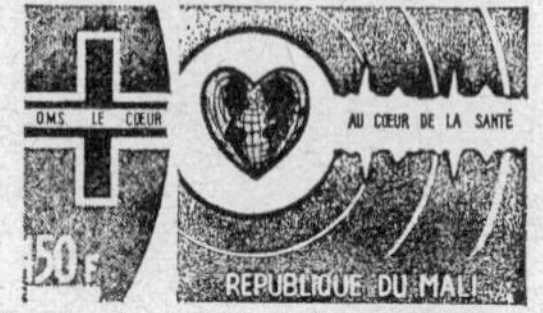

119. Heart and Red Cross Emblems.

1972. Air. World Heart Month.
316. **119.** 150 f. red and blue .. 35 25

120. Football.

1972. Air. Olympic Games, Munich (1st issue). Sports and Munich Buildings.
317. **120.** 50 f. bl., brn. and grn. 12 8
318. – 150 f. bl., brn. and grn. 35 25
319. – 200 f. bl., brn. & grn. 45 25
320. – 300 f. bl., brn. and grn. 70 40
DESIGNS—VERT. 150 f. Judo. 200 f. Hurdling. HORIZ. 300 f. Running.
See also Nos. 357/62.

121. " Apollo 15 " and Lunar Rover.

1972. Air. History of Transport Development.
322. **121.** 150 f. red, grn. & lake 35 35
323. – 250 f. red, blue & grn. 60 35
DESIGN: 250 f. Montgolfier's balloon and Cugnot's steam car.

122. " UIT " on T.V. Screen.

1972. World Telecommunications Day.
324. **122.** 70 f. black, blue & red 15 10

123. Clay Funerary Statue. 124. Samuel Morse, and Early Telegraph.

1972. Mali Archaeology. Multicoloured.
325. 30 f. Type **123** 5 5
326. 40 f. Female Figure (wood-carving) 8 5
327. 50 f. " Warrior " (stone-painting) 12 8
328. 100 f. Wrought-iron ritual figures 25 15

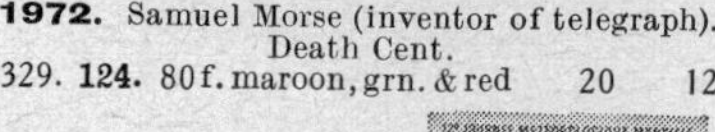

1972. Samuel Morse (inventor of telegraph). Death Cent.
329. **124.** 80 f. maroon, grn. & red 20 12

125. " Cinderella ". 126. Weather Balloon.

1972. Air. Charles Perrault's Fairy Tales.
330. **125.** 70 f. grn., red and brown 15 10
331. – 80 f. brn., red & green 20 12
332. – 150 f. violet, pur. & blue 35 20
DESIGNS: 80 f. " Puss in Boots ". 150 f. " The Sleeping Beauty ".

1972. World Meteorological Day.
333. **126.** 130 f. multicoloured .. 30 20

127. Astronauts and Lunar Rover.

1972. Air. Moon Flight of " Apollo 16 ".
334. **127.** 500 f. brn., violet & grn. 1·10 70

128. Book Year Emblem.

1972. Air. Int. Book Year.
335. **128.** 80 f. gold, green & blue 20 12

129. Sarakole Dance, Kayes. 130. " Learning the Alphabet ".

1972. Traditional Dances. Multicoloured.
336. 10 f. Type **129** 5 5
337. 20 f. Malinke dance, Bamako 5 5
338. 50 f. Hunter's dance, Bougouni 12 5
339. 70 f. Bambara dance, Segou 15 8
340. 80 f. Dogon dance, Sanga .. 20 12
341. 120 f. Targuie dance, Timbukto 30 15

1972. Int. Literacy Day.
342. **130.** 80 f. black and green .. 20 12

131. Statue and Musical Instruments. 132. Club Banner.

1972. First Anthology of Malinenne Music.
343. **131.** 100 f. multicoloured .. 25 15

1972. Air. Bamako Rotary Club. 10th Anniv.
344. **132.** 170 f. purple, blue & red 40 25

133. Aries the Ram.

1972. Signs of the Zodiac.
345. **133.** 15 f. brown & purple 5 5
346. – 15 f. black and brown 5 5
347. – 35 f. blue and red .. 8 5
348. – 35 f. red and green .. 8 5
349. – 40 f. brown and blue 8 5
350. – 40 f. brown and purple 8 5
351. – 45 f. red and blue .. 10 8
352. – 45 f. green and red .. 10 8
353. – 65 f. blue and violet 15 10
354. – 65 f. brown and violet 15 10
355. – 90 f. blue and mauve 20 15
356. – 90 f. green and mauve 20 15
DESIGNS: No. 346, Taurus the Bull. No. 347, Gemini the Twins. No. 348, Cancer the Crab. No. 349, Leo the Lion. No. 350, Virgo the Virgin. No. 351, Libra the Scales. No. 352, Scorpio the Scorpion. No. 353, Saggitarius the Archer. No. 354, Capricornus the Goat. No. 355, Aquarius the Water-carrier. No. 356, Pisces the Fish

1972. Air. Olympic Games, Munich (2nd issue). Sports and Locations of Games since 1952. As Type **120**.
357. 70 f. blue, brown and red .. 15 8
358. 90 f. green, red and blue .. 20 12
359. 140 f. olive, green and brown 30 15
360. 150 f. brn., green and red 35 20
361. 170 f. blue, brn. and purple 40 20
362. 210 f. blue, red and green .. 50 30
DESIGNS—VERT. 70 f. Boxing, Helsinki Games (1952). 150 f. Weightlifting, Tokyo Games (1964) HORIZ. 90 f. Hurdling, Melbourne Games (1950). 140 f. 200 metres, Rome Games (1960). 170 f. Swimming, Mexico Games (1968). 210 f. Throwing the javelin, Munich Games (1972).

1972. Medal Winners, Munich Olympic Games. Nos. 318/20 and 362 optd. with events and names, etc.
363. 150 f. blue, brown & green 35 20
364. 200 f. blue, brown & green 45 30
365. 210 f. blue, red and green .. 45 30
366. 300 f. blue, brown & green 70 40
OVERPRINTS: 150 f. **JUDO RUSKA 2 MEDAILLES D'OR.** 200 f. **STEEPLE KEIN MEDAILLE D'OR.** 210 f. **MEDAILLE D'OR 90 m. 48** 300 f. **100 m.-200m. BORZOV 2 MEDAILLES D'OR.**

134. First Locomotive to arrive at Bamako 1906.

1972. Mali Locomotives (2nd series).
367. **134.** 10 f. blue, green & red 5 5
368. – 30 f. blue, green & brn. 5 5
369. – 60 f. blue, brn. & grn. 15 10
370. – 120 f. maroon, grn. & blk. 30 20
LOCOMOTIVES: 30 f. Locomotive from the Thies-Bamako line, 1920. 60 f. Type " 141 " locomotive, Thies-Bamako line, 1927. 120 f. Alsthom " BB " coupled diesels, Dakar-Bamako line, 1947.

135. Emperor Haile Selassie.

1972. Air. Emperor Haile Selassie. 80th Birth Anniv.
371. **135.** 70 f. multicoloured .. 15 10

136. Balloon, Aircraft and Map.

1972. Air. First Mali Airmail Flight by Balloon. Bamako to Timbukto. Mult.
372. 200 f. Type **136** 45 30
373. 300 f. Balloon, " Concorde " and map .. 65 40

137. High-Jumping.

1973. 2nd African Games, Lagos, Nigeria. Multicoloured.
374. 70 f. Type **137** 15 8
375. 270 f. Throwing the discus 60 35
376. 280 f. Football 65 40

138. 14th-century " Bishop ". 139. Interpol H.Q., Paris.

1973. Air. World Chess Championships, Reykjavik, Iceland.
377. **138.** 100 f. blue & brown .. 20 15
378. – 200 f. brn., red & black 40 30
DESIGN: 200 f. 18th-century " Knight " (Indian elephant).

1973. Int. Criminal Police Organisation (Interpol). 50th Anniv.
379. **139.** 80 f. multicoloured .. 15 10

140. Emblem and Dove with letter. 141. " Fauna Protection " Stamp of 1963.

1973. African Postal Union. Tenth Anniv. (1971).
380. **140.** 70 f. multicoloured .. 15 10

1973. Air. Stamp Day.
381. **141.** 70 f. orge., red & brn. 12 5

142. Astronauts on Moon. 144. Handicapped Africans.

143. Copernicus.

1973. Moon Mission of " Apollo " 17.
382. **142.** 250 f. brown and blue 45 35

1973. Nicholas Copernicus. 500th Birth Anniv.
384. **143.** 300 f. purple and blue 60 40

1973. " Help the Handicapped ".
385. **144.** 70 f. orge., black & red 15 10

145. Dr. G. A. Hansen.

1973. Hansen's Identification of the Leprosy Bacillus. Cent.
386. **145.** 200 f. grn., blk. & red .. 40 25

146. Bentley and Alfa Romeo, 1930.

1973. Le Mans 24 hour Endurance Race. 50th Anniv.
387. **146.** 50 f. grn., orge. & blue 12 10
388. – 100 f. green, blue & red 20 15
389. – 200 f. blue, green & red 40 30
DESIGNS: 100 f. Jaguar and Talbot, 1953. 200 f. Matra and Porsche, 1952.

147. Scouts around Camp-fire.

1973. Int. Scouting Congress, Addis Ababa and Nairobi.
390. **147.** 50 f. brown, red & blue 10 8
391. – 70 f. brown, red & blue 15 10
392. – 80 f. red, brn. & green 15 10
393. – 130 f. grn., blue & brn. 25 20
394. – 270 f. red, violet & grey 50 40
DESIGNS—VERT. 70 f. Scouts Saluting flag. 130 f. Lord Baden-Powell. HORIZ. 80 f. Standard-bearers. 270 f. Map of Africa and Scouts and Guides in ring.

148. Swimming and National Flags.

1973. First Afro-American Sports Meeting, Bamako.
395. **148.** 70 f. green, red & blue 15 10
396. – 80 f. green, red and blue 15 10
397. – 330 f. blue and red .. 65 40
DESIGNS—VERT. 80 f. Throwing the discus and javelin. HORIZ. 330 f. Running.

1973. Pan-African Drought Relief. No. 296 surch. **SECHERESSE SOLIDARITE AFRICAINE** and value.
398. 200 f. on 100 f. multicoloured 40 30

1973. Air. African Fortnight, Brussels. As T **133** of Cameroun.
399. 70 f. violet, blue and brn. 12 8

149. "Perseus" (Cellini). **151.** "Apollo 11" First Landing.

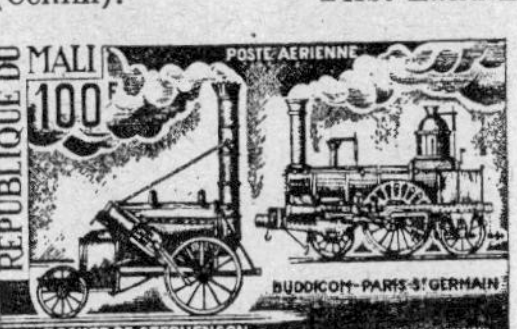

150. Stephenson's "Rocket" and French "Budicom" Locomotive.

1973. Air. Famous Sculptures.
400. **149.** 100 f. green and red .. 20 15
401. – 150 f. maroon and red 25 20
402. – 250 f. green and red .. 45 35
DESIGNS: 150 f. "Pieta" (Michelangelo). 250 f. "Victory of Samothrace".

1973. Air. Famous Locomotives.
403. **150.** 100 f. blk., blue & brn. 20 15
404. – 150 f. multicoloured .. 25 20
405. – 200 f. blue, slate-blue & brown 40 30
DESIGNS: 150 f. Union Pacific and Santa Fe Railroad locomotives. 200 "Mistral" and "Tokaido" trains.

1973. Conquest of the Moon.
406. **151.** 50 f. purple, red & brn. 10 5
407. – 75 f. grey, blue and red 12 8
408. – 100 f. slate-blue, brn. and blue 20 15
409. – 280 f. blue, green & red 50 40
410. – 300 f. blue, red & green 55 45
DESIGNS: 75 f. "Apollo 13" Recovery capsule. 100 f. "Apollo 14" lunar trolley. 280 f. "Apollo 17" lift off from Moon.

152. Picasso. **153.** Pres. Kennedy.

1973. Air. Pablo Picasso (artist). Commem.
411. **152.** 500 f. multicoloured .. 1·00 75

1973. Air. Pres. Kennedy. 10th Death Anniv.
412. **153.** 500 f. black, pur. & gold 1·00 75

154. "The Annunciation" (V. Carpaccio).

1973. Air. Christmas. Multicoloured.
413. 100 f. Type **154** 20 15
414. 200 f. "Virgin of St. Simon" (F. Baroccio) (vert.) .. 35 25
415. 250 f. "Flight into Egypt" (A. Solario) (vert.) .. 45 35

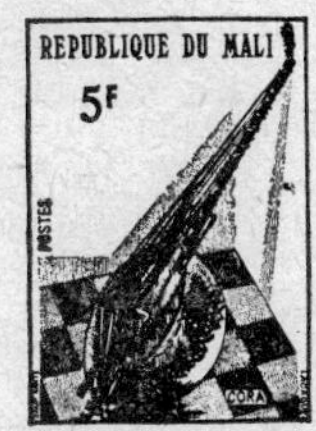

155. Player and Football. **156.** Cora.

1973. Air. World Football Cup Championships, West Germany.
416. **155.** 150 f. red, brn. & grn. 25 20
417. 250 f. grn., brn. & violet 45 35

1973. Musical Instruments.
419. **156.** 5 f. brn., red & green 5 5
420. – 10 f. brown and blue .. 5 5
421. – 15 f. brown, red & yell. 5 5
422. – 20 f. brown and red .. 5 5
423. – 25 f. brn., red & yell. 5 5
424. – 30 f. black and blue .. 8 5
425. – 25 f. sepia, brn. & red 8 5
426. – 40 f. brown and red .. 8 5
DESIGNS—HORIZ. 10 f. Balafon. VERT. 15 f. Djembe. 20 f. Guitar. 25 d. N'Djarka. 30 f. M'Bolon. 35 f. Dozo N'Goni. 40 f. N'Tamani.

157. "Musicians" (mosaic).

1974. Air. Roman Frescoes and Mosaics from Pompeii.
427. **157.** 150 f. red, brown & grey
428. – 250 f. brn., red & orge. 25 20
429. – 350 f. brown, orange and olive-brown .. 45 35
60 50
DESIGNS—VERT. 250 f. "Alexander the Great" (mosaic). 350 f. "Bacchante" (fresco).

MINIMUM PRICE

The minimum price quoted is 5p which represents a handling charge rather than a basis for valuing common stamps. For further notes about prices see introductory pages.

158. Corncob, Worker and "Kibaru" Newspaper. **159.** Sir Winston Churchill.

1974. Rural Press. Second Anniv.
430. **158.** 70 f. brown and green 12 8

1974. Air. Sir Winston Churchill. Birth Cent.
431. **159.** 500 f. black .. .. 1·00 75

160. Chess-pieces on Board.

1974. Air. 21st Chess Olympics. Nice.
432. **160.** 250 f. indigo, brn. & bl. 45 35

161. "The Crucifixion" (Alsace School c 1380).

1974. Air. Easter. Multicoloured.
433. 400 f. Type **161** 70 50
434. 500 f. "The Entombment" (Titian) (horiz.) .. .. 1·00 75

162. Lenin.

1974. Air. Lenin. 50th Death Anniv.
435. **162.** 150 f. purple and violet 25 20

163. Goalkeeper and Globe. **615.** Sailing-ship and Modern Liner.

164. Horse-jumping Scenes.

1974. World Cup Football Championships, West Germany.
436. **163.** 270 f. red, grn. & lilac 50 40
437. – 280 f. blue, brn. & red 50 40
DESIGN: 280 f. World Cup emblem on football.

1974. Air. World Equestrian Championships, La Baule.
438. **164.** 130 f. brn., lilac & blue 25 20

1974. Universal Postal Union. Cent.
439. **165.** 80 f. pur., lilac & brn. 15 10
440. – 90 f. orge., grey & blue 20 15
441. – 270 f. pur., olive & grn. 50 40
DESIGNS: 90 f. Bi-plane and jet airliner. 270 f. Early steam and modern electric trains.
See also Nos. 463/4.

166. "Skylab" over Africa.

1974. Air. Survey of Africa by "Skylab" Space Station.
442. **166.** 200 f. indigo, bl. & orge. 35 25
443. – 250 f. blue, pur. & orge. 45 35
DESIGN: 250 f. Astronaut servicing cameras.

1974. Air. 11th Arab Scout Jamboree, Lebanon. Nos. 391/2 surch. **11e JAMBOREE ARABE AOUT 1974 LIBAN** and value.
444. 130 f. on 70 f. brn., red & bl. 25 20
445. 170 f. on 80 f. bl., grn. & red 30 25

1974. Air. First landing on Moon. Fifth Anniv. Nos. 408/9 surch. **1er DEBARQUEMENT SUR LA LUNE 20-VII-69** and value.
446. 130 f. on 100 f. slate-blue, brown and blue 25 20
447. 300 f. on 280 f. bl., grn. & red 55 45

1974. West Germany's Victory in World Cup Football Championships. Nos. 436/7 surch. **R.F.A. 2 HOLLANDE 1** and value.
448. **163.** 300 f. on 270 f. red, green and lilac .. 55 45
449. – 330 f. on 280 f. blue, brown and red .. 60 50

167. Weaver. **168.** Niger near Gao.

1974. Mail Crafts and Craftsmen. Mult.
450. 50 f. Type **167** 10 8
451. 60 f. Potter 10 8
452. 70 f. Smith 12 8
453. 80 f. Wood-carver 15 10

1974. Mali Views. Multicoloured.
454. 10 f. Type **168** 5 5
455. 20 f. "The Hand of Fatma" (rock formation, Hombori) (vert.) 5 5
456. 40 f. Waterfall, Gouina .. 8 5
457. 70 f. Hill-dwellings, Dogon (vert.) 12 8

169. "C3-PLM" (1906) and "150-P" (1939) Locomotives.

1974. Air. Steam Locomotives.
458. **169.** 90 f. indigo, red & blue 20 15
459. – 120 f. brn., orange-brown and indigo 20 15
460. – 210 f. brn., orge. & blue 40 30
461. – 330 f. blk., grn. & blue 60 50
DESIGNS: 120 f. Baldwin "2-0-2" (1870) and Pacific (1920) locomotives. 210 f. "241-A1" (1925) and Boddicom (1847) locomotives. 330 f. Hudson (1938) and Lagironde (1839) locomotives.

170. Skiing.

1974. Air. Winter Olympics. 50th Anniv.
462. **170.** 300 f. red, blue & grn. 55 45

1974. Berne Postal Convention. Cent. Nos. 439 and 441 surch. **9 OCTOBRE 1974** and value.

463. **165.** 250 f. on 80 f. purple, lilac and brown .. 45 35
464. – 300 f. on 270 f. purple olive and green .. 55 45

171. Mao Tse-tung and Great Wall of China.
172. "The Nativity" (Memling).

1974. Chinese People's Republic. 25th Anniv.

465. **171.** 100 f. blue, red & green 20 15

1974. Air. Christmas. Multicoloured.

466. 290 f. Type **172** 55 45
467. 310 f. "Virgin and Child" (Bourgogne School) .. 55 45
468. 400 f. "Adoration of the Magi" (Schongauer) .. 70 50

173. R. Follereau.

1974. Air. Raoul Follereau, "Apostle of the Lepers".

469. **173.** 200 f. blue 40 30

174. Modern Transport.

1974. Air. Europafrique.

470. **174.** 100 f. grn., brn. & blue 20 15
471. 110 f. bl., vio. & brn... 20 15

175. Dr. Schweitzer.

1975. Dr. Albert Schweitzer. Birth Cent.

472. **175.** 150 f. turq. grn. & blue 35 25

176. Patients making Handicrafts, and Lions International Emblem.

1975. Samanko (Leprosy rehabilitation village). 5th Anniv. Multicoloured.

473. 90 f. Type **176** 20 15
474. 100 f. View of Samanko .. 25 20

177. "The Pilgrims at Emmaus" (Champaigne).

1975. Air. Easter. Multicoloured.

475. 200 f. Type **177** 50 40
476. 300 f. "The Pilgrims at Emmaus" (Veronese).. 75 65
477. 500 f. "Christ in Majesty" (Limoges enamel) (vert.) .. .. 1·25 1·00

178. "Journey to the Centre of the Earth".

1975. Air. Jules Verne. 70th Death Anniv.

478. **178.** 100 f. grn., bl. and brn. 25 20
479. – 170 f. brn., blue and light brown .. 40 30
480. – 190 f. blue, turq. & brn. 45 35
481. – 220 f. brn., pur. & blue 55 45

Designs: 170 f. Jules Verne and "From the Earth to the Moon" 90 f. Giant octopus—'Twenty Thousand Leagues Under the Sea". 220 f. "A Floating City".

179. "Head of Aurora" (Tomb of Medicis).

1975. Air. Michelangelo. 500th Birth Anniv Multicoloured.

482. 400 f. Type **179** 95 85
483. 500 f. "Moses" (marble statue, Rome) .. .. 1·25 1·00

180. "Tetrodon fahaka".

181. Astronaut on Moon.

1976. Fishes (1st series).

484. **180.** 60 f. brn., yell and grn. 15 12
485. – 70 f. blk., brn and grey 15 12
486. – 80 f. yell., oran., green and black 20 15
487. – 90 f. blue, grey & grn. 20 15
488. – 110 f. black and blue.. 25 20

Fishes: 70 f. "Malopterutus electricus". 80 f. "Citharinus latus". 90 f. "Hydrocyon forskali". 110 f. "Lates niloticus".

See also Nos. 544/8.

1975. Air. Soviet–U.S. Space Co-operation.

489. **181.** 290 f. red, blue and blk. 70 60
490. – 300 f. red, blue and blk. 75 65
491. – 370 f. grn., pur. and blk. 90 80

Designs: 300 f. "America and Russia". 370 f. New York and Moscow landmarks.

182. Einstein and Equation.
183. Woman with Bouquet.

1975. Air. Albert Einstein. 20th Death Anniv.

492. **182.** 90 f. blue, pur. & brn. 20 15

See also Nos. 504, 507 and 519.

1975. International Women's Year.

493. **183.** 150 f. red and green .. 35 25

184. Morris "Oxford", 1913.

1975. Early Motor-cars.

494. **184.** 90 f. violet, brn. & blue 20 15
495. – 130 f. red, grey & blue 30 20
496. – 190 f. deep blue, green and blue 45 35
497. – 230 f. brn., blue & red 55 45

Motor-cars: 130 f. Franklin "E", 1907. 190 f. Daimler, 1900. 230 f. Panhard & Levassor, 1895.

185. Scout and Emblem.

1975. Air. "Nordjamb 75" World Scout Jamboree, Norway.

498. **185.** 100 f. blue, brn. & lake 25 20
499. – 150 f. grn., brn. & blue 35 25
500. – 290 f. lake, brn. & blue 70 60

Designs: 150 f., 290 f. Scouts and emblem (different).

186. Lafayette and Battle Scene.

1975. Air. American Revolution. Bicentenary. Multicoloured.

501. 290 f. Type **186** 70 60
502. 300 f. Washington and battle scene 75 65
503. 370 f. De Grasse and sea battle 90 80

1975. Sir Alexander Fleming (scientist). 20th Death Anniv. As T **182**.

504. 150 f. brn., pur. and blue 35 25

187. Olympic Rings "in orbit".

1975. Air. "Pre-Olympic Year".

505. **187.** 350 f. violet and blue 85 75
506. – 400 f. blue 95 85

Designs: 400 f. Emblem of Montreal Olympics (1976).

1975. Andre-Marie Ampere. Birth Bicentenary. As T **182**.

507. 90 f. brown, red & violet 20 15

188. Tristater of Carthage.

1975. Ancient Coins.

508. **188.** 130 f. blk., blue & pur. 30 20
509. – 170 f. blk., grn. & brn. 40 30
510. – 190 f. blk., grn. & red 45 35
511. – 260 f. blk., blue & oran. 60 50

Coins: 170 f. Decadrachm of Syracuse. 190 f. Tetradrachm of Acanthe. 260 f. Didrachm of Eretrie.

1975. Air. "Apollo-Soyuz" Space Link. Nos. 489/91 optd. **ARRIMAGE 17 Juil. 1975.**

512. **181.** 290 f. red, blue & blk. 70 60
513. – 300 f. red, blue & blk. 75 65
514. – 370 f. grn., pur. & blk. 90 80

189. Emblem and U.N. Agencies forming "ONU".

1975. United Nations Charter. 30th Anniv.

515. **189.** 200 f. blue and green 50 40

190. "The Visitation" (Ghirlandaio).

1975. Air. Christmas. Religious Paintings. Multicoloured.

516. 290 f. Type **190** 70 60
517. 300 f. "Nativity" (Fra Filippo Lippi School) 75 65
518. 370 f. "Adoration of the Magi" (Velasquez) .. 90 80

1975. Air. Clement Ader (aviation pioneer). 50th Death Anniv. As T **182**.

519. 100 f. pur., red & blue .. 25 20

191. "Concorde" in Flight.

1976. Air. "Concorde's" First Commercial Flight.

520. **191.** 500 f. multicoloured .. 1·25 1·10

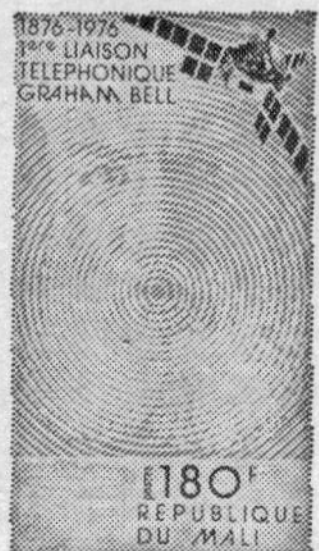

192. Figure-Skating.
193. Alexander Graham Bell.

1976. Air. Winter Olympic Games, Innsbruck. Multicoloured.

521. 120 f. Type **192** 30 25
522. 420 f. Ski-jumping .. 1·00 95
523. 430 f. Skiing (slalom) .. 1·00 95

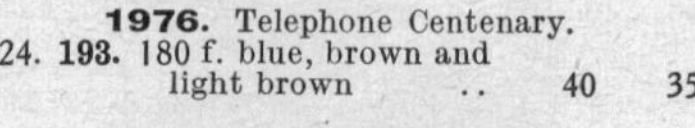

1976. Telephone Centenary.

524. **193.** 180 f. blue, brown and light brown .. 40 35

194. Chameleon.

1976. Reptiles. Multicoloured.

525. 20 f. Type **194** 5 5
526. 30 f. Lizard 8 5
527. 40 f. Tortoise 10 8
528. 90 f. Python 20 15
529. 120 f. Crocodile 30 25

195. Nurse and Patient.

197. Constructing Orbital Space Station.

196. Dr. Adenauer and Cologne Cathedral.

1976. Air. World Health Day.

530.	195.	130 f. multicoloured ..	30	25

1976. Dr. Konrad Adenauer. Birth Centenary.

531.	196.	180 f. maroon & brown	40	35

1976. Air. "The Future in Space".

532.	197.	300 f. deep blue, blue and orange ..	70	65
533.	–	400 f. deep blue, red and maroon	95	90

DESIGN: 400 f. Sun and space-ship with solar batteries.

198. American Eagle and Liberty Bell.

1976. Air. American Revolution. Bicent. and "Interphil '76" Int. Stamp Exn., Philadelphia.

534.	198.	100 f. blue, pur. & blk.	25	20
535.	–	400 f. brn., blue & blk.	95	90
536.	–	440 f. violet, grn. & blk.	1·10	1·00

DESIGNS—HORIZ. 400 f. Ships and American Eagle. VERT. 440 f. Red Indians and American Eagle.

199. Running. 200. Scouts on March.

1976. Air. Olympic Games, Montreal.

537.	199.	200 f. blk., brn. & red	50	45
538.	–	250 f. brn., grn. & blue	60	55
539.	–	300 f. blk., blue & grn.	70	65
540.	–	440 f. blk., blue & grn.	1·10	1·00

DESIGNS: 250 f. Swimming. 300 f. Handball. 440 f. Football.

1976. Air. 1st All-African Scout Jamboree, Nigeria.

541.	200.	140 f. brn., blue & grn.	35	30
542.	–	180 f. brn., grn. & grey	40	35
543.	–	200 f. violet & brown ..	50	45

DESIGNS—HORIZ. 180 f. Scouts tending calf. VERT. 200 f. Scout surveying camp at dusk.

1976. Fishes (2nd series). As Type 180.

544.		100 f. black and blue ..	25	20
545.		120 f. yell., brn. and grn...	30	25
546.		130 f. turq., brn. and blk.	30	25
547.		150 f. yellow, drab & green	35	30
548.		220 f. black, green & brown	55	50

DESIGNS: 100 f. "Synodontis budgetti" 120 f. "Heterobranchus bidorsalis" 130 f. "Tilapia monodi" 150 f. Alestes malerolepidotus" 220 f.

201. Children's Book. 202. "Roi de L'Air".

1976. Literature for Children.

549.	201.	130 f. grey, grn. & red	30	25

1976. "L'Essor" Newspaper Contest.

550.	202.	120 f. multicoloured ..	30	25

203. Fall from Scaffolding.

1976. National Social Insurance. 20th Anniv.

551.	203.	120 f. multicoloured ..	30	25

204. Moenjodaro.

1976. Air. UNESCO "Save Moenjodaro" Campaign.

552.	204.	400 f. pur., blue & blk.	95	90
553.	–	500 f. carm., yell. & blue	1·25	1·10

DESIGN: 500 f. Effigy, animals and remains.

205. Ship, Aircraft and Map.

1976. Air. Europafrique.

554.	205.	200 f. maroon and blue	50	45

206. Cascade of Letters.

1976. U.N. Postal Administration. 25th Anniv.

555.	206.	120 f. orge., grn. & lilac	30	25

OFFICIAL STAMPS

O 1. Dogon Mask.

O 2. Mali Flag and Emblems.

1961.

O 26.	O 1.	1 f. slate-violet ..	5	5
O 27.		2 f. vermilion ..	5	5
O 28.		3 f. slate ..	5	5
O 29.		5 f. turquoise ..	5	5
O 30.		10 f. brown ..	5	5
O 31.		25 f. blue ..	12	8
O 32.		30 f. red ..	15	10
O 33.		50 f. myrtle ..	25	15
O 34.		85 f. maroon ..	40	20
O 35.		100 f. emerald ..	55	30
O 36.		200 f. purple ..	1·10	60

1964. Centre and flag multicoloured; frame colour given.

O 90.	O 2.	1 f. emerald ..	5	5
O 91.		2 f. lavender ..	5	5
O 92.		3 f. slate ..	5	5
O 93.		5 f. purple ..	5	5
O 94.		10 f. blue ..	5	5
O 95.		25 f. ochre ..	10	10
O 96.		30 f. green ..	12	12
O 97.		50 f. orange ..	20	20
O 98.		85 f. brown ..	35	35
O 99.		100 f. red ..	40	40
O 100.		200 f. deep blue ..	70	70

POSTAGE DUE STAMPS

D 1. Bambara Mask.

1961.

D 26.	D 1.	1 f. black	5	5
D 27.		2 f. blue	5	5
D 28.		5 f. mauve	5	5
D 29.		10 f. orange	5	5
D 30.		20 f. blue-green ..	12	12
D 31.		25 f. maroon ..	15	15

D 2. "Polyptychus roseus".

1964. Butterflies. Multicoloured.

D 83.	1 f. Type D 2	5	5
D 84.	1 f. "Deilephila nerii" ..	5	5
D 85.	2 f. "Bunaea alcinoe" ..	5	5
D 86.	2 f. "Gynanisa maja" ..	5	5
D 87.	3 f. "Teracolus eris" ..	5	5
D 88.	3 f. "Colotis antevippe"	5	5
D 89.	5 f. "Manatha microcera"	5	5
D 90.	5 f. "Charaxes epijasius"	5	5
D 91.	10 f. "Hypokopelates otraeda" ..	5	5
D 92.	10 f. "Lipaphnaeus leonina" ..	5	5
D 93.	20 f. "Lobobunaea Christyi" ..	10	10
D 94.	20 f. "Gonimbrasia hecate" ..	10	10
D 95.	25 f. "Hypolimnas misippus" ..	15	15
D 96.	25 f. "Catopsilia florella"	15	15

The two designs in each value are arranged in tete-beche pairs throughout the sheet.

MALTA BC

An island in the Mediterranean Sea, S. of Italy. After a period of self-government under various Constitutions, independence was attained on 21st September, 1964. The island became a republic on 13th December, 1974.

1972. 10 mils = 1 cent.
100 cents = M£1.

1.

2.

1860. Various frames.

18.	1.	½d. yellow	11·00	15·00
20.		½d. green	75	40
22.	–	1d. red	80	75
23.	–	2d. grey	65	80
26.	–	2½d. blue	6·00	80
27.	–	4d. brown	3·00	3·50
28.	–	1s. violet	13·00	10
30.	2.	5s. red	35·00	30·00

6. Harbour of Valletta. 7. Gozo Fishing Boat.

8. Ancient Maltese Galley.

9. "Malta".

10. Shipwreck of St. Paul.

11.

1899.

45.	6.	¼d. brown	55	15
79.		4d. black	6·00	5·50
57.	7.	4½d. brown	6·50	4·50
58.		4½d. orange	3·00	2·50
59.	8.	5d. red	5·00	2·50
60.		5d. green	2·25	2·75
34.	9.	2s. 6d. olive	13·00	12·00
35.	10.	10s. black	35·00	32·00

1902. No. 26 surch. **ONE PENNY.**

36.		1d. on 2½d. blue ..	35·00	40·00

1903.

47.	11.	½d. green	1·00	25
39.		1d. black and red ..	1·25	20
49.		1d. red	70	30
50.		2d. purple and grey ..	2·50	90
51.		2d. grey	90	90
52.		2½d. purple and blue ..	1·40	70
53.		2½d. blue	1·40	50
42.		3d. grey and purple ..	1·00	50
54.		4d. black and brown ..	4·25	4·00
55.		4d. black & red on yellow	2·00	1·60
44.		1s. grey and violet ..	6·50	4·50
62.		1s. black on green ..	3·00	3·00
63.		5s. green & red on yellow	40·00	40·00

12. 13.

14.

15.

1914.

69a.	12.	¼d. brown	20	20
71.		½d. green	60	20
73a.		1d. red	85	30
75.		2d. grey	3·50	2·25
77.		2½d. blue	35	30
78.		3d. purple on yellow ..	4·00	4·00
80.		6d. purple	4·00	4·00
81a.		1s. black on green ..	4·50	5·00
86.	13.	2s. purple & blue on blue	20·00	18·00
88.		5s. green & red on yellow	38·00	40·00
104.	14.	10s. black	£250	£300

1918. Optd. **WAR TAX.**
92. 12. ½d. green 25 20
93. 11. 3d. grey and purple .. 1·75 2·50

1921.
100. 15. 2d. grey .. .. 2·00 60

1922. Optd. **SELF-GOVERNMENT.**
114. 12. ¼d. brown 10 20
106. ½d. green 20 15
116. 1d. red 20 20
117. 15. 2d. grey 45 60
118. 12. 2½d. blue 40 60
108. 3d. purple on yellow .. 70 1·75
109. 6d. purple .. .. 85 1·75
110. 1s. black on green .. 1·40 1·50
120. 13. 2s. purple & blue on blue 16·00 18·00
112. 9. 2s. 6d. olive .. .. 12·00 13·00
113. 13. 5s. green & red on yellow 20·00 25·25
105. 10. 10s. black £110 £100
121. 14. 10s. black .. .. 60·00 70·00

1922. Surch. in words.
122. 15. ¼d. on 2d. grey .. 10 10

16. 17.

1922.
123. 16. ¼d. brown 25 25
124. ½d. green 20 12
125. 1d. orange and purple .. 35 40
126. 1d. violet 35 30
127. 1½d. red 40 15
128. 2d. brown and blue .. 25 20
129. 2½d. blue .. .. 55 1·00
130. 3d. blue .. .. 90 1·00
131. 3d. black on yellow .. 70 95
132. 4d. yellow and blue .. 70 1·00
133. 6d. green and violet .. 80 1·00
134. 17. 1s. blue and brown .. 1·75 1·75
135. 2s. brown and blue .. 4·00 4·50
136. 2s. 6d. purple and black 5·50 6·00
137. 5s. orange and blue .. 7·00 7·00
138. 10s. grey and brown .. 16·00 18·00
140. 16. £1 black and red .. 60·00 70·00

1925 Surch. in words.
141. 16. 2½d. on 3d. blue .. 45 45

1926. Optd. **POSTAGE.**
143. 16. ¼d brown 15 25
144. ½d. green 15 20
145. 1d. violet 15 40
146. 1½d. red 35 35
147. 2d. brown and blue .. 30 40
148. 2½d. blue 40 35
149. 3d. black on yellow .. 45 70
150. 4d. yellow and blue .. 1·00 2·25
151. 6d. green and violet .. 95 60
152. 17. 1s. blue and brown .. 2·75 4·00
153. 2s. brown and blue .. 18·00 20·00
154. 2s. 6d. purple and black 9·00 9·50
155. 5s. orange and blue .. 5·50 8·50
156. 10s. grey and brown .. 10·00 13·00

18.

19. Valetta Harbour.

20. St. Publius.

Designs—As T 19: 2s. Mdina (Notabile). 5s. Ruins at Mnaidra. As T 20: 2s. 6d. Gozo boat. 3s. Statue of Neptune. 10s. St. Paul.

1926. Inscr. "POSTAGE".
157. 18. ¼d. brown 15 12
158. ½d. green 20 12
159. 1d. red 15 20
160. 1½d. brown 30 15
161. 2d. grey .. .. 1·10 1·25
162. 2½d. blue 85 25
162a. 3d. violet .. .. 85 1·10
163. 4d. black and red .. 2·00 2·25
164. 4½d. violet and yellow .. 2·00 2·00
165. 6d. violet and red .. 2·00 2·00
166. 19. 1s. black .. .. 2·00 2·00
167. 20. 1s. 6d. black and green 2·00 2·25
168. – 2s. black and purple .. 5·00 5·00
169. – 2s. 6d. black and red .. 6·00 7·00
170. – 3s. black and blue .. 7·00 7·50
171. – 5s. black and green .. 12·00 14·00
172. – 10s. black and red .. 35·00 40·00

1928. Air. Optd. **AIR MAIL.**
173. 18. 6d. violet and red .. 5·50 6·50

1928. Optd. **POSTAGE AND REVENUE.**
174. 18. ¼d. brown 12 10
175. ½d. green 10 10
176. 1d. red 10 35
177. 1d. brown 35 8
178. 1½d. brown 15 25
179. 1½d. red 40 12
180. 2d. grey .. .. 1·40 1·60
181. 2½d. blue 40 15
182. 3d. violet 70 40
183. 4d. black and red .. 70 1·10
184. 4½d. violet and yellow .. 1·25 1·10
185. 6d. violet and red .. 1·50 1·60
186. 19. 1s. black .. .. 1·25 1·25
187. 20. 1s. 6d. black and green 5·00 6·00
188. – 2s. black and purple .. 6·00 5·50
189. – 2s. 6d. black and red .. 8·00 9·00
190. – 3s. black and blue .. 8·00 8·50
191. – 5s. black and green .. 17·00 22·00
192. – 10s. black and red .. 32·00 38·00

1930. As Nos. 157/72, but inscr. "POSTAGE & REVENUE".
193. ¼d. brown 8 8
194. ½d. green 15 8
195. 1d. brown 12 8
196. 1½d. red 20 8
197. 2d. grey 40 50
198. 2½d. blue 40 15
199. 3d. violet 50 40
200. 4d. black and red .. 70 1·40
201. 4½d. violet and yellow .. 90 1·40
202. 6d. violet and red .. 1·00 1·50
203. 1s. black .. .. 2·50 3·50
204. 1s. 6d. black and green 5·00 5·50
205. 2s. black and purple .. 5·50 7·00
206. 2s. 6d. black and red .. 8·00 9·00
207. 3s. black and blue .. 10·00 13·00
208. 5s. black and green .. 14·00 16·00
209. 10s. black and red .. 40·00 45·00

1935. Silver Jubilee. As T 11 of Antigua.
210. ½d. black and green .. 12 12
211. 2½d. brown and blue .. 60 70
212. 6d. blue and olive .. 3·50 4·00
213. 1s. grey and purple .. 7·50 8·50

1937. Coronation. As T 2 of Aden.
214. ½d. green 8 8
215. 1½d. red 8 10
216. 2½d. blue 35 40

26. Grand Harbour, Valletta. 27. H.M.S. "St. Angelo".

28. Verdala Palace.

1938. Various designs with medallion King George VI.
217. 26. ¼d. brown 8 8
218. 27. ½d. green 12 8
218a. ½d. brown 8 8
219. 28. 1d. brown 25 8
219a. – 1d. green 12 8
220. – 1½d. red 8 8
220a. – 1½d. black 8 8
221. – 2d. black 20 30
221a. – 2d. red 8 8
222. – 2½d. blue 20 30
222a. – 2½d. violet 12 8
223. – 3d. violet 15 40
223a. – 3d. blue 8 8
224. – 4½d. olive and brown .. 30 20
225. – 6d. olive and red .. 25 20
226. – 1s. black 50 50
227. – 1s. 6d. black and olive 1·25 1·75
228. – 2s. green and blue .. 1·25 1·75
229. – 2s. 6d. black and red .. 2·25 2·00
230. – 5s. black and green .. 4·00 4·50
231. – 10s. black and red .. 8·50 8·00

Designs—As T 27/8: vert. 1½d. Hypogeum. Hal Saflieni. 3d. St. John's Co-Cathedral. 6d. Statue of Manoel de Vilhena. 1s. Maltese girl wearing faldetta. 5s. Palace Square, Valletta. 10s. St. Paul. horiz. 2d. Victoria and Citadel Gozo. 2½d. De l'Isle Adam entering Mdina. 4½d. Ruins of Mnajdra. 1s. 6d. St. Publius. 2s. Mdina Cathedral. 2s. 6d. Statue of Neptune.

1946. Victory. As T 4 of Aden.
232. 1d. green 8 8
233. 3d. blue 15 15

1948. Self-Government. As 1938 issue optd. **SELF-GOVERNMENT 1947.**
234. ¼d. brown 8 8
235. ½d. brown 8 8
236. 1d. green 8 8
236a. 1d. grey 8 8
237. 1½d. black 8 8
237a. 1½d. green 8 8
238. 2d. red 8 8
238a. 2d. yellow 8 8
239. 2½d. violet 8 8
239a. 2½d. red 25 25
240. 3d. blue 12 8
240a. 3d. violet 12 8
241. 4½d. olive and brown .. 40 50
241a. 4½d. olive and blue .. 25 25
242. 6d. olive and red .. 12 12
243. 1s. black 50 50
244. 1s. 6d. black and olive 1·10 1·10
245. 2s. green and blue .. 1·25 1·25
246. 2s. 6d. black and red .. 2·00 3·00
247. 5s. black and green .. 4·50 4·50
248. 10s. black and red .. 10·00 10·00

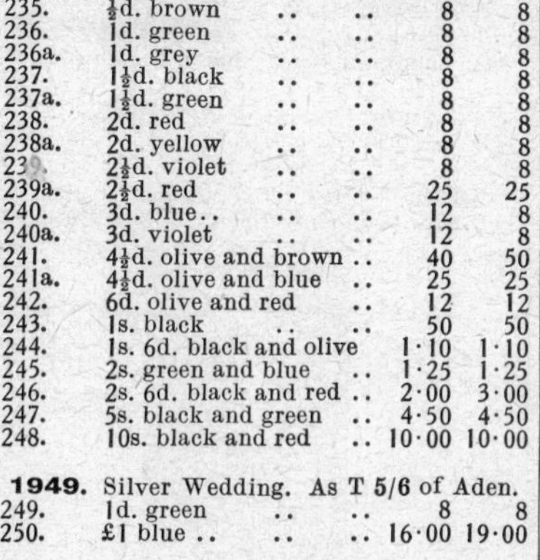

1949. Silver Wedding. As T 5/6 of Aden.
249. 1d. green 8 8
250. £1 blue .. .. 16·00 19·00

1949. U.P.U. As T 14/17 of Antigua.
251. 2½d. violet 12 15
252. 3d. blue 30 30
253. 6d. red 75 55
254. 1s. black .. .. 1·25 1·40

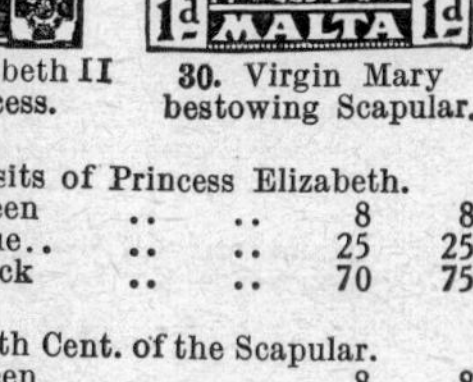

29. Queen Elizabeth II when Princess. 30. Virgin Mary bestowing Scapular.

1950. Visits of Princess Elizabeth.
255. 29. 1d. green 8 8
256. 3d. blue 25 25
257. 1s. black 70 75

1951. 7th Cent. of the Scapular.
258. 30. 1d. green 8 8
259. 3d. violet 12 20
260. 1s. black 85 90

1953. Coronation. As T 7 of Aden.
261 1½d. black and green .. 15 12

31. St. John's Co-Cathedral. 32. Altar-piece, Collegiate Parish Church, Cospicua.

1954. Royal Visit.
262. 31. 3d. violet 15 12

1954. Dogma of the Immaculate Conception. Cent.
263. 32. 1½d. green 5 5
264. 3d. blue 15 10
265. 1s. grey 60 60

33. Monument of the Great Siege, 1565. 34. "Defence of Malta".

1956.
266. 33. ¼d. violet 5 5
267. – ½d. orange 5 5
268. – 1d. black 5 5
269. – 1½d. green 10 8
270. – 2d. sepia 8 8
271. – 2½d. brown 12 10
272. – 3d. red 12 8
273. – 4½d. blue 20 20
274. – 6d. indigo 20 12
275. – 8d. ochre 30 30
276. – 1s. violet 35 35
277. – 1s. 6d. turquoise .. 90 45
278. – 2s. olive .. .. 1·10 70
279. – 2s. 6d. chestnut .. 2·25 1·75
280. – 5s. green .. .. 4·00 3·00
281. – 10s. red .. .. 16·00 12·00
282. – £1 brown .. .. 26·00 22·00

Designs—vert. ¼d. Wignacourt Aqueduct Horsetrough. 1d. Victory Church. 1½d. War Memorial. 2d. Mosta Dome. 3d. King's Scroll. 4½d. Roosevelt's Scroll. 8d. Vedette. 1s. Mdina Gate. 1s. 6d. "Les Gavroches" Statue. 2s. Monument of Christ the King. 2s. 6d. Monument of Grand Master Cottoner. 5s. Grand Master Perellos's Monument. 10s. St. Paul (statue). £1 Baptism of Christ (statue). horiz. 2½d. Auberge de Castile. 6d. Neolithic Temples of Tarxien.

1957. George Cross Commem. Cross in Silver.
283. 34. 1½d. green 10 10
284. – 3d. red 15 15
285. – 1s. brown 35 45

Designs—Horiz. 3d. Searchlights over Malta. Vert. 1s. Bombed buildings.

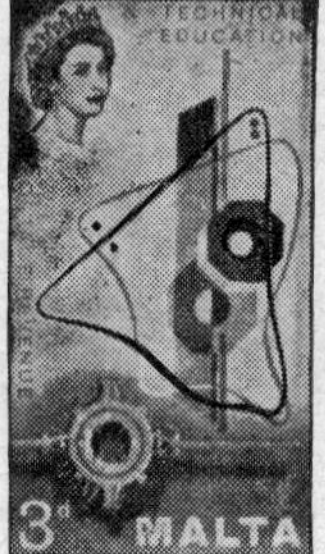

35. "Construction". 36. Sea Raid on Grand Harbour, Valletta.

1958. Technical Education in Malta. Inscr. "TECHNICAL EDUCATION".
286. – 1½d. black and green .. 10 10
287. 35. 3d. black, red and grey 12 12
288. – 1s. grey, purple & black 45 50

Designs—Horiz. 1½d. "Design" (cogwheel, set square, etc.). 1s. Technical School, Paola.

1958. George Cross Commem. Cross in first colour outlined in silver.
289. – 1½d. green and black .. 12 12
290. 36. 3d. red and black .. 12 12
291. – 1s. mauve and black .. 45 50

Designs—Horiz. 1½d. bombed-out family. 1s. searchlight crew.

37. Air Raid Casualties. 38. Shipwreck of St. Paul (after Palombi).

39. Statue of St. Paul, Rabat, Malta.

1959. George Cross Commem.
292. **37.** 1½d. grn., black & gold 10 10
293. – 3d. mauve, black & gold 12 12
294. – 1s. grey, black and gold 50 55
DESIGNS—HORIZ. 3d. "For Gallantry". VERT. 1s. Maltese under bombardment.

1960. Shipwreck of St. Paul (19th Cent.). Insc. as in T **38/9**.
295. **38.** 1½d. blue, gold & brown 12 12
296. – 3d. purple, gold and blue 20 12
297. – 6d. red, gold and grey .. 35 30
298. **38.** 8d. black and gold .. 60 60
299. – 1s. maroon and gold .. 75 75
300. – 2s. 6d. blue, green & gold 3·50 3·00
DESIGNS—As T **38**: 3d. Consecration of St. Publius, First Bishop of Malta. 6d. Departure of St. Paul (after Palombi). As T **39**: 1s. Angel with the "Acts of the Apostles". 2s. 6d. St. Paul with the "Second Epistle to the Corinthians".

40. Stamp of 1860.

1960. Malta Stamp Cent. Stamp in buff and pale blue.
301. **40.** 1½d. green 10 8
302. 3d. red 15 15
303. 6d. blue 45 50

41. George Cross.

1961. George Cross Commem.
304. **41.** 1½d. black, cream & bis. 15 15
305. – 3d. olive-brown and blue 15 12
306. – 1s. ol.-grn., lilac & violet 1·00 1·00
DESIGNS: 3d. and 1s. show George Cross as T **41** over backgrounds with different patterns.

42. "Madonna Damascena". 43. Bruce, Zammit and Microscope.

1962. Great Siege Commem.
307. **42.** 2d. blue 10 10
308. – 3d. red 10 10
309. – 6d. bronze 30 25
310. – 1s. maroon 85 85
DESIGNS: 3d. Great Siege Monument. 6d. Grand Master La Valette. 1s. Assault on Fort St. Elmo.

1963. Freedom from Hunger. As T **10** of Aden.
311. 1s. 6d. sepia .. .. 3·50 2·50

1963. Red Cross Cent. As T **24** of Antigua.
312. 2d. red on black .. 15 12
313. 1s. 6d. red and blue .. 3·25 3·00

1964. Anti-Brucellosis Congress.
316. **43.** 2d. brown, black & green 8 8
317. – 1s. 6d. black and maroon 1·00 1·00
DESIGN: 1s. 6d. Goat and laboratory equipment.

44. "Tending the Sick".

1964. 1st European Catholic Doctors' Congress, Valletta.
318. **44.** 2d. red, blk., gold & blue 12 10
319. – 6d. red, blk., gold & bis. 35 40
320. – 1s. 6d. red, black, gold and violet .. .. 1·00 1·40
DESIGNS: 6d. St. Luke and hospital. 1s. 6d. Sacra Infermeria, Valletta.

45. Dove and British Crown. 47. Neolithic Era.

46. "The Nativity".

1964. Independence.
321. **45.** 2d. olive, red and gold .. 15 12
322. – 3d. brown, red & gold 25 15
323. – 6d. slate, red and gold .. 90 45
324. **45.** 1s. blue, red and gold .. 2·00 1·00
325. – 1s. 6d. indigo, red & gold 5·00 3·00
326. – 2s. 6d. violet-blue, red and gold .. .. 8·00 5·00
DESIGNS: 3d., 1s. 6d. Dove and Pope's Tiara. 6d., 2s. 6d. Dove and U.N. Emblem.

1964. Christmas.
327. **46.** 2d. purple and gold .. 15 12
328. 4d. blue and gold .. 35 30
329. 8d. green and gold .. 1·40 1·25

1965. Multicoloured.
330. ½d. Type **47** 5 5
331. 1d. Punic Era 5 5
332. 1½d. Roman Era 8 8
333. 2d. Proto Christian Era .. 8 8
334. 2½d. Saracenic Era .. 8 8
335. 3d. Siculo Norman Era .. 8 8
336. 4d. Knights of Malta .. 8 8
337. 4½d. Maltese Navy .. 10 10
337a. 5d. Fortifications 15 15
338. 6d. French Occupation .. 10 10

339. 8d. British Rule .. 12 12
339e. 10d. Naval Arsenal .. 30 30
340. 1s. Maltese Corps of the British Army 40 40
341. 1s. 3d. International Eucharistic Congress, 1913 .. 1·00 1·00
342. 1s. 6d. Self-Government, 1921 .. .. 70 70
343. 2s. Gozo Civic Council .. 50 50
344. 2s. 6d. State of Malta .. 90 90
345. 3s. Independence .. .. 1·10 1·10
346. 5s. HAFMED (Allied Forces, Mediterranean) .. .. 1·40 1·40
347. 10s. The Maltese Islands (map) .. .. .. 2·25 2·50
348. £1 Patron Saints .. 4·00 4·50
Nos. 339/48 are larger, 41 × 29 mm. from perf. to perf. and include portrait of Queen Elizabeth II.

48. Dante. 49. Turkish Armada.

1965. Dante's 700th Birth Anniv.
349. **48.** 2d. indigo 8 10
350. 6d. green 30 20
351. 2s. chocolate 80 80

1965. Great Siege. 400th Anniv. Multicoloured.
352. 2d. Turkish camp .. 10 10
353. 3d. Battle scene 15 12
354. 6d. Type **49** 40 30
355. 8d. Arrival of Relief Force 50 45
356. 1s. Grand Master J. de La Valette's Arms 95 90
357. 1s. 6d. "Allegory of Victory" (from mural by M. Preti) 1·00 1·10
358. 2s. 6d. Victory Medal .. 3·25 3·00
SIZES—As T **49**: 1s. SQUARE (32½ × 32½ mm.): others.

50. "The Three Kings".

1965. Christmas.
359. **50.** 1d. slate-purple and red 5 5
360. 4d. slate-purple & blue 80 80
361. 1s. 3d. slate-purple & pur. 1·10 70

51. Sir Winston Churchill.

1966. Churchill Commem.
362. **51.** 2d. black, red and gold 5 5
363. – 3d. green, olive and gold 10 10
364. **51.** 1s. maroon, red and gold 35 40
365. – 1s. 6d. blue, ult. & gold 55 55
DESIGN: 3d., 1s. 6d. Sir Winston Churchill and George Cross.

52. Jean de la Valette.

1966. Valletta. 400th Anniv. Multicoloured.
366. 2d. Type **52** 5 5
367. 3d. Pope Pius V 5 5
368. 6d. Map of Valletta .. 20 20
369. 1s. Francesco Laparelli .. 30 30
370. 2s. 6d. Girolamo Cassar .. 65 70

53. Pres. Kennedy and Memorial.

1966. Pres. Kennedy Commem.
371. **53.** 3d. olive, gold and blask 8 8
372. 1s. 6d. blue, gold & blk. 35 40

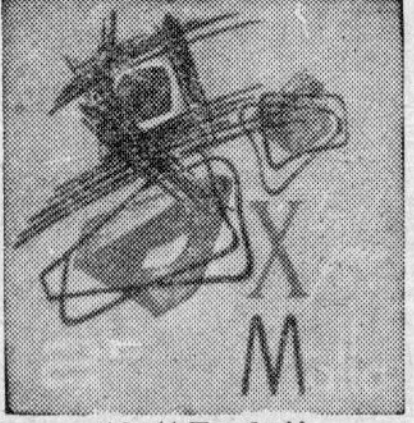

54. "Trade".

1966. 10th Malta Trade Fair.
373. **54.** 2d. multicoloured .. 8 8
374. 8d. multicoloured .. 30 30
375. 1s. 6d. multicoloured .. 90 90

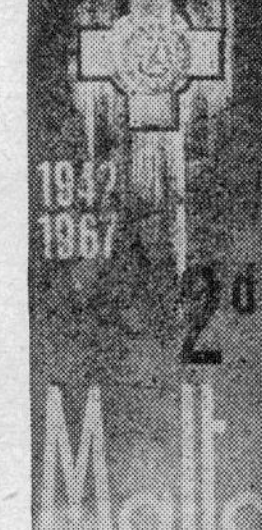

55. "The Child in the Manger". 56. George Cross.

1966. Christmas.
376. **55.** 1d. multicoloured .. 5 5
377. 4d. multicoloured .. 8 8
378. 1s. 3d. multicoloured .. 25 30

1967. George Cross Award to Malta. 25th Anniv.
379. **56.** 2d. multicoloured .. 5 5
380. 4d. multicoloured .. 10 10
381. 3s. multicoloured .. 40 40

57. Crucifixion of St. Peter.

1967. Martyrdom of Saints Peter and Paul. 1,900th Anniv.
382. **57.** 2d. chestnut, orge. & blk. 5 5
383. – 8d. olive, gold and black 15 15
384. – 3s. blue and black .. 45 50
DESIGNS—As T **57**: 3s. Beheading of St. Paul. HORIZ. (47 × 25 mm.): 8d. Open Bible and Episcopal Emblems.

58. "St. Catherine of Siena".

1967. Melchior Gafà (sculptor). 300th Death Anniv. Multicoloured.
385. 2d. Type **58** 5 5
386. 4d. "St. Thomas of Villanova" 8 8
387. 1s. 6d. "Baptism of Christ" (detail) 25 25
388. 2s. 6d. "St. John the Baptist" (from "Baptism of Christ") 40 45

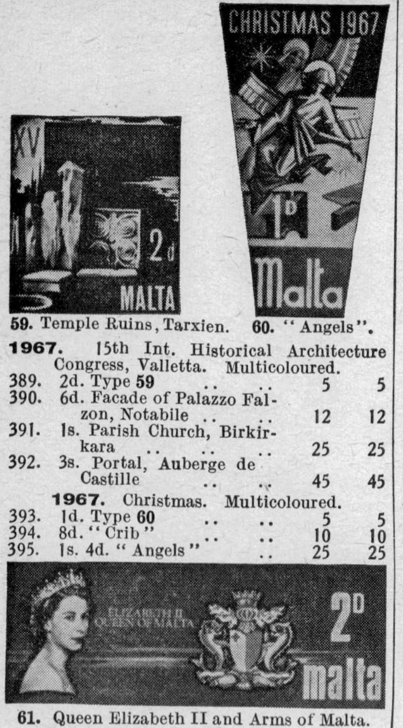

59. Temple Ruins, Tarxien. 60. "Angels".

1967. 15th Int. Historical Architecture Congress, Valletta. Multicoloured.

389. 2d. Type **59** 5 5
390. 6d. Facade of Palazzo Falzon, Notabile 12 12
391. 1s. Parish Church, Birkirkara 25 25
392. 3s. Portal, Auberge de Castille 45 45

1967. Christmas. Multicoloured.

393. 1d. Type **60** 5 5
394. 8d. "Crib" 10 10
395. 1s. 4d. "Angels" .. 25 25

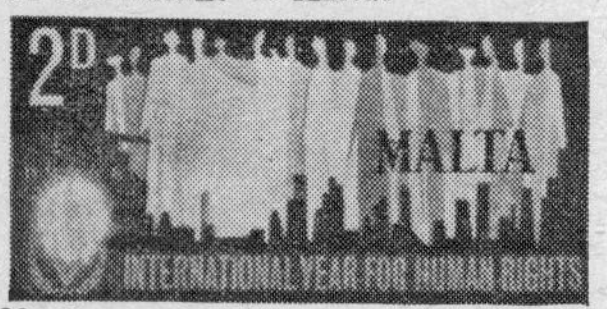

61. Queen Elizabeth II and Arms of Malta.

1967. Royal Visit.

396. **61.** 2d. multicoloured .. 5 5
397. – 4d. black, maroon & gold 12 15
398. – 3s. multicoloured .. 40 45

DESIGNS: VERT. 4d. Queen in Robes of Order of St. Michael and St. George. HORIZ. 3s. Queen and outline of Malta.

62. Human Rights Flame and People.

1968. Human Rights Year. Multicoloured

399. 2d. Type **62** 5 5
400. 6d. Human Rights Flame and People (different).. 12 12
401. 2s. Type **62** (reversed) .. 40 40

63. Fair "Products".

1968. Malta Int. Trade Fair.

402. **63.** 4d. multicoloured .. 5 5
403. 8d. multicoloured .. 12 15
404. 3s. multicoloured .. 45 50

64. Arms of the Order of St. John and La Valette.

1968. Grand Master La Valette. 4th Death Cent. Multicoloured.

405. 1d. Type **64** 5 5
406. 8d. La Valette 12 12
407. 1s. 6d. La Valette's Tomb (28 × 23 mm.) .. 25 25
408. 2s. 6d. Angels and Scroll bearing Date of Death .. 40 40

The 8d., 2s. 6d. are vert.

65. Star of Bethlehem and Angel waking Shepherds.

1968. Christmas. Multicoloured.

409. 1d. Type **65** 5 5
410. 8d. Mary and Joseph with Shepherd watching over Cradle 10 10
411. 1s. 4d. Three Wise Men and Star of Bethlehem .. 25 30

66. "Agriculture". 67. Mahatma Gandhi.

1968. 6th Food and Agricultural Organization Regional Conf. for Europe. Multicoloured.

412. 4d. Type **66** 5 5
413. 1s. F.A.O. Emblem and Coin 20 20
414. 2s. 6d. "Agriculture" sowing Seeds 60 60

1969. Mahatma Gandhi. Birth Cent.

415. **67.** 1s. 6d. brown, blk. & gold 30 30

68. ILO Emblem.

1969. Int. Labour Organisation. 50th Anniv.

416. **68.** 2d. indigo, gold & turq. 5 5
417. 6d. sepia, gold & chest. 15 12

69. Robert Samut.

1969. Robert Samut (composer of Maltese National Anthem). Birth Cent.

418. **69.** 2d. multicoloured .. 12 12

70. Dove of Peace, U.N. Emblem, and Sea-Bed.

1969. United Nations Resolution on Oceanic Resources.

419. **70.** 5d. multicoloured .. 12 12

71. "Swallows" returning to Malta.

1969. Maltese Migrant's Convention.

420. **71.** 10d. black, gold & olive 25 25

72. University Arms and Grand Master de Fonseca (founder).

1969. University of Malta. Bicent.

421. **72.** 2s. multicoloured .. 25 40

73. Flag of Malta and Birds.

1969. Independence. 5th Anniv.

422. – 2d. multicoloured .. 8 8
423. **73.** 5d. black, red and gold 8 8
424. – 10d. black, blue & gold 15 15
425. – 1s. 6d. multicoloured.. 35 35
426. – 2s. 6d. blk., brn. & gold 50 50

DESIGN—SQUARE (31 × 31 mm.). 2d. 1919 War Monument. VERT. 10d. "Tourism". 1s. 6d. U.N. and Council of Europe Emblems. 2s. 6d. "Trade and Industry".

74. Peasants playing Tambourine and Bagpipes.

1969. Christmas. Children's Welfare Fund. Multicoloured.

427. 1d. + 1d. Type **74** .. 8 8
428. 5d. + 1d. Angels playing trumpet and harp .. 12 12
429. 1s. 6d. + 3d. Choir boys singing 40 40

75. "The Beheading of St. John" (Caravaggio) (Illustration reduced. Actual size 56 × 30 mm)

1970. 13th Council of Europe Art Exhibition. Multicoloured.

430. 1d. Type **75** 8 8
431. 2d. "St. John the Baptist" (Mattia Preti) 5 5
432. 5d. Interior of St. John's Co-Cathedral, Valletta 10 10
433. 6d. "Allegory of the Order" (Mattia Preti) 12 12
434. 8d. "St. Jerome" (Caravaggio) 25 25
435. 10d. Articles from the Order of John in Malta .. 25 25
436. 1s. 6d. "The Blessed Gerard receiving Godfrey de Bouillon" (A. de Favray) 40 40
437. 2s. Cape and Stolone (16th-cent.) 50 50

SIZES—HORIZ. 1d., 8d. 56 × 30 mm. 2d., 6d. 45 × 32 mm. 10d., 2s. 63 × 21 mm. 1s. 6d. 45 × 34 mm. SQUARE. 5d. 39 × 39 mm.

76. Artist's Impression of Mt. Fujiyama.

1970. Expo 70.

438. **76.** 2d. multicoloured .. 5 5
439. 5d. multicoloured .. 12 12
440. 3s. mulitcoloured .. 50 50

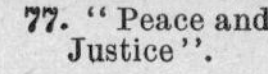

77. "Peace and Justice". 78. Carol-Singers, Church and Star.

1970. United Nations. 25th Anniv.

441. **77.** 2d. multicoloured .. 5 5
442. 5d. multicoloured .. 12 12
443. 2s. 6d. multicoloured.. 45 45

1970. Christmas. Multicoloured.

444. 1d. + ½d. Type **78** .. 5 5
445. 10d. + 2d. Church, Star and Angels with Infant .. 25 25
446. 1s. 6d. + 3d. Church, Star and Nativity Scene .. 45 45

79. Books and Quill.

1971. Literary Anniversaries. Multicoloured.

447. 1s. 6d. Type **79** (De Soldanis (historian) Death Bicent.) 25 25
448. 2s. Dun Karm (poet), books, pens and lamp (Birth Cent.) 30 30

80. Europa Chain. 82. "Centaurea spathulata".

81. "St. Joseph and Angels" (G. Cali).

1971. Europa.

449. **80.** 2d. orange, blk. & olive 5 5
450. 5d. orange, blk. & verm. 10 10
451. 1s. 6d. orge., blk. & slate 45 45

1971. Proclamation of St. Joseph as Patron Saint of Catholic Church. Cent., and Coronation of the Statue of "Our Lady of Victories". 50th Anniv. Multicoloured.

452. 2d. Type **81** 5 5
453. 5d. Statue of "Our Lady of Victories" and Galley.. 8 8
454. 10d. Type **81** 25 25
455. 1s. 6d. As 5d. 40 45

1971. National Plant and Bird of Malta. Multicoloured.

456. 2d. Type **82** 5 5
457. 5d. "Monticola solitarius" (thrush) (horiz.).. .. 8 8
458. 10d. As 5d. 25 25
459. 1s. 6d. Type **82** 45 45

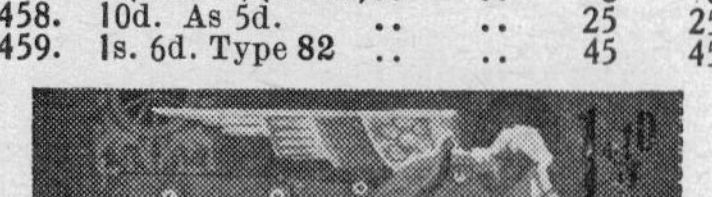

83. Angel. (Illustration reduced. Actual size 59 × 21 mm.).

1971. Christmas. Multicoloured.

460. 1d. + ½d. Type **83** .. 5 5
461. 10d. + 2d. Mary and the Child Jesus 25 25
462. 1s. 6d. + 3d. Joseph lying awake 45 50

84. Heart and W.H.O. Emblem.

1972. World Health Day.

464. **84.** 2d. multicoloured .. 5 5
465. 10d. multicoloured .. 12 12
466. 2s. 6d. multicoloured .. 45 45

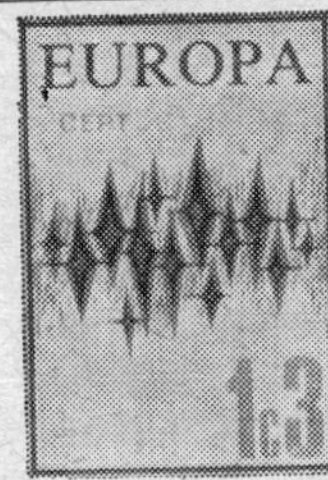

85. Maltese Cross. 86. "Communications".

1972. Decimal Currency. Coins. Mult.

467. 2 m. Type 85 .. .. 5 5
468. 3 m. Bee on Honeycomb .. 5 5
469. 5 m. Earthen lampstand 5 5
470. 1 c. George Cross 5 5
471. 2 c. Classical head .. 8 8
472. 5 c. Ritual altar 20 20
473. 10 c. Grandmaster's galley 45 45
474. 50 c. Great Siege Monument 1·75 1·75

SIZES: 3 m., 2 c. As T 85. 5 m., 1 c., 5 c. 25 × 30 mm. 10 c., 50 c. 31 × 38 mm.

1972. Nos. 337a, 339 and 341 surch.

475. 1 c. 3 m. on 5 d. mult. .. 8 8
476. 3 c. on 8 d. multicoloured .. 10 10
477. 5 c. on 1 s. 3 d. multicoloured 30 30

1972. Europa.

478. 86. 1 c. 3 m. multicoloured 5 5
479. 3 c. multicoloured .. 8 8
480. 5 c. multicoloured .. 15 15
481. 7 c. 5 m. multicoloured 35 35

87. Angel.
(Illustration reduced. Actual size 58 × 22 mm.).

1972. Christmas.

482. 87. 8 m.+2 m. brn., grey and gold 8 8
483. – 3 c.+1 c. purple, violet and gold 15 15
484. – 7 c. 5 m.+1 c. 5 m. indigo, blue & gold .. 30 30

DESIGNS: No. 483, Angel with tambourine. No. 484, Singing angel.

See also Nos. 507/9.

88. Archaeology. 90. Emblem and Woman holding Corn.

89. Europa "Posthorn".

1973. Multicoloured.

486. 2 m. Type 88 .. .. 5 5
487. 4 m. History 5 5
488. 5 m. Folklore 5 5
489. 8 m. Industry 5 5
490. 1 c. Fishing industry .. 5 5
491. 1 c. 3 m. Pottery 5 5
492. 2 c. Agriculture 5 5
493. 3 c. Sport 8 10
494. 4 c. Yacht Marina .. 10 10
495. 5 c. Fiesta 10 12
496. 7 c. 5 m. Regatta .. 15 20
497. 10 c. Voluntary service .. 20 25
498. 50 c. Education .. .. 1·00 1·25
499. £1 Religion .. .. 2·10 2·25
500. £2 Coat of arms (32 × 27 mm.) .. .. .. 4·75 5·00
500a. £2 National Emblem (32 × 27 mm.) .. .. 4·25 4·50

1973. Europa.

501. 89. 3 c. multicoloured .. 8 8
502. 5 c. multicoloured .. 15 15
503. 7 c. 5 m. multicoloured 20 25

1973. Anniversaries.

504. 90. 1 c. 3 m. multicoloured 5 5
505. – 7 c. 5 m. multicoloured 25 25
506. – 10 c. multicoloured .. 35 35

ANNIVERSARIES: 1 c. 3 m., World Food Programme. 10th anniv. 7 c. 5 m., W.H.O. 25th anniv. 10 c. Universal Declaration of Human Rights. 25th Anniv.

1973. Christmas. As T 87. Multicoloured

507. 8 m.+2 m. Angels and organ pipes 5 5
508. 3 c.+1 c. Madonna and Child 25 25
509. 7 c. 5 m.+1 c. 5 m. Buildings and Star 30 35

91. Girolamo Cassar (architect).

1973. Prominent Maltese.

511. 91. 1 c. 3 grn., grey & gold 5 5
512. – 3 c. grn., blue & gold .. 10 10
513. – 5 c. blue, grn. & gold .. 12 15
514. – 7 c. 5 dark blue, blue & gold 20 25
515. – 10 c. purple, dark purple and gold 30 35

DESIGNS: 3 c. Guiseppe Barth (ophthalmologist). 5 c. Nicolo' Isouard (composer). 7 c. 5 John Borg (botanist). 10 c. Antonio Sciortino (sculptor.)

92. "Air Malta" Emblem.

1974. Air. Multicoloured.

516. 3 c. Type 92 .. .. 5 8
517. 4 c. Boeing "707" .. 8 10
518. 5 c. Type 92 .. .. 10 12
519. 7 c. 5 As 4 c. 15 20
520. 20 c. Type 92 .. .. 40 45
521. 25 c. As 4 c. 50 60
522. 35 c. Type 92 .. .. 75 80

93. Prehistoric Sculpture.

1974. Europa.

523. 93. 1 c. 3 pur., blk. & gold 5 5
524. – 3 c. brn., blk. & gold .. 8 8
525. – 5 c. pur., blk. & gold .. 12 15
526. – 7 c. 5 blue, blk. & gold 25 25

DESIGNS—VERT. 3 c. Old Cathedral Door, Mdina. 7 c. 5 "Vetlina" (sculpture by A. Sciortino). HORIZ. 5 c. Silver monstrance.

94. Heinrich von Stephan (founder) and Land Transport.

1974. U.P.U. Centenary.

527. 94. 1 c. 3 grn., blue & orge. 5 5
528. – 5 c. brn., red & green .. 15 15
529. – 7 c. 5 blue, violet & grn. 20 20
530. – 50 c. pur., red & orge... 1·60 1·75

DESIGNS: (each containing portrait as T 94). 5 c. S.S. "Washington" and modern liner. 7 c. 5 Balloon and jet aeroplane. 50 c. U.P.U. Buildings, 1874 and 1974.

95. "The Nativity".

1974. Christmas. Multicoloured.

532. 8 m. + 2 m. Type 95 .. 5 5
533. 3 c + 1 c. "Shepherds" 10 8
534. 5 c. + 1 c. "Shepherds with gifts" 15 15
535. 7 c. 5 + 1 c. 5 "The Magi" 25 25

96. Swearing-in of Prime Minister.

1975. Inauguration of Republic.

536. 96. 1 c. 3 multicoloured .. 5 5
537. – 5 c. red and black .. 12 15
538. – 25 c. multicoloured .. 60 65

DESIGNS: 5 c. Nationl flag. 25 c. Minister of Justice, President and Prime Minister.

97. Mother and Child ("Family Life").

1975. International Women's Year.

539. 97. 1 c. 3 violet and gold .. 5 5
540. – 3 c. blue and gold .. 8 8
541. 97. 5 c. brown and gold .. 12 12
542. – 20 c. brown and gold .. 45 50

DESIGN: 3 c., 20 c. Office Secretary ("Public Life").

98. "Allegory of Malta" (Francesco de Mura).

1975. Europa. Multicoloured.

543. 5 c. Type 98 .. .. 12 15
544. 15 c. "Judith and Holofernes" (Valentin de Boulogne) 35 40

The 15 c. is smaller: 47 × 23 mm.

99. Plan of Ggantija Temple.
(Illustration reduced. Actual size 53 × 22 mm.)

1975. European Architectural Heritage Year.

545. 99. 1 c. 3 black and red .. 5 5
546. – 3 c. purple, red & green 8 10
547. – 5 c. green and red .. 12 15
548. – 25 c. green, red & black 60 70

DESIGNS: 3 c Mdina skyline. 5 c. View of Victoria, Gozo. 25 c. Silhouette of Fort St. Angelo.

100. Farm Animals. 101. "The Right to Work".

1975. Christmas. Multicoloured.

549. 8 m. + 2 m. Type 100 .. 5 5
550. 3 c. + 1 c. Nativity scene (50 × 23 mm.) 8 10
551. 7 c. 5 + 1 c. 5 Approach of the Magi 20 20

1975. Republic. 1st Anniv. Multicoloured.

552. 1 c. 3 Type 101 .. .. 5 5
553. 5 c. "Safeguarding the Environment" 12 15
554. 25 c. National Flag .. 60 70

102. "Festa Tar-Rahal".

1976. Maltese Folklore. Multicoloured.

555. 1 c. 3 Type 102 .. .. 5 5
556. 5 c. "L-Imnarja" (horiz.) 12 15
557. 7 c. 5 "Il-Karnival" (horiz.) 20 25
558. 10 c. "Il-Gimgha L-Kbira" 25 30

103. Waterpolo.

1976. Olympic Games, Montreal. Multicoloured.

559. 1 c. 7 Type 103 .. .. 5 5
560. 5 c. Sailing 12 15
561. 30 c. Athletics 70 75

104. Lace-making.

1976. Europa. Multicoloured.

562. 7 c. Type 104 .. .. 15 20
563. 15 c. Stone carving .. 35 40

105. Nicola Cotoner.

1976. School of Anatomy and Surgery. 300th Anniv. Multicoloured.

564. 2 c. Type 105 .. .. 5 8
565. 5 c. Arm 12 15
566. 7 c. Giuseppe Zammit .. 15 20
567. 11 c. Sacra Infermeria .. 25 30

106. St. John the Baptist and St. Michael.

1976. Christmas. Multicoloured.

568. 1 c.+5 m. Type 106 .. 5 5
569. 5 c.+1 c. Madonna and Child 15 20
570. 7 c.+1 c. 5 St. Christopher and St. Nicholas .. 20 25
571. 10 c.+2 c. Complete painting (32 × 27 mm.) .. 30 35

Nos. 568/71 show portions of "Madonna and Saints" by Domenico di Michelino.

POSTAGE DUE STAMPS

POSTAGE DUE
$\frac{1}{2}$d.
MALTA.

D 1.

D 2.

1925. Imperf.
D 1. D 1. ½d. black 20 35
D 2. 1d. black 30 70
D 3. 1½d. black 50 80
D 4. 2d. black 60 80
D 5. 2½d. black 70 80
D 6. 3d. black on grey .. 80 1·25
D 7. 4d. black on yellow .. 90 1·25
D 8. 6d. black on yellow .. 1·25 1·75
D 9. 1s. black on yellow .. 2·50 3·00
D 10. 1s. 6d. black on yellow 4·00 6·00

1925. Perf.
D 21. D 2. ½d. green 5 5
D 22. 1d. violet 5 5
D 34. 1½d. brown 8 8
D 35. 2d. grey 12 12
D 36. 2½d. orange 12 12
D 37. 3d. blue 12 12
D 38. 4d. olive 20 20
D 39. 6d. purple 30 30
D 40. 1s. black 40 40
D 41. 1s. 6d. red 60 60

D 3. Maltese Lace.

1973.
D 42. D 3. 2 m. brn. & reddish brn. 5 5
D 43. 3 m. orange and red 5 5
D 44. 5 m. pink and red .. 5 5
D 45. 1 c. blue and green .. 5 5
D 46. 2 c. grey and black .. 5 5
D 47. 3 c. light brn. & brn. .. 8 10
D 48. 5 c. dull blue and blue 12 15
D 49. 10 c. lilac and plum .. 25 30

MANAMA O1

A dependency of Ajman.

100 dirhams = 1 riyal.

1966. Nos. 10, 12, 14 and 18 of Ajman surch. **Manama** in English and Arabic and new value.
1. 40 d. on 40 n.p. multicoloured 8 5
2. 70 d. on 70 n.p. multicoloured 15 8
3. 1 r. 50 on 1 r. 50 mult. .. 30 15
4. 10 r. on 10 r. multicoloured 1·90 90

1967. Nos. 170/8 of Ajman optd. **MANAMA** in English and Arabic. (a) Postage.
5. 15 d. blue and brown .. 5 5
6. 30 d. brown and black .. 5 5
7. 50 d. black and brown .. 8 5
8. 70 d. violet and black .. 12 5

(b) Air.
9. 1 r. green and brown .. 15 8
10. 2 r. magenta and black .. 35 15
11. 3 r. black and brown .. 55 25
12. 5 r. chestnut and black .. 90 45
13. 10 r. blue and brown .. 1·75 85

MARIANA ISLANDS O3

A group of Spanish Islands in the Pacific Ocean of which Guam was ceded to the U.S.A. and the others to Germany. The latter are now under U.S. Trusteeship.

100 pfennig = 1 mark.

1899. German stamps optd. **Marianen.**
7. 6. 3 pf. brown .. .. 2·10 11·00
8. 5 pf. green .. .. 2·50 11·00
9. 7. 10 pf. red .. .. 3·50 14·00
10. 20 pf. blue .. .. 5·50 48·00
11. 25 pf. orange .. .. 16·00 55·00
12. 50 pf. brown .. .. 16·00 55·00

1901. "Yacht" key-type inscr. "MARIANEN".
13. N. 3 pf. brown .. 15 35
14. 5 pf. green .. 15 35
15. 10 pf. red .. .. 15 1·40
16. 20 pf. blue .. .. 25 3·00
17. 25 pf. blk. & red on yellow 35 6·00
18. 30 pf. blk. & orge. on buff 35 6·00
19. 40 pf. black and red .. 45 6·00
20. 50 pf. blk. & pur. on buff 55 7·00
21. 80 pf. blk. & red on rose .. 80 9·00
22. O. 1 m. red .. .. 1·10 27·00
23. 2 m. blue .. .. 1·75 30·00
24. 3 m. black .. .. 2·75 55·00
25. 5 m. red and black .. 35·00 £160

MARIENWERDER E2

A district of E. Prussia where a plebiscite was held in 1920. As a result the district remained part of Germany. After the War of 1939-45 it was returned to Poland and reverted to its original name of Kwidzyn.

1.

ILLUSTRATIONS British Commonwealth and all overprints and surcharges are FULL SIZE. Foreign Countries have been reduced to ¾-LINEAR.

1920.
1. 1. 5 pf. green 12 12
2. 10 pf. red 10 10
3. 15 pf. grey 15 15
4. 20 pf. brown 8 8
5. 25 pf. blue 20 20
6. 30 pf. orange 30 30
7. 40 pf. brown 20 20
8. 50 pf. violet 15 15
9. 60 pf. brown .. .. 1·00 1·00
10. 75 pf. brown 30 35
11. 1 m. brown and green .. 25 25
12. 2 m. purple .. .. 1·10 1·25
13. 3 m. red .. .. 1·25 1·40
14. 5 m. blue and red .. 5·50 6·00

1920. Stamps of Germany inscr. "DEUTSCHES REICH" (a) optd. **Commission interalliee Marienwerder** in small letters.
15. 8. 5 pf. green .. .. 5·50 6·00
16. 20 pf. blue .. .. 1·75 2·25
17. 50 pf. black & pur. on buff 60·00 70·00
18. 75 pf. black and green .. 80 90
19. 80 pf. black & red on rose 13·00 18·00
20. 9. 1 m. red .. .. 18·00 22·00

(b) optd. **Commission interalliee Marienwerder** and surch. also.
21. 13. 1 m. on 2 pf. grey .. 5·50 6·00
22. 2 m. on 2½ pf. grey .. 3·00 3·50
23. 8. 3 m. on 3 pf. brown .. 3·00 3·50
24. 13. 5 m. on 7½ pf. orange .. 3·00 3·50

(c) optd. **Commission interalliee Marienwerder** in large lettering.
25. 9. 1 m. red .. .. 1·10 1·50
26. 1 m. 25 green .. .. 1·25 1·50
27. 1 m. 50 brown .. .. 1·75 1·75
28. 10. 2 m. 50 claret .. .. 1·10 1·50

1920. As T 1, with inscription at top changed to "PLEBISCITE".
29. 5 pf. green 70 80
30. 10 pf. red 55 80
31. 15 pf. grey .. .. 2·25 2·75
32. 20 pf. brown 55 55
33. 25 pf. blue .. .. 2·25 2·75
34. 30 pf. orange 25 30
35. 40 pf. brown 15 15
36. 50 pf. violet 35 50
37. 60 pf. brown .. .. 1·00 1·10
38. 75 pf. brown .. .. 1·25 1·50
39. 1 m. brown and green .. 15 20
40. 2 m. purple 30 30
41. 3 m. red 30 35
42. 5 m. blue and red .. 40 50

MARSHALL ISLANDS O3

A group of islands in the Pacific Ocean formerly belonging to Germany. Now under U.S. Trusteeship.

100 pfennig = 1 mark.

1897. Stamps of Germany optd. **Marschall-** (or **Marshall-**) **Inseln.**
5. 6. 3 pf. brown 95 70
6. 5 pf. green .. .. 2·25 1·00
7. 7. 10 pf. red .. .. 4·50 4·50
8. 20 pf. blue .. .. 6·00 6·00
9. 25 pf. orange .. .. 7·00 9·00
10. 50 pf. brown .. .. 12·00 12·00

1901. "Yacht" key types inscr. "MARSHALL INSELN".
11. N. 3 pf. brown 15 55
12. 5 pf. green 15 55
13. 10 pf. red .. .. 15 2·10
14. 20 pf. blue .. .. 25 4·50
15. 25 pf. blk. & red on yell. 35 7·00
16. 30 pf. blk. & orge. on buff 35 7·00
17. 40 pf. black and red .. 35 7·00
18. 50 pf. blk. & pur. on buff 55 9·00
19. 80 pf. blk. & red on rose 80 12·00
20. O. 1 m. red .. .. 1·10 25·00
21. 2 m. blue .. .. 2·00 35·00
22. 3 m. black .. .. 2·75 55·00
23. 5 m. red and black .. 45·00 £160

MARTINIQUE O3

An island in the West Indies, now an overseas department using the stamps of France.

1886. Stamp of French Colonies, "Commerce" type (a) surch. **MARTINIQUE** and value in figures.
3. 9. 01 on 20 c. red on green .. 1·40 1·50
1. 5 on 20 c. red on green .. 5·00 5·00
4. 05 on 20 c. red on green .. 90 65
2. 5 c. on 20 c. red on green .. £1400 £1400
6. 015 on 20 c. red on green .. 6·50 5·50
5. 15 on 20 c. red on green .. 19·00 16·00

(b) surch. **MQE 15c.**
7. 9. 15 c. on 20 c. red on green 13·00 12·00

1888. Stamps of French Colonies. "Commerce" type surch. **MARTINIQUE** and value, thus **01c.**
9. 9. 01 c. on 2 c. brown on yell. 25 20
10. 01 c. on 4 c. claret on grey 90 20
11. 05 c. on 4 c. claret on grey £180 £180
12. 05 c. on 10 c. black on lilac 9·50 5·50
13. 05 c. on 20 c. red on green 2·25 1·90
14. 05 c. on 30 c. brown .. 2·50 2·00
15. 05 c. on 35 c. blk. on yellow 1·90 1·50
16. 05 c. on 40 c. red on yellow 7·00 3·75
17. 15 c. on 4 c. claret on grey £1200 £1100
18. 15 c. on 20 c. red on green 10·00 6·50
19. 15 c. on 25 c. black on red 2·50 1·40
20. 15 c. on 75 c. red .. 15·00 10·00

1891. Postage Due stamps of French Colonies surch. **TIMBRE-POSTE MARTINIQUE** and value in figures.
21. D 1. 05 c. on 5 c. black .. 1·60 1·60
25. 05 c. on 10 c. black .. 75 75
22. 05 c. on 15 c. black .. 1·10 1·00
23. 15 c. on 20 c. black .. 1·50 1·00
24. 15 c. on 30 c. black .. 1·60 1·25

1891. Stamp of French Colonies, "Commerce" type, surch. **TIMBRE-POSTE 01c. MARTINIQUE.**
28. 9. 01 c. on 2 c. brn. on yellow 1·00 85

1892. Stamp of French Colonies, "Commerce" type, surch. **1892 MARTINIQUE** and value in figures.
30. 9. 05 c. on 25 c. blk. on red 7·50 7·00
31. 15 c. on 25 c. blk. on red 2·75 2·75

1892. "Tablet" key-type inscr. "MARTINIQUE".
33. D. 1 c. black on blue .. 5 5
34. 2 c. brown on yellow .. 10 10
35. 4 c. claret on grey .. 20 10
36. 5 c. green 20 5
37. 10 c. black on lilac .. 50 5
47. 10 c. red 25 5
38. 15 c. blue .. .. 2·40 40
48. 15 c. grey .. .. 1·10 8
39. 20 c. red on green .. 1·90 65
40. 25 c. black on red .. 1·60 20
49. 25 c. blue .. .. 1·60 1·60
41. 30 c. brown .. .. 3·50 1·60
50. 35 c. black on yellow .. 1·75 40
42. 40 c. red on yellow .. 3·50 1·25
43. 50 c. red on rose .. 2·75 1·75
51. 50 c. brown on blue .. 2·75 2·50
44. 75 c. brown on orange .. 3·00 2·10
45. 1 f. olive .. .. 2·10 1·25
52. 2 f. violet on rose .. 11·00 11·00
53. 5 f. mauve on lilac .. 14·00 14·00

1904. Surch in figures.
79. D. 05 on 15 c. grey 5 5
80. 05 on 25 c. black on red .. 5 5
54. 10 c. on 30 c. brown .. 75 75
81. 10 on 40 c. red on yellow 20 20
82. 10 on 5 f. mauve on lilac 20 20
55. 10 c. on 5 f. mauve on lilac 1·40 1·40

1904. Surch. **1904. 0f 10.**
56. D. 0 f. 10 on 30 c. brown .. 2·00 2·00
57. 0 f. 10 on 40 c. red on yell. 2·00 2·00
58. 0 f. 10 on 50 c. red on rose 2·00 2·00
59. 0 f. 10 on 75 c. brown on orange .. 1·40 1·40
60. 0 f. 10 on 1 f. olive .. 1·60 1·60
61. 0 f. 10 on 5 f. mauve on lilac .. .. 27·00 27·00

1. Martinique Woman.

3. Woman and Sugar Cane.

2. Fort-de-France.

1908.
62. 1. 1 c. chocolate and brown 5 5
63. 2 c. chocolate and olive .. 5 5
64. 4 c. chocolate and claret 5 5
65. 5 c. chocolate and green 5 5
87. 5 c. chocolate and orange 5 5
66. 10 c. chocolate and red .. 5 5
88. 10 c. olive and green .. 5 5
89. 10 c. red and purple .. 5 5
67. 15 c. red and purple .. 5 5
90. 15 c. olive and green .. 5 5
91. 15 c. orange and blue .. 8 8
68. 20 c. chocolate and lilac .. 5 5
69. 2. 25 c. brown and blue .. 8 8
92. 25 c. brown and orange .. 5 5
93. 30 c. brown and red .. 8 5
94. 30 c. red and claret .. 5 5
95. 30 c. brown 5 5
96. 30 c. green and blue .. 5 5
71. 35 c. lilac 5 5
72. 40 c. brown and olive .. 8 5
73. 45 c. brown 5 5
74. 50 c. brown and red .. 8 8
97. 50 c. brown and blue .. 8 8
98. 50 c. green and red .. 5 5
99. 60 c. red and blue .. 5 5
100. 65 c. brown and mauve .. 20 20
75. 75 c. brown and black .. 5 5
101. 75 c. blue 5 5
102. 75 c. blue and brown .. 30 30
103. 90 c. red 40 40
76. 3. 1 f. brown and red .. 5 5
104. 1 f. blue 5 5
105. 1 f. olive and red .. 20 20
106. 1 f. 10 brown and mauve 35 35
107. 1 f. 50 blue 60 60
77. 2 f. brown and grey .. 30 8
108. 3 f. mauve 55 55
78. 5 f. brown and red .. 1·10 1·10

1916. Surch. **5 c** and red cross.
83. 1. 10 c + 5 c. chocolate & red 20 12

1920. Surch. in figures
115. 1. 0.01 on 2 c. choc. & olive 25 25
109. 0.01 on 15 c. red & purple 5 5
110. 0.02 on 15 c. red & purple 5 5
84. 05 on 1 c. choc. & brown 12 12
111. 0.05 on 15 c. red & purple 5 5
116. 0.05 on 20 c. choc. & lilac 25 25
85. 10 on 2 c. choc. & olive 8 8
118. 2. 0.15 on 30 c. brown & red 1·10 1·10
86. 1. 25 on 15 c. red & purple 10 10
121. 25 c. on 15 c. red & purple 5 5
119. 2. 0.25 on 50 c. brown & red 38·00 35·00
120. 0.25 on 50 c. brown & blue 60 60
122. 3. 25 c. on 2 f. brown & grey 5 5
123. 25 c. on 5 f. brown & red 5 5
112. 2. 60 on 75 c. claret & blue 5 5
113. 65 on 45 c. brown .. 5 5
114. 85 on 75 c. brown & black 10 10
124. 90 c. on 75 c. red .. 25 25
125. 3. 1 f. 25 on 1 f. blue .. 5 5
126. 1 f. 50 on 1 f. blue .. 12 12
127. 3 f. on 5 f. green and red 20 20
128. 10 f. on 5 f. red & green 1·10 1·10
129. 20 f. on 5 f. violet & brown 1·60 1·60

1931. "Colonial Exhibition" key-types. inscr. "MARTINIQUE".
130. E. 40 c. green 30 30
131. F. 50 c. mauve 30 30
132. G. 90 c. red 30 30
133. H. 1 f. 50 blue 30 30

4. Basse Pointe Village.

5. Government House, Fort de France.

6. Martinique Women.

1933.
134. 4. 1 c. red 5 5
135. 5. 2 c. blue 5 5
136. 3 c. purple 5 5
137. 4. 4 c. olive 5 5
138. 5. 5 c. claret 5 5
139. 4. 10 c. black on orange .. 5 5
140. 5. 15 c. black on orange .. 5 5
141. 6. 20 c. lake 5 5
142. 4. 25 c. purple 5 5
143. 5. 30 c. green 5 5
144. 30 c. blue 5 5
145. 6. 35 c. green 5 5
146. 40 c. brown 5 5
147. 5. 45 c. brown 12 10
148. 45 c. green 5 5
149. 50 c. red 5 5
150. 4. 55 c. red 8 8
151. 60 c. blue 5 5
152. 6. 65 c. red on blue .. 5 5
153. 70 c. purple 5 5
154. 4. 75 c. brown 10 10
155. 5. 80 c. violet 5 5
156. 4. 90 c. red 20 12
157. 90 c. purple 5 5
158. 5. 1 f. black on green .. 20 12
159. 1 f. red 5 5
160. 6. 1 f. 25 violet 8 8
161. 1 f. 25 red 5 5
162. 4. 1 f. 40 blue 5 5
163. 5. 1 f. 50 blue 5 5
164. 1 f. 60 brown 5 5
165. 6. 1 f. 75 olive .. .. 1·10 35
166. 1 f. 75 blue 5 5
167. 4. 2 f. blue on green .. 5 5
168. 6. 2 f. 25 blue 5 5
169. 4. 2 f. 50 purple 5 5
170. 6. 3 f. purple 5 5
171. 5 f. red 15 8
172. 4. 10 f. blue 8 8
173. 5. 20 f. red on yellow .. 10 8

7. Belain d'Esnambuc 1635.

8. Schœlcher and Abolition of Slavery, 1848.

1935. West Indies Tercentenary.
174. 7. 40 c. brown 30 30
175. 50 c. red 30 30
176. 1 f. 50 blue .. .. 2·10 2·10
177. 8. 1 f. 75 red .. .. 1·90 1·50
178. 5 f. brown .. .. 1·90 1·50
179. 10 f. green .. .. 1·50 1·25

1937. International Exhibition, Paris. As Nos. 110/15 of Cameroun.
180. 20 c. violet 15 15
181. 30 c. green 15 15
182. 40 c. red 15 15
183. 50 c. brown 20 20
184. 90 c. red 20 20
185. 1 f. 50 blue 20 20

1938. Int. Anti-Cancer Fund. As T **10** of Cameroun.
186. 1 f. 75+50 c. blue .. 1·50 1·50

1939. New York World's Fair. As T **11** of Cameroun.
187. 1 f. 25 red 8 8
188. 2 f. 25 blue 8 8

1939. French Revolution. 150th Anniv. As T **16** of Cameroun.
189. 45 c.+25 c. green.. .. 85 85
190. 70 c.+30 c. brown .. 85 85
191. 90 c.+35 c. orange .. 85 85
192. 1 f. 25+1 f. red 85 85
193. 2 f. 25+2 f. blue .. 85 85

1944. Mutual Aid and Red Cross Funds. As T **19** of Cameroun.
194. 5 f.+20 f. violet 5 5

1945. Eboue. As T **20** of Cameroun.
195. 2 f. black 5 5
196. 25 f. green 10 10

1945. Surch.
197. **5.** 1 f. on 2 c. blue .. 5 5
198. **4.** 2 f. on 4 c. olive .. 5 5
199. **5.** 3 f. on 2 c. blue .. 5 5
200. **6.** 5 f. on 65 c. red on blue.. 10 10
201. 10 f. (DIX f.) on 65 c. red on blue 8 8
202. **5.** 10 f. (VINGT f.) on 3 c. purple 10 10

9. Victor Schœlcher.

1945.
203. **9.** 10 c. blue 5 5
204. 30 c. brown 5 5
205. 40 c. green 5 5
206. 50 c. brown 5 5
207. 60 c. orange 5 5
208. 70 c. brown 5 5
209. 80 c. green 5 5
210. 1 f. blue 5 5
211. 1 f. 20 lilac 5 5
212. 1 f. 50 orange 5 5
213. 2 f. black 5 5
214. 2 f. 40 red 5 5
215. 3 f. pink 5 5
216. 4 f. blue 5 5
217. 4 f. 50 green 5 5
218. 5 f. brown 5 5
219. 10 f. violet 8 8
220. 15 f. red 10 8
221. 20 f. olive 12 12

1945. Air. As T **18** of Cameroun.
222. 50 f. green 8 8
223. 100 f. claret 12 12

1946. Air. Victory. As T **21** of Cameroun.
224. 8 f. blue 20 20

1946. Air. From Chad to the Rhine. As T **22** of Cameroun.
225. 5 f. orange 8 8
226. 10 f. green 8 8
227. 15 f. red 8 8
228. 20 f. brown 10 10
229. 25 f. blue 10 10
230. 50 f. grey 20 20

10. Martinique Woman.

12. Mountains and Palms.

11. Sailing Vessels and Rocks.

13. Flying Boat and West Indians.

1947.
231. **10.** 10 c. lake (postage) .. 5 5
232. 30 c. blue 5 5
233. 50 c. brown 5 5
234. **11.** 60 c. green 5 5
235. 1 f. lake 5 5
236. 1 f. 50 violet 5 5
237. – 2 f. green 8 8
238. – 2 f. 50 brown 8 8
239. – 3 f. blue 8 8
240. – 4 f. brown 5 5
241. – 5 f. green 5 5
242. – 6 f. mauve 5 5
243. – 10 f. blue 8 8
244. – 15 f. lake 20 20
245. – 20 f. brown 20 20
246. **12.** 25 f. violet 20 20
247. 40 f. green 25 25
248. **13.** 50 f. purple (air) .. 60 60
249. – 100 f. green 80 80
250. – 200 f. violet .. .. 3·50 3·50

DESIGNS—HORIZ. As T **11**: 2 f. to 3 f. Gathering sugar cane. 4 f. to 6 f. Mount Pele. 10 f. to 20 f. Fruit products. As T **13**—VERT. 100 f. Aeroplane over landscape. HORIZ. 200 f. Gull in flight.

POSTAGE DUE STAMPS

1927. Postage Due stamps of France optd. **MARTINIQUE.**
D 130. D **2.** 5 c. blue 8 8
D 131. 10 c. brown 8 8
D 132. 20 c. olive 10 10
D 133. 25 c. red 20 20
D 134. 30 c. red 20 20
D 135. 45 c. green 20 20
D 136. 50 c. purple 45 45
D 137. 60 c. green 45 45
D 138. 1 f. claret on yellow 80 80
D 139. 2 f. mauve 80 80
D 140. 3 f. red 80 80

D **1.** Fruit.

D **2.** Map of Martinique.

1933.
D 174. D **1.** 5 c. blue on green 5 5
D 175. 10 c. lake 5 5
D 176. 20 c. blue 15 15
D 177. 25 c. red 15 15
D 178. 30 c. purple 5 5
D 179. 45 c. red on yellow 5 5
D 180. 50 c. brown 10 10
D 181. 60 c. green 10 10
D 182. 1 f. black on orange 25 25
D 183. 2 f. claret 10 10
D 184. 3 f. blue 15 15

1947.
D 251. D **2.** 10 c. blue 5 5
D 252. 30 c. green 5 5
D 253. 50 c. blue 5 5
D 254. 1 f. orange 5 5
D 255. 2 f. purple 5 5
D 256. 3 f. purple 5 5
D 257. 4 f. brown 8 8
D 258. 5 f. red 12 12
D 259. 10 f. black 12 12
D 260. 20 f. green 20 20

MAURITANIA O3

A French colony extending inland to the Sahara, incorporated in French West Africa in 1944. In 1960 Mauritania became an independent Islamic Republic.

1973. 100 cents = 1 ouguiya (um).

1906. "Faidherbe", "Palms" and "Balay" key-types inscr. "MAURITANIE".
1. I. 1 c. grey 5 5
2. 2 c. brown 8 5
3. 4 c. brown on blue .. 20 8
4. 5 c. green 5 5
5. 10 c. red .. .. 1·10 70
6. J. 20 c. black on blue .. 2·10 2·10
7. 25 c. blue .. .. 1·10 1·10
8. 30 c. brown on pink 15·00 11·00
9. 35 c. black on yellow .. 65 60
10. 40 c. red 65 60
11. 45 c. brown on green .. 65 60
12. 50 c. violet 65 60
13. 75 c. green on orange .. 65 60
14. K. 1 f. black .. .. 2·00 1·75
15. 2 f. blue on rose .. 5·00 4·50
16. 5 f. red on yellow .. 22·00 20·00

1. Merchants crossing Desert.

1913.
18. **1.** 1 c. brown and purple .. 5 5
19. 2 c. blue and black .. 5 5
20. 4 c. black and violet .. 5 5
21. 5 c. green 5 5
37. 5 c. red and purple .. 5 5
22. **1.** 10 c. orange and red .. 8 8
38. 10 c. green 5 5
39. 10 c. red on blue .. 5 5
23. 15 c. black on sepia .. 5 5
24. 20 c. orange and brown .. 5 5
25. 25 c. blue 12 12
40. 25 c. red and green .. 5 5
26. 30 c. red and green .. 8 8
41. 30 c. orange and red .. 5 5
42. 30 c. yellow and black .. 5 5
43. 30 c. green 20 20
27. 35 c. violet and brown .. 5 5
44. 35 c. green 5 5
28. 40 c. green and grey .. 30 30
29. 45 c. brown and orange .. 5 5
30. 50 c. red and lilac .. 5 5
45. 50 c. blue 5 5
46. 50 c. blue and green .. 5 5
47. 60 c. violet 5 5
48. 65 c. blue and brown .. 5 5
31. 75 c. brown and blue .. 8 8
49. 85 c. brown and green .. 8 8
50. 90 c. mauve and red .. 20 20
32. 1 f. black and red .. 5 5
51. 1 f. 10 red and violet .. 1·25 1·25
52. 1 f. 25 sepia and blue .. 20 20
53. 1 f. 50 blue 5 5
54. 1 f. 75 red and green .. 5 5
55. 1 f. 75 blue 5 5
33. 2 f. violet and orange .. 10 10
56. 3 f. mauve 12 12
34. 5 f. blue and violet .. 15 15

1915. Surch. **+5 c.**
35. **1.** 10 c.+5 c. orange and red 12 12
36. 15 c.+5 c. black and sepia 8 8

1922. Surch. in figures and bars.
60. **1.** 25 c. on 2 f. violet & orange 8 8
57. 60 on 75 c. violet .. 5 5
58. 65 on 15 c. black and sepia 15 15
59. 85 on 75 c. brown and blue 15 15
61. 90 c. on 75 c. mauve & red 20 20
62. 1 f. 25 on 1 f. blue .. 5 5
63. 1 f. 50 on 1 f. blue .. 12 12
64. 3 f. on 5 f. mauve & brown 85 85
65. 10 f. on 5 f. green & mauve 70 70
66. 20 f. on 5 f. orange & blue 75 75

1931. "Colonial Exhibition" key-types inscr. "MAURITANIE".
67. E. 40 c. green 65 65
68. F. 50 c. mauve 65 65
69. G. 90 c. red 65 65
70. H. 1 f. 50 blue 65 65

1937. Int. Exn., Paris. As Nos. 110/15 of Cameroun.
71. 20 c. violet 10 10
72. 30 c. green 10 10
73. 40 c. red 10 10
74. 50 c. brown 10 10
75. 90 c. red 12 12
76. 1 f. 50 blue 12 12

1938. Int. Anti-Cancer Fund. As T **10** of Cameroun.
76b. 1 f. 75+50 c. blue .. 1·50 1·50

2. Camel and Rider.

3. Moorish Warriors.

4. Encampment.

5. Natives.

1938.
77. **2.** 2 c. purple 5 5
78. 3 c. blue 5 5
79. 4 c. lilac 5 5
80. 5 c. red 5 5
81. 10 c. red 5 5
82. 15 c. violet 5 5
83. **3.** 20 c. red 5 5
84. 25 c. blue 5 5
85. 30 c. purple 5 5
86. 35 c. green 5 5
87. 40 c. red 5 5
88. 45 c. green 5 5
89. 50 c. violet 5 5
90. **4.** 55 c. lilac 5 5
91. 60 c. violet 5 5
92. 65 c. green 5 5
93. 70 c. red 5 5
94. 80 c. blue 12 12
95. 90 c. lilac 5 5
96. 1 f. red 10 10
97. 1 f. green 5 5
98. 1 f. 25 red 8 8
99. 1 f. 40 blue 8 8
100. 1 f. 50 violet 5 5
101. 1 f. 60 brown 8 8
102. **5.** 1 f. 75 blue 12 12
103. 2 f. lilac 15 15
104. 2 f. 25 blue 5 5

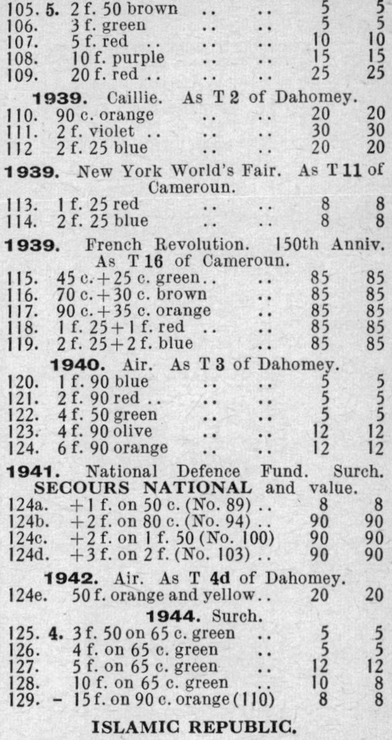

105. **5.** 2 f. 50 brown 5 5
106. 3 f. green 5 5
107. 5 f. red 10 10
108. 10 f. purple 15 15
109. 20 f. red 25 25

1939. Caillie. As T **2** of Dahomey.
110. 90 c. orange 20 20
111. 2 f. violet 30 30
112. 2 f. 25 blue 20 20

1939. New York World's Fair. As T **11** of Cameroun.
113. 1 f. 25 red 8 8
114. 2 f. 25 blue 8 8

1939. French Revolution. 150th Anniv. As T **16** of Cameroun.
115. 45 c.+25 c. green.. .. 85 85
116. 70 c.+30 c. brown .. 85 85
117. 90 c.+35 c. orange .. 85 85
118. 1 f. 25+1 f. red 85 85
119. 2 f. 25+2 f. blue .. 85 85

1940. Air. As T **3** of Dahomey.
120. 1 f. 90 blue 5 5
121. 2 f. 90 red 5 5
122. 4 f. 50 green 5 5
123. 4 f. 90 olive 12 12
124. 6 f. 90 orange 12 12

1941. National Defence Fund. Surch. **SECOURS NATIONAL** and value.
124a. +1 f. on 50 c. (No. 89) .. 8 8
124b. +2 f. on 80 c. (No. 94) .. 90 90
124c. +2 f. on 1 f. 50 (No. 100) 90 90
124d. +3 f. on 2 f. (No. 103) .. 90 90

1942. Air. As T **4d** of Dahomey.
124e. 50 f. orange and yellow .. 20 20

1944. Surch.
125. **4.** 3 f. 50 on 65 c. green .. 5 5
126. 4 f. on 65 c. green .. 5 5
127. 5 f. on 65 c. green .. 12 12
128. 10 f. on 65 c. green .. 10 8
129. – 15 f. on 90 c. orange (110) 8 8

ISLAMIC REPUBLIC.

6. Republican Flag.

7. Pastoral Well.

8. Gull ("Goeland railleur").

1960. Inaug. of Islamic Republic.
130. **6.** 25 f. bistre, green and brown on rose .. 25 20

1960. African Technical Co-operation Commission. 10th Anniv. As T **39** of Cameroun.
131. 25 f. blue and turquoise .. 25 20

1960.
132. **7.** 50 c. pur. & brown (post.) 5 5
133. – 1 f. yellow-brown, red-brown and green .. 5 5
134. – 2 f. chocolate, green & blue 5 5
135. – 3 f. red, sepia & turquoise 5 5
136. – 4 f. buff & yellow-green 5 5
137. – 5 f. choc., brown and red 5 5
138. – 10 f. blue, black & chest. 8 5
139. – 15 f. pur., red, bl. & grn. 12 8
140. – 20 f. brown and green .. 15 8
141. – 25 f. blue and green .. 15 5
142. – 30 f. indigo, vio. & bistre 20 5
143. – 50 f. chestnut and green 40 15
144. – 60 f. purple, red & green 45 20
145. – 85 f. brown, sepia & blue 65 25
146. – 100 f. chestnut, chocolate and blue (air) .. 95 65
147. – 200 f. myrtle, chestnut and sepia .. .. 1·75 1·10
148. **8.** 500 f. sepia, blue & chest. 4·75 2·50

DESIGNS—VERT. (As T **7**) 2 f. Harvesting dates. 5 f. Harvesting millet. 25 f., 30 f. Seated dance. 50 f. "Telmidi" (symbolic figure). 60 f. Metalsmith. 85 f. White oryx. 100 f. Pink flamingo. 200 f. Spoonbill. HORIZ. 3 f. Mountain goat. 4 f. Fennecs. 10 f. Cordwainer. 15 f. Fishing-boat. 20 f. Nomad school.

9. Flag and Map.

1960. Proclamation of Independence.
149. **9.** 25 f. green, choc. & chest. 20 15

1962. Air. "Air Afrique" Airline. As T **44** of Cameroun.
150. 100 f. slate-green, chocolate and bistre 75 55

1962. Malaria Eradication. As T 45 of Cameroun.
151. 25 f.+5 f. olive 25 25

10. U.N. Headquarters and View of Nouakchott.

1962. Admission to U.N.O.
152. 10. 15 f. brn., black & blue 15 15
153. 25 f. brown, myrtle & bl. 20 20
154. 85 f. brown, purple & bl. 65 65

1962. Union of African and Malagasy States. 1st Anniv. As No. 328 of Cameroun.
155. 47. 30 f. blue 25 25

11. Eagle and Crescent over Nouakchott.

1962. 8th Endemic Diseases Eradication Conf., Nouakchott.
156. 11. 30 f. green, brown & blue 25 25

12. Mineral Train.

1962.
157. 12. 50 f. multicoloured .. 40 25

1962. Air. Admission to U.N.O. 1st Anniv. As T 10 but views from different angles and inscr. "1 er ANNIVERSAIRE 27 OCTOBRE 1962".
158. 100 f. blue, brown & turq. 75 65

13. Map and Agriculture.

1962. Independence. 2nd Anniv.
59. 13. 30 f. green and maroon 20 20

14. Congress Representatives.

1962. Unity Congress. 1st Anniv.
160. 14. 25 f. brown, myrtle & bl. 20 15

1962. Freedom from Hunger. As T 51 of Cameroun.
161. 25 f.+5 f. blue, brn. & mar. 25 25

15. Douglas DC-3 Airliner over Nouakchott Airport.

1963. Air. Creation of National Airline.
162. 15. 500 f. myrtle, brn. & bl. 3·75 2·10

16. Open-cast Mining, Zouerate.

1963. Air. Mining Development. Mult.
163. 100 f. T 16.. .. .. 75 40
164. 200 f. Port-Etienne .. 1·50 80

ANIMALS—HORIZ. 1 f. Spotted hyena. 2 f. Baboons. 10 f. Leopard. 15 f. Bongos. 20 f. Anteater. 30 f. Porcupine. 60 f. Chameleon. VERT. 1 f. 50, Cheetah. 5 f. Dromedaries, 25 f. Monkeys. 50 f. Dorcas gazelle.

17. Striped Hyena.

1963. Animals.
165. 17. 50 c. blk., brn. & myrtle 5 5
166. – 1 f. black, blue and buff 5 5
167. – 1 f. 50 brn., olive & mar. 5 5
168. – 2 f. maroon, green & red 5 5
169. – 5 f. yell.-brn., bl. & ochre 5 5
170. – 10 f. black and ochre .. 5 5
171. – 15 f. brn.-pur. & ultram. 8 5
172. – 20 f. yell.-brn., mar. & bl. 10 5
173. – 25 f. ochre, chest. & turq. 12 5
174. – 30 f. bistre, choc. & blue 15 8
175. – 50 f. yellow-brown, brown and green .. 20 8
176. – 60 f. yellow-brown, brown and turquoise 35 12

1963. Air. African and Malagasy Posts and Telecommunications Union. As T 10 of Central African Republic.
177. 85 f. red, buff, choc. & blk. 60 40

DESIGNS: 100 f. "Syncom" satellite. 150 f. "Relay" satellite.

18. "Telstar" Satellite.

1963. Air. Space Telecommunications.
178. 18. 50f. brn., pur. & green 40 35
179. – 100 f. ultramarine, chestnut and red .. 75 55
180. – 150 f. blue-grn. & brown 1·10 90

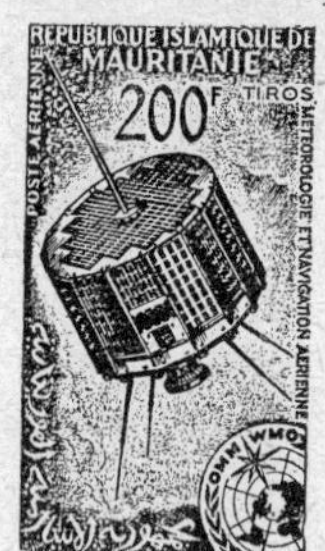

19. "Tiros" Satellite. 20. U.N. Emblem, Sun and Birds.

1963. Air. World Meteorological Day.
181. 19. 200 f. choc., blue & grn. 1·50 1·00

1963. Air. "Air Afrique" 1st Anniv. and "DC-8" Service Inaug. As T 10 of Congo Republic.
182. 25 f. blk., grn., grey & orge. 20 15

1963. Air. Declaration of Human Rights. 15th Anniv.
183. 20. 100 f. blue, violet & pur. 75 60

21. Cogwheels and Wheat. 22. Lichtenstein's Sand-grouse.

1964. Air. European-African Economic Convention.
184. 21. 50 f. multicoloured .. 50 40

1964. Air. Birds.
185. 22. 100 f. ochre,, choc. & grn. 65 30
186. – 200 f. black, brown & bl. 1·25 55
187. – 500 f. slate, red & green 3·25 1·40
DESIGNS: 200 f. African Cormorant. 500 f. Songhawk.

23. Temple, Philae.

1964. Air. Nubian Monuments Preservation.
188. 23. 10 f. brown, black & blue 15 15
189. 25 f. Slate brown & blue 30 30
190. 60 f. choc., brown & blue 60 60

24. W.M.O. Emblem, Sun and Lightning. 25. Radar Antennae and Sun Emblem.

1964. World Meteorological Day.
191. 24. 85 f. blue, orge. & choc. 60 55

1964. Int. Quiet Sun Years.
192. 25. 25 f. red, green and blue 20 15

26. Bowl depicting Horse-racing.

1964. Air. Olympic Games, Tokyo.
193. 26. 15 f. chocolate & bistre 12 8
194. – 50 f. chestnut and blue 35 25
195. – 85 f. brown and red .. 55 40
196. – 100 f. red-brown & grn. 75 50
DESIGNS—VERT. 50 f. Running (vase). 85 f. Wrestling (vase). HORIZ. 100 f. Chariot-racing (bowl).

27. Grey Mullet. 28. Pres. Kennedy.

1964. Marine Fauna.
197. 27. 1 f. green, blue & brown 5 5
198. – 5 f. maroon, grn. & brn. 5 5
199. – 10 f. green, ochre & blue 5 5
200. – 60 f. slate, green & brn. 30 25
DESIGNS—VERT. 5 f. Spiny lobster. 10 f. Meagre. HORIZ. 60 f. Spiny lobster.

1964. French, African and Malagasy Co-operation. As T 500 of France.
201. 25 f. choc., green & mag. 20 15

1964. Air. Pres. Kennedy. 1st Death Anniv.
202. 28. 100 f. multicoloured .. 75 60

29. "Nymphaea lotus".

1965. Mauritanian Flowers.
203. 29. 5 f. green, rose and blue 5 5
204. – 10 f. emer., ochre & pur. 5 5
205. – 20 f. brown, red & sepia 8 8
206. – 45 f. turq.-blue, maroon and slate-green .. 20 15
FLOWERS—VERT. 10 f. "Acacia gommier". 45 f. "Caralluma retrospiciens". HORIZ. 20. f. "Adenium obesum".

30. "Hardine". 31. Abraham Lincoln.

1965. Musical Instruments and Musicians.
207. 30. 2 f. brown, bistre & blue 5 5
208. – 8 f. brown, bistre & red 5 5
209. – 25 f. brown, black & grn. 10 8
210. – 40 f. black, blue & violet 15 12
DESIGNS: 8 f. "Tobol" (drums). 25 f. "Tidinit" ("Violins"). 40 f. Native band.

1965. Abraham Lincoln. Death Cent.
211. 31. 50 f. multicoloured .. 35 15

32. Early Telegraph and Relay Satellite.

1965. Air. I.T.U. Cent.
212. 32. 250 f. grn., mag. & blue 1·90 1·10

33. Palms in the Adrar. 35. Wooden Tea-Service. 34. "Attack on Cancer" (the Crab).

1965. "Tourism and Archaeology". (1st series).
213. 33. 1 f. green, brown & blue 5 5
214. – 4 f. chocolate, red & blue 5 5
215. – 15 f. multicoloured .. 8 5
216. – 60 f. sepia, brn. & green 40 20
DESIGNS—VERT. 4 f. Chinguetti Mosque. HORIZ. 15 f. Clay-pits. 60 f. Carved doorway, Qualata.
See also Nos. 255/8.

1965. Air. Campaign Against Cancer.
217. 34. 100 f. red, blue & ochre 75 30

1965. Native Handicrafts.
218. 35. 3 f. brn., ochre and slate 5 5
219. – 7 f. purple, orge. & blue 5 5
220. – 25 f. brn., black & verm. 12 10
221. – 50 f. red, green & orge. 25 15
DESIGNS—VERT. 7 f. Snuff-box and pipe. 25 f. Damasquine dagger. HORIZ. 50 f. Mederdra chest.

36. Nouakchott Wharf. 37. Sir Winston Churchill.

1965. Mauritanian Development.
222. – 5 f. green and chocolate 5 5
223. 36. 10 f. red, turq. and blue 5 5
224. – 30 f. red, chest. & maroon 20 10
225. – 85 f. violet, lake and blue 55 30
DESIGNS—VERT. 5 f., 30 f. Choum Tunnel. HORIZ. 85 f. Nouakchott Hospital.

1965. Air. Churchill Commem.
226. 37. 200 f. multicoloured .. 1·50 65

DESIGNS—HORIZ. 60 f. Satellite "A 1" and Globe. 90 f. Rocket "Scout" and satellite "FR 1".

38. Rocket "Diamant".

1966. Air. French Satellites.
227. 38. 30 f. green, red and blue 20 12
228. – 60 f. maroon, blue & turq. 45 20
229. – 90 f. lake, violet and blue 65 30

39. Dr. Schweitzer and Hospital Scene.

1966. Air. Schweitzer Commem.
230. **39.** 50 f. multicoloured .. 35 15

40. Stafford, Schirra and "Gemini 6".

1966. Air. Space Flights. Multicoloured.
231. 50 f. Type **40** 35 15
232. 100 f. Borman, Lovell and "Gemini 7" 70 35
233. 200 f. Beliaiev, Leonov and "Voskhod 2" .. .. 1·50 65

41. African Woman and Carved Head.

1966. World Festival of Negro Arts, Dakar.
234. **41.** 10 f. black, chest. & grn. 8 5
235. – 30 f. purple, black & blue 20 12
236. – 60 f. maroon, red & orge. 40 20
DESIGNS: 30 f. Dancers and hands playing cornet. 60 f. Cine-camera and village huts.

42. "Dove" over Map of Africa. **43.** Satellite "D 1".

1966. Air. Organisation of African Unity. (O.A.U.).
237. **42.** 100 f. green, yellow, black and lake .. 70 30

1966. Air. Launching of Satellite "D 1".
238. **43.** 100 f. plum, chest. & blue 70 30

44. Breguet "14".

1966. Air. Early Aircraft.
239. **44.** 50 f. indigo, blue & bistre 40 15
240. – 100 f. green, mar. & blue 70 25
241. – 150 f. turq., brn. & blue 1·00 40
242. – 200 f. indigo, blue & mar. 1·25 45
AIRCRAFT: 100 f. Farman "Goliath". 150 f. Couzinet "Arc-en-Ciel". 200 f. Latecoere "28".

45. "Acacia ehrenbergiana". **47.** "Myrina Silenus".

46. Raft of the Medusa. (after Gericault).

1966. Mauritanian Flowers. Multicoloured.
243. 10 f. Type **45** .. 5 5
244. 15 f. "Schouwia purpurea" 8 5
245. 20 f. "Ipomaea asarifolia" 8 5
246. 25 f. "Grewia bicolor" .. 10 5
247. 30 f. "Pancratium trianthum" .. 12 8
248. 60 f. "Blepharislinariifolia" 25 15

1966. Air. "DC-8" Air Services Inaug. As T **45** of Central African Republic.
249. 30 f. grey, black and red .. 20 8

1966. Air. Shipwreck of the "Medusa". 150th Anniv.
250. **46.** 500 f. multicoloured .. 3·75 1·60

1966. Butterflies. Multicoloured.
251. 5 f. Type **47** 5 5
252. 30 f. "Colotis danae" .. 20 8
253. 45 f. "Hypolimnas misippus" 25 8
254. 60 f. "Danaus chrysippus" 40 15

48. "Hunting" (petroglyph from Tenses Adrar).

1966. Tourism and Archaeology. (2nd series).
255. **48.** 2 f. chestnut and brown 5 5
256. – 3 f. chestnut and blue.. 5 5
257. – 30 f. green and red .. 20 8
258. – 50 f. brn., grn. & mag. 35 20
DESIGNS: 3 f. "Fighting" (petroglyph from Tenses, Adrar). 30 f. Copper jug (from Le Mreyer, Adrar). 50 f. Camel and caravan.

49. Cogwheels and Ears of Wheat.

1966. Air. Europafrique.
259. **49.** 50 f. bl., ind., yell. & red 30 10

50. U.N.E.S.C.O. Emblem.

1966. U.N.E.S.C.O. 20th Anniv.
260. **50.** 30 f. chestnut, yellow, black and green .. 20 8

51. Olympic Village, Grenoble.

1967. Publicity for Olympic Games (1968).
261. – 20 f. brown, blue & grn. 15 5
262. **51.** 30 f. brown, green & blue 20 8
263. – 40 f. brown, maroon & bl. 25 10
264. – 100 f. brown, grn. & blk. 65 30
DESIGNS—VERT. 20 f. Old and new buildings, Mexico City. 40 f. Ice rink, Grenoble, and Olympic torch. HORIZ. 100 f. Olympic stadium, Mexico City.

52. Crowned Crane. **53.** Globe, Rockets and Eye.

1967. Air. Birds. Multicoloured.
265. 100 f. Type **52** 45 25
266. 200 f. Great white heron.. 90 40
267. 500 f. Ostrich .. .. 2·25 1·00

1967. Air. World Fair, Montreal.
268. **53.** 250 f. brn., blue & black 1·50 80

54. Prosopis. **55.** Jamboree Emblem and Scout Kit.

1967. Trees.
269. **54.** 10 f. grn., blue & brown 5 5
270. – 15 f. green, blue & mar. 5 5
271. – 20 f. green, mar. & blue 8 5
272. – 25 f. brown and green.. 10 8
273. – 30 f. brown, green & red 12 10
TREES: 15 f. Jujube. 20 f. Date palm. 25 f. Peltophorum. 30 f. Baobab.

1967. World Scout Jamboree, Idaho.
274. **55.** 60 f. blue, green & brown 45 20
275. – 90 f. blue, green and red 65 30
DESIGN—HORIZ. 90 f. Jamboree emblem and scout.

56. Weaving.

58. Cattle. **57.** Atomic Symbol.

1967. Advancement of Mauritanian Women.
276. **56.** 5 f. red, black and violet 5 5
277. – 10 f. black, violet & grn. 5 5
278. – 20 f. black, purple & blue 8 5
279. – 30 f. blue, black & brown 12 8
280. – 50 f. black, violet & ind. 20 12
DESIGNS—VERT. 10 f. Needlework. 30 f. Laundering. HORIZ. 20 f. Nursing. 50 f. Sewing (with machines).

1967. Air. Int. Atomic Energy Agency.
281. **57.** 200 f. ultram., grn. & red 1·00 55

1967. Campaign for Prevention of Cattle Plague.
282. **58.** 30 f. claret, blue & green 15 8

1967. Air. U.A.M.P.T. 5th Anniv. As T **95** of Cameroun.
283. 100 f. green, brn. & maroon 75 35

59. "Francois of Rimini" (Ingres). **60.** "Hyphaene thebaica".

1967. Air. Jean Ingres (painter). Death Cent. Multicoloured.
284. 90 f. Type **59** 70 30
285. 200 f. "Ingres in his Studio" (Alaux).. .. .. 1·50 65
See also Nos. 306/8.

1967. West African Monetary Union. 5th Anniv. As T **54** of Dahomey.
286. 30 f. grey and orange .. 20 8

1967. Mauritanian Fruits.
287. **60.** 1 f. brown, grn. & purple 5 5
288. – 2 f. yellow, green & brn. 5 5
289. – 3 f. olive, green & violet 5 5
290. – 4 f. red, green & brown 5 5
291. – 5 f. orange, brown & grn. 5 5
FRUITS—HORIZ. 2 f. "Balanites aegyptiaca". 4 f. "Ziziphus lotus". VERT. 3 f. "Adansonia digitata". 5 f. "Phoenix dactylifera".

61. Human Rights Emblem. **62.** Chancellor Adenauer.

1968. Human Rights Year.
292. **61.** 30 f. yellow, grn. & black 15 8
293. 50 f. yellow, brn. & black 30 12

1968. Air. Adenauer Commem.
294. **62.** 100 f. sepia, brn. & blue 70 35

63. Skiing.

1968. Air. Olympic Games, Grenoble and Mexico.
296. **63.** 20 f. purple, indigo & bl. 12 8
297. – 30 f. brown, green & plum 15 8
298. – 50 f. green, blue & ochre 25 15
299. – 100 f. green, verm. & brn. 55 30
DESIGNS—VERT. 30 f. Horse-vaulting. 50 f. Ski-jumping. HORIZ. 100 f. Hurdling.

64. Mosque. Nouakchott.

1968. Tourism. Multicoloured.
300. 30 f. Type **64** 12 8
301. 45 f. Amogjar Pass .. 20 10
302. 90 f. Cavaliers' Tower, Boutilimit 40 20

65. Man and W.H.O. Emblem.

1968. Air. W.H.O. 20th Anniv.
303. **65.** 150 f. blue, purple & brn. 70 40

66. U.N.E.S.C.O. Emblem and "Movement of Water".

1968. Int. Hydrological Decade.
304. **66.** 90 f. green and lake .. 45 20

67. U.P.U. Building, Berne.

1968. Admission of Mauritania to U.P.U.
305. **67.** 30 f. brown and red .. 15 8

1968. Air. Paintings by Ingres. As T **59**. Multicoloured.
306. 100 f. "Man's Torso" .. 45 20
307. 150 f. "The Iliad" .. 65 35
308. 250 f. "The Odyssey" .. 1·10 65

68. Land-yachts crossing Desert.

69. Dr. Martin Luther King.

1968. Land-yacht Racing.
309. **68.** 30 f. blue, yell. & orge. 12 8
310. – 40 f. pur., blue & orge. 15 10
311. – 60 f. emer., yell. & orge. 25 15
DESIGNS—HORIZ. 40 f. Racing on shore. VERT. 60 f. Crew making repairs.

1968. Air. "Apostles of Peace".
312. **69.** 50 f. brown, blue & olive 20 12
313. – 50 f. brown and blue .. 20 12
DESIGN: No. 313, Mahatma Gandhi.

1968. Air. "Philexafrique" Stamp Exn., Abidjan, Ivory Coast, (1969) (1st Issue). As T **109** of Cameroun. Multicoloured.
315. 100 f. "The Surprise Letter" (C. A. Coypel) 70 70

70. Donkey and Foal.

71. Map and I.L.O. Emblem.

1968. Domestic Animals. Multicoloured.
316. 5 f. Type **70** 5 5
317. 10 f. Ewe and lamb .. 5 5
318. 15 f. Camel and calf .. 8 5
319. 30 f. Mare and foal .. 12 8
320. 50 f. Cow and calf .. 20 10
321. 90 f. Goat and kid. .. 40 20

1969. Air. "Philexafrique" Stamp Exn., Abidjan, Ivory Coast (2nd Issue). As T **110** of Cameroun.
322. 50 f. purple, green & brown 35 35
DESIGN: 50 f. Forest scene and stamp of 1938.

1969. Air. Napoleon Bonaparte. Birth Bicent. As T **69** of Dahomey. Multicoloured.
323. 50 f. "Napoleon at the Council of Five Hundred" (Bouchot) 50 30
324. 90 f. "Napoleon's Installation by the Council of State" (Couder) 70 55
325. 250 f. "The Farewell at Fontainebleau" (Vernet) 2·00 1·25

1969. Int. Labour Organisation. 50th Anniv.
326. **71.** 50 f. multicoloured .. 25 12

72. Monitor Lizard.

73. Date-palm Beetle.

1969. Reptiles. Multicoloured.
327. 5 f. Type **72** 5 5
328. 10 f. Horned viper 5 5
329. 30 f. Black-collared cobra 12 8
330. 60 f. Rock python .. 25 12
331. 85 f. Nile crocodile .. 40 30

1969. Date-palms. Protection Campaign.
332. **73.** 30 f. indigo, red & emer. 12 8

74. Camel and Emblem.

1969. Air. African Tourist Year.
333. **74.** 50 f. purple, blue & orge. 25 12

75. Dancers and Baalbek Columns.

1969. Air. Baalbek Festival, Lebanon.
334. **75.** 100 f. brown, red & blue 25 20

76. "Apollo 8" and Moon.

1969. Air. Moon Flight of "Apollo 8". Embossed on gold foil
335. **76.** 1,000 f. gold .. .. 5·50

77. Wolde (marathon).

79. Rahla Headdress.

78. London-Istanbul Route Map.

1969. Air. Gold Medal Winners, Mexico Olympic Games.
336. **77.** 30 f. carmine, brn. & blue 15 10
337. – 70 f. red, brn. & emerald 30 15
338. – 150 f. grn., bis. & carmine 65 40
DESIGNS: 70 f. Beamon (athletics). 150 f. Vera Caslavska (gymnastics).

1969. Air. London–Sydney Motor Rally.
339. **78.** 10 f. brn., blue & purple 5 5
340. – 20 f. brn., blue & purple 10 5
341. – 50 f. brn., blue & purple 25 10
342. – 70 f. brn., blue & purple 35 15
Route—Maps: 20 f. Ankara-Teheran. 50 f. Kandahar-Bombay. 70 f. Perth-Sydney.

1969. African Development Bank. 5th Anniv. As T **118** of Cameroun. Multicoloured.
344. 30 f. brown, green and blue 15 10

1969. Native Handicrafts.
345. – 10 f. brown and purple 5 5
346. **79.** 20 f. red, black and blue 8 5
DESIGN—VERT. 10 f. Pendant.

80. Sea-water Desalination Plant, Nouakchott.

1969. Economic Development.
347. **80.** 10 f. blue, purple and red 5 5
348. – 15 f. black, lake and blue 8 5
349. – 30 f. black, purple & blue 15 8
DESIGNS: 15 f. Fishing quay, Nouadhibou. 30 f. Meat-processing plant, Kaedi.

INDEX

Countries can be quickly located by referring to the index at the end of this volume.

81. Lenin.

82. "Sternocera interrupta".

1970. Lenin. Birth Cent.
350. **81.** 30 f. black, red and blue 15 8

1970. Insects.
351. **82.** 5 f. black, buff & brown 5 5
352. – 10 f. brown, yellow & lake 5 5
353. – 20 f. olive, purple & brn. 10 5
354. – 30 f. violet, grn. & brn. 15 8
355. – 40 f. brown, blue & lake 20 8
INSECTS: 10 f. "Anoplocnemis curvipes". 20 f. "Julodis aequinoctialis". 30 f. "Thermophilum sexmaculatum marginatum". 40 f. "Plocaederus denticornis".

83. Footballers and Hemispheres. 84. Japanese Musician, Emblem and Map on Palette.

1970. World Cup Football Championships, Mexico.
356. **83.** 25 f. multicoloured .. 12 5
357. – 30 f. multicoloured .. 15 8
358. – 70 f. multicoloured .. 30 15
359. – 150 f. multicoloured .. 65 30
DESIGNS: 30 f., 70 f., 150 f. As T **83**, but with different players.

1970. New U.P.U. Headquarters Building. As T **126** of Cameroun.
360. 30 f. red, chocolate & green 15 8

1970. Air. "EXPO 70" World Fair, Osaka, Japan. Multicoloured.
361. 50 f. Type **84** 25 12
362. 75 f. Japanese fan .. 40 20
363. 150 f. Stylised bird, map and boat 80 40

85. U.N. Emblem and Examples of Progress.

1970. Air. United Nations. 25th Anniv.
364. **85.** 100 f. grn., brn. & blue 50 25

86. Vladimir Komarov.

87. Descent of "Apollo 13".

1970. Air. "Lost Heroes of Space" (1st series).
365. **86.** 150 f. brn., oran. & slate 70 30
366. – 150 f. brn., blue and slate 70 30
367. – 150 f. brn., oran. & slate 70 30
HEROES: No. 366, Elliott See. 367, Gagarin. See also Nos. 376/8.

1970. Air. Space Flight of "Apollo 13".
369. **87.** 500 f. red, blue and gold 2·75

88. Woman in Traditional Costume.

89. Arms and State House.

1970. Traditional Costumes. As T **88**.
370. **88.** 10 f. orange and brown 5 5
371. – 30 f. blue, red and brown 12 8
372. – 40 f. brn., purple & red 15 12
373. – 50 f. blue and brown .. 20 15
374. – 70 f. brown, choc & blue 30 20

1970. Air. Independence. Tenth Anniv.
375. **89.** 100 f. multicoloured .. 45 25

1970. Air. "Lost Heroes of Space" (2nd series). As T **86**.
376. 150 f. brn., blue and turq. 70 30
377. 150 f. brown blue & turq. 70 30
378. 150 f. brown blue & orange 70 30
HEROES: No. 376, Roger Chaffee. No. 377, Virgill Grissom. No. 378, Eduard White.

90. Greek Wrestling.

1971. Air. "Pre-Olympics Year".
380. **90.** 100 f. brn., pur. & blue 45 25

91. People of Different Races.

1971. Racial Equality Year.
381. **91.** 30 f. plum, blue & brn. 15 8
382. – 40 f. black, red & blue .. 20 10
DESIGN:—VERT. 40 f. European and African hands.

92. Pres. Nasser.

1971. Air. Pres. Gamal Nasser of Egypt Commem.
383. **92.** 100 f. multicoloured .. 35 25

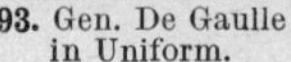

93. Gen. De Gaulle in Uniform.

94. Scout Badge, Scout and Map.

1971. De Gaulle Commem. Multicoloured.
384. 40 f. Type **93** 15 8
385. 100 f. De Gaulle as President of France 45 25

1971. Air. 13th World Scout Jamboree, Asagiri, Japan.
387. **94.** 35 f. multicoloured .. 15 8
388. 40 f. multicoloured .. 20 10
389. 100 f. multicoloured .. 45 25

95. Diesel Locomotive.

1971. Miferma Iron-ore Mines. Multicoloured.
390. 35 f. Iron ore train 15 8
391. 100 f. Type 95 .. .. 45 25
Nos. 390/1 form a composite design.

1971. Air. African and Malagasy Posts and Telecommunications Union. 10th Anniv. As T **153** of Cameroun. Multicoloured.
392. 100 f. U.A.M.P.T. Headquarters, Brazzaville, and Ardin musicians .. 45 25

96. A.P.U. Emblem Airmail Envelope.

1971. Air. African Postal Union. 10th Anniv.
393. **96.** 35 f. multicoloured .. 15 8

97. U.N.I.C.E.F. Emblem and Child.

1971. U.N.I.C.E.F. 25th Anniv.
394. **97.** 35 f. blk., brn. & blue .. 15 8

98. " Moslem King " (c. 1218).

1972. Air. Moslem Miniatures. Multicoloured.
395. 35 f. Type **98** 15 10
396. 40 f. " Enthroned Prince " (Egypt, c. 1334) .. 20 12
397. 100 f. " Pilgrims' Caravan " (Maquamat, Baghdad 1237) .. . 45 25

99. " Quay and Ducal Palace " (Carlevaris)

1972. Air. U.N.E.S.C.O. " Save Venice " Campaign. Multicoloured.
398. 45 f. Type **99** 20 15
399. 100 f. " Grand Canal " (Canaletto) (horiz.) .. 45 25
400. 250 f. " Grand Canal " (Canaletto) (horiz.) .. 1·10 60

100. Hurdling

1972. Air. Olympic Games, Munich.
401. **100.** 75 f. maroon, orange and green .. 35 20
402. 100 f. maroon, bl. & brn. 45 25
403. 200 f. maroon, lake & green 90 45

101. Nurse tending Baby.

102. Samuel Morse and Morse Key.

1972. Mauritanian Red Crescent Fund.
405. **101.** 35 f. + 5 f. multicoloured 20 15

1972. World Telecommunications Day. Multicoloured.
406. 35 f. Type **102** 15 8
407. 40 f. " Relay " and hemispheres 20 12
408. 75 f. Graham Bell 35 20

103. Spirifer Shell.

1972. Fossil Shells. Multicoloured.
409. 25 f. Type **103** 12 5
410. 75 f. Gryphae shell .. 35 20

104. " Luna 16 " and Moon probe.

105. Seal with Young.

1972. Air. Russian Exploration of the Moon.
411. **104.** 75 f. brn., blue & green 35 20
412. – 100 f. brn., grey & violet 45 30
DESIGN—HORIZ. 100 f. " Lunokhod 1 ".

1972. Air. Gold Medal-Winners, Munich. Nos. 401/3 optd. as listed below.
413. **100.** 75 f. maroon, orange and green .. 35 20
414. 100 f. maroon, bl. & brn. 45 30
415. 200 f. maroon, lake & grn. 90 60
OVERPRINTS: 75 f. **110m. HAIES MILBURN MEDAILLE D'OR.** 100 f. **400m. HAIES AKII-BUA MEDAILLE D'OR.** 200 f. **3,000m. STEEPLE KEINO MEDAILLE D'OR.**

1972. West African Monetary Union. 10th Anniv. As Type **109** of Dahomey.
416. 35 f. grey, brn., and green 15 8

1973. Air. Moon Flight of " Apollo 17 ". No. 267 surch. **Apollo XVII Decembre 1972** and value.
417. 250 f. on 500 f. multicoloured 1·10 65

1973. Seals Multicoloured.
418. 40 f. Type **105** (postage) .. 20 10
419. 135 f. Head of seal (air) .. 65 40

106. " Lion and Crocodile " (Delacroix).

1973. Air. Paintings by Delacroix. Mult.
420. 100 f. Type **106** 45 30
421. 250 f. " Lion attacking Wild Boar " .. .. .. 1·10 65

107. " Horns of Plenty ".

1973. World Food Programme. 10th Anniv.
422. **107.** 35 f. multicoloured .. 15 8

108. U.P.U. Monument, Berne and Globe.

1973. World U.P.U. Day.
423. **108.** 100 f. bl., orge. & grn. 45 30

109. Nomad Encampment and Eclipse.

1973. Total Eclipse of the Sun.
424. **109.** 35 f. purple and green 15 8
425. – 40 f. purple, red & blue 20 10
426. – 140 f. purple and red 65 40
DESIGNS—VERT. 40 f. Rocket and " Concorde ". HORIZ. 140 f. Observation team.

1973. " Drought Relief ". African Solidarity. No. 320 optd. **SECHERESSE SOLIDARITE AFRICAINE** and value.
428. 20 u. on 50 f. multicoloured 45 25

1973. African and Malagasy Posts and Telecommunications Union. As Type **182** of Cameroun.
429. 20 u. brn., oran. & brown 45 20

110. Detective making Arrest and Fingerprint.

1973. International Criminal Police Organisation (Interpol). 50th Anniv.
430. **110.** 15 u. vio., red & brn. 35 20

1974. Various stamps surch. with values in new currency.

(a) Postage.

(i) Nos. 345/6.
431. – 27 u. on 10 f. brn. & pur. 55 25
432. **79.** 28 u. on 20 f. red, black and blue .. 55 25

(ii) Nos. 351/5.
433. **82.** 5 u. on 5 f. black, buff and brown .. 10 5
434. – 7 u. on 10 f. brown, yellow and lake .. 15 8
435. – 8 u. on 20 f. olive, pur. and brown .. 15 8
436. – 10 u. on 30 f. violt, purple and brown .. 20 10
437. – 20 u. on 4 f. brown, blue and lake .. 40 20

(iii) Nos. 409/10.
438. **103.** 5 u. on 25 f. mult. .. 10 5
439. – 15 u. on 75 f. mult. .. 30 15

(iv) No. 418.
440. **105.** 8 u. on 40 f. mult. .. 15 8

(b) Air.

(i) Nos. 395/7.
441. **98.** 7 u. on 35 f. mult. .. 15 8
442. – 8 u. on 40 f. mult. .. 15 8
443. – 20 u. on 100 f. mult. .. 40 20

(ii) No. 419.
444. – 27 u. on 135 f. mult. .. 55 25

(iii) Nos. 420/1.
445. **106.** 20 u. on 100 f. mult. .. 40 20
446. – 50 u. on 250 f. mult. .. 1·00 50

(iv) Nos. 424/6.
447. **109.** 7 u. on 35 f. purple and green .. 15 8
448. – 8 u. on 40 f. purple, red and blue .. 15 8
449. – 28 u. on 140 f. purple and red 55 25

111. Footballers.

113. Sir Winston Churchill.

112. Jules Verne and Scenes from Books.

1974. Air. World Cup Football Championships. West Germany.
450. **111.** 7 u. multicoloured .. 15 8
451. 8 u. multicoloured .. 15 8
452. 20 u. multicoloured 40 25

1974. Air. Jules Verne, " Prophet of Space Travel ", and " Skylab " Flights Commem.
454. **112.** 70 u. silver .. .. 1·50
455. – 70 u. silver .. .. 1·50
456. **112.** 250 u. gold .. .. 5·50
457. – 250 u. gold .. .. 5·50
DESIGNS: Nos. 455, 457, " Skylab " in Space.

1974. Air. Sir Winston Churchill. Birth Cent.
458. **113.** 40 u. red and purple 80 50

114. U.P.U. Monument and Globes.

1974. Universal Postal Union. Cent.
459. **114.** 30 u. red, green and deep green .. 60 30
460. 50 u. red, light blue and blue .. .. 1·00 50

115. 5 Ouguiya Coin and Banknote.

1974. Introduction of Ouguiya Currency. First Anniv.
461. **115.** 7 u. blk., grn. & blue 15 8
462. – 8 u. blk., mauve & grn. 15 8
463. – 20 u. blk., blue & red 40 20
DESIGNS: 8 u. 10 ouguiya coin and banknote. 20 u. 20 ouguiya coin and banknote.

116. Lenin.

117. " Two Hunters ".

1974. Air. Lenin. 50th Death Anniv.
464. **116.** 40 u. green and red 80 40

1974. Berne Postal Convention. Nos. 459/60 optd. **9 OCTOBRE 100 ANS D'UNION POSTALE INTERNATIONALE.**
465. **114.** 30 u. red., green and deep green 60 30
466. 50 u. red, light blue and blue .. .. 1·00 50

1975. Nos. 287/91 surch. in new currency.
467. – 1 u. on 5 f. oran., brn. and green 5 5
468. – 2 u. on 4 f. red, grn. and brown 5 5
469. – 3 u. on 2 f. yell., green and brown 5 5
470. **60.** 10 u. on 1 f. brn., grn. and purple 20 15
471. – 12 u. on 3 f. olive, grn. and violet 25 20

1975. Rock-carvings, Zemmour.
472. **117.** 4 u. red and brown .. 8 5
473. – 5 u. purple 10 8
474. – 10 u. blue and light blue 20 15
DESIGNS—VERT: 5 u. Ostrich. HORIZ: 10 u. Elephant.

118. Mauritanian Women.

1975. Air. International Women's Year.
475. **118.** 12 u. pur., brn. & blue 25 20
476. – 40 u. pur., brn. & blue 90 80
DESIGN: 40 u. Head of Mauritanian woman.

119. Combined European and African Heads.

120. Dr. Schweitzer.

1975. Europafrique.
477. **119.** 40 u. brn., red & bistre 90 80

1975. Dr. Albert Schweitzer, Birth Cent.
478. **120.** 60 u. olive, brn. & grn. 1·25 1·00

1975. Pan-African Drought Relief. Nos. 301/2, surch. **SECHERESSE SOLIDARITE AFRICAINE** and value.
479. 15 u. on 45 f. multicoloured 35 25
480. 25 u. on 90 f. multicoloured 55 45

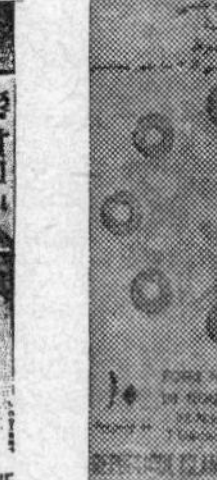

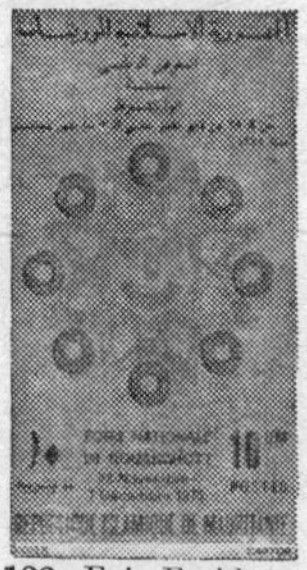

121. Akjoujt Plant and Cameleer.

122. Fair Emblem.

1975. Mining Industry.
481. **121.** 10 u. brn., blue & oran. 20 15
482. – 12 u. blue, red & brn. 25 20
DESIGN: 12 u. Mining operations.

1975. Nouakchott National Fair.
483. **122.** 10 u. multicoloured .. 20 15

123. Throwing the Javelin.

1975. Air. "Pre-Olympic Year". Olympic Games, Montreal (1976).
484. **123.** 50 u. red, grn. & brn. 1·00 95
485. – 52 u. blue, brn. & red 1·10 1·00
DESIGN: 52 u. Running.

124. Commemorative Medal.

1975. Independence. 15th Anniversary. Multicoloured.
486. 10 u. Type **124** 20 15
487. 12 u. Map of Mauritania .. 25 20

125. Soviet Cosmonauts.

1975. "Apollo-Soyuz" Space Link. Mult.
488. 8 u. Type **125** (postage) .. 15 12
489. 10 u. "Soyuz" on launch-pad 20 15
490. 20 u. "Apollo" on launch-pad (air) 40 35
491. 50 u. Cosmonauts meeting astronauts .. .. 1·00 95
492. 60 u. Parachute splashdown 1·25 1·10

126. Foot-soldier of Lauzun's Legion.

1976. American Independence. Bicentenary. Multicoloured.
494. 8 u. Type **126** (postage) .. 15 12
495. 10 u. "Green Mountain" infantryman 20 15
496. 20 u. Lauzun Hussar's officer (air) 40 35
497. 50 u. Artillery officer of 3rd Continental Regiment 1·00 95
498. 60 u. Grenadier of Gatinais' Regiment .. .. 1·25 1·10

1976. Arab Work Charter. 10th Anniversary. No. 408 surch. **10e ANNIVERSAIRE DE LA CHARTE ARABE DU TRAVAIL** in French and Arabic.
500. 12 u. on 75 f. blue, black and green 30 25

127. Commemorative Text on Map.

1976. Reunification of Mauritania.
501. **127.** 10 u. green, lilac and dark green 25 20

128. "Running".

1976. Air. Olympic Games, Montreal.
514. **128.** 10 u. brown, green and violet 25 20
515. – 12 u. brown, green and violet 30 25
516. – 52 u. brown, green and violet .. .. 1·25 1·10
DESIGNS: 12 u. High-jumping. 52 u. Fencing.

129. "LZ 4" at Friedrichshafen.

1976. Zeppelin Airship. 75th Anniv. Multicoloured.
517. 5 u. Type **129** (postage) .. 12 10
518. 10 u. "LZ 10" over German Landscape .. 25 20
519. 12 u. "LZ 13" over Heligoland 30 25
520. 20 u. "LZ 120" and Doctor H. Durr 50 45
521. 50 u. "LZ 127" over Capitol, Washington (air) .. 1·25 1·10
522. 60 u. "LZ 130" crossing Swiss Alps .. .. 1·50 1·40

130. Temple and Bas-relief.

1976. UNESCO. "Save Moendojaro" Campaign.
524. **130.** 15 u. multicoloured .. 35 30

131. Sacred Ibis.

1976. Air. Mauritanian Birds. Multicoloured.
525. 50 u. Type **131** .. .. 1·25 1·10
526. 100 u. Marabou storks (horiz.) .. .. 2·40 2·25
527. 200 u. Martial Eagle .. 4·75 4·50

OFFICIAL STAMPS

O 1. Cross of Trarza.

O 2.

1961.
O 150. **O 1.** 1 f. purple and blue .. 5 5
O 151. 3 f. myrtle and red .. 5 5
O 152. 5 f. brown & emerald 5 5
O 153. 10 f. blue & blue-grn. 5 5
O 154. 15 f. orange and blue 8 8
O 155. 20 f. emer. & myrtle 10 10
O 156. 25 f. crimson & orange 12 12
O 157. 30 f. green & maroon 15 15
O 158. 50 f. sepia and red .. 25 20
O 159. 100 f. blue and orange 45 35
O 160. 200 f. verm. & green 85 65

1976.
O 502. **O 2.** 1 u. multicoloured .. 5 5
O 503. 2 u. multicoloured .. 5 5
O 504. 5 u. multicoloured .. 12 12
O 505. 10 u. multicoloured 25 25
O 506. 12 u. multicoloured 30 30
O 507. 40 u. multicoloured 95 95
O 508. 50 u. multicoloured 1·25 1·25

POSTAGE DUE STAMPS

1906. "Natives" key-type inscr. "MAURITANIE".
D 25. **L.** 5 c. green 25 25
D 26. 10 c. claret 50 45
D 27. 15 c. blue .. .. 1·00 80
D 28. 20 c. black on yellow .. 1·10 90
D 29. 30 c. red .. .. 1·25 1·25
D 30. 50 c. violet .. .. 1·75 1·75
D 31. 60 c. black on yellow .. 1·75 1·50
D 32. 1 f. black .. .. 2·10 2·00

1914. "Figure" key-type inscr. "MAURITANIE".
D 35. **M.** 5 c. green 5 5
D 36. 10 c. red 5 5
D 37. 15 c. grey 5 5
D 38. 20 brown 5 5
D 39. 30 c. blue 5 5
D 40. 50 c. black 12 12
D 41. 60 c. orange 8 8
D 42. 1 f. violet 8 8

1927. Surch. in figures.
D 67. **M.** "2 F." on 1 f. purple .. 25 25
D 68. "3 F." on 1 f. brown .. 25 25

D 1. Qualata Motif.

D 2. Vulture.

1961.
D 150. **D 1.** 1 f. yellow and purple 5 5
D 151. 2 f. grey and red .. 5 5
D 152. 5 f. pink and red .. 5 5
D 153. 10 f. emer. & myrtle 8 8
D 154. 15 f. chestnut & drab 12 10
D 155. 20 f. blue and red .. 15 12
D 156. 25 f. verm. & green 20 15

1963. Birds. Multicoloured.
D 177. 50 c. Type **D 2** 5 5
D 178. 50 c. Crane 5 5
D 179. 1 f. Rose pelican .. 5 5
D 180. 1 f. Garganey (teal) .. 5 5
D 181. 2 f. Oriole 5 5
D 182. 2 f. "Souimanga de Falkenstein" 5 5
D 183. 5 f. Great Snipe 5 5
D 184. 5 f. Shoveler (duck) .. 5 5
D 185. 10 f. Guineafowl .. 5 5
D 186. 10 f. Black stork .. 5 5
D 187. 15 f. Grey heron .. 8 8
D 188. 15 f. White stork .. 8 8
D 189. 20 f. Paradise widow-bird 10 10
D 190. 20 f. Red-legged partridge 10 10
D 191. 25 f. Snipe 12 12
D 192. 25 f. Bustard 12 12

D 3.

1976.
D 509. **D 3.** 1 u. multicoloured .. 5 5
D 510. 3 u. multicoloured .. 8 8
D 511. 10 u. multicoloured 25 25
D 512. 12 u. multicoloured 30 30
D 513. 20 u. multicoloured 50 50

MAURITIUS BC

An island in the Indian Ocean, E. of Madagascar. Attained Self-Government on 1st September, 1967, and became independent on 12th March, 1968.

1878. 100 cents = 1 rupee.

1.

2.

1847. Imperf.
1. **1.** 1d. red £250000 £85000
2. 2d. blue £150000 £85000

1848. Imperf.
23. **2.** 1d. red £550 £200
25. 2d. blue £600 £250

3.

4.

1859. Imperf.
29. **3.** 2d. blue £600 £275

1859. Imperf.
32. **4.** 1d. red £850 £450
34. 2d. blue £675 £250

5.

6.

1854. Surch. **FOUR-PENCE.** Imperf.
35. 5. 4d. green £350 £200

1858. No value on stamps. Imperf.
36. 5. (4d.) green £200 £125
37. (6d.) red .. .. .. 10·00 15·00
38. (9d.) purple £200 £125

1859. Imperf.
42. 6. 6d. blue .. .. .. £200 20·00
44. 6d. black .. .. .. 12·00 12·00
43. 1s. red .. .. .. £800 28·00
45. 1s. green .. .. .. £100 40·00

1862. Perf.
46. 6. 6d. black .. .. .. 10·00 10·00
47. 1s. green £550 £140

7.

8.

1860.
56. 7. 1d. purple .. .. .. 6·00 2·50
57. 1d. brown .. .. .. 8·00 2·75
60. 2d. blue .. .. .. 9·00 2·50
61a. 3d. red .. .. .. 10·00 4·00
62. 4d. red .. .. .. 10·00 2·50
65. 6d. green .. .. .. 13·00 2·50
52. 6d. grey .. .. .. 28·00 18·00
63. 6d. violet .. .. .. 12·00 8·00
53. 9d. purple .. .. .. 20·00 12·00
66. 9d. green .. .. .. 27·00 17·00
67. 8. 10d. claret .. .. .. 18·00 6·00
68. 7. 1s. yellow .. .. .. 22·00 5·50
55. 1s. green .. .. .. 90·00 42·00
70. 1s. blue .. .. .. 25·00 7·00
71. 5s. mauve .. .. .. 25·00 10·00

HALF PENNY (9.)   HALF PENNY (10.)

1876. Surch. with T 9.
76. 7. ½d. on 9d. purple .. .. 2·25 2·75
77. 8. ½d. on 10d. claret .. .. 1·50 3·50

1877. Surch. with T 10.
79. 8. ½d. on 10d. rose .. .. 4·00 5·00

One Penny (11.)   2 CENTS (12.)

1877. Surch. as T 11.
80. 7. 1d. on 4d. red .. .. 5·00 8·00
81. 1s. on 5s. mauve .. .. 38·00 22·00

1878. Surch. as T 12.
83. 8. 2 c. red .. .. .. 2·00 2·25
84. 7. 4 c. on 1d. brown .. 3·50 2·25
85. 8 c. on 2d. blue .. .. 4·00 1·00
86. 13 c. on 3d. red .. .. 2·50 3·00
87. 17 c. on 4d. red .. .. 12·00 1·40
88. 25 c. on 6d. blue .. .. 14·00 2·75
89. 38 c. on 9d. purple .. 7·00 4·00
90. 50 c. on 1s. green .. 7·00 2·00
91. 2 r. 50 on 5s. mauve .. 7·00 3·75

13.

14.

1879. Various frames.
125. 13. 1 c. violet 15 40
101. 2 c. brown .. .. 2·00 2·00
110. 2 c. green 40 30
93. 14. 4 c. orange .. .. 7·00 2·00
111. 4 c. red 25 15
112. – 8 c. blue 65 80
95. – 13 c. grey .. .. 28·00 14·00
126. – 15 c. brown 30 40
127. – 15 c. blue .. .. 1·25 40
113. – 16 c. brown 65 40
96. – 17 c. red .. .. 7·00 2·50
103. – 25 c. olive .. .. 1·15 1·00
98. – 38 c. purple .. .. 30·00 25·00
99. – 50 c. green .. .. 1·40 1·10
114. – 50 c. orange .. .. 6·50 4·00
100. – 2 r. 50 purple .. .. 8·50 7·00

1883. No. 96 surch. **16 CENTS.**
104. 16 c. on 17 c. red .. .. 7·00 6·50

1883. No. 96 surch. **SIXTEEN CENTS.**
107. 16 c. on 17 c. red .. .. 4·00 1·15

1885. No. 98 surch. **2 CENTS** with bar.
108. 2 c. on 38 c. purple .. 13·00 11·00

1887. No. 95 surch. as above without bar.
115. 2 c. on 13 c. grey .. .. 6·00 6·00

1891. Surch. in words with or without bar.
123. 13. 1 c. on 2 c. violet .. 15 40
124. – 1 c. on 16 c. brn. (No. 113) 25 60
117. 14. 2 c. on 4 c. red .. 40 30
118. – 2 c. on 17 c. red (No. 96) 6·50 8·50
119. 7. 2 c. on 38 c. on 9d. (89) 1·10 2·25
120. – 2 c. on 38 c. pur. (No. 98) 2·25 2·75

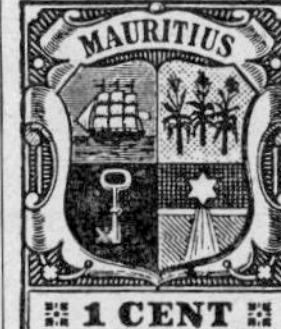

15.

ILLUSTRATIONS British Commonwealth and all overprints and surcharges are FULL SIZE. Foreign Countries have been reduced to ¾-LINEAR.

1895.
128. 15. 1 c. purple and blue .. 15 20
129. 2 c. purple and orange 65 20
130. 3 c. purple 50 50
131. 4 c. purple and green 55 35
131a. 6 c. green and red .. 6·00 55
132. 18 c. green and blue .. 2·25 2·25

16.

1898. Diamond Jubilee.
133. 16. 36 c. orange and blue .. 6·00 6·00

1899. Surch. in figures and words.
137. – 4 c. on 16 c. brn. (No. 113) 40 40
134. 15. 6 c. on 18 c. (No. 132) .. 15 15
142. 12 c. on 18 c. (No. 132) 1·10 3·00
149. 16. 12 c. on 36 c. (No. 133) 1·00 1·25
135. 15 c. on 36 c. (No. 133) 1·60 1·10

17. Admiral M. de Labourdonnais.

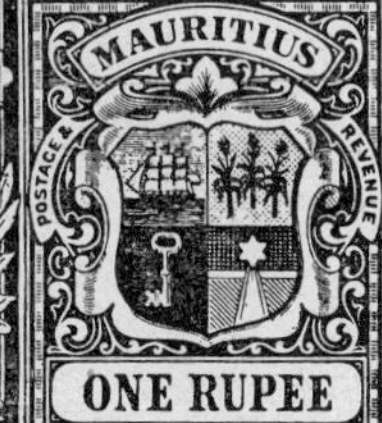

18.

1899. La Bourdonnais. Birth Bicent.
136. 17. 15 c. blue .. .. 4·50 1·60

1900.
138. 15. 1 c. grey and black .. 45 25
139. 2 c. purple 12 12
150. 3 c. green & red on yell. 50 50
140. 4 c. purple & red on yell. 35 35
151. 4 c. green and violet .. 45 75
152. 4 c. black & red on blue 60 8
153. 5 c. purple on buff .. 1·60 7·00
154. 5 c. pur. & blk. on buff 65 75
168. 6 c. purple & red on red 25 8
156. 8 c. grn. & blk. on buff 65 1·60
157. 12 c. black and red .. 75 85
158. 15 c. green and orange .. 3·75 2·00
171. 15 c. blk. & blue on blue 1·60 65
159. 25 c. grn. & red on grn. 1·60 3·50
174. 50 c. green on yellow .. 75 1·60
175. 18. 1 r. grey and red .. 9·00 10·00
162. 2 r. 50 grn. & blk. on bl. 24·00 26·00
163. 5 r. purple & red on red 18·00 20·00

1902. Optd. **Postage & Revenue.**
143. 15. 4 c. purple & red on yell. 25 15
144. 6 c. green and red .. 55 90
145. 15 c. green and orange 35 45
146. – 25 c. olive (No. 103) .. 65 1·25
147. – 50 c. green (No. 99) .. 1·60 80
148. – 2 r. 50 purple (No. 100) 12·00 14·00

19.

20.

1910.
181. 19. 1 c. black 8 8
206. 2 c. brown 15 8
228. 2 c. purple on yellow .. 10 20
183. 3 c. green 20 30
184. 4 c. green and red .. 35 8
208. 4 c. green 30 8
230. 4 c. brown 15 45
186. 19. 6 c. red 25 15
210. 6 c. mauve 25 25
187. 8 c. orange .. .. 40 1·00
211. 10 c. grey .. .. 1·50 2·00
241. 10 c. red 20 15
212. 12 c. red 30 65
232. 12 c. grey 45 75
189. 15 c. blue 40 12
214. 20 c. blue .. .. 1·40 80
234. 20 c. purple .. .. 1·60 1·90

1910.
185. 20. 5 c. grey and red .. 40 80
188. 12 c. grey 25 50
190. 25 c. blk. & red on yell. 2·20 3·50
191. 50 c. purple and black .. 1·75 3·25
192. 1 r. black on green .. 3·00 3·25
193. 2 r. 50 blk. & red on blue 8·50 10·00
194. 5 r. green & red on yell. 18·00 20·00
195. 10 r. green & red on grn. 55·00 60·00

21.

22.

1913.
235. 21. 1 c. black 8 20
236. 2 c. brown 8 8
237. 3 c. green 20 35
238. 4 c. green and red .. 35 30
238b. 4 c. green 25 70
215. 5 c. grey and red .. 8 8
239. 6 c. brown 15 70
240. 8 c. orange 25 70
241. 10 c. red 20 15
216a. 12 c. grey 15 8
217. 12 c. red .. .. 25 1·10
242. 15 c. blue 55 55
243. 20 c. purple 30 90
244. 20 c. blue .. .. 1·40 1·60
218. 25 c. blk. & red on yellow 15 25
219. 50 c. purple and black .. 2·00 1·40
220. 1 r. black on green .. 55 55
221. 2 r. 50 blk. & red on bl. 4·00 1·00
222. 5 r. grn. & red on yellow 12·00 16·00
223. 10 r. green & red on grn. 20·00 26·00

1924. As T 18 but Arms similar to T 19.
224. 50 r. purple and green .. £275 £300

1925. Surch. with figures, words and bar.
225. 19. 3 c. on 4 c. green .. 70 70
226. 10 c. on 12 c. red .. 25 15
227. 15 c. on 20 c. blue .. 30 35

1935. Silver Jubilee. As T 11 of Antigua.
245. 5 c. blue and grey .. 8 8
246. 12 c. green and blue .. 40 25
247. 20 c. brown and blue .. 1·10 90
248. 1 r. grey and purple .. 13·00 13·00

1937. Coronation. As T 2 of Aden.
249. 5 c. violet 8 8
250. 12 c. red 8 8
251. 20 c. blue 8 8

1938.
252. 22. 2 c. grey 8 8
253. 3 c. purple and red .. 8 8
254. 4 c. green 8 10
255aa. 5 c. violet 8 8
256a. 10 c. red 8 8
257. 12 c. orange 8 8
258. 20 c. blue 8 8
259. 25 c. maroon 8 8
260. 1 r. brown 30 30
261. 2 r. 50 violet .. .. 1·00 1·25
262. 5 r. olive .. .. 3·25 3·00
263. 10 r. purple .. .. 4·50 5·50

1946. Victory. As T 4 of Aden.
264. 5 c. violet 5 5
265. 20 c. blue 5 5

23. 1d. "Post Office" Mauritius and King George VI.

1948. First Br. Colonial Stamp Cent.
266. 23. 5 c. orange and mauve 8 8
267. 12 c. orange and green 8 8
268. – 20 c. blue 8 8
269. – 1 r. blue and brown .. 20 20
DESIGN: 20 c., 1 r. As T 23, but showing 2d. "Post Office" Mauritius.

1948. Silver Wedding. As T 5/6 of Aden.
270. 5 c. violet 8 8
271. 10 r. mauve .. .. 4·50 6·50

1949. U.P.U. As T 14/17 of Antigua.
272. 12 c. red 20 35
273. 20 c. blue 20 35
274. 35 c. purple 30 45
275. 1 r. brown 40 50

24. Aloe Plant.

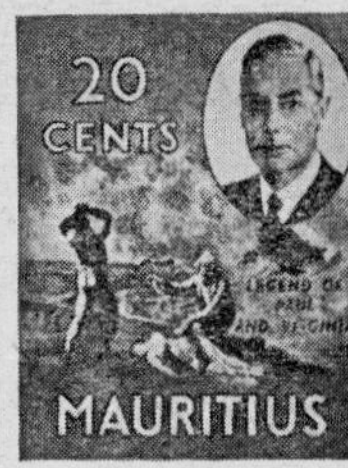

25. "Paul and Virginie".

26. Arms of Mauritius.

1950.
276. – 1 c. purple 12 15
277. – 2 c. red 15 8
278. 24. 3 c. green 25 25
279. – 4 c. green 15 8
280. – 5 c. blue 12 8
281. – 10 c. red 25 25
282. – 12 c. green 15 20
283. 25. 20 c. blue 15 15
284. – 25 c. claret 20 25
285. – 35 c. violet 12 20
286. – 50 c. emerald 20 25
287. – 1 r. brown 95 65
288. – 2 r. 50 orange .. 1·00 1·60
289. – 5 r. brown .. .. 1·60 3·25
290. 27. 10 r. blue .. .. 4·50 4·50
DESIGNS—HORIZ. 1 c. Sugar factory. 2 c. Grand Port. 5 c. Rampart Mountain. 10 c. Transporting cane. 12 c. Dodo and map. 35 c. Government House. 1 r. Mauritius deer. 2 r. 50, Port Louis. 5 r. Beach scene. VERT. 4 c. Tamaring Falls. 25 c. La Bourdonnais Statue. 50 c. Pieter Both Mountain.

1953. Coronation. As T 7 of Aden.
291. 10 c. black and green .. 10 8

27. Historical Museum, Mahebourg.

1953. As 1950 but portrait of Queen Elizabeth II. Designs as for corresponding values except where stated.
293. – 2 c. red 5 5
294. – 3 c. green 5 5
295. – 4 c. purple (as 1 c.) .. 5 5
296. – 5 c. blue 5 8
297. – 10 c. green (as 4 c.) .. 12 10
298. 27. 15 c. red 12 10
299. – 20 c. claret (as 25 c.) .. 12 10
300. – 25 c. blue (as 20 c.) .. 15 10
301. – 35 c. violet 20 12
302. – 50 c. emerald 20 15
302a. – 60 c. green (as 12 c.) .. 35 30
303. – 1 r. sepia 30 25
304. – 2 r. 50 orange .. 1·10 1·10
305. – 5 r. brown .. .. 2·50 2·25
306. – 10 r. blue .. .. 3·00 2·50

28. Queen Elizabeth II and King George II (after Lawrence).

1961. British Post Office in Mauritius. 150th Anniv.
307. 28. 10 c. black and red .. 12 12
308. 20 c. ultramarine & blue 20 20
309. 35 c. black and yellow 30 30
310. 1 r. maroon and green .. 65 65

1963. Freedom from Hunger. As T 10 of Aden.
311. 60 c. violet 35 35

1963. Red Cross Cent. As T 24 of Antigua.
312. 10 c. red and black .. 10 10
313. 60 c. red and blue .. 40 40

29. Grey White-eye.

1965. Birds. Multicoloured.

317. 2 c. Type **29** 5 5
318. 3 c. Rodrigues Fody .. 5 5
319. 4 c. Olive White-eye .. 5 5
340. 5 c. Paradise Flycatcher 5 5
321. 10 c. Mauritius Fody .. 5 8
322. 15 c. Parakeet 8 8
323. 20 c. Cuckoo-shrike .. 10 10
324. 25 c. Kestrel 10 10
341. 35 c. Pink Pigeon .. 25 25
326. 50 c. Bulbul 15 12
327. 60 c. Dutch Pigeon (extinct) 20 20
328. 1 r. Mauritius Dodo (extinct) 40 40
329. 2 r. 50 Rodrigues Solitaire (extinct) 95 95
330. 5 r. Red Rail (extinct) .. 1·75 1·75
331. 10 r. Broad-billed Parrot (extinct) 4·00 4·00

1965. I.T.U. Cent. As T **26** of Antigua.

332. 10 c. orange and green .. 10 10
333. 60 c. yellow and violet .. 30 30

1965. I.C.Y. As T **27** of Antigua.

334. 10 c. purple and turquoise 5 5
335. 60 c. green and lavender .. 30 30

1966. Churchill Commem. As T **28** of Antigua.

336. 2 c. blue 5 5
337. 10 c. green 5 5
338. 60 c. brown 30 30
339. 1 r. violet 60 60

1966. U.N.E.S.C.O. 20th Anniv. As T **33/5** of Antigua.

342. 5 c. vio., red, yell. & orge. 5 5
343. 10 c. yellow, violet & olive 10 10
344. 60 c. black, purple & orange 30 35

30. Red-tailed Tropic Bird.

1967. Self Government. Multicoloured.

345. 2 c. Type **30** 5 5
346. 10 c. Rodrigues Brush-warbler 10 10
347. 60c. Rodrigues Parakeet (extinct) 25 25
348. 1 r. Mauritius Swiftlet .. 35 40

1967. Self Government. Nos. 317/31 optd. SELF GOVERNMENT 1967.

349. **29.** 2 c. multicoloured .. 5 5
350. – 3 c. multicoloured .. 5 5
351. – 4 c. multicoloured .. 5 5
352. – 5 c. multicoloured .. 5 5
353. – 10 c. multicoloured .. 8 5
354. – 15 c. multicoloured .. 8 8
355. – 20 c. multicoloured .. 12 10
356. – 25 c. multicoloured .. 12 12
357. – 35 c. multicoloured .. 15 12
358. – 50 c. multicoloured .. 20 20
359. – 60 c. multicoloured .. 25 25
360. – 1 r. multicoloured .. 40 35
361. – 2 r. 50 multicoloured .. 1·10 1·10
362. – 5 r. multicoloured .. 2·00 2·25
363. – 10 r. multicoloured .. 4·00 4·50

31. Flag of Mauritius.

1968. Independence. Multicoloured.

364. 2 c. Type **31** 5 5
365. 3 c. Arms and Dodo Emblem 8 8
366. 15 c. Type **31** 10 10
367. 20 c. As 3 c. 12 12
368. 60 c. Type **31** 25 25
369. 1 r. As 3 c. 35 35

1968. As Nos. 317/8, 322/3 and 327/8 but background colours changed as below.

370. **29.** 2 c. yellow 8 8
371. – 3 c. cobalt 8 8
372. – 15 c. cinnamon 10 10
373. – 20 c. buff 12 12
374. – 60 c. red 30 30
375. – 1 r. purple 55 55

32. Dominique rescues Paul and Virginie.

1968. Bernardin de St. Pierre's Visit to Mauritius. Multicoloured.

376. 2 c. Type **32** 5 5
377. 15 c. Paul and Virginie Crossing the River .. 8 8
378. 50 c. Visit of Labourdonnais to Madame de la Tour .. 15 15
379. 60 c. Meeting of Paul and Virginie in Confidence .. 25 25
380. 1 r. Departure of Virginie for Europe 45 45
381. 2 r. 50 Bernardin de St. Pierre 1·00 1·00

Nos. 377, 379 and 381 are vert.

33. Batarde.

1969. Multicoloured.

382. 2 c. Type **33** 5 5
383. 3 c. Red Reef Crab .. 5 5
384. 4 c. Episcopal Mitre .. 5 5
385. 5 c. Bourse 10 10
386. 10 c. black, red and flesh (Starfish) 10 10
387. 15 c. ochre, black & cobalt (Sea Urchin) 5 5
388. 20 c. Fiddler Crab .. 10 10
389a. 25 c. red, black and green (Spiny Shrimp) 10 10
390. 30 c. Single Harp Shells, and Double Harp Shell .. 10 10
391. 35 c. Argonaute 12 12
447. 40 c. Nudibranch 5 8
393a. 50 c. Violet and Orange Spider Shells 12 12
449. 60 c. black, red and blue (Blue Marlin) 8 10
450. 75 c. "Conus clytospira" .. 10 12
451. 1 r. Dolphin 15 20
452. 2 r. 50 Spiny Lobster .. 35 40
398a. 5 r. Sacre Chien Rouge .. 1·10 1·10
454. 10 r. Croissant Queue Jaune 1·75 2·00

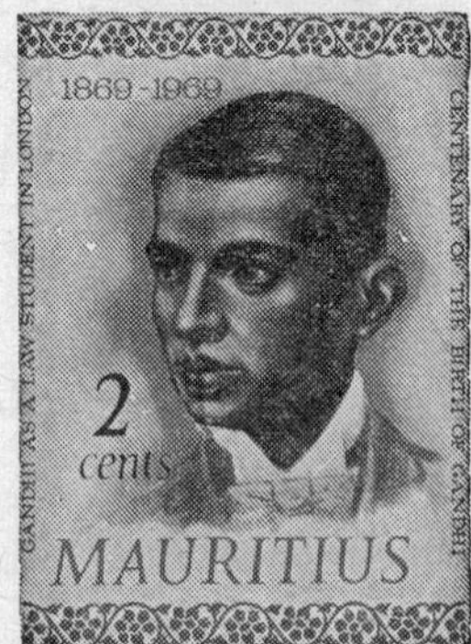

34. Gandhi as Law Student.

1969. Mahatma Gandhi. Birth Cent. Multicoloured.

400. 2 c. Type **34** 5 5
401. 15 c. Gandhi as Stretcher-bearer during Zulu revolt 10 10
402. 50 c. Gandhi as Satyagrahi in South Africa .. 20 20
403. 60 c. Gandhi at No. 10 Downing Street, London 25 25
404. 1 r. Gandhi in Mauritius, 1901 .. .. .. 40 40
405. 2r. 50 Gandhi, "The Apostle of Truth and Non Violence" 85 85

INDEX

Countries can be quickly located by referring to the index at the end of this volume.

35. Three-roller Vertical Mill.

1969. Telfair's Improvements to the Sugar Industry. 150th Anniv. Multicoloured.

407. 2 c. Type **35** 5 5
408. 15 c. Frangournier Cane-crusher (18th cent.) .. 8 8
409. 60 c. Beau Rivage Factory, 1867 .. .. .. 20 20
410. 1 r. Mon Desert-Alma Factory, 1969 .. .. 25 25
411. 2 r. 50 Dr. Charles Telfair 60 65

1970. Expo 70. Nos. 394 and 396 optd. EXPO '70' OSAKA.

413. 60 c. black, red and blue .. 20 20
414. 1 r. multicoloured .. 30 35

36. Morne Plage, Mountain and Lufthansa Airliner.

1970. Lufthansa Flight, Mauritius-Frankfurt. Inaug. Multicoloured.

415. 25 c. Type **36** 10 10
416. 50 c. Airliner and Map (vert.) 15 20

37. Lenin as a Student.

1970. Lenin. Birth Cent.

417. **37.** 15 c. green and silver .. 8 8
418. – 75 c. brown 30 40

DESIGN: 75 c. Lenin as founder of U.S.S.R.

38. 2d. "Post Office" Mauritius and original Post Office.

1970. Port Louis, Old and New. Multicoloured.

419. 5 c. Type **38** 5 5
420. 15 c. G.P.O. Building (built 1870) 8 8
421. 50 c. Mail Coach (c. 1870) 15 15
422. 75 c. Port Louis Harbour (1970) 25 25
423. 2 r. 50 Arrival of Pierre A. de Suffren (1783) .. 70 80

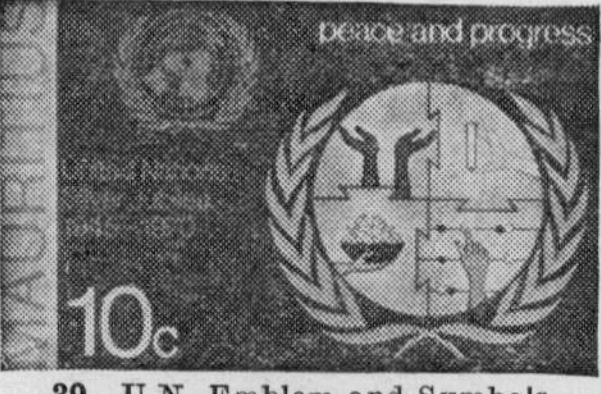

39. U.N. Emblem and Symbols.

1970. U.N. 25th Anniv.

425. **39.** 10 c. multicoloured .. 5 5
426. 60 c. multicoloured .. 20 25

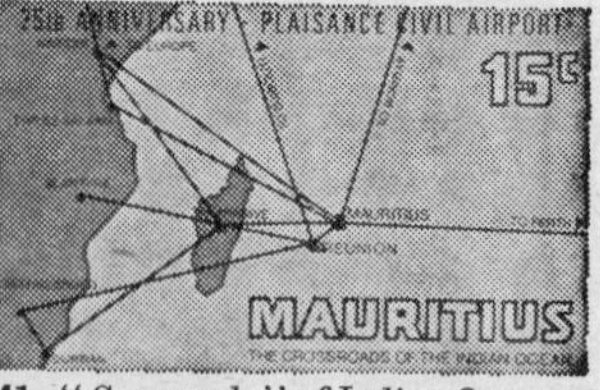

40. Rainbow over Waterfall.

1971. Tourism. Multicoloured.

427. 10 c. Type **40** 5 5
428. 15 c. Trois Mamelles Mountains 8 8
429. 60 c. Beach scene 15 15
430. 2 r. 50 Marine life 65 65

Nos. 427/30 have inscriptions on the reverse.

41. "Crossroads" of Indian Ocean.

1971. Plaisance Airport. 25th Anniv. Multicoloured.

431. 15 c. Type **41** 5 5
432. 60 c. "Boeing 707" and Terminal Buildings .. 15 15
433. 1 r. Air Hostesses on gang-way 25 25
434. 2 r. 50 The "Roland Garros" (plane), Choisy Airfield, 1937 .. .. 80 80

42. Princess Margaret Orthopaedic Centre.

1971. 3rd Commonwealth Medical Conference. Multicoloured.

435. 10 c. Type **42** 5 5
436. 75 c. Operating Theatre in National Hospital .. 15 15

43. Queen Elizabeth II and Prince Philip.

1972. Royal Visit. Multicoloured.

455. 15c. Type **43** 10 10
456. 2r. 50 Queen Elizabeth II (vert.) 80 80

44. Theatre Facade.

1972. Port Louis Theatre. 150th Anniv. Multicoloured.

457. 10 c. Type **44** 5 5
458. 1 r. Theatre auditorium .. 25 25

45. Pirate Dhow.

1972. Pirates and Privateers. Multicoloured.
459. 15 c. Type **45** 5 5
460. 60 c. Treasure chest (vert.) 15 15
461. 1 r. Lememe and "L'Hirondelle" (vert.) 25 25
462. 2 r. 50 Robert Surcouf .. 75 75

46. Mauritius University.

1973. Independence. 5th Anniv. Mult.
463. 15 c. Type **46** 5 5
464. 60 c. Tea Development .. 15 15
465. 1 r. Bank of Mauritius .. 25 25

47. Map and Hands.

1973. O.C.A.M. Conf. Multicoloured.
466. 10 c. O.C.A.M. emblem (horiz.) 5 5
467. 2 r. 50 Type **47** 60 60

O.C.A.M. = Organization Commune Africaine Malgache et Mauricienne.

48. W.H.O. Emblem.

1973. W.H.O. 25th Anniv.
468. **48.** 1 r. multicoloured .. 25 25

49. Meteorological Station, Vacoas.

1973. I.M.O./W.M.O. Cent.
469. **49.** 75 c. multicoloured .. 20 20

50. Capture of the "Kent".

1973. Robert Surcouf (privateer). Birth Bicent.
470. **50.** 60 c. multicoloured .. 20 20

MORE DETAILED LISTS

are given in the Stanley Gibbons Catalogues referred to in the country headings:

BC	British Commonwealth
E1, E2, E3	Europe 1, 2, 3
O1, O2, O3, O4	Overseas 1, 2, 3, 4

51. P. Commerson.

1974. Philibert Commerson (naturalist). Death Bicent.
471. **51.** 2 r. 50 multicoloured .. 55 60

52. Cow being Milked.

1974. Eighth Regional Conf. for Africa, Mauritius.
472. **52.** 60 c. multicoloured .. 15 15

53. Mail Train.

1974. U.P.U. Centenary. Multicoloured.
473. 15 c. Type **53** 5 5
474. 1 r. New G.P.O., Port Louis 20 20

54. "Cottage Life" (F. Leroy).

1975. Aspects of Mauritian Life. Paintings. Multicoloured.
493. 15 c. Type **54** 5 5
494. 60 c. "Milk Seller" (A. Richard) (vert.) .. 12 12
495. 1 r. "Entrance of Port Louis Market" (Thuillier) (horiz.) 20 25
496. 2 r. 50 "Washerwomen" (Max Boulle) 50 55

55. Mace across Map.

1975. French-speaking Parliamentary Assemblies Conf., Port Louis.
497. **55.** 75 c. multicoloured .. 15 15

56. Woman with Lamp. ("The Light of the World").

1976. International Women's Year.
498. **56.** 2 r. 50 multicoloured .. 45 50

57. Parched Landscape.

1976. Drought in Africa. Multicoloured.
499. 50 c. Type **57** 10 10
500. 60 c. Map of Africa and carcass (vert.) 12 12

58. "Pierre Loti", 1953–70.

1976. Mail Carriers to Mauritius. Mult.
501. 10 c. Type **58** 5 5
502. 15 c. "Secunder", 1907 .. 5 5
503. 50 c. "Hindoostan", 1842 8 10
504. 60 c. "St. Geran", 1740 .. 10 10
505. 2 r. 50 "Maen", 1638 .. 40 45

59. "The Flame of Hindi carried across the Seas".

1976. Second World Hindi Convention. Multicoloured.
507. 10 c. Type **59** 5 5
508. 75 c. Type **59** 10 12
509. 1 r. 20 Hindi script .. 20 25

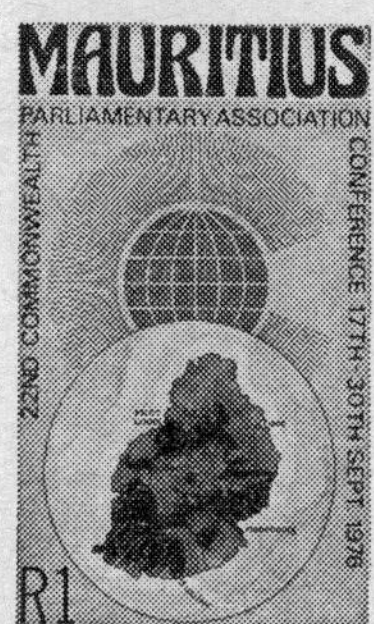

60. Conference Logo and Map of Mauritius.

1976. 22nd Commonwealth Parliamentary Conf. Multicoloured.
510. 1 r. Type **60** 15 20
511. 2 r. Conference logo .. 40 45

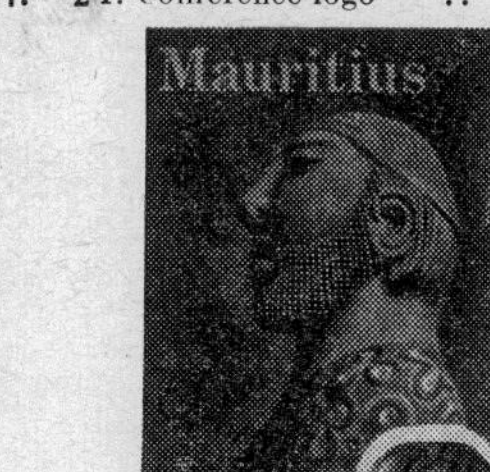

61. King Priest Breastplate.

1976. Moenjodaro Excavations, Pakistan. Multicoloured.
512. 60 c. Type **61** 10 10
513. 1 r. House with well and goblet 15 20
514. 2 r. 50 Terracotta figurine and necklace 40 45

62. Sega Dance.

1977. 2nd World Black and African Festival of Arts and Culture.
515. **62.** 1 r. multicoloured .. 15 20

63. Queen with Sceptre and Rod. (vert.)

1977. Silver Jubilee. Multicoloured.
516. 50 c. The Queen at Mauritius Legislative Assembly .. 8 10
517. 75 c. Type **63** .. 10 12
518. 5 r. Presentation of Sceptre and Rod 80 90

EXPRESS DELIVERY STAMPS.

1903. No. 136 surch. **EXPRESS DELIVERY 15 c.**
E 1. **17.** 15 c. on 15 c. blue .. 2·25 3·00

1903. No. 136 surch. **EXPRESS DELIVERY (INLAND) 15 c.**
E 3. **17.** 15 c. on 15 c. blue .. 1·60 65

1904. T **18** without value in label. (a) Surch. **(FOREIGN) EXPRESS DELIVERY 18 CENTS.**
E 5. **18.** 18 c. green .. .. 1·50 2·00

(b) Surch. **EXPRESS DELIVERY. (INLAND) 15 c.**
E 6. **18.** 15 c. green 85 95

POSTAGE DUE STAMPS

D 1.

1933.
D 1. **D 1.** 2 c. black 8 5
D 2. 4 c. violet 5 5
D 3. 6 c. red 5 8
D 4. 10 c. green 5 8
D 12. 20 c. blue 5 5
D 6. 50 c. purple 30 30
D 7. 1 r. orange 15 20

MAYOTTE O1

One of the Comoro Is. adjacent to Madagascar.

1892. "Tablet" key-type inscr. "MAYOTTE".
1. **D.** 1 c. black on blue .. 5 5
2. 2 c. brown on yellow .. 10 10
3. 4 c. claret on grey .. 15 15
4. 5 c. green 35 20
5. 10 c. black on lilac .. 45 35
15. 10 c. red .. .. 6·50 4·50
6. 15 c. blue 90 55
16. 15 c. grey .. .. 14·00 11·00
7. 20 c. red on green .. 1·60 1·40
8. 25 c. black on red .. 90 75
17. 25 c. blue .. .. 1·00 75
9. 30 c. brown .. .. 1·60 1·40
18. 35 c. black on yellow .. 90 55
10. 40 c. red on yellow .. 1·60 1·40
19. 45 c. black on green .. 1·40 1·00
11. 50 c. red on rose .. 2·75 1·60
20. 50 c. brown on blue .. 1·75 1·60
12. 75 c. brown on orange .. 2·75 2·25
13. 1 f. olive .. .. 2·00 1·60
14. 5 f. mauve on lilac .. 12·00 10·00

1912. Surch. in figures.
21. **D.** 05 on 2 c. brown on yellow 15 15
22. 05 on 4 c. claret on grey 10 10
23. 05 on 15 c. blue .. 10 10

24. D. 05 on 20 c. red on green .. 10 10
25. 05 on 25 c. black on red 12 12
26. 05 on 30 c. brown .. 12 12
27. 10 on 40 c. red on yellow 10 10
28. 10 on 45 c. black on green 5 5
29. 10 on 50 c. red on rose .. 25 25
30. 10 on 75 c. brown on orge. 20 20
31. 10 on 1 f. olive .. 20 20

MECKLENBURG-SCHWERIN E2

In N. Germany. Formerly a Grand Duchy, but now part of East Germany.

48 schillings = 1 thaler.

1.

2.

1856. Imperf.

1. 1. 4/4 s. red .. .. £100 70·00
2. 2. 3 s. yellow .. .. 60·00 32·00
4. 5 s. blue £150 £160

1864. Roul.

6. 1. 4/4 s. red .. .. .. 35·00 35·00
11. 2. 2 s. purple £150 £150
9. 3 s. yellow .. .. £110 75·00
7. 5 s. bistre £100 £180

In No. 6 the bull's head is on a plain instead of a shaded background.

MECKLENBURG-STRELITZ E2

In N. Germany. Formerly a Grand Duchy but now part of East Germany.

30 silbergroschen = 1 thaler.

1

1864. Roul. Various frames.

2. 1. ¼ sgr. orange £100 £1400
3. ⅓ sgr. green .. .. 45·00 £800
6. 1 sch. mauve £180 £2250
7. – 1 sgr. rose .. .. 80·00 £120
9. – 2 sgr. blue .. .. 25·00 £500
11. – 3 sgr. bistre .. .. 25·00 £900

MEMEL E2

A seaport and district on the Baltic Sea, formerly part of Germany. Under Allied control after the 1914-18 war, it was captured and absorbed by Lithuania in 1923 and restored to Germany in 1939. Now part of the Soviet Union.

1920. Stamps of France surch. **MEMEL** in upright capitals and **pfennig** or **mark** with figure of value and bars.

1. 17. 5 pf. on 5 c. green .. 5 5
2. 10 pf. on 10 c. red .. 5 5
3. 20 pf. on 25 c. blue .. 5 5
4. 30 pf. on 30 c. orange .. 5 5
5. 40 pf. on 20 c. chocolate 5 5
6. 50 pf. on 35 c. violet .. 5 12
7. 13. 60 pf. on 40 c. red & blue 12 15
8. 80 pf. on 45 c. grn. & blue 5 10
9. 1 m. on 50 c. brown & lav. 5 5
10. 1 m. 25 on 60 c. vio. & blue 55 80
11. 2 m. on 1 f. red and yellow 5 8
12. 3 m. on 2 f. oran. & grn. 4·00 6·00
13. 3 m. on 5 f. blue & yellow 5·50 7·00
14. 4 m. on 2 f. oran. & green 5 10
15. 10 m. on 5 f. blue & yellow 1·00 1·50
16. 20 m. on 5 f. blue & yell. 11·00 18·00

1920. Stamps of Germany inscr. "DEUTSCHES REICH" optd. **Memel-gebiet** or **Memelgebiet.**

17. 8. 5 pf. green 12 12
18. 10 pf. red .. .. 1·10 2·00
19. 10 pf. orange 10 12
20. 13. 15 pf. purple .. .. 1·10 2·00
21. 8. 20 pf. blue 5 5
22. 30 pf. blk. & oran. on buff 50 55
23. 30 pf. blue 8 12
24. 40 pf. black and red .. 5 5
25. 50 pf. blk. & pur. on buff 5 5
26. 60 pf. olive 20 25
27. 75 pf. black and green .. 1·25 2·00
28. 80 pf. blue 45 65
29. 1 m. red 15 20
30. 1 m. 25 green .. .. 5·50 6·00
31. 1 m. 50 brown .. .. 2·00 2·10
32. 10. 2 m. blue .. .. 90 1·25
33. 2 m. 50 claret .. .. 3·50 3·50

The following are all surch. on stamps of France.

1921. Surch. as 1920 issue but **Pfennig** or **Mark** have capital initials.

34. 13. 60 pf. on 40 c. red & blue 1·00 1·00
35. 3 m. on 60 c. vio. & blue 20 25
36. 10 m. on 5 f. blue & yell. 35 45
37. 20 m. on 45 c. grn. & blue 90 1·00

1921. Stamps of 1920 further surch. in large figures.

40. 17. 15 on 10 pf. on 10 c. red 8 10
41. 15 on 20 pf. on 25 c. blue 12 15
42. 15 on 50 pf. on 35 c. vio. 10 15
43. 60 on 40 pf. on 20 c. choc. 5 5
44. 13. 75 on 60 pf. on 40 c. red and blue 15 20
45. 1,25 on 1 m. on 50 c. brown and lavender .. 8 12
46. 500 on 2 m. on 1 f. red and yellow .. 25 35

1921. Air. Optd. **FLUGPOST** in double-lined letters.

47. 13. 60 pf. on 40 c. red and blue (No. 7) .. .. 14·00 19·00
48. 60 pf. on 40 c. red and blue (No. 34) .. .. 1·25 2·25
49. 80 pf. on 45 c. grn. & blue 90 1·75
50. 1 m. on 50 c. brn. & lav. 70 1·25
51. 2 m. on 1 f. red & yellow 90 1·75
52. 3 m. on 60 c. violet and blue (No. 35) .. .. 90 1·75
53. 4 m. on 2 f. oran. & green 1·25 2·50

1922. Surch. **MEMEL** in slanting capitals and **Pfennig** or **Mark** with figures of value and bars.

54. 17. 5 pf. on 5 c. orange .. 5 5
55. 10 pf. on 10 c. red .. 30 55
56. 10 pf. on 10 c. green .. 5 5
57. 15 pf. on 10 c. green .. 8 10
58. 20 pf. on 20 c. chocolate 1·00 2·00
59. 17. 20 pf. on 25 c. blue .. 1·00 2·00
60. 25 pf. on 5 c. orange .. 5 5
61. 30 pf. on 30 c. red .. 20 55
86. 35 pf. on 35 c. violet .. 5 8
64. 13. 40 pf. on 40 c. red & blue 5 5
62. 15. 50 pf. on 50 c. blue .. 5 8
87. 75 pf. on 15 c. green .. 5 8
63. 17. 75 pf. on 35 c. violet .. 5 8
65. 13. 80 pf. on 45 c. grn. and blue 5 8
88. 17. 1 m. on 25 c. blue .. 5 8
66. 13. 1 m. on 40 c. red and blue 5 8
89. 17. 1½ m. on 30 c. red .. 5 8
67. 13. 1 m. 25 on 60 c. violet & bl. 5 8
68. 1 m. 50 on 45 c. grn. & bl. 5 8
90. 2 m. on 45 c. grn. & blue 5 8
69. 2 m. on 1 f. red & yellow 5 8
91. 2¼ m. on 40 c. red & blue 5 8
92. 2½ m. on 60 c. vio. & bl. 5 15
113. 17. 3 m. on 5 c. orange .. 5 8
70. 13. 3 m. on 60 c. violet & bl. 15 25
93. 4 m. on 45 c. grn. & blue 5 8
71. 5 m. on 1 f. red & yellow 10 12
114. 15. 6 m. on 15 c. green .. 5 12
94. 13. 6 m. on 60 c. vio & blue 5 8
72. 6 m. on 2 f. oran. & grn. 10 12
115. 17. 8 m. on 30 c. red .. 8 15
95. 13. 9 m. on 1 f. red & yellow 5 12
73. 9 m. on 5 f. blue & yellow 12 15
116. 10 m. on 45 c. grn. & bl. 8 12
96. 12 m. on 40 c. red & blue 5 12
117. 20 m. on 40 c. red & bl. 8 12
97. 20 m. on 2 f. oran. & grn. 5 12
118. 30 m. on 60 c. vio. & bl. 8 12
98. 30 m. on 5 f. bl. & yellow 1·00 2·00
119. 40 m. on 1 f. red & yellow 8 12
99. 50 m. on 2 f. oran. & grn. 2·00 4·00
120. 80 m. on 2 f. oran. & grn. 8 12
121. 100 m. on 5 f. bl. & yell. 10 15

1922. Air. Surch. as last (except Nos. 81/2) and optd. **Flugpost** in script letters.

74. 13. 40 pf. on 40 c. red & blue 15 35
75. 80 pf. on 45 c. grn. & bl. 15 35
76. 1 m. on 40 c. red & blue 15 35
77. 1 m. 25 on 60 c. violet and blue 25 60
78. 1 m. 50 on 45 c. green and blue 25 60
79. 2 m. on 1 f. red & yell. 25 60
80. 3 m. on 60 c. violet and blue (No. 70) .. 25 60
81. 3 m. on 60 c. violet and blue (No. 35) .. 40·00 £110
82. 4 m. on 2 f. orange and green (No. 14) .. 25 60
83. 5 m. on 1 f. red & yellow 35 70
84. 6 m. on 2 f. oran. & grn. 35 70
85. 9 m. on 5 f. bl. & yellow 35 70

1922. Air. Surch. as in 1922 and optd. **FLUGPOST** in ordinary capitals.

100. 13. 40 pf. on 40 c. red & bl. 25 90
101. 1 m. on 40 c. red & blue 25 90
102. 1 m. 25 on 60 c. violet and blue 25 90
103. 1 m. 50 on 45 c. green and blue 25 90
104. 2 m. on 1 f. brn. & yellow 25 90
105. 3 m. on 60 c. violet & bl. 25 90
106. 4 m. on 2 f. oran. & grn. 25 90
107. 5 m. on 1 f. brn. & yell. 25 90
108. 6 m. on 2 f. oran. & grn. 25 90
109. 9 m. on 5 f. blue & brn. 25 90

1922. Surch. as in 1922 but with additional surch. **Mark** obliterating **Pfennig.**

110. 17. 10 m. on 10 pf. on 10 c. green (No. 56) .. 25 55
111. 20 m. on 20 pf. on 20 c. chocolate (No. 58) .. 15 25
112. 15. 50 m. on 50 pf. on 50 c. blue (No. 62) .. 30 50

1923. Nos. 64 and 67 with additional surch.

122. 13. (40) Mark on 40 pf. on 40 c. red and blue .. 15 25
123. "80" on 1 m. 25 on 60 c. violet and blue .. 15 25

1923. Nos. 90 and 88 surch. with large figures.

124. 13. 10 on 2 m. on 45 c. green and blue .. 20 45
125. 17. 25 on 1 m. on 25 c. blue 20 45

LITHUANIAN OCCUPATION

The port and district of Memel was captured by Lithuanian forces in 1923 and incorporated in Lithuania.

1.

2.

1923. Surch. **KLAIPEDA (MEMEL)** and value over curved line and **MARKIU.**

1. 1. 10 m. on 5 c. blue .. 8 15
2. 25 m. on 5 c. blue .. 8 15
3. 50 m. on 25 c. red .. 8 15
4. 100 m. on 25 c. red .. 12 20
5. 400 m. on 1 l. brown .. 20 40

1923. Surch. **Klaipeda (Memel)** and value over two straight lines and **Markiu.**

6. 1. 10 m. on 5 c. blue .. 15 35
7. 25 m. on 5 c. blue .. 15 35
8. 50 m. on 25 c. red .. 15 35
9. 100 m. on 25 c. red .. 15 35
10. 400 m. on 1 l. brown .. 20 55
11. 500 m. on 1 l. brown .. 20 55

1923. Surch. **KLAIPEDA (Memel)** and value over four stars and **MARKIU.**

12. 1. 10 m. on 5 c. blue .. 15 25
13. 20 m. on 5 c. blue .. 15 25
14. 25 m. on 24 c. red .. 15 25
15. 50 m. on 25 c. red .. 20 40
16. 100 m. on 1 l. brown .. 25 55
17. 200 m. on 1 l. brown .. 25 55

1923.

18. 2. 10 m. chocolate 5 8
19. 20 m. yellow 5 8
20. 25 m. orange 5 8
21. 40 m. violet 5 8
22. 50 m. green 15 25
23. 100 m. red 8 12
24. 300 m. olive .. .. 80 4·00
25. 400 m. brown 12 20
26. 500 m. purple .. .. 80 4·00
27. 1,000 m. blue 15 25

1923. No. 123 of Memel surch. **Klaipeda,** value and large **M** between bars, sideways.

41. 100 on 80 on 1 m. 25 on 60 c. 1·00 2·00
42. 400 m. on 80 on 1 m. 25 on 60 c. .. .. .. 1·00 2·00
43. 500 m. on 80 on 1 m. 25 on 60 c. .. .. .. 1·00 2·00

3. Memel Port.

4. Memel Arms.

5. Memel Lighthouse.

1923. Uniting of Memel with Lithuania and amalgamation of Memel Harbours.

28. 3. 40 m. olive .. .. 1·00 2·25
29. 50 m. brown .. .. 1·00 2·25
30. 80 m. green .. .. 1·00 2·25
31. 100 m. red .. .. 1·00 2·25
32. 4. 200 m. blue .. .. 1·00 2·25
33. 300 m. brown .. .. 1·00 2·25
34. 400 m. purple .. .. 1·00 2·25
35. 500 m. orange .. .. 1·00 2·25
36. 600 m. olive .. .. 1·00 2·25
37. 5. 800 m. blue .. .. 1·00 2·25
38. 1000 m. purple .. .. 1·00 2·25
39. 2000 m. red .. .. 1·00 2·25
40. 3000 m. green .. .. 1·00 2·25

1923. Surch. (thin figures) in **CENT.** or **LITAS** and bars.

44. 2. 2 c. on 20 m. yellow .. 70 1·40
45. 2 c. on 50 m. green .. 70 70
46. 3 c. on 40 m. violet .. 90 1·00
47. 3 c. on 300 m. olive .. 70 80
48. 5 c. on 100 m. red .. 90 90
49. 5 c. on 300 m. olive .. 90 1·25
50. 10 c. on 400 m. brown .. 1·75 2·50
51. 30 c. on 500 m. purple .. 90 2·10
52. 1 l. on 1000 m. blue .. 3·50 4·50

1923. Surch. (thin figures) in **CENTU** and bars.

53. 2. 2 c. on 300 m. olive .. 90 1·25
54. 3 c. on 300 m. olive .. 90 1·10
55. 10 c. on 25 m. orange .. 90 1·25
56. 15 c. on 25 m. orange .. 90 1·40
57. 20 c. on 500 m. purple .. 1·00 1·75
58. 30 c. on 500 m. purple .. 90 1·75
59. 50 c. on 500 m. purple .. 1·75 2·10

1923. Surch. (thick figures) in **CENT.** or **LITAS** and bars.

60. 2. 2 c. on 10 m. chocolate .. 45 90
61. 2 c. on 20 m. yellow .. 3·50 9·00
62. 2 c. on 50 m. green .. 90 1·75
63. 3 c. on 10 m. chocolate .. 90 1·75
64. 3 c. on 40 m. violet .. 4·50 11·00
65. 5 c. on 100 m. red .. 90 1·75
66. 10 c. on 400 m. brown .. 30·00 60·00
67. 15 c. on 25 m. orange .. 30·00 60·00
68. 50 c. on 1000 m. blue .. 90 1·75
69. 1 l. on 1000 m. blue .. 1·75 3·50

1923. Surch. (thick figures) in **CENT.** or **LITAS.**

70. 3. 15 c. on 40 m. olive .. 1·00 2·50
71. 30 c. on 50 m. brown .. 90 2·40
72. 30 c. on 80 m. green .. 1·00 2·50
73. 30 c. on 100 m. red .. 90 2·40
74. 4. 50 c. on 200 m. blue .. 1·00 2·50
75. 50 c. on 300 m. brown .. 90 2·40
76. 50 c. on 400 m. purple .. 1·00 2·50
77. 50 c. on 500 m. orange .. 90 2·40
78. 1 l. on 600 m. olive .. 1·00 2·50
79. 5. 1 l. on 800 m. blue .. 1·00 2·50
80. 1 l. on 1000 m. purple .. 1·00 2·50
81. 1 l. on 2000 m. red .. 1·00 2·50
82. 1 l. on 3000 m. green .. 1·00 2·50

1923. Surch. in large figures and **Centu** and bars reading upwards.

83. 1. 10 c. on 25 m. on 5 c. blue (No. 2) .. .. 5·50 13·00
84. 15 c. on 100 m. on 25 c. red (No. 4) .. .. 8·00 27·00
85. 30 c. on 400 m. on 1 l. brown (No. 5) .. 1·75 10·00
86. 60 c. on 50 m. on 25 c. red (No. 8) .. .. 7·00 12·00

1923. Surch. in large figures and **CENT.** and bars.

87. 3. 15 c. on 50 m. brown .. 40·00 50·00
88. 25 c. on 100 m. red .. 27·00 35·00
89. 4. 30 c. on 300 m. brown .. 35·00 45·00
90. 60 c. on 500 m. orange .. 22·00 27·00

1923. Surch. in **Centu** or **Centai** between bars.

91. 2. 15 c. on 10 m. chocolate ·25 4·25
92. 15 c. on 20 m. yellow .. 1·25 2·40
93. 15 c. on 25 m. orange .. 1·40 2·75
94. 15 c. on 40 m. violet .. 1·25 2·50
95. 15 c. on 50 m. green .. 90 1·60
96. 15 c. on 100 m. red .. 90 1·60
97. 15 c. on 400 m. brown .. 80 1·50
98. 15 c. on 1000 m. blue .. 18·00 32·00
99. 25 c. on 10 m. chocolate 1·50 3·00
100. 25 c. on 20 m. yellow .. 1·25 2·50
101. 25 c. on 25 m. orange .. 1·40 2·75
102. 25 c. on 40 m. violet .. 1·25 2·50
103. 25 c. on 50 m. green .. 90 1·75
104. 25 c. on 100 m. red .. 90 1·75
105. 25 c. on 400 m. brown .. 80 1·50
106. 25 c. on 1000 m. blue .. 19·00 35·00
107. 30 c. on 10 m. chocolate 2·10 4·00
108. 30 c. on 20 m. yellow .. 1·25 2·50
109. 30 c. on 25 m. orange .. 1·40 2·75
110. 30 c. on 40 m. violet .. 1·25 2·50
111. 30 c. on 50 m. green .. 90 1·75
112. 30 c. on 100 m. red .. 90 1·75
113. 30 c. on 400 m. brown .. 80 1·50
114. 30 c. on 1000 m. blue .. 16·00 30·00

MEXICO O3

A republic of Central America. From 1864-67 an Empire under Maximilian of Austria.

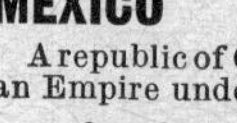

8 reales = 100 centavos = 1 peso.

1. Hidalgo.

2. Hidalgo.

1856. Imperf.

1a. 1. ½ r. blue .. .. .. 3·50 1·50
8. ½ r. black on buff .. .. 5·50 4·50
6. 1 r. orange .. .. .. 3·00 50
9b. 1 r. black on green .. 1·25 75
7b. 2 r. green .. .. .. 2·00 40
10a. 2 r. black on rose .. .. 1·60 60
4a. 4 r. red .. .. .. 8·50 12·00
11b. 4 r. black on yellow .. 9·00 12·00
12. 4 r. rose on yellow .. 17·00 7·00
5c. 8 r. lilac .. .. .. 20·00 22·00
13a. 8 r. black on brown .. 18·00 26·00
14a. 8 r. green on brown .. 20·00 25·00

1864. Perf.

15a. 2. 1 r. red 10
16a. 2 r. blue 10
17a. 4 r. brown 25
18a. 1 p. black 35

3. Arms of Mexico.

4. Emperor Maximilian.

1864. Imperf.

30. 3. 3 c. brown £200 £350
19. ½ r. brown .. .. 45·00 35·00
31. ½ r. purple .. .. 7·00 6·00
31c. ½ r. grey .. .. 7·50 7·00
32b. 1 r. blue .. .. 2·25 1·00
33. 2 r. orange .. .. 1·00 50
34. 4 r. green .. .. 10·00 6·00
35b. 8 r. red .. .. 18·00 11·00

1864. Imperf.

No.	Type	Description	Unused	Used
40.	4.	7 c. purple	40·00	£450
36c.		7 c. grey	4·00	16·00
41.		13 c. blue	1·25	1·50
42.		25 c. orange	75	1·25
39c.		50 c. green	2·25	4·00

5. Hidalgo.  **6.** Hidalgo.  **7.** Hidalgo.

8. Hidalgo.  **9.** Benito Juarez.  **10.**

1868. Imperf. or perf.

No.	Type	Description	Unused	Used
67.	5.	6 c. black on brown ..	2·00	1·10
68.		12 c. black on green ..	50	40
69.		25 c. blue on pink	1·00	25
70b.		50 c. black on yellow ..	16·00	3·00
71.		100 c. black on brown ..	12·00	7·00
76.		100 c. brown on brown ..	13·00	6·50

1872. Imperf. or perf.

No.	Type	Description	Unused	Used
87.	6.	6 c. green	2·25	2·25
88.		12 c. blue	35	25
94.		25 c. red	60	25
90.		50 c. yellow	15·00	4·50
91.		100 c. lilac	12·00	6·50

1874. Various frames. Perf.

No.	Type	Description	Unused	Used
102.	7.	4 c. orange	2·75	2·25
97.	8.	5 c. brown	50	40
98.	7.	10 c. black	30	25
106.		10 c. orange	30	20
99.	8.	25 c. blue	15	10
107.	7.	50 c. green	1·25	1·00
108.		100 c. claret	2·50	2·00

1879.

No.	Type	Description	Unused	Used
115.	9.	1 c. brown	65	85
116.		2 c. violet	55	70
117.		5 c. orange	60	50
118.		10 c. blue	70	40
127.		10 c. brown	1·75	
128.		12 c. brown	1·00	80
129.		18 c. brown	50	2·00
130.		24 c. mauve	1·25	1·00
119.		25 c. red	1·50	1·25
132.		25 c. brown	1·00	
120.		50 c. green	2·25	2·00
134.		50 c. yellow	10·00	15·00
121.		85 c. violet	3·50	3·00
122.		100 c. black	4·00	3·50
137.		100 c. orange	10·00	15·00

1882.

No.	Type	Description	Unused	Used
138.	10.	2 c. green	1·25	80
139.		3 c. red	80	65
140.		6 c. blue	70	50

11. Hidalgo.  **12.**

1884.

No.	Type	Description	Unused	Used
141.	11.	1 c. green	25	5
142.		2 c. green	50	12
157.		2 c. red	1·00	30
143.		3 c. green	80	20
158.		3 c. brown	1·25	30
144.		4 c. green	85	25
159.		4 c. red	2·00	1·25
145.		5 c. green	70	20
160.		5 c. blue	1·00	20
146.		6 c. green	1·25	25
161.		6 c. brown	1·75	35
147.		10 c. green	60	5
162.		10 c. orange	1·25	10
148.		12 c. green	1·50	35
163.		12 c. brown	2·25	60
149.		20 c. green	2·50	15
150.		25 c. green	5·00	30
164.		25 c. blue	8·00	2·00
151.		50 c. green	20	15
152.		1 p. blue	20	20
153.		2 p. blue	25	20
154.		5 p. blue	35·00	15·00
155.		10 p. blue	45·00	22·00

1886.

No.	Type	Description	Unused	Used
196.	12.	1 c. green	5	5
209.		2 c. red	5	5
167.		3 c. lilac	60	40
189.		3 c. red	10	5
198.		3 c. orange	35	20
168.		4 c. lilac	1·00	25
211.		4 c. red	15	15
199.		4 c. orange	35	20
191.		5 c. blue	8	5
170.	12.	6 c. lilac	90	25
213.		6 c. red	8	5
200.		6 c. orange	50	20
171.		10 c. lilac	60	10
193.		10 c. red	5	5
185.		10 c. brown		
201.		10 c. orange	2·00	8
172.		12 c. lilac	1·00	45
215.		12 c. red	1·40	1·40
173.		20 c. lilac	14·00	8·00
194.		20 c. red	35	15
202.		20 c. orange	4·25	55
174.		25 c. lilac	3·50	1·00
217.		25 c. red	20	15
203.		25 c. orange	1·50	35
206.		5 p. red	£100	75·00
207.		10 p. red	£225	£140

13. Foot Postman. 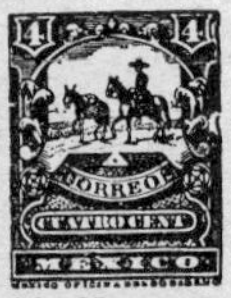 **14.** Mounted Postman and Pack Mules.  **15.** Statue of Cuauhtemoc.

16. Mailcoach.  **17.** Mailtrain.

1895

No.	Type	Description	Unused	Used
253.	13.	1 c. green	10	5
219.		2 c. red	20	10
220.		3 c. brown	20	8
221.	14.	4 c. orange	75	25
257.	15.	5 c. blue	15	5
223.	16.	10 c. purple	20	5
224.	14.	12 c. olive	2·75	1·40
225.	16.	15 c. blue	1·25	25
226.		20 c. red	1·50	25
227.		50 c. mauve	3·25	1·25
228.	17.	1 p. brown	7·00	2·50
229.		5 p. red	25·00	15·00
230.		10 p. blue	45·00	27·00

18.  **19.** Juanacatlan Falls.

20. Popocatepetl.  **21.** Cathedral, Mexico.

1899.

No.	Type	Description	Unused	Used
266.	18.	1 c. green	25	5
276.		1 c. purple	20	5
267.		2 c. red	50	8
277.		2 c. green	30	5
268.		3 c. brown	35	5
278.		4 c. red	60	12
269.		5 c. blue	45	5
279.		5 c. orange	15	5
270.		10 c. brown and purple	90	12
280.		10 c. orange and blue ..	45	8
271.		15 c. purple & lavender	1·10	10
272.		20 c. blue and rose ..	1·25	12
273a.	19.	50 c. black and purple	5·00	40
281.		50 c. black and red ..	8·00	95
274.	20.	1 p. black and blue ..	11·00	60
275.	21.	5 p. black and red ..	35·00	2·25

22. Josefa Ortiz.  **23.** Hidalgo at Dolores.

1910. First Independence Movement. Cent.

No.	Type	Description	Unused	Used
282.	22.	1 c. purple	5	5
283.	–	2 c. green	5	5
284.	–	3 c. brown	15	5
285.	–	4 c. red	35	8
286.	–	5 c. orange	5	5
287.	–	10 c. orange and blue ..	25	5
288.	–	15 c. lake and slate ..	1·90	12
289.	–	20 c. blue and lake ..	85	10
290.	23.	50 c. black and brown ..	1·90	30
291.	–	1 p. black and blue ..	2·75	45
292.	–	5 p. black and claret ..	7·50	1·50

Designs—As T **22**: 2 c. L. Vicario. 3 c. L. Rayon. 4 s. J. Aldama. 5 c. M. Hidalgo. 10 c. Allende. 15 c. E. Gonzalez. 20 c. Abasolo. As T **30**: 1 p. Mass on Mt. of Crosses. 5 p. Capture of Granaditas.

REVOLUTIONARY PROVISIONALS

For full list of the provisional issues made during the Civil War from 1913 onwards, see the Stanley Gibbons' Overseas Catalogue, Volume 3.

CONSTITUTIONALIST GENERAL ISSUES

CT **1.**

1941. "Transitorio".

No.	Type	Description	Unused	Used
CT 1.	CT **1.**	1 c. blue	20	15
CT 2.		2 c. green	20	15
CT 3.		4 c. blue	1·60	70
CT 4.		5 c. green	1·10	35
CT 9.		5 c. green	5	8
CT 5.		10 c. red	10	10
CT 6.		20 c. brown ..	12	12
CT 7.		50 c. red	50	50
CT 8.		1 p. violet	3·00	1·75

The words of value on No. CT 4, are 2 × 14mm and on No. CT 9 are 2½ × 16mm.

1914. Victory of Torreon. Nos. CT 1/7 optd. **Victoria de TORREON ABRIL 2 - 1914.**

No.	Type	Description	Unused	Used
CT 10.	CT **1.**	1 c. blue	16·00	20·00
CT 11.		2 c. green	16·00	20·00
CT 12.		4 c. blue	20·00	20·00
CT 13.		5 c. green	4·00	5·00
CT 14.		10 c. red	16·00	20·00
CT 15.		20 c. brown ..	50·00	
CT 16.		50 c. red	£110	

CT **3.**  CT **4.**

1914. Handstamped with Type CT **3.**

(a) Nos. D 282/6.

No.	Type	Description	Unused	Used
CT 17.	D **1.**	1 c. blue	1·40	1·60
CT 18.		2 c. blue	1·40	1·60
CT 19.		4 c. blue	1·40	1·60
CT 20.		5 c. blue	1·40	1·60
CT 21.		10 c. blue	1·40	1·60

(b) Nos. 282/92.

No.	Type	Description	Unused	Used
CT 22.	22.	1 c. purple	12	12
CT 23.	–	2 c. green	15	15
CT 24.	–	3 c. brown	20	20
CT 25.	–	4 c. red	25	20
CT 26.	–	5 c. orange	10	10
CT 27.	–	10 c. orge. and blue ..	30	25
CT 28.	–	15 c. lake and slate ..	50	45
CT 29.	–	20 c. blue and lake ..	85	75
CT 30.	23.	50 c. black & brown ..	1·25	1·00
CT 31.	–	1 p. black and blue ..	2·10	1·50
CT 32.	–	5 p. black and claret	13·00	9·00

1914.

No.	Type	Description	Unused	Used
CT 33.	CT **4.**	1 c. pink	1·40	1·40
CT 34.		2 c. green	2·00	1·75
CT 35.		3 c. orange ..	2·25	1·75
CT 36.		5 c. red	1·60	1·40
CT 37.		10 c. green	2·25	1·90
CT 38.		25 c. blue	5·50	5·00

CT **5.**

1914. "Denver" issue.

No.	Type	Description	Unused	Used
CT 39.	CT **5.**	1 c. blue	15	15
CT 40.		2 c. green	15	15
CT 41.		3 c. orange ..	20	15
CT 42.		5 c. red	20	15
CT 43.		10 c. red	25	25
CT 44.		15 c. mauve ..	30	30
CT 45.		50 c. yellow ..	60	60
CT 46.		1 p. violet	1·60	1·25

1914. Nos. CT 39/41 surch. **VALE 1914** and value.

No.	Type	Description	Unused	Used
CT 47.	CT **5.**	4 c. on 1 c. blue ..	5·00	5·00
CT 48.		20 c. on 2 c. green ..	5·50	5·00
CT 49.		20 c. on 3 c. orange	5·50	5·00

1914. Optd. **GOBIERNO CONSTITUCIONALISTA.**

(a) Nos. 289 and 281/2.

No.	Type	Description	Unused	Used
CT 50.	–	5 c. orange	12·00	10·00
CT 51.	–	15 c. pur. and lavender	16·00	13·00
CT 52.	–	20 c. blue and rose ..	20·00	14·00

(b) Nos. D 282/6.

No.	Type	Description	Unused	Used
CT 53.	D **1.**	1 c. blue	40	40
CT 54.		2 c. blue	40	40
CT 55.		4 c. blue	2·40	2·40
CT 56.		5 c. blue	2·40	2·40
CT 57.		10 c. blue	40	40

(c) Nos. 282/92.

No.	Type	Description	Unused	Used
CT 58.	22.	1 c. purple	8	8
CT 59.	–	2 c. green	8	8
CT 60.	–	3 c. brown	15	15
CT 61.	–	4 c. red	12	12
CT 62.	–	5 c. orange	5	5
CT 63.	–	10 c. orange & blue ..	8	8
CT 64.	–	15 c. lake and slate ..	20	20
CT 65.	–	20 c. blue and lake ..	25	25
CT 66.	23.	50 c. black and brown	50	40
CT 67.	–	1 p. black and blue ..	1·25	60
CT 68.	–	5 p. black and claret	6·00	2·50

CONVENTIONIST ISSUES.

CV 1.
Villa-Zapata Monogram.

1914. Optd. with Type CV **1.**

(a) Nos. 266/75.

No.	Type	Description	Unused	Used
CV 1.	18.	1 c. green	9·00	
CV 2.		2 c. red	9·00	
CV 3.		3 c. brown	4·50	
CV 4.		5 c. blue	9·00	
CV 5.		10 c. brown & pur. ..	15·00	
CV 6.		15 c. pur. & lavender	4·50	
CV 7.		20 c. blue and rose ..	4·50	
CV 8.	19.	50 c. black and red ..	18·00	
CV 9.	20.	1 p. black and blue ..	24·00	
CV 10.	21.	5 p. black and red ..	50·00	

(b) Nos. 276/80.

No.	Type	Description	Unused	Used
CV 11.	18.	1 c. purple	3·00	
CV 12.		2 c. green	6·50	
CV 13.		4 c. red	11·00	
CV 14.		5 c. orange	1·40	
CV 15.		10 c. orange & blue ..	6·50	

(c) Nos. D 282/6.

No.	Type	Description	Unused	Used
CV 16.	D **1.**	1 c. blue	90	90
CV 17.		2 c. blue	90	90
CV 18.		4 c. blue	90	90
CV 19.		5 c. blue	90	90
CV 20.		10 c. blue	90	90

(d) Nos. 282/92.

No.	Type	Description	Unused	Used
CV 21.	22.	1 c. purple	15	15
CV 22.	–	2 c. green	15	15
CV 23.	–	3 c. brown	15	15
CV 24.	–	4 c. red	55	55
CV 25.	–	5 c. orange	5	5
CV 26.	–	10 c. orange and blue	45	45
CV 27.	–	15 c. lake and slate ..	35	35
CV 28.	–	20 c. blue and lake ..	40	40
CV 29.	23.	50 c. black & brown ..	75	90
CV 30.	–	1 p. black and blue ..	1·25	1·25
CV 31.	–	5 p. black and claret	15·00	12·00

CONSTITUTIONALIST PROVISIONAL ISSUES.

CT **6.**  CT **7.**

1914. Nos. 282/92 handstamped with Type CT **6.**

No.	Type	Description	Unused	Used
CT 69.	22.	1 c. purple	1·50	1·25
CT 70.	–	2 c. green	1·50	1·25
CT 71.	–	3 c. brown	1·50	1·25
CT 72.	–	4 c. red	2·00	1·75
CT 73.	–	5 c. orange	60	60
CT 74.	–	10 c. orange and blue	2·00	1·75
CT 75.	–	15 c. lake and slate ..	2·00	1·75
CT 76.	–	20 c. blue and lake ..	2·40	2·25
CT 77.	23.	50 c. black and brown	6·00	6·00
CT 78.	–	1 p. black and blue ..	10·00	
CT 79.	–	5 p. black & claret ..	27·00	

1915. Optd. with Type CT **7.**

(a) No. 271.

No.	Type	Description	Unused	Used
CT 80.	–	15 c. pur. & lavender	8·00	10·00

(b) No. 279.

No.	Type	Description	Unused	Used
CT 81.	–	5 c. orange	5·00	5·00

(c) Nos. D 282/6.

No.	Type	Description	Unused	Used
CT 82.	D **1.**	1 c. blue	75	
CT 83.		2 c. blue	75	
CT 84.		4 c. blue	75	
CT 85.		5 c. blue	75	
CT 86.		10 c. blue	75	

(d) Nos. 282/92.

No.	Type	Description	Unused	Used
CT 87.	22.	1 c. purple	40	50
CT 88.	–	2 c. green	12	12
CT 89.	–	3 c. brown	15	15
CT 90.	–	4 c. red	45	45
CT 91.	–	5 c. orange	10	8
CT 92.	–	10 c. orange and blue	35	35
CT 93.	–	15 c. lake and slate ..	35	35
CT 94.	–	20 c. blue and lake ..	35	30
CT 95.	23.	50 c. black and brown	1·60	1·25
CT 96.	–	1 p. black and blue ..	3·50	2·00
CT 97.	–	5 p. black and claret	22·00	10·00

24. Arms.  **25.** Cuauhtemoc.  **26.** Zaragoza.

1915. Portraits as T 35. Roul. or perf.
293. 24. 1 c. violet 5 5
294. 25. 2 c. green 5 5
304. 26. 3 c. brown 8 5
305. 4 c. red (Morelos) 10 8
306. 5 c. orange (Madero) 8 5
308. 10 c. blue (Juarez) 5 5

27. Map of Mexico. 28. Lighthouse, Veracruz.

29. Post Office, Mexico City.

1915.
299. 27. 40 c. grey 15 12
433. 40 c. mauve 20 5
300. 28. 1 p. grey and brown 25 12
411. 1 p. grey and blue 3·00 20
301. 29. 5 p. blue and lake 2·25 1·40
412. 5 p. grey and green 2·40 1·50

(30.) 31. Carranza.

1916. Silver Currency. Optd. with T 30.
(a) No. 271.
309. – 15 c. pur. & lavender 32·00 40·00
(b) No. 279.
309a. – 5 c. orange 6·00 5·00
(c) Nos. 282/92.
310. 22. 1 c. purple 25 20
311. – 2 c. green 25 20
312. – 3 c. brown 25 20
313. – 4 c. red 60 60
314. – 5 c. orange 10 8
315. – 10 c. orange and blue 30 20
316. – 15 c. lake and slate 40 30
317. – 20 c. blue and lake 40 40
318. 23. 50 c. black and brown 1·60 1·40
319. – 1 p. black and blue 3·25 1·75
320. – 5 p. black and claret 30·00 15·00
(d) Nos. CT 1/3 and CT 5/8.
320b. CT 1. 1 c. blue 3·50
320c. 2 c. green 55
320d. 4 c. blue 26·00
320e. 10 c. red 20
320f. 20 c. brown 12
320g. 50 c. red 45
320h. 1 p. violet 2·75
(e) Nos. CT 39/46.
321. CT 5. 1 c. blue 40 4·00
322. 2 c. green 40 2·10
323. 3 c. orange 25 2·10
324. 5 c. red 25 2·10
325. 10 c. red 25 1·25
326. 15 c. mauve 25 2·25
327. 50 c. yellow 50 2·50
328. 1 p. violet 4·00 4·00
(f) Nos. CT 58/68.
329. 22. 1 c. purple 25 25
330. – 2 c. green 20 20
331. – 3 c. brown 20 20
332. – 4 c. red 25 25
333. – 5 c. orange 20 8
334. – 10 c. orange and blue 30 20
335. – 15 c. lake and slate 25 20
336. – 20 c. blue and lake 25 25
337. 23. 50 c. black and brown 1·00 95
338. – 1 p. black and blue 1·40 1·25
339. – 5 p. black and claret 14·00 9·50
(g) Nos. CV 21/8.
340. 22. 1 c. purple 1·25 1·25
341. – 2 c. green 20 20
342. – 3 c. brown 35 35
343. – 4 c. red 1·25 1·25
344. – 5 c. orange 30 30
345. – 10 c. orange and blue 1·60 1·50
346. – 15 c. lake and slate 2·10 1·40
347. – 20 c. blue and lake 2·10 1·40
(h) Nos. CT 87/96.
348. 22. 1 c. purple 25 25
349. – 2 c. green 15 15
350. – 3 c. brown 15 15
351. – 4 c. red 25 25
352. – 5 c. orange 10 10
353. – 10 c. orange and blue 15 15
354. – 15 c. lake and slate 15 15
355. – 20 c. blue and rose 35 35
356. 23. 50 c. black and brown 1·25 1·25
357. – 1 p. black and blue 1·40 1·40

1916. Carranza's Triumphal Entry into Mexico City.
358. 31. 10 c. brown 25 20
359. 10 c. blue 2·10 2·10

(32.)

1916. Optd. with Type 32.
(a) Nos. D 282/6.
360. D 1. 5 c. on 1 c. blue 35 35
361. 10 c. on 2 c. blue 35 35
362. 20 c. on 4 c. blue 35 35
363. 25 c. on 15 c. blue 35 35
364. 60 c. on 10 c. blue 25 25
365. 1 p. on 1 c. blue 20 60
366. 1 p. on 2 c. blue 15 60
367. 1 p. on 4 c. blue 15 60
368. 1 p. on 5 c. blue 15 60
369. 1 p. on 10 c. blue 20 60
(b) Nos. 282, 286 and 283.
370. 22. 5 c. on 1 c. purple 8 8
371. 10 c. on 1 c. purple 8 8
372. – 20 c. on 5 c. orange 8 8
373. – 25 c. on 5 c. orange 12 12
374. – 60 c. on 2 c. green 3·25 2·50
(c) Nos. CT 39/40.
375. CT 5. 60 c. on 1 c. blue 1·00 1·25
376. 60 c. on 2 c. green 1·00 1·25
(d) Nos. CT 58, CT 62 and CT 59.
377. 22. 5 c. on 1 c. purple 8 8
378. – 10 c. on 1 c. purple 12 12
379. – 25 c. on 5 c. purple 12 12
380. – 60 c. on 2 c. green 32·00 32·00
(e) No. CV 25.
381. – 25 c. on 5 c. orange 30 30
(f) Nos. CT 87, CT 91 and CT 88.
382. 22. 5 c. on 1 c. purple 1·40 1·25
383. – 10 c. on 1 c. purple 45 45
385. – 25 c. on 5 c. orange 30 30
386. – 60 c. on 2 c. green 25·00

1916. Nos. D 282/6 surch. **GPM** and value.
387. D 1. $2·50 on 1 c. blue 12 12
388. $2·50 on 2 c. blue 1·75 1·75
389. $2·50 on 4 c. blue 80 80
390. $2·50 on 5 c. blue 1·60 1·60
391. $2·50 on 10 c. blue 1·60 1·60

40. Arms. 41. Zaragoza.

1916.
392. 40. 1 c. purple 8 8

1917. Portraits. Roul. or perf.
393. 40. 1 c. violet 8 5
393a. 1 c. grey 20 10
394. – 2 c. green (Vazquez) 8 5
395. – 3 c. brown (Suarez) 8 5
396. – 4 c. red (Carranza) 20 8
397. – 5 c. blue (Herrera) 20 5
398. – 10 c. blue (Madero) 50 5
399. – 20 c. lake (Dominguez) 2·00 20
400. – 30 c. purple (Serdan) 4·00 10
401. – 30 c. black (Serdan) 4·00 20

42. Meeting of Iturbide and Guerrero.

1919. Red Cross Fund. Surch. with cross and premium.
413. 5 c.+3 c. blue (No. 397) 2·00 2·00
414. 10 c.+5 c. blue (No. 398) 2·00 2·00

1921. Declaration of Independence. Cent. Dated "1821 1921".
415. 42. 10 c. brown and blue 1·00 25
416. – 10 p. black and brown 4·50 3·25
DESIGN: 10 p. Entry into Mexico City.

44.

1922. Air.
454. 44. 25 c. sepia and lake 10 8
455. 25 c. sepia and green 10 8
456. 50 c. red and blue 20 12

45. Morelos Monument. 46. Fountain and Aqueduct.

47. Pyramid of the Sun, Teotihuacan. 48. Castle of Chapultepec.

49. Columbus Monument. 50. Benito Juarez.

51. Juarez Colonnade. 52. Monument to Dona Josefa Ortiz de Dominguez.

53. Cuauhtemoc Monument. 54. Ministry of Communications.

55. National Theatre and Palace of Fine Arts.

1923. Roul. or perf.
436. 45. 1 c. brown 8 5
419. 46. 2 c. red 5 5
438. 47. 3 c. brown 5 5
429. 48. 4 c. green 20 5
440. 49. 4 c. green 5 5
441. 5 c. orange 5 5
453. 50. 8 c. orange 5 5
423. 51. 10 c. brown 45 5
442. 53. 10 c. lake 5 5
443. 52. 20 c. blue 10 5
426. 53. 30 c. green 3·25 45
432. 51. 30 c. green 20 5
434. 54. 50 c. brown 12 5
435. 55. 1 p. blue and lake 45 10

56. 58. F. Garcia y Santos.

59. Post Office, Mexico City.

DESIGN — VERT. as T 56: 4 c., 10 c. Map of South America.

1926. 2nd Pan-American Postal Congress Inscr. as in T 56/9.
445. 56. 2 c. red 15 8
446. – 4 c. green 25 20
447. 56. 5 c. orange 15 10
448. – 10 c. red 65 15
449. 58. 20 c. blue 60 35
450. 30 c. green 65 35
451. 40 c. mauve 1·75 55
452. 59. 1 p. blue & red-brown 5·00 2·00

1929. Child Welfare. Optd. **Proteccion a la Infancia.**
457. 45. 1 c. brown 10 5

60. 61. Capt. E. Carranza.

1929. Obligatory Tax. Child Welfare. Rouletted.
459. 60. 1 c. violet 5 5
461. 2 c. green 8 5
462. 5 c. brown 5 5

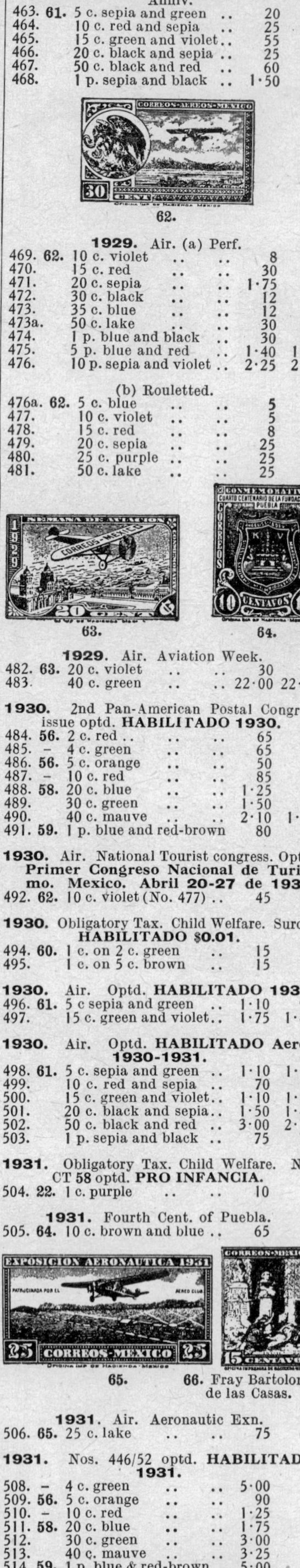

1929. Air. Carranza (airman). 1st Death Anniv.
463. 61. 5 c. sepia and green 20 15
464. 10 c. red and sepia 25 15
465. 15 c. green and violet 55 30
466. 20 c. black and sepia 25 20
467. 50 c. black and red 60 60
468. 1 p. sepia and black 1·50 75

62.

1929. Air. (a) Perf.
469. 62. 10 c. violet 8 8
470. 15 c. red 30 10
471. 20 c. sepia 1·75 8
472. 30 c. black 12 12
473. 35 c. blue 12 12
473a. 50 c. lake 30 30
474. 1 p. blue and black 30 25
475. 5 p. blue and red 1·40 1·25
476. 10 p. sepia and violet 2·25 2·00
(b) Rouletted.
476a. 62. 5 c. blue 5 5
477. 10 c. violet 5 5
478. 15 c. red 8 5
479. 20 c. sepia 25 5
480. 25 c. purple 25 20
481. 50 c. lake 25 20

63. 64.

1929. Air. Aviation Week.
482. 63. 20 c. violet 30 20
483. 40 c. green 22·00 22·00

1930. 2nd Pan-American Postal Congress issue optd. **HABILITADO 1930.**
484. 56. 2 c. red 65 30
485. – 4 c. green 65 30
486. 56. 5 c. orange 50 30
487. – 10 c. red 85 40
488. 58. 20 c. blue 1·25 50
489. 30 c. green 1·50 85
490. 40 c. mauve 2·10 1·10
491. 59. 1 p. blue and red-brown 80 50

1930. Air. National Tourist congress. Optd. **Primer Congreso Nacional de Turismo. Mexico. Abril 20-27 de 1930.**
492. 62. 10 c. violet (No. 477) 45 35

1930. Obligatory Tax. Child Welfare. Surch. **HABILITADO $0.01.**
494. 60. 1 c. on 2 c. green 15 8
495. 1 c. on 5 c. brown 15 8

1930. Air. Optd. **HABILITADO 1930.**
496. 61. 5 c sepia and green 1·10 90
497. 15 c. green and violet 1·75 1·40

1930. Air. Optd. **HABILITADO Aereo 1930-1931.**
498. 61. 5 c. sepia and green 1·10 1·10
499. 10 c. red and sepia 70 70
500. 15 c. green and violet 1·10 1·10
501. 20 c. black and sepia 1·50 1·40
502. 50 c. black and red 3·00 2·75
503. 1 p. sepia and black 75 75

1931. Obligatory Tax. Child Welfare. No. CT 58 optd. **PRO INFANCIA.**
504. 22. 1 c. purple 10 8

1931. Fourth Cent. of Puebla.
505. 64. 10 c. brown and blue 65 15

65. 66. Fray Bartolome de las Casas.

1931. Air. Aeronautic Exn.
506. 65. 25 c. lake 75 65

1931. Nos. 446/52 optd. **HABILITADO 1931.**
508. – 4 c. green 5·00
509. 56. 5 c. orange 90
510. – 10 c. red 1·25
511. 58. 20 c. blue 1·75
512. 30 c. green 3·00
513. 40 c. mauve 3·25
514. 59. 1 p. blue & red-brown 5·00

1931. Air. Surch. **HABILITADO Quince centavos.** Perf. or rouletted.
516. 62. 15 c. on 20 c. sepia 5 5

1932. Air. Surch. in words and figures. Perf. or roul.
517. 65. 20 c. on 25 c. lake .. 10 5
521. 62. 30 c. on 20 c. sepia .. 10 5
519. 44. 40 c. on 25 c. sep. & lake 15 12
520. 40 c. on 25 c. sep. & grn. 5·50 5·50
522. 62. 80 c. on 25 c. (No. 480) 30 25

1932. Air. Carranza. 4th Death Anniv. Optd. **HABILITADO AERO-1932.**
523. 61. 5 c. sepia and green .. 85 55
524. 10 c. red and sepia .. 85 55
525. 15 c. green and violet.. 85 55
526. 20 c. black and sepia .. 85 60
527. 50 c. black and red .. 6·00 6·00

1933. Roul.
528. 66. 15 c. blue 8 5

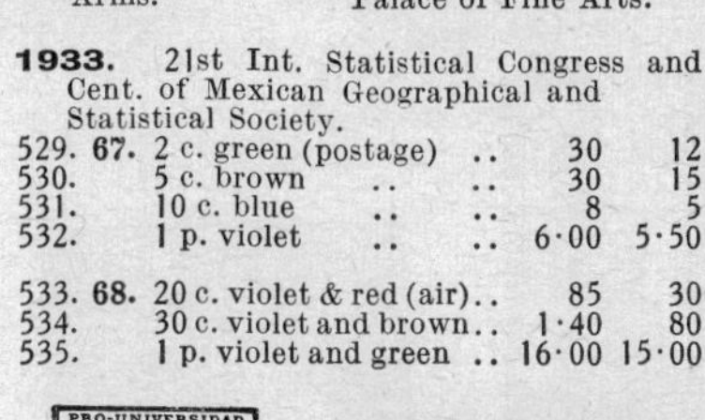
67. Society's Arms. 68. National Theatre and Palace of Fine Arts.

1933. 21st Int. Statistical Congress and Cent. of Mexican Geographical and Statistical Society.
529. 67. 2 c. green (postage) .. 30 12
530. 5 c. brown 30 15
531. 10 c. blue 8 5
532. 1 p. violet .. .. 6·00 5·50

533. 68. 20 c. violet & red (air).. 85 30
534. 30 c. violet and brown.. 1·40 80
535. 1 p. violet and green .. 16·00 15·00

69. Mother and Child. 70. Nevada de Toluca.

1934. National University. Inscr. "PRO-UNIVERSIDAD".
543. 69. 1 c. orange (postage) .. 8 5
544. – 5 c. green 30 10
545. – 10 c. lake 40 12
546. – 20 c. blue .. .. 1·25 60
547. – 30 c. black .. .. 2·40 1·60
548. – 40 c. brown .. .. 3·00 1·60
549. – 50 c. blue .. .. 6·00 4·25
550. – 1 p black and red .. 9·50 8·00
551. – 5 p. brown and black.. 40·00 30·00
552. – 10 p. violet and brown 80·00 60·00
DESIGNS: 5 c. Archer. 10 c. Festive headdress. 20 c. Woman decorating pot. 30 c. Indian and Inca Lily. 40 c. Potter. 50 c. Sculpture. 1 p. Gold craftsman. 5 p. Girl offering fruit. 10 p. Youth burning incense.

553. 70. 20 c. orange (air) .. 1·75 1·00
554. – 30 c. purple & magenta 3·00 2·00
555. – 50 c. brown and green.. 3·50 2·50
556. – 75 c. green and black.. 3·50 3·00
557. – 1 p. blue and green .. 5·00 4·00
558. – 5 p. blue and brown .. 15·00 15·00
559. – 10 p. red and blue .. 26·00 26·00
560. – 20 p. red and brown .. £300 £300
DESIGNS: Aeroplane over 30 c. Pyramids of the Sun and Moon—Teotihuscan. 50 c. Mt. Ajusco. 75 c. Mts. Ixtaccihuatl and Popocatepetl. 1 p. Bridge over R. Papagallo. 5 p. Chapultepec Castle entrance. 10 p. Orizaba Peak, Mt. Citlaltepetl. 20 p. Girl and Aztec calendar stone.

71. Zapoteca Indian Woman. 72. Arms.

1934. Pres. Cardenas' Assumption of Office Designs as T 71 and 72. Imprint "OFICINA IMPRESORA DE HACIENDA-MEXICO" at foot of stamp. (a) Postage.
561. – 1 c. orange 10 5
562. 71. 2 c. green 10 5
563. – 4 c. red 25 8
564. – 5 c. brown 8 5
565. – 10 c. blue 8 5
565a.– 10 c. violet 5 5
566. – 15 c. blue 25 5
567. – 20 c. green 12 5
567a.– 20 c. blue 10 5
568. – 30 c. red 8 5
653. – 30 c. blue 8 5
569. – 40 c. brown 8 5
570. – 50 c. black 10 5
571. 72. 1 p. red and brown .. 15 5
572. – 5 p. violet and orange.. 70 25

DESIGNS: 1 c. Yalalteca Indian. 4 c. Revolution Monument. 5 c. Los Remedios Tower. 10 c. Cross of Palenque. 15 c. Independence Monument, Mexico City. 20 c. Independence Monument, Puebla. 30 c. "Heroic Children" Monument, Mexico City. 40 c. Sacrificial Stone. 50 c. Ruins of Mitla, Oaxaca. 5 p. Mexican "Charro" (Horseman).

73. Mictlantecuhtli. 74. "Native admiration".

(b) Air.
573. 73. 5 c. black 10 5
574. – 10 c. brown 12 5
575. – 15 c. green 12 5
576. – 20 c. red 40 5
577. – 30 c. olive 10 5
577a.– 40 c. blue 30 5
578. – 50 c. green 45 5
579. – 1 p. red and green .. 40 5
580. 74. 5 p. black and red .. 1·10 20
DESIGNS—HORIZ. 10 c. Temple at Quetzalcoatl. 15 c. Aeroplane over Citlaltepetl. 20 c. Popocatepetl. 30 c. Pegasus. 50 c. Uruapan Pottery. 1 p. "Warrior Eagle". VERT. 40 c. Aztec Idol.

75. Tractor. 76. Arms of Chiapas.

1935. Industrial Census.
581. 75. 10 c. violet 75 10

1935. Air. Amelia Earhart Flight to Mexico. No. 576 optd. **AMELIA EARHART VUELO DE BUENA VOLUNTAD MEXICO 1935.**
581a. 20 c. red £700 £750

1935. Annexation of Chiapas Cent.
582. 76. 10 c. blue 10 5

77. E. Zapata. 78. F. I. Madero.

1935. Revolutionary Plans of Ayala and San Luis Potosi. 25th Anniv.
583. 77. 10 c. violet (postage) .. 12 5
584. 78. 20 c. red (air) 10 5

79. Nuevo Laredo Road. 80. Rio Corona Bridge.

1936. Opening of Nuevo Laredo Highway (Mexico City-U.S.A.).
591. – 5 c. red & green (post).. 5 5
592. – 10 c. grey 5 5
593. 79. 20 c. green and brown.. 8 5
DESIGNS—As T 79: 5 c. Symbolical Map of Mexico-U.S.A. road. 10 c. Matalote Bridge.

594. – 10 c. blue (air) .. 10 8
595. 80. 20 c. orange and violet 10 8
596. – 40 c. green and blue .. 25 20
DESIGNS—As T 80: 10 c. Tasquillo Bridge over Rio Tula. 40 c. Guayalejo Bridge.

1936. 1st Congress of Industrial Medicine and Hygeine. Optd. **PRIMER CONGRESO NAL. DE HIGIENE V MED. DEL TRABAJO.**
597. – 10 c. violet (No. 565a.) 8 8

1937. As Nos. 561/4, 565a and 576, but smaller. Imprint at foot changed to "TALLERES DE IMP.(RESION) DE EST.(AMPILLAS) Y VALORES-MEXICO".
708. 1 c. orange (postage) 8 5
709. 2 c. green 8 5
600. 4 c. red 15 5
601. 5 c. brown 15 5
602. 10 c. violet 8 5
603. 20 c. red (air) 5 5

DESIGNS—VERT. 10 c. Peasant revolutionary. 20 c. Preaching revolt. HORIZ. 20 c. Horseman. 40 c. Aeroplane. 1 p. Mounted horseman.
81. Blacksmith.

1938. Carranya's "Plan of Guadelupe". 25th Anniv. Inscr. "CONMEMORATIVO PLAN DE GUADALUPE", etc.
604. 81. 5 c. brown & blk. (post.) 10 5
605. – 10 c. brown 5 5
606. – 20 c. orange and brown 1·10 50
607. – 20 c. blue and red (air).. 10 8
608. – 40 c. red and blue .. 20 10
609. – 1 p. blue and yellow .. 1·40 80

83. Arch of the Revolution. 84. Cathedral and Constitution Square.

1938. 16th Int. Town Planning and Housing Congress, Mexico City. Inscr. as in T 83/4.
610. 83. 5 c. brown (postage) .. 35 25
611. 5 c. olive-brown .. 25 15
612. – 10 c. orange .. .. 1·50 85
613. – 10 c. chocolate .. 5 5
614. – 20 c. black .. .. 1·75 1·25
615. – 20 c. lake 50 30
DESIGNS—As T 83: 10 c. National Theatre. 20 c. Independence Column.

616. 84. 20 c. red (air) 20 10
617. 20 c. violet .. .. 5·50 4·50
619. – 40 c. green .. .. 1·40 1·25
620. – 1 p. slate .. .. 1·60 1·50
621. – 1 p. light blue .. .. 1·60 1·50
DESIGNS—As T 84: 40 c. Chichen Itza Ruins (Yucatan). 1 p. Acapulco Beach.

85. Mosquito and Malaria Victim.

1939. Obligatory Tax. Anti-Malaria Campaign.
721. 85. 1 c. blue.. .. .. 30 5

86. Statue of an Indian. 87. Statue of Woman Pioneer and Child.

1939. Tulsa Philatelic Convention, Oklahoma.
623. 86. 10 c. red (postage) .. 12 5
624. 87. 20 c. brown (air) .. 20 8
625. 40 c. green 55 50
626. 1 p. violet 50 40

88. Mexican Pavilion, New York World's Fair. 89. Morelos Statue on Mexican Pavilion.

1939. Air. F. Sarabia non-stop Flight to New York. Optd. **SARABIA Vuela MEXICO-NUEVA YORK.**
626a. 89. 20 c. blue and red .. 90·00 90·00

1939. New York World's Fair.
627. 88. 10 c. grn. & blue (post.) 20 8
628. 89. 20 c. green (air) .. 25 15
629. 40 c. purple 80 45
630. 1 p. brown and red .. 65 30

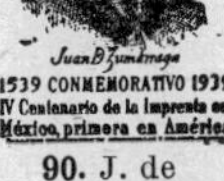

90. J. de Zumarraga. 92. "Building".

93. "Transport".

1939. 400th Anniv. of Printing in Mexico. Inscr. as in T 90.
631. 90. 2 c. black (postage) .. 20 12
632. – 5 c. green 20 8
633. – 10 c. red 5 5
634. – 20 c. blue (air) .. 8 5
635. – 40 c. green 15 5
636. – 1 p. red and brown .. 35 25
DESIGNS: 5 c. First printing works in Mexico. 10 c. Antonio D. Mendoza. 20 c. Book frontispiece. 40 c. Title page of first law book printed in America. 1 p. Oldest Mexican Colophon.

1939. National Census. Inscr. "CENSOS 1939 1940".
637. 92. 2 c. red (postage) .. 20 8
638. – 5 c. green 5 5
639. – 10 c. brown 5 5
640. 93. 20 c. blue (air).. .. 12 8
641. – 40 c. orange 15 8
642. – 1 p. violet and blue .. 45 30
DESIGNS—As T 92: 5 c. "Agriculture". 10 c. "Commerce". As T 93: 40 c. "Industry". 1 p. "Seven Censuses".

94. "Penny Black". 95. Roadside Monument.

1940. First Adhesive Postage Stamps. Cent.
643. 94. 5 c. yell. & black (post.) 35 20
644. 10 c. purple 8 5
645. 20 c. re and blue .. 12 5
646. 1 p. red and grey .. 2·10 1·25
647. 5 p. blue and black .. 20·00 12·00
648. 5 c. green & black (air) 30 25
649. 10 c. blue and brown .. 25 15
650. 20 c. violet and red .. 12 8
651. 1 p. brown and red .. 1·75 1·60
652. 5 p. brown and green .. 30·00 28·00

1940. Opening of Highway from Mexico City to Guadalajara.
654. 95. 6 c. green 8 5

96. Original College at Patzcuaro.

1940. National College of St. Nicholas de Hidalgo. 4th Cent. Inscr. "1540 1940".
655. – 2 c. violet (postage) .. 25 12
656. – 5 c. red 15 5
657. – 10 c. olive 12 5
658. 96. 20 c. emerald (air) .. 12 5
659. – 40 c. orange 20 10
660. – 1 p. violet, brn. & orange 35 25
DESIGNS—VERT. 2 c. V. de Quiroga. 5 c. M. Ocampo. 10 c. St. Nicholas College Arms. 40 c. Former College at Morelia. HORIZ. 1 p. Present College at Morelia.

97. Pirate Galleon.

1940. 400th Anniv. of Campeche. Inscr. as in T 97.
661. – 10 c. red & brown (post.) 65 30
662. 97. 20 c. brown & red (air) 25 15
663. – 40 c. green and black .. 40 25
664. – 1 p. black and blue .. 1·00 70
DESIGNS: 10 c. Campeche City Arms. 40 c. St. Miguel Castel 1 p. Temple of San Francisco.

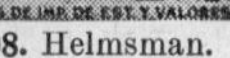

98. Helmsman. 99. Miguel Hidalgo y Costilla.

1941. Inauguration of Pres. Camacho.
665. 98. 2 c. orge. & black (post.) 20 15
666. 5 c. blue and brown .. 55 30
667. 10 c. olive and brown .. 30 15
668. 20 c. grey & orge. (air) .. 30 20
669. 40 c. brown and green .. 60 45
670. 1 p. purple and red .. 80 35

1940. Compulsory Tax. Dolores Hidalgo Memorial Fund.
671. 99. 1 c. red 10 5

100. Javelin throwing. 100a. Dark Nebula in Orion.

1941. National Athletic Meeting.
675. 100. 10 c. green .. .. 1·25 20

1942. Astro-physical Observatory at Tonanzintla, Puebla. Inaug.
676. 100a. 2 c. blue & vio. (post.) 50 15
677. – 5 c. blue .. .. 4·50 70
678. – 10 c. blue and orange 4·50 25
679. – 20 c. blue & grn. (air) 4·50 85
680. – 40 c. blue and red .. 4·50 1·40
681. – 1 p. black and orange 4·50 1·50
DESIGNS: 5 c. Solar Eclipse. 10 c. Spiral Galaxy of the "Hunting Dog". 20 c. Extra-Galactic Nebula in Virgo. 40 c. Ring Nebula in Lyra. 1 p. Russell Diagram

101. Ruins of Chichen-Itza. 102. Montejo University Gateway.

1942. 400th Anniv. of Merida. Inscr. as in T 101/2.
682. 101. 2 c. brown (postage).. 30 20
683. – 5 c. red 30 20
684. – 10 c. violet 30 12
685. – 20 c. blue (air) .. 30 10
686. 102. 40 c. green 45 25
687. – 1 p. red 45 30
DESIGNS: 5 c. Sculptured head. 10 c. Arms of Merida. HORIZ. 20 c., 1 p. Historical building at Merida.

102a. "Mother Earth" 103. Guadalajara.

1942. 2nd Inter-American Agricultural Conf.
688. 102a. 2 c. brown (postage).. 15 15
689. – 5 c. blue 40 25
690. – 10 c. orange 30 12
691. – 20 c. green (air) .. 50 20
692. – 40 c. brown 40 15
693. – 1 p. violet 80 45
DESIGNS: 5 c. Sowing wheat. 10 c. Western Hemisphere carrying torch. 20 c. Corn. 40 c. Coffee. 1 p. Bananas.

1942. Guadalajara. 400th Anniv.
694. – 2 c. brn. & blue (post) 15 12
695. – 5 c. red and black .. 30 15
696. 103. 10 c. blue and red .. 25 10
697. – 20 c. black & grn. (air) 50 20
698. – 40 c. green and olive.. 50 35
699. – 1 p. violet and brown 50 35
DESIGNS—VERT. 2 c. Founders' Monument. 5 c. Government Palace. HORIZ. 20 c. St. Paul's Church, Zapopan. 40 c. Sanctuary of Our Lady of Guadalupe. 1 p. Arms of Guadalajara.

104. Saltillo Athenaeum, Coahuila.

1942. Saltillo Athenaeum. 75th Anniv.
700. 104. 10 c. black 35 8

105. Birthplace of Allende.

1943. San Miguel de Allende. 400th Anniv. of Founding.
701. – 2 c. blue (postage) .. 20 10
702. – 5 c. brown 25 8
703. – 10 c. black 60 20
704. – 20 c. green (air) .. 35 20
705. 105. 40 c. purple 40 15
706. – 1 p. red 60 45
DESIGNS—VERT. 2 c. Cupola de las Monjas. 5 c. Gothic Church. 10 c. Gen. de Allende. HORIZ. 20 c. San Miguel de Allende. 1 p. Church seen through cloisters.

106. "Liberty". 107. Dr. de Castorena. 108. "Flight".

1944.
707. 106. 12 c. brown 5 5

1944. 3rd National Book Fair.
732. 107. 12 c. brown (postage) 12 5
733. – 25 c. green (air) .. 12 5
DESIGN: 25 c. Microphone, book and camera.

1944. Air.
734. 108. 25 c. brown 10 5

109. Hands clasping Globe.

1945. Inter-American Conf.
735. 109. 12 c. red (postage) .. 8 5
736. 1 p. green 15 12
737. 5 p. brown .. .. 1·40 90
738. 10 p. black .. .. 3·00 1·60
739. 25 c. orange (air) .. 5 5
740. 1 p. green 20 15
741. 5 p. blue .. .. 1·00 80
742. 10 p. red .. .. 1·60 1·50
743. 20 p. blue .. .. 4·25 4·25

110.

1945. Reconstruction of La Paz Theatre, San Luis Potosi.
744. 110. 12 c. pur. & blk. (post.) 10 5
745. 1 p. blue and black .. 15 10
746. 5 p. red and black .. 60 50
747. 10 p. green and black 3·50 2·75
748. 30 c. green (air) .. 5 5
749. 1 p. purple and green 15 15
750. 5 p. black and green 60 60
751. 10 p. blue and green.. 1·25 1·25
752. 20 p. green and black.. 3·50 2·75

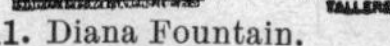
111. Diana Fountain. 112.

1945.
753. 111. 3 c. violet 12 5

1945. Literacy Campaign.
754. 112. 2 c. blue (postage) .. 8 5
755. 6 c. orange 12 5
756. 12 c. blue 8 5
757. 1 p. olive 10 8
758. 5 p. red and black .. 50 50
759. 10 p. green and blue 2·75 1·25
760. 30 c. green (air) .. 8 8
761. 1 p. red 12 12
762. 5 p. blue 60 60
763. 10 p. claret .. .. 1·10 1·10
764. 20 p. brown and green 6·50 6·50

113. Founder of National Post Office. 114. Olive Branch and Globe.

115. Flags of United Nations.

1946. Foundation of Posts in Mexico in 1580.
834. 113. 8 c. black 25 5

1946. U.N.O.
766. 114. 2 c. olive (postage) .. 8 8
767. 6 c. brown 8 5
768. 12 c. blue 5 5
769. 1 p. green 12 10
770. 5 p. red 70 40
771. 10 p. blue .. .. 3·25 2·00
772. 115. 30 c. brown (air) .. 5 5
773. 1 p. grey 15 15
774. 5 p. green and brown 60 60
775. 10 p. brown and sepia 1·40 1·40
776. 20 p. red and slate .. 3·00 2·75

116. Zacatecas. City Arms. 117. Don Genaro Codina and Zacatecas.

1946. Zacatecas. 400th Anniv. Inscr. as in T 116/7.
777. 116. 2 c. brown (postage).. 10 5
778. 12 c. blue 5 5
779. – 1 p. mauve 20 8
780. – 5 p. red 90 60
781. – 10 p. black and blue.. 2·75 1·60
DESIGNS: 1 p. Statue of Gen. Ortega. 5 p. R. L. Velarde. 10 p. F. G. Salinas.
782. – 30 c. grey (air) .. 5 5
783. 117. 1 p. green and brown.. 15 15
784. – 5 p. green and red .. 80 60
785. – 10 p. brown and green 2·50 1·60
PORTRAITS: 30 c. Fr. Margil de Jesus. 5 p. Gen. Enrique Estrada. 10 p. D. Fernando Villal Pando.

118. Pupil learning Vowels. 119. Postman.

1946. Education Plan.
786. 118. 1 c. sepia 5 5

1947.
787. 119. 15 c. blue 5 5

120. Roosevelt and First Mexican Stamp. 121. 10 c. U.S.A. 1847 and Mexican Eagle.

1947. U.S.A. Postage Stamp Cent.
788. 120. 10 c. brown (postage) 35 20
789. – 15 c. green 5 5
790. – 25 c. blue (air) .. 25 15
791. 121. 30 c. black 15 8
792. – 1 p. blue and red .. 40 15
DESIGNS: 15 c. as T 121, but vert. 25 c., 1 p. as T 120 but horiz.

121a. Justo Sierra. 122. Ministry of Communications.

123. Douglas DC4.

DESIGN —HORIZ. 10p. E. Carranza.

1947.
795. 121a. 10 p. green and brown (postage) .. .. 8·00 3·00
796. 122. 20 p. mauve & green.. 2·00 1·40
793. – 10 p. red & brn. (air).. 1·40 1·00
794. 123. 20 p. red and blue .. 2·40 1·60

124. Manuel Rincon. 125. Vicente Suarez.

1947. Battle Centenaries. Portraits of "Child Heroes" etc., inscr. "1er CENTENARIO CHAPULTEPEC ("CHURUBUSCO" or "MOLINO DEL REY") 1847 1947".
797. – 2 c. black (postage) .. 8 5
798. – 5 c. red.. .. 5 5
799. – 10 c. brown .. 5 5
800. – 15 c. green .. 5 5
801. 124. 30 c. olive .. 8 5
802. – 1 p. blue .. 12 8
803. – 5 p. claret and blue .. 70 35
DESIGNS—VERT. 2 c. Francisco Marquez. 5 c. Fernando Montes de Oca. 10 c. Juan Escutin. 15 c. Agustin Melgar. 1 p. Lucas Balderas. 5 p. Flag of San Blas Battalion.

804. 125. 25 c. violet (air) .. 5 5
805. – 30 c. blue 8 5
806. – 50 c. green 10 8
807. – 1 p. violet 12 8
808. – 5 p. brown and blue .. 70 40
DESIGNS—HORIZ. 30 c. Juan de la Barrera. 50 c. Military Academy. 1 p. Pedro Maria Anaya. 5 p. Antonio de Leon.

127. Puebla Cathedral. 128. Dance of the Half Moon.

1950. (a) Postage. As T 127.
835. – 3 c. blue (Doorway) .. 5 5
836. – 5 c. brown (Building) 5 5
1044. – 10 c. green (Archway) 10 5
1045. – 15 c. green (Portrait) 12 5
1290. 127. 20 c. blue 5 5
878. – 30 c. red (Dancer) .. 8 5
1291. – 40 c. orange (Head) .. 5 5
881. – 50 c. blue (Mask) .. 8 5
843. – 1 p. ol.-brn. (Building) 20 5
1048. – 1 p. ol.-grn. (Building) 20 5
1050. – 5 p. blue & grn. (Arms) 1·75 12
885. – 10 p. black and blue (Portrait) .. .. 1·40 40
1051. – 10 p. grey and blue (Portrait) .. .. 2·40 20
886. – 20 p. violet and green (Building) .. .. 2·25 90
1014. – 20 p. violet and black (Building) .. .. 1·75 90
DESIGNS (inscr.): 3 c. "Nuevo Leon". 5 c., 20 p. "Distrito Federal". 10 c. "Morelos". 15 c. "B. Juarez". 30 c. "Michoacan". 40 c. "Tabasco". 50 c. "Veracruz". 1 p. "Hidalgo". 5 p. "Campeche". 10 p. "F. I. Madero".

(b) Air. As T 128.
847. – 5 c. blue (Isthmus) .. 5 5
898. – 10 c. brown (Dancers) 12 5
1052. – 20 c. red (Sculpture) 5 5
850. – 25 c. brown (Masks) 12 5
851. – 30 c. olive (Helmet) 5 5
852. – 35 c. violet (Castle) 8 5
903. – 40 c. blue (Sculpture) 25 5
1053. – 50 c. green (Sculpture) 5 5
1054. – 80 c. claret (Stadium) 8 5
1022. 128. 1 p. green 12 5
907a. – 2 p. brown (Castle) 30 15
908. – 2 p. 25 lake (Masks) 30 20
1017. – 5 p. orange and brown (Building) .. 90 25
895. – 10 p. turq.-bl. & black (Portrait) .. 1·75 40
895a. – 10 p. turq.-grn. & black (Portrait) .. 2·10 30
859. – 20 p. grey and red (Building) .. 2·10 1·25
DESIGNS (inscr.): 5 c. "Guerrero". 10 c. "Oaxaca". 20 c. "Chiapas". 25 c., 2 p. 25, "Michoacan". 30 c. "Cuauhtemoc". 35 c., 2 p. "Guerrero". 40 c. "San Luis Potosi". 50 c. "Chiapas". 80 c. "Aro. Moderna Mex. D.F.". 5 p. "Queretaro". 10 p. "M. Hidalgo". 20 p. "Mex. D.F."

129. Arterial Road. 130. Train and Map.

1950. Opening of Mexican Section of Pan-American Highway. Inscr. "CARRETERA INTERNACIONAL 1950".
860. – 15 c. violet (postage) 8 5
861. 129. 20 c. blue 12 8
862. – 25 c. pink (air) .. 12 8
863. – 35 c. green 8 5
DESIGNS—HORIZ. 15 c. Bridge. 25 c. M. Aleman bridge and map. 35 c. B. Juarez and map.

1950. Mexico-Campeche Rly. Inaug.
864. – 15 c. purple (postage) 8 5
865. 130. 20 c. red 10 5
866. – 25 c. green (air) .. 15 8
867. – 35 c. blue 10 8
DESIGNS—VERT. 15 c. Rail-laying. HORIZ. 25 c. Trains. 35 c. M. Aleman and suspension bridge.

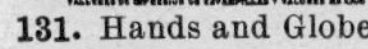

131. Hands and Globe.

DESIGNS—HORIZ. 25 c. Aztec runner. VERT. 50 c. Letters "U.P.U.".

1950. U.P.U. 75th Anniv. Dated "1874-1949".
868. – 50 c. violet (postage) 8 5
869. – 25 c. red (air) .. 10 5
870. 131. 80 c. blue 12 12

132. Miguel Hidalgo. 133.

1953. Hidalgo. Birth Bicent. Inscr. as in T 133.
871. 132. 20 c. sepia & blue (post.) 40 8
872. – 25 c. lake and blue (air) 20 5
873. 133. 35 c. green 20 8
DESIGN—As T 133: 25 c. Full face portrait.

134. Aztec Athlete. 135. View and Mayan Bas-relief.

1954. 7th Central American and Caribbean Games. Inscr. "1954".
918. 134. 20 c. blue & pink (post.) 20 5
919. 135. 25 c. bistre & grn. (air) 25 12
920. – 35 c. turq. & purple .. 25 8
DESIGN—HORIZ. As T 135: 35 c. Stadium.

136. 137.

1954. Mexican National Anthem Cent.
921. 136. 5 c. lilac & blue (post.) 25 5
922. 20 c. brown & purple 12 5
923. 1 p. green and red .. 15 10
924. 137. 25 c. blue & lake (air) 10 5
925. 35 c. maroon and blue 5 5
926. 80 c. green and indigo 8 8

138. Torchbearer and Stadium. 139. Aztec God and Map.

1955. 2nd Pan-American Games, Mexico City. Inscr. "II JUEGOS DEPORTIVOS PANAMERICANOS".
927. 138. 20 c. grn. & brn. (post) 15 5
928. 139. 25 c. blue & brown (air) 25 5
929. – 35 c. brown and red .. 25 8
DESIGN—As T 139: 35 c. Stadium and map.

140. Olin Design.

141. Snake God and Mask.

1956. Mexican Stamp Centenary. Inscr. as in T 140/1.
930. 140. 5 c. grn. & brn. (post.) 12 5
931. – 10 c. blue and grey .. 12 5
932. – 30 c. maroon and red .. 8 5
933. – 50 c. chestnut and blue 8 5
934. – 1 p. black and green .. 15 8
935. – 5 p. sepia and bistre .. 45 30
DESIGNS—As T 140: 10 c. Tohtli bird. 30 c. Zochitl flower. 50 c. Centli corn. 1 p. Mazatl deer. 5 p. Teheutli man's head.

937. 141. 5 c. black (air) .. 12 5
938. – 10 c. blue 12 5
939. – 50 c. purple 8 5
940. – 1 p. violet 10 5
941. – 1 p. 20 magenta .. 10 5
942. – 5 p. turquoise .. 50 30
DESIGNS—As T 141: 10 c. Bell tower, coach and Viceroy Enriquez de Almanza. 50 c. Morelos and cannon. 1 p. Mother, child and mounted horseman. 1 p. 20, Sombrero and spurs. 5 p. Emblems of food and education and pointing hand.

142. Stamp of 1856.

1956. Centenary Int. Philatelic Exn., Mexico City.
944. 142. 30 c. blue and brown .. 15 8

143. F. Zarco. 144. V. Gomez Farias. and M. Ocampo.

1956. Inscr. "CONSTITUYENTE(S) DE 1857".
945. – 25 c. chocolate (postage) 12 5
946. – 45 c. turquoise .. 8 5
947. – 60 c. magenta .. 10 5
948. 143. 70 c. blue 10 5
949. 144. 15 c. blue (air) .. 8 5
950. – 1 p. 20 violet & green 20 12
951. 144. 2 p. 75 purple .. 25 20
DESIGNS—As T 143: 25 c., 45 c. G. Prieto. 60 c. P. Arriaga. As T 144: 1 p. 20, L. Guzman and I. Ramirez.

145. Paricutin Volcano.

1956. Air. 20th Int. Geological Congress.
952. 145. 50 c. violet 8 5

146. Map of C. America and Caribbean.

1956. Air. 4th Inter-American Congress of Caribbean Tourism.
953. 146. 25 c. blue and grey .. 8 5

147. Assembly of 1857. 148. Mexican Eagle and Scales.

1957. 1857 Constitution Cent. Inscr. as in T 147/8.
958. – 30 c. gold & lake (post.) 8 5
959. 147. 1 p. green and sepia .. 12 5
960. 148. 50 c. brn. & green (air) 8 5
961. – 1 p. lilac and blue .. 10 8
DESIGNS—VERT. 30 c. Emblem of Constitution. HORIZ. 1 p. (Air), "Mexico" drafting the Constitution.

149. Globe, Weights and Dials.

1957. Air. Adoption of Metric System in Mexico. Cent.
962. 149. 50 c. black and silver .. 10 5

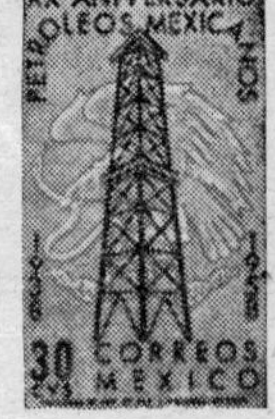

150. Train Disaster. 151. Oil Derrick.

1957. Air. 50th Anniv. of Heroic Death of J. Garcia (engine driver) at Nacozari.
963. 150. 50 c. purple and red .. 8 5

1958. Nationalisation of Oil Industry. 20th Anniv. Inscr. as in T 151.
964. 151. 30 c. blk. & blue (post.) 8 5
965. – 5 p. red and blue .. 45 30
966. – 50 c. grn. & black (air) 8 5
967. – 1 p. black and red .. 12 8
DESIGNS—HORIZ. 50 c. Oil storage tank and "AL SERVICIO DE LA PATRIA" ("At the service of the Fatherland"). 1 p. Oil refinery at night. VERT. 5 p. Map of Mexico and silhouette of oil refinery.

152. "Angel" of the Independence Monument, Mexico City. 153. U.N.E.S.C.O. Headquarters, Paris.

1958. Air. Declaration of Human Rights. 10th Anniv.
968. 152. 50 c. blue 8 5

1959. Inaug. of U.N.E.S.C.O. Headquarters Building.
969. 153. 30 c. black and purple 5 5

154. U.N. Headquarters, New York. 155. President Carranza.

1959. U.N. Economic and Social Council Meeting, Mexico City.
970. 154. 30 c. blue and yellow .. 5 5

1960. "President Carranza Year" (1959) and his Birth Cent.
971. 155. 30 c. mar. & grn. (post.) 5 5
972. – 50 c. vio. & salmon (air) 8 5
DESIGN—HORIZ. 50 c. Inscription "Plan de Guadalupe Constitucion de 1917" and portrait as T 155.

156. Alexander von Humboldt (statue). 157. Alberto Braniff's Aeroplane of 1910, and Britannia 302 Airliner.

1960. Alexander von Humboldt (naturalist). Death Cent.
973. 156. 40 c. green and brown 8 5

1960. Air. Mexican Aviation. 50th Anniv.
974. 157. 50 c. brown and violet 8 5
975. 1 p. brown and green .. 12 8

158. F. I. Madero.

159. Dolores Bell.

160. Children at Desk, University and School Buildings.

1960. Visit to Mexico of Members of Elmhurst Philatelic Society (American Society of Mexican Specialists). Inscr. "HOMENAJE AL COLECCIONISTA".

976. **158.** 10 p. sepia, green and purple (postage) .. 12·00 12·00
977. – 20 p. sepia, green and purple (air) .. .. 25·00 25·00

DESIGN—As No. 1036. 20 p. Building Inscr. "MEX. D.F.".

1960. Independence. 150th Anniv. Inscr. "1810—INDEPENDENCIA—1960".

978. **159.** 30 c. red & grn. (post) 8 5
979. – 1 p. sepia and green .. 12 5
980. – 5 p. blue and maroon 45 35
981. – 50 c. red & grn. (air) .. 8 5
982. – 1 p. 20 sepia and blue 10 8
983. – 5 p. sepia and green .. 45 35

DESIGNS — VERT. No. 952, Independence Column. 953, Hidalgo, Dolores Bell and Mexican Eagle. HORIZ. 954, Mexican Flag. 955, Eagle breaking chain and bell tolling. 956, Dolores Church.

1960. Mexican Revolution. 50th Anniv. Inscr. "REVOLUCION MEXICANA 1910–1960".

984. – 10 c. red, green, brown and black (postage) 12 5
985. – 15 c. chestnut & green 20 5
986. – 20 c. blue and brown .. 15 5
987. – 30 c. violet and sepia .. 8 5
988. **160.** 1 p. slate and maroon 12 8
989. – 5 p. grey and maroon 45 30
990. – 50 c. blk. & blue (air) 8 5
991. – 1 p. green and red .. 10 5
992. – 1 p. 20 sepia and green 12 8
993. – 5 p. bl., ultram. & mve. 45 30

DESIGNS: No. 984, Pastoral scene ($35\frac{1}{2} \times 45\frac{1}{2}$ mm.). As T **160**—VERT. 985, Worker and hospital buildings. 986, Peasant, soldier and marine. 987, Power lines and pylons. 989, Coins, banknotes and bank entrance. HORIZ. 990, Douglas DC-8 airliner. 991, Riggers on oil derrick. 992, Main highway and map. 993 Barrage.

161. Count S. de Revillagigedo.

162. Railway Tunnel.

163. Mosquito Globe and Instruments.

1960. Air. National Census.

994. **161.** 60 c. black and lake .. 12 5

1961. Opening of Chihuahua State Railway Inscr. as in T **162**.

995. **162.** 40 c. blk. & grn. (post) 8 5
996. – 60 c. grey-blue and black (air) .. 10 5
997. – 70 c. black & indigo .. 12 8

DESIGNS—HORIZ. 60 c. Railway track and outline map of Mexico. 70 c. Railway viaduct.

1962. Malaria Eradication.

998. **163.** 40 c. brown and slate-blue 8 5

164. Pres. Goulart.

165. Soldier and Memorial Stone.

1962. Visit of President of Brazil.

999. **164.** 40 c. bistre 15 5

1962. Battle of Puebla Cent. Inscr. "5 DE MAYO 1862-1962".

1000. **165.** 40 c. sepia and green (postage) 8 5
1001. – 1 p. olive and grey-green (air) 12 8

DESIGN—HORIZ. 1 p. Statue of Gen. Zaragoza.

166. Draughtsman and Surveyor.

167. Plumb-line.

1962. National Polytechnic Institute. 25th Anniv.

1002. **166.** 40 c. blue-green and blue (postage) .. 15 5
1003. – 1 p. olive and blue (air) 12 8

DESIGN—HORIZ. 1 p. Scientist and laboratory assistant.

1962. Mental Health.

1004. **167.** 20 c. blue and black 15 5

168. Pres. J. F. Kennedy.

169. Tower and Cogwheels.

1962. Air. Visit of U.S. President.

1005. **168.** 80 c. blue and red .. 30 8

1962. "Century 21" Exn. ("World's Fair"), Seattle.

1006. **169.** 40 c. black and green 8 5

170. Globe and O.E.A. Emblem.

171. Pres. Alessandri.

172. Balloon over Mexico City.

1962. Inter-American Economic and Social Council.

1007. **170.** 40 c. sepia & grey (post.) 8 5
1008. – 1 p. 20 sepia & vio. (air) 12 8

DESIGN—HORIZ. 1 p. 20, Globe, Scroll and O.E.A. emblem.

1962. Visit of President of Chile.

1009. **171.** 20 c. olive-brown .. 15 5

1962. Air. 1st Mexican Balloon Flight Cent.

1010. **172.** 80 c. black and blue 50 12

173. "ALALC" Emblem.

174. Pres. Betancourt.

1963. Air. 2nd "ALALC" Session.

1023. **173.** 80 c. purple & orange 15 8

1963. Visit of President of Venezuela.

1024. **174.** 20 c. slate-blue .. 15 5

175. Petroleum Refinery.

176. Congress Emblem.

1963. Air. Nationalization of Mexican Petroleum Industry. 25th Anniv.

1025. **175.** 80 c. slate and orange 12 8

1963. 19th Int. Chamber of Commerce Congress, Mexico City.

1026. **176.** 40 c. red-brown and black (postage) .. 12 5
1027. – 80 c. black & blue (air) 15 5

DESIGN—HORIZ. 80 c. World map and "C.I.C." emblem.

177. Campaign Emblem.

178. Arms and Mountain.

179. B. Dominguez.

1963. Freedom from Hunger.

1028. **177.** 40 c. red and indigo 15 8

1963. Durango. 4th Centenary.

1029. **178.** 20 c. chocolate and blue 12 5

1963. B. Dominguez (revolutionary). Birth Cent.

1030. **179.** 20 c. olive and green 12 5

180. Exhibition Stamp of 1956.

181. Pres. Tito.

1963. 77th American Philatelic Society Convention, Mexico City.

1031. **180.** 1 p. brown & blue (post) 25 10
1032. – 5 p. red (air) .. 75 45

DESIGN—HORIZ. 5 p. EXMEX "stamp" and "postmark".

1963. Air. Visit of President of Yugoslavia.

1033. **181.** 2 p. olive-grn. & violet 30 20

182. Part of U.I.A. Building.

183. Red Cross on Tree.

184. Pres. Estenssoro.

1963. Air. Int. Architects' Day.

1034. **182.** 80 c. grey and blue .. 15 8

1963. Red Cross Centenary.

1035. **183.** 20 c. red & grey-grn. (postage) 10 5
1036. – 80 c. red & grey-green (air) 25 10

DESIGN—HORIZ. 80 c. Red Cross on dove.

1963. Visit of President of Bolivia.

1037. **184.** 40 c. maroon & choc. 12 5

185. J. M. Morelos

186. "Don Quixote" as skeleton.

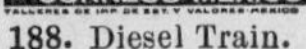

188. Diesel Train.

187. University Arms.

1963. First Anahuac Congress. 150th Anniv.

1038. **185.** 40 c. bronze-grn. & grn. 12 5

1963. Air. Jose Posada (satirical artist). 50th Death Anniv.

1039. **186.** 1 p. 20 black .. 30 12

1963. Sinaloa University. 90th Anniv.

1040. **187.** 40 c. bistre & grey-grn. 12 5

1963. 11th Pan-American Railways Congress, Mexico City.

1041. **188.** 20 c. choc. & blk. (post) 12 5
1042. – 1 p. 20 blue and violet-blue (air) 20 10

DESIGN: 1 p. 20, Steam and diesel locomotives and horse-drawn tramcar.

189. "F.S.T.S.E." Emblem.

190. Mrs. Roosevelt, Flame and U.N. Emblem.

1964. Workers' Statute. 25th Anniv.

1075. **189.** 20 c. sepia and orange 15 8

1964. Air. Declaration of Human Rights. 15th Anniv.

1076. **190.** 80 c. blue and orange 8 5

191. Pres. De Gaulle.

1964. Air. Visit of President of France.

1077. **191.** 2 p. violet-blue & brown 40 20

192. Pres. Kennedy and Pres. A. Lopez Mateos.

1964. Air. Ratification of Chamizal Treaty (1963).

1078. **192.** 80 c. black and blue .. 20 12

193. Queen Juliana and Arms.

194. Academy Emblem.

1964. Air. Visit of Queen Juliana of the Netherlands.

1079. **193.** 20 c. bistre and blue 20 12

1964. National Academy of Medicine. Cent.

1080. **194.** 20 c. gold and black .. 8 5

195. Lieut. Jose Azueto and Cadet V. Uribe.

1964. Air. Heroic Defence of Veracruz. 50th Anniv.

1081. **195.** 40 c. grey-grn. & brown 10 5

196. Arms and World Map.

1964. Air. Int. Bar Assn. Conf., Mexico City.

1082. **196.** 40 c. blue and brown 12 5

197. Colonel G. Mendez. 198. Dr. Jose Rizal. 199. Zacatecas.

1964. Battle of the Jahuactal Tabasco. Cent.
1083. 197. 40 c. blk.-olive & brn. 10 5

1964. 400 Years of Mexican-Philippine Friendship. Inscr. "1564 AMISTAD MEXICANO-FILIPINA 1964".
1084. 198. 20 c. blue & grn. (post) 10 5
1085. – 40 c. indigo and violet 12 5

1086. – 80 c. blue & lt. bl. (air) 25 10
1087. – 2 p. 75 black & yellow 50 30
DESIGNS—As T 198—VERT. 40 c. Legaspi. HORIZ. 80 c. Galleon. LARGER (44 × 36 mm.): 2 p. 75, Ancient map of Pacific Ocean.

1964. Conquest of Zacatecas. 50th Anniv.
1088. 199. 40 c. green and red .. 10 5

200. Morelos Theatre, Aguascalientes. 201. A. M. del Rio.

1965. Aguascalientes Conventon. 50th Anniv.
1089. 200. 20 c. purple and grey 8 5

1965. Andres M. del Rio Commem.
1090. 201. 30 c. black 10 5

202. Netzahualcoyotl Dam. 203. J. Morelos (statue).

1965. Air. Netzahualcoyotl Dam Inaug.
1091. 202. 80 c. slate and maroon 15 8

1965. Constitution. 150th Anniv. (1964).
1092. 203. 40 c. brown and green 12 5

204. Microwave Tower. 205. Fir Trees.

1965. Air. I.T.U. Cent.
1093. 204. 80 c. blue and indigo .. 20 8
1094. – 1 p. 20 green and black 30 10
DESIGN: 1 p. 20, Radio-electric station.

1965. Forest Conservation.
1095. 205. 20 c. green and blue .. 8 5
The inscription "!CUIDALOS!" means "CARE FOR THEM!".

206. I.C.Y. Emblem.

1965. Int. Co-operation Year.
1096. 206. 40 c. brown and green 8 5

207. Camp Fire and Tent.

1965. Air. World Scout Conf., Mexico City.
1097. 207. 80 c. ultramarine & blue 20 8

208. King Baudouin and Queen Fabiola.

1965. Air. Visit of Belgian King and Queen.
1098. 208. 2 p. blue and green .. 30 12

209. Mexican Antiquities and Unisphere. 210. Dante (after R. Sanzio).

1965. Air. New York World's Fair.
1099. 209. 80 c. green and yellow 15 8

1965. Air. Dante's 700th Birth Anniv.
1100. 210. 2 p. red 35 15

211. Sling-thrower. 212. J. M. Morelos y Pavon (leader of independence movement).

1965. Olympic Games (1968) Propaganda. (1st series) Museum pieces.
1101. 211. 20 c. blue & olive (post) 20 5
1102. – 40 c. sepia and cerise 8 5
1103. – 80 c. slate & red (air) 8 5
1104. – 1 p. 20 indigo & blue 10 8
1105. – 2 p. brown & blue .. 20 12
DESIGNS—As T 211—VERT. 40 c. Batsman. HORIZ. 2 p. Ball game. HORIZ. (36 × 20 mm.): 80 c. Fieldsman. 1 p. 20, Scoreboard.

1965. Morelos' Execution. 150th Anniv.
1108. 212. 20 c. black and blue .. 40 40

213. Agricultural Produce. 214. R. Dario (Nicaraguan poet).

1966. Agrarian Reform Law. Cent.
1109. 213. 20 c. red 8 5
1110. – 40 c. black 10 5
DESIGN: 40 c. Emilio Zapata, pioneer of agrarian reform.

1966. Air. Ruben Dario. 50th Death Anniv.
1111. 214. 1 p. 20 sepia 20 8

215. Father A. de Urdaneta and Compass Rose. 216. Flag and Postal Emblem.

217. Brother B. de Las Casas. 218. E.S.I.M.E. Emblem and Diagram.

1966. Air. Father Andres de Urdaneta's Return from the Philippines. 400th Anniv.
1112. 215. 2 p. 75 black 45 20

1966. 9th Postal Union of Americas and Spain Congress (U.P.A.E.), Mexico City.
1113. 216. 40 c. blk. & grn. (post.) 10 5

1114. – 80 c. blk. & mag. (air) 12 8
1115. – 1 p. 20 black and blue 15 10
DESIGNS—VERT. 80 c. Flag and posthorn. HORIZ. 1 p. 20, U.P.A.E. emblem and flag.

1966. Brother Bartolome de Las Casas ("Apostle of the Indies"). 400th Death Anniv.
1116. 217. 20 c. black on buff .. 8 5

1966. Higher School of Mechanical and Electrical Engineering. 50th Anniv.
1117. 218. 20 c. green and grey .. 8 5

219. U Thant and U.N. Emblem.

220. "1966 Friendship Year".

221. F.A.O. Emblem. 222. Running and Jumping.

1966. Air. U.N. Secretary-General U Thant's Visit to Mexico.
1118. 219. 80 c. black and blue.. 15 8

1966. Air. "Year of Friendship" with Central American States.
1119. 220. 80 c. green and red .. 10 8

1966. Int. Rice Year.
1120. 221. 40 c. green 8 5

1966. Olympic Games (1968) Propaganda. (2nd Series).
1121. 222. 20 c. blk. & blue (post.) 8 5
1122. – 40 c. black and lake .. 5 5

1124. – 80 c. blk. & chest. (air) 8 5
1125. – 2 p. 25 black & green 20 10
1126. – 2 p. 75 black & violet 20 12
DESIGNS: 40 c. Wrestling. LARGER (57 × 20 mm.): 80 c. Obstacle race. 2 p. 25, American football. 2 p. 75, Lighting Olympic flame.

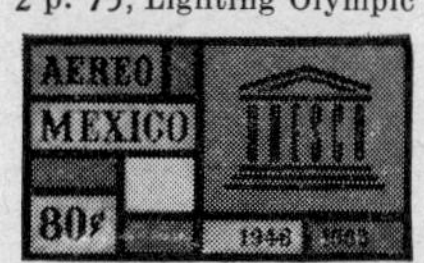

223. U.N.E.S.C.O. Emblem.

1966. Air. U.N.E.S.C.O. 20th Anniv.
1128. 223. 80 c. black, red, yellow and green 12 8

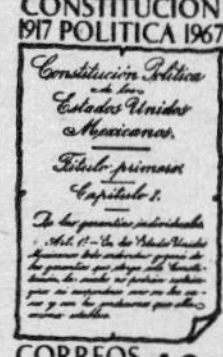

224. Constitution of 1917. 225. Earth and Satellite. 226. Oil Refinery.

1967. Mexican Constitution. 50th Anniv.
1129. 224. 40 c. black (postage) 8 5
1130. – 80 c. brn. & ochre (air) 12 8
DESIGN: 80 c. President V. Carranza.

1967. Air. World Meteorological Day.
1131. 225. 80 c. blue and black 15 10

1967. 7th World Petroleum Congress, Mexico City.
1132. 226. 40 c. black and blue 10 5

227. Nayarit Indian. 228. Degollado Theatre.

1967. Nayarit State. 50th Anniv.
1133. 227. 20 c. black and green 10 5

1967. Degollado Theatre, Guadalajara. Cent.
1134. 228. 40 c. brown and mauve 10 5

229. Mexican Eagle and Crown. 230. School Emblem.

1967. Triumph over the Empire. Cent.
1135. 229. 20 c. black and ochre 8 5

1967. Air. Military Medical School. 50th Anniv.
1136. 230. 80 c. green and yellow 12 8

231. Capt. H. Ruiz Gavino. 232. Marco Polo.

1967. Air. 1st Mexican Airmail Flight, Pachuca-Mexico City. 50th Anniv.
1137. 231. 80 c. brown and black 12 8
1138. – 2 p. brown and black 25 12
DESIGN—HORIZ. 2 p. Biplane.

1967. Air. Int. Tourist Year.
1139. 232 80 c. claret and black 1[illegible] 5

233. Canoeing.

234. A. de Valle-Arizpe (writer).

236. P. Moreno (revolutionary). 235. H. Hertz and J. C. Maxwell.

1967. Olympic Games (1968) Propaganda (3rd Series).
1140. 233. 20 c. blk. & blue (post.) 5 5
1141. – 40 c. black and red .. 8 5
1142. – 50 c. black and green 10 5
1143. – 80 c. black and violet 12 5
1144. – 2 p. black and orange 20 8

1146. – 80 c. black & mag. (air) 8 5
1147. – 1 p. 20 black & green 10 8
1148. – 2 p. black and lemon 20 15
1149. – 5 p. black and yellow 45 30
DESIGNS: 40 c. Basketball. 50 c. Hockey. 80 c. (No. 1143), Cycling. 80 c. (No. 1146), Diving. 1 p. 20, Running. 2 p. (No. 1144), Fencing. 2 p. (No. 1148), Weightlifting. 5 p. Football.

1967. Fuente Athenaeum, Saltillo. Cent.
1151. 234. 20 c. slate and brown 10 5

1967. Air. Int. Telecommunications Plan Conf. Mexico City.
1152. 235. 80 c. green and black 10 5

1967. Pedro Moreno. 150th Death Anniv.
1153. 236. 40 c. black and blue .. 8 5

237. G. Barreda (founder of Preparatory School).

238. Exhibition Emblem.

1968. Nat. Preparatory and Engineering Schools. Cent.
1154. **237.** 40 c. red and blue .. 8 5
1155. – 40 c. blue and black .. 8 5
DESIGN: No. 1115, Staircase, Palace of Mining.

1968 Air. "Efimex '68" Int. Stamp Exn., Mexico City.
1156. **238.** 80 c. green and black 20 8
1157. 2 p. red and black .. 35 15
The emblem reproduces the "Hidalgo" Official stamp design of 1884.

1968. Olympic Games (1968) Propaganda (4th Series). Designs as T **233**, but inscr. "1968".
1158. – 20 c. blk. & olive (post.) 5 5
1159. – 40 c. black and purple 8 5
1160. – 50 c. black & green .. 8 5
1161. – 80 c. black & magenta 12 5
1162. – 1 p. black and brown 60 12
1163. – 2 p. black and grey .. 60 20
1165. – 80 c. black & blue (air) 10 5
1166. – 1 p. black & turquoise 12 8
1167. – 2 p. black and yellow 25 15
1168. – 5 p. black and brown 50 35
DESIGNS: 20 c. Wrestling. 40 c. Various sports. 50 c. Water-polo. 80 c. (No. 1161) Gymnastics. 80 c. (No. 1165) Yachting. 1 p. (No. 1162) Boxing. 1 p. (No. 1166) Rowing. 2 p. (No. 1163) Pistol-shooting. 2 p. (No. 1167) Volley-ball. 5 p. Horse-racing.

239. Dr. Martin Luther King.

1968. Air. Martin Luther King Commem.
1170. **239.** 80 c. black and grey 12 8

240. Olympic Flame. 241. Emblems of Games.

1968. Olympic Games, Mexico.
(i) Inaug. Issue.
1171. **240.** 10 p. multicoloured .. 80 60
(ii) Games Issue. Multicoloured designs as T **240** (20, 40, 50 c. post. and 80 c., 1 p., 2 p. air) or as T **241** (others).
1172. 20 c. Dove of Peace on map (post.) 5 5
1173. 40 c. Stadium 5 5
1174. 50 c. Telecommunications Tower, Mexico City .. 8 5
1175. 2 p. Palace of Sport, Mexico City 20 12
1176. 5 p. Cultural symbols of Games 45 30
1178. 80 c. Dove and Olympic rings (air) 10 5
1179. 1 p. "The Discus-thrower" 12 8
1180. 2 p. Olympic medals .. 20 12
1181. 5 p. Type **241** 50 30
1182. 10 p. Line-pattern based on "Mexico 68" & rings 85 55

Portrait of Father Serra's co-worker was taken in error from a painting showing them both.

242. Arms of Vera Cruz. 243. "Father Palou" (M. Guerrero).

1969. Vera Cruz. 450th Anniv.
1185. **242.** 40 c. multicoloured .. 8 5

1969. Air. Serra Commem. (coloniser of California).
1186. **243.** 80 c. multicoloured .. 10 5
It was intended to depict Father Serra in this design, but the wrong detail of the painting by Guerrero, which showed both priests, was used.

244. Football and Spectators.

1969. Air. World Cup Football Competition. Multicoloured.
1187. 80 c. Type **244** 10 5
1188. 2 p. Foot kicking ball .. 20 12
See also Nos. 1209/10.

245. Underground Train.

1969. Mexican City Underground Railway System. Inaug.
1189. **245.** 40 c. multicoloured .. 5 5

246. Mahatma Gandhi.

247. Footprint on Moon.

1969. Air. Mahatma Gandhi. Birth Cent.
1190. **246.** 80 c. multicoloured .. 10 5

1969. Air. 1st Man on the Moon.
1191. **247.** 2 p. black 20 12

248. Bee and Honeycomb.

249. Acapulco.

250. Red Crosses and Sun.

251. "General Allende" (D. Rivera).

1969. Int. Labour Organization. 50th Anniv.
1192. **248.** 40 c. brn., blue & yell. 5 5

1969. Tourism. (1st series). Multicoloured.
1193. 40 c. "Flying" Dancers and Los Nichos Pyramid, El Tajin (postage) .. 5 5
1194. 80 c. Type **249** (air) .. 10 5
1195. 80 c. Pyramid, Teotihuacan 10 5
1196. 80 c. "El Caracol" (Maya ruin), Yucatan .. 10 5
See also Nos. 1200/3 and 1274/7.

1969. Air. League of Red Cross Societies. 50th Anniv.
1197. **250.** 80 c. multicoloured .. 10 5

1969. General Ignacio Allende ("Father of Mexican Independence"). Birth Bicent.
1198. **251.** 40 c. multicoloured .. 5 5

252. Dish Aerial.

253. Question Marks.

1969. Air. Satellite Communications Station. Tulancingo. Inaug.
1199. **252.** 80 c. multicoloured .. 10 5

1969. Tourism (2nd series). As T **249** but dated "1970". Multicoloured.
1200. 40 c. Puebla Cathedral .. 5 5
1201. 40 c. Anthropological Museum, Mexico City 5 5
1202. 40 c. Belaunzaran street, Guanajuato 5 5
1203. 40 c. Puerto Vallarta .. 5 5

1970. 9th National and 5th Agricultural Census. Multicoloured.
1204. 20 c. Type **253** 5 5
1205. 40 c. Horse's head and agricultural symbols .. 5 5

254. Diagram of Human Eye.

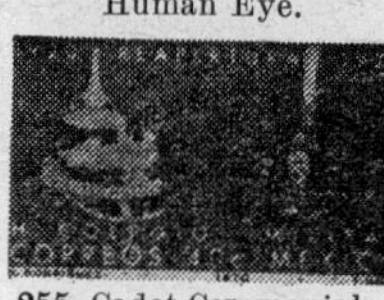

255. Cadet Ceremonial Helmet and Kepi.

256. J. M. P. Suarez.

1970. 21st Int. Ophthalmological Congress, Mexico City.
1206. **254.** 40 c. multicoloured .. 5 5

1970. Military College Reorganization. 50th Anniv.
1207. **255.** 40 c. multicoloured .. 5 5

1970. Jose Maria Pino Suarez (statesman) Birth Cent. (1969).
1208. **256.** 40 c. multicoloured .. 5 5

257. Football and Masks.

258. Composition by Beethoven.

1970. Air. World Cup Football Championships, Mexico. Multicoloured.
1209. 80 c. Type **257** 10 5
1210. 2 p. Football and Mexican idols 20 12

1970. Air. Beethoven Birth Bicent.
1212. **258.** 2 p. multicoloured .. 20 12

259. Arms of Celaya. 260. "General Assembly".

1970. Celaya. 400th Anniv.
1213. **259.** 40 c. multicoloured .. 5 5

1970. Air. United Nations. 25th Anniv.
1214. **260.** 80 c. multicoloured .. 8 5

261. "Eclipse de Sol".

262. "Galileo" (Susterman).

1970. Total Eclipse of the Sun (7.3.70).
1215. **261.** 40 c. black 5 5

1971. Air. Conquest of Space. Early Astronomers. Multicoloured.
1216. 2 p. Type **262** 20 12
1217. 2 p. "Kepler" (unknown artist) 20 12
1218. 2 p. "Sir Isaac Newton" (Kneller) 20 12

263. "Sister Juana" (M. Cabrera).

1971. Air. Mexican Arts and Sciences (1st Series). Paintings. Multicoloured.
1219. 80 c. Type **263** 8 5
1220. 80 c. "El Paricutin" (volcano) (G. Murillo) 8 5
1221. 80 c. "Men and Llamas" (J. C. Orozco) 8 5
1222. 80 c. "Self-portrait" (J. M. Velasco) 8 5
1223. 80 c. "Mayan Warriors" ("Dresden Codex") .. 8 5
See also Nos. 1243/7, 1284/8 and 1323/7.

264. Stamps from Venezuela, Mexico and Colombia.

1971. Air. "Philately for Peace". Latin-American Stamp Exhibitions 1968-70.
1224. **264.** 80 c. multicoloured .. 10 5

265. Lottery Balls.

1971. National Lottery. Bicent.
1225. **265.** 40 c. black and green 5 5

266. "F. Javier Clavijero" (P. Carlin).

1971. Air. Return of the Remains of Francisco Javier Clavijero (historian) to Mexico (1970).
1226. **266.** 2 p. brown and green 20 12

267. Vasco de Quiroga and "Utopia" (O'Gorman).

268. A. Nervo.

1971. Vasco de Quiroga, Archbishop of Michoacan. 500th Birth Anniv.
1227. **267.** 40 c. multicoloured .. 5 5

1971. Amado Nervo (writer). Birth Cent.
1228. **268.** 80 c. multicoloured .. 5 5

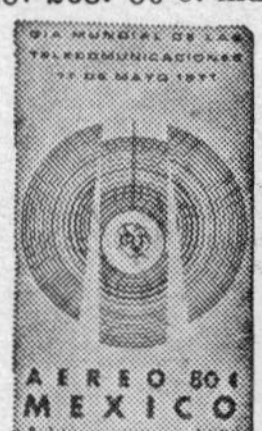

269. I. T. U. Emblem.

270. "M. Matamoros" (D. Rivera).

1971. Air. World Telecommunications Day.
1229. **269.** 80 c. multicoloured .. 8 5

1971. Air. Mariano Matamoros (patriot). Birth Bicent.
1230. **270.** 2 p. multicoloured .. 20 12

271. " General Guerrero ". (O'Gorman). **272.** Loudspeaker and Sound Waves.

1971. Air. Independence from Spain. 150th Anniv.
1231. **271.** 2 p. multicoloured .. 20 12

1971. Radio Broadcasting in Mexico. 50th Anniv.
1232. **272.** 40 c. blk., blue & grn. 5 5

273. Pres. Cardenas and Banners. **274.** Stamps of Venezuela, Mexico, Colombia and Peru.

1971. General Lazaro Cardenas. 1st Death Anniv.
1233. **273.** 40 c. black and lilac .. 5 5

1971. Air. " EXFILIMA 71 " Stamp Exhib. Lima, Peru.
1234. **274.** 80 c. multicoloured .. 8 5

275. Abstract of Circles. **276.** Piano Keyboard.

1971. Air. U.N.E.S.C.O. 25th Anniv.
1235. **275.** 80 c. multicoloured .. 8 5

1971. Agustin Lara (composer). 1st Death Anniv.
1236. **276.** 40 c. blk., blue & yell. 5 5

277. " Mental Patients ". **278.** City Arms of Monterrey.

1971. Air. 5th World Psychiatric Congress, Mexico City.
1237. **277.** 2 p. multicoloured .. 20 12

1971. Monterrey. 375th Anniv.
1238. **278.** 40 c. multicoloured .. 5

279. Durer's Bookplate.

1971. Air. Albrecht Durer (artist). 500th Anniv.
1239. **279.** 2 p. black and brown 20 12

280. Scientific Symbols. **281.** Emblem of Mexican Cardiological Institute.

1972. Air. National Council of Science and Technology. 1st. Anniv.
1240. **280.** 2 p. multicoloured .. 20 12

1972. World Health Month. Multicoloured.
1241. 40 c. Type **281** (postage) 5 5
1242. 80 c. Heart specialists (air) 8 5

1972. Air. Mexican Arts and Sciences (2nd Series). Portraits. As T **263.**
1243. 80 c. brown and black .. 8 5
1244. 80 c. green and black .. 8 5
1245. 80 c. brown and black .. 8 5
1246. 80 c. blue and black .. 8 5
1247. 80 c. red and black .. 8 5
PORTRAITS: No. 1243, King Netzahualcoyotl of Texcoco (patron of the arts). No. 1244, J. R. de Alarcon (lawyer). No. 1245, J. J. Fernandez de Lizardi (writer). No. 1246, E. G. Martinez (poet). No. 1247, R. L. Velarde (author).

282. Rotary Emblems. **283.** Indian Laurel and Fruit.

1972. Air. Rotary Movement in Mexico. 50th Anniv.
1248. **282.** 80 c. multicoloured .. 8 5

1972. Chilpancingo as Capital of Guerrero State. Cent.
1249. **283.** 40 c. blk., gold & grn. 5 5

284. Tread of Rubber Tyre.

1972. Air. Int. Tourist Alliance, Mexico City. 74th Assembly.
1250. **284.** 80 c. black and grey .. 8 5

285. First issue of " Gazetta De Mexico ". **286.** Emblem of Lions Organization.

1972. Publication of " Gazetta De Mexico ". 250th Anniv. (1st newspaper to be published in Latin America).
1251. **285.** 40 c. multicoloured .. 5 5

1972. Lions' Clubs Convention, Mexico City.
1252. **286.** 40 c. multicoloured .. 5 5

287. School Corvette, " Zaragoza ". **288.** Page of Civil Register with Juarez signature.

1972. Naval Academy, Veracruz. 75th Anniv.
1253. **287.** 40 c. multicoloured .. 5 5

1972. Pres. Benito Juarez. Death Cent.
1254. – 20 c. mult. (postage) 5 5
1255. – 40 c. multicoloured .. 5 5
1256. **288.** 80 c. blk. & blue (air) 8 5
1257. – 1 p. 20 multicoloured 12 10
1258. – 2 p. multicoloured .. 20 15
DESIGNS: 20 c. " Margarita Maza de Juarez " (artist unknown). 40 c. " Benito Juarez " (D. Rivera). 1 p. 20 " Benito Juarez " (P. Clave). 2 p. " Benito Juarez " (J. C. Orozco).

290. " Emperor Justinian I" (mosaic). **291.** Atomic Emblem.

1972. Mexican Bar Association. 50th Anniv.
1259. **290.** 40 c. multicoloured .. 5 5

1972. Air. 16th General Conference of Int. Atomic Energy Organization, Mexico City.
1260. **291.** 2p. blk., blue and grey 20 15

292. Caravel on " Stamp ". **293.** " Sobre las Olas " (sheet-music cover by O'Brandstetter).

1972. Stamp Day of the Americas.
1261. **292.** 80 c. violet and brown 8 5

1972. Air. 28th Int. Author's and Composers' Society Congress. Mexico City.
1262. **293.** 80 c. brown 8 5

294. " Mother and Child ". (G. Galvin).

1972. Air. U.N.I.C.E.F. 25th Anniv.
1263. **294.** 80 c. multicoloured .. 8 5

295. " Father Pedro de Gante " (Rodriguez y Arangorti). **296.** Olympic Emblems.

1972. Air. Father Pedro de Gante (founder of first school in Mexico). 400th Death Anniv.
1264. **295.** 2 p. multicoloured .. 20 15

1972. Olympic Games, Munich.
1265. **296.** 40 c. multicoloured (postage) 5 5
1266. – 80 c. multicoloured (air) 8 5
1267. – 2 p. blk., grn. & blue 20 15
DESIGNS—HORIZ. 80 c. " Football ". VERT. 2 p. Similar to Type **296.**

MINIMUM PRICE

The minimum price quoted is 5p which represents a handling charge rather than a basis for valuing common stamps. For further notes about prices see introductory pages.

297. Books on Shelves. **299.** " Footprints on the Americas ".

298. Fish (" Pure Water ").

1972. Int. Book Year.
1268. **297.** 40 c. multicoloured .. 5 5

1972. Anti-Pollution Campaign.
1269. **298.** 40 c. blk. & blue (post.) 5 5
1270. – 80 c. blk. & blue (air) 8 5
DESIGN—VERT. 80 c. Pigeon on cornice " Pure Air ".

1972. Air. Tourist Year of the Americas.
1271. **299.** 80 c. multicoloured 8 5

300. Stamps of Mexico, Colombia, Venezuela, Peru and Brazil.

1973. Air. " EXFILBRA 72 " Stamp Exhibition, Rio de Janeiro, Brazil.
1272. **300.** 80 c. multicoloured .. 8 5

301. " Metlac Viaduct " (J. M. Velasco).

1973. Mexican Railways. Cent.
1273. **301.** 40 c. multicoloured 5 5

302. Ocotlan Abbey.

1973. Tourism (3rd series). Multicoloured.
1274. 40 c. Type **302** (postage) .. 5 5
1275. 40 c. Indian hunting dance, Sonora (vert.) .. 5 5
1276. 80 c. Girl in local costume (vert.) (air) 8 5
1277. 80 c. Sport fishing, Lower California 8 5

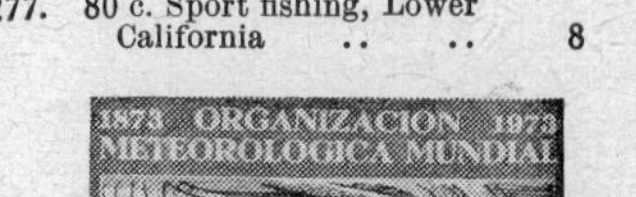

303. " God of the Winds ".

1973. Air. W.M.O. Centenary.
1278. **303.** 80 c. blk., blue & mauve 8 5

304. Copernicus.

305. Cadet.

1973. Air. Copernicus (astronomer). 500th Birth Anniv.
1279. **304.** 80 c. green 8 5

1973. Military College. 150th Anniv.
1280. **305.** 40 c. multicoloured .. 5 5

306. "Francisco Madero" (D. Rivera).

307. A. Narro (founder).

1973. Pres. Francisco Madera. Birth Centenary.
1281. **306.** 40 c. multicoloured .. 5 5

1973. "Antonio Narro" Agricultural School, Saltillo. 50th Anniv.
1282. **307.** 40 c. grey 5 5

308. Statue of San Martin.

309. Carbon Molecules.

1973. Air. Argentina's Gift of San Martin Statue to Mexico City.
1283. **308.** 80 c. multicoloured .. 8 5

1973. Air. "Mexican Arts and Sciences". (3rd series). Astronomers. As T **263**. Mult.
1284. 80 c. green and red .. 8 5
1285. 80 c. multicoloured .. 8 5
1286. 80 c. multicoloured .. 8 5
1287. 80 c. multicoloured .. 8 5
1288. 80 c. multicoloured .. 8 5
DESIGNS: No. 1284, Aztec "Sun" stone. No. 1285, Carlos de Siguenza y Gongora. No. 1286, Francisco Diaz Covarrubias. No. 1287, Joaquin Gallo. No. 1288, Luis Enrique Erro.

1973. Chemical Engineering School. 25th Anniv.
1289. **309.** 40 c. blk., yell. & red 5 5

310. Fist with Pointing Finger.

311. "EXMEX 73" Emblem.

1974. Promotion of Exports.
1294. **310.** 40 c. black and green 5 5

1974. "EXMEX 73" National Stamp Exhibition, Cuernavaca.
1295. **311.** 40 c. black (postage) 5 5
1296. – 80 c. mult. (air) .. 8 5

312. Manuel Ponce.

1974. Manuel M. Ponce (composer). 25th Death Anniv. (1973).
1297. **312.** 40 c. multicoloured .. 5 5

313. Gold Brooch, Mochica Culture.

1974. Air. Exhibition of Peruvian Gold Treasures, Mexico City.
1298. **313.** 80 c. multicoloured .. 8 5

314. C.E.P.A.L. Emblem and Flags.

315. Baggage.

1974. Air. U.N. Economic Commission for Latin America (C.E.P.A.L.). 25th Anniv.
1299. **314.** 80 c. multicoloured .. 8 5

1974. Air. 16th Confederation of Latin American Tourist Organizations (C.O.T.A.L.) Convention, Acapulco.
1300. **315.** 80 c. multicoloured .. 8 5

316. Silver Statuette.

318. "Dancing Dogs" (Indian statuette).

317. "The Enamelled Caserole" (Picasso).

1974. 1st International Silver Fair, Mexico City.
1301. **316.** 40 c. multicoloured .. 5 5

1974. Air. Pablo Picasso (artist). 1st Death Anniv.
1302. **317.** 80 c. multicoloured .. 8 5

1974. 6th Season of Dog Shows.
1303. **318.** 40 c. multicoloured .. 5 5

319. Mariano Azuela

1974. Mariano Azuela (writer). Birth Cent. (1973).
1304. **319.** 40 c. multicoloured .. 5 5

320. Tepotzotlan Viaduct.

1974. National Engineers' Day.
1305. **320.** 40 c. black and blue .. 5 5

321. Dr. R. Robles (surgeon and pioneer in medical research).

1974. World Health Organization. 25th Anniv.
1306. **321.** 40 c. brown and green 5 5

322. U.P.U. Emblem.

1974. "Exfilmex" 74 Inter-American Stamp Exhibition honouring U.P.U., Mexico City.
1307. **322.** 40 c. black and green on yellow (postage) .. 5 5
1308. **322.** 80 c. black and brown on yellow (air) 8 5

323. Demosthenes.

325. Map and Indian Head.

324. Early Biplane.

1974. 2nd Spanish-American Reading and Writing Studies Congress, Mexico City.
1309. **323.** 20 c. green and brown 5 5

1974. Air. "Mexicana" (Mexican Airlines). 50th Anniv. Multicoloured.
1310. 80 c. Type **324** 8 5
1311. 2 p. Jetliner 20 15

1974. Union with Chiapas. 150th Anniv.
1312. **325.** 20 c. green and brown 5 5

326. "Sonar Waves".

1974. Air. 1st International Electrical and Electronic Communications Congress, Mexico City.
1313. **326.** 2 p. multicoloured .. 20 15

327. S. Lerdo de Tejada.

328. Manuscript of Constitution.

1974. Restoration of Senate. Cent.
1314. **327.** 40 c. black and blue .. 5 5

1974. Federal Republic. 150th Anniv.
1315. **328.** 40 c. black and green 5 5

329. Ball in Play.

1974. Air. 8th World Volleyball Championships, Mexico City.
1316. **329.** 2 p. blk., brn. & orge. 20 15

330. F. C. Puerto.

331. Mask, bat and catcher's glove.

1974. Air. Felipe Carrillo Puerto (politician and journalist). Birth Centenary.
1318. **330.** 80 c. brown & green 8 5

1974. Air. Mexican Baseball League. 50th Anniv.
1319. **331.** 80 c. brown and green 8

332. U.P.U. Monument, Berne.

1974. Universal Postal Union. Centenary.
1320. **332.** 40 c. brown & blue (post.) 5 5
1321. – 80 c. multicoloured (air) 8 5
1322. – 2 p. brown & green .. 20 15
DESIGNS: 80 c. Man's face as letter-box, Colonial period. $2 Heinrich von Stephan, founder of U.P.U.

1974. Air. Mexican Arts and Sciences (4th Series). Music and Musicians. As T **263**. Multicoloured.
1323. 80 c. "Musicians"- Mayan painting, Bonampak 5 5
1324. 80 c. First Mexican-printed score, 1556 .. .. 5 5
1325. 80 c. Angela Peralta (soprano and composer) 5 5
1326. 80 c. "Miguel Lerdo de Tejada" (composer) (F. S. Rayon) .. 5 5
1327. 80 c. "Silvestre Revueltas" (composer (bronze by Carlos Bracho) .. 5 5

333. I.W.Y. Emblem.

334. Economic Charter.

1975. Air. International Women's Year.
1328. **333.** 1 p. 60 black and red 10 8

1975. Air. U.N. Declaration of Nations' Economic Rights and Duties.
1329. **334.** 1 p. 60 multicoloured 10 8

335. Jose Marie Mora. **337.** Dr. M. Jimenez.

336. Balsa raft " Acali ".

1975. Federal Republic. 150th Anniv.
1330. **335.** 20 c. multicoloured .. 5 5

1975. Air. Trans-Atlantic Voyage of " Acali ". Canary Islands to Yucatan (1973).
1331. **336.** 80 c. multicoloured .. 5 5

1975. Air. Fifth World Gastroenterological Congress.
1332. **337.** 2 p. multicoloured .. 15 12

338. Merchants with Goods.

1975. Mexican Chamber of Commerce. Cent. (1974).
1333. **338.** 80 c. multicoloured.. 5 5

339. Cervantes. **340.** 4-reales Coin of 1675.

1975. Air. Third International Cervantes Festival, Guanajuato.
1334. **339.** 1 p. 60 red and black 10 8

1975. Air. International Numismatics Convention " Mexico 74 ".
1335. **340.** 1 p. 60 bronze and blue 10 8

341. S. Novo.

1975. Air. Salvador Novo (poet and writer) First Death Anniv.
1336. **341.** 1 p. 60 multicoloured 10 8

342. " Self-portrait " (D. A. Siqueiros).

1975. Air. David Alfaro Siqueiros (painter) First Death Anniv.
1337. **342.** 1 p. 60 multicoloured 10 8

343. " Aldama " (detail from mural by Deigo Rivera).

1975. General Juan Aldama. Birth Cent. (1974).
1338. **343.** 80 c. multicoloured.. 5 5

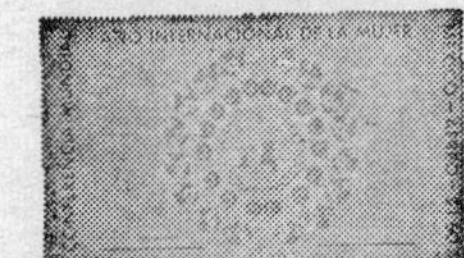

344. U.N. and I.W.Y. Emblems.

1975. Air. International Women's Year and World Conference.
1339. **344** 1 p. 60 blue and pink 10 8

345. " Eagle destroying Serpent " (Duran Codex).

1975. Tenochtitlan (Mexico City). 650th Anniv. Multicoloured.
1340. 80 c. Type **345** (postage) 5 5
1341. 1 p. 60 Arms of Mexico City (air) 10 8

346. Domingo F. Sarmineto. (educator and statesman). **347.** Teacher's Monument, Mexico City.

1975. Air. 1st Int. Congress of " Third World " Educators, Acapulco.
1342. **346.** 1 p. 60 grn. & brown 10 8

1975. Air. Mexican-Lebanese Friendship.
1343. **347.** 4 p. 30 green & brown 30 25

348. Games' Emblem.

1975. Air. 7th Pan-American Games, Mexico City.
1344. **348.** 1 p. 60 multicoloured 10 8

349. J. Carrillo. **350.** Academy Emblem.

1975. Julian Carrillo (composer and violinist) Birth Centenary.
1345. **349.** 80 c. brown and grn. 5 5

1975. Mexican Languages Academy. Cent.
1346. **350.** 80 c. yellow and brn. 5 5

351. University Building.

1975. Guadalajara University. 50th Anniv.
1347. **351.** 80 c. blk., brn. & pink 5 5

352. Dr. Atl. **353.** Road-builders.

1975. Air. Atl (Gerardo Murillo-painter and writer). Birth Centenary.
1348. **352.** 4 p. 30 multicoloured 30 25

1975. " 50 Years of Road Construction " and 15th World Road Congress, Mexico City.
1349. **353.** 80 c. blk. & grn. (post.) 5 5
1350. – 1 p. 60 blk. & blue (air) 10 8
DESIGN: 1 p. 60 Congress emblem.

1975. Air. Mexican Arts and Sciences (5th series). As T **263.** Multicoloured.
1351. 1 p. 60 Title page, F. Hernandez' " History of New Spain " 10 8
1352. 1 p. 60 A. L. Herrera (naturalist) 10 8
1353. 1 p. 60 Page from " Badiano Codex " (Aztec herbal) 10 8
1354. 1 p. 60 A. Rosenblueth Stearns (neurophysiologist) .. 10 8
1355. 1 p. 60 A. A. Duges (botanist and zoologist) .. 10 8

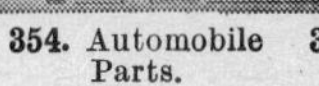

354. Automobile Parts. **355.** Aguascalientes Cathedral.

1975. Mexican Exports. Multicoloured.

1355a.	–	20 c. black (postage)	5	5
1355b.	–	40 c. brown	5	5
1356.	**354.**	50 c. blue	8	5
1357.	–	80 c. red	12	10
1357a.	–	2 p. blue & turquoise	30	25
1358.	–	3 p. brown	45	40
1358a.	–	30 c. bronze (air) ..	5	5
1359.	–	1 p. 60 black & yellow	25	20
1360.	–	1 p. 90 red and green	30	25
1360a.	–	2 p. blue and gold ..	30	25
1361.	–	4 p. 30 mauve & green	65	60
1361a.	–	5 p. 20 black and red	80	75
1361b.	–	5 p. 60 green & yellow	85	80

DESIGNS—POSTAGE. 20 c. Laboratory flasks. 40 c. Cup of coffee. 80 c. Steer marked with beef cuts. 2 p. Seashell. 3 p. Men's shoes. AIR. 30 c. Hammered copper vase. 1 p. 60 Bicycle. 1 p. 90 Valves (petroleum industry). 2 p. Books. 4 p. 30 Strawberry. 5 p. 20 Farm machinery. 5 p. 60 Cotton boll.

1975. Aguascalientes. 400th Anniversary.
1362. **355.** 50 c. black and green 5 5

356. J. T. Bodet. **358.** " Death of Cuauhtemoc " (Chavez Morado).

357. " Fresco " (J. C. Orozco).

1975. Jaime T. Bodet (author and late Director-General of U.N.E.S.C.O.). 1st Death Anniv.
1363. **356.** 80 c. brown and blue 5 5

1975. Mexican Supreme Court of Justice. 150th Anniv.
1364. **357.** 80 c. multicoloured.. 5 5

1975. Emperor Cuauhtemoc. 450th Death Anniversary.
1365. **358.** 80 c. multicoloured.. 5 5

359. Allegory of Irrigation.

1976. Nat. Irrigation Commission. 50th Anniversary.
1366. **359.** 80 c. dark blue & blue 12 10

360. City Gateway.

1976. Leon de los Aldamas, Guanajuato. 400th Anniv.
1367. **360.** 80 c. yellow & purple 12 10

361. Early Telephone. **362.** Gold Coin.

1976. Air. Telephone Centenary.
1368. **361.** 1 p. 60 black and grey 25 20

1976. Air. Int. Numismatics Convention.
1369. **362.** 1 p. 60 gold, brn. & blk. 25 20

363. Rain-God Tlaloc and Calles Dam.

1976. Air. 12th Int. Great Dams Congress.
1370 **363.** 1 p. 60 maroon & green 25 20

364. Perforation Gauge.

1976. Air. "Interphil '76" Int. Stamp Exn., Philadelphia.
1371. **364.** 1 p. 60 blk., red & blue 25 20

365. Rainbow over Industrial Skyline. **366.** Liberty Bell.

1976. Air. HABITAT. U.N. Conf. on Human Settlements.
1372. **365.** 1 p. 60 multicoloured 25 20

1976. Air. American Revolution. Bicent.
1378. **366.** 1 p. 60 blue & magenta 25 20

367. Forest Fire.

1976. Fire Prevention Campaign.
1379. **367.** 80 c. multicoloured .. 12 10

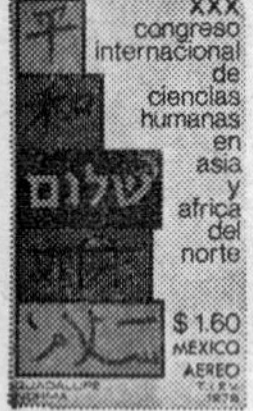

368. Peace Texts. **369.** Children on TV Screen.

1976. 30th Int. Asian and North American Science and Humanities Congress, Mexico City.
1380. **368.** 1 p. 60 multicoloured 25 20

1976. Air. 1st Latin-American Forum on Children's Television.
1381. **369.** 1 p. 60 multicoloured 25 20

370. Scout's Hat. **371.** Exhibition Emblem.

1976. Mexican Boy Scout Movement. 50th Anniv.
1382. **370.** 80 c. olive and brown 12 10

1976. "Mexico Today and Tomorrow" Exhibition.
1383. **371.** 80 c. blk., red & turq. 12 10

372. New Buildings. **373.** Dr. R. Vertiz.

1976. New Military College Buildings. Inaug.
1384. **372.** 50 c. brown and ochre 8 5

1976. Opthalmological Hospital of Our Lady of the Light. Cent.
1385. **373.** 80 c. orange & black 12 10

374. Guadalupe Basilica.

1976. Guadalupe Basilica. Inaug.
1386. **374.** 50 c. bistre and black 8 5

EXPRESS LETTER STAMPS

E 1. Express Service Messenger.

1919.
E 445. E 1. 20 c. black and red 20 8

E 2.

1934.
E 536. E 2. 10 c. blue and red 25 20

E 3. Indian Archer. E 4.

1934. New President's Assumption of Office. Imprint "OFICINA IMPRESORA DE HACIENDA-MEXICO".
E 581. E 3. 10 c. violet 30 10

1938. Imprint "TALLERES DE IMP. DE EST. Y VALORES-MEXICO".
E 610 E 3. 10 c. violet 20 8
E 731. 20 c. orange .. 8 5

1940. Optd. **1940.**
E 665. E 1. 20 c. black and red .. 10 5

1950.
E 860. E 4. 25 c. orange .. 8 5
E 910. – 60 c. green 10 5
DESIGN: 60 c. Hands and letter.

E 5.

E 6.

1956.
E 954. E 5. 35 c. purple .. 8 5
E 1293. 50 c. green .. 5 5
E 956 E 6. 80 c. red .. 12 8
E 1066. 1 p. 20 lilac .. 15 8

E 7. Watch Face.

1976.
E 1373. E 7. 2 p. black & orange 30 25

INSURED LETTER STAMPS

I 1. Safe. I 2. P.O. Treasury Vault.

1935. Inscr. as in Type I 1.
I 583. – 10 c. red 12 8
I 733. – 50 c. blue 10 8
I 734. I 1. 1 p. green 20 12
DESIGNS: 10 c. Bundle of insured letters. 50 c. Registered mailbag.

1950.
I 911. I 2. 20 c. blue 5 5
I 912. 40 c. purple 5 5
I 913. 1 p. green 10 5
I 914. 5 p. grey-green and blue 35 25
I 914a. 5 p. yell.-grn. & ultram. 75 40
I 864. 10 p. blue and red .. 1·00 60

I 3. Padlock.

1976.
I 1374. I 3. 40 c. black and turq. 5 5
I 1375. 1 p. black and turq. 15 12
I 1376. 5 p. black and turq. 75 70
I 1377. 10 p. black and turq. 1·50 1·40

OFFICIAL STAMPS

O 1. Hidalgo.

1884. No value shown.
O 156. O 1. Red 20 15
O 157. Brown 12 8
O 158. Orange 25 12
O 159. Green 20 12
O 160. Blue 30 25

1894. Stamps of 1895 handstamped **OFICIAL.**
O 231. **13.** 1 c. green 45 45
O 232. 2 c. red 50 45
O 233. 3 c. brown 65 45
O 234. **14.** 4 c. orange 65 65
O 235. **15.** 5 c. blue 85 45
O 236. **16.** 10 c. purple 85 35
O 237. **14.** 12 c. olive .. .. 2·00 1·60
O 238. **16.** 15 c. blue .. .. 1·40 1·25
O 239. 20 c. red .. .. 1·40 1·25
O 240. 50 c. mauve .. .. 3·00 2·75
O 241. **17.** 1 p. brown .. .. 11·00 4·75
O 242. 5 p. rose .. .. 35·00 16·00
O 243. 10 p. blue .. .. 60·00 30·00

1899. Stamps of 1899 handstamped **OFICIAL.**
O 276. **18.** 1 c. green .. .. 2·00 35
O 286. 1 c. purple .. .. 1·75 35
O 277. 2 c. red .. .. 2·40 35
O 287. 2 c. green .. .. 2·50 35
O 278. 3 c. brown .. .. 2·40 35
O 288. 4 c. red .. .. 4·00 25
O 279. 4 c. blue .. .. 2·40 45
O 289. 5 c. orange .. .. 3·25 50
O 280. 10 c. brown & purple 3·75 60
O 290. 10 c. orange and blue 4·00 30
O 281. 15 c. purple & lavender 3·75 60
O 282. 20 c. blue and rose .. 4·25 20
O 283. **19.** 50 c. black & purple .. 7·00 2·10
O 291. 50 c. black and red .. 6·00 1·40
O 284. **20.** 1 p. black and blue .. 8·50 1·25
O 285. **21.** 5 p. black and red .. 14·00 4·25

1911. Independence stamps optd. **OFICIAL.**
O 301. **22.** 1 c. purple 45 25
O 302. – 2 c. green 45 25
O 303. – 3 c. brown 60 25
O 304. – 4 c. red 90 25
O 305. – 5 c. orange .. .. 1·25 85
O 306. – 10 c. orge. and blue .. 75 25
O 307. – 15 c. lake and slate .. 1·40 50
O 308. – 20 c. blue and lake .. 1·25 25
O 309. **23.** 50 c. black & brown .. 3·25 1·25
O 310. – 1 p. black and blue .. 5·00 1·75
O 311. – 5 p. black and claret 15·00 5·00

1915. Stamps of 1915 optd. **OFICIAL.**
O 321. **24.** 1 c. violet 12 12
O 322. **25.** 2 c. green 12 12
O 323. **26.** 3 c. brown 12 12
O 324. 4 c. red 12 12
O 325. 5 c. orange 15 15
O 326. 10 c. blue 15 15

1915. Stamps of 1915 optd. **OFICIAL.**
O 318. **27.** 40 c. grey 44 50
O 456. 40 c. mauve 45 40
O 319. **28.** 1 p. grey and brown .. 80 80
O 457. 1 p. grey and blue .. 1·75 1·25
O 320. **29.** 5 p. blue and lake .. 3·50 3·50
O 458. 5 p. grey and green .. 12·00 10·00

1916. Nos. O 301/311 optd. with T **30.**
O 358. **22.** 1 c. purple 75
O 359. – 2 c. green 20
O 360. – 3 c. brown 25
O 361. – 4 c. red 85
O 362. – 5 c. orange 25
O 363. – 10 c. orange and blue 25
O 364. – 15 c. lake and slate .. 25
O 365. – 20 c. blue and lake .. 30
O 366. **23.** 50 c. black and brown 9·50
O 367. – 1 p. black and blue .. 80
O 368. – 5 p. black and claret £160

1918. Stamps of 1917 optd. **OFICIAL.**
O 424. **41.** 1 c. violet 45 30
O 446. 1 c. grey 10 8
O 447. – 2 c. green 10 10
O 448. – 3 c. brown 10 8
O 449. – 4 c. red 45 20
O 450. – 5 c. blue 10 10
O 451. – 10 c. blue 10 10
O 452. – 20 c. lake 30 15
O 454. – 30 c. black 60 30

1923. No. 416 optd. **OFICIAL.**
O 486. 10 p. black and brown 16·00 12·00

1923. Stamps of 1923 optd. **OFICIAL.**
O 471. **45.** 1 c. brown 8 8
O 473. **46.** 2 c. red 8 8
O 475. **47.** 3 c. brown 20 15
O 476. **48.** 4 c. green 20 20
O 461. **49.** 4 c. green 45 40
O 477. 5 c. orange 25 15
O 489. **50.** 8 c. orange 60 50
O 479. **53.** 10 c. lake 20 12
O 480. **52.** 20 c. blue 40 40
O 464. **51.** 30 c. green 12 8
O 467. **54.** 50 c. brown 20 20
O 469. **55.** 1 p. blue and lake .. 1·60 1·10

1929. Air. Optd. **OFICIAL.**
O 501 **62.** 5 c. blue (roul.) .. 15 10
O 502. **63.** 20 c. violet .. 20 20
O 492. **44.** 25 c. sepia and lake 1·25 1·25
O 490. 25 c. sepia and green 65 65

1929. Air. As 1926 Postal Congress stamp optd. **HABILITADO Servicio Oficial Aereo.**
O 493. **56.** 2 c. black .. 12·00 12·00
O 494. – 4 c. black .. 12·00 12·00
O 495. **56.** 5 c. black .. 12·00 12·00
O 496. – 10 c. black .. 12·00 12·00
O 497. **58.** 20 c. black .. 12·00 12·00
O 498. 30 c. black .. 12·00 12·00
O 499. 40 c. black .. 12·00 12·00
O 500. **59.** 1 p. black .. £275 £275

O 2.

1930. Air.
O 503. O 2. 20 c. grey 90 90
O 504. 35 c. violet .. 25 25
O 505. 40 c. blue and brown 30 30
O 506. 70 c. sepia and violet 30 30

1931. Air. Surch. **HABILITADO Quince centavos.**
O 515. O 2. 15 c. on 20 c. grey .. 20 20

1932. Air. Optd. **SERVICIO OFICIAL** in one line. T **62** perf. or roul.
O 532. **62.** 10 c. violet 12 12
O 533. 15 c. red 30 25
O 534. 20 c. sepia 35 25
O 531. **44.** 50 c. red and blue .. 25 25

1932. Stamps of 1923 optd. **SERVICIO OFICIAL** in two lines.

O 535.	45.	1 c. brown	8	8
O 536.	46.	2 c. red	5	5
O 537.	47.	3 c. brown	15	15
O 538.	49.	4 c. green	60	50
O 539.		5 c. red	30	25
O 540.	53.	10 c. lake	30	25
O 541.	52.	20 c. blue	40	40
O 544.	51.	30 c. green	35	35
O 545.	36.	40 c. mauve	40	40
O 546.	54.	50 c. brown	15	15
O 547.	55.	1 p. blue and lake	15	15

1933. Air. Optd. **SERVICIO OFICIAL** in two lines.

O 553.	44.	50 c. red and blue	30	30

1933. Air. Optd. **SERVICIO OFICIAL** in two lines.

O 548.	62.	5 c. blue (No. 476a)	8	8
O 549.		10 c. violet (No. 477)	8	8
O 550.		20 c. sepia (No. 479)	25	25
O 551.		50 c. lake (No. 481)	25	25

1934. Optd. **OFICIAL.**

O 565.	66.	15 c. blue	8	8

1938. Nos. 561/71 optd. **OFICIAL.**

O 622.	1 c. orange	20	20
O 623.	2 c. green	12	12
O 624.	4 c. red	12	12
O 625.	10 c. violet	12	12
O 626.	20 c. blue	20	20
O 627.	30 c. red	20	20
O 628.	40 c. brown	20	20
O 629.	50 c. black	25	25
O 630.	1 p. red and brown	30	30

PARCEL POST STAMPS

P 1. Mail Train.

1941.

P 732.	P 1.	10 c. red	8	5
P 733.		20 c. violet	12	5

P 2. Mail Train.

1951.

P 916.	P 2.	10 c. pink	5	5
P 917.		20 c. violet	8	5

POSTAGE DUE STAMPS

ILLUSTRATIONS British Commonwealth and all overprints and surcharges are FULL SIZE. Foreign Countries have been reduced to ¾-LINEAR.

D 1.

1908.

D 282.	D 1.	1 c. blue	80	80
D 283.		2 c. blue	80	80
D 284.		4 c. blue	80	80
D 285.		5 c. blue	80	80
D 286.		10 c. blue	80	80

MIDDLE CONGO O1

One of three colonies into which Fr. Congo was divided in 1906. Became part of Fr. Equatorial Africa in 1937. Became part of the Congo Republic within the French Community on 28th November, 1958.

1. Leopard in Ambush.

2. Bakalois Woman.

3. Coconut Palms, Libreville.

1907.

1.	1.	1 c. olive and brown	5	5
2.		2 c. violet and brown	5	5
3.		4 c. blue and brown	5	5
4.		5 c. green and blue	5	5
21.		5 c. yellow and blue	5	5
5.		10 c. red and blue	5	5
22.		10 c. green	25	25
6.		15 c. purple and red	15	10
7.		20 c. brown and blue	55	35
8.	2.	25 c. blue and green	8	5
23.		25 c. green and grey	10	10
9.		30 c. brown and green	15	15
24.		30 c. red	10	10
10.		35 c. brown and blue	15	15
11.		40 c. green and brown	12	8
12.		45 c. violet and red	75	50
13.		50 c. green and red	15	15
25.		50 c. blue and green	8	8
14.		75 c. chocolate and blue	1·00	75
15.	3.	1 fr. green and violet	1·60	1·40
16.		2 fr. violet and green	1·00	1·10
17.		5 fr. blue and red	3·75	3·50

1916. Surch. **5 c.** and large red cross.

18.	1.	10 c.+5 c. red and blue	12	10

1916. Surch. **5 c.** and small red cross.

20.	1.	10 c.+5 c. red and blue	5	5

1924. Surch. **AFRIQUE EQUATORIALE FRANCAISE** and value in figures and bars.

26.	3.	25 c. on 2 f. violet & green	5	5
27.		25 c. on 5 f. blue and red	5	5
28.		65 on 1 f. orange & brown	10	10
29.		85 on 1 f. orange & brown	10	10

1926. Surch. with value in figures and bars.

30.	2.	90 on 75 c. red	10	10
31.		1 f. 25 on 1 f. blue	5	5
32.		1 f. 50 on 1 f. blue	15	15
33.		3 f. on 5 f. brown and red	35	25
34.		10 f. on 5 f. orange & green	1·60	1·50
35.		20 f. on 5 f. brn. & purple	1·60	1·50

1924. Optd. **AFRIQUE EQUATORIALE FRANCAISE.**

36.	1.	1 c. olive and brown	5	5
37.		2 c. violet and brown	5	5
38.		4 c. blue and brown	5	5
39.		5 c. yellow and blue	5	5
40.		10 c. green and bl.-grn.	5	5
41.		10 c. red and grey	5	5
42.		15 c. purple and red	5	5
43.		20 c. brown and blue	5	5
44.		20 c. green	5	5
45.		20 c. brown and purple	5	5
46.	2.	25 c. green and grey	5	5
47.		30 c. red	5	5
48.		30 c. grey and violet	5	5
49.		30 c. green	15	12
50.		35 c. brown and blue	5	5
51.		40 c. olive and brown	10	8
52.		45 c. violet and orange	10	8
53.		50 c. blue and green	5	5
54.		50 c. yellow and black	5	5
55.		65 c. brown and blue	40	40
56.		75 c. chocolate and blue	5	5
57.		90 c. red	55	55
58.	3.	1 f. green and violet	10	10
59.		1 f. 10 mauve and brown	40	35
60.		1 f. 50 blue	90	90
61.		2 f. violet and green	12	10
62.		3 f. purple	1·40	1·40
63.		5 f. blue and red	35	30

1931. "Colonial Exhibition" key-types inscr. "MOYEN CONGO".

65.	E.	40 c. green	55	45
66.	F.	50 c. mauve	25	25
67.	G.	90 c. red	35	35
68.	H.	1 f. 50 blue	45	35

4. Mindouli Viaduct.

DESIGN: 40 c. to 1 f. 50, Pasteur Institute, Brazzaville. 1 f. 75 to 20 f. Govt. Building, Brazzaville.

1933.

69.	4.	1 c. chocolate	5	5
70.		2 c. blue	5	5
71.		4 c. olive	5	5
72.		5 c. claret	5	5
73.		10 c. green	5	5
74.		15 c. purple	5	5
75.		20 c. red on rose	1·10	65
76.		25 c. orange	5	5
77.		30 c. green	35	30
78.	–	40 c. brown	25	15
79.	–	45 c. black on green	25	20
80.	–	50 c. purple	12	12
81.	–	65 c. red on green	15	15
82.	–	75 c. black on rose	1·20	90
83.	–	90 c. red	10	10
84.	–	1 f. red	12	8
85.	–	1 f. 25 green	25	25
86.	–	1 f. 50 blue	1·00	55
87.	–	1 f. 75 violet	25	25
88.	–	2 f. olive	20	15
89.	–	3 f. black on red	35	25
90.	–	5 f. grey	2·25	2·25
91.	–	10 f. black	5·00	3·25
92.	–	20 f. brown	3·25	2·25

POSTAGE DUE STAMPS

1928. Postage Due type of France optd. **MOYEN-CONGO A.E.F.**

D 64.	D 2.	5 c. blue	5	5
D 65.		10 c. brown	5	5
D 66.		20 c. olive	10	10
D 67.		25 c. red	10	10
D 68.		30 c. red	10	10
D 69.		45 c. green	15	15
D 70.		50 c. purple	20	20
D 71.		60 c. brown on cream	25	25
D 72.		1 f. claret on cream	30	30
D 73.		2 f. red	30	30
D 74.		3 f. violet	50	50

D 1. Village.

DESIGN: 1 f. to 3 f. Steamer on Congo.

1930.

D 75.	D 1.	5 c. olive and blue	10	10
D 76.		10 c. brown and red	20	20
D 77.		20 c. brown and green	55	55
D 78.		25 c. brown and blue	55	55
D 79.		30 c. green and brown	65	55
D 80.		45 c. olive and green	65	55
D 81.		50 c. brown & mauve	65	55
D 82.		60 c. black and violet	1·00	90
D 83.	–	1 f. black and brown	1·00	90
D 84.	–	1 f. brown & magenta	1·00	90
D 85.	–	3 f. brown and red	1·00	90

D 2. "Le Djoue".

1933.

D 93.	D 2.	5 c. green	5	5
D 94.		10 c. blue on blue	5	5
D 95.		20 c. red on yellow	10	10
D 96.		25 c. claret	10	10
D 97.		30 c. red	10	10
D 98.		45 c. purple	10	10
D 99.		50 c. black	15	15
D 100.		60 c. black on red	45	45
D 101.		1 f. red	55	55
D 102.		2 f. orange	65	65
D 103.		3 f. blue	65	65

For later issues see **FRENCH EQUATORIAL AFRICA.**

MIDDLE EAST FORCES BC

General issues for use in Italian colonies occupied by British Forces: Cyrenaica, Dodecanese Islands, Eritrea, Italian Somaliland and Tripolitania.

1942. Stamps of Gt. Britain optd. **M.E.F.**

M 1.	103.	1d. red	8	25
M 6.		1d. pale red	5	5
M 2.		2d. orange	10	25
M 7.		2d. pale orange	5	5
M 3.		2½d. blue	8	20
M 8.		2½d. light blue	5	5
M 4.		3d. violet	10	15
M 9.		3d. pale violet	5	8
M 10.	104.	5d. brown	5	8
M 11.		6d. purple	5	20
M 12.	105.	9d. olive	25	30
M 13.		1s. brown	20	20
M 14.	106.	2s. 6d. green	60	60
M 15.		5s. red	1·75	3·00
M 16.	–	10s. bright blue (No. 478a)	3·50	3·75

PRICES. Our prices for Nos. M 1/16 in used condition are for stamps with identifiable postmarks of the territories in which they were issued. These stamps were also used in the United Kingdom with official sanction, from the summer of 1950 onwards, and with U.K. postmarks are worth about 25 per cent less.

POSTAGE DUE STAMPS.

1942. Postage Due stamps of Gt. Britain overprinted **M.E.F.**

MD 1.	D 1.	½d. green	5	35
MD 2.		1d. red	5	35
MD 3.		2d. black	30	70
MD 4.		3d. violet	20	70
MD 5.		1s. blue	85	1·75

MODENA E2

A state in Upper Italy, formerly a duchy and now part of Italy. Used stamps of Sardinia after the cessation of its own issues in 1860. Now uses Italian stamps.

100 centesimi = 1 lira.

1. Arms of Este. 2. Cross of Savoy.

1852. Imperf.

9.	1.	5 c. black on green	6·50	9·50
11.		10 c. black on rose	38·00	60·00
4.		15 c. black on yellow	9·00	6·00
5.		25 c. black on buff	9·00	6·50
12.		40 c. black on blue	10·00	45·00
13.		1 l. black on white	6·00	£450

1859. Imperf.

48.	2.	5 c. green	60·00	£160
50.		15 c. brown	55·00	£600
51.		15 c. grey	30·00	
53.		20 c. violet-black	£110	70·00
54.		20 c. lilac	10·00	£170
56.		40 c. red	20·00	£275
58.		80 c. brown	23·00	£3750

NEWSPAPER STAMPS

1853. As T 1, but in the 9 c. value tablet inscr. "B.G. CEN. 9." Imperf.

N 3.	1.	9 c. black on mauve	60·00	30·00
N 4.		10 c. black on lilac	9·00	60·00

ILLUSTRATIONS British Commonwealth and all overprints and surcharges are FULL SIZE. Foreign Countries have been reduced to ¾-LINEAR.

N 1.

1859. Imperf.

N 5.	N 1.	10 c. black	85·00	£325

MOHELI O1

One of the Comoro Is. adjacent to Madagascar.

1906. "Tablet" key-type inscr. "MOHELI".

1.	D.	1 c. black on blue	20	20
2.		2 c. brown on yellow	20	20
3.		4 c. claret on grey	20	20
4.		5 c. green	35	20
5.		10 c. red	45	35
6.		20 c. red on green	90	55
7.		25 c. blue	1·00	45
8.		30 c. brown	1·50	1·10
9.		35 c. black on yellow	55	35
10.		40 c. red on yellow	1·60	1·40
11.		45 c. black on green	7·50	6·00
12.		50 c. brown on blue	2·25	1·10
13.		75 c. brown on orange	2·75	2·25
14.		1 f. olive	2·75	1·75
15.		2 f. violet on red	5·50	4·50
16.		5 f. mauve on lilac	19·00	19·00

1912. Surch. in figures.

17.	D.	05 on 4 c. claret on grey	15	15
18.		05 on 20 c. red on green	45	45
19.		05 on 30 c. brown	15	15
20.		10 on 40 c. red on yellow	15	15
21.		10 on 45 c. black on green	15	15
22.		10 on 50 c. brown on blue	25	25

MONACO E2

A principality on the S. coast of France including the town of Monte Carlo.

100 centimes = 1 French franc.

1. Prince Charles III. 2. Prince Albert. 3. War Widow and Monaco.

1885.

1.	1.	1 c. olive	2·25	2·25
2.		2 c. lilac	8·00	6·50
3.		5 c. blue	10·00	7·50
4.		10 c. brown on yellow	13·00	8·00
5.		15 c. rose	42·00	3·25
6.		25 c. green	£110	11·00
7.		40 c. blue on rose	13·00	9·50
8.		75 c. black on rose	30·00	17·00
9.		1 f. black on yellow	£275	£130
10.		5 f. red on green	£750	£550

1891.

11.	2.	1 c. green	12	12
12.		2 c. lilac	12	12
13a.		5 c. blue	8·50	65
22.		5 c. green	20	12

14. 2. 10 c. brown on yellow .. 24·00 3·75
23. 10 c. red 20 12
15. 15 c. rose .. .. 25·00 95
24. 15 c. brown on yellow .. 50 25
25. 15 c. green .. 80 75
16. 25 c. green .. .. 60·00 6·50
26. 25 c. blue .. .. .. 1·25 35
17. 40 c. blue on pink .. 1·00 55
18. 50 c. brown on orange .. 1·40 80
19. 75 c. brown on buff .. 4·25 2·10
22. 1 f. black on yellow .. 2·50 2·10
21. 5 f. rose on green .. 18·00 14·00
28. 5 f. mauve .. .. 50·00 55·00
29. 5 f. green .. .. 6·50 6·50

1914. Surcharged +5c
30. 2. 10 c.+5 c. red .. .. 1·25 1·00

1919. War Orphans Fund.
31. 3. 2 c.+3 c. mauve .. .. 4·00 4·00
32. 5 c.+5 c. green .. .. 2·25 2·25
33. 15 c.+10 c. red .. .. 2·25 2·25
34. 25 c.+15 c. blue .. .. 7·00 7·00
35. 50 c.+50 c. brn. on orge. 27·00 27·00
36. 1 f.+1 f. black on yellow 95·00 95·00
37. 5 f.+5 f. red £300 £300

1920. Princess Charlotte's Marriage. Nos. 33/7 optd. **20 Mars 1920** or surch. also.
38. 3. 2 c.+3 c. on 15 c.+10 c. 8·50 8·50
39. 2 c.+3 c. on 25 c.+15 c.. 8·50 8·50
40. 2 c+3 c. on 50 c.+50 c... 8·50 8·50
41. 5 c.+5 c. on 1 f.+1 f. .. 8·50 8·50
42. 5 c.+5 c. on 5 f.+5 f. .. 7·50 7·50
43. 15 c.+10 c. red .. .. 4·50 4·50
44. 25 c.+15 c. blue .. .. 1·75 1·50
45. 50 c.+50 c. brn. on orge.. 9·50 9·50
46. 1 f.+1 f. black on yellow 9·50 9·50
47. 5 f.+5 f. red £1400 £1400

1921. Princess Antoinette's Baptism. Optd. **28 Decembre 1920** or surch. also.
48. 2. 5 c. green 12 12
49. 75 c. brown on buff .. 1·75 1·75
50. 2 f. on 5 f. mauve .. 10·00 10·00

1922. Surch.
51. 2. 20 c. on 15 c. green .. 55 35
52. 25 c. on 10 c. red .. 25 25
53. 50 c. on 1 f. black on yellow 2·10 1·60

4. Prince Albert I.

5. Viaduct and St. Devote.

1922.
54. 4. 25 c. brown .. .. 1·90 1·60
55. – 30 c. green 40 30
56. – 30 c. red 25 20
57. 5. 40 c. brown 25 20
58. – 50 c. blue .. .. 1·75 1·75
59. – 60 c. grey 12 12
60. – 1 f. black on yellow .. 12 12
61a.– 2 f. red 20 20
62. – 5 f. brown.. .. 11·00 11·00
63. – 5 f. green on blue .. 2·25 1·90
64. – 10 f. red .. .. 3·75 2·75
DESIGNS—As T 5: 30 c., 50 c. Oceanographic Museum. 60 c., 1 f., 2 f. Rock, Monaco. 5 f., 10 f. Palace, Monaco.

9. Prince Louis.

10. Prince Louis and Palace.

1923.
65. 9. 10 c. green 15 15
66. 15 c. red 35 35
67. 20 c. brown 20 20
68. 25 c. purple 15 15
69. 10. 50 c. blue 12 12

1924. Surch. with new value and bars.
70. 2. 45 c. on 50 c. brn. on oran. 30 30
71. 75 c. on 1 f. black on yell. 15 15
72. 85 c. on 5 f. green.. .. 15 15

11.

12.

13.

14. Viaduct and St. Devote.

1924.
73. 11. 1 c. slate 5 5
74. 2 c. brown 5 5
75. 3 c. magenta 40 30
76. 5 c. orange 8 8
77. 10 c. blue 12 8
78. 12. 15 c. green 8 8
79. 15 c. purple 65 30
80. 20 c. purple 5 5
81. 20 c. red 12 10
82. 25 c. red 5 5
83. 25 c. red on yellow .. 8 8
84. 30 c. orange 8 5
85. 40 c. brown 5 5
86. 40 c. blue 8 5
87. 45 c. black 25 12
88. 13. 50 c. green 10 8
89. 12. 50 c. brown and yellow 8 5
90. 13. 60 c. brown 10 8
91. 12. 60 c. olive and green 8 5
92. 75 c. olive on green .. 8 8
93. 75 c. red on yellow .. 8 8
94. 75 c. black 20 10
95. 80 c. red on yellow .. 15 8
96. 90 c. red on yellow .. 30 20
97. 14. 1 f. black on yellow .. 8 8
98. 1 f. 05 mauve 8 8
99. 1 f. 10 green .. .. 3·50 1·60
100. 12. 1 f. 25 blue 8 8
101. 1 f. 50 blue 50 30
102. – 2 f. sepia and mauve .. 50 40
103. – 3 f. lav. & red on yellow 2·25 1·60
104. – 5 f. red and green .. 2·25 1·60
105. – 10 f. blue and brown .. 3·75 2·75
DESIGN—As T 14: 2 f. to 10 f. Monaco.

1926. Surch.
106. 12. 30 c. on 25 c. red .. 8 5
107. 50 c. on 60 c. ol. on grn. 25 10
108. 14. 50 c. on 1 f. 05 mauve.. 20 15
109. 50 c. on 1 f. 10 green .. 1·10 60
110. 12. 50 c. on 1 f. 25 blue .. 25 15
111. 1 f. 25 on 1 f. blue .. 20 10
112. – 1 f. 50 on 2 f. sepia and mauve (No. 102) .. 65 45

15. Princes Charles III, Louis II and Albert I.

1926. Int. Philatelic Exn.
113. 15. 50 c. red 45 45
114. 1 f. 50 blue 45 45
115. 3 f. violet 45 45

16.

17. Palace Entrance.

18. St. Devote's Church.

19. Prince Louis II.

1933. National Festivity issue.
116. 16. 1 c. plum 5 5
117. 2 c. green 5 5
118. 3 c. purple 5 5
119. 5 c. red 5 5
120. 10 c. blue 5 5
121. 15 c. violet 25 20
122. 17. 15 c. red 25 12
123. 20 c. brown 25 12
124. A. 25 c. sepia 25 15
125. 18. 30 c. green 25 15
126. 19. 40 c. sepia 60 30
127. B 45 c. brown 90 35
128. 19. 50 c. violet 50 12
129. C. 65 c. green 70 20
130. D. 75 c. blue 95 65
131. 19. 90 c. red 95 65
132. 18. 1 f. brown .. .. 5·00 3·25
133. D. 1 f. 25 claret .. .. 1·25 90
134. 19. 1 f. 50 blue .. .. 4·50 2·10
135. A. 1 f. 75 claret .. .. 5·50 1·25
136. 1 f. 75 red .. .. 3·25 1·75
137. B. 2 f. blue .. .. 1·75 1·25
138. 17. 3 f. violet .. .. 2·25 1·75
139. A. 3 f. 50 orange.. .. 12·00 7·50
140. 18. 5 f. purple .. .. 7·00 6·00
141. A. 10 f. blue .. .. 27·00 19·00
142. C. 20 f. black .. .. 50·00 32·00
DESIGNS—As T 17—HORIZ. A. The Prince's Residence. B. The Rock of Monaco. C. Palace Gardens. D. Fortifications and Harbour.
For other stamps in T 16 see Nos. 249, etc.

1933. Air. Surch. with aeroplane and value.
143. – 1 f. 50 on 5 f. red and green (No. 104) .. 8·50 5·50

20. Palace Gardens.

DESIGNS—HORIZ. 90 c. The Rock. 1 f. 50, The Bay of Monaco. VERT. 2 f., 5 f. Prince Louis II.

1927. Charity.
143. 20. 50 c.+50 c. green .. 75 75
144. – 90 c.+90 c. red .. 75 75
145. – 1 f. 50+1 f. 50 blue .. 1·10 1·10
146. – 2 f.+2 f. violet .. 1·75 1·75
147. – 5 f.+5 f. red.. .. 24·00 24·00

1937. Postage Due stamps optd. **POSTES** or surch. also.
149. D 3. 5 c. on 10 c. violet .. 20 20
150. 10 c. violet 25 25
151. 15 c. on 30 c. bistre .. 30 30
152. 20 c. on 30 c. bistre .. 25 30
153. 25 c. on 60 c. red .. 30 30
154. 30 c. bistre 60 60
155. 40 c. on 60 c. red .. 40 40
156. 50 c. on 60 c. red .. 50 50
157. 65 c. on 1 f. blue .. 50 50
158. 85 c. on 1 f. blue .. 50 90
159. 1 f. blue 90 90
160. 2 f. 15 on 2 f. red .. 1·40 1·40
161. 2 f. 25 on 2 f. red .. 1·90 1·90
162. 2 f. 50 on 2 f. red .. 2·25 2·25

22. Prince Louis II.

24. Monaco Hospital.

1938.
164. 22. 55 c. brown 80 40
165. 65 c. violet .. .. 4·00 2·75
166. 70 c. brown 5 5
167. 90 c. violet 5 5
168. 1 f. red .. .. 1·25 1·10
169. 1 f. 25 red 5 5
170. 1 f. 75 blue .. .. 2·25 1·40
171. 2 f. 25 blue 8 8

1938. Anti-Cancer Fund. 40th Anniv. of Discovery of Radium. Inscr. as in T 24.
172. – 65 c.+25 c. green .. 2·75 2·75
173. 24. 1 f. 75+50 c. blue .. 2·75 2·75
DESIGN—VERT. 65 c. Pierre and Marie Curie.

25. The Cathedral.

29. Monaco Harbour.

31. Louis II Stadium.

33. Lucien.

1939.
174. 25. 20 c. mauve 10 10
175. – 25 c. brown 20 12
176. – 30 c. green 12 12
177. – 40 c. red 25 15
178. – 45 c. purple 12 12
179. – 50 c. green 12 12
180. – 60 c. red 20 12
181. – 60 c. green 12 12
182. 29. 70 c. lilac 15 10
183. 75 c. green 12 10
184. – 1 f. black 12 10
185. – 1 f. 30 brown 12 10
186. – 2 f. purple 12 10
187. – 2 f. 50 red .. .. 5·50 3·00
188. – 2 f. 50 blue 20 12
189. 29. 3 f. red 15 12
190. 25. 5 f. blue 50 15
191. – 10 f. green 35 12
192. – 20 f. blue 55 12
DESIGNS—VERT. 25 c., 40 c., 2 f. Place St. Nicholas. 30 c., 60 c., 20 f. Palace Gateway. 50 c., 1 f., 1 f. 30, Palace of Monaco. HORIZ. 45 c., 2 f. 50, 10 f. Aerial view of Monaco.
See also Nos. 251, etc.

1939. Opening of Louis II Stadium, Monaco.
198. 31. 10 f. green .. .. 42·00 38·00

1939. Charity. XVI-XVIII-century portrait designs and view.
199. 33. 5 c.+5 c. black.. .. 20 20
200. – 10 c.+10 c. purple .. 25 25
201. – 45 c.+15 c. green .. 70 70
202. – 70 c.+30 c. mauve .. 1·50 1·50
203. – 90 c.+35 c. violet .. 1·50 1·50
204. – 1 f.+1 f. blue .. .. 6·00 6·00
205. – 2 f.+2 f. red .. .. 7·00 7·00
206. – 2 f. 25+1 f. 25 blue .. 9·00 9·00
207. – 3 f.+3 f. red .. .. 14·00 14·00
208. – 5 f.+5 f. red .. .. 20·00 20·00
DESIGNS—VERT. 10 c. Honore II. 45 c. Louis I. 70 c. Charlotte de Gramont. 90 c. Antoine I. 1 f. Marie de Lorraine. 2 f. Jacques I. 2 f. 25 c. Louise-Hippolyte. 3 f. Honore III. HORIZ. 5 f. The Rock of Monaco.

1939. 8th Int. University Games. As T 31 but inscr. "VIIIeme JEUX UNIVERSITAIRES INTERNATIONAUX 1939".
209. 40 c. green 30 30
210. 70 c. brown 55 55
211. 90 c. violet 55 55
212. 1 f. 25 red 55 55
213. 2 f. 25 blue .. .. 1·10 1·10

1940. Red Cross Ambulance Fund. As Nos. 174/92 in new colours surch. with Red Cross and premium.
214. 25. 20 c.+1 f. violet .. 1·00 1·00
215. – 25 c.+1 f. green .. 1·00 1·00
216. – 30 c.+1 f. red .. 1·00 1·00
217. – 40 c.+1 f. blue .. 1·00 1·00
218. – 45 c.+1 f. red .. 1·00 1·00
219. – 50 c.+1 f. brown .. 1·00 1·00
220. – 60 c.+1 f. green .. 1·00 1·00
221. 29. 75 c.+1 f. black .. 1·00 1·00
222. – 1 f.+1 f. red .. .. 1·00 1·00
223. – 2 f.+1 f. slate .. 1·00 1·00
224. – 2 f. 50+1 f. green .. 3·25 3·25
225. 29. 3 f.+1 f. blue .. 3·75 3·75
226. 25. 5 f.+1 f. black .. 4·00 4·00
227. – 10 f.+5 f. blue .. 4·50 4·50
228. – 20 f.+5 f. maroon .. 5·50 5·50

34. Prince Louis II.

1941.
229. 34. 40 c. red 5 5
230. 80 c. green 5 5
231. 1 f. violet 5 5
232. 1 f. 20 green 5 5
233. 1 f. 50 red 5 5
234. 1 f. 50 violet 5 5
235. 2 f. green 5 5
236. 2 f. 40 red 5 5
237. 2 f. 50 blue 12 12
238. 4 f. blue 5 5

35.

36.

1941. Charity.
239. 35. 25 c.+25 c. purple .. 60 60
240. 36. 50 c.+25 c. brown .. 60 60
241. 75 c.+50 c. purple .. 70 70
242. 35. 1 f.+1 f. blue 70 70
243. 36. 1 f. 50+1 f. 50 red .. 90 90
244. 35. 2 f.+2 f. green .. 90 90
245. 35. 2 f. 50+2 f. blue .. 90 90
246. 35. 3 f.+3 f. brown .. 90 90
247. 36. 5 f.+5 f. green.. .. 1·10 1·10
248. 35. 10 f.+8 f. sepia .. 1·40 1·40

1941. New values and colours.
249. 16. 10 c. black 5 5
250. – 30 c. red (as No. 176).. 12 12
251. 16. 30 c. green 5 5
252. 40 c. red 5 5
253. 50 c. violet 5 5
362. 25. 50 c. brown 5 5
254. 16. 60 c. blue 5 5
363. – 60 c. pink (as No. 175) 8 8
255. 16. 70 c. brown 5 5
256. 25. 80 c. green 5 5
257. – 1 f. brown (as No. 178) 5 5
258. 29. 1 f. 20 blue 12 12
259. – 1 f. 50 blue (as No. 175) 12 12
260. 29. 2 f. blue 5 5
261. – 2 f. grn. (as No. 179) .. 8 8
262. – 3 f. black (as No. 175) .. 5 5
364. – 3 f. purple (as No. 176) 15 12
391. – 3 f. green (as No. 175) 20 15
263. 25. 4 f. mauve 20 20
365. – 4 f. green (as No. 175) 20 15
264. – 4 f. 50 violet (as No. 179) 8 8
265. – 5 f. green (as No. 176) 8 8
392. – 5 f. green (as No. 178) 15 8
393. – 5 f. red (as No. 176).. 15 10
266. – 6 f. violet (as No. 179) 20 20
368. – 8 f. brown (as No. 179) 65 40

267. 25. 10 f. blue 8 10
370. – 10 f. brn. (as No. 179) 80 35
394. 29. 10 f. yellow 30 5
268. 15 f. red 12 10
269. – 20 f. brn. (as No. 178) 12 10
373. – 20 f. red (as No. 178).. 30 12
270. 29. 25 f. green 60 45
374. 25 f. black .. .. 3·75 2·10
397. – 25 f. blue (as No. 176) 3·00 2·00
398. – 25 f. red (as No. 179).. 60 35
399. – 30 f. blue (as No. 176) 1·50 1·25
400. – 35 f. blue (as No. 179) 90 50
401. 25. 40 f. red .. .. 1·50 80
402. – 50 f. violet 90 45
403. – 65 f. violet (as No. 178) 1·75 1·40
404. 25. 70 f. yellow .. .. 1·75 1·40
405. – 75 f. grn. (as No. 175) 4·50 1·75
406. – 85 f. clar. (as No. 175) 1·00 90
407. – 100 f. turquoise (as No. 178) .. .. 1·25 1·25

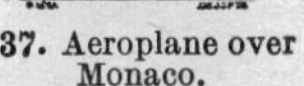

37. Aeroplane over Monaco.

38. Propeller and Palace.

39. Arms, Aeroplane and Globe.

DESIGNS—VERT. 20 f. Pegasus. HORIZ. 50 f. Albatross over Bay of Monaco.

1942. Air.

271. 37. 5 f. green 12 10
272. 10 f. green 12 12
273. 38. 15 f. sepia 12 12
274. – 20 f. red 20 20
275. – 50 f. purple .. .. 1·25 90
276. 39. 100 f. red and purple .. 1·00 60

40. Charles II.

41. Louise-Hippolyte.

1942. National Relief Fund. Royal Personages.

277. – 2 c.+3 c. blue 8 8
278. 40. 5 c.+5 c. red 8 8
279. – 10 c.+5 c. black .. 8 8
280. – 20 c.+10 c. green .. 8 8
281. – 30 c.+30 c. purple .. 8 8
282. 41. 40 c.+40 c. red .. 8 8
283. – 50 c.+50 c. violet .. 8 8
284. – 75 c.+75 c. purple .. 8 8
285. – 1 f.+1 f. green .. 8 8
286. – 1 f. 50+1 f. red .. 8 8
287. – 2 f. 50+2 f. 50 violet .. 60 60
288. – 3 f.+3 f. blue .. 60 60
289. – 5 f.+5 f. sepia .. 65 65
290. – 10 f.+5 f. purple .. 70 70
291. – 20 f.+5 f. blue .. 75 75

PORTRAITS: 2 c. Rainier Grimaldi. 10 c. Jeanne Grimaldi. 20 c. Charles Auguste, Goyon de Matignon. 30 c. Jacques I. 50 c. Charlotte Grimaldi. 75 c. Marie Charles Grimaldi. 1 f. Honore III. 1 f. 50, Honore IV. 2 f. 50, Honore V. 3 f. Florestan I. 5 f. Charles III. 10 f. Albert I. 20 f. Princess Marie-Victoire.

42. Prince Louis II.

43. St. Devote.

44. Blessing the Sea.

45. Arrival of St. Devote at Monaco.

1943.

292. 42. 50 f. violet 35 35

1944. Charity. Festival of St. Devote.

293. 43. 50 c.+50 c. brown .. 5 5
294. – 70 c.+80 c. blue .. 5 5
295. – 80 c.+70 c. green .. 5 5
296. – 1 f.+1 f. purple .. 5 5
297. – 1 f. 50+1 f. 50 red .. 20 20
298. 44. 2 f.+2 f. purple .. 20 20
299. – 5 f.+2 f. violet .. 20 20
300. – 10 f.+40 f. blue .. 20 20
301. 45. 20 f.+60 f. blue .. 2·25 2·25

DESIGNS—VERT. 70 c., 1 f. Various processional scenes. 1 f. 50 Burning the boat. 10 f. Trial scene. HORIZ. 80 c. Procession. 5 f. St. Devote's Church.

1945. Air. As Nos. 272/6 (colours changed) surch.

302. 1 f.+4 f. on 10 f. red .. 8 8
303. 1 f.+4 f. on 15 f. brown 8 8
304. 1 f.+4 f. on 20 f. brown 8 8
305. 1 f.+4 f. on 50 f. blue .. 8 8
306. 1 f.+4 f. on 100 f. purple.. 8 8

46. Prince Louis II. 47.

1946.

361. 46. 30 c. black 12 5
389. 50 c. olive 5 5
390. 1 f. violet 10 8
307. 2 f. 50 green 5 5
308. 3 f. mauve 5 5
366. 5 f. brown 20 10
309. 6 f. red 5 5
367. 6 f. purple 40 12
310. 10 f. blue 5 5
369. 10 f. orange 10 5
371. 12 f. red .. .. 1·00 45
395. 12 f. slate .. .. 1·50 1·00
396. 15 f. lake .. .. 1·50 1·00
372. 18 f. blue .. .. 1·50 1·10
311. 47. 50 f. grey 75 55
312. 100 f. red .. .. 1·25 1·00

48. Child Praying.

49. Nurse and Baby.

1946. Child Welfare Fund.

313. 48. 1 f.+3 f. green .. 12 12
314. 2 f.+4 f. red .. 12 12
315. 4 f.+6 f. blue .. 12 12
316. 5 f.+40 f. mauve .. 20 20
317. 10 f.+60 f. red .. 20 20
318. 15 f.+100 f. blue .. 40 40

1946. Anti-tuberculosis Fund.

319. 49. 2 f.+8 f. blue .. 8 8

1946. Air. Optd. **OPSTE AERIENNE** over aeroplane.

320. 47. 50 f. grey 55 55
321. 100 f. red 90 90

50. Steamship and Chart.

1946. Stamp Day.

322. 50. 3 f.+2 f. blue 5 5

51.

1946. Air.

323. 51. 40 f. red 35 25
324. 50 f. brown 50 30
325. 100 f. green 70 50
326. 200 f. violet .. .. 1·00 70
326a. 300 f. blue .. .. 20·00 15·00
326b. 500 f. green .. .. 11·00 10·00
326c. 1000 f. violet .. .. 22·00 16·00

52. Pres. Roosevelt and Palace of Monaco.

53. Pres. Roosevelt.

1946. President Roosevelt Commem.

327. 53. 10 c. mauve (postage).. 8 8
328. – 30 c. blue 8 8
329. 52. 60 c. green 8 8
330. – 1 f. sepia 25 25
331. – 2 f.+3 f. green .. 35 35
332. – 3 f. violet 45 45
333. – 5 f. red (air) 20 20
334. – 10 f. black 15 15
335. 53. 15 f.+10 f. orange .. 40 40

DESIGNS—HORIZ. 30 c., 5 f. Rock of Monaco. 2 f. Viaduct and Harbour. VERT. 1 f., 3 f., 10 f. Map of Monaco.

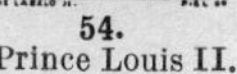

54. Prince Louis II.

55. Pres. Roosevelt, Philatelist.

56. Statue of Liberty and New York Harbour.

57. Prince Charles III.

1947. Participation in the Cent. International Philatelic Exn., New York.

(a) Postage.

336. 54. 10 f. blue 85 85

(b) Air. Dated "1847 1947".

337. 55. 50 c. violet 10 10
338. – 1 f. 50 mauve 12 12
339. – 3 f. orange 15 15
340. – 10 f. blue 70 70
341. 56. 15 f. red 80 80

DESIGNS—HORIZ. As T 55: 1 f. 50, Oceanographic Museum, Monte Carlo. 3 f. G.P.O., New York. As T 56: 10 f. Bay of Monaco.

1948. Stamp Day.

342. 57. 6 f.+4 f. green on blue 8 8

58. Diving.

59. Tennis.

1948. Olympic Games, Wembley. Inscr. "JEUX OLYMPIQUES 1948".

343. – 50 c. green (postage) .. 10 10
344. – 1 f. red 10 10
345. – 2 f. blue 25 25
346. – 2 f. 50 red 30 25
347. 58. 4 f. slate 35 35
348. – 5 f.+5 f. brown (air) .. 2·75 2·75
349 – 6 f.+9 f. violet .. 3·25 3·25
350. 59. 10 f.+15 f. red .. 3·75 3·75
351. – 15 f.+25 f. blue .. 5·50 5·50

DESIGNS—HORIZ. 50 c. Hurdling. 15 f. Yachting. VERT. 1 f. Running. 2 f. Throwing the discus. 2 f. 50, Basket-ball. 5 f. Rowing. 6 f. Ski-ing.

60. The Salmacis Nymph.

61. F. J. Bosio.

1948. Francois Joseph Bosio (sculptor). Death Cent. Inscr. "F. J. BOSIO 1769–1845".

352. 60. 50 c. green (postage) .. 8 8
353. – 1 f. red 8 8
354. – 2 f. blue 10 10
355. – 2 f. 50 violet 15 15
356. 61. 4 f. mauve 20 20
357. – 5 f.+5 f. blue (air) .. 1·40 1·40
358. – 6 f.+9 f. green .. 1·40 1·40
359. – 10 f.+15 f. red .. 2·25 2·25
360. – 15 f.+25 f. brown .. 3·00 3·25

DESIGNS—VERT. 1 f., 5 f. Hercules struggling with Achelous. 2 f., 6 f. Aristaeus (Garden God). 15 f. The Salmacis Nymph (36×48 mm.). HORIZ. 2 f. 50, 10 f. Hyacinthus awaiting his turn to throw a quoit.

62. Tropical Gardens.

63. "Spitzberg".

1949. Prince Albert I. Birth Cent.

375. – 2 f. blue (postage) .. 5 5
376. 62. 3 f. green 12 12
377. – 4 f. brown and blue .. 12 12
378. 63. 5 f. red 12 12
379. – 6 f. violet 20 20
380. – 10 f. sepia 20 20
381. – 12 f. pink 25 25
382. – 18 f. orange and brown 1·10 1·00
383. – 20 f. brown (air) .. 40 40
384. – 25 f. blue 40 40
385. – 40 f. green 45 45
386. – 50 f. green, brn. & blk.. 60 60
387. – 100 f. red .. .. 1·40 1·40
388. – 200 f. orange .. .. 3·25 3·25

DESIGNS—HORIZ. 2 f. Yacht "Hirondelle I". 4 f. Oceanographic Museum, Monaco. 10 f. "Hirondelle II". 12 f. Whale hunting. 18 f. Stone-age drawing of buffalo. 20 f. Proclamation of Constitution, 1911. 25 f. Paris Institute of Palaeontology. 200 f. Coin with effigy of Albert. VERT. 6 f. Statue of Albert. 40 f. Anthropological Museum. 50 f. Prince Albert. 100 f. Oceanographic Institute, Paris.

64. Palace of Monaco and Globe.

1949. U.P.U. 75th Anniv.

410. 64. 5 f. green (postage) .. 10 10
411. 10 f. orange .. .. 1·40 1·40
412. 15 f. red 15 15
413. 25 f. blue (air) 30 30
414. 40 f. sepia and brown.. 45 45
415. 50 f. blue and green .. 50 50
416. 100 f. blue and claret .. 1·25 1·25

65. Prince Rainier III and Monaco Palace.

66. Prince Rainier III.

1950. Accession of Prince Rainier III.

417. **65.** 10 c. pur. & red (post) .. 5 5
418. 50 c. brown & orange .. 5 5
419. 1 f. violet 5 5
420. 5 f. green 30 30
421. 15 f. red 45 45
422. 25 f. blue and green .. 90 90
423. 50 f. lake & blk. (air) .. 1·25 1·00
424. 100 f. blue and brown .. 1·75 1·40

1950.

425. **66.** 50 c. violet 5 5
426. 1 f. brown 8 8
434. 5 f. green 90 90
427. 6 f. green 20 12
428. 8 f. green 65 45
429. 8 f. orange 25 15
435. 10 f. orange .. .. 1·75 1·75
430. 12 f. blue 40 25
431. 15 f. red 50 20
432. 15 f. blue 30 12
433. 18 f. red 80 55

67. Prince Albert I.

68. Edmond and Jules de Goncourt.

1951. Unveilling of Prince Albert Statue.

436. **67.** 15 f. blue .. .. 2·50 2·50

1951. Goncourt Academy. 50th Anniv.

437. **68.** 15 f. purple .. .. 2·25 2·25

69. St. Vincent de Paul.

71. St. Peter's Keys and Papal Bull.

70. Judgment of St. Devote.

1951. Holy Year. Inscr. "ANNO SANTO".

438. **69.** 10 c. blue and red .. 8 8
439. – 50 c. violet and claret .. 8 8
440. **70.** 1 f. green and brown .. 8 8
441. **71.** 2 f. red and purple .. 20 20
442. – 5 f. emerald 25 25
443. – 12 f. violet 35 35
444. – 15 f. red .. .. 1·40 1·40
445. – 20 f. brown .. .. 1·40 1·40
446. – 25 f. blue .. .. 1·75 1·75
447. – 40 f. violet and magenta 2·25 2·25
448. – 50 f. brown and olive .. 2·25 2·25
449. – 100 f. sepia .. .. 7·50 7·50

DESIGNS—TRIANGULAR: 50 c. Pope Pius XII. As T **71**—HORIZ. 5 f. Mosaic. VERT. 12 f. Prince Rainier III in St. Peter's. 15 f. St. Nicholas of Patarc. 20 f. St. Romain. 25 f. St. Charles Borromeo. 40 f. Coliseum. 50 f. Chapel of St. Devote. As T **70.**—VERT. 100 f. Rainier of Westphalia.

72. Wireless Mast and Monaco.

73. Seal of Prince Rainier III.

74. Gallery of Hercules.

1951. Monte Carlo Radio Station.

450. **72.** 1 f. orange, red and blue 10 10
451. 15 f. purple, red & violet 45 30
452. 30 f. brown and blue .. 65 55

1951.

453. **73.** 1 f. violet 20 20
454. 5 f. black 40 40
512. 5 f. violet 35 25
513. 6 f. red 60 40
455. 8 f. claret 90 70
514. 8 f. brown 60 60
456. 15 f. green .. .. 1·25 1·10
515. 15 f. blue 90 90
457. 30 f. blue .. .. 1·60 1·50
516. 30 f. green .. .. 1·25 1·10

1952. Monaco Postal Museum.

460. **74.** 5 f. chestnut and brown 25 25
461. 15 f. violet and purple .. 30 12
462. 30 f. indigo and blue .. 35 35

75. Football.

1953. 15th Olympic Games, Helsinki. Inscr. "HELSINKI 1952".

463. – 1 f. mag. & vio. (postage) 15 15
464. **75.** 2 f. blue and emerald .. 15 15
465. – 3 f. pale and deep blue .. 15 15
466. – 5 f. green and brown .. 40 30
467. – 8 f. red and lake .. 45 40
468. – 15 f. brown, grn. & blue 60 35
469. – 40 f. black (air) .. 3·25 2·25
470. – 50 f. violet .. .. 3·25 2·25
471. – 100 f. green .. .. 3·50 3·00
472. – 200 f. red .. .. 4·00 4·00

DESIGNS: 1 f. Basket-ball. 3 f. Yachting. 5 f. Cycling. 8 f. Gymnastics. 15 f. Louis II. Stadium, Monaco. 40 f. Running. 50 f. Fencing. 10 f. Rifle, target and Arms of Monaco. 200 f. Olympic torch.

76. "Journal Inedit".

1953. Cent. of Publication of Journal by E. and J. de Goncourt.

473. **76.** 5 f. green 25 20
474. 15 f. brown 40 30

77. Physalia, Yacht, Prince Albert, Richet and Portier.

1953. Discovery of Anaphylaxis. 50th Anniv.

475. **77.** 2 f. violet, green & brn. 8 5
476. 5 f. red, lake and green 20 15
477. 15 f. lilac, blue and green 90 70

78. F. C. Ozanam.

79. St. Jean-Baptiste de la Salle.

1954. Ozanam (founder of St. Vincent de Paul Conference). Death Cent.

478. **78.** 1 f. vermilion 5 5
479. – 5 f. blue 15 15
480. **78.** 15 f. black 40 40

DESIGN: 5 f. Sister of Charity.

1954. St. J.-B. de la Salle (educationist.)

481. **79.** 1 f. red 5 5
482. – 5 f. sepia 15 15
483. **79.** 15 f. blue 40 40

DESIGN: 5 f. De la Salle and children.

80. 81. 82. 83. Seal of Prince Rainer III.

1954. Arms.

484. – 50 c. verm., mag. & blk. 5 5
485. – 70 c. red, blue and black 5 5
486. **80.** 60 c. red, green & black 5 5
487. – 1 f. red and blue .. 5 5
488. **81.** 2 f. red, verm. & rose .. 5 5
489. – 3 f. red, emerald & black 5 5
490. **82.** 5 f. red, pur., grn. & blk. 5 5

DESIGNS—HORIZ. 50 c as T **80.** VERT. 70 c., 1 f., 3 r. as T **81.**

1954. Precancelled.

491. **83.** 4 f. red 25 10
492. 5 f. blue 5 5
493. 8 f. green 25 20
494. 8 f. purple 12 5
495. 10 f. green 5 5
496. 12 f. violet 40 25
497. 15 f. orange 25 15
498. 20 f. green 25 20
499. 24 f. brown 90 65
500. 30 f. blue 35 25
501. 40 f. chocolate .. 45 30
502. 45 f. red 45 35
503. 55 f. blue 50 40

See also Nos. 680/3.

84. Lambarene.

85. Dr. Albert Schweitzer.

1955. 80th Birthday of Dr. Schweitzer (Humanitarian).

504. **84.** 2 f. green, turquoise and indigo (postage) .. 8 8
505. **85.** 5 f. blue and emerald .. 40 40
506. – 15 f. purple, blk. & grn. 1·10 1·10
507. – 200 f. slate, green and blue (air) .. .. 7·00 6·50

DESIGNS—As T **85**: 15 f. Lambarene Hospital. HORIZ. (48 × 27 mm.): Schweitzer and jungle scene.

86. Cormorants.

1955. Air.

508a. – 100 f. indigo and blue .. 5·50 3·25
509. – 200 f. black and blue .. 6·50 3·25
510. – 500 f. grey and green .. 7·00 6·50
511a. **86.** 1,000 f. black, turquoise and green .. .. 55·00 55·00

DESIGNS—As T **86**: 100 f. Sea-swallows. 200 f. Seagulls. 500 f. Albatrosses.

87. Eight Starting Points.

88. Prince Rainier III.

1955. 25th Monte Carlo Car Rally.

517. **87.** 100 f. red and brown .. 16·00 16·00

1955.

518. **88.** 6 f. maroon and green .. 8 5
519. 8 f. violet and red .. 8 5
520. 12 f. green and red .. 12 5
521. 15 f. blue and purple .. 20 12
522. 18 f. blue and orange .. 25 15
523. 20 f. turquoise 30 25
524. 25 f. black and orange .. 20 15
525. 30 f. sepia and blue .. 1·10 85
526. 30 f. violet 35 15
527. 35 f. brown 90 40
528. 50 f. lake and green .. 40 30

See also Nos. 627/41.

89. "La Maison a Vapeur".

90. "The 500 Millions of the Begum".

92. U.S.S. "Nautilus".

91. "Around the World in Eighty Days".

1955. Jules Verne (author). 50th Death Anniv. Designs illustrating his works.

529. – 1 f. indigo & brn. (post.) 5 5
530. – 2 f. sepia, indigo & blue 5 5
531. **89.** 3 f. indigo, black & brn. 5 5
532. – 5 f. sepia and red .. 5 5
533. **90.** 6 f. grey and sepia .. 12 12
534. – 8 f. turquoise and olive 20 20
535. – 10 f. sepia, turq. & ind. 55 55
536. **91.** 15 f. vermilion & brown 50 50
537. – 25 f. black and green .. 80 80
538. **92.** 30 f. black, pur. & turq. 2·25 2·25
539. – 200 f. indigo & blue (air) .. 13·00 13·00

DESIGNS—As T **90**—VERT. 1 f. "Five Weeks in a Balloon". HORIZ. 5 f. "Michael Strogoff". 8 f. "Le Superbe Orenoque". As T **89**—HORIZ. 2 f. "A Floating Island". 10 f. "Journey to the Centre of the Earth". 25 f. "20,000 Leagues under the Sea". 200 f. "From Earth to Moon".

93. "The Immaculate Virgin" (F. Brea).

DESIGNS—As T **93**: 10 f. "Madonna" (L Brea). As T **92**: 15f. Bienheureux Rainer.

1955. Marian Year.
540. **93.** 5 f. grn., grey & brown 20 20
541. – 10 f. green, grey & brown 20 20
542. – 15 f. brown and sepia .. 30 30

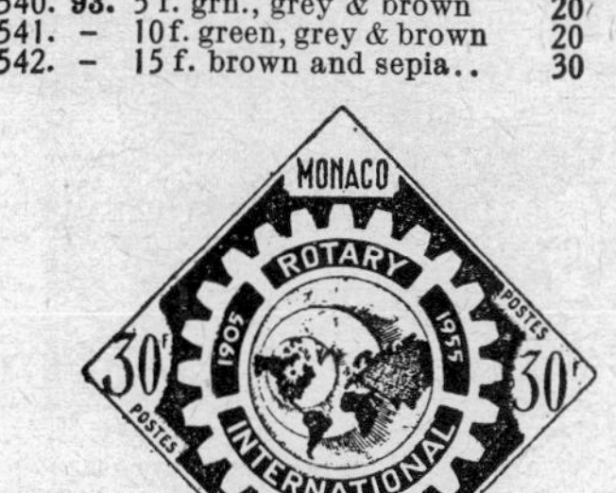
94. Rotary Emblem.

1955. Rotary International. 50th Anniv.
543. **94.** 30 f. blue and yellow .. 55 55

95. George Washington.

97. President Eisenhower.

96. Abraham Lincoln.

1956. New York Int. Philatelic Exn. Inscr "F.I.P.E.X. 1956".
544. **95.** 1 f. purple 5 5
545. – 2 f. purple and maroon 5 5
546. **96.** 3 f. blue and violet .. 5 5
547. **97.** 5 f. lake 8 8
548. – 15 f. chocolate .. 40 40
549. – 30 f. black and blue .. 70 70
550. – 40 f. chocolate 60 60
551. – 50 f. red 60 60
552. – 100 f. green 90 90
DESIGNS—As T **96**: 2 f. F. D. Roosevelt. As T **95**—HORIZ. 15 f. Monaco Palace in the 18th century. 30 f. Landing of Columbus. LARGER (48×36 mm.): 50 f. Aerial view of Monaco Palace in the 18th century. 100 f. Louisiana landscape in 18th century. As T **97**: 40 f. Prince Rainier III.

98.

1956. 7th Winter Olympic Games, Cortina d'Ampezzo and 16th Olympic Games, Melbourne.
553. – 15 f. brn., green & pur. 50 50
554. **98.** 30 f. red .. .. 1·10 1·10
DESIGN: 15 f. "Italia" ski-jump.

1956. Nos. D482/95 with "TIMBRE TAXE" barred out and some surch. also. (a) Postage.
555. 2 f. on 4 f. slate & brown ..
556. 2 f. on 4 f. brown & slate ..
557. 3 f. lake and green ..
558. 3 f. green and lake ..
559. 5 f. on 4 f. slate & brown ..
560. 5 f. on 4 f. brown & slate ..
561. 10 f. on 4 f. slate & brown
562. 10 f. on 4 f. brown & slate
563. 15 f. on 5 f. violet & blue ..
564. 15 f. on 5 f. blue & violet ..
565. 20 f. violet and indigo ..
566. 20 f. indigo and violet ..
567. 25 f. on 20 f. vio. & indigo
568. 25 f. on 20 f. indigo & vio.
569. 30 f. on 10 f. indigo & blue
570. 30 f. on 10 f. blue & indigo
571. 40 f. on 50 f. brown & red
572. 40 f. on 50 f. red & brown
573. 50 f. on 100 f. grn. & mar.
574. 50 f. on 100 f. mar. & grn.

(b) Air. Optd. **POSTE AERIENNE** also.
575. 100 f. on 20 f. violet & ind.
576. 100 f. on 20 f. ind. & violet
Set of 22 (Nos. 555/76) .. 21·00 21·00

99. Route Map from Glasgow.

1956. 26th Monte Carlo Car Rally.
577. **99.** 100 f. brown and red .. 6·50 6·50

100. Princess Grace and Prince Rainier III.

1956. Royal Wedding.
578. **100.** 1 f. blk. & grn. (post.) 5 5
579. 2 f. black and red .. 5 5
580. 3 f. black and blue .. 5 5
581. 5 f. blk. & yell.-grn. .. 5 5
582. 15 f. black and brown 15 15
583. 100 f. brn. & pur. (air) 25 25
584. 200 f. brown & red .. 55 55
585. 500 f. brown & grey .. 1·40 1·40

101. Princess Grace.

102. Princess Grace with Princess Caroline.

1957. Birth of Princess Caroline.
586. **101.** 1 f. grey 5 5
587. 2 f. olive 5 5
588. 3 f. brown 5 5
589. 5 f. crimson 5 5
590. 15 f. pink 5 5
591. 25 f. blue 10 10
592. 30 f. violet 10 10
593. 50 f. red 15 12
594. 75 f. orange 25 25

1958. Birth of Prince Albert.
595. **102.** 100 f. black .. .. 1·40 1·40

103.

104. Route Map from Munich.

1958. Creation of National Order of St. Charles. Cent.
596. **103.** 100 f. lake, green, ochre and red 90 90

1958. 27th Monte Carlo Rally.
597. **104.** 100 f. red, sepia, claret and green .. .. 2·25 2·25

105. Statue of the Holy Virgin and Popes Pius IX and Pius XII.

1958. Apparition of Virgin Mary at Lourdes. Cent. Inscr. "1858–1958".
598. **105.** 1 f. violet-grey & chocolate (postage) 5 5
599. – 2 f. violet and blue .. 5 5
600. – 3 f. sepia and green .. 5 5
601. – 5 f. grey-blue & sepia .. 5 5
602. – 8 f. multicoloured .. 12 12
603. – 10 f. multicoloured .. 12 12
604. – 12 f. multicoloured .. 12 12
605. – 20 f. myrtle & maroon 15 15
606. – 35 f. myrtle, bistre and brown .. 20 20
607. – 50 f. blue, grn. & lake .. 40 40
608. – 65 f. turq. and indigo .. 50 50
609. – 100 f. vio.-grey, myrtle and blue (air) .. 1·00 1·00
610. – 200 f. brn. & chestnut .. 1·40 1·40
DESIGNS—VERT. (26½×36 mm.): 2 f. St. Bernadette. 3 f. St. Bernadette at Bartres. 5 f. The Miracle of Bourriette. 20 f. St. Bernadette at prayer. 35 f. St. Bernadette's canonization. (22 × 36 mm.): 8 f. Stained-glass window representing the Apparition. As T **105**: 50 f. St. Bernadette, Pope Pius XI, Mgr. Laurence and Abbe Peyramale. HORIZ. (48 × 36 mm): 10 f. Lourdes grotto. 12 f. Interior of Lourdes grotto. (36 × 26½ mm.): 65 f. Shrine of St. Bernadette. (48 × 27 mm.): 100 f. Lourdes Basilica. 200 f. Pope Pius X and subterranean interior of basilica.

106. Princess Grace and Clinic.

1959. Opening of new hospital block in "Princess Grace" Clinic, Monaco.
611. **106.** 100 f. grey, choc. & grn. 55 55

107. U.N.E.S.C.O. Headquarters, Paris, and Cultural Emblems.

1959. U.N.E.S.C.O. Headquarters Building Inaug.
612. **107.** 25 f. blue, brown, red and black 15 15
613. – 50 f. turq., blk. & olive 35 35
DESIGN: 50 f. As T **107** but with heads of children and letters of various alphabets in place of the emblems.

108. Route Map from Athens.

109. Prince Rainier and Princess Grace.

1959. 28th Monte Carlo Rally.
614. **108.** 100 f. blue, red and bronze-grn. on blue 2·75 2·75

1959. Air.
615. **109.** 300 f. violet .. .. 2·25 1·75
616. 500 f. blue .. .. 3·25 2·50
See also Nos. 640/1.

110. "Princess Caroline" Carnation.

1959. Flowers.
617. **110.** 5 f. mag., grn. & brown 5 5
618. – 10 f. on 3 f. pink, green and brown .. 8 8
619. – 15 f. on 1 f. yell. & grn. 10 8
620. – 20 f. purple and green 15 15
621. – 25 f. on 6 f. verm., yell.-green and green .. 25 15
622. – 35 f. pink and green .. 30 25
623. – 50 f. green and sepia .. 40 25
624. – 85 f. on 65 f. lavender, bronze-grn. & green 55 50
625. – 100 f. rose and green .. 75 60
FLOWERS—As T **110**: 10 f. "Princess Grace" carnation. 100 f. "Grace of Monaco" rose. VERT. (22×36 mm.): 15 f. Mimosa. 25 f. Geranium. HORIZ. (36×22 mm.): 20 f. Bougainvillaea. 35 f. "Laurier" rose. 50 f. Jasmine. 85 f. Lavender.

(New currency. 100 (old) francs = 1 (new franc.)

111. "Uprooted Tree".

112. Oceanographic Museum.

1960. World Refugee Year.
626. **111.** 25 c. green, blue & blk. 15 15

1960. Prince Rainier types with values in new currency.
627. **88.** 25 c. blk. & orge. (post.) 5 5
628. 30 c. violet 12 5
629. 40 c. red and brown .. 8 5
630. 45 c. brown and grey .. 10 5
631. 50 c. brown and green .. 25 8
632. 50 c. red and brown .. 12 5
633. 60 c. brown and green .. 20 8
634. 60 c. brown and purple 12 8
635. 65 c. blue and brown .. 55 25
636. 70 c. blue and plum .. 15 8
637. 85 c. green and violet .. 20 15
638. 95 c. blue 20 12
639. 1 f. 10 blue and brown 20 15
640. 1 f. 30 brown and red .. 40 40
641. 2 f. 30 purple and orange 55 12
642. **109.** 3 f. violet (air) .. .. 7·50 3·25
643. 5 f. blue .. .. 7·50 5·00

1960.
644. – 5 c. green and blue .. 5 5
645. **112.** 10 c. brown and blue 20 12
646. – 10 c. blue, violet & grn. 5 5
647. – 40 c. mar., grn. & bronze 15 10
648. – 45 c. brn., grn. & blue 15 15
649. – 70 c. brn., red & green 20 15
650. – 80 c. red, green & blue 15 10
651. – 85 c. blk., brn. & grey 30 20
652. – 90 c. brn., bl. & black 25 15
653. – 1 f. brn., grn., blk. & bl. 25 15
654. – 1 f. 15 blk., brn. & blue 25 15
655. – 1 f. 30 brn., grn. & blue 25 15
656. – 1 f. 40 orange grn. & vio. 40 30
DESIGNS—HORIZ. 5 c. Palace of Monaco. 10 c. (No. 646), Aquatic Stadium. 40 c., 45 c., 80 c., 1 f. 40 Aerial view of Palace. 70 c., 85 c., 90 c., 1 f. 15, 1 f. 30, Court of Honour, Monaco Palace. 1 f. Palace floodlit.

112a. St. Devote.

1960. Air.

668. 112a. 2 f. violet and green 75 65
669. 3 f. olive-brown, green and blue .. 1·00 55
670. 5 f. lake .. .. 1·75 1·00
671. 10 f. brown & green .. 3·00 2·75

113. Sea Horse.

114. Route Map from Lisbon.

1960. Marine Life and Plants.

(a) Marine Life.

672. – 1 c. red and blue-green 5 5
673. – 12 c. chest. & violet-blue 5 5
674. 113. 15 c. green & brown-red 15 5
675. – 20 c. red, red-brown, bistre and chestnut 15 5

DESIGNS—HORIZ. 1 c. "Macrocheira kampferi" (crab). 20 c. "Pterois volitans". VERT. 12 c. "Fasciolaria trapezium" (Shell).

(b) Plants.

676. – 2 c. multicoloured .. 5 5
677. – 15 c. orge., choc. & ol. 15 5
678. – 18 c. multicoloured .. 5 5
679. – 20 c. red, olive & brown 15 5

PLANTS—VERT. 2 c. "Selenicereus Gr.". 15 c. "Cereanee". 18 c. "Aloe ciliaris". 20 c. "Nopalea dejecta".

1960. Prince Rainier Seal type with values in new currency. Precancelled.

680. 83. 8 c. purple 12 8
681. 20 c. green 15 8
682. 40 c. chocolate .. 20 15
683. 55 c. blue 30 20

1960. 29th Monte Carlo Rally.

684. 114. 25 c. black, red and blue on blue 80 80

115. Stamps of Monaco 1885, France and Sardinia, 1860.

1960. 1st Monaco Postage Stamp. 75th Anniv.

685. 115. 25 c. bistre, blue & vio. 50 45

116. Aquarium.

1960. Oceanographic Museum, Monaco. 50th Anniv.

686. – 5 c. black, blue & mar. 12 12
687. 116. 10 c. grey, brown & grn. 15 15
688. – 15 c. black, bistre & bl. 15 15
689. – 20 c. blk., blue & mag. 25 25
690. – 25 c. turquoise .. 45 45
691. – 50 c. chocolate and blue 65 65

DESIGNS—VERT. 5 c. Oceanographic Museum (similar to T 112). HORIZ. 15 c. Conference Hall. 20 c. Catch being hauled aboard ship. 25 c. Museum, aquarium and under-water research equipment. 50 c. Prince Albert, "Hirondelle I" and "Princess Alice".

117. Horse-jumping.

1960. Olympic Games.

692. 117. 5 c. choc., red & emer. 8 8
693. – 10 c. brn., blue & green 8 8
694. – 15 c. red, brn. & maroon 12 12
695. – 20 c. blk., blue & green 1·25 1·25
696. – 25 c. mar., turq. & grn. 35 35
697. – 50 c. mar., blue & turq. 60 60

DESIGNS: 10 c. Swimming. 15 c. Long-jumping. 20 c. Throwing the javelin. 25 c. Free-skating. 50 c. Ski-ing.

118. Rally Badge, Old and Modern Cars.

1961. Monte Carlo Rally. 50th Anniv.

698. 118. 1 f. vio., red & chest. 65 65

119. Route Map from Stockholm.

120. Marine-Life.

1961. 30th Monte Carlo Rally.

699. 119. 1 f. red, grn. & violet 65 65

1961. World Aquariological Congress. Orange network background.

700. 120. 25 c. red, sep. & violet 15 15

121. Leper in Town of Middle Ages.

123. Insect within Protective Hand.

122. Semi-submerged Sphinx of Ouadi-es-Saboua.

1961. Sovereign Order of Malta.

701. 121. 25 c. yell., red & brown 15 15

1961. U.N.E.S.C.O. Campaign for Preservation of Nubian Monuments.

702. 122. 50 mar., blue & brown 40 40

1961. Nature Preservation.

703. 123. 25 c. magenta & purple 15 15

124. Chevrolet, 1912.

1961. Veteran Motor Cars.

704. 1 c. chocolate, green and chestnut 5 5
705. 2 c. blue, purple & verm. 5 5
706. 3 c. maroon, black & purple 5 5
707. 4 c. indigo, chocolate and slate-violet 5 5
708. 5 c. myrtle, red and olive .. 5 5
709. 10 c. brown, red & indigo 8 8
710. 15 c. myrtle and turquoise 10 10
711. 20 c. sepia, red and violet 15 15
712. 25 c. violet, red & chocolate 25 25
713. 30 c. lilac and green .. 30 30
714. 45 c. grn., pur. & chestnut 60 60
715. 50 c. blue, red and sepia .. 50 50
716. 65 c. sepia, red and slate .. 60 60
717. 1 f. indigo, red and violet .. 90 90

MOTOR CARS: 1 c. T 124: 2 c. Peugeot, 1898. 3 c. Fiat, 1901. 4 c. Mercedes, 1901. 5 c. Rolls Royce 1903. 10 c. Panhard-Lavassor, 1899. 15 c. Renault, 1898. 20 c. Ford "S", 1908. 25 c. Rochet-Schneider, 1894. 30 c. FN-Herstal, 1901. 45 c. De Dion Bouton, 1900. 50 c. Buick, 1910. 65 c. Delahaye, 1901. 1 f. Cadillac, 1906.

125. Racing Car and Race Route.

1962. 20th Monaco Motor Grand Prix.

718. 125. 1 f. purple 65 65

126. Route Map from Oslo.

1962. 31st Monte Carlo Rally.

719. 126. 1 f. red, bl., mar. & grn. 65 65

127. Louis XII and Lucien Grimaldi.

DESIGNS: 50 c. Parchment bearing declaration of sovereignty. 1 f. Seals of two Sovereigns.

1962. Recognition of Monegasque Sovereignty by Louis XII. 450th Anniv.

720. 127. 25 c. black, red & blue 12 12
721. – 50 c. choc., lake & blue 20 20
722. – 1 f. red, green & brown 40 40

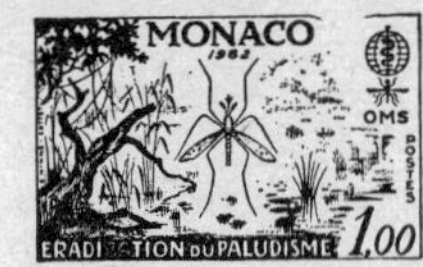

128. Mosquito and Swamp.

1962. Malaria Eradication.

723. 128. 1 f. yellow-grn. & olive 45 45

130. Sun, Bouquet and "Hope Chest".

1962. National Multiple Sclerosis Society, New York.

724. 130. 20 c. multicoloured .. 15 15

131. Harvest Scene.

DESIGN: 2 f. Mercury in flight over Europe.

1962. Europa.

725. 131. 25 c. chestnut, green and blue (postage) .. 12 12
726. 50 c. olive & turquoise .. 25 25
727. 1 f. olive and purple .. 40 40
728. – 2 f. slate, chocolate and green (air) .. 70 55

132. Atomic Symbol and Scientific Centre.

1962. Air. Scientific Centre, Monaco.

729. 132. 10 f. vio., brn. & blue 5·50 5·50

133. Wagtails.

134. Galeazzi's Diving Turret.

1962. Protection of Birds useful to Agriculture.

730. 133. 5 c. yellow, brown & grn. 5 5
731. – 10 c. red, bistre & mar. 5 5
732. – 15 c. pur., yell., grn. & bl. 8 8
733. – 20 c. sepia, green & mve. 8 8
734. – 25 c. black, brown, red and mauve 12 10
735. – 30 c. brn., blue & myrtle 20 15
736. – 45 c. chestnut & violet 25 20
737. – 50 c. black, olive & turq. 35 25
738. – 85 c. vermilion, brown, yellow and green .. 40 40
739. – 1 f. sepia, red & green 50 50

BIRDS: 10 c. Robins. 15 c. Goldfinches, 20 c. Warblers. 25 c. Woodpeckers. 30 c. Nightingale. 45 c. Brown owls. 50 c. Starlings. 85 c. Crossbills. 1 f. White storks.

1962. Underwater Exploration.

740. – 5 c. blk., violet & turq. 5 5
741. 134. 10 c. blue, violet & brn. 5 5
742. – 25 c. bistre, grn. & turq. 10 10
743. – 45 c. black, blue & grn. 25 25
744. – 50 c. olive, bistre & blue 25 25
745. – 85 c. violet-blue & turq. 40 40
746. – 1 f. choc., myrtle & blue 50 50

DESIGNS—HORIZ. 5 c. Divers. 25 c. Williamson's photosphere (1914) and bathyscape "Trieste". 45 c. Klingert's diving-suit (1797) and modern diving-suit. 50 c. Diving saucer 85. c. Fulton's "Nautilus" (1800) and modern submarine. 1 f. Alexander the Great's diving bell and Beebe's bathysphere.

135. Donor's Arm and Globe.

137. Feeding Chicks in Nest.

136. "Ring-a-ring o' Roses".

1962. 3rd Int. Blood Donors' Congress, Monaco.

747. 135. 1 f. crimson, sepia and orange 40 40

1963. U.N. Children's Charter.

748. 136. 5 c. red, blue and ochre 5 5
749. 137. 10 c. emerald, sep. & bl. 5 5
750. – 15 c. ultram., red & emer. 8 8
751. – 20 c. multicoloured .. 12 12
752. – 25 c. blue, pur. & chest. 15 15
753. – 50 c. bl., grn., vio. & mag. 25 25
754. – 95 c. multicoloured .. 30 30
755. – 1 f. maroon, red & turq. 50 50

DESIGNS—As T 136: 1 f. Prince Albert and Princess Caroline. Children's paintings as T 137—HORIZ. 15 c. Children on scales. 50 c. House and child. VERT. 20 c. Sun's rays and children of three races. 25 c. Mother and child. 95 c. Negress and child.

138. Ship's Figurehead.

139. Racing Cars.

1963. Int. Red Cross Cent.
756. **138.** 50 c. red, brown & turq. 25 25
757. – 1 f. myrtle, red, maroon and grey-blue .. 40 40
DESIGN—HORIZ. 1 f. Moynier, Dunant and Dufour.

1963. European Automobile Grand Prix.
758. **139.** 50 c. multicoloured .. 35 20

140. Lions Club Charter.

1963. Founding of Lions Club of Monaco.
759. **140.** 50 c. blue, bistre & violet 30 30

141. Hotel des Postes and U.P.U. Monument.

1963. Paris Postal Conference Cent.
760. **141.** 50 c. lake, grn. & yell. 25 25

142. "Telstar".

1963. 1st Link Trans-Atlantic T.V. Satellite.
761. **142.** 50 c. brown, grn. & pur. 40 40

143. Route Map from Warsaw.

1963. 32nd Monte Carlo Rally.
762. **143.** 1 f. multicoloured .. 55 55

144. Feeding Chicks.

1963. Freedom from Hunger.
763. **144.** 1 f. chestnut, myrtle, olive-brown and blue 40 40

145. Allegory.

1963. Ecumenical Council, Vatican City.
764. **145.** 1 f. turquoise, green and brown-red .. 40 40

146. Henry Ford and Ford "A" Car of 1903.

1963. Henry Ford (motor pioneer). Birth Cent.
765. **146.** 20 c. green and purple 12 12

DESIGN: 50 c. Cyclist passing Desgrange Monument, Col du Galibier, 1963.

147. H. Garin (winner of 1903 race) cycling through village.

1963. 50th "Tour de France" Cycle Race.
766. **147.** 25 c. grn., brn. & blue 12 12
767. – 50 c. sepia, green & blue 20 20

148. P. de Coubertin and Discus-thrower.

1963. Pierre de Coubertin (reviver of Olympic Games). Birth Cent.
768. **148.** 1 f. brown, red & lake 35 35

149. R. Garros and Aircraft.

1963. Air. 1st Aerial Crossing of the Mediterranean Sea. 50th Anniv.
769. **149.** 2 f. sepia and blue .. 70 65

150. Route Map from Paris. **152.** "Europa".

151. Children with Stamp Album.

1963. 33rd Monte Carlo Rally.
770. **150.** 1 f. red, bl.-grn. & blue 55 55

1963. "Scolatex" Int. Stamp Exn., Monaco.
771. **151.** 50 c. ultram., vio. & red 20 20

1963. Europa.
772. **152.** 25 c. brown, red & green 12 10
773. 50 c. sepia, red & blue 25 20

153. Wembley Stadium.

1963. Football Association (British). Cent.
774. **153.** 1 c. violet, green & red 5 5
775. – 2 c. red, black & green 5 5
776. – 3 c. orange, olive & red 5 5
777. – 4 c. blk., red, grn. & bl. 5 5

Multicoloured horiz. designs depicting

(a) "Football Through the Centuries".
778. 10 c. "Calcio", Florence (16th cent.) 5 5
779. 15 c. "Soule", Brittany (19th cent.) 5 5
780. 20 c. English military college (after Cruickshank, 1827) 5 5
781. 25 c. English game (after Overend, 1890) 8 8

(b) "Modern Football".
782. 30 c. Tackling 12 12
783. 50 c. Saving goal 20 20
784. 95 c. Heading ball 45 45
785. 1 f. Corner kick 55 55

DESIGNS—As T **153**: 4 c. Louis II Stadium, Monaco. This stamp is optd. in commemoration of the Association Sportive de Monaco football teams in the French Championships and in the Coupe de France, 1962-63. HORIZ. (36 × 22 mm.): 2 c. Footballer making return kick. 3 c. Goalkeeper saving ball.

Nos. 778/80 and 782/5 were respectively issued together in sheets and arranged in blocks of 4 with a football in the centre of each block.

154. Communications in Ancient Egypt, and Rocket.

1964. "PHILATEC 1964" Int. Stamp Exn., Paris.
786. **154.** 1 f. brown, indigo & bl. 50 50

155. Reproduction of Rally Postcard Design.

1964. 1st Aerial Rally, Monte Carlo. 50th Anniv.
787. 1 c. ol.-brn., bl. & grn. (post.) 5 5
788. 2 c. bistre, brown-red & blue 5 5
789. 3 c. ol.-brn., bl. & yell.-grn. 5 5
790. 4 c. brn.-red, bl.-grn. & blue 5 5
791. 5 c. olive-brown, red & vio. 5 5
792. 10 c. vio., olive-brn. & blue 5 5
793. 15 c. orange, brown & blue 5 5
794. 20 c. sepia, emerald & blue 8 8
795. 25 c. olive-brown, blue & red 12 12
796. 30 c. myrtle, maroon & blue 15 15
797. 45 c. sepia, turquoise & brn. 30 30
798. 50 c. ochre, olive & violet 35 35
799. 65 c. vermilion, slate & turq. 40 40
800. 95 c. blue-green, brown-red and yellow-brown 60 60
801. 1 f. chocolate, bl. & bl.-grn. 60 60
802. 5 f. sep., bl. & brn. (air) .. 2·25 1·75

DESIGNS: 1 c. T **155**. HORIZ. (48 × 27 mm.)—Rally planes: 2 c. Renaux's "Farman". 3 c. Espanet's "Nieuport". 4 c. Moineau's "Breguet". 5 c. Garros' and B. des Moulinais' "Morane-Saulnier". 10 c. Hirth's "Albatros". 15 c. Prevost's "Deperdussin". Famous planes and flights: 20 c. "Vickers-Vimy" (Ross Smith: London-Port Darwin, 1919), 25 c. Douglas,-"Liberty" (U.S. World Flight, 1924). 30 c. Savoia "S-55" (De Pinedo's World Flight, 1925). 45 c. Fokker "F-7" (First Flight over North Pole, Byrd and Bennett, 1925). 50 c. Ryan-"Spirit of St Louis" (First solo crossing of N. Atlantic Lindbergh, 1927). 65 c. "Breguet-19". (Paris—New York, Coste and Bellonte 1930). 95 c. "Late-28" (Dakar—Natal, first S. Atlantic airmail flight, Mermoz, 1930). 1 f. Dornier "DO-X" (Germany—Rio de Janeiro, Christiansen, 1930). 5 f. Convair B-58 "Hustler" (New York—Paris in 3 hours, 19′ 41″ Major Payne, U.S.A.F., 1961).

156. Aquatic Stadium. **157.** Europa "Flower".

1964. Precancelled.
803. **156.** 10 c. red, bl., pur. & blk. 30 5
803a. 15 c. claret, blue, violet and black .. 10 5
804. 25 c. bl.-grn., bl. & blk. 15 5
805. 50 c. vio., turq. & blk. 20 8

The "1962" date has been obliterated with two bars.

See also Nos. 949/51a.

1964. Europa.
806. **157.** 25 c. red, green & indigo 10 8
807. 50 c. brown, bistre & bl. 20 15

158. Weightlifting.

1964. Olympic Games, Tokyo and Innsbruck. Multicoloured.
808. 1 c. Type **158** (postage) .. 5 5
809. 2 c. Judo 5 5
810. 3 c. pole-vaulting 5 5
811. 4 c. Archery 5 5
812. 5 f. Bobsleighing (air) .. 1·75 1·75

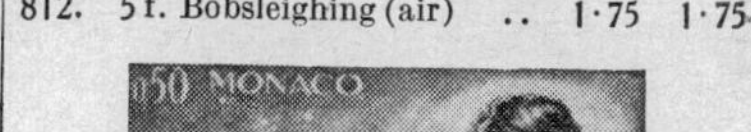

159. Pres. Kennedy and Space Capsule.

1964. Pres. Kennedy Commem.
813. **159.** 50 c. indigo and blue .. 50 50

160. Monaco and Television Set.

1964. 5th Int. Television Festival, Monte Carlo.
814. **160.** 50 c. choc., blue & red 15 15

161. F. Mistral and Statue.

1964. Frederic Mistral (poet). 50th Death Anniv.
815. **161.** 1 f. chestnut and olive 35 35

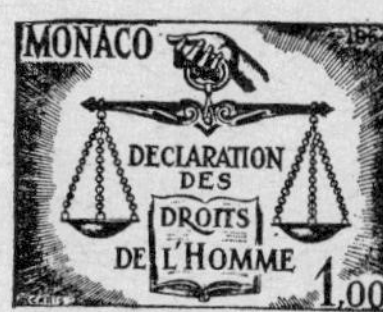

162. Scales of Justice.

1964. Declaration of Human Rights. 15th Anniv.
816. **162.** 1 f. bronze and brown 40 25

163. Route Map from Minsk.

1964. 34th Monte Carlo Rally.
817. **163.** 1 f. choc., turq. & ochre 40 40

164. FIFA Emblem.

1964. Federation Internationale de Football Associations (FIFA). 60th Anniv.
818. 164. 1 f. bistre, blue & red 40 40

165. "Syncom 2" and Globe.

1965. I.T.U. Cent.
819. 165. 5 c. grn. & ult. (post.) 5 5
820. – 10 c. chest., brn. & bl. 5 5
821. – 12 c. mar., red & grey 5 5
822. – 18 c. mar., red & ind. 5 5
823. – 25 c. vio., bis. & mar. 5 5
824. – 30 c. bistre, brn. & sep. 8 8
825. – 50 c. indigo & green 12 12
826. – 60 c. blue and brown 20 20
827. – 70 c. sep., orge. & bl. 20 20
828. – 95 c. blk., indigo & bl. 35 35
829. – 1 f. brown and blue 50 35
830. – 10 f. green, blue and brown (air) .. 3·25 3·25

DESIGNS—As T 165—HORIZ. 10 c. "Echo 2". 18 c. "Lunik 3". 30 c. A. G. Bell and telephone. 50 c. S. Morse and telegraph. 60 c. E. Belin and "belinograph". VERT. 12 c. "Relay". 10 f. Monte Carlo television transmitter. LARGER (48½×27 mm.): 25 c. "Telstar" and Pleumeur-Bodou Station. 70 c. Roman beacon and Chappe's telegraph. 95 c. Cable-laying ships "Great Eastern" and "Alsace". 1 f. E. Branly, G. Marconi and English Channel.

166. Europa "Sprig".

1965. Europa.
831. 166. 30 c. brown and green 12 12
832. 60 c. violet and red .. 25 25

167. Monaco Palace (18th cent.)

1966. Monaco Palace. 750th Anniv.
833. 167. 10 c. violet, grn. & Ind. 5 5
834. – 12 c. bistre, blue & blk. 5 5
835. – 18 c. green, blk. & blue 12 12
836. – 30 c. brn., blk. & ultram. 15 15
837. – 60 c. grn., blue & bistre 20 20
838. – 1 f. 30 brown and green 40 40

DESIGNS (Different views of Palace): 12 c. 17th cent. 18 c. 18th cent. 30 c. 19th cent. 60 c. 19th cent. 1 f. 30, 20th cent.

168. Dante.

1966. Dante's Birth. 700th Anniv.
839. 168. 30 c. green and red .. 25 25
840. – 60 c. indigo, blue & grn. 55 55
841. – 70 c. black, green & red 60 60
842. – 95 c. blue, violet & pur. 1·10 1·10
843. – 1 f. turquoise, greenish blue and blue .. 1·10 1·10

DESIGNS (Scenes from Dante's works): 60 c. Dante harassed by the panther (envy). 70 c. Crossing the 5th circle. 95 c. Punishment of the arrogant. 1 f. Invocation of St. Bernard.

169. "The Nativity".

1966. World Assn. of Children's Friends (A.M.A.D.E.).
844. 169. 30 c. brown 12 12

170. Route Map from London.

1966. 35th Monte Carlo Rally.
845. 170. 1 f. indigo, purple & red 40 40

171. Princess Grace with children.

1966. Air. Princess Stephanie's 1st Birthday.
846. 171. 3 f. brn., blue & violet .. 1·10 1·10

172. Casino in 19th Century.

173. Europa "Ship".

1966. Monte Carlo. Cent.
847. – 12 c. black, red and blue (postage) .. 5 5
848. 172. 25 c. blue, brn., grn. and ultramarine .. 5 5
849. – 30 c. purple, green, brown and blue .. 8 5
850. – 40 c. red, yellow, blue and olive .. 12 8
851. – 60 c. blue, red, purple and green 20 12
852. – 70 c. indigo and lake 20 12
853. – 95 c. black and purple 40 20
854. – 1 f. 30 maroon, brown and chestnut 45 30
855. – 5 f. lake, ochre and blue (air) .. 1·75 1·75

DESIGNS—VERT. 12 c. Prince Charles III. HORIZ. 40 c. Charles III Monument. 95 c. Massenet and Saint-Saens. 1 f. 30, Faure and Ravel. LARGER (48×27 mm.): 30 c. F. Blanc, originator of Monte Carlo, and view of 1860. 60 c. Prince Rainier III and projected esplanade. 70 c. Rene Blum and Diaghilev, ballet character from "Petrouchka". (36×36 mm.): 5 f. Interior of Opera House, 1879.

1966. Europa.
856. 173. 30 c. orange .. 10 8
857. 60 c. green 20 15

174. Prince Rainier and Princess Grace.

176. "Learning to Write".

175. Prince Albert I and Yachts "Hirondelle I" and "Princess Alice".

1966. Air.
858. 174. 2 f. slate and red .. 50 25
859. 3 f. slate and green .. 80 45
860. 5 f. slate and blue .. 1·40 70
860a. 10 f. slate and bistre .. 2·25 1·50
860b. 20 f. brn. & orange 5·00 3·00

1966. 1st Int. Oceanographic History Congress, Monaco.
861. 175. 1 f. lilac and blue .. 35 25

1966. U.N.E.S.C.O. 20th Anniv.
862. 176. 30 c. maroon & magenta 8 5
863. 60 c. brown and blue 15 8

177. T.V. Screen, Cross and Monaco Harbour.

179. W.H.O. Building.

178. "Precontinent III".

1966. 10th Meeting of Int. Catholic Television Assn. (U.N.D.A.), Monaco.
864. 177. 60 c. red, pur. & crim. 15 10

1966. Submarine Research Craft, "Precontinent III". 1st Anniv.
865. 178. 1 f. yellow, brn. & blue 25 20

1966. W.H.O. Headquarters, Geneva. Inaug.
866. 179. 30 c. brn., grn. & blue 8 5
867. 60 c. choc., red & grn 15 8

180. Bugatti, 1931

181. Dog (Egyptian bronze).

1967. 25th Motor Grand Prix, Monaco. Multicoloured. (a) Postage.
868. 1 c. Type 180 .. .. 5 5
869. 2 c. Alfa-Romeo, 1932 .. 5 5
870. 5 c. Mercedes, 1936 .. 5 5
871. 10 c. Maserati, 1948 .. 5 5
872. 18 c. Ferrari, 1955 .. 5 5
873. 20 c. Alfa-Romeo, 1950 .. 8 8
874. 25 c. Maserati, 1957 .. 8 8
875. 30 c. Cooper-Climax, 1958 10 10
876. 40 c. Lotus-Climax, 1960 12 12
877. 50 c. Lotus-Climax, 1961 15 15
878. 60 c. Cooper-Climax, 1962 20 20
879. 70 c. B.R.M., 1963-6 .. 20 20
880. 1 f. Walter Christie, 1907 40 25
881. 2 f. 30 Peugeot, 1910 .. 65 50

(b) Air. Diamond. 50×50 mm.
882. 3 f. black and blue .. 1·00 1·00

DESIGN: Panhard-Phenix, 1895.

1967. Int. Cynological Federation Congress, Monaco.
883. 181. 30 c. black, mar. & grn. 10 8

182. View of Monte Carlo.

1967. Int. Tourist Year.
884. 182. 30 c. brn., grn. & blue 8 5

183. Chessboard.

1967. Int. Chess Grand Prix, Monaco.
885. 183. 60 c. black, plum & blue 20 20

184. Melvin Jones (founder), Lions Emblem and Monte Carlo.

1967. Lions Int. 50th Anniv.
886. 184. 60 c. blue, ult. & choc. 15 12

185. Rotary Emblem and Monte Carlo.

1967. Rotary Int. Convention.
887. 185. 1 f. bistre, blue & green 25 20

186. Fair Buildings.

1967. World Fair, Montreal.
888. 186. 1 f. red, slate and blue 25 20

187. Squiggle on Map of Europe.

188. Cogwheels.

1967. European Migration Committee (C.I.M.E.)
889. 187. 1 f. choc., bistre & blue 25 20

1967. Europa.
890. 188. 30 c. violet, pur. & red 10 8
891. 60 c. green, turq. & emer. 20 15

189. Dredger and Coastal Chart.

1967. 9th Int. Hydrographic Congress, Monaco.
892. 189. 1 f. brown, blue & green 25 20

190. Marie Curie and Scientific Equipment.

1967. Marie Curie. Birth Cent.
893. 190. 1 f. blue, olive & brown 25 20

191. Skiing.

1967. Winter Olympic Games, Grenoble.
894. **191.** 2 f. 30 brn., blue & slate 65 50

192. Prince Rainier I (E Charpentier).

1967. Paintings. "Princes and Princesses of Monaco". Multicoloured.
895. 1 f. Type **192** 85 45
896. 1 f. Lucien Grimaldi (A. di Predis) 85 45

See also Nos. 932/3, 958/9, 1005/6, 1023/4, 1070/1, 1108/9, 1192/3 and 1247/8.

193. Putting the Shot.

1968. Olympic Games, Mexico.
897. **193.** 20 c. blue, brown and green (postage) .. 5 5
898. – 30 c. brn., bl. & plum 10 10
899. – 60 c. blue, pur. & red 15 15
900. – 70 c. red, bl. & ochre 20 15
901. – 1 f. blue, brown and orange-brown .. 35 15
902. – 2 f. 30 ol., bl. & lake 75 65
903. – 3 f. blue, vio. & grn. (air) .. .. 1·00 1·00

DESIGNS: 30 c. High-jumping. 60 c. Gymnastics. 70 c. Water-polo. 1 f. Greco-Roman wrestling. 2 f. 30, Gymnastics (different). 3 f. Hockey.

194. "St. Martin".

1968. Monaco Red Cross. 20th Anniv.
904. **194.** 2 f. 30 blue and brown 65 55

195. "Anemones" (after Raoul Dufy).

196. Insignia of Prince Charles III and Pope Pius IX.

1968. Monte Carlo Floral Exns.
905. **195.** 1 f. multicoloured .. 30 20

1968. "Nullius Diocesis" Abbey. Cent.
906. **196.** 10 c. brown and red .. 5 5
907. – 20 c. red, green & brn. 5 5
908. – 30 c. brown and blue .. 5 5
909. – 60 c. brown, blue & grn. 12 8
910. – 1 f. indigo, bistre & blue 20 15

DESIGNS—VERT. 20 c. "St. Nicholas" (after Louis Brea). 30 c. "St. Benedict" (after Simone Martini). 60 c. Subiaco Abbey. HORIZ. 1 f. Old St. Nicholas' Church (on site of present cathedral).

197. Europa "Key".

1968. Europa.
911. **197.** 30 c. red and orange .. 5 5
912. 60 c. blue and red .. 12 10
913. 1 f. brown and green 25 15

198. Steam Locomotive, Type 030 (1868).

1968. Nice–Monaco Railway. Cent.
914. **198.** 20 c. black, blue & pur. 5 5
915. – 30 c. black, blue & olive 8 5
916. – 60 c. black, blue & ochre 12 8
917. – 70 c. black, vio. & brn. 15 12
918. – 1 f. black, blue and red 20 15
919. – 2 f. 30 blue, blk. & red 65 45

LOCOMOTIVES: 30 c. Steam, Type C–220 (1898). 60 c. Steam, Type 230–C (1910). 70 c. Steam, Type 231–F (1925). 1 f. Steam, Type 241–A (1952). 2 f. 30, Electric, Type BB (1968).

199. Chateaubriand and Combourg Castle.

1968. Chateaubriand (novelist). Birth Cent.
920. **199.** 10 c. plum, grn. & myrtle 5 5
921. – 20 c. violet, pur. & blue 5 5
922. – 25 c. brown, vio. & blue 5 5
923. – 30 c. vio., choc. & brn. 5 5
924. – 60 c. choc., grn. & red 15 8
925. – 2 f. 30 brn., mag. & bl. 55 40

Scenes from Chateaubriand's novels: 20 c. "Le Genie du Christianisme". 25 c. "Rene". 30 c. "Le Dernier Abencerage". 60 c. "Le Martyrs". 2 f. 30, "Atala".

200. Law Courts, Paris, and statues—"La France et la Fidelite".

1968. J. F. Bosio (Monegasque sculptor). Birth Cent.
926. **200.** 20 c. brown and maroon 5 5
927. – 25 c. chocolate and red 5 5
928. – 30 c. ultram. and green 5 5
929. – 60 c. green and myrtle 12 8
930. – 2 f. 30 black and slate 50 40

DESIGNS—VERT. (26 × 36 mm.): 25 c. "Henry IV as a Child". 30 c. "J. F. Bosio" (lithograph). 60 c. "Louis XIV". HORIZ.—As T **200**. 2 f. 30, "Napoleon I, Louis XVIII and Charles X".

201. W.H.O. Emblem.

1968. World Health Organisation. 20th Anniv.
931. **201.** 60 c. multicoloured .. 12 10

1968. Paintings. "Princes and Princesses of Monaco". As T **192**. Multicoloured.
932. 1 f. "Prince Charles II" (after Mimault) .. 20 15
933. 2 f. 30 "Princess Jeanne Grimaldi (Mimault) .. 55 40

202. The Hungarian March.

1969. Hector Berlioz (composer). Death Cent.
934. **202.** 10 c. brown, violet and green (postage) 5 5
935. – 20 c. brn. & magenta 5 5
936. – 25 c. brn., ind. & mag. 5 5
937. – 30 c. blk., grn. & blue 5 5
938. – 40 c. red, blk. & slate 8 5
939. – 50 c. brn., slate & pur. 12 5
940. – 70 c. brn., slate & grn. 15 12
941. – 1 f. blk., mag. & brn. 20 15
942. – 1 f. 15 black & blue 30 25
943. – 2 f. blk., bl. & grn. (air) 70 70

DESIGNS—HORIZ. 20 c. Mephistopheles appears to Faust. 25 c. Auerbach's tavern. 30 c. Sylphs' ballet. 40 c. Minuet of the goblins. 50 c. Marguerite's bedroom. 70 c. "Forests and caverns". 1 f. The journey to Hell. 1 f. 15 Heaven. All scenes from Berlioz's "The Damnation of Faust". VERT. 2 f. Bust of Berlioz.

203. "St. Elisabeth of Hungary".

1969. Monaco Red Cross.
944. **203.** 3 f. indigo, brown & red 65 40

204. "Napoleon I" (P. Delaroche).

1969. Napoleon Bonaparte. Birth Bicent.
945. **204.** 3 f. multicoloured .. 1·10 1·10

205. Colonnade.

206. "Head of Woman" (Da Vinci).

1969. Europa.
946. **205.** 40 c. red and purple .. 12 5
947. 70 c. blue, brown & blk. 15 8
948. 1 f. ochre, brn. & blue 20 15

1969. Precancelled. As Type **156**. No date.
949. 22 c. brown, blue & black 5 5
949a. 26 c. violet, blue & blk. 5 5
949b. 30 c. red, bl., lilac & blk. 8 5
950. 35 c. bl., indigo & blk. 10 5
950a. 45 c. bl., violet, turq. and black 12 5
951. 70 c. black and blue .. 20 10
951a. 90 c. grn., blue & black 25 10

1969. Leonardo da Vinci. 450th Death Anniv.
952. **206.** 30 c. brown 5 5
953. – 40 c. red and brown .. 8 5
954. – 70 c. green 15 8
955. – 80 c. sepia 15 12
956. – 1 f. 15 chestnut .. 25 20
957. – 3 f. brown 65 45

DRAWINGS: 40 c. Self-portrait. 70 c. "Head of an Old Man". 80 c. "Head of St. Madeleine". 1 f. 15 "Man's Head". 3 f. "The Condottiere".

1969. Paintings. "Princes and Princesses of Monaco". As T **192**. Multicoloured.
958. 1 f. "Prince Honore II" (Champaigne) .. 30 15
959. 3 f. "Princess Louise-Hippolyte" (Champaigne) .. 80 50

207. Marine Fauna, King Alfonso XIII of Spain and Prince Albert I of Monaco.

208. I.L.O. Emblem.

1969. Int. Commission for Scientific Exploration of the Mediterranean, Madrid. 50th Anniv.
960. **207.** 40 c. blue and black .. 8 5

1969. Int. Labour Organization. 50th Anniv.
961. **208.** 40 c. multicoloured .. 8 5

209. Aerial View of Monaco and T.V. Camera.

1969. 10th Int. Television Festival.
962. **209.** 40 c. purple, lake & blue 8 5

210. J.C.C. Emblem.

1969. Junior Chamber of Commerce. 25th Anniv.
963. **210.** 40 c. violet-blue, bistre and blue .. 8 5

211. Alphonse Daudet and Scenes from "Lettres".

1969. Daudet's "Lettres de Mon Moulin". Cent.
964. **211.** 30 c. lake, violet & grn. 5 5
965. – 40 c. green, brn. & ult. 8 5
966. – 70 c. brown, agate & vio. 15 8
967. – 80 c. violet, brn. & grn. 15 10
968. – 1 f. 15 brn., orge. & blue 25 15

DESIGNS: (Scenes from the book)—40 c. "Installation" (Daudet writing). 70 c. "Mule, Goat and Wolf". 80 c. "Gaucher's Elixir" and "The Three Low Masses". 1 f. 15 Daudet drinking, "The Old Man" and "The Country Sub-Prefect".

212. Conference Building, Albert I and Rainier III.

1970. Interparliamentary Union's Spring Meeting, Monaco.
969. **212.** 40 c. black, red & mar. 10 5

213. Baby Seal.

1970. Protection of Baby Seals.
970. **213.** 40 c. drab, blue & purple 10 5

214. Japanese Print. **215.** Dobermann.

1970. Expo 70.
971. **214.** 20 c. chocolate, green and carmine .. 8 5
972. – 30 c. brn., buff & green 8 5
973. – 40 c. bistre and violet 10 8
974. – 70 c. grey and red .. 30 25
975. – 1 f. 15 red, grn. & claret 45 40
DESIGNS—VERT. 30 c. Ibises (birds). 40 c. Shinto temple gateway. HORIZ. 70 c. Cherry blossom. 1 f. 15 Monaco Palace and Osaka Castle.

1970. Int. Dog Show, Monte Carlo.
976. **215.** 40 c. black and brown 10 8

216. "Parnassius apollo".

1970. World Federation for Protection of Animals. 20th Anniv.
977. **216.** 30 c. black, red & blue 10 5
978. – 40 c. brown, blue & grn. 12 5
979. – 50 c. brown, ochre & bl. 15 10
980. – 80 c. brown, blue & grn. 20 12
981. – 1 f. choc., bistre & slate 25 15
982. – 1 f. 15 brn., green & blue 30 15
DESIGNS—HORIZ. 40 c. Basque ponies. 50 c. Seal. VERT. 80 c. Izards (antelopes). 1 f. Ospreys. 1 f. 15 Otter.

217. "St. Louis" (King of France).

1970. Monaco Red Cross.
983. **217.** 3 f. green, brown & slate 80 50
See also Nos. 1022, 1041 and 1114.

218. "Roses and Anemones" (Van Gogh).

1970. Monte Carlo Flower Show.
984. **218.** 3 f. multicoloured .. 80 50
See also Nos. 1042 and 1073.

219. Moon Plaque, Presidents Kennedy and Nixon.

1970. 1st Man on the Moon (1969). Multicoloured.
985. 40 c. Type **219** 12 8
986. 80 c. Astronauts on Moon 30 12

220. New U.P.U. Building and Monument. **221.** "Flaming Sun".

1970. New U.P.U. Headquarters Building.
987. **220.** 40 c. brn., black & grn. 10 5

1970. Europa.
988. **221.** 40 c. purple 12 5
989. 80 c. green 20 10
990. 1 f. blue 25 15

222. Camargue Horse.

1970. Horses.
991. **222.** 10 c. slate, olive & blue (postage) 5 5
992. – 20 c. brn., olive and blue 8 5
993. – 30 c. brn., grn. and blue 8 5
994. – 40 c. grey, brn. & slate 10 8
995. – 50 c. brn., olive & blue 15 8
996. – 70 c. brn., orge. & grn. 20 15
997. – 85 c. blue, grn. & olive 25 15
998. – 1 f. 15 black, grn & blue 30 20

999. – 3 f. red, blk., olive and brown (air) 90 70
HORSES—HORIZ. 20 c. Anglo-Arab. 30 c. French saddle-horse. 40 c. Lippizaner. 50 c. Trotter. 70 c. English thoroughbred. 85 c. Arab. 1 f. 15 Barbary. DIAMOND (50 × 50 mm.) 3 f. Rock-drawings of horses in Lascaux grotto.

223. Dumas, D'Artagnan and the Three Musketeers.

1970. Alexandre Dumas (pere) (author). Birth Cent.
1000. **223.** 30 c. slate, brn. & blue 8 5

224. H. Rougier and Bleriot Aircraft.

1970. First Mediterranean Flight. 60th Anniv.
1001. **224.** 40 c. brown, blue & slate 10 8

225. De Lamartine and scene from "Meditations Poetiques".

1970. A. de Lamartine (writer). 150th Birth Anniv.
1002. **225.** 80 c. brn., blue & turq. 20 12

226. Beethoven.

1970. Beethoven Birth Bicent.
1003. **226.** 1 f. 30 brn. and claret 35 20

1970. Modigliani 50th Death Anniv. Vert. painting as T **204**. Multicoloured.
1004. 3 f. "Portrait of Dedie" (Modigliani) 75 60

1970. Paintings. "Princes and Princesses of Monaco". As T **192**.
1005. 1 f. red and black 25 20
1006. 3 f. multicoloured .. 80 50
PORTRAITS: 1 f. "Prince Louis I" (F. de Troy). 3 f. "Princess Charlotte de Gramont" (S. Bourdon).

227. Cocker Spaniel. **228.** Polluted Sea-Bird.

1971. Int. Dog Show, Monte Carlo.
1007. **227.** 50 c. multicoloured .. 12 5
See also No. 1036, 1082, 1119, 1197 and 1218.

1971. Campaign Against Pollution of the Sea.
1008. **228.** 50 c. indigo and blue 12 5

229. Hand holding Emblem.

1971. 7th Int. Blood-Donors Federation Congress.
1009. **229.** 80 c. red, violet & grey 20 12

230. Sextant, Scroll and Underwater Scene.

1971. Int. Hydrographic Bureau. 50th Anniv.
1010. **230.** 80 c. brn., grn. & slate-green 20 12

231. Detail of Michelangelo Sculpture ("The Arts").

1971. U.N.E.S.C.O. 25th Anniv.
1011. **231.** 30 c. brn., blue & vio. 8 5
1012. – 50 c. blue and brown 12 8
1013. – 80 c. brown and green 20 12
1014. – 1 f. 30 green 30 20
DESIGNS—VERT. 50 c. Alchemist and dish aerial ("Science"). 1 f. 30 Prince Pierre of Monaco (National U.N.E.S.C.O. Commission). HORIZ. 80 c. Ancient scribe, book and T.V. screen ("Culture").

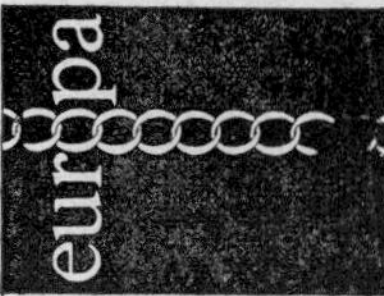

232. Europa Chain.

1971. Europa.
1015. **232.** 50 c. red 12 8
1016. 80 c. blue 20 12
1017. 1 f. 30 green .. 30 20

233. Old Bridge, Sospel.

1971. Protection of Historic Monuments.
1018. **233.** 50 c. brn., blue & grn. 12 5
1019. – 80 c. brn., grn. & grey 20 10
1020. – 1 f. 30 red, grn. & brn. 30 15
1021. – 3 f. slate, blue & olive 70 40
DESIGNS—HORIZ. 80 c. Roquebrune Chateau. 1 f. 30 Grimaldi Chateau, Cagnes-sur-Mer. VERT. 3 f. Roman "Trophy of the Alps", La Turbie.

1971. Monaco Red Cross, As T **217**.
1022. 3 f. brn., olive-brn. & grn. 75 50
DESIGN: 3 f. St. Vincent de Paul.

1972. Paintings. "Princes and Princesses of Monaco". As T **192**. Multicoloured.
1023. 1 f. "Prince Antoine I" (Rigaud) 25 20
1024. 3 f. "Princess Marie de Lorraine" (18th-cent. French School) .. 85 50

234. La Fontaine and Animal Fables (350th Birth Anniv.).

1972. Birth Annivs.
1025. **234.** 50 c. brn., emer. & grn. 12 5
1026. – 1 f. 30 mar., blk. & red 40 20
DESIGNS: 1 f. 30 Baudelaire, nudes and cats (150th Birth Anniv.).

235. Saint-Saens and scene from Opera, "Samson and Delilah".

1972. Camile Saint-Saens (1971). 50th Death Anniv.
1027. **235.** 90 c. brown and sepia 25 12

236. Battle Scene.

1972. Battle of Lepanto (1571). 400th Anniv.
1028. **236.** 1 f. blue, brn. & red .. 25 15

237. "Christ before Pilate" (engraving by Durer).

1972. Albrecht Durer. 500th Birth Anniv. (1971).
1029. **237.** 2 f. black and brown 55 25

238. "The Cradle" (B. Morisot).

1972. Foundation of U.N.I.C.E.F. 25th Anniv. (1971).
1030. **238.** 2 f. multicoloured .. 55 25

239. "Gilles" (Watteau).

1972. Watteau. 250th Death Anniv. (1971).
1031. **239.** 3 f. multicoloured .. 80 50

240. Santa Claus.

1972. Christmas.
1032. **240.** 30 c. red, blue & brn. 8 5
1033. 50 c. red, grn. & orge. 12 8
1034. 90 c. red, blue & brn. 20 12

241. Steam Locomotive and Modern Express.

1972. Int. Railway Union. 50th Anniv.
1035. **241.** 50 c. mar., lilac & red 12 8

1972. Int. Dog Show, Monte Carlo. As T 227. Inscr. "1972".
1036. 60 c. mult. (Great Dane) 15 8

242. "Pollution Kills".

1972. Anti-Pollution Campaign.
1037. **242.** 90 c. brn., grn. & blk. 25 12

243. Ski-jumping.

1972. Winter Olympic Games, Sapporo, Japan.
1038. **243.** 90 c. blk., red & grn. 25 12

244. "Communications". 245. "SS. Giovannie Paolo" (detail Canaletto).

1972. Europa.
1039. **244.** 50 c. blue and orge. 12 8
1040. 90 c. blue and grn. .. 20 12

1972. Monaco Red Cross. As T **217.**
1041. 3 f. brown and plum .. 80 50
DESIGN: 3 f. St. Francis of Assisi.

1972. Monte Carlo Flower Show. As T **218.**
1042. 3 f. multicoloured .. 75 50
DESIGN: 3 f. "Vase of Flowers" (Cezanne).

1972. U.N.E.S.C.O. "Save Venice" Campaign.
1043. **245.** 30 c. red 8 5
1044. – 60 c. violet 20 8
1045. – 2 f. blue 55 25
DESIGNS—(27 × 48 mm.): 60 c. "S. Peitro di Castello". (F. Guradi). As T **245.** 2 f. "Piazzetta S. Marco" (B. Bellotto).

246. Dressage.

1972. Olympic Games, Munich. Equestrian Events.
1046. **246.** 60 c. brn., blue & lake 20 10
1047. – 90 c. lake, brn. & blue 30 20
1048. – 1 f. 10 blue, lake & brn. 40 25
1049. – 1 f. 40 brn., lake & bl. 55 40
DESIGNS 90 c. Cross-Country. 1 f. 50 Show-jumping (wall). 1 f. 40 Show-jumping (parallel bars).

247. Escoffier and Birthplace.

1972. Auguste Escoffier (master chef). 125th Birth Anniv.
1050. **247.** 45 c. black and brown 10 5

248. Drug Addiction. 249. Globe, Birds and Animals.

1972. Campaign Against Drugs.
1051. **248.** 50 c. red, brn. & orange 12 5
1052. 90 c. grn., brn. & blue 20 12

1972. 17th Int. Congress of Zoology, Monaco.
1053. **249.** 30 c. grn., brn. & red 5 5
1054. – 50 c. brn., purple & red 12 8
1055. **249.** 90 c. blue, brn. & red 20 12
DESIGN—HORIZ. 50 c. Similar to Type **249.**

250. Lilies in Vase. 251. "The Nativity" and Child's face.

1972. Monte Carlo Flower Show, 1973 (1st issue). Multicoloured.
1056. 30 c. Type **250** 5 5
1057. 50 c. Bouquet 10 5
1058. 90 c. Flowers in Vase .. 20 12
See also No. 1073.

1972. Christmas.
1059. **251.** 30 c. grey, blue & pur. 5 5
1060. 50 c. red, purple & brn. 12 5
1061. 90 c. violet, plum & violet 20 12

252. Bleriot and Aircraft.

1972. Birth Annivs.
1062. **252.** 30 c. blue and brown 8 5
1063. – 50 c. blue, turquoise and new blue .. 12 5
1064. – 90 c. brown and buff 20 12
DESIGNS AND ANNIVERSARIES: 30 c. (birth cent.). 50 c. Amundsen and polar scene (birth cent). 90 c. Pasteur and laboratory scene (150th birth anniv.).

253. "Gethsemane".

1972. Protection of Historical Monuments. Frescoes by J. Canavesio. Chapel of Notre-Dame des Fontaines, La Brigue.
1065. **253.** 30 c. red 8 5
1066. – 50 c. grey 12 5
1067. – 90 c. green 20 12
1068. – 1 f. 40 red 30 15
1069. – 2 f. purple 55 20
DESIGNS: 50 c. "Christ Outraged". 90 c. "Ascent to Calvary". 1 f. 40 "The Resurrection". 2 f. "The Crucifixion".

1972. "Princes and Princesses of Monaco". As Type **192.** Multicoloured.
1070. 1 f. "Prince Jacques I" (N. Largillière) .. 25 15
1071. 3 f. "Princess Louise-Hippolyte" (J. B. Vanloo Pinx) 75 45

1973. Monte Carlo Flower Show. (2nd issue). As T 218.
1073. 3 f. 50 multicoloured .. 75 40
DESIGN: 3 f. 50 "Bouquet of Flowers" (Ambrosius Bosschaert.)

254. Europa "Posthorn".

1973. Europa.
1074. **254.** 50 c. orange .. 12 5
1075. 90 c. green 20 12

255. Moliere and Characters from "Le Mala de Imaginaire" 257. E. Ducretet, "Les Invalides" and Eiffel Tower.

256. Colette, Cat and Books.

1973. Moliere. 300th Death Anniv.
1076. **255.** 20 c. red, brown & blue 5 5

1973. Birth Annivs.
1077. **256.** 30 c. multicoloured .. 5 5
1078. – 45 c. multicoloured .. 12 5
1079. – 50 c. lilac, purple & bl. 12 5
1080. – 90 c. multicoloured .. 20 12
DESIGNS AND ANNIVERSARIES—HORIZ. 30 c. (nature writer—birth cent.). 45 c. J. H. Fabre and insects (entomologist—150th birth anniv.). 90 c. Sir George Cayley and early flying machines (aviation pioneer—birth bicent.). VERT. 50 c. Blaise Pascal (philosopher and writer—350th birth anniv.).

1973. Eugene Ducretet's First Hertizan Radio Link. 75th Anniv.
1081. **257.** 30 c. maroon and brown 5 5

1973. Int. Dog Show, Monte Carlo. As T **227.** Inscr. "1973". Multicoloured.
1082. 45 c. Alsatian 10 5

258. C. Peguy and Chartres Cathedral.

1973. Charles Peguy. Birth Bicent.
1083. **258.** 50 c. brn., mauve & grey 12 5

259 Telecommunications Equipment. 260. Stage Characters.

1973. 5th World Telecommunications Day.
1084. **259.** 60 c. violet, blue & brn. 12 8

1973. 5th World Amateur Theatre Festival.
1085. **260.** 60 c. mve., blue & red 20 10

261. Ellis and Rugby Tackle.

1973. Founding of Rugby Football by William Webb Ellis. 150th Anniv.
1086. **261.** 90 c. red and brown .. 20 12

262. St. Theresa.

1973. St. Theresa of Lisieux. Birth Cent.
1087. **262.** 1 f. 40 brn., blue and dark blue 30 15

263. Drug Addiction.

1973. Campaign Against Drugs.
1088. **263.** 50 c. red, grn. & blue 12 5
1089. – 50 c. multicoloured .. 12 5
1090. **263.** 90 c. violet, grn. & red 20 10
1091. – 90 c. multicoloured .. 20 12
DESIGN: Nos. 1089, 1091, Children, syringes and addicts.

264. "Institution of the Creche" (Giotto).

1973. St. Francis of Assisi Creche. 750th Anniv.
1092. **264.** 30 c. purple (postage) 5 5
1093. – 45 c. red 10 5
1094. – 50 c. brown .. 12 8
1095. – 1 f. green 20 12
1096. – 2 f. brown 40 20
1097. – 3 f. green (air) .. 65 35
DESIGN–HORIZ. 45 c. "The Nativity" (School of F. Lippi). 50 c. "The Birth of Jesus Christ" (Giotto). VERT. 1 f. "The Nativity" (15th century miniature). 2 f. "The Birth of Jesus" (Fra Angeliso). 3 f. "The Nativity" (Flemish school).

265. Country Picnic.

1973. National Committee for Monegasque Traditions. 50th Anniv.
1098. **265.** 10 c. blue, grn. & brn. 5 5
1099. – 20 c. violet, blue & grn. 5 5
1100. – 30 c. sepia, brn. & grn. 5 5
1101. – 45 c. red, violet & pur. 10 5
1102. – 50 c. blk., red & brn. 12 8
1103. – 60 c. red, violet & blue 12 8
1104. – 1 f. violet, bluish violet and brown 20 12
DESIGNS—VERT. 20 c. Maypole dance. HORIZ. 30 c. "U. Bradi" (local dance). 45 c. St. Jean fire-dance. 50 c. Blessing the Christmas loaf. 60 c. Blessing the sea – Festival of St. Devote. 1 f. Corpus Christi procession.

266. Roses and Strelitzia.

1973. Monte Carlo Flower Show. Mult.
1105. 45 c. Type **266** 10 5
1106. 60 c. Mimosa and myosotis 12 8
1107. 1 f. "Vase of Flowers" (Odilon Redon) .. 20 15

1973. Paintings. "Princesses of Monaco". As Type **192**. Multicoloured.
1108. 2 f. "Charlotte Grimaldi" (in day dress, P. Gobert) 45 20
1109. 2 f. "Charlotte Grimaldi" (in evening dress, P. Gobert) 45 20

267. U.P.U. Emblem and Symbolic Heads.

268. Farman and Aircraft of 1909 and 1919.

1974. Universal Postal Union. Cent.
1111. **268.** 50 c. maroon and brown 12 8
1112. – 70 c. multicoloured .. 20 12
1113. – 1 f. 10 multicoloured 45 30
DESIGNS: 70 c. Hands holding letters. 1 f. 10 "Countries of the World" (famous buildings).

1974. Monaco Red Cross. As Type **217**.
1114. 3 f. blue, green & maroon 80 60
DESIGN: 3 f. St. Bernard of Menthon.

1974. Henri Farman (aviation pioneer). Birth Cent.
1115. **268.** 30 c. brn., pur. & bl. 8 5

269. Marconi, Circuit Plan and Ships.

1974. Guglielmo Marconi (radio pioneer). Birth Cent.
1116. **269.** 40 c. red, dark bl & bl. 12 8

270. Duchesne and "Penicillium glaucum".

1974. Ernest Duchesne (microbiologist). Birth Cent.
1117. **270.** 45 c. black, bl. & pur. 12 8

271. Forest and Engine.

1974. Fernand Forest (motor engineer and inventor). 60th Death Anniv.
1118. **271.** 50 c. pur., red & blk. 12 8

1974. International Dog Show, Monte Carlo. As Type **227**, inscr. "1974".
1119. 60 c. multicoloured .. 15 10
DESIGN: 60 c. Schnauzer.

272. Ronsard and Characters from "Sonnet to Helene".

1974. Pierre de Ronsard (poet). 450th Birth Anniv.
1120. **272.** 70 c. brown and red .. 20 12

273. Sir Winston Churchill (after bust by O. Nemon).

275. "The King of Rome" (Bosio).

274. Interpol Emblem, and Views of Monaco and Vienna.

1974. Sir Winston Churchill. Birth Cent.
1121. **273.** 1 f. brown and grey .. 25 20

1974. 1st Int. Police Judiciary Congress. 60th Anniv., and Int. Criminal Police Organization (Interpol). 50th Anniv.
1122. **274.** 2 f. bl., brn. & grn. .. 55 40

1974. Europa. Sculptures by J. F. Bosio.
1123. **275.** 45 c. green & brown 15 8
1124. – 1 f. 10 bistre-brn. and brown 30 20
DESIGN: 1 f. 10 "Madame Elizabeth".

276. "The Box" (Renoir).

1974. "The Impressionists". Multicoloured.
1126. 1 f. Type **276** 25 15
1127. 1 f. "The Dance Class" (Degas) 25 15
1128. 2 f. "Impression-Sunrise" (Monet) (horiz.) .. 40 30
1129. 2 f. "Entrance to Voisins Village" (Pissarro) (horiz.) 50 30
1130. 2 f. "The Suspended House" (Cezanne) (horiz.) .. 50 30
1131. 2 f. "Floods at Pont Marly" (Sisley) (horiz.) 50 30

277. The Big Cats.

1974. First International Circus Festival.
1132. **277.** 2 c. brown, grn. & bl. 5 5
1133. – 3 c. brown & purple 5 5
1134. – 5 c. blue, brn. & red 5 5
1135. – 45 c. brn., blk. & red 12 5
1136. – 70 c. multicoloured .. 20 12
1137. – 1 f. 10 brn., grn. & red 30 25
1138. – 5 f. green, bl. & brn. 1·40 80
DESIGNS—VERT. 3 c. Performing horses. 45 c. Equestrian act. 1 f. 10 Balancing act. 5 f. Trapeze artists. HORIZ. 5 c. Performing elephants. 70 c. The clowns.

278. Honore II Medal.

1974. Monegasque Numismatic Art. 350th Anniv.
1139. **278.** 60 c. brown & red .. 15 10

279. Underwater Scene.

1974. 24th Congress of the International Commission for the Scientific Exploration of the Mediterranean. Multicoloured.
1140. 45 c. Type **279** 8 5
1141. 70 c. Sea-bed fauna and flora 12 8
1142. 1 f. 10 Sea-bed fauna and flora (different) .. 20 12
Nos. 1141/2 are larger size 48 × 28 mm.

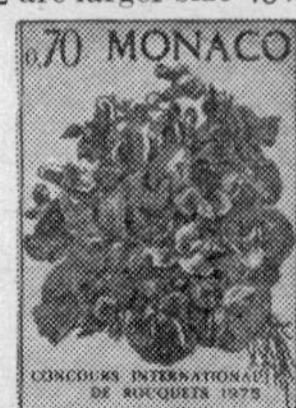

280. Honeysuckle and Violets.

1974. Monte Carlo Flower Show (May, 1975). Multicoloured.
1143. 70 c. Type **280** 12 8
1144. 1 f. 10 Ikebana flower arrangement 20 12
See also Nos. 1204/5.

281. Prince Rainer III. 282.

1974.
1145. **281.** 60 c. black 12 8
1146. 80 c. red 15 10
1147. 1 f. brown 20 12
1148. 1 f. 20 blue 25 15
1149. 2 f. mauve 35 20
1150. **282.** 10 f. blue .. .. 1·90 1·10
1151. 15 f. lake .. .. 2·75 1·60
1152. 20 f. blue .. .. 3·75 2·00

283. Monte Carlo Beach.

284. "Haageocereus chosicensis".

1974.
1153. **283.** 25 c. bl., grn. & brn. 5 5
1154. – 50 c. brown & blue .. 10 5
1155. – 1 f. 40 grn., grey & brn. 25 15
1156. – 1 f. 70 brn., grn. & blue 35 20
1157. – 3 f. brn., grey & grn. 65 30
1158. – 5 f. 50 green, brn. & bl. 1·00 70
DESIGNS—VERT. 50 c. Clock-tower. 1 f. 40 Prince Albert I statue and Museum. 3 f. Fort Antoine. HORIZ. 1 f. 70 Tower of "All the Saints". 5 f. 50 The Condamine.

1975. Cacti. Multicoloured.
1159. 10 c. Type **284** 5 5
1160. 20 c. "Matucana madisoniarum" .. 5 5
1161. 30 c. "Parodia scopaioides" 8 5
1162. 85 c. "Mediolobivia arachnacanthu" .. 20 8
1163. 1 f. 90 "Matucana yanganucensis" .. 40 20
1164. 4 f. "Echinocereus marksianus" 85 50

285. "Portrait of Marin" (P. Florence).

287. "Prologue".

286. "St. Bernardin de Sienne".

1975. Europa.
1165. **285.** 80 c. purple .. 20 12
1166. – 1 f. 20 blue 30 20
DESIGN: 1 f. 20 "St. Devote" (Ludovic Brea).

1975. Monaco Red Cross.
1168. **286.** 4 f. blue and purple 85 50

1975. Bizet's "Carmen". Cent.
1169. **287.** 30 c. blk., vio. & brn. 8 5
1170. – 60 c. brn., grn. & grey 15 10
1171. – 80 c. grn., brn. & blk. 20 12
1172. – 1 f. 40 vio., yell. & brn. 35 20
DESIGNS—HORIZ. 60 c. Lilla Pastias' tavern. 80 c. The smuggler's den. 1 f. 40 "Confrontation" at Seville.

288. Saint-Simon. 289. Dr. Schweitzer.

1975. Louis de Saint-Simon (materialist). 300th Birth Anniv.
1173. **282.** 40 c. blue 12 8

1975. Dr. Schweitzer. Birth Cent.
1174. **289.** 60 c. red and brown 15 10

290. " Stamp " and Calligraphy.

1975. " Arphila 75 " International Stamp Exhibition, Paris.
1175. **290.** 80 c. brown & orange 20 12

291. Seagull and Sunrise.

1975. International Exposition, Okinawa.
1176. **291.** 85 c. multicoloured.. 20 15

292. Pikestaff smashing Crab.

1975. Campaign against Cancer.
1177. **292.** 1 f. multicoloured .. 25 15

293. " Crown of Thorns ".

1975. Holy Year.
1178. **293.** 1 f. 15 lilac, bl. & brn. 30 20

294. Villa Sauber, Monte Carlo.

1975. European Architectural Heritage Year.
1179. **294.** 1 f. 20 grn., brn. & bl. 30 20

295. Head of Woman.

1975. International Women's Year.
1180. **295.** 1 f. 20 multicoloured 30 20

296. Rolls-Royce " Silver Ghost " (1907).

1975. Evolution of the Motor-car.
1181. **296.** 5 c. grey, grn. & yell. 5 5
1182. – 10 c. black and blue 5 5
1183. – 20 c. blue, vio. & blk. 5 5
1184. – 30 c. plum and purple 8 5
1185. – 50 c. blk., vio. & red 10 5
1186. – 60 c. brown and green 12 8
1187. – 80 c. slate and blue.. 15 10
1188. – 85 c. brn., oran. & grn. 20 15
1189. – 1 f. 20 vio., grn. & pur. 25 15
1190. – 1 f. 40 green and blue 25 15
1191. – 5 f. 50 blue, emerald and green .. .. 1·00 70

MOTOR-CARS: 10 c. Hispano-Suiza " h 6B " (1926). 20 c. Isotta Fraschini " 8A " (1928). 30 c. Cord " L–29 ". 50 c. Voisin " V–12 " (1930). 60 c. Duesenberg " SJ " (1933). 80 c. Bugatti " 57–C " (1938). 85 c. Delahaye " 135–M " (1940). 1 f. 20 Cisitalia " Pininfarina " (1946). 1 f. 40 Mercedes-Benz " 300–SL " (1955). 5 f. 50 Lamborghini " Countach " (1974).

1975. Princes and Princesses of Monaco. As T **192**. Multicoloured.
1192. 2 f. " Prince Honore III " 40 25
1193. 4 f. " Princess Catherine de Brignole " 85 50

297. Dog behind Bars. **298.** Maurice Ravel (birth cent.).

1975. Gen. J. P. Delmas de Grammont (author of Animal Protection Code). 125th Birth Anniv.
1194. **297.** 60 c. black and brown 12 8
1195. – 80 c. black and brown 15 10
1196. – 1 f. 20 green & purple 25 15

DESIGNS—VERT. 80 c. Cat in tree. HORIZ. 1 f. 20 Drayman ill-treating horse.

1975. International Dog Show, Monte Carlo. As T **227**, but inscr. " 1975 ". Multicoloured.
1197. 60 c. black and purple.. 12 8

DESIGN: 60 c. French poodle.

1975. Musical Anniversaries.
1198. **298.** 60 c. brown & purple 12 8
1199. – 1 f. 20 black & purple 25 15

DESIGN: 1 f. 20 Johann Strauss the Younger (150th birth anniv.).

299. Circus Clown. **301.** Ampere and Meter.

300. Florin of Honore II (1640).

1975. 2nd International Circus Festival.
1200. **299.** 80 c. multicoloured.. 15 10

1975. Numismatics.
1201. **300.** 80 c. grey and black 15 10

1975. Andre Ampere (physicist). Birth Centenary.
1202. **301.** 85 c. black and blue.. 20 15

302. " Lamentations on the Dead Christ " (Michelangelo).

1975. Michelangelo. 500th Birth Anniv.
1203. **302.** 1 f. 40 olive and black 25 15

1975. Monte Carlo Flower Show (1976). As T **280**. Multicoloured.
1204. 60 c. " Flowers of the Meadow " 12 8
1205. 80 c. Ikebana flower arrangement 15 10

1975. Precancelled. Surch.
1206. 42 c. on 26 c. violet, blue and black (No. 949a) 10 5
1207. 48 c. on 30 c. red, blue, lilac & blk. (No. 949b) 10 8
1208. 70 c. on 45 c. blue, violet, turq. & blk. (No. 950a) 12 8
1209. 1 f. 35 on 90 c. green, blue and black (951a) .. 25 15

303. Prince Pierre of Monaco.

1976. Literary Council of Monaco. 25th Anniversary.
1210. **303.** 10 c. black 5 5
1211. – 20 c. blue and red .. 5 5
1212. – 25 c. blue and red .. 8 5
1213. – 30 c. brown 10 8
1214. – 50 c. blue, blk. and red 15 10
1215. – 60 c. brn., grn. & yell. 20 12
1216. – 80 c. red and black.. 25 15
1217. – 1 f. 20 violet & purple 40 30

COUNCIL MEMBERS—HORIZ. 20 c. A. Maurois and Colette. 25 c. Jean and Jerome Tharaud. 30 c. E. Henriot, M. Pagnol and G. Duhamel. 50 c. Ph. Heriat, J. Supervielle and L. Pierard. 60 c. R. Dorgeles, M. Achard and G. Bauer. 80 c. F. Hellens, A. Billy and Mgr. Grente. 1 f. 20 J. Giono, L. Pasteur Vallery-Radot and M. Garcon.

304. Dachsunds.

1976. Int. Dog Show, Monte Carlo.
1218. **304.** 60 c. multicoloured .. 20 12

305. Bridge Table and Places.

1976. 5th Bridge Olympiad, Monte Carlo.
1219. **305.** 60 c. brn., grn. & red 20 12

306. Bell and Early Telephone.

1976. Telephone Centenary.
1220. **306.** 80 c. brown, light brown and grey 25 15

307. F.I.P. Emblem on Globe.

1976. Federation Internationale de Philatelie. 50th Anniv.
1221. **307.** 1 f. 20 brn., blue & grn. 40 30

308. U.S. Stamp Design of 1926.

1976. American Revolution. Bicentenary.
1222. **308.** 1 f. 70 black & purple 55 45

309. " The Fritillaries " (Van Gogh).

1976. Monte Carlo Flower Show.
1223. **309.** 3 f. multicoloured .. 95 85

310. High-diving. **311.** Decorative Plate.

1976. Olympic Games, Montreal.
1224. **310.** 60 c. brown and blue 20 12
1225. – 80 c. blue, brn. & grn. 25 15
1226. – 85 c. blue, grn. & brn. 25 15
1227. – 1 f. 20 brn., grn. & blue 40 30
1228. – 1 f. 70 brn., blue & grn. 55 45

DESIGNS—VERT. 80 c. Gymnastics. 85 c. Throwing the hammer. HORIZ. 1 f. 20 Sculling. 1 f. 70 Boxing.

1976. Europa. Monegasque Ceramics. Multicoloured.
1230. 80 c. Type **311** 25 20
1231. 1 f. 20 Grape-harvester (statuette) 40 30

312. Palace Tower.

1976. Precancelled.
1233. **312.** 50 c. brown 15 10
1234. 52 c. brown 15 10
1235. 60 c. green 20 12
1236. 62 c. purple 20 12
1237. 90 c. lilac 30 20
1238. 95 c. red 30 20
1239. 1 f. 60 blue 50 40
1240. 1 f. 70 turquoise .. 55 45

313. St. Vincent de Paul. **314.** Marquise de Sevigne.

1976. St. Vincent de Paul Conference. Cent.
1241. **313.** 60 c. blue, brn. & turq. 20 12

1976. Marquise de Sevigne. 350th Birth Anniv.
1242. **314.** 80 c. blk., violet & red 25 15

315. 2 gros coin of Prince Honore II.

1976. " Numismatics ".

1243. **315.** 80 c. grey and green .. 25 20

316. Byrd, Amundsen and Map of North Pole.

1976. First Flights over North Pole. 50th Anniv.

1244. **316.** 85 c. blue, blk. & olive 25 20

317. Gulliver and Lilliputians.

1976. Jonathan Swift's " Voyages of Gulliver ". 250th Anniv.

1245. **317.** 1 f. 20 multicoloured 40 30

318. St. Louise de Marillac.

1976. Monaco Red Cross.

1246. **318.** 4 f. blk., pur. and grn. 1·25 1·00

1976. Princes and Princesses of Monaco. As T **192.**

1247. 2 f. purple 65 55
1248. 4 f. multicoloured .. 1·25 1·00

DESIGNS: 2 f. Prince Honore IV, Princes Louise d'Aumont-Mazarin.

319. Child and Lanterns.

1976. Christmas.

1249. **319.** 1 f. 20 multicoloured 40 30

320. Dagger and Couple in Web.

321. Floral Arrangements by Princess Grace.

1976. Campaign against Drugs.

1250. **320.** 80 c. blue, orange and bronze .. 25 15
1251. 1 f. 20 violet, magenta and bronze .. 40 30

1976. Monte Carlo Flower Show. Mult.

1252. 80 c. Type **321** 25 15
1253. 1 f. Bouquet 30 20

322. Clown juggling with Performers.

1976. International Circus Festival, Monte Carlo.

1254. **322.** 1 f. multicoloured .. 30 20

POSTAGE DUE STAMPS

D 1. D 2. D 3.

1906

D 29. **D 1.** 1 c. olive 5 5
D 30. 5 c. green 20 8
D 31. 10 c. red 10 8
D 32. 10 c. sepia .. .. 85·00 30·00
D 33. 15 c. pur. on cream .. 30 25
D 113. 20 c. bistre on buff 5 5
D 34. 30 c. blue 10 10
D 114. 40 c. magenta .. 5 5
D 35. 50 c. brown on buff 70 65
D 115. 50 c. green 5 5
D 116. 60 c. black 8 8
D 117. 60 c. magenta .. 2·50 2·50
D 118. 1 f. choc. on cream 8 8
D 119. 2 f. red 15 15
D 120. 3 f. rose 15 15
D 121. 5 f. blue 15 15

1910.

D 36. **D 2.** 1 c. olive 8 8
D 37. 10 c. lilac 10 10
D 38. 30 c. bistre .. .. 55·00 42·00

1919. Surch.

D 39. **D 2.** 20 c. on 10 c. lilac .. 30 25
D 40. 40 c. on 30 c. bistre .. 30 25

1925.

D 106. **D 3.** 1 c. olive 5 5
D 107. 10 c. violet 5 5
D 108. 30 c. bistre 5 5
D 109. 60 c. red 5 5
D 110. 1 f. blue .. .. 27·00 16·00
D 111. 2 f. red .. .. 32·00 22·00

1925. Surch. **1 franc a percevoir.**

D 112. **D 1.** 1 f. on 50 c. brown on buff 10 10

D 4. D 5.

1946.

D 327. **D 4.** 10 c. black 5 5
D 328. 30 c. violet 5 5
D 329. 50 c. blue 5 5
D 330. 1 f. green 5 5
D 331. 2 f. brown 5 5
D 332. 3 f. mauve 5 5
D 333. 4 f. red 5 5
D 334. **D 5.** 5 f. brown 5 5
D 335. 10 f. blue 8 8
D 336. 20 f. green 12 12
D 337. 50 f. red and mauve 1·75 1·75
D 338. 100 f. red and green 95 95

D 6. Old Railway Engine.

1953.

D 478. – 1 f. red and green .. 5 5
D 479. – 1 f. green and red .. 5 5
D 480. – 2 f. turquoise & blue 5 5
D 481. – 2 f. blue & turquoise 5 5
D 482. **D 6.** 3 f. lake and green .. 5 5
D 483. – 3 f. green and lake .. 5 5
D 484. – 4 f. slate and brown 5 5
D 485. – 4 f. brown and slate 5 5
D 486. – 5 f. violet and blue .. 10 10
D 487. – 5 f. blue and violet .. 10 10
D 488. – 10 f. indigo and blue 1·90 1·90
D 489. – 10 f. blue and indigo 2·10 2·10
D 490. – 20 f. violet and indigo 55 55
D 491. – 20 f. indigo and violet 55 55
D 492. – 50 f. brown and red 1·60 1·60
D 493. – 50 f. red and brown 1·60 1·60
D 494. – 100 f. grn. & maroon 3·00 3·00
D 495. – 100 f. maroon & grn. 3·00 3·00

TRIANGULAR DESIGNS: Nos. D 478, Pigeons and mobile loft. D 479, " Sikorsky " helicopter. D 480, Sailing ship. D 481, S.S. " United States ". D 483, Streamlined locomotive. D 484, Old monoplane. D 485, " Comet " airliner. D 486, Old motor-car. D 487, " Sabre " racing-car. D 488, Leonardo da Vinci's flying machine. D 489, Postal rocket. D 490, Balloon. D 491, Airship "Graf Zeppelin". D 492, Postilion. D 493, Motor-cycle messenger. D 494, Mailcoach. D 495, Railway mail van.

The two designs in each value are arranged in tete-beche pairs throughout the sheet.

D 7. 18th-Century Felucca.

1960.

D 698. **D 7.** 1 c. brn., grn. & blue 5 5
D 699. – 2 c. sepia, blue & grey-green .. 5 5
D 700. – 5 c. mar., blk. & turq. 5 5
D 701. – 10 c. blk., grn. & blue 5 5
D 702. – 20 c. mar., grn. & blue 12 12
D 703. – 30 c. brn., bl. & grn. 5 5
D 704. – 50 c. bl., brn. & myrtle 20 20
D 705. – 1 f. brn., myrtle & bl. 25 25

DESIGNS: 2 c. Steamboat " La Palmaria ". 5 c. Arrival of first railway train at Monaco. 10 c. 15th-16th-century armed messenger. 20 c. 18th-century postman. 30 c. " The Charles III " (steamboat). 50 c. 17th-century courier. 1 f. Mail-coach (19th-century).

MONGOLIA O3

A republic in Central Asia between China and Russia, independent since 1921.

1924. 100 cents = 1 dollar (Chinese).
1926. 100 mung = 1 tugrik.

1. Eldev-Otchir Symbol. **2.** Soyombo Symbol.

1924. Inscr. in black.

1. **1.** 1 c. brown, pink and grey on bistre .. .. 75 1·00
2. 2 c. brown, blue and rose on brown .. 75 1·00
3. 5 c. grey, rose and yellow 3·50 2·50
4. 10 c. blue & brown on blue 1·00 1·00
5. 20 c. grey, blue and white on blue .. .. 1·75 2·00
6. 50 c. red & orge. on pink 2·50 3·00
7. $1 bistre, red and white on yellow .. .. 5·00 6·00

Stamps vary in size according to the face value.

1926. Fiscal stamps as T **2** optd. **POSTAGE** in frame in English and Mongolian.

8. **2.** 1 c. blue .. .. .. 1·50 1·50
9. 2 c. buff .. .. .. 1·50 1·50
10. 5 c. purple .. .. .. 1·50 1·50
11. 10 c. green .. .. .. 1·50 1·50
12. 20 c. brown .. .. .. 1·50 1·50
13. 50 c. brown and yellow .. 28·00 28·00
14. $1 brown and pink .. 95·00 95·00
15. $5 red and olive .. .. 75·00 £130

Stamps vary in size according to the face value.

3. State Emblem: Soyombo Symbol. Tej. **4.**

1926.

16. **3.** 5 m. black and lilac .. 3·00 3·00
17. 20 m. black and blue .. 2·00 2·00

1926.

18. **4.** 1 m. black and yellow .. 50 75
19. 2 m. black and brown .. 50 75
20. 5 m. black and lilac (A) .. 75 1·00
28. 5 m. black and lilac (B) .. 5·00 4·50
21. 10 m. black and blue .. 75 1·00
30. 20 m. black and blue .. 5·00 4·50
22. 25 m. black and green .. 1·00 85
23. 40 m. black and yellow .. 1·50 1·50
24. 50 m. black and brown .. 2·00 1·75
25. 1 t. black, green & brown 3·50 3·50
26. 3 t. black, yellow and red 7·50 7·50
27. 5 t. black, red and purple 10·00 8·50

In (A) the Arabic numerals are in the upper and in (B) in the lower value tablet.

These stamps vary in size according to the face value.

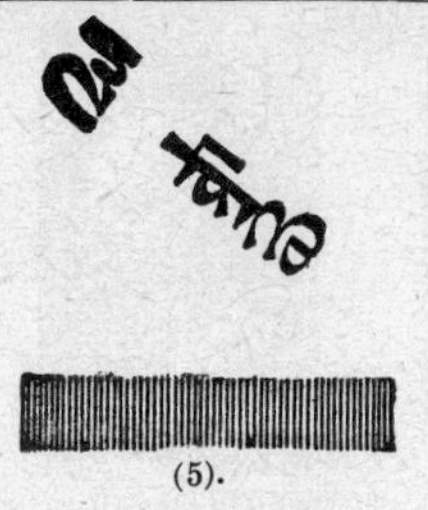
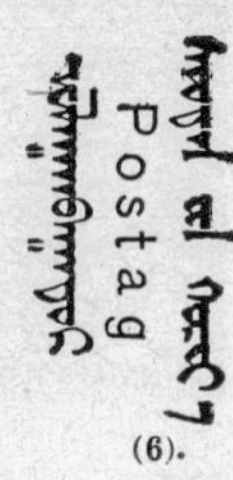

(5). (6).

1926. Surch. as T **5.**

32. **4.** 10 m. on 1 m. blk. & yell. 4·50 3·00
33. 20 m. on 2 m. black & brn. 8·00 6·00
34. 25 m. on 40 m. blk. & yell. 12·00 9·00

1931. Optd. with T **6.**

35. **2.** 1 c. blue .. .. .. 6·00 4·00
36. 2 c. buff .. .. .. 6·00 4·00
37. 5 c. purple .. .. .. 8·00 4·00
38. 10 c. green .. .. .. 8·00 4·00
39. 20 c. brown .. .. .. 9·00 5·00
40. 50 c. brown and yellow .. 30·00 25·00
41. $1 brown and pink .. 60·00 60·00

1931. Surch. **Postage** and value in "Menge".

43. **2.** 5 m. on 5 c. purple .. 8·00 2·50
44. 10 m. on 10 c. green .. 9·00 3·00
45. 20 m. on 20 c. brown .. 13·00 4·00

7. Govt. Building, Ulan Bator. **8.** Sukhe Bator.

9. Lake and Mountain Scenery.

1932.

46. – 1 m. brown 8 15
47. – 2 m. claret 8 15
48. – 5 m. blue 8 15
49. **7.** 10 m. green 10 20
50. – 15 m. brown 10 20
51. – 20 m. red 10 20
52. – 25 m. violet 12 25
53. **8.** 40 m. black 12 25
54. – 50 m. blue 12 25
55. **9.** 1 t. green 25 50
56. – 3 t. violet 30 70
57. – 5 t. brown .. .. 60 1·40
58. – 10 t. blue .. .. 1·75 3·00

DESIGNS—As T **7**: 1 m. Weavers. 5 m. Machinist. As T **8**: 2 m. Telegraphist. 15 m. Revolutionary soldier. 20 m. Mongols learning Latin alphabet. 25 m. Soldier. 50 m. Sukhe Bator's monument. As T **9**: 3 t. Sheep-shearing. 5 t. Camel caravan. 10 t. Lassoing wild horses (after painting by Sampilon).

1941. Stamps of 1932 surch.

58a. 5 m. on 5 t. chocolate ..
58b. 10 m. on 50 m. blue ..
58c. 10 m. on 10 t. ultramarine
58d. 15 m. on 5 t. chocolate ..
58e. 20 m. on 1 t. green ..
58f. 30 m. on 3 t. purple ..

11. Mongol Man. **12.** Camel Caravan.

1943. Network background in similar colour to stamps.

59. **11.** 5 m. green 40 50
60. – 10 m. blue 40 50
61. – 15 m. red 50 75
62. **12.** 20 m. chestnut 75 75
63. – 25 m. brown .. .. 1·25 1·50
64. – 30 m. red .. .. 1·50 2·00
65. – 45 m. purple .. .. 4·00 5·50
66. – 60 m. green .. .. 4·00 5·50

DESIGNS—VERT. 10 m. Mongol woman. 15 m. Soldier. 30 m. Arms of the Republic. 45 m. Portrait of Sukhe Bator, dated 1894–1923. HORIZ. 25 m. Secondary school. 60 m. Pastoral scene.

13. Marshal Kharloin Choibalsan.

15. Victory Medal.

14. Choibalsan and Sukhe Bator.

1945. Choibalsan. 50th Birthday.

67.	13.	1 t. black	1·25	1·10

1946. Independence. 25th Anniv. As T 14/5.

68.	–	30 m. bistre	1·00	1·25
69.	14.	50 m. purple	1·25	1·50
70.	–	60 m. chestnut	1·40	1·60
71.	–	60 m. black	1·40	1·60
72.	15.	80 m. chestnut	1·25	1·40
73.	–	1 t. indigo	3·00	3·50
74.	–	2 t. brown	1·25	1·10

DESIGNS—VERT. (21½ × 32 mm.): 30 m. Choibalsan, aged four. As T 15: 60 m. (No. 71), Choibalsan when young man. 1 t. 25th Anniversary Medal. 2 t. Sukhe Bator. HORIZ. As T 14: 60 m. (No. 70), Choibalsan University.

15a. Flags of Communist Bloc.

1951. Struggle for Peace.

75.	15a.	1 t. red, yell., blue & brn.	2·75	3·00

15b. Lenin (after P. Vasiliev).

17. Sukhe Bator.

16. State Shop.

1951. Honouring Lenin.

76.	15b.	3 t. multicoloured ..	2·25	2·50

1951. Independence. 30th Anniv.

77.	–	15 m. green on azure ..	80	1·00
78.	16.	20 m. orange	80	1·00
79.	–	20 m. bl., red, yell. & orge.	2·25	2·50
80.	–	25 m. blue on azure ..	1·00	1·25
81.	–	30 m. bl., red, yell. & orge.	1·75	2·00
82.	–	40 m. violet on pink ..	1·40	1·60
83.	–	50 m. brown on azure ..	2·75	3·00
84.	–	60 m. black on pink ..	2·25	2·50
85.	17.	2 t. brown	1·90	2·00

DESIGNS—HORIZ. (As T 16): 15 m. Altai Hotel. 40 m. State Theatre, Ulan Bator. 50 m. Pedagogical Institute. (55½ × 26 mm.). 25 m. Choibalsan University. VERT. (As T 17). 20 m. (No. 79), 30 m. Arms and flag. 60 m. Sukhe Bator Monument.

18. School-children.

1952. Culture.

86.	–	5 m. brown on pink ..	35	45
87.	18.	10 m. blue on pink ..	55	55

DESIGN: 5 m. New houses.

19. Choibalsan in National Costume.

20. Choibalsan and Farm Worker.

1953. Marshal Choibalsan. 1st Death Anniv. As T 19/20.

88.	19.	15 m. blue	80	80
89.	20.	15 m. green	80	80
90.	19.	20 m. green	2·00	2·40
91.	20.	20 m. sepia	1·40	1·40
92.	–	20 m. blue	1·40	1·40
93.	–	30 m. sepia	1·90	1·75
94.	–	50 m. brown	1·50	1·75
95.	–	1 t. red	2·00	2·25
96.	–	1 t. maroon	2·00	2·25
97.	–	2 t. red	1·50	1·50
98.	–	3 t. maroon	1·50	1·75
99.	–	5 t. red	2·00	2·25

DESIGNS—VERT. As T 19: 1 t. (No. 96), 2 t. Choibalsan in uniform. (33×48 mm.): 3 t., 5 t. Busts of Choibalsan and Sukhe Bator. (33×46 mm.): 50 m., 1 t. (No. 95), Choibalsan and young pioneer. HORIZ. (48×33 mm.): 20 m. (No. 92), 30 m. Choibalsan and factory hand.

21. Arms of the Republic.

22. Sukhe Bator and Choibalsan.

22a. Lenin.

1954.

100.	21.	10 m. red	5·00	3·50
101.		20 m. red	5·00	3·50
102.		30 m. red	5·00	3·50
103.		40 m. red	5·00	3·50
104.		60 m. red	5·00	3·50

1955.

105.	22.	30 m. green	15	8
106.	–	30 m. blue	25	12
107.	–	30 m. red	15	8
108.	–	40 m. purple	30	15
109.	–	50 m. chestnut ..	35	25
110.	–	1 t. vermilion, orange, blue and red ..	35	60

DESIGNS—HORIZ. 30 m. blue, Lake Khobsogol. 50 m. Choibalsan University. VERT. 30 m. red, Lenin Statue, Ulan Bator. 40 m. Sukhe Bator and dog. 1 t. Arms and flag of the Republic.

1955. Lenin. 85th Birth Anniv.

111.	22a.	2 t. blue	1·50	90

22b. Flags of the Communist Bloc.

23. Arms of the Republic.

1955. Struggle for Peace.

112.	22b.	60 m. vermilion, orge., blue and sepia ..	55	40

1956.

113.	23.	20 m. brown	20	12
114.		30 m. brown	25	15
115.		40 m. blue	30	20
116.		60 m. green	35	25
117.		1 t. red	60	20

23a. Train linking Ulan Bator and Moscow.

1956. Mongol–Soviet Friendship.

118.	23a.	1 t. red, blue, black and yellow ..	80	50
119.	–	2 t. red, orange, blue and yellow ..	1·50	85

DESIGN: 2 t. Flags of Mongolia and Russia.

24. Hunter and Eagle.

25. Arms.

25a. Wrestlers.

1956. Independence. 35th Anniv.

120.	24.	30 m. brown	4·50	4·50
121.	25.	30 m. blue	3·75	3·75
122.	25a.	60 m. green	3·50	3·50
123.	–	60 m. orange	3·50	3·50

DESIGN—As T 24: 60 m. (No. 123), Children. Also inscr. "xxxv".

26.

27.

28. Dove and Globe.

1958. With or without gum.

124.	26.	20 m red	55	55

1958. 13th Congress of Mongol People's Revolutionary Party. With or without gum.

125.	27.	30 m. claret & salmon	1·50	75

1958. As T 25a but without "xxxv". With or without gum.

126.		50 m. brown on pink ..	2·10	1·60

1958. Int. Women's Federation, Vienna. 4th Congress. With or without gum.

127.	28.	60 m. blue	1·50	90

29. Mountain Sheep.

30. Yak.

1958. Mongolian Animals. As T 29/30.

128.	–	30 m. pale blue	55	25
129.	–	30 m. turquoise-blue ..	55	25
130.	29.	30 m. green	55	25
131.		30 m. blue-green ..	55	25
132.	30.	60 m. yellow-brown ..	90	60
133.		60 m. yellow-orange ..	90	60
134.	–	1 t. blue	1·75	1·00
135.	–	1 t. light blue ..	1·50	55
136.	–	1 t. claret	1·75	1·00
137.	–	1 t. red	1·50	70

DESIGNS—VERT. 30 m. (Nos. 128/9), Pelicans. HORIZ. 1 t. (Nos. 134/5), Yak, facing right. 1 t. (Nos. 136/7), Camels.

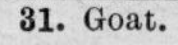

31. Goat.

31a. "Tulaga".

1958. Mongolian Animals.

138.	31.	5 m. sepia and yellow ..	5	5
139.	–	10 m. sepia and green ..	5	5
140.	–	15 m. sepia and lilac ..	5	5
141.	–	20 m. sepia and blue ..	5	5
142.	–	25 m. sepia and red ..	8	5
143.	–	30 m. purple and mauve	10	5
144.	31.	40 m. green	12	5
145.	–	50 m. brown and salmon	20	8
146.	–	60 m. blue	30	12
147.	–	1 t. bistre and yellow ..	50	25

ANIMALS: 10 m., 30 m. Ram. 15 m., 60 m. Stallion. 20 m., 50 m. Bull. 25 m., 1 t. Camel.

1959.

148.	31a.	1 t. red, bl., yell. & blk.	1·00	35

32. Taming a Wild Horse.

1959. Mongolian Sports. Centres and inscriptions multicoloured; frame colours given below.

149.	32.	5 m. yellow and orange	5	5
150.	–	10 m purple	5	5
151.	–	15 m. yellow and green	8	5
152.	–	20 m lake and rose ..	8	5
153.	–	25 m. blue	12	5
154.	–	30 m. yell., grn. & turq.	20	5
155.	–	70 m. red and yellow ..	35	12
156.	–	80 m. purple	65	30

DESIGNS: 10 m. Wrestlers. 15 m Introducing young rider. 20 m. Archer. 25 m. Galloping horseman. 30 m. Archery contest. 70 m. Hunting a wild horse. 80 m. Proclaiming a champion.

33. Child Musician.

DESIGNS — VERT. 10 m. Young wrestlers. 20 m. Youth on horse. 25 m. Artists in national costume. HORIZ. 40 m. Festival parade.

1959. Mongolian Youth Festival (1st issue).

157.	33.	5 m. purple and blue ..	5	5
158.	–	10 m. brown and green	8	5
159.	–	20 m. green and purple	10	5
160.	–	25 m. blue and green ..	20	8
161.	–	40 m. violet and myrtle	25	12

35. Kalmuck Script.

34. Festival Badge.

36. Military Monument.

37. Herdswoman and Lamb.

1959. Mongolian Youth Festival (2nd issue).

162.	34.	30 m. purple and blue ..	25	20

1959. Mongolists' Congress. Designs as T 35 incorporating "MONGOL" in various scripts.

163.	–	30 m. grn., bl., yell. & red	1·75	1·75
164.	–	40 m. red, blue & yellow	1·75	1·75
165.	35.	50 m. grn., bl., yell. & red	2·50	2·50
166.	–	60 m. red, blue & yellow	4·50	4·50
167.	–	1 t. yellow, turq. & orge.	6·00	6·00

SCRIPTS (29½ × 42½ mm.): 30 m. Stylized Uighur. 40 m. Soyombo. 60 m. Square (Pagspa). (21½ × 31 mm.): 1 t. Cyrillic.

1959. Battle of Khalka River. 20th Anniv.

No.	Type	Description	Unused	Used
168.	–	40 m. red, brn. & yellow	20	10
169.	36.	50 m. multicoloured ..	20	10

DESIGN: 40 m. Mounted horseman with flag (emblem), inscr. "AUGUST 1959 HALHIN GOL".

1959. 2nd Meeting of Rural Economy Co-operatives.

No.	Type	Description	Unused	Used
170.	37.	30 m. green	1·25	1·10

38. Sable.

1959. Mongolian Fauna.

No.	Type	Description	Unused	Used
171.	38.	5 m. mar., yell., & blue	8	5
172.	–	10 m. chocolate, red, green and purple ..	8	5
173.	–	15 m. blk., green & red	12	8
174.	–	20 m. mar., blue & red	12	10
175.	–	30 m. myrtle, pur. & grn.	15	12
176.	–	50 m. blk., blue & green	25	12
177.	–	1 t. black, green and red	55	20

ANIMALS—HORIZ. (58×21 mm.): 10 m. Pheasants. 20 m. Otter. 50 m. Saiga antelopes. 1 t. Musk deer. As T 38: 15 m. Muskrat. 30 m. Argali sheep.

39. "Lunik III" in Flight. 41. "Flower" Emblem.

40. Motherhood Badge.

1959. Launching of "Lunik III" Rocket.

No.	Type	Description	Unused	Used
178.	39.	30 m. yellow and violet	30	12
179.	–	50 m. red, green & blue	35	12

DESIGN—HORIZ. 50 m. "Lunik III's" trajectory around the Moon.

1960. Int. Women's Day.

No.	Type	Description	Unused	Used
180.	40.	40 m. bistre and blue ..	20	8
181.	41.	50 m. yell., grn. & blue	25	12

42. Lenin. 43. "Delphinium grandiflorum".

1960. Lenin. 90th Birth Anniv.

No.	Type	Description	Unused	Used
182.	42.	40 m. claret	15	8
183.		50 m. violet	20	10

1960. Mongolian Flowers.

No.	Type	Description	Unused	Used
184.	43.	5 m. blue, grn. & bistre	5	5
185.	–	10 m. red, grn. & orge.	5	5
186.	–	15 m. vio., grn. & bistre	10	5
187.	–	20 m. yellow, bronze-green and olive-green	10	5
188.	–	30 m. vio., bronze-grn. and emerald ..	12	8
189.	–	40 m. orge., grn. & sl.-vio.	15	10
190.	–	50 m. vio., grn. & turq.	25	12
191.	–	1 t. magenta, bronze-grn. & yellow-green ..	75	80

FLOWERS: 10 m. "Tulipa edulis". 15 m. "Polemonium coeruleum". 20 m. "Trollius asiaticus". 30 m. "Campanula glomerata". 40 m. "Parnassia palustris". 50 m. "Geranium pratense". 1 t. "Begonia evansiana".

44. Horse-jumping.

1960. Olympic Games. Inscr. "ROMA 1960" or "ROMA MCMLX". Centres in greenish grey.

No.	Type	Description	Unused	Used
192.	44.	5 m. red, black & turq.	5	5
193.	–	10 m. violet and yellow	5	5
194.	–	15 m. turq., blk. & verm.	8	5
195.	–	20 m. claret and blue ..	10	8
196.	–	30 m. ochre, blk. & green	15	8
197.	–	50 m. blue & blue-green	25	10
198.	–	70 m. grn., blk. & violet	35	20
199.	–	1 t. magenta & yell.-grn.	60	30

DESIGNS—DIAMOND SHAPED: 10 m. Running. 20 m. Wrestling. 50 m. Gymnastics. 1 t. Discus-throwing. As T 44: 15 m. Diving 30 m. Hurdling. 70 m. High-jumping.

45.

1960. Red Cross.

No.	Type	Description	Unused	Used
200.	45.	20 m. red, yellow & blue	20	10

46. Newspapers.

1961. Mongolian Newspaper. "Unen" ("Truth"). 40th Anniv.

No.	Type	Description	Unused	Used
201.	46.	20 m. buff, green & red	12	5
202.		30 m. red, yellow & grn.	20	8

47. Hoopoe ("Upupa epops").

1961. Mongolian Song-birds.

No.	Type	Description	Unused	Used
203.	–	5 m. mauve., blk. & grn.	5	5
204.	47.	10 m. red, blk. & green	5	5
205.	–	15 m. yell., blk. & emer.	10	8
206.	–	20 m. grn., blk. & bistre	10	5
207.	–	50 m. blue, black & red	30	8
208.	–	70 m. yell., blk. & mag.	35	20
209.	–	1 t. magenta, orge. & blk.	45	35

BIRDS—As T 43. 15 m. "Oriolus oriolus". 20 m. "Tetrao urogalloides". Inverted triangulars: 5 m. "Pastor roseus". 50 m. "Eurystomus orientalis". 70 m. "Syrrhaptes tibetanus". 1 t. "Aix galericulata".

48. Foundry Worker. 49. Patrice Lumumba.

1961. World Federation of Trade Unions. 15th Anniv.

No.	Type	Description	Unused	Used
210.	48.	30 m. red and black ..	15	5
211.	–	50 m. red and violet ..	20	8

DESIGN—HORIZ. 50 m. Hemispheres.

1961. Patrice Lumumba Commem.

No.	Type	Description	Unused	Used
212.	49.	30 m. brown	1·40	90
213.		50 m. slate-purple ..	1·40	80

50. Bridge. 51. Gagarin with Capsule.

1961. Independence. 40th Anniv. (1st Issue). Mongolian Modernization.

No.	Type	Description	Unused	Used
214.	50.	5 m. emerald	5	5
215.	–	10 m. blue	8	5
216.	–	15 m. red	8	5
217.	–	20 m. brown	12	5
218.	–	30 m. blue	15	8
219.	–	50 m. green	25	12
220.	–	1 t. violet	45	20

DESIGNS: 10 m. Shoe-maker. 15 m. Store at Ulan Bator. 30 m. Government Building, Ulan Bator. 50 m. Machinist. 1 t. Ancient and modern houses. (59 × 20½ mm.): 20 m. Choibalsan University.

1961. World's First Manned Space Flight. Inscr. as in T 51. Multicoloured.

No.	Type	Description	Unused	Used
221.		20 m. T 51	20	8
222.		30 m. Gagarin in space helmet and globe ..	30	12
223.		50 m. Gagarin making parachute descent ..	45	15
224.		1 t. As 30 m. but positions reversed ..	65	25

The 30 m. and 1 t. are horiz.

52. Postman with Reindeer.

1961. Independence. 40th Anniv. (2nd Issue). Mongolian Postal Service.

No.	Type	Description	Unused	Used
225.	52.	5 m. vermilion, brown and blue (post.) ..	5	5
226.	–	15 m. violet, brn. & bis.	8	5
227.	–	20 m. blue, blk. & green	8	5
228.	–	25 m. vio., bistre & grn.	12	5
229.	–	30 m. grn., blk. & lav.	20	8
230.	–	10 m. orange, black and green (air) ..	5	5
231.	–	50 m. blk., red & turq.	30	10
232.	–	1 t. yell., bl., mar. & red	50	20

DESIGNS—Postman with: 10 m. Horses. 15 m. Camels. 20 m. Yaks. 25 m. Postman on quayside. 30 m. Diesel mail train. 50 m. Mail plane over map. 1 t. Postal emblem.

53. Rams.

1961. Independence. 40th Anniv. (3rd Issue). Animal Husbandry.

No.	Type	Description	Unused	Used
233.	53.	5 m. black, red and blue	5	5
234.	–	10 m. black, green & pur.	5	5
235.	–	15 m. black, red & green	12	5
236.	–	20 m. sepia, bl. & chest.	12	5
237.	–	25 m. black, yell. & grn.	15	5
238.	–	30 m. black, red & violet	15	8
239.	–	40 m. black, grn. & verm.	20	10
240.	–	50 m. black, brown & bl.	20	12
241.	–	1 t. black, violet & olive	40	20

DESIGNS: 10 m. Oxen. 15 m. Camels. 20 m. Pigs and poultry. 25 m. Angora goats. 30 m. Mongolian horses. 40 m. Ewes. 50 m. Cows. 1 t. Combine-harvester.

54. Children Wrestling.

1961. Independence. 40th Anniv. (5th Issue). Mongolian Sports.

No.	Type	Description	Unused	Used
242.	54.	5 m. grn., red., bl. & pink	5	5
243.	–	10 m. sepia, red & green	5	5
244.	–	15 m. pur., blue & yell.	10	5
245.	–	20 m. red, black & green	12	5
246.	–	30 m. mar., grn. & lav.	15	8
247.	–	50 m. indigo, orge. & bl.	35	25
248.	–	1 t. pur., ultram. & grey	75	65

DESIGNS: 10 m. Horse-riding. 15 m. Children on camel and pony. 20 m. Falconry. 30 m. Skiing. 50 m. Archery. 1 t. Dancing.

55. Young Mongol.

1961. Independence. 40th Anniv. (6th Issue). Mongolian Culture.

No.	Type	Description	Unused	Used
249.	55.	5 m. purple and green ..	5	5
250.	–	10 m. blue and red ..	5	5
251.	–	15 m. brown and blue ..	10	5
252.	–	20 m. green and violet ..	12	5
253.	–	30 m. red and blue ..	12	10
254.	–	50 m. violet and bistre ..	20	12
255.	–	70 m. green and magenta	20	12
256.	–	1 t. red and blue ..	45	30

DESIGNS—HORIZ. 10 m. Mongol chief. 70 m. Orchestra. 1 t. Gymnast. VERT. 15 m. Sukhe Bator Monument. 20 m. Young singer. 30 m. Young dancer. 50 m. Dombra-player.

56. Mongol Arms. 57. Congress Emblem.

1961. Arms multicoloured; inscr. in blue; background colours given.

No.	Type	Description	Unused	Used
257.	56.	5 m. salmon	5	5
258.		10 m. lilac	5	5
259.		15 m. brown	8	5
260.		20 m. turquoise	10	5
261.		30 m. ochre	12	8
262.		50 m. mauve	20	10
263.		70 m. olive	30	20
264.		1 t. orange	35	25

1961. 5th World Federation of Trade Unions Congress, Moscow.

No.	Type	Description	Unused	Used
265.	57.	30 m. red, yellow & blue	15	8
266.		50 m. red, yellow & sepia	25	10

58. Dove, Map and Globe.

1962. Admission of Mongolia to U.N.O.

No.	Type	Description	Unused	Used
267.	58.	10 m. multicoloured ..	5	5
268.	–	30 m. multicoloured ..	12	5
269.	–	50 m. multicoloured ..	25	8
270.	–	60 m. multicoloured ..	30	15
271.	–	70 m. multicoloured ..	35	20

DESIGNS: 30 m. U.N. Emblem and Mongol Arms. 50 m. U.N. and Mongol flags. 60 m. U.N. Headquarters and Mongolian Parliament building. 70 m. U.N. and Mongol flags, and Assembly.

59. Football, Globe and Flags.

1962. World Cup Football Championships, Chile. Multicoloured.

272. 10 m. Type **59** 5 5
273. 30 m. Footballers, globe and ball 12 5
274. 50 m. Footballers playing in stadium 30 8
275. 60 m. Goalkeeper saving goal 30 15
276. 70 m. Stadium 40 20

60. D. Natsagdorj. **61.** Torch and Handclasp. **62.** Flags of Mongolia and U.S.S.R.

1962. 3rd Congress of Mongolian Writers.

277. **60.** 30 m. brown 12 5
278. 50 m. green 25 12

See also Nos. 420a/6.

1962. Afro-Asian People's Solidarity.

279. **61.** 20 m. red, black, yellow and green 12 8
280. 30 m. red, black, yellow and blue 20 10

1962. Mongol-Soviet Friendship.

281. **62.** 30 m. red, blue, buff and brown 12 8
282. 50 m. red, blue, buff and ultramarine 20 12

1962. Malaria Eradication. Nos. 184/91 optd. with Campaign emblem and **LUTTE CONTRE LE PALUDISME.**

283. **43.** 5 m. 25 25
284. – 10 m. 25 25
285. – 15 m. 25 25
286. – 20 m. 25 25
287. – 30 m. 25 25
288. – 40 m. 25 25
289. – 50 m. 25 25
290. – 1 t. 25 25

63. Victory Banner.

DESIGNS: 30 m. Engraved lacquer tablets. 50 m. Obelisk. 60 m. Genghis Khan.

1962. Genghis Khan. 800th Birth Anniv.

291. **63.** 20 m. buff, red, gold & bl. 50 50
292. – 30 m. lake, buff, silver and black 90 90
293. – 50 m. black., brn. & red 1·40 1·40
294. – 60 m. buff blue & brown 2·75 2·75

64 Perch.

1962. Fish. Multicoloured.

205. 5 m. T **64** 5 5
296. 10 m. Burbot 5 5
297. 15 m. Arctic Grayling .. 8 5
298. 20 m. Bullhead 10 5
299. 30 m. Pike—perch .. 12 8
300. 50 m. Sturgeon 20 12
301. 70 m. Dace 25 15
302. 1 t. 50 Sculpin 60 40

65. Sukhe Bator.

ILLUSTRATIONS
British Commonwealth and all overprints and surcharges are FULL SIZE. Foreign Countries have been reduced to ¾-LINEAR.

1963. Sukhe Bator. 70th Birth Anniv.

303. **65.** 30 m. blue 12 8
304. 60 m. lake 25 12

66. Dog "Laika" and Rocket.

1963. Space Flights. Multicoloured.

305. 5 m. T **66** 10 5
306. 15 m. Rocket blasting off .. 15 5
307. 25 m. Lunik II (1959) .. 20 8
308. 70 m. Nikolaev and Popovich 50 20
309. 1 t. Mars rocket (1962) .. 65 35

SIZES—As T **66**: 70 m., 1 t. VERT. (21×70 mm.): 15 m., 25 m.

67. Children packing Red Cross Parcels.

1963. Red Cross Cent. Multicoloured.

310. 20 m. Type **67** 8 5
311. 30 m. Blood transfusion .. 12 8
312. 50 m. Doctor treating child 20 10
313. 60 m. Ambulance at street accident 25 12
314. 1 t. 30 Centenary emblem 55 30

68. Karl Marx. **69.** Woman.

1963. Karl Marx. 145th Birth Anniv.

315. **68.** 30 m. blue 12 8
316. 60 m. lake 20 12

1963. 5th World Congress of Democratic Women, Moscow.

317. **69.** 30 m. multicoloured 12 8

70. "Inachis Io L."

1963. Mongolian Butterflies. Multicoloured.

318. 5 m. Type **70** 8 5
319. 10 m. "Gonepteryx rhamni L." 8 5
320. 15 m. "Aglais urticae L." 15 10
321. 20 m. "Parnassius apollo L." 20 12
322. 30 m. "Papilio machaon L." 25 15
323. 60 m. "Agrodiaetus damon Schiff" .. 40 20
324. 1 t. "Limenitis populi L." 60 30

71. Globe and Scales of Justice.

1963. Declaration of Human Rights. 15th Anniv.

325. **71.** 30 m. red, blue & brown 12 8
326. 60 m. black, blue & yell. 25 12

72. "Coprinus comatus".

1964. Mushrooms. Multicoloured.

327. 5 m. Type **72** 5 5
328. 10 m. "Lactarius torminosus" 5 5
329. 15 m. "Psalliota campestris" 10 8
330. 20 m. "Russula delica" .. 12 8
331. 30 m. "Ixocomus granulatus" 20 12
332. 50 m. "Lactarius scobiculatus" 25 15
333. 70 m. "Lactarius deliciosus" 35 20
334. 1 t. "Ixocomus variegatus" 45 25

73. Lenin when a Young Man.

Nos. 335/6 were issued in sheets with se-tenant labels bearing a quotation from Lenin's works.

1964. London Bolshevik (Communist) Party. 60th Anniv.

335. **73.** 30 m. crimson and brown 12 8
336. 50 m. ultramarine & blue 25 12

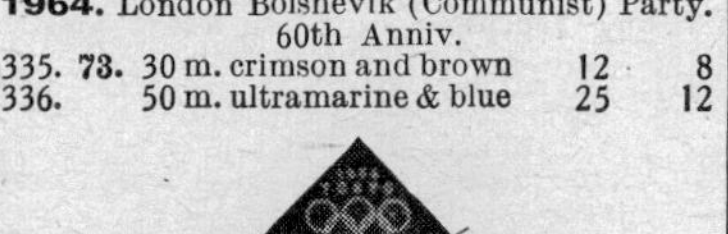

74. Gymnastics.

1964. Olympic Games, Tokyo. Multicoloured.

337. 5 m. Type **74** 5 5
338. 10 m. Throwing the javelin 5 5
339. 15 m. Wrestling 10 5
340. 20 m. Running 12 5
341. 30 m. Horse-jumping .. 15 8
342. 50 m. High-diving .. 20 10
343. 60 m. Cycling 25 15
344. 1 t. Emblem of Tokyo Games 45 20

75. Congress Emblem.

1964. 4th Mongolian Women's Congress.

345. **75.** 30 m. blue, red, gold and green 15 8

76. "Lunik 1".

1964. Space research. Multicoloured.

346. 5 m. Type **76** 5 5
347. 10 m. "Vostoks 1 and 2" 5 5
348. 15 m. "Tiros" 8 5
349. 20 m. "Cosmos" .. 10 5
350. 30 m. "Mars Probe" .. 15 5
351. 60 m. "Luna 4" .. 30 10
352. 80 m. "Echo 2" .. 35 15
353. 1 t. Radio Telescope .. 45 25

The 10 m., 80 m. and 1 t. are horiz., the rest are vert.

77. Horseman and Flag.

1964. Mongolian Constitution. 40th Anniv.

354. **77.** 25 m. multicoloured .. 12 8
355. 50 m. multicoloured .. 20 10

78. Marine Exploration.

1965. Int. Quiet Sun Year. Multicoloured.

356. 5 m. Type **78** (postage) .. 5 5
357. 10 m. Weather balloon .. 5 5
358. 60 m. Northern Lights .. 20 12
359. 80 m. Geomagnetic emblems 25 15
360. 1 t. Globe and I.Q.S.Y. emblem 45 20
361. 15 m. Weather satellite (air) 10 5
362. 20 m. Antarctic exploration 12 5
363. 30 m. Space exploration .. 15 8

79. Horses Grazing.

1965. Mongolian Horses. Multicoloured.

364. 5 m. Type **79** 5 5
365. 10 m. Hunting with falcons 5 5
366. 15 m. Breaking-in wild horse 10 5
367. 20 m. Horses racing .. 12 5
368. 30 m. Horses jumping .. 15 8
369. 60 m. Hunting wolves .. 20 10
370. 80 m. Milking a mare .. 25 12
371. 1 t. Mare and colt 45 20

80. Farm Girl with Lambs.

1965. Mongolian Youth Movement. 40th Anniv.

372. **80.** 5 m. orge., bistre & grn. 5 5
373. – 10 m. bistre, blue & red 5 5
374. – 20 m. ochre, red & violet 12 5
375. – 30 m. lilac, brown & grn. 15 8
376. – 50 m. orge., buff & blue 35 20

DESIGNS: 10 m. Young drummers. 20 m. Children around camp-fire. 30 m. Young wrestlers. 50 m. Emblem.

MINIMUM PRICE

The minimum price quoted is 5p which represents a handling charge rather than a basis for valuing common stamps. For further notes about prices see introductory pages.

81. "Siniperca chua-tsi".

1965. Mongolian Fishes. Multicoloured.

377.	5 m. Type **81**	5	5
378.	10 m. "Brachymistrax lenok"	5	5
379.	15 m. "Acipenser baeri"	8	5
380.	20 m. "Hucho taimen" ..	12	5
381.	30 m. "Pseudobagrus fulvidraco" ..	15	8
382.	60 m. "Parasilurus asotus"	20	10
383.	80 m. "Esox lucius" ..	30	15
384.	1 t. "Perca fluviatilis" ..	50	30

82. Marx and Lenin. **83.** I.T.U. Emblem and Symbols.

1965. Postal Ministers' Congress Peking.

385. **82.**	10 m. black and red ..	12	8

1965. Air. I.T.U. Cent.

386. **83.**	30 m. blue and bistre ..	12	8
387.	50 m. red, bistre & blue	20	10

84. "Martes zibellina".

1966. Mongolian Fur Industry.

388. **84.**	5 m. pur., blk. & yellow	5	5
389. –	10 m. chest., black & grey	5	5
390. –	15 m. brn., black & blue	8	5
391. –	20 m. brown, black, grn. and olive-brown ..	10	5
392. –	30 m. brn., blk & mve.	20	10
393. –	60 m. brown, black & grn.	25	12
394. –	80 m. drab, yellow, black and lavender	45	25
395. –	1 t. blue, black & olive	60	40

DESIGNS (Fur animals)—HORIZ. 10 m. "Vulpes vulpes". 30 m. "Felis manul". 60 m. "Martes foina". VERT. 15 m. "Lutra lutra". 20 m. "Acinonyx jubatus". 80 m. "Mustela ermina". 1 t. Mannequin in fur coat.

85. W.H.O. Building.

1966. W.H.O. Headquarters, Geneva. Inaug.

396. **85.**	30 m. blue, gold & grn.	12	8
397.	50 m. blue, gold and red	20	12

86. Footballers.

1966. World Cup Football Championships. Multicoloured.

398.	10 m. Type **86**	5	5
399.	30 m. Footballers (different)	8	5
400.	60 m. Goalkeeper saving goal	15	8
401.	80 m. Footballers (different)	20	10
402.	1 t. World Cup flag ..	25	15

87. Sukhe Bator and Parliament Buildings, Ulan Bator.

1966. 15th Mongolian Communist Party Congress.

404. **87.**	30 m. multicoloured ..	12	5

88. Wrestling. **89.** State Emblem.

1966. World Wrestling Championships Toledo (Spain). Similar Wrestling designs.

405. **88.**	10 m. blk., mag. & pur.	5	5
406. –	30 m. blk., mag. & grey	8	5
407. –	60 m. blk., mag. & brn.	12	8
408. –	80 m. blk., mag. & lilac	20	10
409. –	1 t. black, mag. & turq.	30	15

1966. Independence. 45th Anniv. Multicoloured.

411.	30 m. Type **89**	12	8
412.	50 m. Sukhe Bator, emblems of agriculture and industry (horiz.) ..	20	10

90. "Physochlaena physaloides". **91.** Child with dove.

1966. Flowers. Multicoloured.

413.	5 m. Type **90**	5	5
414.	10 m. "Allium polyrrhizum"	5	5
415.	15 m. "Lilium tenuifolium"	10	5
416.	20 m. "Thermopsis lanceolata" ..	10	5
417.	30 m. "Amygoalus mongolica"	12	8
418.	60 m. "Caryopteris mongolica"	15	10
419.	80 m. "Piptanthus mogolicus"	20	12
420.	1 t. "Iris bungri" ..	40	20

1966. D. Natsagdorj. 60th Birth Anniv. Nos. 277/8 optd. **1906 1966**.

420a. **62.**	30 m. brown	2·00	2·00
420b.	50 m. green	2·00	2·00

1966. Children's Day. Multicoloured.

421.	10 m. Type **91**	5	5
422.	15 m. Children with reindeer	5	5
423.	20 m. Boys wrestling ..	8	5
424.	30 m. Boy riding horse ..	15	8
425.	60 m. Children on camel ..	20	10
426.	80 m. Shepherd boy with sheep	25	12
427.	1 t. Boy archer	40	15

The 15 m., 30 m. and 80 m. are horiz.

92. "Proton 1".

1966. Space Satellites. Multicoloured.

428.	5 m. "Vostok 1" ..	5	5
429.	10 m. Type **92** ..	5	5
430.	15 m. "Telstar 1" ..	8	5
431.	20 m. "Molniya 1" ..	10	5
432.	30 m. "Syncom 3" ..	15	8
433.	60 m. "Luna 9" ..	20	10
434.	80 m. "Luna 12" ..	20	10
435.	1 t. Mars and photographs taken by "Mariner 4"	45	20

The 5, 15, 20, 30 and 80 m. are vert.

93. Tarbosaurus. **94.** Congress Emblem.

1966. Prehistoric Animals. Multicoloured.

436.	5 m. Type **93**	5	5
437.	10 m. Talararus	5	5
438.	15 m. Protoceratops ..	8	5
439.	20 m. Indricotherium ..	10	5
440.	30 m. Saurolophus ..	15	8
441.	60 m. Mastodon	20	10
442.	80 m. Mongolotherium ..	20	12
443.	1 t. Mammuthus	45	25

1967. 9th Int. Students' Union Congress.

444. **94.**	30 m. ultramarine & blue	12	8
445.	50 m. ultramarine & pink	20	12

95. Sukhe Bator and Mongolian and Soviet Soldiers. **96.** Vietnamese Mother and Child.

1967. October Revolution. 50th Anniv.

446. **95.**	40 m. multicoloured ..	12	8
447. –	60 m. multicoloured ..	20	10

DESIGN: 60 m. Lenin, and soldiers with sword.

1967. Help for Vietnam.

448. **96.**	30 m.+20 m. brown, red and blue ..	20	8
449.	50 m.+30 m. brown, blue and red ..	25	12

97. Figure-skating.

1967. Winter Olympic Games, Grenoble. Multicoloured.

450.	5 m. Type **97** ..	5	5
451.	10 m. Speed-skating ..	5	5
452.	15 m. Ice-hockey ..	10	5
453.	20 m. Ski-jumping ..	12	8
454.	30 m. Bob-sleighing ..	20	8
455.	60 m. Figure-skating (pairs)	25	12
456.	80 m. Downhill skiing ..	35	15

98. Camel and Calf.

1968. Young Animals. Multicoloured.

458.	5 m. Type **98**	5	5
459.	10 m. Yak	5	5
460.	15 m. Lamb	10	5
461.	20 m. Foal	12	8
462.	30 m. Calf	15	8
463.	60 m. Bison	20	10
464.	80 m. Roe deer ..	20	12
465.	1 t. Reindeer	45	20

ЛЭХБ
20 ЖИЛ
WHO

99. "Rosa acicularis". (**99a.**)

1968. Mongolian Berries.

466. **99.**	5 m. ultram. on blue ..	5	5
467. –	10 m. brown on buff ..	5	5
468. –	15 m. emerald on green	10	5
469. –	20 m. red on cream ..	12	5
470. –	30 m. red on pink ..	15	8
471. –	60 m. chestnut on orange	20	8
472. –	80 m. turquoise on blue	20	10
473. –	1 t. red on cream ..	40	15

DESIGNS: 10 m. "Ribes nigrum". 15 m. "Grossularia acicularis". 20 m. "Malus pallasiana". 30 m. "Fragaria orientalis". 60 m. "Ribes altissimum". 80 m. "Vaccinium vitisidaea". 1 t. "Hippophae rhamnoides".

1968. World Health Organization. 20th Anniv. Nos. 396/7 optd. with Type **99a.**

474. **85.**	30 m. blue, gold & grn.	80	70
475.	50 m. blue, gold and red	1·75	1·60

100. Human Rights Emblem. **102.** "Portrait of artist Sharab" (A. Sangatzohyo).

101. "Das Kapital".

1968. Human Rights Year.

476. **100.**	30 m. green and blue ..	10	8

1968 Karl Marx. 150th Birth Anniv. Multicoloured.

477.	30 m. Type **101**	12	8
478.	50 m. Karl Marx	20	10

1968. Mongolian Paintings. Multicoloured.

479.	5 m. Type **102**	10	5
480.	10 m. "On Remote Roads" (A. Sangatzohyo) ..	10	5
481.	15 m. "Camel Calf" (B. Avarzad) ..	15	8
482.	20 m. "The Milk" (B. Avarzad) ..	20	12
483.	30 m. "The Bowman" (B. Gombosuren) ..	25	15
484.	80 m. "Girl Sitting on a Yak" (A. Sangatzohyo)	40	20
485.	1 t. 40 "Cagan Dara Eke" (Janaivajara)	50	40

103. Volley-ball.

1968. Olympic Games, Mexico. Multicoloured.

487.	5 m. Type **103**	5	5
488.	10 m. Wrestling	5	5
489.	15 m. Cycling	10	5
490.	20 m. Throwing the javelin	12	5
491.	30 m. Football	15	8
492.	60 m. Running	20	10
493.	80 m. Gymnastics ..	20	12
494.	1 t. Weightlifting ..	40	15

104. Hammer and Spade.

1968. Darkhan Town Commem.
496. 104. 50 m. orange and blue 12 8

105. Gorky. 106. "Madonna and Child" (Boltraffio).

1968. Maxim Gorky. Birth Cent.
497. 105. 60 m. ochre and blue.. 12 8

1968. Paintings by European Masters in National Gallery, Budapest. Multicoloured.
498. 5 m. Type 106 .. .. 10 5
499. 10 m. "St. Roch healed by an angel" (Moretto of Brescia) 10 5
500. 15 m. "Madonna and Child with St. Anne" (Macchietti) 15 8
501. 20 m. "St. John on Patmos" (Cano) 20 12
502. 30 m. "Young lady with viola da gamba" (Kupetzky) 25 15
503. 80 m. "Study of a head" (Amerling) 40 20
504. 1 t. 40 "The death of Adonis" (Furini) .. 55 40

107. Paavo Nurmi (running).

1969. Olympic Games' Gold-medal Winners. Multicoloured.
506. 5 m. Type 107 .. .. 5 5
507. 10 m. Jessie Owens (running) 5 5
508. 15 m. F. Blankers-Koen (hurdling) 10 5
509. 20 m. Laszlo Papp (boxing) 12 5
510. 30 m. Wilma Rudolph (running) 15 8
511. 60 m. Boris Sahlin (gymnastics) 20 10
512. 80 m. D. Schollander (swimming) 25 12
513. 1 t. A. Nakayama (ring exercises) 45 20

108. Bayit Costume (woman).

1969. Mongolian Costumes. Multicoloured.
515. 5 m. Type 108 .. .. 5 5
516. 10 m. Torgut (man) .. 5 5
517. 15 m. Sakhchin (woman) 10 5
518. 20 m. Khalka (woman) .. 10 5
519. 30 m. Daringanga (woman) 15 8
520. 60 m. Mingat (woman) .. 20 10
521. 80 m. Khalka (man) .. 25 10
522. 1 t. Barga (woman) .. 40 15

109. Emblem and Helicopter Rescue.

1969. Mongolian Red Cross. 30th Anniv.
523. 109. 30 m. red and blue .. 15 8
524. – 50 m. red and violet .. 20 10
DESIGN: 50 m. Shepherd and ambulance.

110. Yellow Lion's-foot.

1969. Landscapes and Flowers. Multicoloured.
525. 5 m. Type 110 .. .. 5 5
526. 10 m. Variegated pink .. 5 5
527. 15 m. Superb pink .. 10 5
528. 20 m. Meadow crane's-bill 12 5
529. 30 m. Mongolian pink .. 15 8
530. 60 m. Asiatic globe-flower 20 10
531. 80 m. Long-lipped larkspur 25 12
532. 1 t. Saxual 45 20

111. "Bullfight" (O. Tsewegdjaw).

1969. Co-operative Movement. 10th Anniv. Paintings in National Gallery, Ulan Bator. Multicoloured.
533. 5 m. Type 111 .. .. 5 5
534. 10 m. "Colts Fighting" (O. Tsewegdjaw) .. 5 5
535. 15 m. "Horse-herd" (A. Sengetsohyo) .. 10 5
536. 20 m. "Camel Caravan" (D. Damdinsuren) .. 12 5
537. 30 m. "On the Steppe" (N. Tsultem) .. 15 8
538. 60 m. "Milking Mares" (O. Tsewegdjaw) .. 20 10
539. 80 m. "Off to School" (B. Avarzad) 25 12
540. 1 t. "After Work" (G. Odon) 45 30

112. Army Crest.

БНМАУ-ыг
тунхагласны
45
жилийн ой
1969—XI—26
(113.)

1969. Victory at Halhin-Gol. 30th Anniv.
542. 112. 50 m. multicoloured .. 12 8

1969. Mongolian People's Republic. 45th Anniv. Optd. with T 113.
544. 89. 30 m. multicoloured .. 80 50
545. – 50 m. multicoloured .. 1·75 75

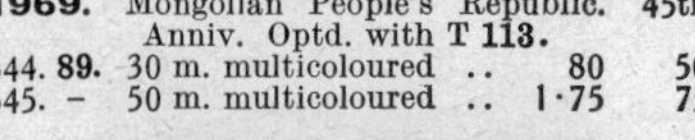

114. "Sputnik 3".

1969. Exploration of Space. Multicoloured.
546. 5 m. Type 114 .. .. 8 5
547. 10 m. "Vostok 1" 8 5
548. 15 m. "Mercury 7" .. 12 8
549. 20 m. Space-walk from "Voskhod 2" 15 8
550. 30 m. "Apollo 8" in Moon orbit 20 10
551. 60 m. Space-walk from "Soyuz 5" 25 12
552. 80 m. "Apollo 12" and Moon landing 35 15

115. Wolf.

1970. Wild Animals. Multicoloured.
554. 5 m. Type 115 .. .. 5 5
555. 10 m. Brown bear .. 5 5
556. 15 m. Lynx 10 5
557. 20 m. Wild Boar 12 8
558. 30 m. Elk 15 8
559. 60 m. Marmot 20 10
560. 80 m. Wild sheep 25 12
561. 1 t. "Hun, Hunter and Hound" (tapestry) .. 45 30

116. "Lenin Centenary" (silk panel, Cerenhuu).

1970. Lenin. Birth Cent. Multicoloured.
562. 20 m. Type 116 .. .. 5 5
563. 50 m. "Mongolians meeting Lenin" (Sangatzohyo) (horiz.) 15 8
564. 1 t. "Lenin" (Mazhig) 30 15

117. "Fairy-tale" Pavilion.

1970. "EXPO 70" World Fair, Osaka, Japan.
565. 117. 1 t. 50 Multicoloured. 55 55
No. 565 was issued with se-tenant tabs depicting various fairy-tales.

118. Footballers.

1970. World Cup Football Championships, Mexico.
567. 118. 10 m. multicoloured .. 5 5
568. – 20 m. multicoloured .. 5 5
569. – 30 m. multicoloured .. 10 5
570. – 50 m. multicoloured .. 12 5
571. – 60 m. multicoloured .. 20 10
572. – 1 t. multicoloured .. 30 12
573. – 1 t. 30 multicoloured .. 40 20
DESIGNS: Nos. 568/73 show different aspects of football, similar to T 118.

119. Buzzard.

1970. Birds of Prey. Multicoloured.
575. 10 m. Type 119 .. .. 5 5
576. 20 m. Tawny owls .. 5 5
577. 30 m. Goshawk 10 5
578. 50 m. White-tailed eagle .. 12 5
579. 60 m. Peregrine falcon .. 25 12
580. 1 t. Kestrels 30 20
581. 1 t. 30 Black kite 50 25

120. Soviet Memorial, Treptow, Berlin. 121. Mongol Archery.

1970. Victory in Second World War. 25th Anniv.
582. 120. 60 m. multicoloured .. 25 12

1970. Mongolian Traditional Life. Mult.
583. 10 m. Type 121 .. .. 10 10
584. 20 m. Bogd gegeen's Palace Ulan Bator 12 12
585. 30 m. Mongol Horseman .. 20 20
586. 40 m. "The White Goddess-Mother" 25 25
587. 50 m. Girl in National costume 30 30
588. 60 m. "Lion's Head" (statue) 35 35
589. 70 m. Dancer's Mask .. 55 55
590. 80 m. Gateway, Bogd-gegeen's Palace .. 60 50

122. I.E.Y. and U.N. Emblems with Flag.

1970. Int. Education Year.
592. 122. 60 m. multicoloured .. 25 12

123. Horseman, "50" and Sunrise.

1970. National Press. 50th Anniv.
593. 123. 30 m. multicoloured .. 20 12

124. "Vostok 2 and 3".

1971. Space Research. Multicoloured.
594. 10 m. Type 124 .. .. 5 5
595. 20 m. Space-walk from "Voskhod 2" 5 5
596. 30 m. "Gemini 6 and 7" .. 8 5
597. 50 m. Docking of "Soyuz 4 and 5" 10 5
598. 60 m. "Soyuz 6, 7 and 8" 12 8
599. 80 m. "Apollo 11" and lunar module 20 10
600. 1 t. "Apollo 13" damaged 25 12
601. 1 t. 30 "Luna 16" .. 35 15
No. 594 is incorrectly dated, "12-15 August 1962" refers to flight of "Vostoks 3 and 4".

125. Sukhe Bator addressing Meeting.

1971. Revolutionary Party. 50th Anniv. Multicoloured.
603. 30 m. Type 125 .. .. 5 5
604. 60 m. Horseman with flag 10 5
605. 90 m. Sukhe Bator with Lenin 20 10
606. 1 t. 20 Mongolians and banner 30 15

126. Tsam Mask.

1971. Mongol Tsam Masks. Diff. designs as T 126.

608. 10 m. multicoloured .. 5 5
609. 20 m. multicoloured .. 5 5
610. 30 m. multicoloured .. 8 5
611. 50 m. multicoloured .. 10 5
612. 60 m. multicoloured .. 12 8
613. 1 t. multicoloured .. 20 8
614. 1 t. 30 multicoloured .. 25 15

127. Banner and Party Emblems.

1971. 16th Revolutionary Party Congress.

615. 127. 60 m. multicoloured .. 12 8

128. Steam Locomotive.

1971. "50 Years of Transport Development". Multicoloured.

616. 20 m. Type 128 .. .. 5 5
617. 30 m. Diesel locomotive .. 5 5
618. 40 m. Russian "Urals" truck 10 5
619. 50 m. Russian "Moskvich 412" car.. .. 15 8
620. 60 m. "PO-2" biplane .. 25 10
621. 80 m. "Antonov AN-24" airliner 30 12
622. 1 t. Lake steamer "Sukhe Bator" 35 15

129. Soldier with Weapon. 130. Emblem and Red Flag.

1971. People's Army and Police. 50th Anniv. Multicoloured.

623. 60 m. Type 129 .. .. 12 8
624. 1 t. 50 Policeman and child 25 20

1971. Revolutionary Youth Movement. 50th Anniv.

625. 130. 60 m. multicoloured .. 12 8

131. Mongolian Flag and Year Emblem.

1971. Racial Equality Year.

626. 131. 60 m. multicoloured .. 12 8

132. "The Woodman and the Tiger".

1971. Mongolian Fairy Tales.

627. 132. 10 m. multicoloured .. 5 5
628. – 20 m. multicoloured .. 5 5
629. – 30 m. multicoloured.. 8 5
630. – 50 m. multicoloured.. 10 5
631. – 60 m. multicoloured.. 12 8
632. – 80 m. multicoloured.. 20 10
633. – 1 t. multicoloured .. 25 15
634. – 1 t. 30 multicoloured.. 35 20

DESIGNS: Various Mongolian Fairy Tales.

133. Yaks.

1971. Livestock Breeding. Multicoloured.

635. 20 m. Type 133 .. .. 5 5
636. 30 m. Camels 5 5
637. 40 m. Sheep 10 5
638. 50 m. Goats 12 8
639. 60 m. Cattle 25 10
640. 80 m. Horses 25 15
641. 1 t. Pony 35 20

134. Cross-country Skiing.

1972. Winter Olympic Games, Sapporo, Japan. Multicoloured.

642. 10 m. Type 134 .. .. 5 5
643. 20 m. Bob-sleighing .. 5 5
644. 30 m. Figure-skating .. 8 5
645. 50 m. Slalom skiing .. 10 5
646. 60 m. Speed-skating .. 12 8
647. 80 m. Downhill skiing .. 20 10
648. 1 t. Ice-hockey 25 15
649. 1 t. 30 Pairs figure-skating 35 20

135. "Horse-breaking".

1972. Paintings by Contemporary Artists from the National Gallery, Ulan Bator. Mult.

651. 10 m. Type 135 .. .. 5 5
652. 20 m. "Camels in the Snow" 5 5
653. 30 m. "Jousting" 8 5
654. 50 m. "Wrestling Match" 10 5
655. 60 m. "Waterfall" .. 12 8
656. 80 m. "Old Musician" .. 20 10
657. 1 t. "Young Musician" .. 25 15
658. 1 t. 30 "Ancient Prophet" 40 20

136. "Calosoma fischeri".

1972. Insects. Multicoloured.

660. 10 m. Type 136. .. .. 5 5
661. 20 m. "Mylabris mongolica" 5 5
662. 30 m. "Sternoplax zichyi" 8 5
663. 50 m. "Rhaebus komarovi" 10 5
664. 60 m. "Meloe centripubens" 12 8
665. 80 m. "Eodorcadion mongolicum" 20 10
666. 1 t. "Platyope maongolica" 25 12
667. 1 t. 30 "Lixus nigrolineatus" 40 20

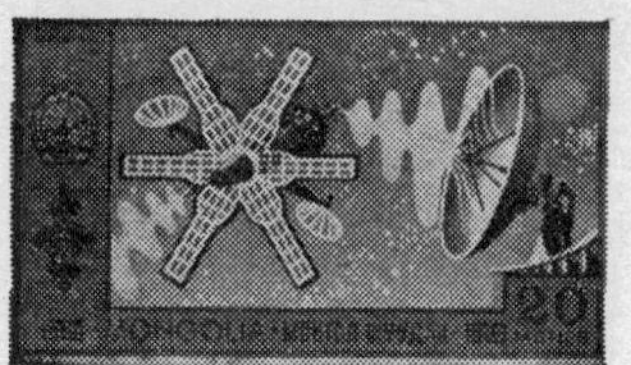

137. Satellite and Dish Aerial ("Telecommunications").

1972. Air. National Achievements. Mult.

669. 20 m. Type 137 .. .. 5 5
670. 30 m. Horse-herd ("Livestock Breeding") 5 5
671. 40 m. Train and aircraft ("Transport") 10 5
672. 50 m. Corncob and farm ("Agriculture").. .. 12 5
673. 60 m. Ambulance and hospital ("Public Health") 15 10
674. 80 m. Actors ("Culture").. 20 12
675. 1 t. Factory ("Industry") 25 15

138. Globe, Flag and Dish Aerial.

1972. Air. World Telecommunications Day.

676. 138. 60 m. multicoloured .. 12 8

139. Running.

1972. Air. Olympic Games, Munich. Mult.

677. 10 m. Type 139 .. .. 5 5
678. 15 m. Boxing 5 5
679. 20 m. Judo 8 5
680. 25 m. High-jumping .. 10 5
681. 30 m. Rifle-shooting .. 12 8
682. 60 m. Wrestling 20 12
683. 80 m. Weightlifting .. 25 15
684. 1 t. Mongolian flag. and Olympic emblems .. 40 20

140. E.C.A.F.E. Emblem.

1972. U.N. Economic Commission for Asia and the Far East. 25th Anniv.

686. 140. 60 m. blue, gold and red 12 8

141. "Eremias argus".

1972. Reptiles. Multicoloured.

687. 10 m. Type 141 .. .. 5 5
688. 15 m. "Bufo raddei" .. 5 5
689. 20 m. "Ancistrodon halys" 8 5
690. 25 m. "Phrynoephalus versicolor" 10 5
691. 30 m. "Rana chensinensis" 12 8
692. 60 m. "Teratoscincus przewalskii" 20 12
693. 80 m. "Taphrometapon lineolatum" 25 15
694. 1 t. "Agama stolizkana" 35 20

142. "Technical Knowledge".

1972. Mongolian State University. 30th Anniv. Multicoloured.

695. 50 m. Type 142 .. .. 12 5
696. 60 m. University building 15 10

143. "Madonna and Child with St. John the Baptist and a Holy Woman" (Bellini).

1972. U.N.E.S.C.O. "Save Venice" Campaign. Venetian Paintings. Multicoloured.

697. 10 m. Type 143 .. .. 5 5
698. 20 m. "The Transfiguration" (Bellini) (vert.) .. 5 5
699. 30 m. "Blessed Virgin with the Child" (Bellini) (vert.) 12 5
700. 50 m. "Presentation of the Christ in the Temple" (Bellini) 15 8
701. 60 m. "St. George" (Bellini) (vert.) .. 20 10
702. 80 m. "Departure of Ursula" (detail, Carpaccio) (vert.) 30 15
703. 1 t. "Departure of Ursula" (detail Carpaccio) .. 35 20

144. Manlay-Bator Ramdinsurren. 145. Kremlin Tower, Moscow.

1972. National Heroes. Multicoloured.

705. 10 m. Type 144 .. .. 5 5
706. 20 m. Ard Ayus in chains (horiz.) 10 5
707. 50 m. Hatan-Bator Magsarzhav 20 10
708. 60 m. Has-Bator on the march (horiz.) 30 15
709. 1 t. Sukhe Bator 40 20

1972. U.S.S.R. 50th Anniv.

710. 145. 60 m. multicoloured .. 12 8

146. Snake and "Mars 1".

1972. Air. Animal Signs of the Mongolian Calendar and Progress in Space Exploration. Multicoloured.

711. 60 m. Type **146** 20 20
712. 60 m. Horse and "Apollo 8" (square) 20 20
713. 60 m. Sheep and "Electron 2" (square) 20 20
714. 60 m. Monkey and "Explorer 6" 20 20
715. 60 m. Dragon and "Mariner 2" 20 20
716. 60 m. Pig and "Cosmos 110" (square) 20 20
717. 60 m. Dog and "Ariel 2" (square) 20 20
718. 60 m. Cockerel and "Venus 1" 20 20
719. 60 m. Hare and "Soyuz 5" 20 20
720. 60 m. Tiger and "Gemini 7" (square) 20 20
721. 60 m. Ox and "Venus 4" (square) 20 20
722. 60 m. Rat and "Apollo 15" lunar rover 20 20

The square designs are size 40 × 40 mm.

147. Swimming Gold Medal (Mark Spitz, U.S.A.).

1972. Gold Medal Winners, Munich Olympic Games. Multicoloured.

723. 5 m. Type **147** 5 5
724. 10 m. High-jumping (Ulrike Meyfarth, West Germany) 5 5
725. 20 m. Gymnastics (Savao Kato, Japan) 10 5
726. 30 m. Show-jumping (Andras Balczo, Hungary) .. 12 8
727. 60 m. Running (Lasse Viren, Finland) 25 12
728. 80 m. Swimming (Shane Gould, Australia) .. 30 15
729. 1 t. Putting the shot (Anatoli Bondarchuk, U.S.S.R.) 1·10 60

148. Monkey on Cycle.

1973. Mongolian Circus. Multicoloured.

731. 5 m. Type **148** 5 5
732. 10 m. Seal with ball .. 5 5
733. 15 m. Bear on mono-wheel 5 5
734. 20 m. Acrobat on camel .. 8 5
735. 30 m. Acrobat on horse .. 12 8
736. 50 m. Clown playing flute 20 12
737. 60 m. Contortionist .. 25 15
738. 1 t. New circus Hall, Ulan Bator 35 20

149. Mounted Postman.

150. Sukhe Bator receiving Traditional Gifts.

1973.

739. **149.** 50 m. brown (postage) 20 12
740. – 60 m. green 25 15
741. – 1 t. purple 35 20
742. – 1 t. 50 blue (air) .. 55 30

DESIGNS: 60 m. Diesel train. 1 t. Mail-truck. 1 t. 50 Airliner.

1973. Sukhe Bator. 80th Birth Anniv. Multicoloured.

743. 10 m. Type **150** 5 5
744. 20 m. Holding reception .. 8 5
745. 50 m. Leading army .. 20 12
746. 60 m. Addressing council 25 15
747. 1 t. Giving audience .. 35 20

151. W.M.O. Emblem and Meteorological Symbols.

1973. World Meteorological Organisation. Cent.

748. **151.** 60 m. multicoloured .. 20 12

152. "Copernicus in his Observatory" (J. Matejko).

1973. Nicholas Copernicus (astronomer). 500th Birth Anniv. Multicoloured.

749. 50 m. "Copernicus" (anon) (vert.) 15 12
750. 60 m. Type **152** 20 15
751. 1 t. "Copernicus" (Jan Matejko) (vert.) .. 30 20

Nos. 749 and 751 are size 25 × 36 mm.

153. Marx and Lenin.

1973. 9th Organisation of Socialist States Postal Ministers Congress, Ulan Bator.

754. **153.** 60 m. multicoloured .. 20 15

154. Russian Stamp and Emblems.

1973. Air Council for Mutual Economic Aid, Posts and Telecommunications Conference, Ulan Bator. Multicoloured.

755. 30 m. Type **154** 10 8
756. 30 m. Mongolia 10 8
757. 30 m. Bulgaria 10 8
758. 30 m. Hungary 10 8
759. 30 m. Czechoslovakia .. 10 8
760. 30 m. German Democratic Republic 10 8
761. 30 m. Cuba 10 8
762. 30 m. Rumania 10 8
763. 30 m. Poland 10 8

155. Shelduck.

1973. Aquatic Birds. Multicoloured.

764. 5 m. Type **155** 5 5
765. 10 m. Black-throated diver 5 5
766. 15 m. Bar-headed goose .. 5 5
767. 30 m. Great crested grebe 10 8
768. 50 m. Mallard 15 12
769. 60 m. Mute swan 20 15
770. 1 t. Scaup duck .. 30 20

156. Weasel.

1973. Small Fur Animals. Multicoloured.

771. 5 m. Type **156** 5 5
772. 10 m. Striped squirrel .. 5 5
773. 15 m. Flying phalanger .. 5 5
774. 20 m. Badger 8 5
775. 30 m. Red squirrel .. 10 8
776. 60 m. Glutton 20 15
777. 80 m. American mink .. 25 20
778. 1 t. Blue hare 30 20

157. Launching "Soyuz" Spacecraft.

1973. Air. "Apollo and Soyuz" Space Programmes. Multicoloured.

779. 5 m. Type **157** 5 5
780. 10 m. "Apollo 8" 5 5
781. 15 m. "Soyuz 4 and 5" linked 5 5
782. 20 m. "Apollo 11" module on Moon 8 5
783. 30 m. "Apollo 14" after splash-down 10 8
784. 50 m. "Soyuz 6, 7 and 8" Triple Flight 15 12
785. 60 m. "Apollo 16" lunar Rover 20 15
786. 1 t. "Lunokhod 1" 30 20

1973. 4th Agricultural Co-operative Congress, Ulan Bator. No. 538 optd. with Mongolian inscription and date.

788 60 m. multicoloured ..

159. Global Emblem.

1973. Czech Review "Problems of Peace and Socialism". 15th Anniv.

789. **159.** 60 m. red, gold and blue 20 15

160. "Aster alpinus".

1973. Mongolian Flowers. Multicoloured.

790. 5 m. Type **160** 5 5
791. 10 m. "Silene mongolica" 5 5
792. 15 m. "Rosa davurica" 5 5
793. 20 m. "Taraxacum mongolicum" 8 5
794. 30 m. "Rhododendron dahuricum" 10 8
795. 50 m. "Clematis tangutica" 15 12
796. 60 m. "Primula sibirica" 20 15
797. 1 t. "Pulsatilla flavescens" 30 20

161. "Limenitus populi".

1973. Butterflies. Multicoloured.

798. 5 m. Type **161** 5 5
799. 10 m. "Arctia hebe" .. 5 5
800. 15 m. "Rhyparia purpurata" 5 5
801. 20 m. "Catocala pacta" .. 8 5
802. 30 m. "Isoceras kaszabi" 10 8
803. 50 m. "Celerio costata" .. 15 12
804. 60 m. "Arctia caja" .. 20 15
805. 1 t. "Diacrisia sannio" .. 30 20

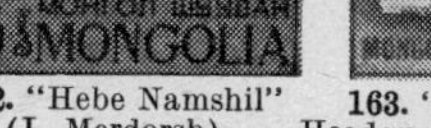

162. "Hebe Namshil" (L. Merdorsh). **163.** "Comecon" Headquarters, Moscow.

1974. Mongolian Opera and Drama. Mult.

806. 15 m. Type **162** 5 5
807. 20 m. "Sive Hiagt" (D. Luvsansharav) (horiz.) 8 5
808. 25 m. "Edre" (D. Namdag) 10 5
809. 30 m. "The Three Khans of Sara-gol" (horiz.) .. 10 8
810. 60 m. "Edre" (different scene) 25 20
811. 1 t. "Edre" (different scene) 30 20

1974. Air. Communist Council for Mutual Economic Aid ("Comecon"). 25th Anniv.
813. **163.** 60 m. multicoloured .. 20 15

164. Government Building and Sukhe Bator Monument, Ulan Bator.

1974. Renaming of Capital as Ulan Bator. 50th Anniv.
814. **164.** 60 m. multicoloured .. 20 15

165. Mounted Courier.

1974. Air. Universal Postal Union. Cent. Multicoloured.
816. 50 m. Type **165** 15 12
817. 50 m. Reindeer mail-sledge 15 12
818. 50 m. Mail-coach 15 12
819. 50 m. Balloon post .. 15 12
820. 50 m. Ferryboat and "AN-2" aircraft 15 12
821. 50 m. Mail-train and P.O. truck 15 12
822. 50 m. Rocket in orbit .. 15 12

166. Performing Horses.

1974. Mongolian Circus (2nd series). Mult.
824. 10 m. Type **166** (postage) 5 5
825. 20 m. Juggler (vert.) .. 8 5
826. 30 m. Elephant on ball (vert.) 10 8
827. 40 m. Performing yak .. 15 10
828. 60 m. Acrobats (vert.) .. 20 15
829. 80 m. Trick cyclist (vert.) 25 20
830. 1 t. Contortionists (vert.) (air) 30 20

167. "Training a Young Horse".

1974. Int. Children's Day. Drawings by Lhamsurem. Multicoloured.
831. 10 m. Type **167** 5 5
832. 20 m. "Boy with Calf" .. 8 5
833. 30 m. "Riding untamed Horse" 10 8
834. 40 m. "Boy with Foal" .. 15 10
835. 60 m. "Girl dancing with Doves" 20 15
836. 80 m. "Wrestling" 25 20
837. 1 t. "Hobby-horse Dance" 30 20

MINIMUM PRICE

The minimum price quoted is 5p which represents a handling charge rather than a basis for valuing common stamps. For further notes about prices see introductory pages.

168. Archer on Foot.

1974. "Nadam" Sports Festival. Mult.
838. 10 m. Type **168** 5 5
839. 20 m. "Kazlodanie" (Kazakh mounted game).. .. 8 5
840. 30 m. Mounted archer .. 10 8
841. 40 m. Horse-racing .. 15 10
842. 60 m. Bucking horse-riding 20 15
843. 80 m. Capturing wild horse 25 20
844. 1 t. Wrestling 30 20

169. Panda ("Ailurus fulgens").

1974. Mongolian Bears. Multicoloured.
845. 10 m. "Ursus horribilis" .. 5 5
846. 20 m. Type **169** 8 5
847. 30 m. "Ailuropoda melanoleucus" (Giant panda).. 10 8
848. 40 m "Ursus arctos". .. 15 10
849. 60 m. "Melursus ursinus" 20 15
850. 80 m. "Selenarctos tibetanua" 25 20
851. 1 t. "Ursus arctos bruinosus" 30 20

170. Stag.

1974. Game Reserves. Fauna. Multicoloured.
852. 10 m. Type **170** 5 5
853. 20 m. Beaver 8 5
854. 30 m. Panther 10 8
855. 40 m. Herring gull .. 15 10
856. 60 m. Roe-deer 20 15
857. 80 m. Mountain sheep .. 25 20
858. 1 t. Young doe 30 30

171. Detail of Buddhist Temple, Palace of Bogdo Gregen.

1974. Mongolian Architecture. Multicoloured.
859. 10 m. Type **171** 5 5
860. 15 m. Buddhist temple (now museum) 5 5
861. 30 m. " Charity " Temple, Ulan Bator 10 8
862. 50 m. Mongolian " yurta " (tent) 20 15
863. 80 m. Arbour in court-yard 25 20

172. Spassky Tower, Moscow, and Sukhe Bator Statue.

173. Proclamation of the Republic.

1974. Brezhnev's Visit to Mongolia.
864. **172.** 60 m. multicoloured .. 20 15

1974. Mongolian People's Republic. 50th Anniv. Multicoloured.
865. 60 m. Type **173** 20 15
866. 60 m. "First Constitution" (embroidery) 20 15
867. 60 m. Mongolian flag .. 20 15

174. Gold Decanter.

1974. Goldsmiths' Treasures of the 19th Century. Multicoloured.
868. 10 m. Type **174** 5 5
869. 20 m. Silver jug 8 5
870. 30 m. Night lamp.. .. 10 8
871. 40 m. Tea jug 15 10
872. 60 m. Candelabra 20 15
873. 80 m. Teapot 25 20
874. 1 t. Silver bowl on stand.. 30 20

175. Lapwing.

1974. Protection of Water and Nature Conservation. Multicoloured.
875. 10 m. Type **175** (postage) 5 5
876. 20 m. Fish 10 8
877. 30 m. Flowers 15 12
878. 40 m. Pelican 20 15
879. 60 m. Fish (different) .. 30 25
880. 80 m. Mink 40 35
881. 1 c. Hydrologist with jar of water (air) 45 40

176. U.S. Mail-coach.

1974. Universal Postal Union. Cent. Mult.
883. 10 m. Type **176** 5 5
884. 20 m. French postal cart.. 10 8
885. 30 m. Changing horses, Russian mail and passenger carriage 15 12
886. 40 m. Swedish postal coach with caterpillar tracks.. 20 15
887. 50 m. First Hungarian mail-van 25 20
888. 60 m. German Daimler-Benz mail-van and trailer .. 30 25
889. 1 t. Mongolian postal courier 45 40

177. Red Flag.

178. Mongolian Woman.

1975. Victory. 30th Anniv.
891. **177.** 60 m. multicoloured .. 30 25

1975. International Women's Year.
892. **178.** 60 m. multicoloured .. 30 25

179. " Zygophyllum xanthoxylon ".

1975. 12th International Botanical Conference. Rare Medicinal Plants. Multicoloured.
893. 10 m. Type **179** 5 5
894. 20 m. "Incarvillea potaninii" 10 8
895. 30 m. " Lancia tibetica ".. 15 12
896. 40 m. " Jurinia mongolica " 20 15
897. 50 m. " Saussurea involucrata " 25 20
898. 60 m. " Allium mongolicum " 30 25
899. 1 t. " Adonis mongolica " 45 40

180. " Soyuz " on Launch-pad.

1975. Air. Joint Soviet-American Space Project. Multicoloured.
900. 10 m. Type **180** 5 5
901. 20 m. Launch of " Apollo " 10 8
902. 30 m. " Apollo " beside " Soyuz " 15 12
903. 40 m. Docking manoeuvre 20 15
904. 50 m. Successful link-up .. 25 20
905. 60 m. " Soyuz " in orbit.. 30 25
906. 1 t. " Apollo " & " Soyuz " encircling earth.. .. 45 40

181. Child and Lamb.

1975. International Children's Day. Puppets. Multicoloured.
908. 10 m. Type **181** 5 5
909. 20 m. Child riding horse .. 10 8
910. 30 m. Child with calf .. 15 12
911. 40 m. Child and " orphan camel " 20 15
912. 50 m. " The obedient yak " 25 20
913. 60 m. Child riding a swan.. 30 25
914. 1 t. Two choristers .. 45 40
See also Nos. 972/8.

MORE DETAILED LISTS

are given in the Stanley Gibbons Catalogues referred to in the country headings:

BC	British Commonwealth
E1, E2, E3	Europe 1, 2, 3
O1, O2, O3, O4	Overseas 1, 2, 3, 4

182. Pioneers tending Tree. 183. Mountain Sheep.

1975. Mongolian Pioneer Organization. 50th Anniv. Multicoloured.

915.	50 m. Type **182**	25	20
916.	60 m. Children's study circle	30	25
917.	1 t. New emblem of Mongolian pioneers	45	40

1975. South Asia Tourist Year.

918. **183.**	1 t. 50 multicoloured ..	70	65

184. Eagle attacking Wolf.

1975. Hunting Scenes. Multicoloured

919.	10 m. Type **184**	5	5
920.	20 m. Lynx-hunting (verb.)	10	8
921.	30 m. Hunter stalking marmots	15	12
922.	40 m. Hunter riding on reindeer (vert.)	20	15
923.	50 m. Shooting wild boar ..	25	20
924.	60 m. Wolf in trap (vert.) ..	30	25
925.	1 t. Hunters with bear ..	45	40

185. "Mesocottus haitej".

1975. Fishes. Multicoloured.

926.	10 m. Type **185**	5	5
927.	20 m "Pseudaspius leptocephalus"	10	8
928.	30 m. "Oreoleucj scus potanini"	15	12
929.	40 m. "Tinca tinca" ..	20	15
930.	50 m. "Coregonus lavaretus pidschian" ..	25	20
931.	60 m. "Erythroculter mongolicus"	30	25
932.	1 t. "Carassius auratus"	45	40

186. "Morin Hur" (musical instrument). 187. Revolutionary with Banner.

1975. Mongolian Handicrafts. Multicoloured.

933.	10 m. Type **186**	5	5
934.	20 m. Mongolian saddle ..	10	8
935.	30 m. Headdress	15	12
936.	40 m. Mongolian boots ..	20	15
937.	50 m. Woman's cap ..	25	20
938.	60 m. Pipe and tobacco-pouch	30	25
939.	1 t. Man's fur hat	45	40

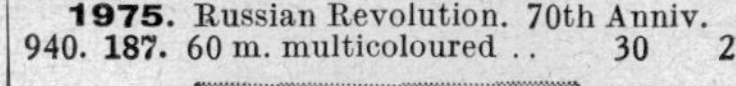

1975. Russian Revolution. 70th Anniv.

940. **187.**	60 m. multicoloured ..	30	25

188. "Taming a Wild Horse".

1975. Mongolian Paintings. Multicoloured.

941.	10 m. Type **188**	5	5
942.	20 m. "Camel Caravan" (horiz.)	10	8
943.	30 m. "Man playing lute"	15	12
944.	40 m. "Woman adjusting headdress" (horiz.) ..	20	15
945.	50 m. "Woman in ceremonial costume"	25	20
946.	60 m. "Woman fetching water"	30	25
947.	1 t. "Woman playing yatga" (musical instrument) ..	45	40

189. Ski-jumping. 190. "House of Young Technicians".

1975. Winter Olympic Games, Innsbruck. Multicoloured.

949.	10 m. Type **198**	5	5
950.	20 m. Ice-hockey	10	8
951.	30 m. Skiing (slalom) ..	15	12
952.	40 m. Bobsleighing ..	20	15
953.	50 m. Rifle-shooting (biathlon)	25	20
954.	60 m. Speed-skating ..	30	25
955.	1 t. Figure-skating ..	45	40

1975. Public Buildings.

957. **190.**	50 m. blue	25	20
958. –	60 m. green	30	25
959. –	1 t. brown	45	40

DESIGNS: 60 m. Hotel, Ulan Bator. 1 t. "Museum of the Revolution".

191. "Molniya" Satellite.

1976. Mongolian Meteorological Office. 40th Anniv.

960. **191.**	60 m. blue and yellow	60	55

192. "National Economy" Star.

1976. 17th Mongolian People's Revolutionary Party Congress, Ulan Bator.

962. **192.**	60 m. red, silver and deep red	60	55

193. Archery.

1976. Olympic Games, Montreal. Multicoloured.

964.	10 m. Type **193**	10	8
965.	20 m. Judo	20	15
966.	30 m. Boxing	30	25
967.	40 m. Gymnastics ..	40	35
968.	60 m. Weightlifting ..	60	55
969.	80 m. High-jumping ..	80	75
970.	1 t. Rifle-shooting ..	1·00	95

1976. Int. Children's Day. Children's Drawings. As T **181**. Multicoloured.

972.	10 m. Gobi Desert landscape	10	8
973.	20 m. Horse-taming ..	20	15
974.	30 m. "Summer Holidays" (horse-riding) ..	30	25
975.	40 m. Pioneer's camp ..	40	35
976.	60 m. Young musician ..	60	55
977.	80 m. Children's party ..	80	75
978.	1 t. Mongolian wrestling ..	1·00	95

194. Cavalry Charge.

1976. Revolution. 55th Anniv. Multicoloured.

979.	60 m. Type **194** (postage)	60	55
980.	60 m. Mongolian and Emblem	60	55
981.	60 m. "Industry and Agriculture" (horiz.) (air) ..	60	55

195. Osprey.

1976. Protected Birds. Multicoloured.

983.	10 m. Type **195**	10	8
984.	20 m. Griffon vulture ..	20	15
985.	40 m. Marsh harrier ..	40	35
986.	60 m. Black vulture ..	60	55
987.	80 m. Golden eagle ..	80	75
988.	1 t. Tawny eagle ..	1·00	95

196. "Rider on Wild Horse".

1976. Mongolian Paintings. Multicoloured.

989.	10 m. Type **196**	10	8
990.	20 m. "The First Nadom"	20	15
991.	30 m. "Harbour on Hubsugal Lake" (horiz.) ..	30	25
992.	40 m. "Awakening on the Steppe" (horiz.) ..	40	35
993.	80 m. "Wrestling" (horiz.)	80	75
994.	1 t. "The Descent" ..	1·00	95

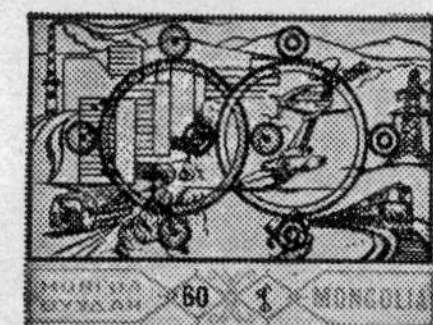

197. Industrial Development.

1976. Mongolian – Soviet Friendship.

995. **197.**	60 m. multicoloured ..	60	55

MONG-TSEU (MENGTSZ) O1

An Indo-Chinese P.O. in Yunnan province, China, closed in 1922.

1903. 100 centimes = 1 franc.
1919. 100 cents = 1 piastre.

Stamps of Indo-China surcharged.

1903. "Tablet" key-type surch. **MONG-TZE** and value in Chinese.

1. D.	1 c. black on blue ..	75	75
2.	2 c. brown on yellow ..	65	65
3.	4 c. claret on grey ..	65	65
4.	5 c. green	65	65
5.	10 c. red	75	75
6.	15 c. grey	90	90
7.	20 c. red on green ..	1·10	1·10
8.	25 c. blue	1·10	1·10
9.	25 c. black on red ..	95·00	95·00
10.	30 c. brown	1·10	1·10
11.	40 c. red on yellow ..	9·00	9·00
12.	50 c. red on rose	50·00	50·00
13.	50 c. brown on blue ..	11·00	11·00
14.	75 c. brown on orange ..	10·00	10·00
15.	1 f. olive	11·00	11·00
16.	5 f. mauve on lilac ..	11·00	11·00

1906. Surch. **Mong-Tseu** and value in Chinese.

17. **1.**	1 c. olive	20	20
18.	2 c. claret on yellow ..	20	20
19.	4 c. purple on grey ..	20	20
20.	5 c. green	25	25
21.	10 c. red	20	20
22.	15 c. brown on blue ..	30	30
23.	20 c. red on green	50	50
24.	25 c. blue	60	60
25.	30 c. brown on cream ..	80	80
26.	35 c. black on yellow ..	70	60
27.	40 c. black on grey ..	70	60
28.	50 c. olive on cream ..	2·25	2·25
29. D.	75 c. brown on orange ..	5·50	5·50
30. **1.**	1 f. green	2·75	2·75
31.	2 f. brown on yellow ..	7·00	7·00
32. D.	5 f. mauve on lilac ..	11·00	11·00
34. **1.**	10 f. red on green	17·00	17·00

1908. Surch. **MONGTSEU** and value in Chinese.

35. **2.**	1 c. black and olive ..	10	10
36.	2 c. black and brown ..	10	10
37.	4 c. black and blue ..	10	10
38.	5 c. black and green ..	12	12
39.	10 c. black and red ..	20	20
40.	15 c. black and violet ..	20	20
41. **3.**	20 c. black and violet ..	55	55
42.	25 c. black and blue ..	75	75
43.	30 c. black and purple ..	30	30
44.	35 c. black and green ..	65	65
45.	40 c. black and brown ..	45	45
46.	50 c. black and red ..	45	45
47. **4.**	75 c. black and orange ..	1·40	1·40
48. –	1 f. black and red	1·75	1·75
49. –	2 f. black and green ..	1·75	1·75
50. –	5 f. black and blue ..	15·00	15·00
51. –	10 f. black and violet ..	17·00	17·00

1919. Nos. 35/51 further surch. in figures and words.

52. **2.**	$\frac{2}{5}$ c. on 1 c. blk. & olive ..	5	5
53.	$\frac{4}{5}$ c. on 2 c. blk. & brn. ..	5	5
54.	$1\frac{3}{5}$ c. on 4 c. black & blue ..	20	20
55.	2 c. on 5 c. black & green ..	8	8
56.	4 c. on 10 c. black & red ..	20	20
57.	6 c. on 15 c. black & violet	20	20
58. **3.**	8 c. on 20 c. black & violet	50	50
59.	10 c. on 25 c. black & blue	40	40
60.	12 c. on 30 c. black & purple	40	40
61.	14 c. on 35 c. black & green	35	35
62.	16 c. on 40 c. black & brown	50	50
63.	20 c. on 50 c. black & red ..	45	45
64. **4.**	30 c. on 75 c. black & orge.	30	30
65. –	40 c. on 1 f. black & red ..	75	75
66. –	80 c. on 2 f. black & green	40	40
67. –	2 p. on 5 f. black & blue ..	20·00	20·00
68. –	4 p. on 10 f. black & violet	2·40	2·40

MONTENEGRO E2

Formerly a monarchy on the Adriatic Sea and now part of Yugoslavia. In Italian and German occupation during 1939-45 war.

1874. 100 novcic = 1 florin.
1902. 100 heller = 1 krone.
1907. 100 para = 1 krone (1910 = 1 perper)

Прослава
1493 1893
Штампарије

1. Prince Nicholas I. (2.)

1874.

45. **1.**	1 n. pale blue	8	8
38.	2 n. yellow	30	30
51.	2 n. green	5	5
39.	3 n. green	12	10
52.	3 n. red	5	5
40.	5 n. red	12	12
13.	5 n. orange	5	5
58.	7 n. mauve	70	60
41.	7 n. pink	12	12
54.	7 n. grey	5	10

42. 1. 10 n. blue 12 12
55. 10 n. purple 5 5
43. 15 n. bistre 20 20
56. 15 n. chocolate 5 8
46. 20 n. brown 5 8
14. 25 n. grey .. .. .. 18·00 15·00
44. 25 n. brown 12 30
57. 25 n. blue 5 15
47. 30 n. brown 5 10
48. 50 n. blue 5 8
49. 1 f. green 8 35
50. 2 f. purple .. .. 15 1·25

1893. Printing in Montenegro. 4th Cent Optd. with T 2.

81. 1. 2 n. yellow .. .. 2·10 60
82. 3 n. green 20 20
83. 5 n. red 12 12
84. 7 n. pink 10 10
86. 10 n. blue 15 15
87. 15 n. bistre 12 12
89. 25 n. brown 20 20

3. Monastery near Cetinje.

1896. Petrovich Njegush Dynasty. Bicent.

90. 3. 1 n. brown and blue .. 5 8
91. 2 n. yellow and purple .. 5 8
92. 3 n. green and brown .. 5 12
93. 5 n. brown and green .. 5 10
94. 10 n. blue and yellow .. 5 10
95. 15 n. green and blue .. 5 15
96. 20 n. blue and green .. 5 15
97. 25 n. yellow and blue .. 5 15
98. 30 n. brown and purple .. 5 25
99. 50 n. slate and red .. 5 35
100. 1 f. slate and pink .. 5 50
101. 2 f. grey and brown .. 5 80

УСТАВ Constitution 1905 (5.) Никола I

4. 6.

1902.

102. 4. 1 h. blue 5 5
103. 2 h. purple 5 8
104. 5 h. green 5 5
105. 10 h. red 8 5
106. 25 h. blue 5 5
107. 50 h. green 5 10
108. 1 k. brown 8 15
109. 2 k. brown 10 30
110. 5 k. orange 15 65

1905. Granting of Constitution. Optd. with T 5.

120. 4. 1 h. blue 5 5
121. 2 h. mauve 5 5
122. 5 h. green 5 5
123. 10 h. red 5 5
124. 25 h. blue 5 5
125. 50 h. green 5 5
126. 1 k. brown 5 5
127. 2 k. brown 5 5
119. 5 k. orange 15 75

1907.

129. 6. 1 p. yellow 5 5
130. 2 p. black 5 5
131. 5 p. green 5 5
132. 10 p. red 5 5
133. 15 p. blue 5 5
134. 20 p. orange 5 5
135. 25 p. blue 5 5
136. 35 p. brown 5 5
137. 50 p. lilac 8 8
138. 1 k. red 5 12
139. 2 k. green 5 15
140. 5 k. brown-red 10 40

7. Nicholas I, when a Youth.

8. Nicholas I and Queen Milena.

9. Crown Prince on Horseback.

10. Nicholas I.

1910. Fiftieth Year of King's Reign.

141. 7. 1 p. black 5 5
142. 8. 2 p. purple 5 5
143. – 5 p. green 5 5
144. – 10 p. red 5 5
145. – 15 p. blue 5 5
146. 8. 20 p. olive-green .. 5 10
147. – 25 p. blue 5 8
148. – 35 p. brown 8 10
149. – 50 p. violet 5 12
150. – 1 per. lake 5 25
151. – 2 per. green 5 35
152. 9. 5 per. blue 10 60

DESIGNS—As T 7: 5 p., 10 p., 25 p., 35 p. Nicholas I in 1910. 15 p. Nicholas I in 1878. 50 p., 1 per., 2 per. Nicholas I in 1890.

1913.

153. 10. 1 p. orange 5 5
154. 2 p. purple 5 5
155. 5 p. green 5 5
156. 10 p. red 5 5
157. 15 p. blue 5 5
158. 20 p. brown 5 5
159. 25 p. blue 5 5
160. 35 p. red 5 15
161. 50 p. blue 5 8
162. 1 per. brown 5 10
163. 2 per. lilac 5 25
164. 5 per green 5 50

ITALIAN OCCUPATION

1941. Stamps of Yugoslavia optd. **Montenegro Црна Гора 17-IV-41-XIX.**

(a) Postage. On Nos. 414, etc.

1. 63. 25 p. black 5 5
2. 1 d. green 5 5
3. 1 d. 50 red 5 5
4. 2 d. mauve 5 5
5. 3 d. brown 5 5
6. 4 d. blue 5 5
7. 5 d. blue 15 30
8. 5 d. 50 violet 15 30
9. 6 d. blue 15 30
10. 8 d. brown 20 40
11. 12 d. violet 15 30
12. 16 d. purple 15 30
13. 20 d. blue .. .. 60·00 75·00
14. 30 d. pink .. .. 27·00 38·00

(b) Air. On Nos. 360/7.

15. 44. 50 p. brown .. .. 1·75 3·00
16. – 1 d. green 45 90
17. – 2 d. blue 45 90
18. 46. 2 d. 50 red .. .. 1·75 3·00
19. 44. 5 d. violet .. .. 15·00 22·00
20. – 10 d. red .. .. 15·00 22·00
21. – 20 d. green .. .. 18·00 27·00
22. 46. 30 d. blue .. .. 15·00 22·00

1941. Stamps of Italy optd. **ЦРНАТОРА**

(a) On Postage stamps of 1929.

28. 69. 5 c. brown 5 5
29. 70. 10 c. brown 5 5
30. 15 c. green 5 5
31. 20 c. red 5 5
32. 25 c. green 5 5
33. 74. 30 c. brown 5 5
34. 50 c. violet 5 5
35. 70. 75 c. red 5 8
36. 1 l. 25 blue 5 5

(b) On Air stamp of 1930.

37. 81. 50 c. brown 5 5

1942. Nos. 416, etc., of Yugoslavia optd. **Governatorato del Montenegro Valore LIRE.**

43. 63. 1 d. green 15 20
44. 1 d. 50 red .. .. 4·50 6·00
45. 3 d. brown 15 20
46. 4 d. blue 20 20
47. 5 d. 50 violet 20 20
48. 6 d. blue 20 25
49. 8 d. brown 20 25
50. 12 d. violet 20 25
51. 16 d. purple 20 25

1942. Air. Nos. 360/7 of Yugoslavia optd. **Governatorato/del/Montenegro/Valore in Lire.**

52. 89. 0. 50 l. brown 20 50
53. – 1 l. green 15 50
54. – 2 l. blue 20 50
55. – 2. 50 l. red 15 50
56. 80. 5 l. violet 20 50
57. – 10 l. brown 30 60
58. – 20 l. green .. .. 27·00 35·00
59. – 30 l. blue .. .. 17·00 22·00

11. Prince Bishop Peter Shepherd and Flock.

1943. National Poem Commemoratives. Each stamp has fragment of poetry inscr. at back.

60. 11. 5 c. violet 5 8
61. – 10 c. green 5 8
62. – 15 c. brown 5 8
63. – 20 c. orange 5 8
64. – 25 c. green 5 8
65. – 50 c. magenta 5 8
66. – 1 l. 25 blue 8 12
67. – 2 l. green 10 15
68. – 5 l. red on buff 35 45
69. – 20 l. purple on grey .. 1·40 1·50

DESIGNS—HORIZ. 10 c. Meadow. 15 c. Country chapel. 20 c. Chiefs Meeting. 25 c., 50 c. Folk-dancing. 1 l. 25, Taking the Oath. 2 l. Procession. 5 l. Interior gathering. VERT. 20 l. Portrait of Prince Bishop Peter.

12. Cetinje.

DESIGNS—HORIZ. 1 l. Coastline. 2 l. Budva. 5 l. Mt. Lovcen. 10 l. Lake of Scutari. VERT. 20 l. Mt. Durmitor.

1943. Air.

70. 12. 50 c. brown 5 5
71. 1 l. blue 5 5
72. 2 l. magenta 5 8
73. 5 l. green 5 15
74. 10 l. purple on buff .. 60 65
75. 20 l. indigo on pink .. 1·50 1·60

GERMAN OCCUPATION

1943. Nos. 419/20 of Yugoslavia surch. **Deutsche Militaer-Verwaltung Montenegro** and new value in lire.

76. 63. 50 c. on 3 d. brown .. 35 35
77. 1 l. on 3 d. brown .. 35 35
78. 1 l. 50 on 3 d. brown .. 35 35
79. 2 l. on 3 d. brown .. 55 55
80. 4 l. on 3 d. brown .. 35 35
81. 5 l. on 4 d. blue .. 55 55
82. 8 l. on 4 d. blue .. 90 90
83. 10 l. on 4 d. blue .. 3·00 3·00
84. 20 l. on 4 d. blue .. 3·50 3·50

1943. Appointment of National Administrative Committee. Optd. **Nationaler Verwaltungsausschuss 10.XI.1943.**

(a) Postage. On Nos. 64/8.

85. 25 c. green 30 40
86. 50 c. magenta 30 40
87. 1 l. 25 blue 30 40
88. 2 l. green 30 40
89. 5 l. red on buff .. .. 55·00 55·00

(b) Air. On Nos. 70/4.

90. 12. 50 c. brown 55 60
91. 1 l. blue 55 60
92. 2 l. magenta 55 60
93. 5 l. green 55 60
94. 10 l. purple on buff .. £475 £550

1944. Refugees Fund. Surch. **Flüchtlingshilfe Montenegro** and new value in German currency.

(a) On Nos. 419/20 of Yugoslavia.

95. 63. 0.15+0.85 Rm. on 3 d. 1·75 1·75
96. 0.15+0.85 Rm. on 4 d. 1·75 1·75

(b) On Nos. 46/9.

97. – 0.15+0.85 Rm. on 25 c. 1·75 1·75
98. – 0.15+1.35 Rm. on 50 c. 1·75 1·75
99. – 0.25+1.75 Rm. on 1 l. 25 1·75 1·75
100. – 0.25+1.75 Rm. on 2 l. 1·75 1·75

(c) Air. On Nos. A 52/4.

101. 12. 0.15+0.85 Rm. on 50 c. 2·40 2·40
102. – 0.25+1.25 Rm. on 1 l. 2·40 2·40
103. – 0.50+1.50 Rm. on 2 l. 2·40 2·40

1944. Red Cross. Surch + **Crveni krst Montenegro** and new value in German currency.

(a) On Nos. 419/20 of Yugoslavia.

104. 63. 0.50+2.50 Rm. on 3 d. 1·10 1·40
105. 0.50+2.50 Rm. on 4 d. 1·10 1·40

(b) On Nos. 46/7.

106. – 0.15+0.85 Rm. on 25 c. 1·10 1·40
107. – 0.15+1.35 Rm. on 50 c. 1·10 1·40

(d) Air. On Nos. 52/4.

108. 12. 0.25+1.75 Rm. on 50 c. 1·10 1·40
109. – 0.25+2.75 Rm. on 1 l. 1·10 1·40
110. – 0.50+2 Rm. on 2 l. 1·10 1·40

ACKNOWLEDGMENT OF RECEIPT STAMPS

A 1. A 2.

1895.

A 90. A 1. 10 n. blue and red .. 8 20

1902.

A 111. A 2. 25 n. orange and red .. 15 25

1905. Optd. with T 5.

A 120. A 2. 25 n. orange and red 12 40

1907. As T 6, but letters "A" and "R" in top corners.

A 141. 6. 25 p. olive 5 12

1913. As T 10, but letters "A" and "R" in top corners.

A 169. 10. 25 p. olive 5 10

POSTAGE DUE STAMPS

D 1. D 2. D 3.

1894.

D 90a. D 1. 1 n red 10 12
D 91. 2 n. green 5 5
D 92. 3 n. orange .. 5 5
D 93. 5 n. green 5 5
D 94. 10 n. purple .. 5 5
D 95. 20 n. blue 5 10
D 96. 30 n. green .. 5 10
D 97. 50 n. pale green .. 5 20

1902.

D 111. D 2. 5 h. orange .. 5 5
D 112. 10 h. olive-green .. 5 5
D 113. 25 h. purple .. 5 10
D 114. 50 h. green .. 5 12
D 115. 1 k. pale green .. 5 20

1905. Optd. with T 5.

D 120. D 2. 5 h. orange .. 5 8
D 121. 10 h. olive-green .. 5 8
D 122. 25 h. purple .. 5 12
D 123. 50 h. green .. 5 15
D 124. 1 k. pale green .. 5 25

1907.

D 141. D 3. 5 p. brown 5 8
D 142. 10 p. violet .. 5 8
D 143. 25 p. red 5 8
D 144. 50 p. green .. 5 8

1913. As T 10 but inscr. "НОРТОМАРКА" at top.

D 165. 5 p. grey 8 15
D 166. 10 p. violet 5 12
D 167. 25 p. blue 5 12
D 168. 50 p. rose 5 12

ITALIAN OCCUPATION

1941. Postage Due stamps of Yugoslavia optd. **Montenegro Црна 17-IV-41-XIX.**

D 23. D 10. 50 p. violet .. 8 10
D 24. 1 d. rose 8 10
D 25. 2 d. blue 8 10
D 26. 5 d. orange .. 1·75 2·50
D 27. 10 d. brown .. 15 20

1942. Postage Due stamps of Italy optd. **ЦРНАТОРА.**

D 38. D 6. 10 c. blue 5 5
D 39. 20 c. red 5 5
D 40. 30 c. orange 5 5
D 41. 50 c. violet 5 5
D 42. 1 l. orange 8 20

MONTSERRAT BC

One of the Leeward Is., Br. W. Indies. Used general issues for Leeward Is. concurrently with Montserrat stamps until 1st July, 1956, when Leeward Is. stamps were withdrawn.

1951. 100 cents = 1 West Indian dollar.

1876. Stamps of Antigua optd. **MONTSERRAT.**

1. 1. 1d. red .. .. .. 9·00 11·00
2. 6d. green .. .. .. 20·00 16·00

1.

1880.

6. 1. ½d. green .. .. .. 1·25 1·75
9. 2½d. red-brown .. .. 50·00 40·00
10. 2½d. blue .. .. 5·50 6·00
5. 4d. blue .. .. .. 55·00 40·00
12. 4d. mauve .. .. 4·00 8·50

2. Device of the Colony. 3.

1903.

24. 2. ½d. green 30 45
15. 1d. grey and red .. 55 55
26. 2d. grey and brown .. 75 1·25
27. 2½d. grey and blue .. 1·10 2·50
28. 3d. orange & brown-purple 1·50 1·75
29. 6d. purple and olive .. 2·00 3·50
30. 1s. green and purple .. 4·50 5·50
21. 2s. green and orange-brown 11·00 14·00
22. 2s. 6d. green and black .. 17·00 22·00
33. 3. 5s. black and red .. 60·00 75·00

1908.

36. 2. 1d. red	85	25
38. 2d. grey	1·25	2·50
39. 2½d. blue	1·75	2·50
40. 3d. purple on yellow	1·10	2·50
43a. 6d. purple	4·50	6·00
44. 1s. black on green	4·50	6·00
45. 2s. purple & blue on blue	14·00	16·00
46. 2s. 6d. blk. & red on blue	16·00	19·00
47. 3. 5s. red & green on yellow	35·00	40·00

1914. As T 3, but portrait of King George V.

48. 5s. red & green on yellow	55·00	75·00

ILLUSTRATIONS British Commonwealth and all overprints and surcharges are FULL SIZE. Foreign Countries have been reduced to ¾-LINEAR.

5.

1916.

63. 5. ½d. brown	20	40
64. ½d. green	15	20
50. 1d. red	30	40
65. 1d. violet	25	25
67. 1½d. yellow	1·75	2·50
68. 1½d. red	25	60
69. 1½d. brown	30	60
70. 2d. grey	65	90
71. 2½d. blue	1·90	2·75
72. 2½d. yellow	1·50	2·25
53. 3d. purple on yellow	1·10	2·25
73. 3d. blue	65	1·40
75. 4d. black & red on yellow	65	1·25
76. 5d. purple and olive	2·75	5·00
77. 6d. purple	90	2·25
78. 1s. black on green	3·50	5·00
79. 2s. pur. and blue on blue	3·00	5·00
80. 2s. 6d. blk. & red on blue	11·00	13·00
81. 3s. green and violet	9·00	11·00
82. 4s. black and red	11·00	14·00
83. 5s. green and red on yellow	16·00	20·00

1917. Optd. **WAR STAMP.**

60. 5. ½d. green	12	25
62. 1½d. black and orange	12	30

6. Plymouth, Montserrat.

1932. Tercentenary issue.

84. 6. ½d. green	60	80
85. 1d. red	60	90
86. 1½d. brown	1·00	1·75
87. 2d. grey	1·10	2·00
88. 2½d. blue	1·25	3·00
89. 3d. orange	2·25	3·50
90. 6d. violet	4·50	6·50
91. 1s. olive-brown	11·00	14·00
92. 2s. 6d. purple	38·00	45·00
93. 5s. chocolate	60·00	70·00

1935. Silver Jubilee. As T 11 of Antigua.

94. 1d. blue and red	45	25
95. 1½d. blue and grey	25	60
96. 2½d. brown and blue	1·40	2·25
97. 1s. grey and purple	5·50	6·00

1937. Coronation. As T 2 of Aden.

98. 1d. red	10	20
99. 1½d. brown	10	20
100. 2½d. blue	15	25

DESIGNS: 1d., 1½d., 2½d. Sea Island cotton. 2d., 6d., 2s. 6d., 10s. Botanic Station.

7. Carr's Bay.

1938. King George VI.

101. ½d. green	12	12
102. – 1d. red	12	12
103a. – 1½d. purple	8	8
104a. – 2d. orange	12	12
105a. – 2½d. blue	8	8
106a. 7. 3d. brown	12	20
107a. – 6d. violet	20	15
108a. 7. 1s. red	40	45
109. – 2s. 6d. blue	1·10	1·00
110a. 7. 5s. red	1·40	1·75
111. – 10s. blue	4·00	5·50
112. 7. £1 black	9·50	11·00

1946. Victory. As T 4 of Aden.

113. 1½d. purple	8	8
114. 3d. brown	8	8

1949. Silver Wedding. As T 5/6 of Aden.

115. 2½d. blue	8	8
116. 5s. red	2·75	4·00

1949. U.P.U. As T 14/17 of Antigua.

117. 2½d. blue	15	25
118. 3d. brown	20	35
119. 6d. purple	55	60
120. 1s. purple	75	90

1951. Inaug. of B.W.I. University College. As T 18/19 of Antigua.

121. 18. 3 c. black and purple	15	15
122. 19. 12 c. black and violet	30	30

8. Government House.

1951.

123. 8. 1 c. black	15	15
124. – 2 c. green	12	15
125. – 3 c. brown	15	15
126. – 4 c. red	15	15
127. – 5 c. violet	15	20
128. – 6 c. brown	20	40
129. – 8 c. blue	30	30
130. – 12 c. blue and chocolate	40	45
131. – 24 c. red and green	80	95
132. – 60 c. black and red	90	1·40
133. – $1·20 green and blue	3·25	3·50
134. – $2·40 black and green	3·25	4·00
135. – $4·80 black and purple	6·00	7·00

DESIGNS: 2 c., $1.20, Sea Island cotton; cultivation. 3 c. Map. 4 c., 24 c. Picking tomatoes. 5 c., 12 c. St. Anthony's Church. 6 c., $4.80, Badge. 8 c., 60 c. Sea Island cotton: ginning. $2.40, Government House (portrait on right).

1953. Coronation. As T 7 of Aden.

136. 2 c. black and green	15	25

1953. As 1951 but portrait of Queen Elizabeth II.

136a. ½ c. violet (As 3 c.) (I)	5	5
136b. ½ c. violet (II)	5	8
137. 1 c. black	5	5
138. 2 c. green	5	5
139. 3 c. brown (I)	8	10
139a. 3 c. brown (II)	8	10
140. 4 c. red	8	8
141. 5 c. violet	8	8
142. 6 c. brown (I)	12	12
142a. 6 c. brown (II)	15	15
143. 8 c. blue	12	12
144. 12 c. blue & chocolate	12	12
145. 24 c. red and green	20	25
145a. 48 c. olive & pur. (As 2 c.)	45	50
146. 60 c. black and red	70	70
147. $1.20 green and blue	1·50	1·75
148. $2.40 black and green	2·50	3·00
149. $4.80 black & purple (I)	9·00	11·00
149a. $4.80 black & purple (II)	6·00	8·00

I. Inscr. "Presidency" II. Inscr. "Colony".

1958. Br. Caribbean Federation. As T 21 of Antigua.

150. 3 c. green	12	12
151. 6 c. blue	20	20
152. 12 c. red	30	30

1963. Freedom from Hunger. As T 10 of Aden.

153. 12 c. violet	40	40

1963. Red Cross Cent. As T 24 of Antigua.

154. 4 c. red and black	12	12
155. 12 c. red and blue	45	50

1964. Shakespeare. 400th Birth Anniv. As T 25 of Antigua.

156. 12 c. indigo	40	40

1965. I.T.U. Cent. As T 26 of Antigua.

158. 4 c. red and violet	12	12
159. 48 c. green and rose	60	65

9. Pineapple.

1965. Multicoloured.

213. 1 c. Type 9	5	5
214. 2 c. Avocado	5	8
215. 3 c. Soursop	8	8
216. 4 c. Pepper	8	8
217. 5 c. Mango	10	10
165. 6 c. Tomato	5	5
166. 8 c. Guava	8	8
218. 10 c. Ochro	20	25
168. 12 c. Lime	12	12
220. 20 c. Orange	40	40
170. 24 c. Banana	20	25
171. 42 c. Onion	65	65
172. 48 c. Cabbage	70	70
173. 60 c. Pawpaw	80	90
174. $1·20 Pumpkin	1·25	1·40
175. $2·40 Sweet potato	2·00	2·00
176. $4·80 Egg plant	4·00	4·00

1965. I.C.Y. As T 27 of Antigua.

177 2 c. purple and turquoise	5	5
178. 12 c. green and lavender	25	25

1966. Churchill Commem. As T 28 of Antigua.

179. 1 c. blue	5	5
180. 2 c. green	5	5
181. 24 c. brown	35	35
182. 42 c. violet	60	70

1966. Royal Visit. As T 29 of Antigua.

183. 14 c. black and blue	20	20
184. 24 c. black and magenta	30	35

1966. W.H.O. Headquarters, Geneva. Inaug. As T 31 of Antigua.

185. 12 c. black, green and blue	15	20
186. 60 c. black, purple & ochre	55	65

1966. U.N.E.S.C.O. 20th Anniv. As T 33/5 of Antigua.

187. 4 c. vio., red, yell. & orge.	8	8
188. 60 c. yellow, violet & olive	50	60
189. $1.80 black, purple & orge.	2·00	2·25

10. Yachting.

1967. Int. Tourist Year. Multicoloured.

190. 5 c. Type 10	5	5
191. 15 c. Waterfall near Chance Mountain	12	12
192. 16 c. "Fishing, skin diving and swimming"	15	15
193. 24 c. Playing golf	30	30

No. 191 is vert.

1968. Nos. 168, 170, 172, 174/6 surch.

219. 15 c. on 12 c. Lime	30	35
221. 25 c. on 24 c. Banana	40	55
196. 50 c. on 48 c. Pawpaw	25	40
197. $1 on $1.20 Pumpkin	70	80
198. $2.50 on $2.40 Sweet potato	1·75	2·00
199. $5 on $4.80 Egg plant	3·50	4·50

11. Sprinting.

1968. Olympic Games, Mexico.

200. 11. 15 c. claret, emer. & gold	10	10
201. – 25 c. blue, orge. & gold	15	15
202. – 50 c. green, red & gold	35	40
203. – $1 multicoloured	70	75

DESIGNS—HORIZ. 25 c. Weightlifting. 50 c. Gymnastics. VERT. $1 Sprinting and Aztec Pillars.

12. Alexander Hamilton.

1968. Human Rights Year. Multicoloured.

204. 5 c. Type 12	5	5
205. 15 c. Albert T. Marryshow	10	10
206. 25 c. William Wilberforce	15	20
207. 50 c. Dag Hammarskjoeld	30	45
208. $1 Dr. Martin Luther King	60	1·00

13. "The Two Trinities" (Murillo).

14. Map showing "CARIFTA" Countries.

1968. Christmas.

209. 13. 5 c. multicoloured	5	5
210. – 15 c. multicoloured	15	15
211. 13. 25 c. multicoloured	25	25
212. – 50 c. multicoloured	40	45

DESIGN: 15 c., 50 c. "The Adoration of the Kings" (detail, Botticelli).

1969. "CARIFTA". 1st Anniv. Multicoloured.

223. 15 c. Type 14	12	12
224. 20 c. Type 14	15	15
225. 35 c. "Strength in Unity"	25	25
226. 50 c. As 35 c.	40	40

Nos. 232/3 are horiz.

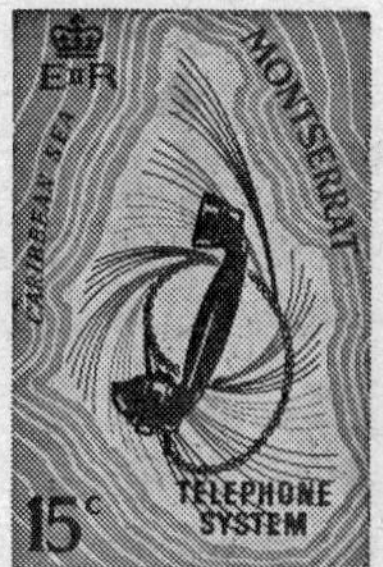

15. Telephone Receiver and Outline of Island.

1969. Development Projects. Multicoloured.

227. 15 c. Type 15	12	12
228. 25 c. School symbols and outline of island	20	20
229. 50 c. Aircraft and outline of island	35	35
230. $1 Electricity pylon and outline of island	60	60

16. Dolphin.

1969. Game Fish. Multicoloured.

231. 5 c. Type 16	5	5
232. 15 c. Atlantic sailfish	15	15
233. 25 c. Blackfin tuna	25	25
234. 40 c. Spanish mackerel	40	40

17. King Caspar before the Virgin and Child (detail) (stained glass window).

1969. Christmas. Paintings multicoloured; frame colours given.

235. 17. 15 c. black, gold & violet	12	12
236. – 25 c. black & vermilion	25	25
237. – 50 c. blk., ultram. & orge.	40	45

DESIGN—HORIZ. 50 c. "Nativity" (Leonard Limosin).

18. "Red Cross Sale".

1970. British Red Cross Cent. Multicoloured.

238. 3 c. Type 18	5	5
239. 4 c. School for deaf children	8	8
240. 15 c. Transport services for disabled	15	15
241. 20 c. Workshop	20	20

19. Red-Footed Booby.

1970. Multicoloured.

242. 1 c. Type **19** 5 5
243. 2 c. Killy Hawk 5 5
244. 3 c. Frigate Bird 5 5
245. 4 c. White Egret 8 8
246. 5 c. Brown Pelican .. 8 8
247. 10 c. Bananaquit.. .. 12 12
248. 15 c. Ani 15 15
301. 20 c. Tropic Bird .. 15 15
250. 25 c. Montserrat Oriole .. 20 20
251. 50 c. Green-Throated Carib 25 30
252. $1 Antillean Crested Hummingbird 40 45
253a. $2.50 Little Blue Heron .. 1·00 1·10
254. $5 Purple-Throated Carib 2·25 2·50
254a. $10 Forest Thrush .. 4·50 5·00

Nos. 250/4, 258 and 260 are vert.

20. "Madonna and Child with Animals" (Durer).

1970. Christmas. Multicoloured.

255. 5 c. Type **20** 5 5
256. 15 c. "The Adoration of the Shepherds" (Domenichino) 12 12
257. 20 c. Type **20** 15 15
258. $1 As 15 c. 65 65

21. War Memorial.

1970. Tourism. Multicoloured.

259. 5 c. Type **21** 5 5
260. 15 c. Plymouth from Fort St. George 12 12
261. 25 c. Carrs Bay 20 20
262. 50 c. Golf Fairway .. 40 40

22. Girl Guide and Badge.

1970. Montserrat Girl Guides. Diamond Jubilee. Multicoloured.

264. 10 c. Type **22** 8 8
265. 15 c. Brownie and Badge .. 12 12
266. 25 c. As 15 c. 25 25
267. 40 c. Type **22** 35 35

23. "Descent from the Cross" (Van Hemessen).

1971. Easter. Multicoloured.

268. 5 c. Type **23** 5 5
269. 15 c. "Noli me tangere" (Orcagna) 12 12
270. 20 c. Type **23** 20 20
271. 40 c. As 15 c. 30 30

24. D.F.C. and D.F.M. in Searchlights.

1971. Commonwealth Ex-Services League. Golden Jubilee. Multicoloured.

272. 10 c. Type **24** 8 8
273. 20 c. M.C., M.M. and jungle patrol 20 20
274. 40 c. D.S.C., D.S.M. and submarine action .. 30 30
275. $1 V.C. and soldier attacking bunker 65 65

25. "The Nativity with Saints" (Romanino).

1971. Christmas. Multicoloured.

276. 5 c. Type **25** 5 5
277. 15 c. "Choir of Angels" (Simon Marmion) .. 10 10
278. 20 c. Type **25** 15 15
279. $1 As 15 c. 70 75

26. Piper "Apache".

1971. Inauguration of L.I.A.T. (Leeward Islands Air Transport). 14th Anniv. Multicoloured.

280. 5 c. Type **26** 5 5
281. 10 c. Beech "Twin Bonanza" 8 8
282. 15 c. De Havilland "Heron" 15 20
283. 20 c. Britten Norman "Islander" .. 15 20
284. 40 c. De Havilland "Twin Otter" 30 35
285. 75 c. Hawker Siddeley "748" 70 75

27. "Chapel of Christ in Gethsemane", Coventry Cathedral.

1972. Easter. Multicoloured.

287. 5 c. Type **27** 5 5
288. 10 c. "The Agony in the Garden" (Bellini) .. 8 8
289. 20 c. Type **27** 15 15
290. 75 c. As 10 c. 60 65

28. Lizard.

1972. Reptiles. Multicoloured.

291. 15 c. Type **28** 10 10
292. 20 c. Mountain Chicken (frog) 12 12
293. 40 c. Iguana (horiz.) .. 25 30
294. $1 Tortoise (horiz. .. 50 50

29. 'Madonna della Seggiola'' (Raphael).

1972. Christmas. Multicoloured.

303. 10 c. Type **29** 8 8
304. 35 c. "Virgin and Child" (Fungai) 20 20
305. 50 c. "Madonna del Magnificat" (Botticelli) .. 35 35
306. $1 "Virgin and Child with St. John" (Botticelli) .. 65 65

1972. Royal Silver Wedding. As T **19** of Ascension but with Lime, Tomatoes and Pawpaw in background.

307. 35 c. pink 20 25
308. $1 blue 60 65

30. "Passiflora herbertiana".

1973. Easter. Passion-flowers. Multicoloured.

309. 20 c. Type **30** 12 12
310. 35 c. "P. vitifolia" .. 20 20
311. 75 c. "P. amabilis" .. 65 65
312. $1 "P. alata-cuerulea" .. 75 75

31. Montserrat Monastery, Spain.

1973. Columbus's Discovery of Montserrat. 480th Anniv. Multicoloured.

313. 10 c. Type **31** 8 8
314. 35 c. Columbus sighting Montserrat 20 20
315. 60 c. Columbus's ship off Montserrat 45 50
316. $1 Island badge and map of voyage 70 75

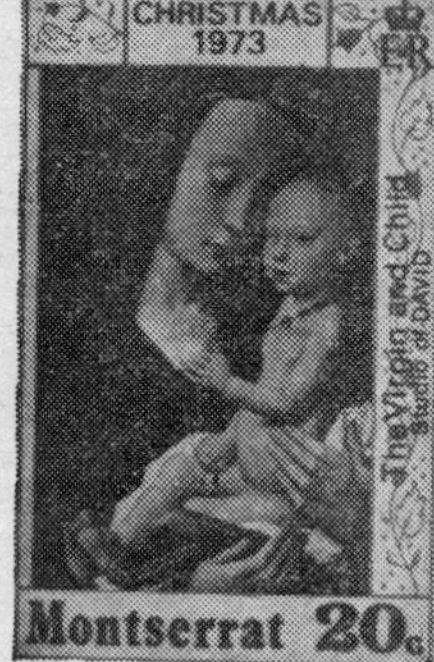

32. "Virgin and Child" (School of Gerard David).

1973. Christmas. Multicoloured.

318. 20 c. Type **32** 12 12
319. 35 c. "The Holy Family with St. John" (Jordaens) 20 20
320. 50 c. "Virgin and Child" (Bellini) 40 40
321. 90 c. "Virgin and Child" (Dolci) 70 75

1973. Royal Wedding. As Type **26** of Anguilla. Multicoloured. Background colours given.

322. 35 c. green 20 20
323. $1 blue 45 50

33. Steel Band.

1974. University of West Indies. 25th Anniv. Multicoloured.

324. 20 c. Type **33** 12 12
325. 35 c. Masqueraders (vert.) 20 20
326. 60 c. Student weaving (vert.) 40 45
327. $1 University Centre, Montserrat 60 65

34. Hands with Letters.

1974. U.P.U. Centenary.

329. **34.** 1 c. multicoloured .. 5 5
330. – 2 c. red, orange & black 5 5
331. **34.** 3 c. multicoloured .. 5 5
332. – 5 c. orge., red & blk. .. 8 8
333. **34.** 50 c. multicoloured 25 30
334. – $1 blue, grn. & blk. .. 55 60

DESIGN: 2 c., 5 c., $1 Figures from U.P.U. Monument.

1974. Various stamps surch.

335. 2 c. on $1 (No. 252) .. 1·25 1·25
336. 5 c. on 50 c. (No. 333) .. 1·50 1·50
337. 10 c. on 60 c. (No. 326) .. 2·50 3·00
338. 20 c. on $1 mult. (No. 252) 2·00 2·25
339. 35 c. on $1 (No. 334) .. 2·00 2·25

35. Churchill and Houses of Parliament.

1974. Sir Winston Churchill. Birth Cent. Multicoloured.

340. 35 c. Type **35** 20 20
341. 70 c. Churchill and Blenheim Palace 35 40

36. Carib "Carbet".

1975. Carib Artefacts.

343. **36.** 5 c. brn., yell. & black.. 5 5
344. – 20 c. blk., brn. & yell... 12 12
345. – 35 c. blk., yell. & brn... 20 20
346. – 70 c. yell., brn. & blk... 35 35

DESIGNS: 20 c. "Caracoli". 35 c. Club or mace. 70 c. Canoe.

Nos. 343/46 also come self-adhesive from booklet panes.

37. One-Bitt Coin.

1975. Local Coinage, 1785-1801.

351. **37.** 5 c. black, blue & silver 5 5
352. – 10 c. black, pink & silver 8 8
353. – 35 c. black, grn. & silver 20 20
354. – $2 black, red & silver.. 80 90

DESIGNS: 10 c. Eighth dollar. 35 c. Quarter dollar. $2 One dollar.

38. 1d. and 6d. Stamps of 1876.

1976. 1st Montserrat Postage Stamp. Centenary.

356. **38.** 5 c. red, green & black.. 5 5
357. – 10 c. yellow, red & black 5 5
358. – 40 c. multicoloured .. 15 15
359. – 55 c. mauve, grn. & blk. 20 20
360. – 70 c. multicoloured 25 25
361. – $1·10 green, blue & black 40 45

DESIGNS: 10 c. G.P.O. and bisected 1d. stamp. 40 c. Bisects on cover. 55 c. G.B. 6d. used in Montserrat and local 6d. of 1876. 70 c. Stamps for 2½d. rate, 1876. $1·10 Packet boat "Antelope" and 6d. stamp.

39. "The Trinity".

1976. Easter. Paintings by Orcagna. Multicoloured.

363. 15 c. Type **39** 5 8
364. 40 c. "The Resurrection" 15 20
365. 55 c. "The Ascension" .. 25 30
366. $1·10 "Pentecost" .. 50 55

1976. Nos. 244, 246 and 247 surch.

368. 2 c. on 5 c. multicoloured 5 5
369. 30 c. on 10 c. multicoloured 12 15
370. 45 c. on 3 c. multicoloured 20 25

40. White Frangipani.

1976. Flowering Trees. Multicoloured.

371. 1 c. Type **40** 5 5
372. 2 c. Cannon-ball tree .. 5 5
373. 3 c. Lignum vitae .. 5 5
374. 5 c. Malay apple 5 5
375. 10 c. Jacaranda 5 5
376. 15 c. Orchid Tree .. 5 5
377. 20 c. Manjak 8 8
378. 25 c. Tamarind .. 10 10
379. 40 c. Flame of the Forest 15 15
380. 55 c. Pink Cassia.. .. 20 20
381. 70 c. Long John 25 30
382. $1 Saman.. .. .. 35 40
383. $2·50 Immortelle.. .. 90 1·00
384. $5 Yellow Poui .. .. 1·75 2·00
385. $10 Flamboyant .. .. 3·50 4·00

41. Mary and Joseph.

1976. Christmas. Multicoloured.

386. 15 c. Type **41** 5 8
387. 20 c. The Shepherds .. 8 10
388. 55 c. Mary and Jesus .. 20 25
389. $1·10 The Magi 45 50

42. Hudson River Review.

1976. American Revolution. Bicent. Multicoloured.

391. 15 c. Type **42** 5 8
392. 40 c. "Raleigh" attacking H.M.S. "Druid" 1776 15 20
393. 75 c. "Raleigh" attacking H.M.S. "Druid" 1776 .. .. 30 35
394. $1·25 Hudson River Review 1976 .. .. 50 55

Nos. 391 and 394 and 392/3 were issued in se-tenant pairs, each pair forming a composite design.

43. The Crowning.

1976. Silver Jubilee. Multicoloured.

396. 30 c. Royal Visit, 1966 .. 12 15
397. 45 c. Firing Salute, Tower of London 20 25
398. $1 Type **43** 40 45

OFFICIAL STAMPS

1976. Various stamps, some already surch. optd. **O.H.M.S.**

O 1. 5 c. multicoloured (No. 246)
O 2. 10 c. multicoloured (No. 247) .. .. ..
O 3. 30 c. on 10 c. multicoloured (No. 369) .. ..
O 4. 45 c. on 3 c. multicoloured (No. 370) .. ..
O 5. $5 multicoloured (No. 254)
O 6. $10 multicoloured (No. 254a) .. ..

These stamps were issued for use on mail from the Monserrat Philatelic Bureau. They were not sold to the public, either unused or used.

1976. Nos. 374/8, 380/2 and 384 optd. **O.H.M.S.**

O 7. 5 c. Malay Apple .. † 5
O 8. 10 c. Jacaranda.. .. † 5
O 9. 15 c. Orchid Tree .. † 5
O 10. 20 c. Manjak .. † 8
O 11. 25 c. Tamarind .. .. † 10
O 12. 55 c. Pink Cassia .. † 25
O 13. 70 c. Long John .. † 30
O 14. $1 Saman .. † 40
O 15. $5 Yellow Poui .. .. † 2·00

Nos. O 7/15 were not available in an unused condition, and were only sold to the public in a used condition.

MOROCCO O3

An independent kingdom, established in 1956, comprising the former French and Spanish International Zones.

A. NORTHERN ZONE.

100 centimos = 1 peseta.

1. Sultan of Morocco.

2. Polytechnic.

1956.

1. **1.** 10 c. brown 5 5
2. – 15 c. brown 5 5
3. **2.** 25 c. violet.. .. .. 5 5
4. – 50 c. green 15 15
5. **1.** 80 c. green 20 20
6. – 2 p. lilac 75 75
7. **2.** 3 p. blue .. .. 1·00 1·00
8. – 10 p. green .. .. 5·00 5·00

DESIGNS—HORIZ. 15 c., 2 p. Villa Sanjurjo harbour. VERT. 50 c., 10 p. Cultural Delegation building, Tetuan.

3. "Constellation" over Lau Dam.

1956. Air.

9. **3.** 25 c. purple 12 12
10. – 1 p. 40 mauve 20 20
11. **3.** 3 p. 40 red 60 60
12. – 4 p. 80 purple 90 90

DESIGN: 1 p. 40, 4 p. 80 "Constellation" over Rio Nekor Bridge.

1957. Independence. 1st Anniv. As T **6** but with Spanish inscriptions and currency.

13. 80 c. green.. .. .. 25 25
14. 1 p. 50 olive 50 50
15. 3 p. claret.. .. .. 1·40 1·40

1957. As T **4** but with Spanish inscriptions and currency.

16. 30 c. indigo and blue .. 5 5
17. 70 c. maroon and brown.. 8 5
18. 80 c. purple 25 10
19. 1 p. 50 lake and emerald.. 15 8
20. 3 p. green.. .. .. 20 10
21. 7 p. red 80 25

1957. Investiture of Prince Moulay el Hassan. As T **8** but with Spanish inscriptions and currency.

22. 80 c. blue 20 10
23. 1 p. 50 green 30 25
24. 3 p. red .. .. .. 1·25 1·10

1957. Nos. 17 and 19 surch.

25. 15 c. on 70 c. mar. & brown 20 15
26. 1 p. 20 on 1 p. 50 lake and emerald.. .. .. 35 20

1957. Coronation of Sultan Sidi Mohammed ben Yusuf. 30th Anniv. As T **9** but with Spanish inscription and currency.

27. 1 p. 20 green and black .. 25 25
28. 1 p. 80 red and black .. 30 30
29. 3 p. violet and black .. 50 50

B. SOUTHERN ZONE

100 centimes = 1 franc.

4. Sultan of Morocco. **5.** Classroom. **6.** Sultan of Morocco.

1956.

30. **4.** 5 f. indigo and blue .. 5 5
31. 10 f. sepia and brown .. 5 5
32. 15 f. lake and green .. 8 5
33. 25 f. purple 15 5
34. 30 f. green 12 5
35. 50 f. red 30 5
36. 70 f. red-brown and sepia 35 5

1956. Education Campaign.

37. – 10 f. violet and purple .. 55 55
38. – 15 f. lake and red .. 65 65
39. **5.** 20 f. green and turquoise 75 75
40. – 30 f. vermilion and lake.. 95 95
41. – 50 f. blue and indigo .. 1·25 1·25

DESIGNS: 10 f. Peasants reading book. 15 f. Two girls reading. 30 f. Child reading to old man. 50 f. Child teaching parents the alphabet.

1957. Independence. 1st Anniv.

42. **6.** 15 f. green 45 45
43. 25 f. olive.. .. .. 55 55
44. 30 f. claret 65 65

7. Emblem over Casablanca. **8.** Crown Prince Moulay el Hassan.

1957. Air. Int. Fair, Casablanca.

45. **7.** 15 f. green and red .. 25 25
46. 25 f. turquoise 30 30
47. 30 f. brown 35 50

1957. Investiture of Crown Prince Moulay el Hassan.

48. **8.** 15 f. blue 35 35
49. 25 f. green 45 45
50. 30 f. red 55 55

9. King Mohammed V.

10. Moroccan Pavilion.

1957. Coronation of King Mohammed V. 30th Anniv.

51. **9.** 15 f. green and black .. 30 30
52. 25 f. red and black .. 35 35
53. 30 f. violet and black .. 45 45

C. ISSUES FOR THE WHOLE OF MOROCCO.

1958. 100 centimes = 1 franc.
1962. 100 francs = 1 dirham.

1958. Brussels Int. Exn.

54. **10.** 15 f. turquoise 10 10
55. 25 f. red 12 12
56. 30 f. indigo 15 15

11. King Mohammed V and U.N.E.S.C.O. Headquarters, Paris.

1958. Inaug. of U.N.E.S.C.O. Headquarters Building, Paris.

57. **11.** 15 f. green 10 10
58. 25 f. lake 12 12
59. 30 f. blue 15 12

12. Ben-Smine Sanatorium.

13. King Mohammed V on Horseback.

1959. "National Aid".

60. **12.** 50 f. bistre, green and red 20 15

1959. King Mohamed V's 50th Birthday.

61. **13.** 15 f. lake 20 15
62. 25 f. blue 30 25
63. 45 f. green 35 30

14. Princess Lailla Amina.

15.

1959. Children's Week.

64. **14.** 15 f. blue 15 12
65. 25 f. green 20 15
66. 45 f. purple 25 20

1960. Meeting of U.N. African Economic Commission, Tangier.

67. **15.** 45 f. green, brn. & violet 40 35

+10 f

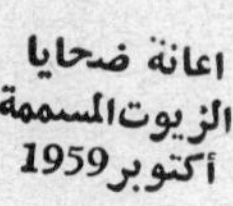

(16.)

17. Arab Refugees.

1960. Adulterated Cooking Oil Victims Relief Fund. Surch. as T **16.**

68. **4.** 5 f. + 10 f. indigo and blue 15 15
69. 10 f. + 10 f. sepia & brown 25 25
70. 15 f. + 10 f. lake and green 35 35
71. 25 f. + 15 f. purple .. 35 35
72. 30 f. + 20 f. green .. 45 45

1960. World Refugee Year.

73. **17.** 15 f. black, green & ochre 12 12
74. – 45 f. green and black .. 20 20

DESIGN: 45 f. "Uprooted tree" and Arab refugees.

18. Marrakesh.

19. Lantern.

1960. Marrakesh. 900th Anniv.

75. **18.** 100 f. grn., brown & blue 55 45

1960. Karaouine University. 1100th Anniv.

76. **19.** 15 f. purple 10 8
77. – 25 f. blue (Fountain) .. 20 12
78. – 30 f. brown (Minaret) .. 25 20
79. – 35 f. black (Frescoes) .. 30 25
80. – 45 f. green (Courtyard) .. 35 30

20. Arab League Centre and King Mohammed V.

اسبوعا التضامن 1380 1960 +5f

(21.)

1960. Arab League Centre, Cairo. Inaug.

81. **20.** 15 f. black and green .. 8 8

1960. Solidarity Fund. Nos. 458/9 of French Protectorate surch. as T **21.**

82. **65.** 15 f. + 3 f. on 18 f. myrtle 20 20
83. +5 f. on 20 f. lake .. 25 25

22. Wrestling.

23. Runner.

1960. Olympic Games.

84. **22.** 5 f. purple, olive-green and violet 5 5
85. – 10 f. choc., blue & brown 5 5
86. – 15 f. brown, blue & emer. 8 5
87. – 20 f. maroon, blue & bis. 10 8
88. – 30 f. brown, violet & red 12 10
89. – 40 f. brown, blue & violet 15 12
90. – 45 f. blue, green & purple 20 15
91. – 70 f. black, blue & choc. 25 20

DESIGNS: 10 f. Gymnastics. 15 f. Cycling. 20 f. Weightlifting. 30 f. Running. 40 f. Boxing. 45 f. Sailing. 70 f. Fencing.

1961. 3rd Pan-Arab Games, Casablanca.

92. **23.** 20 f. green 10 5
93. 30 f. lake 12 8
94. 50 f. blue 25 20

24. Post Office and Letters.

25. King Mohammed V of Morocco and African Map.

26. Lumumba and Congo Map.

1961. African Postal and Telecommunications Conf., Tangier.

95. **24.** 20 f. maroon and mauve 20 12
96. – 30 f. blue-grn. & yell.-grn. 25 15
97. – 90 f. ultramarine & blue 45 30

DESIGNS—VERT. 30 f. Telephone operator. HORIZ. 90 f. "Caravelle" mail-plane over Tangier.

1962. African Charter of Casablanca. 1st Anniv.

98. **25.** 20 f. maroon and buff .. 10 10
99. 30 f. indigo and blue .. 12 12

1962. Patrice Lumumba Commem.

100. **26.** 20 f. black and bistre .. 8 8
101. 30 f. black and brown .. 15 12

27. King Hassan II.

28. "Pupils of the Nation".

1962. Air.

102. **27.** 90 f. black 25 8
103. 1 d. red 25 10
104. 2 d. blue 50 15
105. 3 d. green 75 45
106. 5 d. violet .. .. 1·25 80

1962. Children's Education.

107. **28.** 20 f. indigo, red & green 12 12
108. 30 f. sepia, brown & grn. 20 15
109. 90 f. indigo, mar. & grn. 35 30

1962. Arab League Week. As T **170** of Egypt.

110. 20 f. brown 8 5

29. King Hassan II.

30. Scout with Banner.

1962.

111. **29.** 1 f. olive 5 5
112. 2 f. violet 5 5
113. 5 f. sepia 5 5
114. 10 f. brown 5 5
115. 15 f. blue-green 5 5
116. 20 f. purple (18 × 22 mm.) 8 5
116a. 20 f. pur. (17½ × 23½ mm.) 8 5
116b. 25 f. red 10 5
117. 30 f. green 12 5
117a. 35 f. slate 12 5
117b. 40 f. ultramarine .. 15 5
118. 50 f. maroon 20 5
118a. 60 f. purple 25 5
119. 70 f. blue 25 5
120. 80 f. lake 30 8

1962. 5th Arab Scout Jamboree. Rabat.

121. **30.** 20 f. maroon and blue .. 8 5

31. Campaign Emblem and Swamp.

32. Aquarium and Fish.

فيضانات 1963

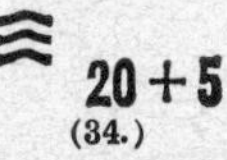

20+5

(34.)

33. Mounted Postman and 1912 Sherifian Stamp.

1962. Malaria Eradication Campaign.

122. **31.** 20 f. indigo and green .. 8 5
123. – 50 f. lake and green .. 20 12

DESIGN—VERT. 50 f. Sword piercing mosquito.

1962. Casablanca Aquarium. Multicoloured.

124. 20 f. Type **32** 12 10
125. 30 f. Aquarium and eel .. 20 15

1962. First National Philatelic Exn., Rabat, and Stamp Day.

126. **33.** 20 f. green and brown .. 15 15
127. – 30 f. black and red .. 25 25
128. – 50 f. bistre and blue .. 30 30

DESIGNS: 30 f. Postman and circular postmark. 50 f. Sultan Hassan I and octagonal postmark. (Both stamps commemorate 70th anniv. of Sherifian post.)

1963. Flood Relief Fund. Surch. as T **34.**

129. **4.** 20 + 5 f. on 5 f. indigo and blue 20 20
130. 30 + 10 f. on 50 f. red .. 30 30

35. King Moulay Ismail (founder).

36. Ibn Batota (voyager).

1963. Ismailia Tercent.

131. **35.** 20 f. sepia 8 8

1963. "Famous Men of Maghreb".

132. **36.** 20 f. maroon 10 10
133. – 20 f. black 10 10
134. – 20 f. myrtle 10 10
134a. **36.** 40 f. ultramarine .. 12 8

PORTRAITS: No. 133, Ibn Khaldoun (historian). 134, Al Idrissi (geographer).

37. Sugar Beet and Refinery.

38. Isis (bas-relief).

1963. Freedom from Hunger.

135. **37.** 20 f. black, brown & grn. 10 8
136. – 50 f. black, brown & blue 20 12

DESIGN—VERT. 50 f. Fisherman and tunny.

1963. Nubian Monuments Preservation.

137. – 20 f. black and grey .. 10 10
138. **38.** 30 f. violet 12 10
139. – 50 f. brown-purple .. 20 15

DESIGNS—HORIZ. 20 f. Heads of Colossi, Abu Simbel. 50 f. Philae Temple.

39. Agadir, before Earthquake.

40. Plan of new Agadir Hospital.

41. Emblems of Morocco and Rabat.

1963. Reconstruction of Agadir.

140. **39.** 20 f. red and blue .. 12 12
141. 30 f. red and blue .. 15 15
142. – 50 f. red and blue .. 25 25

DESIGNS: 30 f. is optd. with large red cross and date of earthquake, 29th February, 1960. 50 f. Reconstructed Agadir.

1963. International Red Cross Centenary.

143. **40.** 30 f. red, silver, black and grey 12 12

1963. Opening of Parliament.

144. **41.** 20 f. red, green, gold and black 10 10

42. Hands breaking Chain.

43. National Flag.

1963 Declaration of Human Rights. 15th Anniv.

145. **42.** 20 f. chest., sepia & green 10 10

1963. Evacuation of Foreign Troops from Morocco.

146. **43.** 20 f. red, green & black 12 12

44. "Moulay Abdurrahman" (after Delacroix).

1964. King Hassan's Coronation. 3rd Anniv.

147. **44.** 1 d. multicoloured .. 1·40 1·10

45. Map, Chart and W.M.O. Emblem.

1964. World Meteorological Day. Mult.
148. 20 f. African weather map (postage) (vert.) .. 10 10
149. 30 f. Type **45** 15 15
150. 90 f. Globe and weather vane (air) (vert.) .. 30 25

46. Fair Entrance.

1964. Air. Casablanca Int. Fair. 20th Anniv.
151. **46.** 1 d. red, drab and blue 35 30

47. Moroccan Pavilion at Fair.

1964. Air. New York World's Fair.
152. **47.** 1 d. multicoloured .. 30 30

48. Children Playing in the Sun. **49.** Olympic Torch.

1964. Postal Employees' Holiday Settlements.
153. **48.** 20 f. multicoloured .. 8 8
154. – 30 f. multicoloured .. 12 12
DESIGN: 30 f. Boy, girl and holiday settlement.

1964. Olympic Games, Tokyo.
155. **49.** 20 f. green, violet & red 10 10
156. 30 f. mar., blue & green 12 12
157. 50 f. red, blue & emerald 20 20

50. Lighthouse and Sultan Mohamed ben Abdurrahman (founder). **51.** Tangier Iris.

1964. Cape Spartel Lighthouse. Cent.
158. **50.** 25 f. multicoloured .. 10 10

1965. Flowers. Multicoloured.
159. 25 f. Type **51** 15 15
160. 40 f. Gladiolus (vert.) .. 20 15
161. 60 f. Caper (horiz.) .. 25 20

52. Return of King Mohamed. **53.** Early Telegraph Receiver.

1965. Return of King Mohamed V from Exile. 10th Anniv.
162. **52.** 25 f. green 10 10

1965. I.T.U. Cent. Multicoloured.
163. 25 f. Type **53** 10 10
164. 40 f. "Syncom" satellite 15 15

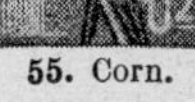

54. I.C.Y. Emblem. **55.** Corn.

1965. Int. Co-operation Year.
165. **54.** 25 f. black and green .. 10 10
166. 60 f. lake 25 25

1965. Seashells. As T **51**. Designs multicoloured; background colours given.
167. 25 f. violet 10 8
168. 25 f. blue 10 8
169. 25 f. yellow 10 8
SEASHELLS: No. 167, "Charonia nodifera". 168, "Pitaria chione". 169, "Cymbium neptuni". Each value issued "tete-beche" horiz. in sheets.

1965. Shellfish. As T **51**. Multicoloured.
170. 25 f. Helmet Crab .. 10 8
171. 40 f. Mantis shrimp .. 15 12
172. 1 d. Royal prawn .. 45 25

1965. Orchids. As T **51**. Multicoloured.
173. 25 f. "Ophrys speculum" (vert.) 10 8
174. 40 f. "Ophrys fusca" (vert.) 15 12
175. 60 f. "Ophrys tenthredinifera" (horiz.) 25 15

1966. Agricultural Products (1st issue).
176. **55.** 25 f. black and ochre 8 5
See also Nos. 188/9 and 211.

56. Flag, Map and Dove.

1966. Independence. 10th Anniv.
177. **56.** 25 f. red and green .. 8 5

57. King Hassan II and Crown.

1966. King Hassan's Coronation. 5th Anniv.
178. **57.** 25 f. blue, green and red 8 5

58. Cross-country Runner.

1966. 53rd "Cross des Nations" (Cross-country Race).
179. **58.** 25 f. green 8 5

59. W.H.O. Building.

1966. W.H.O. Headquarters, Geneva. Inaug.
180. **59.** 25 f. black and purple .. 10 5
181. – 40 f. black and blue .. 15 8
DESIGN: 40 f. W.H.O. Building (different view).

60. King Hassan and Parachutist. **61** Brooch.

1966. Royal Armed Forces. 10th Anniv.
182. **60.** 25 f. black and gold .. 12 12
183. – 40 f. black and gold .. 15 15
DESIGN: 40 f. Crown Prince Hassan kissing hand of King Mohamed.

1966. Palestine Week. As No. 110 but inscr. "SEMAINE DE LA PALESTINE" at foot and dated "1966".
184. 25 f. slate-blue 10 5

1966. Red Cross Seminar. Moroccan Jewellery. Multicoloured.
185. 25 f. + 5 f. Type **61** .. 12 12
186. 40 f. + 10 f. Pendant .. 20 20
See also Nos. 203/4, 245/6, 273/4, 302/3, 323/4, 368/9, 414/15 and 450/1.

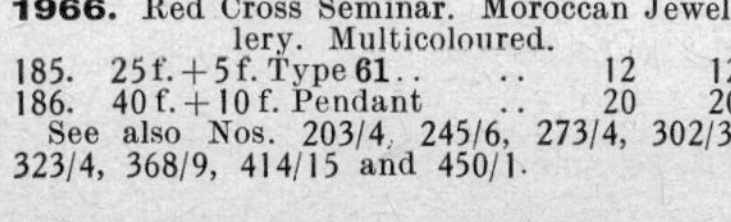

62. Rameses II, Abu Simbel. **63.** Diesel Train.

1966. Air. U.N.E.S.C.O. 20th Anniv.
187. **62.** 1 d. red and yellow .. 25 20

1966. Agricultural Products (2nd and 3rd issue.) Designs as T **55**.
188. 40 f. multicoloured .. 12 8
189. 60 f. multicoloured .. 20 8
DESIGNS—VERT. 40 f. Citrus fruits. HORIZ. 60 f. Olives.

1966. Moroccan Transport. Multicoloured.
(a) Postage. Size as T **63**.
190 25 f. Type **63**. 8 5
191. 40 f. Liner "Maroc" .. 12 8
192. 1 d. Tourist coach .. 30 12
(b) Air. Size $48\times27\frac{1}{2}$ mm.
193. 3 d. "Caravelle" of Royal Air Maroc 75 45

64. Shad.

1967. Fishes. Multicoloured.
194. 25 f. Type **64** 10 5
195. 40 f. Pale bonito 15 8
196. 1 d. Bluefish 30 12

65. Hilton Hotel, Ancient Ruin and Map.

1967. Opening of Hilton Hotel, Rabat.
197. **65.** 25 f. black and blue .. 10 5
198. 1 d. purple and blue .. 30 10

66. Aiit Aadel Dam.

1967. Aiit Aadel Dam. Inaug.
199. **66.** 25 f. grey, blue & green 10 5
200. 40 f. bistre and blue .. 15 8

67. Moroccan Scene and Lions Emblem.

1967. Lions Int. 50th Anniv.
201. **67.** 40 f. blue and gold .. 12 8
202. 1 d. green and gold .. 30 10

1967. Moroccan Red Cross. As T **61**. Multicoloured.
203. 60 f. + 5 f. Necklace .. 15 12
204. 1 d. + 10 f. Two bracelets .. 25 20

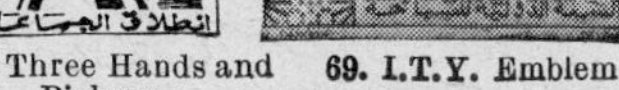

68. Three Hands and Pickaxe. **69.** I.T.Y. Emblem.

1967. Communal Development Campaign.
205. **68.** 25 f. green 10 8

1967. Int. Tourist Year.
206. **69.** 1 d. blue and cobalt .. 25 15

70. Arrow and Map. **71.** Horse-jumping.

1967. Mediterranean Games, Tunis.
207. **70.** 25 f. multicoloured .. 5 5
208. 40 f. multicoloured .. 10 8

1967. Int. Horse Show.
209. **71.** 40 f. multicoloured .. 12 8
210. 1 d. multicoloured .. 30 20

1967. Agricultural Products (4th issue). As T **55**.
211. 40 f. mult. (Cotton plant) 10 8

72. Human Rights Emblem. **73.** Msouffa Woman.

1968. Human Rights Year.
212. **72.** 25 f. slate 10 10
213. 1 d. lake 20 12

1968. Moroccan Costumes. Multicoloured.
214. 10 f. Aiit Moussa or Ali 5 5
215. 15 f. Aiit Mouhad 5 5
216. 25 f. Barquemaster of Rabat-Sale 5 5
217. 25 f. Toursman 5 5
218. 40 f. Toursman 10 5
219. 60 f. Royal Mokhazni .. 15 8
220. 1 d. Type **73** 25 10
221. 1 d. Riff 25 10
222. 1 d. Zemmour 20 10
223. 1 d. Meknassa 20 10

74. King Hassan. **75.** Red Crescent Nurse and Child.

1968.
224. **74.** 1 f. multicoloured .. 5 5
225. 2 f. multicoloured .. 5 5
226. 5 f. multicoloured .. 5 5
227. 10 f. multicoloured .. 5 5
228. 15 f. multicoloured .. 5 5
229. 20 f. multicoloured .. 5 5
230. 25 f. multicoloured .. 5 5
231. 30 f. multicoloured .. 5 5
232. 35 f. multicoloured .. 5 5
233. 40 f. multicoloured .. 8 5
234. 50 f. multicoloured .. 8 5
235. 60 f. multicoloured .. 10 5
236. 70 f. multicoloured .. 12 5
237. 75 f. multicoloured .. 12 5
238. 80 f. multicoloured .. 15 8
239. – 90 f. multicoloured .. 15 8
240. – 1 d. multicoloured .. 20 8
241. – 2 d. multicoloured .. 35 8
242. – 3 d. multicoloured .. 55 12
243. – 5 d. multicoloured .. 85 30
Nos. 239/43 bear a similar portrait of King Hassan, but are larger, $26\frac{1}{2}\times40\frac{1}{2}$ mm.

1968. W.H.O. 20th Anniv.
244. **75.** 25 f. brown, red & blue 5 5
245. 40 f. brown, red & slate 10 5

1968. Red Crescent. Moroccan Jewellery. As T **61**. Multicoloured.
246. 25 f. Pendant brooch .. 10 8
247. 40 f. Bracelet 10 8

76. Rotary Emblem, Conference Building and Map.

1968. Rotary Int. District Conf., Casablanca.
248. **76.** 40 f. gold, ultram. & grn. 10 5
249. 1 d. gold, ultram. & blue 25 12

77. Belt Pattern. **78.** Princess Lalla Meryem.

1968. "The Belts of Fez". Designs showing ornamental patterns.
250. **77.** 25 f. multicoloured .. 5 5
251. – 40 f. multicoloured .. 10 5
252. – 60 f. multicoloured .. 15 8
253. – 1 d. multicoloured .. 25 15

1968. World Children's Day. Multicoloured.
254. 25 f. Type **78** 5 5
255. 40 f. Princess Lalla Asmaa 10 5
256. 1 d. Crown Prince Sidi Mohamed 25 12

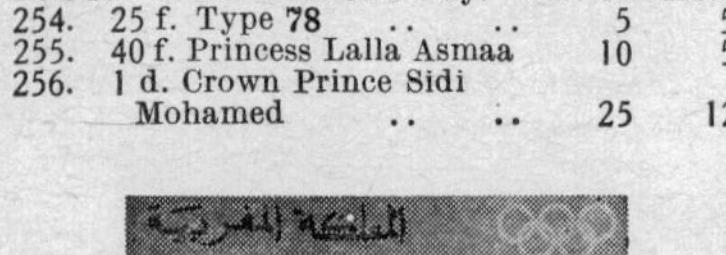

79. Wrestling.

1968. Olympic Games, Mexico. Multicoloured.
257. 15 f. Type **79** 5 5
258. 20 f. Basketball 5 5
259. 25 f. Cycling 5 5
260. 40 f. Boxing 10 5
261. 60 f. Running 15 5
262. 1 d. Football 25 10

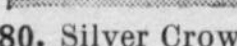

80. Silver Crown. **81.** Costumes of Zagora, South Morocco.

1968. Ancient Moroccan Coins.
263. **80.** 20 f. silver & pur. (post.) 5 5
264. – 25 f. gold and maroon 5 5
265. – 40 f. silver and green .. 10 5
266. – 60 f. gold and red .. 15 8
COINS: 25 f. Gold dinar. 40 f. Silver dirham. 60 f. Gold piece.
See also Nos. 270/1.

1969. Traditional Women's Costumes. Mult.
267. 15 f. Type **81** (postage) .. 5 5
268. 25 f. Aiit Adidou costumes 5 5
269. 1 d. Aiit Ouaouzguit costumes (air) 25 15

1969. Coronation of Hassan II. 8th Anniv. As Type **84** (silver cions).
270. 1 d. silver and blue .. 25 12
271. 5 d. silver and violet .. 1·25 55
COINS: 1 d. One dirham coin of King Mohammed V. 5 d. One dirham coin of King Hassan II.

82. Hands "reading" Braille on Map.

1969. Protection of the Blind Week.
272. **82.** 25 f. + 10 f. mult. .. 8 5

83. "Actor". **84.** King Hassan II.

1969. World Theatre Day.
273. **83.** 1 d. multicoloured .. 25 10

1969. League of Red Cross Societies. 50th Anniv. Moroccan Jewellery as T **61**. Multicoloured.
274. 25 f. + 5 f. Bracelets .. 8 5
275. 40 f. + 10 f. Pendant .. 12 8

1969. King Hassan's 40th Birthday.
276. **84.** 1 d. multicoloured .. 25 10

مؤتمر القمة الاسلامي
الرباط ١٠ رجب 1389

(**85.**) **86.** Mahatma Gandhi.

1969. Islamic Summit Conf., Rabat (1st issue). No. 239 (King Hassan) optd. with Type **85**.
278. 1 d. multicoloured .. 1·00 75

1969. Mahatma Gandhi. Birth Cent.
279. **86.** 40 f. brown and lavender 10 5

87. I.L.O. Emblem.

1969. Int. Labour Organization. 50th Anniv.
280. **87.** 50 f. multicoloured .. 12 5

88. King Hassan on Horseback.

1969. Islamic Summit Conf., Rabat (2nd Issue).
281. **88.** 1 d. multicoloured .. 25 10

89. "Spahi Horseman" (Haram al Glaoui).

1970. Moroccan Art.
282. **89.** 1 d. multicoloured .. 25 10

1970. Flood Victims Relief Fund. Nos. 227/8 surch.
283. **74.** 10 f. + 25 f. multicoloured 50 50
284. 15 f. + 25 f. multicoloured 50 50

90. Drainage System, Fez. **91.** "Dance of the Guedra" (P. Beaulran).

1970. 50th Congress of Public and Municipal Health Officials, Rabat.
285. **90.** 60 f. multicoloured .. 12 5

1970. Folklore Festival, Marrakesh.
286. **91.** 40 f. multicoloured .. 10 5

1970. Red Crescent. Moroccan Jewellery as T **61**. Multicoloured.
287. 25 f. + 5 f. Necklace .. 5 5
288. 50 f. + 10 f. Pendant .. 15 10

1970. Population Census. No. 189 surch. **1970.** Arabic inscr. and new value.
290. 25 f. on 60 f. multicoloured 5 5

92. Dish Aerial, Souk el Arba des Sehoul Communications Station. **93.** Ruddy Shelduck.

1970. Revolution. 17th Anniv.
291. **92.** 1 d. multicoloured .. 25 10

1970. Nature Protection, Wild Birds. Mult.
292. 25 f. Type **93** 5 5
293. 40 f. Houbara bustard .. 8 5

94. I.E.Y. Emblem and Moroccan with Book.

1970. International Education Year.
294. **94.** 60 f. multicoloured .. 8 5

95. Symbols of U.N.

1970. United Nations. 25th Anniv.
295. **95.** 50 f. mult.coloured .. 12 5

96. League Emblem, Map and Laurel.

1970. Arab League. 25th Anniv.
296. **96.** 50 f. multicoloured .. 12 5

97. Olive Grove and Extraction Plant.

1970. World Olive-oil Production Year.
297. **97.** 50 f. blk., brn. & green 12 5

98. Es Sounna Mosque.

1971. Restoration of Es Sounna Mosque Rabat.
298. **98.** 60 f. multicoloured .. 12 5

99. "Heart" within Horse. **100.** King Hassan II and Dam.

1971. European and North African Heart Week.
299. **99.** 50 f. multicoloured .. 12 5

1971. King Hassan's Accession. 10th Anniv.
300. **100.** 25 f. multicoloured .. 5 5

101. Palestine on Globe.

1971. Palestine Week.
302. **101.** 25 f. + 10 f. multicoloured 8 5

1971. Red Crescent. Moroccan Jewellery. As T **61**. Multicoloured.
303. 25 f. + 5 f. Brooch .. 8 5
304. 40 f. + 10 f. Pendant .. 10 8

102. Hands holding Peace Dove.

1971. Racial Equality Year.
305. **102.** 50 f. multicoloured .. 12 5

103. Musical Instrument.

1971. Protection of the Blind Week.
306. **103.** 40 f. + 10 f. mult. .. 12 8

104. Children at Play. **105.** Shah Mohammed Riza of Pahlavi.

1971. International Children's Day.
307. 104. 40 f. multicoloured .. 10 5

1971. Persian Empire. 2,500th Anniv.
308. 105. 1 d. multicoloured .. 25 12

106. Aerial View of Mausoleum.

1971. Mausoleum of Mohammed V. Mult.
309. 25 f. Type 106 .. .. 5 5
310. 50 f. Tomb of Mohammed V 12 5
311. 1 d. Interior of Mausoleum 25 12

107. Football and Emblem. 109. Sun and Landscape.

108. A.P.U. Emblem.

1971. Mediterranean Games, Izmir, Turkey. Multicoloured.
312. 40 f. Type 107 .. .. 10 5
313. 60 f. Athlete and emblem 12 5

1971. Founding of Arab Postal Union at Sofar Conf. 25th Anniv.
314. 108. 25 f. red, blue & light bl. 5 5

1971. Sherifian Phosphates Office. 50th Anniv.
315. 109. 70 f. multicoloured .. 15 12

110. Torch and Book Year Emblem. 111. Lottery Symbol.

1972. Int. Book Year.
316. 110. 1 d. multicoloured .. 25 15

1972. Creation of National Lottery.
317. 111. 25 f. gold, blk. & brn. 5 5

112. Bridge of Sighs. 113. Mizmar (double-horned flute).

1972. U.N.E.S.C.O. "Save Venice" Campaign. Multicoloured.
318. 25 f. Type 112 .. .. 5 5
319. 50 f. St Mark's Basilica (horiz.) 12 8
320. 1 d. Lion of St. Marks (horiz) 25 12

1972. Protection of the Blind.
321 113. 25 f.+10 f. mult. .. 8 5

114. Bridge and Motorway.

1972. 2nd African Highways Conf., Rabat.
322. 114. 75 f. multicoloured .. 15 10

115. Moroccan Stamp of 1969, and Postmark.

1972. Stamp Day.
323. 115. 1 d. multicoloured .. 20 12

1972. Red Crescent. Moroccan Jewellery. As T 61. Multicoloured.
324. 25 f.+5 f. Jewelled bangles 5 5
325. 70 f.+10 f. Filigree pendant 20 12

116. "The Betrothal of Imilchil" (Tayeb Lahlou). 117. Dove on African Map.

1972. Folklore Festival, Marrakesh.
326. 116. 60 f. multicoloured .. 12 8

1972. 9th Organisation of African Unity Summit Conference, Rabat.
327. 117. 25 f. multicoloured .. 5 5

118. Polluted Beach.

1972. U.N. Environmental Conservation Conf., Stockholm.
328. 118. 50 f. multicoloured .. 10 5

119. Running. 120. "Sonchus pinnatifidus".

1972. Olympic Games, Munich.
329. 119. 25 f. red, pink and blk. 5 5
330. – 50 f. violet, lilac & blk. 12 5
331. – 75 f. grn., yellow-grn., and black 15 12
332. – 1 d. blue, light blue and black .. 25 15

DESIGNS: 50 f. Wrestling. 75 f. Football. 1 d. Cycling.

1972. Moroccan Flowers. (1st series). Mult.
333. 25 f. Type 120 .. .. 5 5
334. 40 f. "Amberboa crupinoides" 10 5

See also Nos. 375/6.

121. Gazelle. 122. Rabat Carpet.

1972. Nature Protection. Fauna. Mult.
335. 25 f. Type 121 .. .. 5 5
336. 40 f. Moufflon 10 5

1972. Moroccan Carpets (1st series). Mult.
337. 50 f. Type 122 .. .. 12 5
338. 75 f. Rabat carpet with "star-shaped" centre .. 15 12

See also Nos. 380/1 and 433/4.

123. Mother and Child with U.N. Emblem. 125. Global Weather Map.

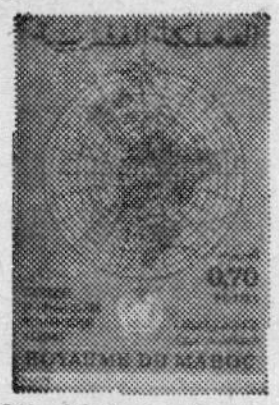

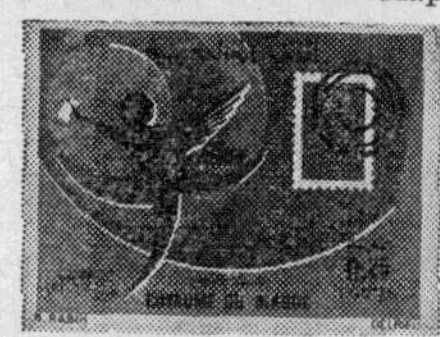
124. "Postman" and "Stamp".

1972. International Children's Day.
339. 123. 75 f. blue, yell. & grn. 15 12

1973. Stamp Day.
340. 124. 25 f. multicoloured .. 5 5

1973. World Meteorological Organization. Cent.
341. 125. 70 f. multicoloured .. 12 8

126. King Hassan and Arms.

1973.
342. 126. 1 f. multicoloured .. 5 5
343. 2 f. multicoloured .. 5 5
344. 5 f. multicoloured .. 5 5
345. 10 f. multicoloured .. 5 5
346. 15 f. multicoloured .. 5 5
347. 20 f. multicoloured .. 5 5
348. 25 f. multicoloured .. 5 5
349. 30 f. multicoloured .. 8 5
350. 35 f. multicoloured .. 8 5
351. 40 f. multicoloured .. 10 5
352. 50 f. multicoloured .. 12 5
353. 60 f. multicoloured .. 15 8
354. 70 f. multicoloured .. 15 10
355. 75 f. multicoloured .. 20 10
356. 80 f. multicoloured .. 20 12
357. 90 f. multicoloured .. 20 12
358. 1 d. multicoloured .. 25 15
359. 2 d. multicoloured .. 45 30
360. 3 d. multicoloured .. 70 45
361. 5 d. mult. (brown background) .. .. 1·25 70
361a. 5 d. mult. (pink background) .. .. 1·25 70

مناظرة
السياحة
1973
(127.)

1973. Nat. Tourist Conf. Nos. 324/5 surch. with T 127.
362. 61. 25 f. on 5 f. multicoloured 8 5
363. 70 f. on 10 f. mult. .. 20 12

On No. 363 the Arabic text is arranged in one line.

128. Tambours.

1973. Protection of the Blind Week.
364. 128. 70 f.+10 f. multicoloured 25 15

129. Kaaba, Mecca, and Mosque, Rabat.

1973. Prophet Mohammed's Birthday.
365. 129. 25 f. multicoloured .. 8 5

130. Roses and M'Gouna.

1973. M'Gouna Rose Festival.
366. 130. 25 f. multicoloured .. 8 5

131. Handclasp and Torch. 132. Folk-dancers.

1973. Organization of African Unity. 10th Anniv.
367. 131. 70 f. multicoloured .. 20 10

1973. Folklore Festival, Marrakesh. Mult.
368. 50 f. Type 132 .. .. 15 8
369. 1 d. Folk-musicians .. 30 15

1973. Red Crescent. Moroccan Jewellery. As T 61. Multicoloured.
370. 25 f.+5 f. Locket.. .. 10 5
371. 70 f.+10 f. Bracelet inlaid with pearls 25 12

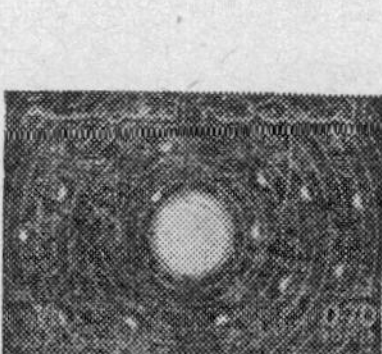

133. Solar System. 134. Microscope.

1973. Nicholas Copernicus. 500th Birth Anniv.
372. 133. 70 f. multicoloured .. 20 10

1973. W.H.O. 25th Anniv.
373. 134. 70 f. multicoloured .. 20 10

135. Interpol Emblem and Fingerprint.

1973. International Criminal Police Organization (Interpol). 50th Anniv.
374. 135. 70 f. multicoloured .. 20 10

1973. Moroccan Flowers. (2nd series). As T 120. Multicoloured.
375. 25 f. "Chrysanthemum carinatum" (horiz.) .. 8 5
376. 1 d. "Amberboa muricata" 30 15

136. Berber Hyena.

1973. Nature Protection. Multicoloured.
377. 25 f. Type 136 .. .. 8 5
378. 40 f. Eleonore's Falcon (vert.) 15 8

137. Map and Arrows.

1973. Meeting of Maghreb Committee for Co-ordination of Posts and Telecommunications, Tunis.
379. 137. 25 f. multicoloured .. 8 5

1973. Moroccan Carpets (2nd series). As Type 122. Multicoloured.
380. 25 f. Carpet from the High Atlas 8 5
381. 70 f. Tazenahht carpet .. 20 10

138. Golf Club and Ball.

المؤتمر الاسلامي - لاهور
1394

(139).

1974. Int. "Hassan II Trophy" Golf Grand Prix, Rabat.
382. 138. 70 f. multicoloured .. 20 10

1974. Islamic Summit Conf., Lahore, Pakistan. No. 281 optd. with Type 139.
383. 1 d. multicoloured .. 30 15

140. Human Rights Emblem.

141. Vanadinite.

1974. Declaration of Human Rights. 25th Anniv. (1973).
384. 140. 70 f. multicoloured .. 20 10

1974. Moroccan Mineral Sources. Mult.
385. 25 f. Type 141 .. .. 8 5
386. 70 f. Erythrine 20 10

142. Marrakesh Minaret.

143. U.P.U. Emblem and Congress Dates.

1974. 173rd District of Rotary Int. Annual Conf., Marrakesh.
387. 142. 70 f. multicoloured .. 20 10

1974. Universal Postal Union. Cent.
388. 143. 25 f. blk., red & green 8 5
389. – 1 d. multicoloured .. 30 15
DESIGN—HORIZ. 1 d. Commemorative scroll.

144. Drummers and Dancers.

1974. 15th Folklore Festival, Marrakesh. Multicoloured.
390. 25 f. Type 144 .. .. 8 5
391. 70 f. Juggler with woman 20 10

MINIMUM PRICE

The minimum price quoted is 5p which represents a handling charge rather than a basis for valuing common stamps. For further notes about prices see introductory pages.

145. Environmental Emblem and Scales.

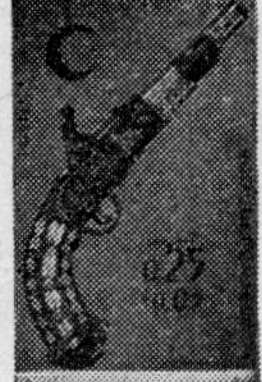

146. Flintlock Pistol.

1974. World Environmental Day.
392. 145. 25 f multicoloured .. 8 5

1974. Red Crescent. Moroccan Firearms. Multicoloured.
397. 25 f. + 5 f. Type 146 .. 10 5
398. 70 f. + 10 f. Gunpowder box 25 12

147. Stamps, Postmark and Magnifier.

الاحصاء الفلاحي

.1,00

(148.)

1974. Stamp Day.
399. 147. 70 f. multicoloured .. 20 10

1974. No. D 393 surch. with Type 148.
400. 1 d. on 5 f. orge., grn. & blk. 30 15

149. Jules Rimet Cup.

150. Erbab.

1974. World Cup Football Championships, Munich.
401. 149. 1 d. multicoloured .. 30 15

1974. Protection of the Blind Week.
402. 150. 70 f. + 10 f. multicoloured 25 12

151. Francolin.

152. Jasmine.

1974. Moroccan Fauna. Multicoloured.
404. 25 f. Type 151 .. .. 8 5
405. 70 f. Leopard 20 10

1974. Moroccan Carpets (3rd series). As Type 122. Multicoloured.
406. 25 f. Zemmour carpet (square pattern) .. 8 5
407. 1 d. Beni M'Guild carpet (diamond pattern) .. 30 15

1975. Moroccan Flora (1st series). Mult.
408. 25 f. Type 152 .. .. 8 5
409. 35 f. Orange lilies 10 5
410. 70 f. Poppies 20 10
411. 90 f. Carnations 25 12
See also Nos. 417/20.

MORE DETAILED LISTS

are given in the Stanley Gibbons Catalogues referred to in the country headings:

BC	British Commonwealth
E1, E2, E3	Europe 1, 2, 3
O1, O2, O3, O4	Overseas 1, 2, 3, 4

153. Aragonite.

154. "The Water-carrier" (Feu Taieb Lalou).

1975. Mineral Rocks, Multicoloured.
412. 50 f. Type 153 .. .. 15 8
413. 1 d. Agate 30 15

1975. Red Crescent. Moroccan Jewellery. As T 61. Multicoloured.
414. 25 f. + 5 f. Pendant .. 8 5
415. 70 f. + 10 f. Earring .. 20 10

1975. "Moroccan Painters".
416. 154. 1 d. multicoloured .. 25 12

1975. Moroccan Flora (2nd series). AS T 152. Multicoloured.
417. 10 f. Daisies 5 5
418. 50 f. Pelargoniums .. 12 5
419. 60 f. Orange blossom .. 15 8
420. 1 d. Pansies 25 12

155. Collector with Stamp Album.

156. Dancer with Rifle.

1975. Stamp Day.
421. 155. 40 f. multicoloured .. 10 5

1975. 16th Nat. Folklore Festival, Marrakesh.
422. 156. 1 d. multicoloured .. 25 12

157. Mandoline.

158. "Animals in Forest" (child's drawing).

1975. Protection of the Blind Week.
423. 157. 1 d. multicoloured .. 25 12

1975. Children's Week.
424. 158. 25 f. multicoloured .. 5 5

159. Games Emplem and Sportsmen.

1975. Mediterranean Games, Algiers.
425. 159. 40 f. multicoloured .. 10 5

160. Bald Ibis.

1975. Moroccan Fauna. Multicoloured.
426. 40 f. Type 160 .. .. 10 5
427. 1 d. Caracal (vert.) .. 25 12

1975. "Green March" (1st issue). Nos. 414/5 optd. 1975 and Arabic inscr.
428. 25 f. (+5 f.) multicoloured 5 5
429. 70 f. (+10 f.) multicoloured 20 10
The premiums on the stamps are obliterated.

161. King Hassan greeting Crowd.

1975. Independence. 20th Anniv. Mult.
430. 40 f. Type 161 .. .. 10 5
431. 1 d. King Hassan (vert.) .. 25 12
432. 1 d. King Hassan wearing fez (vert.) 25 12

1975. Moroccan Carpets (3rd series). As T 122. Multicoloured.
433. 25 f. Ouled Besseba carpet 5 5
434. 1 d. Ait Ouaouzguid carpet 25 12

162. Marchers crossing Desert.

163. Fez Coin of 1883/4.

1975. "Green March" (2nd issue).
435. 162. 40 f. multicoloured .. 10 5

1976. Moroccan Coins (1st series). Multicoloured.
436. 40 f. Type 163 .. .. 10 5
437. 50 f. Rabat coin of 1774/5 12 5
438. 65 f. Sabta coin of 13th/14th centuries 15 8
439. 1 d. Sabta coin of 12th/13th centuries 25 12
See also Nos. 446/8 and 458/63.

164. Interior of Mosque.

1976. Ibn Zaidoun Mosque. Millennium. Multicoloured.
440. 40 f. Type 164 .. .. 10 5
441. 65 f. Interior archways (vert.) 15 8

165. Moroccan Family.

1976. Family Planning.
442. 165. 40 f. multicoloured .. 10 5

166. Bou Anania Street, Fez.

1976. Moroccan Architecture.
443. 166. 1 d. multicoloured .. 25 12

167. Temple Sculpture.

1976. Borobudur Temple Preservation Campaign. Multicoloured.
444. 40 f. Type 167 .. .. 10 5
445. 1 d. View of Temple .. 25 12

1976. Moroccan Coins (2nd series). As Nos. 437/438. Mult.
446. 5 f. As 40 f. 5 5
447. 15 f. As 50 f. 5 5
448. 35 f. As 65 f. 10 5

168. Dome of the Rock, Jerusalem.

1976. Islamic Conference. 6th Anniv.
449. 168. 1 d. multicoloured .. 25 12

1976. Red Crescent, Moroccan Jewellery. As T 61. Multicoloured.
450. 40 f. Jewelled purse .. 10 5
451. 1 d. Jewelled pectoral .. 25 12

169. U.S. and Moroccan Flags.

1976. American Revolution. Bicent. Multicoloured.
452. 40 f. Type 169 .. .. 10 5
453. 1 d. Statue of Liberty and Royal Palace, Rabat, with King Hassan and Washington 25 12

170. Wrestling.

1976. Olympic Games, Montreal. Multicoloured.
454. 35 f. Type 170 .. .. 10 5
455. 40 f. Cycling 10 5
456. 50 f. Boxing 12 5
457. 1 d. Running 75 12

1976. Moroccan Coins (3rd series). As T 163.
458. 5 f. multicoloured .. 5 5
459. 15 f. multicoloured .. 5 5
460. 20 f. multicoloured .. 5 5
461. 30 f. multicoloured .. 8 5
462. 35 f. multicoloured .. 10 5
463. 70 f. multicoloured .. 20 10
DESIGNS: 5 f. to 70 f. Various Moroccan coins.

171. Early and Modern Telephones with Dish Aerial.

1976. Telephone Centenary.
464. 171. 1 d. multicoloured .. 25 12

172. Gold Medallion.

1976. Blind Week.
465. 172. 50 f. multicoloured .. 12 5

POSTAGE DUE STAMPS

D 1.

1965. Values in dirhams.
D 162. D 1. 5 f. green 5 5
D 163. 10 f. brown 5 5
D 164. 20 f. red 5 5
D 165. 30 f. sepia 5 5

D 2. Peaches.

1974.
D 393. – 5 f. orge., grn. & blk. 5 5
D 394. – 10 f. grn., red & blk. 5 5
D 395. – 20 f. green & black 5 5
D 396. D 2. 30 f. orge., grn. & blk. 8 5
DESIGNS—VERT. 5 f. Oranges. 10 f. Cherries. 20 f. Grapes.

MOROCCO AGENCIES BC

Stamps used at British postal agencies in Morocco, N. Africa, the last of which were closed on 30th April, 1957.

I. "GIBRALTAR" PERIOD.

For use at all British Post Offices in Morocco.

All British P.O.s in Morocco were under the control of the Gibraltar P.O. until 1907 when control was assumed by H.M. Postmaster-General.

1898. Stamps of Gibraltar (Queen) optd. **Morocco Agencies.**
9. 2. 5 c. green 8 8
10. 10 c. red 12 8
3. 20 c. olive 65 70
3b. 20 c. olive and brown .. 65 40
4. 25 c. blue 30 25
5. 40 c. brown 30 85
6a. 50 c. lilac .. .. 2·25 2·75
7. 1 p. brown and blue .. 2·50 4·50
8. 2 p. black and red .. 1·50 4·50

1903. Stamps of Gibraltar (King Edward VII) optd. **Morocco Agencies.**
24. 3. 5 c. green 20 15
25. 10 c. purple and red .. 30 12
26. 20 c. green and red .. 85 2·25
20. 25 c. purple & blk. on bl. 40 20
28. 50 c. purple and violet .. 3·50 3·00
29. 1 p. black and red .. 12·00 14·00
30. 2 p. black and blue .. 9·00 8·00

II. BRITISH CURRENCY

On sale at British P.Os throughout Morocco, including Tangier, until 1937.

PRICES. Our prices for used stamps with these overprints are for specimens used in Morocco. These stamps could also be used in the United Kingdom, with official sanction, from the summer of 1950 onwards, and with U.K. postmarks are worth about 25 per cent less.

Stamps of Great Britain optd. **MOROCCO AGENCIES.**

1907. King Edward VII.
31. ½d. yellow-green .. 20 45
32. 1d. red 70 75
33. 2d. green and red .. 70 1·40
34. 4d. green and brown .. 5·50 1·25
35. 4d. orange .. .. 1·00 1·10
36. 6d. purple .. .. 2·00 1·00
37. 1s. green and red .. 4·50 3·00
39. 2s. 6d. purple .. .. 28·00 26·00

1914. King George V.
42. 85. ½d. green 12 20
43. 84. 1d. red 12 10
44. 85. 1½d. brown 70 80
57. 86. 2d. orange 90 70
58. 84. 2½d. blue .. .. 1·10 60
46. 86. 3d. violet 80 30
47. 4d. grey-green 90 40
60. 87. 6d. purple 45 50
49. 88. 1s. brown .. .. 4·50 75
53. 89. 2s. 6d. brown .. 20·00 10·00
74. 5s. red .. .. 9·00 12·00

1935. Silver Jubilee.
62. 100. ½d. green 20 35
63. 1d. red 35 80
64. 1½d. brown .. .. 1·00 1·90
65. 2½d. blue .. .. 1·40 1·75

1935. King George V.
66. 96. 1d. red 20 20
67. 95. 1½d. brown .. .. 70 1·60
68. 97. 2d. orange 15 12
69. 96. 2½d. blue 90 85
70. 97. 3d. violet 15 10
71. 4d. green 20 12
72. 99. 1s. brown 60 45

1936. King Edward VIII.
75. 101. 1d. red 10 10
76. 2½d. blue 12 12

In 1937 unoverprinted Great Britain stamps replaced overprinted **MOROCCO AGENCIES** issues as stocks became exhausted. In 1949 overprinted issues reappeared and were in use at Tetuan (Spanish Zone), the only remaining British P.O. apart from that at Tangier.

1949. King George VI.
77. 103. ½d. pale green .. 8 20
94. ½d. orange 8 12
78. 1d. pale red 8 20
95. 1d. blue 8 12
79. 1½d. pale brown .. 10 30
96. 1½d. green 10 20
80. 2d. pale orange .. 10 30
97. 2d. brown 10 25
81. 2½d. light blue .. 10 30
98. 2½d. red 10 35
82. 3d. pale violet .. 10 20
83. 104. 4d. green 12 20
84. 5d. brown 20 40
85. 6d. purple 15 40
86. 105. 7d. green 20 45
87. 8d. red 20 45
88. 9d. olive 20 55
89. 10d. blue 25 60
90. 11d. plum 70 75
91. 1s. brown 35 70
92. 106. 2s. 6d. green .. 3·25 4·00
93. 5s. red .. .. 7·50 7·50

1951. Pictorials.
99 116. 2s. 6d. green .. 2·00 2·75
100. – 5s. red (No. 510) .. 3·00 5·00

1952. Queen Elizabeth II.
101. 118. ½d. orange 5 5
102. 1d. blue 5 5
103. 1½d. green 5 5
104. 2d. brown 10 10
105. 119. 2½d. red 10 12
106. 4d. blue 20 35
107. 120. 5d. brown 30 40
108. 6d. purple 35 45
109. 121. 8d. magenta .. 60 90
110. 122. 1s. bistre 30 50

III. SPANISH CURRENCY

Stamps surcharged in Spanish currency were sold at British P.Os throughout Morocco until the establishment of the French Zone and the Tangier International Zone, when their use was confined to the Spanish Zone.

Stamps of Great Britain optd. **MOROCCO AGENCIES** or surch. also in Spanish currency.

1907. King Edward VII.
112. 5 c. on ½d. yell-green 10 8
113. 10 c. on 1d. red .. 10 10
114. 15 c. on 1½d. purple and green 20 12
115. 20 c. on 2d. green & red 25 10
116. 25 c. on 2½d. blue .. 45 10
117. 40 c. on 4d. grn. & brn. 70 1·75
118. 40 c. on 4d. orange .. 25 40
119. 50 c. on 5d. pur. & blue 95 30
120. 1 p. on 10d. pur. & red 2·00 2·75
121. 3 p. on 2s. 6d. purple .. 8·50 8·50
122. 6 p. on 5s. red .. 20·00 22·00
123. 12 p. on 10s. blue .. 30·00 26·00

1912. King George V.
126. 82. 5 c. on ½d. green .. 45 8
129. 85. 5 c. on ½d. green .. 25 8
127. 83. 10 c. on 1d. red .. 60 8
131. 85. 15 c. on 1½d. brown .. 12 8

1914. King George V.
128. 85. 3 c. on ½d. green .. 10 75
130. 84. 10 c. on 1d. red .. 12 8
132. 86. 20 c. on 2d. orange .. 20 40
133. 84. 25 c. on 2½d. blue .. 20 10
148. 86. 40 c. on 4d. grey-green 25 25
135. 88. 1 p. on 10d. blue .. 65 1·10
142. 89. 3 p. on 2s. 6d. brown .. 10·00 12·00
136. 6 p. on 5s. red .. 17·00 19·00
141. 12 p. on 10s. blue .. 26·00 28·00

1935. Silver Jubilee.
149. 100. 5 c. on ½d. green .. 12 25
150. 10 c. on 1d. red .. 1·00 1·25
151. 15 c. on 1½d. brown .. 25 1·25
152. 25 c. on 2½d. blue .. 2·00 1·50

1935. King George V.
153. 95. 5 c. on ½d. green .. 10 25
154. 96. 10 c. on 1d. red .. 20 40
155. 95. 15 c. on 1½d. brown .. 2·00 1·40
156. 97. 20 c. on 2d. orange .. 20 25
157. 96. 25 c. on 2½d. blue .. 80 95
158. 97. 40 c. on 4d. green .. 12 40
159. 99. 1 p. on 10d. blue .. 12 15

1936. King Edward VIII.
160. 101. 5 c. on ½d. green .. 8 8
161. 10 c. on 1d. red .. 8 10
162. 15 c. on 1½d. brown .. 10 10
163. 25 c. on 2½d. blue .. 12 10

1937. Coronation.
164. 102. 15 c. on 1½d. brown .. 8 8

1937. King George VI.
165. 103. 5 c. on ½d. green .. 8 8
182. 5 c. on ½d. orange .. 8 15
166. 10 c. on 1d. red .. 8 10
183. 10 c. on 1d. blue .. 8 15
167. 15 c. on 1½d. brown .. 8 10
184. 15 c. on 1½d. green .. 8 15
168. 25 c. on 2½d. blue .. 8 10
185. 25 c. on 2½d. red .. 15 15
169. 104. 40 c. on 4d. green .. 35 35
186. 40 c. on 4d. blue .. 10 30
170. 105. 70 c. on 7d. green .. 15 25
171. 1 p. on 10d. blue .. 15 40

1940. Stamp Cent.
172. 108. 5 c. on ½d. green .. 8 15
173. 10 c. on 1d. red .. 8 15
174. 15 c. on 1½d. brown .. 10 35
175. 25 c. on 2½d. blue .. 12 25

1948. Silver Wedding.
176. 110. 25 c. on 2½d. blue .. 8 8
177. 111. 45 p. on £1 blue .. 6·00 9·50

1948. Olympic Games.
178. 112. 25 c. on 2½d. blue .. 8 15
179. 113. 30 c. on 3d. violet .. 8 15
180. – 60 c. on 6d. purple .. 10 15
181. – 1 p. 20 c. on 1s. brown 25 45

1954. Queen Elizabeth II.
187. 118. 5 c. on ½d. orange .. 5 10
188. 10 c. on 1d. blue .. 8 10
190. 119. 40 c. on 4d. blue .. 20 40

IV. FRENCH CURRENCY.

Stamps surch. in French currency were sold at British P.Os in the French Zone.

Stamps of Great Britain surch. **MOROCCO AGENCIES** and value in French currency.

1917. King George V.
191. 85. 3 c. on ½d. green .. 5 45
192. 5 c. on ½d. green .. 5 5
203. 84. 10 c. on 1d. red .. 8 10
204. 85. 15 c. on 1½d. brown .. 65 65
205. 84. 25 c. on 2½d. blue .. 10 10
206. 86. 40 c. on 4d. grey-grn. 35 20
207. 87. 50 c. on 5d. brown .. 35 10
208. 88. 75 c. on 9d. olive-green 70 10
209. 90 c. on 9d. olive-green 45 80
210. 1 f. on 10d. blue .. 25 12
211. 1 f. 50 c. on 1s. brown 65 1·10
200. 89. 3 f. on 2s. 6d. brown .. 5·00 2·25
201. 6 f. on 5s. red .. 17·00 14·00

1935. Silver Jubilee.
212. 100. 5 c. on ½d. green .. 8 8
213. 10 c. on 1d. red .. 55 80
214. 15 c. on 1½d. brown .. 12 25
215. 25 c. on 2½d. blue .. 20 20

1935. King George V.
216. 95. 5 c. on ½d. green .. 8 8
217. 96. 10 c. on 1d. red .. 8 8
218. 95. 15 c. on 1½d. brown .. 15 15
219. 96. 25 c. on 2½d. blue .. 10 10
220. 97. 40 c. on 4d. green .. 10 10
221. 98. 50 c. on 5d. brown .. 10 10
222. 99. 90 c. on 9d. olive .. 20 20
223. 1 f. on 10d. blue .. 12 12
224. 1 f. 50 c. on 1s. brown 20 20

1936. King Edward VIII.
227. 101. 5 c. on ½d. green .. 8 8
228. 15 c. on 1½d. brown .. 12 8

1937. Coronation.
229. 102. 15 c. on 1½d. brown .. 8 8

1937. King George VI.
230. 103. 5 c. on ½d. green .. 8 10

V. TANGIER INTERNATIONAL ZONE

This Zone was established in 1924 and the first specially overprinted stamps issued in 1927.

PRICES. Our note re U.K. usage (at beginning of Section II) also applies to **TANGIER** optd. stamps.

Stamps of Great Britain optd. **TANGIER.**

1927. King George V.
231. 85. ½d. green 35 8
232. 84. 1d. red 25 8
233. 85. 1½d. brown .. .. 1·25 75
234. 86. 2d. orange 45 10

1934. King George V.
235. 95. ½d. green 40 25
236. 96. 1d. red 80 25
237. 95. 1½d. brown 15 10

1935. Silver Jubilee.
238. 100. ½d. green 25 30
239. 1d. red 65 70
240. 1½d. brown 20 20

1936. King Edward VIII.
241. 101. ½d. green 8 8
242. 1d. red 8 8
243. 1½d. brown 8 8

1937. Coronation.
244. 102. 1½d. brown 8 8

1937. King George VI.
245. 103. ½d. green 8 12
251. ½d. pale green 8 12
280. ½d. orange 8 10
246. 1d. red 8 12
252. 1d. pale red 25 30
281. 1d. blue 8 10
247. 1½d. brown 8 15
282. 1½d. green 8 20
261. 2d. pale orange .. 8 15
283. 2d. brown 10 30
262. 2½d. light blue .. 8 15
284. 2½d. red 10 15
263. 3d. pale violet .. 8 15
264. 104. 4d. green 25 25
285. 4d. blue 20 30
265. 5d. brown 20 40
266. 6d. purple 10 20
267. 105. 7d. green 12 30
268. 8d. red 20 40
269. 9d. olive 12 40
270. 10d. blue 15 40
271. 11d. plum 20 45
272. 1s. brown 20 40
273. 106. 2s. 6d. green .. .. 1·50 2·00
274. 5s. red .. .. 4·00 5·50
275. – 10s. bright blue (No. 478a) .. .. 7·50 9·00

1940 Stamp Cent.
248. 108. ½d. green 8 10
249. 1d. red 10 15
250. 1½d. brown 20 30

1946. Victory.
253. 109. 2½d. blue 15 8
254. – 3d. violet 15 10

1948. Silver Wedding.
255. 110. 2½d. blue 8 8
256. 111. £1 blue .. .. 6·00 9·00

1948. Olympic Games.
257. 112. 2½d. blue 8 8
258. 113. 3d. violet 8 8
259. – 6d. purple 10 10
260. – 1s. brown 15 15

1949. U.P.U.
276. 114. 2½d. blue 8 15
277. 115. 3d. violet 10 20
278. – 6d. purple 12 30
279. – 1s. brown 20 40

1951. Pictorial stamps.
286. 116. 2s. 6d. green 65 75
287. – 5s. red (No. 510) .. 1·10 1·50
288. – 10s. blue (No. 511) .. 3·50 5·50

1952. Queen Elizabeth II.
289. 118. ½d. orange 5 5
290. 1d. blue 5 5
291. 1½d. green 5 5
292. 2d. brown 5 5
317. 2d. pale brown .. 15 25
293. 119. 2½d. red 5 5
294. 3d. lilac 5 8
295. 4d. blue 12 12
296. 120. 5d. brown 30 60
297. 6d. purple 12 10
298. 7d. green 30 60
299. 121. 8d. magenta 30 60
300. 9d. olive 25 25
301. 10d. blue 40 60
302. 11d. plum 40 60
303. 122. 1s. bistre 20 20
304. 1s. 3d. green 25 30
305. 1s. 6d. indigo 30 30

1953. Coronation.
306. 123. 2½d. red 20 25
307. – 4d. ultramarine .. 40 70
308. 124. 1s. 3d. green .. .. 90 1·40
309. – 1s. 6d. blue .. .. 1·00 1·60

1955. Pictorials.
310. 125. 2s. 6d. brown .. .. 1·00 1·50
311. – 5s. red .. .. 2·50 2·75
312. – 10s. blue .. .. 5·00 6·00

1957. British Post Office in Tangier. Cent. Queen Elizabeth II stamps optd. **1857–1957 TANGIER.**
323. 118. ½d. orange 5 5
324. 1d. blue 5 5
325. 1½d. green 5 5
326. 2d. pale brown 5 5
327. 119. 2½d. red 5 5
328. 3d. lilac 5 5
329. 4d. blue 8 8
330. 120. 5d. brown 10 12
331. 6d. purple 12 12
332. 7d. green 20 20
333. 121. 8d. magenta 20 20
334. 9d. olive 20 20
335. 10d. blue 20 20
336. 11d. plum 25 25
337. 122. 1s. bistre 20 20
338. 1s. 3d. green 25 25
339. 1s. 6d. indigo 30 30
340. 125. 2s. 6d. brown .. .. 75 1·50
341. – 5s. red .. .. 1·00 2·00
342. – 10s. blue .. .. 2·50 4·00

MORVI BC

A state of India, Bombay district. Now uses Indian stamps.

12 pies = 1 anna.

1. Maharaja Sir Lakhdirji Waghji. 2.

1931.
8. 1. 3 p. red 15 60
9. 6 p. green 25 70
5. ½ a. blue .. .. 1·00 1·50
6. 1 a. red-brown .. .. 1·50 2·00
10. 1 a. blue .. .. 75 1·50
7. 2 a. brown .. .. 2·50 3·00
11. 2 a. violet .. .. 4·00 6·00

1934.
12. 2. 3 p. red 30 60
13. 6 p. green 35 70
14. 1 a. brown .. .. 60 1·00
15. 2 a. violet .. .. 75 1·50

MOSUL O2; BC

Stamps used by Indian forces in Mesopotamia (now Iraq) at the close of the 1914–18 war.

1919. Turkish Fiscal stamps surch. **POSTAGE I.E.F. D** and value in annas.
1. ½ a. on 1 pi. green and red .. 70 70
2. 1 a. on 20 pa. black on red .. 70 70
4. 2½ a. on 1 pi. mauve & yellow 80 80
5. 3 a. on 20 pa. green .. 80 80
6. 3 a. on 20 pa. green & orange 7·00 8·00
7. 4 a. on 1 pi. violet .. .. 1·50 1·50
8. 8 a. on 10 pa. lake .. .. 2·00 2·00

MOZAMBIQUE O3

Former Overseas Province of Portugal in East Africa, granted independence in 1975.

1876. "Crown" key-type inscr. "MOCAMBIQUE"
1. P. 5 r. black 45 35
2a. 10 r. yellow .. .. 1·50 1·10
19. 10 r. green 35 25
3. 20 r. olive 50 35
20. 20 r. red .. .. .. 90·00 35·00
4a. 25 r. red 20 12
21. 25 r. lilac 60 50
5. 40 r. blue .. .. 6·00 4·00
22. 40 r. yellow 80 70
6. 50 r. green .. .. 17·00 5·50
23. 50 r. blue 30 20
7. 100 r. lilac 30 15
17. 200 r. orange .. .. 1·40 60
9a. 300 r. brown .. .. 1·10 90

1886. "Embossed" key-type inscr. "PROVINCIA DE MOCAMBIQUE".
30. Q. 5 r. black 50 25
32. 10 r. green 50 35
34. 20 r. red 60 40
36. 25 r. mauve .. .. 3·75 50
37. 40 r. brown 65 45
38. 50 r. blue 70 25
40. 100 r. brown 80 20
42. 200 r. violet .. .. 1·50 1·00
43. 300 r. orange .. .. 1·75 1·25

1893. No. 37 surch. **PROVISORIO 5 5.**
53 Q. 5 on 40 r. brown .. 9·00 7·00

1894. "Figures" key-type inscr. "MOCAMBIQUE".
56. R. 5 r. orange 25 20
57. 10 r. mauve 25 20
58. 15 r. brown 30 25
59. 20 r. lilac 40 30
65. 25 r. green 25 12
60. 50 r. blue .. .. 1·60 15
67. 75 r. red 70 50
61. 80 r. green .. .. 1·40 70
62. 100 r. brown on buff .. 80 55
68. 150 r. red on rose .. 2·50 1·90
64. 200 r. blue on blue .. 1·50 1·25
69. 300 r. blue on brown .. 2·00 1·40

1895. "Embossed" key-type of Mozambique optd. **1195 CENTENARIO ANTONINO 1895.**
71. Q. 5 r. black .. .. 3·00 2·00
72. 10 r. green .. .. 3·50 2·50
73. 20 r. red .. .. 4·00 3·50
74. 25 r. mauve .. .. 4·00 3·50
75. 40 r. brown .. .. 4·50 3·50
76. 50 r. blue .. .. 4·50 3·50
77. 100 r. brown .. .. 4·50 3·50
78. 200 r. lilac .. .. 8·00 6·00
79. 300 r. orange .. .. 8·00 6·00

1897. No. 69 surch. **50 reis.**
82. R. 50 r. on 300 r. bl. on brn. 45·00 24·00

1898. Nos. 34 and 37 surch. **MOCAMBIQUE** and value.
83. Q. 2½ r. on 20 r. red .. 4·00 3·50
85. 5 r. on 40 r. brown .. 4·00 3·25

1898. "King Carlos" key-type inscr. "MOCAMBIQUE".
86. S. 2½ r. grey 12 10
87. 5 r. orange 12 10
88. 10 r. green 12 10
89. 15 r. brown 80 45
138. 15 r. green 20 20
90. 20 r. lilac 25 20
91. 25 r. green 25 15
139. 25 r. red 25 10
92. 50 r. blue 30 15
140. 50 r. brown 70 50
141. 65 r. blue .. .. 2·25 1·75
93. 75 r. red .. .. 1·00 80
142. 75 r. purple 70 45
94. 80 r. mauve .. .. 1·00 80
95. 100 r. blue on blue .. 60 25
143. 115 r. brown on pink .. 1·25 1·00
144. 130 r. brown on yellow 1·25 1·00
96. 150 r. brown on yellow 1·00 70
97. 200 r. purple on pink .. 70 60
98. 300 r. blue on pink .. 1·00 70
145. 400 r. blue on yellow .. 1·90 1·50
99. 500 r. black on blue .. 2·25 1·75
100. 700 r. mauve on yellow 3·50 2·75

1902. Various types surch.
146. S. 50 r. on 65 r. blue .. 70 50
101. R. 65 r. on 10 r. mauve .. 1·00 90
102. 65 r. on 15 r. brown .. 1·00 90
105. Q. 65 r. on 20 r. red .. 1·00 90
106. R. 65 r. on 20 r. lilac .. 1·00 90
108. Q. 65 r. on 40 r. brown .. 1·75 1·25
109. 65 r. on 200 r. violet .. 1·00 60
111. V. 115 r. on 2½ r. brown .. 1·00 90
113. Q. 115 r. on 5 r. black .. 60 40
114. R. 115 r. on 5 r. orange .. 1·00 90
115. 115 r. on 25 r. green .. 1·00 90
117. Q. 115 r. on 50 r. blue .. 35 30
120. 130 r. on 25 r. mauve 60 30
121. R. 130 r. on 75 r. red .. 1·00 90
122. 130 r. on 100 r. brown on buff .. .. 1·90 1·90
123. 130 r. on 150 r. red on rose 1·00 80
124. 130 r. on 200 r. bl. on bl. 1·00 80
125. Q. 130 r. on 300 r. orange .. 55 40
128. 400 r. on 10 r. green .. 1·80 1·40
129. R. 400 r. on 50 r. blue .. 35 30
130. 400 r. on 80 r. green .. 35 30
132. Q. 400 r. on 100 r. brown .. 6·50 4·50
133. R. 400 r. on 300 r. blue on brown 35 30

1903. "King Carlos" key-type of Mozambique optd. **PROVISORIO**
134. S. 15 r. brown 35 30
135. 25 r. green 35 30
136. 50 r. blue 60 50
137. 75 r. red .. .. 1·10 80

1911. "King Carlos" key-type of Mozambique optd. **REPUBLICA.**
147. S. 2½ r. grey 12 10
148. 5 r. orange 12 10
149. 10 r. green 35 20
150. 15 r. green 12 10
151. 20 r. lilac 25 20
152. 25 r. red 10 8
153. 50 r. brown 12 8
154. 75 r. purple 20 15
155. 100 r. blue on blue .. 20 15
156. 115 r. brown on pink .. 25 15
157. 130 r. brown on yellow 25 15
158. 200 r. purple on pink .. 40 25
159. 400 r. blue on yellow .. 40 25
160. 500 r. black on blue .. 40 25
161. 700 r. mauve on yellow 40 25

1912. 'King Manoel" key-type inscr. "MOCAMBIQUE" with opt. **REPUBLICA.**
162. T. 2½ r. lilac 10 8
163. 5 r. black 10 8
164. 10 r. green 10 8
165. 20 r. red 12 10
166. 25 r. brown 8 5
167. 50 r. blue 12 10
168. 75 r. brown 12 10
169. 100 r. brown on green 12 10
170. 200 r. green on pink .. 15 12
171. 300 r. black on blue .. 15 15
172. 500 r. brown and olive 40 30

1913. Surch. **REPUBLICA MOCAMBIQUE** and value on "Vasco da Gama" issues of

(a) **Portuguese Colonies.**
173. ¼ on 2½ r. green 35 25
174. ½ c. on 5 r. red 35 25
175. 1 c. on 10 r. purple .. 35 25
176. 2½ c. on 25 r. green .. 35 25
177. 5 c. on 50 r. blue 35 25
178. 7½ c. on 75 r. brown .. 60 45
179. 10 c. on 100 r. brown .. 35 25
180. 15 c. on 150 r. yellow-brn. 35 25

(b) **Macao.**
181. ¼ c. on ½ a. green .. 50 35
182. ½ c. on 1 a. red .. 50 35
183. 1 c. on 2 a. purple .. 50 35
184. 2½ c. on 4 a. green .. 50 35
185. 5 c. on 8 a. blue .. 1·10 80
186. 7½ c. on 12 a brown .. 80 60
187. 10 c. on 16 a. brown .. 50 40
188. 15 c. on 24 a. yellow-brown 50 40

(c) **Timor.**
189. ¼ c. on ½ a. green 50 35
190. ½ c. on 1 a. red 50 35
191. 1 c. on 2 a. purple .. 50 35
192. 2½ c. on 4 a. green .. 50 35
193. 5 c. on 8 a. blue 50 35
194. 7½ c. on 12 a. brown .. 80 60
195. 10 c. on 16 a. brown .. 50 40
196. 15 c. on 24 a. yellow-brown 50 40

1914. "Ceres" key-type inscr. "MOCAMBIQUE".
249c. U. ¼ c. olive 8 8
250. ½ c. black 5 5
251. 1 c. green 5 5
268. 1½ c. brown 8 8
269. 2 c. red 5 5
270. 2 c. grey 8 8
271. 2½ c. violet 5 5
272. 3 c. orange 5 5
273. 4 c. pink 5 5
274. 4½ c. grey 5 5
258. 5 c. blue 5 5
275. 6 c. mauve 5 5
276. 7 c. blue 5 5
277. 7½ c. brown 5 5
278. 8 c. grey 5 5
279. 10 c. brown 8 5
280. 12 c. brown 8 5
281. 12 c. green 8 8
283. 15 c. claret 8 8
284. 20 c. green 8 8
285. 24 c. blue 20 15
286. 25 c. brown 20 15
209. 30 c. brown on green .. 30 20
287. 30 c. green 8 5
295. 30 c. lilac on rose .. 12 10
210. 40 c. brown on rose .. 40 30
288. 40 c. blue 8 5
211. 50 c. orange on pink .. 30 25
289. 50 c. mauve 10 5
297. 60 c. brown on rose .. 12 5
290. 60 c. blue 12 8
291. 60 c. red 15 8
298. 80 c. brown on blue .. 12 10
293. 80 c. red 10 5
299. 1 e. green on blue .. 20 12
264. 1 e. pink 15 10
301. 1 e. blue 15 10
300. 2 e. mauve on rose .. 20 8
302. 2 e. purple 20 8
303. 5 e. yellow-brown .. 1·00 30
304. 10 e. pink .. .. 2·00 90
305. 20 e. green .. .. 5·00 3·00

1915. Nos. 136/7 optd. **REPUBLICA.**
226. S. 50 r. blue 15 15
213. 75 r. red 30 20

1915. Provisional issues of 1902 optd. **REPUBLICA.**
227. S. 50 r. on 65 r. blue .. 15 15
214. V. 115 r. on 2½ r. brown .. 20 12
215. Q. 115. r. on 5 r. black .. 7·00 7·00
229. R. 115 r. on 5 r. orange .. 15 15
230. 115 r. on 25 r. green .. 15 15
231. 130 r. on 75 r. red .. 15 15
220. 130 r. on 100 r. brown on buff 20 12
232. 130 r. on 150 r. red on rose 15 15
233. 130 r. on 200 r. bl. on bl. 15 15
223. 400 r. on 50 r. blue .. 25 20
224. 400 r. on 80 r. green .. 25 20
225. 400 r. on 300 r. bl. on brn. 25 20

1918. Charity Tax stamp surch. **2½ CENTAVOS.** Roul. or perf.
248. C 2. 2½ c. on 5 c. red .. 12 10

1920. Charity Tax stamps surch. **CORREIOS** and value in figures.
306. C 1. 1 c. on 1 c. green .. 10 8
307. C 2. 1½ c. on 5 c. red .. 12 8

1920. Charity Tax stamp surch. **SEIS CENTAVOS.**
308. C 2. 6 c. on 5 c. red 10 8

1921. "Ceres" stamps of 1913 surch.
312. U. 10 c. on ½ c. black .. 15 15
314. 30 c. on 1½ c. brown .. 15 15
316. 50 c. on 4 c. pink .. 12 10
311. 60 c. on 2½ c. violet .. 30 20
328. 70 c. on 2 e. purple .. 15 12
329. 1 e. 40 c. on 2 e. purple 30 15

1922. Charity Tax stamp surch. **2$ 88.**
315. 2. $2 on 5 c. red 25 15

1922. "Ceres" key-type of Lourenzo Marques surch.
309. U. 10 c. on ½ c. black .. 15 15
310. 30 c. on 1½ c. brown .. 15 15

1924. Vasco da Gama. 4th Death Cent. "Ceres" key-type of Mozambique optd. **Vasco da Gama 1924.**
317. U. 80 c. pink 10 10

1925. Nos. 129 and 130 surch. **Republica 40.**
318. R. 40 c. on 400 r. on 50 r. .. 15 12
319. 40 c. on 400 r. on 80 r. .. 15 12

1929. "Due" key-type inscr. "MOCAMBIQUE", optd. **CORREIOS** and bar.
320. W. 50 c. lilac 10 8

1. Mousinho de Albuquerque.

1930. Albuquerque's Victories Commem. Vignette in grey.
321. 1. 50 c. lake and red (Macontene) .. .. 1·25 1·25
322. 50 c. orange and red (Mujenga) .. .. 1·25 1·25
323. 50 c. magenta and brown (Coolela) .. .. 1·25 1·25
324. 50 c. grey and green (Chaimite) .. .. 1·25 1·25
325. 50 c. blue and indigo (Ibrahimo) .. .. 1·25 1·25
326. 50 c. blue and black (Mucuto-muno) .. 1·25 1·25
327. 50 c. violet and lilac (Naguema) .. .. 1·25 1·25

The above were for compulsory use throughout Mozambique in place of ordinary postage stamps on certain days in 1930 and 1931. They are not listed among the Charity Tax stamps as the revenue was not applied to any charitable fund.

3. "Portugal" and Camoens' "Lusiad". 4. New Cathedral Lourenzo Marques.

1933. Value in black or red.
330. 3. 1 c. brown 5 5
331. 5 c. sepia 5 5
332. 10 c. mauve 5 5
333. 15 c. black 5 5
334. 20 c. grey 5 5
335. 30 c. green 5 5
336. 35 c. green 15 15
337. 40 c. red 5 5
338. 45 c. blue 10 8
339. 50 c. brown 8 5
340. 60 c. olive 10 8
341. 70 c. chestnut 10 8
342. 80 c. green 10 8
343. 85 c. red 15 8
344. 1 e. claret 12 5
345. 1 e. 40 blue 50 12
346. 1 e. 75 blue 25 8
347. 2 e. mauve 25 5
348. 5 e. green 50 8
349. 10 e. brown .. .. 1·00 15
350. 20 e. orange .. .. 2·25 20

1938. No. 338 surch. **40 centavos.**
378. 3. 40 c. on 45 c. blue .. 20 12

1938. As 1938 issue of Angola.
351. 3. 1 c. olive (postage) .. 5 5
352. 5 c. brown 5 5
353. 10 c. carmine 5 5
354. 15 c. purple 5 5
355. 20 c. slate 5 5
356. – 30 c. purple 5 5
357. – 35 c. green 12 8
358. – 40 c. brown 12 5
359. – 50 c. mauve 10 5
360. – 60 c. black 10 5
361. – 70 c. violet 12 8
362. – 80 c. orange 12 8
363. – 1 e. red 12 8
364. – 1 e. 75 blue 25 8
365. – 2 e. red 25 8
366. – 5 e. olive .. .. 1·00 15
367. – 10 e. blue .. .. 1·60 25
368. – 20 e. brown .. .. 2·75 30
369. 8. 10 c. red (air) 15 12
370. 20 c. violet 15 15
371. 50 c. orange 25 20
372. 1 e. blue 25 20
373. 2 e. red 45 20
374. 3 e. green 65 20
375. 5 e. brown .. .. 1·00 30
376. 9 e. red .. .. 1·40 40
377. 10 e. mauve .. .. 2·00 50

1938. President Carmona's 2nd Colonial Tour. As T 1 of Cape Verde Islands.
379. 80 c. violet 80 70
380. 1 e. 75 blue .. .. 2·00 1·25
381. 3 e. green .. .. 3·50 1·60
382. 20 e. brown .. .. 16·00 13·00

1944. Exploration of Lourenzo Marques. 400th Anniv.
383. 4. 50 c. brown 25 12
384. 50 c. green 25 12
385. – 1 e. 75 blue 90 20
386. – 20 e. black .. .. 3·50 25

DESIGN—HORIZ. 1 e. 75, 20 e. Town Hall, Lourenzo Marques.

1946. Stamps of 1938 surch.
387. 10 c. on 15 c. purple (post.) 15 12
388. 60 c. on 1 c. 75 blue .. 30 15
389. 3 e. on 5 e. brown (air) .. 2·00 1·00

1947. No. 386 surch.
390. 2 e. on 20 e. black .. 40 15

5.

1946. Air. (a) Inscr. "TAXA RECEBIDA" Values in black.
391. 5. 1 e. 20 red 50 35
392. 1 e. 60 blue 60 45
393. 1 e. 70 purple .. .. 1·00 60
394. 2 e. 90 brown .. .. 1·10 80
395. 3 e. green .. .. 1·10 80

(b) Inscr. "TAXE PERCUE". Values in red or black at bottom, left and right.
397. 4. 50 c. black 35 20
398. 1 e. pink 40 20
399. 3 e. green 80 35
400. 4 e. 50 green .. .. 1·25 50
401. 5 e. lake .. .. 1·40 80
402. 10 e. blue .. .. 4·00 1·60
403. 20 e. violet .. .. 10·00 4·25
404. 50 e. orange .. .. 20·00 9·00

1948. As T 4 but without commem. inscr.
405. 4 e. 50 red 50 12

6. Antonio Enes. 7. R. Pungue at Beira.

1948. Antonio Enes. Birth Cent.
406. 6. 50 c. black and cream .. 20 15
407. 5 e. purple and cream .. 90 30

1948.
408. – 5 c. brown 10 8
409. – 10 c. purple 8 5
410. – 20 c. brown 8 5
411. – 30 c. purple 8 5
412. – 40 c. green 8 5
413. – 50 c. grey 8 5
414. – 60 c. claret 8 5
415. – 80 c. violet 8 5
416. – 1 e. red 15 8
417. – 1 e. 20 grey 15 8
418. 7. 1 e. 50 violet 15 8
419. – 1 e. 75 blue 30 10
420. 7. 2 e. brown 30 8
421. – 2 e. 50 blue 80 8
422. – 3 e. olive 50 8
423. – 3 e. 50 olive 80 12
424. – 5 e. green 80 12
425. – 10 e. brown .. .. 1·50 15
426. – 15 e. red .. .. 3·00 50
427. – 20 e. orange .. .. 3·50 40

DESIGNS—VERT. 5 c., 30 c. Gogogo Peak. 20 c., 40 c. Zumbo River. 50 c., 3 e. 50, Nhanhangare waterfall. HORIZ. 10 c., 1 e. 20, Bridge over Zambesi. 50 c., 80 c. View of Lourenzo Marques. 1 e., 5 e. Gathering coconuts. 1 e. 75, 3 c. Polana beach, Lourenzo Marques. 2 e. 50, 10 e. Bird's eye view of Lourenzo Marques. 15 e., 20 e. Malema River.

1949. Honouring the Statue of Our Lady of Fatima. As T 13 of Angola.
428. 50 c. blue .. .. 1·00 40
429. 1 e. 20 magenta .. 2·50 1·00
430. 4 e. 50 green .. .. 8·50 3·50
431. 20 e. brown .. .. 18·00 5·00

1949. Air. As T 16 of Angola.
432. 50 c. brown 20 12
433. 1 e. 20 violet 30 20
434. 4 e. 50 blue 80 40
435. 5 e. green .. .. 1·50 30
436. 20 e. brown .. .. 3·50 80

1950. 75th Anniv. of U.P.U. As T 7 of Macao.
437. 4 e. 50 blue 90 40

1950. Holy Year. As Angola T 20/1.
438. 1 e. 50 orange 20 8
439. 3 e. blue 40 10

8. "Balistoides conspicillum".

1951. Fish as T 8 in natural colours. Colours given are of the backgrounds. Frames and inscr. in black. Values in red, 20 c., 30 c.; brown, 50 c.; blue 2 e. 50; black, remainder.
440. 5 c. orange 15 12
441. 10 c. blue 8 8
442. 15 c. yellow 30 25
443. 20 c. green 15 8
444. 30 c. grey 12 8
445. 40 c. green 10 5
446. 50 c. buff 10 5
447. 1 e. blue-green 8 5
448. 1 e. 50 olive 8 5
449. 2 e. blue 8 5
450. 2 e. 50 purple-brown .. 20 5
451. 3 e. blue-green 25 8
452. 3 e. 50 green 15 5
453. 4 e. grey 15 12
454. 4 e. 50 green 20 10
455. 5 e. buff 20 5
456. 6 e. pink 25 5
457. 8 e. blue 30 10
458. 9 e. mauve 40 12
459. 10 e. dull purple .. .. 6·50 1·40
460. 15 e. grey .. .. 20·00 7·00
461. 20 e. lemon .. .. 11·00 2·50
462. 30 e. green .. .. 7·50 2·75
463. 50 e. lavender .. .. 18·00 6·00

The 1 e., 6 e. and 8 e. are vert.

1951. Holy Year. As T 23 of Angola.
464. 5 e. red and pink 90 40

9. V. Cordon (colonist). 10. Miguel Bombard Hospital.

1951. Cordon. Birth Cent.
465. 9. 1 e. brown and orange .. 12 10
466. 5 e. black and blue .. 1·10 30

1952. 1st Tropical Medicine Congress. Lisbon.
467. 10. 3 e. orange and blue .. 30 10

11. Air and Sea Transport 12. Missionary.

14. 13. "Papilio demodocus".

1952. 4th African Tourist Congress.
468. 11. 1 e. 50 blue, black, brown and orange 15 8

1953. Missionary Art Exn.
469. 12. 10 c. lake and lilac .. 5 5
470. 1 e. lake and green .. 5 5
471. 5 e. black and blue .. 30 5

1953. Various butterflies and moths in natural colours. Horiz. designs as T 13. Colours given are of the backgrounds. Colours of inscriptions are brown, 20 c., 30 c., 40 c., 80 c., 1 e., 2 e., 7 e., 50; blue 3 e.; green 4 e. 50; black, remainder.
472. 10 c. blue 5 5
473. 15 c. buff 5 5
474. 20 c. green 5 5
475. 30 c. purple 5 5
476. 40 c. brown 5 5
477. 50 c. slate 5 5
478. 80 c. blue 5 5
479. 1 e. blue-green 5 5
480. 1 e. 50 bistre 5 5
481. 2 e. chestnut .. .. 2·40 25
482. 2 e. 30 blue .. .. 1·60 30
483. 2 e. 50 apple .. .. 4·25 30
484. 3 e. claret 90 10
485. 4 e. blue 15 5
486. 4 e. 50 orange 20 5
487. 5 e. blue-green 20 5
488. 6 e. lilac 25 5
489. 7 e. 50 stone .. .. 1·50 20
490. 10 e. pink .. .. 4·00 40
491. 20 e. grey-green .. .. 5·50 40

1953. Philatelic Exn., Lourenzo Marques. Stamps reproduced in original colours.
492. 14. 1 e. indigo, red & brown 25 12
493. 3 e. red, indigo & grey .. 70 25

1953. Portuguese Postage Stamp Cent. As T 27 of Angola.
494. 50 c. sepia, brown and buff 35 30

1954. Sao Paulo. 4th Cent. As T 28 of Angola.
495. 3 e. 50 olive, grey and buff 15 5

15. Map of Mozambique. 16. Arms of Beira. 17. Mousinho de Albuquerque.

1954. Multicoloured map; Mozambique territory in colours given.
496. 15. 10 c. lilac 5 5
497. 20 c. yellow 5 5
498. 50 c. violet 5 5
499. 1 e. orange 8 5
500. 2 e. 30 white 20 5
501. 4 e. salmon 30 10
502. 10 e. green 65 10
503. 20 e. brown .. .. 1·40 25

1954. 1st Philatelic Exn., Manica and Sofala.
504. 16. 1 e. 50 red, gold, silver, green and blue .. 10 5
505. 3 e. 50 red, gold, silver, green and brown .. 15 8

1955. De Albuquerque. Birth Cent. Inscr. "1885 1955".
506. 17. 1 e. black and grey .. 8 5
507. – 2 e. 50 black, blue & buff 10 5

DESIGN: 2 e. 50, Equestrian statue of Albuquerque.

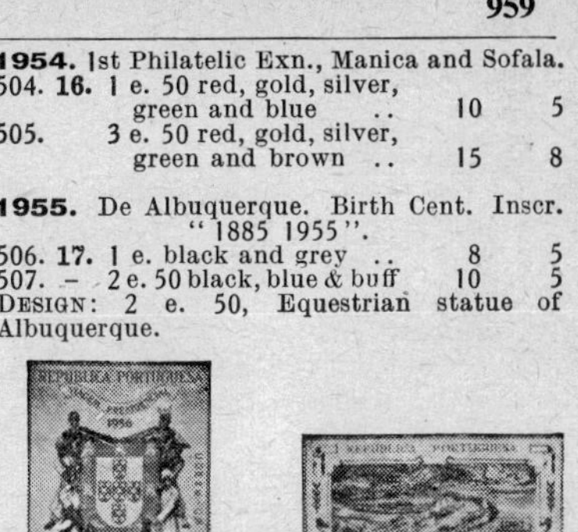

18. Arms and Inhabitants. 19. Beira.

20. Caravel. 21. "Arts and Crafts" (pottery class).

1956. Visit of President to Mozambique. Multicoloured. Background in colours given.
508. 18. 1 e. cream 10 5
509. 2 e. 50 blue 25 8

1957. Beira. 50th Anniv.
510. 19. 2 e. 50 multicoloured .. 30 10

1958. 6th Int. Congress of Tropical Medicine. As T 35 of Angola.
511. 1 e. 50, green, chestnut, sepia and salmon .. 50 35

DESIGN: 1 e. 50, "Strophanthus grandiflorus" (plant).

1958. Brussels Int. Exn. As T 16 of Macao.
512. 3 e. 50 multicoloured .. 15 12

1960. Prince Henry the Navigator. 500th Death Anniv.
513. 20. 5 e. multicoloured .. 20 10

1960. African Technical Co-operation Commission. 10th Anniv.
514. 21. 3 e. multicoloured .. 12 5

22. Arms of Lourenzo Marques. 23. D.H. "Dragon Rapide" and Fokker "Friendship" over Route Map.

1961. Arms. Multicoloured.
515. 5 c. Type 22 .. .. 5 5
516. 15 c. Chibuto 5 5
517. 20 c. Nampula 5 5
518. 30 c. Inhambane 5 5
519. 50 c. Mozambique (city) .. 5 5
520. 1 e. Matola 5 5
521. 1 e. 50, Quelimane .. 10 5
522. 2 e. Mocuba 15 5
523. 2 e. 50, Antonio Enes .. 20 5
524. 3 e. Cabral 25 5
525. 4 e. Manica 15 5
526. 4 e. 50, Pery 20 5
527. 5 e. St. Tiago de Tete .. 30 5
528. 7 e. 50, Porto Amelia .. 50 15
529. 10 e. Chinde 60 12
530. 20 e. Joao Belo .. .. 1·25 20
531. 50 e. Beira .. .. 3·00 60

1962. Sports. As T 41 of Angola. Multicoloured.
532. 50 c. Water-skiing .. 5 5
533. 1 e. Wrestling 20 8
534. 1 e. 50 Gymnastics .. 5 5
535. 2 e. 50 Hockey 10 5
536. 4 e. 50 Net-ball 20 12
537. 15 e. Out-board motor-boat racing 60 40

1962. Malaria Eradication. Mosquito design as T 42 of Angola. Multicoloured.
538. 2 e. 50 "A. funestus" .. 30 12

1962. D.E.T.A. (Mozambique Airline). 25th Anniv.
539. 23. 3 e. multicoloured .. 20 8

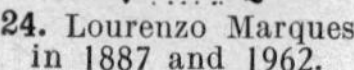

24. Lorenzo Marques in 1887 and 1962. 25. Oil Refinery, Sonarep.

1962. Lourenzo Marques. 75th Anniv.
540. **24.** 1 e. multicoloured .. 20 10

1962. Air. Multicoloured.
541. 1 e. 50 T **25** 20 5
542. 2 e. Salazar Academy .. 10 5
543. 3 e. 50 Port of Lourenzo Marques 25 5
544. 4 e. 50 Salazar Barrage .. 20 5
545. 5 e. Trigo de Morais bridge and Dam 20 5
546. 20 e. Marcelo Caetano Bridge and Dam 80 25
Each design includes an aircraft in flight.

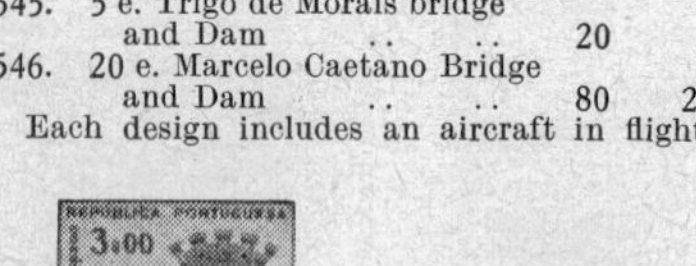

26. Mozambique Arms and statue of Vasco da Gama. 27. Barque, 1430.

1963. City of Mozambique Bicent.
547. **26.** 3 e. multicoloured .. 25 8

1963. T.A.P. Airline. 10th Anniv. As T **4** of Angola.
548. 2 e. 50 multicoloured .. 15 5

1963. Evolution of Sailing Ships. Mult.
549. 10 c. Type **27** 5 5
550. 20 c. Caravel, 1436 .. .. 5 5
551. 30 c. Lateen-rigged caravel, 1460 .. .. 5 5
552. 50 c. "St. Cabriel", 1497 .. 5 5
553. 1 e. Don Manuel's ship, 1498 .. .. 15 5
554. 1 e. 50, Warship, 1500 .. 5 5
555. 2 e. "Flor de la Mar" 1511 8 5
556. 2 e. 50, Caravel "Redonda", 1519 .. .. 10 5
557. 3 e. 50, 800-ton ship, 1520 15 5
558. 4 e. Portuguese-Indian galley, 1521 .. .. 15 8
559. 4 e. 50, "St. Teresa", 1639 20 8
560. 5 e. "Our Lady of Concepcion", 1716 .. .. 35 10
561. 6 e. "Our Lady of Good Success", 1764 .. .. 40 15
562. 7 e. 50, Armed launch, 1788 30 20
563. 8 e. Brigantine "Lebre", 1793 .. .. 35 15
564. 10 e. Corvette "Andorinha", 1799 .. .. 40 20
565. 12 e. 50, Schooner "Maria Teresa," 1829 .. .. 50 35
566. 15 e. "Vasco da Gama", 1841 .. .. 60 30
567. 20 e. Frigate "Don Fernando II", 1843 .. .. 80 40
568. 30 e. "Sagres", 1924 .. 1·25 60
The 2 e. 50, 4 e. and 6 e. to 15 e. are horiz. the rest vert. designs.

1964. National Overseas Bank Centenary. As Angola T **50** but view of Bank building, Lourenzo Marques.
569. 1 e. 50 multicoloured .. 5 5

28. Pres. Tomas. 29. Grand Barge of Joao V.

1964. Presidential Visit.
570. **28.** 2 e. 50 multicoloured .. 15 5

1964. Portuguese Marine, 18th and 19th Centuries. Multicoloured.
571. 15 c. Type **29** 5 5
572. 35 c. Barge of Jose I .. 5 5
573. 1 e. Barge of Alfandega .. 20 5
574. 1 e. 50 Oarsman of 1780 .. 5 5
575. 2 e. 50 Royal Barge, 1780 10 5
576. 5 e. Barge of Carlota Joaquina 20 10
577. 9 e. Miguel's barge .. 40 30
The 1 e. 50, is vert.

1965. I.T.U. Cent. As T **52** of Angola.
578. 1 e. multicoloured .. 12 8

1966. National Revolution. 40th Anniv. As T **56** of Angola, but showing different building. Multicoloured.
579. 1 e. Railway station, Beira and Antonio Enes Academy 5 5

30. Arquebusier, 1560. 31. Sailing ship of 1553.

1967. Portuguese Military Uniforms. Multicoloured.
580. 20 c. Type **30** 5 5
581. 30 c. Arquebusier, 1640 .. 5 5
582. 40 c. Infantryman, 1777 5 5
583. 50 c. Infantry officer, 1777 5 5
584. 80 c. Drummer, 1777 .. 12 5
585. 1 e. Infantry sergeant, 1777 15 5
586. 2 e. Infantry major, 1784 15 5
587. 2 e. 50 Colonial officer, 1788 25 10
588. 3 e. Infantryman, 1789 .. 20 5
589. 5 e. Colonial bugler, 1801 40 10
590. 10 e. Colonial officer, 1807 40 20
591. 15 e. Infantryman, 1817 60 30

1967. Military Naval Assn. Cent. As T **58** of Angola. Multicoloured.
592. 3 e. A. Coutinho and gunboat "Tete" 20 8
593. 10 e. J. Roby and gunboat "Granada" 40 20

1967. Fatima Apparitions. 50th Anniv. As T **59** of Angola.
594. 50 c. "Golden Crown" .. 5 5

1968. Pedro Cabral (explorer). 500th Birth Anniv. As T **63** of Angola. Multicoloured.
595. 1 e. Erecting the Cross at Porto Seguro (horiz.) .. 8 5
596. 1 e. 50 First mission service in Brazil (horiz.) .. 12 5
597. 3 e. Church of Grace, Santarem (vert.) .. 25 5

1969. Admiral Gago Coutinho. Birth Cent. As T **65** of Angola.
598. 70 c. Admiral Gago Coutinho Airport, Lourenzo Marques 5 5

1969. Camoens' Visit to Mozambique. 400th Anniv. Multicoloured.
599. 15 c. Luis de Camoens (poet) 5 5
600. 50 c. Type **31** 5 5
601. 1 e. 50 Map of Mozambique, 1554 (vert.) 5 5
602. 2 e. 50 Chapel of Our Lady of Baluarte 10 5
603. 5 e. Part of the "Lusiad" (poem) (vert.) .. 20 10

1969. Vasco da Gama (explorer). 500th Birth Anniv. As T **66** of Angola. Multicoloured.
604. 1 e. Route map of Da Gama's Voyage to India (horiz.) 5 5

1969. Overseas Administrative Reforms. Cent. As T **67** of Angola.
605. 1 e. 50 multicoloured .. 5 5

1969. Manoel I. 500th Birth Anniv. As T **68** of Angola. Multicoloured.
606. 80 c. Illuminated arms .. 5 5

1970. Marshal Carmona. Birth Cent. As T **70** of Angola.
607. 5 e. Portrait in ceremonial dress 25 10

32. Fossilized Fern.

1971. Rocks, Minerals and Fossils. Mult.
608. 15 c. Type **32** 5 5
609. 50 c. Fossilized snail .. 5 5
610. 1 e. Stibnite 5 5
611. 1 e. 50 Pink beryl 8 5
612. 2 e. Endothiodon and fossil skeleton 10 5
613. 3 e. Tantalocolumbite .. 15 8
614. 3 e. 50 Verdelite 15 10
615. 4 e. Zircon 20 12
616. 10 e. Petrified tree-stump 50 25

33. Mozambique Island in 16th Century. 34. Hurdling and Swimming.

1972. Camoens' "Lusiads" (epic poem). 400th Anniv.
617. **33.** 4 e. multicoloured .. 20 10

1972. Olympic Games, Munich.
618. **34.** 3 e. multicoloured .. 15 10

35. Seaplane "Santa Cruz" at Recife.

1972. 1st Flight, Lisbon-Rio de Janeiro. 50th Anniv.
619. **35.** 1 e. multicoloured .. 5 5

36. Racing Yachts.

1973. World Championships for "Vauriens" Class Yachts. Lourenco Marques.
620. **36.** 1 e. multicoloured .. 5 5
621. – 1 e. 50 multicoloured .. 8 5
622. – 3 e. multicoloured .. 15 8
DESIGNS: Nos. 621/2 similar to Type **36**.

1973. I.M.O./W.M.O. Centenary. As Type **77** of Angola.
623. 2 e. multicoloured 10 5

37. Dish Aerials.

1974. Satellite Communications Station Network. Inaug.
624. **37.** 50 c. multicoloured .. 5 5

38. Bird with "Flag" Wings.

1975. Implementation of Lusaka Agreement.
625. **38.** 1 e. multicoloured .. 5 5
626. 1 e. 50 multicoloured .. 8 8
627. 2 e. multicoloured .. 12 12
628. 3 e. 50 multicoloured .. 20 20
629. 6 e. multicoloured .. 35 35

1975. Independence. Optd. **INDEPENDENCIA 25 Jun 75.**
631. **15.** 10 c. mult. (postage) ..
632. – 40 c. mult. (No. 476) ..
633. **37.** 50 c. multicoloured ..
634. **36.** 1 e. multicoloured ..
635. – 1 e. 50 mult. (No. 621) ..
636. – 2 e. mult. (No. 623) ..
637. – 2 e. 50 mult. (No. 535) ..
638. **34.** 3 e. multicoloured ..
639. – 3 e. mult. (No. 622) ..
640. – 3 e. 50 mult. (No. 614) ..
641. – 4 e. 50 mult. (No. 536) ..
642. – 7 e. 50 mult. (No. 489) ..
643. – 10 e. mult. (No. 616) ..
644. – 15 e. mult. (No. 537) ..
645. **15.** 20 e. multicoloured ..
646. – 3 e. 50 multicoloured (No. 543) (air) ..
647. – 4 e. 50 mult. (No. 544) ..
648. – 5 e. mult. (No. 545) ..
649. – 20 e. mult. (No. 546) ..
Set of 19 .. .. .. 12·00 12·00

39. Workers, Farmer and Children. 40. Farm Worker.

1975. Independence (2nd issue). Mult.
650. 20 c. Type **39** 5 5
651. 30 c. Type **39** 5 5
652. 50 c. Type **39** 5 5
653. 2 e. 50 Type **39** 10 5
654. 4 e. 50 Armed family, workers and dancers .. 25 15
655. 5 e. As No. 654 .. .. 30 15
656. 10 e. As No. 654 .. .. 70 25
657. 50 e. As No. 654 .. .. 3·00 1·50

1976. "Day of Mozambique Women".
659. **40.** 1 e. black and green .. 5 5
660. – 1 e. 50 black and brown 8 5
661. – 2 e. 50 black and blue .. 15 8
662. – 10 e. black and red .. 65 40
DESIGNS: 1 e. 50 Teaching. 2 e. 50 Nurse. 10 e. Mother.

1976. Pres. Kaunda's First Visit to Mozambique. Opt. **PRESIDENTE KENNETH KAUNDA PRIMEIRA VISITA 20/4/1976.**
663. **38.** 2 e. multicoloured .. 10 5
664. 3 e. 50 multicoloured .. 25 15
665. 6 e. multicoloured .. 50 30

41. President Machel's Arrival.

1976. Independence. 1st Anniv. Mult.
666. 50 c. Type **41** 5 5
667. 1 e. Proclamation ceremony 5 5
668. 2 e. 50 Signing ceremony 15 5
669. 7 e. 50 Soldiers on parade 40 40
670. 20 e. Independence flame 1·10 1·10

CHARITY TAX STAMPS

The notes under this heading in Portugal also apply here.

C 1. Arms of Portugal and Mozambique and Allegorical Figures.

C 2. Prow of Gallery of Discoveries and Symbols of Declaration of War.

1916. War Tax Fund. Imperf. roul. or perf.
C 234. C 1. 1 c. green 12 8
C 235. C 2. 5 c. red 15 8

C 3. "Charity". C 4. Society's Emblem.

1920. Restoration of Portugal. 280th Anniv. Wounded Soldiers and Social Assistance Funds
C 309. C 3. ¼ c. olive 70 55
C 310. ½ c. black 70 55
C 311. 1 c. brown 70 55
C 312. 2 c. brown 70 55
C 313. 3 c. lilac 70 55
C 314. 4 c. green 70 55
C 315. – 5 c. green 70 55
C 316. – 6 c. blue 70 55
C 317. – 7½ c. brown 70 55
C 318. – 8 c. yellow 70 55
C 319. – 10 c. lilac 70 55
C 320. – 12 c. pink 70 55
C 321. – 18 c. red 70 55
C 322. – 24 c. brown 70 55
C 323. – 30 c. olive 70 55
C 324. – 40 c. red 70 55
C 325. – 50 c. yellow 70 55
C 326. – 1 c. blue 70 55
DESIGNS: ¼ c. to 4 c. As Type C 3. 5 c. to 12 c. Wounded soldier and nurse. 18 c. to 1 e. Family scene.

1925. Marquis de Pombal stamps of Portugal, but inscr. "MOCAMBIQUE".
C 327. C 4. 15 c. brown 15 12
C 328. – 15 c. brown 15 12
C 329. C 5. 15 c. brown 15 12

1925. Red Cross. Surch. **50 CENTAVOS.**
C 330. C 4. 50 c. yellow and grey 15 12

1926. Surch. **CORREIOS** and value.
C 337. C 4. 5 c. yellow and red .. 40 40
C 338. 10 c. yellow and green 40 40
C 339. 20 c. yellow and grey 60 60
C 340. 30 c. yellow and blue 60 60
C 331. 40 c. yellow and grey 40 40
C 341. 40 c. yellow and violet 60 60
C 332. 50 c. yellow and grey 60 40
C 342. 50 c. yellow and red 60 60
C 333. 60 c. yellow and grey 40 40
C 343. 60 c. yellow & brown 60 60
C 334. 80 c. yellow and grey 40 40
C 344. 80 c. yellow and blue 60 60
C 335. 1 e. yellow and grey 40 40
C 345. 1 e. yellow and olive 60 60
C 336. 2 e. yellow and grey 60 60
C 346. 2 e. yellow and brown 70 70

C 5.

1928. Surch. **CORREIO** and value in black, as in Type C 5.
C 347. C 5. 5 c. yellow and green 80 80
C 348. 10 c. yellow and blue 80 80
C 349. 20 c. yellow and black 80 80
C 350. 30 c. yellow and red 80 80
C 351. 40 c. yellow and claret 80 80
C 352. 50 c. yellow and red 80 80
C 353. 60 c. yellow and brown 80 80
C 354. 80 c. yellow and brown 80 80
C 355. 1 e. yellow and grey 80 80
C 356. 2 e. yellow and red .. 80 80

C 6. C 8. Pelican.

1929. Value in black.
C 357. C 6. 40 c. claret and blue 50 45
C 358. 40 c. violet and red .. 50 45
C 359. 40 c. violet and olive 50 45
C 360. 40 c. red and brown 50 45
C 361. (No value) red & green 50 45
C 362. 40 c. blue and brown 50 45
C 363. 40 c. blue and orange 50 45
C 364. 40 c. claret and green 50 45
C 365. 40 c. black and yellow 90 55
C 366. 40 c. black and brown 1·00 70

C 7. "Charity". (Horiz.).

1942.
C 383. C 7. 50 c. rose and black .. 60 50

1943. Inscr. "Colonia de Mocambique". Value in black.
C 384. C 8. 50 c. vermilion .. 60 20
C 385. 50 c. blue 60 25
C 386. 50 c. violet 60 25
C 387. 50 c. red-brown .. 60 25
C 388. 50 c. yellow-brown .. 60 25
C 389. 50 c. ultramarine .. 60 25
C 390. 50 c. red 60 25
C 393. 50 c. green 60 25

1952. Inscr. "Provincia de Mocambique. Value in black.
C 514. C 8. 50 c. lemon 12 8
C 468. 50 c. orange 20 12
C 469. 50 c. green 20 12
C 470. 50 c. brown 20 12
C 515. 50 c. salmon 12 8

1957. No. C 470 surch.
C 511. C 8. 30 c. on 50 c. brown 15 10

C 9. Women and Children.

C 10. Telegraph Poles and Map.

1963.
C 569. C 9. 30 c. grn., blk. & red 5 5
C 570. 50 c. blk., bistre & red 5 5
C 571. 50 c. blk., pink & red 5 5
C 572. 50 c. blk., green & red 5 5
C 573. 50 c. blk., blue & red 5 5
C 574. 50 c. blk., buff & red 5 5
C 575. 50 c. blk., grey & red 5 5
C 576. 50 c. blk., yell. & red 5 5
C 577. 1 e. grey, blk. & red 5 5
C 578. 1 e. blk., brn. & red 5 5
C 578a. 1 e. blk., mve. & red 5 5

1965. Mozambique Telecommunications Improvement. Inscr. "TELECOMUNICACOES".
C 579. C 10. 30 c. black, pink & vio. 5 5
C 580. – 50 c. black, brn. & bl. 5 5
C 581. C 10. 1 e. blk., orge. & grn. 12 8
DESIGN (19½×36 mm.): 50 c. Telegraph linesman.

A 2 e. 50 in Type C 10 was also issued for compulsory use on telegrams.

NEWSPAPER STAMPS

1893. "Embossed" key-type of Mozambique surch. **JORNAES 2½ 2½.**
N 53. Q. 2½ r. on 40 r. brown .. 5·00 4·50

1893. "Embossed" key-type of Mozambique surch. **JORNAES 2½ REIS.**
N 54. Q. 2½ r. on 40 r. brown .. 22·00 20·00
N 55. 5 r. on 40 r. brown .. 20·00 18·00

1893. "Newspaper" key-type inscr. "MOCAMBIQUE".
N 58. V. 2½ r. brown 15 12

POSTAGE DUE STAMPS

1904. "Due" key-type inscr. "MOCAMBIQUE".
D 146. W. 5 r green 15 12
D 147. 10 r. grey 15 12
D 148. 20 r. brown 15 12
D 149. 30 r. orange 25 15
D 150. 50 r. brown 25 15
D 151. 60 r. brown 50 40
D 152. 100 r. mauve 50 40
D 153. 130 r. blue 25 20
D 154. 200 r. red 30 25
D 155. 500 r. violet 40 30

1911. "Due" key-type of Mozambique optd. **REPUBLICA.**
D 162. W. 5 r. green 10 8
D 163a. 10 r. green 12 10
D 164. 20 r. brown 15 12
D 165. 30 r. orange 15 12
D 166. 50 r. brown 15 12
D 167. 60 r. brown 15 12
D 168. 100 r. mauve 15 12
D 169. 130 r. blue 15 12
D 170. 200 r. red 20 15
D 171. 500 r. violet 20 15

1917. "Due" key-type of Mozambique, but currency changed.
D 246. W. ½ c. green 5 5
D 247. 1 c. grey 5 5
D 248. 2 c. brown 5 5
D 249. 3 c. orange 5 5
D 250. 5 c. brown 5 5
D 251. 6 c. brown 5 5
D 252. 10 c. mauve 5 5
D 253. 13 c. blue 5 5
D 254. 20 c. red 5 5
D 255. 50 c. violet 5 5

1918. Charity Tax stamps. optd. **PORTEADO.**
D 256. C 1. 1 c. green 15 15
D 257. C 2. 5 c. red 15 15

1922. "Ceres" key-type of Lourenzo Marques (½ c., 1½ c.) and of Mozambique (1 c., 2½ c., 4 c.) surch. **PORTEADO** and value and bar.
D 316. U. 5 c. on ½ c. black .. 15 12
D 317. 6 c. on 1 c. green .. 15 12
D 318. 10 c. on 1½ c. brown .. 15 12
D 319. 20 c. on 2½ c. violet .. 15 12
D 320. 50 c. on 4 c. pink .. 15 12

1924. "Ceres" key-type on Mozambique surch. **Porteado** and value.
D 321. U. 20 c. on 30 c. green .. 12 10
D 323. 50 c. on 60 c. blue .. 12 10

1925. Marquis de Pombal tax stamps as Nos. C 24/6, optd. **MULTA.**
D 327. C 4. 30 c. brown .. 15 12
D 328. – 30 c. brown .. 15 12
D 329. C 5. 30 c. brown .. 15 12

1952. As Type D 1 of Macao, but inscr. "MOCAMBIQUE". Numerals in red, name in black (except 50 c. in blue).
D 468. 10 c. crimson and apple 5 5
D 469. 30 c. sepia and pink .. 5 5
D 470. 50 c. black, blue and grey 5 5
D 471. 1 e. blue and olive .. 5 5
D 472. 2 e. green and yellow .. 8 5
D 473. 5 e. chestnut and stone 20 5

MOZAMBIQUE COMPANY O3

The Mozambique Company was responsible until 1942 for the administration of Manica and Sofala territory in Portuguese E. Africa from 1891. Now part of Mozambique.

1892. "Embossed" key-type inscr. "PROVINCA DE MOCAMBIQUE" optd. **COMPA DE MOCAMBIQUE.**
1. Q. 5 r. black 15 12
3. 10 r. green 35 15
2. 20 r. red 45 15
4. 25 r. mauve 25 15
5. 40 r. brown 25 15
6. 50 r. blue 30 15
7. 100 r. brown 40 25
8. 200 r. violet 40 25
9. 300 r. orange 40 25

1. Company's Arms.

ILLUSTRATIONS British Commonwealth and all overprints and surcharges are FULL SIZE. Foreign Countries have been reduced to ¾-LINEAR.

1895. Value in black or red.
15. 2½ r. yellow 10 8
114. 2½ r. grey 40 25
16. 5 r. orange 10 8
18. 10 r. mauve 15 10
115. 10 r. green 30 20
19. 15 r. brown 15 12
116. 15 r. green 30 20
20. 20 r. lilac 15 12
45. 25 r. green 15 12
117. 25 r. red 40 25
46. 50 r. blue 20 15
118. 50 r. brown 30 20
109. 65 r. blue 20 15
25. 75 r. red 20 15
119. 75 r. mauve 50 40
26. 80 r. green 20 25
52. 100 r. brown on buff .. 20 15
120. 100 r. blue on blue .. 50 40
110. 115 r. red on rose .. 20 15
121. 115 r. brown on rose .. 60 50
111. 130 r. green on rose .. 20 15
122. 130 r. brown on yellow .. 60 50
54. 150 r. orange on rose .. 20 15
55. 200 r. blue on blue .. 20 15
123. 200 r. lilac on rose .. 60 50
56. 300 r. blue on brown .. 20 15
112. 400 r. black on blue .. 20 15
124. 400 r. blue on yellow .. 70 65
31. 500 r. black 20 15
125. 500 r. black on blue .. 70 65
113. 700 r. purple on yellow .. 70 60
32. 1000 r. mauve 20 20

1895. Surch. **PROVISORIO 25.**
105. 1. 25 on 75 r. red 25 20
77. 25 on 80 r. green .. 3·25 2·40

1895. No. 6 optd. **PROVISORIO.**
78. Q. 50 r. blue 80 70

1898. Vasco da Gama. Optd. **1498 Centenario da India 1898.**
80. 1. 2½ r. yellow 40 40
81. 5 r. orange 50 50
82. 10 r. mauve 50 40
84. 15 r. brown 50 40
86. 20 r. lilac 70 60
87. 25 r. green .. .. 1·10 75
99. 50 r. blue 60 60
89. 75 r. red .. .. 1·00 1·00
91. 80 r. green .. .. 1·00 80
92. 100 r. brown on buff .. 1·25 1·00
93. 150 r. orange on rose .. 1·25 1·10
94. 200 r. blue on blue .. 1·40 1·25
104. 300 r. blue on brown .. 1·40 1·40

1900. Surch. **25 Reis** and bar.
106. 1. 25 r. on 5 r. orange .. 40 30

1900. Perforated through centre and surch. **50 REIS.**
108. 1. 50 r. on half of 20 r. lilac 15 12

1911. Optd. **REPUBLICA.**
127. 1. 2½ r. grey 20 12
147. 5 r. orange 15 8
148. 10 r. green 10 8
150. 15 r. green 10 8
151. 20 r. lilac 15 10
153. 25 r. red 15 10
155. 50 r. brown 10 8
156. 75 r. mauve 10 8
157. 100 r. blue on blue .. 15 10
159. 115 r. brown on rose .. 25 15
160. 130 r. brown on yellow 30 15
161. 200 r. lilac on rose .. 15 10
162. 400 r. blue on yellow .. 20 12
163. 500 r. black on blue .. 20 12
164. 700 r. purple on yellow 25 15

1916. Surch. **REPUBLICA** and value in figures.
166. 1. ¼ c. on 2½ r. grey .. 10 10
168. ½ c. on 5 r. orange .. 10 10
170. 1 c. on 10 r. green .. 12 12
173. 1½ c. on 15 r. green .. 12 12
175. 2 c. on 20 r. lilac 12 12
177. 2½ c. on 25 r. red 12 12
180. 5 c. on 50 r. brown .. 12 12
181. 7½ c. on 75 r. mauve .. 20 12
182. 10 c. on 100 r. blue on blue 20 15
183. 11½ c. on 115 r. brn. on rose 50 15
184. 13 c. on 130 r. brn. on yell. 50 15
185. 20 c. on 200 r. lilac on rose 30 15
186. 40 c. on 400 r. blue on yell. 30 15
187. 50 c. on 500 r. blk. on blue 35 20
188. 70 c. on 700 r. pur. on yell. 50 30

1917. Red Cross Fund. Optd. **REPUBLICA** and red cross and **31.7 17.**
189. 1. 2½ r. grey .. .. 1·40 1·25
190. 10 r. green .. .. 1·40 1·25
191. 20 r. lilac .. .. 1·75 1·60
192. 50 r. brown .. .. 1·75 1·60
193. 75 r. mauve .. .. 6·50 5·50
194. 100 r. blue .. .. 6·50 5·50
195. 700 r. purple on yellow .. 18·00 16·00

2. Village.

3. Ivory.

4. Native.

5. Tea.

1918. Inscr. "COMPANHIA DE MOCAMBIQUE".
199. 2. ¼ c. green and brown .. 8 8
233. ¼ c. black and olive .. 5 5
200. 3. ½ c. black 8 8
201. – 1 c. black and green .. 8 8
202. – 1½ c. green and black .. 8 8
203. – 2 c. black and red .. 8 8
235. – 2 c. black and grey .. 5 5
204. – 2½ c. black and lilac .. 8 8
236. – 3 c. black and yellow .. 5 5
205. – 4 c. brown and green .. 12 8
237. – 4 c. black and red .. 5 5
227. 2. 4½ c. black and grey .. 12 5
206. – 5 c. black and blue .. 12 10
207. – 6 c. blue and red .. 12 5
238. – 6 c. black and purple .. 10 5
228. – 7 c. black and blue .. 15 8
208. – 7½ c. black, green & orge. 12 12
209. – 8 c. black and lilac .. 12 12
210. – 10 c. black and red .. 10 8
229. – 12 c. black and brown .. 15 8
241. – 12 c. black and green .. 12 5
211. – 15 c. black and red .. 15 12
212. – 20 c. black and green .. 12 10
251. 4. 24 c. black and blue .. 20 15
252. – 25 c. blue and brown .. 20 15
213. – 30 c. black and brown .. 15 12
244. – 30 c. black and green .. 12 5
214. – 40 c. black and green .. 15 12
246. – 40 c. black and blue .. 12 10
258. – 45 c. blue 20 12
215. – 50 c. black and orange .. 15 10
247. – 50 c. black and mauve .. 15 12
230. – 60 c. brown and red .. 15 12
259. – 70 c. brown 20 12
231. – 80 c. brown and blue .. 15 12
248. – 80 c. black and red .. 15 12
253. 4. 85 c. black and red .. 20 12
216. – 1 e. black and green .. 20 15
249. – 1 e. black and blue .. 15 12
254. – 1 e. 40 black and blue .. 20 12
232. – 2 e. violet and red .. 30 15
250. – 2 e. black and lilac .. 25 12
255. – 5 e. blue and brown .. 50 8
256. 4. 10 e. black and red .. 80 25
257. – 20 e. black and green .. 1·10 30
DESIGNS—HORIZ. 1 c., 3 c. Maize field. 2 c. Sugar factory. 5 c., 2 e. Beira. 2 c. Law Court. 40 c. Mangrove swamp. 45 c. Ivory

store. 20 e. R. Zambesi. VERT. 1½ c. Tapping India-rubber. 2½ c. R. Buzi. 4 c. Tobacco field. 6 c. Coffee plantation. 7 c., 15 c. Railroad. 7½ c. Orange trees. 8 c., 12 c. Cotton field. 10 c., 80 c. Sisal plantation. 25 c., 1 e. 40, Beira. 30 c. Coco-palm. 50 c., 60 c. Cattle-breeding. 70 c. Gold-mining. 1 e. Mozambique Co's Arms. 5 e. India-rubber.

1918. Surch. **REPUBLICA** and value.

196. 1. ¼ c. on 700 r. pur. on yell. 20 20
197. 2½ c. on 500 r. blk. on bl. 20 20
198. 5 c. on 400 r. blue on yell. 20 20

1920. Pictorial issue surch.

217. ½ c. on 30 c. (No. 213) .. 1·25 1·00
218. ½ c. on 1 e. (No. 216) .. 1·25 1·00
219. 1½ c. on 2½ c. (No. 204) .. 50 40
220. 1½ c. on 5 c. (No. 206) .. 50 40
221. 2 c. on 2½ c. (No. 204) .. 50 40
222. 4 c. on 20 c. (No. 212) .. 1·00 55
223. 4 c. on 40 c. (No. 214) .. 1·00 55
224. 6 c. on 8 c. (No. 209) .. 1·00 55
225. 6 c. on 50 c. (No. 215) .. 1·00 55

7. Zambesi Bridge.

1935. Opening of Zambesi Bridge.

260. 7. 1 e. black and blue .. 50 45

8. Aeroplane over Beira.

1935. Blantyre-Beira-Salisbury Air route. Inaug.

261. 8. 5 c. black and blue .. 20 15
262. 10 c. black and red .. 20 15
263. 15 c. black and red .. 20 15
264. 20 c. black and green .. 20 15
265. 30 c. black and green .. 20 15
266. 40 c. black and green .. 20 15
267. 45 c. black and blue .. 20 15
268. 50 c. black and purple .. 20 15
269. 60 c. brown and red .. 20 15
270. 80 c. black and red .. 20 15

9. Aeroplane over Beira.

1935. Air.

271. 9. 5 c. black and blue .. 5 5
272. 10 c. black and red .. 5 5
273. 15 c. black and red .. 5 5
274. 20 c. black and green .. 5 5
275. 30 c. black and green .. 5 5
276. 40 c. black and green .. 5 5
277. 45 c. black and blue .. 8 5
278. 50 c. black and purple .. 8 5
279. 60 c. brown and red .. 8 5
280. 80 c. black and red .. 8 5
281. 1 e. black and blue .. 8 5
282. 2 e. black and purple .. 12 5
283. 5 e. blue and brown .. 20 10
284. 10 e. black and red .. 40 30
285. 20 e. black and green .. 80 35

10. Coastal Dhow. 12. Palms at Beira.

11. Crocodile.

1937.

286. – 1 c. violet and green .. 5 5
287. – 5 c. green and blue .. 5 5
288. 10. 10 c. blue and red .. 5 5
289. – 15 c. black and red .. 5 5
290. – 20 c. blue and green .. 5 5
291. – 30 c. blue and green .. 5 5
292. – 40 c. black and green .. 5 5
293. – 45 c. brown and blue .. 5 5
294. 11. 50 c. green and purple .. 5 5
295. – 60 c. blue and red .. 5 5
296. – 70 c. green and brown .. 5 5
297. – 80 c. green and red .. 8 5
298. – 85 c. black and brown .. 5 5
299. – 1 e. black and blue .. 5 5
300. 12. 1 e. 40 c. green and blue 8 5
301. – 2 e. brown and lilac .. 10 5
302. – 5 e. blue and brown .. 20 5
303. – 10 e. black and red .. 40 15
304. – 20 e. purple and green .. 80 30

DESIGNS—VERT. 1 c. Giraffe. 20 c. Zebra. 70 c. Native woman. 10 e. Old Portuguese gate, Sena. 20 e. Arms. HORIZ. 5 c. Native huts. 15 c. S. Caetano fortress, Sofala. 60 c. Leopard. 80 c. Hippopotami. 5 e. Rly. bridge over R Zambesi. TRIANGULAR: 30 c. Python. 40 c. White Rhinoceros. 45 c. Lion. 85 c. Vasco da Gama's ship. 1 e. Native in dug-out canoe. 2 e. Kudu Antelope.

1939. President Carmona's Colonial Tour. Optd. **28-VII-1939 Visita Presidencial.**

305. – 30 c. (No. 291) 20 15
306. – 40 c. (No. 292) 20 15
307. – 45 c. (No. 293) 20 15
308. 11. 50 c. green and purple .. 20 15
309. – 85 c. (No. 298) 20 15
310. – 1 e. (No. 299) 20 15
311. – 2 e. (No. 301) 40 30

13. King Afonso Henriques. 14. "Don John IV" after Alberto de Souza.

1940. Portuguese Independence. 8th Cent.

312. 13. 1 e. 75 blue 25 15

1940. Restoration of Independence. Tercent.

313. 14. 40 c. black and blue .. 15 12
314. 50 c. green and violet 15 12
315. 60 c. blue and red .. 15 12
316. 70 c. green and brown 15 12
317. 80 c. green and red .. 15 12
318. 1 e. black and blue .. 15 12

CHARITY TAX STAMPS

The notes under this heading in Portugal also apply here.

1932. No. 236 surch. **Assistencia Publica 2 Ctvos. 2.**

C 260. 2 c. on 3 c. black & yellow 70 50

C 1. "Charity." C 2.

1934.

C 261. C 1. 2 c. black and mauve 60 45

1940.

C 313. C 2. 2 c. blue and black .. 3·25 3·00

1941. Similar design showing "charity" and family.

C 319. 2 c. red and black .. 3·25 3·00

NEWSPAPER STAMP

1894. "Newspaper" key-type inscr. "MOCAMBIQUE" optd. **COMPA DE MOCAMBIQUE.**

N 1. V. 2½ r. brown 15 12

POSTAGE DUE STAMPS

D 1. D 2.

1906.

D 114. D 1. 5 r. green 8 8
D 115. 10 r. grey 8 8
D 116. 20 r. brown 8 8
D 117. 30 r. orange 15 12
D 118. 50 r. brown 15 12
D 119. 60 r. brown .. .. 1·00 90
D 120. 100 r. mauve 25 20
D 121. 130 r. blue .. .. 2·00 1·10
D 122. 200 r. red 60 30
D 123. 500 r. lilac 90 40

1911. Optd. **REPUBLICA.**

D 166. D 1. 5 r. green 5 5
D 167. 10 r. grey 5 5
D 168. 20 r. brown 5 5
D 169. 30 r. orange 5 5
D 170. 50 r. brown 8 5
D 171. 60 r. brown 12 10
D 172. 100 r. mauve 12 10
D 173. 130 r. blue 25 20
D 174. 200 r. red 25 20
D 175. 500 r. lilac 40 25

1916. Currency changed.

D 189. D 1. ½ c. green 5 5
D 190. 1 c. grey 5 5
D 191. 2 c. brown 5 5
D 192. 3 c. orange 8 8
D 193. 5 c. brown 8 8
D 194. 6 c. brown 10 10
D 195. 10 c. mauve 12 12
D 196. 13 c. blue 25 20
D 197. 20 c. red 25 20
D 198. 50 c. lilac 30 25

1919.

D 217. D 2. ½ c. green 5 5
D 218. 1 c. black 5 5
D 219. 2 c. brown 5 5
D 220. 3 c. orange 5 5
D 221. 5 c. brown 5 5
D 222. 6 c. brown 20 15
D 223. 10 c. claret 20 15
D 224. 13 c. blue 20 20
D 225. 20 c. red 30 15
D 226. 50 c. grey 20 15

MUSCAT BC

Independent Sultanate in Eastern Arabia with Indian and, subsequently, British postal administration.

12 pies = 1 anna. 16 annas = 1 rupee.

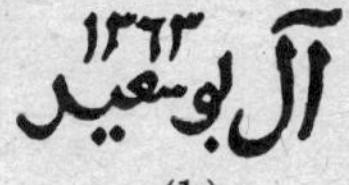

(1.)

1944. Al-Busaid Dynasty Bicent. Stamps of India (King George VI) optd. as T **1**.

1. 78. 3 p. slate 8 10
2. ½ a. mauve 8 10
3. 9 p. green 8 10
4. 1 a. red 8 10
5. 79. 1½ a. plum 8 10
6. 2 a. red 8 10
7. 3 a. violet 8 12
8. 3½ a. blue 8 12
9. 80. 4 a. brown 8 12
10. 6 a. green 10 20
11. 8 a. violet 15 35
12. 12 a. red 20 40
13. – 14 a. purple (No. 277) .. 30 45
14. 77. 1 r. slate and brown .. 35 80
15. 2 r. purple and brown .. 55 1·75

OFFICIAL STAMPS

1944. Al-Busaid Dynasty. Bicent. Official stamps of India optd. as T **1**.

O 1. O 1. 3 p. slate 8 12
O 2. ½ a. purple 8 12
O 3. 9 p. green 8 12
O 4. 1 a. red 8 12
O 5. 1½ a. violet 8 12
O 6. 2 a. orange 8 12
O 7. 2½ a. violet 8 12
O 8. 4 a. brown 8 20
O 9. 8 a. violet 12 35
O 10. 77. 1 r. slate and brown (No. O 138) .. 25 90

For later issues see **BRITISH POSTAL AGENCIES IN EASTERN ARABIA.**

MUSCAT AND OMAN O3

Independent Sultanate in Eastern Arabia. The title of the Sultanate was changed in 1971 to Oman.

64 baizas = 1 rupee.
1970. 1,000 baizas = 1 rial saidi.

1. Sultan's Crest. 2. Nakhal Fort.

1966.

94. 1. 3 b. purple 5 5
95. 5 b. brown 5 5
96. 10 b. chestnut 5 5
97. A. 15 b. black and violet .. 5 5
98. 20 b. black and blue .. 8 5
99. 25 b. black and orange 10 10
100. 2. 30 b. magenta and blue 12 12
101. B. 50 b. green and brown .. 15 15
102. C. 1 r. blue and orange .. 25 25
103. D. 2 r. chestnut and green 60 60
104. E. 5 r. violet and red .. 1·40 1·40
105. F. 10 r. red and violet .. 2·75 2·75

DESIGNS—VERT. (21½ × 25½ mm.); A, Crest and Muscat harbour. HORIZ. (As T 2) B, Samail Fort. C, Sohar Fort. D, Nizwa Fort. E, Matrah Fort. F, Mirani Fort.

3. Mina el Fahal.

1969. 1st Oil Shipment (July 1967). Multicoloured.

106. 20 b. Type 3 .. .. 8 8
107. 25 b. Storage tanks .. 8 8
108. 40 b. Desert oil-rig .. 12 12
109. 1 r. Aerial view from "Gemini 4" 25 25

1970. Designs as issue of 1966, but inscribed in new currency.

110. 1. 5 b. purple 5 5
111. 10 b. brown 5 5
112. 20 b. chestnut 5 5
113. A. 25 b. black and violet .. 5 5
114. 30 b. black and blue .. 8 8
115. 40 b. black and orange .. 10 10
116. 2. 50 b. magenta and blue 12 12
117. B. 75 b. green and brown .. 15 15
118. C. 100 b. blue and orange .. 25 25
119. D. ¼ r. chestnut and green .. 60 60
120. E. ½ r. violet and red .. 1·40 1·40
121. F. 1 r. red and violet .. 2·75 2·75

For later issues see **OMAN.**

NABHA BC

A "Convention" state in the Punjab, India.

Stamps of India optd. **NABHA STATE.**

1885. Queen Victoria. Vert. optd.

1. 14. ½ a. blue-green .. 20 20
2. – 1 a. purple .. 3·00 3·50
3. – 2 a. blue .. 3·00 2·75
4. – 4 a. green (No. 89) .. 6·00
5. – 8 a. mauve .. 22·00
6. – 1 r. grey (No. 79) .. 24·00

1885. Queen Victoria. Horiz. optd.

36. 25. 3 p. red 5 5
14. 14. ½ a. blue-green .. 5 5
15. – 9 p. red 15 15
17. – 1 a. purple .. 5 5
18. – 1½ a. brown .. 8 10
19. – 2 a. blue .. 12 8
22. – 3 a. orange .. 12 10
12. – 4 a. green (No. 89) .. 3·00 3·00
23. – 4 a. green (No. 96) .. 12 8
25. – 6 a. brown (No. 80) .. 40 40
27. – 8 a. mauve .. 30 30
28. – 12 a. purple on red .. 35 35
29. – 1 r. grey (No. 101) .. 1·25 1·25
30. 26. 1 r. green and red .. 50 50
31. 27. 2 r. red and orange .. 10·00 12·00
32. 3 r. brown and green .. 15·00 18·00
33. 5 r. blue and violet .. 18·00 20·00

1903. King Edward VII.

37a. 3 p. grey 5 5
38. ½ a. green (No. 122) .. 5 5
39. 1 a. red (No. 123) .. 10 10
40a. 2 a. lilac 10 10
40b. 2½ a. blue .. .. 9·00
41. 3 a. orange 10 5
42. 4 a. olive 12 12
43. 6 a. yellow-brown .. 20 30
44. 8 a. mauve 25 30
45. 12 a. purple on red .. 40 45
46. 1 r. green and red .. 40 45

1907. As last, but inscr. "INDIA POSTAGE & REVENUE".

47. ½ a. green (No. 149) .. 5 5
48. 1 a. red (No. 150) .. 12 12

1913. King George V. Optd. in two lines.

49. 40. 3 p. grey 5 5
50. 41. ½ a. green 5 5
51. 42. 1 a. red 5 5
59. 1 a. chocolate 5 5
52. 44. 2 a. lilac 5 5
53. 48. 3 a. orange 8 8
54. 49. 4 a. olive 8 8
55. 51. 6 a. yellow-brown .. 8 10
56. 52. 8 a. mauve 12 15
57. 53. 12 a. claret 20 20
58. 54. 1 r. brown and green .. 20 20

1928. King George V. Optd. in one line.

60. 40. 3 p. grey 5 5
61. 41. ½ a. green 5 5
73. 62. ½ a. green 5 5
61a. 63. 9 p. green 5 5
62. 42. 1 a. chocolate 5 5
74. 64. 1 a. chocolate 5 5
63. 65. 1¼ a. mauve 5 5
64. 45. 2 a. lilac 5 5
65. 47. 2½ a. orange 5 5
66. 48. 3 a. blue 8 8

75. 48. 3 a. red 5 5
76. 49. 4 a. olive 5 8
67. 50. 4 a. green 8 12
71. 54. 2 r. red and orange 1·50 2·00
72. 5 r. blue andtpurple 2·50 3·00

1938. King George VI. Nos. 247/63.
77. 74. 3 p. slate 80 30
78. ½ a. brown 15 20
79. 9 p. green 3·00 3·00
80. 1 a. red 8 8
81. 76. 2 a. red 8 10
82. – 2½ a. violet 12 20
83. – 3 a. green 15 25
84. – 3½ a. blue 20 30
85. – 4 a. brown 10 25
86. – 6 a. green 30 60
87. – 8 a. violet 25 60
88. – 12 a. red 60 1·00
89. 77. 1 r. slate and brown 90 1·00
90. 2 r. purple and brown 1·75 2·25
91. 5 r. green and blue 6·00 7·00
92. 10 r. purple and red 12·00 15·00
93. 15 r. brown and green 25·00 30·00
94. 25 r. slate and purple 32·00 35·00

1942. King George VI. Optd. **NABHA** only.
95. 74. 3 p. slate 3·00 60
105. 78. 3 p. slate 8 8
96. 74. ½ a. brown 7·00 4·00
106. 78. ½ a. mauve 8 8
97. 74. 9 p. green 3·00 75
107. 78. 9 p. green 8 8
98. 74. 1 a. red 2·00 75
108. 78. 1 a. red 8 8
109. 79. 1 a. 3 p. bistre 8 8
110. 1½ a. violet 8 8
111. 2 a. red 8 8
112. 3 a. violet 15 25
113. 3½ a. blue 15 25
114. 80. 4 a. brown 20 25
115. 6 a. green 25 40
116. 8 a. violet 20 40
117. 12 a. purple 50 85

OFFICIAL STAMPS

Stamps of Nabha optd. **SERVICE.**

1885. Nos. 1 to 3 (Queen Victoria).
O 1. ½ a. blue-green 15 15
O 2. 1 a. purple 5 5
O 3. 2 a. blue 10·00 10·00

1885. Nos. 14 to 30 (Queen Victoria).
O 6. ½ a. blue-green 5 5
O 7. 1 a. purple 8 5
O 9. 2 a. blue 10 12
O 11. 3 a. orange 45 50
O 13. 4 a. green (No. 12) 15 15
O 15. 6 a. brown 35 45
O 17. 8 a. mauve 25 30
O 18. 12 a. purple on red 2·50 2·50
O 19. 1 r. grey 4·00 5·00
O 20. 1 r. green and red 3·00 4·00

1903. Nos. 37a to 46 (King Edward VII).
O 25. 3 p. grey 12 12
O 26. ½ a. green 5 5
O 27. 1 a. red 5 5
O 29. 2 a. lilac 10 10
O 30. 4 a. olive 15 12
O 32. 8 a. mauve 20 25
O 34. 1 r. green and red 30 50

1907. Nos. 47/8 (King Edward VII inscr. "INDIA POSTAGE & REVENUE").
O 35. ½ a. green 5 5
O 36. 1 a. red 8 10

1913. Nos. 54 and 58, King George V).
O 37. 49. 4 a. olive 4·00
O 38. 54. 1 r. brown and green 15·00

1913. Official stamps of India (King George V), optd. **NABHA STATE.**
O 39. 40. 3 p. grey 5 10
O 40. 41. ½ a. green 5 5
O 41. 42. 1 a. red 5 5
O 42. 44. 2 a. lilac 8 8
O 43. 49. 4 a. olive 10 12
O 44. 52. 8 a. mauve 20 20
O 46. 54. 1 r. brown and green 25 30

1932. Stamps of India (King George V) optd. **NABHA STATE SERVICE.**
O 47. 40. 3 p. grey 5 5
O 50. 64. 1 a. chocolate 5 5
O 50a. 49. 4 a. olive 15 8
O 51. 52. 8 a. mauve 35 50

1938. Stamps of India (King George VI) optd. **NABHA STATE SERVICE.**
O 54. 74. 9 p. green 30 50
O 55. 1 a. red 15 20

1943. Stamps of India (King George VI) optd. **NABHA.**
O 56. O 1. 3 p. slate 8 8
O 57. ½ a. brown 12 12
O 57a. ½ a. purple 8 8
O 58. 9 p. green 8 8
O 59. 1 a. red 8 10
O 61. 1½ a. violet 10 15
O 62. 2 a. orange 10 15
O 64. 4 a. brown 25 30
O 65. 8 a. violet 40 60

1943. Stamps of India (King George VI) optd. **NABHA SERVICE.**
O 66. 77. 1 r. slate and brown 75 1·00
O 67. 2 r. purple and brown 2·50 3·00
O 68. 5 r. green and blue 7·00 7·00

NAGALAND

Labels inscribed "NAGALAND" with currency in cents or chaplees and considered to be propaganda labels.

NANDGAON (RAJNANDGAON) BC

A state of C. India. Now uses Indian stamps.

1. 2.

1892. Imperf.
1. 1. ½ a. blue 75 14·00
2. 2 a. red 6·00 30·00

1893. Imperf.
6. 2. ½ a. green 30 40
8. 1 a. red 1·25 1·50
9. 2 a. red 1·25 1·50

NAPLES E2

A state on the S.W. coast of Central Italy, formerly part of the Kingdom of Sicily, but now part of Italy.

100 grana = 200 tornesi = 1 ducato.

1. Arms under Bourbon Dynasty. 2. Cross of Savoy.

1858. The frames differ in each value. Imperf.
8. 1. ½ t. blue £25000 £2750
1. ½ g. lake £180 50·00
2. 1 g. lake 65·00 9·00
3. 2 g. lake 24·00 2·00
4. 5 g. lake £200 14·00
5. 10 g. lake £400 28·00
6. 20 g. lake £500 £100
7. 50 g. lake £1300 £800

1860. Imperf.
9. 2. ½ t. blue £4500 £900

NATAL BC

On the E. coast of S. Africa. Formerly a British Colony, later a province of the Union of S. Africa.

1.

ILLUSTRATIONS British Commonwealth and all overprints and surcharges are FULL SIZE. Foreign Countries have been reduced to ¾-LINEAR.

1857. Embossed stamps. Various designs.
1. 1. 1d. rose — £650
2. 1d. buff — £350
3. 1d. blue — £450
4. – 3d. rose — £150
5. – 6d. green — £450
6. – 9d. blue — £3000
7. – 1s. buff — £2000

The 3d., 6d., 9d. and 1s. are larger. Beware of reprints.

2. 3.

1859.
19. 2. 1d. red 25·00 7·00
12. 3d. blue 28·00 10·00
13. 6d. grey 45·00 16·00
24. 6d. violet 14·00 10·00

1867.
25. 3. 1s. green 40·00 10·00

1869. Variously optd. **POSTAGE** or **Postage.**
50. 2. 1d. red 22·00 10·00
82. 1d. yellow 12·00 13·00
53. 3d. blue 30·00 14·00
83. 6d. violet 10·00 2·00
84. 3. 1s. green 12·00 2·25

1870. Optd. **POSTAGE** in a curve.
59. 3. 1s. green 11·00 4·00
108. 1s. orange 50 30

1870. Optd. **POSTAGE** twice, reading up and down.
60. 2. 1d. red 20·00 7·00
61. 3d. blue 22·00 7·50
62. 6d violet 40·00 13·00

1873. Optd. **POSTAGE** once, reading up.
63. 3. 1s. purple-brown 22·00 4·25

4. 5.

6.

1874. Queen Victoria. Various frames.
97a. 4. ½d. green 12 12
99. – 1d. red 12 12
107. – 2d. olive 40 30
113. 5. 2½d. blue 35 35
100. – 3d. blue 12·00 5·00
101. – 3d. grey 12 12
102. – 4d. brown 50 30
103. – 6d. lilac 60 40
73. 6. 5s. red 18·00 6·50

1877. No. 99 surch. ½ **HALF.**
85. ½d. on 1d. red 6·00 22·00

POSTAGE Half-penny (7.) POSTAGE. Half-Penny (8.)

1877. Surch. as T 7.
91. 2. ½d. on 1d. yellow 3·25 3·75
92. 1d. on 6d. violet 5·50 1·40
93. 1d. on 6d. red 12·00 5·50

1885. Surch. in words.
104. ½d. on 1d. red (No. 99) 4·00 3·50
105. 2d. on 3d. grey (No. 101) 5·00 3·50
109. 2½d. on 4d. brown (No. 102) 2·00 1·50

1895. No. 23 surch. with T 8
114. 2. ½d. on 6d. violet 35 40

1895. No. 99 surch. **HALF.**
125. HALF on 1d. red 35 40

9.

10.

1902.
146. 9. ½d. green 8 8
147. 1d. red 8 8
129. 1½d. green and black 12 20
149. 2d. red and olive 25 15
131. 2½d. blue 45 45
132. 3d. purple and grey 40 12
152. 4d. red and brown 65 40
134. 5d. black and orange 85 65
135. 6d. green and purple 90 40

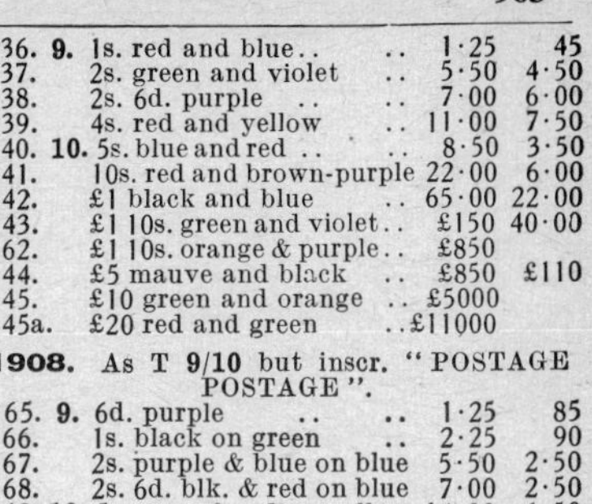

136. 9. 1s. red and blue 1·25 45
137. 2s. green and violet 5·50 4·50
138. 2s. 6d. purple 7·00 6·00
139. 4s. red and yellow 11·00 7·50
140. 10. 5s. blue and red 8·50 3·50
141. 10s. red and brown-purple 22·00 6·00
142. £1 black and blue 65·00 22·00
143. £1 10s. green and violet £150 40·00
162. £1 10s. orange & purple £850
144. £5 mauve and black £850 £110
145. £10 green and orange £5000
145a. £20 red and green £11000

1908. As T 9/10 but inscr. "POSTAGE POSTAGE".
165. 9. 6d. purple 1·25 85
166. 1s. black on green 2·25 90
167. 2s. purple & blue on blue 5·50 2·50
168. 2s. 6d. blk. & red on blue 7·00 2·50
169. 10. 5s. grn., & red on yellow 14·00 6·50
170. 10s. green & red on green 30·00 20·00
171. £1 purple & black on red £130 70·00

OFFICIAL STAMPS

1904. Optd. **OFFICIAL.**
O 1. 9. ½d. green 90 12
O 2. 1d. red 20 12
O 3. 2d. red and olive 2·50 2·25
O 4. 3d. purple and grey 1·00 1·40
O 5. 6d. green and purple 5·00 4·00
O 6. 1s. red and blue 7·50 17·00

NAURU BC

An island in the W. Pacific Ocean, formerly a German possession and then administered by Australia under trusteeship. Became a Republic on the 31st January, 1968.

1966. 100 cents = $1 Australian.

1916. Stamps of Gt. Britain (King George V) optd. **NAURU.**
1. 85. ½d. green 12 20
2. 84. 1d. red 15 30
15. 85. 1½d. brown 3·50 6·00
4. 86. 2d. orange 20 40
6. 84. 2½d. blue 55 65
7. 86. 3d. violet 75 85
8. 4d. grey-green 85 1·40
9. 87. 5d. brown 1·25 1·75
10. 6d. purple 1·50 2·00
11. 88. 9d. black 2·00 2·50
12. 1s. brown 2·50 3·00
25. 89. 2s. 6d. brown 15·00 22·00
22. 5s. red 26·00 35·00
23. 10s. blue 75·00 85·00

1.

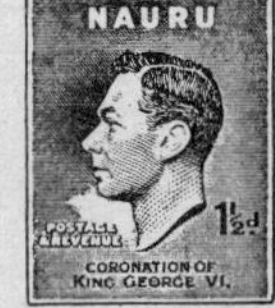

2. King George VI.

1924.
26a. 1. ½d. brown 60 1·00
27. 1d. green 60 1·40
28. 1½d. red 40 80
29. 2d. orange 30 70
30b. 2½d. blue 50 1·10
31a. 3d. blue 50 1·00
32. 4d. green 1·00 1·25
33. 5d. brown 60 90
34. 6d. violet 90 1·40
35. 9d. brown 2·50 3·50
36. 1s. red 2·00 2·50
37. 2s. 6d. green 8·00 9·00
38. 5s. claret 22·00 25·00
39. 10s. yellow 28·00 30·00

1935. Silver Jubilee. Optd. **HIS MAJESTY'S JUBILEE, 1910-1935.**
40. 1. 1½d. red 15 25
41. 2d. orange 30 45
42. 2½d. blue 1·00 80
43. 1s. red 2·00 1·75

1937. Coronation.
44. 2. 1½d. red 8 8
45. 2d. orange 8 10
46. 2½d. blue 8 10
47. 1s. purple 20 20

3. Anibare Bay.

4. "Iyo-calophylium".

5. White Tern.

1954.

48. – ½d. violet 5 5
49. 3. 1d. green 10 10
50. – 3½d. red 12 12
51. – 4d. blue 20 20
52. – 6d. orange 25 25
53. – 9d. claret 40 35
54. – 1s. purple 50 40
55. – 2s. 6d. green .. .. 1·25 1·00
56. – 5s. magenta .. .. 2·75 2·00

DESIGNS—HORIZ. ½d. Nauruan netting fish. 3½d. Loading phosphate from cantilever. 4d. Frigate Bird. 6d. Canoe. 9d. "Domaneab" (Meeting House). 2s. 6d. Buada Lagoon. VERT. 1s. Palm trees. 5s. Map of Nauru.

1963.

57. – 2d. multicoloured .. 8 8
58. – 3d. multicoloured .. 10 10
59. 4. 5d. multicoloured .. 20 20
60. – 8d. black and green .. 30 30
61. – 10d. black.. .. .. 50 40
62. 5. 1s. 3d. blue, black & green 75 70
63. – 2s. 3d. blue .. .. 1·50 90
64. – 3s. 3d. multicoloured .. 2·25 1·50

DESIGNS—As T 5—VERT. 2d. Micronesian Pigeon. As T 4—HORIZ. 3d. Poison Nut. (flower). 8d. Black lizard. 3s. 3d. Reed Warbler. (26 × 29 mm.): 10d. Capparis flower). (26 × 21 mm.): 2s. 3d. Coral pinnacles.

1965. Gallipoli Landing. 50th Anniv. As T **147** of Australia, but slightly larger (22 × 34½ mm.).

65. 5d. sepia, black and green .. 30 30

6. Anibare Bay.

1966. Decimal currency. As earlier issues but with values in cents and dollars as in T **6**. Some colours changed.

66. 6. 1 c. blue 5 5
67. – 2 c. maroon (As No. 48) .. 5 5
68. – 3 c. green (As No. 50) .. 8 8
69. – 4 c. multicoloured (As T **4**) 8 8
70. – 5 c. ultram. (As No. 54) .. 10 10
71. – 7 c. black and chestnut (As No. 60) .. 12 12
72. – 8 c. green (As No. 61) .. 15 15
73. – 10 c. red (As No. 51) .. 20 20
74. – 15 c. blue, black and green (As T **5**) 50 50
75. – 25 c. brown (As No. 63).. 60 60
76. – 30 c. mult. (As No. 58) .. 75 85
77. – 35 c. mult. (As No. 64) .. 1·00 1·25
78. – 50 c. mult. (As No. 57) .. 1·50 1·50
79. – $1 magenta (As No. 56) .. 3·00 3·00

The 25 c. is as No. 63 but larger, 27½ × 25 mm.

1968. Nos. 66/79 optd. **REPUBLIC OF NAURU.**

80. 6. 1 c. blue 5 5
81. – 2 c. maroon 5 5
82. – 3 c. green 8 8
83. – 4 c. multicoloured .. 8 8
84. – 5 c. ultramarine 10 10
85. – 7 c. black and chestnut .. 12 12
86. – 8 c. green 15 15
87. – 10 c. red 20 20
88. – 15 c. blue, black & green 2·50 1·25
89. – 25 c. brown 45 50
90. – 30 c. multicoloured .. 50 65
91. – 35 c. multicoloured .. 90 1·25
92. – 50 c. multicoloured .. 1·40 1·75
93. – $1 magenta .. .. 3·00 3·25

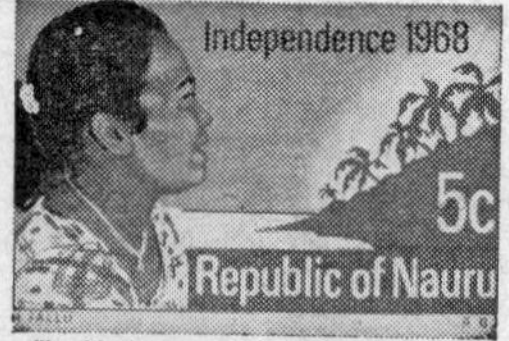

7. "Towards the Sunrise".

1968. Independence.

94. 7. 5 c. black, lilac, yell. & grn. 15 20
95. – 10 c. black, green and blue 25 30

DESIGN: 10 c. Planting Seedling and Map.

8. Flag of Independent Nauru.

1969.

96. 8. 15 c. yellow, orange & blue 30 35

9. Island, "C" and Stars.

1972. South Pacific Commission. 25th Anniv.

97. 9. 25 c. multicoloured .. 55 60

1973. Independence. 5th Anniv. No. 96 optd. **Independence 1968-1973.**

98. 8. 15 c. yellow, orge. & blue 75 75

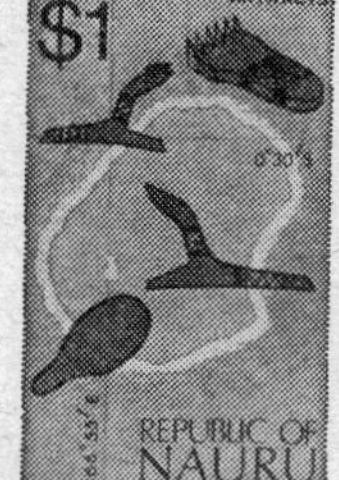

10. Denea. **11.** Artefacts and Map.

1973. Multicoloured.

99. 1 c. Ekwenababae .. 5 5
100. 2 c. Kauwe Iud 5 5
101. 3 c. Rimone 5 5
102. 4 c. Type **10** 5 5
103. 5 c. Erekogo 5 5
104. 7 c. Ikimago (fish) .. 8 8
105. 8 c. Catching flying-fish .. 8 10
106. 10 c. Itsibweb (ball game) 10 12
107. 15 c. Nauruan wrestling .. 12 15
108. 20 c. Snaring Frigate Birds 20 25
109. 25 c. Nauruan girl.. .. 25 30
110. 30 c. Catching Noddy Birds 30 35
111. 50 c. Frigate Birds .. 50 60
112. $1 Type **11** .. .. 1·00 1·10

Nos. 104/106 and 110/11 are horiz. designs.

12. Co-op Store.

1973. Nauru Co-operative Society. 50th Anniv. Multicoloured.

113. 5 c. Type **12** 10 10
114. 25 c. T. Detudamo (founder) 45 45
115. 50 c. N.C.S. trademark (vert.) 85 90

13. Phosphate Mining.

1974. First Contact with the Outside World. 175th Anniv. Multicoloured.

116. 7 c. M.V. "Eignamoiya" .. 12 12
117. 10 c. Type **13** 20 20
118. 15 c. Fokker Friendship "Nauru Chief" 30 30
119. 25 c. Nauruan chief in early times 40 40
120. 35 c. Capt. Fearn and the "Hunter" 55 55
121. 50 c. The "Hunter" off Nauru 90 90

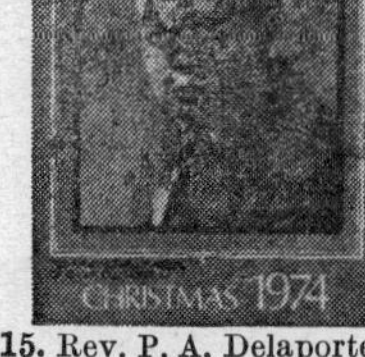

14. Map of Nauru. **15.** Rev. P. A. Delaporte.

1974. U.P.U. Centenary. Multicoloured.

122. 5 c. Type **14** 10 10
123. 8 c. Nauru Post Office .. 12 12
124. 20 c. Nauruan postman .. 35 35
125. $1 U.P.U. Building and Nauruan flag .. .. 1·50 1·60

1974. Christmas and 75th Anniv. of Rev. Delaporte's Arrival.

127. 15. 15 c. multicoloured .. 20 25
128. 20 c. multicoloured .. 35 40

16. Map of Nauru, Lump of Phosphate Rock and Albert Ellis.

1975. Phosphate Mining Anniversaries. Mult.

129. 5 c. Type **16** 10 10
130. 7 c. Coolies and mine .. 12 12
131. 15 c. Electric railway, barges and ship .. 25 25
132. 25 c. Modern ore extraction 35 40

ANNIVERSARIES. 5 c. 75th Anniversary of discovery. 7 c. 70th Anniversary of Mining Agreement. 15 c. 55th Anniversary of British Phosphate Commissioners. 25 c. 5th Anniversary of Nauru Phosphate Corporation.

17. Micronesian Outrigger.

1975. South Pacific Commission Conf., Nauru (1st issue). Multicoloured.

133. 20 c. Type **17** 25 30
134. 20 c. Polynesian double-hull 25 30
135. 20 c. Melanesian outrigger 25 30
136. 20 c. Polynesian outrigger 25 30

18. New Civic Centre.

1975. South Pacific Commission Conf., Nauru (2nd issue). Multicoloured.

137. 30 c, Type **18** 40 45
138. 50 c. Domaneab (meeting-house) .. 70 75

19. "Our Lady" (Yaren Church).

1975. Christmas. Stained-glass Windows. Multicoloured.

139. 5 c. Type **19** 8 8
140. 7 c. "Suffer little children ..." (Orro Church) .. 10 12
141. 15 c. As 7 c. 25 25
142. 25 c. Type **19** 35 40

20. Flowers floating towards Nauru.

1976. Islanders' Return from Truk. 30th Anniv. Multicoloured.

143. 10 c. Type **20** 15 15
144. 14 c. Nauru encircled by garland 20 20
145. 25 c. Reed warbler and maps 35 35
146. 40 c. Arrival of islanders .. 50 55

21. 3d. and 9d. Stamps of 1916.

1976. Nauruan Stamps. 60th Anniv. Multicoloured.

147. 10 c. Type **21** 12 15
148. 15 c. 6d. and 1s. stamps .. 20 25
149. 25 c. 2s.6d. stamp 35 40
150. 50 c. 5s. "Specimen" stamp 65 75

22. "Pandanus Mei" and Nauruan Ship.

1976. South Pacific Forum, Nauru. Multicoloured.

151. 10 c. Type **22** 15 15
152. 20 c. "Tournefortia argentea" and Nauruan aircraft.. 30 35
153. 30 c. "Thespesia populnea" and Nauru Tracking Station 40 45
154. 40 c. "Cordia Subcordata" and produce 55 65

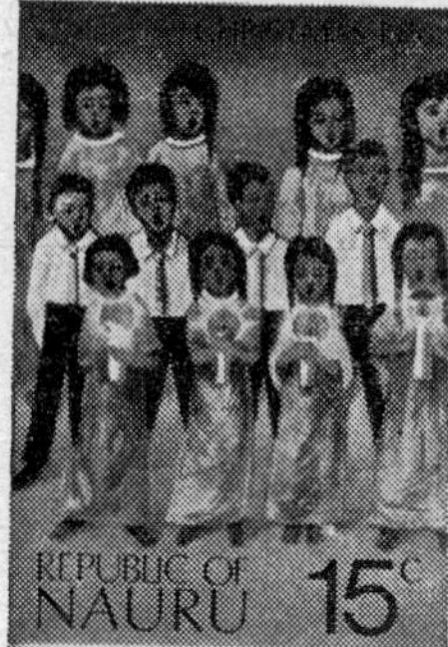

23. Nauruan Choir.

1976. Christmas. Multicoloured.

155. 15 c. Type **23** 20 20
156. 15 c. Nauruan choir .. 20 20
157. 20 c. Angel in white dress 25 30
158. 20 c. Angel in red dress .. 25 30

NAWANAGAR BC

A state of India, Bombay District. Now uses Indian stamps.

6 docra = 1 anna.

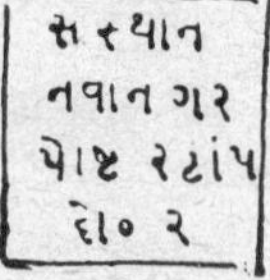

1. Native Sword. **2.**

1877. Imperf. or perf.

1. 1. 1 doc. blue.. .. .. 25 5·00

1880. Imperf.

3a. 2. 1 doc. lilac .. .. 40 1·00
5. 2 doc. green .. .. 60 1·50
6a. 3 doc. yellow .. .. 1·50 2·50

3.

1893. Imperf. or perf.

11. 3. 1 doc. black 12 15
12. 2 doc. green 25 35
13b. 3 doc. yellow 35 50

NEAPOLITAN PROVINCES E2

Temporary issues for Naples and other parts of S. Italy which adhered to the new Kingdom of Italy in 1860.

100 grana = 200 tornesi = 1 ducato.

1.

1861. Embossed. Imperf.

2. 1. ½ t. green .. .. .. 1·40 20·00
6. ½ g. brown .. .. 12·00 45·00
8. 1 g. black .. .. 12·00 4·25
10. 2 g. blue .. .. 4·00 1·60
15. 5 g. red .. .. 9·00 13·00
18. 10 g. orange .. .. 4·75 24·00
19. 20 g. yellow .. .. 32·00 £170
23. 50 g. slate .. .. 2·00 £1200

NEGRI SEMBILAN BC

A state of the Federation of Malaya, incorporated in Malaysia in 1963.

100 cents = 1 dollar (Straits or Malayan).

1891 Stamp of Straits Settlements optd. **Negri Sembilan.**

1. 1. 2 c. rose .. .. .. 90 1·10

1. Tiger. 2.

1891.

2. 1. 1 c. green 90 45
3. 2 c. red .. .. .. 1·25 1·25
4. 5 c. blue .. .. .. 3·25 3·25

1896.

5. 2. 1 c. purple and green .. 90 1·00
6. 2 c. purple and brown .. 3·50 3·00
7. 3 c. purple and red .. 90 40
8. 5 c. purple and yellow .. 1·00 1·75
9. 8 c. purple and blue .. 3·25 3·25
10. 10 c. purple and orange .. 4·50 4·00
11. 15 c. green and violet .. 5·00 3·75
12. 20 c. green and olive .. 7·00 7·00
13. 25 c. green and red .. 8·50 8·50
14. 50 c. green and black .. 12·00 12·00

1898. Surch. in words and bar.

15. 2. 1 c. on 15 c. grn. & violet 17·00 20·00
16. 1. 4 c. on 1 c. green .. 55 1·00
17. 2. 4 c. on 3 c. purple and red 1·25 1·40
18. 1. 4 c. on 5 c. blue .. .. 50 1·00

1898. Surch. in words only.

19. 2. 4 c. on 8 c. purple and blue 1·00 1·10

3. Arms of Negri Sembilan. 4.

1935.

21. 3. 1 c. black 25 15
22. 2 c. green 35 15
23. 2 c. orange 30 60
24. 3 c. green 25 40
25. 4 c. orange 15 15
26. 5 c. brown 20 12
27. 6 c. red .. .. .. 1·00 1·00
28. 6 c. grey .. .. .. 60 3·00
29. 8 c. grey 50 12
30. 10 c. purple 20 15
31. 12 c. blue 50 30
32. 3. 15 c. blue .. .. .. 1·00 2·50
33. 25 c. purple and red .. 40 50
34. 30 c. purple and orange .. 1·00 1·10
35. 40 c. red and purple .. 50 1·25
36. 50 c. black on green .. 1·50 60
37. $1 black and red on blue 75 90
38. $2 green and red .. 7·50 5·50
39. $5 green and red on green 5·00 6·00

1948. Silver Wedding. As T **5/6** of Aden.

40. 10 c. violet 8 8
41. $5 green .. .. .. 5·00 6·00

1949.

42. 4. 1 c. black 5 8
43. 2 c. orange 5 5
44. 3 c. green 8 20
45. 4 c. brown 5 5
46. 5 c. purple 5 10
47. 6 c. grey 5 5
48. 8 c. red 15 30
49. 8 c. green 8 25
50. 10 c. magenta 8 12
51. 12 c. red 10 20
52. 15 c. blue 30 15
53. 20 c. black and green .. 20 40
54. 20 c. blue 20 10
55. 25 c. purple and orange .. 15 12
56. 30 c. red and purpole .. 30 35
57. 35 c. red and purple .. 30 35
58. 40 c. red and purple .. 30 75
89. 50 c. black and blue .. 30 40
60. $1 blue and purple .. 50 35
61. $2 green and red .. 1·50 55
62. $5 green and brown .. 3·50 2·00

1949. U.P.U. As T **14/17** of Antigua.

63. 10 c. purple 10 10
64. 15 c. blue 15 25
65. 25 c. orange 30 35
66. 50 c. black 40 45

1953. Coronation. As T **7** of Aden.

67. 10 c. black and purple .. 8 8

1957. As Nos. 92/102 of Kedah but inset Arms of Negri Sembilan.

68. 1 c. black 5 5
69. 2 c. red 5 5
70. 4 c. sepia 5 5
71. 5 c. lake 5 5
72. 8 c. green 10 10
73. 10 c. sepia 5 5
74. 10 c. maroon 5 5
75. 20 c. blue 10 8
76a. 50 c. black and blue .. 30 15
77. $1 blue and purple .. 55 45
78a. $2 green and red .. 1·00 1·40
79a. $5 brown and green .. 3·00 2·00

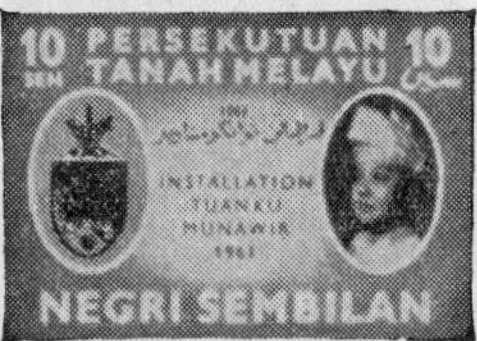

5. Tuanku Munawir.

1961. Installation of Tuanku Munawir as Yang di- Pertuan Besar of Negri Sembilan.

80. 5. 10 c. multicoloured .. 8 8

6. "Vanda hookeriana".

1965. As Nos. 166/72 of Johore but with Arms of Negri Sembilan inset and inscr. "NEGERI SEMBILAN" as in T **6**.

81. 6. 1 c. multicoloured .. 5 5
82. – 2 c. multicoloured .. 5 5
83. – 5 c. multicoloured .. 5 5
84. – 6 c. multicoloured .. 5 5
85. – 10 c. multicoloured .. 5 5
86. – 15 c. multicoloured .. 5 5
87. – 20 c. multicoloured .. 8 8

The higher values used in Negri Sembilan are Nos. 20/7 of Malaysia.

7. Negri Sembilan Crest and Tuanku Ja'afar.

1968. Installation of Tuanku Ja'afar as Yang di-Pertuang Besar of Negri Sembilan.

88. 7. 15 c. multicoloured .. 8 10
89. 50 c. multicoloured .. 30 40

8. Great Orange Tip.

1971. Butterflies. As Nos. 175/81 of Johore, but with Arms of Negri Sembilan inset as T **8**. Multicoloured.

91. – 1 c. multicoloured .. 5 5
92. – 2 c. multicoloured .. 5 5
93. – 5 c. multicoloured .. 5 5
94. – 6 c. multicoloured .. 5 5
95. 8. 10 c. multicoloured .. 5 5
96. – 15 c. multicoloured .. 8 8
97. – 20 c. multicoloured .. 8 8

The higher values in use with this issue are Nos. 64/71 of Malaysia.

NEPAL O3

An independent Kingdom in the Himalayas N. of India.

1881. 16 annas = 1 rupee.
1907. 64 pice = 1 rupee.
1954. 100 paisa = 1 rupee.

1. 2. 3. Siva Mahadeva.

1881. Imperf. or pin-perf.

13. 1. ½ a. brown 55 50
14. ½ a. orange .. .. 20·00 5·00
38. 2. 1 a. blue 50 50
26. 1 a. green .. .. 3·00 4·25
16. 2 a. purple 45 40
39. 2 a. brown 90 40
8. 4 a. green .. .. 1·60 1·60

1907. Various sizes.

51. 3. 2 pice brown 5 5
52. 4 pice green 5 5
59. 8 pice red 5 5
54. 16 pice purple 10 10
55. 24 pice orange 20 15
56. 32 pice blue 30 25
49. 1 r. red 45 30
50. 5 r. black and brown .. 2·50 2·25

4. Swayambhunath. 6. Siva Mahadeva.

5. Sri Guhesori Temple.

DESIGNS—As T **4**: 4 p. Pashupatinath. 6 p. Tri-Chundra College. 8 p. Sri Mahabuddha Temple. 16 p. Sri Krishna Temple. As T **5**: 20 p. View of Katmandu. 32 p. The twenty-two fountains, Balaju.

1949.

64. 4. 2 p. brown 5 5
65. – 4 p. green 5 5
66. – 6 p. pink 8 5
67. – 8 p. red 8 8
68. – 16 p. purple 8 8
69. – 20 p. blue 25 15
70. 5. 24 p. red 12 10
71. – 32 p. blue 35 20
72. 6. 1 r. orange .. .. 1·25 60

7. King Tribhuvana. 8. Map of Nepal.

1954. (a) Size 18×22 mm.

73. 7. 2 p. chocolate 5 5
74. 4 p. green 5 5
75. 6 p. red 5 5
76. 8 p. lilac 8 5
77. 12 p. orange 10 8

(b) Size 25½×29½ mm.

78. 7. 16 p. brown 5 5
79. 20 p. carmine 15 10
80. 24 p. claret 20 12
81. 32 p. blue 30 15
82. 50 p. magenta 40 20
83. 1 r. red 70 35
84. 2 r. chestnut .. .. 1·40 90

(c) Size 30×18 mm.

85. 8. 2 p. chocolate 5 5
86. 4 p. green 5 5
87. 6 p. red 5 5
88. 8 p. lilac 8 5
89. 12 p. orange 10 8

(d) Size 38×21½ mm.

90. 8. 16 p. brown 8 8
91. 20 p. carmine 15 12
92. 24 p. claret 20 12
93. 32 p. blue 35 20
94. 50 p. magenta 50 25
95. 1 r. red 80 45
96. 2 r. chestnut .. .. 1·50 1·10

9. Mechanization of Agriculture. 10. Gate of Hannuman.

1956. Coronation.

97. 9. 4 p. green 10 8
98. – 6 p. red and orange .. 15 8
99. – 8 p. violet 20 10
100. 10. 24 p. red 50 20
101. – 1 r. brown .. .. 10·00 5·00

DESIGNS—VERT. As T **9**: 8 p. Processional elephant. As T **10**: 6 p. Throne. 1 r. King and Queen and mountains.

11. U.N. Emblem and Nepalese Landscape. 12. Nepalese Crown.

1956. Admission into U.N.O. 1st Anniv.

102. 11. 12 p. blue and buff .. 40 20

1957. (a) Size 18×22 mm.

103. 12. 2 p. brown 5 5
104. 4 p. green 5 5
105. 6 p. rose-red 8 5
106. 8 p. lilac 10 8
107. 12 p. orange-red .. 12 8

(b) Size 25½×29½ mm.

108. 12. 16 p. brown 15 10
109. 20 p. carmine-rose .. 20 12
110. 24 p. cerise 25 15
111. 32 p. blue 35 20
112. 50 p. rose 60 30
113. 1 r. salmon .. .. 1·00 45
114. 2 r. yellow-orange .. 2·00 80

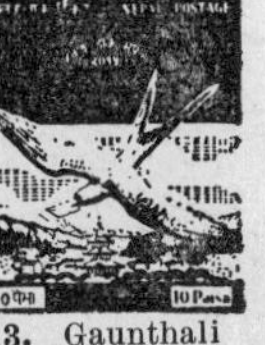

13. Gaunthali carrying Letter. 14. Temple of Lumbini.

1958. Air. Nepalese Internal Airmail Service. Inaug.

115. 13. 10 p. blue 20 15

1958. Human Rights Day.

116. 14. 6 p. yellow 20 12

15. Nepalese Map and Flag.

1959. 1st Nepalese Elections.
117. **15.** 6 p. red and green .. 5 5

16. Vishnu. **17.** Temple Bhaktapur.

1959.
120. **16.** 1 p. chocolate 5 5
121. – 2 p. slate-violet .. 5 5
122. – 4 p. blue 8 5
123. – 6 p. pink 8 5
124. – 8 p. sepia 8 5
125. – 12 p. grey 10 8
126. **17.** 16 p. violet and brown .. 10 8
127. 20 p. lake and blue .. 12 8
128. 24 p. red and myrtle .. 15 10
129. 32 p. blue and lilac .. 20 15
130. 50 p. myrtle and red .. 30 20
131. – 1 r. indigo and brown .. 90 40
132. – 2 r. blue and mauve .. 1·60 1·10
133. – 5 r. red and violet .. 4·50 1·90
DESIGNS—As T **16**—HORIZ. 2 p. Krishna. 8 p. Musk Deer. 12 p. Rhinoceros. VERT. 4 p. Himalayas. 6 p. Gateway, Bhaktapur Palace. As T **17**—VERT. 1 r., 2 r. Pheasant. 5 r. Partridge.

17a. Spinning Wheel. **18.** King Mahendra.

1959. Cottage Industries.
118. **17a.** 2 p. brown 5 5

1959. Admission of Nepal to U.P.U.
119. **18.** 12 p. blue 5 5

19. King Mahendra opening Parliament. **20.** Shri Pashupati Nath.

1959. Opening of 1st Nepalese Parliament.
134. **19.** 6 p. red.. .. .. 20 12

1959. Temple Renovation.
135. **19.** 4 p. green (18×25 mm.) 12 10
136. 8 p. red (21×28½ mm.) 25 15
137. 1 r. blue (24½×33½ mm.) 1·25 60

20a. Children, Pagoda and Mt. Everest. **21.** King Mahendra.

1960. Children's Day.
137a. **20a.** 6 p. blue .. .. 2·50 1·75

1960. King Mahendra's 41st Birthday.
138. **21.** 1 r. purple 50 20
See also Nos. 163/4a.

22. Mt. Everest. **23.** King Tribhuvana.

1960. Mountain Views.
139. – 5 p. sepia and purple .. 5 5
140. **22.** 10 p. purple and blue.. 5 5
141. – 40 p. brown and violet.. 15 12
DESIGNS: 5 p. Machha Puchhre. 40 p. Manaslu (wrongly inscr. "MANSALU").

1961. 10th Democracy Day.
142. **23.** 10 p. salmon & chestnut 5 5

24. Crown Prince Birendra cancelling Children's Day Stamps of 1960. **25.** King Mahendra.

1961. Children's Day.
143. **24.** 12 p. orange .. .. 5·00 5·00

1961. King Mahendra's 42nd Birthday.
144. **25.** 6 p. green 5 5
145. 12 p. blue 8 5
146. 50 p. red 12 10
147. 1 r. brown 30 25

26. Campaign Emblem and House. **27.** King Mahendra on horseback.

1962. Malaria Eradication.
148. **26.** 12 p. blue 5 5
149. – 1 r. orange and red .. 20 20
DESIGN: 1 r. Emblem and Nepalese flag.

1962. King Mahendra's 43rd Birthday.
150. **27.** 10 p. indigo 5 5
151. 15 p. brown 8 5
152. 45 p. chocolate .. 10 10
153. 1 r. olive 30 25

28. Bhana Bhakta Acharya. **29.** King Mahendra. **30.**

1962. Nepalese Poets.
154. **28.** 5 p. brown 5 5
155. – 10 p. turquoise .. 5 5
156. – 40 p. olive 8 5
PORTRAITS: 10 p. Moti Ram Bhakta. 40 p. Sambhu Prasad.

1962.
157. **29.** 1 p. rose 5 5
158. 2 p. blue 5 5
158a. 3 p. grey 5 5
159. 5 p. yellow-brown .. 5 5
160. **30** 10 p. claret 5 5
161. 40 p. brown 8 8
162. 75 p. blue-green .. 8 8
162a.**29.** 75 p. blue-green .. 8 8
163. **21.** 2 r. orange 20 20
164. 5 r. grey-green .. 50 40
164a. 10 r. violet .. .. 1·10 70
No. 158a is smaller, 17½ × 20 mm.

31. Emblems of Learning. **32.**

33. Campaign Symbols. **34.**

1963. U.N.E.S.C.O. "Education for All" Campaign.
165. **31.** 10 p. black 5 5
166. 15 p. brown 5 5
167. 50 p. violet 20 15

1963. National Day.
168. **32.** 5 p. blue 5 5
169. 10 p. brown 5 5
170. 50 p. mauve 8 8
171. 1 r. turquoise 25 15

1963. Freedom from Hunger.
172. **33.** 10 p. orange 5 5
173. 15 p. blue 8 5
174. 50 p. green 15 8
175. 1 r. brown 40 20

1963. Rastruya Panchayat.
176. **34.** 10 p. green 5 5
177. 15 p. purple 5 5
178. 50 p. slate 8 5
179. 1 r. violet 25 15

35. King Mahendra. **36.** King Mahendra and Highway Map.

1963. King Mahendra's 44th Birthday.
180. **35.** 5 p. violet 5 5
181. 10 p. brown 5 5
182. 15 p. green 8 5

1964. East-West Highway Inaug.
183. **36.** 10 p. orange and blue .. 5 5
184. 15 p. orange & violet-bl. 5 5
185. 50 p. brown and green .. 12 8

37. King Mahendra at Microphone. **38.** Crown Prince Birendra.

1964. King Mahendra's 45th Birthday.
186. **37.** 1 p olive-brown .. 5 5
187. 2 p. slate 5 5
188. 2 r. brown 25 15

1964. Crown Prince's 19th Birthday.
189. **38.** 10 p. green 8 8
190. 15 p. brown 12 8

39. Flag, Kukris, Rings and Torch. **40.** Nepalese Family.

1974. Olympic Games, Tokyo.
191. **39.** 10 p. blue, red and pink 5 5

1965. Land Reform.
192. – 2 p. black and green .. 5 5
193. – 5 p. brown and green .. 5 5
194. – 10 p. purple and grey .. 5 5
195. **40.** 15 p brown and yellow 5 5
DESIGNS: 2 p. Farmer and cattle. 5 p. Ears of corn. 10 p. Grain elevator.

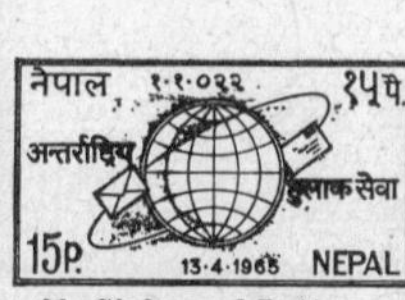

41. Globe and Letters. **42.** King Mahendra.

1965. Introduction of Postal Insurance Scheme.
196. **41.** 15 p. violet 5 5

1965. King Mahendra's 46th Birthday.
197. **42.** 50 p. purple 15 8

43. Four Martyrs. **44.** I.T.U. Emblem.

1965. "Nepalese Martyrs".
198. **43.** 15 p. green 5 5

1965. I.T.U. Cent.
199. **44.** 15 p. black and purple 5 5

45. I.C.Y. Emblem. **46.** Devkota (poet).

48. Flag and King Mahendra.

1965. Int. Co-operation Year.
200. **45.** 1 r. multicoloured .. 20 10

1965. Devkota Commem.
201. **46.** 15 p. brown 5 5

1966. Democracy Day.
202. **48.** 15 p. red & ultramarine 5 5

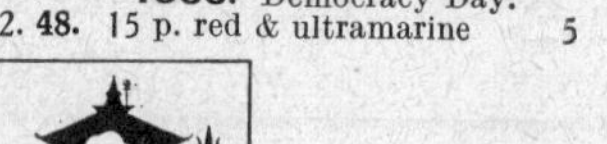

49. Siva Parvati and Pashuvati Temple. **50.** "Stamp" Emblem.

1966. Maha Sita-Ratri Festival.
203. **49.** 15 p. violet 5 5

1966. Nepalese Philatelic Exn.
204. **50.** 15 p. orange and green 5 5

51. King Mahendra. **52.** Queen Mother.

1966. King Mahendra's 47th Birthday.
205. **51.** 15 p. chocolate & ochre 5 5

1966. Queen Mother's 60th Birthday.
206. **52.** 15 p. chestnut 5 5

53. Queen Ratna. **54.** Flute-player and Dancer.

1966. Children's Day.
207. **53.** 15 p. chestnut & yellow 5 5

1966. Krishna Anniv.
208. **54.** 15 p. violet and yellow 5 5

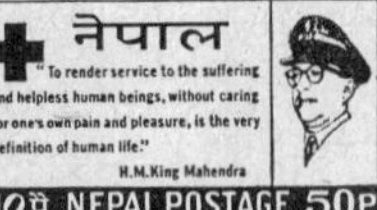

55. "To render service · ·"

1966. Nepalese Red Cross. 1st Anniv.
209. **55.** 50 p. red and green .. 40 15

56. W.H.O. Building. 57. L. Paudyal (poet).

1966. W.H.O. Headquarters Geneva. Inaug.
210. **56.** 1 r. violet 20 10

1966. Lekhnath Paudyal Commem.
211. **57.** 15 p. blue 5 5

58. Rama Navami and Sita. 59. Buddha.

1967. Rama Navami, 2024, birthday of Rama.
212. **58.** 15 p. brown and yellow 5 5

1967. Buddha Jayanti, birthday of Buddha.
213. **59.** 75 p. purple and orange 10 10

60. King Mahendra addressing Nepalese.

1967. King Mahendra's 48th Birthday.
214. **60.** 15 p. brown and blue.. 5 5

61. Queen Ratna and Children. 62. Ama Dablam (mountain).

1967. Children's Day.
215. **61.** 15 p. brown and cream 5 5

1967. Int. Tourist Year.
216. **62.** 5 p. violet (postage) .. 5 5
217. – 65 p. brown 10 8
218. – 1 r. 80 red & blue (air) 30 20
DESIGNS (38×20 mm.): 65 p. Bhaktapur Durbar Square. (35½×25½ mm.). 1 r. 80, Plane over Kathmandu.

63. Open-air Class.

1967. Constitution Day. "Go to the Village" Educational Campaign.
219. **63.** 15 p. multicoloured .. 5 5

64. Crown Prince Birendra (Chief Scout), Camp-fire and Scout Emblem.

1967. World Scouting. Diamond Jubilee.
220. **64.** 15 p. ultramarine .. 5 5

65. Shah Pritvi Narâjan (Founder of kingdom). 66. Arms of Nepal.

1968. Shah Pritvi Commem.
221. **65.** 15 p. blue and red .. 5 5

1968. National Day.
222. **66.** 15 p. blue and red .. 5 5

67. W.H.O. Emblem and Nepalese Flag.

1968. W.H.O. 20th Anniv.
223. **67.** 1 r. 20 blue, red & yellow 20 10

68. Sita and Janaki Temple.

1968. Sita Jayanti.
224. **68.** 15 p. brown and violet 5 5

69. King Mahendra, Mountains and Pheasant.

1968. King Mahendra's 49th Birthday.
225. **69.** 15 p. multicoloured .. 8 5

70. Reproduction of Aerogramme.

1968. Air. Royal Nepalese Airlines. Tenth Anniv.
226. **70.** 15 p. brown and blue 5 5
227. – 65 p. violet-blue .. 10 8
228. – 2 r. 50 blue and orange 35 20
DESIGNS—DIAMOND (25½ × 25½ mm.) 65 p. Route-map. HORIZ. (As T **70**). 2 r. 50, Airliner over Mount Dhaulagiri.

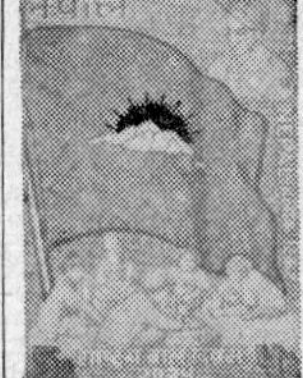

71, Nepalese Flag, Queen Ratna and Children. 72. Human Rights Emblem and Buddha.

1968. Children's Day and Queen Ratna's 41st Birthday.
229. **71.** 5 p. red, yellow & green 5 5

1968. Human Rights Year.
230. **72.** 1 r. red and green .. 20 12

73. Dancers, Flag and Crown Prince Birendra.

1968. Crown Prince Birendra's 24th Birthday, and National Youth Festival.
231. **73.** 25 p. ultramarine .. 8 5

74. King Mahendra, Flags and U.N. Building, New York. 75. Ansu Varma (7th-century ruler).

1969. Nepal's Election to U.N. Security Council.
232. **74.** 1 r. multicoloured .. 20 12

1969. Famous Nepalese.
233. **75.** 15 p. violet and green.. 5 5
234. – 25 p. turquoise.. .. 5 5
235. – 50 p. chestnut 10 8
236. – 1 r. purple and brown.. 15 10
DESIGNS—VERT. 25 p. Ram Shah (7th-century King of Gurkha. 50 p. Bhimsen Thapa (19th-century Prime Minister. HORIZ. 1 r. Bol Bhadra Kunwar (19th-century warrior).

76. I.L.O. Emblem.

1969. Int. Labour Organization. 50th Anniv.
237. **76.** 1 r. brown and red .. 20 10

77. King Mahendra. 79. Queen Ratna, and Child with Toy.

78. King Tribhuvan and Queens.

1969. King Mahendra's 50th Birthday.
238. **77.** 25 p. multicoloured .. 5 5

1969. King Tribhuvan. 64th Birth Anniv.
239. **78.** 25 p. sepia and yellow 5 5

1969. National Children's Day.
240. **79.** 25 p. red and brown .. 5 5

80. Rhododendron. 81. Durga, Goddess of Victory.

1969. Flowers. Multicoloured.
241. 25 p. Type **80** 5 5
242. 25 p. Narcissus 5 5
243. 25 p. Marigold 5 5
244. 25 p. Poinsettia 5 5

1969. Durga Pooja Festival.
245. **81.** 15 p. black and orange 5 5
246. 50 p. violet and brown 10 8

82. Crown Prince Birendra and Princess Aishwarya.

1970. Royal Wedding.
247. **82.** 25 p. multicoloured .. 5 5

83. Produce, Cow and Landscape.

1970. Agricultural Year.
248. **83.** 25 p. multicoloured .. 5 5

85. King Mahendra.

1970. King Mahendra's 51st Birthday.
249. **85.** 50 p. multicoloured .. 5 5

86. Lake Gosainkund.

1970. Nepalese Lakes. Multicoloured.
250. 5 p. Type **86** 5 5
251. 25 p. Lake Phewa Tal .. 5 5
252. 1 r. Lake Rara Daha .. 10 8

87. A.P.Y. Emblem.

1970. Asian Productivity Year.
253. **87.** 1 r. blue 15 10

88. Queen Ratna and Children's Palace, Taulihawa.

1970. National Children's Day.
254. **88.** 25 p. slate and chestnut 5 5

89. U.N. Flag.

1970. United Nations. 25th Anniv.
255. **89.** 25 p. blue and purple.. 5 5

90. New U.P.U. H.Q. Building.

1970. New U.P.U. Headquarters Building.
256. **90.** 2 r. 50 brown 20 15

91. Durbar Square, Patan.

1970 Tourism. Multicoloured.
257. 15 p. Type **91** 5 5
258. 25 p. Bodhnath Stupa (temple) (vert.) 5 5
259. 1 r. Mt. Gauri Shankar .. 12 10

92. Statue of Harihar, Balmiki Ashram. 93. Torch within Spiral.

94. King Mahendra taking Salute. 95. Sweta Bhairab.

1971. Nepalese Religious Art.
260. 92. 25 p. black and brown 5 5

1971. Racial Equality Year.
261. 93. 1 r. red and blue .. 15 10

1971. King Mahendra's 52nd Birthday.
262. 94. 15 p. plum and blue .. 5 5

1971. Bhairab Images.
263. 95. 15 p. brown and chest. 5 5
264. – 25 p. brown & green .. 5 5
265. – 50 p. brown and blue .. 8 5
DESIGNS: 25 p. Mahankal Bhairab. 50 p. Kal Bhairab.

96. Child presenting Queen Ratna with Garland.

1971. National Children's Day.
266. 96. 25 p. multicoloured .. 5 5

97. Iranian and Nepalese Flags on Map.

1971. Persian Empire. 2,500th Anniv.
267. 97. 1 r. multicoloured .. 12 10

98. Mother and Child.

1971. U.N.I.C.E.F. 25th Anniv.
268. 98. 1 r. blue 15 12

99. Mt. Everest. 100. Royal Standard.

1971. Himalayan Peaks. Multicoloured.
269. 25 p. Type 99 .. .. 5 5
270. 1 r. Mt. Kanchenjunga .. 12 10
271. 1 r. 80 Mt. Annapurna I .. 25 20

1972. National Day.
272. 100. 25 p. black and red .. 5 5

101. Araniko and Peking Temple. 102. Open Book.

1972. Araniko (13th-century architect). Commem.
273. 101. 15 p. brown and blue 5 5

1972. Int. Book Year.
274. 102. 2 p. brown and buff .. 5 5
275. 5 p. black and brown 5 5
276. 1 r. black and blue .. 12 12

103. Human Heart.

1972. World Heart Month.
277. 103. 25 p. red and green .. 5 5

104. King Mahendra. 105. King Birendra.

1972. King Mahendra. 1st Death Anniv.
278. 104. 25 p. brown & black .. 5 5

1972. King Birendra's 28th Birthday.
279. 105. 50 p. purple and brown. 8 5

106. Northern Border Costumes. 107. Sri Baburam Acharya (historian).

1973. National Costumes. Multicoloured.
280. 25 p. Type 106 .. .. 5 5
281. 50 p. Hill-dwellers .. 5 5
282. 75 p. Kathmandu Valley 12 10
283. 1 r. Inner Terai 15 12

1973. Sri Baburam Acharya (historian). 85th Birth Anniv.
284. 107. 25 p. drab and red .. 5 5

108. Nepalese Family.

1973. World Health Organization. 25th Anniv.
285. 108. 1 r. blue and brown .. 15 12

109. Birthplace of Buddha, Sumlini.

1973. Tourism. Multicoloured.
286. 25 p. Type 109 .. .. 5 5
287. 75 p. Mt. Makalu .. 10 8
288. 1 r. Gorkha .. 12 10

110. Farm Workers.

1973. World Food Programme. 10th Anniv.
289. 110. 10 p. brown & violet .. 5 5

111. Interpol H.Q., Paris.

1973. Int. Criminal Police Organization (Interpol). 50th Anniv.
290. 111. 25 p. blue and brown 5 5

112. Shri Shom Nath Sigdyal. 113. Cow.

1973. Shri Shom Nath Sigdyal (scholar) 1st Death Anniv.
291. 112. 1 r. 25 violet 15 12

1973. Domestic Animals. Multicoloured.
292. 2 p. Type 113 .. .. 5 5
293. 3 r. 25 Yak 40 35

114. King Birendra.

1974. King Birendra's 29th Birthday.
294. 114. 5 p. brown and black 5 5
295. 15 p. brown and black 5 5
296. 1 r. brown and black 12 10

115. Text of National Anthem. 116. King Janak seated on Throne.

1974. National Day.
297. 115. 25 p. red 5 5
298. – 1 r. green 12 10
DESIGN: 1 r. Anthem musical score.

1974. King Janak Commemoration.
299. 116. 2 r. 50 multicoloured 30 30

117. Emblem and Village.

1974. SOS Children's Village International. 25th Anniv.
300. 117. 25 p. blue and red .. 5 5

118. Football. 119. W.P.Y. Emblem.

1974. Nepalese Games. Multicoloured.
301. 2 p. Type 118 .. .. 5 5
302. 2 r. 75 Baghchal (diagram) 30 30

1974. World Population Year.
303. 119. 5 p. blue and brown .. 5 5

120. U.P.U. Monument, Berne. 121. Brown Butterfly.

1974. Universal Postal Union. Centenary.
304. 120. 1 r. black and green .. 12 10

1974. Nepalese Butterflies.
305. 121. 10 p. multicoloured .. 5 5
306. – 15 p. multicoloured .. 5 5
307. – 1 r. 25 multicoloured 15 12
308. – 1 r. 75 multicoloured 25 20
DESIGNS: Nos. 306/8, Butterflies similar to Type 121.

122. King Birendra. 123. Muktinath.

1974. King Birendra's 30th Birthday.
309. 122. 25 p. black & green .. 5 5

1974. "Visit Nepal". Tourism. Multicoloured
310. 25 p. Type 123 .. .. 5 5
311. 1 r. Peacock window, Bhaktapur (horiz.) 12 10

124. Guheswari Temple.

1975. Coronation of King Birendra. Mult.
312. 25 p. Type 124 .. .. 5 5
313. 50 p. Rara (lake view) .. 8 5
314. 1 r. Throne and sceptre .. 15 12
315. 1 r. 25 Royal Palace, Kathmandu 15 12
316. 1 r. 75 Pashupati Temple 25 20
317. 2 r. 75 King Birendra and Queen 40 35
SIZES—HORIZ. 50 p. 37 × 30 mm. 1 r, 1 r. 25, 2 r. 75 46 × 26 mm. VERT. 1 r. 75 25 × 31 mm.

125. Emblem of Tourism Year.

1975. South Asia Tourism Year. Mult.
319. 2 p. Type 125 .. .. 5 5
320. 25 p. Temple stupa (vert.) 5 5

126. Tiger.

1975. Wildlife Conservation. Multicoloured.
321. 2 p. Type 124 .. .. 5 5
322. 5 p. Deer (" Cervus duvauceli ") (vert.) .. 5 5
323. 1 r. Mountain cat .. 15 12

128. Rupse Falls. 129. King Birendra

1975. Tourism. Multicoloured.
325. 25 p. Type 128 .. .. 5 5
326. 50 p. Kumari (" Living Goddess ") 8 5
327. 2 r. Ganesh Himal (mountain) (horiz.) .. 30 25

1975. King Birendra's 31st Birthday.
328. 129. 25 p. violet and purple 5 5

130. Queen Aishwarya and I.W.Y. Emblem.

1975. International Women's Year.
329. **130.** 1 r. multicoloured .. 15 12

131. Flag and Map. **133.** Flags of Nepal and Colombo Plan.

132. Harvesting Rice.

1976. Nat. Democracy Day. Silver Jubilee.
330. **131.** 2 r. 50 red and blue .. 35 30

1976. Agriculture Year.
331. **132.** 25 p. multicoloured .. 5 5

1976. Colombo Plan. 25th Anniversary.
332. **133.** 1 r. multicoloured .. 12 10

134. Running. **135.** " Dove of Peace ".

1976. Olympic Games, Montreal.
333. **134.** 3 r. 25 black & blue .. 45 40

1976. 5th Non-aligned Countries' Summit Conference.
334. **135.** 5 r. blue, yell. and blk. 65 60

136. Lakhe Dance.

1976. Nepalese Dances. Multicoloured.
335. 10 p. Type **136** 5 5
336. 15 p. Maruni dance .. 5 5
337. 30 p. Jhangad dance .. 5 5
338. 1 r. Sebru dance 12 10

OFFICIAL STAMPS

O 1. Nepalese Arms and Soldiers.

काज सरकारी
(O 2.)

1960. (a) Size 30 × 18 mm.
O 135. **O 1.** 2 p. chocolate .. 5 5
O 136. 4 p. green 5 25
O 137. 6 p. red 5 5
O 138. 8 p. violet 5 5
O 139. 12 p. orange 5 5

(b) Size 38 × 27 mm.
O 140. **O 1.** 16 p. brown .. 5 5
O 141. 24 p. red 8 8
O 142. 32 p. maroon .. 12 10
O 143. 50 p. blue 20 8
O 144. 1 r. red 50 15
O 145. 2 r. orange 80 25

1960. Optd. as Type O 2.
O 139. **21.** 1 r. purple .. .. 5·00 5·00

1961. Optd. with Type O 2.
O 148. **29.** 1 p. red 8 8
O 149. 2 p. blue 12 10
O 150. 5 p. brown 20 20

NETHERLANDS E2

A kingdom in the N.W. of Europe on the North Sea.

100 cents = 1 gulden (florin)

King William III.
1. **2.** **3.**

1852. Imperf.
1. **1.** 5 c. blue .. .. .. £500 16·00
2e. 10 c. red .. .. .. £700 15·00
3b. 15 c. orange .. .. £800 75·00

1864. Perf.
8. **2.** 5 c. blue .. .. .. £200 11·00
9. 10 c. red .. .. .. £275 5·00
10. 15 c. orange .. .. £550 50·00

1867.
39. **3.** 5 c. blue .. .. .. 45·00 55
48. 10 c. red .. .. .. 75·00 1·10
13. 15 c. brown .. .. £300 18·00
14. 20 c. green .. .. £250 11·00
15. 25 c. purple .. .. £650 48·00
16. 50 c. gold .. .. .. £1100 90·00

4. **5.**

1869.
58. **4.** ½ c. brown .. .. 14·00 1·25
53. 1 c. black .. .. £110 45·00
59. 1 c. green .. .. 6·50 60
60. 1½ c. red .. .. 75·00 45·00
61. 2 c. yellow .. .. 30·00 6·50
62. 2½ c. mauve .. .. £250 32·00
91. **5.** 5 c. blue .. .. .. 5·00 10
92. 7½ c. brown .. .. 19·00 11·00
85. 10 c. red .. .. .. 32·00 50
94. 12½ c. grey .. .. 25·00 90
87. 15 c. brown .. .. £190 2·10
96. 20 c. green .. .. £225 2·25
97. 22½ c. green .. .. 38·00 25·00
98. 25 c. lilac .. .. £250 1·75
100. 50 c. bistre .. .. £300 5·00
101. 1 g. violet .. .. £250 15·00
74. – 2 g. 50 blue and red .. £375 55·00
No. 74 is similar to T 5, but larger.

7. **8.** Queen Wilhelmina.

1876.
138d. **7.** ½ c. red .. .. .. 1·90 8
140. 1 c. green .. .. 1·25 8
143. 2 c. yellow .. .. 18·00 1·50
145. 2½ c. mauve .. .. 7·50 12
148. **8.** 3 c. orange .. .. 3·25 65
150. 5 c. blue .. .. .. 1·60 10
154. 7½ c. brown .. .. 11·00 2·50
157. 10 c. red .. .. .. 15·00 45
160. 12½ c. grey .. .. 13·00 40
162. 15 c. brown .. .. 25·00 2·25
166. 20 c. green .. .. 30·00 1·10
168. 22½ c. green .. .. 19·00 7·50
171. 25 c. mauve .. .. 50·00 1·90
172. 50 c. bistre .. .. £250 10·00
176. – 50 c. brown and green .. 45·00 4·50
174. **8.** 1 g. violet .. .. £300 32·00
177. – 1 g. olive and brown .. £110 16·00
178. – 2 g. 50 blue and red .. £325 75·00
179c. – 5 g. brown and green .. £550 £225
Nos. 176 and 177/9c are as T 8, but larger.

10. **11.** Queen Wilhelmina. **12.**

1898. Nos. 187 and 190a also exist imperf.
180. **10.** ½ c. lilac 25 5
181. 1 c. red 55 5
226. 1½ c. blue .. .. 1·25 8
182. 2 c. brown .. .. 2·25 5
183. 2½ c. green .. .. 2·25 5
185. **11.** 3 c. orange .. .. 11·00 2·00
186. 3 c. green 75 5
227. 4 c. claret 85 30
228. 4½ c. mauve .. .. 1·90 2·10
187. 5 c. red .. .. .. 1·00 5
189. 7½ c. brown 40 5
190. 10 c. lilac .. .. 3·75 5
190a. 10 c. grey .. .. 4·50 5
191. 12½ c. blue .. .. 2·10 12
192. 15 c. brown .. .. 55·00 1·50
192a. 15 c. red and blue .. 2·50 10
192b. 17½ c. mauve .. .. 32·00 6·50
192c. 17½ c. brown and blue .. 10·00 30
193. 20 c. green .. .. 65·00 40
193a. 20 c. grey and green .. 6·50 12
194. 22½ c. olive and brown .. 4·50 15
195. 25 c. blue and red .. 4·50 10
230. 30 c. brown and mauve 14·00 12
231. 40 c. orange and green .. 21·00 40
196. 50 c. brown and olive .. 45·00 50
232. 50 c. violet and grey .. 55·00 30
233. 60 c. green and olive .. 21·00 55
205. **12.** 1 g. green .. .. 25·00 12
206. 2½ g. lilac .. .. 65·00 1·90
207. 5 g. claret .. .. £150 3·00
204. 10 g. orange £700 £550

13.

1906. Charity. Society for the Prevention of T.B.
208. **13.** 1 c. + 1 c. red .. .. 1·90 1·25
209. 3 c. + 3 c. green .. 16·00 13·00
210. 5 c. + 5 c. grey .. .. 17·00 4·50

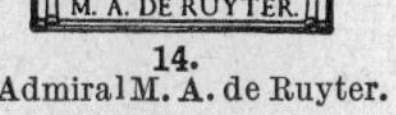

14. Admiral M. A. de Ruyter. **15.** William I.

1907. Admiral de Ruyter. Birth Tercent.
211. **14.** ½ c. blue 40 45
212. 1 c. claret .. .. 1·40 1·50
213. 2½ c. red .. .. 6·50 1·40

1913. Independence Centenary.
214. **15.** 2½ c. green on green .. 25 40
215. – 3 c. yellow on cream .. 45 65
216. – 5 c. red on buff 30 20
217. – 10 c. sepia .. .. 2·00 1·10
218. **14.** 12½ c. blue on blue .. 1·50 1·10
219. – 20 c. brown .. .. 8·50 4·50
220. – 25 c. blue .. .. 9·00 4·50
221. – 50 c. green .. .. 18·00 15·00
222. **15.** 1 g. claret .. .. 30·00 9·50
223. – 2½ g. lilac .. .. 75·00 28·00
224. – 5 g. yellow on cream .. £190 25·00
225. – 10 g. orange £650 £600
DESIGNS: 3 c., 20 c., 2½ g. William II. 5 c., 25 c., 5 g. William III. 10 c., 50 c., 10 g. Queen Wilhelmina.

1919. Surch. **Veertig Cent** (40 c.) or **Zestig Cent** (60 c.).
234. **11.** 40 c. on 30 c. brn. & mve. 19·00 3·00
235. 60 c. on 30 c. brn. & mve. 18·00 2·75

1920. Surch. in figures.
238. **11.** 4 c. on 4½ c. (No. 228) .. 1·00 55
236. **12.** 2 g. 50 on 10 g. (204) .. £120 £110
237. – 2 g. 50 on 10 g. (225) .. £130 55·00

16. **17.**

1921. Air.
239. **16.** 10 c. red .. .. 1·25 65
240. 15 c. green .. .. 3·75 1·25
241. 60 c. blue .. .. 11·00 12

1921.
242. **17.** 5 c. green .. .. 7·50 5
243. 12½ c. red .. .. 9·50 1·25
244. 20 c. blue .. .. 19·00 8

18. Lion in Dutch Garden and Orange Tree. **19.** **20.**

1923.
248. **18.** 1 c. violet 25 40
249. 2 c. orange .. .. 4·00 5
250. **19.** 2½ c. green .. .. 1·00 40
251. **20.** 4 c. blue 75 30

1923.
252. **10.** 2 c. on 1 c. red .. 25 10
253. 2 c. on 1½ c. blue .. 25 10
254. **11.** 10 c. on 3 c. green .. 2·50 5
255. 10 c. on 5 c. red .. 5·00 25
256. 10 c. on 12½ c. blue .. 4·50 30
257. 10 c. on 17½ c. brn. & bl. 1·60 1·90
258. 10 c. on 22½ c. ol. & brn. 1·60 1·90

21. **22.**

1923. Queen's Accession. 25th Anniv.
259. **22.** 2 c. green 5 5
260. **21.** 5 c. green 12 8
261. **22.** 7½ c. lake 12 5
262. 10 c. orange 15 5
263. 20 c. blue .. .. 1·50 25
264. 25 c. yellow .. .. 2·10 40
265. 35 c. orange .. .. 2·50 1·00
266. 50 c. black .. .. 9·50 12
267. **21.** 1 g. red .. .. 18·00 3·25
268. 2½ g. black £150 £130
269. 5 g. blue £130 £100

1923. Surch. **DIENST ZEGAL PORTEN AAN TEEKEN RECHT** and value.
270. **11.** 10 c. on 3 c. (No. 186) .. 50 65
271. 1 g. on 17½ c. (No. 192c) 42·00 11·00

DESIGN: 10 c. Two women.

23.

1923. Charity.
272. **23.** 2 c. + 5 c. bl. on pink .. 10·00 11·00
273. – 10 c. + 5 c. red on pink .. 11·00 11·00

25. Carrier Pigeon. **26.** Queen Wilhelmina.

1924.
330. **25.** ½ c. grey 45 50
423. 1 c. red 5 5
332. 1½ c. mauve 75 5
424a. 1½ c. grey 5 5
425. 2 c. orange 5 5
426a. 2½ c. green .. .. 1·50 5
427. 3 c. green 5 5
427a. 4 c. blue 5 5
428. **26.** 5 c. green 8 5
429. 6 c. brown 8 5
279. 7½ c. yellow 20 5
313. 7½ c. violet .. .. 1·90 5
314. 7½ c. red 12 5
279a. 9 c. orange and black .. 90 65
316. 10 c. red 70 5
430. 10 c. violet .. .. 1·50 5
282. 12½ c. red .. .. 1·10 25
431. 12½ c. blue 12 5
283. 15 c. blue .. .. 3·75 25
343a. 15 c. yellow 40 5
322. 20 c. blue .. .. 4·50 5
434. 21 c. olive .. .. 15·00 45
323. 22½ c. olive .. .. 4·50 90
434a. 22½ c. orange .. .. 7·00 8·00

435. 25 c. green .. .. 2·50 5
325. 27½ c. grey .. .. 2·50 40
326. 30 c. purple .. .. 3·25 5
286a. 35 c. olive .. .. 20·00 4·00
437a. 40 c. brown .. .. 6·50 12
329. 50 c. green .. .. 3·50 12
289. 60 c. violet .. .. 20·00 45
329a. 60 c. black .. .. 15·00 45
301. – 1 g. blue .. .. 5·00 15
302. – 2½ g. red .. .. 45·00 2·50
303. – 5 g. black .. .. 95·00 1·60

The gulden values are as T **26** but larger.
For further stamps in T **25**, see Nos. 546/57.

1924. Int. Philatelic Exn., The Hague.
290. **26.** 10 c. green .. .. 24·00 25·00
291. 15 c. black .. .. 28·00 32·00
292. 35 c. red .. .. 24·00 25·00

28. **29.** **30.**

1924. Dutch Lifeboat Centenary.
293. **28.** 3 c. brown .. .. 80 1·10
294. **29.** 10 c. brown on yellow 4·00 70

1924. Child Welfare.
295. **30.** 2 c.+2 c. green .. 65 85
296. 7½ c.+3½ c. brown .. 3·00 3·50
297. 10 c.+2½ c. red .. 3·00 55

31. Arms of South Holland. **32.** Queen Wilhelmina. **33.** Red Cross Allegory.

1925. Child Welfare. Arms as T **31.**
298. – 2 c.+2 c. grn. & yell... 65 75
299. – 7½ c.+3½ c. vio. & blue 2·50 2·75
300. **31.** 10 c.+2½ c. red & yell. 1·90 25
ARMS: 2 c. North Brabant. 7½ c. Gelderland.

1926. Child Welfare. Arms as T **31.**
350. 2 c.+2 c. red and silver .. 40 30
351. 5 c.+3 c. green and blue .. 1·10 70
352. 10 c.+3 c. red and green .. 1·50 12
353. 15 c.+3 c. yellow & blue .. 4·50 4·50
ARMS: 2 c. Utrecht. 5 c. Zeeland. 10 c. North Holland. 15 c. Friesland.

1927. Dutch Red Cross Society. 60th Anniv.
354. **32.** 2 c.+2 c. red .. .. 1·25 1·25
355. – 3 c.+2 c. green .. .. 3·50 3·75
356. – 5 c.+3 c. blue 40 25
357. – 7½ c.+3½ c. blue .. 2·50 1·00
358. **33.** 15 c.+5 c. red and blue 7·50 7·00
PORTRAITS: 2 c. King William III. 3 c. Queen Emma. 5 c. Henry, Prince Consort.

1927. Child Welfare. Arms as T **31.**
359. 2 c.+2 c. red and lilac .. 25 25
360. 5 c.+3 c. green & yellow .. 1·00 1·00
361. 7½ c.+3½ c. red and black 1·90 12
362. 15 c.+3 c. blue & brown .. 3·75 3·25
ARMS: 2 c. Drente. 5 c. Groningen. 7½ c. Limburg. 15 c. Overyssel.

34. Sculler. **35.** Footballer.

1928. Olympic Games, Amsterdam.
363. **34.** 1½ c.+1 c. green .. 75 50
364. – 2 c.+1 c. purple .. 1·25 75
365. **35.** 3 c.+1 c. green .. 1·25 65
366. – 5 c.+1 c. blue .. 1·40 50
367. – 7½ c.+2½ c. orange .. 1·60 75
368. – 10 c.+2 c. red .. 5·00 3·75
369. – 15 c.+2 c. blue .. 3·25 1·90
370. – 30 c.+3 c. sepia .. 17·00 16·00
DESIGNS—HORIZ. 2 c. Fencer. VERT. 5 c. Yachting. 7½ c. Putting the weight. 10 c. Runner. 15 c. Horseman. 30 c. Boxer.

DESIGN: 75 c. Van der Hoop.

36. Lieut. Koppen.

1928. Air.
371. **36.** 40 c. red 15 20
372. – 75 c. green 15 20

38. J. P. Minckelers. **39.** Mercury.

1928. Child Welfare.
373. **38.** 1½ c.+1½ c. violet .. 30 12
374. – 5 c.+3 c. green .. 55 50
375. – 7½ c.+2½ c. red .. 1·50 12
376. – 12½ c.+3½ c. blue .. 7·00 4·25
PORTRAITS: 5 c. Boerhaave. 7½ c. H. A. Lorentz. 12½ c. G. Huygens.

1929. Air.
377. **39.** 1½ g. black .. .. 1·50 1·10
378. 4½ g. red .. .. 1·00 2·25
379. 7½ g. green .. .. 19·00 2·75

1929. Surch. **21** in large figures.
380. **26.** 21 c. on 22½ c. olive .. 11·00 70

40. "Friendship and Security". **41.** Rembrandt and "De Staalmeester".

1929. Child Welfare.
381. **40.** 1½ c.+1½ c. grey .. 1·25 25
382. 5 c.+3 c. green .. 2·25 55
383. 6 c.+4 c. red .. 1·50 12
384. 12½ c.+3½ c. blue .. 9·00 6·50

1930. Charity. Rembrandt Society.
385. **41.** 5 c.+5 c. green .. 4·50 4·50
386. 6 c.+5 c. black .. 2·50 1·00
387. 12½ c.+5 c. blue .. 7·00 7·00

42. Spring. **43.** **44.** Queen Wilhelmina.

1930. Child Welfare.
388. **42.** 1½ c.+1½ c. red .. 90 20
389. – 5 c.+3 c. green .. 1·40 45
390. – 6 c.+4 c. purple .. 1·40 12
391. – 12½ c.+3½ c. blue .. 9·00 7·00
DESIGNS (allegorical): 5 c. Summer, 6 c. Autumn. 12½ c. Winter.

1931. Gouda Church Restoration Fund.
392. **43.** 1½ c.+1½ c. green .. 8·00 8·00
393. 6 c.+4 c. red .. .. 16·00 15·00

1931.
395. – 70 c. blue and red (post.) 15·00 30
395b. – 80 c. green and red .. 60·00 2·00
394. **44.** 36 c. red and blue (air) .. 6·50 25
DESIGNS: 70 c. Portrait and factory. 80 c. Portrait and shipyard.

46. Mentally Deficient Child **47.** **48.** Gorse (Spring).

1931. Child Welfare.
396. – 1½ c.+1½ c. red & blue .. 1·00 25
397. **46.** 5 c.+3 c. green & pur... 1·50 90
398. – 6 c.+4 c. pur. & grn. .. 1·25 12
399. – 12½ c.+3½ c. bl. & red .. 15·00 11·00
DESIGNS: 1½ c. Deaf mute. 6 c. Blind girl. 12½ c. Sick child.

1932. Tourist Propaganda.
400. **47.** 2½ c.+1½ c. grn. & blk. 2·50 1·25
401. – 6 c.+4 c. grey & black 5·00 1·25
402. – 7½ c.+3½ c. red & blk... 20·00 14·00
403. – 12½ c.+2½ c. bl. & blk. 23·00 14·00
DESIGNS: 2½ c. Windmill and dykes, Kinderdijk. 6 c. Town Hall, Zierikzee. 7½ c. Bridges at Schipluiden and Moerdijk. 12½ c. Tulips.

1932. Child Welfare.
404. **48.** 1½ c.+1½ c. brn. & yell. 1·25 12
405. – 5 c.+3 c. blue & red .. 1·25 65
406. – 6 c.+4 c. grn. & orge... 1·25 12
407. – 12½ c.+3½ c. bl. & orge. 16·00 13·00
DESIGNS—Child and: 5 c. Cornflower (Summer). 6 c. Sunflower (Autumn). 12½ c. Christmas rose. (Winter).

49. Arms of the House of Orange. **50.** William I.

1933. William I of Orange. 4th Birth Cent. T **49** and portraits of William I inscr. "1533", as T **50.**
408. **49.** 1½ c. black 40 5
409. – 5 c. green .. .. 1·10 12
410. **50.** 6 c. purple .. .. 1·90 5
411. – 12½ c. blue .. .. 10·00 2·25

51. Dove of Peace. **52.** Projected Monument at Den Helder. **53.** Hospital-ship "Hope".

1933. Peace Propaganda.
412. **51.** 12½ c. blue .. .. 7·00 15

1933. Charity. Seamen's Fund.
413. **52.** 1½ c.+1½ c. red .. 1·90 65
414. **53.** 5 c.+3 c. green and red 7·00 1·10
415. – 6 c.+4 c. green .. 9·50 95
416. – 12½ c.+3½ c. blue .. 13·00 11·00
DESIGNS: 6 c. Lifeboat. 12½ c. Seaman and Seamen's Home.

56. Monoplane.

1933. Air. Special Flights.
417. **56.** 30 c. green 20 40

57. Child and Star of Epiphany. **58.** Princess Juliana.

1933. Child Welfare.
418. **57.** 1½ c.+1½ c. orge. & grey 90 25
419. 5 c.+3 c. yell. & brn. .. 1·10 40
420. 6 c.+4 c. gold & green .. 1·40 12
421. 12½ c.+3½ c. silver & bl. 15·00 10·00

1934. Charity. Crisis stamps.
438. – 5 c.+4 c. purple .. 7·00 1·50
439. **58.** 6 c.+5 c. blue .. .. 7·00 2·50
DESIGN: 5 c. Queen Wilhelmina.

59. Van Walbeeck's Ship. **61.** Dowager Queen Emma.

1934. Curacao Tercent. Inscr. "1634 1934".
440. – 6 c. black .. .. 2·50 5
441. **59.** 12½ c. blue .. .. 11·00 2·25
DESIGN: 6 c. Willemstad Harbour.

1934. Anti-T.B. Fund.
442. **61.** 6 c.+2 c. blue .. .. 7·00 75

62. Destitute child. **63.** H. D. Guyot.

1934. Child Welfare.
443. **62.** 1½ c.+1½ c. brown .. 1·00 30
444. 5 c.+3 c. red .. 1·40 70
445. 6 c.+4 c. green .. 1·40 12
446. 12½ c.+3½ c. blue .. 14·00 10·00

1935. Cultural and Social Relief Fund.
447. **63.** 1½ c.+1½ c. red .. 1·25 1·50
448. – 5 c.+3 c. brown .. 2·00 2·50
449. – 6 c.+4 c. green .. 3·00 12
450. – 12½ c.+3½ c. blue .. 18·00 2·50
PORTRAITS: 5 c. A. J. M. Diepenbrock. 6 c. F. C. Donders. 12½ c. J. P. Sweelinck.

See also Nos. 456/9, 469/72, 478/82 and 492/6.

64. Aerial map of the Netherlands. **65.** Child picking fruit.

1935. Air. Fund stamp.
451. **64.** 6 c.+4 c. brown .. 13·00 1·75

1935. Child Welfare.
452. **65.** 1½ c.+1½ c. red .. 40 12
453. 5 c.+3 c. green .. 90 75
454. 6 c.+4 c. brown .. 75 12
455. 12½ c.+3½ c. blue .. 13·00 4·00

1936. Cultural and Social Relief Fund. As T **63.**
456. 1½ c.+1½ c. sepia .. 75 65
457. 5 c.+3 c. green .. 2·50 2·25
458. 6 c.+4 c. red .. 1·25 12
459. 12½ c.+3½ c. blue .. 9·50 1·40
PORTRAITS: 1½ c. H. Kammerlingh Onnes. 5 c. D. A. S. Talma. 6 c. Mgr. Dr. H. J. A. M. Schaepman. 12½ c. Desiderius Erasmus.

67. Pallas Athene.

1936. Utrecht University Foundation Tercent. Inscr. "1636 1936".
460. **67.** 6 c. lake .. .. 1·40 12
461. – 12½ c. blue .. .. 2·50 2·75
DESIGN: 12½ c. Gisbert (Gisbertus) Voetius.

68. Child Herald. **69.** "Scout Movement".

1936. Child Welfare.
462. **68.** 1½ c.+1½ c. slate .. 40 12
463. 5 c.+3 c. green .. 1·50 50
464. 6 c.+4 c. brown .. 1·50 12
465. 12½ c.+3½ c. blue .. 8·50 3·00

1937. Scout Jamboree.
466. – 1½ c. black and green .. 12 5
467. **69.** 6 c. brown and black .. 1·25 5
468. – 12½ c. black and blue .. 2·40 65
DESIGNS: 1½ c. Scout Tenderfoot Badge. 12½ c. Hermes.

1937. Cultural and Social Relief Fund. Portraits as T **63.**
469. 1½ c.+1½ c. sepia .. 30 40
470. 5 c.+3 c. green .. 2·50 2·50
471. 6 c.+4 c. purple .. 80 5
472. 12½ c.+3½ c. blue .. 5·50 90
PORTRAITS: 1½ c. Jacob Maris. 5 c. F. de le B. Sylvius. 6 c. J. van den Vondel. 12½ c. A. van Leeuwenhoek.

70. "Laughing Child" by Frans Hals. 71. Queen Wilhelmina.

1937. Child Welfare.

No.	Type	Stamp	Unused	Used
473.	70.	1½ c.+1½ c. black	12	8
474.		3 c.+2 c. green	70	1·00
475.		4 c.+2 c. red	40	30
476.		5 c.+3 c. green	30	5
477.		12½ c.+3½ c. blue	5·00	1·00

1938. Cultural and Social Relief Fund. As T 63.

No.	Type	Stamp	Unused	Used
478.		1½ c.+1½ c. sepia	30	50
479.		3 c.+2 c. green	45	20
480.		4 c.+2 c. red	1·00	1·40
481.		5 c.+3 c. green	1·25	12
482.		12½ c. +3½ c. blue	6·00	70

PORTRAITS: 1½ c. M. van St. Aldegonde. 3 c. O. G. Heldring. 4 c. Maria Tesselschade. 5 c. Rembrandt. 12½ c. H. Boerhaave.

1938. Coronation. 40th Anniv.

No.	Type	Stamp	Unused	Used
483.	71.	1½ c. black	5	5
484.		5 c. red	12	5
485.		12½ c. blue	2·10	65

72. Crow. 73. Boy with flute.

1938. Air. Special Flights.

No.	Type	Stamp	Unused	Used
486.	72.	12½ c. blue and grey	8	20
774.		25 c. blue and grey	30	50

1938. Child Welfare.

No.	Type	Stamp	Unused	Used
487.	73.	1½ c.+1½ c. black	8	5
488.		3 c.+2 c. maroon	30	8
489.		4 c.+2 c. green	45	50
490.		5 c.+3 c. red	25	5
491.		12½ c.+3½ c. blue	4·50	1·25

1939. Cultural and Social Relief Fund. As T 63.

No.	Type	Stamp	Unused	Used
492.		1½ c.+1½ c. brown	40	40
493.		2½ c.+2½ c. green	2·25	1·75
494.		3 c.+3 c. red	65	65
495.		5 c.+3 c. green	1·50	12
496.		12½ c.+3½ c. blue	4·75	65

PORTRAITS: 1½ c. M. Maris. 2½ c. Anton Mauve. 3 c. Gerardus van Swieten. 5 c. Nicolaas Beets. 12½ c. Pieter Stuyvesant.

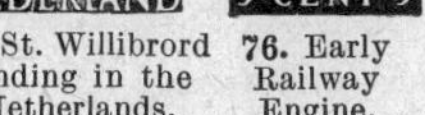

75. St. Willibrord landing in the Netherlands. 76. Early Railway Engine. 77. Child and Cornucopia.

1939. St. Willibrord. 12th Death Cent. Dated "739 1939".

No.	Type	Stamp	Unused	Used
497.	75.	5 c. green	40	5
498.	–	12½ c. blue	2·75	1·50

DESIGN: 12½ c. St. Willibrord when Bishop of Utrecht.

1939. Railways Cent. Inscr. "1839 1939".

No.	Type	Stamp	Unused	Used
499.	76.	5 c. green	65	5
500.	–	12½ c. blue	4·00	2·25

DESIGN: 12½ c. Modern electric locomotive.

1939. Child Welfare.

No.	Type	Stamp	Unused	Used
501.	77.	1½ c.+1½ c. black	12	5
502.		2½ c.+2½ c. green	3·00	1·50
503.		3 c.+3 c. red	40	8
504.		5 c.+3 c. green	75	5
505.		12½ c.+3½ c. blue	2·10	90

78. Queen Wilhelmina. 79. Vincent Van Gogh. 80. Girl with Dandelion.

1940.

No.	Type	Stamp	Unused	Used
506.	78.	5 c. green	5	5
506a.		6 c. brown	15	8
507.		7½ c. red	5	5
508.		10 c. purple	5	5
509.		12½ c. blue	5	5
510.		15 c. blue	8	5
510a.		17½ c. blue	75	25
511.		20 c. violet	12	8
512.		22½ c. olive	30	40
513.		25 c. red	15	5
514.		30 c. ochre	40	10
515.		40 c. green	65	20
515a.		50 c. orange	4·75	30
515b.		60 c. purple	3·75	1·50

1940. Cultural and Social Relief Fund.

No.	Type	Stamp	Unused	Used
516.	79.	1½ c.+1½ c. brown	95	20
517.	–	2½ c.+2½ c. green	1·90	75
518.	–	3 c.+3 c. red	1·60	65
519.	–	5 c.+3 c. green	1·75	12
520.	–	12½ c.+3½ c. blue	3·00	50

PORTRAITS: 2½ c. E. J. Potgieter. 3c. Petrus Camper. 5 c. Jan Steen. 12½ c. Joseph Scaliger.

1940. As No. 519, colour changed. Surch.

No.	Type	Stamp	Unused	Used
521.		7½ c.+2½ c. on 5 c.+3 c. red	30	20

1940. Surch. with large figures and network.

No.	Type	Stamp	Unused	Used
522.	25.	2½ on 3 c. red	65	8
523.		5 on 3 c. green	5	5
534.		7½ on 3 c. red	5	5
525.		10 on 3 c. green	8	5
526.		12½ on 3 c. blue	12	20
527.		17½ on 3 c. green	25	30
528.		20 on 3 c. green	5	5
529.		22½ on 3 c. green	45	50
530.		25 on 3 c. green	20	12
531.		30 on 3 c. green	25	20
532.		40 on 3 c. green	30	30
533.		50 on 3 c. green	45	20
534.		60 on 3 c. green	80	45
535.		70 on 3 c. green	1·50	90
536.		80 on 3 c. green	2·25	2·25
537.		100 on 3 c. green	18·00	19·00
538.		250 on 3 c. green	19·00	21·00
539.		500 on 3 c. green	18·00	19·00

1940. Child Welfare.

No.	Type	Stamp	Unused	Used
540.	80.	1½ c.+1½ c. violet	40	5
541.		2½ c.+2½ c. olive	1·40	30
542.		4 c.+3 c. blue	1·10	40
543.		5 c.+3 c. green	1·10	5
544.		7½ c.+3½ c. red	40	5

1941.

No.	Type	Stamp	Unused	Used
546.	25.	5 c. green	5	5
547.		7½ c. red	5	5
548.		10 c. violet	10	5
549.		12½ c. blue	8	8
550.		15 c. blue	10	8
551.		17½ c. red	8	8
552.		20 c. violet	8	8
553.		22½ c. olive	8	12
554.		25 c. lake	10	8
555.		30 c. brown	2·50	10
556.		40 c. green	10	10
557.		50 c. brown	5	10

82. "Titus Rembrandt." 83. Legionary.

1941. Cultural and Social Relief Fund. As T 79 but inscr. "ZOMERZEGEL 31.12.46".

No.	Type	Stamp	Unused	Used
558.		1½ c.+1½ c. brown	65	12
559.		2½ c.+2½ c. green	50	12
560.		4 c.+3 c. red	50	12
561.		5 c.+3 c. green	70	12
562.		7½ c.+3½ c. purple	70	12

PORTRAITS: 1½ c. Dr. A. Mathijsen. 2½ c. J. Ingenhousz. 4 c. Aagje Deken. 5 c. Johan Bosboom. 7½ c. A. C. W. Staring.

1941. Child Welfare.

No.	Type	Stamp	Unused	Used
563.	82.	1½ c.+1½ c. black	15	12
564.		2½ c.+2½ c. olive	15	12
565.		4 c.+3 c. blue	15	12
566.		5 c.+3 c. green	15	12
567.		7½ c.+3½ c. red	15	12

1942. Netherlands Legion Fund.

No.	Type	Stamp	Unused	Used
568.	83.	7½ c.+2½ c. red	12	12
569.	–	12½ c.+87½ c. blue	4·00	4·50

DESIGN—HORIZ. 12½ c. Legionary with similar inscription.

1943. 1st European Postal Congress. As T 19, but larger, surch. **EUROPEESCHE PTT VEREENIGING 19 OCTOBER 1942 10 CENT.**

No.	Type	Stamp	Unused	Used
570.	19.	10 c. on 2½ c. yellow	5	5

84. Seahorse. 85. M. A. de Ruyter.

1943. Old Germanic Symbols.

No.	Type	Stamp	Unused	Used
571.	84.	1 c. black	5	5
572.	–	1½ c. claret	5	5
573.	–	2 c. blue	5	5
574.	–	2½ c. green	5	5
575.	–	3 c. red	5	5
576.	–	4 c. brown	5	5
577.	–	5 c. olive	5	5

DESIGNS—VERT. 1½ c. Triple crowned tree. 2½ c. Birds in ornamental tree. 4 c. Horse and rider. HORIZ. 2 c. Swans. 3 c. Trees and serpentine roots. 5 c. Prancing horses.

1943. Dutch Naval Heroes.

No.	Type	Stamp	Unused	Used
578.	85.	7½ c. red	5	5
579.	–	10 c. green	5	5
580.	–	12½ c. blue	5	10
581.	–	15 c. violet	5	8
582.	–	17½ c. grey	5	8
583.	–	20 c. brown	5	5
584.	–	22½ c. red	5	12
585.	–	25 c. purple	25	30
586.	–	30 c. blue	5	10
587.	–	40 c. grey	5	12

PORTRAITS: 10 c. Johan Evertsen. 12½ c. M. H. Tromp. 15 c. Piet Hein. 17½ c. W. J. van Gent. 20 c. Witte de With. 22½ c. Cornelis Evertsen. 25 c. Tjerk Hiddes de Fries. 30 c. C. Tromp. 40 c. Evertsen, Junr.

86. Mail Cart. 87. Child and Doll's House.

1943. Stamp Day.

No.	Type	Stamp	Unused	Used
589.	86.	7½ c.+7½ c. red	5	5

1944. Child Welfare and Winter Help Funds. Inscr. "WINTERHULP" (1½ c. and 7½ c.) or "VOLKSDIENST" (others).

No.	Type	Stamp	Unused	Used
590.	87.	1½ c.+3½ c. black	5	8
591.	–	4 c.+3½ c. brown	5	8
592.	–	5 c.+5 c. green	5	8
593.	–	7½ c.+7½ c. red	5	8
594.	–	10 c.+40 c. blue	5	8

DESIGNS: 4 c. Mother and child. 5 c., 10 c. Mother and children. 7½ c. Child and wheatsheaf.

88. Infantryman. 89. Queen Wilhelmina.

1944.

No.	Type	Stamp	Unused	Used
595.	88.	1½ c. black	5	5
596.	–	2½ c. green	5	5
597.	–	3 c. brown	5	5
598.	–	5 c. blue	5	5
599.	89.	7½ c. red	5	5
600.		10 c. orange	8	8
601.		12½ c. blue	8	8
602.		15 c. claret	1·40	1·60
603.		17½ c. green	90	90
604.		20 c. violet	15	15
605.		22½ c. red	40	50
606.		25 c. brown	2·00	1·75
607.		30 c. green	12	12
608.		40 c. purple	1·75	1·90
609.		50 c. mauve	1·00	75

DESIGNS—HORIZ. 2½ c. Merchant ship. 3 c. Airman. VERT. 5 c. Cruiser "De Ruyter".

The above set was originally for use on Netherland warships serving with the Allied Fleet, and was used after liberation in the Netherlands.

93. Lion and Dragon. 94. 95. Queen Wilhelmina.

1945. Liberation.

No.	Type	Stamp	Unused	Used
610.	93.	7½ c. orange	5	5

1945. Child Welfare.

No.	Type	Stamp	Unused	Used
611.	94.	1½ c.+2½ c. grey	12	12
612.		2½ c.+3½ c. green	12	12
613.		5 c.+5 c. brown	12	12
614.		7½ c.+4½ c. red	12	12
615.		12½ c.+5½ c. blue	12	12

1946.

No.	Type	Stamp	Unused	Used
616.	95.	1 g. blue	50	20
617.		2½ g. red	£110	2·00
618.		5 g. green	£110	14·00
619.		10 g. violet	£110	15·00

96. Emblem of Abundance. 97. Princess Irene. 98. Boy on Roundabout.

1946. War Victims' Relief Fund.

No.	Type	Stamp	Unused	Used
620.	96.	1½ c.+3½ c. black	25	20
621.		2½ c.+5 c. green	40	25
622.		5 c.+10 c. violet	50	30
623.		7½ c.+15 c. claret	25	20
624.		12½ c.+37½ c. blue	50	30

1946. Child Welfare.

No.	Type	Stamp	Unused	Used
625.	97.	1½ c.+1½ c. brown	30	25
626.	–	2½ c.+1½ c. green	30	25
627.	97.	4 c.+2 c. claret	40	30
628.	–	5 c.+2 c. brown	30	25
629.	–	7½ c.+2½ c. red	40	12
630.	–	12½ c.+7½ c. blue	30	30

PORTRAITS: 2½ c., 5 c. Princess Margriet. 7½ c., 12½ c. Princess Beatrix.

1946. Child Welfare.

No.	Type	Stamp	Unused	Used
631.	98.	2 c.+2 c. violet	30	25
632.		4 c.+2 c. green	30	30
633.		7½ c.+2½ c. red	30	25
634.		10 c.+5 c. purple	30	12
635.		20 c.+5 c. blue	40	40

99. Numeral. 100. Queen Wilhelmina. 102. Children.

1946.

No.	Type	Stamp	Unused	Used
636.	99.	1 c. red	5	5
637.		2 c. blue	5	5
638		2½ c. orange	7·50	65
638a.		3 c. brown	5	5
639.		4 c. green	15	5
640.	100.	5 c. green	40	5
639a.	99.	5 c. orange	5	5
641.	100.	6 c. black	5	5
642.		6 c. blue	20	5
639c.	99.	6 c. grey	8	5
639d.		7 c. vermilion	8	5
643.	100.	7½ c. lake	5	5
639f.	99.	8 c. purple	8	5
644.	100.	10 c. purple	30	5
645.		12½ c. red	25	25
646.		15 c. violet	1·50	5
647.		20 c. blue	2·00	5
648.		22½ c. olive	40	40
649.		25 c. blue	9·00	5
650.		30 c. orange	4·50	12
651.		35 c. blue	3·75	20
652.		40 c. brown	10·00	20
653.	–	45 c. blue	10·00	7·00
654.	–	50 c. brown	10·00	5
655.	–	60 c. red	10·00	1·10

Nos. 653/5 are as T 100 but have the inscriptions in colour on white ground.

1947. Cultural and Social Relief Fund. As T 79 but inscr. "ZOMERZEGEL 13.12.48".

No.	Type	Stamp	Unused	Used
656.		2 c.+2 c. red	30	30
657.		4 c.+2 c. green	90	45
658.		7½ c.+2½ c. violet	1·00	45
659.		10 c.+5 c. brown	1·00	5
660.		20 c.+5 c. blue	55	40

PORTRAITS: 2 c. H. van Deventer. 4 c. P. C. Hooft. 7½ c. Johan de Witt. 10 c. J. F. van Royen. 20 c. Hugo Grotius.

1947. Child Welfare.

No.	Type	Stamp	Unused	Used
661.	102.	2 c.+2 c. brown	5	5
662.	–	4 c.+2 c. green	80	30
663.	–	7½ c.+2½ c. brown	80	35
664.	–	10 c.+5 c. lake	80	5
665.	102.	20 c.+5 c. blue	75	50

DESIGN: 4 c. to 10 c. Baby.

103. Ridderzaal, The Hague. 104. Queen Wilhelmina.

1948. Cultural and Social Relief Fund.

No.	Type	Stamp	Unused	Used
666.	103.	2 c.+2 c. brown	1·25	15
667.	–	6 c.+4 c. green	1·25	20
668.	–	10 c.+5 c. red	65	10
669.	–	20 c.+5 c. blue	1·25	60

BUILDINGS: 6 c. Palace on the Dam. 10 c. Kneuterdijk Palace. 20 c. Nieuwe Kerk, Amsterdam.

1948. Queen Wilhelmina's Golden Jubilee.
670. **104.** 10 c. red 5 5
671. 20 c. blue 75 75

105. Queen Juliana. **106.** Boy in Canoe.

1948. Coronation.
672. **105.** 10 c. brown 30 5
673. 20 c. blue .. .. 1·10 20

1948. Child Welfare.
674. **106.** 2 c.+2 c. green .. 5 5
675. – 5 c.+3 c. green .. 1·25 45
676. – 6 c.+4 c. grey .. 50 12
677. – 10 c.+5 c. red .. 5 5
678. – 20 c.+8 c. blue .. 1·25 45
DESIGNS: 5 c. Girl swimming. 6 c. Boy on toboggan. 10 c. Girl on swing. 20 c. Boy skating.

DESIGNS: 5 c. Hikers in cornfield. 6 c. Campers by fire. 10 c. Gathering wheat. 20 c. Yachts.

107. Terrace near Beach.

1949. Cultural and Social Relief Fund.
679. **107.** 2 c.+2 c. yell. & blue 75 12
680. – 5 c.+3 c. yell. & blue 1·25 80
681. – 6 c.+4 c. green .. 1·10 30
682. – 10 c.+5 c. yell. & blue 1·00 5
683. – 20 c.+5 c. blue .. 1·50 95

108. Queen Juliana. **109.** **110.** Hands Reaching for Sunflower.

1949.
684. **108.** 5 c. green 40 5
685. 6 c. blue 12 5
686. 10 c. yellow 12 5
687. 12 c. red 40 50
688. 15 c. olive .. .. 1·60 20
689. 20 c. blue .. .. 1·50 5
690. 25 c. brown .. .. 5·00 5
691. 30 c. violet .. .. 2·50 5
692. 35 c. blue .. .. 5·00 8
693. 40 c. purple .. .. 9·00 8
694. 45 c. orange 65 40
695. 45 c. violet .. .. 19·00 12
696. 50 c. green .. .. 3·25 8
697. 60 c. claret .. .. 4·75 8
697a. 75 c. red .. .. 25·00 45
698. **109.** 1 g. red .. .. 2·50 5
699. 2½ g. black .. .. 90·00 90
700. 5 g. brown .. .. £225 2·25
701. 10 g. violet .. .. £180 10·00

1949. Red Cross and Indonesian Relief. Fund.
702. **110.** 2 c.+3 c. yell. & grey 1·25 12
703. 6 c.+4 c. yell. & lake 90 30
704. 10 c.+5 c. yell. & bl. 2·25 12
705. 30 c.+10 c. yell. & brn. 3·75 1·25

111. Posthorns and Globe. **112.** "Autumn".

1949. U.P.U. 75th Anniv.
706. **111.** 10 c. lake 5 5
707. 20 c. blue .. .. 2·25 1·40

1949. Child Welfare Fund. Inscr. "VOOR HET KIND".
708. **112.** 2 c.+3 c. brown .. 5 5
709. – 5 c.+3 c. red .. 1·90 70
710. – 6 c.+4 c. green .. 70 15
711. – 10 c.+5 c. black .. 12 5
712. – 20 c.+7 c. blue .. 1·90 70
DESIGNS: 5 c. "Summer". 6 c. "Spring". 10 c. "Winter". 20 c. "New Year".

113. Resistance Monument. **114.** Moerdyk Bridge.

1950. Cultural and Social Relief Fund. Insc. "ZOMERZEGEL 1950".
713. **113.** 2 c.+2 c. brown .. 1·00 65
714. – 4 c.+2 c. green .. 6·00 4·50
715. – 5 c.+3 c. grey .. 3·75 1·50
716. – 6 c.+4 c. violet .. 1·90 40
717. **114.** 10 c.+5 c. slate .. 1·90 5
718. – 20 c.+5 c. blue .. 6·00 4·25
DESIGNS—VERT. 4 c. Sealing dykes. 5 c. Rotterdam skyscraper. HORIZ.: 6 c. Harvesting. 20 c. Canal boat.

1950. Surch. with bold figure **6**.
719. **100.** 6 c. on 7½ c. lake .. 75 5

115. Good Samaritan. **116.** J. Dousa.

1950. Bombed Churches Fund.
720. **115.** 2 c.+2 c. olive .. 1·00 65
721. 5 c.+3 c. brown .. 11·00 4·50
722. 6 c.+4 c. green .. 2·75 1·00
723. 10 c.+5 c. red .. 3·75 25
724. 20 c.+5 c. blue .. 13·00 11·00

1950. Leyden University. 375th Anniv. Inscr. as in T **116**.
725. **116.** 10 c. olive .. .. 1·90 5
726. – 20 c. blue .. .. 1·90 75
PORTRAIT: 20 c. Jan van Hout.

117. Baby and Bees. **118.** Bergh Castle.

1950. Child Welfare. Inscr. "VOOR HET KIND".
727. **117.** 2 c.+3 c. red 5 5
728. – 5 c.+3 c. olive .. 3·75 1·40
729. – 6 c.+4 c. green .. 1·10 45
730. – 10 c.+5 c. purple .. 5 5
731. – 20 c.+7 c. blue .. 7·50 5·00
DESIGNS: 5 c. Boy and fowl. 6 c. Girl and birds. 10 c. Boy and fish. 20 c. Girl, butterfly and frog.

1951. Cultural and Social Relief Fund. Castles.
732. – 2 c.+2 c. violet .. 1·40 50
733. **118.** 5 c.+3 c. red .. 4·75 3·00
734. – 6 c.+4 c. sepia .. 1·10 30
735. – 10 c.+5 c. green .. 1·75 5
736. – 20 c.+5 c. blue .. 4·75 3·25
DESIGNS—HORIZ. 2 c. Hillenraad. 6 c. Hernen. VERT. 10 c. Rechteren. 20 c. Moermond.

119. Girl and Windmill. **120.** Sea-gull. **121.** Jan van Riebeeck.

1951. Child Welfare.
737. **119.** 2 c.+3 c. green .. 5 5
738. – 5 c.+3 c. indigo .. 3·25 1·75
739. – 6 c.+4 c. brown .. 4·00 45
740. – 10 c.+5 c. lake .. 5 5
741. – 20 c.+7 c. blue .. 4·00 4·00
DESIGNS—Each shows boy or girl: 5 c. Crane. 6 c. Fishing nets. 10 c. Factory chimneys. 20 c. Flats.

1951. Air.
742. **120.** 15 g. grey .. .. £130 65·00
743. 25 g. blue .. .. £130 65·00

1952. Jan van Riebeeck Tercent. and Monument Fund.
744. **121.** 2 c.+3 c. violet .. 1·90 1·10
745. 6 c.+4 c. green .. 2·75 2·25
746. 10 c.+5 c. red .. 3·50 1·75
747. 20 c.+5 c. blue .. 1·90 1·10

122. Miner. **123.** Wild Rose.

1952. State Mines, Limburg. 50th Anniv.
748. **122.** 10 c. blue 95 5

1952. Cultural and Social Relief Fund. Floral designs inscr. "ZOMERZEGEL 1952".
749. **123.** 2 c.+2 c. grn. & red .. 65 45
750. – 5 c.+3 c. yell. & green 90 70
751. – 6 c.+4 c. green & red 90 30
752. – 10 c.+5 c. grn. & orge. 1·40 5
753. – 20 c.+5 c. grn. & blue 9·00 5·50
FLOWERS: 5 c. Marsh Marigold. 6 c. Tulip. 10 c. Marguerite. 20 c. Cornflower.

124. Radio Masts. **125.** Boy Feeding Goat.

1952. 1st Netherlands Postage Stamp and Telegraph Service. Cent. Inscr. "1852. PTT. 1952".
754. – 2 c. violet 25 5
755. **124.** 6 c. red 30 5
756. – 10 c. green 40 5
757. – 20 c. slate .. .. 2·75 1·10
DESIGNS: 2 c. Telegraph poles and train. 10 c. Postman and mansion, 1852. 20 c. Postman and block of flats, 1952.

1952. Int. Postage Stamp Ex., Utrecht ("ITEP"). Nos. 754/7 but colours changed.
757a. – 2 c. brown .. .. 10·00 7·00
757b. **124.** 6 c. green .. .. 10·00 7·00
757c. – 10 c. lake .. .. 10·00 7·00
757d. – 20 c. blue .. .. 10·00 7·00
Nos. 757a/d were sold only in sets at the Exhibition at face + 1 g. entrance fee.

1952. Child Welfare.
758. **125.** 2 c.+3 c. blk. & olive .. 5 5
759. – 5 c.+3 c. blk. & pink 75 50
760. – 6 c.+4 c. blk. & green 1·00 30
761. – 10 c.+5 c. blk. & orge. 5 5
762. – 20 c.+7 c. blk. & blue 5·50 3·25
DESIGNS: 5 c. Girl on donkey. 6 c. Girl and dog. 10 c. Boy and cat. 20 c. Boy and rabbit.

1953. Flood Relief Fund. Surch. **1953 10 c + 10 WATERSNOOD.**
763. **108.** 10 c.+10 c. yellow .. 15 5

126. Hyacinth. **127.** Red Cross.

1953. Cultural and Social Relief Fund.
764. **126.** 2 c.+2 c. grn. & violet 40 25
765. – 5 c.+3 c. grn. & orge. 90 75
766. – 6 c.+4 c. yell. & green 65 30
767. – 10 c.+5 c. grn. & red 1·90 5
768. – 20 c.+5 c. grn. & blue 10·00 6·00
FLOWERS: 5 c. African marigold. 6 c. Daffodil. 10 c. Anemone. 20 c. Dutch iris.

1953. Red Cross Fund. Inscr. "RODE KRUIS".
769. **127.** 2 c.+3 c. red & sepia 25 30
770. – 6 c.+4 c. red & choc. 1·75 1·50
771. – 7 c.+5 c. red & olive 50 30
772. – 10 c.+5 c. red .. 40 5
773. – 25 c.+8 c. red & blue .. 4·75 2·25
DESIGNS: 6 c. Man with lamp. 7 c. Rescue worker in flooded area. 10 c. Nurse giving blood transfusion. 25 c. Red Cross flags.

128. Queen Juliana.

129. Queen Juliana.

131. M. Nijhoff (poet).

130. Girl and Pigeon.

1953.
775. **128.** 10 c. brown 5 5
776. 12 c. turquoise .. 5 5
777. 15 c. red 8 5
777b. 18 c. greenish blue .. 20 5
778. 20 c. slate-purple .. 12 5
778b. 24 c. olive 30 8
779. 25 c. blue 12 5
780. 30 c. orange 40 5
781. 35 c. olive-brown .. 50 5
781a. 37 c. turquoise-blue .. 65 8
782. 40 c. slate 30 5
783. 45 c. red 40 5
784. 50 c. green 30 5
785. 60 c. brown 40 5
785a. 62 c. claret .. .. 3·75 1·90
785b. 70 c. blue 45 5
786. 75 c. purple 45 5
786a. 80 c. violet 50 5
786b. 85 c. green 75 5
786c. 95 c. orange-brown .. 1·40 15
787. **129.** 1 g. red .. .. 5·50 5
788. 2½ g. green .. .. 20·00 5
789. 5 g. black .. .. 3·25 15
790. 10 g. blue .. .. 19·00 50

1953. Child Welfare. Inscr. "VOOR HET KIND".
791. – 2 c.+3 c. blue & yell. 5 5
792. – 5 c.+3 c. lake & green 75 40
793. **130.** 7 c.+5 c. brn. & blue 1·75 50
794. – 10 c.+5 c. lilac & bis. 5 5
795. – 25 c.+8 c. turquoise and pink .. .. 8·50 5·50
DESIGNS: 2 c. Girl, bucket and spade. 5 c. Boy and apple. 10 c. Boy and sailing-boat. 25 c. Girl and tulip.

1954. Cultural and Social Relief Fund.
796. **141.** 2 c.+3 c. blue .. 1·50 1·25
797. – 5 c.+3 c. brown .. 40 40
798. – 7 c.+5 c. red .. 1·90 1·00
799. – 10 c.+5 c. green .. 3·75 12
800. – 25 c.+8 c. purple .. 9·00 7·50
PORTRAITS: 5 c. W Pijper (composer). 7 c. H. P. Berlage (architect). 10 c. J. H. Huizinga (historian). 25 c. Vincent van Gogh (painter).

132. St. Boniface. **133.** Boy and Model Aeroplane.

1954. Martyrdom of St. Boniface. 1200th Anniv.
801. **132.** 10 c. blue .. .. 1·10 5

1954. National Aviation Fund.
802. **133.** 2 c.+2 c. green .. 40 55
803. – 10 c.+4 c. blue .. 1·25 30
PORTRAIT: 10 c. Dr. A. Piesman (aeronautical pioneer).

134. Making Paper-chains. **135.** Queen Juliana.

1954. Child Welfare.
804. **134.** 2 c.+3 c. brown .. 5 5
805. – 5 c.+3 c. olive .. 50 40
806. – 7 c.+5 c. blue .. 65 30
807. – 10 c.+5 c. red .. 5 5
808. – 25 c.+8 c. blue .. 5·00 3·50
DESIGNS—VERT. 5 c. Girl brushing her teeth. 7 c. Boy and toy boat. 10 c. Nurse and child. HORIZ. 25 c. Invalid boy drawing in bed.

1954. Ratification of Statute for the Kingdom.
809. **135.** 10 c. red 12 5

136. Factory, Rotterdam. **137.** "Freedom".

1955. Cultural and Social Relief Fund.
810. **136.** 2 c.+3 c. bistre .. 90 55
811. – 5 c.+3 c. green .. 25 20
812. – 7 c.+5 c. lake .. 90 55
813. – 10 c.+5 c. slate-blue .. 1·25 5
814. – 25 c.+8 c. chocolate .. 8·00 5·00
DESIGNS—HORIZ. 5 c. Post Office, The Hague. 10 c. Town Hall, Hilversum. 25 c. Office Building, The Hague. VERT. 7 c. Stock Exchange, Amsterdam.

1955. Liberation. 10th Anniv.

815. **137.** 10 c. red 35 5

138. Microscope and Emblem of Cancer. **139.** "Willem van Loon" (D. Dirckz).

1955. Queen Wilhelmina Anti-Cancer Fund.

816. **138.** 2 c.+3 c. blk. & red .. 45 40
817. – 5 c.+3 c. green & red 25 25
818. – 7 c.+5 c. purple & red 55 45
819. – 10 c.+5 c. blue and red 50 5
820. – 25 c.+8 c. olive & red 4·25 3·25

1955. Child Welfare Fund.

821. **139.** 2 c.+3 c. green .. 5 5
822. – 5 c.+3 c. red 40 40
823. – 7 c.+5 c. brown .. 1·25 65
824. – 10 c.+5 c. blue .. 5 5
825. – 25 c.+8 c. lilac .. 6·50 4·25

PORTRAITS: 5 c. "Portrait of a Boy" (J. A. Backer). 7 c. "Portrait of a Girl" (unknown). 10 c. "Philips Huygens" (A. Hanneman). 25 c. "Constantin Huygens" (A. Hanneman).

140. "Farmer".

PAINTINGS: 5 c. "Young Tobias with Angel". 7 c. "Persian wearing fur cap". 10 c. "Old Blind Tobias". 25 c. Self-portrait 1639.

1956. Cultural and Social Relief Fund and Rembrandt. 350th Birth Anniv. Details from Rembrandt's paintings inscr. as in T **140**.

826. **140.** 2 c.+3 c. slate .. 1·90 1·50
827. – 5 c.+3 c. olive .. 90 75
828. – 7 c.+5 c. brown .. 2·50 1·40
829. – 10 c.+5 c. green .. 9·00 12
830. – 25 c.+8 c. red-brown 11·00 9·00

141. Yacht. **142.** Amphora. **143.** "Portrait of a Boy" (Pan Scorel).

1956. 16th Olympic Games, Melbourne.

831. **141.** 2 c.+3 c. blk. & blue 25 25
832. – 5 c.+3 c. blk. & yellow 25 25
833. **142.** 7 c.+5 c. blk. & brown 75 50
834. – 10 c.+5 c. blk. & grey 1·25 50
835. – 25 c.+8 c. blk. & green 3·75 3·50

DESIGNS—As T **141**: 5 c. Runner. 10 c. Hockey player. 25 c. Water polo player.

1956. Europa. As T **230** of Belgium.

836. 10 c. black and lake .. 65 5
837. 25 c. black and blue .. 16·00 1·50

1956. Child Welfare Fund. 16th century Dutch Paintings.

838. **143.** 2 c.+3 c. grey & cream 5 5
839. – 5 c.+3 c. ol. & cream 30 35
840. – 7 c.+5 c. mar. & cream 1·60 75
841. – 10 c.+5 c. red & cream 5 5
842. – 25 c.+8 c. bl. & cream 4·00 2·25

PAINTINGS: 5 c. "Portrait of a Boy" (1563). 7 c. "Portrait of a Girl" (1563). 10 c. "Portrait of a Girl" (1590). 25 c. "Portrait of Eechie Pieters" (1592).

144. Trawler. **145.** Admiral de Ruyter.

1957. Cultural and Social Relief Fund. Ships.

843. – 4 c.+3 c. blue .. 65 75
844. – 6 c.+4 c. lilac .. 40 40
845. – 7 c.+5 c. red .. 75 70
846. **144.** 10 c.+8 c. green .. 1·25 5
847. – 30 c.+8 c. brown .. 3·00 3·00

DESIGNS: 4 c. Motor freighter. 6 c. Coaster. 7 c. "Willem Barendsz". 30 c. S.S. "Nieuw Amsterdam".

1957. M. A. de Ruyter. 350th Birth Anniv.

848. **145.** 10 c. orange .. 25 5
849. – 30 c. blue .. 1·50 1·00

DESIGN: 30 c. De Ruyter's flagship, "De Zeven Provincien".

146. Blood Donors' Emblem. **147.** "Europa" Star.

1957. Netherlands Red Cross Society. 90th Anniv. and Red Cross Fund.

850. **146.** 4 c.+3 c. blue & red .. 50 50
851. – 6 c.+4 c. grn. & red 40 40
852. – 7 c.+5 c. red & green 50 40
853. – 10 c.+8 c. red & ochre 50 5
854. – 30 c.+8 c. red & blue 2·10 2·10

DESIGNS: 6 c. Pleasure-ship for the infirm. 7 c. Red Cross. 10 c. Red Cross emblem. 30 c. Red Cross on globe.

1957. Europa.

855. **147.** 10 c. black and blue .. 12 5
856. 30 c. green and blue .. 1·40 1·10

148. Portrait by B. J. Blommers. **149.** Walcheren Costume.

1957. Child Welfare Fund. 19th/20th Century Paintings by Dutch Masters.

857. **148.** 4 c.+4 c. red 5 5
858. – 6 c.+4 c. green .. 1·10 55
859. – 8 c.+4 c. sepia .. 1·50 1·00
860. – 12 c.+9 c. maroon .. 5 5
861. – 30 c.+9 c. blue .. 4·75 4·00

PORTRAITS: Child paintings by W. B. Tholen (6 c.); J. Sluyters (8 c.); M. Maris (12 c.); C. Kruseman (30 c.).

1958. Cultural and Social Relief Fund. Provincial Costumes.

862. **149.** 4 c.+4 c. blue .. 30 40
863. – 6 c.+4 c. ochre .. 50 50
864. – 8 c.+4 c. claret .. 1·60 90
865. – 12 c.+9 c. chestnut .. 55 12
866. – 30 c.+9 c. lilac .. 3·00 2·50

COSTUMES: 6 c. Marken. 8 c. Scheveningen. 12 c. Friesland. 30 c. Volendam.

1958. Surch.

867. **128.** 12 c. on 10 c. brown .. 65 5

1958. Europa. As T **254** of Belgium. Size 22×33 mm.

868. 12 c. blue and red .. 12 5
869. 30 c. red and blue .. 50 50

150. Girl on Stilts and Boy on Tricycle. **151.** Cranes.

1958. Child Welfare Fund. Children's Games.

870. **150.** 4 c.+4 c. blue 5 5
871. – 6 c.+4 c. red 90 55
872. – 8 c.+4 c. green .. 90 55
873. – 12 c.+9 c. vermilion .. 5 5
874. – 30 c.+9 c. indigo .. 3·25 2·50

DESIGNS: 6 c. Boy and girl on scooters. 8 c. Boys playing leap-frog. 12 c. Boys on roller-skates. 30 c. Girl skipping and boy in toy car.

1959. N.A.T.O. 10th Anniv. As T **95** of Luxembourg.

875. 12 c. blue and yellow .. 5 5
876. 30 c. blue and red .. 40 40

1959. Cultural and Social Relief Fund. Prevention of Sea Encroachment.

877. – 4 c.+4 c. blue on green 50 50
878. – 6 c.+4 c. chest. on grey 65 65
879. – 8 c.+4 c. vio. on blue 1·10 75
880. **151.** 12 c.+9 c. grn. on yell. 1·75 12
881. – 30 c.+9 c. blk. on red 3·50 3·00

DESIGNS: 4 c. Tugs and caisson. 6 c. Dredger. 8 c. Labourers making fascine mattresses. 30 c. Sand-spouter and scoop.

1959. Europa. As T **268** of Belgium but size 22×33 mm.

882. 12 c. red 25 5
883. 30 c. green .. .. 1·00 1·00

152. Silhouette of Douglas DC–8 Airliner and World Map. **153.** Child in Play-pen.

1959. K.L.M. (Royal Dutch Airlines). 40th Anniv.

884. **152** 12 c. blue and red .. 12 5
885. – 30 c. blue and green 65 60

DESIGN: 30 c. Silhouette of Douglas DC–8 airliner.

1959. Child Welfare Fund.

886. **153.** 4 c.+4 c. blue & brown 5 5
887. – 6 c.+4 c. brn. & green 95 75
888. – 8 c.+4 c. blue & red .. 1·10 80
889. – 12 c.+9 c. red, black and blue .. 5 5
890. – 30 c.+9 c. turquoise and yellow .. 1·90 1·60

DESIGNS: 6 c. Boy as "Red Indian" with bow and arrow. 8 c. Boy feeding geese. 12 c. Traffic warden escorting children. 30 c. Girl doing homework.

154. Refugee Woman. **155.** White Water-lily.

1960. World Refugee Year.

891. **154.** 12 c.+8 c. maroon .. 25 5
892. 30 c.+10 c. green .. 90 90

1960. Cultural and Social Relief Fund. Flowers.

893. – 4 c.+4 c. red, green and grey .. 30 40
894. – 6 c.+4 c. yellow, green and salmon .. 25 25
895. **155.** 8 c.+4 c. yellow, red, brn., grn. & blue .. 80 65
896. – 12 c.+8 c. red, green and buff .. 90 20
897. – 30 c.+10 c. blue, green and yellow .. 2·50 2·25

FLOWERS—VERT. 4 c. "The Princess" tulip. 6 c. Gorse. 12 c. Poppy 30 c. Blue sea-holly.

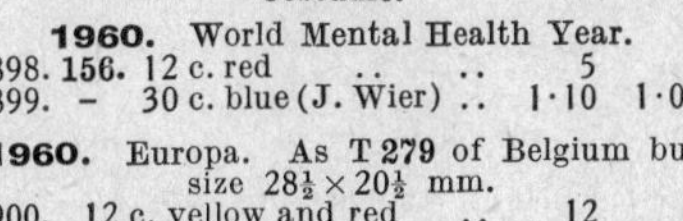

156. J. van der Kolk. **157.** Girl wearing Marken Costume. **158.** Herring Gull.

1960. World Mental Health Year.

898. **156.** 12 c. red 5 5
899. – 30 c. blue (J. Wier) .. 1·10 1·00

1960. Europa. As T **279** of Belgium but size 28½×20½ mm.

900. 12 c. yellow and red .. 12 5
901. 30 c. yellow and indigo .. 1·10 1·10

1960. Child Welfare Fund. Costumes. Multicoloured portraits.

902 **157.** 4 c.+4 c. slate .. 5 5
903. – 6 c.+4 c. ochre .. 75 50
904. – 8 c.+4 c. turquoise .. 1·75 80
905. – 12 c.+9 c. slate-violet 5 5
906. – 30 c.+9 c. grey .. 3·00 2·40

DESIGNS—Costumes of: 6 c. Volendam. 8 c. Bunschoten. 12 c. Hindeloopen. 30 c. Huizen.

1961. Cultural and Social Relief Fund. Beach and Meadow Birds.

907. **158.** 4 c.+4 c. slate & yell. 65 65
908. – 6 c.+4 c. sep. & brown 25 20
909. – 8 c.+4 c. brn. & olive 50 40
910. – 12 c.+8 c. blk. & blue 1·10 20
911. – 30 c.+10 c. blk. & green 1·90 1·75

BIRDS—HORIZ. 6 c. Oyster-catcher. 12 c. Avocet. VERT. 8 c. Curlew. 30 c. Lapwing.

159. Doves. **160.** St. Nicholas.

1961. Europa.

912. **159.** 12 c. brown .. 5 5
913. 30 c. turquoise .. 15 20

1961. Child Welfare.

914. **160.** 4 c.+4 c. red .. 5 5
915. – 6 c.+4 c. blue .. 75 50
916. – 8 c.+4 c. bistre .. 75 65
917. – 12 c.+9 c. green .. 8 5
918. – 30 c.+9 c. orange .. 1·50 1·40

DESIGNS: 6 c. Epiphany. 8 c. Palm Sunday. 12 c. Whitsunday. 30 c. Martinmas.

161. Queen Juliana and Prince Bernhard. **162.** Detail of "The Repast of the Officers of the St. Jorisdoelen" after Frans Hals.

1962. Royal Silver Wedding.

919. **161.** 12 c. red 10 5
920. 30 c. green 55 50

1962. Cultural, Health and Social Welfare Funds.

921. – 4 c.+4 c. green .. 50 45
922. – 6 c.+4 c. black .. 30 40
923. – 8 c.+4 c. maroon .. 65 65
924. – 12 c.+8 c. bistre .. 65 20
925. **162.** 30 c.+10 c. indigo .. 80 90

DESIGNS—HORIZ. 4 c. Roman cat (sculpture). VERT. 6 c. Ammonite fossil. 8 c. Pendulum clock (after principle of Huygens). 12 c. Ship's figure-head.

163. Telephone Dial. **164.** Europa "Tree".

1962. Completion of Netherlands Automatic Telephone System. Inscr. "1962".

926. **163.** 4 c. brn.-red & black 5 5
927. – 12 c. drab and black .. 12 5
928. – 30 c. ochre, bl. & blk. .. 65 75

DESIGNS—VERT. 12 c. Diagram of telephone network. HORIZ. 30 c. Arch and telephone dial.

1962. Europa.

929. **164.** 12 c. blk., yell. & bistre 5 5
930. 30 c. blk., yellow & bl. 40 45

165. "Polder" Landscape (reclaimed area). **166.** Children cooking Meal.

1962.

935. – 4 c. indigo and blue .. 8 5
937. **165.** 6 c. deep green & green 20 5
939. – 10 c. brown-purple .. 5 5

DESIGNS: 4 c. Cooling towers, State mines, Limburg. 10 c. Delta excavation works.

1962. Child Welfare.

940. **166.** 4 c.+4 c. vermilion .. 5 5
941. – 6 c.+4 c. bistre .. 30 30
942. – 8 c.+4 c. blue .. 75 50
943. – 12 c.+9 c. green .. 5 5
944. – 30 c.+9 c. lake .. 1·75 1·40

DESIGNS—Children: 6 c. Cycling. 8 c. Watering flowers. 12 c. Feeding poultry. 30 c. Making music.

167. Ears of Wheat.

169.

168. "Gallery" Windmill.

170. Wayside First Aid Post.

1963. Freedom from Hunger.
945. **167.** 12 c. ochre and blue 5 5
946. 30 c. ochre and red .. 60 65

1963. Cultural, Health and Social Welfare Funds. Windmill types.
947. **168.** 4 c.+4 c. blue 25 30
948. – 6 c.+4 c. violet .. 50 50
949. – 8 c.+4 c. green .. 65 70
950. – 12 c.+8 c. olive-black 90 20
951. – 30 c.+10 c. red .. 1·10 1·25
WINDMILLS—VERT. 6 c. North Holland polder. 12 c. "Post". 30 c. "Wip". HORIZ. 8 c. South Holland polder.

1963. Paris Postal Conference Cent.
952. **169.** 30 c. blue, green & blk. 70 75

1963. Red Cross Fund and Cent. (8 c.).
953. **170.** 4 c.+4 c. blue and red 20 20
954. – 6 c.+4 c. violet and red 12 12
955. – 8 c.+4 c. red & black 50 45
956. – 12 c.+9 c. brn. & red .. 25 5
957. – 30 c.+9 c. grn. & red .. 70 65
DESIGNS: 6 c. "Books" collection-box. 8 c. Crosses. 12 c. "International Aid" (Negro children at meal). 30 c. First aid party tending casualty.

171. "Co-operation". **172.** "Auntie Luce sat on a goose . . .".

1963. Europa.
958. **171.** 12 c. orange and brown 5 5
959. 30 c. orange and green 70 75

1963. Child Welfare.
960. **172.** 4 c.+4 c. ult. & blue .. 5 5
961. – 6 c.+4 c. green & red .. 25 25
962. – 8 c.+4 c. choc. & green 45 30
963. – 12 c.+9 c. vio. & yell. 5 5
964. – 30 c.+8 c. bl. & pink .. 80 75
DESIGNS (Nursery rhymes): 6 c. "In the Hague there lives a count . . .". 8 c. "One day I passed a puppet's fair . . .". 12 c. "Storky, storky, Billy Spoon . . .". 30 c. "Ride on a little pram . . .".

173. William, Prince of Orange, landing at Scheveningen. **174.** Knights' Hall, The Hague.

1963. Kingdom of the Netherlands. 150th Anniv. Inscr. "1813-1963".
965. **173.** 4 c. blk., bistre & blue 5 5
966. 5 c. black, red & bronze 8 5
967. – 12 c. bistre, blue & black 5 5
968. – 30 c. brown-red & black 25 25
DESIGNS: 12 c. Triumvirate: Van Hogendorp, Van Limburg, and Van der Duyn van Maasdam. 30 c. William I taking oath of allegiance.

1964. 1st States-General Meeting. 500th Anniv.
969. **174.** 12 c. black and olvie .. 8 5

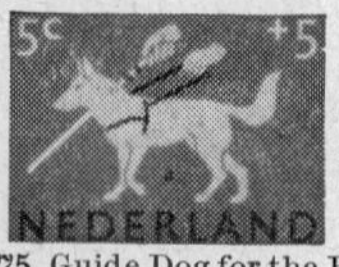

DESIGNS: 8 c. Three deer. 12 c. Three kittens. 30 c. European bison and calf.

175. Guide Dog for the Blind.

1964. Cultural, Health and Social Welfare Funds. Animals.
970. **175.** 5 c.+5 c. red, black and olive 12 12
971. – 8 c.+5 c. brown, black and red 12 12
972. – 12 c.+9 c. black, grey and bistre 15 12
973. – 30 c.+9 c. stone, grey-brn., blk. & blue .. 25 25

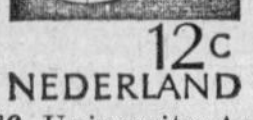

176. University Arms. **177.** Station Signal.

1964. Groningen University. 350th Anniv.
974. **176.** 12 c. slate 5 5
975. – 30 c. brown 12 12
DESIGN: 30 c. "AG" monogram.

1964. Netherlands Railways. 125th Anniv.
976. **177.** 15 c. black and green .. 10 5
977. – 40 c. black and yellow 40 50
DESIGN: 40 c. Electric train at speed.

178. Bible and Dove. **179.** Europa "Flower".

1964. Netherlands Bible Society. 150th Anniv.
978. **178.** 15 c. brown 5 5

1964. Europa.
979. **179.** 15 c. green 8 5
980. 20 c. brown 15 20

1964. "BENELUX". 20th Anniv. As Type **332** of Belgium, but smaller (33 × 22 mm.).
981. 15 c. violet and flesh .. 5 5

180. Young Artist. **181.** Queen Juliana.

1964. Child Welfare.
982. **180.** 7 c.+3 c. blue & green 12 12
983. – 10 c.+5 c. red, pink and green 30 30
984. – 15 c.+10 c. yellow, black and bistre .. 8 5
985. – 20 c.+10 c. red, sepia and magenta .. 30 30
986. – 40 c.+15 c. grn. & blue 30 35
DESIGNS: 10 c. Ballet-dancing. 15 c. Playing the flute. 20 c. Masquerading. 40 c. Toy-making.

1964. Statute for the Kingdom. 10th Anniv.
987. **181.** 15 c. green 5 5

182. "Killed in Action" (Waalwijk) and "Destroyed Town" (Rotterdam) (monuments). **183.** Medal of Knight (Class IV).

1965. "Resistance" Commem.
988. **182.** 7 c. black and red .. 5 5
989. – 15 c. black and olive .. 5 5
990. – 40 c. black and red .. 30 40
MONUMENTS: 15 c. "Docker" (Amsterdam) and "Killed in Action" (Waalwijk). 40 c. "Destroyed Town" (Rotterdam) and "Docker" (Amsterdam).

1965. Military William Order. 150th Anniv.
991. **183.** 1 g. grey 40 40

184. I.T.U. Emblem and "Lines of Communication". **185.** Veere.

1965. I.T.U. Cent.
992. **184.** 20 c. blue and drab .. 12 12
993. 40 c. brown and blue 25 25

1965. Cultural, Health and Social Welfare Funds.
994. **185.** 8 c.+6 c. blk. & yell. 10 10
995. – 10 c.+6 c. blk. & turq. 10 10
996. – 18 c.+12 c. black and salmon 12 10
997. – 20 c.+10 c. blk. & blue 12 15
998. – 40 c.+10 c. blk. & grn. 25 25
DESIGNS (Dutch towns): 10 c. Thorn. 18 c. Drodrecht. 20 c. Staveren. 40 c. Medemblik.

186. Europa "Sprig". **187.** Girl's Head.

1965. Europa.
999. **186.** 18 c. black, red & brn. 8 5
1000. 20 c. black, red & blue 12 15

1965. Child Welfare. Multicoloured.
1001. 8 c.+6 c. T **187** .. 8 5
1002. 10 c.+6 c. Ship .. 25 25
1003. 18 c.+12 c. Boy (vert.) 12 5
1004. 20 c.+10 c. Duck-pond 25 25
1005. 40 c.+10 c. Tractor .. 25 35

188. Marines of 1665 and 1965. **189.** "Help them to a safe Haven" (Queen Juliana).

1965. Marine Corps. Tercent.
1007. **188.** 18 c. blue and red .. 5 5

1966. Intergovernmental Committee for European Migration (I.C.E.M.) Fund.
1008. **189.** 18 c.+7 c. yell. & blk. 20 20
1009. 40 c.+20 c. red and blk. 25 15

190. Writing Materials. **191.** Aircraft in Flight.

1966. Cultural, Health and Social Welfare Funds. Gysbert Japicx Commem. and 200th Anniv. of Netherlands Literary Society. Multicoloured.
1011. 10 c.+5 c. Type **190** .. 10 10
1012. 12 c.+8 c. Part of MS, Japicx's poem "Wobbelke" 15 12
1013. 20 c.+10 c. Part of miniature, "Knight Walewein" 20 15
1014. 25 c.+10 c. Initial "D" and part of MS, novel, "Ferguut" .. 25 35
1015. 40 c.+10 c. 16th-cent. printery (woodcut) 30 30

1966. Air (Special Flights).
1016. **191.** 25 c. multicoloured 15 20

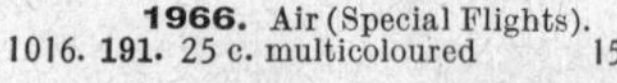

192. Europa "Ship". **193.** Infant.

1966. Europa.
1017. **192.** 20 c. olive and yellow 8 5
1018. 40 c. blue and indigo 20 15

1966. Child Welfare.
1019. **193.** 10 c.+5 c. red & blue 8 5
1020. – 12 c.+8 c. apple & red 8 5
1021. – 20 c.+10 c. bl. & red 10 5
1022. – 25 c.+10 c. pur. & bl. 30 40
1023. – 40 c.+20 c. red & grn. 30 35
DESIGNS: 12 c. Young girl. 20 c. Boy in water. 25 c. Girl with moped. 40 c. Young man with horse.

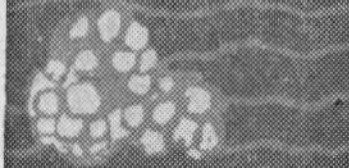

194. Assembly Hall. **195.** Whelk Eggs.

1967. Delft Technological University. 125th Anniv.
1025. **194.** 20 c. sepia and yellow 10 5

1967. Cultural, Health and Social Welfare Funds. Marine Fauna.
1026. **195.** 12 c.+8 c. drab and green 12 12
1027. – 15 c.+10 c. blue & indigo 15 20
1028. – 20 c.+10 c. black, slate, red & grey .. 15 10
1029. – 25 c.+10 c. maroon, bistre and brown .. 25 30
1030. – 45 c.+20 c. orange, red, bistre & drab 30 30
DESIGNS: 15 c. Whelk. 20 c. Mussel. 25 c. Jellyfish. 45 c. Crab.

196. Cogwheels. **197.** Netherlands 5 c. Stamp of 1852.

1967. Europa.
1031. **196.** 20 c. blue 10 5
1032. 45 c. maroon .. 25 25

1967. "Amphilex 67" Stamp Exn., Amsterdam.
1035. **197.** 20 c. blue and black .. 1·60 1·40
1036. – 25 c. red and black .. 1·60 1·40
1037. – 75 c. green and black 1·60 1·40
DESIGNS: 25 c. Netherlands 10 c. stamp of 1864. 75 c. Netherlands 20 c. stamp of 1867.
Nos. 1035/7 were sold at the Exhibition and at post offices at 3 g. 70, which included entrance fee to the Exhibition.

198. "1867-1967". **199.** "Porcupine Lullaby".

1967. Dutch Red Cross. Cent.
1038. 12 c.+8 c. blue and red 10 8
1039. 15 c.+10 c. red .. 20 20
1040. 20 c.+10 c. olive & red .. 15 8
1041. 25 c.+10 c. grn. & red .. 20 25
1042. 45 c.+20 c. grey & red .. 35 40
DESIGNS: 12 c. T **198.** 15 c. Red crosses. 20 c. "NRK" ("Nederlandsche Rood Kruis") in the form of a cross. 25 c. Maltese cross and "red" crosses. 45 c. "100" in the form of a cross.

1967. Child Welfare. Multicoloured.
1043. 12 c.+8 c. Type **199** .. 8 5
1044. 15 c.+10 c. "The Whistling Kettle" 10 5
1045. 20 c.+10 c. "Dikkertje Dap" (giraffe) .. 10 5
1046. 25 c.+10 c. "The Flower-seller" 40 45
1047. 45 c.+20 c. "Pippeloentje" (bear) 45 50

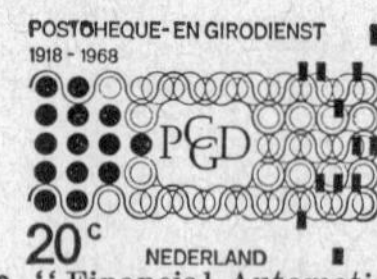

200. "Financial Automation".

1968. Netherlands Postal Cheque and Clearing Service. 50th Anniv.
1049. **200.** 20 c. red, black & yell. 12 5

201. St. Servatius' Bridge, Maastricht. **202.** Europa "Key".

1968. Cultural, Health and Social Welfare Funds. Dutch Bridges.
1050. **201.** 12 c.+8 c. green .. 30 40
1051. – 15 c.+10 c. brown .. 50 55
1052. – 20 c.+10 c. red .. 40 12
1053. – 25 c.+10 c. indigo .. 40 40
1054. – 45 c.+20 c. blue .. 70 70
BRIDGES: 15 c. Magere ("Narrow"), Amsterdam. 20 c. Railway, Culemborg. 25 c. Van Brienenoord, Rotterdam. 45 c. Oosterschelde, Zeeland.

1968. Europa.
1055. 202. 20 c. blue 15 5
1056. 45 c red 45 45

203. "Wilhelmus van Nassouwe". 204. "Wright" Biplane and Cessna Light Aircraft.

1968. Dutch National Anthem, "Wilhelmus". 400th Anniv.
1057. 203. 20 c. red, blue, orge. and grey 20 5

1968. Dutch Aviation Anniversaries.
1058. 12 c. black, red & mauve 12 5
1059. 20 c. black, emerald & grn. 12 5
1060. 45 c. black, blue & green 55 65
DESIGNS AND EVENTS: 12 c. T 204 (Royal Netherlands Aeronautical Assn., 60th anniv. (1967)); 20 c. Fokker "F-2" and "F-29" "Fellowship" aircraft (Royal Netherlands Aircraft Factories "Fokker"), 50th anniv. (1969); 45 c. De Havilland "DH-9" and Douglas "DC-9" aircraft (Royal Dutch Airlines "KLM", 50th anniv. (1969)).

205. "Goblin".

1968. Child Welfare.
1061. 205. 12 c.+8 c. pink, blk. and green .. 10 5
1062. – 15 c.+10 c. pink, blue and black .. 15 5
1063. – 20 c.+10 c. blue, green and black 15 5
1064. – 25 c.+10 c. red, yellow and black .. 1·00 1·10
1065. – 45 c.+20 c. yellow, orange & black.. 1·00 1·10
DESIGNS: 15 c. "Giant"; 20 c. "Witch"; 25 c. "Dragon"; 45 c. "Sorcerer".

206. "I A O" (Internationale Arbeidsorganisatie).

1969. Int. Labour Organisation. 50th Anniv.
1067. 206. 25 c. vermilion & black 20 5
1068. 45 c. ultramarine & blk. 50 50

207. Queen Juliana. 208. Villa, Huis ter Heide (1915).

1969. (a) Type 207.
1069. 207. 25 c. red 10 5
1069b. 30 c. brown 12 5
1070. 35 c. blue 12 5
1071. 40 c. red 15 5
1072. 45 c. blue 15 5
1073. 50 c. purple 20 5
1073a. 55 c. brown 20 5
1074. 60 c. blue 25 5
1075. 70 c. brown 25 5
1076. 75 c. green 25 5
1077. 80 c. red 30 5
1077a. 90 c. grey 35 5
(b) Size 22 × 33 mm.
1078. – 1 g. green 40 5
1079. – 1 g. 25 lake 45 5
1080. – 1 g. 50 brown .. 55 5
1081. 2 g. mauve 75 20
1082. – 2 g. 50 blue .. 95 5
1083. – 5 g. grey .. .. 1·90 30
1084. – 10 g. ultramarine .. 3·75 2·10
DESIGNS: 1 g., 1 g. 25, 1 g. 50, 2 g. 50, 5 g. and 10 g., similar to Type 207.

1969. Cultural, Health and Social Welfare Funds. 20th-century Dutch Architecture.
1085. 208. 12 c.+8 c. blk. & brn. 50 55
1086. – 15 c.+10 c. black, red and blue .. 50 55
1087. – 20 c.+10 c. blk. & vio. 50 55
1088. – 25 c.+10 c. brn. & grn. 70 20
1089. – 45 c.+20 c. black, blue and yellow .. 95 1·00
DESIGNS: 15 c. Private House, Utrecht (1924). 20 c. Open-Air School, Amsterdam (1930). 25 c. Orphanage, Amsterdam (1960). 45 c. Congress Building, The Hague (1969).

209. Colonnade. 210. Stylised "Crab" (of Cancer).

1969. Europa.
1090. 209. 25 c. blue 50 5
1091. 45 c. red 95 70

1969. Queen Wilhelmina Cancer Fund. 20th Anniv.
1092. 210. 12 c.+8 c. violet .. 70 90
1093. 25 c.+10 c. orange .. 1·00 25
1094. 45 c.+20 c. green .. 1·10 1·40

1969. "BENELUX" Customs Union. 25th Anniv. As T 406 of Belgium.
1095. 25 c. red, blue, yell. & blk. 20 5

211. Erasmus. 212. Child with Violin.

1969. Desiderius Erasmus. 500th Birth Anniv.
1096. 211. 25 c. maroon & green 20 5

1969. Child Welfare.
1097. – 12 c.+8 c. black, yellow and blue 10 5
1098. 212. 15 c.+10 c. black and red .. 12 5
1099. – 20 c.+10 c. black, yellow and red.. 1·40 1·40
1100. – 25 c.+10 c. black, red and yellow.. 15 5
1101. – 45 c.+20 c. black, red and green .. 1·40 1·40
DESIGNS—VERT. 12 c. Child with flute. 20 c. Child with drum. HORIZ. 25 c. Three choristers. 45 c. Two dancers.

213. Queen Juliana and "Sunlit Road". 214. Prof. E. M. Meijers (author of Burgerlijk Wetboek).

1969. Statute for the Kingdom. 25th Anniv.
1103. 213. 25 c. multicoloured.. 20 5

1970. Introduction of New Netherlands Civil Code ("Burgerlijk Wetboek").
1104. 214. 25 c. ult., green & blue 20 5

215. Netherlands Pavilion. 216. "Circle to Square".

1970. Expo 70.
1105. 215. 25 c. grey, blue & red 20 5

1970. Cultural, Health and Social Welfare Funds.
1106. 216. 12 c.+8 c. blk. on yell. 55 65
1107. – 15 c.+10 c. black on silver .. 65 65
1108. – 20 c.+10 c. black .. 65 65
1109. – 25 c.+10 c. blk. on bl. 65 40
1110. – 45 c.+20 c. silver-grey 70 75
DESIGNS: 15 c. Parallel planes in cube. 20 c. Overlapping scales. 25 c. Concentric circles in transition. 45 c. Spirals.

17. "V" Symbol. 218. "Flaming Sun".

1970. Liberation. 25th Anniv.
1111. 217. 12 c. red, blue & brown 8 5

1970. Europa.
1112. 218. 25 c. red 12 5
1113. 45 c. blue 55 40

219. "Work and Co-operation". 220. Globe on Plinth.

1970. Inter-Parliamentary Union Conf.
1114. 219. 25 c. green, blk. & grey 25 5

1970. United Nations. 25th Anniv.
1115. 220. 45 c. blk., violet and bl. 45 40

221. Human Heart. 222. Toy Block.

1970. Netherlands Heart Foundation.
1116. 221. 12 c.+8 c. red, black and yellow 45 50
1117. 25 c.+10 c. red, black and mauve 45 30
1118. 45 c.+20 c. red, black & emerald 45 50

1970. Child Welfare. "The Child and the Cube".
1119. 222. 12 c.+8 c. blue, violet and green.. 12 5
1120. – 15 c.+10 c. green, blue and yellow.. 75 75
1121. 222. 20 c.+10 c. magenta, red and violet .. 90 90
1122. – 25 c.+10 c. red, yellow & magenta 25 5
1123. 222. 45 c.+20 c. grey, cream and black 1·10 1·10
DESIGN: 15 c., 25 c. As T 222, but showing underside of block.
The first colours given above are those of the tops or undersides, which are the same as the inscription colours.

223. "Fourteenth Census 1971".

1971. 14th Netherlands Census.
1125. 223. 15 c. purple 8 5

224. "50 years of Adult University Education". 225. Europa Chain.

1971. Cultural, Health and Social Welfare Funds. Other designs show 15th-century wooden statues by unknown artists.
1126. 224. 15 c. + 10 c. blk., red & yellow .. 65 65
1127. – 20 c. + 10 c. blk. & green on green 65 65
1128. – 25 c. + 10 c. blk. & orange on orge. 65 40
1129. – 30 c. + 15 c. blk. and blue on blue 75 80
1130. – 45 c. + 20 c. blk. & red on pink.. 75 80
STATUES: 20 c. "Apostle Paul". 25 c. "Joachim and Ann". 30 c. "John the Baptist and Scribes". 45 c. "Ann, Mary and Christ-Child" (detail).

1971. Europa.
1131. 225. 25 c. yell., red & blk. 12 5
1132. 45 c. yell., blue & blk. 50 30

226. Carnation Symbol of Prince Bernhard Fund. 227. "The Good Earth".

1971. Prince Bernhard's 60th Birthday.
1133. 226. 15 c. yell., grey & blk. 8 5
1134. – 20 c. multicoloured.. 12 12
1135. – 25 c. multicoloured.. 20 5
1136. – 45 c.+20 c. blk., pur. and yellow .. 1·10 1·10
DESIGNS—HORIZ. 20 c. Panda symbol of World Wildlife Fund. VERT. 25 c. Prince Bernhard. 45 c. Statue, Borbudur Temple, Indonesia.

1971. Child Welfare.
1137. 227. 15 c.+10 c. red, purple and black .. 8 5
1138. – 20 c.+10 c. mult. .. 25 25
1139. – 25 c.+10 c. mult. .. 20 8
1140. – 30 c.+15 c. bl., violet and black 75 40
1141. – 45 c.+20 c. blue, green and black .. 85 1·10
DESIGNS—VERT. 20 c. Butterfly. 45 c. Reflecting water. HORIZ. 25 c. Sun waving. 30 c. Moon winking.

228. Delta Map. 229. "Fruit".

1972. Delta Plan.
1143. 228. 20 c. multicoloured.. 12 5

1972. Cultural, Health and Social Welfare Funds. "Floriade Flower Show" (20 c., 25 c.) and "Holland Arts Festival" (30 c., 45 c.). Multicoloured.
1144. 20 c.+10 c. Type 229 .. 50 50
1145. 25 c.+10 c. "Flower" 55 55
1146. 30 c.+15 c. "Sunlitelandscape" 50 30
1147. 45 c.+25 c. "Music" .. 55 55

230. "Communications". 231. "There is more to be done in the world than ever before" (Thorbeche).

1972. Europa.
1148. 230. 30 c. brown and blue 25 5
1149. 45 c. brown and orge. 65 50

1972. J. R. Thorbecke (statesman). Death Cent.
1150. 231. 30 c. black and blue.. 20 5

232. Netherlands Flag. 233. Hurdling.

1972. Netherlands Flag. 400th Anniv.
1151. 232. 20 c. multicoloured .. 25 5
1152. 25 c. multicoloured.. 20 5

1972. Olympic Games, Munich. Mult.
1153. 20 c. Type 233 .. .. 10 8
1154. 30 c. Diving 15 5
1155. 45 c. Cycling 40 40

234. Red Cross.

235. Prince Willem-Alexander.

1972. Netherlands Red Cross.

1156. 234. 5 c. red 5 5
1157. – 20 c.+10 c. red & pink 30 35
1158. – 25 c.+10 c. red & orge. 30 40
1159. – 30 c.+15 c. red & blk. 40 20
1160. – 45 c.+25 c. red & blue 45 45

DESIGNS: 20 c. Accident services. 25 c. Blood transfusion. 30 c. Refugee relief. 45 c. Child care.

1972. Child Welfare. Multicoloured.

1161. 25 c.+15 c. Type 235 .. 15 5
1162. 30 c.+10 c. Prince Johan Friso 50 65
1163. 35 c.+15 c. Prince Constantijn 50 5
1164. 50 c.+20 c. Three Princes 60 75

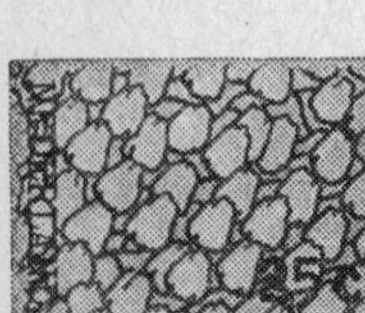

236. Tulips in Bloom.

237. " De Zeven Provincien ".

1973. Tulip Exports.

1166. 236. 25 c. pink, grn. & blk. 12 5

1973. Cultural, Health and Social Welfare Funds. Dutch Ships. Multicoloured.

1167. 25 c.+15 c. Type 237 .. 50 50
1168. 30 c.+10 c. S.S. "W.A. Scholten" 55 55
1169. 35 c.+15 c. S.S. "Veendam" 50 30
1170. 50 c.+20 c. Fishing boat (from etching by R. Nooms) 55 65

238. Europa " Posthorn ".

239. Hockey-players.

1973. Europa.

1171. 238. 35 c. blue 20 5
1172. 50 c. purple .. 40 30

1973. Events and Anniversaries. Mult.

1173. 25 c. Type 239 .. .. 15 5
1174. 30 c. Gymnastics 25 20
1175. 35 c. Dish aerial (horiz.) .. 20 8
1176. 50 c. Rainbow (horiz.) .. 30 20

EVENTS: 25 c. Royal Netherlands Hockey Assn. 75th Anniv. 30 c. World Gymnastics Championships, Rotterdam. 35 c. Satellite ground Station, Burum, Inaug. 50 c. " 100 years of Meteorological Co-operation ".

240. Queen Juliana.

241. "Co-operation".

1973. Queen Juliana's Accession. Silver Jubilee.

1177. 240. 40 c. multicoloured .. 20 5

1973. Int. Development Co-operation.

1178. 241. 40 c. multicoloured .. 20 5

242. "Chess".

243. Eagle in Flight.

1973. Child Welfare.

1179. 242. 25 c.+15 c. red, yellow and black 25 12
1180. – 30 c.+10 c. green, mauve and black .. 45 50
1181. – 40 c.+20 c. yellow, green and black .. 45 5
1182. – 50 c.+20 c. blue, yellow and black .. 65 80

DESIGNS: 30 c. " Noughts and crosses ". 40 c. " Maze ". 50 c. " Dominoes ".

1974. " Nature and Environment ". Mult.

1184. 25 c. Type 243 .. .. 20 5
1185. 25 c. Tree 20 5
1186. 25 c. Fisherman and frog 20 5

244. Bandsmen (World Band Contest, Kerkrade).

245. Football on Pitch.

1974. Cultural, Health and Social Welfare Funds.

1187. 244. 25 c.+15 c. mult. .. 30 30
1188. – 30 c.+10 c. mult. .. 30 30
1189. – 40 c.+20 c. brn., blk. and red 40 25
1190. – 50 c.+20 c. purple, black and red .. 40 45

DESIGNS: 30 c. Dancers and traffic-lights ("Modern Ballet"). 40 c. Herman Heijermans. 50 c. "Kniertje" (character from Heijermans' play "Op hoop van zegan"). The 40 c. and 50 c. commemorate the 50th Death Anniv. of the playwright.

1974. Sporting Events.

1191. 245. 25 c. multicoloured .. 15 5
1192. – 40 c. yell., red & mve. 25 5

DESIGNS AND EVENTS—HORIZ. 25 c. (World Cup Football Championships, West Germany). VERT. 40 c. Hand holding tennis ball (Royal Dutch Lawn Tennis Assn. 75th anniv.).

246. Dutch Cattle.

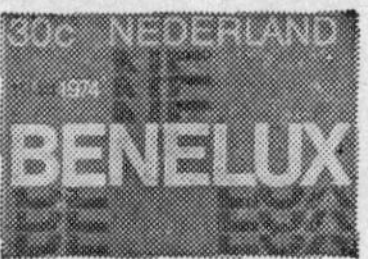

247. "BENELUX".

1974. Anniversaries. Multicoloured.

1193. 25 c. Type 246 .. .. 55 5
1194. 25 c. "Cancer the Crab" 12 5
1195. 40 c. Lifeboat at sea (seen through binoculars) .. 20 5

EVENTS AND ANNIVERSARIES: No. 1193, Netherlands Cattle Herdbook Society. Cent. No. 1194, Queen Wilhelmina Fund (to combat cancer). 25th anniv. No. 1195, "150 Years of Lifesaving Service".

1974. "International" Issue.

1196. 247. 30 c. dark grn., grn. & blue 15 5
1197. – 45c. bl., yell. & blk.. 20 5
1198. – 45 c. bl., silver & dark blue 20 5

DESIGNS—VERT. No. 1197, "Ring" of stars (member countries of Council of Europe. 25th anniv.). No. 1198, NATO emblem (25th anniv.).

248. "Letters and Hands ".

249. Boy with Hoop.

1974. Universal Postal Union. Centenary.

1199. 248. 60 c. multicoloured .. 35 20

1974. "50 Years of Child Welfare Stamps". Turn-of-the-century photographs.

1200. 249. 30 c.+15 c. brn. & blk. 20 12
1201. – 35 c.+20 c. brown .. 30 40
1202. – 45 c.+20 c. black .. 40 12
1203. – 60 c.+20 c. bl. and blk. 45 50

DESIGNS: 35 c. Young girl and baby. 45 c. Two little girls. 60 c. Young girl sitting on balustrade.

250. "Amsterdammers" and Map of City Centre.

251. St. Hubertus (hunting lodge, "De Hoge Veluwe" National Park).

1975. Dutch Anniversaries. Multicoloured.

1205. 30 c. Type 250 .. .. 15 5
1206. 30 c. Synagogue and map 15 5
1207. 35 c. Type 250 .. .. 15 5
1208. 45 c. "Window" in human brain 20 5

ANNIVERSARIES: Nos. 1205, 1207, Amsterdam (700th anniv.). No. 1206, Portuguese-Israelite Synagogue, Amsterdam (300th anniv.). No. 1208, Leiden University and university education (400th anniv.).

1975. Cultural, Health and Social Welfare Funds. Protected Monuments. Multicoloured.

1209. 35 c.+20 c. Type 251 .. 30 25
1210. 40 c.+15 c. Beguinage, Amsterdam (vert.) .. 30 30
1211. 50 c.+20 c. "Kuiperspoort" (Cooper's gate), Middelburg (vert.) 35 35
1212. 60 c.+20 c. Village of Orvelte, Drenthe .. 45 45

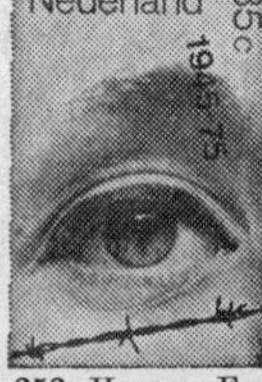

252. Human Eye and Barbed Wire.

253. Company Emblem and "Stad Middelburg".

1975. Liberation. 30th Anniv.

1213. 252. 35 c. black and red .. 20 5

1975. Zeeland Shipping Company. Cent.

1214. 253. 35 c. multicoloured .. 20 5

254. Dr. Schweitzer crossing Lambarene River.

1975. Dr. Schweitzer. Birth Cent.

1215. 254. 50 c. multicoloured .. 25 5

255. Man and Woman on " Playing-card " (" Equality, Education and Peace ").

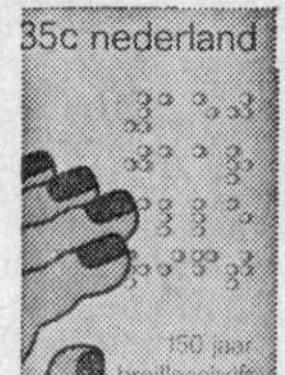

256. " Reading Braille ".

1975. International Events. Multicoloured.

1216. 35 c. Type 255 (Int. Women's Year) .. 20 5
1217. 50 c. Metric scale (Metre Convention centenary) 25 5

1975. Invention of Braille. 150th Anniv.

1218. 256. 35 c. multicoloured .. 20 5

257. Coin " Rubbings ".

1975. Savings Campaign.

1219. 257. 50 c. grey, grn. & blue 25 5

258. " Four Orphans " (" Orphanage, Medemblik ").

1975. Child Welfare. Historic Ornamental Stones. Multicoloured.

1220. 35 c.+15 c. Type 258 .. 20 12
1221. 40 c.+15 c. " Milkmaid " (Alkmaar, formerly Kooltuin) 40 40
1222. 50 c.+25 c. "Four Sons riding on Beyaert" (Amsterdam) 30 12
1223. 60 c.+25 c. "Life at the Orphanage" (Molenstraat, Gorinchem) 45 45

259. Lottery ticket of 18th century.

260.

1976. National Lottery. 250th Anniversary.

1224. 259. 35 c. multicoloured .. 12 5

1976.

1225. 260. 5 c. grey 5 5
1226. 10 c. blue 5 5
1227. 25 c. violet 10 5
1228. 40 c. brown 15 5
1229. 45 c. blue 20 5

261. Hedgehog.

1976. Summer Charity. Nature Protection (1230, 1233) and Anniversaries. Multicoloured.

1230. 40 c.+20 c. Type 261 .. 30 25
1231. 45 c.+20 c. Open book (vert.) 30 25
1232. 55 c.+20 c. People and organization initials .. 35 35
1233. 75 c.+25 c. Frog and spawn (vert.) 45 45

ANNIVERSARIES: No. 1231, Primary education (175th anniv.) and Agricultural education (centenary). No. 1232, Social Security Bank and legislation (75th anniv.).

262. Admiral de Ruyter (Flushing statue).

1976. Admiral Michiel de Ruyter. 300th Death Anniv.

1234. 262. 55 c. multicoloured .. 20 5

263. Groen van Prinsterer.

1976. G. Groen van Prinsterer (statesman). Death Cent.

1235. 263. 55 c. multicoloured .. 20 5

264. Detail of Ancient Calendar.

1976. American Revolution. Bicent.

1236. 264. 75 c. multicoloured .. 30 5

265. Marchers.

1976. Sport and Recreation Anniversaries. Multicoloured.
1237. 40 c. Type **265** .. 20 5
1238. 55 c. Runners "photo-finish" .. 20 5
ANNIVERSARIES: 40 c. 60th Nijmegen Long-Distance March. 55 c. Royal Dutch Athletics Society (75th anniv.).

266. The Art of Printing. **267.** Fishing Boat over Re-claimed Land.

1976. Anniversaries.
1239. **266.** 45 c. red and blue .. 20 5
1240. – 55 c.+25 c. multicoloured 35 35
DESIGNS AND EVENTS: 45 c. Type **266**. (75th Anniv. of Netherlands Printer's organization) 55 c. Rheumatic patient "Within Care" (50th Anniv. of Dutch Anti-Rheumatism Association).

1976. Zuiderzee Project—Reclamation and Urbanization. Multicoloured.
1241. 40 c. Type **267** 20 5
1242. 75 c. Wild duck over dyke 30 5

268. Wilhemina. 5 c. stamp of 1891. **269.** Football.

1976. "Amphilex '77" International Stamp Exhibition, Amsterdam (1977). Stamp Portraits of Queen Wilhemina. Mult.
1243. 55 c.+55 c. Type **268** .. 40 40
1244. 55 c.+55 c. 4½ c. stamp of 1899 .. .. .. 40 40
1245. 55 c.+55 c. 25 c. stamp of 1924 .. .. .. 40 40
1246. 75 c.+75 c. 15 c. stamp of 1940 .. .. .. 60 60
1247. 75 c.+75 c. 25 c. stamp of 1947 .. .. .. 60 60

1976. Child Welfare. Multicoloured.
1248. 40 c.+20 c. Type **269** .. 30 30
1249. 45 c.+20 c. "Boat" .. 30 30
1250. 55 c.+20 c. "Elephant" 35 35
1251. 75 c.+25 c. "Caravan" 45 45

MARINE INSURANCE STAMPS

M 1. Floating Safe.

ILLUSTRATIONS British Commonwealth and all overprints and surcharges are FULL SIZE. Foreign Countries have been reduced to ¾-LINEAR.

1921.
M 238. **M 1.** 15 c. green .. 3·75 32·00
M 239. 60 c. red .. .. 3·75 38·00
M 240. 75 c. brown .. 5·00 45·00
M 241. 1 g. 50 blue .. 90·00 £250
M 242. 2 g. 25 brown .. £190 £350
M 243. 4½ g. black .. £190 £425
M 244. 7½ g. red £225 £650

OFFICIAL STAMPS

1913. Stamps of 1898 optd. **ARMENWET.**
O 214. **10.** 1 c. red .. .. 3·00 1·25
O 215. 1½ c. blue .. .. 90 1·00
O 216. 2 c. brown .. .. 5·00 4·50
O 217. 2½ c. green .. .. 13·00 7·50
O 218. **11.** 3 c. green .. .. 3·00 50
O 219. 5 c. red .. .. 3·25 3·00
O 220. 10 c. grey .. .. 29·00 26·00

POSTAGE DUE STAMPS

TE BETALEN 10 PORT — TE BETALEN 10 CENT PORT
D 1. D 2.

1870.
D 76. **D 1.** 5 c. brn. on yellow .. 28·00 6·50
D 77. 10 c. purple on blue .. 70·00 8·00
For same stamps in other colours, see Netherlands Indies, Nos. D 1/5.

1881.
D 172. **D 2.** 1 c. black & pale blue 5·00 6·50
D 173. 1½ c. black & pl. blue 6·50 7·50
D 174. 2½ c. black & pl. blue 15·00 1·40
D 175. 5 c. black & pl. blue 45·00 1·25
D 176. 10 c. black & pl. blue 50·00 1·25
D 177. 12½ c. black & pl. blue 40·00 10·00
D 178. 15 c. black & pl. blue 45·00 1·25
D 179. 20 c. black & pl. blue 11·00 1·25
D 180. 25 c. black & pl. blue £110 1·10
D 181. 1 g. red and pale blue 40·00 9·50

1895.
D 208. **D 2.** ½ c. black & deep bl. 5 8
D 182. 1 c. black & deep bl. 80 8
D 183. 1½ c. blk. & deep bl. 25 10
D 184. 2½ c. blk. & deep blue 90 10
D 209. 3 c. black & deep bl. 80 55
D 210. 4 c. black & deep bl. 90 1·00
D 185. 5 c. black & deep bl. 6·50 10
D 211. 6½ c. blk. & deep blue 19·00 20·00
D 212. 7½ c. blk. & deep blue 55 30
D 186. 10 c. blk. & deep blue 16·00 20
D 187. 12½ c. blk. & dp. blue 13·00 50
D 188. 15 c. blk. & deep blue 16·00 40
D 189. 20 c. blk. & deep blue 9·00 4·50
D 190. 25 c. blk. & deep blue 19·00 30

1906. Surch.
D 213. **D 2.** 3 c. on 1 g. red and pale blue .. .. 15·00 18·00
D 215. 4 c. on 6½ c. black & deep blue .. 3·25 3·25
D 216. 6½ c. on 20 c. black and deep blue .. 2·50 2·50
D 214. 50 c. on 1 g. red and pale blue .. .. 65·00 55·00

1907. De Ruyter Commem. stamps surch. **PORTZEGEL** and value.
D 217. **14.** ½ c. on 1 c. claret .. 75 90
D 218. 1 c. on 1 c. claret .. 20 20
D 219. 1½ c. on 1 c. claret 25 25
D 220. 2½ c. on 1 c. claret 65 65
D 221. 5 c. on 2½ c. red .. 75 25
D 222. 6½ c. on 2½ c. red .. 1·75 1·75
D 223. 7½ c. on ½ c. blue .. 95 65
D 224. 10 c. on ½ c. blue .. 90 40
D 225. 12½ c. on ½ c. blue .. 2·50 2·50
D 226. 15 c. on 2½ c. red .. 3·25 2·00
D 227. 25 c. on ½ c. blue .. 4·50 4·00
D 228. 50 c. on ½ c. blue .. 23·00 20·00
D 229. 1 g. on ½ c. blue .. 32·00 29·00

1912. Re-issue of Type D 2 in one colour.
D 230. **D 2.** ½ c. blue 5 5
D 231. 1 c. blue 5 5
D 232. 1½ c. blue 50 65
D 233. 2½ c. blue 5 5
D 234. 3 c. blue 20 20
D 235. 4 c. blue 5 5
D 236. 4½ c. blue .. .. 2·00 2·10
D 237. 5 c. blue 5 5
D 238. 5½ c. blue .. .. 2·00 2·10
D 239. 7 c. blue .. .. 1·00 1·10
D 240. 7½ c. blue 90 50
D 241. 10 c. blue 5 5
D 242. 12½ c. blue 8 5
D 243. 15 c. blue 8 5
D 244. 20 c. blue 10 5
D 245. 25 c. blue .. .. 40·00 40
D 246. 50 c. blue 25 8

D 3. D 4.

1921.
D 442. **D 3.** 3 c. blue 5 5
D 445. 6 c. blue 5 5
D 446. 7 c. blue 8 10
D 447. 7½ c. blue 12 15
D 448. 8 c. blue 8 10
D 449. 9 c. blue 12 15
D 247. 11 c. blue .. .. 5·00 1·50
D 451. 12 c. blue 8 8
D 455. 25 c. blue 10 5
D 456. 30 c. blue 15 8
D 458. 1 g. red 45 8

1923. Surch. in white figures in black circle.
D 272. **D 2.** 1 c. on 3 c. blue .. 12 25
D 273. 2½ c. on 7 c. blue .. 12 15
D 274. 25 c. on 1½ c. blue .. 4·50 20
D 275. 25 c. on 7½ c. blue .. 4·50 12

1924. Stamps of 1898 surch. **TE BETALEN PORT** and value in white figures in black circle.
D 295. **11.** 4 c. on 3 c. green .. 50 70
D 296. **10.** 5 c. on 1 c. red .. 12 5
D 297. 10 c. on 1½ c. blue .. 40 8
D 298. **11.** 12½ c. on 5 c. red .. 40 10

1947.
D 656. **D 4.** 1 c. blue 5 5
D 657. 3 c. blue 5 5
D 658. 4 c. blue .. .. 7·50 45
D 659. 5 c. blue 5 5
D 660. 6 c. blue 8 5
D 661. 7 c. blue 8 5
D 662. 8 c. blue 8 5
D 663. 10 c. blue 8 5
D 664. 11 c. blue 12 10
D 665. 12 c. blue 15 10
D 666. 14 c. blue 20 25
D 667. 15 c. blue 20 5
D 668. 16 c. blue 25 25
D 669. 20 c. blue 20 5
D 670. 24 c. blue 30 30
D 671. 25 c. blue 20 5
D 672. 26 c. blue 30 30
D 673. 30 c. blue 25 5
D 674. 35 c. blue 30 5
D 675. 40 c. blue 40 5
D 676. 50 c. blue 45 5
D 677. 60 c. blue 50 15
D 678. 85 c. blue .. .. 9·00 25
D 679. 90 c. blue .. .. 1·25 20
D 680. 95 c. blue .. .. 1·25 20
D 681. 1 g. red .. .. 1·00 5
D 682. 1 g. 75 red .. .. 2·25 10
For stamps as Types **D 4**, but in violet, see under Surinam.

COURT OF INTERNATIONAL JUSTICE

Stamps specially issued for use by the Headquarters of the Court of International Justice. They were not sold to the public in unused condition.

Optd. **COUR PERMANENTE DE JUSTICE INTERNATIONALE.**

1934.
J 1. **25.** 1½ c. mauve .. .. — 40
J 2. 2½ c. green .. .. — 40
J 3. **26.** 7½ c. red .. .. — 65
J 4. **51.** 12½ c. blue .. .. — 11·00
J 7. **26.** 12½ c. blue .. .. — 4·25
J 5. 15 c. yellow .. .. — 75
J 8. 30 c. purple .. .. — 1·25

1940.
J 9. **78.** 7½ c. red .. .. 9·50 3·75
J 10. 12½ c. blue .. .. 9·50 3·75
J 11. 15 c. blue .. .. 9·50 3·75
J 12. 30 c. ochre .. .. 9·50 3·75

1947. Optd. **COUR INTERNATIONALE DE JUSTICE.**
J 13. **78.** 7½ c. red .. .. — 25
J 14. 10 c. purple .. .. — 25
J 15. 12½ c. blue .. .. — 25
J 16. 20 c. violet .. .. — 25
J 17. 25 c. red .. .. — 25

J 1. J 2. Peace Palace, The Hague. J 3. Queen Juliana.

1950.
J 18. **J 1.** 2 c. blue .. .. — 1·10
J 19. 4 c. green .. .. — 1·10

1951.
J 20. **J 2.** 2 c. lake .. .. — 5
J 21. 3 c. blue .. .. — 5
J 22. 4 c. green .. .. — 5
J 23. 5 c. brown .. .. — 5
J 24. **J 3.** 6 c. mauve .. .. — 65
J 25. **J 2.** 6 c. green .. .. — 10
J 26. 7 c. red .. .. — 5
J 27. **J 3.** 10 c. green .. .. — 5
J 28. 12 c. red .. .. — 5
J 29. 15 c. red .. .. — 5
J 30. 20 c. blue .. .. — 8
J 31. 25 c. brown .. .. — 10
J 32. 30 c. purple .. .. — 12
J 33. 1 g. grey .. .. — 40

NETHERLANDS ANTILLES O3

Curacao and other Netherlands islands in the Caribbean Sea. In December 1954 these were placed on an equal footing with Netherlands under the Crown.

1. Galleon. **2.** Alonso de Ojed.

1949. Discovery of Curacao. 450th Anniv.
306. **1.** 6 c. green 80 75
307. **2.** 12½ c. red .. .. 1·25 1·25
308. **1.** 15c. blue .. .. 1·10 75

3. Posthorns and Globe. **4.** Leap-frog.

1949. U.P.U. 75th Anniv.
309. **3.** 6 c. red 80 90
310. 25 c. blue .. .. 1·00 45

1950. As numeral and portrait types of Netherlands but inscr. "NED. ANTILLEN".
325. **99.** 1 c. brown 5 5
226. 1½ c. blue 5 5
327. 2 c. orange 5 5
328. 2½ c. green 30 5
329. 3 c. violet 5 5
329a. 4 c. green 15 12
330. 5 c. red 5 5
311. **108.** 6 c. purple 15 5
311a. 7½ c. brown 75 5
312. 10 c. red 25 5
313. 12½ c. green 30 5
314. 15 c. blue 30 5
315. 20 c. orange 35 5
316. 21 c. black 35 30
316a. 22½ c. green .. .. 1·10 5
317. 25 c. violet 40 5
318. 27½ c. brown 60 45
319. 30 c. sepia 55 5
320. 50 c. olive 75 5
321. **109.** 1½ g. green .. .. 2·25 12
322. 2½ g. chocolate .. 3·75 35
323. 5 g. red .. .. 7·50 2·50
324. 10 g. purple .. 15·00 11·00

1951. Child Welfare.
331. **4.** 1½ c.+1 c. violet .. 75 90
332. – 5 c.+2½ c. brown .. 1·40 1·40
333. – 6 c.+2½ c. blue .. 1·40 1·40
334. – 12½ c.+5 c. red .. 1·40 1·40
335. – 25 c.+10 c. blue-green .. 1·40 1·40
DESIGNS: 5 c. Kite-flying. 6 c. Girl on swing. 12½ c. Girls playing "Oranges and Lemons". 25 c. Bowling hoops.

5. Sea-gull over Ship. **6.** Fort Beekenburg.

1952. Seamen's Welfare Fund. Inscr. "ZEEMANSWELVAREN".
336. **5.** 1½ c.+1 c. green .. 40 40
337. – 6 c.+4 c. brown .. 80 80
338. – 12½ c.+7 c. mauve .. 1·10 1·00
339. – 15 c.+10 c. blue .. 1·25 1·10
340. – 25 c.+15 c. red .. 1·10 90
DESIGNS: 6 c. Sailor and lighthouse. 12½ c. Sailor on ship's prow. 15 c. Vessels in harbour. 25 c. Anchor and compass.

1953. Netherlands Flood Relief Fund No. 321 surch. **22½ Ct.+7½ Ct. WATERSNOOD NEDERLAND 1953.**
341. **109.** 22½ c.+7½ c. on 1½ g... 30 40

1953. Fort Beekenburg. 250th Anniv.
342. **6.** 22½ c. brown 70 12

7. Aruba Beach.

1954. 3rd Caribbean Tourist Assn. Meeting.
343. **7.** 15 c. blue and buff .. 70 60

1954. Ratification of Statue Queen Juliana of the Kingdom. As No. 809 of Netherlands.
344. **135.** 7½ c. olive 30 30

8. "Anglo" Flower.

FLOWERS: 7½ c. White Cayenne. 15 c. "French" flower. 22½ c. Cactus. 25 c. Red Cayenne.

1955. Child Welfare.
435. **8.** 1½ c.+1 c. blue, yellow & turquoise 20 20
346. – 7½ c.+5 c. red, yellow and violet 80 75
347. – 15 c.+5 c. red, grn. & olive 80 85
348. – 22½ c.+7½ c. red, yellow and blue 80 85
349. – 25 c.+10 c. vermilion, yellow and grey .. 85 85

9. Prince Bernhard and Queen Juliana.

1955. Royal Visit.
350. **9.** 7½ c.+2½ c. red.. .. 8 12
351. 22½ c.+7½ c. blue .. 35 35

10. Oil Refinery.

1955. 21st Meeting of Caribbean Commission.
352. – 15 c. blue, green & brown 70 70
353. **10.** 25 c. blue, green & brown 75 75
DESIGN (36×25 mm.): 15 c. Aruba Beach.

11. St. Anne Bay. **12.** Lord Baden-Powell.

1956. Caribbean Commission. 10th Anniv.
354. **11.** 15 c. blue, red and black 12 12

1957. Boy Scout Movement. 50th Anniv.
355. **12.** 6 c.+1½ c. yellow .. 20 25
356. 7½ c.+2½ c. green .. 25 25
357. 15 c.+5 c. red .. 25 30

13. "Dawn of Health".

1957. 1st Caribbean Mental Health Congress, Aruba.
358. **13.** 15 c. black and yellow.. 15 15

14. Saba.

1957. Tourist Publicity. Multicoloured.
359. 7½ c. Type **14** 15 15
360. 15 c. St. Maarten .. 20 20
361. 25 c. St. Eustatius .. 20 20

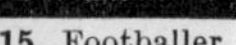

15. Footballer. **16.** Curacao Inter-continental Hotel.

1957. 8th Central American Caribbean Football Championships.
362. **15.** 6 c.+2½ c. orange .. 20 35
363. – 7½ c.+5 c. red .. 35 30
364. – 15 c.+5 c. green .. 40 40
365. – 22½ c.+7½ c. blue .. 40 40
DESIGNS—HORIZ. 7½ c. Caribbean map. VERT.—15 c. Goalkeeper saving ball. 22½ c. Footballers with ball.

1957. Opening of Curacao Inter-continental Hotel.
366. **16.** 15 c. blue 12 12

17. Map of Curacao. **18.** Sparrow Hawk.

1957. Int. Geophysical Year.
367. **17.** 15 c. blue 30 30

1958. Child Welfare. Bird design inscr. "VOOR HET KIND". Multicoloured.
368. 2½ c.+1 c. Type **18** .. 8 12
369. 7½ c.+1½ c. Yellow oriole 25 30
370. 15 c.+2½ c. Doves .. 30 40
371. 22½ c.+2½ c. Curacao parakeet.. .. .. 40 40

19. Flamingoes (Bonaire).

DESIGNS: A. Dutch Colonial houses (Curacao). B. Mountain and palms (Saba). C. Dutch Colonial house (St. Maarten). D. Church tower (Aruba). E. Memorial obelisk (St. Eustatius). F. Town Hall, St. Moarten.

1958.
372. **19.** 6 c. pink and green .. 1·10 5
373. A. 7½ c. yellow and brown 5 5
374. 8 c. yellow and blue .. 5 5
375. B. 10 c. yellow and grey .. 5 5
376. C. 12 c. brown and green 5 8
377. D. 15 c. blue and green .. 5 5
378. E. 20 c. grey and red .. 10 5
379. A. 25 c. green and blue .. 12 5
380. D. 30 c. green and brown 12 5
381. E. 35 c. pink and brown .. 12 5
382. B. 35 c. light blue and blue 15 10
383. C. 40 c. green and mauve 15 5
384. **19.** 50 c. pink and brown .. 20 5
385. E. 55 c. green and red .. 25 5
386. **19.** 65 c. pink and green .. 30 8
387. D. 70 c. orange and purple 30 8
388. **19.** 75 c. pink and violet .. 35 10
389. B. 85 c. green and brown 40 15
390. E. 90 c. orange and blue .. 40 15
391. F. 95 c. yellow and orange 45 20
392. D. 1 g. grey and red .. 50 20
393. A. 1½ g. brown and violet 75 30
394. C. 2½ g. yellow and blue .. 1·25 50
395. B. 5 g. mauve and brown 2·50 1·00
396. **19.** 10 g. pink and blue .. 5·00 2·00

20. **21.** Red Cross and Antilles Map.

1958. Neth. Antilles Radio & Telegraph Administration. 50th Anniv.
397. **20.** 7½ c. lake and blue .. 10 12
398. 15 c. blue and red .. 15 15

1958. Neth. Antilles Red Cross Fund. Cross in red.
399. **21.** 6 c.+2 c. chestnut .. 15 15
400. 7½ c.+2½ c. green .. 20 20
401. 15 c.+5 c. yellow .. 25 25
402. 22½ c. +7½ c. blue .. 30 30

22. Aruba Caribbean Hotel.

1959. Opening of Aruba Caribbean Hotel.
403. **22.** 15 c. red, blue, grn. & yell. 15 15

23. Zeeland.

1959. Curacao Monuments Preservation Fund. Multicoloured.
404. 6 c.+1½ c. Type **23** .. 25 25
405. 7½ c.+2½ c. Saba Island .. 30 35
406. 15 c.+5 c. Malenplein .. 30 35
407. 22½ c.+7½ c. Scharloobrug 30 35
408. 25 c.+7½ c. Brievengat .. 30 35
Nos. 405 and 407/8 are vert.

24. Water-distillation Plant. **25.** Antilles Flag.

27. Mgr. Niewindt. **26.** Fokker plane "Snip" over Caribbean.

1959. Aruba Water-distillation Plant Inaug.
409. **24.** 20 c. blue 20 20

1959. Statute for the Kingdom Ratification. 5th Anniv.
410. **25.** 10 c. red and blue .. 12 12
411. 20 c. red, blue and verm. 15 20
412. 25 c. red, blue and green 20 15

1959. K.L.M. Netherland — Curacao Air Service. 25th Anniv. Inscr. as in T **26**.
413. **26.** 10 c. blue and yellow .. 15 15
414. – 20 c. blue and yellow .. 15 20
415. – 25 c. blue and yellow .. 15 12
416. – 35 c. blue and yellow .. 25 25
DESIGNS: 20 c. 'Plane over Globe. 25 c. Airliner over Handelskade (bridge), Willemstad. 35 c. Airliner at Aruba airport.

1960. Mgr. M. J. Niewindt. Death Cent.
417. **27.** 10 c. purple 15 12
418. 20 c. violet 20 25
419. 25 c. olive 20 15

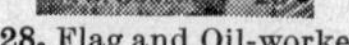

28. Flag and Oil-worker. **29.** Frogman.

1960. Labour Day.
420. **28.** 20 c. multicoloured .. 15 20

1960. Princess Wilhelmina Cancer Relief Fund. Inscr. "KANKERBESTRIJDING".
421. **29.** 10 c.+2 c. blue .. 40 40
422. – 20 c.+3 c. multicoloured 40 40
423. – 25 c.+5 c. red, bl. & blk. 40 40
DESIGNS—HORIZ. 20 c., 25 c. Tropical fishes (different).

30. Child on Bed. **31.** Governor's Salute to "Andrew Doria" at St. Eustatius.

1961. Child Welfare. Inscr. "voor het kind".
424. 6 c.+2 c. black and green 15 15
425. 10 c.+3 c. black and red.. 25 25
426. 20 c.+6 c. black & yellow 25 25
427. 25 c.+8 c. black & orange 25 25
DESIGNS: 6 c. T **30**. 10 c. Girl with doll. 20 c. Boy with bucket. 25 c. Children in classroom.

1961. 1st Salute to the American Flag. 185th Anniv.
428. **31.** 20 c. bl., red, grn. & blk. 25 25

1962. Royal Silver Wedding. As T **161** of Netherlands.
429. 10 c. orange 8 10
430. 25 c. blue 20 20

32. Jaja (nursemaid) and Child. **33.** Knight and World Map.

1962. Cultural Series.
431. – 6 c. chestnut and yellow 5 5
432. – 10 c. multicoloured .. 5 5
433. – 20 c. multicoloured .. 10 8
434. **32.** 25 c. brn., grn. & black 15 12
DESIGNS: 6 c. Corn-masher. 10 c. Benta-player. 20 c. Petju kerchief.

1962. Int. "Candidates" Chess Tournament, Curacao.
436. **33.** 10 c.+5 c. green .. 25 25
437. 20 c.+10 c. red .. 25 30
438. 25 c.+10 c. blue .. 25 30

1963. Freedom from Hunger. No. 378 surch. **TEGEN DE HONGER** wheat sprig and **+10 c.**
439. 20 c.+10 c. grey and red.. 35 35

34. Family Group.

1963. 4th Caribbean Mental Health Congress Curacao.
440. **34.** 20 c. buff and indigo .. 20 25
441. – 25 c. red and blue .. 25 30
DESIGN: 25 c. Egyptian Cross emblem.

35. "Freedom". **36.** Hotel Bonaire.

1963. Abolition of Slavery in Dutch West Indies. Cent.
442. **35.** 25 c. brown and yellow 20 20

1963. Opening of Hotel Bonaire.
443. **36.** 20 c. chocolate .. 12 15

37. Child and Flowers. **38.** Test-tube and Flask.

1963. Child Welfare. Child Art. Mult.
444. 5 c.+2 c. Type **37** .. 10 12
445. 6 c.+3 c. Children and flowers 12 12
446. 10 c.+5 c. Girl with ball.. 15 15
447. 20 c.+10 c. Men with flags 25 30
448. 25 c.+12 c. Schoolboy .. 30 30
Nos. 445/7 are horiz.

1963. Kingdom of the Netherlands. 150th Anniv. As No. 968 of Netherlands, but smaller, size 26×27 mm.
449. 25 c. bronze, red and black 15 20

1963. Chemical Industry, Aruba.
450. **38.** 20 c. red, apple & green 30 40

39. Winged Letter.

1964. 1st U.S.-Curacao Flight. 35th Anniv.
451. **38.** 20 c. red, blue & black.. 20 25
452. – 25 c. red, bl., grn. & blk. 25 30
DESIGN: 25 c. Route map and aircraft of 1929 and 1964.

40. Trinitaria.

1964. Child Welfare. Multicoloured.
453. 6 c.+3 c. Type **40**. .. 10 12
454. 10 c.+5 c. Magdalena .. 20 25
455. 20 c.+10 c. Yellow kelki.. 25 25
456. 25 c.+11 c. Bellisima .. 25 30

41. Caribbean Map. 42. "Six Islands".

1964. 5th Caribbean Council Assembly.
457. **41.** 20 c. yellow, red & blue 15 20

1964. Statute for the Kingdom. 19th Anniv.
458. **42.** 25 c. multicoloured .. 20 20

43. Princess Beatrix. 44. I.T.U. Emblem and Symbols.

1965. Visit of Princess Beatrix.
459. **43.** 25 c. vermilion .. 20 25

1965. I.T.U. Cent.
460. **44.** 10 c. deep blue and blue 15 15

45. Oil Tanker at Curacao.

1965. Curacao's Oil Industry. 50th Anniv. Multicoloured.
461. 10 c. Catalytic cracking plant (vert.) 8 8
462. 20 c. Type **45** 12 12
463. 25 c. Super fractionating plant (vert.) 15 15

46. Flag and Fruit Market, Curacao. 47. Cup Sponges.

1965.
464. **46.** 1 c. ultram., red & grn. 5 5
465. – 2 c. ultram., red & yell. 5 5
466. – 3 c. ultram., red & cobalt 5 5
467. – 4 c. ultram., red & orge. 5 5
468. – 5 c. ultram., red & blue 5 5
469. – 6 c. ultram., red & pink 5 5
DESIGNS (Flag and): 2 c. Divi-divi tree. 3 c. Lace. 4 c. Flamingoes. 5 c. Church. 6 c. Lobster. Each is inscr. with a different place-name.

1965. Child Welfare. Marine Life. Multicoloured.
470. 6 c.+3 c. Type **47** .. 8 10
471. 10 c. +5 c. Cup sponges (diff.) 12 15
472. 20 c.+10 c. Sea anemones on star coral 15 25
473. 25 c.+11 c. Basket sponge and "Brain" coral .. 25 35

48. Marine and Seascape. 49. Love Birds and Wedding Rings.

1965. Marine Corps. Tercent.
474. **48.** 25 c. multicoloured .. 15 15

1966. Intergovernmental Committee for European Migration (I.C.E.M.) Fund. As T **189** of Netherlands.
475. 35 c.+15 c. bistre & brown 30 35

1966. Marriage of Crown Princess Beatrix and Herr Claus von Amsberg.
476. **49.** 25 c. multicoloured .. 15 15

50. Admiral De Ruyter and Map.

1966. Admiral De Ruyter's Visit to St. Eustatius. 300th Anniv.
477. **50.** 25 c. ochre, violet & blue 15 15

51. "Grammar". 52. Cooking.

1966. 25 years of Secondary Education.
478. **51.** 6 c. black, blue & yellow 5 5
479. – 10 c. black, red & green 5 8
480. – 20 c. black, blue & yellow 12 12
481. – 25 c. black red and green 12 12
DESIGNS—The "Free Arts", figures representing: 10 c. "Rhetoric" and "Dialect". 20 c. "Arithmetic" and "Geometry". 25 c. "Astronomy" and "Music".

1966. Child Welfare. Multicoloured.
482. 6 c.+3 c. Type **52** .. 5 5
483. 10 c.+5 c. Nursing .. 8 10
484. 20 c.+10 c. Metal-work fitting 15 15
485. 25 c.+11 c. Ironing .. 20 25

53. Cruiser.

1967. Royal Netherlands Navy League. 60th Anniv.
486. **53.** 6 c. bronze and green .. 5 5
487. – 10 c. ochre and yellow .. 5 5
488. – 20 c. brown and sepia .. 10 10
489. – 25 c. blue and indigo .. 12 12
SHIPS: 12 c. Sailing vessel. 20 c. Tanker. 25 c. Passenger liner.

54. M. C. Piar (patriot). 55. "Heads in Hands".

1967. Manuel Piar. 150th Death Anniv.
490. **54.** 20 c. brown and red .. 12 12

1967. Cultural and Social Welfare Funds.
491. **55.** 6 c.+3 c. black and blue 5 5
492. 10 c.+5 c. black & mag. 8 10
493. 20 c.+10 c. purple .. 15 15
494. 25 c.+11 c. blue .. 20 25

56. "The Turtle and the Monkey". 57. Olympic Flame and Rings.

1967. Child Welfare. "Nanzi" Fairy Tales. Multicoloured.
495. 6 c.+3 c. "Princess Long Nose" (vert.) .. 5 5
496. 10 c.+5 c. Type **56** .. 8 10
497. 20 c.+10 c. "Nanzi (spider) and the Tiger" 15 15
498. 25 c.+11 c. "Shon Arey's Balloon" (vert.) .. 25 25

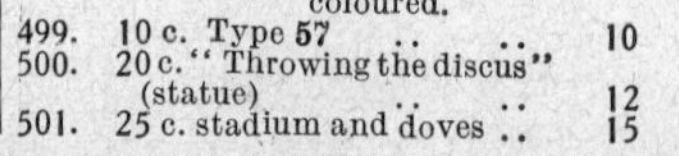

1968. Olympic Games, Mexico. Multicoloured.
499. 10 c. Type **57** 10 10
500. 20 c. "Throwing the discus" (statue) .. 12 12
501. 25 c. stadium and doves .. 15 15

58. "Dance of the Ribbons".

1968. Cultural and Social Relief Funds.
502. **58.** 10 c.+5 c. multicoloured 10 10
503. 15 c.+5 c. multicoloured 12 12
504. 20 c.+10 c. multicoloured 20 20
505. 25 c.+10 c. multicoloured 25 25

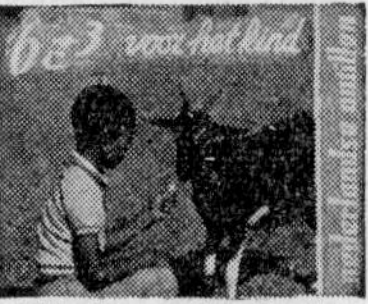

59. Boy with Goat.

1968. Child Welfare. Multicoloured.
506. 6 c.+3 c. Type **59** .. 5 8
507. 10 c.+5 c. Girl with Dog .. 10 12
508. 20 c.+10 c. Boy with Cat 15 20
509. 25 c.+11 c. Girl with Duck 20 25

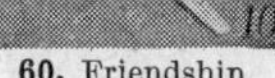

60. Friendship "500" Airliner. 61. Radio Pylon, "Waves" and Map.

1968. Dutch Antilliean Airlines.
510. **60.** 10 c. blue, black & yell. 10 8
511. – 20 c. blue, black & brn. 15 15
512. – 25 c. blue, black & pink 15 15
DESIGNS: 20 c. Douglas "DC–9"; 25 c. Friendship "500" in flight and Douglas "DC–9" on ground.

1969. Opening of Broadcast Relay Station, Bonaire.
513 **61.** 25 c. green and blue .. 15 15

62. "Code of Laws". 63. "Carnival".

1969. Netherlands Antilles' Court of Justice. Cent.
514. **62.** 20 c. grn., gold & apple green 15 15
515. – 25 c. multicoloured .. 15 15
DESIGN: 25 c. "Scales of Justice".

1969. Cultural and Social Antilles' Festivals Relief Funds. Multicoloured.
516. 10 c.+5 c. Type **63** 15 15
517. 15 c.+5 c. "Harvest Festival" 15 15
518. 20 c.+10 c. "San Juan Day" 20 20
519. 25 c.+10 c. "New Year's Day" 25 25

64. I.L.O. Emblem, "Koenoekoe" House and Cacti. 65. Boy playing Guitar.

1969. Int. Labour Organization. 50th Anniv.
520. **64.** 10 c. black and blue .. 5 5
521. 25 c. black and red .. 15 15

1969. Child Welfare.
522. **65.** 6 c.+3 c. violet & orge. 8 10
523. – 10 c.+5 c. emer. & yell. 12 15
524. – 20 c.+10 c. carmine & bl. 20 25
525. – 25 c.+11 c. brn. & pink 30 30
DESIGNS: 10 c. Girl playing recorder. 20 c. Boy playing "marimula". 25 c. Girl playing piano.

1969. Statute for the Kingdom. 25th Anniv. As T **213** of the Netherlands, but inscr. "NEDERLANDSE ANTILLEN".
526. 25 c. multicoloured .. 15 20

66. Radio Station, Bonaire. 67. St. Anna Church, Otrabanda, Curacao.

1970. Trans-World Religious Radio Station, Bonaire. Multicoloured.
527. 10 c. Type **66** 5 5
528. 15 c. Trans-World Radio Emblem 10 10

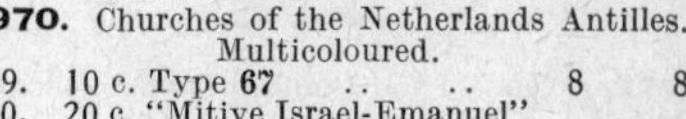

1970. Churches of the Netherlands Antilles. Multicoloured.
529. 10 c. Type **67** 8 8
530. 20 c. "Mitive Israel-Emanuel" Synagogue, Punda, Curacao (horiz.) .. 12 12
531. 25 c. Pulpit, Fort Church, Curacao 15 15

68. "The Press". 69. Mother and Child.

1970. Cultural and Social Relief Funds. "Mass-media". Multicoloured.
532. 10 c.+5 c. Type **68** .. 20 20
533. 15 c.+5 c. "Films" .. 25 25
534. 20 c.+10 c. "Radio" .. 25 25
535. 25 c.+10 c. "Television" 30 30

1970. Child Welfare. Multicoloured.
536. 6 c.+3 c. Type **69** .. 12 12
537. 10 c.+5 c. Child with piggy-bank 20 20
538. 20 c.+10 c. Children wrestling 25 25
539. 25 c.+11 c. "Pick-a-back" 30 30

70. St. Theresia's Church, St. Nicolaas, Aruba. 71. Lions Emblem.

1971. St. Theresia Parish, Aruba. 40th Anniv.
540. **70.** 20 c. multicoloured .. 15 15

1971. Curacao Lions Club. 25th Anniv.
541. **71.** 25 c. multicoloured .. 20 20

72. Charcoal Stove. 73. Admiral Brion.

1971. Cultural and Social Relief Funds. Household Utensils. Multicoloured.
542. 10 c.+5 c. Type **72** .. 15 15
543. 15 c.+5 c. Earthenware water vessel 15 15
544. 20 c.+10 c. Baking oven 20 20
545. 25 c.+10 c. Kitchen implements 25 25

1971. Prince Bernhard's 60th Birthday. Design as No. 1135 of Netherlands.
546. 45 c. multicoloured .. 30 30

1971. Admiral Luis Brion. 150th Death Anniv.
547. **73.** 40 c. multicoloured .. 20 20

74. Bottle Doll. 75. Queen Emma Bridge, Curacao.

1971. Child Welfare. Home-made Toys. Multicoloured.
548. 15 c.+5 c. Type **74** .. 15 15
549. 20 c.+10 c. Prototype cart 15 15
550. 30 c.+15 c. Spinning-tops 20 20

1972. Views of the Islands. Multicoloured.
551. 1 c. Type **75** 5 5
552. 2 c. "The Bottom" (capital of Saba) 5 5
553. 3 c. Flamingoes, Bonaire .. 5 5
554. 4 c. Distillation plant, Aruba 5 5
555. 5 c. Fort Amsterdam, St. Maarten 5 5
556. 6 c. Fort Oranje, St. Eustatius 5 5

76. Ship in Dock. 77. Steel-band.

1972. New Dry Dock Complex, Willemstad. Curacao. Inaug.
557. **76.** 30 c. multicoloured .. 15 15

1972. Cultural and Social Relief Funds, Folklore. Multicoloured.
558. 15 c.+5 c. Type **77** .. 15 15
559. 20 c.+10 c. "Seu" festival 30 30
560. 30 c.+15 c. Drummers .. 30 30

78. J. E. Irausquin. 79. M. F. Da Costa Gomez.

1972. Juan Enrique Irausquin (Antilles statesman). 10th Death Anniversary.
561. **78.** 30 c. red 15 15

1972. Moises F. Da Costa Gomez (statesman). 65th Birth Anniv.
562. **79.** 30 c. black and green 12 12

80. Child playing with Earth. 81. Pedestrian Crossing.

1972. Child Welfare. Multicoloured.
563. 15 c.+5 c. Type **80** .. 20 20
564. 20 c.+10 c. Child playing in water 20 20
565. 30 c.+15 c. Child throwing ball into the air .. 25 25

1973. Cultural and Social Relief Funds. Road Safety.
566. **81.** 12 c.+6 c. multicoloured 15 15
567. – 15 c.+7 c. grn., orge. & red 20 20
568. – 40 c.+20 c. multicoloured 25 25
DESIGNS: 15 c. Road-crossing patrol. 40 c. Traffic lights.

82. William III (stamp portrait of 1873). 83. Map of Leeward Antilles.

1973. Stamp Centenary.
569. **82.** 15 c. lilac, mauve & gold 8 8
570. – 20 c. multicoloured .. 10 10
571. – 30 c. multicoloured .. 15 15
DESIGNS: 20 c. Antilles postman. 30 c. Postal Service emblem.

1973. Telecommunications. Submarine Cable and Microwave Link. Inaug. Mult.
572. 15 c. Type **83** 8 8
573. 30 c. Six stars ("The Antilles") 15 15
574. 45 c. Map of Windward Antilles 20 20

84. Queen Juliana. 85. Jan Eman (statesman).

1973. Queen Juliana's Reign. Silver Jubilee.
576. **84.** 15 c. multicoloured .. 8 8

1973. Jan Eman (Aruba statesman). 16th Death Anniv.
577. **85.** 30 c. black and green .. 15 15

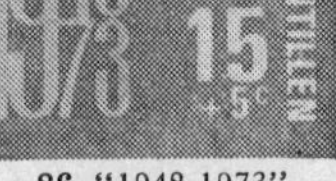

86. "1948-1973". 87. L. B. Scott.

1973. Child Welfare, 1st Child Welfare Stamps. 25th Anniv.
578. **86.** 15 c.+5 c. light green, green and blue .. 10 10
579. – 20 c.+10 c. brown, green and blue .. 15 15
580. – 30 c.+15 c. violet, blue and light blue .. 20 20
DESIGNS: No. 579, Three Children. No. 580, Mother and child.

1974. Lionel B. Scott. 8th Death Anniv.
582. **87.** 30 c. multicoloured .. 15 15

88. Family having meal. 89. Girl combing Hair.

1974. Family Planning Campaign. Mult.
583. 6 c. Type **88** 5 5
584. 12 c. Family at home .. 5 5
585. 15 c. Family in garden .. 8 8

1974. Cultural and Social Relief Funds. "The Younger Generation". Mult.
586. 12 c.+6 c. Type **89** .. 10 10
587. 15 c.+7 c. "Pop dancers" 12 12
588. 40 c.+20 c. Group drummer 30 30

90. Desulphurisation Plant.

1974. Lago Oil Co., Aruba. 50th Anniv. Multicoloured.
589. 15 c. Type **90** 8 8
590. 30 c. Fractionating towers 15 15
591. 45 c. Lago refinery at night 20 20

91. U.P.U. Emblem. 92. "A Carpenter out-ranks a King".

1974. Universal Postal Union. Centenary.
592. **91.** 15 c. gold, grn. & blk... 8 8
593. 30 c. gold, blue & black 15 15

1974. Child Welfare. Children's Songs. Mult.
594. 15 c.+5 c. Type **92** .. 10 10
595. 20 c.+10 c. Footprints ("Let's Do a Ring-dance") .. 15 15
596. 30 c.+15 c. Sun and Moon ("Moon and Sun") .. 20 20

93. Queen Emma Bridge. 94. Ornamental Ventilation Grid.

1975. Antillean Bridges. Multicoloured.
597. 20 c. Type **93** 10 10
598. 30 c. Juliana Bridge .. 15 15
599. 40 c. Wilhelmina Bridge .. 20 20

1975. Cultural and Social Welfare Funds. Art Objects in Stone.
600. **94.** 12 c.+6 c. mult. .. 10 10
601. – 15 c.+7 c. brn. & drab 12 12
602. – 40 c.+20 c. mult. .. 30 30
DESIGNS: 15 c. Tombstone detail. 40 c. Foundation stone.

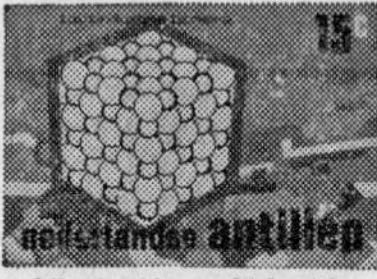

95. Sodium Chloride Molecules.

1975. Bonaire Salt Industry. Multicoloured.
603. 15 c. Type **95** 8 8
604. 20 c. Salt incrustation and blocks 10 10
605. 40 c. Map of salt area (vert.) 20 20

96. Fokker "F-18" and Old Control Tower.

1975. Aruba Airport. 40th Anniv. Mult.
606. 15 c. Type **96** 8 8
607. 30 c. Douglas "DC-9" and modern control tower .. 15 15
608. 40 c. Tail of Boeing "727" and "Princess Beatrix Airport" buildings .. 20 20

97. I.W.Y. Emblem.

1975. International Women's Year. Mult.
609. 6 c. Type **97** 5 5
610. 12 c. "Social Development" 5 5
611. 20 c. "Equality of Sexes" .. 10 10

98. Children making Windmill.

1975. Child Welfare. Multicoloured.
612. 15 c. + 5 c. Type **98** .. 10 10
613. 20 c. + 10 c. Child modelling clay .. 15 15
614. 30 c. + 15 c. Children drawing pictures .. 25 25

99. Beach, Aruba.

1976. Tourism. Multicoloured.
615. 40 c. Type **99** 40 40
616. 40 c. Fish Kiosk, Bonaire 40 40
617. 40 c. "Table Mountain", Curacao 40 40

100. J. A. Abraham (statesman). 101. Dyke and Produce.

1976. Abraham Commemoration.
618. **100.** 30 c. purple on brown 30 30

1976. Agriculture, Animal Husbandry and Fisheries. Multicoloured.
619. 15 c. Type **101** 15 15
620. 35 c. Cattle 35 35
621. 45 c. Fishes 45 45

102. Arm holding Child.

1976. Child Welfare. "Carrying the Child".
622. **102.** 20 c.+10 c. mult. .. 30 30
623. – 25 c.+12 c. mult. .. 40 40
624. – 40 c.+18 c. mult. .. 60 60
DESIGNS—HORIZ. 25 c. VERT. 40 c. Both similar to Type **102** showing arm holding child.

103. Flags and Plaque, Fort Oranje.

1976. First Salute to American Flag. Bicent. Multicoloured.
625. 25 c. Type **103** .. 25 25
626. 40 c. Firing Salute .. 40 40
627. 55 c. Johannes de Graaff, Governor of St. Eustatius 55 55

POSTAGE DUE STAMPS

1952. As Type D 4 of Netherlands but inscr. "NEDERLANDSE ANTILLEN".
D 336. 1 c. green 5 5
D 337. 2½ c. green 15 15
D 338. 5 c. green 5 5
D 339. 6 c. green 5 5
D 340. 7 c. green 5 5
D 341. 8 c. green 5 5
D 342. 9 c. green 5 5
D 343. 10 c. green 5 5
D 344. 12½ c. green 8 8
D 345. 15 c. green 10 10
D 346. 20 c. green 12 12
D 347. 25 c. green 15 5
D 348. 30 c. green 15 15
D 349. 35 c. green 20 20
D 350. 40 c. green 25 25
D 351. 45 c. green 30 30
D 352. 50 c. green 30 30

NETHERLANDS INDIES O2

A former Dutch colony, consisting of numerous settlements in the East Indies, of which the islands of Java and Sumatra and parts of Borneo and New Guinea are the most important. Renamed Indonesia in 1948, Independence was granted during 1950. Netherlands New Guinea remained a Dutch possession until 1962 when it was placed under U.N. control, being incorporated with Indonesia in 1963.

1. King William III. 2.

1864. Imperf.
1. **1.** 10 c. red .. .. .. 95·00 35·00

1868. Perf.
2. **1.** 10 c. red .. .. .. £300 26·00

1870. Perf.
27. 2. 1 c. green .. 1·00 60
29. 2 c. brown .. 2·00 1·25
30. 2½ c. yellow .. 11·00 9·00
3. 5 c. green .. 20·00 1·50
32. 10 c. brown .. 5·00 50
51. 12½ c. grey .. 1·00 5
34. 15 c. bistre .. 6·00 25
35. 20 c. blue .. 32·00 75
36. 25 c. purple .. 6·00 20
55. 30 c. green .. 9·00 1·00
17. 50 c. red .. 5·50 35
38. 2 g. 50 green and purple .. 28·00 6·00

3. 4. Queen Wilhelmina.

1883.
89. 3. 1 c. green .. 20 5
90. 2 c. brown .. 20 5
91. 2½ c. yellow .. 30 25
92. 3 c. mauve .. 30 5
88. 5 c. green .. 9·00 6·00
93. 5 c. blue .. 2·50 5
94. 4. 10 c. brown .. 1·40 5
95. 12½ c. grey .. 3·00 6·50
96. 15 c. bistre .. 4·00 20
97a. 20 c. blue .. 9·00 30
98a. 25 c. mauve .. 8·50 40
99. 30 c. green .. 10·00 60
100. 50 c. red .. 7·50 25
101. 2 g. 50, blue and brown .. 35·00 13·00

1900. Netherlands stamps of 1898 surch. **NED.-INDIE** and value.
111. 11. 10 c. on 10 c. grey .. 60 5
112. 12½ c. on 12½ c. blue .. 80 25
113. 15 c. on 15 c. brown .. 80 8
114. 20 c. on 20 c. green .. 5·00 20
115. 25 c. on 25 c. blue & red 5·00 25
116. 50 c. on 50 c. brn. & olive 8·00 35
117. 12. 2½ g. on 1½ g. lilac .. 17·00 4·00

1902. Surch.
118. 3. ½ on 2 c. brown .. 8 8
119. 2½ on 3 c. mauve .. 8 8

1902. As T 4/6 of Curacao, but inscr. "NEDERLANDSCH-INDIE".
120. ½ c. lilac .. 10 5
121. 1 c. olive .. 10 5
122. 2 c. brown .. 85 5
123. 2½ c. green .. 60 5
124. 3 c. orange .. 55 45
125. 4 c. blue .. 3·50 3·00
126. 5 c. red .. 1·60 5
127. 7½ c. grey .. 70 8
128. 10 c. slate .. 40 5
129. 12½ c. blue .. 50 5
130. 15 c. brown .. 2·50 70
131. 17½ c. bistre .. 1·00 5
132. 20 c. grey .. 65 65
133. 20 c. olive .. 7·50 5
134. 22½ c. olive and brown 1·60 5
135. 25 c. mauve .. 3·00 5
136. 30 c. brown .. 10·00 5
137. 50 c. claret .. 6·50 5
138. 1 g. lilac .. 18·00 10
206. 1 g. lilac on blue .. 16·00 2·50
139. 2½ g. grey .. 22·00 70
207. 2½ g. grey on blue .. 23·00 12·00

1909. No. 130 surch. with horiz. bars.
140. 15 c. brown .. 50 25

1905. No. 132 surch. **10 cent.**
141. 10 c. on 20 c. grey .. 40 40

1908. As 1902, optd. **JAVA.**
142. ½ c. lilac .. 5 5
143. 1 c. olive .. 5 5
144. 2 c. brown .. 60 60
145. 2½ c. green .. 30 5
146. 3 c. orange .. 20 30
147. 5 c. red .. 75 5
148. 7½ c. grey .. 65 65
149. 10 c. slate .. 20 5
150. 12½ c. blue .. 90 25
151. 15 c. brown .. 95 85
152. 17½ c. bistre .. 60 25
153. 20 c. olive .. 3·00 20
154. 22½ c. olive and brown 1·75 85
155. 25 c. mauve .. 1·50 5
156. 30 c. brown .. 9·00 85
157. 50 c. claret .. 5·50 25
158. 1 g. lilac .. 16·00 1·00
159. 2½ g. grey .. 22·00 16·00

1908. As 1902, optd. **BUITEN BEZIT.**
160. ½ c. lilac .. 8 8
161. 1 c. olive .. 12 8
162. 2 c. brown .. 55 90
163. 2½ c. green .. 25 10
164. 3 c. orange .. 20 40
165. 5 c. red .. 60 12
166. 7½ c. grey .. 75 90
167. 10 c. slate .. 20 5
168. 12½ c. blue .. 2·50 90
169. 15 c. brown .. 1·25 60
170. 17½ c. bistre .. 50 40
171. 20 c. olive .. 2·00 60
172. 22½ c. olive and brown .. 1·75 1·50
173. 25 c. mauve .. 1·40 10
174. 30 c. brown .. 5·00 70
175. 50 c. claret .. 2·00 20
176. 1 g. lilac .. 16·00 1·25
177. 2½ g. grey .. 28·00 24·00

1912. As T 7/9 of Curacao, but inscr. "NED. (NEDERL or NEDERLANDSCH) INDIE".
208. 7. ½ c. lilac .. 5 5
209. 1 c. olive .. 5 5
210. 2 c. brown .. 12 5
264. 2 c. grey .. 12 5
211. 2½ c. green .. 40 5
265. 2½ c. rose .. 8 5
212. 3 c. yellow .. 10 5
266. 3 c. green .. 20 5
213. 4 c. blue .. 12 5
267. 4 c. green .. 35 5
268. 4 c. bistre .. 2·50 1·75
214. 5 c. pink .. 25 5
269. 5 c. green .. 30 5
270. 5 c. blue .. 12 5
215. 7½ c. brown .. 12 5
216. 8. 10 c. red .. 15 5
272. 7. 10 c. lilac .. 25 5
217. 8. 12½ c. blue .. 25 5
273. 12½ c. red .. 25 5
274. 15 c. blue .. 2·50 5
218. 17½ c. brown .. 25 5
219. 20 c. green .. 45 5
275. 20 c. blue .. 50 5
276. 20 c. orange .. 4·25 5
220. 22½ c. orange .. 45 25
221. 25 c. mauve .. 50 5
222. 30 c. slate .. 55 5
277. 32½ c. violet and orange 50 5
278. 35 c. brown .. 3·25 20
279. 40 c. green .. 50 5
223. 9. 50 c. green .. 1·40 5
280. 60 c. blue .. 1·40 5
281. 80 c. orange .. 1·75 5
224. 1 g. sepia .. 1·40 5
283. 1 g. 75 lilac .. 5·50 90
225. 2½ g. rose .. 4·75 15

1915. Red Cross. As 1912 surch. with Red Cross and **+5 cts.**
243. 1 c.+5 c. olive (No. 209) 1·75 1·75
244. 5 c.+5 c. pink (No. 214) .. 2·00 2·00
245. 10 c.+5 c. red (No. 216) .. 3·00 3·00

1917. Stamps of 1902 and 1912 surch.
246. ½ c. on 2½ c. (No. 211) .. 5 5
247. 1 c. on 4 c. (No. 213) .. 15 15
250. 12½ c. on 17½ c. (No. 218) 12 5
251. 12½ c. on 22½ c. (No. 220) 15 5
248. 17½ c. on 22½ c. (No. 134) 25 12
252. 20 c. on 22½ c. (No. 220) 15 5
249. 30 c. on 1 g. (No. 138) .. 2·00 50
253. 32½ c. on 50 c. (No 223) .. 70 5
254. 40 c. on 50 c. (No. 223) .. 1·75 15
255. 60 c. on 1 g. (No. 224) .. 3·00 20
256. 80 c. on 1 g. (No. 224) .. 3·50 45

1922. Bandoeng Industrial Fair. Optd. **3de N.I. JAARBEURS BANDOENG 1922.**
285. 7. 1 c. olive .. 2·75 2·00
286. 2 c. brown .. 2·75 2·25
287. 2½ c. rose .. 18·00 18·00
288. 3 c. yellow .. 2·50 2·50
289. 4 c. blue .. 11·00 11·00
290 5 c. green .. 5·00 4·00
291. 7½ c. brown .. 3·00 2·00
292. 10 c. lilac .. 18·00 20·00
293. 8. 12½ c. on 22½ c. orange (No. 251) .. 3·50 2·50
294. 17½ c. brown .. 2·40 2·00
295. 20 c. blue .. 3·50 2·00
Nos. 285/95 were sold at a premium for 3, 4, 5, 6, 8, 9, 10, 12½, 15, 20 and 22 c. respectively.

11. 12.

1923. Queen's Silver Jubilee.
296. 11. 5 c. green .. 5 5
297. 12½ c. red .. 8 5
298. 20 c. indigo .. 15 5
299. 50 c. orange .. 70 30
300. 1 g. purple .. 1·50 20
301. 2½ g. grey .. 10·00 4·00
302. 5 g. brown .. 23·00 30·00

1928. Air. As 1912, surch. **LUCHTPOST** and aeroplane and value.
303. 10 c. on 12½ c. red .. 60 60
304. 20 c. on 25 c. mauve .. 90 1·00
305. 40 c. on 80 c. orange .. 90 70
306. 75 c. on 1 g. sepia .. 50 25
307. 1½ g. on 2½ g. rose .. 2·75 3·00

1928. Air.
308. 12. 10 c. purple .. 12 5
309. 20 c. brown .. 45 30
310. 40 c. red .. 55 30
311. 75 c. green .. 1·25 5
312. 1 g. 50 orange .. 2·00 25

1930. Air. Surch. **30** between bars.
313. 12. 30 c. on 40 c. red .. 40 5

14. Minangkabau compound.

1930. Child Welfare. Centres in brown.
315. – 2 c.+1 c. mauve .. 40 40
316. – 5 c.+2½ c. green .. 1·75 1·00
317. 14. 12½ c.+2½ c. red .. 90 20
318. – 15 c.+5 c. blue .. 2·25 2·00
DESIGNS—VERT. 2 c. Bali Temple. 5 c. Watch-tower. HORIZ. 15 c. Buddhist Temple, Borobudur.

1930. No. 275 surch. **12½** and bars.
319. 8. 12½ c. on 20 c. blue .. 12 5

15. M. P. Pattist in Flight.

1931. Air. 1st Java-Australia mail.
320. 15. 1 g. brown and blue .. 6·00 6·00

16. 17. Ploughing.

1931. Air.
321. 16. 30 c. claret .. 1·60 5
322. 4½ g. blue .. 5·00 1·25
323. 7½ g. green .. 5·50 1·50

1931. Lepers' Colony.
324. 17. 2 c.+1 c. brown .. 1·10 80
325. – 5 c.+2½ c. green .. 2·00 1·40
326. – 12½ c.+2½ c. red .. 1·00 20
327. – 15 c.+4 c. blue .. 3·50 3·00
DESIGNS: 5 c. Fishing. 12½ c. Native actors. 15 c. Native musicians.

1932. Air. Surch. with aeroplane and value.
328. 12. 50 c. on 1 g. 50 c. orange 1·75 12

18. Plaiting Rattan.

DESIGNS: 2 c. Weaving. 12½ c. Textile worker. 15 c. Metal worker.

1932. Salvation Army. Centres in brown.
329. – 2 c.+1 c. purple .. 25 20
330. 18. 5 c.+2½ c. green .. 1·50 1·00
331. – 12½ c.+2½ c. red .. 45 10
332. – 15 c.+5 c. blue .. 1·75 1·50

1933. William I of Orange. 400th Birth Anniv. As Type 50 of the Netherlands, but inscribed "NED-INDIE".
333. 12½ c. red .. 55 5

19. Rice Cultivation. 20. Queen Wilhelmina.

1933.
335. 19. 1 c. violet .. 5 5
336. 2 c. purple .. 8 5
337. 2½ c. bistre .. 8 5
338. 3 c. green .. 8 5
339. 3½ c. grey .. 5 5
340. 4 c. green .. 25 5
401 5 c. blue .. 5 5
342. 7½ c. violet .. 35 5
343. 10 c. red .. 35 5
344. 20. 10 c. red .. 15 5
345. 12½ c. red .. 15 5
404. 15 c. blue .. 5 5
405. 20 c. purple .. 10 5
348. 25 c. green .. 70 5
349. 30 c. blue .. 80 5
350. 32½ c. bistre .. 2·00 2·00
408. 35 c. violet .. 1·00 20
352. 40 c. green .. 70 5
353. 42½ c. yellow .. 70 5
354. – 50 c. blue .. 1·25 5
355. – 60 c. blue .. 1·40 12
356. – 80 c. red .. 1·40 15
357. – 1 g. violet .. 2·00 10
358. – 1 g. 75 green .. 5·00 4·25
414. – 2 g. green .. 11·00 5·50
359. – 2 g. 50 purple .. 7·00 40
415. – 5 g. bistre .. 10·00 2·75
Nos. 354/9 and 414/5 are as T 20 but large (30×30 mm.).

21. Monoplane.

1933. Air. For Special Flights.
360. 21. 30 c. blue .. 20 25

22. Woman and Lotus Blossom. 23. Cavalryman and Wounded Soldier.

1933. Y.M.C.A. Charity.
361. 22. 2 c.+1 c. brn. & purple 50 10
362. – 5 c.+2½ c. brn. & green 1·25 85
363. – 12½ c.+2½ c. brn. & orge. 1·25 10
364. – 15 c.+5 c. brn. & blue 2·00 95
DESIGNS: 5 c. Symbolising the sea of life. 12½ c. Y.M.C.A. emblem. 15 c. Unemployed man.

1934. Surch.
365. 12. 2 c. on 10 c. purple .. 12 20
366. 2 c. on 20 c. brown .. 8 8
367. 16. 2 c. on 30 c. claret .. 15 30
368. 12. 42½ c. on 75 c. green .. 2·00 8
369. 42½ c. on 1 g. 50 orge. .. 2·00 12

1934. Anti-Tuberculosis Fund. As T 61 of Netherlands.
370. 12½ c.+2½ c. brown .. 75 25

1935. Christian Military Home.
371. – 2 c.+1 c. brown & pur. 75 60
372. 23. 5 c.+2½ c. brn. & grn. 2·00 1·75
373. – 12½ c.+2½ c. brn. & orge. 2·00 10
374. – 15 c.+5 c. brn. & blue 2·50 2·40
DESIGNS: 2 c. Engineer chopping wood. 12½ c. Artilleryman and volcano victim. 15 c. Infantry bugler.

24. Dinner-time. 25. Boy Scouts. 26. Sifting Rice.

1936. Salvation Army.
375. 24. 2 c.+1 c. purple .. 60 30
376. 5 c.+1½ c. blue .. 75 50
377. 7½ c.+2½ c. violet .. 70 65
378. 12½ c.+2½ c. orange .. 75 10
379. 15 c.+5 c. blue .. 1·25 90
Nos. 376/9 are as T 24 but larger.

1937. Scout's Jamboree.
380. 25. 7½ c.+2½ c. green .. 90 60
381. 12½ c.+2½ c. red .. 90 30

1937. Nos. 222 and 277 surch. in figures.
382. 10 c. on 30 c. slate .. 85 8
383. 10 c. on 32½ c. vio. & orge. 85 8

1937. Relief Fund. Inscr. "A.S.I.B.".
385. 26. 2 c.+1 c. sepia & orge. 50 40
386. – 3½ c.+1½ c. black .. 50 40
387. – 7½ c.+2½ c. grn. & orge. 50 40
388. – 10 c.+2½ c. red & orge. 65 5
389. – 20 c.+5 c. blue .. 70 50
DESIGNS: 3½ c. Mother and children. 7½ c. Ox-team ploughing rice-field. 10 c. Ox-team and cart. 20 c. Man and woman.

1938 Coronation. 40th Anniv. As T 71 of Netherlands.
390. 2 c. violet .. 5 5
391. 10 c. red .. 10 5
392. 15 c. blue .. 60 35
393. 20 c. red .. 30 12

INDEX

Countries can be quickly located by referring to the index at the end of this volume.

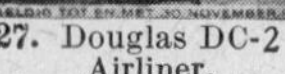

27. Douglas DC-2 Airliner. 28. Nurse and Child.

1938. Air Service Fund. Royal Netherlands Indies Air Lines. 10th Anniv.
394. 27. 17½ c.+5 c. brown .. 50 50
395. – 20 c.+5 c. slate .. 50 30
DESIGNS: 20 c. as T 27, but reverse side of air-liner.

1938. Child Welfare. Inscr. "CENTRAAL MISSIE-BUREAU".
416. 28. 2 c.+1 c. violet.. .. 35 25
417. – 3½ c.+1½ c. green .. 50 50
418. – 7½ c.+2½ c. red.. .. 40 40
419. – 10 c.+2½ c. red.. .. 45 5
420. – 20 c.+5 c. blue.. .. 55 40
DESIGNS: Nurse and child patient with injuries to eye (3½ c.), arm (7½ c.), head (20 c.) and nurse bathing a baby. (10 c.).

29. Group of Natives. 30. European nurse and Patient.

1939. Netherlands Indies Social Bureau and Protestant Church Funds.
421. – 2 c.+1 c. violet .. 15 10
422. – 3½ c.+1½ c. green .. 15 12
423. 29. 7½ c.+2½ c. brown .. 15 10
424. – 10 c.+2½ c. red .. 75 40
425. 30. 10 c.+2½ c. red .. 75 40
426. 20 c.+5 c. blue .. 25 15
DESIGNS—VERT. 2 c. as T 29 but group in European clothes. HORIZ. 3½ c., 10 c. (No. 424) as T 30, but Native nurse and patient.
Nos. 424/5 were issued in sheets showing each type alternately. (Price per pair: £1·25 un. or us.).

1940. Charity. Red Cross Fund. No. 345 surch. with cross and **10+5 ct.**
428. 20. 10 c.+5 c. on 12½ c. red 40 20

31. Queen Wilhelmina. 32. Netherlands Coat of Arms.

1941. As T 78 of Netherlands but inscr. "NED. INDIE" and T 31.
429. – 10 c. red 10 5
430. – 15 c. blue 65 50
431. – 17½ c. orange 20 25
432. – 20 c. mauve .. .. 7·50 9·00
433. – 25 c. green .. .. 10·00 16·00
434. – 30 c. brown 90 35
435. – 35 c. purple .. .. 35·00 70·00
436. – 40 c. green .. .. 3·00 95
437. – 50 c. red 95 30
438. – 60 c. blue 55 25
439. – 80 c. red 60 40
440. – 1 g. violet 80 15
441. – 2 g. green .. .. 4·50 45
442. – 5 g. bistre .. .. 90·00 £200
443. – 10 g. green .. .. 12·00 5·50
444. 31. 25 g. orange .. .. 75·00 38·00
Nos 429/36 measure 18×23 mm., Nos. 437/43 20½×26 mm.

1941. Prince Bernhard and Spitfire Funds.
453. 32. 5 c.+5 c. blue & orange 5 5
454. 10 c.+10 c. blue and red 5 5
455. 1 g.+1 g. blue and grey 4·50 3·50

33. Doctor and Child. 34. Wayangwong Dancer.

1941. Indigent Mohammedans' Relief Fund.
456. 33. 2 c.+1 c. green .. 20 35
457. – 3½ c.+1½ c. brown .. 1·40 1·50
458. – 7½ c.+2½ c. violet .. 90 90
459. – 10 c.+2½ c. red .. 40 10
460. – 15 c.+5 c. blue .. 3·25 1·60
DESIGNS: 3½ c. Native eating rice. 7½ c. Nurse and patient. 10 c. Nurse and children. 15 c. Basket-weaver.

1941.
461. – 2 c. red 5 20
462. – 2½ c. claret 8 10
463. – 3 c. green 10 20
514. – 3 c. red 5 5
464. 34. 4 c. olive 8 15
515. – 4 c. green 5 5
465. – 5 c. blue 5 5
466. – 7½ c. violet 25 5
516. – 7½ c. brown 30 30
DESIGNS (dancers): 2 c., 3 c. (No. 514), Menari. 2½ c. Nias. 3 c. (No. 463), 4 c. (No. 515), Legon. 5 c. Padjoge. 7½ c. (2) Dyak.

35. Paddy Field. 36. Queen Wilhelmina.

1945.
467. 35. 1 c. green 10 5
468. – 2 c. mauve 15 12
469. – 2½ c. purple 10 8
470. – 5 c. blue 5 5
471. – 7½ c. olive 15 5
472. 36. 10 c. brown 5 5
473. 15 c. blue 5 5
474. 17½ c. red 8 5
475. 20 c. purple 8 5
476. 30 c. grey 12 5
477. – 60 c. grey 25 5
478. – 1 g. green 40 5
479. – 2½ g. orange .. .. 1·00 12
DESIGNS—As T 35: 2 c. Lake in W. Java. 2½ c. Medical School, Batavia. 5 c. Seashore. 7½ c. Aeroplane over Bromo Volcano.
Nos. 477/9 are as Type 36 but larger (30×30 mm.).

37. Viaduct near Soekaboemi. 38. Queen Wilhelmina.

1946.
484. 37. 1 c. green 5 5
485. – 2 c. brown 5 5
486. – 2½ c. red 5 5
487. – 5 c. blue 5 5
488. – 7½ c. blue 8 5
DESIGNS: 2 c. Power station. 3 c. Minangkabau house. 5 c. Tondano scene (Celebes). 7½ c. Buddhist Stupas, Java.

1947. Surch. in figures.
502. – 3 c. on 2½ c. red (No. 486) 5 5
503. – 3 c. on 7½ c. bl. (No. 488) 5 5
504. 37. 4 c. on 1 c. green .. 8 5
505. – 45 c. on 60 c. blue (No. 355) 45 40
No. 505 has three bars.

1947. Optd. **1947.**
506. 20. 12½ c. red 5 5
507. 25 c. green 10 5
508. 31. 40 c. green 15 5
509. – 50 c. blue (No. 354) .. 30 15
510. – 80 c. red (No. 356) .. 40 30
511. 31. 2 g. green .. .. 1·50 20
512. 5 g. bistre .. .. 3·50 2·75
The 80 c. has a bar over "1947".

1948. Relief for Victims of the Terror. Surch. **PELITA 15+10 Ct.** and lamp.
513. 20. 15 c.+10 c. on 10 c. red 5 5

1948.
517. 38. 15 c. orange 25 25
518. 20 c. blue 5 5
519. 25 c. green 5 5
520. 40 c. green 10 5
521. 45 c. mauve 15 20
522. 50 c. lake 10 5
523. 80 c. red 10 5
524. 1 g. violet 12 5
525. 10 g. green .. .. 9·00 2·00
526. 25 g. orange .. .. 18·00 17·00
Nos. 524/6 are larger (21×26 mm.).

1948. Queen Wilhelmina's Golden Jubilee. As T 38 but inscr. "1898 1948".
528. 15 c. orange 8 5
529. 20 c. blue 10 5

1948. As T 25 of Curacao.
530. 15 c. red 8 5
531. 20 c. blue 10 5

MARINE INSURANCE STAMPS

1921. As Type M 1 of the Netherlands, but inscribed "NED. INDIE".
M 257. 15 c. green .. .. 1·00 10·00
M 258. 60 c. red .. .. 2·75 16·00
M 259. 75 c. brown .. .. 2·75 18·00
M 260. 1 g. 50 blue .. .. 9·00 70·00
M 261. 2 g. 25 brown .. .. 12·00 £100
M 262. 4½ g. black .. .. 16·00 £150
M 263. 7½ g. red .. .. 55·00 £500

OFFICIAL STAMPS

1911. Stamps of 1883 optd. **D** in white letters in black circle.
O 178. 4. 10 c. brown 45 20
O 179. 12½ c. grey .. .. 80 1·50
O 180. 15 c. bistre 80 80
O 181. 20 c. blue 60 30
O 182. 25 c. mauve .. .. 2·50 2·75
O 183. 50 c. red 40 30
O 184. 2 g. 50, blue and brown 15·00 16·00

1911. Stamps of 1902 (except No. O 185), optd. **DIENST.**
O 186. ½ c. lilac 5 12
O 187. 1 c. olive 5 5
O 188. 2 c. brown 5 5
O 185. 2½ c. yellow (No. 91) .. 25 25
O 189. 2½ c. green 40 45
O 190. 3 c. orange 15 10
O 191. 4 c. blue.. .. 5 5
O 192. 5 c. red 25 25
O 193. 7½ c. grey 80 90
O 194. 10 c. slate 8 5
O 195. 12½ c. blue 65 90
O 196. 15 c. brown 20 20
O 197. 15 c. brown (No. 140).. 12·00
O 198. 17½ c. bistre .. .. 1·10 90
O 199. 20 c. olive 20 15
O 200. 22½ c. olive and brown.. 1·25 1·00
O 201. 25 c. mauve 65 65
O 202. 30 c. brown 30 15
O 203. 50 c. claret .. .. 4·00 2·75
O 204. 1 g. lilac.. .. 1·00 50
O 205. 2½ g. grey .. .. 10·00 11·00

POSTAGE DUE STAMPS

1874 As Postage Due stamps of Netherlands. Colours changed.
D 56. D 1. 5 c. yellow .. .. 60·00 70·00
D 57. 10 c. green on yellow 30·00 20·00
D 59. 15 c. orange on yellow 7·00 5·00
D 60. 20 c. green on blue .. 12·00 2·25

1882. As Type D 1 of Curacao.
D 63. D 1. 2½ c. black and red.. 12 35
D 69. 5 c. black and red .. 8 10
D 65. 10 c. black and red.. 80 1·00
D 70. 15 c. black and red.. 1·00 1·00
D 81. 20 c. black and red.. 28·00 10
D 82. 30 c. black and red.. 60 80
D 72. 40 c. black and red.. 40 60
D 73. 50 c. black and red.. 20 20
D 74. 75 c. black and red.. 15 15

1892. As Type D 2 of Curacao.
D 102. D 2. 2½ c. black and rose 20 10
D 103. 5 c. black and rose 80 5
D 104b. 10 c. black and rose 95 80
D 105. 15 c. black and rose 3·00 60
D 106b. 20 c. black and rose 1·40 25
D 107. 30 c. black and rose 4·50 1·75
D 108. 40 c. black and rose 3·00 45
D 109. 50 c. black and rose 2·00 30
D 110. 75 c. black and rose 4·50 1·10

1913. As Type D 2 of Curacao.
D 226. D 2. 1 c. red 5 30
D 227. 2½ c. red 5 5
D 228. 3½ c. red 5 30
D 229. 5 c. red 5 5
D 230. 7½ c. red 5 5
D 231. 10 c. red 5 5
D 232. 12½ c. red .. .. 1·00 5
D 448. 15 c. red 50 50
D 234. 20 c. red 5 5
D 235. 25 c. red 5 5
D 236. 30 c. red 8 10
D 237. 37½ c. red .. .. 4·00 3·50
D 238. 40 c. red 5 5
D 239. 50 c. red 55 5
D 240. 75 c. red 95 5
D 241. 1 g. red .. .. 1·40 2·00
D 452. 1 g. blue 25 20

1937. Surch. **20.**
D 384. D 2. 20 c. on 37½ c. red 5 10

1946. Optd. **TE BETALEN PORT** or surch. also.
D 480. 2½ c. on 10 c. red (No. 429) 30 30
D 481. 10 c. red (No. 429) .. 45 45
D 482. 20 c. mauve (No. 432) .. 1·25 1·25
D 483. 40 c. green (No. 436) .. 11·00 11·00

1946. As Type D 2 of Curacao.
D 489. D 2. 1 c. violet 25 35
D 527. 2½ c. brown 20 25
D 491. 3½ c. blue 25 30
D 492. 5 c. orange 30 35
D 493. 7½ c. green 30 35
D 494. 10 c. lilac 30 35
D 495. 20 c. blue 30 40
D 496. 25 c. olive 35 45
D 497. 30 c. brown 45 50
D 498. 40 c. green 50 55
D 499. 50 c. yellow 50 55
D 500. 75 c. blue 50 55
D 501. 100 c. green 50 55

For later issues see **INDONESIA.**

NETHERLANDS NEW GUINEA O2

The Western half of the island of New Guinea was governed by the Netherlands until 1962, when control was transferred to the U.N. (see West New Guinea). The territory later became part of Indonesia as West Irian (q.v.).

1950. As numeral and portrait types of Netherlands but inscr. "NIEUW GUINEA".
1. 99. 1 c. grey 8 5
2. 2 c. orange 8 5
3. 2½ c. olive 8 5
4. 3 c. magenta 70 60
5. 4 c. green 70 60
6. 5 c. blue .. .. 1·75 10
7. 7½ c. brown 20 10
8. 10 c. violet 80 10
9. 12½ c. red 80 70
10. 108. 15 c. brown 50 30
11. 20 c. blue 15 5
12. 25 c. red 15 5
13. 30 c. blue 90 15
14. 40 c. green 30 5
15. 45 c. brown 90 30
16. 50 c. orange 30 5
17. 55 c. grey .. .. 1·50 30
18. 80 c. purple .. .. 2·00 1·50
19. 109. 1 g. red .. .. 4·25 5
20. 2 g. brown .. .. 3·75 70
21. 5 g. green .. .. 3·50 55

1953. Netherlands Flood Relief Fund. As last surch. **hulp nederland 1953** and premium.
22. 99. 5 c.+5 c. blue .. 5·00 4·50
23. 108. 15 c.+10 c. brown .. 5·00 4·50
24. 25 c.+10 c. red .. 5·00 4·50

1. Bird of Paradise. 2. Queen Juliana.

1954.
25. 1. 1 c. yellow and red .. 5 5
26. 5 c. yellow and sepia .. 5 5
60. – 7 c. purple blue & chest. 8 15
27. – 10 c. brown and blue .. 8 5
61. – 12 c. purple, blue and green 8 20
28. – 15 c. brown and lemon.. 12 5
62. – 17 c. purple and blue .. 8 12
29. – 20 c. brown and green .. 35 15
30. 2. 25 c. red 10 5
31. 30 c. blue 10 5
32. 40 c. orange .. .. 90 1·25
33. 45 c. olive 30 50
34. 55 c. turquoise 20 5
35. 80 c. violet-grey 35 20
36. 85 c. maroon .. .. 1·10 80
37. 1 g. purple .. .. 1·10 80
DESIGNS: 7 c., 12 c., 17 c. Crown-pigeon. 10 c., 15 c., 20 c. As T 1 but wings outstretched.

1955. Red Cross. As last surch. with cross and premium.
38. 1. 5 c.+5 c. yellow and sepia 55 60
39. – 10 c.+10 c. brown & blue 60 60
40. – 15 c.+10 c. brown & lemon 60 60

3. Child and Native Hut. 4. Papuan Girl and Beach Scene.

1956. Anti-Leprosy Fund.
41. – 5 c.+5 c. green 40 45
42. 3. 10 c.+5 c. maroon 45 50
43. – 25 c.+10 c. blue 50 50
44. 3. 30 c.+10 c. buff 50 50
DESIGN: 5 c., 25 c. Palm-trees and native hut.

1957. Child Welfare Fund.
51. 4. 5 c.+5 c. lake 50 50
52. – 10 c.+5 c. green 50 50
53. 4. 25 c.+10 c. brown 50 50
54. – 30 c.+10 c. blue 50 50
DESIGN: 10 c., 30 c. Papuan child and native hut.

5. Red Cross and Idol. 6. Papuan and Helicopter.

1958. Red Cross Fund.
55. 5. 5 c+5 c. multicoloured 45 50
56. – 10 c.+5 c. multicoloured 45 50
57. 5. 25 c.+10 c. multicoloured 45 50
58. – 30 c.+10 c. multicoloured 45 50
DESIGN: 10 c., 30 c. Red Cross and Asman-Papuan bowl in form of human figure.

1959. Stars Mountains Expedition, 1959.
59. 6. 55 c. brown and blue 60 45

7. "Tecomanthe dendrophila". 8. "Papilio paradisea Stgr.".

1959. Social Welfare. Inscr. "SOCIALE ZORG".
63. 7. 5 c.+5 c. red and green 25 25
64. – 10 c.+5 c. purple, yellow and olive 25 25
65. – 25 c.+10 c. yellow, green and red 30 35
66. – 30 c.+10 c. green & violet 30 35
DESIGNS: 10 c. "Dendrobium attennatum Lindley". 25 c. "Rhododendron zoeileri Warburg". 30 c. "Boea cf. urvillei".

1960. World Refugee Year. As T **154** of Netherlands.
67. 25 c. blue 25 30
68. 30 c. ochre 30 40

1960. Social Welfare Funds. Butterflies.
69. 8. 5 c.+5 c. multicoloured 35 40
70. – 10 c.+5 c. bl., blk. & salmon 35 40
71. – 25 c.+10 c. red, sep. & yell. 35 40
72. – 30 c.+10 c. multicoloured 35 40
BUTTERFLIES: 10 c. "Thysonotis danis Cr.". 25 c. "Cethosia cydippe L." 30 c. "Taeuaris catops Westw.".

9. Council Building, Hollandia. 10. "Scapanes australis Boisd. (Dynastidae)".

1961. Opening of Netherlands New Guinea Council.
73. 9. 25 c. turquoise 15 20
74. 30 c. red 15 20

1961. Social Welfare Funds. Beetles.
75. 10. 5 c.+5 c. multicoloured 15 20
76. – 10 c.+5 c. multicoloured 15 20
77. – 25 c.+10 c. multicoloured 20 20
78. – 30 c.+10 c. multicoloured 20 25
BEETLES: 10 c. "Ectocemus 10-maculatus Montri. (Brenthidae.)" 25 c. "Neolamprina adolphinae Gastro (Lucanidae.)". 30 c. "A spidomorpha aurata Montr. (Cassididae.)".

11. Children's Road Crossing.

1962. Road Safety Campaign. Triangle in red.
79. 11. 25 c. blue 15 20
80. – 30 c. green (Adults at road crossing) 15 20

1962. Silver Wedding of Queen Juliana and Prince Bernhard. As T **161** of Netherlands.
81. 55 c. brown 20 25

12. Shadow of Palm on Beach. 13. Lobster.

1962. 5th South Pacific Conf., Pago Pago Multicoloured.
82. 25 c. Type **12** 15 20
83. 30 c. Palms on beach 15 20

1962. Social Welfare Funds. Shellfish Multicoloured.
84. 5 c.+5 c. Crab (horiz.) 10 10
85. 10 c.+5 c. Type **13** 10 12
86. 25 c.+10 c. Spray lobster 12 15
87. 30 c.+10 c. Shrimp (horiz.) 15 20

POSTAGE DUE STAMPS

1957. As Type D 4 of Netherlands but inscr. "NEDERLANDS NIEUW GUINEA".
D 45. 1 c. red 5 10
D 46. 5 c. red 20 60
D 47. 10 c. red 40 1·00
D 48. 25 c. red 50 40
D 49. 40 c. red 50 45
D 50. 1 g. blue 85 1·60

For later issues see **WEST NEW GUINEA** and **WEST IRIAN**.

NEVIS BC

One of the Leeward Islands, Br. W. Indies. Now uses stamps of St. Christopher, Nevis and Anguilla.

1. 2.

(The design on the stamps refers to a medicinal spring on the island.)

1861. Various frames.
5. 1. 1d. rose 11·00 11·00
15. 1d. red 4·50 5·50
6. 2. 4d. rose 25·00 21·00
12. 4d. orange 35·00 10·00
7. – 6d. grey-lilac 21·00 15·00
13. – 1s green 55·00 14·00

3.

ILLUSTRATIONS
British Commonwealth and all overprints and surcharges are FULL SIZE. Foreign Countries have been reduced to ¾-LINEAR.

1879.
25. 3. ½d. green 1·75 2·00
26. 1d. mauve 25·00 10·00
27. 1d. red 1·40 1·75
28. 2½d. brown 35·00 28·00
29. 2½d. blue 2·10 2·10
30. 4d. blue £110 25·00
31. 4d. grey 2·10 2·10
32. 6d. green £130 £130
33. 6d. brown 10·00 15·00
34. 1s. violet 35·00 85·00

1883. Half of No. 26 surch. **NEVIS ½d.**
36. 3. ½d. on half 1d. mauve 85·00 14·00

NEW BRUNSWICK BC

An eastern province of the Dominion of Canada, whose stamps are now used. Currency, as Canada.

1. Royal Crown and Heraldic Flowers of the United Kingdom.

1851.
2. 1. 3d. red £1500 £200
4. 6d. yellow £2500 £700
6. 1s. mauve £7500 £2500

2. 3. Queen Victoria.

1860.
9. 2. 1 c. purple 6·00 8·00
10. 3. 2 c. orange 6·00 8·00
13. – 5 c. brown £1100
14. – 5 c. green 6·00 6·50
17. – 10 c. red 10·00 11·00
18. – 12½ c. blue 15·00 16·00
19. – 17 c. black 10·00 14·00
DESIGNS—VERT. 5 c. brown, Charles Connell. 5 c. green. 10 c. Queen Victoria. 17 c. King Edward VII when Prince of Wales. HORIZ. 12½ c. Steamship.

NEW CALEDONIA O3

A French Overseas Territory in the S. Pacific, E. of Australia, consisting of New Caledonia and a number of smaller islands.

1. Napoleon III.

1860. Imperf.
1. 1. 10 c. black 22·00

Stamps of French Colonies optd. or surch.

1881. "Peace and Commerce" type surch. **NCE** and value in figures (or **N.C.E.** on No. 5).
5. 8. 05 on 40 c red on yellow 3·35 3·25
8a. 5 on 40 c. red on yellow 1·25 1·25
9a. 5 on 75 c. red 3·75 3·75
11. 5 c. on 1 f. olive £1400 £1300
6a. 25 on 35 c. black on orange 40·00 35·00
7. 25 on 75 c. red 50·00 42·00

1886. "Commerce" type surch. **N.C.E. 5 C.**
10. 9. 5 c. on 1 f. olive 2·75 2·50

1891. "Peace and Commerce" type surch. **N.-C.E. 10 c.** in ornamental frame.
13. 8. 10 c. on 40 c. red on yellow 2·75 2·25

1891. "Commerce" type surch. **N.-C.E. 10 centimes** or without "centimes", in ornamental frame.
15. 9. 10 c. on 30 c. brown 1·40 1·40
14. 10 c. on 40 c. red on yellow 1·60 1·60

1892. "Peace and Commerce" type optd. **NLLE CALEDONIE.**
16. 8. 20 c. red on green 50·00 50·00
17. 35 c. black on orange 5·50 5·00
19. 1 f. olive 32·00 32·00

1892. "Commerce" type optd. **NLLE CALEDONIE.**
20. 9. 5 c. green 1·75 1·25
21. 10 c. black on lilac 11·00 7·00
22. 15 c. blue 10·00 4·50
23. 20 c. red on green 9·00 6·50
24. 25 c. yellow 2·25 1·25
25. 25 c. black on red 11·00 1·75
26. 30 c. brown 8·00 7·00
27. 35 c. black on orange 19·00 19·00
29. 75 c. red 22·00 19·00
30. 1 f. olive 16·00 13·00

1892. "Commerce" type surch. **N-C-E** in ornamental scroll and value in figures.
32. 9. 5 on 20 c. red on green 2·75 1·75
34. 5 on 75 c. red 1·10 90
35. 10 on 1 f. olive 1·25 1·00

1892. "Tablet" key-type inscr. "NLLE CALEDONIE ET DEPENDANCES".
37. D. 1 c. black on blue 5 5
38. 2 c. brown on yellow 10 10
39. 4 c. claret on grey 15 12
55. 5 c. green 10 5
41. 10 c. black on lilac 75 40
56. 10 c. red 80 15
42. 15 c. blue 2·50 8
57. 15 c. grey 1·00 10
43. 20 c. red on green 1·00 1·00
44. 25 c. black on red 1·90 40
58. 25 c. blue 1·40 75
45. 30 c. brown 1·90 1·60
46. 40 c. red on yellow 1·90 1·60
47. 50 c. red 3·75 1·90
59. 50 c. brown on blue (A) 10·00 10·00
60. 50 c. brown on blue (B) 5·50 4·50
48. 75 c. brown on orange 2·25 1·90
49. 1 f. olive 2·75 1·75
(A) has name in red, (B) in blue.

1900. Surch. **N-C-E** in ornamental scroll and **5.**
50. D. 5 on 2 c. brown on yellow 2·40 2·25
51. 5 on 4 c. claret on grey 35 35

1900. Surch. **N.C.E.** and **15** in circle.
52. D. 15 on 30 c. brown 45 45
53. 15 on 75 c. brown on oran. 1·60 1·10
54. 15 on 1 f. olive 2·50 2·50

1902. Surch. **N.-C.E.** and value in figures.
61. D. 5 on 30 c. brown 1·10 1·00
62. 15 on 40 c. red on yellow 90 90

1903. French Occupation. 50th Anniv. Optd. **CINQUANTENAIRE 24 SEPTEMBRE 1853 1903** and eagle.
63. D. 1 c. black on blue 20 20
64. 2 c. brown on yellow 30 20
65. 4 c. claret on grey 45 20
66. 5 c. green 65 45
68. 10 c. black on lilac 85 85
70. 15 c. grey 1·40 65
71. D. 20 c. red on green 2·25 1·75
72. 25 c. black on red 2·25 1·75
73. 30 c. brown 2·75 2·25
74. 40 c. red on yellow 3·25 2·75
75. 50 c. red 4·50 2·75
76. 75 c. brown on orange 7·00 6·00
77. 1 f. olive 9·50 9·50

1903. Nos. 64, etc., further surch. with value in figures within the Jubilee optd.
78. D. 1 on 2 c. brown on yellow 10 10
79. 2 on 4 c. claret on grey 15 15
80. 4 on 5 c. green 20 20
82. 10 on 15 c. grey 30 30
83. 15 on 20 c. red on green 30 30
84. 20 on 25 c. black on red 30 30

2. Kagu. 3.

4.

1905.
85. 2. 1 c. black on green 5 5
86. 2 c. claret 5 5
87. 4 c. blue on orange 5 5
88. 5 c. green 5 5
112. 5 c. blue 5 5
114. 10 c. red 5 5
113. 10 c. green 5 5
90. 15 c. lilac 5 5
91. 3. 20 c. brown 5 5
92. 25 c. blue on green 5 5
115. 25 c. red on yellow 5 5
93. 30 c. brown on orange 5 5
116. 30 c. red 8 8
117. 30 c. orange 5 5
94. 35 c. black on yellow 5 5
95. 40 c. red on green 5 5
96. 45 c. claret 5 5
97. 50 c. red on orange 15 12
118. 50 c. blue 8 8
119. 50 c. grey 5 5
120. 65 c. blue 5 5
98. 75 c. olive 5 5
121. 75 c. blue 5 5
122. 75 c. violet 5 5
99. 4. 1 f. blue on green 5 5
123. 1 f. blue 5 5
100. 2 f. red on blue 15 15
101. 5 f. black on orange 65 60

1912. Surch. in figures.
124. 2. 0.05 on 15 c. lilac 5 5
102. D. 05 on 15 c. grey 8 8
103. 05 on 20 c. red on green 5 5
104. 05 on 30 c. brown 8 8
105. 10 on 40 c. red on yellow 20 20
106. 10 on 50 c. brown on blue 25 25
125. 2. 25 c. on 15 c. lilac 5 5
126. 4. 25 c. on 2 f. red on blue 5 5
127. 25 c. on 5 f. black on orge. 10 10
128. 3. 60 on 75 c. green 5 5
129. 65 on 45 c. claret 5 5
130. 85 on 45 c. claret 5 5
131. 90 on 75 c. red 8 8
132. 4. 1 f. 25 on 1 f. blue 5 5
133. 1 f. 50 on 1 f. blue on blue 8 8
134. 3 f. on 5 f. mauve 10 10
135. 10f. on 5 f. olive 75 75
136. 20 f. on 5 f. red on yellow 1·50 1·50

1915. Surch. with large red cross **5** and **NCE** slanting.
107. 2. 10 c.+5 c. red 10 10

1915. Surch. in figures and small red cross.
109. 2. 10 c.+5 c. red 5 5
110. 15 c.+5 c. lilac 5 5

1918. Surch. **5 CENTIMES.**
111. 2. 5 c. on 15 c. lilac 15 15

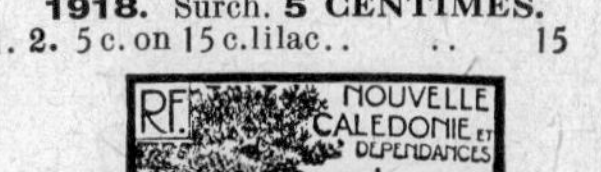

5. Pointe des Paletuviers.

6. Chief's Hut.

7. La Perouse and De Bougainville.

1928.

137. 5. 1 c. blue and purple .. 5 5
138. 2 c. green and brown .. 5 5
139. 3 c. blue and red 5 5
140. 4 c. blue and orange .. 5 5
141. 5 c. brown and blue .. 5 5
142. 10 c. brown and lilac .. 5 5
143. 15 c. blue and brown .. 5 5
144. 20 c. brown and red .. 5 5
145. 25 c. brown and green .. 5 5
146. 6. 30 c. green 5 5
147. 35 c. mauve and black .. 5 5
148. 40 c. olive and red .. 5 5
149. 45 c. red and blue .. 5 5
150. 45 c. green 5 5
151. 50 c. brown and mauve 5 5
152. 55 c. red and blue .. 25 12
153. 60 c. red and blue .. 5 5
154. 65 c. blue and brown .. 5 5
155. 70 c. brown and claret .. 5 5
156. 75 c. olive and blue .. 15 5
157. 80 c. green and maroon 5 5
158. 85 c. brown and green .. 15 8
159. 90 c. red 8 5
160. 90 c. red and brown .. 5 5
161. 7. 1 f. red and brown .. 50 30
162. 1 f. red 10 8
163. 1 f. green and red .. 5 5
164. 1 f. 10 brown and green 1·10 1·00
165. 1 f. 25 green and brown 8 8
166. 1 f. 25 red 5 5
167. 1 f. 40 red and blue .. 5 5
168. 1 f. 50 blue 5 5
169. 1 f. 60 brown and green 8 8
170. 1 f. 75 orange and blue 8 8
171. 1 f. 75 blue 5 5
172. 2 f. brown and orange .. 5 5
173. 2 f. 25 blue 5 5
174. 2 f. 50 brown 5 5
175. 3 f. brown and claret .. 5 5
176. 5 f. brown and blue .. 5 5
177. 10 f. brn. & pur. on pink 15 15
178. 20 f. brown & red on yell. 25 20

1931. "Colonial Exn." key-types.

179. E. 40 c. green 50 50
180. F. 50 c. mauve 50 50
181. G. 90 c. red 50 50
182. H. 1 f. 50 blue 50 50

1932. Paris-Noumea Flight. Optd. with aeroplane and **PARIS-NOUMEA Verneilh-Dove-Munch 5 Avril 1932.**

183. 6. 40 c. olive and red .. 55·00 55·00
184. 50 c. brown and mauve 55·00 55·00

1933. Paris-Noumea Flight. 1st Anniv. Optd. with small aeroplane and **PARIS-NOUMEA Premiere liaison aerienne 5 Avil 1932.**

185. 5. 1 c. blue and purple .. 60 60
186. 2 c. green and brown .. 60 60
187. 4 c. blue and orange .. 60 60
188. 5 c. brown and blue .. 60 60
189. 10 c. brown and lilac .. 60 60
190. 15 c. blue and brown .. 60 60
191. 20 c. brown and red .. 60 60
192. 25 c. brown and green .. 60 60
193. 6. 30 c. green 60 60
194. 35 c. mauve and black .. 60 60
195. 40 c. olive and red .. 60 60
196. 45 c. red and blue .. 60 60
197. 50 c. brown and mauve .. 60 60
198. 70 c. brown and claret .. 70 70
199. 75 c. olive and blue .. 70 70
200. 85 c. brown and green .. 70 70
201. 90 c. red 70 70
202. 7. 1 f. red and brown .. 70 70
203. 1 f. 25 green and brown .. 70 70
204. 1 f. 50 blue 70 70
205. 1 f. 75 orange and blue 70 70
206. 2 f. brown and orange .. 70 70
207. 3 f. brown and claret .. 70 70
208. 5 f. brown and blue .. 70 70
209. 10 f. brn. & pur. on pink 70 70
210. 20 f. brn. & red on yellow 75 75

1937. Int. Exn., Paris. As Nos. 110/15 of Cameroun.

211. 20 c. violet 12 12
212. 30 c. green 12 12
213. 40 c. red 12 12
214. 50 c. brown 12 12
215. 90 c. red 12 12
216. 1 f. 50 blue 12 12

8. Flying-boat over Noumea.

1938. Air.

217. 8. 65 c. violet 5 5
218. 4 f. 50 red 10 10
219. 7 f. green 5 5
220. 9 f. blue 40 40
221. 20 f. orange 20 20
222. 50 f. black 25 25

1938. Int. Anti-Cancer Fund. As T 10 of Cameroun.

223. 1 f. 75+50 c. blue .. 1·00 1·00

1939. New York World's Fair. As T 11 of Cameroun.

224. 1 f. 25 red 8 8
225. 2 f. 25 blue 8 8

1939. French Revolution. 150th Anniv. As T 16 of Cameroun.

226. 45 c.+25 c. green (postage) 90 90
227. 70 c.+30 c. brown .. 90 90
228. 90 c.+35 c. orange .. 90 90
229. 1 f. 25+1 f. red .. 90 90
230. 2 f. 25+2 f. blue 90 90
231. 4 f. 50+4 f. black (air) .. 2·00 2·00

1941. Free French Issue. Optd. **France Libre.**

232. 5. 1 c. blue and purple .. 65 65
233. 2 c. green and brown .. 65 65
234. 3 c. blue and red 65 65
235. 4 c. blue and orange .. 65 65
236. 5 c. brown and blue .. 65 65
237. 10 c. brown and lilac .. 65 65
238. 15 c. blue and brown .. 1·75 1·75
239. 20 c. brown and red .. 1·75 1·75
240. 25 c. brown and green .. 1·75 1·75
241. 6. 30 c. green .. .. 1·75 1·75
242. 35 c. mauve and black .. 1·75 1·75
243. 40 c. olive and red .. 1·75 1·75
244. 45 c. green .. .. 1·75 1·75
245. 50 c. brown and mauve .. 1·75 1·75
246. 55 c. red and blue .. 1·75 1·75
247. 60 c. red and blue .. 1·75 1·75
248. 65 c. blue and brown .. 1·75 1·75
249. 70 c. brown and claret .. 1·75 1·75
250. 75 c. olive and blue .. 1·75 1·75
251. 80 c. green and maroon 1·75 1·75
252. 85 c. brown and green .. 1·75 1·75
253. 90 c. red .. .. 1·75 1·75
254. 7. 1 f. red .. .. .. 1·75 1·75
255. 1 f. 25 green and brown 1·75 1·75
256. 1 f. 40 red and blue .. 1·75 1·75
257. 1 f. 50 blue .. .. 1·75 1·75
258. 1 f. 60 brown and green .. 1·75 1·75
259. 1 f. 75 orange and blue .. 1·75 1·75
260. 2 f. brown and orange .. 1·75 1·75
261. 2 f. 25 blue .. .. 1·75 1·75
262. 2 f. 50 brown .. .. 1·75 1·75
263. 3 f. brown and claret .. 1·75 1·75
264. 5 f. brown and blue .. 1·75 1·75
265. 10 f. brn. & pur. on pink 1·75 1·75
266. 20 f. brn. & red on yellow 1·75 1·75

9. Kagu.

1942. Free French Issue (a) Postage.

267. 9. 5 c. brown 5 5
268. 10 c. blue 5 5
269. 25 c. green 5 5
270. 30 c. red 5 5
271. 40 c. green 5 5
272. 80 c. maroon 5 5
273. 1 f. mauve 5 5
274. 1 f. 50 red 5 5
275. 2 f. black 5 5
276. 2 f. 50 blue 8 8
277. 4 f. violet 8 8
278. 5 f. yellow 8 8
279. 10 f. brown 12 12
280. 20 f. green 20 20

(b) Air. As T 18 of Cameroun.

281. 1 f. orange 5 5
282. 1 f. 50 red 5 5
283. 5 f. maroon 5 5
284. 10 f. black 12 12
285. 25 f. blue 15 15
286. 50 f. green 25 25
287. 100 f. claret 30 30

1944. Mutual Aid and Red Cross Funds. A T 19 of Cameroun.

288. 5 f.+20 f. red 8 8

1945. Eboue. As T 20 of Cameroun.

289. 2 f. black 5 5
290. 25 f. green 15 20

1945. Surch.

291. 9. 50 c. on 5 c. brown .. 5 5
292. 60 c. on 5 c. brown .. 8 8
293. 70 c. on 5 c. brown .. 8 8
294. 1 f. 20 on 5 c. brown .. 5 5
295. 2 f. 40 on 25 c. green .. 5 5
296. 3 f. on 25 c. green .. 8 8
297. 4 f. 50 on 25 c. green .. 12 12
298. 15 f. on 2 f. 50 blue .. 20 20

1946. Air. Victory. As Cameroun T 21.

299. 8 f. blue 12 12

1946. Air. From Chad to the Rhine. As T 22 of Cameroun.

300. 5 f. black 12 12
301. 10 f. red 12 12
302. 15 f. blue 12 12
303. 20 f. brown 15 15
304. 25 f. green 20 20
305. 50 f. purple 30 30

10. Kagu.

11. Chief's Hut.

12. Aeroplane over St. Vincent Bay.

1948. (a) Postage.

306. 10. 10 c. purple and yellow 5 5
307. 30 c. purple and green .. 5 5
308. 40 c. purple and brown 5 5
309. – 50 c. maroon and red .. 5 5
310. – 60 c. brown and yellow 5 5
311. – 80 c. green 5 5
312. – 1 f. violet and orange .. 5 5
313. – 1 f. 20 brown and blue .. 5 5
314. – 1 f. 50 blue & yellow .. 5 5
315. – 2 f. brown and green .. 5 5
316. – 2 f. 40 red and claret .. 5 5
317. – 3 f. violet and orange .. 55 8
318. – 4 f. blue 12 5
319. – 5 f. violet and red .. 15 8
320. – 6 f. brown and yellow .. 15 8
321. – 10 f. blue and orange .. 20 5
322. 11. 15 f. lake and blue .. 25 20
323. 20 f. violet and yellow .. 30 25
324. 25 f. blue and orange .. 40 25

DESIGNS—HORIZ. 50 c. to 80 c. Ducos Sanatorium. 1 f. to 1 f. 50, Porcupine Is. 2 f. to 4 f. Nickel foundry. 5 f. to 10 f. "The Towers of Notre Dame" Rocks.

(b) Air.

325. 12. 50 f. purple and orange 85 65
326. – 100 f. blue and green .. 1·75 85
327. – 200 f. brown and yellow 3·25 1·75

DESIGNS—VERT. 100 f. Aeroplane over landscape. HORIZ. 200 f. Aeroplane over Noumea.

1949. Air. U.P.U. As Cameroun T 25.

328. 10 f. blue., grn., pur. & red 75 75

1950. Colonial Welfare. As Cameroun T 26.

329. 10 f.+2 f. purple & brown 45 45

1952. Military Medal Cent. As Cameroun T 27.

330. 2 f. red, yellow and green 35 35

DESIGNS: 2 f. Mgr. Douarre and church. 6 f. Admiral D'Urville and map. 13 f. Admiral Despointes and view.

13. Admiral D'Entrecasteaux.

1953. French Administration Cent. Inscr. "1853 1953".

331. 13. 1 f. 50 lake and chestnut 20 20
332. – 2 f. indigo and turquoise 20 20
333. – 6 brown, blue and red 45 35
334. – 13 f. blue and green .. 60 45

1954. Air. Liberation. 10th Anniv. As T 29 of Cameroun.

335. 3 f. blue and indigo .. 80 80

14. Towers of Notre-Dame (rocks).

15. Coffee.

16. Transporting Nickel.

1955.

336. 14. 2 f. 50 c. blue, green and sepia (postage) .. 10 8
337. 3 f. blue, brown & green 65 35
338. 15. 9 f. indigo and blue .. 15 8
339. 16. 14 f. blue & brown (air) 45 12
351. – 15 f. green, sepia & red 35 20
352. – 20 f. chest. & grey-green 40 25
353. – 25 f. black, blue & mar. 45 30
354. – 50 f. choc., green & blue 1·00 55
355. – 50 f. brown, green & blue 70 50
356. – 100 f. sep., green & ind. 1·60 85
357. – 200 f. choc., grn. & blue 3·50 2·00

DESIGNS—As T 16—HORIZ. 20 f. Fisherman with net. 20 f. Nautilus. 25 f. Underwater swimmer firing gun at fish. 50 f. (355) Isle of Pines. 100 f. Corbeille de Yate. 200 f. The Carved Rock, Bourail. VERT. 50 f. (354) Yate barrage

17. Dumbea Barrage.

18. "Brachyrus zebra" (fish).

1956. Economic and Social Development Fund.

340. 17. 3 f. green and blue .. 12 10

1958. Tropical Flora. As French Equatorial Africa T 21.

341. 4 f. red, green, yell. & blue 30 10
342. 15 f. red, yellow & green 40 12

DESIGNS—VERT. 4 f. "Xanthostemon". 15 f. "Hibiscus".

1958. Declaration of Human Rights. 10th Anniv. As Comoro Islands T 5.

343. 7 f. red and blue 20 20

1959. (a) Postage. Size as T 18.

344. 18. 1 f. brown and grey .. 5 5
345. – 2 f. blue, mar. & myrtle 10 8
346. – 3 f. red, blue and green 10 8
347. – 4 f. maroon, red & green 15 12
348. – 5 f. bistre, blue & green 15 12
383. – 7 f. orange, brown & blue 20 10
349. – 10 f. salmon, green, turquoise and black 30 20
384. – 10 f. red and blue .. 30 15
385. – 17 f. lake, green & blue 50 35
350. – 26 f. orange, green, brown and blue .. 75 55

(b) Air. Size 48×27 mm.

388. – 13 f. bistre, blk. & orge. 20 15
389. – 15 f. green, olive & ind. 25 20
390. – 25 f. indigo and green .. 40 30

(c) Air. Multicoloured. Size 48×28 mm.

386. – 27 f. "Paracanthuras teuthis" 50 45
387. – 37 f. "Phyllobranchus" 1·00 55

DESIGNS—HORIZ. 2 f. Melanesian pirogues. 3 f. "Lienardella fasciata" (fish). 5 f. Sail Rock, Noumea. 13 f. "Coris angulata" (juvenile) (fish). 15 f. "C. angulata" (fish). 25 f. "C. angulata" (adult) (fish). 26 f. Fluorescent corals. VERT. 4 f. Fisherman with spear. 7 f. "Ascidies polycarpa" (coral). 10 f. (No. 349), "Glaucus" and "Spirographe" (corals). 10 f. (No. 384), "Alcyonium catali" (coral). 17 f. "Crevette hymenocera" (coral).

19. Napoleon III.

20. Port-de-France, 1859

1960. Stamp Cent.

358. 2. 4 f. red 20 12
359. – 5 f. chestnut and lake .. 20 12
360. – 9 f. choc. & blue-green .. 25 15
361. – 12 f. black and blue .. 25 15
362. 19. 13 f. blue 45 55
363. 20. 19 f. red, green & turq. 50 20
364. – 33 f. red, green & blue .. 1·00 55

DESIGNS—As T 20: HORIZ. 5 f. Girl operating cheque-writing machine. 12 f. Telephone receiver and exchange building. 33 f. As T 20 but without stamps in upper corners. VERT. 9 f. Letter-box on tree.

1962. 5th South Pacific Conference, Pago Pago. As T 6 of French Polynesia.

365. 15 f. multicoloured .. 45 35

21. Map and Symbols of Meteorology.

22. "Bikkia fritillarioides".

1962. 3rd Regional Assembly of World Meteorological Association, Noumea.

366. 21. 50 f. multicoloured .. 1·50 1·10

1962. Air. 1st Trans-Atlantic TV Satellite Link. As T 18 of Andorra.

367. 200 f. turq., choc. and blue 3·25 2·25

1963. Freedom from Hunger. As T **8** of Comoro Is.
368. 17 f. blue and maroon .. 50 35

1963. 1st South Pacific Games, Suva. As T **8** of French Polynesia.
369. 1 f. red and grey-green .. 5 5
370. 7 f. brown and steel-blue .. 20 15
371. 10 f. brown and green .. 30 20
372. 27 f. ultram. & deep purple 70 55
DESIGNS: 1 f. Relay-racing. 7 f. Tennis. 10 f. Football. 27 f. Throwing the javelin.

1963. Red Cross Cent. As Type F **2** of New Hebrides.
373. 37 f. red, grey and blue .. 1·00 1·00

1963. Declaration of Human Rights. 15th Anniv. As T **10** of Comoro Islands.
374. 50 f. claret and indigo .. 1·25 1·25

1964. Flowers. Multicoloured.
375. 1 f. "Freycinettia" .. 5 5
376. 2 f. Type **22** 8 5
377. 3 f. "Xanthostemon francii" 10 5
378. 4 f. "Psidiomyrtus locellatus" 12 8
379. 5 f. "Callistemon suberosum" 15 8
380. 7 f. "Montrouziera sphaeroidea" 20 10
381. 10 f. "Ixora collina" 30 15
382. 17 f. "Deplanchea speciosa" 55 25
The 7 f. and 10 f. are horiz.

1964. "PHILATEC 1964" Int. Stamp Exn., Paris. As T **481** of France.
391. 40 f. brown, green & violet 1·25 1·10

23. Houailou Mine.

1964. Air. Nickel Production at Houailou.
392. **23.** 30 f. multicoloured .. 40 25

24. Ancient Greek Wrestling.

1964. Air. Olympic Games, Tokyo.
393. **24.** 10 f. sepia, mag. & green 1·00 85

25. Weather Satellite. 26. Amedee Lighthouse.

1965. Air. World Meteorological Day.
394. **25.** 9 f. multicoloured .. 65 55

1965. Air. I.T.U. Cent. As T **15** of Comoro Islands.
395. 40 f. purple, brown and blue 1·75 1·10

1965. New Caledonia's Adherence to France. 25th Anniv. As T **495** of France but with inscriptions and value changed.
396. 20 f. black, red and blue .. 80 80

1965. Amedee Lighthouse. Inaug.
397. **26.** 8 f. bistre, blue & green 25 10

1966. Air. Launching of 1st French Satellite. As Nos. 1696/7 of France.
398. 8 f. lake, ultram. & turq... 15 12
399. 12 f. lake, ultram. & turq. 20 15

27. Games Emblem. 29. Red-headed Parrot-finch.

28. Noumea, 1866 (after Lebreton).

1966. Publicity for 2nd South Pacific Games, Noumea (December, 1966).
400. **27.** 8 f. black, red and blue 25 12

1966. Air. Launching of Satellite "D1" As T **521** of France.
401. 10 f. brown, blue & chestnut 20 12

1966. Air. Renaming of Port-de-France as Noumea. Cent.
402. **28.** 30 f. slate, red and blue 45 35

1966. Birds. (1st Series). Multicoloured.
403. 1 f. Type **29** (postage) .. 5 5
404. 1 f. Caledonian warbler .. 5 5
405. 2 f. Caledonian whistler .. 5 5
406. 3 f. Giant Imperial pigeon 10 5
407. 3 f. White-collared dove .. 8 5
408. 4 f. Kagu 10 5
409. 5 f. Horned cockatiel .. 12 5
410. 10 f. Honeyeater 25 15
411. 15 f. Friar bird 25 15
412. 30 f. Kingfisher 55 20

413. 27 f. Horned cockatiel (air) (diff.) 45 30
414. 37 f. Scarlet honeyeater .. 55 40
415. 39 f. Green turtle-doves .. 50 35
416. 50 f. Green fruit doves .. 60 40
417. 100 f. Fish eagles .. .. 1·25 80
Nos. 413/4 are 26 × 45½ mm. Nos. 415/7 are 27½ × 48 mm.

30. U.N.E.S.C.O. Allegory.

1966. U.N.E.S.C.O. 20th Anniv.
418. **30.** 16 f. purple, ochre & grn. 45 20

31. High-jumping.

1966. South Pacific Games, Noumea.
419. **31.** 17 f. violet, grn. & lake 35 35
420. – 20 f. green, purple & lake 50 40
421. – 40 f. green, violet & lake 1·00 65
422. – 100 f. pur., turq. & lake 2·40 1·75
DESIGNS: 20 f. Hurdling. 40 f. Running. 100 f. Swimming.

32. Lekine Cliffs.

1967.
424. **32.** 17 f. grey-green, green and blue 40 25

33. Racing Yachts.

1967. Air. 2nd Whangarei-Noumea Yacht Race.
425. **33.** 25 f. red, blue and green 40 25

34. Magenta Stadium.

1967. Sport Centres. Multicoloured.
426. 10 f. Type **34** 25 15
427. 20 f. Ouen-Toro swimming pool 50 30

35. New Caledonian Scenery.

1967. Int. Tourist Year.
428. **35.** 30 f. multicoloured .. 70 45

36. 19th-Cent. Postman.

1967. Stamp Day.
429. **36.** 7 f. red, green & turq... 15 12

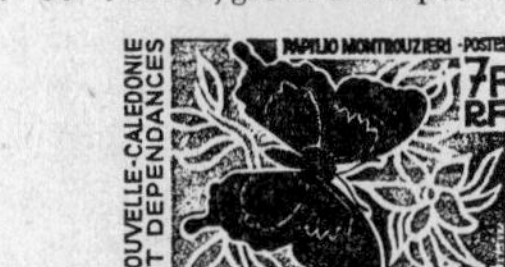

37. "Papilio montrouzieri".

1967. Butterflies.
430. **37.** 7 f. blue, black & emer. (postage) 15 10
431. – 9 f. indigo, brn. & mve. 20 12
432. – 13 f. violet, mar. & brn. 30 20
433. – 15 f. yellow, mar. & blue 35 25

434. – 19 f. orange, brown and green (air) .. 25 15
435. – 29 f. maroon, red & blue 35 25
436. – 85 f. choc., red & yellow 1·10 80
BUTTERFLIES: 9 f. "Polyura clitarchus". 13 f. "Hypolimnas bolina" (male), and 15 f. (female). 19 f. "Danaus plexippus". 29 f. "Hippotion celerio". 85 f. "Delias elipsis". Nos. 434/6 are 48 × 27 mm.

38. Garnierite (mineral), Factory and Jules Garnier.

1967. Air. Garnierite Industry. Cent.
437. **38.** 70 f. sepia, brown, blue and green 85 65

39. Lifou Island.

1967. Air.
438. **39.** 200 f. multicoloured .. 3·00 1·75

40. Skier and Snow-crystal.

1967. Air. Winter Olympic Games, Grenoble.
439. **40.** 100 f. brown, blue & grn. 1·25 85

1968. W.H.O. 20th Anniv. As T **21** of Comoro Islands.
440. 20 f. blue, red and violet .. 50 30

1968. Human Rights Year. As T **23** of Comoro Islands.
441. 12 f. red, green and yellow 30 30

41. Ferrying Mail-van across Tontouta River.

1968. Stamp Day.
442. **41.** 9 f. chocolate, blue & grn. 20 12

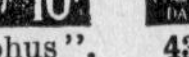

42. "Conus geographus". 43. Dancers.

1968. Seashells.
443. – 1 f. brn., grey & grn. (post.) 5 5
444. – 1 f. maroon and vio. .. 5 5
445. – 2 f. mar., red & blue .. 5 5
446. – 3 f. brown and green .. 5 5
447. – 5 f. red, brn. & violet .. 10 5
448. **42.** 10 f. brn., grey & bl. .. 25 15
449. – 10 f. yell., brn. & red .. 12 8
450. – 10 f. blk., brn. & orge. 10 8
451. – 15 f. red, grey & green 35 15
452. – 21 f. brn., sepia & green 25 12

453. – 22 f. red, brn. & bl. (air) 30 15
454. – 25 f. brown and red .. 25 15
455. – 33 f. brown and blue .. 40 25
456. – 34 f. vio., brn. & orge. 40 20
457. – 39 f. brn., grey & green 50 25
458. – 40 f. blk., brn. & red .. 50 30
459. – 50 f. red, mar. & green 55 40
460. – 60 f. brown and green 80 45
461. – 70 f. brn., grey & violet 85 45
462. – 100 f. brn., blk. & blue 1·40 60
DESIGNS—VERT. 1 f. (No. 443) "Strombus epidromis". 1 f. (No. 444) "Lambis scorpius". 3 f. "Lambis lambis". 10 f. (No. 450) "Strombus variabilis". 22 f. "Strombus sinuatus". 25 f. "Lambis crocata". 34 f. "Strombus vomer". 50 f. "Lambis chiragra". HORIZ. As T **42**. (36 × 22 mm.). 2 f. "Murex haustellum". 5 f. "Murex triremis". 10 f. (No. 449) "Cypraea cribaria". 15 f. "Murex rameux". 21 f. "Cypraea talpe". (48 × 27 mm.). 33 f. "Cypraea argus". 39 f. "Conus lienardi". 40 f. "Conus cabriti". 60 f. "Cypraea mappa". 70 f. "Conus coccineus". 100 f. "Murex noir".

1968. Air.
463. **43.** 60 f. red, blue & green 70 45

44. Rally Car.

1968. 2nd New Caledonian Motor Safari.
464. **44.** 25 f. blue, red and green 60 25

45. Caudron C 600 "Eaglet" and Route-map.

1969. Air. Stamp Day. 30th Anniv. of 1st Noumea-Paris Flight by Martinet and Klein.
465. **45.** 29 f. red, blue & violet 60 35

1969. Air. 1st Flight of "Concorde". As T **27** of Comoro Islands.
466. 100 f. green .. .. 1·75 1·10

46. Cattle-dip.

1969. Cattle-breeding in New Caledonia.
467. **46.** 9 f. brown, green and blue (postage) .. 20 10
468. 25 f. violet, brn. & emer. 60 25

469. – 50 f. mar., red & grn. (air) 65 45
DESIGNS: 25 f. Branding. LARGER (46 × 28 mm.): 50 f. Stockman with herd.

47. Judo.

1969. 3rd South Pacific Games, Port Moresby, Papua New Guinea.
470. **47.** 19 f. pur., blue & red (post.) 35 20
471. – 20 f. black, verm. & grr. 35 20

472. – 30 f. black & blue (air) .. 40 25
473. – 39 f. brn., grn. & black 50 35
DESIGNS—HORIZ. 20 f. Boxing. 30 f. Diving (48 × 28 mm.). VERT. 39 f. Putting the shot (28 × 48 mm.).

1969. Air. Napoleon Bonaparte. Birth Bicent. As T 116 of Cameroun. Multicoloured.
474. 40 f. "Napoleon in Coronation Robes" (Gerard) (vert.) .. .. .. 1·10 90

48. Airliner over Outrigger Canoe.

1969. Air. Noumea-Paris Air Service. 20th Anniv.
475. 48. 50 f. green, brown & blue 60 50

1969. Int. Labour Organization. 50th Anniv. As T 28 of Comoro Islands.
476. 12 f. brown, violet & salmon 15 10

49. "French Wings around the World".

1970. Air. French "Around the World" Air Service. 10th Anniv.
477. 49. 200 f. brn., blue & violet 2·50 1·75

1970. Inaug. of New U.P.U. Headquarters Building. As T 127 of Cameroun.
478. 12 f. red, grey and brown .. 15 12

50. Packet-boat "Natal", 1883.

1970. Stamp Day.
479. 50. 9 f. black, green & blue 15 12

51. Cyclists on Map.

1970. Air. "Tour de Nouvelle Caledonie" Cycle Race.
480. 51. 40 f. brown, blue and light blue 50 30

52. Mt. Fuji and Japanese Express Train.

1970. Air. "EXPO 70" World Fair, Osaka, Japan. Multicoloured.
481. 20 f. Type 52 .. .. 25 15
482. 45 f. "EXPO" emblem, map and Buddha .. 55 30

53. Yachts with Spinnakers.

1971. Air. One Ton Cup Yacht Race Auckland, New Zealand.
483. 53. 20 f. green, red & black 25 20

54. Dumbea Mail Train.

1971. Stamp Day.
484. 54. 10 f. black, green & red 10 5

55. Racing Yachts.

1971. Whangarei-Noumea Ocean Yacht Race.
485. 55. 16 f. turq., green & blue 20 10

56. Lieut.-Col. Broche and Theatre Map.

1971. French Pacific Battalion's Participation in Second World War Mediterranean Campaign. 30th Anniv.
486. 56. 60 f. multicoloured .. 75 50

57. Early Tape Machine.

58. Weightlifting.

1971. World Telecommunications Day.
487. 57. 19 f. orange, pur. & red 25 15

1971. 4th South Pacific Games, Papeete, French Polynesia.
488. 58. 11 f. brn. & red (post.) 12 8
489. – 23 f. violet, red & blue 25 15
490. – 25 f. green & red (air) .. 20 12
491. – 100 f. blue, green & red 1·10 75
DESIGNS—VERT. 23 f. Basketball. HORIZ. (48 × 27 mm.) 25 f. Pole-vaulting. 100 f. Archery.

59. Port de Plaisance, Noumea.

1971. Air.
492. 59. 200 f. multicoloured .. 2·25 1·40

1971. De Gaulle. 1st Death Anniv. As Nos. 1937 and 1940 of France.
493. 34 f. black and plum .. 40 20
494. 100 f. black and plum .. 1·25 75

60. Publicity Leaflet showing Aircraft.

1971. Air. 1st New Caledonia to Australia Flight. 40th Anniv.
495. 60. 90 f. brn., blue & orge. 95 50

61. Downhill Skiing.

1972. Air. Winter Olympic Games, Sapporo, Japan.
496. 61. 50 f. grn., red & blue .. 50 35

62. St. Mark's Basilica, Venice.

1972. Air. U.N.E.S.C.O. "Save Venice" Campaign.
497. 62. 20 f. brn., grn. and bl. 20 10

1972. Air. South Pacific Commission. 25th Anniv. As T 46 of French Polynesia, but inscr. "NOUVELLE-CALEDONIE ET DEPENDANCES".
498. 18 f. multicoloured .. 20 12

63. Breguet Aircraft and Noumea Monument.

1972. Air. 1st Paris-Noumea Flight. 40th Anniv.
499. 63. 110 f. bl., pur. & grn. 1·40 85

64. Pacific Island Dwelling.

65. Carved wooden pillow.

1972. Air. South Pacific Arts Festival, Fiji.
500. 64. 24 f. brn., blue & orange 30 20

1972. Exhibits from Noumea Museum.
501. – 1 f. red, grn. & grey (post.) 5 5
502. 65. 2 f. blk., grn. & dull grn. 5 5
503. – 5 f. multicoloured .. 5 5
504. – 12 f. multicoloured 15 10
505. – 16 f. multicoloured (air) 15 12
506. – 40 f. multicoloured .. 40 35
DESIGNS: 1 f. Goa Door-post. 5 f. Monstrance. 12 f. Tchamba mask. 16 f. Ornamental arrowheads. 40 f. Portico, chief's house.

66. Hurdling over "H" of "MUNICH".

1972. Air. Olympic Games, Munich.
507. 66. 72 f. violet, pur. & blue 85 50

67. New Head Post Office Building, Noumea.

1972. Air.
508. 67. 23 f. brn., blue & green 30 15

68. J.C.I. Emblem.

1972. New Caledonia Junior Chamber of Commerce. 10th Anniv.
509. 68. 12 f. multicoloured .. 12 10

69. Forest Scene.

1973. Air. Landscapes of the East Coast. Multicoloured.
510. 11 f. Type 69 .. .. 12 10
511. 18 f. Beach and palms (vert.) 20 15
512. 21 f. Waterfall and inlet (vert.) 20 15
See also Nos. 534/6.

70. Moliere and Characters.

1973. Air. Moliere. 300th Death Anniv.
513. 70. 50 f. multicoloured .. 60 40

71. Tchamba Mask.

1973.
514. 71. 12 f. mauve (postage) .. 12 5
515. – 23 f. blue (air) 25 12
DESIGN: 23 f. "Concorde" in flight.

72. S.S. "El Kantara" in Panama Canal.

1973. Marseilles-Noumea Service via Panama Canal. 50th Anniversary.
516. 72. 60 f. brown, black & grn. 60 30

73. Globe and Weather Allegory.

1973. World Meteorological Organization. Cent.
517. 73. 80 f. multicoloured .. 80 40

74. "DC-10" in Flight.

1973. Noumea-Paris "DC-10" Air Service. Inaug.
518. 74. 100 f. grn., brn. & blue 1·00 50

75. "Chaetodon melanotus". (daylight colours).

1973. Marine Fauna from Noumea Aquarium. Multicoloured.

519. 8 f. Type **75** (postage) .. 8 5
520. 14 f. "Chaetodon melanotus" (nocturnal colours) .. 15 8
521. 3 f. "Ovula ovum" (air) .. 5 5
522. 32 f. "Acanthurus olivaceus" (adult and young) .. 30 15
523. 32 f. "Hydatina" .. 30 15
524. 37 f. "Dolium perdix" .. 35 20

76. Office Emblem.

1973. Central Schools Co-operation Office. 10th Anniv.

532. **76.** 20 f. blue and yellow .. 20 10

77. New Caledonia Mail-coach, 1880.

1973. Air. Stamp Day.

533. **77.** 15 f. multicoloured .. 15 8

1974. Air. Landscapes of the West Coast. As Type **70**. Multicoloured.

534. 8 f. Beach and palms .. 8 5
535. 22 f. Trees and mountain 20 10
536. 26 f. Trees growing in sea 25 12

78. Centre Building.

1974. Air. Opening of Scientific Studies Centre, Anse-Vata, Noumea.

537. **78.** 50 f. multicoloured .. 50 25

79. "Bird" embracing Flora.

1974. Nature Conservation (1st issue).

538. **79.** 7 f. multicoloured .. 8 5

See also No. 547.

80. 18th-century Sailor.

1974. Air. Discovery and Reconnaissance of New Caledonia and Loyalty Islands.

539. – 20 f. vio. red and blue 20 10
540. – 25 f. grn., brn. & red .. 25 12
541. **80.** 28 f. brn., bl. & grn. .. 25 12
542. – 30 f. bl., brn. & red .. 25 12
543. – 36 f. red, brn. & blue .. 30 15

DESIGNS—HORIZ. 20 f. Captain Cook, "Endeavour" and map of Grand Terre island. 25 f. La Perouse, ship and map of Grand Terre island (reconnaissance of west coast). 30 f. Entrecasteaux, ship and map of Grand Terre island (reconnaissance of west coast). 36 f. Dumont d'Urville, ship and map of Loyalty Islands.

81. "Telecommunications".

1974. Air. Universal Postal Union. Cent.

544. **81.** 95 f. orge., pur. & grey 1·00 50

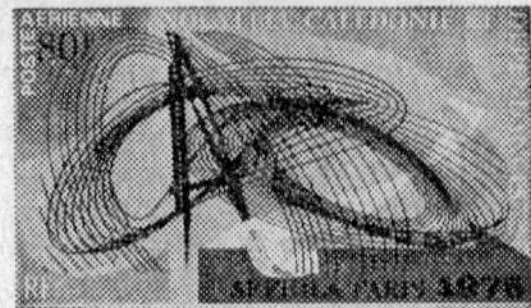

82. "Art" (abstract).

1974. Air. "Arphila 75" Stamp Exhibition, Paris.

545. **82.** 80 f. multicoloured .. 80 40

83. Hotel Chateau-Royal.

1974. Air. Inauguration of Hotel Chateau Royal, Noumea.

546. **82.** 22 f. multicoloured .. 25 12

1975. Protection of Nature (2nd issue). "Stop Bush Fires". As T **79**.

547. 20 f. multicoloured .. 25 12

DESIGNS—VERT. (27 × 49 mm.). 20 f. Animal skull, burnt tree and flaming landscape.

84. "Cricket".

1975. Air. Tourism. Multicoloured.

548. 3 f. Type **84** 5 5
549. 25 f. "Bougna" ceremony 30 15
550. 31 f. "Pilou"–native dance 35 20

85. "Calanthe ceratrifolia".

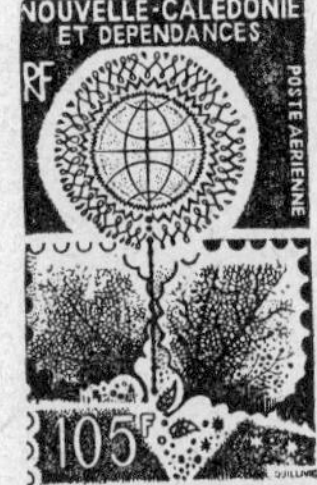

86. Global "Flower".

1975. New Caledonian Orchids. Mult.

551. 8 f. Type **85** (postage) .. 10 5
552. 11 f. "Lyperanthus gigas" 12 5
553. 42 f. "Eriaxis rigida" (air) 50 25

1975. Air. "Arphila 75" International Stamp Exhibition, Paris.

554. **86.** 105 f. purple, grn. & bl. 1·25 65

87. Throwing the Discus.

1975. Air. 5th South Pacific Games, Guam.

555. 24 f. Type **87** 30 15
556. 50 f. Volleyball 60 30

88. Festival Emblem.

89. Birds in Flight.

1975. "Melanesia 2000" Festival, Noumea.

557. **88.** 12 f. multicoloured .. 20 10

1975. Noumea Ornithological Society. 10th Anniv.

558. **89.** 5 f. multicoloured .. 5 5

90. Pres. Pompidou.

92. Brown Booby.

91. Two "Concordes" and Tailfin.

1975. Pompidou Commemoration.

559. **90.** 26 f. grey and green .. 30 15

1976. Air. First Commercial Flight of "Concorde", Paris-Rio de Janeiro.

560. **91.** 147 f. blue and red .. 1·75 85

1976. Ocean Birds. Multicoloured.

561. 1 f. Type **92** 5 5
562. 2 f. Blue-faced booby .. 5 5
563. 8 f. Red-faced booby (vert.) 10 5

93. Festival Emblem.

1976. South Pacific Festival of Arts, Rotorua (New Zealand).

564. **93.** 27 f. multicoloured .. 35 20

94. Lion and Lions' Emblem.

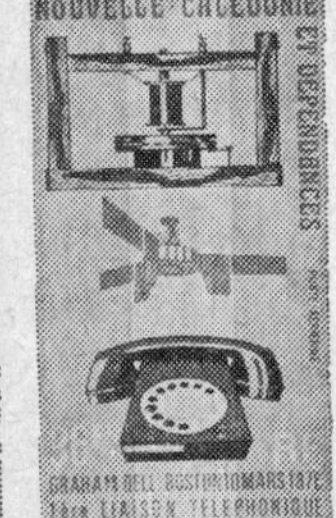

95. Early and Modern Telephones.

1976. Lions Club, Noumea. 15th Anniv.

565. **94.** 49 f. multicoloured .. 65 35

1976. Air. Telephone Centenary.

566. **95.** 36 f. multicoloured .. 45 25

96. Capture of Penbosct.

1976. Air. American Revolution. Bicent.

567. **96.** 24 f. purple and brown 30 15

97. Bandstand.

1976. "Aspects of Old Noumea". Mult.

568. 25 f. Type **97** 35 20
569. 30 f. Monumental fountain (vert.) 40 20

98. Running.

1976. Air. Olympic Games, Montreal.

570. **98.** 33 f. violet, red & purple 45 25

99. "Chick" with Magnifier.

1976. Air. "Philately in Schools", Stamp Exhibition, Noumea.

571. **99.** 42 f. multicoloured .. 55 30

100. Dead Bird and Trees.

1976. Nature Protection.

572. **100.** 20 f. multicoloured .. 25 12

101. South Pacific Heads.

1976. 16th South Pacific Commission Conference.

573. **101.** 20 f. multicoloured .. 25 12

OFFICIAL STAMPS

O 1.

O 2. Carved Head-rest (Noumea Museum).

1958. Inscr. "OFFICIEL".

No.	Type	Description	Unused	Used
O 344.	O 1.	1 f. yellow	5	5
O 345.		3 f. green	5	5
O 346.		4 f. purple	8	5
O 347.		5 f. blue	10	5
O 348.		9 f. black	12	8
O 349.	A.	10 f. violet	15	8
O 350.		13 f. green	20	10
O 351.		15 f. blue	25	12
O 352.		24 f. mauve ..	30	12
O 353.		26 f. orange ..	35	15
O 354.	B.	50 f. green	55	20
O 355.		100 f. brown ..	1·10	35
O 356.		200 f. red	2·25	50

DESIGNS: A, B, Similar designs as Type O 1.

1973.

No.	Type	Description	Unused	Used
O 525.	O 2.	1 f. grn., yell. & blk.	5	5
O 526.		3 f. grn., pink & blk.	5	5
O 527.		4 f. grn., bl. & blk.	5	5
O 528.		5 f. grn., lilac & blk.	5	5
O 529.		9 f. grn., bl. & blk.	10	10
O 530.		10 f. grn., orge. & blk.	10	10
O 531.		12 f. grn., bl. & blk.	12	12

POSTAGE DUE STAMPS

1903. Postage Due stamps of French Colonies optd. **CINQUANTENAIRE 24 SEPTEMBRE 1853 1903** and eagle.

No.	Type	Description	Unused	Used
D 78.	D 1.	5 c. blue	15	15
D 79.		10 c. brown	1·10	90
D 80.		15 c. green	2·75	90
D 81.		30 c. red	1·00	1·60
D 82.		50 c. claret	6·50	2·00
D 83.		60 c. brown and yell.	22·00	5·50
D 84.		1 f. red	1·50	95
D 85.		2 f. brown	£110	£110

D 1.

D 2. Sambar Stag.

D 3. Numeral.

1906.

No.	Type	Description	Unused	Used
D 102.	D 1.	5 c. blue on blue ..	5	5
D 103.		10 c. brown ..	5	5
D 104.		15 c. green	5	5
D 105.		20 c. black on yellow	8	8
D 106.		30 c. red	8	8
D 107.		50 c. blue on cream	10	10
D 108.		60 c. green on blue	12	12
D 109.		1 f. green on cream	15	15

1926. Surch.

No.	Type	Description	Unused	Used
D 137.	D 1.	2 f. on 1 f. mauve ..	25	25
D 138.		3 f. on 1 f. brown ..	25	25

1928.

No.	Type	Description	Unused	Used
D 179.	D 2.	2 c. brown and blue	5	5
D 180.		4 c. green and red ..	5	5
D 181.		5 c. grey and orange	5	5
D 182.		10 c. blue & magenta	5	5
D 183.		15 c. red and olive	5	5
D 184.		20 c. olive and claret	10	10
D 185.		25 c. blue and brown	5	5
D 186.		30 c. olive and green	5	5
D 187.		50 c. red and brown	12	12
D 188.		60 c. red and mauve	8	8
D 189.		1 f. green and blue	12	12
D 190.		2 f. olive and red ..	15	15
D 191.		3 f. brown and violet	25	25

1948.

No.	Type	Description	Unused	Used
D 328.	D 3.	10 c. mauve ..	5	5
D 329.		30 c. brown ..	5	5
D 330.		50 c. green	5	5
D 331.		1 f. brown	5	5
D 332.		2 f. claret	5	5
D 333.		3 f. brown	5	5
D 334.		4 f. blue	5	5
D 335.		5 f. red	8	8
D 336.		10 f. green	12	12
D 337.		20 f. blue	25	25

NEWFOUNDLAND BC

An island off the E. coast of Canada. A British Dominion merged since 1949 with Canada, whose stamps it now uses. Currency as Canada.

1.

2.

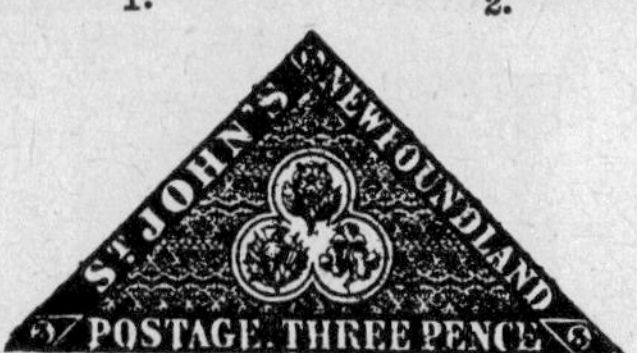

3. Rose, Thistle and Shamrock.

1857. Imperf.

No.	Type	Description	Unused	Used
1.	1.	1d. purple	30·00	55·00
10.	2.	2d. vermilion	£110	£150
11.	3.	3d. green	12·00	45·00
12.	2.	4d. vermilion	£1000	£500
13.	1.	5d. brown	11·00	45·00
14.	2.	6d. vermilion	£1400	£600
7.		6½d. vermilion	£1200	£1500
8.		8d. vermilion	£110	£150
9.		1s. vermilion	£9000	£2500

The frame design of Type 2 differs for each value.

1861. Imperf.

No.	Type	Description	Unused	Used
21.	1.	1d. brown	25·00	80·00
22.	2.	2d. lake	40·00	£180
23.		4d. lake	4·50	40·00
24a.	1.	5d. brown	11·00	80·00
24b.	2.	6d. lake	4·50	50·00
24c.		6½d. lake	15·00	£180
24d.		8d. lake	15·00	£200
24e.		1s. lake	7·00	90·00

8. Prince Consort.

6. Codfish.

7. Seal on Ice-floe.

9. Queen Victoria.

10.

11. Queen Victoria.

1866. Perf. (2 c. also roul.).

No.	Type	Description	Unused	Used
31.	1.	2 c. green	32·00	12·00
26.	7.	5 c. brown	£300	90·00
32.	8.	10 c. black	50·00	15·00
33.	9.	12 c. red-brown	15·00	11·00
29.	10.	13 c. orange	35·00	30·00
30.	11.	24 c. blue	15·00	12·00

12. King Edward VII, when Prince of Wales.

13. Queen Victoria.

1868. Perf. or roul.

No.	Type	Description	Unused	Used
35.	12.	1 c. purple	20·00	15·00
36.		3 c. orange	£120	55·00
37.		3 c. blue	70·00	7·00
38.	7.	5 c. black	80·00	35·00
43.		5 c. blue	90·00	5·50
39.	13.	6 c. rose	5·00	4·50

14. "Newfoundland" Dog.

15. King Edward VII, when Prince of Wales.

16. Codfish.

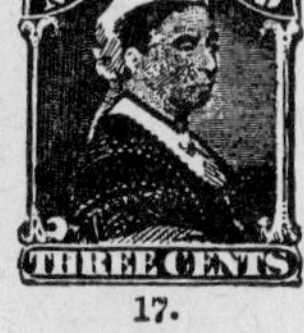

17.

18. Seal on Ice-floe.

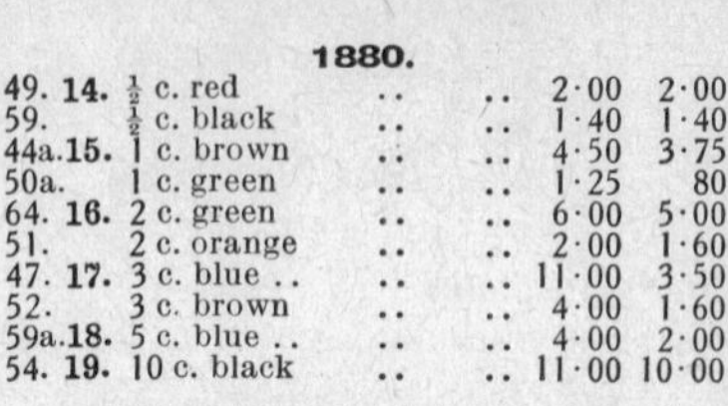

19. Atlantic brigantine.

20. Queen Victoria.

1880.

No.	Type	Description	Unused	Used
49.	14.	½ c. red	2·00	2·00
59.		½ c. black	1·40	1·40
44a.	15.	1 c. brown	4·50	3·75
50a.		1 c. green	1·25	80
64.	16.	2 c. green	6·00	5·00
51.		2 c. orange	2·00	1·60
47.	17.	3 c. blue	11·00	3·50
52.		3 c. brown	4·00	1·60
59a.	18.	5 c. blue	4·00	2·00
54.	19.	10 c. black	11·00	10·00

1890.

No.	Type	Description	Unused	Used
58.	20.	3 c. grey	4·00	12

This stamp on pink paper was stained by sea-water.

21. Queen Victoria.

22. John Cabot.

23. Cape Bonavista, the landfall of Cabot.

24. Caribou hunting.

1897. Discovery of Newfoundland. 400th Anniv. and 60th Year of Queen Victoria's Reign. Dated "1497 1897".

No.	Type	Description	Unused	Used
66.	21.	1 c. green	1·00	1·00
67.	22.	2 c. red	1·00	1·00
68.	23.	3 c. blue	1·25	75
69.	24.	4 c. olive	1·75	1·75
70.	–	5 c. violet	1·75	1·75
71.	–	6 c. chestnut	1·75	1·75
72.	–	8 c. orange	5·00	3·25
73.	–	10 c. brown	6·00	3·25
74.	–	12 c. blue	8·00	3·25
75.	–	15 c. red	7·50	3·50
76.	–	24 c. violet	5·50	4·50
77.	–	30 c. blue	11·00	7·50
78.	–	35 c. red	17·00	16·00
79.	–	60 c. black	5·50	5·50

DESIGNS—As T 23: 5 c. Mining. 6 c. Logging. 8 c. Fishing. 10 c. Cabot's ship, the "Matthew". 15 c. Seals. 24 c. Salmon fishing. 35 c. Iceberg. As T 22: 12 c. Ptarmigan. 30 c. Seal of the Colony. 60 c. Henry VII.

1897. Surch. **ONE CENT** and bar.

No.	Type	Description	Unused	Used
80.	20.	1 c. on 3 c. grey ..	5·00	5·00

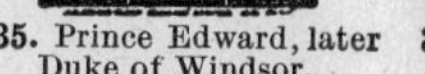
35. Prince Edward, later Duke of Windsor.

36. Queen Victoria.

1897. Royal portraits.

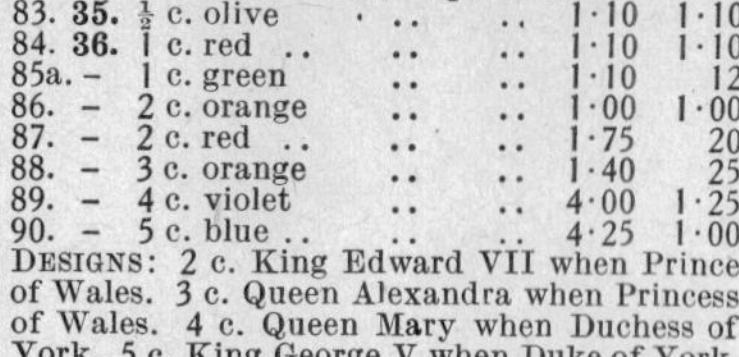

No.	Type	Description	Unused	Used
83.	35.	½ c. olive	1·10	1·10
84.	36.	1 c. red	1·10	1·10
85a.	–	1 c. green	1·10	12
86.	–	2 c. orange	1·00	1·00
87.	–	2 c. red	1·75	20
88.	–	3 c. orange	1·40	25
89.	–	4 c. violet	4·00	1·25
90.	–	5 c. blue	4·25	1·00

DESIGNS: 2 c. King Edward VII when Prince of Wales. 3 c. Queen Alexandra when Princess of Wales. 4 c. Queen Mary when Duchess of York. 5 c. King George V when Duke of York.

41. Map of Newfoundland.

42. King James I.

43. Arms of Colonisation Co.

45. Guy's Ship.

1908.

No.	Type	Description	Unused	Used
94.	41.	2 c. lake	5·00	40

1910. Dated "1610 1910".

No.	Type	Description	Unused	Used
109.	42.	1 c. green	50	40
107.	43.	2 c. red	1·00	45
97.	–	3 c. olive	3·50	4·00
98.	45.	4 c. violet	4·00	4·00
108.	–	5 c. blue	2·50	1·50
100a.	–	6 c. purple	7·00	7·00
101.	–	8 c. bistre	12·00	13·00
102.	–	9 c. green	12·00	13·00
103.	–	10 c. grey	15·00	15·00
104.	–	12 c. plum	15·00	15·00
105.	–	15 c. black	13·00	13·00

DESIGNS—HORIZ. 5 c. Cupids. 8 c. Mosquito. 9 c. Logging camp. 10 c. Paper mills. VERT. 3 c. John Guy. 6 c. Sir Francis Bacon. 12 c. Edward VII. 15 c. George V. (Cupids and Mosquito are places.)

53. Queen Mary.

54. King George V.

63. Seal of Newfoundland.

1911. Coronation.

No.	Type	Description	Unused	Used
117a.	53.	1 c. green	55	12
118.	54.	2 c. red	55	12
119.	–	3 c. chestnut	6·00	6·00
120.	–	4 c. purple	6·00	6·00
121.	–	5 c. blue	3·00	1·00
122.	–	6 c. grey	8·00	8·00
123a.	–	8 c. blue	20·00	20·00
124.	–	9 c. blue	6·00	6·00
125.	–	10 c. green	8·00	8·00
126.	–	12 c. plum	8·00	8·00
127.	63.	15 c. lake	7·00	7·00

PORTRAITS—VERT. As T 53/4: 3 c. Duke of Windsor when Prince of Wales. 4 c. King George VI when Prince Albert. 5 c. Princess Mary, late Princess Royal. 6 c. Duke of Gloucester when Prince Henry. 8 c. Duke of Kent when Prince George. 9 c. Prince John. 10 c. Queen Alexandra. 12 c. Duke of Connaught.

64. Caribou.

Each inscr. with the name of a different action: 1 c. Suvla Bay. 3 c. Gueudecourt. 4 c. Beaumont Hamel. 6 c. Monchy. 10 c. Steenbeck. 15 c. Langemarck. 24 c. Cambrai. 36 c. Combles. The 2 c., 5 c., 8 c. and 12 c. are inscribed "Royal Naval Reserve. Ubique".

1919. Newfoundland Contingent. 1914-18.

130.	64.	1 c. green	50	15
131.		2 c. red	60	20
132a.		3 c. brown	60	12
133.		4 c. mauve	75	45
134.		5 c. blue	1·10	45
135.		6 c. grey	5·00	5·00
136.		8 c. purple	4·50	4·50
137.		10 c. green	3·00	1·50
138.		12 c. orange	12·00	10·00
139.		15 c. blue	6·00	6·00
140.		24 c. brown	9·00	9·00
141.		36 c. olive	6·00	6·00

1919. Air. Hawker Flight. Optd. **FIRST TRANS-ATLANTIC AIR POST April, 1919.**

142.	64.	3 c. brown	£6500	£6000

1919. Air. Alcock Flight. Surch. **Trans-Atlantic AIR POST 1919 ONE DOLLAR.**

143.		$1 on 15 c. red (No. 75)	60·00	60·00

1920. Surch. in words between bars.

144.		2 c. on 30 c. blue (No. 77)	2·25	2·25
146.		3 c. on 35 c. red (No. 78)	2·50	2·50
147.		3 c. on 35 c. red (No. 78)	2·50	2·50

1921. Air. Optd. **AIR MAIL to Halifax N.S. 1921.**

148a.		35 c. red (No. 78)	50·00	40·00

65. Twin Hills, Tors Cove.

67. Statue of Fighting Newfoundlander, St. John's.

1923.

149.	65.	1 c. green	65	12
150.	–	2 c. red	65	12
151.	67.	3 c. brown	65	10
152.	–	4 c. purple	75	55
153.	–	5 c. blue	1·50	65
154.	–	6 c. grey	1·50	1·50
155.	–	8 c. purple	1·40	1·40
156.	–	9 c. grey-green	7·50	7·50
157.	–	10 c. violet	1·75	85
158.	–	11 c. olive	2·25	2·25
159.	–	12 c. lake	2·75	2·75
160.	–	15 c. blue	4·00	4·00
161.	–	20 c. chestnut	3·50	3·50
162.	–	24 c. chocolate	18·00	19·00

DESIGNS—HORIZ. 2 c. South-west Arm, Trinity. 6 c. Upper Steadies, Humber River. 8 c. Quid Vidi, near St. John's. 9 c. Caribou crossing lake. 11 c. Shell Bird Island. 12 c. Mount Moriah, Bay of Islands. 20 c. Placentia. VERT. 4 c. Humber River. 5 c. Coast at Trinity. 10 c. Humber River Canon. 15 c. Humber River, near Little Rapids. 24 c. Topsail Falls.

1927. Air. Optd. **Air Mail DE PINEDO 1927.**

163.		60 c. black (No. 79)	£10000	£5000

79. Newfoundland and Labrador.

80. S.S. "Caribou".

81. King George V and Queen Mary.

82. Duke of Windsor when Prince of Wales.

1928. "Publicity" issue.

180.	79.	1 c. green	75	20
181.	80.	2 c. red	70	12
182.	81.	3 c. chocolate	80	12
183.	82.	4 c. mauve	1·10	35
184.	–	5 c. grey	1·10	40
169.	–	6 c. blue	1·50	1·50
170.	–	8 c. chocolate	2·50	2·50
171.	–	9 c. green	2·75	2·75
188.	–	10 c. violet	1·75	90
173.	–	12 c. lake	1·75	1·75
174.	–	14 c. purple	2·50	2·50
175.	–	15 c. blue	2·75	2·75
176.	–	20 c. black	1·75	1·75
177.	–	28 c. green	6·50	6·50
178.	–	30 c. brown	2·50	3·00

DESIGNS—HORIZ. 5 c. Express train. 6 c. Hotel, St. John's. 8 c. Heart's Content. 10 c. War Memorial, St. John's. 15 c. Trans-Atlantic flight. 20 c. Colonial Building, St. John's. VERT. 9 c., 14 c. Cabot Tower, St. John's. 12 c., 28 c. G.P.O., St. John's. 30 c. Grand Falls, Labrador.

1929. Surch. in words.

179.		3 c. on 6 c. (No. 154)	1·10	1·10

1930. Air. Surch. **Trans-Atlantic AIR MAIL By B.M. "Columbia" September 1930 Fifty Cents.**

191.	64.	50 c. on 36 c. olive	£2000	£2250

92. Aeroplane and Dog-team.

93. Vickers-Vimy Biplane and early Sailing Packet.

94. Routes of historic Trans-Atlantic Flights.

1931. Air.

195.	92.	15 c. brown	1·75	2·00
193.	93.	50 c. green	5·00	6·00
194.	94.	$1 blue	16·00	16·00

95. Codfish.

96. King George V.

98. Duke of Windsor when Prince of Wales.

99. Caribou.

100. Queen Elizabeth II when Princess.

102. Paper Mills.

1932.

209.	95.	1 c. green	60	20
276.		1 c. grey	8	8
210.	96.	2 c. red	50	15
223.		2 c. green	35	10
211.	–	3 c. brown	35	15
212.	98.	4 c. lilac	1·60	50
224.		4 c. red	25	10
213.	99.	5 c. purple	2·25	50
225c.		5 c. violet	40	10
214.	100.	6 c. blue	4·50	4·50
226.	–	7 c. lake	50	60
227.	102.	8 c. red	55	45
283.	–	10 c. brown	50	30
284.	–	14 c. black	75	75
285.	–	15 c. purple	75	75
218.	–	20 c. green	1·00	45
228.	–	24 c. blue	1·25	1·25
219.	–	25 c. grey	1·00	85
220.	–	30 c. blue	7·00	7·50
228a.	–	48 c. brown	2·50	1·50

DESIGNS—VERT. 3 c. Queen Mary. 7 c. Queen Mother when Duchess of York. HORIZ. 10 c. Salmon. 14 c. Newfoundland dog. 15 c. Seal. 20 c. Trans-Atlantic beacon. 24 c. Bell Island. 25 c. Sealing fleet. 30 c., 48 c. Fishing fleet.

1932. Air. Surch. **TRANS-ATLANTIC WEST TO EAST Per Dornier DO-X May, 1932. One Dollar and Fifty Cents.**

221.	94.	$1·50 c. on $1 blue	£130	£130

1933. Optd. **L. & S. Post** ("Land and Sea") between bars.

229.	92.	15 c. brown	2·75	3·50

110. Put to flight.

1933. Air.

230.	110.	5 c. brown	4·00	4·00
231.	–	10 c. yellow	4·50	5·00
232.	–	30 c. blue	9·00	10·00
233.	–	60 c. green	15·00	16·00
234.	–	75 c. brown	16·00	17·00

DESIGNS: 10 c. Land of Heart's Delight. 30 c. Spotting the herd. 60 c. News from home. 75 c. Labrador.

1933. Air. Balbo Trans-Atlantic Mass Formation Flight. No. 234 surch. **1933 GEN. BALBO FLIGHT, $4.50.**

235.		$4.50 on 75 c. brown	£170	£170

115. Sir Humphrey Gilbert.

116. Compton Castle, Devon.

1933. Annexation. 350th Anniv. Dated "1583 1933"

236.	115.	1 c. black	50	30
237.	116.	2 c. green	50	30
238.	–	3 c. orange	75	45
239.	–	4 c. red	75	30
240.	–	5 c. violet	90	45
241.	–	7 c. blue	4·00	4·00
242.	–	8 c. orange	4·00	4·00
243.	–	9 c. blue	3·25	3·25
244.	–	10 c. brown	3·00	1·75
245.	–	14 c. black	6·50	6·50
246.	–	15 c. claret	8·00	8·00
247.	–	20 c. green	4·00	4·50
248.	–	24 c. purple	9·00	9·00
249.	–	32 c. black	10·00	10·00

DESIGNS—VERT. 3 c. Gilbert Coat of Arms. 5 c. Anchor token. 14 c. Royal Arms. 15 c. Gilbert in the "Squirrel". 24 c. Queen Elizabeth. 32 c. Gilbert's statue at Truro. HORIZ. 4 c. Eton College. 7 c. Gilbert commissioned by Elizabeth. 8 c. Fleet leaving Plymouth, 1583. 9 c. Arrival at St. John's. 10 c. Annexation, 5th August, 1583. 20 c. Map of Newfoundland.

1935. Silver Jubilee. As T **11** of Antigua.

250.		4 c. red	40	20
251.		5 c. violet	45	35
252.		7 c. blue	80	60
253.		24 c. olive	1·75	1·50

1937. Coronation. As T **2** of Aden.

254.		2 c. green	15	12
255.		4 c. red	20	12
256.		5 c. purple	35	25

129. Codfish.

1937. Coronation.

257.	129.	1 c. grey	20	10
258.	–	3 c. brown	30	15
259.	–	7 c. blue	35	35
260.	–	8 c. red	55	55
261.	–	10 c. black	75	75
262.	–	14 c. black	1·00	1·00
263.	–	15 c. claret	1·25	1·25
264.	–	20 c. green	1·00	1·00
265.	–	24 c. blue	1·25	1·25
266.	–	25 c. black	1·10	1·10
267.	–	48 c. purple	1·50	1·50

DESIGNS: 3 c. Gulf of St. Lawrence. 7 c. Caribou. 8 c. Corner Brook Paper Mills. 10 c. Salmon. 14 c. Newfoundland Dog. 15 c. Northern Seal. 20 c. Cape Race. 24 c. Bell Island. 25 c. Sealing fleet. 48 c. Bank Fishing fleet.

DESIGNS: 3 c. Queen Mother. 4 c. Queen Elizabeth II, aged 12. 7 c. Queen Mary.

131. King George VI.

1938.

277.	131.	2 c. green	10	5
278.	–	3 c. red	12	5
270.	–	4 c. blue	1·10	12
271.	–	7 c. blue	70	70

135. King George VI and Queen Elizabeth.

1939. Royal Visit.

272.	135.	5 c. blue	50	50

1939. Surch. in figures and triangles.

273.	135.	2 c. on 5 c. blue	75	75
274.		4 c. on 5 c. blue	50	50

136. Grenfell on the "Strathcona".

1941. Sir Wilfred Grenfell's Labrador Mission.

275.	136.	5 c. blue	25	20

137. Memorial University College.

1942.

290.	137.	30 c. red	1·00	75

138. St. John's.

1943. Air.

291.	138.	7 c. blue	25	20

1946. Surch. **TWO CENTS.**

292.	137.	2 c. on 30 c. red	20	25

139. Queen Elizabeth II when Princess.

1947. Princess Elizabeth's 21st Birthday.
293. **139.** 4 c. blue 20 12

140. Cabot off Cape Bonavista.

1947. Cabot's Discovery of Newfoundland. 450th Anniv.
294. **140.** 5 c. violet 20 20

POSTAGE DUE STAMPS

D 1.

1939.
D 1. **D 1.** 1 c. green 60 60
D 2. 2 c. red .. .. 1·25 1·25
D 3. 3 c. blue .. .. 1·25 1·25
D 4. 4 c. orange .. .. 2·25 2·25
D 5. 5 c. brown .. .. 1·00 1·00
D 6. 10 c. purple .. .. 1·00 1·00

NEW GUINEA O2; BC

(Formerly GERMAN NEW GUINEA.)

Formerly a German Colony, part of the island of New Guinea. Occupied by Australian forces during the 1914-18 war and now joined with Papua and administered by the Australian Commonwealth under trusteeship. After the Japanese defeat in 1945 Australian stamps were used until 1952 when the combined issue appeared for Papua and New Guinea (q.v.). The stamps overprinted "N.W. PACIFIC ISLANDS" were also used in Nauru and other ex-German islands.

GERMAN ISSUES

100 pfenning = 1 mark.

1898. Stamps of Germany optd. **Deutsch-Neu-Guinea.**
1. **6.** 3 pf. brown .. .. 5·50 7·00
2. 5 pf. green .. .. 1·25 1·10
3. **7.** 10 pf. red .. .. 2·25 2·40
4. 20 pf. blue .. .. 2·50 3·50
5. 25 pf. orange .. .. 11·00 12·00
6. 50 pf. brown .. .. 11·00 14·00

1901. "Yacht" key-types inscr. "DEUTSCH-NEU-GUINEA".
7. **N.** 3 pf. brown 15 35
8. 5 pf. green .. .. 4·50 55
9. 10 pf. red .. .. 11·00 90
10. 20 pf. blue .. .. 35 1·10
11. **N.** 25 pf. blk. & red on yell. 45 8·00
12. 30 pf. blk. & orge. on buff 45 6·00
13. 40 pf. black and red .. 45 7·00
14. 50 pf. blk. & pur. on buff 60 9·00
15. 80 pf. black & red on rose 1·10 9·50
16. **O.** 1 m. red .. .. 1·25 18·00
17. 2 m. blue .. .. 1·75 24·00
18. 3 m. black .. .. 2·75 45·00
19. 5 m. red and black .. 45·00 £140

BRITISH OCCUPATION

1914. "Yacht" key-types of German New Guinea surch. **G.R.I.** and value in English currency.
16. **N.** 1d. on 3 pf. brown .. 12·00 12·00
17. 1d. on 5 pf. green .. 4·00 4·00
3. 2d. on 10 pf. red .. 9·00 9·00
4. 2d. on 30 pf. blue .. 9·00 9·00
5. 2½d. on 10 pf. red .. 20·00 20·00
6. 2½d. on 20 pf. blue .. 25·00 25·00
22. 3d. on 25 pf. black and red on yellow .. 35·00 35·00
23. 3d. on 30 pf. black and orange on buff .. 40·00 40·00
24. 4d. on 40 pf. black & red 30·00 30·00
25. 5d. on 50 pf. black and purple on buff .. 60·00 60·00
26. 8d. on 80 pf. black and red on rose £150 £150
12. **O.** 1s. on 1 m. red £350 £350
13. 2s. on 2 m. blue £375 £375
14. 3s. on 3 m. black .. £400 £400
15. 5s. on 5 m. red and black £1000 £1000

Nos. 3/4, surch. **1.**
31. **N.** "1" on 2d. on 10 pf. red
32. "1" on 2d. on 20 pf. blue

1.

1914. Registration labels with names of various towns surch. **G.R.I. 3d.**
33. **1.** 3d. black and red .. 40·00 45·00

1914. "Yacht" key-types of German Marshall Islands surch. **G.R.I.** and value in English currency.
50. **N.** 1d. on 3 pf. brown .. 12·00 12·00
51. 1d. on 5 pf. green .. 14·00 14·00
52. 2d. on 10 pf. red .. 4·00 4·00
53. 2d. on 20 pf. blue .. 5·00 5·00
54. 3d. on 25 pf. black and red on yellow £120 £120
55. 3d. on 30 pf. black and orange on buff .. £120 £120
56. 4d. on 40 pf. black & red 25·00 25·00
57. 5d. on 50 pf. black and purple on buff .. 40·00 40·00
58. 8d. on 80 pf. black and red on rose £160 £160
59. **O.** 1s. on 1 m. red £400 £400
60. 2s. on 2 m. blue £275 £275
61. 3s. on 3 m. black .. £700 £800
62. 5s. on 5 m. red and black £1500 £1600

1915. Nos. 52 and 53 surch. **1.**
63. **N.** "1" on 2d. on 10 pf. red 50·00 55·00
64. "1" on 2d. on 20 pf. blue £900 £500

1915. Stamps of Australia optd. **N.W. PACIFIC ISLANDS.**
102. **4.** ½d. green 40 60
103. 1d. red 80 60
120. 1d. violet .. .. .. 90 1·75
73. **1.** 2d. grey .. .. .. 1·10 1·60
121. **4.** 2d. orange .. .. 3·00 3·25
122. 2d. red .. .. .. 1·50 5·00
74. **1.** 2½d. blue .. .. 1·10 1·60
109. 3d. olive .. .. .. 3·00 4·00
70. **4.** 4d. orange .. .. 1·50 1·90
123. 4d. violet .. .. 9·00 10·00
124. 4d. blue .. .. .. 6·00 7·50
72. 5d. brown .. .. 2·25 2·50
88. **1.** 6d. blue .. .. .. 2·50 2·75
89. 9d. violet .. .. .. 2·50 2·75
90. 1s. green .. .. .. 3·00 4·00
97. 2s. brown .. .. .. 7·50 8·00
116. 5s. grey and yellow .. 14·00 15·00
84. 10s. grey and pink .. 35·00 45·00
99. £1 brown and blue .. £160 £170

1918. Nos. 72 and 90 surch. **One Penny.**
100. **4.** 1d. on 5d. brown .. 35·00 30·00
101. **1.** 1d. on 1s. green .. 35·00 30·00

AUSTRALIAN ADMINISTRATION

2. Village.

1925.
125. **2.** ½d. orange .. .. 30 1·00
126. 1d. green .. .. 35 1·00
126a. 1½d. red .. .. 1·00 1·00
127. 2d. claret .. .. 1·25 1·50
128. 3d. blue .. .. 2·00 1·25
129. 4d. olive .. .. 3·00 3·50
130a. 6d. brown .. .. 3·50 5·50
131. 9d. purple .. .. 5·00 6·50
132. 1s. green .. .. 5·00 6·00
133. 2s. lake .. .. 7·00 9·00
134. 5s. brown .. .. 12·00 13·00
135. 10s. red .. .. 22·00 25·00
136. £1 grey .. .. 40·00 45·00

1931. Air. Optd. with aeroplane and **AIR MAIL.**
137. **2.** ½d. orange 20 40
138. 1d. green 30 50
139. 1½d. red .. .. 60 1·40
140. 2d. claret .. .. 70 2·50
141. 3d. blue .. .. 1·10 1·50
142. 4d. olive .. .. 1·50 2·00
143. 6d. brown .. .. 1·60 2·50
144. 9d. purple .. .. 1·75 4·25
145. 1s. green .. .. 3·00 4·50
146. 2s. lake .. .. 5·50 6·00
147. 5s. brown .. .. 11·00 12·00
148. 10s. red .. .. 28·00 30·00
149. £1 grey .. .. 50·00 60·00

3. Bird of Paradise.

1931. Australian Administration. 10th Anniv. Dated "1921-1931".
150. **3.** 1d. green 20 25
151. 1½d. red .. .. 1·75 1·75
152. 2d. claret 75 65
153. 3d. blue 90 90
154. 4d. olive .. .. 2·00 2·50
155. 5d. green .. .. 3·25 2·50
156. 6d. brown .. .. 2·25 2·75
157. 9d. violet .. .. 2·50 3·50
158. 1s. grey .. .. 2·75 3·75
159. 2s. lake .. .. 5·00 5·50
160. 5s. brown .. .. 10·00 11·00
161. 10s. red .. .. 35·00 40·00
162. £1 grey .. .. 60·00 70·00

1931. Air. Optd. with aeroplane and **AIR MAIL.**
163. **3.** ½d. orange 20 30
164. 1d. green 45 50
165. 1½d. red 75 75
166. 2d. claret 80 80
167. 3d. blue .. .. 1·00 1·00
168. 4d. olive .. .. 1·10 1·50
169. 5d. green .. .. 1·50 2·00
170. 6d. brown .. .. 3·00 3·50
171. 9d. violet .. .. 2·75 4·00
172. 1s. grey .. .. 3·00 4·00
173. 2s. lake .. .. 5·00 7·00
174. 5s. brown .. .. 9·00 12·00
175. 10s. red .. .. 40·00 40·00
176. £1 grey .. .. 60·00 60·00

1932. As T **3**, but without dates.
177. 1d. green 20 20
178. 1½d. claret 35 60
179. 2d. red 30 35
179a. 2½d. green .. .. 1·50 3·00
180. 3d. blue 50 60
180a. 3½d. red .. .. 2·75 2·75
181. 4d. olive 60 70
182. 5d. green 70 70
183. 6d. brown .. .. 70 1·00
184. 9d. violet .. .. 3·00 4·50
185. 1s. grey .. .. 1·75 3·25
186. 2s. lake .. .. 3·00 4·00
187. 5s. brown .. .. 9·00 10·00
188. 10s. red .. .. 35·00 35·00
189. £1 grey .. .. 40·00 35·00

1932. Air. T **3**, but without dates, optd. with aeroplane and **AIR MAIL.**
190. ½d. orange 20 20
191. 1d. green 20 25
192. 1½d. mauve 35 50
193. 2d. red 60 50
193a. 2½d. green .. .. 1·00 85
194. 3d. blue 70 45
194a. 3½d. red .. .. 1·50 1·10
195. 4d. olive .. .. 1·00 1·00
196. 5d. green .. .. 1·50 2·00
197. 6d. brown .. .. 1·10 2·25
198. 9d. violet .. .. 2·00 2·50
199. 1s. grey .. .. 2·00 2·00
200. 2s. lake .. .. 3·00 3·50
201. 5s. brown .. .. 9·00 10·00
202. 10s. red .. .. 30·00 28·00
203. £1 grey .. .. 35·00 20·00

4. Bulolo Goldfields.

1935. Air.
204. **4.** £2 violet .. .. 80·00 65·00
205. £5 green £250 £200

1935. Silver Jubilee. Nos. 177 and 179 optd. **HIS MAJESTY'S JUBILEE 1910-1935.**
206. – 1d. green 45 45
207. – 2d. red 75 90

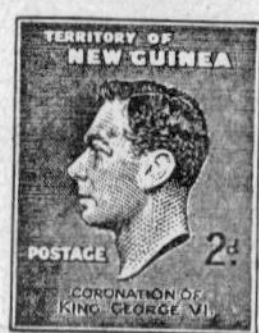

5. King George VI.

ILLUSTRATIONS
British Commonwealth and all overprints and surcharges are FULL SIZE. Foreign Countries have been reduced to ¾-LINEAR.

1937. Coronation.
208. **5.** 2d. red 12 15
209. 3d. blue 12 15
210. 5d. green 15 20
211. 1s. purple 25 35

1939. Air. As T **4**, but inscr. "AIR MAIL POSTAGE".
212. ½d. orange 80 30
213. 1d. green 20 35
214. 1½d. claret .. .. 50 1·00
215. 2d. red .. .. 1·00 1·10
216. 3d. blue .. .. 1·50 1·60
217. 4d. olive .. .. 1·25 1·60
218. 5d. green .. .. 80 1·00
219. 6d. brown .. .. 1·60 2·25
220. 9d. violet .. .. 2·25 3·25
221. 1s. green .. .. 2·75 3·25
222. 2s. red .. .. 10·00 11·00
223. 5s. brown .. .. 17·00 19·00
224. 10s. pink .. .. 45·00 45·00
225. £1 olive .. .. 38·00 40·00

SERVICE STAMPS

1914. Nos. 16 and 17 optd. **O S.**
40. **N.** 1d. on 3 pf. brown .. 75 75
41. 1d. on 4 pf. green .. 1·50 1·50

OFFICIAL STAMPS.

1925. Optd. **O S.**
O 1. **2.** 1d. green .. .. 40 1·00
O 2. 1½d. red .. .. 1·50 2·50
O 3. 2d. claret 65 90
O 4. 3d. blue .. .. 85 1·10
O 5. 4d. olive .. .. 1·00 1·40
O 6. 6d. brown .. .. 2·25 4·50
O 7. 9d. purple .. .. 2·25 5·00
O 8. 1s. green .. .. 2·00 5·00
O 9. 2s. lake .. .. 7·00 12·00

1931. Optd. **O S.**
O 10. **3.** 1d. green .. .. 45 1·00
O 11. 1½d. red .. .. 75 1·10
O 12. 2d. claret .. .. 70 1·10
O 13. 3d. blue .. .. 80 1·25
O 14. 4d. olive .. .. 80 1·75
O 15. 5d. green .. .. 1·10 2·50
O 16. 6d. brown .. .. 2·00 3·75
O 17. 9d. violet .. .. 2·00 3·75
O 18. 1s. grey .. .. 3·50 5·00
O 19. 2s. lake .. .. 6·00 9·00
O 20. 5s. brown .. .. 38·00 55·00

1932. T **3**, but without dates, optd. **O S.**
O 21. 1d. green 20 60
O 22. 1½d. claret 55 75
O 23. 2d. red 55 75
O 24. 2½d. green .. .. 90 1·10
O 25. 3d. blue .. .. 1·25 1·50
O 26. 3½d. red .. .. 1·25 1·75
O 27. 4d. olive .. .. 1·25 1·50
O 28. 5d. green .. .. 1·25 1·50
O 29. 6d. brown .. .. 1·75 3·00
O 30. 9d. violet .. .. 3·00 4·00
O 31. 1s. grey .. .. 4·50 5·50
O 32. 2s. lake .. .. 9·00 11·00
O 33. 5s. brown .. .. 28·00 30·00

For later issues see **PAPUA AND NEW GUINEA.**

NEW HEBRIDES BC; O3

A group of islands in the Pacific Ocean, E. of Australia, under joint administration of Gt. Britain and France,

1938. 100 gold centimes = 1 gold franc.

BRITISH ADMINISTRATION

1908. Stamps of Fiji optd. **NEW HEBRIDES CONDOMINIUM.**
1. **9.** ½d. green 20 75
2. 1d. red 30 75
5. 2d. purple and orange .. 60 75
6. 2½d. purple & blue on blue 60 75
7. 5d. purple and green .. 2·25 2·75
3. 6d. purple and red .. .. 2·25 2·75
3. 1s. green and red .. .. 8·00 10·00

1910. Stamps of Fiji optd. as before.
12. **9.** 2d. grey 40 90
13. 2½d. blue .. .. 50 1·25
15. 6d. purple .. .. 1·00 1·40
16. 1s. black on green .. 1·00 1·75

1. Native Idols, etc.

1911.
18. **1.** ½d. green 45 45
19. 1d. red 60 90
20. 2d. grey .. .. 1·00 1·00
21. 2½d. blue .. .. 65 1·00
24. 5d. green .. .. 80 1·00
25. 6d. purple .. .. 1·10 1·10
26. 1s. black on green .. 1·40 2·00
27. 2s. purple on blue .. 5·00 6·00
28. 5s. green on yellow .. 10·00 11·00

1920. Surch. (a) On T **1**.
40. **1.** 1d. on ½d. green .. 70 3·00
30. 1d. on 5d. green .. 6·00 7·00
31. 1d. on 1s. black on green 1·50 4·00
32. 1d. on 2s. purple on blue 1·50 4·00
33. 1d. on 5s. green on yellow 1·50 4·00
41. 3d. on 1d. red .. .. 1·50 3·00
42. 5d. on 2½d. blue .. 3·00 4·00

(b) On No. F 16 French New Hebrides.
34. **1.** 2d. on 40 c. red on yellow 1·50 4·00

2.

1925.

43. 2. ½d. (5 c.) black 25 45
44. 1d. (10 c.) green 40 55
45. 2d. (20 c.) grey 40 55
46. 2½d. (25 c.) brown .. 55 70
47. 5d. (50 c.) blue 80 80
48. 6d. (60 c.) purple .. 1·25 1·75
49. 1s. (1 f. 25) black on green 1·50 1·75
50. 2s. (2 f. 50) purple on blue 2·75 3·50
51. 5s. (6 f. 25) green on yellow 5·00 6·00

3 Lopevi Islands and Copra Canoe.

1938.

52. 3. 5 c. green 40 45
53. 10 c. orange 65 55
54. 15 c. violet 65 65
55. 20 c. red .. .. .. 75 1·00
56. 25 c. brown .. .. 75 1·00
57. 30 c. blue .. .. .. 90 1·00
58. 40 c. olive .. .. .. 1·10 1·25
59. 50 c. purple .. .. 1·10 80
60. 1 f. red on green .. .. 3·25 3·25
61. 2 f. blue on green .. .. 4·50 4·50
62. 5 f. red on yellow .. .. 10·00 10·00
63. 10 f. violet on blue .. 18·00 18·00

1949. U.P.U. As T 17 of Antigua.

64. 10 c. orange 15 20
65. 15 c. violet 20 20
66. 30 c. blue 30 40
67. 50 c. purple 50 55

4. Outrigger Sailing Canoes.

1953.

68. 4. 5 c. green 5 5
69. 10 c. red 5 5
70. 15 c. yellow 5 8
71. 20 c. blue 8 10
72. – 25 c. olive 10 12
73. – 30 c. brown 15 15
74. – 40 c. sepia 15 20
75. – 50 c. violet 20 20
76. – 1 f. orange 40 45
77. – 2 f. purple .. .. .. 90 1·00
78. – 5 f. red .. .. .. 2·25 2·50

DESIGNS: 25 c. to 50 c. Native carving. 1 f. to 5 f. Two natives outside Hut.

1953. Coronation. As T 7 of Aden.

79. 10 c. black and red 45 60

5. Quiros Caravel and Map.

1956. Condominium. 50th Anniv. Inscr. "1906 1956".

80. 5. 5 c. green 8 8
81. 10 c. red 10 12
82. – 20 c. blue 15 20
83. – 50 c. lilac 40 55

DESIGN: 20 c., 50 c. "Marianne", "Talking Drum" and "Britannia".

6. Port Vila: Iririki Islet.

1957.

84. 6. 5 c. green 5 5
85. 10 c. red 5 5
86. 15 c. yellow 8 8
87. 20 c. blue 10 10
88. – 25 c. olive 12 12
89. – 30 c. brown 15 15
90. – 40 c. sepia 30 30
91. – 50 c. violet 30 30
92. – 1 f. orange 55 55
93. – 2 f. mauve .. .. .. 1·25 1·25
94. – 5 f. black .. .. .. 2·50 2·50

DESIGNS: 25 c. to 50 c. River scene and spear fisherman. 1 f. to 5 f. Woman drinking from coconut.

1963. Freedom from Hunger. As T 10 of Aden.

95. 60 c. green 35 40

1963. Red Cross Cent. As T 24 of Antigua but with British and French cyphers in place of the Queen's portrait.

96. 15 c. red and black .. 15 20
97. 45 c. red and blue 45 60

7. Copra.

1963.

98. – 5 c. lake, brown and blue 5 5
99. – 10 c. brown, buff & green 5 5
100. 7. 15 c. bistre, brown & violet 8 8
101. – 20 c. black, green and blue 8 10
102. – 25 c. violet, brown & red 10 10
103. – 30 c. chestnut, bistre & vio. 25 25
104. – 40 c. red and indigo .. 30 30
105. – 50 c. green, yellow and turquoise-blue 40 40
129. – 60 c. vermilion and blue 25 30
106. – 1 f. red, black and green 60 60
107. – 2 f. black, brown & olive 1·25 1·25
108. – 3 f. multicoloured .. 2·00 2·00
109. – 5 f. blue, indigo and black 3·50 3·50

DESIGNS: 5 c. Exporting manganese, Forari. 10 c. Cocoa beans. 20 c. Fishing from Palikulo Point. 25 c. "Rhinecanthus aculeatus" (fish). 30 c. Nautilus shell. 40 c., 60 c. Sting-fish ("Pterois volitans"). 50 c. "Acanthurus lineatus" (fish). 1 f. Cardinal honey-eater (bird). 2 f. Buff-bellied fly-catcher. 3 f. Thicket Warbler ("Cichlornis grosvenori"). 5 f. White-collared kingfisher.

1965. I.T.U. Cent. As T 26 of Antigua but with British and French cyphers in place of the Queen's portrait.

110. 15 c. red and drab 15 15
111. 60 c. blue and red 45 45

1965. I.C.Y. As T 27 of Antigua but with British and French cyphers in place of the Queen's portrait.

112. 5 c. purple and turquoise .. 5 5
113. 55 c. green and lavender .. 40 45

1966. Churchill Commem. As T 28 of Antigua but with British and French cyphers in place of the Queen's portrait.

114. 5 c. blue 5 5
115. 15 c. green 12 15
116. 25 c. brown 25 25
117. 30 c. violet 30 35

1966. World Cup Football Championships. As T 30 of Antigua but with British and French cyphers in place of the Queen's portrait.

118. 20 c. multicoloured .. 10 12
119. 40 c. multicoloured .. 20 25

1966. W.H.O. Headquarters, Geneva. Inaug. As T 31 of Antigua but with British and French cyphers in place of the Queen's portrait.

120. 25 c. black, green and blue 12 15
121. 60 c. black, purple and ochre 30 30

1966. U.N.E.S.C.O. 20th Anniv. As T 33/5 of Antigua but with British and French cyphers in place of the Queen's portrait.

122. 15 c. multicoloured .. 10 10
123. 30 c. yellow, violet and olive 20 25
124. 45 c. black, purple & orge. 30 30

8. The Coast Watchers. (The above illustration is reduced. Actual size 55½ × 41 mm.)

1967. Pacific War. 25th Anniv. Multicoloured.

125. 15 c. Type 8 .. .. 10 10
126. 25 c. Map of War Zone, U.S. Marine and Australian Soldier 15 15
127. 60 c. H.M.A.S. "Canberra" 40 40
128. 1 f. "Flying Fortress" .. 65 65

9. Globe and Hemispheres.

1968. Bougainville's World Voyage. Bicent.

130. 9. 15 c. emer., violet & red 10 10
131. – 25 c. olive., mar. & ultram. 15 15
132. – 60 c. brown, purple & grn. 25 30

DESIGNS: 25 c. Ships "La Boudeuse" and "L'Etoile", and Map. 60 c. Bougainville, Ship's Figure-head and Bougainvillea Flowers.

10. "Concorde" and Vapour Trails.

1968. Anglo-French "Concorde" Project.

133. 10. 25 c. blue, red & vio.-blue 20 20
134. – 60 c. red, black and blue 35 35

DESIGN: 60 c. "Concorde" in flight.

11. Kauri Pine.

1969. Timber Industry.

135. 11. 20 c. multicoloured .. 20 20

12. Cyphers Flags and Relay Runner.

1969. 3rd South Pacific Games. Port Moresby. Multicoloured.

136. 25 c. Type 12 .. .. 15 15
137. 1 f. Similar to No. 136 .. 50 65

13. Diver on Platform.

1969. Pentecost Island Land Divers. Multicoloured.

138. 15 c. Type 13 .. .. 10 10
139. 25 c. Diver Jumping .. 15 15
140. 1 f. Diver at end of Fall .. 50 50

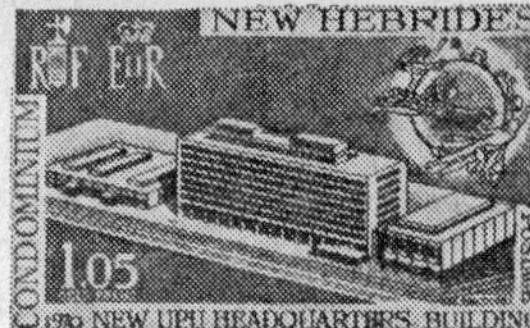

14. New U.P.U. Headquarters Building.

1970. New U.P.U. Headquarters Building.

141. 14. 1 f. 05 slate, orge. & pur. 45 50

15. General de Gaulle.

1970. New Hebrides' Declaration for the Free French Government. 30th Anniv.

142. 15. 65 c. multicoloured .. 25 30
143. 1 f. 10 multicoloured .. 60 65

1970. No. 101 surch.

144. 7. 35 c. on 20 c. black, green and blue 25 30

16. "The Virgin and the Child" (G. Bellini).

1970. Christmas. Multicoloured.

145. 15 c. Type 16 .. .. 10 10
146. 50 c. "The Virgin and the Child" (G. Cima) .. 25 30

1971. Death of General Charles de Gaulle. Nos. 142/3 optd. **1890-1970 IN MEMORIAM 9-11-70.**

147. 15. 65 c. multicoloured .. 40 40
148. 1 f. 10 multicoloured .. 60 60

17. Football.

1971. 4th South Pacific Games, Papeete, French Polynesia.

149. 20 c. Type 17 .. .. 10 12
150. 65 c. Basketball (vert.) .. 35 35

18. Kauri Pine, Cone and Arms of Royal Society.

1971. Royal Society's Expedition to New Hebrides.
151. 18. 65 c. multicoloured .. 30 35

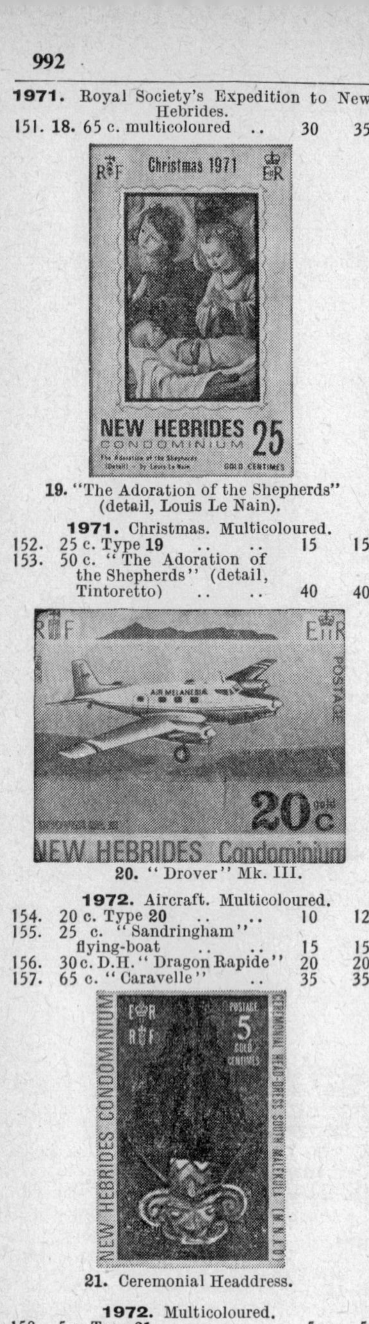

19. "The Adoration of the Shepherds" (detail, Louis Le Nain).

1971. Christmas. Multicoloured.
152. 25 c. Type **19** 15 15
153. 50 c. "The Adoration of the Shepherds" (detail, Tintoretto) 40 40

20. "Drover" Mk. III.

1972. Aircraft. Multicoloured.
154. 20 c. Type **20** 10 12
155. 25 c. "Sandringham" flying-boat 15 15
156. 30 c. D.H. "Dragon Rapide" 20 20
157. 65 c. "Caravelle" .. 35 35

21. Ceremonial Headdress.

1972. Multicoloured.
158. 5 c. Type **21** 5 5
159. 10 c. Baker's pigeon .. 5 5
160. 15 c. Gong and carving .. 5 5
161. 20 c. Royal parrot-finch .. 8 8
162. 25 c. "Cribraria fischeri" (shell) 10 10
163. 30 c. "Oliva rubrolabiata" (shell) 12 12
164. 35 c. Chestnut-bellied Kingfisher 12 15
165. 65 c. "Strombus plicatus" (shell) 25 25
166. 1 f. Gong and carving .. 35 40
167. 2 f. Green Palm Lorikeet.. 65 75
168. 3 f. Ceremonial headdress 1·00 1·25
169. 5 f. Green Snail Shell .. 1·75 2·00

22. "Adoration of the Magi" (Spranger).

1972. Christmas. Multicoloured.
170. 25 c. Type **22** 15 15
171. 70 c. "The Virgin and Child" (Provoost) .. 40 40

1972. Royal Silver Wedding. As T **19** of Ascension but with Royal and French Ciphers in background.
172. 35 c. violet-black.. .. 20 20
173. 65 c. green.. .. .. 40 45

23. "Dendrobium teretifolium".

1973. Orchids. Multicoloured.
174. 25 c. Type **23** 10 10
175. 30 c. "Ephemerantha comata" 15 15
176. 35 c. "Spathoglottis petri" 15 15
177. 65 c. "Dendrobium mohlianum" 30 30

24. New Wharf at Vila.

1973. New Wharf at Vila. Multicoloured.
178. 25 c. Type **24** 12 12
179. 70 c. As T **24** but horiz. format 35 40

25. Wild Horses.

1973. Tanna Island. Multicoloured.
180. 35 c. Type **25** 15 15
181. 70 c. Yasur Volcano .. 35 40

26. Mother and Child.

1973. Christmas. Multicoloured.
182. 35 c. Type **26** 15 15
183. 70 c. Lagoon scene .. 35 40

27. Pacific Dove.

1974. Wild Life. Multicoloured.
184. 25 c. Type **27** 10 10
185. 35 c. Night Swallowtail (butterfly) 15 15
186. 70 c. Green Sea Turtle .. 35 40
187. 1 f. 15 Flying Fox.. .. 45 50

1974. Royal Visit. Nos. 164 and 167 optd. **ROYAL VISIT 1974.**
188. 35 c. multicoloured .. 15 15
189. 2 f. multicoloured.. .. 95 1·00

28. Old Post Office.

1974. Inaug. of New Post Office. Mult.
190. 35 c. Type **28** 15 15
191. 70 c. New Post Office .. 35 40

29. Capt. Cook and Map.

1974. Discovery. Bicent. Multicoloured.
192. 35 c. Type **29** 15 15
193. 35 c. William Wales and beach landing .. 15 15
194. 35 c. William Hodges and island scene 15 15
195. 1 f. 15 Capt. Cook, map and H.M.S. "Resolution" (59 × 34 mm.) 45 45

30. U.P.U. Emblem and Letters.

1974. U.P.U. Centenary.
196. 30. 70 c. multicoloured .. 30 30

31. "Adoration of the Magi" (Velazquez).

1974. Christmas. Multicoloured.
197. 35 c. Type **31** 15 15
198. 70 c. "The Nativity" (Gerard van Honthorst).. .. 30 30

32. Charolais Bull.

1975.
199. 32. 10 f. brown, grn. & blue 3·50 3·75

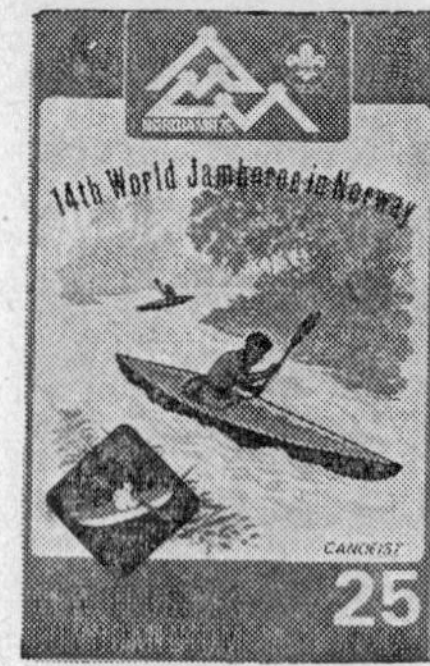

33. Canoeing.

1975. World Scout Jamboree, Norway. Mult.
200. 25 c. Type **33** 10 12
201. 35 c. Preparing meal .. 15 15
202. 1 f. Map-reading 35 40
203. 5 f. Fishing .. .. 1·90 2·40

34. "Pitti Madonna" (Michelangelo).

1975. Christmas. Michelangelo's Sculptures. Multicoloured.
204. 35 c. Type **34** 15 15
205. 70 c. "Bruges Madonna".. 30 35
206. 2 f. 50 "Taddei Madonna" 1·00 1·10

35. "Concorde" in British Airways Livery.

1976. 1st Commercial Flight of "Concorde".
207. 35. 5 f. multicoloured .. 2·00 2·25

36. Telephones of 1876 and 1976.

1976. Telephone Cent. Multicoloured.

208. 25 c. Type **36** 10 12
209. 70 c. Alexander Graham Bell 30 35
210. 1 f. 15 Satellite and Noumea Earth Station 50 55

37. Map of the Islands.

1976. Constitutional Changes. Multicoloured.

211. 25 c. Type **37** 10 12
212. 1 f. View of Santo (horiz.) 40 45
213. 2 f. View of Vila (horiz.) .. 80 90

Nos. 212/13 are smaller, 36 × 26 mm.

38. " The Flight into Egypt " (Lusitano).

1976. Christmas. Multicoloured.

214. 35 c. Type **38** 15 15
215. 70 c. " Adoration of the Shepherds " 30 35
216. 2 f. 50 " Adoration of the Magi " .. .. .. 1·00 1·10

Nos. 215/16 show retables by the Master of Santos-o-Novo.

39. Royal Visit, 1974.

1977. Silver Jubilee. Multicoloured.

217. 35 c. Type **39** 15 15
218. 70 c. Imperial State Crown 30 35
219. 2 f. The Blessing (Coronation) 80 90

POSTAGE DUE STAMPS

1925. Optd. **POSTAGE DUE.**

D 1. **2.** 1d. (10 c.) green .. .. — 45
D 2. 2d. (20 c.) grey .. .. — 50
D 3. 3d. (30 c.) red .. .. — 1·00
D 4. 5d. (50 c.) blue .. .. — 1·25
D 5. 10d. (1 f.) red on blue .. — 1·50
Set of 5 un. .. .. 50·00

1938. Optd. **POSTAGE DUE.**

D 6. **3.** 5 c. green .. .. 90 1·10
D 7. 10 c. orange .. .. 1·00 1·40
D 8. 20 c. red .. .. 1·40 2·25
D 9. 40 c. olive .. .. 2·00 3·00
D 10. **4.** 1 f. red on green .. 5·50 7·00

1953. Optd. **POSTAGE DUE.**

D 11. **4.** 5 c. green 8 8
D 12. 10 c. red 10 12
D 13. 20 c. blue 20 25
D 14. – 40 c. sepia (No. 74) .. 35 35
D 15. – 1 f. orange (No. 76) .. 50 75

1957. Optd. **POSTAGE DUE.**

D 16. **6.** 5 c. green 5 5
D 17. 10 c. red 5 5
D 18. 20 c. blue 12 12
D 19. – 40 c. sepia (No. 90) .. 35 35
D 20. – 1 f. orange (No. 92) .. 75 75

FRENCH ADMINISTRATION

1908. Stamps of New Caledonia optd. **NOUVELLES HEBRIDES.**

F 1. **2.** 5 c. green 40 40
F 2. 10 c. red 60 60
F 3. **3.** 25 c. blue on green .. 60 60
F 4. 50 c. red on green .. 70 70
F 5. **4.** 1 f. blue on green .. 2·25 2·25

1910. Stamps of New Caledonia optd. **NOUVELLES HEBRIDES CONDOMINIUM.**

F 6. **2.** 5 c. green 15 15
F 7. 10 c. red 15 15
F 8. **3.** 25 c. blue on green .. 25 25
F 9. 50 c. red on orange .. 55 55
F 10. **4.** 1 f. blue on green .. 2·10 2·10

The following issues are as stamps of British Administration but inscr. " NOUVELLES HEBRIDES " except where otherwise stated.

1911.

F 11. **1.** 5 c. green 10 10
F 12. 10 c. red 12 12
F 13. 20 c. grey 45 35
F 14. 25 c. blue 65 55
F 15. 30 c. brown on yellow .. 55 45
F 16. 40 c. red on yellow .. 45 45
F 17. 50 c. olive 65 65
F 18. 75 c. orange .. .. 1·10 90
F 19. 1 f. red on blue 55 45
F 20. 2 f. violet .. .. 1·10 1·10
F 21. 5 f. red on green .. 2·00 1·90

1920. Surch. in figures.

F 34. 05 c. on 40 c. red on yell. (No. F. 16) .. .. 4·50 4·50
F 32a. 5 c. on 50 c. red on orge. (No. F 4) £160 £160
F 33. 5 c. on 50 c. red on orge. (No. F 9) 45 45
F 38. 10 c. on 5 c. green (No. F 11) 8 8
F 33a. 10 c. on 25 c. blue on grn. (No. F 8) 12 12
F 35. 20 c. on 30 c. brown on yellow (No. F 15) .. 2·25 2·25
F 39. 30 c. on 10 c. red (No. F 12) 8 8
F 40. 50 c. on 25 c. blue (No. F 14) 75 75

1921. Stamp of New Hebrides (British) surch. in figures.

F 37. 10 c. on 5d. green (No. 24) 2·25 2·25

1925.

F 42. **2.** 5 c. (½d.) black 12 12
F 43. 10 c. (1d.) green .. 8 8
F 44. 20 c. (2d.) grey 8 8
F 45. 25 c. (2½d.) chocolate .. 8 8
F 46. 30 c. (3d.) red 8 8
F 47. 40 c. (4d.) red on yellow 12 12
F 48. 50 c. (5d.) blue 12 12
F 49. 75 c. (7½d.) brown .. 12 12
F 50. 1 f. (10d.) red on blue .. 35 35
F 51. 2 f. (1s. 8d.) violet .. 25 25
F 52. 5 f. (4d.) red on green .. 90 90

1938.

F 53. **3.** 5 c. green 5 5
F 54. 10 c. orange 8 8
F 55. 15 c. violet 8 8
F 56. 20 c. red 12 12
F 57. 25 c. brown 15 15
F 58. 30 c. blue 20 20
F 59. 40 c. olive 30 30
F 60. 50 c. purple 35 35
F 61. 1 f. red on green .. 45 45
F 62. 2 f. blue on green .. 1·00 1·00
F 63. 5 f. red on yellow .. 2·75 2·75
F 64. 10 f. violet on blue .. 6·00 6·00

1941. Free French Issue. As last optd. **France Libre.**

F 65. **3.** 5 c. green .. .. 1·10 1·10
F 66. 10 c. orange .. .. 1·10 1·10
F 67. 15 c. violet .. .. 1·10 1·10
F 68. 20 c. red .. .. 1·10 1·10
F 69. 25 c. brown .. .. 1·40 1·40
F 70. 30 c. blue .. .. 1·40 1·40
F 71. 40 c. olive .. .. 1·40 1·40
F 72. 50 c. purple .. .. 1·40 1·40
F 73. 1 f. red on green .. 1·40 1·40
F 74. 2 f. blue on green .. 1·40 1·40
F 75. 5 f. red on yellow .. 2·10 2·10
F 76. 10 f. violet on blue .. 2·25 2·25

1949. U.P.U. 75th Anniv. As Br. Administration but with inscriptions in French.

F 77. 10 c. orange 25 25
F 78. 15 c. violet 40 40
F 79. 30 c. blue 50 50
F 80. 50 c. purple 75 75

1953.

F 81. **4.** 5 c. green 5 5
F 82. 10 c. red 5 5
F 83. 15 c. yellow 8 8
F 84. 20 c. blue 15 15
F 85. – 25 c. olive 20 20
F 86. – 30 c. brown 20 20
F 87. – 40 c. sepia 30 30
F 88. – 50 c. violet 30 30
F 89. – 1 f. orange 70 70
F 90. – 2 f. purple .. .. 1·60 1·60
F 91. – 5 f. red .. .. 2·75 2·75

1956. 50th Anniv. of Condominium.

F 92. **5.** 5 c. green 25 25
F 93. 10 c. red 25 25
F 94. – 20 c. blue 30 30
F 95. – 50 c. violet 65 65

1957.

F 96. **6.** 5 c. green 5 5
F 97. 10 c. red 5 5
F 98. 15 c. yellow 10 10
F 99. 20 c. blue 10 10
F 100. – 25 c. olive 10 10
F 101. – 30 c. brown 25 25
F 102. – 40 c. sepia 30 30
F 103. – 50 c. violet 35 35
F 104. – 1 f. orange 40 40
F 105. – 2 f. mauve .. .. 1·40 1·40
F 106. – 5 f. black .. .. 1·90 1·90

F 1. Emblem and Globe. **F 2.** Centenary Emblem.

1963. Freedom from Hunger.

F 107. **F 1.** 60 c. green & chestnut 45 45

1963. Red Cross Cent.

F 108. **F 2.** 15 c. red, grey & orge. 20 20
F 109. 45 c. red, grey & bistre 35 35

1963.

F 110. – 5 c. lake, brown & blue 5 5
F 111. – 10 c. brown, buff & grn.* 5 5
F 112. – 10 c. brown, buff & grn. 5 5
F 113. **7.** 15 c. bistre, brn. & vio. 8 8
F 114. – 20 c. black, grn. & blue* 12 12
F 115. – 20 c. black, green & blue 5 5
F 116. – 25 c. violet, brn. & red 10 10
F 117. – 30 c. chest., bis. & vio. 12 10
F 118. – 40 c. red and indigo .. 30 30
F 119. – 50 c. green, yellow and turquoise-blue .. 25 25
F 120. – 60 c. red and blue .. 25 25
F 121. – 1 f. red, black & green 40 40
F 122. – 2 f. black, brown & olive 75 75
F 123. – 3 f. vio., brn., grn. & blk.* 1·40 1·40
F 124. – 3 f. vio., brn., grn. & blk. 80 80
F 125. – 5 f. blue, indigo & blk. 1·75 1·75

The stamps indicated by an asterisk have " RF " wrongly placed on the left.

1965. I.T.U. Cent. As T **15** of Comoro Islands, with British and French cyphers.

F 126. 15 c. blue, emerald & brn. 20 15
F 127. 60 c. cerise, slate & green 55 45

1965. I.C.Y. As Nos. 112/13.

F 128. 5 c. purple and turquoise 12 10
F 129. 55 c. green and lavender 35 35

1966. Churchill Commem. As Nos. 114/17.

F 130. 5 c. black, cerise, gold and blue 5 5
F 131. 15 c. black, cerise, gold and green 10 10
F 132. 25 c. black, cerise, gold and brown 15 15
F 133. 30 c. black, cerise, gold and violet 20 20

1966. World Cup Football Championships. As Nos. 118/19.

F 134. 20 c. vio., olive, lake & brn. 15 15
F 135. 40 c. chocolate, green, lake and chestnut .. 25 25

1966. W.H.O. Headquarters, Geneva. Inaug. As Nos. 120/1.

F 136. 25 c. black, green & blue 12 12
F 137. 60 c. black, mauve & ochre 25 25

1966. U.N.E.S.C.O. 20th Anniv. As Nos. 122/4.

F 138. 15 c. vio., red, yell. & orge. 10 10
F 139. 30 c. yellow, violet & olive 15 15
F 140. 45 c. black, purple & orge. 20 20

1967. Pacific War. 25th Anniv. As Nos. 125/8.

F 141. 15 c. multicoloured .. 10 10
F 142. 25 c. multicoloured .. 15 15
F 143. 60 c. multicoloured .. 25 25
F 144. 1 f. multicoloured .. 45 45

1968. Bougainville's World Voyage. Bicent. As Nos. 130/2.

F 145. 15 c. green, violet & red 5 5
F 146. 25 c. olive, mar. & blue 10 10
F 147. 60 c. brown, pur. & grn. 30 30

1968. Anglo-French " Concorde " Project. As Nos. 133/4.

F 148. 25 c. blue, red & vio.-blue 12 12
F 149. 60 c. red, black and blue 30 30

1969. Timber Industry. As No. 135.

F 150. 20 c. multicoloured .. 8 5

1969. 3rd South Pacific Games, Port Moresby, Papua New Guinea. As Nos. 136/7.

F 151. 25 c. multicoloured .. 10 8
F 152. 1 f. multicoloured .. 35 25

1969. Land Divers of Pentecost Island. As Nos. 138/40.

F 153. 15 c. multicoloured .. 5 5
F 154. 25 c. multicoloured .. 10 8
F 155. 1 f. multicoloured .. 35 30

1970. Inaug. of New U.P.U. Headquarters Building, Berne. As No. 141.

F 156. 1 f. 05 slate, orge. & purple 40 30

1970. New Hebrides' Declaration for the Free French Government. As Nos. 142/3.

F 157. 65 c. multicoloured .. 30 25
F 158. 1 f. 10 multicoloured .. 55 45

1970. No. F 115 surch.

F 159. 35 c. on 20 c. black, green and blue .. 12 10

1970. Christmas. As Nos. 145/6.

F 160. 15 c. multicoloured .. 8 5
F 161. 50 c. multicoloured .. 20 15

1971. Death of General Charles de Gaulle. Nos. F 157/8 optd. **1890-1970 IN MEMORIAM 9-11-70.**

F 162. 65 c. multicoloured .. 25 30
F 163. 1 f. 10 multicoloured .. 45 35

1971. 4th South Pacific Games, Papeete, French Polynesia. As Nos. 149/50.

F 164. 20 c. multicoloured .. 8 5
F 165. 65 c. multicoloured .. 25 20

1971. Royal Society Expedition to New Hebrides. As No. 151.

F 166. 65 c. multicoloured .. 25 20

1971. Christmas. As Nos. 152/3.

F 167. 25 c. multicoloured .. 10 5
F 168. 50 c. multicoloured .. 20 12

1972. Aircraft. As Nos. 154/7.

F 169. 20 c. multicoloured .. 8 5
F 170. 25 c. multicoloured .. 10 8
F 171. 30 c. multicoloured .. 12 8
F 172. 65 c. multicoloured .. 25 20

1972. As Nos. 158/69.

F 173. 5 c. multicoloured .. 5 5
F 174. 10 c. multicoloured .. 5 5
F 175. 15 c. multicoloured .. 5 5
F 176. 20 c. multicoloured .. 8 5
F 177. 25 c. multicoloured .. 10 5
F 178. 30 c. multicoloured .. 10 8
F 179. 35 c. multicoloured .. 12 10
F 180. 65 c. multicoloured .. 20 15
F 181. 1 f. multicoloured .. 35 30
F 182. 2 f. multicoloured .. 70 60
F 183. 3 f. multicoloured .. 1·00 85
F 184. 5 f. multicoloured .. 1·75 1·40

1972. Christmas. As Nos. 170/1.

F 185. 25 c. multicoloured .. 10 8
F 186. 70 c. multicoloured .. 25 20

1972. Royal Silver Wedding. As Nos. 172/3.

F 187. 35 c. multicoloured .. 15 8
F 188. 65 c. multicoloured .. 25 20

1973. Orchids. As Nos. 174/7.

F 189. 25 c. multicoloured .. 10 8
F 190. 30 c. multicoloured .. 12 8
F 191. 35 c. multicoloured .. 15 10
F 192. 65 c. multicoloured .. 25 20

1973. Opening of New Wharf at Villa. As Nos. 178/9.

F 193. 25 c. multicoloured .. 10 8
F 194. 70 c. multicoloured .. 25 20

1973. Tanna Island. As Nos. 180/1.

F 195. 35 c. multicoloured .. 15 10
F 196. 70 c. multicoloured .. 25 20

1973. Christmas. As Nos. 182/3.

F 197. 35 c. multicoloured .. 15 10
F 198. 70 c. multicoloured .. 25 20

1974. Wild Life. As Nos. 184/7.

F 199. **27.** 25 c. multicoloured 8 8
F 200. – 35 c. multicoloured 12 12
F 201. – 70 c. multicoloured 25 25
F 202. – 1 f. 15 multicoloured 35 35

1974. Royal Visit of Queen Elizabeth II. Nos. F 179 and F 182 optd. **ROYAL VISIT 1974.**

F 203. 35 c. multicoloured .. 12 12
F 204. 2 f. multicoloured .. 65 65

1974. New Post Office, Villa. Inaug. As Nos. 190/1.

F 205. 35 c. multicoloured .. 12 12
F 206. 70 c. multicoloured .. 25 25

1974. Rediscovery of New Hebrides by Captain Cook. Bicent. As Nos. 192/5.

F 207. 35 c. multicoloured .. 12 12
F 208. 35 c. multicoloured .. 12 12
F 209. 35 c. multicoloured .. 12 12
F 210. 1 f. 15 multicoloured .. 35 35

1974. Universal Postal Union. Cent. As No. 196.

F 211. 70 c. blue, red & black .. 25 25

1974. Christmas. As Nos. 197/8.

F 212. 35 c. multicoloured .. 12 12
F 213. 70 f. multicoloured .. 25 25

1975. Charolais Bull. As No. 199.

F 214. 10 f. brown, grn. and blue 3·25 3·50

1975. World Scout Jamboree, Norway. As Nos. 200/3.
F 215. 25 c. multicoloured .. 10 12
F 216. 35 c. multicoloured .. 12 15
F 217. 1 f. multicoloured .. 35 40
F 218. 5 f. multicoloured .. 1·90 2·40

1975. Christmas. As Nos. 204/6.
F 219. 35 c. multicoloured .. 15 15
F 220. 70 c. multicoloured .. 30 35
F 221. 2 f. 50 multicoloured .. 1·10 1·10

1976. 1st Commercial Flight of "Concorde". As No. 207, but Concorde in Air France livery.
F 222. 5 f. multicoloured .. 2·00 2·25

1976. Telephone Centenary. As Nos. 208/10.
F 223. 25 c. multicoloured .. 10 12
F 224. 70 c. multicoloured .. 30 35
F 225. 1 f. 15 multicoloured .. 40 40

1976. Constitutional Changes. As Nos. 211/13.
F 226. 25 c. multicoloured .. 10 12
F 227. 1 f. multicoloured .. 40 45
F 228. 2 f. multicoloured .. 80 90

1976. Christmas. Paintings. As Nos. 214/16.
F 229 35 c. multicoloured .. 15 15
F 230. 70 c. multicoloured .. 30 35
F 231. 2 f. 50 multicoloured .. 1·00 1·10

1977. Silver Jubilee. As Nos. 217/9.
F 232. 35 c. multicoloured .. 15 15
F 233. 70 c. multicoloured .. 30 35
F 234. 2 f. multicoloured .. 80 90

POSTAGE DUE STAMPS

1925. Nos. F 32, etc., optd. **CHIFFRE TAXE.**
FD 53. **2.** 10 c. (1d.) green .. 4·50 55
FD 54. 20 c. (2d.) grey .. 4·50 55
FD 55. 30 c. (3d.) red .. 4·50 55
FD 56. 50 c. (5d.) blue .. 4·50 55
FD 57. 1 f. (10d.) red on blue .. 4·50 55

1938. Optd. **CHIFFRE TAXE.**
FD 65. **3.** 5 c. green 20 20
FD 66. 10 c. orange 20 20
FD 67. 20 c. red 25 25
FD 68. 40 c. olive 35 35
FD 69. 1 f. red on green .. 70 70

1941. Free French Issue. As last optd. **France Libre.**
FD 77. **3.** 5 c green 60 60
FD 78. 10 c. orange 60 60
FD 79. 20 c. red 60 60
FD 80. 40 c. olive 60 60
FD 81. 1 f. red on green .. 60 60

1953. Optd. **TIMBRE-TAXE.**
FD 92. **4.** 5 c. green 8 8
FD 93. 10 c. red 10 10
FD 94. 20 c. blue 20 20
FD 95. – 40 c. sepia (No. F 87) 35 35
FD 96. – 1 f. orange (No. F 89) 70 70

1957. Optd. **TIMBRE-TAXE.**
FD 107. **6.** 5 c. green 5 5
FD 108. 10 c. red 5 5
FD 109. 20 c. blue 8 8
FD 110. – 40 c. sepia (No. F 102) 15 15
FD 111. – 1 f. orange (No. F 104) 90 90

NEW REPUBLIC BC

A Boer republic originally part of Zululand. It was incorporated with the S. African Republic in 1888 and annexed to Natal in 1903.

NIEUWE REPUBLIEK 1d 8 NOV 86 ZUID-AFRIKA.

1.

1886. On yellow or blue paper.
2. **1.** 1d. violet .. .. .. 2·25 2·25
73. 2d. violet .. .. .. 2·00 2·00
74. 3d. violet .. .. .. 3·00 3·00
80. 4d. violet .. .. .. 3·00 3·00
81. 6d. violet .. .. .. 2·10 2·10
82. 9d. violet .. .. .. 2·40 2·40
83. 1s. violet .. .. .. 2·40 2·40
77. 1s. 6d. violet .. .. 3·00 3·00
85. 2s. violet .. .. .. 5·50 4·50
86. 2s. 6d. violet .. .. 6·00 6·00
87. 3s. violet .. .. .. 7·50 7·50
88. 4s. violet .. .. .. 3·00 3·00
89. 5s. violet .. .. .. 3·00 3·00
90. 5s. 6d. violet .. .. 3·00 3·00
91. 7s. 6d. violet .. .. 4·50 4·50
92. 10s. violet.. .. .. 3·00 3·00
93. 10s. 6d. violet .. .. 4·50 4·50
46. 12s. violet.. .. .. 80·00
47. 13s. violet.. .. .. 80·00
94. £1 violet .. .. .. 12·00 12·00
95. 30s. violet.. .. .. 23·00

Some stamps are found with Arms embossed in the paper, and others with the Arms and without a date above "ZUID-AFRIKA".

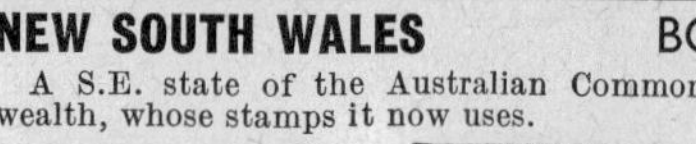

NEW SOUTH WALES BC

A S.E. state of the Australian Commonwealth, whose stamps it now uses.

1. Seal of the Colony.

2.

1850. Imperf.
8. **1.** 1d. red £600 £150
25. 2d. blue .. .. .. £375 70·00
42. 3d. green .. .. .. £600 90·00

1851. Imperf.
82. **2.** 1d. red .. .. .. 38·00 7·50
83. 1d. orange .. .. .. 38·00 7·50
84. 2d. blue .. .. .. 27·00 3·75
87. 3d. green .. .. .. 38·00 12·00
76. 6d. brown .. .. .. £400 75·00
79. 8d. yellow.. .. .. £750 £200

3.

4.

1854. Imperf.
104. **3.** 1d. red .. .. .. 23·00 7·00
107. 2d. blue .. .. .. 27·00 2·75
111. 3d. green.. .. .. £200 38·00
114. **4.** 5d. green.. .. .. £250 £200
116. 6d. grey .. .. .. £110 11·00
122. 6d. brown .. .. .. £120 12·00
126. 8d. orange £1700 £450
128. 1s. red .. .. .. £160 18·00

For these stamps, perf., see No. 154, etc.

5.

1860. Perf.
154. **3.** 1d. red .. .. .. 15·00 3·00
134. 2d. blue .. .. .. 27·00 3·75
226. 3d. green.. .. .. 60 8
243. **4.** 5d. green.. .. .. 45 8
143. 6d. brown .. .. .. 65·00 9·00
165. 6d. violet .. .. .. 11·00 1·50
236. 8d. orange .. .. .. 9·00 80
169. 1s. red .. .. .. 15·00 3·00
297c. **5.** 5s. purple .. .. .. 14·00 5·50

6.

7.

8.

1862. Queen Victoria. Various frames.
223f. **6.** 1d. red 8 5
225g. **7.** 2d. blue.. .. .. 30 8
230c. – 4d. brown .. .. 2·75 20
234. – 6d. lilac.. .. .. 1·50 8
206. – 10d. lilac .. .. 2·00 1·10
237d. – 1s. black .. .. 2·75 20

1871. As No. 206, surch. **NINEPENCE.**
309. 9d. on 10d. brown .. 90 30

1885.
244b. **8.** 5s. green and lilac .. 27·00 12·00
249b. 10s. claret and violet .. 15·00 9·00
246a. £1 claret and lilac .. £150 80·00

13. View of Sydney.

14. Emu.

20. The first Governor, Capt. Arthur Phillip and Lord Carrington, Governor in 1888.

1888. Inscr. "ONE HUNDRED YEARS".
253. **13.** 1d. mauve 30 5
255. **14.** 2d. blue 25 5
257. – 4d. brown 60 5
261. – 6d. red 90 5
262b. – 6d. green .. .. 2·75 1·10
339. – 6d. yellow 45 8
264. – 8d. rose-purple .. 1·50 20
270. – 1s. chocolate .. 1·50 8
277. – 5s. violet .. .. 18·00 7·50
346b. **20.** 20s. blue .. .. 38·00 12·00

DESIGNS—As T **13.** 4d. Capt. Cook. 6d. Queen Victoria and Arms. 8d. Lyre Bird. 1s. Kangaroo. As T **20**: 5s. Map of Australia.

21. Allegorical figure of Australia.

1890.
281. **21.** 2½d. blue 30 8

1891. Types as 1862, but new value and colours, surch. in words.
282. **6.** ½d. on 1d. grey 30 25
283. – 7½d. on 6d. brown .. 80 30
284c.– 12½d. on 1s. red.. .. 75 60

22.

23.

24.

25.

26.

27. Lyre Bird.

1892.
286. **22.** ½d. grey 20 8
298. ½d. green 12 8
300. **23.** 1d. red 15 8
302. **24.** 2d. blue 15 8
296. **25.** 2½d. violet 60 5
303. 2½d. blue 15 8
348. **26.** 9d. brown and blue .. 50 15
345a. **27.** 2s. 6d. green .. .. 1·00 25

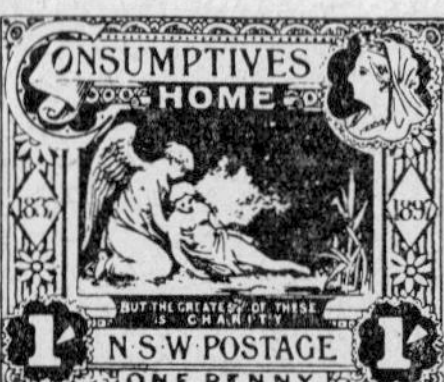

28. (Actual size 47 × 38 mm.)

1897. Charity. Inscr. "CONSUMPTIVES HOME".
287c. **28.** 1d. (1s.) green & brown 15·00 11·00
287d. – 2½d. (2s. 6d.) gold & blue 55·00 60·00

DESIGN—VERT. 2½d. Two female figures.

OFFICIAL STAMPS

1879-92. Various issues optd. **O.S.**

A. Issues of 1854 to 1871.
O 20b. **6.** 1d. red 8 8
O 21c. **7.** 2d. blue 8 8
O 22. **3.** 3d. green 25 8
O 27a. – 4d. brown (No. 230c) 8 8
O 29. **4.** 5d. green 25 25
O 31b. – 6d. lilac (No. 234) .. 12 8
O 32b. **4.** 8d. orange 10 8
O 11. – 9d. on 10d. (No. 309).. 55·00
O 59. – 10d. lilac (No. 206) .. 23·00 27·00
O 33. – 1s. black (No. 237d) .. 12 8
O 18. **5.** 5s. purple .. .. 23·00 23·00

B. Fiscal stamps of 1885.
O 37. **8.** 10 s. claret and violet.. 75·00 45·00
O 38. £1 claret and violet .. £350

C. Issue of 1888 (Nos. 253/346b).
O 39. 1d. muave 8 8
O 41. 2d. blue.. .. .. 8 8
O 43. 4d. brown 8 8
O 44. 6d. red 8 8
O 45. 8d. rose-purple.. .. 12 8
O 46. 1s. chocolate 25 8
O 52. 5s. violet .. .. 11·00 9·00
O 51. 20s. blue £375

D. Issues of 1890 and 1892.
O 58. **22.** ½d. grey 8 8
O 55. **6.** ½d. on 1d. grey .. 1·50 1·50
O 54. **21.** 2½d. blue 8 8
O 56. – 7½d. on 6d. (No. 283) 35 1·50
O 57. – 12½d. on 1s. (No. 284c) 45 1·00

POSTAGE DUE STAMPS

D 1.

ILLUSTRATIONS British Commonwealth and all overprints and surcharges are FULL SIZE. Foreign Countries have been reduced to ¾-LINEAR.

1891.
D 1. **D 1.** ½d. green 15 8
D 2a. 1d. green 15 8
D 3. 2d. green 15 8
D 4. 3d. green 30 12
D 5b. 4d. green 20 8
D 6. 6d. green 35 15
D 7. 8d. green 35 12
D 8. 5s. green .. .. 3·75 75
D 9a. 10s. green .. .. 7·50
D 10b. 20s. green .. .. 6·50 4·00

REGISTRATION STAMPS

R 1.

1856.
88. **R 1.** (6d.) red & bl. (Imp.).. £150 45·00
92. (6d.) orge & bl. (Imp.) £160 38·00
101. (6d.) red & bl. (Perf.).. 14·00 4·50
94. (6d.) orge. & bl. (Perf.) 75·00 12·00

NEW ZEALAND BC

A group of islands in the S. Pacific Ocean. A Commonwealth Dominion.

1967. 100 cents = 1 dollar.

1.

2.

1855. Imperf.
33. **1.** 1d. red .. .. .. 70·00 50·00
34. 1d. orange .. .. .. 75·00 50·00
38. 2d. blue .. .. .. 50·00 35·00
40. 3d. lilac .. .. .. 70·00 50·00
43. 6d. brown .. .. .. 75·00 35·00
45. 1s. green .. .. .. £150 70·00

1862. Perf.
111. **1.** 1d. red .. .. .. 30·00 10·00
112. 1d. orange .. .. .. 65·00 20·00
132. 1d. brown .. .. .. 30·00 10·00
114. 2d. blue .. .. .. 30·00 10·00
133. 2d. orange .. .. .. 30·00 10·00

117.	1.	3d. lilac	25·00	10·00
119.		4d. rose	£150	75·00
120.		4d. yellow	30·00	20·00
122a.		6d. brown	30·00	10·00
135.		6d. blue	30·00	10·00
125.		1s. green	35·00	25·00

1873.

151.	2.	½d. rose	50	10

3.

4.

5.

6.

7.

8.

9.

1874. Inscr. " POSTAGE ".

180.	3.	1d. lilac	6·00	50
181.	4.	2d. red	5·00	50
154.	5.	3d. brown	15·00	10·00
182.	6.	4d. maroon	20·00	8·00
183.	7.	6d. blue	10·00	5·00
184.	8.	1s. green	20·00	5·00
185.	9.	2s. red	£120	£120
186.		5s. grey	£140	£140

10.

11.

12.

20.

1882. Inscr. " POSTAGE & REVENUE".

217	10.	½d. black	55	10
218.	8.	1d. red	1·00	10
228.	7.	2d. mauve	2·00	10
220.	11.	2½d. blue	3·25	1·50
231.	8.	3d. yellow	3·75	1·00
241.	4.	4d. green	3·75	2·00
223.	12.	5d. black	5·00	2·00
242.	6.	6d. brown	8·00	1·50
192.	7.	8d. blue..	10·00	5·50
225.	5.	1s. chestnut	13·00	10·00

1882.

F 90.	20.	2s. blue	3·00	75
F 57.		2s. 6d. brown ..	4·00	75
F 58.		3s. mauve	8·50	1·00
F 102.		5s. green	6·50	1·25
F 66.		10s. brown	20·00	3·25

F 89.	20.	£1 red	40·00	12·00

Nos. F166/77 are revenue stamps authorised for use as postage stamps as there were no other postage stamps available in these denominations. Other values in this and similar types were mainly used for revenue purposes.

21. Mount Cook.

22. Lake Taupo.

24. Lake Wakatipu.

23. Pembroke Peak.

25. Huia Birds.

26. White Terrace, Rotomahana.

27. Otira Gorge and Mount Ruapehu.

28. Kiwi.

29. War Canoe.

30. Pink Terrace, Rotomahana.

31. Keas.

32. Milford Sound.

1898.

246.	21.	½d. deep purple ..	50	12
342.		½d. green	30	15
249.	22.	1d. blue and brown	15	15
251.	23.	2d. lake.. ..	1·75	12
253.	24.	2½d. blue (A)*	1·00	2·75
382.	24.	2½d. blue (B)*	85	30
274.	25.	3d. brown	1·25	35
258.	26.	4d. red	1·40	2·10
391.	27.	5d. brown	4·00	2·00
263.	28.	6d. green	6·00	6·00
362.		6d. red	1·25	60
366.	29.	8d. blue..	2·00	1·25
395.	30.	9d. purple	2·50	2·50
285.	31.	1s. orange	3·00	50
399.	32.	2s. green	8·50	8·50
402.	–	5s. red	35·00	35·00

DESIGN—As T **27**: 5s. Mount Cook.

*Type A of 2½d. is inscribed " WAKITIPU", Type B " WAKATIPU ".

34. N.Z. Contingent, S. African War.

1900.

298.	26.	1d. red	60	8
301.	34.	1½d. brown	95	70
303.	23.	2d. purple	45	15
388.	22.	4d. blue and brown ..	1·40	55

The 1d., 2d. and 4d. are smaller than the illustrations of their respective types.

35.

ILLUSTRATIONS
British Commonwealth and all overprints and surcharges are FULL SIZE.
Foreign Countries have been reduced to ¾-LINEAR.

1901.

415.	35.	1d. red	25	8

36. Te Arawa.

1906. Christchurch Exn. Inscr. "COMMEMORATIVE SERIES OF 1906".

424.	36.	½d. green	15·00	15·00
425.	–	1d. red	15·00	12·00
426.	–	3d. brown and blue ..	50·00	55·00
427.	–	6d. red and green ..	90·00	95·00

DESIGNS: 1d. Maori art. 3d. Landing of Cook. 6d. Annexation of New Zealand.

40.

1907.

441.	40.	1d. red	75	12
442.	25.	3d. brown	3·50	3·00
445.	28.	6d. red	2·75	65
446.	31.	1s. orange	10·00	5·00

The 1d. differs from T **35** in being surface-printed instead of engraved. The circular ornaments in the upper corners are different. The 3d., 6d. and 1s. are much smaller in size than those of the 1898 issue.

41. King Edward VII.

42. Dominion.

1909.

449.	41.	½d. green	20	12
450.	42.	1d. red	15	12
452.	41.	2d. mauve	3·00	65
454		3d. brown	2·25	60
455		4d. orange	2·25	2·25
456		4d. yellow	2·25	1·00
458.		5d. brown	2·50	20
459.		6d. red	4·50	12
461.		8d. blue..	2·25	20
462.		1s. orange	12·00	2·00

1913. Optd. **AUCKLAND EXHIBITION, 1913.**

470.	41.	½d. green	20·00	20·00
471.	42.	1d. red	20·00	20·00
472.	41.	3d. brown	75·00	75·00
473.		6d. red	£110	£110

43. King George V.

1915.

503.	43.	½d. green	40	12
479.		1½d. grey	30	20
506.		1½d. brown	35	12
480.		2d. violet	1·25	2·00
533a.		2d. yellow	95	12
482a.		2½d. blue	65	50
483.		3d. brown	2·25	12
484.		4d. yellow	65	5·50
485.		4d. violet	2·00	12
486a.		4½d. green	4·50	2·75
487a.		5d. blue..	2·25	40
489a.		6d. red	2·00	12
490a.		7½d. brown	1·75	1·95
491.		8d. blue..	1·75	2·25
492.		8d. brown	2·00	40
493a.		9d. green	2·00	40
494.		1s. orange	3·75	12

1915. Optd. **WAR STAMP** and stars.

510.	43.	½d. green	10	8

44.

45.

50. New Zealand.

1920. Victory. Inscr. "VICTORY" or dated "1914 1919" (6d.).

511.	44.	½d. green	20	15
512.	45.	1d. red	25	12
513.	–	1½d. orange	20	15
514.	–	3d. chocolate	5·50	5·00
515.	–	6d. violet	10·00	8·00
516.	–	1s. orange	20·00	22·00

DESIGNS—HORIZ. As T **45**: 1½d. Maori Chief. As T **44**: 3d. British Lion. 1s. King George V. VERT. as T **44**. 6d. "Victory".

1922. Surch.

517.	44.	2d. on ½d. green ..	30	20

1923. Restoration of Penny Postage.

518.	50.	1d. red	8	8

51. View of Exhibition.

1925. Dunedin Exn.

536.	51.	½d. green on green ..	2·00	2·50
537.		1d. red on rose.. ..	2·00	2·50
538.		4d. mauve on mauve ..	35·00	40·00

52. "Admiral" Type.

53. Nurse.

1926.

539.	52.	1d. red	10	8
542.	–	2s. blue	18·00	4·00
541.	–	3s. mauve	30·00	30·00

The 2s. and 3s. are larger (21 × 25 mm.).

1929. Anti-T.B. Fund.

544.	53.	1d.+1d. red	4·00	4·00

1930. Inscr. "HELP PROMOTE HEALTH".

544a.	53.	1d.+1d. red.. ..	12·00	12·00

54. Smiling Boy.

56. "Arms" Type.

55. New Zealand Lake Scenery.

1931. Health stamps.

546.	54.	1d.+1d. red	45·00	45·00
547.		2d.+1d. blue	45·00	45·00

1931. Air.

548.	55.	3d. chocolate	8·00	8·00
549.		4d. purple	8·00	8·00
550.		7d. orange	10·00	10·00

1931. Air. Surch. **FIVE PENCE.**

551.	55.	5d. on 3d. green ..	4·50	4·00

1931. Various frames.

F 145.	56.	1s. 3d. lemon	1·50	1·50
F 146.		1s. 3d. orange ..	3·00	2·00
F 217.		1s. 3d. yellow and black	1·00	20
F 193.		2s. 6d. brown	1·00	20
F 194.		4s. red	2·00	35
F 195.		5s. green	3·00	60
F 196.		6s. red	5·00	1·75
F 197.		7s. blue	5·00	2·25
F 198.		7s. 6d. grey ..	10·00	10·00
F 199.		8s. violet	5·00	2·00
F 200.		9s. orange	5·00	2·75
F 201.		10s. red	5·00	1·25
F 156.		12s. 6d. purple ..	40·00	32·00
F 202.		15s. olive	6·00	4·00
F 203.		£1 pink	8·00	3·00
F 204.		25s. blue	60·00	60·00
F 160.		30s. brown	60·00	42·00
F 161.		35s. yellow	£500	£500
F 206.		£2 violet	15·00	5·00
F 207.		£2 10s. red	80·00	80·00
F 208.		£3 green	25·00	15·00
F 209.		£3 10s. red	£350	£275
F 210.		£4 blue	35·00	18·00
F 167.		£4 10s. grey ..	£225	£225
F 211.		£5 blue	60·00	40·00

57. Hygeia—Goddess of Health.

58. The Path to Health.

1932. Health stamp.

552.	57.	1d.+1d. red	12·00	12·00

1933. Health Stamp.

553.	58.	1d.+1d. red	6·00	6·00

1934. Air. Optd. **TRANS-TASMAN AIR MAIL "FAITH IN AUSTRALIA".**

554.	55.	7d. blue..	7·50	8·50

59. Crusader.

1934. Health stamp.

555.	59.	1d.+1d. red	4·00	5·00

60. Pied Fantail.

62. Maori Woman.

64. Mt. Cook.

65. Maori Girl.

66. Mitre Peak.

68. Harvesting.

70. Maori Panel.

72. Capt. Cook at Poverty Bay.

1935.

556.	60.	½d. green	8	8
557.	–	1d. red	8	8
579.	62.	1½d. brown	35	30
580.	–	2d. orange	8	8
581b.	64.	2½d. brown and grey ..	45	65
582.	65.	3d. brown	1·25	8
583.	66.	4d. black and brown ..	10	8
584.	–	5d. blue..	2·75	20
585b.	68.	6d. red	15	8
586b.	–	8d. brown	40	10
631.	70.	9d. red and black ..	70	20
588.	–	1s. green	65	8
589c.	72.	2s. olive	1·50	25
590b.	–	3s. chocolate and brown	2·00	35

DESIGNS—VERT. Small as T **60**: 1d. Kiwi. 2d. Maori house. 1s. Tui (bird). Larger as T **66**: 8d. Tuatara lizard. HORIZ. As T **64**: 5d. Swordfish. 3s. Mt. Egmont.

74. Bell Block Aerodrome.

1935. Air.

570.	74.	1d. red	30	50
571.		3d. violet	1·50	1·25
572.		6d. blue..	1·50	1·25

75.

1935. Silver Jubilee.

573.	75.	½d. green	8	8
574.		1d. red	8	8
575.		6d. orange	10·00	12·00

76. "The Key to Health."

77. Anzac Cove.

1935. Health Stamp.

576.	76.	1d.+1d. red	1·50	1·50

1936. Charity. Anzac Landing at Gallipoli. 21st Anniv.

591.	77.	½d.+½d. green	25	25
592.		1d.+1d. red	25	25

78. Wool.

1936. Congress of British Empire Chambers of Commerce, Wellington, N.Z. Inscr. as in T **78**.

593.	78.	½d. green	8	8
594.	–	1d. red (Butter) ..	8	8
595.	–	2½d. blue (Sheep) ..	1·00	1·10
596.	–	4d. violet (Apples) ..	1·10	1·40
597.	–	6d. brown (Exports) ..	1·00	1·00

79. Health Camp.

1936. Health stamp.

598.	79.	1d.+1d. red	80	80

80. King George VI and Queen Elizabeth.

1937. Coronation.

599.	80.	1d. red	8	5
600.		2½d. blue	12	15
601.		6d. orange	30	35

81.

82. King George VI.

1937. Children's Health Camps.

602.	81.	1d.+1d. red	1·40	1·40

1938.

603.	82.	½d. green	15	5
604.		½d. orange	5	5
605.		1d. red	30	5
606.		1d. green	5	5
607.		1½d. brown	90	40
608.		1½d. red	5	5
680.		2d. orange	5	5
609.		3d. blue..	5	5
681.		4d. purple	8	5
682.		5d. grey	35	8
683.		6d. red	15	5
684.		8d. violet	35	10
685.		9d. brown	35	8
686b.	–	1s. brown and red ..	25	8
687.	–	1s. 3d. brown and blue	40	8
688.	–	2s. orange and green ..	40	20
689.	–	3s. brown and grey ..	55	25

The shilling values are larger (22×25½ mm.) and "NEW ZEALAND" appears at the top.

83. Children Playing.

84. Beach Ball.

1938. Health stamp.

610.	83.	1d.+1d. red	1·10	1·00

1939. Health stamps. Surch.

611.	84.	1d. on ½d.+½d. green ..	75	1·00
612.		2d. on 1d.+1d. red ..	1·00	1·25

1939. Surch in bold figures.

F212.	56.	3/6 on 3s. 6d. green ..	3·00	2·00
F214.		5/6 on 5s. 6d. lilac ..	6·00	3·00
F215.		11/– on 11s. yellow ..	18·00	10·00
F216.		22/– on 22s. red ..	40·00	35·00
F186.		35/– on 35s. orange ..	30·00	30·00

85. "Endeavour", Chart of N.Z. and Captain Cook.

1940. Cent. of British Sovereignty. Inscr. "CENTENNIAL (OF NEW ZEALAND) 1840-1940".

613.	½d. green	5	5
614.	1d. brown and red ..	8	5
615.	1½d. blue and mauve ..	25	15
616.	2d. green and brown ..	10	5
617.	2½d. green and blue ..	15	25
618.	3d. purple and red ..	75	15
619.	4d. brown and red ..	75	25
620.	5d. blue and brown ..	80	80
621.	6d. green and violet ..	70	20
622.	7d. black and red ..	1·50	2·50
623.	8d. black and red ..	75	45
624.	9d. olive and orange ..	1·60	1·25
625.	1s. green	4·00	1·00

DESIGNS—HORIZ. ½d. Arrival of Maoris. 1½d. Royal portraits. 2d. Abel Tasman, Ship and Chart. 3d. Landing of immigrants. 4d. Road, rail, ocean and air transport. 5d. H.M.S. "Britomart" at Akaroa. 6d. "Dunedin" and "frozen mutton" sea route to London. 7d., 8d. Maori Council. 9d. Gold mining methods, 1861 and 1940. VERT. 2½d. Treaty of Waitangi. 1s. Giant Kauri tree.

1940. Health stamps.

626.	84.	1d.+½d. green ..	80	1·00
627.		2d.+1d. orange ..	1·10	1·40

1941. Surch.

628.	82.	1d. on ½d. green ..	8	5
629.		2d. on 1½d. brown ..	8	5

1941. Health stamps. Optd. **1941.**

632.	84.	1d.+½d. green ..	35	45
633.		2d.+1d. orange ..	50	55

86. Boy and Girl on Swing.

1942. Health stamps.

634.	86.	1d.+½d. green ..	25	30
635.		2d.+1d. orange ..	30	40

87. Queen Elizabeth II when Princess.

1943. Health stamps.

636.	–	1d.+½d. green ..	8	8
637.	87.	2d.+1d. brown ..	8	10

DESIGN: 1d.+½d. Princess Margaret.

1944. Surch. **TENPENCE** between crosses.
662. – 10d. on 1½d. blue and mauve (No. 615) .. 15 15

88. Queen Elizabeth II when Princess and Princess Margaret.

1944. Health Stamps.
663. **88.** 1d.+½d. green .. 5 5
664. 2d.+1d. blue .. 8 8

89. Peter Pan Statue, Kensington Gardens.

1945. Health stamps.
665. **89.** 1d.+½d. green and buff 5 5
666. 2d.+1d. red and buff.. 8 8

90. Lake Matheson.

91. King George VI and Parliament House, Wellington. **92.** St. Paul's Cathedral.

93. R.N.Z.A.F. Badge and Aeroplanes.

94. St. George. **95.** National Memorial Campanile.

1946. Peace Issue.
667. **90.** ½d. green and brown .. 5 5
668. **91.** 1d. green 5 5
669. **92.** 1½d. red 5 5
670. – 2d. purple 5 5
671. **93.** 3d. blue and grey .. 8 5
672. – 4d. green and orange .. 10 10
673. – 5d. green and blue .. 12 10
674. – 6d. brown and red .. 12 12
675. **94.** 8d. black and red .. 15 15
676. – 9d. blue and black .. 25 20
677. **95.** 1s. grey 30 30
DESIGNS—HORIZ. As T **91**: 2d. The Royal Family. As T **94**: 4d. Army (N.Z.) badge, tank and plough. 5d. Navy (anchor) badge, war and trading ships. 6d. N.Z. Coat of Arms, foundry and farm. 9d. Southern Alps and Franz Josef Glacier, seen through chapel window.

96. Soldier helping Child over Stile.

1946. Health stamps.
678. **96.** 1d.+½d. green & orange 5 5
679. 2d.+1d. brown & orge. 8 8

97. Statue of Eros.

1947. Health stamps.
690. **97.** 1d.+½d. green.. .. 5 5
691. 2d.+1d. red 8 8

98. Port Chalmers 1848.

1948. Centenary of Otago. Various designs inscr. "CENTENNIAL OF OTAGO".
692. **98.** 1d. blue and green .. 5 5
693. – 2d. green and brown .. 5 5
694. – 3d. purple 8 8
695. – 6d. black and red .. 15 20
DESIGNS—HORIZ. 2d. Cromwell, Otago. 6d. Otago University. VERT.: 3d. First church, Dunedin.

99. Boy Sunbathing and Children Playing.

1948. Health stamps.
696. **99.** 1d.+½d. blue and green 5 5
697. 2d.+1d. purple and red 8 8

100. Nurse and Child. **101.** Queen Elizabeth II and Prince Charles.

1949. Health stamps.
698. **100.** 1d.+½d. green .. 5 5
699. 2d.+1d. blue.. .. 8 8

1950. As T 56, but without value, surch. **1½d. POSTAGE.**
700. 1½d. red 8 5

1950. Health stamps.
701. **101.** 1d.+½d. green .. 5 5
702. 2d.+1d. purple .. 8 8

102. Cairn on Lyttleton Hills.

1950. Cent. of Canterbury, N.Z.
703. – 1d. green and blue .. 5 5
704. **102.** 2d. red and orange .. 5 5
705. – 3d. blue 8 5
706. – 6d. brown and blue .. 15 20
707. – 1s. purple and blue .. 35 30
DESIGNS—VERT. 1d. Christchurch Cathedral. 3d. J. R. Godley. HORIZ. 6d. Canterbury University College. 1s. Timaru.

103. "Takapuna" class Yachts.

1951. Health stamps.
708. **103.** 1½d.+½d. red & yellow 5 5
709. 2d.+1d. green & yellow 5 5

104. Princess Anne. **105.** Prince Charles.

1952. Health stamps.
710. **104.** 1½d.+½d. red 12 10
711. **105.** 2d.+1d. brown .. 12 10

1952. Surch. in figures.
712. **82.** 1d. on ½d. orange .. 8 10
713. 3d. on 1d. green .. 8 10

106. Queen Elizabeth II. **107a.** Westminster Abbey.

107. The State Coach.

1953. Coronation.
714. – 2d. blue 5 5
715. **106.** 3d. brown 10 8
716. **107.** 4d. red 20 25
717. **107a.** 8d. grey 35 30
718. – 1s. 6d. purple and blue 60 70
DESIGNS—As T **107**: 2d. Queen Elizabeth II and Buckingham Palace. 1s. 6d. Crown and Royal Sceptre.

108. Girl Guides. **109.** Boy Scouts.

1953. Health stamps.
719. **108.** 1½d.+½d. blue .. 8 5
720. **109.** 2d.+1d. green .. 8 5

110. Queen Elizabeth II.

111. Queen Elizabeth II and Duke of Edinburgh.

1953. Royal Visit.
721. **110.** 3d. purple 8 5
722. **111.** 4d. blue 12 15

112.

113. Queen Elizabeth II. **114.**

1953. Small figures of value.
723. **112.** ½d. slate 5 5
724. 1d. orange 5 5
725. 1½d. brown 10 5
726. 2d. green 8 5
727. 3d. vermilion .. 8 5
728. 4d. blue 12 5
729. 6d. purple 35 8
730. 8d. red 30 15
731. **113.** 9d. brown and green 30 10
732. 1s. black and red .. 25 10
733. 1s. 6d. black and blue 50 12
733a. 1s. 9d. black & orange 90 20
733b. **114.** 2s. 6d. brown .. 10·00 4·00
734. 3s. green .. .. 3·50 60
735. 5s. red .. .. 3·50 1·25
736. 10s. blue .. .. 12·00 6·00

115. Young Climber and Mts. Aspiring and Everest. **116.** Maori Mail-carrier.

117. Queen Elizabeth II. **118.** Federation Emblem.

1954. Health stamps.
737. **115.** 1½d.+½d. brown & vio. 10 10
738. 2d.+1d. brn. & indigo 10 10

1955. New Zealand Stamp Cent. Inscr. "1855–1955".
739. **116.** 2d. brown and green.. 8 5
740. **117.** 3d. red.. .. .. 10 5
741. – 4d. black and blue .. 20 20
DESIGN—HORIZ. As T **116**: 4d. Douglas DC 3 Airliner.

1955. Health stamps.
742. **118.** 1½d.+½d. brn. & chest. 10 10
743. 2d.+1d. red and green 12 12
744. 3d.+1d. brown and red 15 15

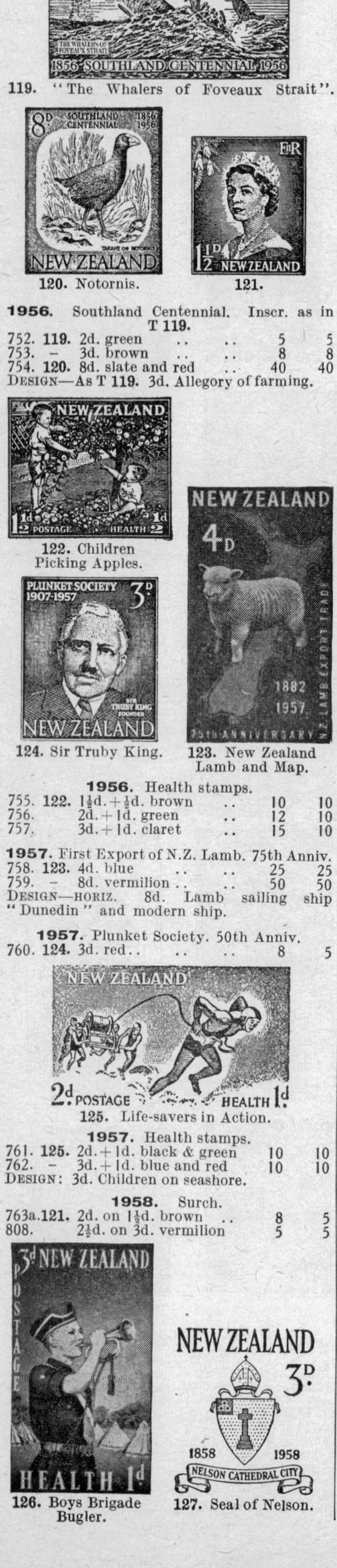

1955. As 1953 but larger figures of value and stars omitted from lower right corner.

745.	121.	1d. orange	5	5
746.		1½d. brown	15	10
747.		2d green	5	5
748.		3d. vermilion ..	15	10
749.		4d. blue	15	8
750.		6d. purple	20	5
751.		8d. chestnut	1·75	1·50

119. "The Whalers of Foveaux Strait".

120. Notornis. 121.

1956. Southland Centennial. Inscr. as in T 119.

752.	119.	2d. green	5	5
753.	–	3d. brown	8	8
754.	120.	8d. slate and red ..	40	40

DESIGN—As T 119. 3d. Allegory of farming.

122. Children Picking Apples.

124. Sir Truby King. 123. New Zealand Lamb and Map.

1956. Health stamps.

755.	122.	1½d.+½d. brown ..	10	10
756.		2d.+1d. green ..	12	10
757.		3d.+1d. claret ..	15	10

1957 First Export of N.Z. Lamb. 75th Anniv.

758.	123.	4d. blue	25	25
759.	–	8d. vermilion ..	50	50

DESIGN—HORIZ. 8d. Lamb sailing ship "Dunedin" and modern ship.

1957. Plunket Society. 50th Anniv.

760.	124.	3d. red	8	5

125. Life-savers in Action.

1957. Health stamps.

761.	125.	2d.+1d. black & green	10	10
762.	–	3d.+1d. blue and red	10	10

DESIGN: 3d. Children on seashore.

1958. Surch.

763a.	121.	2d. on 1½d. brown ..	8	5
808.		2½d. on 3d. vermilion	5	5

126. Boys Brigade Bugler. 127. Seal of Nelson.

1958. Health stamps.

764.	–	2d.+1d. green ..	10	10
765.	126.	3d.+1d. blue ..	10	10

DESIGN: 2d. Girls' Life Brigade cadet.

1958. 1st Air Crossing of Tasman Sea. 30th Anniv. As T 107 of Australia.

766.		6d. blue	30	25

1958. City of Nelson Cent.

767.	127.	3d. red	8	5

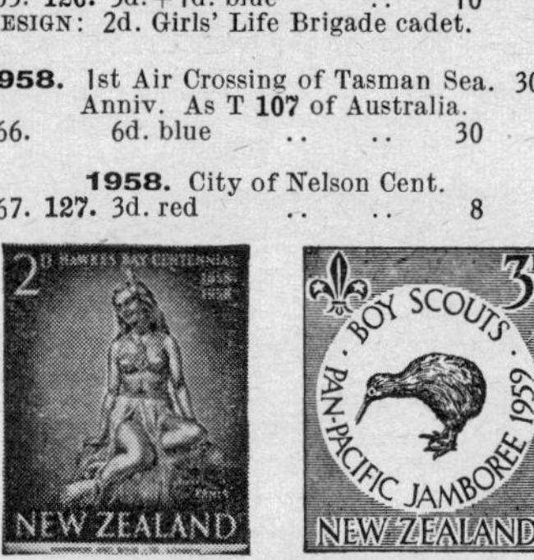

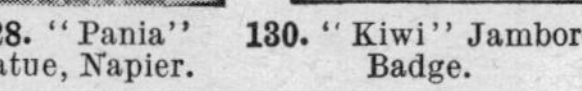

128. "Pania" Statue, Napier. 130. "Kiwi" Jamboree Badge.

129. Gannets on Cape Kidnappers.

1958. Hawke's Bay Province Cent. Inscr. as in T 128.

768.	128.	2d. green	8	5
769.	129.	3d. blue	8	5
770.	–	8d. brown	70	70

DESIGN—As T 128: 8d. Maori sheep-shearer.

1959. Pan-Pacific Scout Jamboree. Auckland.

771.	130.	3d. brown and red ..	10	5

131. Careening H.M. Bark "Endeavour" at Ship Cove.

1959. Marlborough Province Cent. Inscr. as in T 131.

772.	131.	2d. green	10	10
773.	–	3d. blue	8	5
774.	–	8d. brown	65	65

DESIGNS: 3d. Shipping wool. Wairau bar, 1857. 8d. Salt industry, Grassmere.

132. Red Cross Flag.

1959. Red Cross Commem.

775.	132.	3d.+1d. red and blue	15	10

133. Tete (Grey Teal). 134. "The Explorer".

1959. Health stamps.

776.	133.	2d.+1d. yellow, olive and red	10	10
777.	–	3d.+1d. black, pink and blue	15	12

DESIGN: 3d. Poaka (Pied Stilt).

1960. Westland Province Cent.

778.	134.	2d. green	10	8
779.	–	3d. salmon	10	8
780.	–	8d. black	65	65

DESIGNS: 3d. "The Gold Digger". 8d. "The Pioneer Woman".

135. Manuka (Tea Tree). 136. Timber Industry.

137. Tamwha (Maori Rock Drawing). 138. Kotare (Kingfisher).

1960.

781.	135.	½d. green and cerise ..	5	5
782.	–	1d. orange, green, lake and brown	5	5
783.	–	2d. red, black, yellow and green	5	5
784.	–	2½d. red, yellow, black and green	5	5
785.	–	3d. yell., grn., brn. & bl.	10	8
786.	–	4d. pur., buff, grn. & bl.	10	8
787.	–	5d. yell., grn., bk. & vio.	20	10
788.	–	6d. lilac, grn. & bl.-grn.	25	10
788c.	–	7d. red, green & yellow	35	35
789.	–	8d. red, yell., grn. & grey	30	10
790.	–	9d. red and blue ..	30	10
791.	136.	1s. brown and green..	30	10
792.	–	1s. 3d. red, sepia & blue	65	15
793.	–	1s. 6d. olive & chestnut	65	15
794.	–	1s. 9d. brown ..	3·00	45
795.	–	1s. 9d. red, blue, green and yellow	60	25
796.	137.	2 s. black and buff ..	75	15
797.	–	2s. 6d. yellow & brown	1·10	65
798.	–	3s. sepia	12·00	90
799.	–	3s. bistre, blue & green	2·25	80
800.	–	5s. myrtle	4·00	50
801.	–	10s. blue	4·00	3·50
802.	–	£1 magenta	9·00	5·00

DESIGNS—As T 135: 1d. Karaka. 2d. Kowha Ngutu-kaka (Kaka Beak). 2½d. Titoki (plant). 3d. Kowhai. 4d. Puarangi (Hibiscus). 5d. Matua tikumu (Mountain daisy). 6d. Pikiarero (Clematis). 7d. Koromiko. 8d. Rata. As T 136—HORIZ. 9d. National flag. 1s. 9d. Aerial top-dressing. VERT. 1s. 3d. Trout. 1s. 6d. Tiki. As T 137—HORIZ. 2s. 6d. Butter-making. 3s. Tongariro National Park and Chateau. 10s. Tasman Glacier. VERT. 5s. Sutherland Falls. £1, Pohutu Geyser.

1960. Health stamps.

803.	138.	2d.+1d. sepia and blue	15	10
804.	–	3d.+1d. maroon & orge.	15	12

DESIGN: 3d. Kereru (Wood Pigeon).

139. "The Adoration of the Shepherds" (after Rembrandt). 140. Kotuku (White Heron).

1960. Christmas.

805.	139.	2d. red & brn. on cream	1·00	20

1961. Health stamps.

806.	140.	2d.+1d. black & pur.	15	10
807.	–	3d.+1d. sepia & green	15	10

DESIGN: 3d. Karearea (Bush Hawk).

141. "Adoration of the Magi" (Durer).

1961. Christmas.

809.	141.	2½d. multicoloured ..	65	20

142. Morse Key and Port Hills, Lyttleton.

1962. Telegraph Centenary.

810.	142.	3d. sepia and green ..	8	5
811.	–	8d. black and red ..	65	65

DESIGN: 8d. Modern teleprinter.

143. Tieke (Saddleback).

DESIGN: 2½d. Kakarik (Parakeet).

1962. Health stamps.

812.	–	2½d.+1d. multicoloured	15	10
813.	143.	3d.+1d. multicoloured	20	12

144. "Madonna in Prayer" (after Il Sassoferrato). 145. Prince Andrew with book.

1962. Christmas.

814.	144.	2½d. multicoloured ..	50	12

1963. Health stamps.

815.	145.	2½d.+1d. blue ..	15	10
816.	–	3d.+1d. red	20	15

DESIGN: 3d. Prince Andrew.

146. "The Holy Family" (Titian).

1963. Christmas.

817.	146.	2½d. multicoloured ..	15	10

147. Steam Loco. "Pilgrim" and "DG" Diesel Electric Loco.

1963. Railway Cent. Inscr. as in T **147**. Multicoloured.
818. 3d. Type **147** 12 10
819. 1s. 9d. Diesel Express and Mt. Ruapehu .. .. 1·00 1·00

1963. Opening of COMPAC (Trans-Pacific Telephone Cable). As T **143** of Australia.
820. 8d. red, blue, black & yell. 70 70

148. Road Map and Car Steering-wheel.

1964. Road Safety Campaign.
821. **148.** 3d. black, ochre & blue 10 8

149. Tarapunga (gull).

1964. Health stamps. Multicoloured.
822. $2\frac{1}{2}$d. + 1d. Type **149** .. 15 10
823. 3d. + 1d. Korora (penguin) 20 12

150. Rev. S. Marsden taking first Christian service at Rangihoua Bay, 1814.

1964. Christmas.
824. **150.** $2\frac{1}{2}$d. multicoloured .. 20 12

1964. Surch. **7D POSTAGE.**
825. **56.** 7d. on (–) red 15 25

151. Anzac Cove.

1965. Gallipoli Landing. 50th Anniv.
826. **151.** 4d. brown .. 15 15
827. 5d. green and red .. 35 35
The 5d. also has a poppy in the design.

152. I.T.U. Emblem and Symbols.

1965. I.T.U. Cent.
828. **152.** 9d. blue & pale chocolate 25 25

1965. Churchill Commem. As T **149** of Australia.
829. 7d. black, grey and blue .. 25 25

153. Wellington Provincial Council Building.

1965. Government in Wellington. Cent.
830. **153.** 4d. multicoloured .. 8 5

154. Kaka.

1965. Health stamps. Multicoloured.
831. 3d. + 1d. Type **154** .. 12 15
832. 4d. + 1d. Piwakawaka (fantail) 15 12

155. I.C.Y. Emblem.

1965. Int. Co-operation Year.
833. **155.** 4d. red & yellow-olive 8 8

156. "The Two Trinities", after Murillo.

1965. Christmas.
834. **156.** 3d. multicoloured .. 20 12

157. Arms of New Zealand.

1965. 11th Commonwealth Parliamentary Conf. Multicoloured.
835. 4d. Type **157** .. 20 15
836. 9d. Parliament House, Wellington, and Badge 30 20
837. 2s. Wellington from Mt. Victoria .. .. 1·25 1·10

158. "Progress" Arrowhead.

159. Bellbird.

1966. 4th National Scout Jamboree, Trentham.
838. **158.** 4d. gold and green .. 10 5

1966. Health Stamps. Multicoloured.
839. 3d. + 1d. Type **159** .. 10 12
840. 4d. + 1d. Weka (rail) .. 15 12

160. "The Virgin with Child" (after Maratta).
161. Queen Victoria and Queen Elizabeth II.

1966. Christmas.
842. **160.** 3d. multicoloured .. 12 12

1967. New Zealand Post Office Savings Bank. Cent.
843. **161.** 4d. black, gold & mar. 12 5
844. – 9d. multicoloured .. 25 25
DESIGN. 9d. Half-sovereign of 1867 and Commemorative Dollar coin.

162. Manuka (Tea Tree).
163. Running with Ball.

1967. Decimal Currency. Designs as earlier issues, but with values inscr. in decimal currency as T **162**.
845. **162.** $\frac{1}{2}$ c. blue, green & cerise 5 5
846. – 1 c. mult. (No. 782) .. 5 5
847. – 2 c. mult. (No. 783) 5 5
848. – $2\frac{1}{2}$ c. mult. (No. 785) 8 5
849. – 3 c. mult. (No. 786) .. 8 5
850. – 4 c. mult. (No. 787) .. 10 5
851. – 5 c. lilac, olive & green (No. 788) 12 5
852. – 6 c. mult. (No. 788c) 12 8
853. – 7 c. mult. (No. 789) .. 15 8
854. – 8 c. red & blue (No. 790) 15 8
855. **136.** 10 c. brown and green 55 40
856. – 15 c. grn. & brn. (No. 793) 60 75
857. **137.** 20 c. black and buff .. 50 10
858. – 25 c. yell. & brn. (No. 797) 1·50 1·25
859. – 30 c. yellow, green and blue (No. 799) .. 80 45
860. – 50 c. green (No. 800) .. 1·25 35
861. – $1 blue (No. 801) .. 2·75 1·25
862. – $2 magenta (No. 802) 6·00 4·50
For 15 c. in different colours, see No. 874.
F 219. **56.** $4 violet .. .. 5·00 5·00
F 220. $6 emerald .. .. 7·50 7·50
F 221. $8 blue .. .. 10·00 10·00
F 222. $10 ultramarine .. 12·00 12·00

1967. Health Stamps. Rugby Football.
867. $2\frac{1}{2}$ c. + 1 c. multicoloured .. 10 10
868. 3 c. + 1 c. multicoloured .. 12 10
DESIGNS—VERT. $2\frac{1}{2}$ c. T **163**. HORIZ. 3 c. Positioning for Place-kick.

164. Brown Trout.

164a. Forest and Timber.

1967.
870. – 7 c. multicoloured .. 35 25
871a. **164.** $7\frac{1}{2}$ c. multicoloured .. 30 30
872. – 8 c. multicoloured .. 30 25
873. **164a.** 10c. multicoloured .. 30 12
874. – 15 c. grn., myrtle & red 50 30
875. – 18 c. multicoloured .. 45 35
876. – 20 c. multicoloured .. 50 35
877. – 25 c. multicoloured .. 80 45
878. – 28 c. multicoloured .. 60 30
879. – $2 black, ochre & blue 5·00 5·00
DESIGNS: 7 c. Trawler and catch. 8 c. Apples and orchard. 15 c. as No. 793. 18 c. Sheep and the "Woolmark". 20 c. Consignments of beef and herd of cattle. 25 c. Dairy farm, Mt. Egmont and butter consignment. 28 c. Fox Glacier, Westland National Park. $2 as No. 802.

No. 871a was originally issued to commemorate the introduction of the brown trout into New Zealand.

No. 874 is slightly larger than No. 856, measuring 21 × 25 mm. and the inscr. and numerals differ in size.

165. "The Adoration of the Shepherds" (Poussin).
166. Mount Aspiring, Aurora Australis and Southern Cross.

1967. Christmas.
880. **165.** $2\frac{1}{2}$ c. multicoloured .. 12 10

1967. Royal Society of New Zealand. Cent.
881. **166.** 4 c. multicoloured .. 12 12
882. – 8 c. multicoloured .. 25 25
DESIGN: 8 c. Sir James Hector (founder).

167. Open Bible.

1968. Maori Bible. Cent.
883. **167.** 3 c. multicoloured .. 8 8

168. Soldiers and Tank.

1968. New Zealand Armed Forces. Multicoloured.
884. 4 c. Type **168** 10 5
885. 10 c. Airmen, Canberra and "Kittyhawk" Aircraft .. 40 35
886. 28 c. Sailors and Warships 1·00 80

169. Boy Breasting Tape and Olympic Rings.

1968. Health stamps. Multicoloured.
887. $2\frac{1}{2}$ c. + 1 c. Type **169** .. 12 12
888. 3 c. + 1 c. Girl swimming and Olympic Rings .. 15 12

170. Placing Votes in Ballot Box.

171. Human Rights Emblem.

1968. Universal Suffrage in New Zealand. 75th Anniv.

890. **170.** 3 c. ochre, grn. & blue 10 8

1968. Human Rights Year.

891. **171.** 10 c. red, yellow & grn. 30 30

172. "Adoration of the Shepherds" (G. van Honthorst).

1968. Christmas.

892. **172.** 2½ c. multicoloured .. 8 8

173. ILO Emblem.

1969. Int. Labour Organisation. 50th Anniv.

893. **173.** 7 c. black and red .. 25 25

174. Supreme Court, Auckland.

1969. New Zealand Law Society. Cent.

894. **174.** 3 c. multicoloured .. 8 8

895. – 10 c. multicoloured .. 30 30

896. – 18 c. multicoloured 75 60

DESIGNS—VERT. 10 c. Law Society's Coat of Arms. 18 c. "Justice" (from Memorial Window in University of Canterbury).

175. Otago University.

1969. Otago University. Cent. Multicoloured.

897. 3 c. Type **175** 8 8

898. 10 c. Student being conferred with Degree 35 30

The 10 c. is horiz.

176. Boys playing Cricket.

1969. Health Stamps.

899. **176.** 2½ c.+1 c. multicoloured 10 10

900. – 3 c.+1 c. multicoloured 15 15

901. – 4 c.+1 c. brown & ultram. 20 20

DESIGNS—HORIZ. 3 c. Girls playing cricket. VERT. 4 c. Dr. Elizabeth Gunn (founder of 1st Children's Health Camp).

177. Oldest existing House in New Zealand, and Old Stone Mission Store, Kerikeri.

1969. Early European Settlement in New Zealand, and 150th Anniv. of Kerikeri. Multicoloured.

903. 4 c. Type **177** 30 30

904. 6 c. View of Bay of Islands 50 50

178. "The Nativity" (Federico Fiori).

1969. Christmas.

905. **178.** 2½ c. multicoloured .. 10 8

179. Captain Cook, Transit of Venus and "Octant".

1969. Captain Cook's landing in New Zealand. Bicent.

906. **179.** 4 c. black, cerise & blue 12 12

907. – 6 c. green, brown & blk. 20 20

908. – 18 c. brown, grn. & blk. 55 55

909. – 28 c. cerise, blk. & blue 85 85

DESIGNS: 6 c. Sir Joseph Banks (naturalist) and outline of the "Endeavour". 18 c. Dr. Daniel Solander (botanist) and his plant. 28 c. Queen Elizabeth II and Cook's Chart, 1769.

180. Girl in Wheat Field and C.O.R.S.O. Emblem.

1969. C.O.R.S.O. (Council of Organizations for Relief Services Overseas). 25th Anniv. Multicoloured.

911. 7 c. Type **180** 25 25

912. 8 c. Mother feeding her child, dairy herd and C.O.R.S.O. Emblem (horiz.) .. 30 30

181. "Cardigan Bay" (Champion trotter).

1970. Return of "Cardigan Bay" to New Zealand.

913. **181.** 10 c. multicoloured .. 30 30

182. Red Admiral Butterfly.

183. Queen Elizabeth II and New Zealand Coat of Arms.

1970.

914. – ½ c. multicoloured .. 5 5

915. **182.** 1 c. multicoloured .. 5 5

916. – 2 c. multicoloured .. 5 5

917. – 2½ c. multicoloured .. 5 5

918. – 3 c. multicoloured .. 10 5

919. – 4 c. multicoloured .. 10 5

920. – 5 c. multicoloured .. 12 10

921. – 6 c. blackish grn., green and red 15 12

922. – 7 c. multicoloured .. 15 15

923. – 7½ c. multicoloured .. 25 25

924. – 8 c. multicoloured .. 15 12

925. **183.** 10 c. multicoloured .. 20 10

926. – 15 c. brn., blk. & green 20 12

927. – 18 c. grn., brn. & blk. 25 20

928. – 20 c. black and brown 30 15

929. – 23 c. multicoloured .. 25 20

930. – 25 c. multicoloured .. 25 20

931. – 30 c. multicoloured .. 35 25

932. – 50 c. multicoloured .. 50 30

933. – $1 multicoloured .. 95 70

934. – $2 multicoloured .. 1·90 1·25

DESIGNS—As T **182**. ½ c. Glade Copper Butterfly. 2 c. Tussock Butterfly. 2½ c. Magpie Moth. 3 c. Lichen Moth. 4 c. Puriri Moth. 5 c. Scarlet Parrot Fish. 6 c. Sea Horses. 7 c. Leather Jacket (fish). 7½ c. Garfish. 8 c. John Dory (fish). As T **183**. HORIZ. 15 c. Maori fish hook. 20 c. Maori Tattoo pattern. 23 c. Egmont National Park. 50 c. Abel Tasman National Park. $1 Geothermal Power. $2 Agricultural Technology. VERT. 18 c. Maori Club. 25 c. Hauraki Gulf Maritime Park. 30 c. Mt. Cook National Park.

No. 925 was issued on the occasion of the Royal Visit to New Zealand.

184. Geyser Restaurant.

1970. World Fair, Osaka. Multicoloured.

935. 7 c. Type **184** 30 30

936. 8 c. New Zealand Pavilion 30 30

937. 18 c. Bush Walk 50 50

185. U.N. Headquarters Building.

187. "Adoration of the Child" (Correggio).

186. Football.

1970. United Nations. 25th Anniv.

938. **185.** 3 c. multicoloured .. 8 5

939. – 10 c. red and yellow .. 30 25

DESIGN: 10 c. Tractor on horizon.

1970. Health. Multicoloured.

940. 2½ c.+1 c. Netball (vert.) 12 10

941. 3 c.+1 c. Type **186** .. 15 12

1971. Christmas.

943. **187.** 2½ c. multicoloured .. 5 5

944. – 3 c. multicoloured .. 10 10

945. – 10 c. blk., orge. & silver 30 30

DESIGNS: 3 c. Stained Glass Window, Invercargill Presbyterian Church. 10 c. Tower of Roman Catholic Church, Sockburn.

188. Chatham Islands Lily.

1970. Chatham Islands. Multicoloured.

946. 1 c. Type **188** 5 5

947. 2 c. Mollymawk (bird) .. 8 8

189. Country Women's Institutes Emblem.

1971. Country Women's Institutes, and Rotary International in New Zealand. 50th Annivs. Multicoloured.

948. 4 c. Type **189** 12 12

949. 10 c. Rotary emblem and map of New Zealand .. 30 30

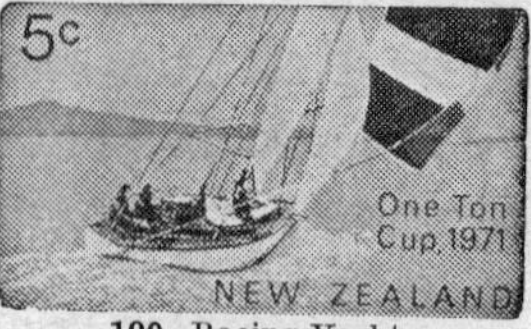

190. Racing Yacht.

1971. One-Ton Cup Racing Trophy. Multicoloured.

950. 5 c. Type **190** 15 15

951. 8 c. One-Ton Cup 30 30

191. Civic Arms of Palmerston North.

1971. City Centenaries. Multicoloured.

952. 3 c. Type **191** 5 5

953. 4 c. Arms of Auckland .. 8 8

954. 5 c. Arms of Invercargill .. 12 12

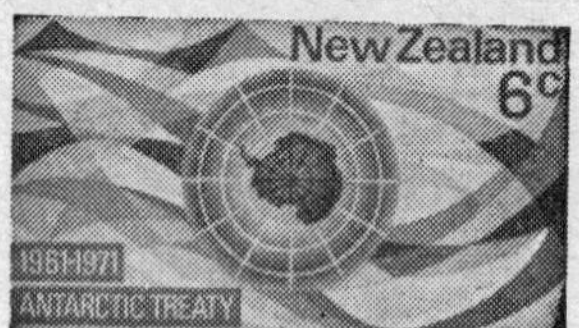

192. Antarctica on Globe.

1971. Antarctic Treaty. 10th Anniv.

955. **192.** 6 c. multicoloured .. 20 20

193. Child on Swing.

1971. U.N.I.C.E.F. 25th Anniv.

956. **193.** 7 c. multicoloured .. 20 20

1971. No. 917 surch.

957. 4 c. on 2½ c. multicoloured 10 8

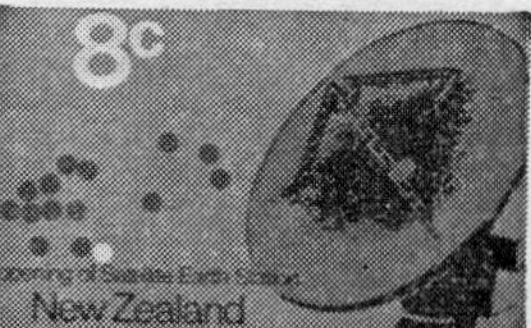

194. Satellite-tracking Aerial.

1971. Opening of Satellite Earth Station.

958. **194.** 8 c. blk., grey and red 20 20

959. – 10 c. blk., green & violet 30 30

DESIGN: 10 c. Satellite.

195. Girls playing Hockey.

1971. Health. Multicoloured.
960. 3 c.+1 c. Type **195** .. 10 12
961. 4 c.+1 c. Boys playing Hockey 12 15
962. 5 c.+1 c. Dental Health .. 20 20

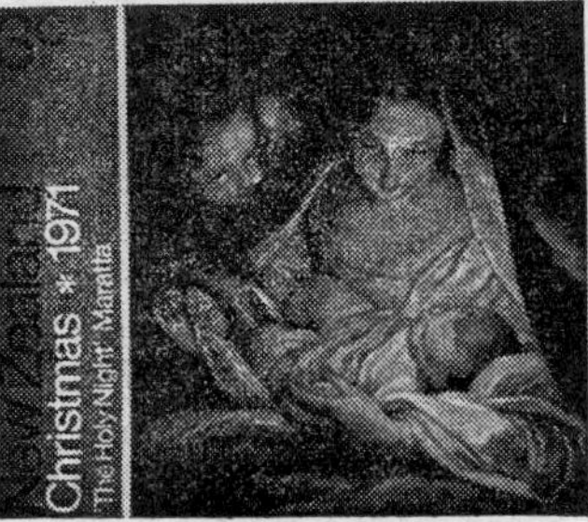

196. "Holy Night" (Maratta).

1971. Christmas. Multicoloured.
964. 3 c. Type **196** 5 5
965. 4 c. Stained-glass window 8 5
966. 10 c. "The Three Kings" 30 30
Nos. 964/6 are smaller, size 21½ × 38 mm.

197. "Tiffany" Rose.

1971. 1st World Rose Convention, Hamilton. Roses. Multicoloured.
967. 2 c. Type **197** 10 10
968. 5 c. "Peace" 25 25
969. 8 c. "Chrysler Imperial" 40 40

198. Lord Rutherford and Alpha Particles.

1971. Lord Rutherford. Birth Cent. Multicoloured.
970. 1 c. Type **198** 5 5
971. 7 c. Lord Rutherford and formula 25 25

199. Benz (1895).

1972. Int. Vintage Car Rally. Multicoloured.
972. 3 c. Type **199** 12 12
973. 4 c. Oldsmobile (1904) .. 25 25
974. 5 c. Ford "Model T" (1914) 25 25
975. 6 c. Cadillac Service car (1915) 30 30
976. 8 c. Chrysler (1924) .. 35 35
977. 10 c. Austin "7" (1923) .. 45 45

200. Wanganui Coat of Arms. **201.** Black Scree Cotula.

1972. Anniversaries.
978. **200.** 3 c. multicoloured .. 5 5
979. – 4 c. orge., brn. & blk. 5 5
980. – 5 c. multicoloured .. 8 8
981. – 8 c. multicoloured .. 15 15
982. – 10 c. multicoloured .. 45 45
DESIGNS AND EVENTS—VERT. 3 c. (Wanganui Council Govt. Cent.). 5 c. De Havilland "Dominie" and Boeing "737" (National Airways Corp. 25th Anniv.). 8 c. French frigate and Maori palisade (landing by Marion du Fresne. Bicent.). HORIZ. 4 c. Postal Union symbol (Asian-Oceanic Postal Union. 10th Anniv.). 10 c. Stone cairn (New Zealand Methodist Church. 150th Anniv.).

1972. Alpine Plants. Multicoloured.
983. 4 c. Type **201** 5 5
984. 6 c. North Island Edelweiss 12 12
985. 8 c. Haast's Buttercup .. 20 20
986. 10 c. Brown Mountain Daisy 45 45

202. Boy playing Tennis. **203.** "Virgin and Child" (Murillo).

1972. Health.
987. **202.** 3 c.+1 c. grey & brown 12 10
988. – 4 c.+1 c. brn., grey & yellow 12 10
DESIGN: No. 988, Girl playing tennis.

1972. Christmas. Multicoloured.
990. 3 c. Type **203** 5 5
991. 5 c. Stained-glass window, St. John's Church, Levin 8 8
992. 10 c. Pohutukawa flower .. 20 20

204. Lake Waikaremoana.

1972. Lake Scenes. Multicoloured.
993. 6 c. Type **204** 20 20
994. 8 c. Lake Hayes 30 30
995. 18 c. Lake Wakatipu .. 80 80
996. 23 c. Lake Rotomahana .. 1·00 1·00

205. Old Pollen Street.

1973. Commemorations.
997. **205.** 3 c. multicoloured .. 5 5
998. – 4 c. multicoloured .. 5 5
999. – 5 c. multicoloured .. 8 8
1000. – 6 c. multicoloured .. 10 10
1001. – 8 c. grey, blue & gold 15 15
1002. – 10 c. multicoloured 20 20
DESIGNS AND EVENTS: 3 c. (Thames Borough. Cent.). 4 c. Coalmining and pasture (Westport Borough. Cent.). 5 c. Cloister (Canterbury University. Cent.) 6 c. Forest, birds and lake (Royal Forest and Bird Protection Society. 50th Anniv.) 8 c. Rowers (Success of N.Z. Rowers in 1972 Olympics). 10 c. Graph and people (E.C.A.F.E. 25th Anniv.).

206. Class "W" Locomotive.

1973. New Zealand Steam Locomotives. Multicoloured.
1003. 3 c. Type **206** 10 10
1004. 4 c. Class "X" 10 10
1005. 5 c. Class "Ab" .. 12 12
1006. 10 c. Class "Ja" .. 40 40

207. "Maori Woman and Child". **208.** Prince Edward.

1973. Paintings by Frances Hodgkins. Multicoloured.
1027. 5 c. Type **207** 10 10
1028. 8 c. "The Hill Top" .. 15 15
1029. 10 c. "Barn in Picardy" 20 20
1030. 18 c. "Self-portrait Still Life" 35 35

1973. Health.
1031. **208.** 3 c.+1 c. green & brn. 8 8
1032. 4 c.+1 c. red & brown 10 8

209. "Tempi Madonna" (Raphael). **210.** Mitre Peak.

1973. Christmas. Multicoloured.
1034. 3 c. Type **209** 5 5
1035. 5 c. "Three Kings" (St. Theresa's Church, Auckland) 10 10
1036. 10 c. Family entering church 25 25

1973. Mountain Scenery. Multicoloured.
1037. 6 c. Type **210** 12 12
1038. 8 c. Mt. Ngauruhoe .. 20 20
1039. 18 c. Mt. Sefton (horiz.) .. 40 40
1040. 23 c. Burnett Range (horiz.) 50 50

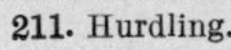

211. Hurdling. **212.** "Spirit of Napier" Fountain.

213. Boeing Seaplane, 1919.

1974. 10th British Commonwealth Games Christchurch.
1041. **211.** 4 c. multicoloured .. 8 8
1042. – 5 c. black and blue 8 8
1043. – 10 c. multicoloured 15 15
1044. – 18 c. multicoloured 40 40
1045. – 23 c. multicoloured 40 40
DESIGNS: 5 c. Ball-player (Paraplegic Games, Dunedin). 10 c. Cycling. 18 c. Rifle-shooting. 23 c. Bowls.

1974. Napier and U.P.U. Cents. Mult.
1047. 4 c. Type **212** 5 5
1048. 5 c. Clock Tower, Berne .. 10 10
1049. 8 c. U.P.U. Monument, Berne 15 15

1974. History of New Zealand Airmail Transport. Multicoloured.
1050. 3 c. Type **213** 5 5
1051. 4 c. Lockheed "Electra", 1937 8 8
1052. 5 c. Bristol Freighter, 1958 8 8
1053. 23 c. Empire "S-30" Flying-boat, 1940 .. 40 40

214. Children, Cat and Dog.

1974. Health.
1054. **214.** 3 c.+1 c. multicoloured. 8 5
1055. – 4 c.+1 c. multicoloured. 8 8
1056. – 5 c.+1 c. multicoloured. 10 8
Nos. 1055/56 are similar to T **214** showing children with pets.

215. "L'Adoration des Mages" (Konrad Witz).

1974. Christmas. Multicoloured.
1058. 3 c. Type **215** 5 5
1059. 5 c. Stained-glass window Old St. Pauls Church, Wellington 10 10
1060. 10 c. Madonna Lily .. 20 20

216. Great Barrier Island.

1974. Off-shore Islands Scenery. Mult.
1061. 6 c. Type **216** 8 8
1062. 8 c. Stewart Island .. 10 10
1063. 18 c. White Island .. 20 20
1064. 23 c. The Brothers .. 30 30

217. Crippled Child.

1975. Anniversaries and Events. Mult.
1065. 3 c. Type **217** 8 8
1066. 5 c. Farming family .. 10 10
1067. 10 c. I.W.Y. symbols .. 20 20
1068. 18 c. Medical School Building, Otago University 30 30

COMMEMORATIONS: 3 c. New Zealand Crippled Children Society. 40th anniv. 5 c. Women's Division, Federated Farmers of New Zealand. 50th anniv. 10 c. International Women's Year. 18 c. Otago Medical School. Centenary.

218. Scow "Lake Erie".

1975. Historic Sailing Ships.
1069. 218. 4 c. black and red .. 5 5
1070. – 5 c. black and blue .. 10 10
1071. – 8 c. black and yellow 12 12
1072. – 10 c. black and yellow 15 15
1073. – 18 c. black & brown .. 25 30
1074. – 23 c. black & lilac .. 30 35

SHIPS: 5 c. Schooner "Herald". 8 c. Brigantine "New Zealander". 10 c. Topsail schooner "Jessie Kelly". 18 c. Barque "Tory". 23 c. Full-rigged clipper "Ragitiki".

219. Lake Sumner Forest Park.

1975. Forest Park Scenes. Multicoloured.
1075. 6 c. Type 219 .. .. 8 8
1076. 8 c. North-west Nelson .. 10 10
1077. 18 c. Kaweka 25 25
1078. 23 c. Coromandel .. 25 25

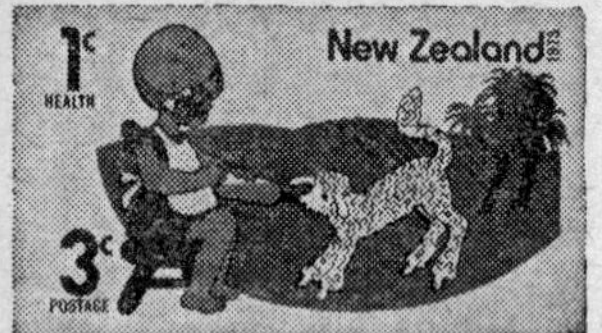

220. Girl feeding Lamb.

1975. Health. Multicoloured.
1079. 3 c.+1 c. Type 220 .. 5 5
1080. 4 c.+1 c. Boy with hen chicks 5 5
1081. 5 c.+1 c. Boy with duck and duckling .. 8 8

221. "Virgin and Child" (Zanobi Machiavelli).

1975. Christmas. Multicoloured.
1083. 3 c. Type 221 .. .. 5 5
1084. 5 c. Stained-glass window, Greendale Church .. 5 5
1085. 10 c. "I saw three ships..." (carol) 12 12

222. "Sterling Silver". 223. Maripi (knife).

1975. Multicoloured.
(a) Garden Roses.
1086. 1 c. Type 222 .. .. 5 5
1087. 2 c. "Lilli Marlene" .. 5 5
1088. 3 c. "Queen Elizabeth" 5 5
1089. 4 c. "Super Star" .. 5 5
1090. 5 c. "Diamond Jubilee" 5 5
1091. 6 c. "Cresset" .. 5 8
1092. 7 c. "Michele Meilland" 8 8
1093. 8 c. "Josephine Bruce" 8 10
1094. 9 c. "Iceberg" 8 10

(b) Maori Artifacts.
1095. 11 c. Type 223 .. .. 10 10
1096. 12 c. Putorino (flute) .. 12 12
1097. 13 c. Wahaika (club) .. 12 15
1098. 14 c. Kotiate (club) .. 15 15

224. Family and League of Mothers Badge.

1976. Anniversaries and Metrification. Mult.
1110. 6 c. Type 224 .. .. 5 5
1111. 7 c. Weight, temperature, linear measure and capacity 5 8
1112. 8 c. Ship, mountain and New Plymouth .. 8 8
1113. 10 c. Two women shaking hands and Y.W.C.A. badge 8 10
1114. 25 c. Map of the world showing cable links .. 20 25

ANNIVERSARIES. 6 c. League of Mothers, 50th Anniversary. 7 c. Metrication. 8 c. Centenary of New Plymouth. 10 c. 50th Anniversary of New Zealand Y.W.C.A. 25 c. Link with International Telecommunications Network, Centenary.

225. Gig.

1976. Vintage Farm Transport. Multicoloured
1115. 6 c. Type 225 .. .. 5 8
1116. 7 c. Thorneycroft lorry .. 8 8
1117. 8 c. Scandi wagon .. 8 10
1118. 9 c. Traction engine .. 10 10
1119. 10 c. Wool wagon .. 10 12
1120. 25 c. Cart 25 30

226. Purakaunui Falls.

1976. Waterfalls. Multicoloured.
1121. 10 c. Type 226 .. .. 10 12
1122. 14 c. Marakopa Falls .. 15 15
1123. 15 c. Bridal Veil Falls .. 15 15
1124. 16 c. Papakorito Falls .. 15 20

227. Boy and Pony.

1976. Health. Multicoloured.
1125. 7 c.+1 c. Type 227 .. 8 10
1126. 8 c.+1 c. Girl and calf .. 10 10
1127. 10 c.+1 c. Girls and bird 12 12

228. "Nativity" (Spanish carving).

1976. Christmas. Multicoloured.
1129. 7 c. Type 228 .. .. 8 8
1130. 11 c. "Resurrection" (stained-glass window, Auckland) (horiz.) .. 10 12
1131. 18 c. Angels (horiz.) .. 20 25

EXPRESS DELIVERY STAMPS

E 1.

1903.
E 1. E 1. 6d. red and violet .. 6·00 4·50

E 2. Express Mail Delivery Van.

1939.
E 7. E 2. 6d. violet 75 75

LIFE INSURANCE DEPARTMENT.

L. 1.

ILLUSTRATIONS
British Commonwealth and all overprints and surcharges are FULL SIZE. Foreign Countries have been reduced to ¾-LINEAR.

1891.
L 16. L 1. ½d. purple .. .. 2·50 45
L 14. 1d. blue .. .. 4·00 10
L 15. 2d. chestnut .. 4·00 85
L 4. 3d. brown .. .. 18·00 5·00
L 5. 6d. green .. .. 25·00 9·00
L 6. 1s. pink .. .. 40·00 18·00

1905. Similar type but "V.R." omitted.
L 24a. ½d. green 40 30
L 22. 1d. blue .. .. 8·50 2·25
L 25b. 1d. red 40 20
L 26. 1½d. black .. .. 4·00 2·00
L 27. 1½d. brown 20 40
L 21. 2d. chestnut .. .. 65·00 8·50
L 28. 2d. purple .. .. 5·00 2·00
L 34. 2d. yellow 85 85
L 30. 3d. orange .. .. 6·00 6·00
L 35. 3d. chocolate .. 5·00 5·00
L 36. 6d. red .. .. 4·00 4·00

L 2. Castlepoint Lighthouse.

1947. Lighthouses.
L 42. L 2. ½d. green and orange 90 80
L 43. – 1d. olive and blue .. 10 8
L 44. – 2d. blue and black .. 15 15
L 45. – 2½d. black and blue .. 85 85
L 46. – 3d. mauve and blue .. 20 20
L 47. – 4d. brown and orange 30 25
L 48. – 6d. brown and blue .. 40 40
L 49. – 1s. brown and blue .. 40 40

LIGHTHOUSES—HORIZ. 1d. Taiaroa. 2d. Cape Palliser. 6d. The Brothers Lighthouse. VERT. 2½d. Cape Campbell. 3d. Eddystone. 4d. Stephens Island. 1s. Cape Brett.

1967. Decimal currency. Stamps of 1947-65 surch.
L 50. 1 c. on 1d. (No. L 43) .. 10 10
L 51. 2 c. on 2½d. (No. L 45) .. 10 10
L 52. 2½ c on 3d. (No. L 46) .. 70 70
L 53. 3 c. on 4d. (No. L 47) .. 35 35
L 54. 5 c. on 6d. (No. L 48) .. 70 70
L 55a. 10 c. on 1s. (No. L 49) .. 45 45

L 3. Moeraki Point Lighthouse.

1969.
L 56. L 3. ½ c. yell , red & violet 1·25 1·25
L 57. – 2½ c. ultra., grn. & buff 5 5
L 58. – 3 c. stone, yell. & brn. 5 5
L 59. – 4 c. grn., ochre & blue 5 5
L 60. – 8 c. multicoloured .. 8 8
L 61. – 10 c. multicoloured .. 10 10
L 62. – 15 c. black, yellow, green and ultram... 15 15

DESIGNS—HORIZ. 2½ c. Pyusegur Point Lighthouse. 4 c. Cape Egmont Lighthouse. VERT. 3 c. Baring Head Lighthouse. 8 c. East Cape. 10 c. Farewell Spit. 15 c. Dog Island Lighthouse.

OFFICIAL STAMPS

Optd. **OFFICIAL.**

1907. Pictorials.
O 59. 21. ½d. green 20 8
O 61. 23. 2d. purple 20 8
O 63. 25. 3d. brown 85 20
O 64. 28. 6d. red .. .. 5·00 2·00
O 65. 31. 1s. orange .. .. 5·00 1·75
O 66. 32. 2s. green .. .. 10·00 4·00
O 67. – 5s. red (No. 402) .. 30·00 20·00

1907. "Universal" type.
O 60c. 35. 1d. red 20 8

1908.
O 70. 40. 1d. red.. .. .. 2·00 20
O 71. 28. 6d. red (No. 445) .. 4·00 2·00

1910. King Edward VII, etc.
O 73. 41. ½d. green 75 8
O 74. 42. 1d. red.. .. .. 20 8
O 76. 41. 3d. brown 85 30
O 78. 6d. red.. .. .. 1·00 80
O 92. 8d. blue .. .. 1·00 1·25
O 79. 1s. orange .. .. 6·00 5·00

1913. Queen Victoria.
O 80. 20. 2s. blue .. .. 3·00 1·25
O 81. 5s. green .. .. 7·50 3·75
O 82. £1 red .. .. 25·00 18·00

1915. King George V.
O 106. 43. ½d. green 8 8
O 88. 1½d. grey 20 8
O 89. 1½d. brown 20 20
O 90. 2d. yellow 15 8
O 110. 3d. brown .. .. 1·10 12
O 94. 43. 4d. violet .. .. 4·00 35
O 95a. 6d. red 20 10
O 96. 8d. brown .. .. 50·00 40·00
O 97. 9d. green .. .. 3·00 4·00
O 98. 1s. orange .. .. 3·00 1·50

1927. King George V.
O 111. 52. 1d. red 20 8
O 112. 2s. blue .. .. 15·00 15·00

1933. "Arms".
O 113. 56. 5 s. green .. .. 80·00 80·00

Optd. **Official.**

1936. "Arms".
O 133a. 56. 5s. green .. .. 3·25 3·25

1936. As 1935.
O 120. 60. ½d. green 15 15
O 121. – 1 c. red (No. 557) .. 10 8
O 122. 62. 1½d. brown 30 40
O 123. – 2d. orange (No. 580) 8 8
O 124. 64. 2½ brown and grey 75 1·50
O 125. 65. 3d. brown .. .. 3·50 25
O 126. 66. 4d. black and brown 50 20
O 127. 68. 6d. red 40 20
O 128. – 8d. brown (No. 586b) 40 20
O 129. 70. 9d. red and black .. 3·00 3·50
O 131. – 1s. green (No. 588) .. 60 20
O 132a. 72. 2s. olive .. .. 4·25 1·75

1938. King George VI.
O 134. 82. ½d. green 10 8
O 135. ½d. orange 8 8
O 136. 1d. red 8 8
O 137. 1d. green 8 8
O 138. 1½d. brown .. .. 1·25 50
O 139. 1½d. red 8 8
O 152. 2d. orange 8 8
O 140. 3d. blue 8 8
O 153. 4d. purple 20 10
O 154. 6d. red 40 20
O 155. 8d. violet 60 25
O 156. 9d. brown .. .. 1·50 1·50
O 157b. – 1s. brn. & red (No. 686b) 2·25 1·00
O 158. – 2s. orange and green (No. 688) .. .. 2·00 75

1940. Centenary stamps.
O 141. ½d. green 8 8
O 142. 1d. brown and red .. 8 8
O 143. 1½d. blue and mauve 15 15
O 144. 2d. green and brown .. 20 8
O 145. 2½d. green and blue .. 8 20
O 146. 3d. purple and red .. 60 25
O 147. 4d. brown and red .. 75 40
O 148. 6d. green and violet .. 1·00 50
O 149. 8d. black and red .. 1·00 1·10
O 150. 9d. olive and red .. 85 75
O 151. 1s. green .. .. 4·50 75

O 1. Queen Elizabeth II.

1954.
O 159. O 1. 1d. orange 12 8
O 160. 1½d. brown 25 40
O 161. 2d. green 30 10
O 162. 2½d. olive 40 30

O 163.	O1.	3d. vermilion	12	8
O 164.		4d. blue	25	10
O 165.		9d. red	40	25
O 166.		1s. purple	40	15
O 167.		3s. slate	8·00	10·00

1959. Surch.

O 169.	O 1.	2½d. on 2d. green	25	25
O 168.		6d. on 1½d. brown	30	30

POSTAGE DUE STAMPS

D 1. D 2.

1899.

D 9.	D 1.	½d. red and green	30	1·00
D 10.		1d. red and green	1·75	15
D 15.		2d. red and green	4·00	1·00
D 12.		3d. red and green	3·00	75
D 16.		4d. red and green	10·00	4·00
D 6.		5d. red and green	5·00	5·00
D 7.		6d. red and green	6·50	6·50
D 2.		8d. red and green	12·00	15·00
D 8.		10d. red and green	12·00	40·00
D 3.		1s. red and green	12·00	15·00
D 4.		2s. red and green	25·00	30·00

1902.

D 18.	D 2.	½d. red and green	30	30
D 30.		1d. red and green	1·00	12
D 31.		2d. red and green	2·00	50
D 32.		3d. red and green	5·00	4·50

D 3.

1939.

D 41.	D 3.	½d. green	25	25
D 42.		1d. red	20	8
D 43.		2d. blue	1·50	20
D 47.		3d. brown	2·50	50

NICARAGUA O3

A republic of Central America independent since 1821.

1862. 100 centavos = 1 peso (paper currency).
1912. 100 centavos de cordoba = 1 peso de cordoba (gold currency).
1925. 100 centavos = 1 cordoba.

1. 2.

1862. Perf. or roul.

13.	1.	1 c. brown	1·00	1·00
4.		2 c. blue	1·25	85
14.		5 c. black	2·00	1·25
18.		10 c. red	1·90	1·25
19.		25 c. green	1·75	1·10

1882.

20.	2.	1 c. green	10	12
21.		2 c. red	10	12
22.		5 c. blue	10	12
23.		10 c. violet	10	30
24.		15 c. yellow	12	1·10
25.		20 c. grey	12	1·25
26.		50 c. violet	15	4·25

3. 4.

1890.

27.	3.	1 c. brown	8	12
28.		2 c. red	8	12
29.		5 c. blue	8	10
30.		10 c. grey	8	12
31.		20 c. red	8	60
32.		50 c. violet	8	2·25
33.		1 p. brown	8	3·25
34.		2 p. green	8	5·00
35.		5 p. red	8	8·00
36.		10 p. orange	8	12·00

1891.

37.	4.	1 c. brown	8	20
38.		2 c. red	8	20
39.		5 c. blue	8	20
40.		10 c. grey	8	30
41.	4.	20 c. lake	8	1·00
42.		50 c. violet	8	2·25
43.		1 p. sepia	8	2·40
44.		2 p. green	8	3·25
45.		5 p. red	8	6·50
46.		10 p. orange	8	8·00

5. First sight of the "New World". 6. 7.

1892. Discovery of America.

47.	5.	1 c. brown	8	12
48.		2 c. red	8	12
49.		5 c. blue	8	10
50.		10 c. grey	8	15
51.		20 c. claret	8	1·25
52.		50 c. violet	8	2·75
53.		1 p. brown	8	2·75
54.		2 p. green	8	4·25
55.		5 p. red	8	6·50
56.		10 p. orange	8	9·00

1893.

57.	6.	1 c. brown	8	12
58.		2 c. red	8	12
59.		5 c. blue	8	12
60.		10 c. grey	8	15
61.		20 c. brown	8	1·10
62.		50 c. violet	8	2·25
63.		1 p. brown	8	3·25
64.		2 p. green	8	4·25
65.		5 p. red	8	5·00
66.		10 p. orange	8	6·50

1894.

67.	7.	1 c. brown	8	12
68.		2 c. red	8	12
69.		5 c. blue	8	12
70.		10 c. grey	8	15
71.		20 c. red	8	1·00
72.		50 c. violet	8	2·00
73.		1 p. brown	8	3·25
74.		2 p. green	8	5·50
75.		5 p. brown	8	6·50
76.		10 p. orange	8	9·00

8. 9. 10.

1895.

77.	8.	1 c. brown	8	10
78.		2 c. red	8	10
79.		5 c. blue	8	10
80.		10 c. grey	8	10
81.		20 c. red	8	50
82.		50 c. violet	8	1·00
83.		1 p. brown	8	2·50
84.		2 p. green	8	3·75
85.		5 p. red	8	5·00
86.		10 p. orange	8	8·00

1896. Date "1896".

90.	9.	1 c. violet	10	50
91.		2 c. green	10	25
92.		5 c. red	10	25
93.		10 c. blue	10	45
94.		20 c. brown	1·00	2·00
95.		50 c. grey	10	3·50
96.		1 p. black	10	5·00
97.		2 p. claret	10	6·50
98.		5 p. blue	10	7·00

1897. As T 9, dated "1897".

99.	9.	1 c. violet	12	20
100.		2 c. green	12	20
101.		5 c. red	12	12
102.		10 c. blue	1·60	45
103.		20 c. brown	80	1·25
104.		50 c. grey	2·25	3·00
105.		1 p. black	2·40	5·00
106.		2 p. rose	6·00	7·00
107.		5 p. blue	6·00	14·00

1898.

108.	10.	1 c. brown	8	8
109.		2 c. grey	8	8
110.		4 c. brown-lake	8	12
122.		5 c. olive	6·00	8
112		10 c. purple	5·00	20
113.		15 c. blue	10	60
114.		20 c. blue	3·25	60
115.		50 c. yellow	3·25	3·00
116.		1 p. blue	12	5·00
117.		2 p. brown	6·00	7·00
118.		5 p. orange	8·00	10·00

11. 12. Mt. Momotombo.

1899.

126.	11.	1 c. green	5	12
127.		2 c. brown	5	12
128.		4 c. red	5	12
129.		5 c. blue	5	12
130.		10 c. orange	5	12
131.		15 c. brown	5	25
132.		20 c. green	5	35
133.		50 c. red	5	1·25
134.		1 p. orange	5	3·00
135.		2 p. violet	5	6·00
136.		5 p. blue	5	6·00

1900.

137.	12.	1 c. claret	10	8
138.		2 c. orange	10	10
139.		3 c. green	12	12
140.		4 c. olive	15	12
184.		5 c. red	12	8
185.		5 c. blue	12	5
142.		6 c. red	2·25	1·00
186.		10 c. mauve	12	5
144.		15 c. blue	1·00	20
145.		20 c. brown	1·00	20
146.		50 c. lake	1·00	40
147.		1 p. yellow	2·75	1·60
148.		2 p. red	1·25	60
149.		5 p. black	1·25	1·00

1901. Surch. **1901** and value.

151.	12.	2 c. on 1 p. yellow	1·25	95
169.		3 c. on 6 c. red	1·40	1·10
163.		4 c. on 6 c. red	1·40	1·00
173.		5 c. on 1 p. yellow	1·25	1·00
168.		10 c. on 2 p. red	1·60	1·25
152.		10 c. on 5 p. black	1·75	1·40
153.		20 c. on 2 p. red	1·60	1·60
176.		20 c. on 5 p. black	1·25	80

1901. Postage Due stamps of 1900 optd. **1901 Correos.**

177.	D 2.	1 c. claret	30	10
178.		2 c. orange	20	12
179.		5 c. blue	30	20
180.		10 c. violet	30	20
181.		20 c. brown	40	30
182.		30 c. green	35	25
183.		50 c. lake	40	35

1902. Surch. **1902** and value.

187.	12.	15 c. on 2 c. orange	40	15
188.		30 c. on 1 c. claret	15	15

13. President Santos Zelaya. 14.

1903. Revolution against Sacaza. 10th Anniv. and 1st election of Pres. Zelaya.

189.	13.	1 c. black and green	15	20
190.		2 c. black and red	35	20
191.		5 c. black and blue	15	10
192.		10 c. black and orange	20	20
193.		15 c. black and lake	20	80
194.		20 c. black and violet	20	80
195.		50 c. black and olive	20	2·00
196.		1 p. black and brown	20	2·40

1903. Surch.

201.	12.	5 c. on 10 c. mauve	1·25	1·25
202.		15 c. on 10 c. mauve	3·00	3·00

1904. Surch. **Vale**, value and wavy lines.

203.	12.	5 c. on 10 c. mauve	12	12
204.		15 c. on 10 c. mauve	12	12

1905.

206.	14.	1 c. green	10	10
207.		2 c. red	10	10
208.		3 c. violet	12	12
280.		3 c. orange	12	10
209.		4 c. orange	12	12
281.		4 c. violet	12	10
282.		5 c. blue	12	10
211.		6 c. grey	15	20
283.		6 c. brown	45	35
212.		10 c. brown	15	20
284.		10 c. lake	15	5
213.		15 c. olive	15	20
285.		15 c. black	30	12
214.		20 c. lake	20	20
286.		20 c. olive	50	20
215.		50 c. orange	2·25	1·60
287.		50 c. green	70	35
216.		1 p. black	35	70
288.		1 p. yellow	70	35
217.		2 p. green	35	1·00
289.		2 p. red	1·25	50
218.		5 p. violet	35	1·25

1906. Surch. **Vale** (or **VALE**) and value in one line.

290.	14.	2 c. on 3 c. orange	15	12
293.		5 c. on 20 c. olive	10	8
247.		10 c. on 2 c. red	20	8
223.		10 c. on 3 c. violet	8	5
248.		10 c. on 4 c. orange	15	12
291.		10 c. on 15 c. black	15	8
250.		10 c. on 20 c. lake	50	30
252.		10 c. on 50 c. orange	50	15
234.		10 c. on 2 p. green	5·50	3·25
235.		10 c. on 5 p. violet	27·00	22·00
226.		15 c. on 1 c. green	10	10
229.	14.	20 c. on 2 c. red	12	10
230.		20 c. on 5 c. blue	15	20
236.		35 c. on 6 c. grey	50	40
232a.		50 c. on 6 c. grey	15	15
238.		1p. on 5 p. violet	13·00	7·50

15. 16. 17.

1908. Fiscal stamps as T 15 optd. **CORREO—1908** or surch. **VALE** and value also.

260.	15.	1 c. on 5 c. yellow	10	8
261.		2 c. on 5 c. yellow	10	8
262.		4 c. on 5 c. yellow	20	8
256.		5 c. yellow	15	12
257.		10 c. blue	10	8
263.		15 c. on 50 c. green	12	10
264.		35 c. on 50 c. green	1·00	25
258.		1 p. brown	1·00	80
259.		2 p. grey	1·10	1·10

1908. Fiscal stamps as T 16 optd. **CORREOS—1908** or surch. **VALE** and value also.

268.	16.	2 c. orange	90	50
269.		4 c. on 2 c. orange	40	25
270.		5 c. on 2 c. orange	35	20
272.		10 c. on 2 c. orange	35	8

1909. Surch. **CORREOS—1909 VALE** and value.

273.	15.	1 c. on 50 c. green	90	50
274.		2 c. on 50 c. green	1·40	60
275.		4 c. on 50 c. green	1·40	60
276.		5 c. on 50 c. green	85	45
277.		10 c. on 50 c. green	30	25

1910. Surch. **Vale** and value in two lines.

296	14.	2 c. on 3 c. orange	15	10
300.		2 c. on 4 c. violet	8	5
301.		5 c. on 20 c. olive	10	8
302.		10 c. on 15 c. black	15	8
303.		10 c. on 50 c. green	8	5
299.		10 c. on 1 p. yellow	12	8
305.		10 c. on 2 p. red	20	20

1911. Surch. **Correos 1911** (or **CORREOS 1911**) and value.

307.	15.	2 c. on 5 p. blue	15	20
312.		5 c. on 2 p. grey	35	35
308.		5 c. on 10 p. pink	20	15
309.		10 c. on 25 c. lilac	10	8
310.		10 c. on 2 p. grey	10	8
311.		35 c. on 1 p. brown	10	10

1911. Surch. **VALE POSTAL de 1911** and value.

313.	15.	5 c. on 25 c. lilac	30	30
314.		5 c. on 50 c. green	1·40	1·40
315.		5 c. on 5 p. blue	2·40	2·40
317.		5 c. on 50 p. red	1·60	1·60
318.		10 c. on 50 c. green	25	20

1911. Railway stamps as T **17**, with fiscal surch. on the front, surch. on back **Vale—cts. CORREO DE 1911**.

319.	17.	2 c. on 5 c. on 2 c. blue	8	10
320.		05 c. on 5 c. on 2 c. blue	8	10
321.		10 c. on 5 c. on 2 c. blue	5	8
322.		15 c. on 10 c. on 1 c. red	8	8

1911. Railway stamps, with fiscal surch. as last, further surch. on front **CORREO** and value.

323b.	17.	2 c. on 10 c. on 1 c. red	20	25
324.		20 c. on 10 c. on 1 c. red	1·00	1·00
325.		50 c. on 10 c. on 1 c. red	2·40	2·40

1911. Railway stamps, with fiscal surch. as last, surch. in addition on front **Correo Vale 1911** and value.

326.	17.	2 c. on 10 c. on 1 c. red	10	10
333.		5 c. on 5 c. on 2 c. blue	10	15
327.		5 c. on 10 c. on 1 c. red	12	12
328.		10 c. on 10 c. on 1 c. red	10	10

1911. Railway stamps, with fiscal surch. on front, surch. in addition **Vale CORREO DE 1911** and value on back.

331.	17.	5 c. on 10 c. on 1 c. red	6·00	
332.		10 c. on 10 c. on 1 c. red	8·00	

19. 20.

1912.

337.	19.	1 c. green	10	8
338.		2 c. red	10	8
339.		3 c. brown	10	8
340.		4 c. purple	10	8
341.		5 c. black and blue	10	8

342. 19. 6 c. brown 10 8
343. 10 c. brown 10 8
344. 15 c. violet 10 8
345. 20 c. brown 10 8
346. 25 c. black and green .. 10 8
347. 20. 35 c. brown and green .. 50 40
348. 19. 50 c. blue 15 12
349. 1 p. orange 35 15
350. 2 p. green 40 25
351. 5 p. black 90 90

1913. Surch. **Vale 15 cts Correos 1913.**
352. 20. 15 c. on 35 c. brn. & grn. 10 8

1913. Surch. **VALE 1913** and value in "centavos de cordoba".
A. On stamps of 1912 issue.
353. 19. ½ c. on 3 c. brown .. 12 12
354. ½ c. on 15 c. violet .. 8 8
355. ½ c. on 1 p. orange .. 10 8
356. 1 c. on 3 c. brown .. 25 25
357. 1 c. on 4 c. purple .. 8 8
358. 1 c. on 50 c. blue .. 8 8
359. 1 c. on 5 p. black .. 8 8
360. 2 c. on 4 c. purple .. 10 10
361. 2 c. on 20 c. brown .. 1·00 1·00
362. 2 c. on 25 c. blk. & grn. 10 10
363. 20. 2 c. on 35 c. brn. & grn. 8 8
364. 19. 2 c. on 50 c. blue .. 8 8
365. 2 c. on 2 p. green .. 8 8
366. 3 c. on 6 c. brown .. 8 8
B. On stamps of 1912 issue (Locomotive type).
367. 18. ½ c on 2 c. red 15 15
368. 1 c. on 3 c. brown .. 8 8
369. 1 c. on 4 c. red 8 8
370. 1 c. on 6 c. claret .. 8 8
371. 1 c. on 20 c. blue .. 8 8
372. 1c. on 25 c. blk. & grn. 8 8
384. 2 c. on 1 c. green .. 60 15
373. 2 c. on 25 c. blk. & grn. 75 75
374. 5 c. on 35 c. blk. & brn. 8 8
375. 5 c. on 50 c. olive .. 8 8
376. 6 c. on 1 p. orange .. 8 8
377. 10 c. on 2 p. brown .. 8 8
378. 1 p. on 5 p. green .. 8 12

1914. No. 352 surch. with new value and **Cordoba** and thick bar over old surch.
385. 20. ½ c. on 15 c. on 35 c. .. 8 8
386. 1 c. on 15 c. on 35 c. .. 10 10

1914. Official stamps of 1913 surch. with new value and thick bar through "OFFICIAL".
387. 19. 1 c. on 25 c. blue .. 15 8
388. 20. 1 c. on 35 c. blue .. 15 8
389. 19. 1 c. on 1 p. blue .. 8 8
391. 2 c. on 50 c. blue .. 15 8
392. 2 c. on 2 p. blue .. 15 8
393. 5 c. on 5 p. blue .. 8 8

21. National Palace, Managua.
22. Cathedral at Leon.

1914. Various frames.
394. 21. ½ c. blue 20 8
395. 1 c. green 20 8
396. 22. 2 c. orange 20 8
915. 21. 3 c. brown 8 5
398. 22. 4 c. red 30 8
399. 21. 5 c. grey 8 5
400. 22. 6 c. sepia .. .. 2·00 1·60
401. 10 c. yellow 20 8
402. 21. 15 c. violet .. .. 1·25 70
403. 22. 20 c. grey .. .. 2·40 1·60
939. 21. 25 c. orange 25 12
405. 22. 50 c. blue 25 15
See also Nos. 465/72, 617/27 and 912/24.

1915. Surch. **VALE 5 cts. de Cordoba 1915.**
406. 22. 5 c. on 6 c. sepia .. 50 25

1918. Stamps of 1914 surch. **Vale— centavos de cordoba.**
407. 22. ½ c. on 6 c. sepia .. 1·40 70
408. ½ c. on 10 c. yellow .. 70 12
409. 21. ½ c. on 15 c. violet .. 70 70
410. ½ c. on 25 c. orange .. 1·75 70
411. 22. ½ c. on 50 c. blue .. 70 10
440. 1 c. on 2 c. orange .. 30 8
413. 21. 1 c. on 3 c. brown .. 70 15
414. 22. 1 c. on 6 c. sepia .. 3·75 1·40
415. 1 c. on 10 c. yellow .. 5·00 3·25
416. 21. 1 c. on 15 c. violet .. 1·25 35
418. 22. 1 c. on 20 c. grey .. 70 12
420. 21. 1 c. on 25 c. orange .. 1·40 40
421. 22. 1 c. on 50 c. blue .. 4·00 2·40
422. 2 c. on 4 c. red .. 70 12
423. 2 c. on 6 c. sepia .. 6·00 3·50
424. 2 c. on 10 c. yellow .. 6·00 2·00
425. 2 c. on 20 c. grey .. 3·50 1·50
426. 21. 2 c. on 25 c. orange .. 1·50 20
427. 22. 5 c. on 6 c. sepia .. 3·00 2·50
428. 21. 5 c. on 15 c. violet .. 1·00 30

1919. Official stamps of 1915 surch. **Vale— centavo de cordoba** and with bar through "OFICIAL".
444. 22. ½ c. on 2 c. blue .. 12 8
445. ½ c. on 4 c. blue .. 30 8
446. 21. 1 c. on 3 c. blue .. 35 12
432. 1 c. on 25 c. blue .. 50 12
433. 22. 2 c. on 50 c. blue .. 50 12
443. 10 c. on 20 c. blue .. 60 25

1921. Official stamps of 1913 optd. **Particular** and wavy lines through "OFICIAL".
441. 19. 1 c. blue 40 25
442. 5 c. blue 40 20

1921. No. 399 surch. **Vale medio centavo.**
447. 21. ½ c. on 5 c. black .. 12 8

1921. Official stamp of 1915 optd. **Particular R de C** and bars.
448. 21. 1 c. blue .. .. 2·40 1·25

1921. Official stamps of 1915 surch. **Vale un centavo R de C** and bars.
449. 21. 1 c. on 5 c. blue .. 60 25
450. 22. 1 c. on 6 c. blue .. 35 12
451. 1 c. on 10 c. blue .. 50 15
452. 21. 1 c. on 15 c. blue .. 80 20

23.
24. Del Valle.

1921. Fiscal stamps as T 23 surch. **R. de C Vale** and new value.
453. 23. 1 c. on 1 c. red & black 8 5
454. 1 c. on 2 c. green & black 8 5
455. 1 c. on 4 c. orge. & black 8 5
456. 1 c. on 15 c. blue & black 8 5
No. 456 is inscr. "TIMBRE TELEGRAFICO".

1921. Independence Cent.
457. – ½ c. black and blue .. 12 12
458. 24. 1 c. black and green .. 12 12
459. – 2 c. black and red .. 12 12
460. – 5 c. black and violet .. 12 12
461. – 10 c. black and orange 12 12
462. – 25 c. black and yellow .. 12 12
463. – 50 c. black and violet .. 12 12
DESIGNS: ½ c. Arce. 2 c. Larreinaga. 5 c. F. Chamorro. 10 c. Jerez. 25 c. J. P. Chamorro. 50 c. Dario.

1922. Surch. **Vale un centavo R. de C.**
464. 22. 1 c. on 10 c. yellow .. 8 5

1922. As Nos. 394, etc., but colours changed.
465. 21. ½ c. green 5 5
466. 1 c. violet 5 5
467. 22. 2 c. red 5 5
468. 21. 3 c. olive 8 8
469. 22. 6 c. brown 8 8
470. 21. 15 c. brown 12 10
471. 22. 20 c. brown 20 10
472. 1 cor. brown 30 20
Nos. 465/72 are size 27×22¾ mm.
For later issues of these types, see Nos. 617/27 and 912/24.

1922. Optd. **R. de C.**
473. 21. 1 c. violet 5 5

1922. Independence issue of 1921 surch. **R. de C. Vale un centavo.**
474. 24. 1 c. on 1 c. black & green 30 25
475. – 1 c. on 5 c. black & vio. 30 30
476. – 1 c. on 10 c. blk. & orge. 30 20
477. – 1 c. on 25 c. black & yell. 30 12
487. – 1 c. on 50 c. black & vio. 12 10

25.
26. F. Hernandez de Cordoba.
27.

1922. Surch. **Nicaragua R. de C. Vale un cent.**
479. 25. 1 c. yellow 5 5
480. 1 c. mauve 5 5
481. 1 c. blue 8 5

1922. Surch. thus: **Vale 0.01 de Cordoba** in two lines.
482. 22. 1 c. on 10 c. yellow .. 35 15
483. 2 c. on 10 c. yellow .. 35 12

1923. Surch. thus: **Vale 2 centavos de cordoba** in three lines.
484. 21. 1 c. on 5 c. black .. 35 8
485. 22. 2 c. on 10 c. yellow .. 35 8

1923. Optd. **Sello Postal.**
486. – ½ c. blk. & bl. (No. 457) 2·40 2·40
487. 24. 1 c. black and green .. 25 20

1923. Independence issue of 1921 surch. **R. de C. Vale un centavo de cordoba.**
488. 1 c. on 2 c. black and red .. 25 25
489. 1 c. on 5 c. black & violet 25 8
490. 1 c. on 10 c. black & orge. 15 10
491. 1 c. on 25 c. black & yellow 20 20
492. 1 c. on 50 c. black & violet 15 8

1923. Fiscal stamp optd. **R. de C.**
493. 23. 1 c. red and black .. 8 5

1924. Optd. **R. de C. 1924** in two lines.
494. 21. 1 c. violet 8 8

1924. Foundation of Leon and Granada. 400th Anniv.
495. 26. 1 c. green 30 8
496. 2 c. red 30 8
497. 5 c. blue 25 12
498. 10 c. brown 20 15

1925. Optd. **R. de C. 1925** in two lines.
499. 21. 1 c. violet 8 5

1927. Optd. **Resello 1927.**
525. 21. ½ c. green 5 5
528. 1 c. violet (No. 466) .. 8 5
555. 1 c. violet (No. 473) .. 8 5
532. 22. 2 c. red 5 5
533. 21. 3 c. green 8 5
537. 22. 4 c. red .. .. 4·00 4·00
539. 21. 5 c. grey 15 8
542. 22. 6 c. brown .. .. 3·00 3·00
543. 10 c. yellow 8 8
545. 21. 15 c. brown 20 12
547. 22. 20 c. brown 8 8
549. 21. 25 c. orange 10 8
551. 22. 50 c. blue 8 5
553. 1 cor. brown 20 8

1928. Optd. **Resello 1928.**
559. 21. ½ c. green 8 8
560. 1 c. violet 5 5
561. 22. 2 c. red 5 5
562. 21. 3 c. green 10 5
563. 22. 4 c. red 5 5
564. 21. 5 c. grey 5 5
565. 22. 6 c. brown 5 5
566. 10 c. yellow 8 5
567. 21. 15 c. brown 8 8
568. 22. 20 c. brown 12 8
569. 21. 25 c. orange 20 8
570. 22. 50 c. blue 30 5
571. 1 cor. brown 45 12

1928. Optd. **Correos 1928.**
574. 21. ½ c. green 5 5
575. 1 c. violet 5 5
576. 3 c. olive 20 8
577. 22. 4 c. red 8 5
578. 21. 5 c. grey 8 8
579. 22. 6 c. brown 10 8
580. 10 c. yellow 12 8
581. 21. 15 c. brown 55 8
582. 22. 20 c. brown 55 8
583. 21. 25 c. orange 55 10
584. 22. 50 c. blue 55 10
585. 1 cor. brown .. .. 1·25 85

1928. No. 577 surch. **Vale 2 cts.**
586. 22. 2 c. on 4 c. red .. 45 10

1928. Fiscal stamp as T 23, but inscr. "TIMBRE TELEGRAFICO" and surch. **Correos 1928 Vale** and new value.
587. 23. 1 c. on 5 c. blue & black 10 8
588. 2 c. on 5 c. blue & black 10 8
589. 3 c. on 5 c. blue & black 10 8

1928. Obligatory Tax. No. 587 additionally optd. **R. de T.**
590. 24. 1 c. on 5 c. blue & black 30 8

1928. As Nos. 465/72 but colours changed.
591. 21. ½ c. red 12 8
592. 1 c. orange 12 8
593. 22. 2 c. green 12 8
594. 21. 3 c. purple 12 8
595. 22. 4 c. brown 12 8
596. 21. 5 c. yellow 12 8
597. 22. 6 c. blue 12 8
598. 10 c. blue 15 12
599. 21. 15 c. red 20 12
600. 22. 20 c. green 30 15
601. 21. 25 c. purple .. .. 6·50 2·00
602. 22. 50 c. brown 80 35
603. 1 cor. violet .. .. 1·60 1·10
See also Nos. 617/27 and 912/24.

1928.
604. 27. 1 c. purple 10 5
647. 1 c. red 12 5
For 1 c. green see No. 925.

1929. Optd. **R. de C.**
605. 21. 1 c. orange 5 5
628. 1 c. olive 8 5

1929. Optd. **Correos 1929.**
606. 21. ½ c. green 8 8

1929. Optd. **Correos 1928.**
607. 26. 10 c. brown 20 20

1929. Fiscal stamps as T 23, but inscr. "TIMBRE TELEGRAFICO". A. Surch. **Correos 1929 R. de C. C$ 0.01** vert.
613. 23. 1 c. on 5 c. blue & black 8 8
B. Surch. **Correos 1929** and value.
611. 23. 1 c. on 10 c. green & blk. 8 8
612. 2 c. on 5 c. blue & black 8 8
C. Surch. **Correos 1929** and value vert. and **R. de C.** or **R. de T.** horiz.
608. 23. 1 c. on 5 c. blue and black (R. de T.) .. 8 8
609. 2 c. on 5 c. blue and black (R. de T.) .. 8 8
610. 2 c. on 5 c. blue and black (R. de C.) .. 5·00 30

1929. Air. Optd. **Correo Aereo 1929. P.A.A.**
614. 21. 25 c. sepia 45 45
615. 25 c. orange 45 45
616. 25 c. violet 45 40

1929. As Nos. 591/603 but colours changed.
617. 21. 1 c. green 5 5
618. 3 c. blue 8 8
619. 22. 4 c. blue 8 8
620. 21. 5 c. brown 10 8
621. 22. 6 c. drab 10 10
622. 10 c. brown 15 8
623. 21. 15 c. red 20 10
624. 22. 20 c. orange 30 12
625. 21. 25 c. violet 8 5
626. 22. 50 c. green 10 8
627. 1 cor. yellow .. .. 1·25 45
See also Nos. 912/24.

28. Mt. Momotombo.
29. G.P.O. Managua.

1929. Air.
629. 28. 15 c. purple 15 15
630. 20 c. green 30 25
631. 25 c. olive 20 15
632. 50 c. sepia 30 25
633. 1 cor. red 50 40
See also Nos. 926/30.

1930. Air. Surch. **Vale** and value.
634. 28. 15 c. on 25 c. olive .. 30 20
635. 20 c. on 25 c. olive .. 30 20

1930. Opening of the G.P.O., Managua.
636. 29. ½ c. sepia 30 30
637. 1 c. red 30 30
638. 2 c. orange 35 35
639. 3 c. orange 40 35
640. 4 c. yellow 40 35
641. 5 c. olive 45 40
642. 6 c. green 45 40
643. 10 c. black 55 50
644. 25 c. blue .. .. 1·40 1·40
645. 50 c. blue .. .. 2·25 1·90
646. 1 cor. violet .. .. 6·00 3·75

1931. Optd. **1931** and thick bar obliterating old overprint "1928".
648. 26. 10 c. brown (No. 607) .. 20 30

1931. No. 607 surch. **C $ 0.02.**
649. 26. 2 c. on 10 c. brown .. 20 12

1931. Optd. **1931** and thick bar.
650. 26. 2 c. on 10 c. brown (641) 20 10

1931. Air. Nos. 614/6 surch. **1931 Vale** and value.
651. 21. 15 c. on 25 c. sepia .. 50·00 50·00
652. 15 c. on 25 c. orange .. 24·00 24·00
653. 15 c. on 25 c. violet .. 5·50 5·50
654. 20 c. on 25 c. violet .. 4·50 4·50

1931. Optd. **1931.**
656. 21. ½ c. green 15 8
657. 1 c. olive 15 8
665. 1 c. orange (No. 605) .. 5 5
658. 22. 2 c. red 15 5
659. 21. 3 c. blue 12 8
660. 5 c. yellow .. .. 1·25 1·25
661. 5 c. sepia 45 20
662. 15 c. orange 45 20
663. 25 c. sepia .. .. 4·00 3·75
664. 25 c. violet .. .. 1·40 1·40

1931. Air. Surch. **1931** and value.
667. 22. 15 c. on 25 c. olive .. 3·00 3·00
668. 15 c. on 50 c. sepia .. 21·00 21·00
669. 15 c. on 1 cor. red .. 65·00 65·00
666. 15 c. on 20 c. on 25 c. olive (No. 635) .. 4·50 4·50

30. Managua G.P.O. before and after the Earthquake.

1932. G.P.O. Reconstruction Fund.
670. 30. ½ c. green (postage) .. 1·00 1·00
671. 1 c. brown .. .. 1·00 1·00
672. 2 c. red .. .. 1·00 1·00
673. 3 c. blue .. .. 1·00 1·00
674. 4 c. blue .. .. 1·00 1·00
675. 5 c. brown .. .. 1·00 1·00
676. 6 c. brown .. .. 1·00 1·00
677. 10 c. brown .. .. 1·00 1·00
678. 15 c. red .. .. 1·00 1·00
679. 20 c. orange .. .. 1·25 1·25
680. 25 c. violet .. .. 1·40 1·40
681. 50 c. green .. .. 2·00 2·00
682. 1 cor. yellow .. .. 4·00 4·00
683. 30. 15 c. mauve (air) .. 1·25 1·25
684. 20 c. green .. .. 1·75 1·75
685. 25 c. brown .. .. 5·00 5·00
686. 50 c. brown .. .. 6·00 6·00
687. 1 cor. red .. .. 10·00 10·00

1932. Air. Surch. **Vale** and value.
688. **28.** 30 c. on 50 c. sepia .. 60 60
689. 35 c. on 50 c. sepia .. 60 60
690. 40 c. on 1 cor. red .. 60 60
691. 55 c. on 1 cor. red .. 60 60
For similar surcharges on these stamps in different colours see Nos. 791/4 and 931/4.

1932. Air. Int. Air Mail Week. Optd. **Semana Correo Aereo Internacional 11-17 Septiembre 1932.**
692. **28.** 15 c. violet .. .. 8·00 8·00

1932. Air. Inaug. of Inland Airmail Service. Surch. **Inauguracion Interior 12 Octubre 1932 Vale C$0.08.**
693. **28.** 8 c. on 1 cor. red .. 4·00 4·00

1932. Air. Optd. **Interior—1932** or surch. **Vale** and value also.
705. **30.** 25 c. brown .. .. 3·75 3·75
706. 32 c. on 50 c. brown .. 3·75 3·75
707. 40 c. on 1 cor. red .. 2·75 2·75

1932. Air. Nos. 671, etc., optd. **Correo Aereo Interior** in one line and **1932**, or surch. **Vale** and value also.
694. **30.** 1 c. brown .. .. 8·00 8·00
695. 2 c. red .. .. .. 8·00 8·00
696. 3 c. blue .. .. 3·75 3·75
697. 4 c. blue .. .. 3·75 3·75
698. 5 c. brown .. .. 3·75 3·75
699. 6 c. brown .. .. 3·75 3·75
700. 8 c. on 10 c. brown .. 3·75 3·75
701. 16 c. on 20 c. orange .. 3·75 3·75
702. 24 c. on 25 c. violet .. 3·75 3·75
703. 50 c. green .. .. 3·75 3·75
704. 1 cor. yellow .. .. 3·75 3·75

1932. Air. Surch. **Correo Aereo Interior—1932** in two lines and **Vale** and value below.
710. **22.** 1 c. on 2 c. red .. 25 25
711. **21.** 2 c. on 3 c. blue .. 25 25
712. **22.** 3 c. on 4 c. blue .. 25 25
713. **21.** 4 c. on 5 c. sepia .. 25 25
714. **22.** 5 c. on 6 c. brown .. 25 25
715. 6 c. on 10 c. brown .. 25 25
716. **21.** 8 c. on 15 c. orange .. 25 25
717. **22.** 16 c. on 20 c. orange .. 25 25
718. **21.** 24 c. on 25 c. violet .. 80 80
719. 25 c. on 25 c. violet .. 80 80
720. **22.** 32 c. on 50 c. green .. 1·00 1·00
721. 40 c. on 50 c. green .. 1·75 1·75
722. 50 c. on 1 cor. yellow .. 1·90 1·90
723. 100 c. on 1 cor. yellow .. 2·40 2·40

32. Wharf at Port San Jorge.

33. La Chocolata Cutting.

DESIGNS—HORIZ. 2 c. El Nacascolo Halt. 5 c. Rivas Station. 10 c. San Juan del Sur. 15 c. (No. 840), Arrival platform at Rivas. 20 c. El Nacascolo. 25 c. La Cuesta cutting. 50 c. San Juan del Sur Quay. 1 cor. El Estero.

T 32, 33 and 35 are ⅔ actual size.

1932. Opening of Rivas Railway.
726. **32.** 1 c. yellow (postage) .. 4·00
727. – 2 c. red .. .. 3·75
728. – 5 c. sepia .. .. 3·75
729. – 10 c. brown .. .. 3·75
730. – 15 c. yellow .. .. 4·00
731. **33.** 15 c. violet (air) .. 6·00
732. – 20 c. green .. .. 6·00
733. – 25 c. brown .. .. 6·00
734. – 50 c. sepia .. .. 6·00
735. – 1 cor. red .. .. 6·00

1932. Surch. **Vale** and value in words.
736. **21.** 1 c. on 3 c. blue .. 12 8
737. **22.** 2 c. on 4 c. blue .. 10 8

35. El Sauce.

1932. Opening of Leon-Sauce Railway.
739. **35.** 1 c. yellow (postage) .. 4·75
740. – 2 c. red .. .. 4·75
741. – 5 c. sepia .. .. 4·75
742. – 10 c. brown .. .. 4·75
743. – 15 c. yellow .. .. 4·75
744. – 15 c. violet (air) .. 6·00
745. – 20 c. green .. .. 6·00
746. – 25 c. brown .. .. 6·00
747. – 50 c. sepia .. .. 6·00
748. – 1 cor. red .. .. 6·00
DESIGNS—HORIZ. 2 c., 15 c. (No. 744), Bridge at Santa Lucia. 5 c. Sanra Lucia. 10 c. Railway construction. 15 c. (No. 743) Santa Lucia cutting. 20 c. Santa Lucia River Halt. 25 c. Malpaicillo Station 50 c. Railway panorama. 1 cor. San Andres.

1933. Surch. **Resello 1933 Vale** and value in words.
749. **21.** 1 c. on 3 c. blue .. 8 8
750. 1 c. on 5 c. sepia .. 8 8
751. **22.** 2 c. on 10 c. brown .. 8 8

36. Flag of the Race.

1933. Columbus' Departure from Palos. 441st Anniv. Roul.
753. **36.** ½ c. green (postage) .. 80 80
754. 1 c. green 65 65
755. 2 c. rose 65 65
756. 3 c. red 65 65
757. 4 c. orange 65 65
758. 5 c. yellow .. .. 1·00 1·00
759. 10 c. red-brown .. 1·00 1·00
760. 15 c. brown .. .. 1·00 1·00
761. 20 c. blue .. .. 1·00 1·00
762. 25 c. blue .. .. 1·00 1·00
763. 30 c. violet .. .. 2·40 2·40
764. 50 c. purple .. .. 2·40 2·40
765. 1 cor. brown .. .. 2·75 2·75
766. **36.** 1 c. brown (air) .. 1·10 1·10
767. 2 c. purple .. .. 1·10 1·10
768. 4 c. violet .. .. 1·75 1·75
769. 5 c. blue .. .. 1·75 1·75
770. 6 c. blue .. .. 1·75 1·75
771. 8 c. red-brown .. 75 75
772. 15 c. brown .. .. 1·10 1·10
773. 20 c. yellow .. .. 1·60 1·60
774. 25 c. orange .. .. 1·60 1·60
775. 50 c. red .. .. 1·75 1·75
776. 1 cor. green .. .. 8·00 8·00

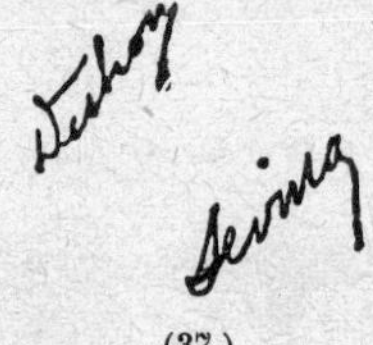
(37.)

1933. Optd. with T 37.
777. **21.** ½ c. green 20 8
778. 1 c. green 8 5
779. **22.** 2 c. red 25 8
780. **21.** 3 c. blue 8 5
781. **22.** 4 c. blue 8 5
782. **21.** 5 c. brown 12 5
783. **22.** 6 c. drab 15 12
784. 10 c. brown 15 8
785. **21.** 15 c. red 20 10
786. **22.** 20 c. orange 25 15
787. **21.** 25 c. violet 25 15
788. **22.** 50 c. green 35 15
789. 1 cor. yellow .. .. 1·40 60

1933. No. 605 optd. with T **37.**
790. **21.** 1 c. orange 10 5

1933. Air. Surch. **Vale** and value.
791. **28.** 30 c. on 50 c. orange .. 15 8
792. 35 c. on 50 c. blue .. 20 12
793. 40 c. on 1 cor. yellow .. 35 8
794. 55 c. on 1 cor. green .. 35 20

38. Lake Xolotlan.

1933. Air. Int. Airmail Week.
795. **38.** 10 c. brown .. .. 1·40 1·40
796. 15 c. violet .. .. 1·40 1·40
797. 25 c. red .. .. 1·40 1·40
798. 50 c. blue .. .. 1·40 1·40

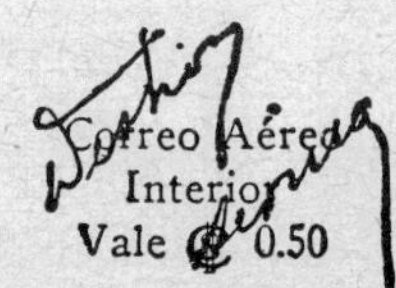

39. (Signatures = Deshon, Sevilla.)

1933. Air. Surch. as T **39.**
799. **22.** 1 c. on 2 c. green .. 8 8
800. **21.** 2 c. on 3 c. olive .. 8 8
801. **22.** 3 c. on 4 c. red .. 8 8
802. **21.** 4 c. on 5 c. blue .. 8 8
803. **22.** 5 c. on 6 c. blue .. 10 10
804. 6 c. on 10 c. sepia .. 8 5
805. **21.** 8 c. on 15 c. brown .. 12 10
806. **22.** 16 c. on 20 c. chocolate 10 10
807. **21.** 24 c. on 25 c. red .. 10 8
808. 25 c. on 25 c. orange .. 15 12
809. **22.** 32 c. on 50 c. violet .. 15 15
810. 40 c. on 50 c. green .. 15 10
811. 50 c. on 1 cor. yellow .. 12 10
812. 1 cor. on 1 cor. red .. 25 20

1933. Obligatory Tax. As No. 647 optd. with T **37.** Colour changed.
813. **27.** 1 c. orange 8 5

1934. Air. Surch. **Servicio Centroamericano Vale 10 centavos.**
814. **28.** 10 c. on 20 c. green .. 20 20
815. 10 c. on 25 c. olive .. 20 20
See also No. 872.

1935. Optd. **Resello 1935.**
(a) Nos. 778/9.
816. **21.** 1 c. green 5 5
817. **22.** 2 c. red 8 5
(b) No. 813 but without T **37** opt.
818. **27.** 1 c. orange 8 5

1935. No. 783 surch. **Vale Medio Centavo.**
819. **22.** ½ c. on 6 c. brown .. 15 8

1935. Optd. with T **37** and **RESELLO-1935** in a box.
820. **21.** ½ c. green 8 8
821. **22.** ½ c. on 6 c. brown (No. 819) 8 8
822. **21.** 1 c. green 10 5
823. **22.** 2 c red 15 5
824. 2 c. red (No. 817) .. 10 5
825. **21.** 3 c. blue 10 8
826. **22.** 4 c. blue 10 8
827. **21.** 5 c. brown 10 5
828. **22.** 6 c. drab 12 8
829. 10 c. brown 20 8
830. **21.** 15 c. red 8 5
831. **22.** 20 c. orange 30 10
832. **21.** 25 c. violet 10 8
833. **22.** 50 c. green 12 10
834. 1 cor. yellow 20 20

1935. Obligatory Tax. No. 605 optd. with **RESELLO-1935** in a box.
835. **21.** 1 c. orange .. .. 20·00

1935. Obligatory Tax. Optd. **RESELLO-1935** in a box.
(a) No. 813 without T **37** optd.
836. **27.** 1 c. orange 15 8
(b) No. 818.
868. **27.** 1 c. orange 12 8

1935. Air. Nos. 799/812 optd. with **RESELLO-1935** in a box.
839. **22.** 1 c. on 2 c. green .. 8 8
840. **21.** 2 c. on 3 c. olive .. 12 12
879. **22.** 3 c. on 4 c. red .. 8 8
880. **21.** 4 c. on 5 c. blue .. 8 8
881. **22.** 5 c. on 6 c. blue .. 8 8
882. 6 c. on 10 c. sepia .. 8 8
883. **21.** 8 c. on 15 c. brown .. 10 10
884. **22.** 16 c. on 20 c. chocolate 10 10
847. **21.** 24 c. on 25 c. red .. 20 15
848. 25 c. on 25 c. orange .. 15 15
849. **22.** 32 c. on 50 c. violet .. 12 12
850. 40 c. on 50 c. green .. 35 30
851. 50 c. on 1 cor. yellow .. 25 20
852. 1 cor. on 1 cor. red .. 80 50

1935. Air. Optd. with **RESELLO-1935** in a box.
(a) Nos. 629/33.
853. **28.** 15 c. purple 35 8
854. 20 c. green 40 40
855. 25 c. green 40 35
856. 50 c. sepia 40 35
857. 1 cor. red 70 35
(b) Nos 791/4.
858. **28.** 30 c. on 50 c. orange .. 40 40
859. 35 c. on 50 c. blue .. 40 30
860. 40 c. on 1 cor. yellow .. 40 35
861. 55 c. on 1 cor. green .. 40 35
(c) Nos. 814/5.
862. **28.** 10 c. on 20 c. green .. £180 £180
863. 10 c. on 25 c. olive .. 30 30

1935. Optd. with **RESELLO-1935** in a box.
864. **21.** ½ c. green (No. 465) .. 8 5
865. 1 c. green (No. 617) .. 8 5
866. **22.** 2 c. red (No. 467) .. 20 5
867. **21.** 3 c. blue (No. 618) .. 8 8

1936. Surch. **Resello 1936 Vale** and value.
869. **21.** 1 c. on 3 c. blue (No. 618) 8 5
870. 2 c. on 5 c. brown (No. 620) 8 8

1936. Air. Surch. **Servicio Centroamericano Vale diez centavos** and **RESELLO-1935** in a box.
871. **28.** 10 c. on 25 c. olive .. 20 20

1936. Air. Nos. 629/30 optd. with **RESELLO-1935** in a box.
872. **28.** 15 c. purple 20 12
873. 20 c. green 20 15

1936. Obligatory Tax. No. 818 optd. **1936.**
874. **27.** 1 c. orange 30 12

1936. Obligatory Tax. No. 605 optd. with T **37** and **1936.**
875. **21.** 1 c. orange 30 12

1936. Air. No. 622 optd. **Correo Aereo Centro-Americano Resello 1936.**
876. **22.** 10 c. brown 10 10

1936. Air. Nos. 799/800 and 805 optd. **Resello 1936.**
885. **22.** 1 c. on 2 c. green .. 12 10
886. **21.** 2 c. on 3 c. olive .. 8 8
887. 8 c. on 15 c. brown .. 15 15

1936. Optd. with or without T **37**, surch. **1936 Vale** and value.
888. **21.** ½ c. on 15 c. red .. 8 8
889. **22.** 1 c. on 4 c. blue .. 10 8
890. **21.** 1 c. on 5 c. brown .. 10 10
891. **22.** 1 c. on 6 c. drab .. 15 12
892. **21.** 1 c. on 15 c. red .. 8 8
893. **22.** 1 c. on 20 c. orange .. 8 8
895. 2 c. on 10 c. brown .. 10 8
896. **21.** 2 c. on 15 c. red .. 45 45
897. **22.** 2 c. on 20 c. orange .. 20 20
898. **21.** 2 c. on 25 c. violet .. 15 8
900. **22.** 2 c. on 50 c. green .. 15 15
901. 2 c. on 1 cor. yellow .. 15 15
902. 3 c. on 4 c. blue .. 25 25

1936. Optd. **Resello 1936.**
903. **21.** 3 c. blue (No. 618) .. 15 12
904. 5 c. brown (No. 620) .. 12 8
905. **22.** 10 c. brown (No. 784) .. 20 20

1936. Air. Surch. **1936 Vale** and value.
906. **28.** 15 c. on 50 c. brown .. 15 15
907. 15 c. on 1 cor. red .. 15 15

1936. Fiscal stamps surch. **RECONSTRUCCION COMUNICACIONES 5 CENTAVOS DE CORDOBA** and further surch. **Vale dos centavos Resello 1936.**
908. **23.** 1 c. on 5 c. green .. 12 8
909. 2 c. on 5 c. green .. 12 8

1936. Obligatory Tax. Fiscal stamps surch. **RECONSTRUCCION COMUNICACIONES 5 CENTAVOS DE CORDOBA** and further surch.
(a) **1936 R. de C. Vale Un Centavo.**
910. **23.** 1 c. on 5 c. green .. 10 8
(b) **Vale un centavo R. de C. 1936.**
911. **23.** 1 c. on 5 c. green .. 15 8

1937. Colours changed. Size 27×22¾ mm.
912. **21.** ½ c. black 8 5
913. 1 c. red 8 5
914. **22.** 2 c. blue 8 5
915. **21.** 3 c. brown 8 5
916. **22.** 4 c. yellow 8 8
917. **21.** 5 c. red 8 8
918. **22.** 6 c. violet 10 8
919. 10 c. green 10 8
920. **21.** 15 c. green 8 8
921. **22.** 20 c. brown 10 8
922. **21.** 25 c. orange 15 8
923. **22.** 50 c. brown 15 12
924. 1 cor. blue 25 20

1937. Obligatory Tax. Colour changed.
925. **27.** 1 c. green 8 5

1937. Air. Colours changed.
926. **28.** 15 c. orange 8 5
927. 20 c. red 10 8
928. 25 c. black 10 8
929. 50 c. violet 25 8
930. 1 cor. orange 50 15

1937. Air. Surch. **Vale** and value. Colours changed.
931. **28.** 30 c. on 50 c. red .. 15 8
932. 35 c. on 50 c. olive .. 20 8
933. 40 c. on 1 cor. green .. 25 8
934. 55 c. on 1 cor. blue .. 30 12

1937. Air. Surch. **Servicio Centro-americano Vale Diez Centavos.**
949. **28.** 10 c. on 1 cor. red .. 12 10

1937. Air. No. 805 (without T **37**) optd. **1937.**
950. **21.** 8 c. on 15 c. brown .. 30 10

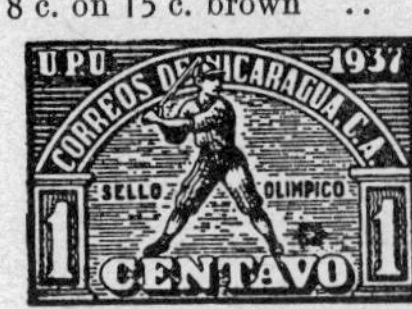

40. Baseball Player.

1937. Obligatory Tax. For 1937 Central American Olympic Games. Optd. with ball in red under "OLIMPICO".
951. **40.** 1 c. red 30 30
952. 1 c. yellow 40 40
953. 1 c. blue 50 50
953a. 1 c. green 60 60

1937. Nos. 799/809 optd. **Habilitado 1937.**
954. **22.** 1 c. on 2 c. green .. 5 5
955. **21.** 2 c. on 3 c. olive .. 5 5
956. **22.** 3 c. on 4 c. red .. 5 5
957. **21.** 4 c. on 5 c. blue .. 5 5
958. **22.** 5 c. on 6 c. blue .. 5 5
959. 6 c. on 10 c. brown .. 5 5
960. **21.** 8 c. on 15 c. brown .. 5 5
961. **22.** 16 c. on 20 c. brown .. 15 12
962. **21.** 24 c. on 25 c. red .. 15 8
963. 25 c. on 25 c. orange .. 15 12
964. **22.** 32 c. on 50 c. violet .. 15 12

41. Presidential Palace, Managua.

1937. Air. Inland.

No.	Type	Description	Unused	Used
965.	41.	1 c. red	8	5
966.		2 c. blue	8	5
967.		3 c. olive	8	5
968.		4 c. black	8	5
969.		5 c. purple	8	5
970.		6 c. brown	8	5
971.		8 c. violet	8	5
972.		16 c. orange	20	12
973.		24 c. yellow	12	10
974.		25 c. green	20	15

42. Nicaragua.

1937. Air. Abroad.

No.	Type	Description	Unused	Used
975.	42.	10 c. green	10	8
976.		15 c. blue	10	8
977.		20 c. yellow	20	10
978.		25 c. violet	20	10
979.		30 c. red	20	12
980.		50 c. orange	20	12
981.		1 cor. olive	50	45

43. Presidential Palace.

1937. Air. Abroad. U.S. Constitution. 150th Anniv.

No.	Type	Description	Unused	Used
982.	–	10 c. blue and green ..	1·60	1·25
983.	43.	15 c. blue and orange ..	1·40	1·00
984.	–	20 c. blue and red ..	60	50
985.	–	25 c. blue and brown ..	70	50
986.	–	30 c. blue and green ..	70	55
987.	–	35 c. blue and yellow ..	35	30
988.	–	40 c. blue and green ..	25	25
989.	–	45 c. blue and purple ..	25	25
990.	–	50 c. blue and mauve ..	25	25
991.	–	55 c. blue and green ..	25	20
992.	–	75 c. blue and green ..	25	25
993.	–	1 cor. claret and blue ..	80	25

DESIGNS: 10 c. Children's Park, Managua. 20 c. S. America. 25 c. C. America. 30 c. N. America. 35 c. Lake Tiscapa. 40 c. Pan American motor-road. 45 c. Priniomi Park. 50 c. Piedrecitas Park. 55 c. San Juan del Sur. 75 c. Rio Tipitapa. 1 cor. Granada landscape.

43a. Diriangen.

1937. Air. Day of the Race.

No.	Type	Description	Unused	Used
993a.	43a.	1 c. green (inland) ..	8	5
993b.		4 c. lake	8	8
993c.		5 c. violet	10	8
993d.		8 c. blue	8	8
993e.	43a.	10 c. brown (abroad)	8	5
993f.		15 c. blue	8	8
993g.		20 c. pink	10	8

44. Letter Carrier.

DESIGNS: 1 c. Mule transport. 2 c. Diligence. 3 c. Sailing boat. 5 c. Steamer. 7½ c. Train.

1938. Postal Administration. 75th Anniv. Inscr. "1862–1937".

No.	Type	Description	Unused	Used
994.	44.	½ c. green	10	8
995.	–	1 c. mauve	10	8
996.	–	2 c. brown	10	8
997.	–	3 c. violet	10	8
998.	–	5 c. blue	10	8
999.	–	7½ c. red	35	20

44a. Gen. Tomas Martinez.

1938. Air. Postal Administration. 75th Anniv.

No.	Type	Description	Unused	Used
999a.	44a.	1 c. black and orange (inland)	12	12
999b.		5 c. black and violet	15	15
999c.		8 c. black and blue ..	15	15
999d.		16 c. black and brown	20	20
999e.		10 c. black and green (abroad)	12	10
999f.	–	15 c. black and blue	15	12
999g.	–	25 c. black and violet	25	25
999h.	–	50 c. black and red ..	30	30

DESIGNS: 10 c. to 50 c. Gen. Anastasio Somoza.

1938. Surch. **1938** and **Vale,** new value in words and **Centavos.**

No.	Type	Description	Unused	Used
1000.	21.	3 c. on 25 c. orange ..	8	5
1001.	22.	5 c. on 50 c. brown ..	8	5
1002.		6 c. on 1 cor. blue ..	8	8

45. Dario Park.

46. Lake Managua.

47. President Somoza.

1939.

No.	Type	Description	Unused	Used
1003.	45.	1½ c. green (postage)..	5	5
1004.		2 c. red	5	5
1005.		3 c. blue	5	5
1006.		6 c. brown	8	8
1007.		7½ c. green	8	5
1008.		10 c. brown	10	8
1009.		15 c. orange	10	8
1010.		25 c. violet	10	8
1011.		50 c. green	12	10
1012.		1 cor. yellow	35	30
1013.	46.	2 c. blue (air: inland)	8	5
1014.		3 c. olive	8	5
1015.		8 c. mauve	8	5
1016.		16 c. orange	12	8
1017.		24 c. yellow	12	10
1018.		32 c. green	12	12
1019.		50 c. red	20	15
1020.	47.	10 c. brown (air: abroad)	8	5
1021.		15 c. blue	8	5
1022.		20 c. yellow	10	10
1023.		25 c. violet	12	12
1024.		30 c. red	15	12
1025.		50 c. orange	25	25
1026.		1 cor. olive	40	35

1939. Nos. 920/1. Surch. **Vale un Centavo 1939.**

No.	Type	Description	Unused	Used
1027.	21.	1 c. on 15 c. green ..	5	5
1028.	22.	1 c. on 20 c. brown ..	5	5

48. Managua Airport.

1939. Air. Will Rogers Commem. Inscr. "WILL ROGERS/1931/1939".

No.	Type	Description	Unused	Used
1029.	48.	1 c. green	5	5
1030.	–	2 c. red	5	5
1031.	–	3 c. blue	5	5
1032.	–	4 c. blue	8	5
1033.	–	5 c. red	5	5

DESIGNS: 2 c. Rogers at Managua. 3 c. Rogers in P.A.A. hut. 4 c. Rogers and U.S. Marines. 5 c. Rogers and street in Managua.

49. Senate House and Pres. Somoza.

1940. Air. President's Visit to U.S.A. Inscr. "AEREO INTERIOR".

No.	Type	Description	Unused	Used
1034.	–	4 c. brown	8	5
1035.	49.	8 c. brown	5	5
1036.	–	16 c. green	8	5
1037.	49.	20 c. mauve	25	20
1038.	–	32 c. red	12	12

(b) Inscr. "CORREO AEREO INTERNACIONAL".

No.	Type	Description	Unused	Used
1039.	–	25 c. blue	12	5
1040.	–	30 c. black	15	5
1041.	49.	50 c. red	30	25
1042.	–	60 c. green	30	25
1043.	–	65 c. brown	15	12
1044.	–	90 c. olive	25	12
1045.	–	1 cor. violet	45	25

DESIGNS: 4 c., 16 c., 25 c., 30 c., 65 c., 90 c. Pres. Somoza addressing Senate. 32 c., 60 c., 1 cor. Portrait of Pres. Somoza between symbols of Nicaragua and New York World's Fair.

50. S. L. Rowe, Statue of Liberty and Union Flags.

1940. Air. Pan-American Union. 50th Anniv.

No.	Type	Description	Unused	Used
1046.	50.	1 cor. 25 blue, yellow, red and orange ..	40	35

51. Earliest Issue and Sir Rowland Hill.

1941. Air. First Adhesive Postage Stamps. Cent.

No.	Type	Description	Unused	Used
1047.	51.	2 cor. brown	5·00	1·25
1048.		3 cor. blue	10·00	2·00
1049.		5 cor. red	20·00	3·00

1941. Surch. **Servicio ordinario/Vale Diez Centavos/de Cordoba.**

No.	Type	Description	Unused	Used
1050.	48.	10 c. on 1 c. green ..	8	5

52. Ruben Dario (poet).

1941. Ruben Dario. 25th Death Anniv.

No.	Type	Description	Unused	Used
1051.	52.	10 c. red (postage) ..	12	8
1052.		20 c. mauve (air) ..	20	8
1053.		35 c. green	20	12
1054.		40 c. orange	25	15
1055.		60 c. blue	45	25

1943. As No. 1050, but **de Cordoba** omitted.

No.	Type	Description	Unused	Used
1056.	48.	10 c. on 1 c. green ..	8	5

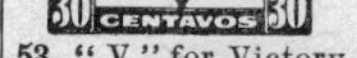

53. "V" for Victory.

54. Red Cross.

55. Red Cross Workers and Wounded.

1943. Victory.

No.	Type	Description	Unused	Used
1057.	53.	10 c. red & violet (post.)	5	5
1058.		30 c. red and brown ..	8	5
1059.		40 c. red and green (air)	10	5
1060.		60 c. red and blue ..	15	5

1944. Air. Int. Red Cross Society. 80th Anniv. Inscr. "1864 1944".

No.	Type	Description	Unused	Used
1061.	54.	25 c. claret	50	20
1062.	–	50 c. bistre	60	35
1063.	55.	1 cor. green	1·25	80

DESIGN—VERT. 50 c. Two Hemispheres.

57. Columbus's Fleet and Lighthouse.

58. Roosevelt as Stamp Collector.

56. Columbus and Lighthouse.

1945. Honouring Columbus's Discovery of America and Erection of Columbus Lighthouse near Trujillo City, Dominican Republic.

No.	Type	Description	Unused	Used
1064.	56.	4 c. blk. & green (post.)	10	8
1065.		6 c. black and orange ..	10	8
1066.		8 c. black and red ..	12	10
1067.		10 c. black and blue ..	15	12
1068.	57.	20 c. grey & green (air)	10	8
1069.		35 c. black and red ..	15	12
1070.		75 c. pink and green	20	15
1071.		90 c. blue and red ..	35	30
1072.		1 cor. blue and black ..	50	20
1073.		2 cor. 50 red and blue ..	1·25	1·10

1946. President Roosevelt Commem. Inscr. "HOMENAJE A ROOSEVELT".

No.	Type	Description	Unused	Used
1074.	58.	4 c. green & black (post)	10	10
1075.	–	8 c. violet and black ..	12	12
1076.	–	10 c. blue and black ..	20	20
1077.	–	16 c. red and black ..	25	25
1078.	–	32 c. brown and black	20	20
1079.	–	50 c. grey and black ..	20	20
1080.	–	25 c. orge. & black (air)	12	12
1081.	–	75 c. red and black ..	15	15
1082.	–	1 cor. green and black	35	35
1083.	–	3 cor. violet and black	1·75	1·75
1084	–	5 cor. blue and black ..	2·25	2·25

DESIGNS—portraying Roosevelt. HORIZ. 8 c., 25 c. with Churchill at the Atlantic Conference. 16 c., 1 cor. with Churchill, De Gaulle and Giraud at the Casablanca Conference. 32 c., 3 cor. with Churchill and Stalin at the Teheran Conference. VERT. 10 c., 75 c. Signing Declaration of War against Japan. 50 c., 5 cor. Head of Roosevelt.

59. Managua Cathedral.

60. G.P.O., Managua.

1947. Managua Cent. Frames in black.

No.	Type	Description	Unused	Used
1085.	59.	4 c. red (postage) ..	10	5
1086.	–	5 c. blue	12	5
1087.	–	6 c. green	12	5
1088.	–	10 c. olive	12	8
1089.	–	75 c. brown	15	12
1090.	–	5 c. violet (air) ..	8	5
1091.	60.	20 c. green	8	5
1092.	–	35 c. orange	10	8
1093.	–	90 c. purple	20	15
1094.	–	1 cor. brown	30	20
1095.	–	2 cor. 50 purple ..	80	60

DESIGNS—POSTAGE (as T 59): 5 c. Health Ministry. 6 c. Municipal Building. 10 c. College. 75 c. G.P.O., Managua. AIR (as T 60): 5 c. College. 35 c. Health Ministry. 90 c. National Bank. 1 cor. Municipal Building. 2 cor. 50, National Palace.

61. San Cristobal Volcano.

62. Ruben Dario Monument, Managua.

1947. (a) Postage.

No.	Type	Description	Unused	Used
1096.	61.	2 c. orange and black ..	5	5
1097.	–	3 c. violet and black ..	5	5
1098.	–	4 c. grey and black ..	8	5
1099.	–	5 c. red and black ..	15	8
1100.	–	6 c. green and black ..	10	8
1101.	–	8 c. brown and black ..	12	8
1102.	–	10 c. red and black ..	15	10
1103.	–	20 c. blue and black ..	20	10
1104.	–	30 c. purple and black	20	10
1105.	–	50 c. claret and black ..	25	12
1106.	–	1 cor. brown and black	25	20

DESIGNS— as T 61: 3 c. Lion on Ruben Dario's tomb, Leon Cathedral. 4 c. Race Stand. 5 c. Soldiers' Monument. 6 c. Sugar cane. 8 c. Tropical fruits. 10 c. Cotton. 20 c. Horses. 30 c. Coffee plant. 50 c. Prize bullock. 1 cor. Agricultural landscape.

(b) Air.

1107. 62. 5 c. red and green .. 5 5
1108. – 6 c. orange and black .. 5 5
1109. – 8 c. brown and red .. 5 5
1110. – 10 c. blue and brown .. 10 8
1111. – 20 c. orange and blue .. 12 8
1112. – 25 c. green and claret .. 15 10
1113. – 35 c. brown and black 12 8
1114. – 50 c. black and violet .. 15 8
1115. – 1 cor. red and black .. 30 15
1116. – 1 cor. 50 green & claret 30 25
1117. – 5 cor. red and brown 2·40 2·00
1118. – 10 cor. brown and violet 1·90 1·60
1119. – 25 cor. yellow and green 4·50 4·00

DESIGNS—as T 62: 6 c. Tapir. 8 c. Highway and Lake Managua. 10 c. Genizaro Dam. 20 c. Ruben Dario Monument, Managua. 25 c. Sulphur Lagoon, Nejapa 35 c. Managua Airport. 50 c. Mouth of Rio Prinzapolka. 1 cor. Thermal Baths, Tipitapa. 1 cor. 50, Rio Tipitapa. 5 cor. Embassy building. 10 cor. Girl carrying basket of fruit. 25 cor. Franklin D. Roosevelt Monument, Managua.

63. Soft-ball. 64. Pole-vaulting.

65. Tennis. 66. National Stadium, Managua.

1949. 10th World Amateur Baseball Championships. Inscr. as in T 63/5.

(a) Postage as T 63/4.

1120. 63. 1 c. brown 8 5
1121. – 2 c. blue 12 8
1122. 64. 3 c. emerald 12 5
1123. – 4 c. purple 8 5
1124. – 5 c. orange 20 8
1125. – 10 c. emerald 20 10
1126. – 15 c. red 25 10
1127. – 25 c. blue 25 12
1128. – 35 c. green 35 12
1129. – 40 c. violet 55 15
1130. – 60 c. black 90 25
1131. – 1 cor. red .. .. 1·25 45
1132. – 2 cor. purple .. .. 1·60 80

DESIGNS—VERT. 2 c. Scout. 5 c. Cycling. 25 c. Boxing. 35 c. Basket-ball. HORIZ. 4 c. Diving. 10 c. Stadium. 15 c. Baseball. 40 c. Yachting. 60 c. Table tennis. 1 cor. Football. 2 cor. Tennis.

(b) Air as T 65.

1133. 65. 1 c. red 8 5
1134. – 2 c. black 8 5
1135. – 3 c. red 8 5
1136. – 4 c. black 5 5
1137. – 5 c. blue 15 5
1138. – 15 c. green 40 8
1139. – 25 c. purple .. .. 1·00 15
1140. – 30 c. brown 80 15
1141. – 40 c. violet 30 15
1142. – 75 c. magenta .. 2·00 1·10
1143. – 1 cor. blue .. .. 2·00 50
1144. – 2 cor. olive .. .. 2·00 80
1145. – 5 cor. green .. .. 2·40 1·00

DESIGNS—SQUARE: 2 c. Football. 3 c. Table tennis. 4 c. Stadium. 5 c. Yachting. 15 c. Basket-ball. 25 c. Boxing. 30 c. Baseball. 40 c. Cycling. 75 c. Diving. 1 cor. Pole-vaulting. 2 cor. Scout. 5 cor. Soft-ball.

1949. Obligatory Tax stamps. Stadium Construction Fund.

1146. 66. 5 c. blue 12 5
1146a. 5 c. red 12 5

67. Rowland Hill. 68. Heinrich von Stephan.

1950. U.P.U. 75th Anniv. Frames in black.

1147. 67. 20 c. red (postage) .. 8 8
1148. – 25 c. green 8 5
1149. – 75 c. blue 30 30
1150. – 80 c. green 20 20
1151. – 4 cor. blue .. .. 1·25 1·25

DESIGNS—VERT. 25 c. Portrait as T 68. 75 c. Monument, Berne. 80 c., 4 cor. Obverse and reverse of Congress Medal.

1152. – 16 c. red (air) 5 5
1153. 68. 20 c. orange 5 5
1154. – 25 c. black 10 8

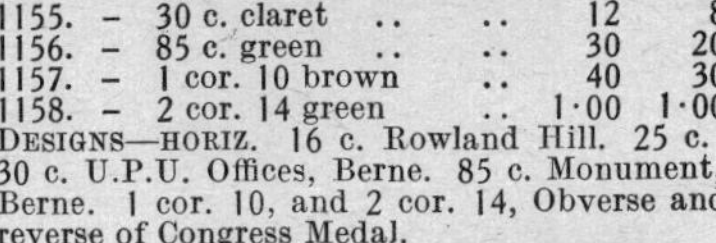

1155. – 30 c. claret 12 8
1156. – 85 c. green 30 20
1157. – 1 cor. 10 brown .. 40 30
1158. – 2 cor. 14 green .. 1·00 1·00

DESIGNS—HORIZ. 16 c. Rowland Hill. 25 c. 30 c. U.P.U. Offices, Berne. 85 c. Monument, Berne. 1 cor. 10, and 2 cor. 14, Obverse and reverse of Congress Medal.

69. Queen Isabella and Columbus' Fleet. 70. Isabella the Catholic.

1952. Isabella the Catholic. 500th Birth Anniv. Inscr. "1451 1951".

1159. – 10 c. magenta (postage) 5 5
1160. 69. 96 c. blue 20 20
1161. – 98 c. red 20 20
1162. – 1 cor. 20 brown .. 25 25
1163. 70. 1 cor. 76 purple .. 30 30
1164. 70. 2 cor. 30 red (air) .. 65 65
1165. – 2 cor. 80 orange .. 60 60
1166. – 3 cor. green 65 65
1167. 69. 3 cor. 30 blue 70 70
1168. – 3 cor. 60 green .. 80 80

DESIGNS—VERT. 10 c., 3 cor. 60 Queen facing right. 98 c., 3 cor. Queen and "Santa Maria". 1 cor. 20, 2 cor. 80 Queen and Map of Americas.

71. O.D.E.C.A. Flag.

1953. Foundation of Organization of Central American States.

1169. 71. 4 c. blue (postage) .. 5 5
1170. – 5 c. green 5 5
1171. – 6 c. brown 5 5
1172. – 15 c. olive 10 8
1173. – 50 c. sepia 12 10
1174. – 20 c. claret (air) .. 8 8
1175. 71. 25 c. blue 8 8
1176. – 30 c. brown 10 8
1177. – 60 c. green 15 12
1178. – 1 cor. purple 35 30

DESIGNS: 5 c., 1 cor. Map of C. America. 6 c., 20 c. Hands holding O.D.E.C.A. arms. 15 c., 30 c. Five Presidents of C. America. 50 c. 60 c. Charter and flags.

72. Pres. Solorzano. 73. Pres. Arguello.

1953. Presidential Series. Portraits in black.

(a) Postage. As T 72.

1179. 72. 4 c. red 5 5
1180. – 6 c. blue (D. M. Chamorro) .. 5 5
1181. – 8 c. brown (Diaz) .. 5 5
1182. – 15 c. red (Somoza) .. 8 5
1183. – 50 c. grn. (E. Chamorro) 12 10

(b) Air. As T 73.

1184. 73. 4 c. red 5 5
1185. – 5 c. orange (Moncada) 5 5
1186. – 20 c. blue (J. B. Sacasa) 5 5
1187. – 25 c. (Zelaya) 5 5
1188. – 30 c. lake (Somoza) .. 8 8
1189. – 35 c. green (Martinez) 8 8
1190. – 40 c. plum (Guzman) 10 10
1191. – 45 c. olive (Cuadra) .. 10 10
1192. – 50 c. red (P.J. Chamorro) .. 10 10
1193. – 60 c. blue (Zavala) .. 12 12
1194. – 85 c. brown (Cardenas) 20 20
1195. – 1 cor. 10 pur. (Carazo) 30 30
1196. – 1 cor. 20 bistre (R. Sacasa) .. 35 35

74. Native Sculptor and U.N. Emblem.

DESIGNS: A, Detail from Nicaragua's Coat of Arms. B, Globe. C, Candle and Nicaragua's Charter. D, Flags of Nicaragua and U.N. E, Torch. F, Trusting hands.

1954. U.N.O. Inscr. "HOMENAJE A LA ONU".

1197. 74. 3 c. drab (postage) .. 8 5
1198. A. 4 c. green 10 5
1199. B. 5 c. emerald 10 5
1200. C. 15 c. green 60 10
1201. D. 1 cor. blue-green .. 50 20
1202. E. 3 c. rose (air) 5 5
1203. F. 4 c. orange 5 5
1204. C. 5 c. red 8 5
1205. D. 30 c. pink 40 8
1206. B. 2 cor. crimson .. 55 40
1207. A. 3 cor. brown .. 1·00 70
1208. 74. 5 cor. maroon .. 1·25 1·10

75. Capt. D. L. Ray. 76. F-86 Sabre-Jet.

1954. National Air Force. Frames in black.

(a) Postage. Frames as T 75.

1209. 75. 1 c. black 5 5
1210. – 2 c. black (F-86 Sabre-Jet) .. 5 5
1211. – 3 c. myrtle (A-20 'plane) 5 5
1212. – 4 c. orge. (B-24 bomber) 5 5
1213. – 5 c. grn. (AT-6 trainer) 8 5
1214. – 15 c. turquoise (Pres. Somoza) .. 10 5
1215. – 1 cor. vio. (Emblem) .. 20 15

(b) Air. Frames as T 76.

1216. – 10 c. black (D. L. Ray) 5 5
1217. 76. 15 c. black .. 5 5
1218. – 20 c. mag. (Emblem) .. 8 5
1219. – 25 c. red (Hangers) .. 10 5
1220. – 30 c. ultramarine (Pres. Somoza) .. 12 5
1221. – 50 c. bl. (AT-6 formation) 30 30
1222. – 1 cor. grn. (P-38 'plane) 25 20

77. Rotary Slogans. 77a.

1955. Rotary Int. 50th Anniv. Inscr. "1905 1955".

1223. 77. 15 c. orange (postage) 5 5
1224. A. 20 c. olive 8 8
1225. B. 35 c. violet 10 10
1226. C. 40 c. red 10 10
1227. D. 90 c. black 15 15
1228. D. 1 c. red (air) 5 5
1229. A. 2 c. blue 5 5
1230. C. 3 c. green 5 5
1231. 77. 4 c. violet 5 5
1232. B. 5 c. brown 5 5
1233. 25 c. turquoise .. 8 8
1234. 77. 30 c. black 8 8
1235. C. 45 c. magenta .. 15 12
1236. A. 50 c. green 12 12
1237. D. 1 cor. blue 25 20

DESIGNS—VERT. A. Clasped hands. B. Rotarian and Nicaraguan flags. D. Paul P. Harris. HORIZ. C. World map and winged emblem.

1956. National Exhibition. Surch. **Conmemoracion Exposicion Nacional Febrero 4-16, 1956** and value.

1238. 5 c. on 6 c. brown (No. 1171) postage .. 5 5
1239. 5 c. on 6 c. blk. & blue (1180) 5 5
1240. 5 c. on 8 c. brn. & blk. (1101) 5 5
1241. 15 c. on 35 c. violet (1225) 8 8
1242. 15 c. on 80 c. grn. & blk. (1150) 8 8
1243. 15 c. on 90 c. black (1227) 8 8
1244. 30 c. on 35 c. black & green (1139) (air) .. 10 8
1245. 30 c. on 45 c. blk. & ol. (1191) 10 8
1246. 30 c. on 45 c. magenta (1235) 12 8
1247. 2 cor. on 5 cor. maroon (1208) 50 40

1956. Obligatory Tax. Social Welfare Fund.

1247a. 77a. 5 c. blue 5 5

78. Gen. J. D. Estrada. 79. President A. Somoza.

1956. Cent. of War of 1856. Inscr. as in T 78.

1248. – 5 c. brown (postage) .. 5 5
1249. – 10 c. lake 5 5
1250. – 15 c. grey 8 5
1251. – 25 c. red 12 10
1252. – 50 c. purple 15 12
1253. 78. 30 c. red (air) 5 5
1254. – 60 c. brown 12 10
1255. – 1 cor. 50 green .. 30 20
1256. – 2 cor. 50 blue .. 40 35
1257. – 10 cor. orange .. 1·90 1·60

DESIGNS—VERT. 5 c. Gen. M. Jerez. 10 c. Gen. F. Chamorro. 50 c. Gen. J. D. Estrada. 1 cor. 50, E. Mangalo. 10 cor. Commodore H. Paulding. HORIZ. 15 c. Battle of San Jocinto. 25 c. Granada in flames. 60 c. Bas-relief. 2 cor. 50, Battle of Rivas.

1957. Air. National Mourning for Pres. A. Somoza. Various frames. Inscr. as in T 79. Centres in black.

1258. – 15 c. black 8 8
1259. – 30 c. indigo 12 12
1260. 79. 2 cor. violet 50 40
1261. – 3 cor. olive .. .. 1·00 1·00
1262. – 5 cor. sepia .. .. 1·40 1·40

80. Scout and Badge. 81. Clasped Hands, Badge and Globe.

1957. Lord Baden-Powell. Birth Cent. Inscr. as in T 80/81.

1263. 80. 10 c. ol. & violet (post.) 5 5
1264. – 15 c. sepia and purple 8 8
1265. – 20 c. brown and blue .. 8 8
1266. – 25 c. brown & turquoise 10 10
1267. – 50 c. olive and red .. 25 25
1268. 81. 3 c. olive and red (air) 8 8
1269. – 4 c. blue and chocolate 8 8
1270. – 5 c. brown and emerald 8 8
1271. – 6 c. drab and violet .. 8 8
1272. – 8 c. red and black .. 8 8
1273. – 30 c. black and green .. 12 12
1274. – 40 c. black and blue .. 12 12
1275. – 75 c. sepia and maroon 25 25
1276. – 85 c. grey and red .. 30 30
1277. – 1 cor. brown and green 30 30

DESIGNS—VERT. 4 c. Scout badge. 5 c., 15 c. Wolf cub. 6 c. Badge and flags. 8 c. Badge and emblems of scouting. 20 c. Scout. 25 c. 1 cor. Lord Baden-Powell. 30 c., 50 c. Joseph A. Harrison. 75 c. Rover Scout. 85 c. Scout. HORIZ. 40 c. Presentation to Pres. Somoza.

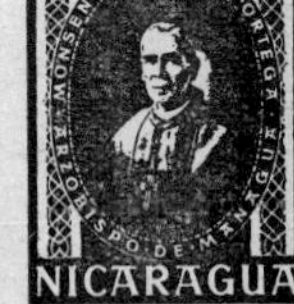

82. Pres. Luis Somoza. 84. Archbishop of Managua.

83. Managua Cathedral.

1957. Election of Pres. Somoza. Portrait in brown. (a) Postage. Oval frame.

1278. 82. 10 c. red 5 5
1279. 15 c. blue 5 5
1280. 35 c. purple 8 8
1281. 50 c. brown 12 12
1282. 75 c. green 25 25

(b) Air. Rectangular frame.

1283. – 20 c. blue 8 8
1284. – 25 c. magenta 8 8
1285. – 30 c. sepia 10 10
1286. – 40 c. turquoise .. 12 12
1287. – 2 cor. violet 50 50

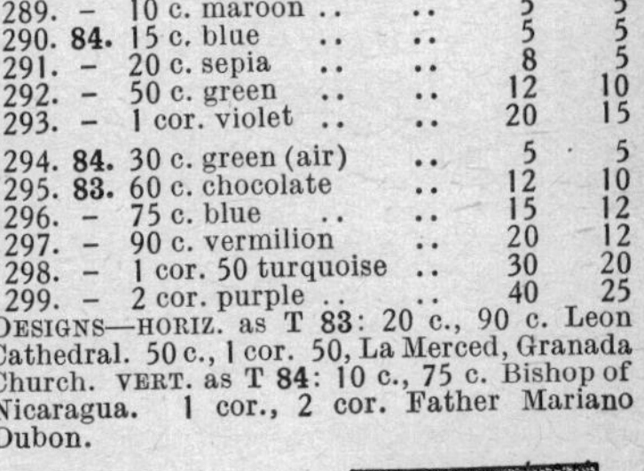

1957. Churches and Priests. Centres in olive.

1288. 83. 5 c. green (postage) .. 5 5
1289. – 10 c. maroon 5 5
1290. 84. 15 c. blue 5 5
1291. – 20 c. sepia 8 5
1292. – 50 c. green 12 10
1293. – 1 cor. violet 20 15
1294. 84. 30 c. green (air) .. 5 5
1295. 83. 60 c. chocolate .. 12 10
1296. – 75 c. blue 15 12
1297. – 90 c. vermilion .. 20 12
1298. – 1 cor. 50 turquoise .. 30 20
1299. – 2 cor. purple 40 25

DESIGNS—HORIZ. as T 83: 20 c., 90 c. Leon Cathedral. 50 c., 1 cor. 50, La Merced, Granada Church. VERT. as T 84: 10 c., 75 c. Bishop of Nicaragua. 1 cor., 2 cor. Father Mariano Dubon.

85. M.S. "Honduras". 86. Exhibition Emblem.

1957. Nicaraguan Merchant Marine Commemoration. Inscr. as in T **85.**

1300. **85.** 4 c. black, blue and myrtle (postage) .. 5 5
1301. – 5 c. vio., blue & choc. 5 5
1302. – 6 c. black, blue & red 5 5
1303. – 10 c. blk., grn. & sepia 5 5
1304. – 15 c. brown, blue & red 8 5
1305. – 50 c. brown, blue & vio. 15 10
1306. – 25 c. purple, blue and ultramarine (air) .. 5 5
1307. – 30 c. grey, buff & brown 8 5
1308. – 50 c. bistre, blue & vio. 10 8
1309. – 60 c. blk., turq. & mar. 12 10
1310. – 1 cor. blk., blue & red 20 15
1311. – 2 cor. 50 brown, blue and black .. 50 35

DESIGNS—HORIZ. 5 c. Gen. A. Somoza, founder of Mamenic (National) Shipping Line and ship. 6 c. M.S. "Guatemala". 10 c. M.S. "Salvador". 15 c. Ship between hemispheres. 25 c. M.S. "Managua". 30 c. Ship's wheel and world map. 50 c. (No. 1305), Hemispheres and ship. 50 c. (No. 1308), Mamenic Shipping Line flag. 60 c. M.S. "Costa Rica". 1 cor. M.S. "Nicarao". 2 cor. 50, Map, ship and flag.

1958. Air. Brussels Int. Exn. Inscr. "EXPOSICION MUNDIAL DE BELGICA 1958".

1312. **86.** 25 c. blk., yell & grn. 8 8
1313. – 30 c. red, yellow, green violet and blue .. 8 8
1314. – 45 c. blk., ochre & blue 12 12
1315. **86.** 1 cor. black, blue and dull purple 25 25
1316. – 2 cor. red, yellow, green and blue .. 40 40
1317. – 10 cor. sepia, purple and blue .. .. 1·75 1·75

DESIGNS—As T **86**: 30 c., 20 cor. Arms of Nicaragua. 45 c., 10 cor. Nicaraguan Pavilion.

87. Emblems of C. American Republics.

88. Arms of La Salle.

1958. 17th Central American Lions Convention. Inscr. as in T **87.** Emblems (5 c., 60 c.) multicoloured; Lions badge (others) in blue, red, yellow (or orange and buff).

1318. **87.** 5 c. blue (postage) .. 5 5
1319. – 10 c. blue and orange 5 5
1320. – 20 c. blue and green .. 5 5
1321. – 50 c. blue and purple .. 12 12
1322. – 75 c. blue and magenta 20 20
1323. – 1 cor. 50, blue, salmon and drab 30 30
1324. – 30 c. blue & orge. (air) 8 5
1325. **87.** 60 c. blue and pink .. 15 8
1326. – 90 c. blue 20 15
1327. – 1 cor. 25 blue and olive 25 20
1328. – 2 cor. blue and green .. 40 35
1329. – 3 cor. blue, red & violet 60 60

DESIGNS—HORIZ. 10 c., 1 cor. 25, Melvin Jones. 20 c., 30 c. Dr. T. A. Arias. 50 c., 90 c. Edward G. Barry. 75 c., 2 cor. Lions emblem. 1 cor. 50, 3 cor. Map of C. American Isthmus.

1958. Brothers of the Nicaraguan Christian Schools Commem. Inscr. as in T **88.**

1330. **88.** 5 c. red, blue & yellow (postage) 5 5
1331. – 10 c. sepia, blue & grn. 5 5
1332. – 15 c. sepia, brn. & bis. 5 5
1333. – 20 c. black, red & bistre 5 5
1334. – 50 c. sepia, orge & bis. 10 10
1335. – 75 c. sepia, turq. & grn. 15 12
1336. – 1 cor. blk., vio. & bistre 25 20
1337. **88.** 30 c. blue, red & yellow (air) 10 8
1338. – 60 c. sepia, pur. & grey 20 15
1339. – 85 c. black, red & blue 20 20
1340. – 90 c. blk., grn. & ochre 25 25
1341. – 1 cor. 25 black, red and ochre 30 30
1342. – 1 cor. 50 sepia, green and grey 35 30
1343. – 1 cor. 75 black, brown and blue 40 35
1344. – 2 cor. sepia, grn. & grey 50 45

DESIGNS—HORIZ. 10 c., 60 c. Managua Teachers Institute. VERT. 15 c., 85 c. De La Salle (founder). 20 c., 90 c. Brother Carlos. 50 c. 1 cor. 50, Brother Antonio. 75 c., 1 cor. 25, Brother Julio. 1 cor., 1 cor. 75, Brother Angeo. 2 cor. Brother Eugenio.

0374411 0636266.

89. U.N. Emblem.

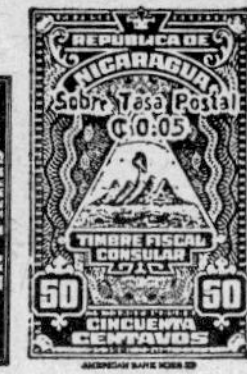
90.

91.

1958. Inaug. of U.N.E.S.C.O. Headquarters Building, Paris. Inscr. as in T **89.**

1345. **89.** 10 c. blue & mag. (post.) 5 5
1346. – 15 c. magenta and blue 5 5
1347. – 25 c. brown and green 8 8
1348. – 40 c. black & vermilion 12 12
1349. – 45 c. mauve and blue .. 15 15
1350. **89.** 50 c. green and brown 20 20
1351. – 60 c. blue & mag. (air) 15 12
1352. – 75 c. brown and green 20 15
1353. – 90 c. green and brown 30 20
1354. – 1 cor. magenta and blue 35 25
1355. – 3 cor. vermilion & black 80 70
1356. – 5 cor. blue and mauve 1·25 1·25

DESIGNS—VERT. 15 c. Aerial view of H.Q. 25 c., 45 c. Facade composed of letters "UNESCO". 40 c. H.Q. and Eiffel Tower. In oval vignettes—60 c., As 15 c.; 75 c., 5 cor., As 25 c.; 90 c., 3 cor. As 40 c.; 1 cor., As T **89.**

1959. Obligatory Tax. Consular Fiscal stamps surch. Serial Nos. in red.

1357. **90.** 5 c. on 50 c. blue .. 8 5
1358. **91.** 5 c. on 50 c. blue .. 8 5

92.

93. Cardinal Spellman with Pope John XXIII.

94. Abraham Lincoln.

1959. Obligatory Tax.

1359. **92.** 5 c. blue 8 5

1959. Cardinal Spellman Commem.

1360. **93.** 5 c. flesh & grn. (post.) 5 5
1361. A. 10 c. multicoloured .. 5 5
1362. B. 15 c. red, blk. & green 5 5
1363. C. 20 c. yellow and indigo 5 5
1364. D. 25 c. red and blue .. 5 5
1365. E. 30 c. bl., red & yell.(air) 8 8
1366. 93. 35 c bronze and orange 10 10
1367. A. 1 cor. multicoloured .. 25 25
1368. B. 1 cor. 5, red and black 30 30
1369. C. 1 cor. 50, yell. & indigo 35 35
1370. D. 2 cor. blue, violet & red 45 45
1371. E. 5 cor. blue, red, yellow and pink .. .. 1·00 1·00

DESIGNS—VERT. A, Cardinal's Arms. B, Cardinal. D, Cardinal wearing sash. HORIZ. C, Cardinal and Cross. E, Flags of Nicaragua, Vatican City and U.S.A.

1960. Abraham Lincoln. 150th Birth Anniv. Portrait in black.

1372. **94.** 5 c. red (postage) .. 5 5
1373. 10 c. green 5 5
1374. 15 c. orange 5 5
1375. 1 cor. maroon .. 20 20
1376. 2 cor. blue 40 40
1377. 30 c. blue (air) .. 8 8
1378. 35 c. red 10 10
1379. 70 c. purple 15 15
1380. 1 cor. 5, green .. 20 20
1381. 1 cor. 50, violet .. 30 30
1382. – 5 cor. ochre and black 90 90

DESIGN—HORIZ. 5 cor. Scroll inscr. "Dar al que necesite—A. Lincoln".

1960. Air. San Jose (Costa Rica) Philatelic Society. 10th Anniv. Optd. **X Aniversario Club Filatelico S. J.—C. R.**

1383. 2 cor. crimson (No. 1206) 40 40
1384. 2 cor. 50 blue (No. 1256) .. 45 45
1385. 3 cor. green (No. 1166) .. 55 55

1960. Red Cross Fund for Chilean Earthquake Relief. Nos. 1372/82 optd. **Resello** and Maltese Cross. Portrait in black.

1386. **94.** 5 c. red (postage) .. 5 5
1387. 10 c. green 5 5
1388. 15 c. orange 5 5
1389. 1 cor. maroon .. 20 20
1390. 2 cor. blue 45 45
1391. 30 c. blue (air) .. 15 15
1392. 35 c. red 15 15
1393. 70 c. purple 20 20
1394. 1 cor. 5 green .. 20 20
1395. 1 cor. 50 violet .. 30 30
1396. 5 cor. ochre and black 90 90

95.

1961. Air. World Refugee Year. Inscr. "ANO MUNDIAL DEL REFUGIADO".

1397. – 2 cor. multicoloured 35 35
1398. **95.** 5 cor. ochre, bl. & grn. 90 90

DESIGN: 2 cor. Procession of refugees.

96. Pres. Roosevelt, Pres. Somoza and an Officer.

1961. Air. Nicaraguan Military Academy. 20th Anniv. Inscr. "1939–1959".

1399. **96.** 20 c. black, flesh, yellow and magenta .. 5 5
1400. – 25 c. red, blue & black 5 5
1401. – 30 c. yellow, flesh, black and blue 8 8
1402. – 35 c. multicoloured .. 8 8
1403. – 40 c. red, bl., yell. & grn. 8 8
1404. – 45 c. black, flesh & rose 10 10
1405. **96.** 60 c. black, flesh, yellow and brown 12 12
1406. – 70 c. red, bl., brn. & blk. 15 15
1407. – 1 cor. 5 black, flesh, yellow and purple .. 20 20
1408. – 1 cor. 50 multicoloured 30 30
1409. – 2 cor. red, blue, yellow and grey 40 40
1410. – 5 cor. blk., flesh & grey 90 90

DESIGNS—VERT. 25 c., 70 c. Flags. 35 c., 1 cor. 50, Standard bearers. 40 c., 2 cor. Pennant and emblem. HORIZ. 30 c., 1 cor. 5, Group of officers. 45 c., 5 cor. Pres. Somoza and Director of Academy.

1961. Air. Consular Fiscal stamps as T **90/1** with serial Nos. in red, surch. **Correo Aereo** and value.

1411. 20 c. on 50 c. blue .. 8 5
1412. 20 c. on 1 cor. olive .. 8 5
1413. 20 c. on 2 cor. green .. 8 5
1414. 20 c. on 3 cor. red .. 8 5
1415. 20c. on 5 cor. vermilion 8 5
1416. 20 c. on 10 cor. violet .. 8 5
1417. 20 c. on 20 cor. chestnut 8 5
1418. 20 c. on 50 cor. brown .. 8 5
1419. 20 c. on 100 cor. lake .. 8 5

97. I.J.C. Emblem and Global Map of the Americas.

98. R. Cabezas.

1961. Air. Junior Chamber of Commerce Congress.

1420. 2 c. blk., yell., grn. & blue 5 5
1421. 3 c. black and yellow .. 5 5
1422. 4 c. green, blue, blk. & yell. 5 5
1423. 5 c. black and red .. 5 5
1424. 6 c. yellow-brown, brown, black and yellow .. 5 5
1425. 10 c. salmon, red, blk. & bl. 5 5
1426. 15 c. black, green and blue 5 5
1427. 30 c. black and blue .. 8 8
1428. 35 c. grn., blue, blk. & red 8 8
1429. 70 c. black, red and yellow 12 12
1430. 1 cor. 5 yellow-brown, brown, black and blue 20 20
1431. 5 cor. grn., red, blk. & bl. 90 90

DESIGNS—HORIZ. 2 c., 15 c. T **97.** 4 c., 35 c. "J.C.I." upon Globe. VERT. 3 c., 30 c. I.J.C. emblem. 5 c., 70 c. Scroll. 6 c., 1 cor. 5. Handclasp. 10 c., 5 cor. Regional map of Nicaragua.

1961. Air. 1st Central American Philatelic Convention, San Salvador. Optd. **Convencion Filatelica - Centro - America - Panama - San Salvador - 27 Julio 1961.**

1432. **50.** 1 cor. 25 blue, yellow, red and orange .. 30 30

1961. Air. Cabezas. Birth Cent.

1433. **98.** 20 c. vio.-blue & orge. 8 8
1434. – 40 c. maroon and blue 10 10
1435. – 45 c. sepia & yell.-grn. 12 12
1436. – 70 c. green & chocolate 15 12
1437. – 2 cor. indigo and pink 35 25
1438. – 10 cor. maroon & turq. 1·75 1·40

DESIGNS—HORIZ. 40 c. Map and view of Cartago. 45 c. 1884 newspaper. 70 c. Assembly outside building. 2 cor. Scroll. 10 cor. Map and view of Masaya.

99. Official Gazettes.

100. "Cattleya skinneri".

1961. Regulation of Postal Rates Cent.

1439. **99.** 5 c. brown & turquoise 5 5
1440. – 10 c. brown and green 5 5
1441. – 15 c. brown and red .. 5 5

DESIGNS: 10 c. Envelopes and postmarks. 15 c. Martinez and Somoza.

1961. Air. Dag Hammarskjoeld Commem. Nos. 1351/6 optd. **Homenaje a Hammarskjold Sept. 18-1961.**

1442. 60 c. blue and magenta .. 25 25
1443. 75 c. brown and green .. 30 30
1444. 90 c. green and brown .. 40 40
1445. 1 cor. magenta and blue .. 40 40
1446. 3 cor. vermilion and black 1·10 1·10
1447. 5 cor. blue and mauve .. 2·00 2·00

1962. Air. Surch. **RESELLO C$ 1.00.**

1448. – 1 cor. on 1 cor. 10 brown (No. 1157) 25 20
1449. **94.** 1 cor. on 1 cor. 5 black and green 25 20

See also Nos. 1498/1500a, 1569/70, 1608/14 and 1669/76.

1962. Obligatory Tax. Nicaraguan Orchids. Multicoloured.

1450. 5 c. T **100** 5 5
1451. 5 c. "Bletia roezlii" .. 5 5
1452. 5 c. "Sobralia pleintha" 5 5
1453. 5 c. "Lycaste macrophylla" 5 5
1454. 5 c. "Schomburgkia tibicinus" 5 5
1455. 5 c. "Maxillaria tenuifolia" 5 5
1456. 5 c. "Stanhopea ecornuta" 5 5
1457. 5 c. "Oncidium ascendens" and "O. cebolleta" .. 5 5
1458. 5 c. "Cycnoches egertonianum" 5 5
1459. 5 c. "Hexisia bidentata" 5 5

101. U.N.E.S.C.O. "Audience".

102. Arms of Nueva Segovia.

1962. Air. U.N.E.S.C.O. 15th Anniv.

1460. **101.** 2 cor. multicoloured 35 25
1461. – 5 cor. multicoloured 90 60

DESIGN: 5 cor. U.N. and U.N.E.S.C.O. emblems.

1962. Air. Malaria Eradication. Nos. 1425, 1428/31 optd. with mosquito surrounded by **LUCHA CONTRA LA MALARIA.**

1462. – 10 c. 15 15
1463. – 35 c. 30 20
1464. – 70 c. 40 30
1465. – 1 cor. 5 .. .. 60 40
1466. – 5 cor. .. .. .. 1·75 1·25

1962. Urban and Provincial Arms. Arms mult.; inscr. black; background colours below.

1467. **102.** 2 c. mauve (postage) 5 5
1468. – 3 c. blue 5 5
1469. – 4 c. lilac 5 5
1470. – 5 c. yellow 5 5
1471. – 6 c. brown 5 5
1472. **102.** 30 c. rose (air) .. 8 5
1473. – 50 c. orange 10 8
1474. – 1 cor. green .. 20 15
1475. – 2 cor. grey 40 30
1476. – 5 cor. blue 90 60

ARMS: 3 c., 50 c. Leon. 4 c., 1 cor. Managua. 5 c., 2 cor. Granada. 6 c., 5 cor. Rivas.

103. Liberty Bell.

104. "Blessing".

1963. Air. Independence. 150th Anniv.
1477. **103.** 30 c. drab, blue & blk. 10 8

1963. Air. St. Vincent de Paul and St. Louise de Marillac. Death Tercent.
1478. – 60 c. black and orange 10 8
1479. **104.** 1 cor. olive & orange 20 15
1480. – 2 cor. black and red.. 40 25
DESIGNS—VERT. 60 c. "Comfort" (St. Louise and woman). HORIZ. 2 cor. St. Vincent and St. Louise.

105. "Map Stamp". **106.** Cross on Globe.

1963. Air. Central American Philatelic Societies Federation Commemoration.
1481. **105.** 1 cor. blue and yellow 20 15

1963. Air. Ecumenical Council, Vatican City.
1482. **106.** 20 c. red and yellow 8 5

107. Ears of Wheat. **108.** Boxing.

1963. Air. Freedom from Hunger.
1483. **107.** 10 c. green & lt. green 5 5
1484. – 25 c. sepia & yellow 8 5
DESIGN: 25 c. Barren tree and campaign emblem.

1963. Air. Sports. Multicoloured.
1485. 2 c. Type **108** 5 5
1486. 3 c. Running 5 5
1487. 4 c. Underwater harpooning 5 5
1488. 5 c. Football 5 5
1489. 6 c. Baseball 5 5
1490. 10 c. Tennis 8 5
1491. 15 c. Cycling 10 8
1492. 20 c. Motor-cycling .. 12 8
1493. 35 c. Chess 15 10
1494. 60 c. Angling 20 12
1495. 1 cor. Table-tennis .. 35 20
1496. 2 cor. Basketball.. .. 55 30
1497. 5 cor. Golf .. .. 1·25 90

1964. Air. Surch. **Resello** or **RESELLO** (1500a) and value.
1498. – 5 c. on 6 c. (No. 1424) 15 8
1499. – 10 c. on 30 c. (No. 1365) 40 12
1500. **94.** 15 c. on 30 c.. .. 60 15
1500a. **88.** 20 c. on 30 c.. .. 8 5
See also Nos. 1448/9, 1569/70, 1608/14 and 1669/76.

1964. Optd. **CORREOS.**
1501. 5 c. mult. (No. 1451) 5 5

109. Flags. **110.** "Alliance Emblem".

1964. Air. "Centro America".
1502. **109.** 40 c. multicoloured .. 8 5

1964. Air. "Alliance for Progress". Multicoloured.
1503. 5 c. Type **110** 5 5
1504. 10 c. Red Cross Post .. 5 5
1505. 15 c. Highway 5 5
1506. 20 c. Ploughing.. .. 5 5
1507. 25 c. Housing 8 8
1508. 30 c. Presidents Somoza and Kennedy and Eugene Black (World Bank) 10 8
1509. 35 c. School and adults 12 8
1510. 40 c. Chimneys 15 10
Nos. 1504/10 are horiz.

111. Map of Member Countries. **112.** Rescue of Wounded Soldier.

1964. Air. Central-American "Common Market". Multicoloured.
1511. 15 c. Type **111** 5 5
1512. 25 c. Ears of wheat .. 5 5
1513. 40 c. Cogwheels .. 8 5
1514. 50 c. Heads of cattle .. 10 8

1964. Air. Olympic Games, Tokyo. Nos. 1485/7, 1489 and 1495/6 optd. **OLIMPIADAS TOKYO-1964.**
1515. 2 c. Type **108** 5 5
1516. 3 c. Running 5 5
1517. 4 c. Underwater harpooning 5 5
1518. 6 c. Japanese fencing .. 5 5
1519. 1 cor. Table-tennis .. 80 80
1520. 2 cor. Basketball .. 1·60 1·60

1965. Air. Red Cross Cent. Multicoloured.
1521. 20 c. Type **112** 5 5
1522. 25 c. Blood transfusion 8 5
1523. 40 c. Red Cross and snowbound town .. 10 8
1524. 10 cor. Red Cross and map of Nicaragua .. 1·60 1·60

113. Statuettes.

1965. Air. Nicaraguan Antiquities. Multicoloured.
1525. 5 c. Type **113** 5 5
1526. 10 c. Totem 5 5
1527. 15 c. Carved dog .. 5 5
1528. 20 c. Composition of "objets d'art" .. 5 5
1529. 25 c. Dish and vase .. 5 5
1530. 30 c. Pestle and mortar.. 5 5
1531. 35 c. Statuettes (different) 5 5
1532. 40 c. Deity 8 5
1533. 50 c. Wine vessel and dish 10 8
1534. 60 c. Bowl and dish .. 12 8
1535. 1 cor. Urn 25 10
The 15, 25, 35 and 60 c. are horiz.

114. Pres. Kennedy. **115.** A. Bello (poet and writer).

1965. Air. Pres. Kennedy Commem.
1536. **114.** 35 c. black and green 8 5
1537. 75 c. black & magenta 15 10
1538. 1 cor. 10 black & blue 25 15
1539. 2 cor. black and brown 50 30

1965. Air. Andres Bello Death Cent.
1540. **115.** 10 c. black & chestnut 5 5
1541. 15 c. black and blue.. 5 5
1542. 45 c. black & purple 8 5
1543. 80 c. black and green 12 10
1544. 1 cor. black & yellow 15 12
1545. 2 cor. black and grey 25 20

1965. 9th Central-American Scout Camporee Nos. 1450/9 optd. with scout badge and **CAMPOREE SCOUT 1965.**
1546. 5 c. multicoloured .. 12 12
1547. 5 c. multicoloured .. 12 12
1548. 5 c. multicoloured .. 12 12
1549. 5 c. multicoloured .. 12 12
1550. 5 c. multicoloured .. 12 12
1551. 5 c. multicoloured .. 12 12
1552. 5 c. multicoloured .. 12 12
1553. 5 c. multicoloured .. 12 12
1554. 5 c. multicoloured .. 12 12
1555. 5 c. multicoloured .. 12 12

116. Sir Winston Churchill. **117.** Pope John XXIII.

1966. Air. Churchill Commem.
1556. **116.** 20 c. magenta & black 5 5
1557. – 35 c. green and black 8 5
1558. – 60 c. ochre and black 10 8
1559. – 75 c. red 12 10
1560. – 1 cor. slate-purple .. 15 12
1561. **116.** 2 cor. violet, lilac & blk. 35 30
1562. – 3 cor. indigo & black 50 45
DESIGNS—HORIZ. 35 c., 1 cor. Churchill broadcasting. VERT. 60 c., 3 cor. Churchill crossing the Rhine. 75 c. Churchill in Hussars' uniform.

1966. Air. Closure of Vatican Ecumenical Council. Multicoloured.
1564. 20 c. Type **117** 5 5
1565. 35 c. Pope Paul VI .. 8 8
1566. 1 cor. Archbishop Gonzalez y Robleto 15 12
1567. 2 cor. St. Peter's, Rome 35 25
1568. 3 cor. Papal arms .. 50 40

1967. Air. Nos. 1533/4 surch. **RESELLO** and value.
1569. 10 c. on 50 c. multicoloured 5 5
1570. 15 c. on 60 c. multicoloured 5 5
See also Nos. 1448/9, 1498/1500a, 1608/14 and 1669/76.

118. Dario and Birthplace.

1967. Air. Ruben Dario (poet). Birth Cent. Designs showing Dario and view. Multicoloured.
1571. 5 c. Type **118** 5 5
1572. 10 c. Monument, Managua 5 5
1573. 20 c. Leon Cathedral (site of Dario's tomb) .. 5 5
1574. 40 c. Allegory of the centaurs 8 8
1575. 75 c. Allegory of the swans 15 12
1576. 1 cor. Roman triumphal march 15 12
1577. 2 cor. St. Francis and the wolf 30 25
1578. 5 cor. "Faith" opposing "Death" 65 55

119. "Megalura peleus".

1967. Air. Butterflies. Multicoloured.
1580. 5 c. "Heliconus petiverana" 5 5
1581. 10 c. "Colaenis julia" .. 5 5
1582. 15 c. Type **119** .. 5 5
1583. 20 c. "Ancyluris jurgensii" 5 5
1584. 25 c. "Thecla regalis" .. 5 5
1585. 30 c. "Doriana thia" .. 5 5
1586. 35 c. "Lymnias pixa" .. 8 5
1587. 40 c. "Metamorpho dido" 10 5
1588. 50 c. "Papilio arcas" .. 10 8
1589. 60 c. "Ananea cleomestra" 12 10
1590. 1 cor. "Vicorina epaphaus" 20 15
1591. 2 cor. "Prepona demophon" 35 25
The 5, 10, 30, 35, 50 c. and 1 cor. are vert.

120. McDivitt and White.

1967. Air. Space Flight of McDivitt and White. Multicoloured.
1592. 5 c. Type **120** 5 5
1593. 10 c. Astronauts and "Gemini 5" on launching pad.. .. 5 5
1594. 15 c. "Gemini 5" and White in Space .. 5 5
1595. 20 c. Recovery operation at sea 5 5
1596. 35 c. Type **120** 5 5
1597. 40 c. As 10 c. 8 8
1598. 75 c. As 15 c. 12 12
1599. 1 cor. As 20 c. 15 15

121. National Flower of Costa Rica.

1967. Air. Central American Economic Integration. 5th Year. Designs showing National Flowers of the Central-American Countries. Multicoloured.
1600. 40 c. Type **121** 8 5
1601. 40 c. Guatemala .. 8 5
1602. 40 c. Honduras 8 5
1603. 40 c. Nicaragua .. 8 5
1604. 40 c. Salvador 8 5

122. Presidents Diaz and Somoza. **123.** Mangoes.

1968. Air. Visit of Pres. Diaz of Mexico.
1605. – 20 c. black 8 5
1606. **122.** 40 c. olive 10 5
1607. – 1 cor. brown.. .. 20 12
DESIGNS—VERT. 20 c. Pres. Somoza greeting Pres. Diaz. 1 cor. Pres. Diaz of Mexico.

1968. Surch. **RESELLO** and value.
1608. – 5 c. on 6 c. (No. 1180) (postage) 5 5
1609. – 5 c. on 6 c. (No. 1471)
1610. – 5 c. on 6 c. (No. 1424) (air) 5 5
1611. – 5 c. on 6 c. (No. 1489) 5 5
1612. **49.** 5 c. on 8 c. (No. 1035) 5 5
1614. – 1 cor. on 1 cor. 50 (No. 1369) 12 12
See also Nos. 1448/9, 1498/1500a, 1569/70 and 1669/76.

1968. Air. Nicaraguan Fruits. Multicoloured.
1615. 5 c. Type **123** 5 5
1616. 10 c. Pineapples .. 5 5
1617. 15 c. Oranges 5 5
1618. 20 c. Pawpaws 5 5
1619. 30 c. Bananas 5 5
1620. 35 c. Avocado pears .. 8 5
1621. 50 c. Water-melons .. 10 5
1622. 75 c. Cashews 15 10
1623. 1 cor. Sapodilla plums .. 20 12
1624. 2 cor. Cocoa beans .. 35 25

124. "The Crucifixion" (Fra Angelico).

1968. Air. Religious Paintings. Multicoloured.
1625. 10 c. Type **124** 5 5
1626. 15 c. "The Last Judgement" (Michelangelo).. .. 5 5
1627. 35 c. "The Beautiful Gardener" (Raphael) .. 8 8
1628. 2 cor. "The Spoilation of Christ" (El Greco) .. 35 35
1629. 3 cor. "The Conception" (Murillo) 50 50
Nos. 1626/9 are vert.

1968. Air. Pope Paul's Visit to Bogota. Nos. 1625/8 optd. **Visita de S. S. Paulo VI C. E. de Bogota 1968.**
1631. **124.** 10 c. multicoloured 5 5
1632. – 15 c. multicoloured 5 5
1633. – 35 c. multicoloured 8 5
1634. – 2 cor. multicoloured 35 30

125. Basketball.

1969. Air. Olympic Games, Mexico. Multicoloured.
1635. 10 c. Type **125** 5 5
1636. 15 c. Fencing 5 5
1637. 20 c. High-diving .. 5 5
1638. 35 c. Running 5 5
1639. 50 c. Hurdling 8 5
1640. 75 c. Weightlifting .. 12 8
1641. 1 cor. Boxing 15 10
1642. 2 cor. Football 30 20
The 15 c., 50 c. and 1 cor. are horiz.

126. " Cichlasoma citrinellum ".

1969. Air. Fishes. Multicoloured.
1644. 10 c. Type **126** 5 5
1645. 15 c. " Cichlasoma nicaraguensis " 5 5
1646. 20 c. " Cyprinus carpio " (carp) 5 5
1647. 30 c. " Lepisosteus tropicus " (gar) 5 5
1648. 35 c. " Xiphias gladius " (swordfish) 8 5
1649. 50 c. "Phylipnus dormitor" 10 8
1650. 75 c. " Tarpon atlanticus " (tarpon) 15 10
1651. 1 cor. " Eulamia nicaraguensis " 30 20
1652. 2 cor "Istiophorus albicans" (sailfish) 45 30
1653. 3 cor. "Pristis antiquorum" (sawfish) .. .. 1·10 80
Nos. 1649/53 are vert.

1969. Air. Various stamps surch. **RESELLO** and value.
1655. 10 c. on 25 c. (No. 1507) .. 5 5
1656. 10 c. on 25 c. (No. 1512) .. 5 5
1657. 15 c. on 25 c. (No. 1529) .. 5 5
1658. 50 c. on 70 c. (No. 1379) .. 8 5

127. Scenery, Tower and Emblem.
128. " Minerals ".

1969. Air. " Hemisfair " (1968) Exn.
1659. **127.** 30 c. ultram. and red 5 5
1660. 35 c. purple and red 8 5
1661. 75 c. red and ultram. 12 8
1662. 1 cor. purple and black 15 10
1663. 2 cor. purple and green 30 20

1969. Various stamps, surch.
(a) Optd. **CORREO.**
1665. 5 c. (No. 1450) 5 5
1666. 5 c. (No. 1453) 5 5
1667. 5 c. (No. 1454) 5 5
1668. 5 c. (No. 1459) 5 5

(b) Optd. **RESELLO** and surch.
1669. 10 c. on 30 c. (No. 1324) .. 5 5
1670. 10 c. on 30 c. (No. 1427) .. 5 5
1671. 10 c. on 25 c. (No. 1529) .. 5 5
1672. 10 c. on 30 c. (No. 1530) .. 5 5
1673. 15 c. on 35 c. (No. 1531) .. 5 5
1674. 20 c. on 30 c. (No. 1307) .. 5 5
1675. 20 c. on 30 c. (No. 1401) .. 5 5
1676. 20 c. on 35 c. (No. 1509) .. 5 5

1969. Air. Nicaraguan Products. Multicoloured.
1677. 5 c. Type **128** 5 5
1678. 10 c. " Fish " 5 5
1679. 15 c. " Bananas " 5 5
1680. 20 c. " Timber " 5 5
1681. 35 c. " Coffee " 5 5
1682. 40 c. "Sugar-cane" 8 5
1683. 60 c. " Cotton " 10 8
1684. 75 c. " Rice and Maize " 12 10
1685. 1 cor. " Tobacco " .. 15 12
1686. 2 cor. " Meat " 30 25

1969. Int. Labour Organization. 50th Anniv. Obligatory tax stamps, Nos. 1450/9, optd., **O.I.T. 1919-1969.**
1687. 5 c. multicoloured .. 5 5
1688. 5 c. multicoloured .. 5 5
1689. 5 c. multicoloured .. 5 5
1690. 5 c. multicoloured .. 5 5
1691. 5 c. multicoloured .. 5 5
1692. 5 c. multicoloured .. 5 5
1693. 5 c. multicoloured .. 5 5
1694. 5 c. multicoloured .. 5 5
1695. 5 c. multicoloured .. 5 5
1696. 5 c. multicoloured .. 5 5
The above stamps are listed in the same order as Nos. 1450/9.

129. Girl carrying "Tinaja".
130. Pele (Brazil).

1970. Air. 8th Inter-American Savings and Loans Conf., Managua.
1697. **129.** 10 c. multicoloured .. 5 5
1698. 15 c. multicoloured 5 5
1699. 20 c. multicoloured .. 5 5
1700. 35 c. multicoloured .. 5 5
1701. 50 c. multicoloured 8 5
1702. 75 c. multicoloured 12 10
1703. 1 cor. multicoloured 15 12
1704. 2 cor. multicoloured 30 25

1970. World Football "Hall of Fame". Poll-winners. Multicoloured.
1705. 5 c. Type **130** (postage) .. 5 5
1706. 10 c. Puskas (Hungary) 5 5
1707. 15 c. Matthews (England) 5 5
1708. 40 c. Di Stefano (Argentina) 8 5
1709. 2 cor. Facchetti (Italy) .. 30 25
1710. 3 cor. Yashin (Russia) .. 45 35
1711. 5 cor. Beckenbauer (West Germany) 75 60
1712. 20 c. Santos (Brazil) (air) 5 5
1713. 80 c. Wright (England) .. 12 10
1714. 1 cor. Flags of 16 World Cup Finalists 15 12
1715. 4 cor. Bozsik (Hungary) 65 50
1716. 5 cor. Charlton (England) 75 60

131. Torii Gate.
132. Module and Astronauts on Moon.

1970. Air. EXPO 70, World Fair, Osaka, Japan.
1717. **131.** 25 c. multicoloured .. 5 5
1718. 30 c. multicoloured .. 5 5
1719. 35 c. multicoloured .. 8 5
1720. 75 c. multicoloured .. 12 10
1721. 1 cor. 50 multicoloured 25 20
1722. 3 cor. multicoloured 45 35

1970. Air. " Apollo 11 " Moon Landing. Multicoloured.
1724. 35 c. Type **132** 5 5
1725. 40 c. Module landing on Moon 8 5
1726. 60 c. Astronauts with U.S. Flag 10 8
1727. 75 c. As 40 c. 12 10
1728. 1 cor. As 60 c. .. 15 12
1729. 2 cor. Type **132** 30 25

133. F. D. Roosevelt.
134. "The Annunciation" (Grunewald).

1970. Air. Franklin D. Roosevelt. 25th Death Anniv.
1730. **133.** 10 c. black .. 5 5
1731. – 15 c. brown and black 5 5
1732. – 20 c. green & black 5 5
1733. **133.** 35 c. purple & black 8 5
1734. – 50 c. brown .. 10 8
1735. **133.** 75 c. blue 12 10
1736. – 1 cor. red 15 12
1737. – 2 cor. black 30 25
PORTRAITS. 15 c., 1 cor. Roosevelt with stamp collection. 20 c., 50 c., 2 cor. Roosevelt (full-face).

1970. Air. Christmas. Paintings. Multicoloured.
1738. 10 c. Type **134** 5 5
1739. 10 c. " The Nativity " (detail, El Greco) .. 5 5
1740. 10 c. " The Adoration of the Magi " (detail, Durer) 5 5
1741. 10 c. " Virgin and Child " (J. van Hemessen) .. 5 5
1742. 10 c. " The Holy Shepherd " (Portuguese School, 16th cent.) 5 5
1743. 15 c. Type **134** .. 5 5
1744. 20 c. As No. 1739 .. 5 5
1745. 35 c. As No. 1740 .. 8 5
1746. 75 c. As No. 1741 .. 12 10
1747. 1 cor. As No. 1742 .. 15 12

1971. Surch. **RESELLO** and new value.
1748. 30 c. on 90 c. black (No. 1227) (postage) .. ..
1749. 10 c. on 1 cor. 5 carmine, blk. & red (No. 1368) (air)
1750. 10 c. on 1 cor. 5 mult. (No. 1407) .. ..
1751. 10 c. on 1 cor. 5 mult. (No. 1430) .. ..
1752. 15 c. on 1 cor. 50 green and red (No. 1116)
1753. 15 c. on 1 cor. 50 green (No. 1255) ..
1754. 15 c. on 1 cor. 50 yellow and blue (No. 1369) ..
1755. 15 c. on 1 cor. 50 black and violet (No. 1381) ..
1756. 20 c. on 85 c. black and red (No. 1276) .. ..
1757. 20 c. on 85 c. black, red and blue (No. 1339) ..
1758. 25 c. on 90 c. black, green and ochre (No. 1440) ..
1759. 30 c. on 1 cor. 10 black and purple (No. 1195) ..
1760. 40 c. on 1 cor. 10 brown and black (No. 1157) ..
1761. 40 c. on 1 cor. 50 mult. (No. 1408) ..
1762. 1 cor. on 1 cor. 10 black and blue (No. 1538) ..

135. Basic Mathematical Equation.

1971. Scientific Formulae. "The Ten Mathematical Equations that changed the Face of the Earth". Multicoloured.
1763. 10 c. Type **135** (postage) 5 5
1764. 15 c. Newton's Law .. 5 5
1765. 20 c. Einstein's Law .. 5 5
1766. 1 cor. Tsiolkovsky's Law 15 12
1767. 2 cor. Maxwell's Law .. 30 25
1768. 25 c. Napier's Law (air) .. 5 5
1769. 30 c. Pythagoras' Law .. 8 5
1770. 40 c. Boltzmann's Law .. 10 8
1771. 1 cor. Broglie's Law .. 15 12
1772. 2 cor. Archimedes' Law .. 30 25

136. Peace Emblem.

1971. " Is There a Formula for Peace? ".
1773. **136.** 10 c. blue and black .. 5 5
1774. 15 c. blue, blk. & vio. 5 5
1775. 20 c. blue, blk. & brn. 5 5
1776. 40 c. blue, blk. & grn. 8 5
1777. 50 c. blue, blk. & pur. 10 8
1778. 80 c. blue, blk. & red 12 10
1779. 1 cor. blue, blk. & grn. 15 12
1780. 2 cor. blue, blk. & vio. 30 25

MINIMUM PRICE

The minimum price quoted is 5p which represents a handling charge rather than a basis for valuing common stamps. For further notes about prices see introductory pages.

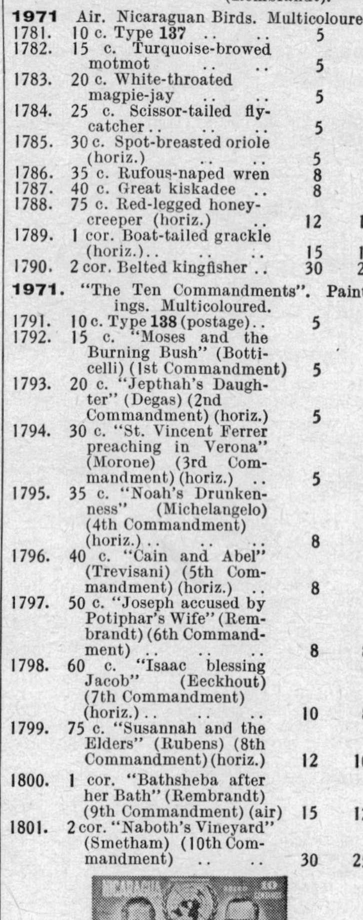
137. Montezuma Oropendola.
138. " Moses with the Tablets of the Law " (Rembrandt).

1971 Air. Nicaraguan Birds. Multicoloured.
1781. 10 c. Type **137** 5 5
1782. 15 c. Turquoise-browed motmot 5 5
1783. 20 c. White-throated magpie-jay 5 5
1784. 25 c. Scissor-tailed fly-catcher 5 5
1785. 30 c. Spot-breasted oriole (horiz.) 5 5
1786. 35 c. Rufous-naped wren 8 5
1787. 40 c. Great kiskadee .. 8 5
1788. 75 c. Red-legged honey-creeper (horiz.) .. 12 10
1789. 1 cor. Boat-tailed grackle (horiz.) 15 12
1790. 2 cor. Belted kingfisher .. 30 25

1971. "The Ten Commandments". Paintings. Multicoloured.
1791. 10 c. Type **138** (postage) .. 5 5
1792. 15 c. "Moses and the Burning Bush" (Botticelli) (1st Commandment) 5 5
1793. 20 c. "Jepthah's Daughter" (Degas) (2nd Commandment) (horiz.) 5 5
1794. 30 c. "St. Vincent Ferrer preaching in Verona" (Morone) (3rd Commandment) (horiz.) .. 5 5
1795. 35 c. "Noah's Drunkenness" (Michelangelo) (4th Commandment) (horiz.) 8 5
1796. 40 c. "Cain and Abel" (Trevisani) (5th Commandment) (horiz.) .. 8 5
1797. 50 c. "Joseph accused by Potiphar's Wife" (Rembrandt) (6th Commandment) 8 8
1798. 60 c. "Isaac blessing Jacob" (Eeckhout) (7th Commandment) (horiz.) 10 8
1799. 75 c. "Susannah and the Elders" (Rubens) (8th Commandment) (horiz.) 12 10
1800. 1 cor. "Bathsheba after her Bath" (Rembrandt) (9th Commandment) (air) 15 12
1801. 2 cor. "Naboth's Vineyard" (Smetham) (10th Commandment) 30 25

139. U Thant and Pres. Somoza.

1971. Air. United Nations. 25th Anniv.
1802. **139.** 10 c. brown and red .. 5 5
1803. 15 c. green and emerald 5 5
1804. 20 c. blue & light blue 5 5
1805. 25 c. red and purple .. 5 5
1806. 30 c. brown & orange 5 5
1807. 40 c. green and grey 8 5
1808. 1 cor. green & sage-grn. 15 12
1809. 2 cor. brn. & light brn. 30 25

1972. Olympic Games, Munich. Nos. 1709, 1711, 1713 and 1716 surch. **OLIMPIADAS MUNICH 1972,** emblem and value or optd. only (5 cor.).
1810. 40 c. on 2 cor. multicoloured (postage) .. 5 5
1811. 50 c. on 3 cor. mult. .. 8 5
1812. 20 c. on 80 c. mult. (air) 5 5
1813. 60 c. on 4 cor. mult. .. 8 5
1814. 5 cor. multicoloured .. 65 60

140. Figurine and Apoyo Site on Map.

1972. Air. Pre-Columbian Art A. H. Heller's Pottery Discoveries. Multicoloured.

1815. 10 c. Type **140** 5 5
1816. 15 c. Cana Castilla .. 5 5
1817. 20 c. Catarina 5 5
1818. 25 c. Santa Helena .. 5 5
1819. 30 c. Mombacho .. 5 5
1820. 35 c. Tisma 5 5
1821. 40 c. El Menco 5 5
1822. 50 c. Los Placeres .. 8 5
1823. 60 c. Masaya 10 8
1824. 80 c. Granada 12 10
1825. 1 cor. Las Mercedes .. 15 12
1826. 2 cor. Nindiri 30 25

141. "Lord Peter Wimsey" (Dorothy Sayers).

1972. Air. International Criminal Police Organization (INTERPOL). 50th Anniv. Famous Fictional Detectives. Mult.

1827. 5 c. Type **141** 5 5
1828. 10 c. "Philip Marlow" (Raymond Chandler) 5 5
1829. 15 c. "Sam Spade" (D. Hammett) 5 5
1830. 20 c. "Perry Mason" (Erle Stanley Gardner) 5 5
1831. 25 c. "Nero Wolfe" (Rex Stout) 5 5
1832. 35 c. "C. Auguste Dupin" (Edgar Allen Poe) .. 5 5
1833. 40 c. "Ellery Queen" (F. Dannay and M. Lee) 5 5
1834. 50 c. "Father Brown" (G. K. Chesterton) .. 8 5
1835. 60 c. "Charlie Chan" (Earl D. Biggers) .. 10 8
1836. 80 c. "Inspector Maigret" (Georges Simenon) .. 12 10
1837. 1 cor. "Hercule Poirot" (Agatha Christie) .. 15 12
1838. 2 cor. "Sherlock Holmes" (A. Conan Doyle) .. 30 25

142. "The Shepherdess and her Brothers".

1972. Air. Christmas. Scenes from Legend of the Christmas Rose. Multicoloured.

1839. 10 c. Type **142** 5 5
1840. 15 c. Adoration of the Wise Men 5 5
1841. 20 c. Shepherdess crying 5 5
1842. 35 c. Angel appears to Shepherdess 5 5
1843. 40 c. Christmas Rose .. 5 5
1844. 60 c. Shepherdess thanks angel for roses.. .. 10 8
1845. 80 c. Shepherdess takes roses to Holy Child .. 12 10
1846. 1 cor. Holy Child receiving roses 15 12
1847. 2 cor. Nativity Scene .. 30 25

143. Sir Walter Raleigh and Ship.

1973. Air. Causes of the American Revolution. Multicoloured.

1849. 10 c. Type **143** 5 5
850. 15 c. Signing "Mayflower Compact" 5 5
1851. 20 c. Acquittal of Peter Zenger (vert.) 5 5
1852. 25 c. Acclaiming American resistance (vert.) .. 5 5
1853. 30 c. Revenue Stamp (vert.) 5 5
1854. 35 c. "Serpent" slogan—"Join or die" 5 5
1855. 40 c. Boston massacre (vert.) 5 5
1856. 50 c. Boston Tea-party .. 8 5
1857. 60 c. Patrick Henry on trial (vert.) 10 8
1858. 75 c. Battle of Bunker Hill 10 8
1859. 80 c. Declaration of Independence 12 10
1860. 1 cor. Liberty Bell .. 15 12
1861. 2 cor. US seal (vert.) .. 30 25

1973. Nos. 1450/54, 1456 and 1458/9 optd. **CORREO.**

1862. **100.** 5 c. multicoloured .. 15 5
1863. – 5 c. multicoloured .. 15 5
1864. – 5 c. multicoloured .. 15 5
1865. – 5 c. multicoloured .. 15 5
1866. – 5 c. multicoloured .. 15 5
1867. – 5 c. multicoloured .. 15 5
1868. – 5 c. multicoloured .. 15 5
1869. – 5 c. multicoloured .. 15 5

144. Baseball, Player and Map. **145.** Givenchy, Paris.

1973. Air. 20th Int., Baseball Championships, Managua (1972).

1870. **144.** 15 c. multicoloured.. 5 5
1871. 20 c. multicoloured.. 5 5
1872. 40 c. multicoloured.. 5 5
1873. 10 cor. multicoloured 1·50 1·25

1973. World-famous Couturiers. Mannequins. Multicoloured.

1875. 1 cor. Type **145** (postage) 15 12
1876. 2 cor. Hartnell, London 25 20
1877. 5 cor. Balmain, Paris .. 65 60
1878. 10 c. Lourdes, Nicaragua (air) 5 5
1879. 15 c. Halston, New York 5 5
1880. 20 c. Pino Lancetti, Rome 5 5
1881. 35 c. Madame Gres, Paris 5 5
1882. 40 c. Irene Galitzene, Rome 5 5
1883. 80 c. Pedro Rodriguez, Barcelona 10 8

146. Diet Chart.

1973. Air. Child Welfare. Multicoloured.

1885. 5 c.+5 c. Type **146** .. 5 5
1886. 10 c.+5 c. Senora Somoza with baby, and Children's Hospital 5 5
1887. 15 c.+5 c. "Childbirth" 5 5
1888. 20 c.+5 c. "Immunisation" 5 5
1889. 30 c.+5 c. Water purification.. .. .. 5 5
1890. 35 c.+5 c. As No. 1886.. 5 5
1891 50 c.+10 c. Alexander Fleming and "Antibiotics" 8 5
1892. 60 c.+15 c. Malaria control 10 8
1893. 70 c.+10 c. Laboratory analysis 10 8
1894. 80 c.+20 c. Gastro-enteritis 15 12
1895. 1 cor.+50 c. As No. 1886 20 15
1896. 2 cor. Pediatric surgery.. 25 20

147. Virginia and Father.

1973. Christmas. "Does Santa Clause exist?" (Virginia O'Hanlon's letter to American "Sun" newspaper). Multicoloured.

1897. 2 c. Type **147** (postage).. 5 5
1898. 3 c. Text of letter .. 5 5
1899. 4 c. Reading the reply .. 5 5
1900. 5 c. Type **147** 5 5
1901. 15 c. As 3 c. 5 5
1902. 20 c. As 4 c. 5 5
1903. 1 cor. Type **147** (air) .. 15 2
1904. 2 cor. As 3 c. 30 5
1905. 4 cor. As 4 c. 60 50

148. Churchill making Speech, 1936.

1974. Sir Winston Churchill. Birth Cent.

1907. **148.** 2 c. mult. (postage).. 5 5
1908. – 3 c. blk., bl. & brn... 5 5
1909. – 4 c. multicoloured .. 5 5
1910. – 5 c. multicoloured .. 5 5
1911. – 10 c. brn., grn. & bl. 5 5
1912. – 5 cor. mult. (air) .. 65 60
1913. – 6 cor. blk. brn. & bl. 90 80

DESIGNS: 3 c. "The Four Churchills" (wartime cartoon). 4 c. Candle, cigar and "Action" stickers. 5 c. Churchill, Roosevelt and Stalin at Yalta. 10 c. Churchill landing in Normandy, 1944. 5 cor. Churchill giving "V" sign. 6 cor. "Bulldog Churchill" (cartoon).

149. Presentation of World Cup to Uruguay, 1930.

1974. World Cup Football Championships. Multicoloured.

1915. 1 c. Type **149** (postage).. 5 5
1916. 2 c. Victorious Italian team, 1934 .. .. 5 5
1917. 3 c. Presentation of World Cup to Italy, 1938 .. 5 5
1918. 4 c. Uruguay's winning goal, 1950 .. .. 5 5
1919. 5 c. Victorious West German team, 1954 .. 5 5
1920. 10 c. Rejoicing Brazilian players, 1958 .. .. 5 5
1921. 15 c. Brazilian player holding World Cup, 1962 .. 5 5
1922. 20 c. Queen Elizabeth II presenting Cup to Bobby Moore, 1966 .. 5 5
1923. 25 c. Victorious Brazilian players, 1970 .. .. 5 5
1924. 10 cor. Football and flags of participating countries, 1974 (air) .. 1·25 1·10

150. "Malachra sp.". **151.** Nicaraguan 7½ c. Stamp of 1938.

1974. Wild Flowers and Cacti. Multicoloured.

1926. 2 c. Type **150** (postage).. 5 5
1927. 3 c. "Paguira insignis" .. 5 5
1928. 4 c. "Convolvulus sp." .. 5 5
1929. 5 c. "Pereschia autumnalis" 5 5
1930. 10 c. "Ipomea tuberosa" 5 5
1931. 15 c. "Hibiscus elatus" .. 5 5
1932. 20 c. "Plumeria acutifolia" 5 5
1933. 1 cor. "Centrosema sp." (air) 15 12
1934. 3 cor. "Hylocereus undatus" 50 0

1974. Universal Postal Union. Cent.

1935. **151.** 2 c. red, grn. & blk. (post.) 5 5
1936. – 3 c. bl., grn. & blk.— 5 5
1937. – 4 c. multicoloured .. 5 5
1938. – 5 c. brn., mve. & blk. 5 5
1939. – 10 c. red, brn. & blk. 5 5
1940. – 20 c. grn., bl. & blk. 5 5
1941. – 40 c. multicoloured (air) 5 5
1942. – 3 cor. grn., blk. & pink 50 40
1943. – 5 cor. bl., blk. & lilac 65 60

DESIGNS—VERT. 3 c. 5 c. stamp of 1938. 5c. 2 c. stamp of 1938. 10 c. 1 c. stamp of 1938. 20 c. ½ c. stamp of 1938. 40 c. 10 c. stamp of 1961. 5 cor. 4 cor. U.P.U. stamp of 1950. HORIZ. 4 c. 10 c. air stamp of 1934. 3 cor. 85 c. U.P.U. air stamp of 1950.

1974. Air. West Germany's Victory in World Cup Football Championships. No. 1924 optd. **TRIUMFADOR ALEMANIA OCCIDENTAL.**

1945. 10 cor. multicoloured .. 1·25 1·10

152. Four-toed Sloth.

1974. Nicaraguan Fauna. Multicoloured.

1947. 1 c. Type **152** (postage).. 5 5
1948. 2 c. Puma 5 5
1949. 3 c. Raccoon 5 5
1950. 4 c. Ocelot 5 5
1951. 5 c. Kinkajou 5 5
1952. 10 c. Coypu 5 5
1953. 15 c. Tajacu (wild pig) .. 5 5
1954. 20 c. Tapir 5 5
1955. 3 cor. Colorado deer (air) 50 40
1956. 5 cor. Jaguar 65 60

153. "Prophet Zacharias" (Michelangelo). **154.** Giovanni Martinelli ("Othello").

1975. Christmas. Michelangelo. 500th Birth Anniv. Multicoloured.

1957. 1 c. Type **153** (postage).. 5 5
1958. 2 c. "Christ amongst the Jews" 5 5
1959. 3 c. "The Creation of Man" (horiz.) .. 5 5
1960. 4 c. Interior of Sistine Chapel, Rome 5 5
1961. 5 c. "Moses" 5 5
1962. 10 c. "Mouscron Madonna" 5 5
1963. 15 c. "David" 5 5
1964. 20 c. "Doni Madonna" 5 5
1965. 50 c. "Madonna of the Staircase" (air) .. 8 5
1966. 80 c. "Pitti Madonna" 12 10
1967. 2 cor. "Christ and Virgin Mary" 30 25
1968. 5 cor. "Michelangelo" (self-portrait) 70 65

1975. Great Opera Singers. Multicoloured.

1970. 1 c. **154** (postage) .. 5 5
1971. 2 c. Tito Gobbi ("Simon Boccanegra") 5 5
1972. 3 c. Lotte Lehmann ("Der Rosenkavalier") .. 5 5
1973. 4 c. Lauritz Melchior ("Parsifal") 5 5
1974. 5 c. Nellie Melba ("La Traviata") 5 5
1975. 15 c. Jussi Bjoerling ("La Boheme") 5 5
1976. 20 c. Birgit Nilsson ("Turandot") .. 5 5
1977. 25 c. Rosa Ponselle ("Norma") (air) .. 5 5
1978. 35 c. Guiseppe de Luca ("Rigoletto") .. 5 5
1979. 40 c. Joan Sutherland ("La Figlia del Reggimento") 5 5
1980. 50 c. Ezio Pinza ("Don Giovanni") 8 5
1981. 60 c. Kirsten Flagstad ("Tristan and Isolde") 8 5
1982. 80 c. Maria Callas ("Tosca") 12 10
1983. 2 cor. Fyodor Chaliapin ("Boris Godunov") .. 30 25
1984. 5 cor. Enrico Caruso ("La Juive") 70 65

155. The First Station. **156.** "The Spirit of 76".

1975. Easter. The 14 Stations of the Cross.

1986. **155.** 1 c. mult. (postage).. 5 5
1987. – 2 c. multicoloured .. 5 5
1988. – 3 c. multicoloured .. 5 5
1989. – 4 c. multicoloured .. 5 5
1990. – 5 c. multicoloured .. 5 5
1991. – 15 c. multicoloured .. 5 5
1992. – 20 c. multicoloured .. 5 5
1993. – 25 c. multicoloured .. 5 5
1994. – 35 c. multicoloured.. 5 5
1995. – 40 c. mult. (air) .. 5 5
1996. – 50 c. multicoloured .. 8 5
1997. – 80 c. multicoloured .. 12 10
1998. – 1 cor. multicoloured 15 12
1999. – 5 cor. multicoloured 70 65

DESIGNS: 2 c. to 5 cor. Different Stations of the Cross.

1975. American Independence. Bicentenary. Multicoloured.

2000. 1 c. Type **156** (postage).. 5 5
2001. 2 c. Pitt addressing Parliament 5 5
2002. 3 c. Paul Revere's Ride (horiz.) 5 5
2003. 4 c. Demolishing statue of George III (horiz.) .. 5 5
2004. 5 c. Boston Massacre .. 5 5

2005. 10 c. Tax stamp and George III 3d. coin (horiz.) 5 5
2006. 15 c. Boston Tea Party (horiz.) 5 5
2007. 20 c. Thomas Jefferson .. 5 5
2008. 25 c. Benjamin Franklin 5 5
2009. 30 c. Signing of Declaration of Independence (horiz.) 5 5
2010. 35 c. Surrender of Cornwallis at Yorktown (horiz.) 5 5
2011. 40 c. Washington's Farewell (horiz.) (air) 5 5
2012. 50 c. Washington addressing Congress (horiz.) .. 8 5
2013. 2 cor. Washington arriving for Presidential Inauguration (horiz.) 30 25
2014. 5 cor. Statue of Liberty & flags 70 65

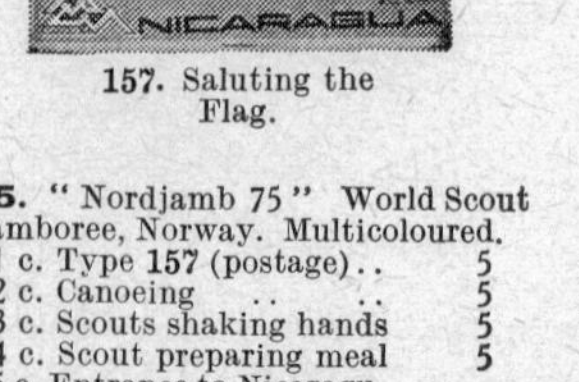

157. Saluting the Flag.

1975. " Nordjamb 75 " World Scout Jamboree, Norway. Multicoloured.

2016. 1 c. Type **157** (postage) .. 5 5
2017. 2 c. Canoeing 5 5
2018. 3 c. Scouts shaking hands 5 5
2019. 4 c. Scout preparing meal 5 5
2020. 5 c. Entrance to Nicaraguan camp 5 5
2021. 20 c. Scouts meeting .. 5 5
2022. 35 c. Aerial view of camp (air) 5 5
2023. 40 c. Scouts making music 5 5
2024. 1 cor. Camp-fire .. 15 12
2025. 10 cor. Lord Baden-Powell 1·40 1·25

158. President Somoza.

159. " Chess-players " (L. Carracci).

1975. President Somoza's New Term of Office, 1974-1981.

2027. **158.** 20 c. mult. (postage) 5 5
2028. 40 c. multicoloured .. 5 5
2029. **158.** 1 cor. mult. (air) .. 15 12
2030. 10 cor. multicoloured 1·40 1·25
2031. 20 cor. multicoloured 2·75 2·50

1975. Chess. Multicoloured.

2032. 1 c. Type **159** (postage) .. 5 5
2033. 2 c. "Arabs playing Chess" (Delacroix) 5 5
2034. 3 c. " Cardinals playing Chess " (V. Marais-Milton) 5 5
2035. 4 c. "Albrecht V and Anna of Austria at Chess" (H. Muelich) (vert.) .. 5 5
2036. 5 c. " Chess game " (Persian manuscript) .. 5 5
2037. 10 c. " Origins of Chess " (India, 1602) 5 5
2038. 15 c. " Napoleon playing Chess in Schonbrunn Palace " (A. Uniechowski) (vert.) 5 5
2039. 20 c. " Chess game " (J. E. Hummel) 5 5
2040. 40 c. "The Chess-players" (T. Eakins) (air) .. 5 5
2041. 2 cor. Fischer-Spasski match, Reykjavik (1972) 30 25
2042. 5 cor. " Shakespeare and Ben Jonson playing Chess " (K. van Mander) 70 65

160. Choir of King's College Cambridge.

1975. Christmas. Famous Choirs. Mult.

2044. 1 c. Type **160** (postage) .. 5 5
2045. 2 c. Abbey Choir, Einsiedeln 5 5
2046. 3 c. Regensburg Cathedral choir 5 5
2047. 4 c. Vienna Boys' choir .. 5 5
2048. 5 c. Sistine Chapel choir .. 5 5
2049. 15 c. Westminster Cathedral choir 5 5
2050. 20 c. Mormon Tabernacle choir 5 5
2051. 50 c. School choir, Montserrat (air) 8 5
2052. 1 cor. St. Florian children's choir 15 12
2053. 2 cor. " Little Singers of the Wooden Cross " (vert.) 30 25
2054. 5 cor. Pope with choristers of Pueri Cantores .. 70 65

161. " The Smoke Signal " (F. Remington).

1976. American Revolution. Bicent. " 200 Years of Progress ". Multicoloured.

2056. 1 c. Type **161** (postage) .. 5 5
2057. 1 c. Space Centre, Cape Kennedy 5 5
2058. 2 c. Lighting candelabra, 1776 .. .. 5 5
2059. 2 c. Edison's lamp and laboratory 5 5
2060. 3 c. " Agriculture 1776 " 5 5
2061. 3 c. " Agriculture 1976 " 5 5
2062. 4 c. Harvard College, 1776 5 5
2063. 4 c. Harvard University, 1976 .. .. .. 5 5
2064. 5 c. Horse and carriage .. 5 5
2065. 5 c. Boeing " 747 " airliner 5 5
2066. 80 c. Philadelphia, 1776 (air) 25 20
2067. 80 c. Washington, 1976 .. 25 20
2068. 2 cor. 75 John Paul Jones' flagship 95 90
2069. 2 cor. 75 Atomic submarine 95 90
2070. 4 cor. Wagon train .. 1·40 1·25
2071. 4 cor. " Amtrak " express train .. .. .. 1·40 1·25

162. Denmark, 1964.

1976. Olympic Games, Victors in Rowing and Sculling. Multicoloured.

2073. 1 c. Type **162** (postage) .. 5 5
2074. 2 c. East Germany 1972 5 5
2075. 3 c. Italy 1968 .. .. 5 5
2076. 4 c. Great Britain 1936 .. 5 5
2077. 5 c. France 1920 (vert.) .. 5 5
2078. 35 c. U.S.A. 1920 (vert.) 12 10
2097. 55 c. Russia 1956 (vert.) (air) 20 15
2080. 70 c. New Zealand 1972 (vert.) 25 20
2081. 90 c. New Zealand 1968 .. 30 25
2082. 20 cor. U.S.A. 1956 .. 6·50 6·00

1976. Air. Olympic Games, Montreal. East German Victory in Rowing Events. No. 2082 optd. **REPUBLICA DEMOCRATICA ALEMANA VENCEDOR EN 1976.**

2084. 20 cor. multicoloured .. 6·50 6·00

SILVER CURRENCY

The following were for use in all places on the Atlantic coast of Nicaragua where the silver currency was in use. This currency was worth about 50 c. to the peso. Earlier issues (overprints on Nicaraguan stamps) were also issued for Zelaya. These are listed in the Stanley Gibbons' Overseas Catalogue volume 3.

1.

1912.

Z 1. **1.** 1 c. green 25 25
Z 2. 2 c. red 12 12
Z 3. 3 c. brown 20 20
Z 4. 4 c. lake 15 15
Z 5. 5 c. blue 20 20
Z 6. 6 c. red 90 90
Z 7. 10 c. grey 15 15
Z 8. 15 c. lilac 12 12
Z 9. 20 c. blue 12 12
Z 10. 25 c. black & green .. 15 15
Z 11. 35 c. black & brown .. 20 20
Z 12. 50 c. green 20 20
Z 13. 1 p. orange 30 30
Z 14. 2 p. brown 85 85
Z 15. 5 p. green .. .. 1·40 1·40

OFFICIAL STAMPS

Overprinted **FRANQUEO OFICIAL.**

1890. Stamps of 1890.

O 37. **3.** 1 c. blue 5 20
O 38. 2 c. blue 5 20
O 39. 5 c. blue 5 25
O 40. 10 c. blue 5 25
O 41. 20 c. blue 5 25
O 42. 50 c. blue 5 35
O 43. 1 p. blue 5 50
O 44. 2 p. blue 5 75
O 45. 5 p. blue .. .. 5 1·40
O 46. 10 p. blue .. .. 5 2·25

1891. Stamps of 1891.

O 47. **4.** 1 c. green 5 25
O 48. 2 c. green 5 25
O 49. 5 c. green 5 25
O 50. 10 c. green 5 25
O 51. 20 c. green 5 35
O 52. 50 c. green 5 50
O 53. 1 p. green 5 65
O 54. 2 p. green 5 75
O 55. 5 p. green .. .. 5 1·10
O 56. 10 p. green .. .. 5 2·10

1892. Stamps of 1892.

O 57. **5.** 1 c. brown 5 15
O 58. 2 c. brown 5 15
O 59. 5 c. brown 5 15
O 60. 10 c. brown 5 15
O 61. 20 c. brown 5 15
O 62. 50 c. brown 5 35
O 63. 1 p. brown 5 55
O 64. 2 p. brown .. .. 5 1·10
O 65. 5 p. brown .. .. 5 1·25
O 66. 10 p. brown .. .. 5 2·10

1893. Stamps of 1893.

O 67. **6.** 1 c. black 5 15
O 68. 2 c. black 5 15
O 69. 5 c. black 5 15
O 70. 10 c. black 5 15
O 71. 20 c. black 5 15
O 72. 25 c. black 5 25
O 73. 50 c. black 5 30
O 74. 1 p. black 5 50
O 75. 2 p. black .. .. 5 1·10
O 76. 5 p. black .. .. 5 1·25
O 77. 10 p. black .. .. 5 2·25

1894. Stamps of 1894.

O 78. **7.** 1 c. orange 5 15
O 79. 2 c. orange 5 15
O 80. 5 c. orange 5 15
O 81. 10 c. orange 5 15
O 82. 20 c. orange 5 30
O 83. 50 c. orange 5 30
O 84. 1 p. orange 5 50
O 85. 2 p. orange .. .. 5 1·00
O 86. 5 p. orange .. .. 5 1·40
O 87. 10 p. orange .. .. 5 1·90

1895. Stamps of 1895.

O 88. **8.** 1 c. green 8 15
O 89. 2 c. green 8 15
O 90. 5 c. green 8 15
O 91. 10 c. green 8 15
O 92. 20 c. green 8 25
O 93. 50 c. green 8 40
O 94. 1 p. green 8 40
O 95. 2 p. green 8 80
O 96. 5 p. green .. .. 8 1·60
O 97. 10 p. green .. .. 8 2·00

1896. Stamps of 1896, dated "1896", optd. **FRANQUEO OFICIAL** in oval frame.

O 99. **9.** 1 c. red .. .. 1·25 1·60
O 100. 2 c. red .. .. 1·25 1·60
O 101. 5 c. red .. .. 1·25 1·60
O 102. 10 c. red .. .. 1·25 1·60
O 103. 20 c. red .. .. 1·50 1·60
O 104. 50 c. red .. .. 1·40 2·00
O 105. 1 p. red .. .. 4·00 4·00
O 106. 2 p. red .. .. 5·50 5·50
O 107. 5 p. red .. .. 6·00 6·00

1896. Nos. D 99/103 handstamped **Franqueo Oficial.**

O 108. **D 1.** 1 c. orange .. .. 2·25
O 109. 2 c. orange .. .. 2·25
O 110. 5 c. orange .. .. 1·75
O 111. 10 c. orange .. .. 1·75
O 112. 20 c. orange .. .. 1·75

1897. Stamps of 1897, dated "1897", optd **FRANQUEO OFICIAL** in oval frame.

O 113. **9.** 1 c. red .. .. 1·25 1·25
O 114. 2 c. red .. .. 1·25 1·25
O 115. 5 c. red .. .. 1·25 1·25
O 116. 10 c. red .. .. 1·40 1·40
O 117. 20 c. red .. .. 1·75 1·75
O 118. 50 c. red .. .. 2·25 2·25
O 119. 1 p. red .. .. 5·50 5·50
O 120. 2 p. red .. .. 5·50 5·50
O 121. 5 p. red .. .. 7·00 7·00

1898. Stamps of 1898 optd. **FRANQUEO OFICIAL** in oval frame.

O 124. **10.** 1 c. red .. .. 1·75 1·75
O 125. 2 c. red .. .. 1·75 1·75
O 126. 4 c. red .. .. 1·75 1·75
O 127. 5 c. red .. .. 1·25 1·25
O 128. 10 c. red .. .. 1·90 1·90
O 129. 15 c. red .. .. 2·75 2·75
O 130. 20 c. red .. .. 2·75 2·75
O 131. 50 c. red .. .. 3·75 3·75
O 132. 1 p. red .. .. 4·50 4·50
O 133. 2 p. red .. .. 5·00 5·00
O 134. 5 p. red .. .. 5·00 5·00

1899. Stamps of 1899 optd. **FRANQUEO OFICIAL** in scroll.

O 137. **11.** 1 c. green 5 40
O 138. 2 c. brown 5 40
O 139. 4 c. red 5 40
O 140. 5 c. blue 5 25
O 141. 10 c. orange 5 40
O 142. 15 c. brown 5 80
O 143. 20 c. green .. .. 5 1·25
O 144. 50 c. red .. .. 5 1·25
O 145. 1 p. orange .. .. 5 4·00
O 146. 2 p. violet .. .. 5 4·00
O 147. 5 p. blue .. .. 5 6·00

O 1

O 2.

1900.

O 148. **O 1.** 1 c. purple 25 25
O 149. 2 c. orange 20 20
O 150. 4 c. olive 25 25
O 151. 5 c. blue 50 20
O 152. 10 c. violet 50 20
O 153. 20 c. brown 40 20
O 154. 50 c. lake 60 20
O 155. 1 p. blue .. .. 1·60 1·25
O 156. 2 p. orange .. .. 1·90 1·90
O 157. 5 p. black .. .. 1·90 1·40

1903. Stamps of 1900 surch. **OFICIAL** and value, with or without ornaments.

O 197. **12.** 1 c. on 10 c. mauve 10 12
O 198. 2 c. on 3 c. green .. 12 15
O 199. 4 c. on 3 c. green .. 50 50
O 200. 4 c. on 10 c. mauve 50 50
O 201. 5 c. on 3 c. green .. 8 8

1903 Surch.

O 202. **O 1.** 10 c. on 20 c. brown 15 10
O 203. 30 c. on 20 c. brown 15 12
O 204. 50 c. on 20 c. brown 30 20

1905.

O 219. **O 2.** 1 c. green 10 10
O 220. 2 c. red 10 10
O 221. 5 c. blue 15 15
O 222. 10 c. brown 15 15
O 223. 20 c. orange 15 15
O 224. 50 c. olive 15 20
O 225. 1 p. lake 15 30
O 226. 2 p. violet 15 40
O 227. 5 p. black 15 55

1907. Surch. thus: **Vale 10 c.**

O 239. **O 2.** 10 c. on 1 c. green .. 50 40
O 241. 10 c. on 2 c. red .. 11·00 9·00
O 243. 20 c. on 2 c. red .. 10·00 7·00
O 245. 50 c. on 1c. green .. 90 60
O 247. 50 c. on 2 c. red .. 10·00 6·00

1907. Surch. thus: **Vale 20 cts** or **Vale $1.00.**

O 249. **O 2.** 20 c. on 2 c. green .. 70 40
O 250. $1 on 2 c. red .. 90 70
O 251. $2 on 2 c. red .. 90 80
O 252. $3 on 2 c. red .. 90 80
O 253. $4 on 5 c. blue .. 1·25 1·00

1907. No. 206 surch. **OFICIAL** and value.

O 256. **14.** 10 c. on 1 c. green .. 3·25 3·00
O 257. 15 c. on 1 c. green .. 3·25 3·00
O 258. 20 c. on 1 c. green .. 3·25 3·00
O 259. 50 c. on 1 c. green .. 3·25 3·00
O 260. 1 p. on 1 c. green .. 3·25 3·25
O 261. 2 p. on 1 c. green .. 3·25 3·25

1907. Fiscal stamps as T 16 surch. thus: **10 cts. CORREOS 1907 OFICIAL 10 cts.**

O 262. **16.** 10 c. on 2 c. orange .. 5 5
O 263. 35 c. on 1 c. blue .. 5 5
O 264. 70 c. on 1 c. blue .. 5 5
O 266. 1 p. on 2 c. orange .. 5 8
O 267. 2 p. on 2 c. orange .. 5 8
O 268. 3 p. on 5 c. brown .. 5 8
O 269. 4 p. on 5 c. brown .. 5 8
O 270. 5 p. on 5 c. brown .. 8 8

1907. Fiscal stamps as T 16 surch. as last but dated **1908.**

O 276. 16. 10 c. on 1 c. blue .. 30 20
O 277. 10 c. on 2 c. orange .. 45 25
O 278. 35 c. on 1 c. blue .. 30 20
O 279. 35 c. on 2 c. orange.. 45 25
O 280. 50 c. on 1 c. blue .. 30 20
O 281. 50 c. on 2 c. orange .. 45 25
O 282. 70 c. on 2 c. orange .. 45 25
O 283. 1 p. on 1 c. blue .. 13·00 12·00
O 284. 1 p. on 2 c. orange .. 45 25
O 285. 2 p. on 1 c. blue .. 45 30
O 286. 2 p. on 2 c. orange .. 50 30

1908. Stamp of 1905 surch. **OFICIAL VALE** and value.

O 271. 14. 10 c. on 3 c. violet .. 4·75 4·75
O 272. 15 c. on 3 c. violet .. 4·75 4·75
O 273. 20 c. on 3 c. violet .. 4·75 4·75
O 274. 35 c. on 3 c. violet .. 4·75 4·75
O 275. 50 c. on 3 c. violet .. 4·75 4·75

1909. Stamps of 1905 optd. **OFICIAL.**

O 290. 14. 10 c. lake 12 8
O 291. 15 c. black 35 30
O 292. 20 c. olive 60 40
O 293. 50 c. green 90 60
O 294. 1 p. yellow .. .. 1·00 70
O 295. 2 p. red .. .. 1·75 1·25

1911. Stamps of 1905 optd. **OFICIAL** and surch. **Vale** and value.

O 296. 14. 5 c. on 3 c. orange .. 2·40 2·40
O 297. 10 c. on 4 c. violet .. 2·00 2·00

1911. Railway coupon stamp surch. **Timber Fiscal Vale 10 ctvs** further surch. **Correo oficial Vale** and new value. Printed in red.

O 334. 17. 10 c. on 10 c. on 1 c. 45 45
O 335. 15 c. on 10 c. on 1 c. 45 45
O 336. 20 c. on 10 c. on 1 c. 45 45
O 337. 50 c. on 10 c. on 1 c. 60 60
O 338. $1 on 10 c. on 1 c. .. 85 85
O 339. $2 on 10 c. on 1 c. .. 1·60 1·60

1912. Railway stamp with postal surch. on back, cancelled, with thick bar and surch. **Correo Oficial 1912** and new value and bar. Printed in red

O 344. 17. 5 c. on 10 c. on 1 c. .. 1·00 1·25
O 345. 10 c. on 10 c. on 1 c. 1·00 1·25
O 346. 15 c. on 10 c. on 1 c. 1·25 1·40
O 347. 20 c. on 10 c. on 1 c. 1·40 1·90
O 353. 35 c. on 10 c. on 1 c. 1·60 1·90
O 354. 50 c. on 10 c. on 1 c. 1·60 1·90
O 355. $1 on 10 c. on 1 c. .. 1·60 1·90

1913. Stamps of 1912 optd. **OFICIAL.**

O 356. 19. 1 c. blue 5 5
O 357. 2 c. blue 5 5
O 358. 3 c. blue 5 5
O 359. 4 c. blue 5 5
O 360. 5 c. blue 5 8
O 361. 6 c. blue 5 10
O 362. 10 c. blue 5 10
O 363. 15 c. blue 5 10
O 364. 20 c. blue 8 12
O 365. 25 c. blue 10 15
O 366. 20. 35 c. blue 15 15
O 367. 19. 50 c. blue .. .. 1·25 1·40
O 368. 1 p. blue 20 25
O 369. 2 p. blue 20 25
O 370. 5 p. blue 30 40

1915. Optd. **OFICIAL.**

O 406. 21. 1 c. blue 8 8
O 407. 22. 2 c. blue 8 8
O 408. 21. 3 c. blue 15 8
O 409. 22. 4 c. blue 8 8
O 410. 21. 5 c. blue 8 8
O 411. 22. 6 c. blue 8 8
O 412. 10 c. blue 10 10
O 413. 21. 15 c. blue 12 12
O 414. 22. 20 c. blue 15 15
O 415. 21. 25 c. blue 15 15
O 416. 22. 50 c. blue 35 35

1925. Optd. **Oficial** or **OFICIAL.**

O 513. 21. ½ c. green 5 5
O 514. 1 c. violet 5 5
O 515. 22. 2 c. red 5 5
O 516. 21. 3 c. olive 5 5
O 517. 22. 4 c. red 5 5
O 518. 21. 5 c. black 5 5
O 519. 22. 6 c. brown 5 5
O 520. 10 c. yellow 5 5
O 521. 21. 15 c. brown 5 5
O 522. 22. 20 c. brown 5 5
O 523. 21. 25 c. orange 8 8
O 524. 22. 50 c. blue 10 10

1929. Air. Official stamps of 1925 additionally optd. **Correo Aereo.**

O 618. 21. 25 c. orange 20 20
O 619. 22. 50 c. blue 40 40

1931. Stamp of 1924 surch. **OFICIAL C$ 0.05 Correos 1928.**

O 651. 26. 5 c. on 10 c. brown .. 20 20

1931. No. 648 additionally surch. **OFICIAL** and value.

O 652. 26. 5 c. on 10 c. brown .. 15 20

1931. Stamps of 1914 optd. **1931** (except 6 c., 10 c.), and also optd **OFICIAL.**

O 670. 21. 1 c. olive (No. 762).. 10 10
O 707. 22. 2 c. red .. .. 3·50 3·50
O 671. 21. 3 c. blue 10 10
O 672. 5 c. sepia 10 10
O 673. 22. 6 c. brown 12 12
O 675. 10 c. brown 12 12
O 674. 10 c. blue (No. 697) 65 65
O 710. 21. 15 c. orange.. .. 50 50
O 711. 25 c. sepia 50 50
O 712. 25 c. violet .. .. 1·00 1·00

1932. Air. Optd. **Correo Aereo OFICIAL** only.

O 688. 21. 15 c. orange 30 30
O 689. 22. 20 c. orange 30 30
O 690. 21. 25 c. violet 30 30
O 691. 22. 50 c. green 50 60
O 692. 1 cor. yellow .. 80 80

1932. Air. Optd. **1931. Correo Aereo OFICIAL.**

O 693. 21. 25 c. sepia .. .. 20·00 20·00

1932. Optd. **OFICIAL.**

O 694. 21. 1 c. olive 5 5
O 695. 22. 2 c. red 5 5
O 696. 21. 3 c. blue 8 5
O 697. 22. 4 c. blue 8 5
O 698. 21. 5 c. Sepia 10 8
O 699. 22. 6 c. brown 12 5
O 700. 10 c. brown 20 12
O 701. 21. 15 c. orange 25 15
O 702. 22. 20 c. orange 40 30
O 703. 21. 25 c. violet .. .. 1·25 30
O 704. 22. 50 c. green 8 8
O 705. 1 cor. yellow 12 12

1933. Columbus's Departure from Palos 441st Anniv. As T 37, but inscr. "CORREO OFICIAL". Roul.

O 777. 1 c. orange 80 80
O 778. 2 c. yellow 80 80
O 779. 3 c. chocolate 80 80
O 780. 4 c. brown 80 80
O 781. 5 c. brown 80 80
O 782. 6 c. blue 80 80
O 783. 10 c. violet .. .. 1·00 1·00
O 784. 15 c. purple .. .. 1·00 1·00
O 785. 20 c. green .. .. 1·00 1·00
O 786. 25 c. green .. .. 1·40 1·40
O 787. 50 c. red .. .. 1·75 1·75
O 788. 1 cor. rose .. .. 3·00 3·00

1933. Optd. with T 37 and **OFICIAL.**

O 814. 21. 1 c. green 5 5
O 815. 22. 2 c. red 5 5
O 816. 21. 3 c. blue 5 5
O 817. 22. 4 c. blue 5 5
O 818. 21. 5 c. brown 5 5
O 819. 22. 6 c. grey 5 5
O 820. 10 c. brown 5 5
O 821. 21. 15 c. red 8 8
O 822. 22. 20 c. orange 8 8
O 823. 21. 25 c. violet 10 10
O 824. 22. 50 c. green 15 15
O 825. 1 cor. yellow 30 30

1933. Air. Optd. with T 37 and **CORREO Aereo OFICIAL.**

O 826. 21. 15 c. violet 12 12
O 827. 22. 20 c. green 12 12
O 828. 21. 25 c. olive 12 12
O 829. 22. 50 c. green 20 20
O 830. 1 cor. red 35 35

1935. Nos. O 814/25 optd. **RESELLO-1935** in a box.

O 864. 21. 1 c. green 5 5
O 865. 22. 2 c. red 5 5
O 866. 21. 3 c. blue 5 5
O 867. 22. 4 c. blue 5 5
O 868. 21. 5 c. brown 5 5
O 869. 22. 6 c. grey 5 5
O 870. 10 c. brown 5 5
O 871. 21. 15 c. red 5 5
O 872. 22. 20 c. orange 8 5
O 873. 21. 25 c. violet 8 8
O 874. 22. 50 c. green 25 25
O 875. 1 cor. yellow.. .. 40 40

1935. Air. Nos. O 826/30 optd. **RESELLO-1935** in a box.

O 877. 21. 15 c. violet 15 15
O 878. 22. 20 c. green 15 15
O 879. 21. 25 c. olive 20 20
O 880. 22. 50 c. green 50 50
O 881. 1 cor. red 50 50

(O 3.)

O 4. Islets in the Great Lake.

1937. Nos. 913, etc., optd. with Type O 3.

O 935. 21. 1 c. red 15 10
O 936. 22. 2 c. blue 15 10
O 937. 21. 3 c. brown 20 15
O 938. 5 c. red 20 15
O 939. 22. 10 c. green 40 25
O 940. 21. 15 c. green 50 30
O 941. 25 c. orange 60 45
O 942. 22. 50 c. brown 90 50
O 943. 1 cor. blue .. .. 1·60 75

1937. Air. Nos. 926/30 optd. with Type O 3.

O 944. 28. 15 c. orange 55 35
O 945. 20 c. red 55 35
O 946. 25 c. black 55 35
O 947. 50 c. violet 55 45
O 948. 1 cor. orange 55 45

1939.

O 1020. O 4. 2 c. red 8 8
O 1021. 3 c. blue 8 8
O 1022. 6 c. brown 8 8
O 1023. 7½ c. green 8 8
O 1024. 10 c. brown 8 8
O 1025. 15 c. orange 8 8
O 1026. 25 c. violet 15 15
O 1027. 50 c. green 25 25

O 5. President Somoza.

1939. Air.

O 1028. O 5. 10 c. brown .. 20 20
O 1029. 15 c. blue 20 20
O 1030. 20 c. yellow 20 20
O 1031. 25 c. violet 20 20
O 1032. 30 c. red 20 20
O 1033. 50 c. orange 45 45
O 1034. 1 cor. olive 75 75

O 6. Managua Airport.

1947. Air.

O 1120. O 6. 5 c. brown and black 5 5
O 1121. – 10 c. blue and black 8 8
O 1122. – 15 c. violet and black 5 5
O 1123. – 20 c. orange & black 10 8
O 1124. – 25 c. blue and black 10 10
O 1125. – 50 c. red and black 10 10
O 1126. – 1 cor. grey and black 25 25
O 1127. – 2 cor. 50 brn. & blk. 60 60

DESIGNS: 10 c. Sulphur Lagoon, Nejapa. 15 c. Ruben Dario Monument, Managua. 20 c. Tapir. 25 c. Genizaro Dam. 50 c. Thermal Baths, Tipitapa. 1 cor. Highway and Lake Managua. 2 cor. 50, Franklin D. Roosevelt Monument, Managua.

O 7. U.P.U. Offices, Berne.

1950. Air. U.P.U. 75th Anniv. Inscr. as in Type O 7. Frames in black.

O 1159. – 5 c. purple .. 5 5
O 1160. – 10 c. green .. 5 5
O 1161. – 25 c. purple .. 8 8
O 1162. O 7. 50 c. orange .. 12 8
O 1163. – 1 cor. blue .. 25 20
O 1164. – 2 cor. 60 black .. 2·00 1·60

DESIGNS—HORIZ. 5 c. Rowland Hill. 10 c. Heinrich von Stephan. 25 c. Standehaus, Berne. 1 cor. Monument, Berne. 2 cor. 60, Congress Medal.

1961. Air. Consular Fiscal stamps as T 90/1 with serial Nos. in red, surch. **Oficial Aereo** and value.

O 1448. 10 c. on 1 cor. olive .. 5 5
O 1449. 15 c. on 20 cor. chestnut 8 5
O 1450. 20 c. on 100 cor. lake 8 5
O 1451. 25 c. on 50 c. blue .. 10 5
O 1452. 35 c. on 50 cor. brown 10 8
O 1453. 50 c. on 3 cor. red .. 10 8
O 1454. 1 cor. on 2 cor. green.. 20 12
O 1455. 2 cor. on 5 cor. vermilion 40 25
O 1456. 5 cor. on 10 cor. violet 90 60

POSTAGE DUE STAMPS

D 1.

D 2.

1896.

D 99. D 1. 1 c. orange 30 60
D 100. 2 c. orange 30 60
D 101. 5 c. orange 30 60
D 102. 10 c. orange .. 30 60
D 103. 20 c. orange .. 30 60
D 104. 30 c. orange .. 30 60
D 105. 50 c. orange .. 30 60

1897.

D 108. D 1. 1 c. violet 30 65
D 109. 2 c. violet 30 65
D 110. 5 c. violet 30 65
D 111. 10 c. violet 30 65
D 112. 20 c. violet 60 90
D 113. 30 c. violet 30 90
D 114. 50 c. violet 30 90

1898.

D 124. D 1. 1 c. green 8 45
D 125. 2 c. green 8 45
D 126. 5 c. green 8 45
D 127. 10 c. green 8 45
D 128. 20 c. green 8 45
D 129. 30 c. green 8 45
D 130. 50 c. green 8 45

1899.

D 137. D 1. 1 c. red 8 45
D 138. 2 c. red 8 45
D 139. 5 c. red 8 45
D 140. 10 c. red 8 45
D 141. 20 c. red 8 45
D 142. 50 c. red 8 45

1900.

D 146. D 2. 1 c. claret 45
D 147. 2 c. orange 45
D 148. 5 c. blue 45
D 149. 10 c. violet 45
D 150. 20 c. brown 45
D 151. 30 c. green 45
D 152. 50 c. lake 45

NIGER O3

Area, South of the Sahara, formerly part of French West Africa. Became a separate territory in 1919 but reverted to the use of French West Africa Stamps from 1944 to 1959. Niger became an autonomous republic of the French Community in 1958, and fully independent in 1960.

100 centimes = 1 franc.

1921. Stamps of Upper Senegal and Niger optd. **TERRITOIRE DU NIGER.**

1. 1. 1 c. violet and purple .. 5 5
2. 2 c. purple and grey .. 5 5
3. 4 c. blue and black .. 5 5
4. 5 c. chocolate and brown 5 5
5. 10 c. green 8 8
25. 10 c. red on blue .. 5 5
6. 15 c. yellow and brown .. 5 5
7. 20 c. black and purple .. 5 5
8. 25 c. green and black .. 5 5
9. 30 c. red and orange .. 5 5
26. 30 c. orange and green .. 5 5
10. 35 c. violet and red .. 5 5
11. 40 c. red and grey .. 5 5
12. 45 c. brown and blue .. 5 5
13. 50 c. blue 5 5
27. 50 c. blue and grey .. 5 5
28. 60 c. red 8 8
14. 75 c. brown and yellow .. 10 10
15. 1 f. purple and brown .. 8 8
16. 2 f. blue and green .. 12 12
17. 5 f. black and violet .. 25 25

1922. Stamps of Upper Senegal and Niger surch. **TERRITOIRE DU NIGER** and value in figures.

18. 1. 25 c. on 15 c. yell. & brown 5 5
19. 25 c. on 2 f. blue & green.. 5 5
20. 25 c. on 5 f. black & violet 5 5
21. 60 on 75 c. violet on pink 5 5
22. 65 on 45 c. brown and blue 20 20
23. 85 c. on 75 c. brown & yell. 25 25
24. 1 f. 25 on 1 f. blue.. .. 5 5

1. Native Wells.

3. Zinder Fortress.

2. Native Craft on the Niger.

1926.

29. 1. 1 c. olive and purple .. 5 5
30. 2 c. red and grey .. 5 5
31. 3 c. brown and mauve .. 5 5
32. 4 c. black and brown .. 5 5
33. 5 c. green and red .. 5 5
34. 10 c. green and blue .. 5 5
35. 15 c. green 5 5
36. 15 c. red and lilac .. 5 5
37. 2. 20 c. brown and green .. 5 5
38. 25 c. red and black .. 5 5
39. 30 c. green 5 5
40. 30 c. mauve and yellow .. 5 5
41. 35 c. blue and red on blue 5 5
42. 35 c. blue-green 5 5
43. 40 c. grey and claret .. 5 5
44. 45 c. mauve and yellow.. 8 8
45. 45 c. green 5 5
46. 50 c. green & red on green 5 5
47. 55 c. brown and red .. 5 5
48. 60 c. brown and red .. 5 5
49. 65 c. red and olive .. 5 5
50. 70 c. red and olive .. 10 10
51. 75 c. mauve & green on red 12 12
52. 80 c. green and claret .. 10 10
53. 90 c. orange and red .. 5 5
54. 90 c. green and red .. 8 8
55. 3. 1 f. green and red .. 90 70
56. 1 f. orange and red .. 8 5
57. 1 f. red and green .. 5 5
58. 1 f. 10 green and brown.. 40 35

59. 3. 1 f. 25 red and green .. 10 10
60. 1 f. 25 orange and red .. 5 5
61. 1 f. 40 brown and mauve 5 5
62. 1 f. 50 blue 5 5
63. 1 f. 60 green and brown.. 8 8
64. 1 f. 75 sepia and mauve.. 30 30
65. 1 f. 75 blue 8 8
66. 2 f. brown and orange .. 5 5
67. 2 f. 25 blue 5 5
68. 2 f. 50 black 5 5
69. 3 f. grey and violet .. 5 5
70. 5 f. black and claret on red 5 5
71. 10 f. red and lilac .. 12 12
72. 20 f. orange and green .. 20 20

1931. "Colonial Exhibition" key types inscr. "NIGER".
73. E. 40 c. green 70 60
74. F. 50 c. mauve 70 60
75. G. 90 c. red 70 70
76. H. 1 f. 50 blue 70 70

1937. International Exn., Paris. As Nos. 110/15 of Cameroun.
77. 20 c. violet 15 15
78. 30 c. green 15 15
79. 40 c. red 15 15
80. 50 c. brown 15 15
81. 90 c. red 15 15
82. 1 f. 50 blue 15 15

1938. Int. Anti-Cancer Fund. As T 10 of Cameroun.
83. 1 f 75+50 c. blue .. 2·75 2·75

1939. Caille. As T 2 of Dahomey.
84. 90 c. orange 12 12
85. 2 f. violet 12 12
86. 2 f. 25 blue 12 12

1939. New York World's Fair. As T 11 of Cameroun.
87. 1 f. 25 red 10 10
88. 2 f. 25 blue 8 8

1939. French Revolution. 150th Anniv. As T 16 of Cameroun.
89. 45 c.+25 c. green .. 85 85
90. 70 c.+30 c. brown .. 85 85
91. 90 c.+35 c. orange .. 85 85
92. 1 f. 25+1 f. red .. 85 85
93. 2 f. 25+2 f. blue.. .. 85 85

1940. Air. As T 3 of Dahomey.
94. 1 f. 90 blue 5 5
95. 2 f. 90 red.. .. .. 5 5
96. 4 f. 50 green 15 15
97. 4 f. 90 olive 5 5
98. 6 f. 90 orange 5 5

1941. National Defence Fund. Surch. **SECOURS NATIONAL** and value.
98a. 1 f. on 50 c. (No. 46) .. 5 5
98b. 2 f. on 80 c. (No. 52) .. 85 85
98c. 2 f. on 1 f. 50 (No. 62) .. 90 90
98d. 3 f. on 2 f. (No. 66) .. 90 90

1942. Air. As T 4d of Dahomey.
98e. 50 f. red and yellow .. 20

4. Giraffes. 5. Game Animals.

1959. Wild Animals and Birds. Inscr. "PROTECTION DE LA FAUNE".
99. – 50 c. turquoise, green and black (postage) 5 5
100. – 1 f. yell., blue, red & grn. 5 5
101. – 2 f. yell., red, blue & grn. 5 5
102. – 5 f. mag., blk. & ol.-brn. 5 5
103. – 7 f. red, blk. & olive-grn. 5 5
104. – 10 f. myrtle, green, chestnut and black .. 8 5
105. – 15 f. sepia and turquoise 10 5
106. – 20 f. black and violet .. 10 5
107. 4. 25 f. chocolate, buff, blue and black 12 5
108. 30 f. brn., bistre & green 20 8
109. – 50 f. indigo and chestnut 20 10
110. – 60 f. sepia & yellow-green 25 15
111. – 85 f. brown and bistre .. 35 20
112. – 100 f. bistre & yell-green 40 25
113. – 200 f. red, purple, blue and olive (air) .. 1·25 75
114. 5. 500 f. green, brn. & blue 2·50 75
DESIGNS—As T 4—HORIZ. 50 c., 10 f. Manatee (sea-cow). VERT. 1 f., 2 f. Crowned cranes. 5 f., 7 f. Jabirus. 15 f., 20 f. Mountain sheep. 50 f., 60 f. Ostriches. 85 f., 100 f. Lion. As T 5—HORIZ. 200 f. Red Bee-eater.

1960. African Technical Co-operation Commission. 10th Anniv. As T 39 of Cameroun.
115. 25 f. brown and ochre .. 30 25

1960. Conseil de l'Entente. 1st Anniv. As T 6 of Dahomey.
116. 25 f. multicoloured .. 30 25

1960. Independence. No. 112 surch. **200 F** and bars and **Independance 3-8-60.**
117. – 200 f. on 100 f. .. 4·50 4·50

6. Pres. Diori Hamani.

1960.
118. 6. 25 f. black and bistre .. 20 15

7. U.N. Emblem and Niger Flag.

1961. Air. Admission into U.N.O. 1st Anniv.
119. 7. 25 f. red, green & orange 25 20
120. 100 f. green, red & emer. 80 60

1962. Air. "Air Afrique" Airline. As T 44 of Cameroun.
121. 100t. violet, black & brown 75 55

1962. Malaria Eradication. As T 45 of Cameroun.
122. 25 f.+5 f. brown 25 25

8. Athletics.

SPORTS — VERT. 15 f. Boxing and cycling. 25 f. Basketball and football.

1962. Abidjan Games, 1961.
123. – 15 f. chocolate, orange green and black .. 12 10
124. – 25 f. chocolate, orange, green and black .. 20 15
125. 8. 85 f. chocolate, orange, green and black .. 65 45

1962. Union of African and Malagasy States. 1st Anniv. As No. 328 of Cameroun.
126. 47. 30 f. magenta 25 20

9. Pres. Hamani and Map. 10. Running.

1962. Republic. 4th Anniv.
127. 9. 25 f. sepia, orange, green, blue and black .. 20 20

1963. Freedom from Hunger. As T 51 of Cameroun.
128. 25 f.+5 f. pur., brn. & olive 25 25

1963. Dakar Games.
129. – 15 f. chocolate and blue 10 8
130. 10. 25 f. red and chocolate 20 15
131. – 45 f. black and green .. 35 25
DESIGNS—HORIZ. 15 f. Swimming. VERT. 45 f. Volleyball.

11. Agadez Mosque.

1963. Air. Admission to U.P.U. 2nd Anniv. Inscr as in T 11. Multicoloured.
132. 50 f T 11 .. .. 40 25
133. 85 f Gaya Bridge .. 65 45
134. 100 f. Presidential Palace, Niamey 75 65

12. Wood-carving.

ILLUSTRATIONS British Commonwealth and all overprints and surcharges are FULL SIZE. Foreign Countries have been reduced to ¾-LINEAR.

1963. Traditional Crafts. Multicoloured.
135. 5 f. Type 12 (postage) .. 5 5
136. 10 f. Skin-tanning .. 8 8
137. 25 f. Goldsmith 20 12
138. 30 f. Mat-making.. .. 25 15
139. 85 f. Potter 65 30
140. 100 f. Canoe-making (air) 65 45
The 10 f. and 30 f. are horiz. and the 100 f. larger (47×27 mm.).

1963. Air. African and Malagasy Posts and Telecommunications Union. As T 10 of Central African Republic.
141. 85 f. red, buff, pale green and green 65 50

1963. Air. Red Cross Centenary. Optd. with cross and **Centenaire de la Croix-Rouge** in red.
142. 7. 25 f. red, green & orange 30 25
143. 100 f. green, red & emerald 1·00 65

13. Costume Museum.

1963. Opening of Costume Museum, Niamey. Vert. costume designs. Multicoloured.
144. 15 f. Berber woman .. 10 5
145. 20 f. Haussa woman .. 15 8
146. 25 f. Tuareg woman .. 20 10
147. 30 f. Tuareg man .. 25 12
148. 60 f. Djerma woman .. 45 30
149. 85 f. Type 13 .. .. 65 40

14. "Europafrique". 16. Man and Globe.

15. Groundnut Cultivation.

1963. Air. European-African Economic Convention.
150. 14. 50 f. brown, yellow, ochre and green .. 55 45

1963. Air. Groundnut Cultivation Campaign.
151. 15. 20 f. blue, chest. & green 15 10
152. – 45 f. chest., blue & green 30 20
153. – 85 f. multicoloured .. 50 35
154. – 100 f. olive, chest. & blue 65 50
DESIGNS: 45 f. Camel transport. 85 f. Fastening sacks. 100 f. Dispatch of groundnuts by lorry.

1963. Air. "Air Afrique" 1st Anniv. and "DC-8" Service Inaug. As T 10 of Congo Republic.
155. 50 f. multicoloured .. 40 30

1963. Declaration of Human Rights. 15th Anniv.
156. 16. 25 f. blue, chest. & green 20 15

17. "Telstar".

1964. Air. Space Telecommunications.
157. 17. 25 f. grey-olive & violet 25 20
158. – 100 f. green and purple 70 70
DESIGN: 100 f. "Relay".

18. "Parkinsonia aculeata". 19. Statue, Abu Simbel.

1964. Flowers. Multicoloured.
159. 5 f. Type 18 .. .. 20 15
160. 10 f. "Russelia equisetiformis" .. 8 5
161. 15 f. "Lantana Camara" 10 5
162. 20 f. "Agyreia nervosa" 15 10
163. 25 f. "Luffa Cylindrica" 20 8
164. 30 f. "Hibiscus rosa-sinensis" .. 25 8
165. 45 f. "Plumieria rubra" 35 15
166. 50 f. "Catharanthus roseus" 40 15
167. 60 f. "Caesalpinia pulcherrima" 45 25
Nos. 164/7 have "REPUBLIQUE DU NIGER" at the top and the value at bottom right.

1964. Air. Nubian Monuments Preservation.
168. 19. 25 f. green and brown.. 25 20
169. 30 f. chestnut and blue 30 25
170. 50 f. blue and maroon.. 55 45

20. Globe and "Tiros" Satellite.

1964. Air. World Meteorological Day.
171. 20. 50 f. choc., blue & emer. 50 40

21. Sun Emblem and Solar Flares. 22. Convoy of Lorries.

1964. International Quiet Sun Years.
172. 21. 30 f. red, violet & sepia 25 20

1964. O.M.N.E.S. (Nigerian Mobile Medica and Sanitary Organisation) Commemoration.
173. 22. 25 f. orge. olive & blue 20 12
174. – 30 f. multicoloured .. 20 12
175. – 50 f. multicoloured .. 30 20
176. – 60 f. purple, orge. & turq. 35 25
DESIGNS: 30 f. Tending children. 50 f. Tending women. 60 f. Open-air laboratory.

23. Rocket, Stars and Stamp Outline.

1964. Air. "PHILATEC 1964" Int. Stamp Exn., Paris.
177. 23. 50 f. magenta and blue 40 40

24. European, African and Symbols of Agriculture and Industry. 25. Pres. Kennedy.

1964. Air. European-African Economic Convention. 1st Anniv.
178. 24. 50 f. red, green, brown and chestnut .. 40 30

1964. Air. Pres. Kennedy. Commem.
179. 25. 100 f. brown, blue, mauve and light blue 75 65

26. Water-polo.

1964. Air. Olympic Games, Tokyo.
180. 26. 60 f. brown, deep green and maroon .. 45 30
181. – 85 f. brown, blue & red 60 40
182. – 100 f. indigo, red & grn. 75 55
183. – 250 f. indigo, yellow-brown and green .. 1·75 1·25
DESIGNS—HORIZ. 85 f. Relay-racing. VERT. 100 f. Throwing the discus. 250 f. Athlete holding Olympic Torch.

1964. French, African and Malagasy Co-operation. As T 500 of France.
184. 50 f. chocolate, oran. & vio. 40 25

27. Azawak Tuareg Encampment.

1964. Native Villages. Multicoloured.
185. 15 f. Type 27 .. .. 10 10
186. 20 f. Songhai hut .. 12 10
187. 25 f. Wogo and Kourtey tents 15 12
188. 30 f. Djerma hut.. .. 20 15
189. 60 f. Sorkawa fishermen's encampment 25 20
190. 85 f. Haussa urban house 50 35

28. Doctors and Patient and Microscope Slide. **29.** Abraham Lincoln

1964. Anti-Leprosy Campaign.
191. 28. 50 f. black, brown, blue and lilac .. 30 25

1965. Abraham Lincoln Death Cent.
192. 29. 50 f. multicoloured .. 30 25

30. Instruction by "Radio-Vision".

1965. "Human Progress". Inscr. as in T 30.
193. 30. 20 f. choc., yell. & blue 15 8
194. – 25 f. sepia, brown & grn. 20 10
195. – 30 f. maroon, red & grn. 25 12
196. – 50 f. maroon, blue & brn. 30 20
DESIGNS: 25 f. Student. 30 f. Adult class. 50 f. Five tribesmen ("Alphabetisation").

31. Ader's Telephone. **32.** Pope John XXIII.

1965. I.T.U. Cent.
197. 31. 25 f. black, lake & grn. 20 15
198. – 30 f. green, purple & red 25 20
199. – 50 f. green, maroon & red 35 25
DESIGNS: 30 f. Wheatstone's telegraph. 50 f. "Telautographe".

1965. Air. Pope John Commem.
200. 32. 100 f. multicoloured .. 75 50

33. Hurdling. **34.** "Capture of Cancer." (the Crab).

1965. 1st African Games, Brazzaville.
201. 33. 10 f. maroon, grn. & brn. 8 5
202. – 15 f. red, brown and grey 10 8
203. – 20 f. maroon, blue & grn. 15 10
204. – 30 f. maroon, grn. & lake 20 12
DESIGNS—VERT. 15 f. Running. 30 f. Long-jumping. HORIZ. 20 f. Pole-vaulting.

1965. Air. Campaign against Cancer.
205. 34. 100 f. brown, black & grn. 70 45

35. Sir Winston Churchill. **36.** Interviewing.

1965. Air. Churchill Commem.
206. 35. 100 f. multicoloured .. 70 45

1965. Radio Club Promotion.
207. 36. 30 f. brown, vio. & grn. 20 10
208. – 45 f. red, black and buff 30 15
209. – 50 f. red, blue, violet and brown 35 20
210. – 60 f. maroon, bl. & ochre 40 25
DESIGNS—VERT. 45 ft. Recording. 50 f. Listening to broadcast. HORIZ. 60 f. Listeners' debate.

37. "Agricultural and Industrial Workers". **38.** Fair Scene and Flags.

1965. Air. Int. Co-operation Year.
211. 37. 50 f. chest., blk. & bistre 35 20

1965. Air. Int. Fair, Niamey.
212. 38. 100 f. black, orange, green and mauve .. 70 50

39. Dr. Schweitzer and Diseased Hands.

1966. Air. Schweitzer Commem.
213. 39. 50 f. multicoloured .. 35 30

40. "Water Distribution and Control".

1966. Int. Hydrological Decennium Inaug.
214. 40. 50 f. blue, orge. & violet 35 25

41. Weather Ship.

1966. Air. 6th World Meteorological Day.
215. 41. 50 f. green, purple & blue 40 25

42. White and "Gemini" Capsule.

1966. Air. Cosmonauts.
216. 42. 50 f. black, brn. & grn. 40 25
217. – 50 f. blue, violet & orge. 40 25
DESIGN: No. 217, Leonov and "Voskhod" capsule.

43. Head-dress and Carvings.

45. Goalkeeper saving ball. **44.** "Diamant" Rocket and Gantry.

1966. World Festival of Negro Arts, Dakar.
218. 43. 30 f. black, chest. & grn. 20 15
219. – 50 f. violet, brown & blue 30 20
220. – 60 f. lake, violet & brn. 35 20
221. – 100 f. black, red & blue 65 25
DESIGNS: 50 f. Carved figures and mosaics. 60 f. Statuettes, drums and arch. 100 f. Handicrafts and church.

1966. Air. French Space Vehicles. Multicoloured designs each showing different Satellites.
222. 45 f. Type 44 .. .. 30 20
223. 60 f. "A 1" (horiz.) .. 45 25
224. 90 f. "FR 1" (horiz.) .. 65 40
225. 100 f. "D 1" (horiz.) .. 75 55

1966. World Cup Football Championships.
226. – 30 f. verm., choc. & blue 20 10
227. 45. 50 f. choc., blue & green 30 12
228. – 60 f. blue, purple & bistre 40 15
DESIGNS—VERT. 30 f. Player dribbling ball. 60 f. Player kicking ball.

47. Parachutist.

46. Cogwheel Emblem and Hemispheres. **48.** Inoculating Cattle.

1966. Air. Europafrique.
229. 46. 50 f. multicoloured .. 35 25

1966. National Armed Forces. 5th Anniv. Multicoloured.
230. 20 f. Type 47 .. 15 8
231. 30 f. Soldiers with standard (vert.) 20 10
232. 45 f. Armoured patrol vehicle (horiz.).. .. 30 15

1966. Air. "DC–8" Air Services. Inaug. As T 81 of Cameroun.
233. 30 f. olive, black and grey 20 15

1966. Campaign for Prevention of Cattle Plague.
234. 48. 45 f. black, chest. & blue 30 15

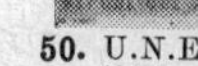

49. "Voskhod 1". **50.** U.N.E.S.C.O. "Tree".

1966. Air. Astronautics.
235. 49. 50 f. blue, indigo and lake 40 20
236. – 100 f. violet, blue & lake 75 40
DESIGN—HORIZ. 100 f. "Gemini 6" and "7".

1966. U.N.E.S.C.O. 20th Anniv.
237. 50. 50 f. black, brown, green and buff 30 15

51. Japanese Gate, Atomic Symbol and Cancer ("The Crab"). **52.** Furnace.

1966. Air. Int. Cancer Congress, Tokyo.
238. 51. 100 f. violet, turquoise, purple and chestnut.. 65 45

1966. Malbaza Cement Works.
239. 52. 10 f. blue, orange & brn. 8 5
240. – 20 f. blue and green .. 12 8
241. – 30 f. brown, grey & blue 15 10
242. – 50 f. indigo, brn. & blue 30 15
DESIGNS—HORIZ. 20 f. Electrical power-house. 30 f. Works and cement silos. 50 f. Installation for handling raw materials.

53. Niamey Mosque.

1967. Air.
243. 53. 100 f. blue, green & grey 70 40

54. Durer (self-portrait).

1967. Air. Paintings. Multicoloured.
244. 50 f. Type 54 .. .. 45 30
245. 100 f. David (self-portrait) 75 65
246. 250 f. Delacroix (self-portrait).. .. .. 1·75 1·10

See also Nos. 271/2 and 277/9.

55. Red-billed Hornbill. **56.** Bob-sleigh Course, Villard-de-Lans.

1967. Birds.
247. **55.** 1 f. bistre, red and green (postage) 5 5
248. – 2 f. black, brown & emer. 5 5
249. – 30 f. red, black, yellow and bistre 15 10
249a. – 40 f. purple, orange and green 15 12
250. – 45 f. brown, green & blue 20 10
251. – 70 f. multicoloured .. 30 20
251a. – 250 f. blue, purple and green (air) (48 × 27 mm.) 1·25 65
BIRDS: 2 f. Pied kingfishers. 30 f. Barbary shrikes. 40 f. Red bishop. 45 f. Orange weaver. 70 f. Small pin-tailed sandgrouse. 250 f. Splendid glossy starlings.

1967. Grenoble—Winter Olympics Town (1968).
252. **56.** 30 f. brown, blue & grn. 20 15
253. – 45 f. brown, blue & grn. 30 20
254. – 60 f. brown, blue & grn. 35 25
255. – 90 f. brown, blue & grn. 55 35
DESIGNS: 45 f. Ski-jump, Autrans. 60 f. Ski-jump, St. Nizier du moucherotte. 90 f. Slalom course, Chamrousse.

57. Family and Lions Emblem.

58. Weather Ship.

1967. Lions Int. 50th Anniv.
256. **57.** 50 f. blue, claret & green 30 20

1967. Air. World Meteorological Day.
257. **58.** 50 f. red, black and blue 35 25

59. View of World Fair.

1967. Air. World Fair, Montreal.
258. **59.** 100 f. black, blue & pur. 70 45

60. I.T.Y. Emblem and Aircraft.

61. Scouts around Camp-fire.

1967. Int. Tourist Year.
259. **60.** 45 f. violet, grn. & pur. 25 20

1967. World Scout Jamboree, Idaho, U.S.A.
260. **61.** 30 f. brown, lake & blue 20 12
261. – 45 f. blue, brn. & orge. 30 20
262. – 80 f. lake, slate & bistre 50 30
DESIGNS—HORIZ. 45 f. Jamboree emblem and scouts. VERT. 80 f. Scout cooking meal.

62. Audio-Visual Centre.

1967. Air. National Audio-Visual Centre, Niamey.
263. **62.** 100 f. violet, blue & grn. 70 35

63. Carrying Patient.

64. "Europafrique".

1967. Nigerian Red Cross.
264. **63.** 45 f. black, red & green 25 12
265. – 50 f. black, red & green 30 12
266. – 60 f. black, red & green 35 15
DESIGNS: 50 f. Nurse with mother and child. 60 f. Doctor giving injection.

1967. Europafrique.
267. **64.** 50 f. multicoloured .. 30 15

65. Dr. Konrad Adenauer.

66. African Women.

1967. Air. Adenauer Commem.
268. **65.** 100 f. brown and blue 65 40

1967. Air. U.A.M.P.T. 5th Anniv. As T **95** of Cameroun.
270. 100 f. violet, green and red 65 40

1967. Air. Jean Ingres (painter). Death Cent. Paintings by Ingres. As T **54**. Multicoloured.
271. 100 f. "Jesus among the Doctors" (horiz.) .. 85 55
272. 150 f. "Jesus restoring the Keys to St. Peter" (vert.) 1·25 90

1967. U.N. Women's Rights Commission.
273. **66.** 50 f. brown, yellow & blue 30 20

1967. West African Monetary Union. 5th Anniv. As T **54** of Dahomey.
274. 30 f. green and purple .. 20 12

67. Nigerian Children.

69. Allegory of Human Rights.

68. O.C.A.M. Emblem.

1967. Air. U.N.I.C.E.F. 21st Anniv.
275. **67.** 100 f. choc., blue & green 65 35

1968. Air, O.C.A.M. Conf., Niamey.
276. **68.** 100 f. orange, green & blue 65 40

1968. Air. Paintings (self-portraits). As T **54**. Multicoloured.
277. 50 f. J.-B. Corot .. 40 30
278. 150 f. Goya .. .. 1·10 50
279. 200 f. Van Gogh .. .. 1·50 85

1968. Human Rights Year.
280. **69.** 50 f. indigo, brown & blue 30 15

70. Breguet "27" Biplane over Lake.

1968. Air. 1st France-Niger Airmail Service. 35th Anniv.
281. **70.** 45 f. blue, green & mag. 25 15
282. – 80 f. slate-bl., brn. & bl. 50 25
283. – 100 f. black, grn. & blue 60 30
DESIGNS: Potez "25 T.O.E." biplane. 80 f. On ground. 100 f. In flight.

INDEX

Countries can be quickly located by referring to the index at the end of this volume.

71. "Joyous Health".

1968. W.H.O. 20th Anniv.
284. **71.** 50 f. indigo, blue & brn. 30 20

72. Cyclists of 1818 and 1968.

1968. Air. Bicycle. 150th Anniv.
285. **72.** 100 f. green and red .. 55 25

73. Beribboned Rope.

1968. Air. Europa-Afrique. 5th Anniv.
286. **73.** 50 f. red, green, black and drab 25 20

74. Fencing.

1968. Air. Olympic Games, Mexico.
287. **74.** 50 f. pur., violet & green 30 20
288. – 100 f. black, mar. & blue 65 30
289. – 150 f. maroon & orange 1·00 60
290. – 200 f. blue, brn. & grn. 1·25 80
DESIGNS—VERT. 100 f. High-diving. 150 f. Weight-lifting. HORIZ. 200 f. Horse-jumping.

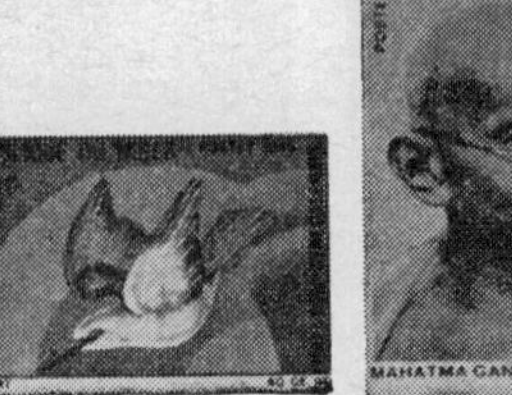

75. Senegal Kingfisher. **76.** Mahatma Gandhi.

1968. Birds. Multicoloured.
292. 5 f. Grey hornbill (postage) 5 5
293. 10 f. Type **75** 5 5
294. 15 f. Senegal coucal .. 8 5
295. 20 f. Long-tailed parrot .. 10 5
296. 25 f. Abyssinian roller .. 8 5
297. 50 f. Cattle egret .. 25 15
298. 100 f. Amethyst starling (air) (27 × 49 mm.) .. 45 30
See also Nos. 375/8 and 567/8.

1968. Air. "Apostles of Non-Violence".
299. **76.** 100 f. black & yellow .. 65 30
300. – 100 f. black & turquoise 65 30
301. – 100 f. black and grey .. 65 30
302. – 100 f. black & orange .. 65 30
PORTRAITS: No. 300, President Kennedy. 301, Martin Luther King. 302, Robert F. Kennedy.

1968. Air. "Philexafrique" Stamp Exn., Abidjan (Ivory Coast, 1969) (1st Issue). As T **109** of Cameroun. Multicoloured.
304. 100 f. "Pare, Minister of the Interior" (J. L. La Neuville) 75 75

77. Arms of the Republic.

1968. Air. Republic. 10th Anniv.
305. **77.** 100 f. multicoloured .. 50 30

1969. Air. Napoleon Bonaparte. Birth Bicent. As T **69** of Dahomey. Multicoloured.
306. 50 f. "Napoleon as First Consul" (Ingres) .. 45 30
307. 100 f. "Napoleon visiting the plague victims of Jaffa" (Gros) 75 55
308. 150 f. "Napoleon Enthroned" (Ingres) .. 1·10 90
309. 200 f. "The French Campaign" (Meissonier) .. 1·50 1·10

1969. Air. "Philexafrique" Stamp Exn., Abidjan, Ivory Coast (2nd Issue). As T **110** of Cameroun.
310. 50 f. brown, blue & orange 35 35
DESIGN. 50 f. Giraffes and stamp of 1926.

78. Plane over Rain-cloud and Anemometer.

1969. Air. World Meteorological Day.
311. **78.** 50 f. blk., blue & green 30 20

79. Workers supporting Globe.

1969. Int. Labour Organisation. 50th Anniv.
312. **79.** 30 f. red and green .. 15 8
313. 50 f. green and red .. 25 15

80. Panhard and Levassor (1909).

1969. Air. Veteran Motor Cars.
314. **80.** 25 f. green 15 10
315. – 45 f. violet, blue & grey 25 15
316. – 50 f. brown, ochre & grey 30 20
317. – 70 f. purple, red & grey 45 30
318. – 100 f. green, brn. & grey 60 40
DESIGNS: 45 f. De Dion Bouton 8 (1904). 50 f. Opel "Doctor-wagen" (1909). 70 f. Daimler (1910). 100 f. Vermorel 12/16 (1912).

81. Man with Red Cross parcel.

82. Mouth and Ear.

1969. League of Red Cross Societies. 50th Anniv.
319. – 45 f. red, brown & blue 25 15
320. – 50 f. red, grey & green 25 15
321. **81.** 70 f. red, brown & ochre 40 20
DESIGNS—VERT.: 45 f. Mother and child. HORIZ. 50 f. Symbolic Figures, Globe and Red Crosses.

1969. 1st "Francophonie" (French Language) Cultural Conf., Niamey.
322. **82.** 100 f. multicoloured .. 55 40

83. School Building.

1969. National School of Administration.
323. **83.** 30 f. black, green & orge. 12 10

1969. Air. 1st Man on the Moon. No. 114 optd. **L'HOMME SUR LA LUNE JUILLET 1969 APOLLO 11** and moon module.
324. **5.** 500 f. grn., brn. & blue .. 3·25 3·25

84. "Apollo 8" and Rocket.

1969. Air. Moon Flight of "Apollo 8". Embossed on gold foil.
325. **84.** 1,000 f. gold .. .. 6·00

1969. African Development Bank. 5th Anniv. As T **118** of Cameroun.
326. 30 f. brown, green & violet 15 12

85. Child and Toys.

1969. Air. Int. Toy Fair, Nuremburg.
327. **85.** 100 f. blue, brown & grn. 55 30

86. Linked Squares.

1969. Air. "Europafrique".
328. **86.** 50 f. yellow, blk. & violet 25 20

87. Trucks crossing Sahara.

1969. Air. "Croisiere Noire" Trans-Africa Expedition. 45th Anniv.
329. **87.** 50 f. brn., violet & mag. 25 15
330. – 100 f. violet, red & blue 50 25
331. – 150 f. maroon, green, blue and ochre .. 70 40
332. – 200 f. green, indigo & blue 1·00 60
Designs: 100 f. Crossing the mountains. 150 f. African children and expedition at Lake Victoria. 200 f. Route Map, European greeting African, and Citroen truck.

1969. Aerial Navigation Security Agency for Africa and Madagascar (A.S.E.C.N.A.). 10th Anniv. As T **121** of Cameroun.
333. 100 f. red 65 40

88. Classical Pavilion.

1970. National Museum.
334. **88.** 30 f. blue, green & brown 20 10
335. – 45 f. blue, green & brown 30 15
336. – 50 f. blue, brown & green 35 15
337. – 70 f. brown, blue & green 45 25
338. – 100 f. brown, blue & grn. 65 40
Designs: 45 f. Temporary Exhibition Pavilion. 50 f. Audio-visual Pavilion. 70 f. Local Musical Instruments Gallery. 100 f. Handicrafts Pavilion.

89. Niger Village and Japanese Pagodas.

90. Hypodermic "Gun" and Map.

1970. Air "EXPO 70" World Fair, Osaka, Japan. (1st issue).
339. **89.** 100 f. multicoloured .. 65 40

1970. One Hundred Million Smallpox Vaccinations in West Africa.
340. **90.** 50 f. blue, purple & green 30 20

91. Education Symbols.

1970. Air. Int. Education Year.
341. **91.** 100 f. slate, red & purple 50 40

92. Footballer.

1970. World Cup Football Competitions, Mexico.
342. **92.** 40 f. emer., choc. & pur. 20 15
343. – 70 f. purple, brown & blue 30 20
344. – 90 f. red and black .. 40 30
Designs: 70 f. Football and Globe. 90 f. Two footballers.

93. Rotary Emblems.

1970. Air. Rotary Int. 65th Anniv.
345. **93.** 100 f. multicoloured 50 40

94. Bay of Naples and Niger Stamp.

1970. Air. 10th "Europafrique" Stamp Exn., Naples.
346. **94.** 100 f. multicoloured .. 45 35

95. Clement Ader, Flying Machine and Modern Aircraft.

1970. Air. Aviation Pioneers.
347. **95.** 50 f. slate, blue & red .. 25 15
348. – 100 f. brn.-red, slate & bl. 50 40
349. – 150 f. ochre, brn. & grn. 70 50
350. – 200 f. carmine, bistre and violet .. .. 1·00 60
351. – 250 f. violet, slate and brown-red .. .. 1·10 70
Designs: 100 f. Montgolfier brothers, balloon and rocket. 150 f. Isaac Newton and gravity diagram. 200 f. Galileo and rocket in planetary system. 250 f. Leonardo da Vinci, flying machine and modern glider.

96. Cathode-ray Tube illuminating Books, Microscope and Globe.

1970. Air. World Telecommunications Day.
352. **96.** 100 f. choc., emer. & red 45 35

1970. New U.P.U. Headquarters Building, Berne. Inaug. As T **126** of Cameroun.
353. 30 f. red, slate & brown .. 25 8
354. 60 f. violet, carmine and ultramarine 30 12

1970. Air. Safe Return of "Apollo 13". Nos. 348 and 350 optd. **Solidarite Spatiale Apollo XIII 11-17 Avril 1970.**
355. 100 f. brown-red, slate and blue 45 30
356. 200 f. carmine, bistre & vio. 90 55

97. U.N. Emblem, Man, Woman and Doves.

1970. Air. United Nations. 25th Anniv.
357. **97.** 100 f. multicoloured .. 45 30
358. 150 f. multicoloured .. 65 50

98. Globe and Heads.

1970. Air. Int. French Language Conference, Niamey. Die-stamped on gold foil.
359. **98.** 250 f. gold and blue .. 1·40

99. European Girl and African Youth.

1970. Air. Renewed "Europafrique" Convention. 1st Anniv.
360. **99.** 50 f. red and green .. 25 15

100. Japanese Girls and "EXPO 70" Skyline.

1970. Air. "EXPO 70" World Fair, Osaka, Japan. (2nd issue).
361. **100.** 100 f. pur., orge. & grn. 45 30
362. – 150 f. blue, brn. & grn. 65 50
Design: 150 f. "No" actor and "EXPO 70" by night.

101. Gymnast on Parallel Bars.

102. Beethoven, Keyboard and Manuscripts.

1970. Air. World Gymnastic Championships, Ljubljana.
363. **101.** 50 f. blue 20 12
364. – 100 f. green 45 20
365. – 150 f. purple 65 35
366. – 200 f. red 90 45
Gymnasts—Horiz. 100 f. Gymnast on vaulting-horse. 150 f. Gymnast in mid-air. Vert. 200 f. Gymnast on rings.

1970. Air. Moon Landing of "Luna 16". Surch. **LUNA 16-Sept. 1970 PREMIERS PRELEVEMENTS AUTOMATIQUES SUR LA LUNE** and value.
367. 100 f. on 150 f. (Nos. 349) 50 25
368. 200 f. on 250 f. (Nos. 351) 1·00 55

1970. Air. Beethoven Birth Bicentenary. Multicoloured.
369. 100 f. Type **102** 50 20
370. 150 f. Beethoven and allegory, "Hymn of Joy" 75 30

104. John F. Kennedy Bridge, Niamey.

1970. Air. 12th Anniv. of the Republic.
371. **104.** 100 f. multicoloured .. 45 25

1971. Birds. Designs similar to T **75**. Multicoloured.
372. 5 f. "Tockus nasutus" .. 5 5
373. 10 f. "Halcyon senegalensis" 5 5
374. 15 f. "Centropus senegalensis" 8 5
375. 20 f. "Psittacula krameri" 8 5
376. 35 f. Paradise whydah .. 15 10
377. 50 f. Buff-backed cattle egret 20 15
The Latin inscription on No. 377 is incorrect, reading "Balbucus ibis" instead of "Bubulcus ibis".

105. Pres. Nasser.

1971. Air. Death of Pres. Gamal Nasser (Egyptian statesman). Multicoloured.
378. 100 f. Type **105** 45 25
379. 200 f. Nasser waving .. 90 70

106. Pres. De Gaulle.

1971. Air. Death of General Charles de Gaulle (French statesman). Embossed on gold foil.
380. **106.** 1000 f. gold .. .. 10·00

107. "MUNICH" and Olympic Rings.

1971. Air. Publicity for 1972 Olympic Games, Munich.
381. **107.** 150 f. pur., blue & grn. 65 45

108. "Apollo 14" leaving Moon.

109. Symbolic Masks.

1971. Air. Moon Mission of "Apollo 14".
382. 108. 250 f. grn., orge. & blue 1·10 65

1971. Air. Racial Equality Year.
383. 109. 100 f. verm., grn. & blue 45 25
384. – 200 f. brn., grn. & ind. 90 60
DESIGN: 200 f. "Peoples" and clover-leaf emblem.

110. Niamey on World Map.

1971. French-speaking Countries Co-operative Agency. 1st Anniv.
385. 110. 40 f. multicoloured .. 15 12

111. African Telecommunications Map.

1971. Air. Pan-African Telecommunications Network.
386. 111. 100 f. multicoloured .. 45 25

112. African Mask and Japanese Stamp.

1971. Air. "PHILATOKYO 71" Int. Stamp Exhibition, Japan.
387. 112. 50 f. olive, mar. & grn. 20 15
388. – 100 f. violet, red & brn. 45 25
DESIGN: 100 f. Japanese scroll painting and Niger stamp.

113. "Longwood House, St. Helena" (C. Vernet).

1971. Air. Napoleon's Death. 150th Anniv. Paintings. Multicoloured.
389. 150 f. Type 113 .. .. 65 25
390. 200 f. "Napoleon's Body on his Camp-bed" (Marryat) 90 65

114. Satellite, Radio Waves, and Globe.

116. Scout Badges and Mount Fuji.

115. Pierre de Coubertin and Discus-throwers.

1971. Air. World Telecommunications Day.
391. 114. 100 f. multicoloured .. 45 25

1971. Air. Modern Olympic Games. 75th Anniv.
392. 115. 50 f. red and blue .. 30 15
393. – 100 f. brn., blue, green and black 65 25
394. – 150 f. blue and purple 1·00 55
DESIGNS—VERT. 100 f. Male and female athletes holding torch. HORIZ. 150 f. Start of race.

1971. 13th World Scout Jamboree, Asagiri, Japan.
395. 116. 35 f. red, pur. & orge. 15 12
396. – 40 f. brn., plum & green 15 12
397. – 45 f. green, red & blue 20 15
398. – 50 f. grn., vio. and red 25 15
DESIGNS—VERT. 40 f. Scouts and badge. 45 f. Scouts converging on Japan. HORIZ. 50 f. "Jamboree" in rope, and marquee.

117. "Apollo 15" on Moon.

1971. Air. Moon Mission of "Apollo 15".
399. 117. 150 f. indigo, vio. & brn. 65 40

118. Europafrique Hemispheres.

1971. Renewed "Europafrique" Convention, Niamey. 2nd Anniv.
400. 118. 50 f. multicoloured .. 30 20

120. Garaya (Hausa).

121. De Gaulle in Uniform.

1971. Musical Instruments.
401. – 25 f. brn., grn. & red .. 10 5
402. – 30 f. brn., vio. & grn... 12 8
403. 120. 35 f. bl., grn. & pur... 15 10
404. – 40 f. brn., orge. & grn. 15 10
405. – 45 f. ochre, brn. & bl. 20 12
406. – 50 f. brn., red & blk... 25 15
DESIGNS: 25 f. Gouroumi (Hausa). 30 f. Molo (Djerma). 40 f. Godjie (Djerma-Sonrai). 45 f. Inzad (Tuareg). 50 f. Kountigui (Sonrai).

1971. Air. Gen. Charles De Gaulle (French statesman). 1st Death Anniv.
407. 121. 250 f. multicoloured .. 1·10 1·00

1971. Air. African and Malagasy Posts and Telecommunications Union. 10th Anniv. As T 153 of Cameroun. Multicoloured.
408. 100 f. U.A.M.P.T. H.Q. and rural scene 45 25

INDEX

Countries can be quickly located by referring to the index at the end of this volume.

122. "Audience with Al Hariri" (Baghdad, 1237).

1971. Air. Moslem Miniatures. Mult.
409. 100 f. Type 122 .. .. 45 25
410. 150 f. "Archangel Israfil" (Iraq, 14th-cent.) (vert.) 65 45
411. 200 f. "Horsemen" (Iraq, 1210) 90 55

123. Louis Armstrong.

124. "Children of All Races".

1971. Air. Death of Louis Armstrong (American jazz musician). Multicoloured.
412. 100 f. Type 123 .. .. 45 25
413. 150 f. Armstrong playing trumpet 65 45

1971. U.N.I.C.E.F. 25th Anniv.
414. 124. 50 f. multicoloured .. 25 12

125. "Adoration of the Magi" (Di Bartolo).

1971. Air. Christmas. Paintings. Mult.
415. 100 f. Type 125 .. .. 45 25
416. 150 f. "The Nativity" (Domenico B. Ghirlandaio) (vert.) 65 45
417. 200 f. "Adoration of the Shepherds" (Perugino) 90 60

126. Presidents Pompidou and Hamani.

1972. Air. Visit of Pres. Pompidou of France.
418. 126. 250 f. multicoloured .. 1·10 70

127. Snow Crystals and Olympic Flame.

1972. Air. Winter Olympic Games, Sapporo, Japan.
419. – 100 f. violet, red & grn. 45 25
420. 127. 150 f. red, pur. & vio. 65 45
DESIGN—VERT. 100 f. Ski "Gate" and cherry blossom.

128. "The Redoubt" (detail, Guardi).

1972. Air. U.N.E.S.C.O. "Save Venice" Campaign.
422. – 50 f. mult. (vert.) .. 25 12
423. – 100 f. mult. (vert.) .. 45 20
424. – 150 f. mult. (vert.) .. 65 30
425. 128. 200 f. multicoloured .. 90 45
DESIGNS: Nos. 422/5 depict various details of Guardi's painting, "The Masked Ball".

129. J. Brahms and Music.

130. Saluting Hand.

1972. Air. Johannes Brahms (composer). 75th Death Anniv.
426. 129. 100 f. grn., myrtle & red 45 20

1972. Air. Int. Scout Seminar, Cotonou.
427. 130. 150 f. vio., blue & orge. 65 35

131. Star Symbol and Open Book.

1972. Int. Book Year.
428. 131. 35 f. purple and green 15 12
429. – 40 f. blue and lake .. 15 12
DESIGN: 40 f. Boy reading, galleon and early aircraft.

132. Heart Operation.

1972. Air. World Heart Month.
430. 132. 100 f. brown and red 45 25

133. Bleriot crossing the Channel, 1909.

1972. Air. Milestones in Aviation History.
431. 133. 50 f. brn., blue & lake 20 12
432. – 75 f. grey, brn. & blue 30 20
433. – 100 f. ultram., blue and purple 45 30
DESIGNS: 75 f. Lindbergh crossing the Atlantic in "Spirit of St. Louis". 100 f. First flight of "Concorde".

134. Satellite and Universe.

1972. Air. World Telecommunications Day.
434. 134. 100 f. brn., purple & red 45 25

135. Boxing.

1972. Air. Olympic Games, Munich. Sports and Munich Buildings.
435. 135. 50 f. brown and blue 20 12
436. – 100 f. brn. and green 45 25
437. – 150 f. brown and red .. 65 35
438. – 200 f. brown & mauve 90 50
DESIGNS—VERT. 100 f. Long-jumping. 150 f. Football. HORIZ. 200 f. Running.

137. A. G. Bell and Telephone.

1972. Air. Alexander Graham Bell (inventor of telephone). 50th Death Anniv.
440. **137.** 100 f. blue, pur. & red 45 25

138. "Europe on Africa" Map.

1972. Air. "Europafrique" Co-operation.
441. **138.** 50 f. red, green & blue 20 12

140. Herdsman and Cattle. 141. Lottery Wheel.

1972. Medicinal Salt-Ponds at In-Gall. Mult.
442. 35 f. Type **140** 15 12
443. 40 f. Cattle in Salt-pond .. 15 12

1972. National Lottery. 6th Anniv.
444. **141.** 35 f. multicoloured .. 15 2

142. Postal Runner.

1972. Air. U.P.U. Day. Postal Transport.
445. **142.** 50 f. brn., grn. & lake 20 15
446. – 100 f. grn., blue & lake 40 25
447. – 150 f. grn., violet & lake 65 35
DESIGNS: 100 f. Rural mail-van. 150 f. Loading mail-plane.

1972. West African Monetary Union. 10th Anniv. As Type **109** of Dahomey.
448. 40 f. grey, violet & brown 15 12

1972. Air. Gold Medal Winners. Munich Olympic Games. Nos. 435/8 optd. with events and names, etc.
449. **135.** 50 f. brown and blue.. 20 12
450. – 100 f. brown and green 40 25
451. – 150 f. brown and red.. 65 35
452. – 200 f. brown and mauve 90 50
OVERPRINTS: 50 f. **WELTER CORREA MEDAILLE D'OR.** 100 f. **TRIPLE SAUT SANEIEV MEDAILLE D'OR.** 150 f. **FOOTBALL POLOGNE MEDAILLE D'OR.** 200 f. **MARATHON SHORTER MEDAILLE D'OR.**

143. "The Crow and the Fox".

1972. Air. Fables of Jean de La Fontaine.
453. **143.** 25 f. blk., brn. & green 12 8
454. – 50 f. brn., grn. & purple 20 15
455. – 75 f. choc., grn. & brn. 30 25
DESIGNS: 50 f. "The Lion and the Rat". 75 f. "The Monkey and the Leopard".

144. Astronauts on Moon.

1972. Air. Moon Flight of "Apollo 17".
456. **144.** 250 f. multicoloured .. 1·10 70

145. Dromedary Race. 146. Pole-vaulting.

1972. Niger Sports.
457. **145.** 35 f. maroon, red & blue 15 12
458. – 40 f. lake, brn. & green 15 12
DESIGN: 40 f. Horse race.

1973. 2nd African Games, Lagos, Nigeria. Multicoloured.
459. 35 f. Type **146** 15 12
460. 40 f. Basketball 15 12
461. 45 f. Boxing 20 15
462. 75 f. Football 35 20

147. "Young Athlete". 148. Knight and Pawn.

1973. Air. Antique Art Treasures.
463. **147.** 50 f. red 20 12
464. – 100 f. violet 40 25
DESIGN: 100 f. "Head of Hermes".

1973. World Chess Championships, Reykjavik, Iceland.
465. **148.** 100 f. grn., blue & red 40 30

149. "Abutilon pannosum". 150. Interpol Badge.

1973. Rare African Flowers. Multicoloured.
466. 30 f. Type **149** 12 10
467. 45 f. "Crotalaria barkae" 20 12
468. 60 f. "Dichrostachys cinerea" 25 20
469. 80 f. "Caralluma decaisneana" 35 25

1973. International Criminal Police Organization (Interpol). 50th Anniv.
470. **150.** 50 f. mulcticoloured .. 20 12

151. Scout with Radio.

1973. Air. Scouting in Niger.
471. **151.** 25 f. brn., grn. & red.. 10 8
472. – 50 f. brn., green & red 20 12
473. – 100 f. brn., grn. & red 40 25
474. – 150 f. brn., grn. & red 60 40
DESIGNS: 50 f. First Aid. 100 f. Care of animals. 150 f. Care of the environment.

152. Hansen and Microscope. 153. Nurse tending Child.

1973. Dr. Hansen's Discovery of Leprosy Bacillus. Cent.
475. **152.** 50 f. brn., grn. & blue 20 12

1973. W.H.O. 25th Anniv.
476. **153.** 50 f. brn., red & blue 20 12

154. "The Crucifixion" (Hugo van der Goes).

1973. Air. Easter. Paintings. Mult.
477. 50 f. Type **154** 20 12
478. 100 f. "The Deposition" (Cima de Conegliano) (horiz.) 40 25
479. 150 f. "Pieta" (Bellini) (horiz.) 60 40

155. Airliner and Mail-van.

1973. Stamp Day.
480. **155.** 100 f. brn., red & green 40 25

156. W.M.O. Emblem and "Weather Conditions".

1973. Air. W.M.O. Cent.
481. **156.** 100 f. brn., red and grn. 40 25

157. "Crouching Lionness" (Delacroix).

1973. Paintings by Delacroix. Multicoloured.
482. 150 f. Type **157** 60 40
483. 200 f. "Tigress and Cub" 80 50

158. Crocodile.

1973. Wild Animals from "Park W".
484. **158.** 25 f. multicoloured .. 10 8
485. – 35 f. grey, gold & blk. 15 10
486. – 40 f. multicoloured .. 15 10
487. – 80 f. multicoloured .. 35 20
DESIGNS: 35 f. Elephant. 40 f. Hippopotamus. 80 f. Wild boar.

159. Eclipse over Mountain.

1973. Total Eclipse of the Sun.
488. **159.** 40 f. violet 15 10

1973. Air. 24th Int. Scouting Congress, Nairobi, Kenya. Nos. 473/4 optd. **24 Conference Mondiale du Scoutisme NAIROBI, 1973.**
489. 100 f. brn., grn. & red .. 40 25
490. 150 f. brn., grn. & red .. 60 40

160. Palomino.

1973. Horse-breeding. Multicoloured.
491. 50 f. Type **160** 20 12
492. 75 f. French trotter .. 35 20
493. 80 f. English thoroughbred 35 20
494. 100 f. Arab thoroughbred 40 25

1973. Pan-African Drought Relief. African Solidarity. No. 436 surch. **SECHERESSE SOLIDARITE AFRICAINE** and value.
495. **140.** 100 f. on 35 f. mult. .. 60 30

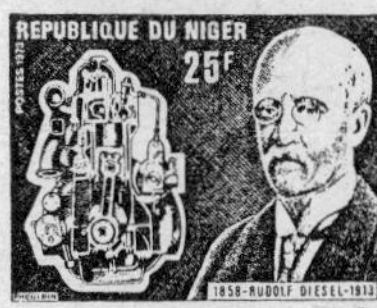

161. Rudolf Diesel and Engine.

1973. Rudolf Diesel (engineer). 60th Death Anniv.
496. **161.** 25 f. bl., mar. & grey 12 8
497. – 50 f. grey, grn. & blue 25 12
498. – 75 f. blue, blk. & mve. 35 20
499. – 125 f. blue, red & grn. 55 30
DESIGNS: 50 f. Type BB-610 ch. diesel locomotive. 75 f. Type 060-DB 1 diesel locomotive. 125 f. Type CC-72004 diesel locomotive.

1973. African and Malagasy Posts and Telecommunications Union. As Type **182** of Cameroun.
500. 100 f. red, green & brown.. 50 25

1973. Air. African Fortnight, Brussels. As Type **183** of Cameroun.
501. 100 f. purple, blue and red 50 25

162. T.V. Set and Class. 163. "Apollo".

1973. Schools Television Service.
502. **162.** 50 f. blk., red and blue 20 10

1973. 3rd Int. French Language and Culture Conf., Liege. No. 385 optd. **3e CONFERENCE DE LA FRANCOPHONIE LIEGE OCTOBRE 1973.**
503. **110.** 40 f. multicoloured .. 20 10

1973. Classical Sculptures.
504. **163.** 50 f. green and brown 25 12
505. – 50 f. black and brown 25 12
506. – 50 f. brown and red .. 25 12
507. – 50 f. purple and red .. 25 12
DESIGNS: No. 505, "Atlas". No. 506, "Hercules". No. 507, "Venus".

164. Bees and Honeycomb.

1973. World Savings Day.
508. **164.** 40 f. brn., red and blue 20 10

165. " Food for the World ". **166.** Copernicus and " Sputnik I ".

1973. Air. World Food Programme. 10th Anniv.
509. **165.** 50 f. violet, red and blue 25 12

1973. Air. Copernicus. 500th Birth Anniv.
510. **166.** 150 f. brn., blue and red 60 30

167. Pres. John Kennedy.

1973. Air. President Kennedy. 10th Death Anniv.
511. **167.** 100 f. multicoloured .. 50 25

168. Kounta Songhai Blanket. **170.** Lenin.

169. Barges on River Niger.

1973. Niger Textiles. Multicoloured.
513. 35 f. Type **168** 15 12
514. 40 f. Tcherka Snghai blanket (horiz.) .. 20 15

1974. Air. Ascent of Niger by " Fleet of Hope ". 1st Anniv.
515. **169.** 50 f. blue, grn. & red .. 25 12
516. – 75 f. pur., blue & green 35 20
DESIGN: 75 f. Tug and barge.

1974. Air. Lenin. 50th Death Anniv.
517. **170.** 50 c. brown 25 12

171. Slalom Skiing.

1974. Air. Winter Olympic Games. 50th Anniv.
518. **171.** 200 f. red, brn. & blue 1·00 50

172. Newly-born Baby.

1974. World Population Year.
519. **172.** 50 f. multicoloured .. 25 12

173. Footballers and "Global" Ball.

1974. Air. World Cup Football Championships, West Germany.
520. **173.** 75 f. vio., blk. & brn... 35 20
521. – 150 f. brn., grn. & bl.-grn. 60 30
522. – 200 f. bl., orge. & grn. 1·00 50
DESIGNS: 150 f., 200 f. Football scenes similar to Type **173**.

174. "The Crucifixion" (Grunewald).

1974. Air. Easter. Paintings. Multicoloured.
524. 50 f. Type **174** 25 12
525. 75 f. "Avignon Pieta" (attributed to E. Quarton) 35 20
526. 125 f. "The Entombment" (G. Isenmann) 55 25

175. Locomotive "230k" (1948) and U.S.A. Loco 2222 (1938).

1974. Famous Railway Locomotives of the Steam Era.
527. **175.** 50 f. grn., blk. & violet 25 12
528. – 75 f. grn., blk. & brn. 35 20
529. – 100 f. grn., brn., blk. & blue 50 25
530. – 150 f. brn., blk. & red 60 35
DESIGNS: 75 f. P.L.M. loco "C 21" (1893). 100 f. U.S.S. loco "220" (1866) and British "231" class loco "Mallard" (1939). 150 f. Seguin locomotive (1829) and Stephenson's "Rocket" (1829).

1974. Council of Accord. 15th Anniv. As Type **131** of Dahomey.
531. 40 f. multicoloured .. 20 15

176. Chess "Knights".

1974. Air 21st Chess Olympics, Nice.
532. **176.** 50 f. brn., blue & indigo 25 12
533. – 75 f. purple, brn. & grn. 35 20
DESIGN: 75 f. Chess "Kings".

177. Marconi and Steam Yacht.

1974. Guglielmo Marconi (radio pioneer). Birth Cent.
534. **177.** 50 f. blue, brn. & mve. 25 12

178. Astronaut on Palm of Hand. **179.** Tree on Palm of Hand.

1974. Air. 1st Landing on Moon. Fifth Anniv.
535. **178.** 150 f. brn., bl. & ind... 60 35

1974. National Tree Week.
536. **179.** 35 f. bl.-grn., yell.-grn. and brown 15 12

180. "The Rhinoceros" (Longhi). **181.** Camel Saddle.

1974. Air. Europafrique.
537. **180.** 250 f. multicoloured .. 1·25 60

1974. Handicrafts.
538. **181.** 40 f. red, bl. & brn. .. 20 15
539. – 50 f. bl., red & brn. .. 25 12
DESIGN: 50 f. Statuettes of horses.

182. Chopin.

1974. Frederic Chopin. 125th Death Anniv.
541. **182.** 100 f. blk., red & blue 50 25

1974. Beethoven's Ninth Symphony Commemoration. As Type **182**.
542. 100 f. lilac, blue & indigo .. 50 25
DESIGN: 100 f. Beethoven.

183. European Woman and Aircraft. **184.** "Skylab" over Africa.

1974. Air. Universal Postal Union. Cent.
543. **183.** 50 f. turq., grn. & pur. 25 12
544. – 100 f. bl., mauve. & ultram. 50 25
545. – 150 f. brn., bl.& indigo 60 35
546. – 200 f. brn., orge.-brn. and red .. .. 1·00 50
DESIGNS: 100 f. Japanese woman and railway locomotives. 150 f. American Indian woman and ships. 200 f. African woman and road transport.

1974. Air. "Skylab" Commemoration.
547. **184.** 100 f. vio., brn. & blue 50 25

185. Don-don Drum. **187.** "Virgin and Child" (Correggio).

186. Tree and Compass Rose.

1974.
548. **185.** 60 f. pur., grn. & red .. 25 12

1974. Tenere Tree (desert landmark). First Death Anniv.
549. **186.** 50 f. brn., blue & ochre 25 12

1974. Air. Christmas. Multicoloured.
550. 100 f. Type **187** 50 25
551. 150 f. "Virgin and Child, and St. Hilary" (F. Lippi) 60 35
552. 200 f. "Virgin and Child" (Murillo) .. .. .. 1·00 50

188. " Apollo " Spacecraft. **189.** European and African Women embracing Globe.

1975. Air. Soviet/US Co-operation in Space.
553. **188.** 50 f. green, red & blue 20 10
554. – 100 f. grey, red & blue 40 20
555. – 150 f. pur., plum & bl. 60 30
DESIGNS: 100 f. Docking in Space. 150 f. " Souyuz " spacecraft.

1975. Air. Europafrique.
556. **189.** 250 f. brn., pur. & red 1·10 55

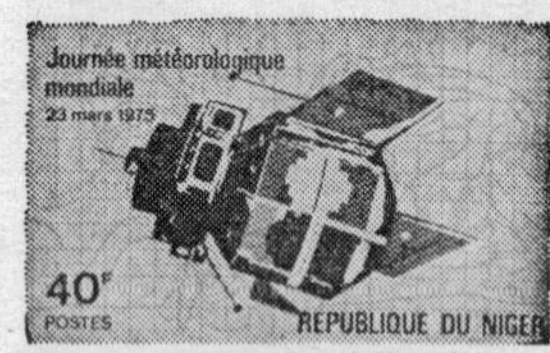

190. Communications Satellite and Weather Map.

1975. World Meteorological Day.
557. **190.** 40 f. red, black & blue 15 8

191. Lt-Col. S. Kountche, Head of State.

1975. Air. Military Coup. 1st Anniv.
558. **191.** 100 f. brown and purple 40 20

192. " Christ in the Garden of Olives ". (Delacoix).

1975. Air. Easter. Multicoloured.
559. 75 Type **192** 30 15
560. 125 f. " The Crucifixion " (El Greco) (vert.) .. 50 25
561. 150 f. " The Resurrection " (Limousin) (vert.) .. 60 30

193. " City of Truro " (G.W.R., England, 1903).

1975. Famous Locomotives. Multicoloured.
562. 50 f. Type **193** 20 10
563. 75 f. " 5003 " (Germany, 1937) 30 15
564. 100 f. " The General " (U.S.A., 1863) 40 20
565. 125 f. " BB-15000 " Electric (France, 1971) 50 25

1975. Birds. As Nos. 296 and 298, but dated " 1975 ". Multicoloured.
567. 25 f. Abyssinian roller (postage) 10 5
568. 100 f. Amethyst starlings (air) 40 20

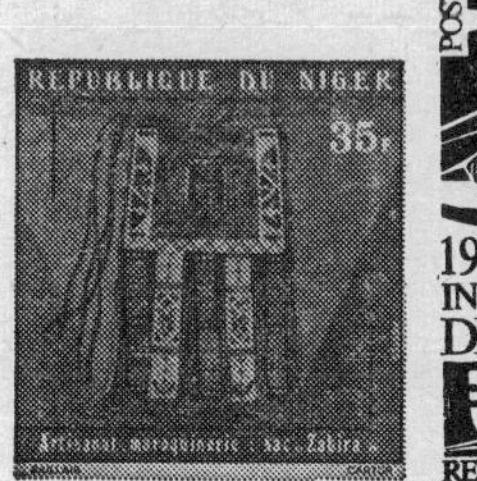

194. " Zabira " Leather Bag. **195.** African Woman and Child.

1975. Niger Handicrafts. Multicoloured.
569. 35 f. Type **194** 15 8
570. 40 f. Chequered rug .. 15 8
571. 45 f. Flower pot 20 10
572. 60 f. Gourd 25 12

1975. International Women's Year.
573. **195.** 50 f. blue, brn. & red 20 10

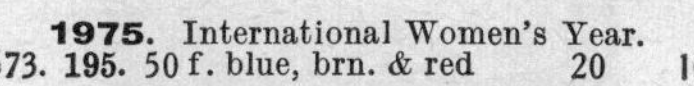

196. Dr. Schweitzer and Lambarene Hospital.

1975. Dr. Albert Schweitzer. Birth Cent.
574. **196.** 100 f. brn., grn. & blk. 40 20

197. Peugeot, 1892.

1975. Early Motor-cars.
575. **197.** 50 f. blue and mauve 20 10
576. – 75 f. purple and blue 30 25
577. – 100 f. mauve and green 40 10
578. – 125 f. green and red .. 50 25
DESIGNS: 75 f. Daimler, 1895. 100 f. Fiat, 1899. 125 f. Cadillac, 1903.

REPUBLIQUE DU NIGER 50F POSTES TETRADRACHME DE LEONTINI 460 AV.JC

198. Tree and Sun. **200.** Leontini Tetradrachme.

199. Boxing.

1975. National Tree Week.
579. **198.** 40 f. grn., oran. and red 15 8

1975. Traditional Sports.
580. **199.** 35 f. brn., oran. & blk. 15 8
581. – 40 f. brn., grn. & blk. 15 8
582. – 45 f. brn., blue & blk. 20 10
583. – 50 f. brn., red and blk. 20 10
DESIGNS—VERT. 40 f. Boxing. 50 f. Wrestling. HORIZ. 45 f. Wrestling.

1975. Ancient Coins.
584. **200.** 50 f. grey, blue & red 20 10
585. – 75 f. grey, blue & mve. 30 15
586. – 100 f. grey, oran. & bl. 40 20
587. – 125 f. grey, pur. & grn. 50 25
COINS: 75 f. Athens tetradrachme. 100 f. Himer diadrachme. 125 f. Gela tetradrachme.

201. Putting the Shot.

1975. Air. " Pre-Olympic Year ". Olympic Games, Montreal (1976).
588. **201.** 150 f. brown and red .. 60 30
589. – 200 f. red, chestnut and brown 85 45
DESIGNS: 200 f. Gymnastics.

202. Starving Family.

1975. Campaign Against Drought.
590. **202.** 40 f. blue, brn. & oran. 15 8
591. – 45 f. brown and blue 20 10
592. – 60 f. blue, grn. & oran. 25 12
DESIGNS: 45 f. Animal skeletons. 60 f. Truck bringing supplies.

203. Merchant's Boat crossing Niger.

1975. Tourism. Multicoloured.
593. 40 f. Type **203** 15 8
594. 45 f. Boubon Camp entrance 20 10
595. 50 f. Boubon Camp view .. 20 10

204. UN Emblem and Peace Dove.

1975. Air. United Nations Organisation. 30th Anniv.
596. **204.** 100 f. light blue & blue 40 20

205. " Virgin of Seville " (Murillo).

1975. Air. Christmas. Multicoloured.
597. 50 f Type **205** 20 10
598. 75 f. " Adoration of the Shepherds " (Tintoretto) (horiz.) 30 15
599. 125 f. " Virgin with Angels " (Master of Burgo d'Osma) 50 25

1975. Air " Apollo-Soyuz " Space Link. Nos. 553/5 optd. **JONCTION 17 Juillet 1975.**
600. **188.** 50 f. grn., red and blue 20 10
601. – 100 f. grey, red & blue 40 20
602. – 150 f purple, plum & bl. 60 30

206. " Ashak ".

1976. Alphabetisation Campaign. Mult.
603. 25 f. Type **206** 10 5
604. 30 f. " Kaska " 12 5
605. 40 f. " Iccee " 15 8
606. 50 f. " Tuuri-nya " .. 20 10
607. 60 f. " Lekki " 25 12

207. Ice-hockey.

1976. Winter Olympic Games, Innsbruck. Multicoloured.
608. 40 f. Type **207** (postage) .. 20 10
609. 50 f. Tobogganing .. 25 12
610. 150 f. Ski-jumping .. 75 35
611. 200 f. Figure-skating (air) 1·00 50
612. 300 f. Cross-country skiing 1·50 75

208. Early Telephone and Satellite.

1976. Telephone Centenary.
614. **208.** 100 f. oran., blue & grn. 50 25

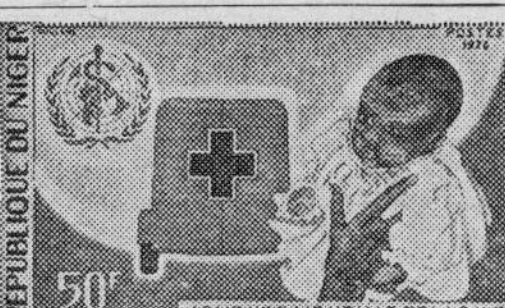

209. Baby and Ambulance.

1976. World Health Day.
615. **209.** 50 f. red, brn. and pur. 25 12

210. Distribution of Provisions.

1976. Take-over by Armed Forces (F.A.N.) 2nd Anniv. Multicoloured.
616. 50 f. Type **210** 25 12
617. 100 f. Soldiers with bull-dozer (horiz.) 50 25

211. Washington crossing the Delaware.

1976. American Revolution. Bicent. Mult.
618. 40 f. Type **211** (postage) .. 20 10
619. 50 f. First soldiers of the Revolution 25 12
620. 150 f. Joseph Warren—martyr of Bunker Hill (air) 75 35
621. 200 f. John Paul Jones aboard the " Bonhomme Richard " .. .. 1·00 50
622. 300 f. Molly Pitcher—heroine of Monmouth .. 1·50 75

212. Zeppelin " LZ-129 " crossing Lake Constance.

1976. Air. Zeppelin Airships. 75th Anniv. Multicoloured.
624. 40 f. Type **212** 20 10
625. 50 f. " LZ-3 " over Wurzberg 25 12
626. 150 f. " L-9 " over Friedrichshafen 75 35
627. 200 f. " LZ-9 " over Rothenburg (vert.) .. .. 1·00 50
628. 300 f. " LZ-130 " over Essen .. .. .. 1·50 75

213. " Europafrique " Symbols.

1976. "Europafrique".
630. **213.** 100 f. multicoloured .. 50 25

214. Plant Cultivation.

1976. Communal Works. Multicoloured.
631. 25 f. Type **214** 12 5
632. 30 f. Harvesting rice .. 15 8

215. Boxing.

1976. Olympic Games, Montreal. Mult.
633. 40 f. Type **215** 20 10
634. 50 f. Basketball 25 12
635. 60 f. Football 30 15
636. 80 f. Cycling 40 20
637. 100 f. Judo 50 25

216. Motobecane '125'.

1976. Motorcycles.
639. **216.** 50 f. violet, brn. & turq. 25 12
640. – 75 f. grn., red & turq. 35 20
641. – 100 f. brn., oran. & pur. 50 25
642. – 125 f. slate, olive & blk. 65 35
DESIGNS: 75 f. Norton "Challenge". 100 f. B.M.W. "903". 125 f. Kawasaki "1000".

217. Cultivation Map.

1976. Operation "Sahel Vert". Mult.
643. 40 f. Type **217** 20 10
644. 45 f. Tending plants (vert.) 25 12
645. 60 f. Planting sapling (vert.) 30 15

218. Basket Making.

1976. Niger Women's Association. Mult.
646. 40 f. Type **218** 20 10
647. 45 f. Hairdressing (horiz.) 25 12
648. 50 f. Making pottery .. 25 12

OFFICIAL STAMPS

O **1.** Djerma Woman.

1962. Figures of value in black.
O 121. O **1.** 1 f. violet 5 5
O 122. 2 f. yellow-green .. 5 5
O 123. 5 f. blue 5 5
O 124. 10 f. red 5 5
O 125. 20 f. ultramarine .. 10 10
O 126. 25 f. orange .. 12 12
O 127. 30 f. blue 12 12
O 128. 35 f. green 15 15
O 129. 40 f. brown.. .. 20 20
O 130. 50 f. slate 25 25
O 131. 60 f. rose 25 25
O 132. 85 f. blue-green .. 35 20
O 133. 100 f. purple .. 45 20
O 134. 200 f. blue 90 50

POSTAGE DUE STAMPS

1921. Postage Due stamps of Upper Senegal and Niger "Figure" key-type optd. **TERRITOIRE DU NIGER.**
D 18. M. 5 c. green 5 5
D 19. 10 c. red 5 5
D 20. 15 c. grey 8 8
D 21. 20 c. brown 8 8
D 22. 30 c. blue 10 10
D 23. 50 c. black 10 10
D 24. 60 c. orange 15 15
D 25. 1 f. violet 20 20

D **1.** Zinder Fort.

1927.
D 73. D **1.** 2 c. red and blue .. 5 5
D 74. 4 c. black and orange 5 5
D 75. 5 c. violet and yellow 5 5
D 76. 10 c. violet and claret 5 5
D 77. 15 c. orange & green 5 5
D 78. 20 c. sepia and red .. 5 5
D 79. 25 c. sepia and black 5 5
D 80. 30 c. grey and violet 12 12
D 81. 50 c. red on green .. 8 8
D 82. 60 c. orange and lilac on blue 8 8
D 83. 1 f. violet & blue on bl. 10 10
D 84. 2 f. mauve and red .. 8 8
D 85. 3 f. blue and brown.. 10 10

DESIGNS: A, Cross of Iferouane. B, Cross of Tahoua.

D **2.** Cross of Agadez.

1962.
D 123. D **2.** 50 c. green 5 5
D 124. 1 f. violet 5 5
D 125. 2 f. myrtle 5 5
D 126. A. 3 f. mauve 5 5
D 127. 5 f. green 5 5
D 128. 10 f. orange 5 5
D 129. B. 15 f. blue 8 8
D 130. 20 f. red 10 10
D 131. 50 f. chocolate .. 20 20

NIGER COAST PROTECTORATE BC

A district on the W. coast of Africa absorbed into S. Nigeria. Now uses stamps of Nigeria.

1892. Stamps of Gt. Britain (Queen Victoria) optd. **BRITISH PROTECTORATE OIL RIVERS.**
1. **54.** ½d. red .. .. .. 1·50 1·90
2. **40.** 1d. lilac .. .. .. 1·50 1·90
3. **56.** 2d. green and red.. .. 2·25 2·25
4. **57.** 2½d. purple and blue .. 1·75 1·60
5. **61.** 5d. purple and blue .. 2·25 3·50
6. **65.** 1s. green .. .. .. 11·00 11·00

1893. Half of No. 2 surch. ½d.
7. **40.** ½d. on half of 1d. lilac .. 32·00 32·00

1893. Nos. 1 to 6 surch. in words or figs.
20. **56.** ½d. on 2d. green and red 38·00 38·00
21. **57.** ½d. on 2½d. pur. on blue 38·00 34·00
38. **56.** 1s. on 2d. green and red 70·00 80·00
40. 5s. on 2d. green and red £2400 £2500
41. **61.** 10s. on 5d. purple & blue £2400 £2500
43. **65.** 20s. on 1s. green ..£30000

1.

2.

1893. Various frames with "OIL RIVERS" barred out and "NIGER COAST" above.
45. **1.** ½d. red .. .. .. 1·00 1·25
46b. 1d. blue .. .. .. 1·25 1·40
47. 2d. green .. .. .. 3·00 3·50
48. 2½d. red .. .. .. 1·00 1·25
49. 5d. grey-lilac .. .. 1·25 2·00
50. 1s. black .. .. .. 4·00 4·00

1894. Surch. with large figures.
58. "½" on half 1d. (No. 46b) £180 50·00
59. "1" on half 2d. (No. 3).. 90·00 70·00

1894. Various frames.
66. **2.** ½d. green 20 20
67. 1d. red 40 50
68. 2d. red 50 50
69. 2½d. blue .. .. .. 60 1·10
70a. 5d. purple.. .. .. 1·75 4·50
71. 6d. brown.. .. .. 2·25 1·60
72. 1s. black .. .. .. 2·25 2·75
73. 2s. 6d. brown .. .. 6·00 9·00
74. 10s. violet.. .. .. 26·00 30·00

1894. No. 67 bisected and surch.
64. **2.** ½d. on half of 1d. red .. £200 50·00

1894. Surch. **ONE HALFPENNY** and bars.
65. **2.** ½d. on 2½d. blue .. 50·00 38·00

NIGERIA BC

A former Br. colony on the W. coast of Africa, comprising the territories of N. and S. Nigeria and Lagos. Now a Federation divided into the three self-governing Regions of Northern Nigeria, Western Nigeria and Eastern Nigeria and the Federal Territory of Lagos. Attained full independence within the Br. Commonwealth in 1960 and became a Federal Republic in 1963.

The Eastern Region (known as Biafra) (q.v) seceded in 1967, remaining independent until overrun by Federal Nigerian troops during Jan. 1970.

1973. 100 kobo = 1 naira.

1.

ILLUSTRATIONS
British Commonwealth and all overprints and surcharges are FULL SIZE. Foreign Countries have been reduced to ¾-LINEAR.

1914.
25a. **1.** ½d. green 10 10
25b. 1d. red 10 10
26. 1½d. orange 35 15
25c. 2d. grey 40 15
27. 2d. chestnut 75 95
28. 2d. chocolate 15 15
4. 2½d. blue 55 30
5. 3d. purple on yellow .. 60 1·10
25d. 3d. violet .. .. 1·10 1·10
29. 3d. blue .. .. .. 1·10 80
20. 4d. black & red on yellow 30 30
25e. 6d. purple.. .. .. 55 80
22. 1s. black on green .. 75 40
9. 2s. 6d. blk. & red on blue 2·50 3·25
10b. 5s. green & red on yellow 6·00 6·50
11a. 10s. green & red on green 15·00 15·00
12. £1 purple & black on red 48·00 50·00

1935. Silver Jubilee. As T **11** of Antigua.
30. 1½d. blue and grey .. 15 15
31. 2d. green and blue .. 20 20
32. 3d. brown and blue .. 40 45
33. 1s. grey and purple .. 1·40 1·75

2. Apapa Wharf.

DESIGNS—VERT. 1d. Cocoa. 1½d. Tin dredger. 2d. Timber industry. 3d. Fishing village. 4d. Cotton ginnery. 6d. Habe Minaret. 1s. Fulani cattle. HORIZ. 5s. Oil palms. 10 s. Niger at Jebba. £1 Canoe pulling.

10. Victoria-Buea Road.

1936.
34. **2.** ½d. green.. .. .. 15 12
35. – 1d. red 15 12
36. – 1½d. brown 20 12
37. – 2d. black.. .. .. 45 25
38. – 3d. blue 60 50
39. – 4d. brown 80 80
40. – 6d. violet 75 55
41. – 1s. olive-green .. .. 2·75 2·50
42. **10.** 2s. 6d. black and blue .. 3·75 4·50
43. – 5 s. black and olive .. 7·00 7·50
44. – 10s. black and grey .. 18·00 20·00
45. – £1 black and orange .. 35·00 35·00

1937. Coronation. As T **2** of Aden.
46. 1d. red 8 8
47. 1½d. brown 10 10
48. 3d. blue 15 20

14. King George VI.

DESIGNS: 2s. 6d., 5s As Nos. 42 and 44 but with portrait of King George VI.

1938.
49. **14.** ½d. green.. .. .. 8 8
50a. 1d. red 8 8
50b. 1d. lilac 8 8
51. 1½d. brown 8 8
52. 2d. black.. .. .. 8 10
52ab. 2d. red 12 10
52a. 2½d. orange 10 20
53. 3d. blue 8 8
53a 3d. black.. .. .. 8 8
54. 4d. orange .. .. 9·00 3·00
54a. 4d. blue 8 12
55a. 6d. violet 10 8
56a. 1s. olive 20 8
57a. 1s. 3d. blue 25 12
58b. – 2s. 6d. black and blue .. 80 55
59a. – 5s. black and orange .. 1·40 90

1946. Victory. As T **4** of Aden.
60. 1½d. brown 8 8
61. 4d. blue 12 15

1948. Silver Wedding. As T **5/6** of Aden.
62. 1d. magenta 8 8
63. 5s. orange .. .. 2·75 3·00

1949. U.P.U. As Antigua T **14/17.**
64. 1d. purple 15 15
65. 3d. blue 20 20
66. 6d. purple 45 35
67. 1s. olive 70 80

1953. Coronation. As T **7** of Aden.
68. 1½d. black and emerald .. 8 5

15. Old Manilla Currency.

16. Victoria Harbour.

17. New and Old Lagos.

1953.

69. 15. ½d. black and orange .. 5 5
70. – 1d. black and bronze .. 5 5
71. – 1½d. blue-green 8 8
72. – 2d. black and ochre .. 8 5
72d.– 2d. slate 8 5
73. – 3d. black and purple .. 8 5
74. – 4d. black and blue .. 8 5
75. – 6d. brown and black .. 10 8
76. – 1s. black and maroon .. 20 10
77. 16. 2s. 6d. black and green .. 50 15
78. – 5s. black and red .. 85 40
79. – 10s. black and brown .. 2·00 45
80. 17. £1 black and violet .. 5·00 1·50

DESIGNS—HORIZ. As T 15: 1d. Bornu horsemen. 1½d. "Groundnuts". 2d. "Tin". 3d. Jebba Bridge and R. Niger. 4d. "Cocoa". 1s., "Timber". As T 16: 5s. "Palm-oil". 10s. "Hides and skins". VERT. as T 15: 6d. Ife bronze.

1956. Royal Visit. No. 72 optd. **ROYAL VISIT 1956.**

81. 2d. black and ochre 8 5

18. Victoria Harbour.

1958. Cent. of Victoria, S. Cameroons.

82. 18. 3d. black and purple .. 8 5

19. Lugard Hall.

1959. Attainment of Self-Government. Northern Region of Nigeria.

83. 19. 3d. black and purple .. 8 5
84. – 1s. black and green .. 25 25

DESIGN: 1s. Kano Mosque.

20. Legislative Building.

1960. Independence Commem.

85. 20. 1d. black and red .. 5 5
86. – 3d. black and blue .. 10 10
87. – 6d. green and brown .. 12 12
88. – 1s. 3d. blue and yellow .. 25 25

DESIGNS—As T 20: 3d. African paddling canoe. 6d. Federal Supreme Court. LARGER (40×24 mm.): 1s. 3d. Dove, torch and map.

21. Groundnuts.

22. Central Bank.

1961.

89 21. ½d. emerald 5 5
90.– 1d. violet 5 5
91.– 1½d. red 8 10
92.– 2d. blue 5 5
93.– 3d. green 5 5
94.– 4d. blue 8 5
95.– 6d. yellow and black .. 8 5
96.– 1s. yellow-green .. 15 5
97.– 1s. 3d. orange .. 25 8
98. 22. 2s. 6d. black and yellow 40 12
99.– 5s. black and emerald .. 1·00 25
100.– 10s. black and blue .. 2·25 75
101.– £1 black and red .. 4·00 2·50

DESIGNS—As T 21: 1d. Coal mining. 1½d. Adult education. 2d. Pottery. 3d. Oyo carver. 4d. Weaving. 6d. Benin mask. 1s. Hornbill. 1s. 3d. Camel train. As T 22: 5s. Nigeria Museum. 10s. Kano Airport. £1, Lagos Railway Station.

23. Globe and Locomotive.

1961. Admission into U.P.U. Inscr. as in T 23.

102. 23. 1d. orange and blue .. 5 5
103. – 3d. olive and black .. 8 8
104. – 1s. 3d. blue and red .. 20 15
105. – 2s. 6d. green and blue 35 35

DESIGNS: Globe and mail-van (3d.); aircraft (1s. 3d.); ship (2s. 6d.).

24. Natural Resources Map.

1961. Independence. 1st Anniv.

106. – 3d. multicoloured .. 5 5
107. 24. 4d. green and orange .. 10 12
108. – 6d. emerald 10 10
109. – 1s. 3d. grey, emer. & bl. 20 20
110. – 2s. 6d. green and blue .. 35 35

DESIGNS—VERT. 3d. Arms HORIZ. 6d. Nigerian eagle. 1s. 3d. Eagles in flight. 2s 6d. Nigerians and flag.

25. "Health".

1962. Lagos Conf. of African and Malagasy States.

111. 25. 1d. bistre 5 5
112. – 3d. purple 8 8
113. – 6d. green 10 10
114. – 1s. brown 15 15
115. – 1s. 3d. blue 20 20

DESIGNS: Map and emblems symbolising Culture (3d.); Commerce (6d.); Communications (1s.); Co-operation (1s. 3d.).

26. Campaign Emblem and Parasites.

1962. Malaria Eradication. Inscr. as in T 26.

116. 26. 3d. green and red .. 5 5
117. – 6d. blue and purple .. 10 10
118. – 1s. 3d. magenta & blue 20 20
119. – 2s. 6d. blue and brown 30 35

DESIGNS (embodying emblem): 6d. Insecticide-spraying. 1s. 3d. Aerial spraying. 2s. 6d. Mother, child and microscope.

27. National Monument.

1962. Independence. 2nd Anniv.

120. 27. 3d. green and blue .. 5 5
121. – 5s. red, green and violet 65 75

DESIGN—VERT. 5s. Benin Bronze.

28. Fair Emblem.

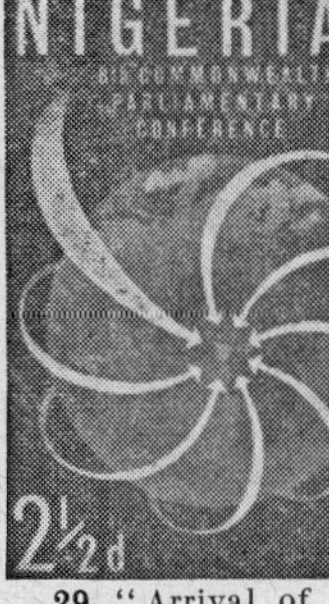

29. "Arrival of Delegates".

1962. Int. Trade Fair, Lagos.

122. 28. 1d. red and olive .. 5 5
123. – 6d. black and red .. 8 8
124. – 1s. black and brown .. 15 15
125. – 2s. 6d. yellow and blue 35 35

DESIGNS—HORIZ. 6d. "Cogwheels of Industry". 1s. "Cornucopia of Commerce". 2s. 6d. Oilwells and tanker.

1962. 8th Commonwealth Parliamentary Conference, Lagos.

126. 29. 2½d. blue 8 8
127. – 4d. indigo and rose .. 8 8
128. – 1s. 3d. sepia and yellow 20 20

DESIGNS—HORIZ. 4d. National Hall. VERT. 1s. 3d. Maccoa Palm Tree.

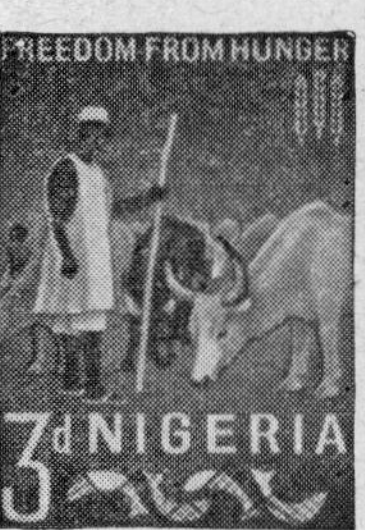

30. Herdsman.  31. Mercury Capsule and Kano Tracking Station.

1963. Freedom from Hunger.

129. 30. 3d. olive 5 5
130. – 6d. magenta 12 12

DESIGN—HORIZ. 6d. Tractor and maize.

1963. "Peaceful Use of Outer Space".

131. 31. 6d. blue & yellow-green 8 8
132. – 1s. 3d. black & blue-grn. 25 25

DESIGN: 1s. 3d. Satellite and Lagos Harbour.

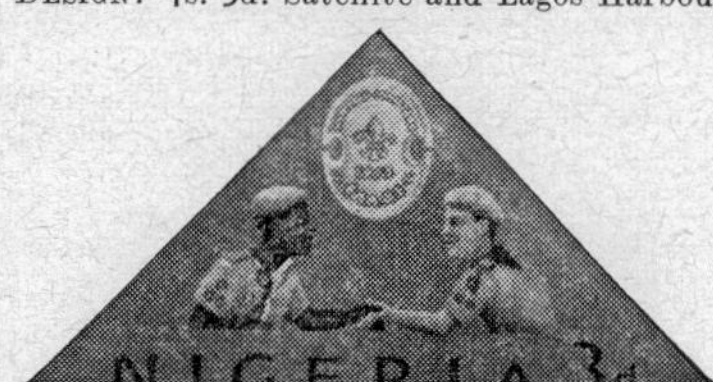

32. Scouts Shaking Hands.
(Illustration reduced: actual size 60×30 mm.).

1963. 11th World Scout Jamboree. Marathon.

133. 32. 3d. red and bronze .. 5 5
134. – 1s. black and red .. 25 25

DESIGN: 1s. Campfire.

33. Emblem and First Aid Team.

1963. Red Cross Cent.

135. 33. 3d. red and blue .. 5 5
136. – 6d. red and green .. 8 8
137. – 1s. 3d. red and sepia .. 20 20

DESIGNS: 6d. Emblem and "Hospital Services". 1s. 3d. Patient ("Medical Services") and emblem.

34. President Azikiwe and State House.

1963. Republic Day.

138. 34. 3d. olive and green .. 5 5
139. 1s. 3d. brown and sepia 20 20
140. 2s. 6d. turquoise & blue 35 35

The buildings on the 1s. 3d. and the 2s. 6d. are the Federal Supreme Court and the Parliament Building respectively.

35. "Freedom of Worship".

1963. Declaration of Human Rights. 15th Anniv.

141. – 3d. red 5 5
142. 35. 6d. green 8 8
143. – 1s. 3d. blue 20 20
144. – 2s. 6d. purple 35 35

DESIGNS—HORIZ. 3d. (Inscr. "1948-1963"), Charter and broken whip. VERT. 1s. 3d. "Freedom from Want". 2s. 6d. "Freedom of Speech".

36. Queen Nefertari.

1964. Nubian Monuments Preservation.

145. 36. 6d. olive and emerald .. 8 8
146. – 2s. 6d. brn. ol. & emer. 35 35

DESIGN: 2s. 6d. Rameses II.

37. President Kennedy.

1964. Pres. Kennedy Memorial Issue.

147. 37. 1s. 3d. lilac and black .. 20 20
148. – 2s. 6d. black, red, blue and green 45 45
149. – 5s. black, blue, red & grn. 85 85

DESIGNS: 2s. 6d. Kennedy and flags. 5s. Kennedy (U.S. Coin Head) and flags.

38. President Azikiwe.

DESIGNS (25×42 mm.): 1s. 3d. Herbert Macaulay. 2s. 6d. King Jaja of Opobo.

1964. Republic. 1st Anniv.

150. 38. 3d. brown 5 5
151. – 1s. 3d. green 20 20
152. – 2s. 6d. grey-green .. 35 35

39. Boxing Gloves.

1964. Olympic Games, Tokyo.
153. **39.** 3d. sepia and green .. 5 5
154. – 6d. emerald and indigo 8 8
155. – 1s. 3d. sepia and olive.. 20 20
156. – 2s. 6d. sepia & chestnut 35 35
DESIGNS—HORIZ. 6d. High-jumping. VERT. 1s. 3d. Running. TRIANGULAR. 2s. 6d. Hurdling (size 60 × 30 mm.)

40. Scouts on Hill-top. **41.** "Telstar".

1965. Nigerian Scout Movement. 50th Anniv.
157. **40.** 1d. brown 5 5
158. – 3d. red, black & emerald 8 8
159. – 6d. red, sepia & green.. 10 10
160. – 1s. 3d. brown, yellow and deep green .. 25 25
DESIGNS: 3d. Scout badge on shield. 6d. Scout badges. 1s. 3d. Chief Scout and Nigerian Scout.

1965. International Quiet Sun Years.
161. **41.** 6d. violet and turquoise 10 10
162. – 1s. 3d. green and lilac.. 30 20
DESIGN: 1s. 3d. Solar Satellite.

42. Native Tomtom and Modern Telephone.

1965. I.T.U. Cent.
163. **42.** 3d. black, red & brown 5 5
164. – 1s. 3d. blk., grn. & blue 20 20
165. – 5s. blk., red, bl. & lt.-bl. 75 75
DESIGNS—VERT. 1s. 3d. Microwave Aerial. HORIZ. 5s. Telecommunications satellite and part of globe.

43. I.C.Y. Emblem and Diesel Locomotive.

1965. Int. Co-operation Year.
166. **43.** 3d. green, red & orange 5 5
167. – 1s. black, blue & lemon 15 15
168. – 2s. 6d. grn., blue & yell. 60 60
DESIGNS: 1s. Students and Lagos Teaching Hospital. 2s. 6d. Kainji (Niger) Dam.

44. Carved Frieze.

1965. Republic. 2nd Anniv.
169. **44.** 3d. black, red & yellow 5 5
170. – 1s. 3d. brown, green & bl. 15 15
171. – 5s. brown, sepia & green 1·00 80
DESIGNS—VERT. 1s. 3d. Stone Images at Ikom. 5s. Tada Bronze.

45. Elephants.

1965. Multicoloured.
172. ½d. Lion and cubs (vert.).. 5 5
173. 1d. Type **45** 5 5
174. 1½d. Splendid Sunbird .. 5 5
175. 2d. Weavers 5 5
176. 3d. Cheetah 5 5
177. 4d. Leopards 20 5
178. 6d. Saddle-billed Stork (vert.) 12 5
179. 9d. Grey Parrots .. 15 10
180. 1s. Kingfisher 20 5
181. 1s. 3d. Crowned Cranes .. 20 15
182. 2s. 6d. Kobs 45 30
183. 5s. Giraffes .. .. 1·00 60
184. 10s. Hippopotamus (vert.) 2·00 1·40
185. £1 Buffalo .. .. 4·00 2·25
Nos. 180/5 are larger, 46×26½ mm.
See also Nos. 220/30.

The 1d., 3d., 4d., 1s. 3d., 2s. 6d., 5s. and £1 exist optd. **F.G.N.** (Federal Government of Nigeria) twice in black. They were prepared in 1968 as official stamps, but the scheme was abandoned. Some stamps held at a Head Post Office were sold in error and passed through the post. The Director of Posts then decided to put limited supplies on sale, but they had no postal validity.

1966. Commonwealth Prime Minister's Meeting, Lagos. Optd. **COMMONWEALTH P. M. MEETING 11. JAN. 1966.**
186. **22.** 2s. 6d. black & yellow 30 35

46. Y.W.C.A. Emblem and H.Q., Lagos.

1966. Nigerian Y.W.C.A.'s Diamond Jubilee.
187. **46.** 4d. orange, blue, chestnut and green 5 5
188. 9d. orange, blue, brown and turquoise .. 15 15

47. Telephone Handset and Linesman.

1966. Republic. 3rd Anniv.
189. – 4d. green 5 5
190. **47.** 1s. 6d. blk., brn. & violet 25 25
191. – 2s. 6d. indigo, blue, yellow and green .. 40 40
DESIGNS—VERT. 4d. Dove and flag. HORIZ. 2s. 6d. Niger Bridge.

48. "Education, Science and Culture".

1966. U.N.E.S.C.O. 20th Anniv.
192. **48.** 4d. black, lake & orange 5 5
193. 1s. 6d. black, lake & turq. 25 25
194. 2s. 6d. black, lake & pink 40 40

49. Children Drinking.

1966. Nigerian Red Cross.
195. **49.** 4d.+1d. blk., violet & red 10 10
196. – 1s. 6d.+3d. multicoloured 35 35
197. – 2s. 6d.+3d. multicoloured 50 50
DESIGNS—VERT. 1s. 6d. Tending patient. HORIZ. 2s. 6d. Tending casualties and Badge.

50. Surveying.

1967. Int. Hydrological Decade. Multicoloured.
198. 4d. Type **50** 5 5
199. 2s. 6d. Water gauge on dam (vert.) 45 45

51. Globe and Weather Satellite.

1967. World Meteorological Day.
200. **51.** 4d. magenta and blue.. 5 5
201. – 1s. 6d. blk., yellow & blue 30 30
DESIGN: 1s. 6d. Passing storm and sun.

52. Eyo Masquerades.

1967. Republic. 4th Anniv. Multicoloured.
202. 4d. Type **52** 5 5
203. 1s. 6d. Crowds watching acrobat 45 45
204. 2s. 6d. Stilt dancer (vert.) 45 60

53. Tending Sick Animal.

1967. Rinderpest Eradication Campaign.
205. **53.** 4d. multicoloured .. 5 5
206. 1s. 6d. multicoloured .. 45 45

54. Smallpox Vaccination.

1968. World Health Organization. 20th Anniv.
207. **54.** 4d. magenta and black 5 5
208. – 1s. 6d. orge., lemon & blk. 30 30
DESIGN: 1s. 6d. African and Mosquito.

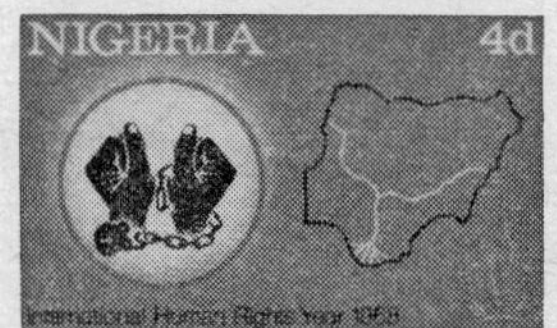

55. Chained Hands and Outline of Nigeria.

1968. Human Rights Year.
209. **55.** 4d. blue, black & yellow 5 5
210. – 1s. 6d. green, red & black 30 30
DESIGN—VERT. 1s. 6d. Nigerian Flag and Human Rights Emblem.

56. Hand grasping at Doves of Freedom.

1968. Federal Republic. 5th Anniv.
211. **56.** 4d. multicoloured .. 5 5
212. 1s. 6d. multicoloured .. 30 30

57. Map of Nigeria and Olympic Rings.

1968. Olympic Games, Mexico.
213. **57.** 4d. black, green and red 5 5
214. – 1s. 6d. multicoloured .. 30 30
DESIGN: 1s. 6d. Nigerian Athletes, Flag and Olympic Rings.

58. G.P.O., Lagos.

1969. Philatelic Service. Inaug.
215. **58.** 4d. black and green .. 5 5
216. 1s. 6d. black and blue.. 40 40

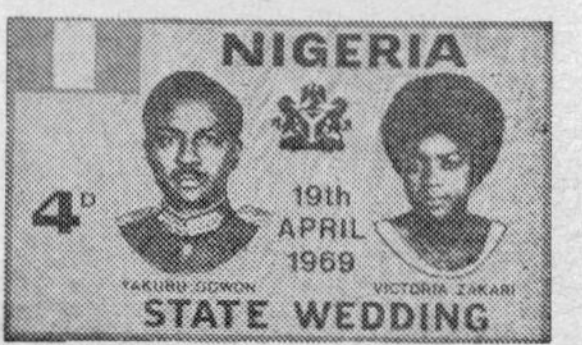

59. Yakubu Gowon and Victoria Zakari.

1969. Wedding of General Gowon.
217. **59.** 4d. chocolate & emerald 5 5
218. 1s. 6d. black & emerald 30 30

1969. As Nos. 172/185, but inscr. "N.S.P. & M. Co. Ltd." (Nigerian Security Printing and Minting Co. Ltd.) at foot.
220. 1d. (As No. 173) 5 5
222. 2d. (As No. 175) 5 5
223. 3d. (As No. 176) 5 5
224. 4d. (As No. 177) 8 5
225. 6d. (As No. 178) 10 8
226. 9d. (As No. 179) 15 10
227. 1s. (As No. 180) 20 12
228. 1s. 3d. (As No. 181) .. 25 15
229. 2s. 6d. (As No. 182) .. 45 35
230. 5s. (As No. 183) .. .. 1·00 75

60. Bank Emblem and "5th Anniversary".

1969. African Development Bank. 5th Anniv.
233. **60.** 4d. orge. black & blue 5 5
234. – 1s. 6d. lemon, black & plum 30 30
DESIGN: 1s. 6d. Bank Emblem and Rays.

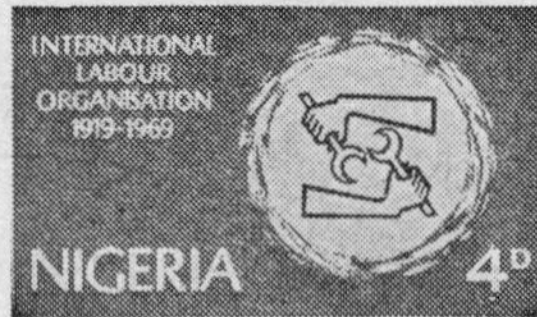

61. I.L.O. Emblem.

1969. I.L.O. 50th Anniv.
235. **61.** 4d. black and violet .. 5 5
236. – 1s. 6d. emerald & black 30 40
DESIGN: 1s. 6d. World map and I.L.O. Emblem.

62. Olumo Rock.

1969. Int. Year of African Tourism.
237. **62.** 4d. multicoloured .. 5 5
238. – 1s. black and emerald.. 15 15
239. – 1s. 6d. multicoloured .. 25 25
DESIGNS—VERT. 1s. Traditional musicians. 1s. 6d. Assob Falls.

63. Symbolic Tree.

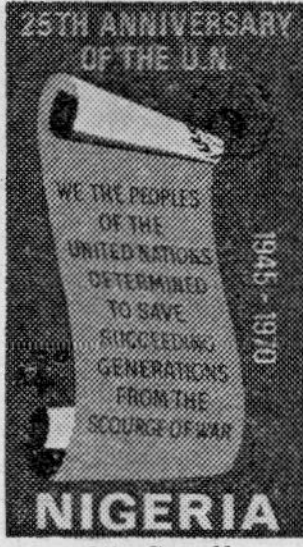

65. Scroll.

64. U.P.U. Headquarters Building.

1970. "Stamp of Destiny". End of Civil War.

240. **63.** 4d. gold, blue and black 5 5
241. – 1s. multicoloured .. 20 20
242. – 1s. 6d. green and black 30 30
243. – 2s. multicoloured .. 40 40

DESIGNS—VERT. 1s. Symbolic Wheel. 1s. 6d. United Nigerians supporting Map. HORIZ. 2s. Symbolic Torch.

1970. New U.P.U. Headquarters Building.

244. **64.** 4d. violet and yellow .. 5 5
245. 1s. 6d. blue and indigo 30 30

1970. United Nations. 25th Anniv.

246. **65.** 4d. brn., buff and black 5 5
247. – 1s. 6d. blue, brown & gold 30 30

DESIGN: 1s. 6d. U.N. Building.

66. Oil Rig.

68. Iibibio Face Mask.

67. Children and Globe.

1970. Independence. 10th Anniv. Multi-coloured.

248. 2d. Type **66** 5 5
249. 4d. University Graduate 5 8
250. 6d. Durbar Horsemen .. 10 10
251. 9d. Servicemen raising Flag 15 15
252. 1s. Footballer 20 20
253. 1s. 6d. Parliament Building 30 30
254. 2s. Kainji Dam 40 40
255. 2s. 6d. Agricultural Produce 50 50

1971. Racial Equality Year. Multicoloured.

256. 4d. Type **67** 5 5
257. 1s. Black and white men uprooting "Racism" (vert.) 15 15
258. 1s. 6d. "The World in Black and White" (vert.) .. 25 25
259. 2s. Black and white men united 40 40

1971. Antiquities of Nigeria.

260. **68.** 4d. black and blue .. 5 5
261. – 1s. 3d. brn. and ochre .. 20 20
262. – 1s. 9d. grn., brn. & yell. 30 30

DESIGN: 1s. 3d. Benin bronze. 1s. 9d. Ife bronze.

HAVE YOU READ THE NOTES AT THE BEGINNING OF THIS CATALOGUE?

These often provide answers to the enquiries we receive.

69. Children and Symbol.

70. Mast and Dish Aerial.

1971. U.N.I.C.E.F. 25th Anniv.

263. **69.** 4d. multicoloured .. 5 5
264. – 1s. 3d. orge., red & brn. 20 20
265. – 1s. 9d. pale greenish bl. & deep greenish blue 30 30

DESIGNS: Each with U.N.I.C.E.F. symbol. 1s. 3d. Mother and child. 1s. 9d. Mother carrying child.

1971. Opening of Nigerian Earth Satellite Station.

266. **70.** 4d. multicoloured .. 5 5
267. – 1s. 3d. grn., blue & blk. 20 20
268. – 1s. 9d. brn., orge. & blk. 30 30
269. – 3s. mauve, blk. & mag. 50 50

DESIGNS: Nos. 267/9, as T **70**, but showing different views of the Satellite Station.

71. Trade Fair Emblem.

73. Nok Style Terracotta Head.

72. Traffic.

1972. All-Africa Trade Fair.

270. **71.** 4d. multicoloured .. 5 5
271. – 1s. 3d. lilac, yell. & gold 20 20
272. – 1s. 9d. yell., orge. & blk. 30 30

DESIGNS—HORIZ. 1s. 3d. Map of Africa with pointers to Nairobi. VERT. 1s. 9d. Africa on globe.

1972. Change to Driving on the Right.

273. **72.** 4d. orge., brn. & black 5 5
274. – 1s. 3d. multicoloured .. 20 20
275. – 1s. 9d. multicoloured .. 30 30
276. – 3s. multicoloured .. 50 50

DESIGNS: 1s. 3d. Roundabout. 1s. 9d. Highway. 3s. Road junction.

1972. All-Nigeria Arts Festival. Mult.

277. 4d. Type **73** 5 5
278. 1s. 3d. Bronze pot from Igbo-Ukwu 25 25
279. 1s. 9d. Bone harpoon (horiz.) 35 35

74. Hides and Skins.

1973.

280. **74.** 1 k. multicoloured .. 5 5
281. – 2 k. multicoloured .. 5 5
292. – 3 k. multicoloured .. 5 5
282a. – 5 k. multicoloured .. 12 8
294. – 7 k. multicoloured .. 12 5
295. – 8 k. multicoloured .. 15 8
283. – 10 k. multicoloured .. 20 12
297. – 12 k. black, grn. & blue 15 12
298. – 15 k. multicoloured .. 30 15
299. – 18 k. multicoloured .. 30 15
300. – 20 k. multicoloured .. 40 20
301. – 25 k. multicoloured .. 40 25
302. – 30 k. multicoloured .. 45 30
303. – 35 k. multicoloured .. 55 35
288. – 50 k. multicoloured .. 1·25 90
305. – 1 n. multicoloured .. 1·50 1·10
306. – 2 n. multicoloured .. 3·00 3·00

DESIGNS-HORIZ. 2 k. Natural gas tanks. 3 k, Cement works. 5 k. Cattle-ranching. 7 k. Timber mill. 8 k. Oil refinery. 10 k. Leopards. Yankari Game Reserve. 12 k. New Civic building. 15 k. Sugar-cane harvesting. 20 k. Vaccine production. 25 k. Modern wharf. 35 k. Textile machinery. 1 n. Eko Bridge. 2 n. Teaching Hospital, Lagos. VERT. 18 k. Palm oil production. 30 k. Argungu Fishing Festival. 50 k. Pottery.

75. Athlete.

1973. Second All-African Games, Lagos.

307. **75.** 5 k. lilac, blue & blk. 8 8
308. – 12 k. multicoloured .. 20 20
309. – 18 k. multicoloured .. 30 30
310. – 25 k. multicoloured .. 40 40

DESIGNS—HORIZ. 12 k. Football. 18 k. Table-tennis. VERT. 25 k. National stadium.

76. All-Africa House, Addis Ababa.

1973. O.A.U. 10th Anniv. Multicoloured.

311. 5 k. Type **76** 10 10
312. 18 k. O.A.U. flag 30 30
313. 30 k. O.A.U. emblem and symbolic flight of ten stairs 45 45

77. Dr. Hansen.

1973. Discovery of Leprosy Bacillus. Cent.

314. **77.** 5 k. + 2 k. brown, pink and black 15 15

78. W.M.O. Emblem and Weather-vane.

1973. I.M.O./W.M.O. Centenary.

315. **78.** 5 k. multicoloured .. 10 10
316. 30 k. multicoloured .. 45 45

79. University Complex.

1973. Ibadan University. 25th Anniv. Multicoloured.

317. 5 k. Type **79** 10 10
318. 12 k. Students' population growth (vert.) 20 20
319. 18 k. Tower and students .. 30 30
320. 30 k. Teaching Hospital .. 45 45

80. Lagos 1d. Stamp of 1874.

1974. Stamp Centenary.

321. – 5 k. grn., orge. & blk... 10 10
322. – 12 k. multicoloured .. 20 20
323. **80.** 18 k. grn., mve. & blk. 30 30
324. – 30 k. multicoloured .. 45 45

DESIGNS: 5 k. Graph of mail traffic growth. 12 k. Northern Nigeria £25 stamp of 1904. 30 k. Forms of mail transport.

81. U.P.U. Emblem on Globe.

1974. U.P.U. Centenary.

325. **81.** 5 k. bl., orge. & blk. .. 10 10
326. – 18 k. multicoloured .. 35 35
327. – 30 k. brn., grn. & blk... 45 45

DESIGNS: 18 k. World transport map. 30 k. U.P.U. emblem and letters.

82. Starving and Well-fed Children.

83. Telex Network and Teleprinter.

1974. Freedom from Hunger Campaign. Mult.

328. 5 k. Type **82** 8 8
329. 12 k. Poultry battery ("More Protein") 20 20
330. 30 k. Water-hoist ("Irrigation increases food production") 45 40

1975. Inauguration of Telex Network.

331. **83.** 5 k. black, oran. & grn. 5 8
332. – 12 k. blk., yell. and brn. 15 20
333. – 18 k. multicoloured .. 25 30
334. – 30 k. multicoloured .. 40 45

DESIGNS: 12 k., 18 k. and 30 k. are as T **83** but with the motifs arranged differently.

84. Queen Amina of Zaria.

85. Alexander Graham Bell.

1975. International Women's Year.

335. **84.** 5 k. grn., yell. and blue 5 8
336. 18 k. pur., blue and mve. 25 30
337. 30 k. multicoloured .. 40 45

1976. Telephone Centenary.

338. **85.** 5 k. multicoloured .. 8 10
339. – 18 k. multicoloured .. 30 35
340. – 25 k. blue, light blue and brown 40 45

DESIGNS—HORIZ. 18 k. Gong and modern telephone system. VERT. 25 k. Telephones, 1876 and 1976.

86. Child Writing.

1976. Universal Primary Education. Launching.

341. **86.** 5 k. yell., violet & mauve 8 10
342. – 18 k. multicoloured .. 30 35
343. – 25 k. multicoloured .. 45 50

DESIGNS—VERT. 18 k. Children entering school. 25 k. Children in class.

87. Festival Emblem.

1976. 2nd World Black and African Festival of Arts and Culture, Nigeria.
344. 87. 5 k. gold and brown .. 8 10
345. – 10 k. brown, yell. & blk. 20 20
346. – 12 k. black, yell. and red 20 25
347. – 18 k. yell., brn. and blk. 30 35
348. – 30 k. red and black .. 55 65
DESIGNS: 10 k. National Arts Theatre. 12 k. African hair-styles. 18 k. Musical instruments. 30 k. "Nigerian arts and crafts".

POSTAGE DUE STAMPS

D 1.

1959.
D 1. D 1. 1d. orange 5 8
D 2. 2d. orange 5 8
D 3. 3d. orange 5 15
D 4. 6d. orange 10 30
D 5. 1s. black 20 45

1961.
D 6. D 1. 1d. red 5 5
D 7. 2d. blue 5 5
D 8. 3d. green 5 8
D 9. 6d. yellow 8 10
D 10. 1s. blue 15 25

1973. As Type D 1.
D 11. 2 k. red 5 5
D 12. 3 k. blue 5 8
D 13. 5 k. yellow 8 8
D 14. 10 k. green 15 20

NIUE BC

One of the Cook Is. group, in the S. Pacific. A dependency of New Zealand, the island achieved local self-government in 1974.

1967. 100 cents = 1 dollar.

1902. T 35 of New Zealand optd. **NIUE** only.
1. 35. 1d. red £140 £140

Stamps of New Zealand surch. **NIUE** and value in native language.

1902. Pictorials of 1898, etc.
8. 21. ½d. green.. .. .. 25 40
9. 35. 1d. red 20 30
2. 24. 2½d. blue (No. 382) .. 45 1·10
13. 25. 3d. brown .. .. 1·10 2·00
14. 28. 6d. red .. .. .. 45 3·00
16. 31. 1s. orange .. .. 3·00 4·50

1911 King Edward VII stamps.
17. 41. ½d. green.. .. .. 25 30
18. 6d. red .. .. .. 2·00 2·75
19. 1s. orange .. .. 3·75 7·00

1917. Dominion and King George V stamps.
21. 42. 1d. red .. .. .. 70 1·75
22. 43. 3d. brown .. .. 24·00 30·00

1917. Stamps of New Zealand (King George V, etc.) optd. **NIUE** only.
23. 43. ½d. green 15 20
24. 42. 1d. red 20 45
25. 43. 1½d. grey 40 75
26. 1½d. brown 30 70
28. 2½d. blue 40 75
27. 3d. brown 40 75
30. 6d. red .. .. 1·25 2·00
31. 1s. orange .. .. 1·50 2·50

1918. Stamps of New Zealand optd. **NIUE.**
33. 20. 2s. blue .. .. .. 10·00 15·00
34. 2s. 6d. brown .. .. 10·00 15·00
35. 5s. green .. .. 12·00 18·00
36. 10s. claret .. .. 50·00 60·00
37. £1 red .. .. .. 95·00 £110

1920. Pictorial types as Cook Islands (1920), but inscr. "NIUE".
38. 4. ½d. black and green .. 20 35
39. – 1d. black and red .. 35 70
40. – 1½d. black and red .. 30 70
46. – 2½d. black and blue .. 45 90
41. – 3d. black and blue .. 45 75
47. 9. 4d. black and violet .. 75 1·25
42. – 6d. brown and green .. 75 1·50
43. – 1s. black and brown .. 1·50 2·50

1927. Admiral type of New Zealand optd. **NIUE.**
49. 52. 2s. blue .. .. 4·50 7·00

1931. No. 40 surch. **TWO PENCE.**
50. 2d. on 1½d. black and red 35 45

1931. Stamps of New Zealand (Arms types) optd. **NIUE.**
83. 56. 2s. 6d. brown .. .. 1·10 1·25
84. 5s. green .. .. 1·25 1·60
85. 10s. red .. .. 4·00 5·00
86. £1 pink .. .. 7·00 8·00

1932. Pictorial stamps as Cook Islands (1932) but inscr. additionally "NIUE".
62. 12. ½d. black and green .. 10 12
63. – 1d. black and red .. 10 10
64. 14. 2d. black and brown .. 10 10
65. – 2½d. black and blue .. 10 20
66. – 4d. black and blue .. 20 20
94. – 6d. black and orange .. 20 20
95. – 1s. black and violet .. 35 50

1935. Silver Jubilee. Nos. 63, 65, 67 and 101, colours changed optd. **SILVER JUBILEE OF KING GEORGE V. 1910-1935.**
69. 1d. red 20 35
70. 2½d. blue.. .. .. 75 1·25
71. 6d. green and orange .. 2·00 2·75

1937. Coronation. New Zealand stamps optd. **NIUE.**
72. 80. 1d. red 8 8
73. 2½d. blue.. .. .. 8 8
74. 6d. orange 15 25

1938. As 1938 issue of Cook Islands, but inscr. "NIUE" "COOK ISLANDS".
75. 20. 1s. black and violet .. 60 60
76. 21. 2s. black and brown .. 80 80
77. – 3s. blue and green .. 1·25 1·25

1940. As T 23 of Cook Islands, but inscr. "NIUE" "COOK ISLANDS".
78. 23. 3d. on 1½d. black & purple 10 10

1946. Peace. New Zealand stamps optd. **NIUE.**
98. 91. 1d. green.. .. .. 5 5
99. – 2d. purple (No. 670) .. 8 10
100. – 6d. brn. & red (No. 674) 8 10
101. 94. 8d. black and red .. 10 12

1. Map of Niue.

2. Capt. Cook's "Resolution".

1950.
113. 1. ½d. orange and blue .. 5 5
114. 2. 1d. brown and green .. 5 5
115. – 2d. black and red .. 8 8
116. – 3d. blue and violet .. 8 8
117. – 4d. olive and maroon .. 10 10
118. – 6d. green and orange .. 15 15
119. – 9d. orange and brown .. 25 25
120. – 1s. purple and black .. 30 30
121. – 2s. brown and green .. 70 30
122. – 3s. blue and black .. 90 1·00
DESIGNS—HORIZ. 2d. Alofi Landing. 3d. Native hut. 4d. Arch of Hikutavake. 6d. Alofi Bay. 1s. Cave, Makefu. VERT. 9d. Spearing fish. 2s. Bananas. 3s. Matapa Chasm.

1953. Coronation. As types of New Zealand but inscr. "NIUE".
123. 106. 3d. brown 10 10
124. 108. 6d. grey 15 20

3.

4. "Pua".

1967. Decimal Currency. (a) Nos. 113/22 surch.
125. 1. ½ c. on ½d. 5 5
126. 2. 1 c. on 1d. 5 5
127. – 2 c. on 2d. 5 5
128. – 2½ c. on 3d. 5 5
129. – 3 c. on 4d. 8 8
130. – 5 c. on 6d. 12 12
131. – 8 c. on 9d. 15 15
132. – 10 c. on 1s. 20 20
133. – 20 c. on 2s. 50 60
134. – 30 c. on 3s. 65 75

(b) Arms type of New Zealand without value, surch. as in T 3.
135. 3. 25 c. brown 45 50
136. 50 c. green .. .. 1·00 1·00
137. $1 magenta .. .. 2·00 2·00
138. $2 pink .. .. 4·00 4·00

1967. Christmas. As T 165 of New Zealand, but inscr. "NIUE".
139. 2½ c. multicoloured .. 10 10

1969. Christmas. As No. 905 of New Zealand but inscr. "NIUE".
140. 2½ c. multicoloured .. 10 10

1969. Flowers. Multicoloured; frame colours given.
141. 4. ½ c. green 5 5
142. – 1 c. red 5 5
143. – 2 c. olive 5 5
144. – 2½ c. brown 5 5
145. – 3 c. blue 5 5
146. – 5 c. red 8 8
147. – 8 c. violet 10 12
148. – 10 c. yellow 15 15
149. – 20 c. blue 30 30
150. – 30 c. green 40 45
DESIGNS: 1 c. "Golden Shower". 2 c. Flamboyant. 2½c. Frangipani. 3 c. Niue Crocus. 5 c. Hibiscus. 8 c. "Passion Fruit". 10 c. "Kampui". 20 c. Queen Elizabeth II (after Anthony Buckley). 30 c. Tapeu Orchid.

5. Kalahimu.

1970. Indigenous Edible Crabs. Multicoloured.
151. 3 c. Type 5 .. .. 5 5
152. 5 c. Kalavi 12 10
153. 30 c. Unga 45 45

1970. Christmas. As T 187 of New Zealand, but inscr. "**NIUE**".
154. 2½ c. multicoloured .. 10 15

6. Native Canoe, and Aircraft over Jungle.

1970. Niue Airport Opening. Multicoloured.
155. 3 c. Type 6.. .. .. 5 5
156. 5 c. Ship, and aircraft over harbour 12 12
157. 8 c. Aircraft over Airport 20 20

7. Polynesian Triller.

1971. Birds. Multicoloured.
158. 5 c. Type 7 .. .. 10 10
159. 10 c. Crimson Crowned Fruit-dove 20 20
160. 20 c. Blue Crowned Lory 40 40

1971. Christmas. As T 196 of New Zealand, but inscr. "Niue".
161. 3 c. multicoloured.. .. 10 10

8. Niuean Boy.

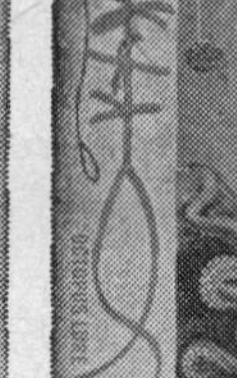

9. Octopus Lure.

1971. Niuean Portraits. Multicoloured.
162. 4 c. Type 8 .. .. 5 5
163. 6 c. Girl with garland .. 10 10
164. 9 c. Man 15 15
165. 14 c. Woman with garland 25 25

1972. South Pacific Arts Festival, Fiji Multicoloured.
166. 3 c. Type 9.. .. .. 5 5
167. 5 c. War weapons.. .. 8 8
168. 10 c. Sika throwing (horiz.) 15 15
169. 25 c. Vivi dance (horiz.) .. 40 40

10. Alofi Wharf.

1972. South Pacific Commission. 25th Anniv. Multicoloured.
170. 4 c. Type 10 .. .. 8 8
171. 5 c. Medical Services .. 10 10
172. 6 c. Schoolchildren .. 12 15
173. 18 c. Dairy cattle .. 35 35

1972. Christmas. As T 203 of New Zealand, but inscr. "NIUE".
174. 3 c. multicoloured.. .. 10 10

11. Kokio.

1973. Fishes. Multicoloured.
175. 8 c. Type 11 .. .. 15 15
176. 10 c. Loi 20 20
177. 15 c. Malau 30 30
178. 20 c. Palu 35 35

12. Flowers (Jan Brueghel). 14. King Fataaiki.

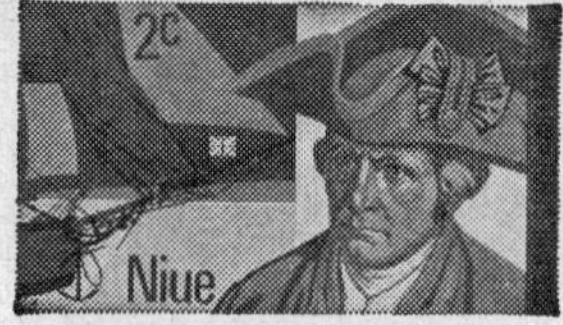

13. Capt. Cook and Bowsprit.

1973. Christmas. Flower studies by the artists listed. Multicoloured.
179. 4 c. Type 12 .. .. 10 10
180. 5 c. Bollongier 10 10
181. 10 c. Ruysch 25 25

1974. Capt. Cook's Visit. Bicent. Mult.
182. 2 c. Type 13 .. .. 5 5
183. 3 c. Niue landing place .. 8 8
184. 8 c. Map of Niue 15 15
185. 20 c. Ensign of 1774 and Administration Building 35 35

1974. Self-Government. Multicoloured.
186. 4 c. Type 14 .. .. 5 5
187. 8 c. Annexation Ceremony, 1900 .. .. 12 15
188. 10 c. Legislative Assembly Chambers (horiz.) .. 15 20
189. 20 c. Village meeting (horiz.) 30 35

15. Decorated Bicycle.

1974. Christmas. Multicoloured.
190. 3 c. Type 15 .. .. 5 5
191. 10 c. Decorated motorcycle 20 20
192. 20 c. Motor transport to church 30 35

16. Children going to Church.

1975. Christmas. Multicoloured.

193. 4 c. Type **16** 5 5
194. 5 c. Child with balloons on bicycle 8 8
195. 10 c. Balloons and gifts on tree 15 15

17. Hotel Buildings.

1975. Opening of Tourist Hotel. Multicoloured.

196. 8 c. Type **17** 8 10
197. 20 c. Ground-plan and buildings 20 25

18. Preparing Ground for Taro.

1976. Food Gathering. Multicoloured.

198. 1 c. Type **18** 5 5
199. 2 c. Planting Taro 5 5
200. 3 c. Banana gathering .. 5 5
201. 4 c. Harvesting a bush plantation 5 5
202. 5 c. Shell fish gathering .. 5 5
203. 10 c. Reef fishing 10 10
204. 20 c. Luku gathering .. 20 20
205. 50 c. Canoe fishing .. 50 55
206. $1 Coconut husking .. 95 1·10
207. $2 Uga gathering .. 1·90 2·25

19. Water.

1976. Utilities. Multicoloured.

208. 10 c. Type **19** 10 12
209. 15 c. Power 15 20
210. 20 c. Telecommunications 20 25

20. Christmas Tree, Alofi.

1976. Christmas. Multicoloured.

211. 9 c. Type **20** 10 10
212. 15 c. Church Service, Avatele 15 20

INDEX

Countries can be quickly located by referring to the index at the end of this volume.

NORFOLK ISLAND BC

A small island East of New South Wales, administered by Australia until 1960 when local government was established.

1966. 100 cents = $1 Australian.

1. Ball Bay.

1947.

1. **1.** ½d. orange 8 8
2. 1d. violet 10 8
3. 1½d. green 15 15
4. 2d. violet 20 20
5. 2½d. red 25 25
6. 3d. brown 30 35
6a. 3d. green .. .. .. 1·75 1·75
7. 4d. claret 35 35
8. 5½d. blue 40 40
9. 6d. brown 50 50
10. 9d. pink 75 75
11. 1s. green 90 90
12. 2s. brown .. .. .. 3·25 2·50
12a. 2s. blue .. .. .. 8·00 8·00

2. "Hibiscus insularis". **3.** Warder's Tower.

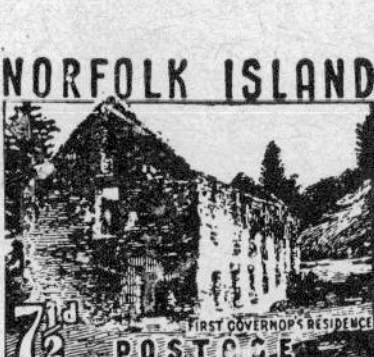

4. First Governor's Residence. **5.** Queen Elizabeth II (after Annigoni) and Cereus.

6. Red-tailed Tropic Bird.

1953.

24. **2.** 1d. green 5 5
25. – 2d. rose and myrtle .. 8 8
26. – 3d. green 15 12
13. **3.** 3½d. lake 60 70
27. – 5d. purple 35 25
14 – 6½d. deep green .. .. 1·10 1·00
15. **4.** 7½d. blue .. .. .. 1·60 1·40
28. – 8d. red 55 55
16. – 8½d. brown .. .. .. 2·00 1·75
29. **5.** 9d. blue 55 55
17. – 10d. violet .. .. .. 1·50 1·25
30. – 10d. brown and violet .. 55 55
31. – 1s. 1d. red 35 35
32. – 2s. sepia .. .. .. 1·10 1·10
33. – 2s. 5d. violet 80 80
34. – 2s. 8d. cinnamon & green 1·00 1·00
18. – 5s. brown .. .. .. 13·00 10·00
35. – 5s. sepia and green .. 2·50 2·00
36. **6.** 10s. emerald .. .. 12·00 12·00

DESIGNS (As T **2/5**)—VERT. 2d. "Lagunaria patersonii". 5d. Lantana. 8d. Red hibiscus. 8½d. Barracks entrance. 10d. Salt House. 1s. 1d. Fringed hibiscus. 2s. Providence petrel. 2s. 5d. Passion-flower. 2s. 8d. Rose-apple. HORIZ. 3d. White tern. 6½d. Airfield. 5s. Bloody Bridge.

7. Norfolk Is. Seal and Pitcairners Landing.

1956. Landing of Pitcairners on Norfolk Is. Cent.

19. **7.** 3d. green 25 30
20. 2s. violet .. .. .. 3·00 3·00

1958. Surch.

21. **4.** 7d. on 7½d. blue .. .. 1·25 1·25
22. – 8d. on 8½d. brown (No. 16) 1·40 1·40

1959. Australian P.O. 150th Anniv. No. 331 of Australia surch. **NORFOLK ISLAND 5D.** in red.

23. **120.** 5d. on 4d. slate .. 80 90

1960. As Nos. 13 and 14/15 but colours changed and surch.

37. **3.** 1s. 1d. on 3½d. blue .. 2·50 2·50
38. 2s. 5d. on 6½d. blue-green 3·00 3·00
39. **4.** 2s. 8d. on 7½d. sepia .. 4·50 4·50

8. Queen Elizabeth II (after Annigoni) and Map.

1960. Introduction of Local Government.

40. **8.** 2s. 8d. purple .. .. 8·00 10·00

1960. Christmas. As No. 338 of Australia.

41. **127.** 5d. magenta .. .. 4·50 5·00

1961. Christmas. As No. 341 of Australia.

42. **130.** 5d. blue .. .. .. 1·25 1·50

9. Tweed Trousers ("Atypichthyslatus").

DESIGNS: 11d. "Trumpeter". 1s. "Po'ov". 1s. 3d. "Dreamfish". 1s. 6d "Hapoeka" ("Promicrops lanceolatus"). 2s. 3d. "Ophie" ("carangidae").

1962.

43. **9.** 6d. sepia, yellow & green 25 25
44. – 11d. orange, brown & blue 50 50
45. – 1s. blue, pink and olive .. 55 55
46. – 1s. 3d. blue, brown & grn. 65 65
47. – 1s. 6d. sepia, violet & blue 90 90
48. – 2s. 3d. blue, red, grn. & yell. 1·25 1·25

1962. Christmas. As No. 345 of Australia.

49. **134.** 5d. blue 60 75

1963. Christmas. As No. 361 of Australia.

50. **142.** 5d. red 60 75

10. Overlooking Kingston.  **11.** Norfolk Pine.

1964. Multicoloured.

51. 5d. Type **10** 20 20
52. 8d. Kingston 30 30
53. 9d. The Arches (Kingston) 35 35
54. 10d. Slaughter Bay .. 40 40

1964. Norfolk Island as Australian Territory. 50th Anniv.

55. **11.** 5d. black, red & orange 30 30
56. 8d. black, red and green 40 40

1964. Christmas. As No. 372 of Australia.

57. **148.** 5d. grn., blue, buff & vio. 85 1·00

1965. Gallipoli Landing. 50th Anniv. As T **147** of Australia, but slightly larger (22×34½ mm.).

58. 5d. brown, black and green 25 25

1965. Christmas. As No. 381 of Australia.

59. **153.** 5d. multicoloured .. 35 30

12. "Hibiscus insularis".

1966. Decimal Currency. As earlier issues but with values in cents and dollars. Surch. in black on silver tablets obliterating old value as in T **12**.

60. **12.** 1 c. on 1d. 8 8
61. – 2 c. on 2d. (No. 25) .. 8 8
62. – 3 c. on 3d. (No. 26) .. 8 8
63. – 4 c. on 5d. (No. 27) .. 10 10
64. – 5 c. on 8d. (No. 28) .. 12 12
65. – 10 c. on 10d. (No. 30) .. 20 20
66. – 15 c. on 1s. 1d. (No. 31) 40 35
67. – 20 c. on 2s (No. 32) .. 50 40
68. – 25 c. on 2s. 5d. (No. 33) 50 50
69. – 30 c. on 2s. 8d. (No. 34) 60 60
70. – 50 c. on 5s. (No. 35) 1·00 1·25
71a. **6.** $1 on 10s. .. .. 3·75 2·75

13. Headstone Bridge.

1966. Multicoloured.

72. 7 c. Type **13** 25 25
73. 9 c. Cemetery Road .. 30 30

14. St. Barnabas' Chapel (interior).

1966. Melanesian Mission. Cent. Mult.

74. 4 c. Type **14** 15 15
75. 25 c. St. Barnabas' Chapel (exterior) 50 50

15. Star over Philip Island.

1966. Christmas.

76. **15.** 4 c. multicoloured .. 12 12

16. H.M.S. "Resolution", 1774.

1967. Multicoloured.

77. 1 c. Type **16** 5 5
78. 2 c. "La Boussole" and "L'Astrolabe", 1788 .. 5 5
79. 3 c. H.M. Brig "Supply", 1788 .. .. .. 5 5
80. 4 c. H.M.S. "Sirius" 1790 8 8
81. 5 c. "The Norfolk" 1798 8 10
82. 7 c. H.M. Survey Cutter "Mermaid", 1825 .. 12 12
83. 9 c. "Lady Franklin", 1853 20 20
84. 10 c. "The Morayshire", 1856 20 20
85. 15 c. "Southern Cross", 1866 35 35
86. 20 c. "The Pitcairn", 1891 50 50
87. 25 c. Norfolk Whaleboat, 1895 .. .. .. 65 65
88. 30 c. H.M.C.S. "Iris", 1907 1·00 1·00
89. 50 c. "The Resolution", 1926 1·25 1·25
90. $1 S.S. "Morinda", 1931 2·75 2·75

1967. Lions Int. 50th Anniv. As T **161** of Australia.

91. 4 c. black, green and yellow 40 40

17. John Adam's Prayer and Candle.

1967. Christmas.

92. **17.** 5 c. black olive and red 15 15

1968. As T 154 of Australia, but inscr. NORFOLK ISLAND.

93. 3 c. black, brown & vermilion 5 5

94. 4 c. black, brown and green 5 5

95. 5 c. black, brown and violet 5 8

95a. 6 c. blk., brn. & lake-brn... 8 10

18. "Skymaster" and "Lancastrian" Aircraft.

1968. 21st Anniv. of QANTAS Air Service. Sydney-Norfolk Island.

96. **18.** 5 c. black, red and blue.. 15 15

97. 7 c. brown, red & turq... 20 20

19. Bethlehem Star and Flowers.

1968. Christmas.

98. **19.** 5 c. multicoloured .. 15 15

20. Captain Cook, Quadrant and Chart of Pacific Ocean.

1969. Bicent of Observation of the transit of Venus across the sun, by Captain Cook from Tahiti.

99. **20.** 10 c. multicoloured .. 30 30

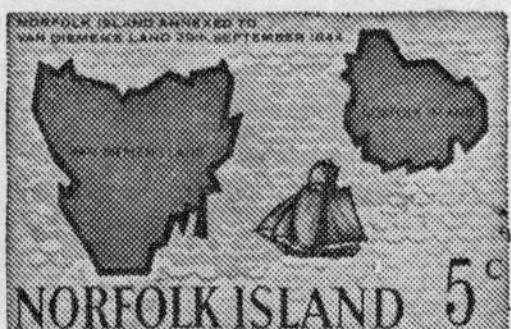

21. Van Dieman's Land, Norfolk Island and Sailing Ship.

1969. Annexation of Norfolk Island to Van Dieman's Land. 125th Anniv.

100. **21.** 5 c. multicoloured .. 12 12

101. 30 c. multicoloured .. 60 60

22. "The Nativity" (carved mother-of-pearl plaque).

1969. Christmas.

102. **22.** 5 c. multicoloured .. 15 20

23. Norfolk Island Fly-eater.

1970. Birds. Multicoloured.

103. 1 c. Norfolk Island Robins 5 5

104. 2 c. Norfolk Island Thick-head 5 5

105. 3 c. Type **23** 8 8

106. 4 c. Long-tailed Cuckoos 8 8

107. 5 c. Norfolk Island Green Parrot 10 10

108. 7 c. Norfolk Island Cater-pillar-catchers 12 15

109. 9 c. Grey-headed Blackbird 15 20

110. 10 c. Norfolk Island Owl 20 20

111. 15 c. Norfolk Island Pigeon 30 30

112. 20 c. White breasted White-eye 35 40

113. 25 c. Philip Island Parrots 45 50

114. 30 c. Norfolk Island Fantail 60 65

115. 45 c. Norfolk Island Starlings .. .. 1·00 1·00

116. 50 c. Red Parrot .. .. 1·25 1·25

117. $1 Norfolk Island King-fisher .. .. 2·50 2·50

Nos. 105/6, 109, 112, 114/5 and 117 are horiz.; the remainder being vert.

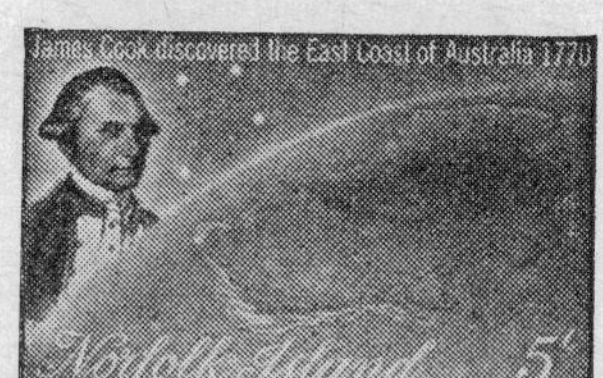

24. Cook and Map of Australia.

1970. Captain Cooks' Discovery of Australia's East Coast. Bicent. Multicoloured.

118. 5 c. Type **24** 12 12

119. 20 c. H.M.S. "Endeavour" and Aborigine 20 25

25. First Christmas Service, 1788.

1970. Christmas.

120. **25.** 5 c. multicoloured .. 15 15

26. Bishop Patteson, and Martyrdom of St. Stephen.

1971. Bishop Patteson. Death Cent. Multicoloured.

121. 6 c. Type **26** 15 15

122. 6 c. Bible, Martyrdom of St. Stephen and knotted palm-frond 15 15

123. 10 c. Bishop Patteson and stained glass 25 25

124. 10 c. Cross and Bishop's Arms 20 20

27. Rose Window, St. Barnabas Chapel.

1971. Christmas.

125. **27.** 6 c. multicoloured .. 15 15

28. Map and Flag.

1972. South Pacific Commission. 25th Anniv.

126. **28.** 7 c. multicoloured .. 40 40

29. Stained-glass Window (All Saints, Norfolk Is.). **30.** Cross and Pines (Stained-glass Window, All Saints Church).

1972. Christmas.

127. **29.** 7 c. multicoloured .. 15 15

1972. First Pitcairner-built Church. Cent.

128. **30.** 12 c. multicoloured .. 20 20

31. "Resolution" in the Antarctic.

1973. Capt. Cook's Crossing of the Antarctic Circle. Bicent.

129. **31.** 35 c. multicoloured .. 65 70

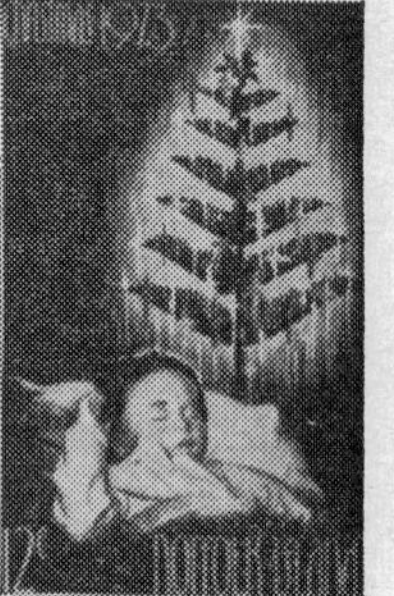

32. Child and Christmas Tree.

1973. Christmas. Multicoloured.

130. 7 c. Type **32** 15 15

131. 12 c. Type **32** 25 25

132. 35 c. Fir trees and star 65 70

33. Protestant Clergyman's Quarters.

1973. Historic Buildings. Multicoloured.

133. 1 c. Type **33** 5 5

134. 2 c. Royal Engineer's Office 5 5

135. 3 c. Double Quarters for Free Overseers 5 5

136. 4 c. Guard House 5 5

137. 5 c. Entrance to Pentagonal Gaol 8 10

138. 7 c. Pentagonal Gaol .. 10 8

139. 8 c. Prisoners' Barracks .. 8 10

140. 10 c. Officer's Quarters, New Military Barracks 15 15

141. 12 c. New Military Barracks 15 15

142. 14 c. Beach Stores 20 20

143. 15 c. The Magazine .. 20 20

144. 20 c. Entrance, Old Military Barracks 25 25

145. 25 c. Old Military Barracks 30 25

146. 30 c. Old Stores (Crankmill) 35 40

147. 50 c. Commissariat Stores 60 65

148. $1 Government House .. 1·40 1·60

34. Royal Couple and Map.

1974. Royal Visit.

149. **34.** 7 c. multicoloured .. 20 20

150. 25 c. multicoloured .. 70 70

35. Chichester's "Madame Elijah".

1974. 1st Aircraft Landing on Norfolk Island.

151. **35.** 14 c. multicoloured .. 55 55

36. "Captain Cook" (Engraving by J. Basire).

1974. Discovery. Bicent. Multicoloured.

152. 7 c. Type **36** 12 12

153. 10 c. "Resolution" (H. Roberts) 20 20

154. 14 c. Norfolk Island Pine 25 25

155. 25 c. "Norfolk Island flax" (G. Raper) 40 40

37. Nativity Scene (Pearl-shell Pew Carving).

1974. Christmas.

156. **37.** 7 c. multicoloured .. 15 15

157. 30 c. multicoloured .. 50 55

MORE DETAILED LISTS

are given in the Stanley Gibbons Catalogues referred to in the country headings:

BC	British Commonwealth
E1, E2, E3	Europe 1, 2, 3
O1, O2, O3, O4	Overseas 1, 2, 3, 4

38. Norfolk Pine.

1974. Universal Postal Union. Centenary. Multicoloured. Imperf. Self-adhesive.

158.	10 c. Type **38**	60	75
159.	15 c. Offshore islands ..	75	1·00
160.	35 c. Island birds ..	2·00	2·25
161.	40 c. Pacific map	2·50	2·75

39. H.M. Survey Cutter "Mermaid".

1975. Second Settlement. 150th Anniv. Multicoloured.

163.	10 c. Type **39**	15	15
164.	35 c. Kingston, 1835 (from painting by T. Seller)	50	50

40. Star on Norfolk Island Pine. **41.** Memorial Cross.

1975. Christmas.

165.	**40.**	10 c. multicoloured ..	15	20
166.		15 c. multicoloured ..	25	30
167.		35 c. multicoloured ..	50	55

1975. St. Barnabas Chapel. Centenary. Multicoloured.

168.	30 c. Type **41**	40	45
169.	60 c. Laying foundation stone, and Chapel n 1975	80	90

42. Launching of " Resolution ".

1975. Launching of the " Resolution ". 50th Anniversary. Multicoloured.

170.	25 c. Type **42**	35	40
171.	45 c. " Resolution " at sea	60	65

43. Whaleship " Charles W. Morgan ".

1976. American Revolution. Bicent. Mult.

172.	18 c. Type **43**	25	25
173.	25 c. Thanksgiving Service	35	40
174.	40 c. " Flying Fortress " over Norfolk Island ..	55	60
175.	45 c. Californian Quail ..	60	70

44. Sea Bird and Sun.

1976. Christmas.

176.	**44.**	18 c. multicoloured ..	25	30
177.		25 c. multicoloured ..	35	40
178.		45 c. multicoloured ..	65	70

45. " Bassaris itea ".

1976. Butterflies and Moths. Multicoloured.

179.	1 c. Type **45**	5	5
183.	5 c. " Leucania loreyimima "	5	5
184.	10 c. " Hypolimnas bolina nerina "	12	15
186.	16 c. " Austrocarea iocephala millsi "	15	20
188.	18 c. " Cleora idiocrossa "	20	20
194.	$1 " Precis villida " ..	1·00	1·25

NORTH BORNEO BC

A territory in the N. of the Island of Borneo in the China Sea, formerly under the administration of the Br. N. Borneo Co. A Crown Colony since 1946. Joined Malaysia in 1963 and renamed Sabah in 1964.

100 cents = 1 dollar (Malayan).

1.

1883. "POSTAGE NORTH BORNEO" at top.

8.	**1.**	½ c. magenta	5·50	11·00
9.		1 c. orange	15·00	23·00
10.		2 c. brown	1·75	1·75
6.		4 c. pink	2·50	5·00
7.		8 c. green	3·50	3·50
13.		10 c. blue	2·40	3·50

1883. Surch. **8 Cents.** vert.

2.	**1.**	8 c. on 2 c. brown	70·00	55·00

1883. Surch. **EIGHT CENTS.**

3.	**1.**	8 c. on 2 c. brown	55·00	23·00

Where there are three price columns, prices in the second column are for postally used stamps and those in the third column are for stamps cancelled with black bars.

2. **3.**

1883.

4.	**2.**	50 c. violet ..	12·00	—	3·00
5.	**3.**	$1 red	11·00	—	2·50

1886. Optd. **and Revenue.**

14.	**1.**	½ c. magenta	7·50	14·00
15.		10 c. blue	18·00	23·00

1886. Surch. in words and figures.

9.	**1.**	3 c. on 4 c. pink ..	7·00	18·00
21.		5 c. on 8 c. green	11·00	21·00

4.

5.

1886. Inscr. "BRITISH NORTH BORNEO"

22.	**4.**	½ c. red	75	1·10	—
24.		1 c. orange ..	40	70	—
25.		2 c. brown ..	55	75	—
26.		4 c. pink	40	80	—
27.		8 c. green	70	1·00	—
28.		10 c. blue	1·25	2·25	—
47.	**5.**	25 c. grey-blue ..	2·25	7·00	12
48.	–	50 c. violet ..	4·50	9·00	12
49.	–	$1 red	4·50	9·00	12
50.	–	$2 green	6·50	11·00	30
36.	–	$5 purple	15·00	18·00	2·25
37.	–	$10 brown ..	24·00	36·00	3·50

The $5 and $10 are much larger than T **5** and show the arms with supporters as in T **3.**

11.

ILLUSTRATIONS British Commonwealth and all overprints and surcharges are FULL SIZE. Foreign Countries have been reduced to ¾-LINEAR.

1888. Inscr. "POSTAGE & REVENUE"

38b.	**11.**	½ c. red	12	25	12
39.		1 c. orange ..	12	20	12
40a.		2 c. brown ..	1·10	70	12
41.		3 c. violet ..	45	45	12
42.		4 c. pink ..	45	45	12
43.		5 c. grey ..	45	45	12
44.		6 c. deep red ..	70	75	15
45.		8 c. green ..	70	75	15
46.		10 c. blue ..	70	75	20

1890. Surch. in words.

51.	**5.**	2 c. on 25 c. grey-blue ..	7·50	6·00
52.		8 c. on 25 c. grey-blue ..	11·00	10·00

1891. Surch. in figures and words.

63.	**11.**	1 c. on 4 c. pink ..	3·75	2·25
64.		1 c. on 5 c. grey ..	1·25	90
54.	**4.**	6 c. on 8 c. green ..	£1200	£1100
55.	**11.**	6 c. on 8 c. green ..	2·25	2·25
56.	**4.**	6 c. on 10 c. blue ..	7·00	3·50
57.	**11.**	6 c. on 10 c. blue ..	12·00	12·00
65.	**5.**	8 c. on 25 c. grey-blue ..	15·00	15·00

12. Dyak Chief.

13. Sambar Stag ("Cervus unicolor").

14. Sago Palm.

15. Argus Pheasant.

16. Arms of the Company.

17. Malay Dhow.

18. Crocodile.

19. View of Mt. Kinabalu.

20. Arms of the Company.

1894.

66.	**12.**	1 c. blk. & yell.-brn. ..	55	75
69.	**13.**	2 c. black and red ..	1·25	1·50
70.	**14.**	3 c. green & mauve ..	90	1·50
72.	**15.**	5 c. black and red ..	1·60	3·00
73a.	**16.**	6 c. black & brown ..	1·50	2·50
74.	**17.**	8 c. black and lilac ..	90	2·10
76.	**18.**	12 c. black & blue ..	8·50	9·50
78.	**19.**	18 c. black & green ..	3·00	4·25
79b.	**20.**	24 c. blue & claret ..	4·50	5·50

NOTE.—The prices in the used column of Nos. 66/79, 92/111, 127/145 and D 2/D 46 are for postally used stamps with circular postmark. Stamps cancelled with bars can be supplied at about one-third of these prices.

1894. As Nos. 47, etc., but inscr. "THE STATE OF NORTH BORNEO".

81.	25 c. grey-blue ..	4·25	5·50	30
82.	50 c. violet	4·25	5·50	30
83.	$1 red	3·00	4·50	40
84.	$2 green	5·00	8·50	40
85.	$5 purple	30·00	40·00	3·50
86.	$10 brown	30·00	37·00	2·10

1895. No. 83 surch. in figures and words.

87.	4 cents on $1 red ..	1·10	1·25	40
88.	10 cents on $1 red	1·50	1·50	40
89.	20 cents on $1 red	1·60	1·60	40
90.	30 cents on $1 red	2·00	2·00	40
91.	40 cents on $1 red	2·25	2·25	50

24. Orang-utan.

28. Bruang or Honey-bear.

30. Borneo Railway Train.

1897. As 1894 issue with insertion of native inscriptions.
92. 12. 1 c. black and yellow-brown .. 1·25 1·10
94a. 13. 2 c. black & red .. 2·10 1·10
95. 2 c. black & grn. .. 2·10 1·10
97. 14. 3 c. grn. & mve. .. 1·10 1·10
98. 24. 4 c. blk. & green .. 1·25 90
99. 4 c. black & red .. 1·25 1·25
100. 15. 5 c. blk. & orge. .. 1·60 1·25
101a. 16. 6 c. blk. & brown .. 1·60 1·25
102b. 17. 8 c. black & lilac .. 1·50 1·25
104. 28. 10 c. brn. & grey .. 5·00 4·00
106. 18. 12 c. blk. & blue .. 7·50 6·00
107. 30. 16 c. grn. & brn. .. 4·50 12·00
108. 19. 18 c. blk. & grn.* .. 2·10 2·10
110. 18 c. blk. & grn.* .. 5·00 4·00
109. 20. 24 c. blue & red* .. 6·00 5·00
111. 24 c. bl. & red* .. 7·00 6·00

* No. 110 is inscribed "POSTAGE & REVENUE" at the sides instead of "POSTAL REVENUE" as in No. 108. No. 111 has the words "POSTAGE & REVENUE" at the sides below the Arms; these words were omitted in No. 109.

1899. Stamps of 1897 and Nos. 81/6 surch. **4 CENTS.**
112. 4 c. on 5 c. black & orange.. 2·50 2·50
113a. 4 c. on 6 c. black & brown.. 2·50 3·50
114. 4 c. on 8 c. black and lilac.. 3·50 2·50
115. 4 c. on 12 c. black and blue 3·50 3·50
116. 4 c. on 18 c. black & grn.(110) 3·50 3·50
117. 4 c. on 24 c. blue & red (111) 3·00 3·00
118. 4 c. on 25 c. grey-blue .. 2·50 3·50
119a. 4 c. on 50 c. violet .. 3·50 3·50
122. 4 c. on $2 green .. 3·50 5·00
125. 4 c. on $5 purple .. 5·00 4·50
126. 4 c. on $10 brown .. 4·50 4·50

1901. Stamps of 1897 and Nos. 81/6 optd. **BRITISH PROTECTORATE.**
127. 1 c. blk. & yell.-brn. .. 80 70
128a. 2 c. black & green .. 70 80
129. 3 c. green and mauve .. 50 80
130a. 4 c. black and red .. 1·10 70
131a. 5 c. black & orange .. 1·25 75
132b. 6 c. black & brown .. 1·00 1·00
133. 8 c. black and lilac .. 1·25 1·25
134. 10 c. brown & grey .. 3·50 1·60
135. 12 c. black and blue .. 6·00 3·75
136. 16 c. green & brown .. 3·00 2·10
137. 18 c. blk. & grn.(110) .. 2·50 2·75
138. 24 c. blue & red (111) .. 4·00 4·50
139. 25 c. grey-blue .. 1·50 3·50
140. 50 c. violet .. 1·80 3·50
142. $1 red .. 5·00 6·50
143. $2 green .. 10·00 12·00
144. $5 purple .. 20·00 23·00
145. $10 brown .. 28·00 28·00

1904. Stamps of 1897 and Nos. 81/6 surch. **4 cents.**
146. 4 c. on 5 c. black & orange 3·50 3·75
147. 4 c. on 6 c. black & brown 1·50 2·00
148. 4 c. on 8 c. black and lilac 4·25 5·00
149a. 4 c. on 12 c. black and blue 5·00 4·25
150. 4 c. on 18 c. blk. & grn.(110) 5·50 5·50
151a. 4 c. on 24 c. bl. and red (111) 3·75 5·00
152. 4 c. on 25 c. grey-blue .. 2·10 3·50
153. 4 c. on 50 c. violet .. 2·10 4·00
154. 4 c. on $1 red .. 3·75 5·00
155. 4 c. on $2 green .. 5·00 5·50
156. 4 c. on $5 purple .. 5·50 6·50
157. 4 c. on $10 brown .. 5·50 6·50

33. Tapir.

34. Traveller's-tree.

45.

(47.)

1909. The 18 c. is surch. **20 CENTS.**
159. 33. 1 c. black & brn. 1·25 40 —
160. 34. 2 c. black & grn. 70 25 12
278. 2 c. blk. & claret 35 30 —
161. – 3 c. black & red 70 40 12
279. – 3 c. black & grn. 1·25 1·00 —
280. – 4 c. black & red 65 15 —
281. – 5 c. black & brn. 1·00 60 —
282. – 6 c. black & olive 1·00 45 —
169. – 8 c. black & red 1·25 60 15
284. – 10 c. black & blue 1·00 30 —
285. – 12 c. black & blue 1·00 65 —
286. – 16 c. black & brn. 1·25 1·00 —
175. – 18 c. black & grn. 5·50 3·75 70
287. – 20 c. on 18 c. blk. and green .. 1·50 1·25 —
288. – 24 blk. & mauve 3·75 3·00 —
178. 45. 25 c. black & grn. 1·60 1·10 —
179. 50 c. blk. & blue 2·50 1·60 —
180. $1 black & brn. 4·50 2·10 —
181. $2 black & lilac 8·50 3·50 —
182. – $5 black & red.. 20·00 13·00 —
294. – $10 blk. & oran. 45·00 45·00 —

Designs—As T 33: 3 c. Railway at Jesselton. 4 c. Sultan of Sulu, his staff and W. C. Cowie, first Chairman of the Company. 5 c. Asiatic elephant. 8 c. Ploughing with buffalo. 24 c. Cassowary. As T 34: 6 c. Rhinoceros. 10 c. Wild boar. 12 c. Cockatoo. 16 c. Hornbill. 18 c. Wild bull. As T 45 but Arms with supporters: $5, $10.

1916. Stamps of 1909 surch.
186. 2 c. on 3 c. black and red.. 1·60 1·50
187. 4 c. on 6 c. black and olive 1·60 1·60
188. 10 c. on 12 c. black & blue 2·50 3·00

1916. Nos. 159, etc., optd. with T **47.**
189. 1 c. black and brown .. 3·50 7·50
203. 2 c. black and green .. 10·00 7·50
204. 3 c. black and red .. 7·00 12·00
192. 4 c. black and red .. 3·50 7·00
193. 5 c. black and brown .. 7·50 14·00
206. 6 c. black and olive .. 6·10 12·00
195. 8 c. black and red .. 7·00 14·00
208. 10 c. black and blue .. 7·00 17·00
209. 12 c. black and blue .. 14·00 27·00
198. 16 c. black and brown .. 15·00 25·00
199. 20 c. on 18 c. black & green 14·00 24·00
200. 24 c. black and mauve .. 21·00 32·00
201. 25 c. black and green .. 70·00 21·40

1918. Nos. 159, etc., surch. **RED CROSS TWO CENTS.**
214. 1 c. black and brown .. 70 2·50
215. 2 c. black and green .. 50 1·50
216. 3 c. black and red .. 1·25 3·00
218. 4 c. black and red .. 50 1·50
219. 5 c. black and brown .. 1·60 3·50
221. 6 c. black and olive .. 1·60 6·50
222. 8 c. black and red .. 1·00 2·75
223. 10 c. black and blue .. 1·60 5·00
224. 12 c. black and blue .. 1·60 5·50
225. 16 c. black and brown .. 2·10 6·50
226. 24 c. black and mauve .. 2·75 6·50
229. 25 c. black and green .. 5·50 12·00
230. 50 c. black and blue .. 5·50 12·00
231. $1 black and brown .. 14·00 20·00
232. $2 black and lilac .. 20·00 37·00
233. $5 black and red.. .. £140 £225
234. $10 black and orange .. £140 £225

The premium of 2 c. on each value was for Red Cross Funds.

1918. Nos. 159, etc., surch. **FOUR CENTS** and a red cross.
235. 1 c. black and brown .. 50 1·25
236. 2 c. black and green .. 70 1·50
237. 3 c. black and red .. 50 1·10
238. 4 c. black and red .. 50 1·00
239. 5 c. black andbrown .. 85 2·10
240. 6 c. black and olive .. 90 3·00
241. 8 c. black and red .. 1·10 2·75
242. 10 c. black and blue .. 1·60 5·00
243. 12 c. black and blue .. 2·00 3·50
244. 16 c. black and brown .. 2·00 5·00
245. 24 c. black and mauve .. 2·75 6·50
246. 25 c. black and green .. 3·00 7·00
248. 50 c. black and blue .. 5·50 10·00
249. $1 black and brown .. 7·00 14·00
250. $2 black and lilac .. 13·00 37·00
251. $5 black and red.. .. 90·00 £150
252. $10 black and orange .. 90·00 £150

The premium of 4 c. on each value was for Red Cross Funds.

1922. Nos. 159, etc., optd. **MALAYA-BORNEO EXHIBITION 1922.**
253. 1 c. black and brown .. 1·10 3·28
255. 2 c. black and green .. 50 2·40
256. 3 c. black and red .. 1·00 2·40
257. 4 c. black and red .. 75 2·10
258. 5 c. black and brown .. 1·25 3·30
260. 6 c. black and green .. 1·10 3·50
261. 8 c. black and red .. 1·50 4·00
263. 10 c. black and blue .. 1·50 5·00
265. 12 c. black and blue .. 1·60 5·00
267. 16 c. black and brown .. 1·10 5·00
268. 20 c. on 18 c. black & green 2·10 6·50
270. 24 c. black and mauve .. 1·60 5·00
273. 25 c. black and green .. 2·25 5·00
275. 50 c. black and blue .. 2·10 6·50

1923. No. 280 surch. **THREE CENTS** and bars.
276. – 3 c. on 4 c. black & red 75 1·00

48. Head of a Murut.

Designs—vert. 6 c. Orang-utan. 10 c. Dyak warrior. $1, $2, $5 Arms. horiz. 25 c. Clouded leopard.

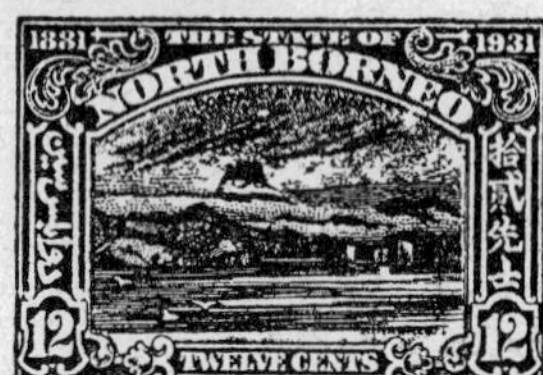

51. Mount Kinabalu.

1931. North Borneo Company. 50th Anniv.
295. 48. 3 c. black and green .. 1·50 1·00
296. – 6 c. black and orange.. 5·50 1·75
297. – 10 c. black and red .. 3·75 3·25
298. 51. 12 c. black and blue .. 2·60 3·25
299. – 25 c. black and violet.. 11·00 13·00
300. – $1 black and green .. 13·00 14·00
301. – $2 black and brown .. 16·00 18·00
302. – $5 black and purple .. 35·00 45·00

55. Buffalo Transport.

56. Cockatoo.

Designs—vert 3c. Native. 4 c. Proboscis monkey. 6 c. Mounted Bajaus. 10 c. Orang-Utan. 15 c. Dyak. $1, $2 Arms. horiz. 8 c. Map of East Indies. 12 c. Murut with blow-pipe. 20 c. River scene. 25 c. Native boat. 50 c. Mt. Kinabalu. $5 Arms with supporters.

1939.
303. 55. 1 c. green and brown .. 15 20
304. 56. 2 c. purple and blue .. 15 15
305. – 3 c. blue and green .. 15 20
306. – 4 c. green and violet .. 35 35
307. – 6 c. blue and claret .. 15 25
308. – 8 c. red 15 25
309. – 10 c. violet and green.. 2·00 1·25
310. – 12 c. green and blue .. 30 1·00
311. – 15 c. green and brown 1·00 1·00
312. – 20 c. violet and blue .. 1·25 1·25
313. – 25 c. green and brown.. 1·25 1·50
314. – 50 c. brown and violet.. 1·50 1·60
315. – $1 brown and red .. 2·40 4·00
316. – $2 violet and olive .. 11·00 14·00
317. – $5 blue.. .. .. 27·00 27·00

1941. Optd. **WAR TAX.**
318. 55. 1 c. green and brown.. 8 12
319. 56. 2 c. purple and blue.. 30 35

1945. British Military Administration. Stamps of 1939 optd. **BMA**
320. 55. 1 c. green and brown .. 30 25
321. 56. 2 c. purple and blue .. 30 25
322. – 3 c. blue and green .. 20 20
323. – 4 c. green and violet .. 2·40 2·40
324. – 6 c. blue and claret .. 25 30
325. – 8 c. red 45 75
326. – 10 c. violet and green .. 75 90
327. – 12 c. green and blue .. 45 60
328. – 15 c. green and brown.. 45 60
329. – 20 c. violet and blue .. 60 70
330. – 25 c. green and brown.. 1·00 90
331. – 50 c. brown and violet.. 1·25 1·60
332. – $1 brown and red .. 6·00 6·00
333. – $2 violet and olive .. 6·00 7·00
334. – $5 blue.. .. .. 6·00 8·00

1947. Stamps of 1939 optd. with Crown over **GR** monogram and bars obliterating "THE STATE OF" and "BRITISH PROTECTORATE".
335. 55. 1 c. green and brown .. 15 15
336. 56. 2 c. purple and blue .. 15 20
337. – 3 c. blue and green .. 15 20
338. – 4 c. green and violet .. 8 8
339. – 6 c. blue and claret .. 15 20
340. – 8 c. red 8 12
341. – 10 c. violet and green .. 15 12
342. – 12 c. green and blue .. 15 20
343. – 15 c. green and brown.. 15 15
344. – 20 c. violet and blue .. 15 25
345. – 25 c. green and brown.. 15 20
346. – 50 c. brown and violet.. 25 35
347. – $1 brown and red .. 35 45
348. – $2 violet and olive .. 1·10 2·00
349. – $5 blue .. .. .. 3·50 5·00

1948. Silver Wedding. As T 5/6 of Aden.
350. 8 c. red 12 15
351. $10 mauve .. .. 6·00 9·00

1949. U.P.U. as T 14/7 of Antigua.
352. 8 c. red 20 15
353. 10 c. brown 20 25
354. 30 c. brown 60 70
355. 55 c. blue .. .. 80 1·00

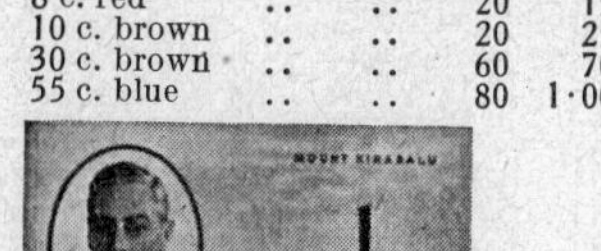

57. Mt. Kinabalu.

58. Coconut Grove.

Designs—vert. 4 c. Hemp-drying. 5 c. Cattle farm. 30 c. Sailing craft. 50 c. Clock tower. $1, Horsemen. horiz. 2 c. Musician. 8 c. Map. 10 c. Logging. 15 c. Sailing craft. 20 c. Chieftain. $2, Murut with blow-pipe. $5, Net fishing. $10, King George VI and arms.

1950.
356. 57. 1 c. chocolate 8 10
357. – 2 c. blue 8 8
358. 58. 3 c. green 8 10
359. – 4 c. purple 8 12
360. – 5 c. violet 20 12
361. – 8 c. red.. .. .. 15 15
362. – 10 c. maroon 12 15
363. – 15 c. blue 20 15
364. – 20 c. brown 30 25
365. – 30 c. buff 35 20
366. – 50 c. red ("JESSLETON").. 40 80
366a. – 50 c. red ("JESSELTON").. 40 80
367. – $1 orange 70 90
368. – $2 green .. .. 1·40 2·00
369. – $5 emerald .. .. 3·25 5·50
370. – $10 blue .. .. 6·50 8·00

1953. Coronation. As T 7 of Aden.
371. 10 c. black and red .. 20 30

1954. As 1950 but with portrait of Queen Elizabeth II.
372. 1 c. chocolate 5 5
373. 2 c. blue 5 5
374. 3 c. green.. .. .. 5 5
375. 4 c. purple 8 8
376. 5 c. violet 8 8
377. 8 c. red 8 8
378. 10 c. maroon 10 10
379. 15 c. blue.. .. .. 20 15
380. 20 c. brown 20 15
381. 30 c. buff 20 15
382. 50 c. red (No. 366a) .. 25 25
383. $1 orange.. .. .. 55 50
384. $2 green.. .. .. 1·50 1·50
385. $5 emerald .. .. 4·50 4·50
386. $10 blue .. .. 7·50 7·50

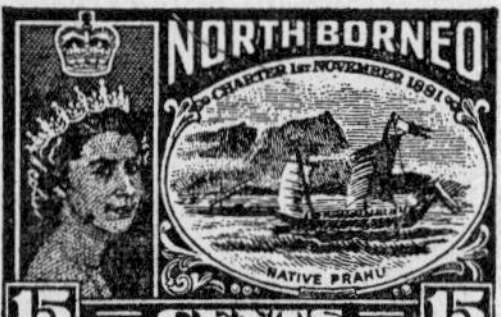

59. Native Prahu.

1956. Foundation of British North Borneo Co. 75th Anniv. Inscr. "CHARTER 1ST NOVEMBER 1881".
387. – 10 c. black and red .. 12 15
388. 59. 15 c. black and brown.. 25 30
389. – 35 c. black and green .. 40 45
390. – $1 black and slate .. 1·00 1·25

Designs—horiz. 10 c. Borneo Railway, 1902. 35 c. Mt. Kinabalu. vert. $1, Arms of Chartered Company.

60. Sambar Stag.

1961.

391. 60. 1 c. emerald & brn-red 5 5
392. – 4 c. olive and orange .. 5 5
393. – 5 c. sepia and violet .. 8 8
394. – 6 c. black and turquoise 10 10
395. – 10 c. green and red .. 12 12
396. – 12 c. brown and myrtle 15 15
397. – 20 c. turquoise and blue 20 15
398. – 25 c. black and red .. 25 30
399. – 30 c. sepia and olive .. 25 20
400. – 35 c. slate and brown .. 30 35
401. – 50 c. emerald & yell-brn. 30 30
402. – 75 c. grey-blue & purple 50 35
403. – $1 brown and green .. 65 50
404. – $2 brown and slate .. 1·50 1·00
405. – $5 emerald and maroon 4·50 3·50
406. – $10 red and blue .. 5·50 6·00

DESIGNS—HORIZ. 4 c. Honey bear. 5 c. Clouded leopard. 6 c. Dusun woman with gong. 10 c. Map of Borneo. 12 c. Tembadau (wild bull). 20 c. Butterfly orchid. 25 c. Sumatran rhinoceros. 30 c. Murut with blow-pipe. 35 c. Mt. Kinabalu. 50 c. Dusun and buffalo transport. 75 c. Bajau horseman. VERT. $1, Orang-utan. $2, Hornbill. $5, Crested wood partridge. $10, Arms of N. Borneo.

1963. Freedom from Hunger. As T 10 of Aden.

407. 12 c. blue 20 20

For Japanese issues see "Japanese Occupation of North Borneo".

POSTAGE DUE STAMPS

Overprinted **POSTAGE DUE.**

1895. Issue of 1894.

D 2. 13. 2 c. black and red .. 1·50 2·00
D 3. 14. 3 c. green and mauve 1·25 2·00
D 4. 15. 5 c. black and red .. 2·00 4·00
D 5a. 16. 6 c. black and brown 1·25 2·75
D 7. 17. 8 c. black and lilac .. 2·25 4·50
D 8b. 18. 12 c. black and blue .. 2·25 4·50
D 10. 19. 18 c. black and green 3·50 7·50
D 11. 20. 24 c. blue and claret .. 2·75

1897. Issue of 1897.

D 12. 13. 2 c. black and red .. 1·10 1·50
D 15. 2 c. black and green .. 1·25 1·50
D 17. 14. 3 c. green and mauve 1·25 1·50
D 18. 4 c. black and red .. 1·00 1·25
D 19. 15. 5 c. black and orange 1·10 1·50
D 20a.16. 6 c. black and brown 75 1·00
D 21a.17. 8 c. black and lilac .. 80 1·00
D 22. 18. 12 c. black and blue .. 2·40 3·00
D 23. 19. 18 c. black and green (No. 108) .. ..
D 24a. 18 c. black and green (No. 110) .. .. 2·40 2·50
D 25. 20. 24 c. blue and red (No. 109) .. .. — 1·60
D 26. 24 c. blue and red (No. 111) .. .. 2·40 3·00

1902. Issue of 1901.

D 47. 1 c. black & yellow-brown 1·60 5·50
D 36. 2 c. black and green .. 50 25
D 37. 3 c. green and mauve .. 50 35
D 38. 4 c. black and red .. 1·10 65
D 39. 5 c. black and orange .. 75 50
D 40. 6 c. black and brown .. 1·60 80
D 41. 8 c. black and lilac .. 2·00 1·10
D 42. 10 c. brown and grey .. 3·50 2·00
D 43. 12 c. black and blue .. 1·60 2·75
D 44. 16 c. green and brown .. 2·00 1·60
D 45. 18 c. black and green .. 1·50 1·50
D 46. 24 c. blue and red .. 2·10 4·00

1920. Issue of 1909.

D 49. 2 c. black and green .. 1·00 1·25
D 57. 2 c. black and claret .. 25 45
D 58. 3 c. black and green .. 25 45
D 59. 4 c. black and red .. 30 45
D 52. 5 c. black and brown .. 75 50
D 53. 6 c. black and olive .. 1·50 1·60
D 54. 8 c. black and red .. 50 45
D 55. 10 c. black and blue .. 1·50 1·60
D 56. 12 c. black and blue .. 2·00 2·75
D 65. 16 c. black and brown .. 2·25 3·00

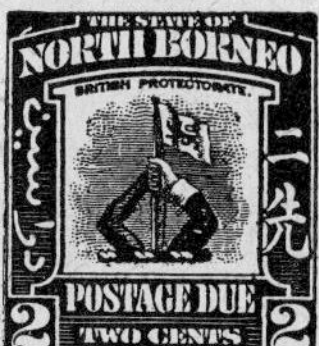

D 1. Crest of the Company.

1939.

D 66. D 1. 2 c. brown .. .. 65 5·50
D 67. 4 c. red .. .. 80 8·00
D 68. 6 c. violet .. .. 1·00 11·00
D 69. 8 c. green .. .. 1·60 14·00
D 70. 10 c. blue .. .. 2·25 15·00

For later issues see **SABAH.**

NORTH GERMAN CONFEDERATION E2

The North German Confederation was set up on 1st January, 1868, and comprised the postal services of Bremen, Brunswick, Hamburg Lubeck, Mecklenburg (both), Oldenburg, Prussia (including Hanover, Schleswig-Holstein with Bergedorf and Thurn and Taxis) and Saxony.

The North German Confederation joined the German Reichspost on 4th May, 1871, and the stamps of Germany were brought into use on 1st January, 1872.

30 groschen = 1 thaler = 60 kreuzer = 1 gulden.

1.

2.

1868. Roul. or perf.

19. 1. ¼ g. purple .. .. 9·00 6·00
22. ⅓ g. green .. .. 2·25 50
23. ½ g. orange .. .. 2·25 50
25. 1 g. red .. .. 1·75 25
27. 2 g. blue .. .. 2·25 30
29. 5 g. bistre .. .. 5·00 1·90
30. – 1 k. green .. .. 7·50 3·75
13. – 2 k. orange .. .. 21·00 17·00
33. – 3 k. red .. .. 3·75 50
36. – 7 k. blue .. .. 6·00 2·50
18. – 18 k. bistre .. .. 20·00 30·00

The 1 k. to 18 k. have the figures in an oval.

1869. Perf.

38. 2. 10 g. grey .. .. £190 32·00
39. – 30 g. blue .. .. £140 55·00

The frame of the 30 g. is rectangular.

OFFICIAL STAMPS

O 1.

1870.

O 40. O 1. ¼ g. black and brown 15·00 28·00
O 41. ⅓ g. black and brown 9·00 10·00
O 42. ½ g. black and brown 1·00 2·00
O 43. 1 g. black and brown 2·00 30
O 44. 2 g. black and brown 3·50 1·50
O 45. 1 k. black and grey .. 21·00 £120
O 46. 2 k. black and grey .. 50·00 £400
O 47. 3 k. black and grey .. 19·00 23·00
O 48. 7 k. black and grey .. 25·00 £120

NORTH INGERMANLAND E2

Stamps issued during temporary independence of this Russian territory, which adjoins Finland.

100 pennia = 1 mark.

1. 18th century Arms. 2. Gathering Crops.

1920.

1. 1. 5 p. green 40 40
2. 10 p. red 40 40
3. 25 p. brown 40 40
4. 50 p. blue 40 40
5. 1 m. black and red .. 5·00 5·00
6. 5 m. black and purple .. 20·00 20·00
7. 10 m. black and brown .. 38·00 38·00

1920. Inscr. as in T 2.

8. – 10 p. blue and green .. 70 90
9. – 30 p. green and brown .. 70 90
10. – 50 p. brown and blue .. 70 90
11. – 80 p. grey and claret .. 70 90
12. 2. 1 m. grey and red .. 4·50 6·00
13. – 5 m. rose and violet .. 3·00 4·00
14. – 10 m. violet and brown .. 3·00 4·00

DESIGNS—VERT. 10 p. Arms. 30 p. Reaper. 50 p. Ploughing. 80 p. Milking. HORIZ. 5 m. Burning church. 10 m. Zither players.

NORTH WEST RUSSIA E3

Issues made for use by the various Anti-bolshevist Armies during the Russian Civil War, 1918-20.

NORTHERN ARMY

1.

1919. As T 1 inscr. "OKCA".

1. 1. 5 k. purple 5
2. 10 k. blue 5
3. 15 k. yellow 5
4. 20 k. red 5
5. 50 k. green 5

NORTH-WESTERN ARMY

Сѣв. Зап.

Армія

(2.)

1919 Arms types of Russia optd. as T 2. Imperf. or perf.

6. 11. 2 k. green 60 90
16. 3 k. red .. .. 90 1·25
7. 5 k. lilac 60 90
8. 12. 10 k. blue .. .. 80 1·25
9. 4. 15 k. blue and purple .. 1·00 2·00
10. 7. 20 k. red and blue .. 2·00 3·25
11. 4. 20 k. on 14 k. red & blue 45·00
12. 25 k. mauve and green .. 2·00 3·25
13. 7. 50 k. green and purple .. 2·00 3·25
14. 8. 1 r. orge. & brn. on brn. 2·00 3·25
17. 5. 3 r. 50 green and red .. 7·00 7·00
18. 13. 5 r. blue on green .. 7·00 7·00
19. 5. 7 r. pink and green .. 20·00 20·00
15. 13. 10 r. grey and red on yell. 15·00 15·00

1919. No. 7 surch.

20. 11. 10 k. on 5 k. claret .. 2·00 3·25

WESTERN ARMY

1919. Stamps of Latvia optd. with Cross of Lorraine in circle with plain background. Imperf. (a) Postage stamps.

21. 1. 3 k. lilac .. .. 2·75 3·50
22. 5 k. red .. .. 2·75 3·50
23. 10 k. blue .. .. 12·00 18·00
24. 20 k. orange .. .. 2·75 3·50
25. 25 k. grey .. .. 2·75 3·50
26. 35 k. brown .. .. 2·75 3·50
27. 50 k. violet .. .. 2·75 3·50
28. 75 k. green .. .. 3·50 4·00

(b) Liberation of Riga issue.

29. 2. 5 k. red .. .. 2·75 3·50
30. 15 k. green .. .. 2·75 3·50
31. 35 k. brown .. .. 3·50 3·75

1919. Stamps of Latvia optd. with Cross of Lorraine in circle with burele background and characters **3. A** (= "Z. A."). Imperf.

(a) Postage stamps.

32. 1. 3 k. lilac .. .. 1·40 2·00
33. 5 k. red .. .. 1·40 2·00
34. 10 k. blue .. .. 16·00 16·00
35. 20 k. orange .. .. 1·60 2·50
36. 25 k. grey .. .. 5·00 6·00
37. 35 k. brown .. .. 3·00 3·50
38. 50 k. violet .. .. 3·00 3·50
39. 75 k. green .. .. 3·00 3·50

(b) Liberation of Riga issue.

40. 2. 5 k. red .. .. 1·25 1·50
41. 15 k. green .. .. 1·25 1·50
42. 35 k. brown .. .. 1·25 1·50

1919. Arms type of Russia surch. with Cross of Lorraine in ornamental frame and **LP** with value in curved frame. Imperf. or perf.

43. 11. 10 k. on 2 k. green .. 25 30
54. 20 k. on 3 k. red .. 40 60
44. 12. 30 k. on 4 k. red .. 50 65
45. 11. 40 k. on 5 k. claret .. 70 1·00
46. 12. 50 k. on 10 k. blue .. 40 50
47. 4. 70 k. on 15 k. blue & pur. 40 50
48. 7. 90 k. on 20 k. red & blue 1·00 1·25
49. 4. 1 r. on 25 k. mve. & grn. 1·00 1·25
50. 4. 1 r. 50 on 35 k. grn. & pur. 4·00 5·00
51. 7. 2 r. on 50 k. grn. & pur. .. 1·00 1·50
52. 4. 4 r. on 70 k. orge. & brn. 2·50 3·50
53. 8. 6 r. on 1 r. orge. & brown 3·25 3·50
56. 5. 10 r. on 3 r. 50 grn. & pur. 7·00 9·00

NORTHERN NIGERIA BC

A Br. Protectorate on the W. coast of Africa in 1914 incorporated in Nigeria, whose stamps it now uses.

1.

2.

1900.

1. 1. ½d. mauve and green .. 30 35
2. 1d. mauve and red .. 80 75
3. 2d. mauve and yellow .. 1·50 2·00
4. 2½d. mauve and blue .. 3·00 3·50
5. 5d. mauve and brown .. 5·00 5·50
6. 6d. mauve and violet .. 5·00 5·50
7. 1s. green and black .. 7·00 7·00
8. 2s. 6d. green and blue .. 35·00
9. 10s. green and brown .. £100

1902. As T 1, but portrait of King Edward VII.

10. ½d. purple and green .. 15 25
11. 1d. purple and red .. 30 20
12. 2d. purple and yellow .. 55 80
13. 2½d. purple and blue .. 35 55
14. 5d. purple and brown .. 90 2·00
15. 6d. purple and violet .. 3·00 3·00
16. 1s. green and black .. 2·25 2·25
17. 2s. 6d. green and blue .. 4·50 6·50
18. 10s. green and brown .. 25·00 25·00

1910. As last. New colours, etc.

28. ½d. green 8 8
29. 1d. red 10 8
30. 2d. grey 60 90
31. 2½d. blue 55 90
32. 3d. purple on yellow .. 45 30
34. 5d. purple and olive .. 90 1·25
36. 1s. black and green .. 90 80
37. 2s. 6d. black & red on blue 6·50 4·00
38. 5s. green & red on yellow 12·00 11·00
39. 10s. green & red on green 20·00 20·00

1912.

40. 2. ½d. green 12 12
41. 1d. red 12 8
42. 2d. grey 40 65
43. 3d. purple on yellow .. 35 45
44. 4d. black & red on yellow 30 30
45. 5d. purple and olive .. 50 65
46. 6d. purple and violet .. 60 90
47. 9d. purple and red .. 65 1·10
48. 1s. black on green .. 85 85
49. 2s. 6d. black & red on blue 4·00 4·00
50. 5s. green & red on yellow 9·50 10·00
51. 10s. green & red on green 14·00 15·00
52. £1 purple and black on red 40·00 30·00

NORTHERN RHODESIA BC

A Br. territory in C. Africa, N. of the Zambesi. From 1954 to 1963 part of the Central African Federation and using the stamps of Rhodesia and Nyasaland (q.v.). A new constitution was introduced on 3rd January, 1964, with internal self-government and independence came on 24th October, 1964, when the country was renamed Zambia (q.v.).

1.

ILLUSTRATIONS British Commonwealth and all overprints and surcharges are FULL SIZE. Foreign Countries have been reduced to ¾-LINEAR.

1925. The shilling values are larger and the view is in first colour.

1. 1. ½d. green 8 8
2. 1d. brown 8 8
3. 1½d. red 8 8
4. 2d. orange 20 10
5. 3d. blue 55 30
6. 4d. violet 65 30
7. 6d. grey 70 25
8. 8d. purple .. .. .. 3·50 5·50
9. 10d. olive .. .. .. 3·50 5·50
10. 1s. orange and black .. 1·50 65
11. 2s. brown and blue .. 5·00 6·00
12. 2s. 6d. black and green .. 4·00 3·50
13. 3s. violet and blue .. 7·00 5·50
14. 5s. grey and violet .. 7·00 5·50
15. 7s. 6d. purple and black .. 30·00 35·00
16. 10s. green and black .. 16·00 16·00
17. 20s. red and purple .. 60·00 65·00

1935. Silver Jubilee. As T 11 of Antigua.

18. 1d. blue and olive .. 15 20
19. 2d. green and blue .. 40 40
20. 3d. brown and blue .. 1·00 1·10
21. 6d. grey and purple .. 1·40 1·50

1937. Coronation. As T 2 of Aden.

22. 1½d. red 8 8
23. 2d. brown 15 15
24. 3d. blue 25 30

1938. As 1925, but with portrait of King George VI facing right and "POSTAGE & REVENUE" omitted.

25. ½d. green 8 8
26. ½d. brown 15 20
27. 1d. brown 8 8
28. 1d. green 30 20
29. 1½d. red .. .. .. 1·10 25
30. 1½d. orange 8 8
31. 2d. orange .. .. .. 9·00 1·50
32. 2d. red 15 15
33. 2d. purple 15 20
34. 3d. blue 15 12
35. 3d. red 25 25
36. 4d. violet 20 8
37. 4½d. blue .. .. .. 80 1·00
38. 6d. grey 25 25
39. 9d. violet .. .. .. 1·00 1·40
40. 1s. orange and black .. 45 12
41. 2s. 6d. black and green .. 1·10 85
42. 3s. violet and blue .. 1·10 90
43. 5s. grey and violet .. 2·00 2·25
44. 10s. green and black .. 3·00 3·50
45. 20s. red and purple .. 7·00 8·00

1946. Victory. As T 4 of Aden.

46.		1½d. orange	8	8
47.		2d. red	10	10

1948. Silver Wedding. As T 5/6 of Aden.

48.		1½d. orange	8	8
49.		20s. claret	6·00	9·00

1949. U.P.U. As T 14/17 of Antigua.

50.		2d. red	15	15
51.		3d. blue	20	25
52.		6d. grey	40	40
53.		1s. orange	75	75

2. Cecil Rhodes and Victoria Falls.

1953. Cecil Rhodes. Birth Cent.

54.	2.	½d. brown	10	10
55.		1d. green	10	10
56.		2d. mauve	10	10
57.		4½d. blue	50	90
58.		1s. orange and black	60	90

1953. Rhodes Centenary Exn. As T 16 of Southern Rhodesia.

59.		6d. violet	25	30

1953. Coronation. As T 7 of Aden.

60.		1½d. black and orange	10	12

1953. As 1938 but with portrait of Queen Elizabeth II facing left.

61.		½d. brown	5	5
62.		1d. green	5	5
63.		1½d. orange	8	8
64.		2d. purple	8	5
65.		3d. red	8	8
66.		4d. violet	10	10
67.		4½d. blue	20	25
68.		6d. grey	15	20
69.		9d. violet	25	35
70.		1s. orange and black	25	20
71.		2s. 6d. black and green	75	1·00
72.		5s. grey and purple	1·50	3·00
73.		10s. green and black	4·00	6·00
74.		20s. red and purple	11·00	13·00

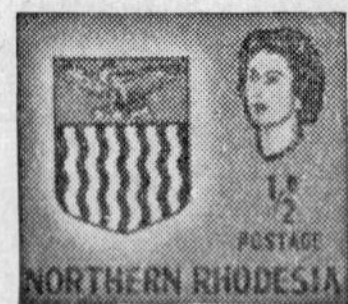

3. Arms.

1963. Arms black, gold and blue; portrait and inscriptions black; background colours given.

75.	3.	½d. violet	5	5
76.		1d. blue	5	5
77.		2d. brown	5	5
78.		3d. yellow	5	5
79.		4d. green	10	10
80.		6d. olive-green	10	10
81.	–	9d. yellow-brown	12	15
82.		1s. slate-purple	15	15
83.		1s. 3d. purple	40	20
84.	–	2s. orange	30	35
85.	–	2s. 6d. maroon	40	50
86.	–	5d. magenta	1·25	2·00
87.	–	10s. mauve	2·00	3·00
88.	–	20s. blue	4·50	8·00

Nos. 84/88 are as T 3 but larger (27 × 23 mm.).

POSTAGE DUE STAMPS

D 1.

D 2.

1929.

D 1a.	D 1.	1d. black	30	30
D 2.		2d. black	40	40
D 3aa.		3d. black	25	35
D 4.		4d. black	70	80

1963.

D 5.	D 2.	1d. orange	10	12
D 6.		2d. blue	12	15
D 7.		3d. lake	15	25
D 8.		4d. ultramarine	20	30
D 9.		6d. purple	30	45
D 10.		1s. green	60	1·00

For later issues see **ZAMBIA.**

NORWAY E2

In 1814 Denmark ceded Norway to Sweden, from 1814 to 1905 the King of Sweden was also King of Norway after which Norway was an independent Kingdom.

1855. 120 skilling = 1 speciedaler.
1877. 100 ore = 1 krone.

1.

2. King Oscar I.

1855. Imperf.

1.	1.	4 s. blue	£2250	55·00

1856. Perf.

4.	2.	2 s. yellow	£150	60·00
6.		3 s. lilac	£120	35·00
7.		4 s. blue	80·00	5·50
11.		8 s. lake	£275	19·00

3. 4.

1863.

12.	3.	2 s. yellow	£190	95·00
13.		3 s. lilac	£250	£140
16.		4 s. blue	35·00	4·25
17.		8 s. pink	£190	21·00
18.		24 s. brown	16·00	50·00

1867.

21.	4.	1 s. black	42·00	19·00
23.		2 s. brown	8·50	28·00
26.		3 s. lilac	£130	32·00
27.		4 s. blue	30·00	2·50
29.		8 s. red	£130	21·00

5.

A

1872. Value in "Skilling".

33.	5.	1 s. green	4·00	12·00
36.		2 s. blue	7·00	23·00
39.		3 s. red	23·00	2·10
42.		4 s. mauve	8·00	19·00
44.		6 s. brown	£140	32·00
45.		7 s. brown	19·00	27·00

1877. Letters without serifs as Type A. Value in "ore".

82.	5.	1 ore grey	2·25	2·75
81.		1 ore olive-brown	7·00	7·00
83.		2 ore brown	80	60
84c.		3 ore orange	27·00	1·60
52.		5 ore blue	23·00	2·75
85c.		5 ore green	23·00	35
86c.		10 ore red	22·00	30
55.		12 ore green	38·00	9·50
75b.		12 ore brown	9·50	6·00
76.		20 ore brown	38·00	4·25
87.		20 ore blue	28·00	35
88.		25 ore mauve	6·00	5·50
61.		35 ore green	7·00	3·75
62.		50 ore maroon	16·00	5·50
63.		60 ore blue	16·00	3·75

6. King Oscar II.

1873.

68.	6.	1 k. green	16·00	5·00
69.		1 k. 50 blue	38·00	25·00
70.		2 k. brown and rose	23·00	16·00

1888. Surch. 2 Ore.

89a.	5.	2 ore on 12 ore brown	80	80

7. With background shading.

B.

1893. Letters with serifs as Type B.

133.	7.	1 ore olive-grey	12	12
134.		2 ore brown	12	12
135.		3 ore orange	20	8
136.		5 ore green	2·25	8
137.		5 ore mauve	25	8
138.		7 ore green	25	8
139.		10 ore red	2·75	8
140.		10 ore green	4·75	12
141.		12 ore violet	40	30
142a.		15 ore brown	2·25	10
143.		15 ore blue	2·25	12
144.		20 ore blue	5·50	8
145.		20 ore sage-green	3·75	12
146.		25 ore mauve	19·00	15
147.		25 ore red	5·50	75
148.		30 ore grey	7·00	12
149.		30 ore blue	3·75	2·75
119.		35 ore green	6·00	2·25
150.		35 ore olive brown	7·00	12
151.		40 ore olive	2·25	12
152.		40 ore blue	9·50	12
153.		50 ore maroon	11·00	12
154.		60 ore blue	14·00	12

See also Nos. 279, etc. and for stamps as T 7 but with unshaded background, see Nos. 413, etc.

1905. Surch.

122.	4.	1 k. on 2 s. brown	19·00	19·00
123.		1 k. 50 on 2 s. brown	38·00	38·00
124.		2 k. on 2 s. brown	23·00	23·00

1906. Surch.

162.	7.	5 ore on 25 ore mauve	25	25
125.	5.	15 ore on 4 s. mauve	1·90	1·60
126.		30 ore on 7 s. brown	4·75	3·75

8. King Haakon VII. 9.

1907.

127.	8.	1 k. green	30·00	17·00
128.		1½ k. blue	40·00	45·00
129.		2 k. red	75·00	38·00

1910.

155a.	9.	1 k. green	70	8
156.		1½ k. blue	1·60	25
157.		2 k. red	2·25	25
158.		5 k. violet	3·75	3·00

10. Constitutional Assembly.

11.

1914. Independence Cent.

159.	10.	5 ore green	60	20
160.		10 ore red	1·40	20
161.		20 ore blue	7·00	3·00

1922.

163.	11.	10 ore green	5·50	20
164.		20 ore purple	9·50	8
165.		25 ore red	19·00	55
166.		45 ore blue	1·40	45

12.

13.

14.

1925. Air. Amundsen's Polar Flight.

167.	12.	2 ore brown	75	75
168.		3 ore orange	1·90	1·90
169.		5 ore mauve	3·75	3·75
170.		10 ore green	5·50	5·50
171.		15 ore blue	4·75	4·75
172.		20 ore mauve	10·00	10·00
173.		25 ore red	1·60	1·60

1925. Annexation of Spitzbergen.

183.	13.	10 ore green	3·00	3·00
184.		15 ore blue	1·90	1·25
185.		20 ore purple	3·75	55
186.		45 ore blue	3·50	2·50

1926. Size 16 × 19½ mm.

187.	14.	10 ore green	55	8
187a.		14 ore orange	95	60
188.		15 ore olive-brown	55	10
189.		20 ore purple	9·50	10
189a.		20 ore red	55	8
190.		25 ore red	5·50	75
190a.		25 ore brown	60	8
190b.		30 ore blue	60	12
191.		35 ore olive-brown	27·00	12
191a.		35 ore violet	1·50	12
192.		40 ore blue	2·25	35
193.		40 ore slate	1·10	12
194.		50 ore claret	1·10	12
195.		60 ore blue	1·10	12

For stamps as T 14 but size 17 × 21 mm., see Nos. 413, etc.

1927. Surcharged with new value and bar.

196.	14.	20 ore on 25 ore red	1·40	70
197.	11.	30 ore on 45 ore blue	7·00	55
198.	13.	30 ore on 45 ore blue	1·40	1·40

15. Akershus Castle.

16. Ibsen.

17. Abel.

1927. Air.

199a.	15.	45 ore blue	2·25	95

For stamp without frame-lines, see No. 295.

1928. Ibsen Centenary

200.	16.	10 ore green	4·50	1·25
201.		15 ore brown	1·90	1·25
202.		20 ore red	2·25	25
203.		30 ore blue	2·25	1·90

1929. Postage Due stamps optd. **Post Frimerke** or **POST** and thick bar.

204.	D 1.	1 ore grey	15	15
205.		4 ore mauve (No. D 96a)	15	15
206.		10 ore green	75	75
207.		15 ore brown	1·50	1·50
208.		20 ore purple	80	60
209.		40 ore blue	1·25	55
210.		50 ore maroon	3·50	2·50
211.		100 ore yellow	1·75	1·10
212.		200 ore violet	3·50	2·40

1929 Abel Centenary.

213.	17.	10 ore green	1·60	50
214.		15 ore brown	1·90	1·10
215.		20 ore red	70	25
216.		30 ore blue	1·60	1·60

1929. Surch. **14 ORE 14.**

217.	4.	14 ore on 2 s. brown	1·40	1·40

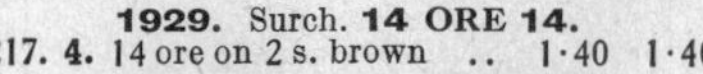

18. St. Olaf.

19. Trondhjem Cathedral.

20. Death of St. Olaf.

1930. St. Olaf. 9th Death Cent.

219.	18.	10 ore green	4·75	25
220.	19.	15 ore sepia and brown	85	35
221.	18.	20 ore red	85	15
222.	20.	30 ore blue	3·75	3·00

21. North Cape.

1930. Norwegian Tourist Assn. Fund. Size 33½ × 21½ mm.

223.	21.	15 ore+25 ore brown	60	60
224.		20 ore+25 ore red	12·00	12·00
225.		30 ore+25 ore blue	35·00	35·00

For smaller stamps in this design see Nos. 265/6, 349/51 and 442/66.

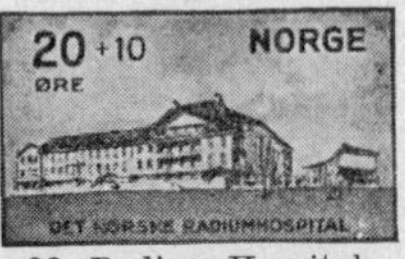

22. Radium Hospital.

1931. Radium Hospital Fund.

226.	22.	20 ore+10 ore red	5·50	2·10

23. Bjornson.

24. L. Holberg.

1932. Bjornstjerne Bjornson. Birth Cent.

227.	23.	10 ore green	5·50	30
228.		15 ore sepia	70	55
229.		20 ore red	60	15
230.		30 ore blue	1·40	1·40

1934. Holberg. 250th Birth Anniv.
231. 24. 10 ore green 70 20
232. 15 ore brown 45 40
233. 20 ore red .. .. 6·00 20
234. 30 ore blue .. .. 1·60 1·40

25. Dr. Nansen. 26. No background shading. 27. King Haakon VII.

1935. Nansen Refugee Fund.
235. 25. 10 ore+10 ore green .. 75 75
236. 15 ore+10 ore brown 3·00 3·00
237. 20 ore+10 ore red .. 75 75
238. 30 ore+10 ore blue .. 4·25 4·25
See also Nos. 275/8.

1937. Air. As T 15 but without surrounding frame-lines.
295. 45 ore blue 35 15

1937.
279. 26. 1 ore olive 5 5
280. 2 ore brown .. 5 5
281. 3 ore orange .. 5 5
282. 5 ore mauve .. 12 8
283. 7 ore green 25 15
284. 10 ore grey 8 8
285. 12 ore violet .. 25 25
414. 15 ore green .. 35 10
415. 15 ore brown .. 10 8
416. 20 ore brown .. 1·50 55
417. 20 ore green .. 8 8

1937. As T 14 but size 17 × 21 mm.
413. 14. 10 ore green 12 8
286. 14 ore orange 60 60
287. 15 ore olive 15 5
288a. 20 ore red 25 5
289. 25 ore brown 45 5
289a. 25 ore vermilion .. 12 5
290. 30 ore blue 45 15
290a. 30 ore grey .. .. 1·50 15
291. 35 ore violet 45 8
292. 40 ore slate 45 8
292a. 40 ore blue 40 8
293. 50 ore claret 45 8
293a. 55 ore orange .. .. 4·50 10
294. 60 ore blue 60 8
294a. 80 ore brown 60 8

1937.
255. 27. 1 k. green 12 12
256. 1 k. 50 blue .. .. 1·10 1·25
257. 2 k. red .. .. 1·10 2·50
258. 5 k. purple .. .. 5·50 15·00

28. Reindeer. 29. Joelster.

1938. Tourist Propaganda.
262. 28. 15 ore brown 35 25
263. – 20 ore red 30 8
264. 29. 30 ore blue 40 25
DESIGN—VERT. 20 ore, Stave Church, Borgund.

1938. Norwegian Tourist Association Fund. As T 21, but reduced to 27½ × 21 mm.
265. 21. 20 ore+25 ore lake .. 2·50 2·50
266. 30 ore+25 ore blue .. 6·00 6·00

30. Queen Maud. 31. Lion Rampant. 32. Dr. Nansen.

1939. Queen Maud Children's Fund.
267. 30. 10 ore+5 ore green .. 45 2·40
268. 15 ore+5 ore brown .. 45 2·40
269. 20 ore+5 ore red .. 45 2·40
270. 30 ore+5 ore blue .. 45 3·00

1940.
271. 31. 1 k. green 85 8
272. 1½ k. blue .. .. 1·10 15
273. 2 k. red .. .. 1·50 55
274. 5 k. purple .. .. 2·50 1·10
See also Nos. 318/21.

1940. National Relief Fund.
275. 32. 10 ore+10 ore green .. 1·10 1·10
276. 15 ore+10 ore brown .. 1·90 1·90
277. 20 ore+10 ore red .. 45 45
278. 30 ore+10 ore blue .. 1·10 1·10

33. Sailing Vessel. 34. Colin Archer and Sailing Vessel.

1941. Halogaland Exhibition and Fishermen's Families Relief Fund.
296. 33. 15 ore+10 ore blue .. 35 1·25

1941. National Lifeboat Institution. 50th Anniv.
297. 34. 10 ore+10 ore green .. 55 55
298. 15 ore+10 ore brown .. 55 55
299. – 20 ore+10 ore red .. 45 45
300. – 30 ore+10 ore blue .. 1·40 1·40
DESIGN—VERT. 20 ore, 30 ore, Lifeboat.

35. Soldier and Flags. 36. Oslo University.

1941. Norwegian Legion Support Fund.
301. 35. 20 ore+80 ore red .. 17·00 27·00

1941. Stamps of 1937 optd. V (=Victory).
302. 26. 1 ore olive 12 60
303. 2 ore brown 12 60
304. 3 ore orange 12 60
305. 5 ore mauve 12 20
306. 7 ore green 45 75
307. 14. 10 ore green 12 15
308. 26. 12 ore violet .. .. 40 1·00
309. 14. 14 ore orange .. 70 1·25
310. 15 ore olive 15 40
311. 20 ore red 12 10
312. 25 ore brown 12 15
313. 30 ore blue 25 40
314. 35 ore violet 25 25
315. 40 ore slate 25 25
316. 50 ore claret 45 75
317. 60 ore blue 45 45
318. 31. 1 k. green 40 12
319. 1½ k. blue .. .. 1·25 2·50
320. 2 k. red .. .. 3·50 7·50
321. 5 k. purple .. .. 8·50 16·00

1941. As No. 413, but with "V" incorporated in the design.
322. 10 ore green .. .. 40 1·90

1941. Foundation Oslo University Building. Cent.
323. 36. 1 k. olive .. .. 12·00 14·00

37. Queen Ragnhild. 38. Snorre Sturlason.

DESIGNS—As T 39. 15 ore Archer. 30 ore Viking ships. 50 ore Spearmen and torchbearers.

39. Battlefield.

1941. Snorre Sturlason (historian). 700th Death Anniv. Inscr. as in T 37/9.
324. 37. 10 ore green 20 10
325. – 15 ore brown 25 25
326. 38. 20 ore red 20 8
327. – 30 ore blue 45 40
328. – 50 ore violet 55 55
329. 39. 60 ore blue 45 40

40. Vidkun Quisling. 41. Rikard Nordraak.

DESIGN—As T 42: 30 ore Mountains across sea and two lines of the National Anthem.

42. Embarkation of the Vikings.

1942.
(a) Without optd.
330. 40. 20 ore+30 ore red .. 1·25 3·50
(b) Optd. **1-2 1942.**
331. 40. 20 ore+30 ore red .. 1·25 3·50

1942. Rikard Nordraak (composer). Birth Cent.
332. 41. 10 ore green 70 70
333. 42. 15 ore brown 70 70
334. 41. 20 ore red 70 70
335. – 30 ore blue 70 70

1942. War Orphans' Relief Fund. As T 40 but inscr. "RIKSTINGET 1942".
336. 20 ore+30 ore red .. 25 1·40

43. J. H. Wessel. 44. Reproduction of Types 40 and 1.

1942. Wessel (poet). Birth Bicent.
337. 43. 15 ore brown 12 12
338. 20 ore red 12 12

1942. European Postal Union, Vienna. Inaug.
339. 44. 20 ore red 20 35
340. 30 ore blue 25 55

45. Destroyer "Sleipner". 46. Edvard Grieg.

1943.
341. 45. 5 ore purple 10 10
342. – 7 ore green 15 15
343. 45. 10 ore green 10 8
344. – 15 ore olive 40 40
345. – 20 ore red 10 8
346. – 30 ore blue 60 60
347. – 40 ore green 45 45
348. – 60 ore blue 45 45
DESIGNS: 7 ore, 30 ore. Ships in convoy. 15 ore Airman. 20 ore "Vi Vil Vinne" (We will win) written on the highway. 40 ore Soldiers on skis. 60 ore King Haakon VII.

For use on correspondence posted at sea on Norwegian merchant ships and (in certain circumstances) from Norwegian camps in Gt. Britain during the German Occupation of Norway. After liberation all values were put on sale in Norway.

1943. Norwegian Tourist Association Fund. As T 21, but smaller (27½×21 mm.).
349. 21. 15 ore+25 ore brown .. 40 40
350. 20 ore+25 ore carmine 60 55
351. 30 ore+25 ore violet .. 1·00 1·00

1943. Grieg (composer). Birth Cent.
352. 46. 10 ore green 15 12
353. 20 ore red 15 12
354. 40 ore olive 25 12
355. 60 ore blue 30 12

47. Soldier's Emblem. 48. Fishing Station.

1943. Soldiers' Relief Fund.
356. 47. 20 ore+30 ore red .. 30 1·75

1943. Winter Relief Fund.
357. 48. 10 ore+10 ore green .. 60 1·25
358. – 20 ore+10 ore red .. 60 2·25
359. – 40 ore+10 ore grey .. 60 1·75
DESIGNS: 20 ore Mountain scenery. 40 ore Winter landscape.

49. Sinking Ship. 50. First North Sea Flight.

1944. Shipwrecked Mariners' Relief Fund.
360. 49. 10 ore+10 ore green .. 45 1·40
361. – 15 ore+10 ore brown .. 45 1·40
362. – 20 ore+10 ore red .. 45 1·40
DESIGNS—HORIZ. 15 ore Aeroplane attacking ship. VERT. 20 ore Sinking of S.S. "Irma".

1944. Tryggve Grans North Sea Flight.
363. 50. 40 ore blue 20 95

51. Girl Spinning. 52. Henrik Wergeland.

1944. Winter Relief Fund. Inscr. as in T 51.
364. 51. 5 ore+10 ore mauve .. 30 80
365. – 10 ore+10 ore green .. 30 1·10
366. – 15 ore+10 ore purple .. 30 1·10
367. – 20 ore+10 ore red .. 30 1·10
DESIGNS: 10 ore Ploughing. 15 ore Tree felling. 20 ore Mother and children.

1945. Wergeland (poet). Death Cent.
369. 52. 10 ore green 20 20
370. 15 ore brown 60 60
371. 20 ore red 12 12

53. Arms. 54. Red Cross Sister. 55. Lion Rampant.

1945.
368. 53. 1½ k. blue 85 35

1945. Red Cross Relief Fund and Norwegian Red Cross Jubilee.
372. 54. 20 ore+10 ore red .. 30 30

1945. National Folklore Museum. 50th Anniv.
373. 55. 10 ore olive 20 12
374. 20 ore red 25 12

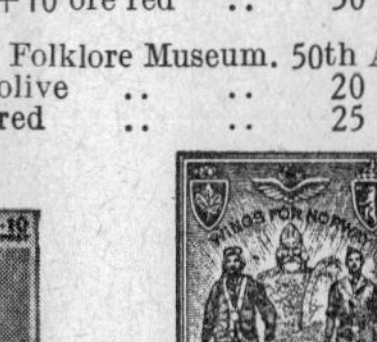

56. King Olav V (when Crown Prince). 57. "R.N.A.F.".

1946. National Relief Fund.
375. 56. 10 ore+10 ore green .. 25 25
376. 15 ore+10 ore brown 25 25
377. 20 ore+10 ore red .. 25 25
378. 30 ore+10 ore blue .. 95 95

1946. Honouring Norwegian Air Force Trained in Canada.
379. 57. 15 ore red 25 25

58. King Haakon. 59. Nansen and Amundsen.

1946.
380. 58. 1 k. green 60 8
381. 1½ k. blue 95 8
382. 2 k. brown .. .. 6·00 8
383. 5 k. violet .. .. 2·25 15

1947. Norwegian Post Office. Tercent.
384. – 5 ore mauve 8 8
385. – 10 ore green 8 8
386. – 15 ore brown 10 8
387. – 25 ore red 12 8
388. – 30 ore grey 30 10
389. – 40 ore blue 30 8
390. – 45 ore violet 75 25
391. – 50 ore brown 30 12
392. 59. 55 ore orange .. .. 2·50 20
393. – 60 ore grey .. .. 1·40 30
394. – 80 ore brown 60 12
DESIGNS: 5 ore Hannibal Sehested. 10 ore "Postal-peasant". 15 ore Admiral Tordenskiold. 25 ore Christian M. Falsen. 30 ore Cleng Peerson. 40 ore Mailboat "Constitutionen". 45 ore First Norwegian locomotive. 50 ore Svend Foyn and whaling ship. 60 ore King Haakon and Queen Maud. 80 ore King Haakon.

60. Petter Dass. 61. King Haakon VII.

1947. Petter Dass (poet). Birth Tercent.
395. **60.** 25 ore red 30 30

1947, 75th Birthday of King Haakon VII.
396. **61.** 25 ore red 30 30

62. Axel Heilberg. **63.** A. L. Kielland.

1948. 50th Anniv. of Norwegian Forestry Society and Birth Cent. of Axel Heilberg (founder).
397. **62.** 25 ore red 20 12
398. 80 ore brown 60 12

1948. Red Cross. Surch. **25+5** and bars.
399. **54.** 25+5 ore on 20+10 ore red 30 30

1949. Stamps of 1937 surch.
400. **14.** 25 ore on 20 ore red .. 40 8
401. 45 ore on 40 ore blue .. 1·40 15

1949. Alexander L. Kielland (author). Birth Cent.
402. **63.** 25 ore red 12 10
403. 40 ore blue 25 15
404. 80 ore brown 40 25

64. Symbolising Universe. **65.** Pigeons and Globe.

1949. U.P.U. 75th Anniv.
405. **64.** 10 ore green and purple 45 45
406. **65.** 25 ore red 45 12
407. – 40 ore blue 30 25
DESIGN—HORIZ. 40 ore signpost and dove.

66. King Haardraade and Oslo Town Hall. **67.** Child with Flowers.

1950. Founding of Oslo. 900th Anniv.
408. **66.** 15 ore green 40 40
409. 25 ore red 20 12
410. 45 ore blue 50 40

1950. Infantile Paralysis Fund.
411. **67.** 25 ore+5 ore red .. 55 45
412. 45 ore+5 ore blue .. 2·10 2·10

69. King Haakon VII. **70.** Arne Garborg.

1950.
418. **69.** 25 ore red 30 5
419. 25 ore grey .. .. 4·50 8
419a. 25 ore green 25 8
420. 30 ore grey .. .. 1·25 20
421. 30 ore red 12 8
422. 35 ore lake .. .. 5·50 8
422a. 35 ore red 85 8
422b. 40 ore purple 40 8
423. 45 ore blue 60 40
424. 50 ore brown 60 8
425. 55 ore orange 60 40
426. 55 ore blue 40 8
427. 60 ore blue 50 8
427a. 65 ore blue 50 10
427b. 70 ore olive .. .. 1·90 8
428. 75 ore brown 60 8
429. 80 ore brown 40 8
430. 90 ore orange 60 8

1951. Garborg (author). Birth Cent.
431. **70.** 25 ore red 25 10
432. 45 ore blue 55 60
433. 80 ore brown 55 15
"NOREG" on the stamps was the spelling advocated by Arne Garborg.

71. Skater. **72.** King Haakon VII.

1951. 6th Winter Olympic Games. Inscr. "OSLO 1952".
434. **71.** 15 ore+5 ore green .. 75 75
435. – 30 ore+10 ore red .. 75 75
436. – 55 ore+20 ore blue .. 3·75 3·75
DESIGNS: 30 ore Ski-jumper. LONGER: 55 ore Winter landscape.

1951. Surch. in figures.
440. **26.** 20 ore on 15 ore green 20 8
437. **69.** 30 ore on 25 ore red .. 30 8

1952. 80th Birthday of King Haakon.
438. **72.** 30 ore red 20 10
439. 55 ore blue 45 45

73. "Supplication". **74.** Medieval Sculpture.

1953. Anti-Cancer Fund.
441. **73.** 30 ore+10 ore red and cream 55 55

1953. Norwegian Tourist Association Fund. As T **21** but smaller (27½×21 mm.).
442. **21.** 20 ore+10 ore green .. 2·25 2·25
464. 25 ore+10 ore green .. 1·25 1·25
443. 30 ore+15 ore red .. 2·75 2·75
465. 35 ore+15 ore red .. 1·25 1·25
444. 55 ore+25 ore blue .. 3·75 3·75
466. 65 ore+25 ore blue .. 1·25 1·25

1953. Archbishopric of Nidaros. 8th Cent.
445. **74.** 30 ore red 20 8

75. 1st. Rly. Engine and Horse-drawn Sledge. **76.** C. T. Nielsen.

1954. Railway Cent. Inscr. "N S B".
446. **75.** 20 ore green 25 20
447. – 30 ore red 40 8
448. – 55 ore blue 45 35
DESIGNS: 30 ore Diesel express train. 55 ore Engine-driver.

1954. Telecommunications in Norway. Cent. Inscr. "1855 1955".
449. **76.** 20 ore black and green.. 25 20
450. – 30 ore red 25 8
451. – 55 ore blue 45 35
DESIGNS: 30 ore Radio towers. 55 ore Telegraph linesman on skis.

77. "Posthorn" Type Stamp.

78. King Haakon and Queen Maud.

79. Crown Princess Martha.

80. Jan Mayen Island.

81. Map of Spitzbergen.

1955. Norwegian Stamp Cent.
452. – 20 ore blue and green.. 20 10
453. **77.** 30 ore carmine and red 25 8
454. – 55 ore blue & grey-blue 50 25
DESIGNS: 20 ore Norway's first stamp. 55 ore "Lion" type stamp.

1955. Postage Stamp Cent. and Int. Stamp Exn., Oslo. Nos. 452/4 with circular opt. **OSLO NORWEX.**
455. – 20 ore blue and green.. 4·75 4·75
456. **77.** 30 ore carmine and red 4·75 4·75
457. – 55 ore blue & grey-blue 4·75 4·75
Nos. 455/7 were only on sale at the Exhibition P.O. at face+1 k. entrance fee.

1955. Golden Jubilee of King Haakon.
458. **78.** 30 ore red 15 8
459. 55 ore blue 40 35

1956. Crown Princess Martha Memorial Fund.
460. **79.** 35 ore+10 ore red .. 75 75
461. 65 ore+10 ore blue .. 1·90 1·90

1956. Northern Countries' Day. As T **69** of Denmark.
462. 35 ore red 95 25
463. 65 ore blue 60 55

1957. Int. Geophysical Year. Inscr. "INTERN. GEOFYSISK AR 1957–1958".
467. **80.** 25 ore green 25 20
468. **81.** 35 ore red and grey .. 20 8
469. – 65 ore green and blue .. 35 25
DESIGN: 65 ore Map of Antarctica showing Queen Maud Land.

82. King Haakon VII. **83.** King Olav V. **84.**

1957. 85th Birthday of King Haakon.
470. **82.** 35 ore red 15 8
471. 65 ore blue 35 35

1958.
472. **83.** 25 ore light green .. 25 5
472a. 25 ore grey-green .. 25 5
473. 30 ore violet .. 25 5
474. 35 ore lake .. 25 5
474a. 35 ore light green .. 25 5
475. 40 ore red .. 25 5
475a. 40 ore grey .. 45 8
476. 45 ore red .. 35 5
477. 50 ore ochre .. 35 5
478. 50 ore red .. 35 5
479. 55 ore grey .. 60 15
480. 60 ore violet .. 60 15
481. 65 ore blue .. 60 15
482. 80 ore brown .. 60 8
483. 85 ore brown .. 60 8
484. 90 ore orange .. 60 8
485. **84.** 1 k. green .. 55 8
486. 1 k. 50 blue .. 70 8
487. 2 k. red .. 90 8
488. 5 k. purple .. 1·90 8
489. 10 k. orange .. 3·50 15

85. Asbjorn Kloster (founder). **86.** Society's Centenary Medal.

1959. Norwegian Temperance Movement Cent.
490. **85.** 45 ore brown 20 8

1959. Royal Norwegian Agricultural Society. 150th Anniv.
491. **86.** 45 ore buff & oran.-red 25 12
492. 90 ore grey and blue .. 1·00 75

87. Sower.

88. White Anemone.

1959. Norwegian Royal College of Agriculture. Cent. Inscr. "NORGES LANDBRUKSHOGSKOLE 1859-1959".
493. **87.** 45 ore black and ochre.. 20 8
494. – 90 ore black and blue.. 45 20
DESIGN—VERT. 90 ore Ears of Corn.

1960. Tuberculosis Relief Funds.
495. **88.** 45 ore+10 ore green and red 75 70
496. – 90 ore+10 ore orange, blue and green .. 2·50 2·50
DESIGN: 90 ore Blue anemone.

89. Society's Original Seal. **90.** Refugee Mother and Child.

1960. Royal Norwegian Society of Scientists Bicent.
497. **89.** 45 ore red 25 10
498. 90 ore blue 50 30

1960. World Refugee Year.
499. **90.** 45 ore+25 ore black and red .. .. 2·25 2·25
500. 90 ore + 25 ore black and blue .. .. 5·50 5·50

91. Viking Ship. **92.** Throwing the Javelin.

1960. Norwegian Ships.
501. **91.** 20 ore black and grey.. 30 25
502. – 25 ore black and green 30 25
503. – 45 ore black and red .. 30 10
504. – 55 ore black and ochre 75 75
505. – 90 ore black and blue.. 60 30
SHIPS: 25 ore Galleon. 45 ore Barque. 55 ore Tanker. 90 ore Liner.

1960. Europa As T **279** of Belgium but size 27½×21 mm.
506. 90 ore blue 40 30

1961. Scandinavian Airlines System (SAS) 10th Anniv. As T **81** of Denmark.
507. 90 ore blue 40 30

1961. Norwegian Sport Cent.
508. **92.** 20 ore ochre 45 15
509. – 25 ore turquoise .. 45 15
510. – 45 ore red 30 8
511. – 90 ore purple 45 20
DESIGNS: 25 ore Skating. 45 ore Ski-jumping. 90 ore Sailing.

93. Hakonshallen Barracks and Rosencrantz Tower.

1961. Hakonshallen. 700th Anniv.
512. **93.** 45 ore black and lake .. 35 8
513. 1 k. black and olive .. 60 15

94. Oslo University. **95.** Nansen.

1961. Oslo University. 150th Anniv.
514. **94.** 45 ore red 25 8
515. 1 k. 50 blue 70 15

1961. Nansen (explorer). Birth Cent.
516. **95.** 45 ore black and red .. 25 8
517. 90 ore black and blue.. 45 35

96. Amundsen, "Fram" and Dog-team. **97.** Frederic Passy and Henri Dunant (Winners of 1901).

1961. Amundsen's Arrival at South Pole. 50th Anniv.
518. **96.** 45 ore red and grey .. 25 8
519. – 90 ore deep & pale blue 45 35
DESIGN: 90 ore Amundsen's party and tent at South Pole.

1961. Nobel Peace Prize.
520. **97.** 45 ore red 25 8
521. 1 k. green 55 15

98. Prof. V. Bjerknes. **99.** Bleriot 'plane, "Start".

1962. Prof. Bjerknes (mathematician). Birth Cent.
522. **98.** 45 ore black and red .. 25 8
523. 1 k. 50 black and blue.. 70 20

1962. Norwegian Aviation. 50th Anniv.
524. **99.** 1 k. 50 sepia and blue .. 75 15

100. Branch of Fir, and Cone. **101.** Europa "Tree".

1962. State Forestry Administration Cent.
525. **100.** 45 ore grey. blk. & sal. 25 20
526. 1 k. grey, black & green 90 15

1962. Europa.
527. **101.** 50 ore red 25 8
528. 90 ore blue 55 25

102. Bosun's Knot. **103.** Camilla Collett. **104.** Boatload of Wheat.

1962.
529. **7.** 5 ore claret 5 5
530. 10 ore slate 5 5
531. 15 ore chestnut .. 5 5
532. 20 ore green 5 5
532a. – 25 ore blue 5 5
533. – 25 ore grey-green .. 5 5
534. – 30 ore drab 40 15
535. – 30 ore green 20 5
536. **102.** 35 ore emerald .. 20 5
537. – 40 ore red 20 5
537a. – 40 ore green 15 5
537b. – 45 ore green 30 30
538. **102.** 50 ore red 20 8
538a. – 50 ore greenish grey .. 20 8
539. – 55 ore chestnut .. 25 15
540. **102.** 60 ore grey-green .. 40 8
540a. 60 ore red 25 8
541. – 65 ore slate-violet .. 40 8
541a. **102.** 65 ore carmine .. 25 8
541b. 70 ore brown 15 8
541c. – 75 ore green 20 8
542. – 80 ore claret 20 8
542a. – 80 ore brown 20 8
543. – 85 ore sepia 20 8
543a. – 85 ore buff 55 8
544. – 90 ore blue 40 15
544a. – 100 ore violet 25 8
544b. – 100 ore red 25 8
544c. – 110 ore red 25 8
544d. – 115 ore brown .. 30 8
544e. – 120 ore blue 30 12
544f. – 125 ore blue 30 8
544g. – 140 ore red 35 20
544h. – 750 ore brown .. 1·10 50

DESIGNS: 25, 40, 90, 100 (2), 110, 120 ore, Runic drawings. 30, 45, 55, 75, 85 ore, Ear of wheat and fish. 65, 80, 140 ore, "Stave" (wooden) church and Aurora Borealis. 115 ore, Fragment of Urnes stave-church. 750 ore, Sigard the Dragon-killer testing sword.

1963. Camilla Collett (author). 150th Birth Anniv.
545. **103.** 50 ore lake .. 20 8
546. 90 ore slate-blue .. 45 35

1963. Freedom from Hunger.
547. **104.** 25 ore bistre 12 8
548. 35 ore green 20 8
549. – 50 ore red 25 8
550. – 90 ore blue 45 35

DESIGN—HORIZ. (37½ × 21 mm.): 50 ore, 90 ore, Boatload of food produce.

105. River Boat. **106.** Ivar Aasen.

1963. Southern–Northern Norwegian Postal Services. Tercent.
551. **105.** 50 ore brown-red .. 55 8
552. – 90 ore blue 60 55

DESIGN: 90 ore, Northern sailing ship.

1963. Ivar Aasen. 150th Birth Anniv.
553. **106.** 50 ore red and grey .. 25 8
554. 90 ore blue and grey 95 35

The note after No. 433 re "NOREG" also applies here.

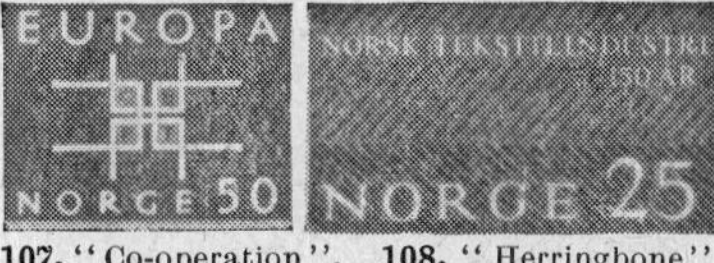

107. "Co-operation". **108.** "Herringbone" Pattern.

1963. Europa.
555. **107.** 50 ore orange and claret 25 8
556. 90 ore green and blue .. 45 35

1963. Norwegian Textile Industry. 150th Anniv.
557. **108.** 25 ore green and bistre 15 10
558. 35 ore blue & turq.-blue 20 12
559. 50 ore purple and red .. 20 8

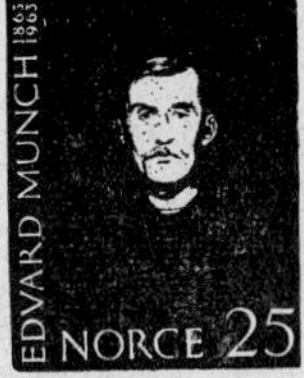

109. Edvard Munch (self-portrait). **110.** Eilert Sundt (founder).

1963. Edvard Munch (painter and engraver). Birth Cent.
560. **109.** 25 ore black 15 8
561. – 35 ore green 20 8
562. – 50 ore maroon .. 25 8
563. – 90 ore blue 45 35

DESIGNS: (Woodcuts)—HORIZ. 35 ore, "Fecundity". 50 ore, "The Solitaries". VERT. 90 ore, "The Girls on the Bridge".

1964. Oslo Workers' Society Centenary.
564. **110.** 25 ore green 15 12
565. – 50 ore maroon .. 25 8

DESIGN: 50 ore, Beehive emblem of O.W.S.

111. C. M. Guldberg and P. Waage (chemists). **112.** Eidsvoll Manor.

1964. Law of Mass Action Centenary.
566. **111.** 35 ore bronze-green .. 25 15
567. 55 ore ochre 40 20

1964. Norwegian Constitution. 150th Anniv.
568. **112.** 50 ore grey and red .. 30 10
569. – 90 ore black and blue 55 55

DESIGN: 90 ore, Storting (Parliament House,) Oslo.

On 1st June, 1964, a stamp depicting the U.N. refugee emblem and inscr. "PORTO BETALT . . . LYKKEBREVET 1964" was put on sale. It had a franking value of 50 ore but was sold for 2 k. 50, the balance being for the Refugee Fund. In addition, each stamp bore a serial number representing participation in a lottery which took place in September. The stamp was on sale until 15th July and had validity until 10th August.

113. Harbour Scene. **114.** Europa "Flower".

1964. Norwegian Seamen's Mission. Cent.
570. **113.** 25 ore green and yellow 20 8
571. 90 ore blue and cream 55 45

1964. Europa.
572. **114.** 90 ore indigo and blue 40 30

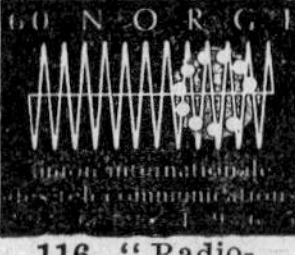

115. H. Anker and O. Arveson (founders). **116.** "Radio-telephone".

1964. Norwegian Folk High Schools. Cent.
573. **115.** 50 ore rose 25 10
574. 90 ore blue 55 55

The note after No. 433 re "NOREG" also applies here.

1965. I.T.U. Cent.
575. **116.** 60 ore maroon .. 25 8
576. – 90 ore slate 45 25

DESIGN: 90 ore, "T.V. transmission".

DESIGN: 60 ore, Norwegian flags.

117. Dove of Peace and Broken Chain.

1965. Liberation. 20th Anniv.
577. **117.** 30 ore + 10 ore brown, green and sepia .. 40 30
578. – 60 ore + 10 ore blue and red 45 25

118. Mountain Landscapes. **119.** Europa "Sprig".

1965. Norwegian Red Cross. Cent.
579. **118.** 60 ore sepia and red .. 25 8
580. – 90 ore slate-blue & red 55 45

DESIGN: 90 ore, Coastal view.

1965. Europa.
581. **119.** 60 ore red 25 8
582. 90 ore blue 45 30

120. St. Sunniva and Bergen Buildings. **121.** Rondane Mountains (after H. Sohiberg).

1965. Harmonien Philharmonic Society. Bicent.
583. – 30 ore black and green 25 12
584. **120.** 90 ore black and blue 45 30

DESIGN—VERT. 30 ore, St. Sunniva.

1965.
585. **121.** 1 k. 50 blue 60 8

122. "Rodoy Skier" (rock carving). **123.** "The Bible".

1966. World Skiing Championships, Oslo. Inscr. "VM OSLO 1966".
586. **122.** 40 ore chocolate .. 30 15
587. – 55 ore green 60 60
588. – 60 ore lake-brown .. 25 8
589. – 90 ore blue 50 30

DESIGNS—HORIZ. 55 ore, Ski jumper. 60 ore, Cross-country skier. VERT. 90 ore, Holmenkollen ski-jumping tower, Oslo.

1966. Norwegian Bible Society. 150th Anniv.
590. **123.** 60 ore red 25 8
591. 90 ore blue 45 20

124. Guilloche Pattern. **125.** J. Sverdrup.

1966. Bank of Norway. 150th Anniv.
592. **124.** 30 ore green 20 12
593. – 60 ore red (Bank bldg.) 25 8

No. 593 is size 27½ × 21 mm.

1966. Johan Sverdrup (statesman). 150th Birth Anniv.
594. **125.** 30 ore green 20 10
595. 60 ore maroon .. 25 8

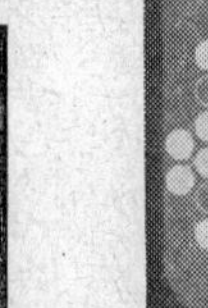

126. Europa "Ship". **127.** Molecules in test-tube.

1966. Europa.
596. **126.** 60 ore red 25 8
597. 90 ore blue 50 35

1966. Birth Cents. of S. Eyde (industrialist) (1966) and K. Birkeland (scientist) (1967) founders of Norwegian Nitrogen Industry.
598. **127.** 40 ore indigo and blue 25 15
599. – 55 ore magenta and red 25 20

DESIGN: 55 ore, Ear of Wheat.

128. E.F.T.A. Emblem. **129.** "Owl" and Three Swords.

1967. European Free Trade Assn.
600. **128.** 60 ore red 25 8
601. 90 ore blue 55 35

1967. Higher Military Training. 150th Anniv.
602. **129.** 60 ore chocolate .. 25 12
603. 90 ore green 55 45

130. Cogwheels. **131.** Johanne Dybwad.

1967. Europa.
604. **130.** 60 ore plum and apple 25 8
605. 90 ore violet and blue 50 35

1967. J. Dybwad (actress). Birth Cent.
606. **131.** 40 ore indigo 20 15
607. 60 ore lake 25 8

132. L. Skrefsrud (missionary and founder). **133.** Climbers on Mountain-top.

1967. Norwegian Santal Mission. Cent.
608. **132.** 60 ore chestnut .. 25 8
609. – 90 ore blue 50 25

DESIGN—HORIZ. 90 ore, Ebenezer Church, Benagaria, Santal, India.

1968. Norwegian Mountain Touring Assn. Cent.
610. **133.** 40 ore maroon .. 30 10
611. – 60 ore lake 30 10
612. – 90 ore blue 55 30

DESIGNS: 60 ore, Mountain cairn and scenery. 90 ore, Glitretind peak.

134. "The Blacksmiths". **135.** A. O. Vinje.

1968. Norwegian Handicrafts.
613. **134.** 65 ore sepia, blk. & red 30 12
614. 90 ore sepia, blk. & blue 50 30

1968. Aasmund Vinje (poet). 150th Birth Anniv.
615. **135.** 50 ore sepia 20 8
616. 65 ore lake 25 8

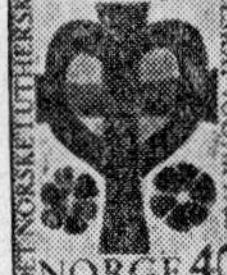

136. Cross and Heart. **137.** Cathinka Guldberg (first deaconess).

1968. Norwegian Lutheran Home Mission Society Cent.
617. **136.** 40 ore lake and emerald 75 20
618. 65 ore lake and violet 25 8

1968. Deaconess House, Oslo Cent.
619. **137.** 50 ore blue 20 15
620. 65 ore red 25 8

138. K. P. Arnoldson and F. Bajer.

1968. Nobel Peace Prize-winners of 1908.
621. **138.** 65 ore brown 25 8
622. 90 ore blue 40 25

1969. Northern Countries' Union. 50th Anniv. Similar to T **125** of Denmark.
623. 65 ore red 25 8
624. 90 ore blue 35 20

139. Transport.

1969. "Rutebok for Norge" ("Communications of Norway"), and Road Safety Campaign. Cent.
625. **139.** 50 ore green 20 10
626. – 65 ore red and green.. 25 8
DESIGN: 65 ore Pedestrian-crossing.

140. Colonnade.

1969. Europa.
627. **140.** 65 ore black and red.. 25 8
628. 90 ore black and blue.. 35 25

141. J. Hjort and Fisheries Emblem. **142.** Traena Islands.

1969. Professor Johan Hjort (fisheries pioneer). Birth Cent.
629. **141.** 40 ore brown and blue 60 15
630. 90 ore blue and green 45 30

1969.
631. **142.** 3 k. 50 black 85 8

143. King Olav V. **144.** "Mother and Child".

1969.
632. **143.** 1 k. olive 25 5
633. 1 k. 50 blue 35 5
634. 2 k. red 50 5
635. 5 k. blue .. .. 1·25 5
636. 10 k. brown .. .. 2·25 25
637. 20 k. sepia .. .. 5·50 30

1969. Gustav Vigeland (sculptor). Birth Cent.
638. **144.** 65 ore black & carmine 30 5
639. – 90 ore black and blue 40 25
DESIGN: 90 ore "Family".

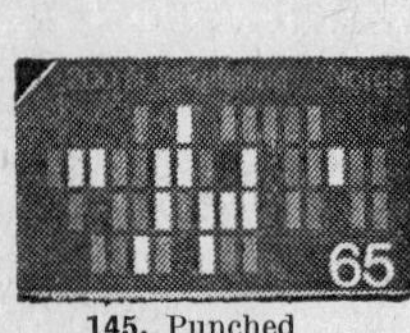

145. Punched Cards. **146.** Queen Maud.

1969. 1st National Census. Bicent. Multicoloured.
640. 65 ore Type **145** .. 25 5
641. 90 ore "People" .. 40 20

1969. Queen Maud. Birth Cent.
642. **146.** 65 ore purple .. 25 8
643. 90 ore ultramarine .. 40 20

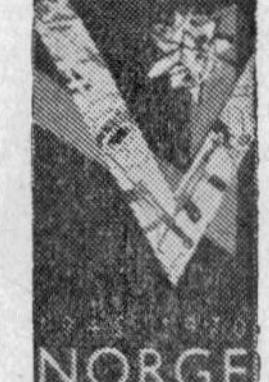

147. Wolf. **148.** "V" Symbol.

1970. Nature Conservation Year.
644. **147.** 40 ore brown and blue 25 12
645. – 60 ore grey and brown 30 15
646. – 70 ore brown and blue 35 8
647. – 100 ore brown and blue 60 20
DESIGNS—VERT. 60 ore "Pulsatilla vernalis" (plant). 70 ore Voringsfossen Falls. HORIZ. 100 ore Sea Eagle ("Haliaeetus albicilla").

1970. Liberation. 25th Anniv.
648. **148.** 70 ore red and violet 75 10
649. – 100 ore ultram. & grn. 60 25
DESIGN—HORIZ. 100 ore Ships in convoy.

149. "Citizens". **150.** Hands reaching for Globe.

1970. Bergen. 900th Anniv.
650. **149.** 40 ore green 35 15
651. – 70 ore claret 70 10
652. – 1 k. blue 60 25
DESIGNS: 70 ore "City in the Mountains". 1 k. "Ships".

1970. United Nations. 25th Anniv.
653. **150.** 70 ore red .. .. 1·00 10
654. 100 ore green 60 25

151. G.O. Sars. **152.** Ball-game.

1970. Norwegian Zoologists.
655. **151.** 40 ore brown 30 15
656. – 50 ore violet 30 12
657. – 70 ore brown 60 8
658. – 100 ore blue 55 25
ZOOLOGISTS: 50 ore, Hans Strom. 70 ore, J. E Gunnerus. 100 ore, Michael Sars.

1970. Central School of Gymnastics, Oslo. Cent.
659. **152.** 50 ore brown and blue 20 10
660. – 70 ore brown and red 60 8
DESIGN—HORIZ. 70 ore, "Leapfrog" exercise.

153. Tonsberg's Seal c. 1340.

1971. Tonsberg. 1100th Anniv.
661. **153.** 70 ore red 30 8
662. 100 ore indigo .. 55 20

154. Parliament House, Oslo.

1971. Introduction of Annual Parliamentary Sessions. Cent.
663. **154.** 70 ore lilac and red .. 30 8
664. 100 ore green and blue 50 25

155. "Helping Hand".

1971. "Help for Refugees".
665. **155.** 50 ore green & black.. 12 5
666. 70 ore red & black .. 15 5

156. "Hauge addressing Followers" (A. Tidemand).

1971. Hans Nielson Hauge (church reformer). Birth Bicent.
667. **156.** 60 ore black .. 15 5
668. 70 ore brown 15 5

157. Bishop welcoming Worshippers.

1971. Oslo Bishopric. 900th Anniv.
669. – 70 ore black and red 15 5
670. **157.** 1 k. black and blue .. 50 25
DESIGN—VERT. 70 ore, Masons building first church.

158. Roald Amundsen and Treaty Emblem. **159.** "The Preacher and the King".

1971. Antarctic Treaty. 10th Anniv.
671. **158.** 100 ore red and blue .. 75 25

1971. Norwegian Folk-tales. Drawings by Erik Werenskiold.
672. – 40 ore black & green.. 25 5
673. **159.** 50 ore black and blue 25 12
674. – 70 ore black and purple 55 5
DESIGNS—VERT. 40 ore, "The Farmer and the Woman". 70 ore, "The Troll and the Girl".

160. Commemorative Emblem. **161.** "Posthorn" Stamp.

1972. Norwegian Savings Banks' 150th Anniv.
675. **160.** 80 ore gold and red .. 25 8
676. 120 ore gold and blue.. 30 20

1972. Norwegian "Posthorn" Stamps. Cent.
677. **161.** 80 ore red and brown 30 8
678. 1 k. blue and violet .. 35 20

162. Alstad "Picture" Stone (detail). **163.** King Haakon VII.

1972. Norway's Unification. 1,100th Anniv.
680. **162.** 50 ore green 30 12
681. – 60 ore brown 15 15
682. – 80 ore red 40 8
683. – 120 ore blue 50 20
DESIGNS: 60 ore, Portal, Hemsedal Church (detail). 80 ore, Animal head-post (Oseberg). 120 ore, Sword-hilt (steinsvik).

1972. King Haakon VII. Birth Cent.
684. **163.** 80 ore red 30 8
685. 120 ore blue 30 20

164. "Joy" (Ingrid Ekrem). **165.** "Maud".

1972. "Youth and Leisure".
686. **164.** 80 ore mauve 35 8
687. – 120 ore blue 50 20
DESIGN: 120 ore, "Solidarity" (Ole Instefjord).

1972. "Interjunex 1972" Stamp Exhib., Oslo. Nos. 686/7 optd. **INTERJUNEX 72.**
688. **164.** 80 ore mauve .. 1·75 1·75
689. – 120 ore blue .. .. 1·75 1·75

1972. Norwegian Polar Ships.
690. **165.** 60 ore olive & green.. 15 8
691. – 80 ore red and black.. 60 8
692. – 120 ore blue and red.. 30 20
DESIGNS: 80 ore, "Fram". 120 ore, "Gjoa".

166. "Little Man". **167.** Dr. Hansen and Bacillus Diagram.

1972. Norwegian Folk Tales. Drawings of trolls by Th. Kittelsen.
693. **166.** 50 ore black and green 20 8
694. – 60 ore black and blue 15 10
695. – 80 ore black and pink 30 8
TROLLS: 60 ore, "The troll who wonders how old he is". 80 ore, "Princess riding on a Bear".

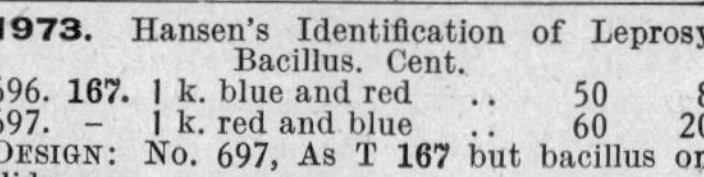

1973. Hansen's Identification of Leprosy Bacillus. Cent.
696. **167.** 1 k. blue and red .. 50 8
697. – 1 k. red and blue .. 60 20
DESIGN: No. 697, As T **167** but bacillus on slide.

168. Europa "Posthorn". **169.** King Olav V.

1973. Europa.
698. **168.** 100 ore red and orange 50 8
699. 140 ore green and blue 35 20

1973. Nordic Countries Postal Co-operation. As T **198** of Sweden.
700. 1 k. multicoloured .. 50 8
701. 1 k. 40 multicoloured .. 35 20

1973. King Olav's 70th Birthday.
702. **169.** 1 k. brown and red .. 25 8
703. 1 k. brown and blue .. 35 20

170. J. Aall. **171.** Bone Carving.

1973. Jacob Aall (industrialist). Birth Cent.
704. **170.** 1 k. purple 25 8
705. 1 k. 40 blue 35 20

1973, Lappish Handicrafts.
706. **171.** 75 ore brown & yellow 20 8
707 – 1 k. red and yellow .. 25 8
708. – 1 k. 40 black and blue 35 20
DESIGNS: 1 k. Detail of weaving. 1 k. 40 Detail of tin-ware.

172. "Viola biflora". **173.** Land Surveying.

1973. Mountain Flowers. Multicoloured.
709. 65 ore Type **172** 30 10
710. 70 ore "Veronica fruticans" 40 15
711. 1 k. "Phyllodoce coerulea" 55 10

1973. Norwegian Geographical Survey. Bicent.
712. **173.** 1 k. red 25 8
713. – 1 k. 40 blue 35 20
DESIGN: 140 ore, Old map of Hestbraepiggene (mountain range).

174. Lindesnes. **175.** "Ferryboat, Hardanger Fjord" (A. Tidemand and H. Gude).

1974. Norwegian Capes.
714. **174.** 1 k. green 25 8
715. – 1 k. 40 blue 35 20
DESIGN: 1 k. 40 North Cape.

1974. Norwegian Paintings. Multicoloured.
716. 1 k. Type **175** 25 8
717. 1 k. 40 "Stugundset from Filefjell" (J. Dahl) .. 35 25

176. Illuminated "M"—Part of Manuscript. **177.** Saw and Conifers.

1974. King Magnus Lagaboter's Legislation. 700th Anniv
718. **176.** 1 k. red and brown .. 40 5
719. – 1 k. 40 blue and brown 35 20
DESIGN: 1 k. 40 King Magnus Lagaboter.

1974. Workers Safeguards.
720. **177.** 85 ore light green, green & lime green.. 30 15
721. – 1 k. red and orange .. 40 12
DESIGN: 1 k. Cogwheel and guard.

178. J. H. L. Vogt. **179.** "Man's Work" (Buildings of the world).

1974. Norwegian Geologists.
722. **178.** 65 ore brn. & grn. .. 15 10
723. – 85 ore brn. & pur. .. 20 10
724. – 1 k. brown & orange.. 25 8
725. – 1 k. 40 brown & blue 35 20
DESIGNS: 85 ore V. M. Goldschmidt. 1 k. Th. Kjerulf. 1 k. 40 W. C. Brogger.

1974. Universal Postal Union. Cent.
726. **179.** 1 k. brown & green .. 25 8
727. – 1 k. 40 blue & brown 35 20
DESIGN: 1 k. 40 "Men, our brethren" (Peoples of the world).

180. "Horseman" (detail from chest of drawers). **181.** Female Skier, 1900.

1974. Norwegian Folk Art. Rose-painting. Multicoloured.
728. 85 ore Type **180** 20 10
729. 1 k. "Bouquet" (detail from cupboard).. .. 25 8

1975. "Norway—Home of Skiing".
730. **181.** 1 k. red and green .. 25 8
731. – 1 k. 40 blue & brown 35 20
DESIGN: 1 k. 40 Male skier making telemark turn.

182. "The Women with Ivies" (wrought-iron gates, Vigeland Park). **183.** Nusfjord Lofoten Islands.

1975. International Women's Year.
732. **182.** 125 ore red 30 8
733. 140 ore blue 35 20

1975. European Architectural Heritage Year.
734. **183.** 100 ore green 25 8
735. 125 ore red 30 8
736. 140 ore blue 35 20

184. Norwegian 1-krone Coin of 1875.

1975. Monetary and Metre Conventions. Cents.
737. **184.** 1 k. 25 red 30 8
738. – 1 k. 40 blue 35 20
DESIGN: 1 k. 40 O.J. Broch (first Director of the International Bureau of Weights and Measures).

185. "Scouting in Summer".

1975. "Homage to Scouting" World Scout Jamboree, Lillehammer. Multicoloured.
739. 125 ore Type **185** .. 30 8
740. 140 ore "Scouting in Winter" 35 20

186. "Colonists' First Home".

1975. Commencement of Emigration to America. 150th Anniv.
741. **186.** 125 ore brown .. 30 8
742. – 140 ore blue 35 20
DESIGNS: 140 ore Cleng Peerson ("Father of Emigration") and text of letter.

187. Temple Mountain. **188.** Television Screen.

1975. Annexation of Spitzbergen. 50th Anniv.
743. **187.** 100 ore grey 25 8
744. 125 ore purple .. 30 8
745. – 140 ore blue 35 20
DESIGNS: 125 ore, Miners leaving pit. 140 ore, Polar bear.

1975. "50 Years of Broadcasting in Norway". Multicoloured.
746. 125 ore Type **188** .. 30 8
747. 140 ore Aerial mast and houses on Globe .. 35 20

189. "The Annunciation". **190.** "Halling" Dance.

1975. Christmas. Vault Paintings from Stave Church, Al. Multicoloured.
748. 80 ore Type **189** 20 5
749. 100 ore "The Visitation" 25 5
750. 125 ore "The Nativity" (28 × 35 mm.).. .. 30 8
751. 140 ore "The Adoration" (28 × 35 mm.).. .. 35 20

1976. Norwegian Folk Dances. Multicoloured.
752. 80 ore Type **190** 20 5
753. 100 ore "Springar" dance 25 5
754. 125 ore "Gangar" dance 30 8

191. Silver Sugar Castor. **193.** "The Pulpit", Lyse Fjord.

192. Bishop's "Mitre" Bowl.

1976. Oslo Museum of Applied Art. Cent.
755. **191.** 125 ore purple and brn. 30 8
756. – 140 ore violet and blue 35 20
DESIGN: 140 ore Glass goblet.

1976. Europa.
757. **192.** 125 ore maroon & pur. 30 5
758. – 140 ore dark blue & blue 35 20
DESIGN: 140 ore Decorative plate.

1976. Norwegian Scenery. Multicoloured.
759. 100 ore Type **193** 25 5
760. 125 ore Blossom-time, Balestrand, Sogne Fjord .. 30 5

194. Social Development Graph, 1876–1976. **195.** Olav Duun by cairn on Dun Mountain.

1976. Norwegian Central Statistics Bureau. Centenary.
761. **194.** 125 ore brown .. 30 5
762. – 200 ore blue 50 20
DESIGN: 200 ore Graph of national productivity.

1976. Olav Duun (novelist). Birth Cent.
763. **195.** 125 ore multicoloured 30 5
764. 140 ore multicoloured 35 20

196. "Slinderbirkin" (T. Fearnley). **197.** Details of "April".

1976. Norwegian Paintings. Multicoloured.
765. 125 ore Type **196**.. .. 30 5
766. 140 ore "Gamle Furutraer" (L. Hertervig) 35 20

1976. Baldish Stave-church Tapestry. Multicoloured.
767. 80 ore Type **197** 20 5
768. 100 ore Detail of "May" 25 5
769. 125 ore "April" and "May" section of tapestry .. 30 5

OFFICIAL STAMPS

O 1. O 2.

1925.
O 187. O **1.** 5 ore mauve 25 25
O 188. 10 ore green 15 8
O 189. 15 ore blue 40 40
O 190. 20 ore purple .. 15 8
O 191. 30 ore slate .. .. 1·25 90
O 192. 40 ore blue 45 25
O 193. 60 ore blue .. .. 1·40 1·25

1929. Surch. **2** twice.
O 219. O **1.** 2 ore on 5 ore mauve 15 15

1933.
O 231. O **2.** 2 ore brown 10 10
O 243. 5 ore purple .. 20 20
O 244. 7 ore orange .. 1·90 1·90
O 245. 10 ore green .. 12 8
O 235. 15 ore olive .. 25 15
O 247. 20 ore red 20 8
O 237. 25 ore chestnut .. 25 15
O 238. 30 ore blue 25 15
O 248. 35 ore mauve .. 30 12
O 249. 40 ore grey 30 10
O 250. 60 ore blue 35 15
O 241. 70 ore chocolate .. 45 45
O 242. 100 ore violet .. 75 60

O 3. O 4. Quisling Emblem.

1937.
O 267. O **3.** 5 ore mauve.. .. 8 5
O 256. 7 ore orange .. 8 5
O 257. 10 ore green .. 8 5
O 270. 15 ore olive .. 15 5
O 271. 20 ore red 8 5
O 260. 25 ore brown .. 25 25
O 273. 25 ore red 15 5
O 261. 30 ore blue 20 5
O 276. 30 ore grey 15 5
O 277. 35 ore purple .. 15 5
O 278. 40 ore grey 20 5
O 279. 40 ore blue 15 5
O 280. 50 ore lilac .. 20 5
O 281. 60 ore blue 25 5
O 282. 100 ore violet .. 40 5
O 283. 200 ore orange .. 1·50 15

1942.
O 336. O **4.** 5 ore mauve 10 25
O 337. 7 ore orange .. 10 30
O 338. 10 ore green .. 8 8
O 339. 15 ore brown .. 70 1·90
O 340. 20 ore red 8 8
O 341. 25 ore brown .. 1·50 2·40
O 342. 30 ore blue .. .. 70 1·90
O 343. 35 ore purple .. 70 2·40
O 344. 40 ore slate 15 15
O 345. 60 ore blue .. .. 70 1·25
O 346. 1 k. blue .. .. 70 2·40

1949. Surch. **25** and bar.
O 402. O **3.** 25 ore on 20 ore red.. 15 10

O 5. O 6.

1951.
O 434. O **5.** 5 ore magenta .. 10 10
O 435. 10 ore grey 8 8
O 436. 15 ore brown .. 10 10
O 437. 30 ore red 12 8
O 438. 35 ore brown .. 20 10
O 439. 60 ore blue 25 10
O 440. 100 ore violet .. 40 12

1955.
O 458. O **6.** 5 ore magenta .. 8 5
O 459. 10 ore slate 8 5
O 460. 15 ore brown .. 8 5
O 461. 20 ore green .. 8 5
O 462. 25 ore green .. 12 5
O 463. 30 ore red 15 5
O 464. 30 ore green .. 8 5
O 465. 35 ore lake .. 15 5
O 466. 40 ore lilac .. 15 5
O 467. 40 ore green 10 5
O 468. 45 ore red 20 5
O 469. 50 ore brown .. 20 5
O 470. 50 ore red .. 20 5
O 471. 50 ore blue 15 5
O 472. 60 ore blue 25 5
O 473. 60 ore red 25 5
O 474. 60 ore green .. 15 5
O 475. 65 ore red 15 5
O 476. 70 ore brown .. 30 5
O 477. 70 ore red 15 5
O 478. 75 ore brown .. 35 35
O 479. 80 ore brown .. 30 5
O 480. 80 ore chestnut .. 20 5
O 481. 90 ore orange .. 25 5
O 482. 1 k. violet .. 25 5
O 483. 2 k. green 50 20
O 484. 5 k. violet .. 1·25 75

POSTAGE DUE STAMPS

D 1.

1889. Inscr. "at betale" and "PORTOMÆRKE"
D 95. D **1.** 1 ore grey 25 25
D 96a. 4 ore mauve 55 40
D 97. 10 ore red .. .. 2·25 25
D 98. 15 ore brown .. 60 25
D 99. 20 ore blue .. .. 1·10 25
D 94. 50 ore maroon .. 2·50 85

1922. Inscr. "a betale" and "PORTOMERKE".
D 162. D **1.** 4 ore mauve .. 3·00 4·75
D 163. 10 ore green .. 60 60
D 164. 20 ore purple .. 2·40 2·40
D 165. 40 ore blue .. 3·75 40
D 166. 100 ore yellow .. 17·00 7·00
D 167. 200 ore violet .. 48·00 14·00

NOSSI-BE O3

An island N.W. of Madagascar, declared a French protectorate in 1840; becoming part of the Madagascan Colony in 1901.

1889. Stamp of French Colonies, "Peace and Commerce" type, surch. in figures.
2. **8.** 25 c. on 40 c. red on yellow £400 £180

1889. Stamps of French Colonies, "Commerce" type, surch. in figures.
3. **9.** 5 c. on 10 c. black on lilac £400 £300
5. 5 c. on 20 c. red on green.. £425 £225
7. 15 on 20 c. red on green.. £250 £140
8. 25 on 30 c. brown .. £300 £160
9. 25 on 40 c. red on yellow.. £200 £120

1890. Stamps of French Colonies, "Commerce" type, surch. **N S B** and value in figures.
10. **9.** 0.25 on 20 c. red on green 50·00 38·00
11. 0.25 on 75 c. red .. 50·00 38·00
12. 0.25 on 1 f. olive .. 50·00 38·00

1893. Stamps of French Colonies, "Commerce" type, surch. **NOSSI-BE** and bar over value in figures.
36. **9.** 25 on 20 c. red on green .. 15·00 3·75
37. 50 on 10 c. black on lilac.. 5·50 4·25
38. 75 on 15 c. blue .. .. 30·00 28·00
39. 1 f. on 5 c. green .. 30·00 25·00

1893. Stamps of French Colonies, "Commerce" type, optd. **Nossi Be.**

No.	Type	Description	Unused	Used
40.	**9.**	10 c. black on lilac ..	1·60	1·10
41.		15 c. blue	1·60	1·25
43.		20 c. red on green ..	10·00	4·25

1894. "Tablet" key-type inscr. "NOSSI-BE".

No.	Type	Description	Unused	Used
44.	D.	1 c. black on blue ..	15	15
45.		2 c. brown on yellow ..	20	20
46.		4 c. claret on grey ..	25	25
47.		5 c. green	45	30
48.		10 c. black on lilac ..	80	65
49.		15 c. blue	85	60
50.		20 c. red on green ..	1·10	70
51.		25 c. black on red ..	1·60	1·10
52.		30 c. brown	1·50	1·25
53.		40 c. red on yellow ..	1·75	1·25
54.		50 c. red	1·60	1·00
55.		75 c. brown on orange ..	4·25	3·50
56.		1 f. olive	1·60	1·25

POSTAGE DUE STAMPS

1891. Stamps of French Colonies, "Commerce" type, surch. **NOSSI-BE chiffre-taxe A PERCEVOIR** and value.

No.	Type	Description	Unused	Used
D 19.	**9.**	0.20 on 1 c. blk. on blue	60·00	42·00
D 20.		0.30 on 2 c. brn. on yell.	60·00	42·00
D 21.		0·35 on 4 c. clar. on grey	60·00	50·00
D 22.		0.35 on 20 c. red on grn.	60·00	50·00
D 23.		0.50 on 30 c. brown ..	19·00	16·00
D 24.		1 F. on 35 c. blk. on oran.	40·00	27·00

1891. Stamps of French Colonies, "Commerce" type, surch. **Nossi-Be A PERCEVOIR** and value.

No.	Type	Description	Unused	Used
D 29.	**9.**	5 c. on 20 c. red on grn.	30·00	30·00
D 33.		0.10 on 5 c. green ..	2·10	1·75
D 30.		10 c. on 15 c. blue ..	30·00	30·00
D 31.		15 c. on 10 c. blk. on lilac	16·00	16·00
D 34.		0.15 on 20 c. red on grn.	2·75	2·75
D 32.		25 c. on 5c. green ..	16·00	16·00
D 35.		0.25 on 75 c. red ..	80·00	70·00

NOVA SCOTIA BC

An eastern province of the Dominion of Canada, whose stamps it now uses.

Currency: As Canada.

1.

2. Emblems of the United Kingdom.

1853. Imperf.

No.	Type	Description	Unused	Used
1.	**1.**	1d. brown	£1500	£300
3.	**2.**	3d. blue	£600	95·00
5.		6d. green	£2500	£325
8.		1s. purple	£9000	£2250

3.

4.

1860. Perf.

No.	Type	Description	Unused	Used
10.	**3.**	1 c. black	1·50	5·00
20.		2 c. purple	3·00	6·00
13.		5 c. blue	70·00	7·00
16.	**4.**	8½ c. green	7·00	9·00
27.		10 c. red	2·00	7·00
27.		12½ c. black	9·00	5·50

NYASALAND PROTECTORATE BC

A Br. Protectorate in C. Africa. Formerly known as Br. Central Africa. From 1954 to 1963 part of the Central African Federation and using the stamps of Rhodesia and Nyasaland (q.v.). From July, 1964, independent within the Commonwealth under its new name of Malawi.

1891. Stamps of Rhodesia optd. **B.C.A.**

No.	Type	Description	Unused	Used
1.	**1.**	1d. black	35	75
2.		2d. green and red ..	60	1·50
3.		4d. brown and black ..	75	1·50
5.		6d. blue	2·50	2·50
6.		8d. red and blue	3·50	7·50
7.		1s. brown	4·00	3·75
8.		2s. red	7·50	8·00
9.		2s. 6d. purple	11·00	11·00
10.		3s. brown and green ..	11·00	11·00
11.		4s. black and red ..	15·00	15·00
12.		5s. yellow	15·00	22·00
13.		10s. green	25·00	40·00
14.	–	£1 blue	£150	£200
15.	–	£2 red	£240	
16.	–	£5 olive	£500	
17.	–	£10 brown	£1200	

1892. Stamps of Rhodesia surch. **B.C.A.** and value in words.

No.	Type	Description	Unused	Used
18.	**1.**	3s. on 4s. black and red ..	75·00	75·00
19.		4s. on 5s. yellow	23·00	23·00

1895. Stamp of Rhodesia surch. **B.C.A. ONE PENNY** and bar.

No.	Type	Description	Unused	Used
20.	**1.**	1d. on 2d. green and red	4·50	8·50

1. Arms of the Protectorate. 2.

1895. The 2s. 6d. and higher values are larger.

No.	Type	Description	Unused	Used
21.	**1.**	1d. black	1·25	1·60
33.		2d. black and green ..	3·50	3·00
34.		4d. black and orange ..	4·00	4·00
35.		6d. black and blue ..	3·50	2·75
36.		1s. black and red ..	5·50	5·50
26.		2s. 6d. black and mauve ..	45·00	27·00
38.		3s. black and yellow ..	16·00	11·00
28.		5s. black and olive ..	45·00	27·00
29.		£1 black and orange ..	£475	£150
40.		£1 black and blue ..	£500	£275
41.		£10 black and orange ..	£2000	£900
31.		£25 black and green ..	£1800	£1200

1897. The 2s. 6d. and higher values are larger.

No.	Type	Description	Unused	Used
43.	**2.**	1d. black and blue ..	60	30
57d.		1d. purple and red ..	45	60
44.		2d. black and yellow ..	35	65
45.		4d. black and red ..	2·10	2·10
57e.		4d. purple and olive ..	2·40	2·75
46.		6d. black and green ..	3·50	3·00
58.		6d. purple and brown ..	3·75	4·00
47.		1s. black and purple ..	2·10	3·00
48.		2s. 6d. black and blue ..	12·00	11·00
49.		3s. black and green ..	80·00	80·00
50.		4s. black and red	16·00	16·00
50a.		10s. black and olive ..	35·00	42·00
51.		£1 black and purple ..	£120	80·00
52.		£10 black and yellow ..	£1800	£900

1898. Surch. **ONE PENNY.**

No.	Type	Description	Unused	Used
53.	**2.**	1d. on 3s. black and green	3·75	4·00

3.

4.

1898.

No.	Type	Description	Unused	Used
56.	**3.**	1d. red and blue (Imperf.)	—	7·00
57.		1d. red and blue (Perf.)	£225	3·50

1903. The 2s. 6d. and higher values are larger.

No.	Type	Description	Unused	Used
59.	**4.**	1d. grey and red	80	20
60.		2d. purple	2·00	90
61.		4d. green and black ..	2·40	2·40
62.		6d. grey and brown ..	2·40	2·40
62a.		1s. grey and blue	2·43	3·50
63.		2s. 6d. green	9·00	9·00
64.		4s. purple	15·00	15·00
65.		10s. green and black ..	27·00	35·00
66.		£1 grey and red	90·00	80·00
67.		£10 grey and blue ..	£1500	£1200

5.

6.

1908.

No.	Type	Description	Unused	Used
73.	**5.**	½d. green	12	30
74.		1d. red	8	12
75.		3d. purple on yellow ..	90	1·10
76.		4d. black & red on yellow	90	1·50
77.		6d. purple	1·50	2·00
72.		1s. black on green ..	1·00	1·50
78.	**6.**	2s. 6d. black & red on blue	9·00	11·00
79.		4s. red and black.. ..	11·00	13·00
80.		10s. green & red on green	30·00	45·00
81.		£1 purple & black on red	£120	£140
82.		£10 purple and blue ..	£2750	

1913. As 1908, but portrait of King George V.

No.	Type	Description	Unused	Used
100.		½d. green	20	12
101.		1d. red	20	15
102.		1½d. orange	5·50	5·50
103.		2d. grey	35	30
89.		2½d. blue	45	50
105.		3d. purple on yellow ..	1·00	50
106.		4d. black and red on yellow	75	90
92.		6d. purple	1·00	1·10
93a.		1s. black on green ..	1·00	1·10
109.		2s. purple and blue on blue	5·50	6·00
94.		2s. 6d. black & red on blue	3·75	4·50
111.		4s. red and black.. ..	4·50	5·00
112.		5s. green & red on yellow	14·00	15·00
96.		10s. green & red on green	16·00	20·00
98.		£1 purple & black on red	35·00	30·00
99.		£10 purple and blue ..	£1100	£675

7. King George V and Symbol of the Protectorate.

1934.

No.	Type	Description	Unused	Used
114.	**7.**	½d. green..	15	15
115.		1d. brown	25	20
116.		1½d. red	45	45
117.		2d. grey	35	35
118.		3d. blue	65	60
119.		4d. magenta	1·00	1·00
120.		6d. violet	80	80
121		9d. olive	1·50	3·00
122.		1s. black and orange ..	1·50	2·75

1935. Silver Jubilee. As T **11** of Antigua.

No.	Type	Description	Unused	Used
123.		1d. blue and grey ..	20	20
124.		2d. green and blue ..	60	60
125.		3d. brown and blue ..	1·60	2·00
126.		1s. grey and purple ..	3·50	4·00

1937. Coronation. As T **2** of Aden.

No.	Type	Description	Unused	Used
127.		½d. green	8	8
128.		1d. brown	8	8
129.		2d grey	20	25

1938. As T **7**, but with head of King George VI and "POSTAGE REVENUE" omitted.

No.	Type	Description	Unused	Used
130.		½d. green	25	10
130a.		½d. brown	8	8
131.		1d. brown	25	10
131a.		1d. green	8	8
132.		1½d. red	50	60
132a.		1½d. grey	15	20
133.		2d. grey	50	25
133a.		2d. red	10	10
134.		3d. blue	8	8
135.		4d. magenta	15	35
136.		6d. violet	15	25
137.		9d. olive	25	80
138.		1s. black and orange ..	30	40

1938. As T **6**, but with head of King George VI facing right.

No.	Type	Description	Unused	Used
139.		2s. purple and blue on blue	70	1·00
140.		2s. 6d. black & red on blue	55	1·00
141.		5s. green & red on yellow	4·50	7·00
142.		10 s. green & red on green	4·00	4·50
143.		£1 purple & black on red	6·00	8·00

8. Lake Nyasa.

9. King's African Rifles.

DESIGNS — HORIZ. 1½d., 6d. Tea estate. 2d., 1s., 10s. Map of Nyasaland. 4d., 2s. 6d. Tobacco. 5s., 20s. Badge of Nyasaland. VERT. 1d. (No. 160), Leopard and sunrise. 3d., 2s. Fishing village.

1945.

No.	Type	Description	Unused	Used
144.	**8.**	½d. black and brown ..	8	8
145.	**9.**	1d. black and green ..	8	8
160.	–	1d. brown and green ..	8	10
146.	–	1½d. black and grey ..	10	8
147.	–	2d. black and red ..	10	8
148.	–	3d. black and blue ..	8	5
149.	–	4d. black and claret ..	12	15
150.	–	6d. black and violet ..	15	8
151.	**8.**	9d. black and olive ..	20	50
152.	–	1s. blue and grey-green	25	12
153.	–	2s. green and maroon ..	70	90
154.	–	2s. 6d. green and blue	90	1·10
155.	–	5s. purple and blue ..	1·40	1·60
156.	–	10s. red and green ..	2·50	3·50
157.	–	20s. red and black ..	5·50	7·00

1946. Victory. As T **4** of Aden.

No.	Type	Description	Unused	Used
158.		1d. green..	8	8
159.		2d. red	8	8

1945. Silver Wedding. As Aden T **5/6.**

No.	Type	Description	Unused	Used
161.		1d. green..	8	8
162.		10s. mauve	4·00	5·50

1949. U.P.U. As T **14/7** of Antigua.

No.	Type	Description	Unused	Used
163.		1d. green..	12	15
164.		3d. blue	25	30
165.		6d. purple	35	45
166.		1s. blue	55	60

10. Arms in 1891 and 1951.

1951. Protectorate Diamond Jubilee.

No.	Type	Description	Unused	Used
167.	**10.**	2d. black and red ..	12	15
168.		3d. black and blue ..	12	20
169.		6d. black and violet ..	25	40
170.		5s. black and indigo ..	2·00	2·50

1953. Rhodes Centenary Exn. As T **16** of Southern Rhodesia.

No.	Type	Description	Unused	Used
171.		6d. violet	30	40

1953. Coronation. As T **7** of Aden.

No.	Type	Description	Unused	Used
172.		2d. black and orange ..	10	12

11. Grading Cotton.

1953. As 1945 but with portrait of Queen Elizabeth II as in T **11**. Designs as for corresponding values except where stated.

No.	Type	Description	Unused	Used
173a.	**8.**	½d. black and brown ..	5	5
174.	–	1d. brown and green (as No. 160)	5	5
175.	–	1½d. black and grey ..	8	25
176.	–	2d. black and orange ..	5	5
177.	**11.**	2½d. green and black ..	10	10
178.	–	3d. black & red (as 4d.)	12	12
179.	–	4½d. black & blue (as 3d.)	20	25
180.	–	6d. black and violet ..	20	25
181.	**8.**	9d. black and olive ..	30	40
182.	–	1s. blue and grey-green	25	30
183.	–	2s. green and claret ..	70	1·25
184.	–	2s. 6d. green and blue	85	1·50
185.	–	5s. purple and blue ..	1·75	3·50
186.	–	10s. red and green ..	5·00	6·00
187.	–	20s. red and black ..	8·00	12·00

12.

1963. Revenue stamps optd. **POSTAGE** as in T **12** or surch. also.

188. **12.** ½d. on 1d. blue 5 8
189. 1d. green 5 8
190. 2d. red 8 10
191. 3d. blue 10 15
192. 6d. maroon 20 20
193. 9d. on 1s. cerise .. 25 30
194. 1s. purple 25 35
195. 2s. 6d. black 55 65
196. 5s. chocolate .. .. 90 1·25
197. 10s. olive .. .. 3·00 3·00
198. £1 violet .. .. 5·00 8·00

13. Mother and Child.

14. Tea Industry.

1964.

199. **13.** ½d. violet 5 8
200. – 1d. black and green .. 10 10
201. – 2d. brown 12 10
202. – 3d. brown, green & bistre 12 10
203. – 4d. blue and yellow .. 12 20
204. **14.** 6d. purple, green & blue 15 15
205. – 1s. brown, blue & yellow 30 25
206. – 1s. 3d. bronze & chestnut 30 25
207. – 2s. 6d. brown and blue 65 75
208. – 5s. bl., grn., yell. & blk. 1·25 1·40
209. – 10s. green, salmon & blk. 3·00 3·50
210. – £1 chocolate and yellow 5·00 6·00

DESIGNS—As T **13**. 1d. Chambo (fish). 2d. Zebu bull. 3d. Groundnuts. 4d. Fishing. As T **14**—HORIZ. 1s. Timber. 1s. 3d. Turkish tobacco industry. 2s. 6d. Cotton industry. 5s. Monkey Bay, Lake Nyasa. 10s. Forestry—Afzelia. VERT. £1, Nyala.

POSTAGE DUE STAMPS

1950. As Type D **1** of Gold Coast, but inscr. "NYASALAND".

D 1. 1d. red 15 30
D 2. 2d. blue 30 60
D 3. 3d. green 45 90
D 4. 4d. purple .. .. .. 60 1·25
D 5. 6d. orange .. .. .. 90 2·00

For later issues see **MALAWI**.

NYASSA COMPANY O3

In 1894 Portugal granted a charter to the Nyassa Company to administer an area in the northern part of Mozambique, including the right to issue its own stamps. The lease was terminated in 1929 and the administration was transferred to Mozambique whose stamps were used there.

1898. "Figures" and "Newspaper" key-types inscr. "MOCAMBIQUE" and optd. **NYASSA.**

1. V. 2½ r. brown 80 80
2. R. 5 r. orange 80 80
3. 10 r. mauve 80 80
4. 15 r. brown 80 80
5. 20 r. lilac 80 80
6. 25 r. green 80 80
7. 50 r. blue 80 80
8. 75 r. red .. .. 1·10 90
9. 80 r. green .. .. 1·10 1·00
10. 100 r. brown on buff .. 1·10 1·00
11. 150 r. red on rose .. 2·40 2·40
12. 200 r. blue on blue .. 1·60 1·60
13. 300 r. blue on brown .. 1·60 1·60

1898. "King Carlos" key-type inscr. "MOCAMBIQUE" and optd. **NYASSA.**

14. S. 2½ r. grey 50 45
15. 5 r. orange 50 45
16. 10 r. green 50 45
17. 15 r. brown 60 50
18. 20 r. lilac 60 50
19. 25 r. green 60 50
20. 50 r. blue 60 50
21. 75 r. red 60 50
22. 80 r. mauve 90 80
23. 100 r. blue on blue .. 90 80
24. 150 r. brown on yellow .. 90 80
25. 200 r. purple on pink .. 90 80
26. 300 r. blue on pink .. 90 80

1. Giraffe. **2.** Camels.

1901.

27. **1.** 2½ r. brown and black .. 40 20
28. 5 r. violet and black .. 40 20
29. 10 r. green and black .. 40 20
30. 15 r. brown and black .. 40 20
31. 20 r. red and black .. 40 20
32. 25 r. orange and black .. 40 20
33. 50 r. blue and black .. 40 20
34. **2.** 75 r. red and black .. 40 20
35. 80 r. mauve and black .. 40 20
36. 100 r. brown and black .. 40 20
37. 150 r. brown and black .. 40 20
38. 200 r. green and black .. 40 20
39. 300 r. green and black .. 40 20

1903. Surch. in figures and words.

40. **2.** 65 r. on 80 r. mauve & blk. 30 25
41. 115 r. on 150 r. brn. & blk. 30 25
42. 130 r. on 300 r. grn. & blk. 30 25

1903. Optd. **PROVISORIO.**

43. **1.** 15 r. brown and black .. 30 25
44. 25 r. orange and black .. 30 25

1910. Optd. **PROVISORIO** and surch. in figures and words.

50. **1.** 5 r. on 2½ r. brown & blk. 40 30
51. **2.** 50 r. on 100 r. brown & blk. 40 30

3. Camels. **5.** The "San Gabriel" Vasco da Gama's Flagship.

1911. Optd. **REPUBLICA.**

53. **3.** 2½ r. violet and black .. 40 25
54. 5 r. black 40 25
55. 10 r. green and black .. 40 25
56. – 20 r. red and black .. 40 25
57. – 25 r. brown and black .. 40 25
58. – 50 r. blue and black .. 40 25
59. – 75 r. brown and black .. 40 25
60. – 100 r. brn. & blk. on green 40 25
61. – 200 r. grn. & blk. on pink 60 50
62. **5.** 300 r. black on blue .. 1·00 80
63. 400 r. brown and black .. 1·10 1·00
64. 500 r. violet and olive .. 1·25 1·10

DESIGNS—HORIZ. 20 r., 25 r., 50 r. Zebra. VERT. 75 r., 100 r., 200 r. Giraffe.

1918. Surch. **REPUBLICA** and value in figures.

65. **1.** ½ c. on 2½ c. brown & black 15·00 12·00
66. ½ c. on 5 r. violet & black 15·00 12·00
67. 1 c. on 10 r. green & black 16·00 12·00
68. 1½ c. on 15 r. brn. & black 1·00 90
69. 2 c. on 20 r. red and black 50 45
70. 3½ c. on 25 r. orge. & black 50 45
71. 5 c. on 50 r. blue & black 50 45
72. **2.** 7½ c. on 75 r. red & black 50 45
73. 8 c. on 80 r. mauve & black 50 45
74. 10 c. on 100 r. brn. & black 50 45
75. 15 c. on 150 r. brn. & blk. 90 80
76. 20 c. on 200 r. grn. & blk. 90 80
77. 30 c. on 300 r. grn. & blk. 1·40 1·10

1919. Nos. 43/4 and 40/2 surch. **REPUBLICA** and value in figures.

78. **1.** 1½ c. on 15 r. brown & blk. 1·75 1·10
79. 3½ c. on 25 r. orge. & blk. 60 50
80. **2.** 40 c. on 65 r. on 80 r. .. 4·00 3·25
81. 50 c. on 115 r. on 150 r. .. 1·00 90
82. 1 e. on 130 r. on 300 r. .. 1·00 90

1921. Stamps of 1911 surch. in figures and words.

83. **3.** ¼ c. on 2½ r. violet & black 60 60
85. ½ c. on 5 r. black .. 60 60
86. 1 c. on 10 r. green & black 60 60
87. **5.** 1½ c. on 300 r. black on blue 60 60
88. – 2 c. on 20 r. red and black 60 60
89. – 2½ c. on 25 r. brown & blk. 60 60
90. **5.** 3 c. on 400 r. brown & blk. 60 60
91. – 5 c. on 50 r. blue and black 60 60
92. – 7½ c. on 75 r. brown & blk. 60 60
93. – 10 c. on 100 r. brown and black on green 60 60
94. **5.** 12 c. on 500 r. violet & olive 60 60
95. – 20 c. on 200 r. green and black on pink 60 60

7. Giraffe. **10.** Zebra.

1921.

96. **7.** ¼ c. purple 40 35
97. ½ c. blue 40 35
98. 1 c. black and green .. 40 35
99. 1½ c. orange and black 40 35
100. – 2 c. black and red .. 40 35
101. – 2½ c. olive and black .. 40 35
102. – 4 c. red and black .. 40 35
103. – 5 c. black and blue .. 40 35
104. – 6 c. violet and black .. 40 35
105. – 7½ c. brown and black 40 35
106. – 8 c. olive and black .. 40 35
107. – 10 c. brown and black .. 40 35
108. – 15 c. red and black .. 40 35
109. – 20 c. blue and black .. 40 35
110. **10.** 30 c. brown and black .. 40 35
111. 40 c. blue and black .. 40 35
112. 50 c. green and black .. 40 35
113. 1 e. brown and black .. 70 40
114. – 2 e. black and brown .. 80 70
115. – 5 e. brown and blue .. 1·00 90

DESIGNS—As T **7**: 2 c. to 6 c. Vasco da Gama. 7½ c. to 20 c. "San Gabriel" (ship). As T **10**: 2 e., 5 e. Native dhow.

CHARITY TAX STAMPS

The notes under this heading in Portugal also apply here.

1925. Marquis de Pombal Commem. Nos. C327/9 of Mozambique optd. **NYASSA.**

C 141. C **4.** 15 c. brown .. 1·75 1·60
C 142. – 15 c. brown .. 1·75 1·60
C 143. C **5.** 15 c. brown .. 1·75 1·60

POSTAGE DUE STAMPS

D **1.** The "San Gabriel".

1924.

D 132. – ½ c. green 80 70
D 133. – 1 c. grey 80 70
D 134. – 2 c. red 80 70
D 135. – 3 c. orange 80 70
D 136. D **1.** 5 c. brown 80 70
D 137. 6 c. brown 80 70
D 138. 10 c. purple .. 80 70
D 139. – 20 c. red 80 70
D 140. – 50 c. violet 80 70

DESIGNS: ½ c., 1 c. Giraffe. 2 c., 3 c. Zebra. 20 c., 50 c. Vasco da Gama.

1925. De Pombal stamps of Mozambique, Nos. D327/9 optd. **NYASSA.**

D 144. C **4.** 30 c. brown .. 2·25 2·00
D 145. – 30 c. brown .. 2·25 2·00
D 146. C **5.** 30 c. brown .. 2·25 2·00

OBOCK O2

A port and district on the Somali Coast, now incorporated in French Somali Coast, and using its stamps.

1892. Stamps of French Colonies, "Commerce" type, optd. **OBOCK** in curve

1. **9.** 1 c. black on blue .. 4·50 4·00
2. 2 c. brown on yellow .. 4·50 4·00
3. 4 c. claret on grey .. 60·00 60·00
4. 5 c. green .. .. 3·50 2·75
5. 10 c. black on lilac .. 10·00 9·50
6. 15 c. blue .. .. 8·50 7·00
7. 25 c. black on red .. 12·00 12·00
8. 35 c. black on orange .. 70·00 70·00
9. 40 c. red on yellow .. 65·00 65·00
10. 75 c. red .. .. 70·00 70·00
11. 1 f. olive .. .. 75·00 75·00

1892. Stamps of French Colonies, "Commerce" type, optd. **OBOCK** in straight line.

12. **9.** 4 c. claret on grey .. 2·50 2·75
13. 5 c. green .. .. 2·50 2·75
14. 10 c. black on lilac .. 3·75 3·25
15. 15 c. blue .. .. 3·75 3·25
16. 20 c. red on green .. 5·50 4·50
17. 25 c. black on red .. 2·25 2·00
18. 40 c. red on yellow .. 7·00 6·00
19. 75 c. red .. .. 50·00 45·00
20. 1 f. olive .. .. 8·50 7·50

1892. Stamp of French Colonies, "Commerce" type, surch. **OBOCK** in straight line and new value.

39. **9.** 1 on 25 c. black on red .. 1·40 1·40
40. 2 on 10 c. black on lilac .. 8·50 7·50
41. 2 on 15 c. blue .. .. 2·00 1·75
42. 4 on 15 c. blue .. .. 2·00 1·75
43. 4 on 25 c. black on red .. 2·75 2·25
44. 5 on 25 c. black on red .. 3·25 2·75
45. 20 on 10 c. black on lilac .. 15·00 13·00
46. 30 on 10 c. black on lilac .. 18·00 16·00
47. 35 on 25 c. black on red .. 14·00 11·00
48. 75 on 1 f. olive .. .. 15·00 14·00
49. 5 f. on 1 f. olive £150 £150

1892. "Tablet" key-type inscr. "OBOCK".

50. D. 1 c. black on blue .. 55 30
51. 2 c. brown on yellow .. 15 12
52. 4 c. claret on grey .. 30 20
53. 5 c. green 45 25
54. 10 c. black on lilac .. 70 45
55. 15 c. blue .. .. 2·25 1·40
56. 20 c. red on green .. 3·75 2·75
57. 25 c. black on red .. 3·50 2·75
58. 30 c. brown .. .. 2·75 1·75
59. 40 c. red on yellow .. 2·75 1·40
60. 50 c. red .. .. 3·00 1·75
61. 75 c. brown on orange .. 3·25 1·75
62. 1 f. olive .. .. 3·50 2·75

1.

1893.

63. **1.** 2 f. grey .. .. .. 7·50 7·00
64. 5 f. red .. .. .. 18·00 17·00

The 5 f. stamp is larger than the 2 f.

2.

3.

1894.

65. **2.** 1 c. black and red 30 30
66. 2 c. claret and green .. 40 40
67. 4 c. claret and orange .. 30 30
68. 5 c. green and brown .. 35 35
69. 10 c. black and green .. 1·50 1·50
70. 15 c. blue and red .. 1·40 1·10
71. 20 c. orange and purple .. 1·40 1·10
72. 25 c. black and blue .. 1·60 1·40
73. 30 c. yellow and green .. 3·25 2·25
74. 40 c. orange and green .. 2·25 1·75
75. 50 c. red and blue .. 1·90 1·40
76. 75 c. lilac and orange .. 1·75 1·10
77. 1 f. olive and purple .. 1·75 1·10
78. **3.** 2 f. orange and lilac .. 18·00 16·00
79. 5 f. red and blue .. 14·00 12·00
80. 10 f. lake and red .. 25·00 22·00
81. 25 f. blue and brown .. £110 £110
82. 50 f. green and lake .. £130 £130

POSTAGE DUE STAMPS

1892. Postage Due stamps of French Colonies optd. **OBOCK** in curved line.

D 21. D **1.** 5 c. black £1200
D 22. 10 c. black .. .. 30·00 30·00
D 23. 30 c. black .. .. 60·00 60·00
D 24. 60 c. black .. .. 65·00 65·00

1892. Postage Due stamps of French Colonies optd. **OBOCK** in straight line.

D 25. D **1.** 1 c. black .. .. 6·00 5·50
D 26. 2 c. black .. .. 4·00 3·50
D 27. 3 c. black .. .. 4·00 3·50
D 28. 4 c. black .. .. 4·00 3·50
D 29. 5 c. black .. .. 1·10 1·10
D 30. 10 c. black .. .. 3·25 3·00
D 31. 15 c. black .. .. 2·25 2·25
D 32. 20 c. black .. .. 2·75 2·10
D 33. 30 c. black .. .. 3·75 3·50
D 34. 40 c. black .. .. 7·00 7·00
D 35. 60 c. black .. .. 7·50 7·00
D 36. 1 f. brown .. .. 30·00 28·00
D 37. 2 f. brown .. .. 30·00 28·00
D 38. 5 f. brown .. .. 65·00 65·00

For later issues see **DJIBOUTI, FRENCH SOMALI COAST** and **FRENCH TERRITORY OF THE AFARS AND THE ISSAS.**

OCEANIC SETTLEMENTS O2

Scattered French islands in the E. Pacific Ocean, including Tahiti and the Marquesas.

For issues after 1956 see under French Polynesia.

INSCRIPTIONS. All stamps are inscribed "ETABLISSEMENTS FRANCAIS DE L'OCEANIE" (in full or abbreviated) or "OCEANIE".

1892. "Tablet" key-type.

No.	Type	Description		
1.	D.	1 c. black on blue	10	10
2.		2 c. brown on yellow	12	10
3.		4 c. claret on grey	12	12
14.		5 c. green	20	15
5.		10 c. black on lilac	2·10	90
15.		10 c. red	20	12
6.		15 c. blue	1·60	55
16.		15 c. grey	45	35
7.		20 c. red on green	1·10	55
8.		25 c. black on red	3·75	1·60
17.		25 c. blue	1·10	55
9.		30 c. brown	1·10	90
18.		35 c. black on yellow	45	25
10.		40 c. red on yellow	8·50	7·00
19.		45 c. black on green	20	20
11.		50 c. red	55	45
20.		50 c. brown on blue	25·00	21·00
12.		75 c. brown on orange	55	45
13.		1 f. olive	1·00	1·00

1\. Vahine Woman. 2. Group of Kanakas.

3\. Valley of Fautaua.

1913.

No.	Type	Description		
21.	1.	1 c. brown and violet	5	5
22.		2 c. black and brown	5	5
23.		4 c. blue and orange	5	5
24.		5 c. green	5	5
46.		5 c. black and blue	5	5
25.		10 c. orange and red	5	5
47.		10 c. green	5	5
48.		10 c. pur. and red on blue	12	12
25a.		15 c. black and orange	5	5
26.		20 c. violet and black	5	5
49.		20 c. green	5	5
50.		20 c. brown and red	8	8
27.	2.	25 c. blue	5	5
51.		25 c. red and violet	5	5
28.		30 c. brown and grey	30	30
52.		30 c. orange and red	10	10
53.		30 c. orange and black	5	5
54.		30 c. green and blue	12	12
29.		35 c. red and green	5	5
30.		40 c. green and black	8	5
31.		45 c. red and orange	8	5
32.		50 c. black and brown	1·00	1·00
55.		50 c. blue	5	5
56.		50 c. blue and grey	5	5
57.		60 c. black and green	5	5
58.		65 c. violet and chocolate	20	20
33.		75 c. violet and purple	12	8
59.		90 c. mauve and red	1·25	1·25
34.	3.	1 f. black and red	10	10
60.		1 f. 10 brown and violet	15	15
61.		1 f. 40 blue and brown	40	40
62.		1 f. 50 blue	1·10	1·10
35.		2 f. green and brown	30	25
36.		5 f. blue and violet	75	55

1915. "Tablet" key-type optd. **E F O 1915** and bar.

No.	Type	Description		
37.	D.	10 c. red	15	12

1915. Red Cross. "Tablet" type surch. **E F O 1915** and bar and **5 c.** and red cross.

No.	Type	Description		
38.	D.	10 c. + 5 c. red	2·00	2·00

1915. Red Cross. Surch. with **5 c** and large red cross.

No.	Type	Description		
40.	1.	10 c. + 5 c. orange and red	20	20

1916. Red Cross. Surch. with **5 c** and small red cross.

No.	Type	Description		
41.	1.	10 c. + 5 c. orange and red	15	15

1916. Surch. in figures.

No.	Type	Description		
42.	1.	10 c. on 15 c. black & orge.	5	5
67.	3.	25 c. on 2 f. green & brown	10	10
68.		25 c. on 5 f. blue and violet	10	10
63.	2.	60 on 75 c. violet and blue	5	5
64.	3.	65 on 1 f. brown and blue	12	12
65.		85 on 1 f. brown and blue	12	12
66.	2.	90 on 75 c. mauve and red	10	10
69.	3.	1 f. 25 on 1 f. blue	10	10
70.		1 f. 50 on 1 f. blue	12	12
71.		20 f. on 5 f. violet & orange	1·60	1·10

1921. Surch. **1921** and value in figures and bar.

No.	Type	Description		
43.	1.	05 on 2 c. black and brown	2·50	2·50
44.	2.	10 on 45 c. red and orange	2·50	2·50
45.	1.	25 on 15 c. black & orange	20	20

1924. Surch. **45 c. 1924.**

No.	Type	Description		
72.	1.	45 c. on 10 c. orange & red	15	15

1926. Surch. in words.

No.	Type	Description		
73.	3.	3 f. on 5 f. blue and grey	12	12
74.		10 f. on 5 f. blk. and green	45	35

4\. Papetoia Bay.

1929.

No.	Type	Description		
75.	4.	3 f. sepia and green	85	85
76.		5 f. sepia and blue	1·10	1·10
77.		10 f. sepia and red	3·25	3·25
78.		20 f. sepia and mauve	4·50	4·50

1931. "Colonial Exn." key-types.

No.	Type	Description		
79.	E.	40 c. green	50	40
80	F.	50 c. mauve	50	45
81	G.	90 c. red	50	45
82.	H.	1 f. 50 blue	55	45

5\. Spearing Fish.

6\. Tahitian Girl.

7\. Native Gods.

1934.

No.	Type	Description		
83.	5.	1 c. black	5	5
84.		2 c. claret	5	5
85.		3 c. blue	5	5
86.		4 c. orange	5	5
87.		5 c. mauve	5	5
88.		10 c. brown	5	5
89.		15 c. green	5	5
90.		20 c. red	5	5
91.	6.	25 c. blue	5	5
92.		30 c. green	10	10
93.		30 c. orange	5	5
94.	7.	35 c. green	25	25
95.	6.	40 c. magenta	5	5
96.		45 c. red	45	45
97.		45 c. green	8	8
98.		50 c. violet	5	5
99.		55 c. blue	30	30
100.		60 c. black	5	5
101.		65 c. brown	25	25
102.		70 c. pink	5	5
103.		75 c. olive	40	40
104.		80 c. purple	5	5
105.		90 c. red	5	5
106.	7.	1 f. brown	5	5
107.		1 f. 25 purple	50	50
108.		1 f. 25 red	5	5
109.		1 f. 40 orange	5	5
110.		1 f. 50 blue	8	8
111.		1 f. 60 violet	5	5
112.		1 f. 75 green	45	45
113.		2 f. red	5	5
114.		2 f. 25 blue	5	5
115.		2 f. 50 black	5	5
116.		3 f. orange	5	5
117.		5 f. magenta	5	5
118.		10 f. green	15	15
119.		20 f. brown	30	30

8\. Flying-boat.

1934. Air.

No.	Type	Description		
120.	8.	5 f. green	5	5

1937 Int. Exn., Paris. As Nos. 110/15 of Cameroun.

No.	Type	Description		
121.		20 c. violet	15	15
122.		30 c. green	15	15
123.		40 c. red	15	15
124.		50 c. brown	15	15
125.		90 c. red	15	15
126.		1 f. 50 blue	15	15

1938. Int. Anti-Cancer Fund. As T 10 of Cameroun.

No.	Type	Description		
127.		1 f. 75+50 c. blue	1·75	1·75

1939. New York World's Fair. As T 11 of Cameroun.

No.	Type	Description		
128.		1 f. 25 red	15	15
129.		2 f. 25 blue	15	15

1939. French Revolution. 150th Anniv. As T 16 of Cameroun.

No.	Type	Description		
130.		15 c.+25 c. green (post.)	1·25	1·25
131.		70 c.+30 c. brown	1·25	1·25
132.		90 c.+35 c. orange	1·25	1·25
133.		1 f. 25+1 f. red	1·25	1·25
134.		2 f. 25+2 f. blue	1·25	1·25
135.		5 f.+4 f. black (air)	2·75	2·75

1941. Free French Issues. Optd. **FRANCE LIBRE.**

(a) Postage stamps of 1922.

No.	Type	Description		
136.	4.	3 f. sepia and green	45	
137.		5 f. sepia and blue	65	
138.		10 f. sepia and red	65	
139.		20 f. sepia and mauve	7·50	

(b) Postage stamps of 1934.

No.	Type	Description		
140.	7.	1 f. brown	30	
141.		2 f. 50 black	30	
142.		3 f. orange	40	
143.		5 f. magenta	45	
144.		10 f. green	3·25	
145.		20 f. brown	2·10	

(c) Air stamp of 1934.

No.	Type	Description		
146.	8.	5 f. green	35	35

9\. Polynesian Travelling Canoe.

1942. Free French Issue. (a) Postage.

No.	Type	Description		
147.	9.	5 c. brown	5	5
148.		10 c. blue	5	5
149.		25 c. green	5	5
150.		30 c. red	5	5
151.		40 c. green	5	5
152.		80 c. maroon	5	5
153.		1 f. mauve	5	5
154.		1 f. 50 red	5	5
155.		2 f. black	5	5
156.		2 f. 50 blue	15	15
157.		4 f. violet	8	8
158.		5 f. yellow	8	8
159.		10 f. brown	10	10
160.		20 f. green	10	10

(b) Air. As T 18 of Cameroun.

No.	Type	Description		
161.		1 f. orange	5	5
162.		1 f. 50 red	5	5
163.		5 f. maroon	8	8
164.		10 f. black	15	15
165.		25 f. blue	15	15
166.		50 f. green	15	15
167.		100 f. claret	25	25

1944. Mutual Aid and Red Cross Funds. As T 19 of Cameroun.

No.	Type	Description		
168.		5 f.+20 f. blue	8	5

1945. Surch. in figures.

No.	Type	Description		
169.	9.	50 c. on 5 c. brown	5	5
170.		60 c. on 5 c. brown	5	5
171.		70 c. on 5 c. brown	5	5
172.		1 f. 20 on 5 c. brown	5	5
173.		2 f. 40 in 25 c. green	5	5
174.		3 f. on 25 c. green	5	5
175.		4 f. 50 on 25 c. green	12	12
176.		15 f. on 2 f. 50 blue	15	15

1945. Eboue. As T 20 of Cameroun.

No.	Type	Description		
177.		2 f. black	5	5
178.		25 f. green	15	15

1946. Air. Victory. As T 21 of Cameroun.

No.	Type	Description		
179.		8 f. green	20	20

1946. Air. From Chad to the Rhine. As T 22 of Cameroun.

No.	Type	Description		
180.		5 f. red	20	20
181.		10 f. brown	20	20
182.		15 f. green	20	20
183.		20 f. red	20	20
184.		25 f. purple	20	20
185.		50 f. black	30	30

10\. Moorea Coastline. 11. Tahitian Girl.

12\. Frigate-bird over Moorea.

1948. (a) Postage as T 10/11.

No.	Type	Description		
186.	10.	10 c. brown	5	5
187.		30 c. green	5	5
188.		40 c. blue	5	5
189.	–	50 c. lake	5	5
190.	–	60 c. olive	5	5
191.	–	80 c. blue	5	5
192.	–	1 f. lake	5	5
193.	–	1 f. 20 blue	5	5
194.	–	1 f. 50 blue	8	5
195.	11.	2 f. brown	8	5
196.		2 f. 40 lake	8	5
197.		3 f. violet	65	12
198.		4 f. blue	10	10
199.		5 f. brown	15	12
200.	–	6 f. blue	15	12
201.	–	9 f. brown, black and red	1·60	1·00
202.	–	10 f. olive	25	10
203.	–	15 f. red	55	40
204.	–	20 f. blue	45	25
205.	–	25 f. brown	55	30

(b) Air. As T 12.

No.	Type	Description		
206.	–	13 f. indigo and blue	85	75
207.	12.	50 f. lake	2·50	1·60
208.	–	100 f. violet	1·90	1·10
209.	–	200 f. blue	5·50	4·00

DESIGNS—VERT. 50 c. to 80 c. Kanaka fishermen. 9 f. Bora-Bora girl. HORIZ. 1 f. to 1 f. 50 Faa Village. 5 f., 6 f., 10 f. Bora-Bora and Pandanus pine. 13 f. Pahia Peak and palms. 15 f. to 25 f. Vahine girls. 100 f. Aeroplane over Moorea. 200 f. Frigate-bird over Maupiti Island.

1949. Air. U.P.U. As T 25 of Cameroun.

No.	Type	Description		
210.		10 f. blue	1·60	1·60

1950. Colonial Welfare. As Cameroun T 26.

No.	Type	Description		
211.		10 f. +2 f. green and blue	40	40

1952. Centenary of Military Medal. As T 27 of Cameroun.

No.	Type	Description		
212.		3 f. violet, yellow & green	75	75

13\. "Nafea" (after Gauguin).

14\. Dry Dock, Papeete.

1953. Air. Gauguin (painter). 50th Death Anniv.

No.	Type	Description		
213.	13.	14 f. sepia, red and turq.	11·00	11·00

1954. Air. Liberation. 10th Anniv. As T 29 of Cameroun.

No.	Type	Description		
214.		3 f. emerald and turquoise	50	50

1956. Economic and Social Development Fund.

No.	Type	Description		
215.	14.	3 f. turquoise	15	12

POSTAGE DUE STAMPS

1926. Postage Due stamps of France optd. **Etablissements Francais de l'Oceanie.**

No.	Type	Description		
D 73.	D 2.	5 c. blue	5	5
D 74.		10 c. brown	8	8
D 75.		20 c. olive	8	8
D 76.		30 c. red	10	10
D 77.		40 c. red	12	12
D 78.		60 c. green	12	12
D 79.		1 f. claret on yellow	15	15
D 80.		2 f. on 1 f. red	20	20
D 81.		3 f. mauve	65	65

D 1. Fautaua Falls.

DESIGN: 1 f. to 3 f. Maori man.

D 2.

1929.

No.	Type	Description		
D 82.	D 1.	5 c. brown and blue	5	5
D 83.		10 c. green and orange	5	5
D 84.		30 c. red and brown	8	8
D 85.		50 c. brown and green	5	5
D 86.		60 c. green and violet	20	20
D 87.	–	1 f. mauve and blue	12	12
D 88.	–	2 f. brown and red	8	8
D 89.	–	3 f. green and blue	8	8

1948.

D 210.	D 2.	10 c. green.. ..	5	5
D 211.		30 c. brown ..	5	5
D 212.		50 c. red	5	5
D 213.		1 f. blue	5	5
D 214.		2 f. green	5	5
D 215.		3 f. red	8	8
D 216.		4 f. violet	12	12
D 217.		5 f. mauve	15	15
D 218.		10 f. blue	35	35
D 219.		20 f. lake	50	50

For later issues see **FRENCH POLYNESIA.**

OLDENBURG E2

A former Grand Duchy in N. Germany. Now part of West Germany.

72 grote = 1 thaler.

1. 2. 3.

1852. Imperf.

1.	1.	⅓ sgr. black on green ..	£350	£450
4.		$\frac{1}{30}$th. black on blue ..	£170	11·00
5.		$\frac{1}{15}$th. black on rose ..	4·25	55·00
8.		$\frac{1}{10}$th. black on yellow ..	£450	50·00

1859. Imperf.

17.	2.	¼ g. orange	£120	£1700
10.		⅓ g. black on green ..	£1100	£1400
19.		⅓ g. green	£200	£425
21.		½ g. brown	£200	£250
11.		1 g. black on blue ..	£350	22·00
23.		1 g. blue	£120	80·00
15.		2 g. black on rose ..	£450	£325
26.		2 g. red	£225	£200
16.		3 g. black on yellow ..	£450	£300
28.		3 g. yellow	£225	£200

1862. Roul.

30.	3.	⅓ g. green	£110	95·00
32.		½ g. orange	85·00	55·00
42.		1 g. red	3·75	28·00
43.		2 g. blue	5·00	£150
39.		3 g. bistre	85·00	23·00

OMAN (SULTANATE) O3

In Jan. 1971, the independent Sultanate of Muscat and Oman was renamed Sultanate of Oman.

NOTE. Labels inscribed "State of Oman" or "Oman Imamate State" are said to have been issued by a rebel administration under the Imam of Oman. There is no convincing evidence that these labels had any postal use within Oman and they are therefore omitted. They can be found, however, used on covers which appear to emanate from Amman and Baghdad.

1000 Baizas = 1 Rial Saidi

1971. Nos. 110/21 of Muscat and Oman optd. **SULTANATE of OMAN** in English and Arabic.

122.	1.	5 b. purple	5	5
123.		10 b. brown	5	5
124.		20 b. brown	5	5
125.	A.	25 b. black and violet ..	8	5
126.		30 b. black and blue ..	10	10
127.		40 b. black and orange..	12	12
128.	2.	50 b. magenta and blue..	15	15
129.	B.	75 b. green and brown..	20	20
130.	C.	100 b. blue and orange..	25	25
131.	D.	¼ r. brown and green ..	65	65
132.	E.	½ r. violet and red ..	1·40	1·40
133.	F.	1 r. red and violet ..	2·75	2·75

4. Sultan Qabus and "Land Development".

1971. National Day. Multicoloured.

134.	10 b. Type 4	5	5
135.	40 b. Sultan in military uniform, and Omanis ("Freedom")	12	12
136.	50 b. Doctors and patients ("Health Services") ..	20	20
137.	100 b. Children in class ("Education")	40	40

1971. No. 94 optd. with **SULTANATE of OMAN** in English and Arabic.

138.	5 b. purple..	8	8

INDEX

Countries can be quickly located by referring to the index at the end of this volume.

5. Child in Class.

1971. U.N.I.C.E.F. 25th Anniv.

139.	5.	50 b. + 25 b. multicoloured	25	20

6. Book Year Emblem.

1972. Int. Book Year.

140.	6.	25 b. multicoloured ..	10	10

1972. Nos. 110/112 optd. with **SULTANATE of OMAN** in English and Arabic.

141.	5 b. purple..	5	5
142.	10 b. brown	5	5
143.	20 b. brown	5	5

سلطنة عمان

25 B ٢٥ ب

(7). 8. Matrah, 1809.

1972. Nos. 102 of Muscat and Oman and 127 of Oman optd. with T 7.

144.	25 b. on 1 r.	5	5
145.	25 b. on 40 b.	5	5

1972.

146.	8.	5 b. multicoloured ..	5	5
147.		10 b. multicoloured ..	5	5
148.		20 b. multicoloured ..	5	5
149.		25 b. multicoloured ..	5	5
150.	–	30 b. multicoloured ..	8	8
151.	–	40 b. multicoloured ..	10	10
152.	–	50 b. multicoloured ..	12	12
153.	–	75 b. multicoloured ..	15	15
154.	–	100 b. multicoloured ..	25	25
155.	–	¼ r. multicoloured ..	55	55
156.	–	½ r. multicoloured ..	1·10	1·10
157.	–	1 r. multicoloured ..	2·25	2·25

DESIGNS—(26 × 21 mm.) Nos. 150/3, Shinas, 1809. (42 × 25 mm.) Nos. 154/7, Muscat, 1809.

9. Government Buildings.

1973. Opening of Ministerial Complex.

170.	9.	25 b. multicoloured ..	8	8
171.		100 b. multicoloured ..	25	25

10. Oman Crafts (boatbuilding).

1973. National Day. Multicoloured.

172.	15 b. Type 10	5	5
173.	50 b. Seeb International Airport	12	12
174.	65 b. Dhow and oil-tanker	15	15
175.	100 b. "Ship of the Desert" (camel)	25	25

11. Aerial View of Port.

1974. Port Qaboos. Inaug.

176.	11.	100 b. multicoloured ..	25	25

12. Map on Open Book.

1974. Illiteracy Eradication Campaign. Mult.

177.	25 b. Type 12	5	5
178.	100 b. Hands reaching for open book (vert.) ..	25	25

13. Sultan Qabus bin Said and Emblems.

1974. Universal Postal Union. Centenary.

179.	13.	100 b. multicoloured ..	25	25

14. Arab Scribe.

1975. "Eradication of Illiteracy".

180.	14.	25 b. multicoloured ..	8	8

15. New Harbour, Mina Raysoot.

1975. National Day. Multicoloured.

181.	30 b. Type 15	10	10
182.	50 b. Stadium and map ..	15	15
183.	75 b. Water Desalination Plant	25	25
184.	100 b. Television Station	30	30
185.	150 b. Satellite Earth Station and map ..	50	50
186.	250 b. Telecommunications Network symbols and map	80	80

16. Arab Woman and Child with Nurse.

1975. International Women's Year. Mult.

187.	75 b. Type 16	25	25
188.	150 b. Mother and children	50	50

ORANGE FREE STATE (ORANGE RIVER COLONY) BC

Br. possession, 1848-54. Independent 1854-99. Annexed by Great Britain, 1900. Later a province of the Union of S. Africa.

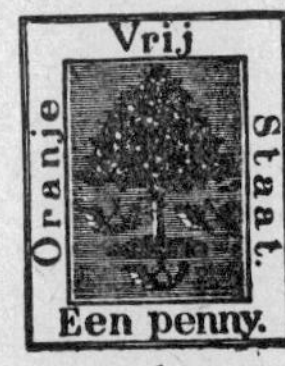

1.

2. King Edward VII, Springbok and Gnu.

1868.

48.	1.	½d. brown..	35	25
85.		½d. orange	20	20
1.		1d. brown..	1·00	20
68.		1d. purple..	20	20
49.		2d. mauve	65	25
51.		3d. blue	1·00	80
18.		4d. blue	2·75	1·00
7.		6d. red	1·50	1·10
9.		1s. orange..	1·50	1·00
87.		1s. brown	1·50	1·00
20.		5s. green	1·00	3·75

1877. Surch in figures.

69.	1.	½d. on 3d. blue	50	65
36.		½d. on 5s. green	1·00	1·10
54.		1d. on 3d. blue	45	45
57.		1d. on 4d. blue	4·50	1·50
22.		1d. on 5s. green	4·00	3·50
53.		2d. on 3d. blue	2·25	1·00
67.		"2½d." on 3d. blue ..	50	30
83.		"2½d " on 3d blue ..	50	50
39.		3d. on 4d. blue	7·50	7·00
10.		"4" on 6d. red	18·00	11·00

1896. Surch. **Halve Penny.**

77.	1.	½d. on 3d. blue	20	20

1900. Surch. **V.R.I.** and value in figures.

112.	1.	½d. orange	20	20
113.		1d. purple	20	20
114.		2d. mauve	20	20
104.		"2½" on 3d. blue (No. 83)	1·50	1·40
117.		3d. blue	20	20
118.		4d. blue	60	50
119.		6d. red	11·00	9·00
120.		6d. blue	35	20
121.		1s. brown	35	45
122.		5s. green	1·50	1·10

1900. Stamps of Cape of Good Hope optd. **ORANGE RIVER COLONY.**

133.	5.	½d. green..	15	12
134.		1d. red	25	25
135.	4.	2½d. blue..	25	25

1902. No. 120 surch. **4d** and bar.

136.	1.	4d. on 6d. blue	25	25

1902. Surch. **E.R.I.** and **6d.**

137.	.	6d. blue	75	75

1902. No. 20 surch. **V.R.I. One Shilling** and star.

138.	1.	1s. on 5s. green	1·60	2·00

1903.

139.	2.	½d. green..	20	12
140.		1d. red	15	12
141.		2d. brown	65	60
142.		2½d. blue..	30	30
143.		3d. mauve	50	30
144.		4d. red and green ..	1·25	1·10
145.		6d. red and mauve ..	90	45
146.		1s. red and brown ..	2·75	80
147.		5s. blue and brown ..	14·00	7·00

ORCHHA BC

A state of C. India. Now uses Indian stamps.

1.

2.

1913. Imperf.

1.	1.	½ a. green	8·00	
2.		1 a. red	9·00	

1914. Imperf.

3.	2.	¼ a. blue	12	20
4.		½ a. green	20	30
5.		1 a. red	70	80
6.		2 a. brown	2·50	2·50
7.		4 a. yellow-brown .. .	4·00	5·00

3. H.H. the Maharaja of Orchha.

1939.

8.	3.	¼ a. brown	10
9.		½ a. green	10
10.		¾ a. blue	10
11.		1 a. red	20
12.		1¼ a. blue	20
13.		1½ a. mauve	30
14.		2 a. red	30

15. 3. 2½ a. green 40
16. 3 a. violet 60
17. 4 a. slate 70
18. 8 a. mauve .. .. 1·50
19. – 1 r. green .. .. .. 2·50
20. – 2 r. violet .. .. .. 8·00
21. – 5 r. orange .. .. 20·00
22. – 10 r. green .. .. 30·00
The rupee values are larger (25 × 30 mm.).

PAHANG BC

A state of the Federation of Malaya, incorporated in Malaysia in 1963.

100 cents = 1 dollar (Straits or Malayan).

1889. Stamps of Straits Settlements optd. **PAHANG.**
4. 1. 2 c. rose .. .. .. 1·75 2·00
2. 8 c. orange £225 £225
3. 5. 10 c. grey .. .. 70·00 70·00

1891. Stamp of Straits Settlements surch. **PAHANG Two CENTS.**
1. 2 c. on 24 c. green .. .. 10·00 11·00

1. Tiger.

2. Tiger.

1891.
11. 1. 1 c. green .. .. .. 90 1·00
12. 2 c. red 45 45
13. 5 c. blue .. .. .. 1·10 1·75

1895.
14. 2. 3 c. purple and red .. 55 40
15. 4 c. purple and red .. 75 65
16. 5 c. purple and yellow .. 3·25 3·50

1897. No. 13 divided, and each half surch.
17. 1. 2 c. on half of 5 c. blue .. £110 90·00
18. 3 c. on half of 5 c. blue .. £110 80·00

1898. Stamps of Perak optd. **Pahang.**
19. 2. 10 c. purple and orange .. 5·00 6·00
20. 25 c. green and red .. 7·00 8·00
21. 50 c. green and black .. 15·00 13·00
22. 50 c. purple and black .. 23·00 19·00
23. 3. $1 green .. .. 20·00 20·00
24. $5 green and blue .. 60·00 60·00

1898. Stamp of Perak surch. **Pahang Four cents.**
25. 2. 4 c. on 8 c. purple & blue 1·50 2·00

1899. No. 15 surch. **Four cents.**
28. 2. 4 c. on 5 c. purple & yellow 4·00 4·00

3. Sultan Sir Abu Bakar. 4.

1935.
29. 3. 1 c. black 10 20
30. 2 c. green 25 20
31. 3 c. green 20 35
32. 4 c. orange 10 20
33. 5 c. brown 30 12
34. 6 c. red .. .. .. 1·00 1·00
35. 8 c. grey 40 10
36. 8 c. red .. .. .. 35 2·00
37. 10 c. purple 15 12
38. 12 c. blue 75 85
39. 15 c. blue .. .. .. 60 2·25
40. 25 c. purple and red .. 75 60
41. 30 c. purple and orange .. 45 75
42. 40 c. red and purple .. 50 1·10
43. 50 c. black on green .. 1·75 80
44. $1 black and red on blue .. 1·25 2·00
45. $2 green and red .. 8·00 8·00
46. $5 green and red on green 4·00 8·00

1948. Silver Wedding. As T 5/6 of Aden.
47. 10 c. violet 8 10
48. $5 green .. .. 6·00 8·00

1949. U.P.U. As T 14/7 of Antigua.
49. 10 c. purple 8 12
50. 15 c. blue 10 20
51. 25 c. orange 25 35
52. 50 c. black 40 55

1950.
53. 4. 1 c. black 5 5
54. 2 c. orange 5 5
55. 3 c. green 20 15
56. 4 c. brown 5 5
57. 5 c. purple 8 5
58. 6 c. grey 8 10
59. 8 c. red 12 20
60. 8 c. green 12 20
61. 10 c. magenta 5 5
62. 12 c. red 15 25
63. 15 c. blue 15 20
64. 20 c. black and green .. 20 40
65. 20 c. blue 25 25
66. 25 c. purple and orange .. 20 12
67. 30 c. red and purple .. 35 30
68. 35 c. red and purple .. 40 45
69. 40 c. red and purple .. 40 70
70. 50 c. black and blue .. 30 20
71. $1 blue and purple .. 70 70
72. $2 green and red .. 1·75 4·00
73. $5 green and brown .. 4·50 5·00

1953. Coronation. As T 7 of Aden.
74. 10 c. black and purple .. 5 5

1957. As Nos. 92/102 of Kedah but inset portrait of Sultan Sir Abu Bakar.
75. 1 c. black 5 5
76. 2 c. red 5 5
77. 4 c. sepia 5 5
78. 5 c. lake 5 5
79. 8 c. green 8 15
80. 10 c. sepia 5 5
81. 10 c. maroon 5 5
82. 20 c. blue 8 8
83a. 50 c. black and blue .. 25 20
84. $1 blue and purple .. 45 35
85a. $2 green and red .. 85 1·00
86. $5 brown and green .. 3·00 3·00

5. " Vanda hookeriana ".

1965. As Nos. 166/172 of Johore but with inset portrait of Sultan Sir Abu Bakar as in T 5.
87. 5. 1 c. multicoloured .. 5 5
88. – 2 c. multicoloured .. 5 5
89. – 5 c. multicoloured .. 5 5
90. – 6 c. multicoloured .. 5 5
91. – 10 c. multicoloured .. 5 5
92. – 15 c. multicoloured .. 8 8
93. – 20 c. multicoloured .. 8 8
The higher values used in Pahang were Nos. 20/7 of Malaysia.

6. Blue Pansy Butterfly.

1971. Butterflies. As Nos. 175/81 of Johore, but with portrait of Sultan Sir Abu Bakar as in T 6.
96. – 1 c. multicoloured .. 5 5
97. – 2 c. multicoloured .. 5 5
98. – 5 c. multicoloured .. 5 5
99. – 6 c. multicoloured .. 5 5
100. – 10 c. multicoloured .. 5 5
101. 6. 15 c. multicoloured .. 8 8
102. – 20 c. multicoloured .. 8 8
The higher values in use with this issue are Nos. 64/71 of Malaysia.

7. Sultan Haji Ahmad Shah.

1975. Installation of the Sultan.
103. 7. 10 c. green, lilac and gold 5 5
104. 15 c. black, yell. and grn. 8 8
105. 50 c. black, blue & green 20 20

HAVE YOU READ THE NOTES AT THE BEGINNING OF THIS CATALOGUE?

These often provide answers to the enquiries we receive.

PAKHOI O1

An Indo-Chinese Post Office in China, closed in 1922.

1903. Stamps of Indo-China, "Tablet", key-type, surch. **PACKHOI** and value in Chinese.
1. D. 1 c. black on blue .. 1·10 1·10
2. 2 c. brown on yellow .. 45 45
3. 4 c. claret on grey .. 30 30
4. 5 c. green 30 30
5. 10 c. red 30 30
6. 15 c. grey 30 30
7. 20 c. red on green .. 60 60
8. 25 c. blue 60 60
9. 25 c. black on red .. 30 30
10. 30 c. brown 70 70
11. 40 c. red on yellow .. 6·50 6·50
12. 50 c. red on rose .. 45·00 45·00
13. 50 c. brown on blue .. 9·00 9·00
14. 75 c. brown on orange .. 8·00 8·00
15. 1 f. olive .. .. 9·00 9·00
16. 5 f. mauve on lilac .. 14·00 14·00

1906. Stamps of Indo-China surch. **PAK-HOI** and value in Chinese.
17. 1. 1 c. olive 25 25
18. 2 c. claret on yellow .. 25 25
19. 4 c. purple on grey .. 25 25
20. 5 c. green 25 25
21. 10 c. red 25 25
22. 15 c. brown on blue .. 75 60
23. 20 c. red on green .. 40 40
24. 25 c. blue 40 40
25. 30 c. brown on cream .. 40 40
26. 35 c. black on yellow .. 40 40
27. 40 c. black on grey .. 40 40
28. 50 c. olive on green .. 80 70
29. D. 75 c. brown on orange .. 8·00 7·00
30. 1. 1 f. green .. .. 4·00 3·75
31. 2 f. brown on yellow .. 5·50 4·50
32. D. 5 f. mauve on lilac .. 16·00 15·00
33. 1. 10 f. red on green .. 16·00 15·00

1908. Stamps of Indo-China (Native types) surch. **PAKHOI** and value in Chinese.
34. 2. 1 c. black and olive .. 5 5
35. 2 c. black and brown .. 8 8
36. 4 c. black and blue .. 10 10
37. 5 c. black and green .. 12 12
38. 10 c. black and red .. 12 12
39. 15 c. black and violet .. 25 25
40. 3. 20 c. black and violet .. 25 25
41. 25 c. black and blue .. 25 25
42. 30 c. black & chocolate .. 40 40
43. 35 c. black and green .. 40 40
44. 40 c. black and brown .. 40 40
45. 50 c. black and red .. 40 40
46. 4. 75 c. black and orange .. 75 75
47. – 1 f. black and red .. 75 75
48. – 2 f. black and green .. 2·40 2·40
49. – 5 f. black and blue .. 12·00 12·00
50. – 10 f. black and violet .. 25·00 25·00

1919. As last surch. in addition in figures and words.
51. 2. ⅖ c. on 1 c. blk. & olive .. 8 8
52. ⅘ c. on 2 c. blk. & brn. .. 8 8
53. 1⅗ on 4 c. blk. & blue .. 10 10
54. 2 c. on 5 c. blk. & green .. 12 12
55. 4 c. on 10 c. black & red .. 50 50
56. 6 c. on 15 c. blk. & violet .. 8 8
57. 3. 8 c. on 20 c. blk. & violet .. 30 30
58. 10 c. on 25 c. blk. & bl. .. 45 45
59. 12 c. on 30 c. blk. & pur. .. 20 20
60. 14 c. on 35 c. blk. & grn. .. 8 8
61. 16 c. on 40 c. blk. & brn. .. 30 30
62. 20 c. on 50 c. blk. & red .. 25 25
63. 4. 30 c. on 75 c. blk. & orge. 25 25
64. – 40 c. on 1 f. blk. & red .. 1·50 1·50
65. – 80 c. on 2 f. blk. & grn. .. 50 50
66. – 2 pi. on 5 f. blk. & blue .. 1·25 1·25
67. – 4 pi. on 10 f. blk. & violet 2·25 2·25

PAKISTAN BC

A Dominion created in 1947 from the partition of India. Became an independent Islamic Republic within the British Commonwealth in 1956. Comprised territory with predominantly Moslem population in Eastern and Western India. The eastern provinces declared their independence of West Pakistan in 1971 and are now known as Bangladesh.

On 30th January, 1972, President Bhutto announced the withdrawal of the Islamic Republic of Pakistan from the British Commonwealth.

1961. 100 paisa = 1 rupee.

1947. King George VI stamps of India optd. **PAKISTAN.**
1. 78. 3 p. slate 5 5
2. ½ a. mauve 5 5
3. 9 p. green 5 5
4. 1 a. red 5 5
5. 79. 1½ a. violet 5 5
6. 2 a. red 5 5
7. 3 a. violet 5 5
8. 79. 3½ a. blue 10 20
9. 80. 4 a. brown 5 5
10. 6 a. green 12 10
11. 8 a. violet 12 5
12. 12 a. purple 20 8
13. – 14 a. purple (No. 277) .. 25 25
14. 77. 1 r. slate and brown .. 25 20
15. 2 r. purple and brown .. 50 30
16. 5 r. green and blue .. 85 50
17. 10 r. purple and red .. 2·20 1·10
18. 15 r. brown and green .. 3·50 2·75
19. 25 r. slate and purple .. 5·50 5·00

1. Constituent Assembly Building, Karachi.

1948. Independence.
20. 1. 1½ a. blue 5 5
21. – 2½ a. green 5 5
22. – 3 a. brown 5 5
23. – 1 r. red 15 15

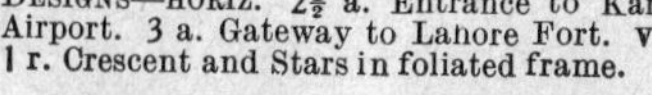

DESIGNS—HORIZ. 2½ a. Entrance to Karachi Airport. 3 a. Gateway to Lahore Fort. VERT. 1 r. Crescent and Stars in foliated frame.

2. Scales of Justice.

3. Lloyd Barrage.

4. Salimullah Hostel, Dacca University.

5. Khyber Pass.

DESIGNS — VERT. As T 2: 1 a., 1½ a., 2 a. Star and Crescent. 6 a., 8 a., 12 a. Karachi Port Trust. HORIZ. As T 4: 3 a., 10 a. Karachi Airport.

1948. Designs with crescent moon pointing to right.
24. 2. 3 p. red 5 5
25. 6 p. violet 5 5
26. 9 p. green 5 5
27. – 1 a. blue 5 5
28. – 1½ a. green 5 5
29. – 2 a. red 5 5
30. 3. 2½ a. green 5 5
31. – 3 a. green 5 5
32. 3. 3½ a. blue 12 10
33. 4 a. brown 10 10
34. – 6 a. blue 5 5
35. – 8 a. black 8 5
36. – 10 a. red 12 12
37. – 12 a. red 10 10
38. 4. 1 r. blue 20 10
39a. 2 r. brown .. .. .. 1·00 50
40a. 5 r. red .. .. .. 1·25 40
41b. 5. 10 r. mauve .. .. .. 1·75 40
42. 15 r. green .. .. .. 2·50 85
210. 25 r. violet .. .. .. 2·10 1·00

6.

1949. Mr. Jinnah's 1st Death Anniv.
44. 6. 1½ a. brown 20 20
45. 3 a. green 20 20
46. 10 a. black 85 85
In No. 46 the inscription reads " QUAID-I-AZAM MOHAMMAD ALI JINNAH ", etc.

1949. As 1948 but with crescent moon pointing to left.
47. – 1 a. blue 5 5
48a.– 1½ a. green 5 5
49a.– 2 a. red 8 5

50. –	3 a. green	10	5
51. –	6 a. blue	20	8
52. –	8 a. black	20	5
53. –	10 a. red	20	20
54. –	12 a. red	30	15

7. Pottery.

DESIGNS—VERT. 3 a., 12 a. Aeroplane and hour-glass. 4 a., 6 a. Saracenic leaf pattern. HORIZ. 8 a., 10 a. Archway and lamp.

1951. Independence. 4th Anniv.

55. 7.	$2\frac{1}{2}$ a. red	5	5
56. –	3 a. purple	5	5
57. 7.	$3\frac{1}{2}$ a. blue (A)	20	20
57a.	$3\frac{1}{2}$ a. blue (B)	12	12
58. –	4 a. green	8	5
59. –	6 a. orange	8	5
60. –	8 a. sepia	10	5
61. –	10 a. violet	10	8
62. –	12 a. slate	15	5

(A) has Arabic fraction on left as in T 7; (B) has it on right. For similar $3\frac{1}{2}$ a. see No. 88.

8. "Scinde Dawk" stamp and Ancient and Modern Transport.

1952. "Scinde Dawk" Issue of India. Cent.

63. 8.	3 a. green on olive ..	25	25
64.	12 a. brown on salmon ..	50	50

9. Kaghan Valley.

DESIGNS—As T 9: HORIZ. 9 p. Mountains, Gilgit. 1 a. Badshahi Mosque, Lahore. VERT. $1\frac{1}{2}$ a. Mausoleum of Emperor Jehangir, Lahore. As T 10: HORIZ. 1 r. Cotton plants, West Pakistan. 2 r. Jute fields and river, East Pakistan.

10. Tea Plantation, East Pakistan.

1954. Independence. 7th Anniv.

65. 9.	6 p. violet	5	5
66. –	9 p. blue	5	15
67. –	1 a. carmine	5	5
68. –	$1\frac{1}{2}$ a. red	5	5
69. 10.	14 a. myrtle	20	10
70. –	1 r. green	25	8
71. –	2 r. orange	40	15

11. View of K2 (Mount Godwin-Austen).

1954. Conquest of K 2.

72. 11.	2 a. violet	12	10

12. Karnaphuli Paper Mill, East Bengal.

DESIGNS: 6 a. Textile mill W. Pakistan. 8 a. Jute mill, E. Pakistan. 12 a. Main Sui gas plant.

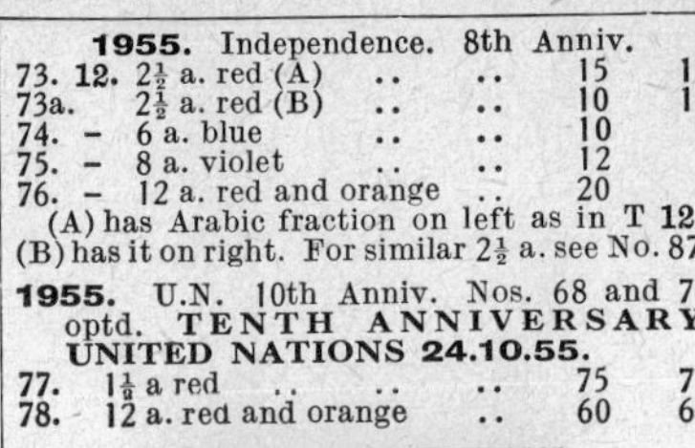

1955. Independence. 8th Anniv.

73. 12.	$2\frac{1}{2}$ a. red (A)	15	15
73a.	$2\frac{1}{2}$ a. red (B)	10	10
74. –	6 a. blue	10	5
75. –	8 a. violet	12	5
76. –	12 a. red and orange ..	20	8

(A) has Arabic fraction on left as in T 12; (B) has it on right. For similar $2\frac{1}{2}$ a. see No. 87.

1955. U.N. 10th Anniv. Nos. 68 and 76 optd. **TENTH ANNIVERSARY, UNITED NATIONS 24.10.55.**

77.	$1\frac{1}{2}$ a red	75	75
78.	12 a. red and orange ..	60	60

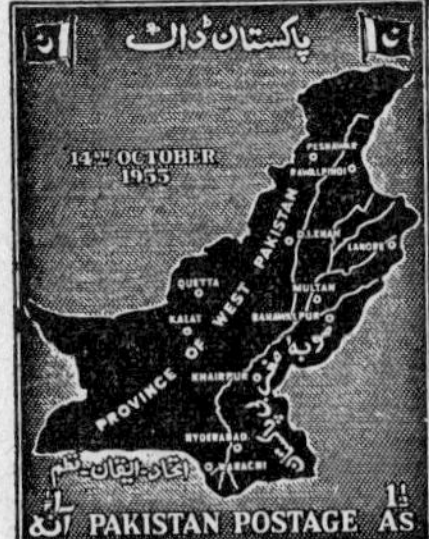

13. Map of W. Pakistan.

1955. West Pakistan Unity.

79. 13.	$1\frac{1}{2}$ a. green	8	8
80.	2 a. brown	10	10
81.	12 a. red	30	30

14. Constituent Assembly Building, Karachi.

1956. Republic Day.

82. 14.	2 a. green	5	5

15.

16. Map of East Pakistan.

1956. 9th Anniv. of Independence.

83. 15.	2 a. red	5	5

1956. 1st Session of National Assembly of Pakistan at Dacca.

84. 16.	$1\frac{1}{2}$ a. green	5	5
85.	2 a. brown	10	10
86.	12 a. red	30	30

17. Orange Tree.

DESIGNS—$2\frac{1}{2}$ a. as T 12 without value in Arabic at right. $3\frac{1}{2}$ a. as T 7 without value in Arabic at right.

1957. Republic. 1st Anniv.

87. –	$2\frac{1}{2}$ a. red	5	5
88. –	$3\frac{1}{2}$ a. blue	5	5
208. 17.	10 r. green and orange ..	85	45

18. Pakistani Flag.

1957. Struggle for Independence (Indian Mutiny). Cent.

90. 18.	$1\frac{1}{2}$ a. green	5	5
91.	12 a. blue	20	20

19. Pakistan Industries.

1957. Independence. 10th Anniv.

92. 19.	$1\frac{1}{2}$ a. blue	5	5
93.	4 a. salmon	12	12
94.	12 a. mauve	25	30

1958. Republic. 2nd Anniv. As T 17.

95.	15 r. red and purple ..	2·25	1·50

DESIGN: 15 r. Coconut tree.

20.

1958. Muhammad Iqbal (poet). 20th Death Anniv.

96. 20.	$1\frac{1}{2}$ a. olive and black ..	5	5
97.	2 a. chestnut and black ..	5	5
98.	14 a. turquoise & black	30	35

21. U.N. Charter and Globe.

1958. Declaration of Human Rights. 10th Anniv.

99. 21.	$1\frac{1}{2}$ a. turquoise ..	5	5
100.	14 a. sepia	25	25

1958. Scout Jamboree. Optd. **PAKISTAN BOY SCOUT 2nd NATIONAL JAMBOREE CHITTAGONG Dec. 58-Jan. 59.**

101. 9.	6 p. violet	5	5
102. –	8 a. violet (No. 75) ..	30	30

1959. Revolution Day. No. 74 optd. **REVOLUTION DAY Oct. 27, 1959.**

103. –	6 a blue	12	12

22. "Centenary of an Idea".

1959. Red Cross Commem.

104. 22.	2 a. red and green ..	5	5
105.	10 a. red and blue ..	15	20

23. Armed Forces Badge.

1960. Armed Forces Day.

106. 23.	2 a. red, blue and green	5	5
107.	14 a. red and blue ..	20	20

24. Map of Pakistan showing Jammu and Kashmir.

1960.

108. 24.	6 p. purple	5	5
109.	2 a. red	5	5
110.	8 a. green	10	8
111.	1 r. blue	20	20

25. "Uprooted Tree".

1960. World Refugee Year.

112. 25.	2 a. red	5	5
113.	10 a. green	15	20

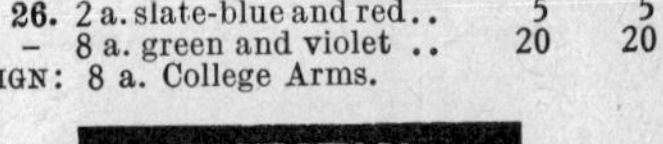

26. Punjab Agricultural College.

1960. Golden Jubilee of Punjab Agricultural College, Lyallpur.

114. 26.	2 a. slate-blue and red ..	5	5
115. –	8 a. green and violet ..	20	20

DESIGN: 8 a. College Arms.

27. "Land Reforms, Rehabilitation and Reconstruction".

1960. Revolution Day.

116. 27.	2 a. green, pink & brown	5	5
117.	14 a. green, yellow & blue	25	25

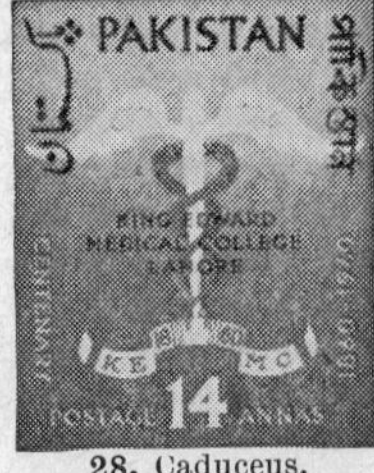

28. Caduceus.

1960. King Edward Medical College, Lahore. Cent.

118. 28.	2 a. yellow, black & blue	5	5
119.	14 a. green, black & red	25	25

29. "Economic Co-operation".

1960. Int. Chamber of Commerce C.A.F.E.A Meeting, Karachi.

120. 29.	14 a. chestnut	25	25

30. Zam-Zama Gun, Lahore. ("Kim's Gun" after Rudyard Kipling.)

1960. 3rd Pakistan Boy Scouts' National Jamboree, Lahore.
121. **30.** 2 a. red, yellow & green 10 8

1961. Surch. in "PAISA".
122. – 1 p. on 1½ a. red (No. 68) 5 5
123. **2.** 2 p. on 3 p. red .. 5 5
124. **24.** 3 p. on 6 p. purple .. 5 5
125. – 7 p. on 1 a. carm. (No. 67) 12 10
126. **24.** 13 p. on 2 a. red .. 15 12
127. **15.** 13 p. on 2 a. red .. 15 12
See also Nos. 262/4.

31. Khyber Pass.

32. Shalimar Gardens, Lahore.

33. Chota Sona Masjid (gateway).

1961.
128. **31.** 1 p. violet 5 5
129. 2 p. red 5 5
172. 3 p. purple 5 5
173. 5 p. blue 5 5
174. 7 p. green 5 5
175. **32.** 10 p. brown 5 5
176. 13 p. slate-violet .. 5 5
176a. 15 p. purple 5 5
176b. 20 p. green 5 5
177. 25 p. blue 5 5
178. 40 p. purple 5 5
179. 50 p. blue-green .. 5 5
180. 75 p. red 5 5
181. 90 p. yellow-green .. 8 5
204. **33.** 1 r. red 8 5
144. 1 r. 25 violet .. 25 12
206. 2 r. orange .. 15 10
144b. 5 r. green .. 1·25 30

1961. Lahore Stamp Exn. Optd. **LAHORE STAMP EXHIBITION 1961** and emblem.
145. **24.** 8 a. green 15 15

34. Warsak Dam and Power Station.

1961. Completion of Warsak Hydro-Electric Project.
146. **34.** 40 p. black and blue .. 10 10

35. Narcissus.

1961. Child Welfare Week.
147. **35.** 13 p. turquoise .. 8 8
148. 90 p. mauve 20 20

36. Ten Roses.

1961. Co-operative Day.
149. **36.** 13 p. red and green .. 5 5
150. 90 p. red and blue .. 20 20

37. Police Crest and "Traffic Control".

1961. Police Cent.
151. **37.** 13 p. silver, black & blue 5 5
152. 40 p. silver, black & red 15 15

RAILWAY CENTENARY 1861-1961
38. Locomotive "Eagle" of 1861.

1961. Railway Cent.
153. **38.** 13 p. green, blk. & yell. 5 5
154. – 50 p. yell., black & green 20 25
DESIGN: 50 p. Diesel locomotive.

1962. Karachi-Dacca Flight. No. 87 surch. with 'plane and **FIRST JET FLIGHT KARACHI-DACCA 13 Paisa.**
155. 13 p. on 2½ a. red .. 8 8

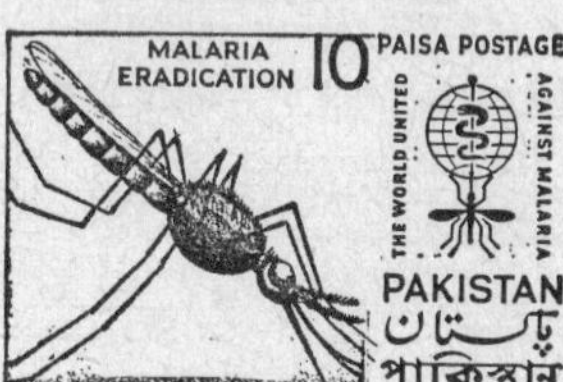

39. Mosquito.

1962. Malaria Eradication.
156. **39.** 10 p. black, yellow & red 5 5
157. – 13 p. black, lemon & red 8 5
DESIGN: 13 p. Mosquito pierced by blade.

40. Pakistan Map and Jasmine.

1962. New Constitution.
158. **40.** 40 p. yellow-green, blue-green and grey .. 15 15

41. Football.

1962. Sports.
159. **41.** 7 p. black and blue .. 5 5
160. – 13 p. black and green .. 5 5
161. – 25 p. black and purple .. 10 10
162. – 40 p. black and brown .. 15 15
DESIGNS: 13 p. Hockey 25 p. Squash. 40 p. Cricket.

42. Marble Fruit Dish and Bahawalpuri Clay Flask.

DESIGNS: 13 p. Sports equipment. 25 p. Camelskin lamp and brassware. 40 p. Wooden powder - bowl and basket - work. 50 p. Inlaid cigarette-box and brassware.

1962. Small Industries.
163. **42.** 7 p. lake 5 5
164. – 13 p. green 10 8
165. – 25 p. violet 10 10
166. – 40 p. yellow-green .. 15 15
167. – 50 p. red 20 20

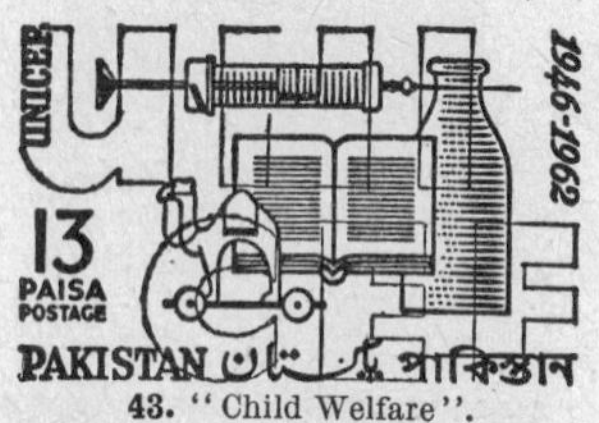

43. "Child Welfare".

1962. U.N.I.C.E.F. 16th Anniv.
168. **43.** 13 p. blk., blue & maroon 5 5
169. 40 p. blk., yell. & turq. 10 12

1963. Pakistan U.N. Force in West Irian. Optd. **U.N. FORCE W. IRIAN.**
182. **32.** 13 p. slate-violet .. 8 5

44. "Dancing" Horse, Camel and Bull.

1963. Nat. Horse and Cattle Show.
183. **44.** 13 p. blue, sepia & pink 8 5

45. Wheat and Tractor.

1963. Freedom from Hunger.
184. **45.** 13 p. orange-brown .. 5 5
185. – 50 p. bistre-brown .. 15 12
DESIGN: 50 p. Lifting rice.

1963. 2nd Int. Stamp Exn., Dacca. Surch. **INTERNATIONAL DACCA STAMP EXHIBITION 1963 13 PAISA** and bars.
186. **24.** 13 p. on 2 a. red .. 10 10

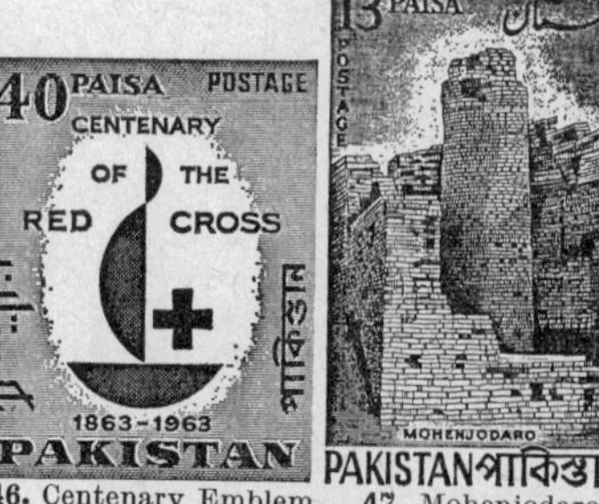

46. Centenary Emblem. 47. Mohenjodaro.

1963. Red Cross Cent.
187. **46.** 40 p. red and olive .. 12 10

1963. Archaeological Series.
188. – 7 p. blue 5 5
189. **47.** 13 p. sepia 10 10
190. – 40 p. red 15 15
191. – 50 p. violet 20 20
DESIGNS—HORIZ. 7 p. Paharpur. 40 p. Taxila. 50 p. Mainamati.

1963. Pakistan Public Works Department Cent. Surch. **100 YEARS OF P.W.D. OCTOBER, 1963 13** and bars.
192. **31.** 13 p. on 3 p. purple .. 8 5

48. Ataturk's Mausoleum.

1963. Kemal Ataturk. 25th Death Anniv.
193. **48.** 50 p. red 20 20

49. Globe and U.N.E.S.C.O. Emblem.

1963. Declaration of Human Rights. 15th Anniv.
194. **49.** 50 p. brown, red & blue 12 8

50. Thermal Power Installations.

1963. Completion of Multan Thermal Power Station.
195. **50.** 13 p. blue 5 5

51. Temple of Thot, Queen Nefertari and Maids.

1964. Nubian Monuments Preservation.
211. **51.** 13 p. blue and red .. 5 5
212. – 50 p. purple and black 20 20
DESIGN: 50 p. Temple of Abu Simbel.

52. "Unisphere" and Pakistan Pavilion.

1964. New York World's Fair.
213. **52.** 13 p. blue 5 5
214. – 1 r. 25 blue and orange 40 40
DESIGN—VERT. 1 r. 25, Pakistan Pavilion on "Unisphere".

53. Shah Abdul Latif's Mausoleum.

1964. Shah Abdul Latif of Bhit. Death Bicent.
215. **53.** 50 p. blue and lake .. 20 20

54. Mausoleum of "Quaid-i-Azam".

1964. Mr. Jinnah ("Quaid-i-Azam"). 16th Death Anniv.
216. **54.** 15 p. green 5 5
217. – 50 p. bronze 20 20
DESIGN: 50p. As T **54**, but 26½ × 31½ mm.

55. Bengali and Urdu Alphabets.

1964. "Universal Childrens' Day".
218. **55.** 15 p. brown 5 8

56. University Building.

1964. 1st Convocation of the West Pakistan University of Engineering and Technology, Lahore.
219. **56.** 15 p. chestnut 5 8

57. "Help the Blind".

1965. Blind Welfare.
220. **57.** 15 p. blue and yellow .. 5 8

58. I.T.U. Emblem and Symbols.

1965. I.T.U. Cent.
221. **58.** 15 p. purple 5 5

59. I.C.Y. Emblem.

1965. Int. Co-operation Year.
222. **59.** 15 p. black and blue .. 5 5
223. 50 p. green and yellow 20 20

60. "Co-operation".

1965. Regional Development Co-operation Pact. 1st Anniv. Multicoloured.
224. 15 p. Type **60** 5 5
225. 50 p. Globe and Flags of Turkey, Iran and Pakistan (54¾ × 30¾ mm.) .. 15 15

61. Soldier and Tanks.

1965. Pakistan Armed Forces. Multicoloured.
226. 7 p. Type **61** 5 5
227. 15 p. Naval Officer and Destroyer 5 5
228. 50 p. Airman and "F-104" Starfighters 20 20

62. Army, Navy and Air Force Crests.

1966. Armed Forces Day.
229. **62.** 15 p. blue, green and buff 12 5

63. Atomic Reactor, Islamabad.

1966. Pakistan's 1st Atomic Reactor. Inaug.
230. **63.** 15 p. black 5 5

64. Bank Crest.

1966. Habib Bank. Silver Jubilee.
231. **64.** 15 p. grn., orge. & sepia 5 5

65. Children.

1966. "Universal Children Day".
232. **65.** 15 p. black, red & yellow 5 5

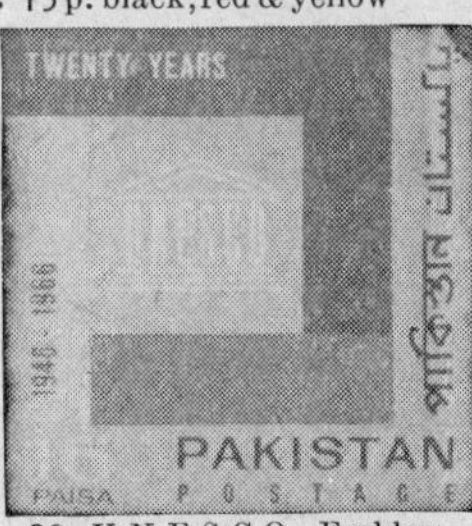

66. U.N.E.S.C.O. Emblem.

1966. U.N.E.S.C.O. 20th Anniv.
233. **66.** 15 p. multicoloured .. 8 8

67. Flag, Secretariat Building and President Ayub.
(Reduced size illustration. Actual size 57 × 27 mm.).

1966. Islamabad (new capital).
234. **67.** 15 p. green, chestnut, blue and brown .. 5 5
235. 50 p. green, chestnut, blue and black .. 12 10

68. Avicenna.

1966. Health and Tibbi Research Institute Foundation.
236. **68.** 15 p. green and salmon 5 5

69. Mohammed Ali Jinnah. **71.** Emblem of Pakistan T.B. Association.

70. Tourist Year Emblem.

1966. Mohammed Ali Jinnah. 50th Birth Anniv.
237. **69.** 15 p. black, orge. & blue 5 5
238. – 50 p. blk., pur. & ultram. 20 20
DESIGN: 50 p. Same portrait as 15 p. but different frame.

1967. Int. Tourist Year.
239. **70.** 15 p. black, blue & brn. 5 8

1967. T.B. Eradication Campaign.
240. **71.** 15 p. red, sepia & chest. 8 5

72. Scout Salute and Badge.

1967. 4th National Scout Jamboree.
241. **72.** 15 p. brown and maroon 10 8

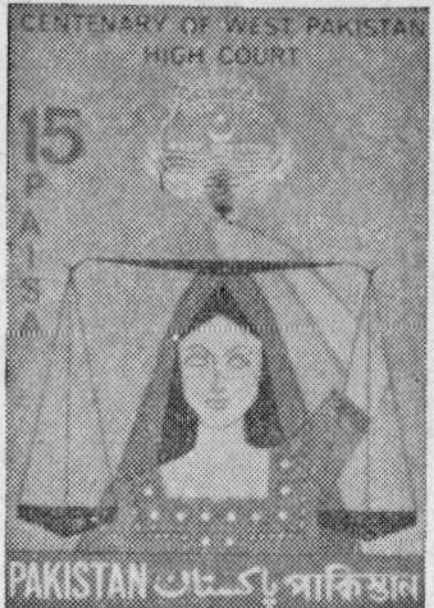

73. "Justice".

1967. West Pakistan High Court. Cent.
242 **73.** 15 p. black, grey, red and blue 10 8

74. Dr. Mohammad Iqbal (philosopher).

1967. Iqbal Commem.
243. **74.** 15 p. sepia and red .. 5 5
244. 1 r. sepia and green .. 30 30

75. Hilal-i-Isteqlal Flag.

1967. Award of Hilal-i-Isteqlal (for valour) to Lahore, Sialkot and Sargodah.
245. **75.** 15 p. green, red & blue 10 8

76. "20th Anniversary".

1967. Independence. 20th Anniv.
246. **76.** 15 p. red and green .. 10 5

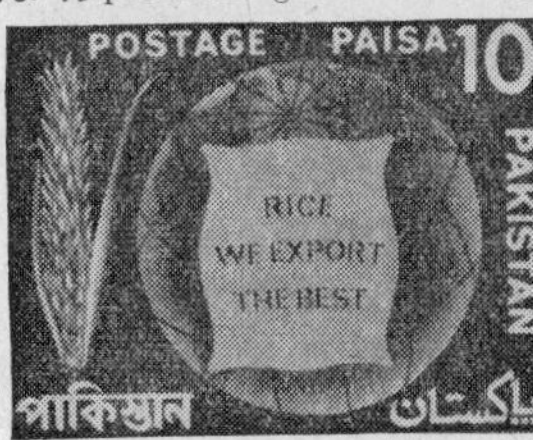

77. "Rice Exports".

1967. Pakistan Exports. Multicoloured.
247. 10 p. Type **77** 5 5
248. 15 p. Cotton plant, yarn and textiles 5 5
249. 50 p. Raw jute, bale and bags 25 20
Nos. 248/9 are vert. and larger 27 × 45 mm.

78. Clay Toys.

1967. Children's Day.
250. **78.** 15 p. multicoloured .. 5 5

79. Shah and Empress of Iran and Gulistan Palace, Teheran.

1967. Coronation of Shah Mohammed Riza Pahlavi and Empress Farah of Iran.
251. **79.** 50 p. purple, blue & ochre 20 20

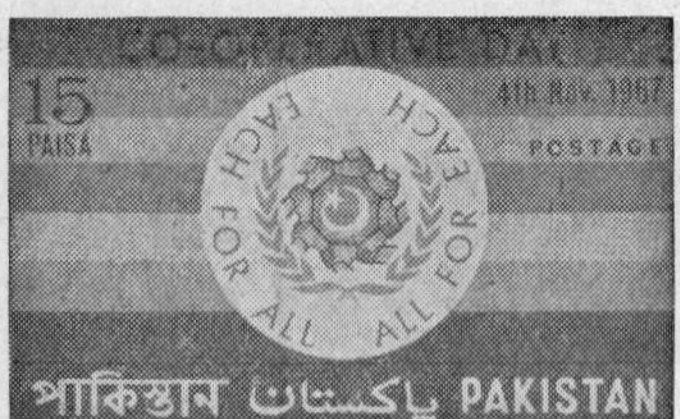

80. "Each For All—All for Each".

1967. Co-operative Day.
252. **80.** 15 p. multicoloured .. 5 5

81. Mangla Dam.

1967. Indus Basin Project.
253. **81.** 15 p. multicoloured .. 5 8

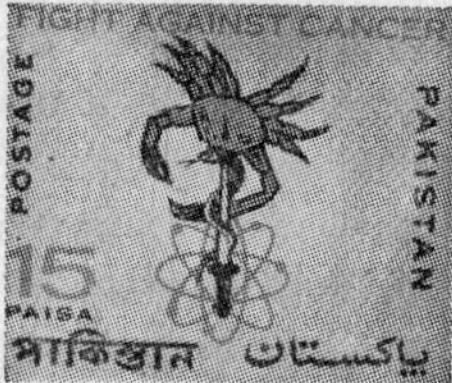

82. Crab Pierced by Sword.

1967. The Fight Against Cancer.
254. **82.** 15 p. red and black .. 5 5

83. Human Rights Emblem.

1968. Human Rights Year.
255. **83.** 15 p. red and blue .. 5 5
256. 50 p. red, yellow & grey 20 20

84. Agricultural University, Mymensingh.

1968. East Pakistan Agricultural University. First Convocation.
257. **84.** 15 p. multicoloured .. 5 8

85. W.H.O. Emblem.

1968. World Health Organization. 20th Anniv.
258. **85.** 15 p. green and red .. 5 5
259. 50 p. orange and indigo 20 20

86. Kazi Nazrul Islam (poet, composer and patriot).

1968. Nazrul Islam Commem.
260. **86.** 15 p. sepia and yellow.. 5 5
261. 50 p. sepia and red .. 20 20

1968. Nos. 56, 74 and 61 surch.
262. 4 p. on 3 a. purple .. 5 5
263. 4 p. on 6 a. blue .. 5 5
264. 60 p. on 10 a. violet .. 30 35

87. Children running with Hoops.

1968. Universal Children's Day.
265. **87.** 15 p. multicoloured .. 5 5

88. National Assembly.

1968. "A Decade of Development".
266. **88.** 10 p. multicoloured .. 5 5
267. – 15 p. multicoloured .. 5 5
268. – 50 p. multicoloured .. 10 10
269. – 60 p. blue, pur. & verm. 15 20

DESIGNS: 15 p. Industry and Agriculture. 50 p. Army, Navy and Air Force. 60 p. Minaret and Atomic Reactor Plant.

89. Chittagong Steel Mill.

1969. Pakistan's 1st Steel Mill, Chittagong.
270. **89.** 15 p. grey, blue and olive 8 5

90. "Family".

1969. Family Planning.
271. **90.** 15 p. purple and blue .. 8 5

91. Olympic Gold Medal and Hockey Player.

1969. Olympic Hockey Champions.
272. **91.** 15 p. blk., gold, grn. & bl. 5 5
273. 1 r. blk., gold, grn. & pink 30 30

92. Mirza Ghalib and Lines of Verse.

1969. Mirza Ghalib (poet). Death Cent.
274. **92.** 15 p. multicoloured .. 5 5
275. 50 p. multicoloured .. 20 20

The lines of verse on No. 275 are different from those in T **92.**

93. Dacca Railway Station.

1969. New Dacca Railway Station. 1st Anniv.
276. **93.** 15 p. multicoloured .. 10 5

94. I.L.O. Emblem and "1919-1969".

1969. I.L.O. 50th Anniv.
277. **94.** 15 p. buff and green .. 5 5
278. 50 p. brown and red .. 30 20

95. Mughal Miniature (Pakistan).

1969. Regional Co-operation for Development. 5th Anniv. Multicoloured.
279. 20 p. Type **95** 5 5
280. 50 p. Safavi miniature (Iran) 12 12
281. 1 r. Ottoman miniature (Turkey) 25 25

96. Eastern Refinery, Chittagong.

1969. 1st East Pakistan Oil Refinery.
282. **96.** 20 p. multicoloured .. 10 5

97. Children playing outside "School". (Reduced size illustration—actual size 52 × 52 mm.).

1969. Universal Children's Day.
283. **97.** 20 p. multicoloured .. 8 5

98. Japanese Doll and P.I.A. Air Routes.

1969. P.I.A. Pearl Route, Dacca-Tokyo. Inaug.
284. **98.** 20 p. multicoloured .. 5 5
285. 50 p. multicoloured .. 15 20

99. "Reflection of Light" Diagram.

1969. Ibn-al-Haitham (physicist). Millenary Commem.
286. **99.** 20 p. black, yell. & blue 8 8

100. Vickers "Vimy" and Karachi Airport.

1969. 1st England-Australia Flight. 50th Anniv.
287. **100.** 50 p. multicoloured .. 15 15

MORE DETAILED LISTS

are given in the Stanley Gibbons Catalogues referred to in the country headings:

BC	British Commonwealth
E1, E2, E3	Europe 1, 2, 3
O1, O2, O3, O4	Overseas 1, 2, 3, 4

101. Flags, Sun Tower and Expo Site Plan.

1970. World Fair, Osaka. Expo 70.
288. **101.** 50 p. multicoloured .. 20 20

102. New U.P.U. Headquarters Building.

1970. New U.P.U. Headquarters Building.
289. **102.** 20 p. multicoloured .. 5 5
290. 50 p. multicoloured .. 25 15

103. U.N. Headquarters Building.

1970. United Nations. 25th Anniv. Multicoloured.
291. 20 p. Type **103** 5 5
292. 50 p. U.N. Emblem .. 20 15

104. I.E.Y. Emblem, Book and Pen.

1970. Int. Education Year.
293. **104.** 20 p. multicoloured .. 5 5
294. 50 p. multicoloured .. 10 10

105. Saiful Malook Lake (Pakistan).

1970. Regional Co-operation for Development. 6th Anniv. Multicoloured.
295. 20 p. Type **105** 5 5
296. 50 p. Seeyo-Se-Pol Bridge, Esfahan (Persia) .. 10 10
297. 1 r. View from Fethiye (Turkey) 20 20

106. Asian Productivity Symbol.

1970. Asian Productivity Year.
298. **106.** 50 p. multicoloured .. 12 15

107. Dr. Maria Montessori.

1970. Dr. Maria Montessori (educationalist). Birth Cent.
299. **107.** 20 p. multicoloured .. 5 5
300. 50 p. multicoloured .. 15 15

108. Tractor and Fertilizer Factory.

1970. Near East F.A.O. Regional Conference, Islamabad.
301. **108.** 20 p. green and brown 5 5

109. Children and Open Book. **110.** Pakistan Flag and Text.

1970. Universal Children's Day.
302. **109.** 20 p. multicoloured .. 5 5

1970. Elections for National Assembly.
303. **110.** 20 p. green and violet 5 5

1970. Elections for Provincial Assemblies. As No. 303, but inscr. "PROVINCIAL ASSEMBLIES".
304. **110.** 20 p. green and red .. 5 5

111. Conference Crest and burning Al-Aqsa Mosque.
(Illustration reduced – Actual size 55 × 33 mm.)

1970. Conference of Islamic Foreign Ministers, Karachi.
305. **111.** 20 p. multicoloured .. 5 5

112. Coastal Embankments.

1971. East Pakistan Coastal Embankments Project.
306. **112.** 20 p. multicoloured .. 5 5

113. Emblem and United Peoples of the World.

1971. Racial Equality Year.
307. **113.** 20 p. multicoloured .. 5 5
308. 50 p. multicoloured .. 12 12

114. Maple Leaf Cement Factory, Daudkhel.

1971. Colombo Plan. 20th Anniv.
309. **114.** 20 p. brn., blk. & violet 5 5

115. Chaharbagh School (Iran).

1971. Regional Co-operation for Development. 7th Anniv. Multicoloured.
310. 10 p. Selimiye Mosque (Turkey) 5 5
311. 20 p. Badshahi Mosque, Lahore 5 5
312. 50 p. Type **115** 15 12

116. Electric Locomotive and Boy with Toy Train. (Illustration reduced. Actual size 56 × 26 mm.)

1971. Universal Children's Day.
313. **116.** 20 p. multicoloured .. 5 5

117. Horseman and Symbols.

1971. Persian Empire. 2500th Anniv.
314. **117.** 10 p. multicoloured .. 5 5
315. 20 p. multicoloured .. 5 5
316. 50 p. multicoloured .. 15 15

118. Hockey-player and Trophy.

1971. World Cup Hockey Tournament.
317. **118.** 20 p. multicoloured .. 5 5

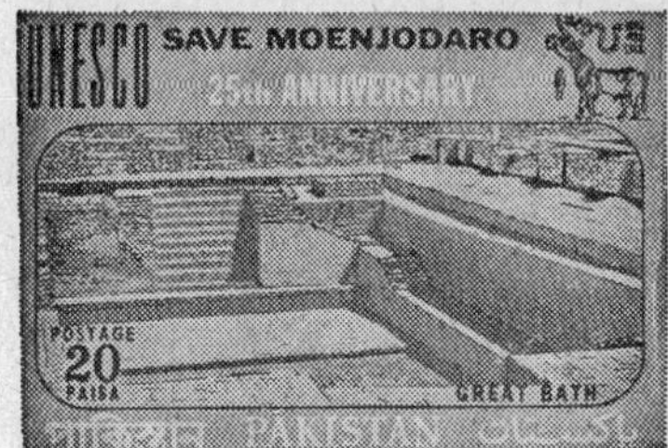

119. Great Bath, Moenjodaro.

1971. U.N.E.S.C.O. 25th Anniv. and Campaign to save the Moenjodaro Excavations.
318. **119.** 20 p. multicoloured .. 5 5

120. U.N.I.C.E.F. Symbol.

1971. U.N.I.C.E.F. 25th Anniv.
319. **120.** 50 p. multicoloured .. 15 15

121. King Hussein and Jordanian Flag.

1971. Hashemite Kingdom of Jordan. 50th Anniv.
320. **121.** 20 p. multicoloured .. 5 5

122. Badge of Hockey Federation and Trophy.

1971. Hockey Championships Victory.
321. 122. 20 p. multicoloured .. 5 5

123. Reading Class.

1972. Int. Book Year.
322. 123. 20 p. multicoloured .. 5 5

124. View of Venice.

1972. U.N.E.S.C.O. Campaign to Save Venice.
323. 124. 20 p. multicoloured .. 5 5

125. E.C.A.F.E. emblem and Discs.

1972. E.C.A.F.E. 25th Anniv.
324. 125. 20 p. multicoloured .. 5 5

126. Human Heart.

1972. World Health Day.
325. 126. 20 p. multicoloured .. 5 5

127. " Only One Earth".

1972. U.N. Conf. on the Human Environment, Stockholm.
326. 127. 20 p. multicoloured .. 5 5

128. " Fisherman " (Cevat Dereli).

1972. Regional Co-operation for Development. 8th Anniv. Multicoloured.
327. 10 p. Type **128** 5 5
328. 20 p. " Iranian Woman " (Behzad) 5 5
329. 50 p. " Will and Power " (A. R. Chughtai) .. 10 12

129. Mohammad Ali Jinnah and Tower.

1972. Independence. 25th Anniv. Mult.
330. 10 p. Type **129** 5 5
331. 20 p. " Land Reform " .. 5 5
332. 20 p. " Labour Reform " .. 5 5
333. 20 p. " Education Policy " 5 5
334. 20 p. " Health Policy " .. 5 5
335. 60 p. State Bank Building 8 10

The 60 p. is 46 × 28 mm.; Nos. 331/4 are 74 × 23½ mm.

130. Donating Blood.

1972. Nat. Blood Transfusion Service.
336. 130. 20 p. multicoloured .. 5 5

131. People and Squares.

1972. Population Census. Cent.
337. 131. 20 p. multicoloured .. 5 5

132. Children from Slums.

1972. Universal Children's Day.
338. 132. 20 p. multicoloured .. 5 5

133. People and Open Book.

1972. Education Week.
339. 133. 20 p. multicoloured .. 5 5

134. Nuclear Power Plant.

1972. Karachi Nuclear Power Plant. Inaug.
340. 134. 20 p. multicoloured .. 5 5

135. Copernicus in Observatory.

1973. Nicholas Copernicus (astronomer), 500th Birth Anniv.
341. 135. 20 p. multicoloured .. 5 5

136. Moenjodaro Excavations.

1973. Moenjodaro Excavations. 50th Anniv.
342. 136. 20 p. multicoloured .. 5 5

137. Elements of Meteorology.

1973. I.M.O./W.M.O. Cent.
343. 137. 10 p. multicoloured .. 5 5

138. Prisoners-of-War.

1973. Prisoners-of-War in India.
344. 138. 1 r. 25 multicoloured 12 15

139. National Assembly Building and Constitution Book.

1973. Constitution Week.
345. 139. 20 p. multicoloured .. 5 5

140. Badge and State Bank Building.

1973. Pakistan State Bank. 25th Anniv.
346. 140. 20 p. multicoloured .. 5 5
347. 1 r. multicoloured .. 12 15

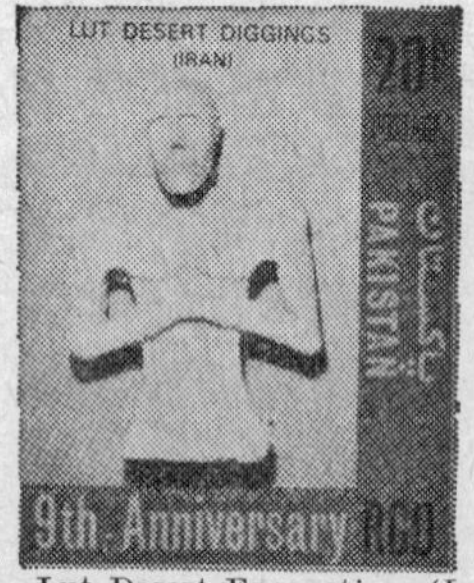

141. Lut Desert Excavations (Iran).

1973. Regional Co-operation for Development 9th Anniv. Multicoloured.
348. 20 p. Type **141** 5 5
349. 60 p. Main Street, Moenjodaro (Pakistan) 8 8
350. 1 r. 25 Mausoleum of Antiochus I (Turkey) .. 12 15

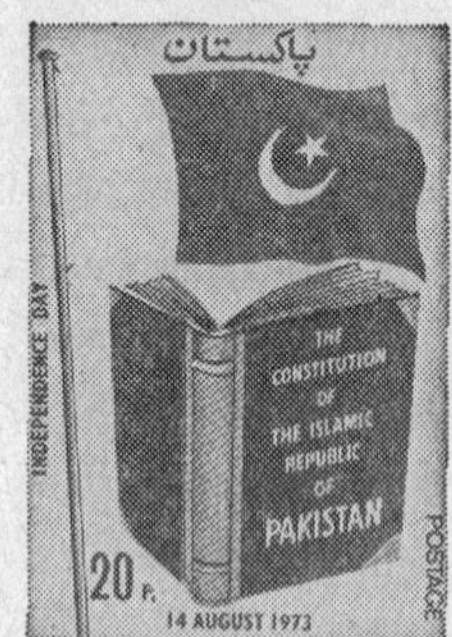

142. Constitution Book and Flag.

1973. Independence Day and Enforcement of the Constitution.
351. 142. 20 p. multicoloured .. 5 5

143. Quaid-i-Azam (Mr. Jinnah).

1973. Mohammad Ali Jinnah. 25th Death Anniv.
352. **143.** 20 p. grn., yell. & blk. 5 5

144. " Wallago attu ".

1973. Fishes. Multicoloured.
353. 10 p. Type **144** 5 5
354. 20 p. " Labeo rohita " .. 5 5
355. 60 p. " Tilapia mossambica " 15 15
356. 1 r. " Catla catla " .. 20 20

145. Children's Education.

1973. Universal Children's Day.
357. **145.** 20 p. multicoloured .. 5 5

146. Harvesting.

1973. World Food Programme. 10th Anniv.
358. **146.** 20 p. multicoloured .. 5 5

147. Ankara and Kemal Ataturk.

1973. Turkish Republic. 50th Anniv.
359. **147.** 50 p. multicoloured .. 8 8

148. Boy Scout. **149.** "Basic Necessities".

1973. National Silver Jubilee Jamboree.
360. **148.** 20 p. multicoloured .. 5 5

1973. Declaration of Human Rights. 25th Anniv.
361. **149.** 20 p. multicoloured .. 5 5

150. Al-Biruni and Nandana Hill.

1973. Al-Biruni Millenium Congress.
362. **150.** 20 p. multicoloured .. 5 5
363. 1 r. 25 multicoloured 12 15

151. Dr. Hansen, Microscope and Bacillus.

1973. Hansen's Discovery of Leprosy Bacillus Cent.
364. **151.** 20 p. multicoloured .. 5 5

152. Family and Emblem.

1974. World Population Year.
365. **152.** 20 p. multicoloured .. 5 5
366. 1 r. 25 multicoloured 12 15

153. Conference Emblem.

1974. Islamic Summit Conference, Lahore. Multicoloured.
367. 20 p. Type **153** 5 5
368. 65 p. Emblem on " Sun " 8 8
No. 368 is larger, size 42 × 30 mm.

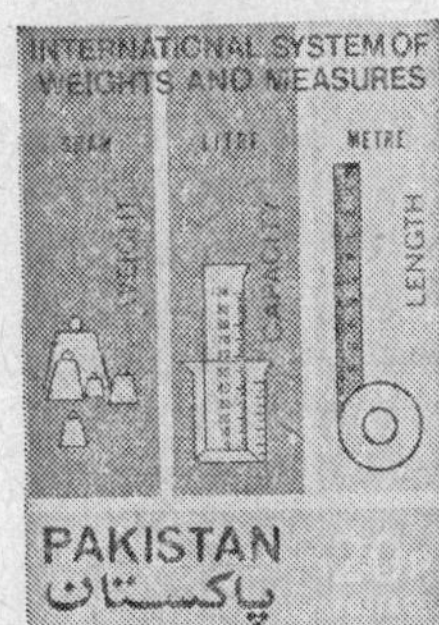

154. Units of Weight and Measurement.

1974. Adoption of Int. Weights and Measures System.
370. **154.** 20 p. multicoloured .. 5 5

155. "Chand Chautai" Carpet, Pakistan.

1974. Regional Co-operation for Development. 10th Anniv. Multicoloured.
371. 20 p. Type **155** 5 5
372. 60 p. Persian carpet, 16th-century 8 8
373. 1 r. Anatolian carpet, 15th-century 12 15

156. Hands protecting Sapling.

1974. Tree Planting Year.
374. **156.** 20 p. multicoloured .. 5 5

157. Torch and Map.

1974. Namibia Day.
375. **157.** 60 p. multicoloured .. 5 5

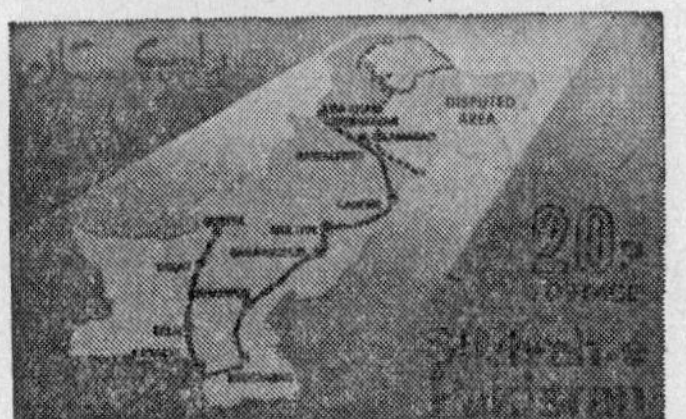

158. Highway Map.

1974. Shahrah-e-Pakistan (Pakistan Highway).
376. **158.** 20 p. multicoloured .. 8 8

159. Boy at Desk.

1974. Universal Children's Day.
377. **159.** 20 p. multicoloured .. 5 5

160. U.P.U. Emblem. **161.** Liaquat Ali Khan.

1974. U.P.U. Centenary. Multicoloured.
378. 20 p. Type **160** 5 5
379. 2 r. 25 U.P.U. emblem, aeroplane and mail-wagon 25 30

1974. Liaquat Ali Khan (First Prime Minister of Pakistan).
381. **161.** 20 p. black and red .. 5 5

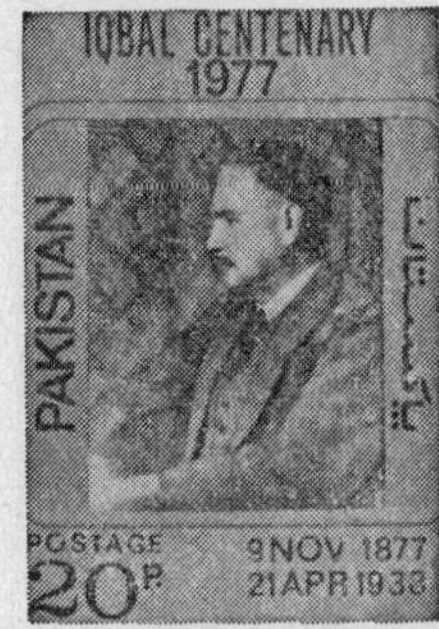

162. Dr. Mohammad Iqbal (poet and philosopher).

1974. Dr. Iqbal. Birth Cent. (1977). (1st issue).
382. **162.** 20 p. multicoloured .. 5 5
See also Nos. 339 and 433.

163. Dr. Schweitzer and River Scene.

1975. Dr. Albert Schweitzer. Birth Cent.
383. **163.** 2 r. 25 multicoloured 25 30

164. Tourism Year Symbol.

1975. South East Asia Tourism Year.
384. **164.** 2 r. 25 multicoloured 25 25

165. Assembly Hall, Flags and Prime Minister Bhutto.

1975. Islamic Summit Conference, Lahore. 1st Anniv.
385. **165.** 20 p. multicoloured .. 5 5
386. 1 r. multicoloured .. 12 12

166. " Scientific Research ".

1975. International Women's Year. Multicoloured.

387. 20 p. Type **166** 5 5
388. 2 r. 25 Girl teaching woman ("Adult Education") 25 30

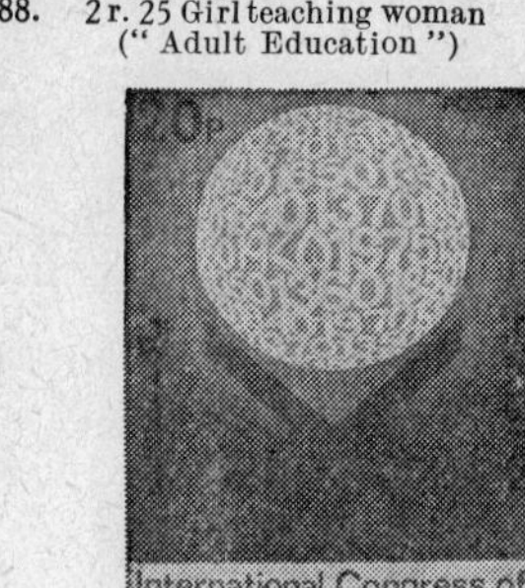

167. "Globe" and Algebraic Symbol.

1975. Int. Congress of Mathematical Sciences, Karachi.

389. **167.** 20 p. multicoloured .. 5 5

168. Pakistani Camel-skin Vase.

1975. Regional Co-operation for Development. 11th Anniversary. Multicoloured.

390. 20 p. Type **168** 5 5
391. 60 p. Iranian tile (horiz.) 5 8
392. 1 r. 25 Turkish porcelain vase 12 15

169. Sapling and Dead Trees.

1975. Tree Planting Year.

393. **169.** 20 p. multicoloured .. 5 5

170. Black Partridge.

1975. Wildlife Protection. (1st series).

394. **170.** 20 p. multicoloured .. 5 5
395. 2 r. 25 multicoloured .. 25 30

See also Nos. 400/1, 411/12 and 417/18.

171. "Today's Girls".

1975. Universal Children's Day.

396. **171.** 20 p. multicoloured .. 5 5

172. Hazrat Amir Khusrau, Sitar and Tabla.

(Reduced size illustration—actual size 74 × 23 mm.)

1975. Hazrat Amir Khusrau (poet and musician). 700th Birth Anniversary.

397. **172.** 20 p. multicoloured .. 5 5
398. 2 r. 25 multicoloured .. 25 30

173. Dr. Mohammad Iqbal.

1975. Dr. Iqbal. Birth Cent. (1977) (2nd issue).

399. **173.** 20 p. multicoloured .. 5 5

174. Urial (wild sheep).

1975. Wildlife Protection (2nd series).

400. **174.** 20 p. multicoloured .. 5 5
401. 3 r. multicoloured .. 30 35

175. Moenjodaro Remains.

1976. "Save Moenjodaro" (1st issue). Multicoloured.

402. 10 p. Type **175** 5 5
403. 20 p. Remains of houses .. 5 5
404. 65 p. Citadel area and stupa 5 5
405. 3 r. Well inside a house .. 30 35
406. 4 r. The "Great Bath" .. 40 45

See also Nos. 414 and 430.

176. Dome and Minaret of the Rauza-e-Mubarak.

1976. Int. Congress on Seerat.

407. **176.** 20 p. multicoloured .. 5 5
408. 3 r. multicoloured .. 30 35

177. Alexander Graham Bell, his Telephone and Modern Dial.

1976. First Telephone Transmission. Cent.

409. **177.** 3 r. multicoloured .. 30 35

178. College Arms within "Sun".

1976. National College of Arts, Lahore. Cent.

410. **178.** 20 p. multicoloured .. 5 5

179. Peacock.

1976. Wildlife Protection (3rd series).

411. **179.** 20 p. multicoloured .. 5 5
412. 3 r. multicoloured .. 30 35

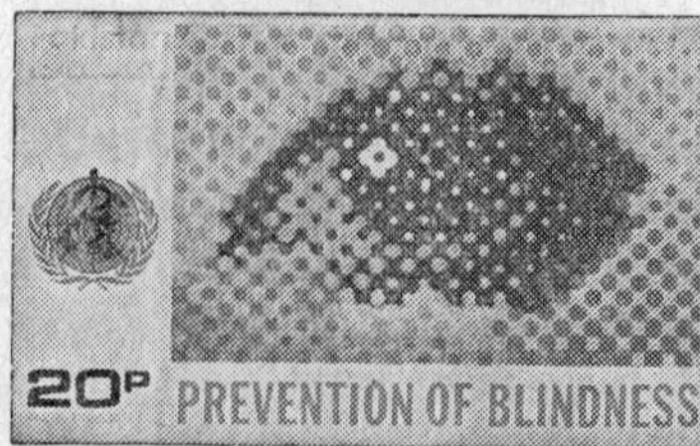

180. Human Eye.

1976. Prevention of Blindness.

413. **180.** 20 p. multicoloured 5 5

181. Unicorn and Ruins.

1976. "Save Moenjodaro" (2nd series).

414. **181.** 20 p. multicoloured .. 5 5

182. Jefferson Memorial.

1976. American Revolution. Bicent. Multicoloured.

415 90 p. Type **182** 8 10
416. 4 r. "Declaration of Independence" .. 40 45

No. 416 is larger, 47 × 36 mm.

183. Ibex.

1976. Wildlife Protection (4th series).

417. **183.** 20 p. multicoloured .. 5 5
418. 3 r. multicoloured .. 30 35

184. Mr. Jinnah.

1976. Regional Co-operation for Development. 12th Anniv. Multicoloured.

419. 20 p. Type **184** 5 5
420. 65 p. Reza Shah the Great 5 8
421. 90 p. Kemal Ataturk .. 8 8

185. Urdu Text. **186.** Quaid-i-Azam (Mr. Jinnah) and Wazir Mansion.

1976. Mr. Jinnah. Birth Centenary (1st issue).

(a) Type **185.**

422. **185.** 5 p. black, blue & yell. 5 5
423. 10 p. black, yell. & pur. 5 5
424. 15 p. black, and blue .. 5 5
425. 1 r. black, yell. & blue 10 12

(b) Type **186.** Background Buildings given. Multicoloured

426. 20 p. Type **186** 5 5
427. 40 p. Sind Madressah 5 5
428. 50 p. Minar Qarardad-e-Pakistan 5 8
429. 3 r. Mausoleum 30 35

187. Dancing-girl, Ruins and King Priest.
(Illustration reduced. Actual size, 64 × 22 mm.)

1976. "Save Moenjodaro" (3rd series).

430.	**187.**	65 p. multicoloured ..	8	8

188. U.N. Racial Discrimination Emblem.

1976. U.N. Decade to Combat Racial Discrimination.

431.	**188.**	65 p. multicoloured ..	8	8

189. Child in Maze and Basic Services.

1976. Universal Children's Day.

432.	**189.**	20 p. multicoloured ..	5	5

190. Verse from "Allama Iqbal".

1976. Dr. Iqbal. Birth Cent. (1977). (3rd issue).

433.	**190.**	20 p. multicoloured ..	5	5

191. Mr. Jinnah giving Scout Salute.

1976. Quaid-i-Azam Centenary Scout Jamboree.

434.	**191.**	20 p. multicoloured ..	5	5

192. Boy and Girl reading.

1976. Children's Literature.

435.	**192.**	20 p. multicoloured ..	5	5

193. Mohammed Ali Jinnah.

1976. Quaid-i-Azam (Mohammed Ali Jinnah) Birth Centenary. (2nd issue).

436.	**193.**	10 r. green and gold ..	1·00	1·10

OFFICIAL STAMPS

1947. King George VI official stamps of India optd. **PAKISTAN.**

O 1.	**O 1.**	3 p. slate	5	5
O 2.		½ a. purple	5	5
O 3.		9 p. green	5	5
O 4.		1 a. red	5	5
O 5.		1½ a. violet	5	5
O 6.		2 a. orange	5	5
O 7.		2½ a. violet	5	5
O 8.		4 a. brown	8	8
O 9.		8 a. violet	12	12
O 10.	**77.**	1 r. slate and brown (No. O 138) ..	15	12
O 11.		2 r. purple and brown (No. O 139) ..	30	25
O 12.		5 r. green and blue (No. O 140) ..	95	90
O 13.		10 r. purple and red (No. O 141) ..	1·75	1·60

1948. Optd. **SERVICE.** Crescent moon pointing to right.

O 14.	**2.**	3 p. red	5	5
O 15.		6 p. violet	5	5
O 37.		9 p. green	5	5
O 17.	–	1 a. blue	5	5
O 18.	–	1½ a. green	5	5
O 19.	–	2 a. red	5	5
O 20.	–	3 a. green	5	5
O 21.	**3.**	4 a. brown	5	5
O 22.	–	8 a. black	10	5
O 23.	**4.**	1 r. blue	15	8
O 24.		2 r. brown	25	15
O 61.		5 r. red	1·00	75
O 26.	**5.**	10 r. mauve	1·50	90

1949. Optd. **SERVICE.** Crescent moon pointing to left.

O 27.	–	1 a. blue	5	5
O 28.	–	1½ a. green	5	5
O 29.	–	2 a. red	5	5
O 30.	–	3 a. green	5	5
O 31.	–	8 a. black	12	10

1951. Independence. 4th Anniv. As Nos. 56, 58 and 60 but inscr. "SERVICE" instead of "PAKISTAN POSTAGE".

O 32.		3 a. purple	5	8
O 33.		4 a. green	8	8
O 34.		8 a. sepia	10	8

1954. 7th Anniv. of Independence. Nos. 65/71 optd. **SERVICE.**

O 45.		6 p violet	5	5
O 46.		9 p. blue	5	5
O 55.		1 a. carmine	5	5
O 56.		1½ a. red	5	5
O 57.		14 a. myrtle	20	8
O 50.		1 r. green	30	20
O 59.		2 r. orange	60	40

1955. 8th Anniv. of Independence. Nos. 74/5 optd. **SERVICE.**

O 63.		6 a. blue	15	15
O 64.		8 a. violet	12	12

1959. 9th Anniv. of Independence. Optd. **SERVICE.**

O 65.	**15.**	2 a. red	8	8

1961. 1st Anniv. of Republic issue optd. **SERVICE.**

O 62.	**17.**	10 r. green and orange	85	85

1961. Optd. **SERVICE.**

O 66.	**24.**	8 a. green	12	12
O 67.		1 r. blue	20	20

1961. New currency. Provisional stamps, Nos. 122, etc., optd. **SERVICE.**

O 68.	–	1 p. on 1½ a. red ..	5	5
O 69.	**2.**	2 p. on 3 p. red ..	5	5
O 70.	**24.**	3 p. on 6 p. purple ..	5	5
O 71.	–	7 p. on 1 a. carmine ..	5	5
O 72.	**24.**	13 p. on 2 a. red ..	5	5
O 73.	**15.**	13 p. on 2 a. red ..	5	5

1961. Definitive issue optd. **SERVICE.**

O 74.	**31.**	1 p. violet	5	5
O 75.		2 p. red	5	5
O 79.		3 p. purple	5	5
O 80.		5 p. blue	5	5
O 81.		7 p. green	5	5
O 82.	**32.**	10 p. brown	5	5
O 97.		13 p. slate-violet ..	5	5
O 98.		15 p. purple	5	5
O 99.		20 p. green	5	5
O 85.		40 p. purple	8	5
O 100.		50 p. blue-green ..	5	5
O 101.		75 p. red	5	5
O 103.	**33.**	1 r. red	8	8
O 104.		2 r. orange	15	12
O 105.		5 r. green	40	30

PALESTINE BC

A territory at the extreme E. of the Mediterranean Sea, captured from the Turks by Great Britain in 1917 and under Military Occupation till 1920, Palestine became a League of Nations Mandate in 1923.

1918. 10 milliemes = 1 piastre.
1927. 1,000 mils = £P1.

1.

5 MILLIEMES

(2.)

1918.

1a.	**1.**	1 p. indigo	£165	£140
3.		1 p. pale blue	1·10	1·10

1918. Surch. with T 2.

4.	**1.**	5 m. on 1 p. pale blue ..	3·00	2·50

3. (4.) (5.)

("E.E.F." = Egyptian Expeditionary Force).

1918.

5.	**3.**	1 m. brown	8	8
6.		2 m. green	10	10
7.		3 m. brown	15	15
8.		4 m. red	15	15
9.		5 m. orange	15	12
10.		1 p. blue	15	5
11.		2 p. olive	25	25
12.		5 p. purple	50	60
13.		9 p. ochre	95	1·60
14.		10 p. blue	85	1·50
15.		20 p. grey	2·75	5·00

Nos. 1/15 were also valid in Transjordan, Cilicia, Northern Egypt and Syria.

1920. Optd. with T 4.

30.	**3.**	1 m. brown	25	35
27.		2 m. green	60	70
32.		3 m. brown	25	35
33.		4 m. red	35	50
29.		5 m. orange	60	40
21.		1 p. blue	40	25
22.		2 p. olive	60	75
23.		5 p. purple	3·00	5·50
24.		9 p. ochre	3·50	9·00
25.		10 p. blue	4·00	8·00
26.		20 p. grey	7·00	14·00

1921. Optd. with T 5 (**PALESTINE** in block type).

60.	**3.**	1 m. brown	15	12
61.		2 m. green	15	15
62.		3 m. brown	15	10
63.		4 m. red	25	25
64.		5 m. orange	25	10
65.		1 p. blue	35	10
66.		2 p. olive	55	25
67.		5 p. purple	2·00	2·75
68.		9 p. ochre	5·00	6·00
69.		10 p. blue	7·00	£180
70.		20 p. grey	20·00	£450

1922. T 3 (design slightly altered) with opt. similar to T **5.**

71.	**3.**	1 m. brown	10	5
72.		2 m. yellow	15	8
73.		3 m. blue	20	5
74.		4 m. red	15	10
75.		5 m. orange	20	5
76.		6 m. green	35	15
77.		7 m. brown	45	12
78.		8 m. red	35	12
79.		1 p. grey	45	10
80.		13 m. blue	40	8
81.		2 p. olive	55	15
82.		5 p. purple	2·50	60
87.		9 p. ochre	6·00	4·50
88.		10 p. blue	4·50	1·25
89.		20 p. violet	6·00	4·00

Where the colours are similar to those of the previous issue, the stamps may be distinguished by the watermark, which is Crown over G v R for Nos. 60 to 70 and Crown over C A for Nos. 71 to 89.

6. Rachel's Tomb. **7.** Dome of the Rock.

8. Citadel, Jerusalem. **9.** Sea of Galilee.

1927.

90.	**6.**	2 m. blue	5	5
91.		3 m. green	5	5
92.	**7.**	4 m. red	75	30
104.		4 m. purple	5	5
93.	**8.**	5 m. orange	5	5
94a.	**7.**	6 m. green	8	8
95.	**8.**	7 m. red	90	25
105.		7 m. violet	5	5
96.	**7.**	8 m. brown	2·40	1·50
106.		8 m. red	5	5
97b.	**6.**	10 m. grey	5	5
98.	**7.**	13 m. blue	1·00	15
107.		13 m. brown	10	5
108a.		15 m. blue	10	5
99a.	**8.**	20 m. olive	8	5
100a.	**9.**	50 m. purple	30	10
101.		90 m. yellow-brown ..	11·00	10·00
102.		100 m. blue	40	8
103b.		200 m. violet	60	40
109.		250 m. brown	45	50
110.		500 m. red	1·00	90
111.		£P1 black	1·50	90

POSTAGE DUE STAMPS

D 1. D 2.

1920.

D 1.	**D 1.**	1 m. brown	7·00	8·00
D 2.		2 m. green	3·75	3·75
D 3.		4 m. red	4·00	4·00
D 4.		8 m. mauve	2·00	2·00
D 5.		13 m. blue	2·25	2·00

1924.

D 6.	**D 2.**	1 m. brown	45	60
D 7.		2 m. yellow ..	50	60
D 8.		4 m. green	55	60
D 9.		8 m. red	70	40
D 10.		13 m. blue	1·25	1·25
D 11.		5 p. violet	2·25	90

1928. As Type D 2, but inscr. "MIL" instead of "MILLIEME".

D 12.	**D 2.**	1 m. brown	12	12
D 13.		2 m. yellow ..	15	20
D 14.		4 m. green	20	20
D 15.		6 m. brown	45	45
D 16.		8 m. red	30	25
D 17.		10 m. grey	30	25
D 18.		13 m. blue	45	50
D 19.		20 m. olive	60	45
D 20.		50 m. violet	60	50

PANAMA O4

Country situated on the C. American isthmus. Formerly a State or Department of Colombia, Panama was proclaimed an independent republic in 1903.

1878. 100 centavos = 1 peso.
1906. 100 centesimos = 1 balboa.

1. Coat of Arms.

2. Map.

1878. Impert. The 50 c. is larger.

1.	**1.**	5 c. green	12·00	12·00
2.		10 c. blue	35·00	35·00
3.		20 c. red	8·00	19·00
4.		50 c. yellow	8·00	

1887. Perf.

5.	**2.**	1 c. black on green ..	45	65
6.		2 c. black on pink ..	45	75
7.		5 c. black on blue ..	45	30
7a.		5 c. black on grey ..	45	30
8.		10 c. black on yellow ..	45	45
9.		20 c. black on lilac ..	60	35
10.		50 c. brown	75	50

3. Map of Panama. **4.**

1892.

12a.**3.** 1 c. green 12 12
12b. 2 c. red 20 15
12c. 5 c. blue 30 25
12d. 10 c. orange 15 15
12e. 20 c. violet 20 15
12f. 50 c. brown 25 20
12g. 1 p. lake 2·75 2·00

1894. Surch. **HABILITADO 1894** and value.
13. **3.** 1 c. on 2 c. red 20 20
15. **2.** 5 c. on 20 c. black on lilac 60 60
18. 10 c. on 50 c. brown 75 75

1903. Optd. **REPUBLICA DE PANAMA.**
70. **3.** 1 c. green 45 45
36. 2 c. red 95 95
37. 5 c. blue 50 50
38. 10 c. orange 75 75
39. 20 c. violet 60 1·10
75. **2.** 50 c. brown 7·50 7·50
40. **3.** 50 c. brown 2·50 2·50
41. 1 p. lake 22·00 22·00

1903. Optd. **PANAMA** twice.
53. **3.** 1 c. green 12 12
54. 2 c. red 12 12
55. 5 c. blue 15 15
56. 10 c. orange 15 15
64. 20 c. violet 55 60
65. 50 c. brown 1·25 1·25
66. 1 p. lake 2·50 2·50

1904. Optd. **Republica de Panama.**
94. **3.** 1 c. green 20 20
97. 2 c. red 25 25
98. 5 c. blue 25 25
99. 10 c. orange 25 25
100. 20 c. violet 30 30
103. **2.** 50 c. brown 1·25 1·25
104. **3.** 1 p. lake 7·50 7·50

1905.
151. **4.** ½ c. orange 20 15
136. 1 c. green 30 30
137. 2 c. red 35 35

1906. Surch. **PANAMA** twice and new value and thick bar.
138. **3.** 1 c. on 20 c. violet 12 12
139. 2 c. on 50 c. brown 12 12
140. 5 c. on 1 p. lake 25 25

5. Panamanian Flag. **6.** Vasco Nunez de Balboa.

7. F. de Cordoba. **8.** Arms of Panama.

9. J. Arosemena. **10.** M. J. Hurtado. **11.** J. de Obaldia.

1906.
142. **5.** ½ c. red, bl., grn. & orge. 25 20
143. **6.** 1 c. black and green 25 20
144. **7.** 2 c. black and red 25 20
145. **8.** 2½ c. red 25 20
146. **9.** 5 c. black and blue 25 20
147. **10.** 8 c. black and purple 50 40
148. **11.** 10 c. black and violet 45 30
149. – 25 c. black and brown 1·25 70
150. – 50 c. black 2·25 1·50
DESIGNS: 25 c. Tomas Herrera. 50 c. Jose de Fabrega.

14. Balboa. **15.** De Cordoba. **16.** Arms.

17. Arosemena. **18.** Hurtado. **19.** Obaldia.

1909.
152. **14.** 1 c. black and green 30 20
153. **15.** 2 c. black and red 30 20
154. **16.** 2½ c. red 35 20
155. **17.** 5 c. black and blue 60 15
156. **18.** 8 c. black and purple 1·90 1·75
157. **19.** 10 c. black and purple 90 45

20. Balboa viewing Pacific Ocean. **21.** Balboa reaches the Pacific.

1913. Discovery of Pacific Ocean. 400th Anniv.
160. **20.** 2½ c. yell.-grn. & grn. 65 65

1915. Panama Exhibition and Opening of Canal.
161. – ½ c. black and olive 20 15
162. – 1 c. black and green 25 20
163. **21.** 2 c. black and red 35 20
164. – 2½ c. black and red 40 30
165. – 3 c. black and violet 40 30
166. – 5 c. black and blue 45 25
167. – 10 c. black and orange 1·10 45
168. – 20 c. black and brown 4·25 1·90
DESIGNS: ½ c. Chorrera Falls. 1 c. Map of Panama Canal. 2½ c. Cathedral Ruins, Old Panama. 3 c. Palace of Arts, National Exhibition. 5 c. Gatun Locks. 10 c. Culebra Cut. 20 c. Archway, S. Domingo Monastery.

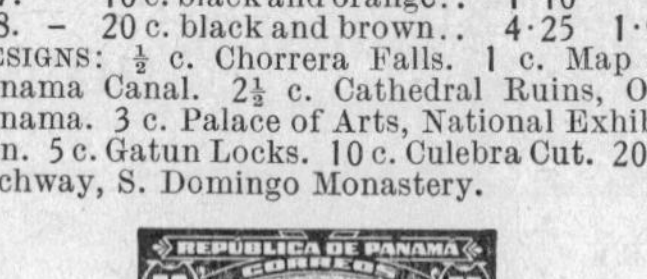

22. Balboa Docks.

1918. Views on Panama Canal.
178. – 12 c. black and violet 5·00 1·90
179. – 15 c. black and blue 2·50 1·10
180. – 24 c. black and brown 4·25 1·50
181. **22.** 50 c. black and orange 4·25 4·25
182. – 1 b. black and violet 6·00 6·00
DESIGNS: 12 c. S.S. "Panama" in Gaillard Cut, north. 15 c. S.S. "Panama" in Gaillard Cut, south. 24 c. S.S. "Cristobal" in Gatun Lock. 1 b. Steamship in San Pedro Miguel Locks.

1919. Founding of City of Panama. 400th Anniv. No. 164 surch. **1519 1919 2 CENTESIMOS 2.**
183. 2 c. on 2½ c. black and red 35 35

23. Arms of Panama. **24.** Vallarino.

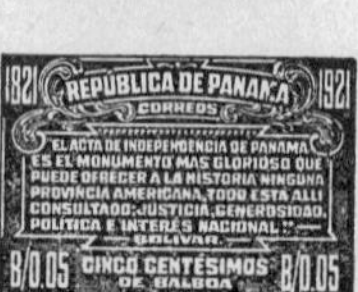

26. Bolivar's speech. **28.** Hurtado.

1921. Independence Cent. Dated "1821 1921".
184. **23.** ½ c. orange 20 15
185. **24.** 1 c. green 20 12
186. – 2 c. red ("Land Gate", Panama City) 25 15
187. **24.** 2½ c. red (Bolivar) 75 65
188. – 3 c. violet (Cervantes Statue) 75 65
189. **26.** 5 c. blue 35 20
190. **24.** 8 c. olive (Carlos Ycaza) 95 90
191. – 10 c. violet (Government House 1821–1921) 80 70
192. – 15 c. blue (Balboa Stat.) 1·00 80
193. – 20 c. brown (Los Santos Church) 1·90 1·75
194. **24.** 24 c. sepia (Herrera) 2·25 1·90
195. – 50 c. black (Fabrega) 3·25 2·50

1921. Manuel Jose Hurtado (writer). Birth Cent.
196. **28.** 2 c. green 35 35

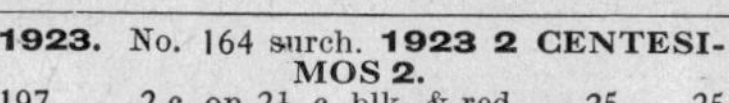

1923. No. 164 surch. **1923 2 CENTESIMOS 2.**
197. 2 c. on 2½ c. blk. & red 25 25

29. **30.** Simon Bolivar.

31. Statue of Bolivar. **32.** Congress Hall, Panama.

1924.
198. **29.** ½ c. orange 5 5
199. 1 c. green 5 5
200. 2 c. red 8 5
201. 5 c. blue 15 5
202. 10 c. violet 20 10
203. 12 c. olive 20 15
204. 15 c. blue 25 15
205. 24 c. brown 55 40
206. 50 c. orange 1·50 90
207. 1 b. black 2·50 1·90

1926. Bolivar Congress.
208. **30.** ½ c. orange 15 12
209. 1 c. green 15 12
210. 2 c. red 25 25
211. 4 c. grey 25 25
212. 5 c. blue 35 25
213. **31.** 8 c. purple 75 65
214. 10 c. violet 65 40
215. 12 c. olive 75 65
216. 15 c. blue 85 75
217. 20 c. brown 1·50 1·25
218. **32.** 24 c. slate 1·90 85
219. 50 c. black 3·00 2·50

34. "Spirit of St. Louis" over Panama.

1928. Lindbergh's Flying Tour.
222. – 2 c. red on rose 50 50
223. **34.** 5 c. blue on green 60 60
DESIGN—VERT. 2 c. "Spirit of St. Louis" and old tower, Panama.

1928. Independence. 25th Anniv. Optd. **1903. NOV 3 BRE 1928.**
224. **28.** 2 c. green 30 25

1929. Air. Optd. **CORREO AEREO** or surch. also. With or without aeroplane.
238. **E 1.** 5 c. on 10 c. orange 50 40
228. 10 c. orange 40 40
268. 10 c. on 20 c. brown 1·10 60
229. 15 c. on 10 c. orange 45 40
269. 20 c. brown 1·00 50
225. 25 c. on 10 c. orange 85 75
230. 25 c. on 20 c. brown 1·90 1·25
239. **22.** 1 b. violet (No. 182) 9·50 9·50

35. **36.**

1930. Air.
231. **35.** 5 c. blue 12 5
232. 5 c. orange 20 8
233. 7 c. red 20 5
234. 8 c. black 20 5
235. 15 c. green 25 5
236. 20 c. red 35 5
237. 25 c. blue 65 65

1930. Air.
244. **36.** 5 c. blue 12 5
245. 10 c. orange 20 15
246. 30 c. violet 5·50 5·00
247. 50 c. red 75 45
248. 1 b. black 5·50 4·25

1930. Bolivar's Death Cent. Surch. **1830-1930 17 DE DICIEMBRE UN CENTESIMO.**
249. **30.** 1 c. on 4 c. grey 25 20

37. Seaplane over old Panama. **38.** Manuel Amador Guerrero.

1931. Air. Opening of service between Panama City and western provinces.
250. **37.** 5 c. blue 95 95

1932. Optd. **HABILITADA** or surch. also.
251. **23.** ½ c. orange (postage) 20 20
252. **30.** ½ c. orange 20 20
253. 1 c. green 20 20
270. **26.** 1 c. on 5 c. blue 25 25
254. **30.** 2 c. red 15 15
255. 5 c. blue 30 25
256. – 10 c. violet (No. 191) 45 25
258. **31.** 10 c. on 12 c. olive 75 45
259. 10 c. on 15 c. blue 40 30
257. 20 c. brown 80 60
260. **35.** 20 c. on 25 c. blue (air) 3·75 45

1932. Dr. Guerrero (first president of republic). Birth Cent.
261. **38.** 2 c. red 25 20

40. National Institute. **(41.)**

1934. National Institute. 25th Anniv. Inscr. "INSTITUTO NACIONAL 1909-1934".
262. – 1 c. green 55 30
263. – 2 c. red 55 30
264. – 5 c. blue 75 60
265. **40.** 10 c. brown 1·25 95
266. – 12 c. green 1·90 1·25
267. – 15 c. blue 3·00 1·75
DESIGNS—VERT. 1 c. J. D. de Obaldia. 2 c. E. A. Morales. 5 c. Sphinx and Quotation from Emerson. HORIZ. 12 c. J. A. Facio. 15 c. R. Arosemena.

1936. Pablo Arosemena. Birth Cent.
(a) Postage. Surch. as T **41**, but without **CORREO AEREO.**
271. **29.** 2 c. on 24 c. brown 25 25
(b) Air. Surch. with T **41.**
272. **29.** 5 c. on 50 c. orange 1·10 1·10

DESIGNS: 1 c. "Panama" (Old tree). 2 c. "La Pollera" (woman in costume). 5 c. Bolivar. 10 c. Ruins of Old Panama Cathedral. 15 c. Garcia y Santos. 20 c. Madden Dam. 25 c. Columbus. 50 c. Gaillard Cut. 1 b. Panama Cathedral.

42. Custom House Ruins, Portobelo.

DESIGNS—HORIZ. 20 c. Panama. 50 c. San Pedro Migue Locks. 1 b. Courts of Justice. VERT. 5 c. Urraca Monument. 30 c. Balboa Monument.

44. "Man's Genius Uniting the Oceans".

1936. 4th Spanish-American Postal Congress (1st issue). Insc. "IV CONGRESO POSTAL AMERICO-ESPANOL".
273. **42.** ½ c. orange (postage) 15 12
274. – 1 c. green 20 15
275. – 2 c. red 20 15
276. – 5 c. blue 20 15
277. – 10 c. violet 30 30
278. – 15 c. blue 45 30
279. – 20 c. red 75 50
280. – 25 c. brown 95 75
281. – 50 c. orange 2·50 1·40
282. – 1 b. black 6·00 4·25
283. – 5 c. blue (air) 35 30
284. **44.** 10 c. orange 50 45
285. – 20 c. red 1·60 1·10
286. – 30 c. violet 2·25 2·10
287. – 50 c. red 5·00 4·00
288. – 1 b. black 6·50 4·75

1937. 4th Spanish-American Postal Congress (2nd issue). Nos. 273/8 optd. **UPU.**
289. **42.** ½ c. orange (postage) 15 15
290. – 1 c. green 15 15
291. – 2 c. red 15 15
292. – 5 c. blue 25 15
293. – 10 c. violet 35 30
294. – 15 c. blue 2·00 1·50
295. – 20 c. red 60 50
296. – 25 c. brown 65 65
297. – 50 c. orange 2·25 1·90
298. – 1 b. black 6·50 5·00
299. – 5 c. blue (air) 30 30
300. **44.** 10 c. orange 45 45
301. – 20 c. red 1·00 90
302. – 30 c. violet 2·50 2·25
303. – 50 c. red 14·00 13·00
304. – 1 b. black 14·00 13·00

1937. Optd. **1937-38.**
305. **30.** ½ c. orange 75 65
306. **24.** 1 c. green 25 15
307. **30.** 1 c. green 25 15
308. **28.** 2 c. green 30 20
309. **30.** 2 c. red 30 20

1937. Surch. **1937-38** and value.
310. **30.** 2 c. on 4 c. grey 25 20
311. **34.** 2 c. on 8 c. olive 25 20
312. **31.** 2 c. on 8 c. purple 25 20
313. 2 c. on 10 c. violet 25 20
314. 2 c. on 12 c. olive 25 20
315. – 2 c. on 15 c. (No. 192) 25 20
316. **24.** 2 c. on 24 c. sepia 25 20
317. 2 c. on 50 c. black 25 20

1937. Air. Optd. **CORREO AEREO** or surch. also.
318. **30.** 5 c. blue 75 75
319. **31.** 5 c. on 15 c. blue 75 75
320. 5 c. on 20 c. brown 75 75
321. **32.** 5 c. on 24 c. slate 75 75
322. **22.** 5 c. on 1 b. blk. & violet 75 75
323. – 10 c. on 10 c. violet (191) 2·25 2·25
324. **32.** 10 c. on 50 c. black 2·25 2·25

45. Fire-Engine.

46. Firemen's Monument. **47.** Fire-Brigade Badge.

1937. Fire Brigade. 50th Anniv. Inscr. "JUBILEO CUERPO DE BOMBEROS".
325. – ½ c. orange (postage) 20 15
326. – 1 c. green 25 15
327. – 2 c. red 25 20
328. **45.** 5 c. blue 30 30
329. **46.** 10 c. violet 50 50
330. – 12 c. green 75 60

331. **47.** 5 c. blue (air) 30 30
332. – 10 c. orange 45 40
333. – 20 c. red 90 70
DESIGNS—VERT. ½ c. R. Arango. 1 c. J. A. Guizado. 10 c. (No. 332), F. Arosemena. 12 c. D. H. Brandon. 20 c. J. G. Duque. HORIZ. 2 c. House on fire.

50. Baseball Player.

1938. Air. C. American and Caribbean Olympic Games. Inscr. as in T **50**.
334. – 1 c. red (Basket-ball) 1·00 25
335. **50.** 2 c. green 1·00 20
336. – 7 c. grey (Swimmer) 1·50 30
337. – 8 c. brown (Boxers) 1·75 40
338. – 15 c. blue (Footballer) 5·00 2·00
The 1 c. and 15 c. are vert., the rest horiz.

1938. Opening of Aguaduice Normal School, Santiago. Optd. **NORMAL DE SANTIAGO JUNIO 5 1938** or surch. also.
340. **29.** 2 c. red (postage) 25 25

341. **36.** 7 c. on 30 c. violet (air) 75 75
342. **35.** 8 c. on 15 c. green 75 75

51. Old Panama Cathedral and Statue of Liberty.

1938. 150th Anniv. of U.S. Constitution. Flags in red, white and blue.
343. **51.** 1 c. blk. & grn. (post.) 25 25
344. 2 c. black and red 35 35
345. 5 c. black and blue 60 30
346. 12 c. black and olive 95 45
347. 15 c. black and blue 1·25 75

348. 7 c. black and grey (air) 25 25
349. 8 c. black and blue 40 40
350. 15 c. black and brown 65 65
351. 50 c. black and orange 7·50 7·50
352. 1 b. black 8·00 8·00

52. Pierre and Marie Curie. **53.** Gatun Lock.

1939. Obligatory Tax. Cancer Research Fund. Dated "1939".
353. **52.** 1 c. red 65 25
354. 1 c. green 65 25
355. 1 c. orange 65 25
356. 1 c. blue 65 25

1939. Opening of Panama Canal. 25th Anniv. Inscr. "XXV ANIVERSARIO DE LA APERTURA DEL CANAL", etc.
357. **53.** ½ c. yellow (postage) 30 10
358. – 1 c. green 40 10
359. – 2 c. red 45 10
360. – 5 c. blue 55 15
361. – 10 c. violet 75 35
362. – 12 c. olive 70 40
363. – 15 c. blue 75 65
364. – 50 c. orange 1·40 1·40
365. – 1 b. brown 2·50 2·50
DESIGNS: 1 c. Pedro Miguel Locks. 2 c. Allegory of canal construction. 5 c. Culebra Cut. 10 c. Ferry-boat. 12 c. Aerial view. 15 c. Gen. Gorgas. 50 c. M. A. Guerrero. 1 b. Woodrow Wilson.

366. – 1 c. red (air) 25 8
367. – 2 c. green 30 10
368. – 5 c. blue 35 15
369. – 10 c. violet 65 25
370. – 15 c. blue 95 30
371. – 20 c. red 2·50 1·25
372. – 50 c. brown 3·25 75
373. – 1 b. black 5·50 3·50
PORTRAITS: 1 c. B. Porras. 2 c. Wm. H. Taft. 5 c. P. J. Sosa. 10 c. L. B. Wise. 15 c. A. Reclus. 20 c. Gen. Goethals. 50 c. F. de Lesseps. 1 b. Theodore Roosevelt.

54. Flags of American Republics. **54a.** "Liberty".

1940. Air. Pan-American Union. 50th Anniv.
374. **54.** 15 c. blue 75 40

1940. Air. No. 370 surch. **55.**
375. 5 c. on 15 c. blue 25 25

No. 363 surch. **AEREO SIETE.**
376. 7 c. on 15 c. blue 50 40

No. 371 surch. **SIETE.**
377. 7 c. on 20 c. red 50 40

No. 374 surch **8—8.**
378. **54.** 8 c. on 15 c. blue 50 40

1941. Obligatory Tax. Cancer Research Fund. Optd. **LUCHA CONTRA EL CANCER.**
379. **29.** 1 c. green 30 25

1941. Enactment of New Constitution. (a) Postage. Optd. **CONSTITUCION 1941.**
380. **29.** ½ c. orange 20 12
381. 1 c. green 20 12
382. 2 c. red 20 15
383. 5 c. blue 25 20
384. 10 c. violet 50 35
385. 15 c. blue 75 65
386. 50 c. orange 2·50 1·50
387. 1 b. black 6·50 4·50

(b) Air. Surch. **CONSTITUCION 1941 AEREO** and value in figures.
388. **E 1.** 7 c. on 10 c. orange 80 85
389. **29.** 15 c. on 24 c. brown 2·25 2·00

(c) Air. Optd. **CONSTITUCION 1941.**
390. **35.** 20 c. red 2·50 1·50
391. **36.** 50 c. red 4·50 3·50
392. 1 b. black 14·00 9·50

1941. Obligatory Tax. Cancer Research Fund. Dated "1940".
393. **52.** 1 c. red 65 20
394. 1 c. green 65 20
395. 1 c. orange 65 20
396. 1 c. blue 65 20

1942. Telegraph stamps as T **54a** optd. or surch. (a) Optd. **CORREOS 1942** and (No. 397) surch. **2c.**
397. 2 c. on 5 c. blue 45 40
398. 10 c. violet 65 65

(b) Air. Optd. **CORREO AEREO 1942.**
399. 20 c. brown 1·75 1·40

55. Flags of Panama and Costa Rica.

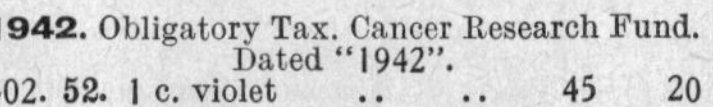

1942. Revised Frontier Agreement between Panama and Costa Rica. First Anniv
400. **55.** 2 c. red (postage) 25 20
401. 15 c. green (air) 95 20

1942. Obligatory Tax. Cancer Research Fund. Dated "1942".
402. **52.** 1 c. violet 45 20

56. Balboa reaches the Pacific.

57. J. D. Arosemena Normal School. **58.** Alejandro Melendez.

1942. (a) Postage stamps.
403. – ½ c. red, blue and violet 5 5
404. – ½ c. blue, orange and red 10 5
405. – 1 c. green 10 5
406. – 1 c. red 5 5
407. – 2 c. red ("ACARRERO") 15 8
408. – 2 c. red ("ACARREO") 40 10
409. – 2 c. black and red 12 8
410. **56.** 5 c. black and blue 20 8
411. – 5 c. blue 20 10
412. – 10 c. orange and red 40 20
413. – 10 c. orange and purple 35 15
414. – 15 c. black and blue 65 15
415. – 15 c. black 35 30
416. – 50 c. black and red 1·50 40
417. – 1 b. black 2·75 75
DESIGNS—VERT. ½ c. National flag. 1 c. Farm girl. 10 c. Golden Altar, Church of St. Jose. 50 c. San Blas Indian woman and child. HORIZ. 2 c. Oxen drawing sugar cart. 15 c. St. Thomas's Hospital. 1 b. National highway.

(b) Air.
418. – 2 c. red 1·25 45
419. – 7 c. red 1·25 20
420. – 8 c. black and brown 15 5
421. – 10 c. black and blue 20 20
422. – 15 c. violet 25 5
423. – 15 c. grey 30 12
424. **57.** 20 c. brown 35 5
425. 20 c. green 30 20
426. – 50 c. green 80 40
427. – 50 c. red 7·50 7·50
428. – 50 c. blue 1·75 1·60
429. – 1 b. orange, yell. & black 1·75 1·10
DESIGNS—HORIZ. 2 c., 7 c. Sword-fish. 8 c., 10 c. Gate of Glory, Porto Bello. 15 c. Taboga Is. 50 c. Fire Brigade H.Q., Panama City. 1 b. Idol (Golden Beast).

1943. Obligatory Tax. Cancer Research Fund. Dated "1943".
433. **52.** 1 c. green 65 25
434. 1 c. red 65 25
435. 1 c. orange 65 25
436. 1 c. blue 65 25

1943. Air.
437. **58.** 3 b. grey 7·50 6·50
438. – 5 b. blue (T. Lefevre) 11·00 9·50

1945. Obligatory Tax. Cancer Research Fund. Dated "1945".
439. **52.** 1 c. red 65 25
440. 1 c. green 65 25
441. 1 c. orange 65 25
442. 1 c. blue 65 25

1946. Obligatory Tax. Cancer Research Fund. Surch. **CANCER B/.0.01 1947.**
443. **29.** 1 c. on ½ c. orange 65 20
444. 1 c. on 1 c. green 65 20
445. – 1 c. on ½ c. red, blue and violet (No. 403) 65 20
446. **29.** 1 c. on 12 c. olive 65 20
447. 1 c. on 24 c. brown 65 20

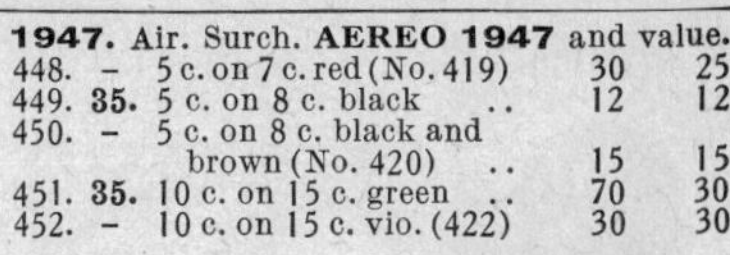

1947. Air. Surch. **AEREO 1947** and value.
448. – 5 c. on 7 c. red (No. 419) 30 25
449. **35.** 5 c. on 8 c. black 12 12
450. – 5 c. on 8 c. black and brown (No. 420) 15 15
451. **35.** 10 c. on 15 c. green 70 30
452. – 10 c. on 15 c. vio. (422) 30 30

59. Flag of Panama. **60.** National Theatre.

1947. National Constitutional Assembly. 2nd Anniv. Inscr. as in T **59.**
453. **59.** 2 c. carmine, red and blue (post.) 12 10
454. – 5 c. blue 20 15
455. **60.** 8 c. violet (air) 45 35
DESIGN—As T **59**: 5 c. Arms of Panama.

1947. Cancer Research Fund. Dated "1947".
456. **51.** 1 c. red 65 20
457. 1 c. green 65 20
458. 1 c. orange 65 20
459. 1 c. blue 65 20

1947. Surch. **HABILITADO CORREOS** and value.
460. **38.** ½ c. on 8 c. black 8 8
461. – ½ c. on 8c. black and brown (No. 420) 8 8
462. – 1 c. on 7 c. red (No. 419) 10 10
463. **60.** 2 c. on 8 c. violet 15 12

1947. Surch. **Habilitada CORREOS B/.0.50.**
464. **29.** 50 c. on 24 c. brown 95 95

61. J. A. Arango. **62.** Firemen's Monument.

1948. Air. Honouring members of the Revolutionary Junta of 1903. Inscr. as in T **61.**
465. – 3 c. black and blue 25 25
466. **61.** 5 c. black and brown 40 35
467. – 10 c. black and orange 40 30
468. – 15 c. black and claret 45 40
469. – 20 c. black and red 75 60
470. – 50 c. black 1·75 1·25
471. – 1 b. black and green 5·50 5·00
472. – 2 b. black and yellow 13·00 11·00
PORTRAITS—HORIZ. 3 c. M. A. Guerrero. 10 c. F. Boyd. 15 c. R. Arias. VERT. 20 c. M. Espinosa. 50 c. C. C. Arosemena. 1 b. N. de Obarrio. 2 b. T. Arias.

1948. Colon Fire Brigade. 50th Anniv. Inscr. as in T **62.**
473. **62.** 5 c. black and red 15 12
474. – 10 c. black and orange 25 15
475. – 20 c. black and blue 45 35
476. – 25 c. black and brown 45 45
477. – 50 c. black and violet 90 45
478. – 1 b. black and green 2·25 1·60
DESIGNS—HORIZ. 10 c. Fire engine. 20 c. Fire hose. 25 c. Fire Brigade Headquarters. VERT. 50 c. Commander Walker. 1 b. First Fire-Brigade Commander.

65. F. D. Roosevelt and J. D. Arosemena. **66.** Roosevelt Monument, Panama.

1948. Air. Homage to F. D. Roosevelt.
479. **65.** 5 c. black and red 15 12
480. – 10 c. orange 25 20
481. **66.** 20 c. green 40 35
482. – 50 c. black and blue 1·10 75
483. – 1 b. black 2·50 1·75
DESIGNS—HORIZ. 10 c. Woman with palm symbolizing "Four Freedoms". 50 c. Map of Panama Canal. VERT. 1 b. Portrait of Roosevelt.

63. Cervantes. 64. Monument to Cervantes.

1948. Cervantes. 400th Birth Anniv.
484. 63. 2 c. black and red (post.) 25 25

485. 64. 5 c. black and blue (air) 20 10
486. – 10 c. black and mauve .. 40 30
DESIGN—HORIZ. 10 c. Don Quixote and Sancho Panza (inscr. as T 64).

1949. Air. Jose Gabriel Duque (philanthropist). Birth Cert. No. 486 optd. **"CENTENARIO DE/JOSE GABRIEL DUQUE"/"18 de Enero de 1949".**
487. 10 c. blk. & mauve .. 50 35

1949. Obligatory Tax. Cancer Research Fund. Surch. **LUCHA CONTRA EL CANCER** and value.
488. 65. 1 c. on 5 c. blk. and red 40 5
489. – 1 c. on 10 c. orange (No. 480) 40 5

1949. Cancer Research Fund. Dated "1949".
504. 52. 1 c. brown 40 20

1949. Incorporation of Chiriqui Province Cent. Stamps of 1930 and 1942 optd. **1849-1949 CHIRIQUI CENTENARIO.**

(a) On postage stamps as No. 407.
(i) Without surch.
491. – 2 c. red 12 10

(ii) Surch. **1 UN CENTESIMO 1** also.
490. – 1 c. on 2 c. red .. 12 10

(b) Air.
492. – 2 c. red (No. 418) .. 12 10
493. 35. 5 c. blue 30 30
494. – 15 c. grey (No. 423) .. 60 45
495. – 50 c. red (No. 427) .. 3·50 2·25

1949. U.P.U. 75th Anniv. Stamps of 1930 and 1942/3 optd. **1874 1949 U.P.U.** No. 625 is also surch. **B/O.25.**
496. – 1 c. grn. (No. 405) (post.) 25 20
497. – 2 c. red (No. 407) .. 35 25
498. 56. 5 c. blue 60 45

499. – 2 c. red (No. 418) (air) .. 25 12
500. 35. 5 c. orange 55 50
501. – 10 c. black and blue (No. 421) 75 75
502. 58. 25 c. on 3 b. grey .. 75 75
503. – 50 c. red (No. 427) .. 4·75 3·00

67. Father Xavier. 68. St. Xavier University.

1949. Founding of St. Xavier University. Bicent.
505. 67. 2 c. blk. & red (post.) .. 25 12
506. 68. 5 c. black & blue (air) 35 12

69. Dr. Carlos J. Finlay. 70. Mosquito.

1950. Dr. Finlay (medical research worker).
507. 69. 2 c. black & red (post.) 35 12

508. 70. 5 c. black & blue (air) .. 3·50 60

1950. San Martin. Death Cent. Optd. **CENTENARIO del General (or Gral.) Jose de San Martin 17 de Agosto de 1950** or surch. also. The 50 c. is optd. **AEREO** as well.
509. – 1 c. grn. (No. 405) (post.) 10 8
510. – 2 c. on ½ c. (No. 404) .. 12 10
511. 56. 5 c. black and blue .. 20 15

512. – 2 c. red (No. 418) (air) .. 30 30
513. 35. 5 c. orange 30 30
514 – 10 c. blk. & bl. (No. 421) 45 45
515 35. 25 c. blue .. .. 1·25 1·00
516 – 50 c. blk. & vio. (No. 477) 2·10 1·75

71. Badge. 72. Stadium.

1950. Obligatory Tax. Physical Culture Fund. Dated "1950".
517. – 1 c. black and red .. 80 45
518. 71. 1 c. black and blue .. 80 45
519. 72. 1 c. black and green .. 80 45
520. – 1 c. black and orange .. 80 45
521. – 1 c. black and violet .. 1·25 45
DESIGNS—VERT. No. 520, as T 72 but medallion changed and incorporating four "F"s. No. 521, Discus thrower. HORIZ. No. 517, as T 72 but front of Stadium.

1951. Jean-Baptiste de La Salle (educational reformer). Birth Tercent. Optd. **Tercer Centenario del Natalicio de San Juan Bautista de La Salle. 1651-1951.**
522. 2 c. black & red (No. 409) 10 10
523. 5 c. blue (No. 411) .. 20 12

1952. Air. Surch. **AEREO 1952** and value.
524. 2 c. on 10 c. black & blue (No. 421) 15 12
525. 5 c. on 10 c. black & blue (No. 421) 25 8
526. 1 b. on 5 b. blue (No. 438) 32·00 25·00

1952. Surch. **1952** and figure of value.
527. 1 c. on ½ c. (No. 404) .. 10 5

Air. Optd. **AEREO** also.
528. 5 c. on 2 c. (No. 408) .. 12 8
529. 25 c. on 10 c. (No. 413) .. 75 55

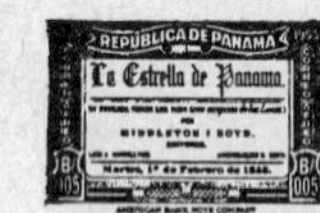

73. Isabella the Catholic. 74. Masthead of "La Estrella".

1952. Isabella the Catholic. 500th Birth Anniv.
530. 73. 1 c. blk. & grn. (postage) 8 5
531. 2 c. black and red .. 10 8
532. 5 c. black and blue .. 12 10
533. 10 c. black and violet .. 25 20

534. 4 c. black & orange (air) 8 8
535. 5 c. black and olive .. 10 10
536. 10 c. black and buff .. 30 20
537. 25 c. black and slate .. 50 30
538. 50 c. black and brown .. 1·25 65
539. 1 b. black .. .. 4·00 3·00

1953. Surch. **B/.0.01 1953.**
540. 1 c. on 10 c. (No. 413) .. 5 5
541. 1 c. on 15 c. blk. (No. 415) 5 5

1953. Air. No. 421 surch. **5 1953.**
542. 5 c. on 10 c. black & blue 35 10

1953. Air. "La Estrella de Panama", Newspaper. Cent.
543. 74. 5 c. red 15 12
544. 10 c. blue 20 20

75. Pres. and Senora Amador Guerrero.

1953. Panama Republic. 50th Anniv. Inscr. "1903 1953".
545. – 2 c. violet (postage) .. 10 5
546. 75. 5 c. orange 12 5
547. – 12 c. purple 20 15
548. – 20 c. indigo 35 20
549. – 50 c. yellow .. .. 1·00 50
550. – 1 b. blue .. .. 2·00 1·25
DESIGNS—VERT. 2 c. Blessing the flag. 50 c. Old Town Hall. HORIZ. 12 c. J. A. Santos and J. De La Ossa. 20 c. Revolutionary council. 1 b. Obverse and reverse of coin.

551. – 2 c. blue (air) 8 5
552. – 5 c. green 10 5
553. – 7 c. grey 20 10
554. – 25 c. black .. .. 2·25 75
555. – 50 c. chocolate .. 1·00 60
556. – 1 b. orange .. .. 3·50 1·50
DESIGNS—VERT. 2 c. Act of Independence. HORIZ. 5 c. Pres. and Senora Remon Cantera. 7 c. Girl in national costume. 25 c. National flower. 50 c. Salazar, Huertas and Domingo. 1 b. National dance.

1954. Surch. in figures.
557. – 3 c. on 1 c. red (No. 406) (postage) 8 5

558. 74. 1 c. on 5 c. red (air) .. 8 5
559. 1 c. on 10 c. blue .. 8 5

76. Gen. Herrera at Conference Table.

DESIGNS — VERT. 3 c. Equestrian statue. HORIZ. 1 b. Cavalry charge.

1954. Gen. Herrera. Death Cent. Inscr. "1854 1954".
560. – 3 c. violet (postage) .. 12 5

561. 76. 6 c. green (air) .. 15 8
562. – 1 b. black and red .. 3·50 2·75

77. Rotary Emblem and Map.

1955. Air. Rotary International. 50th Anniv.
563. 77. 6 c. violet 12 8
564. 21 c. red 50 30
565. 1 b. black .. .. 5·50 4·50

78. Tocumen Airport. 79. President Remon Cantera.

1955.
566. 78. ½ c. brown 5 5

1955. National Mourning for Pres. Remon Cantera.
567. 79 3 c. blk. & pur. (post.) 10 5
568. 6 c. black & violet (air) 12 8

80. V. de la Guardia y Azala and M. Chiaria. 81. F. de Lesseps (engineer).

1955. Cent. of Cocle Province.
569. 80. 5 c. violet 15 5

1955. De Lesseps. 150th Birth Anniv. Inscr. as in T 81.
570. 81. 3 c. lake on pink (post.) 20 5
571. – 25 c. blue on blue .. 55 35
572. – 50 c. violet on lilac .. 1·25 95

573. – 5 c. myrtle on green (air) 15 8
574. – 1 b. black & magenta .. 2·25 1·90
DESIGNS—VERT. 5 c. P. J. Sosa. 50 c. T. Roosevelt. HORIZ. 25 c. First excavations for Panama Canal. 1 b. First ship passing through canal, and De Lesseps.

1955. Air. No. 564 surch.
575. 77. 15 c. on 21 c. red .. 40 30

82. Pres. Eisenhower (United States). 83. Bolivar Statue.

1956. Air. Pan-American Congress, Panama and First Congress. 30th Anniv. Inscr. "1826 CONGRESO DE PANAMA 1956".
576. – 6 c. black and blue .. 30 20
577. – 6 c. black and bistre .. 30 20
578. – 6 c. black and emerald 30 20
579. – 6 c. sepia and green .. 30 20
580. – 6 c. green and yellow .. 30 20
581. – 6 c. green and violet .. 30 20
582. – 6 c. blue and lilac .. 30 20
583. – 6 c. green and purple .. 30 20
584. – 6 c. blue and olive .. 30 20
585. – 6 c. sepia and yellow .. 30 20
586. – 6 c. blue and sepia .. 30 20
587. – 6 c. green and magenta 30 20
588. – 6 c. sepia and red .. 30 20
589. – 6 c. green and blue .. 30 20
590. – 6 c. sepia and blue .. 30 20
591. – 6 c. black and orange .. 30 20
592. – 6 c. sepia and grey .. 30 20
593. – 6 c. black and pink .. 30 20
594. 82. 6 c. blue and red .. 55 30
595. – 6 c. blue and grey .. 30 20
596. – 6 c. green and brown .. 30 20
597. 83. 20 c. grey 55 50
598. – 50 c. green 95 95
599. – 1 b. sepia .. .. 3·25 1·60
PRESIDENTIAL PORTRAITS as T 82: No. 576, Argentina. 577, Bolivia. 578, Brazil. 579, Chile. 580, Colombia. 581, Costa Rica. 582, Cuba. 583, Dominican Republic. 584, Ecuador, 585, Guatemala. 586, Haiti. 587, Honduras. 588, Mexico. 589, Nicaragua. 590, Panama. 591, Paraguay. 592, Peru. 593, Salvador. 595, Uruguay. 596, Venezuela. As T 83—HORIZ. 50 c. Bolivar Hall. VERT. 1 b. Bolivar. Medallion.

84. Arms of Panama City. 85. Dr. C. A. Mendoza.

1956. 6th Inter-American Congress of Municipalities, Panama City. Inscr. as in T 84.
600. 84. 3 c. green (postage) .. 12 5

601. – 25 c. red (air) 50 30
602. – 50 c. black .. .. 1·00 65
DESIGNS: 25 c. Ruins in Old Panama. 50 c. Municipal Building.

1956. Pres. Carlos A. Mendoza. Birth Cent.
604. 85. 10 c. green and red .. 20 12

86. Dr. Belisario Porras.

DESIGNS —HORIZ. 15 c. (No. 605) National Archives 15 c. (No. 608), St. Thomas's Hospital VERT. 5 c. Porras Monument.

1956. Dr. Porras. Birth Cent. Inscr. as in T 86.
605. – 15 c. grey (postage) .. 35 15
606. 86. 25 c. blue and red .. 60 35

607. – 5 c. green (air) .. 10 5
608. – 15 c. red 30 15

87. Isthmus Highway. 88. Manuel E. Batista.

1957. 7th Pan-American Highway Congress. Inscr. as in T 87.
609. 87. 3 c. green (postage) .. 10 5

610. – 10 c. black (air) .. 20 15
611. – 20 c. black and blue .. 75 35
612. – 1 b. green .. .. 2·50 2·25
DESIGNS—VERT. 10 c. Highway under construction. 20 c. Darien Forest. 1 b. Map of Pan-American Highway.

1957. Air. Surch. **1957 X 10 ₵ X.**
614. 79. 10 c. on 6 c. blk. & violet 20 15

1957. Manuel Espinosa Batista (independence leader). Birth Cent.
615. 88. 5 c. blue and green .. 12 8

89. Portobelo Castle. 90. U.N. Emblem.

1957. Air. Buildings. Centres in black.
616. **89.** 10 c. grey 25 15
617. – 10 c. purple 20 15
618. – 10 c. violet 20 15
619. – 10 c. grey and green .. 20 15
620. – 10 c. ultramarine .. 20 15
621. – 10 c. brown 20 15
622. – 10 c. orange 20 15
623. – 10 c. light blue 25 15
624. – 1 b. red .. .. .. 2·40 1·60
DESIGNS—HORIZ. No. 617, San Jeronimo Castle. 618, Portobelo Customs-house. 619, Panama Hotel. 620, Pres. Remon Cantera Stadium. 621, Palace of Justice. 622, Treasury. 623, San Lorenzo Castle. VERT. 624, Jose Remon Clinics.

1957. Surch. **1957** and value.
625. **78.** 1 c. on ½ c. brown .. 5 5
626. 3 c. on ½ c. brown .. 8 5

1958. Air. Surch. **1958** and value.
627. **76.** 5 c. on 6 c. green .. 20 8

1958. Air. United Nations. 10th Anniv. Inscr. as in T **90**.
628. **90.** 10 c. green 25 20
629. 21 c. blue 45 35
630. 50 c. orange .. .. 1·10 60
631. – 1 b. red, blue and grey 3·50 3·25

1958. No. 547 surch. **3 c 1958.**
633. 3 c. on 12 c. purple .. 10 5

91. Flags Emblem.

92. Brazilian Pavilion.

1958. Organization of American States. 10th Anniv. Inscr. "1948 1958". Emblem (T 91) multicoloured within yellow and black circular band; background colours given below.
634. **91.** 1 c. grey (postage) .. 5 5
635. 2 c. green 5 5
636. 3 c. red 8 5
637. 7 c. violet-blue 15 8
638. 5 c. blue (air.) .. 10 5
639. 10 c. red 30 12
640. – 50 c. black, yell. & grey 1·10 65
641. **91.** 1 b. black .. .. 2·25 2·00
DESIGN—VERT. 50 c. Headquarters building.

1958. Brussels. Int. Exn. Inscr. as in T **92**.
642. **92.** 1 c. green & yell. (post.) 5 5
643. – 3 c. green and blue .. 8 5
644. – 5 c. slate and brown .. 12 8
645. – 10 c. chocolate and blue 20 15
646. – 15 c. violet & grey (air) 35 35
647. – 50 c. brown and slate .. 1·25 1·25
648. – 1 b. turquoise and lilac 2·50 2·50
DESIGNS—PAVILIONS—As T **92**: 3 c. Argentina. 5 c. Venezuela. 10 c. Great Britain. 15 c. Vatican City. 50 c. United States. 1 b. Belgium.

93. Pope Pius XII.

94. Children on Farm.

1959. Pope Pius XII Commem. Inscr. as in T **93**.
650. **93.** 3 c. brown (postage) .. 12 5
651. – 5 c. violet (air) 12 12
652. – 30 c. magenta 60 50
653. – 50 c. grey .. .. 1·00 95
PORTRAITS (Pope Pius XII): 5 c. when Cardinal. 30 c. wearing Papal tiara. 50 c. enthroned.

1959. Obligatory Tax. Youth Rehabilitation Institute. Size 35 × 24 mm.
655. **94.** 1 c. grey and red .. 12 5

95. U.N. Headquarters, New York.

96. J. A. Facio.

97. Football.

1959. Declaration of Human Rights. 10th Anniv. Inscr. "X ANIVERSARIO DERECHOS HUMANOS".
656. **95.** 3 c. olive & brown (post.) 10 10
657. – 15 c. green and orange 30 20
658. – 5 c. blue and green (air) 25 12
659. – 10 c. brown and grey .. 25 25
660. – 20 c. slate and brown .. 75 45
661. – 50 c. blue and green .. 2·25 1·10
662. **95.** 1 b. blue and red .. 2·75 2·50
DESIGNS: 5 c., 15 c. Family looking towards light. 10 c., 20 c. U.N. emblem and torch. 50 c. U.N. flag.

1959. 8th Latin-American Economic Commission Congress. Nos. 656/61 optd. **8A REUNION C.E.P.A.L. MAYO 1959** or surch. also.
663. 3 c. olive and brown (post.) 10 10
664. 15 c. green and orange .. 35 25
665. 5 c. blue and green (air) .. 25 15
666. 10 c. brown and grey .. 30 30
667. 20 c. slate and brown .. 70 55
668. 1 b. on 50 c. blue and green 3·25 3·25

1959. National Institute. 50th Anniv. Inscr. as in T **96**.
670. – 3 c. red (postage) .. 5 5
671. – 13 c. green 25 15
672. – 21 c. blue 35 25
673. **96.** 5 c. black (air) .. 8 8
674. – 10 c. black 15 12
DESIGNS—VERT. 3 c. E. A. Morales (founder). 10 c. Ernesto de la Guardia, Jr. 13 c. A. Bravo. HORIZ. 21 c. National Institute Bldg.

1959. Obligatory Tax. Youth Rehabilitation Institute. As No. 655, but colours changed and inscr. "1959".
675. **94.** 1 c. emerald and black 10 5
676. 1 c. blue and black .. 10 5
see also No. 690.

1959. 3rd Pan-American Games, Chicago. Inscr. "III JUEGOS DEPORTIVOS PANAMERICANOS".
677. **97.** 1 c. green & grey (post.) 5 5
678. – 3 c. brown and blue .. 12 5
679. 20 c. brown and green .. 45 35
680. · 5 c. brown & black (air) 15 8
681. · 10 c. brown and grey .. 45 15
682. – 50 c. brown and blue .. 1·60 90
DESIGNS: 3 c. Swimming. 5 c. Boxing. 10 c. Baseball. 20 c. Hurdling. 50 c. Basketball.

1960. Air. World Refugee Year. Nos. 554/6 optd. **NACIONES UNIDAS ANO MUNDIAL, REFUGIADOS. 1959-1960.**
683. 25 c. black 50 50
684. 50 c. chocolate .. 1·10 90
685. 1 b. orange .. .. 2·25 2·25

98. Administration Building.

99. Fencing.

1960. Air. National University. 25th Anniv. Inscr. "UNIVERSIDAD NACIONAL 1935 1960".
686. **98.** 10 c. green 20 15
687. – 21 c. blue 30 25
688. – 25 c. ultramarine .. 45 35
689. – 30 c. black 55 35
DESIGNS: 21 c. Faculty of Science. 25 c. Faculty of Medicine. 30 c. Statue of Dr. Octavio Mendez Pereira (first rector) and Faculty of Law.

1960. Obligatory Tax. Youth Rehabilitation Institute. As No. 655 but smaller (32 × 22 mm.) and inscr. "1960".
690. **94.** 1 c. grey and red .. 8 5

1960. Olympic Games.
691. **99.** 3 c. pur. & violet (post.) 12 5
692. – 5 c. yell.-grn. & bl.-grn. 20 8
693. – 5 c. red and orange (air) 15 12
694. 10 c. blk. & yell.-brown 30 20
695. – 25 c. ultramarine & blue 55 45
696. – 50 c. black and brown .. 1·50 1·10
DESIGNS—VERT. 5 c. (No. 692), Football. (No. 693), Basketball. 25 c. Javelin-throwing. 50 c. Runner with Olympic Flame. HORIZ. 10 c. Cycling.

100. "Population".

DESIGN: 10 c. Two heads and map.

1960. Air. 6th National Census (5 c.) and Central American Census.
698. **100.** 5 c. black 10 8
699. 10 c. brown 15 12

101. Boeing "707" Airliner.

1960. Air.
700. **101.** 5 c. blue 10 10
701. 10 c. green 20 12
702. 20 c. brown 40 25

102. Pastoral Scene.

103. Helen Keller School.

1961. Agricultural Census. (16th April).
703. **102.** 3 c. blue-green .. 8 5

1961. Lions Club. 15th Anniv. Inscr. as in T **103** and with Lions emblem.
705. 3 c. blue (postage) .. 8 5
706. **103.** 5 c. black (air) .. 10 5
707. · 10 c. green 20 12
708. · 21 c. bl., red & yellow 35 25
DESIGNS: 3 c. Nino Hospital. 10 c. Children's Colony, Verano. 21 c. Arms and slogan.

1961. Air. Obligatory Tax. Youth Rehabilitation Fund. Surch. **1c "Rehabilitacion de Menores".**
709. 1 c. on 10 c. black and yell.-brn. (No. 694) 5 5
710. **101.** 1 c. on 10 c. green .. 5 5

1961. Air. Surch. **HABILITADA en** and value.
712. **98.** 1 c. on 10 c. green .. 5 5
713. · 1 b. on 25 c. ultramarine and blue (No. 695) 1·90 1·60

104. Flags of Costa Rica and Panama.

105. Girl using Sewing-machine.

106. Campaign Emblem.

1961. Meeting of Presidents of Costa Rica and Panama.
715. **104.** 3 c. red & blue (post.) 12 5
716. – 1 b. black & gold (air) 1·90 1·60
DESIGN: 1 b. Pres. Chiari of Panama and Pres. Echandi of Costa Rica.

1961. Obligatory Tax. Youth Rehabilitation Fund. Inscr. as in T **105**.
717. **105.** 1 c. violet 5 5
718. 1 c. yellow 5 5
719. 1 c. green 5 5
720. 1 c. blue 5 5
721. 1 c. purple 5 5
722. · 1 c. mauve 5 5
723. – 1 c. grey 5 5
724. – 1 c. blue 5 5
725. – 1 c. orange 5 5
726. 1 c. red 5 5
DESIGN: Nos. 722/6, Boy sawing wood.

1961. Air. Malaria Eradication.
727. **106.** 5 c. + 5 c. red .. 95 75
728. 10 c. + 10 c. blue .. 1·25 1·10
729. 15 c. + 15 c. green .. 1·90 1·90

INDEX

Countries can be quickly located by referring to the index at the end of this volume.

107. Dag Hammarskjoeld.

108. Arms of Panama.

1961. Air. Death of Dag Hammarskjoeld.
730. **107.** 10 c. black and grey .. 25 20

1962. Air. (a) Surch. **"Vale B/.0.15".**
731. **98.** 15 c. on 10 c. green .. 25 20

(b) No. 810 surch. **"XX"** over old value and **"VALE B/.1.00".**
732. 1 b. on 25 c. ultramarine and blue .. .. 1·50 1·25

1962. 3rd Central American Inter-Municipal Co-operation Assembly.
733. **108.** 3 c. red, yellow and blue (postage) 12 5
734. – 5 c. black & blue (air) 20 12
DESIGN—HORIZ. 5 c. City Hall, Colon.

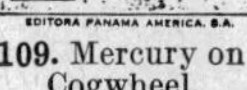
109. Mercury on Cogwheel.

110. Social Security. Hospital.

1962. 1st Industrial Census.
735. **109.** 3 c. red 8 5

1962. Surch. **VALE** and value with old value obliterated.
736. **107.** 10 c. on 5 c. + 5 c. red .. 1·40 1·10
737. 20 c. on 10 c. + 10 c. bl. 2·75 2·00

1962. Opening of Social Security Hospital, Panama City.
738. **110.** 3 c. black and red .. 8 5

111. Colon Cathedral.

113. Col. Glenn and Capsule "Friendship".

112. Thatcher Ferry Bridge nearing completion.

1962. "Freedom of Worship". Inscr. "LIBERTAD DE CULTOS". Centres in black.
739. – 1 c. red and blue (post.) 5 5
740. – 2 c. red and cream .. 5 5
741. – 3 c. blue and cream .. 5 5
742. – 5 c. red and green .. 8 5
743. – 10 c. green and cream 20 12
744. – 10 c. magenta and blue 20 12
745. – 15 c. blue and green .. 25 20
746. **111.** 20 c. red and pink .. 35 25
747. – 25 c. green and pink 45 35
748. – 50 c. blue and pink .. 80 70
749. – 1 b. violet and cream .. 1·90 1·60
DESIGNS—HORIZ. 1 c. San Francisco de Veraguas Church. 3 c. David Cathedral. 25 c. Orthodox Greek Temple. 1 b. Colon Protestant Church. VERT. 2 c. Panama Old Cathedral. 5 c. Nata Church. 10 c. Don Bosco Temple. 15 c. Virgin of Carmen Church. 50 c. Panama Cathedral.

750. – 5 c. violet and flesh (air) 10 5
751. – 7 c. magenta & mauve 12 8
752. – 8 c. violet and blue .. 12 10
753. – 10 c. violet and salmon 20 12
754. – 10 c. green & light purple 20 12
755. – 15 c. red and orange .. 25 25
756. – 21 c. sepia and blue .. 35 30
757. – 25 c. blue and pink .. 35 30
758. – 30 c. magenta and blue 50 40
759. – 50 c. purple and green 1·00 65
760. – 1 b. blue and salmon .. 1·75 1·40

DESIGNS—HORIZ. 5 c. Cristo Rey Church. 7 c. San Miguel Church. 21 c. Canal Zone Synagogue. 25 c. Panama Synagogue. 50 c. Canal Zone Protestant Church. VERT. 8 c. Santuario Church. 10 c. Los Santos Church. 15 c. Santa Ana Church. 30 c. San Francisco Church. 1 b. Canal Zone Catholic Church.

1962. Air. 9th Central American and Caribbean Games, Jamaica. Nos. 693 and 695 optd. **"IX JUEGOS C.A. y DEL CARIBE KINGSTON - 1962"** or surch. also.
762. 5 c. red and orange .. 25 12
764. 10 c. on 25 c. ultram. & bl. 30 20
765. 15 c. on 25 c. ultram. & bl. 45 25
766. 20 c. on 25 c. ultram. & bl. 55 45
763. 25 c. ultram. & blue .. 60 45

1962. Opening of Thatcher Ferry Bridge, Canal Zone.
767. **112.** 3 c. black & red (post.) 10 5
768. – 10 c. black & blue (air) 20 12
DESIGN: 10 c. Completed bridge.

1962. Air. Col. Glenn's Space Flight.
769. **113.** 5 c. red 20 12
770. – 10 c. yellow 35 20
771. – 31 c. blue 80 50
772. – 50 c. green .. .. 1·10 75
DESIGNS—HORIZ. "Friendship": 10 c. Over Earth. 31 c. In space. VERT. 50 c. Col Glenn.

114. U.P.A.E. Emblem.

116. F.A.O. Emblem.

115. Water Exercise.

1963. Air. Postal Union of Americas and Spain. 50th Anniv.
774. **114.** 10 c. gold, blue, black and red 15 12

1963. Panama Fire Brigade. 75th Anniv.
775. **115.** 1 c. blk. & green (post.) 5 5
776. – 3 c. black and blue .. 5 5
777. – 5 c. black and red .. 12 8
778. – 10 c. black & orge. (air) 20 12
779. – 15 c. black and purple 25 20
780. – 21 c. blue, gold and red 50 45
DESIGNS: 3 c. Brigade officers. 5 c. Brigade president and advisory council. 10 c. "China" pump in action, 1887. 15 c. "Cable 14" station and fire-engine. 21 c. Fire Brigade badge.

1963. Air. Red Cross Cent. (1st issue). Nos. 769/71 surch. with red cross **1863 1963** and premium.
781. **109.** 5 c.+5 c. red 75 75
782. – 10 c.+10 c. yellow .. 85 85
783. – 31 c.+15 c. blue .. 1·50 1·50
See also No. 797.

1963. Air. Freedom from Hunger.
784. **116.** 10 c. red and green .. 20 15
785. 15 c. red and blue .. 25 20

1963. Air. 22nd Central American Lions Convention. Optd. **"XXII Convencion. Leonistica Centroamericana Panama 18-21 Abril 1963".**
786. **103.** 5 c. black 12 10

1963. Air. Surch. **HABILITADO Vale B./O.04.**
787. **98.** 4 c. in 10 c. green .. 8 5

1963. Air. Nos. 743 and 769 optd. **AEREO** vert.
790. 10 c. green and cream .. 15 12
791. 20 c. brown and green .. 45 25

1963. Air. Freedom of the Press. No. 693 optd. **LIBERTAD DE PRENSA 29-VIII-63.**
792. 5 c. red and orange .. 12 8

1963. Air. Visit of U.S. Astronauts to Panama. Optd. **"Visita Astronautas Glenn-Schirra Sheppard Cooper a Panama"** or surch. also.
793. **112.** 5 c. red 95 95
794. 10 c. on 5 c. red .. 1·60 1·60

1963. Air. Surch. **HABILITADO 10 c.**
796. **109.** 10 c. on 5 c. red .. 1·75 1·75

1963. Air. Red Cross Centenary (2nd issue). No. 781 surch. **"Centenario Cruz Roja Internacional 10 c.** with premium obliterated.
797. **109.** 10 c. on 5 c.+5 c. red .. 3·50 3·50

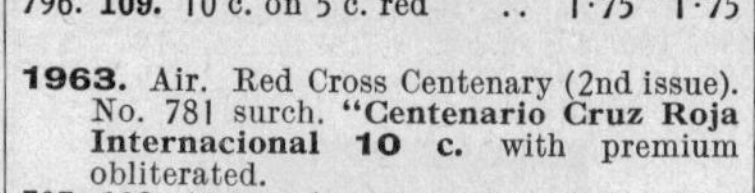

1963. Surch. **VALE** and value.
798. **110.** 4 c. on 3 c. black and red (postage) .. 12 5
799. 4 c. on 3 c. black, blue and cream (No. 741) 12 5
800. **113.** 4 c. on 3 c. blk. & red .. 12 5
801. – 4 c. on 3 c. black and blue (No. 776) .. 12 5
802. **86.** 10 c. on 25 c. blue & red 20 12
803. – 10 c. on 25 c. ultram. (No. 688) (air) .. 20 20

117. Pres. Orlich (Costa Rica) and Flags.

119. Vasco Nunez de Balboa.

118. Innsbruck.

1963. Presidential Reunion, San Jose (Costa Rica). Multicoloured. Presidents and flags of their countries.
804. 1 c. Type 117 (postage) .. 5 5
805. 2 c. Somoza (Nicaragua) .. 5 5
806. 3 c. Villeda (Honduras) .. 5 5
807. 4 c. Chiari (Panama) .. 5 5
808. 5 c. Rivera (El Salvador) (air) 10 10
809. 10 c. Ydigoras (Guatemala) 20 15
810. 21 c. Kennedy (U.S.A.) .. 55 45

1963. Winter Olympic Games, Innsbruck.
811. ½ c. red and blue (postage) 5 5
812. 1 c. red, brown & turquoise 12 5
813. 3 c. red and blue .. 15 12
814. 4 c. red, brown and green .. 20 15
815. 5 c. red, brn. & mve. (air) .. 35 25
816. 15 c. red, brown and blue .. 75 55
817. 21 c. red, brown and myrtle 1·40 1·10
818. 31 c. red, brown & indigo .. 1·60 1·40
DESIGNS: ½ c. (expressed "B/0.005"), 3 c. T 118. 1 c., 4 c. Speed-skating. 15 c. to 31 c. Skiing (slalom).

1964. Discovery of Pacific Ocean. 450th Anniv.
820. **119.** 4 c. grn. on flesh (post). 8 5
821. 10 c. vio. on pink (air) 25 20

120. Boy Scout.

121. St. Paul's Cathedral, London.

1964. Obligatory Tax for Youth Rehabilitation, Institute.
822. **120.** 1 c. cerise 5 5
823. 1 c. brownish grey .. 5 5
824. 1 c. light blue 5 5
825. 1 c. olive 5 5
826. 1 c. reddish violet .. 5 5
827. – 1 c. orange-brown .. 5 5
828. – 1 c. orange 5 5
829. – 1 c. blue-green .. 5 5
830. – 1 c. bluish violet .. 5 5
831. – 1 c. yellow 5 5
DESIGN: Nos. 827/31, Girl guide.

1964. Air. Ecumenical Council, Vatican City (1st issue). Cathedrals. Centres in black.
832. 21 c. red (Type 121) .. 55 45
833. 21 c. blue (Kassa, Hungary) 55 45
834. 21 c. green (Milan) .. 55 45
835. 21 c. black (St. John's, Poland) 55 45
836. 21 c. chocolate (St. Stephen's, Vienna) 55 45
837. 21 c. red-brown (Notre Dame, Paris) 55 45
838. 21 c. violet (Moscow) .. 55 45
839. 21 c. bluish violet (Lima) 55 45
840. 21 c. carmine (Stockholm) 55 45
841. 21 c. magenta (Cologne) .. 55 45
842. 21 c. bis.-brn. (New Delhi) 55 45
843. 21 c. dp. bluish-grn. (Basel) 55 45
844. 21 c. olive-green (Toledo) 55 45
845. 21 c. vermilion (Metropolitan, Athens) 55 45
846. 21 c. yellow-olive (St. Patrick's, New York) .. 55 45
847. 21 c. emerald (Lisbon) .. 55 45
848. 21 c. turquoise-blue (Sofia) 55 45
849. 21 c. deep grey-brown (New Church, Delft, Netherlands) 55 45
850. 21 c. deep sepia (St. George's Patriarchal Church, Istanbul) .. 55 45
851. 21 c. violet-blue (Basilica, Guadalupe, Mexico) .. 55 45
852. 1 b. ultramarine (Panama) 1·60 1·60
853. 2 b. green (St. Peter's, Rome) .. .. .. 3·50 3·50
See Nos. 882, etc.

1964. As Nos. 749 and 760 but colours changed and optd. **HABILITADA.**
855. 1 b. blk., red & blue (post). 1·50 1·50
856. 1 b. blk., grn. & yell. (air) 1·75 1·50

1964. Air. No. 756 surch. **VALE B/.0.50**
857. 50 c. on 21 c. black, sepia and blue 90 65

122. The Discus-thrower.

1964. Olympic Games, Tokyo.
858. ½ c. ("B/0.005") maroon, red, brn. & grn. (post.) .. 5 5
859. 1 c. red, mar., brn. & blue 12 5
860. 5 c. black, red and yellow-olive (air) .. 30 30
861. 10 c. black, red and yellow 45 30
862. 21 c. blk., red, brn. & grn. 95 65
863. 50 c. blk., red, brn. & blue 1·75 1·25
DESIGNS: ½ c. T 122. 1 c. Runner with Olympic Flame. 5 c. to 50 c. Olympic Stadium, Tokyo, and Mt. Fuji.

1964. Air. Nos. 692 and 742 surch. **Aereo B/.0.10.**
865. 10 c. on 5 c. yellow-green and blue-green .. 35 20
866. 10 c. on 5 c. black, red and green 25 20

123. Space Vehicles (Project "Apollo").

1964. Space Exploration. Multicoloured.
867. ½ c. ("B/0.005") Type 123 (postage) .. 12 5
868. 1 c. Rocket and capsule (Project "Gemini") .. 12 5
869. 5 c. W.M. Schirra (air) .. 15 12
870. 10 c. L. G. Cooper .. 30 25
871. 21 c. Schirra's capsule .. 95 75
872. 50 c. Cooper's capsule .. 1·90 1·75

1964. No. 687 surch. **Correos B/.0.10.**
874. 10 c. on 21 c. blue .. 20 15

124. Water-skiing.

1964. Aquatic Sports. Multicoloured.
875. ½ c. ("B/0.005") Type 124 (postage) 5 5
876. 1 c. Underwater-swimming 5 5
877. 5 c. Fishing (air) 20 8
878. 10 c. Sailing (vert.) .. 75 60
879. 21 c. Speedboat racing .. 1·90 1·50
880. 31 c. Water polo at Olympic Games, 1964 .. .. 3·00 2·50

1964. Air. Ecumenical Council, Vatican City (2nd Issue). Stamps of 1st issue optd. **1964.** Centres in black.
882. 21 c. red (No. 832) .. 35 35
883. 21 c. green (No. 834) .. 35 35
884. 21 c. yellow-olive (No. 836) 35 35
885. 21 c. deep sepia (No. 850) 35 35
886. 1 b. ultramarine (No. 852) 1·60 1·60
887. 2 b. green (No. 853) .. 3·50 3·50

125. General View.

126. Mrs. E. Roosevelt.

1964. Air. New York World's Fair.
889. **125.** 5 c. black and yellow 35 35
890. – 10 c. black and red .. 65 65
891. – 15 c. black and green 1·00 95
892. – 21 c. black and blue .. 1·50 1·50
DESIGNS: 10 c., 15 c. Fair pavilions (different). 21 c. Unisphere.

1964. Mrs. Eleanor Roosevelt Commem.
894. **126.** 4 c. black and red on yellow (postage) .. 12 8
895. 20 c. black and green on buff (air) .. 35 35

127. Dag Hammarskjoeld.

128. Pope John XXIII.

1964. Air. U.N. Day.
897. **127.** 21 c. black and blue .. 50 35
898. – 21 c. blue and black .. 50 35
DESIGN: No. 898, U.N. Emblem.

1964. Air. Pope John Commem.
900. **128.** 21 c. black and bistre 50 35
901. – 21 c. mult. (Papal Arms) 50 35

129. Slalom Skiing Medals.

1964. Winter Olympic Winners' Medals. Medals in gold, silver and bronze.
903. **129.** ½ c. ("B/0.005") turquoise (postage) 5 5
904. – 1 c. deep blue 5 5
905. – 2 c. chocolate 10 10
906. – 3 c. magenta 15 12
907. – 4 c. lake 20 15
908. – 5 c. reddish violet (air) 25 25
909. – 6 c. blue 35 35
910. – 7 c. violet 35 35
911. – 10 c. green 50 50
912. – 21 c. red .. .. 1·00 85
913. – 31 c. ultramarine .. 1·50 1·40
DESIGNS—Medals for: 1 c., 7 c. Speed-skating. 2 c., 21 c. Bobsleighing. 3 c., 10 c. Figure-skating. 4 c. Ski-jumping. 5 c., 6 c., 31 c Cross-country skiing. Values in the same design show different medal-winners and country names.

130. Keel-billed Toucan.

1965. Birds. Multicoloured.
915. 1 c. Type **130** (postage) .. 5 5
916. 2 c. Scarlet macaw 5 5
917. 3 c. Red-crowned woodpecker 8 5
918. 4 c. Blue tanager (horiz.) .. 10 8
919. 5 c. Yellow-rumped cacique (horiz.) (air) 12 8
920. 10 c. Crimson-backed tanager (horiz.) 25 15

131. Snapper.

1965. Marine Life. Multicoloured.
921. 1 c. Type **131** (postage) .. 5 5
922. 2 c. Dolphin 5 5
923. 8 c. Shrimp (air) 20 8
924. 12 c. Hammerhead .. 25 12
925. 13 c. Atlantic sailfish .. 30 15
926. 25 c. Seahorse (vert.) .. 65 30

132. Double Daisy and Emblem.

1966. Air. Junior Chamber of Commerce. 50th Anniv. Flowers. Multicoloured: background colour given.
927. **132.** 30 c. magenta .. 50 30
928. – 30 c. flesh (Hibiscus) .. 50 30
929. – 30 c. olive (Mauve orchid) 50 30
930. – 40 c. green (Water lily) 60 40
931. – 40 c. blue (Gladiolus) 60 40
932. – 40 c. pink (White orchid) 60 40
Each design incorporates the Junior Chamber of Commerce Emblem.

1966. Surch. (a) Postage.
933. 13 c. on 25 c. (No. 747) .. 15 12

(b) Air.
934. 3 c. on 5 c. (No. 680) .. 5 5
935. 13 c. on 25 c. (No. 695) .. 15 12

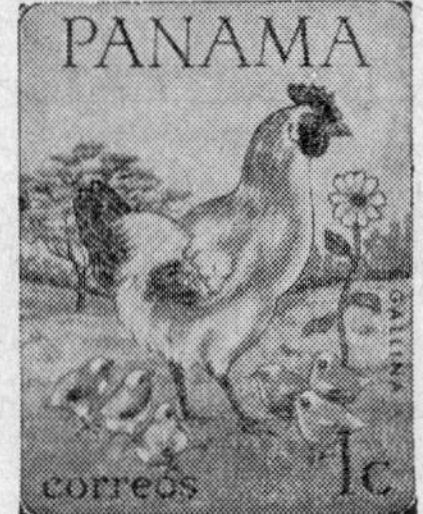

133. Chicken.

1967. Domestic Animals. Multicoloured.
936. 1 c. Type **133** (postage) .. 5 5
937. 3 c. Cockerel 5 5
938. 5 c. Pig (horiz.) 8 5
939. 8 c. Cow (horiz.) 10 5
940. 10 c. Pekingese dog (air) .. 15 8
941. 13 c. Zebu (horiz.) .. 20 8
942. 30 c. Cat 40 15
943. 40 c. Horse (horiz.) .. 60 20

133a. Anherga.

1967. Wild Birds. Multicoloured.
944. ½ c. Type **133a** 5 5
945. 1 c. Quetzal 5 5
946. 3 c. Motmot 8 5
947. 4 c. Toucan (horiz.) .. 10 5
948. 5 c. Macaw 12 5
949. 13 c. Belted Kingfisher .. 30 10

134. "Deer" (F. Marc).

1967. Wild Animals. Paintings. Mult.
950. 1 c. Type **134** (postage) .. 5 5
951. 3 c. "Cougar" (F. Marc) .. 5 5
952. 5 c. "Monkeys" (F. Marc) 8 5
953. 8 c. "Fox" (F. Marc) .. 12 5
954. 10 c. "St. Jerome and the Lion" (Durer) (air) .. 15 8
955. 13 c. "Rabbit" (Durer) .. 20 10
956. 20 c. "Lady with the Ermine" (Da Vinci) 30 12
957. 30 c. "The Hunt" (Delacroix) 50 15
The 3, 10, 13 and 20 c. are vert.

135. Map of Panama and People.

1969. National Population Census.
958. **135.** 5 c. ultramarine .. 8 5
959. – 10 c. purple 15 10
DESIGN—VERT. 10 c. People and map of the Americas.

136. Cogwheel

1969. Rotary Int. in Panama. 50th Anniv.
960. **136.** 13 c. blk., yell. & blue 20 15

137. Cornucopia and Map. **138.** Tower and Map.

1969. 11 October Revolution. 1st Anniv.
961. **137.** 10 c. multicoloured .. 15 8

1969.
962. **138.** 3 c. black and orange 5 5
963. – 5 c. green 8 5
964. – 8 c. brown 12 8
965. – 13 c. black & emerald 20 12
966. – 20 c. brown 30 20
967. – 21 c. yellow 30 20
968. – 25 c. green 35 25
969. – 30 c. black 45 30
970. – 34 c. brown 50 35
971. – 38 c. blue 55 40
972. – 40 c. yellow 60 45
973. – 50 c. black and purple 70 55
974. – 59 c. purple 80 65
DESIGNS—HORIZ. 5 c. Peasants. 13 c. Hotel Continental. 25 c. Del Rey Bridge. 34 c. Panama Cathedral. 38 c. Municipal Palace. 40 c. French Plaza. 50 c. Thatcher Ferry Bridge. 59 c. National Theatre. VERT. 8 c. Nata Church. 20 c. Virgin of Carmen Church. 21 c. Altar, San Jose Church. 30 c. Dr. Arosemena statue.

139. Discus-thrower and Stadium.

1970. 11th Central American and Caribbean Games, Panama (1st series).
975. **139.** 1 c. multicoloured (post.) 5 5
976. 2 c. multicoloured .. 5 5
977. 3 c. multicoloured .. 5 5
978. 5 c. multicoloured .. 8 5
979. 10 c. multicoloured .. 15 10
980. 13 c. multicoloured .. 20 12
981. – 13 c. multicoloured .. 20 12
982. **139.** 25 c. multicoloured .. 35 25
983. 30 c. multicoloured .. 45 30
984. – 13 c. multicoloured (air) 20 12
985. – 30 c. multicoloured .. 45 30
DESIGNS—VERT. No. 981 "Flor del Espiritu Santo" (flowers). 985. Indian girl. HORIZ. 984, Thatcher Ferry Bridge and palm.
See also Nos. 986/94.

140. J. D. Arosemena and Stadium.

1970. Air. 11th Central American and Caribbean Games, Panama (2nd series). Multicoloured.
986. 1 c. Type **140** 5 5
987. 2 c. Type **140** 5 5
988. 3 c. Type **140** 5 5
989. 5 c. Type **140** 8 5
990. 13 c. Basketball 20 12
991. 13 c. New Gymnasium .. 20 12
992. 13 c. Revolution Stadium 20 12
993. 13 c. Panamanian couple in festive costume .. 20 12
994. 30 c. Eternal Flame and stadium 45 30

141. A. Tapia and M. Sosa (first comptrollers).

1971. Panamanian Comptroller-General's Office. 40th Anniv. Multicoloured.
996. 3 c. Comptroller-General's Building (1970) (vert.) .. 5 5
997. 5 c. Type **141** 8 5
998. 8 c. Comptroller-General's emblem (vert.) 12 8
999. 13 c. Comptroller-General's Building (1955-70) .. 20 12

142. "Man and Alligator. **143.** Map on I.E.Y. Emblem.

1971. Indian Handicrafts.
1000. **142.** 8 c. multicoloured .. 15 12

1971. Int. Education Year.
1001. **143.** 1 b. multicoloured .. 1·90 1·25

144. Astronaut on Moon. **145.** Panama Pavilion.

1971. Air. "Apollo 11" and "Apollo 12" Moon Missions. Multicoloured.
1002. 13 c. Type **144** 20 15
1003. 13 c. "Apollo 12" astronauts 20 15

1971. Air. "EXPO 70", World Fair, Osaka, Japan.
1004. **145.** 10 c. multicoloured .. 20 12

146. Conference Text and Emblem.

1971. 9th Inter-American Loan and Savings Assn., Conf., Panama City.
1005. **146.** 25 c. multicoloured .. 65 30

147. Panama Flag.

1971. Air. American Tourist Year. Mult.
1006. 5 c. Type **147** 10 5
1007. 13 c. Map of Panama and Western Hemisphere .. 20 12

148. New U.P.U. H.Q. Building.

1971. New U.P.U. Headquarters Building, Berne. Inaug. Multicoloured.
1008. 8 c. Type **148** 15 8
1009. 30 c. U.P.U. Monument, Berne (vert.) 50 30

149. Cow and Pig.

1972. 3rd Agricultural Census.
1010. **149.** 3 c. multicoloured .. 5 5

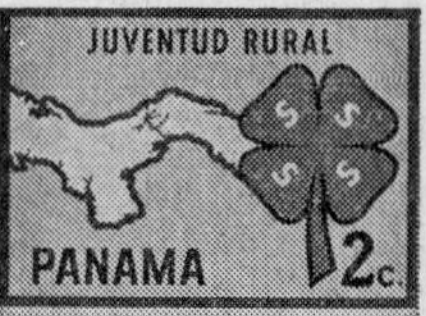

150. Map and "4S" Emblem.

1972. "4S" Programme for Rural Youth.
1011. **150.** 2 c. multicoloured .. 5 5

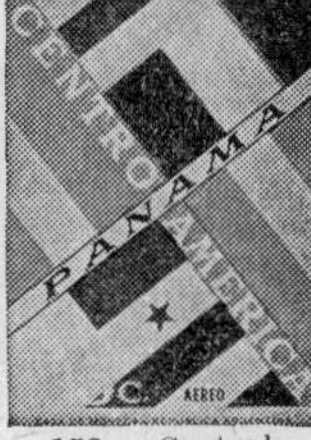

151. Gandhi. **152.** Central American Flags.

1972. Air. Mahatma Gandhi. Birth Cent. (1969).
1012. **151.** 10 c. multicoloured .. 20 10

1971. Air. Central American States' Independence from Spain. 150th Anniv.
1013. **152.** 13 c. multicoloured .. 20 12

153. Early Panama Stamp. **154.** Altar, Nata Church.

1972. Air. 2nd Nat., Philatelic and Numismatic Exhib., Panama.
1014. **153.** 8 c. blue, blk. & red .. 12 8

1972. Air. Nata Church. 450th Anniv.
1015. **154.** 40 c. multicoloured .. 60 45

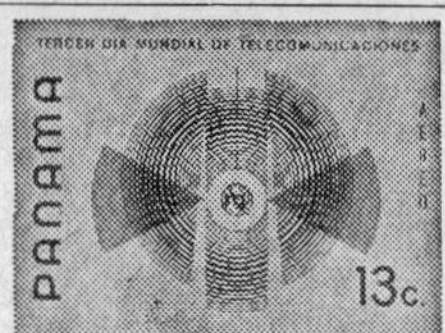

155. Telecommunications Emblem.

1972. Air. World Telecommunications Day.
1016. **155.** 13 c. blk., bl. & light bl. 20 12

156. "Apollo 14" Badge.

1972. Air. Moon Flight of "Apollo 14".
1017. **156.** 13 c. multicoloured .. 20 12

157. Children on See-saw.

1972. U.N.I.C.E.F. 25th Anniv. (1971). Multicoloured.
1018. 1 c. Type **157** (postage) .. 5 5
1019. 5 c. Boy sitting by kerb (vert.) (air) 10 5
1020. 8 c. Indian mother and child (vert.) 15 10
1021. 50 c. U.N.I.C.E.F. emblem (vert.) 75 60

158. Tropical Fruits.

1972. Tourist Publicity. Multicoloured.
1023. 1 c. Type **158** (postage) .. 5 5
1024. 2 c. "Isle of Night" .. 5 5
1025. 3 c. Carnival float (vert.) 5 5
1026. 5 c. San Blas textile (air) 8 5
1027. 8 c. Chaquira (beaded collar) 5 8
1028. 25 c. Ruined fort, Portobello 35 25

159. Map and Flags. 160. Baseball Players.

1973. Obligatory Tax. Panama City Post Office Building Fund. 7th Bolivar Games.
1030. **159.** 1 c. black 5 5

1973. Air. 7th Bolivar Games.
1031. **160.** 8 c. red and yellow .. 12 8
1032. – 10 c. black & blue .. 15 10
1033. – 13 c. multicoloured .. 20 12
1034. – 25 c. blk., red & green 35 25
1035. – 50 c. multicoloured .. 70 50
1036. – 1 b. multicoloured .. 1·50 1·00
DESIGNS—VERT. 10 c. Basketball. 13 c. Flaming torch. HORIZ. 25 c. Boxing. 50 c. Panama map and flag, Games emblem and Bolivar. 1 b. Games' medals.

1973. U.N. Security Council Meeting, Panama City. Various stamps surch. **O.N.U.** in laurel leaf and **CONSEJO DE SEGURIDAD 15-21 Marzo 1973** and value.
1037. 8 c. on 59 c. (No. 974) (postage) 12 8
1038. 10 c. on 1 b. (No. 1001) .. 15 10
1039. 13 c. on 30 c. (No. 969) .. 20 15
1040. 13 c. on 40 c. (No. 1015) (air) 20 12

161. Farming Co-operative.

1973. Obligatory Tax. Post Office Building Fund.
1041. **161.** 1 c. green and red .. 5 5
1042. – 1 c. grey and red .. 5 5
1043. – 1 c. yellow and red .. 5 5
1044. – 1 c. orange and red .. 5 5
1045. – 1 c. blue and red .. 5 5
DESIGNS: No. 1042, Silver coins. No. 1043, V. Lorenzo. No. 1044, Cacique Urraca. No. 1045, Post Office building.
See also Nos. 1061/2.

162. J. D. Crespo (educator).

1973. Famous Panamanians. Multicoloured.
1046. 3 c. Type **162** (postage) .. 5 5
1047. 5 c. Isabel Obaldia (educator) (air) .. 8 5
1048. 8 c. N. V. Jaen (educator) 12 8
1049. 10 c. "Forest Scene" (Roberto Lewis–painter) 15 10
1050. 13 c. R. Miro (poet) .. 20 12
1051. 13 c. "Portrait of a Lady" (M. E. Amador-painter) 20 12
1052. 20 c. "Portrait of a Man" (Isaac Benitez–painter) 30 20
1053. 21 c. M. A. Guerrero (statesman) 30 20
1054. 25 c. Dr. B. Porras (statesman) .. 35 25
1055. 30 c. J. D. Arosemena (statesman) 40 30
1056. 34 c. Dr. O. M. Pereira (writer) 45 35
1057. 38 c. Dr. R. J. Alfaro (writer) 50 40

1973. Air. Isabel Obaldia Professional School. 50th Anniv. Nos. 1047, 1054 and 1056 optd. **1923, 1973 bodas de Oro Escuela Profesional Isabel Herrera Obaldia** and EP emblem.
1058. 5 c. multicoloured .. 10 5
1059. 25 c. multicoloured .. 40 25
1060. 34 c. multicoloured .. 30 35

1974. Obligatory Tax. Post Office Building Fund. As Nos. 1044/5.
1061. 1 c. orange 5 5
1062. 1 c. blue 5 5

1974. Surch. **VALE** and value.
1063. 5 c. on 30 c. black (No. 969) (postage) .. 8 5
1064. 10 c. on 34 c. brown (No. 970) 15 10
1065. 13 c. on 21 c. yellow (No. 967) 20 12
1066. 1 c. on 25 c. mult. (No. 1028) (air) 5 5
1067. 3 c. on 20 c. mult. (No. 1052) 5 5
1068. 8 c. on 38 c. mult. (No. 1057) 12 8
1069. 10 c. on 34 c. mult. (No. 1056) 15 10
1070. 13 c. on 21 c. mult. (No. 1053) 20 12

163. Women's upraised hands.

1975. Air. International Women's Year.
1071. **163.** 17 c. multicoloured .. 25 15

164. Bayano Barrage.

1975. October 1968, Revolution. 7th Anniv.
1073. **291.** 17 c. blk., brn. & blue 30 15
1074. – 27 c. blue and green .. 45 30
1075. – 33 c. multicoloured .. 60 40
DESIGNS—VERT. 27 c. Victoria sugar plant, Veraguas, and sugar cane. HORIZ. 33 c. Tocumen International Airport.

1975. Obligatory Tax. Various stamps surch. **VALE PRO EDIFICIO** and value.
1076. – 1 c. on 30 c. black (No. 969) (postage) 5 5
1077. – 1 c. on 40 c. yellow (No. 972) 5 5
1078. – 1 c. on 50 c. black & purple (No. 973) .. 5 5
1079. – 1 c. on 30 c. mult. (No. 1009) 5 5
1080. **158.** 1 c. on 1 c. multicoloured 5 5
1081. – 1 c. on 2 c. multicoloured (No. 1024) .. 5 5
1082. **154.** 1 c. on 40 c. mult. (air) 5 5
1083. – 1 c. on 25 c. mult. (No. 1028) .. 5 5
1084. – 1 c. on 25 c. mult. (No. 1052) .. 5 5
1085. – 1 c. on 20 c. mult. (No. 1054) .. 5 5
1086. – 1 c. on 30 c. mult. (No. 1055) .. 5 5

1975. Obligatory Tax. Post Office Building Fund. As No. 1045.
1087. 1 c. red 5 5

165. Bolivar and Thatcher Ferry Bridge. 166. "Evibacus princeps".

1976. Panama Congress. 150th Anniv. (1st issue). Multicoloured.
1088. 6 c. Type **165** (postage) .. 12 8
1089. 23 c. Bolivar Statue (air) 35 25
1090. 35 c. Bolivar Hall, Panama City (horiz.) 55 45
1091. 41 c. Bolivar and flag .. 65 55

1976. Marine Fauna. Multicoloured.
1092. 2 c. Type **166** (postage) .. 5 5
1093. 3 c. "Ptitosarcus sinuosus" (vert.) 5 5
1094. 4 c. "Acanthaster planci" 8 5
1095. 7 c. "Oreaster reticultus" 12 8
1096. 17 c. "Diodon hystrix" (vert.) (air) .. 30 20
1097. 27 c. "Pocillopora damicornis" 50 40

167. "Simon Bolivar".

1976. Panama Congress. 150th Anniv. (2nd issue). Designs showing details of Bolivar Monument or flags of Latin-American countries. Multicoloured.
1099. 20 c. Type **167** 35 25
1100. 20 c. Argentina 35 25
1101. 20 c. Bolivar 35 25
1102. 20 c. Brazil 35 25
1103. 20 c. Chile 35 25
1104. 20 c. "Battle scene" .. 35 25
1105. 20 c. Colombia 35 25
1106. 20 c. Costa Rica .. 35 25
1107. 20 c. Cuba 35 25
1108. 20 c. Ecuador 35 25
1109. 20 c. El Salvador .. 35 25
1110. 20 c. Guatemala .. 35 25
1111. 20 c. Guyana 35 25
1112. 20 c. Haiti 35 25
1113. 20 c. "Congress assembly" 35 25
1114. 20 c. "Liberated people" 35 25
1115. 20 c. Hondurus 35 25
1116. 20 c. Jamaica 35 25
1117. 20 c. Mexico 35 25
1118. 20 c. Nicaragua 35 25
1119. 20 c. Panama 35 25
1120. 20 c. Paraguay 35 25
1121. 20 c. Peru 35 25
1122. 20 c. Dominican Republic 35 25
1123. 20 c. "Bolivar and standard-bearer" 35 25
1124. 20 c. Surinam 35 25
1125. 20 c. Trinidad and Tobago 35 25
1126. 20 c. Uruguay 35 25
1127. 20 c. Venezuela 35 25
1128. 20 c. "Indian Delegation" 35 25

ACKNOWLEDGMENT OF RECEIPT STAMPS

ILLUSTRATIONS British Commonwealth and all overprints and surcharges are FULL SIZE. Foreign Countries have been reduced to ¾-LINEAR.

A 1.

1904.
AR 135. A 1. 5 c. blue 30 30

1916. Opt. **A.R.**
AR 177. 16. 2½ c. red 60 60

EXPRESS LETTER STAMPS

1926. Optd. **EXPRESO.**
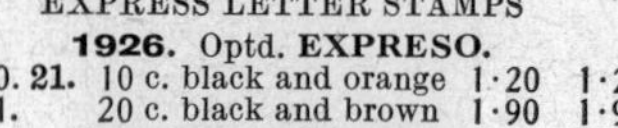
E 220. 21. 10 c. black and orange 1·20 1·20
E 221. 20 c. black and brown 1·90 1·90

E 1. Cyclist Messenger.

1929.
E 226. E 1. 10 c. orange .. 75 75
E 227. 20 c. brown .. 1·25 1·25

POSTAGE DUE STAMPS

D 1. San Geronimo Castle Gate, Portobelo. D 2. Statue of Columbus.

1915.
D 169. D 1. 1 c. brown 35 20
D 170. D 2. 2 c. brown 55 15
D 171. – 4 c. brown 65 75
D 172. – 10 c. brown .. 75 40
DESIGNS—HORIZ. 4 c. House of Deputies. VERT. 10 c. Pedro J. Sosa.
No. D 169, is wrongly inscr. "CASTILLO DE SAN LORENZO CHAGRES".

D 4.

1930.
D 240. D 4. 1 c. green 25 12
D 241. 2 c. red 25 12
D 242. 4 c. blue 30 12
D 243. 10 c. violet 30 25

INSURANCE STAMPS

1942. Surch. **SEGURO POSTAL HABILITADO** and value.
I 430. 5 c. on 1 b. black (No. 373) 15 15
I 431. 10 c. on 1 b. brown (No. 365) 20 20
I 432. 25 c. on 50 b. brown (No. 372) 40 40

REGISTRATION STAMPS

R 1.

1888.
R 12. R 1. 10 c. black on grey .. 2·50 1·25

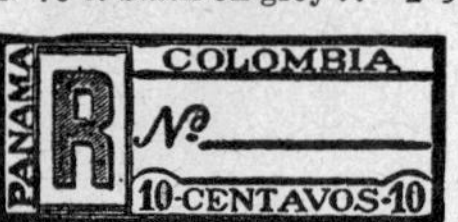

R 2.

1897. Handstamped **R COLON** in circle.
R 22. 3. 10 c. orange .. .. 4·00 4·00

1900.
R 29. R 2. 10 c. black on blue .. 25 25
R 30. 10 c. red .. .. 3·00 4·50

1902. No. R 30 surch. by hand.
R 31. R 2. 20 c. on 10 c. red .. 4·00 4·00

1903. Type R 6 of Colombia. Optd. **REPUBLICA DE PANAMA**
R 42. 20 c. red on blue .. 9·00
R 43. 20 c. blue on blue .. 9·00

1903. Nos. R 42/3 surch.
R 46. 10 c. on 20 c. red on blue 12·00 12·00
R 47. 10 c. on 20 c. blue on blue 15·00 15·00

1904. Optd. **PANAMA.**
R 60. **3.** 10 c. orange 75 75

1904. Type R 6 of Colombia. Surch. **Panama 10** and bar.
R 67. 10 c. on 20 c. red on blue 10·00 10·00
R 68. 10 c. on 20 c. blue on blue 7·50 7·50

1904. Type R 6 of Colombia. Optd. **Republica de Panama.**
R 106. 20 c. red on blue .. 1·00 1·00

R 3.

1904.
R 133. R **3.** 10 c. green 10 10

1916. Stamps of Panama surch. **R 5 cts.**
R 175. **10.** 5 c. on 8 c. blk. & pur. 25 20
R 176. **18.** 5 c. on 8 c. blk. & pur. 20 20

TOO LATE STAMPS

1903. Too Late stamp of Colombia optd. **REPUBLICA DE PANAMA.**
L 44. T **3.** 5 c. violet on red .. 1·25 1·25

L 1.

1904.
L 134. L **1.** 2½ c. red 25 25

1910. Typewritten optd. **Retardo.**
L 158. **16.** 2½ c. red .. .. 32·00 32·00

1910. Optd. **RETARDO.**
L 159. **16.** 2½ c. red .. .. 13·00 13·00

1916. Surch. **RETARDO UN CENTESIMO.**
L 174. **4.** 1 c. on ½ c. orange .. 25 25

PAPAL STATES E2

Parts of Italy under Papal rule till 1870 when they became part of the Kingdom of Italy.

1852. 100 bajocchi = 1 scudo.
1866. 100 centesimi = 1 lira.

1.

2.

1852. Papal insignia as in T **1** and **2** in various shapes and frames. Imperf.
1. ½ b. black on grey .. 75·00 23·00
5. ½ b. black on purple .. 16·00 45·00
10. 1 b. black on green.. .. 28·00 2·50
11. 2 b. black on green.. .. 29·00 1·25
14. 2 b. black on white.. .. 1·60 9·50
15. 3 b. black on brown .. 35·00 7·50
16. 3 b. black on yellow .. 3·25 25·00
17. 4 b. black on brown .. £400 15·00
19. 4 b. black on yellow .. 32·00 15·00
21. 5 b. black on pink .. .. 23·00 1·60
22. 6 b. black on lilac .. .. 75·00 26·00
23. 6 b. black on green.. .. 50·00 7·50
25. 7 b. black on blue .. .. 75·00 15·00
26. 8 b. black on white.. .. 21·00 8·00
28. 50 b. blue £1400 £550
29. 1 s. red £550 £900

1867. Same types. Imperf.
30. 2 c. black on green.. .. 25·00 45·00
32. 3 c. black on grey.. .. £275 £500
33. 5 c. black on blue .. .. 32·00 70·00
34. 10 c. black on orange .. £150 7·50
35. 20 c. black on red .. .. 24·00 10·00
36. 40 c. black on yellow .. 26·00 95·00
37. 80 c. black on pink.. .. 29·00 £140

1868. Same types. Perf.
42. 2 c. black on green.. .. 80 9·00
43. 3 c. black on grey.. .. 10·00 £700
45. 5 c. black on blue .. .. 2·10 8·50
46. 10 c. black on orange .. 12 1·10
51. 20 c. black on red .. .. 50 2·75
49. 20 c. black on purple .. 70 2·75
52. 40 c. black on yellow .. 70 23·00
55. 80 c. black on pink.. .. 3·25 70·00

PAPUA BC

(Formerly **BRITISH NEW GUINEA.**)

The eastern portion of the island of New Guinea, to the N. of Australia, a territory of the Commonwealth of Australia, now combined with New Guinea. Australian stamps were used after the Japanese defeat in 1945 until the combined issue appeared in 1952.

1. Lakatoi (native canoe).

1901.
9. **1.** ½d. black and green .. 1·25 1·40
10. 1d. black and red .. 1·25 1·25
11. 2d. black and violet .. 1·25 1·40
12. 2½d. black and blue .. 3·50 5·50
5. 4d. black and brown .. 9·00 9·00
6. 6d. black and green .. 7·00 9·00
7. 1s. black and orange .. 18·00 20·00
8. 2s. 6d. black and brown.. £200 £190

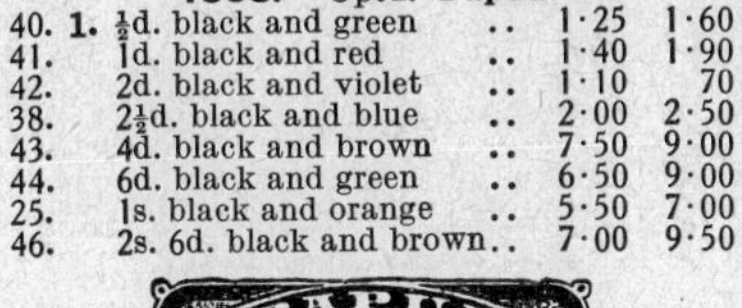

1906. Optd. **Papua.**
40. **1.** ½d. black and green .. 1·25 1·60
41. 1d. black and red .. 1·40 1·90
42. 2d. black and violet .. 1·10 70
38. 2½d. black and blue .. 2·00 2·50
43. 4d. black and brown .. 7·50 9·00
44. 6d. black and green .. 6·50 9·00
25. 1s. black and orange .. 5·50 7·00
46. 2s. 6d. black and brown.. 7·00 9·50

2.

1907.
47. **2.** ½d. black and green .. 55 85
100. 1d. black and red .. 55 20
68. 2d. black and purple .. 1·10 75
62. 2½d. black and blue .. 1·40 1·75
79. 4d. black and brown .. 1·40 2·75
80. 6d. black and green .. 2·25 2·50
81. 1s. black and orange .. 4·00 5·00
83. 2s. 6d. black and brown 11·00 13·00

1911.
84a. **2.** ½d. green.. .. .. 25 40
85. 1d. red 65 25
86. 2d. mauve 45 55
87. 2½d. blue.. .. .. 2·00 2·75
88. 4d. olive .. .. 1·50 2·25
89. 6d. orange-brown .. 1·40 2·50
90. 1s. yellow .. .. 3·25 4·00
91. 2s. 6d. red .. .. 8·50 11·00

1917. Surch. **ONE PENNY.**
93. **2.** 1d. on ½d. green .. 40 35
94. 1d. on 2d. mauve .. 2·50 2·75
95. 1d. on 2½d. blue.. .. 1·00 1·10
96. 1d. on 4d. olive .. 1·00 1·40
97. 1d. on 6d. orange-brown 3·25 3·25
98. 1d. on 2s. 6d. red .. 1·40 2·50

1919.
99. **2.** ½d. green and olive .. 15 12
101. 1½d. blue and brown .. 35 15
102. 2d. brown and purple .. 1·00 55
102a. 2d. brown and red .. 5·00 95
103. 2½d. green and blue .. 1·25 2·75
104. 3d. black and blue-green 70 70
105a. 4d. brown and orange .. 2·25 4·50
106. 5d. grey and brown .. 2·00 2·50
107. 6d. purple .. .. 1·00 1·40
127. 9d. lilac and violet .. 3·00 3·50
108a. 1s. brown and olive .. 1·40 2·25
128. 1s. 3d. lilac and blue .. 5·00 5·00
109a. 2s. 6d. claret and pink .. 7·00 9·00
110. 5s. black and green .. 13·00 12·00
111. 10s. green and blue .. 42·00 45·00

1929. Air. Optd. **AIR MAIL.**
114. **2.** 3d. black and blue-green 1·00 1·40

(3.)

1930. Air. Optd. with T **3.**
118. **2.** 3d. black and blue-green 40 90
119. 6d. purple .. .. 2·25 2·75
120. 1s. brown and olive .. 2·75 3·25

1931. Surch. in words or figs. and words.
122. **2.** 2d. on 1½d. blue & brown 90 1·00
125. 5d. on 1s. brown & olive 60 1·00
126. 9d. on 2s. 6d. clar. & pink 1·50 2·50
123. 1s. 3d. on 5d. black & grn. 1·50 2·00

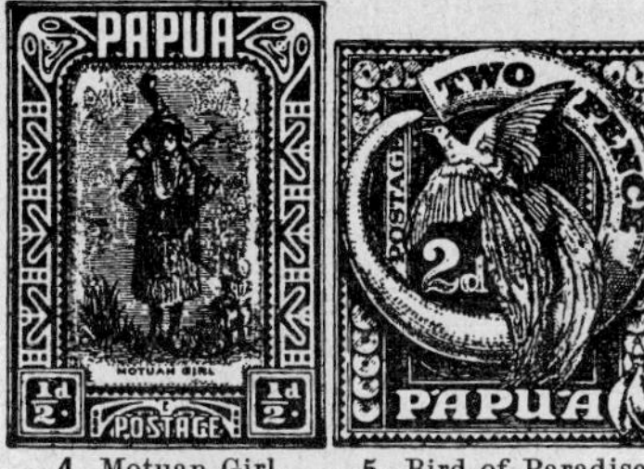

4. Motuan Girl. **5.** Bird of Paradise.

6. Native Mother and Child.

1932.
130. **4.** ½d. black and orange .. 15 15
131. – 1d. black and green .. 10 10
132. – 1½d. black and red .. 55 1·10
133. **5.** 2d. red .. .. .. 1·10 20
134. – 3d. black and blue .. 1·25 2·00
135. **6.** 4d. olive .. .. 1·25 1·90
136. – 5d. black and green .. 1·10 1·25
137. – 6d. brown .. .. 1·75 1·75
138. – 9d. black and violet .. 3·50 4·00
139. – 1s. green .. .. 2·25 3·75
140. – 1s. 3d. black and purple 5·00 6·50
141. – 2s. black and green .. 5·00 6·50
142. – 2s. 6d. black and mauve 9·00 11·00
143. – 5s. black and brown .. 13·00 13·00
144. – 10s. violet .. .. 26·00 32·00
145. – £1 black and grey .. 55·00 50·00

DESIGNS—VERT. as T **4**: 1d. Chieftain's son. 1½d. Tree houses. 3d. Papuan dandy. 5d. Masked dancer. 9d. Shooting fish. 1s. Ceremonial platform. 1s. 3d. Lakatoi. 2s. Papuan art. 2s. 6d. Pottery-making. 5d. Native policeman. £1 Delta house. VERT. as T **5**: 6d. Papuan mother. HORIZ. 10 s. Lighting fire.

7. Hoisting the Union Jack.

1934. Declaration of British Protectorate 50th Anniv. Inscr. "1884 1934".
146. **7.** 1d green 70 85
147. – 2d. red .. .. .. 1·10 1·00
148. **7.** 3d. blue .. .. .. 2·75 2·75
149. – 5d. purple .. .. 5·00 5·50

DESIGN: 2d., 5d. Scene on H.M.S. "Nelson".

1935. Silver Jubilee. Optd. **HIS MAJESTY'S JUBILEE 1910-1935.**
150. – 1d. black & green (No. 131) 25 30
151. **5.** 2d. red 40 55
152. – 3d. black & blue (No. 134) 1·00 1·40
153. – 5d. black & green (No. 136) 3·50 4·00

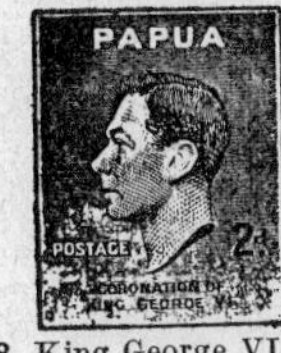

8. King George VI.

ILLUSTRATIONS
British Commonwealth and all overprints and surcharges are FULL SIZE. Foreign Countries have been reduced to ¾-LINEAR.

1937. Coronation.
154. **8.** 1d. green.. .. .. 8 8
155. 2d. red 8 8
156. 3d. blue 12 10
157. 5d. purple 15 15

9. Port Moresby.

1938. Air. Declaration of British Possession 50th Anniv.
158. **9.** 2d. red .. .. .. 55 1·10
159. 3d. blue .. .. .. 1·00 1·40
160. 5d. green .. .. 1·40 1·75
161. 8d. red .. .. .. 3·00 4·00
162. 1s. mauve .. .. 6·00 5·50

10. Natives Poling Rafts.

1399. Air.
163. **10.** 2d. red 70 80
164 3d. blue .. .. 80 1·10
165. 5d. green .. .. 1·40 95
166. 8d. red .. .. .. 2·25 2·75
167. 1s. mauve .. .. 3·50 3·50
168. 1s. 6d. olive .. .. 14·00 16·00

OFFICIAL STAMPS

1931. Optd. **O.S.**
O 1. **2.** ½d. green and olive .. 35 80
O 2a. 1d. black and red .. 20 100
O 3 1½d. blue and brown .. 75 1·75
O 4. 2d. purple and red .. 70 1·75
O 5. 3d. black & blue-green 70 2·75
O 6. 4d. brown and orange.. 95 2·75
O 7. 5d. grey and brown .. 1·50 3·00
O 8. 6d. purple and red .. 2·50 3·50
O 9. 9d. lilac and violet .. 5·50 9·00
O 10. 1s. brown and olive .. 3·50 5·00
O 11. 1s. 3d. lilac and blue .. 8·00 12·00
O 12a. 2s. 6d. claret and pink 8·00 12·00

PAPUA NEW GUINEA BC

Combined territory on the island of New Guinea administered by Australia under trusteeship. Self-government was established during 1973.

1966. 100 cents = $1 Australian.
1975. 100 toea = 1 Kina.

1. Tree-climbing Kangaroo.

2. Kiriwina Chief House.

1952.
1. **1.** ½d. emerald 10 8
2. – 1d. brown 8 5
3. – 2d. blue 15 8
4. – 2½d. orange 50 40
5. – 3d. myrtle 25 10
6. – 3½d. red 25 15
6a. – 3½d. black.. .. .. 2·50 1·25
18. – 4d. vermilion 15 8
19. – 5d. green 15 8
7. **2.** 6½d. purple 45 10
20. – 7d. bronze-green .. .. 1·50 45
8. – 7½d. blue .. .. 4·50 3·00
21. – 8d. blue .. .. 1 50 1·25
9. – 9d. brown.. .. .. 80 40
10. – 1s. green 70 30
11. – 1s. 6d. myrtle .. .. 1·10 45
22. – 1s. 7d. brown .. .. 19·00 16·00
12. – 2s. indigo .. .. 1·75 60
23. – 2s. 5d. vermilion .. .. 2·25 2·25
13. – 2s. 6d. maroon .. .. 1·75 65
24. – 5s. crimson and olive .. 2·25 1·50
14. – 10s. slate .. .. .. 16·00 6·00
15. – £1 brown .. .. 50·00 20·00

DESIGNS—As T **1**: 1d. Buka head-dresses. 2d. Native youth. 2½d. Bird of Paradise. 3d. Native policeman. 3½d. Papuan head-dress. 4d., 5d. Cacao plant. As T **2**, VERT. 7½d. Kiriwina Yam house. 1s. 6d. Rubber tapping. 2s. Sepik dancing masks. 5s. Coffee beans. £1 Native shooting fish. HORIZ. 7d., 8d. Klinki plymill. 9d. Copra making. 1s. Lakatoi (trading canoe). 1s. 7d., 2s. 5d. Cattle. 2s. 6d. Native shepherd and flock. 10s. Map of Papua and New Guinea.

1957. Nos. 4, 1 and 10 surch.
16. – 4d. on 2½d. orange .. 25 20
25. **1.** 5d. on ½d. emerald .. 25 10
17. – 7d. on 1s. green .. 45 35

3. Council Chamber, Port Moresby.

1961. Reconstitution of Legislative Council.

26.	3.	5d. green and yellow ..	80	25
27.		2s. 3d. green and salmon	9·00	9·00

4. Female, Goroka, New Guinea. 6. Female Dancer.

5. Waterfront, Port Moresby.

7. Traffic Policeman.

1961.

28.	4.	1d. lake ..	8	8
29.	–	3d. indigo ..	12	10
47.	5.	8d. green ..	25	25
30.	6.	1s. green ..	2·00	50
31.	–	2s. maroon ..	60	50
48.	–	2s. 3d. blue ..	75	75
32.	7.	3s. green ..	75	60

DESIGNS—As T 4: 3d. Tribal elder, Tari, Papua. As T 5: 2s. 3d. Piaggio P-166 Aircraft landing at Tapini. As T 6: 2s. Male dancer.

8. Campaign Emblem.

1962. Malaria Eradication.

33.	8.	5d. lake and blue ..	25	20
34.		1s. red and sepia ..	1·25	1·25
35.		2s. black and green ..	2·50	2·50

9. Map of South Pacific.

1962. 5th South Pacific Conf., Pago Pago.

36.	9.	5d. red and green	25	25
37.		1s. 6d. violet and yellow	1·25	1·25
38.		2s. 6d. green and blue .	2·75	2·75

SPORTS: No. 40, High jump. No. 41, Runners.

10. Throwing the Javelin.

1962. 7th British Empire and Commonwealth Games, Perth.

39.	10.	5d. brown and blue ..	40	25
40.	–	5d. brown and orange ..	40	25
41.	–	2s. 3d. brown and green	1·75	1·75

Nos. 39/41 are arranged together se-tenant in the sheet.

11. Bird of Paradise. 13. Queen Elizabeth II.

DESIGN—As T 11: 6d. Golden Opossum.

12. Rabaul.

1963.

42.	11.	5d. yellow, chest. & sepia	12	12
43.	–	6d. red, yell-brn. & grey	50	75
44.	12.	10s. multicoloured ..	8·00	7·00
45.	13.	£1 sepia, gold and green	7·00	6·50

1963. Red Cross Cent. As T 138 of Australia.

46.	5d. red, grey and green ..	15	20

14. Games Emblem.

1963. 1st South Pacific Games Suva.

49.	14.	5d. bistre	35	25
50.		1s. green	90	90

15. Watam Head. 16. Casting Vote.

1964. Native Artifacts. Multicoloured.

51.	11d. Type 15	30	30
52.	2s. 5d. Watam Head (diff.)	60	60
53.	2s. 6d. Bosmun Head ..	70	70
54.	5s. Medina Head ..	1·25	1·25

1964. Common Roll Elections.

55.	16.	5d. brown and drab ..	15	15
56.		2s. 3d. brown and blue	80	80

17. "Health Centres". 18. Lawes Six-wired Birds of Paradise.

1964. Health Services.

57.	17.	5d. violet	15	10
58.	–	8d. green	20	20
59.	–	1s. blue	30	30
60.	–	1s. 2d. red	40	40

DESIGNS: 8d. "School Health". 1s. "Infant Child and Maternal Health". 1s. 2d. "Medical Training".

1964. Multicoloured.

61.	1d. Striped Gardener Bowerbird	10	8
62.	3d. New Guinea Regent Bowerbird	12	10
63.	5d. Blue Bird of Paradise ..	12	10
64.	6d. Type 18	15	12
65.	8d. Black-billed Sickle-billed Bird of Paradise ..	20	20
66.	1s. Emperor of Germany Bird of Paradise	30	30
67.	2s. Brown Sickle-billed Bird of Paradise	45	45
68.	2s. 3d. Lesser Bird of Paradise	55	60
69.	3s. Magnificent Bird of Paradise	80	90
70.	5s. Twelve-wired Bird of Paradise	1·60	1·60
71.	10s. Magnificent Rifle Bird	3·00	3·25

Nos. 66/71 are larger (25½ × 36½ mm.).

19. Carved Canoe Prow.

1965. Sepik Canoe Prows in Port Moresby Museum.

72.	19.	4d. multicoloured ..	20	15
73.	–	1s. 3d. multicoloured ..	80	1·00
74.	–	1s. 6d. multicoloured ..	45	45
75.	–	4s. multicoloured ..	1·00	1·25

Each show different carved canoe prows as Type 19.

1965. Gallipoli Landing. 50th Anniv. As T 147 of Australia, but slightly larger (22 × 34½ mm.).

76.	2s. 3d. brown, black and green	60	60

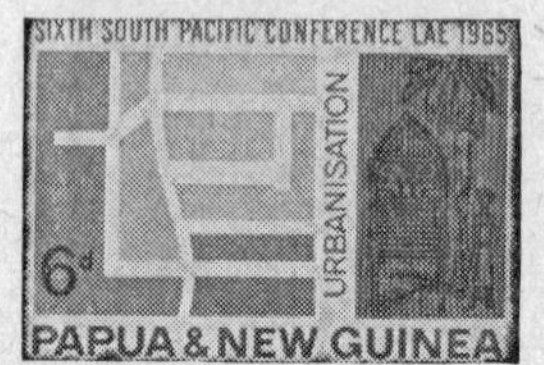

20. Urban Plan and Native House.

1965. 6th South Pacific Conf., Lae.

77.	20.	6d. multicoloured ..	12	12
78.	–	1s. multicoloured ..	30	30

No. 78 is similar to T 20 but with the plan on the right and the house on the left. Also "URBANISATION" reads downwards.

21. Mother and Child.

1965. U.N.O. 20th Anniv.

79.	21.	6d. sepia, blue & turquoise	12	12
80.	–	1s. chest., blue & violet	25	25
81.	–	2s. blue, green and olive	40	40

DESIGNS—VERT. 1s. Globe and U.N. Emblem. 2s. U.N. Emblem and Globes.

22. Blue Emperor.

1966. Decimal Currency. Multicoloured.

82.	1 c. Type 22	5	5
83.	3 c. White-banded Map Butterfly	10	10
84.	4 c. Mountain Swallowtail ..	12	12
85.	5 c. Port Moresby Terinos ..	12	10
86.	10 c. New Guinea Birdwing	25	25
86a.	12 c. Blue Crow (butterfly)	60	60
87.	15 c. Euchenor Butterfly ..	70	70
88.	20 c. White-spotted Parthenos	50	50
89.	25 c. Orange Jezebel ..	70	70
90.	50 c. New Guinea Emperor	1·25	1·00
91.	$1 Blue Spotted Leaf-wing	2·50	2·50
92.	$2 Paradise Birdwing ..	4·50	4·75

Nos. 86/92 are horiz.

23. "Molala Harai". 24. Throwing the Discus.

1966. Folklore. Elema Art.

93.	23.	2 c. black and red ..	5	5
94.	–	7 c. black, yellow and blue	15	15
95.	–	30 c. black, red and green	55	60
96.	–	60 c. black, red & yellow	1·50	1·60

DESIGNS: 7 c. "Marai". 30 c. "Meavia Kivovia". 60 c. "Toivita Tapaivita".

1966. South Pacific Games, Noumea. Multicoloured.

97.	5 c. Type 24	10	10
98.	10 c. Football	25	25
99.	20 c. Tennis	45	4[illegible]

25. "Mucuna novoguineensis".

1966. Flowers. Multicoloured.

100.	5 c. Type 25	15	15
101.	10 c. "Tecomanthe dendrophila"	25	25
102.	20 c. "Rhododendron macgregoriae"	45	45
103.	60 c. "Rhododendron konori"	1·25	1·25

26. "Fine Arts".

1967. Higher Education. Multicoloured.

104.	1 c. Type 26	5	5
105.	3 c. "Surveying" ..	10	10
106.	4 c. "Civil Engineering"	10	10
107.	5 c. "Science"	10	10
108.	20 c. "Law"	40	40

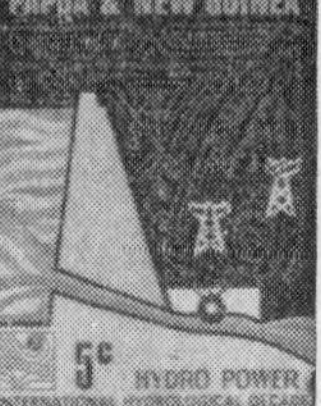

27. "Sagra speciosa". 28. Laloki River.

1967. Fauna Conservation (Beetles). Multicoloured.

109.	5 c. Type 27	10	10
110.	10 c. "Eupholus schoenherri"	25	25
111.	20 c. "Sphingnotus albertisi"	40	35
112.	25 c. "Cyphogastra albertisi"	45	45

1967. Laloki River Hydro-Electric Scheme, and "New Industries". Multicoloured.

113.	5 c. Type 28	10	10
114.	10 c. Pyrethrum	25	25
115.	20 c. Tea Plant	40	40
116.	25 c. Type 28	50	50

29. Air Attack at Milne Bay.

1967. Pacific War. 25th Anniv. Multicoloured.

117.	2 c. Type **29**	5	5
118.	5 c. Kokoda Trail (vert.) ..	10	10
119.	20 c. The Coast Watchers ..	40	35
120.	50 c. Battle of the Coral Sea	95	95

30. Fairy Lory. **31.** Chimbu Head-dress.

1967. Christmas. Territory Parrots. Multicoloured.

121.	5 c. Type **30**	12	12
122.	7 c. Vulturine Parrot ..	20	20
123.	20 c. Dusk-orange Lory ..	50	50
124.	25 c. Edwards' Fig Parrot	60	60

1968. "National Heritage". Designs showing different Head-dresses. Multicoloured.

125.	5 c. Type **31**	12	12
126.	10 c. Southern Highlands (horiz.)	25	25
127.	20 c. Western Highlands (horiz.)	45	45
128.	60 c. Chimbu (different) ..	1·25	1·25

32. 'Hyla thesaurensia'.

1968. Fauna Conservation (Frogs). Multicoloured.

129.	5 c. Type **32**	12	12
130.	10 c. "Hyla iris"	25	25
131.	15 c. "Ceratobatrachus guentheri"	35	35
132.	20 c. "Nyctimystes narinosa"	45	45

33. Human Rights Flame and Papuan Head-dress.

1968. Human Rights Year. Multicoloured.

133.	5 c. Type **33**	12	12
134.	10 c. Human Rights in the World (abstract) ..	25	25

34. Leadership (abstract).

1968. Universal Suffrage. Multicoloured.

135.	20 c. Type **34**	45	45
136.	25 c. Leadership of the Community (abstract) ..	60	60

35. Egg Cowry.

1968. Seashells. Multicoloured.

137.	1 c. Type **35**	5	5
138.	3 c. Lancinated Conch ..	8	8
139.	4 c. Lithograph Cone ..	10	10
140.	5 c. Marbled Cone ..	10	10
141.	7 c. Episcopal Mitre ..	12	15
142.	10 c. Red Volute ..	20	20
143.	12 c. Areola Bonnet ..	25	25
144.	15 c. Scorpion Conch ..	50	30
145.	20 c. Fluted Clam ..	40	40
146.	25 c. Chocolate Flamed Venus Shell	50	50
147.	30 c. Giant Murex ..	70	75
148.	40 c. Chambered Nautilus	80	80
149.	60 c. Pacific Triton ..	1·25	1·25
150.	$1 Emerald Snail ..	2·25	2·25
151.	$2 Glory of the Sea ..	4·00	4·00

36. Tito Myth. **37.** "Fireball"-class Yacht.

1969. Folklore. Elema Art.

152. **36.**	5 c. black, yellow & red	15	15
153. –	5 c. black, yellow & red	15	15
154. –	10 c. black, grey and red	30	30
155. –	10 c. black, grey and red	30	30

DESIGNS: No. 153, Iko Myth. 154, Luvuapo Myth. 155, Miro Myth.

Nos. 152/3 and 154/5 were issued in vert. se-tenant pairs separated by a line of roulette.

1969. Third South Pacific Games, Port Moresby.

156. **37.**	5 c. black	12	12
157. –	10 c. violet	25	25
158. –	20 c. green	45	45

DESIGNS—HORIZ. 10 c. Swimming pool, Boroko. 20 c. Games Arena, Konedobu.

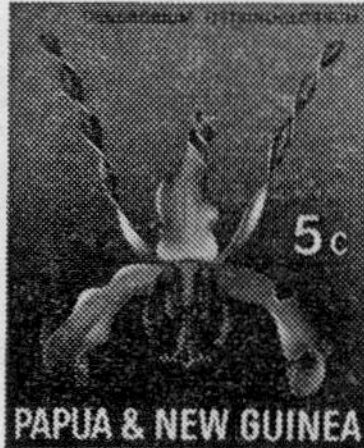

38. "Dendrobium ostrinoglossum". **39.** Bird of Paradise.

1969. Flora Conservation (Orchids). Multicoloured.

159.	5 c. Type **38**	12	12
160.	10 c. "Dendrobium lawesii"	25	25
161.	20 c. "Dendrobium pseudofrigidum"	40	40
162.	30 c. "Dendrobium conanthum"	65	65

1969. Coil Stamps.

162a. **39.**	2 c. blue, blk. & red ..	5	5
163.	5 c. grn., brn. & orange	5	5

40. Native Potter.

1969. I.L.O. 50th Anniv.

164. **40.**	5 c. multicoloured ..	12	10

41. Tareko.

1969. Musical Instruments.

165. **41.**	5 c. multicoloured ..	12	12
166. –	10 c. black, grn. & yellow	25	25
167. –	25 c. blk., yellow & brn.	50	50
168. –	30 c. multicoloured ..	65	65

DESIGNS: 10 c. Garamut. 25 c. viliko. 30 c. Kundu.

42. Prehistoric Ambun Stone.

1970. "National Heritage". Multicoloured.

169.	5 c. Type **42**	12	12
170.	10 c. Masawa canoe of Kula Cicuit	25	25
171.	25 c. Torres' map, 1606 ..	50	50
172.	30 c. H.M.S. "Basilisk" ..	65	65

43. "King of Saxony" Bird of Paradise.

1970. Fauna Conservation. Birds of Paradise. Multicoloured.

173.	5 c. Type **43**	12	12
174.	10 c. "Little King" ..	25	25
175.	15 c. "Augusta Victoria"	35	35
176.	25 c. "Sickle-crested" ..	55	55

44. "D.C. 6B" and Mt. Wilhelm.

1970. Australian and New Guinea Air Services. Multicoloured.

177.	5 c. Type **44**	12	12
178.	5 c. "Lockheed Electra" (turbo-prop), and Mt. Yule	12	12
179.	5 c. Boeing "727" (jet), and Mt. Giluwe ..	12	12
180.	5 c. Fokker "Friendship" and Manam Island ..	12	12
181.	25 c. "D.C. 3." and Matupi Volcano	55	55
182.	30 c. Boeing "707" and Hombrom's Bluff ..	60	65

45. N. Miklouho-Maclay (scientist) and Effigy.

1970. 42nd A.N.Z.A.A.S. Congress, Port Moresby. Multicoloured.

183.	5 c. Type **45**	12	12
184.	10 c. B. Malinowski (anthropologist) and native hut	25	25
185.	15 c. T. Salvadori (ornithologist) and cassowary	40	40
186.	20 c. F. R. R. Schlechter (botonist) and flower ..	50	50

A.N.Z.A.A.S. = Australian-New Zealand Association for the Advancement of Science.

46. Wogeo Island Food Bowl. **47.** Eastern Highlands Dwelling.

1970. Native Artifacts. Multicoloured.

187.	5 c. Type **46**	12	12
188.	10 c. Lime Pot	25	25
189.	15 c. Albom Sago Storage Pot	35	35
190.	30 c. Manus Island Bowl ..	60	60

1971. Native Dwellings. Multicoloured.

191.	5 c. Type **47**	12	12
192.	7 c. Milne Bay Stilt Dwelling	20	20
193.	10 c. Purari Delta Dwelling	30	30
194.	40 c. Sepik Dwelling ..	90	90

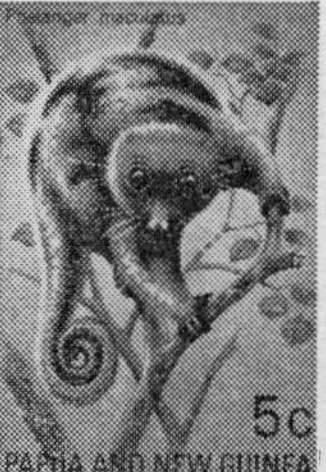

48. Spotted Cuscus. **50.** Bartering Fish for Vegetables.

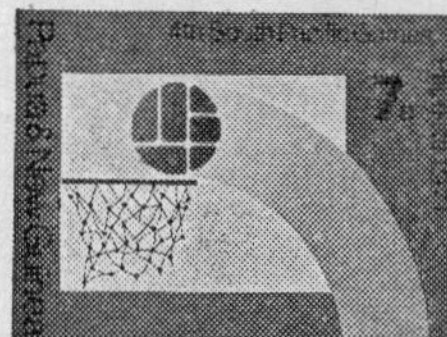

49. "Basketball".

1971. Fauna Conservation. Multicoloured.

195.	5 c. Type **48**	12	12
196.	10 c. Brown and White Striped Possum ..	25	25
197.	15 c. Feather-tailed Possum	30	30
198.	25 c. Spiny Ant-eater (horiz.)	50	50
199.	30 c. Goodfellow's Tree-climbing Kangaroo (horiz.)	65	65

1971. 4th South Pacific Games, Papeete. Multicoloured.

200.	7 c. Type **49**	20	20
201.	14 c. "Sailing"	35	35
202.	21 c. "Boxing"	45	45
203.	28 c. "Athletics"	70	70

1971. Primary Industries. Multicoloured.

204.	7 c. Type **50**	15	15
205.	9 c. Man stacking yams	25	25
206.	14 c. Vegetable market ..	30	30
207.	30 c. Highlanders cultivating garden	70	70

51. Sia Dancer.

1971. Native Dancers. Multicoloured.

208.	7 c. Type **51**	15	15
209.	9 c. Urasena dancer ..	25	25
210.	20 c. Siassi Tubuan dancers (horiz.)	40	40
211.	28 c. Sia dancers (horiz.) ..	70	70

52. Papuan Flag over Australian Flag.

1971. Constitutional Development.

No.	Type	Description		
212.	52.	7 c. multicoloured ..	20	15
213.	–	7 c. multicoloured ..	20	15

DESIGN: No. 213, Crest of Papua and New Guinea and Australian coat of arms.

53. Map of Papua and New Guinea, and Flag of South Pacific Commission.

1972. South Pacific Commission. 25th Anniv.

No.	Type	Description		
214.	53.	15 c. multicoloured ..	35	35
215.	–	15 c. multicoloured ..	35	35

DESIGN: No. 215, Man's face and flag of the Commission.

54. Turtle.

1972. Fauna Conservation (Reptiles). Multicoloured.

216.	7 c. Type **54**	15	15
217.	14 c. Rainforest Dragon ..	45	50
218.	21 c. Green Python ..	45	50
219.	30 c. Salvador's Monitor	55	55

55. Curtiss "Seagull MF-6" and Ship.

1972. Aviation. 50th Anniv. Multicoloured.

220.	7 c. Type **55**	15	12
221.	14 c. De Havilland "37" and native porters ..	45	45
222.	20 c. Junkers "G-31" and gold dredge	45	45
223.	25 c. Junkers "F-13" and mission church	50	50

56. New National Flag.

1972. National Day. Multicoloured.

224.	7 c. Type **56**	12	12
225.	10 c. Native drum	40	40
226.	30 c. Blowing the conch-shell	70	70

57. Rev. Copland King.

1972. Christmas. Missionaries. Mult.

227.	7 c. Type **57**	20	20
228.	7 c. Rev. Dr. Flierl ..	20	20
229.	7 c. Bishop Verjus ..	20	20
230.	7 c. Pastor Ruatoka ..	20	20

58. Mt. Tomavatur Station.

1973. Completion of Telecommunications Project, 1968-72. Multicoloured.

231.	7 c. Type **58**	15	15
232.	7 c. Mt. Kerigomma Station	15	15
233.	7 c. Sattelburg Station ..	15	15
234.	7 c. Wideru Station ..	15	15
235.	9 c. Teleprinter	20	20
236.	30 c. Network map ..	60	60

Nos. 235/6 are larger, 36 × 26 mm.

59. Queen Carol's Bird of Paradise.

1973. Birds of Paradise. Multicoloured.

237.	7 c. Type **59**	20	20
238.	14 c. Decorative	35	35
239.	21 c. Ribbon-tailed ..	60	60
240.	28 c. Princess Stephanie ..	70	70

Nos. 239/40 are size 18 × 49 mm.

60. Wood Carver.

1973. Multicoloured.

241.	1 c. Type **60**	5	5
242.	3 c. Wig-makers	5	5
243.	5 c. Mt. Bagana	8	8
244.	6 c. Pig Exchange ..	10	10
245.	7 c. Coastal village ..	10	12
246.	8 c. Arawe mother ..	10	12
247.	9 c. Fire dancers	10	12
248.	10 c. Tifalmin hunter ..	12	15
249.	14 c. Crocodile hunters ..	20	20
250.	15 c. Mt. Elimbari ..	20	20
251.	20 c. Canoe-racing ..	25	30
252.	21 c. Making sago ..	25	30
253.	25 c. Council House ..	30	35
254.	28 c. Menyamya bowmen	35	40
255.	30 c. Shark-snaring ..	35	40
256.	40 c. Fishing canoes ..	50	55
257.	60 c. Tapa cloth-making ..	75	85
258.	$1 Asaro Mudmen ..	1·75	1·75
259.	$2 Euga "Sing Sing" ..	3·00	3·25

61. Stamps of German New Guinea, 1897. (Illustration reduced. Actual size 55 × 31 mm.).

1973. Papua New Guinea Stamps. 75th Anniv.

No.	Type	Description		
260.	61.	1 c. multicoloured ..	8	8
261.	–	6 c. indigo, blue and silver	20	20
262.	–	7 c. multicoloured ..	25	25
263.	–	9 c. multicoloured ..	35	35
264.	–	25 c. orange and gold ..	80	90
265.	–	30 c. plum and silver ..	1·00	1·10

DESIGNS—As T 61. 6 c. 2 mark stamp of German New Guinea, 1900. 7 c. Surcharged registration label of New Guinea, 1914. 46 × 35 mm. 9 c. Papuan 1 s. stamp, 1901. 45 × 38 mm. 25 c. ½ d. stamp of New Guinea, 1925. 30 c. Papuan 10 s. stamp, 1932.

62. Native Carved Heads.

1973. Self-Government.

No.	Type	Description		
266.	62.	7 c. multicoloured ..	20	20
267.		10 c. multicoloured ..	35	35

63. Queen Elizabeth II (from photo by Karsh).

1974. Royal Visit.

No.	Type	Description		
268.	63.	7 c. multicoloured ..	15	15
269.		30 c. multicoloured ..	55	60

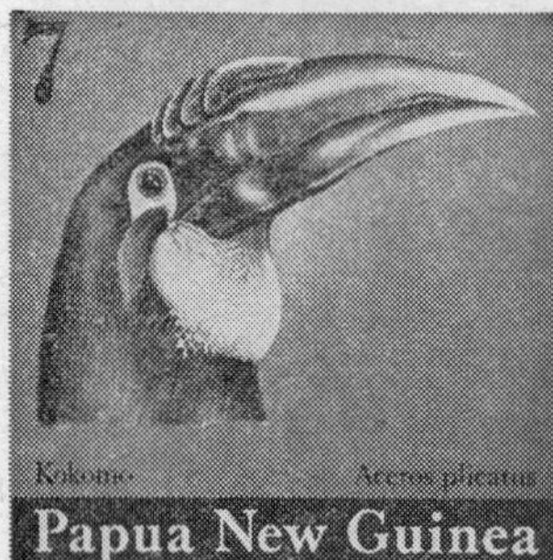

64. Kokomo (Wreathed Hornbill).

1974. Birds' Heads. Multicoloured.

270.	7 c. Type **64**	30	30
271.	10 c. Muruk (Great Cassowary) (33 × 49 mm.)	50	50
272.	30 c. Tarangau (Kapul Eagle)	1·60	1·60

65. "Dendrobium bracteosum".

1974. Flora Conservation. Multicoloured.

273.	7 c. Type **65**	12	12
274.	10 c. "D. anosmum" ..	20	20
275.	20 c. "D. smillieae" ..	35	35
276.	30 c. "D. insigne" ..	45	45

66. Motu Lagatoi.

1974. National Heritage. Canoes. Mult.

277.	7 c. Type **66**	12	12
278.	10 c. Tami tw-master morobe	20	20
279.	25 c. Aramia racing canoe	40	40
280.	30 c. Buka canoe	50	50

67. 1-toea Coin.

1975. New Coinage. Multicoloured.

281.	1 t. Type **67**	5	5
282.	7 t. New 2 t. and 5 t. coins	10	10
283.	10 t. New 10 t. coin ..	15	15
284.	20 t. New 20 t. coin ..	35	35
285.	1 k. New 1 k. coin ..	1·40	1·60

SIZES: 10 t., 20 t. As Type **67**. 7 t., 1 k. 45 × 26 mm.

68. "Ornithoptera alexandrae". **69.** Boxing.

1975. Fauna Conservation (Birdwing Butterflies). Multicoloured.

286.	7 t. Type **68**	10	10
287.	10 t. "O. victoriae regis"	15	15
288.	30 t. "O. allottei" ..	45	45
289.	40 t. "O. chimaera" ..	60	60

1975. 5th South Pacific Games, Guam. Multicoloured.

290.	7 t. Type **69**	10	10
291.	20 t. Running	30	30
292.	25 t. Basketball	35	35
293.	30 t. Swimming	40	40

70. Map and National Flag.

1975. Independence. Multicoloured.

294.	7 t. Type **70**	10	10
295.	30 t. Map and National emblem	40	40

71. M.V. "Bulolo".

1976. Ships of the 1930's. Multicoloured.

297.	7 t. Type **71**	10	10
298.	15 t. M.V. "Macdhui" ..	20	20
299.	25 t. M.V. "Malaita" ..	35	35
300.	60 t. S.S. "Montoro" ..	75	80

72. Rorovana Carvings.

1976. Bougainville Artifacts. Multicoloured.

301.	7 t. Type **72**	10	10
302.	20 t. Upe hats	25	25
303.	25 t. Kapkaps	30	35
304.	30 t. Canoe paddles ..	40	45

73. Rabaul House.

1976. Native Dwellings. Multicoloured.
305. 7 t. Type 73 .. .. 10 12
306. 15 t. Aramia House .. 20 25
307. 30 t. Telefomin house .. 40 45
308. 40 t. Tapini house .. 55 65

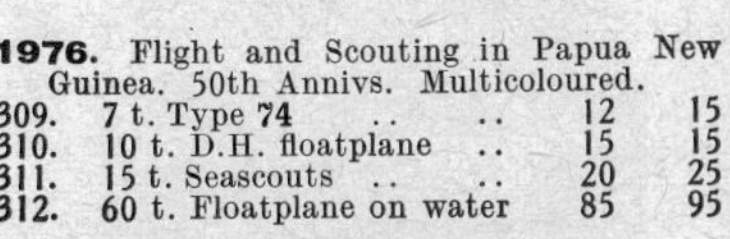

74. Landscouts.

1976. Flight and Scouting in Papua New Guinea. 50th Annivs. Multicoloured.
309. 7 t. Type 74 .. 12 15
310. 10 t. D.H. floatplane .. 15 15
311. 15 t. Seascouts 20 25
312. 60 t. Floatplane on water 85 95

75. Father Ross and New Guinea Highlands.

1976. William Ross Commemoration.
313. 75. 7 t. multicoloured .. 12 15

76. Clouded Rainbow Fish.

1976. Fauna Conservation (Tropical Fish). Multicoloured.
314. 5 t. Type 76 .. .. 8 10
315. 15 t. Emperor or Imperial Angel Fish 20 25
316. 30 t. Freckled Rock Cod .. 40 45
317. 40 t. Threadfin Butterfly Fish 55 65

77. Wasara Headdress.

1977. Multicoloured.
318. 1 k. Type 77 .. 1·40 1·60
319. 2 k. Mekeo headdress .. 2·75 3·00

POSTAGE DUE STAMPS

1960. Stamps of 1952 surch. **POSTAL CHARGES** and value.
D 2. 1 d. on 6½d. purple .. 1·50 1·50
D 3. 3d. on ½d. emerald .. 2·00 2·50
D 1. 6d. on 7½d. blue (A) .. £150 £150
D 4. 6d. on 7½d. blue (B) .. 3·00 4·00
D 5. 1s. 3d. on 3½d. black .. 6·00 8·00
D 6. 3s. on 2½d. orange .. .. 10·00 12·00

In (A) value and "POSTAGE" is obliterated by a solid circle and a series of "IX's" but these are motited in (B).

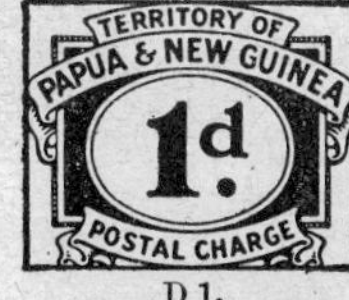

D 1.

1960.
D 7. D 1. 1d. orange 5 5
D 8. 3d. brown 20 20
D 9. 6d. blue 25 25
D 10. 9d. red 40 40
D 11. 1s. green 25 25
D 12. 1s. 3d. violet .. 60 60
D 13. 1s. 6d. pale blue .. 60 60
D 14. 3s. yellow 85 85

PARAGUAY

04

A republic in the centre of S. America independent since 1811.
1870. 8 reales = 1 peso.
1878. 100 centavos = 1 peso.
1944. 100 centimos = 1 guarani.

1. 2.

1870. Various frames. Values in "reales". Imperf.
1. 1. 1 r. red .. .. .. 1·50 1·90
3. 2 r. blue .. .. .. 25·00 35·00
4. 3 r. black .. .. .. 45·00 45·00

1878. Handstamped with large **5.** Imperf.
5. 1. 5 c. on 1 r. red .. .. 22·00 25·00
9. 5 c. on 2 r. blue .. .. 80·00 75·00
7. 5 c. on 3 r. black .. .. 90·00 90·00

1879. Prepared for use but not issued (wrong currency). Values in "reales". Perf.
14. 2. 5 r. orange 20
15. 10 r. brown 25

1879. Values in "centavos". Perf. or imperf.
16. 2. 5 c. brown 65 65
17. 10 c. green 90 90

1881. Handstamped with large figures.
18. 2. 1 on 10 c. green .. .. 3·00 3·00
19. 2 on 10 c. green .. .. 3·00 3·00

1881. As T 1 (various frames), but value in "centavos". Perf.
20. 1. 1 c. blue 20 20
21a. 2 c. red 20 20
22. 4 c. brown 20 20

1884. No. 1 handstamped with large **1.** Imperf.
23. 1. 1 c. on 1 r. red .. .. 1·90 1·90

3. 4.

1884. Perf.
24. 3. 1 c. green 12 12
25. 2 c. red 12 12
26. 5 c. blue 12 12

1887.
32. 4. 1 c. green 10 10
33. 2 c. red 10 10
34. 5 c. blue 20 20
35. 7 c. brown 25 20
36. 10 c. mauve 25 20
37. 15 c. orange 25 20
38. 20 c. rose 25 20
50. 40 c. blue 90 75
51. 60 c. orange 35 35
52. 80 c. blue 30 30
53. 1 p. olive 35 35

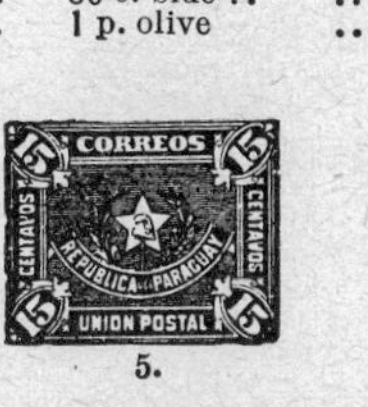

5. 6. C. Rivarola.

1889. Imperf. or perf.
40. 5. 15 c. purple .. .. 1·25 1·25

1892.
42. 6. 1 CENTAVOS grey .. 5 5
54. 1 CENTAVO grey .. 5 5
43. – 2 c. green 8 5
44. – 4 c. red 5 5
57. – 5 c. purple 10 5
46. – 10 c. violet 15 15
47. – 14 c. brown 25 25
48. – 20 c. red 40 40
49. – 30 c. green 60 50
84. – 1 p. blue 25 20

PORTRAITS: 2 c. S. Jovellano, 4 c. J. Bautista Gil. 5 c. H. Uriarte. 10 c. C. Barreiro. 14 c. Gen. B. Caballero. 20 c. P. Escober. 30 c. J. Gonzales. 1 p. J. B. Egusquisa.

1892. Discovery of America. 400th Anniv. Optd. **1492 12 DE OCTUBRE 1892** in oval.
41. – 10 c. violet (No. 46) .. 3·00 1·50

1895. Surch. **PROVISORIO 5.**
59. 4. 5 c. on 7 c. brown .. 12 12

7. 8.

1896. Telegraph stamps as T 7 surch. **CORREOS 5 CENTAVOS** in oval.
60. 7. 5 c. on 2 c. brn., blk. & grey 25 25
61. 5 c. on 4 c. orge., blk. & grey 25 25

1900. Telegraph stamps as T 7 surch. with figures of value twice and bar.
64. 7. 5 c. on 30 c. green, black and grey 65 65
65. 10 c. on 50 c. lilac, black and grey .. .. 1·90 1·90

1898. Surch. **Provisorio 10 Centavos.**
63. 4. 10 c. on 15 c. orange .. 35 35
62. 10 c. on 40 c. blue 20 20

1900.
76. 8. 1 c. green 10 8
77. 2 c. grey 10 8
73. 2 c. red 15 12
68. 3 c. brown 12 12
78. 4 c. blue 10 10
69. 5 c. green 12 12
74. 5 c. brown 15 12
79. 5 c. lilac 12 10
80. 8 c. brown 12 12
81. 10 c. red 15 12
72. 24 c. blue 20 20
82. 28 c. orange 25 20
83. 40 c. blue 25 20

1902. Surch. **Habilitado en** and new values.
88. – 1 c. on 14 c. brown (No. 47) 12 12
91. – 1 c. on 1 p. blue (No. 84) 10 10
86. 8. 5 c. on 8 c. brown (No. 80) 20 20
87. 5 c. on 28 c. orge. (No. 82) 15 15
89. 4. 5 c. on 60 c. orge. (No. 51) 20 20
90. 5 c. on 80 c. blue (No. 52) 15 15
85. 8. 20 c. on 24 c. blue (No. 72) 20 20

9. 10. 11.

1903.
92. 9. 1 c. grey 8 8
93. 2 c. green 10 10
94. 5 c. blue 12 12
95. 10 c. brown 15 12
96. 20 c. red 20 12
97. 30 c. blue 20 15
98. 60 c. violet 65 55

1903.
99. 10. 1 c. green 8 8
100. 2 c. orange 8 8
101. 5 c. blue 12 12
102. 10 c. violet 15 12
103. 20 c. green 45 30
104. 30 c. blue 30 20
105. 60 c. brown 55 45

1904.
106. 11. 10 c. blue 20 20

1904. End of successful Revolt against Govt. (begun in August). Surch. **PAZ 12 Dic. 1904. 30 centavos.**
107. 11. 30 c. on 10 c. blue .. 30 30

12.

13.

1905.
108. 12. 1 c. orange 8 8
109. 1 c. red 8 8
110. 1 c. blue 10 10
112. 2 c. green 8 8
113. 2 c. red 8 8
114. 5 c. blue 10 8
115. 5 c. yellow 10 8
117. 10 c. brown 10 8
118. 10 c. green 8 8
119. 10 c. blue 10 8
120. 20 c. lilac 20 20
121. 20 c. brown 20 20
122. 20 c. green 12 12
123. 30 c. blue 15 12
124. 30 c. grey 15 12
125. 30 c. lilac 25 20
126. 60 c. chocolate 15 15
127. 60 c. brown .. .. 1·40 95
128. 12. 60 c. pink .. .. 1·40 95
129. 13. 1 p. black and red .. 1·40 95
130. 1 p. black and brown 55 30
131. 1 p. black and olive .. 45 30
132. 2 p. black and blue .. 25 25
133. 2 p. black and red .. 30 25
134. 2 p. black and orange .. 30 25
135. 5 p. black and red .. 90 65
136. 5 p. black and grey .. 90 65
137. 5 p. black and olive .. 90 65
138. 10 p. black and brown 90 65
139. 10 p. black and blue .. 90 65
140. 10 p. black & chocolate 95 65
141. 20 p. black and olive .. 2·25 1·90
142. 20 p. black and yellow 2·25 1·90
143. 20 p. black and purple 2·25 1·90

1907. Surch. **Habilitado en** and value and bars.
159. 12. 5 c. on 1 c. blue .. 8 8
144. 5 c. on 2 c. red .. 8 5
145. 5 c. on 2 c. olive .. 12 12
172. 8. 5 c. on 28 c. orange .. 95 95
173. 5 c. on 40 c. blue .. 30 30
161. 12. 5 c. on 60 c. brown .. 10 8
163. 5 c. on 60 c. chocolate 8 8
162. 5 c. on 60 c. pink .. 5 5
175. 20 c. on 1 c. blue .. 12 12
180. 4. 20 c. on 2 c. red .. 1·75 1·75
176. 12. 20 c. on 2 c. red .. 65 65
179. 20 c. on 30 c. lilac .. 15 15
178. 20 c. on 30 c. blue .. 1·40 1·40

1907. Official stamps surch. **Habilitado en** and value and bars. Where not otherwise stated, the design is as T 9, but with "OFICIAL" below the lion.
164. – 5 c. on 10 c. green .. 12 12
149. – 5 c. on 10 c. brown .. 12 12
150. – 5 c. on 10 c. lilac .. 12 12
166. – 5 c. on 20 c. brown .. 25 25
151. – 5 c. on 20 c. green .. 12 12
167. – 5 c. on 20 c. pink .. 25 25
152. – 5 c. on 20 c. lilac .. 10 12
157. 9. 5 c. on 30 c. bl. (No. O 104) 1·10 1·10
154. 5 c. on 30 c. blue .. 35 35
155. – 5 c. on 30 c. yellow .. 5 5
153. – 5 c. on 30 c. grey .. 10 10
158. 9. 5 c. on 60 c. violet (No. O 105) 35 30
156. – 5 c. on 60 c. chestnut .. 8 8
165. – 5 c. on 60 c. chocolate .. 5 5
171. – 5 c. on 60 c. blue .. 5 5
174. 4. 20 c. on 5 c. bl. (No. O 53) 95 95
184. 9. 20 c. on 5 c. bl. (No. O 101) 1·60 1·60

1907. Official stamps, as T 9 and 13, with "OFICIAL" added optd. **Habilitado** and one bar.
146. 5 c. grey 12 12
147. 5 c. blue 25 25
148. 5 c. green 12 12
185. 1 p. black and orange .. 25 25
186. 1 p. black and red .. 50 50

1907. Official stamps, as T 13, with "OFICIAL" added, surch. **Habilitado. 1908 UN CENTAVO** and bar.
187. 1 c. on 1 p. black and red 20 20
188. 1 c. on 1 p. black & lake 15 15
189. 1 c. on 1 p. black & orange 65 65

1909. Optd. **1908.**
190. 12. 1 c. green 5 5
191. 5 c. yellow 8 8
192. 10 c. claret 10 10
193. 20 c. orange 8 8
194. 30 c. red 20 20
195. 60 c. purple 50 20
196. 13. 1 p. blue 12 12

1909. Optd. **1909.**
197. 12. 1 c. blue 5 5
198. 1 c. red 10 10
199. 5 c. green 10 10
200. 5 c. orange 10 10
201. 10 c. rose 10 10
202. 10 c. brown 12 12
203. 20 c. lilac 10 10
204. 20 c. yellow 8 8
205. 30 c. brown 30 30
206. 30 c. blue 25 25

14.

15.

16.

1910.
207. 14. 1 c. brown 5 5
208. 5 c. lilac 5 5
209. 5 c. green 5 5
210. 5 c. blue 5 5
211. 10 c. green 5 5
212. 10 c. violet 8 5
213. 10 c. red 5 5
214. 20 c. red 5 5
215. 50 c. red 25 20
216. 75 c. blue 8 5

1911. No. 216 perf. diagonally and each half used as 20 c.
217. 14. 20 c. (½ of 75 c.) blue .. 5 5

1911. Independence Cent.
218. 15. 1 c. black and olive .. 5 5
219. 2 c. black and blue .. 10 10
220. 5 c. black and red .. 12 10
221. 10 c. brown and blue .. 15 12
222. 20 c. blue and olive .. 15 12
223. 50 c. blue and lilac .. 20 20
224. 75 c. purple and olive .. 20 20

1912. Surch. **Habilitada en VEINTE** and thin bar.
225. 14. 20 c. on 50 c. red .. 15 10

1913.
226. 16. 1 c. black 5 5
227. 2 c. orange 5 5
228. 5 c. mauve 5 5
229. 10 c. green 5 5
230. 20 c. rose 5 5
231. 40 c. red 5 5
232. 75 c. blue 5 5
233. 80 c. yellow 5 5
234. 1 p. blue 10 8
235. 1 p. 25 blue 10 10
236. 3 p. green 20 10

1918. No. D 244 surch. **HABILITADO EN 0.05 1918** and bar.
237. 5 c. on 40 c. brown .. 5 5

1918. Nos. D 239/42 optd. **HABILITADO 1918.**
238. 5 c. brown 5 5
239. 10 c. brown 5 5
240. 20 c. brown 10 8
241. 40 c. brown 10 5

1918. Surch. **HABILITADO EN 0.30 1918** and bar.
242. 16. 30 c. on 40 c. red .. 8 5

1920. Surch. **HABILITADO en,** value and **1920.**
243. 16. 50 c. on 80 c. yellow .. 20 5
244. 1 p. 75 on 3 p. green .. 90 75

1920. Nos. D 243/4 optd. **HABILITADO 1920** or surch. also.
245. 1 p. brown 12 5
246. 1 p. on 1 p. 50 brown .. 25 10

17. Parliament House, Asuncion. 18.

1920. Jubilee of Constitution.
247. 17. 50 c. black and red .. 30 15
248. 1 p. black and blue .. 75 30
249. 1 p. 75 black and blue .. 20 12
250. 3 p. black and orange .. 1·25 20

1920. Surch. **50.**
251. 16. 50 on 75 c. blue .. 25 5

1921. Surch. **50** and two bars.
252. 14. 50 on 75 c. blue .. 12 5
253. 16. 50 on 75 c. blue .. 12 5

1922.
254. 18. 50 c. blue and red .. 12 5
255. 1 p. brown and blue .. 12 5

Between 1922 and 1936 many regular postage stamps were overprinted C (=Campana—country), these being used at post offices outside Asuncion but not for mail sent abroad. The prices quoted are for whichever is the cheapest.

19. Starting-point of Conspirators. 20. Map.

1922. Independence.
256. 19. 1 p. blue 12 10
258. 1 p. blue and red .. 15 10
259. 1 p. grey and purple .. 15 10
260. 1 p. grey and orange .. 20 10
257. 5 p. purple 25 20
261. 5 p. brown and blue .. 35 20
262. 5 p. black and green .. 35 20
263. 5 p. blue and red .. 35 20

1924. Surch. **Habilitado en** value and **1924.**
265. 16. 50 c. on 75 c. blue .. 5 5
266. $1 on 1 p. 25 blue .. 5 5
267. – $1 on 1 p. 50 brown (No. D 244) .. 5 5

1924.
268. 20. 1 p. blue 5 5
269. 2 p. red 10 8
270. 4 p. blue 15 10

21. Gen. Jose E. Diaz. 22. Columbus.

1925.
271. 21. 50 c. red 5 5
272. 1 p. blue 5 5
273. 1 p. green 5 5

1925.
274. 22. 1 p. blue 12 5

1926. Surch. **Habilitado en** and new value.
276. 14. 0.02 on 5 c. blue .. 5 5
275. 1 c. on 5 c. blue .. 5 5
277. 16. 7 c. on 40 c. red .. 5 5
278. 15 c. on 75 c. blue .. 5 5
279. 12. $0.50 on 60 c. purple (No. 195) 5 5
280. – $0.50 on 75 c. blue (No. O 243) .. 5 5
281. – $1.50 on 1 p. 50 brown (No. D 244) 12 10
282. 20. $1.50 on 4 p. blue .. 5 5

23. 24. P. J. Caballero. 25. Map of Paraguay.

28. Cassel Tower, Asuncion. 29. Columbus.

1927.
283 23. 1 c. red 5 5
284. 2 c. orange 5 5
285. 7 c. lilac 5 5
286. 7 c. green 5 5
287. 10 c. green 5 5
288. 10 c. claret 5 5
290. 10 c. blue 5 5
291. 20 c. blue 5 5
292. 20 c. purple 5 5
293. 20 c. violet 5 5
294. 20 c. pink 5 5
295. 50 c. blue 5 5
296. 50 c. red 5 5
297. 50 c. orange 5 5
298. 50 c. grey 5 5
326. 50 c. green 5 5
299. 50 c. mauve 5 5
300. 50 c. rose 5 5
301. 70 c. blue 5 5
302. 24. 1 p. green 5 5
303. 1 p. red 5 5
330. 1 p. claret 5 5
331. 1 p. blue 5 5
304. 1 p. orange 5 5
332. 1 p. violet 5 5
333. 25. 1 p. 50 brown 8 5
334. 1 p. 50 lilac 5 5
307. 1 p. 50 rose 8 5
335. 1 p. 50 blue 5 5
308. 24. 2 p. 50 yellow 8 5
337. – 2 p. 50 violet 5 5
338. – 3 p. grey 10 8
339. – 3 p. red 5 5
311. – 3 p. violet 5 5
312. 28. 5 p. chocolate .. 20 20
340. 5 p. violet 5 5
314. 5 p. orange 10 5
315. 29. 10 p. red 65 25
317. 10 p. blue 65 25
318. 25. 20 p. red .. .. 1·40 1·25
319. 20 p. green .. .. 1·40 1·25
320. 20 p. purple .. .. 1·40 1·25
DESIGNS—As T 24: 2 p. 50, Fulgencio Yegros. 3 p. V. I. Yturbe.

30. Arms of De Espinosa. 31. Pres. Hayes of U.S.A. and Villa Hayes.

1928. Foundation of Asuncion, 1537.
342. 30. 10 p. purple .. .. 1·00 75

1928. Hayes' Decision to award Northern Chaco to Paraguay. 50th Anniv.
343. 31. 10 p. brown .. .. 3·75 1·90
344. 10 p. grey .. .. 3·75 1·90

1929. Air. Surch. **Correo Aereo Habilitado en** and value.
357. 23. $0.95 on 7 c. lilac .. 20 20
358. $1.90 on 20 c. blue .. 20 20
345. – $2.85 on 5 c. purple (No. O 239) .. 1·25 75
348. 24. $3.40 on 3 p. grey .. 2·25 1·90
359. 20. $3.40 on 4 p. blue .. 25 25
360. $4.75 on 4 p. blue .. 50 50
346. – $5.65 on 10 c. green .. (No. O 240) .. 60 30
361. 24. $6.80 on 3 p. grey .. 75 75
349. 20. $6.80 on 4 p. blue .. 2·25 1·25
347. – $11·30 on 50 c. rose (No. O 242) 95 55
350. 28. $17 on 5 p. chocolate (A) 2·25 1·25
362. $17 on 5 p. chocolate (B) 2·50 2·50

On No. 350 (A) the surcharge is in four lines, and on No. 362 (B) it is in three lines.

32.

DESIGNS: 5.65 p. Carrier pigeon. 11.30 p. Stylized aeroplane.

1929. Air.
351. 32. 2.85 p. olive .. .. 1·00 90
352. – 2.85 p. green 45 30
353. – 5.65 p. brown .. .. 1·00 90
354. – 5.65 p. red 65 40
355. – 11.30 p. purple .. .. 1·00 90
356. – 11.30 p. blue 45 40

1930. Air. Optd. **CORREO AEREO** or surch. also in words.
363. 23. 5 c. on 10 c. green .. 5 5
364. 5 c. on 70 c. blue .. 10 10
365. 10 c. green 10 10
366. 20 c. blue 10 10
367. 24. 20 c. on 1 p. red .. 20 20
368. 23. 40 c. on 50 c. orange .. 15 15
369. 24. 1 p. green 55 60
370. 3 p. grey 65 60
371. 29. 6 p. on 10 p. red .. 75 75
372. 25. 10 p. on 20 p. red .. 7·00 7·00
373. 10 p. on 20 p. purple .. 8·00 8·00

35. 37.

1930. Air.
374. 35. 95 c. blue on blue .. 30 25
375. 95 c. red on pink .. 30 25
376. – 1 p. 90 purple on blue .. 30 25
377. – 1 p. 90 rose on pink .. 30 25
378. 37. 6 p. 80 black on blue .. 55 40
379. 6 p. 80 green on pink .. 55 40
DESIGN: 1 p. 90, Asuncion Cathedral.

38. Declaration of Independence. 39.

1930. Air. Independence Day.
380. 38. 2 p. 85 blue 30 25
381. 3 p. 40 green 40 25
382. 4 p. 75 maroon .. 40 25

1930. Red Cross Fund.
383. 39. 1 p. 50+50 c. blue .. 65 50
384. 1 p. 50+50 c. red .. 65 50
385. 1 p. 50+50 c. lilac .. 65 12

40. Portraits of Archbishop Bogarin.

1930. Consecration of Archbishop Bogarin.
386. 40. 1 p. 50 blue 95 65
387. 1 p. 50 claret 95 65
388. 1 p. 50 violet 95 65

1930. Surch **Habilitado en CINCO.**
389. 23. 5 c. on 7 c. green .. 5 5

41. Planned Agricultural College at Ypacavai.

1931. Agricultural College Fund.
390. 41. 1 p. 50+50 c. bl. on rose 20 20

42. Arms of Paraguay.

ILLUSTRATIONS
British Commonwealth and all overprints and surcharges are FULL SIZE. Foreign Countries have been reduced to ¾-LINEAR.

1931. First Paraguay Postage Stamps. 60th Anniv.
391. 42. 10 p. brown 65 25
392. 10 p. red on blue .. 65 25
393. 10 p. blue on red .. 65 25
394. 10 p. grey 45 20
396. 10 p. blue 15 12

43. Gunboat " Paraguay ".

1931. Air. Constitution, 60th Anniv. and Arrival of new Gunboats. Dated " 1870 1930 ".
397. 43. 1 p. claret 15 12
398. 1 p. blue 20 12
399. 2 p. orange 20 15
400. 2 p. brown 20 15
401. 3 p. green 65 40
402. 3 p. blue 45 25
403. 3 p. red 25 25
404. 6 p. green 45 40
405. 6 p. mauve 55 50
406. 6 p. blue 65 35
407. 10 p. red .. .. 1·75 1·25
408. 10 p. green .. .. 1·90 1·50
409. 10 p. brown .. .. 1·25 75
410. 10 p. blue .. .. 1·25 1·00
411. 10 p. pink .. .. 1·60 1·00

1931. A T 43.
412. – 1 p. 50 violet 50 25
413. – 1 p. 50 blue 5 5
DESIGN: Gunboat " Humaita ".

45. War Memorial. 46. Orange Tree and Yerba Mate.

47. Yerba Mate.

48. Palms. 49. Eagle.

1931. Air.
414. 45. 5 c. blue 10 8
415. 5 c. green 8 5
416. 5 c. red 15 5
417. 5 c. purple 5 5
418. 46. 10 c. violet 10 8
419. 10 c. claret 8 5
420. 10 c. brown 8 5
421. 10 c. blue 5 5
422. 47. 20 c. red 10 10
423. 20 c. blue 15 8
424. 20 c. green 15 8
425. 20 c. brown 5 5
426. 48. 40 c. green 12 12
426a. 40 c. blue 12 5
426b. 40 c. red 12 5
427. 49. 80 c. blue 12 8
428. 80 c. green 35 25
428a. 80 c. red 55 20

1931. Air. Optd. **Correo Aereo "Graf Zeppelin"** and airship or surch. also.
429. 20. 3 p. on 4 p. blue .. 7·50 6·50
430. 4 p. blue .. .. 7·50 6·50

50. Farm Colony.

1931. Foundation of San Bernardino. 50th Anniv.
431. 40. 1 p. green 30 15
432. 1 p. red 5 5

1934. New Year. Optd. **FELIZ ANO NUEVO 1932.**

No.	Type	Description	Mint	Used
433.	40.	1p. 50 blue	75	75
434.		1 p. 50 clare	75	75

51. " Graf Zeppelin ".

1932. Air.

No.	Type	Description	Mint	Used
435.	51.	4 p. blue	95	75
436.		8 p. red	1·60	95
437.		12 p. green	1·90	1·25
438.		16 p. purple	2·75	1·90
439.		20 p. brown	2·75	2·25

52. Red Cross H.Q. 53. (Trans: " Has been, is and will be ").

1932. Red Cross Fund.

No.	Type	Description	Mint	Used
440.	52.	50 c.+50 c. pink ..	20	20

1932. Chaco Boundary Dispute.

No.	Type	Description	Mint	Used
441.	53.	1 p. 50 purple	20	20
442.		1 p. 50 brown	10	8
443.		1 p. 50 rose	20	20
444.		1 p. 50 green	8	5
445		1 p. 50 blue	8	5

Nos. 443/5 are optd. with a large **C.**

1932. Surch. **CORREOS FELIZ ANO NUEVO 1933** (trans: " Happy New Year 1933 ") and value.

No.	Type	Description	Mint	Used
446.	51.	50 c. on 4 p. blue ..	50	40
447.		1 p. on 8 p. red ..	50	40
448.		1 p. 50 on 12 p. green..	50	40
449.		2 p. on 16 p. purple ..	50	40
450.		5 p. on 20 p. brown ..	1·10	1·00

54. " Graf Zeppelin " over Paraguay.

55. "Graf Zeppelin" over Atlantic.

1933. Air. " Graf Zeppelin " issue.

No.	Type	Description	Mint	Used
451.	54.	4 p. 50 blue	1·90	95
452.		9 p. red..	2·50	1·25
453.		13 p. 50 green	3·00	2·25
454.	55.	22 p. 50 brown.. ..	7·00	4·25
455.		45 p. violet	11·00	8·00

56. Flag of the Race. 57. G.P.O., Asuncion.

1933. Departure of Columbus from Palos 441st Anniv. Maltese Crosses in violet.

No.	Type	Description	Mint	Used
456.	56.	10 c. olive and claret ..	10	10
457.		20 c. blue and lake ..	10	10
458.		50 c. red and green ..	12	12
459.		1 p. brown and blue ..	12	12
460.		1 p. 50 green and blue ..	12	12
461.		2 p. green and sepia ..	30	30
462.		5 p. lake and olive ..	65	65
463.		10 p. sepia and blue ..	70	70

1934. Air.

No.	Type	Description	Mint	Used
464.	57.	33 p. 75 blue	1·90	1·60
468.		33 p. 75 red	1·90	1·60
466.		33 p. 75 green	1·90	1·25
467.		33 p. 75 brown	1·90	1·25

1934. Air. Optd. **1934.**

No.	Type	Description	Mint	Used
469.	54.	4 p. 50 blue	2·50	1·25
470.		9 p. red	2·50	1·25
471.		13 p. 50 green	3·75	2·50
472.	55.	22 p. 50 brown	11·00	3·00
473.		45 p. violet	9·00	9·00

1935. Air. Optd. **1935.**

No.	Type	Description	Mint	Used
474.	54.	4 p. 50 red	2·50	2·50
475.		9 p. green	3·75	3·75
476.		13 p. 50 brown	5·50	5·50
477.	55.	22 p. 50 purple ..	7·00	7·00
478.		45 p. blue	22·00	22·00

58. Tobacco Plant.

1935. Air.

No.	Type	Description	Mint	Used
479.	58.	17 p. brown	6·50	5·00
480.		17 p. red	6·50	5·00
481.		17 p. blue	6·50	5·00
482.		17 p. green	6·50	5·00

59. Church of the Incarnation.

1935. Air.

No.	Type	Description	Mint	Used
483.	59.	102 p. red	7·00	7·00
485.		102 p. blue	3·25	3·25
486.		102 p. brown	3·25	3·25
487.		102 p. violet	1·60	1·60
487a.		102 p. orange	1·60	1·60

1937. Air. Surch. **Habilitado** and value in figures.

No.	Type	Description	Mint	Used
488.	57.	$24 on 33 p. 75 blue ..	65	65
489.	59.	$65 on 102 p. grey ..	1·75	1·75
490.		$84 on 102 p. green ..	1·75	1·75

60. Arms of Asuncion. 61. Monstrance.

1937. Asuncion. 4th Cent. (1st issue).

No.	Type	Description	Mint	Used
491.	60.	50 c. maroon and violet	5	5
492.		1 p. green and bistre ..	5	5
493.		3 p. blue and red ..	10	8
494.		10 p. yellow and red ..	12	10
495.		20 p. grey and blue ..	20	15

1937. First National Eucharistic Congress.

No.	Type	Description	Mint	Used
496.	61.	1 p. red, yellow & blue	5	5
497.		3 p. red, yellow & blue	5	5
498.		10 p. red, yellow & blue	12	8

62. Oratory of the Virgin of Asuncion. 63. Asuncion.

1938. Asuncion. 4th Cent. (2nd issue).

No.	Type	Description	Mint	Used
499.	62.	5 p. olive	15	8
500.		5 p. red	15	12
501.		11 p. brown	20	12

1939. Air.

No.	Type	Description	Mint	Used
502.	63.	3 p. 40 blue	65	65
503.		3 p. 40 green	45	30
504.		3 p. 40 brown	65	30

DESIGN—VERT. No. 505, C. A. Lopez.

64. J. E. Diaz.

1939. Reburial in National Pantheon of Ashes of C. A. Lopez and J. E. Diaz.

No.	Type	Description	Mint	Used
505.	–	2 p. brown and blue ..	20	12
506.	64.	2 p. brown and blue ..	20	12

DESIGN: Nos. 507/9, Pres. Escobar and Dr. Zubizarreta.

65. Pres Caballero and Senator Decoud.

1939. Asuncion University. 50th Anniv.

No.	Type	Description	Mint	Used
507.	–	50 c. blk. & orge. (post.)	5	5
508.	–	1 p. black and blue ..	12	8
509.	–	2 p. black and red ..	20	12
510.	65.	5 p. black and blue ..	30	15
511.		28 p. black & red (air)..	7·50	6·50
512.		90 p. black & green ..	11·00	9·00

66. Arms. 67. Pres. Baldomir and Flags of Paraguay and Uruguay.

1939. Chaco Boundary Peace Conference, Buenos Aires. (1st issue). Inscr. "PAZ DEL CHACO". Designs as T **67** showing presidents, etc., and flag on right of countries named.

No.	Type	Description	Mint	Used
513.	66.	50 c. blue (postage) ..	10	5
514.	67.	1 p. olive	12	8
515.	A.	2 p. green	15	8
516.	B.	3 p. brown	20	15
517.	C.	5 p. orange	30	20
518.	D.	6 p. violet	55	35
519.	E.	10 p. brown	50	35
520.	F.	1 p. brown (air) ..	10	8
521.	66.	3 p. blue	12	10
522.	E.	5 p. olive	20	12
523.	D.	10 p. violet	15	10
524.	C.	30 p. orange	25	15
525.	B.	50 p. brown	40	30
526.	A.	100 p. green	70	75
527.	67.	200 p. green	4·25	2·75
528.	–	500 p. black	14·00	13·00

DESIGNS: A, Benavides (Peru). B, Eagle (U.S.A.). C, Alessandri (Chile). D, Vargas (Brazil). E. Ortiz (Paraguay). F, Figure of "Peace" (Bolivia). 500 p. (30×40 mm.); Map of Chaco frontiers.

68. Arms of New York. 69. Asuncion-New York Air Route.

1939. New York World's Fair.

No.	Type	Description	Mint	Used
529.	68.	5 p. red (postage) ..	20	20
530.		10 p. blue	35	30
531.		11 p. green	50	45
532.		22 p. grey	65	65
533.	69.	30 p. brown (air) ..	3·75	3·75
534.		80 p. orange	5·50	5·50
535.		90 p. violet	9·50	9·50

70. Soldier. 71. Waterfall.

1940. Chaco Boundary Peace Conference, Buenos Aires. (2nd issue). Inscr. "PAZ DEL CHACO".

No.	Type	Description	Mint	Used
536.	70.	50 c. orange	12	8
537.	–	1 p. purple	15	12
538.	–	3 p. green	20	15
539.	–	5 p. brown	30	15
540.	–	10 p. mauve	35	20
541.	–	20 p. blue	65	35
542.	–	50 p. green	1·40	60
543.	71.	100 p. black	2·50	1·50

DESIGNS as T **70**—VERT. 1 p. Water-carrier. 5 p. Ploughing with oxen. HORIZ. 3 p. Cattle Farming. As T **71**—VERT. 10 p. Fishing in R. Paraguay. HORIZ. 20 p. Bullock-cart. 50 p. Cattle-grazing.

72. Western Hemisphere. 73. First Paraguayan Stamp.

1940. Pan-American Union. 50th Anniv.

No.	Type	Description	Mint	Used
544.	72.	50 c. orange (postage)	8	5
545.		1 p. green	12	8
546.		5 p. blue	20	12
547.		10 p. brown	60	50
548.		20 p. red (air) ..	35	20
549.		70 p. blue	65	25
550.		100 p. green	95	80
551.		500 p. violet	5·00	3·75

1940. Cent. of First Adhesive Postage Stamps. Inscr. " CENTENARIO DEL SELLO POSTAL 1940".

No.	Type	Description	Mint	Used
552.	73.	1 p. purple and green ..	75	30
553.		5 p. brown and green ..	95	45
554.		6 p. blue and brown ..	2·25	75
555.	–	10 p. black and red ..	2·25	1·25

DESIGNS: 5 p. Sir Rowland Hill. 6 p., 10 p. Early Paraguayan stamps.

1940. National Mourning for Pres. Estigarribia. Surch. **7-IX-40/DUELO NACIONAL/5 PESOS** in black border.

No.	Type	Description	Mint	Used
556.	70.	5 p. on 50 c. orange ..	25	25

73a. Dr. Francia. 73b. Our Lady of Asuncion.

1940. Dr. Francia (dictator). Death Cent. Inscr. "1840-20-IX-1940".

No.	Type	Description	Mint	Used
557.	73a.	50 c. red	12	12
558.	–	50 c. purple	12	12
559.	73a.	1 p. green	20	12
560.	–	5 p. blue	35	15

PORTRAIT: Nos. 558 and 560, Francia in his study.

1941. Visit of President Vargas of Brazil. Optd. **Visita al Paragua/Agosto de 1941.**

No.	Type	Description	Mint	Used
560a.		6 p. violet (No. 518) ..	20	20

1941. Charity.

No.	Type	Description	Mint	Used
561.	73b.	7 p.+3 p. brown ..	30	30
562.		7 p.+3 p. violet ..	30	30
563.		7 p.+3 p. red ..	30	30
564.		7 p.+3 p. blue ..	30	30

1942. Nos. 520/2 optd. **Habilitado** and bar(s).

No.	Type	Description	Mint	Used
565.	–	1 p. brown	20	12
566.	65.	3 p. blue	20	12
567.	–	5 p. olive	20	12

74. Arms of Paraguay. 75. Irala's Vision.

1942.

No.	Type	Description	Mint	Used
568.	74.	1 p. green	10	5
569.		1 p. orange	5	5
570.		7 p. blue	8	5
571.		7 p. brown	5	5

For other values as T **74** see Nos. 631, etc.

1942. Asuncion. 4th Cent. Dated " 1541 1941 ".

No.	Type	Description	Mint	Used
572.	–	2 p. green (postage) ..	95	40
573.	75.	5 p. red	95	40
574.	–	7 p. blue	95	40
575.	–	20 p. purple (air) ..	1·25	75
576.	75.	70 p. brown	3·75	1·90
577.	–	500 p. olive	11·00	8·00

DESIGNS—VERT. 2 p., 20 p. Indian hailing ships. 7 p., 500 p. Irala's Arms.

76. Columbus Sighting America.
77. Pres. Morinigo and Symbols of Progress.

1943. Discovery of America. 450th Anniv.
578. 76. 50 c. violet 25 20
579. 1 p. brown 20 12
580. 5 p. green 95 15
581. 7 p. blue 30 15

1943. Three Year Plan.
582. 77. 7 p. blue 10 8
NOTE: From No. 583 onwards, the currency having been changed, the letter "c" in the value description indicates "centimos" instead of "centavos".

1944. St. Juan Earthquake Fund. Surch. **U.P.A.E. Adhesion victimas San Juan y Pueblo Argentino centimos** and bar.
583. – 10 c. on 10 p. brown (No. 519) 35 25

1944. Surch. **Habilitado en un centimo.**
584. 24. 1 c. on 3 p. violet .. 5 5
Design as T 24, but portrait of V. I. Iturbe.

1944. Surch. **1944/5 centimos 5.**
585. 76. 5 c. on 7 p. blue .. 12 5
586. 77. 5 c. on 7 p. blue .. 12 5

79. Primitive Postmen.
81. Jesuit Relics of Colonial Paraguay.

1944.
587. 79. 1 c. black (postage) .. 5 5
588. – 2 c. brown 5 5
589. – 5 c. olive 85 10
590. – 7 c. blue 20 12
591. – 10 c. green 35 25
592. – 15 c. blue 35 25
593. – 50 c. black 65 55
594. – 1 g. red .. .. 1·25 65
DESIGNS—HORIZ. 2 c. Ruins of Humaita Church. 7 c. Marshal Lopez. 1 g. Ytororo Heroes' Monument. VERT. 5 c. Locomotive of 1861. 10 c. Early paddle-steamer. 15 c. Port of Asuncion. 50 c. Meeting place of Independence conspirators.

595. – 1 c. blue (air) 5 5
596. – 2 c. green 12 10
597. – 3 c. purple 10 8
598. – 5 c. green 12 10
599. – 10 c. violet 12 10
600. – 20 c. brown 15 12
601. – 30 c. blue 25 20
602. – 40 c. olive 35 25
603. – 70 c. red 50 45
604. 31. 1 g. orange .. .. 1·50 80
605. – 2 g. brown .. .. 3·00 1·25
606. – 5 g. brown .. .. 8·00 4·75
607. – 10 g. blue .. .. 20·00 13·00
DESIGNS — HORIZ. 1 c. Port of Asuncion. 2 c. First telegraphic apparatus in S. America. 3 c. Early paddle-steamer. 5 c. Meeting Place of Independence conspirators. 10 c. Monument of Antequera. 20 c. Locomotive of 1861. 40 c. Government House. VERT. 30 c. Ytororo Heroes' Monument. 70 c. As T 79 but vert. 2 g. Ruins of Humaita Church. 5 g. Oratory of the Virgin. 10 g. Marsha Lopez.

1945. No. 590 surch. with figures **5** over ornaments deleting old value.
608. 5 c. on 7 c. blue 12 10

82. Clasped Hands and Flags.

1945. President Morinigo's Goodwill Visits. Designs of different sizes inscr. "CONFRATERNIDAD" between crossed flags of Paraguay and another American country, mentioned in brackets. (a) Postage.
609. 82. 1 c. green (Panama) .. 5 5
610. 3 c. claret (Venezuela) .. 10 8
611. 5 c. grey (Ecuador) .. 15 10
612. 2 g. brown (Peru) .. 1·90 1·25

(b) Air).
613. 82. 20 c. orange (Colombia) 30 30
614. 40 c. olive (Bolivia) .. 30 30
615. 70 c. claret (Mexico) .. 45 45
616. 1 g. blue (Chile) .. 65 65
617. 2 g. violet (Brazil) .. 1·00 1·00
618. 5 g. green (Argentina) .. 3·75 3·75
619. 10 g. brown (U.S.A.) .. 11·00 11·00

1945. Surch. **1945 5 Centimos 5.**
620. 76. 5 c. on 7 p. blue .. 15 12
621. 77. 5 c. on 7 p. blue .. 12 12
622. – 5 c. on 7 p. blue (No. 590) 20 12

1945. Surch. **1945** and value.
623. 73b. 2 c. on 7 p.+3 p. brown 10 10
624. 2 c. on 7 p.+3 p. violet 12 10
625. 2 c. on 7 p.+3 p. red .. 10 10
626. 2 c. on 7 p.+3 p. blue 15 10
627. 5 c. on 7 p.+3 p. brown 20 10
628. 5 c. on 7 p.+3 p. violet 20 12
629. 5 c. on 7 p.+3 p. red .. 20 12
630. 5 c. on 7 p.+3 p. blue 20 12

1946. Surch. **1946 5 Centimos 5.**
632. 73b. 5 c. on 7 p.+3 p. violet 35 30
633. 5 c. on 7 p.+3 p. blue 35 30
634. 5 c. on 7 p.+3 p. brown 35 30
635. 5 c. on 7 p.+3 p. red .. 35 30

1946. Air. Surch. **1946 5 Centimos 5.**
636. 5 c. on 20 c. brown (No. 600) 2·50 85
637. 5 c. on 30 c. blue (No. 601) 75 45
638. 5 c. on 40 c. olive (No. 602) 75 45
639. 5 c. on 70 c. red (No. 603) .. 75 45

1946. As Nos. 587/607 but colours changed and some designs smaller.
640. – 1 c. red (postage) .. 5 5
641. – 2 c. violet 8 5
642. 79. 5 c. blue 10 5
643. – 10 c. orange 12 10
644 – 15 c. olive 15 12
645. 81. 50 c. green 45 30
646. – 1 g. blue 95 55
DESIGNS—VERT. 1 c. Early paddle-steamer. 1 g. Meeting place of Independence conspirators. HORIZ. 2 c. First telegraphic apparatus in S. America. 10 c. Monument to Antequera. 15 c. Ytororo Heroes' Monument.

647. – 10 c. red (air) 8 8
648. – 20 c. green 12 12
649. – 1 g. brown 45 45
650. – 5 g. purple .. .. 2·50 2·50
651. – 10 g. red .. .. 7·50 6·00
DESIGNS—VERT. 10 c. Ruins of Humaita Church. HORIZ. 20 c. Port of Asuncion. 1 g. Govt. House. 5 g. Marshall Lopez. 10 g. Oratory of the Virgin.

1946. As T 74 but inscr. "U.P.U." at foot.
631. 74. 5 c. grey 5 5
631a. 5 c. pink 5 5
631b. 5 c. brown 5 5
686. 10 c. blue 5 5
687. 10 c. pink 5 5
631c. 30 c. green 5 5
631d. 30 c. chestnut 5 5
775. 45 c. sage 5 5
631e. 50 c. mauve 5 5
776. 50 c. maroon 5 5
858. 70 c. brown 5 5
777. 90 c. blue 5 5
778. 1 g. violet 12 10
860. 1 g. 50 c. lilac 5 5
779. 2 g. ochre 5 5
780. 2 g. 20 c. magenta .. 5 5
781. 3 g. brown 5 5
782. 4 g. 20 c. green .. 8 5
862. 4 g. 50 blue 8 5
783. 5 g. red 8 5
689. 10 g. orange 35 25
817. 10 g. green 15 12
785. 12 g. 45 c. green .. 20 12
819. 15 g. orange 20 15
786. 20 g. blue 35 30
820. 30 g. bistre 45 30
690. 50 g. pale chocolate .. 1·50 1·10
821. 100 g. grey .. .. 1·60 1·10
See also Nos. 1037/49.

83. Marshal Francisco S. Lopez.
84. Archbishop of Paraguay.

1947. Various frames.
652. 83. 1 c. violet (postage) .. 5 5
653. 2 c. red 5 5
654. 5 c. green 8 5
655. 15 c. blue 10 10
656. 50 c. green 40 40
657. 83. 32 c. red (air) 25 25
658. 64 c. brown 30 30
659. 1 g. blue 35 35
660. 5 g. purple and blue .. 2·25 1·60
661. 10 g. green and red .. 3·00 2·50

1947. Archbishopric of Paraguay. 50th Anniv. Inscr. "CINCUENTENARIO EPISCOPAL 1895 1945".
662. 84. 2 c. slate (postage) .. 5 5
663. – 5 c. red 8 8
664. – 10 c. black 12 10
665. – 15 c. green 25 20
666. – 20 c. black (air) .. 8 5
667. – 30 c. slate 10 10
668. – 40 c. mauve 12 12
669. 84. 70 c. red 25 20
670. – 1 g. lake 30 30
671. – 2 g. red .. .. 1·10 1·10
672. 84. 5 g. slate and red .. 2·50 1·75
673. – 10 g. brown and green .. 5·00 3·75
DESIGNS: 5 c., 20 c., 10 g. Episcopal Arms. 10 c., 30 c., 1 g. Sacred Heart Monument. 15 c., 40 c., 2 g. Archbishop and vision of projected monument.

85. Torchbearer.
86. C. A. Lopez and J. N. Gonzales.

1948. Honouring the "Barefeet" (political party).
674. 85. 5 c. red (postage) .. 5 5
675. 15 c. orange 12 10
676. 85. 69 c. green (air) .. 65 65
677. 5 g. blue .. .. 4·50 3·00

1948 Paraguay's Merchant Fleet. Cent. Centres in black, red and blue.
678. 86. 2 c. orange 5 5
679. 5 c. blue 5 5
680. 10 c. black 5 5
681. 15 c. violet 10 8
682. 50 c. green 15 12
683. 1 g. claret 30 25

1949. Air. National Mourning for Archbishop of Paraguay. Surch. **DUELO NACIONAL 5 CENTIMOS 5.**
684. 84. 5 c. on 70 c. red .. 15 10

1949. Earthquake Victims' Relief Fund No. 667 surch. **AYUDA AL ECUADOR 5+5** and two crosses.
685. 5 c.+5 c. on 30 c. slate .. 10 10

87. "Postal Communications."
88. President Roosevelt.

1950. Air. U.P.U. 75th Anniv.
691. 87. 20 c. violet and green .. 25 25
692. 30 c. brown and purple 25 25
693. 50 c. green and grey .. 50 50
694. 1 g. brown and blue 60 60
695. 5 g. black and red .. 2·10 1·50

1950. Air. Flags in red and blue.
696. 88. 20 c. orange 8 8
697. 30 c. black 10 10
698. 50 c. purple 20 12
699. 1 g. green 30 15
700. 5 g. blue 85 55

1951. First Economic Congress of Paraguay. Surch. **PRIMER CONGRESO DE ENTIDADES ECONOMICAS DEL PARAGUAY 18-IV-1951** and shield over a block of four stamps.
700a. 74. 5 c. pink 25 12
700b. 10 c. blue 25 20
700c. 30 c. green 40 30
Prices are for single stamps. Prices for blocks of four, four times single prices.

89. Columbus Lighthouse.

90. Urn.

1952. Columbus Memorial Lighthouse.
701. 89. 2 c. brown (postage) .. 5 5
702. 5 c. blue 5 5
703. 10 c. pink 5 5
704. 15 c. blue 5 5
705. 20 c. purple 5 5
706. 50 c. orange 12 10
707. 1 g. green 20 10
708. 90. 10 c. blue (air) 5 5
709. 20 c. green 5 5
710. 30 c. purple 5 5
711. 40 c. pink 5 5
712. 50 c. bistre 8 8
713. 1 g. blue 15 10
714. 2 g. orange 35 15
715. 5 g. lake 75 40

91. Isabella the Catholic.
92. S. Pettirossi (aviator).

1952. Air. Isabella the Catholic. 500th Birth Anniv.
716. 91. 1 g. blue 10 8
717. 2 g. brown 15 12
718. 5 g. green 45 25
719. 10 g. purple 80 70

1954. Pettirossi Commem.
720. 92. 5 c. blue (postage) .. 5 5
721. 20 c. red 5 5
722. 50 c. purple 10 5
723. 60 c. violet 15 8
724. 40 c. brown (air) .. 5 5
725. 55 c. green 10 5
726. 80 c. blue 12 8
727. 1 g. 30 slate 45 30

93. San Roque Church, Asuncion.

1954. Air. San Roque Church Cent.
728. 93. 20 c. red 5 5
729. 30 c. maroon 5 5
730. 50 c. blue 5 5
731. 1 g. purple and chestnut 10 8
732. 1 g. black and chestnut 10 8
733. 1 g. green and chestnut 10 8
734. 1 g. orange and chestnut 10 8
735. 5 g. yellow and brown .. 15 15
736. 5 g. olive and brown .. 15 15
737. 5 g. violet and brown .. 15 15
738. 5 g. buff and brown .. 15 15

94. Marshal Lopez, C. A. Lopez and Gen. Caballero.

1954. National Heroes.
739. 94. 5 c. violet (postage) .. 5 5
740. 20 c. ultramarine .. 5 5
741. 50 c. magenta 5 5
742. 1 g. brown 8 8
743. 2 g. green 12 10
744. 5 g. slate-violet (air) .. 15 12
745. 10 g. olive 35 25
746. 20 g. drab 65 50
747. 50 g. salmon .. .. 2·00 50
748. 100 g. blue .. .. 6·00 5·50

95. Presidents Stroessner and Peron.

1955. Visit of President Peron. Flags in red and blue.
749. 95. 5 c. sepia and buff (post) 5 5
750. 10 c. lake and buff .. 5 5
751. 50 c. grey 5 5
752. 1 g. 30 lilac and buff .. 8 8
753. 2 g. 20 blue and buff .. 15 15

754. 95. 60 c. olive and buff (air) 5 5
755. 2 g. green 10 10
756. 3 g. red 15 12
757. 4 g. magenta and buff 20 15

96. Trinidad Campanile.

1955. Sacerdotal Silver Jubilee of Mgr. Rodriguez. Inscr. as in T **96.**

758. **96.** 5 c. ochre (postage) .. 5 5
759. – 20 c. brown 5 5
760. – 50 c. maroon 5 5
761. – 2 g. 50 olive 8 8
762. – 5 g. sepia 15 15
763. – 15 g. blue-green .. 45 45
764. – 25 g. yellow-green .. 75 65

765. **96.** 2 g. blue (air) 5 5
766. – 3 g. olive 8 5
767. – 4 g. green 10 5
768. – 6 g. sepia 15 10
769. – 10 g. red 30 20
770. – 20 g. bistre 45 45
771. – 30 g. myrtle .. .. 1·10 1·00
772. – 50 g. blue .. .. 3·00 1·25

DESIGNS—HORIZ. 20 c., 3 g. Cloisters in Trinidad. 5 g., 10 g. San Cosme Portico. 15 g., 20 g. Church of Jesus. VERT. 50 c., 4 g. Cornice in Santa Maria. 2 g. 50, 6 g. Santa Rosa Tower. 25 g., 30 g. Niche in Trinidad. 50 g. Trinidad Sacristy.

97. Angel and Marching Soldiers.
98. Soldier and Flags.

1957. Chaco Heroes. Inscr. "HOMENAJE A LOS HEROES DEL CHACO". Flags in red, white and blue.

787. **97.** 5 c. green (postage) .. 5 5
788. 10 c. red 5 5
789. 15 c. ultramarine .. 5 5
790. 20 c. maroon 5 5
791. 25 c. black 5 5
792. – 30 c. blue 5 5
793. – 40 c. black 5 5
794. – 50 c. lake 5 5
795. – 1 g. blue-green .. 5 5
796. – 1 g. 30 ultramarine .. 5 5
797. – 1 g. 50 maroon .. 5 5
798. – 2 g. emerald 5 5

799. **98.** 10 c. ultramarine (air) 5 5
800. 15 c. maroon 5 5
801. 20 c. vermilion 5 5
802. 25 c. blue 5 5
803. 50 c. blue-green .. 5 5
804. 1 g. red 5 5
805. 1 g. 30 maroon .. 5 5
806. – 1 g. 50 blue 5 5
807. – 2 g. emerald 5 5
808. – 4 g. 10 vermilion & red 10 10
809. – 5 g. black 10 10
810. – 10 g. blue-green .. 25 20
811. – 25 g. ultramarine .. 55 45

DESIGNS—HORIZ. Nos. 792/8, Man, woman and flags. Nos. 805/11, "Paraguay" and kneeling soldier.

99. R. Gonzalez and St. Ignatius.
100. President Stroessner.

1958. St. Ignatius of Loyola. 4th Cent. Inscr. as in T **99.**

822. **99.** 50 c. green 5 5
823. – 50 c. chocolate .. 5 5
824. – 1 g. 50 violet 5 5
825. – 3 g. blue 10 8
826. **99.** 6 g. 25 rose 20 15

DESIGNS—VERT. 50 c. choc., 3 g. Statue of St. Ignatius. HORIZ. 1 g. 50, Jesuit Fathers' house, Antigua.
See also Nos. 1074/81.

1958. Re-election of Pres. Stroessner. Portrait in black.

827. **100.** 10 c. vermilion (post.) 5 5
828. 15 c. violet 5 5
829. 25 c. green 5 5
830. 30 c. lake 5 5
831. **100.** 50 c. magenta .. 5 5
832. 75 c. blue 5 5
833. 5 g. turquoise .. 8 8
834. 10 g. sepia .. 20 20

835. 12 g. mauve (air) .. 30 30
836. 18 g. orange .. 40 40
837. 23 g. chestnut .. 60 60
838. 36 g. green .. 60 60
839. 50 g. olive .. 90 90
840. 65 g. grey .. .. 1·25 1·25

1959. Nos. 758/72 surch. with star enclosed by palm leaves and value.

841. 1 g. 50 c. on 5 c. ochre (post.) 5 5
842. 1 g. 50 c. on 20 c. brown .. 5 5
843. 1 g. 50 c. on 50 c. maroon .. 5 5
844. 3 g. on 2 g. 50 c. olive .. 10 10
845. 6 g. 25 c. on 5 g. sepia .. 12 12
846. 20 g. on 15 g. blue-green .. 30 30
847. 30 g. on 25 g. yellow-green 50 50

848. 4 g. on 2 g. blue (air) .. 12 8
849. 12 g. 45 c. on 3 g. olive .. 25 15
850. 18 g. 15 c. on 6 g. sepia .. 30 20
851. 23 g. 40 c. on 10 g. red .. 40 25
852. 34 g. 80 c. on 20 g. bistre .. 50 45
853. 36 g. on 4 g. green .. 55 50
854. 43 g. 95 c. on 30 g. myrtle .. 70 65
855. 100 g. on 50 g. blue .. 2·25 1·60

101. U.N. Emblem.
102. U.N. Emblem and Map of Paraguay.

1959. Air. Visit of U.N. Secretary-General.

856. **101.** 5 g. blue and orange .. 70 50

1959. Air. U.N. Day.

857. **102.** 12 g. 45 orange & blue 25 20

103. Football.
104. " Uproote dTree ".

1960. Olympic Games. Inscr. "1960".

863. **103.** 30 c. red & grn. (post.) 5 5
864. 50 c. purple and blue .. 5 5
865. 75 c. bronze-grn. & orge. 5 5
866. 1 g. 50 violet & green .. 5 5

867. – 12 g. 45 blue & red (air) 40 20
868. – 18 g. 15 ol.-grn. & pur. 65 30
869. – 36 g. red and green .. 85 65

DESIGN—AIR: Basketball.

1960. World Refugee Year (1st issue).

870. **104.** 25 c. pink & grn. (post.) 8 5
871. 50 c. green and red .. 10 8
872. 70 c. brown & magenta 35 30
873. 1 g. 50 blue & ultram. 50 35
874. 3 g. grey and brown .. 85 75

875. – 4 g. pink & green (air) 1·25 1·10
876. – 12 g. 45 green and blue 2·50 2·00
877. – 18 g. 15 orange & red .. 3·75 3·00
878. – 23 g. 40 blue and red .. 5·00 4·25

DESIGN—AIR. As T **104** but with "ANO MUNDIAL" insci. below tree.
See also Nos. 971/7.

105. U.N. Emblem.
106. U.N. Emblem and Flags.

1960. "Human Rights." Inscr. "DERECHOS HUMANOS".

879. **105.** 1 g. crim. & blue (post.) 5 5
880. – 3 g. orange and blue .. 8 8
881. – 6 g. orange and green .. 20 20
882. – 20 g. yellow and red .. 50 40

883. **105.** 40 g. blue and red (air) 75 65
884. – 60 g. red and green .. 1·10 1·00
885. – 100 g. red and blue .. 2·25 1·50

DESIGNS: 3 g., 60 g. Hand holding scales. 6 g. Hands breaking chain. 20 g., 100 g. "Freedom flame".

1960. U.N. Day. Flags and inscr. in blue and red.

886. **106.** 30 c. blue (postage) .. 5 5
887. 75 c. yellow 5 5
888. 90 c. mauve 5 5

889. 3 g. orange (air) .. 5 5
890. 4 g. green 8 8

107. Bridge with Arms of Brazil and Paraguay.
108. Timber Truck.

1961. Int. Bridge between Brazil and Paraguay. Inaug.

891. **107.** 15 c. green (postage) .. 5 5
892. 30 c. blue 5 5
893. 50 c. orange 5 5
894. 75 c. blue 5 5
895. 1 g. violet 5 5

896. – 3 g. red (air) 10 10
897. – 12 g. 45 lake 25 20
898. – 18 g. 15 myrtle .. 30 25
899. – 36 g. blue 50 35

DESIGN—HORIZ. Nos. 896/9, Aerial view of bridge.

1961. Paraguayan Progress. Inscr. "PARAGUAY EN MARCHA".

900. **108.** 25 c. red & grn. (post) 5 5
901. – 90 c. yellow and blue .. 5 5
902. – 1 g. crimson and orange 5 5
903. – 2 g. olive-green & pink 8 5
904. – 5 g. violet and emerald 12 10

905. **108.** 12 g. 45 bl. & buff (air) 25 20
906. – 18 g. 15 violet & buff 35 25
907. – 22 g. blue and orange 50 30
908. – 36 g. yell., grn. & blue 70 40

DESIGNS: 90 c., 2 g., 18 g. 15, Timber barge. 1 g., 5 g., 22 g. Radio mast. 36 g. Boeing "707" jetliner.

109. P. J. Caballero, J. G. R. de Francia and F. Yegros.
110. " Chaco Peace ".

1965. Independence. 150th Anniv.

(a) 1st issue.

909. **109.** 30 c. green (postage) .. 5 5
910. 50 c. magenta 5 5
911. 90 c. violet 5 5
912. 1 g. 50 slate-blue .. 5 5
913. 3 g. bistre 8 5
914. 4 g. ultramarine .. 10 5
915. 5 g. brown 12 8

916. 12 g. 45 claret (air) .. 25 20
917. 18 g. 15 blue 40 25
918. 23 g. 40 green .. 50 30
919. – 30 g. violet 55 30
920. 36 g. red 70 40
921. – 44 g. olive-brown .. 75 55

DESIGN: No. 916/21, Scene of declaration of Independence.

(b) 2nd issue. Inscr. "PAZ DEL CHACO".

922. **110.** 25 c. verm. (postage) 5 5
923. 30 c. green 5 5
924. 50 c. brown 5 5
925. 1 g. violet 5 5
926. 2 g. indigo 5 5

927. 3 g. ultramarine (air) .. 20 20
928. – 4 g. purple 20 20
929. – 100 g. green .. .. 1·90 1·25

DESIGN: Nos. 927/9, Clasped hands.

111. Puma.
112. Arms of Paraguay.

(c) 3rd issue.

930. **111.** 75 c. violet (postage) 5 5
931. 1 g. 50 chocolate .. 8 5
932. 4 g. 50 green .. 15 8
933. 10 g. slate-blue .. 30 20

934. – 12 g. 45 purple (air) .. 1·25 60
935. – 18 g. 15 ultramarine .. 1·60 95
936. – 34 g. 80 brown .. 2·75 1·90

DESIGN: Nos. 934/6, Tapir.

(d) 4th issue.

937. **112.** 15 c. ultram. (postage) 5 5
938. 25 c. brown-red .. 5 5
939. 75 c. green 5 5
940. 1 g. red 5 5

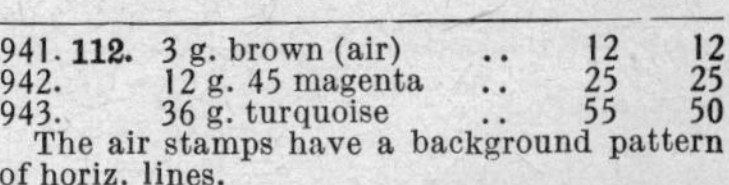

941. **112.** 3 g. brown (air) .. 12 12
942. 12 g. 45 magenta .. 25 25
943. 36 g. turquoise .. 55 50

The air stamps have a background pattern of horiz. lines.

113. Grand Hotel, Guarani.
114. Racquet, Net and Balls.

(e) 5th issue.

944. **113.** 50 c. slate (postage) .. 5 5
945. 1 g. green 5 5
946. 4 g. 50 violet .. 12 5

947. – 3 g. chocolate (air) .. 5 5
948. – 4 g. ultramarine .. 5 5
949. – 18 g. 15 orange .. 30 25
950. – 36 g. crimson .. 50 45

The air stamps are similar to T **113** but inscr. "HOTEL GUARANI" in upper left corner.
See also Nos. 978/85 and 997/1021.

1961. 28th South American Tennis Championships, Asuncion. Centres multicoloured. Border colours given.

951. **114.** 35 c. pink (postage) .. 5 5
952. 75 c. yellow 5 5
953. 1 g. 50 blue 8 5
954. 2 g. 25 turquoise .. 20 8
955. 4 g. grey 30 15

956. 12 g. 45 orange (air) .. 1·25 40
957. 20 g. orange .. .. 1·90 65
958. 50 g. orange .. .. 3·25 1·25

115.

1961. "Europa".

959. **115.** 50 c. red, blue & mauve 5 5
960. 75 c. red, blue & green 5 5
961. 1 g. red, blue & brown 5 5
962. 1 g. 50 red, bl. & lt. bl. 5 5
963. 4 g. 50, red, bl. & yell. 15 15

116. Comm. Alan Shepard.
117.

1961. Commander Shepard's Space Flight.

964. **116.** 10 c. brn. & bl. (post.) .. 12 10
965. 25 c. magenta & blue .. 12 10
966. 50 c. orange & blue .. 12 10
967. 75 c. green and blue .. 12 10

968. – 18 g. 15 bl. & grn. (air) 5·50 4·25
969. – 36 g. blue and orange 5·50 4·25
970. – 50 g. blue & magenta 7·50 5·00

DESIGN—HORIZ. Nos. 968/70, Comm. Shepard and Earth.

1961. World Refugee Year (2nd issue).

971. **117.** 10 c. ultram. and blue (post.) 5 5
972. 25 c. purple & orange .. 5 5
973. 50 c. magenta and pink 8 5
974. 75 c. blue and green .. 12 10

975. – 18 g. 15 red & brn. (air) 1·25 95
976. – 36 g. green and red .. 1·50 1·50
977. – 50 g. orange and green 2·10 1·60

Nos. 975/7 have a different background and frame.

118. Tennis-player
119. Scouts Bugler.

1962. Independence. 150th Anniv. (6th issue) and 28th South American Tennis Championships.
978. **118.** 35 c. blue (postage) .. 5 5
979. 75 c. violet 5 5
980. 1 g. 50 brown 5 5
981 2 g. 25 green .. 5 5

982. – 4 g. red (air) 25 8
983. – 12 g. 45 purple .. 35 20
984. – 20 g. turquoise .. 1·25 35
985. – 50 g. chestnut .. 2·10 90
Nos. 982/5 show tennis-player using back-hand stroke.

1962. Boy Scouts Commem.
986. **119.** 10 c. grn. & pur. (post.) 5 5
987. 20 c. green and red .. 5 5
988. 25 c. grn. & chocolate 5 5
989. 30 c. green and emerald 5 5
990. 50 c. green and indigo 5 5

991. – 12 g. 45 mag. & bl. (air) 40 45
992. – 36 g. mag. & emerald 1·75 1·10
993. – 50 g. mag. & yellow .. 2·50 1·60
DESIGN: Nos. 991/3, Lord Baden-Powell as Chief Scout.

120. Pres. Stroessner and the Duke of Edinburgh.

121. Map of the Americas.

1962. Air. Visit of Duke of Edinburgh.
994. **120.** 12 g. 45 bl., buff & grn. 15 15
995. 18 g. 15 bl., pink & red 25 20
996. 36 g. blue, yell. & brn. 45 35

1962. Independence. 150th Anniv. (7th issue) and Day of the Americas.
997. **121.** 50 c. brn.-orge. (post.) 5 5
998. 75 c. blue 5 5
999. 1 g. violet 5 5
1000. 1 g. 50 green .. 5 5
1001. 4 g. 50 red 12 12

1002. – 20 g. magenta (air) 25 25
1003. – 50 g. orange .. 60 60
DESIGN: 20 g., 50 g. Hands supporting Globe.

122. U.N. Emblem.

1962. Independence. 150th Anniv. (8th issue).
1004. **122.** 50 c. brown (postage) 5 5
1005. 75 c. maroon .. 5 5
1006. 1 g. blue 5 5
1007. 2 g. chestnut .. 5 5

1008. – 12 g. 45 violet (air) 45 30
1009. – 18 g. 15 green .. 55 45
1010. – 23 g. 40 brown-red .. 75 60
1011. – 30 g. red .. .. 1·00 90
DESIGN: Nos. 1008/11, U.N. Headquarters, New York.

123. Mosquito and W.H.O. Emblem.

1962. Malaria Eradication.
1012. **123.** 30 c. blk., blue & pink (postage) 5 5
1013. 50 c. blk., grn. & bistre 5 5
1014. – 75 c. blk., bistre & red 5 5
1015. – 1 g. blk., bis. & emer. 5 5
1016. – 1 g. 50 blk., bis. & brn. 8 5

1017. **123.** 3 g. blk., red & bl. (air) 20 10
1018. 4 g. blk., red & green 30 12
1019. – 12 g. 45 blk., green & olive-brown 45 35
1020. – 18 g. 15 black, red and purple .. .. 1·25 70
1021. – 36 g. blk., blue & red 1·25 1·00
DESIGN: Nos. 1014/16, 1019/21, Mosquito on U N. emblem, and microscope.

INDEX

Countries can be quickly located by referring to the index at the end of this volume.

124. Football Stadium.

125. Freighter.

1962. World Football Championships, Chile.
1022. **124.** 15 c. sep. & yell. (post.) 5 5
1023. 25 c. sepia and green 5 5
1024. 30 c. sepia and violet 5 5
1025. 40 c. sepia and orange 5 5
1026. 50 c. sepia & yell.-grn. 5 5

1027. – 12 g. 45 black, red and violet (air) .. 1·60 65
1028. – 18 g. 15 blk., brn. & vio. 1·60 65
1029. – 36 g. blk., grey & brn. 2·50 1·25
DESIGN—HORIZ. Nos. 1027/9, Footballers and Globe.

1962. Merchant Marine Commem.
1030. **125.** 30 c. brown (postage) 5 5
1031. – 90 c. slate-blue .. 5 5
1032. – 1 g. 50 maroon .. 5 5
1033. – 2 g. green 8 5
1034. – 4 g. 20 blue .. 20 10

1035. – 12 g. 45 red (air) .. 35 15
1036. – 44 g. blue 75 65
DESIGNS—HORIZ. Nos. 1031/4, Various ships. VERT. Nos. 1035/6, Ship's wheel.

1962. As Nos. 631, etc., but with taller figures of value.
1037. **74.** 50 c. slate-blue .. 5 5
1038. 70 c. lilac 5 5
1039. 1 g. 50 violet 5 5
1040. 3 g. blue 10 8
1041. 4 g. 50 brown 5 5
1042. 5 g. mauve 8 5
1043. 10 g. magenta .. 15 15
1044. 12 g. 45 blue 15 5
1045. 15 g. 45 orange-red .. 20 8
1046. 18 g. 15 purple .. 25 20
1047. 20 g. chocolate .. 30 20
1048. 50 g. brown 45 25
1049. 100 g. slate .. .. 1·25 80

126. Gen. A. Stroessner.

127. Popes Paul VI, John XXIII and St. Peter's.

1963. Re-election of Pres. Stroessner to Third Term of Office.
1050. **126.** 50 c. brn. & drab (post.) 5 5
1051. 75 c. brown & pink .. 5 5
1052. 1 g. 50 brn. & mve. .. 10 5

1053. **126.** 12 g. 45 red & pink (air) 1·00 1·00
1054. 18 g. 15 grn. & pink 1·00 1·00
1055. 36 g. vio. and pink .. 1·00 1·00

1964. Popes Paul VI and John XXIII.
1057. **127.** 1 g. 50 yell & red (post.) 5 5
1058. 3 g. green & red .. 8 5
1059. 4 g. brown & red .. 8 5

1060. – 12 g. 45 olive & grn. (air) 30 30
1061. – 18 g. 15 grn. & vio. .. 30 30
1062. – 36 g. green & blue .. 65 65
DESIGNS: Nos. 1060/2, Cathedral, Asuncion.

128. Arms of Paraguay and France.

129. Map of the Americas.

1964. Visit of French President.
1063. **128.** 1 g. 50 brown (postage) 5 5
1064. – 3 g. blue 50 50
1065. **128.** 4 g. grey 8 8

1066. – 12 g. 45 violet (air) .. 20 20
1067. **128.** 18 g. 15 green .. 30 30
1068. – 36 g. red .. .. 1·25 1·25
DESIGNS: 3 g., 12 g. 45, 36 g. Presidents Stroessner and De Gaulle.

1965. 6th Reunion of the Board of Governors of the Inter-American Development Bank. Optd. **Centenario de la Epopeya Nacional 1,864-1,870** as in T **129.**
1069. **129.** 1 g. 50 green (postage) 5 5
1070. 3 g. pink 8 8
1071. 4 g. blue 10 10
1072. **129.** 12 g. 45 brown (air) 20 20
1073. 36 g. violet 65 65
The overprint refers to the National Epic of 1864-70, the war with Argentina, Brazil and Uruguay and this inscription occurs on many other issues from 1965 onwards. Nos. 1068/73 without the overprint were not authorised.

130. R. Gonzalez and St. Ignatius.

1966. Founding of San Ignacio Guazu Monastery. 350th Anniv.
1074. **130.** 15 c. ultram. (post.) 5 5
1075. 25 c. ultramarine .. 5 5
1076. 75 c. ultramarine .. 5 5
1077. 90 c. ultramarine .. 5 5

1078. – 3 g. brown (air) .. 5 5
1079. – 12 g. 45, brown .. 15 12
1080. – 18 g. 15, brown .. 25 20
1081. – 23 g. 40 brown .. 30 25
DESIGNS: Nos. 1078/81, Jesuit Fathers' house, Antigua.

For similar stamps with different inscriptions, see Nos. 822, 824 and 826.

131. Ruben Dario (poet).

132. Lions' Emblem on Globe.

1966. Ruben Dario (poet). 50th Death Anniv.
1082. **131.** 50 c. blue 5 5
1083. 70 c. brown 5 5
1084. 1 g. 50 lake 5 5
1085. 3 g. violet 8 8
1086. 4 g. turquoise .. 10 5
1087. 5 g. black 12 5

1088. 12 g. 45 blue (air) .. 15 12
1089. – 18 g. 15 violet .. 25 15
1090. 23 g. 40 brown .. 30 20
1091. – 36 g. emerald .. 40 30
1092. – 50 g. carmine .. 60 40
DESIGNS: Nos. 1088/92, Open book inscr. "Paraguay de Fuego . . ." by Dario.

1967. Lions Int. 50th Anniv.
1093. **132.** 50 c. violet (postage) 5 5
1094. 70 c. blue 5 5
1095. – 1 g. 50 ultramarine .. 5 5
1096. – 3 g. brown 5 5
1097. – 4 g. blue 5 5
1098. – 5 g. brown 5 5

1099. – 12 g. 45 chocolate (air) 12 10
1100. – 18 g. 15 violet .. 15 12
1101. – 23 g. 40 purple .. 20 15
1102. – 36 g. blue 30 25
1103. – 50 g. cerise 50 45
DESIGNS—VERT. 1 g. 50, 3 g. M. Jones. 4 g., 5 g. Lions headquarters, Chicago. HORIZ. 12 g. 45, 18 g. 15, Library—"Education". 23 g., 36 g., 50 g. Medical laboratory—"Health".

133. W.H.O. Emblem.

1968. World Health Organisation. 20th Anniv.
1104. **133.** 3 g. turquoise (postage) 5 5
1105. 4 g. purple 5 5
1106. 5 g. brown 5 5
1107. 10 g. violet 8 5

1108. – 36 g. brown (air) .. 30 25
1109. – 50 g. cerise 50 45
1110. – 100 g. blue .. 1·00 90
DESIGN—VERT. Nos. 1108/10, W.H.O. emblem on scroll.

134.

135.

1969. World Friendship Week.
1111. **134.** 50 c. red 5 5
1112. 70 c. blue 5 5
1113. 1 g. 50 brown .. 5 5
1114. 3 g. mauve 5 5
1115. 4 g. green 5 5
1116. 5 g. violet 5 5
1117. 10 g. purple 5 5

1969. Air. Campaign for Houses for Teachers.
1118. **135.** 36 g. blue 40 12
1119. 50 g. brown 70 25
1120. 100 g. red .. .. 1·25 40

136. Pres. Lopez.

137. Paraguay 2 r. Stamp of 1870.

1970. Pres. F. Solano Lopez. Death Cent.
1121. **136.** 1 g. brown (postage) 5 5
1122. 2 g. violet 5 5
1123. 3 g. pink 5 5
1124. 4 g. red 5 5
1125. 5 g. blue 8 5
1126. 10 g. green 12 5

1127. **136.** 15 g. blue (air) .. 20 8
1128. 20 g. brown 25 10
1129. 30 g. green 40 15
1130. 40 g. purple 50 20

1970. First Paraguayan Stamps. Cent.
1131. **137.** 1 g. red (postage) .. 5 5
1132. A. 2 g. blue 5 5
1133. B. 3 g. brown 5 5
1134. **137.** 5 g. violet 5 5
1135. A. 10 g. lilac 8 5

1136. B. 15 g. purple (air) .. 20 8
1137. **137.** 30 g. green 40 15
1138. A. 36 g. red 45 20
DESIGNS: First Paraguay stamps. A, 1 r. B, 3 r.

138. Teacher and Pupil.

139. U.N.I.C.E.F. Emblem.

1973. Int. Education Year—U.N.E.S.C.O.
1139. **138.** 3 g. blue (postage) .. 5 5
1140. 5 g. lilac 5 5
1141. 10 g. green 10 5

1142. **138.** 20 g. claret (air) .. 20 8
1143. 25 g. mauve 25 15
1144. 30 g. brown 50 30
1145. 50 g. green .. .. 1·00 65

1973. U.N.I.C.E.F. 25th Anniv.
1146. **139.** 1 g. brown (postage)
1147. 2 g. blue 5 5
1148. 3 g. red 5 5
1149. 4 g. purple 5 5
1150. 5 g. green 5 5
1151. 10 g. maroon .. 10 5

1152. **139.** 20 g. blue (air) .. 20 8
1153. 25 g. green 25 10
1154. 30 g. brown 30 12

140. Acaray Dam.

1973. Tourist Year of the Americas.
1155. **140.** 1 g. brown (postage) 5 5
1156. – 2 g. brown 5 5
1157. – 3 g. blue 8 5
1158. – 5 g. red 15 5
1159. – 10 g. green 30 5

1160. – 20 g. red (air) .. 20 10
1161. – 25 g. grey 25 12
1162. – 50 g. lilac 50 30
1163. 100 g. mauve .. 1·00 50
DESIGNS: 2 g. Marshal Lopez Monument. 3 g. Friendship Bridge. 5 g. Rio Tebicuary Bridge. 10 g. Grand Hotel, Guarani. 20 g. Motor coach. 25 g. Hospital of Institute for Social Service. 50 g. "President Stroessner" (ocean liner). 100 g. "Electra C" airliner.

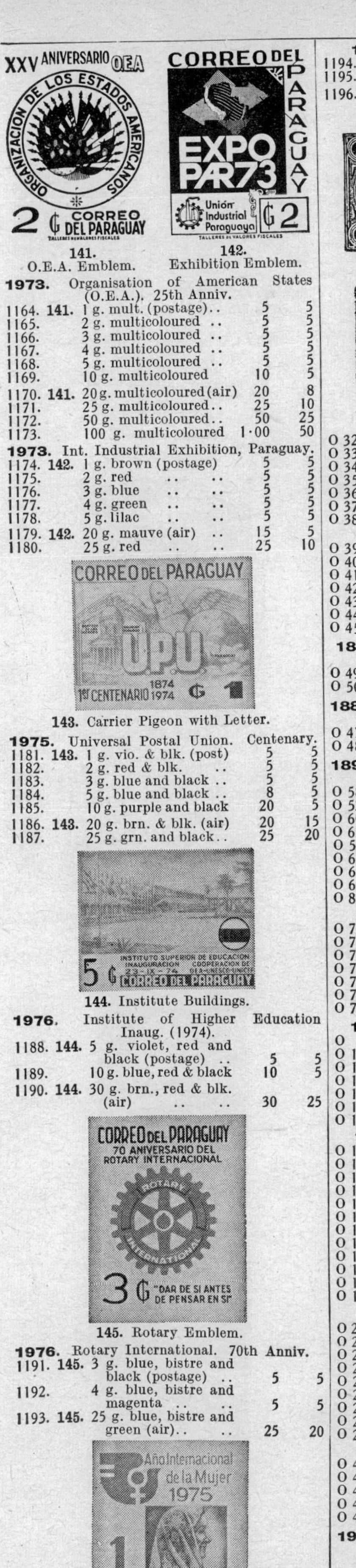

141. O.E.A. Emblem. 142. Exhibition Emblem.

1973. Organisation of American States (O.E.A.). 25th Anniv.
1164. **141.** 1 g. mult. (postage).. 5 5
1165. 2 g. multicoloured .. 5 5
1166. 3 g. multicoloured .. 5 5
1167. 4 g. multicoloured .. 5 5
1168. 5 g. multicoloured .. 5 5
1169. 10 g. multicoloured 10 5
1170. **141.** 20 g. multicoloured (air) 20 8
1171. 25 g. multicoloured.. 25 10
1172. 50 g. multicoloured.. 50 25
1173. 100 g. multicoloured 1·00 50

1973. Int. Industrial Exhibition, Paraguay.
1174. **142.** 1 g. brown (postage) 5 5
1175. 2 g. red 5 5
1176. 3 g. blue 5 5
1177. 4 g. green 5 5
1178. 5 g. lilac 5 5
1179. **142.** 20 g. mauve (air) .. 15 5
1180. 25 g. red 25 10

143. Carrier Pigeon with Letter.

1975. Universal Postal Union. Centenary.
1181. **143.** 1 g. vio. & blk. (post) 5 5
1182. 2 g. red & blk. .. 5 5
1183. 3 g. blue and black .. 5 5
1184. 5 g. blue and black .. 8 5
1185. 10 g. purple and black 20 5
1186. **143.** 20 g. brn. & blk. (air) 20 15
1187. 25 g. grn. and black.. 25 20

144. Institute Buildings.

1976. Institute of Higher Education Inaug. (1974).
1188. **144.** 5 g. violet, red and black (postage) .. 5 5
1189. 10 g. blue, red & black 10 5
1190. **144.** 30 g. brn., red & blk. (air) 30 25

145. Rotary Emblem.

1976. Rotary International. 70th Anniv.
1191. **145.** 3 g. blue, bistre and black (postage) .. 5 5
1192. 4 g. blue, bistre and magenta 5 5
1193. **145.** 25 g. blue, bistre and green (air).. 25 20

146. Woman and I.W.Y. Emblem.

1976. International Women's Year.
1194. **146.** 1 g. brn. & bl. (postage) 5 5
1195. 2 g. brown and red .. 5 5
1196. **146.** 20 g. brn. & grn. (air) 20 15

OFFICIAL STAMPS

O 1. O 2. O 3. O 4.

1886. Various types as O 1/3 optd. **OFICIAL.** (a) Imperf.
O 32. 1 c. orange .. .. 3·00 3·00
O 33. 2 c. violet .. .. 3·00 3·00
O 34. 5 c. orange .. .. 3·00 3·00
O 35. 7 c. green .. .. 3·00 3·00
O 36. 10 c. brown .. .. 3·00 3·00
O 37. 15 c. blue .. .. 3·00 3·00
O 38. 20 c. lake .. .. 3·00 3·00

(b) New colours. Perf.
O 39. 1 c. green 60 60
O 40. 2 c. red 60 60
O 41. 5 c. blue 60 60
O 42. 7 c. orange 60 60
O 43. 10 c. lake 60 60
O 44. 15 c. brown 60 60
O 45. 20 c. blue 60 60

1889. Stamp of 1889 surch. **OFICIAL** and value. Imperf.
O 49. **5.** 3 on 15 c. purple .. 1·90 1·75
O 50. 5 on 15 c. brown .. 1·90 1·75

1889. Stamp of 1889 surch. **OFICIAL** and value. Perf.
O 47. **5.** 1 on 15 c. purple .. 1·90 1·75
O 48. 2 on 15 c. purple .. 1·90 1·75

1890. Stamps of 1887 optd. **OFICIAL** or **Oficial.**
O 58. **4.** 1 c. green 12 12
O 52. 2 c. red 12 12
O 60. 5 c. blue 12 12
O 61. 7 c. brown .. .. 2·25 1·10
O 55. 10 c. mauve 15 15
O 63. 15 c. orange 20 20
O 64. 20 c. rose 25 12
O 65. 50 c. grey 12 12
O 86. 1 p. olive 10 10

1901.
O 73. **O 4.** 1 c. blue 25 25
O 74. 2 c. red 10 10
O 75. 4 c. brown 10 10
O 76. 5 c. green 10 10
O 77. 8 c. brown 8 8
O 78. 10 c. red 12 12
O 79. 20 c. blue 15 15

1903. Stamps of 1903, optd. **OFICIAL.**
O 99. **9.** 1 c. grey 8 5
O 100. 2 c. green 8 8
O 101. 5 c. blue 10 8
O 102. 10 c. brown 8 5
O 103. 20 c. red 8 5
O 104. 30 c. blue 8 5
O 105. 60 c. violet 12 12

1904. As T 12, but inscr. "OFICIAL".
O 106. 1 c. green 15 8
O 107. 1 c. olive 15 8
O 108. 1 c. orange 35 10
O 109. 1 c. red 20 12
O 110. 2 c. orange 12 8
O 111. 2 c. green 12 8
O 112. 2 c. red 65 20
O 113. 2 c. grey 25 20
O 114. 5 c. blue 12 10
O 116. 5 c. grey 90 90
O 117. 10 c. lilac 10 8
O 118. 20 c. lilac 40 40

1913. As T 16, but inscr. "OFICIAL".
O 237. 1 c. grey 5 5
O 238. 2 c. orange 5 5
O 239. 5 c. purple 5 5
O 240. 10 c. green 5 5
O 241. 20 c. rose 5 5
O 242. 50 c. rose 5 5
O 243. 75 c. blue 5 5
O 244. 1 p. blue 5 5
O 245. 2 p. yellow 15 15

1935. Optd. **OFICIAL.**
O 474. **23.** 10 c. blue 5 5
O 475. 50 c. mauve 5 5
O 476. **24.** 1 p. yellow 5 5
O 477. **53.** 1 p. 50 green .. 8 8
O 478. **24.** 2 p. 50 violet .. 8 8

1940. Asuncion University. 50th Anniv As T **67**, inscr. "SERVICIO OFICIAL", but portraits of Pres. Escobar and Dr. Zubizarreta.
O 513. 50 c. black and red .. 5 5
O 514. 1 p. black and red .. 5 5
O 515. 2 p. black and blue .. 5 5
O 516. 5 p. black and blue .. 5 5
O 517. 10 p. black and blue .. 5 5
O 518. 50 p. black and orange 30 30

POSTAGE DUE STAMPS

ILLUSTRATIONS
British Commonwealth and all overprints and surcharges are FULL SIZE.
Foreign Countries have been reduced to ¾-LINEAR.

D 1.

1904.
D 106. **D 1.** 2 c. green 5 5
D 107. 4 c. green 5 5
D 108. 10 c. green 5 5
D 109. 20 c. green 5 5

1913. As T 16, but inscr. "DEFICIENTE".
D 237. 1 c. brown 5 5
D 238. 2 c. brown 5 5
D 239. 5 c. brown 5 5
D 240. 10 c. brown 5 5
D 241. 20 c. brown 5 5
D 242. 40 c. brown 5 5
D 243. 1 p. brown 5 5
D 244. 1 p. 50 brown 8 8

PARMA E2

A former Grand Duchy of N. Italy, united with Sardinia in 1860 and now part of Italy.

100 centesimi = 1 lira.

1. Bourbon "fleur-de-lis". 2. 3.

1852. Imperf.
1. **1.** 5 c. black and yellow .. 15·00 25·00
11. 5 c. yellow £700 £160
4. 10 c. black .. .. 14·00 25·00
6. 15 c. black on rose .. £375 13·00
13. 15 c. red .. .. £1000 38·00
7. 25 c. black on purple .. £1300 38·00
14. 25 c. brown .. .. £2750 55·00
9. 40 c. black on blue .. £325 75·00

1857. Imperf.
17. **2.** 15 c. red .. .. 30·00 £100
19. 25 c. purple .. .. 65·00 32·00
20. 40 c. blue .. .. 11·00 £100

1859. Imperf.
28. **3.** 5 c. green .. .. 90·00 £800
30. 10 c. brown .. .. 42·00 £150
31. 20 c. blue .. .. 75·00 55·00
33. 40 c. red .. .. 45·00 £1400
35. 80 c. yellow £1000

NEWSPAPER STAMPS

1853. As T 3. Imperf.
N 1. **3.** 6 c. black on rose .. 60·00 75·00
N 3. 9 c. black on blue .. 20·00 £5500

PATIALA BC

A "convention" state in the Punjab, India.

1884. Stamps of India (Queen Victoria) with curved opt. **PUTTIALLA STATE** vert.
1. **14.** ½ a. blue-green 20 20
2. – 1 a. purple .. .. 3·00 2·50
3. – 2 a. blue .. .. 1·00 1·25
4. – 4 a. green (No. 89) .. 1·25 1·00
5. – 8 a. mauve .. .. 25·00 26·00
6. – 1 r. grey (No. 101) .. 12·00 12·00

1885. Stamps of India (Queen Victoria optd. **PUTTIALLA STATE** horiz.
7. **14.** ½ a. blue-green 12 12
11. – 1 a. purple 5 5
8. – 2 a. blue 15 12
9. – 4 a. green (No. 89) .. 25 25
12. – 8 a. mauve 20 30
10. – 1 r. grey (No. 101) .. 70 90

Stamps of India optd. **PATIALA STATE.**

1891. Queen Victoria.
32. **25.** 3 p. red 5 5
13. **14.** ½ a. blue-green (No. 84) 5 5
33. ½ a. yellow-green (No. 114) 5 5
14. – 9 p. red 10 12
15. – 1 a. purple 8 5
34. – 1 a. red 5 5
17. – 1½ a. brown 8 10
18. – 2 a. blue 15 8
20. – 3 a. orange 8 10
22. – 4 a. green (No. 96) .. 5 5
24. – 6 a. brown (No. 80) .. 12 8
26. – 8 a. mauve 20 20
27. – 12 a. purple on red .. 30 25
28. **26.** 1 r. green and red .. 1·25 1·25
29. **27.** 2 r. red and orange .. 12·00
30. 3 r. brown and green .. 18·00
31. 5 r. blue and violet .. 25·00

1903. King Edward VII.
36. 3 p. grey 5 5
37. ½ a. green (No. 122) .. 5 5
38. 1 a. red (No. 123) .. 5 5
39. 2 a. lilac 5 5
40. 3 a. orange 5 5
41. 4 a. olive.. .. .. 12 5
42. 6 a. yellow-brown .. 15 12
43. 8 a. mauve 20 15
44. 12 a. purple on red .. 30 35
45. 1 r. green and red .. 35 40

1912. King Edward VII inscr. "INDIA POSTAGE & REVENUE".
46. ½ a. green (No. 149) .. 5 5
47. 1 a. red (No. 150) .. 5 5

1912. King George V. Optd. in two lines.
48. **40.** 3 p. grey 5 5
49. **41.** ½ a. green 5 5
50. **42.** 1 a. red 5 5
61. 1 a. chocolate 5 5
51. **43.** 1½ a. brown (A) .. 15 20
52. **44.** 2 a. lilac 5 5
53. **48.** 3 a. orange 12 8
62. 3 a. blue 10 15
54. **49.** 4 a. olive.. .. .. 10 5
55. **51.** 6 a. yellow-brown .. 20 20
56. **52.** 8 a. mauve 20 20
57. **53.** 12 a. claret 20 20
58. **54.** 1 r. brown and green .. 75 75
59. 2 r. red and orange .. 1·75 1·75
60. 5 r. blue and violet .. 4·00 4·50

1928. King George V. Optd. in one line.
63. **40.** 3 p. grey 5 5
64. **41.** ½ a. green 5 5
75. **62.** ½ a. green 5 5
65. **63.** 9 p. green 5 5
66. **42.** 1 a. chocolate 5 5
76. **64.** 1 a. chocolate 5 5
67. **65.** 1¼ a mauve 5 5
77. **44.** 2 a. orange-red 5 5
68. **45.** 2 a. lilac 5 5
69. **47.** 2½ a. orange 5 5
70. **48.** 3 a. blue 5 5
78. 3 a. red 5 10
71. **50.** 4 a. green 20 15
79. **49.** 4 a. olive.. .. .. 8 12
72. **52.** 8 a. mauve 20 20
73. **54.** 1 r. brown and green .. 50 50
74. 2 r. red and orange .. 1·00 1·25

1937. King George VI. Optd. in one line.
80. **74.** 3 p. slate.. .. .. 5·00 4·00
81. ½ a. brown 20 15
82. 9 p. green 25 20
83. 1 a. red 10 10
84. **76.** 2 a. red 15 15
85. – 2½ a. violet 15 30
86. – 3 a. green 15 30
87. – 3½ a. blue 30 50
88. – 4 a. brown 30 50
89. – 6 a. green 30 75
90. – 8 a. violet 40 75
91. – 12 a. red .. .. 1·00 1·50
92. **77.** 1 r. slate and brown .. 4·00 4·00
93. 2 r. purple and brown .. 4·00 4·00
94. 5 r. green and blue .. 6·00 6·00
95. 10 r. purple and red .. 4·00 12·00
96. 15 r. brown and green .. 20·00 20·00
97. 25 r. slate and purple .. 25·00 30·00

1943. King George VI. Optd. **PATIALA** only. (a) Issue of 1938.
98. **74.** 3 p. slate 80 30
99. ½ a. brown 80 30
100. 9 p. green .. .. 2·50 50
101. 1 a. red .. .. 1·00 50
102. **77.** 1 r. slate and brown .. 75 60

(b) Issue of 1940.
103. **78.** 3 p. slate 8 8
104. ½ a. mauve 8 8
105. 9 p. green 8 8
106. 1 a. red 8 8
107. **79.** 1 a. 3 p. bistre .. 15 20
108. 1½ a. violet 8 8
109. 2 a. red 8 8
110. 3 a. violet 12 15
111. 3½ a. blue 15 30
112. **80.** 4 a. brown 8 25
113. 6 a. green 10 25
114. 8 a. violet 20 30
115. 12 a. purple 30 50

OFFICIAL STAMPS

Overprinted **SERVICE**

1884. Nos. 1 to 3 (Queen Victoria).
O 1. **14.** ½ a. blue-green .. 25 5
O 2. – 1 a. purple 5 5
O 3. – 2 a. blue .. .. 18·00 3·00

1885. Nos. 7, 11 and 8 (Queen Victoria).
O 6. **14.** ½ a. blue-green .. 5 5
O 5. – 1 a. purple 5 5
O 7. – 2 a. blue 5 5

1891. Nos. 13 to 28 and No. 10 Q.V.
O 8. **14.** ½ a. blue-grn. (No. 13) 5 5
O 9. – 1 a. purple 8 5
O 20. – 1 a. red 5 5
O 10. – 2 a. blue 15 10
O 12. – 3 a. orange 5 5
O 13a. – 4 a. green 5 5
O 15. – 6 a. brown 10 10
O 16. – 8 a. mauve 10 10
O 18. – 12 a. purple on red .. 15 15
O 19. – 1 r. grey 20 15
O 21. **26.** 1 r. green and red .. 3·00 4·00

1903. Nos. 36 to 45 (King Edward VII).

O 22. 3 p. grey 5 5
O 24. ½ a. green 5 5
O 25. 1 a. red 5 5
O 26. 2 a. lilac 5 5
O 28. 3 a. orange 35 50
O 29. 4 a. olive 8 10
O 30. 8 a. mauve 10 10
O 32. 1 r. green and red 20 20

1907. Nos. 46/7 (King Edward VII) inscr. "INDIA POSTAGE & REVENUE".

O 33. ½ a. green 5 5
O 34. 1 a. red 5 5

1913. Official stamps of India (King George V) optd. **PATIALA STATE** in two lines.

O 35. **40.** 3 p. grey 5 5
O 36. **41.** ½ a. green 5 5
O 37. **42.** 1 a. red 5 5
O 38. 1 a. chocolate 10 5
O 39. **44.** 2 a. lilac 8 5
O 40. **49.** 4 a. olive 10 10
O 41. **51.** 6 a. yellow-brown 12 15
O 42. **52.** 8 a. mauve 20 12
O 43. **54.** 1 r. brown and green 40 60
O 44. 2 r red and orange 1·25 2·25
O 45. 5 r. blue and violet 3·00 4·00

1927. Postage stamps of India (King George V) optd. **PATIALA STATE SERVICE** in two lines.

O 47. **40.** 3 p. grey 5 5
O 48. **41.** ½ a. green 5 5
O 58. **62.** ½ a. green 5 5
O 49. **42.** 1 a. chocolate 5 5
O 59. **64.** 1 a. chocolate 5 5
O 50. **65.** 1½ a. mauve 5 5
O 51. **45.** 2 a. lilac 8 10
O 61. 2 a. orange-red 5 5
O 60. **44.** 2 a. orange-red 5 5
O 53. **47.** 2½ a. orange 10 10
O 54. **50.** 4 a. green 10 10
O 62. **49.** 4 a. olive 5 5
O 55. **52.** 8 a. mauve 30 30
O 56. **54.** 1 r. brown and green 50 30
O 57. 2 r. red and orange 1·00 1·25

1938. Postage stamps of India (King George VI) optd. **PATIALA STATE SERVICE.**

O 63. **74.** ½ a. brown 40 15
O 64. 9 p. green 6·00 7·00
O 65. 1 a. red 50 15
O 66. **77.** 1 r. slate and brown 80 80
O 67. 2 r. purple and brown 3·00 3·00
O 68. 5 r. green and blue 5·00 5·00

1939. Surch. **1 A SERVICE 1 A.**

O 70. **65.** 1 a. on 1½ a. mauve 15 15

1940. Official stamps of India optd. **PATIALA.**

O 71. O **1.** 3 p. slate 8 8
O 72. ½ a. brown 8 8
O 73. ½ a. purple 8 8
O 74. 9 p. green 8 8
O 75. 1 a. red 8 8
O 76. 1 a. 3 p. bistre 10 8
O 77. 1½ a. violet 8 8
O 78. 2 a. orange 10 10
O 79. 2½ a. violet 15 12
O 80. 4 a. brown 18 20
O 81. 8 a. violet 30 40

1940. Postage stamps of India (King George VI) optd. **PATIALA SERVICE.**

O 82. **77.** 1 r. slate and brown 60 70
O 83. 2 r. purple and brown 1·50 2·50
O 84. 5 r. green and blue 3·50 4·50

PENANG BC

A British Settlement which became a state of the Federation of Malaya, incorporated in Malaysia in 1963.

100 cents = 1 dollar (Straits or Malayan).

1948. Silver Wedding. As T **5/6** of Aden.

1. 10 c. violet 5 8
2. $5 brown 6·00 8·00

1949. As T **17** of Straits Settlements.

3. 1 c. black 5 5
4. 2 c. orange 5 5
5. 3 c. green 8 8
6. 4 c. brown 8 5
7. 5 c. purple 8 10
8. 6 c. grey 5 5
9. 8 c. red 15 30
10. 8 c. green 10 30
11. 10 c. mauve 5 5
12. 12 c. red 12 20
13. 15 c. blue 12 15
14. 20 c. black and green 20 20
15. 20 c. blue 15 12
16. 25 c. purple and orange 12 10
17. 35 c. red and purple 25 35
18. 40 c. red and purple 25 85
19. 50 c. black and blue 25 15
20. $1 blue and purple 60 20
21. $2 green and red 1·00 40
22. $5 green and brown 3·00 1·25

1949. U.P.U. As T **14/7** of Antigua.

23. 10 c. purple 5 5
24. 15 c. blue 8 25
25. 25 c. orange 25 35
26. 50 c. black 40 60

1953. Coronation. As T **7** of Aden.

27. 10 c. black and purple 8 5

1954. As T **1** of Malacca but inscr. "PENANG".

28. 1 c. black 5 8
29. 2 c. orange 5 8
30. 4 c. brown 8 8
31. 5 c. mauve 5 8
32. 6 c. grey 12 12
33. 8 c. green 12 15
34. 10 c. maroon 8 5
35. 12 c. red 12 15
36. 20 c. blue 25 10
37. 25 c. maroon and orange 30 12
38. 30 c. red and purple 35 25
39. 35 c. red and purple 45 35
40. 50 c. black and blue 45 12
41. $1 blue and maroon 65 30
42. $2 green and red 1·40 85
43. $5 green and brown 5·50 2·50

1957. As Nos. 92/102 of Kedah but inset portrait of Queen Elizabeth II.

44. 1 c. black 5 8
45. 2 c. red 5 8
46. 4 c. sepia 5 5
47. 5 c. lake 5 5
48. 8 c. green 8 8
49. 10 c. sepia 5 5
50. 20 c. blue 15 5
51. 50 c. black and blue 25 10
52. $1 blue and purple 60 35
53. $2 green and red 1·50 1·50
54. $5 brown and green 3·00 1·75

1. Copra.

1960. As Nos. 44/54 but with inset Arms of Penang as in T **1.**

55. 1 c. black 5 8
56. 2 c. red 5 8
57. 4 c. sepia 5 5
58. 5 c. lake 5 5
59. 8 c. green 5 8
60. 10 c. maroon 5 5
61. 20 c. blue 8 5
62. 50 c. black and blue 20 5
63. $1 blue and purple 40 20
64. $2 green and red 80 55
65. $5 brown and green 2·25 1·00

2. "Vanda hookeriana".

1965. As Nos. 166/72 of Johore but with Arms of Penang inset and inscr. "PULAU PINANG" as in T **2.**

66. **2.** 1 c. multicoloured 5 5
67. – 2 c. multicoloured 5 5
68. – 5 c. multicoloured 5 5
69. – 6 c. multicoloured 5 5
70. – 10 c. multicoloured 5 5
71. – 15 c. multicoloured 8 5
72. – 20 c. multicoloured 8 8

The higher values used in Panang were Nos. 20/7 of Malaysia.

3. Wanderer.

1971. Butterflies. As Nos. 175/81 of Johore, but with Arms of Penang inset and inscr. "pulau pinang" as in T **3.**

75. – 1 c. multicoloured 5 5
76. – 2 c. multicoloured 5 5
77. – 5 c. multicoloured 5 5
78. – 6 c. multicoloured 5 5
79. – 10 c. multicoloured 5 5
80. – 15 c. multicoloured 8 5
81. **3.** 20 c. multicoloured 8 5

The higher values in use with this issue are Nos. 64/71 of Malaysia.

HAVE YOU READ THE NOTES AT THE BEGINNING OF THIS CATALOGUE?

These often provide answers to the enquiries we receive.

PENRHYN ISLAND BC

One of the Cook Is. in the S. Pacific. A dependency of New Zealand. Used Cook Is. stamps until 1973 when further issues for use in the Northern group of the Cook Is. issues appeared.

A. NEW ZEALAND DEPENDENCY.

1902. Stamps of New Zealand (Pictorials) surch. **PENRHYN ISLANDS** and value in native language.

9. **21.** ½d. green 25 35
10. **35.** 1d. red 25 30
1. **24.** 2½d. blue (No. 253) 35 75
14. **25.** 3d. brown 2·00 3·00
15. **28.** 6d. red 4·00 6·00
17. **31.** 1s. orange 10·00 14·00

1914. Stamps of New Zealand (King Edward VII) surch. **PENRHYN ISLAND** and value in native language.

20. **41.** ½d. green 20 35
22. 6d. red 12·00 15·00
23. 1s. orange 15·00 23·00

1917. Stamps of New Zealand (King George V) optd. **PENRHYN ISLAND.**

28. **43.** ½d. green 20 35
29. 1½d. grey 75 1·10
30. 1½d. brown 25 50
24. 2½d. blue 30 50
31. 3d. brown 60 1·00
26. 6d. red 2·00 3·00
27. 1s. orange 4·50 6·00

1920. Pictorial types as Cook Islands (1920), but inscr. "PENRHYN".

32. **4.** ½d. black and green 25 35
39. – 1d. black and red 50 75
34. – 1½d. black and violet 60 1·00
40. – 2½d. brown and blue 80 2·50
35. – 3d. black and red 75 1·10
36. – 6d. brown and red-brown 1·10 2·50
37. – 1s. black and blue 2·25 4·50

B. PART OF COOK ISLANDS

1973. Nos. 228/9, 231, 233/6, 239/40 and 243/5 of Cook Is. optd. **PENRHYN NORTHERN** or **PENRHYN** ($1).

41. 1 c. multicoloured 8 10
42. 2 c. multicoloured 10 15
43. 3 c. multicoloured 10 15
44. 4 c. multicoloured 12 15
45. 5 c. multicoloured 15 20
46. 6 c. multicoloured 20 25
47. 8 c. multicoloured 50 60
48. 15 c. multicoloured 75 1·00
49. 20 c. multicoloured 1·75 2·00
50. 50 c. multicoloured 3·50 4·00
51. $1 multicoloured 7·00 8·00
52. $2 multicoloured 14·00 16·00

1973. Nos. 452/4 of Cook Is. optd. with **PENRHYN NORTHERN.**

53. **59.** 25 c. multicoloured 1·25 1·40
54. – 30 c. multicoloured 1·50 1·60
55. – 50 c. multicoloured 2·50 2·75

1. "Ostracion sp".

1974. Fishes. Multicoloured.

56. ½ c. Type **1** 5 5
57. 1 c. "Monodactylus argenteus" 5 5
58. 2 c. "Pomacanthus imperatar" 5 5
59. 3 c. "Chelmon rostratus" 5 5
60. 4 c. "Chaetodon ornatissimus" 5 5
61. 5 c. "Chaetodon melanotus" 5 5
62. 8 c. "Chaetodon raffessi" 8 8
63. 10 c. "Chaetodon ephippium" 10 10
64. 20 c. "Pygoplites diacanthus" 20 20
65. 25 c. "Heniochus acuminatus" 25 25
66. 60 c. "Plectorhynchus chaetodonoides" 60 65
67. $1 "Belistipus undulatus" 95 1·10
68. $2 Bird's-eye view of Penrhyn 1·90 2·10
69. $5 Satellite view of Australasia 4·75 5·00

Nos. 68/9 are size 63 × 25 mm.

2. Penrhyn Stamps of 1902.

1974. Universal Postal Union. Centenary. Multicoloured.

70. 25 c. Type **2** 30 35
71. 50 c. Stamps of 1920 55 65

3. "Adoration of the Magi" (Memling).

1974. Christmas. Multicoloured.

72. 5 c. Type **3** 5 5
73. 10 c. "Adoration of the Shepherds" (Hugo van der Goes) 10 12
74. 25 c. "Adoration of the Magi" (Rubens) 30 35
75. 30 c. "The Holy Family" (Borianni) 35 45

4. Churchill giving "V" Sign.

1974. Sir Winston Churchill. Birth Cent.

76. **4.** 30 c. brown and gold 35 45
77. – 50 c. green and gold 55 65

DESIGN: 50 c. Full-face portrait.

1975. "Apollo-Soyuz" Space Project. Optd. **KIA ORANA ASTRONAUTS** and emblem.

78. $5 Satellite view of Australasia 5·00 5·50

5. "Virgin and Child" (T. Bouts).

1975. Christmas. Paintings of the "Virgin and Child" by artists given below. Mult.

79. 7 c. Type **5** 8 10
80. 15 c. Leonardo da Vinci 15 20
81. 35 c. Raphael 35 40

6. "Pieta".

1976. Easter and Michelangelo. 500th Birth Anniversary.

82. **6.** 15 c. brown and gold 15 20
83. – 20 c. lilac and gold 20 25
84. – 35 c. green and gold 40 45

DESIGNS: Nos. 83/4 show different views of the "Pieta".

7. " Washington crossing the Delaware " (E. Leutze).

1976. American Revolution. Bicent. Multicoloured.

86.	30 c.	35	40
87.	30 c. Type 7	35	40
88.	30 c.	35	40
89.	50 c. " The Spirit of '76 "	55	65
90.	50 c. (A. M. Willard)	55	65
91.	50 c.	55	65

Type 7 shows the left-hand stamp of the 30 c. design.

8. Running.

1976. Olympic Games, Montreal. Multicoloured.

93.	25 c. Type 8	30	35
94.	30 c. Long jump	35	40
95.	75 c. Throwing the javelin	80	90

9. " The Flight into Egypt ".

1976. Christmas. Durer Engravings.

97. 9.	7 c. black and silver	8	8
98. –	15 c. blue and silver	15	20
99. –	35 c. violet and silver	35	40

DESIGNS: 15 c. " Adoration of the Shepherds ". 35 c. " The Epiphany ".

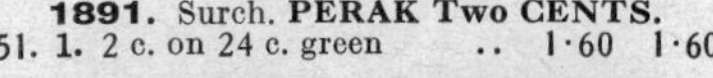

PERAK BC

A state of the Federation of Malaya, incorporated in Malaysia in 1963.

100 cents = 1 dollar (Straits or Malayan).

Stamps of Straits Settlements optd. or surch.

1878. Optd. with crescent, star and **P** in oval.

1. 1.	2 c. brown	£250	£170

1880. Optd. **PERAK.**

10. 1.	2 c. brown	3·00	3·25
16.	2 c. rose	45	55

1883. Surch. **2 CENTS PERAK.**

15. 1.	2 c. on 1 c. rose	50·00	40·00

1886. Surch. **ONE CENT PERAK.**

22. 1.	1 c. on 2 c. rose	5·00	5·00

1886. Surch. **1 CENT PERAK.**

26. 1.	1 c. on 2 c. rose	2·75	4·00

1886. Surch. **One CENT PERAK.**

30. 1.	1 c. on 2 c. rose	25	40

1889. Surch. **PERAK ONE CENT.**

33. 1.	1 c. on 2 c. rose	11·00	10·00

1891. Surch. **PERAK One CENT.**

42. 1.	1 c. on 2 c. rose	35	40
46.	1 c. on 6 c. lilac	4·00	4·00

1891. Surch. **PERAK Two CENTS.**

51. 1.	2 c. on 24 c. green	1·60	1·60

1. Tiger.

2. Tiger.

3. Elephants.

1892.

57. 1.	1 c. green	35	12
58.	2 c. red	50	25
59.	2 c. orange	15	80
60.	5 c. blue	45	80

1895. Surch. **3 CENTS.**

61. 1.	3 c. on 5 c. red	25	50

1895.

62. 2.	1 c. purple and green	20	25
63.	2 c. purple and brown	35	20
64.	3 c. purple and red	60	15
65.	4 c. purple and red	90	1·10
66.	5 c. purple and yellow	85	35
67.	8 c. purple and blue	2·00	40
68.	10 c. purple and orange	2·00	55
69. 2	25 c. green and red	11·00	4·00
70.	50 c. purple and black	8·00	5·00
71.	50 c. green and black	14·00	9·00
72. 3.	$1 green	18·00	13·00
73.	$2 green and red	25·00	19·00
74.	$3 green and yellow	23·00	17·00
75.	$5 green and blue	80·00	38·00
76.	$25 green and orange	£450	£150

1900. Surch. in words.

77. 2.	1 c. on 2 c. purple & brown	15	20
78.	1 c. on 4 c. purple and red	15	30
79.	1 c. on 5 c. purple & yellow	20	40
80.	3 c. on 8 c. purple & blue	50	70
81.	3 c. on 50 c. green & black	40	70
82. 3.	3 c. on $1 green	7·50	8·50
83.	3 c. on $2 green and red	4·25	6·00

4. Sultan Iskandar. 5.

1935.

84. 4.	1 c. black	12	8
85.	2 c. green	8	8
86.	4 c. orange	15	8
87.	5 c. brown	8	8
88.	6 c. red	70	70
89.	8 c. grey	30	12
90.	10 c. purple	8	8
91.	12 c. blue	40	60
92.	25 c. purple and red	35	35
93.	30 c. purple and orange	50	75
94.	40 c. red and purple	1·10	1·40
95.	50 c. black on green	1·10	80
96.	$1 black and red on blue	1·00	90
97.	$2 green and red	3·00	2·50
98.	$5 green and red on green	8·00	6·00

1938.

99. 5.	1 c. black	15	10
100.	2 c. green	35	12
101.	2 c. orange	15	40
102.	3 c. green	15	30
103.	4 c. orange	30	10
104.	5 c. brown	8	8
105.	6 c. red	2·00	10
106.	8 c. grey	35	8
107.	8 c. red	55	1·40
108.	10 c. purple	50	10
109.	12 c. blue	90	90
110.	15 c. blue	70	3·00
111.	25 c. purple and red	2·50	90
112.	30 c. purple and orange	35	70
113.	40 c. red and purple	1·25	90
114.	50 c. black on green	55	60
115.	$1 black and red on blue	5·00	4·00
116.	$2 green and red	10·00	9·00
117.	$5 green and red on green	22·00	24·00

1948. Silver Wedding. As T **5/6** of Aden.

118.	10 c. violet	5	8
119.	$5 green	5·00	7·00

1949. U.P.U. As T **14/7** of Antigua.

120.	10 c. purple	5	5
121.	15 c. blue	8	15
122.	25 c. orange	25	35
123.	50 c. black	50	60

6. Sultan Yussuf 'Izzuddin Shah.

1950.

124. 6.	1 c. black	5	5
125.	2 c. orange	5	5
126.	3 c. green	20	10
127.	4 c. brown	5	5
128.	5 c. purple	5	5
129.	6 c. grey	5	5
130.	8 c. red	12	20
131.	8 c. green	15	20
132.	10 c. purple	8	5
133.	12 c. red	15	20
134.	15 c. blue	20	10
135.	20 c. black and green	20	10
136.	20 c. blue	20	10
137.	25 c. purple and orange	12	8
138.	30 c. red and purple	30	20
139.	35 c. red and purple	25	25
140.	40 c. red and purple	40	40
141. 6.	50 c. black and blue	25	8
142.	$1 blue and purple	70	35
143.	$2 green and red	1·50	70
144.	$5 green and brown	3·50	2·50

1953. Coronation. As T **7** of Aden.

145.	10 c. black and purple	8	5

1957. As Nos. 92/102 of Kedah but portrait of Sultan Yussuf 'Izzuddin Shah.

146.	1 c. black	5	5
147.	2 c. red-orange	5	5
148.	4 c. sepia	5	5
149.	5 c. lake	5	5
150.	8 c. green	8	8
151.	10 c. sepia	5	5
152.	10 c. maroon	5	5
153.	20 c. blue	8	5
154a.	50 c. black and blue	25	10
155.	$1 blue and purple	35	12
156a.	$2 green and red	75	40
157a.	$5 brown and green	1·75	90

7. Sultan Idris Shah.

1963. Installation of Sultan of Perak.

158. 7.	10 c. red, black, blue and yellow	5	5

8. " Vanda hookeriana ".

1965. As Nos. 166/72 of Johore but with inset portrait of Sultan Idris as in T **8.**

159. 8.	1 c. multicoloured	5	5
160. –	2 c. multicoloured	5	5
161. –	5 c. multicoloured	5	5
162. –	6 c. multicoloured	5	5
163. –	10 c. multicoloured	5	5
164. –	15 c. multicoloured	5	5
165. –	20 c. multicoloured	8	8

The higher values used in Perak were Nos. 20/7 of Malaysia.

9. Malayan Jezebel.

1971. Butterflies. As Nos. 175/81 of Johore. but with portrait of Sultan Idris as in T **9.**

168. 9.	1 c. multicoloured	5	5
169. –	2 c. multicoloured	5	5
170. –	5 c. multicoloured	5	5
171. –	6 c. multicoloured	5	5
172. –	10 c. multicoloured	5	5
173. –	15 c. multicoloured	8	8
174. –	20 c. multicoloured	8	8

The higher values in use with this issue are Nos. 64/71 of Malaysia.

OFFICIAL STAMPS

1889. Stamps of Straits Settlements optd. **P.G.S.**

O 1. 1.	2 c. rose	1·10	1·10
O 2.	4 c. brown	2·00	3·00
O 3.	6 c. lilac	6·00	8·00
O 4.	8 c. orange	6·50	8·50
O 5. 5.	10 c. grey	10·00	10·00
O 6. 1.	12 c. blue	20·00	
O 7.	12 c. purple	30·00	
O 9.	24 c. green	20·00	

1894. No. 60 optd. **Service.**

O 10. 1.	5 c. blue	2·50	35

1895. No. 66 optd. **Service.**

O 11. 2.	5 c. purple and yellow	50	12

PERLIS BC

A state of the Federation of Malaya, incorporated in Malaysia in 1963.

100 cents = 1 dollar (Straits or Malayan).

1948. Silver Wedding. As T **5/6** of Aden.

1.	10 c. violet	5	8
2.	$5 brown	5·00	7·00

1949. U.P.U. As T **14/17** of Antigua.

3.	10 c. purple	8	20
4.	15 c. blue	10	30
5.	25 c. orange	25	40
6.	50 c. black	40	55

1. Raja Syed Putra.

1951.

7. 1.	1 c. black	5	8
8.	2 c. orange	5	8
9.	3 c. green	35	40
10.	4 c. brown	5	8
11.	5 c. purple	5	5
12.	6 c. grey	5	8
13.	8 c. red	25	30
14.	8 c. green	30	35
15.	10 c. purple	10	5
16.	12 c. red	10	25
17.	15 c. blue	45	55
18.	20 c. black and green	60	60
19.	20 c. blue	25	25
20.	25 c. purple and orange	25	25
21.	30 c. red and purple	40	45
22.	35 c. red and purple	40	50
23.	40 c. red and purple	55	65
24.	50 c. black and blue	35	35
25.	$1 blue and purple	1·25	1·75
26.	$2 green and red	1·75	2·75
27.	$5 green and brown	4·00	6·00

1953. Coronation. As T **7** of Aden.

28.	10 c. black and purple	15	1

1957. As Nos. 92/102 of Kedah but inset portrait of Raja Syed Putra.

29.	1 c. black	5	5
30.	2 c. red	5	5
31.	4 c. sepia	5	5
32.	5 c. lake	5	5
33.	8 c. green	8	15
34.	10 c. sepia	8	8
35.	10 c. maroon	5	5
36.	20 c. blue	8	8
37a.	50 c. black and blue	20	20
38.	$1 blue and purple	50	65
39.	$2 green and red	95	95
40.	$5 brown and green	2·25	2·25

2. " Vanda hookeriana ".

1965. As Nos. 166/72 of Johore but with inset portrait of Tunku Bendahara Abu Bakar as in T **2.**

41. 2.	1 c. multicoloured	5	5
42. –	2 c. multicoloured	5	5
43. –	5 c. multicoloured	5	5
44. –	6 c. multicoloured	5	5
45. –	10 c. multicoloured	5	5
46. –	15 c. multicoloured	8	8
47. –	20 c. multicoloured	8	10

The higher values used in Perlis were Nos. 20/7 of Malaysia.

3. Black-veined Tiger.

1971. Butterflies. As Nos. 175/81 of Johore, but with portrait of Sultan Syed Putra as in T **3.**

48. –	1 c. multicoloured	5	5
49. 3.	2 c. multicoloured	5	5
50. –	5 c. multicoloured	5	5
51. –	6 c. multicoloured	5	5
52. –	10 c. multicoloured	5	5
53. –	15 c. multicoloured	8	8
54. –	20 c. multicoloured	8	8

The higher values in use with this issue are Nos. 64/71 of Malaysia.

4. Raja Syed Putra.

1971. Installation of Raja Syed Putra. 25th Anniv.

55. **4.** 10 c. multicoloured .. 5 5
56. 15 c. multicoloured .. 5 5
57. 50 c. multicoloured .. 15 15

PERU

O4

A republic on the N.W. coast of S. America independent since 1821.

1857. 8 reales = 1 peso.
1858. 100 centavos = 10 dineros = 5 pesetas = 1 peso.
1874. 100 centavos = 1 sol.

1.

2.

4. Llamas.

1858. T 1 and similar designs with flags below arms. Imperf.

8. **1.** 1 d. blue .. .. .. 30·00 3·00
13. 1 peseta red .. .. 110·00 11·00
5. ½ peso yellow £425 £160

1862. Various frames. Imperf.

14. **2.** 1 d. red .. .. .. 6·00 1·25
20. 1 d. green .. .. .. 4·25 1·25
16. 1 peseta, brown .. .. 35·00 19·00
22. 1 peseta, yellow .. .. 35·00 16·00

1866. Various frames. Perf.

17. **4.** 5 c. green .. .. .. 2·75 75
18. – 10 c. red .. .. .. 2·75 90
19. – 20 c. brown .. .. .. 10·00 3·00

See also Nos. 316/8.

7.

8.

1871. First Railway in Peru (Lima-Chorillos-Callao). 20th Anniv. Imperf.

21a. **7.** 5 c. red .. .. .. 20·00 11·00

1873. Roul. by imperf.

23. **8.** 2 c. blue .. .. .. 9·50 95·00

9. Sun-god.

10.

11.

12.

1874. Various frames. Perf.

24. **9.** 1 c. orange 40 40
25. **10.** 2 c. violet 40 40
26. 5 c. blue 50 25
27. 10 c. green 12 12
28. 20 c. red 65 40
29. **11.** 50 c. green .. .. 1·90 1·25
30. **12.** 1 s. rose 65 65

For further stamps in these types, see Nos. 276, 278/84 and 314/5.

(13.)

(14.)

1880. Optd. with T 13.

36. **9.** 1 c. green 25 25
37. **10.** 2 c. red 40 40
39. 5 c. blue 50 50
40. **11.** 50 c. green .. .. 6·50 5·50
41. **12.** 1 s. rose .. .. 17·00 13·00

1881. Optd. as T 13, but inscr. "LIMA" at foot instead of "PERU".

42. **9.** 1 c. green 40 40
43. **10.** 2 c. red .. .. .. 3·00 3·00
44. 5 c. blue 50 40
45. **11.** 50 c. green .. .. £100 75·00
46. **12.** 1 s. rose .. .. .. 25·00 25·00

1881. Optd. with T 14.

57. **9.** 1 c. orange 20 50
58. **10.** 2 c. violet 20 75
59. 2 c. red .. .. .. 50 1·60
60. 5 c. blue .. .. .. 9·50 16·00
61. 10 c. green 20 60
62. 20 c. red .. .. .. 32·00 38·00

(15.)

(16.)

1882. Optd. with T 14 and 15.

63. **9.** 1 c. green 25 50
64. **10.** 5 c. blue 25 45
66. **11.** 50 c. rose 65 90
67. **12.** 1 s. blue .. .. 1·40 1·90

1883. Optd. with T 15 only.

200. **9.** 1 c. green 50 65
201. **10.** 2 c. red 50 65
202. 5 c. blue 60 75
203. **11.** 50 c. pink .. .. 19·00 22·00
204. **12.** 1 s. blue .. .. 9·50 9·50

1883. Handstamped with T 16 only.

206. **9.** 1 c. orange 40 40
210. **10.** 5 c. blue .. .. 2·00 2·00
211. 10 c. green 25 25
216. **11.** 50 c. green .. .. 1·90 1·75
220. **12.** 1 s. rose .. .. 3·00 2·50

1883. Optd. with T 13 and 16, the inscription in oval reading "PERU".

223. **11.** 50 c. green .. .. 25·00 25·00
225. **12.** 1 s. rose .. .. 32·00 32·00

1883. Optd. with T 13 and 16, the inscription in oval reading "LIMA".

227. **9.** 1 c. green .. .. 1·90 1·90
229. **10.** 2 c. red .. .. 1·25 1·25
232. 5 c. blue .. .. 2·50 2·50
234. **11.** 50 c. green .. .. 32·00 32·00
236. **12.** 1 s. rose .. .. 35·00 35·00

1883. Optd. with T 15 and 16.

238. **9.** 1 c. green 40 40
241. **10.** 2 c. red 25 25
246. 5 c. blue 50 50

1884. Optd. **CORREOS LIMA** and sun.

277. **10.** 5 c. blue 40 25

1886. Re-issue of 1866 and 1874 types.

278. **9.** 1 c. violet 20 20
314. 1 c. red 25 12
279. **10.** 2 c. green 25 12
315. 2 c. blue 25 15
280. 5 c. orange 25 12
316. **4.** 5 c. lake 90 45
281. **10.** 10 c. black 12 12
317. – 10 c. orange (Llamas) .. 50 30
282. **10.** 20 c. blue 90 40
318. – 20 c. blue (Llamas) .. 3·00 1·40
283. **11.** 50 c. rose 60 40
284. **12.** 1 s. brown 40 30

(17. Pres. R. M Bermudez.)

18.

1894. Optd. with T 17.

294. **9.** 1 c. orange 20 20
295. 1 c. green 20 20
296. **10.** 2 c. violet 20 20
297. 2 c. red 20 20
298. 5 c. blue 95 60
299. 10 c. green 20 20
300. **11.** 50 c. green 55 55

1894. Optd. with T 15 and 17.

301. **10.** 2 c. red 20 20
302. 5 c. blue 40 40
303. **11.** 50 c. rose .. .. 8·00 8·00
304. **12.** 1 s. blue .. .. .. 28·00 28·00

1895. Installation of Pres. Pierola.

328. **18.** 1 c. violet 65 65
329. 2 c. green 65 65
330. 5 c. yellow 65 65
331. 10 c. blue 65 65
332. – 20 c. orange 65 65
333. – 50 c. blue .. .. 2·50 2·50
334. – 1 s. lake .. .. 8·00 8·00

Nos. 332/4 are larger (30 × 36 mm.) and the central device is in a frame of laurel.

See also Nos. 352/4.

20. Manco Capac.

21. Pizarro.

22. General de la Mar.

1896.

335. **20.** 1 c. blue 15 15
336. 1 c. green 15 10
337. 2 c. blue 12 10
338. 2 c. red 12 5
339. **21.** 5 c. blue 20 5
340. 5 c. green 20 5
342. 10 c. yellow 35 20
343. 10 c. black 30 8
344. 20 c. orange 75 15
345. **22.** 50 c. red .. .. 1·25 65
346. 1 s. red .. .. 1·90 75
347. 2 s. lake 95 65

1897. No. D 31 optd. **FRANQUEO.**

348. D **1.** 1 c. brown 20 20

23. Suspension Bridge at Paucartambo.

24. Pres. D. Nicolas de Pierola.

1987. Opening of New Postal Building. Dated "1897".

349. **23.** 1 c. blue 35 25
350. – 2 c. brown 35 20
351. **24.** 5 c. red 45 25

DESIGN: 2 c. G.P.O., Lima.

1899. As Nos. 328/34, but vert. inscr. replaced by pearl ornaments.

352. **18.** 22 c. green 20 12
353. – 5 s. red 65 65
354. – 10 s. green .. .. 55·00 70·00

26. President Romana.

27. Admiral Grau.

1900.

357. **26.** 22 c. black and green .. 3·00 65

1901. Advent of the Twentieth Cent.

358. **27.** 1 c. black and green .. 40 20
359. – 2 c. black and red .. 40 20
360. – 5 c. black and lilac .. 40 20

PORTRAITS: 2 c. Col. Bolognesi. 5 c. Pres. Romana.

28. Municipal Board of Health Building.

1905.

361. **28.** 12 c. black and blue .. 25 20

1907. Surch.

362. **28.** 1 c. on 12 c. blk. & blue 12 12
363. 2 c. on 12 c. blk. & blue 25 25

29. Bolognesi Monument.

30. Admiral Grau.

31. Llama.

33. Exhibition Buildings.

35. G.P.O., Lima.

38. Columbus.

1907.

364. **29.** 1 c. black and green .. 12 12
365. **30.** 2 c. purple and red .. 12 12
366. **31.** 4 c. olive .. .. 3·75 50
367. – 5 c. black and blue .. 12 5
368. **33.** 10 c. black and brown 45 35
369. – 20 c. black and green .. 1·75 30
370. **35.** 50 c. black .. 2·50 40
371. – 1 s. green and violet .. 55·00 75
372. – 2 s. black and blue .. 29·00 32·00

DESIGNS—VERT.—As T **30**: 5 c. Statue of Bolivar. (24 × 33 mm.): 2 s. Columbus Monument. HORIZ.—as T **33**: 20 c. Medical School, Lima. (33 × 24 mm.): 1 s. Grandstand, Santa Beatrice Race-course, Lima.

1909. Portraits.

373. – 1 c. grey (Manco Capac) 5 5
374. **38.** 2 c. green 5 5
375. – 4 c. red (Pizarro) .. 10 5
376. – 5 c. purple (San Martin) 5 5
377. – 10 c. blue (Bolivar) .. 12 12
378. – 12 c. blue (de la Mar) .. 30 12
379. – 20 c. brown (Castilla) .. 40 12
380. – 50 c. orange (Grau) .. 80 25
381. – 1 s. black and lake (Bolognesi) .. 1·90 20

See also Nos. 431/5, 439/40, 484/6 and 489.

1913. Surch. **UNION POSTAL 8 Cts. Sud Americana** in oval.

382. **28.** 8 c. on 12 c. black & blue 40 25

1915. As 1896, 1905 and 1907, surch. **1915,** and value.

383. **20.** 1 c. on 1 c. green .. 9·50 9·50
384. **29.** 1 c. on 1 c. black & green 40 40
385. **30.** 1 c. on 2 c. purple & red 65 65
386. **31.** 1 c. on 4 c. olive .. 1·00 1·00
387. **21.** 1 c. on 10 c. black .. 50 50
388. **33.** 1 c. on 10 c. blk. & brn. 20 20
389. 2 c. on 10 c. blk. & brn. 14·00 14·00
390. **28.** 2 c. on 12 c. blk. & blue 12 12
391. – 2 c. on 20 c. black and green (No. 369) .. 4·25 4·35
392. **35.** 2 c. on 50 c. black .. 95 95

1916. Surch. **VALE,** value and **1916.**

393. 1 c. on 12 c. blue (378) .. 10 10
394. 1 c. on 20 c. brown (379) .. 10 10
395. 1 c. on 50 c. orange (380) .. 10 10
396. 2 c. on 4 c. red (375) .. 10 10
397. 10 c. on 1 s. blk. & lake (381) 25 15

1915. Official stamps of 1909 optd. **FRANQUEO 1916** or surch. **VALE 2 Cts** also.

398. O **1.** 1 c. red 10 10
399. 2 c. on 50 c. olive .. 12 12
400. 10 c. brown 15 15

1915. Postage Due stamps of 1909 surch. **FRANQUEO VALE 2 Cts. 1916.**

401. D **3.** 2 c. on 1 c. chocolate 30 30
402. 2 c. on 5 c. chocolate 10 10
403. 2 c. on 10 c. chocolate 10 10
404. 2 c. on 50 c. chocolate 10 10

1917. Surch. **Un Centavo.**

405. 1 c. on 4 c. (No. (375) .. 15 10

1918. Portraits as T **38.**

406. 1 c. blk. & orge. (San Martin) 10 5
407. 2 c. blk. & green (Bolivar) 10 5
408. 4 c. blk. & red (Galvez) .. 12 5
409. 5 c. blk. & blue (Pardo) .. 12 10
410. 8 c. blk. & brown (Grau) .. 25 15
411. 10 c. blk. & blue (Bolognesi) 20 5
412. 12 c. blk. & lilac (Castilla) 30 10
413. 20 c. blk. & green (Caceres) 40 15

See also Nos. 431/5, 439/40. 484/6 and 489.

39. Columbus at Salamanca University. 40. A. B. Leguia.

1918.
414. 39. 50 c. black and brown 95 20
415. – 1 s. black and green 2·50 20
416. – 2 s. black and blue 5·00 35
DESIGNS: 1 s. Funeral of Atahualpa. 2 s. Battle of Arica.

1920. New Constitution.
417. 40. 5 c. black and blue 12 12
418. 5 c. black and brown 15 15

41. 42. Oath of Independence.

44. Admiral Cochrane. 45. J. Olaya.

1921. Independence. Cent. Dated "1821 1921".
419. 41. 1 c. brown (San Martin) 12 8
420. 2 c. green (Arenales) 15 12
421. 4 c. red (Las Heras) 45 30
422. 42. 5 c. brown 15 8
423. 44. 7 c. violet 30 20
424. 41. 10 c. blue (Guisse) 35 25
425. 12 c. black (Vidal) 60 30
426. 20 c. blk. & red (Leguia) 95 60
427. 50 c. violet and purple (S. Martin Monument) 1·90 1·10
428. 42. 1 s. green and red (San Martin and Leguia) 3·75 2·00

1923. Surch. **CINCO Centavos 1923.**
429. 38. 5 c. on 8 c. black and brown (No. 410) 25 20

1924. Surch. **CUATRO Centavos 1924.**
430. 4 c. on 5 c. (No. 409) 15 10

1924. Portraits as T 38. Size 18½×23 mm.
431. 2 c. olive (Rivadeneyra) 12 5
432. 4 c. green (Melgar) 15 5
433. 8 c. black (Iturregui) 30 5
434. 10 c. red (A. B. Leguia) 20 8
435. 15 c. blue (De la Mar) 20 5
439. 1 s. brown (De Saco) 1·90 25
440. 2 s. blue (J. Leguia) 6·50 1·40
See also Nos. 484/6 and 489.

1924. Monuments.
436. 45. 20 c. blue 20 5
437. 20 c. yellow (Olaya) 35 8
438. 50 c. purple (Bellido) 55 10
See also Nos. 484/9.

47. Bolivar. 48.

1924. Battle of Ayacucho. Cent. Portraits of Bolivar. Dated "1824 1924".
441. – 2 c. olive 12 5
442. 47. 4 c. green 15 8
443. 5 c. black 30 8
444. 48. 10 c. red 12 5
445. – 20 c. blue 35 10
446. – 50 c. lilac 80 45
447. – 1 s. brown 2·50 75
448. – 2 s. blue 8·00 4·75

1925. Surch. **DOS Centavos 1925.**
449. 45. 2 c. on 20 c. blue 25 20

1925. Optd. **Plebiscito.**
450. 10 c. red (No. 434) 25 30

49. The Rock of Arica. 52.

1925. Obligatory Tax. Tacna-Arica Plebiscite.
451. 49. 2 c. orange 25 12
452. 5 c. blue 25 12
453. 5 c. red 25 12
454. 5 c. green 20 10
455. – 10 c. brown 80 50
456. – 50 c. green 3·75 3·00
DESIGNS—HORIZ. (39×30 mm.): 10 c. Soldiers with colours. VERT. (27×33 mm.): 50 c. Bolognesi Statue.

1927. Obligatory Tax. Figures of value not encircled.
457. 52. 2 c. orange 20 5
458. 2 c. brown 20 10
459. 2 c. blue 20 10
460. 2 c. violet 10 5
461. 2 c. green 10 5
462. 20 c. red 65 35

1927. Air. Optd. **Servicio Aereo.**
463. 45. 50 c. purple (No. 438) 19·00 15·00

53. Pres. A. B. Leguia. 54. Rock of Arica.

1928. Air.
464. 53. 50 c. green 1·25 25

1928. Obligatory Tax. Plebiscite Fund.
465. 54. 2 c. mauve 12 5

1929. Surch. **Habilitada 2 Cts. 1929.**
466. – 2 c. on 8 c. (No. 410) 30 30
468. 45. 15 c. on 20 c. (No. 437) 45 45

1929. Surch. **Habilitada 2 centavos 1929.**
467. 2 c. on 8 c. (No. 410) 40 40

1930. Optd. **Habilitada Franqueo.**
469. 54. 2 c. mauve 20 20

1930. Surch. **Habilitada 2 Cts. 1930.**
470. 45. 2 c. on 20 c. yellow 15 15

1930. Surch. **Habilitada Franqueo 2 Cts. 1930.**
471. 53. 2 c. on 50 c. green 15 15

55. Arms of Peru. 56. Lima Cathedral.

1930. Sixth (inscribed "seventh") Pan-American Child Congress. Inscr. as in T 55/6.
472. 55. 2 c. green 25 25
473. 56. 5 c. red 75 65
474. – 10 c. blue 50 40
475. – 50 c. brown 8·00 6·50
DESIGNS—HORIZ. 10 c. G.P.O., Lima. VERT. 50 c. Madonna and Child.

1930. Fall of Leguia Govt. No. 434 optd. with Arms of Peru or surch. with new value in four corners also.
477. 2 c. on 10 c. red 5 5
478. 4 c. on 10 c. red 12 12
479. 10 c. red 12 5
476. 15 c. on 10 c. red 15 10

57. Simon Bolivar. 59. Pizarro.

60. The Old Stone Bridge, Lima.

1930. Bolivar's Death Cent.
480. 57. 2 c. brown 25 20
481. 4 c. red 50 30
482. 10 c. green 25 25
483. 15 c. grey 45 45

1930. As T 38 and 45 but smaller (18×22 mm.).
484. – 2 c. olive (Rivadeneyra) 5 5
485. – 4 c. green (Melgar) 8 5
486. – 15 c. blue (De la Mar) 15 5
487. 45. 20 c. yellow (Olaya) 50 15
488. 50 c. purple (Bellido) 50 15
489. – 1 s. brown (De Saco) 65 20

1931. Obligatory Tax. Unemployment Fund. Surch. **Habilitada Pro Desocupados 2 Cts.**
490. 57. 2 c. on 4 c. red 45 30
491. 2 c. on 10 c. green 35 30
492. 2 c. on 15 c. grey 35 30

1931. 1st Peruvian Philatelic Exn.
493. 59. 2 c. slate 1·60 95
494. 4 c. brown 1·60 95
495. 60. 10 c. red 1·50 90
496. 10 c. green and mauve 1·50 90
497. 59. 15 c. green 1·50 90
498. 60. 15 c. red and grey 1·50 90
499. 15 c. blue and orange 1·50 90

61. Manco Capac. 62. Oil Refinery. 63. Arms of Piura.

1931.
500. 61. 2 c. olive 5 5
501. 62. 4 c. green 20 15
502. – 10 c. orange 30 5
503. – 15 c. blue 45 12
504. – 20 c. yellow 85 25
505. – 50 c. lilac 1·25 25
506. – 1 s. brown 3·25 65
DESIGNS—VERT. 10 c. Sugar Plantation. 15 c. Cotton Plantation. 50 c. Copper Mines. 1 s. Llamas. HORIZ. 20 c. Guano Islands.

1932. Piura. 4th Cent.
509. 63. 10 c. blue (postage) 1·90 1·90
510. 15 c. violet 1·90 1·90
511. 50 c. red (air) 19·00 19·00

64. 65. Parakas.

1931. Obligatory Tax. Unemployment Fund.
507. 64. 2 c. green 8 5
508. 2 c. red 8 5

1932. Quaint native designs.
512. 65. 10 c. plum (22×19½ mm.) 10 5
513. – 15 c. lake (25×19½ mm.) 15 10
514. – 50 c. brn. (19½×22 mm.) 45 15
DESIGNS: 15 c. Chimu. 50 c. Inca.

66. Arequipa and El Misti. 67. Pres. Sanchez Cerro.

68. Blacksmith. 69. Monument of 2nd May to Battle of the Maipo.

1932. Constitutional Govt. 1st Anniv.
515. 66. 2 c. blue 12 5
527. 2 c. black 12 5
528. 2 c. green 12 5
516. 4 c. brown 12 5
529. 4 c. orange 12 5
517. 67. 10 c. red 3·75 2·50
530. – 10 c. red 35 5
518. – 15 c. blue 20 5
531. – 15 c. magenta 20 10
519. – 20 c. lake 30 8
532. – 20 c. violet 30 10
520. – 50 c. green 45 12
521. – 1 s. orange 1·10 20
533. – 1 s. chestnut 1·25 30
DESIGNS—VERT. 10 c. (No. 530), Statue of Liberty. 15 c. to 1s. Bolivar Monument, Lima.

1932. Obligatory Tax. Unemployment Fund.
522. 68. 2 c. grey 8 5
523. 2 c. violet 25 5

1933. Obligatory Tax. Unemployment Fund.
524. 69. 2 c. violet 8 5
525. 2 c. orange 8 5
526. 2 c. purple 8 5

70. Fairey Fighter. 71. F. Pizarro.

72. The Inca. 73. Coronation of Huascar.

1934. Air.
534. 70. 2 s. blue 2·75 30
536. 5 s. brown 5·00 55

1934. Obligatory Tax. Unemployment Fund. Optd. **Pro-Desocupados.** (a) In one line.
536. 67. 2 c. green 8 5
585. – 2 c. purple (No. 537) 5 5
(b) In two lines.
566. – 2 c. purple (No. 537) 8 5

1934.
537 – 2 c. purple 12 5
538. – 4 c. green 12 8
539. 71. 10 c. red 20 5
540. 15 c. blue 35 5
541. 73. 20 c. blue 50 8
542. 50 c. brown 65 12
543. 72. 1 s. violet 1·10 30
DESIGN: 2 c., 4 c. show the scene depicted in T 74.

74. City of Ica. 75. Cotton blossom.

1935. Founding of Ica. Tercent.
544. 74. 4 c. black 80 80
545. – 5 c. red 80 80
546. – 10 c. magenta 2·75 1·25
547. – 20 c. green 1·25 1·00
548. 75. 35 c. red 4·50 2·25
549. – 50 c. brown and orange 2·75 2·75
550. – 1 s. red and violet 4·75 4·75
DESIGNS—HORIZ. 5 c., 20 c. Lake De of the Marvellous Cure. 50 c. Don Diego Lopez and King Philip IV of Spain. VERT. 10 c. Grapes. 1 s. Supreme God of the Nazcas.

76. Pizarro and "The Thirteen". 77. Palace of Torre Tagle.

1935. Founding of Lima. 4th Cent.
551. 76. 2 c. brown (postage) 25 15
552. – 4 c. violet 45 30
553. – 10 c. red 30 15
554. – 15 c. blue 65 25
555. 76. 20 c. grey 1·25 45
556. – 50 c. olive-green 1·25 90
557. – 1 s. blue 2·25 1·75
558. – 2 s. brown 6·50 5·50
DESIGNS—HORIZ. 4 c. Lima Cathedral. VERT. 10 c., 50 c. Miss L. S. de Canevaro. 15 c., 2 s. Pizarro. 1 s. The "Tapada" (a veiled woman).

559. – 5 c. green (air) 25 12
560. – 35 c. brown 40 25
561. – 50 c. yellow 50 50
562. – 1 s. purple 75 65
563. 77. 2 s. orange 1·25 1·25
564. – 5 s. purple 8·00 4·75
565. 76. 10 s. blue 19·00 18·00
DESIGNS—HORIZ. 5 c., 5 s. Funeral of Atahualpa. 35 c. Aeroplane near San Cristobal Hill. 50 c., 1 s. Aeroplane over Avenue of Barefoot Friars.

78. "San Cristobal". **79.** Real Felipe Fortifications.

1936. Callao Cent.

567. **78.** 2 c. black (postage) .. 30 15
568. – 4 c. green 30 15
569. – 5 c. brown 30 15
570. – 10 c. blue 30 15
571. – 15 c. green 40 20
572. – 20 c. brown 45 20
573. – 50 c. lilac 75 40
574. – 1 s. olive .. .. 2·75 1·10
575. – 2 s. purple .. .. 4·75 3·00
576. – 5 s. red .. .. 9·50 7·50
577. **79.** 10 s. brown and red .. 16·00 14·00
578. – 35 c. slate (air) .. 5·00 1·50

DESIGNS—HORIZ. 4 c. La Punta Naval College. 5 c. Independence Square, Callao. 10 c. Aerial view of Callao. 15 c. Callao Docks and Custom House. 20 c. Plan of Callao, 1746. 35 c. "La Callao" (early locomotive). 1 s. Packet-boat "Sacramento". VERT. 50 c. D. Jose de la Mar. 2 s. Don Jose de Velasco. 5 s. Fort Maipo and miniature portraits of Galvez and Nunez.

1936. St. Rosa de Lima Cathedral Construction Fund. Optd. "**Ley 8310**".
579. **69.** 2 c. purple 8 5

1936. Surch. **Habilitado** and value in figures and words.
580. – 2 c. on 4 c. green (No. 538) (postage) .. 5 5
581. **73.** 10 c. on 20 c. blue .. 12 12
582. **72.** 10 c. on 1 s. violet .. 20 20
583. **70.** 5 c. on 2 s. blue (air) .. 30 8
584. 25 c. on 5 s. brown .. 65 30

81. Cormorants. **84.** Mailboat "Inca" on Lake Titicaca.

1936.

586. **81.** 2 c. brown (postage) .. 45 12
587. – 4 c. brown 45 15
588. – 10 c. red 15 5
589. – 15 c. blue 40 12
590. – 20 c. black 45 12
591. – 50 c. yellow 95 25
592. – 1 s. purple .. .. 2·25 25
593. – 2 s. blue .. .. 4·00 1·10
594. – 5 s. blue .. .. 5·50 1·60
595. – 10 s. brown and violet 17·00 11·00

DESIGNS—VERT. 4 c. Oil well. 10 c. Inca postal runner. 1 s. G.P.O., Lima. 2 s. M. de Amat y Junyent. 5 s. J. A. de Pando y Riva. 10 s. J. D. Condemarin. HORIZ. 15 c. Paseo de la Republica, Lima. 20 c. Municipal Palace and Natural History Museum. 50 c. University of San Marcos, Lima.
See also Nos. 616/23.

596. – 5 c. green (air) .. 12 5
597. **84.** 15 c. blue 20 8
598. – 20 c. slate .. .. 1·40 25
599. – 30 c. chestnut .. 4·25 55
600. – 35 c. brown .. .. 1·90 1·90
601. – 50 c. yellow 30 25
602. – 70 c. green .. .. 3·00 3·00
603. – 80 c. black .. .. 3·50 3·50
604. – 1 s. blue .. .. 2·25 50
605. – 1 s. 50 brown .. 3·75 3·00
606. – 2 s. blue .. .. 7·50 3·75
607. – 5 s. green .. .. 9·50 1·90
608. – 10 s. brown and red .. 27·00 20·00

DESIGNS—HORIZ. 5 c. La Mar Park. 20 c. Native recorder player and llama. 30 c. Chuquibambilla ram. 35 c. J. Chavez. 50 c. Mining Area. 70 c. Aeroplane over La Punta. 1 s. Train at La Cima. 1 s. 50, Aerodrome at Las Palmas, Lima. 2 s. Mail 'plane. 5 s. Valley of R. Inambari. VERT. 80 c. Infiernillo Canyon, Andes. 10 s. St. Rosa de Lima.
See also Nos. 626/34.

88. St. Rosa de Lima.

ILLUSTRATIONS
British Commonwealth and all overprints and surcharges are FULL SIZE. Foreign Countries have been reduced to ¾-LINEAR.

1937. Obligatory Tax. St. Rosa de Lima Construction Fund.
609. **88.** 2 c. red 5 5

1937. Surch. **Habilit.** and value in figures and words. (a) Postage.
610 1 s. on 2 s. blue (593) .. 1·90 1·50

(b) Air.
611. 15 c. on 30 c. chest. (599) 65 35
612. 15 c. on 35 c. brown (600) 65 30
613. 15 c. on 70 c. green (602) .. 2·50 1·75
614. 25 c. on 80 c. black (603) .. 3·00 1·60
615. 1 s. on 2 s. blue (606) .. 4·25 2·25

1937. As Nos. 586, etc. Colours changed.
616. **81.** 2 c. green (postage) .. 70 12
617. – 4 c. black 20 8
620. – 20 c. brown 15 8
621. – 50 c. grey 50 15
622. – 1 s. blue 95 20
623. – 2 s. violet .. .. 2·25 25
626. – 20 c. olive (air) .. 65 25
627. – 25 c. red (As No. 600) .. 40 10
628. – 30 c. brown .. .. 1·10 25
629. – 50 c. claret 45 12
630. – 70 c. emerald 65 40
631. – 80 c. grey-green .. 90 40
632. – 1 s. brown .. .. 1·90 20
633. – 1 s. 50 orange .. 3·75 25
634. – 2 s. green .. .. 7·00 45

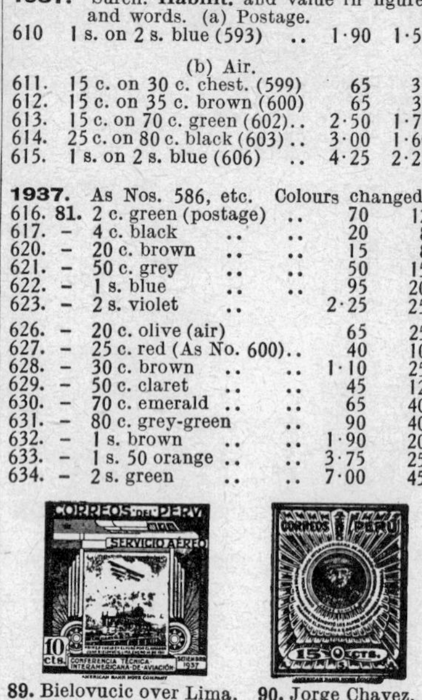

89. Bielovucic over Lima. **90.** Jorge Chavez.

91. Limatambo Airport. **92.** Peruvian Air Routes.

1937. Air. Pan-American Aviation Conf.
635. **89.** 10 c. violet 20 12
636. **90.** 15 c. green 50 10
637. **91.** 25 c. brown 25 10
638. **92.** 1 s. black .. .. 1·60 70

93. "Protection" (by John Q. A. Ward). **94.** Children's Holiday Camp.

1938. Obligatory Tax. Unemployment Fund.
639. **93.** 2 c. brown 8 5

1938. Designs as T **94.**
640. 2 c. green 5 5
641. 4 c. brown 8 5
694. 4 c. chocolate 5 5
642. 10 c. red 15 5
696. 15 c. blue 5 5
727. 15 c. green 5 5
644. 20 c. purple 8 5
740. 20 c. violet 5 5
698. 50 c. green 15 5
741. 50 c. brown 10 5
699. 1 s. claret 65 8
742. 1 s. sepia 20 5
700. 2 s. green 55 8
731. 2 s. blue 55 10
701. 5 s. brown and violet .. 3·25 30
732. 5 s. purple and blue .. 80 35
702. 10 s. blue and black .. 3·25 30
733. 10 s. black and green .. 1·90 55

DESIGNS—VERT. 4 c. (2) Chavin pottery. 10 c. Automobile roads in Andes. 20 c. (2) Industrial Bank of Peru. 1 s. (2) Portrait of Toribio de Luzuriaga. 5 s. (2) Chavin Idol. HORIZ. 15 c. (2) Archaeological Museum, Lima. 50 c. (2) Labourers' homes at Lima. 2 s. (2) Fig Tree. 10 s. (2) Mt. Huascaran.

95. Monument on Junin Plains. **97.** Seal of City of Lima.

1938. Air. As T **95.**
650. 5 c. brown 8 5
734. 5 c. olive 8 5
651. 15 c. brown 8 5
652. 20 c. red 40 10
653. 25 c. green 12 5
654. 30 c. orange 12 5
735. 30 c. red 8 5
655. 50 c. green 30 20
656. 70 c. slate 35 5
736. 70 c. blue 12 5
657. 80 c. olive 90 10
737. 80 c. red 85 12
658. 1 s. grey .. .. 5·00 3·50
738. 1 s. 50 violet 40 30
705. 1 s. 50 purple 30 20
660. 2 s. red and blue .. 1·00 45
661. 5 s. brown .. .. 5·50 50
662. 10 s. blue and olive .. 22·00 16·00

DESIGNS—VERT. 20 c. Rear-Admiral M. Villar. 70 c. Infiernillo Canyon. 2 s. Stele from Chavin Temple. HORIZ. 5 c. People's restaurant, Callao. 25 c. View of Tarma. 30 c. Ica River irrigation system. 50 c. Port of Iquitos. 80 c. Mountain roadway. 1 s. Plaza San Martin, Lima. 1 s. 50, Nat. Radio Station, San Miguel. 5 s. Ministry of Public Works. 10 s. Heroe's Crypt, Lima.

1938. 8th Pan-American Congress, Lima.
663. – 10 c. grey (postage) .. 35 20
664. **97.** 15 c. gold, bl.,red & blk. 55 25
665. – 1 s. brown .. .. 3·75 70

DESIGNS (39×32½ mm.): 10 c. Palace and Square, 1864. 1 s. Palace, 1938.

666. – 25 c. blue (air) .. 65 50
667. – 1 a. 50 lake .. .. 1·90 1·25
668. – 2 s. black .. .. 1·25 85

DESIGNS—VERT. (26×37 mm.): 25 c. Torre Tagle Palace. HORIZ. (39×32½ mm.): 1 s. 50. National Congress Building, Lima. 2 s. Congress Presidents, Ferreyros, Paz Soldan and Arenas.

1940. No. 642 surch. **Habilitada 5 cts.**
669. 5 c. on 10 c. red 10 5

98. National Broadcasting Station.

1941. Optd. **FRANQUEO POSTAL.**
670. **98.** 50 c. yellow .. .. 1·60 12
671. 1 s. violet .. .. 1·60 20
672. 2 s. green .. .. 3·00 3·50
673. 5 s. brown .. .. 13·00 3·00
674. 10 s. mauve .. .. 17·00 3·00

1942. Air. No. 653 surch. **Habilit./O 15.**
675. 15 c. on 25 c. green .. 1·25 5

99. S. American and R. Amazon. **100.** F. de Orellana.

101. Francisco Pizarro. **102.** Samuel Morse.

1943. Discovery of R. Amazon. 400th Anniv.
676. – 2 c. red 5 5
677. **100.** 4 c. grey 8 5
678. **101.** 10 c. brown 12 5
679. **99.** 15 c. blue 40 12
680. – 20 c. olive 15 10
681. – 25 c. orange .. .. 1·10 30
682. **100.** 30 c. claret 20 12
683. **99.** 50 c. green 55 20
685. – 70 c. violet 90 45
686. – 80 c. blue 90 45
687. – 1 s. brown .. .. 1·25 35
688. **101.** 5 s. black .. .. 3·75 2·75

DESIGNS. As T **100**: 2 c., 70 c. Portraits of G. Pizarro and Orellana in medallion. 20 c. 80 c. G. Pizarro. As T **99**: 25 c., 1 s. Orellana's Discovery of the R. Amazon.

1943. Surch. with Arms of Peru (as Nos. 483, etc) above **10 CTVS.**
689. 10 c. on 10 c. red (No. 642) 10 5

1944. Invention of Telegraphy. Cent.
691. **102.** 15 c. blue 12 12
692. 30 c. brown 30 20

1946. Surch. **Habilitada S/o 0.20.**
706. 20 c. on 1 s. mar. (No. 699) 20 8

103.

DESIGNS—VERT. 1 s. Mountain road. 1 s. 35, Forest road. HORIZ. 5s. Road and house.

104.

1947. 1st National Tourist Congress, Lima. Unissued designs inscr. "V Congreso Pan Americano de Carretas 1944" optd. **Habilitada I Congreso Nac. de Turismo Lima—1947.**
707. **103.** 15 c. black and red .. 25 12
708. – 1 s. brown 35 12
709. – 1 s. 35 green 35 25
710. **104.** 3 s. blue 75 50
711. – 5 s. green .. .. 1·50 85

1947. Air. 1st Peruvian Int. Airways Lima-New York Flight. Optd. with **PIA** badge and **PRIMER VUELO LIMA—NUEVA YORK.**
712. – 5 c. brown (No. 650) .. 8 5
713. – 50 c. green (No. 655) .. 12 10

105. Basket-ball Players. **106.** Statue of Admiral Grau.

1948. Air. Olympic Games.
714. – 1 s. blue .. .. 5·00 3·75
715. **105.** 2 s. brown .. .. 7·50 5·50
716. – 5 s. green .. .. 15·00 9·50
717. – 10 s. yellow .. .. 22·00 13·00

No. 714 is inscr. "AEREO" and Nos. 715/7 are optd. **AEREO.**

DESIGNS: 1 s. Map showing air route from Peru to Great Britain. 5 s. Discus thrower. 10 s. Rifleman.

The above stamps exist overprinted **MELBOURNE 1956** but were only valid for postage on one day.

1948. Air. Nos. 653, 656 and 657 surch. **Habilitada S/O** and value.
722. 5 c. on 25 c. green .. 5 5
723. 10 c. on 25 c. green .. 5 5
718. 10 c. on 70 c. slate .. 5 5
719. 15 c. on 70 c. slate .. 10 5
720. 20 c. on 70 c. slate .. 5 5
724. 30 c. on 80 c. olive .. 75 10
721. 55 c. on 70 c. slate .. 12 5

1949.
726. **106.** 10 c. blue and green .. 5 5

106a. **106b.** **106c.** "Education."

1949. Anti-Tuberculosis Fund. Surch. **Decreto Ley No. 18** and value.
724a. **106a.** 3 c. on 4 c. ultram. .. 50 5
724b. **106b.** 3 c. in 10 c. blue .. 50 5

1950. Obligatory Tax. National Education Fund.
738a. **106c.** 3 c. lake (16½×21 mm.) 5 5
897. 3 c. lake (18×21½ mm.) 5 5

107. Park, Lima. 108. Obrero Hospital, Lima.

1951. Air. U.P.U. 75th Anniv. Unissued stamps inscr. "VI CONGRESO DE LA UNION POSTAL DE LAS AMERICAS Y ESPANA–1949" optd. **U.P.U. 1874–1949.**

745. 107. 5 c. green 5 5
746. – 30 c. red and black .. 12 12
747. – 55 c. green 15 12
748. – 95 c. blue-green .. 20 12
749. – 1 s. 50 red 25 25
750. – 2 s. blue 30 30
751. – 5 s. red .. .. 1·40 1·25
752. – 10 s. violet .. .. 3·25 1·90
753. – 20 s. blue and brown 5·50 4·00

DESIGNS: 30 c. Peruvian flag. 55 c. Huancayo Hotel. 95 c. Ancachs Mtns. 1 s. 50, Arequipa Hotel. 2 s. Coaling Jetty. 5 s. Town Hall, Miraflores. 10 s. Congressional Palace. 20 s. Pan-American flags.

1951. Air Surch. **HABILITADA S/O.O.25.**

754. 25 c. on 30 c. red (No. 735) 10 5

1951. Surch. **HABILITADA S/.** and figures.

755. 1 c. on 2 c. (No. 640) .. 5 5
756. 5 c. on 15 c. (No. 727) .. 5 5
757. 10 c. on 15 c. (No. 727) .. 5 5

1951. 5th Pan-American Highways Congress. Unissued "VI CONGRESO DE LA UNION POSTAL" stamps, optd. **V Congreso Panamericano de Carreteras 1951.**

758. – 2 c. green 5 5
759. 108. 4 c. red 5 5
760. – 15 c. grey 8 5
761. – 20 c. sepia 8 5
762. – 50 c. purple 10 5
763. – 1 s. blue 15 8
764. – 2 s. blue 30 10
765. – 5 s. claret 85 35
766. – 10 s. brown .. .. 1·60 65

DESIGNS—HORIZ. 2 c. Aguas Promenade. 50 c. Archiepiscopal Palace, Lima. 1 s. National Judicial Palace. 2 s. Municipal Palace. 5 s. Lake Llanganuco, Ancash. VERT. 15 c. Inca postal runner. 20 c. Old P.O., Lima. 10 s. Machu-Picchu ruins.

109. Father Tomas de San Martin and Capt. J. de Aiaga.

1951. Air. S. Marcos University. 4th Cent. Inscr. "1551 1951".

767. 109. 30 c. black 8 5
768. – 40 c. blue 12 5
769. – 50 c. magenta 12 8
770. – 1 s. 20 green 20 15
771. – 2 s. grey 40 12
772. – 5 s. multicoloured .. 1·10 30

DESIGNS: 40 c. San Marcos University. 50 c. Santo Domingo Convent. 1 s. 20, P. de Peralto Barnuevo, Father Tomas de San Martin and Jose Buquijano. 2 s. Toribio Rodriguez, Jose Hipolito Unanue and Jose Cayetano Heredia. 5 s. University Arms in 1571 and 1735.

110. Engineer's School.

1952. Inscr. "THOMAS DE LA RUE & CO. LTD." at foot. (a) postage.

774. – 2 c. purple 5 5
775 – 5 c. blue-green 5 5
776. – 10 c. olive 5 5
777. – 15 c. grey 5 5
777a. – 15 c. brown 20 5
778. – 20 c. red-brown .. 30 10
779. 110. 25 c. red 5 5
779a. 25 c. green 20 5
780. – 30 c. blue 8 5
780a. – 30 c. red 10 5
781. – 50 c. emerald .. 40 5
781a. – 50 c. plum 15 5
782. – 1 s. brown 25 5
782a. – 1 s. blue 15 5
583. – 2 s. turquoise .. 25 5
783a. – 2 s. grey 30 8

DESIGNS—As T 110: HORIZ. 2 c. Hotel, Tacna. 5 c. Tuna clipper and indigenous fish. 10 c. View of Matarani. 15 c. Locomotive. 30 c. Public Health Ministry. VERT. 20 c. Vicuna (llama). Larger (35×25 mm.): HORIZ. 50 c. Inca maize terraces. 1 s. Inca ruins, Paramonga Fort. 2 s. Agriculture Monument, Lima.

(b) Air.

784. – 40 c. yellow-green .. 5 5
784a. – 40 c. blue-green .. 5 5
785. – 75 c. brown 75 20
785a. – 80 c. brown-red .. 8 5
786. – 1 s. 25 blue 12 12
787. – 1 s. 50 red 20 10
788. – 2 s. 20 grey-blue .. 1·60 20
789. – 3 s. brown .. .. 1·25 30
790. – 5 s. ochre-brown .. 45 20
791. – 10 s. chocolate .. 1·25 35

DESIGNS—As T 110: HORIZ. 40 c. Gunboat "Maranon". 1 s. 50, Housing complex. VERT. 75 c., 80 c. Colony of birds. Larger (35×25 mm.): HORIZ. 1 s. 25, Corpac-Limatambo Airport. 2 s. 20, Inca Observatory, Cusco. 5 s. Garcilaso (portrait). VERT. 3 s. Tobacco plant, leaves and cigarettes. 10 s. Manco Capac Monument (25×37 mm.). For stamps in same designs but inscr. "JOH. ENSCHEDE EN ZONEN-HOLLAND" see Nos. 829, etc.

See also Nos. 867, etc., and 914, etc.

111. Isabella the Catholic.

112. "Santa Maria", "Pinta" and "Nina". 113.

1953. Air. Isabella the Catholic. 500th Birth Anniv.

792. 111. 40 c. red 15 8
793. 112. 1 s. 25 green 30 15
794. 111. 2 s. 15 purple .. 50 25
795. 112. 2 s. 20 black .. 95 30

1954. Obligatory Tax. National Marian Eucharistic Congress Fund. Roul.

796. 113. 5 c. blue and red .. 30 5

114. Gen. M. Perez Jimenez. 115. Arms of Lima and Bordeaux.

1956. Visit of President of Venezuela.

797. 114. 25 c. brown 5 5

1957. Air. Exn. of French Products. Lima.

798. 115. 40 c. lake, blue & green 8 5
799. – 50 c. blk., brn. & grn. 10 5
800. – 1 s. 25 c. indigo, green and blue .. 15 12
801. – 2 s. 20 c. brown & blue 30 25

DESIGNS:—HORIZ. 50 c. Eiffel Tower and Lima Cathedral. 1 s. 25 c. Admiral Dupetit-Thouars and frigate. "La Victorieuse". 2 s. 20 c. Exhibition building, Pres. Prado and Pres. Coty.

116. Provisional 1 r. Stamp of 1857. 117. C. P. Soldan.

1957. Air. First Peruvian Postage Stamp Cent. Inscr. as in T 116.

802. – 5 c. black and grey .. 5 5
803. 116. 10 c. turq. & magenta 5 5
804. – 15 c. brown and green 5 5
805. – 25 c. blue and yellow .. 5 5
806. – 30 c. chestnut & choc. 5 5
807. – 40 c. ochre and black 10 5
808. – 1 s. 25 sepia and blue .. 25 20
809. – 2 s. 20 indigo & verm. 40 35
810. – 5 s. claret and magenta 95 75
811. – 10 s. violet and green .. 1·60 1·25

DESIGNS: 5 c. Pre-stamp Postmarks. 15 c. Provisional 2 r. stamp of 1857. 25 c. 1 d. stamp of 1858. 30 c. 1 p. stamp of 1858. 40 c. ½ peso stamp of 1858. 1 s. 25, Jose Condemarin, Director of Posts. 1857. 2 s. 20 Pres. Ramon Castilla. 5 s. Pres. D. M. Prado. 10 s. Various Peruvian stamps in shield.

1958. Air. Lima-Callao Telegraph Service Cent. Inscr. as in T 117.

812. 117. 40 c. chocolate and rose 5 5
813. – 1 s. green 12 8
814. – 1 s. 25 indigo & maroon 15 12

DESIGNS—VERT. 1 s. Marshal Ramon Castilla. HORIZ. 1 s. 25, Pres. D. M. Prado and view of Callao. No. 814 also commemorates the political centenary of the Province of Callao.

118. Flags of France and Peru. 119. Father Martin de Porras Velasquez.

1958. Air. "Treasures of Peru" Exn., Paris.

815. 118. 50 c. red, bl. & deep bl. 5 5
816. – 65 c. black, lake, ochre and brown .. 10 5
817. – 1 s. 50 brn., mar. & bl. 20 10
818. – 2 s. 50 maroon, turq. and myrtle .. 25 15

DESIGNS—HORIZ. 65 c. Lima Cathedral and girl in national costume. 1 s. 50, Caballero and ancient palace. VERT. 2 s. 50, Natural resources map of Peru.

1958. Air. D. A. Carrion Garcia (patriot) Birth Cent.

819. 119. 60 c. sepia, yellow, black, red & green .. 10 5
820. – 1 s. 20 sepia, yellow, black, red & green .. 12 5
821. – 1 s. 50 sepia, yellow, black, red & green 15 8
822. – 2 s. 20 black 20 15

DESIGNS—VERT. 1 s. 20, D. A. Carrion Garcia. 1 s. 50, J. H. Unanue Pavon. HORIZ. 2 s. 20, Facade of Government Building, Lima.

120. Gen. I. A. Thomas. 121. Association Emblems.

1958. Air. Gen. Thomas. Death Cent.

823. 120. 1 s. 10 mar., red & bis. 15 12
824. 1 s. 20 blk., red & bis. 20 15

1958. Air. Advocates' College Lima. 150th Anniv. Emblems in bistre and blue.

825. 121. 80 c. green 8 5
826. 1 s. 10 red 10 8
827. 1 s. 20 blue 12 10
828. 1 s. 50 purple 15 10

1960. As 1952 but inscr. "JOH. ENSCHEDE EN ZONEN-HOLLAND" at foot.

829. 20 c. red-brown (postage) .. 12 5
830. 30 c. magenta 5 5
831. 50 c. plum 10 5
832. 1 s. blue 12 5
833. 2 s. grey 25 8

834. 80 c. brn.-red (as No. 785) (air) 10 5
835. 3 s. green 45 25
836. 3 s. 80 orange (as No. 788) 1·10 40
837. 5 s. brown 55 40
838. 10 s. vermilion 95 45

122. Piura Arms and Congress Emblem. 123. Refugees in Flight over Plough-team.

1960. Obligatory Tax. 6th National Eucharistic Congress Fund.

839. 122. 10 c. blue, red, green and yellow .. 15 5
839a. 10 c. blue and red .. 25 12

1960. Air. World Refugee Year.

840. 123. 80 c. multicoloured .. 30 30
841. 4 s. 30 multicoloured 65 65

124. Sea Bird bearing Map. 125. Congress Emblem.

1960. Air. Int. Pacific Fair, Lima.

842. 124. 1 s. multicoloured .. 40 25

1960. 6th National Eucharistic Congress, Piura.

843. 125. 50 c. red, black & blue 12 8
844. – 1 s. mult. (Eucharistic symbols) 20 12

126. 1659 Coin.

1961. Air. 1st National Numismatic Exn. Lima. T 126 and similar design.

845. – 1 s. grey and chestnut 12 10
846. 126. 2 s. grey and blue .. 20 15

127. Frigate "Amazonas". 128. Globe, Moon and Stars.

1961. Air. World Tour of Frigate "Amazonas". Cent.

847. 127. 50 c. green and brown 8 5
848. 80 c. red & slate-purple 10 8
849. 1 s. black and green .. 35 12

1961. Air. I.G.Y.

850. 128. 1 s. lemon, red, blue and black 65 40

128. Olympic Torch. 130. "Balloon".

1961. Air. Olympic Games, 1960.

852. 129. 5 c. blue and black .. 55 30
853. 10 s. red and black .. 1·00 65

1961. Christmas and New Year.

854. 130. 20 c. blue 15 5

131. Fair Emblem 132. Symbol of Eucharist.

1961. Air. 2nd Int. Pacific Fair, Lima.

855. 131. 1 s. brown-red, yellow, blue and black .. 20 10

1962. Obligatory Tax. 7th National Eucharistic Congress Fund. Roul.

856. 132. 10 c. blue and yellow .. 5 5

DESIGNS: 2 s. Tupac-Amaru and Hidalgo. 3 s. Presidents Prado and Lopez.

133. Sculptures "Cahuide" and "Cuauhtemoc".

1962. Air. Peruvian Art Treasures Exn., Mexico. 1960. Flags red and green.

859. **133.** 1 s. red 12 5
860. – 2 s. blue-green .. 20 12
861. – 3 s. chocolate .. 30 20

134. Frontier Maps.

1962. Air. Ecuador-Peru Border Agreement 20th Anniv.

862. **134.** 1 s. 30 blk., & red on grey 20 15
863. 1 s. 50 black, red and green and grey .. 20 20
864. 2 s. 50 black, red and blue on grey 30 25

135. The Cedar, Pomabamba. **136.** "Man".

1962. Pomabamba and Pallasca, Ancash. Cent.

865. **135.** 1 s. green & red (post.) 15 10
866. – 1 s. black & drab (air) 10 8

DESIGN: No. 866, Agriculture, mining, etc., Pallasca Ancash ($31\frac{1}{2} \times 22$ mm.).

1962. As Nos. 774/91 but colours and designs changed and new values. Inscr. "THOMAS DE LA RUE & CO. LTD." at foot.

(a) Postage.

867. 20 c. maroon 12 5
868. 30 c. indigo (As No. 776) .. 10 5
869. 40 c. orange (As No. 784).. 10 5
870. 50 c. blue-green 10 5
871. 60 c. black (As No. 774) .. 12 5
872. 1 s. rose 20 10

(b) Air.

873. 1 s. 30 ochre (As No. 785).. 35 20
874. 1 s. 50 claret 25 10
875. 1 s. 80 blue (As No. 777) .. 25 10
876. 2 s. emerald (As No. 783).. 25 12
877. 3 s. purple 35 15
878. 4 s. 30 orange (As No. 788) 60 25
879. 5 s. olive 60 30
880. 10 s. blue .. .. .. 1·00 75

See also Nos. 921/8.

1963. Air. Chavin Excavations Fund. Pottery.

881. – 1 s. + 50 c. drab & pink 10 10
882. – 1 s. 50 + 1 s. drab & bl. 15 15
883. – 3 s. + 2 s. 50 drab & grn. 45 30
884. **136.** 4 s. 30 + 3 s. drab and emerald 55 40
885. – 6 s. + 4 s. drab & olive 80 65

FIGURES—HORIZ. 1 s. "Griffin". 1 s. 50, "Eagle" 3 s. "Cat". VERT. 6 s. "Deity".

137. Campaign and Industrial Emblems. **138.** Henri Dunant and Centenary Emblem.

1963. Freedom from Hunger.

886. **137.** 1 s. bistre & red (post.) 10 5
887. 4 s. 30 bis. & grn. (air) 90 40

1964. Air. Red Cross Cent.

888. **138.** 1 s. 30 + 70 c. mult. .. 20 15
889. 4 s. 30 + 1 s. 70 mult... 50 50

139. Chavez and Wing. **140.** Alliance Emblem.

1964. Air. Jorge Chavez's Trans-Alpine Flight. 50th Anniv.

890. **139.** 5 s. blue, maroon & brn. 55 30

1964. "Alliance for Progress". Emblem black, green and blue.

891. **140.** 40 c. black & yell. (post.) 5 5
892. – 1 s. 30 blk. & mag. (air) 12 12
893. **140.** 3 s. black and blue .. 25 20

DESIGN—HORIZ. 1 s. 30, As T **140**, but with inscription at right.

141. Fair Poster. **142.** Net, Flag and Globe.

1965. Air. Third Int. Pacific Fair, Lima.

894. **141.** 1 s. multicoloured .. 10 5

1965. Air. Women's World Basketball Championships, Lima.

895. **142.** 1 s. 30 violet and red.. 20 8
896. 4 s. 30 bistre and red.. 45 25

143. St. Martin de Porras (anonymous painting). **144.** Fair Emblem.

1965. Air. Canonisation of St. Martin de Porras (1962). Paintings. Multicoloured.

898. 1 s. 30 Type **143** 12 5
899. 1 s. 80 "St. Martin and the Miracle of the Animals" (after painting by Camino Brent) 15 10
900. 4 s. 30 "St. Martin and the Angels" (after painting by Fausto Conti) 40 25

Porras is wrongly spelt "Porres" on the stamps.

1965. 4th Int. Pacific Fair, Lima.

901. **144.** 1 s. 50 black, red, yellow and violet .. 12 8
902. 2 s. 50 black, red, yellow and blue 25 12
903. 3 s. 50 black, red, yell. and green 30 20

145. Father Christmas and Postmarked Envelope. **146.** 2nd May Monument and Battle Scene.

1965. Christmas.

904. **145.** 20 c. black and red .. 10 5
905. 50 c. black and green.. 20 5
906. 1 s. black and blue .. 40 8

The above stamps were valid for postage only on November 2nd. They were subsequently used as postal employees' charity labels.

1966. Obligatory Tax. Journalists' Fund. (a) Surch. **HABILITADO "Fondo del Periodista Peruano" Ley 16078 S/O. 0.10.**

907. **106c.** 10 c. on 3 c. (No. 773) 5 5

(b) Surch. **Habilitado "Fondo del Periodista Peruano" Ley 16078 S/0.10.**

909. **106c.** 10 c. on 3 c. (No. 773) 5 5

1966. Obligatory Tax. Journalists' Fund. No. 856 optd. **Periodista Peruano Ley 16078.**

910. **132.** 10 c. blue and yellow 5 5

1966. Nos. 639 and 773. surch. **XX Habilitado S/.0.10.**

911. **93.** 10 c. on 2 c. brown .. 5 5
912. **106c.** 10 c. on 3 c. lake .. 5 5

1966. Air. Battle of Callao. Cent. Mult.

913. 1 s. 90 Type **146** .. 25 15
914. 3 s. 60 Monument and sculpture 40 25
915. 4 s. 60 Monument and Jose Galvez 65 40

147. Funerary Mask.

1966. Gold Objects of Chimu Culture. Multicoloured.

916. 1 s. 90 + 90 c. Type **147** .. 20 15
917. 2 s. 60 + 1 s. 30 Ceremonial knife (vert.) 25 25
918. 3 s. 60 + 1 s. 80 Ceremonial urn 40 40
919. 4 s. 60 + 2 s. 30 Goblet (vert.) 45 35
920. 20 s. + 10 s. Ear-ring .. 2·25 2·25

1966. As Nos. 867, etc., but inscr. "INA at foot and new values.

921. 20 c. red (postage).. .. 5 5
922. 30 c. indigo 5 5
923. 40 c. orange 5 5
924. 50 c. green.. .. .. 5 5
925. 1 s. rose 10 5
926. 2 s. 60 green (as 783) (air) 20 15
927. 3 s. 60 purple (as 789) .. 25 20
928. 4 s. 60 orange (as 788) .. 30 25

148. Civil Guard Emblem.

1966. Air. Civil Guard Cent.

929. **148.** 90 c. gold, black, red and blue 10 8
930. – 1 s. 90 gold, black and purple 15 12

DESIGN: 1 s. 90. Emblem and activities of Civil Guard.

149. Map and Mountains. **150.** Globe.

1966. Opening of Huinco Hydro-electric Scheme.

931. **149.** 70 c. black, ultramarine and blue (postage).. 8 5
932. 1 s. 90 black, ultram. and violet (air) .. 15 12

1967. Air. Peruvian Photographic Exn., Lima. Multicoloured.

933. 2 s. 60 Sun "carving" .. 20 15
934. 3 s. 60 Map of Peru .. 30 20
935. 4 s. 60 Type **150** 40 25

151. Symbol of Construction. **152.** "St. Rosa" (from painting by A. Medoro).

1967. Six-year Construction Plan.

936. **151.** 90 c. black, gold and magenta (postage).. 8 5
937. **151.** 1 s. 90 black, gold and ochre (air) 15 12

1967. Air. St. Rosa of Lima. 350th Death Anniv. Designs showing portraits of St. Rosa by artists given below. Multicoloured.

938. 1 s. 90 Type **152** .. 15 15
939. 2 s. 60. C. Maratta .. 20 20
940. 3 s. 60 Anon., Cuzquena School 30 20

154. Pen-nib made of Newspaper.

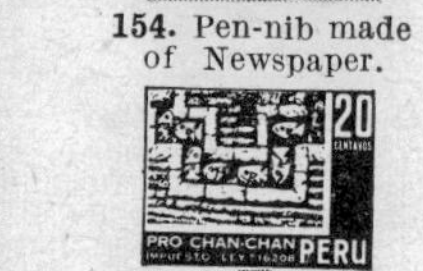

153. Vicuna within Figure "5". **155.** Wall Reliefs (fishes).

1967. 5th Int. Pacific Fair, Lima.

941. **153.** 1 s. black, green and gold (postage) .. 10 5
942. **153.** 1 s. purple, black and gold (air) 10 5

1967. Obligatory Tax. Journalists' Fund.

943. **154.** 10 c. black and red .. 5 5

1967. Obligatory Tax. Chan-Chan Excavation Fund.

944. **155.** 20 c. black and blue .. 5 5
945. – 20 c. black & magenta 5 5
946. – 20 c. black and sepia.. 5 5
947. – 20 c. multicoloured .. 5 5
948. – 20 c. multicoloured .. 5 5
949. – 20 c. black and green 5 5

DESIGNS: No. 945, Ornamental pattern. 946, Carved "bird". 947, Temple on hillside. 948, Corner of Temple. 949, Ornamental pattern (birds).

156. Lions' Emblem. **157.** Nazca Jug.

1967. Air. Lions International. 50th Anniv.

950. **156.** 1 s. 60 violet, bl. & grey 12 10

1968. Air. Ceramic Treasures of Nazca Culture. Designs showing painted pottery jugs. Multicoloured.

951. 1 s. 90 Type **157** 12 10
952. 2 s. 60 Falcon 15 12
953. 3 s. 60 Round jug decorated with bird 20 15
954. 4 s. 60 Two-headed snake 40 30
955. 5 s. 60 Sea Bird 40 30

158. Alligator. **159.** "Antarqui" (Airline Symbol).

1968. Gold Sculptures of Mochica Culture. Multicoloured.

956. 1 s. 90 Type **158** 10 8
957. 2 s. 60 Bird 12 10
958. 3 s. 60 Lizard 20 12
959. 4 s. 60 Bird 20 12
960. 5 s. 60 Jaguar 30 15

Nos. 957 and 959 are vert.

1968. Air. APSA (Peruvian Airlines). 12th Anniv.

961. **159.** 3 s. 60 multicoloured 20 10
962. – 5 s. 60 brown, blk. & red 30 15

DESIGN: 5 s. 60 Alpaca and aircraft symbol.

160. Human Rights Emblem. **161.** "The Discus-thrower".

1968. Air. Human Rights Year.
963. **160.** 6 s. 50 red, grn. & choc. 25 20

1968. Air. Olympic Games, Mexico.
964. **161.** 2 s. 30 brn., ult. & yell. 12 10
965. 3 s. 50 bl., car. & grn. 15 12
966. 5 s. black, blue & pink 45 20
967. 6 s. 50 pur., brn. & blue 35 20
968. 8 s. blue, mag. & lilac 30 15
969. 9 s. violet, grn. & orge. 35 20

161a.

1968. Obligatory Tax. Unissued stamps, surch as in T **161a.**
970. **161a.** 20 c. on 50 c. violet, orange and black . . 5 5
971. 20 c. on 1 s. blue, orange and black . . 5 5

1968. Obligatory Tax. Journalists' Fund. No. 897 surch. **Habilitado Fondo Periodista Peruano Ley 17050** S/. and value.
972. **106c.** 20 c. on 3 c. lake . . 5 5

1968. Christmas. No. 900 surch. **PRO NAVIDAD Veinte Centavos R.S. 5-11-68.**
973. 20 c. on 4 s. 30 multicoloured 20 15

162. **164.** Worker holding Flag.

163. First Peruvian Coin (obverse and reverse).

1969. Unissued Agrarian Reform stamps. Surch. as in T **162.**
974. **162.** 2 s. 50 on 90 c. multicoloured (post.) . . 12 10
975. – 3 s. on 90 c. multicoloured . . 15 12
976. – 4 s. on 90 c. multicoloured . . 20 15
977. – 5 s. 50 on 1 s. 90 multicoloured (air) . . 25 20
978. – 6 s. 50 on 1 s. 90 multicoloured . . 30 25

1969. Air. 1st Peruvian Coinage. 400th Anniv.
979. **163.** 5 s. black, grey and yellow 20 20
980. 5 s. black, grey & green 20 20

1969. Nationalisation of Int. Petroleum Company's Oilfields and Refinery (9 October, 1968).
981. **164.** 2 s. 50 red, green, sepia and yellow . . 10 10
982. 3 s. red, green, sepia and grey . . 12 12
983. 4 s. red, green, sepia and purple . . 20 20
984. 5 s. 50 red, green, sepia and blue . . 20 20

165. Castilla Monument. **166.** Airliner, Globe, and "Kon Tiki" Raft.

1969. Air. President Ramon Castilla. Death Cent.
985. **165.** 5 s. blue and emerald 20 12
986. – 10 s. brown and purple 45 25
DESIGN: (21 × 37 mm.) 10 s. President Castilla.

1969. 1st A.P.S.A. (Peruvian Airlines) Flight to Europe.
987. **166.** 2 s. 50 mult. (postage) 12 8
988. 3 s. multicoloured (air) 12 10
989. 4 s. multicoloured . . 15 12
990. 5 s. 50 multicoloured . . 20 20
991. 6 s. 50 multicoloured . . 30 20

167. Dish Aerial, Satellite and Globe.

1969. Air. Lurin Satellite Telecommunications Station, Lima. Inaug.
992. **167.** 20 s. multicoloured . . 1·00 65

168. Captain Jose A. Quinones Gonzales (military aviator).

1969. Gonzales Commem.
993. **168.** 20 s. mult. (postage) . . 90 55
994. 20 s. multicoloured (air) 85 55

169. W.H.O. Emblem.

1969. Air. World Health Organization (1968). 20th Anniv.
995. **169.** 5 s. gold, chestnut, black and grey 20 12
996. 6 s. 50 gold, blue, black and orange . . 30 25

170. Peasant breaking Chains. **171.** Arms of De La Vega.

1969. Agrarian Reform Law.
998. **170.** 2 s. 50 deep blue, blue and red (post.) . . 12 8
999. 3 s. purple, lilac and black (air) . . 12 10
1000. 4 s. brown and cinnamon 20 12

1969. Air. Garcilaso De La Vega. Commem.
1001. **171.** 2 s. 40 blk., silver & grn. 12 10
1002. – 3 s. 50 black, buff & bl. 15 12
1003. – 5 s. multicoloured . . 20 15
DESIGNS: 3 s. 50 Title page, "Commentarios Reales", Lisbon, 1609. 5 s. Inca Garcilaso de la Vega.

172. Admiral Grau and Warship.

1969. Navy Day.
1005. **172.** 50 s. multicoloured . . 2·10 1·60

173. "6" and Fair Flags.

1969. 6th Int. Pacific Fair, Lima.
1006. **173.** 2 s. 50 mult. (postage) 12 8
1007. 3 s. multicoloured (air) 12 10
1008. 4 s. multicoloured . . 15 12

INDEX

Countries can be quickly located by referring to the index at the end of this volume.

173a. Father Christmas and Greetings Card. **174.** Col. F. Bolognesi and Soldier.

1969. Christmas.
1009. **173a.** 20 c. black and red 15 15
1010. 20 c. black & orange 15 15
1011. 20 c. black & brown 15 15

1969. Army Day.
1012. **174.** 1 s. 20 black, gold and blue (postage) . . 5 5
1013. 50 s. black, gold and brown (air) . . 2·25 1·50

175. Arms of Amazonas.

1970. Air. Republic (1971). 150th Anniv. (1st issue).
1014. **175.** 10 s. multicoloured . . 40 30
See also Nos. 1066/70, 1076/80 and 1081/90.

176. I.L.O. Emblem on Map. **178.** "Puma" Jug.

179. Ministry Building. **177.** "Motherhood".

1970. Air. Int. Labour Organization. 50th Anniv.
1015. **176.** 3 s. ultram. and blue 12 10

1970. Air. U.N.I.C.E.F. Commem.
1016. **177.** 5 s. black and yellow 20 20
1017. 6 s. 50 black and pink 25 25

1970. Vicus Culture. Ceramic Art. Mult.
1018. 2 s. 50 Type **178** (postage) 8 5
1019. 3 s. Squatting warrior (statuette) (air) . . 15 12
1020. 4 s. Animal jug 20 15
1021. 5 s. 50 Twin jugs . . 30 20
1022. 6 s. 50 Woman with jug (statuette) . . 40 25

1970. Ministry of Transport and Communications.
1023. **179.** 40 c. black & purple 5 5
1024. 40 c. black and yellow 5 5
1025. 40 c. black and grey 5 5
1026. 40 c. black and red . . 5 5
1027. 40 c. black and brown 5 5

180. Anchovy. **181.** Telephon and Skyline.

1970. Fishes. Multicoloured.
1028. 2 s. 50 Type **180** (postage) 12 8
1029. 2 s. 50 Hake 12 8
1030. 3 s. Swordfish (air) . . 12 10
1031. 3 s. Yellowfin tuna . . 12 10
1032. 5 s. 50 Wolf-fish . . 25 12

1970. Air. Lima Telephone Service. Nationalisation.
1033. **181.** 5 s. multicoloured . . 25 12
1034. 10 s. multicoloured . . 50 25

182. "Soldier and Farmer". **183.** U.N. Headquarters and Dove.

1970. Unity of Armed Forces and People.
1035. **182.** 2 s. 50 multicoloured (postage) 15 8
1036. 3 s. multicoloured (air) 25 10
1037. 5 s. 50 multicoloured 25 12

1970. Air. United Nations. 25th Anniv.
1038. **183.** 3 s. blue & pale blue 12 10

184. Rotary Emblem.

1970. Air. Lima Rotary Club. 50th Anniv.
1039. **184.** 10 s. gold, red & black 50 25

185. Military Parade (Army Staff College, Chorrillos).

1970. Military, Naval and Air Force Academies. Multicoloured.
1040. 2 s. 50 Type **185** 40 15
1041. 2 s. 50 Parade, Naval Academy, La Punta . . 40 15
1042. 2 s. 50 Parade, Air Force Officer Training School, Las Palmas 40 15

186. Puruchuco, Lima.

1970. Tourism. Multicoloured.
1043. 2 s. 50 Type **186** (postage) 12 8
1044. 3 s. Chan-Chan-Trujillo, La Libertad (air) . . 12 10
1045. 4 s. Sacsayhuaman, Cuzco 20 12
1046. 5 s. 50 Lake Titicaca, Pomata, Puno 25 15
1047. 10 s. Machu-Picchu, Cuzco 50 25
Nos. 1045/7 are vert.

187. Festival Procession.

1970. Air. October Festival, Lima. Multicoloured.

1049. 3 s. Type **187** 12 10
1050. 4 s. "The Cock-fight" (T. Nunez Ureta) .. 20 12
1051. 5 s. 50 Altar, Nazarenas Shrine (vert.) 25 15
1052. 6 s. 50 "The Procession" (J. Vinatea Reinoso) .. 30 20
1053. 8 s. "The Procession" (Jose Sabogal) (vert.) .. 40 20

188. "The Nativity" (Cuzquena School).

1970. Christmas. Paintings by Unknown Artists. Multicoloured.

1054. 1 s. 20 Type **188** 5 5
1055. 1 s. 50 "The Adoration of the Magi" (Cuzquena School) 5 5
1056. 1 s. 80 "The Adoration of the Shepherds" (Peruvian School) .. 8 5

189. "Close Embrace" (petroglyph).

1971. Air. "Gratitude for World Help in Earthquake of May 1970".

1057. **189.** 4 s. olive, black & red 20 12
1058. 5 s. 50 blue, flesh & red 25 15
1059 6 s. 50 slate, blue & red 25 20

190. "St. Rosa de Lima" (F. Laso).

1971. Canonisation of St. Rosa de Lima. 300th Anniv.

1060. **190.** 2 s. 50 multicoloured 10 5

191. Tiahuanacoide Fabric.

1971. Ancient Peruvian Textiles.

1061. **191.** 1 s. 20 mult. (post.) .. 5 5
1062. – 2 s. 50 multicoloured 10 5
1063. – 3 s. multicoloured (air) 15 10
1064. – 4 s. pink, grn. & emer. 20 12
1065. – 5 s. 50 multicoloured 30 15

DESIGNS—HORIZ. 2 s. 50 Chancay fabric. 4 s. Chancay lace. VERT. 3 s. Chancay tapestry. 5 s. 50 Paracas fabric.

192. M. Garcia Pumacahua.

193. "Gojinova" (Nazca Culture).

1971. Independence. 150th Anniv. (2nd issue). National Heroes.

1066. **192.** 1 s. 20 blk. & red (post.) 5 5
1067. – 2 s. 50 black & blue 12 8
1068. – 3 s. blk. & mve. (air) 12 10
1069. – 4 s. black & green .. 20 12
1070. – 5 s. 50 black & brown 25 15

DESIGNS: 2 s. 50 F. Antonio de Zela. 3 s. T. Rodriguez de Mendoza. 4 s. J. P. Viscardo y Guzman. 5 s. 50 J. G. Condorcanqui.

See also Nos. 1076/80.

1971. "Traditional Fisheries of Peru". Piscatorial Ceramics. Multicoloured.

1071. 1 s. 50 Type **193** (post.) 10 5
1072. 3 s. 50 "Bonito" (Chimu Inca) (air) 20 10
1073. 4 s. "Anchoveta" (Mochica) 25 12
1074. 5 s. 50 "Merluza" (Chimu) 25 15
1075. 8 s. 50 "Machete" (Nazca) 50 30

1971. "Precursors of Independence" (3rd issue). As T **192.** Multicoloured.

1076. 1 s. 20 M. Melgar (postage) 5 5
1077. 2 s. 50 J. Baquijano y Carrillo 10 8
1078. 3 s. J. de la Riva Aguero (air) 12 10
1079. 4 s. H. Unanue 15 12
1080. 5 s. 50 F. J. de Luna Pizarro 20 15

194. Liberation Expedition Monument.

195. R. Palma (director).

1971. Independence. 150th Anniv. (4th issue). As T **194.** Multicoloured.

1081. 1 s. 50 M. Bastidas (post.) 8 5
1082. 2 s. J. F. Sanchez Carrion 8 5
1083. 2 s. 50 M. J. Guise .. 10 8
1084. 3 s. F. Vidal (air) 12 10
1085. 3 s. 50 J. de San Martin .. 12 10
1086. 4 s. 50 Type **194** 20 12
1087. 6 s. "Numancia Battalion" (horiz.) (42 × 35 mm.) 20 15
1088. 7 s. 50 Alvarez de Arenales Monument (horiz.) (42 × 39 mm.) 25 20
1089. 9 s. Monument to "La Nacion", Lima (horiz.) (42 × 39 mm.) 30 25
1090. 10 s. "Proclamation of Independence" (horiz.) (46 × 35 mm.) .. 35 25

1971. Air. National Library. 150th Anniv.

1091. **195.** 7 s. 50 black and brn. 25 20

196. Weightlifting.

197. "Gongora portentosa".

1971. Air. 25th World Weightlifting Championships, Huampani, Lima.

1092. **196.** 7 s. 50 black and blue 40 20

1971. Peruvian Flora. (1st series). Orchids. Multicoloured.

1093. 1 s. 50 Type **197** 8 5
1094. 2 s. "Odontoglossum cristatum" 10 5
1095. 2 s. 50 "Mormolyca peruviana" 12 8
1096. 3 s. "Trichocentrum pulchrum" 12 10
1097. 3 s. 50 "Oncidium sanderae" 20 10

See also Nos. 1170/4 and 1206/10.

198. Family and Flag.

199. Warship "Sacramento" of 1821.

1971. Air. October 3rd Revolution. 3rd Anniv.

1098. **198.** 7 s. 50 black, red & bl. 40 20

1971. Air. Peruvian Navy and "Order of the Peruvian Sun". 150th Annivs.

1100. **199.** 7 s. 50 blue and new bl. 30 20
1101. – 7 s. 50 red, gold, green and black 35 20

DESIGN: No. 1110, Order of the Peruvian Sun.

200. "Development and Liberation" (detail).

1971. 2nd Ministerial Meeting of "The 77" Group.

1102. **200.** 1 s. 20 multicoloured (postage) 5 5
1103. – 3 s. 50 multicoloured 15 10
1104. – 50 s. mult. (air) .. 2·50 1·25

DESIGNS—As Type **200.** 3 s. 50, 50 s. Detail from the painting "Development and Liberation".

201. "Plaza de Armas, 1843" (J. Rugendas).

1971. "Exfilima" Stamp Exhib., Lima.

1105. **201.** 3 s. blk. & green .. 15 8
1106. – 3 s. 50 black & pink .. 20 10

DESIGN: 3 s. 50 "Plaza de Armas, 1971" (C. Zeiter).

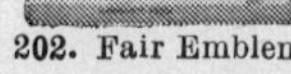

202. Fair Emblem.

203. Army Crest.

1971. Air. 7th Int. Pacific Fair, Lima.

1107. **202.** 4 s. 50 multicoloured 15 10

1971. Peruvian Army. 150th Anniv.

1108. **203.** 8 s. 50 multicoloured 55 20

204. "The Flight into Egypt".

1971. Christmas. Multicoloured.

1109. 1 s. 80 Type **204** .. 12 5
1110. 2 s. 50 "The Magi" .. 20 8
1111. 3 s. "The Nativity" .. 30 10

205. "Fisherman" (J. Ugarte Elespurn).

206. Chimu Idol.

1971. Social Reforms. Paintings. Mult.

1112. 3 s. 50 Type **205** 20 10
1113. 4 s. "Threshing Grain in Cajamarca" (Camilo Blas) 25 10
1114. 6 s. "Huanca Highlanders" (J. Sabogal) .. 40 15

1972. Peruvian Antiquities. Multicoloured.

1115. 3 s. 90 Type **206** .. 20 10
1116. 4 s. Chimu statuette .. 20 10
1117. 4 s. 50 Lambayeque idol 30 10
1118. 5 s. 40 Mochica collar .. 30 12
1119. 6 s. Lambayeque "spider" pendant 30 15

207. "Pseudopriacanthus serrula".

1972. Fishes. Multicoloured.

1120. 1 s. 20 Type **207** (postage) 5 5
1121. 1 s. 50 "Trachichthys mento" 10 5
1122. 2 s. 50 "Trachurus symmetricus murphyi" 12 5
1123. 3 s. "Pontinus furcirhinus" (air) .. 20 10
1124. 5 s. 50 "Bodianus eclancheri 30 12

208. "Peruvian Family" (T. N. Ureta).

1972. Air. Educations Reforms.

1125. **208.** 6 s. 50 mult... .. 25 15

209. Mochica Warrior.

210. White-tailed Trogen.

1972. Peruvian Art (1st series). Mochica Ceramics. Multicoloured.

1126. 1 s. 20 Type **209** 5 5
1127. 1 s. 50 Warrior's head .. 10 5
1128. 2 s. Kneeling deer .. 12 5
1129. 2 s. 50 Warrior's head (different) .. 20 8
1130. 3 s. Kneeling warrior .. 20 10

See also Nos. 1180/4.

1972. Air. Peruvian Birds. Multicoloured.

1131. 2 s. Type **210** .. 12 5
1132. 2 s. 50 Ornate umbrellabird 12 8
1133. 3 s. Peruvian cock-of-the-rock 20 8
1134. 6 s. 50 Cuvier's toucan .. 30 15
1135. 8 s. 50 Common motmot 50 20

211. "The Harvest" (July).

212. "Quipu" (calculator) on Map.

1972. G. Poma de Ayala's "Inca Chronicles". 400th Anniv. Woodcuts.

1136.	211.	2 s. 50 black & red ..	12	8
1137.	–	3 s. black & green ..	15	8
1138.	–	2 s. 50 black and pink	12	8
1139.	–	3 s. black and blue ..	15	8
1140.	–	2 s. 50 black & orange	12	8
1141.	–	3 s. black and lilac ..	20	8
1142.	–	2 s. 50 black & brown	12	8
1143.	–	3 s. black & green ..	15	8
1144.	–	2 s. 50 black & blue	12	8
1145.	–	3 s. black & orange ..	15	8
1146.	–	2 s. 50 black & mauve	12	8
1147.	–	3 s. black & yellow ..	15	8

DESIGNS: No. 1137, "Land Purification" (August). No. 1138, "Sowing" (September). No. 1139, "Invocation of the Rains" (October). No. 1140, "Irrigation" (November). No. 1141, "Rite of the Nobility" (December). No. 1142, "Maize Cultivation Rites" (January). No. 1143, "Ripening of the Maize" (February). No. 1144, "Birds in the maize" (March). No. 1145, "Children as camp-guards" (April). No. 1146, "Gathering the harvest" (May). No. 1147, "Removing the harvest" (June).

1972. Air. "Exfilbra 72" Stamp Exhib., Rio de Janeiro.

1148.	212.	5 s. multicoloured ..	20	15

213. "The Messenger". 214. Catacaos Woman.

1972. Air. Olympic Games, Munich.

1149.	213.	8 s. multicoloured ..	40	20

1972. Air. Provincial Costumes. (1st series). Multicoloured.

1150.	2 s. Tupe girl	10	5
1151.	3 s. 50 Type 214	12	10
1152.	4 s. Conibo Indian ..	15	10
1153.	4 s. 50 Agricultural worker playing "quena" and drum	20	15
1154.	5 s. "Moche" (Trujillo) girl	20	12
1155.	6 s. 50 Ocongate (Cuzco) man and woman	25	20
1156.	8 s. "Chucupana" (Ayacucho) girl	25	20
1157.	8 s. 50 "Cotuncha" (Junin) girl	30	20
1158.	10 s. "Pandilla" dancer ..	40	25

See also Nos. 1248/9.

215. Ruins of Chavin (Ancash).

1972. Air. Julio C. Tello (archaeologist). 25th Death Anniv. Multicoloured.

1159.	1 s. 50 "Stone of the 12 Angles", Cuzco (vert.)	5	5
1160.	3 s. 50 Type 215	20	10
1161.	4 s. Burial-tower, Sillustani (Puno) (vert.) ..	20	10
1162.	5 s. Gateway, Chavin (Ancash)	25	12
1163.	8 s. "Wall of the 3 Windows", Machu Pichu (Cuzco)	40	20

216. "Territorial Waters".

1972. Armed Forces Revolution. 4th Anniv. Multicoloured.

1164.	2 s. Agricultural Workers ("Agrarian Reform") (vert.)	8	5
1165.	2 s. 50 Type 216 ..	10	8
1166.	3 s. Oilrigs ("Nationalisation of Petroleum Industry") (vert.) ..	12	8

MINIMUM PRICE

The minimum price quoted is 5p which represents a handling charge rather than a basis for valuing common stamps. For further notes about prices see introductory pages.

217. "The Holy Family". (wood-carving).

1972. Christmas. Multicoloured.

1167.	1 s. 50 Type 217	5	5
1168.	2 s. "The Holy Family" (carved Huamanga stone) (horiz.)	8	5
1169.	2 s. 50 "The Holy Family" (carved Huamanga stone) ..	10	8

218. "Ipomoea purpurea". 219. Inca Poncho.

1972. Peruvian Flora. (1st series). Mult.

1170.	1 s. 50 Type 218	5	5
1171.	2 s. 50 "Amaryllis ferreyrae"	12	8
1172.	3 s. "Liabum excelsum"	20	10
1173.	3 s. 50 "Bletia catenulata"	25	12
1174.	5 s. "Cantua buxifolia cantuta"	40	15

1973. Air. Ancient Inca Textiles.

1175.	219.	2 s. multicoloured ..	10	5
1176.	–	3 s. 50 multicoloured	12	8
1177.	–	4 s. multicoloured ..	20	8
1178.	–	5 s. multicoloured ..	20	12
1179.	–	8 s. multicoloured ..	30	20

DESIGNS: Nos. 1176/9, similar to T 219.

220. Mochica Cameo and Cups. 221. Andean Condor.

1973. Air. Peruvian Art. (2nd series). Jewelled Antiquities. Multicoloured.

1180.	1 s. 50 Type 220 ..	5	5
1181.	2 s. 50 Gold-plated arms and hands (Lambayeque)	10	8
1182.	4 s. Bronze effigy (Mochica)	15	8
1183.	5 s. Gold pendants (Nazca)	20	15
1184.	8 s. Gold cat (Mochica) ..	30	20

1973. Air. Fauna Protection. (1st series). Multicoloured.

1185.	2 s. 50 Ostrich	10	8
1186.	3 s. 50 Beaver	12	10
1187.	4 s. Type 221	15	10
1188.	5 s. Vicuna	20	15
1189.	6 s. Flamingo	20	15
1190.	8 s. Spectacled bear ..	30	20
1191.	8 s. 50 Mountain dog (horiz.)	25	20
1192.	10 s. Chinchilla (horiz.) ..	35	30

See also Nos. 1245/6.

222. "The Macebearer" (J. Sabogal). 224. "Spanish Viceroy on Horseback"

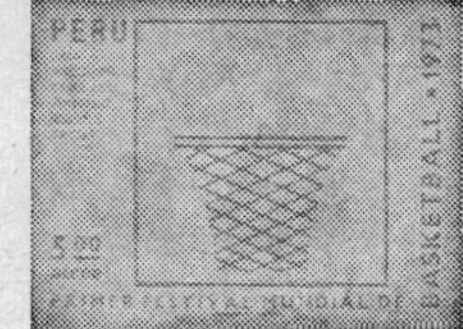

223. Basketball Net and Map.

1973. Air. Peruvian Paintings. Mult.

1193.	1 s. 50 Type 222	5	5
1194.	8 s. "Yananacu Bridge" (E. C. Brent) (horiz.) ..	25	20
1195.	8 s. 50 "Portrait of a Lady" (D. Hernandez)	30	20
1196.	10 s. "Peruvian Birds" (T. N. Ureta)	30	20
1197.	20 s. "The Potter" (F. Laso)	65	50
1198.	50 s. "Boats of Totora" (J. V. Reinoso) (horiz.)	1·60	1·00

1973. Air. 1st World Basketball Festival.

1199.	223.	5 s. green	20	12
1200.		20 s. purple ..	90	50

1973. Pancho Fierro (painter). 170th Birth Anniv. Multicoloured.

1201.	1 s. 50 Type 224	10	5
1202.	2 s. "Peasants"	10	5
1203.	2 s. 50 "Father Abregu"	12	8
1204.	3 s. 50 "Dancers" ..	20	10
1205.	4 s. 50 "Esteban Arredondo on horseback"	25	15

1973. Air. Peruvian Flora. (3rd Series) Orchids. As Type 218. Multicoloured.

1206.	1 s. 50 "Lycaste reichenbachii" ..	5	5
1207.	2 s. 50 "Masdevallia amabilis"	10	8
1208.	3 s. "Sigmatostalix peruviana"	12	10
1209.	3 s. 50 "Porrogossum peruvianum" ..	12	10
1210.	8 s. "Oncidium incarum"	25	20

225. Fair Emblem (poster).

1973. Air. 8th International Pacific Fair, Lima.

1211.	225.	8 s. red, black & grey	30	20

226. Symbol of Flight.

1973. Air. Air Force Officers' School. 50th Anniv.

1212.	226.	8 s. 50 multicoloured	30	20

227. "The Presentation of the Child".

1973. Christmas. Paintings of the Cuzco School. Multicoloured.

1213.	1 s. 50 Type 227	5	5
1214.	2 s. "The Holy Family" (vert.)	8	5
1215.	2 s. 50 "The Adoration of the Kings"	10	8

228. Freighter "Bap Ilo".

1973. Air. National Development. Mult.

1216.	1 s. 50 Type 228	5	5
1217.	2 s. 50 Fishing-boats ..	10	8
1218.	8 s. "Aero Peru" jet aircraft and seagull ..	30	25

229. House of the Mulberry Tree, Arequipa.

1974. Air. "Landscapes and Cities". Mult.

1219.	1 s. 50 Type 229	5	5
1220.	2 s. 50 El Mistu (peak), Arequipa	8	5
1221.	5 s. Giant puya, Cordillera Blanca, Ancash (vert.)	15	12
1222.	6 s. Huascaran (peak), Cordillera Blanca, Ancash	20	15
1223.	8 s. Lake Querococha, Cordillera Blanca, Ancash	30	20

230. Peruvian 2 c. Stamp of 1873. 232. Church of San Jeronimo, Cuzco.

231. Temple of the Three Windows, Machu Picchu.

1974. Stamp Day and 25th Anniv. of Peruvian Philatelic Association.

1224.	230.	6 s. blue and grey ..	20	15

1974. Air. Archaeological Discoveries. Mult.

(a) Cuzco Relics.

1225.	3 s. Type 231 ..	10	5
1226.	5 s. Baths of Tampumacchay	15	12
1227.	10 s. "Kencco"	35	30

(b) Dr. Tello's Discoveries at Chavin de Huantar. Stone carvings.

1228.	3 s. Mythological jaguar	10	5
1229.	5 s. Rodent ("Vizcacha")	15	12
1230.	10 s. Chavin warrior ..	35	30

Nos. 1228/30 are vert. designs.

1974. Air. Architectural Treasures. Mult.

1231.	1 s. 50 Type 232	5	5
1232.	3 s. 50 Cathedral of Santa Catalina, Cajamarca ..	10	8
1233.	5 s. Church of San Pedro, Zepita, Puno (horiz.) ..	15	12
1234.	6 s. Cuzco Cathedral ..	20	15
1235.	8 s. 50 Wall of the Carican-cha, Cuzco	30	20

233. "Colombia" Bridge, Tarapoto-Juanjui Highway.

1974. "Structural Changes". Multicoloured.

1236.	2 s. Type 233	5	5
1237.	8 s. Tayacaja hydro-electric scheme	25	20
1238.	10 s. Tablachaca dam ..	30	20

234. "Battle of Junin" (Felix Yanez).

1974. Battle of Junin. 150th Anniv.

1239.	234.	1 s. 50 mult. (postage)	5	5
1240.		2 s. 50 multicoloured	8	5
1241.	234.	6 s. multicoloured (air)	20	15

235. "Battle of Ayacucho" (F. Yanez).

1974. Battle of Ayacucho. 150th Anniv.

1242. **235.** 2 s. mult. (postage) .. 8 5
1243. 3 s. multicoloured .. 12 10
1244. **235.** 7 s. 50 mult. (air) .. 25 20

1974. Air. Fauna Protection (2nd series). As T **211.** Multicoloured.

1245. 8 s. Colorado monkey .. 25 20
1246. 20 s. As 8 s. 60 45

236. Chimu Gold Mask.

1974. Air. 8th World Mining Congress, Lima.

1247. **236.** 8 s. multicoloured .. 25 20

1974. Air. Provincial Costumes (2nd series). As T **214.** Multicoloured.

1248. 5 s. Horseman in "chalan" (Cajamarca) 15 12
1249. 8 s. 50 As 5 s. 25 20

237. Pedro Paulet and Spacecraft.

1974. Air. Universal Postal Union. Cent. and Pedro E. Paulet (aviation scientist). Birth Cent.

1250. **237.** 8 s. violet and blue .. 25 20

238. La Oroya Metal Works.

1974. Expropriation of Cerro de Pasco Mining Complex.

1251. **238.** 1 s.50 blue and deep blue 5 5
1252. 3 s. red and brown .. 10 5
1253. 4 s. 50 green and slate-green .. 15 10

239. "Capitulation of Ayacucho" (D. Hernandez). **240.** "Virgin and Child".

1974. Air. Spanish Forces' Capitulation at Ayacucho. 150th Anniv.

1254. **239.** 3 s. 50 multicoloured 12 8
1255. 8 s. 50 multicoloured 25 20
1256. 10 s. multicoloured .. 30 20

1974. Christmas. Paintings of the Cuzco School. Multicoloured.

1257. 1 s. 50 Type **240** (postage) 5 5
1258. 6 s. 50 "Holy Family" (air) 20 15

241. "Andean Landscape" (T. Nunez Ureta). **242.** Map and Civic Centre, Lima.

1974. Air. Andean Pact Communications Ministers' Meeting, Cali, Colombia.

1259. **241.** 6 s. 50 multicoloured 20 10

1975. Air. 2nd General Conference of U.N. Organisation for Industrial Development.

1260. **242.** 6 s. black, red & grey 20 15

1975. Air. Nos. 878, 928 and 836 surch.

1261. 2 s. on 4 s. 30 orange .. 8 5
1262. 2 s. 50 on 4 s. 60 orange 8 5
1263. 5 s. on 3 s. 80 orange .. 15 12

243. Lima's Location on World Map.

1975. Air. Foreign Ministers' Conference, Lima.

1264. **243.** 6 s. 50 multicoloured 20 15

244. Maria Parado de Bellido.

1975. "Year of Peruvian Women" and International Women's Year. Multicoloured.

1265. 1 s. 50 Type **244** .. 5 5
1266. 2 s. Micaela Bastidas (vert.) 8 5
1267. 2 s. 50 Juana Alarco de Dammert .. 8 5
1268. 3 s. I.W.Y. emblem (vert.) 10 5

245. Route Map of Flight. **246.** St. Juan Macias.

1975. Air. First "Aero-Peru" Flight, Rio de Janeiro–Lima–Los Angeles.

1269. **245.** 8 s. multicoloured .. 25 20

1975. Canonisation of Juan Macias.

1270. **246.** 5 s. multicoloured .. 15 10

247. Fair Poster. 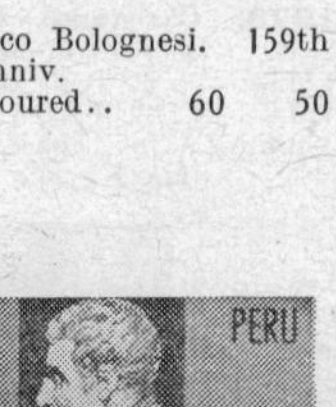 **248.** Col. F. Bolognesi.

1975. Air. 9th Int. Pacific Fair, Lima.

1271. **247.** 6 s. red, brn. & blk. 20 12

1975. Colonel Francisco Bolognesi. 159th Birth Anniv.

1272. **248.** 20 s. multicoloured .. 60 50

249. "Nativity". **250.** Luis Braille.

1976. Air. Christmas (1975).

1273. **249.** 6 s. multicoloured .. 20 12

1976. Braille System for Blind. 150th Anniv.

1274. **250.** 4 s. 50 red, blk. & grey 15 10

1976. Air. Nos. 878 and 926 surch.

1275. 2 s. on 4 s. 30 red 8 5
1276. 5 s. on 4 s. 30 red 15 10
1277. 10 s. on 2 s. 60 green .. 30 20

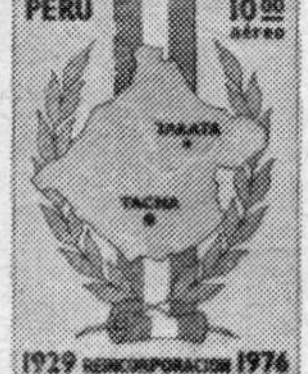

251. Inca Postal Runner. **252.** Map on Riband.

1976. Air. UPAE Congress, Lima.

1278. **251.** 5 s. black, brown & red 15 10

1976. Air. Nos. 836 and 927/8 surch.

1279. 1 s. 50 on 3 s. 60 purple .. 5 5
1280. 2 s. on 3 s. 60 purple .. 5 5
1281. 3 s. on 4 s. 60 orange .. 10 5
1282. 4 s. on 3 s. 80 orange .. 12 8
1283. 6 s. on 4 s. 60 orange .. 20 12
1284. 7 s. on 3 s. 60 purple .. 20 12
1285. 8 s. on 3 s. 60 purple .. 25 15
1286. 50 s. on 3 s. 60 purple .. 1·60 1·40

1976. Air. Nos. 900, 926 and 927 surch.

1287. 2 s. on 4 s. 30 multicoloured 5 5
1288. 4 s. on 2 s. 60 green .. 12 8
1289. 50 s. on 3 s. 60 purple .. 1·60 1·40

1976. Re-incorporation of Tacna.

1290. **252.** 10 s. multicoloured .. 30 20

253. Peruvian Flag. **254.** Police Badge.

1976. Revolution. 1st Anniv.

1291. **253.** 5 s. red, black & grey 15 10

1976. Air. Peruvian Special Police. 54th Anniv.

1292. **254.** 20 s. multicoloured .. 65 55

1976. Air. Nos. 878 and 928 surch.

1293. 5 s. 30 on 4 s. 30 orange .. 15 10
1294. 10 s. on 4 s. 60 orange .. 30 20

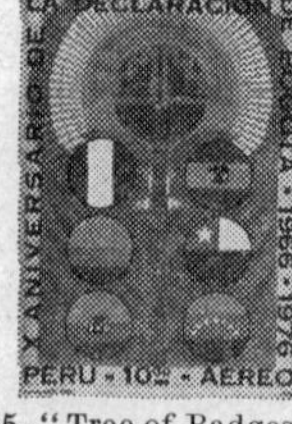

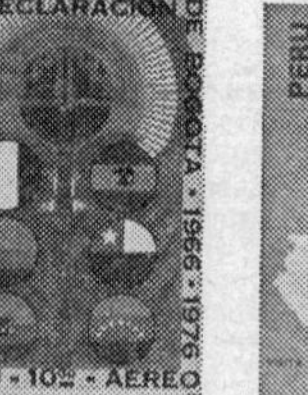

255. "Tree of Badges".  **256.** President P. Losonczi and Map.

1976. Air. Bogota Declaration. 10th Anniv.

1295. **255.** 10 s. multicoloured .. 30 20

1976. Visit of Hungarian President.

1296. **256.** 7 s. black and blue .. 20 12

257. St. Francis of Assisi. **259.** "Nativity".

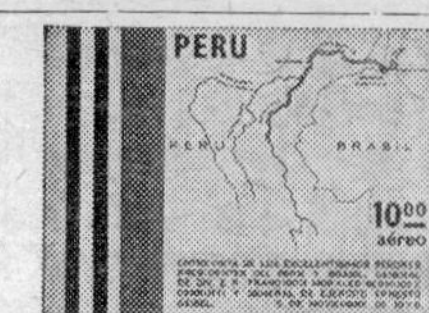

258. Map and National Colours.

1976. St. Francis of Assisi. 750th Death Anniv.

1297. **257.** 5 s. brown and gold .. 15 10

1976. Air. Meeting of Presidents of Peru and Brazil.

1298. **258.** 10 s. multicoloured .. 30 20

1976. Christmas.

1299. **259.** 4 s. multicoloured .. 12 8

EXPRESS LETTER STAMPS

1908. Optd. **EXPRESO.**

E 373. **21.** 10 c. black .. .. 5·00 5·00
E 382. – 10 c. blue (No. 377) 5·00 5·00
E 383. **33.** 10 c. black and brown 7·00 7·00

OFFICIAL STAMPS

1890. Stamps of 1866 optd. **GOBIERNO** in frame.

O 287. **9.** 1 c. violet 60 60
O 324. 1 c. red .. .. 4·25 4·25
O 288. **10.** 2 c. green 60 60
O 325. 2 c. blue .. .. 4·25 4·25
O 289. 5 c. orange 60 60
O 326. **4.** 5 c. lake .. .. 3·00 3·00
O 290. **10.** 10 c. black 45 40
O 291. 20 c. blue .. .. 1·10 1·00
O 327. 20 c. blue (as T **4**) .. 3·00 3·00
O 292. **11.** 50 c. rose .. .. 1·90 1·00
O 293. **12.** 1 s. brown .. .. 2·25 1·60

1894. Stamps of 1894 (with "Head" optd.) optd. **GOBIERNO** in frame.

O 305. **9.** 1 c. orange (No. 294) 8·00 8·00
O 306. 1 c. green (No. 295) 60 50
O 307. **10.** 2 c. violet (No. 296) 60 55
O 308. 2 c. red (No. 297) .. 75 75
O 309. 5 c. blue (No. 298) .. 6·00 6·00
O 310. 10 c. green (No. 299) 1·00 1·60
O 311. **11.** 50 c. green (No. 300) 2·50 2·50

1894. Stamps of 1894 (with "Head" and "Horseshoe" optd.) optd. **GOBIERNO** in frame.

O 312. **10.** 2 c. red (No. 301) .. 80 80
O 313. 5 c. blue (No. 302) .. ·65 65

1896. Stamps of 1896 optd. **GOBIERNO.**

O 348. **20.** 1 c. blue 5 5
O 349. **21.** 10 c. yellow 45 20
O 350. 10 c. black 5 5
O 351. **22.** 50 c. red 20 15

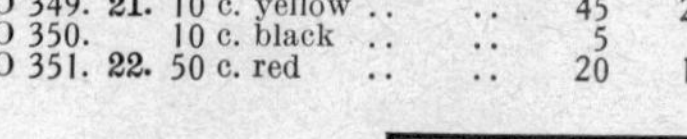
ILLUSTRATIONS British Commonwealth and all overprints and surcharges are FULL SIZE. Foreign Countries have been reduced to ¾-LINEAR.

O 1.

1909.

O 382. **O 1.** 1 c. red 5 5
O 384. 10 c. brown 10 8
O 385. 10 c. plum 12 8
O 386. 50 c. olive 35 15

1935. Optd. **Servicio Oficial.**

O 567. **71.** 10 c. red 8 8

POSTAGE DUE STAMPS

D 1. D 2. D 3.

1874.

D 31. **D 1.** 1 c. brown 10 5
D 32. **D 2.** 5 c. red 12 5
D 33. 10 c. orange 15 10
D 34. 20 c. blue 25 20
D 35. 50 c. brown .. .. 2·75 1·40

1881. Optd. with T 13 ("LIMA" at foot instead of "PERU").
D 47. D 1. 1 c. brown .. .. 1·25 1·25
D 48. D 2. 5 c. red .. .. 2·50 2·50
D 49. 10 c. orange .. .. 2·50 2·50
D 50. 20 c. blue .. .. 6·50 5·00
D 51. 50 c. brown .. 16·00 16·00

1881. Optd. **LIMA CORREOS** in double-lined circle.
D 52. D 1. 1 c. brown .. .. 2·50 2·50
D 53. D 2. 5 c. red .. .. 3·00 3·00
D 54. 10 c. orange .. .. 3·00 3·00
D 55. 20 c. blue .. .. 7·50 7·50
D 56. 50 c. brown .. 19·00 19·00

1883. Optd. with T 13 (inscr. "LIMA" instead of "PERU") and also with T 16.
D 247. D 1. 1 c. brown .. .. 1·25 1·25
D 250. D 2. 5 c. red .. .. 2·50 2·50
D 253. 10 c. orange .. .. 2·50 2·50
D 256. 20 c. blue .. .. 13·00 13·00
D 257. 50 c. brown .. 25·00 25·00

1884. Optd. with T 16 only.
D 259. D 1. 1 c. brown 12 10
D 262. D 2. 5 c. red 15 15
D 267. 10 c. orange 25 15
D 269. 20 c. blue 40 20
D 271. 50 c. brown .. 1·60 75

1894. Optd. **LIMA CORREOS** in double-lined circle and with T 16.
D 275. D 1. 1 c. brown .. .. 3·00 3·00

1896. Optd. **DEFICIT.**
D 348. D 1. 1 c. brown (D 31) .. 12 12
D 349. D 2. 5 c. red (D 32) .. 12 12
D 350. 10 c. orange (D 33) 20 12
D 351. 20 c. blue (D 34) .. 15 12
D 352. 11. 50 c. rose (283) .. 25 25
D 353. 12. 1 s. brown (284) .. 35 35

1899. As T 18, but inscr. "DEFICIT" instead of "FRANQUEO".
D 355. 5 s. green .. .. 25 2·25
D 356. 10 s. brown £140 £170

1902. Surch. **DEFICIT** and value in words.
D 361. – 1 c. on 10 s. (D 356) 20 20
D 362. 19. 5 c. on 10 s. (354) .. 35 35

1902. Surch. **DEFICIT** and value in words.
D 363. D 2. 1 c. on 20 c. (D 34) 20 20
D 364. 5 c. on 20 c. (D 34) 45 45

1909.
D 382. D 3. 1 c. brown 12 5
D 419. 1 c. purple 5 5
D 420. 2 c. purple 8 8
D 570. 2 c. brown 5 5
D 383. 5 c. brown 12 5
D 421. 5 c. purple 15 10
D 384. 10 c. brown .. 10 5
D 422. 10 c. purple .. 15 8
D 571. 10 c. green 25 20
D 385. 50 c. brown .. 25 10
D 423. 50 c. purple .. 80 25
D 424. 1 s. purple .. .. 1·90 1·00
D 425. 2 s. purple .. .. 3·75 1·60

1935. Optd. **Deficit.**
D 568. – 2 c. purple (No. 537) 12 8
D 569. 71. 10 c. red 25 20

PHILIPPINE ISLANDS O4

A group of islands in the China Sea, E. of Asia, ceded by Spain to the United States after the war of 1898. Under Japanese Occupation from 1941 until 1945. The Philippines became fully independent in 1946. An independent Republic since 1946.

1854. 20 cuartos = 1 real.
8 reales = 1 peso plata fuerte.
1864. 100 centimos = 1 peso plata fuerte.
1871. 100 centimos = 1 escudo (= ½ peso).
1872. 100 centimos = 1 peseta (= 1/5 peso).
1876. 1000 milesimas = 100 centavos or centimos = 1 peso.
1899. 100 cents = 1 dollar.
1906. 100 centavos = 1 peso.
1962. 100 sentimos = 1 piso.

A. SPANISH OCCUPATION.

1. 2. 3.
Queen Isabella II.

1854. Imperf.
1. 1. 5 c. orange .. .. £325 70·00
3. 10 c. red .. .. £130 50·00
5. 1 r. blue .. .. £130 48·00
8. 2 r. green .. .. £170 48·00

1859. Imperf.
13. 2. 5 c. orange .. .. 5·50 2·75
14. 10 c. pink .. .. 5·50 4·25

1861. Larger lettering. Imperf.
17. 3. 5 c. orange .. .. 4·50 2·25

4. 5. 6. King Amadeo.

1863. Imperf.
19. 4. 5 c. red .. .. 3·50 2·25
20. 10 c. red .. .. 11·00 7·00
21. 1 r. mauve .. .. £160 90·00
22. 2 r. blue .. .. £140 70·00

1863. Imperf.
23. 5. 1 r. green .. .. 24·00 9·50

1864. As T 10 of Spain, but value in "centimos de peso". Imperf.
26. 3 1/8 c. black on buff .. 1·40 60
27. 6 2/8 c. green on rose .. 1·10 60
28. 12 4/8 c. blue on red .. 2·00 70
30. 25 c. red .. .. 3·50 1·75

1870. As T 16 of Spain, but inscr. "CORREOS" and currency altered. Perf.
37. 5 c. blue .. .. 8·50 1·40
38. 10 c. green .. .. 2·40 95
39. 20 c. brown .. .. 11·00 4·75
40. 40 c. red .. .. 13·00 3·50

1872.
46. 6. 12 c. red .. .. 3·50 95
47. 16 c. blue .. .. 20·00 5·50
48a. 25 c. grey .. .. 2·75 95
49. 62 c. mauve .. .. 7·00 1·75
50. 1 p. 25 brown .. 14·00 4·50

1874. As T 21 of Spain, but inscr. "FILIPINAS".
54. 12 c. lilac .. .. 3·50 1·10
55. 25 c. blue 95 30
56. 62 c. red .. .. 8·00 1·10
57. 1 p. 25 brown .. 29·00 8·50

1876. As T 24 of Spain, but inscr. "FILIPINAS" between rosettes.
58. 2 c. red 60 30
59. 2 c. blue .. .. 29·00 14·00
60. 6 c. orange .. .. 2·75 70
61. 10 c. blue .. .. 1·10 45
62. 12 c. mauve .. .. 2·00 45
63. 20 c. sepia .. .. 4·25 1·40
64. 25 c. green .. .. 2·75 45

1878. As T 24 of Spain, but inscr. "FILIPINAS" without rosettes.
65. 25 m. black .. .. 1·10 25
66. 25 m. green .. .. 14·00 5·50
67. 50 m. purple .. .. 7·00 2·25
68a. (62½ m.) 0.0625 lilac .. 11·00 4·25
69. 100 m. red .. .. 20·00 6·50
70. 100 m. green .. .. 2·25 60
71. 125 m. blue .. .. 1·40 30
72. 200 m. red .. .. 7·00 1·75
74. 250 m. brown .. .. 2·50 60

1877. Surch. **HABILITADO 12 CS P.T.A.** in frame.
75. 12 c. on 2 c. red (No. 58) .. 10·00 3·50
76. 12 c. on 25 m. black (No. 65) .. .. 10·00 3·50

1879. Surch. **CONVENIO UNIVERSAL DE CORREOS HABILITADO** and value in figures and words.
78. 2 c. on 25 m. (No. 66) .. 9·00 2·40
79. 8 c. on 100 m. red (No. 69) 9·00 2·40

1880. "Alfonso XII" key-type inscr. "FILIPINAS".
97. X. 1 c. green 25 10
82a. 2 c. red 12 12
83. 2 4/8 c. brown 70 12
95. 2 4/8 c. blue 12 5
99. 50 m. brown 30 12
85. 5 c. lilac 12 12
100. 6 c. brown .. .. 2·25 70
87. 6 2/8 c. green 60 20
88. 8 c. brown .. .. 1·75 30
89a. 10 c. brown 35 12
90. 10 c. purple .. .. 1·10 95
91. 10 c. green .. .. 70·00 40·00
92. 12 4/8 c. pink 25 12
93. 20 c. brown 35 12
94. 25 c. brown 45 12

1880. "Alfonso XII" key-type inscr. as above with circular surch. **HABILITADO CORREOS** or **HABILITADO U. POSTAL** and value in figures and words.
111. X. 1 c. on 2 4/8 c. blue 25 15
101. 2 c. on 2 4/8 c. brown .. 1·00 55
106. 8 c. on 2 c. red .. 1·75 50
107. 10 cuart. on 2 c. red .. 1·00 70
102. 10 c. on 2 4/8 c. blue .. 1·75 35
112. 16 c. on 2 4/8 c. blue .. 2·75 1·00
103. 20 c. on 8 c. brown .. 2·75 1·00
113. 1 r. on 2 c. red .. .. 1·50 1·10
109. 1 r. on 5 c. lilac .. .. 1·50 70
110. 1 r. on 8 c. brown .. 2·75 1·00
105. 2 r. on 2 4/8 c. blue .. 1·75 45

1880. "Alfonso XII" key-type inscr. as above with circular surch. **UNION GRAL. POSTAL HABILITADO** or **HABILITADO PARA COMUNICACIONES** and new value in oval.
115. X. 2 4/8 c. on 1 c. green .. 60 35
116. 2 4/8 c. on 5 c. lilac .. 40 15
117. 2 4/8 c. on 50 m. brown .. 70 45
118. 2 4/8 c. on 10 c. green .. 40 20
119. 8 c. on 2 4/8 c. blue .. 25 15

1880. "Alfonso XII" key-type inscr. "FILIPAS-IMPRESOS" and surch. **HABILITADO PARA COMUNICACIONES 2 4/8 CMOS** in oval.
120. X. 2 4/8 c. on 1/8 c. green .. 15 8

1889. "Alfonso XII" key-type inscr. "FILIPINAS" and surch. **RECARGO DE CONSUMOS HABILITADO $002 4/8** in oval.
147. X. 2 4/8 c. on 1 c. green .. 5 5
148. 2 4/8 c. on 2 c. red .. 5 5
149. 2 4/8 c. on 2 4/8 c. blue .. 5 5
150. 2 4/8 c. on 5 c. lilac .. 5 5
151. 2 4/8 c. on 50 m. brown .. 5 5
152. 2 4/8 c. on 12 4/8 c. red .. 15 15

1889. No. 120 surch. **RECARGO DE CONSUMOS HABILITADO $002 4/8** in oval.
160. X. 2 4/8 c. on 1/8 c. green .. 5 5

A number of Fiscal and Telegraph stamps were also overprinted for postal use. A full list will be found in Stanley Gibbons's Overseas Catalogue Volume 3.

1890. "Baby" key-type inscr. "FILIPINAS".
176. Y. 1 c. purple 25 12
188. 1 c. red 60 35
197. 1 c. green 35 15
162. 2 c. claret 5 5
177. 2 c. purple 12 5
190. 2 c. brown 8 5
198. 2 c. blue 5 5
163. 2 4/8 c. blue 5 5
178. 2 4/8 c. grey 12 5
165. 5 c. blue 12 5
179. 5 c. green 8 5
199. 5 c. brown .. .. 2·00 85
181. 6 c. purple 12 5
201. 6 c. red 12 12
166. 8 c. green 12 5
182. 8 c. blue 25 12
193. 8 c. brown 8 5
167. 10 c. green 40 12
183. 10 c. red 10 5
202. 10 c. brown 8 5
168. 12 4/8 c. green 5 5
184. 12 4/8 c. orange 12 5
185. 15 c. brown 25 10
195. 15 c. red 15 10
203. 15 c. green 70 35
174. 20 c. red .. .. 2·25 1·40
186. 20 c. brown 45 15
196. 20 c. purple 55 35
204. 20 c. orange 85 35
170. 25 c. brown 85 35
175. 25 c. blue 35 12
205. 40 c. purple .. .. 2·50 85
206. 80 c. claret .. .. 5·50 2·00

1897. "Baby" key-type inscr. "FILIPINAS" and surch. **HABILITADO CORREOS PARA 1897** and value in frame.
212. Y. 5 c. on 5 c. green .. 90 45
208. 15 c. on 15 c. red .. 1·00 45
213. 15 c. on 15 c. brown .. 1·00 45
209. 20 c. on 20 c. purple .. 5·00 3·25
214. 20 c. on 20 c. brown .. 2·00 1·25
210. 20 c. on 25 c. brown .. 3·50 2·25

1897. No. 85 surch. **HABILITADO CORREOS PARA 1897 5 CENTS 1897** in frame.
215. X. 5 c. on 5 c. lilac .. .. 1·40 70

1898. "Curly Head" key-type inscr. "FILIPNAS 1898 y 99".
217. Z. 1 m. brown 5 5
218. 2 m. brown 5 5
219. 3 m. brown 12 5
220. 4 m. brown .. .. 1·10 40
221. 5 m. brown 5 5
222. 1 c. violet 5 5
223. 2 c. green 5 5
224. 3 c. brown 5 5
225. 4 c. orange .. .. 2·00 1·10
226. 5 c. red 12 8
227. 6 c. blue 35 20
228. 8 c. brown 20 12
229. Z. 10 c. red 55 30
230. 15 c. olive 55 25
231. 20 c. claret 55 30
232. 40 c. lilac 35 20
233. 60 c. black .. .. 1·00 45
234. 80 c. brown .. .. 1·10 50
235. 1 p. green .. .. 2·40 1·00
236. 2 p. blue .. .. 4·50 1·75

STAMPS FOR PRINTED MATTER

1886. "Alfonso XII" key-type inscr. "FILIPAS-IMPRESOS".
P 101. X. 1 m. red 12 5
P 102. 1/8 c. green 12 5
P 103. 2 m. blue 12 5
P 104. 5 m. brown 15 5

1890. "Baby" key-type inscr. "FILIPAS-IMPRESOS".
P 171. Y. 1 m. purple 5 5
P 172. 1/8 c. purple 5 5
P 173. 2 m. purple 5 5
P 174. 5 m. purple 5 5

1892. "Baby" key-type inscr. "FILIPAS-IMPRESOS".
P 192. Y. 1 m. green 65 30
P 193. 1/8 c. green 65 20
P 194. 2 m. green 70 45
P 191. 5 m. green .. .. 21·00 7·50

1894. "Baby" key-type inscr. "FILIPAS-IMPRESOS".
P 197. Y. 1 m. grey 5 5
P 198. 1/8 c. brown 5 5
P 199. 2 m. grey 5 5
P 200. 5 m. grey 5 5

1896. "Baby" key-type inscr. "FILIPAS-IMPRESOS".
P 205. Y. 1 m. blue 5 5
P 206. 1/8 c. blue 5 5
P 207. 2 m. brown 12 5
P 208. 5 m. blue 55 35

B. UNITED STATES ADMINISTRATION

1899. United States stamps of 1894 optd. **PHILIPPINES.**
252. 50. 1 c. green (No. 283) .. 70 35
254. 2 c. red (No. 284C) .. 45 30
255. 3 c. violet (No. 271) .. 95 55
256. 4 c. brown (No. 285) .. 2·75 1·10
257. 5 c. blue (No. 286) .. 1·10 45
258. 6 c. brown (No. 287A) 3·75 2·00
259. 8 c. purple (No. 275) .. 4·00 1·40
260. 10 c. brown (No. 289) .. 3·75 1·40
262. 15 c. olive (No. 290) .. 4·25 1·75
263. 50 c. orange (No. 278A) 17·00 8·00
264. $1 black (No. 279) .. 85·00 48·00
266. $2 blue (No. 281) .. £110 48·00
267. $5 green (No. 282) .. £200 £110

1903. United States stamps of 1902 optd. **PHILIPPINES.**
268. 53. 1 c. green 60 15
269. 54. 2 c. red .. .. 1·25 55
270. 55. 3 c. violet .. .. 7·50 3·25
271. 56. 4 c. brown .. .. 10·00 4·50
272. 57. 5 c. blue .. .. 2·00 45
273. 58. 6 c. lake .. .. 7·50 3·50
274. 59. 8 c. violet .. .. 4·25 3·00
275. 60. 10 c. brown .. .. 3·75 1·10
276. 61. 13 c. purple .. .. 5·00 3·50
277. 62. 15 c. olive .. .. 8·50 2·50
278. 63. 50 c. orange .. .. 22·00 5·00
279. 64. $1 black .. .. 85·00 42·00
280. 65. $2 blue £170 £100
281. 66. $5 green £250 £130

1903. United States stamp of 1903 optd. **PHILIPPINES.**
282a. 67. 2 c. red .. .. 1·40 70

7. Rizal.

8. Arms of Manila.

1906. Various portraits as T 7.
337. 7. 2 c. green 5 5
338. 4 c. red (McKinley) .. 5 5
339. 6 c. violet (Magellan) .. 15 5
340. 8 c. brown (Legaspi) .. 12 8
341. 10 c. blue (Lawton) .. 12 5
288. 12 c. lake (Lincoln) .. 2·00 1·10
342. 12 c. orange (Lincoln) .. 15 8
289. 16 c. black (Sampson) .. 1·90 15
344a. 16 c. olive (Sampson) .. 3·50 8
344. 16 c. olive (Dewey) .. 45 8
290. 20 c. brown (Washington) 2·10 15
345. 20 c. oran. (Washington) 20 5
291. 26 c. black (Carriedo) .. 2·10 1·40
346. 26 c. green (Carriedo) .. 30 15
292. 30 c. olive (Franklin) .. 2·50 85
313. 30 c. blue (Franklin) .. 1·40 30
347. 30 c. grey (Franklin) .. 30 5
293. 8. 1 p. orange .. .. 8·00 4·75
315. 1 p. violet .. .. 4·00 25
294. 2 p. black .. .. 8·50 55
316. 2 p. brown .. .. 7·50 40
350. 4 p. blue .. .. 7·00 15
351. 10 p. green .. .. 20·00 2·10

1926. Air. Madrid-Manila Flight. Stamps as last, optd. **AIR MAIL 1926 MADRID-MANILA** and aeroplane propeller.

368. **7.** 2 c. green .. .. 2·00 1·90
369. 4 c. red .. .. .. 2·25 2·10
370. 6 c. violet .. .. 7·00 4·25
371. 8 c. brown .. .. 7·00 4·75
372. 10 c. blue .. .. 7·00 4·75
373. 12 c. orange .. .. 8·50 6·50
375. 16 c. olive (Dewey) .. 8·50 6·50
376. 20 c. orange .. .. 8·50 6·50
377. 26 c. green .. .. 8·50 6·50
378. 30 c. grey .. .. 8·50 6·50
383. **8.** 1 p. violet .. .. 42·00 29·00
379. 2 p. brown .. .. £130 85·00
380. 4 p. blue £200 £130
381. 10 p. green £350 £225

9.

1926. Legislature Palace. Inaug.

384. **9.** 2 c. black and green .. 20 15
385. 4 c. black and red .. 20 20
386. 16 c. black and olive .. 45 45
387. 18 c. black and sepia .. 50 35
388. 20 c. black and orange .. 70 65
389. 24 c. black and grey .. 55 40
390. 1 p. black and mauve .. 8·50 7·00

1928. Air. Stamps of 1906 optd. **L.O.F.** (=London Orient Flight) **1928** and aeroplane.

402. **7.** 2 c. green 25 25
403. 4 c. red 30 30
404. 6 c. violet .. .. 1·00 1·00
405. 8 c. brown .. .. 1·10 1·10
406. 10 c. blue .. .. 1·10 1·10
407. 12 c. orange .. .. 1·40 1·40
408. 16 c. olive (Dewey) .. 1·25 1·25
409. 20 c. yellow .. .. 1·75 1·75
410. 26 c. green .. .. 3·50 3·50
411. 30 c. grey .. .. 3·50 3·50
412. **8.** 1 p. violet .. .. 14·00 14·00

10. Mayon Volcano.

11. Vernal Falls, Yosemite National Park, California, wrongly described on stamp as Pagsanjan Falls.

1932.

424. **10.** 2 c. green 45 20
425. – 4 c. red 30 20
426. – 12 c. orange 45 45
427. **11.** 18 c. red .. .. 8·50 4·75
428. – 20 c. yellow 55 45
429. – 24 c. violet 85 55
430. – 32 c. sepia 85 65

DESIGNS—HORIZ. 4 c. Post Office, Manila. 12 c. Pier No. 7, Manila Bay. 20 c. Rice plantation. 24 c. Rice terraces. 32 c. Bagulo Zigzag.

1932. No. 350 surch. in words in double circle.

431. **8.** 1 p. on 4 p. blue .. 1·25 30
432. 2 p. on 4 p. blue .. 2·25 50

1932. Air. Nos. 424/30 optd. with aeroplane and **ROUND-THE-WORLD FLIGHT VON GRONAU 1932.**

433. 2 c. green 25 25
434. 4 c. red 30 30
435. 12 c. orange 45 45
436. 18 c. red .. .. .. 2·25 2·25
437. 20 c. yellow .. .. 1·25 1·25
438. 24 c. violet .. .. 1·25 1·25
439. 32 c. sepia .. .. .. 1·25 1·25

1933. Air. Stamps of 1906 optd. **F. REIN MADRID - MANILA FLIGHT - 1933** under propeller.

440. **7.** 2 c. green 25 25
441. 4 c. red 30 30
442. 6 c. violet 35 35
443. 8 c. brown 95 95
444. 10 c. blue 75 75
445. 12 c. orange 55 55
446. 16 c. olive (Dewey) .. 60 70
447. 20 c. orange 65 65
448. 26 c. green 85 85
449. 30 c. grey .. .. 1·10 1·10

1933. Air. Nos. 337 and 425/30 optd. with aeroplane with wings inscr. "AIR MAIL".

450. 2 c. green 30 30
451. 4 c. red 8 8
452. 12 c. orange 20 10
453. 20 c. yellow 20 15
454. 24 c. violet 25 20
455. 32 c. sepia 30 25

12. Baseball.

1934. 10th Far Eastern Games. Vert. designs.

456. **12.** 2 c. brown 10 10
457. – 6 c. blue (Tennis) .. 20 20
458. – 16 c. pur. (Basket Ball) 40 40

13. Dr. J. Rizal.

14. Pearl Fishing.

1935. Designs as T 13/14 in various sizes. (Sizes in millimetres).

459. 2 c. red (19×22) 5 5
460. 4 c. green (34×22) .. 5 5
461. 6 c. brown (22½×28) .. 5 5
462. 8 c. violet (34×22) .. 8 8
463. 10 c. red (34×22) 12 12
464. 12 c. black (34×22) .. 10 8
465. 16 c. blue (34×22) .. 10 8
466. 20 c. bistre (19×22) .. 15 5
467. 26 c. blue (34×22) .. 20 20
468. 30 c. red (34×22) .. 20 20
469. 1 p. blk. & orge. (37×27) 1·10 1·10
470. 2 p. blk. & brn. (37×27) 2·25 1·00
471. 4 p. blk. & blue (37×27) 2·25 2·10
472. 5 p. black & grn. (27×37) 4·75 1·25

DESIGNS: 4 c. Woman, Carabao and Rice-stalks. 6 c. Filipino girl. 10 c. Fort Santiago. 12 c. Salt springs. 16 c. Magellan's landing. 20 c. "Juan de la Cruz". 26 c. Rice Terraces. 30 c. Blood Compact. 1 p. Barasoain Church. 2 p. Battle of Manila Bay. 4 p. Montalban Gorge. 5 p. George Washington (after painting by John Faed).

15. "Temples of Human Progress".

1935. Commonwealth. Inaug.

483. **15.** 2 c. red 8 5
484. 6 c. violet 8 8
485. 16 c. blue 15 12
486. 36 c. green 25 25
487. 50 c. brown 40 40

1935. Air. "China Clipper" Trans-Pacific Flight. Optd. **P.I.-U.S. INITIAL FLIGHT 1935** and aeroplane.

488. 10 c. red (No. 463) .. 15 15
489. 30 c. red (No. 468) .. 30 30

16. J. Rizal y Mercado.

17. M. L. Quezon.

1936. Rizal. 75th Birth Anniv.

490. **16.** 2 c. yellow 5 5
491. 6 c. blue 5 5
492. 36 c. brown 30 30

1936. Air. Manila-Madrid Flight. Stamps of 1906 surch. **MANILA—MADRID ARNACAL FLIGHT—1936** and value.

493. **7.** 2 c. on 4 c. red 5 5
494. 6 c. on 12 c. orange .. 8 8
495. 16 c. on 26 c. green .. 15 15

1936. Nos. 459/72 optd. **COMMONWEALTH**

496. 2 c. red 5 5
525. 4 c. green 35 25
526. 6 c. brown 5 5
527. 8 c. violet 5 5
528. 10 c. red 5 5
529. 12 c. black 5 5
530. 16 c. blue 10 5
531. 20 c. bistre 12 5
532. 26 c. blue 15 15
505. 30 c. red 15 8
534. 1 p. black and orange .. 30 15
535. 2 p. black and brown .. 2·00 55
508. 4 p. black and blue .. 8·00 1·40
509. 5 p. black and green .. 1·10 95

1936. Autonomous Government. 1st Anniv.

510. **17.** 2 c. brown 5 5
511. 6 c. green 5 5
512. 12 c. blue 10 8

18. Philippine Is.

19.

1937. 33rd Int. Eucharistic Congress.

513. **18.** 2 c. green 5 5
514. 6 c. brown 8 5
515. 12 c. blue 12 5
516. 20 c. orange 15 8
517. 36 c. violet 30 30
518. 50 c. red 35 30

1937.

522. **19.** 10 p. grey .. .. 2·10 1·40
523. 20 p. brown .. .. 1·10 1·00

1939. 1st Manila Air Mail Exn. Surch. **FIRST AIR MAIL EXHIBITION Feb 17 to 19, 1939** and value.

548. – 8 c. on 26 c. grn. (346) 50 30
549. **19.** 1 p. on 10 p. grey .. 1·60 1·40

1939. Foreign Trade Week. Surch. **FIRST FOREIGN TRADE WEEK MAY 21-27, 1939** and value.

551. – 2 c. on 4 c. green (460) 5 5
552. **7.** 6 c. on 26 c. green (346) 12 12
553. **19.** 50 c. on 20 p. brown .. 55 50

20. Triumphal Arch.

21. Malacanan Palace.

22. Pres. Quezon taking Oath of Office.

1939. Nat. Independence. 4th Anniv.

554. **20.** 2 c. green 5 5
555. 6 c. red 10 5
556. 12 c. blue 15 5
557. **21.** 2 c. green 5 5
558. 6 c. orange 10 5
559. 12 c. red 15 5
560. **22.** 2 c. orange 5 5
561. 6 c. green 10 8
562. 12 c. violet 15 8

23. Jose Rizal.

24 Sailing Vessel and Clipper.

1941.

563. **23.** 2 c. green 5 5
623. 2 c. brown 5 5

In No. 623 the head faces to right.

1941. Air.

566. **24.** 8 c. red 50 40
567. 20 c. blue 55 30
568. 60 c. green 85 55
569. 1 p. sepia 40 35

For Japanese Occupation issues of 1941-45 see **JAPANESE OCCUPATION OF PHILIPPINE ISLANDS.**

1945. Independence Regained. Nos. 496/531, 505, 534 and 522/3 optd. **VICTORY.**

610. 2 c. red 5 5
611. 4 c. green 8 5
612. 6 c. brown 5 5
613. 8 c. violet 10 10
614. 10 c. red 12 8
615. 12 c. black 15 10
616. 16 c. blue 20 8
617. 20 c. bistre 25 8
618. 30 c. red 30 8
619. 1 p. black and orange .. 1·00 25
620. 10 p. grey .. .. .. 20·00 7·00
621. 20 p. brown .. .. 17·00 8·50

C. INDEPENDENT REPUBLIC

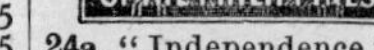
24a. "Independence".

25. Bonifacio Monument.

1946. Proclamation of Independence.

625. **24a.** 2 c. red 15 15
626. 6 c. green 20 15
627. 12 c. blue 35 25

1946. Optd. **PHILIPPINES** at top, **50TH ANNIVERSARY MARTYRDOM** in circle and **OF RIZAL 1896-1946** at foot.

628. **23.** 2 c. brown (No. 623) .. 15 8

1947.

629. – 4 c. brown 8 5
630. **25.** 10 c. red 12 5
631. – 12 c. blue 20 5
632. – 16 c. slate .. .. 1·00 45
633. – 20 c. brown 30 5
634. – 50 c. green 75 35
635. – 1 p. violet .. .. 1·60 30

DESIGNS—VERT. 4 c. Rizal Monument. 50 c. and 1 p. Avenue of Palm Trees. HORIZ. 12 c. Jones Bridge. 16 c. Santa Lucia Gate. 20 c. Mayon Volcano.

26. Manuel L. Quezon.

27. Presidents Quezon and Roosevelt.

28. Pres. Roxas taking Oath of Office.

1947.

636. **26.** 1 c. green 8 5

1947. Independence. 1st Anniv.

638. **28.** 4 c. red 15 15
639. 6 c. green 40 35
640. 16 c. purple 70 45

1947. Air.

641. **27.** 6 c. green 35 35
642. 40 c. orange 70 70
643. 80 c. blue .. .. 2·00 2·00

29. United Nations' Emblem.

30. General MacArthur.

1947. Conference of Economic Commission for Asia and Far East, Baguio. Imperf. or perf.

648. **29.** 4 c. red and pink .. 85 85
649. 6 c. violet & pale violet 1·60 1·60
650. 12 c. bright blue & blue 1·90 1·90

1948. Liberation. 3rd Anniv.

652. **30.** 4 c. violet 30 15
653. 6 c. red 55 55
654. 16 c. blue 70 55

31. Threshing Rice.

32. Dr. Jose Rizal.

1948. United Nations' Food and Agriculture Organization Conference, Baguio.

655. **31.** 2 c. grn. & yell. (postage) 70 30
656. 6 c. brown and yellow .. 1·00 45
657. 18 c. blue & pale blue .. 2·25 1·40
658. **31.** 40 c. red and pink (air) 10·00 4·25

1948.

662. **32.** 2 c. green 5 5

33. Pres. Manuel Roxas.

34. Scout and Badge.

35. Sampaguita National Flower.

1948. President Roxas Mourning Issue.

663. **33.** 2 c. black 15 10
664. 4 c. black 20 15

1948. Philippine Boy Scouts. 25th Anniv. Perf. or imperf.

665. **34.** 2 c. green and brown .. 25 15
666. 4 c. pink and brown .. 30 25

1948. Flower Day.

667. **35.** 3 c. green and black .. 30 20

36. Santos, Tavera and Kalaw.

37. "Doctrina Christiana" (first book published in Philippines).

DESIGN—VERT. 18 c. Title page of Rizal's "Noli Me Tangere".

1949. Library Rebuilding Fund.
671. 36. 4 c.+2 c. brown .. 35 35
672. 37. 6 c.+4 c. violet .. 1·00 1·00
673. – 18 c.+7 c. blue .. 1·75 1·75

38. U.P.U. Monument, Berne.

1949. U.P.U. 75th Anniv.
674. 38. 4 c. green 12 5
675. 6 c. violet 12 5
676. 18 c. blue 40 15

39. General del Pilar at Tirad Pass. 40. Globe.

1949. Gen. Gregorio del Pilar. 50th Death Anniv.
678. 39. 2 c. brown 8 8
679. 4 c. green 20 15

1950. 5th Int. Congress of Junior Chamber of Commerce.
680. 40. 2 c. violet (postage) .. 12 5
681. 6 c. green 15 5
682. 18 c. blue 35 15
683. 30 c. orange (air) .. 35 15
684. 50 c. red 50 15

41. Red Lauan Trees. 42. Franklin D. Roosevelt.

1950. Forestry Service. 15th Anniv.
685. 41. 2 c. green 12 8
686. 4 c. violet 20 15

1950. Philatelic Assn. 25th Anniv.
687. 42. 4 c. sepia 15 10
688. 6 c. pink 25 15
689. 18 c. blue 70 40

43. Lions Emblem. 44. President taking Oath.

1950. "Lions" Int. Convention, Manila.
691. 43. 2 c. orange (postage) .. 35 35
692. 4 c. violet 20 50
693. 30 c. emerald (air) .. 40 35
694. 50 c. blue 50 45

1950. Pres. Quirino's Inaug.
696. 44. 2 c. red 8 8
697. 4 c. purple 8 8
698. 6 c. green 15 12

1950. Surch. ONE CENTAVO.
699. 33. 1 c. on 2 c. green .. 5 5

45. Dove and Map. 46. War Widow and Children.

1950. Baguio Conf.
701. 45. 5 c. green 25 15
702. 6 c. red 20 15
703. 18 c. blue 45 35

1950. War Victims' Relief.
704. 46. 2 c.+2 c. red 8 8
705. – 4 c.+4 c. violet .. 25 25
DESIGN: 4 c. Disabled veteran.

47. Arms of Manila. 48. Soldier and Peasants.

1950. As T 47. Various arms and frames.

(a) Arms inscr. "MANILA".
706. 5 c. violet 35 30
707. 6 c. grey 15 15
708. 18 c. blue 35 30

(b) Arms inscr. "CEBU".
709. 5 c. red 35 30
710. 6 c. brown 15 15
711. 18 c. violet 35 30

(c) Arms inscr. "ZAMBOANGA".
712. 5 c. green 35 30
713. 6 c. chocolate 15 15
714. 18 c. blue 35 30

(d) Arms Inscr. "ILOILO".
715. 5 c. green 35 30
716. 6 c. violet 15 15
717. 18 c. blue 35 30

1951. Guarding Peaceful Labour. Perf. or imperf
718. 48. 5 c. green 12 5
719. 6 c. brown 15 15
720. 18 c. blue 45 45

49. Flag and Emblem. 50. Statue of Liberty.

1951. U.N. Day.
721. 49. 5 c. red 45 20
722. 6 c. green 35 20
723. 18 c. blue 70 50

1951. Human Rights Day.
724. 50. 5 c. green 35 20
725. 6 c. orange 45 35
726. 18 c. blue 70 50

51. Schoolchildren. 52. M. L. Quezon.

1952. Philippine Educational System. 50th Anniv.
727. 51. 5 c. orange 25 20

1952. Portraits.
728. 52. 1 c. brown 5 5
729. – 2 c. black (J. Santos) .. 5 5
730. – 3 c. red (A. Mabini) .. 5 5
731. – 5 c. red (M. H. del Pilar) 5 5
842. – 6 c. blue (Dr. J. Rizal) 5 5
732. – 10 c. blue (Father J. Burgos) .. 12 5
733. – 20 c. red (Lapu-Lapu) 20 5
734. – 25 c. green (Gen. A. Luna) .. 25 5
735. – 50 c. red (C. Arellano) 50 8
736. – 60 c. red (A. Bonifacio) 55 8
737. – 2 p. violet (G. L. Jaena) 2·00 55

53. Aurora A. Quezon.

1952. Fruit Tree Memorial Fund.
742. 53. 5 c.+1 c. blue 8 8
743. 6 c.+2 c. red 25 25
See also No. 925.

54. Milkfish and Map of Oceania. 55. "A Letter from Rizal".

1952. Indo-Pacific Fisheries Council.
744. 54. 5 c. brown 55 35
745. 6 c. blue 40 20

1952. Pan-Asiatic Philatelic Exn., Manila.
746. 55. 5 c. blue (postage) .. 30 8
747. 6 c. brown 30 8
748. 30 c. red (air) 70 55

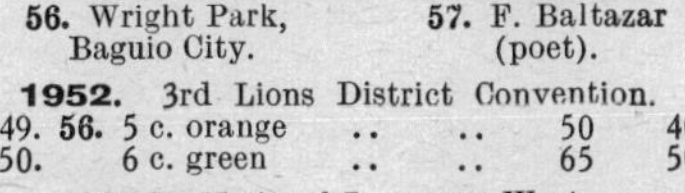

56. Wright Park, Baguio City. 57. F. Baltazar (poet).

1952. 3rd Lions District Convention.
749. 56. 5 c. orange 50 40
750. 6 c. green 65 50

1953. National Language Week.
751. 57. 5 c. olive 25 15

58. "Gateway to the East". 59. Pres. Quirino and Pres. Sukarno.

1953. Int. Fair, Manila.
752. 58. 5 c. blue-green 15 8
753. 6 c. red 15 12

1953. Visit of President to Indonesia. Flags in yellow, blue and red.
754. 59. 5 c. blue, yellow & black 15 8
755. 6 c. green, yell. & black 15 12

60. Doctor examining patient.

1953. Philippines Medical Association. 50th Anniv.
756. 60. 5 c. magenta 30 30
757. 6 c. blue 45 35

1954. Optd. **FIRST NATIONAL BOY SCOUTS JAMBOREE APRIL 23-30 1954** or surch. also.
758. 5 c. red (No. 731) .. 70 70
759. 18 c. on 50 c. grn. (No. 634) 1·25 1·00

61. 1854 Stamp, Magellan and Manila P.O.

1954. 1st Philippines Postage Stamps Cent. Central stamp in orange.
760. 61. 5 c. violet (postage) .. 35 25
761. 18 c. blue 75 70
762. 30 c. green .. .. 1·90 1·40
763. 61. 10 c. sepia (air) 75 70
764. 20 c. bronze-green .. .. 1·10 85
765. 50 c. red .. .. .. 2·75 2·25

62. Diving. 63. "Independence"

1954. 2nd Asian Games, Manila.
766. – 5 c. blue (Discus) .. 65 30
767. 62. 18 c. green 95 65
768. – 30 c. claret (Boxing) .. 1·40 1·25

1954. Surch. **MANILA CONFERENCE OF 1954** and value.
769. 25. 5 c. on 10 c. red 15 8
770. – 18 c. on 20 c. brown (No. 633) 50 45

1954. Independence. Commem.
771. 63. 5 c. lake 15 12
772. 18 c. blue 45 30

64. "The Immaculate Conception" (Murillo). 65. Mayon Volcano.

1954. Marian Year.
773. 64. 5 c. blue 25 15

1955. Rotary International. 50th Anniv.
774. 65. 5 c. blue (postage) .. 15 5
775. 18 c. red 45 35
776. 50 c. green (air) .. 85 65

66. "Labour". 67. Pres. Magsaysay.

1955. Labour-Management Congress, Manila
777. 66. 5 c. brown 25 15

1955. Republic. 9th Anniv.
778. 67. 5 c. blue 12 8
779. 20 c. red 35 35
780. 30 c. green 55 55

ILLUSTRATIONS
British Commonwealth and all overprints and surcharges are FULL SIZE. Foreign Countries have been reduced to ¾-LINEAR.

68. Lt. J. Gozar.

1955. Air. Air Force Heroes.
781. 68. 20 c. violet 35 8
782. – 30 c. red (Lt. C. F. Basa) 40 8
783. 68. 50 c. green 50 8
784. – 70 c. bl. (Lt. C. F. Basa) 85 50

69. Liberty Well.

1956. Artesian Wells for Rural Areas.
785. 69. 5 c. violet 20 20
786. 20 c. green 45 40

1956. 5th Conference of World Confederation of Organizations of the Teaching Profession. No. 731 optd. **WCOTP CONFERENCE MANILA.**
787. 5 c. red 20 20

70. Nurse and War Victims. **71.** Monument (landing marker) in Leyte.

1956. Philippines Red Cross. 50th Anniv.
788. **70.** 5 c. violet and red .. 35 30
789. 20 c. sepia and red .. 35 30

1956. Liberation. Perf. or imperf.
790. **71.** 5 c. red 8 8

72. St. Thomas's University. **73.** Statue of the Sacred Heart.

1956. University of St. Thomas.
791. **72.** 5 c. chocolate and lake 15 12
792. 60 c. brown and mauve 95 95

1956. 2nd National Eucharistic Congress and Cent. of the Feast of the Sacred Heart.
793. **73.** 5 c. olive 15 12
794. 20 c. red 45 45

1956. Surch.
795. 5 c. on 6 c. brown (No. 710) 8 8
796. 5 c. on 6 c. choc. (No. 713) 8 8
797. 5 c. on 6 c. violet (No. 716) 8 8

74. Girl Guide, Badge and Camp. **75.** Pres. Magsaysay.

1957. Girl Guides' Pacific World Camp. Quezon City, and Cent. of Birth of Lord Baden-Powell. Perf. or imperf.
798. **74.** 5 c. indigo 20 15

1957. Death of Pres. Magsaysay.
799. **75.** 5 c. black 8 5

76. S. Osmena (Speaker) and First Philippine Assembly.

1957. First Philippine Assembly. 50th Anniv.
800. **76.** 5 c. green 8 8

77. "The Spoliarium" after Juan Luna.

1957. Juan Luna (painter). Birth Cent.
801. **77.** 5 c. claret 8 8

1957. Inaug. of President C. P. Garcia and Vice-President-elect D. Macapagal. Nos. 732/3 surch. **GARCIA-MACAPAGAL INAUGURATION DEC. 30, 1957** and value
802. 5 c. on 10 c. blue.. .. 12 12
803. 10 c. on 20 c. red.. .. 15 15

78. University of the Philippines.

1958. University of the Philippines. Golden Jubilee.
804. **78.** 5 c. lake 15 8

79. Pres. Garcia. **80.** Main Hospital Building, Quezon Institute.

1958. Republic. 12th Anniv.
805. **79.** 5 c. black, blue, red, gold and salmon .. 8 8
806. 20 c. blk., red, gold & bl. 30 25

1958. Obligatory Tax. T.B. Relief Fund.
807. **80.** 5 c.+5 c. green and red 5 5
808. 10 c.+5 c. violet and red 12 5

81. The Immaculate Conception and Manila Cathedral.

1958. Inaug. of Manila Cathedral.
809. **81.** 5 c. multicoloured .. 15 8

1959. Surch. **One Centavo.**
810. 1 c. on 5 c. red (No. 731) 5 5

1959. Liberation. 14th Anniv. Nos. 704/5 surch.
812. **46.** 1 c. on 2 c.+2 c. verm. 5 5
813. – 6 c. on 4 c.+4 c. violet 8 5

82. Philippines Flag. **83.** Bulacan Seal.

1959. Philippines National Flag Commem.
814. **82.** 6 c. red, blue and yellow 5 5
815. 20 c. red, blue & yellow 15 15

1959. Bulacan Seal and 60th Anniv. of Malolos Constitution.
816. **83.** 6 c. green 5 5
817. 20 c. red 20 15

1959. Capiz Seal and 11th Death Anniv. of Pres. Roxas. As T **83** but with Capiz Seal.
818. 6 c. brown 5 5
819. 25 c. violet 20 15

The shield within the Capiz seal bears the inset portrait of Pres. Roxas.

1959. Bacolod Seal. As **T 83** but with Bacolod Seal.
820. 6 c. green 5 5
821. 10 c. purple 15 8

84. Scout at Camp Fire. **85.** Bohol Sanatorium.

1959. 10th World Scout Jamboree, Manila.
822. **84.** 6 c.+4 c. red on cream (postage) 10 10
823. 6 c.+4 c. red 30 25
824. – 25 c.+5 c. bl. on cream 35 35
825. – 25 c.+5 c. blue .. 45 35
826. – 30 c.+10 c. green (air) 40 35
827. – 70 c.+30 c. brown .. 70 70
828. – 80 c.+20 c. violet .. 95 95

DESIGNS: 25 c. Scout with bow and arrow. 30 c. Scout cycling. 70 c. Scout with model aeroplane. 80 c. Pres. Garcia with scout.

Nos. 823 and 825 were printed *tete-beche*.

1959. Obligatory Tax. T.B. Relief Fund Nos. 807/8 surch. **HELP FIGHT T B** with Cross of Lorraine and value and new design (T **85**).
830. **80.** 3 c.+5 c. on 5 c.+5 c. 8 8
831. 6 c.+5 c. on 10 c.+5 c. 12 8
832. **85.** 6 c.+5 c. green and red 8 8
833. 25 c.+5 c. blue and red 30 25

86. Pagoda and Gardens at Camp John Hay.

1959. Baguio. 50th Anniv.
834. **86.** 6 c. green 8 5
835. 25 c. red 25 15

1959. U.N. Day. Surch. **6 ₵ UNITED NATIONS DAY.**
836. **38.** 6 c. on 18 c. blue .. 8 5

87. Maria Cristina Falls.

1959. World Tourist Conf., Manila.
837. **87.** 6 c. green and violet .. 8 5
838. 30 c. green and sepia .. 25 20

1959. No. 629 surch. **One** and bars.
839. 1 c. on 4 c. brown .. 5 5

88.

1959. Manila Athenaeum (school). Cent.
840. **88.** 6 c. blue 5 5
841. 30 c. red 25 20

89. Book of the Constitution.

1960. Philippines Constitution. 25th Anniv.
844. **89.** 6 c. choc. & gold (post.) 10 5
845. 30 c. blue & silver (air) 20 15

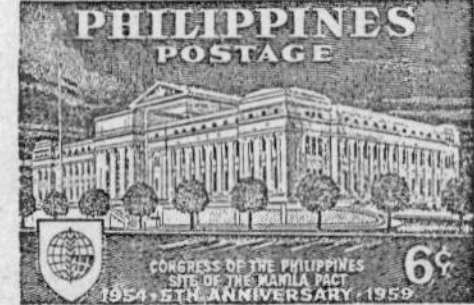

90. Congress Building.

1960. 5th Anniv. of Manila Pact.
846. **90.** 6 c. green 5 5
847. 25 c. orange 25 20

91. Sunset, Manila Bay.

1960. World Refugee Year.
848. **91.** 6 c. multicoloured .. 5 5
849. 25 c. multicoloured .. 25 15

92. Fighter Planes of 1935 and 1960. **93.** Lorraine Cross.

1960. Air. Philippine Air Force. 25th Anniv.
850. **92.** 10 c. red 15 5
851. 20 c. blue 25 15

1960. Surch.
852. **40.** 1 c. on 18 c. blue .. 5 5
853. **63.** 5 c. on 18 c. blue .. 8 5
854. **65.** 5 c. on 18 c. red .. 15 12
855. **61.** 10 c. on 18 c. orge. & bl. 12 8
856. **45.** 10 c. on 18 c. blue .. 15 12

1960. Philippine Tuberculosis Society. 50th Anniv. Lorraine Cross and wreath in red and gold.
857. **93.** 5 c. green 5 5
858. 6 c. blue 8 8

1960. Obligatory Tax. T.B. Relief Fund. Surch. **6+5** and bars and **HELP PREVENT TB.**
859. **80.** 6 c.+5 c. on 5 c.+5 c. green and red .. 12 8

94. Pres. Quezon. **95.** Basketball.

1960.
860. **94.** 1 c. olive 5 5

1960. Olympic Games.
861. **95.** 6 c. brn. & grn. (post.) 10 5
862. – 10 c. chocolate & mauve 15 8
863. – 30 c. sepia & orge. (air) 30 30
864. – 70 c. maroon and blue.. 55 55

DESIGNS: 10 c. Running. 30 c. Rifle-shooting. 70 c. Swimming.

96. Presidents Eisenhower and Garcia.

1960. Visit of President Eisenhower.
865. **96.** 6 c. multicoloured .. 15 10
866. 20 c. multicoloured .. 25 15

97. "Mercury" and Globe.

1961. Manila Postal Conf.
867. **97.** 6 c. orange, gold, blue and black (postage).. 8 8
868. 30 c. orange, gold, green and black (air) .. 25 15

1961. Surch.
869. 20 c. on 25 c. grn. (No. 734) 15 8

1961. 2nd National Scout Jamboree, Zamboanga. Nos. 822/5 surch. **2nd National Boy Scout Jamboree Pasonanca Park** and value.
870. 10 c. on 6 c.+4 c. red on cream 8 8
871. 10 c. on 6 c.+4 c. red .. 12 12
872. 30 c. on 25 c.+5 c. blue on cream 30 30
873. 30 c. on 25 c.+5 c. blue .. 35 35

98. La Salle College.

1961. La Salle College. 50th Anniv.
874. **98.** 6 c. multicoloured .. 5 5
875. 10 c. multicoloured .. 10 5

99. Rizal when student, School and University Buildings.

1961. Dr. Jose Rizal. Birth Cent. Inscr. as in T **99.**
876. **99.** 5 c. multicoloured .. 5 5
877. – 6 c. multicoloured .. 5 5
878. – 10 c. brown and green.. 8 8
879. – 20 c. turquoise & brown 15 15
880. – 30 c. multicoloured .. 25 20

DESIGNS: 6 c. Rizal and birthplace at Calamba, Laguna. 10 c. Rizal, mother and father. 20 c. Rizal extolling Luna and Hidalgo at Madrid. 30 c. Rizal's execution.

1961. Republic. 15th Anniv. Optd. **IKA 15 KAARAWAN Republika ng Pilipinas Hulyo 4, 1961.**
881. **90.** 6 c. green 12 12
882. 25 c. orange 25 25

100. Roxas Memorial T.B. Pavilion.

101. Globe, Plan Emblem and Supporting Hand.

1961. Obligatory Tax. T.B. Relief Fund.
883. **100.** 6 c.+5 c. brown & red 12 8

1961. Admission of Philippines to Colombo Plan. 7th Anniv.
884. **101.** 5 c. orange, green, gold and violet 5 5
885. 6 c. orange, green, gold and blue 5 5

1961. Philippine Amateur Athletic Federation's Golden Jubilee. Surch. with P.A.A.F. monogram and **6 c. PAAF GOLDEN JUBILEE 1911 1961.**
886. **92.** 6 c. in 10 c. red .. 12 12

102. Typist.

1961. Government Employees' Association Commem.
887. **102.** 6 c. violet and brown .. 8 5
888. 10 c. grey-blue & brown 15 10

1961. Inaug. of Pres. Macapagal and Vice Pres. Pelaez. Surch. **MACAPAGAL-PELAEZ DEC. 30, 1961 INAUGURATION 6 c.**
889. 6 c. on 25 c. vio. (No. 819) 8 5

1962. Cross obliterated by Arms and surch. **6 s** and bars.
890. **80.** 6 c. on 5 c.+5 c. green and red 8 5

103. Waling Waling.

104. A. Mabini.

1962. Orchids in natural colours on indigo background.
892. 5 c. T **103** 5 5
893. 6 c. White Mariposa .. 8 8
894. 10 c. "Dendrobium sanderii" 12 12
895. 20 c. Sanggumay 20 20

1962. New Currency.
896. – 1 s. chestnut 5 5
897. **104.** 3 s. red 5 5
898. – 5 s. red 5 5
899. – 6 s. chocolate 5 5
900. – 6 s. blue 5 5
901. – 10 s. purple 8 5
902. – 20 s. blue 12 5
903. – 30 s. red 20 5
904. – 50 s. violet 35 8
905. – 70 s. blue 45 20
906. – 1 p. green 70 15
907. – 1 p. orange 50 25
PORTRAITS: 1 s. M. L. Quezon. 5 s. M. H. del Pilar. 6 s. (2) J. Rizal (different). 10 s. Father J. Burgos. 20 s. Lapu-Lapu. 30 s. Rajah Soliman. 50 s. C. Arellano. 70 s. S. Osmena. 1 p. (No. 906) E. Jacinto. 1 p. (No. 907) J. M. Panganiban.

105. Pres. Macapagal taking Oath.

1962. Independence Day.
915. **105.** 6 s. multicoloured .. 5 5
916. 10 s. multicoloured .. 8 5
917. 30 s. multicoloured .. 25 8

106. Valdes Memorial T.B. Pavilion.

1962. Obligatory Tax Stamps. T.B. Relief Fund. Cross in red.
918. **106.** 6 s.+5 s. slate .. 8 5
919. 30 s.+5 s. ultramarine 25 20
920. 70 s.+5 s. blue .. 55 45

107. Lake Taal.

1962. Malaria Eradication.
921. **107.** 6 s. multicoloured .. 5 5
922. 10 s. multicoloured .. 8 5
923. 70 s. multicoloured .. 50 45

1962. Diego Siland Revolt. Bicent. Surch. **1762 1962 BICENTENNIAL Diego Silang Revolt 20** and ornament.
924. 20 s. on 25 c. grn. (No. 734) 15 8

1962. No. 742 with premium obliterated.
925. **53.** 5 c. blue 5 5

108. Dr. Rizal playing Chess.

1962. Rizal Foundation Fund.
926. **108.** 6 s.+4 s. green & mag. 25 25
927. – 30 s.+5 s. blue & pur. 45 45
DESIGN: 30 s. Dr. Rizal fencing.

1963. Surch.
928. **104.** 1 s. on 3 s. red .. 5 5
929. – 5 s. on 6 s. chocolate (No. 899) .. 5 5

1963. Diego Silang Bicentenary Art and Philatelic Exn., G.P.O., Manila. No. 737 surch. **1763 1963 DIEGO SILANG BICENTENNIAL ARPHEX** and value.
930. 6 c. on 2 p. violet .. 8 5
931. 20 c. on 2 p. violet .. 20 20
932. 70 c. on 2 p. violet .. 50 45

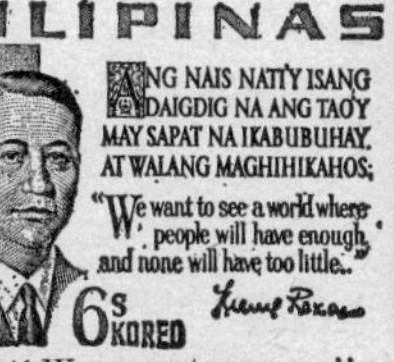

109. "We want to see . . ." (Pres. Roxas).

110. Lorraine Cross on Map.

1963. Presidential Sayings (1st issue).
933. **109.** 6 s. blue and black .. 5 5
934. 30 s. brown and black 25 8
See also Nos. 959/60, 981/2, 1015/6, 1034/5, 1055/6, 1148/9 and 1292/3.

1963. Obligatory Tax. T.B. Relief Fund. Cross in red.
935. **110.** 6 s.+5 s. pink & violet 8 5
936. 10 s.+5 s. pink & grn. 12 8
937. 50 s.+5 s. pink & brn. 45 30

HAVE YOU READ THE NOTES AT THE BEGINNING OF THIS CATALOGUE?

These often provide answers to the enquiries we receive.

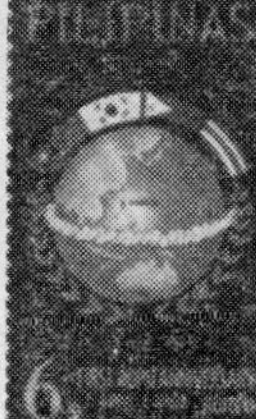

111. Globe and Flags.

112. Centenary Emblem.

1963. Asian-Oceanic Postal Union. 1st Anniv.
938. **111.** 6 s. multicoloured .. 5 5
939. 20 s. multicoloured .. 15 8

1963. Red Cross Centenary. Cross in red.
940. **112.** 5 s. grey and violet .. 5 5
941. 6 s. grey and blue .. 5 5
942. 20 s. grey and green .. 15 8

113. Tinikling.

1963. Folk Dances. Multicoloured.
943. 5 s. Type **113** 5 5
944. 6 s. Pandanggo sa Ilaw .. 8 8
945. 10 s. Itik-Itik 12 12
946. 20 s. Singkil 20 20

114. Pres. Macapagal and Philippine Family.

1963. President's Social-Economic Programme.
947. **114.** 5 s. multicoloured .. 5 5
948. 6 s. multicoloured .. 8 5
949. 20 s. multicoloured .. 15 10

115. Presidents' Meeting.

116. Bonifacio and Flag.

1963. Visit of President Mateos of Mexico.
950. **115.** 6 s. multicoloured .. 5 5
951. 30 s. multicoloured .. 15 8

1963. A. Bonifacio (patriot). Birth Cent.
952. **116.** 5 s. multicoloured .. 5 5
953. 6 s. multicoloured .. 5 5
954. 25 s. multicoloured .. 20 20

117. Harvester.

118. Bamboo Organ, Catholic Church Las Pinas.

1963. Freedom from Hunger.
956. **117.** 6 s. multicoloured (post.) 12 5
957. 30 s. multicoloured (air) 25 12
958. 50 s. multicoloured .. 35 25

1963. Presidential Sayings (2nd issue). As T **109** but with portrait and saying changed.
959. 6 s. black and mauve .. 5 5
960. 30 s. black and green .. 25 8
PORTRAIT AND SAYING: Pres. Magsaysay, "I believe . . .".

1964. Las Pinas Organ Commemoration.
961. **118.** 5 s. multicoloured .. 5 5
962. 6 s. multicoloured .. 5 5
963. 20 s. multicoloured .. 15 8

119. A. Mabini (patriot).

121. S.E.A.T.O. Emblems and Flags.

120. Negros Oriental T.B. Pavilion.

1964. A. Mabini. Birth Cent.
964. **119.** 6 s. gold and violet .. 5 5
965. 10 s. gold and brown .. 8 5
966. 30 s. gold and green .. 15 12

1964. Obligatory Tax. T.B. Relief Fund. Cross in red.
967. **120.** 5 s.+5 s. purple .. 8 5
968. 6 s.+5 s. blue .. 8 5
969. 30 s.+5 s. brown .. 30 20
970. 70 s.+5 s. green .. 55 45

1964. S.E.A.T.O. 10th Anniv.
971. **121.** 6 s. multicoloured .. 5 5
972. 10 s. multicoloured .. 8 5
973. 25 s. multicoloured .. 15 15

122. President Signing the Code.

123. Basketball.

1964. Agricultural Land Reform Code. President and inscr. at foot, brown, rose and sepia.
974. **122.** 3 s. green (postage) .. 5 5
975. 6 s. blue 5 5
976. 30 s. red-brown (air) .. 20 15

1964. Olympic Games, Tokyo. Sport in chocolate. Perf. or imperf.
977. **123.** 6 s. blue and gold .. 5 5
978. – 10 s. pink and gold .. 10 5
979. – 20 s. yellow and gold .. 20 12
980. – 30 s. green and gold .. 25 20
SPORTS: 10 s. Relay-racing. 20 s. Hurdling. 30 s. Football.

1965. Presidential Sayings (3rd issue). As T **109** but with portrait and saying changed.
981. 6 s. black and green .. 5 5
982. 30 s. black and purple .. 25 8
PORTRAIT AND SAYING: Pres. Quirino, "So live . . .".

124. Presidents Luebke and Macapagal.

1965. Visit of President of German Federal Republic.
983. **124.** 6 s. multicoloured .. 5 5
984. 10 s. multicoloured .. 8 5
985. 25 s. multicoloured .. 15 15

125. Meteorological Emblems.

126. Pres. Kennedy.

1965. Philippines Meteorological Services Cent.
986. **125.** 6 s. multicoloured .. 5 5
987. 20 s. multicoloured .. 10 5
988. 50 s. multicoloured .. 35 25

1965. Pres. Kennedy. 48th Birth Anniv.
989. **126.** 6 s. multicoloured .. 10 5
990. 10 s. multicoloured .. 12 5
991. 30 s. multicoloured .. 30 15

127. King Bhumibol and Queen Sirkit, Pres. Macapagal and Wife.

1965. Visit of King and Queen of Thailand.
992. **127.** 2 s. multicoloured .. 5 5
993. 6 s. multicoloured .. 5 5
994. 30 s. multicoloured .. 15 12

128. Princess Beatrix and Mrs. Macapagal.

1965. Visit of Princess Beatrix of the Netherlands.
995. **128.** 2 s. multicoloured .. 5 5
996. 6 s. multicoloured .. 5 5
997. 10 s. multicoloured .. 8 5

1965. Obligatory Tax. T.B. Relief Fund. Surch.
998. **120.** 1 s.+5 s. on 6 s.+5 s. 5 5
999. 3 s.+5 s. on 6 s.+5 s. 8 5

129. Hand holding Cross and Rosary. **130.** Signing Agreement.

1965. Philippines Christianisation. 400th Anniv. Inscr. "1565-1965". Multicoloured.
1000. 3 s. Type **129** (postage) .. 5 5
1001. 6 s. Legaspi-Urdaneta, monument 8 5
1002. 30 s. Baptism of Filipinos by Father Urdaneta (air) .. 15 8
1003. 70 s. "Way of the Cross"—ocean map of Christian voyagers' route, Spain to the Philippines .. 40 20
Nos. 1002/3 are horiz., 48 × 27 mm.

1965. "MAPILINDO" Conf., Manila.
1005. **130.** 6 s. blue, red & yellow 5 5
1006. 10 s. brn., red, yell. & bl. 5 5
1007. 25 s. grn., red, yell. & bl. 15 10
The above stamps depict Pres. Sukarno of Indonesia, former Pres. Macapagal of the Philippines and Prime Minister Tunku Abdul Rahman of Malaysia.

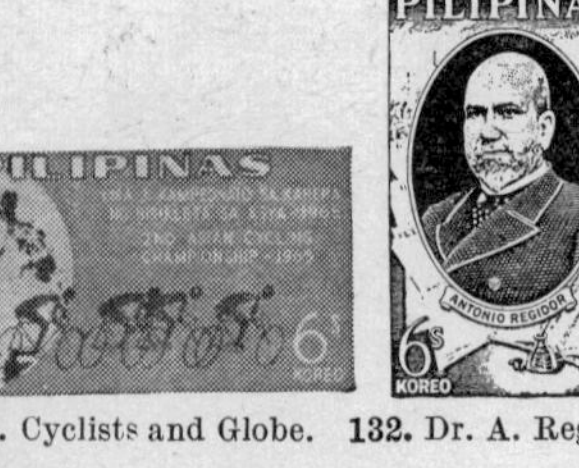

131. Cyclists and Globe. **132.** Dr. A. Regidor.

1965. 2nd Asian Cycling Championships, Philippines.
1008. **131.** 6 s. multicoloured .. 5 5
1009. 10 s. multicoloured .. 8 5
1010. 25 s. multicoloured .. 15 12

1965. Inaug. of Pres. Marcos and Vice-Pres. Lopez. Nos. 926/7 surch. **MARCOS-LOPEZ INAUGURATION DEC. 30, 1965** with value and bars.
1011. **108.** 10 s. on 6 s.+4 s. .. 12 12
1012. – 30 s. on 30 s.+5 s. .. 30 30

1966. Regidor (patriot) Commem.
1013. **132.** 6 s. blue 5 5
1014. 30 s. brown 20 15

1966. Presidential Sayings (4th issue). As T **109** but with portrait and saying changed.
1015. 6 s. black and lake .. 5 5
1016. 30 s. black and blue .. 25 5
PORTRAIT AND SAYING: Pres. Aguinaldo, "Have faith . . .".

1966. Campaign Against Smuggling. No. 900 optd. **HELP ME STOP SMUGGLING Pres. MARCOS.**
1017. – 6 c. blue 5 5

133. Girl Scout.

1966. Philippines Girl Scouts. Silver Jubilee.
1018. **133.** 3 s. multicoloured .. 5 5
1019. 6 s. multicoloured .. 5 5
1020. 20 s. multicoloured .. 12 8

134. Pres. Marcos taking Oath.

1966. Pres. Marcos. Inaug. (1965).
1021. **134.** 6 s. multicoloured .. 5 5
1022. 20 s. multicoloured .. 8 5
1023. 30 s. multicoloured .. 20 15

135. Manila Seal and Historical Scenes.

1966. Introduction of New Seal for Manila.
1024. **135.** 6 s. multicoloured .. 5 5
1025. 30 s. multicoloured .. 15 12

136. Bank Facade and 1-peso Coin.

1966. Philippines National Bank. 50th Anniv.
1026. **136.** 6 s. black, silver, gold and blue 8 5
1027. – 10 s. multicoloured .. 8 5
DESIGN: 10 s. Old and new bank buildings.

137. Bank Building.

1966. Postal Savings Bank. 60th Anniv.
1029. **137.** 6 s. violet, yellow & grn. 5 5
1030. 10 s. claret, yell. & grn. 8 5
1031. 20 s. blue, yell. & grn. 15 10

1966. Manila Summit Conf. Nos. 1021 and 1023 optd. **MANILA SUMMIT CONFERENCE 1966 7 NATIONS** and emblem.
1032. **134.** 6 s. multicoloured .. 5 5
1033. 30 s. multicoloured .. 25 15

1966. Presidential Sayings (5th issue). As T **109** but with portrait and saying changed.
1034. 6 s. black and brown .. 5 5
1035. 30 s. black and blue .. 25 8
PORTRAIT AND SAYING: Pres. Laurel. "No one can love the Filipinos better . . .".

1967. Lions Int. 50th Anniv. Nos. 977/80 optd. **50th ANNIVERSARY LIONS INTERNATIONAL 1967** and emblem. Imperf.
1036. **123.** 6 c. blue and gold .. 5 5
1037. – 10 c. pink and gold .. 10 8
1038. – 20 c. lemon and gold 15 15
1039. – 30 c. green and gold 25 25

138. " Succour " (after painting by F. Amorsolo).

1967. Battle of Bataan. 25th Anniv.
1040. **138.** 5 s. multicoloured .. 5 5
1041. 20 s. multicoloured .. 10 5
1042. 2 p. multicoloured .. 1·00 55

1967. Nos. 900 and 975 surch.
1043. 4 s. on 6 s. blue 5 5
1044. 5 s. on 6 s. blue 5 5

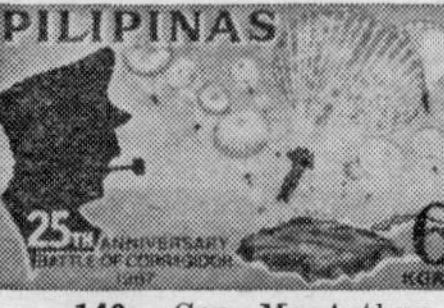

139. Stork-billed Kingfisher. **140.** Gen. MacArthur and Paratroopers landing on Corregidor.

1967. Obligatory Tax. T.B. Relief Fund. Birds. Multicoloured.
1045. 1 s.+5 s. Type **139** .. 5 5
1046. 5 s.+5 s. Luzon hornbill (or kalaw) 8 5
1047. 10 s.+5 s. Monkey-eating eagle 12 8
1048. 30 s.+5 s. Large-billed parrot (or loro) .. 30 30
See also Nos. 1113/6.

1967. Battle of Corregidor. 25th Anniv.
1049. **140.** 6 s. multicoloured .. 8 8
1050. 5 p. multicoloured .. 2·10 1·40

141. Bureau of Posts Building, Manila.

1967. Philippines Bureau of Posts. 65th Anniv.
1051. **141.** 4 s. multicoloured .. 8 8
1052. 20 s. multicoloured .. 8 5
1053. 50 s. multicoloured .. 25 20

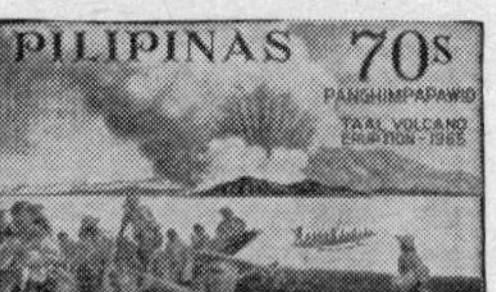

142. Escaping from Eruption.

1967. Obligatory Tax. Taal Volcano Eruption (1965). (1st issue).
1054. **142.** 70 s. multicoloured .. 35 25
For compulsory use on foreign air mail where the rate exceeds 70 s. in aid of Taal Volcano Rehabilitation Committee.
See also No. 1071.

1967. Presidential Sayings (6th issue). As T **109** but with portrait and saying changed.
1055. 10 s. black and blue .. 5 5
1056. 30 s. black and violet .. 25 8
PORTRAIT AND SAYING: Pres. Quezon. "Social justice is far more beneficial . . .".

143. " The Holy Family " (Filipino version).

1967. Christmas.
1057. **143.** 10 s. multicoloured .. 8 5
1058. 40 s. multicoloured .. 25 20

144. Pagoda, Pres. Marcos and Chiang Kai-shek.

1967. China-Philippines Friendship.
1059. **144.** 5 s. multicoloured .. 5 5
1060. – 10 s. multicoloured .. 8 5
1061. – 20 s. multicoloured .. 12 8
DESIGNS: (with portraits of Pres. Marcos and Chiang Kai-shek): 10 s. Gateway, Chinese Garden, Rizal Park, Luneta. 20 s. Chinese Garden, Rizal Park, Luneta.

145. Ayala Avenue, Manila, Inaugural Ceremony and Rotary Badge.

1968. Makati Centre Post Office, Manila. 1st Anniv.
1062. **145.** 10 s. multicoloured .. 8 8
1063. 20 s. multicoloured .. 15 15
1064. 40 s. multicoloured .. 25 25

1968. Surch.
1065. – 5 s. on 6 s. (No. 981) 5 5
1066. – 5 s. on 6 s. (No. 1034) 5 5
1067. **120.** 10 s. on 6 s.+5 s. .. 5 5

146. Calderon, Barasoain Church and Constitution.

1968. Felipe G. Calderon (lawyer and author of Malolos Constitution). Birth Cent.
1068. **146.** 10 s. multicoloured .. 5 5
1069. 40 s. multicoloured .. 20 15
1070. 75 s. multicoloured .. 35 35

147. Eruption. **148.** "Philcomsat", Earth Station and Globe.

1968. Taal Volcano Eruption (1965). (2nd issue).
1071. **147.** 70 s. multicoloured .. 35 25
Two issues were prepared by an American Agency under a contract signed with the Philippine postal authority but at the last moment this contract was cancelled by the Philippine Government. In the meanwhile the stamps had been on sale in the U.S.A. but they were never issued in the Philippine Islands and they had no postal validity.
They comprise a set for the Mexican Olympic Games in the values 1 c., 2 c., 3 c. and 15 c. postage and 50 c., 75 c., 1 p. and 2 p. airmail and an issue in memory of J. F. Kennedy and Robert Kennedy in the values 1 c., 2 c., 3 c., 5 p. and 10 p. as well as 10 p. miniature sheet.

1968. Inaug. of "Philcomsat"—POTC Earth Station, Tanay, Rizal, Luzon.
1072. **148.** 10 s. multicoloured .. 8 8
1073. 40 s. multicoloured .. 25 20
1074. 75 s. multicoloured .. 45 35

149. " Tobacco Production " (mural).

1968. Philippines Tobacco Industry.
1075. **149.** 10 s. multicoloured .. 5 5
1076. 40 s. multicoloured .. 20 15
1077. 70 s. multicoloured .. 35 30

150. "Kudyapi".

1968. St. Cecilia's Day. Musical Instruments. Multicoloured.
1078. 10 s. Type **150** 5 5
1079. 20 s. "Ludag" 10 8
1080. 30 s. "Kulintangan" .. 15 15
1081. 50 s. "Subing" 25 25

151. Concordia College. **152.** Children singing Carols.

1968. Concordia Women's College. Cent.
1082. **151.** 10 s. multicoloured .. 8 5
1083. 20 s. multicoloured .. 12 10
1084. 70 s. multicoloured .. 35 30

1968. Christmas.
1085. **152.** 10 s. multicoloured .. 5 5
1086. 40 s. multicoloured .. 25 20
1087. 75 s. multicoloured .. 45 35

153. Tarsier.

1969. Philippines Fauna. Multicoloured.
1088. 2 s. Type **153** 5 5
1089. 10 s. Tamaraw 5 5
1090. 20 s. Carabao (buffalo) .. 10 8
1091. 75 s. Mouse deer 45 35

154. President Aguinaldo and Cavite Building.

1969. President Amilio Aguinaldo. Birth Cent.
1092. **154.** 10 s. multicoloured .. 8 5
1093. 40 s. multicoloured .. 25 15
1094. 70 s. multicoloured .. 45 35

155. Rotary Emblem and "Bastion of San Andres".

1969. Manila Rotary Club. 50th Anniv.
1095. **155.** 10 s. multicoloured (post.) 8 5
1096. 40 s. multicoloured (air) 20 15
1097. 75 s. multicoloured .. 45 35

156. Senator C. M. Recto. **157.** Jose Rizal College.

1969. Recto Commem.
1098. **156.** 10 s. purple 5 5

1969. Philatelic Week. No. 1051 optd. **PHILATELIC WEEK NOV. 24-30, 1968,** etc.
1099. 4 s. multicoloured .. 5 5

1969. Jose Rizal College, Mandaluyong, Rizal.
1100. **157.** 10 s. multicoloured .. 5 5
1101. 40 s. multicoloured .. 20 15
1102. 50 s. multicoloured .. 25 20

1969. 4th National Boy Scout Jamboree, Palayan City. No. 1019 surch. **4th NATIONAL BOY SCOUT JAMBOREE PALAYAN CITY - MAY, 1959** and value.
1103. **133.** 5 s. on 6 s. multicoloured 5 5

158. Red Cross Emblems and Map. **159.** Pres. and Mrs. Marcos harvesting Rice.

1969. League of Red Cross Societies. 50th Anniv.
1104. **158.** 10 s. red, ultram. & grey 5 5
1105. 40 s. red and blue .. 25 15
1106. 75 s. red, brn. & ochre 35 30

1969. "Rice for Progress".
1107. **159.** 10 s. multicoloured .. 5 5
1108. 40 s. multicoloured .. 25 15
1109. 75 s. multicoloured .. 35 30

160. "The Holy Child of Leyte" (statue).

1969. Return of the "Holy Child of Leyte" to Tacloban. 80th Anniv.
1110. **160.** 5 s. multicoloured (post.) 5 5
1111. 10 s. multicoloured .. 5 5
1112. 40 s. multicoloured (air) 25 15

1969. Obligatory Tax. T.B. Relief Fund. Birds, as Type **139.**
1113. 1 s. + 5 s. Three-toed Woodpecker 5 5
1114. 5 s. + 5 s. Philippine Trogon 8 5
1115. 10 s. + 5 s. Mount Apo Lorikeet 12 8
1116. 40 s. + 5 s. Johnstone's Minivet 30 30

161. Bank Building.

1969. Philippines Development Bank, Makati, Rizal. Inaug.
1117. **161.** 10 s. black, blue & grn. 5 5
1118. 40 s. black, red & grn. 25 15
1119. 75 s. black, brown & grn. 35 30

162. Common Birdwing.

1969. Philippine Butterflies. Multicoloured.
1120. 10 s. Type **162** 5 5
1121. 20 s. Tailed Jay 10 5
1122. 30 s. Red Helen 15 12
1123. 40 s. Birdwing 25 15

163. Children of the World.

1969. Universal Children's Day. 15th Anniv.
1124. **163.** 10 s. multicoloured .. 5 5
1125. 20 s. multicoloured .. 12 8
1126. 30 s. multicoloured .. 15 12

164. Memorial and Outline of Landing.

1969. U.S. Forces' Landing on Leyte. 25th Anniv.
1127. **164.** 5 s. multicoloured .. 5 5
1128. 10 s. multicoloured .. 8 5
1129. 40 s. multicoloured .. 25 15

165. Cultural Centre. **166.** Tandang Sora.

1969. Cultural Centre, Manila.
1130. **165.** 10 s. blue 5 5
1131. 30 s. purple 15 15

1969. Philatelic Week. Nos. 943/6 (Folk Dances) optd. **1969 PHILATELIC WEEK** or optd. and surch.
1132. 5 s. multicoloured .. 5 5
1133. 5 s. on 6 s. multicoloured 5 5
1134. 10 s. multicoloured .. 5 5
1135. 10 s. on 20 s. multicoloured 5 5

1969. Melchora Aquino, "Tandang Sora" (Grand Old Woman of the Revolution). 50th Death Anniv.
1136. **166.** 10 s. multicoloured .. 5 5
1137. 20 s. multicoloured .. 12 5
1138. 30 s. multicoloured .. 15 8

1969. President Marcos. 2nd term Inaug. No. 1021 surch. **PASINAYA, IKA-2 PANUNUNGKULAN PANGULONG FERDINAND E. MARCOS DISYEMBRA 30, 1969.**
1139. **134.** 5 s. on 6 s. multicoloured 5 5

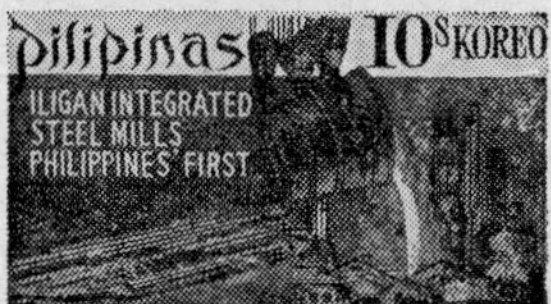

167. Ladle and Steel Mills.

1970. Iligan Integrated Steel Mills.
1140. **167.** 10 s. multicoloured .. 5 5
1141. 20 s. multicoloured .. 12 8
1142. 30 s. multicoloured .. 15 10

1970. Nos. 900, 962 and 964 surch.
1143. – 4 s. on 6 s. blue .. 5 5
1144. **118.** 5 s. on 6 s. multicoloured 5 5
1145. **119.** 5 s. on 6 s. multicoloured 5 5

168. New U.P.U. Headquarters Building.

1970. New U.P.U. Headquarters Building, Berne.
1146. **168.** 10 s. ultram., lemon and blue 5 5
1147. 30 s. ultram., lemon and emerald .. 15 10

1970. Presidential Sayings (7th issue). As T **109** but with portrait and saying changed.
1148. 10 s. black and purple .. 5 5
1149. 40 s. black and emerald .. 25 5
PORTRAIT AND SAYING: Pres. Osmena. "Ante todo el bien de nuestro pueblo".

169. Dona Julia V. de Ortigas and P.T.S. Headquarters.

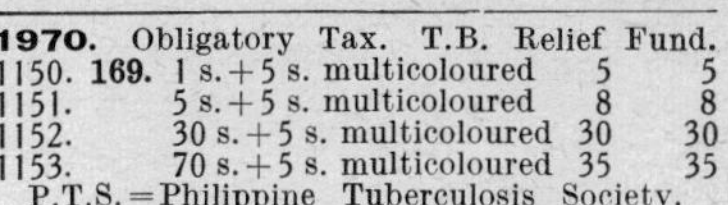

1970. Obligatory Tax. T.B. Relief Fund.
1150. **169.** 1 s. + 5 s. multicoloured 5 5
1151. 5 s. + 5 s. multicoloured 8 8
1152. 30 s. + 5 s. multicoloured 30 30
1153. 70 s. + 5 s. multicoloured 35 35
P.T.S. = Philippine Tuberculosis Society.

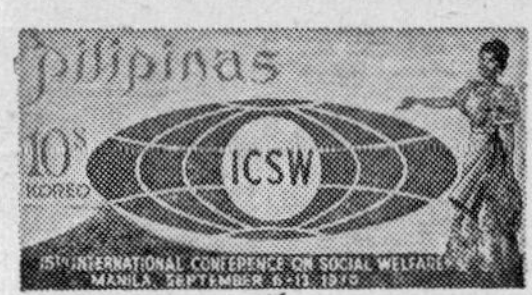

170. I.C.S.W. Emblem.

1970. Int. Conference on Social Welfare.
1154. **170.** 10 s. multicoloured .. 5 5
1155. 20 s. multicoloured .. 10 5
1156. 30 s. multicoloured .. 15 8

171. "Crab" (after sculpture by A. Calder).

1970. "Fight Cancer" Campaign.
1157. **171.** 10 s. multicoloured .. 8 5
1158. 40 s. multicoloured .. 20 12
1159. 50 s. multicoloured .. 25 15

172. Scaled Tridacna.

1970. Seashells. Multicoloured.
1160. 5 s. Type **172** 5 5
1161. 10 s. Royal spiny oyster 5 5
1162. 20 s Venus comb .. 12 8
1163. 40 s. Glory-of-the-Sea cone 25 15

1970. Nos. 986, 1024 and 1026 surch. with new values in figures and letters.
1164. **125.** 4 s. on 6 s. 5 5
1165. **135.** 4 s. on 6 s. 5 5
1166. **136.** 4 s. on 6 s. 5 5

173. The "Hundred Islands" and Ox-cart.

1970. Tourism (1st series). Multicoloured.
1167. 10 s. Type **173** .. 5 5
1168. 20 s. Tree-house, Pasonanca Park, Zamboanga City 10 8
1169. 30 s. "Filipino" (statue) and sugar plantation, Negros Island .. 15 15
1170. 2 p. Calesa (horse-carriage) and Miagao Church, Iloilo 90 45
See also Nos. 1186/9, 1192/5 and 1196/9.

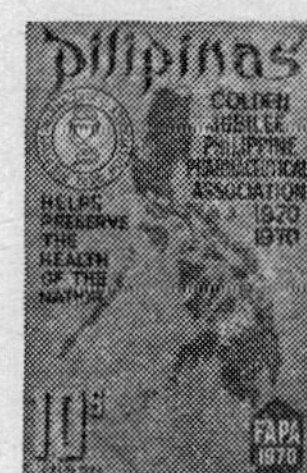

174. Map of the Philippines.

1970. Philippine Pharmaceutical Association. Golden Jubilee.
1171. **174.** 10 s. multicoloured .. 8 5
1172. 50 s. multicoloured .. 25 15

1970. U.P.U./A.O.P.U. Regional Seminar, Manila. No. 938 surch. **UPU-AOPU REGIONAL SEMINAR NOV. 23—DEC. 5, 1970,** and new value.
1173. **111.** 10 s. on 6 s. multicoloured 8 8

1970. Philatelic Week. No. 977 surch. **1970 PHILATELIC WEEK** and new value.
1174. **123.** 10 s. on 6 s. brown, blue and gold .. 5 5

175. Pope Paul VI and Map.

1970. Pope Paul's Visit to the Philippines.
1175. 175. 10 s. multicoloured (postage) 8 5
1176. 30 s. multicoloured .. 15 12
1177. 40 s. multicoloured (air) 25 15

176. Mariano Ponce.

177. P.A.T.A. Horse and Carriage.

1970.
1178. 176. 10 s. red 5 5
1179. – 15 s. brown 5 5
1180. – 40 s. red 15 5
1181. – 1 p. blue 35 15
DESIGNS: 15 s. Josefa Llanes Escoda. 40 s. Gen. Miguel Malvar. 1 p. Julian Felipe.

1970. No. 1178 optd. **G.O.**
1182. 176. 10 s. red 5 5

1971. 20th P.A.T.A. Conference and Workshop, Manila.
1183. 177. 5 s. multicoloured .. 5 5
1184. 10 s. multicoloured .. 8 5
1185. 70 s. multicoloured .. 25 20

1971. Tourism (2nd Series). Views as T 173. Multicoloured.
1186. 10 s. Nayong Pilipino resort 5 5
1187. 20 s. Fish farm, Iloilo .. 10 5
1188. 30 s. Pagsanjan Falls .. 15 15
1189. 5 p. Watch-tower, Punta Cruz .. .. .. 1·75 1·10

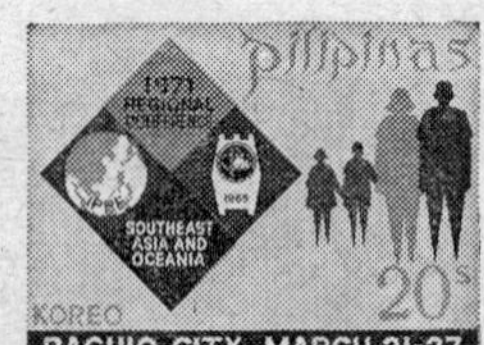

178. Emblem and Family.

1971. Regional Conference of Int. Planned Parenthood Federation for South-East Asia and Oceania.
1190. 178. 20 s. multicoloured 10 5
1191. 40 s. multicoloured 20 12

1971. Tourism (3rd series). As T 173. Multicoloured.
1192. 10 s. Aguinaldo pearl farm 5 5
1193. 20 s. Coral-diving, Davao 10 8
1194. 40 s. Taluksengay Mosque 15 10
1195. 1 p. Ifugao woman and Banaue rice-terraces .. 35 25

1971. Tourism. (4th series). As Type 173. Multicoloured.
1196. 10 s. Cannon and fishing boats, Fort del Pilar .. 5 5
1197. 30 s. Magellan's Cross, Cebu City 10 8
1198. 50 s. "Big Jar", Calamba Laguna (Rizal's birthplace) 15 15
1199. 70 s. Mayon Volcano and diesel train 30 15

1971. Surch in letters and figures.
1200. 136. 5 s. on 6 s. multicoloured 5 5

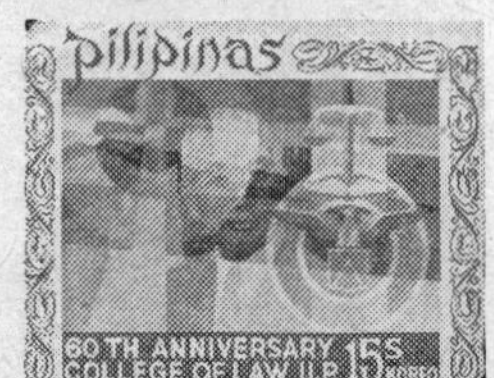

179. G. A. Malcolm (founder) and Law Symbols.

1971. Philippines College of Law. 60th Anniv.
1201. 179. 15 s. mult. (post.) .. 5 5
1202. 179. 1 p. multicoloured (air) 35 35

180. Commemorative Seal.

1971. Manila. 400th Anniv.
1203. 180. 10 s. mult. (postage) 5 5
1204. 180. 1 p. mult. (air) .. 35 35

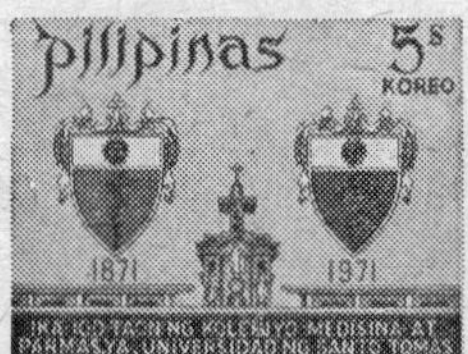

181. Arms of Faculties.

1971. Faculties of Medicine and Surgery, and of Pharmacy, Santo Tomas University. Cents.
1205. 181. 5 s. mult. (postage) .. 5 5
1206. 181. 2 p. mult. (air) .. 75 65

1971. University Presidents' World Congress Manila. Surch. **CONGRESS OF UNIVERSITY PRESIDENTS,** emblems and value.
1207. 137. 5 s. on 6 s. violet, yell. and green 5 5

182. "Our Lady of Guia".

1971. "Our Lady of Guia", Ermita, Manila. 400th Anniv.
1208. 182. 10 s. multicoloured .. 5 5
1209. 75 s. multicoloured .. 30 25

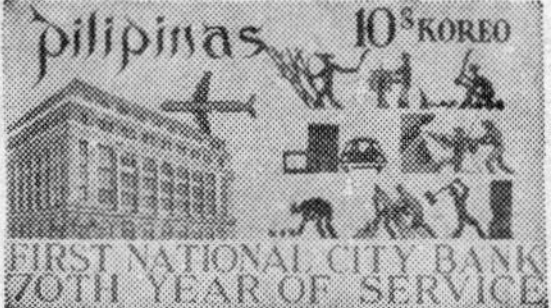

183. Bank and "Customers".

1971. First National City Bank. 70th Anniv.
1210. 183. 10 s. multicoloured .. 5 5
1211. 30 s. multicoloured .. 8 5
1212. 1 p. multicoloured .. 25 12

1971. Surch. in letters and figure.
1213. 132. 4 s. on 6 s. blue .. 5 5
1214. 5 s. on 6 s. blue .. 5 5

1971. Philatelic Week. Surch. **1971-PHILATELIC WEEK** and new value in letters and figure.
1215. 137. 5 s. on 6 s. violet, yellow and green .. 5 5

184. Dish Aerial and Events.

1972. 6th Asian Electronics Conf., Manila (1971) and Related Events.
1216. 184. 5 s. multicoloured .. 5 5
1217. 40 s. multicoloured 15 15

185. Fathers Burgos, Gomez and Zamora.

1972. Martyrdom of Fathers Burgos, Gomez and Zamora. Cent.
1218. 185. 5 s. multicoloured .. 5 5
1219. 60 s. multicoloured 20 20

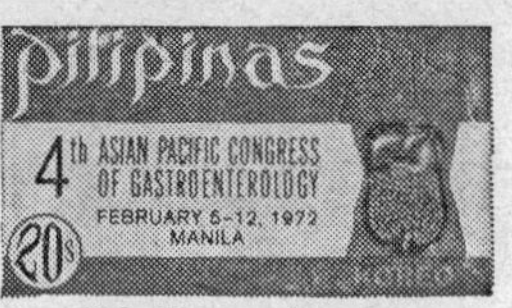

186. Human Organs.

1972. 4th Asian-Pacific Gastro-enterological Congress, Manila.
1220. 186. 20 s. mult. (postage) 10 8
1221. 40 s. mult. (air) .. 20 15

1972. Surch.
1222. 135. 5 s. on 6 s. mult. .. 5 5

1972. No. O 914 with opt. **G.O.** obliterated.
1223. 50 s. violet 20 15

1972. Surch.
1224. 121. 10 s. on 6 s. mult. .. 5 5
1225. 127. 10 s. on 6 s. mult. (No. 993) 5 5
1226. – 10 s. on 6 s. black & lake (No. 1015) .. 8 5

187. Memorial Gardens, Manila.

1972. Tourism. "Visit Asean Lands" Campaign.
1227. 187. 5 s. multicoloured .. 5 5
1228. 50 s. multicoloured .. 15 12
1229. 60 s. multicoloured .. 20 15

188. "KKK" Flag.

1972. Evolution of Philippines' Flag.
1230. 188. 30 s. red and blue .. 8 8
1231. – 30 s. red and blue .. 8 8
1232. – 30 s. red and blue .. 8 8
1233. – 30 s. black and blue 8 8
1234. – 30 s. red and blue .. 8 8
1235. – 30 s. red and blue .. 8 8
1236. – 30 s. red and blue .. 8 8
1237. – 30 s. red and blue .. 8 8
1238. – 30 s. blk., red and blue 8 8
1239. – 30 s. yell., red & blue 8 8
FLAGS: No. 1231, Three "K"s in pyramid. No. 1232, Single "K". No. 1233, "K", skull and crossbones. No. 1234, Three "K"s and sun in triangle. No. 1235, Sun and three "K"s. No. 1236, Ancient Tagalog "K" within sun. No. 1237, Face in sun. No. 1049, Tricolor. No. 1238, Present national flag—sun and stars within triangle, two stripes.

189. Mabol, Santol and Papaya.

1972. Obligatory Tax. T.B. Relief Fund. Fruits. Multicoloured.
1240. 1 s. + 5 s. Type **189** .. 5 5
1241. 10 s. + 5 s. Bananas, balimbang and mangosteen 8 5
1242. 40 s. + 5 s. Guava, mango, duhat and susongkalabac 25 15
1243. 1 p. + 5 s. Orange, pineapple, lanzones and sirhuelas 40 40

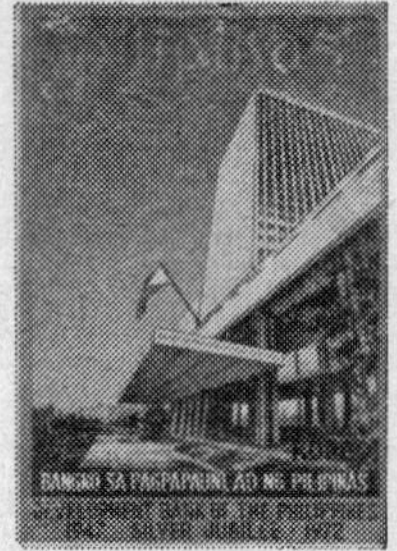

190. "Scarus frenatus".

1972. Fishes. Multicoloured.
1244. 5 s. Type **190** (postage) .. 5 5
1245. 10 s. "Chaetodon kleini" 5 5
1246. 20 s. "Zanclus cornutus" 10 8
1247. 50 s. "Holacanthus bispinosus" (air) .. 20 15

191. Bank Headquarters.

1972. Philippines Development Bank. 25th Anniv.
1248. 191. 10 s. multicoloured 5 5
1249. 20 s. multicoloured 8 5
1250. 60 s. multicoloured 20 15

192. Pope Paul VI.

1972. Pope Paul's Visit to Philippines. 1st Anniv.
1251. 192. 10 s. mult. (postage) 5 5
1252. 50 s. multicoloured .. 20 15
1253. 192. 60 s. multicoloured (air) 25 20

1972. Various stamps surch.
1254. 116. 10 s. on 6 s. (No. 953) 5 5
1255. – 10 s. on 6 s. (No. 959) 5 5
1256. 126. 10 s. on 6 s. (No. 989) 8 5

193. "La Barca de Aqueronte" (Hidalgo).

1972. Stamps and Philatelic Division Philippines Bureau of Posts. 25th Anniv. Filipino Paintings. Multicoloured.
1257. 5 s. Type **193** 5 5
1258. 10 s. "Afternoon Meal of the Rice Workers" (Amorsolo) 5 5
1259. 30 s. "Espana y Filipinas" (Luna) (27 × 60 mm.) .. 15 15
1260. 70 s. "The Song of Maria Clara" (Amorsolo) .. 25 25

194. Lamp, Emblem and Nurse.

1972. Philippine Nurses Assn. 50th Anniv.
1261. 194. 5 s. multicoloured .. 5 5
1262. 10 s. multicoloured .. 5 5
1263. 70 s. multicoloured .. 25 20

195. Heart on Map.

1972. World Heart Month.

1264. **195.** 5 s. red, green & violet 5 5
1265. 10 s. red, green & blue 5 5
1266. 30 s. red, blue & green 12 8

196. "The First Mass" (C. V. Francisco).

1972. 1st Mass in Limasawa (1971). 450th Anniv.

1267. **196.** 10 s. mult. (postage) 5 5
1268. **196.** 60 s. multicoloured (air) 20 15

1972. Asia Pacific Scout Conference, Manila. Various stamps surch. **ASIA PACIFIC SCOUT CONFERENCE NOV. 1972,** and value.

1269. **109.** 10 s. on 6 s. (No. 933) 5 5
1270. **116.** 10 s. on 6 s. (No. 953) 5 5
1271. – 10 s. on 6 s. (No. 981) 5 5

197. Olympic Emblems and Torch.

1972. Olympic Games, Munich.

1272. **197.** 5 s. multicoloured 5 5
1273. 10 s. multicoloured 5 5
1274. 70 s. multicoloured 25 20

1972. Philatelic Week. Nos. 950 and 983 surch. **1972 PHILATELIC WEEK** and value.

1275. **115.** 10 s. on 6 s. mult. 5 5
1276. **124.** 10 s. on 6 s. mult. 5 5

198. Manunggul Burial Jar.

1972. Philippine Archaeological Discoveries. Multicoloured.

1277. 10 s. Type **198** 5 5
1278. 10 s. Ritual earthenware vessel 5 5
1279. 10 s. Metal pot 5 5
1280. 10 s. Earthenware vessel 5 5

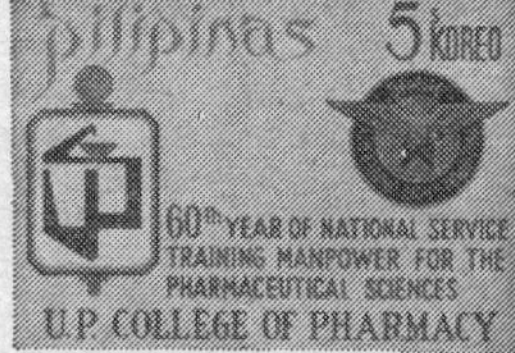

199. Emblems of Pharmacy and University of the Philippines.

1972. Nat. Training for Pharmaceutical Sciences, University of the Philippines. 60th Anniv.

1281. **199.** 5 s. multicoloured 5 5
1282. 10 s. multicoloured 5 5
1283. 30 s. multicoloured 12 12

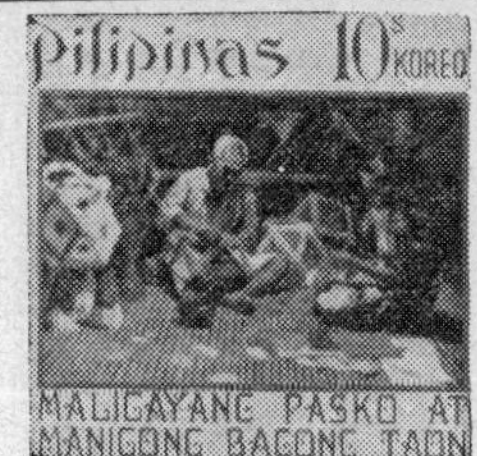

200. "The Lantern-makers" (J. Pineda).

1972. Christmas.

1284. **200.** 10 s. multicoloured 5 5
1285. 30 s. multicoloured 10 8
1286. 50 s. multicoloured 20 15

201. President Roxas and Wife.

1972. Philippines' Red Cross. 25th Anniv.

1287. **201.** 5 s. multicoloured 5 5
1288. 20 s. multicoloured 8 5
1289. 30 s. multicoloured 12 10

1973. Nos. 948 and 1005 surch.

1290. **114.** 10 s. on 6 s. mult. 5 5
1291. **130.** 10 s. on 6 s. mult. 5 5

1973. Presidential Sayings (8th Issue). As T **109**, but with portrait and saying changed.

1292. 10 s. black and yellow 5 5
1293. 30 s. black and mauve 5 5

PORTRAIT AND SAYING: 10 s., 30 s. Pres. Garcia. "I would rather be right than successful".

202. University Building.

1973. St. Louis University, Baguio City. 60th Anniv.

1294. **202.** 5 s. multicoloured 5 5
1295. 10 s. multicoloured 5 5
1296. 75 s. multicoloured 25 25

203. Col. J. Villamor and Air Battle.

1973. Villamor. Commem.

1297. **203.** 10 s. multicoloured 5 5
1298. 2 p. multicoloured 65 65

1973. Various stamps surch.

1299. **137.** 5 s. on 6 s. mult. 5 5
1300. **128.** 5 s. on 6 s. mult. 5 5
1301. **176.** 15 s. on 10 s. red & blk. 5 5

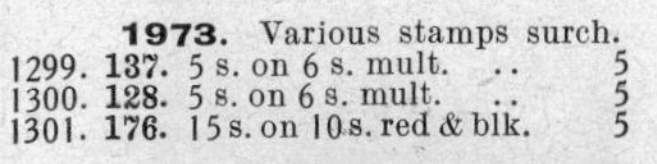

204. Actor and Stage Performance.

1973. 1st "Third-World" Theatre Festival, Manila.

1302. **204.** 5 s. multicoloured 5 5
1303. 10 s. multicoloured 5 5
1304. 50 s. multicoloured 15 12
1305. 70 s. multicoloured 20 15

1973. Pres. Marcos' Anti-Smuggling Campaign. No. 900 surch., with **HELP ME STOP SMUGGLING Pres. MARCOS** and value.

1306. 5 s. on 6 s. blue 5 5

1973. John F. Kennedy. 10th Death Anniv. No. 989 surch.

1307. 5 s. on 6 s. multicoloured 5 5

1973. Compulsory Tax Stamps. T.B. Relief Fund. Nos. 1241/2 surch.

1308. 15 s.+5 s. on 10 s.+5 s. multicoloured 5 5
1309. 60 s.+5 s. on 40 s.+5 s. multicoloured 12 8

205. Proclamation Scenes.

1973. Philippine Independence. 75th Anniv.

1310. **205.** 15 s. multicoloured 5 5
1311. 45 s. multicoloured 15 15
1312. 90 s. multicoloured 30 30

206. M. Agoncillo (maker of first national flag).

207. Sra Imelda Marcos.

1973. Perf. or imperf.

1313. – 15 s. violet 5 5
1314. **206.** 60 s. brown 20 20
1315. – 90 s. blue 25 12
1316. – 1 p. 10 blue 30 15
1317. – 1 p. 50 red 45 35
1318. – 1 p. 50 brown 45 15
1319. – 1 p. 80 green 50 50
1320. – 5 p. blue 1·40 1·40

DESIGNS: 15 s. Gabriela Silang (revolutionary). 90 s. Teodoro Yangco (businessman). 1 p. 10 Pio Valenzuela (physician). 1 p. 50 (No. 1317) Pedro Paterno (revolutionary). 1 p. 50 (No. 1318) Teodora Alonso (mother of Jose Rizal). 1 p. 80 E. Evangelista (revolutionary). 5 p. F. M. Guerrero (writer).

1973. Projects Inaugurated by Sra Imelda Marcos.

1321. **207.** 15 s. multicoloured 5 5
1322. 50 s. multicoloured 15 15
1323. 60 s. multicoloured 15 15

208. Presidential Palace, Manila.

1973. Presidential Palace, Manila.

1324. **208.** 15 s. mult. (postage) 5 5
1325. 50 s. mult. 15 15
1326. **208.** 60 s. mult. (air) 15 15

209. Interpol Emblem.

210. Scouting Activities.

1973. International Criminal Police Organisation. (Interpol). 50th Anniv.

1327. **209.** 15 s. multicoloured 5 5
1328. 65 s. multicoloured 20 15

1973. Golden Jubilee of Philippine Boy Scouts. Perf. or imperf.

1329. **210.** 15 s. brown and green 5 5
1330. – 65 s. blue and brown 20 20

DESIGN: 65 s. Scouts reading brochure.

211. Bank Emblem, Urban and Agricultural Landscapes.

1974. Central Bank of the Philippines 25th Anniv. Multicoloured.

1331. 15 s. Type **211** 5 5
1332. 60 s. Bank building, 1949 15 10
1333. 1 p. 50 Bank complex, 1974 45 25

212. "Maria Clara" Costume.

213. Map of South-East Asia.

1974. U.P.U. Cent. Philippines' Costumes. Multicoloured.

1334. 15 s. Type **212** 5 5
1335. 60 s. "Balintawak" 15 10
1336. 80 s. "Malong" 25 15

1974. Philatelic Week (1973). No. 1303 surch. **1973 PHILATELIC WEEK** and value.

1337. **204.** 15 s. on 10 s. mult. 5 5

1974. Philippine "Lionism". 25th Anniv. Nos. 1297 and 1180 surch. **PHILIPPINE LIONISM 1949-1974,** Lion emblem and value.

1338. **203.** 15 s. on 10 s. mult. 5 5
1339. – 45 s. on 40 s. red 12 8

1974. Asian Paediatrics Congress, Manila. Perf. or imperf.

1340. **213.** 30 s. red and blue 8 5
1341. 1 p. red and green 30 15

214. Gen. Valdes and Hospital.

1974. Obligatory Tax. T.B. Relief Fund. Perf. or imperf.

1342. **214.** 15 s.+5 s. grn. & red 5 5
1343. 1 p. 10+5 s. blue & red 25 25

1974. Nos. 974, 1024 and 1026 surch.

1344. **122.** 5 s. on 3 s. green 5 5
1345. **135.** 5 s. on 6 s. mult. 5 5
1346. **136.** 5 s. on 6 s. mult. 5 5

215. W.P.Y. Emblem.

1974. World Population Year. Perf. or imperf.

1347. **215.** 5 s. black and orange 5 5
1348. 2 p. blue & green 45 30

216. Red Feather Emblem.

1974. Community Chest Movement in the Philippines. 25th Anniv. Perf. or imperf.

1349. **216.** 15 s. red and blue 5 5
1350. 40 s. red and breen 10 5
1351. 45 s. red and brown 10 5

217. Sultan Mohammad Kudarat Map, Ships and Order.

1975. Sultan Kudarat of Mindanao Commem.
1352. **217.** 15 s. multicoloured .. 5 5

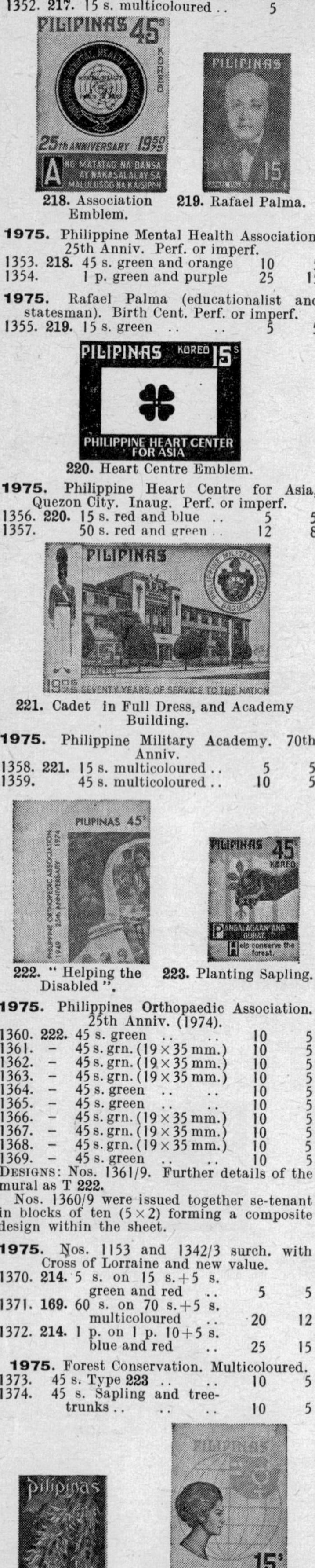

218. Association Emblem. **219.** Rafael Palma.

1975. Philippine Mental Health Association. 25th Anniv. Perf. or imperf.
1353. **218.** 45 s. green and orange 10 5
1354. 1 p. green and purple 25 15

1975. Rafael Palma (educationalist and statesman). Birth Cent. Perf. or imperf.
1355. **219.** 15 s. green 5 5

220. Heart Centre Emblem.

1975. Philippine Heart Centre for Asia, Quezon City. Inaug. Perf. or imperf.
1356. **220.** 15 s. red and blue .. 5 5
1357. 50 s. red and green .. 12 8

221. Cadet in Full Dress, and Academy Building.

1975. Philippine Military Academy. 70th Anniv.
1358. **221.** 15 s. multicoloured .. 5 5
1359. 45 s. multicoloured .. 10 5

222. " Helping the Disabled ". **223.** Planting Sapling.

1975. Philippines Orthopaedic Association. 25th Anniv. (1974).
1360. **222.** 45 s. green 10 5
1361. – 45 s. grn. (19 × 35 mm.) 10 5
1362. – 45 s. grn. (19 × 35 mm.) 10 5
1363. – 45 s. grn. (19 × 35 mm.) 10 5
1364. – 45 s. green 10 5
1365. – 45 s. green 10 5
1366. – 45 s. grn. (19 × 35 mm.) 10 5
1367. – 45 s. grn. (19 × 35 mm.) 10 5
1368. – 45 s. grn. (19 × 35 mm.) 10 5
1369. – 45 s. green 10 5
DESIGNS: Nos. 1361/9. Further details of the mural as T **222**.
Nos. 1360/9 were issued together se-tenant in blocks of ten (5 × 2) forming a composite design within the sheet.

1975. Nos. 1153 and 1342/3 surch. with Cross of Lorraine and new value.
1370. **214.** 5 s. on 15 s. + 5 s. green and red .. 5 5
1371. **169.** 60 s. on 70 s. + 5 s. multicoloured .. 20 12
1372. **214.** 1 p. on 1 p. 10 + 5 s. blue and red .. 25 15

1975. Forest Conservation. Multicoloured.
1373. 45 s. Type **223** 10 5
1374. 45 s. Sapling and tree-trunks 10 5

224. Jade Vine. **225.** Sta. Imelda Marcos and I.W.Y. Emblem.

1975.
1375. **224.** 15 s. multicoloured .. 5 5

1975. International Women's Year.
1376. **225.** 15 s. blk., bl. & deep bl. 5 5
1377. 80 s. black, blue and pink 20 12

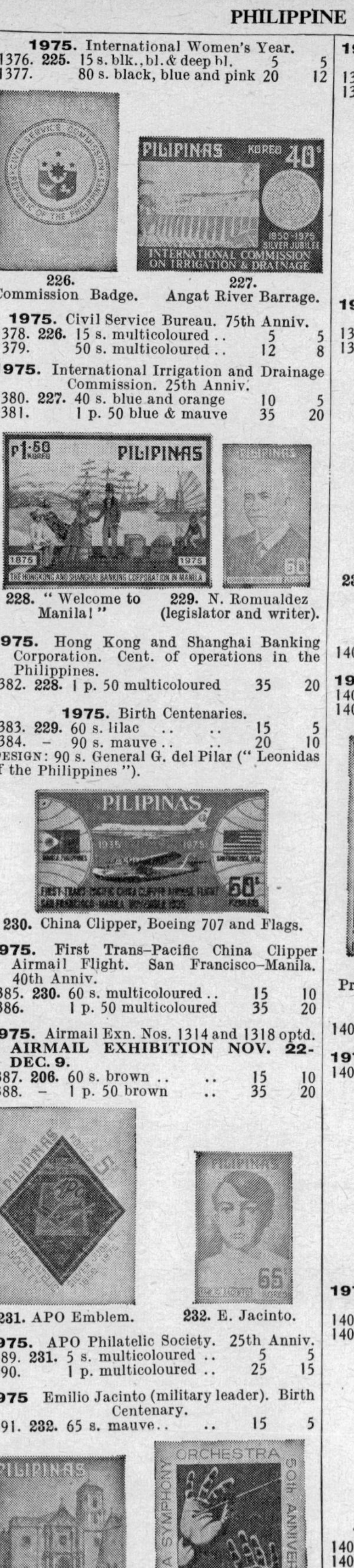

226. Commission Badge. **227.** Angat River Barrage.

1975. Civil Service Bureau. 75th Anniv.
1378. **226.** 15 s. multicoloured .. 5 5
1379. 50 s. multicoloured .. 12 8

1975. International Irrigation and Drainage Commission. 25th Anniv.
1380. **227.** 40 s. blue and orange 10 5
1381. 1 p. 50 blue & mauve 35 20

228. " Welcome to Manila! " **229.** N. Romualdez (legislator and writer).

1975. Hong Kong and Shanghai Banking Corporation. Cent. of operations in the Philippines.
1382. **228.** 1 p. 50 multicoloured 35 20

1975. Birth Centenaries.
1383. **229.** 60 s. lilac 15 5
1384. – 90 s. mauve 20 10
DESIGN: 90 s. General G. del Pilar (" Leonidas of the Philippines ").

230. China Clipper, Boeing 707 and Flags.

1975. First Trans-Pacific China Clipper Airmail Flight. San Francisco–Manila. 40th Anniv.
1385. **230.** 60 s. multicoloured .. 15 10
1386. 1 p. 50 multicoloured 35 20

1975. Airmail Exn. Nos. 1314 and 1318 optd. **AIRMAIL EXHIBITION NOV. 22-DEC. 9.**
1387. **206.** 60 s. brown 15 10
1388. – 1 p. 50 brown .. 35 20

231. APO Emblem. **232.** E. Jacinto.

1975. APO Philatelic Society. 25th Anniv.
1389. **231.** 5 s. multicoloured .. 5 5
1390. 1 p. multicoloured .. 25 15

1975 Emilio Jacinto (military leader). Birth Centenary.
1391. **232.** 65 s. mauve 15 5

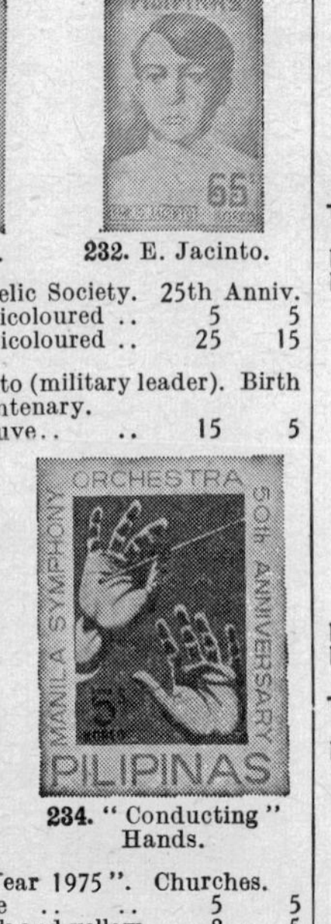

233. San Agustin Church. **234.** " Conducting " Hands.

1975. " Holy Year 1975 ". Churches.
1392. **233.** 20 s. blue 5 5
1393. – 30 s. black and yellow 8 5
1394. – 45 s. red and black .. 12 5
1395. – 60 s. brn., yell. & blk. 15 8
DESIGNS—HORIZ. 30 s. Morong Church. 45 s. Taal Basilica. VERT. 60 s. San Sebastian Church.

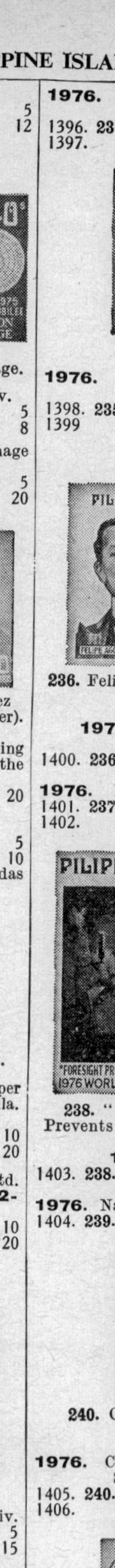

1976. Manila Symphony Orchestra. 50th Anniversary.
1396. **234.** 5 s. multicoloured .. 5 5
1397. 50 s. multicoloured .. 15 8

235. Philippines Airliners.

1976. Philippines Airlines (P.A.L.). 30th Anniversary.
1398. **235.** 60 s. multicoloured .. 20 12
1399 1 p. 50 multicoloured 55 45

236. Felipe Agoncillo. **237.** University Building.

1976. Honouring Felipe Agoncillo (statesman).
1400. **236.** 1 p. black 55

1976. National University. 75th Anniv.
1401. **237.** 45 s. multicoloured .. 15 10
1402. 60 s. multicoloured .. 20 12

238. " Foresight Prevents Blindness ". **239.** Emblem on Book.

1976. World Health Day.
1403. **238.** 15 s. multicoloured .. 5 5

1976. National Archives. 75th Anniversary.
1404. **239.** 1 p. 50 multicoloured 55 45

240. College Emblems and University Tower.

1976. Colleges of Education and Science, Saint Thomas' University.
1405. **240.** 15 s. multicoloured .. 5 5
1406. 50 s. multicoloured .. 20 12

241. College Building.

1976. Maryknoll College. 50th Anniv.
1407. **241.** 15 s. multicoloured .. 5 5
1408. 1 p. 50 multicoloured 55 45

1976. Olympic Games, Montreal. Surch. Montreal 21st Olympics, Canada.
1409. **197.** 15 s. on 10 s. multicoloured 5 5

242. Constabulary Headquarters, Manila.

1976. Philippine Constabulary. 75th Anniv
1410. **242.** 15 s. multicoloured .. 5 5
1411. 60 s. multicoloured .. 20 12

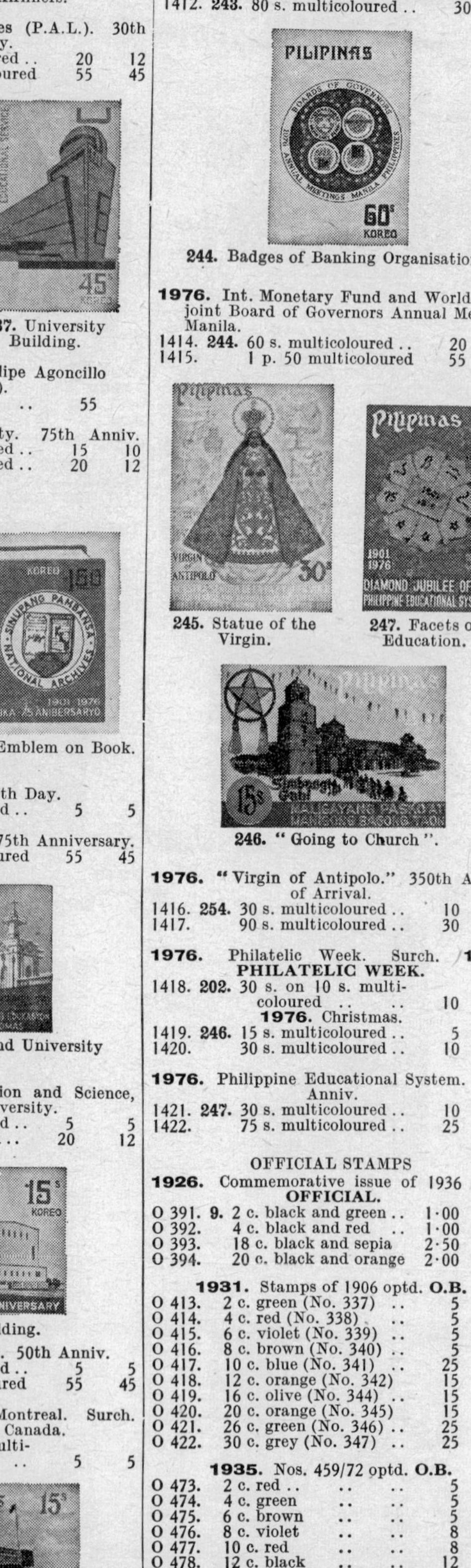

243. Land and Aerial Surveying.

1976. Lands Bureau. Diamond Jubilee.
1412. **243.** 80 s. multicoloured .. 30 20

244. Badges of Banking Organisations.

1976. Int. Monetary Fund and World Bank joint Board of Governors Annual Meeting, Manila.
1414. **244.** 60 s. multicoloured .. 20 12
1415. 1 p. 50 multicoloured 55 45

245. Statue of the Virgin. **247.** Facets of Education.

246. " Going to Church ".

1976. " Virgin of Antipolo." 350th Anniv. of Arrival.
1416. **254.** 30 s. multicoloured .. 10 5
1417. 90 s. multicoloured .. 30 20

1976. Philatelic Week. Surch. **1976 PHILATELIC WEEK.**
1418. **202.** 30 s. on 10 s. multicoloured 10 5

1976. Christmas.
1419. **246.** 15 s. multicoloured .. 5 5
1420. 30 s. multicoloured .. 10 5

1976. Philippine Educational System. 25th Anniv.
1421. **247.** 30 s. multicoloured .. 10 5
1422. 75 s. multicoloured .. 25 15

OFFICIAL STAMPS

1926. Commemorative issue of 1936 optd. **OFFICIAL.**
O 391. **9.** 2 c. black and green .. 1·00 1·00
O 392. 4 c. black and red .. 1·00 95
O 393. 18 c. black and sepia 2·50 1·90
O 394. 20 c. black and orange 2·00 1·00

1931. Stamps of 1906 optd. **O.B.**
O 413. 2 c. green (No. 337) .. 5 5
O 414. 4 c. red (No. 338) .. 5 5
O 415. 6 c. violet (No. 339) .. 5 5
O 416. 8 c. brown (No. 340) .. 5 5
O 417. 10 c. blue (No. 341) .. 25 8
O 418. 12 c. orange (No. 342) .. 15 8
O 419. 16 c. olive (No. 344) .. 15 5
O 420. 20 c. orange (No. 345) .. 15 5
O 421. 26 c. green (No. 346) .. 25 25
O 422. 30 c. grey (No. 347) .. 25 20

1935. Nos. 459/72 optd. **O.B.**
O 473. 2 c. red 5 5
O 474. 4 c. green 5 5
O 475. 6 c. brown 5 5
O 476. 8 c. violet 8 8
O 477. 10 c. red 8 5
O 478. 12 c. black 12 8
O 479. 16 c. blue 12 8
O 480. 20 c. bistre 12 8
O 481. 26 c. blue 25 20
O 482. 30 c. red 25 25

1937. Nos. 459/72 optd. **O.B. COMMONWEALTH.**

O 538.	2 c. red	5	5
O 539.	4 c. green	5	5
O 540.	6 c. brown	8	5
O 541.	8 c. violet	8	5
O 542.	10 c. red	10	5
O 543.	12 c. black	10	10
O 544.	16 c. blue	15	10
O 545.	20 c. bistre	20	20
O 546.	26 c. blue	25	25
O 547.	30 c. red	25	25

1941. Nos. 563 and 623 optd. **O.B.**

O 565. **23.**	2 c. green	5	5
O 624.	2 c. brown	5	5

1948. Various stamps optd. **O.B.**

O 738. **52.**	1 c. brown	5	5
O 668. **33.**	2 c. green	5	5
O 659. –	4 c. brown (No. 629)	8	5
O 639. –	5 c. red (No. 731) ..	8	5
O 843. –	6 c. blue (No. 842) ..	10	5
O 660. **25.**	10 c. red	15	5
O 740. –	10 c. blue (No. 732)	15	5
O 661. –	16 c. slate (No. 632)	1·00	30
O 669. –	20 c. brown (No. 633)	35	10
O 741. –	20 c. red (No. 733) ..	35	5
O 670. –	50 c. green (No. 634)	70	25

1950. Surch. **ONE CENTAVO.**

O 700. **33.**	1 c. on 2 c. grn. (No. O 668)	5	5

1959. No. 810 optd. **O.B.**

O 811.	1 c. on 5 c. red	5	5

1962. Optd. **G.O.**

O 908.	5 s. red (No. 898) ..	5	5
O 909.	6 s. chocolate (No. 899)	5	5
O 910.	6 s. blue (No. 900) ..	5	5
O 911.	10 s. purple (No. 901) ..	8	5
O 912.	20 s. blue (No. 902) ..	12	5
O 913.	30 s. red (No. 903) ..	25	8
O 914.	50 s. violet (No. 904) ..	35	15

POSTAGE DUE STAMPS

1899. Postage Due stamps of United States of 1894 optd. **PHILIPPINES.**

D 268. D **2.**	1 c. red	1·00	65
D 269.	2 c. red	1·00	65
D 270.	3 c. red	2·00	2·00
D 271.	5 c. red	1·10	95
D 272.	10 c. red	2·25	1·90
D 273.	30 c. red	32·00	21·00
D 274.	50 c. red	29·00	21·00

D 1. D 2.

1928.

D 395. D **1.**	4 c. red	8	8
D 396.	6 c. red	8	8
D 397.	8 c. red	8	8
D 398.	10 c. red	10	10
D 399.	12 c. red	12	12
D 400.	16 c. red	15	15
D 401.	20 c. red	10	10

1937. Surch. **3 CVOS. 3.**

D 521. D **1.**	3 c. on 4 c. red ..	15	8

1947.

D 644. D **2.**	3 c. red	10	10
D 645.	4 c. blue	25	25
D 646.	6 c. olive	30	30
D 647	10 c. orange	45	45

SPECIAL DELIVERY STAMPS

1901. Special Delivery stamp of United States of 1888 optd. **PHILIPPINES.**

E 268. S **1.**	10 c. blue (No. E 283)	23·00	23·00

S **1.** Messenger running.

1906.

E 353. S **1.**	20 c. blue	25	15
E 353b.	20 c. violet	25	15

1939. Optd. **COMMONWEALTH.**

E 550. S **1.**	20 c. violet	15	15

1945. Optd. **VICTORY.**

E 622. S **1.**	20 c. vio. (No. E 550)	35	35

S **2.** Cyclist Messenger and Post Office.

1947.

E 651. S **2.**	20 c. purple ..	35	25

S **3.** G.P.O. Manila and Special Delivery of Letters.

1962.

E 891. S **3.**	20 c. magenta ..	30	20

OFFICIAL SPECIAL DELIVERY STAMP

1931. No. E 353b optd. **O.B.**

EO 423.	20 c. violet	35	30

PITCAIRN ISLANDS BC

An island in the Pacific Ocean, nearly midway between Australia and America.

1968. 100 cents = 1 New Zealand dollar.

1. Lt. Bligh and the "Bounty".

1940.

1. –	½d. orange and green ..	15	20
2. –	1d. lilac and mauve ..	15	20
3. –	1½d. grey and red ..	20	25
4. **1.**	2d. green and brown ..	45	60
5. –	3d. green and blue ..	50	70
5a. –	4d. black and green ..	3·50	4·50
6. –	6d. brown and blue ..	75	90
6a. –	8d. olive and magenta ..	3·50	5·50
7. –	1s. violet and grey ..	1·00	6·60
8. –	2s. 6d. green and brown ..	2·25	3·00

DESIGNS—HORIZ. ½d. Oranges. 1d. Fletcher Christian, crew and Pitcairn Is. 1½d. John Adams and house. 3d. Map of Pitcairn Is. and Pacific. 4d. Bounty Bible. 6d. The "Bounty". 8d. School, 1949. 1s. Christian and Pitcairn Is. 2s. 6d. Christian, crew and Pitcairn Coast.

1946. Victory. As T **4** of Aden.

9.	2d. brown	15	20
10.	3d. blue	45	40

1949. Silver Wedding. As T **5/6** of Aden.

11.	1½d. red	30	35
12.	10s. mauve	16·00	22·00

1949. U.P.U. As T **14/17** of Antigua.

13.	2½d. brown	90	1·10
14.	3d. blue	80	1·60
15.	6d. green	2·25	2·75
16.	1s. purple	3·50	4·00

1953. Coronation. As T **7** of Aden.

17.	4d. black and green ..	2·00	3·00

2. Pitcairn Handicrafts.

4d. Type I is inscribed "PITCAIRN SCHOOL"; Type II is inscribed "SCHOOL-TEACHER'S HOUSE".

1957.

18. –	½d. green and mauve ..	8	8
19. –	1d. black and olive ..	15	20
20. –	2d. chocolate and blue ..	20	25
21. **2.**	2½d. chocolate & salmon	35	40
22. –	3d. emerald and blue ..	35	40
23. –	4d. red and blue (I) ..	90	1·00
23a. –	4d. red and blue (II) ..	50	65
24. –	6d. buff and indigo ..	50	65
25. –	8d. olive and lake ..	80	1·00
26. –	1s. black and brown ..	1·00	1·00
27. –	2s. green and orange ..	4·00	4·25
28. –	2s. 6d. ultram and claret	4·50	5·00

DESIGNS—HORIZ. ½d. "Cordyline terminalis". 3d. Bounty Bay. 4d. Pitcairn School. 6d. Map of Pacific. 8d. Islander and landscape. 1s. Model of the "Bounty". 2s. 6d. Launching new whaleboat. VERT. 1d. Map of Pitcairn. 2d. John Adams and Bounty Bible. 2s. Island wheelbarrow and garden scene.

3. Migrant Schooner "Mary Ann".

1961. Return of Pitcairn Islanders. Cent.

29. –	3d. black and yellow ..	50	60
30. –	6d. brown and blue ..	90	1·00
31. **3.**	1s. orange and green ..	1·75	1·90

DESIGNS: 3d. Pitcairn Is. and Simon Young. 6d. Maps of Norfolk and Pitcairn Is.

1963. Freedom from Hunger. As T **10** of Aden.

32.	2s. 6d. blue	4·00	3·50

1963. Red Cross Cent. As T **24** of Antigua.

34.	2d. red and black ..	25	25
35.	2s. 6d. red and blue ..	3·75	4·00

4. Pitcairn Is. Longboat.

5. Queen Elizabeth II.

1964. Multicoloured.

36.	½d. Type **4**	8	8
37.	1d. H.M. Armed Vessel "Bounty"	5	5
38.	2d. "Out from Bounty Bay"	5	8
39.	3d. Frigate Bird	8	8
40.	4d. Fairy Tern	8	10
41.	6d. Pitcairn Sparrow ..	10	12
42.	8d. Austin Bird	15	20
43.	10d. Bosun Birds	25	30
44.	1s. Chicken Bird ..	25	30
45.	1s. 6d. Red Breast ..	35	40
46.	2s. 6d. Ghost Bird	70	75
47.	4s. Wood Pigeon	1·00	1·25
48.	8s. Type **5**	2·25	2·50

1965. I.T.U. Cent. As T **26** of Antigua.

49.	1d mauve and chestnut ..	15	15
50.	2s. 6d. turquoise and blue	3·25	3·50

1965. I.C.Y. As T **27** of Antigua.

51.	1d. purple and turquoise	12	15
52.	1s. 6d. green and lavender	2·00	2·25

1966. Churchill Commem. As T **28** of Antigua.

53.	2d. blue	25	20
54.	3d. green	40	35
55.	6d. brown	1·25	90
56.	1s. violet	2·25	1·75

1966. World Cup Football Championships. As T **30** of Antigua.

57.	4d. violet, grn., lake & brown	15	20
58.	2s. 6d. chocolate, turquoise lake and brown ..	1·00	1·10

1966. W.H.O. Headquarters, Geneva. Inaug. As T **31** of Antigua.

59.	8d. black, green and blue ..	60	60
60.	1s. 6d. black, purple & ochre	1·25	1·25

1966. U.N.E.S.C.O. 20th Anniv As T **33/5** of Antigua.

61.	½d. violet, red, yell. & orge.	8	8
62.	10d. yellow, violet and olive	40	50
63.	2s. black, purple and orange	1·00	1·25

6. Mangarevan, c. 1325.

1976. Pitcairn Islands' Discovery. Bicent. Multicoloured.

64.	½d. Type **6**	5	5
65.	1d. P.F. de Quiros and "San Pedro y Pablo", 1606 ..	5	5
66.	8d. "San Pedro" and "Los Tres Reyes", 1606 ..	15	25
67.	1s. Carteret and H.M.S. "Swallow", 1767 ..	25	40
68.	1s. 6d. "Hercules", 1819 ..	40	60

1967 Decimal Currency. Nos. 36/48 surch. with "Bounty" anchor and value.

69. **4.**	½ c. on ½d. multicoloured ..	5	5
70. –	1 c. on 1d. multicoloured ..	8	8
71. –	2 c. on 2d. multicoloured ..	8	8
72. –	2½ c. on 3d. multicoloured	5	5
73. –	3 c. on 4d. multicoloured ..	8	10
74. –	5 c. on 6d. multicoloured	10	12
75. –	10 c. on 8d. multicoloured	20	25
76. –	15 c. on 10d. multicoloured	40	50
77. –	20 c. on 1s. multicoloured	50	70
78. –	25 c. on 1s. 6d. mult. ..	50	60
79. –	30 c. on 2s. 6d. mult. ..	75	80
80. –	40 c. on 4s. multicoloured	1·00	1·10
81. **5.**	45 c. on 8s. multicoloured	1·25	1·40

7. Bligh and "Bounty's" Launch.

1967. Admiral Bligh. 150th Death Anniv.

82. **7.**	1 c. black, ultram. & blue	5	5
83. –	8 c. black, yellow & mag.	20	25
84. –	20 c. black, brown & buff	45	50

DESIGNS: 8 c. Bligh and Followers cast adrift. 20 c. Bligh's Tomb.

8. Human Rights Emblem.

1968. Int. Human Rights Year.

85. **8.**	1 c. multicoloured ..	5	8
86.	2 c. multicoloured ..	8	12
87.	25 c. multicoloured ..	50	60

9. Miro Wood and Flower.

1968. Handicrafts.

88. **9.**	5 c. multicoloured ..	10	12
89. –	10 c. green, brown & orge.	20	25
90. –	15 c. violet, choc. & salmon	30	35
91. –	20 c. multicoloured ..	45	50

DESIGNS—HORIZ. 10 c. Flying Fish Model. VERT. 15 c. "Hand" Vases. 20 c. Woven Baskets.

10. Microscope and Slides.

1968. World Health Organisation. 20th Anniv.

92. **10.**	2 c. black, turq. & blue	5	5
93. –	20 c. black, orange & pur.	45	50

DESIGN: 20 c. Hypodermic syringe and jars of tablets.

11. Pitcairn Island.

12. Queen Elizabeth II.

1969. Multicoloured.

94.	1 c. Type **11**	10	10
95.	2 c. Captain Bligh and "Bounty" Chronometer	5	5
96.	3 c. "Bounty" Anchor ..	5	5

97. 4 c. Plans and drawing of "Bounty" 5 5
98. 5 c. Breadfruit containers and plant 5 5
99. 6 c. Bounty Bay 5 5
100. 8 c. Pitcairn Longboat .. 8 8
101a. 10 c. Ship Landing Point .. 8 10
102. 15 c. Fletcher Christian's Cave 15 15
103. 20 c. Thursday October Christian's house .. 20 20
104. 25 c. "Flying Fox" cable system 25 25
105. 30 c. Radio Station, Taro Ground 30 35
106. 40 c. "Bounty" Bible .. 35 40
106a. 50 c. Pitcairn Coat-of-Arms 45 50
106b. $1 Type 12 .. .. 90 1·00
The 3 c. and 25 c. are vert.

13. Lantana.

1970. Flowers. Multicoloured.
107. 1 c. Type **13** 5 5
108. 2 c. "Indian Shot" .. 5 8
109. 5 c. Pulau 15 20
110. 25 c. Wild Gladiolus .. 95 1·00

14. Auntie and Ann (grouper).

1970. Fishes. Multicoloured.
111. 5 c. Type **14** .. 12 12
112. 10 c. Dream Fish (rudder fish) 25 30
113. 15 c. Elwyn's Trousers (wrasse) 35 40
114. 20 c. Whistling Daughter (wrasse) .. 50 55

1971. Royal Visit. No. 101 optd **"ROYAL VISIT 1971".**
115. 10 c. multicoloured .. 3·50 3·75

15. Polynesian Rock Carvings.

1971. Polynesian Pitcairn. Multicoloured.
116. 5 c. Type **15** .. 10 10
117. 10 c. Polynesian artifacts (horiz.) 25 30
118. 15 c. Polynesian stone fish-hook (horiz.) 35 40
119. 20 c. Polynesian stone deity 50 55

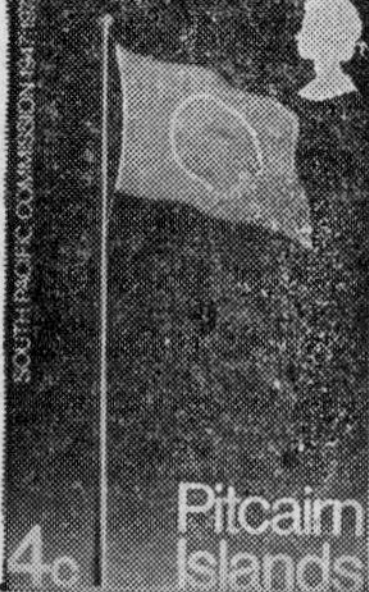

16. Commission Flag. **17.** Rose-apple.

1972. South Pacific Commission. 25th Anniv. Multicoloured.
120. 4 c. Type **16** 10 10
121. 8 c. Young and Elderly (Health) 20 20
122. 18 c. Junior School (Education) 35 40
123. 20 c. Goods Store (Economy) 40 45

1972. Royal Silver Wedding. As T **19** of Ascension but with Bosun Birds and Longboat in background.
124. 4 c. green 20 20
125. 20 c. blue .. .. .. 1·75 1·50

1973. Flowers. Multicoloured.
126. 4 c. Type **17** 8 8
127. 8 c. Mountain-apple .. 20 20
128. 15 c. "Lata" 30 30
129. 20 c. "Dorcas-flower" .. 40 40
130. 35 c. Guava 70 70

1973. Royal Wedding. As T **26** of Anguilla. Multicoloured. Background colours given.
131. 10 c. mauve 20 20
132. 25 c. green 50 60

18. Horn-shells and Mitres.

1974. Shells. Multicoloured.
147. 4 c. Type **18** 8 8
148. 10 c. Dove-shell 20 20
149. 18 c. Limpet and False Limpet 35 35
150. 50 c. Lucine shell .. .. 1·00 1·00

19. Island Post Office.

1974. U.P.U. Centenary.
152. **19.** 4 c. multicoloured .. 8 8
153. – 20 c. pur., brn. & blk. 35 40
154. – 35 c. multicoloured .. 65 70
DESIGNS: 20 c. Pre-stamp letter, 1922. 35 c. Mailship and Pitcairn Longboat.

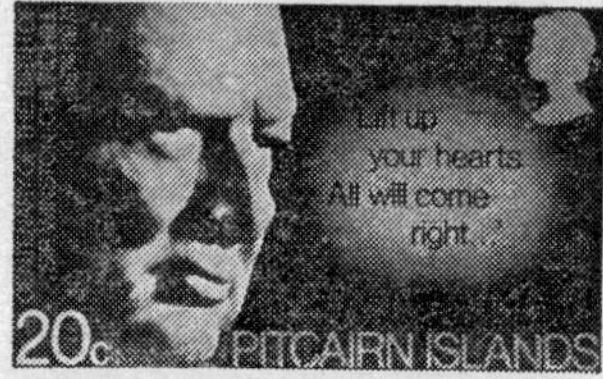

20. Churchill and Text "Lift up your Hearts . . .".

1974. Sir Winston Churchill. Birth Cent.
155. **20.** 20 c. ol., grn. and grey 35 40
156. – 35 c. brn., grn. and grey 55 60
DESIGN: 35 c. Text "Give us the tools . . .".

21. H.M.S. "Seringapatam", 1830.

1975. Mailboats. Multicoloured.
157. 4 c. Type **21** 8 8
158. 10 c. The "Pitcairn", 1890 15 15
159. 18 c. R.M.S. "Athenic", 1904 .. .. 30 30
160. 50 c. S.S. "Gothic", 1948 70 75

22. Pitcairn Wasp.

1975. Pitcairn Insects. Multicoloured.
162. 4 c. Type **22** 5 5
163. 6 c. Grasshopper 10 10
164. 10 c. Moths 15 15
165. 15 c. Devil's Needle .. 20 25
166. 20 c. Banana Moth .. 30 35

23. Fletcher Christian.

1976. American Revolution. Bicent. Mult.
167. 5 c. Type **23** 8 8
168. 10 c. H.M.S. "Bounty" .. 12 12
169. 30 c. George Washington 35 40
170. 50 c. "Mayflower" .. 55 60

24. Chair of Homage.

1977. Silver Jubilee. Multicoloured.
171. 8 c. Prince Philip's visit, 1971 .. .. 8 10
172. 20 c. Type **24** 20 25
173. 50 c. Enthronement .. 55 65

POLAND E2

A country lying between Russia and Germany, originally independent, but divided between Prussia, Austria and Russia in 1772/95. An independent republic since 1918. Occupied by Germany from 1939 to 1945.

1860. 100 kopecks = 1 rouble.
1918. 100 pfennige = 1 mark.
100 halerze = 1 krone.
100 fenigi = 1 mark.
1924. 100 groszy = 1 zloty.

1. Russian Arms. **2.** Statue of Sigismund III.

1860.
1b. **1.** 10 k. blue and red .. £120 40·00

1918. Surch. **POCZTA POLSKA** and value in fen. as in T **2**.
2. **2.** 5 f. on 2 g. brown .. 15 15
3. – 10 f. on 6 g. green .. 8 8
4. – 25 f. on 10 g. red .. 15 15
5. – 50 f. on 20 g. blue .. 35 35
DESIGNS: 6 g. Arms of Warsaw. 10 g. Polish eagle. 20 g. Sobieski Monument.

1918. Stamps of German Occupation of Poland optd. **Poczta Polska** or surch. also.
9. **8.** 3 pf. brown .. .. 3·25 2·40
10. 5 pf. green 5 5
6. **13.** 5 on 2½ pf. grey .. 5 5
7. **8.** 5 on 3 pf. brown .. 70 60
11. 10 pf. red 5 5
12. **13.** 15 pf. violet 5 5
13. **8.** 20 pf. blue 5 5
8. **13.** 25 on 7½ pf. orange .. 8 5
14. **8.** 30 pf. blk. & oran. on buff 5 5
15. 40 pf. black and red .. 12 12
16. 60 pf. purple .. 12 12

1918. Stamps of Austro-Hungarian Military Post (Nos. 69/71) optd. **POLSKA POCZTA** and Polish eagle.
17. 10 h. green .. .. 1·10 1·10
18. 20 h. claret 90 90
19. 45 h. blue 90 90

1918. As stamps of Austro-Hungarian Military Post of 1917 optd. **POLSKA POCZTA** and Polish eagle and (some) surch. also.
20. 3 h. on 3 h. olive .. 3·50 2·75
21. 3 h. on 15 h. red .. 70 70
22. 10 h. on 30 h. green .. 60 60
23. 25 h. on 40 h. olive .. 90 55
24. 45 h. on 60 h. red .. 70 70
25. 45 h. on 80 h. blue .. 1·75 1·75
28. 50 h. green .. .. 3·50 2·25
26. 50 h. on 60 h. red .. 90 90
29. 90 h. violet 90 70

1919. Stamps of Austria optd. **POCZTA POLSKA,** the 80 h. also surch. **25.**
30. **26.** 3 h. violet .. 35·00 32·00
31. 5 h. green .. .. 35·00 32·00
32. 6 h. orange .. .. 2·25 2·25
33. 10 h. claret .. .. 35·00 32·00
34. 12 h. blue .. .. 2·75 2·75
35. **30.** 15 h. red 90 90
36. 20 h. green .. .. 12·00 12·00
37. 25 h. blue £180 £140
49. **28.** 25 on 80 h. brown .. 55 55
38. **30.** 30 h. violet .. .. 27·00 27·00
39. **28.** 40 h. olive .. .. 1·00 1·00
40. 50 h. green 70 70
41. 60 h. blue 60 60
42. 80 h. brown 55 55
43. 90 h. claret £140 £140
44. 1 k. red on yellow .. 70 70
45. **29.** 2 k. blue 70 70
46. 3 k. red .. .. 8·00 8·00
47. 4 k. green .. .. 15·00 15·00
48a. 10 k. violet £1000 £1100

6. **7.** **8.** Agriculture.

9. Ploughing in peace. **10.** Polish Uhlan.

1919. For Northern Poland. Imperf. or perf.
92. **6.** 3 f. brown 5 5
93. 5 f. green 5 5
179. 5 f. blue 5 5
94. 10 f. purple 5 5
180. 10 f. mauve 5 5
95. 15 f. red 5 5
96. **7.** 20 f. blue 5 5
181. 20 f. red 5 5
97. 25 f. olive 5 5
110. 50 f. green 5 5
183. 50 f. orange 5 5
137. **8.** 1 m. violet 5 5
112. 1 m. 50 green 5 5
113. 2 m. brown 5 5
114. **9.** 2 m. 50 brown 5 5
139. 3 m. brown 5 5
140. **10.** 5 m. purple 5 5
141. 6 m. red 5 5
142. 10 m. red 5 5
143. 20 m. green 5 5

1919. 1st Polish Philatelic Exn. and Polish White Cross Fund. Surch. **1 POLSKA WYSTAWA MAREK,** cross and new value. Imperf. or perf.
116. **6.** 5+5 f. green 5 5
117. 10+5 f. purple 5 5
118. 15+5 f. red 5 5
119. **7.** 25+5 f. olive 5 5
120. 50+5 f. green 5 5

1919. For Southern Poland. Value in "halerzy" or "kronen". Imperf. or perf.
68. **6.** 3 h. brown 5 5
69. 5 h. green 5 5
70. 10 h. orange 5 5
71. 15 h. red 5 5
72. **7.** 20 h. brown 5 5
85. 2 h. blue 5 5
86. 50 h. brown 5 5
87. **8.** 1 k. green 5 5
88. 1 k. 50 brown 5 5
89. 2 k. blue 5 5
90. **9.** 2 k. 50 purple 5 5
91. **10.** 5 k. blue 5 5

11.

ILLUSTRATIONS British Commonwealth and all overprints and surcharges are FULL SIZE. Foreign Countries have been reduced to ¾-LINEAR.

1919. Imperf.

50. **11.** 2 h. grey 5 5
51. 3 h. violet 5 5
52. 5 h. green 5 5
53. 6 h. orange .. .. 2·25 2·25
54. 10 h. red 5 5
55. 15 h. brown 5 5
56. 20 h. olive 5 5
57. 25 h. red 5 5
58. 50 h. blue 5 5
59. 70 h. blue 5 5
60. 1 k. red and grey .. 8 8

12.

13. Prime Minister Paderewski.

15. Gen. Pilsudski.

14. A. Trampczynski.

16. Eagle and Ship

18.

1919. 1st Session of Parliament in Liberated Poland. Dated "1919".

121. **12.** 10 f. mauve 5 5
122. **13.** 15 f. red 5 5
123. **14.** 20 f. brown 8 5
125. **15.** 25 f. green 8 8
126. **16.** 50 f. blue 5 5
127. – 1 m. violet 5 5

DESIGN—As T **16**: 1 m. Griffin and fasces.

1920. As T **14**, but smaller (17×20 mm.).

124. **14.** 20 f. brown 5 5

1920.

146. **18.** 40 f. violet 5 5
182. 40 f. brown 5 5
184. 75 f. green 5 5

1920. As T **6**, but value in marks ("Mk").

147. **6.** 1 m. red 5 5
148. 2 m. green 5 5
149. 3 m. blue 5 5
150. 4 m. red 5 5
151. 5 m. purple 5 5
152. 8 m. brown 5 5

1921. Surch. **3 Mk.** and bars.

153. **18.** 3 m. on 40 f. violet .. 5 5

19.
"Peace with Russia".

20.

1921.

165. **19.** 10 m. green 5 5
166. 15 m. brown 5 5
167. 20 m. red 5 5
170. **20.** 25 m. violet and buff .. 5 5
171. 50 m. red and buff .. 5 5
172. 100 m. brown & orange 5 5
173. 200 m. pink and black 5 5
174. 300 m. green 5 5
175. 400 m. brown 5 5
176. 500 m. purple 5 5
177. 1000 m. orange 5 5
178. 2000 m. violet 5 5

1921. Red Cross Surch. with cross and **30 MK.**

154. **10.** 5 m.+30 m. purple .. 60 60
155. 6 m.+30 m. red .. 60 60
156. 10 m.+30 m. red .. 1·00 1·00
157. 20 m.+30 m. green .. 2·25 2·25

21. Sun of Peace.

22. Agriculture.

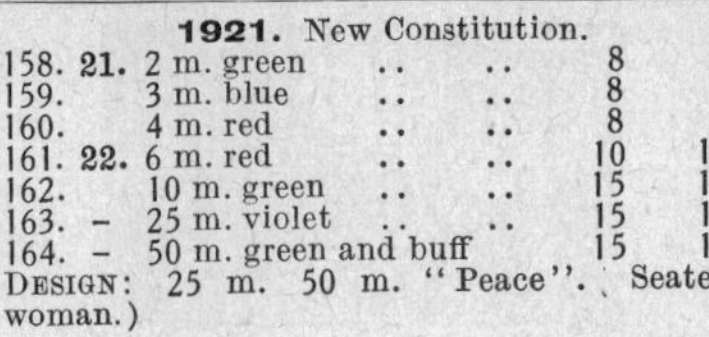

1921. New Constitution.

158. **21.** 2 m. green 8 8
159. 3 m. blue 8 8
160. 4 m. red 8 8
161. **22.** 6 m. red 10 10
162. 10 m. green 15 10
163. – 25 m. violet 15 15
164. – 50 m. green and buff 15 15

DESIGN: 25 m. 50 m. "Peace". Seated woman.)

ILLUSTRATIONS British Commonwealth and all overprints and surcharges are FULL SIZE. Foreign Countries have been reduced to ¾-LINEAR.

24. Silesian Miner.

1922.

185. **24.** 1 m. black 5 5
186. 1 m. 25 green 5 5
187. 2 m. red 5 5
188. 3 m. green 5 5
189. 4 m. blue 5 5
190. 5 m. brown 5 5
191. 6 m. orange 5 5
192. 10 m. brown 5 5
193. 20 m. purple 5 5
194. 50 m. olive 5 8
195. 80 m. red 5 15
196. 100 m. violet 5 15
197. 200 m. orange 5 25
198. 300 m. blue 5 45

25. Copernicus.

27.

1923. Copernicus (astronomer). 450th Birth Anniv. and Konarski (theologian). 150th Death Anniv.

199. **25.** 1,000 m. slate .. 25 10
200. – 3,000 m. brown .. 25 10
201. **25.** 5,000 m. red .. 20 10

DESIGN: 3,000 m. Konarski.

1923. Surch.

202. **20.** 10,000 m. on 25 m. violet and buff 5 5
206. **6.** 20,000 m. on 2 m. green (No. 148) 5 5
204. **19.** 25,000 m. on 20 m. red 5 5
205 50,000 m. on 10 m. grn. 5 5
207. **6.** 100,000 m. on 5 m. purple (No. 151) 5 5

1924.

208. **27.** 10,000 m. purple .. 8 10
209. 20,000 m. green .. 5 5
210. 30,000 m. red 5 5
211. 50,000 m. green .. 8 5
212. 100,000 m. brown .. 5 5
213. 200,000 m. blue .. 5 5
214. 300,000 m. magenta .. 5 5
215. 500,000 m. brown .. 5 15
216. 1,000,000 m. pink .. 10 35
217. 2,000,000 m. green .. 20 60

28.

29. President Wojciechowski.

30.

1924. New Currency.

218. **28.** 1 g. brown 8 5
219. 2 g. brown 12 5
220. 3 g. orange 12 5
221. 5 g. green 15 5
222. 10 g. green 25 5
223. 15 g. red 25 5
224. 20 g. blue 45 5
225. 25 g. claret 45 5
226. 30 g. violet 60 8
227. 40 g. blue 90 8
228. 50 g. purple .. .. 1·10 5
229. **29.** 1 z. red .. .. 1·75 12

1925. National Fund.

230. **30.** 1 g.+50 g. brown .. 3·25 3·25
231. 2 g.+50 g. brown .. 3·25 3·25
232. 3 g.+50 g. orange .. 3·25 3·25
233. 5 g.+50 g. green .. 3·25 3·25
234. 10 g.+50 g. green .. 3·25 3·25
235. 15 g.+50 g. red .. 3·25 3·25
236. 20 g.+50 g. blue .. 3·25 3·25
237. 25 g.+50 g. claret .. 3·25 3·25
238. 30 g.+50 g. violet .. 3·25 3·25
239. 40 g.+50 g. blue .. 3·25 3·25
240. 50 g.+50 g. purple .. 3·25 3·25

31. Holy Gate, Vilna.

32. Town Hall, Poznan.

33. Ship.

1925.

241. **31.** 1 g. brown 5 5
242. – 2 g. olive 8 5
243a. – 3 g. blue 15 5
244a. **32.** 5 g. green 25 5
245a. – 10 g. violet 12 5
246. – 15 g. red 25 5
247. **33.** 20 g. red 40 5
248. **31.** 24 g. blue 90 8
249. – 30 g. blue 80 5
250. – 40 g. blue 90 5
251. **33.** 45 g. mauve .. .. 1·25 5

DESIGNS—VERT. As T **31**: 2 g., 30 g. Sobieski Statue, Lwow. As T **32**: 3 g., 10 g. King Sigismund Monument, Warsaw. HORIZ. 15 g. 40 g. Wawel Castle, Cracow.

34.

35. Chopin.

1925. Air.

252. **34.** 1 g. blue 20 25
253. 2 g. orange 20 25
254. 3 g. brown 20 25
255. 5 g. brown 20 25
256. 10 g. green 45 25
257. 15 g. magenta 60 35
258. 20 g. olive .. .. 2·50 1·10
259. 30 g. red .. .. 1·75 90
260. 45 g. lilac .. .. 2·75 1·75

1927.

261. **35.** 40 g. blue .. .. 3·50 35

36. Pilsudski.

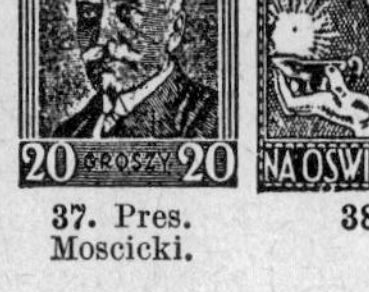
37. Pres. Moscicki.

38.

1927.

262. **36.** 20 g. red 35 5
262a. 25 g. brown 45 5

1927.

263. **37.** 20 g. red 60 5

1927. Educational Funds.

264. **38.** 10 g.+5 g. pur. on grn. 1·00 70
265. 20 g.+5 g. blue on yell. 1·00 70

39. Dr. Karl Kaczkowski.

40. J. Slowacki, poet.

1927. 4th Int. Military Medical Congress, Warsaw.

266. **39.** 10 g. green 45 12
267. 25 g. red 90 25
268. 40 g. blue 90 20

1927. Transfer of Slowacki's remains to Cracow.

269. **40.** 20 g. claret 60 5

41. Pilsudski.

42. Pres. Moscicki.

43. Gen. Joseph Bem.

1928.

272. **41.** 50 g. slate 90 5
272a. 50 g. green .. .. 1·25 5
273. **42.** 1 z. black on cream .. 1·40 5

In 1928 to commem. the Warsaw Philatelic Exn. a miniature sheet consisting of two stamps, one of each value (50 g. and 1 z. sepia) was issued. (Price per sheet un. or us. £35.)

In 1937 to commemorate the visit of King Charles II of Rumania to Poland miniature sheets each consisting of blocks of 4 of T **60**, 25 g. brown, T **41**, 50 g. slate and T **42**, 1 z. black, were issued with arms and special inscriptions in the sheet margins. Price per sheet un. £1·75; us. £1·60.

1928.

271. **43.** 25 g. red 55 5

44. H. Sienkiewicz.

45. Slav God, "Swiatowit".

1928. Henryk Sienkiewicz (author).

274. **44.** 15 g. blue 55 5

1929. National Exn., Poznan.

275. **45.** 25 g. brown 45 5

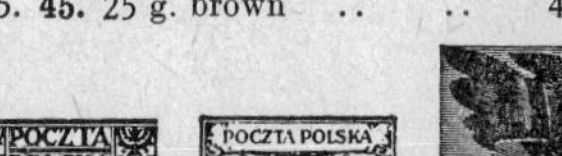

46.

47. King John Sobieski.

48.

1929.

276. **46.** 5 g. violet 5 5
277. 10 g. green 8 5
278. 25 g. brown 10 5

1930. John III Sobieski. Birth Tercent.

279. **47.** 75 g. purple .. .. 1·10 5

1930. Cent. of "November Rising" (29th Nov., 1830).

280. **48.** 5 g. purple 8 5
281. 15 g. blue 15 5
282. 25 g. lake 25 5
283. 30 g. red .. .. 1·60 55

49. Kosciuszko, Washington and Pulaski.

50.

1932. George Washington. Birth Bicent.

284. **49.** 30 g. brown on cream .. 60 5

1932.

284a. **50.** 5 g. violet 5 5
285. 10 g. green 5 5
285a. 15 g. claret 5 5
286. 20 g. grey 12 5
287. 25 g. bistre 15 5
288. 30 g. red 45 5
289. 60 g. blue .. .. 4·50 5

51. Town Hall, Torun.

52. Fr. Zwirko (airman) and St. Wigura (aircraft designer).

1933. 7th Cent. of Torun.

290. **51.** 60 g. blue on cream .. 2·75 12

1933. Torun Philatelic Exn.

293. **51.** 60 g. red on cream .. 2·75 2·75

1933. Victory in Flight round Europe Air Race, 1932.

292. **52.** 30 g. green .. .. 2·75 20

53. Altar-piece carved by Vit Stvosz.

1933. Vit Stvosz. 4th Death Cent.

294. **53.** 80 g. brown on cream .. 3·50 35

54. "Liberation of Vienna".

1933. Relief of Vienna. 250th Anniv.
295. 54. 1 z. 20 blue on cream .. 3·50 1·10

55. Cross of Independence. 56. Marshal Pilsudski and Legion of Fusiliers Badge.

1933. Republic. 15th Anniv.
296. 55. 30 g. red .. .. 1·75 8

1934. Katowice Philatelic Exn. Optd. **Wyst. Filat. 1934 Katowice.**
297. 50. 20 g. grey .. .. 7·00 4·50
298. 30 g. red .. .. 7·00 4·50

1934. Polish Legion. 20th Anniv.
299. 56. 25 g. blue 25 8
300. 30 g. brown 45 5

1934. Int. Air Tournament. Optd. **Challenge 1934.**
301. 34. 20 g. olive .. 3·50 1·40
302. 52. 30 g. green .. 1·75 55

1934. Surch. in figures.
303. 53 25 g. on 80 g. brown on cream .. 1·10 12
304. 50. 55 g. on 60 g. blue .. 2·10 8
305. 54. 1 z. on 1 z. 20 blue on cream .. .. 2·75 90

57. Marshal Pilsudski.

1935. Mourning Issue.
306. 57. 5 g. black 25 5
307. 15 g. black 35 5
308. 25 g. black 60 5
309. 45 g. black 90 25
310. 1 z. black .. .. 2·40 1·10

1935. Optd. **Kopiec Marszalka Pilsudskiego.**
311. 50. 15 g. claret 25 25
312. 56. 25 g. blue 60 15

58. "Dogs' Rock". 59. Pres. Moscicki.

1935.
313. 58. 5 g. violet 8 5
317. – 5 g. violet 8 5
314. – 10 g. green 10 5
318. – 10 g. green 15 5
315. – 15 g. blue 15 5
319. – 15 g. red 70 5
316. – 20 g. black 25 5
320. – 20 g. orange 35 5
321a.– 25 g. green 35 5
322. – 30 g. red 45 5
323a.– 45 g. mauve 70 5
324a.– 50 g. black 90 5
325. – 55 g. blue .. 3·25 5
326. – 1 z. brown .. 1·50 15
327. 59. 3 z. brown 60 70

DESIGNS: 5 g. (No. 317) Cloister, Czestochowa. 10 g. (314) Lake Morskie Oko. 10 g. (318) Docks, Gydnia. 15 g. (315) M./S. "Pilsudski". 15 g. (319) University, Lwow. 20 g. (316) Pieniny-Czorsztyn. 20 g. (320) Administrative Buildings, Katowice. 25 g. Belvedere Palace, Warsaw. 30 g. Castle at Mir. 45 g. Castle at Podhorce. 50 g. Cloth Hall, Cracow. 55 g. Raczynski Library, Poznan. 1 z. Vilna Cathedral.

1936. Moscicki Presidency. 10th Anniv. As T 42, but inscr. "1926. 3. VI. 1936" below design.
328. 42. 1 z. blue .. .. 1·40 55

1936. Gordon-Bennett Balloon Race. Optd. **GORDON-BENNETT 30. VIII. 1936.**
329. 30 g. red (No. 322) .. 3·50 1·75
330. 55 g. blue (No. 325) .. 3·50 1·75

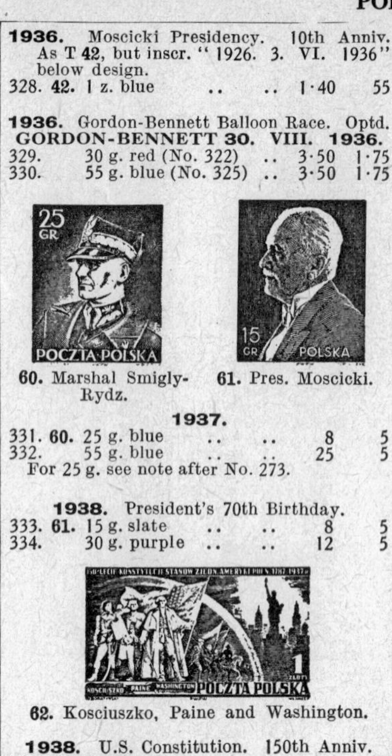

60. Marshal Smigly-Rydz. 61. Pres. Moscicki.

1937.
331. 60. 25 g. blue 8 5
332. 55 g. blue 25 5
For 25 g. see note after No. 273.

1938. President's 70th Birthday.
333. 61. 15 g. slate 8 5
334. 30 g. purple 12 5

62. Kosciuszko, Paine and Washington.

1938. U.S. Constitution. 150th Anniv.
335. 62. 1 z. blue 60 55

63. Wladislaw Jagiello and Jadwiga. 64. Marshal Pilsudski.

1938. Independence. 20th Anniv.
336. – 5 g. orange 5 5
337. – 10 g. green 5 5
338. 63. 15 g. brown (A) .. 8 10
357. 15 g. brown (B) .. 10 5
339. – 20 g. blue 5 5
340. – 25 g. purple 5 5
341. – 30 g. red 12 5
342. – 45 g. black 25 8
343. – 50 g. mauve 15 5
344. – 55 g. blue 15 5
345. – 75 g. green 90 60
346. – 1 z. orange 80 55
347. – 2 z. red .. .. 3·50 1·75
348. 64. 3 z. blue .. .. 3·25 1·75

DESIGNS—VERT. 5 g. Boleslaw the Brave. 10 g. Casimir the Great. 20 g. Casimir Jagellon. 25 g. Sigismund August. 30 g. Stephen Bathory. 45 g. Chodkiewicz and Zolkiewski. 50 g. John III Sobieski. 55 g. Symbol of Constitution of May 3rd, 1791. 75 g. Kosciuszko, Poniatowski and Dabrowski. 1 z. November Uprising, 1830–31. 2 z. Romuald Traugutt.
(A) T 63. (B) as T 63 but crossed swords omitted.

65. Teschen comes to Poland. 66. "Warmth".

1938. Acquisition of Teschen.
349. 65. 25 g. purple 35 8

1938. Winter Relief Fund.
350. 66. 5 g.+5 g. orange .. 12 12
351. 25 g.+10 g. purple .. 35 35
352. 55 g.+15 g. blue .. 55 55

67. Polish Skier.

1939. Int. Ski Championship Zakopane.
353. 67. 15 g. brown 25 8
354. 25 g. purple 35 15
355. 30 g. red 70 35
356. 55 g. blue .. 1·75 90

68. Pilsudski and Polish Legionaries.

1939. 1st Battles of Polish Legions. 25th Anniv.
358. 68. 25 g. purple 35 12

1939-1945. GERMAN OCCUPATION

1939. T 53 of Germany surch. **Deutsche Post OSTEN** and value.
359. 53. 6 g. on 3 pf. brown .. 10 12
360. 8 g. on 4 pf. slate .. 12 15
361. 12 g. on 6 pf. green .. 10 12
362. 16 g. on 8 pf. orange .. 15 20
363. 20 g. on 10 pf. chocolate 10 12
364. 24 g. on 12 pf. red .. 10 10
365. 30 g. on 15 pf. claret .. 15 15
366. 40 g. on 20 pf. blue .. 12 12
367. 50 g. on 25 pf. blue .. 12 15
368. 60 g. on 30 pf. olive .. 12 12
369. 80 g. on 40 pf. mauve .. 20 20
370. 1 z. on 50 pf. blk. & grn. 30 40
371. 2 z. on 100 pf. blk. & yell. 70 80

1940. Surch. **General Gouvernement** and Nazi emblem and value.
372. – 2 g. on 5 g. orge. (No. 336) 5 5
373. – 4 g. on 5 g. orge. (No. 336) 5 5
374. – 6 g. on 10 g. grn. (No. 337) 5 5
375. – 8 g. on 10 g. grn. (No. 337) 5 5
376. – 10 g. on 10 g. green (No. 337) 5 5
377. 63. 12 g. on 15 g. brown (No. 338) 5 5
378. 16 g. on 15 g. brown (No. 338) 5 5
379. 60. 24 g. on 25 g. blue .. 10 10
380. – 24 g. on 25 g. purple (No. 340) 5 5
381. – 30 g. on 30 g. red (No. 341) 5 5
382. 66. 30 g. on 5 g.+5 g. orange 5 5
383. 61. 40 g. on 30 g. purple .. 12 12
384. 66. 40 g. on 25 g.+10 g. pur. 5 5
385. – 50 g. on 50 g. mauve (No. 343) 5 5
386. 60. 50 g. on 55 g. blue .. 5 5
386a. D4 50 g. on 20 g. green .. 15 15
386b 50 g. on 25 g. green .. 1·25 1·25
386c. 50 g. on 30 g. green .. 5·00 5·00
386d. 50 g. on 50 g. green .. 15 15
386e. 50 g. on 1 z. green .. 15 15
387. – 60 g. on 55 g. blue (No. 344) .. .. .. 1·25 1·25
388. – 80 g. on 75 g. green (No. 345) .. .. 1·25 1·25
388a. 66. 1 z. on 55 g.+15 g. blue 1·25 1·25
389. – 1 z. on 1 z. orge. (No. 346) 1·25 1·25
390. – 2 z. on 2 z. red (No. 347) 25 25
391. 64. 3 z. on 3 z. blue .. 40 40
Nos. 386a/e are all postage stamps.

69. Copernicus Memorial, Cracow. 70.

1940.
392. – 6 g. brown 12 15
393. – 8 g. brown 12 15
394. – 8 g. black 8 12
395. – 10 g. green 10 10
396. 69. 12 g. green 12 10
397. 12 g. violet 5 5
398. – 20 g. brown 5 5
399. – 24 g. red 5 5
400. – 30 g. violet 5 5
401. – 30 g. purple 5 5
402. – 40 g. black 5 5
403. – 48 g. brown 5 10
404. – 50 g. blue 5 5
405. – 60 g. olive 12 20
406. – 80 g. violet 5 5
407. – 1 z. purple 55 25
408. – 1 z. green 15 10

DESIGNS: 6 g. Florian Gate, Cracow. 8 g. Castle Keep, Cracow. 10 g. Cracow Gate, Lublin. 20 g. Church of the Dominicans, Cracow. 24 g. Cracow Castle. 30 g. Old Church in Lublin. 40 g. Arcade, Cloth Hall, Cracow. 48 g. Townhall, Sandomir. 50 g. Townhall, Cracow. 60 g. Cracow Castle. 80 g. Notre Dame Church, Cracow. 1 z. Palace, Warsaw.

1940. Red Cross Fund. As last, new colours, surch. with Cross and premium in figures.
409. 12 g.+8 g. olive 10 12
410. 24 g.+16 g. olive .. 12 15
411. 50 g.+50 g. olive .. 30 45
412. 80 g.+80 g. olive .. 45 55

1940. German Occupation. 1st Anniv.
413. 70. 12 g.+38 g. green .. 20 25
414. – 24 g.+26 g. red .. 20 25
415. – 30 g.+20 g. violet .. 30 40
DESIGNS: 24 g. Woman with scarf. 30 g. Fur-capped peasant as T 71.

71. 72. The Rotunda, Cracow.

1940. Winter Relief Fund.
416. 71. 12 g.+8 g. green .. 10 12
417. 24 g.+16 g. red .. 12 15
418. 30 g.+30 g. brown .. 20 20
419. 50 g.+50 g. blue .. 30 40

1941.
421. 72. 2 z. blue 8 8
422. – 4 z. green 12 15
DESIGN: 4 z. Tyniec Monastery.
See also Nos. 456/9.

73. Cracow. 74. Adolf Hitler.

1941.
420. 73 10 z. grey and red .. 40 45

1941.
423. 74. 2 g. grey 5 5
424. 6 g. brown 5 5
425. 8 g. blue 5 5
426. 10 g. green 5 5
427. 12 g. violet 5 5
428. 16 g. orange 5 8
429. 20 g. brown 5 5
430. 24 g. red 5 5
431. 30 g. purple 5 5
432. 32 g. green 5 8
433. 40 g. blue 5 5
434. 48 g. brown 5 8
435. 50 g. blue 5 5
436. 60 g. olive 5 5
437. 80 g. purple 5 5
441. 1 z. green 8 8
442. 1 z. 20 brown 8 8
443. 1 z. 60 blue 8 8

1942. Hitler's 53rd Birthday. As T 74, but premium inserted in design.
444. 30 g.+1 z. purple .. 5 8
445. 50 g.+1 z. blue .. 5 8
446. 1 z. 20+1 z. brown .. 5 8

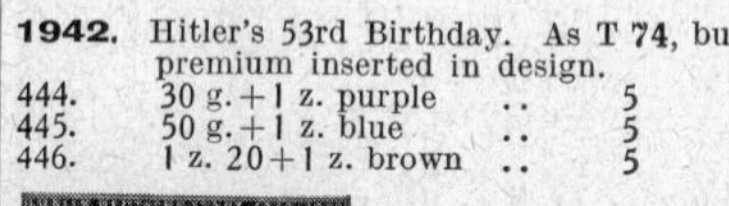

DESIGN: 12 g., 50 g. Lublin, after an ancient engraving.

75. Modern Lublin.

1942. Lublin. 600th Anniv.
447. – 12 g.+8 g. purple .. 5 5
448. 75. 24 g.+6 g. brown .. 5 5
449. – 50 g.+50 g. blue .. 5 5
450. 75. 1 z.+1 z. green .. 5 8

76. Copernicus. 77. Adolf Hitler.

1942. German Occupation. 3rd Anniv.
451. – 12 g.+18 g. violet .. 5 5
452. – 24 g.+26 g. red .. 5 5
453. – 30 g.+30 g. purple .. 5 5
454. – 50 g.+50 g. blue .. 5 5
455. 76. 1 z.+1 z. green .. 12 15
DESIGNS: 12 g. Velt Stoss (Vit Stvosz). 24 g. Hans Durer. 30 g. J. Schuch. 50 g. J. Elsner.

1943. Hitler's 54th Birthday.
456. 77. 12 g.+1 z. violet .. 5 5
457. 24 g.+1 z. red .. 5 5
458. 84 g.+1 z. green .. 5 8

1943. Copernicus. 400th Death Anniv. As No. 455, colour changed, optd. **24 MAI 1543** at left and **24 MAI 1943** at right.
459. 78. 1 z.+1 z. purple .. 12 12

78. Cracow Gate, Lublin. 79. Adolf Hitler.

1943. Nazi Party in German-occupied Poland. 3rd Anniv.
460. **78.** 12 g.+38 g. green .. 5 5
461. – 24 g.+76 g. red .. 5 5
462. – 30 g.+70 g. purple .. 5 5
463. – 50 g.+1 z. blue .. 5 5
464. – 1 z.+2 z. grey .. 5 8
DESIGNS: 24 g. Cloth Hall, Cracow. 30 g. Administrative Building, Radom. 50 g. Bruhl Palace, Warsaw. 1 z. Town hall, Lwow.

1943. As T 72, inscr. "DEUTSCHES REICH GENERALGOUVERNEMENT".
465. **72.** 2 z. green 5 5
466. – 4 z. violet 5 5
467. – 6 z. brown 5 8
468. – 10 z. grey and brown .. 10 12
DESIGNS: 4 z. Tyniec Monastery. 6 z. Lwow. 10 z. Cracow.

1944. Hitler's 55th Birthday.
469. **79.** 12 z.+1 z. green .. 5 5
470. 24 z.+1 z brown .. 5 5
471. 84 z.+1 z. violet .. 5 8

80. Konrad Celtis. **80a.** Cracow Castle.

1944. German Occupation. 5th Anniv.
472. **80.** 12 g.+18 g. green .. 5 5
473. – 24 g.+26 g. red .. 5 5
474. – 30 g.+30 g. purple .. 5 5
475. – 50 g.+50 g. blue .. 5 5
476. – 1 z.+1 z. brown .. 5 5
477. **80a.** 10 z.+10 z. grey & red 2·75 3·25
PORTRAITS: 24 g. A. Schluter. 30 g. H. Boner. 50 g. Augustus the Strong. 1 z. G. Pusch.

1941-45. ISSUES OF EXILED GOVERNMENT IN LONDON.
For correspondence on Polish sea-going vessels and, on certain days, from Polish Military camps in Great Britain.

81. Ruins of Ministry of Finance, Warsaw. **82.** Polish Aeroplanes in Great Britain.

1941.
478. – 5 g. violet 5 5
479. **81.** 10 g. green 12 12
480. – 25 g. grey 25 25
481. – 55 g. blue 40 40
482. – 75 g. olive 65 65
483. – 80 g. red 80 80
484. **82.** 1 z. blue .. .. 1·00 1·00
485. – 1 z. 50 brown .. .. 1·25 1·25
DESIGNS—VERT. 5 g. Ruins of U.S. Embassy, Warsaw. 25 g. Destruction of Mickiewicz Monument, Cracow. 1 z. 50, Polish submarine "Orzel". HORIZ. 55 g. Ruins of Warsaw. 75 g. Polish machine-gunners in Great Britain 80 g. Polish tank in Great Britain.

83. Aeroplane and U-boat. **84.** Merchant Navy.

1943.
486. **83.** 5 g. claret 10 12
487. **84.** 10 g. green 20 8
488. – 25 g. violet 20 25
489. – 55 g. blue 30 35
490. – 75 g. brown 45 50
491. – 80 g. red 50 55
492. – 1 z. olive 60 60
493. – 1 z. 50 black 80 80
DESIGNS—VERT. 25 g. Anti-tank gun in France. 55 g. Poles at Narvik. 1 z. Saboteurs damaging railway line. HORIZ. 75 g. The Tobruk road. 80 g. Gen. Sikorski visiting Polish troops in Middle East. 1 z. 50, Underground newspaper office.

1944. Capture of Montecassino. Nos. 482/5 surch. **MONTE CASSINO 18 V 1944** and value and bars.
494. – 45 g. on 75 g. olive .. 1·25 1·40
495. – 55 g. on 80 g. red .. 1·25 1·40
496. **82.** 80 g. on 1 z. blue .. 1·25 1·40
497. – 1 z. 20 on 1 z. 50 brown 1·25 1·40

85. Polish Partisans.

ILLUSTRATIONS
British Commonwealth and all overprints and surcharges are FULL SIZE.
Foreign Countries have been reduced to ¾-LINEAR.

1945. Survivors of Warsaw Rising Fund.
498. **85.** 1 z.+2 z. green .. 1·40 1·75

1944. INDEPENDENT REPUBLIC.
IMPERF. STAMPS. Many Polish stamps from No. 499 onwards exist imperf. from limited printings.

86. Romuald Traugutt.

PORTRAITS: 50 g. Kosciuszko. 1 z. H. Dabrowski.

1944. National Heroes.
499. **86.** 25 g. red .. .. 7·00 7·00
500. – 50 g. green .. .. 11·00 11·00
501. – 1 z. blue .. .. 11·00 9·00

87. White Eagle. **88.** Grunwald Memorial. Cracow.

1944.
502. **87.** 25 g. red 25 12
503. **88.** 50 g. green 25 8

1944. No. 502 surch. with value **31.XII. 1943** or **1944** and **K.R.N., P.K.W.N.** or **R.T.R.P.**
504. **87.** 1 z. on 25 g. red .. 55 55
505. 2 z. on 25 g. red .. 55 55
506. 3 z. on 25 g. red .. 55 55

1945. 1863 Revolt against Russia. 82nd Anniv. Surch. with value and **22.1.1863.**
507. **86.** 5 z. on 25 g. pink .. 5·50 9·00

1945. Liberation. No. 502 surch. **3 zl.** w town names and dates as indicated.
508. 3 z. on 25 g. Bydgoszcz 23.1.1945 .. .. 90 90
509. 3 z. on 25 g. Czestochowa 17.1.1945 .. .. 90 90
510. 3 z. on 25 g. Gniezno 22.1.1945 .. .. 90 90
511. 3 z. on 25 g. Kalisz 24.1.1945 90 90
512. 3 z. on 25 g. Kielce 15.1.1945 90 90
513. 3 z. on 25 g. Krakow 19.1.1945 .. .. 90 90
514. 3 z. on 25 g. Lodz 19.1.1945 90 90
515. 3 z. on 25 g. Radom 16.1.1945 .. .. 90 90
516. 3 z. on 25 g. Warszawa 17.1.1945 .. .. 90 90
517. 3 z. on 25 g. Zakopane 29.1.1945 .. .. 90 90

89. Flag-bearer and War Victim. **90.** Lodz Factories. **91.** Grunwald Memorial, Cracow.

92. Cloth Hall. **93.** Destroyer.

1945. Liberation of Warsaw.
518. **89.** 5 z. red 80 65

1945. Liberation of Lodz.
519. **90.** 1 z. blue 25 8

1945. Kosciuszko's Oath of Allegiance. 151st Anniv. No. 500 surch. **5 zl. 24.III.1794.**
520. 5 z. on 50 g. green .. 1·75 1·75

1945. Cracow Monuments. Inscr. "19.I.1945".
521. **92.** 50 g. purple 5 5
522. – 1 z. brown 12 5
523. **92.** 2 z. blue 20 8
524. – 3 z. violet 40 12
525. – 5 z. green .. .. 1·10 75
DESIGNS—VERT. 1 z. Kosciuszko Statue. 3 z. Copernicus Memorial. HORIZ. 5 z. Wawel Castle.

1945. 25th Anniv. of Polish Maritime League. Inscr. "LIGA MORSKA".
526. **93.** 50 g.+2 z. orange .. 90 90
527. – 1 z.+3 z. blue 90 90
528. – 2 z.+4 z. red 90 90
529. – 3 z.+5 z. olive 90 90
DESIGNS—VERT. 1 z. Sailing ship. 2 z. Naval ensigns. HORIZ. 3 z. Crane and tower, Gdansk.

94. Town Hall, Poznan.

1945. Postal Employees Congress.
530. **94.** 1 z.+5 z. green .. 3·00 3·50

95. Kosciuszko Memorial, Lodz. **96.** Grunwald 1410.

1945.
531. **95.** 3 z. purple 15 8

1945. Battle of Tannenberg (Grunwald). 535th Anniv.
532. **96.** 5 z. blue .. .. 1·75 2·25

97. Eagle and Manifesto. **98.** Westerplatte.

1945. Liberation. 1st Anniv.
533. **97.** 3 z. red .. .. 3·25 2·75

1945. Defence of Westerplatte. 6th Anniv.
534. **98.** 1 z.+9 z. slate .. 3·00 3·00

1945. Surch. with new value and heavy bars.
535. **88.** 1 z. on 50 g. green .. 20 8
536a. **87.** 1 z. 50 on 25 g. red .. 20 8

99. Crane Tower, Gdansk. **100.** St. John's Cathedral.

1945. Liberation of Gdansk (Danzig). Perf. or imperf.
537. **99.** 1 z. olive 5 5
538. – 2 z. blue 12 5
539. – 3 z. purple 20 5
DESIGNS—VERT. 2 z. Stock Exchange, Gdansk. HORIZ. 3 z. High Gate, Gdansk.

1945. "Warsaw, 1939–1945". Warsaw before and after destruction. Imperf.
540. – 1 z. 50 red 5 5
541. **100.** 3 z. blue 10 5
542. – 3 z. 50 green 20 15
543. – 6 z. grey 10 8
544. – 8 z. brown 12 8
545. – 10 z. purple 25 8
DESIGNS: 1 z. 50, Castle. 3 z. 50, City Hall. 6 z. G.P.O. 8 z. War Ministry. 10 z. Church of the Holy Cross.

101. United Workers.

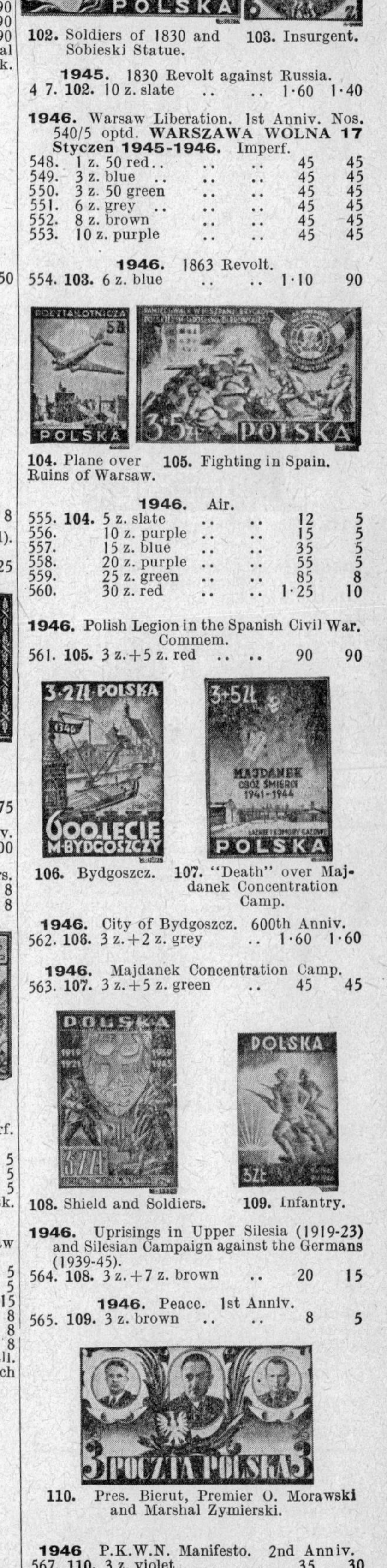

1945. Trades' Union Congress.
546. **101.** 1 z. 50+8 z. 50 slate .. 1·25 1·10

102. Soldiers of 1830 and Sobieski Statue. **103.** Insurgent.

1945. 1830 Revolt against Russia.
547. **102.** 10 z. slate .. .. 1·60 1·40

1946. Warsaw Liberation. 1st Anniv. Nos. 540/5 optd. **WARSZAWA WOLNA 17 Styczen 1945-1946.** Imperf.
548. 1 z. 50 red 45 45
549. 3 z. blue 45 45
550. 3 z. 50 green 45 45
551. 6 z. grey 45 45
552. 8 z. brown 45 45
553. 10 z. purple 45 45

1946. 1863 Revolt.
554. **103.** 6 z. blue .. .. 1·10 90

104. Plane over Ruins of Warsaw. **105.** Fighting in Spain.

1946. Air.
555. **104.** 5 z. slate 12 5
556. 10 z. purple 15 5
557. 15 z. blue 35 5
558. 20 z. purple 55 5
559. 25 z. green 85 8
560. 30 z. red .. .. 1·25 10

1946. Polish Legion in the Spanish Civil War. Commem.
561. **105.** 3 z.+5 z. red 90 90

106. Bydgoszcz. **107.** "Death" over Majdanek Concentration Camp.

1946. City of Bydgoszcz. 600th Anniv.
562. **106.** 3 z.+2 z. grey .. 1·60 1·60

1946. Majdanek Concentration Camp.
563. **107.** 3 z.+5 z. green .. 45 45

108. Shield and Soldiers. **109.** Infantry.

1946. Uprisings in Upper Silesia (1919-23) and Silesian Campaign against the Germans (1939-45).
564. **108.** 3 z.+7 z. brown .. 20 15

1946. Peace. 1st Anniv.
565. **109.** 3 z. brown 8 5

110. Pres. Bierut, Premier O. Morawski and Marshal Zymierski.

1946 P.K.W.N. Manifesto. 2nd Anniv.
567. **110.** 3 z. violet 35 30

111. Polish Coastline.

112. Bedzin Castle.

113. Tombstone of Henry IV

114. Castle of Lanckorona.

1946. Maritime Festival.
566. **111.** 3 z.+7 z. blue .. 30 30

1946. Imperf. (5 z., 10 z.) or perf. (6 z.).
568. **112.** 5 z. olive 5 5
568a. 5 z. brown 5 5
569. **113.** 6 z. black 15 5
570. **114.** 10 z. blue 15 5

115. Crane, Monument and Crane Tower, Gdansk.

1946. Honouring Postal Employees killed in Gdansk fighting.
571. **115.** 3 z.+12 z. slate .. 25 25

115a. Schoolchildren at Desk.

1946. Polish Work for Education and Fund for Int. Bureau of Education.
571a. **115a.** 3 z.+22 z. red .. 15·00 15·00
571b. – 6 z.+24 z. blue .. 15·00 15·00
571c. – 11 z.+19 z. green .. 15·00 15·00
DESIGNS: 6 z. Court of Jagiellonian University, Cracow. 11 z. Gregory Piramowicz (1735-1801), founder of the Education Commission.

116. Stojalowski, Bojko, Stapinski and Witos.

1946. 50th Anniv. of Peasant Movement and Relief Fund.
572. **116.** 5 z.+10 z. green .. 25 20
573. 5 z.+10 z. blue .. 25 20
574. 5 z.+10 z. olive .. 25 20

1947. Opening of Polish Parliament. Surch. +7 **SEJM USTAWODAWCZY 19 1 1947.**
575. **110.** 3 z.+7 z. violet .. 90 90

1947. National Ski Championships, Zakopane. Surch. **5+15 zl. XXII MISTRZOSTWA NARCIARSKIE POLSKI 1947.**
576. **87.** 5+15 z. on 25 g. red 80 90

1947. Surch. **5 ZL** in outlined figure and capital letters between stars.
577. **113.** 5 z. on 6 z. black .. 20 8

INDEX

Countries can be quickly located by referring to the index at the end of this volume.

117. Home of Emil Zegadlowicz.

118. Fr. Chopin (Musician).

120. Wounded Soldier, Nurse and Child.

119. Roguslawski, Modrzejewska and Jaracz (actors).

1947. Emils Zegadlowicz Commem.
578. **117.** 5 z.+15 z. green .. 20 20

1947. Polish Culture. Imperf. or perf.
579. – 1 z. blue 10 5
580. – 1 z. slate 10 5
581. – 2 z. brown 10 5
582. – 2 z. orange 5 5
583. **118.** 3 z. green 25 5
584. 3 z. olive 45 5
585. **119.** 5 z. black 20 5
586. 5 z. sepia 10 5
587. – 6 z. grey 25 5
588. – 6 z. red 15 5
589. – 10 z. grey 25 5
590. – 10 z. blue 15 5
591. – 15 z. violet 70 8
592. – 15 z. brown 55 8
593. – 20 z. black 70 12
594. – 20 z. purple 25 15
PORTRAITS—HORIZ. 1 z. Matejko, Malczewski and Chelmonski (painters). 6 z. Swietochowski, Zeromski and Prus (writers). 15 z. Wyspianski, Slowacki and Kasprowicz (poets). VERT. 2 z. Brother Albert of Cracow. 10 z. Marie Curie (scientist). 20 z. Mickiewicz (poet).

1947. Red Cross Fund.
595. **120.** 5 z.+5 z. grey and red 55 55

122. Steelworker.

123. Brother Albert of Cracow.

1947. Occupations.
596. **122.** 5 z. lake 50 5
597. – 10 z. green 8 5
598. – 15 z. blue 25 5
599. – 20 z. black 30 5
DESIGNS: 10 z. Harvester. 15 z. Fisherman. 20 z. Miner.

1947. Air. Surch. **LOTNICZA** bars and value.
600. **88.** 40 z. on 50 g. green .. 40 25
601. **87.** 50 z. on 25 g. red .. 1·10 80

1947. Winter Relief Fund.
603. **123.** 2 z.+18 z. violet .. 25 25

124. Sagittarius.

125. Chainbreaker.

1948. Air.
604. **124.** 15 z. violet 45 12
605. 25 z. blue 45 5
606. 30 z. brown 45 15
607. 50 z. green .. .. 1·00 15
608. 75 z. black .. .. 1·00 15
609. 100 z. orange .. .. 1·00 15

1948. Revolution Centenaries. Inscr. as in T 125.
610. **125.** 15 z. brown 15 8
611. – 30 z. brown 25 12
612. – 35 z. green 45 20
613. – 60 z. red 55 25
PORTRAITS—HORIZ. 30 z. Generals H. Dembinski and J. Bem. 35 z. S. Worcell, P. Sciezienny and E. Dembowski. 60 z. F. Engels and K. Marx.

126. Insurgents.

127. Wheel and Streamers.

1948. Warsaw Ghetto Revolt. 5th Anniv.
614. **126.** 15 z. black 25 25

1948. Warsaw—Prague Cycle Race.
615. **127.** 15 z. red and blue .. 80 35

128. Cycle Race.

129. Shipbuilding Yard.

1948. Seventh Circuit of Poland.
616. **128.** 3 z. black 25 8
617. 6 z. brown 45 15
618. 15 z. green 60 30

1948. Merchant Marine.
619. **129.** 6 z. violet 15 8
620. – 15 z. red 25 15
621. – 35 z. slate 60 35
DESIGNS—HORIZ. 15 z. Cargo boat. 35 z. Yacht.

130. Firework Display.

131. "Youth".

1948. Wroclaw Exn.
622. **130.** 6 z. blue 8 5
623. 15 z. red 15 5
624. 18 z. claret 55 8
625. 35 z. brown 55 8

1948. Int. Youth Conf., Warsaw.
626. **131.** 15 z. blue 15 5

132. Roadway, St. Anne's Church and Palace.

133. Torun Ramparts and Mail Coach.

1948. Warsaw Reconstruction Fund.
627. **132.** 15 z.+5 z. green .. 8 8

1948. Philatelic Congress, Torun.
628. **133.** 15 z. brown 15 8

ILLUSTRATIONS
British Commonwealth and all overprints and surcharges are FULL SIZE. Foreign Countries have been reduced to ¾-LINEAR.

134. Locomotive, Clock and Winged Wheel.

1948. European Railway Conf.
629. **134.** 18 z. blue .. .. 2·25 1·40

135. President Bierut.

136. Workers and Flag.

1948.
629a. **135.** 2 z. orange .. 5 5
629b. 3 z. emerald .. 5 5
630. 5 z. brown .. 5 5
631. 6 z. black .. 5 5
631a. 10 z. violet .. 8 5
632. 15 z. red .. 15 5
633. 18 z. green .. 25 5
634. 30 z. blue .. 30 5
635. 35 z. purple .. 40 10

1948. Workers' Class Unity Congress.
(a) Dated "8 XII 1948".
636. **136.** 5 z. red 8 5
637. – 15 z. violet 15 12
638. – 25 z. brown 25 15
(b) Dated "XII 1948".
639. **136.** 5 z. plum 25 15
640. – 15 z. blue .. .. 1·20 15
641. – 25 z. green .. .. 1·20 25
DESIGNS: 15 z. Flags and portraits of Engels, Marx, Lenin and Stalin. 25 z. Workers marching and portrait of L. Warynski.

137. Baby.

137a. Pres. Franklin D. Roosevelt.

1948. Anti-tuberculosis Fund. Portraits of babies as T 137.
642. **137.** 3 z.+2 z. green .. 55 55
643. – 5 z.+5 z. brown .. 55 55
644. – 6 z.+4 z. purple .. 55 55
645. – 15 z.+10 z. red .. 45 55

1948. Air. Presidents Roosevelt, Pulaski and Kociuszko.
645a. **137a.** 80 z. violet .. .. 9·00 13·00
645b. – 100 z. purple (Pulaski) 12·00 9·00
645c. – 120 z. blue (Kosciusko) 12·00 9·00

138. "Socialism".

1949. Trades' Union Congress, Warsaw.
646. **138.** 3 z. red 8 5
647. – 5 z. blue 12 8
648. – 15 z. green 25 15
DESIGNS: 5 z. inscr. "PRACA" (Labour), Labourer and tractor. 15 z. inscr. "POKOJ" (Peace), Three labourers.

139. Banks of R. Vistula.

140. Pres. Bierut.

1949. National Liberation Committee. 5th Anniv.
649. **139.** 10 z. black 15 15
650. **140.** 15 z. purple 15 15
651. – 35 z. grey 55 15
DESIGN—VERT. 35 z. Radio station, Raszyn.

141. Mail-coach and Map.

142. Worker and Tractor.

1949. U.P.U. 75th Anniv.
652. **141.** 6 z. violet 35 25
653. – 30 z. blue (Ship) .. 1·00 60
654. – 80 z. green ('Plane) .. 3·00 1·75

1949. Congress of Populist Movement.
655. **142.** 5 z. claret 15 5
656. 10 z. red 8 5
657. 15 z. green 8 5
658. 35 z. brown 45 8

143. Frederick Chopin.

144. Mickiewicz and Pushkin.

145. Postman.

1949. National Celebrities.
659. – 10 z. purple 45 8
660. **143.** 15 z. red 45 15
661. – 35 z. blue 60 25
PORTRAITS: 10 z. Adam Mickiewicz. 35 z. Julius Slowacki.

1949. Polish-Russian Friendship Month.
662. **144.** 15 z. violet 55 20

1950. Postal Workers' Third Congress.
663. **145.** 15 z. purple 30 12

146. Mechanic, Hanger and Aeroplane. **147.** President Bierut. **147a.**

1950. Air.
664. **146.** 500 z. lake .. .. 2·25 1·10

1950. (a) With frame.
665. **147.** 15 z. red 20 5

(b) Without frame. Values in "zloty".
673. **147a.** 5 z. green 5 5
674. 10 z. red 5 5
675. 15 z. blue 25 5
676. 20 z. violet 10 5
677. 25 z. brown 10 5
678. 30 z. claret 15 8
679. 40 z. chocolate .. 20 5
680. 50 z. olive 45 5
For values in "groszy" see Nos. 687/94.

148. J. Marchlewski. **149.** Workers.

1950. Marchlewski (patriot). 25th Death Anniv.
666. **148.** 15 z. grey 20 5

1950. Reconstruction of Warsaw.
667. **149.** 5 zloty brown .. 5 5
695. 15 groszy green .. 5 5

150. Worker and Flag. **151.** Statue.

1950. May Day Manifesto. 60th Anniv. Inscr. "1 MAJ 1890 1950".
668. **150.** 10 z. magenta .. 10 5
669. – 15 z. olive 12 5
DESIGN—VERT. 15 z. Three workers and flag.

1950. Poznan Fair.
670. **151.** 15 z. brown 10 5

152. Dove and Globe. **153.** Labourers.

1950. Int. Peace Conf.
671. **152.** 10 z. green 12 5
672. 15 z. brown 8 5

1950. Six Year Reconstruction Plan.
681. **153.** 15 zloty blue 8 5
696. 45 groszy blue .. 8 5
696b. 75 groszy sepia .. 8 5
696d. 1 z. 15 green .. 8 5
696e. 1 z. 20 red 10 5

154. Hibner, Kniewski, Rutkowski. **155.** Worker and Dove.

1950. Revolutionaries' Execution. 25th Anniv.
682. **154.** 15 z. black 12 5

1950. 1st Polish Peace Congress.
683. **155.** 15 z. green 12 5

REVALUATION SURCHARGES. Following a revaluation of the Polish currency, a large number of definitive and commemorative stamps were locally overprinted "Groszy" or "gr". There are 37 known types of overprint and various colours of overprint. We do not list them as they had only local use, but the following is a list of the stamps which were duly authorised for overprinting:—Nos. 579/94, 596/615 and 619/58. Overprints on other stamps were not authorised.

156. Dove (after Picasso).

1950. 2nd World Peace Congress, Warsaw.
684. **156.** 40 g. blue 12 5
685a. 45 g. claret 12 5

157. General Bem and Battle of Piski.

1950. Bem. Death Cent.
686. **157.** 45 g. blue 80 30

1950. As T **147a.** Values in "groszy".
687. **147a.** 5 g. violet 5 5
688. 10 g. green 5 5
689. 15 g. olive 5 5
690. 25 g. claret 5 5
691. 30 g. red 5 5
692. 40 g. orange 5 5
693. 45 g. blue 30 5
694. 75 g. brown 15 5

158. Woman and Doves. **159.** Battle Scene and J. Dabrowski.

1951. Women's League Congress.
697. **158.** 45 g. red 10 5

1951. Paris Commune. 80th Anniv.
698. **159.** 45 g. green 10 5

1951. Surch. **45 gr.**
699. **156.** 45 g. on 15 z. claret .. 12 5

160. Worker with Flag. **161.** Smelting Works.

1951. Labour Day.
700. **160.** 45 g. red 10 5

1951.
701. **161.** 40 g. blue 5 5
702. 45 g. black 5 5
702a. 60 g. brown 8 5
702b. 90 g. lake 15 5

162. Pioneer and Badge. **163.** St. Staszic.

1951. Int. Children's Day. Insc. "1-VI-51".
703. **162.** 30 g. olive 55 8
704. – 45 g. blue (Boy, girl and map) .. 70 20

1951. 1st Polish Scientific Congress. Inscr. "KONGRES NAUKI POLSKIEJ".
705. **163.** 25 g. red 25 12
706. – 40 g. blue 12 5
707. – 45 g. violet 12 5
708. – 60 g. green 12 5
709. – 1 z. 15 purple 25 12
710. – 1 z. 20 grey 20 5
DESIGNS—As T **163**: 40 g. Marie Curie. 60 g. M. Nencki. 1 z. 15. Copernicus. 1 z. 20, Dove and book. HORIZ. (36×21 mm.): 45 g. Z. Wroblewski and Olszewski.

164. F. Dzerzinsky (politician). **165.** Pres. Bierut, Industry and Agriculture.

1951. 25th Death Anniv. of Dzerzinsky.
711. **164.** 45 g. brown 5 5

1951. People's Republic. 7th Anniv.
712. **165.** 45 g. red 25 5
713. 60 g. green 55 8
714. 90 g. blue 55 5

166. Young People and Globe. **167.** Sports Badge.

1951. 3rd World Youth Festival, Berlin.
715. **166.** 40 g. blue 15 5

1951. Surch. **45 gr.**
716. **147a.** 45 g. on 35 z. orange 10 5

1951. Spartacist Games.
717. **167.** 45 g. green 25 10

168. Stalin. **169.** Chopin and Moniuszko.

1951. Polish-Soviet Friendship.
718. **168.** 45 g. red 5 5
719. 90 g. black 12 5

1951. Polish Musical Festival.
720. **169.** 45 g. black 5 5
721. 90 g. red 12 10

170. Mining Machinery. **171.** Building Modern Flats.

1951. Six Year Plan (Mining).
722. **170.** 90 g. brown 8 5
723. 1 z. 20 blue 8 5
724. 1 z. 20+15 g. orange 8 5

1951. Six Year Plan (Reconstruction).
725. **171.** 30 g. green 5 5
726. 30 g.+15 g. red .. 5 5
727. 1 z. 15 purple 10 5

172. Installing Electric Cables. **173.** M. Nowotko. **174.** Women's Banner.

1951. Six Year Plan (Electrification).
728. **172.** 30 g. black 5 5
729. 45 g. red 5 5
730. 45 g.+15 g. brown .. 5 5

1952. Polish Workers' Party. 10th Anniv.
731. **173.** 45 g.+15 g. lake .. 5 5
732. – 90 g. chocolate .. 12 5
733. – 1 z. 15 orange .. 12 5
PORTRAITS: 90 g. P. Finder. 1 z. 15, M. Fornalska.

1952. Int. Women's Day.
734. **174.** 45 g.+15 g. brown .. 8 5
735. 1 z. 20 red 15 5

175. Gen. Swierczewski. **176.** Aeroplane over Farm.

1952. Gen. Swierczewski. 5th Death Anniv.
736. **175.** 45 g.+15 g. brown .. 12 5
737. 90 g. blue 20 8

1952. Air. Aeroplanes and views. Perf. or imperf.
738. – 55 g. blue (Merchant ships) 5 8
739. **176.** 90 g. green 8 8
740. – 1 z. 40 purple (Warsaw) 15 10
741. – 5 z. black (Steelworks) 40 10

178. Cyclists and City Arms.

177. President Bierut. **179.** Workers and Banner.

1952. Pres. Bierut's 60th Birthday.
742. **177.** 45 g.+15 g. red .. 12 8
743. 90 g. green .. 20 12
744. 1 z. 20+15 g. blue .. 35 8

1952. Warsaw-Berlin-Prague Cycle Race.
745. **178.** 40 g. blue 35 15

1952. Labour Day.
746. **179.** 45 g.+15 g. red .. 5 5
747. 75 g. green 12 5

180. J. I. Kraszewski (writer). **181.** Maria Konopnicka (poetess).

1952. Kraszewski. 140th Birth Anniv.
748. **180.** 25 g. purple 5 5

1952. Maria Konopnicka. 110th Birth Anniv.
749. **181.** 30 g.+15 g. green .. 8 5
750. 1 z. 15 brown 15 5

182. H. Kollataj. **183.** Leonardo da Vinci. **185.** N. V. Gogol

184. President Bierut and Children.

1952. Kollataj (revolutionary). 140th Death Anniv.
751. **182.** 45 g.+15 g. brown .. 8 5
752. 1 z. green 10 5

1952. Leonardo da Vinci. 500th Birth Anniv.
753. **183.** 30 g.+15 g. blue .. 12 5

1952. Int. Children's Day.
754. **184.** 45 g.+15 g. blue .. 20 8

1952. Gogol (Russian writer). Death Cent.
755. **185.** 25 g. green 12 5

186. Cement Works. 187. Swimmers.

1952. Construction of Concrete Works, Wierzbica.
756. 186. 3 z. black 25 5
757. 10 z. red 55 15

1952. Sports Day.
758. 187. 30 g.+15 g. blue .. 55 15
759. – 45 g.+15 g. violet .. 25 8
760. – 1 z. 15 green 35 15
761. – 1 z. 20 red 25 15
DESIGNS: 45 g. Footballers. 1 z. 15 Runners. 1 z. 20 Highjumper.

188. Yachts.

DESIGNS—VERT. 45 g. Sailing-ship. "Dar Pomorza". 90 g. Shipbuilding worker.

1952. Shipbuilders' Day.
762. 188. 30 g.+15 g. green .. 45 15
763. – 45 g.+15 g. blue .. 15 8
764. – 90 g. plum 15 8

189. Young Workers. 190. "New Constitution".

1952. Youth Festival, Warsaw.
765. 189. 30 g.+15 g. green .. 15 12
766. – 45 g.+15 g. red .. 35 8
767. – 90 g. brown 15 15
DESIGNS—HORIZ. 45 g. Girl and boy students. 90 g. Boy bugler.

1952. Adoption of New Constitution.
768. 190. 45 g.+15 g. grn. & brn. 35 8
769. 3 z. violet and brown 15 10

191. L. Warynski. 192. Jaworzno Power Station.

1952. Party "Proletariat". 70th Anniv.
770. 191. 30 g.+15 g. red .. 8 5
771. 45 g.+15 g. brown 15 5

1952. Electricity Power Station, Jaworzno.
772. 192. 45 g.+15 g. red .. 45 5
773. 1 z. black 35 8
774. 1 z. 50 green 35 5

193. Frydman. 194. Pilot and Glider.

1952. Pieniny Mountain Resorts.
775. 193. 45 g.+15 g. purple .. 8 5
776. – 60 g. green (Grywald) 8 5
777. – 1 z. red (Niedzica) .. 35 5

1952. Aviation Day.
778. 194. 30 g.+15 g. green .. 25 5
779. – 45 g.+15 g. red .. 35 5
780. – 90 g. blue 15 10
DESIGNS: 45 g. Pilot and aeroplane. 90 g. Parachutists.

195. Avicenna. 196. Victor Hugo. 197. Shipbuilding.

1952. Avicenna (Arab physician). Birth Millenary.
781. 195. 75 g. red 10 5

1952. Victor Hugo (French author). 150th Birth Anniv.
782. 196. 90 g. brown 12 5

1952. Gdansk Shipyards.
783. 197. 5 g. green 5 5
784. 15 g. red 5 5

198. H. Sienkiewicz (author). 199. Assault on Winter Palace, Petrograd.

1952.
785. 198. 45 g.+15 g. sepia .. 8 5

1952. Russian Revolution. 35th Anniv. Perf. or Imperf.
786. 199. 45 g.+15 g. red .. 35 5
787. 60 g. brown 15 5

200. Lenin. 201. Miner. 202. H. Wieniawski (violinist).

1952. Polish-Soviet Friendship Month.
788. 200. 30 g.+15 g. purple .. 15 5
789. 45 g.+15 g. brown 35 5

1952. Miners' Day.
790. 201. 45 g.+15 g. black .. 5 5
791. 1 z. 20+15 g. brown.. 20 5

1952. 2nd Wieniawski Int. Violin Competition.
792. 202. 30 g.+15 g. green .. 35 8
793. 45 g.+15 g. violet .. 45 5

203. Car Factory, Zeran. 204. Dove of Peace.

1952.
800. – 30 g.+15 g. blue .. 5 5
794. 203. 45 g.+15 g. green .. 5 5
801. – 60 g.+20 g. purple .. 5 5
795. 203. 1 z. 15 brown .. 20 5
DESIGN: 30 g., 60 g. Lorry factory, Lublin.

1952. Peace Congress, Vienna.
796. 204. 30 g. green 15 5
797. 60 g. blue 25 5

205. Soldier and Flag. 206. Karl Marx. 207. Globe and Flag.

1952. Battle of Stalingrad. 10th Anniv.
798. 205. 60 g. red & grey-green 35 5
799. 80 g. red and slate .. 15 5

1953. Marx. 70th Death Anniv.
802. 206. 60 g. blue .. .. 7·00 2·25
803. 80 g. brown .. .. 1·10 25

1953. Labour Day.
804. 207. 60 g. vermilion .. 60 8
805. 80 g. red 12 5

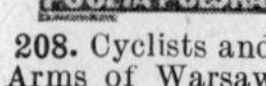

208. Cyclists and Arms of Warsaw. 209. Boxer.

1953. 6th Int. Cycle Race.
806. – 80 g. green 55 12
807. 208. 80 g. brown 55 25
808. – 80 g. red .. .. 1·75 90
DESIGNS: As T 208 but Arms of Berlin (No. 806) or Prague (No. 808).

1953. European Boxing Championship, Warsaw. Inscr. "17–24. V. 1953".
809. 209. 40 g. lake 90 8
810. 80 g. orange .. .. 4·50 1·25
811. – 95 g. purple 90 45
DESIGN: 95 g. Boxing match.

210. Copernicus (after Matejko). 211. Trawler.

1953. Copernicus (astronomer). 480th Birth Anniv. Inscr. "1473–1543".
812. 210. 20 g. brown 35 5
813. – 80 g. grey-blue .. 4·50 90
DESIGN—VERT. 80 g. Portrait and diagram.

1953. Merchant Navy Commem.
814. 211. 80 g. green 15 5
815. – 1 z. 35 blue 60 12
DESIGN: 1 z. 35 Unloading cargo ship.

212. Warsaw Market-place. 213. Students' Badge. 214. Nurse Feeding Baby.

1953. Polish National Day.
816. 212. 20 g. lake 8 5
817. 2 z. 35 blue 70 25

1953. 3rd World Students' Congress, Warsaw. Inscr. "III SWIATOWY KONGRES STUDENTOW". (a) Postage. Perf.
818. – 40 g. brown 8 5
819. 213. 1 z. 35 green 30 5
820. – 1 z. 50 blue 50 15
(b) Air. Imperf.
821. 312. 55 g. plum 55 10
822. 75 g. red 45 15
DESIGNS—HORIZ. 40 g. Students and globe. VERT. 1 z. 50, Woman and dove.

1953. Social Health Service.
823. 214. 80 g. red 70 25
824. – 1 z. 75 green 15 8
DESIGN: 1 z. 75, Nurse, mother and baby.

215. M. Kalinowski. 216. J. Kochanowski.

1913. Polish People's Army. 10th Anniv. Inscr. "1943 1953".
825. 215. 45 g. brown 70 35
826. – 80 g. red 20 5
827. – 1 g. 75 olive 20 5
DESIGNS—HORIZ. 80 g. Russian and Polish soldiers. VERT. 1 z. 75, R. Pazinski.

1953. "Renaissance" Commem. Inscr. "ROK ODRODZENIA".
828. 216. 20 g. brown 5 5
829. – 80 g. purple 12 5
830. – 1 z. 35 indigo.. .. 15 12
DESIGNS–HORIZ. 80 g. Wawel Castle. VERT. 1 z., 3 M. Bej.

217. Cultural Centre. 218. Dunajec Canyon Pieniny Mts.

1953. Reconstruction of Warsaw. Inscr. "WARSZAWA".
831. 217. 80 g. red .. .. 2·10 35
832. – 1 z. 75 blue .. .. 1·10 5
833. – 2 z. purple .. .. 2·10 35
DESIGNS: 1 z. 75, Constitution Place. 2 z. Old City Market, Warsaw.

1953. Tourist Series.
834. – 20 g. lake and blue .. 5 5
835. – 80 g. lilac and green .. 30 20
836. 218. 1 z. 75 green & brown 25 5
837. – 2 z. black and red .. 45 5
DESIGNS—HORIZ. 20 g. Krynica Spa. 2 z. Ciechocinek Spa. VERT. 80 g. Morskie Oko Lake, Tatra Mts.

219. Ski-ing. 220. Infants playing.

1953. Winter Sports.
838. – 80 g. blue 55 8
839. 219. 95 g. green 25 8
840. – 2 z. 85 red .. .. 1·10 35
DESIGNS—VERT. 80 g. Ice-skating. 1 z. 85, Ice-hockey.

1953. Children's Education.
841. 220. 10 g. violet 5 5
842. – 80 g. claret 15 5
843. – 1 z. 50 green .. .. 1·60 55
DESIGNS: 80 g. Girls and school. 1 z. 50, Two girls at desks.

221. Electric Train. 222. Mill Girl.

1954. Electrification of Railways.
844. – 60 g. blue .. .. 1·10 15
845. 221. 80 g. brown 55 12
DESIGN: 60 g. Rear of electric train.

1954. Working Women's Commemoration.
846. 222. 20 g. green 40 25
847. – 40 g. blue 12 5
848. – 80 g. chocolate .. 15 5
DESIGNS: 40 g. Postwoman. 80 g. Woman driving tractor.

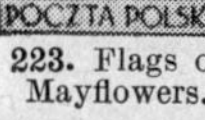

223. Flags of Mayflowers. 224. "Warsaw—Berlin—Prague".

225. Symbols of Labour. 226. Glider and Flags.

1954. Labour Day.
849. 223. 40 g. chocolate .. 25 5
850. 60 g. blue 25 5
851. 80 g. red 15 5

1954. 7th Int. Cycle Race. Inscr. "2–17 MAJ 1954".
852. 224. 80 g. brown 15 5
853. – 80 g. blue (Dove and cycle wheel) .. 25 8

1954. 3rd Trades' Union Congress, Warsaw.
854. 225. 25 g. indigo 10 5
855. 80 g. lake 15 5

1954. Int. Gliding Competition. Inscr. as in T 225.
856. – 45 g. green 25 5
857. 226. 60 g. violet 80 10
858. 60 g. brown 70 5
859. – 1 z. 35 blue 80 20
DESIGNS: 45 g. Glider and clouds in frame. 1 z. 35, Glider and sky.

227. Aeroplane over Paczkow. 228. Fencing.

1954. Air. Inscr. "POCZTA LOTNICZA".
860. 227. 60 g. green 5 5
861. – 80 g. red 8 5
862. – 1 z. 15 black .. 35 8
863. – 1 z. 50 claret 15 5
864. – 1 z. 55 blue 15 5
865. – 1 z. 95 brown .. 20 5
DESIGNS: Aeroplane over—80 g. Kazimierz Dolny. 1 z. 15, Cracow. 1 z. 50, Wroclaw. 1 z. 55, Warsaw. 1 z. 95, Lublin.

1954. 2nd Spartacist Games (1st issue). Inscr. "II OGOLNOPOLSKA SPARTAKIADA".
866. 228. 25 g. purple 35 12
867. – 60 g. turquoise .. 45 5
868. – 1 z. blue 55 8
DESIGNS—VERT. 60 g. Gymnastics. HORIZ. 1 z. Running.

229. Spartacist Games Badge. 230. Battlefield.

1954. 2nd Spartacist Games (2nd issue).
869. 229. 60 g. brown 35 5
870. 1 z. 55 slate 60 12

1954. 10th Anniv. of Liberation and Battle of Studzianki.
871. 230. 60 g. green 70 12
872. – 1 z. blue .. .. 3·25 35
DESIGN—HORIZ. 1 z. Soldier and airman.

231. Steel Works.

1954. People's Republic. 10th Anniv. Inscr. "1944–1954".
873. – 10 g. sepia and brown 8 5
874. – 20 g. myrtle and red .. 8 5
876. 231. 25 g. black and buff .. 8 5
877. – 40 g. chocolate & yellow 15 5
878. – 45 g. purple and mauve 8 5
880. – 60 g. purple and green 8 5
881. – 1 z. 15 blk. & blue-green 1·25 8
882. – 1 z. 40 brown & orange 2·75 45
883. – 1 z. 55 blue and indigo 1·40 25
884. – 2 z. 10 indigo & cobalt 1·40 45
DESIGNS: 10 g. Coal mine. 20 g. Soldier and flag. 40 g. Worker on holiday. 45 g. House-builders. 60 g. Tractor and binder. 1 z. 15, Lublin Castle. 1 z. 40, Customers in bookshop. 1 z. 55, Ship alongside wharf. 2 z. 10, Battle of Lenino.

232. Signal. 233. Picking Apples.

1954. Railway Workers' Day. Inscr. "DZIEN KOLEJARZA".
885. 232. 40 g. blue 60 12
886. – 60 g. black 35 12
DESIGN: 60 g. Night Express.

1954. Polish-Russian Friendship.
887. 233. 40 g. violet 70 15
888. 60 g. black 35 10

234. Elblag. 235. Chopin and Piano.

1954. 500th Anniv. of Return of Pomerania to Poland. Inscr. as in T 234.
889. 234. 20 g. red on blue .. 15 5
890. – 45 g. brown on lemon 15 5
891. – 60 g. green on yellow .. 8 5
892. – 1 z. 40 blue on pink .. 15 5
893. – 1 z. 55 choc. on cream 25 5
VIEWS: 45 g. Gdansk. 60 g. Torun. 1 z. 40, Malbork. 1 z. 55, Olsztyn.

1954. 5th Int. Chopin Music Festival, Warsaw (1st issue).
894. 235. 45 g. brown 12 5
895. 60 g. green 20 5
896. 1 z. blue 55 12

236. Battle Scene.

1954. Kosciuszko's Insurrection. 160th Anniv.
897. 236. 40 g. olive 20 8
898. – 60 g. chocolate .. 30 5
899. – 1 z. 40 black .. 60 15
DESIGNS: 60 g. Kosciuszko on horseback, with insurgents. 1 z. 40, Street battle.

237. Bison. 238. "The Liberator".

1954. Polish Forest Animals. Imperf. or perf.
900. 237. 45 g. brown and green 8 5
901. – 60 g. brown and green 10 5
902. – 1 z. 90 brown and blue 25 5
903. – 3 z. brown & turquoise 35 20
ANIMALS: 60 g. Elk. 1 z. 90, Chamois. 3 z. Beaver.

1955. Liberation of Warsaw. 10th Anniv.
904. 238. 40 g. chocolate .. 15 8
905. – 60 g. blue 15 5
DESIGN: 60 g. "Spirit of Poland".

239. Bust of Chopin (after L. Isler). 240. Mickiewicz Monument.

1955. 5th Int. Chopin Music Festival (2nd issue).
906. 239. 40 g. chocolate .. 8 5
907. 60 g. blue 10 8

1955. Warsaw Monuments (1st issue).
908. – 5 g. green on yellow .. 5 5
909. – 10 g. maroon on yellow 5 5
910. – 15 g. sepia on blue .. 5 5
911. – 20 g. blue on pink .. 5 5
912. – 40 g. violet on violet .. 12 5
913. – 45 g. brown on buff .. 15 8
914. 240. 60 g. blue on stone .. 5 5
915. – 1 z. 55 turquoise on grey 25 10
MONUMENTS: 5 g. "Siren". 10 g. Dzerzhinski Statue. 15 g. King Sigismund III Statue. 20 g. "Brotherhood in Arms". 40 g. Copernicus. 45 g. Marie Curie Statue. 1 z. 55, Kilinski Statue.

241. Flags and Tower. 242. Cycle Wheels and Arms.

1955. Russo-Polish Treaty of Friendship. 10th Anniv.
916. 241. 40 g. red 8 5
917. 40 g. chestnut .. 8 5
918. – 60 g. sepia 8 5
919. – 60 g. turquoise .. 8 5
DESIGN: 60 g. "Statue of Friendship".

1955. 8th Int. Cycle Race.
920. 242. 40 g. brown 10 5
921. – 60 g. blue 8 5
DESIGN: 60 g. "VIII" and doves.

243. Town Hall. Poznan. 244. Festival Emblem.

1955. 24th Int. Fair, Poznan.
922. 243. 40 g. blue 10 5
923. 60 g. red 5 5

1955. Cracow Festival No. 925 is as T 244 but horiz. and inscr. "FESTIWAL SZTUKI", etc.
924. 244. 20 g. ochre, sepia, brown and green 20 5
925. – 40 g. green, black, chestnut and lilac .. 12 5
926. 244. 60 g. brn., blk., red & bl. 12 5

245. "Peace". 246. Motor-cyclists. 247.

1955. 5th Int. Youth Festival, Warsaw. Imperf. or perf.
927. – 25 g. mar., red & yell. 5 5
928. – 40 g. grey and blue .. 8 5
929. – 45 g. lake, red & yellow 8 5
930. – 60 g. black and orange 15 5
931. 245. 60 g. ultram. and blue 15 5
932. 1 z. indigo and blue .. 20 5
DESIGNS: 25 g., 45 g. Pansies and dove. 40 g., 60 g. (No. 930) Dove and tower.

1955. 13th Int. Tatra Mountain Motor-cycle Race.
933. 246. 40 g. brown 10 5
934. 60 g. green 5 5

1955. Polish National Day.
935. 247. 60 g. blue 5 5
936. 60 g. grey 5 5
937. 75 g. green 15 5
938. 75 g. brown 15 5
Nos. 935/6 and 937/8 were printed together in sheets containing alternate vertical rows of each colour se-tenant.

248. Athletes. 249. Szczecin. 250. Peasants and Flag.

1955. 2nd Int. Games. Imperf. or perf.
939. 248. 20 g. brown 5 5
940. – 40 g. purple 8 5
941. – 60 g. blue 12 5
942. – 1 z. red 15 5
943. – 1 z. 35 lilac 20 5
944. – 1 z. 55 green .. 55 12
DESIGNS—VERT. 40 g. Throwing the hammer. 1 z. Net-ball. 1 z. 35, Sculling. 1 z. 55, Swimming. HORIZ. 60 g. Stadium.

1955. Acquisition of Western Territories. 10th Anniv.
945. 249. 25 g. green 5 5
946. – 40 g. red (Wroclaw) .. 8 5
947. – 60 g. bl. (Zielona Gora) 8 5
948. – 95 g. black (Opole) .. 15 10

1955. 1905 Revolution. 50th Anniv.
949. 250. 40 g. brown 8 5
950. 60 g. red 5 5

251. Mickiewicz (poet). 252. Statue.

1955. Mickiewicz. Death Cent.
951. 251. 20 g. brown 5 5
952. 252. 40 g. brown & orange .. 5 5
953. – 60 g. brown and green 8 5
954. – 95 g. black and red .. 15 5
DESIGNS—As T 252: 60 g. Sculptured head. 95 g. Statue.

253. Teacher and Pupil. 254. Rook and Hands. 255. Ice Skates.

1955. Polish Teachers' Union. 50th Anniv.
955. 253. 40 g. brown 12 5
956. – 60 g. blue 15 5
DESIGN: 60 g. Allegory of "Teaching."

1956. 1st World Chess Championship of the Deaf and Dumb.
957. 254. 40 g. lake 15 8
958. – 60 g. blue 10 5
DESIGN: 60 g. Knight and hands.

1956. 11th World Students' Winter Sports Championship.
959. 255. 20 g. black and blue 35 8
960. – 40 g. blue and green .. 35 5
961. – 60 g. red and mauve .. 35 5
DESIGNS: 40 g. Ice-hockey sticks and puck. 60 g. Skis and ski sticks.

256. Officer and Ship. 257. Racing Cyclist.

1956. Merchant Navy.
962. 256. 5 g. green 5 5
963. – 10 g. red (Barges) .. 5 5
964. – 20 g. bl. (Ship in dock) 5 5
965. – 45 g. brown (Ship-building) 12 5
966. – 60 g. bl. (Ships at sea) 10 5

1956. 9th Int. Cycle Race.
967. 257. 40 g. blue 15 8
968. 60 g. green 8 5

258. Lodge, Tatra Mountains. 259. Ghetto Heroes' Monument.

1956. Tourist Propaganda.
969. 258. 30 g. green 5 5
970. – 40 g. brown 8 5
971. – 60 g. blue 25 8
972. – 1 z. 15 purple 30 5
DESIGNS: 40 g. Compass, rucksack and map. 60 g. Canoe and map. 1 z. 15, Skis and mountains.

1956. No. 829 surch.
973. 10 g. on 20 g. purple .. 15 5
974. 40 g. on 80 g. purple .. 10 5
975. 60 g. on 80 g. purple .. 15 5
976. 1 z. 35 on 80 g. purple .. 45 10

1956. Warsaw Monuments (2nd issue).
977. 259. 30 g. black 5 5
978. – 40 g. brown on green 12 5
979. – 1 z. 55 purple on pink 25 5
STATUES: 40 g. King John Sobieski III. 1 z. 55, J. Poniatowski.

260. "Economic Co-operation". 261. Ludwika Wawrzynska (teacher).

1956. Russo-Polish Friendship Month. Inscr. as in T 260.
980. – 40 g. brown and pink 12 5
981. 260. 60 g. red and bistre .. 10 5
DESIGN: 40 g. Polish and Russian dancers.

1956. Ludwika Wawrzynska Commem.
982. 261. 40 g. chocolate .. 15 5
983. 60 g. blue 8 5

262. " Lady with a Weasel " (Leonardo da Vinci).

263. Bee and Hive.

1956. Int. Campaign for Museums.
984. – 40 g. green 90 30
985. – 60 g. violet 55 12
986. **262.** 1 z. 55 sepia 70 12
Designs: 40 g. Niobe (bust). 60 g. Madonna after Vit Stvosz.

1956. Dzierzon. 50th Death Anniv.
987. **263.** 40 g. brown on yellow 12 5
988. – 60 g. brown on yellow 10 5
Design: 60 g. Portrait of Dr. J. Dzierzon.

264. Fencing.

265. 15th-century Postman.

1956. Olympic Game. Inscr. " MELBOURNE 1956 ".
989. **264.** 10 g. brown and slates 5 5
990. – 20 g. lilac and brown 8 5
991. – 25 g. black and blue .. 8 5
992. – 40 g. chocolate & green 10 5
993. – 60 g. sepia and red .. 20 5
994. – 1 z. 55 sepia and violet 80 20
995. – 1 z. 55 brown & orange 35 10
Designs: 20 g. Boxing. 25 g. Rowing. 40 g. Steeplechase. 60 g. Javelin throwing. No. 994, Gymnastics. No. 995, Long jumping (inscr. " 6,35 m ").

1956. Re-opening of Postal Museum, Wroclaw.
996. **265.** 60 g. black on blue .. 45 35

266. Snow Crystals and Skier of 1907.

267. Apple Tree and Globe.

1957. 50 Years of Skiing in Poland.
997. **266.** 40 g. blue 8 5
998. – 60 g. green 8 5
999. – 1 z. purple 15 8
Designs (with snow crystals)—vert. 60 g. Skier jumping. horiz. 1 z. Skier standing.

1957. U.N.O. Commem.
1000. **267.** 5 g. crim. & turquoise 15 8
1001. – 15 g. blue and grey .. 15 8
1002. – 40 g. green and grey .. 20 10
Designs—vert. 15 g. U.N.O. emblem. 40 g. U.N.O. Headquarters, New York.

268. Skier.

269. Winged Letter.

1957. 12th Anniv. of Deaths of Bronislaw Czech and Hanna Marusarzowna (skiers).
1003. **268.** 60 g. brown 15 5
1004. 60 g. blue 10 5

1957. Air. 7th Polish National Philatelic Exn., Warsaw.
1005. **269.** 4 z.+2 z. blue .. 1·10 1·10

270. Foil, Sword and Sabre on Map.

271. Dr. S. Petrycy.

1957. World Youth Fencing Championships, Warsaw.
1006. **270.** 40 g. purple 12 5
1007. – 60 g. red 5 5
1008. – 60 g. blue 5 5
Designs: Nos. 1007/8 are arranged in se-tenant pairs in the sheet and together show two fencers duelling.

1957. Polish Doctors.
1009. **271.** 10 g. sepia and blue .. 5 5
1010. – 20 g. lake and emerald 5 5
1011. – 40 g. black and red .. 5 5
1012. – 60 g. purple and blue 12 5
1013. – 1 z. blue and yellow .. 5 5
1014. – 1 z. 35 sepia and green 5 5
1015. – 2 z. 50 violet and crim. 12 5
1016. – 3 z. olive-brn. & violet 12 5
Portraits: 20 g. Dr. W. Oczko. 40 g. Dr. J. Sniadecki. 60 g. Dr. T. Chalubinski. 1 z. Dr. W. Bieganski. 1 z. 35, Dr. J. Dietl. 2 z. 50, Dr. B Dybowski. 3 z. Dr. H. Jordan.

272. Cycle Wheel and Flower.

273. Fair Emblem.

1957. 10th Int. Cycle Race. Inscr. as in T 272
1017. **272.** 60 g. blue 5 5
1018. – 1 z. 50 red (Cyclist) .. 5 5

1957. 26th Int. Fair, Poznan.
1019. **273.** 60 g. blue 10 5
1020. 2 z. 50 green 5 5

274. " Carlina acaulis ".

275. Fireman.

1957. Polish Flowers.
1021. **274.** 60 g. yell., grn. & grey 5 5
1022. – 60 g. green and blue .. 5 5
1023. – 60 g. olive and grey .. 5 5
1024. – 60 g. yell., red & green 25 5
1025. – 60 g. maroon & green 5 5
Flowers—vert. No. 1022, " Eryngium maritimum ". 1023 " Leontopodium alpinum " (Edelweiss). 1024, " Cypripedium calceolus ". 1025, " Lilium martagon ".

1957. Int. Fire Brigades Conference, Warsaw. Inscr. " KONGRES C.T.I.F. WARSZAWA 1957 ".
1026. **275.** 40 g. black and red .. 5 5
1027. – 60 g. green and red .. 5 5
1028. – 2 z. 50 violet and red 25 5
Designs: 60 g. Flames enveloping child. 2 z. 50, Ear of corn in flames.

276. Town Hall, Leipzig.

277. " The Letter (after Fragonard)."

1957. 4th W.F.T.U. Congress, Leipzig.
1029. **276.** 60 g. violet 5 5

1957. Stamp Day.
1030. **277.** 2 z. 50 green .. 25 5

278. Red Banner.

279. Karol Libelt (founder).

280. H. Wieniawski (violinist).

1957. Russian Revolution. 40th Anniv. Inscr. as in T 278.
1031. **278.** 60 g. red and blue 5 5
1032. – 2 z. 50 brown & black 12 5
Design: 2 z. 50, Lenin Monument, Poronin.

1957. Poznan Scientific Society Cent.
1033. **279.** 60 g. red 5 5

1957. 3rd Wieniawski Int. Violin Competition.
1034. **280.** 2 z. 50 blue 10 5

281. Aeroplane over Steel Works.

282. J. A. Komensky (Comenius).

1957. Air.
1035. **281.** 90 g. black and pink .. 5 5
1036. – 1 z. 50 brown & salmon 5 5
1037. – 3 z. 40 sepia and buff 12 5
1038. – 3 z. 90 brown & yellow 35 15
1039. – 4 z. blue and green .. 15 5
1039a. – 5 z. lake and lavender 25 8
1039b. – 10 z. sepia & turquoise 45 15
1040. – 15 z. violet and blue .. 65 8
1040a. – 20 z. slate-vio. & yell. 90 35
1040b. – 30 z. olive and buff .. 1·40 45
1040c. – 50 z. blue and drab .. 2·75 70
Designs: Aeroplane over: 1 z. 50, Castle Square, Warsaw. 3 z. 40, Old Market, Cracow. 3 z. 90, Szczecin. 4 z. Karconosze Mountains. 5 z. Old Market, Gdansk. 10 z. Liwie Castle. 15 z. Lublin. 20 z. Cable railway, Kasprowy Wierch. 30 z. Porabka Dam. 50 z. M.S. " Batory ".

For stamp as No. 1039b, but printed in slate-purple only, see No. 1095.

1957. Publication of Komensky's " Opera Didactica Omnia ". 3rd Cent.
1041. **282.** 2 z. 50 red 12 5

283. A. Strug (writer).

284. Joseph Conrad and sailing ship " Torrens ".

1957. Andrzej Strug. 20th Death Anniv.
1042. **283.** 2 z. 50 brown .. 12 5

1957. Joseph Conrad (Korzeniowski) author. Birth Cent.
1043. **284.** 60 g. brown on green 5 5
1044. 2 z. 50 blue on pink 15 5

285. Postman of 1558.

286. Town Hall, Biecz.

1958. Polish Postal Service (1st issue). 400th Anniv.
1045. **285.** 2 z. 50, purple & blue 12 5
For similar stamps see Nos. 1063/7.

1958. Ancient Polish Town Halls.
1046. **286.** 20 g. green .. 5 5
1047. – 40 g. brown (Wroclaw) 5 5
1048. – 60 g. blue (Tarnow) (horiz.) .. 5 5
1049. – 2 z. 10 lake (Gdansk) 8 5
1050. – 2 z. 50 vio. (Zamosc) 25 5

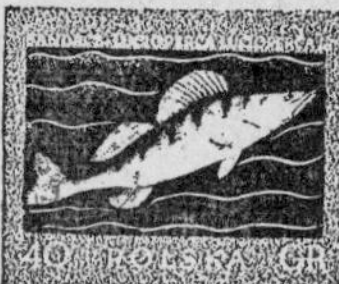

287. Perch.

288. Warsaw University.

1958. Polish Fish.
1051. **287.** 40 g. yell., blk. & blue 5 5
1052. – 60 g. bl., indigo & grn. 5 5
1053. – 2 z. 10 yellow, green, indigo and blue .. 15 5
1054. – 2 z. 50 green, black and violet .. 55 8
1055. – 6 z. 40 brown, red, black and turquoise 35 8
Designs—vert. 60 g. Salmon. 2 z. 10, Pike. 2 z. 50, Trout. horiz. 6 z. 40, Grayling.

1958. Warsaw University. 140th Anniv.
1056. **288.** 2 z. 50 blue 12 5

289. Fair Emblem.

290.

1958. 27th Int. Fair, Poznan.
1057. **289.** 2 z. 50 red and black 12 5

1958. 7th Int. Gliding Championships.
1058. **290.** 60 g. blk. & slate-blue 5 5
1059. – 2 z. 50 black and grey 15 5
Design: 2 z. 50, As T 290 but design in reverse.

291. Armed Postman.

292. Polar Bear Iceberg.

1958. Defence of Gdansk Post Office. 19th Anniv.
1060. **291.** 60 g. blue 5 5

1958. I.G.Y. Inscr. as in T 292.
1061. **292.** 60 g. black 5 5
1062. – 2 z. 50 blue 45 5
Design: 2 z. 50, Sputnik and track of rocket.

293. Tomb of Prosper Prowano (First Polish Postmaster).

294. Envelope Quill and Postmark.

295. Partisans' Cross.

1958. Polish Postal Service (2nd Issue). 400th Anniv. Inscr. " 400 LAT POCZTY POLSKIEJ ".
1063. **293.** 40 g. maroon and blue 15 5
1064. – 60 g. black and lilac .. 5 5
1065. – 95 g. violet and yellow 5 5
1066. – 2 z. 10 blue and grey 8 5
1067. – 3 z. 40 brown & turquoise 8 5
Designs: 60 g. Mail-coach and Church of our Lady, Cracow. 95 g. Mail-coach. 2 z. 10, 16th-century postman. 3 z. 40, Galleon. Nos. 1064/7 show various forms of modern transport in clear silhouette in the background.

1958. Stamp Day.
1068. **290.** 60 g. grn., red & blk. 5 5

1958. Polish People's Army. 15th Anniv. Inscr. " 15-LECIE LUDOWEGO " etc.
1069. **295.** 40 g. buff, black & grn. 5 5
1070. – 60 g. brown, yellow, black and blue .. 5 5
1071. – 2 z. 50 yellow, black, red and green .. 20 5
Designs: 60 g. Virtuti Military Cross. 2 z. 50, Grunwald Cross.

296. "Mail Coach in the Kielce District" (after painting by A. Kedzierskiego). 297. Galleon.

1958. Polish Postal Service. 400th Anniv. Exn.
1072. **296.** 2 z. 50 black on buff . . 45 30

1958. Polish Emigration to America. 350th Anniv. Inscr. "1608" etc.
1073. **297.** 60 g. green 5 5
1074. – 2 z. 50 red (Polish emigrants) 15 8

298. U.N.E.S.C.O. Headquarters, Paris. 299. S. Wyspianski (painter).

1958. Inaug. of U.N.E.S.C.O. Headquarters Building.
1075. **298.** 2 z. 50 black & green 20 5

1958. Famous Poles.
1076. **299.** 60 g. violet 5 5
1077. – 2 z. 50 green 20 8
PORTRAIT: 2 z. 50, S. Moniuszko (composer).

300. "Human Rights". 301. Party Flag. 302. Sailing boat.

1958. Declaration of Human Rights. 10th Anniv.
1078. **300.** 2 z. 50 g. lake & brn. 12 5

1958. Polish Communist Party. 40th Anniv.
1079. **301.** 60 g. red and purple . . 5 5

1959. Sports.
1080. **302.** 40 g. ultram. & blue . . 5 5
1081. – 60 g. maroon & salmon 5 5
1082. – 95 g. maroon & green 15 5
1083. – 2 z. blue and green . . 12 5
DESIGNS: 60 g. Archer. 95 g. Footballers. 2 z. Horseman.

303. The "Guiding Hand". 304. "Amanita phalloides".

1959. 3rd Polish United Workers Party Congress. Inscr. as in T **303**.
1084. **303.** 40 g. blk., brown & red 5 5
1085. – 60 g. multicoloured . . 5 5
1086. – 1 z. 55 multicoloured 8 5
DESIGNS—HORIZ. 60 g. Hammer and ears of corn. VERT. 1 z. 55, Nowa Huta foundry.

1959. Mushrooms of Poland.
1087. **304.** 20 g. yell., brn. & grn. 5 5
1088. – 30 g. red, olive, brown and buff 5 5
1089. – 40 g. red, green, yellow and mauve . . 5 5
1090. – 60 g. yellow, brown, emerald and green 5 5
1091. – 1 z. yellow, brown, green and blue . . 30 5
1092. – 2 z. 50 sep., grn. & bl. 50 12
1093. – 3 z. 40 red, yellow, green and grey . . 55 75
1094. – 5 z. 60 chocolate, green and yellow . . 80 55
MUSHROOMS: 30 g. "Boletus luteus". 40 g. "Boletus edulis". 60 g. "Lactarius deliciosus". 1 z. "Cantharellus cibarius". 2 z. 50, "Psalliota compestris". 3 z. 40, "Amanita muscaria". 5 z. 60, "Boletus scaber"

1959. Air. 65 Years of Philately in Poland and 6th Polish Philatelic Assn. Congress Warsaw. As No. 1039b but in one colour only.
1095. 10 z. slate-purple . . 70 55

305. "Storks" (after Chelmonski). 306. Miner.

1959. Polish Paintings.
1096. **305.** 40 g. green 5 5
1097. – 60 g. maroon . . 12 5
1098. – 1 z. black . . 12 5
1099. – 1 z. 50 sepia . . 30 8
1100. – 6 z. 40 blue . . . . 1·10 35
PAINTINGS—VERT. 60 g. "Motherhood" (Wyspianski). 1 z. "Madame de Romanet" (Rodakowski). 1 z. 50, "Death" (Malczewski). HORIZ. 6 z. 40, "The Sandmen" (Gierymski).

1959. 3rd Int. Miners' Congress, Katowice.
1101. **306.** 2 z. 50 sepia, grn. & bl. 12 5

307. Sheaf of Wheat (Agriculture"). 308. Dr. L. Zamenhof. 309. "Flowering Pink" (Map of Austria).

1959. People's Republic (15th Anniv.). Inscr. "XV LAT PRL".
1102. **307.** 40 g. green and black 5 5
1103. – 60 g. red and black . . 5 5
1104. – 1 z. 50 blue and black 8 5
DESIGNS: 60 g. Crane ("Building"). 1 z. 50, Corinthian column, and book ("Culture and Science").

1959. Int. Esperanto Congress, Warsaw and Birth Cent. of Dr. L. Zamenhof. Inscr. as in T **308**.
1105. **308** 60 g. blk. & grn. on ol. 5 5
1106. – 1z. 5 0 green, red and violet on grey . . 12 5
DESIGN: 1 z. 50, Esperanto Star, and globe.

1959. 7th World Youth Festival, Vienna.
1107. **309.** 60 g. multicoloured on yellow . . 5 5
1108. 2 z. 50 multicoloured on grey 20 5

310. 311. Parliament House, Warsaw.

1959. Polish Airlines "LOT". 30th Anniv.
1109. **310.** 60 g. blue, vio. & black 5 5

1959. 48th Inter-Parliamentary Union Conf., Warsaw.
1110. **311.** 60 g. green, red & blk. 5 5
1111. 2 z. 50 pur., red & blk. 20 5

1959. Baltic States' Int. Philatelic Exn., Gdansk. No. 890 optd. **BALPEXI-GDANSK 1959.**
1112. 45 g. brown on lemon . . 15 5

312. Dove and Globe. 313. Nurse with Bag.

1959. World Peace Movement (10th Anniv.).
1113. **312.** 60 g. grey and blue . . 5 5

1959. Red Cross Commem. Cross in red.
1114. **313.** 40 g. black and green 5 5
1115. – 60 g. brown . . 5 5
1116. – 2 z. 50 blk. & brn.-red 20 10
DESIGNS—VERT. 60 g. Nurse with bottle and bandages. SQUARE (23 × 23 mm.): 2 z. 50, J. H. Dunant.

314. Emblem of Polish-Chinese Friendship Society. 315.

1959. Polish-Chinese Friendship.
1117. **314.** 60 g. red, yellow, blue and violet 10 5
1118. 2 z. 50 red, yellow, blue and green . . 10 5

1959. Stamp Day.
1119. **315.** 60 g. red, grn. & turq. 10 5
1120. 2 z. 50 bl., grn. & red 12 5

316. Sputnik III.

1959. Cosmic Flights.
1121. **316.** 40 g. black and blue 5 5
1122. – 60 g. black and lake 12 8
1123. – 2 z. 50 blue and green 45 25
DESIGNS: 60 g. Rocket "Mieczta" encircling Sun. 2 z. 50, Moon rocket "Lunik II".

317. Schoolgirl. 318. Darwin.

1959. "1000 Schools for Polish Millennium". Inscr. as in T **317**.
1124. **317.** 40 g. sepia and green 5 5
1125. – 60 g. red, black & blue 5 5
DESIGN: 60 g. Children going to school.

1959. Famous Scientists
1126. **318.** 20 g. blue 5 5
1127. – 40 g. olive (Mendeleev) 5 5
1128. – 60 g. purple (Einstein) 5 5
1129. – 1 z. 50 choc. (Pasteur) 8 5
1130. – 1 z. 55 grn. (Newton) 25 5
1131. – 2 z. 50 violet . . (Copernicus) . . 30 8

319. Costumes of Rzeszow. 320.

1959. Provincial Costumes (1st series).
1132. **319.** 20 g. black and myrtle 5 5
1133. **320.** 20 g. black and myrtle 5 5
1134. – 60 g. purple and pink 5 5
1135. – 60 g. purple and pink 5 5
1136. – 1 z. red and blue . . 5 5
1137. – 1 z. red and blue . . 5 5
1138. – 2 z. 50 green and lilac 15 5
1139. – 2 z. 50 green and lilac 15 5
1140. – 5 z. 60 blue & yellow 55 25
1141. – 5 z. 60 blue & yellow 55 25
DESIGNS—Male and female costumes of: Nos. 1134/5, Kurpie. 1136/7, Silesia. 1138/9, Mountain regions. 1140/1, Szamotuly.
See also Nos. 1150/9.

321. Silhouette of Piano. 322. Polish 10 k. Stamp of 1860 and Postmark.

1960. Chopin. 150th Birth Anniv. and Chopin Music Competition, Warsaw. Inscr. "1810–1960".
1142. **321.** 60 g. black and violet 5 5
1143. – 1 z. 50 blk., red & blue 12 5
1144. – 2 z. 50 sepia . . 65 15
DESIGNS—As T **321**: 1 z. 50, Portion of Chopin's music (25 × 39½ mm.).: 2 z. 50, Portrait of Chopin.

1960. Polish Stamp Cent. Inscr. as in T **322**.
1145. **322.** 40 g. red, blue & black 8 5
1146. – 60 g. blue, blk. & vio. 12 5
1147. – 1 z. 35 blue, red & grey 25 12
1148. – 1 z. 55 red, blk. & grn. 40 12
1149. – 2 z. 50, grn., blk. & ol. 60 20
DESIGNS: 1 z. 35, Emblem inscr. "1860 1960". Reproductions of Polish stamps: 60 g. No. 356. 1 z. 55, No. 533. 2 z. 50, No. 1030. With appropriate postmarks.

1960. Provincial Costumes (2nd series). As T **319/20**.
1150. 40 g. red and blue . . 5 5
1151. 40 g. red and blue . . 5 5
1152. 2 z. blue and yellow . . 12 5
1153. 2 z. blue and yellow . . 12 5
1154. 3 z. 10 blue-green and yellow-green 15 5
1155. 3 z. 10 blue-green and yellow-green 15 5
1156. 3 z. 40 brown & blue-grn. 20 5
1157. 3 z. 40 brown & blue-grn. 20 5
1158. 6 z. 50 violet & grey-grn. 35 8
1159. 6 z. 50 violet & grey-grn. 35 8
DESIGNS—Male and female costumes of: Nos. 1150/1, Cracow. 1152/3, Lowicz. 1154/5, Kujawy. 1156/7, Lublin. 1158/9, Lubuski.

323. Throwing the Discus. 324. King Wladislaw's Tomb, Wawel Castle.

1960. Olympic Games, 1960. Rings and inscr. in black.
1160. 60 g. blue (T 323) . . 5 5
1161. 60 g. magenta (Running) 5 5
1162. 60 g. violet (Cycling) . . 5 5
1163. 60 g. blue-green (Horse-jumping) 5 5
1164. 2 z. 30 ult. (Trumpeters) 20 10
1165. 2 z. 50 brown (Boxing) . . 20 10
1166. 2 z. 50 red (Olympic Flame) 20 10
1167. 2 z. 50 emer. (Long-jump) 20 10
The designs all mark Polish successes in previous Olympic Games. The stamps in each denomination are arranged se-tenant in blocks of four (sheets of 60) to form a complete circuit of the stadium track.

1960. Battle of Grunwald. 550th Anniv.
1168. **324.** 60 g. chocolate . . 12 5
1169. – 90 g. bronze-green . . 20 5
1170. – 2 z. 50 black . . 80 20
DESIGNS—As T **324**: 90 g. Proposed Grunwald Monument. HORIZ. (78 × 35½ mm.): 2 z. 50, "Battle of Grunwald" (after painting by Jan Matejko).

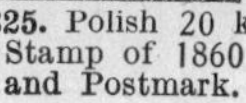

325. Polish 20 k. Stamp of 1860 and Postmark. 326. Ignacy Lukasiewicz (chemist and inventor of petrol lamp).

1960. Int. Philatelic Exn., Warsaw.
1171. **325.** 10 z. + 10 z. red, black and blue . . . . 3·50 3·50

1960. Lukasiewicz Commem. and 5th Pharmaceutical Congress, Poznan.
1172. **326.** 60 g. black & ol.-yell. 5 5

327. "The Annunciation". 328. Paderewski.

1960. Altar Carvings of St. Mary's Church Cracow.

1173. **327.** 20 g. slate-blue .. 5 5
1174. – 30 g. brown 5 5
1175. – 40 g. violet 5 5
1176. – 60 g. grey-green .. 10 5
1177. – 2 z. 50 claret .. 55 12
1178. – 5 z. 60 sepia .. 85 25

DESIGNS: 30 g. "The Nativity". 40 g. "Homage of the Three Kings". 60 g. "The Resurrection". 2 z. 50, "The Ascension". 5 z. 60, "The Descent of the Holy Ghost".

1960. Paderewski. Birth Cent.

1179. **328.** 2 z. 50 black .. 12 5

1960. Stamp Day. Optd. **DZIEN ZNACZKA 1960.**

1180. **322.** 40 g. red, blue & black 45 45

329. Gniezno.

330. Great Bustard ("Otis tardo").

1960. Old Polish Towns as T **329.**

1181. 5 g. brown 5 5
1182. 10 g. blue-green 5 5
1183. 20 g. sepia 5 5
1184. 40 g. red 5 5
1185. 50 g. violet 5 5
1186. 60 g. magenta 5 5
1187. 60 g. blue 5 5
1188. 80 g. blue.. .. .. 5 5
1189. 90 g. brown 5 5
1190. 95 g. olive-black 5 5
1191. 1 z. orange-red & pale lilac 5 5
1192. 1 z. 15 grey-grn. & orange 5 5
1193. 1 z. 35 magenta & pale green 5 5
1194. 1 z. 50 bistre and pale blue 8 5
1195. 1 z. 55 claret & pale yell. 8 5
1196. 2 z. blue and pale lilac .. 10 5
1197. 2 z. 10 sepia & pale yellow 12 5
1198. 2 z. 50 violet & pale green 12 5
1199. 3 z. 10 red and pale grey 55 5
1200. 5 z. 60 slate & grey-green 30 5

TOWNS: 10 g. Cracow. 20 g. Warsaw. 40 g. Poznan. 50 g. Plock. 60 g. magenta, Kalisz. 60 g. blue, Tczew. 80 g. Frombork. 90 g. Torun. 95 g. Puck. 1 z. Slupsk. 1 z. 15. Gdansk. 1 z. 35, Wroclaw. 1 z. 50, Cieszyn. 1 z. 55, Opole. 2 z. Kolobrzeg. 2 z. 10, Legnica. 2 z. 50, Katowice. 3 z. 10, Lodz. 5 z. 60, Walbrzych.

1960. Birds as T **330.** Birds in natural colours. Inscriptions in black. Background colours given.

1201. 10 g. drab 5 5
1202. 20 g. drab 5 5
1203. 30 g. drab 5 5
1204. 40 g. drab 5 5
1205. 50 g. blue-green 8 5
1206. 60 g. blue-green 8 5
1207. 75 g. blue-green 10 5
1208. 90 g. blue-green 15 10
1209. 2 z. 50 stone 45 30
1210. 4 z. stone 60 25
1211. 5 z. 60 stone .. .. 1·25 45
1212. 6 z. 50 stone .. .. 1·60 60

BIRDS: 20 g. Raven. 30 g. Cormorant. 40 g. Stork. 50 g. Owl. 60 g. Sea eagle. 75 g. Golden eagle. 90 g. Harrier eagle. 2 z. 50, Rock thrush. 4 z. Kingfisher. 5 z. 60, Wall creeper. 6 z. 50, Roller.

331. Front page of Newspaper "Proletaryat" (1883).

332. Ice-hockey.

1961. Polish Newspaper Press. Tercent.

1213. – 40 g. grn., blue & blk. 25 5
1214. **331.** 60 g. yell., red & blk. 25 5
1215. – 2 z. 50 bl., vio. & blk. 90 25

DESIGNS—Newspaper front page: 40 g. "Mercuriusz" (first issue, 1661). 2 z. 50, "Rzeczpospolita" (1944).

1961. 1st Winter Military Spartakiad.

1216. **332.** 40 g. blk., yell. & lilac 15 5
1217. – 60 g. black, red, violet-blue and cobalt .. 55 5
1218. – 1 z. olive, black, red, deep and light blue 3·25 80
1219. – 1 z. 50 black, yellow and turquoise .. 45 15

DESIGNS: 60 g. Ski-jumping. 1 z. Rifle-shooting. 1 z. 50, Slalom (ski) racing.

333. Congress Emblem.

334. Yuri Gagarin.

1961. 4th Polish Engineers' Conf.

1220. **333.** 60 g. black and red 5 5

1961. World's First Manned Space Flight.

1221. **334.** 40 g. black, red and brown-red .. 20 5
1222. – 60 g. red., blk. & blue 20 8

DESIGN: 60 g. Globe and star.

335. Fair Emblem.

1961. 3rd Int. Fair, Poznan.

1223. **335.** 40 g. black, red & bl. 5 5
1224. 1 z. 50 blk., bl. & red 10 5

336. King Mieszko I.

1961. Famous Poles (1st issue).

1225. **336.** 60 g. black and blue 5 5
1226. – 60 g. black and claret 5 5
1227. – 60 g. blk. & grey-grn. 5 5
1228. – 60 g. black and violet 12 5
1229. – 60 g. black and brown 5 5
1230. – 60 g. black and olive 5 5

PORTRAITS: No. 1226, King Kazimierz Wielki. 1227, King Kazimiers Jagiellonczyk. 1228, Copernicus. 1229, A. F. Modrzewski. 1230, Kosciuszko.

See also Nos. 1301/6 and 1398/1401.

337. "B 15" Trawler.

1961. Shipbuilding Industry. Multicoloured.

1231. 60 g. T **337** 8 5
1232. 1 z. 55 "B 62" depot ship 15 5
1233. 2 z. 50 "B 471" coaster 25 12
1234. 3 z. 40 "B 55" freighter 45 15
1235. 4 z. "B 54" freighter .. 55 20
1236. 5 z. 60 "B 70" tanker .. 1·60 55

SIZES: 2 z. 50, As T **337.** 5 z. 60, 108×21 mm. Rest, 81×21 mm.

338. Posthorn and Telephone Dial.

339. Opole Seal.

1961. Communications Ministers' Conference, Warsaw.

1237. **338.** 40 g. red, grn. & sl.-bl. 5 5
1238. – 60 g. violet, yellow and slate-purple .. 5 5
1239. – 2 z. 50 ultram., blue and bistre .. 20 5

DESIGNS: 60 g. Posthorn and radar screen. 2 z. 50, Posthorn and conference emblem.

1961. Polish Western Provinces.

1240. 40 g. chocolate on buff .. 5 5
1241. 40 g. chocolate on buff .. 5 5
1242. 60 g. violet on pink .. 5 5
1243. 60 g. violet on pink .. 5 5
1243a. 95 g. green on blue .. 5 5
1243b. 95 g. green on blue .. 5 5
1244. 2 z. 50 sage on green .. 15 5
1245. 2 z. 50 sage on green .. 15 5

DESIGNS—VERT. No. 1240, T **339.** 1242, King Henryk IV's tomb. 1243a, Seal of Conrad II. 1244, Prince Barnim's seal. HORIZ. 1241, Opole cement works. 1243, Wroclaw apartment-house. 1243b, Factory interior, Zielonagora. 1245, Szczecin harbour.

See also Nos. 1308/13.

340. Beribboned Paddle.

341. Titov and Orbit within Star.

1961. 6th European Canoeing Championships. Multicoloured.

1246. 40 g. Two canoes within letter "E" 8 5
1247. 60 g. Two four-seater canoes at finishing post 8 5
1248. 2 z. 50 T **340** 60 12

The 40 g. and 60 g. are horiz.

1961. 2nd Russian Manned Space Flight.

1249. **341.** 40 g. blk., red & pink 10 5
1250. – 60 g. blue and black 10 5

DESIGN: 60 g. Dove and spaceman's orbit around globe.

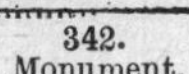

342. Monument.

343. P.K.O. Emblem and Ant.

1961. 3rd Silesian Uprising. 40th Anniv.

1251. **342.** 60 g. grey and green 5 5
1252. – 1 z. 55 grey and blue 10 5

DESIGN: 1 z. 55, Cross of Silesian uprisers.

1961. Savings Month.

1253. 40 g. red, yellow and black 8 5
1254. 60 g. brown, yellow & blk. 8 5
1255. 60 g. blue, violet and pink 8 5
1256. 60 g. green, red and black 8 5
1257. 2 z. 50 mag., grey & black 70 12

DESIGNS: No. 1253, Savings Bank motif. 1254, T **343.** 1255, Bee. 1256, Squirrel. 1257, Savings Bank book.

344. "Mail Cart" (after J. Chelmonski).

1961. Stamp Day and 40th Anniv. of Postal Museum.

1258. **344.** 60 g. chocolate .. 12 5
1259. 60 g. green 12 5

345. Congress Emblem.

346. Emblem of Kopasyni Mining Family, 1284.

347. Child and Syringe.

348. Cogwheel and Wheat.

1961. 5th W.F.T.U. Congress, Moscow.

1260. **345.** 60 g. black 5 5

1961. Millenary of Polish Mining Industry.

1261. **346.** 40 g. purple & orange 5 5
1262. – 60 g. grey-bl. & ultram. 5 5
1263. – 2 z. 50 green and black 20 5

DESIGNS: 60 g. 14th-century seal of Bytom. 2 z. 50, Emblem of Int. Mine Constructors' Congress, Warsaw, 1958.

1961. 15th Anniv. of U.N.I.C.E.F.

1264. **347.** 40 g. black and blue.. 5 5
1265. – 60 g. black and orange 5 5
1266 – 2 z. 50 black & turq. 25 5

DESIGNS—HORIZ. 60 g. Children of three races. VERT. 2 z. 50, Mother and child, and feeding bottle.

1961. 15th Economic Co-operative Council Meeting, Warsaw.

1267. **348.** 40 g. crim., yell. & bl. 5 5
1268. – 60 g. red, bl. & ultram. 5 5

DESIGN: 60 g. Oil pipeline map, E. Europe.

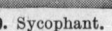

349. Sycophant.

350. Worker with Flag and Dove.

1961. Insects. Multicoloured.

1269. 20 g. T **349** 5 5
1270. 30 g. Violet Ground Beetle 5 5
1271. 40 g. Alpine Longhorn Beetle 5 5
1272. 50 g. European Longhorn Beetle 5 5
1273. 60 g. Ground Beetle .. 5 5
1274. 80 g. Stag Beetle .. 10 5
1275. 1 z. 15 Muse Butterfly .. 15 5
1276. 1 z. 35 Death's Head Hawk Moth 15 5
1277. 1 z. 50 Celadon Swallowtail 15 8
1278. 1 z. 55 Apollo Butterfly.. 15 8
1279. 2 z. 50 Wood Ant .. 60 12
1280. 5 z. 60 Bumble Bee .. 2·25 90

The 20 g. to 80 g. show beetles as T **349** and the rest butterflies in square shape, size 36½ × 36½ mm.

1962. Polish Workers' Party. 20th Anniv.

1281. 60 g. sepia, black & verm. 5 5
1282. 60 g. bistre, black & verm. 5 5
1283. 60 g. vio.-blue, blk. & verm. 5 5
1284. 60 g. bluish grey, black and vermilion 5 5
1285. 60 g. grey-bl., blk. & verm. 5 5

DESIGNS: No. 1281, T **350.** 1282, Steersman. 1283, Worker with hammer. 1284, Soldier with weapon. 1285, Worker with trowel and rifle.

DESIGNS—HORIZ. 60 g. Skier racing. VERT. 1 z. 50. Ski-jumper.

351. Two Skiers Racing.

1962. F.I.S. Int. Ski Championships, Zakopane.

1286. **351.** 40 g. slate-blue, grey and red 5 5
1287. 40 g. grey-blue, brown and red 20 10
1288. – 60 g. slate-blue, grey and red 10 5
1289. – 60 g. grey-blue, brown and red 35 15
1290. – 1 z. 50 slate-blue, grey and red 15 5
1291. – 1 z. 50 vio., grey & red 80 25

352. Majdanek Monument.

1962. Concentration Camp Monuments.

1292. – 40 g. blue 5 5
1293. **352.** 60 g. black 5 5
1294. – 1 z. 50 violet 12 5

DESIGNS—VERT. (20×31 mm.): 40 g. Broken carnations and portion of prison clothing (Auschwitz camp). 1 z. 50, Treblinka monument.

353. Racing Cyclist.

DESIGNS: (74½×22 mm.): 2 z. 50, Cyclists & "XV". As T **353.** 3 z. 40, Arms of Berlin, Prague and Warsaw, and cycle wheel.

1962. 15th Int. Peace Cycle Race.
1295. **353.** 60 g. black and blue . . 8 5
1296. – 2 z. 50 black & yellow 25 5
1297. – 3 z. 40 black & violet 45 8

354. Lenin walking.

355. Gen. K. Swierczewski-Walter Monument.

1962. Lenin's Sojourn in Poland. 50th Anniv. Inscr. "1912–1962".
1298. **354.** 40 g. grn. & pale grn. 5 5
1299. – 60 g. lake and pink . . 5 5
1300. – 2 z. 50 sepia & yellow 12 5
DESIGNS: 60 g. Lenin. 2 z. 50, Lenin wearing cap, and Barbican, Cracow.

1962. Famous Poles (2nd issue). As T **336.**
1301. 60 g. black and grey-green 5 5
1302. 60 g. black and chestnut 5 5
1303. 60 g. black and blue . . 5 5
1304. 60 g. black and bistre . . 5 5
1305. 60 g. blk. & reddish purple 5 5
1306. 60 g. black and blue-green 5 5
PORTRAITS: No. 1301, A. Mickiewicz (poet). 1302, J. Slowacki (poet). 1303, Chopin (composer). 1304, R. Traugutt (patriot). 1305, J. Dabrowski (revolutionary). 1306, Maria Konopnicka (poetess).

1962. Gen. K. Swierczewski-Walter (patriot). 15th Death Anniv.
1307. **355.** 60 g. black . . 5 5

1962. Polish Northern Provinces. As T **339.**
1308. 60 g. slate-violet on blue 5 5
1309. 60 g. slate-violet on blue 5 5
1310. 1 z. 55 sepia on yellow . . 8 5
1311. 1 z. 55 sepia on yellow 8 5
1312. 2 z. 50 slate-blue on grey 20 5
1313. 2 z. 50 slate-blue on grey 20 5
DESIGNS—VERT. No. 1308, Princess Elizabeth's seal. 1310, Gdansk Governor's seal. 1312, Frombork Cathedral. HORIZ. No. 1309, Insulators factory, Szczecinek. 1311, Gdansk shipyard. 1313, Laboratory of Agricultural College, Kortowo.

356. "Crocus scepusiensis" (Borb).

357. "The Poison Well" (after J. Malczewski).

1962. Polish Protected Plants. Plants in natural colours.
1314 **356.** 60 g. yellow 5 5
1315. A. 60 g. cinnamon . . 30 5
1316. B. 60 g. pink 5 5
1317. C. 90 g. yellow-green . . 8 5
1318. D. 90 g. yellow-olive . . 8 5
1319. E. 90 g. green . . 8 5
1320. F. 1 z. 50 grey-blue . . 15 5
1321. G. 1 z. 50 light green . . 15 5
1322. H. 1 z. 50 bluish-green . . 15 5
1323. I. 2 z. 50 grey-green . . 35 25
1324. J. 2 z. 50 turquoise . . 35 25
1325. K. 2 z. 50 violet-blue . . 35 25
PLANTS: A, "Platanthera bifolia" (Rich). B, "Aconitum callibotryon" (Rchb.). C, "Gentiana clusii" (Perr. et Song). D, "Dictamnus albus" (L.). E, "Nymphaea alba" (L.). F, "Daphne mezereum" (L.). G, "Pulsatilla vulgaris" (Mill.). H, "Anemone silvestris" (L.). I, "Trollius europaeus" (L.). J, "Galanthus nivalis" (L.). K, "Adonis vernalis" (L.).

1962. F.I.P. Day (Federation Internationale de Philatelie").
1326. **357.** 60 g. black on cream 8 5

358. Pole Vault.

1962. 7th European Athletic Championships, Belgrade. Multicoloured.
1327. 40 g. T **358** 5 5
1328. 60 g. 400-metres relay . . 5 5
1329. 90 g. Throwing the javelin 5 5
1330. 1 z. Hurdling 5 5
1331. 1 z. 50 High-jumping . . 8 5
1332. 1 z. 55 Throwing the discus 8 5
1333. 2 z. 50 100-metres final . . 15 5
1334. 3 z. 40 Throwing the hammer 45 5

359. Mosquito.

360. Cosmonauts "in flight".

1962. Malaria Eradication.
1335. **359.** 60 g. olive-brown and blue-green . . 5 5
1336. – 1 z. 50 pink, grey, violet and red . . 8 5
1337. – 2 z. 50 orange, green, blue and grey . . 25 5
DESIGNS: 1 z. 50, Malaria parasites in blood, 2 z. 50, Cinchona plant.

1962. 1st "Team" Manned Space Flight.
1338. **360.** 60 g. green, blk. & vio. 10 5
1339. – 2 z. 50 red, black and turquoise 20 8
DESIGN: 2 z. 50, Two stars (representing space-ships) in orbit.

361. "A moment of Determination" (after A. Kamienski).

362. "Mazovian Princes" Mansion, Warsaw.

1962. Stamp Day.
1340. **361.** 60 g. black . . 5 5
1341. 2 z. 50 brown . . 25 8

1962. Polish Democratic Party. 25th Anniv.
1342. **362.** 60 g. black on red . . 5 5

363. Cruiser "Aurora".

1962. Russian Revolution. 45th Anniv.
1343. **363.** 60 g. grey-blue & red 5 5

364. J. Korczak (bust after Dunikowski).

DESIGNS: 60 g. to 5 z. 60, Illustrations from Korczak's children's books.

1962. Janusz Korczak (child educator). 20th Death Anniv. Inscr. as in T **364.**
1344. **364.** 50 g. sepia, bis. & brn. 5 5
1345. – 60 g. multicoloured . . 8 5
1346. – 90 g. multicoloured . . 8 5
1347. – 1 z. multicoloured . . 10 5
1348. – 2 z. 50 multicoloured 30 8
1349. – 5 z. 60 multicoloured 70 20

365. Old Town, Warsaw.

1962. 5th T.U. Congress, Warsaw.
1350. **365.** 3 z. 40 blue, red, black and cream 30 10

366. Master Buncombe.

367. R. Traugutt (insurgent leader).

1962. Maria Konopnicka's Fairy Tale "The Dwarfs and Orphan Mary". Multicoloured.
1351. 40 g. Type **366** 20 8
1352. 60 g. Lardie the Fox and Master Buncombe . . 20 20
1353. 1 z. 50 Bluey the Frog making music 20 8
1354. 1 z. 55 Peter's kitchen . . 20 8
1355. 2 z. 50 Saraband's concert in Nightingale Valley 35 10
1356. 3 z. 40 Orphan Mary and Subearthy 70 35

1963. Cent. of January (1863) Rising.
1357. **367.** 60 g. blk., pink & turq. 5 5

368. Tractor and Wheat.

DESIGNS: 60 g. Millet and hoeing. 2 z. 50, Rice and mechanical harvester.

1963. Freedom from Hunger.
1358. **368.** 40 g. blk., ochre & bl. 5 5
1359. – 60 g. black, green, red and chocolate . . 8 5
1360. – 2 z. 50 black, green, buff and chestnut 30 8

369. Cocker Spaniel.

1963. Dogs.
1361. **369.** 20 g. red, blk. & lilac 5 5
1362. – 30 g. black and red . . 5 5
1363. – 40 g. ochre, blk. & lilac 5 5
1364. – 50 g. ochre, blk. & blue 5 5
1365. – 60 g. black and blue . . 5 5
1366. – 1 z. black and green . . 25 8
1367. – 2 z. 50 brn., yell. & blk. 70 20
1368. – 3 z. 40 blk. & vermilion 1·10 55
1369. – 6 z. 50 black and greenish yellow . . 1·75 1·10
DOGS—HORIZ. 30 g. Sheep-dog. 40 g. Boxer. 2 z. 50, Gun-dog "Ogar". 6 z. 50, Spotted dog. VERT. 50 g. Airedale terrier. 60 g. French bulldog. 1 z. French poodle. 3 z. 40, Podhale sheep-dog.

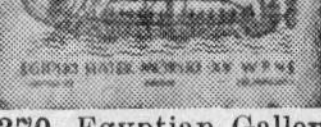
370. Egyptian Galley (15-century B.C.).

371. Insurgent.

1963. Sailing Ships (1st series).
1370. **370.** 5 g. brown on bistre . . 5 5
1371. – 10 g. blue-grn. on grn. 5 5
1372. – 20 g. ultram. on violet 5 5
1373. – 30 g. black on olive . . 5 5
1374. – 40 g. blue on blue . . 5 5
1375. – 60 g. pur. on grey-brn. 8 5
1376. – 1 z. black on blue . . 12 5
1377. – 1 z. 15 green on pink 20 5
SHIPS: 10 g. Phoenician merchantman (15th-cent. B.C.). 20 g. Greek trireme (5th-cent. B.C.). 30 g. Roman merchantman (3rd-cent. A.D.). 40 g. Scandinavian "gokstad" (9th-cent.). 60 g. Hanse "kogge" (14th-cent.). 1 z. "Holk" ship (16th-cent.). 1 z. 15, Mediterranean carrack (15th-cent.).
See also Nos. 1451/66.

1963. Warsaw Ghetto Uprising. 20th Anniv.
1378. **371.** 2 z. 50 slate-purple and pale blue . . 15 5

372. Centenary Emblem.

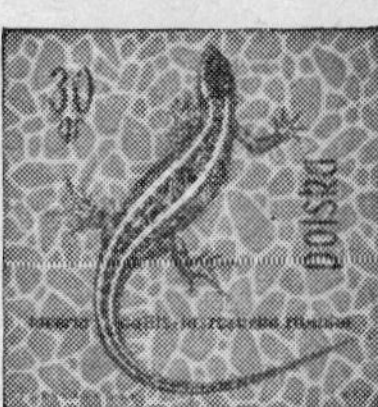

373. Lizard.

1963. Red Cross Cent.
1379. **372.** 2 z. 50 red, blue & yell. 30 8
Issued in sheets with alternate rows inverted.

1963. Protected Reptiles and Amphibians. Reptiles in natural colours: inscr. in black; background colours given.
1380. **373.** 30 g. grey-green . . 5 5
1381. – 40 g. olive . . 5 5
1382. – 50 g. brown . . 5 5
1383. – 60 g. drab . . 5 5
1384. – 90 g. myrtle . . 5 5
1385. – 1 z. 15 grey . . 5 5
1386. – 1 z. 35 grey-blue . . 8 5
1387. – 1 z. 50 blue-green . . 8 5
1388. – 1 z. 55 pale blue . . 15 5
1389. – 2 z. 50 lavender . . 15 12
1390. – 3 z. myrtle . . 45 15
1391. – 3 z. 40 slate-purple 70 20
DESIGNS: 40 g. Copperhead (snake). 50 g. Marsh tortoise. 60 g. Grass snake. 90 g. Blindworm. 1 z. 15, Tree toad. 1 z. 35, Mountain newt. 1 z. 50, Crested newt. 1 z. 55. Green toad. 2 z. 50, "Bombina" toad, 3 z. Salamander. 3 z. 40, "Natterjack" (toad).

374. Epee, foil, rapier and knight's helmet

1963. World Fencing Championships, Gdansk.
1392. **374.** 20 g. yellow and brown 5 5
1393. – 40 g. light blue & blue 5 5
1394. – 60 g. vermilion & red 5 5
1395. – 1 z. 15 light grn. & grn. 8 5
1396. – 1 z. 55 reddish violet and violet . . 20 5
1397. – 6 z. 50 yellow, maroon and bistre-brown 95 12
DESIGNS—HORIZ. Fencers with background of: 40 g. Knights jousting. 60 g. Dragoons in sword-fight. 1 z. 15, 18th-century duellists. 1 z. 55, Old Gdansk. VERT. 6 z. 50, Inscription and Arms of Gdansk.

1963. Famous Poles (3rd issue). As T **336.**
1398. 60 g. black and brown . . 5 5
1399. 60 g. black and sepia . . 5 5
1400. 60 g. black & turquoise-bl. 5 5
1401. 60 g. black and green . . 5 5
PORTRAITS: No. 1398, L. Warynski (patriot). 1399, L. Krzywicki (economist). 1400, M. Sklodowska-Curie (scientist). 1401, K. Swierczewski (patriot).

375. Bykovsky and "Vostock 5".

1963. 2nd "Team" Manned Space Flights.
1402. **375.** 40 g. blk., green & blue 8 5
1403. – 60 g. black, blue & grn. 8 5
1404. – 6 z. 50 green, blue, black and red . . 70 8
DESIGNS: 60 g. Tereshkova and "Vostock 6". 6 z. 50, "Vostocks 5 and 6" in orbit.

376. Basketball.

DESIGNS: 50 g. to 2 z. 50, A T **376** but with ball, players and hands in various positions. 5 z. 60, Hands placing ball in net.

1963. 13th European (Men's) Basketball Championships, Wroclaw.
1405. **376.** 40 g. green, brown, black and yellow . . 5 5
1406. – 50 g. green, blk. & pink 5 5
1407. – 60 g. black, grn. & red 5 5
1408. – 90 g. violet, brown, black and green . . 5 5
1409. – 2 z. 50 black, orange, brown and cobalt . . 15 5
1410. – 5 z. 60 black, cream, green and blue . . 95 8

377. Missile.

1963. Polish People's Army. 20th Anniv. "POLSKA" in red.
1411. 20 g. blk., grey & grey-grn. 5 5
1412. 40 g. green, red and violet 5 5
1413. 60 g. black, grey and blue 5 5
1414. 1 z. 15 blue, orange, red and sepia 8 5
1415. 1 z. 35 black, grey, red and blue-green .. 10 5
1416. 1 z. 55 blk., grey, red & pur. 12 5
1417. 2 z. 50 black, slate, red and yellow-brown .. 15 5
1418. 3 z. grey-green, light grey, red & greenish blue .. 35 10
DESIGNS: 20 g. Type **377**. 40 g. Warship. 60 g. Fighter plane. 1 z. 15, Radar scanner. 1 z. 35, Tank. 1 z. 55, Missile-carrier. 2 z. 50, Amphibious troop-carrier. 3 z. Ancient warrior, modern soldier and two swords.

378. "A Love Letter" (after Czachorsky).

1963. Stamp Day.
1419. **378.** 60 g. brown 10 5

1963. Visit of Soviet Cosmonauts to Poland. Nos. 1402/4 optd. **23-28. X. 1963** and **w Polsce** together with Cosmonauts names.
1420. **375.** 40 g. black, green & bl. 15 5
1421. – 60 g. black, blue & grn. 15 5
1422. – 6 z. 50 green, blue, black and red .. 1·00 15

379. Tsiolkovsky's Rocket and Formula. **380.** Mazurian Horses.

1963. "The Conquest of Space" Inscr. in black.
1423. **379.** 30 g. turquoise-green 5 5
1424. – 40 g. olive 5 5
1425. – 50 g. violet 5 5
1426. – 60 g. brown 5 5
1427. – 1 z. blue-green .. 5 5
1428. – 1 z. 50 red 8 5
1429. – 1 z. 55 blue 8 5
1430. – 2 z. 50 purple .. 15 5
1431. – 5 z. 60 green 55 8
1432. – 6 z. 50 turquoise .. 70 10
DESIGNS: 40 g. "Sputnik 1". 50 g. "Explorer 1". 60 g. Banner carried by "Lunik 2". 1 z. "Lunik 3". 1 z. 50, "Vostock 1". 1 z. 55 "Friendship 7". 2 z. 50, "Vostocks 3 and 4". 5 z. 60, "Mariner 2". 6 z. 50, "Mars 1".

1963. Polish Horse-breeding. Multicoloured.
1433. 20 g. Arab stallion "Comet" 5 5
1434. 30 g. Tarpans (wild horses) 5 5
1435. 40 g. Sokolski horse .. 5 5
1436. 50 g. Arab mares and foals 5 5
1437. 60 g. Type **380** 5 5
1438. 90 g. Steeplechasers .. 8 5
1439. 1 z. 55 Arab stallion "Witez II" 25 5
1440. 2 z. 50 Heads of Arab horse (facing right) 45 5
1441. 4 z. Mixed breeds 60 15
1442. 6 z. 50 Head of Arab horse (facing right) 45 5
SIZES—TRIANGULAR ($55 \times 27\frac{1}{2}$ mm.): 20 g., 30 g., 40 g. HORIZ. (75×26 mm.): 50 g., 90 g., 4 z. VERT. as T **380**: 1 z. 55, 2 z. 50 6 z. 50.

381. Ice-hockey.

ILLUSTRATIONS
British Commonwealth and all overprints and surcharges are FULL SIZE. Foreign Countries have been reduced to $\frac{3}{4}$-LINEAR.

1964. Winter Olympic Games, Innsbruck. Multicoloured.
1443. 20 g. Type **381** 5 5
1444. 30 g. Slalom 5 5
1445. 40 g. Downhill skiing .. 5 5
1446. 60 g. Speed skating .. 5 5
1447. 1 z. Ski-jumping .. 8 5
1448. 2 z. 50 Tobogganing .. 25 8
1449. 5 z. 60 Cross-country skiing 45 10
1450. 6 z. 50 Pairs, figure skating 85 12

1964. Sailing Ships (2nd series). As T **370** but without coloured backgrounds. Some new designs.
1451. **370.** 5 g. chocolate .. 5 5
1452. – 10 g. green .. 5 5
1453. – 20 g. blue 5 5
1454. – 30 g. bronze .. 5 5
1455. – 40 g. blue 5 5
1456. – 60 g. purple 5 5
1457. – 1 z. chestnut .. 8 5
1458. – 1 z. 15 brown .. 8 5
1459. – 1 z. 35 blue .. 8 5
1460. – 1 z. 50 maroon .. 8 5
1461. – 1 z. 55 black .. 8 5
1462. – 2 z. violet 10 5
1463. – 2 z. 10 green 12 5
1464. – 2 z. 50 magenta .. 15 5
1465. – 3 z. olive 20 5
1466. – 3 z. 40 brown .. 30 5
SHIPS—HORIZ. 10 g. to 1 z. 15, As Nos. 1370/7. 1 z. 50, Galleon (16th cent). 2 z. 10, Battleship (18th cent.). 3 z. Clipper (19th cent.). VERT. 1 z. 35, Columbus's caravel. 1 z. 55, Battleship (17th cent.). 2 z. Dutch merchantman (17th cent.). 3 z. 40. Training-ship, "Dar Pomorza".

382. "Flourishing Tree".

DESIGN: No. 1467, Emblem composed of symbols of agriculture and industry.

1964. People's Republic. 20th Anniv. (1st issue).
1467. **382.** 60 g. multicoloured 5 5
1468. – 60 g. black, yell. & red 5 5
See also Nos. 1497/1506.

383. European Cat.

384. Casimir the Great (founder).

1964. Domestic Cats. As T **383**.
1469. 30 g. black & greenish yell. 8 5
1470. 40 g. grey-green, pink, black and orange .. 8 5
1471. 50 g. black, turq. & yellow 10 5
1472. 60 g. multicoloured .. 10 5
1473. 90 g. multicoloured .. 10 8
1474. 1 z. 35 multicoloured .. 12 8
1475. 1 z. 55 sepia, blue, black and ultramarine .. 15 8
1476. 2 z. 50 greenish yellow, black and violet .. 20 12
1477. 3 z. 40 multicoloured .. 70 25
1478. 6 z. 50 multicoloured 1·10 55
CATS—European: 30 g., 40 g., 60 g., 1 z. 55, 2 z. 50, 6 z. 50. Siamese: 50 g. Persian: 90 g., 1 z. 35, 3 z. 40. Nos. 1472/5 are horiz.

1964. Jagiellonian University, Cracow. 600th Anniv.
1479. **384.** 40 g. purple 5 5
1480. – 40 g. green 5 5
1481. – 60 g. violet 5 5
1482. – 60 g. blue 12 5
1483. – 2 z. 50 sepia 20 5
PORTRAITS: No. 1480, H. Kollataj (writer). 1481, J. Dlugosz (geographer and historian). 1482, N. Copernicus (astronomer). 1483 (36×37 mm.), King Jagiello and Queen Jadwiga.

385. Lapwing.

Nos. 1487/9 are vert. (35×48 mm.), the rest as T **385**.

1964. Birds. Multicoloured.
1484. 30 g. Type **385** 5 5
1485. 40 g. Bluethroat 5 5
1486. 50 g. Black-tailed godwit 5 5
1487. 60 g. Osprey 5 5
1488. 90 g. Heron 5 5
1489. 1 z. 35 Little gull .. 20 5
1490. 1 z. 55 Shoveler 20 5
1491. 5 z. 60 Black-throated diver 55 8
1492. 6 z. 50 Great crested grebe 60 12

386. Red Flag on Brick Wall.

1964. 4th Polish United Workers' Party Congress, Warsaw. Inscr. "PZPR". Multicoloured.
1493. 60 g. Type **386** 5 5
1494. 60 g. Beribboned hammer 5 5
1495. 60 g. Hands reaching for Red Flag 5 5
1496. 60 g. Hammer and corn emblems 5 5

387. Factory and Cogwheel.

389. Battle Scene.

388. Gdansk Shipyard.

1964. People's Republic. 20th Anniv. (2nd issue).
1497. **387.** 60 g. black and blue 5 5
1498. – 60 g. black and green 5 5
1499. – 60 g. red and orange 5 5
1500. – 60 g. ultram. & grey 5 5
1501. **388.** 60 g. ultram. & green 5 5
1502. – 60 g. violet & magenta 5 5
1503. – 60 g. sepia & slate-vio. 5 5
1504. – 60 g. bronze & green 5 5
1505. – 60 g. maroon and red 5 5
1506. – 60 g. sepia and yellow 5 5
DESIGNS—As T **387**: No. 1498, Tractor and ear of wheat. 1499, Mask and symbols of the arts. 1500, Atomic symbol and book. As T **388**: No. 1502, Lenin Foundry Nowa Huta. 1503, Cement Works, Chelm. 1504, Turoszow power station. 1505, Petro-chemical plant, Plock. 1506, Tarnobrzeg sulphur mine.

1964. Warsaw Insurrection. 20th Anniv.
1507. **389.** 60 g. multicoloured .. 5 5

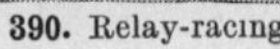
390. Relay-racing.

391. Congress Emblem.

1964. Olympic Games, Tokyo. Multicoloured.
1508. 20 g. Triple-jumping .. 5 5
1509. 40 g. Rowing 5 5
1510. 60 g. Weightlifting .. 5 5
1511. 90 g. Type **390** .. 8 5
1512. 1 z. Boxing 8 5
1513. 2 z. 50 Football 20 5
1514. 5 z. 60 High-jumping (women) 65 10
1515. 6 z. 50 High-diving .. 1·00 15
SIZES: DIAMOND—20 g. to 60 g. SQUARE—90 g. to 2 z. 50. VERT. ($23\frac{1}{2} \times 36$ mm.)—5 z. 60, 6 z. 50.

1964. 15th Int. Astronautical Congress, Warsaw.
1516. **391.** 2 z. 50 black & violet 25 5

392. Hand holding Hammer.

393. S. Zeromski (writer).

1964. 3rd Congress for Freedom and Democracy, Warsaw.
1517. **392.** 60 g. red, black & grn. 5 5

1964. Stefan Zeromski. Birth Cent.
1518. **393.** 60 g. olive-brown .. 5 5

394. Globe and Red Flag.

396. Eleanor Roosevelt.

395. 18th-century Stage Coach (after J. Brodowski).

1964. "First International". Cent.
1519. **394.** 60 g. black and red .. 5 5

1964. Stamp Day.
1520. **395.** 60 g. green 10 5
1521. 60 g. brown 10 5

1964. Eleanor Roosevelt. 80th Birth Anniv.
1522. **396.** 2 z. 50 sepia 15 5

397. Battle of Studzianki (after St. Zoltowski).

1964. "Poland's Struggle" (World War II) (1st issue).
1523. – 40 g. black .. 5 5
1524. – 40 g. slate-violet .. 5 5
1525. – 60 g. indigo 5 5
1526. – 60 g. green .. 5 5
1527. **397.** 60 g. bronze .. 5 5
DESIGNS—VERT. No. 1523, Virtuti Militari Cross. 1524, Westerplatte Memorial, Gdansk. 1525. Bydgoszcz Memorial. HORIZ. No. 1526, Soldiers crossing the Odrai (after St. Zoltowski). See also Nos. 1610/2.

398. Cyclamen.

399. Spacecraft of the Future.

1964. Garden Flowers. Multicoloured.
1528. 20 g. Type **398** 5 5
1529. 30 g. Freesia 5 5
1530. 40 g. Rose 5 5
1531. 50 g. Peony 5 5
1532. 60 g. Lily 5 5
1533. 90 g. Poppy 5 5
1534. 1 z. 35 Tulip 8 5
1535. 1 z. 50 Narcissus .. 8 5
1536. 1 z. 55 Begonia .. 10 5
1537. 2 z. 50 Carnation .. 30 5
1538. 3 z. 40 Iris 50 8
1539. 5 z. 60 Japanese camelia 90 8
Nos. 1534/9 are smaller, $26\frac{1}{2} \times 37$ mm.

1964. Space Research. Multicoloured.
1540. 20 g. Type **399**. .. 5 5
1541. 30 g. Launching rocket 5 5
1542. 40 g. Dog "Laika" and rocket 5 5
1543. 60 g. "Lunik 3" and Moon 8 5
1544. 1 z. 55 Satellite 8 5
1545. 2 z. 50 "Elektron 2" .. 12 5
1546. 5 z. 60 "Mars 1" .. 20 8
1547. 6 z. 50+2 z. Gagarin seated in Capsule .. 60 8

400. "Siren of Warsaw."

1965. Liberation of Warsaw. 20th Anniv.
1548. **400.** 60 g. green 5 5

401. Edaphosaurus.

1965. Prehistoric Animals (1st series). Multicoloured.
1549. 20 g. Type **401** 5 5
1550. 30 g. Cryptocleidus .. 5 5
1551. 40 g. Brontosaurus .. 5 5
1552. 60 g. Mesosaurus .. 5 5
1553. 90 g. Stegosaurus .. 5 5
1554. 1 z. 15 Brachiosaurus .. 8 5
1555. 1 z. 35 Styracosaurus .. 8 5
1556. 3 z. 40 Corythosaurus .. 30 8
1557. 5 z. 60 Rhamphorhynchus 55 12
1558. 6 z. 50 Tyrannosaurus .. 70 25
The 30 g., 60 g., 1 z. 15, 3 z. 40 and 5 z. 60 are vert.
See also Nos. 1639/47.

402. Petro-chemical Works, Plock, and Polish and Soviet Flags.

1965. Polish-Soviet Friendship Treaty. 20th Anniv. Multicoloured.
1559. 60 g. Seal (vert., 27×38½ mm.) 5 5
1560. 60 g. Type **402** 5 5

403. Polish Eagle and Civic Arms.

1965. Return of Western and Northern Territories to Poland. 20th Anniv.
1561. **403.** 60 g. red 5 5

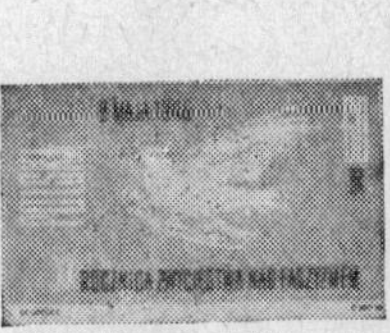

404. Dove of Peace. **405.** I.T.U. Emblem.

1965. Victory. 20th Anniv.
1562. **404.** 60 g. red and black.. 5 5

1965. I.T.U. Cent.
563. **405.** 2 z. 50 blk., vio. & bl. 25 5

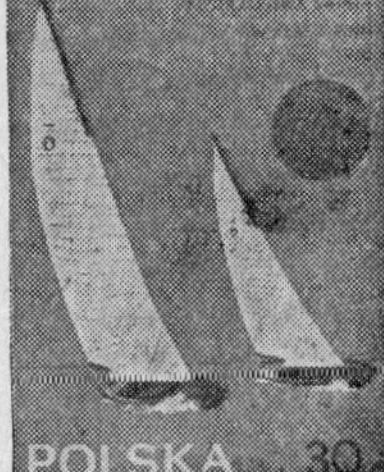

406. Clover-leaf Emblem and "The Friend of the People" (journal). **407.** Yachts of "Dragon" Class.

1965. Polish Popular Movement. 70th Anniv.
1564. **406.** 40 g. green, black, drab and violet .. 5 5
1565. – 60 g. ochre, blue, black and green .. 5 5
DESIGN—HORIZ. 60 g. Ears of Corn and industrial plant.

1965. World Finn Class Sailing Championships, Gdynia. Multicoloured.
1566. 30 g. Type **407** .. 5 5
1567. 40 g. "5·5 m." class .. 5 5
1568. 50 g. "Finn" class .. 5 5
1569. 60 g. "V" class.. .. 5 5
1570. 1 z. 35 "Cadet" class .. 8 5
1571. 4 z. "Star" class .. 35 8
1572. 5 z. 60 "Flying Dutchman" class 55 12
1573. 6 z. 50 "Amethyst" class 60 15
The 50 g., 1 z. 35, 4 z. and 6 z. 50 are horiz.

408. Marx and Lenin. **409.** 17th-Cent. Arms of Warsaw.

410. Heroes Memorial and Old Warsaw Seal.

1965. Postal Minister's Congress, Peking.
1574. **408.** 60 g. black on red .. 5 5

1965. Warsaw. 700th Anniv.
1575. **409.** 5 g. carmine 5 5
1576. – 10 g. green 5 5
1577. – 20 g. ultramarine .. 5 5
1578. – 40 g. brown 5 5
1579. – 60 g. orange 5 5
1580. – 1 z. 50 black.. .. 8 5
1581. – 1 z. 55 blue 10 5
1582. – 2 z. 50 purple .. 20 5
1583. **410.** 3 z. 40 black & bistre 35 25
DESIGNS—As T **409**—VERT. 10 g. 13th-cent. antiques. HORIZ. 20 g. Tombstone of last Masovian dukes. 40 g. Old Town Hall. 60 g. Barbican. 1 z. 50, Arsenal. 1 z. 55, National Theatre. 2 z. 50, Staszic Palace.

411. I.Q.S.Y. Emblem. **412.** "Odontoglossum grande".

1965. Int. Quiet Sun Year. Multicoloured. Background colours given.
1584. **411.** 60 g. ultramarine .. 5 5
1585. 60 g. violet 5 5
1586. – 2 z. 50 red 15 5
1587. – 2 z. 50 brown .. 15 5
1588. – 3 z. 40 orange .. 25 8
1589. – 3 z. 40 olive 25 8
DESIGNS: 2 z. 50, Solar scanner. 3 z. 40, Solar System.

1965. Orchids. Multicoloured.
1590. 20 g. Type **412** 5 5
1591. 30 g. "Cypripedium hibridum" 5 5
1592. 40 g. "Lycaste skinneri" 5 5
1593. 50 g. "Cattleya warszewicza" 5 5
1594. 60 g. "Vanda sanderiana" 5 5
1595. 1 z. 35 "Cypripedium hibridum" 12 5
1596. 4 z. "Sobralia" 35 5
1597. 5 z. 60 "Disa grandiflora" 60 8
1598. 6 z. 50 "Cattleya labiata" 80 15
The 30 g. and 1 z. 35, are different designs.

413. Weightlifting. **414.** "The Post Coach" (after P. Michalowski).

1965. Olympic Games, Tokyo. Polish Winners' Medals. Multicoloured.
1599. 30 g. Type **413** 5 5
1600. 40 g. Boxing 5 5
1601. 50 g. Relay-racing .. 5 5
1602. 60 g. Fencing 5 5
1603. 90 g. Hurdling (women's 80 m.) 8 5
1604. 3 z. 40 Relay-racing (women's) 30 8
1605. 6 z. 50 "Hop, step and jump" 55 12
1606. 7 z. 10 Volleyball (women's) 65 12

1965. Stamp Day.
1607. **414.** 60 g. brown 10 5
1608. – 2 z. 50 green.. .. 20 5
DESIGN: 2 z. 50, "Coach about to leave" (after P. Michalowski).

415. U.N. Emblem. **416.** Memorial, Holy Cross Mountains.

1965. U.N.O. 20th Anniv.
1609. **415.** 2 z. 50 blue 15 5

1965. "Polands Struggle" (World War II) (2nd issue).
1610. **416.** 60 g. brown 5 5
1611. – 60 g. green 5 5
1612. – 60 g. brown 5 5
DESIGNS—VERT. No. 1611, Memorial, Plaszow. HORIZ. 1612, Memorial, Chelm-on-Ner.

417. Wolf.

1965. Forest Animals. Multicoloured.
1613. 20 g. Type **417** 5 5
1614. 30 g. Lynx 5 5
1615. 40 g. Fox 5 5
1616. 50 g. Badger 5 5
1617. 60 g. Brown bear .. 5 5
1618. 1 z. 50 Wild boar .. 8 5
1619. 2 z. 50 Red deer.. .. 15 5
1620. 5 z. 60 European bison.. 55 10
1621. 7 z. 10 Elk 70 15

418. Gig.

1965. Horse-drawn Carriages in Lancut Museum. Multicoloured.
1622. 20 g. Type **418** 5 5
1623. 40 g. Coupe 5 5
1624. 50 g. Ladies' "basket" (trap) 5 5
1625. 60 g. "Vis-a-vis" .. 5 5
1626. 90 g. Cab 8 5
1627. 1 z. 15 Berlinka 8 5
1628. 2 z. 50 Hunting brake .. 25 5
1629. 6 z. 50 Barouche .. 65 12
1630. 7 z. 10 English brake .. 80 15
Nos. 1627/9 are 77×22 mm. and No. 1630 is 104×22 mm.

419. Congress Emblem and Industrial Products.

1966. 5th Polish Technicians' Congress, Katowice.
1631. **419.** 60 g. multicoloured.. 5 5

1966. Industrial Nationalisation. 20th Anniv. Designs similar to T **419**. Multicoloured.
1632. 60 g. Pithead gear (vert.) 5 5
1633. 60 g. Freighter 5 5
1634. 60 g. Petro-chemical works, Plock 5 5
1935. 60 g. Combine-harvester 5 5
1636. 60 g. Electric train .. 5 5
1637. 60 g. Exhibition Hall, 35th Poznan Fair 5 5
1638. 60 g. Crane (vert.) .. 5 5

1966. Prehistoric Animals (2nd series). As T **401**. Multicoloured.
1639. 20 g. Dinichthys.. .. 5 5
1640. 30 g. Eusthenopteron .. 5 5
1641. 40 g. Ichthyostega .. 5 5
1642. 50 g. Mastodonsaurus .. 5 5
1643. 60 g. Cynognathus .. 5 5
1644. 2 z. 50 Archaeopteryx (vert.)
1645. 3 z. 40 Brontotherium .. 25 5
1646. 6 z. 50 Machairodus .. 55 10
1647. 7 z. 10 Mammuthus .. 65 20

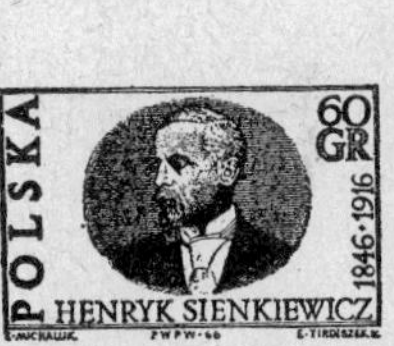

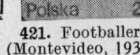

420. H. Sienkiewicz (novelist). **421.** Footballers (Montevideo, 1930).

1966. Henryk Sienkiewicz Commem.
1648. **420.** 60 g. black on buff .. 5 5

1966. World Cup Football Competition.. Multicoloured.
1649. 20 g. Type **421** 5 5
1650. 40 g. Rome, 1934 .. 5 5
1651. 60 g. Paris, 1938.. .. 5 5
1652. 90 g. Rio de Janeiro, 1950 5 5
1653. 1 z. 50 Berne, 1954 .. 10 5
1654. 3 z. 40 Stockholm, 1958.. 30 8
1655. 6 z. 50 Santiago, 1962 .. 55 12
1656. 7 z. 10 "London", 1966 (elimination match, Glasgow, 1965) .. 70 15
Football scenes represent World Cup finals played at the cities stated.

422. Soldier with Flag, and Dove of Peace. **423.** Women's Relay-racing.

1966. Victory. 21st Anniv.
1658. **422.** 60 g. red and black on silver 5 5

1966. 8th European Athletic Championships, Budapest. Multicoloured.

1659. 20 g. Runner starting race .. 5 5
1660. 40 g. Type **423** 5 5
1661. 60 g. Throwing the javelin 5 5
1662. 90 g. Women's hurdles .. 5 5
1663. 1 z. 35 Throwing the discus 8 5
1664. 3 z. 40 Finish of race .. 25 8
1665. 6 z. 50 Throwing the hammer.. .. .. 45 8
1666. 7 z. 10 High-jumping .. 55 12

The 20 g., 60 g., 1 z. 35 and 6 z. 50 are vert.

424. White Eagle.

425. Flowers and Produce.

1966. Polish Millenary (1st issue). Each red and black on gold.

1668. 60 g. Type **424** 5 5
1669. 60 g. Polish flag.. .. 5 5
1670. 2 z. 50 Type **424**.. .. 12 5
1671. 2 z. 50 Polish flag .. 12 5

See also Nos. 1717/18.

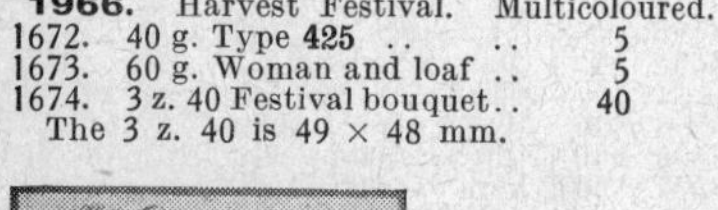

1966. Harvest Festival. Multicoloured.

1672. 40 g. Type **425** 5 5
1673. 60 g. Woman and loaf .. 5 5
1674. 3 z. 40 Festival bouquet.. 40 8

The 3 z. 40 is 49 × 48 mm.

426. Chrysanthemum.

427. Tourist Map.

1966. Flowers. Multicoloured.

1675. 10 g. Type **426** 5 5
1676. 20 g. Poinsettia 5 5
1677. 30 g. Centaury 5 5
1678. 40 g. Rose 5 5
1679. 60 g. Zinnia 5 5
1680. 90 g. Nasturtium .. 8 5
1681. 5 z. 60 Dahlia 45 8
1682. 6 z. 50 Sunflower .. 55 12
1683. 7 z. 10 Magnolia .. 90 15

1966. Tourism.

1684. **427.** 10 g. red 5 5
1685. – 20 g. olive-brown .. 5 5
1686. – 40 g. blue 5 5
1687. – 60 g. brown 5 5
1688. – 60 g. black 5 5
1689. – 1 z. 15 green .. 8 5
1690. – 1 z. 35 vermilion .. 8 5
1691. – 1 z. 55 violet .. 10 5
1692. – 2 z. slate-green .. 12 5

DESIGNS: 20 g. Hela Lighthouse. 40 g. Yacht. 60 g. (No. 1687). Poniatowski Bridge, Warsaw. 60 g. (No. 1688), Mining Academy, Kielce. 1 z. 15, Dunajec Gorge. 1 z. 35, Oal oaks, Rogalin. 1 z. 55, Silesian Planetarium. 2 z. M.S. "Batory".

428. Roman Capital.

1966. Polish Culture Congress.

1693. **428.** 60 g. cerise & chocolate 5 5

DESIGN: 2 z. 50, Stablemen, with horses and dogs.

429. Stable-man with Percherons.

1966. Stamp Day.

1694. **429.** 60 g. sepia 5 5
1695. – 2 z. 50 green .. 12 5

430. Soldier in Action.

1966. Jaroslav Dabrowski Brigade. 30th Anniv.

1696. **430.** 60 g. blk., grn. & red 5 5

431. Woodland Birds.

1966. Woodland Birds. Multicoloured.

1697. 10 g. Type **431** 5 5
1698. 20 g. Green woodpecker 5 5
1699. 30 g. Jay.. .. .. 5 5
1700. 40 g. Golden oriole .. 5 5
1701. 60 g. Hoopoe 5 5
1702. 2 z. 50 Redstart.. .. 15 5
1703. 4 z. Siskin 30 12
1704. 6 z. 50 Chaffinch .. 30 12
1705. 7 z. 10 Great tit.. .. 35 15

432. Ram (ritual statuette)

433. "Vostock 1".

1966. Polish Archaeological Research.

1706. **432.** 60 g. blue 5 5
1707. – 60 g. green 5 5
1708. – 60 g. brown 5 5

DESIGNS—VERT. No. 1707, Plan of Biskupin settlement. HORIZ. No. 1708, Brass implements and ornaments.

1966. Space Research. Multicoloured.

1709. 20 g. Type **433** 5 5
1710. 40 g. "Gemini" .. 5 5
1711. 60 g. "Ariel 2" 5 5
1712. 1 z. 35 "Progon 1" .. 8 5
1713. 1 z. 50 "FR 1".. .. 10 5
1714. 3 z. 40 "Alouette" .. 20 5
1715. 6 z. 50 "San Marco 1" .. 55 8
1716. 7 z. 10 "Luna 9" .. 60 12

434. Polish Eagle and Hammer.

1966. Polish Millenary (2nd issue).

1717. **434.** 40 g. mar., lilac & red 5 5
1718. – 60 g. mar., grn. & red 5 5

DESIGN: 60 g. Polish eagle and agricultural and industrial symbols.

435. Dressage.

1967. Racehorse Breeding in Poland 150th Anniv. Multicoloured.

1719. 10 g. Type **435** 5 5
1720. 20 g. Cross-country racing 5 5
1721. 40 g. Horse-jumping .. 5 5
1722. 60 g. Jumping fence in open country 5 5
1723. 90 g. Horse-trotting .. 8 5
1724. 5 z. 90 Playing polo .. 45 8
1725. 6 z. 60 Stallion "Ofir".. 55 10
1726. 7 z. Stallion "Skowrenek" 65 10

436. Striped Butterfly.

1967. Exotic Fishes. Multicoloured.

1727. 5 g. Type **436** 5 5
1728. 10 g. Imperial Angelfish.. 5 5
1729. 40 g. Banded Butterfly .. 5 5
1730. 60 g. Spotted Triggerfish 5 5
1731. 90 g. Undulate Triggerfish 5 5
1732. 1 z. 50 Picasso Fish .. 8 5
1733. 4 z. 50 Black Eyed Butterfly 30 8
1734. 6 z. 60 Blue Angelfish .. 55 12
1735. 7 z. Saddleback Butterfly 70 20

437. Auschwitz Memorial.

1967. Polish Martyrdom and Resistance, 1939-45.

1736. **437.** 40 g. brown 5 5
1737. – 40 g. black .. 5 5
1738. – 40 g. violet 5 5

DESIGNS—VERT. No. 1737, Auschwitz-Monowitz Memorial. 1738, Memorial guide's emblem.

See also Nos. 1770/2, 1798/9 and 1865/9.

438. Cyclists.

1967. 20th Warsaw-Berlin-Prague Cycle Race.

1739. **438.** 60 g. multicoloured.. 5 5

439. Running.

441. "Arnica montana".

440. Socialist Symbols.

1967. Olympic Games (1968). Multicoloured.

1740. 20 g. Type **439** .. 5 5
1741. 40 g. Horse-jumping .. 5 5
1742. 60 g. Relay-running .. 5 5
1743. 90 g. Weight-lifting .. 5 5
1744. 1 z. 35 Hurdling .. 8 5
1745. 3 z. 40 Gymnastics .. 25 8
1746. 6 z. 60 High-jumping .. 35 12
1747. 7 z. Boxing 55 15

1967. Polish Trade Unions Congress, Warsaw.

1749. **440.** 60 g. multicoloured.. 5 5

1967. Protected Plants. Multicoloured.

1750. 40 g. Type **441** 5 5
1751. 60 g. "Aquilegia vulgaris" 5 5
1752. 3 z. 40 "Gentiana punctata" 20 5
1753. 4 s. 50 "Lycopodium clavatum" 25 5
1754. 5 z. "Iris sibirica" .. 35 5
1755. 10 z. "Azalea pontica" .. 70 15

442. Katowice Memorial.

443. Marie Curie.

1967. Katowice Memorial. Inaug.

1756. **442.** 60 g. multicoloured .. 5 5

1967. Marie Curie. Birth Cent.

1757. **443.** 60 g. lake 5 5
1758. – 60 g. sepia 5 5
1759. – 60 g. violet 5 5

DESIGNS: No. 1758, Marie Curie's Nobel Prize diploma. 1759, Statue of Marie Curie, Warsaw.

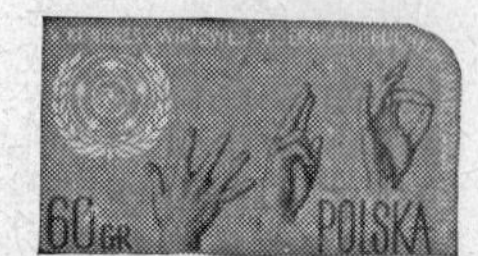

444. "Fifth Congress of the Deaf" (sign language).

1967. 5th World Federation of the Deaf Congress, Warsaw.

1760. **444.** 60 g. black and blue 5 5

445. Bouquet.

1967. "Flowers of the Meadow". Multicoloured.

1761. 20 g. Type **445** 5 5
1762. 40 g. "Papaver rhoeas" 5 5
1763. 60 g. "Convolvulus arvensis" 5 5
1764. 90 g. "Viola tricolor" .. 5 5
1765. 1 z. 15 "Tanacetum vulgare" 5 5
1766. 2 z. 50 "Agrostemma githago" 12 5
1767. 3 z. 40 "Knautia arvensis" 20 8
1768. 4 z. 50 "Anagallis arvensis" 25 8
1769. 7 z. 90 "Cichorium intybus" 60 12

1967. Polish Martyrdom and Resistance, 1939-45 (2nd series). As T **437**.

1770. 40 g. ultramarine .. 5 5
1771. 40 g. green 5 5
1772. 40 g. black 5 5

DESIGNS—HORIZ. No. 1770, Stutthof Memorial. VERT. 1771, Walcz Memorial, 1772, Lodz-Radogoszcz Memorial.

446. "Wilanow Palace" (from painting by W. Kasprzycki).

1967. Stamp Day.

1773. **446.** 60 g. brown and blue 5 5

447. Cruiser "Aurora".

1967. October Revolution. 50th Anniv. Each black, grey and red.

1774. 60 g. Type **447** 5 5
1775. 60 g. Lenin 5 5
1776. 60 g. "Luna 10" 5 5

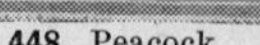

448. Peacock.

449. Kosciuszko.

1967. Butterflies. Multicoloured.
1777. 10 g. Type **448** 5 5
1778. 20 g. Swallowtail .. 5 5
1779. 40 g. Small Tortoise-shell 5 5
1780. 60 g. Camberwell Beauty 5 5
1781. 2 z. Purple Emperor .. 10 5
1782. 2 z. 50 Red Admiral .. 12 5
1783. 3 z. 40 Pale Clouded Yellow 20 5
1784. 4 z. 50 Marbled White .. 30 8
1785. 7 z. 90 Large Blue .. 60 12

1967. Tadeusz Kosciuszko (national hero). 150th Death Anniv.
1786. **449.** 60 g. chocolate & brn. 5 5
1787. 2 z. 50 green and red 12 5

450. "The Lobster" (Jean de Heem).

1967. Famous Paintings.
1788. – 20 g. multicoloured .. 5 5
1789. – 40 g. multicoloured .. 5 5
1790. – 60 g. multicoloured .. 5 5
1791. – 2 z. multicoloured .. 10 5
1792. – 2 z. 50 multicoloured 12 5
1793. – 3 z. 40 multicoloured 25 8
1794. **450.** 4 z. 50 multicoloured 35 12
1795. – 6 z. 60 multicoloured 65 20

DESIGNS (Paintings from the National Museums, Warsaw and Cracow). VERT. 20 g. "Lady with a Weasel" (Leonardo da Vinci). 40 g. "The Polish Lady" (Watteau). 60 g. "Dog Fighting Heron" (A. Hondius). 2 z. "Fowler Tuning Guitar" (J.-B. Greuze). 2 z. 50, "The Tax Collectors" (M. van Reymerswaele). 3 z. 40, "Daria Fiodorowna" (F. S. Rokotov). HORIZ. 6 z. 60, "Parable of the Good Samaritan" (landscape, Rembrandt).

451. W. S. Reymont (novelist).

1967. Reymont. Birth Cent.
1796. **451.** 60 g. sepia, red & ochre 5 5

452. J. M. Ossolinski (medallion) Book and Flag.

1967. Ossolineum Foundation. 150th Anniv.
1797. **452.** 60 g. brown, red & blue 5 5

1967. Polish Martyrdom and Resistance, 1939-45 (3rd series). As T **437**.
1798. 40 g. claret 5 5
1799. 40 g. brown 5 5

DESIGNS—VERT. No. 1798, Zagan Memorial. HORIZ. 1799, Lambinowice-Jencom Memorial.

453. Ice Hockey. 454. "Puss in Boots".

1968. Winter Olympic Games, Grenoble. Multicoloured.
1800. 40 g. Type **453** .. 5 5
1801. 60 g. Ski-jumping .. 5 5
1802. 90 g. Slalom .. 5 5
1803. 1 z. 35 Speed-skating .. 8 5
1804. 1 z. 55 Ski-walking .. 8 5
1805. 2 z. Tobogganing .. 10 5
1806. 7 z. Rifle-shooting on skis 30 12
1807. 7 z. 90 Ski-jumping (different) 55 15

1968. Fairy Tales. Multicoloured.
1808. 20 g. Type **454** 5 5
1809. 40 g. "The Raven and the Fox" 5 5
1810. 60 g. "Mr. Twardowski" 5 5
1811. 2 z. "The Fisherman and the Fish" 10 5
1812. 2 z. 50 "Little Red Riding Hood" 15 5
1813. 3 z. 40 "Cinderella" .. 25 5
1814. 5 z. 50 "The Waif" .. 40 8
1815. 7 z. "Snow-White" .. 60 15

455. "Clianthus dampieri". 456. "Peace" (poster by H. Tomaszewski).

1968. Flowers. Multicoloured.
1816. 10 g. Type **455** 5 5
1817. 20 g. "Passiflora quadrangularis" 5 5
1818. 30 g. "Strelitzia reginae" 5 5
1819. 40 g. "Coryphanta vivipara" 5 5
1820. 60 g. "Odontonia" .. 5 5
1821. 90 g. "Protea cyneroides" 5 5
1822. 4 z.+2 z. "Abutilon" .. 35 10
1823. 8 z.+4 z. "Rosa polyantha" 80 20

1968. 2nd Int. Poster Biennale, Warsaw. Multicoloured.
1824. 60 g. Type **456** 5 5
1825. 2 z. 50 Gounod's "Faust" (poster by Jan Lenica) 12 5

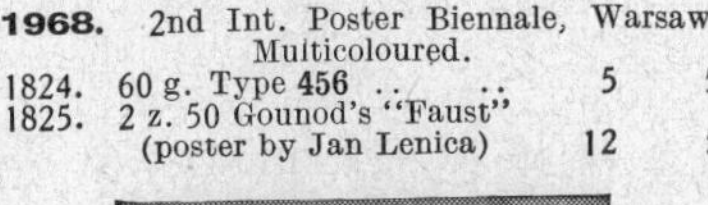

457. "Zephyr" Glider.

1968. 11th World Gliding Championships, Leszno. Gliders. Multicoloured.
1826. 60 g. Type **457** 5 5
1827. 90 g. "Stork" 5 5
1828. 1 z. 50 "Swallow" .. 8 5
1829. 3 z. 40 "Fly" 20 5
1830. 4 z. "Seal" 20 8
1831. 5 z. 50 "Pirate" .. 45 8

458. Child with Stamp. 459. Part of Monument.

1968. "75 years of Polish Philately". Multicoloured.
1832. 60 g. Type **458** 5 5
1833. 60 g. Balloon over Poznan 5 5

1968. Silesian Insurrection Monument. Sosnowiec.
1834. **459.** 60 g. black and purple 5 5

460. Relay-racing.

1968. Olympic Games, Mexico. Multicoloured.
1835. 30 g. Type **460** 5 5
1836. 40 g. Boxing 5 5
1837. 60 g. Basketball 5 5
1838. 90 g. Long-jumping .. 5 5
1839. 2 z. 50 Throwing the javelin 12 5
1840. 3 z. 40 Gymnastics .. 20 5
1841. 4 z. Cycling 20 8
1842. 7 z. 90 Fencing 40 15
1843. 10 z.+5 z. Torch Runner and Aztec bas-relief .. 95 60

The 10 z. is larger, 56×45 mm.

461. "Knight on a Bay Horse" (P. Michalowski).

1968. Polish Paintings (1st Series). Multicoloured.
1844. 40 g. Type **461** 5 5
1845. 60 g. "Fisherman" (L. Wyczolkowski) 5 5
1846. 1 z. 15 "Jewish Women with Lemons" (A. Gierymski) 5 5
1847. 1 z. 35 "Eliza Parenska" (S. Wyspianski) .. 8 5
1848. 1 z. 50 "Manifesto" (W. Weiss) 8 5
1849. 4 z. 50 "Stanczyk" (Jan Matejko) 15 5
1850. 5 z. "Children's Band" (T. Makowski) 40 8
1851. 7 z. "Feast II" (Z. Waliszewski) 55 10

The 4 z. 50, 5 z. and 7 z. are horiz. See also Nos. 1921/8.

462. "September, 1939" (Bylina).

1968. Polish People's Army. Designs show paintings.
1852. 40 g. violet & olive on yell. 5 5
1853. 40 g. ultram. & violet on lilac 5 5
1854. 40 g. green & blue on grey 5 5
1855. 40 g. blk. & chest. on orge. 5 5
1856. 40 g. pur. & green on green 5 5
1857. 60 g. brn. & ultram. on blue 5 5
1858. 60 g. maroon & grn. on grn. 5 5
1859. 60 g. olive & red on pink 5 5
1860. 60 g. green & choc. on red 5 5
1861. 60 g. indigo & turq. on blue 5 5

PAINTINGS AND PAINTERS: No. 1852, T **462**. 1853, "Partisans" (Maciag). 1854, "Lenino" (Bylina). 1855, "Monte Cassino" (Boratynski). 1856, "Tanks before Warsaw" (Garwatowski). 1857, "Neisse River" (Bylina). 1858, "On the Oder" (Mackiewicz). 1859, "In Berlin" (Bylina). 1860, "Blyskawica" ("Lightning"—warship) (Mokwa). 1861, "Pursuit" (fighter planes) (Kulisiewicz).

463. "Party Members" (F. Kowarski).

1968. 5th Workers' Party Congress, Warsaw. Multicoloured designs showing paintings.
1862. 60 g. Type **463** 5 5
1863. 60 g. "Strike" (S. Lentz) 5 5
1864. 60 g. "Manifesto" (W. Weiss) 5 5

(Nos. 1863/4 are vert).

1968. Polish Martyrdom and Resistance. 1939–45 (4th series). As T **437**.
1865. 40 g. grey 5 5
1866. 40 g. brown 5 5
1867. 40 g. sepia 5 5
1868. 40 g. ultramarine .. 5 5
1869. 40 g. lake-brown .. 5 5

DESIGNS—HORIZ. No. 1865, Tomb of Unknown Soldier, Warsaw. 1866, Guerillas' Monument, Kartuzy. VERT. 1867, Insurgents' Monument, Poznan. 1868, People's Guard Insurgents' Monument, Polichno. 1869, Rotunda, Zamosc.

464. "Start of Hunt" (W. Kossak).

1968. Paintings. Hunting Scenes. Multicoloured.
1870. 20 g. Type **464** 5 5
1871. 40 g. "Hunting with Falcon" (J. Kossak) .. 5 5
1872. 60 g. "Wolves' Raid" (A. Wierusz-Kowalski) 5 5
1873. 1 z. 50 "Home-coming with a Bear" (J. Falat) 5 5
1874. 2 z. 50 "The Fox-hunt" (T. Sutherland) .. 10 5
1875. 3 z. 40 "The Boar-hunt" (F. Snyders) 15 5
1876. 4 z. 50 "Hunters' Rest" (W. G. Pierow) .. 35 8
1877. 8 z. 50 "Hunting a Lion in Morocco" (Delacroix) .. 55 15

465. Maltese Dog. 466. House Sign.

1969. Pedigree Dogs. Multicoloured.
1878. 20 g. Type **465** 5 5
1879. 40 g. Wire-haired fox-terrier 5 5
1880. 60 g. Afghan hound .. 5 5
1881. 1 z. 50 Rough-haired terrier 5 5
1882. 2 z. 50 English setter .. 10 5
1883. 3 z. 40 Pekinese 15 5
1884. 4 z. 50 Alsatian 35 8
1885. 8 z. 50 Pointer 55 12

Nos. 1879, 1884 and 1885 are vert.

1969. 9th Polish Democratic Movement Congress.
1886. **466.** 60 g. red, black & grey 5 5

467. "Dove" and Wheat-ears. 468. Running.

1969. 5th Congress of United Popular Party.
1887. **467.** 60 g. multicoloured .. 5 5

1969. Int. Olympic Committee. 75th Anniv. and Polish Olympic Committee Jubilee. Multicoloured.
1888. 10 g. Type **468** 5 5
1889. 20 g. Gymnastics .. 5 5
1890. 40 g. Weightlifting .. 5 5
1891. 60 g. Throwing the javelin 5 5
1892. 2 z. 50+50 g. Throwing the discus 12 5
1893. 3 z. 40+1 z. Running .. 15 5
1894. 4 z.+1 z. 50 Wrestling .. 20 8
1895. 7 z.+2 z. Fencing .. 35 10

469. Pictorial Map of Swictokrzyski National Park.

1969. Tourism (1st Series). Multicoloured.
1896. 40 g. Type **469** 5 5
1897. 60 g. Niedzica Castle (vert.) 5 5
1898. 1 z. 35 Kolobrzeg Lighthouse and yacht 5 5
1899. 1 z. 50 Szczecin Castle and Harbour 8 5
1900. 2 z. 50 Torun and Vistula River 10 5
1901. 3 z. 40 Klodzko Silesia (vert.) 15 5
1902. 4 z. Sulejow 20 5
1903. 4 z. 50 Kazimierz Dolny market-place (vert.) .. 20 8

See also Nos. 1981/5.

470. Route Map and "Opty".

1969. Leonid Teliga's World Voyage in Yacht "Opty".

1904. 470. 60 g. multicoloured .. 5 5

471. Copernicus (after woodcut by T. Stimer) and inscription.

472. "Memory" Flame and Badge.

1969. Copernicus. 500th Birth Anniv. (1973) (1st issue).

1905. 471. 40 g. brn., red & yellow 5 5
1906. – 60 g. blue, red & green 5 5
1907. – 2 z. 50 olive, red & pur. 10 5

DESIGNS: 60 g. Copernicus (after J. Falck) and 15th-century globe. 2 z. 50 Copernicus (after painting by J. Matejko) and diagram of heliocentric system.

See also Nos. 1995/7, 2069/72, 2167/70. 2215/16 and 2217/2221.

1969. 5th National Alert of Polish Pathfinders' Union.

1908. 472. 60 g. black, red & blue 5 5
1909. - 60 g. red, black & green 5 5
1910. – 60 g. black, grn. & red 5 5

DESIGN: No. 1909 "Defence" eagle and badge. 1910 "Labour" map and badge.

473. Coal-miner.

1969. Republic. 25th Anniv. Multicoloured.

1911. 60 g. Frontier Guard and Arms 5 5
1912. 60 g. Plock Petro-chemical Plant 5 5
1913. 60 g. Combine-harvester 5 5
1914. 60 g. Grand Theatre, Warsaw 5 5
1915. 60 g. Curie statue and University, Lublin .. 5 5
1916. 60 g. Type 473 .. 5 5
1917. 60 g. Sulphur-worker .. 5 5
1918. 60 g. Steel-worker .. 5 5
1919. 60 g. Ship-builder .. 2 5

Nos. 1911/5 are vert. and have white arms embossed in the top portion of the stamps.

474. Astronauts and Module on Moon.

1969. 1st Man on the Moon.

1920. 474. 2 z. 50 multicoloured 20 5

475. "Motherhood" (S. Wyspianski).

1969. Polish Paintings. Multicoloured.

1921. 20 g. Type 475 .. .. 5 5
1922. 40 g. "Hamlet" (J. Malczewski) 5 5
1923. 60 g. "Indian Summer" (J. Chelmonski) .. 5 5
1924. 2 z. "Two Girls" (Olga Boznanska) (vert.) .. 12 5
1925. 2 z. 50 "The Sun of May" (J. Mehoffer) (vert.) .. 8 5
1926. 3 z. 40 "Woman combing her Hair" (W. Slewinski) 12 5
1927. 5 z. 50 "Still Life" (J. Pankiewicz) 20 8
1928. 7 z. "Abduction of the King's Daughter" (W. Wojtkiewicz) 50 12

476. "Nike" statue.

478. Krzczonow (Lublin) Costumes.

477. Majdanek Memorial.

1969. 4th Freedom-Fighters Union Congress.

1929. 476. 60 g. red, black & brn. 5 5

1969. Majdanek Memorial. Inaug.

1930. 477. 40 g. black and mauve 5 5

1969. Regional Costumes. Multicoloured.

1931. 40 g. Type 478 .. .. 5 5
1932. 60 g. Lowicz (Lodz) .. 5 5
1933. 1 z. 15 Rozbark (Katowice) 5 5
1934. 1 z. 35 Lower Silesia (Wroclaw) 5 5
1935. 1 z. 50 Opoczno (Lodz) .. 8 5
1936. 4 z. 50 Sacz (Cracow) .. 20 5
1937. 5 z. Highlanders, Cracow 25 5
1938. 7 z. Kurpie (Warsaw) .. 45 8

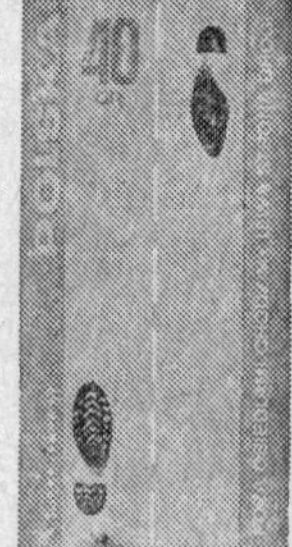

479. "Pedestrians Keep Left".

480. "Welding" and I.L.O. Emblem.

1969. Road Safety. Multicoloured.

1939. 40 g. Type 479 .. .. 5 5
1940. 60 g. "Drive Carefully" (horses on road) .. 5 5
1941. 2 z. 50 "Do Not Dazzle" (cars on road at night) 10 5

1969. Int. Labour Organization. 50th Anniv.

1942. 480. 2 z. 50 blue and gold 12 5

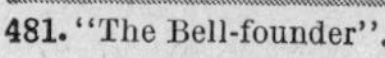

481. "The Bell-founder".

482. "Angel" (19th-century).

1969. Miniatures from Behem's Code of 1505. Multicoloured.

1943. 40 g. Type 481 .. .. 5 5
1944. 60 g. "The Painter" .. 5 5
1945. 1 z. 35 "The Woodcarver" 5 5
1946. 1 z. 55 "The Shoemaker" 8 5
1947. 2 z. 50 "The Cooper" .. 10 5
1948. 3 z. 40 "The Baker" .. 15 5
1949. 4 z. 50 "The Tailor" .. 20 8
1950. 7 z. "The Bowyer" .. 45 12

1969. Polish Folk Sculpture. Multicoloured.

1951. 20 g. Type 482 .. .. 5 5
1952. 40 g. "Sorrowful Christ" (19th-century) .. 5 5
1953. 60 g. "Sorrowful Christ" (19th-cent.) (diff.) .. 5 5
1954. 2 z. "Weeping Woman" (19th-century) .. 8 5
1955. 2 z. 50 "Adam and Eve" (F. Czajkowski) .. 8 5
1956. 3 z. 40 "Girl with Birds" (L. Kudla) .. 12 5
1957. 5 z. 50+1 z. 50 "Choir" (A. Zegadlo) .. 40 8
1958. 7 z.+1 z. "Organ-grinder" (Z. Skretowicz) .. 55 8

Nos. 1957/8 are larger, size 25 × 35 mm.

483. Leopold Staff.

1969. Modern Polish Writers.

1959 483. 40 g. blk., olive & grn. 5 5
1960. – 60 g. blk., red & pink 5 5
1961. – 1 z. 35 blk., royal blue and blue .. 5 5
1962. – 1 z. 50 blk., vio. & lilac 5 5
1963. – 1 z. 55 blk., emerald and green .. 8 5
1964. – 2 z. 50 blk., ultram. and blue .. 10 5
1965. – 3 z. 40 blk., red-brn., and brown .. 15 5

DESIGNS: 60 g. Wladyslaw Broniewski. 1 z. 35, Leon Kruczkowski. 1 z. 50, Julian Tuwim. 1 z. 55, Konstanty Ildefons Galczynski. 2 z. 50, Maria Dabrowska. 3 z. 40, Zofia Nalkowska.

484. Nike Monument.

1970. Liberation of Warsaw. 25th Anniv.

1966. 484. 60 g. multicoloured .. 5 5

485. Early Printing Works and Colour Dots.

486. Mallard.

1970. Printers' Trade Union. Cent.

1967. 485. 60 g. multicoloured 5 5

1970. Game Birds. Multicoloured.

1968. 40 g. Type 486 .. .. 5 5
1969. 60 g. Pheasant 5 5
1970. 1 z. 15 Woodcock .. 5 5
1971. 1 z. 35 Ruff .. 5 5
1972. 1 z. 50 Wood Pigeon .. 5 5
1973. 3 z. 40 Black Grouse .. 8 5
1974. 7 z. Partridge .. 55 10
1975. 8 z. 50 Capercaillie .. 60 15

487. Lenin at Desk.

1970. Lenin. Birth Cent.

1976. 487. 40 g. grey and red .. 5 5
1977. – 60 g. sepia and red .. 5 5
1978. – 2 z. 50 blk. & vermilion 10 5

DESIGNS: 60 g. Lenin addressing meeting. 2 z. 50 Lenin at Party conference.

488. Polish and Russian Soldiers.

1970. Liberation. 25th Anniv.

1980. 488. 60 g. multicoloured .. 5 5

1970. Tourism (2nd Series). As T 469, but with imprint "PWPW 70". Multicoloured.

1981. 60 g. Town Hall, Wroclaw (vert.) 5 5
1982. 60 g. View of Opole .. 5 5
1983. 60 g. Legnice Castle .. 5 5
1984. 60 g. Bolkow Castle .. 5 5
1985. 60 g. Town Hall, Brzeg .. 5 5

489. Polish "Flower".

1970. Annexation of Territory East of the Oder-Neisse Line. 25th Anniv.

1986. 489. 60 g. red, silver and green 5 5

490. Movement Flag.

491. U.P.U. Emblem and New Headquarters.

1970. Peasant Movement. 75th Anniv.

1987. 490. 60 g. multicoloured .. 5 5

1970. New U.P.U. Headquarters Building, Berne.

1988. 491. 2 z. 50 blue and greenish blue .. 10 5

492. Footballers.

493. Hand with "Lamp of Learning".

1970. Gornik Zabre v. Manchester City Final of European Cup-winners Cup Championships.

1989. 492. 60 g. multicoloured .. 5 5

1970. Plock Scientific Society. 150th Anniv.

1990. 493. 60 g. olive, red & black 5 5

494. "Olympic Runners" (from Greek amphora).

495. Copernicus (after miniature by Bacciarelli) and Bologna.

1970. Int. Olympic Academy. 10th Session.
1991. **494.** 60 g. red, yell. & blk. 5 5
1992. – 60 g. vio.-bl., bl. & blk. 5 5
1993. – 60 g. multicoloured .. 5 5
DESIGNS: No. 1992, "The Archer". No. 1993, Modern runners.

1970. Copernicus. 500th Birth Anniv. (1973) (2nd issue).
1995. **495.** 40 g. green, orge. & lilac 5 5
1996. – 60 g. lilac, grn. & yell. 5 5
1997. – 2 z. 50 brown, ultramarine and green .. 10 5
DESIGNS: 60 g. Copernicus (after miniature by Lesseur) and Padua. 2 z. 50, Copernicus (by N. Zinck, after lost Goluchowska portrait) and Ferrara.

496. "Aleksander Orlowski" (self-portrait).

1970. Polish Miniatures. Multicoloured.
1998. 20 g. Type **496** 5 5
1999. 40 g. "Jan Matejko" (self-portrait) .. 5 5
2000. 60 g. "Stefan Batory" (unknown artist) .. 5 5
2001. 2 z. "Maria Leszczynska" (unknown artist) .. 5 5
2002 2 z. 50 "Maria Walewska" (Jacquetot Marie-Victoire) 8 5
2003. 3 z. 40 "Tadeusz Kosciuszko" (Jan Rustem) 5 5
2004. 5 z. 50 "Samuel Linde" (G. Landolfi) 25 8
2005. 7 z. "Michal Oginski" (Windisch Nanette) .. 50 10

497. U.N. Emblem within "Eye".

1970. United Nations. 25th Anniv.
2006. **497.** 2 z. 50 multicoloured 12 5

498. Piano Keyboard and Chopin's Signature. **499.** Population Pictograph.

1970. 8th Int. Chopin Piano Competition.
2007. **498.** 2 z. 50 black & violet 12 5

1970. National Census. Multicoloured.
2008. 40 g. Type **499** 5 5
2009. 60 g. Family in "house" 5 5

500. Destroyer "Piorun".
(Illustration reduced. Actual size 77×23 mm.)

1970. Polish Warships, World War II.
2010. **500.** 40 g. brown 5 5
2011. – 60 g. black 5 5
2012. – 2 z. 50 brown .. 12 5
DESIGNS: 60 g. Submarine "Orzel". 2 z. 50 Destroyer "Garland".

501. "Expressions" (Maria Jarema).

1970. Stamp Day. Contemporary Polish Paintings. Multicoloured.
2013. 20 g. "The Violin-cellist" (J. Nowosielski) (vert.) 5 5
2014. 40 g. "View of Lodz" (B. Liberski) (vert.) .. 5 5
2015. 60 g. "Studio Concert" (W. Taranczewski) (vert.) 5 5
2016. 1 z. 50 "Still Life" (Z. Pronaszko) (vert.) .. 5 5
2017. 2 z. "Hanging-up Washing" (A. Wroblewski) (vert.) 5 5
2018. 3 z. 40 Type **501** 10 5
2019. 4 z. "Canal in the Forest" (P. Potworowski) .. 15 8
2020. 8 z. 50 "The Sun" (W. Strzeminski) .. 45 12

502. "Luna 16 landing on Moon". **503.** "Stag" (detail from "Daniel" tapestry).

1970. Moon Landing of "Luna 16".
2021. **502.** 2 z. 50 multicoloured 12 5

1970. Tapestries in Wawel Castle. Multicoloured.
2022. 60 g. Type **503** 5 5
2023. 1 z. 15 "Stork" (detail) 5 5
2024. 1 z. 35 "Panther fighting Dragon" 5 5
2025. 2 z. "Man's Head" (detail "Deluge" tapestry) .. 8 5
2026. 2 z. 50 "Child with Bird" (detail "Adam Tilling the Soil" tapestry) .. 8 5
2027. 4 z. "God, Adam and Eve" (detail "Happiness in Paradise" tapestry) .. 15 8
2028. 4 z. 50 Royal Monogram tapestry 25 8

504. Training-ship "Dar Pomorza".

1971. Polish Ships. Multicoloured.
2030. 40 g. Type **504** 5 5
2031. 60 g. Liner "Stefan Batory" 5 5
2032. 1 z. 15 Ice-breaker "Perkun" 5 5
2033. 1 z. 35 Salvage-ship "R-1" 5 5
2034. 1 z. 50 Bulk-carrier "Ziemia Szczecinska" 5 5
2035. 2 z. 50 Tanker "Beskidy" 10 5
2036. 5 z. Fast cargo-ship "Hel" 25 5
2037. 8 z. 50 Ferry "Gry" .. 35 12

505. Checiny Castle.

1971. Polish Castles. Multicoloured.
2038. 20 g. Type **505** 5 5
2039. 40 g. Wisnicz 5 5
2040. 60 g. Bedzin 5 5
2041. 2 z. Ogrodzieniec .. 5 5
2042. 2 z. 50 Niedzica 8 5
2043. 3 z. 40 Kwidzyn .. 10 5
2044. 4 z. Pieskowa Skala .. 15 5
2045. 8 z. 50 Lidzbark Warminski 45 12

506. Battle of Pouilly, J. Dabrowski and W. Wroblewski.

1971. Paris Commune. Cent.
2046. **506.** 60 g. brown, blue & red 5 5

507. Plantation.

508. "Bishop Marianos".

1971. Forestry Management. Multicoloured.
2047. 40 g. Type **507** 5 5
2048. 60 g. Forest (vert. 27 × 47 mm.) 5 5
2049. 1 z. 50 Tree-felling (vert.) 5 5

1971. Fresco Discoveries made by Polish Expedition at Faras, Nubia. Multicoloured.
2050. 40 g. Type **508** 5 5
2051. 60 g. "St. Anne" .. 5 5
2052. 1 z. 15 "Archangel Michael" 5 5
2053. 1 z. 35 "The Hermit, Anamon" 5 5
2054. 1 z. 50 "Head of Archangel Michael" 5 5
2055. 4 z. 50 "Evangelists' Cross" 20 5
2056. 5 z. "Christ protecting a noble" 20 5
2057. 7 z. "Archangel Michael" (half-length) 30 10

509. Revolutionaries.

1971. Silesian Insurrection. 50th Anniv.
2058. **509.** 60 g. brown and gold 5 5

510. "Soldiers".

1971. U.N.I.C.E.F. 25th Anniv. Children's Drawings. Multicoloured.
2060. 20 g. "Peacock" (vert.) 5 5
2061. 40 g. Type **510** 5 5
2062. 60 g. "Lady Spring" (vert.) 5 5
2063. 2 z. "Cat and Ball" .. 5 5
2064. 2 z. 50 "Flowers in Jug" (vert.) 8 5
2065. 3 z. 40 "Friendship" .. 10 5
2066. 5 z. 50 "Clown" (vert.) .. 20 8
2067. 7 z. "Strange Planet" .. 40 12

511. Fair Emblem.

512. Copernicus's House, Torun.

1971. 40th Int. Fair, Poznan.
2068. **511.** 60 g. multicoloured .. 5 5

1971. Copernicus. 500th Birth Anniv. (1973). (3rd issue). Multicoloured.
2069. 40 g. Type **512** 5 5
2070. 60 g. College, Cracow (horiz.) 5 5
2071. 2 z. 50 Olsztyn Castle (horiz.) 8 5
2072. 4 z. Frombork Cathedral 15 5

513. Folk Art Pattern.

514. "Head of Worker" (X. Dunikowski).

1971. Folk Art "Paper Cut-outs" showing various patterns.
2073. **513.** 20 g. blk., grn. & blue 5 5
2074. – 40 g. blue, grn. & cream 5 5
2075. – 60 g. brn., blue & grey 5 5
2076. – 1 z. 15 maroon, brn. & buff 5 5
2077. – 1 z. 35 green, red and yellow-green .. 5 5

1971. Modern Polish Sculpture. Multicoloured.
2078. 40 g. Type **514** 5 5
2079. 40 g. "Foundryman" (X. Dunikowski) 5
2080. 60 g. "Miners" (M. Wiecek) 5 5
2081. 60 g. "Harvester" (S. Horno-Poplawski) .. 5 5

515. Congress Emblem and Computer Tapes.

1971. 6th Polish Technical Congress, Warsaw.
2083. **515.** 60 g. violet and red .. 5 5

516. "Angel" (J. Mehoffer). **518.** "P-11C" Fighters.

517. Mrs. Fedorowicz" (W. Pruszkowski).

1971. Stained Glass Windows. Multicoloured.
2084. 20 g. Type **516** 5 5
2085. 40 g. "Lilies" (S. Wyspianski) 5 5
2086. 60 g. "Iris" (S. Wyspianski) 5 5
2087. 1 z. 35 "Apollo" (S. Wyspianski) 5 5
2088. 1 z. 55 "Two Wise Men" (14th-century) 5
2089. 3 z. 40 "The Flight into Egypt" (14th-century) 15 5
2090. 5 z. 50 "Jacob" (14th-century) 25 8
2091. 8 z. 50 + 4 z. "Madonna" (15th-century) .. 55 15

1971. Contemporary Art from National Museum, Cracow. Multicoloured.
2092. 40 g. Type **517** 5 5
2093. 50 g. "Woman with Book" (T. Czyzeski) .. 5 5
2094. 60 g. "Girl with Chrysanthemums" (O. Boznanska) 5 5
2095. 2 z. 50 "Girl in Red Dress" (J. Pankiewicz) (horiz.) 8 5
2096. 3 z. 40 "Reclining Nude" (L. Chwistek) (horiz.) .. 10 5

2097. 4 z. 50 "Strange Garden" (J. Mehoffer) 20 5
2098. 5 z. "Wife in White Hat" (Z. Pronaszko) 25 8
2099. 7 z.+1 z "Seated Nude" (W. Weiss) 55 15

1971. Polish War Planes of World War II. Multicoloured.
2100. 90 g. Type **518** 5 5
2101. 1 z. 50 "Karas" fighter-bombers 8 5
2102. 3 z. 40 "Los" bomber .. 15 5

519. Warsaw Castle (pre-1939).

1971. Reconstruction of Warsaw Castle.
2103. **519.** 60 g. blk., red and gold 5 5

520. Astronauts in Moon Rover. **521.** "Lunokhod 1".

1971. Moon Flight of "Apollo 15".
2104. **520.** 2 z. 50 multicoloured 10 5

1971. Moon Flight of "Lunik 17" and "Lunokhod 1".
2106. **521.** 2 z. 50 multicoloured 10 5

522. Worker at Wheel. **523.** Ship-building.

1971. Polish Workers' Party Congress (a) Party Posters.
2108. **522.** 60 g. red, blue & grey 5 5
2109. – 60 g. red and grey (Worker's head) .. 5 5

(b) Industrial Development. Each in gold and red.
2110. 60 g. Type **523** 5 5
2111. 60 g. Building construction 5 5
2112. 60 g. Combine-harvester 5 5
2113. 60 g. Motor-car production 5 5
2114. 60 g. Pit-head 5 5
2115. 60 g. Petro-chemical plant 5 5

524. "Prunus cerasus".

1971. Flowers of Trees and Shrubs. Multicoloured.
2117. 10 g. Type **524** 5 5
2118. 20 g. "Malus niedzwetzkyana" 5 5
2119. 40 g. "Pyrus L." 5 5
2120. 60 g. "Prunus persica" .. 5 5
2121. 1 z. 15 "Magnolia kobus" 5 5
2122. 1 z. 35 "Crataegus oxyacantha" 5 5
2123. 2 z. 50 "Malus M." .. 8 5
2124. 3 z. 40 "Aesculus carnea" 10 5
2125. 5 z. "Robinia pseudacacia" 25 8
2126. 8 z. 50 "Prunus actum" .. 45 15

525. "Worker" (sculpture, J. Januszkiewicz).

1972. Polish Workers' Party. 30th Anniv.
2127. **525.** 60 g. black and red .. 5 5

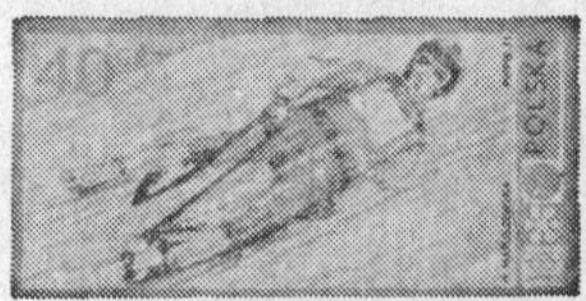

526. Tobogganing.

1972. Winter Olympic Games, Sapporo, Japan. Multicoloured.
2128. 40 g. Type **526** 5 5
2129. 60 g. Slalom (vert.) .. 5 5
2130. 1 z. 65 Biathlon (vert.) .. 5 5
2131. 2 z. 50 Ski-jumping .. 12 5

527. "Heart" and Cardiogram Trace. **528.** Running.

1972. World Heart Month.
2133. **527.** 2 z. 50 multicoloured 10 5

1972. Olympic Games, Munich. Multicoloured.
2134. 20 g. Type **528** 5 5
2135. 30 g. Archery 5 5
2136. 40 g. Boxing 5 5
2137. 60 g. Fencing 5 5
2138. 2 z. 50 Wrestling .. 8 5
2139. 3 z. 40 Weightlifting .. 10 5
2140. 5 z. Cycling 25 5
2141. 8 z. 50 Shooting 40 12

529. Cyclists. **530.** Polish War Memorial, Berlin.

1972. 25th Peace Cycle Race.
2143. **529.** 60 g. multicoloured 5 5

1972. "Victory Day, 1945".
2144. **530.** 60 g. green 5 5

531. "Rodlo" Emblem. **532.** Polish Knight of 972 A.D.

1972. Polish Posts in Germany. 50th Anniv.
2145. **531.** 60 g. ochre, red & grn. 5 5

1972. Battle of Cedynia. Millenium.
2146. **532.** 60 g. multicoloured .. 5 5

533. Cheetah.

1972. Zoo Animals. Multicoloured.
2147. 20 g. Type **533** 5 5
2148. 40 g. Giraffe (vert.) .. 5 5
2149. 60 g. Toco toucan .. 5 5
2150. 1 z. 35 Chimpanzee .. 5 5
2151. 1 z. 65 Gibbon 5 5
2152. 3 z. 40 Crocodile .. 8 5
2153. 4 z. Kangaroo 20 8
2154. 4 z. 50 Tiger (vert.) .. 20 8
2155. 7 z. Zebra 30 12

534. L. Warynsky (founder). **535.** F. Dzierzynski.

1972. Proletarian Party. 90th Anniv.
2156. **534.** 60 g. multicoloured 5 5

1972. Felix Dzierzynski (revolutionary). 95th Birth Anniv.
2157. **535.** 60 g. black and red .. 5 5

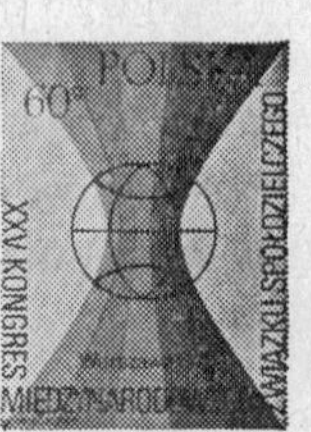

536. Global Emblem. **537.** Scene from "Na Kwaterunku" (ballet).

1972. 25th Co-operative Federation Congress.
2158. **536.** 60 g. multicoloured .. 5 5

1972. Stanislaus Moniuszko (composer). Death Cent. Scenes from Works.
2159. **537.** 10 g. violet and gold 5 5
2160. – 20 g. black and gold .. 5 5
2161. – 40 g. green and gold .. 5 5
2162. – 60 g. blue and gold .. 5 5
2163. – 1 z. 15 blue and gold 5 5
2164. – 1 z. 35 blue and gold 5 5
2165. – 1 z. 55 green and gold 5 5
2166. – 2 z. 50 brown & gold 8 5

DESIGNS: 20 g. "Hrabina" (opera). 40 g. "Strasznydwor" (opera). 60 g. "Halka" (opera). 1 z. 15 "Don Quixote" (ballet). 1 z. 35 "Verbum Nobile". 1 z. 55 "Ideal" (operetta). 2 z. 50 "Paria" (opera).

538. "Copernicus the Astronomer".

1972. Nicolas Copernicus (1973). 500th Birth Anniv. (4th issue).
2167. **538.** 40 g. black and blue .. 5 5
2168. – 60 g. black & orange 5 5
2169. – 2 z. 50 black and red 8 5
2170. – 3 z. 40 black & green 15 5

DESIGNS: 60 g. Copernicus and Polish eagle. 2 z. 50 Copernicus and Medal. 3 z. 40 Copernicus and page of book.

MINIMUM PRICE

The minimum price quoted is 5p which represents a handling charge rather than a basis for valuing common stamps. For further notes about prices see introductory pages.

539. "The Amazon" (P. Michalowski).

1972. Stamp Day. Polish Paintings. Mult.
2172. 30 g. Type **539** 5 5
2173. 40 g. "Ostaffi Laszkiewicz" (J. Matejko) 5 5
2174. 60 g. "Summer Idyll" (W. Gerson) 5 5
2175. 2 z. "The Neapolitan Woman" (A. Kotsis) .. 5 5
2176. 2 z. 50 "Girl Bathing" (P. Szyndler) 5 5
2177. 3 z. 40 "The Princess of Thum" (A. Grottger) .. 12 5
2178. 4 z. "Rhapsody" (S. Wyspianski) 20 5
2179. 8 z. 50+4 z. "Young Woman" (J. Malczewski) (horiz.) .. 60 15

1972. Nos. 1578/9 surch.
2180. 50 g. on 40 g. brown .. 5 5
2181. 90 g. on 40 g. brown .. 5 5
2182. 1 z. on 40 g. brown .. 5 5
2183. 1 z. 50 on 60 g. red .. 5 5
2184. 2 z. 70 on 40 g. brown .. 10 5
2185. 4 z. on 60 g. red .. 15 5
2186. 4 z. 50 on 60 g. red .. 15 5
2187. 4 z. 90 on 60 g. red .. 20 5

540. "The Little Soldier" (E. Piwowarski).

1972. Children's Health Centre.
2188. **540.** 60 g. black & pink .. 5 5

541. "Warsaw Castle" (E. J. Dahlberg, 1656). **542.** Chalet, Dolina Chocholowska.

1972. Restoration of Warsaw Castle.
2189. **541.** 60 g. blk., violet & blue 5 5

1972. Tourism. Mountain Chalets. Mult.
2190. 40 g. Type **542** 5 5
2191. 60 g. Hala Ornak (horiz.) 5 5
2192. 1 z. 55 Hala Gasienicowa 5 5
2193. 1 z. 65 Dolina Pieciu Stawow (horiz.) .. 8 5
2194. 2 z. 50 Morskie Oko .. 10 5

543. Trade Union Banners. **544.** Congress Emblem.

1972. 7th Polish Trade Union Congresses.
2195. **543.** 60 g. multicoloured .. 5 5

1972. 5th Socialist Youth Union Congress.

2196.	544.	60 g. multicoloured . .	5	5

545. Japanese Azalea.

1972. Flowering Shrubs. Multicoloured.

2197.	40 g. Type **545**	5	5
2198.	50 g. Alpine rose	5	5
2199.	60 g. Pomeranian honeysuckle	5	5
2200.	1 z. 65 Chinese quince . .	5	5
2201.	2 z. 50 Korean cranberry	8	5
2202.	3 z. 40 Pontic azalea . .	12	5
2203.	4 z. Delavay's white syringa	20	5
2204.	8 z. 50 Common lilac ("Massena")	45	12

546. Piast Knight (10th-century).

547. Copernicus.

1972. Polish Cavalry Through the Ages. Multicoloured.

2205.	20 g. Type **546**	5	5
2206.	40 g. 13th-century knight	5	5
2207.	60 g. Knight of Wladyslaw Jagiello's Army (15th-century) (horiz.) . .	5	5
2208.	1 z. 35 17th-century hussar	5	5
2209.	4 z. Lancer of National Guard (18th-century) . .	15	5
2210.	4 z. 50 "Congress" cavalry officer	20	5
2211.	5 z. Trooper of Light Cavalry (1939) (horiz.)	20	5
2212.	7 z. Trooper of People's Army (1945)	25	8

1972. Copernicus. 500th Birth Anniv. (5th issue).

2213.	547.	1 z. brown	5	5
2214.		1 z. 50 ochre . .	5	5

548. Statue.

549. "Copernicus as Young Man" (Bacciarelli).

1972. U.S.S.R. 50th Anniv. Multicoloured.

2215.	40 g. Type **548**	5	5
2216.	60 g. Red star and globe	5	5

1973. Copernicus. 500th Birth Anniv. (6th issue). Multicoloured.

2217.	1 z. Type **549**	5	5
2218.	1 z. 50 "Copernicus" (anon)	5	5
2219.	2 z. 70 "Copernicus" (Zinck Nor)	12	5
2220.	4 z. "Copernicus" (from Strassbourg clock) . .	15	5
2221.	4 z. 90 "Copernicus" (Jan Matejko) (horiz.) . .	20	5

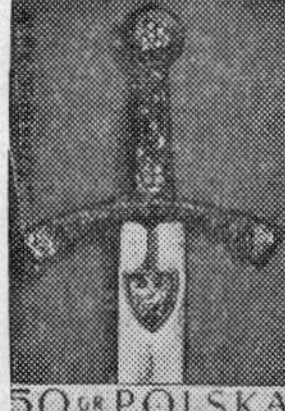

550. Coronation Sword.

551. Statue of Lenin.

1973. Polish Art. Multicoloured.

2222.	50 g. Type **550**	5	5
2223.	1 z. Kruzlowa Madonna (detail)	5	5
2224.	1 z. Armour of hussar . .	5	5
2225.	1 z. 50 Head of Walel (wood)	5	5
2226.	1 z. 50 Silver cockerel . .	5	5
2227.	2 z. 70 Armorial eagle . .	12	5
2228.	4 z. 90 Skarbimierz Madonna	25	8
2229.	8 z. 50 "Portrait of Tenczynski" (anon) . .	40	10

1973. Lenin. 50th Death Anniv. (1974).

2230.	551.	1 z. multicoloured . .	5	5

552. Coded Letter.

1973. Introduction of Postal Codes.

2231.	552.	1 z. multicoloured . .	8	5

553. Wolf.

1973. Game Animals. Multicoloured.

2232.	50 g. Type **553**	5	5
2233.	1 z. Mouflon	5	5
2234.	1 z. 50 Elk	5	5
2235.	2 z. 70 Capercaillie . .	12	5
2236.	3 z. Roe deer	12	5
2237.	4 z. 50 Lynx	20	5
2238.	4 z. 90 Red deer	25	8
2239.	5 z. Wild boar	25	8

554. "Salut".

555. Open Book and Flame.

1973. Cosmic Research. Multicoloured.

2240.	4 z. 90 Type **554**	25	8
2241.	4 z. 90 "Copernicus" (U.S. satellite) . .	25	8

1973. 2nd Polish Science Congress, Warsaw.

2242.	555.	1 z. 50 multicoloured	5	5

556. Ancient Seal of Poznan.

557. M. Nowotko.

1973. "Polska 73" Philatelic Exn., Poznan. Multicoloured.

2243.	1 z. Type **556**	5	5
2244.	1 z. 50 Tombstones of Tomicki	5	5
2245.	2 z. 70 Kalisz paten . .	12	5
2246.	4 z. Bronze gates, Gniezno (horiz.) . .	15	5

1973. Marcel Nowotko (party leader) 80th Birth Anniv.

2249.	557.	1 z. 50 black and red	5	5

558. Cherry Blossom.

1973. Protection of the Environment. Mult.

2250.	50 g. Type **558**	5	5
2251.	90 g. Cattle in meadow . .	5	5
2252.	1 z. Stork on nest . .	5	5
2253.	1 z. 50 Marine life . .	5	5
2254.	2 z. 70 Meadow flora . .	12	5
2255.	4 z. 90 Ocean fauna . .	25	8
2256.	5 z. Forest life . .	25	8
2257.	6 z. 50 Agricultural produce	25	8

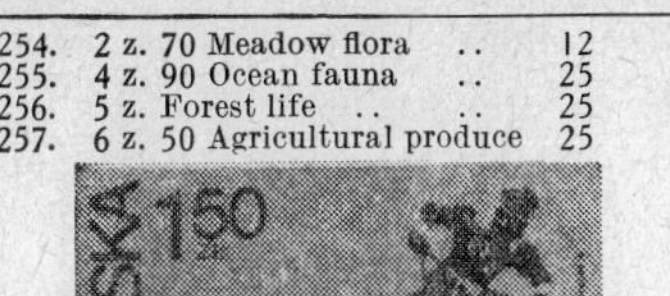

559. Motor-cyclist.

1973. Int. Speedway Race Championships, Chorzow.

2258.	559.	1 z. 50 multicoloured	5	5

560. "Copernicus" (M. Bacciarelli).

1973. Stamp Day.

2259.	560.	4 z. + 2 z. multicoloured	25	8

561. Tank.

1973. People's Army. 30th Anniv. Mult.

2260.	1 z. Type **561**	5	5
2261.	1 z. Jet fighter	5	5
2262.	1 z. 50 Guided missile . .	5	5
2263.	1 z. 50 Destroyer . .	5	5

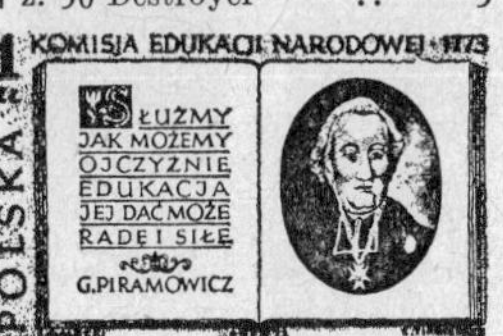

562. G. Piramowicz and Title Page.

1973. Nat. Educational Commission. Bicent.

2264.	562.	1 z. green	5	5
2265.	–	1 z. 50 brown & yell.	5	5

DESIGN: 1 z. 50 J. Sniadecki, H. Kollataj and J. U. Niemcewicz.

563. P. Strzelecki (explorer) and Kangaroo.

1973. Polish Scientists. Multicoloured.

2266.	1 z. Type **563**	5	5
2267.	1 z. H. Arctowski (polar explorer) and penguins	5	5
2268.	1 z. 50 S. Rogozinski (explorer) and "Lucy-Margaret" . .	5	5
2269.	1 z. 50 B. Dybowski (zoologist) and mammal, Lake Baikal	5	5
2270.	2 z. B. Malinowski (anthropologist) and New Guinea dancers . .	8	5
2271.	2 z. 70 S. Drzewiecki (oceanographer) and submarine	12	5
2272.	3 z. E. Strasburger (botanist) and classified plants	12	5
2273.	8 z. I. Domeyko (geologist) and Chilean desert landscape	40	10

INDEX

Countries can be quickly located by referring to the index at the end of this volume.

564. Polish Flag.

565. Jelcz-Berliet Coach.

1973. People's Government. 25th Anniv.

2274.	564.	1 z. 40 red, blue & gold	5	5

1973. Polish Motor Vehicles. Multicoloured.

2275.	50 g. Type **565**	5	5
2276.	90 g. Jelcz "316" truck . .	5	5
2277.	1 z. Polski-Fiat "126p" saloon	5	5
2278.	1 z. 50 Polski-Fiat "125p" saloon and mileage records	5	5
2279.	4 z. Nysa "M-521" utility van	15	5
2280.	4 z. 50 Star "660" truck	20	5

566. Iris.

567. Cottage, Kurpie.

1974. Flowers. Drawings by S. Wyspianski.

2281.	566.	50 g. purple	5	5
2282.	–	1 z. green	5	5
2283.	–	1 z. 50 red	5	5
2284.	–	3 z. violet	12	5
2285.	–	4 z. blue	15	5
2286.	–	4 z. 50 green . .	20	5

FLOWERS: 1 z. Thistle. 1 z. 50 Poppy. 3 z. Asters. 4 z. Pinks. 4 z. 50 Clover.

1974. Wooden Architecture. Multicoloured.

2287.	1 z. Type **567**	5	5
2288.	1 z. 50 Church, Sekowa . .	5	5
2289.	4 z. Town Hall, Sulmierzyce	15	5
2290.	4 z. 50 Church, Lachowice	20	5
2291.	4 z. 90 Windmill, Sobienie Jeziory	20	5
2292.	5 z. Orthodox Church, Ulucz	20	5

568. 19th-century Mailcoach.

569. Cracow Motif.

1974. Centenary of Universal Postal Union.

2293.	568.	1 z. 50 multicoloured	5	5

1974. "SOCPHILEX IV" Int., Stamp Exn., Katowice. Regional Floral Embroideries. Multicoloured.

2294	50 g. Type **569**	5	5
2295.	1 z. 50 Lowicz motif . .	5	5
2296.	4 z. Slask motif	15	5

570. Association Emblem.

571. Soldier and Dove.

1974. Combatants for Liberty and Democracy Association, Warsaw. 5th Congress.

2298.	570.	1 z. 50 red	5	5

1974. Victory over Fascism in Second World War. 29th Anniv.

2299.	571.	1 z. 50 multicoloured	5	5

572. "Comecon" Headquarters, Moscow.

1974. Council for Mutual Economic Aid. 25th Anniv.

2300.	572.	1 z. 50 brn., red & blue	5	5

573. World Cup Emblem.

1974. World Cup Football Championships, West Germany. Multicoloured.
2301. 4 z. 90 Type **573** 20 5
2302. 4 z. 90 Players and Olympic Gold Medal of 1972 .. 20 5

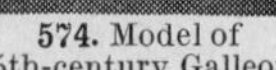

574. Model of 16th-century Galleon. **575.** "Chess" (Title page from book by J. Kochanowski.)

1974. Gdansk Sailing Festival. Polish sailing ships. Multicoloured.
2304. 1 z. Type **574** 5 5
2305. 1 z. 50 Trans-Atlantic sloop "Dal" (1934) .. 5 5
2306. 2 z. 70 Yacht "Opty" (Teliga's circum-navigation, 1969) .. 12 5
2307. 4 z. Training ship "Dar Pomorza" 15 5
2308. 4 z. 90 Yacht "Polonez" (Baranowski's circum-navigation, 1973) .. 20 5

1974. Tenth International Chess Festival Lubin.
2309. **575.** 1 z. black, yell. & brn. 5 5
2310. – 1 z. 50 blk., yell. & grn. 5 5
DESIGN: 1 z. 50 "Education" (D. Chodowski).

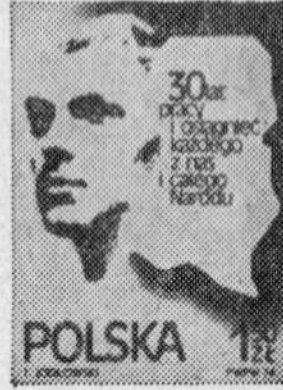

576. Aerial View of Flyover. **577.** Man's Face and Map.

1974. Opening of Lazienkowski Flyover.
2311. **576.** 1 z. 50 multicoloured 5 5

1974. Polish People's Republic. 30th Anniv.
2312. **577.** 1 z. 50 blk., gold & red 5 5
2313. – 1 z. 50 multicoloured 5 5
2314. – 1 z. 50 multicoloured 5 5
DESIGNS—(27 × 38 mm.). Nos. 2313/4 Polish "Eagle".

578. Strawberries.

1974. 19th Int. Horticultural Congress, Warsaw. Fruits, Vegetables and Flowers. Multicoloured.
2316. 50 g. Type **578** 5 5
2317. 90 g. Blackcurrants .. 5 5
2318. 1 z. Apples 5 5
2319. 1 z. 50 Cucumbers .. 5 5
2320. 2 z. 70 Tomatoes .. 12 5
2321. 4 z. 50 Green peas .. 20 5
2322. 4 z. 90 Pansies 20 5
2323. 5 z. Nasturtiums 20 5

579. Department Badge. **580.** "Child in Polish Costume" (L. Orlowski).

1974. Polish Civic Militia and Security Service. 30th Anniv.
2324. **579.** 1 z. 50 multicoloured 5 5

1974. Stamp Day. "The Child in Polish Painting". Multicoloured.
2325. 50 g. Type **580** 5 5
2326. 90 g. "Girl with Pigeon" (anon.) 5 5
2327. 1 z. "Portrait of a Girl" (S. Wyspianski) .. 5 5
2328. 1 z. 50 "The Orphan from Poronin" (W. Slewinski) 5 5
2329. 3 z. "The Peasant Boy" (K. Sichulski) 12 5
2330. 4 z. 50 "The Florence Page" (A. Gierymski) .. 20 5
2331. 4 z. 90 "Tadeusz with a Dog" (artist's son—P. Michalowski) .. 20 5
2332. 6 z. 50 "Youth with Doe" (A. Kotsis) 25 8

581. "The Crib".

1974. "Masterpieces of Polish Art". Mult.
2333. 1 z. Type **581** 5 5
2334. 1 z. 50 "The Flight to Egypt" 5 5
2335. 2 z. "King Zygmunt III Wasa" 8 5
2336. 4 z. "King Jan Olbracht" 15 5

582. Anglers and Fishes. **583.** "Pablo Neruda" (O. Guaysasmin).

1974. Polish Folklore. 16th-century Woodcuts.
2337. **582.** 1 z. black 5 5
2338. – 1 z. 50 blue 5 5
DESIGN: 1 z. 50 Archers and bears.

1974. Pablo Neruda (Chilean poet). 70th Birth Anniv.
2339. **583.** 1 z. 50 multicoloured 5 5

584. Heroes Memorial and Opera House, Warsaw.

1975. Warsaw's Liberation. 30th Anniv.
2340. **584.** 1 z. 50 multicoloured 5 5

585. Lesser Kestrel (male). **586.** Prison Garb and Barbed Wire.

1975. Birds of Prey. Falcons. Multicoloured.
2341. 1 z. Type **585** 5 5
2342. 1 z. Lesser Kestrel (female) 5 5
2343. 1 z. 50 Red-footed Falcon (female) 5 5
2344. 1 z. 50 Red-footed Falcon (male) 5 5
2345. 2 z. Hobby 8 5
2346. 3 z. Kestrel 12 5
2347. 4 z. Merlin 15 5
2348. 8 z. Peregrine Falcon .. 30 10

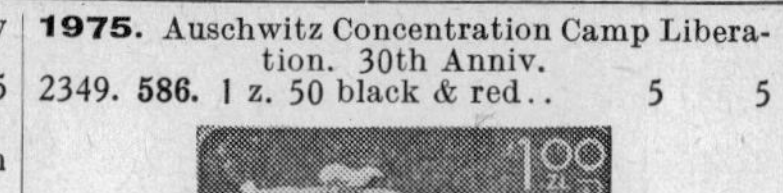

1975. Auschwitz Concentration Camp Liberation. 30th Anniv.
2349. **586.** 1 z. 50 black & red .. 5 5

587. Women's Hurdles.

1975. 6th European Indoor Athletic Championships, Katowice. Multicoloured.
2350. 1 z. Type **587** 5 5
2351. 1 z. 50 Pole vault .. 5 5
2352. 4 z. Hop, step and jump .. 15 5
2353. 4 z. 90 Start of race .. 20 5

588. "St. Anne" (wood-carving) and "Arphila" Emblem.

1975. International Stamp Exhibition, Paris.
2355. **588.** 1 z. 50 multicoloured 10 5

589. Union Emblem.

1975. Amateur Radio Union's International Conference, Warsaw.
2356. **589.** 1 z. 50 multicoloured 10 5

590. Pine and Guide's Badge. **591.** Hand holding Tulips.

1975. Tourism. Mountain Guides' Association. Cent. Multicoloured.
2357. 1 z. Type **590** 5 5
2358. 1 z. Gentians 5 5
2359. 1 z. 50 Sudety Mountains (horiz.) 10 5
2360. 1 z. 50 Branch of yew (horiz.) 10 5
2361. 4 z. Beskidy Mountains 25 8
2362. 4 z. Arnica blossoms .. 25 8

1975. Victory over Fascism. 30th Anniv.
2363. **591.** 1 z. 50 multicoloured 10 5

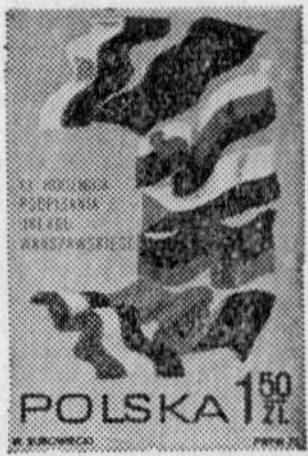

592. Flags of Treaty Countries.

1975. Warsaw Treaty Organization. 20th Anniv.
2364. **592.** 1 z. 50 multicoloured 10 5

593. Hens.

1975. 26th European Zoo-technical Federation Congress, Warsaw. Multicoloured.
2365. 50 g. Type **593** 5 5
2366. 1 z. Geese 5 5
2367. 1 z. 50 Black-and-white cattle 10 5
2368. 2 z. Brown-and-white cow 12 5
2369. 3 z. Wielkopolska horse .. 20 8
2370. 4 z. Pure-bred Arab horses 25 8
2371. 4 z. 50 Pigs 30 10
2372. 5 z. Sheep 30 15

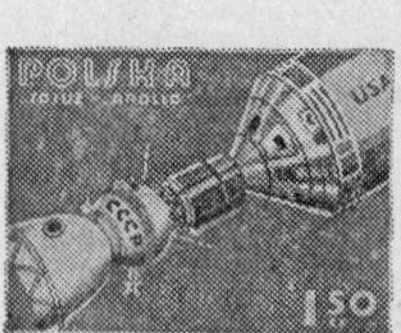

594. Linked Capsules. **595.** Fund Emblem.

1975. "Apollo-Soyuz" Space Project. Multicoloured.
2373. 1 z. 50 Type **594** .. 10 5
2374. 4 z. 90 "Apollo" .. 30 10
2375. 4 z. 90 "Soyuz" .. 30 10

1975. National Health Protection Fund.
2377. **595.** 1 z. 50 bl., blk. & silv. 10 5

596. U.N. Emblem in Sunburst.

1975. United Nations Organization. 30th Anniv.
2378. **596.** 4 z. multicoloured .. 25 8

597. Polish Flag and "E" for "Europe".

1975. European Security and Co-operation Conference, Helsinki.
2379. **597.** 4 z. red, blue & black 25 8

598. "Bolek and Lolek".

1975. Children's Television Characters. Multicoloured.
2380. 50 g. Type **598** 5 5
2381. 1 z. "Jacek" and "Agatka" 5 5
2382. 1 z. 50 "Reksio" (dog) 10 5
2383. 4 z. "Telesfor" (dragon) 25 8

599. I.I.S. Emblem. **600.** Women of Three Races.

1975. International Statistics Institute. 40th Session.
2384. **599.** 1 z. 50 multicoloured 10 5

1975. International Women's Year.
2385. **600.** 1 z. 50 multicoloured 10 5

601. " Albatross " Biplane.

1975. First Polish Airmail Stamps. 50th Anniv. Multicoloured.

2386. 2 z. 40 Type **601** 15 5
2387. 4 z. 90 Tail of " Il-62 " jetliner 30 10

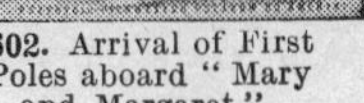

602. Arrival of First Poles aboard " Mary and Margaret ".

603. Frederic Chopin.

1975. American Revolution. Bicent. Poles in American Life. Multicoloured.

2388. 1 z. Type **602** 5 5
2389. 1 z. 50 Polish glass-worker, Jamestown 10 5
2390. 2 z. 70 Helena Modrzejewska (actress) 15 5
2391. 4 z. General Casimir Pulaski 25 8
2392. 6 z. 40 General Tadeusz Kosciuszko 40 15

1975. 9th International Chopin Piano Competition.

2394. **603.** 1 z. 50 blk., lilac & gold 10 5

604. " Self-portrait ".

605. Market Place, Kazimierz Dolny.

1975. Stamp Day. Xawery Dunikowski (sculptor). Birth Cent. Multicoloured.

2395. 50 g. Type **604** 5 5
2396. 1 z. " Breath " (metal sculpture) 5 5
2397. 1 z. 50 " Maternity " (detail of wood sculpture) 10 5
2398. 8 z.+4 z. " Silesian Rising " (stone monument) 75 25

1975. European Architectural Heritage Year.

2399. **605.** 1 z. green 5 5
2400. – 1 z. 50 brown .. 10 5

DESIGN—VERT. 1 z. 50 Town Hall, Zamosc.

606. " Lodz " (Wladyslaw Strzeminski).

608. Symbolic " 7 ".

607. Heraldic Eagle of Henryka IV.

1975. Lodz 75 " Stamp Exhibition.

2401. **606.** 4 z. 50 multicoloured 30 10

1975. Piast Dynasty of Silesia.

2403. **607.** 1 z. green 5 5
2404. – 1 z. 50 brown 10 5
2405. – 4 z. violet 25 8

DESIGNS: 1 z. 50 Seal of Prince Boleslaw of Legnica. 4 z. Coin of last Piast, Jerzy Wilhelm.

1975. 7th Congress of Polish United Workers Party.

2406. **608.** 1 z. multicoloured .. 5 5
2407. – 1 z. 50 red, bl. & silver 10 5

DESIGN: 1 z. 50 Party initials " PZPR ".

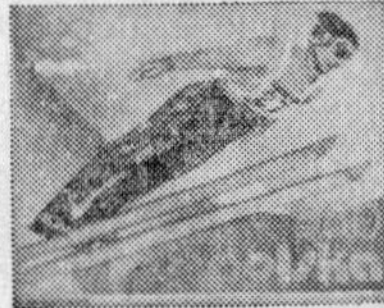

609. Ski-jumping.

1976. Winter Olympic Games, Innsbruck. Multicoloured.

2408. 50 g. Type **609** 5 5
2409. 1 z. Ice-hockey 5 5
2410. 1 z. 50 Downhill skiing .. 10 5
2411. 2 z. Speed skating .. 12 5
2412. 4 z. Tobogganing .. 25 8
2413. 6 z. 40 Biathlon 40 15

610. Richard Trevithick's Steam Engine, 1803.

1976. " History of the Railway Locomotive ". Multicoloured.

2414. 50 g. Type **610** 5 5
2415. 1 z. Murray and Blenkinsop's steam engine, 1810 .. 5 5
2416. 1 z. 50 George Stephensons' " Rocket ", 1829 .. 10 5
2417. 1 z. 50 Polish " Universal " electric Type ET-22 locomotive, 1969 .. 10 5
2418. 2 z. 70 Robert Stephenson's " North Star ", 1837 .. 15 5
2419. 3 z. Joseph Harrison's steam loco, 1840 .. 20 5
2420. 4 z. 50 Thomas Rogers' American locomotive, 1855 .. .. .. 30 10
2421. 4 z. 90 A. Xiezopolski's Polish locomotive, 1922 30 10

611. Members' Flags as Nucleus.

1976. Joint Institute for Nuclear Research (C.M.E.A.). 20th Anniversary.

2422. **611.** 1 z. 50 multicoloured 10 5

612. Early Telephone, Earth Station, " Interkosmos 10 " and " Telstar 1 ".

1976. First Telephone Transmission. Cent.

2423. **612.** 1 z. 50 multicoloured 10 5

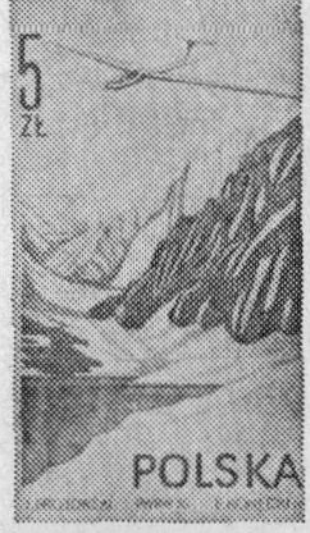

613. " Jantar " Glider over Mountains.

614. Ice-hockey Player.

1976. Air. " Contemporary Aviation ".

2424. **613.** 5 z. blue 30 10
2425. – 10 z. brown 60 25

DESIGN: 10 z. " Mi-6 " transport helicopter.

1976. World and European Ice-hockey Championships, Katowice. Multicoloured.

2426. 1 z. Type **614** 8 5
2427. 1 z. 50 Type **614** reversed 12 5

615. Polish Soldier of U.N. Force.

1976. Polish Troops in U.N. Sinai Force.

2428. **615.** 1 z. 50 multicoloured 12 5

616. Sappers' Monument, Warsaw.

617. " Interphil " Emblem.

1976. Battle Monuments. Multicoloured.

2429. 1 z. Type **616** 8 5
2430. 1 z. Monument to soldiers of 1st Polish Army, Sandau 8 5

1976. " Interphil '76 ". Int. Stamp Exn., Philadelphia.

2431. **617.** 8 z. 40 multicoloured 65 25

618. Wielkopolski Park and Owl.

1976. National Parks. Multicoloured.

2432. 90 g. Type **618** 8 5
2433. 1 z. Wolinski Park and eagle 8 5
2434. 1 z. 50 Slowinski Park and seagull 12 5
2435. 4 z. 50 Bieszczadzki Park and lynx 35 12
2436. 5 z. Ojcowski Park and bat 40 15
2437. 6 z. Kampinoski Park and elk 45 15

619. U.N. H.Q. and Globe.

1976. U.N. Postal Administration. 25th Anniv.

2438. **619.** 8 z. 40 multicoloured 65 25

620. Fencing.

621. Theatre Facade.

1976. Olympic Games, Montreal. Mult.

2439. 50 g. Type **620** 5 5
2440. 1 z. Cycling 8 5
2441. 1 z. 50 Football 12 5
2442. 4 z. 20 Boxing 30 10
2443. 6 z. 90 Weightlifting .. 55 20
2444. 8 z. 40 Running 65 25

1976. Polish Theatre, Poznan. Centenary.

2445. **621.** 1 z. 50 green & orange 12 5

622. A. Czekanowski and Baikal Landscape.

623. " Sphinx ".

1976. A. Czekanowski (geologist). Death Cent.

2447. **622.** 1 z. 50 multicoloured 12 5

1976. Stamp Day. Paintings from Greek Vases, National Museum. Multicoloured.

2448. 1 z. Type **623** 8 5
2449. 1 z. 50 " Mermaid " (horiz.) 12 5
2450. 2 z. " Lion " (horiz.) .. 15 5
2451. 4 z. 20 " Bull " (horiz.) .. 30 10
2452. 4 z. 50 " Goat " (horiz.) .. 35 12
2453. 8 z.+4 z. " Sphinx " (different) 95 30

624. Warszawa " M 20 " car.

1976. Zeran Motor-car Factory, Warsaw. 25th Anniv. Multicoloured.

2454. 1 z. Type **624** 8 5
2455. 1 z. 50 Warszawa " 223 " 12 5
2456. 2 z. Syrena " 104 " .. 15 5
2457. 4 z. 90 Polski – Fiat " 125 P " 40 15

625. Ladle.

1976. First Steel Production from Huta Katowice Plant.

2459. **625.** 1 z. 50 multicoloured 12 5

626. Trade Union Emblem.

627. " Epitaph of Wierzbieto " (painting).

1976. 8th Polish Trade Unions Congress.

2460. **626.** 1 z. 50 oran. & bistre 12 5

1976. Polish Art. Multicoloured.

2461. 1 z. Type **627** 8 5
2462. 6 z. " The Beautiful Madonna " (painted carving) 45 15

628. Tanker "Zawrat", Oil Terminal, Gdansk.

1976. Polish Ports. Multicoloured.
2463. 1 z. Type 628 .. .. 8 5
2464. 1 z. Ferryboat "Gryf" and pier, Gdansk .. 8 5
2465. 1 z. 50 Container ship and wharf, Gdynia .. 12 5
2466. 1 z. 50 "Stefan Bartory", passenger terminal and monument, Gdynia .. 12 5
2467. 2 z. "Ziemia Szczenska" and barge, Szczecin .. 15 5
2468. 4 z. 20 Collier taking on coal, Swinoujscie .. 30 10
2469. 6 z. 90 Liner, lighthouse and hydrofoil, Kolobrzeg 55 20
2470. 8 z. 40 Map of Polish ports 65 25

MILITARY POST

I. Polish Corps in Russia, 1918.

1918. Stamps of Russia optd. **POCZTA. Pol. Korp.** and eagle. Perf. or imperf. (70 k.).
M 1. 11. 3 k. red .. .. 13·00 11·00
M 2. 12. 4 k. red .. .. 13·00 11·00
M 3. 11. 5 k. claret .. .. 5·50 4·50
M 4. 12. 10 k. blue .. .. 5·50 4·50
M 5. 11. 10 k. on 7 k. bl. (No. 151) 55·00 55·00
M 6. 4. 15 k. blue and purple 70 55
M 7. 7. 20 k. red and blue .. 1·40 90
M 8. 4. 25 k. mauve and green 18·00 14·00
M 9. 35 k. green and purple 1·10 70
M 10. 7. 50 k. green and purple 4·00 3·25
M 11. 4. 70 k. orange and brown (No. 166) .. .. 45·00 45·00

1918. Stamps of Russia surch. **Pol. Korp.**, eagle and value. (a) Perf. on Nos. 92/4.
M 12A. 11. 10 k. on 3 k. red .. 65 65
M 13A. 35 k. on 1 k. orange 4·00 4·00
M 14A. 50 k. on 2 k. green 55 55
M 15A. 1 r. on 3 k. red .. 11·00 11·00

(b) Imperf. on Nos. 155/7
M 12B. 11. 10 k. on 3 k. red .. 55 55
M 13B. 35 k. on 1 k. orange 25 25
M 14B. 50 k. on 2 k. green 55 55
M 15B. 1 r. on 3 k. red .. 1·00 1·10

II. Polish Army in Russia, 1942.

M 1. "We Shall Return".

1942.
M 16. M 1. 50 k. brown .. 24·00 40·00

NEWSPAPER STAMPS.

1919. Newspaper stamps of Austria optd. **POCZTA POLSKA.** Imperf.
N 50. N 9. 2 h. brown .. .. 2·25 2·25
N 51. 4 h. green 55 55
N 52. 6 h. blue 45 45
N 53. 10 h. orange .. .. 7·00 7·00
N 54. 30 h. claret .. .. 1·25 1·25

OFFICIAL STAMPS

O 1. O 2.

1920.
O 128. O 1. 3 f. red 5 5
O 129. 5 f. red 5 5
O 130. 10 f. red 5 5
O 131. 15 f. red 5 5
O 132. 25 f. red 5 5
O 133. 50 f. red 5 5
O 134. 100 f. red 5 5
O 135. 150 f. red 5 5
O 136. 200 f. red 5 5
O 137. 300 f. red 5 5
O 138. 600 f. red 5 5

1933. (a) Inscr. "ZWYCZAJNA".
O 295. O 2. (No value) mauve .. 8 5
O 306. (No value) blue .. 5 5

(b) Inscr. "POLECONA".
O 307. O 2. (No value) red .. 5 5

O 3.

1940. (a) Size 31 × 23 mm.
O 392. O 3. 6 g. brown 25 25
O 393. 8 g. grey 25 25
O 394. 10 g. green 25 25
O 395. 12 g. green 40 40
O 396. 20 g. brown 40 40
O 397. 24 g. red .. .. 1·60 80
O 398. 30 g. red 50 50
O 399. 40 g. violet 50 50
O 400. 48 g. olive 75 75
O 401. 50 g. blue 40 40
O 402. 60 g. olive 25 35
O 403. 80 g. purple 25 35

(b) Size 35 × 26 mm.
O 404. 1 z. purple and grey 55 55
O 405. 3 z. brown and grey 55 65
O 406. 5 z. orange and grey 90 1·25

1940. Size 21 × 16 mm.
O 407. O 3. 6 g. brown 5 5
O 408. 8 g. grey 5 5
O 409. 10 g. green 5 5
O 410. 12 g. green 5 5
O 411. 20 g. brown 10 10
O 412. 24 g. red 12 12
O 413. 30 g. red 12 12
O 414. 40 g. violet 15 20
O 415. 50 g. blue 20 20

O 4. O 5. O 6.

1943.
O 456. O 4. 6 g. brown 5 5
O 457. 8 g. blue 5 5
O 458. 10 g. green 5 5
O 459. 12 g. violet 5 5
O 560. 16 g. orange 5 5
O 561. 20 g. olive 5 5
O 562. 24 g. red 5 5
O 563. 30 g. purple 5 5
O 564. 40 g. blue 5 5
O 565. 60 g. olive 5 5
O 566. 80 g. purple 5 8
O 567. 100 g. slate 5 8

1945. No value.

The blue and indigo stamps are inscr. "ZWYKLA" (Ordinary) and the red stamps "POLECONA" (Registered.)

(a) With imprint below design. Perf. or imp.
O 532. O 5. (5 z.) violet-blue .. 5 5
O 533. (10 z.) brown-red .. 10 5

(b) Without imprint below design. Perf.
O 804. O 5. (60 g.) pale blue .. 8 5
O 805. (60 g.) indigo .. 10 5
O 806. (1.55 z.) red .. 12 8

1954. No value.
O 871. O 6. (60 g.) blue .. 8 5
O 872. (1.55 z.) red ("POLECONA") 20 5

POSTAGE DUE STAMPS

1919. Postage Due stamps of Austria optd. **POCZTA POLSKA.**
D 50. D 3. 5 g. red 90 90
D 51. 10 h. red £550 £700
D 52. 15 h. red 55 55
D 53. 20 h. red £160 £160
D 54. 25 h. red .. .. 3·50 3·50
D 55. 30 h. red £275 £225
D 56. 40 h. red .. .. 90·00 90·00
D 57. D 4. 1 k. blue £700 £700
D 58. 5 k. blue £700 £700
D 59. 10 k. blue £1800 £1800

1919. Postage Due Provisionals of Austria optd. **POCZTA POLSKA.**
D 60. 27. 15 on 36 h. (No D 49) 90·00 90·00
D 61. 50 on 42 h. (No D 51) 7·00 7·00

1919. Value in "halerze".
D 92. D 1. 2 h. blue 5 5
D 93. 4 h. blue 5 5
D 94. 5 h. blue 5 5
D 95. 10 h. blue 5 5
D 96. 20 h. blue 5 5
D 97. 30 h. blue 5 5
D 98. 50 h. blue 5 5
D 145. 100 h. blue 5 5
D 147. 500 h. blue 5 5

1919. As Type D 1, but value in "fenigi".
D 128. D 1. 2 f. red 5 5
D 129. 4 f. red 5 5
D 130. 5 f. red 5 5
D 131. 10 f. red 5 5
D 132. 20 f. red 5 5
D 133. 30 f. red 5 5
D 134. 50 f. red 5 5
D 135. 100 f. red 5 5
D 146. 200 f. blue 5 5
D 136. 500 f. red 12 12

1921. Stamps of 1919 surch. with new value and **doplata**. Imperf.
D 154. 11. 6 m. on 15 h. brown 5 8
D 155. 6 m. on 25 h. red .. 5 8
D 156. 20 m. on 10 h. red .. 20 25
D 157. 20 m. on 50 h. blue .. 25 25
D 158. 35 m. on 70 h. blue .. 70 1·10

1921. Value in "marks".
(a) Size 17 × 22 mm.
D 159. D 2. 1 m. blue 5 5
D 160. 2 m. blue 5 5
D 161. 4 m. blue 5 5
D 162. 6 m. blue 5 5
D 163. 8 m. blue 5 5
D 164. 20 m. blue 5 5
D 165. 50 m. blue 5 5
D 166. 100 m. blue 5 5

(b) Size 19 × 24 mm.
D 199. D 2. 50 m. blue 5 5
D 200. 100 m. blue 5 5
D 201. 200 m. blue 5 5
D 202. 500 m. blue 5 5
D 203. 1000 m. blue 5 5
D 204. 2000 m. blue 5 5
D 205. 10,000 m. blue .. 5 5
D 206. 20,000 m. blue .. 5 5
D 207. 30,000 m. blue .. 5 5
D 208. 50,000 m. blue .. 5 5
D 209. 100,000 m. blue .. 5 5
D 210. 200,000 m. blue .. 8 5
D 211. 300,000 m. blue .. 8 5
D 212. 500,000 m. blue .. 15 5
D 213. 1,000,000 m. blue .. 25 5
D 214. 2,000,000 m. blue .. 35 5
D 215. 3,000,000 m. blue .. 55 5

1923. Surch.
D 216. D 2. 10,000 on 8 m. blue 5 5
D 217. 20,000 on 20 m. blue 5 5
D 218. 50,000 on 2 m. blue 8 8

1924. As Type D 2 but value in "groszy", or "zloty". (a) Size 20 × 25½ mm.
D 229. D 2. 1 g. brown 5 5
D 230. 2 g. brown 8 5
D 231. 4 g. brown 8 5
D 232. 6 g. brown 8 5
D 233. 10 g. brown 90 5
D 234. 15 g. brown 90 5
D 235. 20 g. brown .. .. 1·40 5
D 236. 25 g. brown .. .. 1·40 5
D 237. 30 g. brown 35 5
D 238. 40 g. brown 45 5
D 239. 50 g. brown 45 5
D 240. 1 z. brown 35 5
D 241. 2 z. brown 35 5
D 242. 3 z. brown 45 10
D 243. 5 z. brown 45 5

(b) Size 19 × 24 mm.
D 290. D 2. 1 g. brown 5 5
D 291. 2 g. brown 5 5
D 292. 10 g. brown 25 5
D 293. 15 g. brown 35 5
D 294. 20 g. brown 90 5
D 295. 25 g. brown .. .. 6·00 5

1930.
D 280. D 3. 5 g. brown 5 5

1934. Nos. D 79/84 surch.
D 301. D 2. 10 g. on 2 z. brown 5 5
D 302. 15 g. on 2 z. brown 5 5
D 303. 20 g. on 1 z. brown 8 5
D 304. 20 g. on 5 z. brown 35 5
D 305. 25 g. on 40 g. brown 12 8
D 306. 30 g. on 40 g. brown 12 8
D 307. 50 g. on 40 g. brown 15 8
D 308. 50 g. on 3 z. brown 35 5

1934. No. 273 surch. **DOPLATA** and value.
D 309. 10 g. on 1 z. blk. on cream 10 5
D 310. 20 g. on 1 z. blk. on cream 20 5
D 311. 25 g. on 1 z. blk. on cream 15 5

D 1. D 2. D 3. D 4. D 5.

1938.
D 350. D 4. 5 g. green 5 5
D 351. 10 g. green 5 5
D 352. 15 g. green 5 5
D 353. 20 g. green 5 5
D 354. 25 g. green 5 5
D 355. 30 g. green 5 5
D 356. 50 g. green 10 12
D 357. 1 z. green 15 20

1940. German Occupation.
D 420. D 5. 10 g. orange .. 5 12
D 421. 20 g. orange .. 5 15
D 422. 30 g. orange .. 5 25
D 423. 50 g. orange .. 8 60

D 6. D 7.

1945. Size 26 × 19½ mm. Perf.
D 530. D 6. 1 z. brown 5 5
D 531. 2 z. brown 5 5
D 532. 3 z. brown 5 5
D 533. 5 z. brown 10 5

1946. Size 29 × 21½ mm. Perf. or imperf.
D 646. D 6. 1 z. brown 5 5
D 647. 2 z. brown 5 5
D 572. 3 z. brown 5 5
D 573. 5 z. brown 5 5
D 574. 6 z. brown 5 5
D 575. 10 z. brown 5 5
D 576. 15 z. brown 5 5
D 577. 25 z. brown 8 5
D 651. 100 z. brown 15 5
D 652. 150 z. brown 25 5

1950.
D 665. D 7. 5 z. claret 5 5
D 666. 10 z. claret 5 5
D 667. 15 z. claret 5 5
D 668. 20 z. claret 5 5
D 669. 25 z. claret 5 5
D 670. 50 z. claret 8 5
D 671. 100 z. claret 15 8

1951. Value in "groszy" or "zloty".
D 701. D 7. 5 g. claret 5 5
D 702. 10 g. claret 5 5
D 703. 15 g. claret 5 5
D 704. 20 g. claret 5 5
D 705. 25 g. claret 5 5
D 706. 30 g. claret 5 5
D 707. 50 g. claret 5 5
D 708. 60 g. claret 8 5
D 709. 90 g. claret 12 5
D 710. 1 z. claret 15 5
D 711. 2 z. claret 30 8
D 712. 5 z. purple 60 20

1953. As last but with larger figures of value and no imprint below design.
D 804. D 7. 5 g. claret 5 5
D 805. 10 g. claret 5 5
D 806. 15 g. claret 5 5
D 807. 20 g. claret 5 5
D 808. 25 g. claret 5 5
D 809. 30 g. claret 5 5
D 810. 50 g. claret 5 5
D 811. 60 g. claret 5 5
D 812. 90 g. claret 5 5
D 813. 1 z. claret 8 5
D 814. 2 z. claret 12 8

POLISH POST IN DANZIG E1

For Polish post in Danzig, the port through which Poland had access to the sea between the two Great Wars.

Stamps of Poland optd. **PORT GDANSK.**

1925. Issue of 1924.
R 1. 28. 1 g. brown 20 40
R 2. 2 g. brown 30 40
R 3. 3 g. orange 30 40
R 4. 5 g. green .. .. 3·00 1·40
R 5. 10 g. green .. .. 1·10 70
R 6. 15 g. red .. .. 7·50 1·40
R 7. 20 g. blue .. .. 1·10 50
R 8. 25 g. claret .. .. 1·10 50
R 9. 30 g. violet .. .. 1·10 50
R 10. 40 g. blue .. .. 1·10 50
R 11. 50 g. purple .. .. 1·10 50

1926. Issues of 1925-28.
R 14. 32. 5 g. green 70 55
R 15. – 10 g. violet (No. 245a) 70 55
R 16. – 15 g. red (No. 246) .. 1·60 1·25
R 17. 33. 20 g. red .. .. 1·10 60
R 18. 36. 25 g. brown .. .. 1·10 55
R 19. 42. 1 z. black and cream .. 17·00 13·00

1929. Issues of 1928/9.
R 21. 46. 5 g. violet 85 45
R 22. 10 g. green 85 45
R 23. 44. 15 g. blue .. .. 2·00 1·75
R 24. 46. 25 g. brown .. .. 1·10 30

1933. Stamp of 1928 with vert. opt.
R 25. 42. 1 z. black on cream .. 48·00 45·00

1934. Issue of 1932.
R 26. 50. 5 g. violet .. .. 1·60 1·10
R 27. 10 g. green .. .. 17·00 32·00
R 28. 15 g. claret .. .. 1·25 1·10

1936. Issue of 1935.
R 32. 58. 5 g. violet (No. 313) .. 30 35
R 29. – 5 g. violet (No. 317) .. 1·25 85
R 33. – 15 g. blue (No. 315) .. 35 55
R 30. – 15 g. red (No. 319) .. 1·25 1·25
R 31. – 25 g. green (No. 321) 1·25 60

1. Port of Danzig.

ILLUSTRATIONS
British Commonwealth and all overprints and surcharges are FULL SIZE. Foreign Countries have been reduced to ¾-LINEAR.

1938. Polish Independence. 20th Anniv.
R 34. 1. 5 g. orange 35 40
R 35. 15 g. brown 35 40
R 36. 25 g. purple 35 60
R 37. 55 g. blue .. .. 80 1·25

POLISH POST OFFICE IN TURKEY E3

Stamps used for a short period for franking correspondence handed in at the Polish Consulate, Constantinople.

100 fenigi = 1 mark.

1919. Stamps of Poland of 1919 optd. **LEVANT.** Perf.
1. 6. 3 f. brown 35
2. 5 f. green 35
3. 10 f. purple 35
4. 15 f. red 35
5. 20 f. blue 35
6. 25 f. olive 35
7. 50 f. green 35
8. 8. 1 m. violet 70
9. 1 m. 50 green 70
10. 2 m. brown .. .. 1·10
11. 9. 2 m. 50 brown .. 1·10
12. 10. 5 m. purple .. .. 1·10

PONTA DELGADA E1

A district of the Azores, whose stamps were used from 1868, and again after 1905.

1892. As T 9 of Portugal but inscr. "PONTA DELGADA".
6. 5 r. orange 40 35
20. 10 r. mauve 75 60
8. 15 r. brown 85 80
9. 20 r. lilac 85 80
10. 25 r. green 65 25
12. 50 r. blue .. .. 1·10 60
25. 75 r. red .. .. 2·75 2·25
26. 80 r. green .. .. 4·00 3·25
27. 100 r. brown on yellow .. 2·25 2·00
28. 150 r. red on rose .. 13·00 11·00
16. 200 r. blue on blue .. 12·00 8·50
17. 300 r. blue on brown .. 15·00 11·00

1897. "King Carlos" key-types inscr. "PONTA DELGADA".
29. S. 2½ r. grey 20 15
30. 5 r. orange 20 15
31. 10 r. green 20 15
32. 15 r. brown .. .. 1·25 95
45. 15 r. green 35 30
33. 20 r. lilac 55 35
34. 25 r. green 80 30
46. 25 r. red 30 15
35. 50 r. blue 65 40
48. 65 r. blue 35 30
36. 75 r. red .. .. 1·00 90
49. 75 r. brown on yellow .. 3·25 3·00
37. 80 r. mauve 55 50
38. 100 r. blue on blue .. 90 80
50. 115 r. brown on pink .. 60 55
51. 130 r. brown on yellow .. 60 55
39. 150 r. brown on yellow .. 60 55
52. 180 r. black on pink .. 60 55
40. 200 r. purple on pink .. 1·40 1·25
41. 300 r. blue on pink .. 1·50 1·25
42. 500 r. black on blue .. 3·00 2·75

POONCH BC

A state in Kashmir, India. Now uses Indian stamps.

1.

2.

1876. Imperf.
1. 1. 6 pies red .. .. .. — 35·00
2. ½ a. red .. .. .. — £250

1880. Imperf.
32. 1. 1 pice red 15 15
12. 2. ½ a. red 25 30
50. 1 a. red 15 25
52. 2 a. red (22 × 22 mm.) .. 15 30
31. 4 a. red (28 × 27 mm.) .. 75 60

These stamps were printed on various coloured papers.

OFFICIAL STAMPS

1888. Imperf.
O 1. 1. 1 pice black 10 15
O 2. 2. ½ a. black 15 25
O 3. 1 a. black 20
O 4. 2 a. black 25 30
O 5. 4 a. black 50 50

PORT LAGOS E3

French P.O. formerly in Turkey, now closed.

1893. Stamps of France optd. **Port-Lagos** and the three higher values surch. also in figures and words.
75. 10. 5 c. green .. .. 2·75 2·25
76. 10 c. black and lilac .. 4·50 3·25
77. 15 c. blue .. .. 9·00 8·00
78. 1 p. on 25 c. black on red 8·50 7·00
79. 2 p. on 50 c. red .. 14·00 11·00
80. 4 p. on 1 f. olive .. 11·00 10·00

PORT SAID O2

Stamps issued at the French P.O. in this Egyptian seaport.

1902. 100 centimes = 1 franc.
1921. 1,000 milliemes = 1 Egyptian pound.

1899. Stamps of France optd. **PORT-SAID.**
101. 10. 1 c. black on blue .. 10 10
102. 2 c. brown on yellow .. 20 15
103. 3 c. grey 20 12
104. 4 c. lilac on grey .. 20 12
105. 5 c. green .. .. 1·00 50
107. 10 c. black on lilac .. 1·60 1·25
109. 15 c. blue .. .. 1·00 60
110. 20 c. red on green .. 1·50 65
111. 25 c. black on red .. 1·10 25
112. 30 c. brown .. .. 1·25 80
113. 40 c. red on yellow .. 1·25 85
115. 50 c. red .. .. 2·10 1·75
116. 1 f. olive .. .. 2·75 1·10
117. 2 f. brown on blue .. 9·00 7·00
118. 5 f. mauve on lilac .. 15·00 11·00

1899. No. 107 surch.
121. 10. 25 c. on 10 c. blk. on lilac 10·00 1·40

1902. "Blanc", "Mouchon" and "Merson" key-types inscr. "PORT-SAID".
122. A. 1 c. grey 5 5
123. 2 c. claret 5 5
124. 3 c. red 5 5
125. 4 c. brown 5 5
126a. 5 c. green 10 10
127. B. 10 c. red 15 8
128. 15 c. orange 20 15
129. 20 c. claret 15 12
130. 25 c. blue 20 15
131. 30 c. mauve 55 40
132. C. 40 c. red and blue .. 50 40
133. 50 c. brown and lavender 90 65
134. 1 f. red and green .. 1·10 75
135. 2 f. lilac and yellow .. 1·60 1·25
136. 5 f. blue and yellow .. 4·00 3·75

1915. Red Cross. Surch. **5 c.** and red cross.
C 137. B. 10 c. + 5 c. red .. 30 30

1921. Surch. with value in figs and words.
151a. A. 1 m. on 1 c. grey .. 10 10
152. 2 m. on 5 c. green .. 10 10
153. B. 4 m. on 10 c. red .. 25 25
166. A. 5 m. on 1 c. grey .. 1·10 1·10
167. 5 m. on 2 c. claret .. 1·90 1·90
154. 5 m. on 3 c. red .. 1·10 1·10
141. 5 m. on 4 c. brown .. 1·00 1·00
155. B. 6 m. on 15 c. orange .. 40 40
156. 6 m. on 15 c. red .. 2·00 2·00
157. 8 m. on 20 c. claret .. 20 20
168. A. 10 m. on 2 c. claret .. 1·40 1·40
142. 10 m. on 4 c. brown .. 3·25 3·25
158. B. 10 m. on 25 c. blue .. 45 45
159. 10 m. on 30 c. mauve .. 65 65
144. 12 m. on 30 c. mauve .. 5·50 5·50
145. A. 15 m. on 4 c. brown .. 1·00 1·00
169. B. 15 m. on 15 c. orange .. 6·50 6·50
170. 15 m. on 20 c. claret .. 6·00 6·00
146. C. 15 m. on 40 c. red & blue 7·00 7·00
160. 15 m. on 50 c. brn. & lav. 65 65
161. B. 15 m. on 50 c. blue .. 65 65
171. C. 30 m. on 50 c. brn. & lav. 55·00 55·00
162. 30 m. on 1 f. red & green 65 65
172. 60 m. on 50 c. brn. & lav. 60·00 60·00
149. 60 m. on 2 f. lilac & yellow 11·00 11·00
164. 60 m. on 2 f. red & green 1·25 1·25
173. 150 m. on 50 c. brn. & lav. 70·00 70·00
165. 150 m. on 5 f. blue & yell. 1·00 1·00

1925. Surch. with value in figures and words and bars over old value.
174. A. 1 m. on 1 c. grey .. 5 5
175. 2 m. on 5 c. green .. 8 8
176. B. 4 m. on 10 c. red .. 10 10
177. A. 5 m. on 3 c. red .. 12 12
178. B. 6 m. on 15 c. orange .. 12 12
179. 8 m. on 20 c. claret .. 10 10
180. 10 m. on 25 c. blue .. 10 10
181. 15 m. on 50 c. blue .. 10 10
182. C. 30 m. on 1 f. red & green 15 15
183. 60 m. on 2 f. red and green 15 15
184. 150 m. on 5 f. blue & yell. 25 25

1927. "French Sinking Fund" issue. Surch. **+5 Mm Caisse d'Amortissement.**
191. B. 15 m. + 5 m. orange .. 30 30
192. 15 m. + 5 m. lilac .. 30 30
193. 15 m. + 5 m. brown .. 30 30

1927. Altered key-types. Inscr. "Mm" below value.
185. A. 3 m. orange 15 15
186. B. 15 m. blue 20 20
187. 20 m. mauve 25 25
188. C. 50 m. red and green .. 30 30
189. 100 m. blue and yellow 50 50
190. 250 m. green and red .. 1·10 1·10

POSTAGE DUE STAMPS

1921. Postage Due stamps of France surch. in figures and words.
D 174. D 2. 2 m. on 5 c. blue .. 7·50 7·50
D 175. 4 m. on 10 c. brown 7·50 7·50
D 176. 10 m. on 30 c. red .. 7·50 7·50
D 166. 12 m. on 10 c. brown 6·50 6·50
D 167. 15 m. on 5 c. blue .. 8·00 8·00
D 177. 15 m. on 50 c. purple 10·00 10·00
D 168. 30 m. on 20 c. olive 9·50 9·50
D 169. 30 m. on 50 c. purple £600 £600

For 1928 issue, see Alexandria.

PORTUGAL E2

A country on the S.W. coast of Europe, kingdom till 1910, when it became a republic.

1853. 1000 reis = 1 milreis.
1912. 100 centavos = 1 escudo.

1. Queen Maria.

2. King Pedro V.

3. King Luiz.

1853. Various frames. Imperf.
1. 1. 5 r. brown £450 £130
4. 25 r. blue .. .. .. £200 4·00
6. 50 r. green £700 £170
8. 100 r. lilac £2000 £400

1855. Various frames Imperf.
18. 2. 5 r. brown .. .. .. £130 8·00
11. 25 r. blue .. .. .. £180 5·00
22. 25 r. red .. .. .. 70·00 60
13. 50 r. green .. .. .. £130 18·00
15. 100 r. lilac .. .. .. £160 20·00

1862. Various frames. Imperf.
24. 3. 5 r. brown .. .. .. 20·00 2·00
28. 10 r. yellow .. .. .. 30·00 6·00
30. 25 r. red .. .. .. 20·00 60
32. 50 r. green .. .. .. £120 20·00
34. 100 r. lilac .. .. .. £160 20·00

4. King Luiz.

5.

1866. With curved value labels. Imperf
35. 4. 5 r. black .. .. .. 24·00 3·25
36. 10 r. yellow .. .. .. 55·00 15·00
38. 20 r. olive .. .. .. 45·00 14·00
39. 25 r. red .. .. .. 50·00 80
41. 50 r. green .. .. .. 60·00 15·00
43. 80 r. orange .. .. .. 70·00 16·00
45. 100 r. purple .. .. .. 75·00 18·00
46. 120 r. blue .. .. .. 75·00 15·00

1867. With curved value labels. Perf.
52. 4. 5 r. black .. .. .. 26·00 6·00
54. 10 r. yellow .. .. .. 70·00 14·00
56. 20 r. olive .. .. .. 95·00 24·00
57. 25 r. red .. .. .. 12·00 60
60. 50 r. green .. .. .. 75·00 14·00
61. 80 r. orange .. .. .. £100 27·00
62. 100 r. lilac .. .. .. 90·00 14·00
64. 120 r. blue .. .. .. 70·00 13·00
67. 240 r. mauve .. .. .. £300 90·00

1870. With straight value labels. Perf.
102. 5. 5 r. black .. .. .. 9·00 1·25
70. 10 r. yellow .. .. .. 12·00 3·50
134. 10 r. green .. .. .. 15·00 2·00
136. 15 r. brown .. .. .. 14·00 2·00
76. 20 r. olive .. .. .. 12·00 1·60
143a. 20 r. red .. .. .. 50·00 7·00
113. 25 r. red .. .. .. 4·00 40
83. 50 r. green .. .. .. 20·00 1·75
86. 50 r. blue .. .. .. 50·00 8·00
148. 80 r. orange .. .. .. 24·00 1·60
153. 100 r. mauve .. .. .. 12·00 1·40
93. 120 r. blue .. .. .. 55·00 15·00
150. 150 r. blue .. .. .. 60·00 20·00
155. 150 r. yellow .. .. .. 32·00 3·50
99. 240 r. mauve £550 £300
175. 300 r. mauve .. .. .. 30·00 7·50
128. 1000 r. black .. .. .. 50·00 13·00

6. King Luiz.

7.

1880. Various frames for T 6.
178. 6. 5 r. black .. .. .. 4·50 80
181. 25 r. grey .. .. .. 4·00 30
183. 25 r. brown .. .. .. 4·00 30
180. 7. 25 r. grey .. .. .. 16·00 2·00
184. 6. 50 r. blue .. .. .. 70·00 4·00

8. King Luiz.

9. King Carlos.

1882. Various frames.
229. 8. 5 r. black .. .. .. 1·50 25
230. 10 r. green .. .. .. 4·00 60
232. 20 r. red .. .. .. 8·00 2·00
222. 25 r. brown .. .. .. 4·00 30
234. 25 r. mauve .. .. .. 4·00 20
236. 50 r. blue .. .. .. 7·00 40
216. 500 r. black .. .. .. £120 60·00
217. 500 r. mauve .. .. .. 50·00 10·00

1892.
270. 9. 5 r. orange 90 20
239. 10 r. mauve .. .. .. 3·50 80
241. 15 r. brown .. .. .. 3·00 1·00
242. 20 r. lilac .. .. .. 4·00 1·00
275. 25 r. green .. .. .. 4·00 20
277. 50 r. blue .. .. .. 7·00 80
245. 75 r. red .. .. .. 24·00 1·60
247. 80 r. green .. .. .. 14·00 6·00
248. 100 r. brown on yellow .. 15·00 1·40
265. 150 r. red on rose .. 32·00 8·00
252. 200 r. blue on blue .. 32·00 8·00
267. 300 r. blue on brown .. 30·00 8·00

1892. Optd. **PROVISORIO.**
284. 8. 5 r. black .. .. .. 2·00 60
285. 10 r. green .. .. .. 2·40 1·00
286. 5. 15 r. brown .. .. .. 2·50 1·60
290. 8. 20 r. red .. .. .. 5·00 2·40
291. 25 r. mauve .. .. .. 2·75 1·00
292. 50 r. blue .. .. .. 13·00 9·00
293. 5. 80 r. orange .. .. .. 20·00 15·00

1893. Optd. **1893. PROVISORIO** or surch. also.
302. 8. 5 r. black .. .. .. 3·50 2·00
303. 10 r. green .. .. .. 4·00 2·00
304. 20 r. red .. .. .. 10·00 8·00
309. 20 r. on 25 r. mauve .. 8·50 5·00
305. 25 r. mauve .. .. .. 16·00 14·00
306. 50 r. blue .. .. .. 22·00 16·00
310. 5. 50 r. on 80 r. orange .. 30·00 20·00
312. 75 r. on 80 r. orange .. 18·00 12·00
308. 80 r. orange .. .. .. 20·00 16·00

10. Prince Henry's Ship.

DESIGNS: 25 r. to 100 r. Prince Henry's fleet. 150 r. to 1000 r. Prince Henry's studies.

1894. Prince Henry the Navigator. 500th Birth Anniv.
314. 10. 5 r. orange .. .. .. 1·00 40
315. 10 r. red .. .. .. 1·40 60
316. 15 r. brown .. .. .. 2·00 80
317. 20 r. violet .. .. .. 2·25 80
318. – 25 r. green .. .. .. 1·40 40
319. – 50 r. blue .. .. .. 4·00 1·25
320. – 75 r. red .. .. .. 6·00 3·00
321. – 80 r. green .. .. .. 10·00 3·00
322. – 100 r. brown on buff .. 6·00 1·75
323. – 150 r. red .. .. .. 16·00 6·00
324. – 300 r. blue on buff .. 16·00 7·00
325. – 500 r. purple .. .. .. 42·00 15·00
326. – 1000 r. black .. .. .. 50·00 16·00

13. St. Anthony's Vision.

15. St. Anthony ascending into Heaven.

1895. St. Anthony (Patron Saint). 700th Birth Anniv.
327. 13. 2½ r. black .. .. .. 1·00 50
328. – 5 r. orange .. .. .. 1·25 80
329. – 10 r. mauve .. .. .. 3·00 1·75
330. – 15 r. brown .. .. .. 3·50 2·50
331. – 20 r. grey .. .. .. 3·50 2·50
332. – 25 r. purple and green .. 1·60 90
333. 15. 50 r. brown and blue .. 10·00 6·00
334. – 75 r. brown and red .. 13·00 10·00
335. – 80 r. brown and green .. 16·00 13·00
336. – 100 r. black and brown 14·00 10·00
337. – 150 r. red and brown .. 30·00 16·00
338. – 200 r. blue and brown .. 35·00 32·00
339. – 300 r. black and brown 55·00 35·00
340. – 500 r. brown and green 85·00 70·00
341. – 1,000 r. lilac and green £170 95·00

DESIGNS — HORIZ. 5 r. to 25 r. St. Anthony preaching to fishes. VERT. 150 r. to 1,000 r. St. Anthony from picture in Academy of Fine Arts, Paris.

ILLUSTRATIONS British Commonwealth and all overprints and surcharges are FULL SIZE. Foreign Countries have been reduced to ¾-LINEAR.

17. King Carlos.

1895.

342. **17.** 2½ r. grey 8 5
343. 5 r. orange 5 5
347. 10 r. green 5 5
349. 15 r. green .. .. 4·00 50
350. 15 r. brown .. .. 10·00 1·00
351. 20 r. violet 10 5
352. 25 r. green .. .. 9·00 5
354. 25 r. red 5 5
357. 50 r. blue 10 5
359. 65 r. blue 15 8
360. 75 r. red .. .. 17·00 40
362. 75 r. brown on yellow .. 25 15
363. 80 r. mauve 40 35
365. 100 r. blue on blue .. 20 10
366. 115 r. brown on pink .. 30 25
367. 130 r. brown 40 30
368. 150 r. brown on yellow 18·00 5·00
369. 180 r. grey on pink .. 90 60
370. 200 r. purple on pink .. 60 15
372. 300 r. blue on pink .. 90 30
373. 500 r. black on blue .. 1·25 70

18. Departure of Fleet.

DESIGNS—HORIZ. 5 r. Arrival at Calicut. 10 r. Embarkation at Rastello. 100 r. Flagship "San Gabriel". 150 r. Vasco da Gama. VERT. 75 r. Archangel Gabriel.

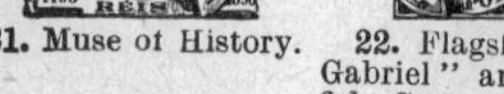

21. Muse of History. **22.** Flagship "San Gabriel" and portraits of da Gama and Camoens.

1898. Vasco da Gama. 4th cent. of Discovery of Route to India.

378. **18.** 2½ r. green 50 30
379. – 5 r. red 50 30
380. – 10 r. purple .. .. 2·50 80
381. **21.** 25 r. green .. .. 2·25 30
382. **22.** 50 r. blue .. .. 3·50 90
383. – 75 r. brown .. .. 8·50 3·50
384. – 100 r. brown .. .. 8·50 3·00
385. – 150 r. brown .. .. 12·00 6·00

26. King Manoel. **27.**

1910.

390. **26.** 2½ r. violet 10 8
391. 5 r. black 10 8
392. 10 r. green 15 12
393. 15 r. brown 60 40
394. 20 r. red 30 20
395. 25 r. brown 15 8
396. 50 r. blue 50 35
397. 75 r. brown .. .. 2·00 1·75
398. 80 r. grey .. .. 1·00 70
399. 100 r. brown on green 3·25 1·75
400. 200 r. green on pink .. 90 70
401. 300 r. black on blue .. 1·25 1·00
402. **27.** 500 r. brown and olive .. 2·50 1·75
403. 1,000 r. black and blue 7·50 6·00

1910. Optd. **REPUBLICA.**

404. **26.** 2½ r. violet 15 10
405. 5 r. black 15 10
406. 10 r. green .. .. 1·00 30
407. 15 r. brown 20 15
408. 20 r. red .. .. 1·40 80
409. 25 r. brown 40 5
410. 50 r. blue .. .. 1·75 80
411. 75 r. brown .. .. 2·75 1·50
412. 80 r. grey 70 50
413. 100 r. brown on green .. 80 50
414. 200 r. green on pink .. 80 40
415. 300 r. black on blue .. 1·00 80
416. **27.** 500 r. brown and olive .. 2·75 1·75
417. 1,000 r. black and blue 5·00 3·75

1911. Optd. **REPUBLICA** or surch. also.

441. **18.** 2½ r. green 20 12
442a. D **1.** 5 r. black 20 15
443a. 10 r. mauve 30 25
444. – 15 r. on 5 r. red (379) 20 15
445a. D **1.** 20 r. orange .. .. 1·50 90
446. **21.** 25 r. green 20 15
447. **22.** 50 r. blue .. .. 1·00 50
448. – 75 r. brown (No. 383) 9·50 7·50
449. – 80 r. on 150 r. (385) .. 1·75 1·40
450. – 100 r. brown (No. 384) 1·25 60
451. D **1.** 200 r. brown on buff 10·00 8·00
452. 300 r. on 50 r. grey .. 8·00 7·00
453. 500 r. on 100 r. red .. 3·50 2·50
454. – 1,000 r. on 10 r. (380) 7·50 6·00

1911. Vasco da Gama stamps of Madeira optd. **REPUBLICA** or surch. also.

455. 2½ r. green 70 50
456. 15 r. on 5 r. red 70 50
457. 25 r. green .. .. 1·25 60
458. 50 r. blue .. .. 2·50 1·60
459. 75 r. brown .. .. 2·50 1·60
460. 80 r on 150 r. brown .. 2·75 1·60
461. 100 r. brown .. .. 6·50 3·00
462. 1,000 r. on 10 r. purple .. 5·50 4·00

28. Ceres. **29.**

1912.

513. **28.** ¼ c. olive 5 5
485. ½ c. black 5 5
486. 1 c. green 40 5
515. 1 c. brown 5 5
488. 1½ c. brown .. .. 1·75 40
489. 1½ c. green 5 5
490. 2 c. red .. .. 1·75 20
517. 2 c. yellow 5 5
702. 2 c. chocolate 5 5
492. 2½ c. lilac 5 5
521. 3 c. red 5 5
703. 3 c. blue 5 5
495. 3½ c. green 5 5
496. 4 c. green 5 5
704. 4 c. orange 5 5
497. 5 c. blue .. .. 1·40 8
705. 5 c. brown 5 5
527. 6 c. claret 5 5
815. 6 c. brown 5 5
500. 7½ c. brown .. .. 1·40 15
501. 7½ c. blue 5 5
530. 8 c. grey 5 5
531. 8 c. green 10 5
532. 8 c. orange 10 5
503. 10 c. brown 5 5
533. 10 c. red 5 5
504. 12 c. grey 30 20
534. 12 c. green 12 10
535. 13½ c. blue 15 12
481. 14 c. blue on yellow .. 30 30
536. 14 c. purple 10 8
505. 15 c. maroon 60 20
537. 15 c. black 5 5
709. 16 c. blue 5 5
474a. 20 c. brown on green .. 3·50 40
475. 20 c. brown on buff .. 3·00 50
539. 20 c. chocolate 20 5
540. 20 c. green 12 10
541. 20 c. drab 8 5
542. 24 c. turquoise 12 8
543. 25 c. pink 5 5
710. 25 c. grey 5 5
819. 25 c. green 12 10
476. 30 c. brown on rose .. 30·00 3·50
477. 30 c. brown on yellow .. 1·25 20
545. 30 c. brown 12 8
711. 32 c. green 10 8
548. 36 c. red 15 5
549. 40 c. blue 15 12
550. 40 c. sepia 15 10
712. 40 c. green 8 5
713. 48 c. pink 20 15
478. 50 c. orange on salmon 2·75 50
553. 50 c. yellow 10 5
824. 50 c. brown 40 25
554. 60 c. blue 25 12
715. 64 c. blue 20 15
556. 75 c. pink 70 50
826. 75 c. red 40 25
510 80 c. pink 20 12
558. 80 c. violet 25 8
827. 80 c. green 50 15
559. 90 c. blue 30 15
717. 96 c. red 60 40
480. 1 e. green on blue .. 3·00 60
561. 1 e. lilac 30 12
565. 1 e. blue 80 50
566. 1 e. slate-purple .. 60 30
562. 1 e. 10 brown 40 30
563. 1 e. 20 green 30 25
719. 1 e. 20 ochre .. .. 1·75 10
830. 1 e. 20 chocolate .. 40 20
831. 1 e. 25 blue 40 30
569. 1 e. 50 lilac .. .. 1·75 50
720. 1 e. 60 blue 70 10
721. 2 e. green .. .. 3·00 10
833. 2 e. purple .. .. 3·50 1·75
572. 2 e. 40 green .. 24·00 18·00
573. 3 e. pink .. .. 16·00 11·00
722. 3 e. 20 bronze .. .. 1·10 30
723. 4 e. 50 yellow .. .. 1·10 30
575. 5 e. turquoise-green .. 4·50 1·60
724. 5 e. brown .. .. 15·00 30
576. 10 e. rose .. .. 14·00 2·75
725. 10 e. red .. .. 1·75 30
577. 20 e. blue .. .. 48·00 27·00

1923. Trans-Atlantic Flight.

578. **29.** 1 c. brown 5 5
579. 2 c. orange 5 5
580. 3 c. blue 5 5
581. 4 c. green 5 5
582. 5 c. brown 5 5
583. 10 c. brown 5 5
584. 15 c. black 5 5
585. 20 c. green 5 5
586. 25 c. red 5 5
587. 30 c. brown 30 30
588. 40 c. brown 5 5
589. 50 c. yellow 5 5
590. 75 c. purple 8 8
591. 1 e. blue 12 12
592. 1 e. 50 olive-grey .. 20 20
593. 2 e. green 25 25

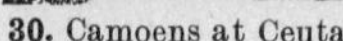

30. Camoens at Ceuta. **31.** Saving the "Lusiad".

1924. Camoens (poet). 4th Birth Cent. Dated "1524–1924".

600. **30.** 2 c. blue 8 8
601. 3 c. orange 8 8
602. 4 c. grey 8 8
603. 5 c. green 8 8
604. 6 c. red 8 8
605. **31.** 8 c. brown 10 8
606. 10 c. violet 10 8
607. 15 c. olive 12 10
608. 16 c. purple 12 10
609. 20 c. orange 12 10
610. – 25 c. mauve 12 10
611. – 30 c. brown 12 10
612. – 32 c. green 20 20
613. – 40 c. blue 12 10
614. – 48 c. purple 30 25
615. – 50 c. red 30 25
616. – 64 c. green 30 30
617. – 75 c. violet 30 30
618. – 80 c. brown 30 30
619. – 96 c. red 30 30
620. – 1 e. blue 40 30
621. – 1 e. 20 brown 40 35
622. – 1 e. 50 red 40 35
623. – 1 e. 60 blue 50 35
624. – 2 e. green 50 35
625. – 2 e. 40 green on green 90 75
626. – 3 e. blue on blue .. 90 75
627. – 3 e. 20 black on green 90 75
628. – 4 e. 50 black on yellow 1·25 1·10
629. – 10 e. brown on rose .. 1·75 1·60
630. – 20 e. violet on mauve .. 2·75 2·50

DESIGNS—VERT. 25 c. to 48 c. Camoens. 50 c. to 96 c. 1st Edition of "Lusiad". 20 e. Monument to Camoens. HORIZ. 1 e. to 2 e. Death of Camoens. 2 e. 40 to 10 e. Tomb of Camoens.

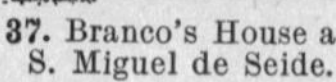

37. Branco's House at S. Miguel de Seide. **39.** Camilo Castelo Branco.

1925. Branco (novelist). Birth Cent. Dated "1825–1925".

631. **37.** 2 c. orange 10 8
632. 3 c. green 10 8
633. 4 c. blue 10 8
634. 5 c. red 10 8
635. 6 c. purple 10 8
636. 8 c. brown 10 8
637. A. 10 c. blue 10 8
638. **39.** 15 c. olive 15 10
639. A. 16 c. orange 15 10
640. 20 c. violet 15 10
641. **39.** 25 c. red 15 10
642. A. 30 c. brown 15 10
643. 32 c. green 20 15
644. **39.** 40 c. black and green .. 12 10
645 A. 48 c. maroon 40 35
646. B. 50 c. green 40 25
647. 64 c. brown 75 60
648. 75 c. grey 40 30
649. **39.** 80 c. brown 40 30
650. B. 96 c. red 80 70
651. 1 e. violet 50 40
652. 1 e. 20 green 75 60
653. C. 1 e. 50 blue on blue 5·50 4·50
654. **39.** 1 e. 60 blue .. .. 1·40 80
655. C. 2 e. green on green .. 1·25 70
656. 2 e. 40 red on orange .. 9·00 7·50
657. 3 e. red on blue .. 9·00 7·50
658. 3 e. 20 black on green .. 9·00 7·50
659. **39.** 4 e. 50 black and red .. 4·75 1·75
660. C. 10 e. brown on buff .. 5·50 1·75
661. D. 20 e. black on orange .. 7·00 80

DESIGNS—HORIZ. A, Branco's study. VERT. B. Teresa de Albuquerque. C, Mariana and Joao da Cruz. D, Simao de Botelho.

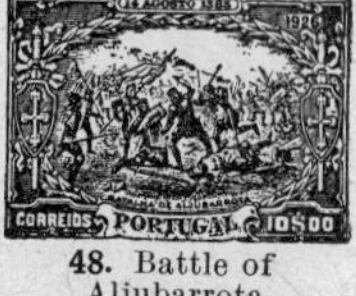

47. Afonso I, first King of Portugal 1140. **48.** Battle of Aljubarrota.

50. Battle of Montijo. **49.** Goncalo Mendes de Maia.

1926. 1st Independence issue. Dated 1926. Centres in black.

671. **47.** 2 c. orange 10 8
672. – 3 c. blue 10 8
673. **47.** 4 c. green 10 8
674. – 5 c. brown 10 8
675. **47.** 6 c. orange 10 8
676. – 15 c. green 15 10
677. **47.** 16 c. blue 40 30
678. **48.** 20 c. violet 40 30
679. – 25 c. red 30 20
680. **48.** 32 c. green 40 30
681. – 40 c. brown 15 12
682. – 46 c. red 90 60
683. – 50 c. olive .. .. 1·10 60
684. – 64 c. green .. .. 1·00 80
685. – 75 c. red .. .. 1·10 80
686. – 96 c. red .. .. 1·90 1·60
687. – 1 e. violet .. .. 2·50 2·00
688. **48.** 1 e. 60 blue .. .. 3·00 2·40
689. – 3 e. purple .. .. 7·00 6·00
690. – 4 e. 50 green .. .. 6·00 5·50
691. **43.** 10 e. red .. .. 12·00 11·00

DESIGNS—VERT. 25 c., 40 c., 50 c., 75 c. Philippa de Vilhena arms her sons, 64 c., 1 e. Don John IV, 1640. 96 c., 3 e., 4 e. 50, Independence Monument, Lisbon. HORIZ. 3 c. 5 c., 15 c., 46 c. Monastery of Don John I.

1926. 1st Independence issue surch. Centres in black.

692. 2 c. on 5 c. brown .. 50 50
693. 2 c. on 46 c. red 50 50
694. 2 c. on 64 c. green 50 50
695. 3 c. on 75 c. red 50 50
696. 3 c. on 96 c. red 50 50
697. 3 c. on 1 e. violet 50 50
698. 4 c. on 1 e. 60 blue .. .. 1·25 1·25
699. 4 c. on 3 e. purple .. .. 1·25 1·25
700. 6 c. on 4 e. 50 green .. 1·25 1·25
701. 6 c. on 10 e. red .. .. 1·25 1·25

1927. 2nd Independence issue. Dated 1927. Centres in black.

726. **49.** 2 c. brown 10 10
727. – 3 c. blue 10 10
728. **49.** 4 c. orange 10 10
729. – 5 c. brown 10 10
730. **50.** 6 c. brown 12 10
731. – 15 c. brown 15 15
732. – 16 c. blue 30 25
733. **49.** 25 c. grey 30 25
734. **50.** 32 c. green 70 65
735 – 40 c. green 20 15
736. **49.** 48 c. red .. .. 1·90 1·50
737. – 80 c. violet .. .. 1·60 1·40
738. – 96 c. red .. .. 2·75 2·40
739. – 1 e. 60 blue .. .. 2·75 2·25
740. – 4 e. 50 yellow .. .. 5·00 4·50

DESIGNS—HORIZ. 3 c., 15 c., 80 c. Guimaraens Castle. VERT. 5 c., 16 c., 1 e. 60, Joao das Regras. 40 c., 96 c. Brites de Almeida. 4 e. 50, J. P. Ribeiro.

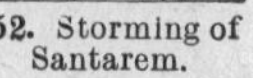

52. Storming of Santarem. **53.** Battle of Atoleiros.

1928. 3rd Independence issue. Dated 1928. Centres in black.

742. – 2 c. blue 10 10
743. – 3 c. green 10 10
744. – 4 c. red 10 10
745. – 5 c. olive 10 10
746. – 6 c. brown 10 10

747. 52. 15 c. grey 30 25
748. – 16 c. purple 30 25
749. – 25 c. blue 40 30
750. – 32 c. green 70 60
751. 53. 40 c. brown 25 20
752. – 50 c. red .. .. 1·60 1·25
753. 52. 80 c. grey .. .. 2·00 1·75
754. – 96 c. red .. .. 2·50 2·00
755. 53. 1 e. mauve .. .. 6·50 6·50
756. – 1 e. 60 blue .. .. 2·00 2·25
757. – 4 e. 50 yellow .. .. 2·25 1·90

DESIGNS—VERT. 2 c., 25 c., 1 e. 60, G. Paes. 6 c., 32 c., 96 c. Joana de Gouveia. 4 e. 50, M. de Albuquerque. HORIZ. 4 c., 16 c., 50 c. Battle of Rolica.

1928. Surch.

758. 28. 4 c. on 8 c. orange .. 10 5
759. 4 c. on 30 c. brown .. 8 5
761. 10 c. on ¼ c. olive .. 12 10
762. 10 c. on ½ c. black .. 12 10
764. 10 c. on 1 c. brown .. 12 8
765. 10 c. on 4 c. green .. 15 10
766. 10 c. on 4 c. orange .. 12 10
767. 10 c. on 5 c. olive .. 12 10
769. 15 c. on 16 c. blue .. 15 15
770. 15 c. on 20 c. chocolate 8·50 8·00
771. 15 c. on 20 c. drab .. 15 10
772. 15 c. on 24 c. turquoise 15 12
773. 15 c. on 25 c. pink .. 12 10
774. 15 c. on 25 c. drab .. 15 10
775. 16 c. on 32 c. green .. 15 15
777. 40 c. on 2 c. yellow .. 12 10
779. 40 c. on 2 c. chocolate 15 10
780. 40 c. on 3 c. blue .. 15 8
783. 40 c. on 50 c. yellow .. 15 10
784. 40 c. on 60 c. blue .. 25 20
785. 40 c. on 64 c. blue .. 40 30
786. 40 c. on 75 c. pink .. 40 30
787. 40 c. on 80 c. violet .. 20 12
788. 40 c. on 90 c. blue .. 40 30
789. 40 c. on 1 e. slate-purple 25 12
790. 40 c. on 1 e. 10 brown .. 20 12
793. 80 c. on 6 c. claret .. 20 12
794. 80 c. on 6 c. brown .. 25 15
796. 80 c. on 48 c. pink .. 40 30
797. 80 c. on 1 e. 50 lilac .. 40 25
798. 96 c. on 1 e. 20 green .. 1·10 1·00
799. 96 c. on 1 e. 20 ochre .. 1·25 90
800. 1 $ 60 on 2 e. green .. 1·10 1·00
802. 1 $ 60 on 3 e. 20 bronze 2·00 1·75
804. 1 $ 60 on 20 e. blue .. 2·50 2·00

1929. Optd. **Revalidado.**

805. 28. 10 c. red 12 10
806. 15 c. black 15 12
807. 40 c. sepia 15 12
808. 40 c. green 15 12
810. 96 c. red .. .. 1·00 90
811. 1 e. 60 blue .. .. 2·00 1·75

1929. Telegraph stamp surch. **CORREIO 1 $ 60** and bars.

812. – 1 $ 60 on 5 c. brown .. 1·50 1·25

54. Camoen's poem " Lusiad ".

1931.

835. 54. 4 c. brown 5 5
836. 5 c. deep brown 5 5
837. 6 c. grey 5 5
838. 10 c. purple 5 5
839. 15 c. black 5 5
840. 16 c. blue 25 8
841. 25 c. green 80 25
841a. 25 c. blue .. .. 1·00 5
841b. 30 c. green 50 5
842. 40 c. red .. .. 1·60 5
843. 48 c. brown 10 5
844. 50 c. brown 5 5
845. 75 c. red 70 30
846. 80 c. green 5 5
846a. 95 c. red .. .. 3·00 1·10
847. 1 e. claret .. .. 5·00 5
848. 1 e. 20 olive 12 5
849. 1 e. 25 blue 5 5
849a 1 e. 60 blue .. .. 5·00 50
849b 1 e. 75 blue 5 5
850. 2 e. violet 8 5
851. 4 e. 50 orange 20 5
852. 5 e. green 20 5

55. St. Anthony's Birthplace.

56. Lisbon Cathedral. 57. Don Nuno Alvares Pereira. 58. President Carmona.

1931. St. Anthony. 7th Death Cent.

853. 55. 15 c. purple 30 20
854. – 25 c. green 30 20
855. 56. 40 c. brown 30 20
856. – 75 c. red .. .. 3·00 2·50
857. – 1 e. 25 grey .. .. 7·50 4·00
858. – 4 e. 50 purple .. .. 4·50 1·25

DESIGNS—VERT. 25 c. Saint's baptismal font. 75 c. St. Anthony. 1 e. 25 Santa Cruz Cathedral, Coimbra. HORIZ. 4 e. 50, Saint's tomb, Padua.

1931. Pereira. 5th Death Cent.

859. 57. 15 c. black 50 30
860. 25 c. green and black .. 50 30
861. 40 c. orange 50 20
862. 75 c. red .. .. 4·50 3·75
863. 1 e. 25 blue .. .. 6·00 4·00
864. 4 e. 50 green and brown 30·00 10·00

1933. Pereira issue of 1931 surch.

865. 57. 15 c. on 40 c. orange .. 30 25
866. 40 c. on 15 c. black .. 1·25 1·00
867. 40 c. on 25 c. grn. & blk. 40 25
868. 40 c. on 75 c. red .. 2·00 1·60
869. 40 c. on 1 e. 25 blue .. 2·00 1·60
870. 40 c. on 4 e. 50 green and brown .. .. 2·00 1·50

1933. St. Anthony issue of 1931 surch.

871. 56. 15 c. on 40 c. brown .. 50 20
872. 55. 40 c. on 15 c. purple .. 80 20
873. – 40 c. on 25 c. green .. 80 30
874. – 40 c. on 75 c. red .. 1·75 1·60
875. – 40 c. on 1 e. 25 grey .. 1·75 1·60
876. – 40 c. on 4 e. 50 purple .. 1·75 1·50

1934.

877. 58. 40 c. violet .. .. 3·25 5

59. Woman. 60. Queen Maria.

1934. Colonial Exhibition.

878. 59. 25 c. olive .. .. 1·00 25
879. 40 c. red .. .. 3·75 15
880. 1 e. 60 blue .. .. 6·50 4·00

1935. 1st Portuguese Philatelic Exhibition.

881. 60. 40 c. red 40 5

61. Temple of Diana at Evora. 62. Prince Henry the Navigator.

63. " All for the Nation ". 64. Coimbra Cathedral.

1935.

882. 61. 4 c. black 5 5
883. 5 c. blue 5 5
884. 6 c. brown 5 5
885. 62. 10 c. green 20 5
886. 15 c. brown 5 5
887. 63. 25 c. blue 50 5
888. 40 c. brown 5 5
889. 1 e. red 5 5
890. 64. 1 e. 75 blue .. .. 17·00 40
890a. 63. 10 e. slate 40 20
890b. 20 e. green 80 25

65. Shield and Propeller. 66. Symbol of Medicine.

1937. Air.

891. 65. 1 e. 50 blue 35 15
892. 1 e. 75 red 65 15
893. 2 e. 50 red 60 15
893a. 3 e. blue .. .. 2·50 1·90
893b. 4 e. green .. .. 3·00 2·50
894. 5 e. claret 80 20
895. 10 e. maroon .. .. 1·60 20
895a. 15 e. orange .. .. 4·50 2·25
896. 20 e. purple .. .. 3·50 70
896a. 50 e. red .. .. 50·00 15·00

1937. Medical and Surgical Colleges at Lisbon and Oporto. Cent.

897. 66. 25 c. blue .. .. 2·00 30

67. Gil Vicente. 68. Grapes. 69. Cross of Aviz.

1937. Gil Vicente (poet). 4th Death Cent.

898. 67. 40 c. brown .. .. 4·00 5
899. 1 e. red 20 5

1938. Wine and Raisin Congress.

900. 63. 15 c. violet 60 20
901. 25 c. brown .. .. 1·00 50
902. 40 c. mauve .. .. 1·90 10
903. 1 e. 75 blue .. .. 6·50 4·75

1940. Portuguese Legion.

904. 69. 5 c. yellow 12 8
905. 10 c. violet 20 8
906. 15 c. blue 20 8
907. 25 c. brown .. .. 2·00 25
908. 40 c. green .. .. 4·50 5
909. 80 c. green 20 12
910. 1 e. red .. .. 7·00 35
911. 1 e. 75 blue .. .. 1·75 50

70. Portuguese World Exhibition. 71. Sir Rowland Hill.

1940. Independence Cent. and Restoration of Monarchy.

912. 70. 10 c. red 10 5
913. – 15 c. blue 10 5
914. – 25 c. olive 30 15
915. – 35 c. green 20 15
916. – 40 c. sepia 30 5
917. 70. 80 c. purple 20 15
918. – 1 e. red 70 20
919. – 1 e. 75 blue 60 35

DESIGNS—VERT. 15 c., 35 c. Statue of Don John IV. 25 c., 1 e. Monument of Discoveries, Belem. 40 c., 1 e. 75 Afonso Henriques.

1940. First Adhesive Postage Stamps Cent.

920. 71. 15 c. purple 25 8
921. 25 c. red 25 12
922. 35 c. green 20 15
923. 40 c. purple 20 5
924. 50 c. green .. .. 1·75 90
925. 80 c. blue 25 15
926. 1 e. red .. .. 1·10 60
927. 1 e. 75 blue .. .. 1·10 70

72. Fish-woman of Nazare. 73. Caravel.

1941. Costumes.

932. 72. 4 c. green 5 5
933. – 5 c. brown 10 5
934. – 10 c. purple 15 5
935. – 15 c. green 10 5
936. – 25 c. purple 15 8
937. – 40 c. green 5 5
938. – 80 c. blue 25 20
939. – 1 e. red 90 30
940. – 1 e. 75 blue 90 50
941. – 2 e. orange .. .. 3·50 2·75

DESIGNS: 5 c. Woman from Coimbra. 10 c. Vine-grower of Saloio. 15 c. Fish-woman of Lisbon. 25 c. Woman of Olhao. 40 c. Woman of Aveiro. 80 c. Shepherdess of Madeira. 1 e. Spinner of Viana do Castelo. 1 e. 75, Horse-breeder of Ribatejo. 2 e. Reaper of Alentejo.

1943.

942. 73. 5 c. black 5 5
943. 10 c. red 5 5
944. 15 c. grey 5 5
945. 20 c. violet 5 5
946 30 c. brown 5 5
947. 35 c. green 5 5
948. 50 c. purple 10 5
948a. 80 c. green 90 15
949 73. 1 e. red 80 5
949a. 1 e. lilac 50 5
949b. 1 e. 20 red .. .. 1·10 5
949c. 1 e. 50 olive .. .. 4·25 8
950. 1 e. 75 blue .. .. 2·75 12
950a. 1 e. 80 orange .. .. 4·75 50
951. 2 e. claret 25 5
951a. 2 e. blue .. .. 1·00 5
952. 2 e. 50 red 30 5
953. 3 e. 50 blue .. .. 2·50 12
953a. 4 e. orange .. .. 3·75 20
954. 5 e. salmon 20 5
954a. 6 e. emerald .. .. 5·50 40
954b. 7 e. 50 green .. .. 3·00 30
955. 10 e. grey 40 5
956. 15 e. green 60 12
957. 20 e. grey-olive .. .. 11·00 8
958. 50 e. orange .. .. 45·00 20

74. Labourer. 75. Mounted Postal Courier.

1943. Agricultural Science. 1st Congress.

959. 74. 10 c. blue 12 8
960. 50 c. red 12 8

1944. 3rd National Philatelic Exn., Lisbon.

961. 75. 10 c. plum 10 8
962. 50 c. violet 20 8
963. 1 e. red 40 15
964. 1 e. 75 blue 30 15

76. Felix Avellar Brotero. 77. Brotero's Statue, Coimbra.

1944. Brotero (botanist). Birth Cent.

965. 76. 10 c. brown 12 8
966. 77. 50 c. green 35 8
967. 1 e. red 60 30
968. 76. 1 e. 75 blue 45 40

78. Vasco da Gama. 79. President Carmona.

1945. Portuguese Navigators.

969. – 10 c. brown 5 5
970. – 30 c. orange 5 5
971. – 35 c. green 15 12
972. 78. 50 c. olive 15 8
973. – 1 e. red 80 15
974. – 1 e. 75 blue 60 45
975. – 2 e. black 70 40
976. – 3 e. 50 red .. .. 1·10 70

PORTRAITS: 10 c. Gil Eannes. 30 c. J. G. Zraco. 35 c. Bartolomeu Dias. 1 e. P. A. Cabral. 1 e. 75, F. de Magalhaes (Magellan) 2 e. Frey Goncalo Velho. 3 e. 50 Diogo Cao.

1945.

977. 79. 10 c. violet 5 5
978. 30 c. brown 5 5
979. 35 c. green 5 8
980. 50 c. olive 12 5
981. 1 e. red 55 15
982. 1 e. 75 blue .. .. 1·00 50
983. 2 e. maroon .. .. 3·50 70
984. 3 e. 50 slate .. .. 2·50 80

80. 81. Almourol Castle.

1945. Naval School Cent.

985. 80. 10 c. brown 5 5
986. 50 c. green 5 5
987. 1 e. red 40 20
988. 1 e. 75 c. blue 70 55

1946. Portuguese Castles.
989. – 10 c. purple 5 5
990. – 30 c. brown 10 5
991. – 35 c. olive 10 10
992. – 50 c. grey 10 5
993. **81.** 1 e. red 90 25
994. – 1 e. 75 c. blue .. 1·00 60
995. – 2 e. green .. 2·50 60
996. – 3 e. 50 c. brown .. 1·75 90
DESIGNS: Castles at Silves (10 c.), Leiria (30 c.), Feira (35 c.), Guimaraes (50 c.), Lisbon (1 e. 75 c.), Braganza (2 e.) and Ourem (3 e. 50 c.).

82. "Decree Founding National Bank". **83.** Madonna and Child.

1946. Bank of Portugal Cent.
997. **82.** 50 c. blue 5 5

1946. Proclamation of St. Mary of Castile as Patron Saint of Portugal. Tercent.
998. **83.** 30 c. grey 20 12
999. 50 c. green 20 8
1000. 1 e. red 80 30
1001. 1 e. 75 blue .. .. 1·10 60

84. Caramulo Shepherdess. **85.** Surrender of the Keys of Lisbon.

1947. Regional Costumes.
1002. **84.** 10 c. mauve 5 5
1003. – 30 c. red 5 5
1004. – 35 c. green 8 5
1005. – 50 c. brown 20 5
1006. – 1 e. red .. .. 1·40 15
1007. – 1 e. 75 blue .. .. 1·50 70
1008. – 2 e. blue .. .. 3·50 70
1009. – 3 e. 50 green .. 2·40 80
COSTUMES: 30 c. "Malpique" 35 c. "Monsanto". 50 c. "Avintes". 1 e. "Maia". 1 e. 75, "Algarve". 2 e. "Miranda do Douro". 3 e. 50, "Acores".

1947. Recapture of Lisbon from the Moors. 8th Cent.
1010. **85.** 5 c. green 5 12
1011. 20 c. red 12 10
1012. 50 c. violet 20 5
1013. 1 e. 75 blue .. .. 1·10 1·00
1014. 2 e. 50 brown .. .. 1·90 1·50
1015. 3 e. 50 black .. .. 2·50 2·00

86. St. Joao de Brito. **87.**

1948. St. Joao de Brito. 3rd Birth Cent.
1016. **86.** 30 c. green 10 5
1017. **87.** 50 c. brown 12 5
1018. **86.** 1 e. red .. .. 1·25 55
1019. **87.** 1 e. 75 blue .. .. 1·25 70

88. "Engineering" and "Architecture". **89.** King John I.

1948. Exhibition of Public Works, and National Congress of Engineering and Architecture.
1020. **88.** 50 c. claret 5 5

1949. Portraits.
1021. **89.** 10 c. violet 5 5
1022. – 30 c. green 8 8
1023. – 35 c. olive 10 10
1024. – 50 c. blue 40 12
1025. – 1 e. red 35 12
1026. – 1 e. 75 purple .. 2·50 1·50
1027. – 2 e. blue .. .. 1·40 40
1028. – 3 e. 50 chocolate .. 3·50 2·40
PORTRAITS: 30 c. Queen Philippa. 35 c. Prince Ferdinand. 50 c. Prince Henry the Navigator. 1 e. Nuno Alvares. 1 e. 75, Joao da Regras. 2 e. Fernao Lopes. 3 e. 50, Alphonso Domingues.

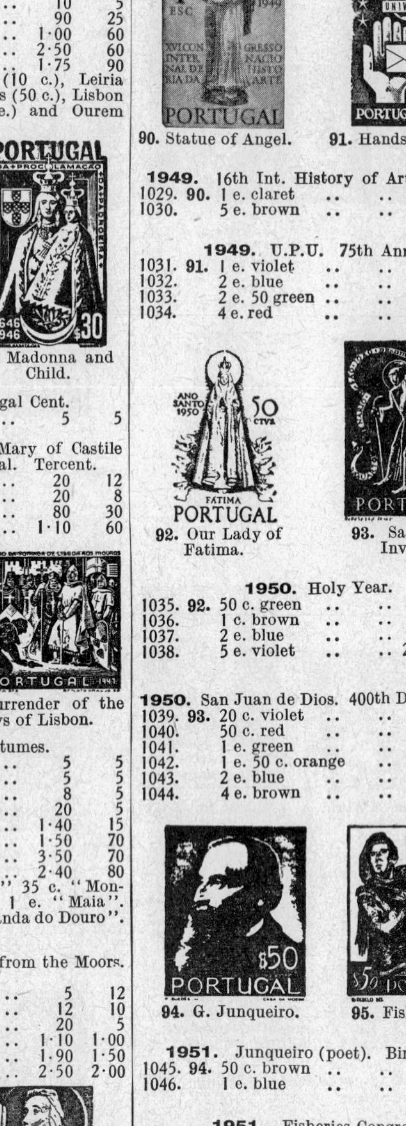

90. Statue of Angel. **91.** Hands and Letter.

1949. 16th Int. History of Art Congress.
1029. **90.** 1 e. claret 80 5
1030. 5 e. brown 20 8

1949. U.P.U. 75th Anniv.
1031. **91.** 1 e. violet 20 5
1032. 2 e. blue 40 12
1033. 2 e. 50 green 90 20
1034. 4 e. red .. .. 2·00 80

92. Our Lady of Fatima. **93.** Saint and Invalid.

1950. Holy Year.
1035. **92.** 50 c. green 50 10
1036. 1 c. brown .. .. 1·00 8
1037. 2 e. blue .. .. 1·50 20
1038. 5 e. violet .. .. 22·00 7·50

1950. San Juan de Dios. 400th Death Anniv.
1039. **93.** 20 c. violet 15 12
1040. 50 c. red 25 10
1041. 1 e. green 30 5
1042. 1 e. 50 c. orange .. 2·50 80
1043. 2 e. blue .. .. 2·00 50
1044. 4 e. brown .. .. 4·50 1·60

94. G. Junqueiro. **95.** Fisherman.

1951. Junqueiro (poet). Birth Cent.
1045. **94.** 50 c. brown 60 20
1046. 1 e. blue 15 8

1951. Fisheries Congress.
1047. **95.** 50 c. green on buff .. 70 40
1048. 1 e. purple on buff .. 5 5

96. Dove and Olive Branch. **97.** 15th Century Colonists.

1951. End of Holy Year. Inscr. "ANO SANTO 1951".
1049. **96.** 20 c. brown 10 8
1050. 90 c. olive 45 30
1051. – 1 e. maroon 50 5
1052. – 2 e. 30 blue-green .. 60 30
PORTRAIT: 1 e., 2 e. 30. Pope Pius XII.

1951. Colonization of Terceira, Azores. 5th Cent.
1053. **97.** 50 c. blue 50 20
1054. 1 e. brown 40 15

98. Revolutionaries. **99.** King John VI Coach.

1951. National Revolution. 25th Anniv.
1055. **98.** 1 e. maroon 50 5
1056. 2 e. 30 indigo 10 12

1952. National Coach Museum.
1057. – 10 c. purple 5 5
1058. **99.** 20 c. olive 5 5
1059. – 50 c. green 20 5
1060. – 90 c. emerald 12 8
1061. – 1 e. orange 50 5
1062. – 1 e. 40 rose .. .. 1·00 70
1063. **99.** 1 e. 50 brown .. .. 1·50 50
1064. – 2 e. 30 blue 10 10
DESIGNS (coaches of): 10 c., 90 c. King Philip II. 50 c., 1 e. 40, Pope Clement XI. 1 e., 2 e. 30, King Joseph I.

100. "N.A.T.O." **101.** Hockey Players.

1952. N.A.T.O. 3rd Anniv.
1065. **100.** 1 e. green .. .. 2·00 5
1066. 3 e. 50 blue .. .. 28·00 9·50

1952. 8th World Roller-skating Hockey Championship.
1067. **101.** 1 e. black and blue .. 1·25 10
1068. 3 e. 50 black & brown 2·75 1·25

102. Prof. G. Teixeira. **103.** Marshal Carmona Bridge.

1952. Prof. Teixeira (mathematician). Birth Cent.
1069. **102.** 1 e. red 30 5
1070. 2 e. 30 blue .. .. 1·25 1·10

1952. Ministry of Public Works. Cent.
1071. **103.** 1 e. chocolate on cream 20 5
1072. – 1 e. 40 lilac on cream 2·40 2·10
1073. – 2 e. green on cream .. 1·25 50
1074. – 3 e. 50 blue on cream 1·00 75
DESIGNS: 1 e. 40, 28th May Stadium, Braga. 2 e. Coimbra University. 3 e. 50, Salazar Barrage.

104. St. Francis Xavier. **105.** Medieval Knight.

1952. St. Francis Xavier. 400th Death Anniv.
1075. **104.** 1 e. green 35 5
1076. 2 e. red 65 20
1077. 3 e. 50 blue .. .. 4·00 1·60
1078. 5 e. lilac .. .. 4·50 1·25

1953.
1079. **105.** 5 c. bronze on yellow 5 5
1080. 10 c. purple on pink .. 5 5
1081. 20 c. orange on yellow 5 5
1081a. 30 c. purple on buff .. 5 5
1082. 50 c. black 5 5
1083. 90 c. green on yellow 50 5
1084. 1 e. lake on pink .. 5 5
1085. 1 e. 40 red 60 5
1086. 1 e. 50 red on yellow 10 5
1087. 2 e. black 8 5
1088. 2 e. 30 blue .. .. 1·00 5
1089. 2 e. 50 black on pink 12 5
1090. 5 e. purple on yellow 20 5
1091. 10 e. blue on yellow .. 70 5
1091a. 10 e. green on yellow 55 5
1092. 20 e. brown on yellow 1·25 5
1093. 50 e. lilac .. .. 3·00 15

106. St. Martin Dume. **107.** G. Gomes Fernandes (fire-brigade chief).

1953. Landing of Dume on Iberian Peninsula. 14th Cent.
1094. **106.** 1 e. black and grey .. 60 5
1095. 3 e. 50 sepia & yellow 3·50 1·60

1953. Fernandes. Birth Cent.
1096. **107.** 1 e. purple and cream 60 5
1097. 2 e. 30 blue and cream 2·40 1·60

108. Club Emblem. **109.** Princess St. Joan.

1953. Portuguese Automobile Club. 50th Anniv.
1098. **108.** 1 e. green 60 5
1099. 3 e. 50 brown .. .. 2·40 1·40

1953. Princess St. Joan. 5th Birth Cent.
1100. **109.** 1 e. green .. .. 1·00 5
1101. 3 e. 50 blue .. .. 4·00 2·10

ILLUSTRATIONS
British Commonwealth and all overprints and surcharges are FULL SIZE. Foreign Countries have been reduced to ¾-LINEAR.

110. Queen Maria II.

1953. Portuguese Stamp Cent. Bottom panel in gold.
1102. **110.** 50 c. lake 5 5
1103. 1 e. brown 5 5
1104. 1 e. 40 purple .. 80 50
1105. 2 e. 30 blue .. .. 1·00 60
1106. 3 e. 50 blue .. .. 1·40 85
1107. 4 e. 50 gold .. .. 1·00 40
1108. 5 e. olive .. .. 2·00 40
1109. 20 e. violet .. .. 18·00 1·25

111. **112.** Open Book.

1954. Trade Secretariat. 150th Anniv.
1110. **111.** 1 e. blue 30 5
1111. 1 e. 50 brown 40 20

1954. People's Education Plan.
1112. **112.** 50 c. blue 8 5
1113. 1 e. red 12 5
1114. 2 e. green 80 15
1115. 2 e. 50 brown .. .. 1·10 45

113. Cadet and College Banner. **114.** Father Manuel da Nobrega.

1954. Military College. 150th Anniv.
1116. **113.** 1 e. brown and green 20 5
1117. 3 e. 50 blue and green 50 30

1954. Sao Paulo. 4th Cent.
1118. **114.** 1 e. brown 30 5
1119. 2 e. 30 blue .. .. 2·40 1·50
1120. 3 e. 50 grey-green .. 2·00 60
1121. 5 e. green .. .. 3·25 90

115. King Sancho I. **116.** Telegraph Poles.

1955. Portuguese Kings.
1122. – 10 c. purple 5 5
1123. **115.** 20 c. grey-green .. 5 5
1124. – 50 c. turquoise .. 15 5
1125. – 90 c. blue-green .. 30 30
1126. – 1 e. brown 25 5
1127. – 1 e. 40 red 80 70
1128. – 1 e. 50 olive 70 40
1129. – 2 e. salmon .. .. 1·25 80
1130. – 2 e. 30 blue 90 70
KINGS: 10 c. Afonso I. 50 c. Afonso II. 90 c. Sancho II. 1 e. Afonso III. 1 e. 40, Diniz. 1 e. 50, Afonso IV. 2 e. Pedro I. 2 e. 30, Fernando.

1955. Electric Telegraph System in Portugal. Cent.
1131. **116.** 1 e. red and yellow 20 10
1132. 2 e. 30 blue and green 1·25 70
1133. 3 e. 50 green & yellow 1·40 60

117. A. J. Ferreira da Silva (teacher). **118.** 1856 Locomotive.

1956. Da Silva. Birth Cent.
1134. **117.** 1 e. blue 20 5
1135. 2 e. 30 green .. 1·50 80

1956. Portuguese Railways. Cent.
1136. **118.** 1 e. olive 15 5
1137. – 1 e. 50 blue & turquoise 45 25
1138. – 2 e. chestnut & bistre 1·25 40
1139. **118.** 2 e. 50 brown .. 1·10 55
DESIGN: 1 e. 50, 2 e. 1956 electric locomotive.

119. Madonna and Child. **120.** Almeida Garrett (after Barata Feyo).

1956. Mothers' Day.
1140. **119.** 1 e. sage and green .. 20 5
1141. 1 e. 50 olive & brown 30 12

1957. Almeida Garrett (writer) Commem.
1142. **120.** 1 e. brown 20 5
1143. 2 e. 30 violet .. 1·25 90
1144. 3 e. 50 green.. .. 50 20
1145. 5 e. red .. .. 3·50 1·25

121. Cesario Verde (poet). **122.** Exhibition Emblem.

1957. Cesario Verde Commem.
1146. **121.** 1 e. brn., buff & olive 40 5
1147. 3 e. 30 blk., ol. & sage 30 20

1958. Brussels International Exhibition.
1148. **122.** 1 e. red, yellow, blue and green 35 5
1149. 3 e. 30 red, yellow, blu and brown .. 60 40

123. St. Elizabeth. **124.** Institute of Tropical Medicine, Lisbon.

1958. St. Elizabeth and St. Teotonio Commem.
1150. **123.** 1 e. lake and cream .. 20 5
1151. – 2 e. green and cream 30 10
1152. **123.** 2 e. 50 violet & cream 90 12
1153. – 5 e. brown and cream 1·00 15
PORTRAIT: 2 e., 5 e. St. Teotonio.

1958. 6th Int. Congress of Tropical Medicine.
1154. **124.** 1 e. green and drab.. 40 5
1155. 2 e. 50 blue and grey 1·10 20

125. Merchant Ship. **126.** Queen Leonora.

128. **127.** Arms of Aveiro.

1958. 2nd National Merchant Navy Congress.
1156. **125.** 1 e. brn., ochre & sepia 40 5
1157. 4 e. 50 vio., lav. & blue 20 20

1958. Queen Leonora. 500th Birth Anniv. Frames and ornaments in bistre, inscriptions and value tablet in black.
1158. **126.** 1 e. blue and chestnut 12 5
1159. 1 e. 50 blue 70 12
1160. 2 e. 30 blue and green 60 20
1161. 4 e. 10 blue and grey 20 15

1959. Millenary of Aveiro.
1162. **127.** 1 e. purple, grey, gold and silver 20 5
1163. 5 e. green, grey, gold and silver .. 1·60 20

1960. N.A.T.O. 10th Anniv.
1164. **128.** 1 e. black and lilac .. 40 5
1165. 3 e. 50 black and grey 1·10 80

129. "Doorway to Peace". **130.** Glider.

1960. World Refugee Year. Symbol in black.
1166. **129.** 20 c. yell., lemon & brn. 5 5
1167. 1 e. yell., green & blue 25 5
1168. 1 e. 80 yellow and green 8 8

1960. Portuguese Aero Club. 50th Anniv. Inscr. as in T **130**. Multicoloured.
1169. 1 e. T **130** 5 5
1170. 1 e. 50 Light monoplane 40 15
1171. 2 e. Aircraft & parachutes 50 20
1172. 2 e. Model aircraft .. 55 15

131. Padre Cruz (after M. Barata). **132.** University Seal.

1960. Padre Cruz. Death Cent.
1173. **131.** 1 e. brown 10 5
1174. 4 e. 30 blue .. .. 1·10 1·00

1960. Evora University. 400th Anniv.
1175. **132.** 50 c. blue 8 5
1176. 1 e. brown and yellow 12 5
1177. 1 e. 40 claret .. 30 15

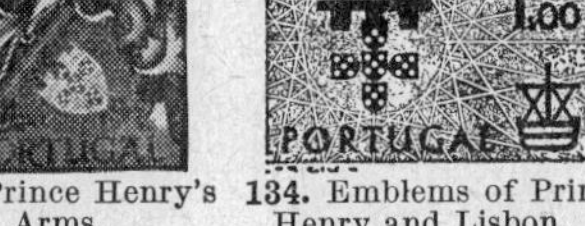

133. Prince Henry's Arms. **134.** Emblems of Prince Henry and Lisbon.

1960. Prince Henry the Navigator. 5th Death Cent. Multicoloured.
1178. 1 e. T **133**. 10 5
1179. 2 e. 50 Caravel 80 15
1180. 3 e. 50 Prince Henry .. 1·00 40
1181. 5 e. Motto.. .. .. 1·60 20
1182. 8 e. Sloop 30 25
1183. 10 e. Map showing Sagres 2·50 75

1960. Europa. As T **279** of Belgium, but size 31×21 mm.
1184. 1 e. light blue and blue .. 10 5
1185. 3 e. 50, red and lake .. 1·10 80

1960. 5th National Philatelic Exn. Lisbon.
1186. **134.** 1 e. blue, black and sage-green 20 5
1187. 3 e. 30 blue, black and olive .. .. 2·00 1·10

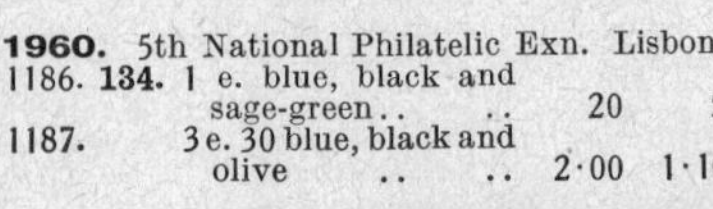

135. Portuguese Flag. **136.** King Pedro V.

1960. Republic. 50th Anniv.
1188. **135.** 1 e. red, green, orange and black 12 5

1961. Lisbon University Faculty of Letters. Cent.
1189. **136.** 1 e. green and sepia.. 20 5
1190. 6 e. 50 sepia and blue 60 30

137. Arms of Setubal. **138.**

1961. Setubal City Cent.
1191. **137.** 1 e. multicoloured .. 15 5
1192. 4 e. 30 multicoloured 1·10 1·10

1961. Europa.
1193. **138.** 1 e. blue 10 5
1194. 1 e. 50 green .. 50 40
1195. 3 e. 50 pink and lake 60 60

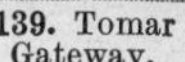

139. Tomar Gateway. **140.** National Guardsman.

1961. 8th Cent. of Tomar.
1196. **139.** 1 e. multicoloured .. 12 5
1197. – 3 e. 50 multicoloured 40 25
DESIGN: 3 e. 50, As T **139** but with ornamental background.

1962. National Republican Guard. 50th Anniv.
1198. **140.** 1 e. multicoloured .. 8 5
1199. 2 e. multicoloured .. 50 12
1200. 2 e. 50 multicoloured 45 12

141. St. Gabriel (Patron Saint of Telecommunications). **142.** Scout Badge and Tents.

1962. St. Gabriel Commem.
1201. **141.** 1 e. choc., grn. & olive 20 5
1202. 3 e. 50 grn., choc. & ol. 15 15

1962. 18th Int. Scout Conference (1961). Tent centres in black; frames in grey.
1203. **142.** 20 c. multicoloured.. 5 5
1204. 50 c. multicoloured.. 5 5
1205. 1 e. multicoloured .. 35 5
1206. 2 e. 50 multicoloured 80 5
1207. 3 e. 50 multicoloured 15 12
1208. 6 e. 50 multicoloured 25 25

143. Children with Ball. **144.** Europa "Honeycomb".

1962. 10th Int. Paediatrics Congress, Lisbon. Centres in black.
1209. – 50 c. yellow & grey-grn. 5 5
1210. – 1 e. yellow & bluish grey 25 5
1211. **143.** 2 e. 80 yellow & chestnut 12 12
1212. – 3 e. 50 yellow & mauve 40 20
DESIGNS: 50 c. Children with book. 1 e. Child being inoculated. 3 e. 50, Baby being weighed.

1962. Europa. "EUROPA" in gold.
1213. **144.** 1 e. ultramarine & blue 15 5
1214. 1 e. 50 deep grn. & grn. 30 10
1215. 3 e. 50 choc. & purple 15 15

145. St. Zenon (the Courier). **146.** Benifica Emblem and European Cup.

1962. Stamp Day. Saint in yellow and flesh.
1216. **145.** 1 e. black and maroon 10 5
1217. 2 e. black and myrtle 30 15
1218. 2 e. 80 black and bistre 35 35

1963. Benifica Club's Double Victory in European Football Cup Championships (1961-62).
1219. **146.** 1 e. red, brown-red, gold and black .. 30 8
1220. 4 e. 30 chestnut, sepia, gold and black .. 15 15

147. Campaign Emblem.

148. Mailcoach. **149.** St. Vincent de Paul.

1963. Freedom from Hunger.
1221. **147.** 1 e. gold, blue, black and grey .. 15 5
1222. 3 e. 30 gold, green, black and olive .. 15 15
1223. 3 e. 50 gold, crimson, black and red .. 60 20

1963. Paris Postal Conference Cent.
1224. **148.** 1 e. blue, light blue and grey .. 15 5
1225. 1 e. 50 brown, yellow-brown, pink & bistre 30 8
1226. 5 e. red-brown, lilac and orange-brown .. 20 15

1963. St. Vincent de Paul. Death Tercent. Inscr. in gold.
1227. **149.** 20 c. ultram. and blue 5 5
1228. 1 e. indigo and grey.. 15 5
1229. 2 e. 80 black and green 30 20
1230. 5 e. grey and magenta 90 20

150. Medieval Knight. **151.** Europa "Dove".

1963. Military Order of Avis. 800th Anniv.
1231. **150.** 1 e. multicoloured .. 12 5
1232. 1 e. 50 multicoloured 5 5
1233. 2 e. 50 multicoloured 50 15

1963. Europa.
1234. **151.** 1 e. drab, blue & black 10 5
1235. 2 e. 50 drab, grn. & blk. 35 15
1236. 3 e. 50 drab, red & blk. 40 25

152. "Supersonic Flight". **153.** Pharmacist's Jar.

1963. T.A.P. Airline. 10th Anniv.
1237. **152.** 1 e. blue & deep blue 15 5
1238. 2 e. 50 green & blk.-grn. 35 15
1239. 3 e. 50 orange and red 50 20

1964. 400th Anniv. of Publication of "Coloquios dos Simples" (Dissertations on Indian herbs and drugs) by Dr. G. d'Orta.
1240. **153.** 50 c. brown, blk. & bis. 10 5
1241. 1 e. lake, black & brown 20 5
1242. 4 e. 30 slate-blue, black and grey 60 40

154. Bank Emblem. **155.** Sameiro Shrine (Braga).

1964. National Overseas Bank Cent.
1243. 154. 1 e. yellow, olive & ind. 10 5
1244. 2 e. 50 yell., olive & grn. 35 12
1245. 3e. 50 yell., olive & brn. 35 25

1964. Sameiro Shrine Cent.
1246. 155. 1 e. yell., drab & chest. 12 5
1247. 2 e. yellow, drab & brn. 35 15
1248. 5 e. yellow, green & ult. 50 25

156. Europa "Flower". 157. Sun and Globe.

1964. Europa.
1249. 156. 1 e. indigo, light blue and blue .. 12 5
1250. 3 e. 50 brown, orange-brown & brown-pur. 40 20
1251. 4 e. 30 bronze, yellow-green and green .. 55 40

1964. International Quiet Sun Years.
1252. 157. 1 e. bistre, green, yellow and black .. 12 5
1253. 8 e. orange, green, yellow and black .. 60 20

158. Olympic "Rings". 159. E. Coelho (founder).

161. Dom Fernando I (second Duke of Braganca). 160. Traffic Signals.

1964. Olympic Games, Tokyo.
1254. 158. 20 c. multicoloured .. 5 5
1255. 1 e. multicoloured .. 15 5
1256. 1 e. 50 multicoloured 30 12
1257. 6 e. 50 multicoloured 55 35

1964. "Diario de Noticias" (newspaper). Cent.
1258. 159. 1 e. multicoloured .. 12 5
1259. 5 e. multicoloured .. 75 30

1965. 1st National Traffic Congress. Lisbon.
1260. 160. 1 e. yellow, red & green 10 5
1261. 3 e. 30 green, red & yell. 50 40
1262. 3 e. 50 red, yell. & grn. 60 20

1965. Braganca. 500th Anniv.
1263. 161. 1 e. brown and black 10 5
1264. 10 e. green and black 90 35

162. Angel and Gateway. 163. I.T.U. Emblem.

1965. Capture of Coimbra from the Moors. 900th Anniv.
1265. 162. 1 e. multicoloured .. 10 5
1266. 2 e. 50 multicoloured 30 10
1267. 5 e. multicoloured .. 60 25

1965. I.T.U. Cent.
1268. 163. 1 e. olive and brown .. 12 5
1269. 3 e. 50 maroon & green 40 15
1270. 6 e. 50 blue & green .. 50 40

164. C. Gulbenkian. 165. Red Cross Emblem.

1965. Calouste Gulbenkian (oil industry pioneer and philanthropist). 10th Death Anniv.
1271. 164. 1 e. multicoloured .. 15 5
1272. 8 e. multicoloured .. 65 30

1965. Portuguese Red Cross Cent.
1273. 165. 1 e. red, green & black 8 5
1274. 4 e. red, olive and black 30 15
1275. 4 e. 30 red, brown & blk. 1·00 1·00

166. Europa "Sprig". 167. Fighter Aircraft.

1965. Europa.
1276. 166. 1 e. turq., blk. & blue 8 5
1277. 3 e. 50 flesh, sep. & lake 45 15
1278. 4 e. 30 apple, blk. & grn. 50 40

1965. Portuguese Air Force. 50th Anniv.
1279. 167. 1 e. red, green & olive 10 5
1280. 2 e. red, green & brown 30 8
1281. 5 e. red, green and blue 60 20

168. 169. Monogram of Christ.

1965. Gil Vicente (poet and dramatist). 500th Birth Anniv. Designs depicting characters from Vicente's poems.
1282. 168. 20 c. multicoloured .. 5 5
1283. – 1 e. multicoloured .. 10 5
1284. – 2 e. 50 multicoloured 40 5
1285. – 6 e. 50 multicoloured 45 40

1966. Int. Committee for the Defence of Christian Civilisation Congress, Lisbon.
1286. 169. 1 e. violet, gold & bistre 20 5
1287. 3 e. 30 blk., gold & pur. 90 60
1288. 5 e. black, gold & lake 90 30

170. Emblems of Agriculture, Construction and Industry. 171. Giraldo the "Fearless".

1966. National Revolution. 40th Anniv.
1289. 170. 1 e. blk., blue & grey 10 5
1290. 3 e. 50 brown & bistre 40 15
1291. 4 e. mar., lake & pink 40 20

1966. Reconquest of Evora. 800th Anniv.
1292. 171. 1 e. multicoloured .. 20 5
1293. 8 e. multicoloured .. 60 30

172. Salazar Bridge. 173. Europa "Ship".

1966. Salazar Bridge, Lisbon. Inaug.
1294. 172. 1 e. red and gold .. 10 5
1295. 2 e. 50 ultram. & gold 50 15
1296. – 2 e. 80 ultram. & silver 40 35
1297. – 4 e. 30 green & silver 60 40
DESIGN—VERT. 2 e. 80, 4 e. 30, Salazar Bridge (different view).

1966. Europa.
1298. 173. 1 e. multicoloured .. 10 5
1299. 3 e. 50 multicoloured 40 15
1300. 4 e. 50 multicoloured 50 35

174. C. Pestana (bacteriologist). 175. Bocage (poet).

1966. Portuguese Scientists. Portraits in brown and bistre; background colours given.
1301. 174. 20 c. grey-green .. 5 5
1302. – 50 c. orange .. 5 5
1303. – 1 e. olive-yellow .. 10 5
1304. – 1 e. 50 cinnamon .. 15 5
1305. – 2 e. brown .. 40 5
1306. – 2 e. 50 green .. 50 15
1307. – 2 e. 80 salmon .. 40 35
1308. – 4 e. 30 blue .. 40 35
SCIENTISTS: 50 c. E. Moniz (neurologist). 1 e. E.A.P. Coutinho (botanist). 1 e. 50, J. C. da Serra (botanist). 2 e. R. Jorge (hygienist and anthropologist). 2 e. 50, J. L. de Vasconcelos (ethnologist). 2 e. 80, M. Lemos (medical historian). 4 e. 30, J. A. Serrano (anatomist).

1966. Manuel M. B. du Bocage. Birth Bicent. (1965).
1309. 175. 1 e. black, grn. & bistre 10 5
1310. 2 e. black, grn. & brn. 30 8
1311. 6 e. black, grn. & grey 50 30

176. Cogwheels. 177. Adoration of the Virgin.

1967. Europa.
1312. 176. 1 e. ultram., blk. & bl. 10 5
1313. 3 e. 50 brown, black and salmon .. 30 12
1314. 4 e. 30 bronze, black and green 40 35

1967. Fatima Apparitions. 50th Anniv. Multicoloured.
1315. 1 e. Type 177 .. .. 8 5
1316. 2 e. 80 Fatima Church .. 30 30
1317. 3 e. 50 Virgin of Fatima .. 35 15
1318. 4 e. Chapel of the Apparitions 40 15

178. Roman Senators. 179. Lisnave Shipyard.

1967. New Civil Law Code.
1319. 178. 1 e. lake and gold .. 10 5
1320. 2 e. 50 blue and gold 35 10
1321. 4 e. 30 green and gold 35 30

1967. Lisnave Shipyard, Lisbon. Inaug.
1322. 178. 1 e. multicoloured .. 8 5
1323. – 2 e. 80 multicoloured 30 25
1324. 178. 3 e. 50 multicoloured 40 15
1325. – 4 e. 30 multicoloured 35 35
DESIGN: 2 e. 80, 4 e. 30, Section of ship's hull and location map.

180. Serpent Symbol. 181. Flags of EFTA Countries.

1967. 6th Rheumatological Congress Lisbon.
1326. 180. 1 e. multicoloured .. 10 5
1327. 2 e. multicoloured .. 30 15
1328. 5 e. multicoloured .. 60 20

1967. European Free Trade Assn.
1329. 181. 1 e. multicoloured .. 8 5
1330. 3 e. 50 multicoloured 35 20
1331. 4 e. 30 multicoloured 50 35

182. Tombstones. 183. Bento de Goes.

1967. Abolition of Death Penalty in Portugal. Cent.
1332. 182. 1 e. olive 10 5
1333. 2 e brown 30 10
1334 5 e green 60 20

1968. Bento de Goes Commem.
1335. 183. 1 e. indigo, maroon and green 15 5
1336. 8 e. purple, grn. & brn. 50 25

184. Europa "Key". 185. "Maternal Love".

1968. Europa.
1337. 184. 1 e. multicoloured .. 10 5
1338. 3 e. 50 multicoloured 30 15
1339. 4 e. 30 multicoloured 50 35

1968. Organization of Mothers for National Education (O.M.E.N.) 30th Anniv.
1340. 185. 1 e. black, orge. & drab 10 5
1341. 2 e. black, orge. & pink 30 10
1342. 5 e. black, orge. & blue 60 20

186. "Victory over Disease".

1968. World Health Organization. 20th Anniv.
1343. 386. 1 e. multicoloured .. 8 5
1344. 3 e. 50 multicoloured 35 12
1345. 4 e. 30 multicoloured 80 70

187. Vineyard, Girao.

1968. "Lubrapex 1968" Stamp Exn. "Madeira—Pearl of the Atlantic". Multicoloured.
1346. 50 c. Type 187 .. .. 5 5
1347. 1 e. Firework display .. 8 5
1348. 1 e. 50 Landscape .. 20 5
1349. 2 e. 80 J. Fernandes Vieira (liberator of Pernambuco) 40 40
1350. 3 e. 50 Embroidery .. 60 15
1351. 4 e. 30 J. Goncalves Zarco (navigator) .. .. 1·00 80
1352. 20 e. "Muschia aurea" 2·00 60
The 2 e. 80 to 20 e. are vert.
Nos. 1346/52 have tri-lingual captions (Portuguese, French and English) printed on the back.

188. Pedro Alvares Cabral (from medallion).

1969. Pedro Alvares Cabral (explorer). 500th Birth Anniv.
1353. 188. 1 e. blue 10 5
1354. – 3 e. 50 purple .. 70 15
1355. – 6 e. 50 multicoloured 1·00 45
DESIGNS—VERT. 3 e. 50 Cabral's arms. HORIZ. 6 e. 50 Cabral's fleet (from contemporary documents).

189. Colonnade. 190. King Joseph I.

1969. Europa.
1356. 189. 1 e. multicoloured .. 10 5
1357. 3 e. 50 multicoloured 30 15
1358. 4 e. 30 multicoloured 40 35

1969. National Press. Cent.
1359. 190. 1 e. multicoloured .. 10 5
1360. 2 e. multicoloured .. 30 8
1361. 8 e. multicoloured .. 60 30

191. I.L.O. Emblem.

192. J. R. Cabrilho (navigator and coloniser).

1969. Int. Labour Organization. 50th Anniv.
1362. **191.** 1 e. multicoloured .. 8 5
1363. 3 e. 50 multicoloured 30 12
1364. 4 e. 30 multicoloured 50 35

1969. San Diego (California). Bicent.
1365. **192.** 1 e. bronze, yell. & grn. 10 5
1366. 2 e. 50 brown & blue 30 8
1367. 6 e. 50 brown & green 50 25

193. Vianna da Motta.

1969. Jose Vianna da Motta (concert pianist). Birth Cent. (1968).
1368. **193.** 1 e. multicoloured .. 12 5
1369. 9 e. multicoloured .. 45 40

194. Coutinho and Seaplane.

1969. Gago Coutinho (aviator). Birth Cent. Multicoloured.
1370. 1 e. Type **194** 8 5
1371. 2 e. 80 Coutinho & Sextant 30 20
1372. 3 e. 30 Type **194**.. .. 35 25
1373. 4 e. 30 As No. 1371 .. 40 25

195. Vasco da Gama.

1969. Vasco da Gama. 500th Birth Anniv. Multicoloured.
1374. 1 e. Type **195** 8 5
1375. 2 e. 80 Arms of Vasco da Gama 35 20
1376. 3 e. 50 Route map .. 70 20
1377. 4 e. Vasca da Gama's fleet 70 20
Nos. 1374/7 have descriptive captions in three languages; Portuguese, French and English, printed on the backs.

196. "Flaming Sun".

197. Distillation Plant and Pipelines.

1970. Europa.
1378. **196.** 1 e. cream and blue.. 8 5
1379. 3 e. 50 cream and brn. 30 20
1380. 4 e. 30 cream and green 40 30

1970. Porto Oil Refinery. Inaug.
1381. **197.** 1 e. blue 10 5
1382. – 2 e. 80 black & green 30 20
1383. **197.** 3 e. 30 olive .. 40 25
1384. – 6 e. brown 40 25
DESIGN: 2 e. 80, 6 e. Catalytic cracking plant and pipelines.

198. Marshal Carmona (from sculpture by L. de Almedia).

1970. Marshal Carmona. Birth Cent.
1385. **198.** 1 e. green 8 5
1386. 2 e. 50 blue and red.. 35 5
1387. 7 e. blue 30 25

199. Station Badge.

200. Emblem within Cultural Symbol.

1970. Plant Breeding Station. 25th Anniv.
1388. **199.** 1 e. multicoloured .. 8 5
1389. 2 e. 50 multicoloured 40 10
1390. 5 e. multicoloured .. 45 10

1970. Expo 70. Multicoloured.
1391. 1 e. Compass and Expo emblem (postage) .. 8 5
1392. 5 e. Christian Symbol and emblem 40 10
1393. 6 e. 50 Symbolic initials and emblem 50 35
1394. 3 e. 50 Type **200** (air) .. 30 5

201. Wheel and Star.

1970. Cities' Centenaries. Multicoloured.
1395. 1 e. Type **201** (Covilha).. 8 5
1396. 2 e. 80 Ram and weaving frame 25 15
1397. 1 e. Castle (Santarem) .. 8 5
1398. 4 e. Two knights.. .. 30 15

202. Cableship laying Cable.

1970. Portugal-England Submarine Telegraph Cable. Cent.
1399. **202.** 1 e. black, blue & grn. 8 5
1400. 2 e. 50 black, green and cream 30 8
1401. – 2 e. 80 multicoloured 30 25
1402. – 4 e. multicoloured .. 40 15
DESIGN: 2 e. 80, 4 e. Cable cross-section.

203. Harvesting Grapes.

204. Mountain Windmill, Bussaco Hills.

1970. Port Wine Industry. Multicoloured.
1403. 50 c. Type **203** 5 5
1404. 1 e. Harvester and jug 10 5
1405. 3 e. 50 Wine-glass and barge 35 5
1406. 7 e. Wine-bottle and casks 35 25

1971. Portuguese Windmills.
1407. **204.** 20 c. red, blk. & brn. 5 5
1408. – 50 c. brn., blk. & blue 5 5
1409. – 1 e. pur., blk. and grey 8 5
1410. – 2 e. brn., blk. & mauve 20 5
1411. – 3 e. 30 brn., black & yellow-brown .. 35 20
1412. – 5 e. brn., blk. & green 50 12
WINDMILLS: 50 c. Beira Litoral Province. 1 e. "Saloio" type, Estremadura Province. 2 e. St. Miguel, Azores. 3 e. 30 Porto Santo, Madeira. 5 e. Pico, Azores.
Nos. 1407/12 were issued with tri-lingual descriptions on the reverse.

205. Europa Chain.

206. F. Franco.

1971. Europa.
1413. **205.** 1 e. grn. blue & blk. 10 5
1414. 3 e. 50 yell., brn. & blk. 30 5
1415. 7 e. 50 brn., grn. & blk. 30 25

1971. Portuguese Sculptors.
1416. **206.** 20 c. black 5 5
1417. – 1 e. brown 8 5
1418. – 1 e. 50 brown .. 12 5
1419. – 2 e. 50 blue 30 5
1420. – 3 e. 50 red 30 5
1421. – 4 e. green 40 12
DESIGNS: 1 e. A. Lopes. 1 e. 50 A. de Costa Mota. 2 e. 50 R. Gameiro. 3 e. 50 J. Simoes de Almeida (the Younger). 4 e. F. dos Santos.

207. Pres. Salazar.

208. Wolframite.

1971. Pres. Antonio Salazar Commemoration.
1422. **207.** 1 e. brn., green & orge. 10 5
1423. 5 e. brn., pur. & orge. 40 8
1424. 10 e. brn., blue & orge. 70 15

1971. 1st Spanish-Portuguese-American Congress of Economic Geology. Multicoloured.
1425. 1 e. Type **208** 8 5
1426. 2 e. 50 Arsenopyrite .. 35 5
1427. 3 e. 50 Beryllium .. 12 5
1428. 6 e. 50 Chalcopyrite .. 25 20

209. Town Gate.

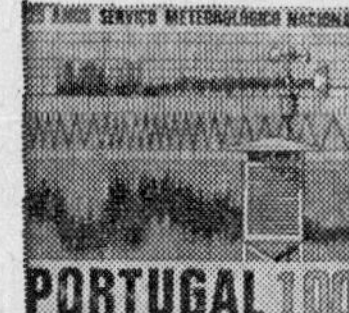

210. Weather Equipment.

1971. Castelo Branco. Bicent. Multicoloured.
1429. 1 e. Type **209** 10 5
1430. 3 e. Town square and monument 35 10
1431. 12 e. 50 Arms of Castelo Branco. (horiz.) .. 50 40

1971. Portuguese Meteorological Service. 25th Anniv. Multicoloured.
1432. 1 e. Type **210** 8 5
1433. 4 e. Weather balloon .. 30 12
1434. 6 e. 50 Weather satellite 35 20

211. Drowning Missionaries.

212. Man and his Habitat.
213. Clerigos Tower, Oporto.

1971. Martyrdom of Brazil Missionaries. 400th Anniv.
1435. **211.** 1 e. blk., blue & grey 8 5
1436. 3 e. 30 blk., pur. & brn. 25 20
1437. 4 e. 80 blk., grn. & olive 40 30

1971. Nature Protection. Multicoloured.
1438. 1 e. Type **212** 8 5
1349. 3 e. 30 Conservation, Horses and trees ("Earth").. 15 12
1440. 3 e. 50 Birds ("The Atmosphere") .. 15 5
1441. 4 e. 50 Fishes ("Water") 55 20

1972. Buildings and Views.
1442. – 5 c. grey, grn. & blk. 5 5
1442a. – 10 c. grn., blk. & blue 5 5
1442b. – 30 c. yell., ochre & brn. 5 5
1443. – 50 c. blk., brn. & grn. 5 5
1444. **213.** 1 e. blk., brn. & grn. 5 5
1445. – 1 e. 50 blk., brn. & bl. 5 5
1445a. – 2 e. blk., brn. & red.. 8 5
1446. – 2 e. 50 multicoloured 10 5
1447. – 3 c. brn., yell. & blk. 12 5
1448. – 3 e. 50 multicoloured 15 5
1448a. – 4 e. 50 blk., brn. & blue 15 5
1448b. – 4 e. 50 blk., brn. & grn. 15 5
1448c. – 5 e. grn., brn. & blk. 15 5
1448d. – 6 e. brn., blk. & grn. 20 5
1448e. – 7 e. 50 blk., grn. & orge. 25 8
1449. – 8 e. multicoloured .. 30 8
1450. – 10 e. multicoloured .. 40 8
1451. – 20 e. multicoloured .. 80 10
1452. – 50 e. black, brn. & bl. 2·00 40
1453. – 100 e. multicoloured 4·00 60
DESIGNS: 5 c. Aguas Livres aqueduct, Lisbon. 10 c. Lima Bridge. 30 c. Interior of Monastery, Alcobaca. 50 c. Coimbra University. 1 e. 50 Belem Tower, Lisbon. 2 e. "Domus Municipalis", Braganza. 2 e. 50 Castle, Vila de Feira. 3 e. Misericord House, Vianado Castelo. 3 e. 50 Window, Tomar Convent. 4 e. New Gate, Braga. 4 e. 50 Dolmen of Carrazeda. 5 e. Roman Temple, Evora. 6 e. Monastery, Leca do Balio. 7 e. 50 Almourol Castle. 8 e. Ducal Palace, Guimaraes. LARGER (31 × 22 mm.). 10 e. Cape Girao. 20 e. Episcopal Garden. Castelo Branco. 50 e. Town Palace, Sintra, 100 e. Seven Cities' Lake, St. Miguel, Azores.

214. Arms of Pinhel.

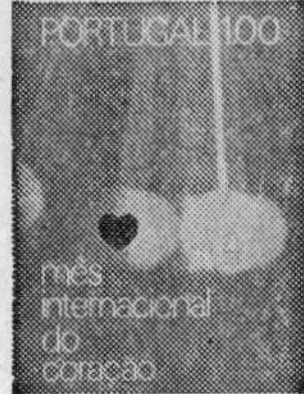

215. Heart and Pendulum.

1972. Pinhel's Status as a City. Bicent. Multicoloured.
1464. 1 e. Type **214** 5 5
1465. 2 e. 50 Balustrade (vert.) 30 5
1466. 7 e. 50 Lantern on pedestal (vert.) 30 20

1972. World Heart Month.
1467. **215.** 1 e. red and lilac .. 5 5
1468. – 4 e. red and green .. 40 10
1469. – 9 e. red and brown .. 35 30
DESIGNS: 4 e. Heart in spiral. 9 e. Heart and cardiogram trace.

216. "Communications".

217. Container Truck.

1972. Europa.
1470. **216.** 1 e. multicoloured .. 8 5
1471. 3 e. 50 multicoloured 12 5
1472. 6 e. multicoloured .. 25 20

1972. 13th Int. Road Transport Union Congress, Estoril. Multicoloured.
1473. 1 e. Type **217** 5 5
1474. 4 e. 50 Roof of taxi-cab.. 30 15
1475. 8 e. Motor-coach.. .. 30 20

218. Football.

1972. Olympic Games, Munich. Mult.
1476. 50 c. Type **218** 5 5
1477. 1 e. Running 5 5
1478. 1 e. 50 Horse-jumping .. 12 5
1479. 3 e. 50 Swimming .. 12 5
1480. 4 e. 50 Sailing 30 12
1481. 5 e. Gymnastics 40 12

219. Marquis of Pombal.

220. Tome de Sousa.

1972. Pombaline University Reforms. Multicoloured.
1482. 1 e. Type **219** 5 5
1483. 2 e. 50 "The Sciences" (emblems) 25 8
1484. 8 e. Arms of Coimbra University 30 25

1972. Brazil's Independence. 150th Anniv. Multicoloured.
1485. 1 e. Type **220** 8 5
1486. 2 e. 50 Jose Bonifacio .. 20 5
1487. 3 e. 50 Dom Pedro IV .. 12 5
1488. 6 e. Dove and globe .. 25 20

221. Cabral, Coutinho and Seaplane.

1972. 1st Flight, Lisbon-Rio de Janeiro. 50th Anniv. Multicoloured.

1489. 1 e. Type **221** 5 5
1490. 2 e. 50 Route-map .. 25 5
1491. 2 e. 80 Type **221** 12 10
1492. 3 e. 80 As 2 e. 50 .. .. 15 12

222. Camoens.

1972. Camoens "Lusiads" (epic poem). 400th Anniv. Multicoloured.

1493. 1 e. Type **222** 8 5
1494. 3 e. "Saved from the sea" 12 5
1495. 10 e. "Encounter with Adamstor" 40 25

223. Graph and Computer Tapes.

1973. Portugese Productivity Conf., Lisbon. Multicoloured.

1496. 1 e. Type **223** 5 5
1497. 4 e. Computer scale .. 30 8
1498. 9 e. Graphs chart 35 30

224. Europa "Posthorn". 226. Child Running.

225. Pres. Medici and Arms.

1973. Europa.

1499. **224.** 1 e. multicoloured .. 5 5
1500. 4 e. multicoloured .. 30 8
1501. 6 e. multicoloured .. 25 20

1973. Visit of Pres. Medici of Brazil.

1502. **225.** 1 e. multicoloured .. 5 5
1503. 2 e. multicoloured .. 12 10
1504. 3 e. 50 multicoloured 15 8
1505. 4 e. 80 multicoloured 20 15

1973. "For the Child".

1506. **226.** 1 e. blue and brown .. 5 5
1507. – 4 e. brown and violet 25 8
1508. – 7 e. 50 brown & orge. 30 20

DESIGNS: 4 e. Child running (to right). 7 e. 50 Child jumping.

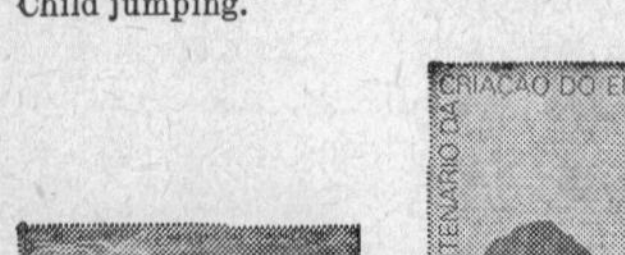

227. Transport and Weather map. 228. Child and Written Text.

1973. Ministry of Communications. 25th Anniv. Multicoloured.

1509. 1 e. Type **227** 5 5
1510. 3 e. 80 "Telecommunications" 15 10
1511. 6 e. "Postal Services" .. 25 15

1973. Primary State School Education. Bicent. Multicoloured.

1512. 1 e. Type **228** 5 5
1513. 4 e. 50 Page of children's primer 15 12
1514. 5 e. 30 "Schooldays" (child's drawing) (horiz.) 20 15
1515. 8 e. "Teacher and children" (horiz.) 30 20

229. Early Tram-car. 230. League Badge.

1973. Oporto's Public Transport System. Multicoloured.

1516. 1 e. Horse-drawn tram-car 5 5
1517. 3 e. 50 Modern omnibus .. 12 5
1518. 7 e. 50 Type **229** 30 20

Nos. 1516/17, 31×32 mm.

1973. Servicemen's League. 50th Anniv. Multicoloured.

1519. 1 e. Type **230** 5 5
1520. 2 e. 50 Servicemen .. 10 5
1521. 11 e. Awards and medals 55 30

231. Death of Nuno Gonzalves. 232. Damiao de Gois.

1973. Defence of Faria Castle by the Alcaide, Gonzalo Nunes. 600th Anniv.

1522. **231.** 1 e. green and yellow 5 5
1523. 10 e. purple and yellow 40 25

1974. Damiao de Gois (scholar and diplomat). 400th Death Anniv. Multicoloured.

1524. 1 e. Type **232** 5 5
1525. 4 e. 50 Title-page of Chronicles of "Prince Dom Joao" 20 12
1526. 7 e. 50 Lute and "Dodecahordon" score .. 30 20

233. "The Exile" (A. Soares dos Reis). 234. Light Emission.

1974. Europa.

1527. **233.** 1 e. green, blue & olive 5 5
1528. 4 e. green, red & yellow 15 12
1529. 6 e. dark grn., grn & blue 25 15

1974. Satellite Communications Station Network. Inaug.

1530. **234.** 1 e. 50 green 5 5
1531. – 4 e. 50 blue 20 8
1532. – 5 e. 30 purple .. 25 15

DESIGNS: 4 e. 50 Spiral Waves. 5 e. 30 Satellite and Earth.

235. "Wireless Telegraphy".

1974. Guglielmo Marconi (radio pioneer). Birth Cent.

1533. **235.** 1 e. 50 multicoloured 5 5
1534. – 3 e. 50 multicoloured 15 5
1535. – 10 e. multiticoloured 40 25

DESIGNS—VERT. Nos. 1534/5, Radio waves similar to Type **235**.

236. Mounted Postman and Mail-van. 237. Luisa Todi (opera-singer).

1974. Universal Postal Union. Cent. Mult.

1536. 1 e. 50 Type **236** 5 5
1537. 2 e. Hand with letters .. 10 5
1538. 3 e. 30 Mail-ships old and new 15 8
1539. 4 e. 50 Carrier-pigeon and plane 20 12
1540. 5 e. 30 Hand with letters (different) 25 15
1541. 20 e. Locomotives old and new .. .. .. 1·00 50

1974. Portuguese Musicians.

1542. **237.** 1 e. 50 purple .. 5 5
1543. – 2 e. red 10 5
1544. – 2 e. 50 brown .. 10 5
1545. – 3 e. blue 12 5
1546. – 5 e. 30 green 25 10
1547. – 11 e. purple 55 30

PORTRAITS: 2 e. J. D. Bomtempo (composer). 2 e. 50 C. Seixas (organist and harpsicordist). 3 e. D. Lobo (chorus-master). 5 e. 30 J. de Sousa Carvalho (composer and teacher). 11 e. M. Portugal (composer and musical director).

238. Arms of Beja.

1974. Beja. 2,000th Anniv. Multicoloured.

1548. 1 e. 50 Type **238** 5 5
1549. 3 e. 50 Beja's inhabitants "through the ages" .. 15 5
1550. 7 e. Site of Beja seen through Moorish arches 30 15

239. "The Annunciation". 240. Rainbow and Dove.

1974. Christmas. Multicoloured.

1551. 1 e. 50 Type **239** 5 5
1552. 4 e. 50 "The Nativity" .. 25 15
1553. 10 e. "The Flight into Egypt" 60 30

1974. Armed Forces' Movement of 25 April 1974.

1554. **240.** 1 e. 50 multicoloured 5 5
1555. 3 e. 50 multicoloured 15 5
1556. 5 e. multicoloured .. 25 15

241. Egas Moniz. 242. Farmer and Soldier.

1974. Professor Egas Moniz (brain surgeon). Birth Centenary.

1557. **241.** 1 e. 50 brown & orge. 5 5
1558. – 3 e. 30 orge. & brown 15 5
1559. – 10 e. grey and blue .. 50 30

DESIGNS: 3 e. 30 Leucotomy probe and Nobel Prize medal (1949). 10 e. Cerebral angiograph (1927).

1975. Cultural Progress and Citizens' Guidance Campaign.

1560. **242.** 1 e. 50 multicoloured 5 5
1561. 3 e. multicoloured .. 15 5
1562. 4 e. 50 multicoloured 20 15

243. Hands and Dove of Peace.

1975. 25th April Movement. First Anniv. Multicoloured.

1563. 1 e. 50 Type **243** .. 5 5
1564. 4 e. 50 "Black" hands and dove 20 15
1565. 10 e. Peace dove and olive branch 45 30

244. "The Hand of God".

1975. Holy Year. Multicoloured.

1566. 1 e. 50 Type **244** .. 5 5
1567. 4 e. 50 "Hand with Crucifix" 20 15
1568. 10 e. "Holy Dove" .. 45 30

245. "The Horseman of the Apocalypse" (detail from ancient manuscript).

1975. Europa. Multicoloured.

1569. 1 e. 50 Type **245** .. 5 5
1570 10 e. "Fernando Pessoa" (poet) (A. Negreiros) 45 30

246. Parliament Building.

1975. Opening of Constituent Assembly.

1571. **246.** 2 e. black, red & yell. 8 5
1572. 20 e. olive, grn. & yell. 90 40

247. Hiking. 248. "Planting Tree".

1975. 36th Rally of International Camping and Caravanning Federation. Multicoloured.

1573. 2 e Type **247** 8 5
1574 4 e. 50 Boating and swimming .. 20 15
1575. 5 e. 30 Caravanning .. 25 15

1975. United Nations. 30th Anniv. Multicoloured.

1576. 2 e. Type **248** 8 5
1577. 4 e. 50 "Releasing peace dove" 20 15
1578. 20 e. "Harvesting corn" 90 40

249. Da Vinci's Glider, and Rocket Launch.

1975. 26th International Astronautical Federation Congress, Lisbon. Multicoloured.

1579. 2 e. Type **249** 8 5
1580. 4 e. 50 "Apollo-Soyuz" space link 20 15
1581. 5 e. 30 Astronautical pioneers—"Goddard, Pelterie, Oberth and Tsiolkovsky" .. 25 15
1582. 10 e. Space panorama of events (66×29 mm.) .. 45 30

250. "Surveying the Land".

1975. Lisbon Geographical Society. Centenary. Multicoloured.

1583. 2 e. Type **250** 8 5
1584. 8 e. "Surveying the Sea" 35 20
1585. 10 e. Globe and people .. 45 30

251. Symbolic Arch.

1975. European Architectural Heritage Year. Multicoloured.

1586. 2 e. Type **251** 8 5
1587. 8 e. Plan of stylised residence 35 20
1588. 10 e. Hand protecting classical building from development .. 45 30

252. Nurse in Hospital Ward.

1975. International Women's Year. Mult.

1589. 50 c. Type **252** 5 5
1590. 2 e. Woman harvesting wheat 8 5
1591. 3 e. 50 Female secretary in office 15 10
1592. 8 e. Woman in factory .. 35 20

253. Pen-nib as Ploughshare.

1976. Portugese Society of Writers. 50th Anniversary.

1594. **253.** 3 e. blue and red .. 15 10
1595. 20 e. red and blue .. 90 60

254. Graham Bell's Telephone.

1976. First Telephone Transmission. Cent.

1596. 3 e. Type **254** 15 10
1597. 10 e. 50 Alexander Graham Bell 45 30

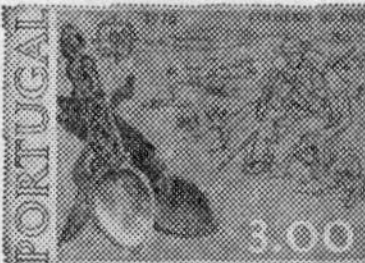

255. Insets of Industrial Progress. **256.** Carved Olive-wood Spoon.

1976. Nat. Production Campaign.

1598. **255.** 50 c. brown 5 5
1599. – 1 e. green 5 5

DESIGN: 1 e. Inserts of consumer goods.

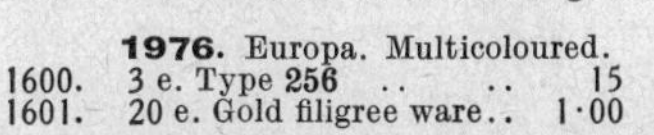

1976. Europa. Multicoloured.

1600. 3 e. Type **256** 15 10
1601. 20 e. Gold filigree ware .. 1·00 90

257. "Stamp Designing".

1976. "Interphil '76". Int. Stamp Exn., Philadelphia. Multicoloured.

1602. 3 e. Type **257** 15 10
1603. 7 e. 50 "Stamp Display" 40 30
1604. 10 e. "Stamp Printing" 50 40

258. King Fernando promulgating Law.

1976. Law of "Sesmarias" (Uncultivated Land). 600th Anniv. Multicoloured.

1605. 3 e. Type **258** 15 10
1606. 5 e. Ploughshare and farmers repelling hunters .. 25 15
1607. 10 e. Harvesting scene .. 50 40

259. Runner with Torch.

1976. Olympic Games, Montreal. Mult.

1608. 3 e. Type **259** 15 10
1609. 7 e. Women's relay .. 35 25
1610. 10 e. 50 Olympic flame .. 55 45

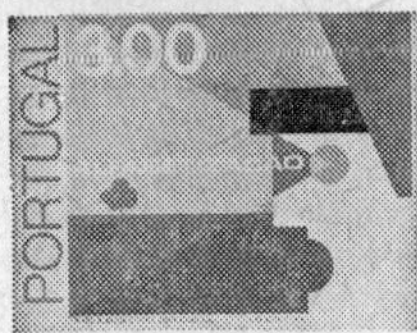

260. "Speaking on Land".

1976. Literacy Campaign. Multicoloured.

1611. 3 e. Type **260** 15 10
1612. 3 e. "Speaking at sea" .. 15 10
1613. 3 e. "Speaking in town" 15 10
1614. 3 e. "Speaking in industry" 15 10

261. Azure-winged Magpie. **262.** Exhibition Hall.

1976. "Portucale '77" Thermatic Stamp Exhibition, Oporto. Multicoloured.

1615. 3 e. Type **261** 15 10
1616. 5 e. Lynx 25 15
1617. 7 e. Portuguese cherry laurel 35 25
1618. 10 e. Little wild carnation 50 40

1976. 6th Luso-Brazilian Philatelic Exhibition. Multicoloured.

1619. 3 e. Type **262** 15 10
1620. 20 e. Lubrapex emblem on "Stamp" .. .. 1·00 90

263. Bank Symbol.

1976. Portuguese Trust Fund Bank. Centenary.

1622. **263.** 3 e. multicoloured .. 15 10
1623. 7 e. multicoloured .. 35 25
1624. 15 e. multicoloured .. 75 65

264. Sheep Grazing. **265.** "Liberty".

1976. European Wetlands Year and Protection of Humid Zones. Multicoloured.

1625. 1 e. Type **264** 5 5
1626. 3 e. Drainage of marshes 15 10
1627. 5 e. Fishes in sea .. 25 15
1628. 10 e. Protection of wild-fowl 50 40

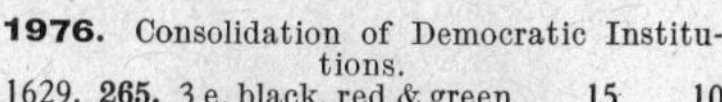

1976. Consolidation of Democratic Institutions.

1629. **265.** 3 e. black, red & green 15 10

266. Mother examining Child's Eyes.

1976. World Health Day. Multicoloured.

1630. 3 e. Type **266** 15 10
1631. 5 e. Welder (occupational hazard) 25 15
1632. 10 e. Blind person reading Braille 50 40

267. Hydro-electric Power.

1976. Uses of Natural Energy. Mult.

1633. 1 e. Type **267** 5 5
1634. 4 e. Fossil fuel (oil) .. 20 12
1635. 5 e. Geo-thermic sources 25 15
1636. 10 e. Wind power .. 50 40
1637. 15 e. Solar energy .. 75 65

CHARITY TAX STAMPS

Used on certain days of the year as an additional postal tax on internal letters. Other values in some of the types were for use on telegrams only. The proceeds were devoted to public charities. If one was not affixed in addition to the ordinary postage, postage due stamps were used to collect the deficiency and the fine.

1911. Optd. **ASSISTENCIA.**

C 455. **26.** 10 r. grn. (No. 406) 70 40
C 484. **28.** 1 c. green (No. 486) 75 40

C 1. "Lisbon". **C 2.** "Charity".

1913. Lisbon Fetes.

C 485. **C 1.** 1 c. green 20 12

1915. For poor people.

C 486. **C 2.** 1 c. red 12 8
C 669. 15 c. red 15 12

1924. Surch. **15 ctvs.**

C 594. **C 2.** 15 c. on 1 c. red .. 30 15

C 3. Muse of History. **C 6.** Hurdler.

C 4. Monument to de Pombal. **C 5.** Marquis de Pombal.

1925. Portuguese Army in Flanders, 1484 and 1918.

C 662. **C 3.** 10 c. red 20 15
C 663. 10 c. green 20 15
C 664. 10 c. blue 20 15
C 665. 10 c. brown .. 20 15

1925. Marquis de Pombal Commem.

C 666. **C 4.** 15 c. blue 25 20
C 667. – 15 c. blue 30 25
C 668. **C 5.** 15 c. blue 8 5

DESIGN: No. C 667. Planning reconstruction of Lisbon.

1928. Olympic Games.

C 741. **C 6.** 15 c. black and red 1·60 1·60

NEWSPAPER STAMPS

N 1. **N 2.**

1876.

N 177. **N 1.** 2 r. black .. .. 2·40 2·00
N 184. **N 2.** 2½ r. olive .. .. 1·10 12
N 187. 2½ r. yellow-brown 1·10 12

OFFICIAL STAMPS

1938. Optd. **OFICIAL.**

O 900. **68.** 40 c. brown .. 5 5

O 1.

1952.

O 1069. **O 1.** (No value) blk. & buff 5 5

PARCEL POST STAMPS.

P 1.

1920.

P 578. **P 1.** 1 c. brown 5 5
P 579. 2 c. orange 5 5
P 580. 5 c. brown 5 5
P 581. 10 c. brown .. 10 5
P 582. 20 c. blue 12 5
P 583. 40 c. red 12 5
P 584. 50 c. black 20 12
P 585. 60 c. blue 20 12
P 586. 70 c. brown .. 80 70
P 587. 80 c. blue 80 70
P 588. 90 c. violet .. 80 70
P 590. 1 e. green 70 30
P 591. 2 e. lilac 90 30
P 592. 3 e. olive .. .. 1·00 40
P 593. 4 e. blue .. .. 1·90 60
P 594. 5 e. lilac .. .. 2·75 60
P 595. 10 e. brown .. 6·00 1·60

P 2.

1936.

P 891. **P 2.** 50 c. grey 10 5
P 892. 1 e. brown 10 5
P 893. 1 e. 50 violet .. 10 5
P 894. 2 e. claret 30 5
P 895. 2 e. 50 olive .. 40 5
P 896. 4 e. 50 maroon .. 60 5
P 897. 5 e. violet 60 10
P 898. 10 e. orange .. 1·50 20

POSTAGE DUE STAMPS

D 1. Da Gama received by the Zamorin of Calicut. **D 2.**

1898.

D 386. D 1. 5 r. black .. .. 1·50 90
D 387. 10 r. mauve .. 2·00 1·10
D 388. 20 r. orange .. 3·00 1·50
D 389. 50 r. grey .. 5·50 2·50
D 390. 100 r. red .. 14·00 10·00
D 391. 200 r. brown .. 18·00 11·00

1904.

D 392. D 2. 5 r. brown .. 12 10
D 393. 10 r. orange .. 50 25
D 394. 20 r. mauve .. 1·60 80
D 395. 30 r. green .. 70 50
D 396. 40 r. lilac .. 80 50
D 397. 50 r. red .. 5·00 60
D 398. 100 r. blue .. 1·50 90

1911. Optd. **REPUBLICA.**

D 418. D 2. 5 r. brown .. 10 10
D 419. 10 r. orange .. 12 12
D 420. 20 r. mauve .. 12 12
D 421 30 r. green .. 12 12
D 422. 40 r. lilac .. 12 12
D 423. 50 r. red .. 50 40
D 424. 100 r. blue .. 65 55

1915. As Type D 2, but value in centavos.

D 491. D 2. ½ c. brown 5 5
D 498. 1 c. orange .. 5 5
D 493. 2 c. claret .. 5 5
D 499. 3 c. green .. 5 5
D 500. 4 c. lilac .. 5 5
D 501. 5 c. red .. 5 5
D 497. 10 c. blue .. 5 5

1921.

D 578. D 2. ½ c. green .. 5 5
D 579. 4 c. green .. 5 5
D 580. 8 c. green .. 5 5
D 581. 10 c. green .. 10 10
D 582. 12 c. green .. 5 5
D 583. 16 c. green .. 8 5
D 584. 20 c. green .. 10 5
D 585. 24 c. green .. 8 5
D 586. 32 c. green .. 8 5
D 587. 36 c. green .. 8 5
D 588. 40 c. green .. 12 10
D 589. 48 c. green .. 10 8
D 590. 50 c. green .. 12 8
D 591. 60 c. green .. 12 8
D 592. 72 c. green .. 10 8
D 593. 80 c. green .. 50 12
D 594. 1 e. 20 green .. 30 12

D 3. D 4.

1925. Great War Commemorative.

D 662. D 3. 20 c. brown .. 12 10

1925. De Pombal types optd. **MULTA.**

D 663. C 4. 30 c. blue 25 20
D 664. – 30 c. blue 25 20
D 665. C 5. 30 c. blue 25 20

1928. Olympic Games.

D 741. D 4. 30 c. black and red .. 1·50 1·50

D 5. D 6. D 7.

1932.

D 865. D 5. 5 c. buff 5 5
D 866. 10 c. blue 5 5
D 867. 20 c. pink 8 5
D 868. 30 c. blue 5 5
D 869. 40 c. green 5 5
D 870. 50 c. grey 5 5
D 871. 60 c. pink 5 5
D 872. 80 c. claret .. 70 10
D 873. 1 e. 20 green .. 45 30

1940.

D 912. D 6. 5 c. brown .. 5 5
D 913. 10 c. lilac .. 5 5
D 914. 20 c. red .. 5 5
D 925. 30 c. violet .. 5 5
D 916. 40 c. mauve .. 5 5
D 917. 50 c. blue .. 5 5
D 928. 60 c. green .. 5 5
D 929. 80 c. red .. 10 5
D 930. 1 e. brown .. 10 5
D 931. 2 e. mauve .. 20 5
D 922. 5 e. orange .. 40 12

1967.

D 1312. D 7. 10 c. brn., yell. & oran. 5 5
D 1313. 20 c. mar., yell. & ochre 5 5
D 1314. 30 c. brown, yellow and orange-yellow 5 5
D 1315. 40 c. mar., yell. & bistre 5 5
D 1316. 50 c. indigo, blue and light blue 5 5
D 1317. 60 c. olive, blue & turq. 5 5
D 1318. 80 c. indigo, blue and light blue 5 5
D 1319. 1 e. indigo, blue & ult. 5 5
D 1320. 2 e. olive, apple & grn. 8 5
D 1320a. 3 e. grey, grn. & yell. 12 5
D 1320b. 4 e. grey, grn. & yell. 15 5
D 1321. 5 e. choc., mve. & clar. 20 5
D 1321a. 9 e. slate, vio. & mve. 35 20
D 1321b. 10 e. slate, vio. & lilac 40 25
D 1321c. 20 e. brn., red & lilac 80 65

PORTUGUESE COLONIES 04

General Issues for the Portuguese possessions in Africa; Angola, Cape Verde Islands, Guinea, Lourenco Marques, Mozambique, Congo, St. Thomas and Prince Is. and Zambezia.

1898. Vasco da Gama issue of Portugal as Nos. 378/85, but inscr. " AFRICA ".

1. 2½ r. green 30 25
2. 5 r. red 30 25
3. 10 r. purple 30 25
4. 25 r. green 25 25
5. 50 r. blue 30 30
6. 75 r. brown .. .. .. 1·25 1·10
7. 100 r. brown .. .. .. 1·00 80
8. 150 r. yellow-brown .. 1·25 1·00

CHARITY TAX STAMP

C 1.

1919. Fiscal stamps optd. **TAXA DE GUERRA.**

C 1. C 1. 1 c. black and green .. 15 15
C 2. 5 c. green 15 15

POSTAGE DUE STAMPS

D 1.

1945. Value in black.

D 1. D 1. 10 c. claret 10 10
D 2. 20 c. purple 10 10
D 3. 30 c. blue 10 10
D 4. 40 c. brown 10 10
D 5. 50 c. lilac 10 10
D 6. 1 e. brown 12 12
D 7. 2 e. green 20 20
D 8. 3 e. red 40 35
D 9. 5 e. yellow 85 50

PORTUGUESE CONGO 01

The area known as Portuguese Congo, now called Cabinda, was the part of Angola north of the River Congo. It issued its own stamps from 1894 until 1920.

1894. " Figures " key-type inscr. " CONGO ".

8. R. 5 r. orange 30 20
9. 10 r. mauve 70 30
10. 15 r. brown .. .. 1·00 90
12. 20 r. lilac .. .. 1·00 80
13. 25 r. green 30 30
22. 50 r. blue .. .. 1·10 70
5. 75 r. red .. .. 1·60 1·40
6. 80 r. green .. .. 2·40 2·25
7. 100 r. brown on yellow .. 1·50 1·10
17. 150 r. red on rose .. 2·75 2·50
18. 200 r. blue on blue .. 2·75 2·50
19. 300 r. blue on brown .. 3·50 3·00

1898. " King Carlos " key-type inscr. " CONGO ".

24. S. 2½ r. grey 10 8
25. 5 r. orange 10 8
26. 10 r. green 15 12
27. 15 r. brown 15 40
66. 15 r. green 20 20
28. 20 r. lilac 35 25
29. 25 r. green 60 40
67. 25 r. red 35 20
30. 50 r. blue 75 60
68. 50 r. brown 90 55
69. 65 r. blue .. .. 2·25 2·00
31. 75 r. red .. .. 1·10 1·00
70. 75 r. purple .. .. 1·00 80
32. 80 r. mauve .. .. 1·10 1·00
33. 100 r. blue on blue .. 80 80
71. 115 r. brown on pink .. 1·75 1·60
72. 130 r. brown on yellow .. 1·75 1·60
34. 150 r. brown on yellow .. 1·25 1·10
35. 200 r. purple on pink .. 1·50 1·40
36. 300 r. blue on pink .. 1·25 1·10
73. 400 r. blue on yellow .. 2·50 2·10
37. 500 r. black on blue .. 3·00 2·75
38. 700 r. mauve on yellow .. 5·00 4·50

1902. Surch.

74. S. 50 r. on 65 r. blue .. 1·25 90
40. R. 65 r. on 15 r. brown .. 1·50 1·25
41. 65 r. on 20 r. lilac .. 1·50 1·25
44. 65 r. on 25 r. green .. 1·40 1·10
46. 65 r. on 300 r. blue on brn. 1·60 1·25
50. V. 115 r. on 2½ r. brown .. 1·40 1·25
47. R. 115 r. on 10 r. mauve .. 1·50 1·25
49. 115 r. on 50 r. blue .. 1·40 1·25
53. 130 r. on 5 r. orange .. 1·40 1·25
54. 130 r. on 75 r. red .. 1·40 1·25
57. 130 r. on 100 r. brown on yellow .. 1·40 1·25
58. 400 r. on 80 r. green .. 60 45
60. 400 r. on 150 r. red on rose 50 40
61. 400 r. on 200 r. blue on blue .. 50 40

1902. " King Carlos " key-type of Portuguese Congo optd. **PROVISORIO.**

62. S. 15 r. brown 50 40
63. 25 r. green 50 40
64. 50 r. blue 60 45
65. 75 r. red .. .. 1·00 70

1911. " King Carlos " key-type of Angola, optd. **REPUBLICA** and **CONGO** with bar (200 r. also surch.).

75. S. 2½ r. grey 25 20
76. 5 r. orange 35 35
77. 10 r. green 35 35
78. 15 r. green 45 40
79. 25 r. on 200 r. purple on pink 50 40

1911. " King Carlos " key-type of Portuguese Congo optd. **REPUBLICA.**

80. S. 2½ r. grey 8 5
81. 5 r. orange 12 10
82. 10 r. green 12 10
83. 15 r. green 12 10
84. 20 r. lilac 12 10
85. 25 r. red 12 10
86. 50 r. brown 12 10
87. 75 r. purple 15 12
88. 100 r. blue on blue .. 20 15
89. 115 r. brown on pink .. 25 20
90. 130 r. brown on yellow .. 25 20
143. 200 r. purple on pink .. 30 25
92. 400 r. blue on yellow .. 55 40
93. 500 r. black on blue .. 55 40
94. 700 r. mauve on yellow .. 70 50

1913. Surch. **REPUBLICA CONGO** and value on " Vasco da Gama " stamps of

(a) Portuguese Colonies.

95. ¼ c. on 2½ r. green .. 45 40
96. ½ c. on 5 r. red .. 45 40
97. 1 c. on 10 r. purple .. 45 40
98. 2½ c. on 25 r. green .. 45 40
99. 5 c. on 50 r. blue .. 45 40
100. 7½ c. on 75 r. brown .. 55 40
101. 10 c. on 100 r. brown .. 55 40
102. 15 c. on 150 r. yellow-brown 70 50

(b) Macao.

103. ¼ c. on ½ a. green .. 60 50
104. ½ c. on 1 a. red .. 60 50
105. 1 c. on 2 a. purple .. 60 50
106. 2½ c. on 4 a. green .. 60 50
107. 5 c. on 8 a. blue .. 60 50
108. 7½ c. on 12 a. brown .. 90 80
109. 10 c. on 16 a. brown .. 75 60
110. 15 c. on 24 a. yellow-brown 75 60

(c) Timor.

111. ¼ c. on ½ a. green .. 60 50
112. ½ c. on 1 a. red .. 60 50
113. 1 c. on 2 a. purple .. 60 50
114. 2½ c. on 4 a. green .. 60 50
115. 5 c. on 8 a. blue .. 60 50
116. 7½ c. on 12 a. brown .. 90 90
117. 10 c. on 16 a. brown .. 75 60
118. 15 c. on 24 a. yellow-brown 75 60

1914. " Ceres " key-type inscr. " CONGO ".

135. U. ¼ c. olive 15 8
120. ½ c. black 20 20
121. 1 c. green 80 50
122. 1½ c. brown 60 35
136. 2 c. red 15 8
124. 2½ c. violet 15 15
125. 5 c. blue 40 20
126. 7½ c. brown 50 35
127. 8 c. black 50 40
128. 10 c. brown 50 40
129. 15 c. claret 60 40
130. 20 c. green 60 40
131. 30 c. brown on green .. 70 50
132. 40 c. brown on rose .. 80 60
133. 50 c. orange on pink .. 80 70
134. 1 e. green on blue .. 1·10 90

1914. " King Carlos " key-type of Portuguese Congo optd. **PROVISORIO** and **REPUBLICA.**

146. S. 15 r. brown (No. 62) .. 15 10
147. 50 r. blue (No. 64) .. 15 10
140. 75 r. red (No. 65) .. 35 25

1914. Provisional stamps of 1902 optd. **REPUBLICA.**

148. S. 50 r. on 65 r. blue .. 15 12
150. V. 115 r. on 2½ r. brown .. 12 10
151. R. 115 r. on 10 r. mauve .. 12 10
154. 115 r. on 50 r. blue .. 12 10
156. 130 r. on 5 r. orange .. 15 12
157. 130 r. on 75 r. red .. 50 25
159 130 r. on 100 r. brown on yellow .. 20 12

NEWSPAPER STAMP

1894. " Newspaper " key-type inscr. " CONGO ".

N 24. V 2½ r. brown 30 25

PORTUGUESE GUINEA 04

A former Portuguese territory, W. coast of Africa, with adjacent islands. Used stamps of Cape Verde from 1877 until 1881. In Sept. 1974 the territory became independent and was renamed Guinea-Bissau.

1881. " Crown " key-type inscr. " CABO VERDE " and optd. **GUINE.**

19. P. 5 r. black .. .. 1·60 1·50
20. 10 r. yellow .. .. 30·00 23·00
31. 10 r. green .. .. 2·00 1·50
21. 20 r. olive .. .. 1·40 90
32. 20 r. red .. .. 2·00 1·50
13. 25 r. red 90 65
28. 25 r. lilac 85 45
23. 40 r. blue .. .. 40·00 32·00
29. 40 r. yellow 60 50
15. 50 r. green .. .. 40·00 30·00
30. 50 r. blue .. .. 1·60 85
16. 100 r. lilac .. .. 1·90 1·75
17. 200 r. orange .. .. 3·00 2·25
18. 300 r. brown .. .. 5·50 4·00

1886. As T 8 of Portugal but inscr. " GUINE PORTUGUEZA ".

35. 5 r. black 95 85
36. 10 r. green .. .. 1·75 1·25
37. 20 r. red .. .. 1·90 1·50
38. 25. r. mauve .. .. 1·90 1·60
46. 40 r. brown .. .. 2·10 1·75
40. 50 r. blue .. .. 2·50 1·60
47. 80 r. grey .. .. 3·50 2·75
48. 100 r. brown .. .. 3·75 2·75
43. 200 r. lilac .. .. 7·00 4·50
44. 300 r. orange .. .. 10·00 7·50

1893. " Figures " key-type inscr. " GUINE ".

50. R. 5 r. yellow 60 50
51. 10 r. mauve 60 55
52. 15 r. brown 75 60
53. 20 r. lilac 75 60
54. 25 r. green 75 60
55. 50 r. blue .. .. 1·25 80
57. 75 r. red .. .. 3·25 3·00
58. 80 r. green .. .. 3·25 3·00
59. 100 r. brown on buff .. 3·25 3·00
60. 150 r. red on rose .. 4·50 3·75
61. 200 r. blue on blue .. 4·50 3·75
62. 300 r. blue on brown .. 5·50 4·25

1898. " King Carlos " key-type inscr. " GUINE ".

65. S. 2½ r. grey 15 15
66. 5 r. orange 15 15
67. 10 r. green 15 15
68. 15 r. brown .. .. 1·10 55
114. 15 r. green 60 35
69. 20 r. lilac 50 30
70. 25 r. green 75 40
115. 25 r. red 35 30
71. 50 r. blue .. .. 1·10 50
116. 50 r. brown 85 70
117. 65 r. blue .. .. 2·75 2·10
72. 75 r. red .. .. 3·75 2·10
118. 75 r. purple .. .. 1·00 75
73. 80 r. mauve .. .. 1·40 90
74. 100 r. blue on blue .. 90 50
119. 115 r. brown on pink .. 2·50 1·90
120. 130 r. brown on yellow .. 2·50 1·90
75. 150 r. brown on yellow .. 2·40 1·50
76. 200 r. purple on pink .. 2·40 1·50
77. 300 r. blue on pink .. 1·90 1·25
121. 400 r. blue on yellow .. 2·50 2·10
78. 500 r. black on blue .. 3·50 2·10
79. 700 r. mauve on yellow .. 5·00 3·50

1902. Surch.

122. S. 50 r. on 65 r. blue .. 90 80
81. – 65 r. on 10 r. grn. (No. 36) 2·00 1·40
84. R. 65 r. on 10 r. mauve .. 1·75 1·40
85. 65 r. on 15 r. brown .. 1·75 1·40
82. – 65 r. on 20 r. red (No. 37) 2·00 1·40
86. R. 65 r. on 20 r. lilac .. 1·75 1·40
83. – 65 r. on 25 r. mve. (No. 38) 2·00 1·40
87. R. 65 r. on 50 r. blue .. 1·40 1·10
96. V. 115 r. on 2½ r. brown .. 1·90 1·40
93. R. 115 r. on 5 r. yellow .. 1·90 1·40
95. 115 r. on 25 r. green .. 1·75 1·50
89. – 115 r. on 40 r. brn. (No. 46) 1·75 1·25
91. – 115 r. on 50 r. blue (No. 40) 1·75 1·25
92. – 115 r. on 300 r. orange (No. 44) .. 2·00 1·75
98. – 130 r. on 80 r. grey (No. 47) 2·25 1·90
100. – 130 r. on 100 r. brown (No. 48) .. 2·25 1·90
102. R. 130 r. on 150 r. red on rose 1·90 1·50
103. 130 r. on 200 r. blue on blue 1·90 1·50
104. 130 r. on 300 r. bl. on brn. 1·90 1·50
105. – 400 r. on 5 r. blk. (No. 35) 9·50 8·00
107. R. 400 r. on 75 r. red 65 40
108. 400 r. on 80 r. green 65 40
109. 400 r. on 100 r. brn. on buff 65 40
106. 400 r. on 200 r. lilac (No. 43) .. .. 4·00 3·00

1902. " King Carlos " key-type of Portuguese Guinea optd. **PROVISORIO.**

110. S. 15 r. brown 60 50
111. 25 r. green 60 50
112. 50 r. blue 90 60
113. 75 r. red .. .. 1·90 1·75

1911. " King Carlos " key-type of Portuguese Guinea optd. **REPUBLICA.**

123. S. 2½ r. grey 25 20
124. 5 r. orange 25 20
125. 10 r. green 35 30
126. 15 r. green 35 30
127. 20 r. lilac 35 30
128. 25 r. red 35 30
129. 50 r. brown 30 25
130. 75 r. purple 30 25
131. 100 r. blue on blue .. 35 30
132. 115 r. brown on pink .. 35 30
133. 130 r. brown on yellow .. 35 30
134. 200 r. purple on pink .. 1·75 1·40
135. 400 r. blue on yellow .. 85 75
136. 500 r. black on blue .. 85 75
137. 700 r. mauve on yellow 1·25 1·00

1913. Surch. **REPUBLICA GUINE** and value on " Vasco da Gama " stamps of

(a) Portuguese Colonies.

138. ¼ c. on 2½ r. green .. 85 75
139. ½ c. on 5 r. red .. 85 75
140. 1 c. on 10 r. purple .. 85 75
141. 2½ c. on 25 r. green .. 85 75
142. 5 c. on 50 r. blue .. 85 75
143. 7½ c. on 75 r. brown .. 1·40 1·10
144. 10 c. on 100 r. brown .. 85 75
145. 15 c. on 150 r. yellow-brown 1·75 1·50

(b) Macao.
146. ¼ c. on ½ a. green .. .. 1·10 1·00
147. ½ c. on 1 a. red .. .. 1·10 1·00
148. 1 c. on 2 a. purple .. .. 1·10 1·00
149. 2½ c. on 4 a. green .. .. 1·10 1·00
150. 5 c. on 8 a. blue .. .. 1·10 1·00
151. 7½ c. on 12 a. brown .. .. 1·25 1·10
152. 10 c. on 16 a. brown .. .. 1·10 1·00
153. 15 c. on 24 a. yellow-brown 1·10 1·00

(c) Timor.
154. ¼ c. on ½ a. green .. .. 1·10 1·00
155. ½ c. on 1 a. red .. .. 1·10 1·00
156. 1 c. on 2 a. purple .. .. 1·10 1·00
157. 2½ c. on 4 a. green .. .. 1·10 1·00
158. 5 c. on 8 a. blue .. .. 1·10 1·00
159. 7½ c. on 12 a. brown .. .. 1·25 1·10
160. 10 c. on 16 a. brown .. 1·10 90
161. 15 c. on 24 a. yellow-brown 1·10 1·00

1913. "King Carlos" key-type of Portuguese Guinea optd. **PROVISORIO** and **REPUBLICA.**
184. S. 15 r. brown 25 20
185. 50 r. blue 25 20
164. 75 r. red .. .. 2·10 1·90

1914. "Ceres" key-type inscr. "GUINE".
208. U. ¼ c. olive 5 5
209. ½ c. black 5 5
210. 1 c. green 5 5
211. 1½ c. brown 8 5
212. 2 c. red 8 5
213. 2 c. grey 10 8
214. 2½ c. violet 5 5
215. 3 c. orange 8 5
216. 4 c. red 8 5
217. 4½ c. grey 8 5
218. 5 c. blue 5 5
219. 6 c. mauve 8 5
220. 7 c. blue 12 10
221. 7½ c. brown 10 8
222. 8 c. black 10 8
223. 10 c. brown 8 8
224. 12 c. green 25 15
225. 15 c. claret 20 5
226. 20 c. green 8 8
227. 24 c. blue 85 70
228. 25 c. brown 85 70
180. 30 c. brown on green .. 2·25 1·40
229. 30 c. green 20 12
181. 40 c. brown on rose .. 1·00 85
230. 40 c. blue 20 12
182. 50 c. orange on pink .. 1·10 90
231. 50 c. mauve 20 20
232. 60 c. blue 30 25
233. 60 c. red 50 35
234. 80 c. red 50 30
183. 1 e. green on blue .. 1·10 90
236. 1 e. pink 75 50
235. 1 e. blue 75 50
237. 2 e. purple 85 75
238. 5 e. brown .. .. 2·00 1·75
239. 10 e. pink .. .. 4·25 3·25
240. 20 e. green .. .. 8·50 6·50

1915. Provisional stamps of 1902 optd. **REPUBLICA.**
186. S. 50 r. on 65 r. blue .. 25 20
187. V. 115 r. on 2½ r. brown .. 60 35
190. R. 115 r. on 5 r. yellow .. 35 30
191. 115 r. on 25 r. green .. 35 30
192. – 115 r. on 40 r. brown (89) 35 30
194. – 115 r. on 50 r. bl. (No. 91) 35 30
196. – 130 r. on 80 r. grey (98) 1·10 90
197. – 130 r. on 100 r. brn. (100) 1·10 90
199. R. 130 r. on 150 r. red on rose 35 30
200. 130 r. on 200 r. bl. on bl. 35 30
201. 130 r. on 300 r. bl. on brn. 35 30

1920. Surch.
241. U. 4 c. on ½ c. olive .. 1·75 90
242. 6 c. on ½ c. black .. 1·10 90
243. S. 12 c. on 115 r. brown on pink (No. 132) .. 1·90 1·50

1925. Stamps of 1902 optd. **Republica** and surch.
244. R. 40 c. on 400 r. on 75 r. red 35 30
245. 40 c. on 400 r. on 80 r. grn. 35 30
246. 40 c. on 400 r. on 100 r. brown on buff .. 35 30

1931. "Ceres" key-type of Portuguese Guinea surch.
247. U. 50 c. on 60 c. red .. 60 50
248. 70 c. on 80 c. red .. 75 60
249. 1 e. 40 on 2 e. purpl .. 1·60 1·25

1933. As T 2 of Angola (new "Ceres" type). but inscr. "GUINE".
251. 1 c. brown 5 5
252. 5 c. sepia 5 5
253. 10 c. mauve 8 5
254. 15 c. black 8 5
255. 20 c. grey 8 8
256. 30 c. green 8 8
257. 40 c. red 12 8
258. 45 c. blue 30 12
259. 50 c. brown 30 20
260. 60 c. olive 30 20
261. 70 c. brown 40 25
262. 80 c. green 40 25
263. 85 c. red 60 50
264. 1 e. claret 50 35
265. 1 e. 40 blue 85 75
266. 2 e. mauve 75 35
267. 5 e. green .. .. 1·90 1·40
268. 10 e. bistre .. .. 3·00 2·25
269. 20 e. orange .. .. 9·00 6·50

1938. As T 3 and 8 of Angola but inscr. "GUINE".
270. 3. 1 c. olive (postage) .. 5 5
271. 5 c. brown 8 8
272. 10 c. red 8 8
273. 15 c. purple 12 10
274. 20 c. slate 25 20
275. – 30 c. purple 25 20
276. – 35 c. green 25 20
277. – 40 c. brown 25 20
278. – 50 c. mauve 25 20
279. – 60 c. black 25 20
280. – 70 c. violet 25 20
281. – 80 c. orange 35 25
282. – 1 e. red 35 25
283. – 1 e. 75 blue 50 35
284. – 2 e. red 90 50
285. – 5 e. olive .. .. 1·90 1·25
286. – 10 e. blue .. .. 3·00 1·40
287. – 20 e. brown .. .. 6·00 2·25
288. 8. 10 c. red (air) 40 35
289. 20 c. violet 40 35
290. 50 c. orange 50 40
291. 1 e. blue 55 40
292. 2 e. red .. .. 2·10 1·75
293. 3 e. green .. .. 1·10 90
294. 5 e. brown .. .. 1·75 1·10
295. 9 e. red .. .. 2·40 1·75
296. 10 e. mauve .. .. 2·50 1·25

3. Cacheu Castle.

4. Nuno Tristao.

1946. Discovery of Port. Guinea. 5th Cent. Inscr. as in T 3/4.
297. 3. 30 c. black 45 40
298. 4. 50 c. green 30 25
299. 50 c. purple 30 25
300. – 1 e. 75 blue .. .. 1·40 1·00
301. – 3 e. 50 red .. .. 2·25 1·40
302. – 5 e. brown .. .. 6·00 3·00
303. – 20 e. violet .. .. 8·50 5·50
DESIGNS—VERT. 1 e. 75, Pres. Grant. 3 e. 50, T. Pinto. 5 c. H. Barreto. HORIZ. 20 e. Church at Bissau.

5. Native Huts.

6. Native Youth.

1948.
304. 5. 5 c. brown 12 12
305. – 10 c. purple .. .. 1·50 85
306. 6. 20 c. magenta 40 35
307. – 35 c. green 40 35
308. – 50 c. red 15 12
309. – 70 c. blue 45 35
310. – 80 c. green 50 40
311. – 1 c. red 50 25
312. – 1 e. 75 blue .. .. 3·50 2·00
313. – 2 e. blue .. .. 6·00 75
314. 6. 3 c. 50 brown .. .. 1·60 1·00
315. – 5 e. slate .. .. 2·10 1·10
316. – 20 e. violet .. .. 5·50 2·75
DESIGNS: 10 c. Bird. 35 c., 5 e. Woman. 50 c. Musician. 70 c. Man. 80 c. 20 e. Girl. 1 c., 2 e. Drummer. 1 e. 75, Antelope.

1948. Statue of Our Lady of Fatima. As T 13 of Angola.
317. 50 c. olive .. .. 3·25 2·75

1949. U.P.U. 75th Anniv. As T 18 of Angola.
318. 2 e. orange .. .. 3·00 1·75

1950. Holy Year. As T 20/1 of Angola.
319. 1 e. claret .. .. 1·25 65
320. 3 e. green .. .. 1·75 1·00

1951. Holy Year. As T 23 of Angola.
321. 1 e. brown and buff .. 50 40

7. Doctor treating Patient.

8. Exhibition Entrance.

1952. 1st Tropical Medicine Congress, Lisbon.
322. 7. 50 c. chocolate and purple 25 20

1953. Missionary Art Exhibition.
323. 8. 10 c. lake and olive .. 5 5
324. 50 c. blue and ochre .. 35 20
325. 3 e black and salmon .. 50 35

9. "Analeptes Trifasciata".

10. Barreto's Statue at Bissau.

1953. Insects. Multicoloured.
326. 5 c. Type 9 .. .. 5 5
327. 10 c. "Callidea panaethiopica kirk" 5 5
328. 30 c. "Craspedophorus brevicollis" 8 8
329. 50 c. "Anthia nimrod" .. 10 5
330. 70 c. "Platypria luctuosa" 25 15
331. 1 e. "Acanthophorus maculatus" 25 20
332. 2 e. "Cordylomera nitidipennis" 75 20
333. 3 e. "Lycus latissimus" 1·25 40
334. 5 e. "Cicindeia Brunet" 1·60 60
335. 10 e. "Colluris dimidiata" 2·75 1·00

1953. Portuguese Stamp Cent. As T 27 of Angola.
336. 50 c. grey and yellow .. 65 50

1954. 4th Cent. of Sao Paulo. As T 28 of Angola.
337. 1 e. blk., mauve & lavender 5 5

1955. Presidential Visit. As T 8 of Cape Verde Is.
338. 1 e. multicoloured .. 5 5
339. 2 e. 50 multicoloured .. 25 10

1958. Brussels Int. Exn. As T 34 of Angola.
340. 2 e. 50 multicoloured .. 30 15

1958. 6th Int. Congress of Tropical Medicine As T 35 of Angola.
341. 5 e. grn., brn., red & ochre 1·25 60
DESIGN: 5 e. "Maytenus senegalensis" (plant).

1959. H. Barreto (statesman). Death Cent.
342. 10. 2 e. 50 olive-green, red, blue and brown .. 12 5

11. Compass.

12. "Medical Services" (village hospital).

1960. Prince Henry the Navigator. 500th Death Anniv.
343. 11. 2 e. 50 multicoloured .. 12 5

1960. African Technical Co-operation Commission. 10th Anniv.
344. 12. 1 e. 50 multicoloured .. 15 8

1962. Sports. As T 41 of Angola. Mult.
345. 50 c. Motor-racing .. 5 5
346. 1 e. Tennis 20 5
347. 1 e. 50 Putting the shot .. 8 8
348. 2 e. 50 Wrestling 12 8
349. 3 e. 50 Shooting 20 10
350. 15 e. Volley-ball 75 50

1962. Malaria Eradication. Mosquito design as T 42 of Angola. Multicoloured.
351. 2 e.50 "A. gambiae" .. 45 25

13. "Causus rhombeatus".

1963. Snakes. Multicoloured.
352. 20 c. "Naja nigricollis" .. 12 8
353. 35 c. "Pithon sebae" .. 12 10
354. 70 c. "Dispholidus typus" 35 25
355. 80 c. "Dendroaspis viridis" 35 25
356. 1 e. 50 "Grayia smythii" 50 10
357. 2 e. T 13 .. .. 25 8
358. 2 e. 50 "Philothamnus irregularis" 85 10
359. 3 e. 50 "Boaedon lineatus" 20 20
360. 4 e. "Lycophidium semicinctum" 20 20
361. 5 e. "Bitis lachesis" .. 25 25
362. 15 e. "Psammophis elegans" 75 85
363. 20 e. "Dasypeltis scaber" 1·00 85
The 2 e. and 20 e. are horiz., the rest vert.

1963. T.A.P. Airline. 10th Anniv. As T 48 of Angola.
364. 2 e. 50 multicoloured .. 30 12

1964. National Overseas Bank Centenary. As Angola T 50, but portrait of J. de A. Corvo.
365. 2 e. 50 multicoloured .. 35 12

1965. I.T.U. Cent. As T 52 of Angola.
366. 2 e. 50 multicoloured .. 1·00 50

14. Soldier, 1548.

1966. Portuguese Military Uniforms. Multicoloured.
367. 25 c. Type 14 .. .. 10 8
368. 40 c. Arquebusier, 1578 .. 12 8
369. 60 c. Arquebusier, 1640 .. 20 10
370. 1 e. Grenadier, 1721 .. 50 20
371. 2 e. 50 Captain of Fusiliers, 1740 .. .. 1·00 50
372. 4 e. 50 Infantryman, 1740 1·10 90
373. 7 e. 50 Sergeant-major, 1762 1·50 90
374. 10 e. Engineer's officer, 1806 1·25 70

1966. National Revolution. 40th Anniv. As T 56 of Angola, but showing different building. Multicoloured.
375. 2 e. 50 B.C. Lopes School and Bissau Hospital .. 12 5

1967. Military Naval Assn. Cent. As T 58 of Angola. Multicoloured.
376. 50 c. O. Muzanty and cruiser "Republica" .. 5 5
377. 1 e. A. de Cerqueira and destroyer "Guadiana" 20 8

1967. Fatima Apparitions. 50th Anniv. As T 80 of Angola.
378. 50 c. multicoloured .. 5 5
DESIGN: 50 c. Chapel of the Apparitions and Monument of the Holy Spirit.

1968. Visit of Pres. Tomás of Portugal. As T 15 of Cape Verde Islands.
396. 1 e. multicoloured 5 5

1968. Pedro Cabral (explorer). 500th Birth Anniv. As T 63 of Angola. Multicoloured.
397. 2 e. 50 Cabral's arms (vert.) 30 5

1969. Admiral Gago Coutinho. Birth Cent. As T 65 of Angola. Multicoloured.
409. 1 e. Admiral Countinho's astrolabe 5 5

1969. Vasco da Gama (explorer). 500th Birth Anniv. As T 66 of Angola. Multicoloured.
410. 2 e. 50 Arms of Vasco da Gama (vert.) 12 5

1969. Overseas Administrative Reforms. Cent. as T 67 of Angola.
411. 50 c. multicoloured .. 5 5

1969. Manuel I. 500th Birth Anniv. As T 68 of Angola. Multicoloured.
412. 2 e. Arms of Manoel I .. 10 5

15. Ulysses Grant and Square, Bolama.

16. Camoens.

1970. Arbitral Judgment on Sovereignty of Bolama. Cent.
413. 15. 2 e. 50 multicoloured .. 20 8

1970. Marshal Carmona. Birth Cent. As T 70 of Angola.
414. 1 e. 50 Portrait wearing cap and cloak 8 5

1972. Camoens' "The Lusiads" (epic poem). 400th Anniv.
422. 16. 50 c. multicoloured .. 5 5

17. Weightlifting and Hammer-throwing.

1972. Olympic Games, Munich.
423. 17. 2 e. 50 multicoloured .. 12 5

18. Seaplane "Lusitania" taking-off from Lisbon.

1972. 1st Flight, Lisbon-Rio de Janeiro. 50th Anniv.
424. 18. 1 e. multicoloured .. 5 5

1973. I.M.O./W.M.O. Centenary. As Type 77 of Angola.
425. 2 e. multicoloured 10 5

CHARITY TAX STAMPS

The notes under this heading in Portugal also apply here.

1919. Fiscal stamp as T 2 of Macao, optd. **REPUBLICA** and **TAXA DE GUERRA**.
C 241. 10 r. brn., buff & blk. 7·00 4·75

1925. Marquis de Pombal Commem. stamps of Portugal, but inscr. "GUINE".
C 247. C 4. 15 c. red 25 20
C 248. – 15 c. red 25 20
C 249. C 5. 15 c. red 25 20

C 1. C 3. C 4. C 2.

1934.
C 270. C 1. 50 c. brn. & grn. 2·00 1·60

1938.
C 299. C 2. 30 c. blk. & mar. 12 10
C 297. 50 c. yellow 1·75 1·50
C 298. 50 c. brn. & grn. 1·75 1·50
C 300. 50 c. blk. & yell. 60 35
C 301. 50 c. brn. & yell. 1·40 1·00
C 302. 2 e. 50 blk. & blue 12 10
C 303. 5 e. blk. & grn. 25 20
C 304. 10 e. blk. & blue 45 40

Nos. C 302/4 were used at several small post offices as ordinary postage stamps during a temporary shortage. Nos. C 297, 300/304 are smaller (20½ × 25 mm.).

1967. National Defence. No gum.
C 379. C 3. 50 c. red & blk. 60 15
C 380. 1 e. red, grn. & blk. 70 30
C 381. 5 e. red, grey & blk. 1·25 1·25
C 382. 10 e. red, bl. & blk. 3·75 3·75

1967. National Defence. No gum.
C 383. C 4. 50 c. verm., red & blk. 5 5
C 384. 1 e. verm., grn. & blk. 5 5
C 385. 5 e. verm., grey & blk. 30 30
C 386. 10 e. verm., bl. & blk. 60 60

C 5. Carved Statuette of Woman. C 8. Hands grasping Sword.

1967. Guinean Artifacts from Bissau Museum. Multicoloured.
C 387. 50 c. Type C 5 5 5
C 388. 1 e. "Tree of life" (carving) 10 10
C 389. 2 e. Cow-headed statuette 20 20
C 390. 2 e. 50 "The Magistrate" (statuette) 40 40
C 391. 5 e. "Kneeling Servant" (statuette) 35 35
C 392. 10 e. Stylized pelican (carving) 60 60

The 1 e. is horiz.

1968. No. C 389 but inscr. "TOCADOR DE BOMBOLON" surch.
C 394. 50 c. on 2 e. multicoloured 12 12
C 395. 1 e. on 2 e. multicoloured 12 12

1969. National Defence.
C 398. C 8. 50 c. multicoloured 5 5
C 399. 1 e. multicoloured 8 8
C 400. 2 e. multicoloured 12 12
C 401. 2 e. 50 multicoloured 20 20
C 402. 3 e. multicoloured 20 20
C 403. 4 e. multicoloured 25 25
C 404. 5 e. multicoloured 35 35
C 405. 8 e. multicoloured 40 40
C 406. 9 e. multicoloured 40 40
C 407. 10 e. multicoloured 50 50
C 408. 15 e. multicoloured 85 85

NOTE—30, 50 and 100 e. stamps in the same design were for fiscal use only.

C 9. Mother and Children.

1971.
C 415. C 9. 50 c. multicoloured 5 5
C 416. 1 e. multicoloured 5 5
C 417. 2 e. multicoloured 10 10
C 418. 3 e. multicoloured 15 15
C 419. 4 e. multicoloured 20 20
C 420. 5 e. multicoloured 25 25
C 421. 10 e. multicoloured 50 50

Higher values were intended for fiscal use.

NEWSPAPER STAMP

1893. "Newspaper" key-type inscr. "GUINE".
N 50. V. 2½ r. brown 30 25

POSTAGE DUE STAMPS

1904. "Due" key-type inscr. "GUINE".
D 122. W. 5 r. green 30 25
D 123. 10 r. grey 30 25
D 124. 20 r. brown 30 25
D 125. 30 r. orange 60 35
D 126. 50 r. brown 60 35
D 127. 60 r. brown 1·10 75
D 128. 100 r. mauve 1·10 75
D 129. 130 r. blue 1·10 75
D 130. 200 r. red 1·25 1·00
D 131. 500 r. lilac 3·00 2·10

1911. "Due" key-type of Portuguese Guinea optd. **REPUBLICA**.
D 138. W. 5 r. green 20 12
D 139. 10 r. grey 20 12
D 140. 20 r. brown 25 20
D 141. 30 r. orange 25 20
D 142. 50 r. brown 20 15
D 143. 60 r. brown 50 40
D 144. 100 r. mauve 75 50
D 145. 130 r. blue 60 30
D 146. 200 r. red 75 60
D 147. 500 r. lilac 50 35

1921. "Due" key-type of Portuguese Guinea. Currency changed.
D 244. W. ½ c. green 8 5
D 245. 1 c. grey 8 5
D 246. 2 c. brown 8 5
D 247. 3 c. orange 8 5
D 248. 5 c. brown 8 5
D 249. 6 c. brown 8 5
D 250. 10 c. mauve 10 8
D 251. 13 c. blue 10 8
D 252. 20 c. red 10 8
D 253. 50 c. grey 12 10

1925. Marquis de Pombal stamps, as Nos. C 247/9, optd. **MULTA**.
D 254. C 4. 30 c. red 25 20
D 255. – 30 c. red 25 20
D 256. C 5. 30 c. red 25 20

1952. As Type D 1 of Macao, but inscr. "GUINE PORTUGUESA". Numerals in red, name in black (except 2 e. in blue).
D 323. 10 c. green and pink 5 5
D 324. 30 c. violet and grey 5 5
D 325. 50 c. green and lemon 5 5
D 326. 1 e. blue and grey 5 5
D 327. 2 e. black and olive 10 5
D 328. 5 e. brown and orange 25 15

PORTUGUESE INDIA O4

Portuguese territories on the W. coast of India, consisting of Goa, Damao and Diu. Became part of India in December, 1961.

1871. 1,000 reis = 1 milreis.
1882. 12 reis = 1 tanga. 16 tangas = 1 rupia.
1959. 100 centavos = 1 escudo.

1. 2.

1871. Perf.
35. 1. 10 r. black 1·60 1·40
33a. 15 r. pink 3·25 2·75
26. 20 r. red 3·00 2·40
13. 40 r. blue 14·00 11·00
22. 100 r. green 18·00 16·00
23. 200 r. yellow 48·00 38·00
27. 300 r. purple 32·00 28·00
28. 600 r. purple 35·00 32·00
29. 900 r. purple 35·00 32·00

1877. Star above value. Perf. or imperf.
241. 2. 1½ r. black 50 45
242. 4½ r. olive 3·75 2·75
243. 6 r. green 3·75 1·75
48. 10 r. black 6·00 4·00
49. 15 r. red 7·00 5·00
50. 20 r. red 3·25 3·00
51. 40 r. blue 8·00 7·00
52. 100 r. green 16·00 14·00
53. 200 r. yellow 15·00 13·00
54. 300 r. purple 20·00 14·00
55. 600 r. purple 26·00 18·00
56. 900 r. purple 27·00 22·00

1877. "Crown" key-type inscr. "INDIA PORTUGUEZA". Perf.
57. P. 5 r. black 80 70
58. 10 r. yellow 1·60 1·10
74. 10 r. green 2·25 1·75
59. 20 r. olive 1·50 90
60. 25 r. red 2·50 2·25
79. 25 r. grey 4·75 3·00
80. 25 r. purple 5·00 4·50
69. 40 r. blue 6·50 5·50
81. 40 r. yellow 6·00 5·00
70. 50 r. green 6·00 5·00
77. P. 50 r. blue 7·00 6·00
63. 100 r. lilac 3·25 3·00
64. 200 r. orange 6·00 5·00
73. 300 r. brown 8·50 6·50

1881. Surch. in figures.
213. 1. 1½ on 10 r. black — 90·00
90. 1½ on 20 r. red 21·00 12·00
91. 2. 1½ on 20 r. red 45·00 32·00
219. 1. 4½ on 40 r. blue 5·00 5·00
223. 4½ on 100 r. green 6·50 6·50
96. 5 on 10 r. black 2·00 1·50
98. 2. 5 on 10 r. black 11·00 8·50
101. 1. 5 on 15 r. pink 40 40
106. 5 on 20 r. red 45 40
108. 2. 5 on 20 r. red 1·50 1·50
224. 1. 6 on 20 r. red
228. 6 on 100 r. green 48·00 40·00
230. 6 on 200 r. yellow — 35·00
233. 2. 6 on 200 r. yellow £120

1881. "Crown" key-type of Portuguese India surch. in figures.
109. P. 1½ on 5 r. black 20 20
110. 1½ on 10 r. green 40 35
111. 1½ on 20 r. olive 3·25 2·50
157. 1½ on 25 r. grey 11·00 10·00
113. 1½ on 100 r. lilac 11·00 9·50
114. 4½ on 5 r. black 1·60 1·50
115. 4½ on 10 r. green 60·00 60·00
116. 4½ on 20 r. olive 80 70
117. 4½ on 25 r. purple 4·00 3·75
118. 4½ on 100 r. lilac 15·00 13·00
119a. 6 on 10 r. yellow 13·00 10·00
120. 6 on 10 r. green 1·50 1·40
121. 6 on 20 r. olive 4·25 3·00
167. 6 on 25 r. grey 6·50 4·25
123. 6 on 25 r. purple 80 70
124. 6 on 40 r. blue 32·00 24·00
170. 6 on 40 r. yellow 5·00 4·00
171. 6 on 50 r. green 6·00 5·00
172. 6 on 50 r. blue 12·00 9·00
128. 1 t. on 10 r. green 50·00 45·00
129. 1 t. on 20 r. olive 15·00 13·00
130. 1 t. on 25 r. grey 11·00 7·00
176. 1 t. on 25 r. purple 1·90 1·60
132. 1 t. on 40 r. blue 3·50 2·40
133. 1 t. on 50 r. green 10·00 8·00
134. 1 t. on 50 r. blue 5·00 4·00
136. 1 t. on 100 r. lilac 2·50 2·00
137. 1 t. on 200 r. orange 9·00 8·00
139. 2 t. on 25 r. purple 4·00 3·50
182. 2 t. on 25 r. grey 5·00 3·75
184. 2 t. on 40 r. blue 9·50 8·50
185. 2 t. on 40 r. yellow 7·50 6·50
142. 2 t. on 50 r. green 5·00 5·00
187. 2 t. on 50 r. blue 24·00 22·00
144. 2 t. on 100 r. lilac 2·25 2·00
145. 2 t. on 200 r. orange 6·00 5·00
189. 2 t. on 300 r. brown 6·00 5·00
146. 4 t. on 10 r. green 3·00 2·75
191. 4 t. on 50 r. green 3·50 3·00
192. 4 t. on 200 r. orange 9·50 8·50
193. 8 t. on 20 r. olive 7·00 5·50
194. 8 t. on 25 r. red 65·00 55·00
151. 8 t. on 40 r. blue 15·00 10·00
196. 8 t. on 100 r. lilac 8·00 4·75
197. 8 t. on 200 r. orange 4·00 3·75
198. 8 t. on 300 r. brown 7·00 5·50

1881. "Crown" key-type of Portuguese India.
204II. P. 1½ r. black 10 5
205I. 4½ r. olive 12 5
206I. 6 r. green 12 5
207I. 1 t. red 12 5
208I. 2 t. blue 10 5
209I. 4 t. purple 60 45
210I. 8 t. orange 75 40

1886. "Embossed" key-type inscr. "INDIA PORTUGUEZA".
244. Q. 1½ r. black 60 30
245. 4½ r. olive 60 30
246. 6 r. green 60 30
247. 1 t. red 80 40
248. 2 t. blue 1·60 80
249. 4 t. lilac 1·60 80
250. 8 t. orange 1·60 80

1895. "Figures" key-type inscr. "INDIA".
271. R. 1½ r. black 40 25
259. 4½ r. orange 40 20
273. 6 r. green 50 20
274. 9 r. lilac 1·40 1·25
260. 1 t. blue 65 40
261. 2 t. red 55 30
262. 4 t. blue 70 40
270. 8 t. lilac 1·40 90

1898. Vasco da Gama stamps of Portugal T 18, etc., but inscr. "INDIA".
275. 1½ r. green 30 20
276. 4½ r. red 30 20
277. 6 r. purple 35 25
278. 9 r. green 45 30
279. 1 t. blue 60 45
280. 2 t. brown 70 60
281. 4 t. brown 80 65
282. 8 t. yellow-brown 1·25 85

1898. "King Carlos" key-type inscr. "INDIA".
323. S. 1 r. grey 8 5
283. 1½ r. orange 10 5
324. 1½ r. grey 12 8
325. 2 r. orange 10 5
326. 2½ r. brown 12 10
327. 3 r. blue 10 5
284. 4½ r. green 40 25
285. 6 r. brown 40 25
328. 6 r. green 12 8
286. 9 r. lilac 40 25
287. 1 t. green 40 25
329. 1 t. red 12 8
288. 2 t. blue 40 12
330. 2 t. brown 80 40
331. S. 2½ t. blue 1·90 1·40
289. 4 t. blue on blue 1·00 30
332. 5 t. brown on yellow 70 60
290. 8 t. purple on pink 80 60
291. 12 t. blue on pink 1·25 90
334. 12 t. green on pink 1·40 1·10
292. 1 rp. black on blue 1·60 1·25
335. 1 rp. blue on yellow 2·40 1·60
293. 2 rp. mauve on yellow 3·00 1·90
336. 2 rp. black on yellow 4·00 3·00

1900. No. 288 surch. **1½ Reis.**
295. S. 1½ r. on 2 t. blue 60 30

1902. Surch.
299. R. 1 r. on 6 r. green 15 12
298. Q. 1 r. on 2 t. blue 25 15
300. 2 r. on 4½ r. olive 15 12
301. R. 2 r. on 8 t. lilac 15 12
302. Q. 2½ r. on 6 r. green 15 12
303. R. 2½ r. on 9 r. lilac 15 12
305. 3 r. on 4½ r. orange 50 40
304. Q. 3 r. on 1 t. red 15 12
306. R. 3 r. on 1 t. blue 45 35
337. S. 2 t. on 2½ t. blue 60 50
307. Q. 2½ t. on 1½ r. black 55 45
312. R. 2½ t. on 1½ r. black 60 25
309. Q. 2½ t. on 4 t. lilac 65 45
315. R. 5 t. on 2 t. red 50 30
317. 5 t. on 4 t. blue 50 30
314. Q. 5 t. on 8 t. orange 35 25

1902. Optd. **PROVISORIO.**
319. S. 6 r. brown (No. 285) 40 20
320. 1 t. green (No. 287) 40 20
321. 2 t. blue (No. 288) 40 20

1911. "King Carlos" key-type of Portuguese India. optd. **REPUBLICA.**
338. S. 1 r. grey 5 5
339. 1½ r. grey 8 5
340. 2 r. orange 8 5
341. 2½ r. brown 12 5
342. 3 r. blue 12 5
343. 4½ r. green 15 12
344. 6 r. green 10 5
345. 9 r. lilac 12 5
346. 1 t. red 15 10
347. 2 t. brown 15 10
348. 4 t. blue on blue 40 30
349. 5 t. brown on yellow 50 40
350. 8 t. purple on pink 1·25 90
351. 12 t. green on rose 1·25 90
352. 1 rp. blue on yellow 1·75 1·50
353. 2 rp. black on yellow 2·40 1·75
404. 2 rp. mauve on yellow 3·25 2·75

Both unused and used prices for the following three issues (Nos. 371 to 386) are for entire stamps showing both halves.

1911. "King Carlos" key-type of Portuguese India bisected by perforation, and each half surch.
371. S. 1 r. on 2 r. orange 10 8
372. 1 r. on 1 t. red 10 8
378. 1 r. on 5 t. brown on yell. 80 70
374. 1½ r. on 2½ r. brown 35 25
354. 1½ r. on 4½ r. green 2·00 1·50
355. 1½ r. on 9 r. lilac 20 15
356. 1½ r. on 4 t. blue on blue 20 15
375. 2 r. on 2½ r. brown 15 10
357. 2 r. on 4 t. blue on blue 25 20
376. 3 r. on 2½ r. brown 15 10
377. 3 r. on 2 t. brown 20 12
358. 6 r. on 4½ r. green 25 20
359d. 6 r. on 9 r. lilac 20 15
379. 6 r. on 8 t. purple on pink 40 25

1912. Stamps of 1902 bisected by perf., and each half surch.
360. S. 1 r. on 5 t. on 2 t. red 3·00 2·50
361. 1 r. on 5 t. on 4 t. blue 2·25 1·75
363. Q. 1 r. on 5 t. on 8 t. orange 1·00 70
364. 2 r. on 2½ r. on 6 r. green 1·00 70
365. R. 2 r. on 2½ r. on 9 r. lilac 3·50 3·00
366. 3 r. on 5 t. on 2 t. red 2·40 1·75
367. 3 r. on 5 t. on 4 t. blue 2·50 1·75
370. Q. 3 r. on 5 t. on 8 t. orange 1·00 70

1912. "King Carlos" key-type of Portuguese India, optd **REPUBLICA**, bisected by perf., and each half surch.
380. S. 1 r. on 1 r. grey 10 8
381. 1 r. on 2 r. orange 10 8
382. 1 r. on 1 t. red 15 12
383. 1 r. on 5 t. brown on yell. 15 15
384. 1½ r. on 4½ r. green 20 15
385. 3 r. on 2 t. brown 3·00 2·50
386. 6 r. on 9 r. lilac 20 20

1913. Nos. 275/82 optd. **REPUBLICA.**
389. 1½ r. green 15 12
390. 4½ r. red 15 12
391. 6 r. purple 20 20
392. 9 r. green 20 15
393. 1 t. blue 20 20
394. 2 t. brown 50 40
395. 4 t. brown 40 20
396. 8 t. yellow-brown 55 35

1914. Stamps of 1902 optd. **REPUBLICA.**
406. R. 2 r. on 8 t. lilac 1·60 1·40
407. Q. 2½ r. on 6 r. green 25 20
459. S. 2 t. on 2½ t. blue 30 25
408. R. 5 t. on 2 t. red 1·25 1·00
409. 5 t. on 4 t. blue 1·10 1·00
460. Q. 5 t. on 8 t. orange 50 40

1914. Nos. 320/1 optd. **REPUBLICA.**
415. S. 1 t. green 2·25 1·50
458. 2 t. blue 20 20

1914. "King Carlos" key-type of Portuguese India optd. **REPUBLICA** and surch.
423. S. 1½ r. on 4½ r. green 15 12
424. 1½ r. on 9 r. lilac 20 15
425. 1½ r. on 12 t. grn. on pink 20 15
426. 3 r. on 1 t. red 15 12
427. 3 r. on 2 t. brown 90 80
428. 3 r. on 8 t. purple on pink 70 60
429. 3 r. on 1 rp. blue on yellow 15 12
430. 3 r. on 2 rp. blk. on yellow 30 25

1914. Nos. 390 and 392/6 surch.
433. 1½ on 4½ r. red 15 12
434. 1½ r. on 9 r. green 20 15
435. 3 r. on 1 t. blue 15 12
436. 3 r. on 2 t. brown 30 20
437. 3 r. on 4 t. brown 12 10
438. 3 r. on 8 t. yellow-brown 60 40

1914. Bisected provisional stamps of 1912 optd. **REPUBLICA.**
417. S. 1 r. on 2 r. (No. 371) 1·50 1·25
418. 1½ r. on 4½ r. (No. 354) 1·50 1·25
419. 3 r. on 2 t. (No. 377) 1·00 90
420. 6 r. on 4½ r. (No. 358) 30 25
421. 6 r. on 9 r. (No. 359) 55 45
422. 6 r. on 8 t. (No. 379) 55 45
Prices for the above issue are for entire stamps showing both halves.

1914. "Ceres" key-type inscr. "INDIA".
461. U. 1 r. olive 5 5
471. 1½ r. green 5 5
441. 2 r. black 12 5
464. 2½ r. green 8 5
465. 3 r. lilac 5 5
474. 4 r. blue 35 20
444. 4½ r. brown 15 10
445. 5 r. green 15 10
477. 6 r. brown 5 5
447. 9 r. blue 20 12
448. 10 r. red 15 12
468. 1 t. violet 8 5
481. 1½ t. green 30 20
469. 2 t. blue 20 5
483. 2½ t. blue 20 12
451. 3 t. brown 25 12
484. 3 t. 4 brown 1·00 70
485. 4 t. grey 40 10
453. 8 t. claret 1·60 1·40
454. 12 t. brown on green 1·40 1·10
455. 1 rup. brown on rose 6·00 3·75
487. 1 rup. brown 1·60 1·60
456. 2 rup. orange on pink 4·00 3·25
488. 2 rup. yellow 2·40 1·60
457. 3 rup. green on blue 4·25 3·25
489. 3 rup. green 4·00 2·50
490. 5 rup. red 5·50 4·50

1922. "Ceres" key-type of Portuguese India surch. with new value.
496. U. 1½ r. on 8 t. claret 25 12
492. 1½ r. on 2 r. black 12 10
497. 2½ t. on 3 t. 4 brown 2·10 1·60

3. Vasco da Gama and "San Gabriel".

1925. Vasco da Gama. 4th Cent.
493. **3.** 6 r. brown 80 70
494. 1 t. purple 1·00 80

4. Signature of St. Francis. **6.** "Portugal" and "San Gabriel".

1931. St. Francis Xavier Exhibition. Inscr. as in T **4.**
498. – 1 r. green 30 25
499. **4.** 2 r. brown 30 25
500. – 6 r. purple 40 40
501. – 1½ t. brown 1·50 1·10
502. – 2 t. blue 2·40 1·75
503. – 2½ t. red 2·75 2·00
DESIGNS—VERT. 1 r. Monument to St. Francis. 6 r. St. Francis. 1½ t. St. Francis and Cross. 2½ t. St. Francis' Tomb. HORIZ. 2 t. Bom Jesus Church, Goa.

1933.
504. **6.** 1 r. brown 5 5
505. 2 r. sepia 5 5
506. 4 r. mauve 5 5
507. 6 r. green 5 5
508 8 r. black 8 5
509. 1 t. grey 8 5
510. 1½ t. red 10 5
511. 2 t. brown 12 5
512. 2½ t. blue 20 8
513. 3 t. blue 25 10
514. 5 t. orange 25 10
515. 1 rp. olive 1·10 40
516. 2 rp. red 2·00 1·00
517. 3 rp. orange 3·00 1·50
518. 5 rp. green 5·00 2·50

1938. As T 3 and 8 of Angola, but inscr. "ESTADO DA INDIA".
519. **3.** 1 r. olive (postage) 5 5
520. 2 r. brown 5 5
521. 3 r. violet 8 5
522. 6 r. green 8 5
523. – 10 r. red 15 10
524. – 1 t. mauve 15 10
525. – 1½ t. red 15 12
526. – 2 t. orange 15 12
527. – 2½ t. blue 15 12
528. – 3 t. slate 20 12
529. – 5 t. purple 25 12
530. – 1 rp. red 1·10 25
531. – 2 rp. olive 2·00 80
532. – 3 rp. blue 3·00 1·75
533. – 5 rp. brown 4·50 2·25

534. **8.** 1 t. red (air) 35 20
535. 2½ t. violet 50 20
536. 3½ t. orange 50 20
537. 4½ t. blue 50 20
538. 7 t. red 60 25
539. 7½ t. green 60 25
540. 9 t. brown 90 40
541. 11 t. mauve 90 40

1942. Surch.
549. **6.** 1 r. on 8 r. black 30 20
546. 1 r. on 5 t. orange 35 25
550. 2 r. on 8 r. black 20 15
547. 3 r. on 1½ t. red 30 25
551. 3 r. on 2 t. brown 30 25
552. 3 r. on 3 rp. orange 60 50
553. 6 r. on 2½ t. blue 65 50
554. 6 r. on 3 t. blue 65 50
542. 1 t. on 1½ t. red 80 70
548. 1 t. on 2 t. brown 60 50
543. 1 t. on 1 rp. olive 80 70
544. 1 t. on 2 rp. red 80 70
545. 1 t. on 5 rp. green 80 70

7. St. Francis Xavier. **8.** D. Joao de Castro. **9.** Our Lady of Fatima.

1946. Portraits and view.
555. **7.** 1 r. black 15 12
556. – 2 r. claret 15 12
557. – 6 r. bistre 15 12
558. – 7 r. violet 70 35
559. – 9 r. brown 70 35
560. – 1 t. green 40 25
561. – 3½ t. blue 50 35
562. – 1 rp. brown 1·10 50
DESIGNS: 2 r. Luis de Camoens. 6 r. Garcia de Orta. 7 r. Beato Joao Brito. 9 r. Viceregal Archway. 1 t. Afonso de Albuquerque. 3½ t. Vasco da Gama. 1 rp. D. Francisco de Almeida.

1948. Portraits.
564. **8.** 3 r. blue 30 20
565. – 1 t. green 30 20
566. – 1½ t. violet 70 50
567. – 2½ t. red 70 50
568. – 7½ t. brown 90 60
PORTRAITS: 1 t. St. Francis Xavier. 1½ t. P. Jose Vaz. 2½ t. D. Luis d'Ataide. 7½ t. Duarte Pacheco Pereira.

1948. Statue of Our Lady of Fatima. As T **13** of Angola.
570. 1 t. green 1·60 1·50

1949. Statue of Our Lady of Fatima.
571. **9.** 1 r. blue 45 35
572. 3 r. yellow 45 35
573. 9 r. pink 90 60
574. 2 t. green 1·60 70
575. 9 t. orange 1·90 80
576. 2 rp. brown 2·50 1·10
577. 5 rp. olive and black 4·50 2·50
578. 8 rp. violet and blue 11·00 4·50

1949. U.P.U. 75th Anniv. As T **7** of Macao.
579. 2½ t. red 1·10 1·00

1950. Holy Year. As T **20/1** of Angola.
580. **20.** 1 r. bistre 20 10
588. 1 r. red 8 5
589. 2 r. green 10 8
590. **21.** 3 r. chocolate 10 8
591. **20.** 6 r. grey 12 10
592. **21.** 9 r. pink 12 10
593. **20.** 1 t. blue 12 10
581. **21.** 2 t. olive 30 15
594. 2 t. yellow 12 8
595. **20.** 4 t. brown 15 8

1950. Nos. 523 and 527 surch.
582. 1 real on 10 r. red 12 10
583. 1 real on 2½ t. blue 8 8
584. 2 reis on 10 r. red 12 10
585. 3 reis on 2½ t. blue 8 8
586. 6 reis on 2½ t. blue 8 8
587. 1 tanga on 2½ t. blue 8 8

1951. Holy Year. As T **23** of Angola.
596. 1 rp. blue and lavender 50 25

10. Father Jose Vaz. **11.** Goa Medical School.

1951. Jose Vaz. 300th Birth Anniv.
597. **10.** 1 r. grey 5 5
598. – 2 r. orange and brown 5 5
599. **10.** 3 r. black 12 5
600. – 1 t. blue and indigo 5 5
601. **10.** 2 t. claret 5 5
602. – 3 t. olive and black 5 5
603. **10.** 9 t. blue and indigo 20 8
604. – 10 t. mauve 20 5
605. – 12 t. sepia and black 30 12
DESIGNS—Inscr. "1651 1951": 2 r., 1 t., 3 t., 10 t. Sancoale Church Ruins. 12 t. Veneravel Altar.

1952. 1st Tropical Medicine Congress, Lisbon.
606. **11.** 4½ t. blue and black 70 30

1952. St. Francis Xavier. 4th Death Cent. As Nos. 452/4 of Macao but without lined background.
607. 6 r. blk., red, yell., gold & bl. 12 5
608. 2 t. blk., red, bl., gold & yell. 20 12
609. 5 t. olive, silver and magenta 70 25

12. Stamp of 1871. **13.** St. Francis Xavier. **14.** Virgin.

1952. Philatelic Exn., Goa.
612. **12.** 3 t. black
613. **13.** 5 t. black and lilac
Strip of 3 containing label 4·00 4·00
Nos. 612/13 were printed together in sheets comprising two rows of stamps (one row of each value), *tete-beche*, separated by a row of square, grey labels, inscr. "GOA—1952", etc.

1953. Missionary Art Exn.
614. **14.** 6 r. black and blue 8 5
615. 1 t. brown and buff 8 5
616. 3 t. lilac and olive 30 20

1953. Portuguese Postage Stamp Cent. As T **27** of Angola.
617. 1 t. blue and green 30 25

15. Dr. Gama Pinto. **16.** Academy Buildings.

1954. Dr. Gama Pinto. Birth Cent.
618. **15.** 3 r. sage-green and grey 5 5
619. 2 t. black and indigo 8 5

1954. Sao Paulo. 4th Cent. As T **28** of Angola.
620. 2 t. blk., bl. & light blue 8 5

1954. Afonso de Albuquerque National Academy. Cent.
621. **16.** 9 t. blk., red, grn. & blue 20 12

17. Mgr. Dalgado.

18. M. A. de Sousa.

20. Map of Becaim. **19.** F. de Almeida.

1955. Mgr. Dalgado. Birth Cent.
622. **17.** 1 r. magenta, black, grey green and red 8 5
623 1 t. magenta, black, pink, green and maroon 15 5

1956. Portuguese Settlements in India. 450th Anniv. Multicoloured vert. designs.
(a) Famous Men. As T **18.**
624. 6 r. M. A. de Sousa 5 5
625. 1½ t. F. N. Xavier 5 5
626. 4 t. A. V. Lourenco 8 5
627. 8 t. Father Jose Vaz 15 10
628. 9 t. M. G. de Heredia 20 12
629. 2 rp. A. C. Pacheco 60 30
(b) Viceroys. As T **19.**
630. 3 r. F. de Almeida 8 5
631. 9 r. A. de Albuquerque 12 8
632. 1 t. Vasco da Gama 12 8
633. 3 t. N. de Cunha 5 5
634. 10 t. J. de Castro 15 12
635. 3 rp. C. de Braganca 90 40
(c) Settlements. As T **20.**
636. 2 t. Bacaim 40 12
637. 2½ t. Mombaim 12 5
638. 3½ t. Damao 30 15
639. 5 t. Diu 10 5
640. 12 t. Cochim 25 15
641. 1 rp. Goa 40 25

21. Map of Damao. Dadra and Nagar Aveli Districts. **22.** Arms of Vasco da Gama.

1957. Centres multicoloured.
642. **21.** 3 r. grey 5 5
643. 6 r. green 5 5
644. 3 t. pink 5 5
645. 6 t. blue 10 10
646. 11 t. bistre 20 15
647. 2 rp. lilac 60 35
648. 3 rp. yellow 90 70
649. 5 rp. claret 1·10 1·00

1958. Heraldic Arms of Famous Men. Multicoloured designs.
650. 2 r. Type **22** 5 5
651. 6 r. Lopo Soares de Albergaria 5 5
652. 9 r. D. Francisco de Almeida 5 5
653. 1 t. Garcia de Noronha 5 5
654. 4 t. D. Afonso de Albuquerque 12 5
655. 5 t. D. Joao de Castro 12 8
656. 11 t. D. Luis de Ataide 20 12
657. 1 rp. Nuno da Cunha 30 20

1958. 6th Int. Congress of Tropical Medicine. As T **35** of Angola.
658. 5 t. grn., red, sepia & grey 30 20
DESIGN: 5 t. "Holarrhena antidysenterica" (plant).

1958. Brussels Int. Exn. As T **16** of Macao.
659. 1 rp. multicoloured 30 25

1959. Surch. in new currency.
60. – 5 c. on 2 r. (No. 650) 5 5
661. **21.** 10 c. on 3 r. grey 5 5
662. – 15 c. on 6 r. (No. 651) 5 5
663. – 20 c. on 9 r. (No. 652) 5 5
664. – 30 c. on 1 t. (No. 653) 5 5
681. – 40 c. on 1½ t. (No. 566) 5 5
682. – 40 c. on 1½ t. (No. 625) 5 5
683. – 40 c. on 2 t. (No. 620) 20 10
665. – 40 c. on 2 t. (No. 636) 8 5
666. – 40 c. on 2½ t. (No. 637) 20 10
667. – 40 c. on 3½ t. (No. 638) 10 5
668. **21.** 50 c. on 3 t. pink 8 5
684. **14.** 80 c. on 3 t. lilac & olive 8 5
669. – 80 c. on 3 t. (No. 633) 10 8
685. – 80 c. on 3½ t. (No. 561) 5 5
686. – 80 c. on 5 t. (No. 658) 5 5
670. – 80 c. on 10 t. (No. 634) 20 12
687. – 80 c. on 1 rp. (No. 659) 30 20
671. – 80 c. on 3 rp. (No. 635) 30 20
672. – 1 e. on 4 t. (No. 654) 5 5
673. – 1 e. 50 on 5 t. (No. 655) 8 5
674. **21.** 2 e. on 6 t. blue 8 5
675. – 2 e. 50 on 11 t. bistre 10 5
676. – 4 e. on 11 t. (No. 656) 15 10
677. – 4 e. 50 on 1 rp. (No. 657) 20 12
678. **21.** 5 e. on 2 rp. lilac 20 15
679. 10 e. on 3 rp. yellow 40 30
680. 30 e. on 5 rp. claret 1·25 50

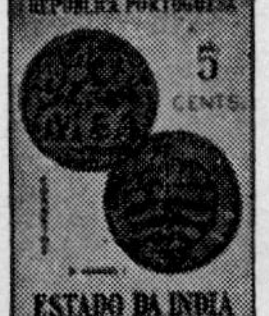

23. Coins of Manoel I. **24.** Prince Henry's Arms.

1959. Portuguese Indian Coins. As T 23 showing both sides of each coin. "CORREOS" and value in red; country name, etc., and frame in black. Colours of coin and background given.

688. 5 c. gold and blue .. 5 5
689. 10 c. gold and brown .. 5 5
690. 15 c. silver and green .. 5 5
691. 30 c. silver and salmon .. 5 5
692. 40 c. silver and yellow .. 5 5
693. 50 c. silver and lilac .. 5 5
694. 60 c. silver and green .. 5 5
695. 80 c. silver and blue .. 5 5
696. 1 e. silver-grey and orange 5 5
697. 1 e. 50 silver and blue .. 5 5
698. 2 e. gold and turquoise .. 8 5
699. 2 e. 50 gold and stone .. 10 5
700. 3 e. silver and yellow .. 12 8
701. 4 e. silver and pink .. 15 8
702. 4 e. 40 pink, black & yellow 15 12
703. 5 e. silver and lavender .. 20 15
704. 10 e. silver and yellow .. 40 20
705. 20 e. silver and buff .. 80 50
706. 30 e. pink, black & emerald 1·25 90
707. 50 e. silver and grey .. 2·00 1·75

COINS (of various rulers): 10 c. Joao III. 15 c. Sebastiao. 30 c. Felipe I. 40 c. Felipe II. 50 c. Felipe III. 60 c. Joao IV. 80 c. Afonso VI. 1 e. Pedro II. 1 e. 50, Joao V. 2 e. Jose I. 2 e. 50, Maria I. 3 e. Prince Regent Joao. 4 e. Pedro IV. 4 e. 40, Miguel. 5 e. Maria II. 10 e. Pedro V. 20 e. Luis I. 30 e. Carlos I. 50 e. Republic.

1960. Prince Henry the Navigator. 500th Death Anniv.

708. 24. 3 e. multicoloured .. 12 10

The 1962 sports set and malaria eradication stamp similar to those for the other territories were ready for issue when Portuguese India was occupied but they were not put on sale there.

CHARITY TAX STAMPS

The notes under this heading in Portugal also apply here.

1919. Fiscal stamp. Type C 1 of Portuguese Africa optd. **TAXA DE GUERRA.**

C 491. Rps. 0:00:05, 48 green .. 12 10
C 492. Rps. 0:02:03, 43 green .. 35 25

1925. Marquis de Pombal Commem. stamps of Portugal, but inscr. "INDIA".

C 495. C 4. 6 r. red 12 12
C 496. – 6 r. red 12 12
C 497. C 5. 6 r. red 12 12

C 1. Mother and Child. C 2. Mother and Child.

1948. (a) Inscr. "ASSISTENCIA PUBLICA".

C 571. C 1. 6 r. apple 50 30
C 572. 6 r. yellow 35 25
C 573. 1 t. red 50 30
C 574. 1 t. orange 50 35
C 575. 1 t. green 60 40

(b) Inscr. "PROVEDORIA DE ASSISTENCIA PUBLICA".

C 607. C 1. 1 t. grey 60 40

1951. Surch. **1 tanga.**

C 606. C 1. 1 t. on 6 r. red .. 35 20

1953. Optd. **"Revalidado" P.A.P.** and dotted line.

C 617. C 1. 1 t. red .. .. 1·00 70

1953. Surch. as in Type C 2.

C 624. C 2. 1 t. on 4 t. blue .. 2·00 1·60

C 3. Mother and Child. C 4. Arms and Needy People.

1956.

C 625. C 3. 1 t. black, green & red 25 20
C 626. 1 t. blue, salmon & grn. 30 20

1957. Surch.

C 650. C 3. 6 r. on 1 t. black, green and red 30 20

1959. Surch.

C 688. C 3. 20 c. on 1 t. blue, salmon and green 15 15
C 689. 40 c. on 1 t. blue, salmon and green 15 15

1960.

C 709. C 4. 20 c. brown and red 12 10

POSTAGE DUE STAMPS

1904. "Due" key-type inscr. "INDIA".

D 337. W. 2 r. green 5 5
D 338. 3 r. green 8 5
D 339. 4 r. orange 8 5
D 340. 5 r. black 8 5
D 341. 6 r. grey 10 8
D 342. 9 r. brown 12 10
D 343. 1 t. orange 12 10
D 344. 2 t. brown 30 20
D 345. 5 t. blue 40 30
D 346. 10 t. red 60 40
D 347. 1 rp. lilac .. .. 1·25 90

1911. Nos. D 337/47 optd. **REPUBLICA.**

D 354. W. 2 r. green 5 5
D 355. 3 r. green 5 5
D 356. 4 r. orange 5 5
D 357. 5 r. black 5 5
D 358. 6 r. grey 5 5
D 359. 9 r. brown 10 5
D 360. 1 t. orange 12 5
D 361. 2 t. brown 15 12
D 362. 5 t. blue 25 15
D 363. 10 t. red 50 40
D 364. 1 rp. lilac 85 60

1925. Marquis de Pombal stamps, as Nos. C 495/7, optd. **MULTA.**

D 495. C 4. 1 t. red 12 12
D 496. – 1 t. red 12 12
D 497. C 5. 1 t. red 12 12

1943. Stamps of 1933 surch. **Porteado** and new value.

D 549. 6. 3 r. on 2½ t. blue .. 25 20
D 550. 6 r. on 3 t. blue .. 35 25
D 551. 1 t. on 5 t. orange .. 70 50

1945. As Type D 1 of Portuguese Colonies, but optd. **ESTADO DA INDIA.**

D 555. 2 r. red 10 8
D 556. 3 r. blue 10 8
D 557. 4 r. yellow 10 8
D 558. 6 r. green 10 8
D 559. 1 t. brown 10 8
D 560. 2 t. brown 10 8

1951. Surch. **Porteado** and new value and bar.

D 588. 2 rs. on 7 r. (No. 558) .. 12 10
D 589. 3 rs. on 7 r. (No. 558) .. 12 10
D 590. 1 t. on 1 rp. (No. 562) .. 12 10
D 591. 2 t. on 1 rp. (No. 562) .. 12 10

1952. As Type D 1 of Macao, but inscr. "INDIA PORTUGUESA". Numerals in red, name in black.

D 606. 2 r. olive and brown .. 5 5
D 607. 3 r. black and green .. 5 5
D 608. 6 r. blue and turquoise 5 5
D 609. 1 t. red and grey .. 5 5
D 610. 2 t. orange, green & grey 5 5
D 611. 10 t. blue, grn. & yellow 70 50

1959. Nos. D 606/8 and D 610/11 surch. in new currency.

D 688. 5 c. on 2 r. olive & brown 8 8
D 689. 10 c. on 3 r. blk. & grn. 8 8
D 690. 15 c. on 6 r. blue & turq. 12 12
D 691. 60 c. on 2 t. orge, green and grey .. 50 50
D 692. 60 c. on 10 t. blue, green and yellow 90 90

PRINCE EDWARD ISLAND BC

An island off the E. coast of Canada, now a province of that Dominion, whose stamps it uses. Currency: as Canada.

1. 2.

1861. Queen's portrait in various frames. Values in pence.

9. 1. 1 d. orange .. .. 4·50 6·00
28. 2d. red .. .. .. 3·00 4·00
30. 3d. blue .. .. .. 3·00 4·50
31. 4d. black .. .. .. 1·75 14·00
18. 6d. green .. .. .. 9·00 9·00
20. 9d. mauve .. .. .. 8·00 8·00

1870.

32. 2. 4½d. (3d. stg.) brown .. 7·00 14·00

3.

ILLUSTRATIONS British Commonwealth and all overprints and surcharges are FULL SIZE. Foreign Countries have been reduced to ¾-LINEAR.

1872. Queen's portrait in various frames. Values in cents.

44. 3. 1 c. orange .. .. 85 3·25
38. 2 c. blue .. .. .. 1·25 9·00
37. 3 c. red .. .. .. 1·75 3·50
39. 4 c. green .. .. .. 70 7·00
41. 6 c. black .. .. .. 80 4·50
42. 12 c. mauve .. .. 85 11·00

PRUSSIA E2

Formerly a kingdom in the N. of Germany. In 1867 it became part of the North German Confederation.

1850. 12 pfenige = 1 silbergroschen.
30 silbergroschen = 1 thaler.
1867. 60 kreuzer = 1 gulden.

1. Frederick William IV. 2. 3.

1850. Imperf.

14. 1. 4 pf. green .. .. 38·00 15·00
4. 6 pf. red .. .. .. 45·00 21·00
5. 1 sgr. black on rose .. 42·00 2·50
16. 1 sgr. rose .. .. 19·00 1·25
6. 2 sgr. black on blue .. 55·00 5·50
18. 2 sgr. blue .. .. 55·00 8·00
8. 3 sgr. black on yellow .. 55·00 3·75
21. 3 sgr. yellow .. .. 40·00 7·50

1861. Roul.

24. 2. 3 pf. lilac .. .. 8·50 11·00
26. 4 pf. green .. .. 5·00 4·00
28. 6 pf. orange .. .. 5·00 7·50
31. 3. 1 sgr. red .. .. 1·60 20
35. 2 sgr. blue .. .. 3·75 40
36. 3 sgr. brown .. .. 4·00 75

4. 5.

1866. Printed in reverse on back of specially treated transparent paper. Roul.

38. 4. 10 sgr. rose .. .. 30·00 35·00
39. – 30 sgr. blue .. .. 45·00 £100

The 30 sgr. has the value in a square.

1867. Roul.

40. 5. 1 k. green .. .. 12·00 18·00
42. 2 k. orange .. .. 20·00 38·00
43. 3 k. red .. .. 11·00 10·00
45. 6 k. blue .. .. 11·00 18·00
46. 9 k. bistre .. .. 15·00 20·00

PUERTO RICO O4

A W. Indian island, ceded by Spain to the United States after the war of 1898. Until 1873 stamps of Cuba were in use. Now uses stamps of the U.S.A.

1873. 100 centimos = 1 peseta.
1881. 1000 milesimas = 100 centavos = 1 peso.
1898. 100 cents = 1 dollar.

A. SPANISH OCCUPATION

(1.)

1873. Nos. 53/5 of Cuba optd. with T 1.

1. 25 c. de p. lilac .. .. 6·50 35
3. 50 c. de p. brown .. .. 14·00 1·10
4. 1 p. brown .. .. .. 25·00 2·50

1874. No. 57 of Cuba with opt. similar to T 1. (Two separate characters.)

5. 25 c. de p. blue .. .. 3·50 55

1875. Nos. 61/3 of Cuba with opt. similar to T 1. (Two separate characters.)

6. 25 c. de p. blue .. .. 3·25 50
7. 50 c. de p. green .. .. 4·75 70
8. 1 p. brown .. .. 16·00 3·00

1876. Nos. 65b/7 of Cuba with opt. similar to T 1. (Two separate characters.)

9. 25 c. de p. lilac 70 35
10. 50 c. de p. blue .. .. 1·75 70
11. 1 p. black .. .. .. 4·50 1·40

1876. Nos. 65b/7 of Cuba with opt. as last, but characters joined.

12. 25 c. de p. lilac .. .. 2·50 35
13. 1 p. black .. .. .. 7·00 2·25

1877. As T 24 of Spain, but inscr. "PTO-RICO 1877".

14. 5 c. brown .. .. .. 1·25 45
15. 10 c. red .. .. .. 2·50 60
16. 15 c. green .. .. .. 3·25 1·40
17. 25 c. blue .. .. .. 1·40 20
18. 50 c. brown .. .. .. 1·75 55

1878. As T 24 of Spain, but inscr. "PTO-RICO 1878".

19. 5 c. olive .. .. .. 3·00 2·25
20. 10 c. brown .. .. 20·00 11·00
21. 25 c. green 35 20
22. 50 c. blue .. .. .. 1·10 35
23a. 1 p. brown .. .. .. 3·50 2·00

1879. As T 24 of Spain, but inscr. "PTO-RICO 1879".

24. 5 c. claret .. .. .. 1·60 95
25. 10 c. brown .. .. .. 1·60 95
26. 15 c. black .. .. .. 1·60 95
27. 25 c. blue 55 20
28. 50 c. green .. .. .. 1·50 70
29. 1 p. grey .. .. .. 4·00 2·25

1880. "Alfonso XII" key-type inscr. "PUERTO-RICO 1880".

30. X. ¼ c. green .. .. 4·50 2·25
31. ½ c. red .. .. .. 1·10 45
32. 1 c. claret .. .. 1·60 1·10
33. 2 c. grey .. .. .. 1·10 70
34. 3 c. orange .. .. 1·25 70
35. 4 c. black .. .. 1·25 70
36. 5 c. green 55 30
37. 10 c. red 70 45
38. 15 c. brown .. .. 1·10 55
39. 25 c. lilac 55 20
40. 40 c. grey .. .. 1·60 30
41. 50 c. brown .. .. 2·25 1·10
42. 1 p. olive .. .. 4·50 1·40

1881. "Alfonso XII" key-type inscr. "PUERTO-RICO 1881".

43. X. ½ m. red 10 5
45. 1 m. violet 10 8
46. 2 m. red 20 10
47. 4 m. green 25 10
48. 6 m. claret 25 15
49. 8 m. blue 50 25
50. 1 c. green 55 25
51. 2 c. red 70 35
52. 3 c. brown .. .. 1·75 80
53. 5 c. lilac 60 8
54. 8 c. brown .. .. 1·00 20
55. 10 c. lilac .. .. 3·25 90
56. 20 c. olive .. .. 4·00 1·10

1882. "Alfonso XII" key-type inscr. "PUERTO-RICO".

57. X. ½ m. pink 8 8
58. 1 m. claret 8 8
59. 2 m. mauve 8 8
60. 4 m. claret 8 8
61. 6 m. brown 10 8
62. 8 m. green 10 8
63. 1 c. green 8 8
64. 2 c. red 20 8
65. 3 c. yellow 50 30
66. 5 c. lilac .. .. 1·75 25
67. 8 c. brown 50 8
68. 10 c. green 50 10
69. 20 c. grey 70 10
70. 40 c. blue .. .. 4·50 1·40
71. 80 c. brown .. .. 5·00 1·75

1884. "Alfonso XII" key-type inscr. "PUERTO-RICO".

73. X. ½ m. claret 8 8
74. 1 m. pink 8 8
76. 3 c. brown 40 15

1890. "Baby" key-type inscr. "PUERTO-RICO".

80. Y. ½ m. black 10 5
81. 1 m. green 15 5
82. 2 m. claret 10 5
83. 4 m. black .. .. 3·00 1·25
84. 6 m. brown .. .. 4·75 2·50
85. 8 m. brown .. .. 6·50 4·75
86. 1 c. brown 10 5
87. 2 c. purple 55 20
88. 3 c. indigo .. .. 1·40 20
89. 5 c. purple .. .. 3·00 15
90. 8 c. blue .. .. 3·00 50
91. 10 c. red 90 25
122. 20 c. red .. .. 1·00 70
93. 40 c. orange .. .. 10·00 6·50
94. 80 c. green .. .. 45·00 22·00

1891. "Baby" key-type inscr. "PUERTO-RICO".

95. Y. ½ m. grey 5 5
96. 1 m. purple 5 5
97. 2 m. purple 5 5
98. 4 m. blue 5 5
99. 6 m. red 5 5
100. 8 m. green 8 5
101. 1 c. green 15 8
102. 2 c. chocolate 25 8
103. 3 c. orange 20 5
104. 5 c. green 15 5
105. 8 c. brown 8 5
106. 10 c. claret 20 8
107. 20 c. mauve 30 15
108. 40 c. blue 70 35
109. 80 c. orange .. .. 1·75 1·10

2. Landing of Columbus.

1893. Discovery of America. 4th Cent.
110. 2. 3 c. green .. .. 25·00 4·25

1893. "Baby" key-type inscr. "PUERTO-RICO".
111. Y. ½ m. brown 5 5
112. 1 m. blue 5 5
113. 2 m. red 5 5
114. 4 m. brown 5 5
115. 1 c. purple 70 8
116. 2 c. lilac 30 10
117. 3 c. grey 70 8
118. 4 c. blue 20 8
120. 6 c. orange 10 5
121. 8 c. purple .. .. 1·10 20
122. 20 c. rose 15 8
123. 40 c. claret 90 45

1896. "Baby" key-type inscr. "PUERTO RICO".
124. Y. ½ m. purple 5 5
125. 1 m. brown 5 5
126. 2 m. green 5 5
127. 4 m. green 15 10
128. 1 c. claret 10 5
129. 2 c. brown 10 5
130. 3 c. blue .. .. 1·75 10
131. 3 c. brown 8 5
132. 4 c. grey 15 5
133. 5 c. blue 8 5
134. 6 c. lilac 8 5
135. 8 c. red 35 15
136. 20 c. grey 70 15
137. 40 c. red 70 35
138. 80 c. black .. .. 3·75 2·10

1898. "Curly Head" key-type inscr. "PTO. RICO 1898 y 99".
139. Z. 1 m. brown 5 5
140. 2 m. brown 5 5
141. 3 m. brown 5 5
142. 4 m. brown 50 20
143. 5 m. brown 5 5
144. 1 c. violet 5 5
145. 2 c. green 5 5
146. 3 c. brown 5 5
147. 4 c. orange 50 35
148. 5 c. red 5 5
149. 6 c. blue 8 5
150. 8 c. brown 8 5
151. 10 c. red 8 5
152. 15 c. olive 8 5
153. 20 c. claret 30 20
154. 40 c. lilac 35 35
155. 60 c. black 35 35
156. 80 c. brown 70 70
157. 1 p. green .. .. 1·40 1·10
158. 2 p. blue .. .. 3·25 1·75

1898. "Baby" key-type inscr. "PUERTO RICO" and optd. **Habilitado PARA 1898 y '99.**
159. Y. ½ m. purple .. .. 1·75 1·10
160. 1 m. brown 8 5
161. 2 m. green 5 5
162. 4 m. green 5 5
163. 1 c. claret 5 5
164. 2 c. brown 5 5
165. 3 c. blue .. .. 3·50 1·75
166. 3 c. brown 20 8
167. 4 c. grey 8 8
168. 4 c. blue .. .. 2·25 1·40
169. 5 c. blue 8 8
171. 5 c. green .. .. 1·10 70
172. 6 c. lilac 8 5
173a. 8 c. red 15 15
174. 20 c. grey 12 12
175. 40 c. red 20 15
176. 80 c. black .. .. 3·50 2·50

WAR TAX STAMPS

1898. Baby" key type inscr. "PUERTO RICO" and "Curly Head" key type inscr. "PTO. RICO 1898 y 99", optd. **IMPUESTO DE GUERRA** or surch. also.
W 177. Y. 1 m. blue 55 35
W 178. 1 m. brown .. .. 1·40 1·10
W 179. 2 m. red .. .. 3·00 1·50
W 180. 2 m. green .. .. 1·75 1·40
W 181. 4 m. green .. .. 2·25 2·00
W 182a. 1 c. brown .. .. 1·40 90
W 183. 1 c. claret .. .. 2·50 2·25
W 184. 2 c. purple 8 5
W 185. 2 c. red 8 5
W 186. 2 c. lilac 20 20
W 187. 2 c. brown 8 5
W 192. 2 c. on 2 m. red .. 8 5
W 193c. 2 c. on 5 c. green .. 50 35
W 188. 3 c. orange .. .. 2·25 2·25
W 194. 3 c. on 10 c. red .. 2·75 2·25
W 195. 4 c. on 20 c. red .. 2·75 2·25
W 189. 5 c. green 8 5
W 196. 5 c. on ½ m. brown .. 1·10 55
W 197a. 5 c. on 1 m. purple .. 5 5
W 198. 5 c. on 1 m. blue .. 10 10
W 199. Z. 5 c. on 1 m. brown .. 90 90
W 200. Y. 5 c. on 5 c. green .. 1·25 90
W 191. 8 c. purple .. .. 4·50 3·50

B. UNITED STATES OCCUPATION

1899. 1894 stamps of United States optd. **PORTO RICO.**
202. 50. 1 c. green (No. 283) .. 80 30
203. 2 c. red (No. 284c) .. 80 15
204. 5 c. blue (No. 286) .. 90 50
205. 8 c. purple (No. 275) .. 3·00 2·40
206. 10 c. brown (No. 289).. 1·90 1·00

1900. As last but optd. **PUERTO RICO.**
210. 50. 1 c. green (No. 283) .. 55 30
212. 2 c. red (No. 284c) .. 60 25

POSTAGE DUE STAMPS

1899. Postage Due stamps of United States of 1894 optd. **PORTO RICO.**
D 207. D 2. 1 c. red .. .. 2·00 1·40
D 208. 2 c. red .. .. 1·90 1·40
D 209. 10 c. red .. .. 14·00 8·00

QATAR BC; O4

An independent Arab Shaikhdom with British postal administration until May 23, 1963; later issues by the Qatar Post Department. The stamps of Muscat were formerly used at the Capital, Doha and at Umm Said.

100 naye paise = 1 rupee.
1966. 100 dirhams = 1 riyal.

Stamps of Great Britain surcharged **QATAR** and value in Indian currency.

1957. Queen Elizabeth II and pictorials.
1. 120. 1 n.p. on 5d. brown .. 5 5
2. 118. 3 n.p. on ½d. orange .. 5 5
3. 6 n.p. on 1d. blue .. 5 5
4. 9 n.p. on 1½d. green .. 5 5
5. 12 n.p. on 2d. pale brown 5 5
6. 119. 15 n.p. on 2½d. red .. 5 5
7. 20 n.p. on 3d. lilac .. 5 5
8. 25 n.p. on 4d. blue .. 15 20
9. 129. 40 n.p. on 6d. purple .. 15 10
10. 121. 50 n.p. on 9d. olive .. 15 20
11. 122. 75 n.p. on 1s. 3d. green 25 25
12. 1 r. on 1s. 6d. indigo 20 20
13. 125. 2 r. on 2s. 6d. brown 90 1·60
14. – 5 r. on 5s. red .. 3·00 3·50
15. – 10 r. on 10s. blue .. 5·50 6·00

1957. World Scout Jubilee Jamboree.
16. 126. 15 n.p. on 2½d. red .. 12 12
17. 127. 25 n.p. on 4d. blue .. 20 25
18. – 75 n.p. on 1s. 3d. green 35 40

1. Shaikh Ahmad bin Ali al Thani.

2. Falcon.

3. Oil Derrick.

1961.
27. 1. 5 n.p. rose.. .. .. 5 10
28. 15 n.p. black 5 10
29. 20 n.p. purple 5 10
30. 30 n.p. green 8 10
31. 2. 40 n.p. red 8 10
32. 50 n.p. sepia 12 20
33. – 75 n.p. blue 15 25
34. 3. 1 r. red 20 25
35. 2 r. blue 40 50
36. – 5 r. green .. .. 1·00 1·25
37. – 10 r. black .. .. 2·00 2·50

DESIGNS—As T 2: 75 n.p. Dhow. As T 3: 5 r., 10 r. Mosque.

1964. Olympic Games, Tokyo. Optd. **1964** Olympic Rings and Arabic inscr. or surch. also.
38. 2. 50 n.p. sepia 60 60
39. – 75 n.p. blue (No. 33) .. 85 85
40. – 1 r. on 10 r. black (No. 37) 1·10 1·10
41. 3. 2 r. blue .. .. 2·00 2·00
42. 5 r. green (No. 36) .. 4·00 4·00

1964. Pres. Kennedy Commem. Optd. **John F. Kennedy 1917-1963** in English and Arabic or surch. also.
43. 2. 50 n.p. sepia 60 60
44. – 75 n.p. blue (No. 33) .. 85 85
45. – 1 r. on 10 r. black (No. 37) 1·10 1·10
46. 3. 2 r. blue .. .. 2·00 2·00
47. – 5 r. green (No. 36) .. 4·00 4·00

4. Colonnade, Temple of Isis.

5. Scouts on Parade.

1965. Nubian Monuments Preservation. Multicoloured.
48. 1 n.p. Type 4 .. .. 5 5
49. 2 n.p. Temple of Isis, Philae 5 5
50. 3 n.p. Trajan's Kiosk, Philae 5 5
51. 1 r. As 3 n.p. 30 30
52. 1 r. 50 As 2 n.p. .. 45 45
53. 2 r. Type 4 .. .. .. 60 60

1965. Qatar Scouts.
54. – 1 n.p. brown and green .. 5 5
55. – 2 n.p. blue and chestnut.. 5 5
56. – 3 n.p. blue and green .. 5 5
57. – 4 n.p. brown and blue .. 5 5
58. – 5 n.p. blue and turquoise 5 5
59. 5. 30 n.p. multicoloured .. 8 8
60. 40 n.p. multicoloured .. 12 12
61. 1 r. multicoloured .. 25 25

DESIGNS—TRIANGULAR (60×30 mm.): 1 n.p., 4 n.p. Qatar Scout badge. 2 n.p., 3 n.p., 5 n.p. Ruler, badge, palms and camp.

6. "Telstar" and Eiffel Tower.

1965. I.T.U. Cent.
62. 6. 1 n.p. chestnut and blue 5 5
63. – 2 n.p. brown and blue .. 5 5
64. – 3 n.p. violet and green .. 5 5
65. – 4 n.p. blue and chestnut.. 5 5
66. 6. 5 n.p. ochre and violet .. 5 5
67. – 40 n.p. black and crimson 12 12
68. – 50 n.p. ochre and green .. 15 15
69. – 1 r. red and green.. .. 25 25

DESIGNS: 2 n.p., 1 r. "Syncom 2" and pagoda. 3 n.p., 40 n.p. "Relay" and radar scanner. 4 n.p., 50 n.p. Post Office Tower (London), Globe and satellites.

7. Triggerfish.

1965. Fish of the Arabian Gulf. Mult.
70. 1 n.p. Type 7 .. .. 5 5
71. 2 n.p. Butterfly sweetlip .. 5 5
72. 3 n.p. Saddle-spot butterfly fish 5 5
73. 4 n.p. Threadfin butterfly fish 5 5
74. 5 n.p. Mahomet's lancet fish 5 5
75. 15 n.p. Paradise fish .. 5 5
76. 20 n.p. Sailfin tang.. .. 5 5
77. 30 n.p. Thousand-spotted grouper 8 8
78. 40 n.p. Regal angelfish .. 12 12
79. 50 n.p. As 2 n.p. .. 15 15
80. 75 n.p. Type 7 .. .. 20 20
81. 1 r. As 30 n.p. 25 25
82. 2 r. As 20 n.p. 50 50
83. 3 r. As 15 n.p. 80 80
84. 4 r. As 5 n.p. .. .. 1·10 1·10
85. 5 r. As 4 n.p. .. .. 1·40 1·40
86. 10 r. As 3 n.p. .. .. 2·75 2·75

8. Basketball.

1966. Pan-Arab Games, Cairo (1965).
87. 8. 1 r. black, grey and red .. 30 30
88. – 1 r. brown and green .. 30 30
89. – 1 r. red and blue.. .. 30 30
90. – 1 r. green and indigo .. 30 30
91. – 1 r. blue and brown .. 30 30

SPORTS: No. 88, Horse-jumping. 89, Running. 90, Football. 91, Weightlifting.

1966. Space Rendezvous. Nos. 62/9 optd. **SPACE RENDEZVOUS 15th DECEMBER 1965** in English and Arabic and two space capsules.
92. 6. 1 n.p. chestnut and blue.. 5 5
93. – 2 n.p. brown and blue .. 5 5
94. – 3 n.p. violet and green .. 5 5
95. – 4 n.p. blue and chestnut.. 5 5
96. 8 5 n.p. ochre and violet .. 5 5
97. – 40 n.p. black and crimson 10 10
98. – 50 n.p. ochre and green .. 12 12
99. – 1 r. red and green .. 25 25

9. Shaikh Ahmad.

1966. Gold and Silver Coinage. Circular designs, embossed on gold (G) or silver (S) foil, backed with "Walsall Security Paper" inscr. in English and Arabic. Imperf.

(a) Diameter 1½ in.
101. 9. 1 n.p. bistre & purple (S) 5 5
102. – 3 n.p. black & orange (S) 5 5
103. 9. 4 n.p. violet and red (G) 5 5
104. – 5 n.p. emer. & cerise (G) 5 5

(b) Diameter 2⅜ in.
105. 9. 10 n.p. brown & violet (S) 5 5
106. – 40 n.p. vermilion & bl.(S) 10 10
107. 9. 70 n.p. blue & ultram. (G) 15 15
108. – 80 n.p. cerise & green (G) 20 20

(c) Diameter 2 $\frac{5}{16}$ in.
109. 9. 1 r. magenta & black (S) 25 25
110. – 2 r. green and purple (S) 50 50
111. 9. 5 r. purple & orange (G) 1·25 1·25
112. – 10 r. ultram. & red (G) .. 2·50 2·50

The 1, 4, 10, 70 n.p. and 1 and 5r. each show the obverse side of the coins as T 9. The remainder show the reverse side of the coins (Shaikh's seal.)

10. I.C.Y. and U.N. Emblems.

11. Pres. Kennedy and New York Skyline.

1966. Int. Co-operation Year.
113. 10. 40 n.p. brn., violet & blue 12 12
114. A. 40 n.p. violet, sep. & turq. 12 12
115. B. 40 n.p. blue, brn. & violet 12 12
116. C. 40 n.p. turq., violet & bl. 12 12

DESIGNS: A, Pres. Kennedy, I.C.Y. emblem and U.N. Headquarters. B, Dag Hammarskjoeld and U.N. General Assembly. C, Nehru and dove.

Nos. 113/6 were issued together in blocks of four, each sheet containing four blocks separated by gutter margins. Subsequently the sheets were reissued perf. and imperf. with the opt. **U.N. 20TH ANNIVERSARY** on the stamps. The gutter margins were also printed in various designs, face values and opt.

1966. Pres. Kennedy Commem. Multicoloured.
118. 10 n.p. Type 11 .. .. 5 5
119. 30 n.p. Pres. Kennedy and Cape Kennedy 8 8
120. 60 n.p. Pres. Kennedy and Statue of Liberty .. 15 15
121. 70 n.p. Type 11 .. .. 20 20
122. 80 n.p. As 30 n.p... .. 20 20
123. 1 r. As 60 n.p. 25 25

12. Horse-jumping.

1966. Olympic Games Preparation (Mexico). Multicoloured.

125. 1 n.p. Type **12** 5 5
126. 4 n.p. Running 5 5
127. 5 n.p. Throwing the javelin 5 5
128. 70 n.p. Type **12** 20 20
129. 80 n.p. Running 20 20
130. 90 n.p. Throwing the javelin 25 25

13. J. A. Lovell and Capsule.

1966. American Astronauts. Each design showing space-craft and Astronaut. Multicoloured.

132. 5 n.p. Type **13** 5 5
133. 10 n.p. T. P. Stafford 5 5
134. 15 n.p. A. B. Shephard 5 5
135. 20 n.p. J. H. Glenn 5 5
136. 30 n.p. M. Scott Carpenter 8 8
137. 40 n.p. W. M. Schirra 10 10
138. 50 n.p. V. I. Grissom 12 12
139. 60 n.p. L. G. Cooper 15 15

Nos. 132/4 are diamond-shaped as T **13**, the remainder are horiz. designs (56 × 25 mm.).

1966. Various stamps with currency names changed to dirhams and riyals by overprinting in English and Arabic.

(i) Nos. 27/37 (Definitives).

141. 5 d. on 5 n.p. 5 5
142. 15 d. on 15 n.p. 5 5
143. 20 d. on 20 n.p. 5 5
144. 30 d. on 30 n.p. 8 8
145. 40 d. on 40 n.p. 10 10
146. 50 d. on 50 n.p. 12 12
147. 75 d. on 75 n.p. 20 20
148. 1 r. on 1 r. 25 25
149. 2 r. on 2 r. 45 45
150. 5 r. on 5 r. 1·25 1·25
151. 10 r. on 10 r. 2·50 2·50

(ii) Nos. 70/86 (Fish).

152. 1 d. on 1 n.p. 5 5
153. 2 d. on 2 n.p. 5 5
154. 3 d. on 3 n.p. 5 5
155. 4 d. on 4 n.p. 5 5
156. 5 d. on 5 n.p. 5 5
157. 15 d. on 15 n.p. 5 5
158. 20 d. on 20 n.p. 5 5
159. 30 d. on 30 n.p. 8 8
160. 40 d. on 40 n.p. 10 10
161. 50 d. on 50 n.p. 12 12
162. 75 d. on 75 n.p. 20 20
163. 1 r. on 1 r. 25 25
164. 2 r. on 2 r. 45 45
165. 3 r. on 3 r. 75 75
166. 4 r. on 4 r. 1·00 1·00
167. 5 r. on 5 r. 1·25 1·25
168. 10 r. on 10 r. 2·50 2·50

14. National Library, Doha.

1966. Education Day. Multicoloured.

169. 2 n.p. Type **14** 5 5
170. 3 n.p. School and playing field 5 5
171. 5 n.p. School and gardens 5 5
172. 1 r. Type **14** 25 25
173. 2 r. As 3 n.p. 50 50
174. 3 r. As 5 n.p. 75 75

15. Palace, Doha.

16. Jules Rimet Trophy and "football" globe.

1966. Currency expressed in naye paise and rupees. Multicoloured.

175. 2 n.p. Type **15** 5 5
176. 3 n.p. Gulf Street, Shahra Al-Khalij 5 5
177. 10 n.p. Doha airport 5 5
178. 15 n.p. Garden, Rayan 5 5
179. 20 n.p. Head Post Office, Doha 5 5
180. 30 n.p. Mosque, Doha (vert.) 8 8
181. 40 n.p. Shaikh Ahmad 10 10
182. 50 n.p. Type **15** 12 12
183. 60 n.p. As 3 n.p. 15 15
184. 70 n.p. As 10 n.p. 20 20
185. 80 n.p. As 15 n.p. 25 25
186. 90 n.p. As 20 n.p. 30 30
187. 1 r. As 30 n.p. (vert.) 30 30
188. 2 r. As 40 n.p. 60 60

1966. World Football Cup Championships, England.

189. – 60 n.p. mult. (postage) 25 25
190. **16.** 70 n.p. multicoloured 30 30
191. – 80 n.p. multicoloured 40 40
192. – 90 n.p. multicoloured 50 50
193. – 1 n.p. blue (air) 5 5
194. – 2 n.p. blue 5 5
195. – 3 n.p. blue 8 8
196. – 4 n.p. blue 10 10

DESIGNS: No. 189, Hands holding Jules Rimet Trophy. No. 191, Footballers and globe. No. 192, Wembley stadium. Nos. 193/6, Jules Rimet Trophy.

17. A.P.U. Emblem.

19. Traffic Lights.

18. "Apollo" Spacecraft.

1967. Admission of Qatar to Arab Postal Union.

198. **17.** 70 d. brown & violet 20 20
199. 80 d. brown & blue 25 25

1967. U.S. "Apollo" Space Missions. Mult.

200. 5 d. Astronauts on Moon 5 5
201. 10 d. Type **18** 5 5
202. 20 d. Landing module on Moon 5 5
203. 30 d. Blast-off from Moon 8 8
204. 40 d. "Saturn 5" rocket 10 10
205. 70 d. As 5 d. 20 20
206. 80 d. Type **18** 25 25
207. 1 r. As 20 d. 30 30
208. 1 r. 20 As 30 d. 35 35
209. 2 r. As 40 d. 50 50

1967. Traffic Day.

211. **19.** 20 d. multicoloured 5 5
212. 30 d. multicoloured 8 8
213. 50 d. multicoloured 12 12
214. 1 r. multicoloured 25 25

20. Brownsea Island and Jamboree Camp, Idaho.

1967. Diamond Jubilee of Scout Movement and World Scout Jamboree, Idaho. Multicoloured.

215. 1 d. Type **20** 5 5
216. 2 d. Lord Baden-Powell 5 5
217. 3 d. Pony-trekking 5 5
218. 5 d. Canoeing 5 5
219. 15 d. Swimming 5 5
220. 75 d. Rock-climbing 20 20
221. 2 r. World Jamboree emblem 50 50

21. Viking Ship (from Bayeux tapestry).

1967. Famous Navigators' Ships. Multicoloured.

222. 1 d. Type **21** 5 5
223. 2 d. "Santa Maria" (Columbus) 5 5
224. 3 d. "San Gabriel" (Vasco da Gama) 5 5
225. 75 d. "Victoria" (Magellan) 20 20
226. 1 r. "Golden Hind" (Drake) 25 25
227. 2 r. "Gipsy Moth IV" (Chichester) 50 50

22. Arab Scribe.

1968. Qatar Postage Stamps. 10th Anniv. Multicoloured.

228. 1 d. Type **22** 5 5
229. 2 d. Pigeon Post 5 5
230. 3 d. Mounted postman 5 5
231. 60 d. Canoe postman 15 15
232. 1 r. 25, Camel postman 30 30
233. 2 r. Letter-writing and Qatar 1 n.p. stamp of 1957 50 50

The 2 d. and 60 d. are vert.

23. Human Rights Emblem and Barbed Wire.

1968. Human Rights Year. Multicoloured designs embodying Human Rights emblem.

234. 1 d. Type **23** 5 5
235. 2 d. Arab refugees 5 5
236. 3 d. Scales of justice 5 5
237. 60 d. Opening doors 15 15
238. 1 r. 25, Family (vert.) 30 30
239. 2 r. Human rights 50 50

24. Shaikh Ahmad. **26.**

25. Dhow.

1968.

240. **24.** 5 d. green and blue 5 5
241. 10 d. brown and blue 5 5
242. 20 d. red and black 5 5
243. 25 d. green and purple 8 8
244. **25.** 35 d. grn., blue and pink 8 8
245. – 40 d. purple, bl. & orge. 10 10
246. – 60 d. brown, bl. & violet 15 15
247. – 70 d. black, blue & green 20 20
248. – 1 r. ult., lemon & emer. 25 25
249. – 1 r. 25 blue and flesh 30 30
250. – 1 r. 50 grn., blue & pur. 35 35
251. **26.** 2 r. blue, brn. & cinnamon 45 45
252. 5 r. purple and green 1·00 1·10
253. 10 r. brn., ultram. & blue 2·25 2·25

DESIGNS: As T **25**. 40 d. Water purification plant. 60 d. Oil jetty. 70 d. Qatar mosque. 1 r. Palace, Doha. 1 r. 25 Doha fort. 1 r. 50 Falcon.

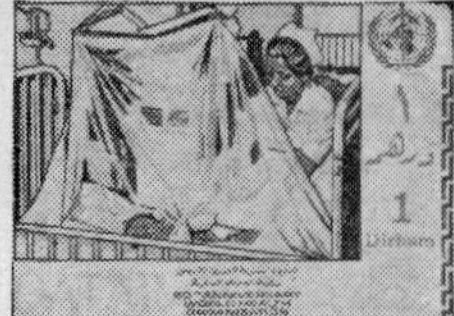

27. Maternity Ward.

1968. W.H.O. 20th Anniv. Multicoloured.

258. 1 d. Type **27** 5 5
259. 2 d. Operating theatre 5 5
260. 3 d. Dental surgery 5 5
261. 60 d. Oxygen treatment 15 15
262. 1 r. 25 Laboratory 30 30
263. 2 r. State Hospital, Qatar 45 45

28. Olympic Flame and Runner.

1968. Olympic Games. Mexico. Multicoloured.

264. 1 d. Throwing the discus 5 5
265. 2 d. Type **28** 5 5
266. 3 d. "68", Rings and gymnast 5 5
267. 60 d. Weightlifting and Flame 15 15
268. 1 r. 25 "Flame" in mosaic pattern (vert.) 30 30
269. 2 r. "Cock" emblem 45 45

29. U.N. Emblem and Flags.

1968. United Nations Day. Multicoloured.

270. 1 d. Type **29** 5 5
271. 4 d. Dove of Peace and world map 5 5
272. 5 d. U.N. Headquarters and flags 5 5
273. 60 d. Teacher and class 15 15
274. 1 r. 50 Agricultural workers 35 35
275. 2 r. U Thant and U.N. Assembly 50 50

30. Fishing Vessel Ross Rayyan.

1969. Progress in Qatar. Multicoloured.

276. 1 d. Type **30** 5 5
277. 4 d. Primary school 5 5
278. 5 d. Doha International Airport 5 5
279. 60 d. Cement factory and road-making 15 15
280. 1 r. 50 Power station and pylon 35 35
281. 2 r. Housing estate 50 50

31. Armoured Cars.

1969. Qatar Security Forces. Multicoloured.

282. 1 d. Type **31** 5 5
283. 2 d. Traffic control 5 5
284. 3 d. Trooping helicopter 5 5
285. 60 d. Section of military band 15 15
286. 1 r. 25 Field gun 30 30
287. 2 r. Mounted police 50 50

32. Tanker at Mooring.

1969. Qatar's Oil Industry. Multicoloured.
288. 1 d. Type 32 .. .. 5 5
289. 2 d. Training school .. 5 5
290. 3 d. Offshore drilling rig .. 5 5
291. 60 d. Storage tanks, Halul 15 15
292. 1 r. 50 Topping plant .. 35 35
293. 2 r. Various tankers 1890–1968 .. .. .. 50 50

33. "Guest-house" and Boat-building.

1969. 10th Scout Jamboree, Qatar. Multicoloured.
294. 1 d. Type 33 .. .. 5 5
295. 2 d. Scouts at work .. 5 5
296. 3 d. Review and March Past 5 5
297. 60 d. Interior gateway .. 15 15
298. 1 r. 25 Camp Entrance .. 30 30
299. 2 r. Hoisting Flag, and Shaikh Ahmad 50 50

34. Neil Armstrong.

1969. 1st Man on the Moon. Multicoloured.
301. 1 d. Type 34 .. .. 5 5
302. 2 d. Edward Aldrin .. 5 5
303. 3 d. Michael Collins .. 5 5
304. 60 d. Astronaut on Moon 15 15
305. 1 r. 25 Take-off from Moon 30 30
306. 2 r. Splashdown (horiz.) .. 50 50

35. Airliner and Mail-van.

1970. Admission to U.P.U. Multicoloured.
307. 1 d. Type 35 .. .. 5 5
308. 2 d. Ocean liner 5 5
309. 3 d. Loading mail-van .. 5 5
310. 60 d. G.P.O. Doha .. 15 15
311. 1 r. 25 U.P.U. Building, Berne 30 30
312. 2 r. U.P.U. Monument, Berne (detail) .. 50 50

36. League Emblem, Flag and Map.

1970. Arab League. Silver Jubilee.
313. 36. 35 d. multicoloured .. 8 8
314. 60 d. multicoloured .. 15 15
315. 1 r. 25 multicoloured .. 30 30
316. 1 r. 50 multicoloured .. 35 35

37. "VC-10" on Runway.

1970. 1st Gulf Aviation "VC-10" Flight, Doha–London. Multicoloured.
317. 1 d. Type 37 .. .. 5 5
318. 2 d. Falcon and "VC-10" 5 5
319. 3 d. Tail view of "VC-10" 5 5
320. 60 d. Gulf Aviation emblem on map 15 15
321. 1 r. 25 "VC-10" over Doha 30 30
322. 2 r. Tail assembly of "VC-10" 50 50

38. "Space Achievements".

1970. Int. Education Year.
323. 38. 35 d. multicoloured .. 8 8
324. 60 d. multicoloured .. 15 15

39. Freesias.

41. Globe, "25" and U.N. Emblem.

40. Toyahama Fishermen with Giant "Fish".

1970. Qatar Flowers. Multicoloured.
325. 1 d. Type 39 .. .. 5 5
326. 2 d. Azaleas 5 5
327. 3 d. Ixia 5 5
328. 60 d. Amaryllises .. 15 15
329. 1 r. 25 Cinerarias 30 30
330. 2 r. Roses 50 50

1970. "EXPO 70". World Fair, Osaka. Multicoloured.
331. 1 d. Type 40 .. .. 5 5
332. 2 d. Expo emblem and map of Japan 5 5
333. 3 d. Fisherman on Shikoku beach 5 5
334. 60 d. Expo emblem and Mt. Fuji 10 10
335. 1 r. 50 Gateway to Shinto Shrine 25 25
336. 2 r. Expo Tower and Mt. Fuji 35 35
Nos. 333, 334 and 336 are vert.

1970. United Nations. 25th Anniv. Multicoloured.
337. 1 d. Type 41 .. .. 5 5
338. 2 d. Flowers in gun-barrel 5 5
339. 3 d. Anniversary cake .. 5 5
340. 35 d. "The U.N. Agencies" 8 8
341. 1 r. 50 "Trumpet fanfare" 35 35
342. 2 r. "World friendship" 50 50

42. Al Jahez (philosopher), and Ancient Globe.

1971. Famous Men of Islam. Multicoloured.
343. 1 d. Type 42 .. .. 5 5
344. 2 d. Saladdin (soldier), palace and weapons .. 5 5
345. 3 d. Al Farabi (philosopher and musician), instruments and view .. 5
346. 35 d. Iben Al Haithum (scientist), palace and emblems 8 8
347. 1 r. 50 Al Motanabbi (poet), symbols and desert .. 35 35
348. 2 r. Iben Sinah (astronomer), "Gods of profession" and ancient globe .. 90 90

43. Cormorant and Water Plants.

1971. Qatar Fauna and Flora. Multicoloured.
349. 1 d. Type 43 .. .. 5 5
350. 2 d. Lizard and prickly pear 5 5
351. 3 d. Flamingoes and palms 5 5
352. 60 d. Oryx and yucca .. 15 15
353. 1 r. 25 Gazelle and desert dandelion 30 30
354. 2 r. Camel, palm and bronzed chenopod 50 50

44. Satellite Earth Station, Goonhilly.

1971. World Telecommunications Day. Multicoloured.
355. 1 d. Type 44 .. .. 5 5
356. 2 d. Cable-laying ship .. 5 5
357. 3 d. Post Office Tower and T.V. control-room .. 5 5
358. 4 d. Modern telephones .. 5 5
359. 5 d. Video-phone equipment 5 5
360. 35 d. As 3 d. 8 8
361. 75 d. As 5 d. 20 25
362. 3 r. Telex machine .. 75 70

45. Arab Child reading Book.

46. A.P.U. Emblem.

1971. Education Day. 10th Anniv.
363. 45. 35 d. multicoloured .. 8 8
364. 55 d. multicoloured .. 15 15
365. 75 d. multicoloured .. 20 20

1971. Arab Postal Union. 25th Anniv.
366. 46. 35 d. multicoloured .. 8 8
367. 55 d. multicoloured .. 15 15
368. 75 d. multicoloured .. 20 20
369. 1 r. 25 multicoloured .. 30 30

47. "Hammering Racism".

1971. Racial Equality Year. Multicoloured.
370. 1 d. Type 47 .. .. 5 5
371. 2 d. "Pushing back racism" 5 5
372. 3 d. War-wounded .. 5 5
373. 4 d. Working together (vert.) 5 5
374. 5 d. Playing together (vert.) 5 5
375. 35 d. Racial "tidal-wave" 8 8
376. 75 d. Type 47 .. .. 20 20
377. 3 r. As 2 d. 75 75

48. Nurse and Child.

1971. U.N.I.C.E.F. 25th Anniv. Multicoloured.
378. 1 d. Mother and child (vert.) 5 5
379. 2 d. Child's face 5 5
380. 3 d. Child with book (vert.) 5 5
381. 4 d. Type 48 .. .. 5 5
382. 5 d. Mother and baby .. 5 5
383. 35 d. Child with daffodil (vert.) 8 8
384. 75 d. As 3 d. 20 20
385. 3 r. As 1 d. 75 75

49. Shaikh Ahmad and Flags of Arab League and Qatar.

1971. Independence.
386. 49. 35 d. multicoloured .. 8 8
387. – 75 d. multicoloured .. 20 20
388. – 1 r. 25 blk., pink & brn. 30 30
389. – 3 r. multicoloured .. 75 75
DESIGNS—HORIZ. 75 d. As Type 49, but with U.N. flag in place of Arab League flag. VERT. 1 r. 25 Shaikh Ahmad. 3 r. Handclasp.

1972. Provisionals. Nos. 328/30 surch. with value in English and Arabic.
391. 10 d. on 60 d. mult. .. 5 5
392. 1 r. on 1 r. 25 mult. .. 25 25
393. 5 r. on 2 r. multicoloured 1·25 1·25

50. Roller.

51. Shaikh Khalifa bin Hamad al-Thaini.

1972. Birds. Multicoloured.
394. 1 d. Type 50 .. .. 5 5
395. 2 d. Kingfisher 5 5
396. 3 d. Rock thrush .. 5 5
397. 4 d. Caspian tern 5 5
398. 5 d. Hoopoe 5 5
399. 35 d. Bee-eater 8 8
400. 75 d. Golden oriole .. 20 20
401. 3 r. Peregrine falcon .. 75 75

1972.
402. 51. 5 d. blue and violet .. 5 5
403. 10 d. red and brown .. 5 5
404. 35 d. green and orge. .. 8 8
405. 55 d. purple and grn... 12 12
406. 75 d. purple and blue 20 20
407. – 1 r. black & brown .. 25 25
408. – 1 r. 25 black and grn... 30 30
409. – 5 r. black and blue .. 1·25 1·25
410. – 10 r. black and scarlet 2·50 2·50
The rupee values are larger, size 27 × 32 mm.

52. Book Year Emblem.

1972. Int. Book Year.
411. 52. 35 d. black and blue .. 8 8
412. 55 d. black and brown 12 12
413. 75 d. black and green.. 20 20
414. 1 r. 25 black and lilac.. 30 30

53. Football.

1972. Olympic Games, Mexico. Depicting sportsmen's hands or feet. Multicoloured.
415. 1 d. Type 53 .. .. 5 5
416. 2 d. Running (foot on starting block) 5 5
417. 3 d. Cycling (hand) .. 5 5
418. 4 d. Gymnastics (hand) .. 5 5
419. 5 d. Basketball (hand) .. 5 5
420. 35 d. Discus (hand) .. 8 8
421. 75 d. Type 53 .. .. 20 20
422. 3 r. As 2 d... .. 75 75

54. Underwater Pipeline Construction.

1972. "Oil from the Sea". Multicoloured.

424. 1 d. Drilling (vert.) 5 5
425. 4 d. Type **54** 5 5
426. 5 d. Offshore rig 5 5
427. 35 d. Underwater "prospecting" for oil 8 8
428. 75 d. As 1 d. 20 20
429. 3 r. As 5 d. 75 75

55. Administrative Building.

1972. Independence Day. Multicoloured.

430. 10 d. Type **55** 5 5
431. 35 d. Handclasp and Arab League flag 8 8
432. 75 d. Handclasp and U.N. flag 20 20
433. 1 r. 25 Shaikh Khalifa .. 30 30

56. Dish Aerial, Satellite and Telephone (I.T.U.).

1972. United Nations Day. Multicoloured.

435. 1 d. Type **56** 5 5
436. 2 d. Archaeological team (U.N.E.S.C.O.) 5 5
437. 3 d. Tractor, produce and helicopter (F.A.O.) .. 5 5
438. 4 d. Children with books (U.N.I.C.E.F.) .. 5 5
439. 5 d. Weather satellite (W.M.O.) 5 5
440. 25 d. Construction workers (I.L.O.) 5 5
441. 55 d. Child care (W.H.O.) .. 12 12
442. 1 r. Mail-plane and van (U.P.U.) 25 25

57. Emblem and Flags.

1972. Arab States Civil Aviation Council, Qatar. 10th Session.

443. **57.** 25 d. multicoloured .. 5 5
444. 30 d. multicoloured .. 8 8

58. Housing Development.

1973. Shaikh Khalifa's Accession. 1st Anniv. Multicoloured.

455. 2 d. Road construction .. 5 5
456. 3 d. Type **58** 5 5
457. 4 d. Hospital operating theatre 5 5
458. 5 d. Telephone exchange .. 5 5
459. 15 d. School classroom .. 5 5
460. 20 d. Television studio .. 5 5
461. 35 d. Shaikh Khalifa .. 8 8
462. 55 d. Gulf Hotel, Doha .. 12 12
463. 1 r. Industrial plant .. 25 25
464. 1 r. 35 Flour mills .. 35 35

59. Aerial Crop-spraying.

1973. W.H.O. 25th Anniv. Multicoloured.

465. 2 d. Type **59** 5 5
466. 3 d. Drugs and syringe .. 5 5
467. 4 d. Woman in wheelchair (Prevention of polio) .. 5 5
468. 5 d. Mosquito (Malaria control) 5 5
469. 55 d. Mental patient (Mental Health Research) .. 12 12
470. 1 r. Dead trees (Anti-pollution) 25 25

60. Shaikh Khalifa. **61.** Clock Tower, Doha.

1973.

445. **60.** 5 d. multicoloured .. 5 5
446. 10 d. multicoloured .. 5 5
447. 20 d. multicoloured .. 5 5
448. 25 d. multicoloured .. 5 5
449. 35 d. multicoloured .. 8 8
450. 55 d. multicoloured .. 10 10
451. **61.** 75 d. multicoloured .. 15 15
452. – 1 r. multicoloured .. 20 20
453. – 5 r. multicoloured .. 1·00 1·00
454. – 10 r. multicoloured .. 2·00 2·00

Nos. 452/4 are as Type **60**, but size 27 × 32 mm.

62. Weather Ship.

1973. World Meteorological Organization Cent. Multicoloured.

471. 2 d. Type **62** 5 5
472. 3 d. Launching radio-sonde balloon 5 5
473. 4 d. Weather plane .. 5 5
474. 5 d. Meteorological station 5 5
475. 10 d. Met. aircraft taking-off 5 5
476. 1 r. "Nimbus 1" 20 20
477. 1 r. 55 Rocket on launch-pad 30 30

63. Handclasp.

1973. Independence Day. 2nd Anniv. Mult.

478. 15 d. Type **63** 5 5
479. 35 d. Agriculture 8 8
480. 55 d. Government building 10 10
481. 1 r. 35 View of Doha .. 25 25
482. 1 r. 55 Illuminated fountain 30 30

64. Child planting Sapling (U.N.E.S.C.O.).

1973. United Nations Day. Multicoloured.

483. 2 d. Type **64** 5 5
484. 4 d. U.N. H.Q., New York and flags 5 5
485. 5 d. Building construction (I.L.O.) 5 5
486. 35 d. Nurses in dispensary (W.H.O.) 8 8
487. 1 r. 35 Radar control (I.T.U.) 25 25
488. 3 r. Inspection of wheat and cattle (F.A.O.) .. 60 60

65. "Open Gates".

1973. Declaration of Human Rights. 25th Anniv. Multicoloured.

489. 2 d. Type **65** 5 5
490. 4 d. Freedom marchers .. 5 5
491. 5 d. "Equality of Man" .. 5 5
492. 35 d. Primary education .. 8 8
493. 1 r. 35 General Assembly, U.N. 25 25
494. 3 r. Flame emblem (vert.) 60 60

66. New Flyover, Doha.

1974. Shaikh Khalifa's Accession. 2nd Anniv. Multicoloured.

495. 2 d. Type **66** 5 5
496. 3 d. Education symbol .. 5 5
497. 5 d. Gas plant 5 5
498. 35 d. Gulf Hotel, Doha .. 8 8
499. 1 r. 55 Space communications station 30 30
500. 2 r. 25 Shaikh Khalifa .. 45 45

67. Camel Caravan and Articulated Mail-van.

1974. Universal Postal Union. Cent. Mult.

501. 2 d. Type **67** 5 5
502. 3 d. Early mail wagon and modern express train .. 5 5
503. 10 d. Packet steamer and modern mail-ship .. 5 5
504. 35 d. Early and modern mail-planes 8 8
505. 75 d. Manual and mechanised mail-sorting 15 15
506. 1 r. 25 Early and modern P.O. sales counters .. 25 25

68. Doha Hospital.

1974. World Population Year. Multicoloured.

507. 5 d. Type **68** 5 5
508. 10 d. W.P.Y. emblem .. 5 5
509. 15 d. Emblem within wreath 5 5
510. 35 d. World population map 8 8
511. 1 r. 75 New-born infants and clock ("a birth every minute") 30 30
512. 2 r. 25 "Ideal Family" group 45 45

69. Television Station.

1974. Independence Day. 3rd Anniv. Mult.

513. 5 d. Type **69** 5 5
514. 10 d. Doha palace .. 5 5
515. 15 d. Teachers' College .. 5 5
516. 75 d. Clock Tower and Mosque 15 15
517. 1 r. 55 Roundabout and surroundings 30 30
518. 2 r. Shaikh Khalifa .. 45 45

70. Operating Theatre (W.H.O.).

1974. United Nations Day.

519. **70.** 5 d. orge., mve. & blk. .. 5 5
520. – 10 d. orge., red & blk. .. 5 5
521. – 20 d. bl., grn. & blk. .. 5 5
522. – 25 d. bl., brn. & blk. .. 5 5
523. – 1 r. 75 bl., red & blk. .. 40 40
524. – 2 r. bl., orge. & blk. .. 40 40

DESIGNS: 10 d. Satellite earth station (I.T.U.). 20 d. Tractor (F.A.O.). 25 d. Classroom (U.N.E.S.C.O.). 1 r. 75 African open-air court ("Human Rights"). 2 r. U.P.U. and U.N. emblems (U.P.U.).

71. Gulf Aviation "VC-10" Airliner.

1974. Arab Civil Aviation Day.

525. **71.** 20 d. multicoloured .. 8 8
526. – 25 d. bl., grn. & yellow 8 8
527. – 30 d. multicoloured .. 8 8
528. – 50 d. red, grn. & maroon 12 12

DESIGNS: 25 d. Doha airport. 30 d., 50 d. Flags of Qatar and the Arab League.

72. Clock-tower, Qatar.

1974. Tourism. Multicoloured.

529. 5 d. Type **72** 5 5
530. 10 d. Birds and Shara'o Island (horiz.) 5 5
531. 15 d. Fort Zubara (horiz.) 5 5
532. 35 d. Yachts and Gulf Hotel (horiz.) 8 8
533. 55 d. Qatar by night (horiz.) 12 12
534. 75 d. Arabian oryx (horiz.) 15 15
535. 1 r. 25 Khor al-Udeid (horiz.) 25 25
536. 1 r. 75 Ruins, Wakrah (horiz.) 40 40

73. Traffic Roundabout, Doha.

1975. Amir's Accession. 3rd Anniv. Multicoloured.

537. 10 d. Type **73** 5 5
538. 35 d. Oil pipelines .. 8 8
539. 55 d. Laying offshore pipelines 12 12
540. 1 r. Oil refinery 25 25
541. 1 r. 35 Shaikh Khalifa (vert.) 30 30
542. 1 r. 55. As 1 r. 35 .. 35 35

74. Flintlock Pistol.

1975. National Museum Opening. Multicoloured.

543. 2 d. Type **74** 5 5
544. 3 d. Arabesque-pattern mosaic 5 5
545. 35 d. Museum buildings .. 8 8
546. 75 d. Museum archway (vert.) 20 20
547. 1 r. 25 Flint tools .. 30 30
548. 3 r. Gold necklace and pendant (vert.) .. 75 75

75. Policeman and Road Signs.

1975. Traffic Week. Multicoloured.

549.		5 d. Type **75**	5	5
550.		15 d. Traffic arrows and signal lights	5	5
551.		35 d. Type **75**	8	8
552.		55 d. As 15 d.	12	12

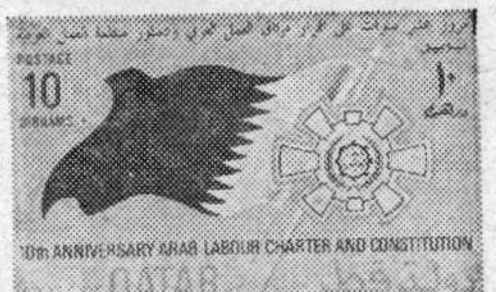

76. Flag and Emblem.

1975. Arab Labour Charter and Constitution. 10th Anniv.

553.	**76.**	10 d. multicoloured ..	5	5
554.		35 d. multicoloured ..	8	8
555.		1 r. multicoloured ..	25	25

77. Government Building, Doha.

1975. Independence. 4th Anniv. Mult.

556.		5 d. Type **77**	5	5
557.		15 d. Museum and clock tower, Doha	5	5
558.		35 d. Constitution-Arabic text (vert.)	8	8
559		55 d. Ruler and flag (vert.)	12	12
560.		75 d. Constitution-English text (vert.)	20	20
561.		1 r. 25. As 55 d... ..	30	30

78. Telecommunications Satellite (I.T.U.).

1975. United Nations. 30th Anniv. Multicoloured.

562.		5 d. Type **78**	5	5
563.		15 d. U.N. Headquarters, New York	5	5
564.		35 d. U.P.U. emblem and map	8	8
565.		1 r. Doctors tending child (U.N.I.C.E.F.) ..	25	25
566.		1 r. 25 Bulldozer (I.L.O.)	30	30
567.		2 r. Students in class (U.N.E.S.C.O.).. ..	45	45

79. Fertilizer Plant.

1975. Qatar Industry. Multicoloured.

568.		5 d. Type **79**	5	5
569.		10 d. Flour Mills (vert.) ..	5	5
570.		35 d. Natural Gas plant ..	12	12
571.		75 d. Oil refinery	20	20
572.		1 r. 25 Cement works ..	30	30
573.		1 r. 55 Steel mills	40	40

80. Modern Building, Doha.

1976. Amir's Accession. 4th Anniversary.

574.	**80.**	5 d. multicoloured ..	5	5
575.	–	10 d. multicoloured ..	5	5
576.	–	35 d. multicoloured ..	15	15
577.	–	55 d. multicoloured ..	20	20
578.	–	75 d. multicoloured ..	30	30
579.	–	1 r. 55 multicoloured ..	60	60

DESIGNS: Nos. 574/6 show public buildings etc. Nos. 577/8 show the Amir with flag.

81. Tracking Aerial. **82.** Early and Modern Telephones.

1976. Satellite Earth Station. Opening. Multicoloured.

580.		35 d. Type **81**	15	15
581.		55 d. "Intelsat" satellite	20	20
582.		75 d. Type **81**	30	30
583.		1 r. As 55 d.	40	40

1976. Telephone Centenary.

584.	**82.**	1 r. multicoloured ..	40	40
585.		1 r. 35 multicoloured ..	55	55

82. Tournament Emblem. **85.** Football.

84. Qatar Dhows.

1976. 4th Arabian Gulf Football Cup Tournament. Multicoloured.

586.		5 d. Type **83**	5	5
587.		10 d. Qatar Stadium ..	5	5
588.		35 d. Type **83**	15	15
589.		55 d. Two players with ball	20	20
590.		75 d. Player with ball ..	30	30
591.		1 r. 25 As 10 d.	50	50

1976. Arab Dhows.

592.	**84.**	10 d. multicoloured ..	5	5
593.	–	35 d. multicoloured ..	15	15
594.	–	80 d. multicoloured ..	30	30
595.	–	1 r. 25 multicoloured..	50	50
596.	–	1 r. 50 multicoloured..	60	60
597.	–	2 r. multicoloured ..	80	80

DESIGNS: As T **84** showing local craft.

1976. Olympic Games, Montreal. Mult.

598.		5 d. Type **85**	5	5
599.		10 d. Sailing	5	5
600.		35 d. Horse-jumping ..	15	15
601.		80 d. Boxing	30	30
602.		1 r. 25 Weightlifting ..	50	50
603.		1 r. 50 Basketball ..	60	60

86. Urban Housing Development.

1976. HABITAT. U.N. Conf. on Human Settlements. Multicoloured.

604.		10 d. Type **86**	5	5
605.		35 d. U.N. and HABITAT emblems	15	15
606.		80 d. Communal housing development	30	30
607.		1 r. 25 Shaikh Khalifa ..	50	50

87. Sandpiper.

1976. Birds. Multicoloured.

608.		5 d. Type **87**	5	5
609.		10 d. Tern	5	5
610.		35 d. Hawk	15	15
611.		80 d. Flamingo (vert.) ..	30	30
612.		1 r. Rock thrush (vert.)..	40	40
613.		2 r. Falcon (vert.).. ..	80	80

88. Ruler and Flag.

1976. Independence. 5th Anniv. Mult.

614.		5 d. Type **88**	5	5
615.		10 d. Type **88**	5	5
616.		40 d. Doha buildings (horiz.)	15	15
617.		80 d. As 40 d.	30	30
618.		1 r. 25 Off-shore oil-rig (horiz.)	50	50
619.		1 r. 50 U.N. and Qatar Emblems (horiz.) ..	60	60

89. U.N. Emblem.

1976. United Nations Day.

620.	**89.**	2 r. multicoloured ..	80	80
621.		3 r. multicoloured ..	1·25	1·25

POSTAGE DUE STAMPS

D 1.

1968.

D 254.	**D 1.**	5 d. blue	5	5
D 255.		10 d. red	5	5
D 256.		20 d. green	5	5
D 257.		30 d. lilac	8	8

QUEENSLAND

BC

The N.E. state of the Commonwealth of Australia whose stamps it now uses.

1. 2.

1860. Imperf.

1.	**1.**	1d. red	£700	£300
2.		2d. blue	£1600	£650
3.		6d. green	£1500	£300

1860. Perf.

96.	**1.**	1d. red	14·00	2·25
94.		1d. orange	12·00	1·10
99.		2d. blue	5·50	35
16.		3d. brown	8·00	9·00
65.		3d. olive	26·00	1·50
53.		4d. grey	40·00	6·00
55.		4d. lilac	13·00	3·00
103.	**1.**	4d. yellow	95·00	3·50
27.		6d. green..	16·00	3·50
108.		1s. purple	14·00	2·75
29.		1s. grey	26·00	4·25
119.		2s. blue	9·00	6·00
121.		2s. 6d. red	17·00	6·00
58.		5s. red	40·00	13·00
123.		5s. yellow	12·00	6·00
125.		10s. brown	60·00	22·00
127.		20s. rose	60·00	17·00

1879.

136.	**2.**	1d. brown	1·50	55
138.		1d. orange	1·50	55
140.		1d. red	1·50	30
143.		2d. blue	2·25	25
146.		4d. yellow	3·50	55
147.		6d. green..	4·25	85
150.		1s. mauve	3·50	2·00

1880. No. 136 surch. **Half-penny.**

151.	**2.**	½d. on 1d. brown ..	14·00	12·00

3. 4.

5. 6.

1882.

152.	**3.**	2s. blue	12·00	6·00
162.		2s. 6d. orange	9·00	6·50
163.		5s. red	9·00	7·00
164.		10s. brown	12·00	11·00
165.		£1 green	26·00	10·00

1882. Shaded background round head.

184.	**4.**	½d. green..	45	5
206.	**5.**	1d. orange	8	5
204.		2d. blue	25	5
191.	**6.**	2½d. red	45	5
192.	**5.**	3d. brown	45	10
193.		4d. yellow	50	12
170.		6d. green..	85	8
173.		1s. mauve	1·10	12
197.		2s. brown	2·75	45

7.

8. 9.

1895. Head on white background.

208.	**7.**	½d. green..	8	5
211.	**8.**	1d. orange	25	5
212.		2d. blue	25	5
214.	**9.**	2½d. red	1·10	25
215.		5d. brown	85	25

10. 12.

1896.

229.	**10.**	1d. red	8	5

1897. Same designs, but figures in all four corners, as T **12**.

231. ½d. green 25 10
288. 1d. red 12 5
234. 2d. blue 12 5
236. 2½d. red .. .. .. 1·00 45
238. 2½d. purple on blue .. 30 5
241. 3d. brown 40 8
244. 4d. yellow 55 12
294. 4d. black 40 25
246. 5d. brown 40 8
249. 6d. green 60 10
251. 1s. mauve .. .. 1·00 40
254. 2s. green .. .. .. 2·00 80

14.

16. 15.

1899.

287. **14.** ½d. green 12 5

1900. S. African War Charity. Inscr. "PATRIOTIC FUND 1900".

264a. **15.** 1d. (1s.) mauve .. 32·00 35·00
264b. – 2d. (2s.) violet (horiz.) 55·00 65·00

1903.

265. **16.** 9d. brown and blue .. 1·75 45

REGISTRATION STAMP

1861. Inscr. "REGISTERED".

20. **1.** (No value) yellow .. 6·00 11·00

QUELIMANE O3

A district of Portuguese E. Africa, now part of Mozambique, whose stamps it now uses.

1913. Surch. **REPUBLICA QUELIMANE** and new value on "Vasco da Gama" stamps of (a) Portuguese Colonies.

1. ¼ c. on 2½ r. green 60 40
2. ½ c. on 5 r. red 60 40
3. 1 c. on 10 r. purple .. 60 40
4. 2½ c. on 25 r. green .. 60 40
5. 5 c. on 50 r. blue 60 40
6. 7½ c. on 75 r. brown .. 80 60
7. 10 c. on 100 r. brown .. 60 40
8. 15 c. on 150 r. yellow-brown 60 40

(b) Macao.

9. ¼ c. on ½ a. green 60 40
10. ½ c. on 1 a. red 60 40
11. 1 c. on 2 a. purple 60 40
12. 2½ c. on 4 a. green 60 40
13. 5 c. on 8 a. blue 60 40
14. 7½ c. on 12 a. brown .. 80 60
15. 10 c. on 16 a. brown .. 60 40
16. 15 c. on 24 a. yellow-brown 60 40

(c) Timor.

17. ¼ c. on ½ a. green 60 40
18. ½ c. on 1 a. red 60 40
19. 1 c. on 2 a. purple 60 40
20. 2½ c. on 4 a. green 60 40
21. 5 c. on 8 a. blue 60 40
22. 7½ c. on 12 a. brown .. 80 60
23. 10 c. on 16 a. brown .. 60 40
24. 15 c. on 24 a. yellow-brown 60 40

1914. "Ceres" key-type inscr. "QUELIMANE".

25. U. ¼ c. olive 30 25
26. ½ c. black 55 40
42. 1 c. green 40 35
28. 1½ c. brown 60 50
29. 2 c. red 60 50
30. 2½ c. violet 20 15
31. 5 c. blue 35 30
43. 7½ c. brown 40 35
33. 8 c. black 55 45
44. 10 c. brown 40 35
35. 15 c. claret 70 55
45. 20 c. green 40 35
37. 30 c. brown on green .. 90 70
38. 40 c. brown on rose .. 90 70
39. 50 c. orange on pink .. 90 70
40. 1 e. green on blue .. 90 70

MORE DETAILED LISTS

are given in the Stanley Gibbons Catalogues referred to in the country headings:

BC British Commonwealth
E1, E2, E3 Europe 1, 2, 3
O1, O2, O3, O4 Overseas 1, 2, 3, 4

RAJASTHAN BC

Formed in 1948 from states in Rajputana, India, which included Bundi, Jaipur and Kishangarh whose separate posts functioned until 1 April, 1950. Now uses Indian stamps.

BUNDI

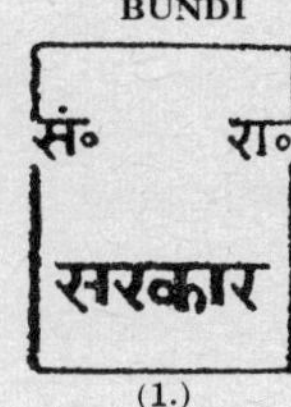

(1.)

1949. Nos. 86/92 of Bundi handstamped or optd. by machine with T **1**.

1. **4.** ¼ a. green 20
2. ½ a. violet 30
3. 1 a. green 30
11. – 2 a. red .. .. 60 3·50
12. – 4 a. orange .. .. 40 3·50
6. – 8 a. blue 70
14. – 1 r. brown .. .. 2·50

Nos. 1, 2, 3 and 6 used are worth about three times the unused prices.

JAIPUR

राजस्थान

RAJASTHAN

(2.)

1949. Stamps of Jaipur optd. with T **2**.

15. **6.** ¼ a. black & brown-purple 50 1·50
16. ½ a. black and violet .. 60 1·50
17. ¾ a. black and orange .. 60 1·50
18. 1 a. black and blue .. 1·00 1·50
19. 2 a. black and orange .. 1·00 2·25
20. 2½ a. black and red .. 1·00 4·00
21. 3 a. black and green .. 1·10 4·00
22. 4 a. black and green .. 1·50 6·00
23 6 a. black and blue .. 1·50 6·00
24. 8 a. black and brown .. 4·50 7·00
25. 1 r. black and bistre .. 6·00 20·00

KISHANGARH

1949. Stamps of Kishangarh handstamped with T **1**.

(a) On stamps of 1899.

26. **2.** ¼ a. pink .. .. ..
27. ½ a. blue .. .. 12·00
28. 1 a. lilac .. .. .. 8·00
30. 4 a. chocolate .. .. 13·00
31. 1 r. green .. .. ..
32. 5 r. mauve .. ..

(b) On stamps of 1904.

33. **6.** ½ a. chestnut .. .. 8·00
34. 4 a. brown .. .. 10·00
35. **2.** 8 a. grey .. .. .. 18·00
36. **6.** 8 a. violet .. .. 9·00
37. 1 r. green .. .. .. 13·00
38. 2 r. yellow .. .. 13·00
39. 5 r. chocolate .. .. 13·00

(c) On stamps of 1912.

40. **7.** ½ a. green .. .. 4·00 4·00
41. 1 a. red .. .. .. 4·00 5·00
43. 2 a. purple .. .. 65 2·25
44. 4 a. blue .. .. .. 9·00
45. 8 a. brown .. .. 2·50
46. 1 r. mauve .. .. 7·00
47. 2 r. green .. .. .. 7·00
48 5 r. brown .. .. 20·00

(d) On stamps of 1928.

55. **9.** ¼ a. blue .. .. 10·00 10·00
57. ½ a. green .. .. 4·00 4·00
58. – 1 a. red .. .. .. 5·50 6·50
60. – 2 a. purple .. .. 6·50 5·50
61. **9.** 4 a. brown .. .. 35 1·00
62. 8 a. violet .. .. 4·00
63. 1 r. green .. .. .. 4·00
53. 2 r. yellow .. .. 13·00
54. 5 r. claret .. .. 13·00

RAJPIPLA BC

A state of Bombay, India. Now uses Indian stamps.

1.

2.

1880

1. **1.** 1 p. blue .. .. .. 40 1·25
2. **2.** 2 a. green .. .. .. 3·25 4·00
3. 4 a. red .. .. .. 2·50 3·00

RAS AL KHAIMA O4

Arab Shaikhdom in the Arabian Gulf.

Ras al Khaima joined the United Arab Emirates in February, 1972. U.A.E. stamps were used in the shaikhdom from 1st January, 1973.

100 naye paise = 1 rupee.
1966. 100 dirhams = 1 riyal.

1. Shaikh Saqr bin Mohammed al Qasimi.

2. Dhow.

1964.

1. **1.** 5 n.p. brown and black .. 5 5
2. 15 n.p. blue and black .. 5 5
3. – 30 n.p. yellow and black .. 8 8
4. – 40 n.p. blue and black .. 12 12
5. – 75 n.p. red and black .. 25 25
6. **2.** 1 r. brown and green .. 25 25
7. 2 r. brown and violet .. 55 55
8. 5 r. brown and slate .. 1·75 1·75

DESIGNS: As T **1**—VERT. 30 n.p. to 75 n.p. Seven palms.

3. Pres. Kennedy inspecting "Friendship 7".

1965. Pres. Kennedy Commem.

9. **3.** 2 r. blue and ochre .. 65 65
10. – 3 r. blue and ochre .. 90 90
11. – 4 r. blue and ochre .. 1·10 1·10

DESIGNS—HORIZ. 3 r. Kennedy and wife. VERT. 4 r. Kennedy and flame of remembrance.

4. Sir Winston Churchill and Houses of Parliament.

1965. Churchill Commem.

12. **4.** 2 r. blue and ochre .. 65 65
13. – 3 r. blue and ochre .. 90 90
14. – 4 r. blue and ochre .. 1·10 1·10

DESIGNS—HORIZ. 3 r. Churchill and Pres. Roosevelt. 4 r. Churchill, and Heads of State at his funeral.

1965. Olympic Games, Tokyo (1964). Optd. **OLYMPIC TOKYO 1964** in English and Arabic, and Olympic "rings".

15. **2.** 1 r. brown and green .. 25 25
16. 2 r. brown and violet .. 55 55
17. 5 r. brown and slate .. 1·60 1·60

1965. Abraham Lincoln. Death Cent. Optd. **ABRAHAM LINCOLN 1809-1865** in English and Arabic.

18. **2.** 1 r. brown and green .. 25 25
19. 2 r. brown and violet .. 55 55
20. 5 r. brown and slate .. 1·60 1·60

1965. Pres. Roosevelt. 20th Death Anniv. Optd. **FRANKLIN D. ROOSEVELT 1882-1945.** in English and Arabic.

21. **2.** 1 r. brown and green .. 25 25
22. 2 r. brown and violet .. 55 55
23. 5 r. brown and slate .. 1·60 1·60

5. Satellite and Tracking Station.

1966. I.T.U. Cent. Multicoloured.

24. 15 n.p. Type **5** 5 5
25. 50 n.p. Post Office Tower, London, "Telstar" and tracking gantry .. 15 15
26. 85 n.p. Rocket on launching-pad and "Relay" .. 25 25
27. 1 r. Type **5** 30 30
28. 2 r. As 50 n.p. 60 60
29. 3 r. As 85 n.p. .. 90 90

6. Swimming.

7. Carpenter.

1966. Pan-Arab Games, Cairo (1965).

31. A. 1 n.p. brown, pink & grn. 5 5
32. B. 2 n.p. black, grey & emer. 5 5
33. C. 3 n.p. brown pink & green 5 5
34. D. 4 n.p. brown, pink & pur. 5 5
35. A. 5 n.p. black, grey & orge. 5 5
36. **6.** 10 n.p. brown, pink & blue 5 5
37. B. 25 n.p. brown, pink & cinn. 8 8
38. C. 50 n.p. black, grey & violet 15 15
39. D. 75 n.p. black, grey & blue 25 25
40. **6.** 1 r. black, grey & turquoise 50 50

DESIGNS: A, Running. B, Boxing. C, Football. D, Fencing.

1966. American Astronauts.

42. **7.** 25 n.p. black, gold & purple 8 8
43. – 50 n.p. black, silver & brn. 15 15
44. – 75 n.p. blk., silver & turq. 25 25
45. – 1 r. black, silver & bistre 40 40
46. – 2 r. black, silver & mag. 80 80
47. – 3 r. black, gold and green 1·25 1·10
48. – 4 r. black, gold and red .. 1·60 1·40
49. – 5 r. black, gold and blue 2·00 1·75

ASTRONAUTS: 50 n.p. Glenn. 75 n.p. Shephard. 1 r. Cooper. 2 r. Grissom. 3 r. Schirra. 4 r. Stafford. 5 r. Lovell.

8. Shaikh Sabah of Kuwait and Shaikh Saqr of Ras al Khaima.

1966. Int. Co-operation Year.

51. **8.** 1 r. black and brown .. 25 25
52. A. 1 r. black and lilac .. 25 25
53. B. 1 r. black and red .. 25 25
54. C. 1 r. black and turquoise .. 25 25
55. D. 1 r. black and olive .. 25 25
56. E. 1 r. black and yellow .. 25 25
57. F. 1 r. black and orange .. 25 25
58. G. 1 r. black and blue .. 25 25

SHAIKH SAQR AND WORLD LEADERS: A, Shaikh Ahmad of Qatar. B, Pres. Nasser. C, King Hussein. D, Pres. Johnson. E, Pres. De Gaulle. F, Pope Paul VI. G, Prime Minister, Harold Wilson.

NEW CURRENCY SURCHARGES. During the latter half of 1966 various issues appeared surcharged in dirhams and riyals. The 1964 definitives with this surcharge are listed below as there is considerable evidence of their postal use. Nos. 24/58 also exist with these surcharges.

In August 1966 Nos. 1/14, 24/9 and 51/8 appeared surcharged in fils and rupees. As Ras al Khaima did not adopt this currency their status is uncertain.

1966. Nos. 1/8 with currency names changed to dirhams and riyals by overprinting in English and Arabic.

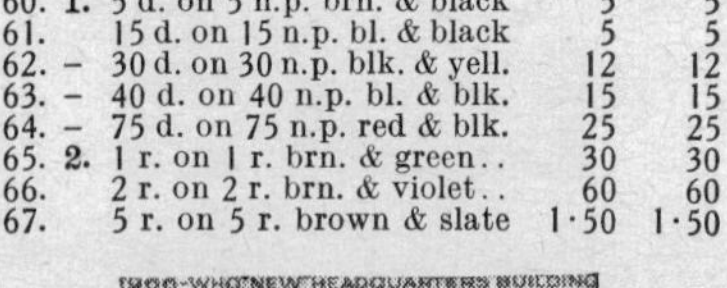

60. **1.** 5 d. on 5 n.p. brn. & black 5 5
61. 15 d. on 15 n.p. bl. & black 5 5
62. – 30 d. on 30 n.p. blk. & yell. 12 12
63. – 40 d. on 40 n.p. bl. & blk. 15 15
64. – 75 d. on 75 n.p. red & blk. 25 25
65. **2.** 1 r. on 1 r. brn. & green .. 30 30
66. 2 r. on 2 r. brn. & violet .. 60 60
67. 5 r. on 5 r. brown & slate 1·50 1·50

9. W.H.O. Building and Flowers.

1966. W.H.O. Headquarters, Geneva. Inaug.

68. **9.** 15 d. multicoloured (post.) 5 5
69. – 35 d. multicoloured .. 12 12
70. **9.** 50 d. multicoloured (air) .. 15 15
71. – 3 r. multicoloured .. 90 90

DESIGN: 35 d., 3 r. As T **9** but with red instead of yellow flower at left.

10. Queen Elizabeth II presenting Jules Rimet Cup to Bobby Moore, Captain of England Team.

1966. Air. England's Victory in World Cup Football Championships. Multicoloured.
73. 1 r. Wembley Stadium .. 30 30
74. 2 r. Goalkeeper saving ball 60 60
75. 3 r. Footballers with ball .. 90 90
76. 4 r. Type **10** .. 1·25 1·25

APPENDIX. Further issues for 1967-72 are recorded in the Appendix at the end of this catalogue.

For later issues see **UNITED ARAB EMIRATES.**

REUNION

04

An island in the Indian Ocean, E. of Madagascar, now an overseas department of France.

1.

1852. Imperf.
1. **1.** 15 c. black on blue .. £4000 £2500
2. 30 c. black on blue .. £4000 £2500

1885. Stamps of French Colonies surch. "**R**" and value in figures. Imperf.
5. **4.** 5 c. on 30 c. brown .. 6·50 5·50
7. **8.** 5 c. on 30 c. brown .. 80 80
3. **1.** 5 c. on 40 c. orange .. 55·00 55·00
6. **6.** 5 c. on 40 c. orange .. 4·75 3·50
8. **8.** 5 c. on 40 c. red on yellow 13·00 10·00
9. 10 c. on 40 c. red on yellow 1·60 1·25
10. 20 c. on 30 c. brown .. 7·50 5·50
4. **1.** 25 c. on 40 c. orange .. 6·50 4·25

1891. Stamps of French Colonies optd. **REUNION.**
17. **9.** 1 c. black on blue .. 50 40
18. 2 c. brown on yellow .. 60 50
19. 4 c. brown on grey .. 1·25 85
20. 5 c. green .. .. 1·10 85
21. 10 c. black on lilac .. 3·25 65
22. 15 c. blue .. .. 6·00 45
23. 20 c. red on green .. 4·50 3·25
24. 25 c. black on red .. 4·50 55
13. **8.** 30 c. brown .. .. 5·00 3·75
25a. **9.** 35 c. black on yellow .. 3·25 2·10
11. **6.** 40 c. orange .. .. 75·00 65·00
14. **8.** 40 c. red on yellow .. 3·25 2·75
26. **9.** 40 c. red on yellow .. 11·00 8·00
15. **8.** 75 c. red .. .. 65·00 60·00
27. **9.** 75 c. red .. .. 90·00 85·00
12. **7.** 80 c. red .. .. 6·00 5·50
16. **8.** 1 f. olive .. .. 5·50 5·50
28. **9.** 1 f. olive .. .. 85·00 75·00

1891. No. 23 surch. in figures.
29. **9.** 02 c. on 20 c. red on green 1·10 1·10
31. 2 on 20 c. red on green .. 25 25
30. 15 c. on 20 c. red on green 1·75 1·75

1892. "Tablet" key-type inscr. "REUNION".
34. D. 1 c. black on blue .. 8 8
35. 2 c. brown on yellow .. 10 8
36. 4 c. claret on grey .. 10 8
50. 5 c. green 15 8
38. 10 c. black on lilac .. 65 8
51. 10 c. red 25 10
39. 15 c. blue .. .. 2·75 15
52. 15 c. grey 65 5
40. 20 c. red on green .. 1·60 1·25
41. 25 c. black on red .. 1·60 20
53. 25 c. blue .. .. 3·25 3·00
42. 30 c. brown .. .. 2·75 1·25
43. 40 c. red on yellow .. 3·25 2·10
44. 50 c. red .. .. 7·00 3·25
54. 50 c. brown on blue (A) .. 6·50 6·00
55. 50 c. brown on blue (B) .. 7·00 5·50
45. 75 c. brown on orange .. 5·50 5·00
46. 1 f. olive .. .. 3·75 2·40
Type (A) has name in red, Type (B) in blue.

1893. Stamp of French Colonies, "Commerce" type, surch. in figures.
47. **9.** 2 c. on 20 c. red on green .. 25 25

1901. "Tablet" key-type surch. in figures.
56. D. 5 c. on 40 c. red on yellow 35 35
57. 5 c. on 50 c. red 50 50
58. 15 c. on 75 c. brn. on orge. 1·50 1·50
59. 15 c. on 1 f. olive .. 1·50 1·50

2. Map of Reunion.

3. View of Saint-Denis and Arms of Colony.

4. View of St. Pierre and Crater Dolomieu.

1907.
60. **2.** 1 c. red and lilac .. 5 5
61. 2 c. blue and brown .. 5 5
62. 4 c. red and olive .. 5 5
63. 5 c. red and green .. 5 5
92. 5 c. violet and yellow .. 5 5
64. 10 c. green and red .. 15 5
93. 10 c. green 5 5
94. 10 c. red & brown on blue 5 5
65. 15 c. blue and black .. 5 5
95. 15 c. green 5 5
96. 15 c. red and blue .. 5 5
66. **3.** 20 c. green and olive .. 5 5
67. 25 c. brown and blue .. 30 15
97. 25 c. blue and brown .. 5 5
68. 30 c. green and brown .. 5 5
98. 30 c. red 5 5
99. 30 c. red and grey .. 5 5
100. 30 c. green 10 8
69. 35 c. blue and brown .. 10 5
101. 40 c. brown and olive .. 5 5
70. 45 c. red and violet .. 10 5
102. 45 c. red and claret .. 5 5
71. 50 c. blue and brown .. 20 10
104. 50 c. blue 5 5
105. 50 c. violet and yellow .. 5 5
106. 60 c. brown and blue .. 5 5
107. 65 c. blue and violet .. 8 8
72. 75 c. red 5 5
108. 75 c. purple and brown .. 25 20
109. 90 c. red 95 85
73. **4.** 1 f. blue and brown .. 5 5
110. 1 f. blue 5 5
111. 1 f. lilac and brown .. 10 8
112. 1 f. 10 mauve and brown 10 8
113. 1 f. 50 blue .. .. 1·10 1·00
74. 2 f. green and red .. 50 20
114. 3 f. mauve on red .. 1·10 1·00
75. 5 f. brown and red .. 95 40

1912. "Tablet" key-type surch.
76. D. 05 on 2 c. brown on yell. 5 5
77. 05 on 15 c. grey .. 5 5
78. 05 on 20 c. red on green 10 10
79. 05 on 25 c. black on red 5 5
80. 05 on 30 c. brown .. 5 5
81. 10 on 40 c. red on yellow 5 5
82. 10 on 50 c. brown on blue 35 35
83. 10 on 75 c. brn. on orge. 1·00 1·00

1915. Red Cross. Surch. **5 c** and large red cross.
88. **2.** 10 c.+5 c. green and red 8 8

1916. Surch. **5 c** and small red cross.
90. **2.** 10 c.+5 c. green and red 5 5

1917. Surch. in figures.
91. **2.** 0.01 on 4 c. red and olive 15 15
124. **4.** 25 c. on 5 f. brown & red 10 10
115. **3.** 40 on 20 c. yellow & green 5 5
116. 50 on 45 c. red and claret 12 8
118. 50 on 65 c. blue and violet 8 8
119. 60 on 75 c. red .. 5 5
120. **2.** 65 on 15 c. blue & black 12 12
121. 85 on 15 c. blue & black 12 12
122. **3.** 85 on 75 c. red .. 12 12
123. 90 on 75 c. red .. 12 12
125. **4.** 1 f. 25 on 1 f. blue 5 5
126. 1 f. 50 on 1 f. blue 8 8
127. 3 f. on 5 f. blue and red .. 30 12
128. 10 f. on 5 f. lake & green 2·00 1·75
129. 20 f. on 5 f. red & brown 2·50 1·90

1931. "Colonial Exhibition" key-types inscr. "REUNION".
130. E. 40 c. green 30 30
131. F. 50 c. mauve 45 45
132. G. 90 c. red 45 45
133. H. 1 f. 50 blue 55 65

5. Cascade, Salazie.

6. Anchain Peak, Salazie.

7. Leon Dierx Museum, Saint-Denis.

8.

1933.
134. **5.** 1 c. purple 5 5
135. 2 c. sepia 5 5
136. 3 c. mauve 5 5
137. 4 c. olive 5 5
138. 5 c. orange 5 5
139. 10 c. blue 5 5
140. 15 c. black 5 5
141. 20 c. blue 5 5
142. 25 c. brown 5 5
143. 30 c. green 5 5
144. **6.** 35 c. green 5 5
145. 40 c. blue 5 5
146. 40 c. sepia 5 5
147. 45 c. mauve 5 5
148. 45 c. green 5 5
149. 50 c. red 5 5
150. 55 c. orange 5 5
151. 60 c. blue 5 5
152. 65 c. olive 15 5
153. 70 c. olive 5 5
154. 75 c. sepia 45 40
155. 80 c. black 5 5
156. 90 c. red 25 20
157. 90 c. purple 5 5
158. 1 f. green 15 5
159. 1 f. red 10 5
160. 1 f. black 5 5
161. **7.** 1 f. 25 brown 5 5
162. 1 f. 25 red 10 10
163. **5.** 1 f. 40 blue 5 5
164. **7.** 1 f. 50 blue 5 5
165. **5.** 1 f. 60 red 8 8
166. **7.** 1 f. 75 olive 8 5
167. **5.** 1 f. 75 blue 5 5
168. **7.** 2 f. red 5 5
169. **5.** 2 f. 25 blue 20 20
170. 2 f. 50 brown 8 8
171. **7.** 3 f. violet 5 5
172. 5 f. mauve 5 5
173. 10 f. blue 10 10
174. 20 f. brown 15 15

1937. Air. Pioneer Flight from Reunion to France by Laurent, Lenier and Touge. Optd. **REUNION - FRANCE par avion "ROLAND GARROS".**
174a. **6.** 50 c. red .. .. 50·00 40·00

1937. International Exhibition, Paris. As Nos. 110/15 of Cameroun.
175. 20 c. violet 20 20
176. 30 c. green 20 20
177. 40 c. red 20 20
178. 50 c. brown 20 20
179. 90 c. red 20 20
180. 1 f. 50 blue 20 20

1938. Air.
181. **8.** 3 f. 65 blue and red .. 5 5
182. 6 f. 65 brown and red .. 5 5
183. 9 f. 65 red and blue .. 5 5
184. 12 f. 65 brown and green 15 15

1938. Int. Anti-Cancer Fund. As T **10** of Cameroun.
185. 1 f. 75+50 c. blue .. 2·25 2·25

1939. New York World's Fair. As T **11** of Cameroun.
186. 1 f. 25 red 8 8
187. 2 f. 25 blue 8 8

1939. 150th Anniv. of French Revolution. As T **16** of Cameroun.
188. 45 c.+25 c. green (postage) 1·40 1·40
189. 70 c.+30 c. brown .. 1·40 1·40
190. 90 c.+35 c. orange .. 1·40 1·40
191. 1 f. 25+1 f. red .. 1·40 1·40
192. 2 f. 25+2 f. blue .. 1·40 1·40
193. 3 f. 65+4 f. black (air) 2·25 2·25

1943. Surch.
194. **6.** 1 f. on 65 c. olive .. 15 5

1943. Optd. **France Libre.**
198. **5.** 1 c. purple (postage) .. 5 5
199. 2 c. sepia 5 5
200. 3 c. mauve 5 5
195. **2.** 4 c. red and olive .. 35 35
201. **5.** 4 c. olive 5 5
202. 5 c. orange 5 5
203. 10 c. blue 5 5
204. 15 c. black 5 5
205. 20 c. blue 5 5
206. 25 c. brown 5 5
207. 30 c. green 5 5
208. **6.** 35 c. green 5 5
209. 40 c. blue 5 5
210. 40 c. sepia 5 5
211. 45 c. mauve 5 5
212. 45 c. green 5 5
213. 50 c. red 5 5
214. 55 c. orange 5 5
215. 60 c. blue 15 15
216. 65 c. olive 5 5
217. 70 c. green 12 12
196. **3.** 75 c. red 12 12
218. **6.** 75 c. sepia 35 35
219. 80 c. black 5 5
220. 90 c. violet 5 5
221. 1 f. green 10 10
222. 1 f. red 12 12
223. 1 f. black 10 10
240. 1 f. on 65 c. olive .. 8 8
224. **7.** 1 f. 25 brown 10 10
225. 1 f. 25 red 12 12
238. – 1 f. 25 red (No. 186) .. 20 20
226. **5.** 1 f. 40 blue 12 12
227. **7.** 1 f. 50 blue 5 5
228. **5.** 1 f. 60 red 12 12
229. **7.** 1 f. 75 olive 5 5
230. **5.** 1 f. 75 blue 20 20
231. **7.** 2 f. red 5 5
239. – 2 f. 25 blue (No. 187) .. 20 20
232. **5.** 2 f. 25 blue 15 15
233. 2 f. 50 brown 30 30
234. **7.** 3 f. violet 5 5
197. **4.** 5 f. brown and red .. 4·50 4·50
235. **7.** 5 f. mauve 10 10
236. 10 f. blue 50 50
237. 20 f. brown .. .. 1·00 1·00
241. **8.** 3 f. 65 blue & red (air) .. 35 35
242. 6 f. 65 brown and red .. 35 35
243. 9 f. 65 red and blue .. 35 35
244. 12 f. 65 brown and green 35 35

9. Chief Products.

1943. Free French Issue.
245. **9.** 5 c. brown 5 5
246. 10 c. blue 5 5
247. 25 c. green 5 5
248. 30 c. red 5 5
249. 40 c. green 5 5
250. 80 c. mauve 5 5
251. 1 f. maroon 5 5
252. 1 f. 50 red 5 5
253. 2 f. black 5 5
254. 2 f. 50 blue 5 5
255. 4 f. violet 5 5
256. 5 f. yellow 5 5
257. 10 f. brown 12 12
258. 20 f. green 15 15

1944. Free French Administration. Air. As T **18** of Cameroun.
259. 1 f. orange 5 5
260. 1 f. 50 red 5 5
261. 5 f. maroon 5 5
262. 10 f. black 5 5
263. 25 f. blue 5 5
264. 50 f. green 5 5
265. 100 f. claret 15 15

1944. Mutual Air and Red Cross Funds. As T **19** of Cameroun.
266. 5 f.+20 f. black 8 8

1945. Eboue. As T **20** of Cameroun.
267. 2 f. black 5 5
268. 25 f. green 8 8

1945. Surch.
269. **9.** 50 c. on 5 c. brown .. 5 5
270. 60 c. on 5 c. brown .. 5 5
271. 70 c. on 5 c. brown .. 5 5
272. 1 f. 20 on 5 c. brown .. 5 5
273. 2 f. 40 on 25 c. green .. 5 5
274. 3 f. on 25 c. green .. 5 5
275. 4 f. 50 on 25 c. green .. 5 5
276. 15 f. on 2 f. 50 blue .. 10 10

1946. Air. Victory. As T **21** of Cameroun.
277. 8 f. grey 8 8

1946. Air. From Chad to the Rhine. As T **22** of Cameroun.
278. 5 f. red 15 15
279. 10 f. violet 15 15
280. 15 f. black 15 15
281. 20 f. red 20 20
282. 25 f. blue 20 20
283. 50 f. green 25 25

10. Cliffs.

11. Banana Tree and Cliff.

12. Mountain Landscape.

13. Shadow of Aeroplane over Coast.

1947.
284. **10.** 10 c. orge. & grn. (post.) .. 5 5
285. 30 c. orange and blue .. 5 5
286. 40 c. orange and brown 5 5
287. – 50 c. brown and green .. 5 5
288. – 60 c. brown and blue .. 5 5
289. – 80 c. olive and brown .. 5 5
290. – 1 f. purple and blue .. 5 5
291. – 1 f. 20 grey and green .. 5 5
292. – 1 f. 50 purple & orange 5 5
293. **11.** 2 f. blue and green .. 5 5
294. 3 f. purple and green .. 5 5
295. 3 f. 60 red 5 5

296. **11.** 4 f. blue and brown .. 5 5
297. **12.** 5 f. mauve and brown.. 5 5
298. 6 f. blue and brown .. 8 8
299. 10 f. orange and blue .. 15 12
300. – 15 f. purple and blue .. 45 35
301. – 20 f. blue and orange .. 55 45
302. – 25 f. brown and mauve 60 55
303. **13.** 50 f. green & grey (air) 1·40 1·10
304. – 100 f. orange and brown 1·75 1·75
305. – 200 f. blue and orange .. 2·25 2·25

DESIGNS—VERT. (20×37 mm.). 50 c. to 80 c. Cutting sugar cane. 1 f. to 1 f. 50, Cascade. (28×50 mm.). 100 f. Aeroplane over Reunion. HORIZ. (37×20 mm.). 15 f. to 25 f. Ship approaching Reunion. (50×28 mm.). 200 f. Reunion from the air.

1949. Stamps of France surch. **CFA** and value in African francs. (a) Postage.
(i) Small Arms, Ceres, Marianne, Harvester and "France" types.

308. 10 c. on 30 c. (No. 972) .. 5 5
342. 10 c. on 50 c. (No. 1050) .. 5 5
309. 30 c. on 50 c. (No. 973) .. 8 5
306. 50 c. on 1 f. (Ceres) .. 8 5
347. 50 c. on 1 f. (Bearn) .. 5 5
354. 50 c. on 1 f. (Poitou) .. 5 5
376. 50 c. on 1 f. (Venaissin) .. 5 5
307. 60 c. on 2 f. (No. 914) .. 1·10 20
343. 1 f. on 2 f. (Auvergne) .. 1·75 1·00
348. 1 f. on 2 f. (Touraine) .. 20 10
355. 1 f. on 2 f. (Champagne) .. 5 5
364. 1 f. on 2 f. (Angoumois) .. 5 5
314. 1 f. on 3 f. (No. 999) .. 15 10
315. 2 f. on 4 f. (No. 1001) .. 30 10
316. 2 f. on 5 f. green (No. 921) 1·50 10
317. 2 f. on 5 f. violet (No. 1004b) 20 8
381. 2 f. on 6 f. (No. 1198b) .. 5 5
318. 2 f. 50 on 5 f. (No. 1004) .. 2·50 2·25
319. 3 f. on 6 f. red (No. 923) .. 20 5
320. 3 f. on 6 f. green (No. 1005a) 90 40
321. 4 f. on 10 f. (No. 1007) .. 10 5
382. 4 f. on 12 f. (No. 1200a) .. 40 20
383. 5 f. on 10 f. (No. 1199c) .. 15 8
322. 6 f. on 12 f. blue (No. 1007a) 40 5
323. 6 f. on 12 f. orange (1007b) 35 25
331. 9 f. on 18 f. (No. 1007e) .. 35 35
384. 10 f. on 20 f. (No. 1238b).. 10 8
385. 12 f. on 25 f. (No. 1238c).. 40 5

(ii) Large pictorial types.

358. 2 f. on 6 f. (Lourdes) .. 5 5
369. 2 f. on 6 f. (Bordelaise) .. 20 15
351. 3 f. on 6 f. (No. 1168) .. 10 5
359. 3 f. on 8 f. (Seine) .. 20 5
370. 3 f. on 8 f. (Marseille) .. 12 5
387. 3 f. on 10 f. (No. 1351) .. 5 5
360. 4 f. on 10 f. (Royan) .. 20 8
371. 4 f. on 10 f. (Nice) .. 12 5
372. 5 f. on 12 f. (No. 1265) .. 25 5
310. 5 f. on 20 f. (Finistere) .. 50 12
344. 5 f. on 20 f. (Comminges) 1·00 30
349. 5 f. on 20 f. (Chambord) .. 15 8
361. 6 f. on 12 f. (No. 1208) .. 20 8
373. 6 f. on 18 f. (Uzerche) .. 12 5
388. 6 f. on 18 f. (Beynac) .. 15 5
311. 7 f. on 12 f. (No. 979) .. 90 55
386. 7 f. on 15 f. (No. 1335) .. 15 5
312. 8 f. on 25 f. (Nancy) .. 2·00 60
346. 8 f. on 25 f. (Wandrille) .. 35 12
377. 8 f. on 30 f. (No. 1297) .. 45 5
350. 8 f. on 40 f. (Bigorre) .. 95 8
352. 8 f. on 40 f. (Cristaux) .. 1·10 8
356. 8 f. on 40 f. (Canoe) .. 3·00 1·00
362. 9 f. on 18 f. (No. 1210) .. 1·75 1·25
389. 9 f. on 25 f. (No. 1353) .. 15 8
378. 9 f. on 40 f. (No. 1298) .. 30 25
363. 10 f. on 20 f. (No. 1211) .. 45 8
313. 10 f. on 25 f. (Nancy) .. 25 10
374. 10 f. on 25 f. (Brouage) .. 90 45
325. 11 f. on 18 f. (No. 1022) .. 90 60
346. 15 f. on 30 f. (No. 1068b) 40 8
379. 15 f. on 50 f. (No. 1299) .. 45 25
390. 17 f. on 35 f. (No. 1354) .. 55 12
367. 17 f. on 70 f. (No. 1268b) 30 20
391. 20 f. on 50 f. (No. 1355) .. 20 10
357. 20 f. on 75 f. (Hippisme).. 8·00 5·50
353. 20 f. on 75 f. (Fleurs) .. 1·10 12
380. 20 f. on 75 f. (1300) .. 55 20
392. 25 f. on 85 f. (No. 1356a) 45 20

(b) Air.

326. 20 f. on 40 f. (Centaur) .. 45 20
327. 25 f. on 50 f. (Iris) .. 50 25
328. 50 f. on 100 f. (Jupiter) .. 1·10 90
365. 50 f. on 100 f. (Mystere IV) 55 15
329. 100 f. on 200 f. (Apollo) .. 7·50 6·00
330. 100 f. on 200 f. (Bordeaux) 13·00 6·50
366. 100 f. on 200 f. (Noratlas) 1·10 25
331. 200 f. on 500 f. (Marseille) 8·00 6·50
367. 200 f. on 500 f. (Magister) 6·50 5·00
393. 200 f. on 500 f. (Caravelle) 2·25 1·10
332. 500 f. on 1000 f. (Paris) .. 55·00 55·00
368. 500 f. on 1000 f. (Provence) 5·50 4·50
394. 500 f. on 1000 f. (Alouette) 6·00 3·25

1960. "New franc" stamps of France surch. **CFA** and value. (a) Postage.

415. 1 f. on 2 c. (No. 1498b) .. 5 5
416. 2 f. on 5 c. (No. 1499) .. 5 5
417. 2 f. on 5 c. (No. 1499a) .. 5 5
448. 2 f. on 5 c. (No. 1700) .. 5 5
398. 5 f. on 10 c. (No. 1453) .. 5 5
418. 5 f. on 10 c. (No. 1499b).. 5 5
419. 6 f. on 18 c. (No. 1499e) .. 5 5
395. 7 f. on 15 c. (No. 1461) .. 20 5
413. 7 f. on 15 c. (No. 1541) .. 5 5
400. 10 f. on 20 c. (No. 1455) .. 5 5
442. 10 f. on 20 c. (No. 1513) .. 5 5
458. 10 f. on 20 c. (No. 1735) 5 5
401. 12 f. on 25 c. (No. 1494) .. 8 5
420. 15 f. on 30 c. (No. 1499f) .. 8 5
413. 20 f. on 40 c. (No. 1654) .. 15 8
414. 20 f. on 45 c. (No. 1545) .. 20 15
396. 20 f. on 50 c. (No. 1464) .. 1·75 65
436. 25 f. or 50 c. (No. 1684) .. 15 5
435. 30 f. on 60 c. (No. 1621) .. 15 20
437. 30 f. on 60 c. (No. 1685) .. 20 15
432. 35 f. on 70 c. (No. 1655) .. 20 15
469. 45 f. (No. 1931) 20 15
397. 50 f. on 1 f. (No. 1467) .. 45 20
438. 50 f. on 1 f. (No. 1688) .. 25 20
470. 50 f. on 1 f. 10 (No. 1932).. 25 15

(b) Air.

402. 100 f. on 2 f. (No. 1457) 80 40
403. 100 f. on 2 f. (No. 1457b) 45 20
404. 200 f. on 5 f. (No. 1459) 1·10 70
405. 500 f. on 10 f. (No. 1460) 2·75 1·75

1962. Red Cross stamps of France (Nos. 1593/4) surch. **CFA** and value.

409. 10 f. + 5 f. on 20 c. + 10 c... 55 55
410. 12 f. + 5 f. on 25 c. + 10 c... 55 55

1962. Satellite Link stamps of France surch. **CFA** and value.

411. 12 f. on 25 c. (No. 1587) .. 20 15
412. 25 f. on 50 c. (No. 1588) .. 20 15

1963. Red Cross stamps of France. Nos. 1627/8) surch. **CFA** and value.

421. 10 f. + 5 f. on 20 c. + 10 c... 65 65
422. 12 f. + 5 f. on 25 c. + 10 c... 65 65

1964. "PHILATEC 1964" Int. Stamp Exhibition stamp of France surch. **CFA** and value.

423. 12 f. on 25 c. (No. 1629) .. 20 12

1964. Red Cross stamps of France. (Nos. 1665/6) surch. **CFA** and value.

433. 10 f. + 5 f. on 20 c. + 10 c. 35 35
434. 12 f. + 5 f. on 25 c. + 10 c. 35 35

1965. Colonisation of Reunion. Tercent. As No. 1692 of France, but additionally inscr. "CFA".

439. 15 f. blue and red 15 5

1965. Red Cross stamps of France (Nos. 1698/9) surch. **CFA** and value.

440. 12 f. + 5 f. on 25 c. + 10 c... 30 30
441. 15 f. + 5 f. on 30 c. + 10 c... 30 30

1966. Launching of 1st French Satellite. Nos. 1696/7 (plus se-tenant label) of France surch. **CFA** and value.

443. 15 f. on 30 c. blue, greenish blue and indigo 10 5
444. 30 f. on 60 c. blue, greenish blue and indigo 20 15

1966. Red Cross stamps of France (Nos 1733/4 surch. **CFA** and value.

445. 12 f. + 5 f. on 25 c. + 10 c. 25 25
446. 15 f. + 5 f. on 30 c. + 10 c. 25 25

1967. World Fair, Montreal. No. 1747 of France surch. **CFA** and value.

447. 30 f. on 60 c. 15 8

1967. Lions Int. 50th Anniv. No. 1766 of France surch. **CFA** and value.

449. 20 f. on 40 c. 12 5

1967. Red Cross. Nos. 1772/3 of France surch. **CFA** and value.

450. 12 f. + 5 f. on 25 c. + 10 c... 20 20
451. 15 f. + 5 f. on 30 c. + 10 c... 20 20

1968. French Polar Exploration. No. 1806 of France surch. **CFA** and value.

452. 20 f. on 40 c. 20 8

1968. Red Cross stamps of France (Nos. 1812/3) surch. **CFA** and value.

453. 12 f. + 5 f. on 25 c. + 10 c. 20 20
454. 15 f. + 5 f. on 30 c. + 10 c. 20 20

1969. Stamp Day. No. 1824 of France, surch. **CFA** and value.

455. 15 f. + 5 f. on 30 c. + 10 c. 12 12

1969. Nos. 1768a/b of France, surch **CFA** and value.

456. 15 f. on 30 c. green .. 5 5
457. 20 f. on 40 c. cerise .. 8 5

1969. Napoleon Bonaparte. Birth Bicent. No. 1845 of France surch. **CFA** and value.

459. 35 f. on 70 c. green, violet and blue 25 15

1969. Red Cross stamps of France (Nos. 1853/4) surch. **CFA** and value.

460. 20 f. + 7 f. on 40 c. + 15 c... 20 20
461. 20 f. + 7 f. on 40 c. + 15 c... 20 20

1970. Stamp Day. No. 1866 of France surch **CFA** and value.

462. 20 f. + 5 f. on 40 c. + 10 c. 20 15

1970. Red Cross. Nos. 1895/96 of France surch. **CFA** and value.

463. 20 f. + 7 f. on 40 c. + 15 c. 45 45
464. 20 f. + 7 f. on 40 c. + 15 c. 45 45

1971. No. 1905/6a of France surch. **CFA** and value.

465. 25 f. on 50 c. red 8 8
502. 30 f. on 60 f. green .. 15 12
503. 40 f. on 80 f. red 20 15

1971. Stamp Day. No. 1919 of France surch. **CFA** and value.

466. 25 f. + 5 f. on 50 c. + 10 c. 12 12

1971. "Antoinette". No. 1920 of France surch. **CFA** and value.

467. 40 f. on 80 c. 20 15

1971. No. 1928 of France (Rural Aid) surch. **CFA** and value.

468. **629.** 15 f. on 40 c. 8 5

1971. 1st Meeting of Crafts Guilds Association 40th Anniv. No. 1935 of France surch. **CFA** and value.

471. **631.** 45 c. on 90 c. purple & red 25 15

14. Reunion Chameleon.

1971. Nature Protection.

472. **14.** 25 f. grn., brn. & yellow 12 8

1971. De Gaulle Commem. As Nos 1937/40 of France, but with face value in CFA francs.

473. 25 f. black 12 12
474. 25 f. blue 12 12
475. 25 f. red 12 12
476. 25 f. black 12 12

DESIGNS: No. 473, De Gaulle in uniform (June, 1940). No. 474, De Gaulle at Brazzaville, 1944. No. 475, De Gaulle in Paris, 1944. No. 476, De Gaulle as President of the French Republic, 1970.

1971. Nos. 1942/3 of France (Red Cross Fund) surch. **CFA** and value.

477. 15 f. + 5 f. on 30 c. + 10 c. 20 20
478. 25 f. + 5 f. on 50 c. + 10 c... 20 20

1972. Discovery of Crozet Islands and Kerguelen (French Southern and Antarctic Territories). Bicent. As T **636** of France, but with face value in CFA francs.

479. 45 f. blk., bl. & orge-brn... 25 15

1972. No. 1956 of France, surch. **CFA** and value.

480. **639.** 25 f. + 5 f. on 50 c. + 10 c. blue, drab & yell. 15 12

1972. No. 1966 of France (Blood Donors) surch. **CFA** and value.

481. **643.** 15 f. on 40 c. red .. 5 5

1972. Air. No. 1890 of France (Duarat and Vanier) surch **CFA** and value.

482. **613.** 200 f. on 5 f. brn., grn. and blue 75 40

1972. Postal Codes. Nos. 1969/70 of France surch. **CFA** and value.

483. **646.** 15 f. on 30 c. red, black and green 5 5
484. 25 f. on 50 c. yellow, black and red .. 12 10

1972. Red Cross Fund. Nos. 1979/80 of France surch **CFA** and value.

485. **653.** 15 f. + 5 f. on 30 c. + 10 c. 8 5
486. 25 f. + 5 f. on 50 c. + 10 c. 15 12

1973. Stamp Day. No. 1996 of France surch. **CFA** and value.

487. **659.** 25 f. + 5 f. on 50 c. + 10 c. 15 15

1973. No. 2011 of France surch. **CFA** and value.

488. **667.** 45 f. on 90 c. green, violet and blue .. 20 15

1973. No. 2008 of France surch. **CFA** and value.

489. 50 f. on 1 f. grn., brn. & bl. 20 15

1973. No. 1960 of France surch. **CFA** and value.

490. 100 f. on 2 f. mar. & green 45 25

1973. No. 2021/2 of France surch. **CFA** and value.

491. **673.** 30 f. + 10 f. on 30 c. + 10 c. green and red 12 12
492. – 50 f. + 10 f. on 50 c. + 10 c. black and red .. 15 15

1973. No. 2026 of France surch. **CFA** and value.

494. **677.** 25 f. on 50 c. brown, blue and purple .. 12 12

1974. Stamp Day. No. 2031 surch. **CFA** and value.

495. **679.** 25 f. + 5 f. on 50 c. + 10 c. 12 12

1974. French Art. No. 2035/7a surch. **CFA** and value.

496. 100 f. on 2 f. multicoloured 45 25
497. 100 f. on 2 f. multicoloured 45 25
498. 100 f. on 2 f. brown and blue 45 25
499. 100 f. on 2 f. multicoloured 45 25

1974. French Lifeboat Service. No. 2041 surch. **CFA** and value.

500. **583.** 45 f. on 90 c. blue, red and brown 30 20

1974. Universal Postal Union. Centenary. No. 2056 surch **CFA** and value.

501. **691.** 60 f. on 1 f. 20 grn., red and blue .. 30 20

1974. Red Cross Fund. 'The Seasons" Nos. 2058/9 surch. **CFA** and value.

504. **693.** 30 f. + 7 f. on 60 c. + 15 c... .. .. 20 20
505. – 40 f. + 7 f. on 80 c. + 15 c... .. .. 20 20

From 1st January 1975 the CFA franc was replaced by the French Metropolitan franc, and Reunion subsequently used unsurcharged stamps of France.

POSTAGE DUE STAMPS

D 1.

D 2.

1889. Imperf.

D 11. **D 1.** 5 c. black .. .. 3·25 1·10
D 12. 10 c. black .. .. 3·50 1·25
D 13. 15 c. black .. .. 8·00 4·50
D 14. 20 c. black .. .. 6·50 3·75
D 15. 30 c. black .. .. 4·25 2·25

1907. Perf.

D 76. **D 2.** 5 c. red on yellow .. 5 5
D 77. 10 c. blue 5 5
D 78. 15 c. black on grey .. 5 5
D 79. 20 c. red 5 5
D 80. 30 c. green 8 8
D 81. 50 c. red on green .. 15 15
D 82. 60 c. red on blue .. 12 12
D 83. 1 f. lilac 25 25

1927. Surch.

D 130. **D 2.** 2 f. on 1 f. red .. 60 60
D 131. 3 f. on 1 f. brown .. 60 60

D 3. Arms of Reunion. D 4.

1933.

D 175. **D 3.** 5 c. purple 5 5
D 176. 10 c. green 5 5
D 177. 15 c. brown .. 5 5
D 178. 20 c. orange .. 5 5
D 179. 30 c. olive 5 5
D 180. 50 c. blue 8 8
D 181. 60 c. sepia 10 10
D 182. 1 f. violet 5 5
D 183. 2 f. blue 5 5
D 184. 3 f. red 5 5

1947.

D 306. **D 4.** 10 c. mauve .. 5 5
D 307. 30 c. brown .. 5 5
D 308. 50 c. green 5 5
D 309. 1 f. brown 5 5
D 310. 2 f. claret 5 5
D 311. 3 f. brown 5 5
D 312. 4 f. blue 15 15
D 313. 5 f. red 15 15
D 314. 10 f. green 15 15
D 315. 20 f. blue 20 20

1949. As Type D 5 of France, but inscr. "TIMBRE TAXE" surch. **CFA** and value.

D 333. 10 c. on 1 f. blue .. 5 5
D 334. 50 c. on 2 f. blue .. 5 5
D 235. 1 f. on 3 f. red 5 5
D 336. 2 f. on 4 f. violet .. 5 5
D 337. 3 f. on 5 f. pink .. 20 8
D 338. 5 f. on 10 f. red .. 5 5
D 339. 10 f. on 20 f. brown .. 20 15
D 340. 20 f. on 50 f. green .. 1·10 70
D 341. 50 f. on 100 f. green .. 1·75 1·10

1962. Type of France surch. **CFA** and value.

D 406. **D 6.** 1 f. on 5 c. magenta 20 20
D 407. 10 f. on 20 c. brown 35 35
D 408. 20 f. on 50 c. slate-grn. 70 70

1964. Nos. D 1650/4 and D 1656/7 of France surch. **CFA** and value.

D 424. – 1 f. on 5 c... .. 5 5
D 425. – 5 f. on 10 c. .. 5 5
D 426. **D 7.** 7 f. on 15 c. .. 5 5
D 427. – 10 f. on 20 c. .. 5 5
D 428. – 15 f. on 30 c. .. 8 8
D 429. – 20 f. on 50 c. .. 10 10
D 430. – 50 f. on 1 f. .. 20 20

RHODESIA BC

A Br. territory in S. Central Africa, formerly administered by the Br. S. Africa Co., and in 1924 divided into the territories of N. and S. Rhodesia which issued their own stamps (q.v.).

1. Arms of the Company.

1890. The pound values are larger.

18. 1. ½d. blue and red .. .. 1·00 1·00
1. 1d. black .. .. .. 3·00 1·50
20. 2d. green and red .. 1·75 1·00
21. 3d. black and green .. 1·75 1·50
22. 4d. brown and black .. 1·75 1·50
3. 6d. blue .. .. .. 6·00 3·00
23. 8d. red and blue .. .. 1·75 1·75
4. 1s. brown .. .. .. 10·00 7·00
5. 2s. red .. .. .. 12·00 9·00
6. 2s 6d. purple .. .. 11·00 11·00
25. 3s. brown and green .. 25·00 30·00
26. 4s. black and red .. .. 11·00 15·00
8. 5s. yellow .. .. .. 20·00 18·00
9. 10s. green .. .. .. 30·00 35·00
10. – £1 blue .. .. .. 80·00 80·00
11. – £2 red .. .. .. £200 80·00
12. – £5 green £1000 £250
13. – £10 brown £1500 £400

1891. Surch. in figures.

14. 1. ½d. on 6d. blue .. .. 40·00 45·00
15. 2d. on 6d. blue .. .. 35·00 60·00
16. 4d. on 6d. blue .. .. 45·00 70·00
17. 8d. on 1s. brown .. .. 45·00 70·00

3. 4.

1896. The ends of ribbons containing motto cross the animals' legs.

41. 3. ½d. grey and mauve .. 60 1·00
42. 1d. red and green .. 50 1·00
30. 2d. brown and mauve .. 1·75 1·00
31. 3d. brown and blue .. 1·00 1·00
45. 4d. blue and mauve .. 1·00 50
46. 6d. mauve and red .. 1·00 1·00
34. 8d. green & mauve on buff 1·00 1·00
35. 1s. green and blue .. 2·50 1·50
47. 2s. blue and green on buff 6·00 1·75
48. 2s. 6d. brn. & pur. on yell. 7·00 8·00
36. 3s. green & mauve on blue 10·00 10·00
37. 4s. red and blue on green 9·00 8·00
49. 5s. brown and green .. 10·00 10·00
50. 10s. grey and red on rose .. 22·00 22·00

1896. Surch. in words.

51. 1. 1d. on 3d. black and green £125 £200
52. 1d. on 4s. black and red .. £110 80·00
53. 3d. on 5s. yellow . 70·00 90·00

1896. Cape of Good Hope stamps optd. **BRITISH SOUTH AFRICA COMPANY.**

58. 4. ½d. black (No. 48) .. 2·00 3·00
59. 5. 1d. red (No. 58a) .. 2·00 3·00
60. 4. 2d. brown (No. 60) .. 3·00 2·50
61. 3d. claret (No. 40) .. 12·00 15·00
62. 4d. blue (No. 51) .. 5·00 5·00
63. 3. 6d. violet (No. 52a) .. 16·00 18·00
64. 4. 1s. yellow (No. 65) .. 30·00 40·00

1897. The ends of motto ribbons do not cross the animals' legs.

66. 4. ½d. grey and mauve .. 75 1·00
67. 1d. red and green .. 1·25 1·50
68. 2d. brown and mauve .. 1·00 1·00
69. 3d. brown and blue .. 1·00 1·00
70. 4d. blue and mauve .. 1·25 1·10
71. 6d. mauve and red .. 1·25 2·00
72. 8d. grn. and mve. on buff 2·25 1·75
73. £1 black & brown on green £200 £120

5.

6.

1898. Nos. 90/3 are larger (24×28½ mm.).

75. 5. ½ green 30 10
77. 1d. red 30 10
79. 2d. brown 60 10
80. 2½d. blue .. .. .. 1·00 15
81. 3d. claret .. .. .. 1·50 1·25
82. 4d. olive .. .. .. 1·25 20
83. 6d. purple .. .. .. 1·50 1·00
84. 6. 1s. brown .. .. .. 1·75 1·00
85. 2s. 6d. grey .. .. 4·50 1·75
86. 3s. violet .. .. .. 2·50 1·50
87. 5s. orange .. .. .. 7·00 3·00
88. 7s. 6d. black .. .. 11·00 11·00
89. 10s. green .. .. .. 5·00 4·00
90. – £1 purple .. .. .. 60·00 12·00
91. – £2 chocolate .. .. 30·00 10·00
92. – £5 blue £3000 £1250
93. – £10 lilac £2000 £1250
93a.– £20 brown £2500

7. Victoria Falls.

1905. Visit of British Assn. and Opening of Victoria Falls Bridge across Zambesi.

94. 7. 1d. red .. .. .. 1·00 1·00
95. 2½d. blue .. .. .. 2·50 2·50
96. 5d. claret .. .. .. 5·00 7·00
97. 1s. green .. .. .. 5·00 7·00
98. 2s. 6d. black .. .. 20·00 25·00
99. 5s. violet .. .. .. 13·00 15·00

1909. Optd. **RHODESIA** or surch. also.

100. 5. ½d. green 15 10
101. 1d. red 15 10
102. 2d. brown 75 50
103. 2½d. blue 20 20
104. 3d. claret 70 50
105. 4d. olive .. .. .. 1·00 50
114. 5d. on 6d. purple .. 1·75 1·75
106b. 6d. purple .. .. .. 1·10 50
116. 6. 7½d. on 2s. 6d. grey .. 1·50 1·50
117a. 10d. on 3s. violet .. 1·50 1·50
107. 1s. brown .. .. .. 1·50 50
118. 2s. on 5s. orange .. .. 3·50 3·50
108. 2s 6d. grey .. .. .. 4·50 3·00
109. 3s. violet .. .. .. 4·50 4·50
110. 5s. orange .. .. .. 7·50 5·00
111. 7s. 6d. black .. .. 10·00 5·00
112. 10s. green .. .. .. 7·00 7·00
113. – £1 purple .. .. .. 30·00 15·00
113c.– £2 chocolate £1600 £100

8.

1910.

119. 8. ½d. green .. .. .. 1·00 25
123. 1d. red .. .. .. 1·00 10
129. 2d. black and grey .. 4·50 1·75
131a. 2½d. blue .. .. .. 4·50 4·00
134. 3d. purple and yellow .. 4·00 2·00
140. 4d. black and orange .. 4·00 4·00
141a. 5d. purple and olive .. 8·00 7·00
144. 6d. purple and mauve .. 5·00 4·00
148. 8d. black and purple .. 30·00 12·00
149. 10d. red and purple .. 10·00 15·00
152. 1s. black and green .. 6·00 3·00
153. 2s. black and blue .. 15·00 12·00
157. 2s. 6d. black and red .. 80·00 90·00
158a. 3s. green and violet .. £250 £150
159. 5s. red and green .. 60·00 65·00
161. 7s. 6d. red and blue .. £175 £175
163. 10s. green and orange .. £175 £100
165. £1 red and black .. £200 £110

9.

ILLUSTRATIONS British Commonwealth and all overprints and surcharges are FULL SIZE. Foreign Countries have been reduced to ¾-LINEAR.

1913.

282. 9. ½d. green .. .. .. 1·00 10
190. 1d. red 30 10
197. 1½d. brown 30 10
256. 2d. black and grey .. 60 50
200. 2½d. blue .. .. .. 1·00 1·25
223. 3d. black and yellow .. 1·00 50
261. 4d. black and orange .. 2·50 75
264. 5d. black and green .. 1·25 1·50
295. 6d. black and mauve .. 75 40
230. 8d. violet and green .. 3·50 3·00
247. 10d. blue and red .. 2·00 2·50
300. 1s. black and blue .. 90 1·00
273. 2s. black and brown .. 3·50 3·00

236. 9. 2s. 6d. blue and brown .. 6·50 2·50
304. 3s. brown and blue .. 7·00 4·00
239. 5s. blue and green .. 10·00 8·00
252. 7s. 6d. mauve and grey .. 20·00 25·00
241. 10s. red and green .. 30·00 32·00
242. £1 black and purple .. £150 £140

1917. Surch. **Half Penny.**

281. 9. ½d. on 1s. red 40 75

RHODESIA

The following stamps are for the former Southern Rhodesia, renamed Rhodesia.

10. "Telecommunications".

1965. I.T.U. Cent.

351. 10. 6d. violet and olive .. 15 15
352. 1s. 3d. violet and lilac .. 35 35
353. 2s. 6d. violet and brown 55 60

11. Bangala Dam.

1965. Water Conservation. Multicoloured

354. 3d. Type 11 .. .. 10 10
355. 4d. Irrigation Canal .. 12 20
356. 2s. 6d. Cutting Sugar Cane 55 65

12. Sir Winston Churchill, Quill, Sword and Houses of Parliament.

1965. Churchill Commem.

357. 12. 1s. 3d. black and blue .. 70 80

UNILATERAL DECLARATION OF INDEPENDENCE.

11 November 1965.

1969. 100 cents = $1.

13. Coat of Arms.

1965. "Independence".

358. 13. 2s. 6d. multicoloured .. 40 40

1966. Optd. **INDEPENDENCE 11th November 1965.** (a) On Nos. 92/105 of Southern Rhodesia.

359. 21. ½d. yellow, green & blue 5 5
360. – 1d. violet and ochre .. 5 5
361. – 2d. yellow and violet 5 5
362. – 3d. chocolate and blue .. 5 8
363. – 4d. orange and green .. 8 8
364. 22. 6d. red, yellow & green 10 10
365. – 9d. brown, yellow & grn. 12 15
366. – 1s. green and ochre .. 20 20
367. – 1s. 3d. red, violet & grn. 25 25
368. – 2s. blue and ochre .. 50 50
369. – 2s. 6d. blue and red .. 35 45
370. 23. 5s. brown, yellow, blue and green .. .. 3·50 5·00
371. – 10s. blk., ochre, bl. & red 2·50 3·00
372. – £1 brn., grn., ochre & red 4·50 5·50

(b) On No. 357 Surch. also.

373. 12. 5s. on 1s. 3d. black & blue 12·00 14·00

14. Emeralds.

1966. As Nos. 92/8 and 100/105 of Southern Rhodesia, but inscr. "RHODESIA" as in T 14. Some designs and colours changed.

374. – 1d. violet and ochre .. 5 5
375. – 2d. orange and green (As No. 96) .. 5 5
376. – 3d. chocolate and blue .. 8 5
377. 14. 4d. green and sepia .. 10 10
378. 22. 6d. red, yellow & green 10 10
379. – 9d. yellow and violet (As No. 94) .. 15 15
380. 21. 1s. yellow, green & blue 15 12
381. – 1s. 3d. blue and ochre (As No. 101) .. 30 25
382. – 1s. 6d. brown, yellow and green (As No. 98) .. 35 30
383. – 2s. red, violet and green (As No. 100) 35 50
384. – 2s. 6d. blue, red & turq. 50 50
385. 23. 5s. brown, yellow, blue and green 85 85
386. – 10s. blk., ochre, bl. & red 1·60 1·90
387. – £1 brn., grn., ochre & red 3·50 4·00

Nos. 379/80 are in larger format as T 22.

Stamps in these designs were later printed locally. These vary only slightly from the above in details and shade.

For Nos. 376, 380 and 382/4 in dual currency see Nos. 408/12.

NOTE. The stamps which have been issued since 1966, when sanctions were imposed, are listed purely for reference purposes.

At the time of going to press sanctions remain in force and the importation of these stamps is illegal. In the event of trade being resumed prices will be published in "Stamp Monthly".

15. Zeederberg Coach, c. 1895.

1966. 28th Congress of Southern Africa Philatelic Federation ("Rhopex").

388. 15. 3d. multicoloured ..
389. – 9d. multicoloured ..
390. – 1s. 6d. blue and black ..
391. – 2s. 6d. pink, grn. & blk.

DESIGNS: 9d. Sir Rowland Hill. 1s. 6d. The Penny Black. 2s. 6d. Rhodesian stamp of 1892 (No. 12).

16. De Havilland "Rapide" (1946).

1966. Central African Airways. 20th Anniv.

393. 16. 6d. multicoloured ..
394. – 1s. 3d. multicoloured ..
395. – 2s. 6d. multicoloured ..
396. – 5s. black and blue ..

AIRCRAFT: 1s. 3d. Douglas "D.C.3" (1953). 2s 6d. Vickers "Viscount" (1956). 5s. Modern jet.

17. Kudu.

1967. Dual Currency Issue. As Nos. 376, 380 and 382/4 but value in dual currency as T 17.

408. 17. 3d./2½ c. brn. & blue ..
409. – 1s./10 c. yellow, green and blue (No. 380) ..
410. – 1s. 6d./15 c. brown, yellow & green (No. 382)
411. – 2s./20 c. red, violet and green (No. 383) ..
412. – 2s. 6d./25 c. ultram., red and blue (No. 384) ..

18. Dr. Jameson (administrator).

1967. Famous Rhodesians (1st series). Dr. Jameson. 50th Death Anniv.
413. **18.** 1s. 6d. multicoloured ..
See also 426, 430, 457, 458, 469, 480, 488 and 513.

19. Soapstone Sculpture (Joram Mariga).

1967. Opening of Rhodes National Gallery. 10th Anniv.
414. **19.** 3d. brn., green & black
415. – 9d. blue, brn. & black
416. – 1s. 3d. multicoloured ..
417. – 2s. 6d. multicoloured ..
DESIGNS: 9d. "The Burgher of Calais" (detail, Rodin). 1s. 3d. "Totem" (Roberto Crippa). 2s. 6d. "John the Baptist" (Tosini).

20. Baobab Tree.

1967. Nature Conservation.
418. **20.** 4d. brown and black..
419. – 4d. green and black ..
420. – 4d. grey and black ..
421. – 4d. orange and black ..
DESIGNS—HORIZ. No. 419, White Rhino. No. 420, Elephants. VERT. No. 421, Wild Gladiolis.

21. Wooden Hand Plough.

1968. 15th World Ploughing Contest, Norton, Rhodesia.
422. **21.** 3d. orange, red & brn...
423. – 9d. multicoloured ..
424. – 1s. 6d. multicoloured ..
425. – 2s. 6d. multicoloured ..
DESIGNS: 9d. Early wheel plough. 1s. 6d. Steam powered tractor, and ploughs. 2s. 6d. Modern tractor, and plough.

22. Alfred Beit (national benefactor).

1968. Famous Rhodesians. (2nd issue).
426. **22.** 1s. 6d. orge., blk. & brn.

23. Raising the Flag, Bulawayo, 1893.

1968. Matabeleland. 75th Anniv.
427. **23.** 3d. orge., red-orge., & blk.
428. – 8d. multicoloured ..
429. – 1s. 6d. grn., emerald & blackish-green ..

DESIGNS: 9d. View and coat-of-arms of Bulawayo. 1s. 6d. Allan Wilson (combatant in the Matabele War).

24. Sir William Henry Milton (administrator).

1969. Famous Rhodesians (3rd issue).
430. **24.** 1s. 6d. multicoloured ..

25. 2 ft. Gauge Locomotive (1899).

1969. Opening of Beira-Salisbury Railway. 70th Anniv. Multicoloured.
431. 3d. Type **25** .. ..
432. 9d. Steam loco (1904) ..
433. 1s. 6d. Articulated loco (1950)
434. 2s. 6d. Diesel-electric (1955)

26. Low Level Bridge.

1969. Bridges of Rhodesia. Multicoloured.
435. 3d. Type **26** .. ..
436. 9d. Mpudzi bridge ..
437. 1s. 6d. Umniati bridge ..
438. 2s. 6d. Birchenough bridge

27. Harvesting Wheat. **28.** Devil's Cataract Victoria Falls.

1970. Decimal Currency.
439. **27.** 1 c. multicoloured ..
440. – 2 c. multicoloured ..
441. – 2½ c. greenish-bl., bl. & blk.
441a. – 3 c. multicoloured ..
442. – 3½ c. multicoloured ..
442b. – 4 c. multicoloured ..
443. – 5 c. multicoloured ..
443a. – 6 c. multicoloured ..
443b. **28.** 7½ c. multicoloured ..
444. 8 c. multicoloured ..
445. – 10 c. multicoloured ..
446. – 12½ c. multicoloured ..
446a. – 14 c. multicoloured ..
447. – 15 c. multicoloured ..
448. – 20 c. multicoloured ..
449. – 25 c. orge., grey & blk.
450. – 50 c. turquoise & blue
451. – $1 blue, turq. & black
452. – $2 multicoloured ..
DESIGNS: Size as Type **27**. 2 c. Pouring molten metal. 2½ c. Zimbabwe Ruins. 3 c. Articulated lorry. 3½ c., 4 c. Statue of Cecil Rhodes. 5 c. Mine headgear. 6 c. Hydrofoil "Seaflight". Size as Type **28**. 10 c. Yachting on Lake McIlwaine. 12½ c. Hippo in river. 14 c., 15 c. Kariba Dam. 20 c. Irrigation canal. Larger (31×26 mm.). 25 c. Bateleur eagles. 50 c. Radar antenna and Vickers "Viscount". $1 "Air Rescue". $2 Rhodesian flag.

29. Despatch Rider, c. 1890.

1970. Posts and Telecommunications Corporation. Inaug. Multicoloured.
453. 2½ c. Type **29** .. ..
454. 3½ c. Loading mail at Salisbury airport ..
455. 15 c. Constructing telegraph line, c. 1890 ..
456. 25 c. Telephone and modern telecommunications equipment .. .. ..

30. Mother Patrick (Dominican nurse and teacher).

1971. Famous Rhodesians (4th issue).
457. **30.** 15 c. multicoloured ..

31. Fredrick Courteney, Selous (Big-game hunter, explorer and pioneer).

1971. Famous Rhodesians (5th issue).
458. **31.** 15 c. multicoloured ..

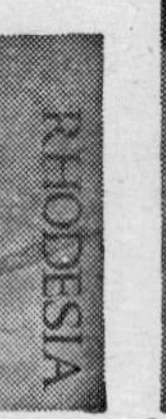

32. African Hoopoe. **33.** Porphyrite Granite.

1971. Birds of Rhodesia. Multicoloured.
459. 2 c. Type **32** .. ..
460. 2½ c. Half-collared Kingfisher (horiz.) .. ..
461. 5 c. Golden-breasted Bunting .. .. ..
462. 7½ c. Carmine-Bee-eater ..
463. 8 c. Red-eyed Bulbul ..
464. 25 c. Wattled Plover (horiz.)

1971. "Granite 71" Geological Symposium. Multicoloured.
465. 2½ c. Type **33**
466. 7½ c. Muscovite mica seen through microscope ..
467. 15 c. Granite seen through microscope .. ..
468. 25 c. Geological map of Rhodesia.. .. ..

34. Dr. Robert Moffat (missionary).

1972. Famous Rhodesians (6th issue).
469. **34.** 13 c. multicoloured ..

35. Bird ("Be Airwise").

1972. "Prevent Pollution". Mult.
470. 2½ c. Type **35** .. ..
471. 3½ c. Antelope ("Be Countrywise").. ..
472. 7 c. Fish ("Be Waterwise")
473. 13 c. City ("Be Citywise")

36. "The Three Kings". **38.** W.M.O. Emblem.

37. Dr. David Livingstone.

1972. Christmas.
477. **36.** 2 c. multicoloured ..
478. 5 c. multicoloured ..
479. 13 c. multicoloured ..

1973. Famous Rhodesians (7th issue).
480. **37.** 14 c. multicoloured ..

1973. I.M.O./W.M.O. Centenary.
481. **38.** 3 c. multicoloured ..
482. 14 c. multicoloured ..
483. 25 c. multicoloured ..

39. Arms of Rhodesia.

1973. Responsible Government. 50th Anniv.
484. **39.** 2½ c. multicoloured ..
485. 4 c. multicoloured ..
486. 7½ c. multicoloured ..
487. 14 c. multicoloured ..

40. George Pauling (Construction engineer).

1974. Famous Rhodesians (8th issue).
488. **40.** 14 c. multicoloured ..

41. Kudu. **42.** Thunbergia.

43. Pearl Charaxes.

1974. Multicoloured.

(a) Antelopes.

489. 1 c. Type **41** .. ..
490. 2½ c. Eland .. ..
491. 3 c. Roan Antelope ..
492. 4 c. Reedbuck .. ..
493. 5 c. Bushbuck .. ..

(b) Wild Flowers.

494. 6 c. Type **42** .. ..
495. 7½ c. Flame Lily .. ..
496. 8 c. As 7½ c. .. ..
497. 10 c. Devil Thorn .. ..
498. 12 c. Hibiscus .. ..
499. 12½ c. Pink Sabi Star ..
500. 14 c. Wild Pimpernel ..
501. 15 c. As 12½ c. .. ..
502. 16 c. As 14 c. .. ..

(c) Butterflies.

503. 20 c. Type **43** .. ..
504. 24 c. Yellow Pansy ..
505. 25 c. As 24 c. .. ..
506. 50 c. Queen Purple Tip ..
507. $1 Large Striped Swordtail
508. $2 Guinea Fowl Butterfly

44. Collecting Mail.

1974. U.P.U. Centenary. Multicoloured.

509. 3 c. Type **44** .. ..
510. 4 c. Sorting mail .. ..
511. 7½ c. Mail delivery ..
512. 14 c. Weighing parcel ..

45. Thomas Baines (artist).

1975. Famous Rhodesians (9th issue).

513. **45.** 14 c. multicoloured ..

46. " Euphorbia confinalis ". **48.** Telephones, 1876 and 1976.

47. Prevention of Head Injuries.

1975. Int. Succulent Congress, Salisbury (" Aloe '75 "). Multicoloured.

514. 2½ c. Type **46** .. ..
515. 3 c. " Aloe excelsa " ..
516. 4 c. " Hoodia lugardii " ..
517. 7½ c. " Aloe ortholopha "
518. 14 c. " Aloe musapana "
519. 25 c. " Aloe saponaria "

1975. Occupational Safety. Multicoloured.

520. 2½ c. Type **47** .. ..
521. 4 c. Bandaged hand and gloved hand .. ..
522. 7½ c. Broken glass and eye
523. 14 c. Blind man and welder with protective mask ..

1976. Telephone Centenary.

524. **48.** 3 c. grey and blue ..
525. – 14 c. black and brown ..

DESIGN: 14 c. Alexander Graham Bell.

1976. Nos. 495, 500 and 505 surch.

526. 8 c. on 7½ c. multicoloured
527. 16 c. on 14 c. multicoloured
528. 24 c. on 25 c. multicoloured

49. Roan Antelope.

1976. Vulnerable Wildlife. Multicoloured.

529. 4 c. Type **49** .. ..
530. 6 c. Brown Hyena ..
531. 8 c. Wild Dog .. ..
532. 16 c. Cheetah .. ..

50. Msasa.

1976. Trees of Rhodesia. Multicoloured.

533. 4 c. Type **50** .. ..
534. 6 c. Red Mahogany ..
535. 8 c. Mukwa .. ..
536. 16 c. Rhodesian Teak ..

POSTAGE DUE STAMPS

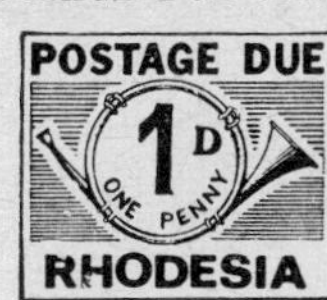

D 1.

1965. Roul.

D 1a. D **1.**	1d. red	8	10
D 2.	2d. blue	8	8
D 3.	4d. green	5	8
D 4.	6d. plum	10	15

D 2. Zimbabwe Bird (soapstone sculpture).

1966.

D 5. D **2.** 1d. red .. ..
D 6. 2d. blue .. ..
D 7. 4d. green .. ..
D 8. 6d. violet .. ..
D 9. 1s. brown .. ..
D 10. 2s. black .. ..

1970. Decimal Currency. As Type D 2 but larger (26 × 22½ mm.).

D 11. D **2.** 1 c. green .. ..
D 12. 2 c. blue .. ..
D 13. 5 c. violet .. ..
D 14. 6 c. yellow .. ..
D 15. 10 c. red .. ..

RHODESIA AND NYASALAND BC

Stamps for the Central African Federation of Northern and Southern Rhodesia and Nyasaland Protectorate. The stamps of the Federation were withdrawn on 19th February, 1964, when all three constituent territories had resumed issuing their own stamps.

1. Queen Elizabeth II. **2.**

1954.

1. **1.**	½d. vermilion	5	5
2.	1d. blue	5	5
3.	2d. green	5	5
3a.	2½d. ochre	12	12
4.	3d. red	10	8
5.	4d. brown	20	15
6.	4½d. green	25	30
7.	6d. purple	30	15
8.	9d. violet	35	40
9.	1s. grey	30	15
10. **2.**	1s. 3d. vermilion & blue ..	30	12
11.	2s. blue and brown ..	45	35
12.	2s. 6d. black and red ..	75	65
13.	5s. violet and olive	1·50	80
14. –	10s. blue-green and orange	4·00	3·00
15. –	£1 olive and lake ..	11·00	5·00

The 10s. and £1 are as T 2 but larger (31 × 17 mm.) and have the name at top and foliage on either side of portrait.

3. Aeroplane over Falls. **4.** Livingstone and Falls.

1955. Discovery of Victoria Falls. Cent.

16. **3.**	3d. blue and turquoise ..	12	12
17. **4.**	1s. purple and blue ..	50	60

5. Tea Picking. **6.** Lake Bangweulu.

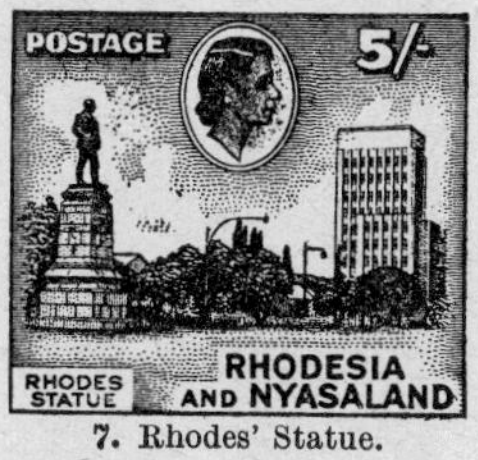

7. Rhodes' Statue.

1959.

18. **5.**	½d. black and emerald ..	5	8
19. –	1d. red and black ..	5	5
20. –	2d. violet and buff ..	5	5
21. –	2½d. purple and grey-blue	12	20
22. –	3d. black and blue ..	8	5
23. **6.**	4d. maroon and olive ..	12	10
24. –	6d. blue and myrtle ..	15	10
24a. –	9d. chestnut and violet ..	45	65
25. –	1s. green and blue ..	25	12
26. –	1s. 3d. emerald & chocolate	40	12
27. –	2s. grey-green and red ..	60	50
28. –	2s. 6d. blue and buff ..	75	50
29. **7.**	5s. chocolate & yell.-green	1·25	1·00
30. –	10s. bistre and red ..	2·50	3·00
31. –	£1 black and violet ..	5·50	7·00

DESIGNS—As T 5: VERT. 1d. V.H.F. mast. 2d. Copper mining. 2½d. Fairbridge Memorial. HORIZ. 3d. Rhodes' grave. As T 6: VERT. 6d. Eastern Cataract, Victoria Falls. HORIZ. 9d. Rhodesian railway trains. 1s. Tobacco. 1s. 3d Lake Nyasa. 2s. Chirundu Bridge. 2s. 6d. Salisbury Airport. As T 7: HORIZ. 10s. Mlanje. £1 Federal Coat of Arms.

8. Kariba Gorge, 1955.

1960. Opening of Kariba Hydro-Electric Scheme.

32. **8.**	3d. myrtle and orange ..	20	12
33. –	6d. brown & yellow-brown	30	30
34. –	1s. slate-blue and green ..	40	45
35. –	1s. 3d. blue and brown ..	60	45
36. –	2s. 6d. slate-purple and red	1·75	2·00
37. –	5s. violet and turquoise ..	4·00	5·00

DESIGNS: 6d. 330 k.V. power lines. 1s. Barrage wall. 1s. 3d. Barrage and lake. 2s. 6d. Interior of power station. 5s. Queen Mother and barrage wall (inscr. " ROYAL OPENING ").

9. Miner Drilling.

1961. 7th Commonwealth Mining and Metallurgical Congress.

38. **9.**	6d. olive-green and brown	25	30
39. –	1s 3d. black and blue ..	50	45

DESIGN: 1s. 3d. Surface installations, Nchanga mine.

10. D.H. " Hercules " on Rhodesian Air-strip.

1962. 1st London-Rhodesian Airmail Service. 30th Anniv.

40. **10.**	6d. green and red ..	20	20
41. –	1s. 3d. blue, blk. & yell.	40	45
42. –	2s. 6d. red and violet ..	85	1·00

DESIGNS: 1s. 3d. Empire " C " Class flying-boat taking-off from Zambesi. 2s. 6d. D.H. " Comet " at Salisbury Airport.

11. Tobacco Plant.

DESIGNS: 6d. Tobacco field. 1s. 3d. Auction floor. 2s. 6d. Cured tobacco.

1963. World Tobacco Congress, Salisbury.

43. **11.**	3d. green and olive ..	10	12
44. –	6d. green, brown & blue	15	20
45. –	1s. 3d. chestnut and indigo	35	35
46. –	2s. 6d. yellow and brown	80	1·10

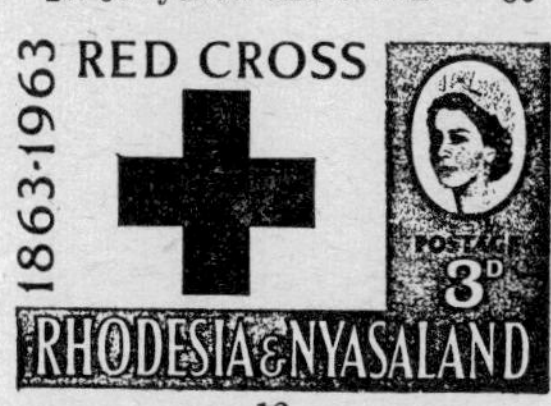

12.

1963. Red Cross Cent.

47. **12.**	3d. red	10	10

13. African " Round Table " Emblem.

1963. World Council of Young Men's Service Clubs, Salisbury.
48. 13. 6d. black, gold and green 20 25
49. 1s. 3d. gold, black, green and lilac .. 35 45

POSTAGE DUE STAMPS

D 1.

1961.
D 1. D 1. 1d. vermilion .. 10 10
D 2. 2d. violet-blue .. 12 20
D 3. 4d. green .. 30 50
D 4. 6d. purple 30 50

RIAU-LINGGA ARCHIPELAGO O2

A group of islands E. of Sumatra and S. of Singapore. Part of Indonesia.

1954. Optd. **RIAU** in double-lined letters.
A. On stamps of Indonesia.
1. 56. 5 s. red
2. 7½ s. green
3. 10 s. blue
4. 15 s. violet
5. 20 s. red
6. 25 s. green
7. 57. 30 s. red
8. 35 s. violet
9. 40 s. green
10. 45 s. purple
11. 50 s. brown
12. 58. 60 s. brown
13. 70 s. grey
14. 75 s. blue
15. 80 s. purple
16. 90 s. green
B. On Netherlands Indies Nos. 566/71.
17. – 1 r. violet
18. – 2 r. green
19. – 3 r. purple
20. – 5 r. brown
21. – 10 r. black
22. – 25 r. brown
Set of 22 .. .. 90·00 £120

Stamps of Indonesia overprinted.

1957. Optd. **RIAU** in bold letters.
23. 73. 10 s. brown
24. – 25 s. maroon (No. 717)
25. – 50 s. bistre (No. 722)
Set of 3 .. .. 20·00 25·00

1958. Optd. **RIAU** in double-lined letters
26. 73. 5 s. grey-blue
27. 10 s. brown (No. 714)
28. 15 s. purple (No. 715)
29. – 20 s. green (No. 716)
30. – 25 s. maroon (No. 717)
31. – 30 s. orange (No. 718)
32. – 50 s. bistre (No. 722)
Set of 7 .. .. 1·50 2·00

1960. Optd. **RIAU** in double-lined letters.
33. 59. 1 r. 25 orange
34. 1 r. 50 brown
35. 2 r. 50 lake
36. 4 r. olive
37. 6 r. purple
38. 15 r. yellow
39. 20 r. slate
40. 40 r. green
41. 50 r. violet
Set of 9 .. .. 4·50 7·00

RIO DE ORO O4

A Spanish territory on the W. Coast of N. Africa, renamed Spanish Sahara in 1924.

1905. "Curly Head" key-type inscr. "COLONIA DE RIO DE ORO".
1. Z. 1 c. green 1·40 75
2. 2 c. red 1·40 75
3. 3 c. black 1·40 75
4. 4 c. brown 1·40 75
5. 5 c. red 1·40 75
6. 10 c. grey 1·40 75
7. 15 c. brown 1·40 75
8. 25 c. blue 16·00 5·50
9. 50 c. green 8·00 2·75
10. 75 c. violet 11·00 3·50
11. 1 p. brown 5·50 1·50
12. 2 p. orange 17·00 6·50
13. 3 p. lilac 11·00 3·25
14. 4 p. green 15·00 4·50
15. 5 p. blue 30·00 11·00
16. 10 p. red 30·00 11·00

1906. "Curly Head" key-type surch. **HABILITADO PARA 15 CENTS** in circle.
17. Z. 15 c. on 25 c. blue .. 35·00 11·00

1. 2. 3.

1907.
18. 1. 1 c. claret 1·25 60
19. 2 c. black 1·25 60
20. 3 c. brown 1·25 60
21. 4 c. red 1·25 60
22. 5 c. brown 1·25 60
23. 10 c. brown 1·25 60
24. 15 c. blue 1·25 60
25. 25 c. green 1·25 60
26. 50 c. purple 1·25 60
27. 75 c. brown 1·25 60
28. 1 p. orange 1·40 60
29. 2 p. lilac 95 60
30. 3 p. green 1·10 60
31. 4 p. blue 2·00 70
32. 5 p. red 2·10 1·00
33. 10 p. green 2·40 1·60

1907. Nos. 9/10 surch. **1907 10 Cens.**
34. Z. 10 c. on 50 c. green .. 8·00 3·00
35. 10 c. on 75 c. violet .. 7·00 3·00

1908. No. 12 surch. **1908** and value.
36. Z. 2 c. on 2 p. orange .. 6·50 3·00
37. 1. 10 c. on 50 c. purple .. 7·00 3·00

1908. Surch. **HABILITADO PARA 15 CENTS** in circle.
38. 1. 15 c. on 25 c. green .. 5·00 1·40
39. 15 c. on 75 c. brown .. 6·00 1·75
40. 15 c. on 1 p. orange .. 6·00 1·75
70. 15 c. on 3 p. green .. 3·50 1·10
72. 15 c. on 5 p. red .. 3·00 90

1908. Large Fiscal stamp inscr. "TERRITORIOS ESPANOLES DEL AFRICA OCCIDENTAL" surch. **HABILITADO PARA CORREOS RIO DE ORO 5 CENS.** Imperf.
45. 5 c. on 50 c. green .. 11·00 4·50

Prices of No. 45 are for stamps with control number on back. Stamps without are worth about half.

1909.
47. 2. 1 c. red 25 20
48. 2 c. orange 25 20
49. 5 c. green 25 20
50. 10 c. red 25 20
51. 15 c. green 25 20
52. 20 c. purple 40 30
53. 25 c. blue 40 30
54. 30 c. red 40 30
55. 40 c. brown 40 30
56. 50 c. purple 55 30
57. 1 p. brown 90 55
58. 4 p. red 1·25 95
59. 10 p. claret 2·25 1·60

1910. Nos. 13/16 surch. **1910** and value.
60. Z. 10 c. on 5 p. blue .. 7·00 3·50
62. 10 c. on 10 p. red .. 7·00 3·50
65. 15 c. on 3 p. lilac .. 7·00 3·50
66. 15 c. on 4 p. green .. 7·00 3·50

1911. Surch. with value in figs. and words.
67. 1. 2 c. on 4 p. blue .. 3·50 1·10
68. 5 c. on 10 p. green .. 3·50 1·10
69. 10 c. on 2 p. lilac .. 3·50 1·10
70. 10 c. on 3 p. green .. 11·00 3·25

1912.
73. 3. 1 c. red 10 8
74. 2 c. lilac 10 8
75. 5 c. green 10 8
76. 10 c. red 10 8
77. 15 c. brown 10 8
78. 20 c. brown 10 8
79. 25 c. blue 10 8
80. 30 c. lilac 10 8
81. 40 c. green 10 8
82. 50 c. red 10 8
83. 1 p. red 55 20
84. 4 p. claret 1·25 70
85. 10 p. brown 1·75 1·00

This set was also issued overprinted **1917**.

4. 5. 6.

1914.
86. 4. 1 c. brown 10 8
87. 2 c. purple 10 8
88. 5 c. green 10 8
89. 10 c. red 10 8
90. 15 c. orange 10 8
91. 20 c. red 10 8
92. 25 c. blue 10 8
93. 30 c. green 10 8
94. 40 c. orange 10 10
95. 50 c. brown 10 10
96. 1 p. lilac 55 35
97. 4 p. red 1·25 60
98. 10 p. violet 1·75 95

1919.
112. 5. 1 c. brown 20 12
113. 2 c. purple 20 12
114. 5 c. green 20 12
115. 10 c. red 20 12
116. 15 c. orange 20 12
117. 20 c. orange 20 12
118. 5. 25 c. blue 20 12
119. 30 c. green 20 12
120. 40 c. orange 20 12
121. 50 c. brown 20 12
122. 1 p. lilac 1·10 55
123. 4 p. red 1·75 90
124. 10 p. violet 2·50 1·40

1920.
125. 6. 1 c. purple 20 12
126. 2 c. red 20 12
127. 5 c. red 20 12
128. 10 c. purple 20 12
129. 15 c. brown 20 12
130. 20 c. green 20 12
131. 25 c. orange 20 12
132. 30 c. blue 90 70
133. 40 c. orange 55 25
134. 50 c. purple 55 25
135. 1 p. green 55 25
136. 4 p. red 1·25 70
137. 10 p. brown 2·25 1·40

1921. As T 1 of La Aguera, but inscr. "RIO DE ORO".
138. 1 c. yellow 20 10
139. 2 c. brown 20 10
140. 5 c. green 20 10
141. 10 c. red 20 10
142. 15 c. green 20 10
143. 20 c. blue 20 10
144. 25 c. blue 20 12
145. 30 c. red 40 25
146. 40 c. violet 40 25
147. 50 c. orange 40 25
148. 1 p. mauve 1·10 55
149. 4 p. claret 1·75 1·10
150. 10 p. brown 2·50 1·40

For later issues see **SPANISH SAHARA**.

RIO MUNI O2

A coastal settlement between Cameroun and Gabon, formerly using the stamps of Spanish Guinea. On 12th October, 1968, became independent and joined Fernando Poo to become Equatorial Guinea.

1. Native Boy reading Book. 2. Cactus. 3. Bishop Juan de Ribera.

1960.
1. 1. 25 c. violet-grey 5 5
2. 50 c. drab 5 5
3. 75 c. chocolate 5 5
4. 1 p. red 5 5
5. 1 p. 50 turquoise 5 5
6. 2 p. purple 10 5
7. 3 p. blue 25 5
8. 5 p. brown 50 8
9. 10 p. olive 1·00 15

1960. Child Welfare Fund. Plant designs inscr. "PRO-INFANCIA 1960".
10. 2. 10 c.+5 c. claret 5 5
11. – 15 c.+5 c. brown 5 5
12. – 35 c. myrtle 5 5
13. 2. 80 c. blue-green 5 5

DESIGNS: 15 c. Sprig with berries. 35 c. Quina plant.

1960. Colonial Stamp Day. Inscr. "DIA DEL SELLO 1960".
14. 3. 10 c.+5 c. lake 5 5
15. – 20 c.+5 c. myrtle 5 5
16. – 30 c.+10 c. olive-brown 5 5
17. 3. 50 c.+20 c. brown 5 5

DESIGNS: 20 c. Portrait of man (after Velasquez). 30 c. Statue.

4. Mandrill with Banana.

DESIGN—VERT. 25 c. Elephant.

1961. Child Welfare. Inscr. "PRO-INFANCIA 1961".
18. 4. 10 c.+5 c. lake 5 5
19. – 25 c.+10 c. violet 5 5
20. 4. 80 c.+20 c. green 5 5

5. 6. Statuette.

7. Girl wearing Headdress.

8. Buffalo.

1961. 25th Anniv. of Gen. Franco as Head of State.
21. – 25 c. violet-grey 5 5
22. 5. 50 c. olive-brown 5 5
23. – 70 c. green 5 5
24. 5. 1 p. orange 5 5

DESIGNS: 25 c. Map. 70 c. Govt. Building.

1961. Stamp Day. Inscr. "DIA DEL SELLO 1961".
25. 6. 10 c.+5 c. lake 5 5
26. – 25 c.+10 c. purple 5 5
27. 6. 30 c.+10 c. olive-brown 5 5
28. – 1 p.+10 c. orange 5 5

DESIGN: 25 c., 1 p. Figure holding offering.

1962. Child Welfare. Inscr. "PRO-INFANCIA 1962".
29. 7. 25 c. violet 5 5
30. – 50 c. green 5 5
31. 7. 1 p. chestnut 5 5

DESIGN: 50 c. Native mask.

1962. Stamp Day. Inscr. "DIA DEL SELLO 1962".
32. 8. 15 c. olive 5 5
33. – 35 c. purple 5 5
34. 8. 1 p. orange-red 8 5

DESIGN—VERT. 35 c. Gorilla.

9. Statuette. 10. "Blessing". 11. Child at Prayer.

1963. Seville Flood Relief.
35. 9. 50 c. green 5 5
36. 1 p. orange-red 5 5

1963. Child Welfare. Inscr. "PRO-INFANCIA 1963".
37. – 25 c. violet 5 5
38. 10. 50 c. olive 5 5
39. – 1 p. orange-red 5 5

DESIGN: 25 c., 1 p. Priest.

1963. "For Barcelona".
40. 11. 50 c. blue-green 5 5
41. 1 p. red-brown 5 5

12. Copal Flower. 13. Scaly Anteater.

14. "Goliath" Frog. 15. Woman.

1964. Stamp Day. Inscr. "DIA DEL SELLO 1963".
42. 12. 25 c. violet 5 5
43. – 50 c. turquoise 5 5
44. 12. 1 p. red 5 5

FLOWER—HORIZ. 50 c. Cinchona blossom.

1964. Child Welfare. Inscr. "PRO-INFANCIA 1964".
45. 13. 25 c. violet 5 5
46. – 50 c. olive (Chameleon) 5 5
47. 13. 1 p. chestnut 5 5

1964. Wild Life. As T 13 but without "PRO INFANCIA" inscription.
48. 15 c. yellow-brown 5 5
49. 25 c. violet 5 5
50. 50 c. olive 8 5
51. 70 c. green 8 5
52. 1 p. red-brown 25 5
53. 1 p. 50 turquoise-green 25 5
54. 3 p. blue 30 5
55. 5 p. brown 1·00 25
56. 10 p. green 2·25 50

ANIMALS: 15 c., 70 c., 3 p. Crocodile. 25 c., 1 p., 5 p. Leopard. 50 c., 1 p. 50, 10 p. Rhinoceros.

1964. Stamp Day.

57. 14. 50 c. bronze 5 5
58. – 1 p. lake 5 5
59. 14. 1 p. 50 green 5 5

DESIGN—VERT. 1 p. Guinea hen.

1965. End of Spanish Civil War. 25th Anniv. Inscr. "XXV ANOS DE PAZ".

60. 15. 50 c. green 5 5
61. – 1 p. orange-red 5 5
62. – 1 p. 50 turquoise 5 5

DESIGNS: 1 p. Nurse. 1 p. 50, Logging.

16. "Goliathus goliathus".

1965. Child Welfare. Insects.

63. 16. 50 c. green 5 5
64. – 1 p. brown 5 5
65. 16. 1 p. 50 black 5 5

DESIGN: 1 p. "Acridoxena hewaniana".

17. Cheetah and Arms of Rio Muni.

1965. Stamp Day.

66. – 50 c. grey 5 5
67. 17. 1 p. sepia 12 5
68. – 2 p. 50 violet 60 30

DESIGN—VERT. 50 c., 2 p. 50, Jungle pheasant.

18. Elephant and Parrot.

1966. Child Welfare.

69. 18. 50 c. brown 5 5
70. 1 p. lilac 5 5
71. – 1 p. 50 blue 5 5

DESIGN: 1 p. 50 African and lion.

19. "Hyemoschus aquaticus" (water deer). 20 Flowers.

1966. Stamp Day.

72. 19. 10 c. sepia and ochre 5 5
73. – 40 c. brown and lemon 5 5
74. 19. 1 p. 50 violet and red 5 5
75. – 4 p. blue and green 8 8

DESIGN—VERT. 40 c., 4 p. "Smutsia gigantea" (pangolin).

1967. Child Welfare. Similar Floral designs.

76. 20. 10 c. yellow, olive & green 5 5
77. – 40 c. green, black & mag. 5 5
78. 20. 1 p. 50 red and blue 5 5
79. – 4 p. black and green 8 8

21. Marsh Hog.

1967. Stamp Day.

80. 21. 1 p. chestnut and brown 5 5
81. – 1 p. 50 brown and green 5 5
82. – 3 p. 50 brown and green 8 8

DESIGNS—VERT. 1 p. 50, Potto (West African lemur). HORIZ. 3 p. 50, Tiger-cat.

1968. Child Welfare. Signs of the Zodiac. As T 26 of Fernando Poo.

83. 1 p. magenta on yellow 5 5
84. 1 p. 50 brown on pink 5 5
85. 2 p. 50 violet on yellow 8 8

DESIGNS: 1 p. Crab (Cancer). 1 p. 50 Bull (Taurus). 2 p. 50 Twins (Gemini).

ROMAGNA E2

One of the Papal states, now part of Italy. Stamps issued prior to the annexation by Sardinia.

100 bajocchi = 1 scudo.

ILLUSTRATIONS British Commonwealth and all overprints and surcharges are FULL SIZE. Foreign Countries have been reduced to ¾-LINEAR.

1.

1859. Imperf.

2. 1. ½ b. black on yellow 6·50 £100
3. 1 b. black on grey 6·50 48·00
4. 2 b. black on buff 8·00 48·00
5. 3 b. black on green 9·00 £120
6. 4 b. black on brown 90·00 42·00
7. 5 b. black on lilac 8·00 £180
8. 6 b. black on green 65·00 £2500
9. 8 b. black on rose 45·00 £550
10. 20 b. black on grey 45·00 £1000

ROSS DEPENDENCY BC

A dependency of New Zealand in the Antarctic on the Ross Sea.

DESIGNS—HORIZ. as T1: 3d. H.M.S. "Erebus". 4d. Shackleton and Scott.

1. Map of Ross Dep. and N.Z. 2. Queen Elizabeth II.

1957.

1. – 3d. indigo 15 20
2. – 4d. red 25 30
3. 1. 8d. red and blue 35 40
4. 2. 1s. 6d. purple 80 90

3. H.M.S. "Erebus".

1968. Nos. 1/4 with values inscr. in decimal currency as T 3.

5. 3. 2 c. indigo 12 15
6. – 3 c. red 20 25
7. 1. 7 c. red & ultramarine 30 30
8. 2. 15 c. purple 65 70

4. Skua.

5. Scott Base.

1972.

9. 4. 3 c. blk., grey and blue 5 5
10. – 4 c. black, blue and violet 5 8
11. – 5 c. black, grey and lilac 5 10
12. – 8 c. black, grey & brown 8 15
13. 5. 10 c. black, green and slate-green 10 20
14. – 18 c. black, violet and bright violet 20 30

DESIGNS: Size as T 4. 4 c. "Hercules" aeroplane at Williams Field. 5 c. Shackleton's Hut. 8 c. Supply ship H.M.N.Z.S. "Endeavour". Size as T 5. 18 c. Tabular ice floe.

ROUAD ISLAND (ARWAD) O4

An island in the E. Mediterranean off the coast of Syria. A French P.O. was established there during 1916.

1916. "Blanc" and "Mouchon" key-types inscr. "LEVANT" and optd. **ILE ROUAD** vert.

1. A. 5 c. green 80·00 40·00
2. B. 10 c. red 80·00 40·00
3. 1 pi. on 25 c. blue 80·00 40·00

1916. "Blanc," "Mouchon" and "Merson" key-types inscr. "LEVANT" and optd. **ILE ROUAD** horiz.

4. A. 1 c. grey 8 8
5. 2 c. claret 10 10
6. 3 c. red 10 10
7. 5 c. green 12 12
8. B. 10 c. red 20 20
9. 15 c. orange 25 25
10. 20 c. claret 25 25
11. 1 p. on 25 c. blue 30 30
12. 30 c. mauve 45 45
13. C. 40 c. red and blue 45 45
15. 2 p. on 50 c. brown & lav. 80 80
16. 4 p. on 1 f. red and yellow 80 80
17. 20 p. on 5 f. blue & yellow 4·00 4·00

RUANDA-URUNDI O4

Part of German E. Africa, including Ruanda and Urundi, occupied by Belgian forces during the war of 1914-18 and a Trust Territory administered by Belgium until 1 July, 1962. The territory then became two separate independent states, named Rwanda and Burundi.

1916. Stamps of Belgian Congo of 1915 optd. **EST AFRICAIN ALLEMAND OCCUPATION BELGE** and also in Flemish.

15. 13. 5 c. black and green 12 8
16. 14. 10 c. black and red 20 15
17. 5. 15 c. black and green 10 8
18. 15. 25 c. black and blue 75 60
19. 7. 40 c. black and lake 1·75 1·25
20. 8. 50 c. black and lake 1·90 1·25
21. 9. 1 f. black and olive 25 20
22. 11. 5 f. black and orange 35 35

1918. Belgian Congo Red Cross stamps of 1918 optd. **A. O.**

23. 13. 5 c.+10 c. blue & green 5 5
24. 14. 10 c.+15 c. blue and red 5 5
25. 5. 15 c.+20 c. blue & green 5 5
26. 15. 25 c.+25 c. blue 5 5
27. 7. 40 c.+40 c. blue and lake 8 8
28. 8. 50 c.+50 c. blue and lake 8 8
29. 9. 1 f.+1 f. blue and olive 60 60
30. 11. 5 f.+5 f. blue and orange 1·40 1·40
31. 12. 10 f.+10 f. blue & green 16·00 16·00

1922. Stamps of 1916 surch.

32. 8. 5 c. on 50 c. black & lake 15 15
33. 13. 10 c. on 5 c. black & green 15 15
34. 7. 25 c. on 40 c. black & lake 25 20
35. 14. 30 c. on 10 c. black & red 8 8
36. 15. 50 c. on 25 c. black & blue 12 12

1924. Belgian Congo stamps of 1923 optd. **RUANDA URUNDI** in two lines close together or in one line (45 c. and 60 c.).

37. A. 5 c. yellow 5 5
38. B. 10 c. green 5 5
39. C. 15 c. brown 5 5
40. D. 20 c. olive 5 5
41. E. 20 c. green 8 8
42. F. 25 c. brown 12 10
43. 20. 30 c. red 10 10
44. 30 c. olive 10 8
45. D. 40 c. purple 15 15
62. 21. 45 c. purple 20 15
46. G. 50 c. blue 10 10
47. 50 c. orange 20 10
63. 21. 60 c. lake 20 15
48. E. 75 c. orange 12 12
49. 75 c. blue 12 12
50. H. 1 f. brown 15 15
51. 1 f. blue 20 12
52. I. 3 f. brown 1·00 75
53. J. 5 f. slate 2·10 1·40
54. K. 10 f. black 4·75 3·00

1925. Stamp of Belgian Congo, optd. **RUANDA-URUNDI.** Inscriptions in French or in Flemish.

61. 23. 25 c.+25 c. black and red 10 10

1927. Belgian Congo stamps of 1923 optd. **RUANDA URUNDI** in two lines, wide apart.

64. B. 10 c. green 8 8
65. C. 15 c. brown 25 25
66. 20. 35 c. green 12 10
67. 75 c. red 15 12
68. H. 1 f. red 25 15
69. D. 1 f. 25 blue 20 20
70. 1 f. 50 blue 25 15
71. 1 f. 75 blue 35 30

1927. No. 144 of Belgian Congo optd. **RUANDA URUNDI.**

72. 1 f. 75 on 1 f. 50 blue 20 15

1930. Native Fund stamps of Belgian Congo (Nos. 160/8), optd. **RUANDA URUNDI.**

73. 10 c.+5 c. red 10 10
74. 20 c.+10 c. brown 20 20
75. 35 c.+15 c. green 50 45
76. 60 c.+30 c. purple 55 50
77. 1 f.+50 c. red 60 55
78. 1 f. 75+75 c. blue 75 70
79. 3 f. 50+1 f. 50 lake 1·75 1·60
80. 5 f.+2 f. 50 brown 1·50 1·50
81. 10 f.+5 f. black 1·60 1·60

1931. Nos. 68 and 71 surch.

82. H. 1 f. 25 on 1 f. red 70 35
83. D. 2 f. on 1 f. 75 blue 80 50

1. Mountain Scenery. 2. Cowherds.

1931.

84. – 5 c. claret 5 5
85. 1. 10 c. grey 5 5
86. – 15 c. red 8 5
87. – 25 c. purple 5 5
88. 2. 40 c. green 10 10
89. – 50 c. violet 5 5
90. – 60 c. claret 5 5
91. – 75 c. black 5 5
92. – 1 f. red 5 5
93. – 1 f. 25 brown 8 8
94. – 1 f. 50 purple 5 5
95. – 2 f. blue 12 10
96. – 2 f. 50 blue 12 12
97. – 3 f. 25 purple 10 10
98. – 4 f. red 20 20
99. – 5 f. grey 15 15
100. – 10 f. purple 25 20
101. – 20 f. brown 85 75

DESIGNS—HORIZ. 15 c. Warrior. 25 c. Chieftain's kraal. 50 c. Head of buffalo. 1 f. Wives of Urundi chiefs. 1 f. 50, 2 f. Wooden pot hewer. 2 f. 50, 3 f. 25, Leather-workers. 4 f. Watubu potter. VERT. 5 c., 60 c. Native porter. 75 c. Native greeting. 1 f. 25, Mother and child. 5 f. Ruanda dancer. 10 f. Warriors. 20 f. Native prince.

1934. King Albert Mourning stamps. As T 32 of Belgian Congo.

102. – 1 f. 50 black 25 25

1936. Charity. Queen Astrid Fund. As T34 of Belgian Congo.

103. – 1 f. 25+5 c. brown 25 20
104. – 1 f. 50+10 c. red 25 20
105. – 2 f. 50+25 c. blue 35 35

1941. Stamps of Belgian Congo optd. **RUANDA URUNDI.**

106. 37. 10 c. grey 2·50 2·50
107. 1 f. 75 orange 1·10 1·10
108. 2 f. 75 blue 1·10 1·10

1941. Ruanda-Urundi stamps of 1931 surch.

109. 2. 5 c. on 40 c. green 1·25 1·25
110. – 60 c. on 50 c. violet 85 85
111. – 2 f. 50 on 1 f. 50 purple 85 85
112. – 3 f. 25 on 2 f. blue 4·00 4·00

1941. Stamps of Belgian Congo optd. **RUANDA URUNDI** and surch. also.

113. – 5 c. on 1 f. 50 black and chocolate (No. 222) 8 8
114. – 75 c. on 90 c. brown and red (No. 221) 35 35
115. 37. 2 f. 50 on 10 f. red 60 60

1942. War Relief. As Nos. 246/7 of Belgian Congo.

116. 10 f.+40 f. blue 90 95
117. 10 f.+40 f. red 90 95

1942. Nos. 107/8 of Ruanda-Urundi surch.

118. 37. 75 c. on 1 f. 75 orange 60 60
119. 2 f. 50 on 2 f. 75 blue 1·25 1·25

1942. As T 39/40 of Belgian Congo.

120. 39. 5 c. red 5 5
121. 10 c. olive 5 5
122. 15 c. brown 5 5
123. 20 c. blue 5 5
124. 25 c. purple 5 5
125. 30 c. blue 5 5
126. 50 c. green 5 5
127. 60 c. brown 5 5
128. – 75 c. black and violet 5 5
129. – 1 f. black and brown 8 5
130. – 1 f. 25 black and red 12 8
131. 40. 1 f. 75 brown 25 15
132. 2 f. orange 25 12
133. 2 f. 50 red 25 8
134. – 3 f. 50 olive 25 12
135. – 5 f. orange 25 15
136. – 6 f. blue 25 15
137. – 7 f. black 25 20
138. – 10 f. brown 45 25
139. – 20 f. black and brown 70 50
140. – 50 f. black and red 85 60
141. – 100 f. black and green 1·90 1·75

DESIGNS—VERT. As T 39: 75 c. to 1 f. 25 and 100 f. Head of chief. 3 f. 50 to 10 f. and 50 f. Askari sentry. 20 f. Zebra head.

1944. Red Cross Fund. Nos. 126, 130, 131 and 134 surch. **Au profit de la Croix Rouge Ten voordeele van het Roode Kruis** and premium.

147. 39. 50 c.+50 f. green 75 75
148. – 1 f. 25+100 f. blk. & red 1·00 1·00
149. 40. 1 f. 75+100 f. brown 75 75
150. – 3 f. 50+100 f. olive 1·00 1·00

1948. Native Art designs as T **43** of Belgian Congo.
151. 10 c. orange 5 5
152. 15 c. blue 5 5
153. 20 c. blue 5 5
154. 25 c. red 10 10
155. 40 c. mauve 5 5
156. 50 c. olive 5 5
157. 70 c. green 5 5
158. 75 c. mauve 5 5
159. 1 f. purple and orange .. 8 5
160. 1 f. 25 mauve and blue .. 8 5
161. 1 f. 50 mauve and olive .. 15 12
162. 2 f. claret and red .. 10 5
163. 2 f. 50 green and brown .. 10 5
164. 3 f. 50 green and blue .. 10 8
165. 5 f. claret and brown .. 15 8
166. 6 f. green and orange .. 20 8
167. 10 f. brown and violet .. 25 12
168. 20 f. purple and red .. 45 25
169. 50 f. black and brown .. 1·10 50
170. 100 f. black and red .. 2·00 1·10

1949. Surch.
171. 3 f. on 2 f. 50 (No. 163) .. 10 5
172. 4 f. on 6 f. (No. 166) .. 12 8
173. 6 f. 50 on 6 f. (No. 166) .. 15 10

1953. St. Francis Xavier. 400th Death Anniv. As T **48** of Belgian Congo.
174. 1 f. 50, black and blue .. 20 20

1953. Flowers. As T **47** of Belgian Congo. Flowers in natural colours. Colours of backgrounds and inscriptions given.
175. 10 c. yellow and purple .. 5 5
176. 15 c. green and red .. 5 5
177. 20 c. grey and green .. 5 5
178. 25 c. orange and green .. 5 5
179. 40 c. salmon and green .. 5 5
180. 50 c. turquoise and red .. 5 5
181. 60 c. purple and green .. 8 5
182. 75 c. grey and lake .. 8 5
183. 1 f. lemon and red .. 12 5
184. 1 f. 25 blue and green .. 20 15
185. 1 f. 50 green and violet .. 12 5
186. 2 f. yellow, buff and olive .. 85 5
187. 3 f. pink and green .. 25 5
188. 4 f. lavender and sepia .. 25 5
189. 5 f. green and purple .. 35 8
190. 7 f. brown and green .. 45 15
191. 8 f. yellow and green .. 55 20
192. 10 f. olive and purple .. 75 20
193. 20 f. red and blue .. .. 1·40 30

1955. As Nos. 323/6 of Belgian Congo.
194. **51.** 1 f. 50, black and red .. 12 5
195. – 3 f. black and green .. 12 5
196. – 4 f. 50 black and blue .. 15 10
197. – 6 f. 50 black and maroon 20 12

1956. Mozart. Birth Bicent. As T **226/7** of Belgium.
198. **226.** 4 f. 50+1 f. 50 violet 50 55
199. **227.** 6 f. 50+2 f. 50 maroon 75 80

1957. Red Cross Fund. As T **53** of Belgian Congo.
200. 3 f.+50 c. indigo 30 30
201. 4 f. 50 c.+50 c. green .. 40 40
202. 6 f. 50 c.+50 c. brown .. 50 50

1959. Fauna. As T **55** of Belgian Congo.
203. 10 c. black, red and brown 5 5
204. 20 c. black and green .. 5 5
205. 40 c. black, ol.-blk. & mag. 5 5
206. 50 c. brown, yellow & green 5 5
207. 1 f. black, blue and brown 5 5
208. 1 f. 50 black and orange .. 10 5
209. 2 f. black, brown & turquoise 5 5
210. 3 f. black, red and brown .. 8 5
211. 5 f. brown, blk., grn. & yell. 12 5
212. 6 f. 50 brown, yell. & red .. 15 5
213. 8 f. black, magenta & blue 30 12
214. 10 f. brn., blk., mag. & yell. 25 10

DESIGNS—VERT. 10 c., 1 f. Gorilla. 40 c., 2 f. Colobus monkey. HORIZ. 20 c., 1 f. 50, Black buffaloes. 50 c., 6 f. 50, Impala. 3 f., 8 f. Elephants. 5 f., 10 f. Eland and zebras.

1960. African Technical Co-operation Commission. 10th Anniv. As T **57** of Belgian Congo. Inscr. in French or Flemish.
222. 3 f. salmon and blue .. 10 8

1960. Child Welfare Fund. As Nos. 355/9 of Belgian Congo.
223. **58.** 50 c.+25 c. slate-blue and red 5 5
224. – 1 f. 50+50 c. lake & blk. 10 10
225. – 2 f.+1 f. black and red 12 12
226. – 3 f.+1 f. 25 verm. & grn. 55 60
227. – 6 f. 50+3 f. 50 bronze green and red .. 55 60

1960. No. 210 surch.
228. 3 f. 50 on 3 f. blk., red & brn. 15 5

DESIGN: 50 f. Lion and lioness.

3. Leopard.

1961.
229. **3.** 20 f. yellow, black, red and blue-green .. 35 25
230. – 50 f. bistre, black, blue and vermilion 85 60

DESIGNS: 1 f., 5 f. Side view of Cathedral. 1 f. 50, 6 f. 50, Stained glass windows.

4. Usumbura Cathedral.

1961. Usumbura Cathedral Fund.
231. **4.** 50 c.+25 c. brown & buff 5 5
232. – 1 f.+50 c. green .. 5 5
233. – 1 f. 50+75 c. mult. .. 5 5
234. **4.** 3 f. 50+1 f. 50 blue .. 10 10
235. – 5 f.+2 f. red and orange 20 20
236. – 6 f. 50+3 f. multicoloured 25 25

POSTAGE DUE STAMPS

1924. Postage Due stamps of Belgian Congo optd. **RUANDA URUNDI.**
D 55. **D 1.** 5 c. sepia 5 5
D 56. 10 c. red 5 5
D 57. 15 c. violet 5 5
D 58. 30 c. green 10 12
D 59. 50 c. blue 12 15
D 60. 1 f. slate 20 20

1943. Postage Due stamps of Belgian Congo optd. **RUANDA URUNDI.**
D 142. **D 2.** 10 c. olive 5 5
D 143. 20 c. blue 5 5
D 144. 50 c. green 5 5
D 145. 1 f. brown 10 10
D 146. 2 f. orange 12 12

1959. Postage Due stamps of Belgian Congo optd. **RUANDA URUNDI.**
D 215. **D 3.** 10 c. brown 5 5
D 216. 20 c. maroon .. 5 5
D 217. 50 c. green 5 5
D 218. 1 f. blue 8 8
D 219. 2 f. red 10 10
D 220. 4 f. violet 20 20
D 221. 6 f. blue 25 25

For later issues see **BURUNDI** and **RWANDA.**

RUMANIA E3

A republic in S.E. Europe, bordering on the Black Sea, originally a kingdom formed by the union of Moldavia and Wallachia.

1858. 40 parale = 1 piastre.
1867. 100 bani = 1 leu.

MOLDAVIA

1. 2.

1858. Imperf.
1. **1.** 27 p. black on rose .. £4000 £1000
2. 54 p. blue on green .. £800 £400
3. 81 p. blue on blue .. £4000 £4500
4. 108 p. blue on pink .. £3000 £900

1858. Imperf.
15. **2.** 5 p. black .. .. 10·00
13. 40 p. blue .. .. 15·00 10·00
14. 80 p. red .. .. 75·00 30·00

RUMANIA

3.

1862. Imperf.
29. **3.** 3 p. yellow .. .. 5·00 25·00
30. 6 p. red .. .. 4·00 17·00
31. 30 p. blue .. .. 7·00 3·50

4. Prince Cuza. 5. Prince Carol. 6.

1865. Imperf.
49a. **4.** 2 p. orange .. .. 3·75 18·00
46. 5 p. blue .. .. 1·25 35·00
48. 20 p. red .. .. 70 1·00

1866. Imperf.
60. **5.** 2 p. black on yellow .. 50 4·00
61. 5 p. black on blue .. 3·75 65·00
62. 20 p. black on rose .. 40 60

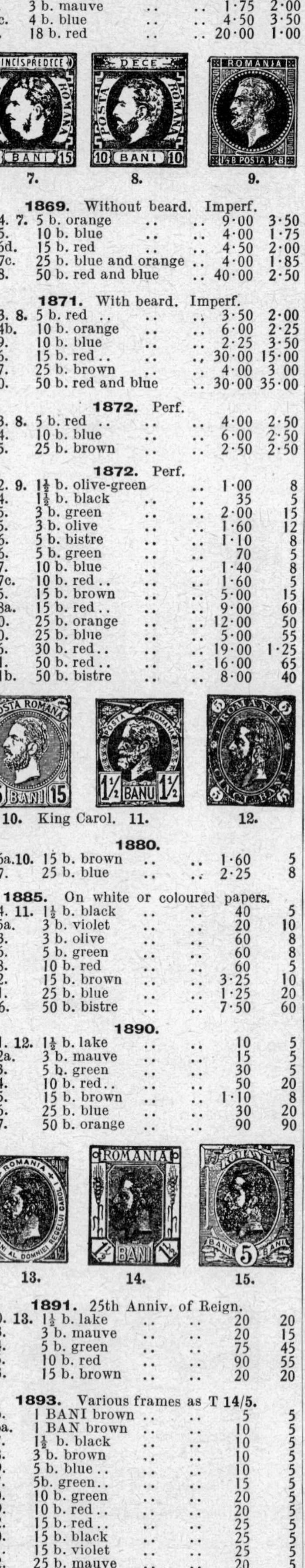

1868. Imperf.
71. **6.** 2 b. orange .. .. 1·25 80
72. 3 b. mauve .. .. 1·75 2·00
66c. 4 b. blue .. .. 4·50 3·50
67. 18 b. red .. .. 20·00 1·00

7. 8. 9.

1869. Without beard. Imperf.
74. **7.** 5 b. orange .. .. 9·00 3·50
75. 10 b. blue .. .. 4·00 1·75
76d. 15 b. red .. .. 4·50 2·00
77c. 25 b. blue and orange .. 4·00 1·85
78. 50 b. red and blue .. 40·00 2·50

1871. With beard. Imperf.
83. **8.** 5 b. red .. .. 3·50 2·00
84b. 10 b. orange .. .. 6·00 2·25
99. 10 b. blue .. .. 2·25 3·50
86. 15 b. red .. .. 30·00 15·00
87. 25 b. brown .. .. 4·00 3 00
100. 50 b. red and blue .. 30·00 35·00

1872. Perf.
93. **8.** 5 b. red .. .. 4·00 2·50
94. 10 b. blue .. .. 6·00 2·50
95. 25 b. brown .. .. 2·50 2·50

1872. Perf.
112. **9.** $1\frac{1}{2}$ b. olive-green .. 1·00 8
124. $1\frac{1}{2}$ b. black 35 5
105. 3 b. green .. .. 2·00 15
125. 3 b. olive .. .. 1·60 12
106. 5 b. bistre .. .. 1·10 8
126. 5 b. green 70 5
107. 10 b. blue .. .. 1·40 8
127c. 10 b. red .. .. 1·60 5
115. 15 b. brown .. .. 5·00 15
128a. 15 b. red .. .. 9·00 60
110. 25 b. orange .. .. 12·00 50
130. 25 b. blue .. .. 5·00 55
116. 30 b. red .. .. 19·00 1·25
111. 50 b. red .. .. 16·00 65
131b. 50 b. bistre .. .. 8·00 40

10. King Carol. 11. 12.

1880.
146a. **10.** 15 b. brown .. .. 1·60 5
147. 25 b. blue .. .. 2·25 8

1885. On white or coloured papers.
174. **11.** $1\frac{1}{2}$ b. black 40 5
165a. 3 b. violet 20 10
163. 3 b. olive 60 8
166. 5 b. green 60 8
168. 10 b. red 60 5
182. 15 b. brown .. .. 3·25 10
171. 25 b. blue .. .. 1·25 20
186. 50 b. bistre .. .. 7·50 60

1890.
271. **12.** $1\frac{1}{2}$ b. lake 10 5
272a. 3 b. mauve 15 5
273. 5 b. green 30 5
254. 10 b. red 50 20
255. 15 b. brown .. .. 1·10 8
306. 25 b. blue 30 20
307. 50 b. orange 90 90

13. 14. 15.

1891. 25th Anniv. of Reign.
300. **13.** $1\frac{1}{2}$ b. lake 20 20
293. 3 b. mauve 20 15
294. 5 b. green 75 45
295. 10 b. red 90 55
303. 15 b. brown 20 20

1893. Various frames as T **14/5.**
396. 1 BANI brown 5 5
316a. 1 BAN brown 10 5
317. $1\frac{1}{2}$ b. black 10 5
318. 3 b. brown 10 5
319. 5 b. blue 10 5
417. 5 b. green 15 5
320. 10 b. green 20 5
399. 10 b. red 20 5
332. 15 b. red 25 5
400. 15 b. black 25 5
431. 15 b. violet 25 5
322. 25 b. mauve 20 5
401a. 25 b. blue 20 5
323. 40 b. green .. .. 1·75 5
334. 50 b. orange .. .. 1·75 5
414. 1 l. rose and brown .. 4·50 8
326. 2 l. brown and orange .. 5·00 20
See also Nos. 427 etc.

16. Four-in-hand Postal Coach.

17. New Post Office, Bucharest.

1903. Opening of New Post Office in 1901.
464. **16.** 1 b. brown 25 15
465. 3 b. claret 30 15
466. 5 b. green 45 15
467. 10 b. rose 40 15
468. 15 b. black 30 15
472. **17.** 15 b. black 80 50
469. **16.** 25 b. blue .. .. 1·75 1·00
473. **17.** 25 b. blue .. .. 2·40 1·10
470. **16.** 40 b. green .. .. 2·10 1·00
474. **17.** 40 b. green .. .. 2·50 1·10
471. **16.** 50 b. orange .. .. 2·50 1·00
475. **17.** 50 b. orange .. .. 2·50 1·10
476. 1 l. brown .. .. 2·50 1·10
477. 2 l. red .. .. 6·50 3·25
478. 5 l. lilac .. .. 8·00 4·00
See also No. 1275.

1905. Various frames as T **14/5.**
427. 1 ban black 8 5
627. $1\frac{1}{2}$ b. yellow 15 5
703. 40 b. brown 8 5
705. 50 b. red 10 5
432. 1 l. black and green .. 3·00 8
706. 1 l. green 30 5
433. 2 l. black and brown .. 2·00 30
707. 2 l. orange 50 10

18. Queen of Rumania spinning.

19. Queen of Rumania weaving.

1906. Charity.
481. **18.** 3 b. (+7) brown .. 35 10
482. 5 b. (+10) green .. 35 10
483. 10 b. (+10) red .. 1·25 60
484. 15 b. (+10) purple .. 70 40

1906. Charity.
485. **19.** 3 b. (+7) brown .. 35 10
486. 5 b. (+10) green .. 35 10
487. 10 b. (+10) red .. 1·25 60
488. 15 b. (+10) lilac .. 70 40

20. Queen of Rumania nursing wounded Soldier.

21.

1906. Charity.
489. **20.** 3 b. (+7) brown .. 35 10
490. 5 b. (+10) green .. 35 10
491. 10 b. (+10) red .. 1·25 60
492. 15 b. (+10) purple .. 70 40

1906. Kingdom. 25th Anniv.
493. **21.** 1 b. black and bistre .. 5 5
494. 3 b. black and brown .. 25 5
495. 5 b. black and green .. 5 5
496. 10 b. black and red .. 5 5
497. 15 b. black and violet .. 12 5
498. 25 b. black and blue .. 1·25 70
499. 40 b. black and brown .. 25 5
500. 50 b. black and brown .. 25 8
501. 1 l. black and red .. 30 10
502. 2 l. black and orange .. 25 12

22. Prince Carol at Battle of Calafat.

23.

1906. 40 Years' Rule of Prince and King Dated "1906".

503.	–	1 b. black and bistre ..	5	5
504.	–	3 b. black and brown ..	8	5
505.	22.	5 b. black and green ..	20	5
506.	–	10 b. black and red	5	5
507.	–	15 b. black and violet..	8	5
508.	–	25 b. black and blue ..	30	5
508a.	–	25 b. black and green ..	50	30
509.	–	40 b. black and brown..	12	5
510.	–	50 b. black and brown..	12	10
511.	–	1 l. black and red ..	12	12
512.	–	2 l. black and orange ..	12	12

DESIGNS—HORIZ. 1 b. Prince Carol taking oath of allegiance in 1866. 3 b. Prince in carriage. 10 b. Meeting of Prince and Osman Pasha, 1878. 15 b. Carol when Prince in 1866 and King in 1906. 25 b. Rumanian Army crossing Danube, 1877. 40 b. Triumphal entry into Bucharest, 1878. 50 b. Prince at head of Army in 1877. 1 l. King Carol at Cathedral in 1896. 2 l. King at shrine of S. Nicholas, 1904.

1906. Charity.

513.	23.	3 b. (+7) brown, bistre and blue	25	15
514.		5 b. (+10) green, rose and bistre	25	15
515.		10 b. (+10) red, bistre and blue	50	30
516.		15 b. (+10) violet, bistre and blue	1·10	45

24. Peasant ploughing and Angel.

1906. Jubilee Exhibition, Bucharest.

517.	24.	5 b. black and green ..	60	40
518.		10 b. black and red ..	60	40
519.	–	15 b. black and violet..	75	45
520.	–	25 b. black and blue ..	75	45
521.	–	30 b. brown and red ..	75	45
522.	–	40 b. brown and green	75	45
523.	–	50 b. black and orange..	75	45
524.	–	75 b. sepia and brown..	75	45
525.	–	1 l. 50 brown & mauve..	5·00	2·50
526.		2 l. 50 brown and yell...	3·25	1·75
527.	–	3 l. brn. & orge.-brn. ..	3·25	1·75

DESIGNS—HORIZ. 15 b., 25 b. Exhibition Building. VERT. 30 b., 40 b. Farmhouse. 50 b., 75 b. (different). Royal Family pavilion. 1 l. 50, 2 l. 50 King Carol on horseback. 3 l. Queen Elisabeth (Carmen Silva).

25. Princess Maria and Children receiving a Poor Family conducted by an Angel.

1907. Charity

528.	25.	3 b. (+7) brown ..	1·00	70
529.		5 b. (+10) brown & grn.	50	25
530.		10 b. (+10) brown & red	50	20
531.		15 b. (+10) brown & bl.	50	20

26. 27.

1908.

575.	26.	5 b. green	20	5
562.		10 b. red	10	5
577.		15 b. violet	1·25	5
564.		25 b. blue	20	5
579.		40 b. green	12	5
702.		40 b. sepia	40	10
566.		50 b. orange	12	5
705.		50 b. red	10	5
581.		1 l. brown	15	5
582.		2 l. red	80	40

1908.

583.	27.	1 b. black	5	5
590.		3 b. brown	5	5
585.		5 b. green	5	5
592.		10 b. red	5	5
599.		15 b. violet	1·60	75
594.		15 b. olive	5	5
692.		15 b. brown	8	5

28. 29.

30. Troops crossing Danube.

31. Mircea the Great (1387) and King Carol (1913).

1913. Acquisition of Southern Dobruja.

626.	28.	1 b. black	10	5
627.	29.	3 b. brown and grey ..	15	5
628.	30.	5 b. black and green ..	10	5
629.	–	10 b. black and orange	10	5
630.	31.	15 b. violet and brown	15	5
631.	–	25 b. brown and blue ..	30	10
632.	30.	40 b. claret and brown	50	10
633.	29.	50 b. blue and yellow ..	1·10	40
634.		1 l. brown and blue ..	2·00	90
635.		2 l. rose and red ..	4·00	2·50

DESIGNS—HORIZ. As T 30: 10 b. Town of Constantza. 25 b. Church and School in Dobruja.

1918. Surch. **25. BANI.**

657.	27.	25 b. on 1 b. black ..	20	20

1918. Optd. **1918.**

662.	27.	5 b. green	5	5
663.		10 b. red	5	5

TRANSYLVANIA

The Eastern portion of Hungary. Union with Rumania proclaimed in December 1918, and the final frontiers settled by the Treaty of Trianon, 4th June, 1920.

The following issues for Transylvania (Nos. 747/858) were valid throughout Rumania

(32.)

(33.)

(The "F" stands for King Ferdinand and "P.T.T." for Posts, Telegraphs and Telephones).

The values "BANI", "LEU" or "LEI" appear above or below the monogram.

A. Issues for Cluj (Kolozsvar of Klausenburg).

1919. Various stamps of Hungary optd. as T 32.

(a) Flood Relief Charity stamps of 1913.

747.	3.	1 l. on 1 f. grey ..	6·00	6·00
748.		1 l. on 2 f. yellow ..	18·00	18·00
749.		1 l. on 3 f. orange ..	8·00	8·00
750.		1 l. on 5 f. green ..	50	50
751.		1 l. on 10 f. red ..	50	50
752.		1 l. on 12 f. lilac on yell.	2·10	2·10
753.		1 l. on 16 f. green ..	95	1·10
754.		1 l. on 25 f. blue ..	17·00	17·00
755.		1 l. on 35 f. purple ..	95	1·10
756.	4.	1 l. on 1 k. red	18·00	18 00

(b) War Charity stamps of 1916.

757.	6.	10 (+2) b. red	5	5
758.	–	15 (+2) b. violet ..	5	5
759.	8.	40 (+2) b. lake ..	5	5

(c) Harvesters and Parliament Types.

760.	11.	2 b. brown	5	5
761.		3 b. claret	5	5
762.		5 b. green	5	5
763.		6 b. blue	5	5
764.		10 b. red	30·00	30·00
765.		15 b. violet (No. 244)	90	90
766.		15 b. violet	5	5
767.		25 b. blue	5	5
768.		35 b. brown	5	5
769.		40 b. olive	5	5
770.	12.	50 b. purple	5	5
771.		75 b. blue	5	5
772.		80 b. green	5	5
773.		1 l. lake.. ..	5	5
774.		2 l. brown	8	8
775.		3 l. grey and violet ..	50	50
776.		5 l. brown	40	40
777.		10 l. lilac and brown ..	60	60

(d) Karl and Zita stamps.

778.	13.	10 b. red	9·00	9·00
779.		15 b. violet	2·50	2·50
780.		20 b. brown	5	5
781.		25 b. blue	15	15
782.	14.	40 b. olive	5	5

B. Issues for Oradea (Nagyvarad, Grosswardein).

1919. Various stamps of Hungary optd. as T 33.

(a) "Turul" Type.

794.	3.	2 b. yellow	90	90
795.		3 b. orange	2·25	2·25
796.		6 b. drab.. ..	20	25
797.		16 b. green	6·00	6·00
798.		50 b. lake on blue ..	25	25
799.		70 b. brown and green	4·00	4·50

(b) Flood Relief Charity stamps of 1913.

800.	3.	1 l. on 1 f. grey ..	30	30
801.		1 l. on 2 f. yellow ..	1·25	1·40
802.		1 l. on 3 f. orange ..	30	30
803.		1 l. on 5 l. green ..	10	10
804.		1 l. on 6 f. drab ..	30	30
805.		1 l. on 10 f. red ..	8	8
806.		1 l. on 12 f. lilac on yell.	14·00	14·00
807.		1 l. on 16 f. green ..	35	35
808.		1 l. on 20 f. brown ..	2·00	2·00
809.		1 l. on 25 f. blue ..	90	1·00
810.		1 l. on 35 f. purple ..	90	1·00

(c) War Charity stamp of 1915.

811.	3.	5+2 b. green (No. 173)..	1·25	1·25

(d) War Charity stamps of 1916.

812.	6.	10 (+2) b. red	12	12
813.	–	15 (+2) b. violet ..	5	5
814.	8.	40 (+2) b. lake	5	5

(e) Harvesters and Parliament Types.

815.	11.	2 b. brown	5	5
816.		3 b. claret	5	5
817.		5 b. green	5	5
818.		6 b. blue	10	10
819.		10 b. red	12	12
820.		15 b. violet (No. 244)..	25·00	25·00
821.		15 b. violet	5	5
822.		20 b. brown	2·75	2·75
823.		25 b. blue	8	8
824.		35 b. brown	8	8
825.		40 b. olive	5	5
826.	12.	50 b. purple	8	8
827.		75 b. blue	5	5
828.		80 b. green	5	5
829.		1 l. lake.. ..	10	10
830.		2 l. brown	8	8
831.		3 l. grey and violet ..	70	90
832.		5 l. brown	30	30
833.		10 l. lilac and brown ..	30	30

(f) Charles and Zita stamps.

834.	13.	10 b. red	50	50
835.		20 b. brown	8	8
836.		25 b. blue	10	10
837.	14.	40 b. olive	10	10

The following (Nos. 838/58) are also optd. **KOZTARSASAG.**

(g) Harvesters and Parliament Types.

838.	11.	2 b. brown	45	45
839.		3 b. claret	5	5
840.		4 b. slate	5	5
841.		5 b. green	8	8
842.		6 b. blue	40	40
843.		10 b. red	3·75	3·75
844.		20 b. brown	30	30
845.		40 b. olive	8	8
846.	12.	1 l. lake.. ..	5	5
847.		3 l. grey and violet ..	10	10
848.		5 l. brown	80	90

(h) Charles and Zita stamps.

849.	13.	10 b. red	32·00	32·00
850.		20 b. brown	60	60
851.		25 b. blue	15	20
852.	14.	50 b. purple	5	5

(k) Harvesters and Parliament Types inscr. "MAGYAR POSTA".

853.	11.	5 b. green	5	5
854.		10 b. red	5	5
855.		20 b. brown	8	8
856.		25 b. blue	20	20
857.		40 b. olive	30	30
858.	12.	5 l. brown	1·50	1·50

(35.) King Ferdinand's Monogram.

36. King Ferdinand. 37.

1919. Recovery of Transylvania and Return of King of Rumania to Bucharest. Optd. with T 35.

873.	27.	1 b. black	5	5
874.		5 b. green	10	8
878a.		10 b. red	5	5

1920.

891.	36.	1 b. black	5	5
892.		5 b. green	5	5
893.		10 b. red	5	5
882.		15 b. brown	10	5
895.		25 b. blue	8	5
896.		25 b. brown	5	5
910.		40 b. brown	10	8
898.		50 b. pink	8	5
887.		1 l. green	8	5
900.		1 l. red	8	5
889.		2 l. orange	10	10
902.		2 l. blue	10	5
903.		2 l. red	25	25

1922.

923.	37.	3 b. black	5	5
924.		5 b. black	5	5
925.		10 b. green	5	5
926.		25 b. brown	5	5
927.		25 b. red	5	5
928.		30 b. violet	5	5
929.		50 b. yellow	5	5
930.		60 b. green	5	5
931.		1 l. violet	5	5
932.		2 l. red	8	5
933a.		2 l. green	5	5
934.	37.	3 l. blue	8	5
935a.		3 l. brown	5	5
937.		3 l. red	5	5
936a.		3 l. pink	5	8
938.		5 l. green	15	5
939b.		5 l. brown	5	5
940.		6 l. blue	12	5
941.		6 l. red	20	10
942.		6 l. olive	12	5
943.		7 l. 50 blue	10	5
944.		10 l. blue	10	5

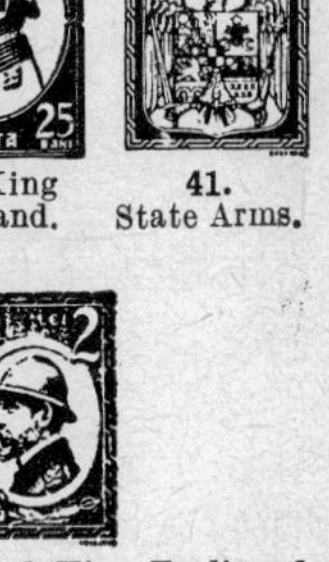

39. Cathedral of Alba Julia. 40. King Ferdinand. 41. State Arms.

43. Michael the Brave and King Ferdinand.

1922. Coronation.

1032.	39.	5 b. black	5	5
1033	40.	25 b. brown	5	5
1034.	41.	50 b. green	5	5
1035.	–	1 l. olive	5	5
1036.	43.	2 l. red	5	5
1037.	–	3 l. blue	35	15
1050.	–	6 l. violet	85	85

DESIGNS—As T 40: 1 l. Queen Marie as a nurse. 3 l. Portrait of King, but rectangular frame. Larger (21×33 mm.): 6 l. Queen Marie in coronation robes.

46. King Ferdinand.

47. Map of Rumania.

1926. King's 60th Birthday. Imperf. or perf.

1051.	46.	10 b. green	8	8
1052.		25 b. orange	5	5
1053.		50 b. brown	5	5
1054.		1 l. violet	5	5
1055.		2 l. green	5	5
1056.		3 l. red	5	5
1057.		5 l. sepia	5	5
1058.		6 l. olive	5	5
1059.		9 l. grey	5	5
1060.		10 l. blue	5	5

1927. Rumanian Geographical Society. 50th Anniv.

1061.	47.	1+9 l. violet	35	30
1062.	–	2+8 l. green	35	30
1063.	–	3+7 l. red	35	30
1064.	–	5+5 l. blue	35	30
1065.	–	6+4 l. olive	50	30

DESIGNS: 2 l. Stephen the Great. 3 l. Michael the Brave. 5 l. Carol and Ferdinand. 6 l. Adam Clisi Monument.

52. King Carol and King Ferdinand.

DESIGNS—HORIZ. 30 b., 2 l., 3 l., 5 l. King Ferdinand. VERT. 50 b., 4 l., 4 l. 50, 6 l. King Ferdinand as in T 52.

1927. Independence. 50th Anniv.

1066.	52.	25 b. claret	5	5
1067.	–	30 b. black	5	5
1068.	–	50 b. green	5	5
1069.	52.	1 l. blue	5	5
1070.	–	2 l. green	5	5
1071.	–	3 l. purple	5	5
1072.	–	4 l. brown	12	10
1073.	–	4 l. 50 chestnut ..	80	60
1074.	–	5 l. brown	8	5
1075.	–	6 l. red.. ..	35	15
1076.	52.	7 l. 50 blue	15	12
1077.	–	10 l. blue	15	12

55. King Michael. 56.

1928.

1080. **55.** 25 b. black 5 5
1081. 30 b. pink 8 5
1082. 50 b. olive 5 5

(a) Size 19×25 mm.

1083. **56.** 1 l. purple 5 5
1084. 2 l. green 5 5
1085. 3 l. red 8 5
1086. 5 l. brown 8 5
1087. 7 l. 50 blue 50 5
1088. 10 l. blue 35 5

(b) Size 18×23 mm.

1129. **56.** 1 l. purple 5 5
1130. 2 l. green 12 5
1131. 3 l. red 45 5
1132. 7 l. 50 blue 35 5
1133. 10 l. blue 85 55

DESIGNS: 3 l., 5 l., 20 l. Hotin Fortress. 7 l. 50, 10 l. Alba Fortress.

57. Bessarabian Parliament House.

1928. Annexation of Bessarabia. 10th Anniv.

1092. **57.** 1 l. green 15 8
1093. – 2 l. brown 15 12
1094. – 3 l. sepia 15 8
1095. – 5 l. lake 15 12
1096. – 7 l. 50 blue 20 15
1097. – 10 l. blue 45 30
1098. – 20 l. violet 60 40

58. Spad S 33 Biplane.

1928. Air.

1099. **58.** 1 l. chocolate 90 55
1100. 2 l. blue 90 55
1101. 5 l. red 90 55

DESIGNS: 2 l. Constanza Harbour and Carol Lighthouse. 5 l., 7 l. 50, Adam Clisi Monument. 10 l., 20 l. Cernavoda Bridge over the Danube.

59. King Carol and King Michael.

1928. Acquisition of Northern Dobruja. 50th Anniv. Inscr. "1878 POSTA 1928".

1102. **59.** 1 l. green 12 8
1103. – 2 l. chocolate 12 8
1104. **59.** 3 l. grey 12 8
1105. – 5 l. mauve 15 8
1106. – 7 l. 50 blue 15 8
1107. – 10 l. blue 20 20
1108. – 20 l. red 45 30

63. **64.** The Union.

1929. Union of Rumania and Transylvania. 10th Anniv.

1109. **63.** 1 l. purple 12 12
1110. **64.** 2 l. green 15 12
1111. – 3 l. brown 15 15
1112. – 4 l. red 20 12
1113. – 5 l. orange 20 12
1114. – 10 l. blue 45 30

DESIGNS—HORIZ. 1 l. Ferdinand I, Stephen the Great, Michael the Brave, Hunyadi and Brancoveanu. 10 l. Ferdinand I. VERT. 2 l. Union. 3 l. Avram Jancu. 4 l. King Michael the Brave. 5 l. Bran Castle.

1930. Stamps of King Michael optd. **8 IUNIE 1930**. (Accession of Carol II.)

1134. **55.** 25 b. black (postage) .. 5 5
1135. 30 b. pink 5 5
1136. 50 b. olive 5 5
1142. **56.** 1 l. purple (No. 1129) 5 5
1143. 2 l. green (No. 1130) .. 5 5
1144. 3 l. red (No. 1131) .. 5 5
1137. 5 l. brown 8 5
1140. 7 l. 50 blue (No. 1087) 55 5
1145. 7 l. 50 blue (No. 1132) 20 5
1138. 10 l. blue (No. 1088) .. 85 20
1146. 10 l. blue (No. 1133) 20 5
1147. **58.** 1 l. chocolate (air) .. 1·10 90
1148. 2 l. blue .. .. 1·10 90
1149. 5 l. red .. .. 1·10 90

66. **67.** King Carol II. **69.**

1930.

1172. **66.** 25 b. black 5 5
1173. 50 b. brown 8 5
1174. 1 l. violet 5 5
1175. 2 l. green 12 5
1176. **67.** 3 l. red 15 5
1177. 4 l. orange 15 5
1178. 6 l. claret 15 5
1179. 7 l. 50 blue 20 5
1180. – 10 l. blue 25 5
1181. – 16 l. green 85 5
1182. – 20 l. yellow 50 5

DESIGN: 10 l. to 20 l. Portrait as T **66**, but in plain circle, with "ROMANIA" at top.

1930. Air.

1183. **69.** 1 l. violet on blue .. 35 12
1184. 2 l. green on blue .. 35 12
1185. 5 l. brown on blue .. 65 20
1186. 10 l. blue on blue .. 90 35

70. Map of Rumania. **71.** Woman with Census Paper. **72.** King Carol II.

1930. National Census.

1187. **70.** 1 l. violet 20 5
1188. **71.** 2 l. green 20 12
1189. 4 l. orange 20 5
1190. 6 l. claret 45 5

1931.

1191. **72.** 30 l. blue and olive .. 15 8
1192. 50 l. blue and red .. 40 15
1193. 100 l. blue and green 85 40

73. King Carol II.

74. King Carol I. **75.** Kings Carol II, Ferdinand I, & Carol I.

1931. Rumanian Monarchy. 50th Anniv. Inscr. "1881-1931".

1200. **73.** 1 l. violet 25 8
1201. **74.** 2 l. green 25 12
1202. – 6 l. claret .. .. 1·25 25
1203. **75.** 10 l. blue .. .. 1·40 45
1204. – 20 l. orange .. .. 4·00 1·20

DESIGNS—As T **73**: 6 l. King Carol II, facing right. As T **74**: 20 l. King Ferdinand I.

DESIGNS: 10 l. Monitor "Lascar Catargiu". 16 l. Monitor "Ardeal". 20 l. Destroyer "Regele Ferdinand".

76. Naval Cadet Ship "Mircea".

1931. Rumanian Navy. 50th Anniv. Inscr. "1881-1931".

1205. **76.** 6 l. claret 80 35
1206. – 10 l. blue 90 45
1207. – 16 l. green .. .. 1·60 45
1208. – 20 l. orange 65 45

77. Bayonet Attack. **80.** King Carol I.

81. Infantry Attack. **82.** King Ferdinand I.

1931. Rumanian Army Cent.

1209. **77.** 25 b. black 20 12
1210. – 50 b. brown 20 12
1211. – 1 l. violet 20 12
1212. **80.** 2 l. green 35 12
1213. **81.** 3 l. red 55 35
1214. **82.** 7 l. 50 blue 65 35
1215. – 16 l. green .. .. 1·60 55

DESIGNS: 50 b. Infantryman, 1870. (20×33 mm.). 1 l. Infantry and drummer, 1830 (23×36 mm.). 16 l. King Carol II in uniform with plumed helmet. (21×34 mm.).

84. Scouts' Encampment. **85.** Farman.

1931 Rumanian Boy Scouts' Exn. Fund.

1221. **84.** 1 l.+1 l. red 80 55
1222. – 2 l.+2 l. green 80 55
1223. – 3 l.+3 l. blue 80 55
1224. – 4 l.+4 l. sepia .. .. 1·00 55
1225. – 6 l.+6 l. brown .. .. 1·10 55

DESIGNS—VERT. As T **84**. 3 l. Recruiting (22×37½ mm.): 2 l. Rescue work. (22×41½ mm.): Prince Nicholas. 6 l. King Carol II in Scoutmaster's uniform.

1931. Air.

1226. **85.** 2 l. green 15 5
1227. – 3 l. red 20 8
1228. – 5 l. brown 20 10
1229. – 10 l. blue 80 15
1230. – 20 l. violet .. .. 1·60 30

DESIGNS: 3 l. Farman III. 5 l. Farman F 60 "Goliath". 10 l. Farman III.
The 20 l. is smaller and shows three aeroplanes.

87. Kings Carol II, Ferdinand I, and Carol I. **91.** Alexander the Good.

1931.

1231. **87.** 16 l. green .. .. 1·60 10

1932. Alexander I, Prince of Moldavia. 500th Death Anniv.

1232. **91.** 6 l. claret .. .. 1·50 85

92. King Carol II.

1932.

1248. **92.** 10 l. blue .. .. 1·60 12

93. Semaphore signaller. **94.** Camp fire.

1932. Boy Scouts' Jamboree Fund.

1256. – 25 b.+25 b. green .. 1·00 45
1257. **93.** 50 b.+50 b. blue .. 1·00 80
1258. – 1 l.+1 l. green .. 1·00 45
1259. **94.** 2 l.+2 l. red .. 2·00 1·10
1260. – 3 l.+3 l. blue .. 5·00 2·25
1261. – 6 l.+6 l. brown .. 3·25 2·25

DESIGNS—VERT. as T **93**. 25 b. Scouts in camp. 1 l. On the trail. 3 l. King Carol II 9 l. King Carol and King Michael when a Prince.

95. Cantacuzino and Gregory Chika.

1932. 9th Int. Medical Congress.

1262. **95.** 1 l. red .. .. 1·60 55
1263. – 6 l. orange .. .. 3·25 1·10
1264. – 10 l. blue .. .. 3·25 1·10

DESIGNS: 6 l. Congress in session. 10 l. Hygeia and Æsculapius.

96. Tuberculosis Sanatorium.

1932. Postal Employees' Fund.

1265. **96.** 4 l.+1 l. green .. 80 50
1266. – 6 l.+1 l. brown .. 80 50
1267. – 10 l.+1 l. blue .. 1·25 65

DESIGNS—VERT. 6 l. War Memorial Tablet. HORIZ. 10 l. Convalescent Home.

97. "Bull's head". **98.** Dolphins. **99.** Arms.

1932. First Moldavian Stamps. 75th Anniv. Imperf.

1268. **97.** 25 b. black 20 12
1269. – 1 l. purple 20 12
1270. **98.** 2 l. green 35 12
1271. – 3 l. red 35 15
1272. **99.** 6 l. claret 55 20
1273. – 7 l. 50 blue .. .. 1·10 30
1274. – 10 l. blue .. .. 2·75 65

DESIGNS—As T **98**. 1 l. Lion rampant and bridge. 3 l. Eagle and castles. 7 l. 50, Eagle. 10 l. Bull's head.

1932. 30th Anniv. of G.P.O., Bucharest. As T **16**, but smaller.

1275. 16 l. green .. .. 2·00 65

DESIGNS: 50 b. Trajan at the completion of bridge over the Danube. 1 l. Arrival of Prince Carol at Turnu-Severin. 2 l. Trajan's Bridge.

100. Ruins of Trajan's Bridge: Arms of Turnu-Severin and Tower of Severus.

1933. Founding of Turnu-Severin. Cent.

1279. **100.** 25 b. green 12 8
1280. – 50 b. blue 20 12
1281. – 1 l. sepia 20 12
1282. – 2 l. green 35 8

DESIGNS: 3 l. Eagle and medallion portraits of Kings Carol I, Ferdinand I and Carol II. 6 l. Pelesch Castle.

101. Carmen Sylva and King Carol I.

1933. Construction of Pelesch Castle, Sinaia. 50th Anniv.

1283. **101.** 1 l. violet 35 15
1284. – 3 l. brown 40 15
1285. – 6 l. red 40 20

102. Weaver. **103.** King Carol II.

1934. Rumanian Women's Exhibition. Inscr. "L.N.F.R. MUNCA NOASTRA ROMANEASC".

1286. – 1 l.+1 l. brown .. 45 20
1287. **102.** 2 l.+1 l. blue .. 45 20
1288. – 3 l.+1 l. green .. 45 20

DESIGNS—VERT. 1 l. Wayside shrine. 3 l. Spinner.

1934. Mamaia Jamboree Fund. Nos 1256/61. Optd. **MAMAIA 1934** and Arms of Constanza.

1289. – 25 b.+25 b. green .. 55 35
1290. **93.** 50 b.+50 b. blue .. 1·10 55
1291. – 1 l.+1 l. green .. 1·10 65
1292. **94.** 2 l.+2 l. red .. .. 1·60 65
1293. – 3 l.+3 l. blue .. .. 2·75 1·60
1294. – 6 l.+6 l. brown .. 4·00 3·25

1934.

1295. – 50 b. brown 8 5
1296. **103.** 2 l. green 12 5
1297. 4 l. orange 15 8
1298. – 6 l. lake .. .. 1·00 5

DESIGNS: 50 b. Profile portrait of King Carol II in civilian clothes. 6 l. King Carol in plumed helmet.

104. "Grapes for Health".

105. Crisan, Horia and Closca.

106. Boy Scouts.

107. King Carol II.

1934. Bucharest Fruit Exhibition. Inscr. as in T **104.**

1299. **104.** 1 l. green 55 20
1300. – 2 l. brown 55 20

DESIGN: 2 l. Woman with fruit.

1935. 150th Anniv. of Death of Three Rumanian Martyrs. Portraits inscr. "MARTIR AL NEAMULUI 1785".

1301. **105.** 1 l. violet 20 12
1302. – 2 l. green (Crisan) 20 12
1303. – 6 l. brown (Closca) .. 55 20
1304. – 10 l. blue (Horia) 55 20

1935. Accession of Carol II. 5th Anniv. Inscr. "O.E.T.R.".

1305. – 25 b. black 65 35
1306. – 1 l. violet .. .. 1·40 55
1307. **106.** 2 l. green .. .. 1·60 80
1308. **107.** 6 l.+1 l. brown .. 2·00 1·10
1309. – 10 l.+2 l. blue .. 3·25 1·60

DESIGNS—VERT. 25 b. Scout saluting (21½×33 mm.). 1 l. Bugler (21½×30½ mm.). HORIZ. 10 l. Colour party (29×21½ mm.).

1935. Portraits as T **103** but additionally inscr. "POSTA".

1310. – 25 b. black 5 5
1311. – 50 b. brown 5 5
1312. – 1 l. violet 5 5
1313. **103.** 2 l. green 5 5
1315. – 3 l. red 5 5
1316. – 3 l. blue 5 5
1317. **103.** 4 l. orange 30 5
1318. – 5 l. red 5 5
1319. – 6 l. lake 15 5
1320. – 7 l. 50 blue 15 5
1321. – 8 l. purple 5 5
1322. **103.** 9 l. blue 12 8
1323. – 10 l. blue 8 5
1324. – 12 l. blue 30 15
1325. – 15 l. brown 12 8
1326. – 16 l. green 30 5
1327. – 20 l. orange 15 5
1328. – 24 l. red 30 12

PORTRAITS—IN PROFILE: 25 b., 15 l. In naval uniform. 50 b., 3 l., 8 l., 10 l. In civilian clothes. THREE-QUARTER FACE: 1 l., 5 l., 7 l. 50. In civilian clothes. FULL FACE: 6 l., 12 l., 16 l., 20 l., 24 l. In plumed helmet.

108. King Carol II.

109. Oltenia Peasant Girl.

1936. Bucharest Exn. and 70th Anniv. of Hohenzollern-Sigmaringen Dynasty.

1329. **108.** 6 l.+1 l. red 30 12

1936. 6th Anniv. of Accession of Carol II. Inscr. "O.E.T.R. 8 IUNIE 1936".

1330. **109.** 50 b.+50 b. brown .. 20 12
1331. – 1 l.+1 l. violet .. 20 12
1332. – 2 l.+1 l. green .. 20 12
1333. – 3 l.+1 l. red 20 12
1334. – 4 l.+2 l. red 45 20
1335. – 6 l.+3 l. grey .. 45 20
1336. – 10 l.+5 l. blue .. 90 45

DESIGNS (costumes of following districts)—VERT. 1 l. Banat. 4 l. Gorj. 6 l. Neamz. HORIZ. 2 l. Saliste. 3 l. Hateg. 10 l. Suceava (Bukovina).

110. Brasov Jamboree Badge.

111. S.S. "Regele Carol".

1936. National Scout Jamboree, Brasov. Inscr. as in T **110.**

1337. – 1 l.+1 l. blue .. 1·10 65
1338. – 3 l.+3 l. grey .. 1·10 80
1339. **110.** 6 l.+6 l. red .. .. 1·10 80

DESIGNS: 1 l. National Scout Badge. 3 l. Tenderfoot Badge.

1936. First Marine Exhibition, Bucharest. Inscr. as in T **111.**

1343. – 1 l.+1 l. violet .. 1·10 55
1344. – 3 l.+2 l. blue .. 1·10 55
1345. **111.** 6 l.+3 l. red .. .. 1·40 85

DESIGNS: 1 l. Submarine "Delfinul". 3 l. Naval Cadet Ship "Mircea".

1936. 18th Anniv. of Annexation of Transylvania and 16th Anniv. of Foundation of "Little Entente" Nos. 1320 and 1323 optd. **CEHOSLOVACIA YUGOSLAVIA 1920-1936.**

1346. 7 l. 50 blue .. .. 1·40 1·10
1347. 10 l. blue .. .. .. 1·40 1·10

112. Creanga's Birthplace.

1937. Ion Creanga (poet). Birth Cent.

1348. **112.** 2 l. green 15 15
1349. – 3 l. red 20 15
1350. **112.** 4 l. violet 35 20
1351. – 6 l. brown 40 35

DESIGN: 3 l., 6 l. Portrait of Creanga (37×22 mm.).

113. Footballers.

1937. Accession of Carol II. 7th Anniv. Inscr. "8 IUNIE 1937" and "U.F.S.R.".

1352. **113.** 25 b.+25 b. olive .. 12 8
1353. – 50 b.+50 b. brown .. 15 8
1354. – 1 l.+50 b. violet .. 15 8
1355. – 2 l.+1 l. green .. 15 8
1356. – 3 l.+1 l. claret .. 20 8
1357. – 4 l.+1 l. red 35 8
1358. – 6 l.+2 l. brown .. 65 15
1359. – 10 l.+4 l. blue .. 1·00 65

DESIGNS—HORIZ. 50 b. Swimmer. 3 l. King Carol II hunting. 10 l. U.F.S.R. Inaugural Meeting. VERT. 1 l. Javelin thrower. 2 l. Skier. 4 l. Rowing. 6 l. Steeplechaser.

Premium in aid of the Federation of Rumanian Sports Clubs (U.F.S.R.).

114. Curtea de Arges Cathedral.

115. Hurdling.

1937. "Little Entente".

1360. **114.** 7 l. 50 blue 85 40
1361. 10 l. blue .. .. 1·10 30

1937. 8th Balkan Games, Bucharest. Inscr. as in T **115.**

1362. – 1 l.+1 l. violet .. 35 15
1363. – 2 l.+1 l. green .. 35 15
1364. **115.** 4 l.+1 l. red .. 35 15
1365. – 6 l.+1 l. brown .. 45 20
1366. – 10 l.+1 l. blue .. 1·40 65

DESIGNS: 1 l. Sprinting. 2 l. Throwing the javelin. 6 l. Breasting the tape. 10 l. High-jumping.

116. Arms of Rumania, Greece, Turkey and Yugoslavia.

117. King Carol II.

119. Dimitrie Cantemir.

118. King Carol II. and Provincial Arms.

1938. Balkan Entente.

1368. **116.** 7 l. 50 blue 55 40
1369. 10 l. blue 85 40

1938. New Constitution. Profile portraits of King inscr. "27 FEBRUARIE 1938". 6 l. shows Arms also.

1370. **117.** 3 l. red 12 5
1371. – 6 l. brown 15 5
1372. – 10 l. blue 15 12

1938. Fund for Bucharest Exhibition celebrating 20th Anniv. of Annexation of Provinces.

1373. **118.** 6 l.+1 l. magenta .. 15 12

1938. Boy Scouts' Fund. 8th Anniv. of Accession of Carol II. Inscr. "STRAJA TARII 8 IUNIE 1938".

1374. **119.** 25 b.+25 b. olive .. 5 5
1375. – 50 b.+50 b. brown .. 5 5
1376. – 1 l.+1 l. violet .. 5 5
1377. – 2 l.+2 l. green .. 12 5
1378. – 3 l.+2 l. mauve .. 12 5
1379. – 4 l.+2 l. red 15 5
1380. – 6 l.+2 l. brown .. 15 8
1381. – 7 l. 50 blue 20 8
1382. – 10 l. blue 35 12
1383. – 16 l. green 45 30
1384. – 20 l. red 55 35

PORTRAITS: 50 b. Maria Doamna. 1 l. Mircea the Great. 2 l. Constantin Brancoveanu. 3 l. Stephen the Great. 4 l. Prince Cuza. 6 l. Michael the Brave. 7 l. 50, Queen Elisabeth. 10 l. King Carol II. 16 l. King Ferdinand I. 20 l. King Carol I.

120. "Escorting Prisoners" (Russo-Turkish War 1877-78).

DESIGNS—HORIZ. 4 l. "Returning from Market." VERT. 1 l. "The Spring" (woman). 6 l. "Rodica, the Water Carrier." 10 l. Self portrait.

1938. Nicholas Grigorescu (painter). Birth cent. Reproductions of paintings inscr. "1838 N(ICOLAE) GRIGORESCU 1938".

1385. – 1 l.+1 l. blue .. 15 15
1386. **120.** 2 l.+1 l. green .. 20 15
1387. – 4 l.+1 l. red 20 20
1388. – 6 l.+1 l. claret .. 55 25
1389. – 10 l.+1 l. blue .. 85 35

121. Prince Carol in Royal Carriage.

1939. King Carol I. Birth cent.

1390. **121.** 25 b. black 5 5
1391. – 50 b. brown 5 5
1392. – 1 l. violet 5 5
1393. – 1 l. 50 green 5 5
1394. – 2 l. blue 5 5
1395. – 3 l. red 5 5
1396. – 4 l. claret 5 5
1397. – 5 l. black 5 5
1398. – 7 l. black 5 5
1399. – 8 l. blue 5 5
1400. – 10 l. mauve 8 5
1401. – 12 l. blue 8 5
1402. – 15 l. blue 12 5
1403. – 16 l. green 30 15

DESIGNS—HORIZ. 50 b. Prince Carol at Battle of Calafat. 1 l. 50, Sigmaringen and Pelesch Castles. 15 l. Carol I, Queen Elizabeth and Arms of Rumania. VERT. 1 l. Examining plans for restoring Curtea de Arges Monastery. 2 l. Carol I and Queen Elizabeth. 3 l. Carol I at age of 8. 4 l. In 1866. 5 l. in 1877. 7 l. Equestrian Statue. 8 l. Leading troops in 1878. 10 l. In General's uniform. 12 l. Bust. 16 l. Restored Monastery of Curtea de Arges.

122. Rumanian Pavilion. N.Y. Fair.

123. Eminescu, after painting by Joano Basarab.

1939. New York World's Fair.

1407. **122.** 6 l. lake 15 15
1408. – 12 l. blue 15 15

DESIGN: 12 l. Another view of Pavilion.

1939. Michael Eminescu (poet). 50th Death Anniv.

1409. **123.** 5 l. black 15 12
1410 – 7 l. red 15 12

DESIGN: 7 l. Eminescu in later years.

124. St. George and Dragon.

125. Railway engines of 1869 and 1939.

1939. 9th Anniv. of Accession of Carol II and Boy Scouts' Fund.

1411. **124.** 25 b.+25 b. grey .. 12 5
1412. 50 b.+50 b. brown 12 5
1413. 1 l.+1 l. blue .. 12 5
1414. 2 l.+2 l. green .. 12 5
1415. 3 l.+2 l. purple .. 12 5
1416. 4 l.+2 l. orange .. 12 5
1417. 6 l.+2 l. red 12 5
1418. 8 l. grey 12 5
1419. 10 l. blue 20 8
1420. 12 l. blue 20 8
1421. 16 l. green 35 35

1939. Rumanian Railways. 70th Anniv.

1422. **125.** 1 l. violet 12 5
1423. – 4 l. red 12 5
1424. – 5 l. grey 12 5
1425. – 7 l. mauve 15 8
1426. – 12 l. blue 25 12
1427. – 15 l. green 65 30

DESIGNS—HORIZ. 4 l. Steam train crossing railway-bridge. 15 l. Railway Headquarters. VERT. 5 l., 7 l. Train leaving station. 12 l. Electric train crossing railway bridge.

1940. Balkan Entente. As T **68** of Yugoslavia, but with Arms rearranged.

1428. 12 l. blue 35 15
1429. 16 l. blue 35 15

126. King Carol II.

127. King Carol II.

1940. Aviation Fund.

1430. **126.** 1 l.+50 b. green .. 5 5
1431. 2 l. 50+50 b. green .. 5 5
1432. 3 l.+1 l. red 8 5
1433. 3 l. 50+50 b. brown .. 12 5
1434. 4 l.+1 l. orange .. 15 5
1435. 6 l.+1 l. blue .. 20 8
1436. 9 l.+1 l. blue .. 25 15
1437. 14 l.+1 l. green .. 40 15

1940. Charity. 10th Anniv. of Accession of Carol II. Royal portraits, dated "1930 1940 8 IUNIE".

1438. **127.** 1 l.+50 b. purple .. 12 5
1439. – 4 l.+1 l. brown .. 12 5
1440. – 6 l.+1 l. blue .. 15 5
1441. – 8 l. red 15 8
1442. – 16 l. blue 30 8
1443. – 32 l. brown 45 20

PORTRAITS: 1 l., 4 l. left profile. 6 l., 16 l. in steel helmet. 8 l. in military uniform. 32 l. in flying helmet.

128. The Iron Gates of the Danube.

1940. Charity. 10th Anniv. of Accession of Carol II and Boy Scouts' Fund. Inscr. "STRAJA TARII 8 IUNIE 1940".

1444. 128. 1 l.+1 l. violet .. 12 5
1445. – 2 l.+1 l. brown .. 12 5
1446. – 3 l.+1 l. green .. 15 8
1447. – 4 l.+1 l. black .. 15 8
1448. – 5 l.+1 l. orange .. 15 12
1449. – 8 l.+1 l. red 15 12
1450. – 12 l.+2 l. blue .. 35 20
1451. – 16 l.+2 l. grey .. 45 30

DESIGNS—HORIZ. 3 l. Hotin Fortress. 4 l. Hurez Monastery. VERT. 2 l. Greco-Roman ruins. 5 l. Church in Suceava. 8 l. Alba Julia Cathedral. 12 l. Village Church, Transylvania. 16 l. Triumphal Arch, Bucharest.

129. King Michael. 130.

1940.

1455. 129. 25 b. green 5 5
1456. 50 b. olive 5 5
1457. 1 l. violet 5 5
1458. 2 l. orange 5 5
1608. 3 l. brown 5 5
1609. 3 l. 50 brown 5 5
1459. 4 l. grey 5 5
1611. 4 l. 50 brown 5 5
1460. 5 l. pink 5 5
1613. 6 l. 50 violet.. .. 5 5
1461. 7 l. blue 5 5
1615. 10 l. mauve 5 5
1616. 11 l. blue 5 5
1463. 12 l. blue 5 5
1464. 13 l. purple 5 5
1618. 15 l. blue 5 5
1619. 16 l. blue 5 5
1620. 20 l. brown 5 5
1621. 29 l. blue 15 8
1467. 30 l. green 5 5
1468. 50 l. brown 5 5
1469. 100 l. brown 5 5

1940. Aviation Fund.

1470. 130. 1 l.+50 b. green .. 5 5
1471. 2 l.+50 b. green .. 5 5
1472. 2 l. 50+50 b. green.. 5 5
1473. 3 l.+1 l. violet .. 5 5
1474. 3 l. 50+50 b. pink .. 8 8
1475. 4 l.+50 b. red .. 5 5
1476. 4 l.+1 l. brown .. 5 5
1477. 5 l.+1 l. red.. .. 20 8
1478. 6 l.+1 l. blue .. 5 5
1479. 7 l.+1 l. green .. 8 5
1480. 8 l.+1 l. violet .. 8 5
1481. 12 l.+1 l. brown .. 8 5
1482. 14 l.+1 l. blue .. 15 5
1483. 19 l.+1 l. mauve .. 20 5

131. Codreanu (founder) 132.

1940. "Iron Guard" Fund.

1484. 131. 7 l.+30 l. grn. (post.) 1·25 1·00
1485. 132. 20 l.+5 l. green (air) 15 15

133. Ion Mota. 134. Library.

1941. Marin and Mota (legionaries killed in Spain).

1486. – 7 l.+7 l. red.. .. 15 15
1487. 133. 15 l.+15 l. blue .. 40 35

PORTRAIT: 7 l. Vasile Marin.

1941. Carol I Endowment Fund. Inscr. "1891 1941".

1488. – 1 l. 50+43 l. 50 violet 15 15
1489. 134. 2 l.+43 l. red .. 15 15
1490. – 7 l.+38 l. red .. 15 15
1491. – 10 l.+35 l. green .. 15 15
1492. – 16 l.+29 l. brown .. 20 20

DESIGNS. 1 l. 50, Ex-libris. 7 l. Foundation building and equestrian statue. 10 l. Foundation stone. 16 l. Kings Michael and Carol I.

1941. Occupation of Cernauti. Nos. 1488/92 optd. **CERNAUTI 5 Iulie 1941.**

1493. – 1 l. 50+43 l. 50 violet 35 35
1494 134. 2 l.+43 l. red .. 35 35
1495. – 7 l.+38 l. red .. 35 35
1496. – 10 l.+35 l. green .. 35 35
1497. – 16 l.+29 l. brown .. 35 35

1941. Occupation of Chisinau. Nos. 1488/92 optd. **CHISINAU 16 Iulie 1941.**

1498. – 1 l. 50+43 l. 50 violet 35 35
1499. 134. 2 l.+43 l. red .. 35 35
1500. – 7 l.+38 l. red .. 35 35
1501. – 10 l.+35 l. green .. 35 35
1502. – 16 l.+29 l. brown .. 35 35

135. "Charity". 136. Prince Voda.

1941. Red Cross Fund. Cross in red.

1503. 135. 1 l. 50+38 l. 50 vio. 20 20
1504. 2 l.+38 l. red .. 20 20
1505. 5 l.+35 l. olive .. 20 20
1506. 7 l.+33 l. brown .. 20 20
1507. 10 l.+30 l. blue .. 35 20

1941. Conquest of Transdniestria.

1572. 136. 3 l. orange 5 5
1509. 6 l. brown 5 5
1510. 12 l. violet 5 5
1511. 24 l. blue 8 5

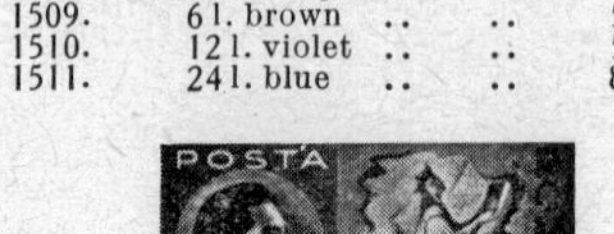

137. King Michael and Stephen the Great.

1941. Charity. Inscr. "RAZBOIUL SFANT CONTRA BOLSEVISMULUI".

1512. 137. 10 l.+30 l. blue .. 15 15
1513. – 12 l.+28 l. red .. 15 15
1514. – 16 l.+24 l. brown .. 15 15
1515. – 20 l.+20 l. violet .. 15 15

DESIGNS: 12 l. Hotin and Akkerman Fortresses. 16 l. Arms and helmeted soldiers. 20 l. Bayonet charge and Arms of Rumania.

1941. Fall of Odessa. Nos. 1512/15 optd. **ODESA/16 Oct. 1941.**

1517. 137. 10 l.+30 l. blue .. 15 15
1518. – 12 l.+28 l. red .. 15 15
1519. – 16 l.+24 l. brown .. 20 20
1520. – 20 l.+20 l. violet .. 20 20

138. Hotin Fortress, Bessarabia. 139. Milisaut Monastery, Bukovina.

1941. Restoration of Bessarabia and Bukovina (Suceava). Inscr. "BASARABIA" or "BUCOVINA".

1522. – 25 b. red 5 5
1523. 138. 50 b. brown 5 5
1524. – 1 l. violet 5 5
1525. – 1 l. 50 green 5 5
1526. – 2 l. brown 5 5
1527. – 3 l. olive 5 5
1528. – 5 l. olive 5 5
1529. – 5 l. 50 brown.. .. 5 5
1530. – 6 l. 50 mauve .. 5 5
1531. 138. 9 l. 50 grey 8 5
1532. – 10 l. purple 5 5
1533. 139. 13 l. blue 5 5
1534. – 17 l. brown 8 5
1535. – 26 l. green 12 8
1536. – 39 l. blue 15 15
1537. – 130 l. yellow 70 35

VIEWS—VERT. 25 b., 5 l. Paraclis Hotin. 3 l. Dragomirna. HORIZ. 1 l., 17 l. Sucevita. 1 l. 50, Soroca, 2 l., 5 l. 50, Tighina. 6 l. 50, Cetatea Alba. 10 l., 130 l. Putna. 26 l. St. Nicolae, Suceava. 39 l. Monastery, Rughi.

1941. Winter Relief Fund. Inscr. "BASARABIA" or "BUCOVINA".

1538. – 3 l.+50 b. red .. 5 5
1539. – 5 l. 50+50 b. orange 5 5
1540. – 5 l. 50+1 l. black .. 5 5
1541. – 6 l. 50+1 l. brown .. 5 5
1542. – 8 l.+1 l. blue .. 5 5
1543. 139. 9 l. 50+1 l. blue .. 8 8
1544. – 10 l. 50+1 l. blue .. 10 8
1545. – 16 l.+1 l. mauve .. 20 10
1546. 138. 25 l.+1 l. grey .. 30 20

VIEWS—HORIZ. 3 l. Sucevita. 5 l. 50 (1539), Monastery, Rughi. 5 l. 50 (1540), Tighina. 6 l. 50, Soroca. 8 l. St. Nicolae, Suceava. 10 l. 50, Putna. 16 l. Cetatea Alba.

140. Titu Maiorescu. 141. Arms of Bukovina.

1942. Prisoners of War Relief Fund through International Education Office, Geneva.

1549. 140. 9 l.+11 l. violet .. 15 15
1550. 20 l.+20 l. brown .. 15 15
1551. 20 l.+30 l. blue .. 15 15

1942. Liberation of Bukovina. 1st Anniv. Inscr. "BUCOVINA UN AN DE LA DESROBIRE".

1553. 141. 9 l.+41 l. red .. 20 20
1554. – 18 l.+32 l. blue .. 20 20
1555. – 20 l.+30 l. red .. 20 20

ARMORIAL DESIGNS: 18 l. Castle. 20 l. Mounds and crosses.

142. Map of Bessarabia, King Michael, Antonescu, Hitler and Mussolini. 143. Statue of Miron Costin, Jassy.

1942. Liberation of Bessarabia. 1st Anniv. Inscr. "BASARABIA UN AN DE LA DESROBIRE".

1556. 142. 9 l.+41 l. brown .. 20 20
1557. – 18 l.+32 l. olive .. 20 20
1558. – 20 l.+30 l. blue .. 20 20

DESIGNS—VERT. 18 l. King Michael and Marshal Antonescu below miniature of King Stephen. HORIZ. 20 l. Marching soldiers and miniature of Marshal Antonescu.

1942. Incorporation of Transdniestria. 1st Anniv.

1559. 143. 6 l.+44 l. brown .. 20 20
1560. 12 l.+38 l. violet .. 20 20
1561. 24 l.+26 l. blue .. 20 20

144. A. Muresanu. 146. Nurse and wounded Soldier.

145. Avram Iancu. 147. Sword.

1942. A. Muresanu (novelist). 80th Death Anniv.

1562. 144. 5 l.+5 l. violet .. 15 15

1943. Fund for Statue of Iancu (national hero).

1563. 145. 16 l.+4 l. brown .. 20 20

1943. Red Cross Charity. Cross in red

1564. 146. 12 l.+88 l. red .. 15 15
1565. 16 l.+84 l. blue .. 15 15
1566. 20 l.+80 l. olive .. 15 15

1943. Charity. 2nd Year of War. Inscr. "22 JUNIE 1941 22 JUNIE 1943".

1568. 147. 36 l.+164 l. brown .. 90 90
1569. – 62 l.+138 l. blue .. 90 90
1570. – 76 l.+124 l. red .. 90 90

DESIGNS: 62 l. Sword severing chain. 76 l. Angel protecting soldier and family.

148. Petru Maior. 149. King Michael and Marshal Antonescu.

1943. Transylvanian Refugees' Fund (1st issue).

1576. 148. 16 l.+134 l. red .. 15 15
1577. – 32 l.+118 l. blue .. 15 15
1578. – 36 l.+114 l. purple .. 15 15
1579. – 62 l.+138 l. red .. 15 15
1580. – 91 l.+109 l. brown .. 30 15

PORTRAITS—VERT. 32 l. C. Sincai. 36 l. T. Cipariu. 91 l. Cosbuc. HORIZ. 62 l. Horia, Closca and Crisan.

See also Nos. 1584/8.

1943. Charity. 3rd Anniv. of King Michael's Reign.

1581. 149. 16 l.+24 l. blue .. 20 20

150. Sports Shield. 151. Calafat, 1877.

1943. Charity. Sports Week.

1582. 150. 16 l.+24 l. blue .. 20 15
1583. 16 l.+24 l. brown .. 20 15

1943. Transylvanian Refugees' Fund (2nd issue). Portraits as T **148**.

1584. 16 l.+134 l. mauve .. 15 15
1585. 51 l.+99 l. orange .. 15 15
1586. 56 l.+144 l. red 15 15
1587. 76 l.+124 l. blue .. 15 15
1588. 77 l.+123 l. brown .. 15 15

PORTRAITS—VERT. 16 l. S. Michu. 51 l. G. Lazar. 56 l. O. Goga. 76 l. S. Barnutiu. 77 l. A. Sarguna.

1943. National Artillery Cent. Inscr. "1843-1943".

1596. 151. 1 l.+1 l. brown .. 5 5
1597. – 2 l.+2 l. violet .. 5 5
1598. – 3 l. 50+3 l. 50 blue 5 5
1599. – 4 l.+4 l. mauve .. 5 5
1600. – 5 l.+5 l. orange .. 5 5
1601. – 6 l. 50+6 l. 50 blue 10 5
1602. – 7 l.+7 l. purple .. 15 10
1603. – 20 l.+20 l. red .. 20 15

DESIGNS—HORIZ.: (1 l. to 7 l. inscr. battle scenes): 2 l. "1916-1918". 3 l. 50, Stalingrad. 4 l. Crossing R. Tisza. 5 l. Odessa. 6 l. 50, Caucasus. 7 l. Sevastopol. 20 l. Bibescu and King Michael.

152. Insignia of the Association.

1943. National Engineers' Assn. 25th Anniv.

1624. 152. 21 l.+29 l. brown .. 20 15

153. Posthorn and Transport.

1944. Postal Employees' Relief Fund and 200th Anniv. of National Postal Service.

(a) Without opt.

1625. 153. 1 l.+49 l. red .. 30 30
1626. – 2 l.+48 l. mauve .. 30 30
1627. – 4 l.+46 l. blue .. 30 30
1628. – 10 l.+40 l. brown .. 30 30

(b) Optd. **1744 1944.**

1631. 153. 1 l.+49 l. red .. 65 65
1632. – 2 l.+48 l. mauve .. 65 65
1633. – 4 l.+46 l. blue .. 65 65
1634. – 10 l.+40 l. brown .. 65 65

DESIGNS—HORIZ. 2 l. Mail van and eight horses. 4 l. Chariot. VERT. 10 l. Horseman and Globe.

154. Dr. Cretzulescu. **155.** Rugby Footballer.

1944. Medicinal Teaching in Rumania. Cent.
1637. **154.** 35 l.+65 l. blue 15 15

1944. Foundation of National Rugby Football Association. 30th Anniv.
1638. **155.** 16 l.+184 l. red 1·00 80

156. Stefan Tomsa Church, Radaseni. **157.** Fruit Pickers.

1944. Cultural Fund. Town of Radaseni Inscr. "RADASENI".
1639. **156.** 5 l.+145 l. blue 15 12
1640. – 12 l.+138 l. red 15 12
1641. **157.** 15 l.+135 l. orange 15 12
1642. – 32 l.+118 l. brown 15 12
DESIGNS—HORIZ. 12 l. Agricultural Institution. 32 l. School.

158. Queen Helen. **159.** King Michael and Carol I Foundation, Bucharest.

1945. Red Cross Relief Fund. Portrait in black on yellow and Cross in red.
1643. **158** 4 l. 50+5 l. 50 violet 8 8
1644. 10 l.+40 l. brown 8 8
1645. 15 l.+75 l. blue 10 10
1646. 20 l.+80 l. red 10 10

1945. King Carol I Foundation Fund.
1647. **159.** 20 l.+180 l. orange 8 10
1648. 25 l.+175 l. slate 8 10
1649. 35 l.+165 l. brown 8 10
1650. 75 l.+125 l. violet 8 10
Nos. 1647/50 were printed in sheets of four.

160. Andrei Saguna. **161.** Andrei Muresanu.

1945. Liberation of Northern Transylvania. Inscr. "1944".
1652. **160.** 25 b. red 8 8
1653. **161.** 50 b. orange 8 8
1654. – 4 l. 50 brown 8 8
1655. – 11 l. blue 8 8
1656. – 15 l. green 12 12
1657. – 31 l. violet 12 12
1658. – 35 l. grey 12 12
1659. – 41 l. olive 12 12
1660. – 55 l. brown 12 12
1661. – 61 l. mauve 12 12
1662. – 75 l.+75 l. brown 12 12
DESIGNS—HORIZ. 4 l. 50, Samuel Micu. 31 l. George Lazar. 55 l. Three Heroes. 61 l. Petru Major. 75 l. King Ferdinand and King Michael. VERT. 11 l. George Sincai. 15 l. Michael the Brave. 35 l. Avram Iancu. 41 l. Simeon Barnutiu.

162. King Michael. **163.**

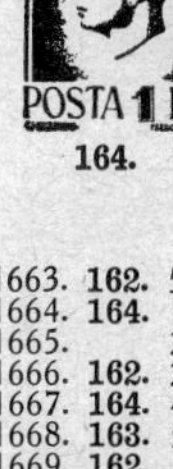

164. King Michael. **165.**

1945.
1663. **162.** 50 b. grey 5 5
1664. **164.** 1 l. brown 5 5
1665. 2 l. violet 5 5
1666. **162.** 2 l. brown 5 5
1667. **164.** 4 l. green 5 5
1668. **163.** 5 l. mauve 5 5
1669. **162.** 10 l. blue 5 5
1670. 10 l. brown 5 5
1671. **164.** 10 l. brown 5 5
1672. **162.** 15 l. mauve 5 5
1673. 20 l. blue 5 5
1674. 20 l. lilac 5 5
1675. **163.** 20 l. purple 5 5
1676. 25 l. red 5 5
1677. 35 l. brown 5 5
1678. 40 l. red 5 5
1679. **164.** 50 l. blue 5 5
1680. 55 l. red 5 5
1681. **163.** 75 l. green 5 5
1682. **165.** 80 l. orange 5 5
1683. 80 l. blue 5 5
1684. **162.** 80 l. blue 5 5
1685. **165.** 100 l. brown 5 5
1686. **162.** 137 l. green 5 5
1687. **165.** 160 l. green 5 5
1688. 160 l. violet 5 5
1689. 200 l. green 5 5
1690. 200 l. red 5 5
1691. **164.** 200 l. red 5 5
1692. **165.** 300 l. blue 5 5
1693. 360 l. brown 5 5
1694. 400 l. violet 5 5
1695. **164.** 400 l. red 5 5
1696. **165.** 480 l. brown 5 5
1697. **162.** 500 l. mauve 5 5
1698. **165.** 600 l. green 5 5
1699. **163.** 860 l. brown 5 5
1700. **165.** 1000 l. green 5 5
1701. **162.** 1500 l. green 5 5
1702. **165.** 2400 l. lilac 5 5
1703. **164.** 2500 l. blue 5 5
1704. **165.** 3700 l. blue 5 5
1705. **162.** 5000 l. grey 5 5
1706. 8000 l. green 5 5
1707. **165.** 10000 l. brown 5 5

166. N. Jorga. **167.** Books and Torch.

1945. War Victims' Relief Fund. Inscr. as in T **166.**
1708. – 12 l.+188 l. blue 12 12
1709. – 16 l.+184 l. brown 12 12
1710. **166.** 20 l.+180 l. brown 12 12
1711. – 32 l.+168 l. red 12 12
1712. – 35 l.+165 l. blue 12 12
1713. – 36 l.+164 l. violet 12 12
PORTRAITS: 12 l. I. G. Duca. 16 l. Virgil Madgearu. 32 l. Ilie Pintilie. 35 l. Bernath Andrei. 36 l. Filimon Sarbu.

1945. Charity. First Rumanian-Soviet Congress Fund. Inscr. "ARLUS".
1715. **167.** 20 l.+80 l. olive 15 15
1716. – 35 l.+165 l. red 15 15
1717. – 75 l.+225 l. blue 15 15
1718. – 80 l.+420 l. brown 15 15
DESIGNS: 35 l. Soviet and Rumanian flags. 75 l. Drawn curtain revealing Kremlin. 80 l. T. Vladimirescu and A. Nevsky.

168. Karl Marx. **169.** Postman.

1945. Trade Union Congress, Bucharest. Inscr. as in T **168.** Perf. or Imperf.
1720. **168.** 75 l.+425 l. red 40 40
1723. 75 l.+425 l. b.ue 50 50
1721. – 120 l.+380 l. blue 40 40
1724. – 120 l.+380 l. brown 50 50
1722. – 155 l.+445 l. brown 40 40
1725. – 155 l.+445 l. red 50 50
PORTRAITS: 120 l. Engels. 155 l. Lenin.

1945. Postal Employees. Inscr. "MUNCA P.T.T.".
1726. **169.** 100 l. brown 15 15
1727. 100 l. olive 15 15
1728. – 150 l. brown 15 15
1729. – 150 l. red 15 15
1730. – 250 l. olive 20 20
1731. – 250 l. blue 20 20
1732. – 500 l. mauve 1·60 1·60
DESIGNS: 150 l. Telegraphist. 250 l. Lineman. 500 l. Post Office, Bucharest.
Nos. 1726/32 were printed in sheets of four.

170. Discus Throwing. **171.** Agricultural and Industrial Workers.

1945. Charity. With shield inscr. "O.S.P.". Perf. or imperf.
1733. **170.** 12 l.+188 l. olive (post.) 55 55
1738. 12 l.+188 l. orange 55 55
1734. – 16 l.+184 l. blue 55 55
1739. – 16 l.+184 l. purple 55 55
1735. – 20 l.+180 l. green 55 55
1740. – 20 l.+180 l. violet 55 55
1736. – 32 l.+168 l. mauve 55 55
1741. – 32 l.+168 l. green 55 55
1737. – 35 l.+165 l. blue 55 55
1742. – 35 l.+165 l. olive 55 55
1743. – 200 l.+1000 l. bl. (air) 2·25 2·25
DESIGNS: 16 l. Diving. 20 l. Skiing. 32 l. Volleyball. 35 l. Sport and work. Larger design—200 l. Mail-plane and bird.

1945. Rumanian Armistice with Russia. 1st Anniv.
1744. **171.** 100 l.+400 l. red 5 5
1745. – 200 l.+800 l. blue 8 8
DESIGN: 200 l. King Michael, "Agriculture" and "Industry".

172. T. Vladimirescu. **173.** I. Ionescu, G. Titeica, A. G. Idachimescu and V. Cristescu.

1945. Charity. Patriotic Defence Fund Inscr. "APARAREA PATRIOTICA."
1746. – 20 l.+580 l. brown 55 55
1747. – 20 l.+580 l. mauve 55 55
1748. – 40 l.+560 l. blue 55 55
1749. – 40 l.+560 l. green 55 55
1750. – 55 l.+545 l. red 55 55
1751. – 55 l.+545 l. brown 55 55
1752. **172.** 60 l.+540 l. blue 55 55
1753. 60 l.+540 l. brown 55 55
1754. – 80 l.+520 l. red 55 55
1755. – 80 l.+520 l. mauve 55 55
1756. – 100 l.+500 l. green 55 55
1757. – 100 l.+500 l. brown 55 55
DESIGNS—HORIZ. 20 l. "Political Amesty". 40 l. "Military Amnesty". 55 l. "Agrarian Amnesty". 100 l. King Michael and "Reconstruction". VERT. 80 l. Nicholas Horia, soldier and flag.

1945. Founding of Journal of Mathematics. 50th Anniv.
1759. **173.** 2 l. brown 5 5
1760. – 80 l. grey 8 5
DESIGN: 80 l. Allegory of Learning.

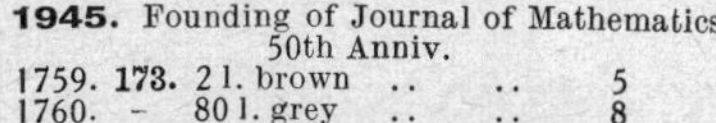

174. Cernavoda Bridge.

1945. Cernavoda Bridge. 50th Anniv.
1761. **174.** 80 l. black 8 5

175. Electric Train.

DESIGNS—HORIZ. As T **175**: 20 l. Coats of arms. 25 l. Arterial road. 55 l. Oil wells. 100 l. "Agriculture".

176.

1945. Charity. 16th Congress of Rumanian Engineers. Inscr. as in T **175.** Perf. or imperf. (a) Postage.
1762. **175.** 10 l.+490 l. olive 15 15
1763. 10 l.+490 l. blue 15 15
1764. – 20 l.+480 l. brown 15 15
1765. – 20 l.+480 l. violet 15 15
1766. – 25 l.+475 l. purple 15 15
1767. – 25 l.+475 l. green 15 15
1768. – 55 l.+445 l. blue 15 15
1769. – 55 l.+445 l. grey 15 15
1770. – 100 l.+400 l. brown 15 15
1771. – 100 l.+400 l. mauve 15 15
(b) Air. Symbolical design as T **176.** Imperf.
1772. **176.** 80 l.+420 l. grey 20 20
1773. 200 l.+800 l. blue 20 20

177. Globe and Clasped Hands.

DESIGNS: 160 l. Globe and Dove of Peace. 320 l. Hand and hammer. 440 l. Scaffolding and flags.

1945. Charity. World Trade Union Congress, Paris. Symbolical designs inscr. "CONFERINTA MONDIALA SINDICALA DIN-PARIS 25 SEPTEMVRE 1945".
1776. **177.** 80 l.+920 l. mauve 1·40 1·40
1777. – 160 l.+1840 l. brown 1·40 1·40
1778. – 320 l.+1680 l. violet 1·40 1·40
1779. – 440 l.+2560 l. green 1·40 1·40

1946. Nos. 1444/5 surch. in figures.
1780. 10 l.+90 l. on 100 l.+400 l. 15 15
1781. 10 l.+90 l. on 200 l.+800 l. 15 15
1782. 20 l.+80 l. on 100 l.+400 l. 15 15
1783. 20 l.+80 l. on 200 l.+800 l. 15 15
1784. 80 l.+120 l. on 100 l.+400 l. 15 15
1785. 80 l.+120 l. on 200 l.+800 l. 15 15
1786. 100 l.+150 l. on 100 l.+400 l. 15 15
1787. 100 l.+150 l. on 200 l.+800 l. 15 15

178. The Sower.

179. Distribution of Title Deeds. **180.**

1946. Agrarian Reform. Inscr. "REFORMA AGRARA".
1788. – 80 l. blue 5 5
1789. **178.** 50 l.+450 l. red 5 5
1790. **179.** 100 l.+900 l. purple 5 5
1791. – 200 l.+800 l. orange 5 5
1792. – 400 l.+1600 l. green 5 5
DESIGNS—VERT. 80 l. Blacksmith and ploughman. HORIZ. 200 l. Ox-drawn farm wagon. 400 l. Plough and tractor.

1946. Philharmonic Orchestra. 25th Anniv. Inscr. "FILARMONICA".
1794. **180.** 10 l. blue 5 5
1795. – 20 l. brown 5 5
1796. – 55 l. green 5 5
1797. – 80 l. violet 8 8
1798. – 160 l. orange 5 5
1799. **180.** 200 l.+800 l. red 30 30
1800. – 350 l.+1650 l. blue 30 30
DESIGNS: 20 l., 55 l., 160 l. "XXV" and musical score. 80 l., 350 l. G. Enescu.

181. Building worker. **182.** Sower.

1946. Labour Day. Designs of workers inscr. "ZIUA MUNCII".
1803. **181.** 10 l. claret 5 5
1804. 10 l. green 12 12
1805. 20 l. blue 12 12
1806. 20 l. brown 5 5
1807. 200 l. red 5 5

1946. Youth Issue.
1809. 182. 10 l.+100 l. red & brn. 5 5
1810. – 10 l.+200 l. pur. & blue 65 65
1811. – 80 l.+200 l. brn. & pur. 5 5
1812. – 80 l.+300 l. mve. & brn. 5 5
1813. – 200 l.+400 l. red & grn. 8 8
DESIGNS—VERT. 10 l.+200 l. Hurdling. 80 l.+200 l. Student. 80 l.+300 l. Worker and factory. 200 l.+400 l. Marching with flag.

183. Aviator and Aeroplanes. 184. Football.

1946. Air. Youth Issue.
1814. – 200 l. blue and green 40 40
1815. 183. 500 l. blue and orange 40 40
DESIGN: 200 l. Aeroplane grounded.

1946. Sports, designs inscr. "O.S.P." Perf. or imperf.
1816. 184. 10 l. blue (postage).. 15 15
1817. – 20 l. red 15 15
1818. – 50 l. violet 15 15
1819. – 80 l. brown 15 15
1820. – 160 l.+1340 l. green.. 20 20
1821. – 300 l. red (air) .. 40 40
1822. – 300 l.+1200 l. blue.. 40 40
DESIGNS: 20 l. Diving. 50 l. Running. 80 l. Mountaineering. 160 l. Ski-jumping. 300 l., 300 l.+1,200 l. Flying.

185. "Traditional Ties". 186. Banat Girl holding Distaff.

1946. Rumanian-Soviet Friendship Pact.
1824. 185. 80 l. brown 5 5
1825. – 100 l. blue 5 5
1826. – 300 l. grey 5 5
1827. – 300 l.+1200 l. red .. 8 5
DESIGNS: 100 l. Guitar, book and mask. 300 l. Ear of wheat and factory. 300 l.+1,200 l. Dove of Peace.
No. 1827 also exists imperf.

1946. Charity. Women's Democratic Federation.
1829. – 80 l. olive 5 5
1830. 186. 80 l.+320 l. red .. 5 5
1831. – 140 l.+360 l. orange 5 5
1832. – 300 l.+450 l. green 5 5
1833. – 600 l.+900 l. blue .. 8 8
DESIGNS: 80 l. Girl and handloom. 140 l. Wallachian girl and wheatsheaf. 300 l. Transylvanian horsewoman. 600 l. Moldavian girl carrying water from a well.

187. King Michael and Food Transport.

1947. Social Relief Fund.
1845. – 300 l. olive .. 5 5
1846. 187. 600 l. magenta .. 5 5
1847. – 1500 l.+3500 l. orge. 5 5
1848. – 3700 l.+5300 l. violet 8 8
DESIGNS—VERT: 300 l. Loaf of bread and hungry child. 1500 l. Angel bringing food and clothing to destitute people. 3700 l. Loaf of bread and starving family.

188. King Michael and Chariot. 189. Symbols of Labour and Clasped Hands.

1947. Peace.
1850. 188. 300 l. purple.. .. 5 5
1851. – 600 l. brown .. 5 5
1852. – 3000 l. blue .. 5 5
1853. – 7200 l. green .. 8 8
DESIGNS—VERT. 600 l. Winged figure of Peace. 3000 l. Flags of four Allied Nations. 7200 l. Dove of Peace.

1947. Trades' Union Congress.
1854. 189. 200 l. blue (postage).. 12 12
1855. 300 l. orange .. 12 12
1856. 600 l. red 12 12
1857. – 1100 l. blue (air) .. 15 15
DESIGN (22×37 mm.): 1100 l. as T 189 with aeroplane at top.

190. Worker and Torch. 191. King Michael.

1947. Air. Trades Union Congress. Imperf.
1858. 190. 3000 l.+7000 l. choc. 20 20

1947.
1865. 191. 1000 l. blue .. 5 5
1869. 3000 l. blue .. 5 5
1866. 5500 l. green .. 5 5
1870. 7200 l. mauve .. 5 5
1871. 15000 l. blue .. 5 5
1867. 20000 l. brown .. 5 5
1872. 21000 l. mauve .. 5 5
1873. 36000 l. violet .. 5 5
1868. 50000 l. orange .. 5 5
Nos. 1865/8 are size 18×21½ mm. and Nos 1869/73 are 25×30 mm.

192. Symbolical of "Learning".

1947. Charity. People's Culture.
1859. – 200 l.+200 l. blue .. 5 5
1860. – 300 l.+300 l. brown 5 5
1861. – 600 l.+600 l. green 5 5
1862. – 1200 l.+1200 l. blue 5 5
1863. 192. 1500 l.+1500 l. claret 5 5
DESIGNS—HORIZ. 200 l. Boys' reading class. 300 l. Girls' school. 600 l. Engineering classroom. 1200 l. School building.

193. N. Grigorescu. 193a. Douglas DC3 over Land.

1947. Charity. Institute of Rumanian-Soviet Studies.
1874. – 1500 l.+1500 l. pur. (postage) 5 5
1875. – 1500 l.+1500 l. orge. 5 5
1876. – 1500 l.+1500 l. green 5 5
1877. 193. 1500 l.+1500 l. blue 5 5
1878. – 1500 l.+1500 l. blue 5 5
1879. – 1500 l.+1500 l. lake 5 5
1880. – 1500 l.+1500 l. red.. 5 5
1881. – 1500 l.+1500 l. brn. 5 5
1882. 193a. 15000 l.+15000 l. green (air) 12 12
PORTRAITS: No. 1874, Petru Movila. 1875, V. Babes. 1876, M. Eminescu. 1878, P. Tchaikovsky. 1879, M. Lomonosov. 1880, A. Pushkin. 1881, L. Y. Repin.
No. 1882 is imperf.

194. Miner. 195. Douglas DC4 over Black Sea.

1947. Charity. Labour Day.
1883. 194. 1000 l.+1000 l. olive 5 5
1884. – 1500 l.+1500 l. brown 5 5
1885. – 2000 l.+2000 l. blue 5 5
1886. – 2500 l.+2500 l. mve. 5 5
1887. – 3000 l.+3000 l. red.. 5 5
DESIGNS: 1500 l. Peasant. 2000 l. Peasant woman. 2500 l. Intellectual. 3000 l. Factory worker.

1947. Air. Labour Day.
1888. – 3000 l. red 8 5
1889. – 3000 l. green .. 8 5
1890. – 3000 l. brown .. 8 5
1891. 195. 3000 l.+12,000 l. bl. 20 20
DESIGNS—(24½×30 mm.): No. 1888, Four parachutes. 1889, Air Force Monument. 1890, Aeroplane over landscape.

(New currency 1 (new) leu = 100 (old) lei.)

196. Timber Barges. 197. Tractor.

1947. Designs with medallion portrait of King Michael.
1892. – 50 b. orange .. 5 5
1893. 196. 1 l. brown 5 5
1894. – 2 l. blue 5 5
1895. – 3 l. red .. 5 5
1896. – 5 l. blue .. 8 5
1897. – 10 l. blue .. 15 5
1898. – 12 l. violet .. 15 5
1899. – 15 l. blue .. 25 5
1900. – 20 l. brown .. 30 8
1901. – 32 l. brown.. .. 60 20
1902. – 36 l. lake .. 60 20
DESIGNS: 50 b. Harvesting. 2 l. River Danube. 3 l. Reshitza Industries. 5 l. Curtea de Arges Cathedral. 10 l. Royal Palace, Bucharest. 12 l., 36 l. Cernavoda Bridge. 15 l., 32 l. Port of Constanza. 20 l. Oil Wells, Prahova.

1947. Balkan Games. Surch **2+3 LEI C.B.A. 1947** and bar.
1903. 191. 2+3 l. on 36,000 l. vio. 30 20

1947. 17th Congress of General Assn. of Rumanian Engineers. With monogram as in T 197.
1904. 197. 1 l.+1 l. claret (post.) 5 5
1905. – 2 l.+2 l. brown .. 8 8
1906. – 3 l.+3 l. violet .. 8 8
1907. – 4 l.+4 l. olive .. 12 12
1908. – 5 l.+5 l. blue (air) .. 60 30
DESIGNS: 2 l. Sawmill. 3 l. Refinery. 4 l. Steel mill. 5 l. Aeroplane over mountains.

1947. Charity. Soviet-Rumanian Amity. As No. 1869 surch. **ARLUS 1-7.XI 1947 +5.** Imperf.
1909. 5 l.+5 l. blue 15 15

198. Behive. 199. Food Convoy.

1947. Savings Day.
1910. 198. 12 l. red 15 8

1947. Patriotic Defence.
1911. 199. 1 l.+1 l. blue .. 5 5
1912. – 2 l.+2 l. brown .. 5 5
1913. – 3 l.+3 l. claret .. 5 5
1914. – 4 l.+4 l. blue .. 8 5
1915. – 5 l.+5 l. red.. .. 12 8
SYMBOLIC DESIGNS—HORIZ. 2 l. Soldiers' parcels. 3 l. Modern hospital. 4 l. Hungry children. VERT. 5 l. Manacled wrist and flag.

DESIGNS—HORIZ. 2 l. Industrial and Agricultural workers. 11 l. Aeroplane over meeting.
200. Allegory of Work.

1947. Charity. Trades' Union Congress, Bucharest. Inscr. "C.G.M. 1947".
1916. – 2 l.+10 l. red (post).. 8 8
1917. 200. 7 l.+10 l. black .. 12 10
1918. – 11 l. red and blue (air) 20 12

201. Map of Rumania.

1948. Census of 1948.
1925. 201. 12 l. blue 15 5

202. Printing Works and Press.

1948. Rumanian State Printing Works. 75th Anniv.
1926. 202. 6 l. violet 50 25
1927. 7 l. 50 green .. 15 5

203. Discus Thrower. 204. 'Plane over Running Track.

1948. Balkan Games, 1947. Inscr. as in T 203. Imperf. or perf.
1928. 203. 1 l.+1 l. brown (post.) 12 5
1929. – 2 l.+2 l. claret .. 15 8
1930. – 5 l.+5 l. blue .. 30 15
1931. 204. 7 l.+7 l. violet (air) 60 30
1932. 10 l.+10 l. green .. 70 70
DESIGNS: 2 l. Runner. 5 l. Heads of two young athletes.

1948. Nos. 1892/1902 optd. **RPR** (Republica Populara Romana).
1933. 50 b. orange .. 5 5
1934. 1 l. brown 5 5
1935. 2 l. blue .. 10 5
1936. 3 l. red .. 8 5
1937. 5 l. blue .. 12 5
1938. 10 l. blue .. 20 5
1939. 12 l. violet .. 40 8
1940. 15 l. blue .. 45 5
1941. 20 l. brown .. 55 12
1942. 32 l. brown .. 1·25 65
1943. 36 l. lake .. .. 1·25 1·50

DESIGNS: As T 205. 3 l. Peasant girl and wheatsheaf. 5 l. Student and book. TRIANGULAR: 8 l. Youths bearing Filimon Sarbu banner. HORIZ. (larger): 12 l. Aeroplane and swallows.
205. Industrial Worker.

1948. Young Workers' Union. Imperf. or perf.
1954. 205. 2 l.+2 l. blue (post) 8 5
1955. – 3 l.+3 l. green .. 12 8
1956. – 5 l.+5 l. brown .. 15 12
1957. – 8 l.+8 l. claret .. 20 20
1958. – 12 l.+12 l. blue (air) 50 35

206. "Friendship". 207. "New Constitution".

209. Aviator and Aeroplane. 208. Globe and Banner.

1948. Rumanian-Bulgarian Amity.
1959. 206. 32 l. brown 30 8

1948. New Constitution.
1960. 207. 1 l. red 12 5
1961. 2 l. orange 15 5
1962. 12 l. blue 55 20

1948. Labour Day.
1963. 208. 8 l.+8 l. red (postage) 55 55
1964. – 10 l.+10 l. green .. 55 55
1965. – 12 l.+12 l. brown .. 55 55

1966. **209.** 20 l.+20 l. blue (air) 2·75 2·25
DESIGNS—HORIZ. 10 l. Peasants and mountains. VERT. 12 l. Worker and factory.

210. Soldiers cutting Barbed Wire.

211. Nicolas Balcescu.

212. Five Portraits.

213. Proclamation of Islaz.

1948. Army Day.
1967. – 1 l. 50+1 l. 50 red (postage) 20 20
1968. **210.** 2 l.+2 l. purple .. 20 20
1969. – 4 l.+4 l. brown .. 20 20
1970. – 7 l. 50+7 l. 50 black 45 45
1971. – 8 l.+8 l. violet .. 45 45

1972. – 3 l.+3 l. blue (air) .. 55 45
1973. – 5 l.+5 l. blue .. 80 65
DESIGNS—VERT. 1 l. 50, Infantry. 3 l. Fighter aircraft. 5 l. Bomber aircraft. HORIZ. 4 l. Artillery. 7 l. 50, Tank. 8 l. Destroyer.

1948. Cent. of 1848 Revolution. Dated "1848 1948".
1974. **211.** 2 l.+2 l. purple .. 20 15
1975. **212.** 5 l.+5 l. violet .. 20 15
1976. **213.** 11 l. red 20 20
1977. – 10 l.+10 l. green .. 20 15
1978. – 36 l.+18 l. blue .. 45 30
DESIGNS—As T **211**—HORIZ. 10 l. Balcescu, Petofi, Iancu Barnutiu, Baritin and Murcu. VERT. 36 l. Balcescu, Kogalniceanu, Alecsandri and Cuza.

214. Emblem of Republic.

1948.
2023. **214.** 50 b. red 5 5
1980. 0.50 l. red 5 5
1981. 1 l. brown 5 5
1982. 2 l. green 5 5
1983. 3 l. grey 5 5
1984. 4 l. brown 12 5
1985. 5 l. blue 15 5
2028. 5 l. violet 20 5
1986. 10 l. blue 50 5
No. 2023 is inscribed "BANI 0.50" (=½ bani) and in No. 1980 this was corrected to "LEI 0.50".

215. Glider Meeting.

216. Sailing Ships.

1948. Air Force and Navy Day. (a) Air Force (vert.).
1987. **215.** 2 l.+2 l. blue .. 55 35
1988. – 5 l.+5 l. violet .. 55 35
1989. – 8 l.+8 l. red .. 65 35
1990. – 10 l.+10 l. brown .. 55 35

(b) Navy (horiz.).
1991. **216.** 2 l.+2 l. green .. 30 30
1992. – 5 l.+5 l. grey .. 40 30
1993. – 8 l.+8 l. blue .. 40 30
1994. – 10 l.+10 l. red .. 45 40
DESIGNS—AIR FORCE: 5 l. Early aircraft. 8 l. 'Plane and tractor. 10 l. Transport 'plane. NAVY: 5 l. Brig. "Mircea". 8 l. Steamship on Danube. 10 l. Liner "Transylvania".

1948. Surch.
1995. **206.** 31 l. on 32 l. brown 30 8

217. Newspapers and Torch.

218. Soviet Soldiers' Monument.

1948. Press week. Inscr. as in T **217**. Imperf. or perf.
1997. **217.** 5 l.+5 l. red 20 20
1996. 10 l. brown 12 8
1998. – 10 l.+10 l. violet .. 25 20
1999. – 15 l.+15 l. blue .. 25 20
DESIGNS—HORIZ. 10 l. (No. 1998), Flag, torch and ink-well. VERT. 15 l. Alexander Sahia (journalist).

1948. Rumanian-Russian Amity.
2000. **218.** 10 l. red (postage) .. 15 15
2001. – 10 l.+10 l. green .. 40 40
2002. – 15 l.+15 l. blue .. 40 40
2003. – 20 l.+20 l. blue (air) 1·10 85
DESIGNS—VERT. 10 l. (No. 2001), Badge of Arlus. 15 l. Kremlin. HORIZ. 20 l. Twin-engined aircraft.

219. Aeroplane and Emblem of Republic.

DESIGNS: 50 l. Workers in a field. 100 l. Forms of transport (train, ship, etc.).

1948. Air. Designs showing aircraft.
2004. **219.** 30 l. red 20 5
2005. – 50 l. green 20 5
2006. – 100 l. blue 55 15

220. Lorry.

DESIGNS: 1 l. Dockers loading ship. 11 l. Aeroplane. 15 l. Train.

1948. Work on Communications.
2007. – 1 l.+1 l. black & grn. 30 25
2008. **220.** 3 l.+3 l. black & brn. 30 25
2009. – 11 l.+11 l. blk. & blue 45 35
2010. – 15 l.+15 l. blk. & red 45 35

221. Nicolas Balcescu.

222. Hands Breaking Chain.

1948.
2012. **221.** 20 l. red 20 5

1948. People's Republic. 1st Anniv.
2013. **222.** 5 l. red 8 5

223. Runners.

DESIGNS—HORIZ. 10 l. Parade of athletes with flags. VERT. 20 l. Boy flying model aeroplane.

1948. National Sport Organization. Imperf. or perf.
2014. **223.** 5 l.+5 l. green (post.) 90 90
2017. 5 l.+5 l. brown .. 90 90
2015. – 10 l.+10 l. violet .. 1·40 1·40
2018. – 10 l.+10 l. red .. 1·40 1·40
2016. – 20 l.+20 l. blue (air) 4·50 2·75
2019. – 20 l.+20 l. green .. 4·50 2·75

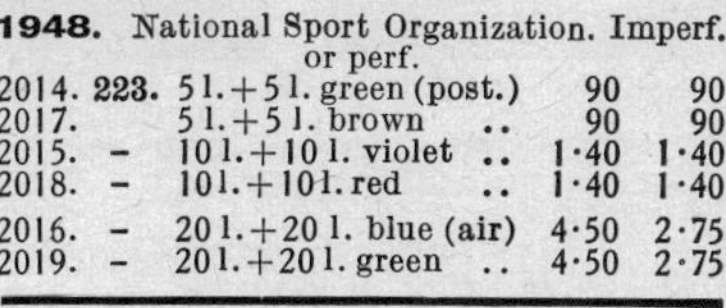

224. Lenin.

225. Dancers.

1949. Lenin. 25th Death Anniv. Perf. or Imperf.
2020. **224.** 20 l. black 15 5

1949. Union of Rumanian Principalities. 90th Anniv.
2021. **225.** 10 l. blue 15 5

226. I. C. Frimu and Revolutionaries.

227. A. S. Pushkin.

1949. I. C. Frimu. 30th Death Anniv. Perf. or imperf.
2022. **226.** 20 l. red 15 5

1949. A. S. Pushkin (poet). 150th Birth Anniv.
2030. **227.** 11 l red 15 5
2031. 30 l. green 35 20

228. Globe and Posthorn.

229. Forms of Transport.

1949. U.P.U. 75th Anniv.
2032. **228.** 20 l. brown 85 55
2033. **229.** 30 l. blue 65 55

230. Russians entering Bucharest.

1949. Russian Army's Entry into Bucharest. 5th Anniv. Perf. or imperf.
2034. **230.** 50 l. brown on green 40 15

231. "Rumanian-Soviet Amity".

1949. Rumanian-Soviet Friendship Week. Perf. or imperf.
2035. **231.** 20 l. red 15 12

232. Forms of Transport.

233. Joseph Stalin.

1949. Int. Congress of Transport Unions. Perf. or imperf.
2036. **232.** 11 l. blue 15 8
2037. 20 l. red 20 15

1949. Stalin's 76th Birthday. Perf. or imperf.
2038. **233.** 31 l. black 25 12

234. "The Third Letter".

235. Michael Eminescu.

1950. Eminescu (poet). Birth Cent. Inscr "MIHAIL EMINESCU 1850 1950".
2040. **234.** 11 l. green 15 8
2041. – 11 l. brown 15 8
2042. – 11 l. rose 15 8
2043. – 11 l. violet 15 8
2044. **235.** 11 l. blue 20 12
DESIGNS (scenes representing poems): No. 2041, "Angel and Demon". 2042, "Ruler and Proletariat". 2043, "Life".

232. "Dragaica Fair".

237. I. Andreescu.

1950. Andreescu (painter). Birth Cent. Inscr. "I. Andreescu".

(a) Perf.
2045. **236.** 5 l. olive 12 5
2047. – 20 l. brown 30 15

(b) Perf. or imperf.
2046. **237.** 11 l. blne 20 12
DESIGN—HORIZ. 20 l. Village well.

238. Factory and Graph.

239. Worker and Flag.

1950. State Plan, 1950. Inscr. "PLANUL DU STAT 1950".
2048. **238.** 11 l. red 12 5
2049. – 31 l. violet 35 20
DESIGN: 31 l. Tractor and factories. No. 2048 exists imperf.

1950. Labour Day. Perf. or imperf.
2050. **239.** 31 l. orange 15 8

240. Emblem of Republic.

241. Trumpeter and Drummer.

1950.
2051. **240.** 50 b. black 8 5
2052. 1 l. red 5 5
2053. 2 l. grey 5 5
2054. 3 l. purple 5 5
2055. 4 l. mauve 5 5
2056. 5 l. claret 5 5
2057. 6 l. green 8 5
2058. 7 l. brown 8 5
2059. 7 l. 50 blue 12 5
2060. 10 l. brown 15 5
2061. 11 l. red 20 5
2062. 15 l. blue 15 5
2063. 20 l. green 25 5
2064. 31 l. green 35 5
2065. 36 l. brown 35 15
For stamps as T **240** but with inscriptions in white, see Nos. 2240, etc., and Nos. 2277/8.

1950. Rumanian Pioneers Organisation. 1st Anniv.
2074. **241.** 8 l. blue 20 15
2075. – 11 l. purple 15 15
2076. – 31 l. red 55 20
DESIGNS: 11 l. Children reading. 31 l. Youth parade.

242. Engineer.

243. Vlaicu and Aeroplane.

244. Mother and Child.

1950. Industrial Nationalisation.
2077. **242.** 11 l. red 15 8
2078. 11 l. blue 15 8
2079. 11 l. brown 15 8
2080. 11 l. olive 15 8

1950. 1st Flight by A. Vlaicu. 40th Anniv.
2081. **243.** 3 l. green 15 5
2082. 6 l. blue 15 5
2083. 8 l. blue 20 8

1950. Peace Congress, Bucharest.
2084. **244.** 11 l. red 20 12
2085. – 20 l. brown 20 8
DESIGN: 20 l. Lathe operator.

245. Statue and Flags.

246. Students and Badge.

1950. Rumanian-Soviet Amity.
2086. **245.** 30 l. brown 30 10

1950. Rumanian-Hungarian Amity. Optd. **TRAIASCA PREITENIA ROMANO-MAGHIARAL.**
2087. **240.** 15 l. blue 15 8

1950. G.M.A. Complex Sports Facilities. Designs incorporating badge.
2088. – 3 l. red 25 15
2089. **246.** 5 l. brown 20 8
2090. – 5 l. blue 20 8
2091. – 11 l. green 30 12
2092. – 31 l. olive 45 30
DESIGNS: 3 l. Agriculture and Industry. 11 l. Runners. 31 l. Gymnasts.

247.

248. Ski-jumper.

1950. 3rd Soviet-Rumanian Congress.
2093. **247.** 11 l. red 12 8
2094. 11 l. blue 12 8

1951. Winter Sports.
2095. **248.** 4 l. chocolate .. 15 8
2096. – 5 l. red 20 15
2097. – 11 l. blue 20 15
2098. – 20 l. brown 45 35
2099. – 31 l. green 75 40
DESIGNS: 5 l. Skater. 11 l. Skier. 20 l. Ice-hockey. 31 l. Tobogganing.

249. Peasant and Tractor.

DESIGN—VERT. 11 l. Engineer and machine.

1951. Agricultural and Industrial Exhibition.
2100. – 11 l. brown 5 5
2101. **249.** 31 l. blue 20 12

250. Star of the Republic.

251. Youth Camp.

1951. Orders and Medals. Perf. or imperf.
2102. – 2 l. grey 5 5
2103. – 4 l. blue 5 5
2104. – 11 l. red 8 5
2105. **250.** 35 l. brown 30 5
DESIGNS: 2 l. Medal of Work. 4 l. As T **250** but with different centre to star and with ribbon at top. 11 l. Order of Work.

1951. Rumanian Pioneer Organisation. 2nd Anniv.
2106. **251.** 1 l. green 15 5
2107. – 11 l. blue 35 5
2108. – 35 l. red 60 15
DESIGNS—VERT. 11 l. Children meeting Stalin. HORIZ. 35 l. Decorating boy on parade.

252. Woman and Flags.

253. Ion Negulici.

1951. Int. Women's Day. Perf. or imperf.
2109. **252.** 11 l. brown 12 5

1951. Negulici (painter). Death Cent.
2110. **253.** 35 l. red 55 20

254. Cyclists.

255. F. Sarbu.

1951. Rumanian Cycle Race.
2111. **254.** 11 l. brown 50 20

1951. Sarbu (patriot). 10th Death Anniv.
2112. **255.** 11 l. sepia 15 5

256. "Revolutionary Rumania".

257. Students.

1951. Rosenthal (painter). Death Cent.
2113. **256.** 11 l. green 30 15
2114. 11 l. orange 30 15
2115. – 11 l. brown 30 15
2116. – 11 l. violet 30 15
DESIGN—VERT. Nos. 2115/16, Portrait of a woman.

1951. 3rd World Youth Festival. Berlin.
2117. **257.** 1 l. red 12 5
2118. – 5 l. blue 15 5
2119. – 11 l. purple 30 12
DESIGNS: 5 l. Girl, boy and flag. 11 l. Young people around globe.

258. Soldier and Pithead.

259. "Scanteia" Building.

1951. Miners' Day.
2120. **258.** 5 l. blue 15 5
2121. – 11 l. mauve 15 5
DESIGN: 11 l. Miner and pithead.

1951. "Scanteia" (Communist newspaper). 20th Anniv.
2122. **259.** 11 l. blue 15 5

260. Order of Defence.

261. Oil Refinery.

1951. Liberation Day.
2123. **260.** 10 l. red 15 8

1951. Five Year Plan. Dated "1951 1955".
2124. **261.** 1 l. olive (postage) .. 5 5
2125. – 2 l. chocolate .. 5 5
2126. – 3 l. red 8 5
2127. – 4 l. brown 12 5
2128. – 5 l. green 12 5
2129. – 6 l. blue 55 40
2130. – 7 l. emerald 20 8
2131. – 8 l. brown 20 8
2132. – 11 l. blue 20 5
2133. – 35 l. violet 50 15
2134. – 30 l. green (air) .. 55 40
2135. – 50 l. brown 65 35
DESIGNS: 2 l. Miner and pithead. 3 l. Soldier and pylons. 4 l. Steel furnace. 5 l. Combine-harvester. 6 l. Canal construction. 7 l. Threshing machine. 8 l. Sanatorium. 11 l. Dam and pylons. 30 l. Potato planting. 35 l. Factory. 50 l. Ship, loco and 'plane.

262. Orchestra and Dancers.

263. Soldier and Arms.

1951. Music Festival.
2136. **262.** 11 l. brown 20 8
2137. – 11 l. blue (Mixed Choir) 20 8
2138. – 11 l. mauve (Lyre and dove) (vert.) .. 20 8

1951. Army Day.
2139. **263.** 11 l. blue 15 5

264. Arms of U.S.S.R. and Rumania.

265. P. Tcancenco.

1951. Rumanian-Soviet Friendship.
2140. **264.** 4 l. brown on buff .. 12 5
2141. 35 l. orange .. 40 20

1951. Tcancenco (revolutionary). 25th Death Anniv.
2142. **265.** 10 l. olive 15 5

266. Open Book "1907". 267. I. L. Caragiale.

1952. Caragiale (writer). Birth Cent.

(a) Unissued values surch.
2143. **266.** 20 b. on 11 l. red .. 15 5
2144. – 55 b. on 11 l. green .. 20 5
2145. **267.** 75 b. on 11 l. blue .. 20 8

(b) Without surch.
2146. **266.** 55 b. red 15 5
2147. – 55 b. green 20 5
2148. **267.** 55 b. blue 20 5
2149. – 1 l. brown 30 20
DESIGNS—HORIZ. Nos. 2144, 2147, Profile of Caragiale. 1 l. Caragiale addressing assembly.

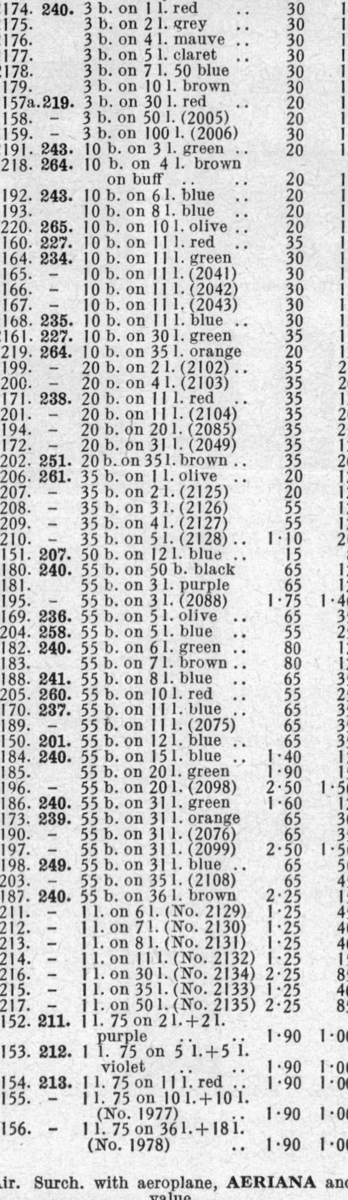

1952. Currency revalued. Surch.
2174. **240.** 3 b. on 1 l. red .. 30 12
2175. 3 b. on 2 l. grey .. 30 12
2176. 3 b. on 4 l. mauve .. 30 12
2177. 3 b. on 5 l. claret .. 30 12
2178. 3 b. on 7 l. 50 blue 30 12
2179. 3 b. on 10 l. brown 30 12
2157a. **219.** 3 b. on 30 l. red .. 20 15
2158. – 3 b. on 50 l. (2005) 20 15
2159. – 3 b. on 100 l. (2006) 30 15
2191. **243.** 10 b. on 3 l. green .. 20 12
2218. **264.** 10 b. on 4 l. brown on buff 20 12
2192. **243.** 10 b. on 6 l. blue .. 20 12
2193. 10 b. on 8 l. blue .. 20 12
2220. **265.** 10 b. on 10 l. olive .. 20 12
2160. **227.** 10 b. on 11 l. red .. 35 15
2164. **234.** 10 b. on 11 l. green 30 15
2165. – 10 b. on 11 l. (2041) 30 15
2166. – 10 b. on 11 l. (2042) 30 15
2167. – 10 b. on 11 l. (2043) 30 15
2168. **235.** 10 b. on 11 l. blue .. 30 15
2161. **227.** 10 b. on 30 l. green 35 15
2219. **264.** 10 b. on 35 l. orange 20 12
2199. – 20 b. on 2 l. (2102) .. 35 20
2200. – 20 b. on 4 l. (2103) 35 20
2171. **238.** 20 b. on 11 l. red .. 35 12
2201. – 20 b. on 11 l. (2104) 35 20
2194. – 20 b. on 20 l. (2085) 35 25
2172. – 20 b. on 31 l. (2049) 35 12
2202. **251.** 20 b. on 35 l. brown .. 35 20
2206. **261.** 35 b. on 1 l. olive .. 20 12
2207. – 35 b. on 2 l. (2125) 20 12
2208. – 35 b. on 3 l. (2126) 55 12
2209. – 35 b. on 4 l. (2127) 55 12
2210. – 35 b. on 5 l. (2128) .. 1·10 20
2151. **207.** 50 b. on 12 l. blue .. 15 8
2180. **240.** 55 b. on 50 b. black 65 12
2181. 55 b. on 3 l. purple 65 12
2195. – 55 b. on 3 l. (2088) 1·75 1·40
2169. **236.** 55 b. on 5 l. olive .. 65 35
2204. **258.** 55 b. on 5 l. blue .. 55 25
2182. **240.** 55 b. on 6 l. green .. 80 12
2183. 55 b. on 7 l. brown .. 80 12
2188. **241.** 55 b. on 8 l. blue .. 65 35
2205. **260.** 55 b. on 10 l. red .. 55 25
2170. **237.** 55 b. on 11 l. blue .. 65 35
2189. – 55 b. on 11 l. (2075) 65 35
2150. **201.** 55 b. on 12 l. blue .. 65 35
2184. **240.** 55 b. on 15 l. blue .. 1·40 12
2185. 55 b. on 20 l. green 1·90 15
2196. – 55 b. on 20 l. (2098) 2·50 1·50
2186. **240.** 55 b. on 31 l. green 1·60 12
2173. **239.** 55 b. on 31 l. orange 65 30
2190. – 55 b. on 31 l. (2076) 65 35
2197. – 55 b. on 31 l. (2099) 2·50 1·50
2198. **249.** 55 b. on 31 l. blue .. 65 50
2203. – 55 b. on 35 l. (2108) 65 45
2187. **240.** 55 b. on 36 l. brown 2·25 15
2211. – 1 l. on 6 l. (No. 2129) 1·25 45
2212. – 1 l. on 7 l. (No. 2130) 1·25 40
2213. – 1 l. on 8 l. (No. 2131) 1·25 40
2214. – 1 l. on 11 l. (No. 2132) 1·25 15
2216. – 1 l. on 30 l. (No. 2134) 2·25 85
2215. – 1 l. on 35 l. (No. 2133) 1·25 40
2217. – 1 l. on 50 l. (No. 2135) 2·25 85
2152. **211.** 1 l. 75 on 2 l.+2 l. purple .. .. 1·90 1·00
2153. **212.** 1 l. 75 on 5 l.+5 l. violet .. .. 1·90 1·00
2154. **213.** 1 l. 75 on 11 l. red .. 1·90 1·00
2155. – 1 l. 75 on 10 l.+10 l. (No. 1977) .. 1·90 1·00
2156. – 1 l. 75 on 36 l.+18 l. (No. 1978) .. 1·90 1·00

Air. Surch. with aeroplane, **AERIANA** and value.
2162. **228.** 3 l. on 20 l. brown .. 2·75 1·60
2163. **229.** 5 l. on 30 l. blue .. 2·75 1·60

268. Railwayman.

269. Gogol and character from "Taras Bulba".

1952. Railway Day.
2229. **268.** 55 b. brown 35 5

1952. Gogol (Russian writer). Death Cent.
2230. **269.** 55 b. blue 40 15
2231. – 1 l. 75 olive 50 20
DESIGN—VERT. 1 l. 75, Gogol and open book.

270. Maternity Medal. 271. I. P. Pavlov.

1952. Int. Women's Day.
2232. **270.** 20 b. blue and purple 12 5
2233. – 55 b. brn. & chestnut 20 8
2234. – 1 l. 75 brown and red 45 15
MEDALS: 55 b. "Glory of Maternity" medal. 1 l. 75, "Mother Heroine" medal.

1952. Rumanian-Soviet Medical Congress.

2235. **271.** 1 l. brown 40 8

272. Hammer and Sickle Medal.

273. Boy and Girl Pioneers.

1952. Labour Day.

2236. **272.** 55 b. brown 35 8

1952. Rumanian Pioneers Organisation. 3rd Anniv.

2237. **273.** 20 b. chestnut .. 35 5

2238. – 55 b. green 35 5

2239. – 1 l. 75 blue 55 15

DESIGNS—VERT. 55 b. Pioneer nature-study group. HORIZ. 1 l. 75, Worker and pioneers.

1952. As T 240 but with figures and inscriptions in white. Bani values size $20\frac{1}{4} \times 24\frac{1}{2}$ mm., lei values size $24\frac{1}{2} \times 29\frac{1}{2}$ mm.

2240. **240.** 3 b. orange 5 5

2241. 5 b. red 5 5

2242. 7 b. green 8 5

2243. 10 b. brown 8 5

2244. 20 b. blue 10 5

2245. 35 b. sepia 12 5

2246. 50 b. green 15 5

2247. 55 b. violet 30 5

2248. 1 l. 10 brown .. 50 5

2249. 1 l. 75 violet.. .. 1·90 5

2250. 2 l. olive 85 5

2251. 2 l. 35 brown .. 1·10 8

2252. 2 l. 55 orange .. 1·40 8

2253. 3 l. green .. .. 1·60 8

2254. 5 l. red .. .. 1·60 20

For similar stamps with star added at top of emblem, see Nos. 2277/8.

274. "Smirdan" (after Grigorescu).

275. Leonardo da Vinci.

1952. 75th Anniv. of Independence.

2255. **274.** 50 b. lake 20 5

2256. – 1 l. 10 b. blue .. 35 10

DESIGN—HORIZ. 1 l. 10 b. Rumanian and Russian soldiers.

1952. 500th Anniv. of Birth of Leonardo da Vinci.

2257. **275.** 55 b. violet 95 20

276 Miner.

277. Students' Union Badge.

1952. Miners' Day.

2258. **276.** 20 b. red 15 5

2259. 55 b. violet 30 5

1952. Int. Students' Union Council. Bucharest.

2260. **277.** 10 b. blue 5 5

2261. – 20 b. orange 20 5

2262. – 55 b. green .. .. 1·40 15

2263. – 1 l. 75 red 60 15

DESIGNS—HORIZ. 20 b. Student in laboratory (35×22 mm). 1 l. 75, Six students dancing (30×24 mm.). VERT. 55 b. Students playing football (24×30 mm.).

278. Soldier, Sailor and Airman.

279. Statue and Flags.

280. Workers and Views of Russia and Rumania (after N. Parlius).

1952. Army Day.

2264. **278.** 55 b. blue 20 5

1952. Rumanian-Soviet Friendship.

2265. **279.** 55 b. red 55 5

2266. **280.** 1 l. 75 brown .. 80 10

281. Rowing.

282. N. Balcescu (after C. Tattarescu).

1952. Physical Culture.

2267. **281.** 20 b. blue 65 8

2268. – 1 l. 75 red (Athletes) 1·40 30

1954. Balcescu (revolutionary). Death Cent.

2269. **282.** 55 b. grey 45 8

2270. 1 l. 75 olive 95 25

283. Emblem and Flags.

284.

1952. New Constitution.

2271. **283.** 55 b. green 35 8

1952. People's Republic. 5th Anniv.

2272. **284.** 55 b. blue, green, yellow and red .. 55 15

285. Millo, Caragiale and Mme. Romanescu.

286. Foundry Worker.

1953. Caragiale National Theatre. Cent.

2273. **285.** 55 b. blue 55 12

1953. 3rd Industrial and Agricultural Congress.

2274. **286.** 55 b. green 15 5

2275. – 55 b. orange 12 5

2276. – 55 b. brown 20 8

DESIGNS—HORIZ. No. 2275, Farm workers and tractor. No. 2276, Workman, refinery and oil wells.

1953. As Nos. 2240, etc., but with star added at top of emblem.

2277. **240.** 5 b. red 5 5

2278. 55 b. purple 15 5

287. "The Strikers of Grivitsa" (after Nazarev).

1953. Grivitsa Strike. 20th Anniv.

2279. **287.** 55 b. brown 30 8

288.

1953. Treaty of Friendship with Russia. 5th Anniv.

2280. **288.** 55 b. brown on blue 45 5

289. Table Tennis Badge.

290. Oltenian Carpet.

1953. 20th World Table Tennis Championship, Bucharest.

2281 **289.** 55 b. green 90 20

2282. 55 b. brown 90 20

1953. Rumanian Art.

2283. – 10 b. green 15 5

2284. – 20 b. brown 15 5

2285. – 35 b. violet 30 5

2286. – 55 b. blue 50 5

2287. **290.** 1 l. purple 55 5

DESIGNS—VERT. 10 b. Pottery. 20 b. Campulung peasant girl. 55 b. Apuseni Mountain peasant girl. HORIZ. 35 b. National dance.

291. Karl Marx.

292. Pioneers Planting Tree.

1953. Karl Marx. 70th Death Anniv.

2288. **291.** 1 l. 55 brown .. 55 12

1953. Rumanian Pioneer Organization. 4th Anniv.

2289. **292.** 35 b. green 15 5

2290. – 55 b. blue 30 8

2291. – 1 l. 75 brown .. 65 20

DESIGNS—VERT. 55 b. Boy and girl flying model gliders. HORIZ. 1 l. 75, Pioneers and instructor.

293. Women and Flags.

ILLUSTRATIONS
British Commonwealth and all overprints and surcharges are FULL SIZE. Foreign Countries have been reduced to ¾-LINEAR.

1953. 3rd World Congress of Women.

2292. **293.** 55 b. brown 35 8

294.

295. Cornfield and Forest.

1953. 4th World Youth Festival.

2293. **294.** 20 b. orange 20 5

2294. – 55 b. blue 25 5

2295. – 65 b. red 25 12

2296. – 1 l. 75 purple .. 60 20

DESIGNS—VERT. 55 b. Students releasing dove over globe. HORIZ. 65 b. Girl presenting bouquet. 1 l. 75, Folk dancers.

1953. Forestry Month.

2297. – 20 b. blue 20 8

2298. **295.** 38 b. green 35 15

2299. – 55 b. brown 55 12

DESIGNS—VERT. 20 b. Waterfall and trees. 55 b. Forestry worker.

296. V. V. Mayakovsky.

297. Miner.

1953. Mayakovsky (Russian poet). 60th Birth Anniv.

2300. **296.** 55 b. brown 35 8

1953. Miners' Day.

2301. **297.** 1 l. 55 indigo .. 55 12

298. Telephonist, G.P.O. and P.O. Worker.

299.

1953. Construction of G.P.O. 50th Anniv.

2302. **298.** 20 b. brown 8 5

2303. – 55 b. olive 15 5

2304. – 1 l. blue 30 8

2305. – 1 l. 55 lake 40 15

DESIGNS: 55 b. Postwoman and G.P.O. 1 l. G.P.O., radio-transmitter and map. 1 l. 55, Telegraphist, G.P.O. and teletypist.

1953. Liberation. 9th Anniv.

2306. **299.** 55 b. brown 30 5

300. Soldier and Flag.

301. Girl and Model Glider.

1953. Army Day.

2307. **300.** 55 b. olive 30 5

1953. Aerial Sports.

2308. **301.** 10 b. green & orange 55 12

2309. – 20 b. olive & chestnut 85 12

2310. – 55 b. purple and red 1·40 20

2311. – 1 l. 75 brown & pur. 1·60 35

DESIGNS: 20 b. Parachutists. 55 b. Glider and pilot. 1 l. 75, Monoplane.

302. Workman, Girl and Flags.

303. "Unity".

1953. Rumanian-Soviet Friendship.

2312. **302.** 55 b. brown 15 5

2313. – 1 l. 55 lake 35 15

DESIGN: 1 l. 55, Spasski Tower and Volga-Don canal.

1953. 3rd World Trades' Union Congress.

2314. **303.** 55 b. olive 20 5

2315. – 1 l. 25 red 35 15

DESIGN—VERT. 1 l. 25, Workers, flags and globe.

304. C. Porumbescu.

305. Agricultural Machinery.

1953. Porumbescu (composer). Birth Cent.

2316. **304.** 55 b. lilac 85 8

1953. Agricultural designs.

2317. **305.** 10 b. olive 5 5

2318. – 35 b. green 20 5

2319. – 2 l. 55 brown .. 1·75 45

DESIGNS: 35 b. Tractor drawing disc harrows, 2 l. 55, Cows grazing.

306. A. Vlaicu.

307. Lenin.

1953. Vlaicu (pioneer aviator). 40th Death Anniv.
2320. **306.** 50 b. blue 30 5

1954. Lenin. 30th Death Anniv.
2321. **307.** 55 b. brown 20 5

308. Stag. **309.** Calimanesti.

1954. Forestry Month.
2322. **308.** 20 b. brown on yellow 3·00 15
2323. – 55 b. violet on yellow 35 15
2324. 1 l. 75 blue on yellow 1·25 25
DESIGNS: 55 b. Pioneers planting tree. 1 l. 75, Forest.

1954. Workers' Rest Homes
2325. **309.** 5 b. black on yellow .. 5 5
2326. – 1 l. 55 black on blue .. 40 8
2327. – 2 l. green on pink .. 45 12
2328. – 2 l. 35 sepia on green 80 25
2329. – 2 l. 55 brown on green 80 35
DESIGNS: 1 l. 55 Siniai. 2 l. Predeal. 2 l. 35, Tusnad. 2 l. 55 Govora.

310. O. Bancila. **311.** Child and Dove of Peace.

1954. Bancila (painter). 10th Death Anniv.
2330. **310.** 55 b. green and brown 40 15

1954. Int. Children's Day.
2331. **311.** 55 b. brown 30 8

312. Girl Pioneer feeding Calf. **313.** Stephen the Great.

1954. Rumanian Pioneer Organization. 5th Anniv.
2332. **312.** 20 b. black 8 5
2333. – 55 b. blue 25 5
2334. – 1 l. 75 red 65 15
DESIGNS: 55 b. Girl Pioneers harvesting. 1 l. 75, Young Pioneers examining globe.

1954. Stephen the Great. 450th Death Anniv.
2335. **313.** 55 b. chocolate .. 35 10

314. Miner operating Coal-cutter. **315.** Dr. V. Babes.

1954. Miners' Day.
2336. **314.** 1 l. 75 black 55 15

1954. Babes (pathologist). Birth Cent.
2337. **315.** 55 b. red 40 8

316. Sailor and Flag. **317.** Dedication Tablet.

1954. Navy Day.
2338. **316.** 55 b. blue 30 8

1954. Mutual Aid Organization. 5th Anniv. Inscr. "1949–AUGUST–1954".
2339. – 20 b. violet 8 5
2340. **317.** 55 b. brown 25 8
DESIGN: 20 b. Man receiving money from counter clerk.

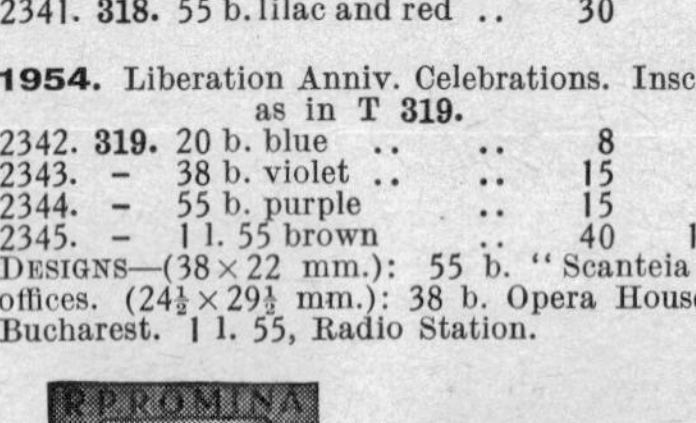

318. Liberation Monument. **319.** Recreation Centre.

1954. Liberation. 10th Anniv.
2341. **318.** 55 b. lilac and red .. 30 5

1954. Liberation Anniv. Celebrations. Inscr. as in T **319.**
2342. **319.** 20 b. blue 8 5
2343. – 38 b. violet 15 8
2344. – 55 b. purple .. 15 5
2345. – 1 l. 55 brown .. 40 15
DESIGNS—(38 × 22 mm.): 55 b. "Scanteia" offices. (24½ × 29½ mm.): 38 b. Opera House, Bucharest. 1 l. 55, Radio Station.

320. Airman. **321.** Chemical Plant and Oil Derricks.

1954. Aviation Day.
2346. **320.** 55 b. blue 30 8

1954. Int. Chemical and Petroleum Workers Conference, Bucharest.
2347. **321.** 55 b. black 35 8

322. Dragon Pillar, Peking. **323.** T. Neculuta.

1954. Chinese Culture Week.
2348. **322.** 55 b. black on yellow 35 8

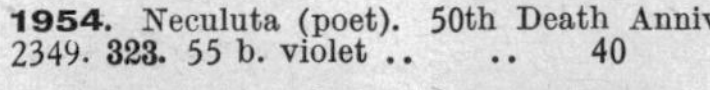

1954. Neculuta (poet). 50th Death Anniv.
2349. **323.** 55 b. violet 40 8

324. ARLUS Badge. **325.** Friendship.

1954. "ARLUS" 10th Anniv. and Rumanian-Russian Friendship.
2350. **324.** 55 b. red 15 5
2351. **325.** 65 b. purple 25 8

326. G. Tattarescu (painter). **327.** B. Iscovescu (painter).

1954. Tattarescu. 60th Death Anniv.
2352. **326.** 55 b. red 30 8

1954. Iscovescu. Death Cent.
2353. **327.** 1 l. 75 brown 80 12

328. Teleprinter. **329.** Wild Boar.

1954. Cent. of Telecommunications in Rumania.
2354. **328.** 50 b. lilac 30 8

1955. Forestry Month. Inscr. "LUNA PADURII 1955".
2355. **329.** 35 b. brown .. .. 1·60 12
2356. – 65 b. blue 45 15
2357. – 1 l. 20 red 65 15
DESIGNS: 65 b. Tree planting. 1 l. 20, Logging.

330. Airman. **331.** Clasped Hands.

1955. Occupations.
2358. – 3 b. blue 5 5
2359. – 5 b. violet 5 5
2360. **330.** 10 b. chocolate .. 5 5
2361. – 20 b. magenta .. 5 5
2362. 30 b. ultramarine .. 8 5
2363. – 35 b. turquoise .. 8 5
2364. – 40 b. indigo 10 5
2365. – 55 b. olive 12 5
2366. – 1 l. violet 25 5
2367. – 1 l. 55 lake 50 5
2368. – 2 l. 35 buff 80 20
2369. – 2 l. 55 myrtle .. 80 15
DESIGNS: 3 b. Scientist. 5 b. Foundryman. 20 b. Miner. 30 b. Tractor driver. 35 b. Schoolboy. 40 b. Girl student. 5 b. Bricklayer. 1 l. Sailor. 1 l. 55, Millgirl. 2 l. 35, Soldier. 2 l. 55, Telegraph linesman.

1955. Int. Conference of Municipal Workers, Vienna.
2370. **331.** 25 b. red 15 5

332. Lenin. **333.** Dove and Globe.

1955. Lenin. 85th Birth Anniv. Portraits of Lenin.
2371. **332.** 20 b. sepia and bistre 12 5
2372. – 55 b. brown (full-face) 15 8
2373. – 1 l. lake and red (half length) .. 30 10

1955. Peace Congress, Helsinki.
2374. **333.** 55 b. blue 30 5

334. War Memorial, Berlin. **335.** Children and Dove.

1955. Victory over Germany. 10th Anniv.
2375. **334.** 55 b. blue 30 5

1955. Int. Children's Day.
2376. **335.** 55 b. brown 25 5

336. "Service". **337.** People's Art Museum.

1955. European Volley-ball Championships. Inscr. as in T **236.**
2377. – 55 b. purple on pink 85 20
2378. **236.** 1 l. 75 red on yellow .. 1·90 45
DESIGN: 55 b. Volley-ball players.

1955. Bucharest Museums.
2379. – 20 b. magenta .. 5 5
2380. – 55 b. brown 15 5
2381. **237.** 1 l. 20 black .. 35 15
2382. – 1 l. 75 green .. 45 15
2383. – 2 l. 55 purple .. 65 35
MUSEUMS—(30 × 24½ mm.): 20 b. Theodor Aman. 2 l. 55, Simu. (34 × 23 mm.): 55 b. Lenin-Stalin. 1 l. 75, Republican Art.

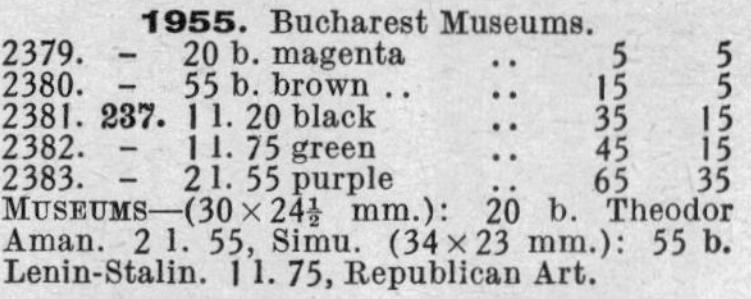

338. Mother and Child. **339.** "Nature Study".

1955. 1st World Mothers' Congress, Lausanne.
2384. **338.** 55 b. blue 20 8

1955. 5th Anniv. of Pioneer Headquarters, Bucharest. Inscr. as in T **339.**
2385. – 10 b. blue 5 5
2386. **339.** 20 b. green 15 5
2387. – 55 b. maroon .. 55 8
DESIGNS: 10 b. Model railway. 55 b. Headquarters building.

340. Coxed Four. **341.** A. Pann.

1955. Women's European Rowing Championships, Bucharest.
2388. **340.** 55 b. green .. .. 1·60 25
2389. – 1 l. blue (Woman sculler) .. .. 2·25 35

1955. Rumanian Writers.
2390. – 55 b. blue 30 12
2391. – 55 b. slate 30 12
2392. **341.** 55 b. olive 30 12
2393. – 55 b. violet 30 12
2394. – 55 b. purple 30 12
PORTRAITS—No. 2390, D. Cantemir. 2391, M. Dosoftei. 2393, S. C. Cantacuzino. 2394, E. Vacarescu.

342. Marksman. **343.** Fire Engine.

1955. European Sharpshooting Championship.
2395. **342.** 1 l. choc. & pale brn. 1·25 30

1955. Firemen's Day.
2396. **343.** 55 b. red 25 8

344. **345.** Spraying Fruit Trees.

1955. W.F.T.U. 10th Anniv. Inscr. as in T **344.**
2397. **344.** 55 b. olive 20 5
2398. – 1 l. blue 30 5
DESIGN: 1 l. Workers and flag.

1955. Fruit and Vegetable Cultivation.
2399. **345.** 10 b. green 12 5
2400. – 20 b. red 12 5
2401. – 55 b. blue 50 8
2402. – 1 l. lake 50 20
DESIGNS: 20 b. Fruit picking. 55 b. Harvesting grapes. 1 l. Gathering vegetables.

INDEX

Countries can be quickly located by referring to the index at the end of this volume.

346.

347. I. V. Michurin.

1955. 4th A.R.L.U.S. Congress.
2403. 346. 20 b. blue and buff 20 5

1955. Michurin (Russian botanist). Birth Centenary.
2404. 347. 55 b. blue 30 8

348. Cotton.

349. Sheep and Shepherd blowing Bucium.

1955.
2405. – 10 b. pur. (Sugar beet) 20 5
2406. 348. 20 b. grey 25 5
2407. – 55 b. blue (Linseed).. 55 15
2408. – 1 l. 55 brown (Sunflower) .. .. 1·25 30

1955.
2409. 349. 5 b. brown & green.. 15 5
2410. – 10 b. violet and bistre 20 5
2411. – 35 b. brown & salmon 65 20
2412. – 55 b. brown & bistre 95 30
DESIGNS: 10 b. Pigs and farm girl. 35 b. Cows and dairy maid. 55 b. Horse and groom.

350. Schiller.

351. Bank and Book.

1955. Famous Writers.
2413. – 20 b. indigo 12 5
2414. – 55 b. blue 25 8
2415. 350. 1 l. grey 35 15
2416. – 1 l. 55 brown .. 55 15
2417. – 1 l. 75 violet.. .. 95 25
2418. – 2 l. lake .. .. 1·10 30
PORTRAITS: 20 b. Hans Andersen. 55 b. Mickiewicz. 1 l. 55, Montesquieu. 1 l. 75, Walt Whitman. 2 l. Cervantes.

1955. Savings Bank.
2419. 351. 55 b. blue 20 8
2420. 55 b. violet 55 35

352. Family.

353. Hare.

1956. National Census. Inscr. as in T 352.
2421. – 55 b. orange 15 8
2422. 352. 1 l. 75 brown & green 55 20
DESIGN: 55 b. "21 FEBRUARIE 1956" in circle.

1956. Wild Life.
2423. 353. 20 b. black and green 15 5
2424. – 20 b. black and olive 15 20
2425. – 35 b. black and blue.. 20 20
2426. – 50 b. sepia and blue.. 30 20
2427. – 55 b. green and bistre 20 20
2428. – 55 b. brown & turquoise 20 20
2429. – 1 l. lake and green .. 45 20
2430. – 1 l. 55 lake and blue.. 55 20
2431. – 1 l. 75 sepia and green 65 20
2432. – 2 l. sepia and blue .. 2·75 1·40
2433. – 3 l. 25 black & green 2·10 1·40
2434. – 4 l. 25 sep. & salmon 3·25 2·25
DESIGNS—VERT. No. 2424, Bustard. 35 b. Trout. 1 l. 55, Squirrel. 1 l. 75, Grouse. 4 l. 25, Deer. HORIZ. 50 b. Wild boar. No. 2427, Pheasant. No. 2428, Bear. 1 l. Lynx. 2 l. Black mountain goat. 3 l. 25, Wild duck.
See also Nos. 2474/85.

354. Insurgents.

355. Boy and Globe.

1956. Paris Commune. 85th Anniv.
2435. 354. 55 b. vermilion 20 5

1956. Int. Children's Day.
2436. 355. 55 b. violet 40 8

356. Red Cross Nurse.

357. Tree.

1956. 2nd Rumanian Red Cross Congress.
2437. 356. 55 b. olive and red .. 45 8

1956. Forestry Month.
2438. 357. 20 b. slate on green.. 35 5
2439. – 55 b. black on green.. 55 8
DESIGN: 55 b. Lumber train.

358. Woman Speaking.

359. Academy Buildings.

1956. Int. Women's Congress, Bucharest.
2440. 358. 55 b. green 30 8

1956. Rumanian People's Academy. 90th Anniv.
2441. 359. 55 b. green and buff.. 30 8

ILLUSTRATIONS
British Commonwealth and all overprints and surcharges are FULL SIZE. Foreign Countries have been reduced to ¾-LINEAR.

360. T. Vuia and Early and Modern Aeroplanes.

1956. 1st Flight by Vuia (pioneer airman). 50th Anniv.
2442. 360. 55 b. sepia and olive 30 8

361. Georgescu and Statues.

362. Farm Girl.

1956. Georgescu (sculptor). Birth Cent.
2443. 361. 55 b. green and brown 25 8

1956. Collective Farming. 5th Anniv.
(a) Inscr. "1951-1956".
2444. 362. 55 b. plum .. .. 1·40 1·00
(b) Inscr. "1949–1956".
2445. 362. 55 b. plum 30 8

363. Cabbage Butterfly.

364. Striker.

1956. Insect Pests.
2446. 363. 10 b. cream, black and violet 30 5
2447. – 55 b. orange & sepia 55 5
2448. – 1 l. 75 lake and olive 1·60 80
2449. – 1 l. 75 choc. and olive 1·10 30
PESTS: 55 b. Colorado beetle. 1 l. 75 (2) May-bug.

1956. Dockers' Strike at Galatz. 50th Anniv.
2450. 364. 55 b. brown on pink 20 5

365. Newspaper.

366. Maxim Gorky.

1956. Newspaper " Scanteia ". 25th Anniv.
2451. 365. 55 b. blue 20 5

1956. Maxim Gorky. 20th Death Anniv.
2452. 366. 55 b. brown.. .. 25 8

367. T. Aman (painter).

368. Snowdrops and Polyanthus.

1956. Aman. 125th Birth Anniv.
2453. 367. 55 b. grey 30 8

1956. Flowers. Designs multicoloured. Colours of backgrounds given.
2454. 368. 5 b. blue 15 5
2455. – 55 b. black 40 12
2456. – 1 l. 75 indigo .. 90 20
2457. – 3 l. green .. .. 1·40 35
FLOWERS: 55 b. Daffodil and violets. 1 l. 75, Antirrhinums and campanulas. 3 l. Poppies and lilies of the valley.

369. Janos Hunyadi.

370. Olympic Flame.

1956. Hunyadi. 500th Death Anniv.
2458. 369. 55 b. violet 30 8

1956 Olympic Games.
2459. 370. 20 b. red 15 5
2460. – 55 b. blue 20 8
2461. – 1 l. magenta.. .. 45 12
2462. – 1 l. 55 turquoise .. 55 15
2463. – 1 l. 75 violet.. .. 60 30
DESIGNS: 55 b. Water-polo. 1 l. Ice-skating. 1 l. 55, Canoeing. 1 l. 75, High-jumping.

371. George Bernard Shaw.

372. Aeroplane over City.

1956. Cultural Anniversaries.
2464. – 20 b. blue (Franklin) 25 5
2465. – 35 b. clar. (Toyo Oda) 12 5
2466. 371. 40 b. chocolate .. 12 5
2467. – 50 b. sepia (I. Franco) 12 5
2468. – 55 b. olive (Curie) .. 50 10
2469. – 1 l. turquoise (Ibsen) 35 5
2470. – 1 l. 55 violet (Dostoievsky) .. 45 10
2471. – 1 l. 75 blue (Heine).. 55 20
2472. – 2 l. 55 pur. (Mozart).. 90 15
2473. – 3 l. 25 indigo (Rembrandt) .. 1·10 25

1956. Wild Life. As Nos. 2423/34 but colours changed. Imperf.
2474. 20 b. brown and green.. 12 5
2475. 20 b. black and blue .. 12 5
2476. 35 b. black and blue .. 12 5
2477. 50 b. black and brown.. 15 12
2478. 55 b. black and violet .. 15 12
2479. 55 b. brown and green .. 15 15
2480. 1 l. brown and blue .. 30 20
2481. 1 l. 55 brn. & yell.-brn. .. 45 20
2482. 1 l. 75 purple & green .. 85 20
2483. 2 l. black and blue .. 95 85
2484. 3 l. 25 brown and green.. 1·60 1·40
2485. 4 l. 25 brown and violet.. 2·25 1·60

1956. Air. Multicoloured designs embodying aeroplanes and views.
2486. 372. 20 b. City 12 5
2487. – 55 b. Mountains .. 15 5
2488. – 1 l. 75 Cornfield .. 55 12
2489. – 2 l. 55 Seashore .. 65 20

373. Georgi Enescu.

374. " Rebels " (after O. Bancila).

1956. Enescu (musician). 75th Birth Anniv.
2490. – 55 b. blue 25 8
2491. 373. 1 l. 75 maroon .. 70 15
DESIGN: 55 b. Enescu when a child, holding violin.

1957. Peasant Revolt. 50th Anniv.
2492. 374. 55 b. slate 20 5

375. Stephen the Great.

376. Dr. G. Marinescu and Institute of Medicine.

1957. Accession of Stephen the Great. 500th Anniv.
2493. 375. 55 b. brown 35 5
2494. 55 b. olive 20 5

1957. National Congress of Medical Sciences, Bucharest and Cent. of Medical and Pharmaceutical Teaching in Bucharest (1 l. 75).
2495. 376. 20 b. green 8 5
2496. – 35 b. chocolate .. 15 5
2497. – 55 b. purple 20 8
2498. – 1 l. 75 red and blue.. 65 20
DESIGNS: 35 b. Dr. I. Cantacuzino and Cantacuzino Institue. 55 b. Dr. V. Babes and Babes Institute. 1 l. 75 (66 × 23 mm.), Drs. N. Kretzulescu and C. Dairla, and Faculty of Medicine, Bucharest.

377. Gymnast and Spectator.

378. Emblems of Atomic Energy.

1957. 1st European Women's Gymnastic Championships, Bucharest.
2499. 377. 20 b. green 12 5
2500. – 35 b. red 20 8
2501. – 55 b. blue 45 8
2502. – 1 l. 75 purple .. 1·25 20
DESIGNS—HORIZ. 35 b. High jumping. 55 b. Vaulting over horse. VERT. 1 l. 75, Acrobatics.

1957. 2nd A.S.I.T. Congress.
2503. 378. 55 b. brown 40 8
2504. 55 b. blue 40 15

379. Dove and Handle-bars.

380. Rhododendron.

1957. 10th Int. Cycle Race.
2505. 379. 20 b. blue 8 5
2506. – 55 b. sepia 25 12
DESIGN: 55 b. Racing cyclist.

1957. Flowers of the Carpathian Mountains.
2513. **380.** 5 b. red and grey .. 5 5
2514. – 10 b. green and grey .. 5 5
2515. – 20 b. orange and grey .. 8 5
2516. – 35 b. olive and grey .. 15 8
2517. – 55 b. blue and grey .. 20 12
2518. – 1 l. red and grey .. 85 15
2519. – 1 l. 55 yellow and grey 1·10 20
2520. – 1 l. 75 violet and grey 1·40 30
FLOWERS: 10 b. Daphne. 20 b. Lily. 35 b. Edelweiss. 55 b. Gentian. 1 l. Dianthus. 1 l. 55, Primula. 1 l. 75, Anemone.

381. N. Grigorescu.

DESIGNS—HORIZ. 20 b. Country scene. 1 l. 75, Battle scene.

1957. Grigorescu (painter). 50th Death Anniv.
2521. – 20 b. green 15 5
2522. **381.** 55 b. brown 30 8
2523. – 1 l. 75 blue .. .. 1·10 20

382. Festival Visitors. 383. Festival Emblem.

1957. 6th World Youth Festival, Moscow.
2524. **382.** 20 b. purple 8 5
2525. – 55 b. green 20 5
2526. **383.** 1 l. orange 40 15
2527. – 1 l. 75 blue 65 20
DESIGNS: 55 b. Girl with flags. (22 × 38 mm.). 1 l. 75, Dancers (49 × 20 mm.).

384. Warship. 385. "The Trumpeter" (after N. Grigorescu).

1957. Navy Day.
2528. **384.** 1 l. 75 blue 55 12

1957. War of Independence. 80th. Anniv.
2529. **385.** 20 b. violet 20 5

386. Soldiers Advancing. 387. Child with Dove.

1957. Battle of Marasesti. 40th Anniv.
2530. **386.** 1 l. 75 brown .. 50 8

1957. Red Cross.
2531. **387.** 55 b. green and red .. 35 5

388. Sprinter and Bird. 389. Ovid.

1957. Int. Athletic Championships, Bucharest.
2532. **388.** 20 b. black and blue .. 15 5
2533. – 55 b. black and yellow 25 8
2534. 1 l. 75 black and red .. 70 15
DESIGNS: 55 b. Javelin-thrower and bull. 1 l. 75, Runner and stag.

1957. Ovid (Latin poet). Birth Bimillenary.
2535. **389.** 1 l. 75 blue 70 15

390. Congress Emblem. 391. Oil Refinery, 1957.

1957. 4th W.F.T.U. Congress, Leipzig.
2536. **390.** 55 b. blue 20 5

1957. Rumanian Petroleum Industry Cent.
2537. **391.** 20 b. brown 12 5
2538. 20 b. blue 12 5
2539. – 55 b. slate-purple .. 20 5
DESIGN: 55 b. Oil production, 1857: horse-operated borer.

392. Lenin, Youth and Girl. 393. Artificial Satellite encircling Globe.

1957. Russian Revolution. 40th Anniv. Inscr. "1917 1957".
2540. **392.** 10 b. red 5 5
2541. – 35 b. purple 15 5
2542. – 55 b. brown 20 5
DESIGNS—HORIZ. 35 b. Lenin and flags. 55 b. Statue of Lenin.

1957. Air. Launching of Artificial Satellite by Russia. Inscr. "SATELITII ARTIFICIALI".
2543. **393.** 25 b. green 30 5
2545. 25 b. blue 30 5
2544. – 3 l. 75 green .. .. 1·40 30
2546. – 3 l. 75 blue .. .. 1·40 30
DESIGN: 3 l. 75 (2), Satellite's orbit around Globe.
See also Nos. 2593/6.

394. Peasant Soldiers. 395. Endre Ady.

1957. Bobilna Revolution. 520th Anniv. Inscr. as in T **394.**
2547. **394.** 50 b. maroon .. 15 5
2548. – 55 b. slate 20 5
DESIGN—VERT. 55 b. Bobilna Memorial.

1957. Endre Ady (Hungarian poet). 80th Birth Anniv.
2549. **395.** 55 b. olive 25 5

395a. "Laika" & Satellite. 396. Wading Bird.

1957. Launching of Dog "Laika" in artificial satellite.
2550. **395a.** 1 l. 20 brown & green 95 35
2551. 1 l. 20 brown and blue 95 35

1957. Fauna of the Danube Delta.
2552. **396.** 5 b. grey & brn. (post). 5 5
2553. – 10 b. orange and green 5 5
2554. – 20 b. orange and red 5 5
2555. – 50 b. orange and green 15 5
2556. – 55 b. blue and maroon 15 5
2557. – 1 l. 30 orange & violet 55 10
2558. – 3 l. 30 grey & bl. (air) 90 20
2559. – 5 l. orange and red .. 1·60 30
DESIGNS—VERT. 10 b. Egret. 20 b. "Lopatar". 50 b. Fish. HORIZ. 55 b. White bear. 1 l. 30, Pelican. 3 l. 30, Seagull. 5 l. Vulture.

397. Emblem of Republic and Flags.

1957. People's Republic. 10th Anniv. Inscr. as in T **397.**
2560. **397.** 25 b. buff, red & blue 12 5
2561. – 55 b. yellow .. 20 5
2562. – 1 l. 20 red .. 15 15
DESIGNS: 55 b. Emblem, Industry and Agriculture. 1 l. 20, Emblem, the Arts and Sport.

398. Republican Flag. 399. "Telecommunications".

1958. Strike at Grivita. 25th Anniv.
2563. **398.** 1 l. red & brn. on buff 30 8
2564. 1 l. red & blue on buff 30 8

1958. Communist Postal Conference, Moscow. Inscr. as in T **399.**
2565. **399.** 55 b. violet 20 5
2566. – 1 l. 75 purple .. 45 15
DESIGN: 1 l. 75, Telegraph pole and pylons carrying lines.

400. N. Balcescu. 401. Fencer.

1958. Rumanian Writers.
2567. **400.** 5 b. indigo 5 5
2568. – 10 b. black (Ion Creanga) 5 5
2569. – 35 b. blue (Vlahuta) 10 5
2570. – 55 b. choc. (Eminescu) 15 10
2571. – 1 l. 75 sepia (Alecsandri) .. 45 10
2572. – 2 l. myrtle (Delavrancea) .. 55 20

1958. World Youth Fencing Championships, Bucharest.
2573. **401.** 1 l. 75 magenta .. 70 12

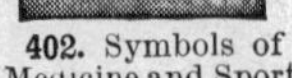

402. Symbols of Medicine and Sport. 403.

1958. Sports Doctors' Service. 25th Anniv.
2574. **402.** 1 l. 20 red and green 50 12

1958. 4th Int. Congress of Democratic Women.
2575. **403.** 55 b. blue 20 8

404. Linnaeus. 405. "Lepiota procera".

1958. Cultural Celebrities. Inscr. "MARILE ANIVERSARI CULTURALE 1957".
2576. **404.** 10 b. green .. 5 5
2577. – 20 b. brown (Comte) 8 5
2578. – 40 b. purple (Blake) 12 5
2579. – 55 b. blue (Glinka) .. 15 8
2580. – 1 l. plum (Longfellow) 30 10
2581. – 1 l. 75 bl. (Goldoni) .. 50 15
2582. – 2 l. olive-brown (Comenius) 80 20

1958. Mushrooms. As T **405.**
2583. **405.** 5 b. brn., light brn. & grey-blue 5 5
2584. – 10 b. brown, buff and bronze 5 5
2585. – 20 b. red, yell. & grey 5 5
2586. – 30 b. brn.-orge., orge. and green 8 5
2587. – 35 b. brn., light brn. and blue 10 5
2588. – 55 b. sepia, red & grn. 20 8
2589. – 1 l. brn., buff & turq. 35 12
2590. – 1 l. 55 pink, drab & grey 55 15
2591. – 1 l. 75 brown, buff and emerald 65 15
2592. – 2 l. yellow, brown and blue-green .. .. 1·00 35
MUSHROOMS: 10 b. "Clavaria aurea". 20 b. "Amanita caesarea". 30 b. "Lactarius deliciosus". 35 b. "Armillaria mellea". 55 b. "Coprinus comatus". 1 l. "Morchella conica". 1 l. 55, "Psalliota campestris". 1 l. 75, "Boletus edulis". 2 l. "Cantharellus cibarius".

1958. Brussels International Exhibition. Nos. 2543/4 and 2545/6 optd. **EXPOZITIA BRUXELLES 1958** and star or with star only.
2593. **393.** 25 b. green 45 12
2594. 25 b. blue 45 12
2595. – 1 l. 75 green .. .. 5·00 1·40
2596. – 1 l. 75 blue .. .. 5·00 1·40

406. Emil Racovita (scientist), Antarctic Map and Ship.

1958. Racovita Commem. Inscr. "1868 1947".
2597. **406.** 55 b. indigo and blue 35 12
2598. – 1 l. 20 violet and olive 35 8
DESIGN: 1 l. 20 Racovita and grotto.

407. Sputnik encircling Globe. 408. Servicemen's Statue.

1958. Air. Launching of Third Artificial Satellite by Russia.
2599. **407.** 3 l. 25 buff and indigo 1·40 12

1958. Army Day.
2600. **408.** 55 b. brown (postage) 12 5
2601. – 75 b. purple 15 5
2602. – 1 l. 75 blue 35 8
2603. – 3 l. 30 violet (air) .. 65 35
DESIGNS: 75 b. Soldier guarding industrial plant. 1 l. 75, Sailor hoisting flag. 3 l. 30, Pilot and aircraft.

409. Costumes of Oltenia. 410.

1958. Provincial Costumes. Female and male costumes as T **409/10.**
2604. **409.** 35 b. red and black on yellow 8 5
2605. **410.** 35 b. red and black on yellow 8 5
2606. – 40 b. red and brown on drab 12 5
2607. – 40 b. red and brown on drab 12 5
2608. – 50 b. red and brown on lilac 12 5
2609. – 50 b. red and brown on lilac 12 5
2610. – 55 b. red and brown on grey 20 8
2611. – 55 b. red and brown on grey 20 8
2612. – 1 l. red & brn. on pink 35 10
2613. – 1 l. red & brn. on pink 35 10
2614. – 1 l. 75 red and brown on blue 55 20
2615. – 1 l. 75 red and brown on blue 55 20

PROVINCES: Nos. 2606/7 Tara Oasului. 2608/9, Transylvania. 2610/11, Muntenia. 2612/3, Banat. 2614/5, Moldova.

411. Stamp Printer. 412. Runner.

1958. Rumanian Stamp Centenary. Inscr. "1858 1958".
2617. 411. 35 b. ultramarine .. 8 5
2618. – 55 b. brown 15 5
2619. – 1 l. 20 blue 35 12
2620. – 1 l. 30 plum 40 15
2621. – 1 l. 55 sepia 50 20
2622. – 1 l. 75 claret 65 20
2623. – 2 l. violet 80 30
2624. – 3 l. 30 brown .. .. 1·60 55
DESIGNS: 55 b. Scissors and Moldavian stamps of 1858. 1 l. 20, Driver with whip and mail coach. 1 l. 30, Postman with horn and mounted courier. 1 l. 55 to 3 l. 30, Moldavian stamps of 1858 (Nos. 1/4).

1958. 3rd Youth Spartacist Games.
2627. 412. 1 l. brown 40 12

413. Revolutionary Emblem. 414. Boy Bugler.

1958. Workers' Revolution. 40th Anniv.
2628. 413. 55 b. red 20 5

1958. Education Reform. 10th Anniv.
2629. 414. 55 b. red 20 5

415. Alexander Cuza. 416. First Cosmic Rocket.

1959. Union of Rumanian Provinces. Cent.
2630. 415. 1 l. 75 b. indigo .. 40 12

1959. Air. Launching of 1st Cosmic Rocket.
2631. 416. 3 l. 25 b. bl. on salmon 1·90 55

417. Charles Darwin. 418. Maize.

1959. Cultural Anniversaries.
2633. 417. 55 b. black (postage) 20 8
2634. – 55 b. blue (Robert Burns) 20 8
2635. – 55 b. red (Popov) .. 35 8
2636. – 55 b. purple (Sholem Aleichem) 20 8
2637. – 55 b. brown (Handel) 35 8
2638. – 3 l. 25 b. blue (Joliot-Curie) (air) .. 1·40 40

1959. Collective Farming in Rumania. 10th Anniv.
2639. 418. 55 b. green 35 5
2640. – 55 b. orange .. 35 5
2641. – 55 b. purple .. 35 5
2642. – 55 b. olive 35 5
2643. – 55 b. red-brown .. 35 5
2644. – 55 b. yellow-brown .. 35 5
2645. – 55 b. grey-blue .. 25 5
2646. – 55 b. bistre-brown .. 25 5
2647. – 5 l. crimson .. .. 1·40 30
DESIGNS—VERT. No. 2640, Sunflower with bee 2641, Sugar beet. HORIZ. 2642, Sheep, 2643, Cattle, 2644, Rooster and hens. 2645, Farm tractor, 2646, Farm wagon and horses. 2647 (38×26½ mm.), Farmer and wife, and wheat-field within figure "10".

419. Rock Thrush. 420.

1959. Air. Birds in natural colours. Inscriptions in grey. Colours of value tablets and backgrounds given.
2648. 419. 10 b. grey on buff .. 5 5
2649. – 20 b. grey on grey .. 5 5
2650. – 35 b. grey on greyish 8 5
2651. – 40 b. red on pinkish .. 12 5
2652. – 55 b. grey on greenish 15 5
2653. – 55 b. grey on cream .. 15 5
2654. – 55 b. green on azure .. 15 5
2655. – 1 l. red on yellow .. 35 15
2656. – 1 l. 55 red on pinkish 55 15
2657. – 5 l. grey on greenish 1·60 45
BIRDS—HORIZ. 20 b. Golden Oriole. 1 l. 55, Long-tailed Tit. 5 l. Wall Creeper. VERT. 35 b. Lapwing. 40 b. Swallow. 55 b. No. 2652, Great Spotted Woodpecker. 2653, Goldfinch. 2654, Great Tit. 1 l. Bullfinch.

1959. 7th World Youth Festival, Vienna. Inscr. "26 VII-4 VIII 1959".
2658. 420. 1 l. blue 20 8
2659. – 1 l. 60 red 45 12
DESIGN: 1 l. 60, Folk-dancer in national costume.

421. Workers and Banners. (422.)

1959. Liberation. 15th Anniv.
2660. 421. 55 b. chocolate, red, yellow and blue .. 20 5

1959. Air. Landing of Russian Rocket on the Moon. Surch. **h. 00.02'.24" 14-IX-1959. PRIMA RACHETA COSMICA IN LUNA 5 LEI** in red.
2662. 416. 5 l. on 3 l. 25 blue on salmon .. .. 2·75 1·10

1959. 8th Balkan Games. Optd. with T 422 in silver.
2663. 412. 1 l. brown .. .. 1·10 1·10

423. Peace Building, Bucharest.

1959. Bucharest. 500th Anniv. Inscr. as in T 423.
2664. – 20 b. black and blue .. 12 10
2665. 423. 40 b. black and brown 20 5
2666. – 55 b. black and bistre 20 5
2667. – 55 b. black and purple 20 8
2668. – 1 l. 55 black and lilac 45 15
2669. – 1 l. 75 black & turquoise 1·00 30
DESIGNS—HORI. 20 b. Prince Vlad Tepes and Charter. 55 b. (No. 2666), Athanaeum. 55 b. (No. 2667), "Scanteia" Printing House. 1 l. 55, Opera House. 1 l. 75, "23 August" Stadium.

424. Football. 425. Atomic Icebreaker "Lenin".

1959. International Sport. Multicoloured.
2671. 20 b. Type 424 (postage) 8 5
2672. 35 b. Motor-cycle racing 15 5
2673. 40 b. Ice-hockey 15 5
2674. 55 b. Handball 15 8
2675. 1 l. Horse-jumping .. 35 15
2676. 1 l. 50 Boxing 50 15
2677. 1 l. 55 Rugby football .. 55 20
2678. 1 l. 60 Tennis 55 20
2679. 2 l. 80 Hydroplaning (air) 1·10 35
The 35 b., 40 b., 1 l. 55, 1 l. 60 and 2 l. 80 values are horizontal designs.

1959. Launching of Atomic Icebreaker "Lenin".
2680. 425. 1 l. 75 violet 65 12

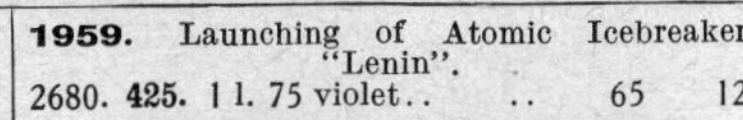

426. Stamp Album and Magnifier.

1959. Stamp Day.
2681. 426. 1 l. 60 (+40 b.) blue 55 25

427. Foxglove. 428. Cuza University.

1959. Medicinal Flowers. Multicoloured.
2682. 20 b. Type 427 .. .. 5 5
2683. 40 b. Peppermint .. 12 10
2684. 55 b. Camomile .. 35 5
2685. 55 b. Cornflower .. 30 5
2686. 1 l. Autumn crocus .. 30 15
2687. 1 l. 20 Monk's-hood .. 35 20
2688. 1 l. 55 Red poppy .. 40 20
2689. 1 l. 60 Linden 45 15
2690. 1 l. 75 Wild rose .. 55 25
2691. 3 l. 20 Adonis .. .. 1·10 45

1959. Cent. of Cuza University, Jassy.
2692. 428. 55 b. chocolate .. 20 8

429. Rocket, Dog and Rabbit. 430. G. Cosbuc.

1959. Air. Cosmic Rocket Flight.
2693. 429. 1 l. 55 blue .. .. 1·60 45
2694. – 1 l. 60 ultramarine on cream .. .. 1·00 35
2695. – 1 l. 75 blue .. .. 1·10 35
DESIGNS—HORIZ. (52×29½ mm.): 1 l. 60, Picture of "invisible" side of the Moon, with lists of place-names in Rumanian and Russian VERT. (as T 429): 1 l. 75, Lunik III's trajectory around the Moon.

1960. Rumanian Authors.
2696. 430. 20 b. indigo 8 5
2697. – 40 b. purple 15 5
2698. – 50 b. brown 15 5
2699. – 55 b. maroon 20 5
2700. – 1 l. violet 40 8
2701. – 1 l. 55 blue 55 12
PORTRAITS: 40 b. I. L. Caragiale. 50 b. G. Alexandrescu. 55 b. A. Donici. 1 l. C. Negruzzi. 1 l. 55. D. Bolintineanu.

431. Huchen (Danube salmon). 432.

1960. Rumanian Fauna
2702. 431. 20 b. blue (postage) .. 8 5
2703. – 55 b. choc. (Tortoise) 20 5
2704. – 1 l. 20 lilac (White duck) 35 12
2705. – 1 l. 30 blue (Golden eagle) (air) 35 12
2706. – 1 l. 75 grn. (Wild cock) 45 15
2707. – 2 l. red (Bearded vulture) 55 15

1960. Int. Women's Day. 50th Anniv.
2708. 432. 55 b. blue 25 8

433. Lenin (after painting by M. A. Gerasimov). 434. "Victory".

1960. Lenin. 90th Birth Anniv.
2709. 433. 40 b. purple 15 5
2710. – 55 b. blue (Statue of Lenin by Boris Curogea) 15 5

1960. Victory. 15th Anniv. Inscr. "Ziua Victoriei 1945 1946".
2712. 434. 40 b. blue 15 5
2714. 40 b. purple 30 20
2713. – 55 b. blue 20 8
2715. – 55 b. purple 35 30
DESIGN: 55 b. Statue of soldier with flag.

435. Rocket Flight.

1960. Air. Launching of Soviet Rocket.
2716. 435. 55 b. blue 55 12

436. Diving. 437. Gymnastics

1960. Olympic Games, Rome (1st issue). Multicoloured.
2717. 40 b. Type 436 .. 35 15
2718. 55 b. Gymnastics .. 35 20
2719. 1 l. 20 High-jumping .. 55 30
2720. 1 l. 60 Boxing 65 35
2721. 2 l. 45 Canoeing 90 65
2722. 3 l. 70 Canoeing .. .. 5·50 5·50
Nos. 2717/9 and 2720/1 are arranged together in "brickwork" fashion, se tenant in sheets, forming complete overall patterns of the Olympic rings.

1960. Olympic Games, Rome (2nd issue).
2723. – 20 b. grey-blue .. 12 5
2724. 437. 40 b. maroon .. 15 5
2725. – 55 b. blue 15 8
2726. – 1 l. red 25 15
2727. – 1 l. 60 purple .. 45 25
2728. – 2 l. lilac 55 35
DESIGNS: 20 b. Diving. 55 b. High-jumping. 1 l. Boxing. 1 l. 60, Canoeing. 2 l. Football.

438. Industrial Scholars. 439. Vlaicu and Aeroplane.

440. Ambulance 'Plane. 441. Pilot and Aeroplanes.

1960.
2731. 438. 3 b. magenta (post.) .. 5 5
2732. – 5 b. olive-brown .. 5 5
2733. – 10 b. slate-purple .. 5 5
2734. – 20 b. violet-blue .. 5 5
2735. – 30 b. vermilion .. 8 5
2736. – 35 b. red 8 5

2737. – 40 b. yellow-brown .. 8 5
2738. – 50 b. blue-violet .. 8 5
2739. – 55 b. blue 10 5
2740. – 60 b. emerald .. 10 5
2741. – 75 b. olive 15 5
2742. – 1 l. red 35 10
2743. – 1 l. 20 black 20 5
2744. – 1 l. 50 purple.. .. 25 5
2745. – 1 l. 55 blue-green .. 25 5
2746. – 1 l. 60 blue 35 12
2747. – 1 l. 75 brown.. .. 35 5
2748. – 2 l. sepia 40 5
2749. – 2 l. 40 violet.. .. 50 5
2750. – 3 l. grey-blue.. .. 55 5
2751. – 3 l. 20 blue (air) 65 35

DESIGNS—VERT. 5 b. Diesel train. 10 b. Dam. 20 b. Miner. 30 b. Doctor. 35 b. Textile worker. 50 b. Children at play. 55 b. Timber tractor. 1 l. Atomic reactor. 1 l. 20, Petroleum refinery. 1 l. 50, Iron-works. 1 l. 75, Mason. 2 l. Road-roller. 2 l. 40, Chemist. 3 l. Radio communications and television. HORIZ. 40 b. Grand piano and books. 60 b. Combine harvester. 75 b. Cattle-shed. 1 l. 55, Dock scene. 1 l. 60 Runner. 3 l. 30, Baneasa Airport, Bucharest.

1960. 1st Flight by A. Vlaicu. 50th Anniv. and Aviation Day.

2752. 439. 10 b. brown & yellow 5 5
2753. – 20 b. brown & orange 5 5
2754. 440. 35 b. red 8 5
2755. – 40 b. violet 12 5
2756. 441. 55 b. blue 15 5
2757. – 1 l. 60 multicoloured 40 20
2758. – 1 l. 75 multicoloured 55 20

DESIGNS—HORIZ. 20 b. Vlaicu in flying helmet and aeroplane. 40 b. Aeroplane spraying crops. (59×22 mm.). 1 l. 60 Airliner and airport control tower. 1 l. 75 Parachute descents.

442. Worker and Emblem.

1960. 3rd Workers' Party Congress.

2759. 442. 55 b. orge.-red & carm. 15 5

443. Tolstoy.

444. Tomis (Constantza)

1960. Cultural Anniversaries.

2760. 10 b. purple (T 443) .. 5 5
2761. 20 b. olive (Mark Twain) 8 5
2762. 35 b. blue (K. Hokusai).. 12 5
2763. 40 b. grey-grn. (De Musset) 12 5
2764. 55 b. chocolate (Defoe).. 15 5
2765. 1 l. blue-grn. (J. Bolyai).. 20 5
2766. 1 l. 20 claret (Chekhov).. 30 8
2767. 1 l. 55 slate (R. Koch).. 35 8
2768. 1 l. 75 brown (Chopin) .. 45 10

1960. Black Sea Resorts. Multicoloured.

2769. 20 b. T 444 (postage) .. 5 5
2770. 35 b. Constanta 8 5
2771. 40 b. V. Roaita 12 5
2772. 55 b. Mangalia 15 5
2773. 1 l. Eforie.. .. .. 30 10
2774. 1 l. 60 Eforie (different).. 45 15
2775. 2 l. Mamaia (air).. .. 40 20

445. Globe and Flags in form of puppet.

446. Children tobogganing.

1960. Int. Puppet Theatre Festival, Bucharest. Designs (24×28½ mm., except 20 b.) show puppets. Multicoloured.

2776. 20 b. T 445 .. .. 8 5
2777. 40 b. Petrushka 15 5
2778. 55 b. Punch 15 5
2779. 1 l. Kaspar 30 5
2780. 1 l. 20 Tindarica 30 10
2781. 1 l. 75 Vasilache.. .. 40 15

1960. Village Children's Games. Multicoloured.

2782. 20 b. T 446 .. .. 5 5
2783. 35 b. "Oina" (ball-game) 8 5
2784. 55 b. Ice-skating.. .. 15 5
2785. 1 l Running 20 8
2786. 1 l. 75 Swimming .. 40 10

The 20 b. and 1 l. are vert. and the rest horiz.

447. "Saturnia pyri" (moth).

1960. Air. Butterflies and Moths. Multicoloured.

2787. 10 b. Type 447 .. .. 5 5
2788. 20 b. "Limenitus Populi" 5 5
2789. 40 b. "Chrisophanus virgaureae" 8 5
2790. 55 b. "Papilio machaon" 15 5
2791. 1 l. 60 "Acherontia atropus" 45 15
2792. 1 l. 75 "Apatura iris" .. 65 20

SIZES—Triangular (36½×21½ mm.). 20 b., 40 b. VERT. (23½×34 mm.). 55 b., 1 l. 60. HORIZ. (34×23½ mm.). 1 l. 75.

448. Striker and Flag.

1960. General Strike. 40th Anniv.

2793. 448. 55 b. red and lake .. 15 5

449. Compass Points and Airliner.

1960. Air. Stamp Day.

2794. 449. 55 b. (+45 b.) blue.. 35 15

450. "XV", Globe and "Peace" Riband.

1960. World Democratic Youth Federation. 15th Anniv.

2795. 450. 55 b. yellow and blue 15 5

451. Herrings.

452. Woman tending Vine (Cotnari).

1960. Fish Culture. Fish in actual colours. Background colours given.

2796. – 10 b. turquoise .. 5 5
2797. – 20 b. violet-blue .. 5 5
2798. – 40 b. yellow .. 8 5
2799. 451. 55 b. slate 15 5
2800. – 1 l. claret 30 8
2801. – 1 l. 20 blue 40 12
2802. – 1 l. 60 olive 50 15

FISHES: 10 b. Carp. 20 b. Coal-fish. 40 b. Turbot. 1 l. Silurus. 1 l. 20, Sturgeon. 1 l. 60, Cod.

1960. Rumanian Vineyards. Multicoloured.

2803. 20 b. Dragasani 5 5
2804. 30 b. Dealul Mare (horiz.) 8 5
2805. 40 b. Odobesti (horiz.) .. 8 5
2806. 55 b. Type 452 .. .. 12 5
2807. 75 b. Tirnave 20 5
2808. 1 l. Minis 30 15
2809. 1 l. 20 Murfatlar.. .. 45 10

453. "Furnaceman" (after I. Irimescu).

454. Slalom Racer.

1961. Rumanian Sculptures.

2811. 453. 5 b. red 5 5
2812. – 10 b. violet 5 5
2813. – 20 b. black 5 5
2814. – 40 b. bistre-brown .. 8 5
2815. – 50 b. chocolate .. 12 5
2816. – 55 b. brown-red .. 15 5
2817. – 1 l. purple 30 8
2818. – 1 l. 55 blue 35 8
2819. – 1 l. 75 myrtle .. 40 8

SCULPTURES—VERT. 10 b. "Gh. Doja" (I. Vlad). 20 b. "Reunion" (B. Caragea). 40 b. "Enescu" (G. Anghel). 50 b. "Eminescu" (C. Baraschi). 1 l. "Peace" (I. Jalea). 1 l. 55, "Constructive Socialism" (C. Medrea). 1 l. 75, "Birth of an Idea" (A. Szobotka). HORIZ. 55 b. "Peasant Uprising, 1907" (M. Constantinescu).

1961. Air. Rumanian Winter Sports. 50th Anniv. Inscr. "1961". (a) Perf.

2820. – 10 b. olive and grey.. 5 5
2821. 454. 20 b. brn.-red & grey 5 5
2822. – 25 b. turquoise & grey 5 5
2823. – 40 b. violet and grey 10 5
2824. – 55 b. blue and grey .. 15 5
2825. – 1 l. crimson and grey 20 12
2826. – 1 l. 55 brown and grey 40 15

(b) Imperf.

2827. – 10 b. blue and grey.. 5 5
2828. 454. 20 b. brown and grey 8 5
2829. – 25 b. olive and grey.. 10 8
2830. – 40 b. crimson & grey 15 12
2831. – 55 b. turquoise & grey 20 15
2832. – 1 l. violet and grey .. 40 40
2833. – 1 l. 55 brn.-red & grey 85 85

DESIGNS—HORIZ. Skier: racing (10 b.), jumping (55 b), walking (1 l. 55). VERT. 25 b. Skiers climbing slope. 40 b. Toboggan. 1 l. Rock-climber.

455. P. Poni (chemist).

456. Yuri Gagarin in Capsule.

1961. Rumanian Scientists. Inscr. "1961". Portraits in black-brown.

2834. 455 10 b. ultram. & pink 5 5
2835. – 20 b. mar. & ol.-yell. 8 5
2836. – 55 b. red and blue .. 12 5
2837. – 1 l. 55 vio. & brn.-orge. 35 8

PORTRAITS: 20 b. A. Saligny (engineer). 55 b. C. Budeanu (electrical engineer). 1 l. 55, G. Titeica (mathematician).

1961. Air. World's First Manned Space Flight. Inscr. "12.IV.1961". (a) Perf.

2838. – 1 l. 35 blue 40 15
2839. 456. 3 l. 20 ultramarine .. 70 35

(b) Imperf

2840. 456. 3 l. 20 red .. .. 1·60 85

DESIGN—VERT. 1 l. 35, Yuri Gagarin.

457. Freighter "Galati".

1961. Merchant Navy. Multicoloured.

2841. 20 b. T 457 .. .. 5 5
2842. 40 b. Liner "Oltenita" 8 5
2843. 55 b. Hydroboat "Tomis" 15 5
2844. 1 l. Tramp ship "Arad" 20 5
2845. 1 l. 55 Tugboat "N. Cristea" 35 8
2846. 1 l. 75 Freighter "Dobrogea" 40 15

458. Red Flag with Marx, Engels and Lenin.

1961. Rumanian Communist Party 40th Anniv. Inscr. "1921–1961".

2847. 458. 35 b. multicoloured.. 8 5
2848. – 55 b. red, grey, maroon and yellow 15 5

DESIGN: 55 b. Two bill-posters.

459. Eclipse over Scanteia Building and Observatory.
460. Roe.

1961. Air. Solar Eclipse. Inscr. as in T 459.

2850. – 1 l. 60 ultramarine .. 45 20
2851. 459. 1 l. 75 blue 45 25

DESIGN: 1 l. 60, Eclipse over Palace Square, Bucharest.

1961. Forest Animals. Inscr. "1961". Multicoloured.

2852. 10 b. T 460 .. .. 5 5
2853. 20 b. Lynx 5 5
2854. 35 b. Wild boar 8 5
2855. 40 b. Bear 12 5
2856. 55 b. Stag 15 5
2857. 75 b. Fox 20 8
2858. 1 l. Goat 30 8
2859. 1 l. 55 Hare 40 12
2860. 1 l. 75 Badger 70 15
2861. 2 l. Roebuck .. 1·00 30

The 20, 35, 40 and 75 b. are horiz. and the rest vert.

461. George Enescu.

1961. 2nd Int. George Enescu Festival.

2862. 461. 3 l. lavender & choc. 70 35

462. Gagarin and Titov.
463. Iris.

1961. Air. 2nd Soviet Space Flight.

2863. – 55 b. blue 15 8
2864. – 1 l. 35 violet.. .. 35 15
2865. 462. 1 l. 75 red 50 20

DESIGNS—VERT. 55 b. "Vostok-2" in flight. 1 l. 35, G. S. Titov.

1961. Bucharest Botanical Gardens Cent. Flowers in natural colours. Background and inscription colours given. Perf. or imperf.

2866. – 10 b. yellow & brown 5 5
2867. – 20 b. yell.-grn. & crim. 5 5
2868. – 25 b. blue, grn. & red 8 5
2869. – 35 b. lilac and slate.. 8 5
2870. 463. 40 b. yellow & violet 10 5
2871. – 55 b. blue & ultram. 15 5
2872. – 1 l. orange and blue.. 20 8
2873. – 1 l. 20 cobalt & brown 35 12
2874. – 1 l. 55 chest. & lake.. 45 15

FLOWERS—HORIZ. 10 b. Primula. 35 b. Opuntia. 1 l. Hepatica. VERT. 20 b. Dianthus. 25 b. Peony. 55 b. Ranunculus. 1 l. 20, Poppy. 1 l. 55, Gentian.

464. Cobza Player.

465. Heraclides.

1961. Musicians. Multicoloured.

2876. 10 b. Pan piper 5 5
2877. 20 b. Alpenhorn player.. 5 5
2878. 40 b. Flautist 10 5
2879. 55 b. T 464 .. .. 20 5
2880. 60 b. Bagpiper 25 8
2881. 1 l. Cembalo player .. 35 12

The 20 b. is horiz. and the rest vert.

1961. Cultural Anniversaries. Inscr. as in T **465**.
2882. 10 b. maroon (T **465**) .. 5 5
2883. 20 b. brown (Sir Francis Bacon) 5 5
2884. 40 b. green (Tagore) .. 8 5
2885. 55 b. red (Sarmiento) .. 12 5
2886. 1 l. 35 blue (Von Kleist) 35 8
2887. 1 l. 75 vio. (Lomonosov) 50 15

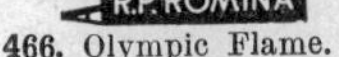

466. Olympic Flame. **468.** Tower Building, Republic Palace Square, Bucharest.

467. "Stamps Round the World".

1961. Olympic Games 1960, Gold Medal Awards. Inscr. "MELBOURNE 1956" or "ROMA 1960". Perf. or imperf.
2888. – 10 b. turq. & ochre .. 5 5
2889. **466.** 20 b. red 5 5
2890. – 20 b. grey 5 5
2891. – 35 b. brown and ochre 8 5
2892. – 40 b. purple & ochre 10 5
2893. – 55 b. ultramarine .. 15 8
2894. – 55 b. blue 20 8
2895. – 55 b. brn.-red & ochre 20 8
2896. – 1 l. 35 blue and ochre 50 15
2897. – 1 l. 75 red and ochre 65 35

DESIGNS (Medals)—DIAMOND: 10 b. Boxing. 35 b. Pistol-shooting. 40 b. Rifle-shooting. 55 b. (No. 2895), Wrestling. 1 l. 35, High-Jumping. VERT. as T **466**: 20 b. (No. 2890). Diving. 55 b. (No. 2893), Water-polo. 55 b. (No. 2894), Women's high-jumping. HORIZ. (45×33 mm.): 1 l. 75, Canoeing.

1961. Air. Stamp Day.
2899. **467.** 55 b. (+45 b.) blue, brown and red .. 35 20

1961. Air. Modern Rumanian Architecture. Multicoloured.
2900. 20 b. T **468** 5 5
2901. 40 b. Constantza Railway Station 8 5
2902. 55 b. Congress Hall, Republic Palace, Bucharest 12 5
2903. 75 b. Rolling mill, Hunedoara 15 8
2904. 1 l. Apartment blocks, Bucharest 20 8
2905. 1 l. 20 Circus Building, Bucharest 35 8
2906. 1 l. 75 Workers' Club, Mangalia 50 20

The 40 b. to 1 l. 75 are horiz.

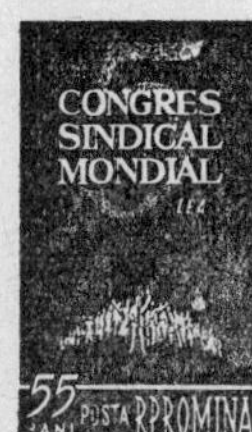

469. U.N. Emblem. **470.** Workers with Flags.

1961. U.N.O. 15th Anniv. Perf. or imperf.
2907. – 20 b. multicoloured.. 12 5
2908. – 40 b. multicoloured.. 12 5
2909. **469.** 55 b. multicoloured.. 15 5

DESIGNS (bearing U.N. emblem): 20 b. Peace dove over Eastern Europe. 40 b. Peace dove and youths of three races.

1961. 5th W.F.T.U. Congress, Moscow.
2910. **470.** 55 b. red 20 5

471. Cock and Savings Book. **472.** Footballer.

1962. Savings Day. Inscr. "1962".
2911. **471.** 40 b. pink, red, ol. & bl. 12 5
2912. – 55 b. black, red, yellow and blue .. 12 5

DESIGN: 55 b. Savings Bank book, bee and "honeycombs" of agriculture, housing and industry.

1962. European Junior Football Competition, Bucharest.
2913. **472.** 55 b. chest. & yell-grn. 20 8

473. Ear of Corn, Map and Tractor. **474.** Handball-player.

1962. Completion of Agricultural Collectivisation Project. Inscr. "1962".
2914. **473.** 40 b. red and orange 8 5
2915. – 55 b. lake & yellow .. 12 5
2916. – 1 l. 55 yell., red & bl. 35 12

DESIGNS: 55 b. Commemorative medal. 1 l. 55, Wheatsheaf, and hammer and sickle emblem

1962. Women's World Handball Championships, Bucharest.
2917. **474.** 55 b. violet & yellow 20 8

475. Canoe Race. **476.** J. J. Rousseau.

1962. Boating and Sailing. Inscr. "1962".

(a) Perf.
2918. **475.** 10 b. blue & magenta 5 5
2919. – 20 b. blue and olive.. 5 5
2920. – 40 b. blue & brown .. 8 5
2921. – 55 b. bl. & ultramarine 10 5
2922. – 1 l. blue and red .. 25 8
2923. – 1 l. 20 blue & purple.. 30 8
2924. – 1 l. 55 blue & orange 35 15
2925. – 3 l. blue and violet.. 65 20

(b) Imperf. Colours changed.
2926. **475.** 10 b. blue & ultram... 5 5
2927. – 20 b. blue & magenta 8 5
2928. – 40 b. blue & orange.. 8 5
2929. – 55 b. blue and olive.. 12 5
2930. – 1 l. blue and brown.. 30 20
2931. – 1 l. 20 blue & violet.. 40 25
2932. – 1 l. 55 blue and red.. 45 35
2933. – 3 l. blue and purple.. 1·25 45

DESIGNS: 20 b. Kayak. 40 b. Racing "eight". 55 b. Sculling. 1 l. Yachting. 1 l. 20, Motor-boats. 1 l. 55, Sailing. 3 l. Canoe slalom.

1962. Cultural Anniversaries (writers). Inscr. as in T **476**.
2934. **476.** 40 b. olive 8 5
2935. – 55 b. lake 12 5
2936. – 1 l. 75 blue 35 10

WRITERS: 55 b. I. L. Caragiale. 1 l. 75, A. I. Herzen.

477. Flags and Globes. **478.** T. Vuia (aviator).

1962. World Youth Festival, Helsinki.
2938. **477.** 55 b. blue, red, yellow and green 20 8

1962. Rumanian Celebrities.
2939. **478.** 15 b. brown 5 5
2940. – 20 b. claret 5 5
2941. – 35 b. purple 8 5
2942. – 40 b. indigo 12 5
2943. – 55 b. blue 12 5
2944. – 1 l. ultramarine .. 20 5
2945. – 1 l. 20 red 20 8
2946. – 1 l. 35 blue-green .. 35 8
2947. – 1 l. 55 violet.. .. 55 10

PORTRAITS: 20 b. A. Davila (writer). 35 b. V. Pirvan (archaeologist). 40 b. I. Negulici (painter). 55 b. G. Cobilcescu (geologist). 1 l. Dr. Marinescu. 1 l. 20, Dr. Cantacuzino. 1 l. 35, Dr. V. Babes. 1 l. 55, Dr. C. Levaditi.

479. Anglers by Pond.

1962. Fishing Sport. Multicoloured.
2948. 10 b. Rod-fishing in boats 8 5
2949. 25 b. Line-fishing in mountain pool .. 8 5
2950. 40 b. T **479** 12 5
2951. 55 b. Anglers on beach .. 12 5
2952. 75 b. Line-fishing in mountain stream .. 15 5
2953. 1 l. Shore-fishing .. 20 8
2954. 1 l. 75 Freshwater-fishing 35 15
2955. 3 l. 25 Fishing in Danube delta 65 35

480. Doves and "Space" Stamps of 1957/58. **481.** "Vostoks 3 and 4" in Orbit.

1962. Air. Cosmic Flights.
2956. **480.** 35 b. brown 12 5
2957. – 55 b. green 15 8
2958. – 1 l. 35 blue 45 20
2959. – 1 l. 75 red 60 30

DESIGNS—Dove and: 55 b. "Space" stamps of 1959. 1 l. 35, "Space" stamps of 1957 ("Laika"), 1959 and 1960. 1 l. 75, "Spacemen" stamps of 1961.

1962. Rumanian Victory in European Junior Football Competition, Bucharest. Surch. **1962. Campioana Europeana 2 lei.**
2961. **472.** 2 l. on 55 b. chestnut and yellow-green .. 80 45

1962. Rumanian Victory in Women's World Handball Championships, Bucharest. Surch. **Campioana Mondiala 5 lei**
2962. **474.** 5 l. on 55 b. violet and yellow .. .. 1·75 95

1962. Air. 1st "Team" Manned Space Flight.
2963. – 55 b. violet 15 5
2964. **481.** 1 l. 60 blue 50 15
2965. – 1 l. 75 purple.. .. 55 15

DESIGNS: 55 b. Cosmonaut Nikolaev. 1 l. 75, Cosmonaut Popovich.

482. Child and Butterfly. **483.** Pottery.

1962. Children.
2966. **482.** 20 b. blue, brown & red 5 5
2967. – 30 b. yellow, blue and brown-red .. 5 5
2968. – 40 b. grey-blue, red and turquoise .. 10 5
2969. – 55 b. olive, blue & red 12 5
2970. – 1 l. 20 red, sep. & ultram. 25 8
2971. – 1 l. 55 ochre, ult. & red 35 8

DESIGNS—VERT. 30 b. Girl feeding dove. 40 b. Boy with model yacht. 1 l. 20, Boy violinist and girl pianist. HORIZ. 55 b. Girl teaching boy to write. 1 l. 55, Pioneers around camp-fire.

1962. 4th Sample Fair, Bucharest. Inscr. "AL IV—LEA PAVILION DE MOSTRE —BUCURESTI 1962". Multicoloured.
2972. 5 b. T **483** (postage) .. 5 5
2973. 10 b. Preserved foodstuffs 5 5
2974. 20 b. Chemical products 5 5
2975. 40 b. Ceramics 8 5
2976. 55 b. Leather goods .. 15 5
2977. 75 b. Textiles 15 5
2978. 1 l. Furniture and fabrics 25 8
2979. 1 l. 20 Office equipment.. 35 8
2980. 1 l. 55 Needlework .. 45 12
2981. 1 l. 60 Fair pavilion (air) 65 20

The 1 l. 60 is horiz., the rest vert.

484. Lenin and Red Flag.

1962. Russian Revolution. 45th Anniv.
2982. **484.** 55 b. brown, red & blue 15 5

485. "The Coachmen" (after Szatmay).

1962. Air. Stamp Day and 1st Rumanian Stamps. Cent.
2983. **485.** 55 b. (+45 b.) black and blue 40 20

DESIGNS — HORIZ. 40 b. Ram. 1 l. 55, Heifer. 1 l. 75, Sows. VERT. 55 b. Bull. 1 l. Pig. 1 l. 35, Cow.

486. Lamb.

1962. Prime Farm Stock.
2984. **486.** 20 b. black and blue.. 5 5
2985. – 40 b. sep., yell. & blue 8 5
2986. – 55 b. myrtle, buff and orange 12 5
2987. – 1 l. brown, buff & grey 20 8
2988. – 1 l. 35 brn., blk. & grn. 30 10
2989. – 1 l. 55 sep., black & red 35 12
2990. – 1 l. 75 chestnut, cream and blue 45 15

The 55 b. to 1 l. 35 are vert., the rest horiz.

488. Strikers.

487. Arms, Industry and Agriculture. **489.** Tractor-driver.

1962. People's Republic. 15th Anniv.
2991 **487.** 1 l. 55 multicoloured 45 12

1963. Grivitsa Strike. 30th Anniv.
2992. **488.** 1 l. 75 multicoloured 40 15

1963. Freedom from Hunger.
2993. **489.** 40 b. blue 8 5
2994. – 55 b. brown 12 5
2995. – 1 l. 55 red 30 12
2996. – 1 l. 75 green.. .. 35 15

DESIGNS (each with F.A.O. emblem): 55 b. Girl harvester. 1 l. 55, Child with beaker of milk. 1 l. 75, Girl vintager.

1963. Air. Rumanian Philatelists' Conference, Bucharest. No. 2983, optd. **A.F.R.** surrounded by **CONFERINTA PE TARA BUCURESTI 30-III-1963** in diamond shape.
2997. **485.** 55 b. (+45 b.) black and blue 45 35

The opt. is applied in the middle of the se-tenant pair—stamp and 45 b. label.

490. Sighisoara Glass Factory. **491.** Tomatoes.

1963. Air. "Socialist Achievements".
2998. **490.** 30 b. blue and red .. 5 5
2999. – 40 b. myrtle & violet 8 5
3000. – 55 b. claret & ultram. 10 5
3001. – 1 l. violet and brown 20 8
3002. – 1 l. 55 red and blue .. 30 10
3003. – 1 l. 75 ultram. & pur. 30 15
DESIGNS: 40 b. Govora soda works. 55 b. Tirgul-Jiu wood factory. 1 l. Savinesti chemical works. 1 l. 55, Hunedoara metal works. 1 l. 75, Brazi thermic power station.

1963. Vegetable Culture. Multicoloured.
3004. 35 b. T **491** 8 5
3005. 40 b. Hot peppers .. 8 5
3006. 55 b. Radishes.. .. 12 5
3007. 75 b. Aubergines .. 15 8
3008. 1 l. 20 Mild peppers .. 40 12
3009. 3 l. 25 Cucumbers (horiz.) 85 35

492. Moon Rocket "Luna 4". **493.** Chick.

1963. Air. Launching of Soviet Moon Rocket "Luna 4". The 1 l. 75 is imperf.
3010. **492.** 55 b. red and blue .. 15 5
3011. 1 l. 75 red and violet 50 15

1963. Domestic Poultry.
3012. **493.** 20 b. yellow and blue 5 5
3013. – 30 b. red, blue & drab 8 5
3014. – 40 b. blue, orange and orange-brown .. 8 5
3015. – 55 b. red, bistre, blue and turquoise .. 12 5
3016. – 70 b. blue, red & pur. 15 5
3017. – 1 l. red, slate and blue 20 10
3018. – 1 l. 35 red, blue & ochre 30 12
3019. – 3 l. 20 red, violet, blue and green 65 35
POULTRY: 30 b. Cockerel. 40 b. Duck. 55 b. White Leghorn. 70 b. Goose. 1 l. Rooster. 1 l. 35, Turkey (cock). 3 l. 20, Turkey (hen).

494. Diving. **495.** Congress Emblem

1963. Swimming. Bodies in drab.
3020. **494.** 25 b. green and brown 5 5
3021. – 30 b. yellow and olive 8 5
3022. – 55 b. red & grsh.-blue 10 5
3023. – 1 l. red and green .. 20 12
3024. – 1 l. 35 magenta & blue 25 12
3025. – 1 l. 55 orange & violet 30 12
3026. – 2 l. yellow & magenta 40 20
DESIGNS—HORIZ. 30 b. Crawl. 55 b. Butterfly 1 l. Back-stroke. 1 l. 35, Breast-stroke. VERT. 1 l. 55, Swallow-diving. 2 l. Water-polo.

1963. Int. Women's Congress, Moscow.
3027. **495.** 55 b. blue 15 5

496. Bykovsky and Globe.

DESIGN: 1 l. 75, Tereshkova and globe.

1963. Air. 2nd "Team" Manned Space Flights.
3028. **496.** 55 b. blue 15 5
3029. – 1 l. 75 red 35 15

497. Steam Locomotive. **498.** W. M. Thackeray (writer).

1963. Air. Transport. Multicoloured.
3031. 40 b. Type **497** 12 5
3032. 55 b. Diesel freight locomotive.. .. .. 15 5
3033. 75 b. Trolley bus .. 20 8
3034. 1 l. 35 Motor ship .. 30 15
3035. 1 l. 75 Airliner 40 15

1963. Cultural Anniversaries. Inscr. "MARILE ANNIVERSARI CULTURALE 1963".
3036. **498.** 40 b. black and lilac 8 5
3037. – 50 b. black and brown 8 5
3038. – 55 b. black and olive 10 8
3039. – 1 l. 55 black and red 30 8
3040. – 1 l. 75 black and blue 35 8
PORTRAITS: 50 b. Delacroix (painter). 55 b. G. Marinescu (physician). 1 l. 55, G. Verdi (composer). 1 l. 75, K. Stanislavsky (theatrical producer).

499. Walnuts. **500.** Volleyball.

1963. Fruits and Nuts. Multicoloured.
3041. 10 b. Type **499** .. 5 5
3042. 20 b. Plums 5 5
3043. 40 b. Peaches 8 5
3044. 55 b. Strawberries .. 12 5
3045. 1 l. Grapes 20 8
3046. 1 l. 55 Apples 35 12
3047. 1 l. 60 Cherries 40 12
3048. 1 l. 75 Pears 45 12

1963. Air. Aurel Vlaicu (aviation pioneer). 50th Death Anniv. No. 2752 surch. **1913-1963. 50 ani de la moarte 1,75 lei.**
3049. **439.** 1 l. 75 on 10 b. chocolate and yellow .. 45 20

1963. European Volleyball Championships.
3050. **500.** 5 b. magenta and grey 5 5
3051. – 40 b. blue and grey .. 8 5
3052. – 55 b. turquoise & grey 12 5
3053. – 1 l. 75 chestnut & grey 30 15
3054. – 3 l. 20 violet and grey 65 35
DESIGNS: 40 b. to 1 l. 75, Various scenes of play at net. 3 l. 20, European Cup.

501. Rumanian 1 l. 55 "Centenary" stamp of 1958.

1963. Air. Stamp Day and 15th U.P.U. Congress. Inscr. "AL XV-LEA CONGRESS", etc.
3055. **501.** 20 b. sepia & light blue 5 5
3056. – 40 b. blue & magenta 8 5
3057. – 55 b. lake and blue .. 15 8
3058. – 1 l. 20 violet and buff 30 15
3059. – 1 l. 55 olive and red .. 40 15
3060. – 1 l. 60+50 b. green, red, bistre and grey .. 70 30
DESIGNS (Rumanian stamps): 40 b. (1 l. 20) "Laika", 1957 (blue). 55 b. (3 l. 20) "Gagarin") 1961. 1 l. 20 (55 b.) "Nikolaev" and (1 l. 75. "Popovich", 1962. 1 l. 55 (55 b.) "Postwoman", 1953. 1 l. 60, U.P.U. Monument, Berne, Globe, map of Rumania and aircraft (36½×27 mm.)

502. Ski-jumping.

1963. Winter Olympic Games, Innsbruck. 1964. (a) Perf.
3061. **502.** 10 b. blue and red .. 5 5
3062. – 20 b. brown and blue 10 5
3063. – 40 b. brown and green 20 5
3064. – 55 b. brown & violet 25 5
3065. – 60 b. blue & orge.-brn. 25 5
3066. – 75 b. blue and magenta 40 5
3067. – 1 l. ultram. and ochre 55 5
3068. – 1 l. 20 ultram. & turq. 60 5

(b) Imperf. Colours changed.
3069. **502.** 10 b. brown and green 60 50
3070. – 20 b. brown and violet 60 50
3071. – 40 b. blue and red .. 60 50
3072. – 55 b. brown and blue 60 50
3073. – 60 b. ultram. & turq. 60 50
3074. – 75 b. ultram. and ochre 60 50
3075. – 1 l. blue and magenta 60 50
3076. – 1 l. 20 bl. & orge.-brn. 60 50
DESIGNS: 20 b. Ice-skating. 40 b. Ice-hockey, 55 b. Figure-skating. 60 b. Slalom. 75 b. Rifle-shooting on skis. 1 l. Bobsleigh. 1 l. 20. Skiing.

503. Cone, Fern and Conifer. **504.** Silk Moth.

1963. Reafforestation Campaign. 18th Anniv.
3078. **503.** 55 b. green 15 5
3079. – 1 l. 75 blue 35 15
DESIGN: 1 l. 75, Chestnut trees.

1963. Bee-keeping and Silkworm-breeding. Multicoloured.
3080. 10 b. Type **504** 5 5
3081. 20 b. Moth emerging from chrysalis 5 5
3082. 40 b. Silkworm 8 5
3083. 55 b. Bee 15 5
3084. 60 b. } Bee extracting 20 5
3085. 1 l. 20 } nectar from 30 10
3086. 1 l. 35 } various flowers 40 12
3087. 1 l. 60 } (diff. designs) 55 15
The 55 b. to 1 l. 60 are horiz.

505. Carved Pillar. **507.** G. Stephanescu.

506. Gagarin.

1963. Village Museum, Bucharest.
3088. **505.** 20 b. purple 5 5
3089. – 40 b. blue 8 5
3090. – 55 b. slate-violet .. 12 5
3091. – 75 b. green 15 5
3092. – 1 l. claret and brown 20 8
3093. – 1 l. 20 bronze-green.. 25 8
3094. – 1 l. 75 blue and brown 50 12
DESIGNS: Various Rumanian peasant houses. The 40 b. and 55 b. are horiz., the rest vert.

1964. Air. "Space Navigation". Soviet flag, red and yellow; U.S. flag, red and blue; backgrounds, light blue; portrait and inscription colours below. (a) Perf.
3095. **506.** 5 b. ultramarine .. 5 5
3096. – 10 b. violet 5 5
3097. – 20 b. bronze.. .. 8 5
3098. – 35 b. slate 12 5
3099. – 40 b. bluish violet .. 12 8
3100. – 55 b. bluish violet .. 15 8
3101. – 60 b. sepia 20 10
3102. – 75 b. blue 30 12
3103. – 1 l. purple 40 20
3104. – 1 l. 40 purple 50 25

(b) Imperf. Colours changed.
3105. **506.** 5 b. violet 5 5
3106. – 10 b. ultramarine .. 8 5
3107. – 20 b. slate 15 8
3108. – 35 b. bronze .. 30 15
3109. – 40 b. purple 40 20
3110. – 55 b. purple 50 25
3111. – 60 b. blue 50 30
3112. – 75 b. sepia 60 40
3113. – 1 l. bluish violet .. 70 60
3114. – 1 l. 40 bluish violet 1·10 70
PORTRAITS (with flags of their countries)—As T **506**: 10 b. G. Titov. 20 b. J. Glenn. 35 b. S. Carpenter. 60 b. W. Schirra. 75 b. G. Cooper. SQUARE (35×34 mm.): 40 b. A. Nikolaev. 55 b. P. Popovich. 1 l. V. Bykovsky. 1 l. 40, V. Tereshkova.

1964. Rumanian Opera Singers and their stage roles. Portraits in brown.
3116. **507.** 10 b. olive 5 5
3117. – 20 b. ultramarine .. 5 5
3118. – 35 b. green 8 5
3119. – 40 b. light blue .. 8 5
3120. – 55 b. magenta .. 10 5
3121. – 75 b. reddish violet.. 15 5
3122. – 1 l. blue 25 8
3123. – 1 l. 35 violet.. .. 35 10
3124. – 1 l. 55 red 45 12
SINGERS: 20 b. Elena Teodorini. 35 b. I. Bajenaru. 40 b. D. Popovici. 55 b. Hariclea Darclee. 75 b. G. Folescu. 1 l. J. Athanasiu. 1 l. 35. T. Grosavescu. 1 l. 55, N. Leonard.

508. Prof. G. M. Murgoci. **509.** "Ascalaphus macaronius" (moth).

1964. 8th Int. Soil Congress, Bucharest.
3125. **508.** 1 l. 60 indigo, ochre and blue 35 15

1964. Rumanian Insects. Multicoloured.
3126. 5 b. Type **509** 5 5
3127. 10 b. "Ammophila sabulosa" (flying ant) .. 5 5
3128. 35 b. "Scolia maculata" (wasp) 8 5
3129. 40 b. "Rhyparioides metelkana" (moth) .. 8 5
3130. 55 b. "Lymantria dispar" (moth) 12 5
3131. 1 l. 20 "Kanetisa circe" (butterfly) 30 10
3132. 1 l. 55 "C. Fabricii malachiticus" (beetle) .. 35 15
3133. 1 l. 75 "Procerus gigas" (horned beetle).. .. 40 15

510. "Nicotiana alata". **511.** Cross Country.

1964. Rumanian Flowers. Multicoloured.
3134. 10 b. Type **510** 5 5
3135. 20 b. "Pelargonium" .. 5 5
3136. 40 b. "Fuchsia gracilis" 8 5
3137. 55 b. "Chrysanthemum indicum" 15 5
3138. 75 b. "Dahlia hybrida" 15 5
3139. 1 l. "Lilium croceum".. 20 8
3140. 1 l. 25 "Hosta ovata" .. 25 10
3141. 1 l. 55 "Tagetes erectus" 40 15

1964. Horsemanship.
3142. – 40 b. crimson, black, purple and blue .. 8 5
3143. **511.** 55 b. brn., red & lilac 12 5
3144. – 1 l. 35 brn., red & grn. 25 15
3145. – 1 l. 55 mag., blue & bis. 45 15
DESIGNS—HORIZ. 40 b. Show jumping. 1 l. 55, Horse-race. VERT. 1 l. 35, Dressage.

512. Scorpionfish. **513.** M. Eminescu (poet).

1964. Constantza Aquarium. Fish designs. Multicoloured.
3146. 5 b. Type **512** .. 5 5
3147. 10 b. Blenny .. 5 5
3148. 20 b. Mackerel .. 5 5
3149. 40 b. Nisetru Sturgeon 8 5
3150. 50 b. Seahorse .. 10 5
3151. 55 b. Gurnard .. 12 5
3152. 1 l. Bekuga Sturgeon 20 8
3153. 3 l. 20 Sting Ray .. 65 25

1964. Cultural Anniversaries. Portraits in brown.
3154. 5 b. green (Type **513**) .. 5 5
3155. 20 b. lake (I. Creanga) .. 5 5
3156. 35 b. red (E. Girleanu) .. 8 5
3157. 55 b. bistre (Michelangelo) 12 5
3158. 1 l. 20 blue (Galileo) .. 20 10
3159. 1 l. 75 violet (Shakespeare) 35 12
Nos. 3154/5 commemorate 75th anniv. of death. No. 3156, 50th anniv. of death. No. 3157, 400th anniv. of death. Nos. 3158/9 400th anniv. of birth. Creanga and Girleanu were writers.

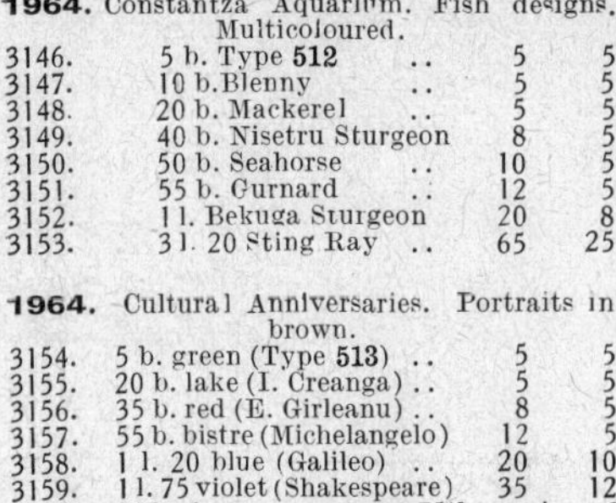

514. Cheile Bicazului (gorge). **515.** High-jumping.

1964. Mountain resorts.
3160. **514.** 40 b. lake 8 5
3161. – 55 b. blue 15 5
3162. – 1 l. maroon 20 8
3163. – 1 l. 35 sepia 30 10
3164. – 1 l. 75 green 40 12
DESIGNS—VERT. 55 b. Cabin on Lake Bilea. 1 l. Polana Brasov ski-lift. 1 l. 75, Alpine Hotel. HORIZ. 1 l. 35, Lake Bicaz.

1964. Balkan Games. Inscr. as in T **515**. Multicoloured.
3165. 30 b. Type **515** .. 5 5
3166. 40 b. Throwing the javelin 12 5
3167. 55 b. Running .. 15 8
3168. 1 l. Throwing the discus 30 12
3169. 1 l. 20, Hurdling .. 40 15
3170. 1 l. 55, Flags of competing countries (24 × 44 mm.) 50 15

516. Arms and Flag.

1964. Liberation. 20th Anniv. Inscr. "1944 1964". Multicoloured.
3171. 55 b. Type **516** .. 8 5
3172. 60 b. Industrial plant .. 8 5
3173. 75 b. Harvest scene .. 12 5
3174. 1 l. 20, Apartment houses 20 8
Nos. 3172/4 are horiz.

517. High-jumping.

1964. Olympic Games, Tokyo. Multicoloured. (a) Perf.
3176. 20 b. Type **517** 5 5
3177. 30 b. Wrestling 8 5
3178. 35 b. Volley-ball 10 5
3179. 40 b. Canoeing 12 5
3180. 55 b. Fencing 15 8
3181. 1 l. 20, Gymnastics .. 35 15
3182. 1 l. 35, Football 35 15
3183. 1 l. 55, Rifle-shooting .. 45 20

(b) Imperf. Colours changed and new values.
3184. 20 b. Type **517** 8 5
3185. 30 b. Wrestling 10 8
3186. 35 b. Volley-ball 15 8
3187. 40 b. Canoeing 15 8
3188. 55 b. Fencing 20 15
3189. 1 l. 60, Gymnastics .. 60 40
3190. 2 l. Football 70 45
3191. 2 l. 40, Rifle-shooting .. 85 55

518. George Enescu. **519.** Python.

520. Brincoveanu, Cantacuzino, Lazar and Academy. **521.** Soldier.

1964. 3rd Int. Georgi Enescu Festival.
3193. **518.** 10 b. green 5 5
3194. – 55 b. maroon .. 10 5
3195. – 1 l. 60 brown-purple 30 10
3196. – 1 l. 75 blue .. 40 15
DESIGNS (Portraits of Enescu): 55 b. At piano. 1 l. 60, Medallion. 1 l. 75, When an old man.

1964. Bucharest Zoo. Multicoloured.
3197. 5 b. Type **519** 5 5
3198. 10 b. Black swans .. 5 5
3199. 35 b. Ostriches 8 5
3200. 40 b. Crowned cranes .. 8 5
3201. 55 b. Tigers 15 8
3202. 1 l. Lions 30 12
3203. 1 l. 55, Zebras 45 15
3204. 2 l. Camels 65 20

1964. Anniversaries. Multicoloured.
3205. 20 b. Type **520** 5 5
3206. 40 b. Cuza and seal .. 8 5
3207. 55 b. Emblems and the Arts (vert.) 10 5
3208. 75 b. Laboratory workers and class 12 5
3209. 1 l. Savings Bank building 15 8
Events, etc.: 20 b. 270th Anniv. of Domneasca Academy. 40 b. and 75 b. Bucharest University Cent. 55 b. "Fine Arts" Cent. (emblems are masks, curtains, piano keyboard, harp, palette and brushes). 1 l. Savings Bank Cent.

1964. Army Day. Cent.
3210. **521.** 55 b. blue & lt. blue .. 15 5

No. 3211 is a two-part design, the two parts being arranged vert. imperf. between.

522. Post Offices of 19th and 20th Centuries.

1964. Air. Stamp Day.
3211. **522.** 1 l. 60 + 40 b. blue red and yellow .. 35 20

523. Canoeing Medal (1956). **524.** Strawberries.

1964. Olympic Games—Rumanian Gold Medal Awards. Medals in brown and bistre (Nos. 3218/19 and 3226/7 in sepia and gold). (a) Perf.
3212. **523.** 20 b. red and blue .. 5 5
3213. – 30 b. green and blue 12 5
3214. – 35 b. turquoise & blue 15 8
3215. – 40 b. lilac and blue .. 15 8
3216. – 55 b. orange and blue 20 8
3217. – 1 l. 20 green and blue 40 20
3218. – 1 l. 35 brown and blue 50 30
3219. – 1 l. 55 mauve and blue 65 30

(b) Imperf. Colours changed and new values.
3220. **523.** 20 b. orange and blue 8 5
3221. – 30 b. turquoise & blue 15 8
3222. – 35 b. green and blue 15 8
3223. – 40 b. green and blue 20 12
3224. – 55 b. red and blue .. 25 15
3225. – 1 l. 60 lilac and blue .. 70 40
3226. – 2 l. mauve and blue .. 95 60
3227. – 2 l. 40 brown and blue 1·10 70
MEDALS: 30 b. Boxing (1956). 35 b. Pistol-shooting (1956). 40 b. High-jumping (1960). 55 b. Wrestling (1960). 1 l. 20, 1 l. 60, Rifle-shooting (1960). 1 l. 35, 2 l. High-jumping (1964). 1 l. 55, 2 l. 40, Throwing the javelin (1964).

1964. Forest Fruits. Multicoloured.
3229. 5 b. Type **524** 5 5
3230. 35 b. Blackberries .. 8 5
3231. 40 b. Raspberries .. 8 5
3232. 55 b. Rosehips 12 5
3233. 1 l. 20, Blueberries .. 25 8
3234. 1 l. 35, Cornelian cherries 30 10
3235. 1 l. 55, Hazel nuts .. 40 12
3236. 2 l. 55, Cherries 55 20

525. "Syncom 3". **526.** U.N. Headquarters, New York.

1965. Space Navigation. Multicoloured.
3237. 30 b. Type **525** 12 5
3238. 40 b. "Syncom 3" (different view) .. 12 5
3239. 55 b. "Ranger 7" .. 15 5
3240. 1 l. "Ranger 7" (different view) 30 8
3241. 1 l. 20 "Voskhod 1" .. 35 12
3242. 5 l. Feoktistov, Komarov and Yegorov, and "Voskhod 1" ($52\frac{1}{2} \times 29\frac{1}{2}$ mm.) 1·25 65
Nos. 3239/42 are horiz.

1965. U.N.O. 20th Anniv.
3243. **526.** 55 b. gold, blue & red 30 5
3244. – 1 l. 60 gold, blue, yellow and red .. 55 15
DESIGN: 1 l. 60, Arms and U.N. emblem on Rumanian flag.

527. Tortoise ("Testudo graeca").

1965. Reptiles. Multicoloured.
3245. 5 b. Type **527** 5 5
3246. 10 b. "Lacerta taurica" 5 5
3247. 20 b. "Lacerta trilineata" 5 5
3248. 40 b. "Alepharus kitalbelli" .. 8 5
3249. 55 b. "Anguis fragilis" 8 5
3250. 60 b. "Vipera ammodytes" 12 5
3251. 1 l. "Eremias arguta" .. 20 8
3252. 1 l. 20, "Vipera ursinii" 25 8
3253. 1 l. 35, "Coluber jugularis" .. 35 10
3254. 3 l. 25, "Elaphe quatuorlineata" .. 85 30

528. Tabby Cat. **529.** Ion Bianu (philologist).

1965. Domestic Cats. Multicoloured.
3255. 5 b. Type **528** 5 5
3256. 10 b. Ginger tomcat .. 5 5
3257. 40 b. White Persians .. 8 5
3258. 55 b. Kittens with shoe .. 10 5
3259. 60 b. Kitten with ball of wool 12 8
3260. 75 b. Cat and two kittens 20 10
3261. 1 l. 35, Siamese 30 35
3262. 3 l. 25, Heads of three cats (62 × 29 mm.) .. .. 1·10 60
Nos. 3257/61 are vert.

1965. Space Flight of "Ranger 9" (24.3.65). No. 3240 surch. **RANGER 9 24-3-1965 5 Lei** and floral emblem over old value.
3263. 5 l. on 1 l. multicoloured 6·00 7·00

1965. Cultural Anniversaries. Portraits in sepia.
3264. **529.** 40 l. blue 5 5
3265. – 55 b. ochre 8 5
3266. – 60 b. purple 12 8
3267. – 1 l. red 20 15
3268. – 1 l. 35 olive 35 20
3269. – 1 l. 75 vermilion .. 45 20
PORTRAITS, etc.: 40 b. (30th death anniv.). 55 b. A. Bacalbasa (writer: birth cent.). 60 b. V. Conta (philosopher: 120th birth anniv.). 1 l. Jean Sibelius (composer: birth cent.). 1 l. 35, Horace (poet: birth bimillenary). 1 l. 75, Dante (poet: 700th birth anniv.).

530. I.T.U. Emblem and Symbols.

1965. I.T.U. Cent.
3270. **530.** 1 l. 75 blue 50 30

531. Derdap Gorge (The Iron Gate).

1965. Derdap Hydro-Electric Project Inaug.
3271. **531.** 30 b. (25 d.) green and grey 12 8
3272. – 55 b. (50 d.) red & grey 20 15
DESIGN: 55 b. Derdap Dam.
Nos. 3271/72 were issued simultaneously in Yugoslavia.

532. Rifleman. **533.** "Fat-Frumos and the Beast".

1965. European Shooting Championships, Bucharest. Multicoloured. (a) Perf.
3274. 20 b. Type **532** .. 5 5
3275. 40 b. Prone rifleman .. 8 5
3276. 55 b. Pistol-shooting .. 12 5
3277. 1 l. "Free" pistol-shooting 20 15
3278. 1 l. 60 Standing rifleman 30 15
3279. 2 l. Various marksmen .. 40 30

(b) Imperf. Colours changed and new values.
3280. 40 b. Prone rifleman .. 8 5
3281. 55 b. Pistol-shooting .. 12 8
3282. 1 l. "Free" pistol-shooting 20 12
3283. 1 l. 60 Standing rifleman 35 15
3284. 3 l. 25 Type **532** 70 35
3285. 5 l. Various marksmen .. 1·10 60
Apart from T **532** the designs are horiz., the 2 l. and 5 l. being larger ($51\frac{1}{2} \times 28\frac{1}{2}$ mm.).

1965. Rumanian Fairy Tales. Multicoloured.
3286. 20 b. Type **533** 5 5
3287. 40 b. "Fat-Frumos and Ileana Cosinzeana" .. 5 5
3288. 55 b. "Harap Alb" (horse-man and bear) .. 10 5
3289. 1 l. "The Moralist Wolf" 20 5
3290. 1 l. 35 "The Ox and the Calf" 45 8
3291. 2 l. "The Bear and the Wolf" (drawing a sledge) 65 15

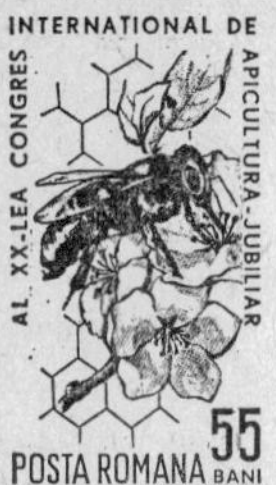

534. Bee on Flowers. **535.** Beliaiev, Leonov, "Voskhod 2" and Leonov in Space.

1965. 20th Int. Bee-keeping Associations Federation ("Apimondia") Congress, Bucharest.

3292. **534.** 55 b. black, red & yell. 20 8
3293. – 1 l. 60 black, green, buff and blue .. 35 20

DESIGN—HORIZ. 1 l. 60, Congress Hall.

1965. Space Achievements. Multicoloured.

3294. 5 b. "Proton 1" .. 5 5
3295. 10 b. "Sonda 3" (horiz.) 5 5
3296. 15 b. "Monia 1" .. 5 5
3297. 1 l. 75 Type **535** .. 45 15
3298. 2 l. 40 "Early Bird" satellite 65 30
3299. 3 l. 20 "Gemini 3" and astronauts in capsule .. 1·10 35
3300. 3 l. 25 "Mariner 4" .. 1·10 30
3301. 5 l. "Gemini 5" (horiz.) 1·50 45

536. Marx and Lenin. **538.** V. Alecsandri (poet).

537. Quail.

1965. Postal Ministers' Congress, Peking.

3302. **536.** 55 b. multicoloured .. 15 5

1965. Migratory Birds. Multicoloured.

3303. 5 b. Type **537** 5 5
3304. 10 b. Woodcock 5 5
3305. 20 b. Snipe 15 5
3306. 40 b. Turtle dove .. 8 5
3307. 55 b. Mallard 10 5
3308. 60 b. White-fronted goose 15 5
3309. 1 l. Crane 30 12
3310. 1 l. 20 Glossy ibis .. 40 15
3311. 1 l. 35 Mute swan .. 45 15
3312. 3 l. 25 White pelican .. 1·10 40

The 3 l. 25, is vert., 32 × 73 mm.

1965. Vasile Alecsandri. 75th Death Anniv.

3313. **538.** 55 b. multicoloured .. 15 5

539. "Nymphaea zanzibariensis".

1965. Cluj Botanical Gardens. Multicoloured.

3314. 5 b. "Strelitzia reginae" (crane flower) .. 5 5
3315. 10 b. "Stanhopea tigrina" (orchid) 5 5
3316. 20 b. "Paphiopedilum insigne" (orchid) .. 5 5
3317. 30 b. Type **539** 5 5
3318. 40 b. "Ferocactus glaucescens" (cactus) .. 8 5
3319. 55 b. "Gossypium arboreum" 12 5
3320. 1 l. "Hibiscus rosa sinensis" 20 5
3321. 1 l. 35 "Gloxinia hibrida" 30 8
3322. 1 l. 75 "Victoria amazonica" (Victoria Regis lily) .. 45 12
3323. 2 l. 30 Hibiscus, crane flower, water lilt and botanical building (52 × 29½ mm.) 65 15

The 5 b., 10 b., 20 b. and 1 l. 35 are vert.

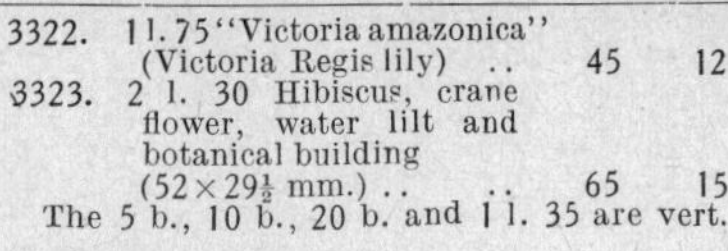

540. Running. **542.** Pigeon on TV Aerial.

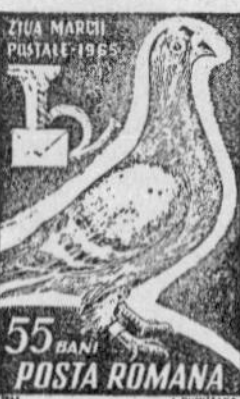

541. Pigeon and Horseman.

1965. Spartacist Games. Multicoloured.

3324. 55 b. Type **540** 12 5
3325. 1 l. 55 Football 35 15
3326. 1 l. 75 Diving 40 15
3327. 2 l. Mountaineering (inscr. "TURISM") 55 20
3328. 5 l. Canoeing (inscr. "CAMPIONATELE EUROPENE 1965") (horiz.) .. .. 1·40 35

1965. Stamp Day.

3329. **541.** 55 b. + 45 b. blue and magenta 15 8
3330. **542.** 1 l. chocolate & green 20 8
3331. – 1 l. 75 choc. and green 50 12

DESIGN: As T **542**. 1 l. 75. Pigeon in flight. No. 3329 is a two-part design arranged horiz. imperf. between.

543. Chamois.

1965. "Hunting Trophies".

3332. **543.** 55 b. brn., yell. & mve. 12 5
3333. – 1 l. brown, grn. & red 20 12
3334. – 1 l. 60 brn., bl. & orge. 30 15
3335. – 1 l. 75 brn., red & grn. 40 15
3336. – 3 l. 20 sepia, gold, orge. & grn. (49 × 37 mm.) 95 30

DESIGNS: 1 l. Brown bear. 1 l. 60, Stag. 1 l. 75, Wild boar. 3 l. 20, Trophy and antlers.

544. Dachshund.

1965. Hunting Dogs. Multicoloured.

3337. 5 b. Type **544** 5 5
3338. 10 b. Spaniel 5 5
3339. 40 b. Retriever with snipe 12 5
3340. 55 b. Fox terrier 15 8
3341. 60 b. Red setter 20 12
3342. 75 b. White setter .. 30 15
3343. 1 l. 55 Pointers 55 15
3344. 3 l. 25 Duck-shooting with retriever .. .. .. 1·60 30

SIZES—DIAMOND (47½ × 47½ mm.): 10 b. to 75 b. HORIZ. (43½ × 29 mm.): 1 l. 55, 3 l. 25.

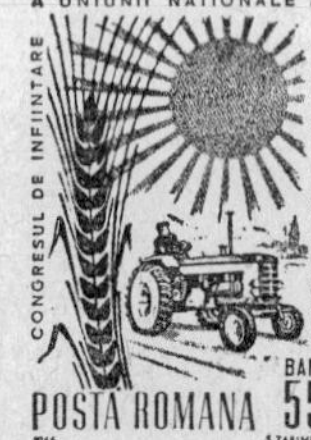

545. Pawn and Globe. **546.** Tractor, Corn and Sun.

1966. World Chess Championships, Cuba. Multicoloured.

3345. 20 b. Type **545** 5 5
3346. 40 b. Jester and "Bishop" 12 5
3347. 55 b. Knight and "Rook" 15 5
3348. 1 l. Knight and "Rook" .. 25 12
3349. 1 l. 60 Type **545** 55 15
3350. 3 l. 25 Jester and "Bishop" 1·60 55

1966. Co-operative Farming Union Congress.

3351. **546.** 55 b. green and yellow 8 5

547. G. Gheorghiu-Dej (Head of State). **548.** Congress Emblem.

1966. G. Gheorghiu-Dej. Death Anniv.

3352. **547.** 55 b. black and gold 15 5

1966. Communist Youth Union Congress.

3354. **548.** 55 b. red and yellow .. 8 5

549. Dance of Moldova.

1966. Rumanian Folk-dancing.

3355. **549.** 30 b. black and purple 5 5
3356. – 40 b. black and red .. 8 5
3357. – 55 b. black & turquoise 12 8
3358. – 1 l. black and lake .. 30 8
3359. – 1 l. 60 black and blue 55 12
3360. – 2 l. black and green .. 90 30

DANCES OF: 40 b. Oltenia. 55 b. Maramures. 1 l. Muntenia. 1 l. 60, Banat. 2 l. Transylvania.

550. Footballers. **551.** "Agriculture and Industry".

1966. World Cup Football Championships.

3361. **550.** 5 b. multicoloured .. 5 5
3362. – 10 b. multicoloured .. 5 5
3363. – 15 b. multicoloured .. 5 5
3364. – 55 b. multicoloured .. 40 20
3365. – 1 l. 75 multicoloured 70 40
3366. – 4 l. multicoloured .. 1·75 85

DESIGNS: 10 b. to 1 l. 75 Various footballers as T **550**. 4 l. Jules Rimet Cup.

1966. Trade Union Congress, Bucharest.

3368. **551.** 55 b. red, blue, yellow and grey 10 5

552. Red-breasted Fly-catcher. **553.** "Venus 3".

1966. Song Birds. Multicoloured.

3369. 5 b. Type **552** 5 5
3370. 10 b. Crossbill 5 5
3371. 15 b. Great reed warbler 5 5
3372. 20 b. Redstart 5 5
3373. 55 b. Robin 15 8
3374. 1 l. 20 White-spotted blue-throat 35 15
3375. 1 l. 55 Yellow wagtail .. 45 20
3376. 3 l. 20 Penduline tit .. 1·40 35

1966. Space Achievements. Multicoloured.

3377. 10 b. Type **553** 5 5
3378. 20 b. "FR 1" satellite .. 5 5
3379. 1 l. 60 "Luna 9" 35 15
3380. 5 l. "Gemini 6" and "7" 1·40 40

554. U. Nestor (birth cent.). **556.** "Hottonia palustris".

555. "House" (after Petrascu).

1966. Cultural Annivs.

3381. – 5 b. ultram., blk. & grn. 5 5
3382. – 10 b. grn., blk. & crim. 5 5
3383. **554.** 20 b. pur., blk. & grn. 5 5
3384. – 40 b. brn., blk. & blue 8 5
3385. – 55 b. grn., blk. & chest. 10 5
3386. – 1 l. vio., blk. & bistre 20 8
3387. – 1 l. 35 olive, blk. & bl. 20 12
3388. – 1 l. 60 pur., blk. & grn. 25 15
3389. – 1 l. 75 pur., blk. & orge. 35 15
3390. – 3 l. 25 lake, blk. & bl. 85 20

PORTRAITS: 5 b. G. Cosbuc (birth cent.). 10 b. G. Sincai (150th death anniv.). 40 b. A. Pumnul (death cent.). 55 b. S. Luchian (50th death anniv.). 1 l. Sun Yat-sen (birth cent.). 1 l. 35, G. W. Leibnitz (250th death anniv.). 1 l. 60, R. Rolland (birth cent.). 1 l. 75, I. Ghica (150th birth anniv.). 3 l. 25, S. C. Cantacuzino (250th death anniv.).

1966. Paintings in National Gallery, Bucharest. Multicoloured.

3391. 5 b. Type **555** 30 15
3392. 10 b. "Peasant Girl" (Grigorescu) 30 15
3393. 20 b. "Midday Rest" (Rescu) 30 15
3394. 55 b. "Portrait of a Man" (Van Eyck) 30 15
3395. 1 l. 55 "The 2nd Class Compartment" (Daumier) .. .. 1·10 65
3396. 3 l. 25 "The Blessing" (El Greco) .. .. 2·75 1·40

The 10 b., 55 b. and 3 l. 25 are vert.

See also Nos. 3450/55, 3543/8, 3583/8, 3631/6, 3658/63, 3756/61 and 3779/84.

1966. Aquatic Flora. Multicoloured.

3397. 5 b. Type **556** 5 5
3398. 10 b. "Ceratophtllum submersum" 5 5
3399. 20 b. "Aldrovanda vesiculosa" 5 5
3400. 40 b. "Callitriche verna" 8 5
3401. 55 b. "Vallisneria spiralis" 12 5
3402. 1 l. "Elodea canadensis" 30 12
3403. 1 l. 55 "Hippuris vulgaris" 35 20
3404. 3 l. 25 "Myriophyllum spicatum" (28 × 49½ mm.) 1·10 35

557. Diagram showing one metre in relation to quadrant of Earth **558.** "Medicine".

1966. Metric System in Rumania. Cent.

3405. **557.** 55 b. ultram. & chest. 15 8
3406. – 1 l. violet and green 30 15

DESIGN: 1 l. Metric abbreviations and globe.

1966. Rumanian Academy. Cent.

3407. **558.** 40 b. black, blue, gold and lilac 12 5
3408. – 55 b. red, bistre, gold and grey 12 5
3409. – 1 l. brn., gold & blue 35 8
3410. – 3 l. brn., gold & yell. 65 20

DESIGNS—As T **558**. 55 b. "Science" (formula). VERT. (22½ × 33½): 1 l. Gold medal. HORIZ. (67 × 27 mm.): 3 l. I. Radulescu, M. Kogalniceanu and. T Savulescu.

559. Putna Monastery.

1966. Putna Monastery. 500th Anniv.
3411. **559.** 2 l. multicoloured .. 40 8

560. Crayfish.

1966. Crustaceans and Molluscs. Multicoloured.
3412. 5 b. Type **560** 5 5
3413. 10 b. Netted Dog Whelk (vert.) 5 5
3414. 20 b. Marbled Rock Crab 5 5
3415. 40 b. Lapidary Snail .. 8 5
3416. 55 b. Brown Lipped Snail 8 5
3417. 1 l. 35 Mediterranean Mussel 35 15
3418. 1 l. 75 Pord Snail .. 40 20
3419. 3 l. 25 Swan Mussel .. 1·25 35

561. Bucharest and Mail-coach.

1966. Stamp Day.
3420. **561.** 55 b.+45 b. purple, yellow, grn. & blue 30 10
No. 3420 is a two-part design arranged horiz. imperf. between.

562. "Ursus spelaeus".

1966. Prehistoric Animals.
3421. **562.** 5 b. ult., brn. & grn. 5 5
3422. – 10 b. violet, bis. & grn. 5 5
3423. – 15 b. brn., mar. & grn. 5 5
3424. – 55 b. vio., bistre & grn. 15 5
3425. – 1 l. 55 blue, brn. & grn. 40 15
3426. – 4 l. mag., bistre & grn. 1·40 45
ANIMALS: 10 b. "Mamuthus trogontherii". 15 b. "Bison priscus". 55 b. "Archidiscodon". 1 l. 55, "Megaceros eurycerus" (43×27 mm.). 4 l. "Deinotherium gigantissimum".

563. "Sputnik 1" orbiting Globe.

1967. 10 years of Space Achievements. Multicoloured.
3427. 10 b. Type **563** (postage) 5 5
3428. 20 b. Gagarin and "Vostok 1" 5 5
3429. 25 b. Tereshkova ("Vostok 6") 5 5
3430. 40 b. Nikolaiev and Popovich ("Vostok 3" and "4") 12 5
3431. 55 b. Leonov in space ("Voskhod 2") .. 20 5
3432. 1 l. 20 "Early Bird" (air) 20 12
3433. 1 l. 55 Photo transmission ("Mariner 4") .. 35 15
3434. 3 l. 25 Space rendezvous ("Gemini 6" and "7") 55 35
3435. 5 l. Space link-up ("Gemini 8").. .. 1·10 50

564. Barn Owl.

1967. Birds of Prey. Multicoloured.
3442. 10 b. Type **564** 5 5
3443. 20 b. Eagle owl 5 5
3444. 40 b. Saker falcon .. 5 5
3445. 55 b. Egyptian vulture .. 8 5
3446. 75 b. Osprey 15 8
3447. 1 l. Griffon vulture .. 15 12
3448. 1 l. 20 Bearded vulture or lammergeyer 20 15
3449. 1 l. 75 Black vulture .. 50 20

565. "Washerwomen" (after I. Steriadi).

1967. Paintings.
3450. – 10 b. blue, gold & red 5 5
3451. **565.** 20 b. grn., gold & ochre 5 5
3452. – 40 b. red, gold & blue 5 5
3453. – 1 l. 55 pur., gold & blue 45 20
3454. – 3 l. 20 brn., gold & grn. 60 30
3455. – 5 l. brn., gold & orge. 1·60 80
PAINTINGS—VERT. 10 b. "Model in Fancy Dress" (I. Andreescu). 40 b. "Peasants Weaving" (S. Dimitrescu). 1 l. 55, "Venus and Cupid" (L. Cranach). 5 l. "Haman beseeching Esther" (Rembrandt). HORIZ. 3 l. 20, "Hercules and the Lion" (Rubens).

566. Woman's Head. **568.** "Infantryman" (after Grigorescu).

567. Copper and Silver Coins of 1867.

1967. C. Brancusi (sculptor). 10th Death Anniv. Designs showing Sculptures.
3456. **566.** 5 b. brown, yell. & red 5 5
3457. – 10 b. blk., grn. & violet 5 5
3458. – 20 b. black, green & red 5 5
3459. – 40 b. black, red & grn. 8 5
3460. – 55 b. blk., olive & blue 15 8
3461. – 1 l. 20, brown, violet and orange .. 20 15
3462. – 3 l. 25 black, green and magenta .. 55 35

1967. Rumanian Monetary System. Cent.
3463. **567.** 55 b. multicoloured.. 12 5
3464. – 1 l. 20 multicoloured 30 15
DESIGN: 1 l. 20, Obverse and reverse of modern silver coin (1966).

1967. Independence. 90th Anniv.
3465. **568.** 55 b. multicoloured.. 30 12

HAVE YOU READ THE NOTES AT THE BEGINNING OF THIS CATALOGUE?

These often provide answers to the enquiries we receive.

569. Peasants attacking (after O. Bancila). **570.** "Centaurea pinnatifida".

1967. Peasant Rising. 60th Anniv.
3466. **569.** 40 b. multicoloured.. 15 12
3467. – 1 l. 55 multicoloured 55 35
DESIGN—HORIZ. 1 l. 55, Peasants marching (after S. Luchian).

1967. Carpathian Flora. Multicoloured.
3468. 20 b. Type **570** 5 5
3469. 40 b. "Erysimum transsilvanicum" 8 5
3470. 55 b. "Aquilegia transsivanica" 12 8
3471. 1 l. 20 "Viola alpina" .. 20 12
3472. 1 l. 75 "Campanula carpatica".. .. .. 35 15
3473. 4 l. "Dryas octopetala" (horiz.).. .. .. 80 45

571. Towers, Sibiu.

1967. Historic Monuments and Int. Tourist Year. Multicoloured.
3474. 20 b. Type **571** 5 5
3475. 40 b. Castle at Cris .. 8 5
3476. 55 b. Wooden church, Plopis 12 8
3477. 1 l. 60 Ruins, Neamtului 30 20
3478. 1 l. 75 Mogosoaia Palace, Bucharest 30 20
3479. 2 l. 25 Church, Voronet.. 40 30
No. 3479 is horiz., 48½×36 mm.

572. "The Marasesti Attack" (from painting by E. Stoica).

1967. Battles of Marasesti, Marasti and Oituz. 50th Anniv.
3481. **572.** 55 b. brn., blue & grey 15 8

573. D. Lipatti (composer and pianist: 50th birth anniv.). **574.** Wrestling.

1967. Cultural Annivs.
3482. **573.** 10 b. vio., bl. & black 5 5
3483. – 20 b. blue, brn. & blk. 5 5
3484. – 40 b. chest., turq. & blk. 5 5
3485. – 55 b. brown, red & blk. 8 5
3486. – 1 l. 20 brn., olive & blk. 20 8
3487. – 1 l. 75 grn., bl. & blk. 30 12
DESIGNS: 20 b. A. Orascu (architect: 150th birth anniv.). 40 b. G. Antipa (zoologist: birth cent.). 55 b. M. Kogalniceanu (politician: 150th birth anniv.). 1 l. 20, Jonathan Swift (300th birth anniv.). 1 l. 75, Marie Curie (birth cent.).

1967. World Wrestling Championships, Bucharest. Designs showing wrestlers and globes.
3488. **574.** 10 b. multicoloured.. 5 5
3489. – 20 b. mult. (horiz.).. 5 5
3490. – 55 b. multicoloured.. 8 5
3491. – 1 l. 20 multicoloured 20 12
3492. – 2 l. mult. (horiz.) .. 35 20

575. Inscription on Globe.

1967. Int. Linguists' Congress, Bucharest.
3493. **575.** 1 l. 60 ultramarine, red and blue .. 30

576. Academy.

1967. Book Academy, Bucharest. Cent.
3494. **576.** 55 b. slate, brn. & blue 12 5

577. Dancing on Ice. **578.** Curtea de Arges Monastery.

1967. Winter Olympic Games, Grenoble. Multicoloured.
3495. 20 b. Type **577** 5 5
3496. 40 b. Skiing 5 5
3497. 55 b. Bobsleighing .. 8 5
3498. 1 l. Downhill skiing .. 15 10
3499. 1 l. 55 Ice-hockey .. 30 15
3500. 2 l. Games emblem .. 35 15
3501. 2 l. 30 Ski-jumping .. 40 20

1967. Curtea de Arges Monastery. 450th Anniv.
3503. **578.** 55 b. multicoloured.. 15 5

579. Karl Marx and Title Page. **580.** Lenin.

1967. Karl Marx's "Das Kapital". Cent.
3504. **579.** 40 b. black, yell. & red 8 5

1967. October Revolution. 50th Anniv.
3505. **580.** 1 l. 20 blk., gold & red 20 8

581. Arms of Rumania. **582.** Telephone Dial and Map.

1967. (a) T **581**.
3506. **581.** 40 b. ultramarine .. 8 5
3507. 55 b. yellow 8 5
3508. 1 l. 60 red 30 5

(b) T **582** and similar designs.
3509. – 5 b. green 5 5
3510. – 10 b. red 5 5
3511. – 20 b. grey 5 5
3512. – 35 b. indigo 5 5
3513. – 40 b. ultramarine .. 8 5
3514. – 50 b. orange 8 5
3515. – 55 b. red 8 5
3516. – 60 b. chestnut .. 10 5
3517. – 1 l. green 15 5
3518. – 1 l. 20 violet.. .. 20 5
3519. – 1 l. 35 blue 20 5
3520. – 1 l. 50 red 25 5
3521. – 1 l. 55 brown .. 25 5

3522. – 1 l. 75 emerald .. 30 5
3523. – 2 l. yellow 30 5
3524. – 2 l. 40 blue 35 5
3525. 582. 3 l. turquoise 40 5
3526. – 3 l. 20 ochre 55 5
3527. – 3 l. 25 ultramarine .. 55 5
3528. – 4 l. magenta .. 65 5
3529. – 5 l. violet 85 8

DESIGNS—HORIZ. (23 × 17 mm.). 5 b. "Carpati" lorry. 20 b. Railway T.P.O. coach. 35 b. Light aircraft. 60 b. Electric parcels truck. As T 582 (29 × 23 mm.). 1 l. 20, Motor-coach. 1 l. 35, Helicopter. 1 l. 75, Lakeside highway. 2 l. Postal van. 3 l. 20 Tarom airliner. 4 l. Electric train. 5 l. Telex instrument and world map. VERT. (17 × 23 mm.). 10 b. Posthorn and telephone emblem. 40 b. Power Pylons. 50 b. Telephone handset. 55 b. Dam. (23 × 29 mm.). 1 l. Diesel train. 1 l. 50, Trolley-bus. 1 l. 55, Radio Station. 2 l. 40 T.V. relay station. 3 l. 25, Liner "Transilvania".

No. 3525 also commemorates the 40th Anniv. of the Automatic Telephone Service.

For Nos. 3517/29 in smaller format see Nos. 3842/57.

583. "Crossing the River Buzau" (lithograph by Raffet) (actual size 93 × 30 mm.).

1967. Stamp Day.

3530. 583. 55 b. + 45 b. indigo and ochre 20 15

584. Monorail Train and Globe. 585. Arms and Industrial Scene.

1967. World Fair, Montreal. Multicoloured.

3531. 55 b. Type 584 .. .. 8 5
3532. 1 l. Expo emblem within atomic symbol 15 5
3533. 1 l. 60 Gold cup and world map 30 8
3534. 2 l. Expo emblem .. 35 20

1967. Republic. 20th Anniv. Multicoloured.

3535. 40 b. Type 585 .. .. 5 5
3536. 55 b. Arms of Rumania .. 8 5
3537. 1 l. 60 Rumanian flag .. 20 12
3538. 1 l. 75 Arms and cultural emblems 25 15

The 1 l. 60, is 34 × 48 mm.

586. Flying Ambulance.

1968. Air. Rumanian Aviation.

3539. – 40 b. multicoloured .. 8 5
3540. 586. 55 b. multicoloured .. 12 5
3541. – 1 l. multicoloured .. 15 12
3542. – 2 l. 40 multicoloured 40 30

DESIGNS—VERT. 40 b. Crop-spraying aircraft. 1 l. "Aviasan" emblem and aircraft. 2 l. 40 M. Zorileanu (pioneer aviator) and biplane.

587. "Angelica and Medor" (S. Ricci).

1968. Paintings in Rumanian Galleries. Multicoloured.

3543. 40 b. "Young Woman" (Misu Pop) 12 8
3544. 55 b. "Little Girl in Red Scarf" (N. Grigorescu) 12 8
3545. 1 l. "Old Nicholas, the Cobzaplayer" (S. Luchian) 20 12
3546. 1 l. 60 "Man with Skull" (Dierick Bouts) 35 20
3547. 2 l. 40 Type 587 .. .. 45 35
3548. 3 l. 20 "Ecce Homo" (Titian) 70 40

Nos. 3543/6 and 3548 are vert.

See also Nos. 3583/8, 3631/6, 3658/63, 3756/61 and 3779/84.

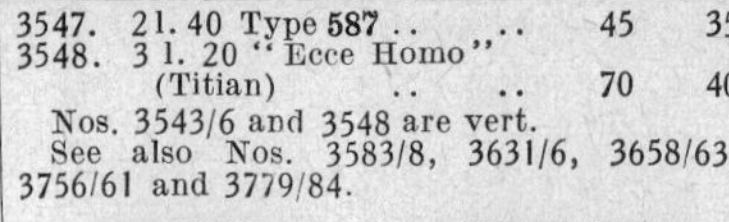

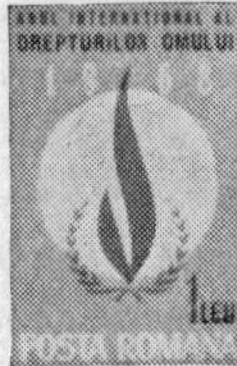

588. Human Rights Emblem. 589. W.H.O. Emblem.

1968. Human Rights Year.

3551. 588. 1 l. multicoloured .. 15 5

1968. W.H.O. 20th Anniv.

3552. 589. 1 l. 60 multicoloured 30 8

590. "The Hunter" (after N. Grigorescu).

1968. Hunting Congress, Mamaia.

3553. 590. 1 l. 60 multicoloured 30 8

591. Pioneers and Liberation Monument.

1968. Young Pioneers. Multicoloured.

3554. 5 b. Type 591 .. .. 5 5
3555. 40 b. Receiving scarves .. 8 5
3556. 55 b. With models .. 12 5
3557. 1 l. Operating radio sets 20 8
3558. 1 l. 60 Folk-dancing .. 30 9
3559. 2 l. 40 In camp 45 15

592. Prince Mircea. 593. Ion Ionescu de la Brad (scholar).

1968. Prince Mircea (the Old). 550th Death Anniv.

3560. 592. 1 l. 60 multicoloured 30 8

1968. Cultural Annivs.

3561. 593. 40 b. multicoloured .. 8 5
3562. – 55 b. multicoloured .. 10 5

Portraits and Annivs.: 40 b. T 593 (150th Birth Anniv.). 55 b. Emil Racovita (scientist: Birth Cent.).

594. "Pelargonium zonale Ait". 596. Throwing the Javelin.

595. "Nicolae Balcescu" (G. Tattarescu).

1968. Garden Geraniums. Multicoloured.

3563. 10 b. Type 594 .. .. 5 5
3564. 20 b. "Pelargonium zonale Ait" 5 5
3565. 40 b. "Pelargonium zonale Ait" 8 5
3566. 55 b. "Pelargonium zonale Ait" 10 5
3567. 60 b. "Pelargonium grandiflorum Hort" .. 12 8
3568. 1 l. 20 "Pelargonium peltatum Hort" .. 20 8
3569. 1 l. 35 "Pelargonium peltatum Hort" .. 25 10
3570. 1 l. 60 "Pelargonium grandiflorum Hort" .. 30 15

Nos. 3563/6, 3567 and 3570, 3568/9 respectively are different varieties of the same species.

1968. 1848 Revolution. 120th Anniv. Paintings. Multicoloured.

3571. 55 b. Type 595 .. .. 12 5
3572. 1 l. 20 "Avram Iancu" (B. Iscovescu) .. 20 8
3573. 1 l. 60 "Vasile Alecsandri" (N. Livaditti) .. 30 15

1968. Olympic Games, Mexico. Multicoloured.

3574. 10 b. Type 596 .. .. 5 5
3575. 20 b. Diving 5 5
3576. 40 b. Volleyball .. 8 5
3577. 55 b. Boxing 10 5
3578. 60 b. Wrestling 12 8
3579. 1 l. 20 Fencing 20 8
3580. 1 l. 35 Punting .. 25 12
3581. 1 l. 60 Football 30 15

1968. Paintings in the Fine Arts Museum, Bucarest. Multicoloured. As T 587.

3583. 10 b. "The Awakening of Rumania" (G. Tattarescu) (28 × 49 mm.) .. 5 5
3584. 20 b. "Composition" (Teodorescu Sionion) .. 8 5
3585. 35 b. "The Judgment of Paris" (H. van Balen) 12 5
3586. 60 b. "The Mystical Betrothal of St. Catherine" (L. Sustris) .. 15 5
3587. 1 l. 75 "Mary with the Child Jesus" (J. van Bylert) 15 8
3588. 3 l. "The Summer" (J. Jordaens) 55 35

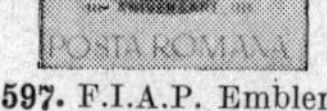

597. F.I.A.P. Emblem within "Lens". 598. Academy and Harp.

1968. International Federation of Photographic Art. (F.I.A.P.). 20th Anniv.

3589. 597. 1 l. 60 multicoloured 30 12

1968. Georges Enescu Philharmonic Academy Cent.

3590. 598. 55 b. multicoloured .. 12 5

599. Triumph of Trajan. (Roman metope).

1968. Historic Monuments.

3591. 599. 10 b. grn., blue & red 5 5
3592. – 40 b. bl., brn. & car. 8 5
3593. – 55 b. vio., brn. & grn. 8 5
3594. – 1 l. 20 purple, slate and ochre 20 15
3595. – 1 l. 55 bl., grn. & pur. 30 15
3596. – 1 l. 75 brown, bistre and orange 35 15

DESIGNS—HORIZ. 40 b. Monastery Church, Moldovita. 55 b. Monastery Church, Cezia. 1 l. 20 Tower and Church, Tirgoviste. 1 l. 55 Palace of Culture, Jassy. 1 l. 75 Corvinus Castle, Hunedoara.

600. Old Bucharest (18th-century painting). (Actual size 76 × 29 mm.).

1969. Stamp Day.

3597. 600. 55 b. + 45 b. mult. .. 20 15

601. "Entry of Michael the Brave into Alba Julia" (E. Stoica).

1968. Union of Transylvania with Rumania. 50th Anniv. Multicoloured.

3598. 55 b. Type 601 .. .. 12 8
3599. 1 l. "Union Dance" (T. Aman) 20 8
3600. 1 l. 75 "Alba Julia Assembly" 30 15

602. Swan. 603. Neamtz Costume (female).

1968. Fauna of Nature Reservations. Multicoloured.

3602. 10 b. Type 602 .. .. 5 5
3603. 20 b. Black-winged stilt .. 5 5
3604. 40 b. Shelduck 8 5
3605. 55 b. Great white heron .. 10 5
3606. 60 b. Golden eagle .. 12 5
3607. 1 l. 20 Great bustard .. 20 12
3608. 1 l. 35 Carpathian chamois 25 12
3609. 1 l. 60 Bison 30 15

1968. Provincial Costumes (1st Series). Multicoloured.

3610. 5 b. Type 603 .. .. 5 5
3611. 40 b. Neamtz (male) .. 8 5
3612. 55 b. Hunedoara (female) 8 5
3613. 1 l. Hunedoara (male) .. 15 8
3614. 1 l. 60 Brasov (female) .. 35 15
3615. 2 l. 40 Brasov (male) .. 45 15

See also Nos. 3617/22.

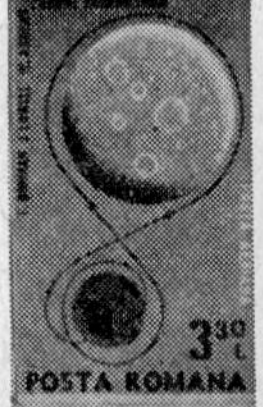

604. Earth, Moon and Orbital Track of "Apollo 8". 605. Fencing.

1969. Air. Flight of "Apollo 8" around the Moon.

3616. 604. 3 l. 30 blk., silver & bl. 55 50

1969. Provincial Costumes (2nd Series). As T 603. Multicoloured.

3617. 5 b. Doli (female) .. 5 5
3618. 40 b. Doli (male) .. 8 5
3619. 55 b. Arges (female) .. 12 5
3620. 1 l. Arges (male) .. 20 8
3621. 1 l. 60 Timisoara (female) 30 12
3622. 2 l. 40 Timisoara (male) .. 45 15

1969. Sports.

3623. 605. 10 b. grey, blk. & brn. 5 5
3624. – 20 b. grey, blk. & vio. 5 5
3625. – 40 b. grey, blk. & blue 8 5
3626. – 55 b. grey, blk. & red 8 5
3627. – 1 l. grey, blk. & green 15 8
3628. – 1 l. 20 grey, blk. & bl. 20 8
3629. – 1 l. 60 grey, blk. & red 25 15
3630. – 2 l. 40 grey, blk. & grn. 40 20

DESIGNS: 20 b. Throwing the javelin. 40 b. Canoeing. 55 b. Boxing. 1 l. Volleyball. 1 l. 20 Swimming. 1 l. 60 Wrestling. 2 l. 40 Football.

1969. Nude Paintings in the National Gallery. As T **587**. Multicoloured.

3631. 10 b. "Nude" 5 5
3632. 20 b. "Nude" (T. Pallady) 5 5
3633. 35 b. "Nude" (N. Tonitza) 8 5
3634. 60 b. "Venus and Cupid" (Flemish School) .. 12 8
3635. 1 l. 75 "Diana and Endymion" (M. Liberi) .. 35 15
3636. 3 l. "The Three Graces" (J. H. von Achen) .. 55 30

SIZES: VERT. (36 × 49 mm.)—10 b., 35 b., 60 b., 1 l. 75. (27 × 49 mm.)—3 l. HORIZ. (49 × 36 mm.)—20 b.

606. "Soyuz 4" and "Soyuz 5".

607. I.L.O. Emblem.

1969. Air. Space Link-up of "Soyuz 4" and "Soyuz 5".

3638. **606.** 3 l. 30 multicoloured 55 20

1969. Int. Labour Office. 50th Anniv.

3639. **607.** 55 b. multicoloured .. 10 5

608. Stylised Head.

610. Referee introducing Boxers.

609. Posthorn.

1969. Inter-European Cultural and Economic Co-operation.

3640. **608.** 55 b. multicoloured .. 10 5
3641. 1 l. 50 multicoloured 30 12

1969. Postal Ministers' Conf., Bucharest.

3642. **609.** 55 b. ultram. and blue 10 5

1969. European Boxing Championships, Bucharest. Multicoloured.

3643. 35 b. Type **610** 8 5
3644. 40 b. Sparring 8 5
3645. 55 b. Leading with Punch 12 5
3646. 1 l. 75 Declaring the Winner 35 15

611. "Apatura ilia".

1969. Butterflies. Multicoloured.

3647. 5 b. Type **611** 5 5
3648. 10 b. "Prosperpinus prosperina" 5 5
3649. 20 b. "Colias erate" .. 5 5
3650. 40 b. "Pericallia matronula" 8 5
3651. 55 b. "Argynnis laodice" 8 5
3652. 1 l. "Callimorpha quadripunctaria" 15 8
3653. 1 l. 20 "Anthocaris cardamines" 20 12
3654. 2 l. 40 "Meleageria daphnis" 55 20

612. "Apollo 9" and Module over Earth.

613. Astronaut and Module on Moon.

1969. Air. "Apollo" Moon Flights. Multicoloured.

3655. 60 b. Type **612** 12 8
3656. 2 l. 40 "Apollo 10" and module approaching Moon (vert.) 45 30

1969. Air. 1st Man on the Moon.

3657. **613.** 3 l. 30 multicoloured 60 35

1969. Paintings in the National Gallery, Bucharest. Multicoloured. As T **587**.

3658. 10 b. "Venetian Senator" (School of Tintoretto) .. 5 5
3659. 20 b. "Sofia Kretzulescu" (G. Tattarescu) .. 5 5
3660. 35 b. "Philip IV" (Velazquez) 5 5
3661. 60 b. "Man Reading" (Memling) 12 5
3662. 1 l. 75 "Lady D'Aguesseau" (Vigee-Lebrun) 35 15
3663. 3 l. "Portrait of a Woman" (Rembrandt) 60 30

614. Communist Flag.

615. Symbols of Learning.

1969. 10th Rumanian Communist Party Congress.

3665. **614.** 55 b. multicoloured .. 10 5

1969. National "Economic Achievements" Exn., Bucharest. Multicoloured.

3666. 35 b. Type **615** 8 5
3667. 40 b. Symbols of Agriculture and Science 8 5
3668. 1 l. 75 Symbols of Industry 35 15

616. Liberation Emblem.

617. Juggling on Trick-cycle.

1969. Liberation. 25th Anniv. Multicoloured.

3669. 10 b. Type **616** 5 5
3670. 55 b. Crane and Trowel .. 10 5
3671. 60 b. Flags on scaffolding 12 5

1969. Rumanian State Circus. Multicoloured.

3672. 10 b. Type **617** 5 5
3673. 20 b. Clown 5 5
3674. 35 b. Trapeze artists .. 5 5
3675. 60 b. Equestrian act .. 12 5
3676. 1 l. 75 High-wire act .. 35 15
3677. 3 l. Performing tiger .. 60 30

618. Forces Memorial.

1969. "Army Day" and 25th Anniv. of People's Army.

3678. **618.** 55 b. black, gold & red 12 5

619. Trains of 1869 and 1969.

1969. Rumanian Railways. Cent.

3679. **619.** 55 b. multicoloured .. 12 5

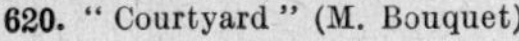

620. "Courtyard" (M. Bouquet).

1969. Stamp Day.

3680. **620.** 55 b.+45 b. mult... 20 15

621. Branesti Mask.

622. "Apollo 12" above Moon.

1969. Folklore Masks. Multicoloured.

3681. 40 b. Type **621** 8 5
3682. 55 b. Tudora mask .. 12 8
3683. 1 l. 55 Birsesti mask .. 35 12
3684. 1 l. 75 Rudaria mask .. 35 20

1969. Moon landing of "Apollo 12".

3685. **622.** 1 l. 50 multicoloured 25 10

623. "Three Kings" (Voronet Monastery).

1969. Frescoes from Northern Moldavian Monasteries (1st series). Multicoloured.

3686. 10 b. Type **623** 5 5
3687. 20 b. "Three Kings" (Sucevita) 5 5
3688. 35 b. "Holy Child in Manger" (Voronet) .. 5 5
3689. 60 b. "Ship" (Sucevita) .. 12 5
3690. 1 l. 75 "Walled City" (Moldovita) 35 15
3691. 3 l. "Pastoral Scene" (Voronet) 60 30

The 60 b. and 3 l. are vert.
See also Nos. 3736/42 and 3872/8.

624. "Old Mother Goose", Capra.

1969. New Year Children's Celebrations. Multicoloured.

3692. 40 b. Type **624** 8 5
3693. 55 b. Decorated tree, Sorcova 12 8
3694. 1 l. 50 Drummers, Buhaiul 30 12
3695. 2 l. 40 Singer and bell-ringer, Plugusurol .. 50 20

625. Hockey-players and Emblem.

626. "Pulsatilla pratensis".

1970. World Ice-hockey Championships. Multicoloured.

3696. 20 b. Type **625** 5 5
3697. 55 b. Goalkeeper .. 12 5
3698. 1 l. 20 Two players .. 25 8
3699. 2 l. 40 Goal-mouth melee 50 20

1970. Flowers. Multicoloured.

3700. 5 b. Type **626** 5 5
3701. 10 b. "Adonis vernalis" 5 5
3702. 20 b. "Carduus nutans" 5 5
3703. 40 b. "Amygdalus nana" 8 5
3704. 55 b. "Iris pumilla" .. 12 5
3705. 1 l. "Linum hirsutum" 20 12
3706. 1 l. 20 "Salvia aethiopis" 25 15
3707. 2 l. 40 "Paeonia tenuifolia" 50 25

627. Japanese Woodcut.

629. "Camille" (Monet) and Maximum Card.

628. BAC "1-11" in flight.

1970. World Fair, Osaka, Japan. Expo 70. Multicoloured.

3714. 20 b. Type **627** 5 5
3715. 1 l. Japanese pagoda (29 × 92 mm) 20 12

1970. Rumanian Civil Aviation. 50th Anniv. Multicoloured.

3717. 60 b. Type **628** 12 5
3718. 2 l. Tail of BAC "1-11" 45 20

1970. Maximafila Franco-Rumanian Philatelic Exn., Bucharest.

3719. **629.** 1 l. 50 multicoloured 30 5

630. "Prince Alexander Cuza" (Szathmary).

631. Lenin.

1970. Prince Alexander Cuza. 150th Birth Anniv.

3720. **630.** 55 b. multicoloured .. 12 5

1970. Lenin. Birth Cent.

3721. **631.** 40 b. multicoloured .. 8 5

632. "Co-operation" Map.

633. Victory Monument, Bucharest.

1970. Inter-European Cultural and Economic Co-operation.

3722. **632.** 40 b. green, chestnut and black 8 5
3723. 1 l. 50 blue, brn. & blk. 30 20

1970. Liberation. 25th Anniv.

3724. **633.** 55 b. multicoloured .. 12 5

634. Greek Silver Drachma. 5th-cent B.C.

1970. Ancient Coins.

3725. 634. 10 b. black and ultramarine .. 5 5
3726. – 20 b. black and red .. 5 5
3727. – 35 b. bronze and green 8 5
3728. – 60 b. black and brown 12 5
3729. – 1 l. 75 black and blue 35 8
3730. – 3 l. blk. & cerise .. 50 15

DESIGNS—HORIZ: 20 b. Getic-Dacian silver didrachm, 2nd-1st-cent B.C. 35 b. Copper sestertius of Trajan, 106 A.D. 60 b. Mircea ducat, 1400, 1 l. 75 Silver groschen of Stephen the Great. 1460. VERT. 3 l. Brasov klippe-thaler, 1601.

635. Footballers and Ball.

1970. World Cup Football Championships, Mexico.

3731. 635. 40 b. multicoloured .. 8 5
3732. – 55 b. multicoloured .. 12 5
3733. – 1 l. 75 multicoloured .. 40 10
3734. – 3 l. 30 multicoloured 60 15

DESIGNS: Nos. 3732/4, various football scenes as T 635.

636. "Prince Petru Rares qand Family" (Moldovita).

637. "Apollo 13" Splashdown.

1970. Frescoes from Northern Moldavian Monasteries (2nd Series). Multicoloured.

3736. 10 b. Type 636 .. .. 5 5
3737. 20 p. "Metropolitan Grigore Rosca" (Voronet) 5 5
3738. 40 b. "Alexander the Good and Family" (Sucevita) 8 5
3739. 55 b. } Scenes from "The Last Judgement" (Voronet) 12 8
3740. 1 l. 75 } .. 35 10
3741. 3 l. "St. Anthony" (Voronet) 50 15

The 20 b. is smaller, 28 × 48 mm.

1970. Air. Space Flight of "Apollo 13".

3743. 637. 1 l. 50 multicoloured 30 30

638. Engels.

639. Exhibition Hall.

1970. Friedrich Engels. 150th Birth Anniv.

3744. 638. 1 l. 50 multicoloured 25 5

1970. National Events. Multicoloured.

3745. 35 b. "Iron Gates" Dam 12 5
3746. 55 b. Freighter and flag .. 8 5
3747. 1 l. 50 Type 639 .. .. 25 5

EVENTS: 35 b. Danube navigation projects. 55 b. 75th Anniv. of Rumanian Merchant Marine. 1 l. 50 1st International Fair, Bucharest.

640. New Headquarters Building.

1970. New U.P.U. Headquarters Building, Berne.

3748. 640. 1 l. 50 green and blue 25 5

641. Education Year Emblem.

642. "Iceberg".

1970. Int. Education Year.

3749. 641. 55 b. plum, blk. & red 12 5

1970. Roses. Multicoloured.

3750. 20 b. Type 642 .. .. 5 5
3751. 35 b. "Wiener Charme" 8 5
3752. 55 b. "Pink Lustre" .. 12 5
3753. 1 l. "Piccadilly" .. 20 10
3754. 1 l. 50 "Orange Delbard" 30 12
3755. 2 l. 40 "Sibelius" .. 45 15

643. "Spaniel and Pheasant" (J. B. Oudry).

644. Refugee Woman and Child.

1970. Paintings in Rumanian Galleries. Multicoloured. Sizes in millimetres.

3756. 10 b. "The Hunt" (D. Brandi) (38 × 50) .. 5 5
3757. 20 b. Type 643 .. .. 5 5
3758. 35 b. "The Hunt" (Jan Fyt) (38 × 50) 8 5
3769. 60 b. "After the Chase" (Jordaens) (As T 643) .. 15 8
3760. 1 l. 75 "The Game Dealer" (F. Snyders) (50 × 38) .. 25 12
3761. 3 l. "The Hunt" (A. de Gryeff) (As T 643) .. 55 15

1970. Danube Flood Victims (1st Issue).

3763. 644. 55 b. blk., blue & grn. (postage) 12 5
3764. – 1 l. 50 multicoloured 25 10
3765. – 1 l. 75 multicoloured 40 15
3766. – 60 b. black, drab and blue (air) 12 5

DESIGNS: 60 b. Helicopter rescue. 1 l. 50, Red Cross post. 1 l. 75, Building reconstruction. See also No. 3777.

645. U.N. Emblem.

647. Beethoven.

646. Arab Horse.

1970. United Nations. 25th Anniv.

3767. 645. 1 l. 50 multicoloured 25 5

1970. Horses. Multicoloured.

3768. 20 b. Type 646 .. .. 5 5
3769. 35 b. American trotter .. 8 5
3770. 55 b. "Ghidran" .. 12 5
3771. 1 l. "Hutul" 20 12
3772. 1 l. 50 Thoroughbred .. 30 20
3773. 2 l. 40 Lippizaner .. 45 20

1970. Beethoven. Birth Bicent.

3774. 647. 55 b. multicoloured .. 10 5

648. "Mail-cart in the Snow" (E. Volkers) (Illustration reduced. Actual size 75 × 33 mm.)

1970. Stamp Day.

3775. 648. 55 b. + 45 b. multicoloured 12 5

649. Coanda's Model Aircraft.

1970. Air. 1st Experimental Rocket-powered Flight. 60th Anniv.

3776. 649. 60 b. multicoloured .. 12 5

650. "The Flood" (abstract, Joan Miro).

1970. Danube Flood Victims (2nd Issue).

3777. 650. 3 l. multicoloured .. 60 60

651. "Sight" (G. Coques).

1970. Paintings from the Bruckenthal Museum, Sibiu. Multicoloured.

3779. 10 b. Type 651 .. .. 5 5
3780. 20 b. "Hearing" .. 5 5
3781. 35 b. "Smell" 8 5
3782. 60 b. "Taste" 15 8
3783. 1 l. 75 "Touch" 35 12
3784. 3 l. Bruckenthal Museum 55 20

Nos. 3779/84 show a series of pictures by Coques entitled "The Five Senses".

652. T. Vladimirescu (T. Aman).

654. Alsatian.

653. "Three Races".

1971. Tudor Vladimirescu (Wallachian revolutionary). 150th Death Anniv.

3786. 652. 1 l. 50 multicoloured 30 8

1971. Racial Equality Year.

3787. 653. 1 l. 50 multicoloured 30 8

1971. Dogs. Multicoloured.

3788. 20 b. Type 654 .. .. 8 5
3789. 35 b. Bulldog 12 5
3790. 55 b. Fox terrier 20 8
3791. 1 l. Setter 20 12
3792. 1 l. 50 Cocker spaniel .. 30 15
3793. 2 l. 40 Poodle 45 30

655. "Luna 16" leaving Moon.

656. Proclamation of Commune.

1971. Air. Moon Missions of "Luna 16" and "Luna 17". Multicoloured.

3794. 3 l. 30 Type 655 .. .. 55 55
3795. 3 l. 30 "Lunokhod 1" on Moon 55 55

1971 Paris Commune. Cent.

3796. 656. 40 b. multicoloured .. 8 5

657. Astronaut and Moon Trolley.

659. "Toadstool" Rocks, Babele.

658. "Three Fists" Emblem and Flags.

1971. Air. Moon Mission of "Apollo 14".

3797. 657. 3 l. 30 multicoloured 55 55

1971. Trade Union Congress, Bucharest.

3798. 658. 55 b. multicoloured .. 10 5

1971. Tourism. Multicoloured.

3799. 10 b. Gorge, Cheile Bicazului (vert.) .. 5 5
3800. 40 b. Type 659 .. .. 8 5
3801. 55 b. Winter resort, Poiana Brasov 10 5
3802. 1 l. Holiday scene, Danube delta 20 8
3803. 1 l. 50 Hotel, Baile Sovata 40 15
3804. 2 l. 40 Venus, Jupiter and Neptune Hotels, Black Sea (77 × 29 mm.) .. 45 20

660. "Arrows".

661. Museum Building.

1971. Inter-European Cultural and Economic Co-operation. Multicoloured.

3805. 55 b. Type 660 .. .. 12 5
3806. 1 l. 75 Stylised map of Europe 30 15

1971. Historical Museum, Bucharest.

3807. 661. 55 b. multicoloured .. 8 5

662. "The Secret Printing-press" (S. Szonyi). 663. "Motra Tone" (K. Idromeno).

1971. Rumanian Communist Party. 50th Anniv. Multicoloured.

3808. 35 b. Type **662** 5 5
3809. 40 b. Emblem and red flags (horiz.) 8 5
3810. 55 b. "The Builders" (A. Anastasiu) 10 5

1971. "Balkanfila III". Int. Stamp Exhib., Bucharest. Multicoloured.

3811. 1 l. 20+60 b. Type **663** .. 30 15
3812. 1 l. 20+60 b. "Maid" (V. Dimitrov-Maystora) 30 15
3813. 1 l. 20+60 b. "Rosa Botzaris" (J. Stieler) .. 30 15
3814. 1 l. 20+60 b. "Portrait of a Lady" (K. Ivanovic) 30 15
3815. 1 l. 20+60 b. "Argeseanca" (C. Popp de Szathmary) 30 15
3816. 1 l. 20+60 b. "Woman in Modern Dress" (C. Ibrahim) 30 15

Each stamp has a premium-carrying "tab" as shown in Type **663**.

664. "Phyllocactus phyllanthoides".

1971. Flowers. Multicoloured.

3818. 20 b. "Punica grantum" 5 5
3819. 35 b. "Calceolus speciosum" 8 5
3820. 55 b. "Life jagra" .. 12 5
3821. 1 l. "Mimulus luteus" .. 20 8
3822. 1 l. 50 "Convolvulus tricolor" 30 15
3823. 2 l. 40 Type **664** 55 30

Nos. 3818/22 are vertical.

665. "Venus and Cupid" (Il Vecchio).

1971. Paintings of Nudes. Multicoloured.

3824. 10 b. "Nude" (J. Iser) (vert.) 5 5
3825. 29 b. "Nude" (C. Ressu) (vert.) 5 5
3826. 35 b. "Nude" (N. Grigorescu) (vert.) 5 5
3827. 60 b. "Odalisque" (Delacroix) 12 5
3828. 1 l. 75 "Nude in Landscape" (Renoir) .. 35 15
3829. 3 l. Type **665** 55 30

The 20 b. is smaller, 29 × 50 mm.

666. Astronauts and Lunar Rover on Moon.

1971. Air Moon Flight of "Apollo 15".

3833. **666.** 1 l. 50 multicoloured (blue background) 30 30

No. 3833 also exists imperforate, with background colour changed to green, from a restricted printing.

667. "Fishing-Boats" (M. W. Arnold).

1971. Marine Paintings. Multicoloured.

3835. 10 b. "Coastal Storm" (B. Peters) 5 5
3836. 20 b. "Seascape" (I. Backhuysen) 5 5
3837. 35 b. "Boat in Stormy Seas" (A. van de Eertvelt) 8 5
3838. 60 b. Type **667** 12 5
3839. 1 l. 75 "Seascape" (I. K. Aivazovsky) 30 15
3840. 3 l. "Fishing-boats, Braila" (J. A. Steriadi) 55 30

1971. As Nos. 3517/29 and three new designs but in smaller format, 17 × 23 or 23 × 17 mm.

3842. 1 l. green 15 5
3843. 1 l. 20 violet 15 8
3844. 1 l. 35 blue 20 8
3845. 1 l. 50 red 20 12
3846. 1 l. 55 brown 20 12
3847. 1 l. 75 green 25 12
3848. 2 l. green 30 15
3849. 2 l. 40 blue 35 15
3850. 3 l. blue 45 20
3851. 3 l. 20 brown 45 20
3852. 3 l. 25 blue 45 20
3853. 3 l. 60 blue 55 20
3854. 4 l. mauve 60 20
3855. 4 l. 80 blue 70 30
3856. 5 l. violet 70 35
3857. 6 l. mauve 90 35

NEW DESIGNS—VERT. 3 l. 60, Clearing letter-box. 4 l. 80, Postman on round. 6 l. Postal Ministry, Bucharest.

668. "Neagoe Basarab" (fresco, Curtea de Arges). 669. "T. Pallady" (self portrait).

1971. Prince Neagoe Basarab, Regent of Wallachia. 450th Death Anniv.

3858. **668.** 60 b. multicoloured .. 12 5

1971. Artists Anniversaries.

3859. **669.** 40 b. multicoloured .. 8 5
3860. – 55 b. blk., stone & gold 8 5
3861. – 1 l. 50 blk. stone & gold 25 15
3862. – 2 l. 40 multicoloured 40 15

DESIGNS: 40 b. (Birth centenary). 55 b. "B. Cellini" (400th Death anniv.), 1 l. 50, "Watteau" (self-portrait) (250th Death anniv.). 2 l. 40, "Durer" (self-portrait) (500th Birth anniv.)

670. Persian Text and Seal. 671. Figure-skating.

1971. Persian Empire. 2500th Anniv.

3863. **670.** 55 b. multicoloured .. 8 5

1971. Winter Olympic Games, Sapporo, Japan (1972). Multicoloured.

3864. 10 b. Type **671** 5 5
3865. 20 b. Ice-hockey 5 5
3866. 40 b. Biathlon 10 5
3867. 55 b. Bobsleighing .. 10 5
3868. 1 l. 75 Downhill skiing .. 30 15
3869. 3 l. Games emblem .. 55 30

672. "Lady with Letter" (Sava Hentia).

1971. Stamp Day.

3871 **672.** 1 l. 10+90 b. mult. 35 15

673. "St. George and the Dragon" (Moldovita).

1971. Frescoes from Northern Moldavian Monasteries (3rd series). Multicoloured.

3872. 10 b. Type **673** 5 5
3873. 20 b. "Three Kings and Angel" (Moldovita) .. 5 5
3874. 40 b. "The Crucifixion" (Moldovita) 8 5
3875. 55 b. "Trial" (Voronet) .. 12 5
3876. 1 l. 75 "Death of a Martyr" (Vovonet) .. 30 15
3877. 3 l. "King and Court" (Arborea) 55 30

674. Matei Millo (dramatist). 675. Magellan and Ships (450th Death Anniv.).

1971. Famous Rumanians. Multicoloured.

3879. 55 b. Type **674** 12 5
3880. 1 l. Nicolae Iorga (historian) 15 8

ANNIVERSARIES: 55 b. 75th Death Anniv. 1 l. Birth Cent.

1971. Scientific Annivs.

3881. **675.** 40 b. mauve, bl. & grn. 8 5
3882. – 55 b. blue, grn. & lilac 10 5
3883. – 1 l. multicoloured .. 15 8
3884. – 1 l. 50 grn., bl. & brn. 25 12

DESIGNS AND ANNIVERSARIES: 55 b. Kepler and observatory (400th Birth Anniv.). 1 l. Gargarin, rocket and Globe (10th anniv. of first manned space flight). 1 l. 50 Lord Rutherford and atomic symbol (Birth cent.).

676. Lynx Cubs.

1972. Young Wild Animals. Multicoloured.

3885. 20 b. Type **676** 5 5
3886. 35 b. Fox cubs 8 5
3887. 55 b. Fallow deer fawns .. 10 5
3888. 1 l. Wild piglets 20 5
3889. 1 l. 50 Wolf cubs 30 5
3890. 2 l. 40 Brown bear cubs .. 45 10

677. U.T.C. Emblem. 679. Crossed Arrows.

678. Wrestling.

1972. Communist Youth Union (U.T.C.) 50th Anniv.

3891. **677.** 55 b. multicoloured .. 8 5

1972. Olympic Games, Munich (1st issue). Multicoloured.

3892. 10 b. Type **678** 5 5
3893. 20 b. Canoeing 5 5
3894. 55 b. Football 5 5
3895. 1 l. 55 High-jumping .. 15 5
3896. 2 l. 90 Boxing 30 15
3897. 6 l. 70 Volleyball .. 55 35

See also Nos. 3915/20 and 3923.

1972. Inter-European Cultural and Economic Co-operation.

3899. – 1 l. 75 gold, blk. & pur. 30 5
3900. **679.** 2 l. 90 gold, blk. & grn. 50 15

DESIGN: 1 l. 75 Stylised map of Europe.

680. Astronauts in Lunar Rover. 681. Modern Trains and Symbol.

1972. Air. Moon Flight of "Apollo 16".

3901. **680.** 3 l. blue, grn. & pink 25 15

1972. Int. Railway Union. 50th Anniv.

3902. **681.** 55 b. multicoloured .. 8 5

682. "Paeonia romanica".

1972. Scarce Rumanian Flowers.

3904. **682.** 20 b. multicoloured .. 5 5
3905. – 40 b. pur., grn. & brn. 5 5
3906. – 55 b. brown and blue 8 5
3907. – 60 b. red, green and bright green .. 12 5
3908. – 1 l. 35 multicoloured 20 5
3909. – 2 l. 90 multicoloured 45 15

DESIGNS: 40 b. "Dianthus callizonus". 55 b. Leontopadium alpinum". 60 b. "Nigritella rubra". 1 l. 35 "Narcissus stellaris". 2 l. 90 "Cypripedium calceolus".

683. Saligny Bridge, Cernavoda.

1972. Danube Bridges. Multicoloured.

3910. 1 l. 35 Type **683** 15 5
3911. 1 l. 75 Giurgeni Bridge, Vadul Oii 20 5
3912. 2 l. 75 Prieteniei Bridge, Giurgiu-Russe 30 10

684. North Railway Station, Bucharest, 1872.

1972. North Railway Station, Bucharest. Cent.

3913. **684.** 55 b. multicoloured .. 8 5

685. Water-polo.

1972. Olympic Games, Munich. (2nd Issue). Multicoloured.

3914. 10 b. Type **685** 5 5
3915. 20 b. Pistol-shooting .. 5 5
3916. 55 b. Throwing the discus 8 5
3917. 1 l. 55 Gymnastics .. 15 5
3918. 2 l. 75 Canoeing 30 5
3919. 6 l. 40 Fencing 55 25

686. " E. Stoenescu " (S. Popescu).

1972. Rumanian Art. Portraits and Self-portraits. Multicoloured.

3921. 55 b. Type **686** 5 5
3922. 1 l. 75 " O. Bancila " (self-portrait) 15 5
3923. 2 l. 90 " Gh. Petrascu " (self-portrait) 30 5
3924. 6 l. 50 " J. Andreescu " (self-portrait) 55 20

689. Runner with Flame.

1972. Olympic Games, Munich (3rd Issue). Olympic Flame.

3928. **689.** 55b. pur. & blue on silver 8 5

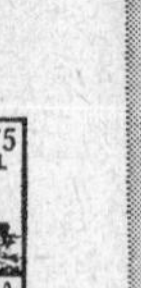

690. Sphinx Rock, Mt. Bucegi.

691. Satu Mare.

1972.

3929. – 1 l. 85 violet (postage) 12 5
3930. **690.** 2 l. 75 grey 20 5
3931. – 3 l. 35 red 25 5
3932. – 3 l. 45 green 25 5
3933. – 5 l. 15 blue 35 5
3934. – 5 l. 60 green 40 5
3935. – 6 l. 20 purple .. 40 5
3936. – 6 l. 40 brown .. 45 5
3937. – 6 l. 80 red 50 5
3938. – 7 l. 05 black 50 5
3939. – 8 l. 45 red 55 5
3940. – 9 l. 05 green 60 5
3941. – 9 l. 10 blue 60 5
3942. – 9 l. 85 green 65 5
3943. – 10 l. brown 65 5
3944. – 11 l. 90 purple .. 80 5
3945. – 12 l. 75 violet .. 85 5
3946. – 13 l. 30 red 90 5
3947. – 16 l. 20 green .. 1·10 5
3948. – 14 l. 60 blue (air) .. 1·00 5

DESIGNS—HORIZ. As Type **690.** 3 l. 45 Sinaia Castle. 5 l. 15 Hydro-electric power station, Arges. 6 l. 40 Hunidoara Castle. 6 l. 80 Polytechnic complex. 9 l. 05 Coliseum, Sarmisegetuza. 9 l. 10 Hydro-electric power station, Iron Gate (29×21 mm.). 11 l. 90 Place of the Republic, Bucharest. 13 l. 30 City Gate, Alba Iulia. 14 l. 60 Otopeni Airport. VERT. As Type **690.** 1 l. 85 Cluj Cathedral. 3 l. 35 Heroes' Monument, Bucharest. 5 l. 60 Iasi-Biserica. 6 l. 20 Bran Castle. 7 l. 05 Biserica Neagra, Brasnov. 8 l. 45 Roman building, Bucharest. 9 l. 85 Decebal's statue, Cetatea Deva. (20×30 mm.). 10 l. City Hall Tower, Sibiu. 12 l. 75 T.V. Building, Bucharest. 16 l. 20 Clock Tower, Sighisoara.

1972. Satu Mare. Millenium.

3949. **691.** 55 b. multicoloured .. 8 5

692. Davis Cup on Racquet.

1972. Final of Davis Cup Championships 1972, Bucharest.

3950. **692.** 2 l. 75 multicoloured 50 12

694. Fencing and Bronze Medals.

696. Flags and " 25 ".

695. " Travelling Romanies " (E. Volkers).

1972. Munich Olympic Games' Medals.

3958. **694.** 10 b. multicoloured .. 5 5
3959. – 20 b. multicoloured .. 5 5
3960. – 35 b. multicoloured .. 5 5
3961. – 1 l. 45 grey, pur. & pink 15 5
3962. – 2 l. 75 grey, brn. & ochre 30 5
3963. – 6 l. 20 multicoloured 55 20

DESIGNS: 20 b. Handball and bronze medal. 35 b. Boxing and silver medal. 1 l. 45 Hurdling and silver medal. 2 l. 75 Pistol-shooting, silver and bronze medals. 6 l. 20 Wrestling and two gold medals.

1972. Stamp Day.

3965. **695.** 1 l. 10+90 b. mult... 35 12

1972. Proclamation of Republic. 25th Anniv. Multicoloured.

3966. 55 b. Type **696** 5 5
3967. 1 l. 20 Arms and "25" .. 10 5
3968. 1 l. 75 Industrial scene and " 25 " 35 20

697. " Apollo 1, 2, 3 ".

698. Bee-eater.

1973. " Apollo " Moon Flights. Mult.

3969. 10 b. Type **697** .. 5 5
3970. 35 b. Grissom, Chaffee and White 5 5
3971. 40 b. " Apollo 4, 5, 6 " .. 5 5
3972. 55 b. " Apollo 7, 8 " .. 5 5
3973. 1 l. " Apollo 9, 10 " .. 8 5
3974. 1 l. 20 " Apollo 11, 12 " .. 12 5
3975. 1 l. 85 " Apollo 13, 14 " .. 20 5
3976. 2 l. 75 " Apollo 15, 16 " .. 25 10
3977. 3 l. 60 " Apollo 17 " .. 35 12

1973. Protection of Nature. Multicoloured.

(a) Birds.

3979. 1 l. 40 Type **698** .. 12 5
3980. 1 l. 85 Red-breasted goose 15 5
3981. 2 l. 75 Penduline tit .. 20 10

(b) Flowers.

3982. 1 l. 40 Marsh marigold .. 12 5
3983. 1 l. 85 Martagon lily .. 15 5
3984. 2 l. 75 Gentian 20 10

699. Copernicus.

700. Suceava Costume (female).

1973. Copernicus. 500th Birth Anniv.

3985. **699.** 2 l. 75 multicoloured 25 12

1973. Regional Costumes. Multicoloured.

3986. 10 b. Type **700** 5 5
3987. 40 b. Suceava (male) .. 5 5
3988. 55 b. Harghila (female) 5 5
3989. 1 l. 75 Harghila (male) .. 15 5
3990. 2 l. 75 Gorj (female) .. 25 5
3991. 6 l. 40 Gorj (male) .. 60 25

701. D. Paciurea (sculptor).

702. Map of Europe.

1973. Cultural Celebrities. Multicoloured.

3992. 10 b. Type **701** 5 5
3993. 40 b. I. Slavici (writer) .. 5 5
3994. 55 b. G. Lazar (writer) .. 5 5
3995. 6 l. 40 A. Flechtenmacher (composer) 60 25

1973. Inter-European Cultural and Economic Co-operation.

3996. **702.** 3 l. 35 gold, blue & pur. 25 25
3997. – 3 l. 60 gold & purple 25 25

DESIGN: 3 l. 60 Symbol of collaboration.

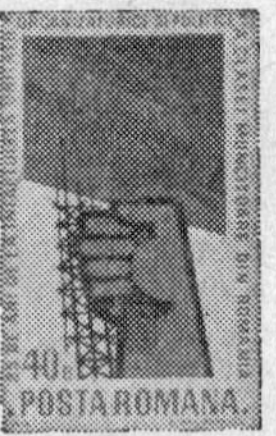

703. Hand with Hammer and Sickle.

704. W.M.O. Emblem and Weather Satellite.

1973. Anniversaries. Multicoloured.

3999. 40 b. Type **703** .. 5 5
4000. 55 b. Flags and bayonets 5 5
4001. 1 l. 75 Prince Cuza .. 15 5

EVENTS: 40 b. Rumanian Workers and Peasants Party. 25th Anniv. 55 b. National Anti-Fascist Committee. 40th Anniv. 1 l. 75 Prince Alexander Cuza. Death Cent.

1973. I.M.O./W.M.O. Centenary.

4002. **704.** 2 l. multicoloured .. 20 5

705. "Dimitri Ralet" (anon).

706. Prince Dimitri Cantemir.

1973. " Socfilex III " Stamp Exhibition, Bucharest. Portrait Paintings. Mult.

4003. 40 b. Type **705** 5 5
4004. 60 b. " Enacheta Vacarescu " (A. Chladek) 5 5
4005. 1 l. 55 " Dimitri Aman " (C. Lecca) 12 5
4006. 4 l.+2 l. " Barbat at his Desk " (B. Iscovescu) 60 25

1973. Dimitri Cantemir, Prince of Moldavia (writer). 300th Birth Anniv. Mult.

4008. **706.** 1 l. 75 multicoloured 15

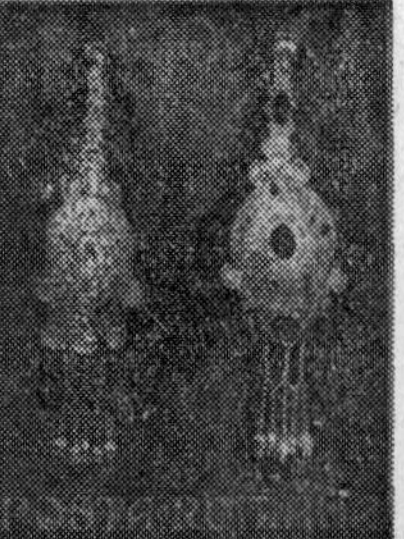

707. Fibular Brooches.

687. Aurel Vlaicu and Flying-Machine.

688. Rotary stamp-printing Press.

1972. Air. Rumanian Aviation Pioneers. Multicoloured.

3925. 60 b. Type **687** 12 8
3926. 3 l. Traian Vuja and flying-machine 45 35

1972. State Stamp-printing Works. Cent.

3927. **688.** 55 b. multicoloured 8 5

693. " Venice " (G. Petrascu).

1972. Paintings of Venice. Multicoloured.

3951. 10 b. Type **693** 5 5
3952. 20b. " Marina " (Darascu) 5 5
3953. 55 b. " Moliberi Palace " (Petrascu) 5 5
3954. 1 l. 55 " Venice " (Bunescu) 15 5
3955. 2 l. 75 " Venetian Palace " (Darascu) 30 5
3956. 6 l. 40 " Venice " (Bunesca) (different) .. 55 20

1973. Treasures of Pietrosa. Multicoloured.
4010. 10 b. Type **707** 5 5
4011. 20 b. Golden figurine and bowl (horiz.) 5 5
4012. 55 b. Gold oil flask .. 5 5
4013. 1 l. 55 Brooch and bracelets (horiz.) 12 5
4014. 2 l. 75 Gold platter .. 20 10
4015. 6 l. 80 Filgree cup-holder (horiz.).. .. .. 60 25

708. Oboga Jar. **709.** "Postilion" (A. Verona).

1973. Rumanian Ceramics. Multicoloured.
4018. 10 b. Type **708** 5 5
4019. 20 b. Vama dish and jug.. 5 5
4020. 55 b. Magiena bowl .. 5 5
4021. 1 l. 55 Sibiu Saschiz jug and dish 12 5
4022. 2 l. 75 Pisc pot and dish.. 20 10
4023. 6 l. 80 Oboga "bird" vessel 60 25

1973. Stamp Day.
4024. **709.** 1 l. 10+90 b. mult... 20 5

710. "Textile Workers" (G. Saru). **711.** Town Hall, Craiova.

1973. Paintings showing Workers. Mult.
4025. 10 b. Type **710** 5 5
4026. 20 b. "Construction Site" (M. Buncscu) (horiz.).. 5 5
4027. 55 b. "Shipyard Workers" (H. Catargi) (horiz.) .. 5 5
4028. 1 l. 55 "Working Man" (H. Catargi) 12 5
4029. 2 l. 75 "Miners" (A. Phoebus) 20 10
4030. 6 l. 80 "The Spinner" (N. Grigorescu) 60 25

1974.

(a) Buildings.
4032. **711.** 5 b. red 5 5
4033. – 10 b. blue 5 5
4034. – 20 b. orange 5 5
4035. – 35 b. green 5 5
4036. – 40 b. violet 5 5
4037. – 50 b. blue 5 5
4038. – 55 b. brown 5 5
4039. – 60 b. red 5 5
4040. – 1 l. blue 8 5
4041. – 1 l. 20 green .. 10 5

(b) Ships.
4042. – 1 l. 35 black.. .. 12 5
4043. – 1 l. 45 blue 12 5
4044. – 1 l. 50 red 12 5
4045. – 1 l. 55 blue 15 5
4046. – 1 l. 75 green 15 5
4047. – 2 l. 20 blue 15 5
4048. – 3 l. 65 lilac 25 12
4049. – 4 l. 70 purple.. .. 50 25

DESIGNS—VERT. 10 b. "Column of Infinity", Tirgu Jiu. 40 b. Romanesque church, Densus. 50 b. Reformed Church, Dej. 1 l. Curtea de Arges Monastery. HORIZ. 20 b. Heroes' Monument, Merasesti. 35 b. Citadel, Risnov. 55 b. Castle, Maldarasti. 60 b. National Theatre, Jassy. 1 l. 20 Fortress and church, Tirgu Mures. 1 l. 35 Danube tug. 1 l. 45 Freighter "Dimbovita". 1 l. 50 Cruise-ship "Muntenis". 1 l. 55 Training-ship "Mircea". 1 l. 75 Motorship "Transilvania". 2 l. 20 Ore-carrier "Oltul". 3 l. 65 Trawler "Mures". 4 l. 70 Oil-tanker "Arges".

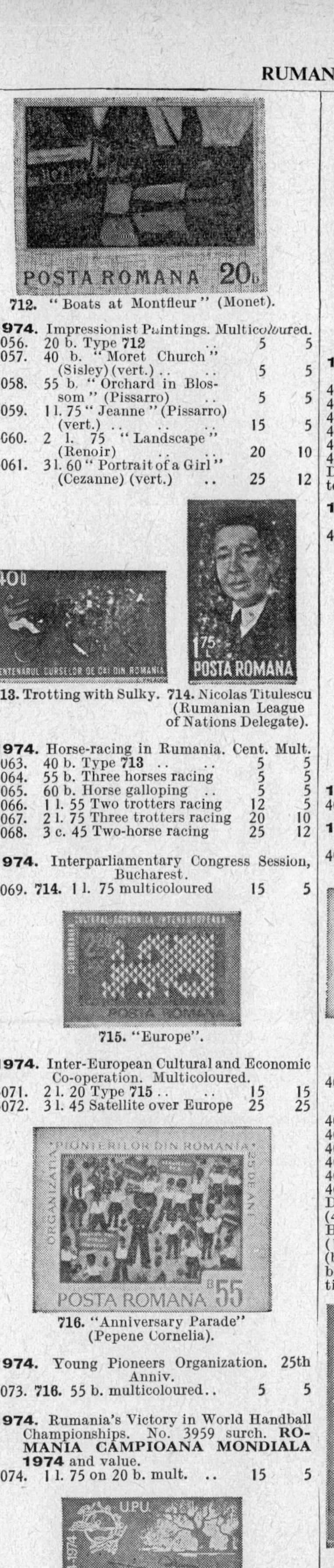

712. "Boats at Montfleur" (Monet).

1974. Impressionist Paintings. Multicoloured.
4056. 20 b. Type **712** 5 5
4057. 40 b. "Moret Church" (Sisley) (vert.) 5 5
4058. 55 b. "Orchard in Blossom" (Pissarro) .. 5 5
4059. 1 l. 75 "Jeanne" (Pissarro) (vert.) 15 5
4060. 2 l. 75 "Landscape" (Renoir) 20 10
4061. 3 l. 60 "Portrait of a Girl" (Cezanne) (vert.) .. 25 12

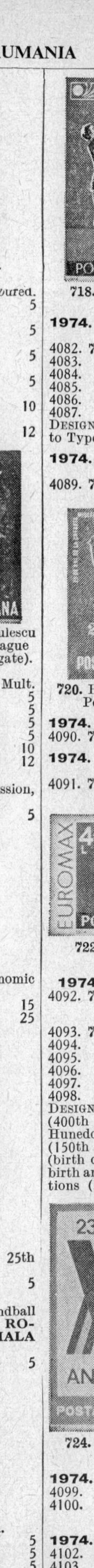

713. Trotting with Sulky. **714.** Nicolas Titulescu (Rumanian League of Nations Delegate).

1974. Horse-racing in Rumania. Cent. Mult.
4063. 40 b. Type **713** 5 5
4064. 55 b. Three horses racing 5 5
4065. 60 b. Horse galloping .. 5 5
4066. 1 l. 55 Two trotters racing 12 5
4067. 2 l. 75 Three trotters racing 20 10
4068. 3 c. 45 Two-horse racing 25 12

1974. Interparliamentary Congress Session, Bucharest.
4069. **714.** 1 l. 75 multicoloured 15 5

715. "Europe".

1974. Inter-European Cultural and Economic Co-operation. Multicoloured.
4071. 2 l. 20 Type **715** 15 15
4072. 3 l. 45 Satellite over Europe 25 25

716. "Anniversary Parade" (Pepene Cornelia).

1974. Young Pioneers Organization. 25th Anniv.
4073. **716.** 55 b. multicoloured.. 5 5

1974. Rumania's Victory in World Handball Championships. No. 3959 surch. **ROMANIA CAMPIOANA MONDIALA 1974** and value.
4074. 1 l. 75 on 20 b. mult. .. 15 5

717. Postal Motor-launch.

1974. U.P.U. Cent. Multicoloured.
4075. 20 b. Type **717** 5 5
4076. 40 b. Loading mail-train 5 5
4077. 55 b. Loading mail-plane 5 5
4078. 1 l. 75 Rural postman delivering letter .. 15 5
4079. 2 l. 75 Town postman delivering letter .. 20 10
4080. 3 l. 60 Young stamp collectors 25 12

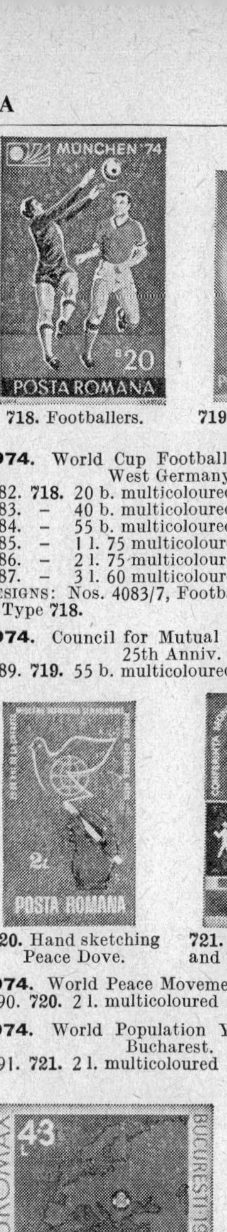

718. Footballers. **719.** Anniversary Emblem.

1974. World Cup Football Championships, West Germany.
4082. **718.** 20 b. multicoloured.. 5 5
4083. – 40 b. multicoloured.. 5 5
4084. – 55 b. multicoloured.. 5 5
4085. – 1 l. 75 multicoloured 15 5
4086. – 2 l. 75 multicoloured 20 10
4087. – 3 l. 60 multicoloured 25 12

DESIGNS: Nos. 4083/7, Football scenes similar to Type **718**.

1974. Council for Mutual Economic Aid. 25th Anniv.
4089. **719.** 55 b. multicoloured.. 5 5

720. Hand sketching Peace Dove. **721.** U.N. Emblem and "Five Races".

1974. World Peace Movement. 25th Anniv.
4090. **720.** 2 l. multicoloured .. 20 5

1974. World Population Year Conference, Bucharest.
4091. **721.** 2 l. multicoloured .. 20 5

722. Map of Europe. **723.** Prince John of Wallachia.

1974. "Euromax" Exhibition, Bucharest.
4092. **722.** 4 l.+3 l. yell., red & blue 60 25

1974. Anniversaries.
4093. **723.** 20 b. blue 5 5
4094. – 55 b. red 5 5
4095. – 1 l. blue 8 5
4096. – 1 l. 10 brown .. 10 5
4097. – 1 l. 30 purple .. 10 5
4098. – 1 l. 40 violet.. .. 12 5

DESIGNS AND ANNIVERSARIES—VERT. 20 b. (400th anniv.). 1 l. Iron and Steel Works, Hunedoara (220th anniv.). 1 l. 10 Avram Iancu (150th birth anniv.). 1 l. 30 Dr. C. I. Parhon (birth cent.). 1 l. 40 Dosoftei (savant) (350th birth anniv.). HORIZ. 55 b. Soldier and Installations (Rumanian Army Day. 30th anniv.).

724. "XXX" in Flags. **725.** "Centaurea nervosa".

1974. Liberation. 30th Anniv. Mult.
4099. 40 b. Type **724** 5 5
4100. 55 b. Soldiers, citizens and flags (horiz.) 5 5

1974. "Save Nature". Wild Flowers. Mult.
4102. 20 b. Type **725** 5 5
4103. 40 b. "Fritillaria montana" 5 5
4104. 55 b. "Taxus baccata" .. 5 5
4105. 1 l. 75 "Rhododendron kotschyi" 15 5
4106. 2 l. 75 "Eritrichium nanum" 20 10
4107. 3 l. 60 "Dianthus spiculifolius" 25 12

726. Bust of Isis.

1974. Rumanian Archaeology. Multicoloured.
4108. 20 b. Type **726** 5 5
4109. 40 b. Glykon serpent (sculpture) 5 5
4110. 55 b. Head of Emperor Traianus Decius (bronze) 5 5
4111. 1 l. 75 Rumanian Woman (statue).. .. .. 15 5
4112. 2 l. 75 Mithras (sculptured relief) 20 10
4113. 3 l. 60 Rumanian citizen (statue).. .. .. 25 12

727. Sibiu.

1974. Stamp Day.
4114. **727.** 2 l. 10+1 l. 90 mult. 40 15

1974. "Nationala 74" Stamp Exhibition. No. 4114 optd. **EXPOZITIA FILATELICA "NATIONALA '74" 15-24 noiembrie Bucuresti.**
4115. **727.** 2 l. 10+1 l. 90 mult. 40 15

728. Party Emblem.

1974. 11th Rumanian Communist Party Congress, Bucharest.
4116. **728.** 55 b. multicoloured.. 5 5
4117. – 1 l. multicoloured .. 8 5

DESIGN: 1 l. Similar to Type **728**, showing party emblem and curtain.

729. "The Discus-thrower" (Myron).

1974. Rumanian Olympic Committee. 60th Anniv.
4118. **729.** 2 l. multicoloured .. 20 5

730. "Skylab". **731.** Dr. Schweitzer.

1974. "Skylab" Space Laboratory.
4119. **730.** 2 l. 50 multicoloured 20 5

1974. Dr. Albert Schweitzer. Birth Cent.
4120. **731.** 40 b. brown 5 5

732. Handball Players. 734. Flaming Torch.

733. "Rocks and Birches" (Andreescu).

1975. World University Handball Championships.

4121. 732. 55 b. multicoloured.. 5 5
4122. – 1 l. 75 multicoloured 15 5
4123. – 2 l. 20 multicoloured 20 5

DESIGNS: 1 l. 75, 2 l. 20 similar designs to Type 732.
No. 4122 is vert.

1975. Paintings by Ion Andreescu. Mult.

4124. 20 b. Type 733 .. .. 5 5
4125. 40 b. "Peasant Woman with Green Kerchief".. 5 5
4126. 55 b. "Winter in the Forest".. .. .. 5 5
4127. 1 l. 75 "Winter in Barbizon" (horiz.).. .. 15 5
4128. 2 l. 75 Self-portrait .. 20 10
4129. 3 l. 90 "Main Road" (horiz.) 25 12

1975. Socialist Republic. Tenth Anniv.

4130. 734. 40 b. multicoloured.. 5 5

735. "Battle of the High Bridge" (O. Obedeanu).

1975. Victory over the Turks at High Bridge. 500th Anniv.

4131. 735. 55 b multicoloured.. 8 5

736. "Peasant Woman Spinning" (N. Grigorescu). 737. "Michelangelo" (self-portrait).

1975. International Women's Year.

4132. 736. 55 b multicoloured.. 8 5

1975. Michelangelo 500th Birth Anniv.

4133. 737. 5 l. multicoloured .. 60 30

738. Mitsui Children's Science Pavilion.

1975. International Exposition, Okinawa.

4135. 738. 4 l. multicoloured .. 50 25

739. "Peonies" (N. Tonitza).

1975. Inter-European Cultural and Economic Co-operation. Multicoloured.

4136. 2 l. 20 Type 739 .. 25 12
4137. 3 l. 45 "Chrysanthemums" (St. Luchian) 40 20

740. Dove with Coded Letter.

1975. Introduction of Postal Codes.

4138. 740. 55 b. multicoloured.. 8 5

741. Emblem on Globe.

1975. Metre Convention. Cent.

4139. 741. 1 l. 85 multicoloured 25 12

742. M. Eminescu and Museum.

1975. Mihail Eminescu (poet). 125th Birth Anniv.

4140. 742. 55 b. multicoloured.. 8 5

743. Commemorative Tablet and Coins.

1975. Alba-Iulia. Bimillenary.

4141. 743. 55 b. multicoloured.. 8 5

744. Ana Ipatescu. 745. Emperor Trajan.

1975. Ana Ipatescu (revolutionary). Death Cent.

4143. 744. 55 b. mauve.. .. 8 5

1975. European Protection of Monuments Year.

4144. 745. 55 b. black & brown 8 5
4145. – 1 l. 20 black and blue 15 8
4146. – 1 l. 55 black & green 20 10
4147. – 1 l. 75 sepia, blk. & red 25 12
4148. – 2 l. sepia, blk. & yell. 25 12
4149. – 2 l. 25 sepia, blk. & bl. 25 12

DESIGNS—VERT. 1 l. 20 Trajan's Column, Rome. 1 l. 55 Decebel. 10 l. Roman remains, Gradiste. HORIZ: 1 l. 75 Remains and "reconstruction" of Imperial monument, Adam Clissi. 2 l. Excavations, Turnu-Severin. 2 l. 25 Remains and drawing of Emperor Trajan's Bridge.

746. "Apollo" and "Soyuz" in Orbit.

1975. Air. "Apollo-Soyuz" Space Link. Multicoloured.

4151. 1 l. 75 Type 746 .. 25 12
4152. 3 l. 25 "Apollo" and "Soyuz" linked together 40 20

747. "Michael the Brave" (Sadeler).

1975. First Political Union of Rumanian States. 575th Anniv. Multicoloured.

4153. 55 b. Type 747 .. .. 8 5
4154. 1 l. 20 "Ottoman envoys bringing gifts to Michael the Brave" (T. Aman) (horiz.) 15 8
4155. 2 l. 75 "Michael the Brave at Calugareni" (T. Aman).. .. .. 35 15

748. "Delphinium consolida". 749. Policeman using Pocket Radio.

1975. Flowers. Multicoloured.

4158. 20 b. Type 748.. .. 5 5
4159. 40 b. "Papaver dubium" 5 5
4160. 55 b. "Xeranthemum annuum" 8 5
4161. 1 l. 75 "Helianthemum nummularium" .. 25 12
4162. 2 l. 75 "Salvia pratensis" 35 15
4163. 3 l. 60 "Cickorium intybus" 45 20

1975. International Philatelic Fair, Riccione (Italy). Optd. **Ricione—Italia 23-25 August 1975.**

4164. 737. 5 l. multicoloured .. 60 30

1975.

4165. 749. 55 b. blue 8 5

750. Text on Map.

1975. First Documentary Attestations of Daco-Getian Settlements. Annivs. Multicoloured.

4166. 20 b. Type 750 .. .. 5 5
4167. 55 b. Map showing location of Pelendava (1750th) and Craiova (500th) (horiz.) .. 8 5
4168. 1 l. Text As T 750, but diff. map .. 12 5

751. Muntenia Carpet.

1975. Rumanian Carpets. Multicoloured.

4169. 20 b. Type 751 .. .. 5 5
4170. 40 b. Banat 5 5
4171. 55 b. Oltenia 8 5
4172. 1 l. 75 Moldova 25 12
4173. 2 l. 75 Oltenia (different) 35 15
4174. 3 l. 60 Maramures .. 45 20

752. Minibus.

1976. Rumanian Motor Vehicles. Multicoloured.

4175. 20 b. Type 752 .. .. 5 5
4176. 40 b. 19 A L P tanker lorry 5 5
4177. 55 b. A R O 240 field car 8 5
4178. 1 l. 75 R. 8135 l lorry .. 25 12
4179. 2 l. 75 Dacia 1300 saloon car 35 15
4180. 3 l. 60 R. 19215 D F K tipper truck 45 20

753. Head Post Office, Bucharest.

1975. Stamp Day. Multicoloured.

4181. 1 l. 50+1 l. 50 Type 753 35 20
4182. 2 l. 10+1 l. 90 Aerial view of G.P.O. 50 30

754. Tobogganing.

1976. Winter Olympic Games, Innsbruck. Multicoloured.

4184. 20 b. Type 754 .. .. 5 5
4185. 40 b. Rifle-shooting (biathlon) (vert.) 5 5
4186. 55 b. Downhill skiing (slalom) 8 5
4187. 1 l. 75 Ski-jumping .. 25 12
4188. 2 l. 75 Figure-skating (women's) .. 40 20
4189. 3 l. 60 Ice-hockey .. 55 25

755. "Washington at Valley Forge" (Tergo).

1976. American Revolution. Bicent. Multicoloured.

4191. 20 b. Type 755 .. .. 5 5
4192. 40 b. "Washington at Trenton" (Trumbull) (vert.) 5 5
4193. 55 b. "Washington crossing the Delaware" (Leutze) 8 5
4194. 1 l. 75 "Capture of the Hessians" (Trumbull) 25 12
4195. 2 l. 75 "Jefferson" (Sully) (vert.) 40 20
4196. 3 l. 60 "Surrender of Cornwallis at Yorktown" (Trumbull) 55 25

756. " Prayer ".

1976. C. Brancusi (sculptor). Birth Cent. Mult.

4198. 55 b. Type **756** 8 5
4199. 1 l. 75 Architectural Assembly, Tg. Jiu .. 25 12
4200. 3 l. 60 C. Brancusi .. 55 25

757. Anton Davidoglu (mathematician). **759.** Dr. C. Davila.

758. Inscribed Tablets.

1976. Anniversaries. Multicoloured.

4201. 40 b. Type **757** (birth centenary) 5 5
4202. 55 b. Prince Vlad Tepes (500th death anniv.).. 8 5
4203. 1 l. 20 Costache Negri (patriot-death centenary) 20 10
4204. 1 l. 75 Gallery, Archives Museum (50th anniv.) 25 12

1976. Daco-Roman Archaelogical Discoveries. Multicoloured.

4205. 20 b. Type **758** 5 5
4206. 40 b. Roman sculptures 5 5
4207. 55 b. Dacian coins and pottery 8 5
4208. 1 l. 75 Dacian pottery.. 25 12
4209. 2 l. 75 Roman Altar and spears 40 20
4210. 3 l. 60 Vase and spears.. 55 25

1976. Rumanian Red Cross Centenary. Multicoloured.

4212. 55 b. Type **759** 8 5
4213. 1 l. 75 Red Cross Nurse.. 25 12
4214. 2 l. 20 First aid.. .. 35 15
4215. 3 l. 35 Blood donors .. 50 25

760. Gymnastics.

1976. Olympic Games, Montreal. Mult.

4216. 20 b. Type **760** 5 5
4217. 40 b. Boxing 5 5
4218. 55 b. Netball 8 5
4219. 1 l. 75 Rowing (horiz.).. 25 12
4220. 2 l. 75 Gymnastics (different) (horiz.) .. 40 20
4221. 3 l. 60 Canoeing (horiz.).. 55 25

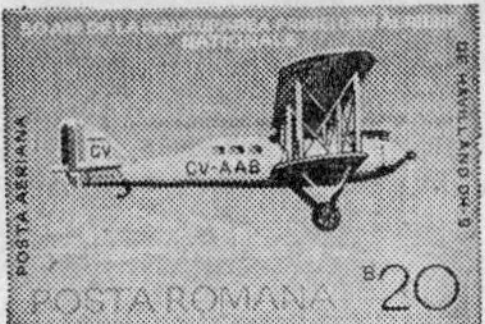

761. De Haviland D.H.-9.

1976. TAROM (State airline). 50th Anniv.

4223. 20 b. Type **761** 5 5
4224. 40 b. I.C.A.R. " Commercial " monoplane.. 5 5
4225. 60 b. Douglas " DC "-3.. 10 5
4226. 1 l. 75 Antonov " AN "-24 25 12
4227. 2 l. 75 Ilyushin " LL "-62 40 20
4228. 3 l. 60 Boeing " 707 " .. 55 25

762. Daco-Getian Statuette.

1976. Bazau State. 1600th Anniv.

4229. **762.** 55 b. multicoloured.. 8 5

763. Vase with Portrait of King Decebalus. **764.** Arms of Rumania.

1976. Inter-European Cultural and Economic Collaboration. Multicoloured.

4230. 2 l. 20 Type **736** .. 35 15
4231. 3 l. 45 Vase with portrait of King Michael the Bold 50 25

1976.

4232. **764.** 1 l. 75 multicoloured 25 12

1976. Philatelic Exhibition, Bucharest. No. 4200 surch. +**1.80 L EXPOZITIA FILATELICA, BUCURESTI. 12-19-IV, 1976.**

4233. 3 l. 60+1 l. 80 multicoloured 80 40

765. " Carnations and Oranges ".

1976. Floral Paintings by Stefan Luchian. Multicoloured.

4234. 20 b. Type **765** 5 5
4235. 40 b. " Flower Arrangement " 5 5
4236. 55 b. " Immortelles " .. 8 5
4237. 1 l. 75 " Roses in Vase " 25 12
4238. 2 l. 75 " Cornflowers ".. 40 20
4239. 3 l. 60 " Carnations in Vase ".. .. 55 25

766. Milan Cathedral.

1976. " Italia '76 " International Philatelic Exhibition, Milan.

4240. **766.** 4 l. 75 multicoloured 70 35

767. Gymnastics. (Bronze Medal). **768.** " Elena Cuza " (T. Aman).

1976. Olympic Games, Montreal. Rumanian Medal Winners. Multicoloured.

4241. 20 b. Type **767** 5 5
4242. 40 b. Fencing (Bronze Medal).. .. .. 5 5
4243. 55 b. Javelin (Bronze Medal).. .. .. 8 5
4244. 1 l. 75 Handball (Silver Medal).. .. .. 25 12
4245. 2 l. 75 Boxing (Silver and Bronze Medals) (horiz.) 40 20
4246. 3 l. 60 Wrestling (Silver and Bronze Medals) (horiz.) 55 25
4247. 5 l. 70 Nadi Comaneci (gymnastics – 3 Gold, 1 Silver and 1 Bronze Medals) 85 40

1976. Stamp Day.

4249. **768.** 2 l. 10+1 l. 90 multicoloured 60 30

POSTAL TAX STAMPS

The following stamps were for compulsory use at certain times on inland mail to raise money for various funds. In some instances where the stamps were not applied the appropriate Postal Tax Postage Due stamps were applied.

Other denominations exist but these were purely for revenue purposes and were not applied to postal matter.

Soldiers Families Fund.

1915. Optd. **TIMBRU DE AJUTOR.**

T 638. **27.** 5 b. green 5 5
T 639. 10 b. red 5 5

T 1. The Queen Weaving. **T 2.** " Charity "

1916.

T 649. **T 1.** 5 b. black 5 5
T 710. 5 b. green 5 5
T 650. 10 b. brown 5 5
T 711. 10 b. black 5 5

The 50 b. and 1, 2, 5 and 50 l. in similar designs were only used fiscally.

1918. Optd. **1918.**

T 671. **27.** 5 b. green (No. T 638) 10·00 10·00
T 667. **T 1.** 5 b. black 8 8
T 672. **27.** 10 b. red (No. T 639) 10·00 10·00
T 668. **T 1.** 10 b. brown .. 8 8

1921. Social Welfare.

T 978. **T 2.** 10 b. green .. 5 5
T 979. 25 b. black .. 5 5

Aviation Fund.

T 3. **T 4.**

1931.

T 1216. **T 3.** 50 b. green .. 5 5
T 1217. 1 l. brown .. 5 5
T 1218. 2 l. blue .. 5 5

1932.

T 1252. **T 4.** 50 b. green .. 5 5
T 1253. 1 l. purple.. .. 5 5
T 1254. 2 l. blue 5 5

Stamps as T 4 but inscr. "FONDUL AVIATIEI" were only for fiscal use. Nos. T 1253/4 could only be used fiscally after 1937.

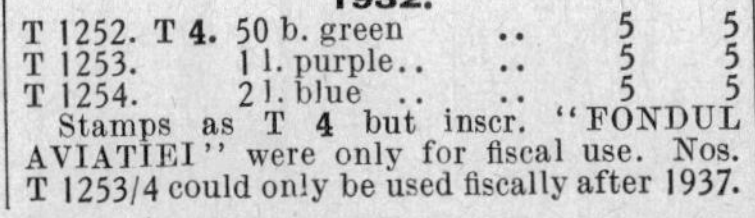

T 5. **T 6.** " Aviation "

1932. Cultural Fund.

T 1276. **T 5.** 2 l. blue 12 5
T 1277. 2 l. Brown .. 8 5

These were for compulsory use on postcards.

1936.

T 1340. **T 6.** 50 b. green .. 5 5
T 1341. 1 l. brown .. 5 5
T 1342. 2 l. blue .. 5 5

Other stamps inscr. "FONDUL AVIATIEI" were only for fiscal use.

T 7. King Michael. **T 8.** Destitute Children.

1943.

T 1589. **T 7.** 50 b. orange .. 5 5
T 1590. 1 l. lilac .. 5 5
T 1591. 2 l. brown .. 5 5
T 1592. 4 l. blue .. 5 5
T 1593 5 l. violet .. 5 5
T 1594. 8 l. green .. 5 5
T 1595. 10 l. brown .. 5 5

1945. Child Welfare Fund.

T 1758. **T 8.** 40 l. blue .. 8 8

Invalids, Widows and Orphans Fund.

1947. Fiscal stamps (22×18½ mm.), perf. vert. through centre surch. **IOVR** and value.

T 1923. 1 l. on 2 l. red.. .. 5 5
T 1924. 5 l. on 1 l. green .. 5 5

1948. Vert. designs (approx. 18½×22 mm.) inscr. "I.O.V.R.".

T 1948. 1 l. red 5 5
T 1949. 1 l. violet 5 5
T 1950. 2 l. blue 8 8
T 1951. 5 l. yellow 25 25

NEWSPAPER STAMPS.

1919. Transylvania. Cluj Issue. No. N 136 of Hungary optd. as **T 44.**

N 783. **N 3.** 2 b. orange .. 5 5

1919. Transylvania. Oradea Issue. No. 136 of Hungary optd. as **T 45.**

N 859. **N 3.** 2 b. orange .. 8 8

EXPRESS LETTER STAMPS.

1919. Transylvania. Cluj Issue. No. E 245 of Hungary optd. as **T 44.**

E 784. **E 1.** 2 b. olive and red 5 5

1919. Transylvania. Oradea Issue. No. E 245 of Hungary optd. as **T 45.**

E 860. **E 1.** 2 b. olive and red .. 8 8

SAVINGS BANK STAMPS.

1919. Transylvania. Cluj Issue. No. B 199 of Hungary optd. as **T 44.**

B 785. **B 1.** 10 b. dull purple .. 8 8

1919. Transylvania. Oradea Issue. No. B 199 of Hungary optd. as **T 45.**

B 861. **B 1.** 10 b. purple .. 8 8

OFFICIAL STAMPS

O 1. Rumanian Eagle and National Flag. **O 2.**

1929.

O 1115. **O 1.** 25 b. orange .. 5 5
O 1116. 50 b. brown .. 5 5
O 1117. 1 l. violet .. 5 5
O 1118. 2 l. green .. 5 5
O 1119. 3 l. red .. 5 5
O 1120. 4 l. olive .. 5 5
O 1121. 6 l. blue .. 25 5
O 1122. 10 l. blue .. 5 5
O 1123. 25 l. claret .. 20 5
O 1124. 50 l. violet .. 50 25

1930. Optd. **8 IUNIE 1930.**

O 1150. **O 1.** 25 b. orange .. 5 5
O 1151. 50 b. brown .. 5 5
O 1152. 1 l. violet .. 5 5
O 1153. 2 l. green .. 5 5

O 1165. O1. 3 l. red 5 5
O 1154. 4 l. olive 5 5
O 1160. 6 l. blue 5 5
O 1161. 10 l. blue 5 5
O 1156. 25 l. claret .. 40 8
O 1157. 50 l. violet .. 65 10

1831.
O 1194 O 2. 25 b. black .. 5 5
O 1195 1 l. purple .. 5 5
O 1196 2 l. green .. 12 5
O 1197 3 l. red .. 12 5
O 1247 6 l. claret .. 20 15

PARCEL POST STAMPS

1895. As Type D 1 but inscr. at top "TAXA DE FACTAGIU".
P 353. 25 b. brown 90 10
P 479. 25 b. red 40 8

1928. Surch. **FACTAJ 5 LEI.**
P 1078. 37. 5 l. on 10 b. green 15 5

POSTAGE DUE STAMPS

A. Ordinary Postage Due Stamps.

D 1. D 2.

1881.
D 152. D 1. 2 b. brown 40 20
D 153. 5 b. brown .. .. 2·00 35
D 200. 10 b. brown .. 1·25 12
D 201. 30 b. brown .. 1·00 12
D 156. 50 b. brown .. 2·00 40
D 157. 60 b. brown .. 2·10 60

1887.
D 448. D 1. 2 b. green 10 5
D 551. 5 b. green 5 5
D 558. 10 b. green .. 5 5
D 553. 30 b. green .. 8 5
D 452. 50 b. green .. 35 8
D 245. 60 b. green .. 1·25 50

1911.
D 617. D 2. 2 b. blue on yellow 5 5
D 618. 5 b. blue on yellow 5 5
D 619. 10 b. blue on yellow 5 5
D 604. 15 b. blue on yellow 8 5
D 621. 20 b. blue on yellow 5 5
D 622. 30 b. blue on yellow 5 5
D 623. 50 b. blue on yellow 5 5
D 624. 60 b. blue on yellow 5 5
D 609. 2 l. blue on yellow 15 8

1918. Optd. **TAXA DE PLATA.**
D 675. 27. 5 b. green 8 8
D 676. 10 b. red 8 8

1918. Re-issue of Type D 2. On greenish or white paper.
D 1001. D 2. 5 b. black .. 5 5
D 722. 10 b. black .. 5 5
D 734a. 20 b. black .. 5 5
D 735. 30 b. black .. 5 5
D 736. 50 b. black .. 5 5
D 998. 60 b. black .. 8 5
D 1007. 1 l. black .. 10 5
D 1010. 2 l. black .. 15 5
D 991. 3 l. black .. 8 5
D 992. 6 l. black .. 8 5
D 1547. 50 l. black .. 5 5
D 1548. 100 l. black .. 5 5

1919. Transylvania. Cluj Issue. No. D 190 etc. of Hungary optd. as T **44.**
D 786. D 1. 1 b. red and green .. 40·00 40·00
D 787. 2 b. red and green .. 8 8
D 788. 5 b. red and green .. 8·00 8·00
D 789. 10 b. red and green .. 8 8
D 790. 15 b. red and green .. 2·10 2·10
D 791. 20 b. red and green .. 8 8
D 792. 30 b. red and green .. 4·50 4·50
D 793. 50 b. red and green .. 1·90 1·90

1919. Transylvania. Oradea Issue. No. D 190, etc. of Hungary optd. as T **45.**
D 861. D 1. 1 b. red and green 8·00 8·00
D 862. 2 b. red and green .. 5 5
D 863. 5 b. red and green .. 1·25 1·25
D 865. 10 b. red and green .. 5 5
D 866. 12 b. red and green .. 20 20
D 867. 15 b. red and green .. 20 20
D 868. 20 b. red and green .. 5 5
D 869. 30 b. red and green .. 20 20

1930. Optd. **8 IUNIE 1930.**
D 1168. D 2. 1 l. black .. 5 5
D 1169. 2 l. black .. 5 5
D 1170. 3 l. black .. 8 5
D 1171. 6 l. black .. 12 5

D 4. D 5.

1932.
D 1249. D 4. 1 l. black .. 5 5
D 1250. 2 l. black .. 5 5
D 1251. 3 l. black .. 5 5
D 1252. 6 l. black .. 5 5
D 1835. 20 l. black .. 5 5
D 1839. 50 l. black .. 5 5
D 1840. D 4. 80 l. black .. 5 5
D 1841. 100 l. black .. 5 5
D 1842. 200 l. black .. 5 5
D 1843. 500 l. black .. 5 5
D 1844. 5000 l. black .. 15 12

1947. Type D 5 perforated down centre (without opt.).
Un. pair
D 1919. 2 l. red 5
D 1920. 4 l. blue 8
D 1921. 5 l. black 8
D 1922. 10 l. brown 15

The left half of Nos. D 1919/22, showing Crown, served as a receipt and was stuck in the postman's book and so does not come postally used.

1948. Nos. D 1919/22, optd. as in Type D **5.**
Un. pair. Us. pair.
D 1944. 2 l. red 5 5
D 1945. 4 l. blue 5 5
D 1946. 5 l. black 8 5
D 1947. 10 l. brown .. 12 8

D 6.
Badge. Postwoman.

1950. Un. pair. Us. pair.
D 2066. D 6. 2 l. vermilion .. 5 5
D 2067. 4 l. blue 8 8
D 2068. 5 l. green .. 12 8
D 2069. 10 l. brown .. 15 15

1952. Currency revalued. Nos. D 2066/9 surch. thus: **4 Bani** on each half.
Un. pair. Us. pair.
D 2221. D 6. 4 b. on 2 l. vermilion 5 5
D 2222. 10 b. on 4 l. blue 5 5
D 2223. 20 b. on 5 l. green 8 8
D 2224. 50 b. on 10 l. brown 15 15

D 7.
G.P.O. Bucharest. Posthorn.

1957. Un. pair. Us. pair.
D 2507. D 7. 3 b. black .. 5 5
D 2508. 5 b. orange .. 5 5
D 2509. 10 b. purple .. 5 5
D 2510. 20 b. red .. 5 5
D 2511. 40 b. green .. 10 5
D 2512. 1 l. blue .. 25 10

D 8.

1967. Un. pair. Us. pair.
D 3436. D 8. 3 b. green .. 5 5
D 3437. 5 b. blue .. 5 5
D 3438. 10 b. magenta .. 5 5
D 3439. 20 b. red .. 5 5
D 3440. 40 b. brown .. 5 5
D 3441. 1 l. violet .. 15 5

D 9.

1974. Un pair Us. pair
D 4050. D 9. 5 b. blue .. 5 5
D 4051. 10 b. green .. 5 5
D 4052. – 20 b. red .. 5 5
D 4053. – 40 b. violet .. 10 5
D 4054. – 50 b. brown .. 10 5
D 4055. – 1 l. orange .. 15 5

DESIGNS: 20 b., 40 b. Dove with letter and Hermes with posthorn. 50 b., 1 l. G.P.O., Bucharest and emblem with mail-van.

B. Postal Tax Due Stamps.

1915. Optd. **TIMBRU DE AJUTOR.**
TD 643. D 2. 5 b. blue on yellow 10 5
TD 644. 10 b. blue on yellow 5 5

TD 1.

TD 2.

1917. Green or white paper.
TD 655. TD 1. 5 b. brown .. 30 12
TD 743. 5 b. red .. 5 5
TD 654. 10 b. red .. 10 10
TD 741. 10 b. brown .. 8 8

1918. Optd. **TAXA DE PLATA.**
TD 680. TD 1. 5 b. black .. 8 8
TD 681. 10 b. brown .. 8 8

1922. As Type TD 1, but inscr. "ASSISTENTA SOCIALA". On green or white paper.
TD 1028. 10 b. brown 5 5
TD 1029. 20 b. brown 5 5
TD 1030. 25 b. brown 5 5
TD 1031. 50 b. brown 5 5

1931. Aviation Fund. Optd. **TIMBRUL AVIATIEI.**
TD 1219. D 2. 1 l. black .. 5 5
TD 1220. 2 l. black .. 5 5

1932.
TD 1278. TD 2. 3 l. black .. 12 5

RUMANIAN OCCUPATION OF HUNGARY E2

BANAT BACSKA

The following stamps were issued by the Temesvar postal authorities between the period of the Serbian evacuation and the Rumanian occupation. This area was later divided, the Western part going to Yugoslavia and the Eastern part going to Rumania.

100 filler = 1 korona.

1919. Stamps of Hungary optd. **Banat Bacska 1919.**

(a) "Turul" Type.
1. 3. 50 f. lake on blue .. 3·75 3·75

(b) War Charity stamps of 1916.
2. 6. 10 f. (+2 f.) red .. 10 10
3. – 15 f. (+2 f.) violet .. 10 10
4. 8. 40 f. (+2 f.) lake .. 10 10

(c) Harvesters and Parliament Types.
5. 11. 2 f. brown .. 10 10
6. 3 f. claret .. 10 10
7. 5 f. green .. 10 10
8. 6 f. blue .. 10 10
9. 15 f. violet .. 10 10
10. 35 f. brown .. 5·50 5·50
11. 12. 50 f. purple .. 3·75 3·75
12. 75 f. blue .. 10 10
13. 80 f. green .. 10 10
14. 1 k. lake .. 10 10
15. 2 k. brown .. 10 10
16. 3 k. grey and violet .. 4·00 4·00
17. 5 k. brown .. 25 25
18. 10 k. lilac and brown .. 65 65

(d) Karl and Zita stamps.
19. 13. 10 f. red .. 10 10
20. 20 f. brown .. 10 10
21. 25 f. blue .. 10 10
22. 14. 40 f. olive .. 10 10
23. 50 f. purple .. 10 10

(e) Harvesters Type inscr. "MAGYAR POSTA"
24. 11. 10 f. red .. 2·50 2·50
25. 20 f. brown .. 2·10 2·10
26. 25 f. blue .. 4·25 4·25

The following (Nos. 27/39) are also optd. **KOZTARSASAG**

(f) Harvesters and Parliament Types.
27. 11. 4 f. slate .. 10 10
28. 5 f. green .. 10 10
29. 6 f. blue .. 10 10
30. 10 f. red .. 1·90 1·90
31. 20 f. brown .. 1·90 1·90
32. 40 f. olive .. 10 10
33. 12. 1 k. lake .. 10 10
34. 2 k. brown .. 2·25 2·50
35. 3 k. grey and violet .. 2·25 2·50
36. 5 k. brown .. 2·50 2·50
37. 10 k. lilac and brown .. 2·75 2·75

(g) Karl portrait stamps.
38. 13. 15 f. violet .. 1·00 1·00
39. 25 f. blue .. 1·00 1·00

(h) Serbian Occupation of Temesvar stamps.
40. 11. 10 f. on 2 f. brown 40 40
41. 6. 45 f. on 10 f. (+2 f.) red 40 40
42. 11. 1 k. 50 in 15 f. violet .. 40 40

NEWSPAPER STAMP

1919. No. N 136 optd. **Banat Bacska 1919.**
N 43. N 3. (2 f.) orange .. 15 15

EXPRESS LETTER STAMP

1919. No. E 245 optd. as above, and surch.
E 44. E 1. 30 f. on 2 f. olive & red 80 80

SAVINGS BANK STAMP.

1919. No. B 199 optd. as above, and surch.
B 45. B 1. 50 f. on 10 f. purple 80 80

POSTAGE DUE STAMPS

1919. Nos. D 191 etc. optd. as above.
D 46. D 1. 2 f. red and green .. 25 25
D 47. 10 f. red and green .. 25 25
D 48. 15 f. red and green .. 4·00 4·00
D 49. 20 f. red and green 25 25
D 50. 30 f. red and green .. 2·50 2·50
D 51. 50 f. black and green 3·50 3·50

DEBRECEN

This area was later returned to Hungary.
100 filler = 1 korona.

(1.)

1919. Stamps of Hungary optd. with T 1, or surch. in addition.

(a) "Turul" Type.
1. 3. 2 f. yellow .. .. 1·75 1·75
2. 3 f. orange .. .. 3·50 3·50
3. 6 f. drab 90 90

(b) War Charity stamps of 1915.
4. 3. 2 f.+2 f. yellow (No. 171) .. 3·50 3·50
5. 3 f.+2 f. orange (No. 172) .. 3·50 3·50

(c) War Charity stamps of 1916.
6. 6. 10 f. (+2 f.) red .. 5 5
7. – 15 f. (+2 f.) violet .. 20 25
8. 8. 40 f. (+2 f.) lake .. 12 12

(d) Harvesters and Parliament Types.
9. 11. 2 f. brown .. 8 5
10. 3 f. claret .. 8 5
11. 5 f. green .. 12 12
12. 6 f. blue .. 8 8
13. 10 f. red (No. 243) .. 4·25 4·25
14. 15 f. violet (No. 244) .. 4·25 4·25
15. 15 f. violet .. 8 8
16. 20 f. brown .. 2·75 2·75
17. 25 f. blue .. 25 25
18. 35 f. brown .. 1·90 1·90
19. 35 f. on 3 f. claret .. 10 10
20. 40 f. olive .. 15 15
21. 45 f. on 2 f. brown .. 10 10
22. 12. 50 f. purple .. 25 25
23. 75 f. blue .. 10 10
24. 80 f. green .. 15 15
25. 1 k. lake .. 30 30
26. 2 k. brown .. 10 10
27. 3 k. grey and violet .. 1·60 1·60
28. 3 k. on 75 f. blue .. 30 30
29. 5 k. brown .. 1·60 1·60
30. 5 l. on 75 f. blue .. 15 15
31. 10 k. lilac and brown .. 4·50 4·50
32. 10 k. on 80 f. green .. 40 40

(e) Karl and Zita stamps.
33. 13. 10 f. red .. 1·40 1·40
34. 15 f. violet .. 1·75 1·75
35. 20 f. brown .. 20 20
36. 25 f. blue .. 20 20
37. 14. 40 f. olive .. 10 10
38. 50 f. purple .. 1·25 1·25

(f) Harvesters and Parliament Types inscr. "MAGYAR POSTA".
39. 11. 5 f. green .. 8 8
40. 6 f. blue .. 40 40
41. 10 f. red .. 8 8
42. 20 f. brown .. 8 8
43. 25 f. blue .. 8 8
44. 45 f. orange .. 35 35
45. 5 k. brown .. £100

The following (Nos. 46/64) are also optd. **KOZTARSASAG.**

(g) Harvesters and Parliament Types.
46. 11. 2 f. brown .. 10 10
47. 3 f. claret .. 1·75 1·75
48. 4 f. slate .. 8 8
49. 5 f. green .. 8 8
50. 10 f. red .. 70 70
51. 20 f. brown .. 12 12
52. 40 f. olive .. 8 8
53. 12. 1 k. lake .. 8 10
54. 2 k. brown .. 1·75 1·75
55. 3 k. grey and violet .. 60 60
56. 5 k. brown .. 18·00 18·00

(h) War Charity stamps of 1916.
57. 6. 10 f. (+2 f.) red .. 40 40
58. – 15 f. (+2 f.) violet .. 4·50 4·50
59. 8. 40 f. (+2 f.) lake .. 50 50

(k) Karl and Zita stamps.
60. 13. 10 f. red .. 20 20
61. 15 f. violet .. 55 55
62. 20 f. brown .. 2·25 2·25
63. 25 f. blue .. 8 8
64. 14. 50 f. purple .. 5 5

2.

3.

1920. Types 2 and 3 and similar design, optd. with inscr. as T 1 but in circle.

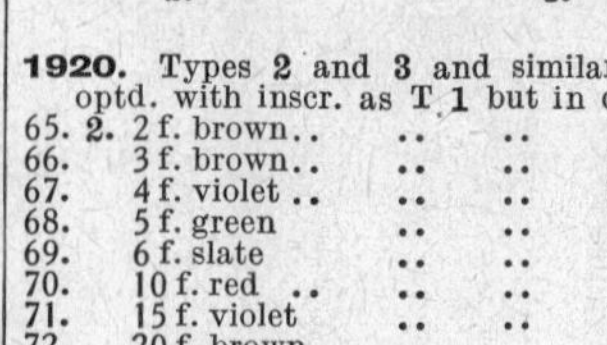

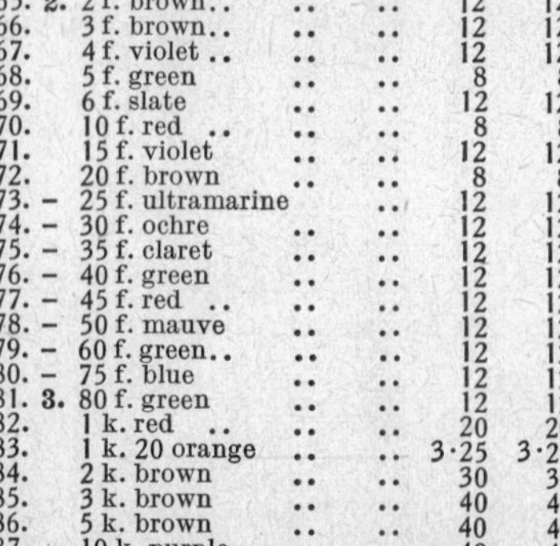

65. 2. 2 f. brown 12 12
66. 3 f. brown 12 12
67. 4 f. violet 12 12
68. 5 f. green 8 8
69. 6 f. slate 12 12
70. 10 f. red 8 8
71. 15 f. violet 12 12
72. 20 f. brown 8 8
73. – 25 f. ultramarine .. 12 12
74. – 30 f. ochre .. 12 12
75. – 35 f. claret .. 12 12
76. – 40 f. green .. 12 12
77. – 45 f. red .. 12 12
78. – 50 f. mauve .. 12 12
79. – 60 f. green .. 12 12
80. – 75 f. blue .. 12 12
81. 3. 80 f. green .. 12 12
82. 1 k. red .. 20 20
83. 1 k. 20 orange .. 3·25 3·25
84. 2 k. brown .. 30 30
85. 3 k. brown .. 40 40
86. 5 k. brown .. 40 40
87. 10 k. purple .. 40 40

DESIGN: Nos. 73/80, Horseman using lasso.

4.

1920. War Charity. Type 4 with circular opt., and "Segely belyeg" at top.
88. **4.** 20 f. green 10 10
89. 20 f. green on blue .. 35 35
90. 50 f. brown 12 12
91. 50 brown on magenta .. 12 12
92. 1 k. green 15 15
93. 1 k. green on green .. 20 20
94. 2 k. green 30 30

NEWSPAPER STAMP

1919. No. N 136 optd. with T **1.**
N 65. N **3.** 2 f. olive and red .. 8 8

EXPRESS LETTER STAMP

1919. No. E 245 optd. with T **1.**
E 66. E **1.** (2 f.) orange .. 10 10

SAVINGS BANK STAMP

1919. No. B 199 optd. with T **1.**
B 67. B **1.** 10 f. purple .. .. 2·75 2·75

POSTAGE DUE STAMPS

1919. Nos. D 190 etc. optd. with T **1.**
D 68. D **1.** 1 f. red and green 2·50 2·50
D 69. 2 f. red and green .. 8 8
D 70. 5 f. red and green .. 22·00 22·00
D 71. 6 f. red and green .. 1·60 1·60
D 72. 10 f. red and green .. 8 8
D 73. 12 f. red and green 6·50 6·50
D 74. 15 f. red and green .. 25 25
D 75. 20 f. red and green .. 25 25
D 76. 30 f. red and green .. 25 25

The following (Nos. D 77/82) are also optd. **KOZTARSASAG.**
D 77. D **1.** 2 f. red and green .. 50 50
D 78. 3 f. red and green .. 50 50
D 79. 10 f. red and green .. 50 50
D 80. 20 f. red and green .. 50 50
D 81. 40 f. red and green .. 50 50
D 82. 50 f. red and green .. 50 50

D 1.

1920.
D 95. D **1.** 5 f. green 8 8
D 96. 10 f. green 8 8
D 97. 20 f. green 8 8
D 98. 30 f. green 8 8
D 99. 40 f. green 8 8

TEMESVAR

After being occupied by Serbia this area was then occupied by Rumania. It later became part of Rumania and was renamed Timisoara.

100 filler = 1 korona.

(1.) (2.)

1919. Stamps of Hungary surch. as T 1/2 (Nos. 6 and 7), with value only (Nos. 8 and 9) or with **KORONA** and value (No. 10).

(a) Harvesters Type.
6. **11.** 30 on 2 f. brown 10 10
7. 1 k. on 4 f. slate (optd. **KOZTARSASAG**) .. 10 10
8. 150 on 3 f. claret .. 12 12
9. 150 on 5 f. green .. 12 12

(b) Express Letter Stamp.
10. E **1.** 3 KORONA on 2 f. olive and red 15 15

POSTAGE DUE STAMPS

1919. Charity stamp surch. **PORTO** and value.
D 11. – 40 PORTO on 15 + (2 f.) violet (No. 265) .. 12 12

(D 1.)

1919. Postage Due stamps surch. with T D **1.**
D 12. D **1.** 60 on 2 f. red and green 30 30
D 13. 60 on 10 f. red and green 25 25

RUMANIAN POST OFFICES ABROAD E3

Rumanian P.O.s in the Turkish Empire including Constantinople. Now closed.

I. IN TURKISH EMPIRE

1896. Stamps of Rumania of 1893 surch. in "PARAS".
9. 10 pa. on 5 b. blue (No. 345a) 3·50 3·50
10. 20 pa. on 10 b. grn. (No. 346) 3·50 3·50
11. 1 pi. on 25 b. mve. (No. 351) 3·50 3·50

II. IN CONSTANTINOPLE

(1.)

1919. Stamps of Rumania of 1893–1908 optd. with T **1.**
10. **27.** 5 b. green 8 10
11. 10 b. red 10 12
7. 15 b. brown 12 12
13. – 25 b. blue (No. 411) .. 10 10
14. – 40 b. brown (No. 555a) .. 45 45

1919. Charity stamp of Rumania of 1916 optd. with T **1.**
16. **32.** 5 b. green 25 25

RUSSIA E3

A country in the E. of Europe and N. Asia, an empire till 1917 when forerunner of the present Union of Soviet Socialist Republics (U.S.S.R.) was formed.

100 kopecks = 1 rouble.

1.

1a.

2.

1858. Imperf.
1. **1.** 10 k. blue and brown .. £1000 £110

1858. Perf.
21. **1.** 10 k. blue and brown .. 9·00 12
22. 20 k. orange and blue .. 20·00 2·50
23. 30 k. green and red .. 25·00 5·00

1863.
8. **1a.** 5 k. black and blue .. 5·00 25·00
No. 8 was first issued as a local but was later authorised for general use.

1864.
18a. **3.** 1 k. black and yellow .. 1·10 20
30. 2 k. black and red .. 1·75 20
19b. 3 k. black and green .. 1·75 20
20. 5 k. black and lilac .. 2·00 20

1875.
31. **2.** 7 k. red and grey .. 1·75 15
32. 8 k. red and grey .. 2·50 25
33. 10 k. blue and brown .. 8·50 1·50
34. 20 k. orange and blue .. 11·00 1·00

3.

4.

5.

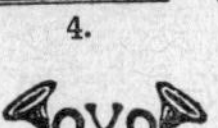
6. No thunderbolts.

1883. Posthorns in design without thunderbolts, as T **6.**

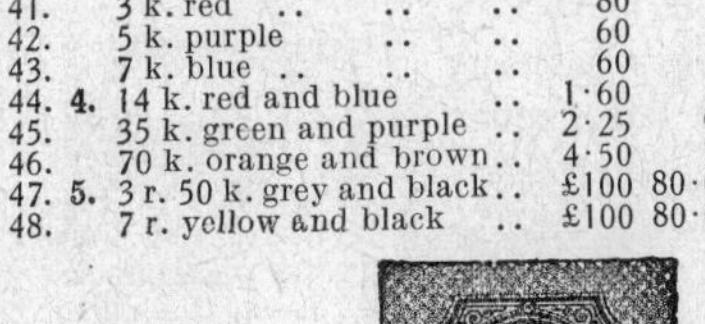

38. **3.** 1 k. orange 35 12
39. 2 k. green 70 12
41. 3 k. red 80 12
42. 5 k. purple 60 12
43. 7 k. blue 60 5
44. **4.** 14 k. red and blue .. 1·60 12
45. 35 k. green and purple .. 2·25 90
46. 70 k. orange and brown .. 4·50 75
47. **5.** 3 r. 50 k. grey and black .. £100 80·00
48. 7 r. yellow and black .. £100 80·00

7.

8.

9. With thunderbolts.

1889. Posthorns in design with thunderbolts, as T **9.** Perf.
50. **3.** 1 k. orange 8 5
51a. 2 k. green 8 5
52. 3 k. red 10 5
53. **7.** 4 k. red 20 5
54. **3.** 5 k. purple 12 5
55. 7 k. blue 8 5
56. **7.** 10 k. blue 20 5
99. **4.** 14 k. red and blue .. 5 5
100. 15 k. blue and purple .. 5 5
116. **7.** 20 k. red and blue .. 8 5
102. **4.** 25 k. violet and green .. 5 5
103. 35 k. green and purple .. 5 5
119. **7.** 50 k. green and purple .. 12 15
105. **4.** 70 k. orange and brown .. 15 5
121A. **8.** 1 r. orange and brown .. 5 5
79. **5.** 3 r. 50 grey and black .. 2·75 1·25
122A. 3 r. 50 green and claret .. 15 20
80. 7 r. yellow and black .. 1·90 1·00
124bA. 7 r. pink and green .. 20 20
For imperf. stamps, see Nos 107B/125aB.

10. Admiral Kornilov Monument, Sevastopol.

DESIGNS: 5 (8) k. Minin and Pozharsk Monument, Moscow. 7(10) k. Peter the Great Statue, Leningrad. 10 (13) k. Alexander II Monument and Kremlin, Moscow.

1905. War Charity (Russo-Japanese War).
88. **10.** 3 (6) k. brn., red & green 1·10 1·00
82. – 5 (8) k. purple and yellow 80 70
83. – 7 (10) k. blue and red .. 1·00 90
84. – 10 (13) k. blue & yellow 1·40 1·10

11.

12.

13.

1906.
92. **11.** 1 k. orange 8 5
93. 2 k. green 5 5
94. 3 k. red 5 5
95. **12.** 4 k. red 5 5
96. **11.** 5 k. claret 5 5
97. 7 k. blue 5 5
98a. **12.** 10 k. blue 5 5
123A. **13.** 5 r. blue and green .. 30 30
125aA. 10 r. grey, red & yellow .. 45 30
For imperf. stamps, see Nos. 107B/125aB.

14. Nicholas II.

15. Elizabeth.

16. The Kremlin.

DESIGNS—HORIZ. 2 r. Winter Palace. 3 r. Castle Romanov. VERT. 5 r. Nicholas II (23 × 29 mm.).

1913. Romanov Dynasty Tercent. Views as T **16.** and portrait as T **15.**
126. 1 k. orange (Peter I) .. 5 5
127. 2 k. green (Alexander II) .. 5 5
128. 3 k. red (Alexander III) .. 5 5
129. 4 k. red (Peter I) .. 5 5
130. 7 k. brown 5 5
131. 10 k. blue (Nicholas II) .. 15 5
132. 14 k. green (Katherine II) .. 12 5
133. 15 k. brown (Nicholas I) .. 40 12
134. 20 k. olive (Alexander I) .. 45 10
135. 25 k. claret (Alexei Michaelovich) 55 20
136. 35 k. green & violet (Paul I) 55 20
137. 50 k. grey and brown .. 65 20
138. 70 k. brown and green (Michael Feodorovich) .. 1·00 45
139. 1 r. green .. .. 2·25 45
140. 2 r. brown .. .. 3·00 1·40
141. 3 r. violet .. .. 3·50 1·75
142. 5 r. brown .. .. 3·50 3·00

20. Russian hero, Ilya Murometz.

DESIGNS: 3 k. Cossack shaking girl's hand. 7 k. Symbolical of Russia surrounded by her children. 10 k. St. George and Dragon.

1914. War Charity.
143. **20.** 1 (2) k. grn. & red on yell. 10 12
144. 3 (4) k. grn. & red on rose 10 12
145. 7 (8) k. green and brown on buff 12 15
161. 10 (11) k. brown and blue on blue 8 12

1915. As last. Colours changed.
159. **20.** 1 (2) k. grey and brown 12 20
160. 3 (4) k. black and red 12 12
157. 7 (8) k. green and brown 2·25
158. 10 (11) k. brown & blue 10 12

21.

22.

1
КОПѢЙКА.
Имѣетъ
хожденіе на-
равнѣ съ мѣд-
ной монетой.

23.

24. Cutting the fetters.

1915. Nos. 131, 133 and 134 printed on card with inscription on back as T **21.**
165. 10 k. blue 20 70
166. 15 k. brown 20 70
167. 20 k. olive 20 70

1916. Various types surch.
168. **11.** 10 k. on 7 k. blue .. 8 5
170. – 10 k. on 7 k. brown (130) 8 5
169. **4.** 20 k. on 14 k. red and blue (No. 99) .. 8 8
171. – 20 k. on 14k. green (132) 15 12

1917. Various earlier types, but imperf.
107B. **11.** 1 k. orange 5 5
108B. 2 k. green 5 5
109B. 3 k. red 5 5
110B. **12.** 4 k. red 5 5
111B. **11.** 5 k. claret 5 5
113B. **12.** 10 k. blue .. .. 4·50 9·00
115dB. **4.** 15 k. bl. & pur. (115A) 5 5
116B. **7.** 20 k. red and blue .. 8 20
117B. **4.** 25 k. mve. & grn. (102) 45 2·25
118B. 35 k. grn. & pur. (118A) 5 15
119B. **7.** 50 k. grn. & purple .. 12 15
120B. **4.** 70 k. orange and brn. (No. 105) 5 15
121B. **8.** 1 r. orange & brown 5 5
122aB. **5.** 3 r. 50 k. grn. & claret 5 5
123aB. **13.** 5 r. blue on green .. 20 35
124aB. **5.** 7 r. pink and green .. 45 60
125aB. **13.** 10 r. grey & red on yell. 9·00 7·00

1917. Types of 1913 printed on card and surch. on back as T **22** or **23**, or with figure "1" or "2" in addition on front.
172. **22.** 1 k. orange (No. 126) .. 6·50 11·00
175. 1 k. on 1 k. orange (126) 20 1·25
177. **23.** 1 k. on 1 k. orange (126) 20 90
173. **22.** 2 k. green (No. 127) .. 11·00 18·00
176. 2 k. on 2 k. green (127) 20 1·60
178. **23.** 2 k. on 2 k. green (127) 25 90
174. **22.** 3 k. red (No. 128) .. 20 1·10
179. **23.** 3 k. red (No. 128) .. 15 1·10

1917.
187. **24.** 35 k. blue 8 55
188. 70 k. brown 8 55

25. Agriculture and Industry.

26. Triumph of Revolution.

27. Agriculture.

28. Industry.

29. Science and Arts.

31.

30. Industry.

1921. Imperf.
195. **27.** 1 r. orange 20 35
196. 2 r. brown 20 35
197. **28.** 5 r. blue 12 25
198. **25.** 20 r. blue .. .. 90 1·25
199a.**26.** 40 r. blue 55 65
214a.**27.** 100 r. yellow 5 5
215. 200 r. brown 5 5
216. **29.** 250 r. lilac 5 5
217. **27.** 300 r. green 5 5
218. **28.** 500 r. blue 5 12
219b. 1000 r. red 5 5
256. **30.** 5000 r. violet .. 25 45
257a.**25.** 7500 r. blue 5 5
259. 7500 r. blue on buff .. 12 20
258. **30.** 10,000 r. blue .. .. 2·00 2·50
260. 22,500 r. purple on buff 15 20

1921. October Revolution. 4th Anniv. Imperf.
227. **31.** 100 r. yellow 5 15
228. 250 r. violet 5 15
229. 1000 r. red 10 35

32. Famine Relief Work.

33.

Р. С. Ф. С. Р.
ГОЛОДАЮЩИМ
250 р.+250 р.
(34.)

1921. Charity. Volga Famine. Imperf.
230. **32.** 2250 r. green .. .. 1·40 2·75
231. 2250 r. red .. .. 80 1·60
232. 2250 r. brown .. .. 1·60 4·00
233. **33.** 2250 r. blue .. .. 3·00 5·00

1922. Surch. Imperf.
239. **27.** 5000 r. on 1 r. orange .. 15 35
235. 5000 r. on 2 r. brown .. 20 45
236. **28.** 5000 r. on 5 r. blue .. 15 45
237. **25.** 5000 r. on 20 r. blue .. 25 65
243. **26.** 10,000 r. on 40 r. blue .. 35 50

1922. Famine Relief. Surch. as T **34.** Perf.
245. **24.** 100 r.+100 r. on 70 k. brown .. 10 20
247. 250 r.+250 r. on 25 k. bl. 10 20

1922. Surch. with new value and diagonally. Imperf.

РУБ.

250. **29.** 7500 r. on 250 r. lilac .. 5 5
251. 100,000 r. on 250 r. lilac 5 8

35.

1922. Rostov-on-Don issue. Famine Relief. Inscr. as in T **35.** Various sizes. Imperf.
261. **35.** 2 T. (2000 r.) green .. 3·75 5·00
262. – 2 T (2000 r.) red .. 6·00 6·00
263. – 4 T (4000 r.) red .. 6·00 7·00
264. – 6 T. (6000 r. green .. 6 00 7·00

DESIGNS: 2 T. red, Worker and family (35×42 mm.). 4 T. Clasped hands (triangular, 57 mm. each side). 6 T Sower (29×59 mm.).

РСФСР
Филателия
–детям
19-8-22
(39. "Philately—for the children".)

1922. Optd. with T **39.** Perf. or Imperf.
273. **11.** 1 k. orange .. .. 27·00 45·00
274. 2 k. green .. .. 3·50 7·00
275. 3 k. red .. .. .. 2·25 4·50
276. 5 k. claret .. .. 2·25 4·50
277. **12.** 10 k. blue .. .. 2·75 5·50

40.

41.

1922. October Revolution. 5th Anniv. Imperf.
279. **40.** 5 r. black and yellow .. 8 10
280. 10 r. black and brown .. 8 10
281. 25 r. black and purple .. 15 35
282. 27 r. black and red .. 55 1·10
283. 45 r. black and blue .. 45 90

1922. Air. Optd. with aeroplane. Imperf.
284. **40.** 45 r. black and green .. 3·25 5·50

1922. Famine Relief. Imperf.
285. **41.** 20 r.+5 r. mauve .. 8 12
286. – 20 r.+5 r. violet .. 8 12
287. – 20 r.+5 r. blue .. 8 12
288. – 20 r.+5 r. blue .. 1·10 2·75

DESIGNS—HORIZ. No. 286, Steamship. No. 287, Train. VERT. No. 288, Aeroplane.

Р.40Р.
(45.)

46. Worker.

47. Soldier.

1922. Surch. as T **45.** Imperf. or perf.
289. **7.** 5 r. on 20 k. red and blue 65 1·10
290. **4.** 20 r. on 15 k. blue & pur. 80 1·40
291. 20 r. on 70 k. orange and brown (No. 105) .. 8 15
292. **7.** 30 r. on 50 k. grn. & pur. 75 1·10
293. **4.** 40 r. on 15 k. bl. & pur. 8 8
294. 100 r. on 15 k. bl. & pur. 8 8
295. 200 r. on 15 k. bl. & pur. 8 8

1922. Imperf. or perf.
303. **46.** 10 r. blue 5 5
304. **47.** 50 r. brown 5 5
305. 70 r. purple 5 5
306. 100 r. red 5 5

1 мая
1923 г. Филателия—
Трудящимея,
1 р.+1 р.
(43.)

1923. Charity. Surch. as T **48.** Imperf.
315. **40.** 1 r.+1 r. on 10 r. black and brown .. .. 3·25 5·00
317. **29.** 2 r.+2 r. on 250 r. lilac 3·25 5·50
318. **30.** 4 r.+4 r. on 5000 r. vio. 3·25 5·50

49. Worker.

50. Peasant.

51. Soldier.

1923. Perf.
320. **51.** 3 r. red 8 8
321. **49.** 4 r. brown 8 8
322. **50.** 5 r. blue 8 8
323. **51.** 10 r. grey 10 10
324. 20 r. purple 20 20

52. Reaper.

54. Tractor.

1923. Agricultural Exn., Moscow. Imperf or perf.
325. **52.** 1 r. brown .. .. 65 1·10
326. – 2 r green .. .. 65 1·10
327. **54.** 5 r. blue .. .. 90 1·40
328. – 7 r. red .. .. .. 1·10 1·75

DESIGNS—As T **52:** 2 r. Sower. 7 r. Exhibition buildings.

56. Worker.

57. Peasant.

58. Soldier.

59.

60.

61.

1923. Perf. (some values also imperf.).
430. **56.** 1 k. yellow 20 10
359. **57.** 2 k. green 20 10
360. **58.** 3 k. brown 20 10
361. **56.** 4 k. red 12 5
434. 5 k. purple 20 10
435. **57.** 6 k. blue 25 15
364. **58.** 7 k. brown 55 10
437. **56.** 8 k. olive 55 10
366. **57.** 9 k. red 45 35
367. **58.** 10 k. blue 20 8
385. **56.** 14 k. grey 65 12
386. **57.** 15 k. yellow 65 65
442. **58.** 18 k. violet 90 20
443. **56.** 20 k. green 85 12
444. **57.** 30 k. violet .. .. 1·40 20
445. **58.** 40 k. grey .. .. 1·60 35
446. **57.** 50 k. brown .. .. 1·75 35
447. **58.** 1 r. red and brown .. 2·25 35
375. **59.** 2 r. green and red .. 2·75 45
392. **60.** 3 r. green and brown .. 6·50 1·40
450. **61.** 5 r. brown and blue .. 8·50 2·25

62. Lenin.

63.

1924. Lenin Mourning. Imperf. or perf.
405. **62.** 3 k. black and red .. 70 45
406. 6 k. black and red .. 70 35
407. 12 k. black and red .. 70 35
408. 20 k. black and red .. 1·10 65

1924. Air. Surch. Imperf.
417. **63.** 5 k. on 3 r. blue .. 1·00 65
418. 10 k. on 5 r. green .. 1·00 65
419. 15 k. on 1 r. brown .. 80 55
420. 20 k. on 10 r. red .. 80 55

С.С.С.Р.
пострадавшему
от наводнения
Ленинграду.
3 к.+10 к.
(64. Trans. "For the victims of the flood in Leningrad".)

65. Lenin Mausoleum, Moscow.

1924. Leningrad Flood Relief. Surch. as T **64.** Imperf.
421. **27.** 3+10 k. on 100 r. yell. 50 55
422. 7+20 k. on 200 r. brown 40 55
423. 14+30 k. on 300 r. grn. 55 1·25
424. **28.** 12+40 k. on 500 r. blue 1·50 1·50
425. 20+50 k. on 1000 r. red 90 1·40

1925. Lenin. 1st Death Anniv. Imperf. or perf.
426. **65.** 7 k. blue .. .. 1·40 70
427. 14 k. olive .. .. 1·60 1·10
428. 20 k. red .. .. 1·60 1·40
429. 40 k. brown .. .. 1·75 1·60

66. Lenin.

ILLUSTRATIONS
British Commonwealth and all overprints and surcharges are FULL SIZE. Foreign Countries have been reduced to ¾-LINEAR.

1925.
451. **66.** 1 r. brown .. .. 3·25 1·10
452. 2 r. sepia .. .. 5·50 1·75
850. 3 r. green .. .. 9·00 2·25
851. 5 r. brown .. .. 8·00 1·75
852. 10 r. blue .. .. 8·00 3·50

67. Prof. Lomonosov and Academy of Sciences, Leningrad.

68. Popov (Wireless Pioneer).

1925. Academy of Sciences. Bicent.
456b. **67.** 3 k. brown .. .. 2·25 1·10
457. 15 k. olive .. .. 2·75 1·10

1925. Popov. 20th Death Anniv.
458. **68.** 7 k. blue .. .. 1·10 80
459. 14 k. olive .. .. 2·25 1·00

69. Decembrist Exiles.

70. St. Petersburg Riots, Dec. 1825.

1925. Decembrist Rebellion Cent. Inscr. "1825–1925". Imperf. or perf.
466. **69.** 3 k. green 85 85
467. **70.** 7 k. brown .. .. 1·00 1·00
468. – 14 k. red .. .. 1·50 1·50

DESIGN—VERT. 14 k. Medallion with heads of Rileyev, Pestel, Muraviev-Apostol, Bestuzhev-Riumin and Kakhovski.

74. Moscow Barricade.

75.

1925. 1905 Rebellion. 20th Anniv. Inscr. "1905–1925". Imperf. or perf.
463a. – 3 k. green 90 80
464c. – 7 k. brown .. .. 1·10 1·10
462. **74.** 14 k. red .. .. 1·40 1·10

DESIGNS—VERT. 3 k. Postal rioters. 7 k. Orator and mob.

1962. Int. Esperanto Congress.
471. **75.** 7 k. red and green .. 1·40 1·00
472. 14 k. violet and green .. 1·75 65

76. Waifs.

77. Lenin when a Child.

ПОЧТОВАЯ
МАРКА
КОП. 8 КОП.
(78).

1926. Child Welfare.
473. **76.** 10 k. brown 25 15
474. **77.** 20 k. blue 40 35

1927. Same type with new inscriptions.
475. **76.** 8 k.+2 k. green .. 20 15
476. **77.** 18 k.+2 k. red .. 55 30

1927. Postage Due stamps surch. with T 78.

484. D 2. 8 k. on 1 k. red .. 35 70
485. 8 k. on 2 k. violet .. 35 70
493. 8 k. on 3 k. blue .. 55 55
494. 8 k. on 7 k. yellow .. 35 35
484b. 8 k. on 8 k. green .. 30 45
494d. 8 k. on 10 k. blue .. 35 45
494f. 8 k. on 14 k. brown .. 35 70

1927. Various types of 7 k. surch. **8 KOIL.** (Some values imperf. or perf.).

495. **58.** 8 k. on 7 k. brown .. 55 45
523. **68.** 8 k. on 7 k. blue .. 1·10 1·60
527. **70.** 8 k. on 7 k. brown .. 1·10 1·60
524. – 8 k. on 7 k. brown (No. 464c) 1·10 1·60
526. **75.** 8 k. on 7 k. red & green 3·25 4·50

79. Dr. Zamenhof.

1927. Esperanto (Leningrad Congress). 40th Anniv. Imperf. or perf.

498. **79.** 14 k. green and brown 1·75 90

80.

1927. 1st Int. Air Post Congress, The Hague.

499. **80.** 10 k. blue and brown .. 3·25 2·75
500. 15 k. red and olive .. 4·00 3·00

81. Worker, Soldier and Peasant. **84.** Sailor and Worker.

82. Allegory of Revolution.

1927. October Revolution. 10th Anniv.

501. **81.** 3 k. red 80 45
502. **82.** 5 k. brown .. .. 2·25 1·10
503. – 7 k. green .. .. 2·75 1·60
504. **84.** 8 k. black and brown .. 1·10 55
505. – 14 k. red and blue .. 2·25 80
506. – 18 k. blue .. .. 1·60 55
507. – 28 k. brown .. .. 5·00 2·75

DESIGNS—HORIZ. as T **82.** 7 k. Smolny Institute. 14 k. Map of Russia inscr. "C.C.C.P.". 18 k. Various Russian races. 28 k. Worker, soldier and peasant.

88. Worker. **89.** Peasant. **90.** Lenin.

1927.

508. **88.** 1 k. orange 35 20
509. **89.** 2 k. green 35 10
510. **88.** 4 k. blue 35 10
511. **89.** 5 k. brown 35 10
512. 7 k. red .. .. .. 1·60 55
513. **88.** 8 k. green 80 10
514. 10 k. brown 65 10
515. **90.** 14 k. green 90 20
516. 18 k. olive 90 20
517. 18 k. blue .. .. 1·60 35
518. **89.** 20 k. olive .. .. 1·25 20
519. **88.** 40 k. red .. .. 2·00 35
520. **89.** 50 k. blue .. .. 2·75 55
521. **88.** 70 k. olive .. .. 4·00 65
522. **89.** 80 k. orange .. .. 5·50 2·25

91. Infantryman and Kremlin.

DESIGNS: 14 k. Salior and cruiser "Aurora". 18 k. Cavalryman. 28 k. Airman.

1928. Red Army. 10th Anniv. Dated "1918–1928".

529. **91.** 8 k. brown 60 10
530. – 14 k. blue .. .. 1·00 20
531. – 18 k. red .. .. 1·00 55
532. – 28 k. green .. .. 1·60 1·00

95. Young Factory Workers. **97.** Trumpeter sounding the Assembly.

1929. Child Welfare.

536. **95.** 10 k.+2 k. brn. & sepia 90 65
537. – 20 k.+2 k. blue & sepia 65 45

DESIGN: 20 k. Children in harvest field.

1929. First All-Russian Gathering of Pioneers.

538. **97.** 10 k. brown .. .. 4·00 1·60
539. 14 k. blue .. .. 2·25 1·10

98. Worker. **99.** Factory Girl. **100.** Peasant. **101.** Farm Girl.

102. Guardsman. **102a.** Miner. **103.** Worker, Soldier and Peasant. **104.** Lenin.

105. Steel foundryman. **106.** Infantryman. **107.** Airman. **107a.** Arms of U.S.S.R.

107b. Furnaceman. **107c.** Farm Girl. **108.** Central Telegraph Office, Moscow.

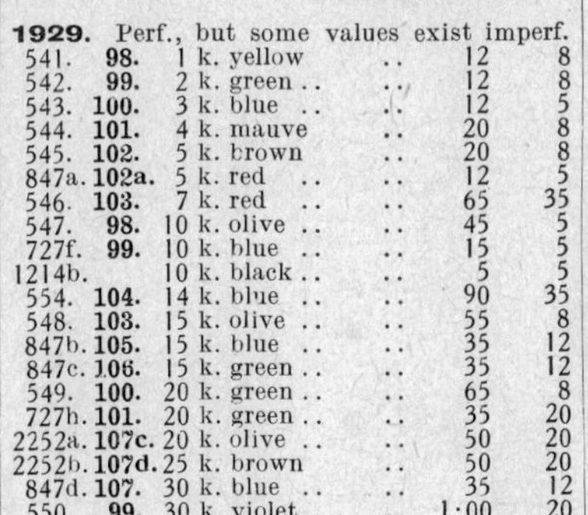

107d. Architect. **109.** Lenin Hydro-electric Power Station.

1929. Perf., but some values exist imperf.

541. **98.** 1 k. yellow 12 8
542. **99.** 2 k. green 12 8
543. **100.** 3 k. blue 12 5
544. **101.** 4 k. mauve 20 8
545. **102.** 5 k. brown 20 8
847a. **102a.** 5 k. red 12 5
546. **103.** 7 k. red 65 35
547. **98.** 10 k. olive 45 5
727f. **99.** 10 k. blue 15 5
1214b. 10 k. black 5 5
554. **104.** 14 k. blue 90 35
548. **103.** 15 k. olive 55 8
847b. **105.** 15 k. blue 35 12
847c. **106.** 15 k. green 35 12
549. **100.** 20 k. green 65 8
727h. **101.** 20 k. green 35 20
2252a. **107c.** 20 k. olive 35 20
2252b. **107d.** 25 k. brown 50 20
847d. **107.** 30 k. blue 35 12
550. **99.** 30 k. violet .. .. 1·00 20
727l. **104.** 40 k. blue 55 20
727m. **101.** 50 k. brown 45 20
847e. **107a.** 60 k. red 60 25
2253. **107b.** 60 k. red .. .. 1·00 20
2253a. 60 k. blue .. .. 1·50 40
552. **102.** 70 k. red .. .. 1·75 80
553. **100.** 80 k. brown .. .. 1·10 80
561. **108.** 1 r. blue .. .. 1·10 45
562. **109.** 3 r. brown and green 4·50 1·60

Nos. 727f, 1214b and 550 show the factory girl without factory in background. Nos. 549, 727m, 552, 553 have designs like those shown but with unshaded background.

110. "Industry". **111.** "More metal, more machines."

1929. Industrial Loan Propaganda.

563. **110.** 5 k. brown .. .. 1·40 65
564. – 10 k. olive .. .. 1·60 90
565. **111.** 20 k. green .. .. 3·25 1·60
566. – 28 k. violet .. .. 2·25 1·40

DESIGNS—HORIZ. 10 k. Tractors. VERT. 28 k. Blast Furnace and graph of Pig-iron output.

1930. Child Welfare.

567. **95.** 10 k.+2 k. olive .. 45 35
568. – 20 k.+2 k. green (as No. 537) 65 55

112.

DESIGNS — Dated "1919 1929": 5 k. Cavalry charge. 10 k. Cavalry charging. 14 k. (not dated) Cavalry and map.

1930. 1st Red Cavalry. 10th Anniv.

569. **112.** 2 k. green .. .. 1·40 80
570. – 5 k. brown .. .. 1·40 80
571. – 10 k. olive .. .. 3·00 1·10
572. – 14 k. blue and red .. 1·10 65

117. Group of Soviet Pupils.

1930. Educational Exhibition, Leningrad.

573. **117.** 10 k. olive 50 35

118.

1930. Air. "Graf-Zeppelin" Friedrichshaven–Moscow Flight.

574. **118.** 40 k. blue .. .. 6·50 3·50
575. 80 k. red .. .. 6·50 3·50

121. Cruiser "Potemkin".

DESIGNS–HORIZ. 5 k. Barricade and rebels. VERT. 10 k. Red Flag at Presnaja barricade.

1930. 25th Anniv. of 1905 Rebellion. Imperf. or perf.

576. **121.** 3 k. red 90 25
577. – 5 k. blue 90 40
578. – 10 k. red and green .. 1·75 55

124. From the Tundra (reindeer) to the Steppes (camel).

DESIGNS—As T **125**: 50 k. Above the North Pole. As T **124**: 1 r. Airship construction. VERT. 20 k. Zeppelin above Lenin's Mausoleum.

125. Above Dnieprostroi Dam.

1931. Airship Construction Fund. Imperf. or perf. (a) Air.

579. **124.** 10 k. violet .. .. 4·00 2·25
580. **125.** 15 k. grey-blue .. .. 8·00 4·00
581. – 20 k. red .. .. 5·50 2·75
582. – 50 k. sepia .. .. 3·25 1·60
583. – 1 r. green .. .. 4·50 2·75

(b) Air Express.

592. **125.** 15 k. grey-black .. 1·10 45

129. Ice breaker "Malygin".

1931. Air. "Graf Zeppelin" North Pole Flight. Imperf. or perf.

584. **129.** 30 k. purple .. .. 5·50 3·25
585. 35 k. green .. .. 5·50 3·25
586. 1 r. black .. .. 6·50 4·50
587. 2 r. blue .. .. 6·50 4·50

130. Polar Region and Ice-breaker "Sibiriakoff".

1932. Air. 2nd Int. Polar Year and Franz Joseph's Land to Archangel Flight.

588. **130.** 50 k. red .. .. 11·00 5·50
589. 1 r. green .. .. 9·00 5·50

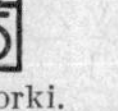

131. Maxim Gorki. **132.** Storming the Winter Palace.

1932. Publication of "Makar Chadra". 40th Anniv.

590. **131.** 15 k. sepia .. .. 2·75 1·75
591. 35 k. blue .. .. 6·50 4·50

1932. October Revolution. 15th Anniv.

593. – 3 k. violet 35 20
594. **132.** 5 k. brown 35 20
595. – 10 k. blue .. .. 1·10 65
596. – 15 k. green 65 45
597. 20 k. red 90 80
598. – 30 k. slate .. .. 2·25 1·00
599. – 35 k. brown .. .. 21·00 13·00

DESIGNS—HORIZ. 10 k. Dnieper Dam. 15 k. Harvesting with combines. 20 k. Industrial Works, Magnitogorsk. 30 k. Siberians listening to Moscow broadcast. VERT. 3 k. Lenin's arrival in Petrograd. 35 k. People of the World hailing Lenin.

134. "Liberation".

ILLUSTRATIONS
British Commonwealth and all overprints and surcharges are FULL SIZE. Foreign Countries have been reduced to ¾-LINEAR.

1932. Int. Revolutionaries' Relief Organization. 10th Anniv.

600. **134.** 50 k. red .. .. 2·75 1·40

135. Museum of Fine Arts.

1932. 1st All-Russian Philatelic Exn., Moscow.

601. **135.** 15 k. brown .. .. 4·50 4·50
602. 35 k. blue .. .. 13·00 9·00

136. Trier, Marx's Birthplace.

DESIGNS–VERT. 10 k. Marx's grave, Highgate Cemetery. 35 k. Marx.

1933. Marx. 50th Death Anniv. Inscr. "1818–1883–1933".
603. **136.** 3 k. green .. .. 1·10 30
604. – 10 k. sepia .. .. 2·25 1·00
605. – 35 k. purple .. .. 6·00 2·40

1933. Leningrad Philatelic Exn. Surch. **LENINGRAD 1933** in Russian characters and premium.
606. **135.** 15 k.+30 k. black .. 14·00 9·00
607. 35 k.+70 k. blue .. 22·00 10·00

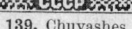

139. Chuvashes.

140. Lesghians.

1933. Ethnographical Issue. Racial types. Inscr. "noyma".
608. **139.** 1 k. chocolate (Kazakhs) 55 15
609. **140.** 2 k. blue 55 15
610. **139.** 3 k. green (Crimean Tatars) 45 15
611. 4 k. chocolate (Byro-Bidjans) 35 30
612. **140.** 5 k. claret (Tungus) .. 50 25
613. 6 k. blue (Buriats) .. 35 15
614. **139.** 7 k. choc. (Chechens) 35 15
615. 8 k. red (Abkhasians) 50 25
616. 9 k. blue (Georgians) .. 1·00 30
617. 10 k. sepia (Samoyedes) 1·40 55
618. **140.** 14 k. green (Yakuts) .. 1·10 25
619. – 15 k. purple (Ukrainians) .. 1·60 50
620. – 15 k. black (Uzbeks) .. 1·25 25
621. – 15 k. blue (Tadzhiks) 1·25 20
622. – 15 k. chocolate (Transcaucasians) .. 1·10 25
623. – 15 k. green (White Russians) .. 1·10 25
624. – 15 k. orange (Great Russians) .. 1·10 25
625. – 15 k. red (Turkmen) .. 1·60 50
626. **139.** 20 k. blue (Koriaks) .. 3·00 80
627. 30 k. claret (Bashkirs) 3·00 60
628. 35 k. brown .. 5·50 90

SIZES: Nos. 619/24, 48 × 22 mm. No. 625, 22 × 48 mm.

143. V. V. Vorovsky.

1933. Soviet Martyrs' issue. Dated "1933", "1934" or "1935".
629. **143.** 1 k. green .. 55 20
718. – 2 k. violet (Frunze) .. 1·10 20
630. – 3 k. blue (Volodarsky) 85 35
719. – 4 k. purple (Bauman) 1·60 20
631. – 5 k. sepia (Uritzky) .. 1·75 90
632. – 10 k. blue (Sverdlov) 8·00 3·25
633. – 15 k. red (Nogin) 9·00 4·50
720. – 40 k. brown (Kirov) .. 3·25 90

144. The Stratostat, "U S.S.R"

145. Massed Standard Bearers.

1932. Stratoshere record (19,000 metres).
634. **144.** 5 k. blue .. .. 35·00 5·00
635. 10 k. red .. .. 27·00 5·00
636. 20 k. violet .. .. 13·00 5·00

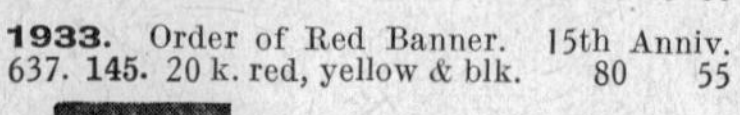

1933. Order of Red Banner. 15th Anniv.
637. **145.** 20 k. red, yellow & blk. 80 55

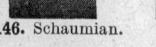

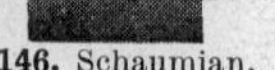
146. Schaumian.

147. Aeroplane over Oilfield.

1934. Death of 26 Baku Commissars. 15th Anniv. Inscr. "26".
638. **146.** 4 k. chocolate .. 2·25 70
639. – 5 k. black .. .. 2·25 70
640. – 20 k. violet .. .. 1·40 70
641. – 35 k. blue .. .. 7·50 1·75
642. – 40 k. red .. .. 5·00 3·25

DESIGNS: 5 k. Commissar Dzhaparidze. HORIZ. 20 k. The 26 condemned commissars. 35 k. Monument in Baku. 40 k. Workman, peasant and soldier.

1934. Air. 10th Anniv. of Soviet Civil Aviation and U.S.S.R. Airmail Service.
643. – 5 k. blue .. .. 5·50 1·40
644. **147.** 10 k. green .. .. 5·50 1·40
645. – 20 k. red .. .. 8·50 3·00
646. – 50 k. blue .. .. 18·00 4·50
647. – 80 k. violet .. .. 11·00 3·00

DESIGNS: 'Plane over:—5 k. Furnaces at Kusnetzk. 20 k. Harvesters. 50 k. Volga-Moscow Canal. 80 k. Steamer in the Arctic.

148. New Lenin Mausoleum. **149.** Fedorov Monument. Moscow, between Hand and Rotary Presses.

1934. Lenin. 10th Death Anniv.
648. **148.** 5 k. brown 70 15
649. 10 k. blue .. .. 2·00 90
650. 15 k. red .. .. 1·60 65
651. 20 k. green .. .. 1·60 80
652. 35 k. brown .. .. 3·25 1·10

1934. Ivan Fedorov. 350th Death Anniv.
653. **149.** 20 k. red .. .. 2·75 1·10
654. 40 k. blue .. .. 4·50 1·60

151. Dmitri Mendeleiev.

152. A. V. vasenko and Stratostat "Osoviachim".

1934. Dmitri Mendeleiev (chemist). Birth Cent. Dated "1834-1934"
655. – 5 k. green .. .. 2·00 55
656. **151.** 10 k. brown .. .. 6·50 1·40
657. 15 k. red .. .. 5·50 1·10
658. – 20 k. violet .. .. 3·00 1·10

DESIGN—VERT. 5 k., 20 k. Mendeleiev seated.

1934. Air. Stratosphere Disaster Victims.
659. – 5 k. purple .. .. 10·00 3·25
660. **152.** 10 k. brown .. .. 22·00 3·25
661. – 20 k. violet .. .. 25·00 4·25
1042. – 1 r. green .. .. 3·25 75
1043. **152.** 1 r. green .. .. 3·25 75
1044. – 1 r. blue .. .. 3·25 75

DESIGNS: 5 k., 1 r. (No. 1042). N. D. Usyiskin. 20 k., 1 r. (No. 1044). P. O. Fedosienko.

The 1 r values, issued in 1944, commemorated the 10th anniv. of the disaster.

153. Airship. "Pravda".

1934. Airship Travel Propaganda.
662. **153.** 5 k. red .. .. 3·75 65
663. – 10 k. lake .. .. 4·50 1·10
664. – 15 k. brown .. .. 4·50 3·00
665. – 20 k. black .. .. 12·00 2·25
666. – 30 k. blue .. .. 27·00 6·00

DESIGNS—HORIZ. 10 k. Airship landing. 15 k. Airship "Voroshilov". 30 k. Airship "Lenin" and route map. VERT. 20 k. Airship's gondolas and mooring mast.

DESIGN—VERT. 1 k. Lenin aged 3.3 k. Lenin as student. 5 k. Lenin as man. 10 k. Lenin as orator. HORIZ. 20 k. Red demonstration, Lenin Mausoleum.

156. Stalin and Marchers inspired by Lenin.

157. "War Clouds".

1934. "Ten years without Lenin". Portraits inscr. "1924-1934".
667. – 1 k. black and blue .. 1·40 65
668. – 3 k. black and blue .. 1·40 80
669. – 5 k. black and blue .. 3·25 1·40
670. – 10 k. black and blue .. 2·25 1·40
671. – 20 k. blue and orange 4·50 2·25
672. **156.** 30 k. red and orange .. 16·00 5·50

1935. Anti-War. Inscr. "1914-1934".
673. **157.** 5 k. black .. .. 1·60 90
674. – 10 k. blue .. .. 3·25 1·75
675. – 15 k. green .. .. 6·50 2·25
676. – 20 k. brown .. .. 4·50 2·50
677. – 35 k. red .. .. 16·00 6·00

DESIGNS: 10 k. "Flight from a burning village". 15 k. "Before and after war". 20 k. "Ploughing with the sword. 35 k. "Comradeship".

158. Capt. Voronin and "Chelyuskin".

1935. Air. "Chelyuskin" Rescue.
678. **158.** 1 k. orange .. .. 2·25 70
679. – 3 k. red .. .. 3·25 90
680. – 5 k. green .. .. 2·75 90
681. – 10 k. brown .. .. 3·25 1·25
682. – 15 k. black .. .. 4·50 1·25
683. – 20 k. purple .. .. 6·50 2·25
684. – 25 k. blue .. .. 16·00 4·50
685. – 30 k. green .. .. 22·00 5·50
686. – 40 k. violet .. .. 14·00 2·75
687. **158.** 50 k. blue .. .. 18·00 4·50

DESIGNS—HORIZ. 3 k. Prof. Schmidt and Schmidt Camp. 50 k. Schmidt Camp Deserted. VERT. 5 k. A. V. Liapidevski. 10 k. S. A. Levanevski. 15 k. M. G. Slepnev. 20 k. I. V. Doronin. 25 k. M. V. Vodopianov. 30 k. V. S. Molokov. 40 k. N. P. Kamanin.

160. Underground Station.

DESIGNS–HORIZ. as T **160**: 5 k. Excavating tunnel. 10 k. Section of roadway, escalator and station. 20 k. ($48\frac{1}{2}$ × 23 mm.) Train in station.

1935. Opening of Moscow Underground.
688. – 5 k. orange .. .. 2·25 90
689. – 10 k. blue .. .. 3·25 1·40
690. **160.** 15 k. red .. .. 13·00 4·50
691. – 20 k. green .. .. 4·50 2·25

162. Rowing.

1935. Spartacist Games.
692. – 1 k. blue and orange .. 2·75 1·10
693. – 2 k. blue and black .. 2·75 1·10
694. **162.** 3 k. brown and green 4·50 2·25
695. – 4 k. blue and red .. 2·75 1·40
696. – 5 k. brown and violet 2·75 1·40
697. – 10 k. purple and red .. 9·00 3·25
698. – 15 k. brown and black 14·00 5·50
699. – 20 k. blue and brown 14·00 4·50
700. – 35 k. brown and blue 20·00 9·00
701. – 40 k. red and brown .. 18·00 7·00

DESIGNS: 1 k. Running. 2 k. Diving. 4 k. Football. 5 k. Ski-running. 10 k. Cycling. 15 k. Lawn-tennis. 20 k. Skating. 35 k. Hurdling. 40 k. Parade of Athletes.

163. Friedrich Engels.

164. "Lion Hunt"

1935. F. Engels. 40th Death Anniv.
702. **163.** 5 k. red .. .. 4·50 35
703. 10 k. green .. .. 2·25 80
704. 15 k. blue .. .. 4·50 1·00
705. 20 k. black .. .. 2·75 2·40

1935. Air. Moscow – San Francisco via North Pole Flight. Surch. in Russian characters.
706. 1 r. on 10 k. brown (No. 681) 50·00 60·00

1935. 3rd Int. Congress of Persian Art and Archaeology, Leningrad.
707. **164.** 5 k. orange .. .. 2·40 70
708. 10 k. green .. .. 2·40 90
709. 15 k. violet .. .. 3·25 1·75
710. 35 k. black .. .. 4·75 2·40

165. Kalinin.

166. Tolstoy in 1910

1935. Pres. Kalinin's 60th Birthday. Autographed portraits inscr. "1875-1935".
711. – 3 k. purple 25 25
712. – 5 k. green 40 30
713. – 10 k. blue 55 40
714. **165.** 20 k. brown .. .. 1·00 60

DESIGNS: Kalinin as machine worker (3 k.), harvester (5 k.), orator (10 k.), and a recent portrait (20 k.).

1935. Tolstoy. 25th Death Anniv. Inscr. "1910-1935".
715. – 3 k. violet and black .. 45 25
716. **166.** 10 k. brown and blue .. 90 40
717. – 20 k. brown and green 2·00 1·00

DESIGNS: 3 k. Tolstoy in 1860. 20 k. Monument in Moscow.

167. Pioneers securing Letter-box.

DESIGNS: 3 k., 5 k. Pioneer preventing another from throwing stones. 10 k. Pioneers disentangling kite-line from telegraph wires. 15 k. Girl pioneer saluting.

1936. Pioneer Movement.
721. **167.** 1 k. green 65 20
722. 2 k. red 65 35
723. – 3 k. blue .. .. 1·10 35
724. – 5 k. red .. .. 1·10 35
725. – 10 k. blue .. .. 1·75 55
726. – 15 k. brown .. .. 2·75 1·10

168. A. N. Dobroliubov.

169. A. S. Pushkin.

1936. Dobroliubov. Birth Cent.
727. **168.** 10 k. purple .. 1·00 35

1937. A. S. Pushkin (poet). Death Cent.
728. **169.** 10 k. brown 20 15
729. 20 k. green 35 20
730. 40 k. claret 65 20
731. – 50 k. blue 80 35
732. – 80 k. red .. .. 1·10 35
733. – 1 r. green .. .. 1·75 55

DESIGN: 50 k. to 1 r., Pushkin's Monument.

171. Meyerhold Theatre.

172. F. E. Dzerzhinsky.

1937. 1st Soviet Architectural Congress.
734. 171. 3 k. claret 65 15
735. – 5 k. lake 65 15
736. 171. 10 k. brown .. .. 1·00 20
737. – 15 k. black .. .. 1·10 20
738. – 20 k. olive 65 35
739. – 30 k. black 65 45
740. – 40 k. violet .. .. 1·10 65
741. – 50 k. brown .. .. 1·40 1·40
DESIGNS: 5 k., 15 k. G.P.O. 20 k., 50 k. Red Army Theatre. 30 k. Hotel Moscow. 40 k. Palace of Soviets.

1937. F. E. Dzerzhinsky. 10th Death Anniv.
742. 172. 10 k. brown 20 20
743. 20 k. green 35 30
744. 40 k. claret 90 45
745. 80 k. red .. .. 1·10 45

SIZES: 20 k. to 50 k., 45 × 25 mm. 80 k. 1 r., 60 × 24½ mm.

173. Aeroplane.

1937. Air. Air Force Exn. Aeroplane designs as T 173.
746. 173. 10 k. black and brown 75 20
747. 20 k. black and green 75 20
748. 30 k. black and brown 90 20
749. 40 k. black and purple 1·40 50
750. 50 k. black and violet 2·25 80
751. 80 k. brown and blue.. 1·75 1·00
752. 1 r. black and purple.. 6·00 1·50

174. Arms of Ukraine. 175. Arms of U.S.S.R.

1937. New U.S.S.R. Constitution. Arms of Constituent Republics.
753. – 20 k. blue (Armenia).. 80 20
754. – 20 k. purple (Azerbaijan) 80 20
755. – 20 k. brown (White Russia) 80 20
756. – 20 k. red (Georgia) .. 80 20
757. – 20 k. green (Kazakhstan) 80 20
758. – 20 k. green (Kirkhizia) 80 20
759. – 20 k. claret (Tadzhikistan) 80 20
760. – 20 k. red (Turkmenistan) 80 20
761. 174. 20 k. red (Ukraine) .. 80 20
762. – 20 k. orange (Uzbekistan) 80 20
763. – 20 k. blue (R.S.F.S.R.) 80 20
764. 175. 40 k. red 90 75

167. Sculptured group on Pavilion. 177. Russian Pavilion, Paris Exhibition. 178. Shota Rustaveli.

1933. Paris Int. Exn.
765. 176. 5 k. red 20 12
766. 177. 20 k. red 40 20
767. 176. 50 k. blue 75 35

1938. 750th Anniv of Poem "Knight in Tiger Skin".
768. 178. 20 k. green 65 20

179. Route of North Pole Flight. 180. Infantryman.

1938. North Pole Flight.
769. 179. 10 k. black and purple 1·10 15
770. 20 k. black and blue.. 1·40 25
771. – 40 k. red and green .. 3·50 80
772. – 80 k. red .. .. 1·00 60
DESIGN: 40 k., 80 k. Soviet Flag at N. Pole.

1938. Red Army. 20th Anniv.
773. 180. 10 k. black and red .. 20 8
774. – 20 k. black and red .. 35 10
775. – 30 k. black, red & blue 55 15
776. – 40 k. black, red & blue 90 35
777. – 50 k. black and red .. 1·10 45
778. – 80 k. black and red .. 1·75 75
779. – 1 r. black and red .. 45 20
DESIGNS—VERT. 20 k. Tank driver. 30 k. Sailor. 40 k. Airman. 50 k. Artilleryman. HORIZ. 80 k. Stalin reviewing cavalry. 1 r. Machine-gunners.

182. Polar Flight Heroes. 183.

1938. 1st Polar Flight.
780. 182. 10 k. red and black .. 80 30
781. 20 k. red and black .. 1·10 30
782. 40 k. red and brown .. 2·25 50
783. 50 k. red and purple .. 3·75 70

1938. 2nd Polar Flight.
784. 183. 10 k. maroon .. .. 1·75 25
785. 20 k. black .. .. 2·25 50
786. 50 k. purple .. .. 2·75 80

DESIGN—VERT. 30 k., 50 k. Survivors with funnel and rigging.

185. Rescue Ships approaching Survivors.

1938. Rescue of Papanin's North Pole Meteorological Party.
787. 185. 10 k. purple .. .. 1·60 35
788. 20 k. blue .. .. 1·60 50
789. – 30 k. brown .. .. 4·00 60
790. – 50 k. blue .. .. 4·00 90

187. Nurse weighing Baby. 188. Children visiting Statue of Lenin.

1938. Soviet Union Children.
791. 187. 10 k. blue 65 20
792. 188. 15 k. blue 65 25
793. – 20 k. purple 90 25
794. – 30 k. claret .. .. 1·10 45
795. – 40 k. brown .. .. 1·40 60
796. – 50 k. blue .. .. 1·75 75
797. – 80 k. green .. .. 2·75 75
DESIGNS—HORIZ. 20 k., 40 k. Biology class. 30 k. Health camp. 50 k., 80 k. Young inventors at play.

189. Crimean Landscape.

1938. Russian Landscapes.
798. 189. 5 k. black 55 30
799. A. 5 k. brown 55 30
800. B. 10 k. green 80 30
801. C. 10 k. brown 80 30
802. D. 15 k. black 90 45
803. A. 15 k. black 90 45
804. E. 20 k. brown .. .. 1·40 45
805. C. 30 k. black .. .. 1·40 55
806. F. 40 k. brown .. .. 2·00 65
807. G. 50 k. green .. .. 2·00 1·40
808. H. 80 k. brown .. .. 3·50 1·40
809. I. 1 r. green .. .. 5·50 1·90
DESIGNS—HORIZ. A. Yalta (two views). B. Caucasian military road. E. Crimean rest-house. F. Alupka. H. Crimea. I. Swallows'-Nest Castle. VERT. C. Crimea (two views). D. Swallows' Nest Castle. G. Gursuf Park.

190. Schoolchildren and Model Aeroplane. 191. Underground Railway.

1938. Int. Aviation Records.
810. 190. 5 k. purple 90 45
811. – 10 k. brown 90 45
812. – 15 k. red .. .. 1·25 45
813. – 20 k. blue .. .. 1·25 45
814. – 30 k. claret .. .. 2·25 65
815. – 40 k. blue .. .. 2·75 65
816. – 50 k. green .. .. 5·50 90
817. – 80 k. brown .. .. 4·00 1·50
818. – 1 r. green .. .. 6·00 1·25
DESIGNS—HORIZ. 10 k. Glider in flight. 40 k. Seaplane landing. 1 r. Transport aeroplane. VERT. 15 k. Captive observation balloon. 20 k. Airship over Kremlin. 30 k. Parachutists. 50 k. Balloon in flight. 80 k. Stratospheric balloon.

1938. Moscow Underground Railway. Extension.
819. – 10 k. violet 45 20
820. – 15 k. brown 65 20
821. – 20 k. black 65 20
822. – 30 k. violet 90 35
823. 191. 40 k. black 90 55
824. – 50 k. brown 90 65
DESIGNS—VERT. 10 k. "Mayakovsky Square". 15 k. "Sokol Terminus". 20 k. "Kiev". HORIZ. 30 k. "Dynamo Stadium". 50 k "Revolution Square".

192. Miner and Pneumatic Drill. 193. Diving.

1938. Federation of Young Lenin Communists. 20th Anniv.
825. 192. 20 k. blue 65 35
826. – 30 k. maroon 90 35
827. – 40 k. purple .. .. 1·10 35
828. – 50 k. red .. .. 1·60 65
829. – 80 k. blue .. .. 3·50 90
DESIGNS—VERT. 20 k. Girl parachutist. 50 k. Students and University. HORIZ. 40 k. Harvesting. 80 k. Airman and Sailor.

1938. Sports.
830. 193. 5 k. red .. .. 1·75 20
831. – 10 k. black .. .. 1·75 35
832. – 15 k. brown .. .. 2·25 45
833. – 20 k. green .. .. 2·25 65
834. – 30 k. purple .. .. 6·00 80
835. – 40 k. green .. .. 7·00 90
836. – 50 k. blue .. .. 4·00 1·00
837. – 80 k. blue .. .. 3·50 1·40
DESIGNS: 10 k. Discus throwing. 15 k. Tennis. 20 k. Motor-cycling. 30 k. Skiing. 40 k. Sprinting. 50 k. Football. 80 k. Athletic parade.

194. Council of People's Commissars Headquarters and Hotel Moscow.

1939. New Moscow. Architectural design as T 194.
838. – 10 k. brown 45 30
839. 194. 20 k. green 55 40
840. – 30 k. purple 70 55
841. – 40 k. blue .. .. 1·40 65
842. – 50 k. claret .. .. 2·25 1·10
843. – 80 k. olive .. .. 2·25 1·10
844. – 1 r. blue .. .. 4·00 1·40
DESIGNS—HORIZ. 10 k. Gorky Avenue. 30 k. Lenin Library. 40 k. Suspension and 50 k. Arched Bridges over River Moskva. 80 k. Khimki River Station. VERT. 1 r. Dynamo Underground Station.

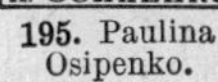

195. Paulina Osipenko. 197. Russian Pavilion, N.Y. Fair.

1939. Women's Moscow-Far East Flight. Inscr. as in T 195.
845. 195. 15 k. green .. .. 1·40 35
846. – 30 k. purple .. .. 1·40 55
847. – 60 k. red .. .. 2·75 90
PORTRAITS: 30 k. Marina Raskova. 60 k. Valentina Grisodubova.

1939. New York World's Fair.
848. – 30 k. red and black .. 55 35
849. 197. 50 k. brown and blue 80 55
DESIGN—VERT. (26×41½ mm.): 30 k. Russian Sculpture, N.Y. Fair (man holding aloft star).

198. T. G. Shevchenko in early Manhood. 199. Milkmaid.

1939. Shevchenko (Ukrainian poet and painter). 125th Birth Anniv. Inscr. "1814 1939".
853. 198. 15 k. black and brown 60 40
854. – 30 k. black and red .. 85 35
855. – 60 k. brown and green 1·60 1·10
DESIGNS: 30 k. Last portrait of Shevchenko. 60 k. Monument to Shevchenko, Kharkov.

1939. All Union Agricultural Fair. Inscr. as in T 199.
856. 199. 10 k. red 45 12
857. – 15 k. red 45 12
858. – 20 k. slate 45 12
859. – 30 k. orange 45 20
860. – 30 k. violet 45 12
861. – 45 k. green 55 25
862. – 50 k. brown 70 35
863. – 60 k. violet .. .. 1·40 60
864. – 80 k. violet .. .. 1·00 40
865. – 1 r. blue .. .. 2·25 60
DESIGNS—HORIZ. 15 k. Harvesting. 20 k. Sheep farming. 30 k. (No. 860) Agricultural Fair Pavilion. VERT. 30 k. (No. 859) Agricultural Fair Emblem. 45 k. Gathering cotton. 50 k. Thoroughbred horses. 60 k. "Agricultural Wealth". 80 k. Girl with sugar-beet. 1 r. Trapper.

1939. Aviation Day. Nos. 811 814/6 and 818 (colours changed) optd. **18 ABRYCTA** in Russian characters.
866. 190. 10 k. red .. .. 1·00 20
867. 30 k. blue .. .. 1·00 20
868. 40 k. green .. .. 1·00 20
869. 50 k. violet .. .. 2·10 45
870. 1 r. brown .. .. 2·75 1·10

1939. Surch.
871. 101. 30 k. on 4 k. mauve .. 3·25 2·75

200. Saltykov-Schedrin. 201. Kislovodsk Sanatorium.

1939. M. E. Saltykov-Schedrin (writer and satirist). 50th Death Anniv. Dated "1889 1959".
872. 200. 15 k. claret 35 15
873. – 30 k. green 55 30
874. 200. 45 k. brown 90 35
875. – 60 k. blue .. .. 1·40 45
DESIGN: 30 k., 60 k. Saltykov-Schedrin in later years.

1939. Caucasian Health Resorts.
876. 201. 5 k. brown 25 12
877. – 10 k. red 25 12
878. – 15 k. green 25 12
879. – 20 k. green 40 12
880. – 30 k. blue 40 12
881. – 50 k. black 65 35
882. – 60 k. maroon 90 40
883. – 80 k. red .. .. 1·25 50
DESIGNS: 10 k., 15 k., 30 k., 50 k., 80 k. Sochi Convalescent Homes. 20 k. Abkhazia Sanatorium. 60 k. Sukumi Rest Home.

202. M. I. Lermontov. 203. N. G. Chernyshevsky.

1939. Lermontov (poet and novelist). 125th Birth Anniv.

884.	202.	15 k. brown and blue ..	55	25
885.	–	30 k. black and green	1·25	40
886.	–	45 k. blue and red ..	90	65

1939. N. G. Chernyshevsky (writer and politician). 50th Death Anniv.

887.	203.	15 k. green	35	10
888.		30 k. violet	35	20
889.		60 k. green	1·00	45

204. A. P. Chekhov.   205. Welcoming Soviet Troops.

1940. Chekhov (playwright). 80th Birth Anniv.

890.	204.	10 k. green	20	10
891.		15 k. blue	20	10
892.	–	20 k. violet	25	20
893.	–	30 k. brown	90	35

DESIGN: 20 k., 30 k. Chekhov with hat on.

1940. Occupation of Eastern Poland.

893a.	205.	10 k. red	35	10
894.	–	30 k. green	35	10
895.	–	50 k. black	90	20
896.	–	60 k. blue	90	25
897.	–	1 r. red	1·60	65

DESIGNS: 30 k. Villagers welcoming tank crew. 50 k., 60 k. Soldier distributing newspapers to crowd. 1 r. People waving to column of tanks.

206. Ice-breaker "G. Sedov" and Badigin and Trofimov.   207. V. V. Mayakovsky.

1940. Polar research.

898.	–	15 k. green	90	15
899.	206.	30 k. violet	1·60	30
900.	–	50 k. brown	1·40	35
901.	–	1 r. blue	3·00	80

DESIGNS: 15 k. Ice-breaker "Joseph Stalin" and Papanin and Beloussov. 50 k. Badigin and Papanin meeting. LARGER (45×25 mm.): 1 r. Route of "George Sedov".

1940. Mayakovsky (poet). 10th Death Anniv.

902.	207.	15 k. red	20	10
903.		30 k. brown	40	20
904.	–	60 k. violet	50	35
905.	–	80 k. blue	40	35

DESIGN—VERT. 60 k., 80 k. Mayakovsky in profile wearing a cap.

208. K. A. Timiryasev.   209. Relay Runner.

1940. Timiryasew (scientist). 20th Death Anniv.

906.	–	10 k. blue	20	10
907.	–	15 k. violet	20	20
908.	208.	30 k. brown	20	20
909.	–	60 k. green	1·40	40

DESIGNS—HORIZ. 10 k. Timiryasev and Academy of Agricultural Sciences, Moscow. 15 k. Timiryasev in laboratory. VERT. 60 k. Timiryasev's monument, Moscow.

1940. 2nd All Union Physical Culture Festival.

910.	209.	15 k. red	90	25
911.	–	30 k. purple	1·40	40
912.	–	50 k. blue	2·50	45
913.	–	60 k. blue	2·75	35
914.	–	1 r. green	4·50	90

DESIGNS—HORIZ. 30 k. Girls' parade. 60 k. Skiing. 1 r. Grenade-throwing. VERT. 50 k. Children and sports badges.

210. Tchaikovsky and Passage from his "Fourth Symphony".   211. Central Regions Pavilion.

1940. Tchaikovsky (composer). Birth Cent. Inscr. "1840 1940".

915.	–	15 k. green	45	15
916.	210.	20 k. brown	45	15
917.		30 k. blue	45	35
918.	–	50 k. red	55	45
919.	–	60 k. red	65	55

DESIGNS: 15 k., 50 k. Tchaikovsky's house at Klin. 60 k. Tchaikovsky and excerpt from "Eugene Onegin".

920. ПАВИЛЬОН «ПОВОЛЖЬЕ»
921. ПАВИЛЬОН «ДАЛЬНИЙ ВОСТОК»
922. ПОРТАЛ ПАВИЛЬОНА „ЛЕНИНГРАД И СЕВЕРО-ВОСТОК РСФСР"
923. ПАВИЛЬОН МОСКОВСКОЙ, РЯЗАНСКОЙ И ТУЛЬСКОЙ ОБЛ.
924. ПАВИЛЬОН УКРАИНСКОЙ ССР
925. ПАВИЛЬОН БЕЛОРУССКОЙ ССР
926. ПАВИЛЬОН АЗЕРБАЙДЖАНСКОЙ ССР
927. ПАВИЛЬОН ГРУЗИНСКОЙ ССР
928. ПАВИЛЬОН АРМЯНСКОЙ ССР
929. „У ВХОДА В ПАВИЛЬОН УЗБЕКСКОЙ ССР"
930. ПАВИЛЬОН ТУРКМЕНСКОЙ ССР
931. ПАВИЛЬОН ТАДЖИКСКОЙ ССР
932. ПАВИЛЬОН КИРГИЗСКОЙ ССР
933. ПАВИЛЬОН КАРЕЛО-ФИНСКОЙ ССР
934. ПАВИЛЬОН КАЗАХСКОЙ ССР
935. ГЛАВНЫЙ ПАВИЛЬОН
936. ПАВИЛЬОН МЕХАНИЗАЦИИ

(211a.)

1940. All-Union Agricultural Fair. Coloured reproductions of Soviet Pavilions in green frames as T 211. Inscriptions as in T 211a.

920.	10 k. Volga Provinces (RSFSR)	80	25
921.	15 k. Siberia (RSFSR) ..	80	25
922.	30 k. Arctic Regions (RSFSR)	90	45
923.	30 k. Three Central Regions (RSFSR)	90	45
924.	30 k. Ukranian SSR ..	90	45
925.	30 k. Byelorussian SSR ..	90	45
926.	30 k. Azerbaijan SSR ..	90	45
927.	30 k. Georgian SSR ..	90	45
928.	30 k. Armenian SSR ..	90	45
929.	30 k. Uzbek SSR	1·40	45
930.	30 k. Turkmen SSR ..	90	45
931.	30 k. Tadzhik SSR ..	90	45
932.	30 k. Kirghiz SSR ..	90	45
933.	30 k. Karelo-Finnish SSR	1·40	45
934.	30 k. Kazakh SSR ..	1·40	45
935.	50 k. Main Pavilion ..	1·40	1·10
936.	60 k. Mechanization Pavilion and the statue of Stalin	1·75	1·40

Nos. 920/1, 927 and 930 are horiz.

212. Grenade Thrower.   213. Railway Bridge and Moscow-Volga Canal.

1940. Wrangel's Defeat at Perekop (Crimea). 20th Anniv. Perf. or imperf.

937.	–	10 k. green	55	15
938.	212.	15 k. red	25	10
939.	–	30 k. brown and red ..	35	10
940.	–	50 k. purple	25	20
941.	–	60 k. blue	55	35
942.	–	1 r. black	1·10	45

DESIGNS—VERT. 10 k. Red Army Heroes' Monument. 30 k. Map of Perekop and portrait of M. V. Frunze. 1 r. Victorious soldier. HORIZ.: 50 k. Soldiers crossing R. Sivash. 60 k. Army H.Q. at Stroganovka.

1941. Industrial and Agricultural Records.

943.	–	10 k. blue	20	15
944a.	–	15 k. mauve	25	15
945a.	213.	20 k. blue	20	15
946.	–	30 k. brown	25	30
947.	–	50 k. sepia	25	45
948.	–	60 k. sepia	50	35
949.	–	1 r. green	1·00	1·10

DESIGNS—VERT. 10 k. Coal-miners and pithead. 15 k. Blast furnace. 1 r. Oil derricks and refinery. HORIZ. 30 k. Locomotives. 50 k. Harvesting machine and elevator. 60 k. Ballbearing vehicles.

214. Red Army Ski Corps.   215. Marshal Suvorov.

1941. Red Army. 23rd Anniv. Designs with Hammer, Sickle and Star Symbol.

950a.	214.	5 k. violet	65	12
951.	–	10 k. blue	65	12
952.	–	15 k. green	35	12
953a.	–	20 k. red	35	12
954a.	–	30 k. brown	25	12
955a.	–	45 k. green	90	55
956.	–	50 k. blue	45	65
957.	–	1 r. green	65	90
957b.	–	3 r. green	4·50	1·75

DESIGNS—VERT. 10 k. Sailor. 20 k. Cavalry. 30 k. Automatic Rifle Squad. 50 k. Airman. 1 r., 3 r. Marshal's star. HORIZ. 15 k. Artillery. 45 k. Cavalryman clearing a hurdle.

1941. Battle of Ismail. 150th Anniv.

965.	–	10 k. green	35	20
966.	–	15 k. red	55	20
967.	215.	30 k. blue	90	25
968.		1 r. sepia	1·60	65

DESIGN: 10 k., 15 k. Storming of Ismail.

216. N. E. Zhukovsky and Air Force Academy.

DESIGNS—VERT. 15 k. Zhukovsky. 50 k. Zhukovsky lecturing.

1941. Zhukovsky (scientist). 20th Death Anniv.

958.	–	15 k. blue	45	12
959.	216.	30 k. red	45	20
960.	–	50 k. claret	65	45

217. Thoroughbred Horses.   218. Arms of Karelo-Finnish S.S.R.

1941. Kirghiz S.S.R. 15th Anniv.

961.	217.	15 k. sepia	55	20
962.	–	30 k. violet	1·10	35

DESIGN: 30 k. Coal-miner and colliery.

1941. Karelo-Finnish Republic. 1st Anniv.

963.	218.	30 k. red	35	20
964.		45 k. green	55	45

219. Spasski Tower, Kremlin.   220. "Razin on the Volga".

1941.

970.	219.	1 r. red	40	20
971.	–	2 r. orange	1·10	45

DESIGN—HORIZ. 2 r. Kremlin Palace.

1941. Surikov (artist). 25th Death Anniv.

972.	–	20 k. black	1·40	55
973.	220.	30 k. red	2·00	80
974.	–	50 k. purple	4·00	1·40
975.	220.	1 r. green	6·00	2·00
976.	–	2 r. brown	11·00	2·40

DESIGNS—VERT. 20 k., 50 k. "Suvoroy's march through Alps, 1799". 2 r. Surikov.

221. Lenin Museum.   222. M. I. Lermontov.

1941. Lenin Museum. 5th Anniv.

977.	221.	15 k. red	1·60	1·10
978.	–	30 k. violet on mauve	5·00	2·25
979.	221.	45 k. green	2·25	1·10
980.	–	1 r. red on rose ..	4·50	3·75

DESIGN: 30 k., 1 r. Museum exterior.

1941. M. I. Lermontov (poet and novelist). Death Cent.

981.	222.	15 k. green	1·75	1·75
982.		30 k. violet	2·25	2·25

223. Reproduction of Poster.   224. Mass Enlistment.

1941. Mobilization.

983a.	223.	30 k. red	9·00	7·00

1941. National Defence.

984.	224.	30 k. blue	17·00	17·00

225. Alishir Navoi.   226. Lt. Talalikhin Ramming Enemy Aeroplane.

227. Five Heroes.   228. Anti-tank Gun.

1942. 5th Cent. of poet Mir Ali Shir (Alishir Navoi).

985a.	225.	30 k. sepia	2·25	1·40
986.		1 r. purple	4·00	2·25

1942. Russian Heroes.

987.	226.	20 k. blue	20	8
988.	A.	30 k. grey	20	10
989.	B.	30 k. black	20	10
990.	C.	30 k. black	20	20
991.	D.	30 k. black	20	20
1048c.	226.	30 k. grey	65	25
1048d.	A.	30 k. blue	65	25
1048e.	C.	30 k. green	65	25
1048f.	D.	30 k. purple	65	25
1048g.	227.	30 k. blue	65	25
992.	C.	1 r. green	2·25	1·00
993.	D.	2 r. green	4·50	1·60

DESIGNS: A. Capt. Gastello and burning aeroplane diving into enemy petrol tanks. B. Maj-Gen. Dovator and Cossack cavalry in action. C. Shura Chekalin guerilla fighting. D. Zoya Kosmodemyanskaya being led to death.

1942. War Episodes.

994.	228.	20 k. brown	55	35
995.	–	30 k. blue	55	35
996.	–	30 k. green	55	35
997.	–	30 k. red	55	35
998.	–	60 k. slate	1·10	50
999.	–	1 r. brown	2·75	85

DESIGNS—HORIZ. 30 k. (No. 996), Guerilla fighter. 30 k. (No. 997), Munition-Worker. 1 r. Machine-gunners. VERT. 30 k. (No. 995), Signallers. 60 k. Defenders of Leningrad.

229. Distributing Gifts to Soldiers.   230. Munition Workers.

1942. War Episodes (2nd Issue).

1000.	229.	20 k. blue	45	20
1001.	–	20 k. purple	45	20
1002.	–	30 k. purple	65	35
1003.	–	45 k. red	1·25	80
1004.	–	45 k. blue	1·25	80

DESIGNS—VERT. No. 1001, Aeroplane destroying tank. 30 k. Food packers. No. 1002, Woman sewing. No. 1004, Anti-aircraft gun. See also Nos. 1012/16.

1943. Russian Revolution. 25th Anniv.
1005. 230. 5 k. brown 55 12
1006. – 10 k. brown 55 12
1007. – 15 k. blue 55 12
1008. – 20 k. blue 55 12
1009. – 30 k. brown 55 12
1010. – 60 k. brown .. .. 1·10 35
1011. – 1 r. red .. .. 1·50 45
1012. – 2 r. brown .. .. 2·40 80
DESIGNS: 10 k. Lorry convoy. 15 k. Troops and Lenin's banner. 20 k. Leningrad seen through an archway. 30 k. Spassky Tower, Lenin and Stalin. 60 k. Tank parade. 1 r. Lenin speaking. 2 r. Star of Order of Lenin.

231. Nurses and Wounded Soldier.  **232.** Routes of Bering's Voyages.

1943. War Episodes (3rd Issue).
1013. 231. 30 k. green 65 25
1014. – 30 k. green (Scouts) 65 25
1015. – 30 k. brown (Mine-thrower) .. 65 25
1016. – 60 k. green (Anti-tank troops) 65 25
1017. – 60 k. blue (Sniper) .. 65 25

1943. V. Bering (explorer). Death Bicent.
1018. – 30 k. blue 55 15
1019. 232. 60 k. grey .. .. 1·10 15
1020. – 1 r. green .. .. 1·60 45
1021. 232. 2 r. brown .. .. 2·75 85
DESIGN: 30 k., 1 r. Mt. St. Ilya.

233. Maxim Gorky.

1943. Maxim Gorki. 75th Birth Anniv.
1022. 233. 30 k. green 35 5
1023. 60 k. blue 45 15

234. Order of the Great Patriotic War.  **a.** Order of Suvorov.

1943. War Orders and Medals (1st series), Medals with ribbon attached.
1024. 234. 1 r. black .. .. 1·10 45
1025. a. 10 r. olive .. .. 4·50 2·75
See also Nos. 1051/8, 1089/94, 1097/99a, 1172/86, 1197/1204 and 1776/80a.

235. Karl Marx.  **236.** Naval Landing Party.

1943. Marx. 125th Birth Anniv.
1026. 235. 30 k. blue 45 10
1027. 60 k. green 65 12

1943. Red Army and Navy. 25th Anniv.
1028. 236. 20 k. brown 10 8
1029. – 30 k. green 10 12
1030. – 60 k. green 45 25
1031. 236. 3 r. blue .. .. 1·60 40
DESIGNS: 30 k. Sailors and anti-aircraft gun. 60 k. Tanks and infantry.

237. Ivan Turgenev.  **238.** Loading a Gun.

1943. Turgenev (novelist). 125th Birth Anniv.
1031a. 237. 30 k. green .. .. 5·00 2·40
1032. 60 k. violet .. .. 6·00 3·25

1943. Young Communist League. 25th Anniv.
1033. 238. 15 k. blue 20 10
1034. – 20 k. orange 20 10
1035. – 30 k. brown and red .. 35 10
1036. – 1 r. green 45 15
1037. – 2 r. green .. .. 1·40 30
DESIGNS 20 k. Tank and banner. 30 k. Bayonet fighter and flag. 1 r. Infantrymen. 2 r. Grenade thrower.

239. V. V. Mayakovsky.  **240.** Memorial Tablet and Allied Flags.

1943. Mayakovsky (poet). 50th Birth Anniv.
1038. 239. 30 k. orange 30 8
1039. 60 k. blue 45 15

1943. Teheran Three Power Conf. and 26th Anniv. of Revolution.
1040. 240. 30 k. black 45 15
1041. 3 r. blue .. .. 2·25 90

241. Defence of Odessa.

АВИАПОЧТА
1944 г.
1 РУБЛЬ
(242.)

1944. Liberation of Russian Towns.
1045. – 30 k. brown and red 45 15
1046. – 30 k. blue 45 15
1047. – 30 k. green 45 15
1048. 241. 30 k. green 45 15
DESIGNS: No. 1045 Stalingrad. No. 1046 Sebastopol. No. 1047 Leningrad.

1944. Air. Surch. as T 242.
1049. 226. 1 r. on 30 k. grey .. 65 20
1050. – 1 r. on 30 k. blue (No. 1048b) 65 20

243. Order of Kutusov.

b. Order of Patriotic War. **c.** Order of Alexander Nevsky. **d.** Order of Suvorov. **e.** Order of Kutusov.

1944. War Orders and Medals (2nd series). Various Stars without ribbons showing as Types **b** to **e**. Perf. or imperf.
(a) Frames as T 243.
1051. b 15 k. red 10 5
1042. c 20 k. blue 15 5
1053. d. 30 k. green 20 8
1054. e 60 k. red 45 15
(b) Frames as T 234.
1055. b 1 r. black 35 15
1056. c 3 r. blue .. .. 1·25 20
1057. e 5 r. green .. .. 1·75 35
1058. d 10 r. red .. .. 3·25 80

245. Lenin Mausoleum and Red Square, Moscow.

1944. "Twenty Years without Lenin". As Nos. 667/72, but inscr. "1924–1944", and T 245.
1059. – 30 k. black and blue 12 8
1060. 156. 30 k. red and orange 12 8
1061. – 45 k. black and blue 25 10
1062. – 50 k. black and blue 25 10
1063. – 60 k. black and blue 30 15
1064. 245. 1 r. brown and blue 55 30
1065. 156. 3 r. black and orange 1·60 65
DESIGNS—VERT. Lenin at 3 years of age. (No. 1059; at school (45 k.); as man (50 k.); as orator (60 k.).

246. Allied Flags.  **247.** Rimsky-Korsakov.

1944. 14th June (Allied Nations' Day).
1066. 246. 60 k. black, red & blue 90 20
1067. 3 r. blue and red .. 3·50 65

1944. Rimsky-Korsakov (composer). Birth Cent. Imperf. or perf.
1068. 247. 30 k. grey 10 5
1069. 60 k. green 20 5
1070. 1 r. green 45 8
1071. 3 r. mauve .. .. 1·00 15

248. Nuradilov and Machine-gun.  **249.** Polivanova and Kovshova.

1944. War Heroes.
1072. 248. 30 k. green 20 15
1073. – 60 k. violet 40 15
1074. – 60 k. blue 40 15
1075. 249. 60 k. green 65 35
1076. – 60 k. black 65 35
DESIGNS: No. 1073, Matrosov defending a snow-trench. 1074, Luzak hurling a hand-grenade. 1076, B. Safonev, medals and aerial battle over the sea.

250. S. A. Chaplygin.  **251.** V. I. Chapayev.

1944. S. A. Chaplygin (scientist). 75th Birth Anniv.
1077. 250. 30 k. grey 30 8
1078. 1 r. brown 55 15

1944. Heroes of 1918 Civil War.
1079. 251. 30 k. green 65 12
1080. – 30 k. black (N. Shchors) 65 12
1081. – 30 k. emerald (S. Lazo) 65 12
For 40 k. stamp as T 251, see No. 1531.

252. Ilya Yenmovich Repin.  **243.** "Reply of the Cossacks to Sultan Mahmoud IV".

1944. I. Y. Repin (artist). Birth Cent. Imperf. or perf.
1082. 252. 30 k. green 45 8
1083. 253. 50 k. green 45 8
1084. 60 k. blue 45 8
1085. 252. 1 r. brown 65 15
1086. 253. 2 r. violet .. .. 1·60 25

254. I. A. Krylov.

1944. Krylov (fabulist). Death Cent.
1087. 254. 30 k. brown 20 8
1088. 1 r. blue 55 20

f. Partisans' Medal. **g.** Medal for Bravery. **h.** Order of Bogdan Chmielnitsky. **j.** Order of Victory.

k. Order of Uchakof. **l.** Order of Nakhimov.

1945. War Orders and Medals (3rd series). Frame as T 243 with various centres as Types **f** to **l**. Perf. or imperf.
1089. f 15 k. black 35 5
1090. g 30 k. blue 55 8
1091. h 45 k. blue 55 12
1092. j 60 k. red 90 15
1093. k 1 r. blue .. .. 1·10 30
1094. l 1 r. green .. .. 1·10 30

255. A. S. Griboyedov.  **256.** Soldier.

1945. Griboyedov (author). 150th Birth Anniv.
1095. 255. 30 k. green 65 12
1096 60 k. purple .. .. 1·00 20

1945. War Orders and Medals (4th series). Frames as T 234. Various centres.
1097. g 1 r. black 90 35
1098. h 2 r. black .. .. 2·25 65
1098a. 2 r. purple .. .. 22·00 9·00
1098b. h 2 r. olive .. .. 4·00 1·00
1099. 3 r. red .. .. 1·60 45
1099a. 3 r. purple .. .. 5·00 45

1945. Relief of Stalingrad.
1100. 256. 60 k. black and red .. 80 45
1101. 3 r. black and red .. 1·40 80

258. Standard-Bearer.  **259.** Infantry v. Tank.

1945. Red Army Victories.
1102. 258. 20 k. green, red & black 10 10
1103. 259. 30 k. black and red .. 15 10
1104. – 1 r. green and red .. 85 55
DESIGN—HORIZ. 1 r. Infantry charge.

260. Attack.  **261.** Badge and Guns.

1945. Liberation of Russian Soil.
1105. 260. 30 k. blue 15 10
1106. – 60 k. red 50 20
1107. – 1 r. green 85 55
DESIGNS: 60 k. Welcoming troops. 1 r. Grenade thrower.

1945. Red Guards Commem.
1108. 261. 60 k. red 60 8

262. Barricade.

DESIGNS: 30 k. Tanks in Red Square, Moscow. 1 r. Aerial battle and searchlights.

1945. Battle of Moscow.
1109. – 30 k. blue 20 30
1110. 262. 60 k. black 35 30
1111. 1 r. black 80 45

263. Prof. Lomonosov and Academy of Sciences, Leningrad.

1945. Academy of Sciences. 220th Anniv.
1112. – 30 k. blue 45 10
1113. 263. 2 r. black .. .. 1·60 45
DESIGN—VERT. 30 k. Moscow Academy, inscr. "1725-1945".

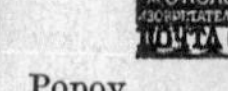

264. Popov. 265.

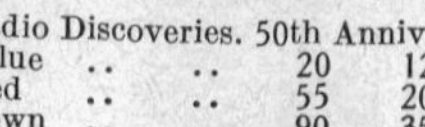

1945. Popov's Radio Discoveries. 50th Anniv.
1114. 264. 30 k. blue 20 12
1115. 60 k. red 55 20
1116. 265. 1 r. brown 90 35

266. Motherhood Medal. 267.

1945. Orders and Medals of Motherhood. Imperf. or perf.
1117. 266. 20 k. brown on blue.. 15 5
1118. – 30 k. brown on green 20 12
1119. – 60 k. red 55 15
1120. 267. 1 r. black on green .. 80 15
1121. – 2 r. blue .. .. 1·60 30
1122. – 3 r. red on blue .. 2·75 90
DESIGNS: 30 k., 2 r. Order of Motherhood Glory. 60 k., 3 r. Order of Heroine-Mother.

268. Petliakov-2 Dive Bombers. 269. Ilyushin-2 Bombers.

270. Petliakov-8 Bombers.

1945. Air. Aviation Day.
1123. 268. 1 r. brown .. .. 1·00 40
1124. 269. 1 r. brown .. .. 1·00 40
1125. – 1 r. red .. .. 1·00 40
1126. – 1 r. black .. .. 1·00 40
1127. – 1 r. blue .. .. 1·00 40
1128. – 1 r. green .. .. 1·00 40
1129. 270. 1 r. grey .. .. 1·00 40
1130. – 1 r. brown .. .. 1·00 40
1131. – 1 r. red .. .. 1·00 40
DESIGNS—As T 269: No. 1125, Lavochkin-7 fighter shooting tail off enemy 'plane. 1126, Iliushin-4 bomber dropping bombs. 1127, Tupolev-2 bombers in flight. 1128, Polikarhov-2 biplane. As T 270: 1130, Iakovlev-3 fighter destroying enemy fighter. 1131, Iakovlev-9 fighter destroying enemy twin-engined 'plane.
See also Nos. 1163/71.

ПРАЗДНИК
ПОБЕДЫ

9 мая
1945 года
(270a.)

1945. VE Day. No. 1101 optd. with T 270a.
1132. – 3 r. red .. .. 1·40 20

271. Lenin. 272.

1945. Lenin. 75th Birth Anniv.
1133. 271 30 k. blue 20 8
1134. – 50 k. brown 45 8
1135. – 60 k. red 45 20
1136. 272 1 r. black 65 20
1137. – 3 r. brown .. .. 2·25 45
DESIGNS—VERT. (inscr. "1870–1945"): 50 k. Lenin at desk. 60 k. Lenin making a speech. 3 r. Portrait of Lenin.

273. Prince Michael Kutusov. 274. A. I. Herzen.

1945. Kutusov (military leader). Birth Bicent.
1138. 273. 30 k. blue 45 15
1139. 60 k. brown 90 40

1945. Herzen (author and critic). 75th Death Anniv.
1140. 274. 30 k. brown 20 15
1141. 2 r. black .. .. 1·10 30

275. I. I. Mechnikov. 276. Friedrich Engels.

1945. Mechnikov (biologist). Birth Cent.
1142. 275. 30 k. brown 35 12
1143. 1 r. black 65 20

1945. Engels. 125th Birth Anniv.
1144. 276. 30 k. brown 45 12
1145. 60 k. green 65 25

277. Observer and Guns. 278. Heavy Guns.

1945. Artillery Day.
1146. 277. 30 k. brown 30 20
1147. 278. 60 k. black .. .. 1·00 35

279. Tank Production.

DESIGNS: 30 k. Harvesting. 60 k. Aeroplane designing. 1 r. Firework display.

1945. Home Front.
1148. 279. 20 k. blue and brown 55 12
1149. – 30 k. black and brown 55 20
1150. – 60 k. brown and green 90 35
1151. – 1 r. blue and brown .. 1·40 45

280. Victory Medal. 281. Soldier with Victory Flag.

1946. Victory Issue.
1152. 280. 30 k. violet 20 10
1153. 30 k. brown 20 10
1154. 60 k. black 35 15
1155. 60 k. brown 35 15
1156. 281. 60 k. black and red .. 90 35

282. Arms of U.S.S.R. 283. Kremlin, Moscow.

1946. Supreme Soviet Elections.
1157. 282. 30 k. red 15 8
1158. 283. 45 k. red 20 10
1159. 282. 60 k. green 45 20

284. Tank Parade.

285. Infantry Parade.

1946. Red Army and Navy. 28th Anniv.
1160. 284. 60 k. brown 50 12
1161. 2 r. violet .. .. 1·10 35
1162. 285. 3 r. black and red .. 2·50 55

1946. Air. As Nos. 1123/31.
1163. – 5 k. violet (as No. 1130) 20 20
1164. 268. 10 k. red 20 20
1165. 269. 15 k. red 20 20
1166. 270. 15 k. green 20 20
1167. – 20 k. black (as No. 1127) 20 20
1168. – 30 k. vio. (as No. 1131) 35 20
1169. – 30 k. brown (as No. 1134) 35 20
1170. – 50 k. blue (as No. 1127) 55 35
1171. – 60 k. blue (as No. 1131) 65 35

A B C D
E F G H
J K L M

N O P

1946. War Orders with Medals (5th Series). Frames as T 243 with various centres as Types A to P.
1172. A. 60 k. red 65 35
1173. B. 60 k. red 65 35
1174. C. 60 k. green 65 35
1175. D. 60 k. green 65 35
1176. E. 60 k. green 65 35
1177. F. 60 k. blue 65 35
1178. G. 60 k. blue 65 35
1179. H. 60 k. violet 65 35
1180. J. 60 k. purple 65 35
1181. K. 60 k. brown 65 35
1182. L. 60 k. brown 65 35
1183. M. 60 k. purple 65 35
1184. N. 60 k. claret 65 35
1185. O. 60 k. blue 65 35
1186. P. 60 k. purple 65 35

287. P. L. Chebyshev. 288. Maxim Gorky.

1946. Chebyshev (mathematician). 125th Birth Anniv.
1187. 287. 30 k. brown 20 10
1188. 60 k. black 35 20

1946. Death of President Kalinin. As T 165, but inscr. "3-VI-1946".
1189. 20 k. black 40 15

1946. Gorky. 10th Death Anniv. T 288 and similar design.
1190. 288. 30 k. brown 20 8
1191. – 60 k. green 40 12

289. Gagri.

DESIGNS — HORIZ. 15 k. Sukumi. 45 k. New Athos. VERT. 30 k. (No. 1194) Sochi.

1946. Health Resorts.
1192. – 15 k. brown 12 8
1193. 289. 30 k. green 35 8
1194. – 30 k. green 35 8
1195. – 45 k. brown 55 20

290. Stalin and Parade of Athletes. R.

1946. Sports Festival.
1196. 290. 30 k. green .. .. 3·25 1·40

1946. War Medals (6th Series). Frames as T 234. with various centres.
1197. R. 1 r. red 90 40
1198. B. 1 r. green 90 40
1199. C. 1 r. brown 90 40
1200. D. 1 r. blue 90 40
1201. G. 1 r. slate 90 40
1202. H. 1 r. slaret 90 40
1203. K. 1 r. purple 90 40
1204. L. 1 r. red 90 40

292. Moscow Opera House. 293. Tanks in Red Square.

1946. Moscow Buildings.
1205. – 5 k. brown 12 8
1206. 292. 10 k. grey 12 12
1207. – 15 k. brown 12 12
1208. – 20 k. brown 20 12
1209. – 45 k. green 35 30
1210. – 50 k. brown 45 30
1211. – 60 k. violet 55 40
1212. – 1 r. brown 80 40
DESIGNS—VERT. 5 k. Church of Ivan the Great and Kremlin. 1 r. Spassky Tower (larger). HORIZ. 15 k. Hotel Moscow. 20 k. Theatre and Sverdlov Square. 45 k. As 5 k. but horiz. 50 k. Lenin Museum. 60 k. St. Basil's Cathedral and Spassky Tower (larger).

1946. Heroes of Tank Engagements.
1213. 293. 30 k. green 45 15
1214. 60 k. brown 90 35

294. "Iron".

DESIGNS — HORIZ. 5 k. Combine harvester. 15 k. Coal trucks. VERT. 10 k. Oil derricks and refinery. 20 k. Steel works.

1946. 4th Stalin "Five-Year Reconstruction Plan". Agriculture and Industry.
1215. – 5 k. olive 15 8
1216. – 10 k. green 15 8
1217. – 15 k. brown 35 12
1218. – 20 k. violet 45 12
1219. 294. 30 k. brown 55 25

295. Soviet Postage Stamps.

1946. Soviet Postal Service. 25th Anniv.
1220. – 15 k. black and red .. 50 20
1221. – 30 k. brown and green 75 35
1222. **295.** 60 k. black and green 1·40 65
DESIGNS: 15 k. (48½ × 23 m.) Stamps on map of U.S.S.R. 30 k. (33 × 22½ mm.) Reproduction of T 26.

296. Lenin and Stalin. **297.** N. A. Nekrasov.

1946. Russian Revolution. 29th Anniv. Imperf. or perf.
1223. **296.** 30 k. orange.. .. 85 25
1224. 30 k. green 85 25

1946. Nekrasov (poet). 125th Birth Anniv.
1225. **297.** 30 k. black 20 12
1226. 60 k. brown 45 15

298. Stalin Prize Medal.

ILLUSTRATIONS British Commonwealth and all overprints and surcharges are FULL SIZE. Foreign Countries have been reduced to ¾-LINEAR.

1946. Stalin Prize.
1227. **298.** 30 k. sepia 75 20

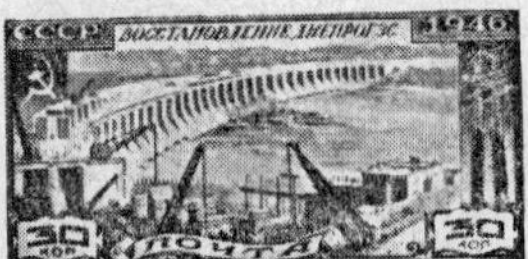

299. Dnieperprostroi Dam.

1946. Restoration of Dnieperprostroi Hydro-Electric Power Station.
1228. **299.** 30 k. black 45 20
1229. 60 k. blue 90 40

300. A. Karpinsky. **301.** N. E. Zhukovsky.

1947. Karpinsky (geologist). Birth Cent.
1230. **300.** 30 k. green 40 20
1231. 50 k. black 80 40

1947. Zhukovsky (scientist). Birth Cent.
1232. **301.** 30 k. black 15 8
1233. 60 k. blue 35 15

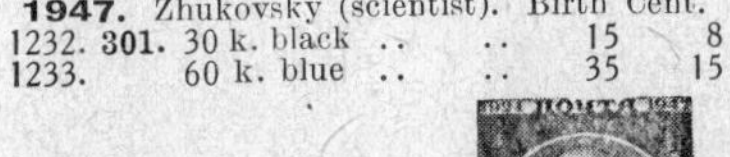

302. Lenin Mausoleum. **303.** Lenin.

1947. Lenin. 23rd Death Anniv.
1234. **302.** 30 k. green 20 12
1235. 30 k. blue 20 12
1236. **303.** 50 k. brown 90 20
For similar designs inscr. "1924/1948" see Nos. 1334/6.

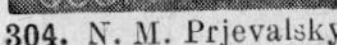

304. N. M. Prjevalsky. **305.** Arms of R.S.F.S.R.

306. Arms of U.S.S.R.

1947. Soviet Geographical Society. Cent.
1237. – 20 k. sepia 45 12
1238. – 20 k. blue 45 12
1239. **304.** 60 k. olive 90 35
1240. 60 k. sepia 90 35
DESIGN: 20 k. Miniature portrait of F. P. Litke and sailing vessel.

1947. Supreme Soviet Elections. Arms of Constituent Republics. As T **305.**
1241. **305.** 30 k. red (R.S.F.S.R.) 45 30
1242. – 30 k. brown (Armenia) 45 30
1243. **305.** 30 k. bistre (Azerbaijan) 45 30
1244. – 30 k. olive (White Russia) 45 30
1245. – 30 k. grey (Estonia).. 45 30
1246. – 30 k. lake (Georgia).. 45 30
1247. – 30 k. purple (Karelo-Finnish S.S.R.) .. 45 30
1248. – 30 k. orange (Kazakhistan) 45 30
1249. – 30 k. purple (Kirghizia) 45 30
1250. – 30 k. yell.-brn. (Latvia) 45 30
1251. – 30 k. grey-green (Lithu- 45 30
ania) 45 30
1252. – 30 k. maroon (Moldavia) 45 30
1253. – 30 k. bl.-grn. (Tadzhikistan) 45 30
1254. – 30 k. black (Turkmenistan) 45 30
1255. – 30 k. blue (Ukraine).. 45 30
1256. – 30 k. olive-brn. (Uzbekistan) 45 30
1257. **306.** 1 r. red, blue, gold and brown .. .. 1·40 35
A Hammer and Sickle in the centre of No. 1247 and at the base of No. 1249 should assist identification.

307. Russian Soldier. **308.** Alexander S. Pushkin.

1947. Soviet Army. 29th Anniv. Inscr. "XXIX". Perf. or imperf.
1258. **307.** 20 k. black 20 10
1259. – 30 k. blue 35 15
1260. – 30 k. brown 35 15
DESIGNS—VERT. No. 1259, Military cadet. HORIZ. No. 1260, Soldier, Sailor and Airman.

1947. Pushkin (poet). 110th Death Anniv.
1261. **308.** 30 k. black 35 1
1262. 50 k. green 50 3

309. Schoolroom. **310.** Women Students and Banner.

1947. Int. Women's Day.
1263. **309.** 15 k. blue 90 65
1264. **310.** 30 k. red .. .. 1·40 90

311. Moscow Council Building.

1947. Moscow Soviet. 30th Anniv. Perf. or imperf.
1265. **311.** 30 k. red, blue & blk. 90 35

312. May Day Procession. **313.** Soviet Aircraft and Flag.

1947. May Day.
1266. **312.** 30 k. red 45 20
1267. 1 r. green 90 45

1947. "Day of the Wing".
1268. **313.** 30 k. violet 45 12
1269. 1 r. blue 90 20

314. Yakromsky Lock.

1947. Volga-Moscow Canal. 10th Anniv. Inscr. "1937-1947".
1270. – 30 k. black 30 8
1271. **314.** 30 k. lake 30 8
1272. – 45 k. red 40 15
1273. – 50 k. blue 50 35
1274. – 60 k. red 55 35
1275. – 1 r. violet .. .. 1·40 35
DESIGNS—HORIZ. 30 k. (No. 1270), Karamyshevsky Dam. 45 k. Yakromsky Pumping Station. 50 k. Kimry Pier. 1 r. Lock. No. 8. VERT. 60 k. Map of Volga-Moscow Canal.

800 лет Москвы
1147—1947 гг.

(315.)

316. Izmailovsky Railway Station.

1947. 8th Cent. of Moscow (1st issue). Optd. as T **315.**
1276. 20 k. brown (No. 1208) 20 15
1277. 50 k. brown (No. 1210) 45 35
1278. 60 k. violet (No. 1211) 65 40
1279. 1 r. brown (No. 1212) 1·40 55

1947. Opening of New Moscow Underground Stations. Inscr. "M".
1280. **316.** 30 k. blue 20 8
1281. – 30 k. brown 20 8
1282. – 45 k. brown 45 12
1283. – 45 k. violet 45 12
1284. – 60 k. green 65 20
1285. – 60 k. red 65 20
DESIGNS—HORIZ. No. 1281, Electric power house. 1282, Falcon station. 1283, Stalinsky station. 1284, Kiev station. VERT. 1285, Mayakovsky station.

317. Crimea Bridge, Moscow.

1947. 8th Cent. of Moscow (2nd issue). Inscr. "800" and "1147-1947".
1286. **317.** 5 k. brown and blue 8 12
1287. – 10 k. black and brown 20 12
1288. – 30 k. slate 35 15
1289. – 30 k. blue 35 15
1290. – 30 k. brown 35 15
1291. – 30 k. green 35 15
1292. – 30 k. green 35 15
1293. – 50 k. green 55 40
1294. – 60 k. blue 65 45
1295. – 60 k. black and brown 65 45
1296. – 1 r. purple 90 55
Centre in yellow, red and blue.
1297. – 1 r. blue .. .. 1·75 55
1298. – 2 r. red .. .. 2·75 90
1299. – 3 r. blue .. .. 4·00 1·40
1300. – 5 r. blue .. .. 5·00 3·00
DESIGNS—VERT. 10 k. Gorky Street, Moscow. 30 k. (No. 1292), Pushkin Place. 60 k. (1294). 2 r. Kremlin. 1 r. (1296), "Old Moscow" after Vasnetsov. 1 r. (1297), St. Basil Cathedral. HORIZ. 30 k. (1288), Kiev station. 30 k. (1289), Kazan station. 30 k. (1290), Central Telegraph Offices. 30 k. (1291), Kaluga Street. 50 k. Kremlin. 60 k. (1295) (54½ × 24½ mm.) Kremlin. 3 r. Kremlin. 5 r. Government Buildings.

318. "Ritz", Gagri. **319.** "Zapadugol", Sochi.

1947. U.S.S.R. Health Resorts.
(a) Vertical.
1301. **318.** 30 k. green 35 10
1302. – 30 k. green (Sukhumi) 35 10
(b) Horizontal.
1303. **319.** 30 k. black 35 10
1304. – 30 k. brown ("New Riviera", Sochi) .. 35 10
1305. – 30 k. purple ("Voroshilov", Sochi) .. 35 10
1306. – 30 k. violet ("Gubripsh", Sukhumi) .. 35 10
1307. – 30 k. blue ("Kemeri", Riga) 35 10
1308. – 30 k. orange-brown ("Abkhazia", Novy Aphon) 35 10
1309. – 30 k. olive ("Krestyansky", Livadia) .. 35 10
1310. – 30 k. ultram. ("Kirov", Kislovodsk) .. 35 10

320. 1917 Revolution.

1947. Revolution. 30th Anniv. Inscr. "1917–1947 XXX". Perf. or imperf.
1311. **320.** 30 k. black and red.. 20 5
1312. – 50 k. blue and red .. 40 12
1313. **320.** 60 k. black and red .. 50 20
1314. – 60 k. brown and red.. 50 20
1315. – 1 r. black and red .. 90 25
1316. – 2 r. green and red .. 1·90 55
DESIGNS: 50 k., 1 r. "Industry". 60 k. (No. 1314) 2 r. "Agriculture".

321. Oil Refinery. **322.** Spasky Tower, Kremlin.

1947. Post-War Five Year Plan. Horiz. industrial designs. All dated "1947" except No. 1324. Perf. or imperf.
1317. **321.** 15 k. brown 12 5
1318. – 20 k. sepia (Foundry) 20 8
1319. **321.** 30 k. purple 25 8
1320. – 30 k. green (Harvesting machines) .. 25 8
1321. – 30 k. brown (Tractor) 25 8
1322. – 30 k. sepia (Tractors) 25 8
1323. – 60 k. bistre (Harvesting machines) .. 55 25
1324. – 60 k. purple (Builders) 55 25
1325. – 1 r. orange (Foundry) 1·10 45
1326. – 1 r. red (Tractor) .. 1·10 45
1327. – 1 r. violet (Tractors) 1·10 45

1947.
1328. **322.** 60 k. red .. .. 1·00 30
1329a. 1 r. red .. .. 1·40 12

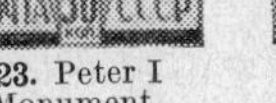

323. Peter I Monument. **324.** Peter and Paul Fortress.

1948. Relief of Leningrad. 5th Anniv. Dated "1947r".
1330. – 30 k. violet 20 8
1331. **323.** 50 k. green 45 12
1332. **324.** 60 k. black 80 20
1333. – 1 r. violet .. .. 1·10 45
DESIGNS—HORIZ. 30 k. Winter Palace. 1 r. Smolny Institute.

1948. Lenin. 24th Death Anniv. As issue of 1947, but dated "1924 1948".
1334. **302.** 30 k. violet 25 8
1335. 60 k. blue 60 20
1336. **303.** 60 k. green 60 20

325. Government Building, Kiev.

DESIGNS: 50 k. Dnieperprostroi Dam. 60 k. Wheatfield and granary. 1 r. Foundry and Colliery.

1948. 30th Anniversary of Ukrainian S.S.R. Various designs inscr. "XXX" and "1917-1947".

1337. **325.** 30 k. blue 25 12
1338. – 50 k. violet 50 15
1339. – 60 k. brown 75 30
1340. – 1 r. sepia .. .. 1·25 55

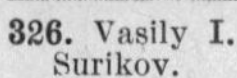

326. Vasily I. Surikov.

327. Skiing.

1948. Surikov (artist). Birth Cent.

1341. **326.** 30 k. brown 35 12
1342. 60 k. green 55 20

1948. R.S.F.S.R. Games. Various designs.

1343. **327.** 15 k. blue 55 8
1344. – 20 k. blue .. .. 1·00 20

DESIGN—VERT.: 20 k. Motor cyclist crossing stream.

328. Artillery.

329. Bulganin and Military School.

1948. Founding of Soviet Defence Forces and of Civil War. 30th Anniv.

(a) Various designs with arms and inscr. "1918 XXX 1948".

1345. **328.** 30 k. brown 60 20
1346. – 30 k. grey 60 20
1347. – 30 k. blue 60 20
1348. **329.** 60 k. brown .. .. 1·60 35

DESIGNS—VERT.: No. 1346, Navy. HORIZ. No. 1347, Air Force.

(b) Various portraits of Civil War Heroes as Nos. 1079/81.

1349. **253.** 60 k. brown (Chapayev) 90 40
1350. – 60 k. green (Shchors) 90 40
1351. – 60 k. blue (Lazo) .. 90 40

330. Karl Marx and Friedrich Engels.

ILLUSTRATIONS
British Commonwealth and all overprints and surcharges are FULL SIZE. Foreign Countries have been reduced to ¾-LINEAR.

1948. Publication of "Communist Manifesto". Cent.

1352. **330.** 30 k. black 20 8
1353. 50 k. brown 35 12

331. Miner.

332. Arms of U.S.S.R.

333. Spasski Tower, Kremlin.

1948. Various designs.

1354. **331.** 5 k. black 35 35
1355. – 10 k. violet (sailor) .. 35 35
1356. – 15 k. blue (Airman) .. 90 65
1361i. **331.** 15 k. grey 50 25
1357. – 20 k. brown (Farm Girl) .. .. 1·10 45
1361j. – 20 k. green (Farm Girl) 50 25
1361k. – 25 k. grey-blue (Airman) 60 25
1358. **332.** 30 k. brown .. 1·75 80
1361l. – 30 k. brn. (Scientist) 75 40

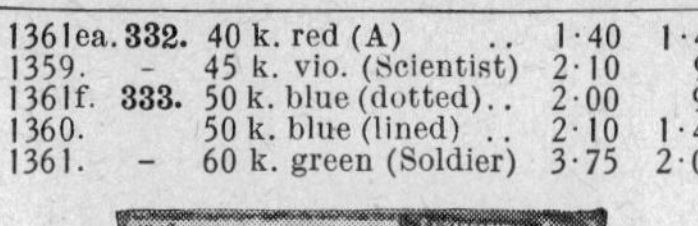

1361ea. **332.** 40 k. red (A) .. 1·40 1·40
1359. – 45 k. vio. (Scientist) 2·10 90
1361f. **333.** 50 k. blue (dotted) .. 2·00 90
1360. 50 k. blue (lined) .. 2·10 1·40
1361. – 60 k. green (Soldier) 3·75 2·00

334. Parade of Workers.

1948. May Day.

1362. **334.** 30 k. red 50 12
1363. 60 k. blue .. .. 1·00 25

335. V. G. Belinsky (philosopher).

1948. Belinsky. Death Cent.

1364. **335.** 30 k. brown 60 8
1365. 50 k. green 60 15
1366. 60 k. violet 90 35

336. A. N. Ostrovsky.

337.

1948. Ostrovsky (dramatist). 125th Birth Anniv.

1367. **336.** 30 k. green 45 20
1368. **337.** 60 k. brown 65 30
1369. 1 r. violet .. .. 1·60 50

338. I. I. Shishkin.

340. Factories.

339. Landscape.

1948. Shishkin (landscape painter). 50th Death Anniv.

1370. **338.** 30 k. brown & green 55 8
1371. **339.** 50 k. yellow, red & bl. 90 15
1372. – 60 k. yellow, red, blue and brown .. 1·40 20
1373. **338.** 1 r. blue and brown .. 1·60 40

DESIGN—HORIZ. 60 k. Bears in a forest.

1948. Leningrad Workers' Four Year Plan.

1374. **340.** 15 k. brown and red 35 25
1375. – 30 k. black and red .. 45 40
1376. **340.** 60 k. brown and red 1·40 1·00

DESIGN—HORIZ. (40×22 mm.): 30 k. Proclamation to Leningrad workers.

341. Arms and People of the U.S.S.R.

342. Caterpillar drawing Seed Drills.

1948. U.S.S.R. 25th Anniv.

1377. **341.** 30 k. black and red .. 50 20
1378. 60 k. olive and red .. 1·00 40

1948. Five Year Agricultural Plan.

1379. **342.** 30 k. red 25 15
1380. – 30 k. green 25 15
1381. – 45 k. brown 40 20
1382. **342.** 50 k. black 50 20
1383. – 60 k. green 60 25
1384. – 60 k. green 60 25
1385. – 1 r. violet .. .. 1·75 50

DESIGNS: 30 k. (No. 1380), 1 r. Harvesting sugar beet. 45 k., 60 k. (No. 1383), Gathering cotton. 60 k. (No. 1384), Harvesting machine.

1948. Aviation Day. Optd. **ΗΙΟΗЬ 1948 roAa.**

1386. **313.** 30 k. violet .. .. 2·00 65
1387. 1 r. blue .. .. 2·00 65

343. Miners.

344. A. A. Zhdanov.

1948. Miners' Day.

1388. **343.** 30 k. blue 35 12
1389. – 60 k. violet 65 20
1390. – 1 r. green .. .. 1·00 35

DESIGNS: 60 k. Inside a coal mine. 1 r. Miner's emblem.

1948. Death of A. A. Zhdanov (statesman).

1391. **344.** 40 k. blue 90 20

345. Sailor.

346. Football.

1948. Navy Day.

1392. **345.** 30 k. green 35 20
1393. 60 k. blue 55 40

1948. Sports.

1394. – 15 k. violet 35 12
1395. **346.** 30 k. brown 65 15
1396. – 45 k. brown 60 20
1397. – 50 k. blue .. .. 1·40 35

DESIGNS—VERT. 15 k. Running. 50 k. Diving. HORIZ. 45 k. Speedboat racing.

347. Tank and Drivers.

348. Horses and Groom.

1948. Tank Drivers' Day.

1398. **347.** 30 k. black 50 20
1399. – 1 r. red .. .. 1·25 35

DESIGN: 1 r. Parade of tanks.

1948. Five Year Livestock Development Plan.

1400. **348.** 30 k. black 35 12
1401. – 60 k. green 95 30
1402. **348.** 1 r. brown .. .. 1·40 40

DESIGN: 60 k. Dairy farming.

349. Railway Locomotive.

350. Iron Pipe Manufacture.

1948. Five Year Transport Plan.

1403. **349.** 30 k. brown 30 12
1404. 50 k. green 65 30
1405. – 60 k. blue 90 40
1406. – 1 r. violet .. .. 1·40 55

DESIGNS: 60 k. Road traffic. 1 r. Steamships.

1948. Five Year Rolled-iron, Steel and Machine-building Plan.

1407. – 30 k. violet 35 12
1408. – 30 k. purple 35 12
1409. – 50 k. brown 60 20
1410. – 50 k. black 60 20
1411. – 60 k. brown 80 25
1412. **350.** 60 k. red 80 25
1413. 1 r. blue .. .. 1·40 50

DESIGNS—HORIZ. Nos. 1407, 1410, Foundry. 1408/9, Pouring molten metal. 1411, Group of machines.

351. K. Abovyan.

352. Miner.

1948. Khachatur Abovyan (writer). Death Cent.

1414. **351.** 40 k. purple 60 30
1415. 50 k. green 65 35

1948. Five Year Coal-mining and Oil Extraction Plan.

1416. **352.** 30 k. black 45 12
1417. 60 k. brown 90 35
1418. – 60 k. brown 90 35
1419. – 1 r. green .. .. 1·75 55

DESIGN: Nos. 1418/9, Oil wells and tanker train.

353. Farhatz Power Station.

354. Flying Model Aeroplanes.

1948. Five Year Electrification Plan.

1420. **353.** 30 k. green 35 12
1421. – 60 k. red .. .. 1·00 30
1422. **353.** 1 r. red .. .. 1·40 60

DESIGN: 60 k. Zoversk Power Station.

1948. School Children's Summer Vacation.

1423. **354.** 30 k. green .. .. 1·40 65
1424. – 45 k. red .. .. 1·75 1·00
1425. – 45 k. violet .. .. 1·75 1·00
1426. – 60 k. blue .. .. 2·25 1·40
1427. – 1 r. blue .. .. 7·00 2·25

DESIGNS—VERT. No. 1424, Boy and Girl saluting. 60 k. Boy trumpeter. HORIZ. No. 1425, Children marching. 1 r. Children round camp fire.

355. Children in School.

356. U.S.S.R. Flag.

1948. Lenin's Young Communist League 30th Anniv. Inscr. "1918 1948 XXX".

1428. – 20 k. purple 65 35
1429. – 25 k. red .. .. 1·10 35
1430. – 40 k. brown and red 1·75 65
1431. **355.** 50 k. green .. .. 2·75 1·00
1432. **356.** 1 r. red, blue, yellow and black .. .. 5·00 1·60
1433. – 2 r. violet .. .. 11·00 3·25

DESIGNS—HORIZ. 20 k. Youth parade. VERT. 25 k. Peasant girl. 40 k. Youths and flag. 2 r. Industrial worker.

357. Interior of Theatre.

358. Searchlights over Moscow.

1948. Moscow Arts Theatre. 50th Anniv.

1434. **357.** 50 k. blue 65 20
1435. – 1 r. purple .. .. 1·10 60

DESIGN: 1 r. Portraits and early theatre.

1948. October Revolution. 31st Anniv.

1436. **358.** 40 k. red 65 45
1437. 1 r. green .. .. 1·40 90

359. Artillery Barrage. **360.** Tournament Building.

1948. Artillery Day.

1438. **359.** 30 k. blue 65 35
1439. 1 r. red 1·40 65

1948. 16th World Chess Championship.

1440. **360.** 30 k. blue 55 12
1441. – 40 k. violet 1·60 20
1442. **360.** 50 k. brown 1·90 35

DESIGN—VERT. 40 k. Chessboard and Castle.

361. Stasov and Building.

1948. Stasov (architect). Death Cent.

1443. – 40 k. brown 50 25
1444. **361.** 1 r. black 1·25 40

DESIGN—VERT. Portrait of Stasov.

362. **363.** Statue of Sverdlov.

1948. Air Force Day.

1445. **362.** 1 r. blue 2·75 1·10

1948. Sverdlovsk City. 225th Anniv. Inscr. "225". Imperf. or Perf.

1446. **363.** 30 k. blue 30 12
1447. – 40 k. purple 40 15
1448. **363.** 1 r. green 1·00 40

DESIGN: 40 k. View of Sverdlovsk.

364. Sukhumi **365.** State Emblem.

1948. Views of Crimea and Caucasus.

1449. **364.** 40 k. green 50 15
1450. – 40 k. violet 50 15
1451. – 40 k. mauve 50 15
1452. – 40 k. brown 50 15
1453. – 40 k. purple 50 15
1454. – 40 k. green 50 15
1455. – 40 k. blue 50 15
1456. – 40 k. green 50 15

DESIGNS—VERT. No. 1450, Gardens, Sochi. 1451, Eagle-topped monument, Pyatigorsk. 1452, Cliffs, Crimea. HORIZ. 1453, Gardens, Sochi. 1454, Garden-bordered road, Sochi. 1455, Colonnade, Kislovodsk. 1456, Sea and palms, Gagri.

1949. Byelorussian Soviet Republic. 30th Anniv.

1457. **365.** 40 k. red 55 20
1458. 1 r. green 1·10 50

366. M. V. Lomonosov. **367.** Lenin Mausoleum.

1949. Establishment of Lomonosov Museum.

1459. **366.** 40 k. brown 55 35
1460. 50 k. green 90 35
1461. – 1 r. blue 1·90 65

DESIGN—HORIZ. 1 r. Lomonosov Museum.

1949. Lenin. 25th Death Anniv.

1462. **367.** 40 k. green and red 90 80
1463. 1 r. brown and red 2·00 1·60

DESIGN: 40 k. Ice-covered Cape.

368. Dezhnev's ship and route.

1949. Dezhnev's Exploration of Bering Strait. Tercent. Inscr. "300", etc.

1464. – 40 k. olive 1·40 65
1465. **368.** 1 r. black 2·75 1·40

369. "Women in Industry". **370.** Admiral S. O. Makarov.

1949. Int. Women's Day.

1466. **369.** 20 k. violet 20 8
1467. – 25 k. blue 30 8
1468. – 40 k. red 45 12
1469. – 50 k. grey 55 20
1470. – 50 k. brown 55 20
1471. – 1 r. green 1·40 30
1472. – 2 r. red 2·25 55

DESIGNS—HORIZ. 25 k. Kindergarten. 50 k. grey, Woman teacher. 50 k. brown, Women in field. 1 r. Women sports champions. VERT. 40 k., 2 r. Woman broadcasting.

1949. Admiral S. O. Makarov (naval scientist). Birth Cent.

1473. **370.** 40 k. blue 50 35
1474. 1 r. red 1·40 1·00

371. Soldier. **372.** Kirov Military Medical Academy.

1949. Soviet Army. 31st Anniv.

1475. **371.** 40 k. red 2·00 1·00

1949. Kirov Military Medical Academy. 150th Anniv.

1476. **372.** 40 k. red 50 30
1477. – 50 k. blue 65 40
1478. **372.** 1 r. green 1·60 1·00

DESIGN — HORIZ. 50 k. Three miniature portraits of eminent professors and Kirov Academy.

373. V. R. Williams. **373a.** Three Russians with Flag.

1949. V. R. Williams (agricultural scientist).

1479. **373.** 25 k. green 65 45
1480. 50 k. brown 1·10 90

1949. Labour Day.

1481. **373a.** 40 k. red 35 30
1482. 1 r. green 90 55

374. Newspapers and Books. **375.** A. S. Popov and Radio Equipment.

1949. Press Day. Inscr. "5 MAR 1949".

1483. **374.** 40 k. red 45 40
1484. – 1 r. violet 1·50 70

DESIGN: 1 r. Man and boy reading newspaper

1949. Radio Day.

1485. **375.** 40 k. violet 80 20
1486. – 50 k. brown 1·50 40
1487. **375.** 1 r. green 2·40 90

DESIGN—HORIZ. 50 k. Popov demonstrating receiver to Admiral Makarov.

376. Alexander S. Pushkin. **377.** Pushkin reading "Epistle to Decembrists".

1949. Pushkin (poet). 150th Birth Anniv.

1488. **376.** 25 k. black and slate 20 12
1489. – 40 k. black and brown 75 30
1490. **377.** 40 k. purple and red 75 30
1491. – 1 r. slate and brown 1·50 90
1492. **377.** 2 r. blue and brown 2·40 1·40

DESIGNS—VERT. No. 1489, Pushkin portrait after Kiprensky. HORIZ. 1 r. Pushkin museum. Horizontal rows of Nos. 1490 and 1492 contain stamps and labels alternately.

378. Cargo Vessel. **379.** L. V. Michurin.

1949. "Krasnoe Sormovo" Machine and Ship-building Works Cent.

1493. **378.** 40 k. blue 1·00 90
1494. – 1 r. brown (Tanker) 2·40 1·10

1949. Honouring I. V. Michurin (agricultural scientist).

1495. **379.** 40 k. blue 50 25
1496. 1 r. green 1·25 65

380. Yachting. **381.** V. V. Dokuchaev.

1949. National Sports.

1497. **380.** 20 k. blue 35 8
1498. – 25 k. green 45 8
1499. – 30 k. violet 55 8
1500. – 40 k. brown 75 12
1501. – 40 k. green 75 12
1502. – 50 k. slate 75 20
1503. – 1 r. red 1·60 35
1504. – 2 r. black 2·75 65

DESIGNS: 25 k. Canoeing. 30 k. Swimming. 40 k. (No. 1500), Cycling. 40 k. (No. 1501), Football. 50 k. Mountaineering. 1 r. Parachuting. 2 r. High-jumping.

1949. Honouring V. V. Dokuchaev (soil research scientist).

1505. **381.** 40 k. brown 40 15
1506. 1 r. green 95 35

382. V. I. Bazhenov. **383.** A. N. Radischev.

1949. V. I. Bazhenov (architect). 150th Death Anniv.

1507. **382.** 40 k. violet 60 35
1508. 1 r. brown 1·00 65

1949. A. N. Radischev (writer). Birth Bicent.

1509. **383.** 40 k. green 65 35
1510. 1 r. black 1·10 65

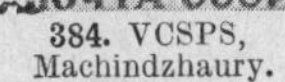

384. VCSPS, Machindzhaury. **385.** I. P. Pavlov.

1949. State Sanatoria. Designs showing various buildings.

1511. **384.** 40 k. green 50 15
1512. – 40 k. chocolate 50 15
1513. – 40 k. violet 50 15
1514. – 40 k. black 50 15
1515. – 40 k. red 50 15
1516. – 40 k. blue 50 15
1517. – 40 k. sepia 50 15
1518. – 40 k. brown 50 15
1519. – 40 k. green 50 15
1520. – 40 k. orange 50 15

DESIGNS—HORIZ. No. 1512, VCSPS No. 41, Zheleznovodsk. 1513, Energetics, Hosta. 1514, VCSPS No. 3, Kislovodsk. 1515, VCSPS No. 3, Hosta. 1516, State Theatre, Sochi. 1517, Clinical, Chaltubo. 1518, Frunze, Sochi. 1519, VCSPS No. 1, Kislovodsk. 1520, Communications, Hosta.

1949. I. P. Pavlov (scientist). Birth Cent.

1521. **385.** 40 k. brown 40 12
1522. 1 r. black 1·00 30

386. Globe and Letters.

1949. U.P.U. 75th Anniv. Perf. or Imperf.

1523. **386.** 40 k. blue and brown 65 20
1524. 50 k. violet and blue 65 20

387. Tree-planting Machines.

388. Map of S.W. Russia.

1949. Forestry and Field Conservancy.

1525. **387.** 25 k. green 40 20
1526. – 40 k. violet 50 25
1527. **388.** 40 k. green and black 50 25
1528. – 50 k. blue 80 25
1529. **387.** 1 r. black 1·50 65
1530. – 2 r. brown 3·25 1·60

DESIGNS ($33 \times 22\frac{1}{2}$ mm.): 40 k. violet, Harvesters. 50 k. River scene. ($33 \times 19\frac{1}{2}$ mm.): 2 r. Old man and children.

1949. Chapayev (military strategist). 30th Death Anniv.

1531. **251.** 40 k. brown 1·60 1·10

389. Nikitin. **390.** Malyi Theatre, Moscow.

1949. Nikitin (poet). 125th Birth Anniv.

1532. **389.** 40 k. brown 40 15
1533. 1 r. blue 95 35

1949. Malyi Theatre, Moscow. 125th Anniv.

1534. **390.** 40 k. green 40 12
1535. 50 k. red 40 12
1536. – 1 r. brown 1·00 30

DESIGN: 1 r. Five portraits.

ILLUSTRATIONS
British Commonwealth and all overprints and surcharges are FULL SIZE. Foreign Countries have been reduced to ¾-LINEAR.

391. Crowd with Banner.

1949. October Revolution. 32nd Anniv.

1537. 391. 40 k. red 50 45
1538. 1 r. green .. .. 1·10 90

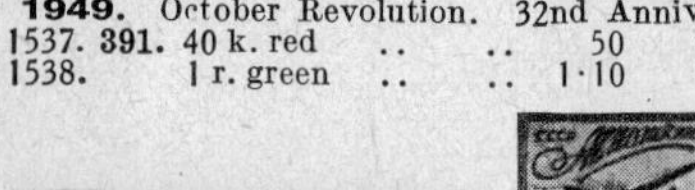

392. Sheep and Cows. 393. Aeroplane over Building.

394. Aeroplanes and Map.

1949. Encouragement of Cattle-breeding.

1539. 392. 40 k. brown 50 15
1540. 1 r. violet .. .. 1·00 35

1949. Air. Aerial views and map.

1541. 393. 50 k. brown on yellow 1·10 65
1542. – 60 k. chocolate on buff 1·60 90
1543. – 1 r. orange on yellow 2·75 1·40
1544. – 1 r. brown on buff .. 2·75 1·40
1545. – 1 r. blue on blue .. 2·75 1·40
1546. 394. 1 r. blue, red and grey 5·50 2·75
1547. – 2 r. red on blue .. 8·00 3·25
1548. – 3 r. green on blue .. 10·00 6·50

DESIGNS—As T. 393—HORIZ. 60 k., 1 r. (No. 1543). VERT. 1 r. (Nos. 1544/5), 2 r., 3 r.

395. Ski-Jumper. 396. Diesel Train.

1949. National Sports.

1549. 395. 20 k. green 45 8
1550. – 40 k. orange 90 10
1551. – 50 k. blue .. .. 1·10 10
1552. – 1 r. red .. .. 2·50 25
1553. – 2 r. violet .. .. 4·25 80

DESIGNS: 40 k. Girl gymnast. 50 k. Ice hockey. 1 r. Weight-lifting. 2 r. Shooting wolves.

1949. Modern Railway Transport Development.

1554. – 25 k. red 35 10
1555. 396. 40 k. violet 60 20
1556. – 50 k. brown 90 20
1557. 396. 1 r. green .. .. 1·75 65

DESIGNS: 25 k. Electric train. 50 k. Steam train.

397. Arms of U.S.S.R.

398. Government Building.

1949. Constitution Day.

1558. 397. 40 k. red .. .. 2·00 1·10

1949. Republic of Tadzhikstan. 20th Anniv.

1559. – 20 k. blue 20 5
1560. – 25 k. green 25 5
1561. 398. 40 k. red 35 12
1562. – 50 k. violet 50 12
1563. 398. 1 r. black 90 35

DESIGNS: 20 k. Textile mills. 25 k. Irrigation canal. 50 k. Medical University.

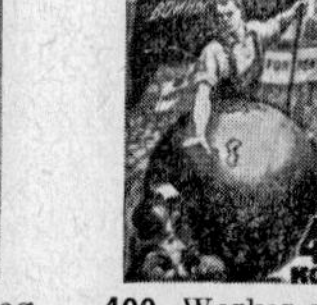

399. People with Flag. 400. Worker and Globe.

1949. Republics of West Ukraine and West Byelorussia. 10th Anniv.

1564. 399. 40 k. red .. .. 1·40 65
1565. – 40 k. orange .. .. 1·40 65

DESIGN—VERT. No. 1565, Ukrainians and flag.

1949. Peace Propaganda.

1566. 400. 40 k. red 50 20
1567. 50 k. blue 50 20

DESIGNS: 20 k. Teachers' College. 25 k. State Theatre. 40 k. violet, Street in Tashkent. 1 r. Map of Fergan Canal. 2 r. Knigonyarsk Dam.

401. Government Buildings, Tashkent.

1950. Uzbek Republic. 25th Anniv. Designs, in similar frames.

1568. – 20 k. blue 20 8
1569. – 25 k. black 20 8
1570. 401. 40 k. red 50 15
1571. – 40 k. violet 50 15
1572. – 1 r. green .. .. 1·25 40
1573. – 2 r. brown .. .. 2·50 75

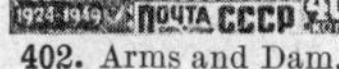

402. Arms and Dam. 403. Statue of Lenin.

1950. Turkmen Republic. 25th Anniv. Designs, in similar frames. Inscr. "XXV 1924 1949".

1574. – 25 k. black 30 12
1575. 402. 40 k. brown 50 20
1576. – 50 k. green 60 50
1577. 402. 1 r. violet .. .. 1·50 1·10

DESIGNS: 25 k. Ashkhabad. 50 k. Carpet weavers.

1950. Lenin. 26th Death Anniv. Inscr. "1924 1950".

1578. 403. 40 k. brown and grey 55 12
1579. – 50 k. red, brn. & grn. 80 30
1580. – 1 r. buff, green & brn. 1·50 45

DESIGNS—HORIZ. 50 k. Lenin's Office, Kremlin. 1 r. Lenin Museum.

404. Film Show. 405. Voter.

1950. Soviet Film Industry. 30th Anniv.

1581. 404. 25 k. brown .. .. 4·00 2·75

1950. Supreme Soviet Elections. Inscr. "12 МАРТА 1950".

1582. 405. 40 k. green on yellow 60 30
1583. – 1 r. red .. .. 1·50 60

DESIGN: 1 r. Kremlin and flags.

406. Statue of Morozov. 407. Lenin Central Museum.

1950. Unveiling of Monument to Pavlik Morozov (model Soviet youth).

1584. 406. 40 k. black and red .. 80 45
1585. 1 r. green and red .. 1·60 90

1950. Moscow Museums. Buildings inscr. "МОСКВА 1949".

1586. 407. 40 k. brown-olive .. 65 15
1587. – 40 k. claret .. 65 15
1588. – 40 k. blue-green .. 65 15
1589. – 40 k. brown .. 65 15
1590. – 40 k. magenta .. 65 15
1591. – 40 k. blue (no tree) 65 15
1592. – 40 k. red-brown .. 65 15
1593. – 40 k. blue (with tree) 65 15
1594. – 40 k. red .. 65 15

DESIGNS—HORIZ. (33½ × 23½ mm.): No. 1587, Revolution Museum. 1588, Tretiakovsky Gallery. 1589, History Museum. 1591, Polytechnic Museum. 1593, Oriental Museum. (39½ × 26½ mm.): 1590, Pictorial Arts Museum. VERT. (22½ × 33½ mm.): 1592, Biological Museum. 1594, Zoological Museum.

408. Hemispheres and Wireless Mast.

1950. Int. Congress of P.T.T. and Radio Trade Unions, London.

1595. 408. 40 k. green on blue .. 1·40 65
1596. 50 k. blue on blue .. 1·40 65

409. Workers. 410. A. S. Shcherbakov. 411. Statue.

1950. Labour Day.

1597. 409. 40 k. red and black .. 80 80
1598. – 1 r. red and black .. 1·90 1·25

DESIGN—HORIZ. 1 r. Banners and Kremlin.

1950. 5th Anniv. of Death of Shcherbakov (statesman).

1599. 410. 40 k. black 55 20
1600. 1 r. green on pink .. 1·10 55

1950. 5th Anniv. of German Defeat.

1606. 411. 40 k. red and sepia .. 1·10 90
1607. – 1 r. red .. .. 1·60 1·40

DESIGN (22½ × 33 mm.): 1 r. Victory medal.

412. Marshal Suvorov. 413. Sowing on Collective Farm.

1950. Marshal Suvorov. 150th Death Anniv. Inscr. "1800 1950".

1601. 412. 40 k. blue on pink .. 65 25
1602. – 50 k. brown on pink .. 1·00 55
1603. – 60 k. black on blue .. 90 90
1604. 412. 1 r. brown on yellow 1·50 1·10
1605. – 2 r. green .. .. 2·75 2·25

DESIGNS—VERT. 50 k. Battle (32½ × 47 mm.). 60 k. Medal and soldiers (24½ × 39½ mm.). 2 r. Suvorov in cloak (19½ × 33½ mm.).

1950. Agricultural Workers. Inscr. "1950".

1608. – 40 k. green on blue .. 55 12
1609. 413. 40 k. brown on buff .. 55 12
1610. 1 r. blue on yellow .. 1·00 45

DESIGN: No. 1608, Students.

414. G. M. Dimitrov. 415. Baku Opera House.

1950. Dimitrov. 1st Death Anniv.

1611. 414. 40 k. black on yellow 60 20
1612. 1 r. black on red .. 1·50 55

1950. Azerbaijan S.S.R. 30th Anniv. Inscr. "1920 1950".

1613. 415. 25 k. green on yellow 40 15
1614. – 40 k. brown on red .. 70 20
1615. – 1 r. black on buff .. 1·50 65

DESIGNS: 40 k. Science Academy. 1 r. Stalin Avenue, Baku.

416. Lenin Street. 417. Kaluzhskaya Station.

1950. Stalingrad Reconstruction.

1616. – 20 k. blue 35 20
1617. 416. 40 k. green 60 55
1618. – 50 k. orange .. .. 90 1·00
1619. – 1 r. black .. .. 2·10 1·40

DESIGNS—VERT. 20 k. Victory Cinema. HORIZ. 50 k. Gorki Theatre. 1 r. Tank Memorial.

1950. Underground Railway Stations, Inscr. "M".

1620. 417. 40 k. green on buff .. 50 15
1621. A. 40 k. red 50 15
1622. B. 40 k. blue on buff .. 50 15
1623. C. 1 r. brown on yellow 1·40 40
1624. D. 1 r. violet on blue .. 1·40 40
1625. A. 1 r. green on yellow .. 1·40 40
1626. E. 1 r. black on buff .. 1·40 40

DESIGNS—HORIZ. (34 × 22½ mm.): A. Culture Park. B. Taganskaya. C. Kurskaya. D. Paveletskaya. (34 × 18½ mm.): E. Taganskaya.

418. National Flags and Civilians.

1950. Unconquerable Democracy. Flags in red, blue and yellow.

1627. 418. 40 k. black 50 15
1628. 50 k. brown .. .. 1·00 25
1629. 1 r. green .. .. 1·50 50

419. Trade Union Building. 420. Marite Melnikaite.

1950. Latvian S.S.R. 10th Anniv. Inscr. "1940 1950".

1630. 419. 25 k. chocolate .. 35 12
1631. – 40 k. red 40 35
1632. – 50 k. green 85 35
1633. – 60 k. blue .. .. 1·00 35
1634. – 1 r. violet .. .. 1·50 80
1635. – 2 r. chocolate .. 3·00 1·40

DESIGNS—VERT. 40 k. Council Offices. 50 k. Rainis' Monument. 2 r. Academy of Sciences. HORIZ. 60 k. National Theatre. 1 r. University, Riga.

1950. Lithuanian S.S.R. 10th Anniv. Inscr. "1940 1950".

1636. – 25 k. blue 30 15
1637. 420. 40 k. chocolate .. 80 40
1638. – 1 r. red .. .. 1·60 1·40

DESIGNS—HORIZ. 25 k. Academy of Sciences. 1 r. Cabinet Council Offices.

421. Stalingrad Square, Tallinn. 422. Signing Peace Appeal.

1950. Estonian S.S.R. 10th Anniv. Inscr. "1940 1950".

1639. 421. 25 k. green 40 20
1640. – 40 k. red 60 40
1641. – 50 k. blue on yellow .. 85 60
1642. – 1 r. chocolate on blue 1·60 1·60

DESIGNS—HORIZ. 40 k. Tallinn Theatre. 50 k. Government Building. VERT. 1 r. Victor Kingsiev.

1950. Peace Conf.

1643. 422. 40 k. red on buff .. 55 20
1644. – 40 k. black 60 20
1645. – 50 k. red .. .. 1·00 35
1646. 422. 1 r. chocolate on buff 1·40 75

DESIGNS—VERT. 40 k. black, Children and teacher. 50 k. Procession.

423. Bellingshausan, Lazarev and Globe. 424. M. V. Frunze.

1950. 1st Antarctic Expedition. 130th Anniv. Inscr. "1820 1950".

1647. 423. 40 k. red on blue .. 5·50 5·00
1648. – 1 r. violet on blue .. 11·00 5·00

DESIGN—VERT. 1 r. Map and ships.

1950. Frunze (strategist). 25th Death Anniv.
1649. **424.** 40 k. blue on buff .. 1·00 55
1650. 1 r. chocolate on blue 2·25 1·00

425. M. I. Kalinin.

426. Picking Grapes.

1950. Kalinin (statesman). 75th Birth Anniv.
1651. **425.** 40 k. green 65 35
1652. 1 r. brown .. .. 1·60 80
1653. 5 r. violet .. .. 4·50 1·75

1950. Armenian S.S.R. 30th Anniv.
1654. **426.** 20 k. blue on buff .. 40 20
1655. – 40 k. orange on blue .. 75 55
1656. – 1 r. black on yellow .. 1·90 1·90
DESIGNS—HORIZ. (33 × 16 mm.): 40 k. Government Offices. VERT ($21\frac{1}{2}$ × 33 mm.): 1 r. G.M. Sundukian (dramatist).

427. Kotelnicheskaya Quay.

СССР ПОЧТА 1 Р.
428. Spassky Tower, Kremlin.

1950. Moscow Building Projects.
1657. **427.** 1 r. brown on buff .. 9·00 5·00
1658. – 1 r. black on buff .. 9·00 5·00
1659. – 1 r. chocolate on blue 9·00 5·00
1660. – 1 r. green on yellow 9·00 5·00
1661. – 1 r. blue on buff .. 9·00 5·00
1662. – 1 r. black .. .. 9·00 5·00
1663. – 1 r. orange .. .. 9·00 5·00
1664. – 1 r. green on blue .. 9·00 5·00
DESIGNS—HORIZ. No. 1659, Vosstaniya Square. 1660, Moscow University. 1662, Dorogomilovskaya Quay. 1664, Smolenskaya Sq. VERT. 1658, Krasnye Vorota. 1661, Komsomolskaya Sq. 1663, Zariadie.

1950. October Revolution. 33rd Anniv.
1665. **428.** 1 r. red, yell. & green 4·00 1·75

429. "Golden Autumn".

PORTRAIT: 50 k. Levitan seated.

1950. Levitan (painter). 50th Death Anniv. 40 k. multicoloured centre. 50 k. inscr. "1900 1950".
1666. **429.** 40 k. blue .. .. 1·50 50
1667. – 50 k. chocolate .. 1·75 50

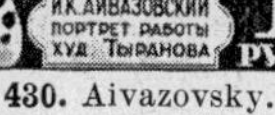

430. Aivazovsky.

431. "Iskra" and "Pravda".

1950. Aivazovsky (painter). 50th Death Anniv. Multicoloured centres.
1668. – 40 k. brown .. .. 1·75 12
1669. – 50 k. brown .. .. 1·75 20
1670. **430.** 1 r. blue .. .. 3·00 55
PAINTINGS—HORIZ. 40 k. "Black Sea". 50 k. "Ninth Wave".

1950. Newspaper "Iskra". 50th Anniv. Inscr. "1900 1950".
1671. – 40 k. red and black .. 4·50 2·25
1672. **431.** 1 r. red and black .. 5·50 2·75
DESIGN: 40 k. As T **431** without Lenin and Stalin.

432. Government Offices.

DESIGN: 1 r. Opera House, Alma-Ata.

1950 Kazakh S.S.R. 30th Anniv.
1673. **432.** 40 k. black on blue .. 80 25
1674. – 1 r. brown on yellow 1·50 55

433. Decembrists and Senatskaya Square, Leningrad.

1950. December Rising. 125th Anniv.
1675. **433.** 1 r. choc. on yellow .. 3·25 2·25

434. Govt. Offices, Tirana.

435. Greeting Soviet Troops.

1951. Friendship with Albania.
1676. **434.** 40 k. green on blue .. 4·00 2·75

1951. Friendship with Bulgaria.
1677. **435.** 25 k. black on blue .. 50 50
1678. – 40 k. orange on pink 1·25 1·25
1679. – 60 k. sepia on pink .. 1·60 1·60
DESIGNS: 40 k. Lenin Square, Sofia. 60 k. Monument to Soviet fighters, Kolarovgrad.

436. Lenin at Razliv.

1951. Lenin. 27th Death Anniv. Multi-coloured centres.
1680. **436.** 40 k. green 80 12
1681. – 1 r. blue .. .. 1·50 20
DESIGN: 1 r. Lenin and young Communists.

437. Horses.

437a. Gathering Lemons.

1951. Kirghiz S.S.R. 25th Anniv. Inscr. "XXV".
1682. **437.** 25 k. sepia on blue .. 65 45
1683. – 40 k. green on blue .. 80 65
DESIGN ($33 \times 22\frac{1}{2}$ mm.): 40 k. Government Offices, Frunze.

1951. Georgia S.S.R. 30th Anniv. Dated "1951 r.".
1683a. – 20 k. grn. on yellow 35 20
1683b. **437a.** 25 k. orange & pur. 55 20
1683c. – 40 k. brn. on blue 1·10 55
1683d. – 1 r. green & brown 2·75 1·60
DESIGNS—VERT. 20 k. Theatre, Tiflis. HORIZ. 40 k. Main thoroughfare, Tiflis. 1 r. Plucking tea.

438. University, Ulan-Bator.

1951. Friendship with Mongolia.
1684. **438.** 25 k. violet on pink .. 1·10 35
1685. – 40 k. orange on yellow 1·60 55
1686. – 1 r. blue, red, cream and brown .. 3·50 1·75
DESIGNS—HORIZ. ($37\frac{1}{2}$ × 25 mm.): 40 k. State Theatre, Ulan-Bator. VERT. ($22 \times 33\frac{1}{2}$ mm.): 1 r. State Emblem and Mongolian Flag.

439. D. A. Furmanov.

440. Soviet Soldiers Memorial, Berlin.

1951. D. A. Furmanov (writer). 25th Death Anniv.
1687. **439.** 40 k. brown on blue .. 80 80
1688. – 1 r. black on pink .. 1·10 1·10
DESIGN—HORIZ. 1 r. Furmanov writing.

1951. Stockholm Peace Appeal.
1689. **440** 40 k. green and red .. 1·40 90
1690. 1 r. black and red .. 2·75 2·00

441. Kirov Factory.

1951. Kirov Factory, Leningrad. 150th Anniv.
1691. **441.** 40 k. brown on yellow 2·00 1·10

442. Bolshoi State Theatre.

1951. State Theatre. 175th Anniv. Inscr. "175 ΔET".
1692. **442.** 40 k. multicoloured .. 1·75 25
1693. – 1 r. multicoloured .. 3·00 50
DESIGN: 1 r. Medallion portraits of Glinka, Tchaikovsky, Moussorgsky, Rimsky-Korsakov, Borodin and theatre.

443. National Museum.

444. Harvesting.

1951. Hungarian Peoples' Republic. Buildings in Budapest.
1694. – 25 k. green 40 12
1695. – 40 k. blue 55 30
1696. **443.** 60 k. black 90 95
1697. – 1 r. black on pink .. 1·60 1·10
DESIGNS—HORIZ. 25 k. Liberty Bridge. 40 k. Parliament bldgs. VERT. Liberation Monument.

1951. Agricultural scenes.
1698. **444.** 25 k. green 50 12
1699. – 40 k. green on blue 60 15
1700. – 1 r. brown on yellow 1·25 40
1701. – 2 r. green on pink .. 3·00 60
DESIGNS: 40 k. Apiary. 1 r. Gathering citrus fruit. 2 r. Harvesting cotton.

445. M. I. Kalinin.

ПОЧТА СССР 1926-1951 Ф.Э.ДЗЕРЖИНСКИЙ 40 коп
446. F. E. Dzerzhinsky.

1951. Pres. Kalinin. 5th Death Anniv.
1702. – 20 k. sepia and brown 15 10
1703. **445.** 40 k. choc. and green 50 15
1704. – 1 r. black and blue .. 95 35
DESIGNS—HORIZ. 20 k. Kalinin Museum. VERT. 1 r. Kalinin Statue.

1951. Dzerzhinsky (founder of Cheka). 25th Death Anniv.
1705. **446.** 40 k. red 85 45
1706. – 1 r. black (portrait in uniform) .. .. 1·50 1·00

447. P. K. Kozlov.

448. Kalinnikov.

1951. Russian Scientists.
1707. **447.** 40 k. orange 80 12
1708. – 40 k. orange on pink 80 12
1709. – 40 k. orange on blue 2·00 35
1710. – 40 k. brown 80 12
1711. – 40 k. brown on pink (facing left) .. 2·00 35
1712. – 40 k. brown on pink (facing right) .. 80 12
1713. – 40 k. grey 80 12
1714. – 40 k. grey on pink .. 80 12
1715. – 40 k. grey on blue .. 80 12
1716. – 40 k. green 80 12
1717. – 40 k. green on pink .. 80 12
1718. – 40 k. blue 80 12
1719. – 40 k. deep blue on pink 80 12
1720. – 40 k. blue on blue .. 80 12
1721. – 40 k. violet 80 12
1722. – 40 k. violet on pink 80 12
PORTRAITS: No. 1708, N. N. Miklukho-Maklai. 1709, A. M. Butlerov. 1710, N. I. Lobachevsky. 1711, K. A. Timiriazev. 1712, N. S. Kurnakov. 1713, P. N. Yablochkov 1714, A. N. Severtsov. 1715, K. E. Tsiolkovsky. 1716, A. N. Lodygin. 1717, A. O. Stoletov. 1718, P. N. Lebedev. 1719, A. O. Kovalevsky. 1720, D. I. Mendeleev. 1721, S. P. Krasheninnikov. 1722, S. V. Kovalevskaya.

1951. Russian Composers.
1723. **448.** 40 k. grey on pink .. 4·00 1·75
1724. – 40 k. brown on pink .. 3·25 1·75
PORTRAIT: No. 1724, Aliablev and bar of music.

449. Aviation Society Badge.

450. V. M. Vasnetsov (painter).

1951. Aviation Development.
1725. **449.** 40 k. multicoloured .. 70 12
1726. – 60 k. multicoloured .. 1·00 20
1727. – 1 r. multicoloured .. 1·50 35
1728. – 2 r. multicoloured .. 3·00 65
DESIGNS—VERT. 60 k. Boys and model gliders. 1 r. Parachutists descending. HORIZ. (45 × 25 mm.): 2 r. Three aeroplanes.

1951. Vasnetsov. 25th Death Anniv.
1729. **450.** 40 k. brown and blue 1·10 20
1730. – 1 r. grn. & yell. (frame) 2·00 50
DESIGN—(47 × 33 mm.): 1 r. Multicoloured painting—"Three Heroes".

451. Lenin, Stalin and Dnieperprostroi Dam.

DESIGN: 1 r. Lenin, Stalin and Spasski Tower.

1951. October Revolution. 34th Anniv. Dated "1917-1951".
1731. **451.** 40 k. blue and red .. 1·40 90
1732. – 1 r. brown and red .. 3·00 1·60

INDEX

Countries can be quickly located by referring to the index at the end of this volume.

452. Volga-Don Canal.

1951. Construction of Hydro-electric Power Stations.
1733. – 20 k. multicoloured .. 85 35
1734. **452.** 30 k. multicoloured .. 1·10 45
1735. – 40 k. multicoloured .. 1·75 80
1736. – 60 k. multicoloured .. 2·25 1·00
1737. – 1 r. multicoloured .. 4·00 1·90
DESIGNS—VERT. (32 × 47 mm.): 20 k. Khakhovsky power station. HORIZ. (47 × 32 mm.): 40 k. Stalingrad dam. 60 k. Excavator and map of Turkmen canal. 1 r. Kuibyshev power station.

453. Signing Peace Petition.

454. M. V. Ostrogradsky (mathematician).

1951. 3rd U.S.S.R. Peace Conf.
1738. **453.** 40 k. red and sepia .. 2·25 1·60

1951. Ostrogradsky. 150th Birth Anniv.
1739. **454.** 40 k. sepia on pink .. 3·00 95

455. Zhizka Monument, Prague.

456. Volkhovsky Hydro-electric Station and Lenin Monument.

1951. Friendship with Czechoslovakia.
1740. **455.** 20 k. blue on pink .. 40 15
1741. – 25 k. red on lemon .. 50 20
1742. – 40 k. orange on orange 80 40
1743. – 60 k. grey .. .. 1·25 90
1744. – 1 r. grey .. .. 2·10 1·75
DESIGNS—VERT. 25 k. Soviet Army Monument, Ostrava. 40 k. J. Fucik. 60 k. Smetana Museum, Prague. HORIZ. 1 r. Soviet Soldiers Monument, Prague.

1951. Lenin Volkhovsky Hydro-electric Station. 25th Anniv.
1745. **456.** 40 k. yellow and blue 55 12
1746. 1 r. yellow and violet 1·50 30

457. Lenin when a Student.

458. P. P. Semenov-Tian-Shansky

1952. Lenin. 28th Death Anniv. Multicoloured centres.
1747. **457.** 40 k. green 85 45
1748. – 60 k. blue .. .. 1·10 55
1749. – 1 r. brown .. .. 1·40 65
DESIGNS—HORIZ. 60 k. Lenin and children. 1 r. Lenin talking to peasants.

1952. Semenov-Tian-Shansky (scientist). 125th Birth Anniv.
1750. **458.** 1 r. sepia on blue .. 2·00 90

459. Skaters.

460. V. O. Kovalevsky (scientist).

1952. Winter Sports.
1751. **459.** 40 k. multicoloured .. 90 20
1752. – 60 k. mult. (skiers) .. 1·60 25

1952. Kovalevsky (scientist). Birth Cent.
1753. **460.** 40 k. sepia on yellow 1·00 90

461. Gogol and character from "Taras Bulba".

1952. Gogol (writer). Death Cent.
1754. **461.** 40 k. black on blue .. 80 10
1755. – 60 k. brown and black 1·00 15
1756. – 1 r. multicoloured .. 1·50 60
DESIGNS: 60 k. Gogol and Belinsky. 1 r. Gogol and Ukranian peasants.

462. G. K. Ordzhonikidze (statesman).

463. Workpeople and Flag.

1952. Ordzhonikidze. 15th Death Anniv.
1757. **462.** 40 k. green on pink .. 60 20
1758. 1 r. black on blue .. 1·25 45

1952. Stalin Constitution. 15th Anniv.
1759. **463.** 40 k. red and black on cream .. .. 1·40 80
1760. – 40 k. red and green on green .. .. 1·40 80
1761. – 40 k. red and brown on blue .. .. 1·40 80
1762. – 40 k. red and black .. 1·40 80
DESIGNS—HORIZ. No. 1760, Recreation centre. 1761, Old people and banners. VERT. 1762, Schoolgirl and Spassky Tower Kremlin.

464. Novikov-Priboy and Warship.

465. Victor Hugo (author).

1952. Novikov-Priboy (writer). 75th Birth Anniv.
1763. **464.** 40 k. slate, yell. & grn. 60 20

1952. Victor Hugo. 150th Birth Anniv.
1764. **465.** 40 k. blk., blue & brn. 50 15

466. Salavat Yulaev.

467. G. Y. Sedov.

1952. Yulaev (Bashkirian hero). Birth Bicent.
1765. **466.** 40 k. red on pink .. 50 20

1952. Sedov (Arctic explorer). 75th Birth Anniv.
1766. **467.** 40 k. sepia, blue & grn. 2·75 1·25

468. Arms and Rumanian Flag.
469. V. A. Zhukovsky.
470. K. P. Bryullov.

1952. Friendship with Rumania.
1767. **468.** 40 k. yellow, red, blue and brown .. 80 35
1768. – 60 k. green on pink .. 1·00 55
1769. – 1 r. blue .. .. 1·60 90
DESIGNS—VERT. 60 k. Soviet Soldiers' Monument, Bucharest. HORIZ. 1 r. University Square, Bucharest.

1952. Zhukovsky (poet). Death Cent.
1770. **469.** 40 k. black on blue .. 35 15

1952. Bryullov (artist). Death Cent.
1771. **470.** 40 k. green on blue 35 15

471. N. P. Ogarev.

472. G. I. Uspensky.

1952. Ogarev (revolutionary writer). 75th Death Anniv.
1772. **471.** 40 k. green 35 12

1952. Uspensky (writer). 50th Death Anniv.
1773. **472.** 40 k. sepia and indigo 35 12

473. Admiral Nakhimov.

474. Tartu University.

1952. Admiral Nakhimov. 150th Birth Anniv.
1774. **473.** 40 k. multicoloured .. 1·10 55

1952. Extension of Tartu University. 150th Anniv.
1775. **474.** 40 k. black on salmon 1·00 45

1952. War Orders and Medals (7th series). Frame as T **234** with various centres.
1776. F. 1 r. sepia .. .. 2·25 1·10
1777. P. 2 r. red .. .. 1·75 90
1778. J. 3 r. violet .. .. 1·75 1·10
1779a. A. 5 r. lake .. .. 2·75 90
1780a. E. 10 r. red .. .. 6·50 3·25

475. Kayum Nasyri.

476. A. N. Radischev.

1952. Nasyri (educationist). 50th Death Anniv.
1781. **475.** 40 k. brown on yellow 1·10 1·10

1952. Radischev (writer). 150th Death Anniv.
1782. **476.** 40 k. black and red .. 55 25

477. Entrance to Volga-Don Canal.

478. P. A. Fedotov.

1952. October Revolution. 35th Anniv. Inscr. "1917–1952".
1783. **477.** 40 k. yellow, red, black and blue .. 1·10 1·10
1784. – 1 r. yell., red & brn. 2·25 1·60
DESIGN: 1 r. Lenin, Stalin, Spasski Tower and flags.

1952. Fedotov (painter). Death Cent.
1785. **478.** 40 k. sepia and lake .. 1·00 25

479. V. D. Polenov.

481. A. I. Odoyevsky.

480. "Moscow Courtyard" (painting).

1952. Polenov (painter). 25th Death Anniv. Multicoloured centre (1 r.).
1786. **479.** 40 k. lake and buff .. 60 20
1787. **480.** 1 r. blue and grey .. 1·50 45

1952. Odoyevsky (poet). 150th Birth Anniv.
1788. **481.** 40 k. black and red .. 50 20

482. Mamin-Sibiriak.

483. V. M. Bekhterev.

1952. Mamin-Sibiriak (writer). Birth Cent.
1789. **482.** 40 k. green on yellow 50 20

1952. Bekhterev (psychiatrist). 25th Death Anniv.
1790. **483.** 40 k. blk., grey & blue 55 15

484. Komsomolskaya Koltsevaya Station.

1952. Underground stations. Multicoloured centres.
1791. – 40 k. violet 65 20
1792. – 40 k. blue 65 20
1793. – 40 k. grey 65 20
1794. **484.** 40 k. green 65 20
STATIONS: No. 1791, Byelorussia Koltsevaya. 1792. Botanical Gardens. 1793, Novoslobodskaya.

485. U.S.S.R. Arms and Flags.

486. Lenin and Flags.

1952. U.S.S.R. 30th Anniv.
1795. **485.** 1 r. brown, red & green 2·00 80

1953. Lenin. 29th Death Anniv.
1796. **486.** 40 k. multicoloured 2·25 90

487. Peace Prize Medal. **488.** V. V. Kuibyshev.

1953. Stalin Peace Prize.
1797. **487.** 40 k. yell., blue & brn. 2·25 1·10

1953. Kuibyshev (statesman). 65th Birth Anniv.
1798. **488.** 40 k. black and lake 75 50

489. V. V. Mayakovsky. **490.** N. G. Chernyshevsky.

1953. Mayakovsky (poet). 60th Birth Anniv.
1799. **489.** 40 k. black and red .. 65 20

1953. Chernyshevsky (writer). 125th Birth Anniv.
1800. **490** 40 k. brown and buff 60 35

491. Volga Lighthouse.

1953. Views of Volga-Don Canal. Multicoloured.
1801. 40 k. T **491** 70 15
1802. 40 k. Lock No. 9 .. 70 15
1803. 40 k. Lock No. 13 .. 70 15
1804. 40 k. Lock No. 15 .. 70 15
1805. 40 k. Tsymljanskaja hydro-electric station .. 70 15
1806. 1 r. M.V. "Joseph Stalin" 1·10 50

492. V. G. Korolenko. **493.** Tolstoy.

1953. Korolenko (writer). Birth Cent.
1807. **492.** 40 k. brown 50 12

1953. Tolstoy. 125th Birth Anniv.
1808. **493.** 1 r. sepia .. .. 1·40 60

494. Lomonosov University and Students. **495.** Peoples of the U.S.S.R.

1953. 35th Anniv. of "Komsomol" (Russian Youth Organization).
1809. **494.** 40 k. red, yellow, blue and brown .. 90 30
1810. – 1 r. red, yell. & blue 1·90 55
DESIGN—VERT. 1 r. Four medals and "Komsomol" badge.

1953. 36th Anniv. of Russian Revolution.
1811. **495.** 40 k. brn., red & buff 1·50 55
1812. – 60 k. brn., red & buff 3·25 3·25
DESIGN—VERT. 60 k. Lenin and Stalin in Smolny Institute, 1917.

496. Lenin Medallion. **497.** Lenin Statue.

498. Peter I Monument.

1953. Communist Party. 50th Anniv.
1813. **496.** 40 k. multicoloured .. 2·00 1·10

1953. Views of Lenigrad as T **497/8.**
1814. **497.** 40 k. black on yellow 55 45
1815. 40 k. brown on pink 55 20
1816. – 40 k. brown on lemon 55 45
1817. – 40 k. black on buff 55 20
1818. **498.** 1 r. brown on blue .. 1·75 1·25
1819. – 1 r. violet on lemon 1·50 45
1820. – 1 r. green on pink .. 1·75 1·25
1821. – 1 r. brown on blue .. 1·50 45
DESIGNS—As T **497**: Nos. 1816/7, Admiralty. As T **498**: 1820/1, Smolny Institute.

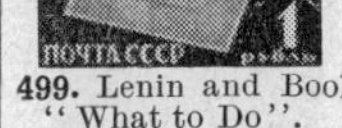

499. Lenin and Book "What to Do". **500.** Pioneers and Moscow University Model.

1953. 2nd Social Democratic Workers' Party Congress. 50th Anniv.
1822. **499.** 1 r. brown and red .. 3·00 1·00

1953. Peace Propaganda.
1823. **500.** 40 k. brown, red and slate .. .. .. 1·10 65

501. A. S. Griboyedov. **502.** Kremlin.

1954. Griboyedov (author). 125th Death Anniv.
1824. **501.** 40 k. maroon on buff 55 15
1825. 1 r. black on green .. 80 25

1954. General Election.
1826. **502.** 40 k. slate and red .. 90 45

503. V. P. Chkalov. **504.** Lenin in Smolny Institute.

1954. 50th Birthday of Chkalov (aviator).
1827. **503.** 1 r. brn., blue & grey 2·00 35

1954. Lenin. 30th Death Anniv. Inscr. "1924-1954". Nos. 1829/32 are multicoloured.
1828. – 40 k. brown, salmon, red and brown .. 80 35
1829. **504.** 40 k. (38 × 26 mm.) .. 80 35
1830. – 40 k. (38 × 26 mm.) .. 80 35
1831. – 40 k. (48 × 35 mm.) .. 80 35
1832. – 40 k. (48 × 35 mm.) .. 80 35

DESIGNS—VERT. No. 1828. Lenin. HORIZ. 1830. Cottage Museum, Ulyanovsk. 1831, Lenin addressing revolutionaries. 1832, Lenin and other students in Kazan University.

505. Stalin. **506.** Supreme Soviet Buildings in Kiev and Moscow.

1954. Stalin. 1st Death Anniv.
1833. **505.** 40 k. brown 85 20

1954. Reunion of Ukraine with Russia. Tercent. Multicoloured. (a) Designs as T **506** inscr. "1654-1954".
1834. 40 k. Type **506** 50 8
1835. 40 k. Shevchenko Memorial, Kharkhov (vert.) .. 50 8
1836. 40 k. State Opera House, Kiev 50 8
1837. 40 k. Shevchenko University, Kiev 50 8
1838. 40 k. Academy of Sciences, Kiev 55 8
1839. 60 k. Bogdan Chmielnitski Memorial, Kiev (vert.) 55 15
1840. 1 r. Flags of R.S.F.S.R. and Ukrainian S.S.R. (vert.) .. .. 1·25 20
1841. 1 r. Shevchenko Monument, Kanev (vert.) .. 90 35
1842. 1 r. Pereyasaavskaya Rada .. .. 1·25 20

(b) No. 1098b optd. with five lines of Cyrillic characters as inscr. at top of T **506.**
1843. **h.** 2 r. green .. .. 2·25 80

507. Running.

DESIGNS—HORIZ. Nos. 1845/50, Yachting, Cycling, Swimming, Hurdling, Mountaineering, and Ski-ing resp. VERT. No. 1851, Basketball.

1954. Sports. Frames in chestnut.
1844. **507.** 40 k. black and stone 65 12
1845. – 40 k. black and blue 65 12
1846. – 40 k. sepia and buff 65 12
1847. – 40 k. black and blue 65 12
1848. – 40 k. black 65 12
1849. – 1 r. grey and blue .. 1·60 35
1850. – 1 r. black and blue .. 1·60 35
1851. – 1 r. sepia and drab .. 1·60 35

508. Cattle. **509.** A. P. Chekhov.

1954. Agriculture.
1852. **508.** 40 k. blue, brown & cream 90 20
1853. – 40 k. grn., brn. & buff 80 20
1854. – 40 k. black, blue and emerald 80 20
DESIGNS: No. 1853, Potato cultivation. 1854, Collective-farm hydro-electric station.

1954. Chekhov (writer). 50th Death Anniv.
1855. **509.** 40 k. brown & green .. 60 20

510. **511.** M. I. Glinka.

1954. Rebuilding of Pulkov Observatory.
1856. **510.** 40 k. blk., bl. & violet 3·25 80

1954. Glinka (composer). 150th Birth Anniv.
1857. **511.** 40 k. sepia, rose and claret 65 20
1858. – 60 k. multicoloured .. 1·00 35
DESIGN—HORIZ. (38 × 25½ mm.): 60 k. Young Glinka playing piano to friends Pushkin and Zhukovsky.

512. Exhibition Emblem. **513.** N. A. Ostrovsky.

1954. Agricultural Exhibition. Nos. 1860/4 multicoloured.
1859. **512.** 40 k. bistre, orange, brown and green .. 55 20
1860. – 40 k. (41 × 30½ mm.) 55 20
1861. – 40 k. (41 × 30½ mm.) 55 20
1862. – 40 k. (40 × 30 mm.) .. 55 20
1863. – 1 r. (41 × 33 mm.) .. 1·60 65
1864. – 1 r. (29 × 41 mm.) .. 1·60 65
DESIGNS—HORIZ. No. 1860 Agriculture Pavilion. 1861, Cattle-breeding Pavilion. 1862, Mechanization Pavilion. 1863, Exhibition entrance. VERT. 1864, Main Pavilion.

1954. Ostrovsky (writer). 50th Birth Anniv.
1865. **513.** 40 k. red, yellow, black and brown .. 50 15

514. Monument. **515.** Marx, Engels, Lenin and Stalin.

1954. Defence of Sevastopol Cent.
1866. **514.** 40 k. blk., drab & grn. 65 20
1867. – 60 k. blk., brn. & buff 90 25
1868. – 1 r. black, brown, buff and olive .. .. 1·75 55
DESIGNS—HORIZ. 60 k. Defenders of Sevastopol. VERT. 1 r. Admiral Nakhimov.

1954. Russian Revolution. 37th Anniv.
1869. **515.** 1 r. brown, red & orge. 1·40 55

ILLUSTRATIONS
British Commonwealth and all overprints and surcharges are FULL SIZE. Foreign Countries have been reduced to ¾-LINEAR.

516. Kazan University.

1954. Kazan University. 150th Anniv.
1870. **516.** 40 k. blue on blue . 55 20
1871. 60 k. claret 80 35

517. Salomea Neris (poetess).

1954. Salomea Neris. 50th Birth Anniv.
1872. **517.** 40 k. multicoloured .. 65 15

518. Cultivating Vegetables. **519.** Stalin.

1954. Agriculture. Multicoloured.
1873. 40 k. Type **518** 80 20
1874. 40 k. Tractor and plough 80 20
1875. 40 k. Harvesting flax .. 80 20
1876. 60 k. Harvesting sunflowers 1·25 35
SIZES: Nos. 1873/4. 38½ × 24 mm. Nos. 1875/6, 48½ × 25 mm.

1954. Stalin. 75th Birth Anniv.
1877. **519.** 40 k. purple 80 20
1878. 1 r. blue .. .. 1·75 50

520. Rubinstein.

521. V. M. Garshin.

1954. Rubinstein (composer). 125th Birth Anniv.
1879. **520.** 40 k. black & purple 65 20

1955. Garshin (writer). Birth Cent.
1880. **521.** 40 k. blk., brn. & grn. 55 20

522. Aeroplane over Landscape.

523. K. A. Savitsky and "Construction of Railroad".

1955. Air.
1881. – 1 r. multicoloured .. 1·10 20
1882. **522.** 2 r. black and green .. 1·90 35
DESIGN: 1 r. Aeroplane over coastline.

1955. Savitsky (painter). 50th Death Anniv. Multicoloured centre.
1883. **523.** 40 k. brown 65 20

524. Clasped Hands.

525. Pushkin and Mickiewicz.

1955. W.F.T.U. Int. Conference.
1884. **524.** 50 k. multicoloured .. 45 12

1955. Russo-Polish Friendship Agreement. 10th Anniv.
1885. **525.** 40 k. multicoloured .. 1·10 20
1886. – 40 k. black .. .. 1·10 20
1887. – 1 r. multicoloured .. 2·25 70
1888. – 1 r. multicoloured .. 2·25 70
DESIGNS: No. 1886, "Brotherhood in Arms" Monument, Warsaw (26½×39 mm.). 1887, Palace of Science, Warsaw (37½×25½ mm.) 1888, Copernicus and Matejko (39×26½ mm.).

526. Lenin at Shushinskoe.

527. Schiller.

1955. Lenin. 85th Birth Anniv. Inscr. "1870 1955". Multicoloured centres.
1889. **526.** 60 k. brown-red .. 1·10 35
1890. – 1 r. brown-red .. 1·60 50
1891. – 1 r. red .. .. 1·60 50
DESIGNS: No. 1890, Lenin in secret printing house (26½×39 mm.). As T **526**: 1891, Lenin and Krupskaya at Gorki.

1955. Schiller (poet). 150th Death Anniv.
1892. **527.** 40 k. brown 55 15

528. Aeroplane over Globe.

529. V. Mayakovsky.

1955. Air.
1893. **528.** 2 r. brown .. .. 2·25 40
1894. 2 r. blue .. .. 2·25 40

1955. Mayakovsky (poet). 25th Death Anniv.
1895. **529.** 40 k. multicoloured .. 75 25

530. Tadzhik S.S.R. Pavilion.

1955. Agricultural Exhibition. Pavilions of provinces of the U.S.S.R. as T **530** inscr. "BCXB". Multicoloured designs with green frames.
1896. 40 k. R.S.F.S.R. .. 50 15
1897. 40 k. Byelorussian S.S.R. 50 15
1898. 40 k. Tadzhik S.S.R. 50 15
1899. 40 k. Azerbaijan S.S.R... 50 15
1900. 40 k. Latvian S.S.R. .. 50 15
1901. 40 k. Lithuanian S.S.R. 50 15
1902. 40 k. Karelo-Finnish S.S.R. .. 50 15
1903. 40 k. Estonian S.S.R. .. 50 15
1904. 40 k. Armenian S.S.R. .. 50 15
1905. 40 k. Ukrainian S.S.R. .. 50 15
1906. 40 k. Georgian S.S.R. .. 50 15
1907. 40 k. Kazakh S.S.R. .. 50 15
1908. 40 k. Turkmen S.S.R. 50 15
1909. 40 k. Kirghiz S.S.R. .. 50 15
1910. 40 k. Uzbek S.S.R. .. 50 15
1911. 40 k. Moldavian S.S.R... 50 15

531. M. V. Lomonosov and Building.

1955. Lomonosov University Bicent. Inscr. "1755 1955". Multicoloured.
1912. 40 k. Type **531** 60 15
1913. 1 r. Lomonosov University 1·10 25

532. Venetsianov and "The Labours of Spring".

1955. Venetsianov (painter). 175th Birth Anniv. Multicoloured centre.
1914. **532.** 1 r. black .. .. 1·60 35

533. A. Lyadov (composer).

1955. Lyadov. Birth Cent.
1915. **533.** 40 k. brown, ochre and black 55 15

534. A. A. Popov.

535. Lenin.

536. Revolution Scene.

1955. Popov's Radio Discoveries. 60th Anniv. Multicoloured centres.
1916. **534.** 40 k. blue 80 12
1917. 1 r. brown .. .. 1·40 20

1955. Russian Revolution. 38th Anniv. No. 1920 as T **536** and similarly inscr.
1918. **535.** 40 k. multicoloured .. 80 20
1919. **536.** 40 k. multicoloured .. 80 20
1920. – 1 r. multicoloured .. 2·00 55
DESIGN: 1 r. Lenin speaking to revolutionaries.

„Сев. полюс“
— Москва
1955 г.
(537.)

538. Magnitogorsk.

1955. Air. Opening of North Pole Scientific Stations. Nos. 1881/2 optd. with T **537**.
1921. – 1 r. multicoloured .. 1·75 1·75
1922. **522.** 2 r. black and green .. 3·50 3·50

1955. Magnitogorsk. 25th Anniv.
1923. **538.** 40 k. multicoloured .. 50 20

539. Helicopter over Station.

540. F. I. Shubin (sculptor).

1955. North Pole Scientific Stations.
1924. **539.** 40 k. multicoloured .. 65 25
1925. 60 k. multicoloured .. 1·00 45
1926. – 1 r. multicoloured .. 1·60 60
DESIGN: 1 r. Meteorologist taking observations.

1955. Shubin. 150th Death Anniv.
1927. **540.** 40 k. multicoloured .. 50 15
1928. 1 r. multicoloured .. 85 25

541. A. N. Krylov (scientist).

542. Racing.

1956. Krylov. 10th Anniv.
1929. **541.** 40 k. multicoloured .. 45 15

1956. Int. Horse Racing.
1930. **542.** 40 k. brown .. 35 12
1931. 60 k. green 55 25
1932. – 1 r. blue and purple 90 40
DESIGN (33½ × 25 mm.): 1 r. Trotting.

543. Badge and Stadium.

544. Atomic Power Station.

1956. 5th Spartacist Games.
1933. **543.** 1 r. green and purple 80 20

1956. Foundation of Atomic Power Station of Russian Academy of Sciences.
1934. **544.** 25 k. yellow, blue, red and green .. 45 12
1935. – 60 k. yellow, turquoise and brown .. 1·10 20
1936. **544.** 1 r. yell., red & blue 1·75 35
DESIGN: 60 k. Top of atomic reactor.

545. Statue of Lenin.

1956. 20th Communist Party Congress.
1937. **545.** 40 k. multicoloured .. 60 15
1938. 1 r. multicoloured .. 1·00 35

546. K. Abovyan (Armenian writer).

547. Revolutionaries.

1956. Khatchatur Abovyan. 150th Birth Anniv.
1939. **546.** 40 k. black on blue .. 65 15

1956. 1905 Revolution. 50th Anniv.
1940. **547.** 40 k. multicoloured .. 15 5

548.

1941. ПАВИЛЬОН «УРАЛ»
1942. ПАВИЛЬОН СЕВЕРО-ВОСТОЧНЫХ ОБЛАСТЕЙ
1943. ПАВИЛЬОН ЦЕНТРАЛЬНЫХ ЧЕРНОЗЕМНЫХ ОБЛАСТЕЙ
1944. ПАВИЛЬОН «ЛЕНИНГРАД • СЕВЕРО-ЗАПАД»
1945. ПАВИЛЬОН МОСКОВСКОЙ, ТУЛЬСКОЙ, КАЛУЖСКОЙ, РЯЗАНСКОЙ И БРЯНСКОЙ ОБЛАСТЕЙ
1946. ПАВИЛЬОН БАШКИРСКОЙ АССР
1947. ПАВИЛЬОН ДАЛЬНЕГО ВОСТОКА
1948. ПАВИЛЬОН ТАТАРСКОЙ АССР
1949. ПАВИЛЬОН ЦЕНТРАЛЬНЫХ ОБЛАСТЕЙ
1950. ПАВИЛЬОН ЮНЫХ НАТУРАЛИСТОВ
1951. ПАВИЛЬОН СЕВЕРНОГО КАВКАЗА
1952. ПАВИЛЬОН «СИБИРЬ»
1953. ПАВИЛЬОН «ПОВОЛЖЬЕ»

548a.

1956. Agricultural Exn. Multicoloured reproductions of Pavilions of various U.S.S.R. regions as T **548** with inscriptions as in T **548a**. Inscr. "BCXB".
1941. 1 r. Ural 70 20
1942. 1 r. North East 70 20
1943. 1 r. Black Sea 70 20
1944. 1 r. Leningrad 70 20
1945. 1 r. Moscow-Tula-Kaluga-Ryazan-Bryansk .. 70 20
1946. 1 r. Bashkhir 70 20
1947. 1 r. Far East 70 20
1948. 1 r. Tatar 70 20
1949. 1 r. Central Asia 70 20
1950. 1 r. Young Naturalists .. 70 20
1951. 1 r. North Caucasus .. 70 20
1952. 1 r. Siberia 70 20
1953. 1 r. Volga 70 20

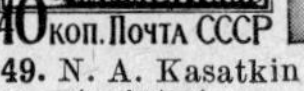
549. N. A. Kasatkin (painter).

550. Arkhipov and painting "On the Oka River".

1956. Kasatkin Commemoration.
1954. **549.** 40 k. red 35 12

1956. Arkhipov Commemoration.
1955. **550.** 40 k. multicoloured.. 40 20
1956. – 1 r. multicoloured.. 95 30

551. I. P. Kulibin (inventor).

552. "Fowler" (after Perov).

1956. Kulibin. 220th Birth Anniv.
1957. **551.** 40 k. multicoloured.. 65 20

1956. Perov Commemoration. Inscr. "1956". Multicoloured centres.
1958. – 40 k. green 65 20
1959. **552.** 1 r. brown .. .. 1·40 40
1960. – 1 r. chestnut.. .. 1·40 40
DESIGNS—VERT. 40 k. V. G. Perov. HORIZ. No. 1960, "Hunters Resting" (after Perov).

553. Lenin speaking.

554. N. I. Lobachevsky.

1956. Lenin. 86th Birth Anniv.
1961. **553.** 40 k. multicoloured.. 1·00 20

1956. Lobachevsky (mathematician). Death Cent.
1962. **554.** 40 k. sepia 35 12

555. Student Nurses.

DESIGN—(37½ × 25½ mm.): No. 1964, Nurse and textile factory.

1956. Red Cross.
1963. **555.** 40 k. red, blue & brn. 50 20
1964. – 40 k. red, olive & turq. 50 20

556.

557. I. M. Sechenov (scientist).

1956. Air. Opening of North Pole Scientific Station No. 6.
1965. **556.** 1 r. multicoloured .. 1·75 50

1956. Sechenov Commemoration.
1966. **557.** 40 k. multicoloured.. 85 20

558. V. K. Arseniev (writer).

559. I. V. Michurin.

1956. Arseniev Commemoration.
967. **558.** 40 k. blk., vio. & pink 35 12

1956. Michurin (naturalist). Birth Cent. Inscr. "1855–1955". Multicoloured centres.
1968. **559.** 25 k. sepia 20 8
1969. – 60 k. green 50 20
1970. **559.** 1 r. blue .. .. 1·00 40
DESIGN (47½ × 26½ mm.): 60 k. Michurin and children.

560. A. K. Savrasov (painter).

561. N. K. Krupskaya (Lenin's wife).

1956. Savrasov Commemoration.
1971. **560.** 1 r. sepia and yellow 85 35

1956. Russian Women Writers.

(a) Krupskaya.
1972. **561.** 40 k. sepia, blk. & blue 60 10

(b) Lesya Ukrainka.
2005. – 40 k. blk., brn. & olive 35 15

(c) Julia Zemaite.
2027. – 40 k. olive & brown.. 50 15

(d) Clara Zetkin. Birth Cent.
2115. – 40 k. brn., slate & blk. 25 12

(e) Rosa Luxemburg.
2169. – 40 k. brown and blue 50 12

562. S. M. Kirov.

563. A. A. Blok (poet).

1956. Kirov (statesman). 70th Birth Anniv.
1973. **562.** 40 k. multicoloured.. 45 15

1956. Blok Commemoration.
1974. **563.** 40 k. brn., blk. & olive 50 12

564. N. S. Leskov.

565. Factory Building.

1956. Leskov (writer). 125th Birth Anniv.
1975. **564.** 40 k. multicoloured.. 30 15
1976. – 1 r. multicoloured .. 80 35

1956. Rostov Agricultural Machinery Works. 25th Anniv.
1977. **565.** 40 k. multicoloured.. 45 12

566. G. N. Fedstova (actress).

1956. Russian Actresses.

(a) Fedstova.
1978. **566.** 40 k. brn. & mauve.. 45 15

(b) M. N. Ermolova.
2159. – 40 k. brown and violet 35 12

567. P. M. Tretiakov and Art Gallery.

DESIGN—VERT No. 1980 "Rooks have arrived" (painting by Savrasov).

1956. Tretiakov Art Gallery Cent. Inscr. "1856 1956". Centres multicoloured.
1979. **567.** 40 k. black and green 85 20
1980. – 40 k. black and brown 85 20

568. Relay-race.

ILLUSTRATIONS British Commonwealth and all overprints and surcharges are FULL SIZE. Foreign Countries have been reduced to ¾-LINEAR.

1956. Spartacist Games.
1981. **568.** 10 k. red 12 5
1982. – 25 k. brown 20 5
1983. – 25 k. brn., blue & grn. 20 5
1984. – 25 k. blue 20 5
1985. – 40 k. blue 30 8
1986. – 40 k. green 30 8
1987. – 40 k. sepia and green 30 8
1988. – 40 k. brown and green 30 8
1989. – 40 k. red and green.. 30 8
1990. – 40 k. chestnut .. 30 8
1991. – 40 k. multicoloured 30 8
1992. – 60 k. violet 50 20
1993. – 60 k. violet 50 20
1994. – 1 r. brown 80 35
DESIGNS—VERT. No. 1982, Volley-ball, 1983, Swimming. 1984, Rowing. 1985, Diving. 1989, Flag and stadium. 1990, Tennis. 1991, Medal. 1992, Boxing. HORIZ. 1986, Cycle racing. 1987, Fencing. 1988, Football. 1993, Gymnastics. 1994, Net-ball.

569. Parachutist Landing.

570. Construction Work.

1956. 3rd World Parachute-jumping Competition.
1995. **569.** 40 k. multicoloured.. 35 12

1956. Builders' Day. Insc. as in T **570.**
1996. **570.** 40 k. orange 35 12
1997. – 60 k. brown 35 12
1998. – 1 r. blue 55 25
DESIGNS: 60 k. Plant construction. 1 r. Dam construction.

571. I. Y. Repin and "Volga River Boatmen" (painting).

572. "Reply of the Cossacks to Sultan Mahmoud IV" (painting).

1956. Repin Commemoration (painter).
1999. **571.** 40 k. multicoloured.. 1·00 25
2000. **572.** 1 r. multicoloured .. 2·25 40

573. Robert Burns.

574. Ivan Franko.

1956. Burns (Scots poet). 160th Death Anniv.
2001. **573.** 40 k. brown .. .. 1·75 80
2002. 40 k. sepia and blue 1·10 60

1956. Franko (writer). Birth Cent. (1st issue).
2003. **574.** 40 k. maroon .. 25 8
2004. 1 r. blue 60 15
See also No. 2037.

576. M. Aivazov (farmer.)

577. Statue of Nestor.

1956. 148th Birthday of Aivazov.

(a) Wrongly inscr. "МЧХАМЕД" (Muhamed).
2006. **576.** 40 k. green .. .. 4·00 1·75

(b) Corrected to "МАХМЧД" (Makmud).
2006a. **576.** 40 k. green .. .. 4·00 2·25

1956. Nestor (historian). 900th Birth Anniv.
2007. **577.** 40 k. multicoloured.. 65 12
2008. 1 r. multicoloured .. 1·25 30

578. A. A. Ivanov.

579.

1956. Ivanov (painter). 150th Birth Anniv.
2009. **578.** 40 k. brown and grey 40 15

1956. Agriculture. Multicoloured.
2010. **579.** 10 k. Feeding poultry 12 5
2011. – 10 k. Harvesting .. 12 5
2012. – 25 k. Gathering maize 30 12
2013. – 40 k. Maize field .. 60 20
2014. – 40 k. Tractor station 60 20
2015. – 40 k. Cattle grazing 60 20
2016. – 40 k. "Agriculture and industry" .. 60 20
SIZES: Nos. 2010, 2014/5, 37 × 25½ mm. Nos. 2011/3, 37 × 28 mm. No. 2016, 37 × 21 mm.

580. Mozart.

581. Mirny Base and Ships.

1956. Cultural Anniversaries.
2017. 40 k. blue (Type **580**) .. 50 12
2018. 40 k. emerald (Curie) .. 50 12
2019. 40 k. violet (Heine) .. 50 12
2020. 40 k. brown (Ibsen) .. 50 12
2021. 40 k. green (Dostoievsky) 50 12
2022. 40 k. chestnut (Franklin) 50 12
2023. 40 k. black (Shaw) .. 1·00 12
2024. 40 k. orange (Sesshu-Toyo Oda) 50 12
2025. 40 k. black (Rembrandt) 50 12
Nos. 2022/5 are larger (25 × 38 mm.).

1956. Soviet Scientific Antarctic Expedition.
2026. **581.** 40 k. turq., red & slate 1·25 50

583. F. A. Bredikin.

584. G. I. Kotovsky.

1956. Bredikin (astronomer). 125th Birth Anniv.
2028. **583.** 40 k. multicoloured.. 2·25 40

1956. Kotovsky (military leader). 75th Birth Anniv.
2029. **584.** 40 k. magenta .. 1·00 65

585. Shatura Power Station.

585a. Marshal Suvorov.

1956. Shatura Power Station. 30th Anniv.
2030. **585.** 40 k. multicoloured 35 15

1956. Marshal Suvorov. 225th Birth Anniv.
2031. **585a.** 40 k. lake and orge. 45 15
2032. 1 r. choc. and olive 90 30
2033. 3 r. black and choc. 2·75 90

586. Kryakutni's Ascent.

1956. First Balloon Flight by Kryakutni. 225th Anniv.
2034. **586.** 40 k. multicoloured .. 65 25

587. A. M. Vasnetsov (artist), "Dawn at the Voskresenski Gate".

1956. Vasnetsov (artist). 30th Death Anniv.
2035. **587.** 40 k. multicoloured .. 55 30

588. Y. M. Shokalsky. 589. Ivan Franko.

1956. Shokalsky (oceanographer). Birth Cent.
2036. **588.** 40 k. brown and blue 1·00 20

1956. Franko (writer). Birth Cent. (2nd issue).
2037. **589.** 40 k. green 25 12

590. Indian Temple and Books. 591. F. G. Volkov (actor) and State Theatre.

1956. Kalidasa (Indian poet) Commem.
2038. **590.** 40 k. red 25 12

1956. Leningrad State Theatre. Bicent.
2039. **591.** 40 k. blk., claret & yell. 35 12

592. Lomonosov and St. Petersburg University.

1956. Russian writers.
2040. **592.** 40 k. red, olive, green and sepia 60 20
2041. – 40 k. red, sepia, pink and black 60 20
2042. – 40 k. brown and blue 60 20
2043. – 40 k. olive, brn. & blk. 60 20
2044. – 40 k. sepia and turq. 60 20
2045. – 40 k. purple & brown 60 20
2046. – 40 k. olive and blue .. 60 20

Designs: No. 2041, Gorky and scene from "Mother" (novel). 2042, Pushkin and "Bronze Horseman" (statue). 2043, Rustavely and episode from "The Knight in the Tiger Skin" (poem). 2044, Tolstoy and scene from "War and Peace" (novel). 2045, V. G. Belinsky and titles of literary works. 2046, M. Y. Lermontov and Daryal Pass.

See also Nos. 2076, 2089/90, 2256, 2316/22 and 2458.

593. Vitus Bering and Routes of his Voyages. 594. Dimitri Mendeleiev.

1956. Bering (explorer). 275th Birth Anniv.
2047. **593.** 40 k. multicoloured .. 1·25 40

1957. Mendeleiev (chemist). 50th Death Anniv.
2048. **594.** 40 k. brown and grey 75 25

595. M. I. Glinka. 596. Youth Festival Emblem.

1957. Glinka (composer). Death Cent. Multicoloured.
2049. 40 k. Type **595** .. .. 1·00 12
2050. 1 r. Scene from Glinka's Opera "Ivan Susanin" 1·60 35

1957. All-Union Festival of Soviet Youth.
2051. **596.** 40 k. multicoloured .. 20 8

597. Ice-Hockey Player. 598. Youth Festival Emblem and Pigeon.

1957. 23rd World and 35th European Ice-Hockey Championships, Moscow.
2052. – 25 k. violet 80 8
2053. **597.** 40 k. blue 70 12
2054. – 60 k. green 80 12

Designs: 25 k. Championship emblem. 60 k. Goal-keeper.

1957. 6th World Youth Festival, Moscow. (1st issue). Perf. or imperf.
2055. **598.** 40 k. multicoloured .. 20 8
2056. 60 k. multicoloured .. 35 12

See also Nos. 2084/7.

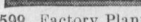

599. Factory Plant. 600. Spotted Deer.

1957. "Red Proletariat" Plant, Moscow. Cent.
2057. **599.** 40 k. multicoloured .. 50 15

1957. Russian Wildlife. Multicoloured.
2057a. 10 k. Game bird .. 20 8
2058. 15 k. Black grouse .. 20 8
2058a. 15 k. Polar bear .. 40 20
2059. 20 k. Type **600** .. 40 8
2059a. 20 k. Hare 20 8
2059b. 25 k. Siberian tiger .. 35 12
2059c. 25 k. Siberian wild horse 35 12
2060. 30 k. Duck 40 12
2061. 30 k. Bison 40 12
2062. 40 k. Elk 90 30
2063. 40 k. Sable 90 30
2063a. 40 k. Squirrel 50 12
2063b. 40 k. Marten 50 12
2063c. 60 k. Grouse 55 20
2063d. 1 r. White swan .. 80 35

Nos. 2058/a, 2059a/62, 2063a/b and 2063d, are horiz.

See also Nos. 2534/6.

601. Vologda Lace-making. 602. G. V. Plekhanov.

1957. Regional Handicrafts. Multicoloured.
2064. 40 k. Moscow wood-carving 35 12
2065. 40 k. Woman engraving vase 35 12
2066. 40 k. Type **601** 35 12
2067. 40 k. Northern bone-carving 35 20
2067a. 40 k. Wood-block engraving 45 20
2067b. 40 k. Turkmen carpet-weaving 45 20

1957. Plekhanov (politician). Birth Cent.
2068. **602.** 40 k. plum 50 20

603. A. N. Bakh. 604. L. Euler.

1957. Bakh (bio-chemist). Birth Cent.
2069. **603.** 40 k. multicoloured .. 65 20

1957. Euler (mathematician). 250th Birth Anniv.
2070. **604** 40 k. black and purple 1·00 12

605. Lenin in Meditation. 606. Dr. William Harvey.

1957. Lenin. 87th Birth Anniv. Multicoloured
2071. 40 k. Type **605** 45 12
2072. 40 k. Lenin carrying pole 45 12
2073. 40 k. Talking with soldier and sailor 45 12

1957. Harvey (physician). Death Tercent.
2074. **606.** 40 k. brown 50 20

607. M. A. Balakirev (composer). 608. 12th-Century Narrator.

1957. Balakirev. 120th Birth Anniv.
2075. **607.** 40 k. black 45 20

1957. "The Tale of the Host of Igor".
2076. **608.** 40 k. multicoloured .. 45 20

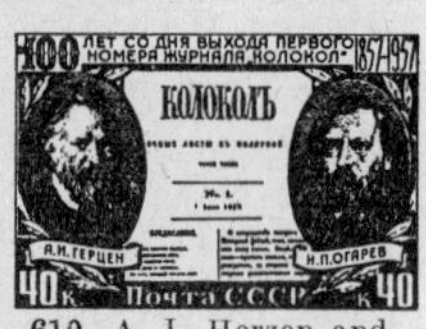

609. Agricultural Medal. 610. A. I. Herzen and N. P. Ogarev (writers).

1957. Cultivation of Virgin Soil.
2077. **609.** 40 k. multicoloured .. 50 8

1957. Publication of the Magazine "Kolokol". Cent.
2078. **610.** 40 k. brn., blk. & indigo 50 12

611. Monument.

250 лет Ленинграда

(612.)

613. Youths with Banner.

1957. Leningrad. 250th Anniv. Vert. designs as T **611** and stamps as Nos. 1818 and 1820 optd. as T **612**.
2079. **611.** 40 k. green 30 8
2080. – 40 k. violet 30 8
2081. – 40 k. brown 30 8
2082. **498.** 1 r. brown on green .. 1·00 35
2083. – 1 r. green on salmon 1·00 35

Designs: No. 2080, Main thoroughfare, Leningrad. No. 2081, Lenin Statue.

1957. 6th World Youth Festival, Moscow (2nd issue). Multicoloured. Perf. or imperf.
2084. 10 k. Type **613** .. 8 5
2084a. 20 k. Sculptor with statue 15 5
2085. 25 k. Type **613** 15 5
2086. 40 k. Dancers 20 8
2087. 1 r. Festival emblem and fireworks over Moscow State University .. 45 15

614. A. M. Lyapunov. 615. T. G. Shevchenko and Scene from Book.

1957. Lyapunov (mathematician). Birth Cent.
2088. **614.** 40 k. brown 50 15

1957. 19th-Cent. Writers. Multicoloured.
2089. 40 k. Type **615** 25 8
2090. 40 k. N. G. Chernyshevsky and scene from book .. 25 8

616. Henry Fielding. 617. Racing Cyclists.

1957. Fielding (novelist). 250th Birth Anniv.
2091. **616.** 40 k. multicoloured .. 35 15

1957. 10th Int. Cycle Race.
2092. **617.** 40 k. multicoloured .. 35 20

618. Interior of Observatory.

Designs — vert. No. 2094, Meteor in sky. 2095, ($14\frac{1}{2} \times 22$ mm.). Rocket in sky. 2095a, Meteorology; radar scanner and balloon. 2095b, Geo-magnetism; non magnetic sailing ship. 2095c, Northern Lights and recording instrument.

See also Nos. 2371/2373a.

1957. Int. Geophysical Year (1st issue).
2093. **618.** 40 k. brown, yellow and blue 75 20
2094. – 40 k. indigo, yellow and blue .. .. 1·40 25
2095. – 40 k. vio. & lavender 1·10 35
2095a. – 40 k. blue 65 20
2095b. – 40 k. green 65 20
2095c. – 40 k. yellow and blue 65 20

619. Gymnast.

1957. 3rd Int. Youth Games.
2096. **619.** 20 k. chestnut & blue 15 5
2097. – 25 k. claret and green 20 8
2098. – 40 k. violet and red .. 25 15
2099. – 40 k. olive, red & grn. 25 15
2100. – 60 k. chocolate & blue 55 20
DESIGNS—As T **619**: No. 2097, Wrestlers. 2098, Young athletes. 2099, Moscow Stadium. 2100, Javelin-thrower.

620. Football. **621.** Yanka Kupala.

1957. Russian Successes at Olympic Games, Melbourne.
2101. – 20 k. brn., blue & blk. 12 5
2102. – 20 k. claret & green 12 5
2103. – 25 k. blue and orange 12 8
2104. **620.** 40 k. magenta, blue, yellow and black 25 12
2105. – 40 k. sepia and purple 25 12
2106. – 60 k. brown and violet 55 20
DESIGNS—VERT. No. 2101, Javelin-throwing. 2102, Running. 2103, Gymnastics. 2105, Boxing. 2106, Weight-lifting.

1957. Kupala (poet). 75th Birth Anniv.
2107. **621.** 40 k. sepia 50 20

622. Moscow State University. **623.** Lenin Library.

1957. 6th World Youth Festival, Moscow (3rd issue).
2108. – 40 k. black & brown 35 12
2109. – 40 k. black and purple 35 12
2110. – 1 r. black and blue .. 1·00 20
2111. **622.** 1 r. black and red .. 1·00 20
DESIGNS—HORIZ. No. 2108, Kremlin. 2109, Stadium. 2110, Bolshoi State Theatre.

1957. Int. Philatelic Exn., Moscow. Perf. or imperf.
2112. **623.** 40 k. turquoise .. 50 15

624. Dove of Peace encircling Globe. **625.** P. Beranger.

1957. " Defence of Peace ".
2113. **624.** 40 k. multicoloured .. 65 20
2114. 1 r. multicoloured .. 1·00 45

1957. Beranger (French poet). Death Cent.
2116. **625.** 40 k. green 25 5

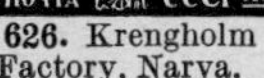

626. Krengholm Factory, Narva. **627.** Factory Plant and Statue of Lenin.

1957. Krengholm Textile Factory, Narva, Estonia. Cent.
2117. **626.** 40 k. sepia 40 12

1957. Crasny Vyborzhetz Plant, Leningrad. Cent.
2118. **627.** 40 k. blue 40 12

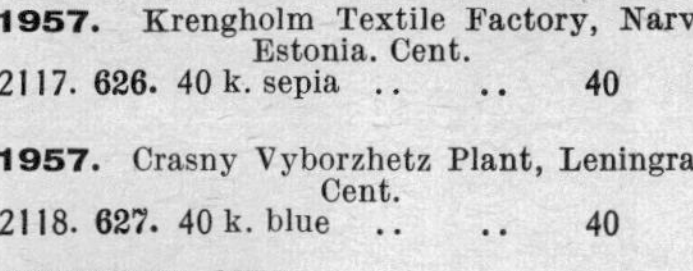

628. V. V. Stasov (Art Critic). **629.** Pigeon with Letter.

1957. Stasov. 50th Death Anniv.
2119. **628.** 40 k. sepia 65 15
2120. 1 r. indigo .. .. 1·00 20

1957. Int. Correspondence Week.
2121. **629.** 40 k. blue 30 15
2122. 60 k. purple 45 20

630. K. E. Tsiolkovsky. **631.** Congress Emblem.

1957. Tsiolkovsky (scientist). Birth Cent.
2123. **630.** 40 k. multicoloured .. 2·00 50

1957. 4th World T.U.C., Leipzig.
2124. **631.** 40 k. blue on blue .. 35 12

632. Students. **633.** Workers and Emblem. **634.** Lenin.

1957. Russian Revolution. 40th Anniv. Inscr. " 1917-1957 ". (a) 1st Issue. As T **632**. Multicoloured. Perf. or imperf.
2125. 10 k. Type **632** 5 5
2126. 40 k. Railway worker .. 20 8
2127. 40 k. Portrait of Lenin on banner 20 8
2128. 40 k. Lenin and workers with banners 20 8
2129. 60 k. Harvester (horiz.) .. 35 12

(b) 2nd Issue. As T **633**, designs representing the Soviet Republics. Multicoloured.
2130. **633.** 40 k. Ukraine .. 20 10
2131. – 40 k. Estonia .. 20 10
2132. – 40 k. Uzbekistan .. 20 10
2133. – 40 k. R.S.F.S.R. .. 20 10
2134. – 40 k. Byelorussia .. 20 10
2135. – 40 k. Lithuania .. 20 10
2136. – 40 k. Armenia .. 20 10
2137. – 40 k. Azerbaijan .. 20 10
2138. – 40 k. Georgia .. 20 10
2139. – 40 k. Kirghizia .. 20 10
2140. – 40 k. Turkmenistan 20 10
2141. – 40 k. Tadzhikistan .. 20 10
2142. – 40 k. Kazakhstan .. 20 10
2143. – 40 k. Latvia .. 20 10
2144. – 40 k. Moldavia .. 20 10

(c) 3rd Issue. As T **634**.
2145. **634.** 40 k. blue 25 12
2146. – 60 k. red 35 20
DESIGN—HORIZ. 60 k. Lenin at desk.

635. Satellite encircling Globe. **636.** Meteor Falling.

1957. Launching of 1st Artificial Satellite.
2147. **635.** 40 k. indigo on blue 2·00 35
2148. 40 k. blue .. .. 2·00 35

1957. Sikhote-Alin Meteor.
2149. **636.** 40 k. multicoloured .. 1·00 35

4/X-57 г. Первый в мире искусств. спутник Земли
(**638.**)

637. Kuibyshev Power Station Turbine. **639.** Soviet War Memorial, Berlin.

1957. All-Union Industrial Exhibition (1st issue).
2150. **637.** 40 k. chestnut .. 25 8

1957. First Artificial Satellite of the World. Optd. with T **638**.
2151. **630.** 40 k. multicoloured .. 13·00 6·50

1957. Academy of Arts, Moscow. Bicent. Inscr. " 1757 1957 ".
2152. – 40 k. black on salmon 15 5
2153. **639.** 60 k. black 30 10
2154. – 1 r. black on pink .. 55 15
DESIGNS—($25\frac{1}{2} \times 37\frac{1}{2}$ mm.): 40 k. Academy and portraits of Bryullov, Repin and Surikov. ($21\frac{1}{2} \times 32$ mm.): 1 r. Worker and Peasant Memorial, Moscow.

640. Arms of Ukraine. **641.** Garibaldi.

1957. Ukraine S.S.R. 40th Anniv.
2155. **640.** 40 k. multicoloured .. 20 8

1957. Garibaldi. 150th Birth Anniv.
2156. **641.** 40 k. pur., mar. & grn. 45 20

642. Edward Grieg. **643.** Borovikovsky.

1957. Grieg (composer). 50th Death Anniv.
2157. **642.** 40 k. black on salmon 25 15

1957. Borovikovsky (painter). Birth Bicent.
2158. **643.** 40 k. brown 25 15

644. Y. Kolas. **645.** U. N. Kapsukas. **646.** G. Z. Bashindzhagian.

1957. Jacob Kolas (poet). 75th Birth Anniv.
2160. **644.** 40 k. black 45 20

1957. Kapsukas (Communist Party leader) Commem.
2161. **645.** 40 k. brown 45 20

1957. Bashindzhagian (artist) Commem.
2162. **646.** 40 k. brown 45 20

647. Kuibishev Hydro-electric Station. **648.** Allegory of Progress.

1957. Kuibishev Hydro-electric Station. 40th Anniv.
2163. **647.** 40 k. blue on flesh .. 25 12

1957. Launching of 2nd Artificial Satellite
2164. **648.** 20 k. red and black .. 35 5
2165. 40 k. green and black 55 12
2166. 60 k. brown & black 65 20
2167. 1 r. blue and black .. 1·10 30

649. Allegory of Industry. **650.** Tsi Bai-Shi.

1958. All-Union Industrial Exn. (2nd issue).
2168. **649.** 60 k. red, blk. & lav. 35 12

1958. Tsi Bai-Shi (Chinese artist) Commem.
2170. **650.** 40 k. violet 40 20

651. Linnaeus Carl von Linne). **652.** A. N. Tolstoy.

1958. Linnaeus. 250th Birth Anniv.
2171. **651.** 40 k. sepia 45 25

1958. Tolstoy (writer). 75th Birth Anniv.
2172. **652.** 40 k. bistre 35 12

653. Soldier, Sailor and Airman. **654.** E. Charents. **655.** Henry W. Longfellow.

1958. Red Army. 40th Anniv. Multicoloured.
2173. 25 k. Battle of Narva, 1918 12 5
2174. 40 k. T **653** 20 8
2175. 40 k. Soldier and blast-furnaceman 20 8
2176. 40 k. Soldier and sailor .. 20 8
2177. 60 k. Storming the Reichstag, 1945 .. .. 50 15
Nos. 2175/6 are vert., rest horiz.

1958. Charents (Armenian poet) Commem.
2178. **654.** 40 k. brown 55 35

1958. Longfellow. 150th Birth Anniv.
2179. **655.** 40 k. black 55 35

656. William Blake. **657.** Tchaikovsky. **658.** Admiral Rudnev and Cruiser " Varyag ".

1958. William Blake. Birth Bicent.
2180. **656.** 40 k. black 55 35

1958. Tchaikovsky Int. Music Competition, Moscow. Inscr. " 1958 ".
2181. **657.** 40 k. multicoloured .. 20 12
2182. – 40 k. multicoloured .. 20 12
2183. – 1 r. lake and green .. 65 25
DESIGNS—HORIZ. No. 2182, Scene from "Swan Lake" ballet. VERT. 2183, Pianist, violinist and inset portrait of Tchaikovsky.

1958. Admiral Rudnev. 45th Death Anniv.
2184. **658.** 40 k. multicoloured .. 65 25

659. Gorky (writer). **660.** Congress Emblem and Spassky Tower, Kremlin.

1958. Gorky Commem.
2185. **659.** 40 k. multicoloured .. 50 15

1958. 13th Young Communists' League Congress, Moscow.
2186. **660.** 40 k. violet on pink .. 35 12
2187. 60 k. red on flesh .. 55 20

661. Russian Pavilion.
662. J. A. Komensky ("Comenius").

1958. Brussels Int. Exn. Perf or imperf.
2188. **661.** 10 k. multicoloured .. 12 5
2189. 40 k. multicoloured .. 20 12

1958. Komensky Commem.
2190. **662.** 40 k. green 50 20

663. Lenin.

200 лет Академии художеств СССР. 1957
(664.)

1958. Lenin Commem.
2191. **663.** 40 k. indigo 20 8
2192. 60 k. red 30 15
2193. 1 r. brown 60 25

1958. Russian Academy of Artists. Bicent. Optd. with T **664.**
2194. **504.** 40 k. multicoloured .. 2·25 65

665. C. Goldoni (Italian dramatist).
666. Lenin Bonus Medal.
667. Karl Marx.

1958. C. Goldoni. 250th Birth Anniv.
2195. **665.** 40 k. sepia and blue .. 35 15

1958. Lenin Bonus Medal.
2196. **666.** 40 k. red, yellow & brn. 35 15

1958. Karl Marx Commem.
2197. **667.** 40 k. sepia 8 5
2198. 60 k. blue 30 12
2199. 1 r. red 65 20

668. Federation Emblem.
669. Radio Beacon, Aircraft and Ship.

1958. 4th Int. Women's Federation Congress.
2200. **668.** 40 k. blue and black 15 5
2201. 60 k. ultram. & black 30 8

1958. Radio Day.
2202. **669.** 40 k. green and red .. 90 20

670. Chavchavadze (poet).
671. Flags of Communist Countries.

1958. Chavchavadze Commem.
2203. **670.** 40 k. black and blue 20 8

1958. Communist Postal Conf., Moscow.
2204. **671.** 40 k. multicoloured (A) 2·50 65
2205. 40 k. multicoloured (B) 2·00 20
Central flag to left of inscription is in red, white and mauve. (A) has red at top and white at foot, (B) is vice versa.

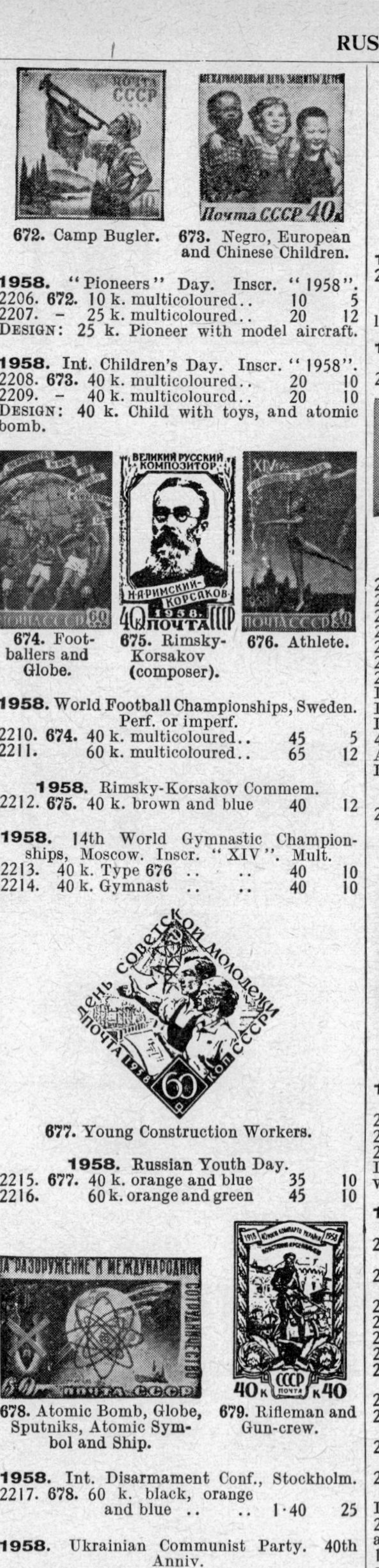

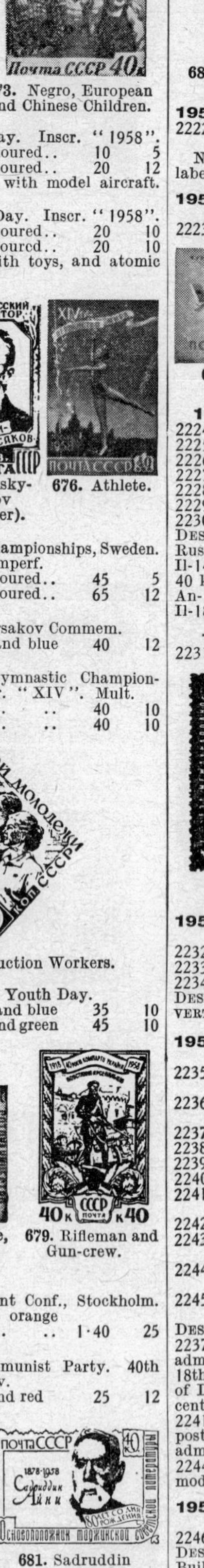

672. Camp Bugler.
673. Negro, European and Chinese Children.

1958. "Pioneers" Day. Inscr. "1958".
2206. **672.** 10 k. multicoloured .. 10 5
2207. – 25 k. multicoloured .. 20 12
DESIGN: 25 k. Pioneer with model aircraft.

1958. Int. Children's Day. Inscr. "1958".
2208. **673.** 40 k. multicoloured .. 20 10
2209. – 40 k. multicoloured .. 20 10
DESIGN: 40 k. Child with toys, and atomic bomb.

674. Footballers and Globe.
675. Rimsky-Korsakov (composer).
676. Athlete.

1958. World Football Championships, Sweden. Perf. or imperf.
2210. **674.** 40 k. multicoloured .. 45 5
2211. 60 k. multicoloured .. 65 12

1958. Rimsky-Korsakov Commem.
2212. **675.** 40 k. brown and blue 40 12

1958. 14th World Gymnastic Championships, Moscow. Inscr. "XIV". Mult.
2213. 40 k. Type **676** 40 10
2214. 40 k. Gymnast 40 10

677. Young Construction Workers.

1958. Russian Youth Day.
2215. **677.** 40 k. orange and blue 35 10
2216. 60 k. orange and green 45 10

678. Atomic Bomb, Globe, Sputniks, Atomic Symbol and Ship.
679. Rifleman and Gun-crew.

1958. Int. Disarmament Conf., Stockholm.
2217. **678.** 60 k. black, orange and blue .. .. 1·40 25

1958. Ukrainian Communist Party. 40th Anniv.
2218. **679.** 40 k. violet and red 25 12

680. "V" and Silhouette of Moscow State University.

681. Sadruddin Aini.

1958. 5th Int. Architects Union Congress, Moscow.
2219. **680.** 40 k. blue and red .. 25 8
2220. – 60 k. red, purple, blue and green 40 15
DESIGN—VERT. 60 k. "U.I.A. Moscow 1958" in square panel of bricks and "V" in background.

1958. Sadruddin Aini (Tadjik writer). 80th Birth Anniv.
2221. **681.** 40 k. red, black & buff 20 8

682. Third Artificial Satellite.

683. Conference Emblem.

1958. Launching of 3rd Artificial Satellite.
2222. **682.** 40 k. red, violet-blue and green .. .. 1·00 25
No. 2222 was issued with a commemorative label attached se-tenant in sheets.

1958. 1st World T.U. Young Workers' Conf., Prague.
2223. **683.** 40 k. blue and purple 20 8

684. Tu-110 Jet Airliner.

685. L. A. Kulik (scientist).

1958. Civil Aviation. Perf. or imperf.
2224. – 20 k. blk., red & ultram. 20 8
2225. – 40 k. blk., red & grn. 30 12
2226. – 40 k. blk., red & blue 30 12
2227. – 60 k. red, buff & blue 40 15
2228. **684.** 60 k. black and red .. 40 15
2229. – 1 r. blk., red & orange 65 35
2230. – 2 r. blk., red & purple 65 35
DESIGNS: 60 k. (No. 2227), Global air routes. Russian aircraft flying across globe: 20 k. Il-14 airliner. 40 k. (2225), Tu-104 jet airliner. 40 k. (2226), Tu-114 turbo-prop airliner. 1 r. An-10 "Ukraina" turbo-prop airliner. 2 r. Il-18 turbo-prop airliner.

1958. Tunguz Meteor. 50th Anniv.
2231. **685.** 40 k. multicoloured .. 1·00 25

686. Crimea Observatory.

687. 15th-century Scribe.

1958. 10th Int. Astronomical Union Congress, Moscow.
2232. **686.** 40 k. turq. & brown .. 45 8
2233. – 60 k. yell., vio. & blue 55 12
2234. – 1 r. brown and blue .. 65 20
DESIGNS—HORIZ. 60 k. Moscow University. VERT. 1 r. Telescope of Moscow Observatory.

1958. 1st Russian Postage Stamp Cent. Inscr. "1858 1958".
2235. **687.** 10 k. black, mauve, red and yellow .. 8 5
2236. – 10 k. black, mauve, red and yellow .. 8 5
2237. – 25 k. blue, blk. & grn. 12 5
2238. – 25 k. black and blue .. 12 5
2239. – 40 k. brn., pur. & sep. 20 8
2240. – 40 k. lake and sepia .. 20 8
2241. – 40 k. black, orange and red .. 20 8
2242. – 60 k. turq., blk. & vio. 30 12
2243. – 60 k. black, turquoise and purple .. 30 12
2244. – 1 r. brown, yellow, grey and mauve .. 50 20
2245. – 1 r. purple, black and orange .. 50 20
DESIGNS—HORIZ. No. 2236, 16th-century courier. 2237, Ordin-Nastchokin (17th-century postal administrator) and postal sleigh coach. 2238, 18th-century mail coach. 2239, Reproduction of Lenin portrait stamp of 1947. 2240, 19th-century postal troika (three horse sleigh). 2241, Russian Tu-104 jet airliner. 2242, Parcel post train. 2243, V. L. Podbielsky (postal administrator 1918-20) and postal scenes. 2244, Parcel post aircraft. 2245, Globe and modern forms of mail transport.

1958. Stamp Cent. Philatelic Exhib., Leningrad.
2246. 40 k. brn. & chestnut .. 25 12
DESIGN—VERT. 40 k. Facade of Exhibition Building.

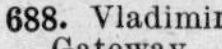
688. Vladimir Gateway.

689. M. Chigorin (chess-player).

1958. Town of Vladimir, 850th Anniv. Multicoloured.
2247. 40 k. Type **688** 15 10
2248. 60 k. Street scene in Vladimir 35 20

1958. Chigorin. 50th Death Anniv.
2249. **689.** 40 k. green and black 40 8

690. Red Cross Nurse and Patient.

1958. Red Cross and Crescent Societies. 40th Anniv. Inscr. with red cross and crescent and "1918 1958".
2254. **690.** 40 k. multicoloured .. 40 15
2255. – 40 k. red, yellow and bistre 40 15
DESIGN: No. 2255, Convalescent home.

691. M. Saltykov-Schedrin (writer) and scene from one of his works

692. V. Kapnist (poet).

1958. M. Saltykov-Schedrin Commem.
2256. **691.** 40 k. black & maroon 35 12
For similar stamps see Nos. 2316/22 and 2458.

1958. V. Kapnist. Birth Bicent.
2257. **692.** 40 k. black and blue .. 25 8

693. Erivan, Armenia.

1958. Republican Capitals.
2258. 40 k. brown (T **693**) .. 20 12
2259. 40 k. redd.-vio. (Baku, Azerbaijan) .. 20 12
2260. 40 k. sepia (Minsk, Byelorussia) .. 20 12
2261. 40 k. ultramarine (Tiflis, Georgia) 20 12
2262. 40 k. green (Tallinn, Estonia) 20 12
2263. 40 k. blue-green (Alma-Ata, Kazakhstan) .. 20 12
2264. 40 k. grey-blue (Frunze, Kirghizia) .. 20 12
2265. 40 k. chest. (Riga, Latvia) 20 12
2266. 40 k. red (Vilna, Lithuania) 20 12
2267. 40 k. bistre (Kishinev, Moldavian S.S.R.) .. 20 12
2268. 40 k. violet (Moscow, R.S.F.S.R.) 20 12
2269. 40 k. blue (Stalinabad, Tadzhikistan) 20 12
2270. 40 k. myrtle (Ashkhabad, Turkmenistan) 20 12
2271. 40 k. mag. (Kiev, Ukraine) 20 12
2272. 40 k. black (Tashkent), Uzbekistan) 20 12
See also No. 2940.

694. Open book, torch, lyre and flowers.

695. Rudaki (poet and musician).

1958. Asian-African Writers' Conf., Tashkent.
2273. **694.** 40 k. orange, black and olive 25 12

1958. Rudaki. 1100th Birth. Anniv.
2274. **695.** 40 k. multicoloured .. 25 12

696. Mounted Georgian (statue).

697. Chelyabinsk Tractor Plant.

1958. Founding of Tiflis (Georgian Capital). 1500th Anniv.
2275. **696.** multicoloured .. 45 15

1958. Industrial Plants. 25th Anniv. Inscr. "1933 1958".
2276. **697.** 40 k. green & yellow 20 10
2277. – 40 k. blue & pale blue 20 10
2278. – 40 k. lake & pale orge. 20 10
DESIGNS: No. 2277. Ural machine-construction plant. No. 2278. Zaporozhe foundry plant.

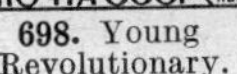

698. Young Revolutionary. **699.** Marx and Lenin (bas-relief).

1958. Young Communists League. 40th. Anniv. Inscr. "1918 1958". Multicoloured.
2279. 10 k. T **698** 8 5
2280. 20 k. Riveters 12 5
2281. 25 k. Soldier 20 8
2282. 40 k. Harvester 35 12
2283. 60 k. Builder 45 15
2284. 1 r. Students 90 45

1958. October Revolution. 41st Anniv. Inscr. "1958".
2285. **699.** 40 k. blk., yell. & red 20 12
2286. – 1 r. multicoloured .. 40 20
DESIGN—HORIZ. 1 r. Lenin with student, peasant and miner.

700. "Human Rights". **701.** Serge Esenin.

1958. Declaration of Human Rights. 10th Anniv.
2287. **700.** 60 k. blue, blk. & buff 20 8

1958. Serge Esenin (poet). 30th Death Anniv.
2288. **701.** 40 k. multicoloured .. 35 12

702. Kuan Han-Ching (Chinese playwright). **703.** G. K. Ordzhonikidze (statesman). **704.** John Milton (poet).

1958. Kuan Han-Ching Commem.
2289. **702.** 40 k. black and blue 35 12

1958. Ordzhonikidze. 21st Death Anniv.
2290. **703.** 40 k. multicoloured .. 30 12

1958. John Milton. 350th Birth Anniv.
2291. **704.** 40 k. sepia 30 12

705. Lenin's Statue, Minsk. **706.** Fuzuli (poet). **707.** Census Emblem.

1958. Byelorussian Republic. 40th Anniv.
2292. **705.** 40 k. brown, buff, grey and red .. 40 12

1958. Fuzuli Commem.
2293. **706.** 40 k. bistre & turquoise 50 12

1958. All-Union Census, 1959. Multicoloured.
2294. 40 k. Type **707** 20 8
2295. 40 k. Census official with workers' family .. 20 8

708. Eleonora Duse. **709.** Rulie (naturalist).

1958. Eleonora Duse (Italian actress). Birth Cent.
2296. **708.** 40 k. blk., grey & grn. 50 12

1958. Rulie (naturalist). Death Cent.
2297. **709.** 40 k. black and blue 25 12

710. Atomic Icebreaker "Lenin". **711.** Moon Rocket and Sputniks.

1958. All-Union Industrial Exn. Mult.
2298. 40 k. Type **710** 75 15
2299. 60 k. TE 3 Diesel locomotive 80 25

1959. 21st Communist Party Congress, Moscow.
2300. – 40 k. multicoloured .. 35 8
2301. – 60 k. multicoloured .. 45 20
2302. **711.** 1 r. multicoloured .. 1·40 30
DESIGNS: 40 k. Lenin, Red Banner and Kremlin view. 60 k. Workers beside Lenin hydro-electric plant, Volga River.

712. E. Torricelli. **713.** Ice-skater. **714.** Charles Darwin.

1959. Torricelli (physicist). 350th Birth Anniv.
2303. **712.** 40 k. black and green 60 12

1959. Women's World Ice-skating Championships, Sverdlovsk.
2304. **713.** 25 k. multicoloured .. 25 8
2305. 40 k. black, bl. & grey 40 12

1959. Charles Darwin (naturalist). 150th Birth Anniv.
2306. **714.** 40 k. brown and blue 40 12

Победа баскетбольной команды СССР. Чили 1959 г.

715. N. Gamaleya. **716.** Sholem Aleichem. **(717.)**

1959. Gamaleya (microbiologist). Birth Cent.
2307. **715.** 40 k. black and red .. 35 12

1959. Aleichem (Jewish writer). Birth Cent.
2308. **716.** 40 k. chocolate .. 25 12

1959. Russian (Unofficial) Victory in World Basketball Championships, Chile. No. 1851 optd. with T **717.**
2309. – 1 r. sepia and drab .. 5·00 3·50

1959. Robert Burns. Birth Bicent. Optd. **1759 1959.**
2310. **573.** 40 k. sepia and blue .. 4·00 3·25

718. Selma Lagerlof. **719.** P. Cvirka. **720.** F. Joliot-Curie (scientist).

1959. Selma Lagerlof (Swedish writer). Birth Cent.
2311. **718.** 40 k. black, brown and cream 35 12

1959. Cvirka (poet). 50th Birth Anniv.
2312. **719.** 40 k. black and red on yellow 20 12

1959. Joliot-Curie Commem.
2313. **720.** 40 k. black and turq. 60 20

721. Popov and Polar Sea Rescue. **722.** Saadi (Persian poet).

1959. A. S. Popov (radio pioneer). Birth Cent. Inscr. "1859 1959".
2314. **721.** 40 k. brown, black and grey-blue .. 65 15
2315. – 60 k. brown, black, blue and red .. 85 25
DESIGN: 60 k. Popov and radio tower.

1959. Writers as T **691**. Inscr. "1959".
2316. 40 k. grey, black and red 55 10
2317. 40 k. brown, sepia & yell. 55 10
2318. 40 k. brown & slate-violet 55 10
2319. 40 k. black, bl., yell. & mar. 55 10
2320. 40 k. black, olive & yellow 55 10
2321. 40 k. brown, violet, blue, green and yellow .. 55 10
2322. 40 k. slate and violet .. 55 10
PORTRAITS (with scenes from works): No. 2316, Chekhov. 2317, Krylov. 2318, Ostrovsky. 2319, Gryboedov. 2320, Gogol. 2321, Aksakov. 2322, Kolitzov.

1959. Saadi Commem.
2323. **722.** 40 k. black and blue .. 25 12

723. Orbeliani (writer). **724.** Ogata Korin.

1959. Orbeliani Commem.
2324. **723.** 40 k. black and red .. 25 12

1959. Ogatha Korin (Japanese artist). Birth Tercent.
2325. **724.** 40 k. multicoloured .. 1·00 50

725. Liner on Odessa-Batum Service.

1959. Russian Shipping. Multicoloured. Liners on various services.
2326. 10 k. Vladivostock-Kamchatka 5 5
2327. 20 k. Odessa-Latakia .. 12 5
2328. 40 k. T **725** 20 5
2329. 40 k. Murmansk-Tyksi .. 20 10
2330. 60 k. Leaving Leningrad 30 10
2331. 1 r. Leningrad-London .. 45 20

726. Trajectory of Moon Rocket. **727.** Lenin.

1959. Launching of Moon Rocket. Inscr. "2-1-1959".
2332. **726.** 40 k. brown and pink 55 20
2333. – 40 k. blue & light blue 55 20
DESIGN: No. 2333, Preliminary route of moon rocket after launching.

1959. Lenin. 89th Birth Anniv.
2334. **727.** 40 k. sepia 25 12

728. M. Cachin. **729.** Youths with Banner. **730.** A. von Humboldt.

1959. Marcel Cachin (French communist leader). 90th Birth. Anniv.
2335. **728.** 60 k. sepia 25 12

1959. World Peace Movement. 10th Anniv.
2336. **729.** 40 k. multicoloured .. 20 8

1959. Alexander von Humboldt (German naturalist). Death Cent.
2337. **730.** 40 k. sepia and violet 55 15

731. Haydn. **732.** Mountain-Climbing.

1959. Haydn (composer). 150th Death Anniv.
2338. **731.** 40 k. sepia and blue .. 25 12

1959. Tourist Publicity. Multicoloured.
2339. **732.** 40 k. Type **732** .. 25 8
2340. – 40 k. Map-reading .. 25 8
2341. – 40 k. Skiing 25 8
2342. – 40 k. Canoieng .. 25 8
No. 2342 is horiz., the rest vert.

733. Exhibition Emblem and New York Coliseum. **734.** Statue of Repin (painter).

1959. Russian Scientific, Technological and Cultural Exn., New York.
2343. **733.** 20 k. multicoloured .. 8 5
2344. 40 k. multicoloured .. 20 8

1959. Cultural Celebrities. Inscr. "1959". Statues in black.
2345. **734.** 10 k. ochre 5 5
2346. – 10 k. vermilion .. 10 5
2347. – 20 k. lilac 10 5
2348. – 25 k. turquoise .. 20 12
2349. – 60 k. green 35 12
2350. – 1 r. blue 35 12
STATUES: 10 k. (No. 2346), Lenin. 20 k. V. Mayakovsky (poet). 25 k. Pushkin. 60 k. Gorky. 1 r. Tchaikovsky.

735. Sturgeon. **736.** Louis Braille.

1959. Fisheries Protection.
2350a. – 20 k. black & blue .. 12 5
2350b. – 25 k. brown & lilac .. 20 5
2351. **735.** 40 k. black & turq. .. 25 8
2351a. – 40 k. purple & mauve 35 8
2352. – 60 k. black and blue 40 12
DESIGNS: 20 k. Perch. 25 k. Fur seals. 40 k. (No. 2351a), Five salmon. 60 k. One salmon.

1959. Braille (inventor of Braille). 150th Birth Anniv.
2353. **736.** 60 k. brn., yell. & turq. 20 8

737. Musa Djalil (patriot).
738. Vaulting.

1959. Djalil Commem.
2354. **737.** 40 k. black & violet .. 25 12

1959. 2nd Russian Spartakiad. Inscr. " 1959 ".
2355. **738.** 15 k. grey and purple 20 5
2356. – 25 k. grey, brn. & grn. 20 8
2357. – 30 k. olive and red .. 30 12
2358. – 60 k. grey, blue & yell. 40 20
DESIGNS—HORIZ. 25 k. Running. 60 k. Water-polo. VERT. 30 k. Athletes supporting Spartakiad emblem.

739.
740. Steel Worker.

1959. 2nd Int. T. U. Conference, Leipzig.
2359. **739.** 40 k. red, blue & yell. 25 12

1959. Seven Year Plan.
2360. – 10 k. red, blue & vio. 8 5
2361. – 10 k. crim. red & yell. 8 5
2362. – 15 k. red, yell. & brn. 12 5
2363. – 15 k. brn., grn. & bistre 12 5
2364. – 20 k. red, yell. & grn. 15 5
2365. – 20 k. red, grey, yellow and green 15 5
2366. – 30 k. red, flesh & pur. 12 5
2366a. – 30 k. red, lilac, green, purple and brown .. 20 8
2367. **740.** 40 k. orge., yell. & bl. 20 8
2368. – 40 k. red, pink & blue 20 10
2369. – 60 k. red, blue & yell. 30 10
2370. – 60 k. red, buff & blue 35 12
DESIGNS: No. 2360, Chemist. 2361, Spassky Tower, hammer and sickle. 2362, Builder's labourer. 2363, Farm girl. 2364, Machine-minder. 2365, Tractor-driver. 2366, Oil technician. 2366a, Cloth production. 2368. Coal miner. 2369, Iron moulder. 2370, Power station.

741. Glaciologist.
742. Novgorod.

1959. Int. Geophysical Year (2nd issue). Inset globe and date " 1959 ".
2371. **741.** 10 k. turquoise .. 35 8
2372. – 25 k. red and blue .. 65 20
2373. – 40 k. red and blue .. 65 20
2373a. – 1 r. blue and yellow .. 1·25 40
DESIGNS: 25 k. Oceanographic survey-ship " Vitjaz ". 40 k. Antarctic map and camp. 1 r. Observatory and rocket.

1959. 11th Cent. of Novgorod.
2374. **742.** 40 k. red, sepia & blue 25 12

743. Schoolboys in Workshop.
744. Exhibition Emblem.

1959. Industrial Training Scheme for School-leavers. Inscr. " 1959 ".
2375. **743.** 40 k. violet 10 5
2376. – 1 r. blue 40 15
DESIGN: 1 r. Children at night-school.

1959. All-Union Exhibition.
2377. **744.** 40 k. multicoloured .. 25 12

DESIGN: 40 k. Russian miner and Chinese foundryman.

745. Russian and Chinese Students.

1959. Chinese Peoples' Republic. 10th Anniv.
2378. **745.** 20 k. multicoloured .. 15 5
2379. – 40 k. multicoloured .. 35 12

746. Postwoman.
747. Mahtumkuli.

1959. Int. Correspondence Week.
2380. **746.** 40 k. multicoloured .. 15 5
2381. 60 k. multicoloured .. 35 10

1959. Mahtumkuli (Turkestan writer). 225th Birth Anniv.
2382. **747.** 40 k. brown 25 12

748. Arms and Workers of East Germany.
749. Lunik 3's trajectory around the Moon.

1959. German Democratic Republic. 10th Anniv.
2383. **748.** 40 k. red, yellow, olive and brown .. 15 5
2384. – 60 k. maroon & cream 20 8
DESIGN—VERT. 60 k. Town Hall, East Berlin.

1959. Launching of " Lunik 3 ".
2385. **749.** 40 k. violet .. .. 1·00 20

750. Republican Arms and Emblems.
751. Red Square, Moscow.

1959. Tadzhikistan Republic. 30th Anniv.
2386. **750.** 40 k. red, yellow, green and black .. 25 12

1959. October Revolution. 42nd Anniv.
2387. **751.** 40 k. red 20 10

752. Capitol, Washington and Kremlin, Moscow.

1959. Visit of Russian Prime Minister to U.S.A.
2388. **752.** 60 k. blue and yellow 25 12

DESIGNS: 25 k. " Frogman ". 40 k. Racing motor-cyclist. 60 k. Parachutist.

753. Helicopter.

1959. Military Sports.
2389. **753.** 10 k. claret & violet 5 5
2390. – 25 k. brown and blue 12 5
2391. – 40 k. indigo & brown 20 8
2392. – 60 k. bistre and blue 30 12

754. Track of Moon Rocket.
755. Statue and aerial view of Budapest.

1959. Landing of Russian Rocket on Moon Inscr. " 14.IX.1959 ". Multicoloured.
2393. 40 k. Type **754** .. 55 25
2394. 40 k. Diagram of flight trajectory 55 25

1959. Hungarian Republic Commem. Multicoloured.
2395. 20 k. Petofi (Hungarian poet) (horiz.) 12 5
2396. 40 k. Type **755** 25 12

758. Manolis Glezos (Greek Communist).

1959. Glezos Commem.
2397. **758.** 40 k. brown and blue 5·00 3·25

756. A. Voskresensky (chemist).
757. River Chusovaya.

1959. Voskresensky Commem.
2398. **756.** 40 k. brown and blue 25 12

1959. Tourist Publicity. Inscr. " 1959 ".
2399. **757.** 10 k. violet 5 5
2400. – 10 k. magenta .. 5 5
2401. – 25 k. blue 12 5
2402. – 25 k. red 12 5
2403. – 25 k. olive 12 5
2404. – 40 k. claret 15 5
2405. – 60 k. turquoise .. 30 12
2406. – 1 r. green .. 40 20
2407. – 1 r. orange 40 20
DESIGNS: No. 2400, Riza Lake, Caucasus. 2401, River Lena. 2402, Iskanderkuly Lake. 2403, Coastal region. 2404, Lake Baikal. 2405 Beluha Mountains, Altay. 2406, Hibinsky Mountain. 2407, Gursuff region, Crimea.

759. " The Trumpeters of the First Horse Army " (after Grekov).

1959. Russian Cavalry. 40th Anniv.
2408. **759.** 40 k. multicoloured .. 40 12

760. A. P. Chekhov and Moscow Residence.
761. M. V. Frunze.

1960. Chekhov (writer). Birth Cent.
2409. **760.** 20 k. red, drab and violet 12 5
2410. – 40 k. brn., bl. & sepia 25 8
DESIGN: 40 k. Chekhov and Yalta residence.

1960. M. V. Frunze (military leader). 75th Birth Anniv.
2411. **761.** 40 k. brown 25 12

762. G. N. Gabrichevsky.
763. Vera Komissarzhevskaya.

1960. G. N. Gabrichevsky (microbiologist). Birth Cent.
2412. **762.** 40 k. brown & violet 25 12

1960. V. F. Komissarzhevskaya (actress). 50th Death Anniv.
2413. **763.** 40 k. brown 20 8

DESIGNS: 10 k. Ice-hockey. 25 k. Ice-skating. 40 k. Ski-ing. 1 r. Ski-jumping.

764. Free-skating.

1960. Winter Olympic Games.
2414. – 10 k. blue and orange 5 5
2415. – 25 k. blue, black, green and red .. 10 5
2416. – 40 k. orge., bl. & pur. 15 5
2417. **764.** 60 k. vio., brn. & grn. 25 12
2418. – 1 r. blue, orange-red and green 50 20

765. Timur Frunze and Air Battle.
766. Helicopter over Kremlin.

1960. War Heroes. Multicoloured.
2419. 40 k. Type **765** 25 12
2420. 1 r. Gen. Cherniakovksy and battle scene .. 60 25

1960. Air.
2421. **766.** 60 k. blue 60 20

767. Women of various Races.
768. " Swords into Ploughshares ".

1960. Int. Women's Day. 50th Anniv.
2422. **767.** 40 k. multicoloured .. 20 8

1960. Presentation of Statue by Russia to U.N.
2423. **768.** 40 k. yellow, bistre and blue .. 20 8

15 лет освобождения Венгрии
(769)

770. Lenin when a Child.

1960. Liberation of Hungary. 15th Anniv. Optd. with T **769**.
2424. **755.** 40 k. multicoloured .. 2·75 2·00

1960. Lenin. 90th Birth Anniv. Multicoloured. Portraits of Lenin.
2425. 10 k. T **770** 5 5
2426. 20 k. L. holding child .. 8 5
2427. 30 k. L. and revolutionary scenes 12 5
2428. 40 k. L. with party banners 20 8
2429. 60 k. L. and industrial scenes 40 10
2430. 1 r. L. with globe and rejoicing people .. 65 15

771. Lunik 3 photographing Moon.
772. Government House, Baku.

1960. Flight of Lunik 3. Inscr. "7.X.1959".
2431. **771.** 40 k. yellow and blue 65 35
2432. – 60 k. yell., blue & ind. 1·00 35
DESIGN: 60 k. Lunar map.

1960. Azerbaijan Republic. 40th Anniv.
2433. **772.** 40 k. brn., bis. & yell. 20 8

773. "Fraternization" (after Pokorny). **774.** Furnaceman.

1960. Czechoslovak Republic. 15th Anniv. Inscr. "1960".
2434. **773.** 40 k. black and blue 12 5
2435. – 60 k. sepia & yellow 20 5
DESIGN: 60 k. Charles Bridge, Prague.

1960. Completion of First Year of Seven Year Plan.
2436. **774.** 40 k. brown & verm. 20 8

775. Popov Museum, Leningrad.

1960. Radio Day.
2437. **775.** 40 k. multicoloured.. 20 8

776. Robert Schumann (composer). **777.** Y. M. Sverdlov (statesman).

1960. Schumann. 150th Birth Anniv.
2438. **776.** 40 k. black and blue 20 8

1960. Y. M. Sverdlov. 75th Birth Anniv.
2439. **777.** 40 k. sepia & chestnut 20 8

778. Magnifier and Stamp.

1960. Philatelists Day.
2440. **778.** 60 k. multicoloured.. 55 12

779. Petrozavodsk (Karelian Republic).

1960. Capitals of Autonomous Republics. 1st Issue.
2441. **779.** 40 k. blue-green .. 25 10
2442. – 40 k. ultramarine .. 25 10
2443. – 40 k. green .. 25 10
2444. – 40 k. brown-purple.. 25 10
2445. – 40 k. brown-red .. 25 10
2446. – 40 k. deep blue .. 20 10
2447. – 40 k. chestnut .. 20 10
2448. – 40 k. brown 20 10
2449. – 40 k. carmine-red .. 20 10
2450. – 40 k. sepia 20 10
CAPITALS: Nos. 2442, Batumi (Adzharian). 2443, Izhevsk (Udmurt). 2444, Grozny (Chechen-Ingush). 2445, Gheboksary (Chuvash). 2446, Yakutsk (Yakut). 2447, Ordzhonikidze (North Ossetian). 2448, Nukus (Kara-Kalpak). 2449, Makhachkala (Daghestan). 2450, Yoshkar-Ola (Mari).
See also Nos. 2586/92 and 2703/5.

780. Children of Different Races. **781.** Rocket.

1960. Int. Children's Day. Inscr. "1960". Multicoloured.
2451. 10 k. T **780** 8 5
2452. 20 k. Children on farm .. 12 5
2453. 25 k. Children with snowman 20 8
2454. 40 k. Children in zoo .. 30 8

1960. Karelian Autonomous Republic. 40th Anniv. Optd. **40 aer KACCP 8.VI.1960.**
2455. **779.** 40 k. blue-green .. 1·00 35

1960. Launching of Cosmic Rocket on May 15th.
2456. **781.** 40 k. red and blue .. 1·10 35

782. I.F.A.C. Emblem.

1960. 1st Int. Automation Control Federation Congress, Moscow.
2457. **782.** 60 k. brown & yellow 20 10

1960. Kosta Hetagurov Commem. As T **691**. Inscr. "1960".
2458. 40 k. sepia & grey-blue.. 20 10
DESIGN: 40 k. Portrait of Hetagurov and scene from his works.

783. Industrial Plant.

DESIGN: 40 k. Industrial plant (different view).

1960. First Plant Construction of Seven Year Plan.
2459. **783.** 25 k. black and blue 10 5
2460. – 40 k. black and lake 20 8

784. Capstans and Cogwheel. **785.** Vilna (Lithuania).

1960. Industrial Mass-Production Plant.
2461. **784.** 40 k. blue-green .. 25 10
2462. – 40 k. purple (Factory plant) 25 10

1960. Baltic Soviet Republics. Mult.
2463. 40 k. Type **785** 20 8
2464. 40 k. Riga (Latvia) .. 20 8
2465. 40 k. Tallinn (Estonia) .. 20 8

786. Running.

Международная ярмарка в Риччоне

(**787.**)

1960. Olympic Games. Inscr. "1960". Multicoloured.
2466. 5 k. T **786** 5 5
2467. 10 k. Wrestling 8 5
2468. 15 k. Basketball .. 10 5
2469. 20 k. Weightlifting .. 12 5
2470. 25 k. Boxing 15 5
2471. 40 k. High-diving .. 20 8
2472. 40 k. Fencing 20 8
2473. 40 k. Gymnastics .. 20 8
2474. 60 k. Canoeing 40 12
2475. 1 r. Horse-jumping .. 75 20

1960. Moldavian Republic. 20th Anniv.
2476. 40 k. multicoloured .. 20 8
DESIGN: 40 k. Kishinev (capital).

1960. Int. Exhibition, Riccione. No. 2471 optd. with T **787**.
2477. 40 k. multicoloured .. 4·50 2·75

788. "Agriculture and Industry". **789.** G. H. Minkh (epidemiologist).

1960. Vietnam Democratic Republic. 15th Anniv. Inscr. "1960".
2478. 40 k. Type **788** 20 5
2479. 60 k. Book Museum, Hanoi (vert.) 25 10

1960. G. H. Minkh. 125th Birth Anniv.
2480. **789.** 60 k. sepia and bistre 25 12

790. "March" (after I. Levitan).

1960. I. Levitan (painter). Birth Cent.
2481. **790.** 40 k. black and olive 45 12

791. "Forest" (after Shishkin).

1960. 5th World Forestry Congress, Seattle.
2482. **791.** 1 r. brown .. .. 1·40 35

792. Addressing Letter.

1960. Int. Correspondence Week.
2483. **792.** 40 k. multicoloured.. 15 5
2484. 60 k. multicoloured.. 35 10

793. Kremlin, Dogs "Belka" and "Strelka", and Rocket Trajectory.

1960. Cosmic Rocket Flight of August 1960.
2485. **793.** 40 k. purple & yellow 55 12
2486. 1 r. blue and orange.. 1·10 30

794. Globes. **795.** People of Kazakhstan.

1960. W.F.T.U. 15th Anniv.
2487. **794.** 60 k. bl., drab & lilac 20 8

1960. Kazak Soviet Republic. 40th Anniv.
2488. **795.** 40 k. multicoloured.. 20 8

796. River-boat "Karl Marx". **797.** A. N. Voronikhin and Leningrad Cathedral.

1960. River Navigation. River-boats. Multicoloured.
2489. 25 k. T **796** 25 5
2490. 40 k. "Lenin" 35 8
2491. 60 k. "Rocket" 60 20

1960. A. N. Voronikhin (architect). Birth Bicent.
2492. **797.** 40 k. black and grey 25 12

798. Motor Coach. **799.** J. S. Gogebashvily.

1960. Russian Motor Industry.
2493. – 25 k. black and blue 20 5
2494. – 40 k. blue and olive 35 8
2495. – 60 k. red & turquoise 55 12
2496. **798** 1 r. multicoloured .. 1·10 25
DESIGNS: 25 k. Lorry. 40 k. "Volga" car. 60 k. "Moskvitch" car.

1960. J. S. Gogebashvily (teacher). 120th Birth Anniv.
2497. **799.** 40 k. black and lake 25 12

800. Industrial Plant and Power Station. **801.** Federation Emblem.

1960. October Revolution. 43rd Anniv.
2498. **800.** 40 k. multicoloured.. 45 12

1960. Int. Federation of Democratic Women. 15th Anniv.
2499. **801.** 60 k. red and slate .. 20 8

40 лет Удмуртской АССР 4/XI 1960.

802. Youth of Three Races. (**803**).

1960. World Youth Federation. 15th Anniv.
2500. **802.** 60 k. multicoloured.. 20 8

1960. Udmurt Republic. 40th Anniv. No. 2443 optd. with T **803**.
2501. 40 k. green .. .. 1·10 35

804. Tolstoy and his Moscow Residence. **805.** Government House, Erivan.

1960. Tolstoy. 50th Death Anniv. Inscr. "1960".
2502. **804.** 20 k. brown, black, violet and blue .. 12 5
2503. – 40 k. brn., sep. & bl. 25 8
2504. – 60 k. brown, black, orange and maroon 50 20
DESIGNS—HORIZ. 40 k. Tolstoy and his country estate. VERT. 60 k. Full-face portrait.

1960. Armenian Republic. 40th Anniv.
2505. **805.** 40 k. multicoloured.. 20 8

806. Students and University. **807.** Tulip ("T. Kaufmanniana R.").

1960. Opening of Friendship University, Moscow.
2506. **806.** 40 k. maroon .. 20 10

1960. Russian Flowers. Multicoloured.
2507. 20 k. T **807** 10 5
2508. 20 k. Autumn crocus .. 10 5
2509. 25 k. Marsh marigold .. 12 5
2510. 40 k. Tulip 20 5
2511. 40 k. Panax 20 5
2512. 60 k. Hypericum .. 25 12
2513. 60 k. Iris.. .. .. 25 12
2514. 1 r. Wild Rose 45 15

808. Engels. **809.** Mark Twain.

1960. Engels. 140th Birth Anniv.
2515. **808.** 60 k. grey 65 20

1960. Mark Twain. 125th Birth Anniv.
2516. **809.** 40 k. bistre & orange 1·40 65

810. N. Pirogov. **811.** Chopin.

1960. N. Pirogov (surgeon). 150th Birth Anniv.
2517. **810.** 40 k. sepia & green.. 20 8

1960. Chopin Commem.
2518. **811.** 40 k. bistre and buff 45 10

812. North Korean Flag and Emblem. **813.** Lithuanian Costumes.

1960. Korean Liberation. 15th Anniv.
2519. **812.** 40 k. multicoloured.. 20 8

1960. Provincial Costumes. (1st issue). Inscr. " 1960 ".
2520. **813.** 10 k. red, buff, blue and brown .. 12 5
2521. – 60 k. purple, brown, buff and green .. 55 12
DESIGN: 60 k. Uzbek costumes.
See also Nos. 2537/45, 2796 and 2835/8.

814. A. Tseretely (Georgian poet).

1960. A. Tseretely. 120th Birth Anniv.
2522. **814.** 40 k. maroon and lilac 35 10

Currency Revalued.
10 (old) Kopeks = 1 (new) Kopeck

815. Worker. **816.** "Russian and Ludmilla."

1961. Inscr. " 1961 ".
2523. **815.** 1 k. bistre 12 10
2524. – 2 k. green 10 10
2525. – 3 k. violet 50 10
2526. – 4 k. red 20 10
2526a. – 4 k. brown 20 12
2527. – 6 k. red .. .. 1·10 15
2528. – 6 k. claret 40 10
2529. – 10 k. orange.. .. 65 10
2533. – 12 k. purple.. .. 65 10
2530. – 16 k. blue .. .. 1·00 10
DESIGNS: 2 k. Combine-harvester. 3 k. Cosmic rocket. 4 k. Soviet Arms and Flag. 6 k. Spasski Tower and Kremlin. 10 k. Workers' Statue. 12 k. Monument and Spasski Tower. 16 k. Aircraft over power-station.

1961. Russian Wild Life. As T **600** but inscr. " 1961 ". Centres in natural colours. Frame colours given.
2534. 1 k. sepia (Brown bear).. 12 5
2535. 6 k. black (Beaver) .. 40 5
2536. 10 k. black (Roebuck) .. 50 12
The 1 k. is vert. and the rest horiz.

1961. Provincial Costumes (2nd issue). As T **813** but inscr. " 1961 ".
2537. 2 k. verm., brn. & stone 12 5
2538. 2 k. red, buff, brn. & blk. 12 5
2539. 3 k. red, brn., bis. & blue 20 5
2540. 3 k. red, ochre, brn. & blk. 20 5
2541. 3 k. red, grn., bis. & brn. 20 5
2542. 4 k. brown, red, buff, black and grey .. 20 5
2543. 6 k. red, yellow, cobalt, black, sepia & green .. 35 8
2544. 10 k. sep., red, bis. & olive 50 10
2545. 12 k. red, blue, blk. & sep. 40 12
COSTUMES: No. 2537, Moldavia. 2538, Georgia. 2539, Ukraine. 2540, Byelorussia. 2541, Kazakhs. 2542, Koryaks. 2543, Russia. 2544, Armenia. 2545, Estonia.

1961. Scenes from Russian Fairy Tales. Multicoloured.
2546. 1 k. " Geese-Swans " .. 10 5
2547. 3 k. " The Fox, the Hare and the Cock " .. 30 8
2548. 4 k. " The Little Humpbacked Horse " .. 15 5
2549. 6 k. " The Muzhik and the Bear " 35 12
2550. 10 k. Type **816** 45 20

817. Lenin, Map and Power Station.

1961. State Electricity Plan. 40th Anniv.
2551. **817.** 4 k. brn., yell. & blue 15 5
2552. 10 k. black, maroon and salmon .. 35 12

818. Tractor. **819.** N. A. Dobroliubov.

1961. Soviet Agricultural Achievements. Inscr. " 1961 ".
2553. – 3 k. magenta & blue 15 8
2554. **818.** 4 k. black and green 15 5
2555. – 6 k. brown and blue 20 5
2556. – 10 k. maroon & olive 35 12
DESIGNS: 3 k. Dairy herd. 6 k. Agricultural machinery. 10 k. Fruit Picking.

1961. N. A. Dobroliubov (writer). 125th Birth Anniv.
2557. **819.** 4 k. buff, blk. & blue 20 12

820. N. D. Zelinsky.

1961. N. D. Zelinsky (chemist). Birth Cent.
2558. **820.** 4 k. maroon & mauve 20 12

821. Georgian Republican Flag.

1961. Georgian Republic. 40th Anniv.
2559. **821.** 4 k. multicoloured .. 15 8

822. Sgt. Miroshnichenko and Battle.

1961. Miroshnichenko (war hero).
2560. **822.** 4 k. indigo & maroon 15 8
See also Nos. 2664/5.

823. T. G. Shevchenko and Birthplace. **824.** A. Rubliov.

1961. T. G. Shevchenko (Ukrainian Poet and painter). Death Cent. Inscr. "1961".
2561. **823.** 3 k. brown & violet.. 12 5
2562. – 6 k. maroon & green 25 8
DESIGN: 6 k. Portrait of Shevchenko in old age, pen, book and candle.
See also No. 2956/62.

1961. Rubiliov (painter). 600th Birth Anniv.
2563. **824.** 4 k. brn., blk., buff & bl. 20 10

825. Statue of Shevchenko (poet). **826.** N. V. Sklifosovsky.

1961. Cultural Celebrities.
2564. – 2 k. sepia and blue .. 12 5
2565. **825.** 4 k. chestnut & black 15 10
2566. – 4 k. sepia and purple 12 5
DESIGNS: 2 k. Shchors Monument, Kiev. 4 k. (No. 2566), Kotovsky Monument, Kishinev.

1961. N. V. Sklifosovsky (surgeon). 125th Birth Anniv.
2567. **826.** 4 k. black and blue.. 15 5

827. Robert Koch. **828.** Zither-player and Folk Dancers.

1961. Robert Koch (German microbiologist). 50th Death Anniv.
2568. **827.** 6 k. sepia 20 5

1961. Russian National Choir. 50th Anniv.
2569. **828.** 4 k. red, yellow, violet and black .. 15 5

829. " Popular Science ".

1961. " Vokrug Sveta " (science magazine) Cent.
2570. **829.** 6 k. sepia, blue and ultramarine .. 65 20

4 коп.

имени
Патриса
Лумумбы
1961 г.
(**831.**)

830. Venus Rocket.

1961. Launching of Venus Rocket.
2571. **830.** 6 k. orange and blue 55 12
2572. – 10 k. blue and yellow 95 25
DESIGN: 10 k. Capsule and flight route.

1961. Lumumba Commem. Surch. with T **831**.
2573. **806.** 4 k. on 40 k. maroon 65 35

832. African breaking Chains.

1961. Africa Freedom Day. Inscr. " 1961 ".
2574. **832.** 4 k. multicoloured .. 10 5
2575. – 6 k. pur., orge. & blue 20 8
DESIGN: 6 k. Hands clasping torch of freedom and map.

833. Yuri Gagarin. **843.** Lenin.

1961. World's First Manned Space Flight. Inscr. " 12-IV-1961 ". Perf. or imperf.
2576. **833.** 3 k. blue 15 5
2577. – 6 k. blue, vio. & red 25 10
2578. – 10 k. red, grn. & brn. 40 12
DESIGNS (37×26 mm.): 6 k. Rocket and Spassky Tower. 10 k. Rocket, Gagarin in space helmet and Kremlin.

1961. Lenin. 91st Birth Anniv.
2579. **834.** 4 k. blk., salm. & red 20 10

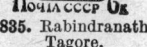

835. Rabindranath Tagore. **836.** Garibaldi.

1961. Tagore (Indian writer). Birth Cent.
2580. **835.** 6 k. blk., bistre & rose 25 10

1961. Int. Labour Exhibition, Turin.
2581. – 4 k salmon and red .. 15 5
2582. **836.** 6 k. salmon and lilac 30 5
DESIGN: 6 k. Statue.

837. Lenin. **838.** Patrice Lumumba.

1961.
2583. **837.** 20 k. green and brown 80 40
2584. – 30 k. indigo & brown 1·40 70
2585. – 50 k. red and brown 2·25 1·50
PORTRAITS (Lenin): 30 k. In cap. 50 k. Profile.

1961. Capitals of Autonomous Republics. 2nd issue. As T **779**.
2586. 4 k. deep violet 12 5
2587. 4 k. blue 12 5
2588. 4 k. orange 12 5
2589. 4 k. black 12 5
2590. 4 k. lake 12 5
2591. 4 k. green 12 5
2592. 4 k. deep purple .. 12 5
CAPITALS: No. 2586, Nalchik (Kabarda-Balkar). 2587, Ulan-Ude (Buryat). 2588, Sukhumi (Abkhazia). 2589, Syktyrkar (Komi). 2590, Nakhichevan (Nakhichevan). 2591, Rodina Cinema, Elista (Kalmyk). 2592, Ufa (Bashkiria).

1961. Lumumba Commem.
2593. **838.** 2 k. multicoloured .. 12 5

839. Kindergarten. **840.** " Chernushka " and Sputnik 4.

1961. Int. Children's Day.
2594. **839.** 2 k. blue and orange 8 5
2595. – 3 k. violet and ochre 12 5
2596. – 4 k. drab and red .. 20 5
DESIGNS—HORIZ. 3 k. Children in Pioneer camp. VERT. 4 k. Children with toys and pets.

1961. 4th and 5th Sputnik Flights.
2597. – 2 k. blk., blue & vio. 20 8
2598. **840.** 4 k. turquoise & blue 45 12
DESIGN—HORIZ. 2 k. Dog " Zvezdochka ", Sputnik 5 and Controller (inscr. " 25.III.1961 ").

841. V. G. Belinsky. **842.**

1961. Belinsky (writer). 150th Birth Anniv.
2599. **841.** 4 k. black and red .. 20 8

1961. Soviet Hydrometereological Service. 40th Anniv.
2600. **842.** 6 k. multicoloured .. 25 12

843. D. M. Karbishev.

844. Glider.

1961. Lieut.-Gen. Karbishev (war hero).
2601. **843.** 4 k. black, red & yell. 10 5

1961. Soviet Spartakiad.
2602. **844.** 4 k. red and grey .. 15 5
2603. – 6 k. red and slate .. 30 10
2604. – 10 k. red and slate .. 55 20
DESIGNS: 6 k. Hydro-plane. 10 k. Motor-cyclist.

845. Sukhe Bator Monument and Govt. Buildings, Ulan Bator.

846. S. I. Vavilov.

1961. Mongolian People's Republic. 40th Anniv.
2605. **845.** 4 k. multicoloured .. 20 8

1961. Vavilov (scientist). 70th Birthday.
2606. **846.** 4 k. sepia, bis. & grn. 15 5

847. V. Pshavela.

848. "Youth Activities".

1961. Pshavela (Georgian poet). Birth Cent.
2607. **847.** 4 k. sepia and cream 15 5

1961. World Youth Forum.
2608. – 2 k. sepia and orange 8 5
2609. – 4 k. green and lilac .. 15 5
2610. **848.** 6 k. blue and ochre .. 25 8
DESIGNS—HORIZ. 2 k. Youths pushing Tank into river. VERT. 4 k. "Youths and progress".

849.

850.

1961. 5th Int. Biochemical Congress, Moscow.
2611. **849.** 6 k. red, blk., bl. & grey 25 5

1961. Cent. of "Kalevipoeg" (Estonian Saga).
2612. **850.** 4 k. yell., turq. & blk. 15 5

851. Javelin Thrower.

1961. 7th Soviet Trade Union Sports.
2613. **851.** 6 k. red 20 5

852. A. D. Zakharov.

1961. Zakharov (architect). Birth Bicent.
2614. **852.** 4 k. buff, sepia & blue 20 5

853. Counter-attack.

854. Union. Emblem.

1961. War of 1941-45 (1st issue). Inscr. "1961".
2615. **853.** 4 k. multicoloured .. 15 5
2616. – 4 k. multicoloured .. 15 5
2617. – 4 k. indigo and brown 15 5
DESIGNS: No. 2616, Sailor with bayonet. 2617, Soldier with tommy-gun
See also Nos. 2717 and 2851/5.

1961. Int. Union of Students. 15th Anniv.
2617a. **854.** 6 k. violet and red .. 20 5

855. Stamps Commemorating Industry.

1961. 40th Anniv. of First Soviet Stamp. Centres multicoloured.
2618. **855.** 2 k. ochre and brown 12 5
2619. – 4 k. blue and indigo .. 20 5
2620. – 6 k. green and olive .. 30 5
2621. – 10 k. buff and sepia .. 45 10
DESIGNS (Stamps commemorating): 4 k. Electrification. 6 k. Peace. 10 k. Atomic energy.

856. Titov and "Voskhod 2".

1961. 2nd Manned Space Flight. Perf. or imperf.
2622. – 4 k. blue and purple 20 8
2623. **856.** 6 k. orge., grn. & brn. 35 12
DESIGN: 4 k. Space pilot and globe.

857. Angara River Bridge.

1961. Tercent. of Irkutsk, Siberia.
2624. **857.** 4 k. black, lilac & bis. 12 5

858. Letters and Mail Transport.

1961. International Correspondence Week.
2625. **858.** 4 k. black & magenta 15 5

859. Workers and Banners.

1961. 22nd Communist Party Congress (1st issue).
2626. **859.** 2 k. brn., yell. & verm. 8 5
2627. – 3 k. blue and orange 45 5
2628. – 4 k. red, buff & mar. 20 5
2629. – 4 k. orge., blk. & mag. 20 5
2630. – 4 k. sepia, brn. & red 20 12
DESIGNS: No. 2627, Moscow University and obelisk. 2628, Combine-harvester. 2629, Workmen and machinery. 2630, Worker and slogan.

860. Soviet Monument, Berlin.

861. Adult Education.

1961. Int. Federation of Resistance. 10th Anniv.
2631. **860.** 4 k. grey and red .. 15 5

1961. Communist Labour Teams.
2632. – 2 k. pur. & red on buff 10 5
2633. **861.** 3 k. sepia & red on buff 12 5
2634. – 4 k. bl. & red on cream 12 5
DESIGNS: 2 k. Worker at machine. 4 k. Workers round piano.

862. Rocket and Globes.

1961. Cosmic Flights. Aluminium-surfaced paper.
2635. **862.** 1 r. red & blk. on silver 6·50 9·00

864. A. Imanov (Kazakh leader).

XXII съезд
КПСС
(863.)

865. Liszt, Piano and Music.

1961. 22nd Communist Party Congress. 2nd issue). Optd. with T **863.**
2636. **862.** 1 r. red & blk. on silver 6·50 9·00

1961. Imanov commem.
2637. **864.** 4 k. sepia, brn. & grn. 15 5

1961. Liszt. 150th Birth Anniv.
2638. **865.** 4 k. sepia, mar. & yell. 20 5

866. Flags, Rocket and Skyline.

1961. October Revolution. 44th Anniv.
2639. **866.** 4 k. red, mar. & yell. 12 5

867. Congress Emblem.

868. M. V. Lomonosov and Lomonosov University.

1961. 5th W.F.T.U. Congress, Moscow. Inscr. "MOCKBA 1961".
2640. **867.** 2 k. red and bistre .. 5 5
2641. – 2 k. violet and grey .. 5 5
2642. – 4 k. chest., mar. & bl. 15 5
2643. – 4 k. red, blue & violet 12 5
2644. **867.** 6 k. red, bistre & grn. 25 10
2645. – 6 k. blue, pur. & bis. 20 8
DESIGNS—HORIZ. Nos. 2641, 2645, Negro breaking chains. VERT. 2642, Hand holding hammer. 2643, Hands holding globe.

1961. Lomonosov (scientist). 250th Birth Anniv. Inscr. "1961".
2646. **868.** 4 k. sepia, grn. & blue 15 5
2647. – 6 k. indigo, buff & grn. 25 8
2648. – 10 k. brown, indigo & maroon 55 12
DESIGNS—VERT. 6 k. Lomonosov at desk. HORIZ. 10 k. Lomonosov, his birthplace, and Leningrad Academy of Science.

869. Power-station Workers.

870. Scene from "Romeo and Juliet".

1961. Young Builders of Seven Year Plan. Inser. "1961".
2649. **869.** 3 k. slate, chest. & red 12 5
2650. – 4 k. choc., blue & red 15 8
2651. – 6 k. slate, brn. & red 20 5
DESIGNS: 4 k. Welders. 6 k. Engineer with theodolite.

1961. Russian Ballet (1st issue). Inscr. "1961". Multicoloured.
2652. 6 k. Type **870** 25 8
2653. 10 k. Scene from "Swan Lake" 45 12
See also Nos. 2666/7.

871. Hammer and Sickle.

872. A. Pumpur.

1961. Soviet Constitution. 25th Anniv.
2654. **871.** 4 k. lake, yell. & red .. 15 5

1961. Pumpur (Lettish poet). 120th Birth Anniv.
2655. **872.** 4 k. maroon and grey 15 5

1961. Air. Surch. **1961 r. 6 kon.** and bars.
2656. **766.** 6 k. on 60 k. blue .. 55 12

873. "Bulgarian Achievements".

1961. Bulgarian Republic. 15th Anniv.
2657. **873.** 4 k. multicoloured .. 15 5

874. Nansen and "Fram".

1961. Nansen (explorer). Birth Cent.
2658. **874.** 6 k. sepia, blue & blk. 40 10

875. M. Dolivo-Dobrovolsky.

876. A. S. Pushkin.

1962. Dolivo-Dobrovolsky (electrical engineer). Birth Cent.
2659. **875.** 4 k. blue and bistre .. 12 5

1962. Pushkin (poet). 125th Death Anniv.
2660. **876.** 4 k. black, red & buff 15 5

877. Soviet Woman.

1962. Soviet Women Commem.
2661. **877.** 4 k. black, bis. & orge. 12 5

878. People's Dancers.

1962. Soviet People's Dance Ensemble. 25th Anniv.
2662. **878.** 4 k. brown and red... 15 5

879. Skaters.

СОВЕТСКИЕ КОНЬКОБЕЖЦЫ—
ЧЕМПИОНЫ
МИРА
(880.)

1962. Ice-skating Championships, Moscow.
2663. **879.** 4 k. blue and orange 20 8

1962. War Heroes. As T **822** but inscr. "1962".
2664. 4 k. brown and grey-blue 20 5
2665. 6 k. blue-green and brown 40 10
DESIGNS: 4 k. Lieut. Shalandin, tanks and 'planes. 6 k. Capt. Gadzhiev, submarine and sinking ship.

1962. Russian Ballet (2nd issue). As **870** but inscr. "1962".
2666. 2 k. multicoloured .. 12 5
2667. 3 k. multicoloured .. 20 5
DESIGNS: Scenes from—2 k. "Red Flower" (Glier). 3 k. "Paris Flame" (Prokofiev).

1962. Soviet Victory in Ice-skating Championships. Optd. with T **880**.
2668. **879.** 4 k. blue and orange 1·25 65

881. Ski-ing.

1962. 1st People's Winter Games, Sverdlovsk.
2669. **881.** 4 k. violet and red .. 15 5
2670. – 6 k. turquoise & pur. 20 8
2671. – 10 k. red, black & bl. 40 12
DESIGNS. 6 k. Ice-hockey. 10 k. Figure-skating.

882. A. I. Herzen. **883.** Lenin on Banner.

1962. A. I. Herzen (writer). 150th Birth Anniv.
2672. **882.** 4 k. flesh, black & bl. 12 5

1962. 14th Leninist Young Communist League Congress. Inscr. "1962".
2673. **883.** 4 k. red, yell. & mar. 10 5
2674. – 6 k. mar., orge. & bl. 20 5
DESIGN—HORIZ. 6 k. Lenin on flag.

884. Rocket and Globe. **885.** Tchaikovsky (after sculpture by Z. M. Vilensky).

1962. World's First Manned Space Flight. 1st. Anniv. Perf. or imperf.
2675. **884.** 10 k. multicoloured .. 35 12

1962. 2nd Int. Tchaikovsky Music Competition.
2676. **885.** 4 k. drab, black & bl. 15 5

886. Youth of Three Races. **887.** The Ulyanov (Lenin's) Family.

1962. Int. Day of Solidarity of Youth against Colonialism.
2677. **886.** 6 k. multicoloured .. 20 5

1962. Lenin. 92nd Birth Anniv.
2678. **887.** 4 k. sepia, grey & red 20 5
2679. – 10 k. slate-purple, black and lake .. 55 12
DESIGN: 10 k. Lenin.

888. "Cosmos 3". **889.** Charles Dickens.

1962. Cosmic Research. Launching of Earth Satellite "Cosmos III".
2680. **888.** 6 k. blk., vio. & blue 40 12

1962. Charles Dickens. 150th Birth Anniv.
2681. **889.** 6 k. purple, turquoise and olive-brown .. 25 5

890. J. J. Rousseau. **891.** Karl Marx Monument, Moscow.

1962. Rousseau. 250th Birth Anniv.
2682. **890.** 6 k. bistre, grey & pur. 25 5

1962. Karl Marx Commem.
2683. **891.** 4 k. grey and blue .. 15 5

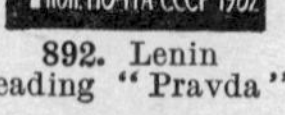

892. Lenin reading "Pravda". **893.** Mosquito and Campaign Emblem.

1962. "Pravda" Newspaper. 50th Anniv.
2684. **892.** 4 k. maroon, brown-red and buff .. 10 5
2685. – 4 k. multicoloured .. 10 5
2686. – 4 k. multicoloured .. 10 5
DESIGNS (25 × 38 mm.): No. 2685, Statuary and front page of first issue of "Pravda". 2686, Lenin and modern front page of "Pravda".

1962. Malaria Eradication. Perf. (6 k. also imperf.).
2687. **893.** 4 k. black, turq. & red 20 5
2688. 6 k. black, grn. & red 25 5

894. Building Model Rocket.

1962. All-Union Lenin Pioneer Organization. 40th Anniv. Designs embody Pioneer badge. Multicoloured.
2689. 2 k. Lenin and Pioneers giving Oath 5 5
2690. 3 k. L. Golikov and V. Kotik (pioneer heroes) 8 5
2691. 4 k. T **894.** 10 5
2692. 4 k. Hygiene education .. 10 5
2693. 6 k. Pioneers marching .. 20 8

896. Ski-jumping.
895. M. Mashtotz.

898. Cycle Racing. **897.** I. Goncharov.

1962. Mesrop Mashtotz (author of Armenian Alphabet). 1600th Birth Anniv.
2694. **895.** 4 k. brown and yellow 12 5

1962. F.I.S. Int. Ski Championships, Zakopane (Poland).
2695. **896.** 2 k. red, choc. & blue 5 5
2696. – 10 k. blue, black & red 25 12

1962. I. Goncharov (writer). 150th Birth Anniv.
2697. **897.** 4 k. brown and grey 15 5

1962. Summer Sports Championships.
2698. **898.** 2 k. blk., red & brown 8 5
2699. – 4 k. blk., yell. & chest. 12 5
2700. – 10 k. blk., lemon & bl. 25 8
2701. – 12 k. brown, yell. & bl. 35 12
2702. – 16 k. red, violet, black and green 45 12
DESIGNS—VERT. 4 k. Volleyball. 10 k. Rowing. 16 k. Horse-jumping. HORIZ. 12 k. Football (goal-keeper).

1962. Capitals of Autonomous Republics. 3rd issue. As T **779**.
2703. 4 k. black 12 5
2704. 4 k. purple 12 5
2705. 4 k. emerald 12 5
CAPITALS: No. 2703, Kazan (Tartar). 2704, Kizyl (Tuva). 2705, Saransk (Mordoa).

DESIGN: No. 2707, Modern library building.

899. Lenin Library, 1862.

1962. Lenin Library Cent.
2706. **899.** 4 k. black and slate .. 12 5
2707. – 4 k. black and slate .. 12 5

900. Fur Bourse, Leningrad, and Ermine.

1962. Fur Bourse Commem.
2708. **900.** 6 k. multicoloured .. 25 8

901. Pasteur. **902.** Youth and Girl with Book.

1962. Pasteur's Sterilisation Process Cent.
2709. **901.** 6 k. chestnut & black 20 5

1962. Communist Party Programme. Mult.
2710. 2 k. Type **902** 5 5
2711. 4 k. Workers of three races and dove 12 5

903. Hands breaking Bomb. **904.** Y. Kupala and Y. Kolas.

1962. World Peace Congress, Moscow.
2712. **903.** 6 k. bistre, blk. & blue 15 5

1962. Byelorussian Poets Commem.
2713. **904.** 4 k. brn.-red & yellow 12 5

905. Sabir. **906.** Congress Emblem.

1962. Sabir (Azerbaijan poet). Birth Cent.
2714. **905.** 4 k. sepia, buff & blue 15 5

1962. 8th Anti-Cancer Congress, Moscow.
2715. **906.** 6 k. red, black & blue 20 5

907. N. N. Zinin (chemist). **908.** V. Nesterov (painter).

1962. N. N. Zinin. 150th Birth Anniv.
2716. **907.** 4 k. sepia and violet .. 12 5

1962. War of 1941-45 (2nd issue). As T **853** inscr. "1962".
2717. 4 k. multicoloured .. 20 5
DESIGN: Sailor throwing petrol bomb.

1962. Russian Artists.
2718. **908.** 4 k. brown, flesh, blue and black 15 5
2719. – 4 k. sepia, mar. & grey 15 5
2720. – 4 k. black & chestnut 15 5
PORTRAITS—VERT. No. 2719, I. N. Kramska (painter). HORIZ. No. 2220, J. D. Shadr (sculptor).

909. "Vostok-2". **910.** Nikolaev and "Vostok-3".

1962. Titov's Space Flight. 1st Anniv. Perf. or imperf.
2721. **909.** 10 k. pur., blk. & blue 45 10
2722. 10 k. orge., blk. & blue 45 10

1962. 1st "Team" Manned Space Flight. Perf. or imperf.
2723. **910.** 4 k. brown, red & blue 20 8
2724. – 4 k. brown, red & blue 20 8
2725. – 6 k. multicoloured .. 45 12
DESIGNS: No. 2724, As T **910** but with Popovich and "Vostok-4". 2725 (47 × 28½ mm.), Cosmonauts in flight.

911. House of Friendship.

1962. People's House of Friendship, Moscow.
2726. **911.** 6 k. grey and blue .. 20 5

912. Lomonosov University and Atomic Symbols.

1962. "Atoms for Peace".
2727. **912.** 4 k. multicoloured .. 12 5
2728. – 6 k. multicoloured .. 15 5
DESIGN: 6 k. Map of Russia, Atomic symbol and "Peace" in ten languages.

913. Sazan and Bream. **914.** F. E. Dzerzhinsky (politician).

1962. Fish Preservation Campaign.
2729. **913.** 4 k. yell., vio. & blue 20 5
2730. – 6 k. blue, black & orge. 15 5
DESIGN: 6 k. Freshwater salmon.

1962. Dzerzhinsky. 85th Birth Anniv.
2731. **914.** 4 k. blue and olive .. 12 5

915. O. Henry (American writer).

1962. O. Henry. Birth Cent.
2732. **915.** 6 k. blk., brown & yell. 20 5

916. Field-Marshals Barclay de Tolly, Kutusov and Bagration.

1962. Patriotic War of 1812. 150th Anniv.
2733. **916.** 3 k. brown 20 5
2734. – 4 k. blue 20 8
2735. – 6 k. slate 35 12
2736. – 10 k. violet 55 15
DESIGNS: 4 k. Davidov and partisans. 6 k. Battle of Borodino. 10 k. Partisans escorting French prisoners-of-war.

917. Vinnitsa.

918. Transport, "Stamp" and "Postmark".

919. Cedar.

1962. Vinnitsa. 6th Cent.
2737. **917.** 4 k. black and bistre 12 5

1962. Int. Correspondence Week.
2738. **918.** 4 k. blk., mag. & turq. 15 5

1962. Nikitsky Botanical Gardens. 150th Anniv. Multicoloured.
2739. 3 k. T **919** 12 5
2740. 4 k. "Vostok-2" canna (plant) 12 5
2741. 6 k. Strawberry tree (arbutus) 20 8
2742. 10 k. "Road to the Stars" chrysanthemum .. 40 12

920. Builder.

921. "Sputnik 1".

923. Harvester.

922. M. Ahundov.

1962. "The Russian People". Multicoloured.
2743. 4 k. T **920** 12 5
2744. 4 k. Textile worker 12 5
2745. 4 k. Surgeon 12 5
2746. 4 k. Farm girl 12 5
2747. 4 k. Physical training instructor 12 5
2748. 4 k. Housewife 12 5
2749. 4 k. Rambler 12 5

1962. Launching of "Sputnik 1". 5th Anniv.
2750. **921.** 10 k. multicoloured .. 35 8

1962. M. Ahundov (poet). 150th Birth Anniv.
2751. **922.** 4 k. sepia and green 12 5

1962. "Settlers on Virgin Lands". Multicoloured.
2752. 4 k. T **923** 20 12
2753. 4 k. Surveyor, tractors and map 20 12
2754. 4 k. Pioneers with flag .. 20 12

924. N. Burdenko.

DESIGN: 4 k. V. Filatov (wearing beret).

1962. Soviet Scientists. Inscr. "1962". Multicoloured.
2755. **924.** 4 k. Type **924** .. 12 5
2756. – 4 k. V. Filatov (wearing beret) .. 12 5

925. Lenin Mausoleum.

1962. Lenin. 92nd Birth Anniv.
2757. **925.** 5 k. multicoloured .. 15 5

926. Worker with Banner.

927. "Towards the Stars".

ЗЕМЛЯ—МАРС
1.XI.
(**928.**)

1962. October Revolution. 45th Anniv.
2758. **926.** 4 k. multicoloured .. 15 5

1962. Space Flights Commem. Perf. or imperf.
2759. **927.** 6 k. black, brn. & blue 30 12
2760. 10 k. ult., bis. & violet 40 20

1962. Launching of Rocket to Mars (1st issue). Optd with T **928.**
2761. **927.** 10 k. ult., bis. & violet 1·50 60

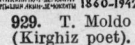

929. T. Moldo (Kirghiz poet).

930. Hammer and Sickle.

1962. Poet's Anniversaries.
2762. **929.** 4 k. black & brn.-red 15 5
2763. – 4 k. black and blue .. 15 5
DESIGN: No. 2763, Sayat-Nova (Armenian poet) with musical instrument.

1962. U.S.S.R. 40th Anniv.
2764. **930.** 4 k. red and crimson 12 5

931. Mars Rocket in Space. (Actual size $73\frac{1}{2} \times 27\frac{1}{2}$ mm.).

1962. Launching of Rocket to Mars 2nd issue).
2765. **931.** 10 k. violet and red .. 55 20

932. Chemical Industry and Statistics.

1962. 22nd Communist Party Congress. "Achievements of the People". Multicoloured.
2766. 4 k. T **932** 15 5
2767. 4 k. Engineering (machinery and atomic symbol) .. 15 5
2768. 4 k. Hydro-electric power 15 5
2769. 4 k. Agriculture (harvester) 15 8
2770. 4 k. Engineering (surveyor and welder) .. 15 8
2771. 4 k. Communications (telephone installation) 15 8
2772. 4 k. Heavy industry (furnace) .. 15 8
2773. 4 k. Transport (signalman, etc.) 15 8
2774. 4 k. Dairy-farming (milkmaid, etc.) 15 8
All the designs show production targets relating to 1980.

933. Chessmen.

935. V. K. Blucher (military commander).

934. Four Soviet Cosmonauts (actual size 151 × 70 mm.).

1962. 30th Soviet Chess Championships Erivan.
2775. **933.** 4 k. black and ochre 25 10

1962. Soviet Cosmonauts Commem. Perf. or imperf.
2776. **934.** 1 r. black and blue .. 3·25 1·50

1962. V. K. Blucher Commem.
2777. **935.** 4 k. multicoloured .. 12 5

936. V. N. Podbelsky.

937. A. Gaidar.

1962. V. N. Podbelsky (statesman). 75th Birth Anniv.
2778. **936.** 4 k. slate-vio. & chest. 12 5

1962. Soviet Writers.
2779. **937.** 4 k. buff, blk. & blue 12 5
2780. – 4 k. yellow, chocolate, brown and grey .. 12 5
DESIGN: No. 2780, A. S. Makharenko.

938. Dove and Christmas Tree.

1962. New Year. Perf. or imperf.
2781. **938.** 4 k. multicoloured .. 15 5

939. D. N. Pryanishnikov. (agricultural chemist).

940. Rose-coloured Starlings.

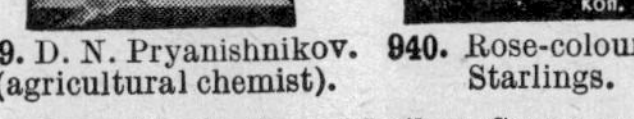

1962. D. N. Pryanishnikov Commem.
2782. **939.** 4 k. multicoloured .. 12 5

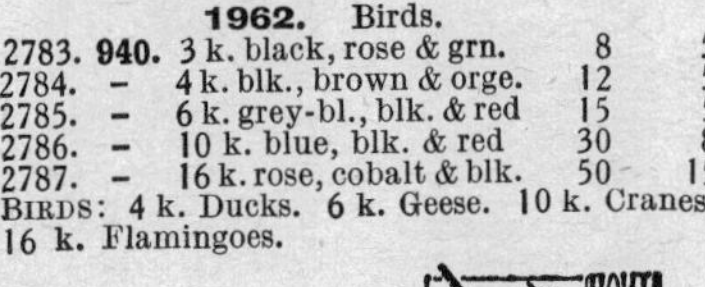

1962. Birds.
2783. **940.** 3 k. black, rose & grn. 8 5
2784. – 4 k. blk., brown & orge. 12 5
2785. – 6 k. grey-bl., blk. & red 15 5
2786. – 10 k. blue, blk. & red 30 8
2787. – 16 k. rose, cobalt & blk. 50 15
BIRDS: 4 k. Ducks. 6 k. Geese. 10 k. Cranes. 16 k. Flamingoes.

941. F.I.R. Emblem and Handclasp.

942. Badge and York Fighter 'Planes.

1962. 4th Int. Federation of Resistance Heroes Congress.
2788. **941.** 4 k. violet and red .. 10 5
2789. 6 k. turquoise and red 15 5

1962. French Air Force "Normandy-Niemen" Unit. 20th Anniv.
2790. **942.** 6 k. red, green & buff 25 5

943. Map and Savings Book.

DESIGN: 6 k. As T **943** but with people and figure "53" in place of symbols and "70" within map.

1962. Soviet Savings Banks. 40th Anniv.
2791. **943.** 4 k. multicoloured .. 12 5
2792. – 6 k. multicoloured .. 20 5

944. Rustovsky Plant.

1962. Heavy Industries.
2793. **944.** 4 k. black, pale blue and blue 20 5
2794. – 4 k. black, blue-green and yellow-green .. 20 5
2795. – 4 k. black, light blue and grey-blue .. 20 5
POWER STATIONS: No. 2794, Bratskaya. 2795, Volzhskaya.

1962. Provincial Costumes (3rd issue). As T **813.** Inscr. "1962".
2796. 3 k. red, brown and drab 15 5
COSTUME: 3 k. Latvia.

945. K. S. Stanislavsky (actor).

946. A. S. Serafimovich (writer).

1963. Russian Stage Celebrities.
2797. **945.** 4 k. grn. on pale grn. 12 5
2798. – 4 k. brown 12 5
2799. – 4 k. brown 12 5
PORTRAITS AND ANNIVERSARIES: No. 2797 (birth cent.). No. 2798, M. S. Schepkin (actor, death cent.). No. 2799, V. D. Durov (animal trainer and circus artiste, birth cent.).

1963. Russian Writers and Poets.
2800. **946.** 4 k. brn., sepia & mve. 12 5
2801. – 4 k. brown and pur. 12 5
2802. – 4 k. brn., red-brn. & buff 12 5
2803. – 4 k. brown & green .. 12 5
2804. – 4 k. brn., sepia & mve. 12 5
2805. – 4 k. multicoloured .. 12 5
PORTRAITS AND ANNIVERSARIES: No. 2800, (birth cent.). 2801, D. Bednii (80th birth anniv.). 2802, G. I. Uspensky (120th birth anniv.). 2803, N. P. Ogarev (150th birth anniv.). 2804, V. J. Bryusov (90th birth anniv.). 2805, F. V. Gladkov (80th birth anniv.).

947. Children in Nursery.

948. Dolls and Toys.

1963. Child Welfare.
2806. **947.** 4 k. chestnut, black and orange-brown 15 5
2807. – 4 k. pur., blue & orge. 15 5
2808. – 4 k. bistre, red & grn. 15 5
2809. – 4 k. purple, red & orge. 15 5
DESIGNS: No. 2807, Children with nurse. 2808, Young pioneers. 2809, Students at desk and trainee at lathe.

1963. Decorative Arts. Multicoloured.
2810. 4 k. T **948** 15 5
2811. 6 k. Pottery 20 5
2812. 10 k. Books 40 12
2813. 12 k. Porcelain 55 15

949. Ilyushin Il-62 Airliner.

DESIGNS: 12 k. "Aeroflot" emblem. 16 k. Tu-104 airliner.

1963. "Aeroflot" Airline. 40th Anniv.
2814. **949.** 10 k. blk., brown & red 35 5
2815. – 12 k. black, red, brown and blue 50 12
2816. – 16 k. red, blk. & blue 60 20

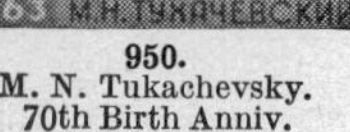

950. M. N. Tukachevsky. 70th Birth Anniv.
951. M. A. Pavlov (scientist).

1963. Red Army and War Heroes. 45th Anniversary.
2817. **950.** 4 k. green & turquoise 12 5
2818. – 4 k. black & chestnut 12 5
2819. – 4 k. sepia and blue .. 12 5
2820. – 4 k. black and claret 12 5
2821. – 4 k. violet & magenta 12 5
DESIGNS (Army heroes and battle scenes): No. 2818, U. M. Avetusjan. 2819, A. M. Matrosov. 2820, J. V. Panfilov. 2821, Y. F. Fabriscius.

1963. Academy of Sciences Members.
2822. **951.** 4 k. bl., grey & brown 12 5
2823. – 4 k. brown & slate-grn. 12 5
2824. – 4 k. flesh, yellow, brown and slate-violet .. 15 5
2825. – 4 k. sep., red & indigo 15 5
2826. – 4 k. brown, slate-vio., red and bistre .. 15 5
PORTRAITS: No. 2823, I. V. Kurchatov. 2824, V. I. Vernadsky. LARGER. ($23\frac{1}{2} \times 30$ mm.). 2825, A. Krylov. 2826, V. Obroutchev. All commemorate birth centenaries except No. 2823 (60th anniv. of birth).

Советские хоккеисты— чемпионы мира и Европы. Стокгольм. 1963 г.

952. Games Emblem.
953.

1963. 5th Soviet T.U. Winter Sports.
2827. **952.** 4 k. orge., blk. & blue 20 5

1963. Soviet Victory in Swedish Ice Hockey Championships. No. 2670 optd. with T **953**.
2828. 6 k. turquoise and purple 90 20

954. V. Kingisepp.
955. R. M. Blauman.

1963. Victor Kingisepp (Estonian Communist Party leader). 75th Birth Anniv.
2829. **954.** 4 k. chocolate and blue 15 5

1963. Rudolf Blauman (Latvian writer). Birth Cent.
2830. **955.** 4 k. maroon and blue 15 5

956. Globe and Flowers.
957. Lenin.

1963. "World without Arms and Wars". Perf. or imperf.
2831. **956.** 4 k. green, blue & red 10 5
2832. – 6 k. lilac, green & red 15 5
2833. – 10 k. violet, blue & red 20 8
DESIGNS: 6 k. Atomic emblem and pylon. 10 k. Sun and rocket.

1963. Lenin. 93rd Birth Anniv.
2834. **957.** 4 k. brown and red .. 20 5

1963. Provincial Costumes (4th issue). As T **813**. Inscr. "1963".
2835. 3 k. red, yell. blk. & ochre 20 5
2836. 4 k. red, yell., sepia & green 25 5
2837. 4 k. red, blue, chocolate and yellow-brown .. 25 5
2838. 4 k. rose, pur., ochre & sep. 25 5
COSTUMES: No. 2835, Tadzhikistan. 2836, Azerbaijan. 2837, Kirkghizia. 2838, Turkmenistan.

958. "Luna 4" Rocket.
959. Woman and Lido.

1963. Launching of "Luna 4" Space Rocket. Perf. or imperf.
2839. **958.** 6 k. red, black & blue 20 12
See also No. 3250.

1963. World Health Day. 15th Anniv. Multicoloured.
2840. 2 k. T **959** 8 5
2841. 4 k. Man and stadium .. 12 5
2842. 10 k. Child and school .. 30 8

960. Sputniks and Globe.

1963. "Cosmonautics Day".
2843. **960.** 10 k. blue, blk. & pur. 20 8
2844. – 10 k. purple, blk. & bl. 20 8
2845. – 10 k. red, black & yell. 20 8
DESIGNS: No. 2844, "Vostok-1" and Moon. 2845, Space rocket and Sun.

962. Cuban Horsemen with Flag.

1963. Cuban-Soviet Friendship.
2846. **962.** 4 k. black, red & blue 15 5
2847. – 6 k. black, blue & red 30 8
2848. – 10 k. blue, red & black 35 12
DESIGNS: 6 k. Hands, weapon, book and flag. 10 k. Crane, hoisting tractor and flags.

963. J. Gashek.
964. Karl Marx.

1963. Jaroslav Gashek (writer). 40th Death Anniv.
2849. **963.** 4 k. black 12 5

1963. Karl Marx. 80th Death Anniv.
2850. **964.** 4 k. black and brown 15 5

1963. War of 1941-45 (3rd issue). As T **853** inscr. "1963".
2851. 4 k. multicoloured .. 12 5
2852. 4 k. multicoloured .. 12 5
2853. 4 k. multicoloured .. 12 5
2854. 4 k. sepia and red .. 12 5
2855. 6 k. olive, black and red 20 5
DESIGNS: No. 2851, Woman making shells (Defence of Leningrad, 1942). 2852, Soldier in winter kit with tommy-gun (20th anniv. of Battle of the Volga). No. 2853, Soldiers attacking (Liberation of Kiev, 1943). 2854, Tanks and map indicating Battle of Kursk, 1943. 2855, Tank commander and tanks.

965. International P.O. Building.
967. Wagner.

968. Boxers on "Glove".
966. Medal and Chessmen.

1963. Opening of Int. Post Office, Moscow.
2856. **965.** 6 k. brown and blue 20 5

1963. World Champions Title Chess Match, Moscow. Perf. or imperf.
2857. **966.** 4 k. yellow, green, black and turquoise 15 5
2858. – 6 k. blue, mag. & ult. 20 5
2859. – 16 k. blk., mag. & pur. 55 12
DESIGNS: 6 k. Chessboard and men. 16 k. Building and chessmen.

1963. Wagner and Verdi (composers). 150th Birth Anniv.
2860. **967.** 4 k. black and red .. 15 5
2861. – 4 k. maroon and red .. 20 5
DESIGN: No. 2861, Verdi.

1963. 15th European Boxing Championships, Moscow. Multicoloured.
2862. 4 k. Type **968** 15 5
2863. 6 k. Referee and winning boxer on "glove" .. 25 5

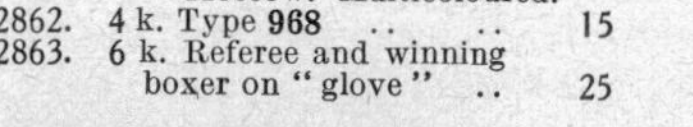

Всемирный конгресс женщин.

969. Bykovsky and "Vostok 5".
(970.)

1963. Second "Team" Manned Space Flights (1st issue). Perf. or imperf.
2864. **969.** 6 k. brown and purple 20 8
2865. – 6 k. red and green .. 20 8
2866. – 10 k. red and blue .. 40 15
DESIGNS: No. 2865, Tereshkova and "Vostok 6". No. 2866. Allegory—"Man and Woman in Space".

1963. Int. Women's Congress, Moscow. Optd. with T **970**.
2867. **956.** 4 k. green, blue & red 30 15

971. Globe, Film and Camera.
972. V. Mayakovsky.

1963. Int. Film Festival, Moscow.
2868. **971.** 4 k. blue, blk. & ol.-brn. 15 5

1963. Mayakovsky (poet). 70th Birth Anniv.
2869. **972.** 4 k. brown 20 5

973. Tereshkova.
974. Cycling.

1963. 2nd "Team" Manned Space Flights (2nd issue). Multicoloured.
2870. 4 k. Bykovsky 20 12
2871. 4 k. Tereshkova 20 12
2872. 10 k. Type **973** 90 20

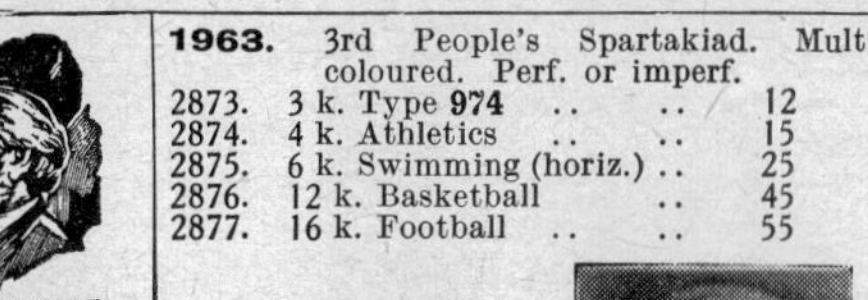

1963. 3rd People's Spartakiad. Multicoloured. Perf. or imperf.
2873. 3 k. Type **974** 12 5
2874. 4 k. Athletics .. 15 5
2875. 6 k. Swimming (horiz.) .. 25 8
2876. 12 k. Basketball .. 45 12
2877. 16 k. Football 55 15

975. Ice-hockey Player.
976. Lenin.

1963. Russian Ice Hockey Championships.
2878. **975.** 6 k. grey-blue and red 35 12

1963. 1st Socialist Party Congress 60th Anniv.
2879. **976.** 4 k. black and red .. 20 5

977. Ship and Crate.
978. Guibozo (polo).

1963. Red Cross Cent.
2880. **977.** 6 k. red and green .. 35 5
2881. – 12 k. red and ultram. 50 12
DESIGN: 12 k. Centenary emblem.

1963. Regional Sports.
2882. – 3 k. bistre, brown, red and blue .. 15 5
2883. **978.** 4 k. black, red & ochre 20 5
2884. – 6 k. red, sepia & yell. 25 10
2885. – 10 k. black, brown & olive-brown .. 40 12
DESIGNS—HORIZ. 3 k. Lapp reindeer-racing. 6 k. Buryat archery. VERT. 10 k. Armenian wrestling.

979. A. Mozhaisky and Model Aeroplane.

1963. Aviation Celebrities.
2886. **979.** 6 k. black and blue .. 35 8
2887. – 10 k. black and blue .. 45 12
2888. – 16 k. black and blue .. 65 15
DESIGNS: 10 k. P. Nesterov and "looping the loop". 16 k. N. Shukovsky and "aerodynamics".

981. S. S. Gulak-Artemovsky (poet).
982. O. Kobilanskaya (writer).

1963. Celebrities.
2889. **981.** 4 k. black and red .. 15 5
2890. – 4 k. brown & purple 15 5
2891. – 4 k. brown and violet 15 5
2892. **982.** 4 k. mauve & brown 15 5
2893. – 4 k. mauve and green 15 5
DESIGNS AND ANNIVERSARIES—As T **981**: No. 2889, 150th birth anniv. No. 2893, M. I. Petraskas (Lithuanian composer) and scene from one of works (90th birth anniv.). As T **982**: No. 2890, G. D. Eristavi (writer, death cent., 1964). No. 2891, A. S. Dargomizhsky (composer, 150th birth anniv.). No. 2892 (birth cent.).

983. Antarctic Map and Ship.
985. E. O. Paton.

984. Letters and Transport.

1963. Arctic and Antarctic Research. Multicoloured.

2894. 3 k. Type **983** 12 10
2895. 4 k. Convoy of snow tractors and map 20 10
2896. 6 k. Globe and aircraft at polar base 35 15
2897. 12 k. Polar ships and whale 65 20

1963. Int. Correspondence Week.

2898. **984.** 4 k. vio., orge. & blk. 15 5

1963. Paton (engineer). 10th Death Anniv.

2899. **985.** 4 k. black, red & blue 15 5

986. D. Diderot. **987.** "Peace and Progress".

1963. Denis Diderot (French philosopher). 250th Birth Anniv.

2900. **986.** 4 k. brn., blue & bistre 20 8

1963. "Peace – Brotherhood – Liberty – Labour". All black, red and lake.

2901. 4 k. Type **987** 15 5
2902. 4 k. "The Plan" .. 15 5
2903. 4 k. "Intellectual Work" 15 5
2904. 4 k. "People's Union" .. 15 5
2905. 4 k. "Nations' Elite" .. 15 5
2906. 4 k. "The Family" .. 15 5

988. Academy of Sciences, Frunze.

1963. Union of Kirghizia and Russia. Cent.

2907. **988.** 4 k. blue, yellow & red 12 5

990. Lenin and Congress Building. **991.** Menchnikov.

1963. 13th Soviet Trade Unions Congress, Moscow.

2908. **990.** 4 k. red and black .. 12 5
2909. 4 k. red and black .. 12 5

DESIGN: No. 2909, Lenin with man and woman workers.

1963. Pasteur Institute, Paris. 75th Anniv

2910. **991.** 4 k. green and bistre 12 5
2911. – 6 k. violet and bistre 20 5
2912. – 12 k. blue and bistre 45 12

PORTRAITS: 6 k. Pasteur. 12 k. Calmette.

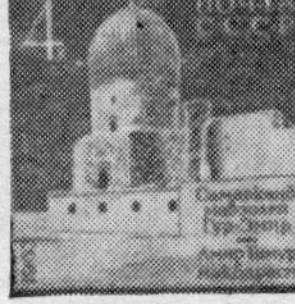

992. Cruiser "Aurora" and Rockets. **993.** Gur Emi Mausoleum.

1963. October Revolution. 46th Anniv.

2913. **992.** 4 k. blk., orange & lake 20 5
2914. 4 k. black, fluorescent red and lake .. 20 5

1963. Ancient Samarkand Buildings. Multicoloured.

2915. 4 k. Type **993** 20 5
2916. 4 k. Schachi-Zinda Mosque 20 5
2917. 6 k. Registan Square (55 × 28½ mm.) 40 8

994. Inscription, Globe and Kremlin. **995.** Pushkin Monument, Kiev.

1963. Signing of Nuclear Test-Ban Treaty, Moscow.

2918. **994.** 6 k. violet and pale blue 25 8

1963.

2919. **995.** 4 k. sepia 12 5

997. V. G. Shukhov, and Tower. **998.** Y. M. Steklov and "Izvestia".

1963. Shukhov (engineer). 110th Birth Anniv.

2920. **997.** 4 k. black and green 12 5

1963. Steklov (first editor of "Izvestia"). 90th Birth Anniv.

2921. **998.** 4 k. black and magenta 12 5

999. Buildings and Emblems of Moscow (and U.S.S.R.) and Prague (and Czechoslovakia).

1963. Soviet-Czech Friendship Treaty. 20th Anniv.

2922. **999.** 6 k. red, bistre & blue 20 5

1000. F. A. Poletaev (soldier) and Medals.

1963. Poletaev Commem.

2923. **1000.** 4 k. multicoloured .. 15 5

1003. J. Grimau (Spanish Communist). **1004.** Rockets.

1963. Grimau Commem.

2924. **1003.** 6 k. slate-violet, red and cream .. 20 5

1963. New Year (1st issue).

2925. **1004.** 6 k. multicoloured .. 20 5

1005. "Happy New Year". **1008.** Topaz.

1963. New Year (2nd issue).

2926. **1005.** 4 k. red, blue & grn. 12 5
2927. 6 k. red, blue and green 20 5

1963. "Precious Stones of the Urals". Multicoloured.

2928. 2 k. Type **1008** 10 5
2929. 4 k. Jasper 20 5
2930. 6 k. Amethyst 25 8
2931. 10 k. Emerald 40 12
2932. 12 k. Ruby 55 15
2933. 16 k. Malachite 65 20

1009. Sputnik 7.

1963. "First in Space". Gold, vermilion and grey.

2934. 10 k. Type **1009** 30 10
2935. 10 k. Moon-landing .. 30 10
2936. 10 k. Back of Moon .. 30 10
2937. 10 k. Vostok I 30 10
2938. 10 k. Twin flight 30 10
2939. 10 k. Seagull (first woman in space) .. 30 10

1010. Dushanbe (formerly "Stalinabad" 1929–62), Tadzhikistan.

1963. Dushanbe Commem.

2940. **1010.** 4 k. slate-blue .. 12 5

1012. Flame and Rainbow. **1013.** F. A Sergeev ("Artyem").

1963. Declaration of Human Rights. 15th Anniv.

2941. **1012.** 6 k. multicoloured .. 20 5

1963. Sergeev (revolutionary). 80th Birth Anniv.

2942. **1013.** 4 k. sepia and red .. 12 5

1014. Sun and Globe. **1015.** K. Donelaitis.

1964. International Quiet Sun Year.

2943. – 4 k. black, orge. & mag. 15 5
2944. **1014.** 6 k. blue, yellow and red 20 5
2945. – 10 k. vio-blue, red & blue 25 10

DESIGNS—HORIZ. 4 k. Giant telescope and Sun. 10 k. Globe and Sun.

1964. K. Donelaitis (Lithuanian poet). 250th Birth Anniv.

2946. **1015.** 4 k. black & myrtle 12 5

1016. Speed-skating.

DESIGNS: 2 k. T **1016**. 4 k. Skiing 6 k. Game emblem. 10 k. Rifle - shooting (biathlon). 12 k. Figure - skating (pairs).

1964. Winter Olympic Games, Innsbruck.

2947. 2 k. black, magenta & blue 5 5
2948. 4 k. black, blue & magenta 10 5
2949. 6 k. red, black and blue .. 15 5
2950. 10 k. blk., magenta & grn. 25 10
2951. 12 k. black, green & mag. 25 10

1017. A. S. Golubkina and Statue. **1018.** "Agriculture".

1020. Shevchenko's Statue.

150 років з дня народження. 1964 р. (**1019.**)

1964. A. Golubkina (sculptress). Birth Cent.

2952. **1017.** 4 k. sepia and grey 15 5

1964. Heavy Chemical Industries. Multicoloured.

2953. 4 k. Type **1018** 12 5
2954. 4 k. "Textiles" 12 5
2955. 4 k. "Tyre Production" 12 5

1964. T. G. Shevchenko (Ukrainian poet and painter). 150th Birth Anniv. No. 2561 optd. with T **1019** and designs as T **1020** inscr. "1814–1861".

2956. **823.** 3 k. brown & violet 12 5
2959. **1020.** 4 k. green 12 5
2960. 4 k. claret .. 20 5
2961. – 6 k. indigo 20 5
2962. – 6 k. chestnut .. 20 5
2957. – 10 k. violet & brown 25 10
2958. – 10 k. sepia & bistre 25 10

DESIGNS: 6 k. Shevchenko in fur hat. 10 k. Bareheaded.

1021. K. S. Zaslonov.

1964. Soviet Heroes.

2963. **1021.** 4 k. sepia and brown 12 5
2964. – 4 k. slate-pur. & blue 12 5
2965. – 4 k. grey-blue & red 12 5
2966. – 4 k. sep. & grey-blue 12 5

PORTRAITS: No. 2964, N. A. Vilkov. 2965, J. V. Smirnov. 2966, V. Khoruyaya.

DESIGN: 6 k. Federov statue, books and newspapers.

1022. Federov printing the first Russian book, "Apostle".

1964. First Russian Printed Book. 400th Anniv. Inscr. "1964".

2967. **1022.** 4 k. black, yellow, red and green .. 12 5
2968. – 6 k. black, yellow, green and red .. 20 5

Слава советским спортсменам— победителям IX зимней Олимпиады! (**1023.**)

1024. Ice-hockey Player.

1964. Winter Olympic Games. Soviet Medal-winners. (a) Nos. 2947/51 optd. with T **1023** or similarly.

2969. 2 k. black, magenta & blue 8 5
2970. 4 k. black, blue & magenta 12 5
2971. 6 k. red, black and blue .. 20 5
2972. 10 k. black, magenta & grn. 25 10
2973. 12 k. black, green & mag. 30 12

(b) New designs.

2974. **1024.** 3 k. red, black & turq. 10 5
2975. – 16 k. orange & brown 45 15

DESIGN: 16 k. Gold medal and inscr.—"Triumph of Soviet Sport—11 Gold, 8 silver, 6 Bronze Medals".

1025. Militiaman and Factory Guard. **1026.** Lighthouse, Odessa, and Sailor.

1964. "Public Security".
2976. **1025.** 4 k. blue, red & black 12 5

1964. Liberation of Odessa and Leningrad. 20th Anniv. Multicoloured.
2977. 4 k. Type **1026** 12 5
2978. 4 k. Lenin, Statue, Leningrad 12 5

1027. Sputniks. **1028.** N. I. Kibalchich.

1964. "The Way to the Stars". Imperf. or perf.

(a) Cosmonautics. As T **1027**.
2979. 4 k. green, black and red 20 5
2980. 6 k. black, blue and red .. 25 8
2981. 12 k. turq., brown & black 50 20
DESIGNS: 6 k. "Mars I" space station. 12 k. Gagarin and space capsule.

(b) Rocket Construction Pioneers. As T **1028**.
2982. 10 k. black, grn. & violet 35 10
2983. 10 k. black, emerald and red 35 10
2984. 10 k. black, bluish green and red 35 10
2985. 10 k. black and blue .. 50 12
DESIGNS: No. 2982, T **1028**. 2983, F. Zander. 2984. K. E. Tsiolkovsky. 2985, Pioneers' medallion and Saransk memorial.

1029. Lenin.

1964. Lenin. 94th Birth Anniv.
2986. **1029.** 4 k. blk., buff & mag. 12 5

1030. Shakespeare (400th Birth Anniv.).

1964. Cultural Annivs.
2987. – 6 k. yell., brn. & sepia 35 10
2988. **1030.** 10 k. brn. & olive-brn. 40 10
2989. – 12 k. green & brown 65 20
DESIGNS AND ANNIVERSARIES: 6 k. Michelangelo (400th death anniv.). 12 k. Galileo (400th birth anniv.).

1031. Crop-watering Machine and Produce.

1964. "Irrigation".
2990. **1031.** 4 k. multicoloured .. 12 5

1032. Gamarnik.

1964. Y. B. Gamarnik (Soviet Army Commander). 70th Birth Anniv.
2991. **1032.** 4 k. sepia, blue & blk. 12 5

1033. D. I. Gulia (Abhazian poet).

1964. Cultural Annivs.
2992. **1033.** 4 k. black, green and light green 12 5
2993. – 4 k. blk., verm. & red 12 5
2994. – 4 k. blk., brn. & bistre 12 5
2995. – 4 k. blk., yell. & brn. 12 5
2996. – 4 k. multicoloured .. 12 5
2997. – 4 k. blk., yell. & brn. 15 5
DESIGNS: No. 2993, Nijazi (Uzbek writer, composer and painter). No. 2994, S. Seifullin (Kazakh poet). 2995, M. M. Kotsyubinsky (writer). No. 2996, S. Nazaryan (Armenian writer). No. 2997, T. Satylganov (Kirghiz poet).

1034. A. Gaidar.

1964. Writers A. P. Gaider and N. A. Ostrovsky. 60th Birth Annivs.
2998. **1034.** 4 k. red and blue .. 12 5
2999. – 4 k. lake & bronze-grn. 12 5
DESIGN: No. 2999, N. Ostrovsky and battle scene.

150 лет вхождения
в состав России
1964

(**1035.**)

1964. Union of Azerbaijan and Russia. Surch. with T **1035**.
3000. 772. 4 k. on 40 k. brown, bistre and yellow .. 50 20

1036. Rumanian Woman and Emblems on Map. **1037.** Elephant.

1964. Rumanian—Soviet Friendship Treaty. 20th Anniv.
3001. **1036.** 6 k. multicoloured .. 20 8

1964. Moscow Zoo Cent. Multicoloured. Imperf. or perf.
3002. 1 k. Type **1037** 5 5
3003. 2 k. Giant Panda 5 5
3004. 4 k. Polar bear 8 5
3005. 6 k. Elk 20 5
3006. 10 k. Pelican 25 8
3007. 12 k. Tiger 30 10
3008. 16 k. Eagle 45 15
The 2 k. and 12 k. are horiz.; the 4 k. and 10 k. are "square", approx. $26\frac{1}{2} \times 28$ mm.

1038. Flag and Obelisk. **1039.** Leningrad G.P.O.

1964. Liberation of Byelorussia. 20th Anniv.
3009. **1038.** 4 k. multicoloured .. 12 5

1964. Leningrad's Postal Service. 250th Anniv.
3010. **1039.** 4 k. blk., bistre & red 12 5

1040. Maize. **1041.** Map of Poland and Emblems.

1964. Agricultural Crops. Multicoloured. Imperf. or perf.
3011. 2 k. Type **1040** 5 5
3012. 3 k. Wheat 8 5
3013. 4 k. Potatoes 10 5
3014. 6 k. Peas 15 5
3015. 10 k. Sugar beet 25 8
3016. 12 k. Cotton 30 10
3017. 16 k. Flax 45 12

1964. Polish People's Republic. 20th Anniv.
3018. **1041.** 6 k. multicoloured .. 20 5

1042. Horse-jumping. **1043.** M. Thorez (French Communist leader).

1964. Olympic Games, Tokyo. Imperf. or perf.
3019. 3 k. multicoloured .. 5 5
3020. 4 k. red black & yellow .. 8 5
3021. 6 k. red, black and blue .. 15 5
3022. 10 k. red, blk. & blue-grn. 25 8
3023. 12 k. red, black and grey 30 10
3024. 16 k. violet, red and blue 50 12
DESIGNS: 3 k. T **1042**. 4 k. Weightlifting. 6 k. Pole-vaulting. 10 k. Canoeing. 12 k. Gymnastics. 16 k. Fencing.

1964. Maurice Thorez Commem.
3025. **1043.** 4 k. black and red .. 15 5

1044. Three Races. **1045.** Jawaharial Nehru.

1964. Int. Anthropologists and Ethnographers Congress, Moscow.
3026. **1044.** 6 k. black and yellow 20 8

1964. Nehru Commem.
3027. **1045.** 4 k. brown and slate 20 8

1046. Globe and Banner. **1047.** A. V. Vishnevsky (surgeon).

1964. "First International". Cent.
3028. 4 k. red, bistre and blue 12 5
3029. 4 k. red, olive and black 12 5
3030. 4 k. drab, red and lake .. 12 5
3031. 4 k. red, black and blue .. 12 5
3032. 4 k. multicoloured .. 12 5
DESIGNS: No. 3028 T **1046**. 3029, Communist Party manifesto. 3030, Marx and Engels. 3031, Chain-breaker. 3032, Lenin.

1964. "Outstanding Soviet Physicians".
3033. 4 k. brown and slate-pur. 12 5
3034. 4 k. sepia, red & yellow 12 5
3035. 4 k. brown, blue & bistre 15 5
DESIGNS: No. 3033, T **1047**. 3034, N. A. Semashko (public health pioneer). Both are 90th birth anniversaries. 3035, D. I. Ivanovsky and siphon.

1048. Bulgarian Flag, Rose and Emblems. **1049.** P. Togliatti (Italian Communist leader).

1964. Bulgarian People's Republic. 20th Anniv.
3036. **1048.** 6 k. red, green & drab 20 8

1964. Togliatti Commem.
3037. **1049.** 4 k. black and red .. 15 5

1052. Globe and Letters.

1964. Int. Correspondence Week.
3038. **1052.** 4 k. mauve, bl. & brn. 12 5

1053. Soviet and Yugoslav Soldiers. **1054.** D.D.R. Emblem, Ship and Industrial Plants.

1964. Liberation of Belgrade. 20th Anniv
3039. **1053.** 6 k. multicoloured .. 20 5

1964. German Democratic Republic. 15th Anniv.
3040. **1054.** 6 k. multicoloured .. 25 5

1055. Woman holding Bowl of Produce (Moldovian Republic).

40 лет Советскому Таджикистану
1964 год

(**1056.**)

1964. Soviet Republics. 40th Anniv.
(a) Inscr. "1964" or "1924 1964" (Nos. 3038/40).
3041. **1055.** 4 k. brown, grn. & red 12 5
3042. – 4 k. multicoloured .. 12 5
3043. – 4 k. red, pur. & yell. 12 5

(b) Optd. with T **1056**.
3044. **1010.** 4 k. slate-blue .. 25 8
DESIGNS—VERT. No. 3042, Women holding Arms (Turkmenistan). No. 3043, Man and Woman holding produce (Uzbekistan). No. 3044, commemorates the Tadzhikistan Republic.

1057. Yegorov.

1964. Three-manned Space Flight. (a) Portraits in black, orange and turquoise.
3045. 4 k. Type **1057** 15 5
3046. 4 k. Feoktistov 15 5
3047. 4 k. Komarov 15 5
These can be identified by the close proximation of the Russian names on the stamps to the English versions.

(b) Designs $73\frac{1}{2} \times 22\frac{1}{2}$ mm.
3048. 6 k. purple and violet .. 25 8
3049. 10 k. violet & ultramarine 45 10
DESIGNS: 6 k. The three cosmonauts. 10 k. Spaceship "Voskhod I".

1058. Soldier and Flags. **1060.** Lermontov's Birthplace.

1964. Liberation of Ukraine. 20th Anniv.
3050. **1058.** 4 k. multicoloured .. 12 5

1964. M. Lermontov (poet). 150th Birth Anniv.
3051. **1060.** 4 k. violet 10 5
3052. – 6 k. black 20 5
3053. – 10 k. brown and flesh 30 8
DESIGNS: 6 k. Lermontov. 10 k. Lermontov talking with Belinsky.

1061. Hammer and Sickle. **1062.** N. K. Krupskaya (Lenin's wife).

1964. October Revolution. 47th Anniv.
3054. **1061.** 4 k. multicoloured .. 12 5

1964. Birth Anniversaries.
3055. **1062.** 4 k. multicoloured .. 12 5
3056. – 4 k. multicoloured .. 12 5
DESIGNS, etc.: No. 3055 (95th anniv.). 3056, A. Yelizarova-Ulianova (Lenin's sister) (cent.).

1063. Mongolian Woman and Lamb. **1065.** Mushrooms.

1964. Mongolian People's Republic. 40th Anniv.
3057. **1063.** 4 k. multicoloured .. 20 8

1964. Mushrooms. Various designs as T **1065**. Imperf. or perf.
3058. **1065.** 2 k. multicoloured .. 8 5
3059. – 4 k. multicoloured 12 5
3060. – 6 k. multicoloured .. 15 5
3061. – 10 k. multicoloured 20 10
3062. – 12 k. multicoloured 40 12

1066. A. Dovzhenko (film producer). **1067.** Christmas Tree Star and Globe.

1068. V. Y. Struve (scientist). **1069.** S. V. Ivanov (painter) and Skiers.

1964. A. Dovzhenko. 70th Birth Anniv.
3063. **1066.** 4 k. blue and grey .. 12 5

1964. New Year.
3064. **1067.** 4 k. multicoloured .. 15 5

1964. V. Struve (scientist). Death Cent.
3065. **1068.** 4 k. sepia and blue 25 5

1964. S. Ivanov (painter). Birth Cent.
3066. **1069.** 4 k. brown and black 25 5

1070. Scene from Film.

1964. "Chapayev" Film. 30th Anniv.
3067. **1070.** 6 k. black and green 20 5

1071. Test-tubes, Jar and Agricultural Scenes.

1964. Chemistry for the National Economy.
3068. **1071.** 4 k. purple and olive 12 5
3069. – 6 k. black and blue .. 20 5
DESIGN: 6 k. Chemical plant.
See also Nos. 2953/5.

1072. Berries. **1073.** Library.

1964. Woodland Fruits. Multicoloured.
3070. 1 k. Type **1072** 10 5
3071. 3 k. Bilberries 12 5
3072. 4 k. Rowanberries .. 15 5
3073. 10 k. Blackberries .. 25 8
3074. 16 k. Cranberries .. 30 12

1964. Academy of Sciences Library, Leningrad. 250th Anniv.
3075. **1073.** 4 k. black, grn. & red 12 5

1074. Congress Palace and Spassky Tower. **1075.** Mt. Khan-Tengri.

1964.
3076. **1074.** 1 r. indigo .. .. 3·25 1·10

1964. Mountaineering. Multicoloured.
3077. 4 k. Type **1075** .. 5 5
3078. 6 k. Mt. Kazbeck (horiz.) 20 5
3079. 12 k. Mt. Ushba 35 10

1077. Helmet.

1964. Kremlin Treasures. Multicoloured.
3080. 4 k. Type **1077** .. 20 5
3081. 6 k. Quiver 35 8
3082. 10 k. Coronation headgear 45 12
3083. 12 k. Ladle 55 15
3084. 16 k. Bowl 65 20

1078. I. M. Sivko. **1079.** Dante.

1965. War Heroes.
3085. **1078.** 4 k. black & violet .. 12 5
3086. – 4 k. sepia and blue .. 12 5
DESIGN: No. 3086, General I. S. Polbin.

1965. Dante. 700th Birth Anniv.
3087. **1079.** 4 k. black, bistre and maroon 25 5

1080. Blood Donor. **1081.** N. P. Kravkov (pharmacologist).

1965. Blood Donors. Multicoloured.
3088. 4 k. Type **1080** .. 12 5
3089. 4 k. Hand holding red carnation .. 12 5

1965. N. Kravkov. Birth Cent.
3090. **1081.** 4 k. multicoloured .. 12 5

1082. Figure-skaters. **1083.** Alsatian.

1965. European Figure-skating Championships, Moscow.
3091. **1082.** 6 k. red, black & grn. 20 8
See also No. 3108.

1965. World Ice-hockey Championships, Moscow. Design similar to T **1082** but depicting ice-hockey players.
3092. 4 k. red, blue and bistre .. 10 5

1965. Hunting and Service Dogs. Multicoloured.
3093. 1 k. Hound (horiz.) .. 5 5
3097. 2 k. Setter (horiz.) .. 5 5
3098. 3 k. Type **1083** 8 5
3099. 4 k. Fox terrier (horiz.)* 12 5
3100. 4 k. Pointer (horiz.)* .. 12 5
3101. 6 k. Borzol (horiz.) .. 20 5
3102. 6 k. Sheepdog 20 5
3094. 10 k. Collie 25 10
3095. 12 k. Husky (horiz.) .. 30 12
3096. 16 k. Caucasian sheepdog 35 15
*No. 3099, value in green, 3100, value in orange.

1084. R. Sorge (Soviet secret agent).

1965. Richard Sorge Commem.
3103. **1084.** 4 k. black and red .. 20 8

1085. I T.U. Emblem and Telecommunications Symbols.

1965. I.T.U. Cent.
3104. **1085.** 6 k. violet and blue 35 5

1965. Ice-hockey Championships. Optd. **ТАМПЕРЕ 1965 г.**
3105. **975.** 6 k. grey-blue and red 35 8

1086. Leonov in Space.

1965. Space Flight of "Voskhod 2" (1st issue.) Imperf. or perf.
3106. **1086.** 10 k. orge., blk. & bl. 30 10
See also Nos. 3138/9.

(**1087.**) **1088.** Soldier and Woman.

1965. Soviet Victory in European Figure-skating Championships. Optd. with T **1087**.
3108. **1082.** 6 k. red, blk. & grn. 35 20

1965. 20th Anniversaries.
3109. **1088.** 6 k. multicoloured .. 15 5
3110. – 6 k. multicoloured .. 15 5
3111. – 6 k. ochre and red .. 15 5
3112. – 6 k. multicoloured .. 20 5
3113. – 6 k. multicoloured .. 20 5
DESIGNS: No. 3109, T **1088** (Czech Liberation). 3110, Statue and emblems of development (Friendship with Hungary). 3111, Polish and Soviet arms (Polish-Soviet Friendship Treaty). 3112, Viennese buildings and Russian soldier (Freeing of Vienna). 3113, Liberation medal, Polish flag and building reconstruction (Freeing of Warsaw).
See also Nos. 3182 and 3232.

1089. Statue, Rockets and Globe. **1090.** Rockets and Radio-telescope.

1965. National Cosmonautics Day. Nos. 3117/18 on aluminium-surfaced paper.
3114. **1089.** 4 k. green, blk. & red 20 5
3115. – 12 k. pur., fluorescent red and blue .. 40 10
3116. – 16 k. blue, black, fluorescent red and green 50 15
3117. **1090.** 20 k. red, black and green on silver .. 1·40 65
3118. – 20 k. red, black and blue on silver .. 1·40 65
DESIGNS: 12 k. Statue and Globe. 16 k. Rockets and Globe. No. 3118, Globe, satellite and cosmonauts.

1091. Lenin.

1965. Lenin's 95th Birth Anniv.
3119. **1091.** 10 k. indigo, black and brown .. 35 8

1092. Poppies. **1093.** Red Flag, Reichstag Building and Broken Swastika.

1965. Flowers.
3120. **1092.** 1 k. red, lake & grn. 5 5
3121. – 3 k. yell., brn. & grn. 8 5
3122. – 4 k. lilac, blk. & grn. 10 5
3123. – 6 k. red, deep green and green 20 5
3124. – 10 k. yell., mar. & grn. 35 8
FLOWERS: 3 k. Marguerite. 4 k. Peony. 6 k. Carnation. 10 k. Tulips.

1965. Victory. 20th Anniv.
3125. **1093.** 1 k. blk., gold & red 8 5
3126. – 2 k. red, black & gold 12 5
3127. – 3 k. blue and gold .. 20 8
3128. – 4 k. violet and gold .. 25 10
3129. – 4 k. green and gold .. 25 10
3130. – 6 k. mag., brn. & gold 45 12
3131. – 10 k. pur., choc. & gold 80 15
3132. – 12 k. blk., red & gold 85 20
3133. – 16 k. claret and gold 1·00 20
3134. – 20 k. blk., red & gold 1·60 40

DESIGNS: 2 k. Soviet mother holding manifesto. 3 k. "The Battle for Moscow". 4 k. (No. 3128), "Partisan Mother". 4 k. (No. 3129), "Red Army Soldiers and Partisans". 6 k. Soldiers and flag. 10 k. "Mourning the Fallen Hero". 12 k. Soldier and worker holding bomb. 16 k. Victory celebrations. Red Square, Moscow 20 k. Soldier and machines of war.

1094. Marx and Lenin.

No. 3136 is similar in design to those issued by China and Hungary for the Postal Ministers' Congress, Peking, but this event is not mentioned on the stamp or in the Soviet philatelic bulletins.

1965. Marxism and Leninism.
3136. **1094.** 6 k. black and red .. 20 5

1095. Bolshoi Theatre.

1965. Int. Theatre Day.
3137. **1095.** 6 k. ochre, blk. & turq. 25 5

1096. Leonov.

1097. Y. Sverdlov (revolutionary).

1965. "Voskhod 2" Space Flight (2nd issue).
3138. **1096.** 6 k. violet and silver 15 5
3139. – 6 k. purple and silver 15 5
DESIGN: No. 3139, Beliaiev.

1965. 80th Birth Annivs.
3140. **1097.** 4 k. black & chestnut 12 5
3141. – 4 k. black and violet 12 5
PORTRAIT: No. 3141, J. Akhunbabaev (statesman).

1098. Otto Grotewohl (1st death anniv.).

1099. Telecommunications Satellites.

1965. Annivs. of Grotewohl and Thorez (Communist leaders).
3142. **1098.** 4 k. black & purple 15 5
3143. – 6 k. brown and red 20 5
DESIGN: 6 k. Maurice Thorez (65th birth anniv.).

1965. Int. Co-operation Year. Multicoloured.
3144. 3 k. Type **1099** 10 5
3145. 6 k. Star and sputnik .. 20 5
3146. 6 k. Foundry ladle, iron works and map of India 20 5
No. 3145 signifies peaceful uses of atomic energy and No. 3146 co-operation with India.

1100. Conf. Emblem, Chemical Plant and Symbols.

1102. V. Ivanov and Armoured Train.

1101. Serov (painter).

1965. 20th IUPAC Conf., Moscow.
3147. **1100.** 4 k. fluorescent red, black and turquoise 12 5

1965. V. A. Serov. Birth Cent. Inscr. "1965".
3148. **1101.** 4 k. black, chestnut and pale stone .. 55 12
3149. – 6 k. black and drab 80 20
DESIGN: 6 k. Full length portrait of Chaliapin (singer) by Serov.

1965. Famous Writers.
3150. **1102.** 4 k. black and purple 12 5
3151. – 4 k. black and violet 12 5
3152. – 4 k. black and blue .. 12 5
3153. – 4 k. black and grey .. 12 5
3154. – 4 k. blk., red & green 12 5
3155. – 4 k. black and brown 15 5
WRITERS AND ANNIVERSARIES: No. 3150, (70th birth anniv.). No. 3151, A. Kunanbaev and military parade. No. 3152, J. Rainis (Lettish poet: 90th birth anniv.). No. 3153, E. J. Vilde (Estonian author): 90th birth anniv.). No. 3154, M. Ch. Abegjan (Armenian writer and critic: 90th birth anniv.). No. 3155, M. L. Kropivnitsky and scene from play (Ukrainian playwright).

1103. Festival Emblem.

1965. Film Festival, Moscow.
3156. **1103.** 6 k. blk., gold & blue 15 5

1104. Concert Arena, Tallinn.

1105. Hand holding "Peace Flower".

1965. Incorporation of Estonia, Lithuania and Latvia in the U.S.S.R. 25th Anniv.
3157. **1104.** 4 k. multicoloured .. 12 5
3158. – 4 k. brown and red .. 12 5
3159. – 4 k. brn., red & blue 12 5
DESIGNS—VERT. No. 3158, Lithuanian girl and Arms. HORIZ. No. 3159, Latvian Flag and Arms.

1965. Peace Issue.
3160. **1105.** 6 k. yell., blk. & blue 15 5

1107. "Potemkin" Sailors' Monument, Odessa.

1965. 1905 Rebellion. 60th Anniv.
3161. **1107.** 4 k. blue and red .. 12 5
3162. – 4 k. grn., blk. & red 12 5
3163. – 4 k. grn., blk. & red 12 5
3164. – 4 k. brn., blk. & red 12 5
DESIGNS: No. 3162, Demonstrator up lamp-post. 3163, Defeated rebels. 3164, Troops at street barricade.

1108. G. G. Dej (Rumanian Communist).

1109. Power Station.

1965. G. Georgri-Dej Commem.
3165. **1108.** 4 k. black and red .. 12 5

1965. Industrial Progress.
3166. **1109.** 1 k. black, bistre, green and blue .. 5 5
3167. – 2 k. blk., orge. & yell. 8 5
3168. – 3 k. violet, yellow and ochre 10 5
3169. – 4 k. indigo, blue & red 20 5
3170. – 6 k. blue and bistre 20 5
3171. – 10 k. brown, yellow and orange .. 35 8
3172. – 12 k. turquoise & red 40 10
3173. – 16 k. pur., blue & blk. 80 15
DESIGNS: 2 k. Steel works. 3 k. Chemical works and formula. 4 k. Machine tools production. 6 k. Building construction. 10 k. Agriculture. 12 k. Communications and transport. 16 k. Scientific research.

1110. Relay Racing.

1111. Gymnastics.

1965. Trade Unions Spartakiad. Multicoloured.
3174. 4 k. Type **1110** 12 5
3175. 4 k. Gymnastics 12 5
3176. 4 k. Cycling 12 5

1965. Schoolchildren's Spartakiad.
3177. **1111.** 4 k. red & ultram. .. 12 5
3178. – 6 k. red, brn. & turq. 15 5
DESIGN: 6 k. Cycle-racing.

1112. Javelin-throwing and Running.

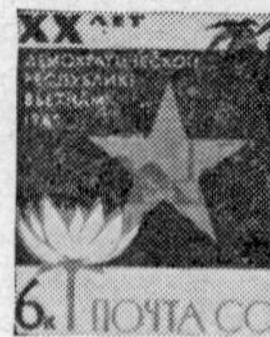

1113. Star, Palms and Lotus.

1965. American-Soviet Athletic Meeting. Kiev.
3179. **1112.** 4 k. red, brn. & lilac 10 5
3180. – 6 k. red, brown & grn. 20 5
3181. – 10 k. red, brn. & slate 30 10
DESIGNS: 6 k. High-jumping and putting the shot. 10 k. Throwing the hammer and hurdling.

1965. North Vietnamese People's Republic. 20th Anniv.
3182. **1113.** 6 k. multicoloured .. 15 5

1114. Worker with Hammer (World T.U. Federation).

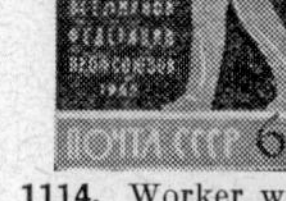

1116. P. K. Sternberg (astronomer: birth cent.).

1965. Int. Organisations. 20th Anniv.
3183. **1114.** 6 k. drab and plum 20 5
3184. – 6 k. brn., verm. & bl. 20 5
3185. – 6 k. cinnamon & turq. 20 5
DESIGNS: No. 3184, Torch and heads of three races (World Democratic Youth Federation). 3185, Woman holding dove (Int. Democratic Women's Federation).

1965. Scientists' Annivs.
3186. **1116.** 4 k. brown & ultram. 12 5
3187. – 4 k. black and purple 12 5
3188. – 4 k. blk., mar. & yell. 12 5
PORTRAITS: No. 3187, Ch. Valikhanov (scientific writer: death cent.). 3188, V. A. Kistyakovsky (scientist: birth cent.).

1117. Battleship "Potemkin".

1965. "Soviet Cinema Art". Designs showing scenes from films. Multicoloured.
3189. 4 k. Type **1117** 12 5
3190. 6 k. "Young Guard" .. 20 5
3191. 12 k. "A Soldier's Ballad" 40 12

1118. Mounted Postman and Map.

1965. History of the Russian Post Office.
3192. **1118.** 1 k. grn., chest. & vio. 12 5
3193. – 1 k. sep., ochre & grey 12 5
3194. – 2 k. brn., bl. & lilac 8 5
3195. – 4 k. blk., ochre & purr 20 5
3196. – 6 k. blk., grn. & brn. 25 8
3197. – 12 k. sepia, brn. & bl. 45 15
3198. – 16 k. plum, red & grey 50 20
DESIGNS: No. 3193, Mailcoach and map. 2 k. Early steam train and ship. 4 k. Mail-lorry and map. 6 k. Diesel train and various transport. 12 k. Moscow Post Office—electronic facing, sorting and cancelling machines. 16 k. Airport and Lenin.

1119. Sailing Ships in Antarctic.

1965. Polar Research Annivs.
3199. – 4 k. black, orge. & bl. 20 5
3200. – 4 k. black, orge. & bl. 20 5
3201. – 6 k. sepia and violet 25 5
3202. **1119.** 10 k. blk., drab & red 30 10
3203. – 16 k. blk., viol & brn. 45 15
DESIGNS—HORIZ. ($37\frac{1}{2} \times 25\frac{1}{2}$ mm.): No. 3199, Icebreakers "Taimir" and "Vaigitch" in Arctic (50th Anniv.). 3200, Atomic icebreaker "Lenin". 6 k. Dikson settlement (50th anniv.). 16 k. "Vostok" Antarctic station. SQUARE. 10 k. T **1119** (Lazarev Bellingshausen Expedition. 145th anniv.).

1120. Agricultural Academy.

1965. Academy of Agricultural Sciences, Moscow. Cent.
3205. **1120.** 4 k. vio., red & drab 15 5

1121. N. Poussin (self-portrait).

1122. Kremlin

1965. Nicolas Poussin (French painter). 300th Death Anniv.
3207. **1121.** 4 k. multicoloured .. 15 5

1965. New Year.
3208. **1122.** 4 k. vermilion, silver and black .. 20 5

1123. M. I. Kalinin (statesman).

1965. Kalinin. 90th Birth Anniv.
3209. **1123.** 4 k. lake and red .. 12 5

1124. Klyuchevski Volcano.

1965. Soviet Volcanoes. Multicoloured.
3210. 4 k. Type **1124** 15 5
3211. 12 k. Karumski Volcano (vert.) 40 10
3212. 16 k. Koryakski Volcano 55 15

1125. Oktyabrskaya Station, Moscow.

1965. Soviet Metro Stations.
3213. **1125.** 6 k. blue 20 5
3214. – 6 k. brown 20 5
3215. – 6 k. sepia 20 5
3216. – 6 k. green 20 5
STATIONS: No. 3214, Leninski Prospekt, Moscow. 3215, Moskovian Gate, Leningrad. 3216, Bolshevik Factory, Kiev.

1126. Buzzard. **1127.** "Red Star" (medal) and Scenes of Odessa.

1965. Birds of Prey. Birds in black.
3217. **1126.** 1 k. olive-grey .. 5 5
3218. – 2 k. brown 8 5
3219. – 3 k. olive 10 5
3220. – 4 k. drab 12 5
3221. – 10 k. purple-brown 30 8
3222. – 12 k. blue 40 10
3223. – 14 k. slate-blue .. 45 12
3224. – 16 k. brown-purple 45 15
BIRDS—VERT. 2 k. Kestrel. 3 k. Steppe eagle. 4 k. Kite. 10 k. Peregrine. 16 k. Gyr falcon. HORIZ. 12 k. Golden eagle. 14 k. Bearded vulture (or lammergeyer).

1965. Heroic Soviet Towns. Multicoloured.
3225. 10 k. Type **1127** 25 8
3226. 10 k. Leningrad 25 8
3227. 10 k. Kiev 25 8
3228. 10 k. Moscow 25 8
3229. 10 k. Brest-Litovak .. 25 8
3230. 10 k. Volgograd 25 8
3231. 10 k. Sebastopol 25 8

1128. Flag, Map and Parliament Building, Belgrade.

1965. Yugoslavia Republic. 20th Anniv.
3232. **1128.** 6 k. multicoloured .. 15 5

1129. Tu-134 Jet-Airliner.

1965. Soviet Civil Aviation. Multicoloured.
3233. 6 k. Type **1129** 25 5
3234. 10 k. An-24 .. .. 40 8
3235. 12 k. Mi-10 (helicopter) .. 40 10
3236. 16 k. Be-10 (flying-boat) 60 15
3237. 20 k. "Antey" turboprop 70 20

1130. "The Proposal of Marriage", after P. Fedotov (150th Birth Anniv.).

1965. Soviet Painters' Annivs.
3238. – 12 k. black and red 55 15
3239. **1130** 16 k. blue and red 80 25
DESIGN—VERT. 12 k. "A Collective Farm Watchman" (after S. Gerasimov: 80th Birth Anniv.).

1131. Crystallography Congress Emblem.

1966. Int. Congresses, Moscow.
3240. **1131.** 6 k. blk., bl. & bistre 20 5
3241. – 6 k. black, red & blue 20 5
3242. – 6 k. purple, slate-purple and black 20 5
3243. – 6 k. black and blue .. 15 5
3244. – 6 k. blk., red & yell. 15 5
CONGRESS EMBLEMS: No. 3241, Microbiology. 3242, Poultry-raising. 3243, Oceanography. No. 3244, Mathematics.

1132. 19th-cent. Statuettes.

1966. Dmitrov Ceramic Works. Bicent. Multicoloured.
3245. 6 k. Type **1132** 15 5
3246. 10 k. Modern tea-set .. 30 10

1133. Rolland and Scene from Novel. **1134.** Mongol Horseman.

1966. Romain Rolland (French writer). Birth Cent. and Eugene Potier (French poet). 150th Birth Anniv.
3247. **1133.** 4 k. chestnut & blue 12 5
3248. – 4 k. brn., red and blk. 12 5
DESIGN: No. 3248, Potier and revolutionary scene.

1966. Soviet-Mongolian Treaty. 20th Anniv.
3249. **1134.** 4 k. multicoloured .. 12 5

„ЛУНА-9"—НА ЛУНЕ!
3.2.1966
(**1135.**)

1966. Landing of "Luna 9" Rocket on Moon. Optd. with T **1135.**
3250. **958.** 6 k. red, black & blue 60 20

1136. M.V. "Ob".

1966. Soviet Antarctic Expedition. 10th Anniv.
3251. **1136.** 10 k. lake and silver 40 15
3252. – 10 k. lake, silver & bl. 40 15
3253. – 10 k. lake, silver & bl. 40 15
DESIGNS—TRIANGULAR: No. 3252, Snow vehicle. DIAMOND: 3253, Antarctic Map. This stamp is partly perf. across the centre.

1137. M. Dyalil and Scene from Poem.

1966. Writers.
3254. **1137.** 4 k. black and brn. 12 5
3255. – 4 k. black and grn. 12 5
3256. – 4 k. black & green 12 5
WRITERS: No. 3254 (Azerbaijan writer: 60th birth anniv.). No. 3255, Akpb Akopyan (Armenian poet: birth cent.). No. 3256, Djalil Mamedkulizade (Azerbaijan writer: birth cent.).

1138. Lenin (after bust by Kibalnikov).

1966. Lenin's 96th Birth Anniv.
3257. **1138.** 10 k. gold and green 65 10
3258. 10 k. silver and red 50 12

1139. N. Ilyin. **1140.** Scene from "Alive and Dead".

1966. Soviet Heroes.
3259. **1139.** 4 k. violet and red .. 12 5
3260. – 4 k. lilac and blue .. 12 5
3261. – 4 k. sepia and green 12 5
PORTRAITS: No. 3260, G. Kravchenko. 3261, A. Uglovsky.

1966. Soviet Cinema Art.
3262. **1140.** 4 k. blk., grn. & red 10 5
3263. – 10 k. black and blue 20 8
DESIGN: 10 k. Scene from "Hamlet".

1141. Kremlin and Inscription.

Учредительная конференция
Всесоюзного общества
филателистов. 1966
(**1142.**)

1966. 23rd CPSU Conf., Moscow.
3264. **1141.** 4 k. gold, red & blue 12 5

1966. Philatelists All-Union Society Conf. No. 3198 optd. with T **1142.**
3265. 16 k. plum, red and grey 80 20

1143. Ice-Skating.

1966. 2nd People's Winter Spartakiad.
3266. **1143.** 4 k. ultram., red & ol. 12 5
3267. – 6 k. red, lake & lilac 20 5
3268. – 10 k. lake, red & blue 40 8
DESIGNS: Inscription, emblem and—6 k. Ice-hockey. 10 k. Skiing. Nos. 3266/8 are each perf. across the centre.

1144. M. V. "Alexander Pushkin". **1145.** Government Building, Frunze.

1966. Soviet Transport.
3269. – 4 k. multicoloured .. 12 5
3270. – 6 k. multicoloured .. 15 5
3271. – 10 k. multicoloured 35 8
3272. **1144.** 12 k. multicoloured 35 8
3273. – 16 k. multicoloured 45 12
DESIGNS—HORIZ. 4 k. Electric train. 6 k. Map of Lenin Volga-Baltic canal system. 16 k. Silhouette of liner on Globe. VERT. 10 k. Canal lock. Nos. 3271/3 Commemorates the Inaug. of Leningrad-Montreal Sea Service.

1966. Kirghizia. 40th Anniv.
3274. **1145.** 4 k. red 12 5

1146. S. M. Kirov (80th Birth Anniv.) **1147.** A. Fersman (mineralogist).

1966. Soviet Personalities.
3275. **1146.** 4 k. brown 12 5
3276. – 4 k. green 12 5
3277. – 4 k. violet 12 5
PORTRAITS: No. 3276, G. Ordzhonikidze (80th birth anniv.). 3277, Ton Yakir (military commander, 70th birth anniv.).

1966. Soviet Scientists. Multicoloured. Colours of name-panels below.
3279. **1147.** 4 k. blue 15 5
3280. – 4 k. brown 15 5
3281. – 4 k. violet 15 5
3282. – 4 k. brown & blue .. 15 5
PORTRAITS: No. 3280, D. Zabolotny (microbiologist). 3281, M. Shatelen (electrical engineer). No. 3282, O. Y. Shmidt (arctic explorer).

„Луна-10"—XXIII съезду КПСС
(**1148.**)

1966. Launching of "Luna 10". As No. 3284, but imperf., optd with T **1148.**
3283. **1149.** 10 k. multicoloured 25 10

1149. Arrowheads, "Luna 9" and Orbit.

1966. Cosmonautics Day. Multicoloured.
3284. 10 k. Type **1149** 25 8
3285. 12 k. Rocket-launching and different orbit .. 35 12

1150. "Lightning I" in Orbit. **1151.** Ernst Thalmann (80th birth anniv.)

1966. Launching of "Lightning I". Inscr. "23–IV–1965".
3286. **1150.** 10 k. multicoloured 25 10

1966. Prominent Leaders.
3287. **1151.** 6 k. claret 20 5
3288. – 6 k. violet 15 5
3289. – 6 k. brown 15 5
PORTRAITS: No. 3288, W. Pieck (90th birth anniv.). 3289, Sun Yat-sen (birth cent.).

1153. Spaceman and Soldier.

1966. 15th Young Communist League Congress.
3290. 1153. 4 k. black & cerise .. 12 5

1154. Ice-hockey player.

1966. Soviet Victory in World Ice-hockey Championships.
3291. 1154. 10 k. multicoloured 30 8

1155. N. I. Kuznetsov. 1156. Tchaikovsky.

1966. War Heroes. Guerilla Fighters.
3292. 1155. 4 k. black and green 12 5
3293. 4 k. black and yellow 12 5
3294. 4 k black and blue 12 5
3295. 4 k. black and mag. 12 5
3296. 4 k. black and violet 12 5
PORTRAITS: No. 3293, I. Sudmalis. 3294, A. Morozova. 3295. F. Strelets. 3296 T. Bumazhkov.

1966. 3rd Int. Tchaikovsky Music Competition, Moscow.
3297. – 4 k. black red & yell. 10 5
3298. 1156. 6 k. black, red & yell. 20 5
3299. – 16 k. blk., red & blue 45 15
DESIGNS: 4 k. Moscow State Conservatoire of Music. 16 k. Tchaikovsky's house and museum, Klin.

1157. Running.

1966. Sports Events.
3300. 1157. 4 k. brn., olive & grn. 10 5
3301. – 6 k. blk., bis. & orge. 20 5
3302. – 12 k. blk., bistre & bl. 30 8
DESIGNS: 6 k. Weightlifting. 12 k. Wrestling.

1159. Gold Medal and Chess Pieces.

1966. World Chess Title Match.
3303. 1159. 6 k. multicoloured .. 20 5

INDEX

Countries can be quickly located by referring to the index at the end of this volume.

1160. Jules Rimet Cup and Football.

1966. World Cup Football Championships and World Fencing Championships.
3304. 1160. 4 k. blk., gold & verm. 12 5
3305. 6 k. multicoloured .. 20 5
3306. 12 k. multicoloured 35 10
3307. 16 k. multicoloured 55 15
DESIGNS: 6 k. Footballers. 12 k. Fencers. 16 k. Fencing emblems and Globe.

1161. Sable, Lake Baikal and Animals (Reduced size illustration. Actual size 80×26 mm.).

1966. Barguzin Nature Reserve.
3308. 1161. 4 k. black and blue 12 5
3309. – 6 k. black & maroon 20 5
DESIGN: 6 k. Map of Reserve, and bear.
See also No. 3465.

1162. Lotus Plants. 1163. "Venus 3"—Medal, Globe and Flight Trajectory.

1966. Sukhumi Botanical Gardens. 125th Anniv.
3310. 1162. 3 k. cerise, yell. & grn. 8 5
3311. – 6 k. bistre, sep. & bl. 20 5
3312. – 12 k. cerise, green and turquoise .. 25 10
DESIGNS: 6 k. Palms and cypresses. 12 k. Water-lilies.

1966. Space Achievements.
3313. 1163. 6 k. blk., silver & red 20 8
3314. – 6 k. indigo, bl. & brn. 20 8
3315. – 6 k. ochre and blue 20 8
3316. – 6 k. multicoloured .. 25 5
3317. – 6 k. pink, mve. & blk. 25 5
DESIGNS: No. 3314, Space-dogs, Ugolek and Veterok. No. 3315, "Luna 10". No. 3316, "Molniya 1". No. 3317, "Luna 2's" pennant, Earth and Moon.

1164. Itkol.

1966. Tourist Resorts. Multicoloured.
3318. 1 k. Type 1164 .. 5 5
3319. 4 k. Motor-ship on the Volga .. 12 5
3320. 6 k. Archway, Leningrad 20 5
3321. 10 k. Kislovodsk .. 25 8
3322. 12 k. Ismail Samani Mausoleum Bokhara .. 45 10
3323. 16 k. Sochi (Black Sea) .. 55 12
The 6 k. is 27½×28 mm.

1166. Congress Emblem. 1167. Peace Dove and Japanese Crane.

1966. 7th Consumers' Co-operative Societies' Congress, Moscow.
3325. 1166. 4 k. yellow & brown 12 5

1966. Soviet-Japanese Meeting, Khabarovsk.
3326. 1167. 6 k. black and red .. 20 8

1168. Scene from poem "The Knight in the Tiger's Skin", after I. Toidze.

1966. Shota Rustaveli (Georgian poet). 800th Birth Anniv.
3327. 1168. 3 k. black on green 10 5
3328. – 4 k. sepia on yellow 12 5
3329. – 6 k. black on blue .. 25 5
DESIGNS: 4 k. Rustaveli, after bas-relief by Y. Nikoladze. 6 k. "Avtandil at a Mountain Spring", after engraving by S. Kabuladze.

1169. Arms, Moscow Skyline and Fireworks. 1170. Trawler, Net and Map of Lake Baikal.

1966. October Revolution. 49th Anniv.
3331. 1169. 4 k. multicoloured .. 10 5

1966. Fish Resources of Lake Baikal. Multicoloured.
3332. 2 k. Grayling 5 5
3333. 4 k. Sturgeon 8 5
3334. 6 k. Type 1170 .. .. 12 5
3335. 10 k. "Omul" 20 8
3336. 12 k. "Sig" (salmon) .. 25 12
The 2, 4, 10 and 12 k. are horiz.

1171. "Agriculture and Industry".

1966. 23rd Communist Party Congress.
3337. 1171. 4 k. silver & chestnut 10 5
3338. – 4 k. silver and blue .. 10 5
3339. – 4 k. silver and red .. 10 5
3340. – 4 k. silver & verm... 10 5
3341. – 4 k. silver and green 10 5
DESIGNS (MAP AS T 1171 WITH SYMBOLS OF): No. 3338, "Communications and Transport". 3339, "Education and Technology". 3340, "Increased Productivity". 3341, "Power Resources".

1172. Government Buildings, Kishinev.

1966. Kishinev (Moldavian Republic). 500th Anniv.
3342. 1172. 4 k. multicoloured .. 12 5

1173. Clouds, Rain and Decade Emblem. 1174. Nikitin Monument, Map and Ship.

1966. Int. Hydrological Decade.
3343. 1173. 6 k. multicoloured .. 15 5

1966. Nikitin's Voyage to India.
3344. 1174. 4 k. blk., grn. & yell. 12 5

1175. Scene from "Nargiz".

1966. Azerbaijan Operas.
3345. 1175. 4 k. ochre and black 15 5
3346. – 4 k. green and black 15 5
DESIGN: No. 3346, Scene from "Kehzoglu".

1176. "Luna 9" and Moon. 1177. Agricultural and Chemical Symbols.

1966.
3347. – 1 k. brown 5 5
3348. 1176. 2 k. violet 5 5
3349. – 3 k. purple 5 5
3350. – 4 k. vermilion .. 8 5
3351. – 6 k. blue 15 5
3352. – 10 k. olive .. 20 8
3353. – 12 k. brown .. 30 8
3354. – 16 k. ultramarine .. 35 12
3355. – 20 k. red, blue & drab 45 15
3566. – 20 k. red 65 20
3356. 1177. 30 k. green .. 65 25
3357. – 50 k. ult., blue & grey 1·10 45
3568. – 50 k. ultramarine .. 1·60 50
3358. – 1 r. brown and red .. 3·75 1·00
3569. – 1 r. brown and black 2·25 90
DESIGNS. As T 1176: 1 k. Palace of Congresses, Kremlin. 3 k. Youth, girl and Lenin emblem. 4 k. Arms and hammer and sickle emblem. 6 k. "Communications"—airliner and sputnik. 10 k. Soldier and star emblem. 12 k. Furnaceman. 16 k. Girl with dove. As T 1177. 20 k. Worker's demonstration and flower. 50 k. Postal communications. 1 r. Lenin and Industrial emblems.

1178. "Presenting Arms". 1180. Campaign Meeting.

1966. People's Voluntary Corps. 25th Anniv.
3359. 1178. 4 k. chocolate & red 12 5

1966 "Hands off Vietnam".
3360. 1180. 6 k. multicoloured .. 20 5

1181. Servicemen.

1966. Spanish Civil War. 30th Anniv.
3361. 1181. 6 k. blk., red & ochre 15 5

1182. Ostankino TV Tower, "Molniya 1" (satellite) and "1967". 1184. Statue, Tank and Medal. 1185. Cervantes and Don Quixote.

1183. Flight Diagram.

1966. New Year and "October Revolution. 50th Year".
3362. **1182.** 4 k. multicoloured.. 12 5

1966. Space Flight and Moon landing of "Luna 9".
3363. **1183.** 10 k. black & silver 25 15
3364. – 10 k. red and silver 25 15
3365. – 10 k. black and silver 25 15
DESIGNS—SQUARE (25 × 25 mm.). No. 3364, Arms of Russia and Lunar pennant. HORIZ. 3365, "Lunar 9" on Moon's surface.

1966. Battle of Moscow. 25th Anniv.
3366. – 4 k. chestnut .. 12 5
3367. **1184.** 6 k. ochre and sepia 15 5
3368. – 10 k. yellow & brown 25 8
DESIGNS—HORIZ. (60×28 mm.): 4 k. Soviet troops advancing. 10 k. "Moscow at peace"—Kremlin, Sun and "Defence of Moscow" medal.

1966. Cervantes. 350th Death Anniv.
3369. **1185.** 6 k. brown, green and emerald 15 5

1187. Bering's Ship and Map of Komandor Islands.

1966. Soviet Far Eastern Territories. Multi-coloured.
3370. 1 k. Type **1187** 5 5
3371. 2 k. Medny Island and map 8 5
3372. 4 k. Petropavlovsk Harbour, Kamchatka .. 12 5
3373. 6 k. Geyser, Kamchatka (vert.) 20 5
3374. 10 k. Avatchinskaya Bay, Kamchatka 30 8
3375. 12 k. Fur seals, Bering Is. 40 10
3376. 16 k. Guillemot colony, Kurile Islands 45 15

1189. "The Lute Player" (Caravaggio).

1966. Art Treasures of the Hermitage Museum, Leningrad.
3377. – 4 k. black on yellow 12 5
3378. – 6 k. black on grey 20 5
3379. – 10 k. black on lilac.. 25 8
3380. – 12 k. black on green 35 10
3381. **1189.** 16 k. black on buff.. 40 15
DESIGNS—HORIZ. 4 k. "Golden Stag" (from Scythian battle-shield (6th cent. B.C.). VERT. 6 k. Persian silver jug (5th cent. A.D.). 10 k. Statue of Voltaire (Houdon, 1781). 12 k. Malachite vase (Urals, 1840).

1190. Sea-water Distilling Apparatus.

1967. World Fair, Montreal.
3382. **1190.** 4 k. blk., silver & grn. 10 5
3383. – 6 k. multicoloured.. 20 5
3384. – 10 k. multicoloured 25 10
DESIGNS—VERT. 6 k. "Atomic Energy" (explosion and symbol). HORIZ. 10 k. Space-station "Proton I".

1191. Lieut. B. I. Sizov. **1193.** Cine-camera and Film "Flower".

1192. Woman's Face amid Flowers.

1967. War Heroes.
3386. **1191.** 4 k. brown on yellow 12 5
3387. – 4 k. brown on drab.. 12 5
DESIGN: No. 3387, Private V. V. Khodyrev.

1967. Int. Women's Day.
3388. **1192.** 4 k. red, violet & grn. 12 5

1967. 5th Int. Film Festival, Moscow.
3389. **1193.** 6 k. multicoloured.. 15 5

1194. Factory Ship.

1967. Soviet Fishing Industry. Each black, red, drab and blue.
3390. 6 k. Type **1194** 20 5
3391. 6 k. Refrigerator ship .. 20 5
3392. 6 k. Crab-canning ship .. 20 5
3393. 6 k. Trawler 20 5
3394. 6 k. Black Sea seiner .. 20 5

11·5. Newspaper Cuttings, Hammer and Sickle. **1196.** I.S.O. Congress Emblem.

1967. Newspaper "Isvestia". 50th Anniv.
3395. **1195.** 4 k. multicoloured.. 12 5

1967. Moscow Congresses.
3396. 6 k. turq.. black & blue .. 15 5
3397. 6 k. red, black and blue.. 15 5
DESIGNS: No. 3396, T **1196** (7th Congress of Int. Standards Assn. "I.S.O."). 3397, "V" emblem of 5th Int. Mining Congress.

1197. I.T.Y. Emblem.

1967. Int. Tourist Year.
3398. **1197.** 4 k. blk., silver & blue 12 5

Вена - 1967
(1198.) **1200.** "Lenin as Schoolboy".

1199. A. A. Leonov in Space.

1967. Soviet Victory in World Ice-hockey Championships (1967). No. 3291 optd. with T **1198**.
3399. **1154.** 10 k. multicoloured 30 12

1967. Cosmonautics Day. Multicoloured.
3400. 4 k. Type **1199** 12 5
3401. 10 k. Rocket-launching from space-pad .. 30 8
3402. 16 k. "Luna 10" over Moon 40 15

1967. Lenin's 97th Birth Anniv.
3403. **1200.** 2 k. sepia, yell. & grn. 12 5
3404. – 3 k. brown and lake 20 5
3405. – 4 k. green, yellow and olive.. .. 25 5
3406. – 6 k. silver, blk. & bl. 45 8
3407. – 10 k. bl., blk. & silver 85 10
3408. – 10 k. black and gold 25 10
SCULPTURES—VERT. 3 k. Lenin's monument, Ulyanovsk. 6 k. Lenin's bust (after Neroda). 10 k. "Lenin as Leader" (after Andreiev), HORIZ. 4 k. "Lenin at Razliv" (after Pinchuk).

1201. M. F. Shmyrev. **1203.** Marshal Biryuzov.

1202. Transport crossing Ice on Lake Ladoga.

1967. War Heroes.
3409. **1201.** 4 k. brown & chestnut 10 5
3410. – 4 k. brown & ultram. 10 5
3411. – 4 k. brown and violet 10 5
DESIGNS: No. 3410, Major-General S. V. Rudnev. 3411, First Lieut. M. S. Kharchenke.

1967. Siege of Leningrad, 1941-42.
3412. **1202.** 4 k. grey, red & cream 10 5

1967. Biryuzov Commem.
3413. **1203.** 4 k. green and yellow 10 5

1204. Minsk Old and New. **1205.** Red Cross and Tulip.

1967. Minsk. 900th Anniv.
3414. **1204.** 4 k. green and black 10 5

1967. Russian Red Cross. Cent.
3415. **1205.** 4 k. red and ochre.. 10 5

1206. Russian Stamps of 1918 and 1967.

1967. U.S.S.R. 50th Anniv. Philatelic Exn. Moscow.
3416. **1206.** 20 k green and blue 50 20

1207. Komsomolsk-on-Amur and Map. **1208.** Motor-cyclist (International Motor Rally, Moscow).

1967. Komsomolsk-on-Amur. 35th Anniv.
3418. **1207.** 4 k. brown and red.. 20 5

1967. Sports and Pastimes. Int. Events.
3419. – 1 k. brn. bistre & grn. 5 5
3420. – 2 k. lake-brown .. 5 5
3421. – 3 k. ultramarine .. 8 5
3422. – 4 k. turquoise-blue 10 5
3423. – 6 k. purple and bistre 12 8
3424. **1208.** 10 k. purple and lilac 30 10
DESIGNS AND EVENTS: 1 k. Draughts-board and players (World Draughts Championships). 2 k. Throwing the javelin. 3 k. Running. 4 k. Long-jumping (all preliminary events for Europa Cup Games). 6 k. Gymnast (World Gymnastics Championships).

1209. G. D. Gai (soldier). **1210.** Games Emblem and Cup.

1967. Commander G. D. Gai Commem.
3426. **1209.** 4 k. black and red.. 12 5

1967. Celebrating 50th Anniv. of October Revolution. Schoolchildren's Games, Leningrad.
3427. **1210.** 4 k. red, blk. & silver 12 5

1211. Spartakiad Emblem and Cup.

1967. 4th People's Spartakiad.
3428. 4 k. black, red and silver 10 5
3429. 4 k. black, red and silver 10 5
3430. 4 k. black, red and silver 10 5
3431. 4 k. black, red and silver 10 5
DESIGNS: Each with Cup. No. 3428, T **1211**. 3429, Gymnastics. 3430, Diving. 3431, Cycling.

1212. V. G. Klochkov (Soviet hero).

1967. Klochkov Commem.
3432. **1212.** 4 k. black and red.. 10 5

1213. Crest, Flag and Capital of Moldavia.

1214. Telecommunications Symbols.

Inscr. at foot as shown above.

1967. October Revolution. 50th Anniv. (1st Issue.) Designs showing crests, flags and capitals of the Soviet Republics. Multicoloured.

3433. 4 k. Armenia 10 5
3434. 4 k. Azerbaijan 10 5
3435. 4 k. Byelorussia 10 5
3436. 4 k. Estonia 10 5
3437. 4 k. Georgia 10 5
3438. 4 k. Kazakhstan 10 5
3439. 4 k. Kirghizia 10 5
3440. 4 k. Latvia 10 5
3441. 4 k. Lithuania 10 5
3442. 4 k. Type **1213** 10 5
3443. 4 k. Russia 10 5
3444. 4 k. Tadzhikistan 10 5
3445. 4 k. Turkmenistan 10 5
3446. 4 k. Ukraine 10 5
3447. 4 k. Uzbekistan 10 5
3448. 4 k. Soviet Arms 10 5

No. 3448 is size 47 × 32 mm.

1967. "Progress of Communism".

3449. **1214.** 4 k. red, pur. & silver 15 5

1215. Japanese Crane and Dove.

1967. Soviet-Japanese Friendship.

3450. **1215.** 16 k. sepia, blk. & red 40 12

1216. Karl Marx and Title Page.

1967. Karl Marx's "Das Kapital". Cent.

3451. **1216.** 4 k. brown and red .. 15 5

1217. Blue Fox.

1219. Krasnodon Memorial.

1218. Ice-skating.

1967. Fur-bearing Animals.

3452. **1217.** 2 k. cobalt, blk. & brn. 8 5
3453. – 4 k. blue, blk. & drab 12 5
3454. – 6 k. ochre, blk. & grn. 20 5
3455. – 10 k. brn., blk. & grn. 25 5
3456. – 12 k. black, ochre and violet .. 30 8
3457. – 16 k. sepia, blk. & yell. 35 12
3458. – 20 k. brown, black & turquoise 40 15

DESIGNS—VERT. 4 k. Silver Fox. 12 k. Ermine. 16 k. Sable. HORIZ. 6 k. Red Fox. 10 k. Musk-rat (musquash). 20 k. Otter.

1967. Winter Olympic Games, Grenoble (1968). Multicoloured.

3459. 2 k. Type **1218** 5 5
3460. 3 k. Ski-jumping .. 12 5
3461. 4 k. Games emblem .. 12 5
3462. 10 k. Ice-hockey 30 8
3463. 12 k. Skiing 40 12

The 4 k. is vert.

1967. Krasnodon Defence. 25th Anniv.

3464. **1219.** 4 k. blk., yell. & pur. 8 5

1219a. Map and Snow Leopard. (Reduced size illustration. Actual size 80 × 26 mm.).

1967. Cedar Fall Nature Reserve.

3465. **1219a.** 10 k. black and bistre 30 10

1220. Badge and Fighter Aircraft.

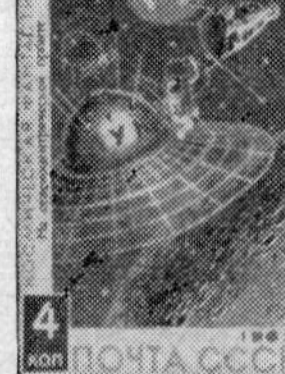

1222. Cosmonauts in Space.

1221. Militiaman and Soviet Crest.

1967. French "Normandie-Niemen" Fighter Squadron. 25th Anniv.

3466. **1220.** 6 k. red, blue & gold 15 5

1967. Soviet Militia. 50th Anniv.

3467. **1221.** 4 k. red & ultram. .. 12 5

1967. Space Exploration. Multicoloured.

3468. 4 k. Type **1222** 12 5
3469. 6 k. Men on the Moon .. 20 5
3470. 10 k. Cosmic vehicle .. 30 8
3471. 12 k. Planetary landscape 40 10
3472. 16 k. Imaginary spacecraft 45 15

The 6 k. and 12 k. are horiz.

1223. Red Star and Soviet Crest.

1967. October Revolution. 50th Anniv. (2nd Issue.) "50 Heroic Years". Designs showing paintings and Soviet Arms. Multicoloured.

3473. 4 k. Type **1223** .. 12 5
3474. 4 k. "Lenin addressing Congress" (Serov—1955) .. 12 5
3475. 4 k. "Lenin explaining the Goerlo map" (Schmatko—1957) .. 12 5
3476. 4 k. "The First Cavalry" (Grekov—1924) .. 12 5
3477. 4 k. "Students" (Yoganson—1928) .. 12 5
3478. 4 k. "People's Friendship" (Karpov—1924) .. 12 5
3479. 4 k. "Dawn of the Five-Year Plan" (construction work, Romas—1934) 12 5
3480. 4 k. "Farmers' Holiday" (Gerasimov—1937) .. 12 5
3481. 4 k. "Victory in World War II" (Korolev—1965) .. 12 5
3482. 4 k. "Builders of Communism" (Merpert and Skriokov—1965) .. 12 5

1224. S. Katayama (founder Japanese Communist Party).

1225. T.V. Tower, of Moscow.

1967. Katayama Commem.

3484. **1224.** 6 k. green 15 5

1967. Opening of Ostankino T.V. Tower, Moscow.

3486. **1225.** 16 k. black, silver and orange .. 40 15

1226. Yurmala.

1967. Baltic Health Resorts. Multicoloured.

3487. 4 k. Type **1226** .. 10 5
3488. 6 k. Narva 15 5
3489. 10 k. Druskinikai .. 20 8
3490. 12 k. Zelenogradsk (vert.) 25 10
3491. 16 k. Svetlogorsk (vert.) 35 15

1227. K.G.B. Emblem.

1228. Moscow View.

1967. State Security Commission (K.G.B.). 50th Anniv.

3492. **1227.** 4 k. red, silver & ult. 12 5

1967. New Year.

3493. **1228.** 4 k. brown, pink and silver 12 5

1229. Revolutionaries at Kharkov, and Monument.

1967. Ukraine Republic. 50th Anniv.

3494. **1229.** 4 k. multicoloured .. 10 5
3495. – 6 k. multicoloured .. 15 5
3496. – 10 k. multicoloured 20 10

DESIGNS: 6 k. Hammer and sickle, and industrial and agricultural scenes. 10 k. Unknown Soldier's monument, Kiev, and young Ukrainians with welcoming bread and salt.

1230. Kremlin Towers.

1232. Unknown Soldier's Tomb, Kremlin.

1231. Moscow Badge, Lenin's Tomb and Rockets.

1967. Kremlin Buildings.

3497. **1230.** 4 k. brn., pur. & grn. 12 5
3498. – 6 k. brn., grn. & yell. 20 5
3499. – 10 k. brown and slate 30 8
3500. – 12 k. green, violet and cream .. 35 10
3501. – 16 k. brown, red and cinnamon .. 40 15

DESIGNS—HORIZ. 6 k. Cathedral of the Annunciation. VERT. 10 k. Towers (different). 12 k. Ivan the Great's bell-tower. 16 k. Spassky tower and gateway.

1967. "50 Years of Communist Development".

3502. **1231.** 4 k. lake 10 5
3503. – 4 k. brown 10 5
3504. – 4 k. green 10 5
3505. – 4 k. blue 10 5
3506. – 4 k. deep blue .. 10 5

DESIGNS—HORIZ. No. 3503, Computer-tape, cogwheel and industrial scene. 3504, Ear of wheat and grain silo. 3505, Microscope, radar antennae and Moscow University. VERT. 3506, T.V. Tower, ship, railway bridge and jetliner.

1967. "Unknown Soldier" Commem.

3507. **1232.** 4 k. scarlet .. 10 5

1233. "The Interrogation" (Yoganson).

1967. Paintings in the Tretyakov Gallery Moscow. Multicoloured.

3508. 3 k. Type **1233** 10 5
3509. 4 k. "The Sea-shore" (Aivazovsky) 12 5
3510. 4 k. "The Lace-maker" (Tropinin) (vert.) .. 12 5
3511. 6 k. "The Bakery" (Yablonskaya) 20 5
3512. 6 k. "Alexander Nevsky" (part of triptych by Korin) (vert.) .. 20 5
3513. 6 k. "Boyarynia Morozov's Farewell" (Surikov) .. 20 5
3514. 10 k. "The Swan Maiden" (Vrubel) (vert.) .. 35 10
3515 10 k. "The Arrest" (Repin) 35 10
3516. 16 k. "Moscow Suburb in February" (Nissky) 45 15

Nos. 3511/3 are larger 60 × 34 mm.

1234. Congress Emblem. 1235. Lieut. S. G. Baikov.

1968. 14th Soviet Trade Unions Congress, Moscow.
3517. **1234.** 6 k. red and green .. 15 5

1968. War Heroes.
3518. **1235.** 4 k. black and blue.. 10 5
3519. – 4 k. blue and green.. 10 5
3520. – 4 k. black and red.. 10 5
PORTRAITS: No. 3519, Lieut. P. L. Guchenko. 3520, A. A. Pokaltchuk.

1236. Racehorses. 1237. M. Ulyanova.

1968. Soviet Horse-Breeding.
3521. **1236.** 4 k. blk., pur. & blue 10 5
3522. – 6 k. black, blue & red 20 5
3523. – 10 k. blk., brn. & turq. 25 8
3524. – 12 k. blk., grn. & brn. 35 10
3525. – 16 k. blk., red & grn. 45 15
DESIGNS (each with horse's head and horses "in the field"). VERT. 6 k. Show horses. 12 k. Show-jumpers. HORIZ. 10 k. Trotters. 16 k. Hunters.

1968. M. I. Ulyanova (Lenin's sister). 90th Birth Anniv.
3526. **1237.** 4 k. blue and green.. 10 5

1238. Red Star and Forces' Flags.

1968. Soviet Armed Forces. 50th Anniv. Multicoloured.
3527. 4 k. Type **1238** 10 5
3528. 4 k. Lenin addressing recruits 10 5
3529. 4 k. Recruiting poster and volunteers 10 5
3530. 4 k. Red Army entering Vladivostok, 1922, and monument 10 5
3531. 4 k. Dnieper Dam and statue "On Guard".. 10 5
3532. 4 k. "Liberators" poster and tanks in the Ukraine 10 5
3533. 4 k. "To the West" poster and retreating Germans fording river 10 5
3534. 4 k. Stalingrad battle monument and German prisoners-of-war .. 10 5
3535. 4 k. Victory parade, Red Square, Moscow, and monument, Treptow (Berlin) 10 5
3536. 4 k. Rockets, tank, warships and Red Flag .. 10 5
Nos. 3527 and 3536 are vert. The rest are horiz.

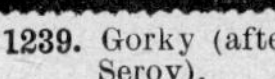

1239. Gorky (after Serov). 1240. Fireman and Appliances.

1968. Maxim Gorky (writer). Birth Cent.
3538. **1239.** 4 k. brown and drab 10 5

1968. Soviet Fire Services. 50th Anniv.
3539. **1240.** 4 k. black and red.. 10 5

1241. Linked Satellites. 1242. N. N. Popudrenko.

1968. Space Link of "Cosmos" Satellites.
3540. **1241.** 6 k. blk., gold & pur. 15 5

1968. War Heroes.
3541. **1242.** 4 k. black and green 10 5
3542. – 4 k. black and lilac.. 10 5
DESIGN: No. 3542, P. P. Vershigora.

1243. Protective Hand. 1245. Lenin.

1244. Cosmonaut filming in Space.

1968. "Solidarity with Vietnam".
3543. **1243.** 6 k. multicoloured.. 15 5

1968. Cosmonautics Day. Multicoloured.
3544. 4 k. Type **1244** 15 5
3545. 6 k. Satellite link in Space 20 5
3546. 10 k. Venus probe .. 40 15

1968. Lenin's 98th Birth Anniv.
3547. **1245.** 4 k. multicoloured.. 10 5
3548. – 4 k. blk., red & gold 10 5
3549. – 4 k. brn., red & gold 10 5
DESIGNS: No. 3548, Lenin speaking in Red Square. No. 3549, Lenin in peaked cap speaking from lorry during parade.

1246. A. Navoi. 1247. Karl Marx.

1968. Alisher Navoi (Uzbek poet). 525th Birth Anniv.
3550. **1246.** 4 k. brown 10 5

1968. Karl Marx. 150th Birth Anniv.
3551. **1247.** 4 k. black and red.. 12 5

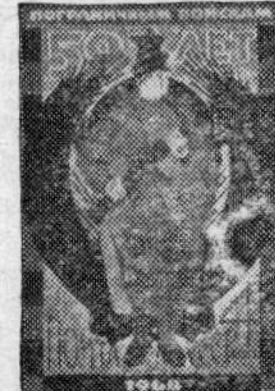

1248. Frontier Guard. 1249. Gem and Congress Emblem. (8th Enriching Minerals Congress).

1968. Soviet Frontier Guards. 50th Anniv. Multicoloured.
3552. 4 k. Type **1248** 10 5
3553. 6 k. Jubilee badge .. 15 5

1968. "Int. Congresses and Assemblies".
3554. **1249.** 6 k. deep blue, new blue and green .. 15 5
3555. – 6 k. gold, orge. & brn 15 5
3556. – 6 k. gold, black & red 15 5
3557. – 6 k. multicoloured.. 15 5
DESIGNS: No. 3555, Power stations, pylon and emblem (7th World Power Conference). No. 3556, Beetle and emblem (13th Entomological Congress. No. 3557, Roses and emblem (4th Congress on Volatile Oils).

1250. S. Aini (Tadzhik writer). 1252. "Kiev Uprising" (after V. Boroday).

1251. Congress Emblem and Postrider.

1968. Sadriddin Aini. 90th Birth Anniv.
3570. **1250.** 4 k. maroon & bistre 10 5

1968. Meeting of UPU Consultative Commission, Moscow.
3571. **1251.** 6 k. red and grey .. 15 5
3572. – 6 k. red and yellow 15 5
DESIGN: No. 3572, Emblem and transport.

1968. Ukraine Communist Party. 50th Anniv.
3573. **1252.** 4 k. red, pur. & gold 10 5

1253. Athletes and "50". 1254. Handball.

1968. Young Communist League's Games. 50th Anniv.
3574. **1253.** 4 k. red, drab & yell. 10 5

1968. Various Sports Events.
3575. **1254.** 2 k. multicoloured.. 8 5
3576. – 4 k. multicoloured 10 5
3577. – 6 k. multicoloured.. 15 5
3578. – 10 k. red, blk. & bistre 20 8
3579. – 12 k. multicoloured 30 10
DESIGNS AND EVENTS—VERT. T **1254** (World Handball Games, Moscow). 6 k. Sailing (20th Baltic Regatta). 10 k. Football (Russian soccer. 70th anniv.). HORIZ. 4 k. Table-tennis (All-European Juvenile Competitions). 12 k. Underwater swimming (European Underwater Sports Championships, Alushta, Ukraine).

1255. Girl Gymnasts. 1256. Gediminas Tower, Vilnius (Vilna).

1968. Olympic Games, Mexico. Backgrounds in gold.
3580. **1255.** 4 k. turq. and blue 12 5
3581. – 6 k. violet and red.. 20 5
3582. – 10 k. yellow-green and blue-green .. 30 8
3583. – 12 k. brown & orge. 35 8
3584. – 16 k. blue and pink 40 12
DESIGNS: 6 k. Weightlifting. 10 k. Rowing. 12 k. Women's Hurdles. 16 k. Fencing match.

1968. Soviet Lithuania. 50th Anniv.
3586. **1256.** 4 k. red, drab & pur. 10 5

1257. Tbilisi University. 1258. "Death of Laocoon and his sons" (from sculpture by Agesandre, Polidor and Asinodor).

1968. Tbilisi University. 50th Anniv.
3587. **1257.** 4 k. beige and green 10 5

1968. "Promote Solidarity with the Greek Democrats".
3588. **1258.** 6 k. drab, maroon and chocolate .. 1·75 1·75

1259. Cavalryman.

1968. Young Communists' League. 50th Anniv. Multicoloured.
3589. 2 k. Type **1259** 8 5
3590. 3 k. Young workers .. 8 5
3591. 4 k. Army officer .. 10 5
3592. 6 k. Construction workers 15 5
3593. 10 k. Agricultural workers 20 8

1260. Institute and Molecular Structure.

1968. N. S. Kurnakov Institute of Chemistry 50th Anniv.
3595. **1260.** 4 k. purple, black and ultramarine.. 10 5

1261. Letter.

1968. Int. Correspondence Week and Stamp Day.
3596. **1261.** 4 k. brn., red & lake 10 5
3597. – 4 k. indigo, ochre and ultramarine .. 10 5
DESIGN: No. 3597, Russian stamps.

1262. "The 26 Baku Commissars" (statue by Makarov). 1263. T. Antikainen (Finnish Communist Leader).

1968. Execution of 26 Baku Commissars. 50th Anniv.
3598. **1262.** 4 k. multicoloured.. 10 5

1968. 70th Birthday of T. Antikainen.
3599. **1263.** 6 k. sepia and grey.. 15 5

1264. Liner, "Ivan Franko". 1266. P. P. Postyshev (1887-1940).

1265. Order of the October Revolution.

1968. Soviet Merchant Marine.
3600. **1264.** 6 k. red, ultramarine and blue 15 5

1968. October Revolution. 51st Anniv.
3601. **1265.** 4 k. multicoloured.. 15 5

1968. Soviet Personalities.
3602. **1266.** 4 k. black 12 5
3603. – 4 k. black 12 5
3604. – 4 k. black 12 5
DESIGNS: No. 3603, S. G. Shaumian (1878–1918). 3604, A. Ikramov (1898–1938).

1267. Statuette of Warrior and Ararat Mountains.

1268. I. S. Turgenev (writer).

1968. Erivan. (Armenian capital). 2,750th Anniv.
3605. **1267.** 4 k. black and brown on grey 8 5
3606. – 12 k. brown & sepia on yellow .. 25 10
DESIGN: 12 k. Sasunsky Monument.

1968. Ivan Turgenev. 150th Birth Anniv.
3607. **1268.** 4 k. green 10 5

1269. Bison and Zebra.

1968. Fauna. Soviet Wildlife Reservations. Multicoloured.
3608. 4 k. Type **1269** 12 5
3609. 4 k. Purple gallinule and lotus 12 5
3610. 6 k. White herons .. 15 5
3611. 6 k. Ostrich and pheasant 15 5
3612. 10 k. Llama and antelope 30 10
3613. 10 k. Glossy ibis and spoonbill 30 10
Nos. 3610/11 are vert.

1270. Building and Equipment.

1968. Lenin Radio-laboratory, Gorky. 50th Anniv.
3614. **1270** 4 k. blue and ochre 10 5

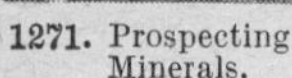

1271. Prospecting for Minerals.

1272. Djety-Oguz, Kirghizia.

1968. Geology Day. Multicoloured.
3615. 4 k. Type **1271** 15 5
3616. 6 k. "Tracking down" metals 10 5
3617. 10 k. Oil derrick.. .. 25 8

1968. Central Asian Spas. Multicoloured.
3618. 4 k. Type **1272** 10 5
3619. 4 k. Borovoe, Kazakhstan 10 5
3620. 6 k. Issyik kul, Kirghizia 15 5
3621. 6 k. Borovoe, Kazakhstan 15 5
Nos. 3619/20 are horiz.

1273. Silver Medal, "Philatec", Paris, 1964.

1968. Awards to Soviet Post Office at Foreign Stamp Exns.
3622. 4 k. black, silver and red 12 5
3623. 6 k. black, gold and blue 20 5
3624. 10 k. black, gold & blue.. 25 8
3625. 12 k. blk., silver & turq. 30 8
3626. 16 k. blk., gold & verm... 35 12
3627. 20 k. black, gold and blue 40 15
3628. 30 k. blk., gold & chest. 60 25
DESIGNS: 4 k. Type **1273**. 6 k. Plaque, "Debria", Berlin, 1959. 10 k. Cup and medals, Riccione, 1952, 1968. 12 k. Diploma and medal, "Thematic Biennale", Buenos Aires, 1965. 16 k. Trophies and medals, Rome, 1952, 1954. 20 k. Medals and plaques, "Wipa", Vienna. 1966. 30 k. Glass trophies, Prague, 1950, 1955. 1962.

1274. V. K. Lebedinsky.

1275. Soldier with Flag.

1968. Lebedinsky (physicist). Birth Cent.
3629. **1274.** 4 k. multicoloured.. 10 5

1968. Estonian Workers' Commune. 50th Anniv.
3630. **1275.** 4 k. black and red.. 10 5

1276. Moscow Buildings and Fir Branch.

1968. New Year.
3632. **1276.** 4 k. multicoloured.. 10 5

1277. G. Beregovoi (cosmonaut).

1278. Electric Train, Map and Emblem.

1968. Flight of "Soyuz 3".
3633. **1277.** 10 k. blk., red & blue 20 8

1968. Soviet Railways.
3634. **1278.** 4 k. orge. & magenta 8 5
3635. – 10 k. brown & green 20 8
DESIGN: 10 k. Track-laying train.

INDEX

Countries can be quickly located by referring to the index at the end of this volume.

1279. Red Flag, Newspapers and Monument.

1280. "The Reapers" (Venezianov).

1968. Byelorussian Communist Party. 50th Anniv.
3636. **1279.** 4 k. black, brn. & red 10 5

1968. Paintings in State Museum, Leningrad. Multicoloured.
3637. 1 k. Type **1280** 5 5
3638. 2 k. "The Last Days or Pompeii" (Bryullov) .. 10 5
3639. 3 k. "A Knight at the Crossroads" (Vaznetzov) .. 12 5
3640. 4 k. "Conquering a Town in Winter" (Surikov).. 15 5
3641. 6 k. "The Lake" (Levitan) 20 5
3642. 10 k. "The Year 1919: Alarm" (Petrov-Vodkin) 30 8
3643. 16 k. "The Defence of Sebastopol" (Deineka) 35 15
3644. 20 k. "Homer's Bust" (Korzhev) 40 20
3645. 30 k. "The Celebration in Uritsky Square" (Kustodiev) 60 30
3646. 50 k. "The Duel between Peresvet and Chelumbey" (Avilov).. .. 1·00 45
Nos. 3638/41, 3643, 3645/6 are horiz. designs, size 61 × 28 mm.

1281. House, Onega Region.

1283. "Declaration of Republic".

1282. Flags and Order of October Revolution.

1968. Soviet Architecture.
3647. **1281.** 3 k. brown on buff 10 5
3648. – 4 k. green on yellow 12 5
3649. – 6 k. violet on grey 15 5
3650. – 10 k. ultram. on green 20 8
3651. – 12 k. red on drab .. 25 8
3652. – 16 k. black on yellow 35 12
DESIGNS: 4 k. Farmhouse door, Gorky region. 6 k. Wooden Church, Kishi. 10 k. Citadel, Rostov-Yaroslavl. 12 k. Entrance gate, Tsaritzino. 16 k. Master-builder Rossi's Street, Leningrad.

1968. N. G. Markin (1893–1918) (revolutionary). 50th Death Anniv. As T **1266**.
3653. 4 k. black 10 5

1968. Komsomol Youth Organisation. 50th Anniv.
3654. **1282.** 12 k. multicoloured 30 8

1969. Byelorussian Republic. 50th Anniv. Multicoloured.
3655. 2 k. Type **1283** 5 5
3656. 4 k. Partisans at war, 1941–45 .. .. 8 5
3657. 6 k. Reconstruction workers 12 5

1284. Red Guards in Riga (statue).

1285. University Building.

1969. Unsuccessful Soviet attempt to seize Latvia. 50th Anniv.
3658. **1284.** 4 k. red and orange 8 5

1969. Leningrad University. 150th Anniv.
3660. **1285.** 10 k. black and lake 20 8

1286. I. A. Krylov (fabulist).

1287. N. D. Filchenkov.

1969. Ivan Krylov. Birth Bicent.
3661. **1286.** 4 k. multicoloured.. 8 5

1969. War Heroes.
3662. **1287.** 4 k. sepia and red 10 5
3663. – 4 k. sepia and green 10 5
DESIGN: No. 3663, A. A. Kosmodemiansky.

1288. "The Wheel Turns Round Again" (sculpture, Z. Kisfaludi-Strob).

1969. 1st Hungarian Soviet Republic. 50th Anniv.
3664. **1288.** 6 k. blk., red & green 12 5

1289. Crest and Symbols of Petro-chemical Industry.

1969. Bashkir Soviet Republic. 50th Anniv.
3665. **1289.** 4 k. multicoloured.. 8 5

1290. "Vostok 1" on Launching-pad.

1969. Cosmonautics' Day. Multicoloured.
3666. 10 k. Type **1290** .. 20 8
3667. 10 k. "Zond 5" in Lunar orbit (horiz.) .. 20 8
3668. 10 k. S. P. Korolev (space scientist) (horiz.) .. 20 8

1291. Lenin University, Kazan.

1969. Buildings connected with Lenin. Multicoloured.
3670. 4 k. Type **1291** 8 5
3671. 4 k. Lenin Museum, Kuibyshev 8 5
3672. 4 k. Lenin Museum, Pskov 8 5
3673. 4 k. Hunting-lodge, Shushenskaya 8 5
3674. 4 k. "Hay Hut", Razliv.. 8 5
3675. 4 k. Lenin Museum, Gorky Park, Leningrad .. 8 5
3676. 4 k. Smolny Institute, Leningrad 8 5
3677. 4 k. Lenin's Office, Kremlin 8 5
3678. 4 k. Lenin Museum, Ulyanovsk 8 5
3679. 4 k. Lenin Museum, Ulyanovsk (rear view) 8 5

1292. Telephone and Radio Set.

1969. VEF Electrical Works, Riga. 50th Anniv.
3680. **1292.** 10 k. brown and red 20 5

1293. I.L.O. Emblem.

1969. Int. Labour Organisation. 50th Anniv.
3681. **1293.** 6 k. gold and red .. 10 5

1294. Otakar Jaros. **1295.** P. E. Dybenko.

1969. Otakar Jaros (Czech war hero). Commem.
3682. **1294.** 4 k. black and blue .. 10 5

1969. Soviet Personalities. (80th birth Annivs.).
3683. **1295.** 4 k. red 8 5
3684. – 4 k. blue 8 5
DESIGN: No. 3684, S. V. Kosior (1889-1939).

1296. S. Stalsky.

1969. Suleiman Stalsky (Dagestan poet). Birth Cent.
3685. **1296.** 4 k. grn. & brown .. 8 5

1297. "Clear Glade" Rose. **1298.** Scientific Centre.

1969. Academy of Sciences' Botanical Gardens. Multicoloured.
3686. 2 k. Type **1297** .. 5 5
3687. 4 k. "Slender" lily .. 8 5
3688. 10 k. "Cattleya hybr" orchid 20 5
3689. 12 k. "Leaves' Fall" dahlia 25 10
3690. 14 k. "Ural Girl" gladiolus 25 12

1969. Ukraine Academy of Sciences. 50th Anniv.
3691. **1298.** 4 k. purple & yellow 8 5

1299. Gold Medal within Film "Flower". **1300.** Congress Emblem.

1969. Cine and Ballet Events, Moscow. Multicoloured.
3692. 6 k. Type **1299** (6th Int. Cinema Festival) .. 12 5
3693. 6 k. Ballet-dancers (1st Int. Ballet Competitions) .. 12 5

1969. 3rd Int. Protozoologists Congress, Leningrad.
3694. **1300.** 6 k. multicoloured .. 12 5

1301. Estonian Singer.

1969. Estonian Choir Festival. Cent.
3695. **1301.** 4 k. red and ochre .. 8 5

1302. Mendeleiev and Formulae.

1969. Mendeleiev's Periodic Law of Elements. Cent.
3696. **1302.** 6 k. brown and red 20 8

1303. Peace Banner and World Landmarks. **1304.** Rocket on Laser Beam, and Moon.

1969. World Peace Movement. 20th Anniv.
3698. **1303.** 10 k. multicoloured 20 8

1969. "50 Years of Soviet Inventions".
3699. **1304.** 4 k. red, black & silver 8 5

1305. I. Kotliarovsky.

Стокгольм 1969
(1306.)

1969. Ivan Kotliarovsky (Ukrainian writer). Birth Bicent.
3700. **1305.** 4 k. black, red & grn. 8 5

1969. Soviet Ice-hockey Victory in World Championships, Stockholm. No. 2821 optd. with T **1306**.
3701. **881.** 6 k. turquoise & purple 1·40 60

1307. Monument and Campaign map. **1308.** Hands holding Torch, and Bulgarian Arms.

1969. Byelorussian Liberation. 25th Anniv.
3702. **1307.** 4 k. red, purple & olive 8 5

1969. Bulgarian and Polish Peoples' Republics. 25th Anniv.
3703. **1308.** 6 k. multicoloured .. 10 5
3704. – 6 k. red and ochre .. 10 5
DESIGN: No. 3704, Polish map, flag and arms.

1309. Registan Square, Samarkand.

1969. Samarkand. 2,500th Anniv. Multicoloured.
3705. 4 k. Type **1309** 10 5
3706. 6 k. Intourist Hotel, Samarkand .. 15 5

1310. Liberation Monument, Nikolaev. **1311.** Volleyball.

1969. Liberation of Nikolaev. 25th Anniv.
3707. **1310.** 4 k. red, violet & blk. 8 5

1969. Int. Sporting Events.
3708. **1311.** 4 k. red, brn. & orge. 8 5
3709. – 6 k. multicoloured .. 12 5
DESIGN AND EVENTS: 4 k. (European Junior Championships). 6 k. Canoeing (European Championships).

1312. M. Munkacsy and detail of painting, "Peasant Woman churning Butter". **1313.** Miner's Statue, Donetsk.

1969. Michaly Munkacsy (Hungarian painter). 125th Birth Anniv.
3710. **1312.** 6 k. blk., orge. & brn. 15 5

1969. Donetsk. Cent.
3711. **1313.** 4 k. magenta & grey 8 5

1314. "Horse-drawn Machine-guns" (M. Grekov).

1969. 1st Cavalry Army. 50th Anniv.
3712. **1314.** 4 k. brown and red 12 5

1315. Ilya Repin (self-portrait). **1316.** Running.

1969. Ilya Repin (painter). 125th Birth Anniv. Multicoloured.
3713. 4 k. "Barge-haulers on the Volga" 15 5
3714. 6 k. "Unexpected" .. 20 10
3715. 10 k. Type **1315** .. 25 10
3716. 12 k. "The Confession" 35 10
3717. 16 k. "Dnieper Cossacks" 40 15

1969. 9th Trade Unions' Games, Moscow.
3718. **1316.** 4 k. blk., grn. & red 8 5
3719. – 10 k. blk., blue & grn. 20 8
DESIGN: 10 k. Gymnastics.

1317. V. L. Komarov. **1318.** O. Tumanyan and Landscape.

1969. V. L. Komarov (botanist). Birth Cent.
3721. **1317.** 4 k. brown and olive 10 5

1969. O. Tumanyan (Armenian poet). Birth Cent.
3722. **1318.** 10 k. black and blue 20 8

1319. Turkoman Drinking-horn (2nd-cent. B.C.). **1320.** Mahatma Gandhi.

1969. Oriental Art Treasures, State Museum of Oriental Art, Moscow. Multicoloured.
3723. 4 k. Type **1319** .. 12 5
3724. 6 k. Simurg vessel, Persia (13th-cent.) 20 5
3725. 12 k. Statuette, Korea (8th-cent.) 30 10
3726. 16 k. Bodhisatva statuette, Tibet (7th-cent.) .. 35 15
3727. 20 k. Ebisu statuette, Japan (17th-cent.) .. 45 20

1969. Mahatma Gandhi. Birth Cent.
3728. **1320.** 6 k. brown 15 5

1321. Black Stork at Nest.

1969. Byelovezhaskaya Pushcha State Reservation. Multicoloured.
3729. 4 k. Type **1321** 10 5
3730. 6 k. Deer and calf .. 15 8
3731. 10 k. Bison 30 12
3732. 12 k. Lynx and cubs .. 30 12
3733. 16 k. Wild boar and piglets 35 15
No. 3731 is larger, 76 × 24 mm.

1322. "Komitas" and Rural Scene.

1969. "Komitas" (S. Sogomonyan, Armenian composer). Birth Cent.
3734. **1322.** 6 k. black, flesh & grey 12 5

1323. S. Gritsevets (fighter pilot). **1324.** I. Pavlov (after portrait by A. Yar-Kravchenko).

1969. Soviet War Heroes.
3735. **1323.** 4 k. black and grn. 8 5
3736. – 4 k. brn., red & yell. 8 5
3737. – 4 k. brown and green 8 5
DESIGNS: As T **1323**. No. 3737, Lisa Chaikina (partisan). (35½ × 24 mm.): No. 3736, A. Cheponis, Y. Alexonis and G. Boris (Kaunas resistance fighters).

1969. Ivan P. Pavlov (physiologist). 120th Birth Anniv.
3738. **1324.** 4 k. multicoloured .. 8 5

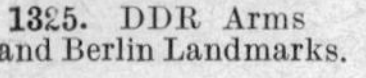

1325. DDR Arms and Berlin Landmarks.

1326. A. V. Koltsov (from portrait by A. Yar-Kravchenko.

1969. German Democratic Republic. 20th Anniv.
3739. **1325.** 6 k. multicoloured . . 15 5

1969. A. Koltzov (poet). 160th Birth Anniv.
3740. **1326.** 4 k. brown and blue 8 5

1327. Ukraine Arms and Memorial.

1328. Kremlin, and Hammer and Sickle.

1969. Ukraine Liberation. 25th Anniv.
3741. **1327.** 4 k. red and gold . . 10 5

1969. October Revolution. 52nd Anniv.
3742. **1328.** 4 k. multicoloured . . 8 5

1329. Shonin and Kubasov ("Soyuz 6").

1969. Cosmonauts' Meeting, Moscow.
3744. **1329.** 10 k. olive and gold 20 8
3745. – 10 k. olive and gold 20 8
3746. – 10 k. olive and gold 20 8
DESIGNS: No. 3745, Filipchenko, Volkov and Gorbatko ("Soyuz 7"). 3746, Shatalov and Elisyev ("Soyuz 8").

1330. Lenin as Youth, and Emblems.

1331. Corps Emblem on Red Star.

1969. Lenin's Birth Centenary Youth Philatelic Exn., Kiev.
3747. **1330.** 4 k. lake and pink . . 8 5

1969. Red Army Communications Corps. 50th Anniv.
3748. **1331.** 4 k. red, brn. & bistre 8 5

1332. "Male and Female Farmworkers" (sculptured group, V. Mukhina), and title page.

1969. 3rd Soviet Collective Farmers' Congress, Moscow.
3749. **1332.** 4 k. brown and gold 8 5

1333. "Vasilissa, the Beauty".

1969. Russian Fairy Tales. Multicoloured.
3750. 4 k. Type **1333** 12 10
3751. 10 k. "Maria Morevna" (folk tale) . . 25 20
3752. 16 k. "The Golden Cockerel" (Pushkin) (horiz.) 40 35
3753. 20 k. "Finist, the Fine Fellow" (folk tale) . . 45 40
3754. 50 k. "The Tsar" (Pushkin) . . . . 1·00 95

1334. Venus Plaque and Radio-telescope.

1969. Space Exploration.
3755. **1334.** 4 k. red, brn. & blk. 8 5
3756. – 6 k. pur., grey & blk. 12 5
3757. – 10 k. multicoloured 30 8
DESIGNS: 6 k. Space station and capsule in orbit. 10 k. Photograph of the Earth taken by "Zond 7".

1335. Soviet and Afghan Flags.

1336. Red Star and Arms.

1969. U.S.S.R.-Afghanistan Diplomatic Relations. 50th Anniv.
3759. **1335.** 6 k. red, blk. & grn. 12 5

1969. Coil Stamp.
3760. **1336.** 4 k. red 12 5

1337. "Mig" Fighters of 1940 and 1969.

1969. "30 Years of MIG Aircraft".
3761. **1337.** 6 k. blk., grey & red 25 5

1338. Lenin.

1969. New Year.
3762. **1338.** 4 k. multicoloured . . 8 5

1339. ANT-2" Aircraft.

1969. Development of Soviet Civil Aviation.
3763. **1339.** 2 k. multicoloured . . 5 5
3764. – 3 k. multicoloured . . 8 5
3765. – 4 k. multicoloured . . 8 5
3766. – 6 k. blk., red & pur. 12 5
3767. – 10 k. multicoloured 20 8
3768. – 12 k. multicoloured 25 8
3769. – 16 k. multicoloured 35 12
3770. – 20 k. multicoloured 40 15
AIRCRAFT: 3 k. "Po-2 (U-2)". 4 k. "ANT-9". 6 k. "ZAGI 1-EA" helicopter. 10 k. "ANT-20 Maxim Gorky". 12 k. "TU-104". 16 k. "MI-10" helicopter. 20 k. "Il-62".

1341. Model Aircraft.

1969. Technical Sports.
3772. **1341.** 3 k. purple . . 8 5
3773. – 4 k. green 10 5
3774. – 6 k. orange-red . . 15 5
DESIGNS: 4 k. Speedboat racing. 6 k. Parachuting.

1342. Rumanian Arms and Soviet Memorial, Bucharest.

1343. TV Tower, Ostankino.

1969. Rumanian Liberation. 25th Anniv.
3775. **1342.** 6 k. red and brown 15 5

1969. Television Tower, Ostankino, Moscow.
3776. **1343.** 10 k. multicoloured 20 10

1344. "Lenin" (from sculpture by N. Andreev).

1970. V. I. Lenin. Birth Cent. (1st Issue). Multicoloured.
3777. 4 k. Type **1344** 12 5
3778. 4 k. "Marxist meeting, Petrograd" (A. Moravov) 12 5
3779. 4 k. "Second R.S.D.R.P. Congress" (Y. Vinogradov) . . 12 5
3780. 4 k. "First day of Soviet Power" (F. Morodov) . . 12 5
3781. 4 k. "Visiting Lenin" (F. Morodov) 12 5
3782. 4 k. "Conversation with Ilyich" (A. Shirokov) . . 12 5
3783. 4 k. "May Day 1920" (I. Brodsky) 12 5
3784. 4 k. "With Lenin" (V. Serov) 12 5
3785. 4 k. "Conquerors of the Cosmos" (A. Deyneka) 12 5
3786. 4 k. "A. Korentsov, Y. Merkoulov, V. Bourakov) 12 5

1345. F. V. Sychkov and painting "Tobogganing".

1970. F. V. Sychkov (artist). Birth Cent.
3787. **1345.** 4 k. blue and brown 8 5

1346. Sailing Ships and Antarctic Map.

1347. V. I. Peshekhonov.

1970. Antarctic Expedition by Bellinghausen and Lazarev. 150th Anniv.
3788. **1346.** 4 k. turquoise, mag. and blue 10 5
3789. – 16 k. red, grn. & pur. 35 12
DESIGN: 16 k. Modern polar-station and map.

1970. Soviet War Heroes.
3790. **1347.** 4 k. pur. & slate-black 8 5
3791. – 4 k. brown & olive-brn. 8 5
DESIGN: No. 3791, V. B. Borshoev (1906-1945).

1348. Emblem of Geographical Society.

1349. "The Torch of Peace" (A. Dumpe).

1970. Russian Geographical Society. 125th Anniv.
3792. **1348.** 6 k. multicoloured . . 12 5

1970. Int. Women's Solidarity Day. 60th Anniv.
3793. **1349.** 6 k. drab & bl.-grn. 12 5

1350. Ivan Bazhov (folk hero) and Crafts.

1351. Lenin.

1970. World Fair "Expo 70", Osaka, Japan.
3794. **1350.** 4 k. blk., red and grn. 8 5
3795. – 6 k. silver, red & blk. 12 5
3796. – 10 k. multicoloured 20 8
DESIGNS: 6 k. U.S.S.R. Pavilion. 10 k. Boy and model toys.

1970. Lenin Birth Cent. All-Union Philatelic Exhib., Moscow.
3798. **1351.** 4 k. blk., gold & red 8 5

1352. Friendship Tree.

1970. Friendship Tree, Sochi.
3800. **1352.** 10 k. multicoloured 35 8

1353. Ice-Hockey Players.

1970. World Ice-Hockey Championships, Stockholm, Sweden.
3801. **1353.** 6 k. green and blue 35 5

1354. Hammer, Sickle and Azerbaijan Emblems.

1970. Soviet Republics. 50th Anniv.
3802. **1354.** 4 k. red and gold .. 8 5
3803. – 4 k. brown & silver.. 8 5
3804. – 4 k. purple and gold 8 5
DESIGNS: No. 3803, Woman and motifs of Armenia. No. 3804, Woman and emblems of Kazakh Republic.

1355. Worker and Book. **1356.** D. N. Medvedev.

1970. U.N.E.S.C.O. "Lenin Centenary" Symposium.
3805. **1355.** 6 k. ochre and lake.. 12 5

1970. War Heroes.
3806. **1356.** 4 k. chocolate .. 8 5
3807. – 4 k. brown.. .. 8 5
PORTRAIT: No. 3807, K. P. Orlovsky.

(1357.) **1358.** Hungarian Arms and Budapest View.

1970. Russian Victory in World Ice-hockey Championships, Stockholm. No. 3801 optd. with T **1357**.
3808. **1353.** 6 k. green and blue.. 25 5

1970. Hungarian and Czech Liberation. 25th Anniv. Multicoloured.
3809. 6 k. Type **1358** 15 5
3810. 6 k. Czech Arms and Prague view 12 5

1359. Cosmonauts' Emblem. **1360.** Lenin, 1890.

1970. Cosmonautics Day.
3811. **1359.** 6 k. multicoloured.. 15 5

1970. Lenin. Birth Cent. (2nd Issue).
3812. **1360.** 2 k. green 5 5
3813. – 2 k. olive 5 5
3814. – 4 k. ultramarine .. 8 5
3815. – 4 k. lake 8 5
3816. – 6 k. brown 12 5
3817. – 6 k. lake 12 5
3818. – 10 k. purple .. 20 10
3819. – 10 k. sepia 20 10
3820. – 12 k. black and silver 25 12
3821. – 12 k. red and gold.. 25 12
PORTRAITS OF LENIN: No. 3813, Period, 1893-1900. 3814, Period, 1900-03. 3815, As an emigrant. 3816, In 1917. 3817, Period of Revolution. 3818, In 1918. 3819, In 1920. 3820, Bas-relief. 3821, Sculpture by Kolesnikov.

1362. Order of Victory. **1363.** Komsomol Badge.

1970. Victory in Second World War. 25th Anniv.
3823. **1362.** 1 k. gold, grey & pur. 5 5
3824. – 2 k. pur., brn. & gold 5 5
3825. – 3 k. red, blk. & gold 5 5
3826. – 4 k. red, brn. & gold 8 5
3827. – 10 k. gold, red & pur. 20 8
DESIGNS: 2 k. Eternal Flame. 3 k. Treptow Monument, Berlin. 4 k. Home Defence Order. 10 k. Hero of the Soviet Union and Hero of Socialist Labour medals.

1970. Young Communist League (Komsomol). 16th Congress.
3829. **1363.** 4 k. multicoloured.. 8 5

1364. Sculptured Head of Lenin.

1970. World Youth Meeting for Lenin. Birth Cent.
3830. **1364.** 6 k. red 12 5

1365. "Young Workers" and Federation Emblem.

1970. World Democratic Youth Federation. 25th Anniv.
3831. **1365.** 6 k. black and blue.. 12 5

1366. Arms and Government Building, Kazan.

1970. Soviet Republics. 50th Anniv. Dated "1970".
3832. **1366.** 4 k. blue 8 5
3833. – 4 k. green 8 5
3834. – 4 k. red 8 5
3835. – 4 k. brown 8 5
3836. – 4 k. green 8 5
3837. – 4 k. brown 8 5
DESIGNS: No. 3832 (Tatar Republic). 3833, State emblem and Government building (Karelian Republic). 3834, Russian Federation emblem and Supreme Soviet building (Chuvash Republic). 3835, Russian Federation emblem and Supreme Soviet building (Kalmuk Republic). 3836, Russian Federation and Supreme Soviet building (Udmurt Republic). 3837, State emblem and Government building (Mari republic).
See also Nos. 3903/7, 4052/3, 4175, 4253, 4298 and 4367.

1367. Gymnast on Bar (World Championships, Yugoslavia). **1368.** "Swords into Ploughshares" (sculpture by E. Vuchetich).

1970. Int. Sporting Events.
3838. **1367.** 10 k. red and drab.. 20 8
3839. – 16 k. brown & green 35 12
DESIGN: 16 k. Three footballers (World Cup Championships, Mexico).

1970. United Nations. 25th Anniv.
3840. **1368.** 12 k. purple and green 25 8

1369. Cosmonauts and Soyuz 9". **1370.** F. Engels.

1970. Space Flight by "Soyuz 9".
3841. **1369.** 10 k. black, red & pur. 20 8

1970. Friedrich Engels. 150th Birth Anniv.
3842. **1370.** 4 k. agate and red.. 8 5

1371. Cruiser "Aurora".

1970. Soviet Warships.
3843. **1371.** 3 k. pink, lilac & blk. 10 5
3844. – 4 k. black and yellow 12 5
3845. – 10 k. blue and mauve 25 8
3846. – 12 k. brown and buff 35 10
3847. – 20 k. pur., blue & turq. 50 20
WARSHIPS: 4 k. Guided-missile cruiser "Grozny". 10 k. Cruiser "October Revolution". 12 k. Guided-missile cruiser "Varyag". 20 k. Atomic submarine "Lenin Komsomol".

1372. Soviet and Polish Workers. **1373.** Allegory of the Sciences.

1970. Soviet-Polish Friendship Treaty. 25th Anniv.
3848. **1372.** 6 k. verm. and blue 12 5

1970. 13th Int. Historical Sciences Congress, Moscow.
3849. **1373.** 4 k. multicoloured.. 8 5

1374. Mandarin Ducks. **1375.** Magnifying Glass, "Stamp" and Covers.

1970. Fauna of Sikhote-Alin Nature Reserve. Multicoloured.
3850. 4 k. Type **1374** 10 5
3851. 6 k. Marten 20 5
3852. 10 k. Black bear (vert.) 20 8
3853. 16 k. Elk.. .. .. 35 12
3854. 20 k. Tiger 45 15

1970. 2nd U.S.S.R. Philatelic Society Conference, Moscow.
3855. **1375.** 4 k. silver and red.. 8 5

1376. V. I. Kidwidze. **1377.** University Building.

1970. V. J. Kidvidze (Civil War hero). 75th Birth Anniv.
3856. **1376.** 4 k. brown.. .. 8 5

1970. Erivan University. 50th Anniv.
3857. **1377.** 4 k. red and blue .. 8 5

1378. Lenin Badge. **1379.** Library Book-plate.

1970. Pioneer Youth Organisation.
3858. **1378.** 1 k. gold, red & grey 5 5
3859. – 2 k. grey and brown 5 5
3860. – 4 k. multicoloured.. 8 5
DESIGNS: 2 k. "Lenin with Children" (sculpture). 4 k. Red Star, Pioneer emblem.

1970. Vilnius (Vilna) University Library (Lithuania). 400th Anniv.
3861. **1379.** 4 k. blk., grey & silver 8 5

1380. Woman with Bouquet.

1970. Int. Democratic Women's Federation. 25th Anniv.
3862. **1380.** 6 k. brown and blue 12 5

1381. Milkmaid and Cows. ("Livestock").

1970. Soviet Agricultural. Multicoloured.
3863. 4 k. Type **1381** .. 8 5
3864. 4 k. Driver, tractor and harvester ("Mechanisation") 8 5
3865. 4 k. Lock-operator and canal ("Irrigation and Chemical Research").. 8 5

1382. Lenin addressing Meeting.

1970. October Revolution. 53rd Anniv.
3866. **1382.** 4. k. gold and red .. 8 5

50 лет
ленинскому плану
ГОЭЛРО • 1970
(1383.)

1970. GOELRO Electrification Plan. 50th Anniv. No. 3475 optd. with T **1383**.
3868. 4 k. multicoloured .. 12 5

1384. Spassky Tower, Kremlin. **1385.** A. A. Baikov.

1970. New Year.
3869. **1384.** 6 k. multicoloured.. 12 5

1970. A. A. Baikov (metallurgic scientist) Birth Cent.
3870. **1385.** 4 k. black and brown 8 5

1386. A. D. Tsyurupa. **1387.** Church, Red Square, Moscow.

1970. A. D. Tsyurupa (Vice-Chairman of Soviet People's Commissars). Birth Cent.
3871. **1386.** 4 k. brown and yellow 8 5

1970. Tourism.
3872. **1387.** 4 k. multicoloured .. 8 5
3873. – 6 k. blue, indigo & brn. 12 5
3874. – 10 k. brown and green 20 8
3875. – 12 k. multicoloured 25 8
3876. – 14 k. blue, red & brn. 25 10
3877. – 16 k. multicoloured 40 12
DESIGNS: 6 k. Scene from "Swan Lake". 10 k. Deer. 12 k. Souvenir handicrafts. 14 k. "Swords into Ploughshares" (sculpture by E. Vuchetich). 16 k. Tourist and camera.

1388. Camomile.

1970. Flowers. Multicoloured.
3878. 4 k. Type **1388** 8 5
3879. 6 k. Dahlia 10 5
3880. 10 k. Phlox 20 8
3881. 12 k. Aster 20 8
3882. 16 k. Clematis 35 15

1389. African Woman and Child. **1390.** Beethoven (after Holzschnitt).

1970. U.N. Declaration on Colonial Independence. 10th Anniv.
3883. **1389.** 10 k. brown and blue 20 8

1970. Beethoven. Birth Bicent.
3884. **1390.** 10 k. maroon on red 25 8

1391. "Luna 16" in Flight. **1392.** Speed-Skating.

1970. Flight of "Luna 16".
3885. **1391.** 10 k. green .. 20 8
3886. – 10 k. purple .. 20 8
3887. – 10 k. green 20 8
DESIGNS: No. 3886, "Luna 16" on Moon's surface. No. 3887, Parachute descent.

1970. Trade-Unions' Winter Games (1971).
3889. **1392.** 4 k. blue, red & grey 8 5
3890. – 10 k. grn., brn. & grey 20 8
DESIGN: 10 k. Skiing.

1393. "The Conestabile Madonna" (Raphael).

1970. Foreign Paintings in Soviet Galleries. Multicoloured.
3891. 3 k. Type **1393** .. 5 5
3892. 4 k. "Saints Peter and Paul" (El Greco) .. 8 5
3893. 10 k. "Perseus and Andromeda" (Rubens) horiz.) 20 8
3894. 12 k. "The Return of the Prodigal Son" (Rembrandt) 25 8
3895. 16 k. "Family Portrait" (Van Dyck) 30 12
3896. 20 k. "The Actress Jeanne Samary" (Renoir) 40 20
3897. 30 k. "Woman with Fruit" (Gauguin) .. 65 25
See also Nos. 4064/70.

1394. Harry Pollitt. **1395.** "75" Emblem.

1970. H. Pollitt (British Communist). 80th Birth Anniv.
3899. **1394.** 10 k. brn. & purple 20 8

1970. Int. Co-operative Alliance. 75th Anniv.
3900. **1395.** 12 k. red and green 20 8

1396. Sculptured Head, Lenin.

1971. 24th Soviet Union Communist Party Congress.
3901. **1396.** 4 k. red and gold .. 8 5

1397. "50", State Emblem and Flag. **1398.** Genua Fortress and Cranes.

1971. Georgian Soviet Republic. 50th Anniv.
3902. **1397.** 4 k. multicoloured .. 8 5

1971. Soviet Republics. 50th Anniv. Similar designs to T **1366**, but dated "1971".
3903. 4 k. turquoise 8 5
3904. 4 k. red 5 5
3905. 4 k. red 5 5
3906. 4 k. blue 5 5
3907. 4 k. green 5 5
DESIGNS: No. 3903, Russian Federation Arms and Supreme Soviet building (Dagestan Republic). 3904, National emblem and symbols of agriculture and industry (Abkhazian Republic). 3905, Arms produce and industry (Adjarian Republic). 3906, Arms and State building (Kabardino-Balkar Republic). 3907, Arms, industrial products and Government building (Komi Republic).

1971. Feodosia (Crimean city). 2,500th Anniv.
3908. **1398.** 10 k. multicoloured 20 8

1399. Palace of Culture, Kiev. **1400.** "Features of National Economy".

1971. 24th Ukraine Communist Party Congress, Kiev.
3909. **1399.** 4 k. multicoloured 8 5

1971. Soviet State Planning Organisation. 50th Anniv.
3910. **1400.** 6 k. red and brown .. 10 5

1401. N. Gubin, I. Chernykh and S. Kossinov (dive-bomber crew).

1971. Soviet Air Force Heroes.
3911. **1401.** 4 k. brown & green .. 8 5

1402. Gipsy Dance.

1971. State Folk-dance Ensemble. Mult.
3912. 10 k. Type **1402** 20 8
3913. 10 k. Russian "Summer" dance (women in circle) 20 8
3914. 10 k. Ukraine "Gopak" dance (dancer leaping) 20 8
3915. 10 k. Adjar "Khorumi" dance (with drummer) 20 8
3916. 10 k. "On the Ice" (ballet) 20 8

1403. L. Ukrainka.

1971. L. Ukrainka (Ukrainian writer). Birth Cent.
3917. **1403.** 4 k. red and brown .. 8 5

1404. "Luna 17" Module on Moon. **1405.** Fighting at the Barricades.

1971. Soviet Moon Exploration.
3918. **1404.** 10 k. brown and vio. 20 8
3919. – 12 k. brown & blue 35 8
3920. – 12 k. brown & blue 35 8
3921. – 16 k. brown & violet 45 12
DESIGNS: No. 3919, Control room and radio-telescope. No. 3920, Moon trench. No. 3921, "Lunokhod 1" Moon-vehicle.

1971. Paris Commune. Cent.
3923. **1405.** 6 k. blk., brn. & red 10 5

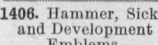

1406. Hammer, Sickle and Development Emblems. **1408.** E. Birznieks-Upitis.

1407. Gagarin Medal, Spaceships and Planets.

1971. 24th Soviet Communist Party Congress. Moscow.
3924. **1406.** 6 k. red, bistre & brn. 10 5

1971. First Manned Space Flight (1st issue). 10th Anniv., and Cosmonauts' Day.
3925. **1407.** 10 k. ol., yell. & brn. 30 8
3926. – 12 k pur., bl. & slate 35 8
DESIGN: 12 k. Spaceship over Globe and economic symbols.

1971. E. Birznieks-Upitis (Lettish writer). Birth Cent.
3927. **1408.** 4 k. red and green .. 8 5

1409. Bee on Flower.

1971. 23rd Int. Bee-keeping Congress, Moscow.
3928. **1409.** 6 k. multicoloured .. 10 5

1410. Memorial Building.

1971. Lenin Memorial Building, Ulyanovsk.
3930. **1410.** 4 k. yellow & red .. 8 5

1411. Lieut-Col. N. I. Vlasov. **1412.** Khafiz Shirazi.

1971. Victory in 2nd World War. 26th Anniv.
3931. **1411.** 4 k. brown & green 8 5

1971. Khafiz Shirazi (Tadzhik writer). 650th Birth Anniv.
3932. **1412.** 4 k. multicoloured .. 8 5

1413. "Gaz-66" Truck.

1971. Soviet Motor Vehicles.
3933. **1413.** 2 k. multicoloured .. 5 5
3934. – 3 k. multicoloured .. 8 5
3935. – 4 k. blue, blk. & lilac 12 5
3936. – 4 k. grn., mar. & drab 12 5
3937. – 10 k. red, blk. & lilac 20 8
DESIGNS: 3 k. "BelAZ-540" tipper-truck. 4 k. (3935) "Moskvich-412" 4-door saloon. 4 k. (3936) "Zaporozhez ZAZ-968" 2-door saloon. 10 k. "Volga GAZ-24" saloon.

1414. A. A. Bogomolets. **1415.** Commemorative Scroll.

1971. A. A. Bogomolets (medical scientist). 90th Birth Anniv.
3938. **1414.** 4 k. blk., pink & orge. 8 5

1971. Int. Moscow Congresses.
3939. **1415.** 6 k. brown & green .. 12 5
3940. – 6 k. multicoloured .. 12 5
3941. – 6 k. multicoloured .. 12 5
DESIGNS AND EVENTS—HORIZ. No. 3939, (13th Science History Congress). No. 3940, Oil derrick and symbols (8th World Oil Congress). VERT. No. 3941, Satellite over Globe (15th General Assembly of Geodesics and Geophysics Union).

1416. Sukhe Bator's Statue, Ulan Bator.

1971. Mongolian People's Republic. 50th Anniv.

3942. **1416.** 6 k. grey, gold & red 10 5

1417. Defence Monument. **1418.** Treaty Emblem.

1971. Defence of Liepaja. 30th Anniv.

3943. **1417.** 4 k. brn., blk. & grey 8 5

1971. Antarctic Treaty. 10th Anniv., and Soviet Hydrometeorological Service. 50th Anniv.

3944. **1418.** 6 k. ultram., blk. & bl. 25 8

3945. – 10 k. violet, blk. & red 35 10

DESIGN: 10 k. Hydrometeorological map.

1419. "Motherland" (sculpture by E. Vouchetich). **1420.** Throwing the Discus.

1971. "Federation Internationale des Resistants". 20th Anniv.

3946. **1419.** 6 k. green and red .. 10 5

1971. 5th Summer Spartakiad.

3947. **1420.** 3 k. blue on pink .. 5 5

3948. – 4 k. green on flesh 8 5

3949. – 6 k. brown on green 12 5

3950. – 10 k. purple on blue 20 8

3951. – 12 k. brown on yell. 25 8

DESIGNS: 4 k. Archery. 6 k. Horse-riding (dressage). 10 k. Basketball. 12 k. Wrestling

1421. "The Washerwoman" (Chardin).

1971. Museum Paintings. Multicoloured.

3952. 2 k. "Benois Madonna" (Leonardo da Vinci) (vert.) 5 5

3953. 4 k. "Mary Magdalen" (Titian) (vert.) .. 10 5

3954. 10 k. Type **1421** 25 8

3955. 12 k. "Young Man with gloves" (Hals) (vert.) 25 10

3956. 14 k. "Tancred and Arminia" (Poussin) .. 30 10

3957. 16 k. "Portrait of Young Girl" (Murillo) (vert.) 35 12

3958. 20 k. "Child with ball" (Picasso) (vert.) .. 45 20

1422. Lenin Badge and Kazakh Flag.

1971. Kazakh Communist Youth Association. 50th Anniv.

3959. **1422.** 4 k. brown, red & bl. 8 5

1423. Posthorn within Star. **1424.** A. Spendiazov (Armenian composer) (after M. Sarian).

1971. Int. Correspondence Week.

3960. **1423.** 4 k. black, blue & grn. 8 5

1971. Birth Annivs. Multicoloured.

3961. 4 k. Type **1424** (Birth Centenary) 8 5

3962. 4 k. N. Nekrasov (J. Kramskoi) (poet) (150th birth anniv.) 8 5

3963. 10 k. M. Dostoievsky (W. Perov) (writer) (150th birth anniv.) 20 8

1425. Z. Paliashvili. **1426.** Emblem, Gorky Kremlin and Hydrofoil.

1971. Z. Paliashvili (Georgian composer). Birth Cent.

3964. **1425.** 4 k. brown 8 5

1971. Gorky (formerly Nizhni-Novgorod). 750th Anniv. (1st issue).

3965. **1426.** 16 k. multicoloured 35 12

1427. Students and Globe.

1971. Int. Students' Federation. 25th Anniv.

3966. **1427.** 6 k. blue, red and brn. 10 5

1428. Dolphins.

1429. Star and Miners' Order.

1431. Maxim Gorky Statue and View. **1430.** Lord Rutherford and Atomic Formula.

1971. Marine Fauna. Multicoloured.

3967. 4 k. Type **1428** 8 5

3968. 6 k. Sea otter 12 5

3969. 10 k. Narwhal 20 8

3970. 12 k. Walrus 25 8

3971. 14 k. Seal 25 10

1971. Coal Discovery in Donetz Basin. 250th Anniv.

3972. **1429.** 4 k. red, brown & blk. 8 5

1971. Lord Rutherford (physicist). Birth Cent.

3973. **1430.** 6 k. brown & purple 15 10

1971. Gorky (formerly Nizhni-Novgorod) 750th Anniv. (2nd issue).

3974. **1431.** 4 k. multicoloured .. 8 5

1432. Santa Claus in Troika.

1971. New Year.

3975. **1432.** 10 k. red, gold & blk. 20 8

1433. Workers and Marx Books. ("Int. Socialist Solidarity").

1971. 24th Soviet Union Communist Party Congress Resolutions.

3976. **1433.** 4 k. blue, ultram. & red 8 5

3977. – 4 k. red, yell. & brn. 8 5

3978. – 4 k. lilac, blk. & red 8 5

3979. – 4 k. bistre, brn. & red 8 5

3980. – 4 k. red, grn. & yellow 8 5

DESIGNS: No. 3977, Farmworkers and wheat-field ("Agricultural Production"). 3978, Factory production line ("Increased Productivity"). 3979, Heavy industry ("Industrial Expansion"). 3980, Family in department store ("National Welfare").

1434. "Meeting" (V. Makovsky). **1435.** V. V. Vorovsky.

1971. Travelling Art Exhibitions Cent. Paintings by Russian Artists. Multicoloured.

3982. 2 k. Type **1434** 5 5

3983. 4 k. "Girl Student" (N. Yaroshenko) 8 5

3984. 6 k. "Woman Miner" (N. Kasatkin) 12 5

3985. 10 k. "Harvesters" (G. Myasoyedov) (horiz.) 20 10

3986. 16 k. "Country Road" (A. Savrasov) 35 12

3987. 20 k. "Pine Forest" (I. Shiskin) (horiz.) .. 40 15

See also Nos. 4063/9.

1971. V. V. Vorovsky (diplomat). Birth Cent.

3989. **1435.** 4 k. brown 8 5

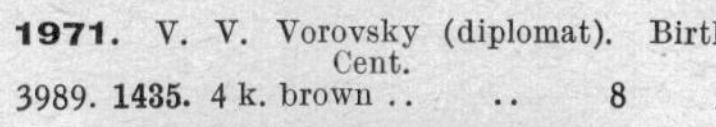

1436. Dobrovolsky, Volkov and Pataiev.

1971. "Soyuz II" Cosmonauts Commem.

3990. **1436.** 4 k. black, pur. & orge. 8 5

1437. Order of the Revolution and Building Construction.

1971. October Revolution. 54th Anniv.

3991. **1437.** 4 k. multicoloured .. 8 5

1438. B. Shtchukin (actor) and scene from "The Man with the Rifle". **1439.** D. Dzhabaiev (A. Yar-Krauchenko).

1971. Vakhtangov Theatre, Moscow. 50th Anniv.

3992. – 10 k. red and crimson 20 8

3993. **1438.** 10 k. yellow & brn. 20 8

3994. – 10 k. orange & brn. 20 8

DESIGNS—VERT. No. 3992, E. Vakhtangov (founder) and characters from "Princess Turandot". HORIZ. No. 3994, R. Simonov (director) and scene from "Cyrano de Bergerac".

1971. Dzhambul Dzhabaiev (Kazakh poet). 125th Birth Anniv.

3995. **1439.** 4 k. brn., yell. & orge. 8 5

1440. Pskov Kremlin.

1971. Historical Buildings. Multicoloured.

3996. 3 k. Type **1440** 5 5

3997. 4 k. Novgorod kremlin .. 8 5

3998. 6 k. Smolensk fortress .. 12 5

3999. 10 k. Kolumna kremlin .. 20 8

1441. William Foster (American Communist).

1971. Foster. 90th Birth Anniv.

4001. **1441.** 10 k. black & brown 5·50 8·00

4002. 10 k. black & brown 20 10

No. 4001, shows the incorrect date of death "1968". No. 4002, shows the correct date, "1961".

1442. A. Fadeiev and Scene from novel, "The Rout".

1971. Alexandre Fadeiev (writer). 75th Birth Anniv.

4003. **1442.** 4 k. orange & blue 5 5

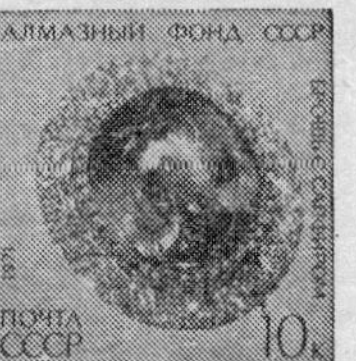

1443. Sapphire Brooch.

1971. Diamonds and Jewels. Multicoloured.

4004. 10 k. Type **1443** .. 20 8

4005. 10 k. "Shah" diamond 20 8

4006. 10 k. "Narcissi" diamond brooch 20 8

4007. 20 k. Amethyst pendant 40 15

4008. 20 k. "Rose" platinum and diamond brooch .. 40 15

4009. 30 k. Pearl and diamond pendant 65 20

1444. Vanda Orchid. **1446.** Ice-hockey Players.

1445.

1971. Tropical Flowers. Multicoloured.

4010. 1 k. Type **1444** 5 5
4011. 2 k. " Anturium sherzerium " 5 5
4012. 4 k. " Cactus epiphyllum " 5 5
4013. 12 k. Amaryllis 25 8
4014. 14 k. " Medinilla magnifica " 30 12

1971. History of the Russian Navy (1st series). Multicoloured.

4016. 1 k. Type **1445** 5 5
4017. 4 k. Battleship " Oriol ", 1712 (vert.) 8 5
4018. 10 k. Battleship "Poltava", 1712 (vert.) 20 8
4019. 12 k. Battleship " Ingermanland ", 1715 (vert.) 25 8
4020. 16 k. Steam-frigate " Vladimir ", 1848 .. 35 12

See also Nos. 4117/21, 4209/13 and 4303/6.

1971. Soviet Ice-hockey. 25th Anniv.

4021. **1446.** 6 k. multicoloured .. 25 5

1447. Baku Oil Installations. **1448.** G. M. Krzhizhanovsky.

1971. Baku Oil Industry.

4022. **1447.** 4 k. blk., red and blue 8 5

1972. G. M. Krzhizhanovsky (scientist). Birth Cent.

4023. **1448.** 4 k. brown 8 5

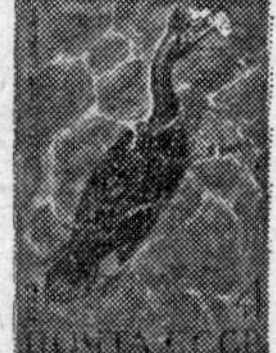

1449. A. N. Scriabin. **1450.** Shag.

1972. A. N. Scriabin (composer). Birth Cent.

4024. **1449.** 4 k. blue and green 8 5

1972. Sea Birds. Multicoloured.

4025. 4 k. Type **1450** 8 5
4026. 6 k. Ross's gull (horiz.) .. 12 5
4027. 10 k. Pair of Barnacle geese 20 8
4028. 12 k. Pair of Spectacled eiders (horiz.) 25 8
4029. 16 k. Mediterranean gull 35 15

1451. Speed-skating. **1452.** Heart Emblem.

1972. Winter Olympic Games, Sapporo, Japan. Multicoloured.

4030. 4 k. Type **1451** 8 5
4031. 6 k. Figure-skating .. 10 5
4032. 10 k. Ice-hockey .. 20 8
4033. 12 k. Ski-jumping .. 25 8
4034. 16 k. Cross-country skiing 30 12

1972. World Heart Month.

4036. **1452.** 4 k. red and green .. 8 5

1453. Fair Emblem. **1454.** Labour Emblems.

1972. Soviet Participation in Leipzig Fair. 50th Anniv.

4037. **1453.** 16 k. gold and red .. 35 12

1972. 15th Soviet Trade Unions Congress, Moscow.

4038. **1454.** 4 k. brn., red & pink 8 5

1455. "Aloe arborescens". **1456.** Alexandra M. Kollonai (diplomat).

1972. Medicinal Plants. Multicoloured.

4039. 1 k. Type **1455** 5 5
4040. 2 k. "Glaucium flavum" 5 5
4041. 4 k. "Senecio platyphylloides" 8 5
4042. 6 k. "Orthosiphon stamineus" 12 5
4043. 10 k. "Solanum laciniatum" 25 8

1972. Soviet Celebrities.

4044. **1456.** 4 k. chestnut .. 5 5
4045. – 4 k. lake .. 5 5
4046. – 4 k. bistre .. 5 5

CELEBRITIES: No. 4045, G. Chicherin (Foreign Affairs Commissar). No. 4046, "Kamo" (S. A. Ter-Petrosyan—revolutionary).

1457. "Salyut" Space-station and "Soyuz" Spacecraft.

1972. Cosmonautics Day. Multicoloured.

4048. 6 k. Type **1457** 12 5
4049. 6 k. "Mars 2" approaching Mars 12 5
4050. 16 k. Capsule, "Mars 3" .. 35 20

1458. Factory and Products.

1972. Izhory Factory. 250th Anniv.

4051. **1458.** 4 k. pur. and silver 10 5

1972. Soviet Republics. 50th Anniv. Design similar to T **1366**, but dated "1972".

4052. 4 k. blue 5 5
4053. 4 k. red 5 5

DESIGN: No. 4052, State emblem and natural resources (Yakut Republic). No. 4053, Arms, agriculture and industry (Checheno-Ingush Republic).

1459. Sobinov and scene from "Eugene Onegin".

1972. L. Sobinov (singer). Birth Cent.

4054. **1459.** 10 k. brown 20 8

1460. Symbol of Knowledge and Children reading Books.

1972. Int. Book Year.

4055. **1460.** 6 k. multicoloured .. 10 5

1461. P. Morosov (pioneer) and Pioneers Saluting.

1972. Pioneer Organisation. 50th Anniv.

4056. **1461.** 1 k. multicoloured .. 5 5
4057. – 2 k. pur., red & grn. 5 5
4058. – 3 k. blue, red & brn. 5 5
4059. – 4 k. red, blue & grn. 5 5

DESIGNS: 2 k. Girl laboratory worker and Pioneers with book. 3 k. Pioneer Palace, Chukotka, and Pioneers at work. 4 k. Pioneer parade.

1462. Pioneer Trumpeter.

1972. " 50th Anniv. of Pioneer Movement " Youth Philatelic Exhib. Minsk.

4061. **1462.** 4 k. mar., red & yell. 5 5

1463. " World Security ".

1972. European Security Conference, Brussels.

4062. **1463.** 6 k. blue, turq. & gold 35 35

1464. M. S. Ordubady. **1465.** G. Dimitrov.

1972. M. S. Ordubady (Azerbaijan writer). Birth Cent.

4063. **1464.** 4 k. pur. & orange .. 5 5

1972. Russian Paintings. As T **1393**, but dated " 1972 ". Multicoloured.

4064. 2 k. " Cossack Hetman " (I. Nikitin) 5 5
4065. 4 k. " F. Volkov " (A. Lossenko) 8 5
4066. 6 k. " V. Majkov " (F. Rokotov) 10 5
4067. 10 k. " N. Novikov " (D. Levitsky) 20 8
4068. 12 k. " G. Derzhavin " (V. Borovikovsky) .. 20 8
4069. 16 k. " Peasants' Dinner " (M. Shibanov) (horiz.) .. 30 12
4070. 20 k. " Moscow View " (F. Alexeiev) (horiz.) .. 40 15

1972. Georgi Dimitrov (Bulgarian statesman). 90th Birth Anniv.

4071. **1465.** 6 k. brn. & bistre .. 12 5

1466. Congress Building and Emblem.

1972. 9th Int. Gerontology Congress, Kiev.

4072. **1466.** 6 k. brown and blue 12 5

1467. Fencing.

1972. Olympic Games, Munich.

4073. **1467.** 4 k. purple & gold .. 8 5
4074. – 6 k. green and gold 10 5
4075. – 10 k. blue and gold 20 8
4076. – 14 k. blue and gold 25 10
4077. – 16 k. red and gold .. 30 15

DESIGNS: 6 k. Gymnastics. 10 k. Canoeing. 14 k. Boxing. 16 k. Running.

1468. Amundsen, Airship "Norge" and Northern Lights. **1469.** Market-place, Lvov (Lemberg).

1972. Roald Amundsen (Polar explorer). Birth Cent.

4079. **1468.** 6 k. blue and brown 15 5

1972. Ukraine's Architectural Monuments. Multicoloured.

4080. 4 k. Type **1469** 5 5
4081. 6 k. 17th-century house, Tchernigov (horiz.) .. 10 5
4082. 10 k. Kovnirovsky building, Kiev (horiz.) .. 15 8
4083. 16 k. Kamenetz-Podolsk Castle 25 12

1470. Indian Flag and Asokan Capital. **1471.** Liberation Monument and Cavalry.

1972. India's Independence. 25th Anniv.

4084. **1470.** 6 k. red, blue & green 10 5

1972. Liberation of Far Eastern Territories. 50th Anniv.

4085. **1471.** 3 k. grey, orge. & red 5 5
4086. – 4 k. grey, yell. & ochre 5 5
4087. – 6 k. grey, pink & red 10 5

DESIGNS: 4 k. " Labour with Peace " (statue). 6 k. " Sailor holding Anchor " (statue).

1472. Miners' Day Emblem.

1972. Miners' Day. 25th Anniv.

4088. **1472.** 4 k. red, blk. & violet 5 5

1473. " The Milk-seller's Family " (Le Nain).

1972. Paintings by Foreign Artists in Hermitage Gallery, Leningrad. Multicoloured.

4089. 4 k. " Breakfast " (Velasquez) 8 5
4090. 6 k. Type **1473** 12 5
4091. 10 k. " Boy with Dog " (Murillo) 20 8

4092. 16 k. "The Capricious Girl" (Watteau) .. 35 12
4093. 20 k. "Moroccan with Horse" (Delacroix) .. 40 15
Nos. 4091/93 are vert.

1474. "Sputnik I".

1972. "Cosmic Era". 15th Anniv. Mult.
4095. 6 k. Type **1474** 10 5
4096. 6 k. Launching rocket .. 10 5
4097. 6 k. "Lunokhod" vehicle 10 5
4098. 6 k. "Man in space" .. 10 5
4099. 6 k. "Luna" auto-station 10 5
4100. 6 k. Touch-down on Venus 10 5

1475. K. Mardjanishevili.

1476. Museum Emblem.

1972. K. Mardjanishevili (Georgian actor). Birth Cent.
4101. **1475.** 4 k. green 5 5

1972. Popov Communications Museum. Cent.
4102. **1476.** 4 k. multicoloured.. 5 5

1477. Exhibition Labels.

1972. U.S.S.R. 50th Anniv. Philatelic Exhib.
4103. **1477.** 4 k. red & blk. on yell. 5 5

1478. Lenin.

1972. October Revolution. 55th Anniv.
4104. **1478.** 4 k. red and gold .. 5 5

1479. Militia Badge and Soviet Flag.

1480. Arms of U.S.S.R.

1972. Soviet Militia. 55th Anniv.
4105. **1479.** 4 k. multicoloured.. 5 5

1972. U.S.S.R. 50th Anniversary.
4106. **1480.** 4 k. gold, mar. & red 8 5
4107. – 4 k. gold, red & brn. 8 5
4108. – 4 k. gold, mar. & grn. 8 5
4109. – 4 k. gold, pur. & grey 8 5
4110. – 4 k. gold, mar. & grey 8 5
DESIGNS: No. 4107, Lenin and banner. No. 4108, Arms and Kremlin. N. 4109, Arms and industrial scenes. No. 4110, Arms, worker and open books.

1481. Emblem of U.S.S.R.

1482. Insurance Book.

1972. U.S.S.R. Victories in Olympic Games, Munich. Multicoloured.
4112. 20 k. Type **1481** 35 15
4113. 30 k. Olympic Medals .. 50 20

1972. "50 Years of Soviet Insurance".
4115. **1482.** 4 k. blue and purple 5 5

1483. Kremlin and Snowflakes.

1485. "G. Skovoroda" (P. Mesheryakov).

1484. "Petr Velikiye" (Peter the Great).

1972. New Year.
4116. **1483.** 6 k. multicoloured.. 5 5

1972. History of the Russian Navy (2nd series). Multicoloured.
4117. 2 k. Type **1484** 5 5
4118. 3 k. "Varyag" 8 5
4119. 4 k. "Potemkin" .. 10 5
4120. 6 k. "Ochakov" .. 12 5
4121. 10 k. "Amur" 25 10

1972. Grigory S. Skovoroda. 250th Birth Anniv.
4122. **1485.** 4 k. blue 5 5

1486. "Meeting of Village Party Members" (E. M. Cheptsov).

1972. "History of Russian Painting". Multicoloured.
4123. 2 k. Type **1486** 5 5
4124. 4 k. "Pioneer Girl with Books" (N. A. Kasatkine) (vert.) 8 5
4125. 6 k. "Party Delegate" (G. G. Ryazhsky) (vert.) 12 5
4126. 10 k. "End of Winter-Midday" (K. F. Yuon) 15 10
4127. 16 k. "Partisan Lunev" (N. I. Strunnikov) (vert.) 25 15
4128. 20 k. "Self-portrait" (I. E. Grabarj) (vert.) .. 40 20

1487. Child reading Safety Code.

1488. Emblem of Technology.

1972. Road Safety Campaign.
4130. **1487.** 4 k. black, blue & red 5 5

1972. Polytechnic Museum, Moscow. Cent.
4131. **1488.** 4 k. multicoloured.. 5 5

1489. "Venus 8" and Parachute.

1972. Space Research.
4132. **1489.** 6 k. blue, blk. & mar. 10 5

1490. Solidarity Emblem.

1973. Asian and African People's Solidarity Organisation. 15th Anniv.
4134. **1490.** 10 k. bl., red & brn. 15 5

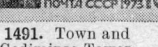

1491. Town and Gediminas Tower.

1492. J. V. Babushkin.

1973. Vilnius (Vilna). 650th Anniv.
4135. **1491.** 10 k. red, black & grn. 15 5

1973. J. V. Babushkin (revolutionary). Birth Cent.
4136. **1492.** 4 k. black 5 5

1493. "Tu-154" Jetliner.

1973. Soviet Civil Aviation. 50th Anniv.
4137. **1493.** 6 k. multicoloured.. 10 5

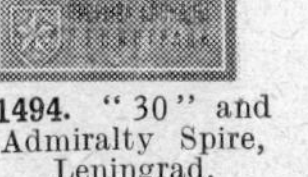
1494. "30" and Admiralty Spire, Leningrad.

1495. Portrait and Masks (Mayakovsky Theatre).

1973. Relief of Leningrad Blockade. 30th Anniv.
4138. **1494.** 4 k. blk., orange & brn. 5 5

1973. Moscow Theatres. 50th Anniv.
4139. **1495.** 10 k. multicoloured 15 5
4140. – 10 k. red and blue.. 15 5
DESIGN: No. 4140, Commemorative panel (Mossoviet Theatre).

1496. M. Prishvin.

1973. Mikhail Prishvin (writer). Birth Cent.
4141. **1496.** 4 k. multicoloured.. 5 5

1497. Soldier and Allegory.

1973. Stalingrad Victory. 30th Anniv. Detail from Heroes' Memorial.
4142. **1497.** 3 k. multicoloured.. 5 5
4143. – 4 k. yellow and black 5 5
4144. – 10 k. green and black 15 10
4145. – 12 k. red and black 20 10
DESIGNS—HORIZ. 4 k. Memorial statues. 10 k. Mother mourning for child. VERT. 12 k. Hand with upraised torch.

1498. Copernicus and Planetary Chart.

1973. Copernicus. 500th Birth Anniv.
4147. **1498.** 10 k. brown and blue 30 10

1499. "Chaliapin" (K'Korovin).

1973. F. Chaliapin (opera singer). Birth Cent.
4148. **1499.** 10 k. multicoloured 15 10

1500. Ice-hockey Players.

1501. Athletes.

1973. World Ice-hockey Championships, Moscow.
4149. **1500.** 10 k. brn., bl. & gold 20 8

1973. Central Red Army Sports Club. 50th Anniv.
4151. **1501.** 4 k. multicoloured.. 5 5

1502. Red Star, Tank, and Map.

1503. N. E. Bauman.

1973. Battle of Kursk. 30th Anniv.
4152. **1502.** 4 k. red and grey .. 5 5

1973. Nikolai Bauman (revolutionary). Birth Cent.
4153. **1503.** 4 k. brown 5 5

1504. Red Cross and Red Crescent.

1973. International Co-operation.

4154. **1504.** 4 k. red, green & blk. 5 5
4155. – 6 k. blue and red .. 10 5
4156. – 16 k. multicoloured 25 15

DESIGNS AND EVENTS: 4 k. (Soviet Red Cross and Red Crescent Societies Union. 50th Anniv.). 6 k. Mask, emblem and theatre curtain (15th Int., Theatre Institution Congress). 16 k. Floral emblem (10th World Festival of Youth, Berlin).

1505. A. N. Ostrovsky (V. Perov). 1506. Satellites.

1973. Alexander Ostrovsky (writer). 150th Birth Anniv.

4157. **1505.** 4 k. multicoloured .. 5 5

1973. Cosmonauts Day. Multicoloured.

4158. 6 k. Type **1506** .. 12 5
4159. 6 k. " Lunokhod 2 " .. 12 5

1507. " Guitarist " (Tropinin). 1508. Athlete. and Emblems.

1973. History of Russian Painting. Mult.

4162. 2 k. Type **1507** 5 5
4163. 4 k. " The Young Widow " (Fedotov) 8 5
4164. 6 k. " Self-portrait " (Kipresky) 10 5
4165. 10 k. " An Afternoon in Italy " (Brullov) .. 20 10
4166. 12 k " That's My Father's Dinner !" (boy with dog —Venetsianov) .. 25 8
4167. 16 k. " Lower Gallery of Albane " (Ivanov) .. 35 15
4168. 20 k. " Ermak conquering Siberia " (Sourikov) .. 45 20

1973. Dynamo Sports Club. 50th Anniv.

4169. **1508.** 4 k. multicoloured 5 5

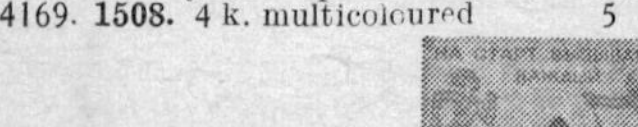

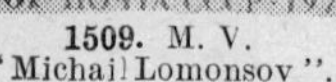

1509. M. V. " Michail Lomonsov ". 1511. Emblem and Sports.

1510. E. T. Krenkel and Polar Scenes.

1973. Leningrad-New York Trans-Atlantic Service. Inaug.

4171. **1509.** 16 k. multicoloured 25 15

1973. E. T. Krenkel (Polar explorer). 70th Birth Anniv.

4172. **1510.** 4 k. brown and blue 5 5

1973. " Sport for Everyone ".

4173. **1511.** 4 k. multicoloured .. 5 5

1512. Girls' Choir.

1973. Centenary of Latvian Singing Festival.

4174. **1512.** 10 k. multicoloured 15 10

1973. Republic. 50th Anniv. Design similar to Type **1366**, but dated "1973".

4175. 4 k. blue 5 5

DESIGN: No. 4175, Arms and industries of Buriat.

1513. Throwing the Hammer.

1973. Universiade Games, Moscow. Mult.

4176. 2 k. Type **1513** 5 5
4177. 3 k. Gymnastics .. 5 5
4178. 4 k. Swimming .. 5 5
4179. 16 k. Fencing 25 15

1514. Bison.

1973. Soviet Fauna. Multicoloured.

(a) Caucasus Reserve.

4182. 1 k. Type **1514** 5 5
4183. 3 k. Mountain sheep .. 5 5
4184. 4 k. Mountain partridges 5 5

(b) Voronezh Reserve. (50th Anniv.).

4185. 6 k. Beaver with young .. 10 5
4186. 10 k. Deer with young .. 15 8

1515. Lenin, Banner and Membership Card.

1973. 2nd Soviet Social Democratic Workers' Party Congress. 70th Anniv.

4187. **1515.** 4 k. multicoloured .. 5 5

1516. A.R. al-Biruni. 1518. "The Sculpture" (P. D. Korin).

1517. Schaumburg Palace, Bonn and Spassky Tower, Moscow.

1973. Abu Reihan al-Biruni (astronomer and mathematician). Millennium.

4188. **1516.** 6 k. brown 10 5

1973. General Secretary Leonid Brezhnev's Visits to West Germany, France and U.S.A. Multicoloured.

4189. 10 k. Type **1517** 20 8
4190. 10 k. Eiffel Tower, Paris and Spassky Tower .. 20 8
4191. 10 k. White House, Washington and Spassky Tower 20 8

See also No. 4257.

1973. History of Russian Paintings. Mult.

4193. 2 k. Type **1518** 5 5
4194. 4 k. "Farm-workers' Supper" (A. A. Plastov) 5 5
4195. 6 k. "Letter from the Battle front" (A. Laktionov) .. 10 5
4196. 10 k. "Mountain Landscape" (M. S. Saryan) 15 8
4197. 16 k. "Wedding on Tomorrow's Street" (Y. Pimenov) .. 25 12
4198. 20 k. "Ice Hockey" (A. Deineka) 30 20

1519. Lenin Museum. 1520. Y. Steklov.

1973. Lenin Museum, Tashkent, Inaug.

4200. **1519.** 4 k. multicoloured .. 5 5

1973. Y. Steklov (statesman). Birth Cent.

4201. **1520.** 4 k. brn., red and pink 5 5

1521. " The Eternal Pen " 1522. " Oplopanax elatum ".

1973. Afro-Asian Writers' Conf., Alma-Ata.

4202. **1521.** 6 k. multicoloured .. 10 5

1973. Medicinal Plants. Multicoloured.

4203. 1 k. Type **1522** 5 5
4204. 2 k. "Panax ginseng" .. 5 5
4205. 4 k. "Orchis macolata" .. 5 5
4206. 10 k. "Arnica montana" 15 8
4207. 12 k. "Convallaria majalis" 20 8

1523. I. Nasimi.

1973. Imadeddin Nasimi (Azerbaijan poet).

4208. **1523.** 4 k. brown 5 5

1524. Cruiser "Kirov".

1973. Warships of Russian Navy (3rd series). Multicoloured.

4209. 3 k. Type **1524** 5 5
4210. 4 k. Battleship "Oktobrskaya Revolyutsiya" .. 5 5
4211. 6 k. Submarine "Krasnogvardeets" .. 10 5
4212. 10 k. Destroyer "Soobrazitelny" .. 15 10
4213. 16 k. Cruiser "Krasny Kavkas" 25 15

1525. Pugachev and Battle Scene.

1973. Peasant War. Bicent.

4214. **1525.** 4 k. multicoloured .. 5 5

1526. Red Flag encircling Globe.

1973. "Problems of Peace and Socialism" Review. 15th Anniv.

4215. **1526.** 6 k. red, gold & green 10 5

1527. Institute Building.

1973. Leningrad Mining Institute. Bicent.

4216. **1527.** 4 k. multicoloured .. 5 5

1528. Laurel and Hemispheres. 1529. Elena Stasova.

1973. World Congress " Peaceful Forces " Moscow.

4217. **1528.** 6 k. multicoloured .. 10 5

1973. Elena Stasova (party official). Birth Cent.

4218. **1529.** 4 k. mauve 5 5

1530. Order of People's Friendship. 1531. Marshal Malinovsky.

1973. Foundation of Order of People's Friendship.

4219. **1530.** 4 k. multicoloured .. 5 5

1973. Marshal R. Malinovsky. 75th Birth Anniv.

4220. **1531.** 4 k. grey 5 5

1532. Workers and Red Guard. 1533. D. Cantemir.

1973. Sverdlovsk. 250th Anniv.

4221. **1532.** 4 k. blk., gold and red 5 5

1973. Dmitri Cantemir (Moldavian scientist and encyclopaedist). 300th Birth Anniv.

4222. **1533.** 4 k. red 5 5

1534. Pres. Allende of Chile.

1973. Allende Commemoration.
4223. **1534.** 6 k. black and brn. 10 5

1535. Kremlin. **1536.** N. Narimanov.

1973. New Year.
4224. **1535.** 6 k. multicoloured.. 10 5

1973. Nariman Narimanov (Azerbaijan politician). Birth Cent.
4225. **1536.** 4 k. green 5 5

1537. "Russobalt" Touring Car (1909).

1973. History of Soviet Motor Industry. (1st series). Multicoloured.
4226. 2 k. Type **1537** 5 5
4227. 3 k. "AMO-F15" lorry (1924) 5 5
4228. 4 k. Spartak "Nami-1" tourer (1927) .. 5 5
4229. 12 k. Yaroslavsky "Ya-6" bus (1929) .. 20 10
4230. 16 k. Gorkovsky "GAZ-A" tourer (1932) 25 12
See also Nos. 4293/7, 4397/401 and 4512/16.

1538. "Game and Lobster" (Sneiders).

1973. Museum Paintings. Multicoloured.
4231. 4 k. Type **1538** 5 5
4232. 6 k. "Young Woman with Ear-rings" (Rembrandt) (vert.) 10 5
4233. 10 k. "Sick Woman and Physician" (Steen) (vert.) 15 8
4234. 12 k. "Attributes of Art" (Chardin) .. 20 10
4235. 14 k. "Lady in a Garden" (Monet) .. 25 15
4236. 16 k. "Village Lovers" (Bastien-Lepage) (vert.) 25 15
4237. 20 k. "Girl with Fan" (Renoir) (vert.) .. 30 20

1539. Great Sea Gate, Tallin (Estonia). **1540.** Picasso.

1973. Historical Buildings. Multicoloured.
4239. 4 k. Type **1539** .. 5 5
4240. 4 k. Dome, Cathedral and organ-pipes, Riga (Latvia) 5 5
4241. 4 k. Traku Castle (Lithuania) 5 5
4242. 10 k. Town Hall, Tallin 15 8

1973. Picasso Commemoration.
4243. **1540.** 6 k. multicoloured 10 5

1541. I. G. Petrovsky (mathematician and Rector of Moscow University).

1973. Petrovsky Commemoration.
4244. **1541.** 4 k. multicoloured.. 5 5

1542. Text and Flags.

1973. Brezhnev's Visit to India.
4245. **1542.** 4 k. multicoloured.. 5 5

1543. Soviet Soldier and Title Page. **1545.** Oil Workers.

1544. Siege Monument and Peter the Great Statue, Leningrad.

1974. "Red Star" Newspaper. 50th Anniv.
4246. **1543.** 4 k. blk., red and gold 5 5

1974. Soviet Victory in Battle for Leningrad. 30th Anniv.
4247. **1544.** 4 k. multicoloured.. 5 5

1974. Tyumen Oil-fields. 10th Anniv.
4248. **1545.** 4 k. red and blue .. 5 5

1546. "Comecon" Headquarters, Moscow. **1547.** Skaters and Stadium.

1974. Council for Mutual Economic Aid. 25th Anniv.
4249. **1546.** 16 k. multicoloured 25 10

1974. European Women's Ice-skating Championships, Medeo, Alma-Ata.
4250. **1547.** 6 k. red, blue and slate-blue .. 8 5

1548. Commemorative Text. **1549.** L. A. Artsimovitch (physicist).

1974. Russian Academy of Sciences. 250th Anniv.
4251. **1548.** 10 k. multicoloured 15 10

1974. Artsimovitch Commemoration.
4252. **1549.** 4 k. brown and green 5 5

1974. Soviet Republics. 50th Anniv. Design similar to Type **1366**, but dated "1974".
4253. 4 k. brown 5 5
DESIGN: No. 4253, Arms and industries of Nahichevan.

1550. K. D. Ushinsky. **1551.** M. D. Millionschikov.

1974. K. D. Ushinsky (educationalist). 150th Birth Anniv.
4254. **1550.** 4 k. brown and grn. 5 5

1974. M. D. Millionschikov (scientist). 1st Death Anniv.
4255. **1551.** 4 k. brown, pink & grn. 5 5

1552. Spartakiad Emblem. **1553.** Young Workers and Emblem.

1974. 3rd Winter Spartakiad Games.
4256. **1552.** 10 k. multicoloured 15 10

1974. General Secretary Leonid Brezhnev's Visit to Cuba. As Type **1517** but showing Kremlin, Revolution Square, Havana and Flags.
4257. 4 k. multicoloured .. 5 5

1974. Scientific and Technical Youth Work Review.
4258. **1553.** 4 k. multicoloured.. 5 5

1554. Theatre Facade. **1555.** Globe and Meteorological Activities.

1974. Azerbaijan Drama Theatre, Baku. Cent.
4259. **1554.** 6 k. brown, red & orge. 10 5

1974. Cosmonautics Day.
4260. **1555.** 6 k. blue, red & vio. 10 5
4261. – 10 k. brn., red & blue 15 8
4262. – 10 k. blk. red & yell. 15 8
DESIGNS: No. 4261, V. G. Lazarev and O. G. Makarov, and launch of "Soyuz 12". No. 4262, P. I. Klimuk and V. V. Lebedev, and "Soyuz 13".

1556. "Odessa by Moonlight" (Aivazovsky).

1974. Marine Paintings by Ivan Aivazovsky. Multicoloured.
4263. 2 k. Type **1556** 5 5
4264. 4 k. "Battle of Chesma" (vert.) 5 5
4265. 6 k. "St. George's Monastery" 10 5
4266. 10 k. "Storm at Sea" .. 15 8
4267. 12 k. "Rainbow" .. 20 12
4268. 16 k. "Shipwreck" .. 25 15

1557. Young Communists.

1974. 17th Young Communist's League Congress and 50th Anniv. of Lenin's naming the "Comsomol" (No. 4271). Mult.
4270. 4 k. Type **1557** 5 5
4271. 4 k. "Lenin" (from sculpture by V. Tsigal) 5 5

1558. Swallow ("Atmosphere"). **1559.** "Cobble-stone" (sculpture, I. D. Shadra).

1974. "EXPO 74" World Fair, Spokane, U.S.A. "Preserve the Environment".
4273. **1558.** 4 k. blk., red & lilac 5 5
4274. – 6 k. yell., blk. & blue 10 5
4275. – 10 k. blk., vio. & red 15 8
4276. – 16 k. bl., grn. & blk. 25 12
4277. – 20 k. blk., brn. & orge. 30 15
DESIGNS: 6 k. Fish and globe ("The Sea"). 10 k. Crystals ("The Earth"). 16 k. Rose bush ("Flora"). 20 k. Young fawn ("Fauna").

1974. Central Museum of the Revolution. 50th Anniv.
4279. **1559.** 4 k. grn., red & gold 5 5

1560. Congress Emblem within Lucerne Grass. **1562.** Tchaikovsky and Competition Emblem.

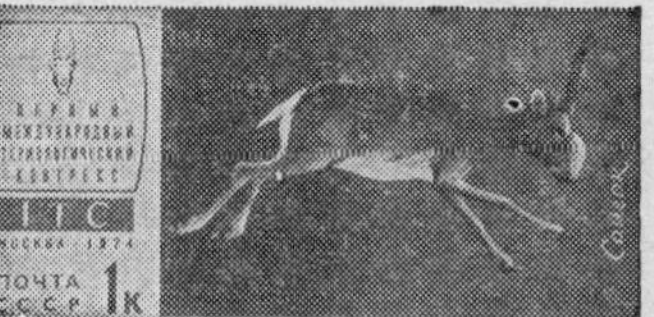

1561. Saigak Antelope.

1974. 12th Int. Congress of Meadow Cultivation, Moscow
4280. **1560.** 4 k. red, grn. & dark-grn. 5 5

1974. 1st Int. Theriological Congress, Moscow. Fauna. Multicoloured.
4281. 1 k. Type **1561** 5 5
4282. 3 k. Wild ass 5 5
4283. 4 k. Musk-rat 5 5
4284. 6 k. Fur seal 10 5
4285. 10 k. Greenland whale .. 15 8

1974. 5th Int. Tchaikovsky Music Competition.
4286. **1562.** 6 k blk., vio. & grn. 8 5

1563. Marshal F. I. Tolbukhin. **1565.** Runner and Emblem.

1564. K. Stanislavsky, V. Nemirovich-Danchenko and Theatre Curtain.

1974. Marshal F. I. Tolbukhin. 80th Birth Anniv.
4288. **1563.** 4 k. green 5 5

1974. Moscow Arts Festival. 75th Anniv.
4289. **1564.** 10 k. multicoloured 15 8

1974. 13th Soviet Schools Spartakiad, Alma Ata.
4290. **1565.** 4 k. multicoloured.. 5 5

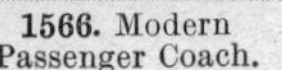
1566. Modern Passenger Coach.

1567. Shield and Monument on Battle Map.

1974. Egorov Railway Wagon Works, Leningrad. Cent.
4291. **1566.** 4 k. multicoloured . . 5 5

1974. Liberation of Byelorussia. 30th Anniv.
4292. **1567.** 4 k. multicoloured . . 5 5
See also No. 4301.

1974. History of Soviet Motor Industry (2nd series). As Type **1537.** Multicoloured.
4293. 2 k. Gorkovsky "GAZ-AA" lorry (1932) 5 5
4294. 3 k. Gorkovsky "GAZ-03-30" bus (1933) 5 5
4295. 4 k. Moscow Auto Works "ZIS-5" lorry (1933) . . 5 5
4296. 14 k. Moscow Auto Works "ZIS-8" bus (1933) . . 25 10
4297. 16 k. Moscow Auto Works "ZIS-101" saloon car (1936) 25 12
See also Nos. 4226/30 and 4397/410.

1974. Soviet Republics. 50th Anniv. As Type **1366**, date "1974".
4298. 4 k. red 5 5
DESIGN: 4 k. Arms and industries of North Ossetian Republic.
No. 4298 also commemorates the 200th anniv. of Ossetia's merger with Russia.

1568. Liberation Monument and Skyline.

1570. Admiral Issakov.

1569. Warsaw Monument and Flag.

1974. Poltava. 800th Anniv.
4299. **1568.** 4 k. red and brown . . 5 5

1974. Polish People's Republic. 30th Anniv.
4300. **1569.** 6 k. brown and red 10 5

1974. Liberation of Ukraine. 30th Anniv. As Type **1567**, but background details and colours changed.
4301. 4 k. multicoloured . . 5 5

1974. Admiral I. S. Issakov. 80th Birth Anniv.
4302. **1570.** 4 k .blue 5 5

1571. Mine-layer.

1974. History of the Russian Navy (4th series). Modern Warships. Multicoloured.
4303. 3 k. Type **1571** 5 5
4304. 4 k. Landing-ship . . 5 5
4305. 6 k. Helicopter-carrier . . 10 5
4306. 16 k. Anti-submarine destroyer 25 12

HAVE YOU READ THE NOTES AT THE BEGINNING OF THIS CATALOGUE?

These often provide answers to the enquiries we receive.

1572. Pentathlon Sports. 1573. D. Ulyanov.

1974. World Modern Pentathlon Championships, Moscow.
4307. **1572.** 16 k. brn., gold & blue 25 12

1974. D. Ulyanov (Lenin's brother). Birth Centenary.
4308. **1573.** 4 k. green 5 5

1574. V. Menzhinsky. 1576. Marshal Budenny.

1575. "Flowers in Basket" (W. Kontchalovski).

1974. V. Menzhinsky (statesman). Birth Cent.
4309. **1574.** 4 k. maroon . . 5 5

1974. Soviet Paintings. Multicoloured.
4310. 4 k. Type **1575** 5 5
4311. 6 k. "Towards the Wind" (sailing) (E. Kalnins) . . 10 5
4312. 10 k. "Spring" (young woman) (O. Zardarjan) 15 8
4313. 16 k. "Northern Harbour" (G. Nissky) . . 20 10
4314. 20 k. "Daughter of the Soviet Kirghitz" (S. Tchnikov) (vert.) . . 25 12

1974. Budenny Commemoration.
4315. **1576.** 4 k. green 5 5

1577. Title Page. 1578. Soviet Memorial, Bucharest, and Flags.

1974. First Russian Primer. 400th Anniv.
4316. **1577.** 4 k. red, blk. & gold 5 5

1974. Liberation of Rumania. 30th Anniv.
4317. **1578.** 6 k. blue, yell. & red 10 5

1579. Ancient and Modern Vitebsk.

1974. Millenary of Vitebsk.
4318. **1579.** 4 k. red and green . . 5 5

1580. Flag and Emblems of Kirghizia. 1581. Bulgarian Arms and Flags.

1974. Soviet Republics (named). 50th Anniv. Flags and Agricultural/Industrial Emblems Multicoloured. Background colours given.
4319. **1580.** 4 k. blue 8 5
4320. – 4 k. maroon . . 8 5
4321. – 4 k. light blue . . 8 5
4322. – 4 k. yellow 8 5
4323. – 4 k. green 8 5
DESIGNS: No. 4320, Moldavian republic. No. 4321, Tadzhikistan republic. No. 4322, Turkmenistan republic. No. 4323, Uzbekistan republic.

1974. Bulgarian Revolution. 30th Anniv.
4324. **1581.** 6 k. multicoloured . . 10 5

1582. DDR Crest and Soviet War Memorial, Treptow (Berlin). 1583. Theatre Building.

1974. German Democratic Republic. 25th Anniv.
4325. **1582.** 6 k. multicoloured . . 10 5

1974. State Maly Theatre, Moscow. 150th Anniv.
4327. **1583.** 4 k. multicoloured . . 5 5

1584. "Guests from Overseas" (Viking ship).

1974. Nikolai K. Rorich (painter). Birth Centenary.
4328. **1584.** 6 k. multicoloured . . 10 5

1585. U.P.U. Monument, Berne.

1974. Universal Postal Union. Cent. Mult.
4329. 10 k. Type **1585** 15 8
4330. 10 k. U.P.U. H.Q., Berne 15 8
4331. 10 k. Emblem, letters, early mailcoach and rocket . . 15 8

1586. Orders of Labour Glory.

1974. October Revolution. 57th Anniv. Mult.
4333. 4 k. Type **1586** 5 5
4334. 4 k. Kamaz lorry (vert.) 5 5
4335. 4 k. Nurek hydro-electric power station and dam (vert.) 5 5

1587. "Exploration of Mars".

1974. Soviet Space Flights. Multicoloured
4336. 6 k. Type **1587** 10 5
4337. 10 k. Cosmonauts Popovich and Artchunin ("Soyuz 14") 15 8
4338. 10 k. Cosmonauts Sarafanov and Demin ("Soyuz 15") 15 8
SIZES—VERT. No. 4337, 24×36 mm. HORIZ. No. 4338, 36×24 mm.

1588. Mongolian Crest. 1589. Commemorative Text.

1974. Mongolian People's Republic. 50th Anniv.
4339. **1588.** 6 k. multicoloured . . 10 5

1974. Estonian Liberation. 30th Anniv.
4340. **1589.** 4 k. multicoloured . . 5 5

1590. Ships and Pennant.

1974. Soviet Merchant Marine. 50th Anniv.
4341. **1590.** 4 k. multicoloured . . 5 5

1591. Clock on Kremlin's Spassky Tower.

1974. New Year.
4342. **1591.** 4 k. multicoloured . . 5 5

1592. "The Market Place" (Beuckelaar).

1974. Foreign Paintings in Soviet Museums. Multicoloured.
4343. 4 k. Type **1592** 5 5
4344. 6 k. "Woman selling Fish" (Pieters) 10 5
4345. 10 k. "A Goblet of Lemonade" (Terborsh) 15 8
4346. 14 k. "Girl at Work" (Metsu) 25 10
4347. 16 k. "Saying Grace" (Chardin) 25 12
4348. 20 k. "The Spoilt Child" (Greuze) 30 15
Nos. 4344/8 are vertical designs.

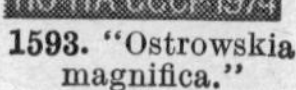

1593. "Ostrowskia magnifica." 1594. I. S. Nikitin.

1974. Soviet Flora. Multicoloured.
4350. 1 k. Type **1593** 5 5
4351. 2 k. "Paeonia intermedia" 5 5
4352. 4 k. "Roemeria refracta" 5 5
4353. 10 k. "Tulipa dasystemon" 15 8
4354. 12 k. "Dianthus versicolor" 20 8

1974. I. S. Nikitin (poet). 150th Birth Anniv.
4355. **1594.** 4 k. blk., grn. & olive 5 5

1595. Pediment of Mint Building.

1974. Leningrad Mint. 250th Anniv.
4356. **1595.** 6 k. multicoloured .. 10 5

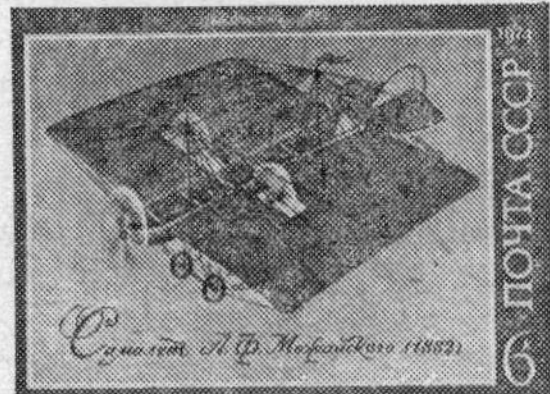
1596. Mozhaisky's Monoplane, 1882.

1974. Pioneer Russian Aircraft. Multi-coloured.
4357. 6 k. Type **1596** 10 5
4358. 6 k. Grizidubov's biplane No. 2, 1910 .. .. 10 5
4359. 6 k. Sikorsky "A" biplane, 1910 .. .. .. 10 5
4360. 6 k. Sikorsky "Vityaz" multi-engine biplane, 1913 .. .. .. 10 5
4361. 6 k. Grigorovich's flying-boat, 1914 .. .. 10 5

1597. Komsomol Badge and Rotary Press.

1975. "Komsomolskaya Pravda" (youth newspaper) and "Pionerskaya Pravda" (children's magazine). 50th Anniv. Mult.
4363. 4 k. Type **1597** 5 5
4364. 4 k. Commemorative scroll (vert.) 5 5

1598. Emblem and Sportsmen.

1975. 8th Trade Unions' and 5th Military Winter Spartakiads. Multicoloured.
4365. 4 k. Emblem and skiers (vert.) 5 5
4366. 16 k. Type **1598** 25 12

1975. Soviet Republics. 50th Anniv. Designs similar to Type **1366**, but dated "1975".
4367. 4 k. green 5 5
DESIGN: No. 4367, Arms, industries and produce of Kara-Kalpak Republic.

1599. "David".

1975. Michelangelo. 500th Birth Anniv.
4368. **1599.** 4 k. bluish grn. & grn. 5 5
4369. – 6 k. red and brown 10 5
4370. – 10 k. bluish grn. & grn. 15 8
4371. – 14 k. brown 25 10
4372. – 20 k. bluish grn. & grn. 30 15
4373. – 30 k. brown 50 20
DESIGNS: 6 k. "Kneeling Boy". 10 k. "Rebellious Slave". 14 k. "The Creation of Adam". 20 k. "Staircase of Laurentiana Library, Florence". 30 k. "Christ and the Virgin".

1600. A. F. Mozhaisky and Aircraft.

1975. A. F. Mozhaisky (aircraft designers). 150th Birth Anniv.
4375. **1600.** 6 k. blue and brown 10 5

1601. Convention Emblem.

1975. International Metric Convention. Cent.
4376. **1601.** 6 k. orge., bl. & blk. 10 5

1602. Spartakiad Emblem.

1975. Sixth Summer Spartakiad.
4377. **1602.** 6 k. blk., red & silver 10 5

1603. Towers of Charles' Bridge, Prague.

1604. Liberation Monument and Parliament Buildings, Budapest.

1975. Liberation of Czechoslovakia and Hungary. 30th Anniv.
4378. **1603.** 6 k. bl., gold & red .. 10 5
4379. **1604.** 6 k. grn., red & gold 10 5

1605. French and Soviet Flags.

1606. Yuri Gagarin.

1975. Establishment of Franco-Soviet Relations. 50th Anniv.
4380. **1605.** 6 k. multicoloured .. 10 5

1975. Cosmonautics Day. Multicoloured.
4381. 6 k. Type **1606** 10 5
4382. 10 k. Gubarev and Grechko (horiz.) 15 8
4383. 16 k. Filipchecko and Rukavishnikov (horiz.) 25 12

1607. Flags of Member Countries.

1609. Head of Lenin.

1608. Communications Emblem and Exhibition Hall.

1975. Warsaw Treaty. 20th Anniv.
4384. **1607.** 6 k. multicoloured .. 10 5

1975. "Communication 75" Exhibition, Sokolniki Park, Moscow.
4385. **1608.** 6 k. red, blue and silver 10 5

1975. "Soviet People's Victory in Great Patriotic War". 30th Anniv. Multi-coloured.
4386. 4 k. Type **1609** .. 8 5
4387. 4 k. Eternal flame and guard of honour .. 8 5
4388. 4 k. Woman making ammunition 8 5
4389. 4 k. Armed partisans .. 8 5
4390. 4 k. Liberation by Soviet solider 8 5
4391. 4 k. Soldier with weapon and banner 8 5

1610. "Lenin" (V. G. Tsiplakov).

1611. Memorial Dates.

1975. Lenin. 105th Birth Anniv.
4393. **1610.** 4 k. multicoloured .. 8 5

1975. "Sotsfilex 75" Stamp Exhibition.
4394. **1611.** 6 k. multicoloured .. 10 5

1612. "Apollo" and "Soyuz" Space Link.

1975. Joint Soviet-American Space Project. (1st issue).
4396. **1612.** 20 k. multicoloured 35 15
See also Nos. 4410/13.

1975. History of Soviet Motor Industry (3rd series). As T **1537.** Multicoloured.
4397. 2 k. Gorkovsky "GAZ-M1" saloon (1936) .. 5 5
4398. 3 k. Yaroslavsky "YAG-6" lorry (1936) .. 5 5
4399. 4 k. Moscow Auto Works "ZIS-16" coach (1938) 8 5
4400. 12 k. Moscow KIM Works "KIM-10" saloon (1940) 20 10
4401. 16 k. Gorkovsky "GAZ-67B" utility car (1943) 25 12

1613. Canal and Emblem.

1614. Soviet-Polish Arms and Flags.

1975. Ninth International Irrigation Congress, Moscow.
4402. **1613.** 6 k. multicoloured .. 10 5

1975. Soviet-Polish Friendship. 30th Anniv.
4403. **1614.** 6 k. multicoloured .. 10 5

MINIMUM PRICE

The minimum price quoted is 5p which represents a handling charge rather than a basis for valuing common stamps. For further notes about prices see introductory pages.

1615. Leonov's "Space-walk".

1616. Y. M. Sverdlov.

1975. Cosmonaut's First "Walk in Space". Tenth Anniv.
4404. **1615.** 6 k. multicoloured .. 10 5

1975. Yakov Sverdlov (Communist leader and statesman). 90th Birth Anniv.
4405. **1616.** 4 k. brn., buff & silv. 8 5

1617. Emblem and Countryside.

1975. Eighth International Congress for Conservation of Plants, Moscow.
4406. **1617.** 6 k. multicoloured .. 10 5

1618. Stylised Flower.

1975. 12th International Botanical Congress. Leningrad.
4407. **1618.** 6 k. multicoloured .. 10 5

1619. Festival Emblem and Film Strip.

1975. 9th International Film Festival, Moscow.
4409. **1619.** 6 k. multicoloured .. 10 5

1620. "Apollo" and "Soyuz" Crew.

1975. Joint Soviet-American Space Project (2nd issue). Multicoloured
4410. 10 k. Type **1620** 15 8
4411. 12 k. Docking manoeuvre 20 10
4412. 12 k. Successful link-up .. 20 10
4413. 16 k. Launch of "Soyuz" (vert.) 25 12

1621. Sturgeon.

1975. International Exposition, Okinawa. Fauna of the Oceans. Multicoloured.
4415. 3 k. Type **1621** 5 5
4416. 4 k. Mollusc 8 5
4417. 6 k. Eel 10 5
4418. 10 k. Wild duck .. 15 8
4419. 16 k. Crab 25 12
4420. 20 k. "Chrysiptera hollisi" (fish) 35 15

1622. "Parade in Red Square, Moscow" (K. F. Iuon).

1975. Soviet Paintings. Multicoloured.

4422. 1 k. Type **1622** 5 5
4423. 2 k. "Winter morning in Industrial Moscow" (K. F. Iuon) 5 5
4424. 6 k. "Soldiers with captured Guns" (I. I. Lansere) 10 5
4425. 10 k. "Excavating the Metro Tunnel" (I. I. Lansere) 15 8
4426. 16 k. "A. H. Pushkin and N. N. Pushkina at Palace Ball" (N. P. Ulyanov) (vert.) .. 25 12
4427. 20 k. "Loriston at Kutosov's Headquarters" (N. P. Ulyanov) .. 35 15

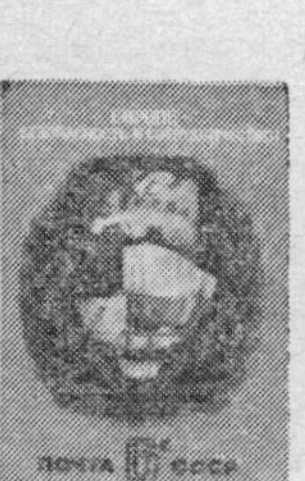

1623. Conference Emblem. **1624.** A. Isaakjan.

1975. European Security and Co-operation Conference, Helsinki.

4428. **1623.** 6 k. blk., gold & blue 10 5

1975. Avetic Isaakjan (Armenian poet). Birth Cent.

4429. **1624.** 4 k. multicoloured .. 8 5

1625. M. K. Ciurlionis. **1626.** Jacques Duclos (French Communist leader).

1975. M. K. Ciurlionis (Lithuanian composer). Birth Cent.

4430. **1625.** 4 k. multicoloured .. 8 5

1975. Duclos Memorial.

4431. **1626.** 6 k. purple and silver 10 5

1627. Farabi (after A. Leontiev). **1628.** Sandpiper.

1975. Farabi (Persian philosopher). 1100th Birth Anniv.

4432. **1627.** 6 k. multicoloured .. 10 5

1975. Berezinsky and Stolby Nature Reserves. 50th Anniv. Soviet Fauna. Multicoloured.

4433. 1 k. Type **1628** 5 5
4434. 4 k. Altai roebuck .. 8 5
4435. 6 k. Siberian marten .. 10 5
4436. 10 k. Capercailzie .. 15 8
4437. 16 k. Badger 25 12

1629. Korean Badge and Flags. **1631.** S. A. Esenin.

1630. Cosmonauts, and "Soyuz 18" linked with "Salyut 4".

1975. Korean Liberation and Vietnam Democratic Republic. 30th Annivs. Multicoloured.

4438. 6 k. Type **1629** 10 5
4439. 6 k. Vietnamese badge and flags 10 5

1975. Space Flight of "Soyuz 18".

4440. **1630.** 10 k. black 15 8

1975. S. A. Esenin (poet). 80th Birth Anniv.

4441. **1631.** 6 k. multicoloured .. 10 5

1632. Standardisation Symbols.

1975. Soviet Standardisation Committee. 50th Anniv.

4442. **1632.** 4 k. multicoloured .. 8 5

1633. Astrakhan Lamb. **1634.** M. P. Konchalovsky.

1975. Third International Astrakhan Lamb Breeding Symposium.

4443. **1633.** 6 k. multicoloured .. 10 5

1975. M. P. Konchalovsky (therapeutist). Birth Cent.

4444. **1634.** 4 k. brown and red 8 5

1635. Exhibition Emblem. **1636.** Emblem and Rose.

1975. Third All-Union Youth Philatelic Exhibition, Erevan

4445. **1635.** 4 k. red, black & blue 8 5

1975. International Women's Year.

4446. **1636.** 6 k. red, blue & turq. 10 5

1637. Parliament Buildings, Belgrade. **1638.** Favorsky's Motif for Title-page of 1938 Reprint.

1975. Yugoslav Republic. 30th Anniv.

4447. **1637.** 6 k. multicoloured .. 10 5

1975. Publication of "Slovo o polku Igoreve". 175th Anniv.

4448. **1638.** 4 k. red, blk. and brn. 8 5

1639. M. I. Kalinen. **1640.** A. V. Lunacharsky.

1975. M. I. Kalinen (statesman) and A. V. Lunacharsky (politician). Birth Cents.

4449. **1639.** 4 k. brown 8 5
4450. **1640.** 4 k. brown 8 5

1641. Revolutionary Torch.

1975. Russian 1905 Revolution. 70th Anniv.

4451. **1641.** 4 k. red and brown 8 5

1642. Terrain of Baikal-Amur Railway. **1644.** Star of Spassky Tower.

1643. "The Decembrists in Senate Square" (D. N. Kardovsky). (Illustration reduced. Actual size 70×33 mm.)

1975. October Revolution. 58th Anniv. Multicoloured.

4452. 4 k. Type **1642** .. 8 5
4453. 4 k. Rolling mill, Novolipetsk steel plant (vert.) 8 5
4454. 4 k. Formula and ammonia plant, Nevynomyssk chemical works (vert.) 8 5

1975. Decembrists' Revolt. 150th Anniv.

4455. **1643.** 4 k. multicoloured .. 8 5

1975. New Year.

4456. **1644.** 4 k. multicoloured .. 8 5

1645. "Village Street".

1975. F. A. Vassiliev (painter). 125th Birth Anniv. Multicoloured.

4457. 2 k. Type **1645** 5 5
4458. 5 k. "Forest Path" .. 8 5
4459. 6 k. "After the Thunderstorm" 10 5
4460. 10 k. "Forest Marsh" (horiz.) 15 8
4461. 12 k. "In the Crimean Mountains" 20 12
4462. 16 k. "Wet Meadow" (horiz.) 25 15

1646. Spacecraft and Lenin Plaque.

1975. Space Flights of "Venus 9" and "Venus 10".

4464. **1646.** 10 k. multicoloured 15 8

1647. G. Sudukyan.

1975. G. Sudukyan (Armenian playwright). 150th Birth Anniv.

4465. **1647.** 4 k. multicoloured .. 8 5

1648. "Papaveraceae polare". **1649.** A. L. Mints.

1975. Soviet Flora. Multicoloured.

4466. 4 k. Type **1648** 8 5
4467. 6 k. "Trollius europaeus" 10 5
4468. 10 k. "Anemone ranunculoides" 15 8
4469. 12 k. "Anemone silvestris" 20 10
4470. 16 k. "Eminium lehemannii" 25 12

1975. A. L. Mints (scientist) Commemoration.

4471. **1649.** 4 k. brown and gold 8 5

1650. "Demon" (A. Kochupalov). **1651.** Pres. Pieck.

1976. Folk Minitature from Palekh Village. (1st series). Multicoloured.

4472. 4 k. Type **1650** 8 5
4473. 6 k. "The Snow Maiden" (T. Zubkova) 10 5
4474. 10 k. "Vasilisa the Beautiful" (I. Vakurov) .. 15 8
4475. 16 k. "Summer" (K. Kukulieva) .. 25 12
4476. 20 k. "Fisherman and Goldfish" (I. Vakurov) (horiz.) 35 15

See also Nos. 4553/7.

1975. Wilhelm Pieck (East German statesman). Birth Cent.

4477. **1651.** 6 k. black 10 5

1652. M. Saltikov-Tchedrin. **1653.** Congress Emblem.

1976. M. Saltikov-Tchedrin (writer). 150th Birth Anniv.
4478. **1652.** 4 k. multicoloured .. 8 5

1976. 25th Communist Party Congress, Moscow (1st issue).
4479. **1653.** 4 k. multicoloured .. 8 5
See also Nos. 4489 and 4548/52.

1654. Lenin Statue, Kiev. **1655.** Ice-hockey.

1976. 25th Ukraine Communist Party Congress, Kiev.
4481. **1654.** 4 k. black, red & blue 8 5

1976. Winter Olympic Games, Innsbruck. Multicoloured.
4482. 2 k. Type **1655** 5 5
4483. 4 k. Cross-country skiing 8 5
4484. 6 k. Pairs figure-skating 10 5
4485. 10 k. Speed skating .. 15 8
4486. 20 k. Tobogganing .. 35 15

1656. Marshal Voroshilov. **1657.** Palace of Congress, Kremlin and Flag.

1976 Marshal Clement Voroshilov 95th Birth Anniv.
4488. **1656.** 4 k. green 8 5

1976. 25th Communist Party Congress, Moscow (2nd issue).
4489. **1657.** 20 k. multicoloured 30 15

1658. " Lenin on Red Square " (Vasiliev).

1976. Lenin. 106th Birth Anniv.
4490. **1658.** 4 k. multicoloured .. 8 5

1659. Atomic Symbol.

1976. Joint Institute of Nuclear Research, Dybna. 20th Anniv.
4491. **1659.** 6 k. multicoloured .. 10 5

1660. Bolshoi Theatre.

1976. Bolshoi Theatre. Bicentenary.
4493. **1660.** 10 k. multicoloured 15 8

1661. " Back from the Fair " (Konchalovsky).

1976. P. P. Konchalovsky (painter). Birth Cent. Multicoloured.
4494. 1 k. Type **1661** 5 5
4495. 2 k. " The Green Glass " 5 5
4496. 6 k. " Peaches " 10 5
4497. 16 k. " Meat, Game and Vegetables by the Window " .. 25 12
4498. 20 k. " P. P. Konchalovsky " (self-portrait) .. 35 15

1662. " Vostok " and " Soyuz " docking with " Salyut ".

1976. First Manned Space Flight. 15th Anniv. Multicoloured.
4499. 4 k. Type **1662** 5 5
4500. 6 k. " Meteor " and " Molniya " 10 5
4501. 10 k. Cosmonauts aboard " Salyut " 15 8
4502. 12 k. " Interkosmos " and docking of " Soyuz " and " Apollo " .. 20 8

1663. I. A. Dzhavakhishvili. **1664.** S. Vurgun.

1976. I. A Dzhavakhishvili (scientist). Birth Cent.
4504. **1663.** 4 k. multicoloured .. 8 5

1976. Samed Vurgun (Azerbaijan poet). 70th Birth Anniv.
4505. **1664.** 4 k. multicoloured .. 8 5

1665. Couple and Banner. **1666.** F.I.P. Emblem.

1976. First All-Union Amateur Art Festival.
4506. **1665.** 4 k. multicoloured .. 8 5

1976. " Federation Internationale de Philatelie ". 50th Anniversary.
4507. **1666.** 6 k. blue and red .. 10 5

1667. Bicentenary Emblem. **1668.** N. N. Burdenko.

1976. Dnepropetrovsk. Bicentenary.
4509. **1667.** 4 k. gold, blk. & blue 8 5

1976. N. N. Burdenko (neurologist). Birth Cent.
4510. **1668.** 4 k. brown and red .. 8 5

1669. K. A. Trenev. **1671.** Electric Trains.

1670. Canoeing.

1976. K. A. Trenev (playwright). Birth Cent.
4511. **1669.** 4 k. multicoloured .. 8 5

1976. History of Soviet Motor Industry. (4th series). As Type **1537.** Multicoloured.
4512. 2 k. Moscow Auto Works " ZIS-110 " saloon car 5 5
4513. 3 k. Gorkovsky " GAZ-51 " lorry 5 5
4514. 4 k. Gorkovsky " GAZ-M20 " " Pobeda " saloon car 8 5
4515. 12 k. Moscow Auto Works " ZIS-150 " lorry .. 20 8
4516. 16 k. Moscow Auto Works " ZIS-154 " bus .. 25 12

1976. Olympic Games, Montreal. Multicoloured.
4517. 4 k. Type **1670** 8 5
4518. 6 k. Basketball (vert.) .. 10 5
4519. 10 k. Graeco-Roman wrestling 15 8
4520. 14 k. Discus-throwing (vert.) 20 10
4521. 16 k. Rifle-shooting .. 25 12

1976. Soviet Railway Electrification. 50th Anniv.
4523. **1671.** 4 k. red, grn. & blk. 8 5

1672. L. Pavlichenko and Order of Gold Star. **1673.** L. E. Rekabarren.

1976. Ljudmila Pavlichenko (war heroine). 60th Birth Anniv.
4524. **1672.** 4 k. brn., yell. & silver 8 5

1976. Luis Rekabarren (founder of Chilean Communist Party). Birth Centenary.
4525. **1673.** 6 k. blk., red & gold 10 5

1674. " Fresh Partner ".

1976. Russian Art. Paintings by P. A. Fedotov. Mult.
4526. 2 k. Type **1674** 5 5
4527. 4 k. " Fastidious Fiancee " (horiz.) 8 5
4528. 6 k. " Aristocrat's Breakfast " 10 5
4529. 10 k. " The Gamblers " (horiz.) 15 8
4530. 16 k. " The Outing " .. 25 12

1680. Text and Flags. **1682.** UNESCO Emblem (Soviet version).

1681. Cosmonauts Volynov and Zholobov.

1976. Soviet–Indian Friendship.
4545. **1680.** 4 k. multicoloured .. 8 5

1976. Space Flight of " Soyuz 21 ".
4546. **1681.** 10 k. brn., turq. & blk. 15 8

1976. UNESCO. 30th Anniv.
4547. **1682.** 16 k. brn., bistre & bl. 25 12

1683. " Industry ".

1976. 25th Communist Party Congress (3rd issue). Multicoloured.
4548. 4 k. Type **1683** 8 5
4549. 4 k. " Farming " .. 8 5
4550. 4 k. " Science and Space Technology " .. 8 5
4551. 4 k. " Transport and Communications " .. .8 5
4552. 4 k. " International Co-operation " 8 5

1675. S. S. Nametkin. **1676.** Marx and Lenin.

1976. Sergei Nametkin (chemist). Birth Centenary.
4532. **1675.** 4 k. multicoloured .. 8 5

1976. " Proletarian Solidarity ".
4533. **1676.** 20 k. lake 35 15
4534. – 30 k. red 50 25
4535. – 50 k. brown .. 85 40
4536. – 1 r. blue .. .. 1·75 80
DESIGNS: 30 k. CMEA Building and text. 50 k. Lenin. 1 r. " Science "–globe and sputniks.

1677. Squacco Heron. **1678.** Dove of Peace with Laurel.

1976. Soviet Nature Reserves. Birds. Multicoloured.

4537. 1 k. Type **1677** 5 5
4538. 3 k. Common loon .. 5 5
4539. 4 k. Coot.. .. .. 8 5
4540. 6 k. Puffin 10 5
4541. 10 k. Seagull 15 8

1976. Stockholm Appeal. " Stop Arms Race ".
4542. **1678.** 4 k. blue, yell. & gold 8 5

1679. Federation Emblem.

1976. Int. Resistance Movement Federation. 25th Anniv.
4543. **1679.** 6 k. gold, blk. & blue 10 5

1684. " The Ploughman ".

1976. Folk Miniatures, Palekh Art Museum (2nd series). Multicoloured.

4553. 2 k. Type **1684** 5 5
4554. 4 k. " The Search " (I. Markichev) 8 5
4555. 12 k. " The Firebird " (A. Kotuchin) 20 8
4556. 14 k. " Folk Festival " (A. Vatagin) 20 8
4557. 20 k. " Victory " (I. Vakurov) 35 15

1685. D. Shostakovitch. **1686.** Marshal Zhukov.

1976. Dmitri Shostakovitch (composer). 70th Birth Anniv.
4558. **1685.** 6 k. blue 10 5

1976. 80th Birth Anniversaries.
4559. **1686.** 4 k. green 8 5
4560. – 4 k. brown 8 5
DESIGN: No. 4560 Marshal Rokossovsky.

1687. " Interkosmos 14 " Satellite. **1688.** V. I. Dal.

1976. Space Research. Multicoloured.

4561. 6 k. Type **1687** 10 5
4562. 10 k. " Aryabhata " (India's first satellite) 15 8
4563. 12 k. " Apollo " and " Soyuz 19 " 20 8
4564. 16 k. " Aureole " (French) satellite 25 12
4565. 20 k. " Apollo " and " Soyuz " docking, " Interkosmos 14 " and " Aureole " .. 35 15

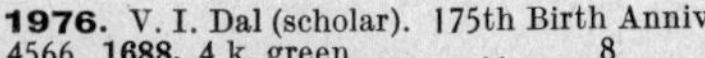

1976. V. I. Dal (scholar). 175th Birth Anniv.
4566. **1688.** 4 k. green 8 5

1689. Turbine (Electric Power).

1976. October Revolution. 59th Anniv. Multicoloured.

4567. 4 k. Type **1689** 8 5
4568. 4 k. Looms (Balashovo Waterproof Fabrics).. 8 5
4569. 4 k. Mechanical drain laying (" Agriculture ").. 8 5

1690. Emblem of Medicine. **1691.** M. A. Novinsky.

1976. Petrov Institute of Cancer Research. 50th Anniv.
4570. **1690.** 4 k. multicoloured .. 8 5

1976. Novinsky (cancer researcher) Commemoration.
4571. **1691.** 4 k. brn., blue & buff 8 5

1692. " Gakkel VII ".

1976. Russian Aircraft Industry, 1911–14. Multicoloured.

4572. 3 k. Type **1692** 5 5
4573. 6 k. Gakkel IX monoplane 10 5
4574. 12 k. Steglau's No. 2 biplane 20 8
4575. 14 k. Dybovsky's " Dolphin " monoplane .. 20 8
4576. 16 k. " Ilya ", Muromet's 4-engine biplane .. 25 12

1693. Sharoyan's Saffron.

1976. Flora of Caucasus. Multicoloured.

4577. 1 k. Type **1693** 5 5
4578. 2 k. " Pulsatilla aurea " 5 5
4579. 3 k. " Gentiana lutea ".. 5 5
4580. 4 k. " Aquilegia olimpica " 8 5
4581. 6 k. " Fritellaria flavus " 10 5

1694. New Years Greeting.

1976. New Year.
4582. **1694.** 4 k. multicoloured .. 8 5

1695. " Parable of the Vineyard."

1976. Rembrandt. 350th Birth Anniv. Multicoloured.

4583. 4 k. Type **1695** 8 5
4584. 6 k. " Danae " 10 5
4585. 10 k. " David and Jonathan " (vert.) .. 15 8
4586. 14 k. " The Holy Family " (vert.) 20 8
4587. 20 k. " Adrian " (vert.).. 35 15

1696. " Luna 24 " and Emblem. **1697.** Armed Forces Order.

1976. Space Flight of " Luna 24 ".
4589. **1696.** 10 k. multicoloured 15 8

1976.

4590. **1697.** 1 k. green 5 5
4591. – 2 k. purple 5 5
4592. – 3 k. red 5 5
4593. – 4 k. red 8 5
4594. – 6 k. turquoise .. 10 5
4595. – 10 k. green 15 8
4596. – 12 k. blue 20 8
4597. – 16 k. green 25 12

DESIGNS: 2 k. " Heroes " medals. 3 k. Workers monument. 4 k. Soviet arms. 6 k. " TU 154 " aircraft. (Postal Communications). 10 k. " Reputation for Work " order. 12 k. Gagarin (Space Exploration). 16 k. Lenin medal.

1698. " Pilot."

1976. Soviet Ice-breakers. Multicoloured.

4598. 4 k. Type **1698** 8 5
4599. 6 k. " Ermak " (vert.) .. 10 5
4600. 10 k. " Fedor Litke " .. 15 8
4601. 16 k. " Vladmir Il'ich " (vert.) 25 12
4602. 20 k. " Krasin ".. .. 35 15

1699. Bykovsky, Aksenov and " Raduga " Experiment.

1976. Space Flight of " Soyuz 22 ".
4603. **1699.** 10 k. grn., blue & red 15 8

1700. Hands holding Torch.

1976. Olympic Games, Moscow (1980). Multicoloured.

4604. 4 k.+2 k. Type **1700** .. 10 8
4605. 10 k.+5 k. Emblem of Moscow Games .. 25 20
4606. 16 k.+6 k. As 10 k. .. 40 35

1701. " Red Banner " Emblem and Star. **1702.** Kotolev Medal.

1977. Red Banner (Forces Voluntary Society). 50th Anniv.
4608. **1701.** 4 k. multicoloured .. 8 5

1977. S. P. Korolev (scientist and rocket pioneer). 70th Birth Anniv.
4609. **1702.** 4 k. gold, blk. & blue 8 5

1703. Global Emblem.

1977. World Peace Congress, Moscow.
4610. **1703.** 4 k. gold. utram. & bl. 8 5

1704. G. Y. Sedov and S.S. " Stefan Foka ".

1977. G. Y. Sedov (polar explorer) Birth Cent.
4611. **1704.** 4 k. multicoloured .. 8 5

1705. Banner, Monument and Front Page. **1706.** Ship on Globe.

1977. Newspaper " Izvestiya ". 60th Anniv.
4612. **1705.** 4 k. blk., red & silver 8 5

1977. International Navigation Congress, Leningrad.
4613. **1706.** 6 k. blue, blk. & gold 10 5

1707. Palace of Congress. **1708.** Marshal Govorov.

1977. 16th Soviet Trade Unions Congress.
4614. **1707.** 4 k. gold, blk. & red 8 5

1977. Marshal Govorov. 80th Birth Anniv.
4615. **1708.** 4 k. brown 8 5

1709. Emblem, Text and Academy.

1977. Grechko Naval Academy, Leningrad. 150th Anniv.
4616. **1709.** 6 k. multicoloured .. 10 5

1710. Jeanne Labourbe.

1711. Queen and Knights.

1977. Jeanne Labourbe. (French communist). Birth Cent.
4617. **1710.** 4 k. multicoloured .. 8 5

1977. 4th European Chess Championships, Moscow.
4618. **1711.** 6 k. multicoloured .. 10 5

1712. Cosmonauts Zudov and Rozhdestvensky.

1977. " Soyuz 23 " Space Flight.
4619. **1712.** 10 k. multicoloured 15 8

EXPRESS STAMPS

E 1.

DESIGNS — HORIZ. 10 k. Express motor-van. 80 k. Express locomotive.

1932. Inscr. " EXPRES ".
E 588. E **1.** 5 k. sepia .. .. 1·00 55
E 589. – 10 k. purple .. 1·75 55
E 590. – 80 k. green .. 3·50 2·25

POSTAGE DUE STAMPS

Доплата
1 коп.
ЗОЛОТОМ.
(D 1.)

D 2.

1924. Surch. as Type D 1.
D 401. **24.** 1 k. on 35 k. blue .. 5 20
D 402. 3 k. on 35 k. blue .. 5 20
D 403. 5 k. on 35 k. blue .. 5 20
D 404. 8 k. on 35 k. blue .. 5 20
D 405. 10 k. on 35 k. blue .. 5 35
D 406. 12 k. on 70 k. brown 5 20
D 407. 14 k. on 35 k. blue .. 5 20
D 408. 32 k. on 35 k. blue .. 5 35
D 409. 40 k. on 35 k. blue .. 10 35

1924. Surch. in Russian characters resembling **AONNATA 1 KON.**
D 421. **27.** 1 k. on 100 r. yellow 70 80

1925.
D 464. D **2.** 1 k. red 10 10
D 465. 2 k. violet 10 10
D 466. 3 k. blue 10 10
D 467. 7 k. yellow .. 12 12
D 468. 8 k. green 12 12
D 469. 10 k. blue 20 20
D 470. 14 k. brown .. 30 30

RUSSIAN POST OFFICES IN CHINA O1

Russian Post Offices were opened in various towns in Manchuria and China from 1870 onwards.

1899. 100 kopecks = 1 rouble.
1917. 100 cents = 1 dollar (Chinese).

(1.)

1899. Arms types (with thunderbolts) of Russia optd. with T **1.**
1. **3.** 1 k. orange 10 10
2. 2 k. green 10 10
3. 3 k. red 10 10
9. **7.** 4 k. red 20 20
4. **3.** 5 k. purple 10 10
5. 7 k. blue 20 20
6. **7.** 10 k. blue 20 20
30. **4.** 14 k. red and blue .. 20 20
31. 15 k. blue and brown .. 12 12
32. **7.** 20 k. red and blue .. 12 12
33. **4.** 25 k. violet and green .. 10 10
34. 35 k. green and purple .. 10 10
35. **7.** 50 k. green and purple .. 12 12
36. **4.** 70 k. orange and brown .. 12 12
37. **8.** 1 r. orange and brown .. 35 35
20. **5.** 3 r. 50 grey and black .. 3·50 3·50
21. **13.** 5 r. blue and grn. on grn. 2·00 2·00
22. **5.** 7 r. yellow and black .. 3·50 3·50
23. **13.** 10 r. grey and red on yell. 11·00 11·00

1910. Arms of types of Russia optd. with T **1.**
24. **11.** 1 k. orange 10 10
25. 2 k. green 10 10
26. 3 k. red 10 10
27. **12.** 4 k. red 10 10
28. **11.** 7 k. blue 10 10
29. **12.** 10 k. blue 10 10

1917. Arms types of Russia surch. in "cents" and "dollars" diagonally in one line.
42. **11.** 1 c. on 1 k. orange .. 8 45
43. 2 c. on 2 k. green 8 45
44. 3 c. on 3 k. red 8 45
45. **12.** 4 c. on 4 k. red 8 45
46. **11.** 5 c. on 5 k. lilac .. 12 1·10
47. **11.** 10 c. on 10 k. blue .. 12 1·10
48. **4.** 14 c. on 14 k. red & blue 20 1·10
49. 15 c. on 15 k. blue & pur. 12 1·10
50. **7.** 20 c. on 20 k. red & blue 10 1·10
51. **4.** 25 c. on 25 k. violet & grn. 10 1·10
52. 35 c. on 35 k. grn. & pur. 20 1·40
53. **7.** 50 c. on 50 k. grn. & pur. 20 1·40
54. **4.** 70 c. on 70 k. orge. & brn. 20 1·40
55. **8.** 1 d. on 1 r. orge & brn. on brown .. .. 20 1·75
39. **4.** 3 d. 50 on 3 r. 50 grey and black .. .. .. 1·75 4·50
40. **13.** 5 d. on 5 r. blue and green 1·60 6·50
41. **5.** 7 d. on 7 r. yellow & black 1·00 4·50
57. **13.** 10 d. on 10 r. grey, red and yellow .. 5·50 14·00

1920. Arms types of Russia surch. in "cents" in two lines.
65. **11.** 1 c. on 1 k. orange .. 2·25 2·75
59. 2 c. on 2 k. green .. 1·75 2·25
60. 3 c. on 3 k. red .. .. 1·75 2·25
61. **12.** 4 c. on 4 k. red .. .. 2·25 2·75
62. **11.** 5 c. on 5 k. lilac .. .. 2·75 3·25
63. **12.** 10 c. on 10 k. blue .. 11·00 13·00
64. **11.** 10 c. on 10 k. on 7 k. blue 13·00 16·00

RUSSIAN POST OFFICES IN CRETE E1

(RETHYMNON PROVINCE)

4 metallik = 1 grosion. (Turkish piastre).

The Russian Postal Service operated from 13 May to 29 July 1899.

There issues were optd, with circular control marks as shown on T **3/4**. Prices are for stamps with these marks, but unused examples without them are known.

1.

2.

1899. Imperf.
1. 1. **1** m. blue .. .. .. 8·50 8·50
2. 2. **1** m. green .. .. 3·25 3·25
3. 2 m. red .. .. .. 50·00 42·00
4. 2 m. green .. .. 3·25 3·25

3.

4.

1899. Without stars in oval.
5. **3.** 1 m. pink .. .. .. 9·00 8·50
6. 2 m. pink .. .. .. 9·00 8·50
7. 1 g. pink .. .. .. 9·00 8·50
8. 1 m. blue .. .. .. 9·00 8·50
9. 2 m. blue .. .. .. 9·00 8·50
10. 1 g. blue .. .. .. 9·00 8·50
11. 1 m. green .. .. 9·00 8·50
12. 2 m. green .. .. 9·00 8·50
13. 1 g. green .. .. 9·00 8·50
14. 1 m. red .. .. .. 9·00 8·50
15. 2 m. red .. .. .. 9·00 8·50
16. 1 g. red .. .. .. 9·00 8·50
17. 1 m. orange .. .. 9·00 8·50
18. 2 m. orange .. .. 9·00 8·50
19. 1 g. orange .. .. 9·00 8·50
20. 1 m. yellow .. .. 9·00 8·50
21. 2 m. yellow .. .. 9·00 8·50
22. 1 g. yellow .. .. 9·00 8·50
23. 1 m. black £140 £140
24. 2 m. black £140 £140
25. 1 g. black £140 £140

1899. Starred at each side.
26. **4.** 1 m. pink .. .. .. 4·25 4·25
27. 2 m. pink .. .. .. 4·25 4·25
28. 1 g. pink .. .. .. 4·25 4·25
29. 1 m. blue .. .. .. 4·25 4·25
30. 2 m. blue .. .. .. 4·25 4·25
31. 1 g. blue .. .. .. 4·25 4·25
32. 1 m. green .. .. 4·25 4·25
33. 2 m. green .. .. 4·25 4·25
34. 1 g. green .. .. 4·25 4·25
35. 1 m. red .. .. .. 4·25 4·25
36. 2 m. red .. .. .. 4·25 4·25
37. 1 g. red .. .. .. 4·25 4·25

RUSSIAN POST OFFICES IN TURKEY E3

General issues for Russian P.Os in the Turkish Empire and stamps specially overprinted for use at particular offices.

1863. 100 kopecks = 1 rouble.
1900. 40 paras = 1 piastre.

1.

1863. Imperf.
2a. **1.** 6 k. blue .. .. .. 45·00 £180

2.

3.

1865. Imperf.
4. **2.** 2 k. brown and blue .. £180 £160
5. 20 k. blue and red £275 £180

1865. Imperf.
6. **3.** 2 k. red and blue .. .. 5·50 6·00
7. 20 k. blue and red .. .. 12·00 12·00

4.

5.

1868. Perf.
14a. **4.** 1 k. brown .. .. 2·25 1·40
11. 3 k. green .. .. 5·50 2·75
16. 5 k. blue .. .. .. 1·10 55
17a. 10 k. red and green .. 55 25

1876. Surch. with large figures of value.
24. **4.** 7 k. on 10 k. red & green 22·00 13·00
22. 8 k. on 10 k. red & green 18·00 11·00

1879.
26. **4.** 1 k. black and yellow .. 90 55
32. 1 k. orange 8 8
27. 2 k. black and red .. 1·10 70
33. 2 k. green 12 12
34. 5 k. purple 60 35
28. 7 k. red and grey .. 1·75 45
35. 7 k. blue 35 12

1900. Arms types of Russia surch. in " paras " or " piastres ".
36. **3.** 4 pa. on 1 k. orange .. 5 5
40. 10 pa. on 2 k. green .. 8 8
41. **7.** 20 pa. on 4 k. red .. 8 8
42. **3.** 20 pa. on 5 k. purple .. 8 8
43. **7.** 1 pi. on 10 k. blue .. 5 5
44. 2 pi. on 20 k. red and blue 15 15
45. 5 pi. on 50 k. green & pur. 55 55
46. **4.** 7 pi. on 70 k. orge. & brown 70 70
56. **8.** 10 pi. on 1 r. orge. & brown 20 20
48. **5.** 35 pi. on 3 r. 50 grey & blk. 2·75 2·75
49. 70 pi. on 7 r. yellow & blk. 3·50 3·50

1909. As T **7, 8** and **5** of Russia, but ship and date in centre as T **5**, and surch. in " paras " or " piastres ".
57. **7.** 5 pa. on 1 k. orange .. 8 8
58. 10 pa. on 2 k. red .. 12 12
59. 20 pa. on 4 k. red .. 20 20
60. 1 pi. on 10 k. blue .. 25 25
61. 5 pi. on 50 k. green & pur. 55 55
62. 7 pi. on 70 k. orge. & brn. 90 90
63. **8.** 10 pi. on 1 r. orge. & brn. 1·10 1·10
64. **5.** 35 pi. on 3 r. 50 grn. & brn. 3·50 3·50
65. 70 pi. on 7 r. pink & green 6·00 6·00

The above stamps exist overprinted for Constantinople, Jaffa, Jerusalem, Kerassunde, Mount Athos, Salonika, Smyrna, Trebizonde, Beyrouth, Dardanelles, Mytilene and Rizeh. For full list see Stanley Gibbons' Europe Catalogue, Vol. 3 under Turkish Empire.

1910. Arms type of Russia surch. with value in " paras " or " piastres ".
50. **11.** 5 pa. on 1 k. orange .. 5 5
51. 10 pa. on 2 k. green .. 5 5
201. 15 pa. on 3 k. red .. 5 5
52. **12.** 20 pa. on 4 k. red .. 5 5
181. **11.** 20 pa. on 5 k. claret .. 5 5
53. **12.** 1 pi. on 10 k. blue .. 5 5
182. **4.** $1\frac{1}{2}$ pi. on 15 k. blue & pur. 5 5
183. **7.** 2 pi. on 20 k. red and blue 5 5
184. **4.** $2\frac{1}{2}$ pi. on 25 k. mauve and green 8 8
185. $3\frac{1}{2}$ pi. on 35 k. grn. & pur. 10 10
202. **13.** 50 pi. on 5 r. blue & green 1·40 1·40
203. 100 pi. on 10 r. grey, red and yellow .. 3·50 3·50

1913. Romanov types of Russia surch.
186. 5 pa. on 1 k. orange (No. 107) 5 5
187. 10 pa. on 2 k. green .. 5 5
188. 15 pa. on 3 k. red .. 5 5
189. 20 pa. on 4 k. red .. 5 5
190. 1 pi. on 10 k. blue .. 8 8
191. $1\frac{1}{2}$ pi. on 15 k. brown 15 15
192. 2 pi. on 20 k. olive 15 15
193. $2\frac{1}{2}$ pi. on 25 k. claret 25 25
194. $3\frac{1}{2}$ pi. on 35 k. grn. & violet 55 55
195. 5 pi. on 50 k. grey & brown 60 60
196. 7 pi. on 70 k. brown & green 2·75 2·75
197. 10 pi. on 1 r. green .. 2·75 2·75
198. 20 pi. on 2 r. brown .. 55 55
199. 30 pi. on 3 r. violet .. 70 70
200. 50 pi. on 5 r. brown .. 29·00 32·00

RWANDA O4

100 centimes = 1 franc.

An independent republic established on 1st July, 1962, formerly part of Ruanda-Urundi.

1. Pres. Kayibanda and Map.

1962. Independence.
1. **1.** 10 c. sepia and green .. 5 5
2. – 40 c. sepia and purple .. 5 5
3. **1.** 1 f. sepia and slate-blue .. 45 20
4. – 1 f. 50 sepia and brown .. 5 5
5. **1.** 3 f. 50 sepia and orange .. 8 5
6. – 6 f. 50 sepia & viol-blue .. 12 5
7. **1.** 10 f. sepia and olive .. 15 5
8. – 20 f. sepia and red .. 30 12

DESIGN: Nos. 2, 4, 6, 8, are as T 1 but with halo around Rwanda on map in place of " R ".

1963. Admission to U.N. No. 204 of Ruanda-Urundi with coloured frame obliterating old inscr. (colours below), and surch. **Admission a l'O.N.U. 18-9-1962 REPUBLIQUE RWANDAISE** and new value.
9. 3 f. 50 on 3 f. silver-grey .. 8 8
10. 6 f. 50 on 3 f. silver-pink .. 55 55
11. 10 f. on 3 f. silver-blue .. 15 15
12. 20 f. on 3 f. silver 30 30

1963. Flowers issue of Ruanda-Urundi (Nos. 178. etc.) optd. **REPUBLIQUE RWANDAISE** or surch. also in various coloured panels over old inscriptions and values. Flowers in natural colours.

13. 25 c. orange and green .. 5 5
14. 40 c. salmon and green .. 5 5
15. 60 c. purple and green .. 5 5
16. 1 f. 25 blue and green .. 45 45
17. 1 f. 50 green and iol .. 40 40
18. 2 f. on 1 f. 50 green & violet 55 55
19. 4 f. on 1 f. 50 green & violet 55 55
20. 5 f. green and purple .. 55 55
21. 7 f. brown and green .. 55 55
22. 10 f. olive and purple .. 55 55

The coloured panels are in various shades of silver except No. 19 which is in blue.

2. Ears of Wheat and Native Implements.

1963. Freedom from Hunger.

23. 2. 2 f. brown and emerald 5 5
24. 4 f. magenta and blue .. 8 5
25. 7 f. red and grey .. 12 5
26. 10 f. olive-green & yellow 40 25

3. Coffee.

4. Postal Services Emblem.

6. Child Care.

5. Emblems.

1963. Independence. 1st Anniv.

27. 3. 10 c. brown & ultramarine 5 5
28. – 20 c. yellow and indigo .. 5 5
29. – 30 c. green and orange .. 5 5
30. 3. 40 c. brown and blue-green 5 5
31. – 1 f. yellow and maroon .. 5 5
32. – 2 f. green and blue .. 40 30
33. 3. 4 f. brown and red .. 5 5
34. – 7 f. yellow and green .. 10 5
35. – 10 f. green and violet .. 15 8

DESIGNS: 20 c., 1 f., 7 f. Bananas. 30 c., 2 f., 10 f. Tea.

1963. African and Malagasian Postal and Telecommunications Union. As T 10 of Central African Republic but with "AERIENNE" omitted.

36. 14 f. multicoloured.. .. 40 40

1963. Admission of Rwanda to U.P.U.

37. 4. 50 c. ultramarine and pink 5 5
38. 1 f. 50 brown and blue .. 35 30
39. 3 f. purple and grey .. 5 5
40. 20 f. green and yellow .. 25 15

1963. Declaration of Human Rights. 15th Anniv.

41. 5. 5 f. red 8 5
42. 6 f. violet 30 20
43. 10 f. blue 15 8

1963. Red Cross Centenary.

44. 6. 10 c. multicoloured .. 5 5
45. – 20 c. multicoloured .. 5 5
46. – 30 c. multicoloured .. 5 5
47. – 40 c. choc., red and violet 5 5
48. 6. 2 f. multicoloured .. 40 35
49. – 7 f. multicoloured .. 12 8
50. – 10 f. choc., red and brown 15 10
51. – 20 f. choc., red & orange 30 12

DESIGNS—HORIZ. 20 c., 7 f. Patient having blood test. 40 c., 20 f. Stretcher-party. VERT. 30 c.. 10 f. Doctor examining child.

7. Map and Hydraulic Pump.

8. Boy with Crutch.

9. Running.

1964. World Meteorological Day.

52. 7. 3 f. sepia, blue and green 5 5
53. 7 f. sepia, blue and rose .. 20 12
54. 10 f. sepia, blue and orange 25 20

1964. Stamps of Ruanda-Urundi optd. **REPUBLIQUE RWANDAISE** or surch. also in black over coloured metallic panels obliterating old inscription or value.

55. 10 c. on 20 c. (No. 204) .. 5 5
56. 20 c. (No. 204) 5 5
57. 30 c. on 1 f. 50 (No. 208) .. 5 5
58. 40 c. (No. 205) 5 5
59. 50 c. (No. 206) 5 5
60. 1 f. (No. 207) 5 5
61. 2 f. (No. 209) 5 5
62. 3 f. (No. 210) 5 5
63. 4 f. on 3 f. 50 on 3 f. (No. 228) 10 5
64. 5 f. (No. 211) 8 5
65. 7 f. 50 on 6 f. 50 (No. 212) 15 5
66. 8 f. (No. 213) .. .. 1·40 1·10
67. 10 f. (No. 214) 20 8
68. 20 f. (No. 224) 40 20
69. 50 f. (No. 230) 80 55

1964. Gatagara Re-education Centre.

70. 8. 10 c. sepia and violet .. 5 5
71. – 40 c. sepia and blue .. 5 5
72. – 4 f. sepia and chestnut .. 8 5
73. 8. 7 f. 50 sepia and green .. 15 12
74. – 8 f. sepia and bistre .. 65 50
75. – 10 f. sepia and purple .. 20 15

DESIGNS—HORIZ. 40 c., 8 f. Children operating sewing-machines. VERT. 4 f., 10 f. Crippled child on crutches.

1964. Olympic Games, Tokyo. Sportsmen in slate.

76. 9. 10 c. slate-blue 5 5
77. – 20 c. red 5 5
78. – 30 c. turquoise 5 5
79. – 40 c. brown 5 5
80. 9. 4 f. blue 5 5
81. – 5 f. green 90 85
82. – 20 f. purple 25 20
83. – 50 f. grey 55 50

DESIGNS—VERT. 20 c., 5 f. Basketball. 40 c., 50 f. Football. HORIZ. 30 c., 20 f. High-jumping

10. Faculties of "Letters" and "Sciences".

11. Abraham Lincoln.

1965. National University. Multicoloured.

84. 10 c. Type 10 .. .. 5 5
85. 20 c. Student with microscope and building ("Medicine") 5 5
86. 30 c. Scales of Justice, Hand of Law ("Social Sciences" and "Normal High School") 5 5
87. 40 c. University buildings.. 5 5
88. 5 f. Type 10.. .. .. 8 5
89. 7 f. As 20 c. 10 8
90. 10 f. As 30 c.. .. .. 60 55
91. 12 f. As 40 c.. .. .. 15 10

The 20 c., 40 c., 7 f. and 12 f. are horiz.

1965. Abraham Lincoln. Death Cent.

92. 11. 10 c. green and red .. 5 5
93. 20 c. brown and blue .. 5 5
94. 30 c. violet and red .. 5 5
95. 40 c. blue and brown .. 5 5
96. 9 f. chestnut & purple .. 12 8
97. 40 f. slate-purple & green 1·00 45

12. Marabou Storks.

13. "Telstar" Satellite.

1965. Kagera National Park. Multicoloured.

98. 10 c. Type 12 .. .. 5 5
99. 20 c. Zebras 5 5
100. 30 c. Impalas 5 5
101. 40 c. Crowned cranes, hippopotami and storks .. 5 5
102. 1 f. Buffaloes 5 5
103. 3 f. Wild dogs 5 5
104. 5 f. Baboons .. .. 2·00 70
105. 10 f. Elephant and map .. 12 5
106. 40 f. Cormorants and anhingas 50 20
107. 100 f. Lions .. .. 1·25 30

SIZES: As T 12—VERT. 30 c., 1 f., 5 f. HORIZ. 20 c., 40 c., 3 f., 10 f. LARGER (45×25½ mm.): 40 f., 100 f.

1965. I.T.U. Cent. Multicoloured.

108. 10 c. Type 13 .. .. 5 5
109. 40 c. "Syncom" satellite .. 5 5
110. 4 f. 50 Type 13 .. .. 75 25
111. 50 f. "Syncom" satellite .. 60 12

14. "Colotis aurigineus".

15. Cattle and I.C.Y. emblem.

1965. Rwanda Butterflies. Multicoloured.

112. 10 c. "Papilio bromius".. 5 5
113. 15 c. "Papilio hesperus".. 5 5
114. 20 c. Type 14 .. .. 5 5
115. 30 c. "Amphicallia pactolicus" 5 5
116. 35 c. "Lobobunaea phaedusa" 5 5
117. 40 c. "Papilio jacksoni ruandana" 5 5
118. 1 f. 50 "Papilio dardanus dardanus" .. 5 5
119. 3 f. "Amaurina elliotti".. 95 30
120. 4 f. "Colias electo pseudohecate" 55 25
121. 10 f. "Bunaea alcinoe" .. 12 8
122. 50 f. "Athletes gigas" .. 40 15
123. 100 f. "Charaxes ansorgei R." .. .. 1·10 30

The 10 c., 30 c., 35 c., 3 f., 4 f. and 100 f. are vert.

1965. Int. Co-operation Year.

124. 15. 10 c. green and yellow.. 5 5
125. – 40 c. brown, blue & grn. 5 5
126. – 4 f. 50 grn., brn. & yell. 60 25
127. – 45 f. purple and brown 50 20

DESIGNS: 40 c. Crater lake and giant plants. 4 f. 50 Gazelle and candelabra tree. 45 f. Mt. Ruwenzori. Each with I.C.Y. emblem.

16. Pres. Kennedy, Globe and Satellites.

17. Madonna and Child.

1965. Pres. Kennedy's Death. 2nd Anniv.

128. 16. 10 c. brown and green.. 5 5
129. 40 c. brown and cerise.. 5 5
130. 50 c. brown and blue .. 5 5
131. 1 f. brown and olive .. 5 5
132. 8 f. brown and violet .. 75 70
133. 50 f. brown and grey .. 60 55

1965. Christmas.

134. 17. 10 c. green and gold .. 5 5
135. 40 c. brown and gold .. 5 5
136. 50 c. blue and gold .. 5 5
137. 4 f. black and gold .. 45 40
138. 6 f. violet and gold .. 8 8
139. 30 f. chocolate and gold 35 35

18. Father Damien.

1966. World Leprosy Day.

140. 18. 10 c. blue and brown .. 5 5
141. – 40 c. red and blue .. 5 5
142. 18. 4 f. 50 slate and green 12 5
143. – 45 f. brown and red .. 1·00 60

DESIGNS: 40 c., 45 f. Dr. Schweitzer.

19. Pope Paul, Rome and New York.

1966. Pope Paul's Visit to U.N. Organisation.

144. 19. 10 c. indigo and brown 5 5
145. – 40 c. indigo and blue .. 5 5
146. 19. 4 f. 50 indigo & purple.. 70 60
147. – 50 f. indigo and green.. 65 55

DESIGNS: 40 c., 50 f. Pope Paul, Arms and U.N. emblem.

20. "Echinops amplexicaulis" and "E. bequaertii".

1966. Flowers. Multicoloured.

148. 10 c. Type 20 .. .. 5 5
149. 20 c. "Haemanthus multiflorus" 5 5
150. 30 c. "Helichrysum ericirosenii" 5 5
151. 40 c. "Carissa edulis" .. 5 5
152. 1 f. "Spathodea campanulata" 5 5
153. 3 f. "Habenaria praestans" 5 5
154. 5 f. "Aloe lateritia" .. 2·00 1·25
155. 10 f. "Ammocharis tinneana" 15 10
156. 40 f. "Erythrina abyssinica" 50 25
157. 100 f. "Capparis tomentosa" 1·25 75

The 20 c., 40 c., 1 f., 3 f., 5 f. and 10 f. are vert.

21. W.H.O. Building.

1966. W.H.O. Headquarters, Geneva. Inaug.

159. 21. 2 f. olive 5 5
160. 3 f. red 10 10
161. 5 f. blue 5 5

22. Football.

23. Mother and Child within flames.

1966. "Youth and Sports".

162. 22. 10 c. blk., blue & green 5 5
163. – 20 c. black, green & red 5 5
164. – 30 c. black, purple & blue 5 5
165. 22. 40 c. blk. green & bistre 5 5
166. – 9 f. black, purple & grey 12 8
167. – 50 f. black, blue & pur. 65 60

DESIGNS: 20 c., 9 f. Basketball. 30 c., 50 f. Volleyball.

1966. Nuclear Disarmament.

168. 23. 20 c. brown, red & mve. 5 5
169. 30 c. brown, red & green.. 5 5
170. 50 c. brown, red & cobalt 5 5
171. 6 f. brown, red & yellow 5 5
172. 15 f. brown, red & turq. 20 20
173. 18 f. brown, red & lav... 25 20

24. Football.

25. Yellow-breasted Helmet-shrike and Mikeno Volcano.

1966. World Cup Football Championships.
174. **24.** 20 c. blue and orange .. 5 5
175. 30 c. blue and violet .. 5 5
176. 50 c. blue and green .. 5 5
177. 6 f. blue and magenta .. 10 5
178. 12 f. blue and brown .. 30 15
179. 25 f. indigo and blue .. 50 35

1966. Rwanda Scenery.
180. **25.** 10 c. green 5 5
181. – 40 c. lake 5 5
182. – 4 f. 50 ultramarine .. 35 25
183. – 55 f. purple 40 25
DESIGNS—VERT. 40 c. Nyamilanga Falls. 55 f. Rusumu Falls. HORIZ. 4 f. 50, Gahinga and Muhabura Volcanoes, and giant plants.

26. U.N.E.S.C.O. and Cultural Emblems.

1966. U.N.E.S.C.O. 20th Anniv.
184. **26.** 20 c. magenta and blue 5 5
185. – 30 c. turquoise & black 5 5
186. – 50 c. brown and black .. 5 5
187. – 1 f. violet and black 5 5
188. **26.** 5 f. green and brown .. 5 5
189. – 10 f. brown and black .. 10 5
190. – 15 f. purple and blue .. 30 15
191. – 50 f. blue and black .. 35 25
DESIGNS: 30 c., 10 f. "Animal" primer. 50 c., 15 f. Atomic symbol and drill operator. 1 f., 50 f. Nubian monuments partly submerged in the Nile.

27. Head of Mamba.

1967. Snakes. Multicoloured.
192. 20 c. Type **27** 5 5
193. 30 c. Python 5 5
194. 50 c. "Bitis gabonica" .. 5 5
195. 1 f. "Naja melanoleuca" .. 5 5
196. 3 f. Head of python .. 5 5
197. 5 f. "Psammophis sibilans" 8 8
198. 20 f. "Dendroaspis jamesoni kaimosae" .. 40 40
199. 70 f. "Dasypeltis scabra" .. 60 50
The 30 c., 1 f., 5 f. and 70 f. are vert.

28. Girders and Tea Flower.

1967. Ntaruka Hydro-Electric Project.
200. **28.** 20 c. blue and purple .. 5 5
201. – 30 c. brown and black .. 5 5
202. – 50 c. violet and brown .. 5 5
203. **28.** 4 f. maroon and green .. 5 5
204. – 25 f. green and violet .. 20 20
205. – 50 f. brown and blue .. 55 55
DESIGNS: 30 c., 25 f. Power conductors and pyrethrum flowers. 50 c., 50 f. Barrage and coffee-beans.

29. "St. Martin" (after Van Dyck).

1967. Paintings.
208. **29.** 20 c. blk., gold & violet 5 5
209. – 40 c. black, gold & grn. 5 5
210. – 60 c. black, gold & red 5 5
211. – 80 c. black, gold & blue 5 5
212. **29.** 9 f. black, gold & brown 50 25
213. – 15 f. black, gold & verm. 15 10
214. – 18 f. blk., gold & bronze 20 10
215. – 26 f. black, gold & lake 25 20
PAINTINGS—HORIZ. 40 c., 15 f. "Rebecca and Eliezer" (Murillo). 80 c., 26 f. "Job and his Friends" (attributed to Il Calabrese). VERT. 60 c., 18 f. "St. Christopher" (D. Bouts).

30. Rwanda "Round Table" Emblem and Zebra's Head.

1967. Rwanda "Round Table" Fund for Charitable Works. Each with "Round Table" Emblem. Multicoloured.
216. 20 c. Type **30** 5 5
217. 40 c. Elephant's head .. 5 5
218. 60 c. Buffalo's head .. 5 5
219. 80 c. Kudu's head .. 5 5
220. 18 f. Ear of wheat .. 20 10
221. 100 f. Palm .. .. 1·10 45

31. "Africa Place" and Dancers.

1967. World Fair, Montreal.
222. **31.** 20 c. blue and sepia .. 5 5
223. – 30 c. purple and sepia 5 5
224. – 50 c. orange and sepia 5 5
225. – 1 f. green and sepia .. 5 5
226. – 3 f. violet and sepia .. 5 5
227. **31.** 15 f. green and sepia .. 12 8
228. – 34 f. cerise and sepia .. 35 20
229. – 40 f. turquoise and sepia 45 20
DESIGNS: "Africa Place" (two different views used alternately in order of value): 30 c., 3 f. Drum and handicrafts. 50 c., 40 f. Dancers leaping. 1 f., 34 f. Spears, shields and weapons.

1967. Air. U.A.M.P.T. 5th Anniv. As T **95** of Cameroun.
230. 6 f. slate, brown and lake 8 5
231. 18 f. purple and brown .. 25 20
232. 30 f. red, green and blue .. 40 35

32. Zebra's Head and Lions' Emblem.

1967. Lions Int. 50th Anniv.
233. **32.** 20 c. black, blue & violet 5 5
234. 80 c. black, blue & green 5 5
235. 1 f. black, blue and red 5 5
236. 8 f. black, blue & brown 8 8
237. 10 f. black, blue & ult. 10 10
238. 50 f. black, blue & green 55 55

33. Senegal Kingfisher.

1967. Birds of Rwanda. Multicoloured.
239. 20 c. Red bishop 5 5
240. 40 c. Type **33** 5 5
241. 60 c. Red-billed dioch .. 5 5
242. 80 c. Pied barber 5 5
243. 2 f. Pin-tailed whydah .. 5 5
244. 3 f. Solitary cuckoo .. 5 5
245. 18 f. Green wood-hoopoe (or kakelaar) .. 25 20
246. 25 f. Lafresnay's bee-eater 30 25
247. 80 f. Regal sunbird .. 85 80
248. 100 f. Fan-tailed whydah .. 1·25 1·10
The 20 c., 60 c., 2 f., 18 f. and 80 f. are vert.

34. Running, and Mexican Antiquities.

1968. Olympic Games, Mexico. (1st Issue). Multicoloured.
250. 20 c. Type **34** 5 5
251. 40 c. Hammer-throwing .. 5 5
252. 60 c. Hurdling 5 5
253. 80 c. Javelin-throwing .. 5 5
254. 8 f. Football (vert.) .. 10 10
255. 10 f. Mexican horseman and cacti (vert.) 12 12
256. 12 f. Hockey (vert.) .. 15 15
257. 18 f. Cathedral (vert.) .. 20 20
258. 20 f. Boxing (vert.) .. 20 20
259. 30 f. Mexico City (vert.) .. 35 35
The 20 c. to 80 c. include Mexican Antiquities in their designs.

35. "Diaphananthe fragrantissima".

1968. Flowers. Multicoloured.
261. 20 c. Type **35** 5 5
262. 40 c. "Phaeomeria speciosa" 5 5
263. 60 c. "Ravenala madagascariensis" 5 5
264. 80 c. "Costus afer" .. 5 5
265. 2 f. "Musa sapientum" .. 5 5
266. 3 f. "Carica papaya" .. 5 5
267. 18 f. "Clerodendron sp." .. 20 20
268. 25 f. "Ipomoea batatae" 25 25
269. 80 f. Baobab flower .. 90 90
270. 100 f. "Passiflora caerulea" 1·10 1·10

36. Horse-jumping. 37. Tuareg (Algeria).

1968. Olympic Games, Mexico (2nd Issue).
271. **36.** 20 c. brown and orange 5 5
272. – 40 c. brown & turquoise 5 5
273. – 60 c. brown and purple 5 5
274. – 80 c. brown and blue .. 5 5
275. – 38 f. brown & vermilion 35 35
276. – 60 f. brown and green .. 70 70
SPORTS: 40 c. Japanese wrestling. 60 c. Fencing. 80 c. High-jumping. 38 f. High-diving. 60 f. Weightlifting. Each design also represents the location of previous Olympics as at left in Type **36**.

1968. African National Costumes (1st Series). Multicoloured.
277. 30 c. Type **37** 5 5
278. 40 c. Upper Volta 5 5
279. 60 c. Senegal 5 5
280. 70 c. Rwanda 5 5
281. 8 f. Morocco 8 8
282. 20 f. Nigeria 20 20
283. 40 f. Zambia 40 40
284. 50 f. Kenya 50 50
See also Nos. 345/52.

1968. Air. "Philexafrique" Stamp Exn., Abidjan (Ivory Coast, 1969) (1st Issue). As T **109** of Cameroun.
286. 100 f. "Alexandre Lenoir" (J. L. David) .. .. 1·25 1·25

38. Rwanda Scene and Stamp of Ruanda-Urundi (1953).

1969. Air. "Philexafrique" Stamp Exn. (2nd Issue).
287. **38.** 50 f. multicoloured .. 60 60

39. "The Musical Angels" (Van Eyck). 40. Tuareg Tribesmen.

1969. "Paintings and Music". Multicoloured.
288. 20 c. Type **39** (postage) .. 5 5
289. 40 c. "The Angels' Concert" (M. Grunewald) .. 5 5
290. 60 c. "The Singing Boy" (Frans Hals) 5 5
291. 80 c. "The Lute-player" (G. Terborch) 5 5
292. 2 f. "The Fifer" (Manet) .. 5 5
293. 6 f. "Young Girls at the Piano" (Renoir) .. 8 8
294. 50 f. "The Music Lesson" (Fragonard) (air) .. 50 50
295. 100 f. "Angels Playing their Musical Instruments" (Memling) .. .. 1·10 1·10
The 100 f. is horiz.

1969. African Headdresses (1st series). Multicoloured.
297. 20 c. Type **40** 5 5
298. 40 c. Young Ovambo woman 5 5
299. 60 c. Ancient Guinean and Middle Congo festival head-dresses .. 5 5
300. 80 c. Guinean "Dagger" dancer 5 5
301. 8 f. Nigerian Muslims .. 10 10
302. 20 f. Luba dancer, Kabondo (Congo) 25 25
303. 40 f. Senegalese and Gambian women .. 50 50
304. 80 f. Rwanda dancer .. 1·00 1·00
See also Nos. 408/15.

41. "The Moneylender and his Wife" (Quentin Metsys).

1969. African Development Bank. 5th Anniv.
305. **41.** 30 f. mult. on silver .. 35 30
306. – 70 f. mult. on gold .. 90 85
DESIGN: 70 f. "The Moneylender and his Wife" (Van Reymerswaele).

42. Pyrethrum. 43. Revolutionary.

1969. Medicinal Plants. Multicoloured.
308. 20 c. Type **42** 5 5
309. 40 c. Aloes 5 5
310. 60 c. Cola 5 5
311. 80 c. Coca 5 5
312. 3 f. Hagenia 5 5
313. 75 f. Cassia 85 85
314. 80 f. Cinchona .. 95 95
315. 100 f. Tephrosia .. .. 1·10 1·10

1969. Revolution. 10th Anniv.
316. **43.** 6 f. multicoloured .. 8 8
317. 18 f. multicoloured .. 20 20
318. 40 f. multicoloured .. 45 45

44. " Napoleon on Horseback " (David).

1969. Napoleon Bonaparte. Birth Bicent. Multicoloured. Portraits of Napoleon. Artists name given.

320. 20 c. Type **44** 5 5
321. 40 c. Debret 5 5
322. 60 c. Gautherot 5 5
323. 80 c. Ingres 5 5
324. 8 f. Pajou 12 12
325. 20 f. Gros 25 25
326. 40 f. Gros 50 50
327. 80 f. David 95 95

45. " The Quarryman " (O. Bonnevalle).

1969. Int. Labour Organization. 50th Anniv. Multicoloured.

328. 20 c. Type **45** 5 5
329. 40 c. " Ploughing " (detail, Brueghel's " Descent of Icarus ") 5 5
330. 60 c. " The Fisherman " (C. Meunier) 5 5
331. 80 c. " Ostend Slipway " (J. van Noten) 5 5
332. 8 f. " The Cook " (P. Aertsen) 10 10
333. 10 f. " Vulcan's Blacksmiths " (Velazquez) 12 12
334. 50 f. " Hiercheuse " (C. Meunier) 55 55
335. 70 f. " The Miner " (P. Paulus) 80 80

Nos. 330, 332 and 334/5 are vert.

46. " The Derby at Epsom " (Gericault).

1970. Paintings of Horses. Multicoloured.

336. 20 c. Type **46** 5 5
337. 40 c. " Horses leaving the Sea " (Delacroix) 5 5
338. 60 c. " Charles V at Muhlberg " (Titian) 5 5
339. 80 c. " To the Races, Amateur Jockeys " (Degas) 5 5
340. 8 f. " Horsemen at Rest " (Wouwermans) 10 10
341. 20 f. " Officer of the Imperial Guard " (Gericault) 25 25
342. 40 f. " Horse and Dromedary " (Bonnevalle) 50 50
343. 80 f. " The Prodigal Child " (Rubens) 95 95

Nos. 338 and 341 are vert.

1970. African National Costumes (2nd series). As T **37**. Multicoloured.

345. 20 c. Tharaka Meru woman 5 5
346. 30 c. Niger flautist 5 5
347. 50 c. Tunisian water-carrier 5 5
348. 1 f. Kano ceremonial (Nigeria) 5 5
349. 3 f. Mali troubador .. 5 5
350. 5 f. Quipongo, Angola women 5 5
351. 50 f. Mauritanian at prayer 60 60
352. 90 f. Sinehatiali dancers, Ivory Coast .. .. 1·00 1·00

47. Footballer attacking Goal.

1970. World Cup Football Championships, Mexico.

353. **47.** 20 c. multicoloured .. 5 5
354. – 30 c. multicoloured .. 5 5
355. – 50 c. multicoloured .. 5 5
356. – 1 f. multicoloured .. 5 5
357. – 6 f. multicoloured .. 8 8
358. – 18 f. multicoloured .. 25 25
359. – 30 f. multicoloured .. 40 40
360. – 90 f. multicoloured .. 1·10 1·10

Nos. 354/60 show footballers in various positions, similar to T **47.**

48. Flowers and Peacock.

1970. "EXPO 70", World Fair, Osaka, Japan. Multicoloured.

361. 20 c. Type **48** 5 5
362. 30 c. Torii gate and " Hibiscus " (Yashuda) 5 5
363. 50 c. Dancer and " Musician " (Katayama) 5 5
364. 1 f. Sun Tower and " Warrior " .. 5 5
365. 3 f. House and " Seated Buddha " .. 5 5
366. 5 f. Pagoda and " Head of Girl " (Yamakawa) 5 5
367. 20 f. Greeting and " Imperial Palace " .. 25 25
368. 70 f. Expo emblem and " Horseman " .. 85 85

49. Two Young Gorillas.

1970. Gorillas of the Mountains.

369. **49.** 20 c. black and green .. 5 5
370. – 40 c. black, brn. & pur. 5 5
371. – 60 c. black, blue & brn. 5 5
372. – 80 c. blk., orge. & brn. 5 5
373. – 1 f. black and magenta 5 5
374. – 2 f. black, yellow, grn., brown and blue .. 5 5
375. – 15 f. black and sepia .. 15 15
376. – 100 f. black, brn. & blue 1·25 1·25

GORILLA—VERT. 40 c. Squatting. 80 c. Beating chest. 2 f. Eating banana. 100 f. With young. HORIZ. 60 c. Walking. 1 f. With family. 15 f. Heads.

50. Cinchona Bark.

1970. Discovery of Quinine. 150th Anniv. Multicoloured.

377. 20 c. Type **50** 5 5
378. 80 c. Pharmaceutical equipment 5 5
379. 1 f. Anopheles mosquito .. 5 5
380. 3 f. Malaria patient and nurse 5 5
381. 25 f. " Attack " on mosquito 30 30
382. 70 f. Pelletier and Caventou (discoverers of quinine) 85 85

51. Rocket in Flight.

1970. Moon Missions. Multicoloured.

383. 20 c. Type **51** 5 5
384. 30 c. Separation during orbit 5 5
385. 50 c. Spaceship above the moon 5 5
386. 1 f. Module and astronauts on moon 5 5
387. 3 f. Take-off from the moon 5 5
388. 5 f. Return journey to earth 8 8
389. 10 f. Final separation before landing 12 12
390. 80 f. Splashdown .. .. 1·00 1·00

52. F. D. Roosevelt and " Brassocattleya olympia alba ". **53.** Pope Paul VI.

1970. F. D. Roosevelt. 25th Death Anniv. Portraits and Orchids.

391. **52.** 20 c. brown, blue & black 5 5
392. – 30 c. brown, red & black 5 5
393. – 50 c. brown, orange & blk. 5 5
394. – 1 f. brown, green & black 5 5
395. – 2 f. green, brn. and blk. 5 5
396. – 6 f. green, purple & blk. 5 5
397. – 30 f. green, blue & black 40 40
398. – 60 f. green, red & black 80 80

ORCHIDS: 30 c. " Laeliocattleya callistoglossa ". 50 c. " Chondrorrhyncha ". 1 f. " Paphiopedilum ". 2 f. " Cymbidium hybride ". 6 f. " Cattleya labiata ". 30 f. " Dendrobium nobile ". 60 f. " Laelia gouldiana ".

1970. 1st Vatican Council. Cent.

400. **53.** 10 c. brown and gold .. 5 5
401. – 20 c. green and gold .. 5 5
402. – 30 c. lake and gold .. 5 5
403. – 40 c. blue and gold .. 5 5
404. – 1 f. violet and gold .. 5 5
405. – 18 f. purple and gold .. 20 20
406. – 20 f. orange and gold .. 25 25
407. – 60 f. brown and gold .. 75 75

POPES: 20 c. John XXIII. 30 c. Pius XII. 40 c. Pius XI. 1 f. Benedict XV. 18 f. Pius X. 20 f. Leo XIII. 60 f. Pius IX.

1971. African Headdresses (2nd series). Multicoloured designs as T **40.**

408. 20 c. Rendille woman .. 5 5
409. 30 c. Chad woman .. 5 5
410. 50 c. Bororo man (Niger) .. 5 5
411. 1 f. Masai man (Kenya) .. 5 5
412. 5 f. Air girl (Niger) .. 5 5
413. 18 f. Rwanda woman .. 20 20
414. 25 f. Mauritania man .. 30 30
415. 50 f. Rwanda girls .. 60 60

54. '' Beethoven '' (C. Horneman).

1971. Beethoven. Birth Cent. (1970). Portraits and funeral scene by various artists. Multicoloured.

418. 20 c. Type **54** 5 5
419. 30 c. K. Stieler 5 5
420. 50 c. F. Schimon 5 5
421. 3 f. H. Best 5 5
422. 6 f. W. Fassbender .. 8 8
423. 90 f. " Beethoven's Burial " (Stober) .. .. .. 1·10 1·10

55. Horse-jumping.

1971. Olympic Games, Munich (1972). (1st issue).

424. **55.** 20 c. gold and black .. 5 5
425. – 30 c. gold and purple .. 5 5
426. – 50 c. gold and violet .. 5 5
427. – 1 f. gold and green .. 5 5
428. – 8 f. gold and red .. 10 10
429. – 10 f. gold and violet .. 15 15
430. – 20 f. gold and brown .. 25 25
431. – 60 f. gold and green .. 75 75

DESIGNS: 30 c. Running (start). 50 c. Basketball. 1 f. High-jumping. 8 f. Boxing. 10 f. Pole-vaulting. 20 f. Wrestling. 60 f. Gymnastics.

See also Nos. 490/7.

1971. Air. U.A.M.P.T. 10th Anniv. As T **153** of Cameroun. Multicoloured.

432. 100 f. U.A.M.P.T. H.Q. and Rwandaise woman and child .. .. .. 1·25 1·25

56. " Durer " (self-portrait).

1971. Durer. 500th Birth Anniv. Paintings. Multicoloured.

434. 20 c. " Adam " 5 5
435. 30 c. " Eve " 5 5
436. 50 c. " Portrait of H. Holzschuhur " .. 5 5
437. 1 f. " Mourning the Dead Christ " 5 5
438. 3 f. " Madonna and Child " 5 5
439. 5 f. " St. Eustace " .. 8 8
440. 20 f. " St. Paul and St. Mark " 25 25
441. 70 f. Type **56** 85 85

57. Astronauts in Moon Rover.

1972. Moon Mission of "Apollo 15".

442. **57.** 600 f. gold .. .. 12·00

58. Participation in Sport.

1972. National Guard. Multicoloured.

443. 4 f. Type **58** 5 5
444. 6 f. Transport of emergency supplies 5 5
445. 15 f. Helicopter transport for the sick .. 15 15
446. 25 f. Participation in health service .. 30 30
447. 50 f. Guard, map and emblem (vert.) 60 60

59. Ice-hockey.

1972. Winter Olympic Games, Sapporo, Japan. Multicoloured.
448. 20 c. Type **59** 5 5
449. 30 c. Speed-skating .. 5 5
450. 50 c. Ski-jumping .. 5 5
451. 1 f. Figure-skating .. 5 5
452. 6 f. Cross-country skiing .. 5 5
453. 12 f. Slalom 12 12
454. 20 f. Tobogganing .. 25 25
455. 60 f. Downhill skiing .. 75 75

60. Gazelles and Monkey.

1972. Akagera National Park. Multicoloured.
456. 20 c. Type **60** 5 5
457. 30 c. Buffalo 5 5
458. 50 c. Zebra 5 5
459. 1 f. Rhinoceros 5 5
460. 2 f. Wart-hogs 5 5
461. 6 f. Hippopotamus .. 8 8
462. 18 f. Hyenas 20 20
463. 32 f. Guineafowl .. 40 40
464. 60 f. Antelopes 75 75
465. 80 f. Lion and lioness .. 1·00 1·00

61. Family supporting Flag. **62.** Orange-breasted Sunbirds.

1972. Referendum. 10th Anniv.
466. **61.** 6 f. multicoloured .. 5 5
467. 18 f. multicoloured .. 20 20
468. 60 f. multicoloured .. 75 75

1972. Rwanda Birds Multicoloured.
469. 20 c. Common waxbills .. 5 5
470. 30 c. Malachite sunbird .. 5 5
471. 50 c. Type **62** 5 5
472. 1 f. Lesser double-collared sunbird 5 5
473. 4 f. Puff-backed shrike .. 5 5
474. 6 f. Red bishops 5 5
475. 10 f. Scarlet-chested sunbird 12 12
476. 18 f. Red-headed amadinas 25 25
477. 60 f. Crimson-breasted shrike 75 75
478. 100 f. African golden oriole 1·25 1·25

63. King Baudouin and Queen Fabiola with President and Mrs. Kayibanda in Rwanda.

1972. "Belgica 72" Stamp Exhib., Brussels.
479. – 18 f. multicoloured .. 25 25
480. – 22 f. multicoloured .. 30 30
481. **63.** 40 f. blue, blk. & gold .. 55 55

DESIGNS: 18 f. Rwanda village. 22 f. View of Bruges.

Nos. 479/80 are smaller, size 39 × 36 mm.

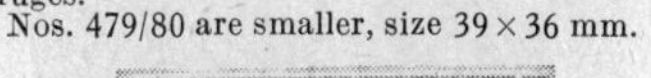

64. Announcement of Independence.

1972. Independence. 10th Anniv.
482. **64.** 20 c. green and gold .. 5 5
483. – 30 c. purple and gold .. 5 5
484. – 50 c. sepia and gold .. 5 5
485. – 6 f. blue and gold .. 8 8
486. – 10 f. maroon and gold .. 12 12
487. – 15 f. blue and gold .. 20 20
488. – 18 f. brown and gold .. 25 25
489. – 50 f. green and gold .. 60 60

DESIGNS—HORIZ. 30 c. Promotion ceremony, officers of the National Guard. 50 c. Pres. Kayibanda, wife and family. 6 f. Pres. Kayibanda casting vote in legislative elections. 10 f. Pres. and Mrs. Kayibanda at "Festival of Justice". 15 f. President and members of National Assembly. 18 f. Investiture of Pres. Kayibanda. VERT. 50 f. President Kayibanda.

65. Horse-jumping.

1972. Olympic Games, Munich. (2nd issue).
490. **65.** 20 c. green and gold .. 5 5
491. – 30 c. violet and gold .. 5 5
492. – 50 c. green and gold .. 5 5
493. – 1 f. maroon and gold .. 5 5
494. – 6 f. black and gold .. 8 8
495. – 18 f. brown and gold .. 20 20
496. – 30 f. violet and gold .. 35 35
497. – 44 f. blue and gold .. 50 50

DESIGNS: 30 c. Hockey. 50 c. Football. 1 f. Long-jumping. 6 f. Cycling. 18 f. Sailing. 30 f. Hurdling. 44 f. Gymnastics.

66. Runners.

1972. Racial Equality Year. "Working Together". Multicoloured.
498. 20 c. Type **63** 5 5
499. 30 c. Musicians 5 5
500. 50 c. Ballet dancers .. 5 5
501. 1 f. Medical team in operating theatre 5 5
502. 6 f. Weaver and painter .. 8 8
503. 18 f. Children in class .. 20 20
504. 24 f. Laboratory technicians 30 30
505. 50 f. U.N. emblem and hands of four races 60 60

67. "Phymateus brunneri".

1973. Rwanda Insects. Multicoloured.
507. 20 c. Type **67** 5 5
508. 30 c. "Diopsisfumipennis" (vert.) 5 5
509. 50 c. "Kitoko alberti" .. 5 5
510. 1 f. "Archibracon fasciatus" (vert.) 5 5
511. 2 f. "Ornithacris cyanea imperialis" 5 5
512. 6 f. "Clitodaca fenestralis" (vert.) 8 8
513. 18 f. "Senaspis oesacus" 20 20
514. 22 f. "Phonoctonus grandis" (vert.) 30 30
515. 70 f. "Loba leopardina" .. 90 90
516. 100 f. "Ceratocoris distortus" (vert.) .. .. 1·25 1·25

68. "Emile Zola" (Manet). **69.** Longombe.

1973. Int. Book Year. "Readers and Writers". Paintings and portraits. Mult.
518. 20 c. Type **68** 5 5
519. 30 c. "Rembrandt's Mother" (Rembrandt) .. 5 5
520. 50 c. "St. Jerome removing Thorn from Lion's paw" (Colantonio) 5 5
521. 1 f. "St. Peter and St. Paul" (El Greco) .. 5 5
522. 2 f. "Virgin and Child" (Van der Weyden) .. 5 5
523. 6 f. "St. Jerome in his Cell" (Antonella de Messina) 8 8
524. 40 f. St. Barbara" (Master of Flemalle) 55 55
525. 100 f. "Don Quixote" (O. Bonnevalle) .. 1·25 1·25

1973. Musical Instruments. Multicoloured.
527. 20 c. Type **69** 5 5
528. 30 c. Horn 5 5
529. 50 c. "Xylophone" .. 5 5
530. 1 f. "Harp" 5 5
531. 4 f. Alur horns 5 5
532. 6 f. Horn, bells and drum .. 8 8
533. 18 f. Drums 20 20
534. 90 f. Gourds .. .. 1·10 1·10

70. "Rubens and Isabelle Brandt" (Rubens). **71.** Map of Africa and Doves.

1973. "IBRA" Stamp Exhibition, Munich. Famous Paintings. Multicoloured.
535. 20 c. Type **70** 5 5
536. 30 c. "Portrait of a Lady" (Cranach the Younger) .. 5 5
537. 50 c. "Woman peeling Turnips" (Chardin) .. 5 5
538. 1 f. "Abduction of the Daughters of Leucippe" (Rubens) 5 5
539. 2 f. "Virgin and Child" (Lippi) 5 5
540. 6 f. "Boys eating Fruit" (Murillo) 8 8
541. 40 f. "The Sickness of Love" (Steen) .. 55 55
542. 100 f. "Jesus divested of His Garments" (El Greco) 1·25 1·25

1973. O.A.U. 10th Anniv. Multicoloured.
544. 6 f. Type **71** 8 8
545. 94 f. Map of Africa and hands .. .. .. 1·10 1·10

1973. Pan-African Drought Relief. Nos. 308/13 and 315 optd. **SECHERESSE SOLIDARITE AFRICAINE** and No. 315 additionally surch.
546. **42.** 20 c. multicoloured .. 5 5
547. – 40 c. multicoloured .. 5 5
548. – 60 c. multicoloured .. 5 5
549. – 80 c. multicoloured .. 5 5
550. – 3 f. multicoloured .. 5 5
551. – 75 f. multicoloured .. 90 90
552. – 100 f. + 50 f. mult. .. 1·90 1·90

72. "Distichodus sexfasciatus".

1973. Fishes. Multicoloured.
553. 20 c. Type **72** 5 5
554. 30 c. "Hydrocyon forkalii" 5 5
555. 50 c. "Synodontis angelicus" 5 5
556. 1 f. "Tilapia nilotica" .. 5 5
557. 2 f. "Protopterus aethiopicus" 5 5
558. 6 f. "Pareutropius mandevillei" 8 8
559. 40 f. "Phenacogrammus interruptus" 55 55
560. 150 f. "Julidochromis ornatus" .. .. 1·90 1·90

1973. U.A.M.P.T. 12th Anniv. As Type **182** of Cameroun.
562. 100 f. blue, brown, mauve 1·25 1·25

1973. African Fortnight, Brussels. Nos. 408/15 optd. **QUINZAINE AFRICAINE BRUXELLES 15/30 SEPT. 1973** and globe.
563. 20 c. multicoloured .. 5 5
564. 30 c. multicoloured .. 5 5
565. 50 c. multicoloured .. 5 5
566. 1 f. multicoloured .. 5 5
567. 5 f. multicoloured .. 5 5
568. 18 f. multicoloured .. 20 20
569. 25 f. multicoloured .. 30 30
570. 50 f. multicoloured .. 60 60

1973. Air. Congress of French-speaking Nations, Liege. No. 432 optd. **LIEGE ACCUEILLE LES PAYS DE LANGUE FRANCAISE 1973** (No. 562) or congress emblem (No. 563).
571. 100 f. multicoloured .. 1·25 1·25
572. 100 f. multicoloured .. 1·25 1·25

1973. Declaration of Human Rights. 25th Anniv. Nos. 443/7 optd. with Human Rights emblem.
574. **58.** 4 f. multicoloured .. 5 5
575. – 6 f. multicoloured .. 8 8
576. – 15 f. multicoloured .. 15 15
577. – 25 f. multicoloured .. 30 30
578. – 50 f. multicoloured .. 60 60

73. Copernicus and Astrolabe. **74.** Pres. Habyarimana.

1973. Copernicus. 500th Birth Anniv. Mult.
580. 20 c. Type **73** 5 5
581. 30 c. Copernicus 5 5
582. 50 c. Copernicus and heliocentric system 5 5
583. 1 f. Type **73** 5 5
584. 18 f. As 30 c. 20 20
585. 80 f. As 50 c. .. .. 1·10 1·10

1974. "New Regime".
587. **74.** 1 f. brown, black & buff 5 5
588. 2 f. brown, black & blue 5 5
589. 5 f. brown, black & red 5 5
590. 6 f. brown, black & blue 8 8
591. 26 f. brown, black & lilac 30 30
592. 60 f. brown, black & green 70 70

75. Yugoslavia v Zaire. **77.** "Diane de Poitiers" (Fontainebleau School).

76. Marconi's Yacht "Electra".

1974. World Cup Football Championships, West Germany. Players represent specified teams. Multicoloured.
594. 20 c. Type **75** 5 5
595. 40 c. Netherlands v Sweden 5 5
596. 60 c. West Germany v Australia 5 5
597. 80 c. Haiti v Argentina .. 5 5
598. 2 f. Brazil v Scotland .. 5 5
599. 6 f. Bulgaria v Uruguay .. 8 8
600. 40 f. Italy v Poland 45 45
601. 50 f. Chile v East Germany 55 55

1974. Guglielmo Marconi (radio pioneer). Birth Cent. Multicoloured.
602. 20 c. Type **76** 5 5
603. 30 c. Steamer "Carlo Alberto" 5 5
604. 50 c. Marconi's telegraph equipment 5 5
605. 4 f. "Global Telecommunications" 5 5
606. 35 f. Early radio receiver 40 40
607. 60 f. Marconi and Poldhu radio station 70 70

1974. Int. Stamp Exhibitions "Stockholmia" and "Internaba". Paintings from Stockholm and Basle. Multicoloured.
609. 20 c. Type **77** 5 5
610. 30 c. "The Flute-player" (J. Loyster) 5 5
611. 50 c. "Virgin Mary and Child" (G. David) .. 5 5
612. 1 f. "The Triumph of Venus" (F. Boucher) 5 5
613. 10 f. "Harlequin Seated" (P. Oicasso) 10 10
614. 18 f. "Virgin and Child" (15th-century) 20 20
615. 20 f. "The Beheading of St. John" (H. Fries) .. 20 20
616. 50 f. "The Daughter of Andersdotter" (J. Huckert) 45 45

78. Monastic Messenger. **79.** Head of Uganda Kobo.

1974. Universal Postal Union. Cent. Mult.
619. 20 c. Type **78** 5 5
620. 30 c. Inca messenger 5 5
621. 50 c. Moroccan postman 5 5
622. 1 f. Indian postman 5 5
623. 18 f. Polynesian postman 15 15
624. 80 f. Early Rwanda messenger with horn and drum 70 70

1974. Revolution. 15th Anniv. Nos. 316/18 optd. **1974 15e ANNIVERSAIRE.**
625. **43.** 6 f. multicoloured
626. 18 f. multicoloured
627. 40 f. multicoloured

1974. African Development Bank. 10th Anniv. Nos. 305/6 optd. **1974 10e ANNIVERSAIRE.**
629. **41.** 30 f. multicoloured 20 20
630. – 70 f. multicoloured 50 50

1975. Antelopes. Multicoloured.
631. 20 c. Type **79** 5 5
632. 30 c. Bongo with calf (horiz.) 5 5
633. 50 c. Roan antelope and Black buck heads 5 5
634. 1 f. Young Sututunga antelopes (horiz.) 5 5
635. 4 f. Great Kudu 5 5
636. 10 f. Impala family (horiz.) 10 10
637. 34 f. Waterbuck head 40 40
638. 100 f. Derby eland (horiz.) 1·00 1·00

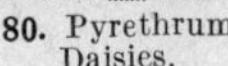

80. Pyrethrum Daisies.

82. Globe and Emblem.

81. White Pelicans.

1975. Agricultural Labour Year. Multicoloured.
642. 20 c. Type **80** 5 5
643. 30 c. Tea plant 5 5
644. 50 c. Coffee berries 5 5
645. 4 f. Bananas 5 5
646. 10 f. Maize 15 15
647. 12 f. Sorghum 20 20
648. 26 f. Rice 40 40
649. 47 f Coffee cultivation 70 70

1975. Holy Year. Nos. 400/7 optd **1975 ANNEE SAINTE.**
652. **53.** 10 c. brown and gold 5 5
653. – 20 c. green and gold 5 5
654. – 30 c. lake and gold 5 5
655. – 40 c. blue and gold 5 5
656. – 1 f. violet and gold 5 5
657. – 18 f. purple and gold 25 25
658. – 20 f. orange and gold 30 30
659 – 60 f. brown and gold 90 90

1975. Aquatic Birds. Multicoloured.
660. 20 c. Type **81** 5 5
661. 30 c. Malachite kingfisher 5 5
662. 50 c. Great herons 5 5
663. 1 f African jabirus 5 5
664. 4 f. African jacana 5 5
665. 10 f Red anhingas 15 15
666. 34 f. Sacred ibis and bronze-mantled ibis 50 50
667. 80 f. Hartlaub's duck 1·25 1·25

1975. World Population Year (1974). Multicoloured.
669. 20 f. Type **82** 30 30
670. 26 f. Population graph 40 40
671. 34 f. Symbolic doorway 50 50

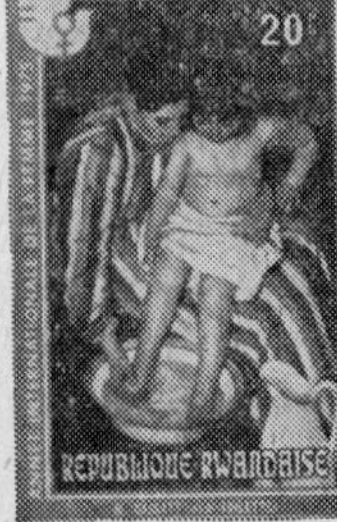

83. " La Toilette " (M. Cassatt).

84. " Letters ".

1975. International Women's Year. Multicoloured.
672. 20 c. Type **83** 5 5
673. 30 c. " Mother and Child " (G. Melchers) 5 5
674. 50 c. " The Milk Jug " (Vermeer) 5 5
675. 1 f. " The Water-carrier " (Goya) 5 5
676. 8 f. Coffee-picking 12 12
677. 12 f. Laboratory technician 20 20
678. 18 f. Rwandaise mother and child 25 25
679. 60 f. Woman carrying water-jug 90 90

1975. National University. Tenth Anniv. The Faculties. Multicoloured.
681. 20 c. Type **84** 5 5
682. 30 c. " Medicine " 5 5
683. 1 f. 50 " Jurisprudence " 5 5
684. 18 f. " Science " 25 25
685. 26 f. " Commerce " 40 40
686. 34 f. University Building, Kigali 50 50

85. Cattle at Pool, and " Impatiens stuhlmannii " (plant).

1975. Protection of Nature. Multicoloured.
688. 20 c. Type **85** 5 5
689. 30 c Euphorbis " candelabra " and savannah bush 5 5
690. 50 c. Bush fire and " Tapinanthus prunifolius " 5 5
691. 5 f. Lake Bulera and " Nymphaea lotus " 8 8
692. 8 f. Soil erosion and " Protea madiensis " 12 12
693. 10 f. Protected marshland and " Melanthera brownei " 15 15
694. 26 f. Giant lobelias and groundsel 40 40
695. 100 f. Sabyinyo volcano and " Polystachya kermesina " 1·50 1·50

1975. " Solidarity ". Drought Emergency. Nos. 345/52 optd. or surch. **SECHERESSE SOLIDARITE 1975** (both words share same capital letter).
696. 20 c. multicoloured 5 5
697. 30 c. multicoloured 5 5
698. 50 c. multicoloured 5 5
699. 1 f. multicoloured 5 5
700. 3 f. multicoloured 5 5
701. 5 f. multicoloured 8 8
702. 50 f.+25 f. multicoloured 1·10 1·10
703. 90 f.+25 f. multicoloured 1·75 1·75

86. Loading Aircraft.

1975. Year of Increased Production. Multicoloured.
704. 20 c. Type **86** 5 5
705. 30 c. Coffee—packing plant 5 5
706. 50 c. Lathe—operator 5 5
707. 10 f. Farmer with hoe (vert.) 15 15
708. 35 f. Coffee—picking (vert.) 55 55
709. 54 f. Mechanical plough 80 80

87. African Woman with Basket on Head.

1975. " Themabelga " Stamp Exhibition, Brussels. African Folklore.
710. **87.** 20 c. multicoloured 5 5
711. – 30 c. multicoloured 5 5
712. – 50 c. multicoloured 5 5
713. – 1 f. multicoloured 5 5
714. – 5 f. multicoloured 8 8
715. – 7 f. multicoloured 10 10
716. – 35 f. multicoloured 55 55
717. – 51 f. multicoloured 80 80
DESIGNS: 30 c. to 51 f. Various Rwanda costumes.

88. Dr. Schweitzer, Piano Keyboard and Music.

1976. World Leprosy Day.
719. **88.** 20 c. lilac, brn. and blk. 5 5
720. – 30 c. lilac, grn. and blk. 5 5
721. – 50 c. lilac, brn. and blk. 5 5
722. – 1 f. lilac, pur. and blk. 5 5
723. **88.** 3 f. lilac, blue and black 5 5
724. – 5 f. lilac, brn. and black 10 10
725. – 10 f. lilac, blue and blk. 20 20
726. – 80 f. lilac, red and black 1·60 1·60
DESIGNS: Dr. Schweitzer and: 30 c. Lambarene Hospital. 50 c. Organ pipes and music. 1 f. Lambarene residence. 5 f. As 30 c. 10 f. As 50 c. 80 f. As 1 f.

89. " Surrender at Yorktown ".

1976. American Revolution. Bicent. Multicoloured.
727. 20 c. Type **89** 5 5
728. 30 c. " The Sergeant-Instructor at Valley Forge " 5 5
729. 50 c. " Presentation of Captured Yorktown Flags to Congress " 5 5
730. 1 f. " Washington and his Staff at Fort Lee " 5 5
731. 18 f. " Washington boarding a British warship " 35 35
732. 26 f. " Washington studies Battle-plans " 50 50
733. 34 f. " Washington firing a Cannon " 70 70
734. 40 f. " Crossing the Delaware " 80 80

90. Sister Yohana. **91.** Sailing.

1976. Catholic Church in Rwanda. 75th Anniv. Multicoloured.
736. 20 c. Type **90** 5 5
737. 30 c. Abdon Sabakati 5 5
738. 50 c. Father Alphonse Brard 5 5
739. 4 f. Abbe Balthazar Gafuku 8 8
740. 10 f. Monseigneur Bigirumwami 20 20
741. 25 f. Save Catholic Church (horiz.) 50 50
742. 60 f. Kabgayi Catholic Cathedral (horiz.) 1·25 1·25

1976. Olympic Games, Montreal (1st issue).
743. **91.** 20 c. brown and green 5 5
744. – 30 c. blue and green 5 5
745. – 50 c. black and green 5 5
746. – 1 f. violet and green 5 5
747. – 10 f. blue and green 20 20
748. – 18 f. brown and green 35 35
749. – 29 f. purple and green 60 60
750. – 51 f. deep green & green 1·00 1·00
DESIGNS: 30 c. Horse-jumping. 50 c. Long-jumping. 1 f. Hockey. 10 f. Swimming. 18 f. Football. 29 f. Boxing. 51 f. Gymnastics.
See also Nos. 767/74.

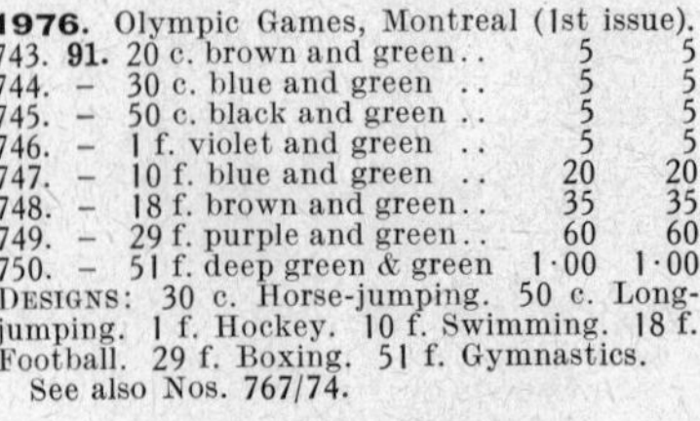

92. Bell's Experimental Telephone and Manual Switchboard.

1976. Telephone Centenary.
751. **92.** 20 c. brown and blue 5 5
752. – 30 c. blue and violet 5 5
753. – 50 c. brown and blue 5 5
754. – 1 f. orange and blue 5 5
755. – 4 f. mauve and blue 8 8
756. – 8 f. green and blue 15 15
757. – 26 f. red and blue 50 50
758. – 60 f. lilac and blue 1·25 1·25
DESIGNS: 30 c. Early telephone and man making call. 50 c. Early telephone and woman making call. 1 f. Early telephone and exchange building. 4 f. Alexander Graham Bell and " candlestick " telephone. 8 f. Rwanda subscriber and dial telephone. 26 f. Dish aerial, satellite and modern hand-set. 60 f. Rwanda, PTT building, operator and push-button telephone.

1976. Declaration of American Independence. Bicent. Nos. 727/34 optd. **INDEPENDENCE DAY** and Bicentennial Emblem.
759. **89.** 20 c. multicoloured 5 5
760. – 30 c. multicoloured 5 5
761. – 50 c. multicoloured 5 5
762. 1 f. multicoloured 5 5
763. – 18 f. multicoloured 35 35
764. – 26 f. multicoloured 50 50
765. – 34 f. multicoloured 70 70
766. – 40 f. multicoloured 80 80

93. Football.

1976. Olympic Games, Montreal (2nd issue) Multicoloured.
767. 20 c. Type **93** 5 5
768. 30 c. Rifle-shooting 5 5
769. 50 c. Canoeing 5 5
770. 1 f. Gymnastics 5 5
771. 10 f. Weightlifting 20 20
772. 12 f. Swimming 25 25
773. 26 f. Horse-riding 50 50
774. 50 f. Throwing the hammer 1·00 1·00

94. Emblem and Launches.

1976. " Apollo – Soyuz " Space Mission. Multicoloured.
776. 20 c. Type **94** 5 5
777. 30 c. " Soyuz " rocket 5 5
778. 50 c. " Apollo " rocket 5 5
779. 1 f. " Apollo " after separation 5 5
780. 2 f. Approach to link-up 5 5
781. 12 f. Spacecraft linked 25 25
782. 30 f. Sectional view of interiors 60 60
783. 54 f. " Apollo " splashdown 1·10 1·10

95. " Eulophia cucullata ".

96. Hands embracing. " Cultural Collaboration ".

1976. Rwandaise Orchids. Multicoloured.
784. 20 c. Type **95** 5 5
785. 30 c. " Eulophia streptopetala " 5 5
786. 50 c. " Disa stairsii " 5 5
787. 1 f. " Aerangis kotschyana " 5 5
788. 10 f. " Eulophia abyssinica " 20 20
789. 12 f. " Bonatea steudneri " 25 25
790. 26 f. " Ansellia gigantea " 50 50
791. 50 f. " Eulophia angelonsis " 1·00 1·00

1977. World Leprosy Day. Nos. 719/26 optd. with JOURNEE MONDIALE 1977.
793. **88.** 20 c. lilac, brown & black 5 5
794. – 30 c. lilac, green & black 5 5
795. – 50 c. lilac, brown & black 5 5
796. – 1 f. lilac, purple & black 5 5
797. **88.** 5 f. lilac, brown & black 10 10
798. – 10 f. lilac, brown & black 20 20
799. – 80 f. lilac, red and black 1·60 1·60

1977. 10th OCAM Summit Meeting, Kigali. Multicoloured.

801.		10 f. Type **96**	20	20
802.		26 f. Hands embracing "Technical Collaboration"	50	50
803.		64 f. Hands embracing "Economic Collaboration"	1·25	1·25

RYUKYU ISLANDS O2

Group of islands between Japan and Formosa formerly Japanese until occupied by U.S. forces in 1945. After a period of military rule they became semi-autonomous under U.S. administration. The Amami Oshima group reverted to Japan in December, 1953. The remaining islands were returned to Japan on 15 May, 1972. Japanese stamps are now in use.

1948. 100 sen = 1 yen.
1958. 100 cents = U.S. $1.

1. Cycad Palm. **2.** Tribute Junk.

1948.

1.	**1.**	5 s. purple	1·75	1·00
2.	–	10 s. green	2·00	1·25
3.	**1.**	20 s. green	2·25	1·25
4.	**2.**	30 s. red	1·75	1·60
5.	–	40 s. purple	1·75	1·60
6.	**2.**	50 s. blue	2·00	2·00
7.	–	1 y. blue	2·25	2·00

DESIGNS: 10 s., 40 s. Easter lily. 1 y. Farmer with hoe.

3. Shi-Shi Roof Tiles. **4.** Dove over Ryukyu Is. Map.

1950.

8.	**3.**	50 s. red	10	8
10.	–	1 y. blue	1·40	35
11.	–	2 y. purple	5·00	1·40
12.	–	3 y. red	11·00	3·00
13.	–	4 y. slate	3·00	1·10
14.	–	5 y. green	5·00	1·75

DESIGNS: 1 y. Shuri Woman. 2 y. Former Okinawa Palace, Shuri. 3 y. Dragon's head. 4 y. Okinawa women. 5 y. Sea-shells.

1950. Air.

15.	**4.**	8 y. blue	24·00	7·00
16.		12 y. green	20·00	7·00
17.		16 y. red	16·00	6·00

5. University and Shuri Castle. **6.** Pine Tree.

1951. Ryukyu University. Inaug.

19.	**5.**	3 y. brown	20·00	8·00

1951. Afforestation Week.

20.	**6.**	3 y. green	20·00	8·00

改訂
*
10圓

7. Flying Goddess. (**8.**)

1951. Air.

21.	**7.**	13 y. blue	90	25
22.		18 y. green	1·60	90
23.		30 y. magenta	2·00	50
24.		40 y. purple	3·00	70
25.		50 y. orange	4·00	1·10

1952. Surch. as T **8.**

27.	**8.**	10 y. on 50 s. red	4·00	2·25
29.	–	100 y. on 2 y. pur. (No. 11)	£600	£350

9. Dove and Bean Seedling. **10.** Madanbashi Bridge.

1952. Establishment of Ryukyuan Govt.

30.	**9**	3 y. lake	40·00	9·00

1952.

31.	**10**	1 y. red	10	8
32.	–	2 y. green	12	8
33.	–	3 y. blue	20	8
34.	–	6 y. blue	1·75	1·00
35.	–	10 y. red	70	20
36.	–	30 y. olive	1·75	80
37.	–	50 y. purple	3·75	80
38.	–	100 y. claret	6·00	55

DESIGNS: 2 y. Presence Chamber, Shuri Palace. 3 y. Shuri Gate. 6 y. Sogenji Temple Wall. 10 y. Bensaitendo Temple. 30 y. Sonohyamutake Gate. 50 y. Tamaudun Mausoleum, Shuri. 100 y. Hosho-chai bridge.

11. Reception at Shuri Castle.

12. Perry and American Fleet at Naha Harbour. **13.** Chofu Ota and Matrix.

1953. Visit of Commodore Perry. Cent.

39.	**11.**	3 y. purple	6·00	2·25
40.	**12.**	6 y. blue	1·00	1·00

1953. 3rd Press Week.

41.	**13.**	4 y. brown	5·00	1·75

14. Wine Flask to fit around Waist. **15.** Shigo Toma and Pen-nib.

1954.

42.	**14.**	4 y. brown	35	8
43.	–	15 y. red	1·00	20
44.	–	20 y. orange	1·50	60

DESIGNS: 15 y. Lacquer bowl. 20 y. Textile pattern.

1954. 4th Press Week.

45.	**15.**	4 y. blue	5·50	1·75

16. Noguni Shrine and Sweet Potatoes. **17.**

1955. Introduction of Sweet Potato Plant. 350th Anniv.

46.	**16.**	4 y. blue	5·00	2·00

1956. Afforestation Week.

47.	**17.**	4 y. green	5·00	2·00

18. Nidotekito Dance. **19.** Telephone and Dial.

1956. National Dances.

48.	–	5 y. purple	55	20
49.	–	8 y. violet	70	55
50.	**18.**	14 y. brown	1·10	80

DESIGNS: 5 y. Willow dance. 8 y. Straw-hat dance.

1956. Telephone Dialling System Inaug.

51.	**19.**	4 y. violet	8·00	2·75

20. Floral Garland. **21.** Flying Goddess.

1956. New Year.

52.	**20.**	2 y. multicoloured	1·10	45

1957. Air.

53.	**21.**	15 y. blue-green	1·00	30
54.		20 y. lake	2·75	1·10
55.		35 y. yellow-green	5·00	1·25
56.		45 y. brown	6·50	2·00
57.		60 y grey	9·00	3·00

22. Rocket "Pencils". **23.** Phoenix.

1957. 7th Press Week.

58.	**22.**	4 y. blue	65	45

1957. New Year.

59.	**23.**	2 y. red, gold, yell. & blue	15	10

24. Various Ryukyu Postage Stamps. **25.** Stylized Dollar sign over Yen Symbol.

1958. First Postage Stamps of Ryukyu Is. 10th Anniv.

60.	**24.**	4 y. brn., grey, pur. & bl.	35	15

1958.

61.	**25.**	½ c. yellow	10	5
62.		1 c. green	10	5
63.		2 c. grey-blue	12	5
64.		3 c. red	12	5
65.		4 c. emerald	35	10
66.		5 c. brown	90	10
67.		10 c. turquoise-blue	2·25	12
68.		25 c. lavender	2·00	25
69.		50 c. grey	3·25	40
70.		$1 purple	4·25	70

26. Gateway of Courtesy.

1958.

71.	**26.**	3 c. multicoloured	70	20

27. Lion Dance. **28.** Trees.

1958. New Year.

72.	**27.**	1½ c. multicoloured	15	10

1959. Afforestation Week.

73.	**28.**	3 c. multicoloured	65	40

29. Yonaguni Moth. **30.** Hibiscus.

1959. Japanese Biological Teachers' Conf., Okinawa.

74.	**29.**	3 c. multicoloured	1·40	70

1959. Multicoloured.

(a) Inscr. as in T **30**.

75.		½ c. Type **30**	12	5
76.		3 c. Tropical fish	50	10
77.		8 c. Sea-shells	2·25	60
78.		13 c. Butterfly	1·00	60
79.		17 c. Jellyfish	7·00	2·25

(b) Inscr. smaller and 13 c. with design with value at right.

87.		½ c. Type **30**	12	5
88.		3 c. As No. 76	70	8
89.		8 c. As No. 77	50	30
90.		13 c. As No. 78	70	40
91.		17 c. As No. 79	2·25	95

31. Yakazi (Ryukyuan Toy).

改訂 9¢

32.)

1959. New Year.

80.	**31.**	1½ c. multicoloured	40	12

1959. Air. Surch. as T **32**.

81.	**21.**	9 c. on 15 y. blue-green	1·00	25
82.		14 c. on 20 y. lake	2·00	1·00
83.		19 c. on 35 y. yell.-green	3·00	1·40
84.		27 c. on 45 y. brown	4·50	1·60
85.		35 c. on 60 y. grey	5·50	2·00

33. University Badge. **34.** "Manjuru".

1960. University of the Ryukyus. 10th Anniv.

86.	**33.**	3 c. multicoloured	80	50

1960. Air. Surch.

92.	**14.**	9 c. on 4 y. brown	1·90	10
93.	–	14 c. on 5 y. pur. (No. 48)	1·00	60
94.	–	19 c. on 15 y. red (No. 43)	1·60	80
95.	**18.**	27 c. on 14 y. brown	2·50	1·50
96.	–	35 c. on 20 y. orge. (No. 44)	3·00	1·60

1960. Ryukyun Dances. Multicoloured.

(a) Inscr. as in T **34**.

97.		1 c. Type **34**	1·00	20
98.		2½ c. "Inohabushi"	80	20
99.		5 c. "Hatomabushi"	60	20
100.		10 c. "Hanafu"	80	20

(b) As T **34** but additionally inscr. "RYUKYUS".

107.		1 c. Type **34**	10	5
108.		2½ c. As No. 98	10	5
109.		4 c. "Nu-Fwa-Bushi" Dancer	10	5
110.		5 c. As No. 99	10	5
111.		10 c. As No. 100	20	5
112.		20 c. "Shuden"	50	15
113.		25 c. "Haodori"	60	20
114.		50 c. "Nobori Kuduchi"	1·00	25
115.		$1 "Koteibushi"	2·00	30

35. Start of Race.

1960. 8th Kyusku Athletic Meeting.

101.	–	3 c. red, green and blue	3·50	75
102.	**35.**	8 c. grey-green & orange	80	70

DESIGN: 3 c. Torch and coastal scene.

36. Heron and Rising Sun. **37.** Bull Fight.

1960. National Census.

103.	**36.**	3 c. brown	3·50	80

1960. New Year.

104.	**37.**	1½ c. chocolate, buff & bl.	1·25	20

38. Native Pine Tree.

1961. Afforestation Week.

105.	**38.**	3 c. multicoloured	1·10	50

39. Naha, Junk, Liner and City Seal.

1961. Naha City. 40th Anniv.

106. **39.** 3 c. turquoise .. .. 1·60 70

40. Flying Goddess. 41. White Silver Temple.

1961. Air.

116. **40.** 9 c. multicoloured .. 30 5

117. – 14 c. multicoloured .. 40 30

118. – 19 c. multicoloured .. 50 30

119. – 27 c. multicoloured .. 70 40

120. – 35 c. multicoloured .. 90 30

DESIGNS: 14 c. Flying goddess playing flute. 19 c., 27 c. Wind gods. 35 c. Flying goddess over trees.

1961. Unification of Itoman District and Takamine, Kanegushiku and Miwa Villages.

121. **41.** 3 c. brown 70 50

43. Sunrise and Eagles.

42. Books and Bird.

44. Govt. Building, Steps and Trees. 45. Shurei Gate and Campaign Emblem.

1961. Ryukyu Book Week. 10th Anniv.

122. **42.** 3 c. multicoloured .. 70 50

1961. New Year.

123. **43.** $1\frac{1}{2}$ c. red, black and gold 1·75 20

1962. Ryukyu Government. 10th Anniv.

124. **44.** $1\frac{1}{2}$ c. multicoloured .. 40 20

125. – 3 c. grey, green and red 50 30

DESIGN: 3 c. Government Building.

1962. Malaria Eradication.

126. – 3 c. multicoloured .. 40 30

127. **45.** 8 c. indigo, red and ochre 80 70

DESIGN: 3 c. "Anopheles Hycanus sinensis" mosquito.

46. Windmill, Dolls and Horse. 47. "Hibiscus liliaceus".

1962. Children's Day.

128. **46.** 3 c. multicoloured .. 1·00 50

1962. Ryukyu Flowers. Multicoloured.

129. ½ c. Type **47** 5 5

142. $1\frac{1}{2}$ c. "Etithyllum strictum" 10 5

130. 2 c. "Lxora chinensis" .. 10 5

131. 3. c. "Erythrina indica" 20 5

132. 3 c. "Caesulpinia rulcherrima" 10 5

133. 8 c. "Schima mertensiana" 30 10

134. 13 c. "Impatiens balsamina" 40 20

135. 15 c. "Hamaomoto" (herb) 50 20

136. 17 c. "Alpinia speciosa".. 50 20

No. 142 is smaller, $18\frac{3}{4} \times 22\frac{1}{2}$ mm.

48. Akaeware Bowl.

1962. Philatelic Week.

137. **48.** 3 c. multicoloured .. 2·50 90

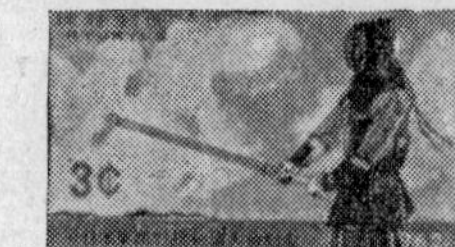

49. Kendo (Japanese Fencing).

1962. All-Japan Kendo Meeting.

138. **49.** 3 c. multicoloured .. 3·00 80

50. "Hare and Water" (textile design). 51. Reaching Maturity (clay relief).

1962. New Year.

139. **50.** $1\frac{1}{2}$ c. multicoloured .. 70 12

1963. Adults' Day.

140. **51.** 3 c. gold, black and blue 50 30

52. Trees and Wooded Hills. 53. Okinawa Highway.

1963. Afforestation Week.

141. **52.** 3 c. multicoloured .. 60 25

1963. Opening of Okinawa Highway.

143. **53.** 3 c. multicoloured .. 70 25

54. Hawks over Islands. 55. Shioya Bridge.

1963. Bird Week.

144. **54.** 3 c. multicoloured .. 70 25

1963. Shioya Bridge, Okinawa, Opening.

145. **55.** 3 c. multicoloured .. 70 30

56. Lacquerware Bowl. 57. Jetliner and Shurei Gate.

1963. Philatelic Week.

146. **56.** 3 c. multicoloured .. 2·00 65

1963. Air.

147. **57.** $5\frac{1}{2}$ c. multicoloured .. 12 8

148. – 7 c. black, red and blue 15 8

DESIGN: 7 c. Jetliner over sea.

58. Map and Emblem. 59. Nakagusuku Castle Ruins.

1963. Meeting of Junior International Chamber, Naha.

149. **58.** 3 c. multicoloured .. 60 25

1963. Ancient Buildings Protection Week.

150. **59.** 3 c. multicoloured .. 60 25

60. Flame. 61. Bingata "dragon" (textile design).

1963. Declaration of Human Rights. 15th Anniv.

151. **60.** 3 c. multicoloured .. 55 25

1963. New Year.

152. **61.** $1\frac{1}{2}$ c. multicoloured .. 25 10

62. Carnation. 63. Pineapples and Sugar-cane.

1964. Mothers' Day.

153. **62.** 3 c. multicoloured .. 35 20

1964. Agricultural Census.

154. **63.** 3 c. multicoloured .. 30 20

64. Hand-woven Sash. 65. Girl Scout and Emblem.

1964. Philatelic Week.

155. **64.** 3 c. multicoloured .. 40 20

1964. Ryukyu Girl Scouts. 10th Anniv.

156. **65.** 3 c. multicoloured .. 20 15

66. Transmitting Tower. 67. Shuri Gate and Olympic Torch.

1964. Ryukyu-Japan Microwave Link. Inaug.

157. **66.** 3 c. green and black .. 50 35

158. – 8 c. blue and black .. 90 75

DESIGN: 8 c. "Bowl" receiving aerial. Both stamps have "1963" cancelled by bars and "1964" inserted in black.

1964. Passage of Olympic Torch through Okinawa.

159. **67.** 3 c. multicoloured .. 20 10

68. "Naihanchi" (Karate stance). 69. "Miyara Dunchi" (old Ryukyuan residence).

1964. Karate ("self defence"). Multicoloured.

160. 3 c. Type **68** 40 12

161. 3 c. "Makiwara"—Karate training (with wooden pole) 30 10

162. 3 c. "Kumite" exercise .. 30 10

1964. Ancient Buildings Protection Week.

163. **69.** 3 c. multicoloured .. 20 10

70. Bingata "snake" (textile design). 71. Boy Scouts, Badge and Shurei Gate.

1964. New Year.

164. **70.** $1\frac{1}{2}$ c. multicoloured .. 20 8

1965. Ryukyu Islands Boy Scouts. 10th Anniv.

165. **71.** 3 c. multicoloured .. 40 10

72. "Samisen" (musical instrument).

74. Kin Power Station.

75. I.C.Y. Emblem and "Globe". 73. Stadium.

1965. Philatelic Week.

166. **72.** 3 c. multicoloured .. 40 10

1965. Completion of Onoyama Sports Ground.

167. **73.** 3 c. multicoloured .. 20 10

1965. Completion of Kin Power Plant.

168. **74.** 3 c. multicoloured .. 15 10

1965. Int. Co-operation Year and 20th Anniv. of U.N.O.

169. **75.** 3 c. multicoloured. .. 12 8

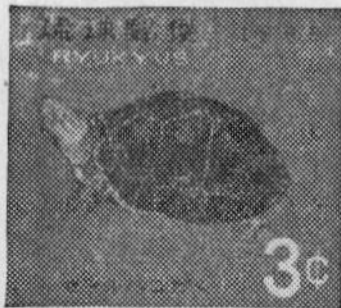

76. City Hall, Naha. 77. Semaruhakogame Turtle.

1965. Completion of Naha City Hall.

170. **76.** 3 c. multicoloured .. 12 8

1965. Ryukyuan Turtles. Multicoloured.

171. 3 c. Type **77** 25 8

172. 3 c. Taimai or hawk's-bill turtle 20 8

173. 3 c. Yamagame or hill tortoise 20 8

78. Bingata "horse" (textile design). 79. Woodpecker.

1965. New Year.

174. **78.** $1\frac{1}{2}$ c. multicoloured .. 10 8

1966. "Natural Monument" (Wildlife). Multicoloured.

175. 3 c. Type **79** 20 10

176. 3 c. Japanese deer .. 20 10

177. 3 c. Dugong 20 10

80. "Swallow". 81. Lilies and Ruins.

1966. Bird Week.

178. **80.** 3 c. multicoloured .. 12 8

1966. Memorial Day (Battle of Okinawa).

179. **81.** 3 c. multicoloured .. 10 8

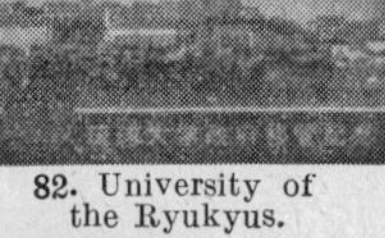

82. University of the Ryukyus.

83. Lacquer Box.

84. Ryukyuan-tiled House. 85. "GRI" Museum Shuri.

1966. Transfer of University of the Ryukyus to Government Administration.
180. **82.** 3 c. multicoloured .. 10 8

1966. Philatelic Week.
181. **83.** 3 c. multicoloured .. 12 8

1966. U.N.E.S.C.O. 20th Anniv.
182. **84.** 3 c. multicoloured .. 10 8

1966. Completion of Government Museum, Shuri.
183. **85.** 3 c. multicoloured .. 10 8

86. Nakasone-Tuimya Tomb.
87. Bingata "ram" (textile design).

1966. Ancient Buildings Protection Week.
184. **86.** 3 c. multicoloured .. 10 8

1966. New Year.
185. **87.** 1½ c. multicoloured .. 10 8

88. Clown Fish.
89. Tsuboya Urn.

1966. Tropical Fish. Multicoloured.
186. 3 c. Type **88** 20 10
187. 3 c. Box fish 20 10
188. 3 c. Forceps Fish 20 10
189. 3 c. Spotted Triggerfish .. 20 10
190. 3 c. Saddleback Butterfly 20 10

1967. Philatelic Week.
191. **89.** 3 c. multicoloured .. 15 10

90. Episcopal Mitre.
91. Roof Tiles and Emblem.

1967. Sea-shells. Multicoloured.
192. 3 c. Type **90** 20 10
193. 3 c. Venus Comb Murex .. 20 10
194. 3 c. Chiragra Spider Conch 20 10
195. 3 c. Green Turban.. .. 20 10
196. 3 c. Bubble Conch .. 40 10

1967. Int. Tourist Year.
197. **91.** 3 c. multicoloured .. 12 8

92. Mobile Clinic.
93. Hojo Bridge, Enkaku.

1967. Anti-T.B. Assn. 15th Anniv.
198. **92.** 3 c. multicoloured .. 12 8

1967. Ancient Buildings Protection Week.
199. **93.** 3 c. multicoloured .. 12 8

94. Bingata "monkey" (textile design).
95. T.V. Tower and Map.

1967. New Year.
200. **94.** 1½ c. multicoloured .. 12 8

1967. Opening of T.V. Broadcasting Stations in Miyako and Yaeyama.
201. **95.** 3 c. multicoloured .. 12 8

96. Dr. Nakachi and Assistant.
97. Medicine Case (after Sokei Dana).

1968. 1st Ryukyu Vaccination (by Dr. Kijin Nakachi). 120th Anniv.
202. **98.** 3 c. multicoloured .. 12 8

1968. Philatelic Week.
203. **97.** 3 c. multicoloured .. 40 10

98. Young Man, Book, Map and Library.

1968. Library Week.
204. **98.** 3 c. multicoloured .. 30 10

99. Postmen with Ryukyu Stamp of 1948.

1968. 1st Ryukyu Islands' Stamps. 20th Anniv.
205. **99.** 3 c. multicoloured .. 30 10

100. Temple Gate.
101. Old Man Dancing.

1968. Restoration of Enkaku Temple Gate.
206. **100.** 3 c. multicoloured .. 30 10

1968. Old People's Day.
207. **101.** 3 c. multicoloured .. 30 10

102. "Mictyris longicarpus".

1968. Crabs. Multicoloured.
208. 3 c. Type **102** 40 10
209. 3 c. "Uca dubia" 40 10
210. 3 c. "Baptozius vinosus" 40 10
211. 3 c. "Cardisoma carnifex" 40 10
212. 3 c. "Ocypode ceratophthalma" 40 10

103. Saraswati Pavilion.
104. Softball Tennis-player.

1968. Ancient Buildings Protection Week.
213. **103.** 3 c. multicoloured .. 30 10

1968. 35th All-Japan East v. West Men's Softball Tennis Tournament. Ohnoyama.
214. **104.** 3 c. multicoloured .. 30 10

105. Bingata "Cock" (textile design).
106. Boxer.

1968. New Year.
215. **105.** 1½ c. multicoloured .. 12 8

1969. 20th All-Japan Boxing Championships.
216. **106.** 3 c. multicoloured .. 30 10

107. Inkwell Screen.
108. U.H.F. Antennae and Map.

1969. Philatelic Week.
217. **107.** 3 c. multicoloured .. 30 10

1969. Okinawa-Sakishima U.H.F. Radio Service. Inaug.
218. **108.** 3 c. multicoloured .. 12 8

109. "Gate of Courtesy".
110. "Tug of War" Festival.

1969. 22nd All-Japan Formative Education Study Conf., Naha.
219. **109.** 3 c. multicoloured .. 12 8

1969. Folklore. Multicoloured.
220. 3 c. Type **110** 40 10
221. 3 c. "Hari" canoe race .. 40 10
222. 3 c. "Izaiho" religious ceremony 40 10
223. 3 c. "Ushideiku" Dance 40 10
224. 3 c. "Sea God" Dance .. 40 10

1969. No. 131 surch.
225. ½ c. on 3 c. multicoloured.. 10 10

111. Nakamura-Ke.

1969. Ancient Buildings Protection Week.
226. **111.** 3 c. multicoloured .. 15 8

112. Kyuzo Toyama and Map.
113. Bingata "dog and flowers" (textile design).

1969. Toyama's Ryukyu-Hawaii Emigration Project. 70th Anniv.
227. **112.** 3 c. multicoloured .. 25 10

No. 227 has "1970" cancelled by bars and "1969" inserted in black.

1969. New Year.
228. **113.** 1½ c. multicoloured .. 12 8

114. Sake Flask.
115. "Shushin-Kaneiri".

116/19.

1970. Philatelic Week.
229. **114.** 3 c. multicoloured .. 25 10

1970. "Kumi-Odori" Ryukyu Theatre. Mult.
230. 3 c. Type **115** 40 10
231. 3 c. "Chu-nusudu" (**116**) 40 10
232. 3 c. "Mekarushi" (**117**) .. 40 10
233. 3 c. "Nidotichiuchi" (**118**) 40 10
234. 3 c. "Kokonomaki" (**119**) 40 10

120. Observatory.
121. Noboru Jahana (politician).

122. "Population".
123. "Great Cycad of Une".

1970. Completion of Underwater Observatory Busena-Misaki, Nago.
240. **120.** 3 c. multicoloured .. 15 8

1970. Famous Ryukyuans.
241. **121.** 3 c. red 30 10
242. – 3 c. green 30 10
243. – 3 c. black 30 10

PORTRAITS: No. 242, Saion Gushichan Bunjaku (statesman). No. 243, Choho Giwan (regent).

1970. Population Census.
244. **122.** 3 c. multicoloured .. 12 8

1970. Ancient Buildings Protection Week.
245. **123.** 3 c. multicoloured .. 20 10

124. Ryukyu Islands, Flag and Japanese Diet.
125. "Wild Boar" (Bingata textile design).

1970. Election of Ryukyu Representatives to the Japanese Diet.
246. **124.** 3 c. multicoloured .. 70 15

1970. New Year.
247. **125.** 1½ c. multicoloured .. 10 5

126. "Jibata" (hand-loom).
127. "Filature" (spinning-wheel).

128. Farm-worker wearing "shurunnu" coat and "kubagasa" Hat.
129. Woman using "shiri-usni" (rice huller).

130. Fisherman's "Umi-Fujo" (box) and "Yuyui" (bailer).

1971. Ryukyu Handicrafts.
248. **126.** 3 c. multicoloured .. 25 8
249. **127.** 3 c. multicoloured .. 25 8
250. **128.** 3 c. multicoloured .. 25 8
251. **129.** 3 c. multicoloured .. 25 8
252. **130.** 3 c. multicoloured .. 25 8

131. "Taku" (container).
133. Restored Battlefield, Okinawa.

132. Civic Emblem with Old and New City Views.

1971. Philatelic Week.
253. **131.** 3 c. multicoloured .. 20 8

1971. Naha's City Status. 50th Anniv.
254. **132.** 3 c. multicoloured .. 15 8

1971. Government Parks. Multicoloured.
255. 3 c. Type **133** 12 8
256. 3 c. Haneji inland sea .. 12 8
257. 4 c. Yabuchi island .. 12 8

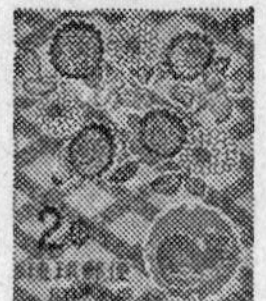

134. Deva King Torinji Temple. 135. " Rat " Bingata textile pattern).

1971. Ancient Buildings Protection Week.
258. **134.** 4 c. multicoloured .. 12 8

1971. New Year.
259. **135.** 2 c. multicoloured .. 10 5

136. Student Nurse and Candle. 137. Islands and Sunset.

1971. Nurses' Training Scheme. 25th Anniv.
260. **136.** 4 c. multicoloured .. 12 8

1972. Maritime Scenery. Multicoloured.
261. 5 c. Type **137** 20 10
262. 5 c. Coral reef 20 10
263. 5 c. Islands and sea-birds .. 20 10

138. Dove, US and Japanese Flags. 139. Yushbin (ceremonial sake container).

1972. Ratification of Treaty for Return of Ryukyu Islands to Japan.
264. **138.** 5 c. multicoloured .. 20 10

1972. Philatelic Week.
265. **139.** 5 c. multicoloured .. 20 10

SPECIAL DELIVERY STAMP

E 1. Sea horse.

1951.
E 18. S **1.** 5 y. blue .. .. 14·00 5·00

SAAR E3

A German territory to the S.E. of Luxembourg. Occupied by France under League of Nations control from 1920 to 1935. Following a plebiscite, Saar returned to Germany in 1935 when German stamps were used until the French occupation in 1945 when Nos. F 1/13 of Germany replaced them followed by Nos. 203, etc. The territory was autonomous under French protection until it again returned to Germany at the end of 1956 following a national referendum. Issues from 1957 were authorised by the German Federal Republic pending the adoption of German currency on July 6th, 1959, after which West German stamps were used.

1920. German stamps inscr. " DEUTSCHES REICH " optd. **Sarre** and bar.
1. **13.** 2 pf. grey .. .. 90 1·25
2. 2½ p. grey .. .. 3·00 1·75
3. **8.** 3 pf. brown 75 55
4. 5 pf. green 10 8
5. **13.** 7½ pf. orange 30 25
6. **8.** 10 pf. red 8 8
7. **13.** 15 pf. violet 8 8
8. **8.** 20 pf. blue 8 8
9. 25 pf. blk. & red on yell. 5·00 3·50
10. 30 pf. blk. & or. on buff 7·50 7·50
11. **13.** 35 pf. brown 25 20
12. **8.** 40 pf. black and red .. 30 25
13. 50 pf. blk. & pur. on buff 20 20
14. 60 pf. purple 40 30
15. 75 pf. black and green .. 30 20
16. 80 pf. blk. & red on rose £140 75·00
17a. **9.** 1 m. red .. .. .. 16·00 15·00

1920. Bavarian stamps optd. **Sarre** or **SARRE** and bars.
18. **9.** 5 pf. green 40 30
19. 10 pf. red 50 45
20a. 15 pf. red 65 65
21. 20 pf. blue 65 50
22. 25 pf. grey .. .. 5·00 3·00
23. 30 pf. orange .. .. 5·00 2·75
24. 40 pf. olive .. .. 5·00 3·00
25. 50 pf. brown 65 55
26. 60 pf. green .. .. 1·00 1·00
27. **10.** 1 m. brown .. .. 11·00 7·50
28. 2 m. violet .. .. 50·00 50·00
29. 3 m. red .. .. .. 75·00 75·00
30. – 5 m. blue (No. 192) .. £500 £300
31. – 10 m. green (No. 193) .. £100 90·00

1920. German stamps inscr. " DEUTSCHES REICH " optd. **SAARBEBIET.**
32. **8.** 5 pf. green 15 12
33. 5 pf. brown 35 25
34. 10 pf. red 15 12
35. 10 pf. orange 25 12
36. **13.** 15 pf. violet 15 12
37. **8.** 20 pf. blue 15 12
38. 20 pf. green 30 20
39. 30 pf. blk. & orge. on buff 20 12
40. 30 pf. blue 45 40
41. 40 pf. black and red .. 20 12
42. 40 pf. red 65 35
43. 50 pf. blk. & pur. on buff 20 20
44. 60 pf. purple 25 20
45. 75 pf. black and green .. 25 20
46. **9.** 1 m. 25 green .. .. 1·00 60
47. 1 m. 50 brown .. .. 1·00 60
48. **10.** 2 m. 50 claret .. .. 1·50 1·75
49. **8.** 4 m. red and black .. 5·50 3·75

1920. Stamps of Germany optd. as above and surch.
50. **8.** 20 on 75 pf. blk. & grn. 35 25
51. **13.** 5 m. on 15 pf. purple .. 3·75 3·50
52. 10 m. on 15 pf. purple .. 4·75 4·00

1. Miner.

2. Pit-head.

3. Burbach Steelworks.

1921.
53. – 5 pf. violet and olive .. 15 8
54. **1.** 10 pf. orange and blue .. 15 8
55. – 20 pf. blue and green .. 20 10
56. – 25 pf. blue and brown .. 20 12
57. – 30 pf. brown and green .. 20 12
58. – 40 pf. red 20 12
59. – 50 pf. black and grey .. 50 45
60. – 60 pf. brown and red .. 65 45
61. – 80 pf. blue 50 35
62. – 1 m. black and red .. 60 30
63. **2.** 1 m. 25 green and brown .. 75 50
64. – 2 m. black and orange .. 2·00 1·10
65. – 3 m. black and brown .. 2·50 1·50
66. – 5 m. violet and yellow .. 4·00 4·50
67. – 10 m. brown and green .. 6·50 5·50
68. **3.** 25 m. blue, black and red 20·00 14·00

Designs—As T **2** horiz. 5 pf. Mill above Mettlach. 20 pf. Pit-head at Reding. 25 f. River at Saarbrucken. 30 pf. Saar at Mettlach. 40 pf. Slag-heap, Volklingen. 50 pf. Signal gantry, Saarbrucken. 60 pf. "Old Bridge", Saarbrucken. 1 m. Wire-rope Railway. 2 m. Town Hall, Saarbrucken. 3 m. Pottery, Mettlach. 5 m. St. Ludwig's Church. 10 m. Chief Magistrate's and Saar Commissioner's Offices. vert. 60 pf. Gothic Chapel, Mettlach.

1921. Nos. 55/68 surch. in new currency.
70. 3 c. on 20 pf. blue & green 25 12
71. 5 c. on 25 pf. blue and brown 15 25
72. 10 c. on 30 pf. brown & green 25 20
73. 15 c. on 40 pf. red 30 20
74. 20 c. on 50 pf. black & grey 25 10
75. 25 c. on 60 pf. brown & red 30 12
76. 30 c. on 80 pf. blue .. 75 30
77. 40 c. on 1 m. black and red 1·25 30
78. 50 c. on 1 m. green & brown 2·00 50
79. 75 c. on 2 m. black & orange 2·50 65
80. 1 f. on 3 m. black and brown 2·50 1·10
81. 2 f. on 5 m. violet & yellow 6·50 2·00
82. 3 f. on 10 m. brown & green 9·00 5·00
83. 5 f. on 25 m. blue, blk. & red 16·00 11·00

1922. Larger designs (except 5 f.) and values in French currency.
84. 3 c. olive (as No. 62) .. 30 20
85. 5 c. blk. & orge (as No. 54) 20 5
86. 10 c. green (as No. 61) .. 25 5
87. 15 c. brown (as No. 62) .. 35 5
98. 15 c. orange (as No. 62) .. 1·90 5
88. 20 c. bl. & yell. (as No. 64) 1·00 5
89. 25 c. red & yell. (as No. 64) 4·50 1·10
100. 25 c. pur. & yell. (as No. 64) 1·25 10
90. 30 c. red & yell. (as No. 58) 35 10
91. 40 c. brn. & yell. (as No. 65) 50 5
92. 50 c. bl. & yell. (as No. 56) 40 5
93. 75 c. grn. & yell. (as No. 65) 10·00 7·50
101. 75 c. blk. & yell. (as No. 65) 6·50 90
94. 1 f. lake (as No. 66) .. 1·00 25
95. 2 f. violet (as No. 63) .. 2·25 1·10
96. 3 f. grn. & orge. (as No. 60) 2·25 1·10
97. 5 f. brn. & choc.)as No. 68) 14·00 13·00

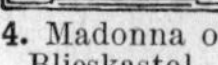

4. Madonna of Blieskastel. 5. Army Medical Service.

1925.
102. **4.** 45 c. plum .. .. 2·50 1·25
103. 10 f. brn. (31 × 36 mm.) 10·00 8·50

1926. Charity.
104. **5.** 20 c. + 20 c. olive .. 6·50 5·00
105. – 40 c. + 40 c. brown .. 7·50 6·50
106. – 50 c. + 50 c. orange .. 7·50 5·00
107. – 1 f. 50 + 1 f. 50 blue .. 14·00 15·00

Design: 40 c. Nurse and patient. 50 c. Children at a spring. 1 f. 50 Maternity Nursing Service.

7. Tholey Abbey.

1926.
108. – 10 c. brown 25 8
109. – 15 c. green 60 50
110. – 20 c. orange 55 8
111. **7.** 25 c. blue 75 20
112. – 30 c. green 50 8
113. – 40 c. sepia 75 8
114. **7.** 50 c. lake 90 8
114a. – 60 c. orange .. .. 1·40 8
115. – 75 c. purple 75 8
116. – 80 c. orange .. .. 3·00 2·50
116a. – 90 c. red .. .. 7·00 6·50
117. – 1 f. violet .. .. 1·10 20
118. – 1 f. 50 blue .. .. 1·60 20
119. – 2 f. red .. .. 1·60 20
120. – 3 f. olive .. .. 3·00 50
121. – 5 f. brown .. .. 9·00 3·75

Designs—vert.: 10 c., 30 c. St. Jean market-place, Saarbrucken. horiz.: 15 c., 75 c. Saar Valley near Gudingen. 20 c., 40 c., 90 c. View from Saarlouis fortifications. 60 c., 80 c., 1 f. Colliery Shafthead. 1 f. 50 c., 2 f., 3 f., 5 f. Burbach Steelworks.

1927. Charity. Optd. **1927-28.**
122. **5.** 20 c. + 20 c. olive .. 9·00 5·00
123. 40 c. + 40 c. brown .. 9·00 7·50
124. 50 c. + 50 c. orange .. 7·50 4·50
125. 1 f. 50 + 1 f. 50 blue .. 11·00 15·00

8. Aeroplane over Saarbrucken. 9. "The blind beggar," by Dyckmanns.

1928. Air.
126. **8.** 50 c. red .. .. 3·00 1·10
127. 1 f. violet .. .. 5·00 1·50

1928. Christmas Charity.
128. **9.** 40 c. + 40 c. brown .. 7·50 11·00
129. 50 c. + 50 c. claret .. 7·50 11·00
130. 1 f. + 1 f. violet .. 7·50 11·00
131. – 1 f. 50 + 1 f. 50 blue .. 7·50 11·00
132. – 2 f. + 2 f. red .. .. 7·50 11·00
133. – 3 f. + 3 f. olive .. .. 7·50 11·00
134. – 10 f. + 10 f. brown .. £350 £375

Designs: 1 f. 50, 2 f. 3 f. "Alms-giving" by Schiestl. 10 f. "Charity" by Raphael (picture in circle).

10. "Orphaned" by H. Kaulbach. 11. "The safety-man". 12. St. Martin.

1929. Christmas Charity.
135. **10.** 40 c. + 15 c. green .. 1·90 1·50
136. 50 c. + 20 c. red .. 4·50 2·50
137. 1 f. + 50 c. plum .. 4·50 3·00
138. – 1 f. 50 + 75 c. blue .. 4·50 3·00
139. – 2 f. + 1 f. red .. .. 4·50 3·00
140. – 3 f. + 2 f. green .. 7·00 7·50
141. – 10 f. + 8 f. brown .. 35·00 32·00

Designs: 1 f. 50, 2 f., 3 f. " St. Ottilla " by V. Feuerstein. 10 f. " The Little Madonna " by Ferruzzio.

1930. Nos. 114 and 116 surch.
141a. **7.** 40 c. on 50 c. lake .. 1·25 65
142. – 60 c. on 80 c. orange .. 1·25 1·00

1931. Christmas Charity (1930 issue).
143. **11.** 40 c. + 15 c. brown .. 5·00 4·25
144. 60 c. + 20 c. orange .. 5·00 4·25
145. – 1 f. + 50 c. red .. .. 7·50 6·50
146. **11.** 1 f. 50 + 75 c. blue .. 7·50 6·50
147. – 2 f. + 1 f. brown .. 7·50 6·50
148. – 3 f. + 2 f. green .. .. 10·00 6·50
149. – 10 f. + 10 f. brown .. 60·00 42·00

Designs: 1 f., 2 f., 3 f. "The Good Samaritan". 10 f. " At the Window ".

1931. Christmas Charity.
150. **12.** 40 c. + 15 c. brown .. 10·00 7·50
151. 60 c. + 20 c. red .. 10·00 7·50
152. 1 f. + 50 c. claret .. 12·00 14·00
153. – 1 f. 50 + 75 c. blue .. 15·00 14·00
154. – 2 f. + 1 f. red .. .. 17·00 14·00
155. – 3 f. + 2 f. green .. 22·00 20·00
156. – 5 f. + 5 f. brown .. 60·00 60·00

Designs: 1 f. 50, 2 f., 3 f. " Charity ". 5 f. " The widow's mite ".

13. Saar Airport.

14. Kirkel Castle Ruins.

17. " Love ". 16. Scene of the Disaster.

1932. Air.
157. **13.** 60 c. red .. .. 6·50 1·75
158. 5 fr. brown .. .. 35·00 25·00

1932. Christmas Charity.
159. **14.** 40 c. + 15 c. brown .. 6·50 6·50
160. – 60 c. + 20 c. red .. 6·50 6·50
161. – 1 f. + 50 c. purple .. 13·00 13·00
162. – 1 f. 50 + 75 c. blue .. 19·00 19·00
163. – 2 f. + 1 f. red .. 19·00 19·00
164. – 3 f. + 2 f. green .. 38·00 38·00
165. – 5 f. + 5 f. brown .. 75·00 75·00

Designs—vert. 60 c. Blieskastel Church. 1 f. Ottweiler Church. 1 f. 50, St. Michael's Church, Saarbrucken. 2 f. Cathedral and fountain, St. Wendel. 3 f. St. John's Church, Saarbrucken. horiz. 5 f. Kerpen Castle, Illingen.

1933. Neunkirchen Explosion Disaster.
166. **16.** 60 c. + 60 c. orange .. 13·00 7·50
167. 3 f. + 3 f. green .. 30·00 20·00
168. 5 f. + 5 f. brown .. 32·00 30·00

1934. Christmas Charity.
169. **17.** 40 c. + 15 c. brown .. 4·50 4·50
170. – 60 c. + 20 c. red .. 4·50 4·50
171. – 1 f. + 50 c. mauve .. 6·50 6·50
172. – 1 f. 50 c + 75 c. blue 13·00 13·00
173. – 2 f. + 1 f. red .. .. 9·00 9·00
174. – 3 f. + 2 f. green .. 11·00 11·00
175. – 5 f. + 5 f. brown .. 24·00 24·00

Designs: 60 c. " Solicitude ". 1 f. " Peace ". 1 f. 50 c. " Consolation ". 2 f. " Welfare ". 3 f. " Truth ". 5 f. " Prayer ".

1934. Saar Plebiscite. Optd. **VOLKSABSTIMMUNG 1935.**

(a) Postage. On Nos. 108/15, 116a/21 and 103.
176. – 10 c. brown 40 25
177. – 15 c. green 40 25
178. – 20 c. orange 25 15
179. **7.** 25 c. blue 70 50
180. – 30 c. green 25 20
181. – 40 c. sepia 30 25
182. **7.** 50 c. lake 55 50
183. – 60 c. orange 30 25
184. – 75 c. purple 65 65
185. – 90 c. red 70 65
186. – 1 f. violet 75 65
187. – 1 f. 50 c. blue .. 1·75 1·60
188. – 2 f. red .. .. 2·00 1·90
189. – 3 f. olive .. .. 3·00 2·50
190. – 5 f. brown .. .. 15·00 11·00
191. **4.** 10 f. brown .. .. 16·00 16·00

(b) Air. On Nos. 126/7 and 157/8.

192. 8. 50 c. red .. .. 5·00 3·25
193. 13. 60 c. red .. .. 2·00 1·10
194. 8. 1 f. violet .. .. 4·50 3·75
195. 13. 5 f. brown .. .. 7·50 5·00

(c) Charity. On Nos. 169/75.

196. 17. 40 c.+15 c. brown .. 2·50 2·50
197. – 60 c.+20 c. red .. 2·50 2·50
198. – 1 f.+50 c. mauve .. 6·50 6·50
199. – 1 f. 50 c.+75 c. blue .. 6·50 6·50
200. – 2 f.+1 f. red .. .. 9·00 9·00
201. – 3 f.+2 f. green .. 7·50 7·50
202. – 5 f.+5 f. brown .. 11·00 11·00

FRENCH OCCUPATION

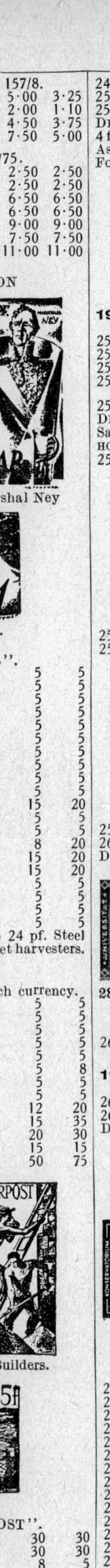

18. Coal-miner. 19. Marshal Ney

20. Loop of the Saar.

1947. Inscr. "SAAR".

203. 18. 2 pf. grey 5 5
204. 3 pf. orange 5 5
205. 6 pf. green 5 5
206. 8 pf. red 5 5
207. 10 pf. mauve 5 5
208. 12 pf. green 5 5
209. – 15 pf. brown 5 5
210. – 16 pf. blue 5 5
211. – 20 pf. lake 5 5
212. – 24 pf. brown 5 5
213. – 25 pf. mauve 15 20
214. – 30 pf. green 5 5
215. – 40 pf. brown 5 5
216. – 45 pf. red 8 20
217. – 50 pf. violet 15 20
218. – 60 pf. violet 15 20
219. – 75 pf. blue 5 5
220. – 80 pf. orange 5 5
221. 19. 84 pf. brown 5 5
222. 20. 1 m. green 5 5

DESIGNS—SMALL SIZE: 15 pf. to 24 pf. Steel workers. 25 pf. to 50 pf. Sugar Beet harvesters. 60 pf. to 80 pf. Mettlach Abbey.

1947. As last surch. in French currency.

223. 18. 10 c. on 2 pf. grey .. 5 5
224. 60 c. on 3 pf. orange .. 5 5
225. 1 f. on 10 pf. mauve .. 5 5
226. 2 f. on 12 pf. green .. 5 5
227. – 3 f. on 15 pf. brown .. 5 5
228. – 4 f. on 16 pf. blue .. 5 8
229. – 5 f. on 20 pf. lake .. 5 5
230. – 6 f. on 24 pf. brown .. 5 5
231. – 9 f. on 30 pf. green .. 12 20
232. – 10 f. on 50 pf. violet .. 15 35
233. – 14 f. on 60 pf. violet .. 20 30
234. 19. 20 f. on 84 pf. brown .. 15 15
235. 20. 50 f. on 1 m. green .. 50 75

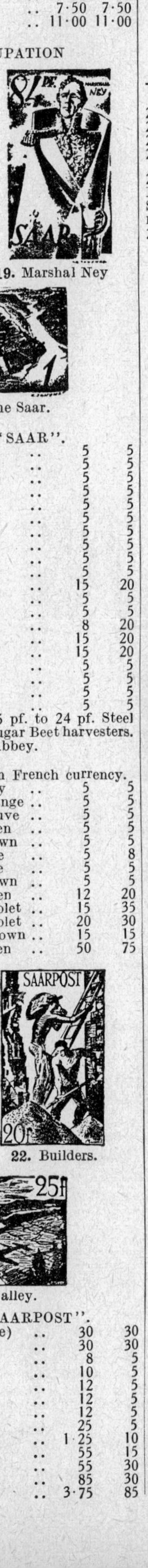

21. Clasped Hands. 22. Builders.

23. Saar Valley.

1948. Inscr. "SAARPOST".

236. 21. 10 c. red (postage) .. 30 30
237. 60 c. blue 30 30
238. 1 f. black 8 5
239. – 2 f. red 10 5
240. – 3 f. brown 12 5
241. – 4 f. red 12 5
242. – 5 f. violet 12 5
243. – 6 f. red 25 5
244. – 9 f. blue .. .. 1·25 10
245. – 10 f. blue 55 15
246. – 14 f. purple 55 30
247. 22. 20 f. red 85 30
248. – 50 f. blue .. .. 3·75 85
249. 23. 25 f. red (air) .. .. 2·50 1·50
250. 50 f. blue .. .. 1·40 1·10
251. 200 f. red .. .. 6·50 7·50

DESIGNS—As T 21: 2 f., 3 f. Man's head. 4 f., 5 f. Woman's head. 6 f., 9 f. Miner's head. As T 22: 10 f. Blast-furnace chimney. 14 f. Foundry. 50 f. Facade of Mettlach Abbey.

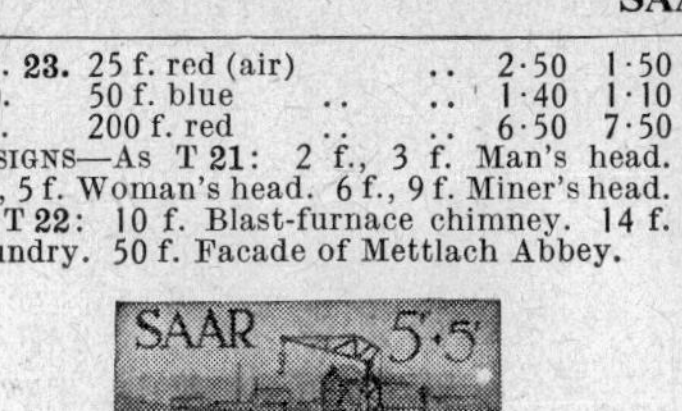

24. Flooded Industrial Area.

1948. Charity. Flood Disaster. Flood scenes. Inscr. as in T 24.

252. 5 f.+5 f. green (post.) .. 1·75 1·90
253. 6 f.+4 f. purple .. .. 1·75 1·90
254. 12 f.+8 f. red .. .. 2·00 2·25
255. 18 f.+12 f. blue .. .. 2·75 3·00
256. 25 f.+15 f. brown (air) .. 8·50 10·00

DESIGNS—VERT. 6 f. Floods in St. Johann, Saarbrucken. 18 f. Flooded street, Saarbrucken. HORIZ. 12 f. Landtag building, Saarbrucken. 25 f. Floods at Ensdorf, Saarlouis.

26. Map of Saarland.

1948. Constitution. 1st Anniv.

257. 26. 10 f. red 75 75
258. 25 f. blue .. .. 1·25 1·50

27. Hikers and Ludweiler Hostel.

1949 Youth Hostels Fund.

259. 27. 8 f.+5 f. brown .. 45 50
260. – 10 f.+7 f. green .. 75 95

DESIGN: 10 f. Hikers and Weisskirchen hostel.

28. Chemical Research. 29. Mare and foal.

1949. Saar University

261. 28. 15 f. red .. .. 1·40 12

1949. Day of the Horse. Inscr. "TAG DES PFERDES 1949".

262. 29. 15 f.+5 f. red .. .. 3·75 4·50
263. – 25 f.+15 f. blue .. 4·00 5·50

DESIGN: 25 f. Two horses in steeple-chase.

30. Beethoven. 31. "Typography". 32. Labourer and Foundry.

1949.

264. – 10 c. purple 10 5
265. 30. 60 c. black 10 5
266. – 1 f. lake 40 5
267. – 3 f. brown 50 5
268. – 5 f. violet 70 5
269. – 6 f. green 40 5
270. – 8 f. olive 25 5
271. 31. 10 f. orange 70 5
272. – 12 f. green .. .. 3·25 5
273. – 15 f. red .. .. 1·60 5
274. – 18 f. magenta .. .. 1·10 75
275. 32. 20 f. grey 60 5
276. – 25 f. blue .. .. 5·00 5
277. – 30 f. lake .. .. 3·50 8
278. – 45 f. purple .. .. 1·75 8
279. – 60 f. green .. .. 1·75 40
280. – 100 f. sepia .. .. 2·50 50

DESIGNS—As T 31: 10 c. Building. 1 f. Engineering. 3 f. Cog-wheels and factory. 5 f. Slag heap. 6 f. Colliery. 8 f. Post-horn. 12 f. Pottery. 15 f. Colliery. 18 f. Mettlach pottery. As T 32. HORIZ. 25 f. Furnace worker. 30 f. Saarbrucken. 45 f. "Giant's Boot". 100 f. Wiebelskirchen. VERT. 60 f. Landsweiler.

33. Detail from "Moses Striking the Rock" (Murillo). 34. Adolf Kolping. 35. P. Wust (philosopher).

1949. National Relief Fund.

281. 33. 8 f.+2 f. blue .. .. 2·50 2·50
282. – 12 f.+3 f. green .. 3·00 3·00
283. – 15 f. +5 f. claret .. 4·00 4·50
284. – 25 f.+10 f. blue .. 7·00 7·50
285. – 50 f.+20 f. purple .. 11·00 16·00

DESIGNS—VERT. 12 f. "Our Lord healing the Paralytic" (Murillo). 15 f. "The Sick Child" (Metsu). 25 f. "St. Thomas of Villanueva (Murillo). 50 f. "Madonna of Blieskastel".

1950. Honouring Kolping (miners' padre).

286. 34. 15 f.+5 f. lake .. 7·50 8·50

1950. Peter Wust. 10th Death Anniv.

287. 35. 15 f. lake .. .. 2·00 2·00

36. Mail Coach.

1950. Stamp Day.

288. 36. 15 f.+5 f. brn. & red 22·00 28·00

37. "Food for the Hungry". 38. St. Peter. 39. Town Hall, Ottweiler.

1950. Red Cross Fund.

289. 37. 25 f.+10 f. lake & red 6·50 9·00

1950. Holy Year.

290. 38. 12 f. green .. .. 1·40 1·60
291. 15 f. red .. .. 1·60 1·90
292. 25 f. blue .. .. 3·25 3·50

1950. 400th Anniv. of Ottweiler.

293. 39. 10 f. brown .. .. 1·50 1·60

40.

1950. Saar's Admission to Council of Europe.

294. 40. 25 f. blue (postage) .. 7·50 2·00
295. 200 f. lake (air) .. .. 65·00 65·00

41. St. Lutwinus Enters Monastery.

DESIGNS: 12 f. Lutwinus builds Mettlach Abbey. 15 f. Lutwinus as Abbot. 25 f. Bishop Lutwinus confirming children at Rheims. 50 f. Lutwinus helping needy.

1950. National Relief Fund. Inscr. "VOLKSHILFE".

296. 41. 8 f.+2 f. sepia .. 3·00 3·25
297. – 12 f.+3 f. green .. 3·00 3·25
298. – 15 f.+5 f. brown .. 3·50 3·75
299. – 25 f.+10 f. blue .. 5·00 6·50
300. 50 f.+20 f. claret .. 7·50 11·00

42. Orphans. 44. Allegory.

43. Mail-carriers, 1760.

1951. Red Cross Fund.

301. 42. 25 f.+10 f. green & red 4·50 5·50

1951. Stamp Day.

302. 43. 15 f. purple .. 1·50 1·90

1951. Trade Fair.

303. 44. 15 f. green .. 1·25 1·50

45. Flowers and Building. 46. Calvin and Luther.

1951. Horticultural Show, Bexbach.

304. 45. 15 f. green .. .. 1·00 40

1951. Reformation in Saar. 375th Anniv.

305. 46. 15 f.+5 f. brown .. 1·00 1·10

47. "The Good Mother" (Lepicie). 48. Postilion.

1951. National Relief Fund. Inscr. "VOLKSHILFE 1951".

306. 47. 12 f.+3 f. green .. 2·00 2·50
307. – 15 f.+5 f. violet .. 2·10 2·75
308. – 18 f.+7 f. lake .. 2·25 3·25
309. – 30 f.+10 f. blue .. 3·75 4·25
310. – 50 f.+20 f. brown .. 8·50 10·00

PAINTINGS—VERT. 18 f. "Outside the Theatre" (Kampf). 18 f. "Sisters of Charity" (Browne). 30 f. "The Good Samaritan" (Bassano). 50 f. "St. Martin and the Poor" (Van Dyck).

1952. Stamp Day.

311. 48. 30 f.+10 f. blue .. 4·00 4·25

49. Athlete bearing Olympic Flame. 50. Globe and Emblem.

1952. 15th Olympic Games, Helsinki. Inscr. "OLYMPISCHE SPIELE 1952".

312. 49. 15 f.+5 f. green .. 1·25 1·50
313. – 30 f.+5 f. blue .. 1·25 1·60

DESIGN: 30 f. Globe and hand holding laurel sprig.

1952. Saar Fair.

314. 50. 15 f. maroon .. .. 1·00 40

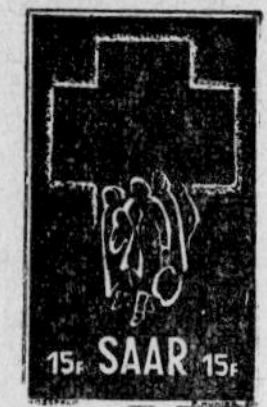
51. Red Cross and Refugees

52. G.P.O., Saarbrucken.

1952. Red Cross Week.
315. 51. 15 f. red .. .. 1·00 40

1952. (A) Without inscr. below design. (B) With inscr.
316. – 1 f. green (B) 5 5
317. – 2 f. violet 5 5
318. – 3 f. red 5 5
319. 52. 5 f. blue-green (A) .. 1·25 5
320. – 5 f. blue-green (B) .. 5 5
321. – 6 f. maroon 8 5
322. – 10 f. olive 12 5
323. 52. 12 f. emerald (B) .. 10 5
324. – 15 f. sepia (A) .. .. 3·75 5
325. – 15 f. sepia (B) .. .. 1·00 5
326. – 15 f. carmine (B) .. 8 5
327. – 18 f. purple 25 50
329. – 30 f. blue 20 20
334. – 500 f. lake .. .. 3·25 5·00
DESIGNS—HORIZ. 1 f., 15 f. (3) Colliery shaft-head. 2 f., 10 f. Ludwigs High School, Saarbrucken. 3 f., 18 f. Gersweiler Bridge. 6 f. Mettlach Bridge. 30 f. University Library, Saarbrucken. VERT. 500 f. St. Ludwi's Church, Saarbrucken.

53. "Count Stroganov as a Boy" (Greuze).

54. Fair Symbol.

1952. National Relief Fund. Paintings inscr. "VOLKSHILFE 1952".
335. 53. 15 f. + 5 f. sepia .. 1·25 1·40
336. – 18 f. + 7 f. lake .. 1·50 1·60
337. – 30 f. + 10 f. blue .. 2·00 2·50
PAINTINGS: 18 f. "The Holy Shepherd" (Murillo). 30 f. Portrait of a Boy (Kraus).

1953. Saar Fair.
338. 54. 15 f. blue 95 40

55. Postilions.

56. Henri Dunant.

1953. Stamp Day.
339. 55. 15 f. blue .. .. 1·50 1·75

1953. Red Cross Week and 125th Anniv. of Birth of Dunant (the founder).
340. 56. 15 f. + 5 f. brown & red 1·10 1·40

57. "Painter's Young Son" (Rubens).

58. St. Benedict Blessing St. Maurus.

1953. National Relief Fund. Paintings inscr. "VOLKSHILFE 1953".
341. – 15 f. + 5 f. purple .. 1·00 1·00
342. – 18 f. + 7 f. lake .. 1·00 1·00
343. 57. 30 f. + 10 f. olive .. 1·50 1·75
DESIGNS—VERT. 15 f. "Clarice Strozzi" (Titian). HORIZ. 18 f. "Painter's Children" (Rubens).

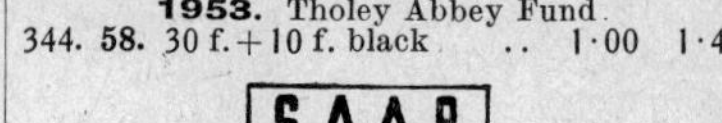
1953. Tholey Abbey Fund
344. 58. 30 f. + 10 f. black .. 1·00 1·40

59. Saar Fair.

1954. Saar Fair.
345. 59. 15 f. green .. 60 35

60. Postal Motor Coach.

1954. Stamp Day.
346. 60. 15 f. red .. .. 1·50 1·75

61. Red Cross and Child.

62. Madonna and Child (Holbein).

1954. Red Cross Week.
347. 61. 15 f. + 5 f. chocolate .. 1·00 1·10

1954. Marian Year. Vert. portraits of Madonna and Child as T 62.
348. 5 f. red 40 45
349. 10 f. green 50 60
350. 15 f. blue 75 90

63. "Street Urchin with a Melon" (Murillo).

64. Cyclist and Flag.

65. Rotary Emblem and Industrial Plant.

1954. National Relief Fund. Paintings inscr. "VOLKSHILFE 1954".
351. 63. 5 f. + 3 f. red 25 30
352. – 10 f. + 5 f. green .. 30 35
353. – 15 f. + 7 f. violet .. 40 45
DESIGNS: 10 f. "Maria de Medici" (A. Bronzino). 15 f. "Baron Emil von Maucler" (J. F. Dietrich).

1955. World Cross-Country Cycle Race.
354. 64. 15 f. blue, red and black 12 15

1955. Rotary Int. 50th Anniv.
355. 65. 15 f. chestnut 12 15

66. Exhibitors' Flags.

67. Nurse and Baby.

1955. Saar. Fair
356. 66. 15 f. yell., bl. & grn. 15 20

1955. Red Cross Week.
357. 67. 15 f. + 5 f. black & red 15 20

68. Postman.

69. "Mother".

1955. Stamp Day.
358. 68. 15 f. maroon 35 45

1955. Referendum. Optd. **VOLKSBEFRAGUNG 1955.**
359. 15 f. carmine (No. 326) .. 10 12
360. 18 f. purple (No. 327) .. 12 15
361. 30 f. blue (No. 329) .. 25 25

1955. National Relief Fund. Durer paintings inscr. as in T 69.
362. 69. 5 f. + 3 f. green .. 20 20
363. – 10 f. + 5 f. olive .. 40 45
364. – 15 f. + 7 f. bistre .. 50 55
PAINTINGS: 10 f. "The Praying Hands". 15 f. "The Old Man from Antwerp".

70.

71. Radio Tower.

1956. Saar Fair.
365. 70. 15 f. green and lake .. 10 12

1956. Stamp Day.
366. 71. 15 f. green 10 12

72. Casualty Station.

73.

1956. Red Cross Week.
367. 72. 15 f. + 5 f. brown .. 10 12

1956. Olympic Games.
368. 73. 12 f. + 3 f. blue & green 12 12
369. 15 f. + 5 f. sepia & mar. 12 15

74. Winterberg Memorial.

75. "Portrait of Lucrezia Crivelli" (Leonardo).

1956. Winterberg Memorial Reconstruction Fund.
370. 74. 5 f. + 2 f. green .. 8 8
371. 12 f. + 3 f. mauve .. 10 12
372. 15 f. + 5 f. brown .. 10 12

1956. National Relief Fund. Inscr. as in T 75.
373. 75. 5 f. + 3 f. blue .. 5 5
374. – 10 f. + 5 f. lake .. 12 15
375. – 15 f. + 7 f. green .. 20 20
PAINTINGS—VERT. 10 f. "Saskia" (Rembrandt). 15 f. "Lady Playing Spinet" (Floris).

RETURN TO GERMANY

76. Arms of the Saar.

77. President Heuss.

1957. Return of the Saar to Germany.
376. 76. 15 f. slate and orange .. 5 8

1957. (a) Without "F" after figure of value
377. 77. 1 f. green 5 5
378. 2 f. violet 5 5
379. 3 f. brown 5 5
380. 4 f. magenta 8 12
381. 5 f. olive 5 5
382. 6 f. red 5 10
383. 10 f. grey 5 5
384. 12 f. orange 5 5
385. 15 f. turquoise 5 5
386. 18 f. red 25 40
387. 25 f. mauve 12 12
388. 30 f. purple 12 15
389. 45 f. olive 25 60
390. 50 f. chocolate .. 25 25
391. 60 f. red 35 50
392. 70 f. salmon 50 55
393. 80 f. olive 50 65
394. 90 f. grey 65 90
395. 100 f. red ($24 \times 29\frac{1}{2}$ mm.) 75 1·00
396. 200 f. lilac ($24 \times 29\frac{1}{2}$ mm.) 1·50 2·25

(b) With "F" after figure of value.
406. 77. 1 f. slate 5 5
407. 3 f. blue 5 5
408. 5 f. olive 5 5
409. 6 f. brown 5 5
410. 10 f. violet 5 5
411. 12 f. chestnut 5 5
412. 15 f. green 8 10
413. 18 f. grey 35 50
414. 20 f. olive 30 35
415. 25 f. chestnut 20 15
416. 30 f. mauve 20 15
417. 35 f. brown 30 35
418. 45 f. turquoise 30 50
419. 50 f. brown 30 35
420. 70 f. green 35 65
421. 80 f. blue 35 65
422. 90 f. red 65 75
423. 100 f. yellow 65 75
424. 200 f. green .. .. 1·50 2·50
425. 300 f. blue .. .. 1·90 2·50
Nos. 423/5 are larger, $24\frac{1}{2} \times 29\frac{1}{2}$ mm.

78. Iron Foundry.

79. Arms of Merzig and St. Pierre Church.

1957. Saar Fair.
397. 78. 15 f. lake and sepia .. 8 10

1957. Merzig Cent.
398. 79. 15 f. blue 8 10

The following stamps (except where otherwise indicated) are as types of West Germany but inscribed "SAARLAND" and with values in French currency. The Type numbers quoted are those of Germany. In some instances the colours are changed.

1957. Europa.
399. 276. 20 f. orange and yellow 25 30
400. 35 f. violet and pink .. 30 35

1957. Humanitarian Relief Fund.
401. 277. 6 f. + 4 f. blk. & brn. 5 5
402. – 12 f. + 6 f. blk. & grn. 8 8
403. – 15 f. + 7 f. blk. & red 12 12
404. – 30 f. + 10 f. blk. & bl. 20 20

1957. Int. Correspondence Week.
405. 279. 15 f. black and red .. 8 10

1958. Wilhelm Busch (caricaturist).
426. 284. 12 f. olive and black .. 5 5
427. – 15 f. red and black .. 12 12

1958. Forest Fires Prevention Campaign.
428. 285. 15 f. black and red .. 8 8

1958. Rudolf Diesel (engineer).
429. 286. 12 f. turquoise .. 5 8

1958. Berlin Students' Fund.
430. 287. 12 f. + 6 f. brown, black and green .. 8 8
431. – 15 f. + 7 f. brown, green and red .. 12 12

80. Saarbrucken Town Hall and Fair Emblem.

81. Homburg.

1958. Saar Fair.
432. 80. 15 f. claret 8 8

1958. Homburg. 4th Cent.
433. 81. 15 f. olive-green .. 8 8

1958. German Gymnastics.
434. 292. 12 f. black, grn. & grey 8 8

1958. Herman Schulze-Delitzsch.
435. 293. 12 f. green .. 5 8

1958. Europa. As Nos. 1212/13
436. 12 f. blue and green .. 25 30
437. 30 f. red and blue.. .. 30 35

1958. Humanitarian Relief and Welfare Funds.
438. 294. 6 f.+4 f. brown .. 5 5
439. 295. 12 f.+6 f. red, yellow and green .. 8 8
440. – 15 f.+7 f. blue, green and red 15 15
441. – 30 f.+10 f. yellow, green and blue .. 20 25

1959. Jakob Fugger.
442. 297. 15 f. black & brn.-red 8 8

82. Hands holding Crates. 83. Saarbrucken.

1959. Saar Fair.
443. 82. 15 f. lake 10 10

1959. Greater Saarbrucken. 50th Anniv.
444. 83. 15 f. blue 8 8

1959. Alexander von Humboldt.
445. 299. 15 f. blue 10 10

OFFICIAL STAMPS

1922. Nos. 84 to 94 optd. **DIENSTMARKE.**
O 98. 3 c. olive 60 65
O 99. 5 c. black and orange .. 25 10
O 100. 10 c. green 20 8
O 101. 15 c. brown 20 10
O 109. 15 c. orange 40 15
O 102. 20 c. violet and yellow 25 8
O 110. 20 c. blue and yellow .. 40 15
O 103. 25 c. red and yellow .. 1·50 35
O 111. 25 c. purple and yellow 40 15
O 104. 30 c. purple and yellow 20 8
O 105. 40 c. brown and yellow 30 8
O 106. 50 c. blue and yellow .. 45 8
O 112. 75 c. green and yellow.. 1·00 75
O 108a. 1 f. lake .. .. 6·50 2·75

1927. Nos. 108/15, 117 and 119 optd. **DIENSTMARKE.**
O 128. 10 c. brown .. .. 1·10 1·00
O 129. 15 c. green .. .. 1·60 2·75
O 130. 20 c. orange .. .. 1·10 75
O 131. 25 c. blue .. .. 1·75 2·00
O 122. 30 c. green .. .. 1·75 25
O 133. 40 c. sepia .. .. 1·10 15
O 134. 50 c. lake .. .. 1·10 15
O 135. 60 c. orange 70 15
O 125. 75 c. purple .. .. 1·10 30
O 126. 1 f. violet .. .. 1·25 15
O 138. 2 f. red .. .. 1·25 15

O 1. Arms.

1949.
O 264 O 1. 10 c. red 20 25
O 265. 30 c. black 15 15
O 266. 1 f. green 10 10
O 267. 2 f. orange 65 65
O 268. 5 f. blue 20 15
O 269. 10 f. black 40 40
O 270. 12 f. lilac .. .. 1·60 2·00
O 271. 15 f. blue 50 12
O 272. 20 f. green 80 50
O 273. 30 f. mauve .. .. 1·10 1·10
O 274. 50 f. violet .. .. 1·10 1·25
O 275. 100 f. brown .. 19·00 25·00

SABAH BC

Formerly North Borneo, now part of Malaysia.
100 cents = 1 Malaysian dollar.

1964. Nos. 391/406 of North Borneo optd. **SABAH.**
408. 1 c. emerald & brown-red.. 5 5
409. 4 c. olive and orange .. 5 5
410. 5 c. sepia and violet .. 5 5
411. 6 c. black and turquoise .. 8 8
412. 10 c. green and red .. 10 8
413. 12 c. brown and myrtle .. 10 10
414. 20 c. turquoise and blue .. 15 20
415. 25 c. black and red .. 25 25
416. 30 c. sepia and olive .. 30 30
417. 35 c. slate and brown .. 40 35
418. 50 c. emerald & yellow-brn. 40 35
419. 75 c. grey-blue and purple 60 50
420. $1 brown and green .. 60 50
421. $2 brown and slate .. 1·25 1·40
422. $5 emerald and maroon .. 3·00 2·50
423. $10 red and blue .. 7·50 9·00

1. "Vanda hookeriana".

1965. As No. 166/72 of Johore but with Arms of Sabah inset as in T 1.
424. 1. 1 c. multicoloured .. 5 5
425. – 2 c. multicoloured .. 5 5
426. – 5 c. multicoloured .. 5 5
427. – 6 c. multicoloured .. 8 8
428. – 10 c. multicoloured .. 10 10
429. – 15 c. multicoloured .. 15 12
430. – 20 c. multicoloured .. 12 12
The higher values used in Sabah were Nos. 20/7 of Malaysia.

2. Great Orange Tip.

1971. Butterflies. As Nos. 175/81 of Johore, but with Sabah Arms inset as T 2.
432. – 1 c. multicoloured .. 5 5
433. – 2 c. multicoloured .. 5 5
434. – 5 c. multicoloured .. 5 5
435. – 6 c. multicoloured .. 8 5
436. 2. 10 c. multicoloured .. 5 5
437. – 15 c. multicoloured .. 8 8
438. – 20 c. multicoloured .. 10 10
The higher values in use with this issue are Nos. 64/71 of Malaysia.

ST. CHRISTOPHER BC

One of the Leeward Is. Stamps superseded in 1890 by Leeward Islands general issue.

ILLUSTRATIONS British Commonwealth and all overprints and surcharges are FULL SIZE. Foreign Countries have been reduced to ¾-LINEAR.

1.

1870.
11. 1. ½d. green 60 70
7. 1d. magenta .. .. 18·00 5·50
13. 1d. red 45 60
14. 2½d. red-brown .. .. 60·00 28·00
16. 2½d. blue .. .. .. 1·50 1·75
10. 4d. blue .. .. .. 50·00 11·00
18. 4d. grey .. .. .. 1·10 1·25
8. 6d. green .. .. .. 11·00 6·00
19. 6d. olive .. .. .. 60·00 60·00
20. 1s. mauve.. .. .. 60·00 55·00

1885. Surch. in words.
22. 1. ½d. on half of 1d. rose .. 9·00 15·00
26. 1d. on ½d. green .. .. 14·00 15·00
28. 1d. on 2½d. blue .. .. 14·00 18·00
24. 1d. on 6d. green .. .. 7·00 12·00
23. 4d. on 6d. green .. 16·00 20·00

1886. Surch. in figures.
25. 1. 4d. on 6d. green .. .. 20·00 35·00

ST. HELENA BC

An island in the S. Atlantic Ocean, W. of Africa.

1.

2.

The early stamps of St. Helena, other than the 6d. were formed by printing the 6d. in various colours and surcharging it with new values in words or (in the case of the 2½d.) in figures.

1856. Imperf.
4. 1. 1d. on 6d. red .. .. 35·00 27·00
5. 4d. on 6d. red .. .. £170 65·00
1. 6d. blue .. .. .. £100 48·00

1861. Perf.
36. 1. ½d. on 6d. green .. 65 80
38. 1d. on 6d. red .. 1·25 1·25
39. 2d. on 6d. yellow.. .. 1·25 1·40
40. 2½d. on 6d. blue .. .. 1·25 2·00
41. 3d. on 6d. purple .. 1·25 1·60
22. 4d. on 6d. red .. .. 18·00 11·00
43a. 4d. on 6d. brown .. 4·50 3·25
33. 6d. blue .. .. .. 26·00 8·00
44. 6d. grey .. .. .. 4·50 4·00
25. 1s. on 6d. green .. 8·00 5·00
18a. 5s. on 6d. yellow .. 11·00 14·00

1890.
46. 2. ½d. green .. .. .. 75 1·00
47. 1d. red .. .. .. 1·40 1·40
48. 1½d. brown and green .. 1·50 1·50
49. 2d. yellow .. .. .. 1·60 2·40
50. 2½d. brown .. .. .. 2·25 3·00
51. 5d. violet .. .. .. 5·00 7·00
52. 10d. brown .. .. .. 7·00 9·00

3.

4. Government House.

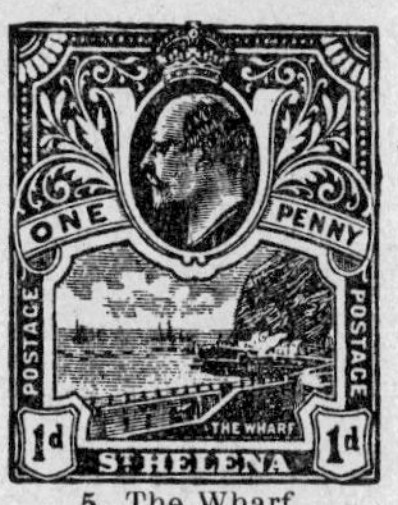

5. The Wharf.

1902. Inscr. "POSTAGE POSTAGE".
53. 3. ½d. green 30 50
54. 1d. red .. .. .. 80 1·10

1903.
55. 4. ½d. brown and green .. 60 90
56. 5. 1d. black and red .. 40·00 30·00
57. 4. 2d. black and green .. 4·00 4·00
58. 5. 8d. black and brown .. 7·50 8·50
59. 4. 1s. brown and orange .. 7·00 10·00
60. 5. 2s. black and violet .. 12·00 14·00

1908. Inscr. "POSTAGE & REVENUE".
64. 3. 2½d. blue .. .. .. 80 1·25
66. 4d. black and red on yellow 80 1·40
67. 6d. purple .. .. 1·25 2·50
71. 10s. green & red on green £110 £150

1912. As T 4/5, but with medallion of King George V.
72. 4. ½d. black and green .. 15 15
73. 5. 1d. black and red .. 25 45
89. 1d. green .. .. .. 40 1·40
74. 1½d. black and orange .. 80 1·40
90. 1½d. red .. .. .. 2·75 4·50
75. 4. 2d. black and grey .. 1·00 1·40
76. 5. 2½d. black and blue .. 1·00 1·75
77. 4. 3d. black & purple on yell. 1·25 1·75
91. 3d. blue .. .. .. 5·00 7·00
78. 5. 8d. black and purple .. 4·00 6·00
79. 4. 1s. black on green .. 6·00 9·00
80. 5. 2s. black and blue on blue 11·00 14·00
81. 3s. black and violet .. 17·00 20·00

8.

9. Badge of St. Helena.

1912. Inscr. "POSTAGE & REVENUE".
83. 8. 4d. black & red on yellow 1·40 5·00
84. 6d. purple .. .. 1·50 5·00

1913. Inscr. "POSTAGE POSTAGE".
85. 8. 4d. black & red on yellow 1·50 2·75
86. 6d. purple .. .. 3·50 7·00

1916. Surch. **WAR TAX ONE PENNY.**
87. 1d.+1d. black & red (No. 73) 20 40

1919. Surch. **WAR TAX 1d.**
88. 1d.+1d.black & red (No. 73) 15 15

1922.
97. 9. ½d. black.. .. .. 15 15
98. 1d. black and green .. 25 15
99. 1½d. red .. .. 70 1·00
100. 2d. black and grey .. 55 55
101. 3d. blue 40 70
92. 4d. black on yellow .. 1·25 2·00
103. 5d. green & red on green 1·10 1·60
104. 6d. black and purple .. 95 1·60
105. 8d. black and violet .. 1·75 2·50
106. 1s. black and brown .. 1·40 3·00
107. 1s. 6d. black and green .. 5·00 7·50
108. 2s. purple & blue on blue 5·00 7·50
109. 2s.6d. black & red on yell. 5·00 8·00
95. 5s. black & green on yell. 14·00 17·00
111. 7s. 6d. black and orange 22·00 32·00
112. 10s. black and green .. 35·00 35·00
113. 15s. black & pur. on blue £250 £350
96. £1 black & purple on red £100 £130

10. Lot and Lot's wife.

1934. British Colonization Cent.
114. 10. ½d. black and purple .. 30 45
115. – 1d. black and green .. 65 75
116. – 1½d. black and red .. 1·10 1·25
117. – 2d. black and orange .. 1·40 1·60
118. – 3d. black and blue .. 2·50 2·75
119. – 6d. black and blue .. 4·00 4·50
120. – 1s. black and brown .. 7·50 11·00
121. – 2s. 6d. black and red .. 17·00 22·00
122. – 5s. black and brown .. 26·00 32·00
123. – 10s. black and purple .. 70·00 85·00
DESIGNS—HORIZ. 1d. "Plantation". 1½d. Map of St. Helena. 2d. Quay, Jamestown. 3d. James Valley. 6d. Jamestown. 1s. Mundens Promontory. 5s. High Knoll. 10s. Badge of St. Helena. VERT. 2s. 6d. St. Helena.

1935. Silver Jubilee. As T 11 of Antigua.
124. 1½d. blue and red .. 30 40
125. 2d. blue and grey .. 60 70
126. 6d. green and blue .. 3·00 3·25
127. 1s. grey and purple .. 7·00 7·50

1937. Coronation. As T 2 of Aden.
128. 1d. green 10 12
129. 2d. orange 25 20
130. 3d. blue.. .. .. 25 25

20. Badge of St. Helena.

1938.
131. 20. ½d. violet 10 12
132. 1d. green .. .. 3·50 3·00
132a. 1d. orange 10 12
149. 1d. black and green .. 25 40
133. 1½d. red 10 12
150. 1½d. black and red .. 40 60
134. 2d. orange 12 12
151. 2d. black and red .. 40 60
135. 3d. blue.. .. .. 14·00 7·50
135a. 3d. grey 20 25
135b. 4d. blue 25 30
136. 6d. blue.. .. .. 20 30
136a. 8d. green .. .. .. 80 1·40
137. 1s. brown 55 70
138. 2s. 6d. maroon .. .. 1·50 2·00
139. 5s. brown .. .. .. 2·50 3·00
140. 10s. purple .. .. 5·00 6·00

1946. Victory. As T 4 of Aden.
141. 2d. orange 12 12
142. 4d. blue.. .. .. 12 15

1948. Silver Wedding. As T 5/6 of Aden.
143. 3d. black 10 12
144. 10s. blue .. .. 4·00 5·50

1949. U.P.U. As T 14/7 of Antigua.
145. 3d. red 10 20
146. 4d. blue.. .. .. 25 30
147. 6d. olive 60 70
148. 1s. black .. .. .. 95 1·10

1953. Coronation. As T 7 of Aden.
152. 3d. black and lilac .. 75 1·00

21. The Colony's Badge.

1953.

153. 21. ½d. black and emerald.. 5 5
154. – 1d. black and green .. 5 8
155. – 1½d. black and purple 10 10
156. – 2d. black and claret .. 15 15
157. – 2½d. black and vermilion 15 15
158. – 3d. black and brown .. 20 20
159. – 4d. black and blue .. 25 25
160. – 6d. black and violet .. 25 30
161. – 7d. black 35 35
162. – 1s. black and red .. 60 60
163. – 2s. 6d. black and violet 2·75 2·75
164. – 5s. black and sepia .. 4·00 4·50
165. – 10s. black and yellow .. 13·00 13·00

DESIGNS—HORIZ. 1d. Flax plantation. 2d. Lace making. 2½d. Drying flax. 3d. Wire Bird. 4d. Flagstaff and the Barn (hills). 6d. Donkeys carrying flax. 7d. Map. 1s. The Castle. 2s. 6d. Cutting flax. 5s. Jamestown. 10s. Longwood House. VERT. 1½d. Heartshaped Waterfall.

22. Stamp of 1856.

1956. Cent. of First St. Helena Postage Stamp.

166. 22. 3d. blue and red .. 25 25
167. 4d. blue and brown .. 35 35
168. 6d. blue and purple .. 70 70

23. "London" off James Bay.

1959. Settlement. Tercent.

169. – 3d. black and red .. 25 25
170. 23. 6d. emerald and slate-bl. 45 50
171. – 1s. black and orange .. 70 80

DESIGNS—HORIZ. 3d. Arms of East India Company. 1s. Commemoration Stone.

1961. Tristan Relief Fund. Nos. 46 and 49/51 of Tristan da Cunha surch. **ST. HELENA Tristan Relief** and premium.

172. 2½ c.+3d. black and red..
173. 5 c.+6d. black and blue ..
174. 7½ c.+9d. black and rose..
175. 10 c.+1s. black and brown
Set of 4 .. ..£1100 £600

24. Cunning Fish.

25. Queen Elizabeth II with Prince Andrew (after Cecil Beaton).

1961.

176a. 24. 1d. blue, vio., yell. & red 5 5
177. – 1½d. yellow, green, black and drab 5 5
178. – 2d. red and grey .. 8 8
179a. – 3d. bl., blk., pink & ind. 15 20
180. – 4½d. yellow-green, green, brown and grey .. 12 15
181a. – 6d. red, sepia and olive 15 20
182. – 7d. brown, black & vio. 15 20
183. – 10d. maroon and blue.. 25 30
184. – 1s. lemon, grn. & brown 25 30
185. – 1s. 6d. grey & slate-blue 60 70
186. – 2s. 6d. red, yell. & turq. 60 80
187. – 5s. yellow, brown & grn. 1·50 1·50
188. – 10s. red, black and blue 2·50 3·00
189a. 25. £1 chocolate and blue.. 5·00 6·00

DESIGNS—As T 24—VERT. 1½d. Cape Canary. 3d. Queen Elizabeth II. 4½d. Red-wood Flower. 6d. "Red Bird" (Weaver). 1s. Gum-wood Flower. 1s. 6d. Fairy Tern. 5s. Night-blooming Cereus. HORIZ. 2d. Brittle Starfish. 7d. Trumpet Fish. 10d. Feather Starfish. 2s. 6d. Orange Starfish. 10s. Deep-water Bull's-eye.

1963. Freedom from Hunger. As T **10** of Aden.

190. 1s. 6d. blue .. .. 2·50 2·00

1963. Red Cross Cent. As T **24** of Antigua.

191. 3d. red and black.. .. 30 30
192. 1s. 6d. red and blue .. 2·75 2·50

1965. 1st Local Post. Optd. **FIRST LOCAL POST 4th JANUARY 1965.**

193. 24. 1d. 10 10
194. 3d. (No. 179a) 12 12
195. 6d. (No. 181a) 20 20
196. 1s. 6d. (No. 185) .. 45 45

1965. I.T.U. Cent. As T **26** of Antigua.

197. 3d. blue and brown .. 30 30
198. 6d. purple and green .. 60 60

1965. I.C.Y. As T **27** of Antigua.

199. 1d. purple and turquoise.. 12 12
200. 6d. green and lavender .. 80 70

1966. Churchill Commem. As T **28** of Antigua.

201. 1d. blue 10 10
202. 3d. green 25 25
203. 6d. brown 50 50
204. 1s. 6d. violet .. .. 1·60 1·60

1966. World Cup Football Championships. As T **30** of Antigua.

205. 3d. violet, grn., lake & brn. 20 20
206. 6d. choc., turq., lake & brn. 50 50

1966. W.H.O. Headquarters, Geneva. Inaug. As T **31** of Antigua.

207. 3d. black, green and blue 20 20
208. 1s. 6d. black, purple & ochre 95 1·00

1966. U.N.E.S.C.O. 20th Anniv. As T **33/5** of Antigua.

209. 3d. violet, red, yell. & orge. 25 25
210. 6d. yellow, violet and olive 45 45
211. 1s. 6d. black, purple & orge. 1·50 1·25

26. Badge of St. Helena.

1967. New Constitution

212. 26. 1s. multicoloured .. 35 30
213. 2s. 6d. multicoloured .. 75 60

27. Fire of London.

1967. 300th Anniv. of Arrival of Settlers after Great Fire of London.

214. 27. 1d. red and black .. 8 5
215. – 3d. ultramarine & black 15 15
216. – 6d. violet and black .. 30 30
217. – 1s. 6d. green and black 60 60

DESIGNS: 3d. East Indiaman "Charles". 6d. Settlers landing at Jamestown. 1s. 6d. Settlers clearing scrub.

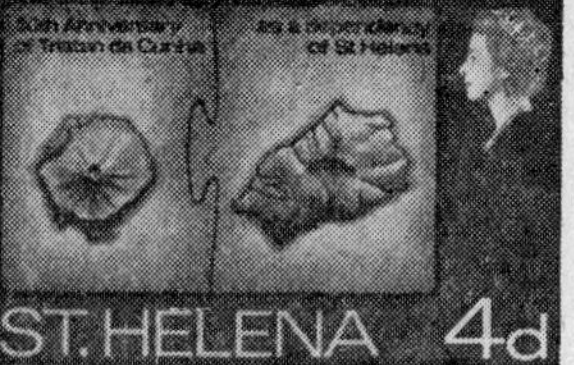

28. Interlocking Maps of Tristan and St. Helena.

1968. Tristan da Cunha as a Dependency of St. Helena. 30th Anniv.

218. 28. 4d. purple and chocolate 10 10
219. – 8d. olive and brown .. 20 20
220. 28. 1s. 9d. ultram. & choc. 40 40
221. – 2s. 3d. blue & brown .. 60 60

DESIGN: 8d. and 2s. 3d. Interlocking Maps of Tristan and St. Helena (different).

29. Queen Elizabeth and Sir Hudson Lowe.

1968. Abolition of Slavery in St. Helena. 150th Anniv.

222. 29. 3d. multicoloured .. 12 12
223. 9d. multicoloured .. 20 25
224. – 1s. 6d. multicoloured .. 40 45
225. – 2s. 6d. multicoloured .. 70 65

DESIGN: Nos. 224 and 225, Queen Elizabeth and Sir George Bingham.

30. Road Construction.

1968. Multicoloured.

226. ½d. Type **30** 8 8
227. 1d. Electricity Development 5 5
228. 1½d. Dental Unit 5 5
229. 2d. Pest Control 8 8
230. 3d. Flats in Jamestown .. 10 10
231. 4d. Pasture and Livestock Improvement .. 12 12
232. 6d. Schools Broadcasting 15 20
233. 8d. County Cottages .. 15 20
234. 10d. New School Buildings 25 25
235. 1s. Reafforestation .. 25 30
236. 1s. 6d. Heavy Lift Crane.. 35 40
237. 2s. 6d. Lady Field Children's Home .. 50 60
238. 5s. Agricultural Training.. 90 1·10
239. 10s. New General Hospital 1·75 2·00
274. £1 Lifeboat "John Dutton" 2·25 2·50

PLANTS SHOWN: ½d., 4d., 1s. 6d. Blue gum Eucalyptus. 1d., 6d., 2s. 6d. Cabbage-tree. 1½d., 8d., 5s. St. Helena Redwood. 2d., 10d., 10s. Scrubweed. 3d., 1s., £1 Tree-fern.

31. Brig "Perseverance".

1969. Mail Communications. Multicoloured.

241. 4d. Type **31** 10 10
242. 8d. R.M.S. "Dane" .. 20 20
243. 1s. 9d. S.S. "Llandovery Castle" 40 40
244. 2s. 3d. R.M.S. "Good Hope Castle" 60 60

32. W.O. and Drummer of the 53rd Foot, 1815.

1969. Military Uniforms. Multicoloured.

245. 6d. Type **32** 12 12
246. 8d. Officer and Surgeon, 20th Foot, 1816 .. 20 25
247. 1s. 8d. Drum Major, 66th Foot, 1816, and Royal Artillery Officer, 1920 .. 45 50
248. 2s. 6d. Private, 91st Foot, and 1832, 2nd Corporal, Royal Sappers and Miners 75 80

33. Dickens, Mr. Pickwick and Job Trotter ("Pickwick Papers").

1970. Charles Dickens. Death Cent. Multicoloured.

249. 4d. Type **33** 10 10
250. 8d. Mr. Bumble and Oliver ("Oliver Twist") .. 20 20
251. 1s. 6d. Sairey Gamp and Mark Tapley ("Martin Chuzzlewit") 40 40
252. 2s. 6d. Jo and Mr. Turveydrop ("Bleak House") 70 70

All designs include a portrait of Dickens as T **33**.

34. "Kiss of Life".

1970. British Red Cross. Cent.

253. 34. 6d. bistre, verm. & blk. 10 10
254. – 9d. green, verm. & blk. 15 20
255. – 1s. 9d. grey, verm. & blk. 40 40
256. – 2s. 3d. lilac, vermilion and black .. 45 50

DESIGNS: 9d. Nurse with girl in wheelchair. 1s. 9d. Nurse bandaging child's knee. 2s. 3d. Red Cross emblem.

35. Officer's Shako Plate (20th Foot).

1970. Military Equipment (1st issue). Multicoloured.

257. 4d. Type **35** 12 12
258. 9d. Officer's Breast Plate (66th Foot) 30 35
259. 1s. 3d. Officer's Full Dress Shako (91st Foot) .. 45 50
260. 2s. 11d. Ensign's Shako (53rd Foot) .. .. 1·10 1·25

See also Nos. 281/4, 285/8 and 291/4.

36. Electricity Development.

1971. Decimal Currency. Designs as Nos. 227/39. inscr. as T **36**.

261. ½p. multicoloured .. 5 5
262. 1p. multicoloured .. 5 5
263. 1½p. multicoloured .. 5 5
264. 2p. multicoloured .. 8 8
265. 2½p. multicoloured .. 8 8
266. 3½p. multicoloured .. 10 10
267. 4½p. multicoloured .. 12 15
268. 5p. multicoloured .. 20 25
269. 7½p. multicoloured .. 12 15
270. 10p. multicoloured .. 20 25
271. 12½p. multicoloured .. 20 25
272. 25p. multicoloured .. 45 50
273. 50p. multicoloured .. 1·00 1·10

37. St. Helena holding the "True Cross".

1971. Easter.
275. **37.** 2p. multicoloured .. 10 10
276. 5p. multicoloured .. 20 20
277. 7½p. multicoloured .. 35 35
278. 12½p. multicoloured .. 60 65

38. Napoleon (after painting by David), and Tomb on St. Helena.

1971. Napoleon. 150th Death Anniv. Multicoloured.
279. 2p. Type **38** 15 15
280. 34p. Napoleon at St. Helena (after painting by Delaroche) .. .. 1·25 1·40

1971. Military Equipment (2nd issue). As T **35**. Multicoloured.
281. 1½p. Artillery Private's hanger 8 8
282. 4p. Baker rifle and socket bayonet 20 20
283. 6p. Infantry Officer's sword 30 30
284. 22½p. Baker rifle and sword bayonet .. .. .. 1·00 1·00

1972. Military Equipment (3rd issue). As T **35**. Multicoloured.
285. 2p. multicoloured .. 8 10
286. 5p. lilac, blue and black .. 20 20
287. 7½p. multicoloured 30 35
288. 12½p. sepia, brn. & black .. 50 55
DESIGNS: 2p. Royal Sappers and Miners breast-plate, post 1823. 5p. Infantry sergeant's spontoon, c. 1830. 7½p. Royal Artillery Officer's breast-plate, c. 1830. 12½p. English military pistol, c. 1800.

1972. Royal Silver Wedding. As T **19** of Ascension but with Wire Bird and White Fairy Tern in background.
289. 2p. green 10 15
290. 16p. brown 75 85

1973. Military Equipment (4th issue). As Type **35**. Multicoloured.
291. 2p. Other Rank's shako, 53rd Foot, 1815 .. .. 8 10
292. 5p. Band and Drums sword, 1830 .. .. .. 20 25
293. 7½p. Royal Sappers and Miners Officer's hat, 1830 35 35
294. 12½p. General's sword, 1831 60 65

1973. Royal Wedding. As T **26** of Anguilla. Multicoloured. Background colours given.
295. 2p. blue 10 12
296. 18p. green 50 55

39. "Westminster" and "Claudine" Beached, 1849.

1973. East India Company Charter. Tercentenary. Multicoloured.
297. 1½p. Type **39** 8 8
298. 4p. "True Briton", 1790 15 15
299. 6p. "General Goddard" in action, 1795 .. .. 20 25
300. 22½p. "Kent" burning in the Bay of Biscay, 1825, 75 80

40. U.P.U. Emblem and Ships.

1974. U.P.U. Centenary. Multicoloured.
301. 5p. Type **40** 20 20
302. 25p. U.P.U. emblem and letters 60 65

41. Churchill as Sailor Boy, and Blenheim Palace.

1974. Sir Winston Churchill. Birth Cent.
304. **41.** 5p. multicoloured .. 15 15
305. – 25p. black, pink & purple 55 60
DESIGN: 25 p. Churchill and River Thames.

42. Capt. Cook and H.M.S. "Resolution".

1975. Capt. Cook's Return to St. Helena. Bicent. Multicoloured.
307. 5p. Type **42** 15 15
308. 25p. Capt. Cook and Jamestown 50 55

43. "Mellissia begonifolia" (tree).

1975. Publication of "St. Helena" by J. C. Melliss. Centenary. Multicoloured.
310. 2p. Type **43** 8 8
311. 5p. "Mellissius adumbratus" (beetle) 12 15
312. 12p. "Aegialitis sanctaehelenae" (bird) (horiz.) 25 30
313. 25p. "Scorpaenia mellissii" (fish) (horiz.) 50 55

44. £1 Note.

1976. Currency Notes. First Issue. Mult.
314. 8p. Type **44** 20 25
315. 33p. £5 Note 65 70

45. 1d. Stamp of 1863.

1976. Festival of Stamps, London.
316. **45.** 5p. brn., blk. and pink .. 12 15
317. – 8p. blk., grn. & lt. grn. 20 25
318. – 25p. multicoloured .. 50 55
DESIGNS—VERT. 8p. 1d. stamp of 1922. HORIZ. 25p. Mail carrier "Good Hope Castle".

46. High Knoll, 1806.

1976. Views of St. Helena. Multicoloured.
319. 1p. Type **46** 5 5
320. 3p. The Friar Rock, 1815 5 5
321. 5p. The Column Lot, 1815 8 10
322. 6p. Sandy Bay Valley, 1809 10 12
323. 8p. Scene from Castle Davis, 1815 .. .. .. 15 15
324. 9p. The Briars, 1815 .. 15 20
325. 10p. Plantation House, 1821 20 20
326. 15p. Longwood House, 1821 25 30
327. 18p. St. Paul's Church .. 30 35
328. 26p. St. James's Valley, 1815 .. .. .. 45 50
329. 40p. St. Mathew's Church, 1860 .. .. .. 70 80
330. £1 St. Helena, 1815 .. 1·75 2·00
331. £2 Sugar Loaf Hill, 1821 .. 3·50 4·00
Nos. 330/1 are larger, 47 × 34 mm.

47. Duke of Edinburgh paying Homage.

1977. Silver Jubilee. Multicoloured.
332. 8p. Royal Visit, 1947 .. 15 20
333. 15p. Queen's sceptre with dove 30 35
334. 26p. Type **47** 55 65

ST. KITTS-NEVIS BC

Islands of the Leeward Is., Br. W. Indies. The general issues for Leeward Is. were in concurrent use until 1st July, 1956. From 1952 the stamps are inscribed "St. Christopher, Nevis and Anguilla". Achieved Associated Statehood on 27th February, 1967.

1951. 100 cents = 1 West Indian dollar.

1. Christopher Columbus.

2. Medicinal Spring.

1903.
1. **1.** ½d. purple and green .. 1·40 1·10
12. ½d. green 40 60
2. **2.** 1d. grey and red .. .. 1·50 40
14a. 1d. red 40 30
15. **1.** 2d. purple and brown .. 85 1·50
4. 2½d. black and blue .. 7·50 5·00
17. 2½d. blue 75 80
18. **2.** 3d. green and orange .. 1·50 1·75
6. **1.** 6d. black and purple .. 4·50 5·50
20. 1s. green and orange .. 2·25 5·00
8. **2.** 2s. green and black .. 9·00 6·50
9. **1.** 2s. 6d. black and violet .. 13·00 17·00
10. **2.** 5s. purple and green .. 25·00 28·00

1916. Optd. WAR TAX.
22. **1.** ½d. green 12 15

1918. Optd. WAR STAMP.
23. **1.** 1½d. orange 12 20

3.

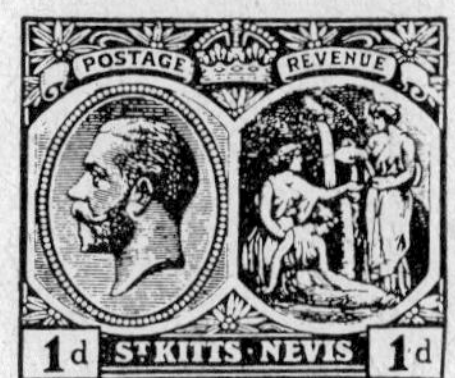

4.

1920.
37. **3.** ½d. green 15 20
38. **4.** 1d. red 20 25
39a. 1d. violet 20 15
26. **3.** 1½d. yellow 40 70
40. 1½d. red 60 75
40a. 1½d. brown 25 30
41. **4.** 2d. grey 25 30
44a. **3.** 2½d. blue .. .. .. 1·10 75
43. 2½d. brown .. .. 55 1·75
45a. **4.** 3d. purple on yellow .. 70 1·10
45. 3d. blue .. .. .. 55 1·10
46. **3.** 6d. purple and mauve .. 1·10 1·75
31. **4.** 1s. black on green .. 1·10 2·75
32. **3.** 2s. purple & blue on blue 5·50 6·00
33. **4.** 2s. 6d. black & red on blue 6·00 9·00
34. **3.** 5s. green & red on yellow 7·50 13·00
35. **4.** 10s. green & red on green 17·00 22·00
36. **3.** £1 purple and black on red 95·00 £130

5. Old Road Bay and Mount Misery.

1923. Tercent. Commem.
48. **5.** ½d. black and green .. 90 1·00
49. 1d. black and violet .. 90 1·00
50. 1½d. black and red .. 1·40 2·00
51. 2d. black and grey .. 1·40 2·00
52. 2½d. black and brown .. 2·25 3·00
53. 3d. black and blue .. 2·50 4·50
54. 6d. black and purple .. 5·00 7·00
55. 1s. black and green .. 7·00 10·00
56. 2s. black and blue on blue 13·00 17·00
57. 2s. 6d. black & red on blue 18·00 20·00
59. 5s. black and red on yellow 75·00 £120
58. 10s. black and red on .reen £130 £225
60. £1 black and purple on red £450 £650

1935. Silver Jubilee. As T **11** of Antigua.
61. 1d. blue and red 20 25
62. 1½d. blue and grey .. 25 40
63. 2½d. brown and blue .. 55 90
64. 1s. grey and purple .. 2·25 2·75

1937. Coronation. As T **2** of Aden.
65. 1d. red 12 12
66. 1½d. brown 12 12
67. 2½d. blue 15 35
Nos. 61/7 are inscribed "ST. CHRISTOPHER NEVIS".

6. King George VI. **7.** King George VI and Medicinal Spring.

8. King George VI and Anguilla Island.

1938.

68a. 6. ½d. green 8 10
69a. 1d. red 8 10
70. 1½d. orange 8 8
71a. 7. 2d. red and grey .. .. 4·00 3·75
72a. 6. 2½d. blue 10 8
73a. 7. 3d. purple and red .. 65 80
74ab. – 6d. green and purple .. 40 35
75a. 7. 1s. black and green .. 45 45
76a. 2s. 6d. black and red .. 1·10 2·25
77a. –. 5s. green and red .. .. 2·75 3·00
77b. 8. 10s. black and blue .. 5·50 7·00
77c. £1 black and brown .. 8·00 11·00

The 6d. and 5s. are as T **7**, but with the Christopher Columbus device as in T **3**.

1946. Victory As T **4** of Aden.

78. 1½d. orange 8 8
79. 3d. red 8 8

1949. Silver Wedding. As T **5/6** of Aden.

80. 2½d. blue 8 8
81. 5s. red .. .. .. 3·00 4·00

1949. U.P.U. As T **14/7** of Antigua.

82. 2½d. blue 12 20
83. 3d. red 20 40
84. 6d. magenta 55 75
85. 1s. green 80 95

1950. Br. Settlement in Anguilla. Tercent. Optd. **ANGUILLA TERCENTENARY 1650-1950.**

86. 6. 1d. red 8 8
87. 1½d. orange 8 8
88. 2½d. blue 10 10
89. 7. 3d. purple and red .. 8 10
90. – 6d. green & purple (No. 74ab) 25 30
91. 7. 1s. black and green .. 40 40

1951. B.W.I. University College. Inaug. As T **18/9** of Antigua.

92. 18. 3 c. black and orange .. 15 20
93. 19. 12 c. green and mauve .. 25 30

ST. CHRISTOPHER, NEVIS AND ANGUILLA

9. Bath House and Spa.

1952.

94. 9. 1 c. green and ochre .. 15 15
95. – 2 c. green 20 20
96. – 3 c. red and violet .. 20 25
97. – 4 c. red 25 25
98. – 5 c. blue and grey .. 25 30
99. 6 c. blue 30 25
100. – 12 c. blue and brown .. 40 30
101. – 24 c. black and red .. 50 40
102. – 48 c. olive and chocolate .. 90 1·25
103. – 60 c. ochre and green .. 1·10 2·00
104. – $1.20 green and blue .. 2·75 2·50
105. – $4.80 green and red .. 7·00 7·50

DESIGNS—HORIZ. 2 c. Warner Park. 4 c. Brimstone Hill. 5 c. Nevis from the sea. 6 c. Pinney's Beach. 24 c. Old Road Bay. 48 c. Sea Island cotton. 60 c. The Treasury. $1.20 Salt pond. $4.80 Sugar factory. VERT. 3 c. Map of the islands. 12 c. Sir Thomas Warner's tomb.

1953. Coronation. As T **7** of Aden.

106. 2 c. black and green .. 12 20

1954. As 1952 but with portrait of Queen Elizabeth II.

106a. ½ c. olive (as $1.20) .. 5 5
107. 1 c. green and ochre .. 5 5
108. 2 c. green 5 5
109. 3 c. red and violet .. 8 8
110. 4 c. red 8 8
111. 5 c. blue and grey .. 10 10
112. 6 c. blue 15 15
112a. 8 c. black 12 12
113. 12 c. blue and brown .. 12 12
114. 24 c. black and red .. 25 25
115. 48 c. olive and chocolate 50 60
116. 60 c. ochre and green .. 70 85
117. $1.20 green and blue .. 1·50 2·00
117a. $2.40 black and orange .. 4·00 5·00
118. $4.80 green and red .. 8·00 10·00

DESIGNS (new values)—VERT. 8 c. Sombrero Lighthouse. HORIZ. $2.40 Map of Anguilla and Dependencies.

10. Alexander Hamilton and View of Nevis.

1956. Alexander Hamilton. Birth Bicent.

119. 10. 24 c. green and blue .. 35 40

1958. British Caribbean Federation. As T **21** of Antigua.

120. 3 c. green 10 12
121. 6 c. blue 15 20
122. 12 c. red 30 35

11. 1d. Nevis Stamp of 1861.

1961. Nevis Stamp Cent.

123. 11. 2 c. dull rose and green 10 12
124. 8 c. rose and blue .. 20 20
125. 12 c. grey-lilac and red 30 30
126. 24 c. green and orange 40 50

The 8 c., 12 c. and 24 c. show the original 4d., 6d. and 1s. stamps of Nevis respectively.

1963. Red Cross Cent. As T **24** of Antigua.

127. 3 c. red and black .. 12 12
128. 12 c. red and blue .. 65 65

12. Loading Sugar Cane, St. Kitts.

1963. Multicoloured.

129. ½ c. New Lighthouse Sombrero 5 5
130. 1 c. Type **12** 5 5
131. 2 c. Pall Mall Square, Basseterre 5 5
132. 3 c. Gateway, Brimstone Hill Fort, St. Kitts .. 5 5
133. 4 c. Nelson's Spring, Nevis 5 5
134. 5 c. Grammar School, St. Kitts 8 8
135. 6 c. Crater, Mt. Misery, St. Kitts 10 10
136. 10 c. Hibiscus 10 10
137. 15 c. Sea Island cotton, Nevis 12 12
138. 20 c. Boat-building, Anguilla 15 15
139. 25 c. White-crowned pigeon 25 20
140. 50 c. St. George's Church Tower, Basseterre .. 40 40
141. 60 c. Alexander Hamilton 40 35
142. $1 Map of St. Kitts-Nevis 75 75
143. $2.50 Map of Anguilla .. 2·00 2·75
144. $5 Arms of St. Christopher, Nevis and Anguilla .. 4·00 4·00

The ½, 2, 3, 15, 25, 60 c., $1 and $5 are vert. the rest horiz.

1964. Arts Festival. Optd. **ARTS FESTIVAL ST. KITTS 1964.**

145. 3 c. mult. (No. 132) .. 8 8
146. 25 c. mult. (No. 139) .. 25 30

1965. I.T.U. Cent. As T **26** of Antigua.

147. 2 c. bistre and red .. 8 8
148. 50 c. blue and olive .. 60 65

1965. I.C.Y. As T **27** of Antigua.

149. 2 c. purple and turquoise 10 10
150. 25 c. green and lavender .. 30 35

1966. Churchill Commem. As T **28** of Antigua.

151. ½ c. blue 5 5
152. 3 c. green 5 8
153. 15 c. brown 25 30
154. 25 c. violet 45 50

1966. Royal Visit. As T **29** of Antigua.

155. 3 c. black and blue .. 5 8
156. 25 c. black and magenta .. 30 35

1966. World Cup Football Championships. As T **30** of Antigua.

157. 6 c. violet, grn., lake & brn. 5 8
158. 25 c. choc., turq., lake & brn. 30 35

13. Festival Emblem.

1966. Arts Festival.

159. 13. 3 c. blk., buff, grn. & gold 5 10
160. 25 c. black, buff, green and silver 25 30

1966. W.H.O. Headquarters, Geneva. Inaug. As T **31** of Antigua.

161. 3 c. black, green and blue .. 5 8
162. 40 c. black, purple & ochre 40 45

1966. U.N.E.S.C.O. 20th Anniv. As T **33/5** of Antigua.

163. 3 c. violet, red, yell. & orge. 5 5
164. 6 c. yellow, violet and olive 8 8
165. 40 c. black, purple and orge. 45 45

14. Government Headquarters, Basseterre.

1967. Statehood. Multicoloured.

182. 3 c. Type **14** 5 8
183. 10 c. National Flag .. 10 12
184. 25 c. Coat of Arms .. 30 35

15. John Wesley and Cross.

1967. West Indies Methodist Conf.

185. 15. 3 c. black, cerise & violet 5 5
186. – 25 c. black, turq. & blue 25 25
187. – 40 c. black, yell. & orge. 35 40

DESIGNS: 25 c. Charles Wesley and cross. 40 c. Thomas Coke and cross.

16. "Herald" Aircraft over Merchant Ship.

1968. Caribbean Free Trade Area.

188. 16. 25 c. multicoloured .. 20 25
189. 50 c. multicoloured .. 35 40

17. Dr. Martin Luther King.

18. "The Mystical Nativity" (Botticelli).

1968. Martin Luther King Commem.

190. 17. 50 c. multicoloured .. 40 40

1968. Christmas.

191. 18. 12 c. multicoloured .. 12 12
192. – 25 c. multicoloured .. 20 25
193. 18. 40 c. multicoloured .. 25 35
194. – 50 c. multicoloured .. 40 45

DESIGN: 25 c., 50 c. "The Adoration of the Magi" (Rubens).

19. Tarpon.

1968. Fishes.

195. 19. 6 c. multicoloured .. 10 10
196. – 12 c. black, green & blue 12 15
197. – 40 c. multicoloured .. 30 30
198. – 50 c. multicoloured .. 35 35

FISHES: 12 c. Garfish. 40 c. Horse eye Jack. 50 c. Redsnapper.

20. The Warner Badge and Islands.

1969. Sir Thomas Warner Commem. Multicoloured.

199. 20 c. Type **20** 20 20
200. 25 c. Sir Thomas Warner's tomb 25 25
201. 40 c. Charles I's Commission 35 35

21. "The Adoration of the Kings" (Mostaert).

22. Pirates and Treasure at Frigate Bay.

1969. Christmas. Multicoloured.

202. 10 c. Type **21** 10 10
203. 25 c. As 10 c. 25 25
204. 40 c. "The Adoration of the Kings" (Geertgen) .. 35 35
205. 50 c. As 40 c. 40 45

1970. Multicoloured (except ½ c.).

206. ½ c. Type **22** (black, orange and emerald) 5 5
207. 1 c. English Two-decker warship, 1650 .. .. 5 5
208. 2 c. Naval flags of colonising nations 5 5

209. 3 c. Rapier hilt (17th-cent.) 5 5
210. 4 c. Portuguese caravels (16th-cent.) 5 5
211. 5 c. Sir Henry Morgan and fireships, 1669 5 5
212. 6 c. L'Ollonois and pirate carack (16th-cent.) 8 8
213. 10 c. 17th-century smugglers' ship 10 10
214. 15 c. "Piece of Eight" 20 20
215. 20 c. Cannon (17th-cent.) 20 20
279. 25 c. Humphrey Cole's astrolabe, 1574 8 10
280. 50 c. Flintlock pistol (17th-cent.) 20 20
218. 60 c. Dutch Flute (17th-cent.) 25 30
282. $1 Capt. Bartholomew Roberts and his crew's death sentence 35 40
220. $2.50 Railing Piece (gun) (16th-cent.) 90 1·00
221. $5 Drake, Hawkins and sea battle 1·75 1·90
284. $10 The Apprehension of Blackbeard (Edward Teach) 3·50 4·00

Nos. 210/13, 215, 217, 220/1 and 284 are horiz.

23. Graveyard Scene ("Great Expectations").

1970. Charles Dickens. Death Cent.

222. **23.** 4 c. brown, gold & green 10 10
223. – 20 c. brn., gold and purple 25 25
224. – 25 c. brown, gold & green 30 30
225. – 40 c. brown, gold & blue 50 50

DESIGNS—HORIZ. 20 c. Miss Havisham and Pip ("Great Expectations"). VERT. 25 c. Dickens' Birthplace. 40 c. Charles Dickens.

24. Local Steel Band.

1970. Festival of Arts. Multicoloured.

226. 20 c. Type **24** 15 15
227. 25 c. Local string band 20 20
228. 40 c. Scene from "A Midsummer Night's Dream" 35 35

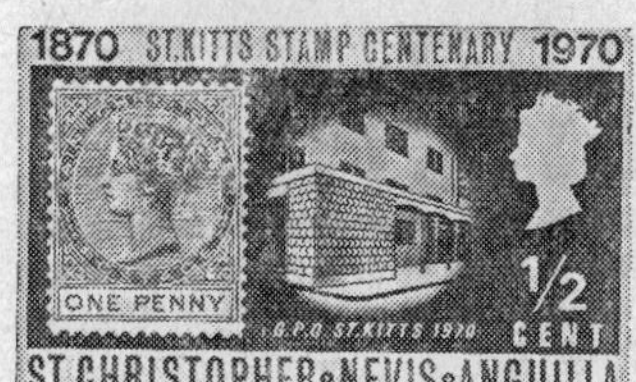

25. 1d. Stamp of 1870 and Post Office, 1970.

1970. Stamp Cent.

229. **25.** ½ c. green and red 8 8
230. – 20 c. blue, green & red 20 20
231. – 25 c. purple, grn. & red 25 25
232. – 50 c. red, green and blk. 1·00 1·00

DESIGNS: 20 c., 25 c., 1d. and 6d. stamps of 1870. 50 c. 6d. stamp of 1870 and early postmark.

26. "Adoration of the Shepherds" (Frans Floris).

1970. Christmas. Multicoloured.

233. 3 c. Type **26** 5 5
234. 20 c. "The Holy Family" (Van Dyck) 20 20
235. 25 c. As 20 c. 25 25
236. 40 c. Type **26** 35 40

27. Monkey Fiddle.

1971. Flowers. Multicoloured.

237. ½ c. Type **27** 5 5
238. 20 c. Tropical Mountain Violet 20 20
239. 30 c. Trailing Morning Glory 25 25
240. 50 c. Fringed Epidendrum 40 45

28. Royal Poinciana.

1971. Philippe de Poincy Commem. Multicoloured.

241. 20 c. Type **28** 20 20
242. 30 c. Chateau de Poincy 30 30
243. 50 c. De Poincy's badge (vert.) 40 40

29. The East Yorks.

1971. Siege of Brimstone Hill, 1782. Multicoloured.

244. ½ c. Type **29** 5 5
245. 20 c. Royal Artillery 20 20
246. 30 c. French infantry 30 35
247. 50 c. The Royal Scots 55 60

30. "Crucifixion" (Massys).

1972. Easter.

248. **30.** 4 c. multicoloured 5 5
249. 20 c. multicoloured 15 20
250. 30 c. multicoloured 25 30
251. 40 c. multicoloured 35 40

31. "Virgin and Child" (Bergognone).

1972. Christmas. Multicoloured.

252. 3 c. Type **31** 5 5
253. 20 c. "Adoration of the Kings" (J. Bassano) (horiz.) 20 20
254. 25 c. "Adoration of the Shepherds" (Domenichino) 25 25
255. 40 c. "Virgin and Child" (Fiorenzo) 40 40

1972. Royal Silver Wedding. As T **19** of Ascension, but with Pelicans in background.

256. 20 c. red 20 20
257. 25 c. blue 25 25

32. Landing on St. Christopher 1623.

1973. Sir Thomas Warner's Landing on St. Christopher. 350th Anniv. Multicoloured.

258. 4 c. Type **32** 5 5
259. 25 c. Growing tobacco 20 20
260. 40 c. Building fort at Old Road 35 40
261. $2. 50 Sir Thomas Warner's ship 1·90 2·00

33. "The Last Supper" (Titian).

1973. Easter. Paintings of "The Last Supper" by the artists listed. Mult.

262. 4 c. Type **33** 5 5
263. 25 c. Ascribed to Roberti 20 25
264. $2. 50 Juan de Juanes (horiz.) 1·75 1·75

1973. Royal Visit Nos. 258/61 optd. **VISIT OF HRH THE PRINCE OF WALES 1973.**

265. **32.** 4 c. multicoloured 5 5
266. – 25 c. multicoloured 15 15
267. – 40 c. multicoloured 25 25
268. – $2. 50 multicoloured 2·50 2·75

MINIMUM PRICE

The minimum price quoted is 5p which represents a handling charge rather than a basis for valuing common stamps. For further notes about prices see introductory pages.

34. Harbour Scene and 2d. Stamp of 1903.

1973. 1st St. Kitts-Nevis Stamps. 70th Anniv. Multicoloured.

285. 4 c. Type **34** 5 5
286. 25 c. Sugar-mill and 1d. stamp of 1903 25 25
287. 40 c. Unloading boat and ½d. stamp of 1903 35 40
288. $2·50 Rock-carvings and 3d. stamp of 1903 1·90 2·00

1973. Royal Wedding. As T **26** of Anguilla. Multicoloured. Background colours given.

290. 25 c. green 20 20
291. 40 c. brown 30 30

35. "Virgin and Child" (Murillo).

1973. Christmas. Paintings of "The Holy Family" by the artists listed. Mult.

292. 4 c. Type **35** 5 5
293. 40 c. Mengs 30 30
294. 60 c. Sassoferrato 40 40
295. $1 Filippino Lippi (horiz.) 55 60

36. "Christ Carrying the Cross" (S. del Piombo).

1974. Easter. Multicoloured.

296. 4 c. Type **36** 5 5
297. 25 c. "The Crucifixion" (Goya) 20 20
298. 40 c. "Trinity" (Ribera) 30 30
299. $2·50 "The Deposition" (Fra Bartolomeo) (horiz.) 1·50 1·75

37. University Centre, St. Kitts.

1974. University of West Indies. 25th Anniv. Multicoloured.

300. 10 c. Type **37** 10 10
301. $1 As Type **37** but showing different buildings 55 60

38. Hands reaching for Globe.

1974. Family Planning.

303. **38.** 4 c. brn., blue & black . . 5 5
304. – 25 c. multicoloured . . 15 20
305. – 40 c. multicoloured . . 25 30
306. – $2.50 multicoloured . . 1·40 1·50

DESIGNS—HORIZ. 25 c. Instruction by nurses. $2.50 Emblem and globe on scales. VERT. 40 c. Family group.

39. Churchill as Army Lieutenant.

1974. Sir Winston Churchill. Birth Cent. Multicoloured.

307. 4 c. Type **39** 5 5
308. 25 c. Churchill as Prime Minister 15 20
309. 40 c. Churchill as Knight of the Garter 25 30
310. 60 c. Churchill's statue, London 30 35

40. " The Last Supper " (Dore).

1975. Easter. Paintings by Dore. Mult.

314. 4 c. Type **40** 5 5
315. 25 c. " Christ Mocked " . . 15 15
316. 40 c. " Jesus Falling beneath the Cross " 20 25
317. $1 " The Erection of the Cross " 45 50

41. E.C.C.A. H.Q. Buildings, Basseterre.

1975. Opening of East Caribbean Currency Authority's Headquarters.

318. **41.** 12 c. multicoloured . . 8 8
319. – 25 c. multicoloured . . 12 15
320. – 40 c. red, silver and grey 20 25
321. – 45 c. multicoloured . . 25 25

DESIGNS: 25 c. Specimen one-dollar banknote. 40 c. Half-dollar of 1801 and current 4-dollar coin. 45 c. Coins of 1801 and 1960.

42. Evangeline Booth (Salvation Army General).

1975. International Women's Year. Multicoloured.

338. 4 c. Type **42** 5 5
339. 25 c. Sylvia Pankhurst . . 12 15
340. 40 c. Marie Curie 20 25
341. $2·50 Lady Annie Allen (teacher and guider) . . 1·25 1·40

43. Golfer.

1975. Opening of Frigate Bay Golf Course.

342. **43.** 4 c. black and red . . 5 5
343. 25 c. black and yellow . . 12 15
344. 40 c. black and green . . 20 25
345. $1 black and blue . . 40 45

44. " St. Paul " (Sacchi Pier Francesco).

1975. Christmas. Religious Paintings. Mult.

346. 25 c. Type **44** 12 15
347. 40 c. " St. James " (Bonifazio di Pitati) 15 20
348. 45 c. " St. John " (Mola) . . 20 25
349. $1 " St. John " (Raphael) 45 50

45. " Crucifixion " (detail).

1976. Easter. Stained Glass Windows. Mult.

350. 4 c. } Type **45** . . 5 5
351. 4 c. } . . 5 5
352. 4 c. } . . 5 5
353. 25 c. " Last Supper " . . 12 15
354. 40 c. " Last Supper " . . 20 25
355. $1 " Baptism of Christ " 40 45

Type **45** shows the left-hand stamp of the 4 c. design.

Nos. 353/5 are size 27 × 35 mm.

1976. West Indian Victory in World Cricket Cup. As Nos. 559/60 of Barbados.

356. 12 c. Map of the Caribbean 8 8
357. 40 c. Prudential Cup . . 20 20

46. Crispus Attucks and the Boston Massacre.

1976. American Revolution. Bicent. Multicoloured.

359. 20 c. Type **46** 10 10
360. 40 c. Alexander Hamilton and Battle of Yorktown 20 20
361. 45 c. Jefferson and Declaration of Independence . . 20 20
362. $1 Washington and the Crossing of the Delaware 40 45

47. " The Nativity " (Sforza Book of Hours).

1976. Christmas. Multicoloured.

363. 20 c. Type **47** 8 10
364. 40 c. " Virgin and Child with St. John " (Pintoricchio) 15 20
365. 45 c. " Our Lady of Good Children " (Ford Maddox-Brown) 20 20
366. $1 " Little Hands Outstretched to Bless " (M. Tarrant) 40 45

48. Royal Visit, 1966.

1977. Silver Jubilee. Multicoloured.

367. 50 c. Type **48** 20 25
368. 55 c. The Sceptre 25 25
369. $1·50 Bishops paying homage 60 70

ST. LUCIA BC

One of the Windward Is., Br. W. Indies Achieved Associated Statehood on 1st March 1967.

1949. 100 cents = 1 West Indian dollar.

1.

HALFPENNY
(2.)

1860. No value on stamps.

5. **1.** (1d.) red . . . . . . 25·00 35·00
11. (1d.) black . . . . 10·00 10·00
7. (4d.) blue . . . . . . 75·00 80·00
16. (4d.) yellow . . . . 28·00 15·00
8. (6d.) green £150 £140
17a. (6d.) violet . . . . 30·00 15·00
18a. (1s.) orange . . . . 75·00 15·00

1881. With value added by surch. as T 2.

25. **1.** ½d. green . . . . . . 10·00 12·00
26. 1d. black . . . . . . 9·00 9·00
24. 2½d. red . . . . . . 10·00 10·00
27. 4d. yellow . . . . . . 60·00 20·00
28. 6d. violet . . . . . . 18·00 18·00
29. 1s. orange . . . . . . £100 75·00

3.

4.

1882.

43. **3.** ½d. green 12 15
32. 1d. red . . . . . . 7·00 7·00
46. 2½d. blue . . . . . . 1·00 25
48. 4d. brown . . . . . . 1·75 2·00
35. 6d. lilac £120 £110
36. 1s. brown . . . . . . £110 60·00

1886.

44. **3.** 1d. mauve 40 15
45. 2d. blue and orange . . 1·10 1·10
47. 3d. mauve and green . . 2·00 2·25
41. 6d. mauve and blue . . 4·25 6·50
50. 1s. mauve and red . . 2·25 4·00
51. 5s. mauve and orange . . 11·00 16·00
52. 10s. mauve and black . . 23·00 24·00

1891. Surch. in words.

56. **3.** ½d. on 3d. mauve & green 18·00 15·00
55. 1d. on 4d. brown . . . . 3·00 3·00

1891. Surch. in figures.

54. **3.** ½d. on half 6d. (No. 41) . . 8·00 8·00

1902.

64. **4.** ½d. purple and green . . 35 40
66. 1d. purple and red . . 35 12
68. 2½d. purple and blue . . 1·90 3·00
70. 3d. purple and yellow . . 2·25 4·00
72. 6d. purple . . . . . . 4·00 5·00
62. 1s. green and black . . 5·00 6·00
76. 5s. green and red . . . . 15·00 18·00

5. The Pitons.

6.

7.

8.

1902. Discovery. 400th Anniv.

63. **5.** 2d. green and brown . . 2·75 4·00

1907.

65. **4.** ½d. green 25 15
67. 1d. red 35 12
69. 2½d. blue . . . . . . 1·50 2·25
71. 3d. purple on yellow . . 90 2·50
75. 1s. black on green . . 5·50 7·00
77. 5s. green & red on yellow 18·00 22·00

1912.

91. **6.** ½d. green 12 10
79b. 1d. red 70 25
93. 1d. brown 20 12
94. **8.** 1½d. red 25 45
95. **7.** 2d. grey 20 15
96. **6.** 2½d. blue . . . . . . 95 1·10
97. 2½d. orange . . . . 4·00 4·50
82. 3d. purple on yellow . . 65 1·10
99a. 3d. blue . . . . . . 90 1·40
101. **8.** 4d. black & red on yellow 55 1·90
102. **6.** 6d. purple . . . . 1·10 2·50
85a. 1s. black on green . . 3·00 3·50
103. 1s. brown . . . . . . 1·40 3·00
104. **7.** 2s. 6d. black & red on blue 5·50 9·50
105. **6.** 5s. green & red on yellow 11·00 14·00

1916. Optd. WAR TAX in two lines.

89. **6.** 1d. red . . . . . . 1·60 2·75

1916. Optd. WAR TAX in one line.

90. **6.** 1d. red 8 8

1935. Silver Jubilee. As T **11** of Antigua.

109. ½d. black and green . . 15 25
110. 2d. blue and grey . . 40 65
111. 2½d. brown and blue . . 75 1·10
112. 1s. grey and purple . . 2·50 3·00

9. Port Castries.

1936. King George V.
113. 9. ½d. black and green .. 15 12
114. – 1d. black and brown .. 12 12
115. – 1½d. black and red .. 15 20
116. 9. 2d. black and grey .. 15 25
117. – 2½d. black and blue .. 25 30
118. – 3d. black and green .. 60 70
119. 9. 4d. black and brown .. 40 65
120. – 6d. black and orange .. 60 80
121. – 1s. black and blue .. 80 1·75
122. – 2s. 6d. black and blue .. 4·50 5·50
123. – 5s. black and violet .. 5·00 7·00
124. – 10s. black and red .. 18·00 22·00
DESIGNS—HORIZ. 1d., 2½d., 6d. Columbus Square, Castries. 1s. Fort Rodney, Pigeon Island. 5s. Govt. House. 10s. Badge of Colony. VERT. 1½d., 3d. Ventine Falls. 2s. 6d. Inniskilling Monument.

1937. Coronation. As T 2 of Aden.
125. 1d. violet 8 8
126. 1½d. red 8 8
127. 2½d. blue 8 8

16. King George VI.

DESIGNS — HORIZ. As T 17: 1s. Govt. House. 2s. The Pitons. 5s. Loading bananas. VERT. 10s. Device of St. Lucia as T 18.

17. Columbus Square.

1938. King George VI.
128. 16. ½d. green 10 8
129a. 1d. violet 8 8
129b. 1d. red 10 8
130. 1½d. red 10 8
131a. 2d. grey 8 8
132a. 2½d. blue 8 8
132b. 2½d. violet 8 8
133a. 3d. orange 10 8
133b. 3½d. blue 10 10
134. 17. 6d. red 50 50
134b.16. 8d. brown 30 40
135. – 1s. brown 55 55
136. – 2s. blue and red .. 1·10 1·10
136a.16. 3s. purple .. .. 1·90 2·75
137. – 5s. black and purple .. 1·60 2·75
138. – 10s. black on yellow .. 2·75 4·00
141. 16. £1 brown .. .. 8·00 8·50

1946. Victory. As T 4 of Aden.
142. 1d. violet 8 8
143. 3½d. blue 10 8

1948. Silver Wedding. As T 5/6 of Aden
144. 1d. red 8 8
145. £1 purple .. .. 6·50 8·00

18. Device of St. Lucia.

19. Phoenix rising from Flames.

1949. New Currency.
146. 16. 1 c. green 8 8
147. 2 c. magenta 8 8
148. 3 c. red 8 10
149. 4 c. grey 8 8
150. 5 c. violet 8 8
151. 6 c. orange 8 8
152. 7 c. blue 8 8
153. 12 c. claret 20 30
154. 16 c. brown 20 15
155. 18. 24 c. blue 25 25
156. 48 c. olive 90 80
157. $1.20 purple .. .. 1·10 1·40
158. $2.40 green .. .. 2·75 3·75
159. $4.80 red .. .. 5·50 6·00

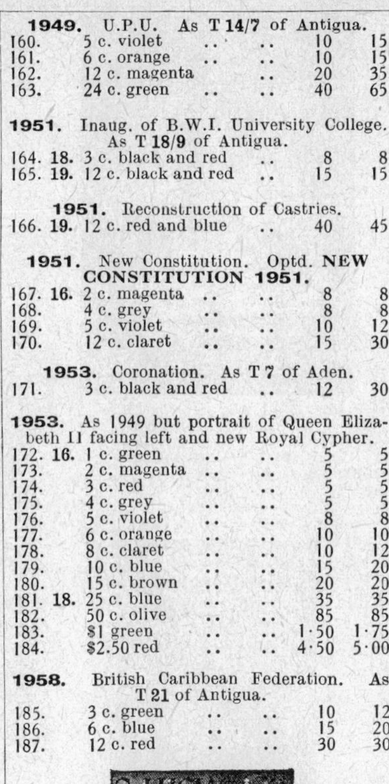

1949. U.P.U. As T 14/7 of Antigua.
160. 5 c. violet 10 15
161. 6 c. orange 10 15
162. 12 c. magenta 20 35
163. 24 c. green 40 65

1951. Inaug. of B.W.I. University College. As T 18/9 of Antigua.
164. 18. 3 c. black and red .. 8 8
165. 19. 12 c. black and red .. 15 15

1951. Reconstruction of Castries.
166. 19. 12 c. red and blue .. 40 45

1951. New Constitution. Optd. NEW CONSTITUTION 1951.
167. 16. 2 c. magenta 8 8
168. 4 c. grey 8 8
169. 5 c. violet 10 12
170. 12 c. claret 15 30

1953. Coronation. As T 7 of Aden.
171. 3 c. black and red .. 12 30

1953. As 1949 but portrait of Queen Elizabeth II facing left and new Royal Cypher.
172. 16. 1 c. green 5 5
173. 2 c. magenta 5 5
174. 3 c. red 5 5
175. 4 c. grey 5 5
176. 5 c. violet 8 8
177. 6 c. orange 10 10
178. 8 c. claret 10 12
179. 10 c. blue 15 20
180. 15 c. brown 20 20
181. 18. 25 c. blue 35 35
182. 50 c. olive 85 85
183. $1 green .. .. 1·50 1·75
184. $2.50 red .. .. 4·50 5·00

1958. British Caribbean Federation. As T 21 of Antigua.
185. 3 c. green 10 12
186. 6 c. blue 15 20
187. 12 c. red 30 30

20. Columbus's "Santa Maria" off the Pitons.

1960. New Constitution for the Windward and Leeward Islands.
188. 20. 8 c. red 25 25
189. 10 c. orange 30 30
190. 25 c. blue 45 50

21. Stamp of 1860.

1960. Stamp Cent.
191. 21. 5 c. red and blue .. 25 25
192. 16 c. blue & yellow-green 40 40
193. 25 c. green and red .. 55 60

1963. Freedom from Hunger. As T 10 of Aden.
194. 25 c. green 45 45

1963. Red Cross Cent. As T 24 of Antigua.
195. 4 c. red and black .. 10 10
196. 25 c. red and blue .. 60 65

22. Queen Elizabeth II. 23.

24. Fishing Boats.

1964.
197. 22. 1 c. red 5 5
198. 2 c. violet 5 5
199. 4 c. green 5 5
200. 5 c. blue 8 8
201. 6 c. brown 8 8
202. 23. 8 c. multicoloured .. 10 10
203. 10 c. multicoloured .. 12 12
204. 24. 12 c. multicoloured .. 15 15
257. – 15 c. multicoloured .. 20 20
206. – 25 c. multicoloured .. 35 30
207. – 35 c. blue and buff .. 60 45
208. – 50 c. multicoloured .. 65 80
209. – $1 multicoloured .. 1·75 1·75
210. – $2.50 multicoloured .. 3·50 3·00
DESIGNS—As T 24: HORIZ. 15 c. Pigeon Island. 25 c. Reduit Beach. VERT. $1, Vigie Beach. As T 24 but "E. II R" in place of portrait: HORIZ. 35 c. Castries Harbour. 50 c. The Pitons. As T 23: $2·50, Queen Elizabeth II, head and shoulders.

1964. Shakespeare. 400th Birth Anniv. As T 25 of Antigua.
211. 10 c. green 20 25

1965. I.T.U. Cent. As T 26 of Antigua.
212. 2 c. mauve and magenta .. 8 10
213. 50 c. lilac and green .. 65 70

1965. I.C.Y. As T 27 of Antigua.
214. 1 c. purple and turquoise .. 5 5
215. 15 c. green and lavender .. 35 40

1966. Churchill Commem. As T 28 of Antigua.
216. 4 c. blue 8 10
217. 6 c. green 10 10
218. 25 c. brown 30 35
219. 35 c. violet 45 50

1966. Royal Visit. As T 29 of Antigua.
220. 4 c. black and blue .. 8 10
221. 25 c. black and magenta .. 35 40

1966. World Cup Football Championships. As T 30 of Antigua.
222. 4 c. multicoloured .. 8 10
223. 25 c. multicoloured .. 25 30

1966. W.H.O. Headquarters, Geneva. Inaug. As T 31 of Antigua.
224. 4 c. black, green and blue .. 8 8
225. 25 c. black, purple & ochre 35 40

1966. U.N.E.S.C.O. 20th Anniv. As T 33/5 of Antigua.
226. 4 c. multicoloured 8 8
227. 12 c. yellow, violet & olive 15 15
228. 25 c. black, purple & orge. 35 40

25. Map of St. Lucia.

1967. Statehood. Nos. 198, 202/9 and 257 optd. STATEHOOD 1st MARCH, 1967.

(a) Postage.
229. 22. 2 c. violet 8 8
230. 5 c. blue 8 8
231. 6 c. brown 10 10
232. 23. 8 c. multicoloured .. 12 12
233. 10 c. multicoloured .. 15 15
234. 24. 12 c. multicoloured .. 20 20
235. – 15 c. multicoloured .. 25 30
236. – 25 c. multicoloured .. 40 45
237. – 35 c. blue and buff .. 55 60
238. – 50 c. multicoloured .. 75 85
239. – $1 multicoloured .. 1·50 1·75

(b) Air.
240. 25. 15 c. blue 15 20

26. "Madonna, Child and St. John" (Raphael).

1967. Christmas.
241. 26. 4 c. multicoloured .. 10 10
242. 25 c. multicoloured .. 30 35

27. Batsman and Sir Frederick Clarke (Governor).

1968. M.C.C.'s West Indies Tour.
243. 27. 10 c. multicoloured .. 10 10
244. 35 c. multicoloured .. 30 35

28. The Crucifixion (after Raphael). 29. Dr. Martin Luther King.

1968. Easter Commem.
245. 28. 10 c. multicoloured .. 8 8
246. – 15 c. multicoloured .. 10 10
247. 28. 25 c. multicoloured .. 20 20
248. – 35 c. multicoloured .. 25 25
DESIGN: 15 c., 35 c. "Noli me tangere" (detail by Titian).

1968. Martin Luther King Commem.
250. 29. 25 c. blue, black & flesh 25 25
251. 35 c. blue, black & flesh 30 30

30. "Virgin and Child in Glory" (Murillo).

1968. Christmas.
252. 30. 5 c. multicoloured .. 5 5
253. – 10 c. multicoloured .. 10 10
254. 30. 25 c. multicoloured .. 25 25
255. – 35 c. multicoloured .. 30 35
DESIGN: 10 c., 35 c. "Virgin and Child" (Murillo).

31. Humming bird.

1969. Birds.

256. **31.** 10 c. multicoloured .. 8 8
257. – 15 c. multicoloured .. 12 12
258. **31.** 25 c. multicoloured .. 25 25
259. – 35 c. multicoloured .. 30 35

DESIGN: 15 c., 35 c. St. Lucia Parrot.

32. "Ecce Homo" (Reni).

1969. Easter Commem. Multicoloured.

260. 10 c. Type **32** 10 10
261. 15 c. "Resurrection of Christ" (Sodoma) .. 15 15
262. 25 c. Type **32** 25 25
263. 35 c. As the 15 c. 30 30

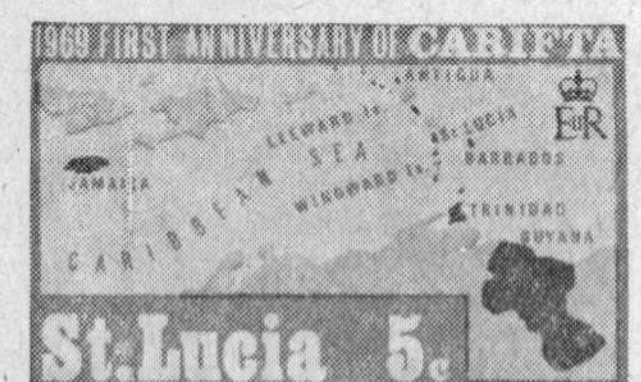

33. Map showing "CARIFTA" Countries.

1969. "CARIFTA". 1st Anniv.

264. **33.** 5 c. multicoloured .. 5 5
265. 10 c. multicoloured .. 8 8
266. – 25 c. multicoloured .. 20 20
267. – 35 c. multicoloured .. 30 35

DESIGN: 25 c., 35 c. Handclasp and names of "CARIFTA" countries.

34. Emperor Napoleon and Empress Josephine.

1969. Napoleon Bonaparte. Birth Bicent.

268. **34.** 15 c. multicoloured .. 10 12
269. 25 c. multicoloured .. 20 20
270. 35 c. multicoloured .. 30 30
271. 50 c. multicoloured . 40 45

35. "Virgin and Child" (Delaroche).

1969. Christmas. Paintings. Multicoloured; background colours given.

272. **35.** 5 c. gold and purple .. 5 5
273. – 10 c. gold and blue .. 8 8
274. **35.** 25 c. gold and red .. 25 25
275. – 35 c. gold and green .. 30 35

DESIGN: 10 c. and 35 c. "Holy Family" (Rubens).

36. House of Assembly.

1970. Multicoloured.

276. 1 c. Type **36** 5 5
277. 2 c. Roman Catholic Cathedral 5 5
278. 4 c. The Boulevard, Castries 8 8
279. 5 c. Castries Harbour .. 5 5
280. 6 c. Sulphur Springs .. 5 5
281. 10 c. Vigie Airport .. 8 8
282. 12 c. Reduit Beach .. 8 8
283. 15 c. Pigeon Island .. 10 10
284. 25 c. The Pitons and yacht 15 15
285. 35 c. Marigot Bay.. .. 20 20
286. 50 c. Diamond Waterfall.. 25 25
287. $1 Flag of St. Lucia .. 40 45
288. $2.50 St. Lucia Coat of Arms 1·10 1·25
289. $5 Queen Elizabeth II .. 2·25 2·50
289a. $10 Map of St. Lucia .. 4·50 5·00

Nos. 286/9a are vert.

37. "The Sealing of the Tomb" (Hogarth).

1970. Easter. Multicoloured.

290. 25 c. Type **37** 30 30
291. 35 c. "The Three Marys at the Tomb" (Hogarth).. 40 40
292. $1 "The Ascension" (Hogarth) .. .. 1·10 1·25

The $1 is larger (39×54 mm.).

Nos. 290/2 were issued in a triptych, with the $1 value 10 mm. higher than the other values.

38. Charles Dickens and Dickensian Characters.

1970. Charles Dickens. Death Cent.

293. **38.** 1 c. multicoloured .. 5 5
294. 25 c. multicoloured .. 25 25
295. 35 c. multicoloured .. 30 30
296. 50 c. multicoloured .. 40 40

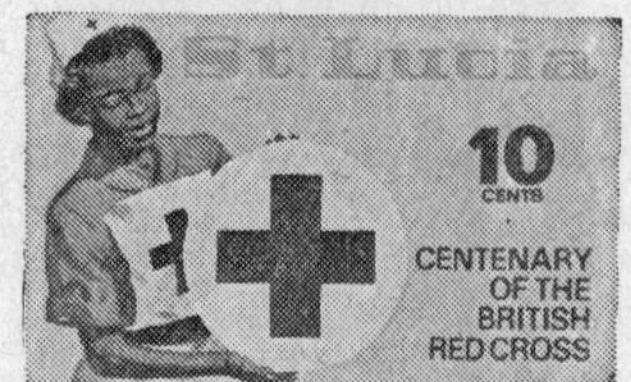

39. Nurse and Emblem.

1970. British Red Cross. Cent. Multicoloured.

297. 10 c. Type **39** 8 8
298. 15 c. Flags of Great Britain, Red Cross and St. Lucia 10 12
299. 25 c. Type **39** 15 20
300. 35 c. As 15 c. 25 30

40. "Madonna with the Lilies" (Luca della Robbia).

1970. Christmas.

301. **40.** 5 c. multicoloured .. 10 10
302. 10 c. multicoloured .. 12 12
303. 35 c. multicoloured .. 30 35
304. 40 c. multicoloured .. 35 40

41. "Christ on the Cross" (Rubens).

1971. Easter. Multicoloured.

305. 10 c. Type **41** 10 10
306. 15 c. "Descent from the Cross" (Rubens) .. 12 12
307. 35 c. Type **41** 30 30
308. 40 c. As 15 c. 30 35

42. Moule a Chique Lighthouse.

1971. Beane Field Airport Opening. Multicoloured.

309. 5 c. Type **42** 8 8
310. 25 c. Aircraft landing at Beane Field 25 30

43. Morne Fortune.

44. Morne Fortune, Modern View.

1971. Old and New Views of St. Lucia. Multicoloured.

311. 5 c. Type **43** 5 5
312. 5 c. Type **44** 5 5
313. 10 c. } Castries City .. 10 10
314. 10 c. } .. 10 10
315. 25 c. } Pigeon Island .. 20 20
316. 25 c. } .. 20 20
317. 50 c. } View from grounds 40 40
318. 50 c. } of Govt. House .. 40 40

Each value of this issue was printed horizontally and vertically se-tenant in two designs showing respectively old and new views of St. Lucia.

45. "Virgin and Child" (Verrocchio).

1971. Christmas. Multicoloured.

319. 5 c. Type **45** 5 5
320. 10 c. "Virgin and Child" (Morando) 8 8
321. 35 c. "Virgin and Child" (Battista) 30 30
322. 40 c. Type **45** 40 45

46. "St. Lucia" (Dolci School) and Coat of Arms.

1971. National Day.

323. **46.** 5 c. multicoloured .. 5 5
324. 10 c. multicoloured .. 8 8
325. 25 c. multicoloured .. 30 30
326. 50 c. multicoloured .. 40 45

47. "The Dead Christ Mourned" (Carracci).

1972. Easter. Multicoloured.

327. 10 c. Type **47** 8 8
328. 25 c. "Angels weeping over the dead Christ" (Guercino) 20 20
329. 35 c. Type **47** 25 25
330. 50 c. As 25 c. 40 45

48. Science Block and Teachers' College.

1972. Morne Educational Complex. Multicoloured.

331. 5 c. Type **48** 5 5
332. 15 c. University Centre .. 12 12
333. 25 c. Secondary School .. 15 20
334. 35 c. Technical College .. 30 30

49. Steamship Stamp and Map.

1972. 1st Postal Service by St. Lucia Steam Conveyance Co. Ltd. Cent.

335. 49. 5 c. multicoloured .. 10 10
336. – 10 c. blue, mauve & blk. 15 15
337. – 35 c. red, blue and black 30 30
338. – 50 c. multicoloured .. 40 40

DESIGNS: 10 c. Steamship stamp and Castries Harbour. 35 c. Steamship stamp and Soufriere. 50 c. Steamship stamps.

50. "The Holy Family" (Sebastiano Ricci).

1972. Christmas.

339. 50. 5 c. multicoloured .. 5 5
340. 10 c. multicoloured .. 8 8
341. 35 c. multicoloured .. 30 30
342. 40 c. multicoloured .. 35 35

1972. Royal Silver Wedding. As T 19 of Ascension, but with Arms and St. Lucia Parrot in background.

343. 15 c. red 20 25
344. 35 c. green 35 40

51. Week-day Headdress. 52. Coat of arms.

1973. Local Headdresses. Multicoloured.

345. 5 c. Type 51 .. .. 5 5
346. 10 c. Formal style .. 10 10
347. 25 c. Unmarried girl's style 25 25
348. 50 c. Ceremonial style .. 40 40

1973.

349. 52. 5 c. green 5 5
350. 10 c. blue 5 8
351. 25 c. brown 12 12

53. H.M.S. "St. Lucia".

1973. Old Ships. Multicoloured.

352. 15 c. Type 53 .. .. 12 12
353. 35 c. H.M.S. "Prince of Wales" 30 30
354. 50 c. "Oliph Blossom" .. 40 40
355. $1 H.M.S. "Rose" .. 70 75

54. Plantation and Flower.

1973. Banana Industry. Multicoloured.

357. 5 c. Type 54 .. .. 5 5
358. 15 c. Aerial spraying .. 15 15
359. 35 c. Boxing plant .. 30 30
360. 50 c. Loading a boat .. 40 40

55. "The Virgin with Child" (Maratta).

1973. Christmas. Multicoloured.

361. 5 c. Type 55 .. .. 5 5
362. 15 c. "Virgin in the Meadow" (Raphael) .. 12 12
363. 35 c. "The Holy Family" (Bronzino) 20 25
364. 50 c. "Madonna of the Pear" (Durer) 35 35

1973. Royal Wedding. As T 26 of Anguilla. Multicoloured. Background colours given.

365. 40 c. green 20 25
366. 50 c. lilac 25 30

56. "The Betrayal".

1974. Easter. Multicoloured.

369. 5 c. Type 56 .. .. 5 5
370. 35 c. "The Way to Calvary" 20 20
371. 80 c. "The Deposition" 45 50
372. $1 "The Resurrection" 55 60

57. 3-Escalins Coins, 1798.

1974. Coins of Old St. Lucia. Multicoloured.

374. 15 c. Type 57 .. .. 10 10
375. 35 c. 6-escalins coins, 1798 20 20
376. 40 c. 2-livres, 5-sols coins, 1813 .. .. 25 25
377. $1 6-livres, 15-sols coins, 1813 .. .. .. 50 50

58. Baron de Laborie. 59. "Virgin and Child" (Andrea del Verrocchio).

1974. Past Governors of St. Lucia. Mult.

379. 5 c. Type 58 .. .. 5 5
380. 35 c. Sir John Moore .. 20 20
381. 80 c. Sir Dudley Hill .. 40 45
382. $1 Sir Frederick Clarke .. 45 50

1974. Christmas. Multicoloured.

384. 5 c. Type 59 .. .. 5 5
385. 35 c. "Virgin and Child" (Andrea della Robbia) .. 20 20
386. 80 c. "Madonna and Child" (Luca della Robbia) .. 40 45
387. $1 "Virgin and Child" (Rossellino) 45 50

60. Churchill and Montgomery.

1974. Sir Winston Churchill. Birth Centenary. Multicoloured.

389. 5 c. Type 60 .. .. 5 5
390. $1 Churchill and Truman 45 50

61. "The Crucifixion" (Van der Weyden).

1975. Easter. Multicoloured.

391. 5 c. Type 61 .. .. 5 5
392. 35 c. "Noli me tangere" (Romano) 15 20
393. 80 c. "The Crucifixion" (Gallego) 35 40
394. $1 "Noli me tangere" (Correggio) 45 50

62. "Nativity" (French Book of Hours).

1975. Christmas. Multicoloured.

399. 5 c. Type 62 .. .. 5 5
400. 10 c. } "Epiphany scene" 8 8
402. 10 c. } (stained glass 8 8
402. 10 c. } window' .. 8 8
403. 40 c. "Nativity" (Hastings Book of Hours) .. 20 20
404. $1 "Virgin and Child" (Bergognone) 40 45

63. War Vessel "Hanna".

1975. American Revolution. Bicent. Ships. Multicoloured.

406. ½ c. Type 63 .. .. 5 5
407. 1 c. Mail Packet "Prince of Orange" 5 5
408. 2 c. H.M.S. "Edward" .. 5 5
409. 5 c. Merchantman "Millern" 5 5
410. 15 c. Lugger "Surprise" 8 10
411. 35 c. H.M.S. "Serapis" .. 15 20
412. 50 c. Frigate "Randolph" 25 25
413. $1 Frigate "Alliance" .. 40 45

64. Laughing Gull.

1976. Multicoloured.

415. 1 c. Type 64 .. .. 5 5
416. 2 c. Little Blue Heron .. 5 5
417. 4 c. Belted Kingfisher .. 5 5
418. 5 c. St. Lucia Parrot .. 5 5
419. 6 c. St. Lucia Oriole .. 5 5
420. 8 c. Trembler 5 5
421. 10 c. Sparrow Hawk .. 5 5
422. 12 c. Red-billed Tropicbird 5 5
423. 15 c. Common Gallinule .. 5 5
424. 25 c. Brown Noddy .. 10 10
425. 35 c. Sooty Tern 12 15
426. 50 c. Osprey 20 20
427. $1 White Breasted Thrasher 35 40
428. $2·50 St. Lucia Black Finch 90 1·00
429. $5 Ramier .. .. 1·75 2·00
430. $10 Caribbean Elaenia .. 3·50 4·00

1976. West Indian Victory in World Cricket Cup. As Nos. 559/60 of Barbados.

431. 50 c. Caribbean map .. 20 25
432. $1 Prudential Cup .. 40 45

65. H.M.S. "Ceres".

1976. Royal Naval Crests. Multicoloured.

434. 10 c. Type 65 .. .. 5 5
435. 20 c. H.M.S. "Pelican" .. 8 10
436. 40 c. H.M.S. "Ganges" .. 15 20
437. $2 H.M.S. "Ariadne" .. 80 90

66. "Madonna and Child" (Murillo).

1976. Christmas. Multicoloured.

438. 10 c. Type 66 .. .. 5 5
439. 20 c. "Virgin and Child" (Costa) 8 10
440. 50 c. "Madonna and Child" (Isenbrandt) 20 25
441. $2 "Madonna and Child with St. John" (Murillo) 80 90

67. Queen Elizabeth II.

1977. Silver Jubilee.
442. 67. 10 c. multicoloured 5 5
443. 20 c. multicoloured 8 10
444. 40 c. multicoloured 15 20
445. $2 multicoloured 80 90

POSTAGE DUE STAMPS

D 1.

1931.
D 1. D 1. 1d. black on blue 40 40
D 2. 2d. black on yellow 60 60

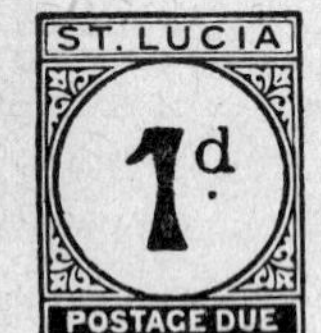

D 2. D 3.

1933.
D 3. D 2. 1d. black 25 25
D 4. 2d. black 40 40
D 5. 4d. black 40 45
D 6. 8d. black 50 55

1949.
D 11. D 3. 2 c. black 8 8
D 12. 4 c. black 8 8
D 9a. 8 c. black 8 8
D 10a. 16 c. black 10 10

STE. MARIE DE MADAGASCAR O3

An island off the east coast of Madagascar. From 1898 used the stamps of Madagascar and Dependencies.

1894. "Tablet" key-type inscr. "STE MARIE DE MADAGASCAR".
1. D. 1 c. black on blue 5 5
2. 2 c. brown on yellow 15 15
3 4 c. claret on grey 45 30
4. 5 c. green 75 45
5. 10 c. black on lilac 1·10 1·10
6. 15 c. blue 4·25 3·75
7. 20 c. red on green 2·75 2·75
8. 25 c. black on red 3·25 2·10
9. 30 c. brown 1·25 1·00
10. 40 c. red on yellow 1·60 1·25
11. 50 c. red 6·50 5·00
12. 75 c. brown on orange 8·50 5·50
13. 1 f. olive 4·25 3·75

ST. PIERRE ET MIQUELON O4

A group of French islands off the S. coast of Newfoundland.

1885. Stamps of French Colonies surch. **SPM** or **spm** and value in figures.
1. 9. 5 on 2 c. brown on yellow £800 £425
4. 5 on 4 c. claret on grey 45·00 30·00
8. 05 on 20 c. red on green 3·50 3·00
9. 8. 05 on 35 c. black on yellow 14·00 11·00
5. 05 on 40 c. red on yellow 17·00 9·00
10a. 05 on 75 c. red 45·00 28·00
11. 05 on 1 f. olive 3·00 2·25
6. 10 on 40 c. red on yellow 3·25 2·75
15. 9. 15 c. on 30 c. brown 4·50 3·25
16. 15 c. on 35 c. blk. on yellow £100 60·00
7. 8. 15 c. on 40 c. red on yellow 3·25 2·75
18. 9. 15 c. on 40 c. red on yellow 11·00 8·00
3. 8. 25 on 1 f. olive £600 £350

1891. Stamps of French Colonies, "Commerce" type, optd. **ST-PIERRE M-on.**
19. 9. 1 c. black on blue 1·10 1·10
24. 2 c. brown on yellow 1·25 1·00
25. 4 c. claret on grey 1·25 1·10
26. 5 c. green 1·25 1·00
27. 10 c. black on lilac 1·90 1·90
28. 15 c. blue 2·75 1·50
29. 20 c. red on green 12·00 10·00
30. 25 c. black on red 3·75 2·75
31. 30 c. brown 16·00 14·00
32. 35 c. black on yellow 65·00 55·00
33. 40 c. red on yellow 11·00 8·00
34. 75 c. red 17·00 14·00
35. 1 f. olive 11·00 9·00

1891. Stamps of French Colonies, "Commerce" type optd. **ST-PIERRE M-on** and surch. in figures and words either side of opt.
36. 9. 1 c. on 5 c. green 1·25 1·10
37. 1 c. on 10 c. black on lilac 1·40 1·25
38. 1 c. on 25 c. black on red 90 65
39. 2 c. on 10 c. black on lilac 90 65
40. 2 c. on 15 c. blue 70 70
41. 2 c. on 25 c. black on red 70 70
42. 4 c. on 20 c. red on green 70 70
43. 4 c. on 25 c. black on red 70 70
44. 4 c. on 30 c. brown 2·25 1·90
45. 4 c. on 40 c. red on yellow 2·75 2·00

1892. Stamps of French Colonies, "Commerce" type, optd. **ST-PIERRE M-on** and surch. in figures through opt.
49. 9. 1 on 5 c. green 1·10 1·10
46. 1 on 25 c. black on red 60 60
50. 2 on 5 c. green 1·10 1·10
47. 2 on 25 c. black on red 60 60
51. 4 on 5 c. green 1·10 1·10
48. 4 on 25 c. black on red 60 60

1892. Postage Due stamps of French Colonies optd. **ST-PIERRE M-on** between the letters **T** and **P.**
52. D 1. 10 c. black 5·00 5·00
53. 20 c. black 2·75 2·75
54. 30 c. black 4·00 3·25
55. 40 c. black 4·00 3·25
56. 60 c. black 17·00 13·00
57. 1 f. brown 22·00 18·00
58. 2 f. brown 35·00 30·00
59. 5 f. brown 65·00 60·00

1892. "Tablet" key-type inscr. "ST. PIERRE ET MIQUELON".
60. D. 1 c. black on blue 5 5
61. 2 c. brown on yellow 10 10
62. 4 c. claret on grey 20 20
73. 5 c. green 30 25
64. 10 c. black on lilac 40 35
74. 10 c. red 30 8
65. 15 c. blue 1·10 20
75. 15 c. grey 8·00 7·50
66. 20 c. red on green 2·25 1·75
67. 25 c. black on red 1·40 20
76. 25 c. blue 1·50 1·40
68. 30 c. brown 1·00 45
77. 35 c. black on yellow 55 45
69. 40 c. red on yellow 65 50
70. 50 c. red 5·50 4·50
78. 50 c. brown on blue 4·50 4·00
71. 75 c. brown on orange 4·00 3·25
72. 1 f. olive 2·75 1·75

1. Fisherman.

2. Sea-gull.

3. Fishing Boat.

1909.
79. 1. 1 c. brown and orange 5 5
80. 2 c. blue and brown 5 5
81. 4 c. brown and violet 5 5
82. 5 c. olive and green 5 5
109. 5 c. black and blue 5 5
83. 10 c. red 5 5
110. 10 c. olive and green 5 5
111. 10 c. mauve and bistre 5 5
84. 15 c. red and purple 5 5
85. 20 c. purple and brown 10 8
86. 2. 25 c. blue 12 12
112. 25 c. green and brown 5 5
87. 30 c. chocolate & orange 8 8
113. 30 c. red 5 5
114. 2. 30 c. blue and lake 5 5
115. 30 c. green 5 5
88. 35 c. chocolate and green 5 5
89. 40 c. green and chocolate 25 15
90. 45 c. green and violet 5 5
91. 50 c. green and brown 10 12
116. 50 c. blue 5 5
117. 50 c. purple and brown 5 5
118. 60 c. red and blue 5 5
119. 65 c. brown and mauve 15 15
92. 75 c. olive and brown 8 8
120. 90 c. red 2·25 2·25
93. 3. 1 f. blue and green 30 25
121. 1 f. 10 red and green 25 25
122. 1 f. 50 blue 90 90
94. 2 f. brown and violet 40 35
123. 3 f. mauve on red 90 90
95. 5 f. green and chocolate 1·40 95

1912. "Tablet" issue surch. in figures.
96. D. 05 on 2 c. brown on yell. 12 12
97. 05 on 4 c. claret on grey 5 5
98. 05 on 15 c. blue 5 5
99. 05 on 20 c. red on green 5 5
100. 05 on 25 c. black on red 5 5
101. 05 on 30 c. brown 5 5
102. 05 on 35 c. black on yell. 8 8
103. 10 on 40 c. red on yellow 5 5
104. 10 on 50 c. red 5 5
105. 10 on 75 c. brn. on orange 12 12
106. 10 on 1 f. olive 12 12

1915. Surch. **5 c.** and red cross.
107. 1. 10 c.+5 c. red 5 5
108. 15 c.+5 c. red & purple 5 5

1924. Surch. in figures and bars.
124. 1. 25 c. on 15 c. red & pur. 5 5
125. 3. 25 c. on 2 f. brn. & violet 5 5
126. 25 c. on 5 f. grn. & choc. 5 5
127. 2. 65 on 45 c. green & violet 10 10
128. 85 on 75 c. olive & brown 5 5
129. 90 c. on 75 c. red 20 20
130. 3. 1 f. 25 on 1 f. blue 5 5
131. 1 f. 50 on 1 f. blue 15 15
132. 3 f. on 5 f. mve. & black 25 25
133. 10 f. on 5 f. green & red 2·75 2·75
134. 20 f. on 5 f. red and violet 3·00 3·00

1931. "Colonial Exn." key-types inscr. "ST. PIERRE ET MIQUELON".
135. E. 40 c. green 35 35
136. F. 50 c. mauve 35 35
137. G. 90 c. red 35 35
138. H. 1 f. 50 blue 35 35

4. St. Pierre and Miquelon Map. 5. Lighthouse.

6. Trawler.

1932.
139. 4. 1 c. blue and purple 5 5
140. 5. 2 c. green and black 5 5
141. 6. 4 c. brown and red 5 5
142. 5 c. brown and mauve 5 5
143. 5. 10 c. black and purple 5 5
144. 15 c. mauve and blue 8 8
145. 4. 20 c. red and black 10 10
146. 25 c. green and mauve 5 5
147. 6. 30 c. green and olive 12 12
148. 40 c. brown and blue 8 8
149. 5. 45 c. green and red 10 10
150. 50 c. green and brown 8 8
151. 6. 65 c. red and brown 15 15
152. 4. 75 c. red and green 15 15
153. 90 c. red 15 15
154. 6. 1 f. red and brown 12 12
155. 4. 1 f. 25 red and blue 20 20
156. 1 f. 50 blue 20 20
157. 6. 1 f. 75 brown and black 25 25
158. 2 f. green and black 70 70
159. 5. 3 f. brown and green 90 90
160. 5 f. brown and red 1·90 1·90
161. 6. 10 f. mauve and green 5·50 5·50
162. 4. 20 f. green and red 5·50 5·50

1934. Cartier's Discovery of Canada. 4th Cent. Optd. **JACQUES CARTIER 1534-1934.**
163. 5. 50 c. green and brown 20 20
164. 4. 75 c. red and green 30 30
165. 1 f. 50 blue 30 30
166. 6. 1 f. 75 brown and black 30 30
167. 5. 5 f. brown and red 3·75 3·75

1937. Int. Exn., Paris. As Nos. 110/15 of Cameroun.
168. 20 c. violet 20 20
169. 30 c. green 20 20
170. 40 c. red 20 20
171. 50 c. brown 20 20
172. 90 c. red 20 20
173. 1 f. 50 blue 20 20

1938. Int. Anti-Cancer Fund. As T **10** of Cameroun.
174. 1 f. 75+50 c. blue 1·75 1·75

7. Dog Team.

DESIGNS: 30 c. to 70 c. St. Pierre Harbour. 80 c. to 1 f. 75, Turtle Lighthouse. 2 f. to 20 f. Soldiers' Cove, Langlade.

1938.
175. 7. 2 c. green 5 5
176. 3 c. brown 5 5
177. 4 c. purple 5 5
178. 5 c. red 5 5
179. 10 c. brown 5 5
180. 15 c. purple 5 5
181. 20 c. violet 5 5
182. 25 c. blue 15 15
183. – 30 c. purple 5 5
184. – 35 c. green 5 5
185. – 40 c. blue 5 5
186. – 45 c. green 5 5
187. – 50 c. red 5 5
188. – 55 c. blue 35 35
189. – 60 c. violet 5 5
190. – 65 c. brown 35 35
191. – 70 c. orange 5 5
192. – 80 c. violet 8 8
193. – 90 c. blue 8 5
194. – 1 f. red 70 70
195. – 1 f. olive 5 5
196. – 1 f. 25 red 10 10
197. – 1 f. 40 brown 5 5
198. – 1 f. 50 green 5 5
199. – 1 f. 60 purple 5 5
200. – 1 f. 75 blue 12 12
201. – 2 f. purple 5 5
202. – 2 f. 25 blue 5 5
203. – 2 f. 50 orange 5 5
204. – 3 f. brown 5 5
205. – 5 f. red 8 8
206. – 10 f. blue 8 8
207. – 20 f. olive 10 10

1939. New York World's Fair. As T **11** of Cameroun.
208. 1 f. 25 red 12 12
209. 2 f. 25 blue 12 12

1939. French Revolution. 150th Anniv. As T **16** of Cameroun.
210. 45 c.+25 c. green 85 85
211. 70 c.+30 c. brown 85 85
212. 90 c.+35 c. orange 85 85
213. 1 f. 25+1 f. red 85 85
214. 2 f. 25+2 f. blue 85 85

1941. Free French Plebiscite. Stamps of 1938 optd. **Noel 1941 FRANCE LIBRE F. N. F. L.**
215. 7. 10 c. brown 5·00 5·00
216. 20 c. violet 5·00 5·00
217. 25 c. blue 5·00 5·00
218. – 40 c. blue 5·00 5·00
219. – 45 c. green 5·00 5·00
220. – 65 c. brown 5·00 5·00
221. – 70 c. orange 5·00 5·00
222. – 80 c. violet 5·00 5·00
223. – 90 c. blue 5·00 5·00
224. – 1 f. green 5·00 5·00
225. – 1 f. 25 red 5·00 5·00
226. – 1 f. 40 brown 5·00 5·00
227. – 1 f. 60 purple 5·00 5·00
228. – 1 f. 75 blue 5·00 5·00
229. – 2 f. purple 5·00 5·00
230. – 2 f. 25 blue 5·50 5·50
231. – 2 f. 50 orange 5·50 5·50
232. – 3 f. brown 5·50 5·50
233. 7. 10 f. on 10 c. brown 10·00 10·00
234. – 20 f. on 90 c. blue 10·00 10·00

"F.N.F.L." = Forces Navales Francaises Libres (Free French Naval Forces).

1941. Various stamps optd. **FRANCE LIBRE/F.N.F.L.** or surch also.

(a) Nos. 111 and 114.
245. 1. 10 c. mauve and bistre £150 £150
246. 2. 30 c. blue and lake £150 £150

(b) On stamps of 1932.
247. 5. 2 c. green and black 32·00 32·00
248. 6. 4 c. brown and red 5·50 5·50
249. 5 c. brown and mauve £110 £110
250. 40 c. brown and blue 2·25 2·25
251. 5. 45 c. green and red 22·00 22·00
252. 50 c. green and brown 65 65
253. 6. 65 c. red and brown 5·50 5·50
254. 1 f. red and brown 60·00 60·00
255. 1 f. 75 brown and black 1·00 1·00
256. 2 f. green and black 1·00 1·00
257. 5. 5 f. brown and red 50·00 50·00
258. 6. 5 f. on 1 f. 75 brn. & blk. 1·10 1·10

(c) On stamps of 1938.

259. 7. 2 c. green .. .. 60·00 60·00
260. 3 c. brown .. .. 18·00 18·00
261. 4 c. purple .. .. 14·00 14·00
262. 5 c. red £130 £130
263. 10 c. brown .. .. 2·25 2·25
264. 15 c. purple £200 £200
265. 20 c. violet .. .. 25·00 25·00
266. 20 c. on 10 c. brown .. 80 80
267. 25 c. blue .. .. 2·25 2·25
268. 30 c. on 10 c. brown .. 1·10 1·10
269. – 35 c. green £110 £110
270. – 40 c. blue .. .. 2·25 2·25
271. – 45 c. green .. .. 2·25 2·25
272. – 55 c. blue £900 £900
273. – 60 c. violet .. .. 80·00 80·00
274. – 60 c. on 90 c. blue .. 1·40 1·40
275. – 65 c. brown .. .. 2·25 2·25
276. – 70 c. orange .. .. 4·00 4·00
277. – 80 c. violet .. .. 55·00 55·00
278. – 90 c. blue .. .. 2·75 2·75
279. – 1 f. green .. .. 2·25 2·25
280. – 1 f. 25 red .. .. 2·25 2·25
281. – 1 f. 40 brown .. .. 2·25 2·25
282. – 1 f. 50 green £100 £100
283. – 1 f. 50 on 90 c. blue .. 1·40 1·40
284. – 1 f. 60 purple .. .. 1·75 1·75
285. – 2 f. purple .. .. 8·00 8·00
286. – 2 f. 25 blue .. .. 1·75 1·75
287. – 2 f. 50 orange .. .. 2·25 2·25
288. 7. 2 f. 50 on 10 c. brown .. 2·25 2·25
289. – 3 f. brown £1000 £1000
290. – 5 f. red £325 £325
291. 7. 10 f. on 10 c. brown .. 8·00 8·00
292. – 20 f. olive £170 £170
293. – 20 f. on 90 c. blue .. 8·00 8·00

(d) On Nos. 208/9.

294. 1 f. 25 red .. .. .. 1·10 1·10
295. 2 f. 25 blue .. .. .. 1·10 1·10
296. 2 f. 50 on 1 f. 25 red .. 1·75 1·75
297. 3 f. on 2 f. 25 blue .. 1·75 1·75

1942. Stamps of 1932 optd. **FRANCE LIBRE F. N. F. L.** or surch also.

304. 4. 20 c. red and black .. 40·00 40·00
305. 75 c. red and green .. 2·25 2·25
306. 1 f. 25 red and blue .. 2·25 2·25
307. 1 f. 50 blue .. .. 55·00 55·00
308. 10 f. on 1 f. 25 red & blue 3·25 3·25
309. 20 f. on 75 c. red & green 5·50 5·50

1942. Social Welfare Fund. Nos. 279 and 287 further surch. **OEUVRES SOCIALES,** cross and premium.

320. 1 f. + 50 c. green .. .. 4·00 4·00
321. 2 f. 50 + 1 f. orange .. 4·00 4·00

8.

1942. (a) Postage.

322. 8. 5 c. blue 5 5
323. 10 c. red 5 5
324. 25 c. green 5 5
325. 30 c. black 5 5
326. 40 c. blue 5 5
327. 60 c. brown 5 5
328. 1 f. mauve 5 5
329. 1 f. 50 red 5 5
330. 2 f. brown 5 5
331. 2 f. 50 blue 5 5
332. 4 f. orange 5 5
333. 5 f. purple 5 5
334. 10 f. blue 10 10
335. 20 f. green 12 12

(b) Air. As T 18 of Cameroun.

336. 1 f. orange 5 5
337. 1 f. 50 red 5 5
338. 5 f. maroon 5 5
339. 10 f. black 5 5
340. 25 f. blue 5 5
341. 50 f. green 20 25
342. 100 f. claret 25 20

1944. Mutual Aid and Red Cross Funds. As T 19 of Cameroun.

343. 5 f. + 20 f. blue 12 12

1945. Eboue. As T 20 of Cameroun.

344. 2 f. black 5 5
345. 25 f. green 8 8

1945. Surch.

346. 8. 50 c. on 5 c. blue 5 5
347. 70 c. on 5 c. blue 5 5
348. 80 c. on 5 c. blue 5 5
349. 1 f. 20 on 5 c. blue 5 5
350. 2 f. 40 on 25 c. green .. 5 5
351. 3 f. on 25 c. green 5 5
352. 4 f. 50 on 25 c. green .. 5 5
353. 15 f. on 2 f. 50 blue .. 15 15

1946. Air. Victory. As T 21 of Cameroun.

354. 8 f. claret 10 10

1946. Air. From Chad to the Rhine. As T 22 of Cameroun.

355. 5 f. red 8 8
356. 10 f. lilac 8 8
357. 15 f. black 10 10
358. 20 f. violet 12 12
359. 25 f. brown 12 12
360. 50 f. black 15 15

9. Soldiers' Cove, Langlade.

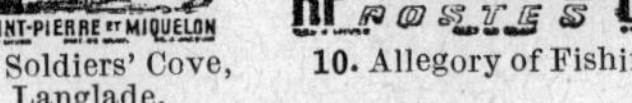

10. Allegory of Fishing.

11. Aircraft and Wrecked Vessel.

1947.

361. 9. 10 c. brown (postage) .. 5 5
362. 30 c. violet 5 5
363. 40 c. purple 5 5
364. 50 c. blue 5 5
365. 10. 60 c. red 5 5
366. 80 c. blue 5 5
367. 1 f. green 5 5
368. – 1 f. 20 green 5 5
369. – 1 f. 50 black 5 5
370. – 2 f. red 5 5
371. – 3 f. violet 10 10
372. – 3 f. 60 red 8 8
373. – 4 f. purple 5 5
374. – 5 f. yellow 8 8
375. – 6 f. blue 10 10
376. – 8 f. sepia 12 8
377. – 10 f. green 15 15
378. – 15 f. green 25 25
379. – 17 f. blue 25 12
380. – 20 f. red 20 20
381. – 25 f. blue 20 20
382. – 50 f. green and red (air) 45 45
383. 11. 100 f. green 65 65
384. – 200 f. blue and red .. 1·40 90

DESIGNS—As T 10: 1 f. 20 to 2 f. Cross and fishermen. 3 f. to 4 f. Weighing fish. 5 f., 6 f., 10 f. Fishing trawler. 8 f., 17 f. Arctic fox. 15 f. 20 f., 25 f. Windswept mountain landscape. As T 11: 50 f. Aircraft and fishing village. 200 f. Aircraft and snow-bound sailing vessel.

1949. Air. U.P.U. as T 25 of Cameroun.

395. 25 f. multicoloured .. 1·10 1·10

1950. Colonial Welfare. As Cameroun T 26.

396. 10 f. + 2 f. red and brown .. 30 30

1952. Military Medal. Cent. As T 27 of Cameroun.

397. 8 f. blue, yellow and green 70 70

1954. Air. Liberation. 10th Anniv. As T 29 of Cameroun.

398. 15 f. red and brown .. 45 45

12. Refrigeration Plant.

13. Codfish.

DESIGNS — HORIZ. As T 12/13: 4 f., 10 f. Lighthouse and fishing craft. 20 f. Ice hockey players. 25 f. Minks. As T 14: 100 f. "Caravelle" airliner over St. Pierre and Miquelon. 500 f. Aeroplane over St. Pierre port.

14. Dog and Coastal Scene.

1955.

399. 12. 30 c. blue (postage) .. 5 5
400. 13. 40 c. brown and blue .. 5 5
401. 12. 50 c. sepia, grey & black 5 5
402. 13. 1 f. sepia and green .. 5 5
403. 2 f. indigo and blue .. 5 5
404. 12. 3 f. plum 5 5
405. – 4 f. plum, red and lake 5 5
406. – 10 f. brown, blue & turq.. 8 5
407. – 20 f. lake, turquoise, green and black .. 20 15
408. – 25 f. brn., grn. & indigo 35 30
409. 12. 40 f. turquoise 30 15
410. 14. 50 f. black, blue & grey (air) 85 55
411. – 100 f. black and grey .. 1·00 45
412. – 500 f. indigo and blue .. 3·75 2·00

15. Fishing Vessel.

17. "Cypripedium acaule".

16. Flaming Torches.

1956. Economic and Social Development Fund.

413. 15. 15 f. sepia and brown .. 12 8

1958. Declaration of Human Rights. 10th Anniv. As T 5 of Comoro Is.

414. 20 f. brown and blue .. 20 15

1959. Tropical Flora. As T 21 of French Equatorial Africa.

415. 5 f. violet, grn., red & yell. 15 10

DESIGN: 5 f. "Picea".

1959. Air. Adoption of Constitution.

416. 16. 200 f. grn., lake & violet 1·25 55

1962. Flowers.

417. 17. 25 f. purple, orange and green (postage) .. 20 15
418. – 50 f. crimson and green 35 20
419. – 100 f. orange, red and green (air) .. 65 25

DESIGNS—VERT. 50 f. "Calopogon pulchellus". HORIZ. (48 × 27 mm.): 100 f. "Sarracenia purpurea".

18. Submarine "Surcouf" and Map.

1962. Air. Adherence to Gen. de Gaulle (Free French Government). 20th Anniv.

420. 18. 500 f. black, blue & red 10·00 9·00

1962. Air. 1st Trans-Atlantic TV Satellite Link. As T 18 of Andorra.

421. 50 f. brown, myrtle & sep. 55 45

19. Eider Ducks.

20. Dr. A. Calmette.

1963. Birds.

422. 19. 50 c. yell.-brn., blk. & bl. 5 5
423. – 1 f. chest., magenta & blue 5 5
424. – 2 f. brown, blk. & indigo 5 5
425. – 6 f. yell.-brn., bl. & turq. 8 5

BIRDS: 1 f. Ptarmigan. 2 f. Ringed plovers. 6 f. Blue-winged teal.

1963. Dr. Albert Calmette (bacteriologist). Birth Cent.

426. 20. 30 f. chocolate and blue 20 15

21. Landing of Governor.

1963. Air. Arrival of First Governor (Dangeac) in St. Pierre and Miquelon. Bicent.

427. 21. 200 f. blue, grn. & choc. 1·25 80

1963. Red Cross Cent. As Type F 2 of New Hebrides.

428. 25 f. red, green and ultram. 40 25

1963. Declaration of Human Rights. 15th Anniv. As T 10 of Comoro Islands.

429. 20 f. orange, maroon & blue 25 20

1964. "PHILATEC 1964" Int. Stamp Exn., Paris. As T 481 of France.

430. 60 f. blue, green and maroon 60 60

22. Rabbits.

ANIMALS: 4 f. Fox. 5 f. Roebucks. 34 f. Charolais bull.

1964. Fauna.

431. 22. 3 f. choc., brown & green 5 5
432. – 4 f. sepia, blue and green 5 5
433. – 5 f. brown, sepia & blue 5 5
434. – 34 f. brown, green & blue 25 15

23. Airliner and Map.

1964. Air. 1st St. Pierre-New York Airmail Flight.

435. 23. 100 f. brown and blue .. 1·10 90

1965. Air. I.T.U. Cent. As T 15 of Comoro Islands.

436. 40 f. blue, purple and brown 1·00 75

1966. Air. Launching of 1st French Satellite. As Nos. 1696/7 (plus se-tenant label) of France.

437. 25 f. brown, blue and red .. 70 55
438. 30 f. brown, blue and red .. 70 55

1966. Air. Launching of Satellite "D1". As T 521 of France.

439. 48 f. blue, green and lake .. 45 40

24. Arrival of Settlers.

1966. Air. Return of Islands to France. 150th Anniv.

440. 24. 100 f. multicoloured .. 65 45

25. "Journal Officiel" and Old and New Printing Presses.

27. Freighter and Harbour Plan.

26. Map and Fishing-boats.

1966. Air. "Journal Officiel" Printing Works. Cent.

441. 25. 60 f. plum, lake and blue 50 45

1967. Air. Pres. De Gaulle's Voyage.

442. 26. 25 f. brown, blue & red 1·00 85
443. – 100 f. blue, turq. & pur. 2·10 1·60

DESIGN: 100 f. Maps and cruiser "Richelieu".

1967. Opening of St. Pierre's New Harbour.

444. 27. 48 f. brown, blue & red 35 25

28. Map and Control Tower.

1967. Opening of St. Pierre Airport.
445. **28.** 30 f. multicoloured .. 20 12

29. T.V. Receiver, Aerial and Map.

30. Speed-skating.

31. J. D. Cassini (discover of group), Compasses and Chart.

1967. Television Service. Inaug.
446. **29.** 40 f. red, green & olive 25 15

1968. Air. Winter Olympic Games, Grenoble. Multicoloured.
447. 50 f. Type **30** 35 20
448. 60 f. Ice-hockey goalkeeper 40 25

1968. W.H.O. 20th Anniv. As T **21** of Comoro Islands.
449. 10 f. red, yellow and blue 10 8

1968. Famous Visitors to St. Pierre and Miquelon. (1st series.)
450. **31.** 4 f. brown, yellow & lake 10 10
451. – 6 f. chest., bl., yell. & grn. 15 15
452. – 15 f. chest., yell., red & bl. 25 25
453. – 25 f. chest., yell., bl. & sep. 35 35
CELEBRITIES: 6 f. Rene de Chateaubriand (colonist) and ship. 15 f. Prince de Joinville (governor) and ships. 25 f. Admiral Gauchet and flagship (Isle of Dogs expedition).

1968. Human Rights Year. As T **23** of Comoro Islands.
454. 20 f. vermilion, blue & yell. 15 8

32. War Memorial, St. Pierre.

1968. Air. Armistice. 50th Anniv.
455. **32.** 500 f. multicoloured .. 3·50 2·25

1969. Air. 1st Flight of "Concorde". As T **27** of Comoro Islands.
456. 34 f. brown & olive-brown 65 40

33. Mountain Stream, Langlade.

1969. Tourism.
457. **33.** 5 f. brn., bl. & grn. (post.) 5 5
458. – 15 f. brown, green & blue 10 5
459. – 50 f. mar., ol. & bl. (air) 40 30
460. – 100 f. brn., ind. & blue .. 80 55
DESIGNS: 15 f. River-bank, Debon, Langlade. 50 f. Wild Horses, Miquelon. 100 f. Gathering wood, Miquelon. The 50 f. and 100 f. are larger (48 × 27 mm.).

34. Treasury.

1969. Public Buildings and Monuments.
461. **34.** 10 f. black, red and blue 8 5
462. – 25 f. red, ultram. & blue 15 5
463. – 30 f. brown, green & blue 20 10
464. – 60 f. black, red and blue 40 25
DESIGNS: 25 f. Maritime Fisheries Scientific and Technical Institute. 30 f. Unknown Sailor's Monument. 60 f. St. Christopher's College.

35. "L'Estoile" and Granville, 1690.

1969. Maritime Links with France.
465. **35.** 34 f. lake, green and emerald (postage) .. 30 20
466. – 40 f. green, red & bistre 35 25
467. – 48 f. multicoloured .. 40 30
468. – 200 f. black, lake and emerald (air) .. 1·40 75
DESIGNS—As Type **35**. 40 f. "La Jolie" and St. Jean de Luz, 1750. 48 f. "Le Juste" and La Rochelle, 1860. (48 × 27 mm.). 200 f. "L'Esperance" and St. Malo, 1600.

36. Pierre Loti (explorer and writer), Ship and Book Titles.

1969. Air. Loti Commem.
469. **36.** 200 f. brown, blue & ochre 2·00 1·40

37. Seals.

1969. Marine Animals.
470. **37.** 1 f. brn., purple & lake 5 5
471. – 3 f. indigo, green and red 5 5
472. – 4 f. green, brown and red 5 5
473. – 6 f. violet, emer. and red 8 8
DESIGNS: 3 f. Sperm whales. 4 f. Pilot whales. 6 f. Dolphins.

1969. Int. Labour Organization. 50th Anniv. As T **28** of Comoro Islands.
474. 20 f. brown, slate & salmon 15 8

1970. New U.P.U. Headquarters Building, Berne. As T **126** of Cameroun.
475. 25 f. brown, blue & claret 15 8
476. 34 f. slate, brown & purple 20 10

38. Rocket and Japanese Women.

40. "Rubus chamaemorus".

39. Rowing Fours.

1970. Air. World Fair "EXPO 70", Osaka, Japan.
477. **38.** 34 f. brn., lake & indigo 20 15
478. – 85 f. indigo, red & orge. 45 25
DESIGN–HORIZ. 85 f. "Mountain Landscape" (Y. Taikan) and Expo "star".

1970. World Rowing Championships. St. Catherine, Canada.
479. **39.** 20 f. brn., bl. & pale bl. 10 5

1970. Fruit Plants.
480. **40.** 3 f. green, pur. & brn. 5 5
481. – 4 f. yell., red and green 5 5
482. – 5 f. rose, green & violet 8 5
483. – 6 f. violet, green & purple 8 8
PLANTS: 4 f. "Fragaria vesca". 5 f. "Rubus idaeus". 6 f. "Vaccinium myrtillus".

41. Ewe and Lamb.

1970. Live-stock Breeding.
484. **41.** 15 f. brown, purple & grn. 8 5
485. – 30 f. brn., grey and green 15 10
486. – 34 f. brn., purple & green 20 10
487. – 48 f. maroon, brn. & bl. 25 12
DESIGNS: 30 f. Animal quarantine station. 34 f. Charolaise bull. 48 f. Refrigeration plant and trawler.

42. Etienne Francois. Duke of Choiseul, and ships.

1970. Air. Celebrities of St. Pierre and Miquelon (2nd series).
488. **42.** 25 f. brown, blue & pur. 15 8
489. – 50 f. brown, purple & grn. 30 12
490. – 60 f. brown, green & pur. 40 15
DESIGNS: 50 f. Jacques Cartier and landing scene. 60 f. Sebastien Le Gonard de Sourdeval and ships.

43. "St. Francis of Assisi", 1900.

1971. Fisheries' Protection Vessels.
491. **43.** 30 f. red, blue & turq... 15 8
492. – 35 f. brn., grn. & blue.. 20 10
493. – 40 f. brn., blue & green 20 10
494. – 80 f. blk., grn. & blue.. 40 15
DESIGNS: 35 f. "St. Jehanne", 1920. 40 f. "L'Aventure, 1950. 80 f. "Commandant Bourdais", 1970.

44. "Aconit".

1971. Allegiance to Free French Movement. 30th Anniv. French Naval Patrol Vessels.
495. **44.** 22 f. blk., green & blue 20 15
496. – 25 f. brn., grn.-bl. & bl. 25 20
497. – 50 f. blk., grn.-bl. & bl. 45 35
DESIGNS: 25 f. "Alysse". 50 f. "Mimosa".

45. Ship's Bell.

46. Haddock.

1971. St. Pierre Museum. Multicoloured.
498. 20 f. Type **45** 10 8
499. 45 f. Navigational instruments and charts (horiz.) 25 15

1971. De Gaulle. First Death Anniv. As Nos. 1937 and 1940 of France.
500. 35 f. black and red .. 20 10
501. 45 f. black and red .. 30 25

1972. Ocean Fish.
502. **46.** 2 f. red and blue .. 5 5
503. – 3 f. brown and green .. 5 5
504. – 5 f. red and blue .. 5 5
505. – 10 f. grn. and emerald 5 5
DESIGNS: 3 f. Dab. 5 f. Sea perch. 10 f. Cod.

47. De Gaulle and Servicemen.

1972. Air. General De Gaulle Commem.
506. **47.** 100 f. brn., grn. & pur. 55 30

48. Long-tailed Ducks. 50. Swimming Pool.

49. Montcalm and Ships.

1973. Currency Revaluation.
507. **48.** 6 c. brn., pur. & blue (post.) 5 5
508. – 10 c. blk., red & blue .. 5 5
509. – 20 c. brn., ultram. & blue 5 5
510. **48.** 40 c. brn., grn. & violet 8 5
511. – 70 c. blk., red & gr en.. 15 5
512. – 90 c. brn., pur. & blue.. 20 10
513. **49.** 1 f. 60 violet, indigo and blue (air) 25 15
514. – 2 f. pur., green & violet 30 20
515. – 4 f. green, mauve & brn. 60 50
DESIGNS—As T **48**, 10 c., 70 c. Puffins. 20 c., 90 c. Snowy owls. As T **49**. HORIZ. 4 f. La Salle, map and ships. VERT. 2 f. Frontenac and various scenes.

1973. St. Pierre Cultural Centre. Inaug.
521. **50.** 60 c. brn., blue and red 10 5
522. – 1 f. purple, orge. and blue 20 10
DESIGN: 1 f. Centre building.

51. "Transall C-160" in flight.

1973. Air.
523. **51.** 10 f. multicoloured .. 1·75 1·00

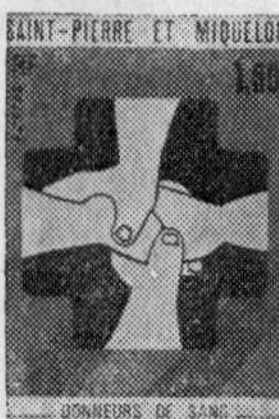

52. Met. Balloon and Weather Ship.

54. Clasped Hands on Red Cross.

53. Gull with Letter.

1974. World Meteorological Day.
524. **52.** 1 f. 60 blue, green & red 30 20

1974. Universal Postal Union. Centenary.
525. **53.** 70 c. ultram., blue & brn. 15 8
526. 90 c. blue, red & brown 20 10

1974. Campaign for Blood Donors.
527. **54.** 1 f. 50 multicoloured .. 30 15

55. Arms and Map of Islands.

1974. Air.
528. **55.** 2 f. multicoloured .. 40 25

56. Banknotes in "Fish" Money-box. **57.** Copernicus and Famous Scientists.

1974. St. Pierre Savings Bank. Centenary.
529. **56.** 50 c. brown, blue & black 10 5

1974. Air. Nicholas Copernicus (astronomer). 500th Birth Anniv. (1973).
530. **57.** 4 f. violet, red and blue 80 50

58. St. Pierre Church and Sea-gull.

1974. Island Churches.
531. **58.** 6 c. black, brn. & green 5 5
532. – 10 c. ind., blue & brown 5 5
533. – 20 c. multicoloured .. 5 5
DESIGNS: 10 c. Miquelon Church and fish. 20 c. Our Lady of the Seamen Church and fishermen.

59. " Vanessa atalanta ". **60.** Codfish and " Fisherman " Stamp of 1909.

1975. Butterflies. Multicoloured.
534. 1 f. Type **59** 20 10
535. 1 f. 20 " Danaus plexippus " 25 12

1975. Air. " Arphila 75 " International Stamp Exhibition, Paris.
536. **60.** 4 f. red, indigo and blue 90 45

61. " Pottery " – Potter's Wheel and Ware. **62.** Pointe-Plate Lighthouse and Sea-birds.

1975. Artisan Handicrafts.
537. **61.** 50 c. pur., brn. and grn. 10 5
538. – 60 c. blue and yellow .. 12 5
DESIGNS: 60 c. " Sculpture "—wood-carving of Virgin and Child.

1975. Lighthouses.
539. **62.** 6 c. black, violet & green 5 5
540. – 10 c. purple, green & slate 5 5
541. – 20 c. brn., indigo & blue 5 5
DESIGNS: 10 c. Galantry Lighthouse and auks. 20 c. Cap Blanc Lighthouse and dolphin.

MORE DETAILED LISTS

are given in the Stanley Gibbons Catalogues referred to in the country headings:

BC	British Commonwealth
E1, E2, E3	Europe 1, 2, 3
O1, O2, O3, O4	Overseas 1, 2, 3, 4

63. Judo.

1975. Air. " Pre-Olympic Year ". Olympic Games Montreal (1976).
542. **63.** 1 f. 90 blue, red & violet 40 20

64. " Concorde " in Flight.

1976. Air. " Concorde's " First Commercial Flight.
543. **64.** 10 f indigo, blue & red 2·25 1·10

1976. Pompidou Commemoration. As T **73** of French Polynesia.
544. 1 f. 10 grey and maroon .. 25 12

65. Alexander Graham Bell and Early Telephone.

1976. Air. Telephone Centenary.
545. **65.** 5 f. blue, orange and red 1·10 55

66. Washington and Lafayette.

1976. American Revolution. Bicent.
546. **66.** 1 f. multicoloured .. 25 12

67. Basketball.

1976. Olympic Games, Montreal.
547. **67.** 10 c. sepia, turq. & brn. 5 5
548. – 2 f. 50 turq., grn. & emer. 60 30
DESIGN—HORIZ. 2 f. 50 Swimming.

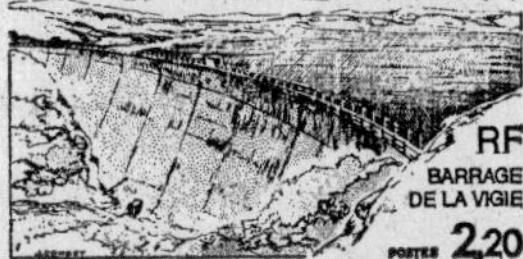

68. Vigie Dam.

1976.
549. **68.** 2 f. 20 brn., blue & turq. 50 25

69. " Croix de Lorraine."

1976. Fishing Vessels. Multicoloured.
550. 1 f. 20 Type **69** 30 15
551. 1 f. 40 " Geolette " .. 35 20

PARCEL POST STAMPS

1901. Optd. **COLIS POSTAUX.**
P 79. D. 10 c. black on lilac .. 6·50 6·50

1901. Optd. **Colis Postaux.**
P 80. D. 10 c. red .. .. 1·60 1·60

1917. Nos. 83 and 85 optd. **Colis Postaux.**
P 109. **1.** 10 c. red 25 25
P 110. 20 c. purple and brown 12 12

1941. Free French Plebiscite. No. P 110 optd. **Noel 1941. FRANCE LIBRE F. N. F. L.**
P 303. **1.** 20 c. purple and brown 65·00 65·00

POSTAGE DUE STAMPS

1892. Postage Due stamps of French Colonies optd. **ST-PIERRE M-on.**
D 60. **D 1.** 5 c. black .. .. 5·50 5·00
D 61. 10 c. black .. .. 2·25 2·25
D 62. 15 c. black .. .. 2·00 2·00
D 63. 20 c. black .. .. 1·90 1·90
D 64. 30 c. black .. .. 1·90 1·90
D 65. 40 c. black .. .. 1·10 1·10
D 66. 60 c. black .. .. 8·50 8·50
D 67. 1 f. brown .. .. 16·00 16·00
D 68. 2 f. brown .. .. 16·00 16·00

1925. Postage Due type of France. Optd. **SAINT - PIERRE - ET - MIQUELON** or surch. also **centimes a percevoir and** value in figures.
D 135. **D 2.** 5 c. blue 5 5
D 136. 10 c. brown 5 5
D 137. 20 c. olive 5 5
D 138. 25 c. red 5 5
D 139. 30 c. red 5 5
D 140. 45 c. green 5 5
D 141. 50 c. claret 20 20
D 142. 60 c. on 50 c. brown 12 12
D 143. 1 f. claret 15 15
D 144. 2 f. on 1 f. red .. 25 25
D 145. 3 f. mauve 90 90

D 1. Newfoundland Dog. **D 2.** Codfish.

1932.
D 163. **D 1.** 5 c. black and blue 10 10
D 164. 10 c. black & green 10 10
D 165. 20 c. black and red 15 15
D 166. 25 c. black and purple 15 15
D 167. 30 c. black & orange 35 35
D 168. 45 c. black and blue 45 45
D 169. 50 c. black and green 60 60
D 170. 60 c. black and red 75 75
D 171. 1 f. black and brown 1·50 1·50
D 172. 2 f. black and purple 2·75 2·75
D 173. 3 f. black and brown 3·00 3·00

1938.
D 208. **D 2.** 5 c. black 5 5
D 209. 10 c. purple .. 5 5
D 210. 15 c. green 5 5
D 211. 20 c. blue 5 5
D 212. 30 c. red 5 5
D 213. 50 c. green 5 5
D 214. 60 c. blue 5 5
D 215. 1 f. red 5 5
D 216. 2 f. brown 30 30
D 217. 3 f. violet 30 30

1941. Free French Plebiscite. Nos. D 208/17 optd. **NOEL 1941 F N F L.**
D 235. **D 2.** 5 c. black .. .. 2·25 2·25
D 236. 10 c. purple .. 2·25 2·25
D 237. 15 c. green .. .. 2·25 2·25
D 238. 20 c. blue .. .. 2·25 2·25
D 239. **D 2.** 30 c. red .. .. 2·25 2·25
D 240. 50 c. green .. .. 2·75 2·75
D 241. 60 c. blue .. .. 5·50 5·50
D 242. 1 f. red .. .. 8·00 8·00
D 243. 2 f. brown .. .. 8·00 8·00
D 244. 3 f. violet .. .. 8·00 8·00

1941. Postage Due stamps of 1932 optd. **Noel 1941 FRANCE LIBRE F. N. F. L.** or surch also.
D 298. **D 1.** 25 c. blk. & pur. .. 28·00 28·00
D 299. 30 c. blk. & orange 28·00 28·00
D 300. 50 c. blk. & green .. 95·00 95·00
D 301. 2 f. blk. & purple .. 2·75 2·75
D 302. 3 f. on 2 f. blk. & pur. 1·60 1·60

1941. Free French Plebiscite. Nos. D 208/17 optd. **FRANCE LIBRE F. N. F. L.**
D 310. **D 2.** 5 c. black .. .. 2·25 2·25
D 311. 10 c. purple 40 40
D 312. 15 c. green .. 40 40
D 313. 20 c. blue .. 40 40
D 314. 30 c. red .. 40 40
D 315. 50 c. green .. 40 40
D 316. 60 c. blue .. 40 40
D 317. 1 f. red .. 50 50
D 318. 2 f. brown .. 50 50
D 319. 3 f. violet .. .. 42·00 42·00

D 3. **D 4.** Newfoundland Dog and Shipwreck Scene.

1947.
D 385. **D 3.** 10 c. orange .. 5 5
D 386. 30 c. blue 5 5
D 387. 50 c. green 5 5
D 388. 1 f. red 5 5
D 389. 2 f. green 5 5
D 390. 3 f. violet 5 5
D 391. 4 f. brown 5 5
D 392. 5 f. green 5 5
D 393. 10 f. black 5 5
D 394. 20 f. red 12 12

1973.
D 516. **D 4.** 2 c. black and brown 5 5
D 517. 10 c. black and violet 5 5
D 518. 20 c. black and blue 5 5
D 519. 30 c. black and brown 8 8
D 520. 1 f. black and blue 30 30

ST. THOMAS AND PRINCE IS. O4

Two islands in the Gulf of Guinea off the West coast of Africa which became independent of Portugal in 1975.

1870. " Crown " key-type inscr. " S. THOME E PRINCIPE ".
17. **P.** 5 r. black 70 60
9. 10 r. orange .. .. 3·25 2·50
29. 10 r. green .. .. 1·75 1·25
20. 20 r. olive 80 70

30. **P.** 20 r. red 70 65
11b. 25 r. red 50 35
31. 25 r. lilac 35 25
12. 40 r. blue .. .. 1·60 1·40
32. 40 r. yellow .. .. 1·40 1·25
5. 50 r. green .. .. 5·00 3·25
33. 50 r. blue 60 50
26. 100 r. lilac .. .. 2·10 1·90
15. 200 r. orange .. .. 2·40 2·00
27. 300 r. brown .. .. 2·50 2·25

1887. " Embossed " key-type inscr. " S. THOME E PRINCIPE ".
41. **Q.** 5 r. black .. .. 1·10 70
42. 10 r. green .. .. 1·10 70
43. 20 r. red .. .. 1·25 1·00
44. 25 r. mauve 80 40
45. 40 r. brown .. .. 1·25 1·00
40. 50 r. blue .. .. 1·25 70
47. 100 r. brown .. .. 1·10 70
48. 200 r. lilac .. .. 4·00 3·25
49. 300 r. orange .. .. 3·50 3·25

1889. Stamps of 1887 surch.
50. **Q.** 5 r. on 10 r. green .. 5·00 4·00
51. 5 r. on 20 r. red .. .. 5·00 4·00
52. 50 r. on 40 r. brown .. 20·00 15·00

1895. " Figures " key-type inscr. " S. THOME E PRINCIPE ".
60. **R.** 5 r. yellow 30 25
61. 10 r. mauve 40 40
53. 15 r. brown 60 40
54. 20 r. lilac 60 40
62. 25 r. green 60 15
63. 50 r. blue 60 15

55. R. 75 r. red 1·40 1·10
64. 80 r. green 2·50 2·40
56. 100 r. brown on buff 1·25 1·00
57. 150 r. red on rose 1·75 1·60
58. 200 r. blue on blue 2·40 2·00
59. 300 r. blue on brown 2·75 2·40

1898. "King Carlos" key-type inscr. "S. THOME E PRINCIPE".
66. S. 2½ r. grey 12 10
67. 5 r. orange 12 10
68. 10 r. green 15 12
69. 15 r. brown 40 35
113. 15 r. green 40 20
70. 20 r. lilac 20 15
71. 25 r. green 20 15
114. 25 r. red 40 20
72. 50 r. blue 25 15
115. 50 r. brown 1·00 75
116. 65 r. blue 2·10 1·50
73. 75 r. red 2·10 1·10
117. 75 r. purple 60 45
74. 80 r. mauve 1·10 1·00
75. 100 r. blue on blue 60 40
118. 115 r. brown on pink 1·60 1·40
119. 130 r. brown on yellow 1·60 1·40
76. 150 r. brown on yellow 80 60
77. 200 r. purple on pink 1·10 50
78. 300 r. blue on pink 1·10 1·10
120. 400 r. blue on yellow 2·40 2·00
79. 500 r. black on blue 1·60 1·10
80. 700 r. mauve on yellow 2·50 1·60

1902. Surch. with new value.
121. S. 50 r. on 65 r. blue 80 60
85. R. 65 r. on 5 r. yellow 1·10 1·00
86. 65 r. on 10 r. mauve 1·10 1·00
87. 65 r. on 15 r. brown 1·10 1·00
88. Q. 65 r. on 20 r. red 1·10 1·00
81. R. 65 r. on 20 r. lilac 1·10 1·00
83. Q. 65 r. on 25 r. mauve 1·25 1·10
84. 65 r. on 100 r. brown 1·25 1·10
90. 115 r. on 10 r. green 1·10 1·00
92. R. 115 r. on 25 r. green 1·10 1·00
89. P. 115 r. on 50 r. green 1·50 1·40
93. R. 115 r. on 150 r. red on rose 1·10 1·00
94. 115 r. on 200 r. blue on bl. 1·10 1·00
91. Q. 115 r. on 300 r. orange 1·10 1·00
95. 130 r. on 5 r. black 1·60 1·50
98. R. 130 r. on 75 r. red 1·25 1·10
99. 130 r. on 100 r. brn. on buff 1·60 1·50
97. Q. 130 r. on 200 r. lilac 1·10 1·00
100. R. 130 r. on 300 r. blue on brown 1·10 1·00
108. V. 400 r. on 2½ r. brown 25 25
101. P. 400 r. on 10 r. orange 7·00 5·00
102. Q. 400 r. on 40 r. brown 3·50 2·75
103. 400 r. on 50 r. blue 4·00 3·50
105. R. 400 r. on 50 r. blue 25 25
107. 400 r. on 80 r. green 25 25

1903. Stamps of 1898 optd. **PROVISORIO.**
109. S. 15 r. brown 40 30
110. 25 r. green 40 30
111. 50 r. blue 45 25
112. 75 r. red 1·25 1·00

1911. Stamps of 1898 optd. **REPUBLICA.**
122. S. 2½ r. grey 12 10
123. 5 r. orange 12 10
124. 10 r. green 12 10
125. 15 r. green 12 10
126. 20 r. lilac 12 10
127. 25 r. red 15 10
128. 50 r. brown 12 8
129. 75 r. purple 12 10
130. 100 r. blue on blue 15 10
131. 115 r. brown on pink 20 15
132. 130 r. brown on yellow 20 15
133. 200 r. purple on pink 1·10 80
134. 400 r. blue on yellow 40 30
135. 500 r. black on blue 40 30
136. 700 r. mauve on yellow 40 30

1912. "King Manoel" key-type inscr. "S. THOME E. PRINCIPE" and optd. **REPUBLICA.**
137. T. 2½ r. lilac 10 8
138. 5 r. black 12 8
139. 10 r. green 12 8
140. 20 r. red 20 12
141. 25 r. brown 15 12
142. 50 r. blue 15 12
143. 75 r. brown 15 12
144. 100 r. brown on green 15 12
145. 200 r. green on pink 40 25
146. 300 r. black on blue 40 30

1913. Nos. 109 and 111/2 optd. **REPUBLICA.**
185. S. 15 r. brown 40 30
186. 50 r. blue 45 35
272. 75 r. red 1·40 1·10

1913. Stamps of 1902 optd. **REPUBLICA.**
244. S. 50 r. on 65 r blue 75 60
188. Q. 115 r. on 10 r. green 80 65
246. R. 115 r. on 25 r. green 15 15
164. P. 115 r. on 50 r. green 14·00 12·00
247. R. 115 r. on 150 r. red on rose 15 15
248. 115 r. on 200 r. blue on blue 15 15
249. Q. 115 r. on 300 r. orange 80 65
250. 130 r. on 5 r. black 1·25 1·00
251. R. 130 r. on 75 r. red 50 50
252. 130 r. on 100 r. brown on buff 50 50
253. Q. 130 r. on 200 r. lilac 50 50
254. R. 130 r. on 300 r. blue on brown 25 20
197. V. 400 r. on 2½ r. brown 70 65
168. Q. 400 r. on 50 r. blue 8·50 6·50
169. R. 400 r. on 50 r. blue 1·10 80
202. 400 r. on 80 r. green 80 70

1913. Surch. **REPUBLICA S. TOME E PRINCIPE** and new value on "Vasco da Gama" stamps of

(a) **Portuguese Colonies.**
203. ¼ c. on 2½ r. green 40 30
204. ½ c. on 5 r. red 40 30
205. 1 c. on 10 r. purple 40 30
206. 2½ c. on 25 r. green 40 30
207. 5 c. on 50 r. blue 40 30
208. 7½ c. on 75 r. brown 60 50
209. 10 c. on 100 r. brown 40 30
210. 15 c. on 150 r. yellow-brown 40 30

(b) **Macao.**
211. ¼ c. on ½ c. green 60 45
212. ½ c. on 1 a. red 60 45
213. 1 c. on 2 a. purple 60 45
124. 2½ c. on 4 a. green 60 45
215. 5 c. on 8 a. blue 60 45
216. 7½ c. on 12 a. brown 80 70
217. 10 c. on 16 a. brown 60 45
218. 15 c. on 24 a. yellow-brown 60 45

(c) **Timor.**
219. ¼ c. on ½ a. green 60 45
220. ½ c. on 1 a. red 60 45
221. 1 c. on 2 a. purple 60 45
222. 2½ c. on 4 a. green 60 45
223. 5 c. on 8 a. blue 75 60
224. 7½ c. on 12 a. brown 75 60
225. 10 c. on 16 a. brown 60 40
226. 15 c. on 24 a. yellow-brown 60 40

1914. "Ceres" key-type inscr. "S. TOME E PRINCIPE".
280a. U. ¼ c. olive 5 5
281. ½ c. black 5 5
282. 1 c. green 5 5
283. 1½ c. brown 5 5
284. 2 c. red 5 5
285. 2 c. grey 8 8
286. 2½ c. violet 5 5
287. 3 c. orange 10 8
288. 4 c. claret 10 8
289. 4½ c. grey 10 8
290. 5 c. blue 5 5
291. 6 c. mauve 10 8
292. 7 c. blue 10 8
293. 7½ c. brown 8 5
294. 8 c. grey 8 5
295. 10 c. brown 5 5
296. 12 c. green 12 10
297. 15 c. claret 8 5
298. 20 c. green 10 8
299. 24 c. blue 20 20
300. 25 c. brown 20 20
239. 30 c. brown on green 40 35
301. 30 c. green 12 10
240. 40 c. brown on rose 40 35
302. 40 c. blue 12 10
241. 50 c. orange on pink 1·10 90
303. 50 c. mauve 12 10
304. 60 c. blue 12 10
305. 60 c. pink 20 12
306. 80 c. red 20 12
242. 1 e. green on blue 90 75
307. 1 e. pink 25 15
308. 1 e. blue 25 15
309. 2 e. purple 50 25
310. 5 e. brown 1·75 1·25
311. 10 e. pink 4·00 2·75
312. 20 e. green 8·50 4·50

1919. "King Carlos" key-type of St. Thomas and Prince Islands surch. **PROVISORIO** and **REPUBLICA** and new value.
255. S. 2½ r. on 15 r. brown 15 12

1919. "King Carlos" key-type of St. Thomas and Prince Islands surch. **REPUBLICA** and new value.
256. S. ½ c. on 2½ r. grey 1·25 1·10
257. 1 c. on 2½ r. grey 70 55
258. 2½ c. on 2½ r. grey 25 20

1919. "Ceres" key-types of St. Thomas and Prince Islands surch.
259. U. ½ c. on ¼ c. olive 50 45
260. 2 c. on ¼ c. olive 50 45
261. 2½ c. on ¼ c. olive 1·90 1·50

1919. "Ceres" key-type of St. Thomas and Prince Islands surch. **$04 Centavos** and with old value blocked out.
262. U. 4 c. on 2½ c. violet 15 12

1923. Stamps of 1913 surch. **REPUBLICA DEZ CENTAVOS** and bars.
313. R. 10 c. on 115 r. on 24 r. green 12 12
314. 10 c. on 115 r. on 150 r. red on rose 12 12
316. 10 c. on 115 r. on 200 r. blue on blue 20 12
317. R. 10 c. on 130 r. on 75 r. red 12 12
318. 10 c. on 130 r. on 100 r. brown on buff 12 12
319. 10 c. on 130 r. on 300 r. blue on brown 12 12

1925. Stamps of 1902 surch **Republica 40 C.** and bars over original surcharge.
321. V. 40 c. on 400 r. on 2½ r. brn 15 12
322. R. 40 c. on 400 r. on 80 r. grn. 15 12

1931. Nos. 307 and 309 surch.
323. U. 70 c. on 1 e. pink 35 25
324. 1 e. 40 on 2 e. purple 40 35

1934. As T 2 of Angola (new "Ceres" type).
325. 2. 1 c. brown 5 5
326. 5 c. sepia 5 5
327. 10 c. mauve 5 5
328. 15 c. black 8 5
329. 20 c. grey 8 5
330. 30 c. green 5 5
331. 40 c. red 10 5
332. 45 c. blue 12 10
333. 50 c. brown 10 8
334. 60 c. olive 12 10
335. 70 c. brown 12 10
336. 80 c. green 12 10
337. 85 c. red 50 40
338. 1 e. claret 12 10
339. 1 e. 40 blue 40 20
340. 2 e. mauve 50 20
341. 5 e. green 1·60 70
342. 10 e. brown 2·50 1·40
343. 20 e. orange 5·00 2·75

1938. As T 3 and 8 of Angola, but inscr. "S. TOME".
344. 3. 1 c. olive (postage) 5 5
345. 5 c. brown 10 8
346. 10 c. red 10 8
347. 15 c. purple 10 8
348. 20 c. slate 10 8
349. – 30 c. purple 12 10
350. – 35 c. green 15 12
351. – 40 c. brown 15 12
352. – 50 c. mauve 15 12
353. – 60 c. black 15 12
354. – 70 c. violet 15 12
355. – 80 c. orange 15 12
356. – 1 e. red 25 20
357. – 1 e. 75 blue 60 30
358. – 2 e. red 3·00 2·40
359. – 5 e. olive 2·00 1·50
360. – 10 e. blue 3·00 2·00
361. – 20 e. brown 4·25 2·50

362. 8. 10 c. red (air) 20·00 17·00
363. 20 c. violet 14·00 13·00
364. 50 c. orange 1·10 90
365. 1 e. blue 1·60 1·50
366. 2 e. red 2·40 2·25
367. 3 e. green 2·75 2·75
368. 5 e. brown 5·00 4·50
369. 9 e. red 5·00 4·50
370. 10 e. mauve 5·00 4·50

1938. President's Colonial Tour. As T 9 of Angola.
371. 9. 80 c. green 80 70
372. 1 e. 75 blue 2·10 1·40
373. 20 e. brown 12·00 8·00

1939. As T 3 and 8 of Angola, but inscr. "S. TOME e PRINCIPE".
374. 3. 1 c. olive (postage) 5 5
375. 5 c. brown 5 5
376. 10 c. red 8 8
377. 15 c. purple 10 8
378. 20 c. slate 10 8
379. – 30 c. purple 15 12
380. – 35 c. green 15 12
381. – 40 c. brown 15 12
382. – 50 c. mauve 15 12
383. – 60 c. black 15 12
384. – 70 c. violet 15 12
385. – 80 c. orange 15 12
386. – 1 e. red 25 15
387. – 1 e. 75 blue 35 15
388. – 2 e. red 40 30
389. – 5 e. olive 1·25 80
390. – 10 e. blue 2·00 1·00
391. – 20 e. brown 3·25 1·50

392. 8. 10 c. red (air) 15 12
393. 20 c. violet 15 12
394. 50 c. orange 15 12
395. 1 e. blue 15 12
396. 2 e. red 50 30
397. 3 e. green 60 40
398. 5 e. brown 1·10 1·00
399. 9 e. red 2·00 1·50
400. 10 e. mauve 2·00 1·50

1. Cola Nuts. 2. Doctor examining Patients.

1948. Fruits.
401. 1. 5 c. black and yellow 20 15
402. – 10 c. black and salmon 20 15
403. – 30 c. black and grey 1·00 75
404. – 50 c. brown and yellow 1·10 75
405. – 1 e. red 1·75 1·10
406. – 1 e. 75 blue and grey 3·00 2·00
407. – 2 e. black and green 2·00 1·10
408. – 5 e. brown and mauve 6·00 4·25
409. – 10 e. black and mauve 8·00 7·00
410. – 20 e. black and grey 19·00 15·00
DESIGNS: 10 c. Bread-fruit. 30 c. Custard-apple. 50 c. Cocoa. 1 e. Coffee. 1 e. 75, Bunch of dendem. 2 e. Abacate. 5 e. Pineapple. 10 e. Mango. 20 e. Coconuts.

1948. Honouring the Statue of Our Lady of Fatima. As T 13 of Angola.
411. 50 c. violet 2·50 2·00

1949. U.P.U. 75th Anniv. As T 18 of Angola.
412. 3 e. 50 black 4·25 3·00

1950. Holy Year. As T 20/1 of Angola.
413. 2 e. 50 blue 1·40 1·00
414. 4 e. orange 2·50 1·75

1951. Holy Year. As T 23 of Angola.
415. 4 e. indigo and blue 1·00 50

1952. 1st Tropical Medicine Congress, Lisbon.
416. 2. 10 c. blue and chocolate 12 10

3. J. de Santarem. 4. Cloisters Monastery.

1952. Portuguese Navigators. Multicoloured centres. Frame colours given below.
417. 3. 10 c. brown on flesh 5 5
418. – 30 c. green on green 5 5
419. – 50 c. grey on grey 5 5
420. – 1 e. blue on blue 5 5
421. – 2 e. maroon on purple 8 5
422. – 3 e. 50 sepia on brown 12 8
PORTRAITS: 30 c. P. Escobar. 50 c. F. de Po. 2 e. A. Esteves. 2 e. L. Goncalves. 3 e. 50, M. Fernandes.

1953. Missionary Art Exhibition.
423. 4. 10 c. sepia and green 5 5
424. 50 c. brown and orange 10 8
425. 3 e. indigo and blue 35 20

1953. Cent. of First Portuguese Postage Stamps. As T 27 of Angola.
426. 50 c. blue, chest. & orange 30 15

1954. Presidential Visit. As T 29 of Angola.
427. 15 c. indigo, red, green, blue and black 10 8
428. 5 e. brown, red and green 40 35

1954. 4th Cent. of Sao Paulo. As T 28 of Angola.
429. 2 e. 50 black, blue and slate 20 12

1958. Brussels Int. Exn. As T 34 of Angola.
430. 2 e. 50 c. multicoloured 30 10

1958. 6th Int. Congress of Tropical Medicines. As T 35 of Angola.
431. 5 e. green, yell., sep., brn. and olive 1·00 55
DESIGN: 5 e. "Cassia occidentalis" (plant).

5. Points of Compass. 6. "Religion" (village church).

1960. Prince Henry the Navigator. 500th Death Anniv.
432. 5. 10 e. multicoloured 40 20

1960. African Technical Co-operation Commission. 10th Anniv.
433. 6. 1 e. 50 multicoloured 20 12

1962. Sports. As T 41 of Angola. Multicoloured.
434. 50 c. Fishing 5 5
435. 1 e. Gymnastics 12 5
436. 1 e. 50 Handball 5 5
437. 2 e. Yachting 8 5
438. 2 e. 50 Running 20 10
439. 20 e. Skin-diving 80 40

1962. Malaria Eradication. Mosquito design as T 42 of Angola. Multicoloured.
440. 2 e. 50 "A. gambiae" .. 35 20

1963. T.A.P. Airline. 10th Anniv. As T 48 of Angola.
441. 1 e. 50 multicoloured .. 15 12

1964. National Overseas Bank Centenary. As Angola T 50 but portrait of F. de O. Chamico.
442. 2 e. 50 multicoloured .. 20 12

1965. I.T.U. Cent. As T 52 of Angola.
443. 2 e. 50 multicoloured .. 60 25

7. Infantry Officer 1788. 8. Pero Escobar and Joao de Santarem.

1965. Portuguese Military Uniforms. Multicoloured.
444. 20 c. Type 7 .. .. 8 8
445. 35 c. Infantry sergeant, 1788 8 8
446. 40 c. Infantry corporal, 1788 12 12
447. 1 e. Infantryman, 1788 .. 45 20
448. 2 e. 50 Artillery officer, 1806 45 25
449. 5 e. Light Infantryman, 1811 90 50
450. 7 e. 50 Infantry sapper, 1833 1·10 90
451. 10 e. Lancers officer, 1834 1·40 1·10

1966. National Revolution. 40th Anniv. As T 56 of Angola, but showing different building. Multicoloured.
452. 4 e. Arts and Crafts School and Anti-T.B. Clinic .. 15 10

1967. Military Naval Assn. Cent. As T 58 of Angola. Multicoloured.
453. 1 e. 50 C. Rodrigues and corvette "Vasco da Gama" 12 12
454. 2 e. 50 A. Kopke, microscope and "Glossina palalis" (insect) 20 12

1967. Fatima Apparitions. 50th Anniv. As T 59 of Angola.
455. 2 e. 50 multicoloured .. 12 5
DESIGN: 2 e. 50, Apparition appearing to children and Valinhos Monument.

1968. Pedro Cabral (explorer). 500th Birth Anniv. As T 63 of Angola. Multicoloured.
456. 1 e. 50 Medal of the Jeronimos' Monastery (vert.) .. 15 8

1969. Admiral Gago Coutinho. Birth Cent. As T 65 of Angola. Multicoloured.
457. 2 e. Island route-map and monument (vert.) .. 20 8

1969. Vasco da Gama (explorer). 500th Birth Anniv. As T 66 of Angola. Multicoloured.
458. 2 e. 50 Da Gama's fleet, and fireship (vert.) .. 10 8

1969. Overseas Administrative Reforms. Cent. As T 67 of Angola.
459. 2 e. 50 multicoloured .. 10 8

1969. Manoel I. 500th Birth Anniv. As T 68 of Angola. Multicoloured.
460. 4 e. Manoel Gate, Guarda See 15 8

1969. Discovery of St. Thomas and Prince Islands. 500th Anniv.
461. 8. 2 e. 50 multicoloured .. 10 5

9. President A. Tomas. 10. Stamps on Coffee Plant.

1970. Presidential Visit.
462. 9. 2 e. 50 multicoloured .. 10 5

1970. Marshal Carmona. Birth Cent. Multicoloured as T 70 of Angola.
463. 5 e. Portrait in Marshal's uniform .. 20 10

1970. Stamp Centenary. Multicoloured.
464. 1 e. Type 10 .. .. 8 5
465. 1 e. 50 G.P.O. St. Thomas (horiz.) .. 12 5
466. 2 e. 50 Se Cathedral, St. Thomas .. 25 8

11. "Descent from the Cross" and Ship at St. Thomas. 12. Running and Throwing the Javelin.

1972. Camoens' "Lusaid". 400th Anniv.
467. 11. 20 e. multicoloured .. 85 45

1972. Olympic Games, Munich.
468. 12. 1 e. 50 multicoloured .. 8 5

13. Seaplane "Lusitania" and Warship off Rock of Sao Pedro.

1972. 1st Flight, Lisbon-Rio de Janeiro. 50th Anniv.
469. 13. 2 e. 50 multicoloured .. 10 5

1973. World Meteorological Organization. Centenary. As Type 77 of Angola.
470. 5 e. multicoloured .. 20 8

14. Flags of Portugal and St. Thomas and Prince.

1975. Argel Agreement. First Anniv.
471. 14. 3 e. multicoloured .. 20 20
472. 10 e. multicoloured .. 60 60
473. 20 e. multicoloured .. 1·25 1·25
474. 50 e. multicoloured .. 3·00 3·00

15. Erecting Flag.

1975. Independence Proclamation.
475. 15. 1 e. 50 multicoloured .. 8 8
476. 4 e. multicoloured .. 25 25
477. 7 e. 50 multicoloured .. 45 45
478. 20 e. multicoloured .. 1·25 1·25
479. 50 e. multicoloured .. 3·00 3·00

16. Diagram and Hand.

1976. National Restoration Fund.
480. 16. 1 e. multicoloured .. 5 5
481. 1 e. 50 multicoloured .. 8 8
482. 2 e. multicoloured .. 12 12

CHARITY TAX STAMPS

The notes under this heading in Portugal also apply here.

1925. Marquis de Pombal Commem. Stamps of Portugal, but inscr. "S. TOME E PRINCIPE".
C 323. C 4. 15 c. orange .. 15 12
C 324. – 15 c. orange .. 15 12
C 325. C 5. 15 c. orange .. 15 12

1946. Fiscal stamps as in Type C 1 of Portuguese Africa surch.
C 401. 50 c. on 1 e. green .. 2·00
C 402. 50 c. on 4 e. red .. 3·75
C 403. 1 e. on 4 e. red .. .. 3·75
C 404. 1 e. on 5 e. red .. .. 3·75
C 405. 1 e. on 6 e. green .. 2·00
C 406. 1 e. on 7 e. green .. 2·00
C 409. 1 e. on 10 e. red .. 3·75
C 410. 1 e. 50 on 7 e. green .. 2·40
C 411. 1 e. 50 on 8 e. green .. 3·00
C 412. 2 e. 50 on 7 c. green .. 2·00
C 413. 2 e. 50 on 9 e. green .. 2·00
C 414. 2 e. 50 on 10 e. green .. 2·00

C 1. Arms.

ILLUSTRATIONS
British Commonwealth and all overprints and surcharges are FULL SIZE. Foreign Countries have been reduced to ¾-LINEAR.

1948. Value in black.
C 415. C 1. 50 c. green 25 20
C 416. 1 e. red 50 30
C 417. 1 e. green 25 20
C 418. 1 e. 50 brown .. 50 30

1965. (a) Surch. **"um escudo 1 $00"** and two heavy bars.
C 452. C 1. 1 e. on 5 e. yellow .. 3·00 2·40

(b) Surch. **"Um escudo".**
C 453. C 1. 1 e. on 1 e. green .. 50 40

(c) as No. C 417 but inscr. "UM ESCUDO at foot, surch. **"1 $00".**
C 454. C 1. 1 e. on 1 e. green .. 30 30

(d) inscr. "Cinco escudos 5 $00" further surch. **"Um escudo 1 $00".**
C 455. C 1. 1 e. on 5 e. yellow .. 15 15

NEWSPAPER STAMPS

1892. Nos. 41/3 surch. 2½ **RS.**
N 53. Q. 2½ r. on 5 r. black .. 9·00 7·00
N 54. 2½ r. on 10 r. green .. 10·00 9·50
N 55. 2½ r. on 20 r. red .. 12·00 7·50

1893. "Newspaper" key-type inscr. "S. THOME E PRINCIPE".
N 59. V. 2½ r. brown 30 20

1899. No. N 59 optd. **PROVISORIO.**
N 81. V. 2½ r. brown .. 4·50 1·60

POSTAGE DUE STAMPS

1904. "Due" key-typed inscr. "S. THOME E PRINCIPE"
D 121. W. 5 r. green 30 25
D 122. 10 r. grey 40 35
D 123. 20 r. brown 40 35
D 124. 30 r. orange .. 40 35
D 125. 50 r. brown .. 70 70
D 126. 60 r. brown .. 80 70
D 127. 100 r. mauve .. 1·10 1·00
D 128. 130 r. blue .. 1·10 1·00
D 129. 200 r. red .. 1·60 1·25
D 130. 500 r. lilac .. 2·25 1·90

1911. As last optd. **REPUBLICA.**
D 137. W. 5 r. green .. 8 8
D 138. 10 r. grey .. 8 8
D 139. 20 r. brown .. 10 10
D 140. 30 r. orange .. 10 10
D 141. 50 r. brown .. 12 10
D 142. 60 r. brown .. 30 20
D 143. 100 r. mauve .. 30 20
D 144. 130 r. blue .. 30 20
D 145. 200 r. red .. 30 20
D 146. 500 r. lilac .. 50 40

1921. "Due" key-type inscr. "S. TOME E PRINCIPE" or "S. THOME E PRINCIPE". Currency changed.
D 313. W. ½ c. green 5 5
D 314. 1 c. grey 5 5
D 315. 2 c. brown .. 5 5
D 316. 3 c. orange .. 5 5
D 317. 5 c. brown .. 8 5
D 318. 6 c. brown .. 8 5
D 319. 10 c. mauve .. 8 5
D 320. 13 c. blue .. 8 5
D 321. 20 c. red .. 8 8
D 322. 50 c. lilac .. 12 12

1925. As Nos. C 323/5 optd. **MULTA.**
D 323. C 4. 30 c. orange .. 8 5
D 324. – 30 c. orange .. 8 5
D 325. C 5. 30 c. orange .. 8 5

1952. As Type D 1 of Macao, but inscr. "S. TOMÉ E PRINCIPE". Numerals in red, name in black.
D 417. 10 c. brown and yellow 5 5
D 418. 30 c. brown and blue .. 5 5
D 419. 50 c. blue and pink .. 5 5
D 420. 1 e. blue and olive .. 5 5
D 421. 2 e. green and orange .. 8 5
D 422. 5 e. brown and lilac .. 20 12

ST. VINCENT BC

One of the Windward Is., Br. W. Indies.

1949. 100 cents = 1 West Indian dollar.

1.

2.

3.

1861.
36. 1. ½d. orange .. .. 4·50 3·50
47. ½d. green 45 15
48b. 2. 1d. red 65 25
15. 1d. black .. .. 20·00 11·00
29. 1d. olive .. .. 35·00 7·00
39. 1d. drab .. .. 7·50 3·50
61. 2½d. blue .. .. 1·10 2·50
43. 4d. blue .. .. 80·00 9·00
56. 4d. yellow .. .. 80·00 1·40
51. 4d. brown .. .. 9·00 3·00
62. 5d. sepia .. .. 3·50 4·50
4. 6d. green .. .. 33·00 11·00
57. 6d. violet .. .. 1·10 1·90
11. 1s. grey .. .. £110 60·00
13. 1s. blue .. .. £170 55·00
14. 1s. brown .. .. £200 80·00
17. 1s. rose .. .. £325 70·00
58. 1s. orange .. .. 3·00 4·50
53a. 3. 5s. red .. .. 12·00 9·00

1880. Surch. in figures.
33. 2. ½d. on half 6d. green .. 70·00 70·00
28. 1d. on half 6d. green .. £150 £100

1881. Surch. in words
34. 2. 1d. on 6d. green .. £160 £120
63. 3d. on 1d. mauve .. 2·75 3·00
60a. 5d. on 6d. red .. 65 90

1881. Surch. in figures.
54. 2. 2½d. on 4d. brown .. 20·00 22·00
35. 4d. on 1s. orange .. £450 £325

1882. Surch. in figures and words.
40. 2. 2½d. on 1d. red .. 4·00 2·00
55a. 2½d. on 1d. blue .. 50 25
59. 5d. on 4d. brown .. 3·75 4·00

1885. No. 40 surch. **1d.** and bars.
46. 2. 1d. on 2½d. on 1d. red .. 5·00 5·50

4.

5. Seal of the Colony.

1899.
67. 4. ½d. mauve and green .. 25 30
68. 1d. mauve and red .. 1·25 45
69. 2½d. mauve and blue .. 1·60 3·25
70. 3d. mauve and green .. 2·25 2·25
71. 4d. mauve and orange .. 1·60 4·00
72. 5d. mauve and black .. 3·50 5·50
73. 6d. mauve and brown .. 5·00 7·00
74. 1s. green and red .. 9·00 11·00
75. 5s. green and blue .. 25·00 30·00

1902. As T 4, but portrait of King Edward VII.
85. ½d. purple and green .. 15 25
77. 1d. purple and red .. 25 10
78. 2d. purple and black .. 1·40 1·75
79. 2½d. purple and blue .. 2·25 2·50
80. 3d. purple and green .. 3·00 3·00
81. 6d. purple and brown .. 4·00 5·00
90. 1s. green and red .. 5·50 7·00
83. 2s. green and violet .. 12·00 15·00
91. 2s. purple & blue on blue 14·00 17·00
84. 5s. green and blue .. 22·00 25·00
92. 5s. green and red on yellow 19·00 22·00
93. £1 purple and black on red £170 £225

1907.
94. 5. ½d. green 20 25
95. 1d. red 70 45
96. 2d. orange .. .. 1·10 1·90
97. 2½d. blue .. .. .. 3·50 4·00
98. 3d. violet .. .. .. 4·50 7·00

6. Seal of the Colony. 7.

1909.
102. 6. ½d. green 30 35
103. 1d. red 15 15
104. 2d. grey 80 40
105. 2½d. blue .. .. .. 80 1·90
106. 3d. purple on yellow .. 1·10 1·40
107. 6d. purple .. .. 1·60 3·00
101. 1s. black on green .. 3·50 4·50
139. 2s. blue and purple .. 4·30 6·00
119. 5s. red and green .. 8·00 11·00
141. £1 mauve and black .. 50·00 65·00

1913.
131. 7. ½d. green 8 8
109. 1d. red 25 12
132b. 1½d. brown 20 20
133. 2d. grey 12 12
133a. 2½d. blue 25 30
135. 3d. purple on yellow .. 70 90
134. 3d. blue .. .. .. 1·40 2·00
113. 4d. red on yellow .. 45 1·10
136. 5d. green .. .. .. 85 1·75
115. 6d. claret .. .. 1·10 1·50
116. 1s. black on green .. 1·75 3·00
138. 1s. brown .. .. 1·10 2·00

1915. Surch. **ONE PENNY.**
121. 7. 1d. on 1s. black on green 1·10 4·00

1916. Optd. **WAR STAMP** in two lines.
124. 7. 1d. red 70 90

1916. Optd. **WAR STAMP** in one line.
128. 7. 1d. red 10 20

1935. Silver Jubilee. As T 11 of Antigua.
142. 1d. blue and red 15 20
143. 1½d. blue and grey .. 25 30
144. 2½d. brown and blue .. 80 1·00
145. 1s. grey and purple .. 2·00 3·00

1937. Coronation. As T 2 of Aden.
146. 1d. violet 8 8
147. 1½d. red 10 10
148. 2½d. blue 25 25

8. 9. Young's Island and Fort Duvernette.

1938.
149. 8. ½d. blue and green .. 10 8
150. 9. 1d. blue and brown .. 8 8
151. – 1½ d. green and red .. 8 8
152. 8. 2d. green and black .. 40 40
153. – 2½ d. black and green .. 8 8
153a. – 2½d. green and brown .. 8 8
154. 8. 3d. orange and purple .. 10 8
154a. – 3½d. blue and green .. 25 25
155. 8. 6d. black and red .. 30 25
156. – 1s. purple and green .. 50 30
157. 8. 2s. blue and purple .. 1·10 85
157a. 2s. 6d. brown and blue 1·10 1·90
158. 5s. red and green .. 1·90 2·50
158a. 10 s. violet and brown 3·50 3·50
159. £1 purple and black .. 7·00 7·00
DESIGNS—HORIZ. 1½d. Kingstown and Fort Charlotte. 2½d. (No. 153) and 3½d. Bathing Beach at Villa. 2½d. (No. 153a) and 1s. Victoria Park, Kingstown.

1946. Victory. As T 4 of Aden.
160. 1½d. red 8 8
161. 3½d. blue 8 8

1948. Silver Wedding. As T 5/6 of Aden.
162. 1½d. red 8 8
163. £1 mauve .. .. .. 7·00 9·00

1949. As 1938 issue, but values in cents and dollars.
164. 8. 1 c. blue and green .. 8 10
164a. 1 c. green and black .. 8 10
165. 9. 2 c. blue and brown .. 8 10
166. – 3 c. green and red .. 10 12
166a. 8. 3 c. orange and purple .. 8 10
167. 4 c. green and black .. 8 12
167a. 4 c. blue and green .. 8 10
168. – 5 c. green and brown .. 8 10
169. 8. 6 c. orange and purple .. 12 15
169a. – 6 c. green and red .. 8 10
170. – 7 c. black and blue .. 15 35
170a. – 10 c. black & blue-green 20 35
171. 8. 12 c. black and red .. 20 35
172. – 24 c. purple and green .. 40 55
173. 8. 48 c. blue and purple .. 80 1·50
174. 60 c. brown and blue .. 90 1·75
175. $1.20 red and green .. 3·50 4·00
176. $2.40 violet and brown 4·50 4·50
177. $4.80 purple and black 5·50 6·00
DESIGNS—HORIZ. 3 c. (No. 166), 6 c. (No. 169a) Kingstown and Fort Charlotte. 5 c., 24 c. Victoria Park, Kingstown. 7 c., 10 c. Bathing Beach at Villa.

1949. U.P.U As T 14/7 of Antigua.
178. 5 c. blue 12 12
179. 6 c. purple 12 12
180. 12 c. magenta 35 35
181. 24 c. green 60 70

1951. Inaug. of B.W.I. University College. As T 18/19 of Antigua.
182. 18. 3 c. green and red .. 12 8
183. 19. 12 c. black and purple 15 15

1951. New Constitution. Optd. **NEW CONSTITUTION 1951.**
184. – 3 c. green and red (No. 166) 25 30
185. 8. 4 c. green and black .. 25 30
186. – 5 c. grn. & brn. (No. 168) 20 30
187. 8. 12 c. black and red .. 20 35

1953. Coronation. As T 7 of Aden.
188. 4 c. black and green .. 25 30

10. 11.

1955.
189. 10. 1 c. orange 5 5
190. 2 c. blue 8 8
191. 3 c. grey 8 8
192. 4 c. brown 10 10
193. 5 c. red 12 15
194. 10 c. lilac 20 25
195. 15 c. blue 20 20
196. 20 c. green 30 35
197. 25 c. sepia 50 60
198. 11. 50 c. brown 80 90
199. $1 green .. .. 2·25 2·75
200. $2.50 blue .. .. 5·50 7·00

1958. British Caribbean Federation. As T 21 of Antigua.
201. 3 c. green 10 12
202. 6 c. blue 20 20
203. 12 c. red 30 30

1963. Freedom from Hunger. As T 10 of Aden.
204. 8 c. violet 80 65

1963. Red Cross Cent. As T 24 of Antigua.
205. 4 c. red and black .. 35 30
206. 8 c. red and blue .. 85 75

12. Scout Badge and Proficiency Badges. 13. Doric Temple and Pond.

1964. St. Vincent Boy Scouts Assn. 50th Anniv.
221. 12. 1 c. green and brown .. 5 5
222. 4 c. blue and purple .. 10 10
223. 20 c. yellow and violet .. 25 25
224. 50 c. red and green .. 60 60

1965. Botanic Gardens. Bicent. Multicoloured.
225. 1 c. Tropical Fruits .. 5 5
226. 4 c. Breadfruit and the "Providence" .. 8 8
227. 25 c. Type 13 .. 30 30
228. 40 c. Talipot Palm and Doric Temple .. 60 55

1965. I.T.U. Cent. As T 26 of Antigua.
229. 4 c. blue and green .. 10 12
230. 48 c. ochre and orange .. 80 75

14. Boat-building, Bequia (inscr. "BEQUIA").

1965. Multicoloured.
231. 1 c. Type 14 .. .. 5 5
231a. 1 c. Type 14 (inscr. "BEQUIA") .. 10 10
232. 2 c. Friendship Beach, Bequia 5 5
233. 3 c. Terminal Building, Arnos Vale Airport .. 5 5
261. 4 c. Woman with Bananas 15 15
235. 5 c. Crater Lake .. 8 8
236. 6 c. Carib Stone .. 8 8
237. 8 c. Arrowroot .. 8 8
238. 10 c. Owia Salt Pond .. 10 10
239. 12 c. Deep Water Wharf .. 12 12
240. 20 c. Sea Island Cotton .. 20 20
241. 25 c. Map of St. Vincent and Islands .. 25 25
242. 50 c. Breadfruit .. 50 50
243. $1 Baleine Falls .. 1·00 1·00
244. $2.50 St. Vincent Parrot .. 2·25 2·25
245. $5 Arms of St. Vincent .. 3·75 4·00
Nos. 261, 236/7 and 240/5 vert.

1966. Churchill Commem. As T 28 of Antigua.
246. 1 c. blue 5 5
247. 4 c. green 8 8
248. 20 c. brown 35 35
249. 40 c. violet 65 60

1966. Royal Visit. As T 29 of Antigua.
250. 4 c. black and blue .. 8 8
251. 25 c. black and magenta .. 60 50

1966. W.H.O. Headquarters, Geneva. Inaug. As T 31 of Antigua.
252. 4 c. black, green and blue .. 8 8
253. 25 c. black, purple & ochre 60 55

1966. U.N.E.S.C.O. 20th Anniv. As T 33/5 of Antigua.
254. 4 c. violet, red, yell. & orge. 8 8
255. 8 c. yellow, violet & olive 20 20
256. 25 c. black, purple & orge. 55 55

15. Coastal View of Mount Coke Area.

1967. Autonomous Methodist Church. Multicoloured.
257. 2 c. Type 15 .. .. 5 5
258. 8 c. Kingstown Methodist Church 8 8
259. 25 c. First Licence to perform Marriages .. 20 20
260. 35 c. Conference Arms .. 35 30

16. Meteorological Institute.

1968. World Meteorological Day.
262. 16. 4 c. multicoloured .. 5 5
263. 25 c. multicoloured .. 25 25
264. 35 c. multicoloured .. 30 30

17. Martin Luther King and Cotton Pickers.

1968. Dr. Martin Luther King Commem.
265. 17. 5 c. multicoloured .. 8 8
266. 25 c. multicoloured .. 25 25
267. 35 c. multicoloured .. 35 25

18. Speaker addressing Demonstrators.

1968. Human Rights Year.
268. 18. 3 c. multicoloured .. 5 5
269. – 35 c. blue 30 35
DESIGN: 35 c. Scales of Justice and Human Rights Emblem.

19. Male Masquerader.

1969. St. Vincent Carnival.
270. 19. 1 c. multicoloured .. 5 5
271. – 5 c. red and brown .. 8 8
272. – 8 c. multicoloured .. 12 12
273. – 25 c. multicoloured .. 35 35
DESIGNS: 5 c. Steel Bandsman. 8 c. Carnival Revellers. 25 c. Queen of Bands.

1969. Methodist Conf. Nos. 241, 257/8 and 260 optd. **METHODIST CONFERENCE MAY 1969.**
274. 15. 2 c. multicoloured .. 8 8
275. – 8 c. multicoloured .. 15 15
276. – 25 c. multicoloured .. 40 40
277. – 35 c. multicoloured .. 5·00 4·25

20. "Strength in Unity".

1969. "CARIFTA". 1st Anniv.
278. 20. 2 c. black, buff and red 5 5
279. – 5 c. multicoloured .. 5 5
280. 20. 8 c. black, buff & green 10 10
281. – 25 c. multicoloured .. 35 30
DESIGN—VERT. 5 c., 25 c. Map.

21. Flag of St. Vincent.

1969. Statehood.
282. 21. 4 c. multicoloured .. 5 5
283. – 10 c. multicoloured .. 15 15
284. – 50 c. grey, black & orange 50 50
DESIGNS: 10 c. Battle scene with insets of Petroglyph and Carib Chief Chatoyer. 50 c. Carib House with maces and scales.

22. House Wren.

1970. Multicoloured.
285. ½ c. Type **22** 5 5
286. 1 c. Green Heron 10 10
287. 2 c. Bullfinches 5 5
288. 3 c. St. Vincent Parrots .. 8 8
289. 4 c. Soufriere Bird .. 8 8
290. 5 c. Ramier Pigeon .. 15 15
291. 6 c. Bananaquits 12 12
292. 8 c. Hummingbird .. 8 8
293. 10 c. Mangrove Cuckoo .. 12 12
370. 12 c. Black Hawk .. 5 5
371. 20 c. Bare-eyed Thrush .. 8 10
296. 25 c. Prince 20 20
297. 50 c. Blue Hooded Euphonia 30 35
298. $1 Barn Owl .. 50 60
299. $2.50 Crested Elaenia .. 1·50 1·75
300. $5 Ruddy Quail Dove .. 3·00 3·25
Nos. 286/8, 291/2, 371, 297 and 300 are horiz.

23. "DHC-6", Twin Otter.

1970. Regular Air Services. 20th Anniv. Multicoloured.
301. 5 c. Type **23** 8 10
302. 8 c. "Grumman Goose" .. 15 15
303. 10 c. Hawker Siddeley "HS-748" 35 35
304. 25 c. Douglas "DC-3" .. 80 80

24. "Children's Nursery".

1970. British Red Cross Cent. Multicoloured.
305. 3 c. Type **24** 5 5
306. 5 c. "First Aid" 5 5
307. 12 c. "Voluntary Aid Detachment" 20 20
308. 25 c. "Blood Transfusion" 35 35

25. Stained-glass Window.

1970. St. George's Cathedral, Kingstown. 150th Anniv.
309. ½ c. Type **25** 5 5
310. 5 c. St. George's Cathedral 5 5
311. 25 c. Tower, St. George's Cathedral 25 25
312. 35 c. Interior, St. George's Cathedral 35 35
313. 50 c. Type **25** 50 50
Nos. 310 and 312 are horiz.

26. "The Adoration of the Shepherds" (Le Nain).

1970. Christmas. Multicoloured.
314. 8 c. "The Virgin and Child" (G. Bellini) (vert.) 10 10
315. 25 c. Type **26** 25 25
316. 35 c. As 8 c. 35 35
317. 50 c. Type **26** 55 50

27. New Post Office and 6d. Stamps of 1861.

1971. 1st St. Vincent Stamps. 110th Anniv. Multicoloured.
318. 2 c. Type **27** 8 8
319. 4 c. 1d. stamp of 1861 and new Post Office 10 10
320. 25 c. Type **27** 30 25
321. $1 As 4 c. .. .. 1·10 1·10

28. Trust Seal and Wildlife.

1971. St. Vincent's National Trust. Multicoloured.
322. 12 c. Type **28** 10 10
323. 30 c. Old Cannon, Fort Charlotte 30 30
324. 40 c. Type **28** 40 40
325. 45 c. As 30 c. 45 45

29. "Madonna appearing to St. Anthony" (Tiepolo).

1971. Christmas. Multicoloured.
326. 5 c. Type **29** 5 5
327. 10 c. "The Holy Family with Angels" (detail, Pietro da Cortona) .. 12 12
328. 25 c. Type **29** 30 25
329. $1 As 10 c... .. .. 1·25 1·25

30. Careening.

1971. The Grenadines of St. Vincent. Multicoloured.
330. 1 c. Type **30** 5 5
331. 5 c. Seine fishermen .. 5 5
332. 6 c. Map of the Grenadines 8 8
333. 15 c. Type **30** 20 20
334. 20 c. As 5 c. 25 25
335. 50 c. As 6 c. 70 60

31. Private, Grenadier Company, 32nd Foot (1764).

1972. Military Uniforms.
337. **31.** 12 c. multicoloured .. 15 12
338. – 30 c. multicoloured .. 35 35
339. – 50 c. multicoloured .. 65 60
DESIGNS: 30 c. Officer, Battalion Company, 31st. Foot (1772). 50 c. Private, Grenadier Company, 6th Foot (1772).

32. Breadnut Fruit.

1972. Fruit. Multicoloured.
340. 3 c. Type **32** 5 5
341. 5 c. Pawpaw 8 5
342. 12 c. Plumrose or Roseapple 20 15
343. 25 c. Mango 40 35

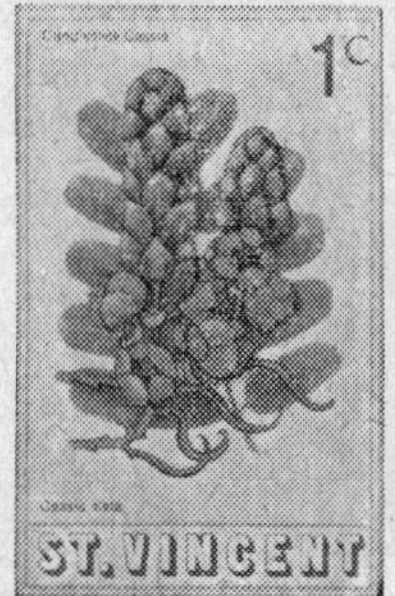

33. Candlestick Cassia.

1972. Flowers. Multicoloured.
344. 1 c. Type **33** 5 5
345. 30 c. Lobster Claw .. 40 35
346. 40 c. White Trumpet .. 45 45
347. $1 Soufriere tree .. 1·00 1·00

34. Sir Charles Brisbane and Coat-of-arms.

1972. Sir Charles Brisbane. Birth Bicent.
348. **34.** 20 c. brn., gold & red-brn. 25 20
349. – 30 c. yellow, mauve & blk. 35 40
350. – $1 multicoloured .. 1·00 75
DESIGNS: 30 c. H.M.S. "Arethusa". $1 H.M.S. "Blake".

1972. Royal Silver Wedding. As T **19** of Ascension, but with Arrowroot and Breadfruit in background.
352. 30 c. brown 30 25
353. $1 green 85 75

35. Sighting of St. Vincent.

1973. Columbus's Visit to the West Indies 475th Anniv. Multicoloured.
354. 5 c. Type **35** 8 8
355. 12 c. Caribs watching Columbus's fleet .. 12 12
356. 30 c. Christopher Columbus 35 35
357. 50 c. "Santa Maria" .. 60 60

36. "The Last Supper" (French stained-glass Window).

1973. Easter.
358. **36.** 15 c. multicoloured .. 12 12
359. – 60 c. multicoloured .. 50 50
360. – $1 multicoloured .. 90 90
Nos. 358/60 are in the form of a triptych which make a composite design depicting "The Last Supper".

37. William Wilberforce and Poster.

1973. William Wilberforce. 140th Death Anniv. Multicoloured.
369. 30 c. Type **37** 30 20
370. 40 c. Slaves cutting cane .. 40 30
371. 50 c. Wilberforce and medallion 50 40

38. P.P.F. Symbol.

1973. International Planned Parenthood Federation. 21st Anniv. Multicoloured.
372. 12 c. Type **38** 12 10
373. 40 c. "IPPF" and symbol 45 45

1973. Royal Wedding. As T **26** of Anguilla. Multicoloured. Background colours given.
374. 50 c. blue 30 35
375. 70 c. green 40 45

39. Administration Block, Mona.

1973. West Indies University. 25th Anniv. Multicoloured.

376. 5 c. Type **39** 5 5
377. 10 c. University Centre, Kingston 8 8
378. 30 c. Aerial view, Mona University 25 25
379. $1 University coat-of-arms (vert.) 60 60

1973. Nos. 297, 292 and 298 surch.

380. 30 c. on 50 c. multicoloured 20 20
381. 40 c. on 8 c. multicoloured 30 30
382. $10 on $1 multicoloured .. 4·50 4·75

40. "The Descent from the Cross" (Sansovino).

1974. Easter. Multicoloured.

383. 5 c. Type **40** 5 5
384. 30 c. "The Deposition" (English, 14th-century) 20 25
385. 40 c. "Pieta" (Fernandez) 20 25
386. $1 "The Resurrection" (French, 16th-century) 50 55

41. "Istra".

1974. Cruise Ships. Multicoloured.

387. 15 c. Type **41** 8 10
388. 20 c. "Oceanic" 12 12
389. 30 c. "Alexander Pushkin" 20 20
390. $1 "Europa" 50 55

42. U.P.U. Emblem.

1974. U.P.U. Centenary. Multicoloured.

392. 5 c. Type **42** 5 5
393. 12 c. Globe within posthorn 10 10
394. 60 c. Map of St. Vincent and hand-cancelling .. 30 35
395. 90 c. Map of the World .. 50 55

43. Royal Tern.

1974. Multicoloured.

396. 30 c. Type **43** 12 15
397. 40 c. Brown pelican .. 15 20
398. $10 Frigatebird .. .. 4·00 4·25

44. Scout Badge and Emblems.

1974. Diamond Jubile of Scout Movement in St. Vincent.

399. **44.** 10 c. multicoloured .. 8 8
400. 25 c. multicoloured .. 20 20
401. 45 c. multicoloured .. 25 25
402. $1 multicoloured .. 50 55

45. Sir Winston Churchill.

1974. Sir Winston Churchill. Birth Cent. Multicoloured.

403. 25 c. Type **45** 20 20
404. 35 c. Churchill in military uniform 20 25
405. 45 c. Churchill in naval uniform 25 25
406. $1 Churchill in air force uniform 50 55

46. The Shepherds.

1974. Christmas.

407. **46.** 3 c. blue and black .. 5 5
408. – 3 c. blue and black .. 5 5
409. – 3 c. blue and black .. 5 5
410. – 3 c. blue and black .. 5 5
411. **46.** 8 c. green and black .. 8 8
412. – 35 c. pink and black .. 20 25
413. – 45 c. brown and black 25 25
414. – $1 mauve and black .. 50 55

DESIGNS: Nos. 408, 411, Mary and crib. Nos. 409, 413, Joseph, Ox and Ass. Nos. 410, 414, The Three Kings.

47. Faces.

1975. Kingstown "Carnival '75" Multicoloured.

415. 1 c. Type **47** 5 5
416. 15 c. Pineapple women .. 10 10
417. 25 c. King of the Bands .. 15 15
418. 35 c. Carnival dancers .. 20 20
419. 45 c. Queen of the Bands 20 25
420. $1·25 "African Splendour" 55 60

48. French Angelfish.

1975. Multicoloured.

422. 1 c. Type **48** 5 5
423. 2 c. Spotfin Butterfly-fish 5 5
424. 3 c. Horse-eyed Jack .. 5 5
425. 4 c. Mackerel 5 5
426. 5 c. French Grunt .. 5 5
427. 6 c. Spotted Goatfish .. 5 5
428. 8 c. Ballyhoo 5 5
429. 10 c. Sperm Whale .. 5 5
430. 12 c. Humpback Whale .. 5 5
431. 15 c. Cowfish 5 5
432. 15 c. Skipjack 5 5
433. 20 c. Queen Angelfish .. 8 8
434. 25 c. Princess Parrotfish .. 10 10
435. 35 c. Red Hind 12 15
436. 45 c. Atlantic Flying-fish 15 20
437. 50 c. Porkfish 20 20
438. 70 c. Albacore 25 30
439. 90 c. Pompano 35 35
440. $1 Queen Triggerfish .. 35 40
441. $2·50 Sailfish .. .. 1·00 1·10
442. $5 Dolphin Fish .. .. 1·75 2·00
443. $10 Blue Marlin .. .. 3·50 3·75

49. Cutting Bananas.

1975. Banana Industry. Multicoloured.

447. 25 c. Type **49** 12 12
448. 35 c. Packaging Station, La Croix 15 15
449. 45 c. Cleaning and boxing 20 20
450. 70 c. Shipping bananas aboard "Geeste Tide" 30 35

50. Snorkel Diving.

1975. Tourism. Multicoloured.

451. 15 c. Type **50** 8 8
452. 20 c. Aquaduct Golf Course 10 10
453. 35 c. Steel Band at Mariner's Inn 15 15
454. 45 c. Sunbathing at Young Island 20 20
455. $1·25 Yachting Marina .. 50 55

51. George Washington, John Adams, Thomas Jefferson and James Madison.

1975. American Independence Bicentennial.

456. **51.** ½ c. black and mauve .. 5 5
457. – 1 c. black and green .. 5 5
458. – 1½ c. black and mauve 5 5
459. – 5 c. black and green .. 5 5
460. – 10 c. black and blue .. 8 8
461. – 25 c. black and yellow .. 15 15
462. – 35 c. black and blue .. 15 15
463. – 45 c. black and red .. 20 20
464. – $1 black and orange .. 40 45
465. – $2 black and green .. 80 90

PRESIDENTS: 1 c. Monroe, Quincy Adams, Jackson, van Buren. 1½ c. W. Harrison, Tyler, Polk, Taylor. 5 c. Fillmore, Pierce, Buchanan, Lincoln. 10 c. Andrew Johnson, Grant, Hayes, Garfield. 25 c. Arthur, Cleveland, B. Harrison, McKinley. 35 c. Theodore Roosevelt, Taft, Wilson, Harding. 45 c. Coolidge, Hoover, Franklin Roosevelt, Truman, $1 Eisenhower, Kennedy, Lyndon Johnson, Nixon. $2 Pres. Ford and White House.

52/3. " Shepherds ".
(Illustration reduced. Actual size, 36 × 56 mm.)

1975. Christmas.

467. – 3 c. black and mauve .. 5 5
468. – 3 c. black and mauve .. 5 5
469. – 3 c. black and mauve .. 5 5
470. – 3 c. black and mauve .. 5 5
471. – 8 c. black and blue .. 5 5
472. – 8 c. black and blue .. 5 5
473. – 35 c. black and yellow .. 15 15
474. – 35 c. black and yellow .. 15 15
475. **52.** 45 c. black and green .. 20 20
476. **53.** 45 c. black and green .. 20 20
477. – $1 black and purple .. 40 45
478. – $1 black and purple .. 40 45

DESIGNS: No. 467, " Star of Bethlehem ". No. 468, " Holy Trinity ". No. 469, As T **52.** No. 470, " Three Kings ". No. 471/2, As No. 467. No. 473/4, As No. 468. No. 475/6, T **52/3.** No. 477/8, As No. 470. The two designs of each value (Nos. 471/8) differ in that the longest side is at the top and at the foot respectively, as in T **52/3.**

54. Carnival Dancers.

1976. Kingstown " Carnival '76 ". Mult.

479. 1 c. Type **54** 5 5
480. 2 c. Humpty-Dumpty people 5 5
481. 5 c. Smiling faces 5 5
482. 35 c. Dragon worshippers 15 20
483. 45 c. Carnival tableau .. 20 25
484. $1·25 Bumble-bee dancers 50 55

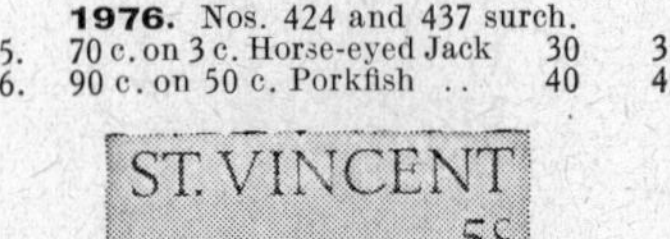

1976. Nos. 424 and 437 surch.

485. 70 c. on 3 c. Horse-eyed Jack 30 35
486. 90 c. on 50 c. Porkfish .. 40 45

55. Blue-headed Hummingbird and Yellow Hibiscus.

1976. Hummingbirds and Hibiscuses. Mult.

487. 5 c. Type **55** 5 5
488. 10 c. Crested Hummingbird and Pink Hibiscus .. 5 5
489. 35 c. Purple-throated Carib and White Hibiscus .. 15 15
490. 45 c. Blue-headed Hummingbird and Red Hibiscus 20 20
491. $1·25 Green-throated Carib and Peach Hibiscus .. 50 60

1976. West Indian Victory in World Cricket Cup. As Nos. 559/60 of Barbados.

492. 15 c. Map of the Caribbean 5 8
493. 45 c. Prudential Cup .. 20 20

56. St. Mary's R.C. Church, Kingstown.

1976. Christmas. Multicoloured.
494. 35 c. Type **56** 15 15
495. 45 c. Anglican Church, Georgetown 20 20
496. 50 c. Methodist Church, Georgetown 20 20
497. $1·25 St. George's Anglican Cathedral, Kingstown .. 50 60

SAMOA BC; O4

Islands in the W. Pacific administered jointly from 1889–99 by Gt. Britain, Germany and the U.S.A. In 1899 the eastern islands were assigned to the U.S.A. and the western to Germany. The latter were occupied by British forces in 1914 and were taken over by New Zealand, under mandate, in 1920. W. Samoa was under United Nations trusteeship but became independent on 1st January, 1962.

1900-1914. 100 pfenning = 1 mark.
1967. 100 sene or cents = 1 tale or dollar.

I INDEPENDENT KINGDOM.

1.

2. Palm trees.

3. King Malletoa.

4.

1877.
15. **1.** 1d. blue .. .. .. 10·00 10·00
16. 3d. red .. .. .. 14·00 15·00
6. 6d. violet .. .. .. 15·00 20·00
20. 9d. brown .. .. .. 15·00 20·00
7c. 1s. yellow .. .. .. 20·00 30·00
8. 2s. brown .. .. .. 32·00 30·00
14. 5s. green £100 £110

The majority of the stamps of T 1 found in old collections are worthless reprints. A 2d. stamp exists but was never issued.

1886.
27. **2.** ½d. purple-brown 15 10
88. ½d. green 25 25
73. 1d. green .. .. .. 1·00 1·00
89. 1d. brown 25 25
36. 2d. orange 15 10
44. **3.** 2½d. red 20 10
82. 2½d. black .. .. .. 75 1·00
93. **2.** 4d. blue 30 30
71. **4.** 5d. red 50 50
62. **2.** 6d. lake .. .. .. 1·00 1·00
63. 1s. red .. .. .. 1·50 1·00
64b. 2s. 6d. violet .. .. 1·50 1·50

1893. Surch. **FIVE PENCE** and bar.
65. **2.** 5d. on 4d. blue .. .. 10·00 10·00

1893. Surch. **5d.** and bar.
69. **2.** 5d. on 4d. blue 50 10

1895. Surch. **Surcharged** and value in figures.
73. **2.** 1½d. on 2d. orange .. 1·00 1·00
84. 2½d. on 1d. green 30 30
83. 2½d. on 1s. red .. .. 1·50 1·50
87. 2½d. on 2s. 6d. violet .. 2·00 2·00

1895. Surch. R **3d.**
79. **2.** 3d. on 2d. orange .. .. 1·00 1·25

1899. Optd. **PROVISIONAL GOVT.**
90. **2.** ½d. green 10 10
91. 1d. red-brown 10 10
92. 2d. orange 10 10
93. 4d. blue 30 30
94. **4.** 5d. red 50 50
95. **2.** 6d. lake 75 75
96. 1s. red .. .. .. 1·50 1·50
97. 2s. 6d. violet .. .. 3·00 3·00

II GERMAN COLONY.

1900. Stamps of Germany optd. **Samoa.**
1. **6.** 3 pf. brown .. .. 2·10 3·00
2. 5 pf. green .. .. 3·00 4·50
3. **7.** 10 pf. red .. .. 2·25 4·50
4. 20 pf. blue .. .. 4·50 11·00
5. 25 pf. orange .. .. 12·00 15·00
6. 50 pf. brown .. .. 12·00 15·00

1901. "Yacht" key-types inscr. "SAMOA".
7. **N.** 3 pf. brown 15 25
8. 5 pf. green 45 25
9. 10 pf. red 45 25
10. 20 pf. blue 25 90
11. 25 pf. blk. & red on yellow 45 4·50
12. 30 pf. blk. & orge. on buff 45 4·50
13. 40 pf. black and red .. 45 4·50
14. 50 pf. blk. & pur. on buff 60 4·50
15. 80 pf. black & red on rose 95 11·00
16. **O.** 1 m. red .. .. 1·40 18·00
17. 2 m. blue .. .. 2·00 27·00
18. 3 m. black .. .. 2·75 40·00
19. 5 m. red and black .. 42·00 £130

III NEW ZEALAND DEPENDENCY (under Mandate from League of Nations and United Nations).

1914. "Yacht" key-types of German Cameroons surch. **G.R.I.** and value in British currency.
101. **N.** ½d. on 3 pf. brown .. 4·00 3·00
102. ½d. on 5 pf. green .. 10·00 5·00
103. 1d. on 10 pf. red .. 38·00 15·00
104. 2½d. on 20 pf. blue .. 13·00 5·50
105. 3d. on 25 pf. black and red on yellow .. 25·00 15·00
106. 4d. on 30 pf. black and orange on buff .. 35·00 22·00
107. 5d. on 40 pf. black & red 35·00 30·00
108. 6d. on 50 pf. black and purple on buff .. 20·00 10·00
109. 9d. on 80 pf. black and red on rose .. 75·00 38·00
110. **O.** 1s. on 1 m. red .. £900 £900
112. 2s. on 2 m. blue .. £850 £800
113. 3s. on 3 m. black .. £400 £400
114. 5s. on 5 m. red and black £450 £400

1914. Stamps of New Zealand (King Edward VII) optd. **SAMOA.**
115. **41.** ½d. green 15 20
116. **42.** 1d. red 15 12
117. **41.** 2d. mauve 55 60
118. **24.** 2½d. blue .. .. 90 1·10
119. **41.** 6d. red .. .. 1·10 1·40
121. 1s. red .. .. 2·75 3·50

1914. Large stamps of New Zealand (Queen Victoria) optd. **SAMOA.**
127. **20.** 2s. blue .. .. 3·50 4·50
123. 2s. 6d. brown .. .. 3·50 4·00
129. 3s. violet .. .. 4·50 9·00
130. 5s. green .. .. 6·00 7·50
125. 10s. brown .. .. 18·00 20·00
132. £1 red .. .. 38·00 42·00

1916. Stamps of New Zealand (King George V) overprinted **SAMOA.**
134. **43.** ½d. green 12 15
135. 1½d. grey 15 20
136. 1½d. brown 15 40
137. 2d. yellow 20 15
139a. 2½d. blue 25 40
140. 3d. brown 30 65
141. 6d. red .. .. 85 1·10
142a. 1s. red .. .. 1·10 1·50

1920. Stamps of New Zealand (Victory issue. Nos. 511/16) optd. **SAMOA.**
143. **44.** ½d. green 20 25
144. **45.** 1d. red 20 40
145. – 1½d. orange 55 70
146. – 3d. chocolate .. .. 70 1·75
147. – 6d. violet .. .. 1·75 2·50
148. – 1s. orange .. .. 2·75 4·00

5. Native Hut.

ILLUSTRATIONS
British Commonwealth and all overprints and surcharges are FULL SIZE. Foreign Countries have been reduced to ¾-LINEAR.

1921.
153. **5.** ½d. green 20 25
154. 1d. lake 12 10
151. 1½d. brown 20 75
156. 2d. yellow 90 25
157. 2½d. blue 40 75
158. 3d. sepia 70 85
159. 4d. violet 70 90
160. 5d. blue .. .. 75 1·60
161. 6d. red .. .. 1·00 1·60
162. 8d. brown .. .. 1·40 2·75
163. 9d. olive .. .. 1·40 2·75
164. 1s. red .. .. 2·00 4·00

1926. Stamps of New Zealand (King George V) overprinted **SAMOA.**
167. **52.** 2s. blue .. .. 2·50 4·50
168. 3s. mauve .. .. 3·50 5·00

1932. Stamps of New Zealand (Arms type) optd. **SAMOA.**
171. **56.** 2s. 6d. brown .. 10·00 12·00
172. 5s. green .. .. 15·00 20·00
173. 10 s. red .. .. 28·00 35·00
174. £1 pink .. .. 35·00 40·00
175. £2 violet £200
176. £5 blue £700

1935. Silver Jubilee. Stamps of 1921 optd. **SILVER JUBILEE OF KING GEORGE V 1910-1935.**
177. **5.** 1d. lake 20 35
178. 2½d. blue 55 90
179. 6d. red .. .. 2·50 3·00

6. Samoan Girl with Kava Bowl.

7. Apia.

1935.
180. **6.** ½d. green 12 8
181. **7.** 1d. black and red .. 12 8
182. – 2d. black and orange .. 12 12
183. – 2½d. black and blue .. 12 8
184. – 4d. grey and brown .. 25 15
205. – 5d. brown and blue .. 25 40
185. – 6d. magenta 25 20
186. – 1s. violet and brown .. 50 30
187. – 2s. green and purple .. 80 65
188. – 3s. blue and orange .. 1·10 1·10

DESIGNS—HORIZ. 2d. River scene. 4d. Samoan canoe and house. 5d. Apia post office. 6d. R. L. Stevenson's home, "Vailima". 1s. Stevenson's tomb. VERT. 2½d. Samoan chief and wife. 2s. Lake Lanuto'o. 3s. Falefa Falls.

1935. Stamps of New Zealand (Arms types) optd. **WESTERN SAMOA.**
207. **56.** 2s. 6d. brown .. 85 2·00
208. 5s. green .. .. 2·00 4·00
209. 10s. red .. .. 6·00 8·00
210. £1 pink .. .. 20·00 28·00
211. 30s. brown .. .. 45·00 65·00
212. £2 violet .. .. 55·00 75·00
213. £3 green .. .. 65·00 £100
214. £5 blue £140 £200

8. Coastal Scene.

11. Robert Louis Stevenson.

1939. New Zealand Control. 25th Anniv.
195. **8.** 1d. olive and red .. 25 30
196. – 1½d. blue and brown .. 40 45
197. – 2½d. brown and blue .. 1·25 1·40
198. **11.** 7d. violet and green .. 3·00 3·00

DESIGNS—HORIZ. 1½d. Map of Western Samoa. 2½d. Samoan dancing party.

12. A Samoan Chief.

13. Making Siapo Cloth.

14. Native House and Flags.

1940. Surch.
199. **12.** 3d. on 1½d. brown .. 8 8

1946. Peace stamps of New Zealand optd. **WESTERN SAMOA.**
215. **91.** 1d. green 8 8
216. – 2d. purple (No. 670) .. 8 8
217. – 6d. brown and red (674) 10 15
218. **94.** 8d. black and red .. 10 20

1952.
219. **13.** ½d. claret and brown .. 8 8
220. **14.** 1d. olive and green .. 8 10
221. – 2d. red 10 12
222. – 3d. blue and indigo .. 12 15
223. – 5d. brown and green .. 15 20
224. – 6d. blue and magenta .. 20 20
225. – 8d. red 30 30
226. – 1s. sepia and blue .. 35 35
227. – 2s. brown 65 65
228. – 3s. chocolate and olive .. 1·40 1·40

DESIGNS: As T 13—VERT. 2d. Seal of Samoa. 5d. Manumea (pigeon). HORIZ. 1s. Thatching native hut. As T 14—HORIZ. 3d. Malifa Falls, wrongly inscr. on stamp "Aleisa Falls". 6d. Bonito fishing canoe. 8d. Cacao harvesting. 2s. Preparing copra. VERT. 3s. Samoan chieftainess.

1953. Coronation. As Types of New Zealand.
229. **106.** 2d. brown 12 12
230. **108.** 6d. grey 25 30

15. Map of Samoa and the Mace.

1958. Samoan Parliament. Inaug. Inscr. "FONO FOU 1958" and "SAMOA I SISIFO".
236. – 4d. red (As T 14) .. 20 20
237. – 6d. violet (As No. 221) 25 25
238. **15.** 1s. blue 30 35

IV INDEPENDENT STATE.

16. Samoan Fine Mat.

DESIGNS — HORIZ. 2d. Samoa College. 3d. Public library. 4d. Fono house. 6d. Map of Samoa. 8d. Airport. 1s. 3d. "Vailima". 2s. 6d. Samoan flag. 5s. Samoan Seal. VERT. 1s. Samoan orator.

1962. Independence.
257. **16.** 1d. brown and rose .. 15 20
240. – 2d. brn., grn., yell. & red 5 5
241. – 3d. brown green & blue 8 8
242. – 4d. magenta, yellow, blue and black .. 12 15
260. 6d. yellow and blue .. 15 20
261. – 8d. bl.-grn., grn. & blue 20 25
262. – 1s. brown and green .. 25 25
246. – 1s. 3d. green and blue .. 30 35
247. – 2s. 6d. red and ultram. 55 65
248. – 5s. ultramarine, yellow, red and drab .. 1·40 1·60

17. Seal and Joint Heads of State.

1963. Independence. 1st Anniv.
249. **17.** 1d. sepia and green .. 5 5
250. 4d. sepia and blue .. 8 10
251. 8d. sepia and pink .. 15 20
252. 2 s. sepia and orange .. 40 45

18. Signing the Treaty.

1964. New Zealand-Samoa Treaty of Friendship. 2nd Anniv.
253. **18.** 1d. multicoloured .. 5 5
254. 8d. multicoloured .. 12 15
255. 2s. multicoloured .. 30 35
256. 3s. multicoloured .. 40 35

19. Tropic Bird.

1965. Air.
263. **19.** 8d. black, orge & blue 12 15
264. – 2s. black and blue .. 35 35

DESIGN: 2s. Flying Fish.

20. Aerial View of Deep Sea Wharf.

1966. Opening of 1st Deep Sea Wharf, Apia. Multicoloured.

265. 1d. Type **20** 5 5
266. 8d. Aerial View of Wharf and Bay .. 12 15
267. 2s. Aerial View of Wharf and Bay 30 35
268. 3s. Type **20** 45 45

21. W.H.O. Building.

1966. W.H.O. Headquarters, Geneva. Inaug.

269. **21.** 3d. ochre, blue and slate 5 5
270. – 4d. blue, yell., grn. & brn. 8 8
271. **21.** 6d. lilac, green & olive .. 10 12
272. – 1s. blue, yellow, green and turquoise 20 25

DESIGNS: 4d. and 1s. W.H.O. Building on flag.

1966. Hurricane Relief Fund. No. 261 surch. **HURRICANE RELIEF** and value.

273. 8d. + 6d. blue-green, green and blue 25 25

22. Hon. Tuatagaloa L.S. (Minister of Justice).

1967. Independence. 5th Anniv.

274. **22.** 3d. sepia and violet .. 8 10
275. – 8d. sepia and blue .. 15 15
276. – 2s. sepia and olive .. 30 35
277. – 3s. sepia and magenta 45 45

DESIGNS: 8d. Hon. F. C. F. Nelson (Minister of Works, Marine and Civil Aviation). 2s. Hon. To'omata T.L. (Minister of Lands). 3s. Hon. Fa'alava'au G. (Minister of Post Office, Radio and Broadcasting).

23. Samoan Fales (houses), 1890.

1967. Mulinu'u as Seat of Government. Cent.

278. **23.** 8d. multicoloured .. 12 15
279. – 1s. multicoloured .. 20 25

DESIGN: 1s. Fono (Parliament) House, 1967.

24. Wattled Honey-eater.

1967. Decimal Currency. Multicoloured.

280. 1 s. Type **24** 5 5
281. 2 s. Pacific Pigeon .. 5 5
282. 3 s. Samoan Starling .. 8 8
283. 5 s. Samoan Broadbill .. 10 10
284. 7 s. Red-headed Parrot-finch 12 12
285. 10 s. Purple Swamp-hen 20 20
286. 20 s. Barn Owl .. 35 40
287. 25 s. Tooth-billed Pigeon .. 40 45
288. 50 s. Island Thrush .. 80 85
289. $1 Samoan Fantail .. 1·75 2·00
289a. $2 Mao .. .. .. 3·50 4·00
289b. $4 Samoan White Eye .. 7·00 7·50

25. Nurse and Child.

1967. South Pacific Health Service. Mult.

290. 3 s. Type **25** 8 8
291. 7 s. Leprosarium 12 12
292. 20 s. Mobile X-ray Unit .. 30 35
293. 25 s Apia Hospital .. 40 45

26. Thomas Trood.

1968. Independence. 6th Anniv. Multicoloured.

294. 2 s. Type **26** 5 5
295. 7 s. Dr. Wilhelm Solf .. 12 12
296. 20 s. J. C. Williams .. 30 35
297. 25 s. Fritz Marquardt .. 40 45

27. Cocoa.

1968. Agricultural Development.

298. **27.** 3 s. brown, green & black 8 8
299. – 5 s. green, yellow & brn. 12 12
300. – 10 s. red, brown & yellow 20 20
301. – 20 s. bistre, yell. & olive 30 35

DESIGNS: 5 s. Breadfruit. 10 s. Copra. 20 s. Bananas.

28. Women Weaving Mats.

1968. South Pacific Commission. 21st Anniv. Multicoloured.

302. 7 s. Type **28** 12 12
303. 20 s. Palm Trees and Bay 35 35
304. 25 s. Sheltered Cove .. 40 45

1968. Kingsford-Smith's Trans-Pacific Flight. 40th Anniv. No. 285 surch. **1928-1968 KINGSFORD-SMITH TRANS-PACIFIC FLIGHT** and new value.

305. 20 s. on 10 s. multicoloured 40 45

29. Bougainville's Route.

1968. Bougainville's Visit to Samoa. Bicent.

306. **29.** 3 s. blue and black .. 8 8
307. – 7 s. ochre and black .. 12 15
308. – 20 s. multicoloured .. 35 35
309. – 25 s. multicoloured .. 40 45

DESIGNS: 7 s. Louis de Bougainville. 20 s. Bougainvillea Flower. 25 s. Ships "La Boudeuse" and "L'Etoile".

30. Globe and Human Rights Emblem.

1968. Human Rights Year.

310. **30.** 7 s. blue, brown & gold 12 15
311. 20 s. orge., green & gold 30 35
312. 25 s. violet, grn. & gold 40 45

31. Dr. Martin Luther King.

32. Polynesian Version of Madonna and Child.

1968. Martin Luther King. Commem.

313. **31.** 7 s. black and green .. 12 15
314. 20 s. black and purple .. 35 35

1968. Christmas.

315. **32.** 1 s. multicoloured .. 5 5
316. 3 s. multicoloured .. 8 8
317. 20 s. multicoloured .. 35 35
318. 30 s. multicoloured .. 50 55

33. Frangipani—"Plumeria acuminata".

1969. Independence. 7th Anniv. Multicoloured.

319. 2 s. Type **33** 5 5
320. 7 s. Hibiscus (vert.) .. 12 15
321. 20 s. Red-Ginger (vert.) .. 30 35
322. 30 s. Moso'oi 50 55

34. R. L. Stevenson and "Treasure Island".

1969. Robert Louis Stevenson. 75th Death Anniv. Multicoloured.

323. 3 s. Type **34** 8 8
324. 7 s. R. L. Stevenson and "Kidnapped" 15 15
325. 20 s. R. L. Stevenson and "Dr. Jekyll and Mr. Hyde" 35 40
326. 22 s. R. L. Stevenson and Weir of Hermiston .. 45 50

35. Weightlifting.

1969. 3rd South Pacific Games, Port Moresby.

327. **35.** 3 s. black and green .. 8 8
328. – 20 s. black and blue .. 35 40
329. – 22 s. black and orange .. 40 45

DESIGNS: 20 s. Yachting. 22 s. Boxing.

36. U.S. Astronaut on the Moon and the Splashdown near Samoa Islands.

1969. 1st Man on the Moon.

330. **36.** 7 s. multicoloured .. 15 15
331. 20 s. multicoloured .. 35 55

37. "Virgin and Child" (Murillo).

1969. Christmas. Multicoloured.

332. 1 s. Type **37** 5 5
333. 3 s. "The Holy Family" (El Greco) 8 8
334. 20 s. "The Nativity" (El Greco) 35 40
335. 30 s. "The Adoration of the Magi" (detail) (Velazquez) 50 55

38. Seventh Day Adventist's Sanatorium, Apia.

1970. Independence. 8th Anniv.

337. **38.** 2 s. brown, slate & black 5 5
338. – 7 s. violet, buff & black 12 15
339. – 20 s. rose, lilac & black 30 35
340. – 22 s. green, buff & black 35 40

DESIGNS—HORIZ. 7 s. Rev. Father Violette and Roman Catholic Cathedral, Apia. 22 s. John Williams, 1797-1839, and London Missionary Society Church, Sapapali'i. VERT. 20 s. Mormon Church of Latter Day Saints, Tuasivi-on-Safotulafai.

39. Wreck of S.M.S. "Adler".

1970. Great Apia Hurricane of 1889. Multicoloured.

341. 5 s. Type **39** 12 12
342. 7 s. U.S.S. "Nipsic" .. 20 20
343. 10 s. H.M.S. "Calliope" .. 30 30
344. 20 s. Apia after the hurricane 60 65

40. Sir Gordon Taylor's "Frigate Bird III".

1970. Air. Multicoloured.

345. 3 s. Type **40** 5 5
346. 7 c. Polynesian Airlines "DC-3" 15 15
347. 20 s. Pan-American Airways "Samoan Clipper" 45 45
348. 30 s. Air Samoa Britten-Norman "Islander" .. 65 65

41. Kendal's Chronometer and Cook's Sextant.

1970. Cook's Exploration of the Pacific.

349. **41.** 1 s. red silver and black 5 5
350. – 2 s. multicoloured .. 8 8
351. – 10 s. black, blue & gold 40 40
352. – 30 s. multicoloured .. 60 60

DESIGNS-VERT. 2 s. Cook's Statue, Whitby. 10 s. Cook's Head. HORIZ. 30 s. Cook, H.M.S. "Endeavour" and Island (83×25 mm.).

42. "Peace for the World" (F. B. Eccles).

1970. Christmas. Multicoloured.

353. 2 s. Type **42** 5 5
354. 3 s. "The Holy Family" (W. E. Jahnke) .. 8 8
355. 20 s. "Mother and Child" (F. B. Eccles) 40 40
356. 30 c. "Prince of Peace" (Meleane Fe'ao).. .. 60 60

43. Pope Paul VI.

1970. Visit of Pope Paul to Samoa.

358. **43.** 8 s. black and blue .. 15 15
359. 20 s. black and red .. 40 40

44. Native and Tree.

1971. Timber Industry. Multicoloured.

360. 3 s. Type **44** 8 8
361. 8 s. Bulldozer in clearing.. 15 15
362. 20 s. Log in Sawmill .. 40 40
363. 22 s. Floating Logs, and Harbour. 45 45

The 8 s. and 20 s. are horiz.

45. Siva Dance.

1971. Tourism. Multicoloured.

365. 5 s. Type **45** 10 10
366. 7 s. Samoan cricket .. 12 15
367. 8 s. Hideaway Hotel .. 15 15
368. 10 s. Aggie Grey and her hotel 20 25

46. "Queen Salamasina".

1971. Myths and Legends of Old Samoa (1st series). Multicoloured.

369. 3 s. Type **46** 8 8
370. 8 s. "Lu and his Sacred Hens" 15 15
371. 10 s. "God Tagaloa fishes Samoa from the sea" .. 20 20
372. 22 s. "Mount Vaea and the Pool of Tears" 45 45

See also Nos. 426/9.

47. "The Virgin and Child" (Bellini).

1971. Christmas.

373. **47.** 2 s. multicoloured .. 5 5
374. 3 s. multicoloured .. 8 8
375. – 20 s. multicoloured .. 40 40
376. – 30 s. multicoloured .. 60 60

DESIGN: 20 s., 30 s. "The Virgin and Child with St. Anne and John the Baptist" (Leonardo da Vinci).

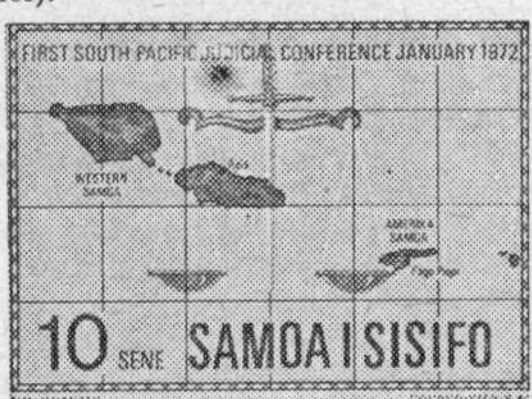

48. Map and Scales of Justice.

1972. First South Pacific Judicial Conference.

377. **48.** 10 s. multicoloured .. 20 25

HAVE YOU READ THE NOTES AT THE BEGINNING OF THIS CATALOGUE?

These often provide answers to the enquiries we receive.

49. Asau Wharf, Savaii.

1972. Independence. 10th Anniv. Multicoloured.

378. 1 s. Type **49** 5 5
379. 8 s. Parliament Building 15 15
380. 10 s. Mothers' Centre .. 20 20
381. 22 s. Vailima Residence and Rulers 35 40

50. Flags of Member Countries.

1972. South Pacific Commission. 25th Anniv. Multicoloured.

382. 3 s. Type **50** 8 8
383. 7 s. Flag and Afoafouvale Misimoa (Sec. Gen.) .. 15 15
384. 8 s. H.Q. building, Noumea (horiz.) 15 15
385. 10 s. Flags and area map (horiz.) 20 25

51. Expedition Ships.

1972. Sighting of Western Samoa by Jacob Roggeveen. 250th Anniv. Multicoloured.

386. 2 c. Type **51** 5 5
387. 8 s. Ships in storm (horiz.) 15 15
388. 10 s. Ships passing island (horiz.) 20 20
389. 30 s. Route of Voyage (horiz.) (87×24 mm.) .. 50 55

52. Bull Conch.

1972. Multicoloured.

390. 1 s. Type **52** 5 5
391. 2 s. Rhinoceros Beetle .. 5 5
392. 3 s. Skipjack (fish) .. 5 5
393. 4 s. Painted Crab.. .. 5 5
394. 5 s. Butterfly Fish .. 5 8
395. 7 s. Samoan Monarch (butterfly) 8 10
396. 10 s. Triton Shell.. .. 12 12
397. 20 s. Jewel Beetle.. .. 25 25
398. 50 s. Spiny Lobster .. 60 65
399. $1 Hawkmouth .. .. 1·25 1·40
399a. $2 Green Turtle .. .. 2·40 2·50
399b. $4 Black Marlin .. .. 4·75 5·00
399c. $5 Green Tree Lizard .. 6·50 7·00

53. "The Ascension".

1972. Christmas. Multicoloured.

400. 1 s. Type **53** 5 5
401. 4 s. "The Blessed Virgin, and Infant Christ" .. 8 8
402. 10 s. "St. Andrew blessing Samoan canoe" .. 20 20
403. 30 s. "The Good Shepherd" 60 60

54. Erecting a Tent.

1973. Boy Scout Movement. Multicoloured.

405. 2 s. Saluting the flag .. 5 5
406. 3 s. First-aid 8 8
407. 8 s. Type **54** 15 15
408. 20 s. Samoan action-song 40 40

55. Airport and Hawker Siddeley "748" taking-off.

1973. Air. Multicoloured.

409. 8 s. Type **55** 10 10
410. 10 s. Hawker Siddeley "748" in flight .. 12 12
411. 12 s. Hawker Siddeley "748" on runway .. 15 15
412. 22 s. "B.A.C. 1-11" aircraft 25 30

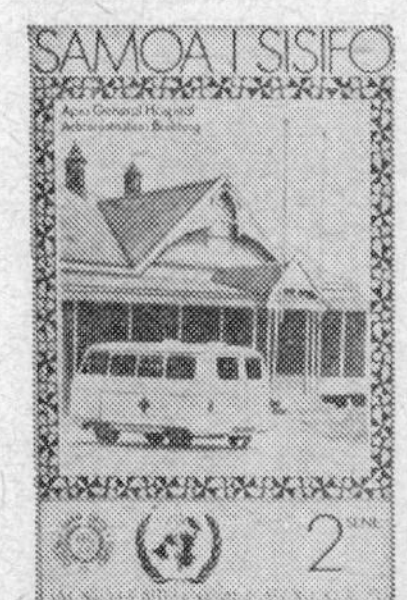

56. Apia General Hospital.

1973. W.H.O. 25th Anniv. Multicoloured.

413. 2 s. Type **56** 5 5
414. 8 s. Baby clinic 15 15
415. 20 s. Filariasis research .. 35 35
416. 22 s. Family welfare .. 35 40

57. Mother and Child, and Map.

1973. Christmas. Multicoloured.

417. 3 s. Type **57** 8 8
418. 4 s. Mother and Child, and village 10 10
419. 10 s. Mother and child, and beach 20 20
420. 30 s. Samoan stable .. 50 55

58. Boxing.

1973. Commonwealth Games, Christchurch. Multicoloured.

422. 8 s. Type **58** 15 15
423. 10 s. Weight-lifting .. 20 25
424. 20 s. Bowls.. .. .. 35 35
425. 30 s. Athletics stadium .. 50 55

1974. Myths and Legends of Old Samoa (2nd series). As Type **46**. Multicoloured.

426. 2 s. Tigilau and sacred dove 8 8
427. 8 s. Pili, his sons and fishing net 15 15
428. 20 s. Sina and the origin of the coconut 30 35
429. 30 s. The warrior, Nafanua 50 55

59. Mail-van at Faleolo Airport.

1974. U.P.U. Centenary. Multicoloured.

430. 8 s. Type **59** 15 15
431. 20 s. Ship and Apia Wharf 30 35
432. 22 s. Early Post Office, Apia, and letter 35 40
433. 50 s. William Willis and sailing-raft (87 × 29 mm.) 80 85

60. "Holy Family" (Sebastiano).

1974. Christmas. Multicoloured.

435. 3 s. Type **60** 8 8
436. 4 s. "Virgin and Child with Saints" (Lotto) 10 10
437. 10 s. "Madonna and Child with St. John" (Titian) 20 20
438. 30 s. "Adoration of the Shepherds" (Rubens) .. 50 55

61. Winged Passion Flower.

1975. Tropical Flowers. Multicoloured.

440. 8 s. Type **61** 15 15
441. 20 s. Gardenia (vert.) .. 30 35
442. 22 s. "Barringtonia samoensis" (vert.) .. 35 40
443. 30 s. Malay apple 50 55

62. "Joyita" loading at Apia.

1975. "Interpex 1975" Stamp Exhibition, New York, and "Joyita" Mystery. Mult.

444. 1 s. Type **62** 5 5
445. 8 s. "Joyita" sails for Tokelau Islands .. 15 15
446. 20 s. Taking to rafts .. 30 35
447. 25 s. "Joyita" abandoned 35 40
448. 50 s. Discovery of "Joyita" north of Fiji 75 80

63. " Pate " Drum.

1975. Musical Instruments. Multicoloured.

450. 8 s. Type **63** 15 15
451. 20 s. " Lali " drum .. 30 35
452. 22 s. " Logo " drum .. 35 40
453. 30 s. " Pu " shell horn .. 45 50

64. " Mother and Child " (Meleane Fe'ao).

1975. Christmas. Multicoloured.

454. 3 s. Type **64** 8 8
455. 4 s. " The Saviour " (Polataia Tuigamala) .. 8 8
456. 10 s. " A Star is Born " (Iosua Toafa) 20 20
457. 30 s. " Madonna and Child " (Ernesto Coter) .. 45 50

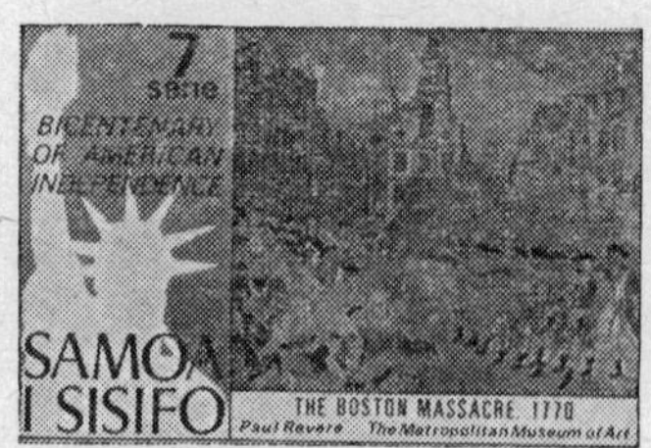

65. " The Boston Massacre " (Paul Revere).

1976. American Revolution. Bicent. Multicoloured.

459. 7 s. Type **65** 12 12
460. 8 s. " The Declaration of Independence " (John Turnbull) 15 15
461. 20 s. " The Ship that Sank in Victory " (J. L. G. Ferris) 30 35
462. 22 s. " Pitt addressing the Commons " (R. A. Hickel) 35 40
463. 50 s. " Battle of Princeton " (William Mercer) .. 75 80

66. Mullet Fishing.

1976. Fishing. Multicoloured.

465. 10 s. Type **66** 15 20
466. 12 s. Fish traps 20 25
467. 22 s. Samoan fisherman .. 35 40
468. 50 s. Net fishing 75 80

67. Boxing.

1976. Olympic Games, Montreal. Mult.

470. 10 s. Type **67** 15 20
471. 12 s. Wrestling 20 25
472. 22 s. Javelin 35 40
473. 50 s. Weightlifting .. 75 80

68. Mary and Joseph going to Bethlehem.

1976. Christmas. Multicoloured.

474. 3 s. Type **68** 5 8
475. 5 s. The Shepherds .. 8 10
476. 22 s. The Holy Family .. 30 35
477. 50 s. The Magi 65 75

69. Queen Elizabeth and View of Apia.

1977. Silver Jubilee and Royal Visit. Mult.

479. 12 s. Type **69** 15 20
480. 26 s. Presentation of Spurs of Chivalry 35 40
481. 32 s. Queen and Royal Yacht " Britannia " 40 45
482. 50 s. Queen leaving Abbey 65 75

SAN MARINO E3

An independent Republic lying near the E. coast of the Italian peninsula.

100 centesimi = 1 lira.

1. **2.**

1877.

1. **1.** 2 c. green .. .. .. 3·25 80
18. 2 c. blue .. .. .. 3·25 1·60
32. 2 c. red .. .. .. 3·00 1·60
2. **2.** 5 c. yellow .. .. 21·00 3·25
19. 5 c. olive .. .. .. 1·25 75
33. 5 c. green .. .. .. 1·25 75
3. 10 c. blue .. .. .. 32·00 2·75
20. 10 c. green .. .. 1·25 80
34. 10 c. red .. .. 1·25 80
21. 15 c. lake .. .. .. 42·00 9·00
4. 20 c. red .. .. 4·25 80
35. 20 c. lilac .. .. .. 2·10 1·25
5. 25 c. claret .. .. 30·00 3·75
36. 25 c. blue .. .. .. 1·25 1·00
6. 30 c. brown .. .. £160 15·00
22. 30 c. yellow .. .. 1·60 1·60
7. 40 c. mauve .. .. £170 15·00
23. 40 c. brown .. .. 1·25 1·75
24. 45 c. green .. .. 1·25 1·60
25. 65 c. brown .. .. 1·25 1·60
26. 1 l. red and yellow .. £600 £160
37. 1 l. blue £600 £160
27. 2 l. brown and buff .. 21·00 17·00
28. 5 l. lake and blue .. 50·00 32·00

1892. Surch. **Cmi.** and figure of value.

10c. **2.** 5 c. on 10 c. blue.. .. 20·00 3·75
12. 5 c. on 30 c. brown .. £160 21·00
16. 10 c. on 20 c. red .. 12·00 1·25

1892. Surch. **10 10.**

17. **2.** 10 c. on 20 c. red .. 65·00 1·75

3. Government Palace. **4.**

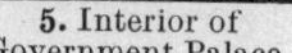

5. Interior of Government Palace. **6.** Statue of Liberty.

1894. Opening of new Govt. Palace and Installation of New Regent.

29. **3.** 25 c. chocolate and blue.. 80 30
30. **4.** 50 c. chocolate and red .. 6·00 90
31. **5.** 1 l. chocolate and green.. 6·00 1·25

1899.

38. **6.** 2 c. brown 80 60
39. 5 c. orange .. .. 1·25 85

See also Nos. 86/91.

7. **8.** Mt. Titano.

1903.

40. **7.** 2 c. lilac .. .. .. 5·00 40
41. **8.** 5 c. green .. .. .. 1·25 12
42. 10 c. red .. .. .. 1·25 15
43. 20 c. orange .. .. 25·00 5·00
44. 25 c. blue .. .. .. 3·25 80
45. 30 c. lake .. .. .. 2·50 1·40
46. 40 c. red .. .. .. 3·25 1·40
47. 45 c. yellow .. .. 3·25 1·60
48. 65 c. brown .. .. 2·50 1·40
49. 1 l. olive .. .. .. 4·25 2·10
50. 2 l. violet .. .. .. £300 65·00
51. 5 l. slate .. .. .. 32·00 29·00

See also Nos. 73, etc.

1905. Surch. **1905 15.**
52. **8.** 15 c. on 20 c. orange .. 3·75 1·25

9. 10. 11. Statue of Liberty.

1907.
53a. **9.** 1 c. brown 40 40
54. **10.** 15 c. grey .. .. 8·00 80

1917. For Combatants. Surch. **1917 Pro combattenti** and value.
55. **7.** 25 c. on 2 c. lilac .. 1·25 85
56. **8.** 50 c. on 2 l. violet .. 23·00 20·00

1918. Surch. **Cent. 20 1918.**
57. **10.** 20 c. on 15 c. grey .. 2·10 1·00

1918. War Casualties Fund. Inscr. as in T **11.**
58. **11.** 2 c. (+5 c.) blk. & lilac 20 20
59. 5 c. (+5 c.) black & grn. 20 20
60. 10 c. (+5 c.) blk. & red 20 20
61. 20 c. (+5 c.) blk. & orge. 20 20
62. 25 c. (+5 c.) blk. & blue 30 30
63. 45 c. (+5 c.) blk. & brn. 30 30
64. – 1 l. (+5 c.) blk. & green 7·00 5·50
65. – 2 l. (+5 c.) blk. & lilac 4·50 4·25
66. – 3 l. (+5 c.) blk. & red 4·25 4·25
DESIGN—HORIZ. 1 l., 2 l., 3 l. San Marino.

1918. Italian Victory over Austria and Premium for War Casualties Fund. Optd. **3 Novembre. 1918.**
67. **11.** 20 c. (+5 c.) blk. & orge. 80 80
68. 25 c. (+5 c.) blk. & bl. 80 80
69. 45 c. (+5 c.) blk. & brn. 80 80
70. – 1 l. (+5 c.) blk. & green 1·25 1·25
71. – 2 l. (+5 c.) blk. & lilac 4·25 3·25
72. – 3 l. (+5 c.) black & red 3·25 3·25

1921.
73. **7.** 2 c. brown 5 5
74. **8.** 5 c. olive 8 8
111. 5 c. claret 8 8
112. 10 c. olive 8 8
75. 10 c. orange 8 8
76. 15 c. green 8 8
113. 15 c. purple 8 8
77. 20 c. brown 8 8
114. 20 c. green 8 8
78. 25 c. grey 12 12
115. 25 c. violet 10 10
79. 30 c. mauve 12 12
116. 30 c. orange 20 12
117. 40 c. brown 8 8
81. 50 c. purple 25 25
118. 50 c. grey 12 12
119. 60 c. red 20 20
82. 80 c. blue 25 25
83. 90 c. brown 25 25
120. 1 l. blue 20 20
85. 2 l. red .. .. 8·00 5·00
121. 2 l. green .. .. 2·50 2·10
122. 5 l. blue .. .. 9·00 7·00

1922. Re-issue of T **6.**
86. **6.** 2 c. purple 8 8
87. 5 c. olive 8 8
88. 10 c. brown 8 8
89. 20 c. brown 20 20
90. 25 c. blue 45 30
91. 45 c. lake 90 65

13. Arbe (Rab). 14. St. Marinus.

1923. Delivery of Italian Flag flown on Arbe to San Marino.
92. **13.** 50 c. olive 35 30

1923. San Marino Mutual Aid Society.
93. **14.** 30 c. brown 30 30

15. Mt. Titano. 16. "Liberty". 17.

1923. Red Cross.
94. **15.** 5 c. +5 c. olive .. 20 20
95. 10 c. +5 c. orange .. 20 20
96. 15 c. +5 c. green .. 20 20
97. 25 c. +5 c. lake .. 40 25
98. 40 c. +5 c. purple .. 70 55
99. 50 c. +5 c. grey .. 90 40
100. **16.** 1 l. +5 c. blue and black 1·60 70

1923. San Marino Volunteers in the Great War.
101. **17.** 1 l. brown .. .. 6·00 4·25

18. Garibaldi. 19.

1924. Garibaldi's Refuge in San Marino. 75th Anniv.
102. **18.** 30 c. purple 40 30
103. 50 c. brown 35 25
104 60 c. lake 80 60
105. **19.** 1 l. blue .. .. 1·00 70
106. 2 l. green .. .. 1·75 1·10

1924. Red Cross stamps of 1918 surch.
107. **11.** 30 c. on 45 c. blk. & brn. 40 20
108. – 60 c. on 1 l. blk. & grn. 1·60 1·40
109. – 1 l. on 2 l. black & lilac 5·50 4·50
110. – 2 l. on 3 l. black & red 4·50 4·25

1926. Surch.
123. **8.** 75 c. on 80 c. blue .. 40 40
124. 1 l. 20 on 90 c. brown .. 40 40
125. 1 l. 25 on 90 c. brown .. 1·25 80
126. 2 l. 50 on 80 c. blue .. 2·00 1·60

20. Antonio Onofri. 21. San Marino War Memorial.

1926. Onofri. Death Cent.
127. **20.** 10 c. black and blue .. 15 12
128. 20 c. black and olive.. 60 40
129. 45 c. black and violet.. 45 35
130. 65 c. black and green.. 30 15
131. 1 l. black and orange.. 1·25 75
132. 2 l. black and claret .. 1·40 1·00

1926. No. E 92 surch. **Lire 1,85.**
133. **8.** 1 l. 85 on 60 c. violet .. 55 40

1927. Surch.
134. **20.** 1 l. 25 on 1 l. blk. & orge. 80 80
135. 2 l. 50 on 2 l. blk. & clar. 1·60 1·60
136. 5 l. on 2 l. blk. & claret 26·00 22·00

1927. Unissued Express stamp (No. 115 surch. **ESPRESSO 50**) ruled through and surch. **L.1.75.**
137. **8.** 1 l. 75 on 50 c. on 25 c. vio. 90 90

1927. War Cenotaph Commem.
138. **21.** 50 c. purple 80 60
139. 1 l. 25 blue .. .. 1·60 1·00
140. 10 l. black .. .. 21·00 12·00

22. Franciscan Convent and Capucin Church.

1928. St. Francis of Assisi. 700th Death Anniv. Inscr. "VII CENTENARIO FRANCESCANO".
141. **22.** 50 c. red .. .. 15·00 80
142. 1 l. 25 blue .. .. 1·75 2·10
143. – 2 l. 50 brown .. .. 1·75 2·10
144. – 5 l. violet .. .. 15·00 7·50
DESIGN: 2 l. 50, 5 l. Death of St. Francis.

24. La Rocca Fortress. 25. Government Palace. 26. Statue of Liberty.

1929.
145. **24.** 5 c. blue and maroon .. 8 5
146 10 c. mauve and blue .. 8 5
147. 15 c. green and orange.. 8 5
148. 20 c. red and blue .. 8 5
149. 25 c. black and green .. 8 5
150. 30 c. red and grey .. 8 8
151. 50 c. green and purple.. 8 5
152. 75 c. grey and red .. 8 8
153. **25.** 1 l. green and brown .. 8 8
154. 1 l. 25 black and blue .. 8 8
155. 1 l. 75 orange and green 55 45
156. 2 l. red and blue .. 12 12
157. 2 l. 50 blue and red .. 15 15
158. 3 l. blue and orange .. 20 20
159. 3 l. 70 brown and green 45 45
160. **26.** 5 l. green and violet .. 60 60
161. 10 l. blue and brown .. 2·50 2·50
162. 15 l. purple and green.. 25·00 25·00
163. 20 l. red and blue .. £140 80·00

27. Mt. Titano. 28. G.P.O., San Marino.

1931. Air.
164. **27.** 50 c. green 40 40
165. 80 c. red 80 80
166. 1 l. brown 80 80
167. 2 l. purple .. .. 1·25 1·25
168. 2 l. 60 blue .. .. 8·50 8·50
169. 3 l. grey .. .. 9·50 9·50
170. 5 l. olive .. .. 2·10 2·10
171. 7 l. 70 sepia .. .. 2·75 2·75
172. 9 l. orange .. .. 4·00 4·00
173. 10 l. blue .. .. £190 95·00

1932. New G.P.O. Inaug.
174. **28.** 20 c. green .. .. 1·50 60
175. 50 c. red .. .. 2·40 80
176. 1 l. 25 blue .. .. 90·00 35·00
177. 1 l. 75 brown .. .. 38·00 21·00
178. 2 l. 75 violet .. .. 8·00 8·00

29. San Marino Railway Station.

1932. Opening of Electric Railway between San Marino and Rimini.
179. **29.** 20 c. green 80 70
180. 50 c. red .. .. 1·25 1·10
181. 1 l. 25 blue .. .. 2·10 1·90
182. 5 l. brown .. .. 35·00 25·00

30. Garibaldi.

DESIGN: 75 c. to 5 l. Garibaldi's arrival at San Marino.

1932. Garibaldi. 50th Death Anniv. Dated "1882-1932".
183. **30.** 10 c. brown 40 40
184. 20 c. violet 40 40
185. 25 c. green 80 80
186. 50 c. brown .. .. 3·25 3·25
187. – 75 c. red .. .. 3·25 3·25
188. – 1 l. 25 blue .. .. 3·25 3·25
189. – 2 l. 75 orange .. .. 9·00 9·00
190. – 5 l. olive .. .. £140 80·00

1933. Air. "Graf Zeppelin". Surch. **ZEPPELIN 1933** under airship and new value.
191. **27.** 3 l. on 50 c. orange .. 85 17·00
192. 5 l. on 80 c. olive .. 27·00 17·00
193. 10 l. on 1 l. blue .. 27·00 17·00
194. 12 l. on 2 l. brown .. 27·00 17·00
195. 15 l. on 2 l. 60 red .. 27·00 17·00
196. 20 l. on 3 l. green .. 27·00 17·00

1933. 20th Italian Philatelic Congress. Optd. **28 MAGGIO 1933 CONVEGNO FILATELICO** and surch.
197. **28.** 25 c. on 2 l. 75 violet 80 60
198. 50 c. on 1 l. 75 brown.. 3·25 1·90
199. 75 c. on 2 l. 75 violet .. 8·50 5·50
200. 1 l. 25 on 1 l. 75 brown £200 £110

1934. Philatelic Exn. Surch. **12-27 APRILE 1934 MOSTRA FILATELICA** and value with wheel.
201. **28.** 25 c. on 1 l. 25 blue .. 55 40
202. 50 c. on 1 l. 75 brown.. 70 60
203. 75 c. on 50 c. red .. 5·00 4·25
204. 1 l. 25 on 20 c. green .. 25·00 15·00

1934. Surch. with value and wheel.
205. **28.** 3 l. 70 on 1 l. 25 blue .. 65·00 40·00
206. 3 l. 70 on 2 l. 75 violet.. 65·00 40·00

32. Ascent to Mt. Titano. 33. Melchiorre Delfico.

1935. San Marino Fascist Party. 12th Anniv.
207. **32.** 5 c. black and brown .. 12 12
208. 10 c. black and violet .. 12 12
209. 20 c. black and orange.. 12 12
210. 25 c. black and green .. 12 12
211. 50 c. black and bistre .. 35 30
212. 75 c. black and lake .. 80 60
213. 1 l. 25 black and blue .. 3·25 2·25

1935. Delfico (historian of San Marino). Death Cent.
214. **33.** 5 c. black and claret .. 20 12
215. 7½ c. black and brown.. 20 12
216. 10 c. black and green .. 20 12
217. 15 c. black and red .. 4·25 65
218. 20 c. black and orange 20 12
219. 25 c. black and green .. 20 12
220. – 30 c. black and violet .. 20 15
221. – 50 c. black & olive-green 2·10 30
222. – 75 c. black and red .. 7·50 2·50
223. – 1 l. 25 black and blue.. 2·10 1·25
224. – 1 l. 50 black and brown 17·00 8·00
225. – 1 l. 75 black and orange 17·00 8·00
DESIGN—(25 × 35 mm.): 30 c. to 1 l. 75, Statue of Delfico.

1936. Surch. (a) Postage.
226. **20.** 80 c. on 45 c. blk. & vio. 3·25 2·50
227. 80 c. on 65 c. blk. & grn. 3·25 2·50
228. **22.** 2 l. 05 on 1 l. 25 blue .. 3·25 2·50
229. 2 l. 75 on 2 l. 50 brown.. 27·00 22·00

(b) Air.
230. **27.** 75 c. on 50 c. green .. 2·50 1·90
231. 75 c. on 80 c. red .. 12·00 9·00

1941. Surch.
233. **8.** 10 c. on 15 c. purple .. 8 8
234. 10 c. on 30 c. orange .. 12 12

1942. Air. Surch. **Lire 10** and bars.
235. **27.** 10 l. on 2 l. 60 blue .. 65·00 65·00
236. 10 l. on 3 l. grey .. 8·50 8·50

36. Gajarda Tower, Arbe, and Flags of Italy and San Marino. 37. Arbe Harbour.

39. Printing Press. 40. Newspapers.

1942. Restoration of Italian Flag to Arbe.
237. **36.** 10 c. red & bistre (post.) 8 8
238. 15 c. red and brown .. 8 8
239. 20 c. grey and olive .. 8 8
240. 25 c. blue and green .. 8 8
241. 50 c. brown and red .. 8 8
242. 75 c. grey and red .. 8 8
243. **37.** 1 l. 25 grey and blue .. 8 8
244. 1 l. 75 grey and brown.. 15 15
245. 2 l. 75 blue and bistre 25 25
246. 5 l. brown and green .. 4·25 4·25

247. – 25 c. grey & brn. (air).. 8 8
248. – 50 c. brown and green.. 8 8
249. – 75 c. brown and blue.. 8 8
250. – 1 l. brown and bistre.. 25 25
251. – 5 l. blue and bistre .. 5·00 5·00
DESIGN—As T **36** inscr. "1923 1941"—Air: Granda Belfry, Arbe.

1942. Italian Philatelic Congress. Surch. **GIORNATA FILATELICA RIMINI—SAN MARINO 3 AGOSTO 1942 (1641 d. F.R.)** and value in figures.
252. **36.** 30 c. on 10 c. red & bistre 8 8

1942. Surch.
253. **36.** 30 c. on 20 c. grey & olive 8 8
254. – 20 l. on 75 c. black and red (No. 222) .. 22·00 16·00

1943. Press Propaganda.
255. **39.** 10 c. green 8 8
256. 15 c. brown 8 8
257. 20 c. brown 8 8

258. 39. 30 c. purple 8 8
259. 50 c. blue 8 8
260. 75 c. red 8 8
261. 40. 1 l. 25 blue 8 8
262. 1 l. 75 violet 12 12
263. 5 l. blue 50 50
264. 10 l. brown .. .. 6·00 5·50

1943. Philatelic Exn. Optd. **GIORNATA FILATELICA RIMINI SAN MARINO 5 LUGLIO 1943 (1642 d. F.R.).**
265. 39. 30 c. purple 8 8
266. 50 c. blue 8 8

41. Gateway.  43. Map of San Marino.

1943. Fall of Fascism. Unissued series for 20th Anniv. of Fascism optd. **28 LVGLIO 1943 1642 d. F.R.** and bars cancelling commemorative inscription.
267. 41. 5 c. brown (postage) .. 8 8
268. 10 c. orange 8 8
269. 20 c. blue 8 8
270. 25 c. green 8 8
271. 30 c. claret 8 8
272. 50 c. violet 8 8
273. 75 c. red 8 8
274. – 1 l. 25 blue 8 8
275. – 1 l. 75 orange 8 8
276. – 2 l. 75 brown 15 15
277. – 5 l. green 80 80
278. – 10 l. violet .. .. 1·10 1·10
279. – 20 l. blue .. .. 2·10 2·10
280. 43. 25 c. brown (air) 8 8
281. 50 c. red 8 8
282. 75 c. brown 8 8
283. 1 l. purple 8 8
284. 2 l. blue 8 8
285. 5 l. orange 30 30
286. 10 l. green 55 55
287. 20 l. black .. .. 3·75 3·75
DESIGN—As T 41: 1 l. 25 to 20 l. War Memorial.

1943. Provisional Govt. Optd. **GOVERNO PROVVISORIO** over ornamentation.
288. 41. 5 c. brown (postage) .. 8 8
289. 10 c. orange 8 8
290. 20 c. blue 8 8
291. 25 c. green 8 8
292. 30 c. claret 8 8
293. 50 c. violet 8 8
294. 75 c. red 8 8
295. – 1 l. 25 blue 8 8
296. – 1 l. 75 orange 35 35
297. – 5 l. green .. .. 1·25 1·25
298. – 20 l. blue .. .. 2·75 2·75
299. 43. 25 c. brown (air) 8 8
300. 50 c. red 8 8
301. 75 c. brown 8 8
302. 1 l. purple 8 8
303. 5 l. orange 90 90
304. 20 l. black .. .. 3·75 3·75

44. St. Marinus.  46. Govt. Palace.

45. Mt. Titano.  47. Govt. Palace.

1944.
305. 44. 20 l. + 10 l. brn. (post.) 1·40 1·40
306. 45. 20 l. + 10 l. olive (air) .. 1·40 1·40

1945. Government Palace. 50th Anniv.
307. 46. 25 l. purple (postage) .. 9·00 9·00
308. 47. 25 l. brown (air) .. 9·00 9·00

48. Arms of Montegiardino.  49. Arms of San Marino.

1945. Arms types.
309. – 10 c. blue 5 5
310. 48. 20 c. red 5 5
311. – 40 c. orange 5 5
312. 48. 60 c. slate 5 5
313. – 80 c. green 5 5
314. – 1 l. red 5 5
315. – 1 l. 20 violet 5 5
316. – 2 l. brown 8 8
317. – 3 l. blue 8 8
317a. – 4 l. orange 30 20
318. – 5 l. brown 12 8
319. – 10 l. red and brown .. 2·75 80
318a. – 15 l. blue .. .. 1·60 1·00
320. – 20 l. red and blue .. 4·50 1·00
321. – 20 l. brown and blue .. 2·75 1·00
322. 48. 25 l. blue and brown .. 2·75 1·00
323. 49. 50 l. blue and olive .. 9·00 5·00
DESIGNS (Arms of San Marino and villages in the Republic):—10 c., 1 l., 1 l. 20, 15 l. Faetano. 40 c., 5 l. San Marino. 80 c., 2 l., 3 l., 4 l. Fiorentino. 10 l. Borgomaggiore. 20 l. (2) Serravalle.

50. U.N.R.R.A. Aid for San Marino.

1946. U.N.R.R.A.
324. 50. 100 l. red, purple and orange .. 7·50 6·50

1946. Stamp Day. Surch. **L. 10.**
325. 49. 50 l. + 10 l. blue & olive 5·50 3·25

51. Aeroplane and Mt. Titano.

53. Aeroplane over Globe.  52. Aeroplanes over Mt. Titano.

1946. Air.
326. – 25 c. grey 5 5
327. 51. 75 c. orange 5 5
328. – 1 l. brown 5 5
329. 51. 2 l. green 5 5
330. 3 l. violet 5 5
331. 52. 5 l. blue 8 8
332. – 10 l. red 15 12
335. 52. 20 l. claret 40 40
333. 35 l. red .. .. 1·00 1·00
336. 50 l. olive .. .. 1·90 1·90
334. 53. 100 l. brown .. .. 1·25 80
DESIGN: 25 c., 1 l., 10 l. Wings over Mt. Titano.

1946. National Philatelic Convention. Nos. 330/2 but colours changed and without "POSTA AEREA" surch. **CONVEGNO FILATELICO 30 NOVEMBRE 1946** and premium.
336a. 51. 3 l. + 25 l. brown .. 40 40
336b. 52. 5 l. + 25 l. orange .. 40 40
336c. – 10 l. + 50 l. blue .. 3·00 2·50

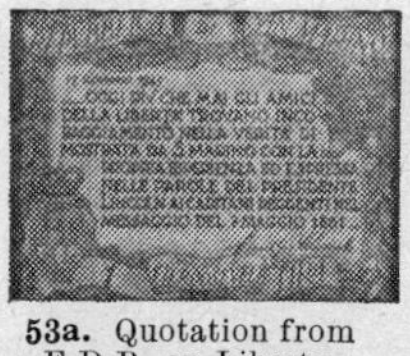

53a. Quotation from F.D.R. on Liberty.  53b. Franklin D. Roosevelt.

1947. In Memory of President Franklin D. Roosevelt.
336d. 53a. 1 l. brn. & ochre (post.) 8 8
336e. 53b. 2 l. brown and blue 8 8
336f. – 5 l. multicoloured .. 8 8
336g. – 15 l. multicoloured .. 12 12
336h. 53a. 50 l. brown and red 45 25
336i. 53b. 100 l. brown and violet 1·50 70
DESIGN—HORIZ.: 5 l., 15 l. Roosevelt and flags of San Marino and U.S.A.
336j. – 1 l. brn. & blue (air) .. 8 8
336k. – 2 l. brown and red .. 8 8
336l. – 5 l. multicoloured .. 8 8
336m. – 20 l. brown and purple 8 8
336n. – 31 l. brn. & orange .. 12 12
336o. – 50 l. brown and red .. 25 25
336p. – 100 l. brown and blue 60 60
336q. – 200 l. multicoloured .. 14·00 9·00
DESIGNS—HORIZ. 1 l., 31 l., 50 l. Roosevelt and eagle. 2 l., 20 l., 100 l. Roosevelt and San Marino arms. VERT. 5 l., 200 l. Roosevelt and flags of San Marino and U.S.A.

1947. Surch. in figures.
336r. 53a. 3 on 1 l. brown and ochre (postage) .. 20 15
336s. 53b. 4 on 2 l. brown and bl. 20 15
336t. – 6 on 5 l. multicoloured (No. 336f) .. 20 15
336u. – 3 on 1 l. brown and blue (No. 336j) (air) 20 15
336v. – 4 on 2 l. brown and red (No. 336k) .. 20 20
336w. – 6 on 5 l. multicoloured (No. 336l) .. 30 30

1947. No. 317a surch.
337. 6 l. on 4 l. orange 20 8
338. 21 l. on 4 l. orange .. 1·00 55

54. St. Marinus founding Republic.  55. Mt. Titano, Statue of Liberty and 1847 U.S.A. Stamp.

56. Mt. Titano and 1847 U.S.A. Stamp.

1947. Reconstruction.
339. 54. 1 l. mve. & grn. (post.) 8 8
340. 2 l. olive and mauve .. 8 8
341. 4 l. green and brown .. 8 8
342. 10 l. blue and orange .. 12 12
343. 25 l. mauve and red .. 1·60 1·60
344. 50 l. brown and green .. 7·50 4·50
345. 25 l. blue & orge (air) .. 1·75 1·00
346. 50 l. blue and brown .. 2·50 1·90
Nos. 343/6 are larger (24 × 32 mm.) and have two rows of ornaments forming the frame.

1947. Air. Rimini Philatelic Exn. Optd. **Giornata Filatelica Rimini-San Marino 18 Luglio 1947.**
347. 53. 100 l. brown .. .. 1·50 1·00

1947. Reconstruction. Surch. + and value in figures.
348. 54. 1 + 1 l. mauve & green .. 8 8
349. 1 + 2 l. mauve & green .. 8 8
350. 1 + 3 l. mauve & green .. 8 8
351. 1 + 4 l. mauve & green .. 8 8
352. 1 + 5 l. mauve & green .. 8 8
353. 2 + 1 l. olive & mauve .. 8 8
354. 2 + 2 l. olive & mauve .. 8 8
355. 2 + 3 l. olive & mauve .. 8 8
356. 2 + 4 l. olive & mauve .. 8 8
357. 2 + 5 l. olive & mauve .. 8 8
358. 4 + 1 l. green & brown .. 1·25 1·25
359. 4 + 2 l. green & brown .. 1·25 2·25

1947. Cent. of 1st U.S.A. Postage Stamp Inscr. as in T 55.
360. 55. 2 l. brn. & pur. (post) 8 8
361. – 3 l. grey, red and blue 8 8
362. 55. 6 l. green and blue .. 10 10
363. – 15 l. violet, red and blue 60 60
364. – 35 l. brown, red and blue 1·25 1·25
365. – 50 l. green, red and blue 2·10 2·10
366. 56. 100 l. brn. & vio. (air) 12·00 4·50
DESIGNS: 3 l., 35 l. U.S.A. stamps, 5 c. and 10 c., 1847 and 90 c., 1869 and flags of U.S.A. and San Marino. 15 l., 50 l. Similar but differently arranged.

57. Worker and San Marino Flag.

1948. Workers' Issue.
367. 57. 5 l. brown 10 10
368. 8 l. green 20 20
369. 30 l. red 40 40
370. 50 l. brown and mauve 90 90
371. 100 l. blue and violet .. 30·00 16·00

1948. Surch. **L100** between circular ornaments.
372. 33. 100 l. on 15 c. blk. & red 29·00 16·00

1948. Air. Surch. **POSTA AEREA 200.**
373. 54. 200 l. on 25 l. mauve and red (No. 343) 21·00 15·00

58. Faetano.  59. Mt. Titano.

60. Guaita Tower.

DESIGNS—As T 58:—HORIZ. A. Guaita Tower and walls. B. Serravalle and Mt. Titano. C. Franciscan Convent and Capuckin Church. D. Ramparts. VERT. E. Castle and Mt. Titano. F. Government Palace.

1949. National Scenes.
374. A. 1 l. blue and black .. 5 5
375. B. 2 l. red and purple .. 5 5
376. 58. 3 l. blue and violet .. 5 5
377. C. 4 l. violet and black .. 5 5
378. A. 5 l. brown and purple .. 5 5
491. D. 5 l. brown and blue .. 5 5
379. 58. 6 l. black and blue .. 8 8
380. 59. 8 l. brown and sepia .. 8 8
381. 60. 10 l. blue and black .. 10 8
578. E. 10 l. green and orange 8 5
382. B. 12 l. violet and red .. 25 15
383. C. 15 l. red and violet .. 35 25
493. F. 15 l. red and green .. 15 8
383a. 58. 20 l. brown and blue .. 5·00 1·40
494. D. 25 l. violet and brown 20 8
384. A. 35 l. violet and green .. 80 60
495. E. 35 l. red and lilac .. 40 20
797. D. 40 l. red and lilac .. 5 5
385. B. 50 l. brown and red .. 1·00 80
385a. C. 55 l. green and blue .. 10·00 7·00
798. E. 90 l. blue and black .. 12 12
386. 59. 100 l. green and black 32·00 19·00
799. F. 140 l. orange and violet 25 20
387. 60. 200 l. brown and blue 40·00 25·00
See also Nos. 522a/7a.

1949. Stamp Day. Optd. **Gionata Filatelica San Marino - Riccione 28-6-1949.**
388. 54. 1 l. mauve and green .. 8 8
389. 2 l. olive and mauve .. 8 8

61. Anita Garibaldi.  62. Garibaldi.

63. Garibaldi in San Marino.

PORTRAITS—VERT. 1 l., 20 l. Francesco Nullo. 4 l., 15 l. Ugo Bassi.

1949. Garibaldi's Retreat from Rome.
(a) Postage. Portraits inscr. as in T 61/2.
(i) Size 22 × 28 mm.
390. – 1 l. red and black .. 8 8
391. 61. 2 l. blue and brown .. 8 8
392. 62. 3 l. green and red .. 8 8
393. – 4 l. chocolate and blue .. 8 8

(ii) Size 27 × 37 mm.
394. 61. 5 l. chocolate and violet 12 12
395. – 15 l. blue and red .. 30 25
396. – 20 l. red and blue .. 60 60
397. 62. 50 l. blue and brown .. 11·00 5·50

(b) Air. (i) Size 28 × 22 mm.
398. 63. 2 l. blue and brown .. 8 8
399. 3 l. black and green .. 8 8
400. 5 l. green and blue .. 8 8

(ii) Size 37×27 mm.
401. **63.** 25 l. violet and green .. 3·00 2·25
402. 65 l. black and green .. 9·00 4·00

64. Mail-coach and Mt. Titano.

1949. U.P.U. 75th Anniv.
403. **64.** 100 l. pur. & blue (post.) 13·00 11·00

404. 200 l. blue (air) .. 3·75 2·75
405. 300 l. brown and lake .. 11·00 9·00

65. Mt. Titano from Serravalle.

67a. Flag, 'Plane and Mt. Titano. **66.** Second and Guaita Towers.

67. Guaita Tower.

1950. Air. Views.
406. **65.** 2 l. green and violet .. 5 5
407. – 3 l. brown and blue .. 5 5
408. **66.** 5 l. red and brown .. 5 5
409. – 10 l. blue and green .. 20 12
410. – 15 l. violet and black .. 15 25
411. – 55 l. green and blue .. 40 35
412. **65.** 100 l. black and red .. 65 65
413. **66.** 250 l. brown and violet 15·00 8·50
415. **67.** 500 l. pur., grn. & blue 50·00 40·00
414. 500 l. brown and green 75·00 48·00
423. **67a.** 1,000 l. blue & brown .. £160 £100
DESIGNS—As T **65**, HORIZ. 3 l., Distantview of Domagnano. 10 l. Domagnano. 15 l. San Marino from St. Mustiola. As T **66**., VERT. 55 l. Borgo Maggiore.
No. 415 is larger, size 47 × 33 mm.

1950. Air. 28th Milan Fair. As Nos. 408, 410 and 411 but in different colours, optd. **XXVIII FIERA INTERNAZIONALE DI MILANO APRILE 1950.**
416. 5 l. green and blue .. 20 20
417. 15 l. black and red .. 40 40
418. 55 l. brown and violet .. 4·25 3·50

68. Government Palace. **69.** "Columbus at the Council of Salamanca" (after Barabino).

1951. Red Cross.
419. **68.** 25 l. pur., red & brown 2·10 1·25
420. – 75 l. sepia, red & brown 4·50 3·75
421. – 100 l. black, red & brown 10·00 8·50
DESIGNS: 75 l. (horiz.) Archway of Murata Nuova. 100 l. (vert.). Guaita Tower.

1951. Air. Stamp Day. No. 415 surch. **Giornata Filatelica San Marino-Riccione 20-8-1951.** and new value.
422. **67.** 300 l. on 500 l. purple, green and blue .. 30·00 25·00

1951. Air. Italian Flood Relief. Surch. **Pro-alluvionati italiani 1951 L. 100** and bars.
424. **66.** 100 l. on 250 l. brown and violet .. 7·50 5·00

1952. Columbus.
425. **69.** 1 l. chestnut and bronze (postage) 8 8
426. – 2 l. sepia and violet .. 8 8
427. – 3 l. violet and brown .. 8 8
428. – 4 l. blue and chestnut .. 8 8
429. – 5 l. green and blue .. 8 8
430. – 10 l. sepia and black .. 20 20
431. – 15 l. red and black .. 35 35
432. – 20 l. blue and green .. 50 50
433. – 25 l. purple and brown 1·00 65
434. **69.** 60 l. brown and violet .. 4·25 2·50
435. – 80 l. grey and black .. 10·00 4·25
436. – 200 l. green and blue .. 25·00 12·00

437. – 200 l. blue & black (air) .. 20·00 8·00
DESIGNS—HORIZ. 2 l., 25 l. Columbus and "Santa Maria". 3 l., 10 l., 20 l. Landing in America. 4 l., 15 l., 80 l. Red Indians and American settlers. 5 l., 200 l. (No. 436), Columbus and map of America. 200 l. (No. 437), Columbus, Statue of Liberty and skyscrapers.

1952. Trieste Fair. As Columbus issue of 1952 optd. **FIERA DI TRIESTE 1952.**
438. 1 l. vio. & brn. (postage) 8 8
439. 2 l. red and black .. 8 8
440. 3 l. green and blue .. 8 8
441. 4 l. sepia and black .. 8 8
442. 5 l. mauve and violet 20 15
443. 10 l. blue and brown .. 2·40 1·40
444. 15 l. brown and blue .. 3·75 2·25

445. 200 l. brn. & blk. (air) .. 17·00 8·00

70. Rose.

71. Cyclamen, Rose, San Marino and Riccione.

1952. Air. Philatelic Exn.
446. – 1 l. purple and violet .. 8 8
447. – 2 l. green and blue .. 8 8
448. **70.** 3 l. vermilion & sepia .. 8 8
449. **71.** 5 l. brown and purple .. 12 12
450. 25 l. green and violet .. 50 50
451. 200 l. green, blue, claret, purple and red .. 25·00 15·00
DESIGNS—As T **70**: 1 l. Cyclamen. 2 l. San Marino and Riccione.

72. Aeroplane over San Marino.

DESIGN: 75 l. 'Plane over Mt. Titano.

1952. Air. Aerial Survey of San Marino.
452. **72.** 25 l. green .. .. 1·25 1·00
453. – 75 l. violet and brown .. 3·25 3·00

73. Discus Throwing.

74. Tennis.

DESIGNS—As T **73**: 3 l. Running. As T **74**: HORIZ. 4 l. Cycling. 5 l. Football. 100 l. Roller-skating. 200 l. Ski-ing. VERT. 10 l. Model glider flying. 25 l. Shooting.

1953. Sports.
454. **73.** 1 l. blk. & brn. (postage) 8 8
455. **74.** 2 l. brown and black .. 8 8
456. – 3 l. blue-green and black 8 8
457. – 4 l. blue and green .. 8 8
458. – 5 l. green and brown .. 12 12
459. – 10 l. red and blue .. 30 30
460. – 25 l. brown and black .. 1·00 1·00
461. – 100 l. grey and brown .. 2·50 2·50

462. – 200 l. blue-green and green (air) .. 35·00 21·00

1953. Stamp Day and Philatelic Exn. As No. 461 but colour changed, optd. **GIORNATA FILATELICA S. MARINO-RICCIONE 24 AGOSTO 1953.**
463. 100 l. green and blue .. 20·00 8·00

75. Narcissus.

FLOWERS: 2 l. "Parrot" tulip. 3 l. Oleander. 4 l. Cornflower. 5 l. Carnation. 10 l. Iris. 25 l. Cyclamen. 80 l. Geranium. 100 l. Rose.

1953. Flowers.
464. **75.** 1 l. blue, green & yellow 8 8
465. – 2 l. blue, green & yellow 8 8
466. – 3 l. blue, green & yellow 8 8
467. – 4 l. blue, green & yellow 8 8
468. – 5 l. green and red .. 12 12
469. – 10 l. blue, green & yellow 70 40
470. – 25 l. blue, green and red 2·75 1·60
471. – 80 l. blue, green & verm. 10·00 5·00
472. – 100 l. blue, green & red 19·00 9·00

76. Aeroplane over Mt. Titano.

1954. Air.
473. **76.** 1000 l. sepia and blue .. 50·00 25·00

77. Walking. **78.** Statue of Liberty.

1954. Sports.
474. **77.** 1 l. magenta and violet 8 8
475. – 2 l. violet and green .. 8 8
476. – 3 l. chestnut and brown 8 8
477. – 4 l. blue 8 8
478. – 5 l. sepia and green .. 8 8
479. – 8 l. lilac and mauve .. 12 12
480. – 12 l. red and black .. 12 12
481. – 25 l. green and blue .. 60 40
482. **77.** 80 l. turquoise and blue 1·25 80
483. – 200 l. brown and lilac .. 5·00 2·50
484. – 250 l. black, chestnut, lake and sepia .. 20·00 15·00
DESIGNS—HORIZ. 2 l. Fencing. 3 l. Boxing. 5 l. Motor-cycle racing. 8 l. Throwing the javelin. 12 l. Car racing. VERT. 4 l., 200 l., 250 l. Gymnastics. 25 l. Wrestling.

1954.
485. **78.** 20 l. blue & brn. (post.) 65 40
486. 60 l. green and red .. 1·25 1·50

487. 120 l. brown & blue (air) 1·90 80

79. Hurdling.

80. Yacht.

81. Ice-skating. **82.** Pointer.

1955. Air. 1st Int. Exn. of Olympic Stamps. Inscr. as in T **79**.
488. **79.** 80 l. black and red .. 1·25 1·00
489. – 120 l. red and green .. 2·00 1·75
DESIGN—HORIZ. 120 l. Relay racing.

1955. 7th Int. Philatelic Exn.
490. **80.** 100 l. black and blue .. 4·25 2·50

1955. Winter Olympic Games, Cortina D'Ampezzo.
496. **81.** 1 l. brown & yell. (post.) 8 8
497. – 2 l. blue and red .. 8 8
498. – 3 l. black and brown .. 8 8
499. – 4 l. brown and green .. 8 8
500. – 5 l. blue and red .. 10 10
501. – 10 l. blue and pink .. 40 30
502. – 25 l. black and red .. 80 40
503. – 50 l. brown and blue .. 1·25 1·00
504. – 100 l. black and green .. 4·00 2·75

505. – 200 l. blk. & orge. (air) .. 13·00 7·50
DESIGNS—HORIZ. 2 l., 25 l. Skiing. 3 l., 50 l. Bob-sleighing. 5 l., 100 l. Ice-hockey. 200 l. Ski-jumping. VERT. 4 l. Slalom racing. 10 l. Figure skating.

1956. Winter Relief Fund. As T **57** but additionally inscr. "ASSISTENZA INVERNALE".
506. 50 l. green .. .. .. 4·25 2·50

1956. 50th Anniv. of "Arengo" (San Marino Parliament). As T **57** but additionally inscr. "50° ANNIVERSARIO ARENGO 25 MARZO 1906".
507. 50 l. blue .. .. .. 4·25 2·50

1956. Dogs. 25 l. to 100 l. have multicoloured centres.
508. **82.** 1 l. brown and blue .. 8 8
509. – 2 l. grey and red .. 8 8
510. – 3 l. brown and blue .. 8 8
511. – 4 l. grey and turquoise 8 8
512. – 5 l. brown and red .. 8 8
513. – 10 l. brown and blue .. 20 15
514. – 25 l. grey-blue .. 35 25
515. – 60 l. red 80 60
516. – 80 l. grey-blue .. 1·60 1·00
517. – 100 l. red .. .. 5·50 3·75
DOGS: 2 l. Borzoi. 3 l. Sheepdog. 4 l. Greyhound. 5 l. Boxer. 10 l. Great Dane. 25 l. Irish Setter. 60 l. Alsatian. 80 l. Scotch Collie. 100 l. Foxhound.

1956. Philatelic Exn. As T **80** but inscr. "1956".
518. **80.** 100 l. sepia & turquoise 1·90 1·25

1956. Int. Philatelic Congress. Designs as 1949 (Nos. 491 etc.) but larger and inscr. "CONGRESSO INTERNAZ. PERITI FILATELICI SAN MARINO SALSOMAGGIORE 6-8 OTTOBRE 1956".
519. E. 20 l. sepia and blue .. 40 20
520. D. 80 l. red and violet .. 1·75 1·00
521. F. 100 l. green and orange 3·00 1·60
SIZES—$26\frac{1}{2}$ × 37 mm., 20 l., 100 l. $36\frac{1}{2}$ x 27 mm., 80 l.

1956. Air. No. 504 optd. with an aeroplane and **POSTA AEREA.**
522. 100 l. black and green .. 1·60 1·40

1957. National scenes as T **58**.
522a. 1 l. blue-green and green 5 5
523. 2 l. red and green .. 5 5
524. 3 l. brown and blue .. 5 5
524a. 4 l. blue and sepia .. 1·25 60
794. 5 l. brown and blue .. 5 5
795. 10 l. green and black .. 5 5
796. 15 l. violet and sepia .. 5 5
525. 20 l. blue-green and green 20 5
525a. 30 l. violet and brown .. 1·00 30
526. 60 l. violet and brown .. 1·60 80
526a. 115 l. brown and blue .. 60 50
527. 125 l. blue and sepia .. 55 40
527a. 500 l. black and green .. 45·00 21·00
DESIGNS—HORIZ. 1 l., 5 l., 60 l. San Marino from Hospital Avenue. VERT. 2 l., 115 l. Borgo Maggiore Church. 3 l., 10 l., 30 l. Town Gate, San Marino. 40 l., 15 l., 125 l. San Marino from southern wall. 20 l., 115 l. Borgo Maggiore Marketplace. ($37\frac{1}{2}$ × 28 mm.): 500 l. Panorama of San Marino.

83. Marguerites. **84.** St. Marinus Statue and Fair Entrance.

1957. Flowers as T **83** in natural colours. Background colour blue (Nos. 528/32), rest multicoloured.
528. 1 l. T **83** 5 5
529. 2 l. Polyanthuses 5 5
530. 3 l. Lilies 5 5
531. 4 l. Orchid 5 5
532. 5 l. Lilies of the Valley .. 5 5
533. 10 l. Poppies 5 5
534. 25 l. Pansies 12 12
535. 60 l. Gladiolus 30 25
536. 80 l. Wild Roses 55 40
537. 100 l. Anemones .. .. 1·40 1·00

1957. Garibaldi. 150th Birth Anniv. As T **61/2** but inscr. "COMMEMORAZIONE 150° NASCITA G. GARIBALDI 1807 1957".
(a) Size 22 × 28 mm.
538. **61.** 2 l. blue and violet .. 5 5
539. – 3 l. green and red (as No. 390) 5 5
540. **62.** 5 l. sepia and brown .. 5 5
(b) Size 27 × 37 mm.
541. – 15 l. violet and blue (as No. 395) 8 8
542. – 25 l. black and green (as No. 396) 15 12
543. **61.** 50 l. brown and violet 1·50 80
544. **62.** 100 l. violet and brown 1·50 80
Nos. 543/4 were printed se-tenant alternately throughout the sheet.

1958. 36th Milan Fair.
545. **84.** 15 l. yell. & blue (post.) 15 12
546. – 60 l. green and red .. 65 35

547. – 125 l. blue & brn. (air) 2·50 80
DESIGNS—HORIZ. 60 l. Italian pavilion and giant arch. VERT. 125 l. Helicopter and aeroplane over fair.

85. Exhibition Emblem, Atomium and Mt. Titano. **86.** View of San Marino.

88. Naples 10 grana stamp of 1858, and Bay of Naples. **87.** Wheat.

1958. Brussels Int. Exn.

548. **85.** 40 l. sepia and green .. 40 20
549. 60 l. lake and blue .. 70 25

1958. Air.

550. **86.** 200 l. blue and brown .. 4·25 3·75
551. – 300 l. violet and red .. 4·25 3·75

DESIGN: 300 l. Mt. Titano.

1958. Fruit and Agricultural Products.

552. **87.** 1 l. yellow and blue .. 5 5
553. – 2 l. red and green .. 5 5
554. – 3 l. yellow and blue .. 5 5
555. – 4 l. red and green .. 5 5
556. – 5 l. yellow, grn. & blue 5 5
557. **87.** 15 l. buff and blue .. 8 8
558. – 25 l. multicoloured .. 8 8
559. – 40 l. multicoloured .. 12 12
560. – 80 l. multicoloured .. 60 50
561. – 125 l. multicoloured .. 2·00 1·25

DESIGNS: 2 l., 125 l. Maize. 3 l., 80 l. Grapes. 4 l., 25 l. Peaches. 5 l., 40 l. Plums.

1958. First Naples Postage Stamps Cent.

562. **88.** 25 l. brn. & blue (post.) 20 15

563. 125 l. brown & bistre-brown (air) .. 1·40 80

The Naples stamp on No. 563 is the 50 gr.

89. Seagull. **90.** P. de Coubertin.

1959. Air. Native Birds.

564. **89.** 5 l. black and green .. 5 5
565. – 10 l. salmon, blk. & blue 5 5
566. – 15 l. multicoloured .. 8 8
567. – 120 l. multicoloured .. 30 25
568. – 250 l. blk., yell. & green 2·00 1·25

BIRDS: 10 l. Falcon. 15 l. Wild duck. 120 l. Dove. 250 l. Swallow.

1959. Pre-Olympic Games Issue.

569. **90.** 2 l. blk., & ches. (post.) 5 5
570. – 3 l. sepia and mauve .. 5 5
571. – 5 l. green and blue .. 8 8
572. – 30 l. black and violet .. 10 8
573. – 60 l. sepia and green .. 10 8
574. – 80 l. green and lake .. 12 12

575. – 120 l. brown (air) .. 2·00 1·50

PORTRAITS—As T **90**: 3 l. A. Bonacossa. 5 l. A. Brundage. 30 l. C. Mantu. 60 l. J. S. Edstrom. 80 l. De Baillet-Latour. HORIZ. (36×21½ mm.): 120 l. De Coubertin and Olympic Flame. All, except the founder, De Coubertin, are executives of the Olympic Games Committee.

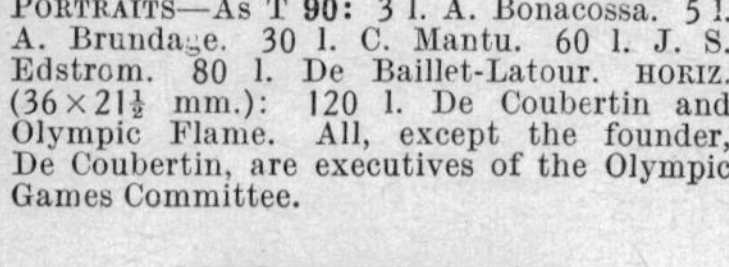

91. Vickers "Viscount" over Mt. Titano.

1959. Air "Alitalia" Inaugural Flight, Rimini-London.

576. **91.** 120 l. violet .. .. 1·50 1·25

93. Abraham Lincoln and Scroll.

1959. Abraham Lincoln's 150th Birth Anniv. Inscr. "ABRAMO LINCOLN 1809–1959".

577. **93.** 5 l. brn. & sepia (post.) 5 5
578. – 10 l. green and blue .. 5 5
579. – 15 l. grey and green .. 10 10
580. – 70 l. violet .. .. 1·00 60

581. – 200 l. blue (air) .. 5·50 2·75

DESIGNS—Portraits of Lincoln with: HORIZ. 10 l. Map of San Marino. 15 l. Govt. Palace, San Marino. 200 l. Mt. Titano. VERT. 70 l. Mt. Titano.

94. 1859 Romagna ½ b. stamp and Arch of Augustus, Rimini. **95.** Portal of Messina Cathedral and ½ gr. Sicily stamp.

1959. Romagna Stamp Centenary Inscr. "1859–1959".

582. **94.** 30 l. brn., & sepia (post.) 25 15

583. – 120 l. grn. & blk. (air) 1·25 80

DESIGN: 120 l. 1859 Romagna 3 b. stamp and view of Bologna.

1959. Turin University Commem. Inscr. "UNIVERSIADE TORINO 1959".

584. **73.** 30 l. orange 80 40

1959. Sicily Stamp Centenary. Inscr. as in T **95**.

585. **95.** 1 l. brn. & yell. (post.) .. 5 5
586. – 2 l. red and olive .. 5 5
587. – 3 l. slate-blue and blue 5 5
588. – 4 l. brown and red .. 5 5
589. – 5 l. mauve and blue .. 5 5
590. – 25 l. multicoloured .. 35 12
591. – 60 l. multicoloured .. 30 15

592. – 200 l. multicoloured (air) 85 55

DESIGNS—VERT. 2 l. Selinunte Temple (1 gr.). 3 l. Erice Church (2 gr.). 4 l. "Concordia" Temple, Agrigento (5 gr.). 5 l. "Castor and Pollux" Temple, Agrigento (10 gr.). 25 l. "St. John of the Hermits" Church, Palermo (20 gr.). HORIZ. 60 l. Taormina (50 gr.). 200 l. Bay of Palermo (50 gr.).

96. Golden Oriole. **97.** Putting the Shot.

1960. Birds.

593. **96.** 1 l. yell., olive and blue 5 5
594. – 2 l. brown, red and green 5 5
595. – 3 l. red, brown and green 5 5
596. – 4 l. black, brown & grn. 5 5
597. – 5 l. red, brown and green 5 5
598. – 10 l. multicoloured .. 8 8
599. – 25 l. multicoloured .. 15 15
600. – 60 l. multicoloured .. 75 50
601. – 80 l. multicoloured .. 2·40 1·60
602. – 110 l. multicoloured .. 2·40 1·75

DESIGNS—VERT. 2 l. Nightingale. 4 l. Hoopoe. 10 l. Goldfinch. 25 l. Kingfisher. 80 l. Green woodpecker. 110 l. Red-breasted flycatcher. HORIZ. 3 l. Woodcock. 5 l. Red-legged partridge. 60 l. Pheasant.

1960. Olympic Games. Inscr. "ROMA 1960".

603. **97.** 1 l. violet & crim. (post.) 5 5
604. – 2 l. orange and black .. 5 5
605. – 3 l. violet & bistre-brn. 5 5
606. – 4 l. brown and red .. 5 5
607. – 5 l. blue and brown .. 5 5
608. – 10 l. blue and chestnut 5 5
609. – 15 l. violet and green .. 5 5
610. – 25 l. orange & blue-grn. 8 8
611. – 60 l. orange & grey-green 10 10
612. – 110 l. red, black & green 25 15

613. – 20 l. violet (air) .. 5 5
614. – 40 l. red and brown .. 12 12
615. – 80 l. yellow and blue .. 20 15
616. – 125 l. sepia and red .. 35 30

DESIGNS—VERT. 2 l. Gymnastics. 3 l. Long-distance walking. 4 l. Boxing. 10 l. Cycling. 20 l. Handball. 40 l. Athletics. 60 l. Football. HORIZ. 5 l. Fencing. 15 l. Hockey. 25 l. Rowing. 80 l. Diving. 110 l. Horse-jumping. 125 l. Rifle-shooting.

98. Melvin Jones (founder) and Lions International H.Q.

1960. Lions International Commem.

617. – 30 l. brn. & violet (post.) 8 8
618. **98.** 45 l. chestnut and violet 15 15
619. – 60 l. red and blue .. 8 8
620. – 115 l. green and black .. 30 30
621. – 150 l. brown and violet 1·00 60

622. – 200 l. blue & green (air) 5·50 2·75

DESIGNS—VERT. 30 l. Mt. Titano. 60 l. Government Palace. HORIZ. 115 l. Pres. Clarence Sturim. 150 l. Vice-Pres. F. E. Davis. 200 l. Globe. All designs except T **98** bear the Lions emblem.

99. Riccione. **100.** "Youth with basket of fruit" (after Caravaggio).

1960. 12th Riccione-San Marino Stamp Day. Centres multicoloured.

623. **99.** 30 l. red postage) .. 30 25

624. 125 l. blue (air) .. .. 1·50 1·25

1960. Michelangelo Merisi da Caravaggio (painter). 350th Death Anniv.

625. **100.** 200 l. multicoloured .. 13·00 4·25

101. Hunting Deer.

1961. Hunting (1st issue). Historical Scenes.

626. **101.** 1 l. blue and magenta 5 5
627. – 2 l. red and sepia .. 5 5
628. – 3 l. black and red .. 5 5
629. – 4 l. red and blue .. 5 5
630. – 5 l. brown and green .. 5 5
631. – 10 l. violet and orange 8 8
632. – 30 l. blue, grn. & yellow 12 12
633. – 60 l. red, brown, ochre and black 25 25
634. – 70 l. red, purple, green and black 40 40
635. – 115 l. violet, blue, purple and black .. 1·40 1·40

DESIGNS—VERT. 2 l. 16th-cent. falconer. 10 l. 16th-cent. falconer (mounted). 60 l. 17th-cent. hunter with rifle and dog. HORIZ. 3 l. 16th-cent. boar-hunt. 4 l. Duck-shooting with crossbow (16th-cent.). 5 l. 16th-cent. stag-hunt with bow and arrow. 30 l. 17th-cent. huntsman with horn and dogs. 70 l. 18th-cent. hunter and beater. 115 l. Duck-shooting with bow and arrow (18th-cent.).

See also Nos. 679/88.

102. Agusta-Bell 47-J "Ranger" Helicopter near Mt. Titano.

1961. Air.

636. **102.** 1,000 l. red .. .. 32·00 16·00

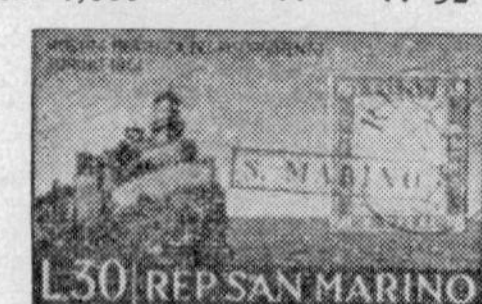

103. Guaita Tower, Mt. Titano and 1858 Sardinian Stamp.

1961. Italian Independence Cent. Philatelic Exn., Turin.

637. **103.** 30 l. ochre, orange, blue and indigo .. .. 1·00 55
638. 70 l. ochre, orange, black and blue .. .. 2·10 1·00
639. 200 l. ochre, orange, blue and black .. .. 1·00 55

104. Mt. Titano. **105.** King Enzo's Palace, Bologna.

1961. Europa.

640. **104.** 500 l. green & brown 3·25 2·75

1961. Bologna Stamp Exhibition. Inscr. "BOLOGNA".

641. **105.** 30 l. black and blue .. 15 12
642. – 70 l. black and myrtle 35 25
643. – 100 l. black and brown 75 50

DESIGNS: 70 l. Gateway of Merchant's Palace. 100 l. Towers of Garisenda and Asinelli, Bologna.

106. Duryea—U.S.A., 1892.

1962. Veteran Motor Cars.

644. 1 l. blue and brown .. 5 5
645. 2 l. orange and blue .. 5 5
646. 3 l. orange and black .. 5 5
647. 4 l. red and black .. 5 5
648. 5 l. orange and violet .. 5 5
649. 10 l. orange and black .. 5 5
650. 15 l. red and black .. 5 5
651. 20 l. blue and black .. 5 5
652. 25 l. orange and black .. 8 8
653. 30 l. buff and black .. 8 8
654. 50 l. mauve and black .. 8 8
655. 70 l. green and black .. 15 15
656. 100 l. red, yellow and black 20 20
657. 115 l. grn., orange & black 25 25
658. 150 l. yellow, orge. & blk. 50 50

MOTOR CARS—HORIZ. 1 l. T **106**. 2 l. Panhard and Levassor, 1895. 3 l. Peugeot "Vis-a-vis", 1895. 4 l. Daimler, 1899. 10 l. Decauville, 1900. 15 l. Wolseley, 1901. 20 l. Benz, 1902. 25 l. Napier, 1903. 50 l. Oldsmobile, 1904. 100 l. Isotta Fraschini, 1908. 115 l. Bianchi, 1910. 150 l. Alfa, 1910. VERT. F.I.A.T., 1899. 30 l. White, 1903. 70 l. Renault, 1904.

107. Wright "Flyer". **108.** Roping Down.

1962. "Vintage" Aircraft.

659. 1 l. black and yellow .. 5 5
660. 2 l. brown and green .. 5 5
661. 3 l. chestnut & grey-green 5 5
662. 4 l. black and yellow-brown 5 5
663. 5 l. red and blue 5 5
664. 10 l. chestnut & blue-green 5 5
665. 30 l. yellow-brown and blue 8 8
666. 60 l. yellow-brn. & slate-vio. 15 15
667. 70 l. black and orange .. 20 20
668. 115 l. yell.-brn., blk. & grn. 75 55

DESIGNS—Aircraft constructed and flown by: 1 l. T **107**. 2 l. Ernest Archdeacon. 3 l. Albert and Emile Bonnet-Labranche. 4 l. Glenn Curtiss. 5 l. Henri Farman. 10 l. Louis Blériot. 30 l. Hubert Latham. 60 l. Alberto Santos-Dumont. 70 l. Alliott Verdon-Roe. 115 l. Faccioli.

1962. Mountaineering.

669. 1 l. yellow-brown and black 5 5
670. 2 l. blue-green and black .. 5 5
671. 3 l. purple and black .. 5 5
672. 4 l. blue and black .. 5 5
673. 5 l. orange and black .. 5 5
674. 15 l. yellow and black .. 15 12
675. 30 l. red and black .. 15 12
676. 40 l. blue and black .. 8 8
677. 85 l. green and black .. 20 15
678. 115 l. violet-blue and black 75 55

DESIGNS: 1 l. T **108**. 2. Sassolungo. 3 l. Mt. Titano. 4 l. Three Lavaredo peaks. 5 l. The Matterhorn. 15 l. Skier. 30 l. Climber negotiating overhang. 40 l. Step-cutting in ice. 85 l. Aiguille du Geant. 115 l. Citadel of Mt. Titano.

109. Hunter and Retriever.

1962. Hunting (2nd issue). Modern scenes.
679. 1 l. dull purple & yell.-green .. 5 5
680. 2 l. indigo and orange .. 5 5
681. 3 l. black and blue .. 5 5
682. 4 l. sepia and brown .. 5 5
683. 5 l. choc. & yellow-green .. 5 5
684. 15 l. black and chestnut .. 8 8
685. 50. l. sepia and green .. 8 8
686. 70 l. blue-green and red .. 12 12
687. 100 l. black and red .. 35 25
688. 150 l. green and lilac .. 70 45
DESIGNS—HORIZ. 1 l. T **109**. Hunting: 3 l. Marsh ducks (with decoys). 4 l. Deer. 5 l. Grey partridge. 15 l. Lapwing. 50 l. Partridge. 70 l. Marsh geese. 100 l. Wild boar. VERT. 2 l. Huntsman and hounds. 140 l. Hunter shooting pheasant.

110. Arrows encircling "Europa".

112. "The Fornarina" (or "The Veiled Woman").

111. Egyptian Ship, about 2,000 B.C.

113. Saracen Game, Arezzo.

1962. Europa.
689. **110.** 200 l. red and black .. 1·25 60

1963. Historical Ships.
690. 1 l. grey-blue and orange .. 5 5
691. 2 l. sepia and purple .. 5 5
692. 3 l. sepia and mauve .. 5 5
693. 4 l. dull purple and grey .. 5 5
694. 5 l. sepia and yellow .. 5 5
695. 10 l. choc. and yellow-green .. 8 8
696. 30 l. sepia and blue .. 30 20
697. 60 l. ultram. & yellow-green .. 20 15
698. 70 l. red and black .. 30 25
699. 115 l. brown and blue .. 1·60 95
DESIGNS—HORIZ. 1 l. T **111**. 2 l. Greek vessel (5th-cent. B.C.). 3 l. Roman trireme (1st-cent. B.C.). 4 l. Viking ship. 5 l. The "Santa Maria". 30 l. Galley (about 1600). 115 l. Frigate of 1850. VERT. 10 l. Galleon (about 1550). 60 l. English ship "Sovereign of the Seas" (1637). 70 l. Danish ship (about 1750).

1963. Paintings by Raphael. Multicoloured.
700. 30 l. T **112** .. .. 1·25 65
701. 70 l. Self-portrait .. 8 8
702. 100 l. Sistine Madonna (detail of woman praying) .. 20 15
703. 200 l. "Portrait of a Young Woman" (Maddalena Strozzi) .. 75 65
The 200 l. is larger (27 × 44 mm.).

1963. Ancient Tournaments.
704. **113.** 1 l. magenta 5 5
705. – 2 l. slate 5 5
706. – 3 l. black 5 5
707. – 4 l. violet 5 5
708. – 5 l. reddish violet .. 5 5
709. – 10 l. green 5 5
710. – 30 l. brown 12 12
711. – 60 l. slate-blue .. 8 8
712. – 70 l. bistre-brown .. 12 12
713. – 115 l. black 30 30
TOURNAMENTS—HORIZ. 2 l. 14th-century, French cavaliers. 4 l. 15th-century, Presenting arms to an English cavalier. 30 l. Quintana game, Foligno. 70 l. 15th-century, Cavaliers (from castle mural, Malpaga). VERT. 3 l. Crossbow Championships, Gubbio. 5 l. 16th-century, Cavaliers, Florence. 10 l. Quintana game, Ascoli Piceno. 60 l. Palio (horse-race), Siena. 115 l. 13th century. The Crusades: cavaliers' challenge.

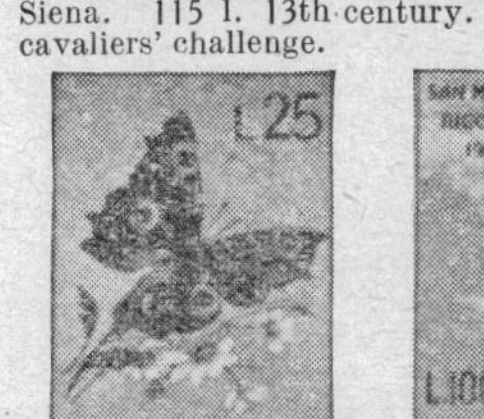

114. Butterfly. **115.** Corner of Government Palace, San Marino.

1963. Butterflies. Various designs as T **114**.
714. **114.** 25 l. multicoloured .. 5 5
715. – 30 l. multicoloured .. 8 8
716. – 60 l. multicoloured .. 8 8
717. – 70 l. multicoloured .. 20 20
718. – 115 l. multicoloured .. 30 30

1963. San Marino—Riccione Stamp Fair.
719. **115.** 100 l. black and blue .. 50 40
720. – 100 l. blue and sepia .. 25 15
DESIGN: No. 720 Fountain, Riccione.

116. Pole Vaulting.

117. "E" and Flag of San Marino.

1963. Olympic Games, Tokyo (1964).
721. – 1 l. maroon and orange .. 5 5
722. **116.** 2 l. sepia and green .. 5 5
723. – 3 l. sepia and blue .. 5 5
724. – 4 l. sepia and blue .. 5 5
725. – 5 l. sepia and red .. 5 5
726. – 10 l. maroon and purple .. 5 5
727. – 30 l. maroon and grey .. 5 5
728. – 60 l. sepia and yellow .. 8 8
729. – 70 l. sepia and blue .. 8 8
730. – 115 l. sepia and green .. 20 20
SPORTS—HORIZ. 1 l. Hurdling. 3 l. Relay-racing. 4 l. High-jumping. 5 l. Football. 10 l. High-jumping (women). 60 l. Throwing the javelin. 70 l. Water-polo. 115 l. Throwing the hammer VERT. 30 l. Throwing the discus.
See also Nos. 743/52.

1963. Europa.
731. **117.** 200 l. blue and brown .. 30 30

118. Tupolev "TU-104A".

119. Running.

1963. Air. Contemporary Aircraft.
732. **118.** 5 l. maroon & turq. .. 5 5
733. – 10 l. blue and red .. 5 5
734. – 15 l. red and violet .. 5 5
735. – 25 l. red and violet .. 8 8
736. – 50 l. red and turquoise .. 10 10
737. – 75 l. orange & green .. 12 12
738. – 120 l. red and blue .. 55 55
739. – 200 l. black and yellow .. 20 20
740. – 300 l. black and orange .. 35 35
741. – 500 l. multicoloured .. 6·00 2·50
742. – 1000 l. multicoloured .. 5·00 2·00
AIRCRAFT—HORIZ. 15 l. Douglas "DC-8". 25 l. Boeing "707". 50 l. Vickers "Viscount 837". 120 l. Vickers "VC-10". 200 l. D. H. "Comet 4 C". 300 l. Boeing "727". 1000 l. Boeing "707". VERT. 10 l. Boeing "707". 75 l. "Caravelle". 500 l. Rolls Royce "Dart" turbo-prop engine.

1964. Olympic Games, Tokyo. Inscr. "TOKIO 1964".
743. **119.** 1 l. brown and green .. 5 5
744. – 2 l. red-brown & sepia .. 5 5
745. – 3 l. yellow-brown & blk. .. 5 5
746. – 4 l. slate-blue & verm. .. 5 5
747. – 5 l. sepia and blue .. 5 5
748. – 15 l. purple and orange .. 5 5
749. – 30 l. violet-blue & blue .. 5 5
750. – 70 l. chestnut & green .. 12 12
751. – 120 l. chestnut and blue .. 15 15
752. – 150 l. purple and red .. 35 35
DESIGNS—VERT. 2 l. Gymnastics. 3 l. Basket-ball. 120 l. Cycling. 150 l. Fencing. HORIZ. 4 l. Pistol-shooting. 5 l. Rowing. 15 l. Long-jumping. 30 l. Diving. 70 l. Sprinting.

1964. "Towards Tokyo" Sports Stamp Exn. Rimini. As Nos. 749/50, but inscr. "VERSO TOKIO" and colours changed.
753. 30 l. grey-blue & reddish vio. .. 15 15
754. 70 l. chestnut & turq.-blue .. 20 20

120. Murray-Blenkinsop Locomotive (1812).

1964. "Story of the Locomotive".
755. **120.** 1 l. black and buff .. 5 5
756. – 2 l. black and green .. 5 5
757. – 3 l. black and violet .. 5 5
758. – 4 l. black and yellow .. 5 5
759. – 5 l. black and salmon .. 5 5
760. – 15 l. black and green .. 5 5
761. – 20 l. black and pink .. 5 5
762. – 50 l. black & vio.-blue .. 8 8
763. – 90 l. black and orange .. 15 15
764. – 110 l. black and blue .. 55 55
LOCOMOTIVES: 2 l. "Puffing Billy" (1813). 3 l. "Locomotion 1" (1825). 4 l. "Rocket" (1829). 5 l. "Lion" (1838). 15 l. "Bayard". (1839). 20 l. "Crampton" (1849). 50 l. "Little England" (1851). 90 l. "Spitfire" (c. 1860). 110 l. "Rogers" (c. 1865).

121. Baseball Players.

1964. 7th European Baseball Championships Milan.
765. **121.** 30 l. sepia and green .. 12 12
766. – 70 l. black and cerise .. 20 20
DESIGN: 70 l. Player pitching ball.

122. "E" and Part of Globe.

123. Pres. Kennedy giving Inaugural Address.

124. Cyclists at Government Palace.

1964. Europa.
767. **122.** 200 l. red, blue & lt. bl. .. 40 40

1964. Pres. Kennedy. 1st Death Anniv.
768. **123.** 70 l. multicoloured .. 20 20
769. – 130 l. multicoloured .. 30 30
DESIGN—VERT. 130 l. Kennedy and U.S. flag.

1965. Cycle Tour of Italy.
770. **124.** 30 l. sepia 12 12
771. – 70 l. purple 8 8
772. – 200 l. red 20 20
DESIGNS:—Cyclists passing: 70 l. "The Rock". 200 l. Mt. Titano.

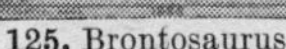
125. Brontosaurus.

126. "Castles" on Chessboard.

1965. Prehistoric Animals.
773. **125.** 1 l. maroon and green .. 5 5
774. – 2 l. black and blue .. 5 5
775. – 3 l. yellow and green .. 5 5
776. – 4 l. brown and blue .. 5 5
777. – 5 l. maroon and green .. 5 5
778. – 10 l. maroon and green .. 5 5
779. – 75 l. blue and turquoise .. 20 20
780. – 100 l. maroon & green .. 30 30
781. – 200 l. maroon & green .. 65 65
ANIMALS—VERT. 2 l. Brachyosaurus. HORIZ. 3 l. Pteranodon. 4 l. Elasmosaurus. 5 l. Tyrannosaurus. 10 l. Stegosaurus. 75 l. Thaumatosaurus. 100 l. Iguanodon. 200 l. Triceratops.

1965. Europa.
782. **126.** 200 l. multicoloured .. 30 30

127. Dante.

DESIGNS: 90 l. "Hell". 130 l. "Purgatory". 140 l. "Paradise".

1965. Dante's 700th Birth Anniv.
783. **127.** 40 l. sepia and indigo .. 15 15
784. – 90 l. sepia and red .. 10 10
785. – 130 l. sepia and brown .. 12 12
786. – 140 l. sepia and blue .. 30 30

128. Mt. Titano and Flags.

1965. Visit of Pres. Saragat of Italy.
787. **128.** 115 l. multicoloured .. 15 15

129. Trotting.

1966. Equestrian Sports. Multicoloured.
788. 10 l. Type **129** 5 5
789. 20 l. Cross-country racing .. 5 5
790. 40 l. Horse-jumping .. 5 5
791. 70 l. Horse-racing 8 8
792. 90 l. Steeple-chasing .. 10 10
793. 170 l. Polo 20 20
The 20 l. and 170 l. are vert.

130. "La Bella".

1966. Paintings by Titian. Multicoloured.
800. 40 l. Type **130** 8 8
801. 90 l. "The Three Graces" .. 15 15
802. 100 l. "The Three Graces" .. 15 15
803. 170 l. "Sacred and Profane Love" 30 30
The 90 l. and 100 l. show different details rom the picture.

131. Stone Bass.

1966. Fishes. Multicoloured.
804. 1 l. Type **131** 5 5
805. 2 l. Cuckoo Wrasse .. 5 5
806. 3 l. Common Dolphin .. 5 5
807. 4 l. John Dory 5 5
808. 1 l. Octopus 5 5
809. 10 l. Orange Scorpion fish .. 5 5
810. 40 l. Electric Ray .. 5 5
811. 90 l. Medusa 10 10
812. 115 l. Seahorse 12 12
813. 130 l. Dentex 15 15
The 5, 40, 90 and 115 l. are vert.

132. Our Lady of Europe.

133. Peony.

1966. Europa.
814. **132.** 200 l. multicoloured .. 20 20

1967. Flowers. Multicoloured.
815. 5 l. Type **133** 5 5
816. 10 l. Campanula 5 5
817. 15 l. Pyrenean poppy .. 5 5
818. 20 l. Purple deadnettle .. 5 5
819. 40 l. Hemerocallis .. 5 5
820. 140 l. Gentian .. 15 15
821. 170 l. Thistle 15 15
Each flower has a different background view of Mt. Titano.

134. "St. Marinus".

135. Map of Europe.

1967. Paintings by G. F. Barbieri ("Guercino"). Multicoloured.

822. 40 l. Type **134** 5 5
823. 170 l. "St. Francis" .. 15 15
824. 190 l. "Return of the Prodigal Son" 35 35

The 190 l. is horiz. (44×36½ mm.).

1967. Europa.

825. **135.** 200 l. green & chestnut 20 20

136. "Amanita caesarea".

137. Salisbury Cathedral.

1967. Fungi. Multicoloured.

826. 5 l. Type **136** 5 5
825. 15 l "Clitopilus prunulus" 5 5
828. 20 l. "Lepiota procera" 5 5
829. 40 l. "Boletus edulis" .. 5 5
830. 50 l. "Russula paludosa" 5 5
831. 170 l. "Lyophyllum georgii" 20 20

1967. Gothic Cathedrals.

832. – 20 l. violet on cream .. 5 5
833. – 40 l. green on cream .. 5 5
834. – 80 l. blue on cream .. 15 12
835. **137.** 90 l. sepia on cream .. 8 8
836. – 170 l. red on cream .. 15 15

DESIGNS: 20 l. Amiens. 40 l. Siena. 80 l. Toledo. 170 l. Cologne.

138. Cimabue Crucifix, Florence.

1967. Christmas.

837. **138.** 300 l. brown and violet 35 30

139. Arms of San Marino.

140. Europa "Key".

1968. Arms. Multicoloured.

838. 2 l. Type **189** 5 5
839. 3 l. Penna Rossa .. 5 5
840. 5 l. Fiorentino 5 5
841. 10 l. Montecerreto .. 5 5
842. 25 l. Serravalle 5 5
843. 35 l. Montegiardino .. 5 5
844. 50 l. Faetano 5 5
845. 90 l. Borgo Maggiore .. 10 10
846. 180 l. Montelupo .. 30 30
847. 500 l. State crest 50 50

1968. Europa.

848. **140.** 250 l. brown 30 25

141. "The Battle of San Romano" (detail, P. Uccello).

1968. Paolo Uccello Commem.

849. **141.** 50 l. black on lilac .. 5 5
850. – 90 l. black on lilac .. 8 8
851. – 130 l. black on lilac .. 12 12
852. – 230 l. black on pink .. 30 30

All stamps show details of "The Battle of San Romano". The 90 l. is vert.

142. "The Nativity" (detail, Botticelli).

1968. Christmas.

853. **142.** 50 l. deep ultramarine 5 5
854. 90 l. deep claret .. 10 10
855. 180 l. blackish brown 20 20

143. "Peace".

1969. "The Good Government"—Fresco, by A. Lorenzetti.

856. **143.** 50 l. blue 5 5
857. – 80 l. sepia 15 15
858. – 90 l. violet 8 8
859. – 180 l. claret 15 15

DESIGNS—VERT. 80 l. "Justice". 90 l. "Temperance". HORIZ. 180 l. View of Siena.

144. "Young Soldier" (Bramante).

1969. Donato Bramante (architect and painter). 525th Birth Anniv. Multicoloured.

860. 50 l. Type **144** 8 8
861. 90 l. "Old Soldier" (Bramante) 12 12

145. Colonnade.

1969. Europa.

862. **145.** 50 l. green 8 8
863. 180 l. purple 20 15

146. Benched Carriage ("Char-a-banc").

1969. Horses and Carriages. Multicoloured.

864. 5 l. Type **146** 5 5
865. 10 l. Barouche 5 5
866. 25 l. Private Drag .. 5 5
867. 40 l. Hansom Cab .. 5 5
868. 50 l. Curricle 5 5
869. 90 l. Wagonette 10 10
870. 180 l. Spider Phaeton .. 25 25

147. Mt. Titano.

148. "Faith".

1969. Paintings by R. Viola. Multicoloured.

871. 20 l. Type **147** 5 5
872. 180 l. Pier at Rimini .. 20 20
873. 200 l. Pier at Riccione (horiz.) 30 30

1969. Christmas. "The Theological Virtues", after Raphael.

874. **148.** 20 l. violet and orange 5 5
875. – 180 l. violet and green 20 20
876. – 200 l. violet and buff .. 25 25

DESIGNS: 180 l. "Hope". 200 l. "Charity".

149. "Aries".

1970. Signs of the Zodiac. Multicoloured.

877. 1 l. Type **149** 5 5
878. 2 l. "Taurus" 5 5
879. 3 l. "Gemini" 5 5
880. 4 l. "Cancer" 5 5
881. 5 l. "Leo" 5 5
882. 10 l. "Virgo" 5 5
883. 15 l. "Libra" 5 5
884. 20 l. "Scorpio" 5 5
885. 70 l. "Sagittarius" .. 8 8
886. 90 l. "Capricorn" .. 10 10
887. 100 l. "Aquarius" .. 15 15
888. 180 l. "Pisces" .. .. 1·50 1·50

150. "Flaming Sun".

152. St. Francis' Gate.

151. "The Fleet in the Bay of Naples" (Brueghel).

1970. Europa.

889. **150.** 90 l. red and green .. 10 10
890. 180 l. red and yellow 30 30

1970. 10th Europa Stamp Exn., Naples.

891. **151.** 230 l. multicoloured .. 35 35

1970. Rotary Int. 65th Anniv. and San Marino Rotary Club 10th Anniv. Multicoloured.

892. 180 l. Type **152** 20 20
893. 220 l. "Rocco" Fort, Mt. Titano 30 30

153. "Girl with Mandoline".

154. "Black Pete".

1970. Paintings by Tiepolo.

894. 50 l. Type **153.** 15 15
895. 180 l. "Girl with Parrot" 30 30
896. 220 l. "Rinaldo and Armida Surprised" .. 35 35

SIZES: 180 l. As T **153.** 220 l. 57×37 mm.

1970. Walt Disney Commemoration. Cartoon Characters. Multicoloured.

897. 1 l. Type **154** 5 5
898. 2 l. "Gyro Gearloose" 5 5
899. 3 l. "Pluto" .. 5 5
900. 4 l. "Minnie Mouse" .. 5 5
901. 5 l. "Donald Duck" .. 5 5
902. 10 l. "Goofy" 5 5
903. 15 l. "Scrooge McDuck" 5 5
904. 50 l. "Donald Duck's Nephews" .. 12 12
905. 90 l. "Mickey Mouse" .. 25 25
906. 220 l. Walt Disney and scene from "The Jungle Book" (horiz.) .. .. 4·00 4·00

155. "Customs House, Venice".

1971. "Save Venice" Campaign. Paintings by Canaletto. Multicoloured.

907. 20 l. Type **155** 5 5
908. 180 l. "Grand Canal, Balbi Palace and Rialto Bridge, Venice" 30 30
909. 200 l. "St. Mark's and Doge's Palace" .. 35 35

156. Congress Building and San Marino flag.

1971. Italian Philatelic Press Union Congress, San Marino. Multicoloured.

910. 20 l. Type **156** 5 5
911. 90 l. Palace door and emblems 10 10
912. 180 l. Type **156** 30 30

157. Europa Chain.

159. "Hemerocallis hydrida".

158. "Duck" Jug with "Lasa" Decoration.

1971. Europa.

913. **157.** 50 l. blue and yellow 12 12
914. 90 l. orange and blue 25 25

1971. Etruscan Art.
915. **158.** 50 l. black & orange .. 5 5
916. – 80 l. black and green .. 12 12
917. – 90 l. black and green .. 15 15
918. – 180 l. black and orange 30 30
DESIGNS—VERT. 80 l. Head of Hermes (bust). 90 l. Man and Wife (relief on sarcophagus). HORIZ. 180 l. Chimera (bronze).

1971. Flowers. Multicoloured.
919. 1 l. Type **159** 5 5
920. 2 l. "Phlox paniculata" 5 5
921. 3 l. "Dianthus plumarius" 5 5
922. 4 l. "Trollius europaeus" 5 5
923. 5 l. "Centaurea dealbata" 5 5
924. 10 l. "Paeonia lactiflora" 5 5
925. 15 l. "Helleborus niger" 5 5
926. 50 l. "Anemone pulsatilla" 5 5
927. 90 l. "Gaillardia aristats" 10 10
928. 220 l. "Aster dumosus" 30 30

160. "Primavera" (detail, Botticelli).

1972. Botticelli Commem. Details of Botticelli's "Primavera" (Allegory of Spring).
929. – 50 l. multicoloured .. 8 8
930. **160.** 180 l. multicoloured .. 40 40
931. – 220 l. multicoloured .. 50 50
SIZE: 50 l., 220 l. 21 × 37 mm.

161. "Communications". **162.** "Taming the Bear".

1972. Europa.
932. **161.** 50 l. multicoloured .. 12 12
933. 90 l. multicoloured .. 20 20

1972. "Life of St. Marinus". 16th-century Paintings from former Government Palace.
934. **162.** 25 l. black and brown 5 5
935. – 55 l. black and pink .. 8 8
936. – 100 l. black and blue 12 12
937. – 130 l. black and green 30 30
DESIGNS: 55 l. "The Conversion of Donna Felicissima". 100 l. "Hostile archers turned to stone". 130 l. "Mount Titano given to St. Marinus".

163. Italian Sparrow. **164.** "Healthy Man".

1972. Birds. Multicoloured.
938. 1 l. Type **163** 5 5
939. 2 l. Firecrest 5 5
940. 3 l. Blue tit 5 5
941. 4 l. Cretolan bunting .. 5 5
942. 5 l. Bluethroat 5 5
943. 10 l. Bullfinch 5 5
944. 25 l. Linnet 5 5
945. 50 l. Black-eared wheatear 8 8
946. 90 l. Sardinian Warbler .. 12 12
947. 220 l. Greenfinch .. 30 30

1972. World Health Month. Multicoloured.
948. 50 l. Type **164** 10 10
949. 90 l. "Sick Man" 15 15

165. Veterans Emblem. **166.** Plane over Mt. Titano.

1972. "Veterans of Philately" Award of Italian Philatelic Federation.
950. **165.** 25 l. gold and blue .. 10 10

1972. Air.
951. **166.** 1000 l. multicoloured .. 2·75 2·50

167. Five-cent Coin of 1864.

1972. San Marino Coinage.
952. **167.** 5 l. bronze, blk. & grey 5 5
953. – 10 l. bronze, blk. & orge. 5 5
954. – 15 l. silver, blk. & red 5 5
955. – 20 l. silver, blk. & pur. 5 5
956. – 25 l. silver, blk. & blue 5 5
957. – 50 l. silver, blk. & blue 5 5
958. – 55 l. silver, blk. & ochre 8 8
959. – 220 l. gold, blk. & green 40 35
COINS (obverse and reverse on each stamp): 10 l. 10 c. of 1935. 15 l. 1 l. of 1906. 20 l. 5 l. of 1898. 25 l. 5 l. of 1937. 50 l. 10 l. of 1932. 55 l. 20 l. of 1938. 220 l. 20 l. of 1925.

168. New York, 1673.

1973. "Interpex" Stamp Exhibition, New York.
960. **168.** 200 l. multicoloured .. 60 55
961. – 300 l. pur., blue & blk. 80 70
DESIGN: 300 l. New York, 1973.

169. Printing Press. **170.** "Sportsman".

1973. Tourist Press Congress.
962. **169.** 50 l. multicoloured .. 12 12

1973. Youth Games.
963. **170.** 100 l. multicoloured .. 15 15

171. Europa "Posthorn". **172.** Grapes.

1973. Europa.
964. **171.** 20 l. pink, grn. & purple 5 5
965. 180 l. blue, red & purple 35 35

1973. Fruits. Multicoloured.
966. 1 l. Type **172** 5 5
967. 2 l. Manderines 5 5
968. 3 l. Apples 5 5
969. 4 l. Plums 5 5
970. 5 l. Strawberries 5 5
971. 10 l. Pears 5 5
972. 25 l. Cherries 5 5
973. 50 l. Pomegranate .. 5 5
974. 90 l. Apricots 10 10
975 200 l. Peaches 40 40

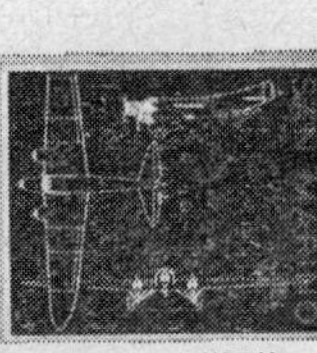

173. Couzinet "70" Arc-en-Ciel. **174.** Serra valle.

1973. "Story of the Aeroplane". Mult.
976. 25 l. Type **173** 5 5
977. 55 l. Macchi "MC-72/181" "Castoldi" 8 8
978. 60 l. Anthony "Ant-9" .. 8 8
979. 90 l. Ryan "NX-211" "Spirit of St Louis" 12 12
980. 220 l. Handley Page "HP-42E" 30 30

1973. Crossbowman of Italian Castles. Multicoloured
981. 5 l. Type **174** 5 5
982. 10 l. Pennarossa 5 5
983. 15 a. Montegiardino (drummer) 5 5
984. 20 l. Fiorentino (trumpeter) 5 5
985. 30 l. Montecerreto .. 5 5
986. 40 l. Borgo Maggiore .. 5 5
987. 50 l. The Guata (trumpeter) 5 5
988. 80 l. Faetano 10 10
989. 220 l. Montelupo .. 35 35

175. "Adoration of the Magi" (detail). **176.** Combat Shield, (16th century).

1973. Christmas. Gentile da Fabriano. 600th Birth Anniv. Portions of Gentile's altarpiece "Adoration of the Magi" (Uffizi Gallery). As Type **175**.
990. **175.** 5 l. multicoloured .. 5 5
991. – 30 l. multicoloured .. 5 5
992. – 115 l. multicoloured .. 15 15
993. – 250 l. multicoloured .. 55 55

1974. Ancient Weapons from "Cesta" Museum, San Marino.
994. **176.** 5 l. blk. brn. & grn... 5 5
995. – 10 l. blk., blue & brn. 5 5
996. – 15 l. blk., blue & light bl. 5 5
997. – 20 l. blk., bl. & brn... 5 5
998. – 30 l. blk., brn. & blue 5 5
999. – 50 l. blk., blue & pink 8 8
1000. – 80 l. blk., blue & lilac 12 12
1001. – 250 l. blk. & yellow.. 35 35
DESIGNS: 10 l. German armour (16th century). 15 l. Crested morion (16th century). 20 l. Horse head-armour (15th-16th century). 30 l. Italian morion with crest (16th-17th century). 50 l. Gauntlets and sword pommel (16th century). 80 l. Sallet helmet (16th century). 250 l. Sforza shield (16th century).

177. "The Joy of Living" (Emilio Greco).

1974. Europa. Sculpture.
1002. **177.** 100 l. black and brown 15 15
1003. – 200 l. black and green 35 35
DESIGN: 200 l. Head and shoulders detail of sculpture depicted in Type **177**.

178. "Sea and Mountains". **179.** Arms of Sunsepolcro.

1974. San-Marino-Riccione Stamp Fair.
1004. **178.** 50 l. multicoloured .. 8 8

1974. 9th Crossbow Tournament, San Marino. Multicoloured.
1005. 15 l. Type **179** 5 5
1006. 20 l. Massa Marittima .. 5 5
1007. 50 l. San Marino 5 5
1008. 115 l. Gubbio 15 15
1009. 300 l. Lucca 60 60

180. U.P.U. Emblem and Shadow.

1974. Universal Postal Union. Cent.
1010. **180.** 50 l. multicoloured .. 5 5
1011. 90 l. multicoloured .. 12 12

181. Sailplane.

1974. Air. Gliding in Italy. 50th Anniv.
1012. **181.** 40 l. blue, grn. & brn. 5 5
1013. 120 l. bl., light bl. & vio. 12 12
1014. 500 l. vio., mve. & red 60 60

182. Mt. Titano and Text of Hymn.

1974. Niccolo Tommaseo (writer). Death Cent.
1015. **182.** 50 l. grn., red & pale grn. 5 5
1016. – 150 l. blk., bl. & yell. 20 20
DESIGN: 150 l. Tommaseo in old age.

183. "Madonna and Child" (4th century painting on wood by unknown artist).

1974. Christmas.
1017. **183.** 250 l. multicoloured 30 30

184. "Dancing Scene".

1975. Etruscan Tomb Paintings. Mult.
1018. 20 l. Type **184** 5 5
1019. 30 l. "Chariot Race" .. 5 5
1020. 180 l. "Achilles and Troilus" 25 25
1021. 220 l. "Dancers" 30 30

185. San Marino "Tunnel". **186.** "The Blessing".

1975. "Escape of the Hundred Thousand". (Refuge for Italian wartime refugees). 30th Anniv.
1022. **185.** 50 l. multicoloured .. 8 8

1975. Europa. Details from "St. Marinus" by "Guercino" (G. F. Barbieri). Multicoloured.
1023. 100 l. Type **186** 15 15
1024. 200 l. "St. Marinus" .. 30 30

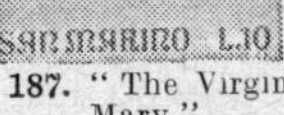

187. "The Virgin Mary". **188.** Head of Aphrodite.

1975. Holy Year. Details from Scrovegni Chapel Frescoes by Giotto. Multicoloured.
1025. 10 l. Type **187** 5 5
1026. 40 l. "Virgin and Child" 5 5
1027. 50 l. "Heads of Angels" 8 8
1028. 100 l. "Mary Magdalene" (horiz.) 15 15
1029. 500 l. "Heads of Saints" (horiz.) 75 75

1975. Europa Stamp Exhibition, Naples.
1030. **188.** 50 l. blk., vio. & grey 8 8

189. Congress Emblem.

1975. "Eurocophar" International Pharmaceutical Congress, San Marino.
1031. **189.** 100 l. multicoloured 15 15

190. "Tokyo 1835" (after Hiroshige).

1975. "Worlds Most Important Cities". Tokyo. Multicoloured.
1032. 200 l. Type **190** 30 30
1033. 300 l. "Tokyo 1975" (same view) 45 45

191. "Woman on Balcony". **192.** "Head of the Child".

1975. International Women's Year. Multicoloured.
1034. 50 l. Type **191** 8 8
1035 150 l. "Heads of Two Women" (horiz.) .. 25 25
1036. 230 l. "Profile of Girl" 35 35

1975. Christmas. Multicoloured.
1037. 50 l. Type **192** 8 8
1038. 100 l. "Head of Virgin" 15 15
1039. 250 l. "Doni Madonna" 35 35

193. "Modesty". **194.** Capitol, Washington.

1976. "The Civil Virtues".
1040. **193.** 10 l. black and brown 5 5
1041. – 20 l. black and lilac 5 5
1042. – 50 l. black and green 8 8
1043. – 100 l. black and red 15 15
1044. – 150 l. black and violet 75 25
1045. 220 l. black and grey 30 30
1046. – 250 l. black and yellow 35 35
1047. – 300 l. black and blue 45 45
1048. – 500 l. black and buff 75 75
1049. – 1000 l. black and blue 1·50 1·50
VIRTUES: 20 l. "Temperance". 50 l. "Fortitude". 100 l. "Altruism". 150 l. "Hope". 220 l. "Prudence". 250 l. "Justice". 300 l. "Faith". 500 l. "Honesty". 1000 l. "Industry".

1976. American Revolution. Bicent. Mult.
1050. 70 l. Type **194** 10 10
1051. 150 l. Statue of Liberty .. 25 25
1052. 180 l. Independence Hall, Philadelphia 30 30

195. Games Emblem and Maple Leaf.

1976 Olympic Games, Montreal.
1053. **195.** 150 l. black and red .. 25 25

196. Decorative Plate.

1976. Europa. Multicoloured.
1054. 150 l. Type **196** 25 25
1055. 180 l. Silver plate .. 30 30

197. Doves as "Flower".

1976. Social Welfare Union. Centenary.
1056. **197.** 150 l. multicoloured. 25 25

198. Children of Three Races. **199.** "San Marino".

1976. UNESCO. 30th Anniv.
1057. **198.** 180 l. orange and blue 30 30
1058. 220 l. ochre and black 35 35

1976. "Italia '76" International Stamp Exhibition, Milan.
1059. **199.** 150 l. multicoloured 25 25

200. "The Annunciation".

1976. Christmas. Titian Paintings. Mult.
1060. 150 l. Type **200** 25 25
1061. 300 l. "The Nativity" .. 50 50

EXPRESS LETTER STAMPS

E 1.

1907.
E 53. E **1.** 25 c. red .. .. 7·50 1·25

1923. Optd. **ESPRESSO.**
E 92. **8.** 60 c. violet 50 40

1923. Surch. **Cent. 60.**
E 93. E **1.** 60 c. on 25 c. red .. 30 30

E 2.

1923. Red Cross.
E 101. E **2.** 60 c.+5 c. red .. 1·25 1·00

1926. No. E 92 surch. **Lire 1,25.**
E 134. **8.** 1 l. 25 on 60 c. violet 75 75

1927. No. E 93 surch. **L. 1,25** and bars over old surch.
E 138. E **1.** 1 l. 25 on 60 c. on 25 c. red 55 55

E **3.** Statue of Liberty and View of San Marino.

1929. As Type E **3**, without "UNION POSTALE UNIVERSELLE" and inscr. "ESPRESSO".
E 164. E **3.** 1 l. 25 green .. 30 12

1929. Optd. **UNION POSTALE UNIVERSELLE** as in Type E **3.**
E 165. E **3.** 2 l. 50 blue .. .. 1·40 1·25

E **4.**

1943.
E 305. E **4.** 1 l. 25 green .. 5 5
E 306. 2 l. 50 orange .. 10 10

E **5.** Mt. Titano.

1945.
E 307. E **5.** 2 l. 50 green .. 8 8
E 308. 5 l. orange .. 15 15
E 309. 5 l. red 40 15
E 310. 10 l. blue .. .. 1·25 80
E 419. 60 l. red .. .. 8·00 4·00

E **6.** Pegasus and Mt. Titano.

1946.
E 337. E **6.** 30 l. blue 80 75
E 420. 80 l. blue .. .. 8·00 4·00

1947. Surch.
E 339. E **5.** 15 l. on 5 l. red .. 8 8
E 340. 15 l. on 10 l. blue .. 8 8
E 374. E **6.** 35 l. on 30 l. blue .. 18·00 8·50
E 341. 60 l. on 30 l. blue .. 4·00 1·60
E 545. E **5.** 75 l. on 60 l. red .. 2·00 1·40
E 375. E **6.** 80 l. on 30 l. blue .. 12·00 6·50
E 546. 100 l. on 80 l. blue 2·00 1·40
E 783. E **7.** 120 l. on 75 l. black and yellow .. 15 15
E 784. 135 l. on 100 l. black and orange .. 20 20

E **7.** Crossbow and Three "Castles".

1966.
E 800. E **7.** 75 l. black and yellow 8 8
E 801. 80 l. black and purple 10 10
E 802. 100 l. black & orange 12 12
No. E 800 has crossbow in white without shadows.

PARCEL POST STAMPS

P 1.

1928.
P 145. P **1.** 5 c. purple and blue .. 5 5
P 146. 10 c. blue .. 5 5
P 147. 20 c. black and blue .. 5 5
P 148. 25 c. red and blue .. 5 5
P 149. 30 c. blue .. 5 5
P 150. 50 c. orange and blue 5 5
P 151. 60 c. red and blue .. 5 5
P 152. 1 l. violet and red .. 5 5
P 153. 2 l. green and red .. 8 8
P 154. 3 l. bistre and red .. 12 12
P 155. 4 l. grey and red .. 15 15
P 156. 10 l. mauve and red .. 75 75
P 157. 12 l. lake and red .. 1·40 1·40
P 158. 15 l. olive and red .. 6·00 6·00
P 159. 20 l. purple and red .. 7·50 7·50

1945. Perf. vert. between halves of each stamp.
P 309. P **1.** 5 c. purple and red .. 5 5
P 310. 10 c. brown and black 5 5
P 311. 20 c. red and green .. 5 5
P 312. 25 c. yellow and black 5 5
P 313. 30 c. mauve and red .. 5 5
P 314. 50 c. violet and black 5 5
P 315. 60 c. red and black .. 5 5
P 316. 1 l. brown and blue .. 5 5
P 317. 2 l. brown and blue .. 5 5
P 318. 3 l. grey and brown .. 5 5
P 319. 4 l. green and brown 5 5
P 320. 10 l. grey and violet .. 8 8
P 321. 12 l. green and blue .. 1·10 1·10
P 322. 15 l. green and violet 1·40 1·40
P 323. 20 l. violet and brown 1·90 1·90
P 324. 25 l. red and blue .. 17·00 4·25
P 771. 50 l. yellow and red .. 8 8
P 773. 300 l. violet and lake 40 40
P 526. 500 l. sepia and red .. 5·00 2·50
P 775. 1000 l. green and brn. 1·25 1·25

1948. Nos. P324 and P771 surch. in figures and wavy lines on each half of design.
P 374. P **1.** 100 l. on 50 l. .. 32·00 8·00
P 375. 200 l. on 25 l. .. 70·00 16·00
Used prices are for complete stamps as illustrated. Half stamps are worth about one-third of these prices.

POSTAGE DUE STAMPS

D **1.** D **2.**

1897.
D 38. D **1.** 5 c. brown and green 5 5
D 39. 10 c. brown and green 8 8
D 40. 30 c. brown and green 15 15
D 41. 50 c. brown and green 50 50
D 42. 60 c. brown and green 1·60 1·60
D 43. 1 l. brown and rose .. 55 45
D 44. 3 l. brown and rose .. 2·75 2·75
D 45. 5 l. brown and rose .. 10·00 4·50
D 46. 10 l. brown and rose 2·50 2·10

1924.
D 107. D **1.** 5 c. brown and red .. 5 8
D 108. 10 c. brown and red .. 5 8
D 109. 30 c. brown and red .. 5 8
D 110. 50 c. brown and red .. 5 8
D 111. 60 c. brown and red .. 80 80
D 112. 1 l. brown and green 80 80
D 113. 3 l. brown and green 3·25 3·25
D 114. 5 l. brown and green 3·25 3·25
D 115. 10 l. brown and green 60·00 50·00

1925.
D 116. D **1.** 5 c. brown and blue 5 5
D 118. 10 c. brown and blue 5 5
D 119. 15 c. brown and blue 5 5
D 120. 20 c. brown and blue 5 5
D 121. 25 c. brown and blue 12 8
D 122. 30 c. brown and blue 5 5
D 123. 40 c. brown and blue 90 55
D 124. 50 c. brown and blue 8 8
D 125. 60 c. brown and blue 25 25
D 126. 1 l. brown and orange 1·40 15
D 127. 2 l. brown and orange 50 30
D 128. 3 l. brown and orange 20·00 8·00
D 129. 5 l. brown and orange 4·00 2·10
D 130. 10 l. brown & orange 6·50 2·50
D 131. 15 l. brown & orange 40 40
D 132. 25 l. brown & orange 12·00 6·50
D 133. 30 l. brown & orange 6·00 2·50
D 134. 50 l. brown & orange 6·00 2·75

1931. As Type D **1**, but with centre obliterated in black and new values superimposed in silver.
D 164. D **1.** 15 c. on 5 c. blue .. 12 12
D 165. 15 c. on 10 c. blue .. 12 12
D 166. 15 c. on 30 c. blue .. 12 12
D 167. 20 c. on 5 c. blue .. 8 8
D 168. 20 c. on 10 c. blue .. 8 8
D 169. 20 c. on 30 c. blue .. 8 8
D 170. 25 c. on 5 c. blue 80 40
D 171. 25 c. on 10 c. blue .. 80 40
D 172. 25 c. on 30 c. blue .. 7·00 2·50
D 173. 40 c. on 5 c. blue .. 40 15
D 174. 40 c. on 10 c. blue .. 40 15
D 175. 40 c. on 30 c. blue .. 60 20
D 176. 2 l. on 5 c. blue .. 15·00 8·50
D 177. 2 l. on 10 c. blue .. 25·00 12·00
D 178. 2 l. on 30 c. blue .. 20·00 10·00

1936. Surch. in figures and words and bars. D 232/8 and D 242 are brown and blue; the rest brown and orange.
D 233. D **1.** 10 c. on 5 c. .. 40 35
D 234. 25 c. on 30 c. .. 6·00 4·00
D 236. 50 c. on 5 c. .. 1·25 60
D 237. D **1.** 1 l. on 30 c. .. 12·00 2·10
D 238. 1 l. on 40 c. .. 4·50 1·75
D 239. 1 l. on 3 l. .. 9·00 1·40
D 240. 1 l. on 25 l. .. 29·00 3·00
D 241. 2 l. on 15 l. .. 12·00 3·00
D 242. 3 l. on 20 c. .. 10·00 4·00
D 243. 25 l. on 50 l. .. 2·10 80

1945.

D 309. D 2. 5 c. green 5 5
D 310. 10 c. brown 5 5
D 311. 15 c. red 5 5
D 312. 20 c. blue 5 5
D 313. 25 c. violet 5 5
D 314. 30 c. mauve 5 5
D 315. 40 c. yellow 5 5
D 316. 50 c. slate 5 5
D 317. 60 c. brown 5 5
D 318. 1 l. orange 5 5
D 319. 2 l. red 5 5
D 320. 5 l. violet 5 5
D 321. 10 l. blue 12 12
D 322. 20 l. green 8·00 4·00
D 323. 25 l. brown 9·00 4·50
D 324. 50 l. brown 11·00 5·50

SANTANDER O1

One of the states of the Granadine Confederation.

A department of Colombia from 1886, now uses Colombian stamps.

1. 2.

1884. Imperf.

1. 1. 1 c. blue 15 15
2. 5 c. red 30 25
3. 10 c. violet 50 50

1886. Imperf.

4. 2. 1 c. blue 40 40
5. 5 c. red 12 12
6. 10 c. lilac 20 20

1887. T 1 but inscr. "REPUBLICA DE COLOMBIA". Imperf.

7. 1 c. blue 12 12
8. 5 c. red 45 45
9. 10 c. violet 1·50 1·50

3. 4.

5. 6. 7.

1890. Perf.

10. 3. 1 c. blue 12 12
11. 4. 5 c. red 60 60
12. 5. 10 c. violet 25 25

1895.

14. 6. 5 c. red on buff 35 30

1895.

15. 7. 5 c. brown 40 40
16. 5 c. green 40 40

9. 10. 11.

1899.

17. 9. 1 c. black on green 20 20
18. 10. 5 c. black on rose 20 20
19. 11. 10 c. blue 30 30

12.

1903. Fiscal stamp as T 12 optd. **Provisional Correos de Santander.** Imperf.

21. 12. 50 c. red 20 20

SARAWAK BC

Formerly an independent state on the N. coast of Borneo under British protection. Under Japanese occupation from 1941 until 1945. A Crown Colony from 1946 until September, 1963, when it became a state of the Federation of Malaysia.

100 cents = 1 dollar (Malayan or Malaysian).

1. Sir James Brooke. 2. Sir Charles Brooke.

1869.

1. 1. 3 c. brown on yellow 15·00 50·00

1871.

3. 2. 2 c. mauve on lilac 1·00 2·00
3. 3 c. brown on yellow 1·00 1·50
4. 4 c. brown on yellow 1·25 1·00
6. 6 c. green on green 1·00 1·25
6. 8 c. blue on blue 1·50 2·00
7. 12 c. red on red 2·50 2·50

3. Sir Charles Brooke. 4.

1888.

8. 3. 1 c. mauve and black 60 75
9. 2 c. mauve and red 1·25 75
10. 3 c. mauve and blue 50 75
11. 4 c. mauve and yellow 3·50 4·50
12. 5 c. mauve and green 2·50 1·50
13. 6 c. mauve and brown 3·00 4·50
14. 8 c. green and red 1·25 1·50
15. 10 c. green and violet 5·50 5·00
16. 12 c. green and blue 1·00 2·25
17. 16 c. green and orange 6·00 6·00
18. 25 c. green and brown 6·00 6·00
19. 32 c. green and black 6·00 7·00
20. 50 c. green 7·00 8·00
21. $1 green and black 11·00 12·00

1889. Surch. in words or figures.

27. 2. 1 c. on 3 c. brown on yell. 50 75
23. 3. 1 c. on 3 c. mauve & blue 2·00 3·00
24. 2 c. on 8 c. green and red 1·50 3·00
25. 5 c. on 12 c. green & blue 10·00 11·00

1895. Various frames.

28c. 4. 2 c. red 1·50 2·00
29. 4 c. black 2·00 1·50
30. 6 c. violet 3·00 4·00
31. 8 c. green 4·00 5·00

1899. Surch. in figures and words.

32. 2. 2 c. on 3 c. brown on yell. 75 1·50
33. 2 c. on 12 c. red on red 80 1·25
34. 4 c. on 6 c. green on green 7·00 8·00
35. 4 c. on 8 c. blue on blue 1·50 2·50

1899. As T 3, but inscr. "POSTAGE POSTAGE".

36. 1 c. blue and red 35 25
37. 2 c. green 20 12
38. 3 c. purple 60 10
39a. 4 c. red 1·50 10
40. 8 c. yellow and black 1·25 1·10
41. 10 c. blue 1·40 20
42. 12 c. mauve 2·00 1·25
43. 16 c. red-brown and green 2·00 1·50
44. 20 c. olive and mauve 2·50 3·50
45. 25 c. brown and blue 2·50 3·50
46. 50 c. olive and red 6·00 7·00
47. $1 red and green 11·00 12·00

5. Sir Charles Vyner Brooke. 6.

1918.

50. 5. 1 c. blue and red 12 15
51. 2 c. green 30 25
77. 2 c. purple 25 12
52. 3 c. purple 70 80
64. 3 c. green 20 20
53. 4 c. red 70 60
65. 4 c. purple 20 12
66. 5 c. orange 12 40
81. 6 c. claret 40 20
54. 8 c. yellow and black 90 2·00
68. 5. 8 c. red 70 1·00
55. 10 c. blue 75 1·60
83. 10 c. black 60 1·00
56. 12 c. purple 1·00 2·00
84. 12 c. blue 85 1·00
85. 16 c. brown and green 85 1·00
86. 20 c. olive and lilac 85 1·00
87. 25 c. brown and blue 95 1·10
88. 30 c. brown and blue 2·25 1·40
60. 50 c. olive and red 1·60 2·00
61. $1 red and green 4·00 5·00

1923. Surch. in words.

72. 5. 1 c. on 10 c. blue 5·00 6·50
73. 2 c. on 12 c. purple 1·60 3·00

1932.

91. 6. 1 c. blue 30 15
92. 2 c. green 30 15
93. 3 c. violet 40 15
94. 4 c. orange 20 8
95. 5 c. claret 40 12
96. 6 c. red 1·10 2·00
97. 8 c. yellow 70 90
98. 10 c. black 75 1·50
99. 12 c. blue 80 1·50
100. 15 c. brown 1·10 2·25
101. 20 c. orange and violet 1·10 2·00
102. 25 c. yell. and red-brown 2·00 2·75
103. 30 c. brown and red 2·00 3·00
104. 50 c. red and olive 2·50 3·25
105. $1 green and red 4·50 6·00

ILLUSTRATIONS British Commonwealth and all overprints and surcharges are FULL SIZE. Foreign Countries have been reduced to ¾-LINEAR.

7. Sir Charles Vyner Brooke.

1934.

106. 7. 1 c. purple 10 8
107. 2 c. green 8 8
107a. 2 c. black 30 50
108. 3 c. black 8 8
108a. 3 c. green 12 25
109. 4 c. purple 15 8
110. 5 c. violet 8 8
111. 6 c. red 10 20
111a. 6 c. brown 15 45
112. 8 c. brown 8 10
112a. 8 c. red 15 12
113. 10 c. red 35 35
114. 12 c. blue 20 35
114a. 12 c. orange 20 1·40
115. 15 c. orange 15 1·00
115a. 15 c. blue 25 1·25
116. 20 c. green and red 45 45
117. 25 c. violet and orange 20 40
118. 30 c. brown and violet 40 80
119. 50 c. violet and red 80 80
120. $1 red and brown 90 90
121. $2 purple and violet 2·00 4·00
122. $3 red and green 3·00 4·00
123. $4 blue and red 4·00 6·00
124. $5 red and brown 7·00 9·00
125. $10 black and yellow 12·00 14·00

1945. Optd. **BMA.**

126. 7. 1 c. purple 8 10
127. 2 c. black 8 8
128. 3 c. green 8 10
129. 4 c. purple 8 8
130. 5 c. violet 15 30
131. 6 c. brown 25 45
132. 8 c. red 1·60 2·25
133. 10 c. red 25 40
134. 12 c. orange 30 90
135. 15 c. blue 30 15
136. 20 c. green and red 50 1·00
137. 25 c. violet and orange 45 1·10
138. 30 c. brown and violet 50 1·60
139. 50 c. violet and red 45 25
140. $1 red and brown 80 1·10
141. $2 purple and violet 2·00 2·50
142. $3 red and green 2·00 3·25
143. $4 blue and red 3·00 3·25
144. $5 red and brown 12·00 12·00
145. $10 black and yellow 14·00 16·00

8. Sir James Brooke, Sir Chas. Vyner Brooke and Sir Charles Brooke.

1946. Centenary Issue.

146. 8. 8 c. red 10 20
147. 15 c. blue 30 35
148. 50 c. black and red 55 90
149. $1 black and brown 2·75 4·00

1947. Optd. with the Royal Cypher.

150. 7. 1 c. purple 8 8
151. 2 c. black 8 8
152. 3 c. green 8 8
153. 4 c. purple 10 10
154. 6 c. brown 10 12
155. 8 c. red 8 8
156. 10 c. red 10 10
157. 7. 12 c. orange 8 15
158. 15 c. blue 8 12
159. 20 c. green and red 20 30
160. 25 c. violet and orange 15 12
161. 50 c. violet and red 10 12
162. $1 red and brown 40 65
163. $2 purple and violet 90 1·10
164. $5 red and brown 2·00 2·50

1948. Silver Wedding. As T 5/6 of Aden.

165. 8 c. red 12 12
166. $5 brown 4·00 6·50

1949. U.P.U. As T 14/17 of Antigua.

167. 8 c. red 12 15
168. 15 c. blue 20 25
169. 25 c. green 25 45
170. 50 c. violet 75 85

9. Troides Brookiana.

10. Tarsier. 11. Kayan Tomb.

1950.

171. 9. 1 c. black 10 10
172. 10. 2 c. orange 12 10
173. 11. 3 c. green 12 15
174. – 4 c. brown 12 8
175. – 6 c. blue 12 10
176. – 8 c. red 12 8
177. – 10 c. orange 35 55
186. – 10 c. orange 8 8
178. – 12 c. violet 20 25
179. – 15 c. blue 15 8
180. – 20 c. brown and orange 20 8
181. – 25 c. green and red 25 8
182. – 50 c. brown and violet 35 15
183. – $1 green and brown 60 35
184. – $2 blue and red 1·25 1·60
185. – $5 black, yellow, red and purple 3·00 3·50

DESIGNS—VERT. 4 c. Kayan boy and girl. 6 c. Beadwork. 50 c. Iban woman. HORIZ. 8 c. Dyak dancer. 10 c. (No. 177) Scaly ant-eater. 10 c. (No. 186), Map of Sarawak. 12 c. Kenyah boys. 15 c. Fire making. 20 c. Kelemantan rice barn. 25 c. Pepper vines. $1 Kelabit smithy. $2 Map of Sarawak. $5 Arms of Sarawak.

1953. Coronation. As T 7 of Aden.

187. 10 c. black and blue 30 35

12. Barong Panau.

13. Queen Elizabeth II. 14. Queen Elizabeth II (after Annigoni).

1955.

204. – 1 c. green 5 5
205. – 2 c. orange 5 8
190. – 4 c. brown 5 5
206. – 6 c. blue 12 25
192. – 8 c. red 10 10
193. – 10 c. green 10 10
194. 12. 12 c. plum 12 12
195. – 15 c. blue 20 15
196. – 20 c. olive and brown 20 12
197. – 25 c. sepia and green 25 20
198. 13. 30 c. brown and lilac 25 10
199. 50 c. black and red 25 20
200. 14. $1 myrtle and chestnut 50 50
201. $2 violet and green 1·50 1·50
202. – $5 blk., yell., red & pur. 3·50 3·50

DESIGNS—As T 12 —VERT. 1 c. Logging. 2 c. Young Orang-Utan. 4 c. Kayan dancing. HORIZ. 6 c. Hornbill. 8 c. Shield with spears. 10 c. Kenyah ceremonial carving. 15 c. Turtles. 20 c. Melanau basket-making. 25 c. Astana, Kuching. $5, Arms of Sarawak.

1963. Freedom from Hunger. As T 10 of Aden.

203.		12 c. sepia	20	25

15. "Vanda hookeriana".

1965. As Nos. 166/72 of Johore but with Arms of Sarawak inset as in T **15**.

212.	**15.**	1 c. multicoloured	5	5
213.	–	2 c. multicoloured	5	5
214.	–	5 c. multicoloured	5	5
215.	–	6 c. multicoloured	5	5
216.	–	10 c. multicoloured	8	5
217.	–	15 c. multicoloured	8	10
218.	–	20 c. multicoloured	10	10

The higher values used in Sarawak were Nos. 20/7 of Malaysia.

16. Blue Pansy Butterfly.

1971. Butterflies. As Nos. 175/81 of Johore but with Sarawak Arms as in T **16**.

219.	–	1 c. multicoloured	5	5
220.	–	2 c. multicoloured	5	5
221.	–	5 c. multicoloured	5	5
222.	–	6 c. multicoloured	5	5
223.	–	10 c. multicoloured	5	5
224.	**16.**	15 c. multicoloured	8	8
225.	–	20 c. multicoloured	10	10

The higher values in use with this issue are Nos. 64/71 of Malaysia.

For Japanese issue see "Japanese Occupation of Sarawak".

SARDINIA E2

A former Italian kingdom, including the island of Sardinia, a large part of the mainland and parts of what is now S.E. France. The Kingdom of Italy was formed by the adhesion of other Italian states to Sardinia, whose king became the first ruler of united Italy.

100 centesimi = 1 lira.

1. Victor Emmanuel II. **2.**

1851. Imperf.

1.	**1.**	5 c. black	£500	£350
3.		20 c. blue	£550	50·00
5.		40 c. rose	£600	£650

1853. Embossed on coloured paper. Imperf.

9.	**1.**	5 c. green	£500	£200
10.		20 c. blue	£700	45·00
11.		40 c. rose	£500	£190

1854. Embossed on white paper. Imperf.

13.	**1.**	5 c. green	£3000	£150
15.		20 c. blue	£1200	35·00
18.		40 c. red	—	£500

1855. Head embossed. Imperf.

27.	**2.**	5 c. olive-green	1·00	2·75
28.		5 c. green	55	2·75
37.		10 c. yellow	8·00	1·75
40.		10 c. brown	25	1·25
34.		10 c. grey	16·00	2·25
48.		20 c. blue	2·50	1·75
55.		40 c. red	45	6·00
60.		80 c. yellow	80	35·00
61.		3 l. bronze	40·00	£650

For T 2 perf., see Italy Nos. 1/4.

NEWSPAPER STAMPS

N **1.**

1861. Numerals embossed. Imperf.

N 1.	N **1.**	1 c. black	15	40
N 2.		2 c. black	5·00	6·50

For 2 c. stamps of similar types in yellow see Italy No. N 5.

SASENO E1

An island off the W. coast of Albania, temporarily occupied by Italy.

1923. Stamps of Italy optd. **SASENO.**

1.	**24.**	10 c. red	25	55
2.		15 c. grey	25	55
3.	**25.**	20 c. orange	25	55
4.	**26.**	25 c. blue	25	55
5.		30 c. brown	25	55
6.		50 c. mauve	25	55
7.		60 c. red	90	1·50
8.	**23.**	1 l. brown and green	90	1·50

SAUDI ARABIA O4

Formerly under Turkish rule, the Hejaz became an independent kingdom in 1916, but was conquered by the Sultan of Nejd in 1926 who became King of Hejaz and Nejd when combined issues of stamps were used. In 1932 the name of the state was changed to the Saudi Arabian Kingdom.

1916. 40 paras = 1 piastre.
1929. 110 guerche = 10 riyal = 1 gold sovereign.
1952. 440 guerche = 40 riyal = 1 gold sovereign.
1960. 100 halalah = 20 guerche = 1 riyal. 1 piastre = 1 guerche.
1977. 100 halalas = 1 rial.

A. HEJAZ

1.

1916. As T **1** (various Arabic designs). Perf. or roul.

11.		1 pa. purple	35	35
12.		⅛ pi. yellow	35	35
13.		¼ pi. green	35	35
14.		½ pi red	35	35
15.		1 pi. blue	35	35
16.		2 pl. claret	1·50	1·50

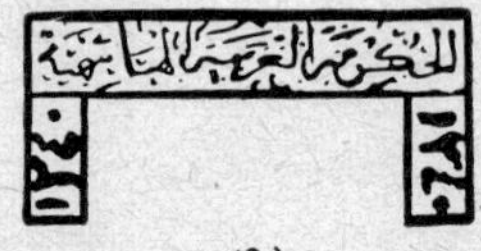

(**2.**)

1921. Nos. 11 to 16 optd. with T **2.**

21.		1 pa. purple	1·50	1·50
22.		⅛ pi. yellow	1·50	1·50
23.		¼ pi. green	50	50
24.		½ pi. red	50	50
26.		1 pi. blue	1·00	1·50
28.		2 pi. claret	75	75

T 2 also exists without the frame-lines.

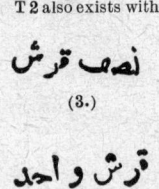

(**3.**)

(**4.**) **5.**

1921. No. 25 surch. with T **3** (½ pi.) or T **4** (1 pi.).

29.		½ pi. on 1 pa. purple	10·00	10·00
30.		1 pi. on 1 pa. purple	10·00	10·00

1922.

39.	**5.**	⅛ pi. brown	15	15
40.		¼ pi. green	15	15
41.		½ pi. red	15	15
42.		1 pi. blue	15	15
43.		1½ pi. violet	15	15
44.		2 pi. orange	15	15
45.		3 pi. brown	15	15
46.		5 pi. olive	15	15
58.		10 pi. brown and mauve	50	

(6.)

(7.) (8.)

1923. Surch. with T **6** (¼ pi.) or T **7** (10 pi.).

48.	**5.**	¼ pi. on ⅛ pi. brown	1·50	1·50
49.		10 pi. on 5 pi. olive	1·50	1·50

1924. Proclamation of King Hassan as Caliph. Optd. with T **8.**

50.	**5.**	⅛ pi. brown	40	
51.		½ pi. red	40	40
52.		1 pi. blue	40	40
53.		1½ pi. violet	40	40
54.		2 pi. orange	40	40
55.		3 pi. brown	40	40
56.		5 pi. olive	40	40

(**9.** "Hejaz Government. 4th October, 1924".)

1925. Nos. 11 to 16 optd. with T **9.**

66.		1 pa. purple	75	
67.		⅛ pi. yellow	75	
60.		¼ pi. green	1·00	1·00
71.		½ pi. red	1·25	
84.		½ pi. on 1 pa. pur. (No. 29)	7·50	
65.		1 pi. blue	1·50	
85.		1 pi. on 1 pa. pur. (No. 30)	6·50	
74.		2 pi. claret	1·00	

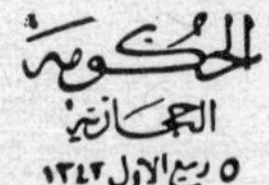

(**10.** "Hejaz Government, 4th October, 1924".)

1925. Optd. with T **10.**

105.		⅛ pi. brown	25	
96.		¼ pi. green	50	
106.		½ pi. red	25	
98.		1 pi. blue	25	
99.		1½ pi. violet	25	
100.		2 pi. orange	25	
101.		3 pi. brown	25	
103.		5 pi. olive	25	
104.		10 pi. brown and mauve	75	

1925. Nos. 50/6 optd. with T **10.**

136.	**5.**	⅛ pi. brown	75	
144.		½ pi. red	75	
138.		1 pi. blue	75	
139.		1½ pi. violet	1·00	
134.		2 pi. orange	1·50	
146.		3 pi. brown	1·00	
142.		5 pi. olive	75	

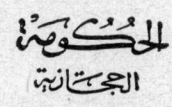

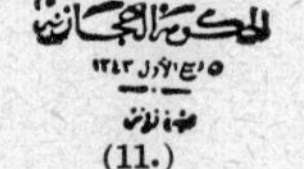

(**11.**) (**12.**)

1925. Stamps of 1922 surch. as Type **11.**

148.	**5.**	¼ pi. on ⅛ pi. brown	75	
149.		¼ pi. on ½ pi. red	1·50	
150.		1 pi. on 2 pi. orange	75	
151.		1 pi. on 3 pi. brown	1·00	
153.		10 pi. on 5 pi. olive	1·50	

1925. Nos. 148/53 further surch. with values in larger type as Type **12.**

154.	**5.**	¼ pi. on ¼ pi. on ⅛ pi. brown	75	
155.		¼ pi. on ¼ pi. on ½ pi. red	75	
156.		¼ pi. on 1 pi. on 2 pi. orge.		
157.		1 pi. on 1 pi. on 2 pi. orge.	1·00	
158.		1 pi. on 1 pi. on 3 pi. brn.	1·00	
160.		10 pi. on 10 pi. on 5 pi. olive	1·00	

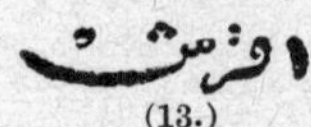

(**13.**)

1925. Stamps of 1922 surch. as T **13.**

165.	**5.**	⅛ pi. on ½ pi. red	25	
166.		¼ pi. on ½ pi. red	25	
167.		1 pi. on ½ pi. red	25	
161.		1 pi. on 1½ pi. violet	25	
162.		1 pi. on 2 pi. orange	25	
163.		1 pi. on 3 pi. brown	30	
171.		10 pi. on 5 pi. olive	50	

14.

(**15.**)

1925. As T **14** (various Arabic designs) optd. with T **15.**

177.		⅛ pi. brown	10	
178.		¼ pi. blue	10	
179.		½ pi. red	10	
180.		1 pi. green	15	
181.		1½ pi. orange	15	
182.		2 pi. blue	15	
183.		3 pi. olive	15	
184.		5 pi. brown	15	
185.		10 pi. green and red	25	

B. NEJD

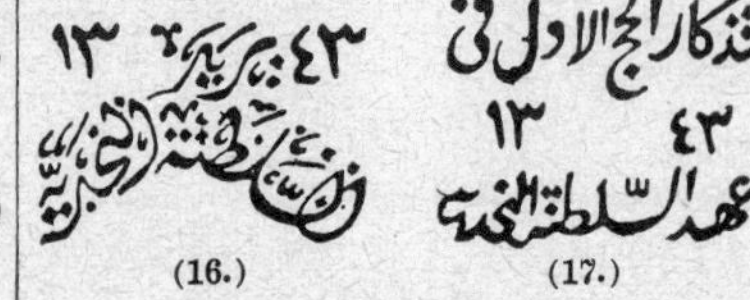

(**16.**) (**17.**)

A number of Hejaz and Turkish postage stamps and Hejaz fiscal stamps were overprinted with T **16** and **17** and similar types during the early period of the Nejd Sultanate, but are rarely seen by general collectors. A full list will be found in Stanley Gibbons' Overseas Catalogue, Vol. 4.

C. HEJAZ-NEJD

18. **19.**

1926.

254.	**18.**	¼ pi violet	30	
261.		¼ pi. orange	30	
255.		½ pi. grey	30	
262.		½ pi. green	15	
256.		1 pi. blue	30	
263.		1 pi. red	15	
257.	**19.**	2 pi. green	30	
264.		2 pi. violet	15	
259.		3 pi red	30	
265.		3 pi. blue	15	
260.		5 pi claret	30	
266.		5 pi. brown	20	

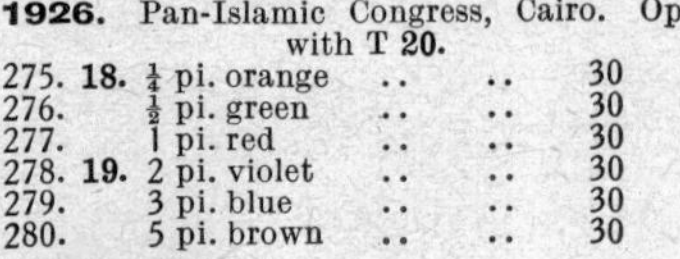

(**20.**). "Islamic Congress, 1 June, 1926".

1926. Pan-Islamic Congress, Cairo. Optd. with T **20.**

275.	**18.**	¼ pi. orange	30	
276.		½ pi. green	30	
277.		1 pi. red	30	
278.	**19.**	2 pi. violet	30	
279.		3 pi. blue	30	
280.		5 pi. brown	30	

21.

(**22.** "25th Rajab 1345").

1926.

284.	**21.**	⅛ pi. brown	20	5
285.		¼ pi. green	20	5
286.		½ pi. red	20	5
287.		1 pi. purple	20	8
288.		1½ pi. blue	30	5
289.		3 pi. olive	60	8
290.		5 pi. brown	1·25	8
291.		10 pi. chocolate	3·00	25

1927. Establishment of Kingdom. Optd. with T **22.**

294.	**21.**	⅛ pi. brown	40	40
295.		¼ pi. green	40	40
296.		½ pi. red	40	40
297.		1 pi. purple	40	40
298.		1½ pi. blue	40	40
299.		3 pi. olive	40	40
300.		5 pi. brown	40	40
301.		10 pi. chocolate	40	40

23. **24.**

1929.

302.	**23.**	1¾ g. blue	75	8
303.		20 g. violet	1·25	20
304.		30 g. green	1·90	25

1930. King Ibn Saud's Accession. Fourth Anniv.

305.	24.	½ g. red	40	40
306.		1½ g. violet	40	40
307.		1¾ g. blue	45	45
308.		3½ g. green	50	50
309.		5 g. purple	60	60

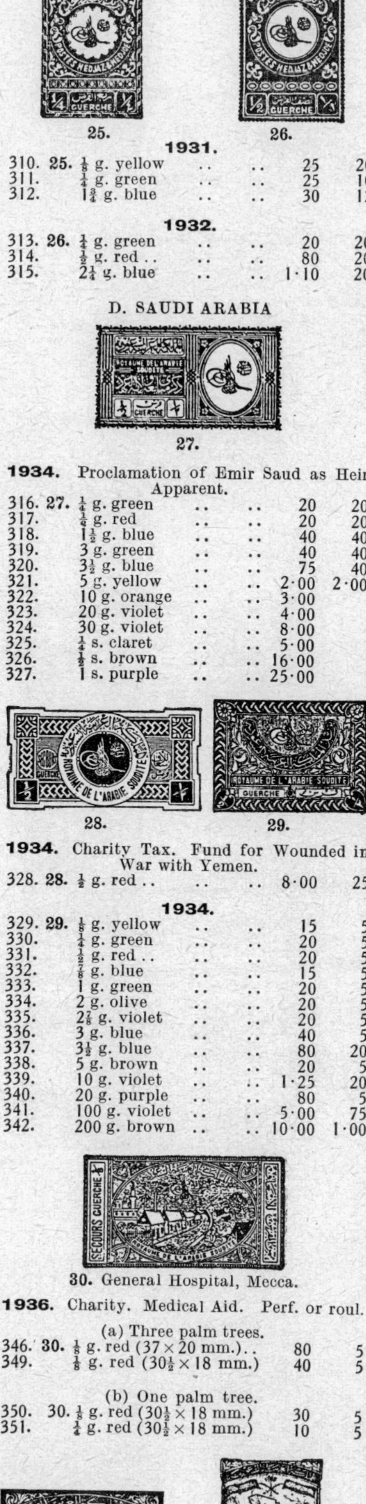

25. 26.

1931.

310.	25.	⅛ g. yellow	25	20
311.		¼ g. green	25	10
312.		1¾ g. blue	30	12

1932.

313.	26.	¼ g. green	20	20
314.		½ g. red	80	20
315.		2¼ g. blue	1·10	20

D. SAUDI ARABIA

27.

1934. Proclamation of Emir Saud as Heir Apparent.

316.	27.	¼ g. green	20	20
317.		½ g. red	20	20
318.		1½ g. blue	40	40
319.		3 g. green	40	40
320.		3½ g. blue	75	40
321.		5 g. yellow	2·00	2·00
322.		10 g. orange	3·00	
323.		20 g. violet	4·00	
324.		30 g. violet	8·00	
325.		¼ s. claret	5·00	
326.		½ s. brown	16·00	
327.		1 s. purple	25·00	

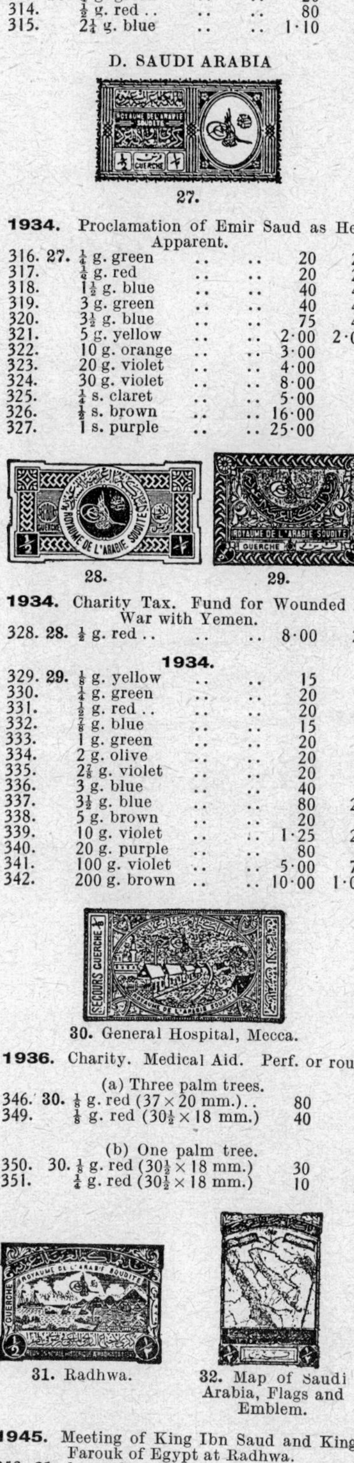

28. 29.

1934. Charity Tax. Fund for Wounded in War with Yemen.

328.	28.	½ g. red	8·00	25

1934.

329.	29.	⅛ g. yellow	15	5
330.		¼ g. green	20	5
331.		½ g. red	20	5
332.		⅞ g. blue	15	5
333.		1 g. green	20	5
334.		2 g. olive	20	5
335.		2⅞ g. violet	20	5
336.		3 g. blue	40	5
337.		3½ g. blue	80	20
338.		5 g. brown	20	5
339.		10 g. violet	1·25	20
340.		20 g. purple	80	5
341.		100 g. violet	5·00	75
342.		200 g. brown	10·00	1·00

30. General Hospital, Mecca.

1936. Charity. Medical Aid. Perf. or roul.

(a) Three palm trees.

346.	30.	⅛ g. red (37 × 20 mm.) ..	80	5
349.		⅛ g. red (30½ × 18 mm.)	40	5

(b) One palm tree.

350.	30.	⅛ g. red (30½ × 18 mm.)	30	5
351.		¼ g. red (30½ × 18 mm.)	10	5

31. Radhwa.

32. Map of Saudi Arabia, Flags and Emblem.

1945. Meeting of King Ibn Saud and King Farouk of Egypt at Radhwa.

352.	31.	½ g. red	20	20
353.		3 g. blue	40	40
354.		5 g. violet	80	80
355.		10 g. purple	2·00	1·25

1946. Return of King Ibn Saud from Egypt.

356a.	32.	½ g. mauve	40	8

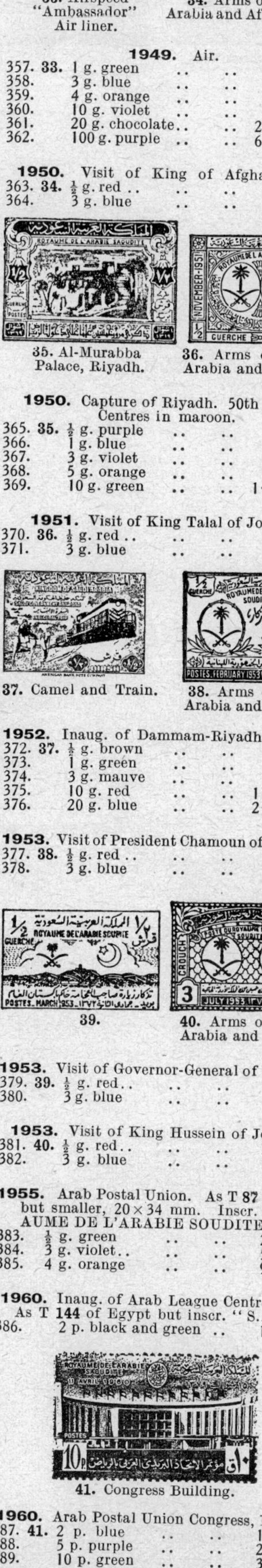

33. Airspeed "Ambassador" Air liner.

34. Arms of Saudi Arabia and Afghanistan.

1949. Air.

357.	33.	1 g. green	20	5
358.		3 g. blue	30	5
359.		4 g. orange	30	5
360.		10 g. violet	80	8
361.		20 g. chocolate	2·00	10
362.		100 g. purple	6 00	1·00

1950. Visit of King of Afghanistan.

363.	34.	½ g. red	20	8
364.		3 g. blue	30	15

35. Al-Murabba Palace, Riyadh.

36. Arms of Saudi Arabia and Jordan.

1950. Capture of Riyadh. 50th Anniv. Centres in maroon.

365.	35.	½ g. purple	15	8
366.		1 g. blue	20	10
367.		3 g. violet	30	12
368.		5 g. orange	60	20
369.		10 g. green	1·25	40

1951. Visit of King Talal of Jordan.

370.	36.	½ g. red	15	8
371.		3 g. blue	30	12

37. Camel and Train.

38. Arms of Saudi Arabia and Lebanon.

1952. Inaug. of Dammam-Riyadh Railway.

372.	37.	½ g. brown	8	8
373.		1 g. green	10	10
374.		3 g. mauve	15	15
375.		10 g. red	1·00	50
376.		20 g. blue	2·00	1·25

1953. Visit of President Chamoun of Lebanon.

377.	38.	½ g. red	20	10
378.		3 g. blue	35	25

39.

40. Arms of Saudi Arabia and Jordan.

1953. Visit of Governor-General of Pakistan.

379.	39.	½ g. red	20	10
380.		3 g. blue	35	25

1953. Visit of King Hussein of Jordan.

381.	40.	½ g. red	20	10
382.		3 g. blue	35	25

1955. Arab Postal Union. As T **87** of Egypt but smaller, 20 × 34 mm. Inscr. "ROYAUME DE L'ARABIE SOUDITE" at top.

383.		½ g. green	20	10
384.		3 g. violet	55	30
385.		4 g. orange	90	60

1960. Inaug. of Arab League Centre, Cairo. As T **144** of Egypt but inscr. "S.A.K.".

386.		2 p. black and green ..	15	8

41. Congress Building.

1960. Arab Postal Union Congress, Riyadh.

387.	41.	2 p. blue	10	8
388.		5 p. purple	20	10
389.		10 p. green	35	15

42. Radio Mast and Globe.

43. Refugee Camp.

1960. Direct Wireless Service. Inaug.

390.	42.	2 p. red and black ..	10	8
391.		5 p. purple and claret ..	20	8
392.		10 p. indigo and blue ..	30	12

1960. World Refugee Year.

393.	43.	2 p. blue	8	8
394.		8 p. violet	20	15
395.		10 p. green	25	20

44. Gas Oil Plant.

45. Wadi Hanifa Dam, Near Riyadh.

46. Convair 440.

(I).

(II).

1960. Cartouche of King Saud as Type **1.** Size 27½ × 22 mm. (a) Postage. (i) Type **44.**

396.	½ p. orange and claret ..	5	5
397.	1 p. red and blue	5	5
398.	2 p. blue and red	5	5
399.	3 p. emerald and violet ..	8	5
400.	4 p. purple and green ..	8	5
401.	5 p. lake and maroon ..	10	8
402.	6 p. lilac and chestnut ..	12	10
403.	7 p. myrtle and violet ..	10	8
404.	8 p. black and green ..	12	8
405.	9 p. brown and blue ..	12	8
406.	10 p. red and blue ..	15	8
407.	20 p. black and brown ..	25	10
408.	50 p. green and brown ..	1·75	50
409.	75 p. maroon and red ..	2·75	60
410.	100 p. chocolate and blue	3·50	90
411.	200 p. bronze and black ..	7·00	1·90

(ii) Type **45.**

412.	½ p. orange and brown ..	5	5
413.	1 p. purple and olive ..	5	5
414.	2 p. sepia and blue ..	5	5
415.	3 p. blue and sepia ..	8	5
416.	4 p. chestnut and brown	8	5
417.	5 p. maroon and sepia ..	10	8
418.	6 p. red and black ..	10	10
419.	7 p. olive and red ..	12	10
420.	8 p. maroon and blue ..	12	10
421.	9 p. red and brown ..	12	10
422.	10 p. lake and green ..	15	8
423.	20 p. green and brown ..	25	10
424.	50 p. brown and black ..	1·75	50
425.	75 p. grey and brown ..	2·75	60
426.	100 p. turquoise and blue	3·50	90
427.	200 p. green and purple ..	7·00	1·90

(b) Air. T **46.**

428.	1 p. green and lilac ..	5	5
429.	2 p. purple and green ..	5	5
430.	3 p. blue and magenta ..	5	5
431.	4 p. purple and blue ..	8	5
432.	5 p. red and yellow-green ..	8	5
433.	6 p. grey and chestnut ..	10	8
434.	8 p. olive and red	12	8
435.	9 p. red-brown and violet	12	8
436.	10 p. chocolate and purple	20	10
437.	15 p. brown and blue ..	30	12
438.	20 p. emerald and chestnut	30	10
439.	30 p. turquoise and bistre	1·25	60
440.	50 p. indigo and green ..	1·60	40
441.	100 p. brown and grey ..	3·50	1·00
442.	200 p. black and purple ..	7·00	1·75

See also Nos. 487/92, 529/610 and 660/744.

47. Globe, Pylon and Telegraph Pole.

1960. Arab Telecommunications Union Commemoration.

443.	47.	3 p. purple	8	8
444.		6 p. black	20	12
445.		8 p. brown	25	15

47a. Dammam Port. 48. Campaign Emblem.

1961. Opening of Dammam Port Extension.

446.	47a.	3 p. violet	8	5
447.		6 p. blue	15	10
448.		8 p. green	20	15

1962. Arab League Week. As T **170** of Egypt.

449.	3 p. bronze-green ..	8	8
450.	6 p. cerise	15	15
451.	8 p. black-green	25	20

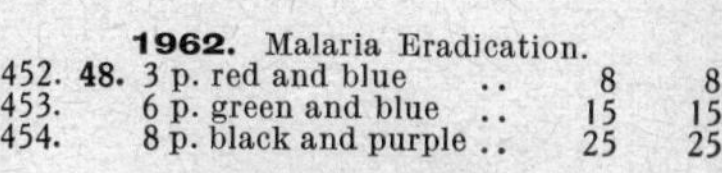

1962. Malaria Eradication.

452.	48.	3 p. red and blue ..	8	8
453.		6 p. green and blue ..	15	15
454.		8 p. black and purple ..	25	25

49. Koran.

1963. Islamic Institute, Medina. 1st Anniv.

456.	49.	2½ p. purple and salmon	5	5
457.		7½ p. blue and green ..	8	8
458.		9½ p. green and black ..	20	15

50. Emblem within Hands.

51. Boeing "707" over Airport.

1963. Freedom from Hunger.

459.	50.	2½ p. magenta and salmon	8	5
460.		7½ p. purple and pink ..	15	12
461.		9 p. chestnut and blue ..	20	15

1963. Opening of Dhahran Airport and Jet Service Inaug.

462.	51.	1 p. slate-vio. & orge.-brn.	5	5
463.		3½ p. blue and green ..	10	8
464.		6 p. yellow-green & red	20	12
465.		7½ p. magenta and blue	20	12
466.		9½ p. red & slate-violet	30	20

1963. As T **44/6** but redrawn in larger format (29 × 23 mm.). Cartouche of King Saud as Type I.

(a) Postage. (i) T **44.**

487.	½ p. orange and red ..	5	5
488.	1 p. orange and blue ..	5	5

(ii) T **45.**

489.	½ p. orange and bistre ..	5	5

(b) Air. T **46.**

490.	3 p. blue and red	5	5
491.	10 p. chocolate and black	15	8
492.	20 p. green and brown ..	35	10

Nos. 487/92 are widely spaced in the sheets, thus producing wide margins.

52. "Flame of Freedom".

1964. Declaration of Human Rights. 15th Anniv.

493.	52.	3 p. blue, violet & salmon	10	8
494.		6 p. bl., grn. & pale blue	12	12
495.		9 p. blue, brown & flesh	20	20

53. Arms and King Faisal.

1964. Installation of King Faisal.

496.	53.	4 p. blue and green ..	12	10

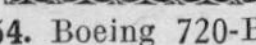

54. Boeing 720-B.

54a. Kaaba, Mecca.

1964. As T 44/5 but completely redrawn (Arabic inscr. closer to top frame) and T 54. Smaller size, 26¾ × 21¾ mm. Cartouche of King Saud as Type I.

(a) Postage. (i) Type **44**.

No.	Description	Unused	Used
529.	1 p. red and blue.. ..	5	5
530.	2 p. blue and red.. ..	5	5
531.	3 p. emerald and violet ..	5	5
532.	4 p. purple and green ..	5	5
533.	5 p. lake and maroon ..	1·00	1·00
534.	6 p. chocolate and brown	8	5
535.	7 p. green and lilac ..	8	5
536.	8 p. black and green ..	10	5
537.	9 p. brown and blue ..	35	5
538.	10 p. red and blue ..	12	5
539.	11 p. orange and green ..	15	12
540.	12 p. green and ochre ..	15	12
541.	13 p. blue and cerise ..	20	15
542.	14 p. chestnut and lilac ..	20	15
543	15 p. brown and cerise ..	20	20
544.	16 p. vermilion and green	25	20
545.	17 p. brown and cerise ..	25	20
546.	18 p. blue and black ..	30	25
547.	19 p. yellow and brown ..	30	25
548.	20 p. black and brown ..	30	12
549.	23 p. red and orange ..	35	25
550.	24 p. yellow and green ..	35	30
551.	26 p. chestnut and purple	40	35
552.	27 p. black and red ..	40	35
553.	31 p. red and turquoise ..	45	40
554.	33 p. black and brown ..	50	40
555.	50 p. green and brown ..	70	50
556.	200 p. green and slate ..	2·75	65

(ii) Type **45**.

No.	Description	Unused	Used
557.	1 p. purple and olive ..	5	5
558.	2 p. sepia and blue ..	5	5
559.	3 p. blue and sepia ..	5	5
560.	4 p. chestnut and brown	5	5
561.	5 p. purple and black ..	8	5
562.	6 p. red and black ..	10	5
563.	7 p. black and brown ..	10	5
564.	8 p. agate and blue ..	1·25	10
565.	9 p. vermilion and brown	15	5
566.	10 p. brown and green ..	15	5
567.	11 p. green and red ..	15	12
568.	12 p. blue and orange ..	15	12
569.	13 p. cerise and olive ..	20	15
570.	14 p. green and brown ..	20	15
571.	15 p. green and sepia ..	20	15
572.	16 p. red and lilac ..	25	20
573.	17 p. blue and purple ..	25	20
574.	18 p. blue and emerald ..	30	25
575.	19 p. ochre and black ..	30	25
576.	20 p. green and chocolate	30	15
577.	23 p. purple and chocolate	35	30
578.	24 p. blue and vermilion..	35	30
579.	26 p. yellow and olive ..	40	35
580.	27 p. maroon and blue ..	40	35
581.	31 p. blue and black ..	45	40
582.	33 p. purple and green ..	50	45
583.	100 p. turq. and blue ..	1·25	60
584.	200 p. green & purple ..	2·50	75

(b) Air. Type **54**.

No.	Description	Unused	Used
585.	1 p. green and purple ..	1·60	5
586.	2 p. purple and green ..	5	5
587.	3 p. blue and red	5	5
588.	4 p. purple and blue ..	5	5
589.	5 p. red and green ..	5	5
590.	6 p. slate and brown ..	10	5
591.	7 p. green and magenta ..	10	5
592.	8 p. olive and red.. ..	12	5
593.	9 p. chestnut and violet ..	15	5
594.	10 p. maroon and black ..	15	5
595.	11 p. buff and emerald ..	5·00	
596.	12 p. grey and orange ..	15	12
597.	13 p. green and myrtle ..	20	15
598.	14 p. orange and blue ..	20	15
599.	15 p. brown and blue ..	20	15
600.	16 p. blue and black ..	25	20
601.	17 p. brown and ochre ..	25	20
602.	18 p. green and blue ..	30	25
603.	19 p. orange and magenta	30	25
604.	20 p. emerald and brown	40	25
605.	23 p. ochre and green ..	35	30
606.	24 p. sepia and ultramarine	40	30
607.	26 p. green and vermilion	40	35
608.	27 p. green and sepia ..	40	35
609.	31 p. red and magenta ..	45	40
610.	33 p. purple and vermilion	50	45

1965. Moslem League Conf., Mecca.

No.	Type	Description	Unused	Used
611.	54a.	4 p. black and brown	8	5
612.		6 p. black and mauve	10	8
613.		10 p. black and green	15	12

55. Arms of Saudi Arabia and Tunisia.

1965. Visit of President Bourguiba of Tunisia.

No.	Type	Description	Unused	Used
614.	55.	4 p. silver and magenta	8	5
615.		8 p. silver and violet ..	15	12
616.		10 p. silver and blue ..	20	15

56. Highway.

1965. Opening of Arafat–Taif Highway.

No.	Type	Description	Unused	Used
617.	56.	2 p. black and red ..	5	5
618.		4 p. black and blue ..	8	8
619.		6 p. black and violet ..	10	8
620.		8 p. black and green ..	15	12

57. I.C.Y. Emblem.

1965. Int. Co-operation Year.

No.	Type	Description	Unused	Used
621.	57.	1 p. brown and yellow..	5	5
622.		2 p. green and salmon..	5	5
623.		3 p. olive and blue ..	8	8
624.		4 p. black and olive ..	10	10
625.		10 p. purple and orange	20	20

58. I.T.U. Symbol and Emblems.

1965. I.T.U. Cent.

No.	Type	Description	Unused	Used
626.	58.	3 p. black and blue ..	5	5
627.		4 p. green and violet ..	10	10
628.		8 p. brown & emerald..	15	15
629.		10 p. green and orange	20	20

59. Lamp and Burning Library.

1966. Burning of Algiers Library.

No.	Type	Description	Unused	Used
630.	59.	1 p. vermilion	5	5
631.		2 p. red	5	5
632.		3 p. purple	8	8
633.		4 p. violet	10	10
634.		5 p. magenta	12	12
635.		6 p. red	20	15

60. A.P.U. Emblem.

62. Scout Badges.

63. W.H.O. Building.

61. Dagger on Deir Yasin, Palestine.

1966. Arab Postal Union. 10th Anniv. (in 1964).

No.	Type	Description	Unused	Used
636.	60.	3 p. olive and plum ..	5	5
637.		4 p. olive and blue ..	8	8
638.		6 p. olive and maroon..	12	10
639.		7 p. olive and green ..	12	10

1966. Deir Yasin Massacre.

No.	Type	Description	Unused	Used
640.	61.	2 p. black and green ..	5	5
641.		4 p. black and brown ..	8	8
642.		6 p. black and blue ..	10	10
643.		8 p. black and orange ..	12	12

1966. Arab Scout Jamboree.

No.	Type	Description	Unused	Used
644.	62.	4 p. green, grey, black and yellow	8	8
645.		8 p. orange, blue, black and yellow	15	12
646.		10 p. blue, pink, black and yellow	20	15

1966. W.H.O. Headquarters, Geneva. Inaug.

No.	Type	Description	Unused	Used
647.	63.	4 p. multicoloured ..	8	8
648.		6 p. multicoloured ..	12	10
649.		10 p. multicoloured ..	20	15

64. U.N.E.S.C.O. Emblem.

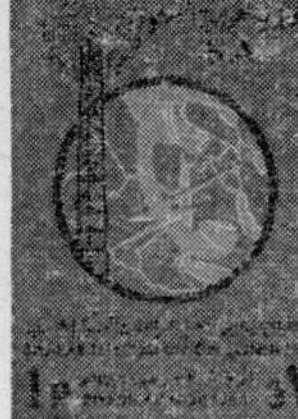
65. Radio Mast, Telephone and Map.

1966. U.N.E.S.C.O. 20th Anniv.

No.	Type	Description	Unused	Used
650.	64.	1 p. multicoloured ..	5	5
651.		2 p. multicoloured ..	5	5
652.		3 p. multicoloured ..	5	5
653.		4 p. multicoloured ..	8	8
654.		10 p. multicoloured ..	20	12

1966. 8th Arab Telecommunications Union Congress, Riyadh.

No.	Type	Description	Unused	Used
655.	65.	1 p. red, yell., blk. & blue	5	5
656.		2 p. red, yell., blk. & lilac	5	5
657.		4 p. red, yell., blk. & pur.	8	8
658.		6 p. red, yell., blk. & ol.	12	10
659.		7 p. red, yell., blk. & grn.	15	12

1966. As 1964 issue, but with cartouche of King Faisal as Type II (see above No. 396).

(a) Postage. (i) Type **44**.

No.	Description	Unused	Used
660.	1 p. red and blue	5	5
661.	2 p. blue and red	5	5
662.	3 p. green and violet ..	5	5
663.	4 p. purple and green ..	5	5
664.	5 p. brown and purple ..	8	5
665.	6 p. chocolate and brown	10	5
666.	7 p. green and lilac ..	10	5
667.	8 p. green and blue-green	12	5
668.	9 p. brown and blue ..	12	5
669.	10 p. red and blue ..	15	5
670.	11 p. orange and green ..	15	12
671.	12 p. green and brown ..	20	15
672.	13 p. blue and red ..	20	15
673.	14 p. brown and lilac ..	20	15
674.	15 p. brown and red ..	20	20
675.	16 p. red and green ..	25	20
676.	18 p. blue and black ..	30	25
677.	19 p. yellow and brown ..	30	12
678.	20 p. brown and yellow-brown	30	12
679.	23 p. red and orange ..	35	30
680.	24 p. yellow and green ..	35	30
682.	27 p. black and red ..	40	35
683.	31 p. red and green ..	45	40
684.	33 p. black and brown ..	50	45
686.	100 p. black and blue ..	1·25	50
687.	200 p. green and black ..	2·50	70

(ii) Type **45**.

No.	Description	Unused	Used
688.	1 p. purple and green ..	5	5
689.	2 p. brown and blue ..	5	5
690.	3 p. blue and brown ..	5	5
691.	4 p. orange and brown ..	5	5
692.	5 p. purple and black ..	8	5
693.	6 p. red and black ..	10	5
694.	7 p. black and brown ..	12	5
695.	8 p. brown and blue ..	12	5
696.	9 p. red and brown ..	12	5
697.	10 p. brown and green ..	15	8
698.	11 p. green and red ..	15	8
699.	12 p. purple and orange ..	20	10
700.	13 p. red and green ..	20	10
701.	14 p. green and brown ..	25	20
702.	15 p. green and brown ..	20	15
703.	16 p. lilac and red ..	25	20
704.	17 p. blue and purple ..	25	12
705.	18 p. blue and green ..	25	20
706.	19 p. brown and black ..	25	12
707.	20 p. green and brown ..	30	12
708.	23 p. purple and brown ..	35	15
708a.	24 p. blue and red ..	40	35
709.	26 p. brown and green ..	40	35
711.	27 p. purple and blue ..	40	35
712.	33 p. purple and green ..	50	45
713.	50 p. brown and black ..	60	30
714.	100 p. blue and deep blue	1·25	50
715.	200 p. green and purple ..	2·50	70

(b) Air. Type **54**.

No.	Description	Unused	Used
716.	1 p. green and purple ..	5	5
717.	2 p. purple and green ..	5	5
718.	3 p. blue and red.. ..	5	5
719.	4 p. purple and blue ..	5	5
720.	5 p. red and green ..	5	5
721.	6 p. grey and brown ..	10	5
722.	7 p. green and mauve ..	10	5
723.	8 p. green and red ..	12	5
724.	9 p. brown and violet ..	12	5
725.	10 p. brown and black ..	15	5
726.	11 p. brown and green ..	15	12
728.	13 p. green and myrtle ..	20	15
729.	14 p. orange and blue ..	25	20
730.	15 p. brown and blue ..	20	20
731.	16 p. blue and black ..	25	20
732.	17 p. brown and yellow..	25	20
733.	18 p. green and blue ..	25	20
734.	19 p. orange and mauve..	30	20
735.	20 p. green and brown ..	30	20
736.	23 p. brown and green ..	35	30
737.	24 p. brown and blue ..	35	30
741.	33 p. purple and red ..	50	40
744.	200 p. black and purple..	2·40	60

66. Moot Emblem.

67. Meteorological Apparatus.

1967. 2nd Rover Moot, Mecca.

No.	Type	Description	Unused	Used
745.	66.	1 p. multicoloured ..	5	5
746.		2 p. multicoloured ..	5	5
747.		3 p. multicoloured ..	8	5
748.		4 p. multicoloured ..	10	5
749.		10 p. multicoloured ..	25	10

1967. World Meteorological Day.

No.	Type	Description	Unused	Used
750.	67.	1 p. magenta	5	5
751.		2 p. violet	5	5
752.		3 p. olive	5	5
753.		4 p. green	8	5
754.		10 p. blue	15	10

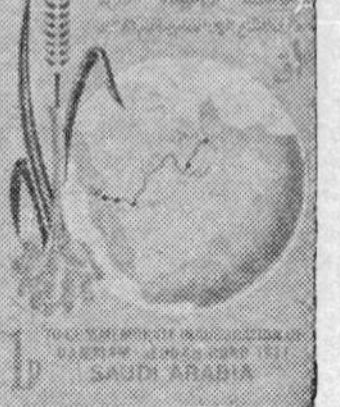

68. Route Map.

69. The Prophet's Mosque, Medina.

70. Prophet's Mosque Extension.

71. Ancient Wall Tomb, Madayin Saleh.

72. Colonnade, Sacred Mosque, Mecca.

73. Camels and Oil Derrick.

74. Arab Stallion.

75. Holy Ka'aba, Mecca

1968. Dammam—Jeddah Highway. Inaug.

No.	Type	Description	Unused	Used
834.	68.	1 p. multicoloured ..	5	5
835.		2 p. multicoloured ..	5	5
836.		3 p. multicoloured ..	5	5
837.		4 p. multicoloured ..	8	8
838.		10 p. multicoloured ..	15	15

1968.

(a) Type **69**.

No.	Type	Description	Unused	Used
839.	69.	1 p. green and orange..	5	5
840.		2 p. green and brown ..	8	5
857.		3 p. green and violet ..	5	5
858.		4 p. green and green ..	10	5
843.		5 p. green and purple ..	12	5
860.		6 p. green and black ..	50	30
948.		10 p. green and brown	20	5
863.		20 p. green and brown	70	40
864.		50 p. green and purple	1·25	85
865.		100 p. green and blue..		
866.		200 p. green and red ..	5·00	3·50

(b) Type **70**.

No.	Type	Description	Unused	Used
933.	70.	1 p. green and orange..	5	5
934.		2 p. green and brown ..	5	5
867.		3 p. green and black ..	8	5
868.		4 p. green and red ..	10	5
851.		5 p. green and red ..	12	5
852.		6 p. green and blue ..	15	5
870a.		8 p. green and red ..	20	5
853.		10 p. green and brown	25	5
940.		20 p. green and violet..	50	20

(c) Type **71**.

No.	Type	Description	Unused	Used
876.	71.	2 p. brown and blue ..	15	15
878.		4 p. cinnamon and brown	10	5
880.		7 p. brown and orange	20	10
881.		10 p. brown and green	70	35
883.		20 p. brown and purple	50	20

(d) Type **72.**

887. **72.** 3 p. grey and red .. 25 25
888. 4 p. grey and green .. 10 5
891. 10 p. grey and purple .. 70 35

(e) Type **73.**

898. **73.** 4 p. red and lilac .. 30 25
901. 10 p. red and blue .. 55 40

(f) Type **74.**

908. **74.** 4 p. brown and purple 10 5
911. 10 p. brown and black 50 25
912. 14 p. brown and blue .. 70 45
913. 20 p. brown and green 50 10

(g) Type **75.**

1016. **75.** 4 p. black and green .. 10 5
920. 6 p. black and purple 15 5
924. 8 p. black and red .. 20 5
1008. 10 p. black and red .. 50 25

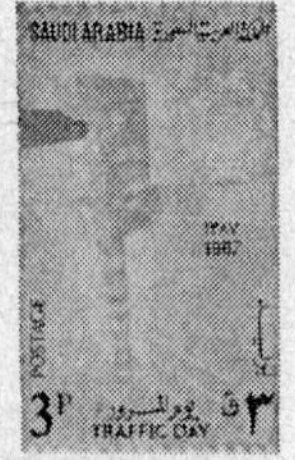

76. Falcon. **77.** Traffic Signals.

1968. Air.

1022. **76.** 1 p. brown and green 5 5
1023. 4 p. orange and red .. 10 5
1024. 10 p. brown and blue 25 5
1025. 20 p. brown and green 40 8

1969. Traffic Day.

1026. **77.** 3 p. red, green and blue 5 5
1027. 4 p. red, green & brown 8 5
1028. 10 p. red, green & purple 25 15

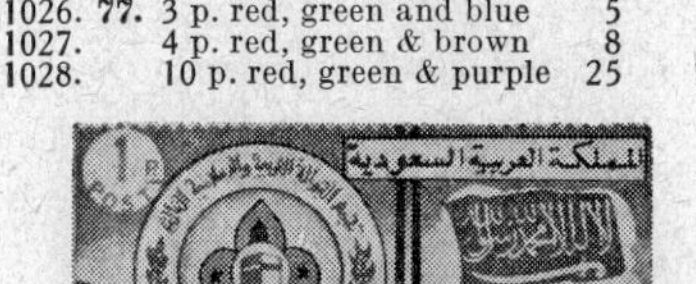

78. Scout Emblem, Camp and Flag.

1969. 3rd Arab Rover Moot, Mecca.

1029. **78.** 1 p. multicoloured .. 5 5
1030. 4 p. multicoloured .. 8 5
1031. 10 p. multicoloured .. 25 15

79. W.H.O. Emblem.

1969. World Health Organization (1968). 20th Anniv.

1032. **79.** 4 p. multicoloured .. 10 5

80. Conference Emblem. **81.** Satellite, Dish Aerial and Open Book.

1970. Islamic Foreign Ministers' Conf., Jeddah

1033. **80.** 4 p. black and blue .. 10 5
1034. 10 p. black and ochre 20 15

1970. World Telecommunications Day.

1035. **81.** 4 p. blue, magenta and ultramarine .. 10 5
1036. 10 p. blue, magenta & grn. 15 15

82. Steel Rolling-mill. **83.** Emblem and Arab Archway.

1970. First Arabian Steel Rolling-mill. Inaug. (1967).

1037. **82.** 3 p. multicoloured .. 5 5
1038. 4 p. multicoloured .. 8 5
1039. 10 p. multicoloured .. 15 15

1971. 4th Int. Rover Moot.

1049. **83.** 10 p. multicoloured .. 25 25

84. Global Emblem.

1971. World Telecommunications Day.

1050. **84.** 4 p. black & blue .. 8 5
1051. 10 p. black and lilac .. 15 15

85. University "Tower" Emblem. **86.** I.E.Y. Emblem.

1971. King Abdul Aziz National University. 4th Anniv.

1052. **85.** 3 p. black and green .. 5 5
1053. 4 p. black and brown 8 5
1054. 10 p. black and blue .. 15 15

1971. Int. Education Year (1970).

1055. **86.** 4 p. brown and green 10 5

87. Arab League Emblem. **88.** O.P.E.C. Emblem.

1971. Arab Propaganda Week.

1056. **87.** 10 p. multicoloured .. 15 15

1971. O.P.E.C. 10th Anniv.

1057. **88.** 4 p. blue 10 5

O.P.E.C. = Organisation of Petroleum Exporting Countries.

89. Globe. **91.** Writing in Book.

90. Telephone within Dial.

1972. World Telecommunications Day.

1058. **89.** 4 p. multicoloured .. 10 5

1972. Automatic Telephone System (1969). Inaug.

1059. **90.** 1 p. black, green & red 5 5
1060. 4 p. black, bl.-grn. & grn. 10 5
1061. 5 p. blk., grn. & mauve 10 5
1062. 10 p. blk., grn. & brown 15 15

1973. World Literacy Day (1972).

1063. **91.** 10 p. multicoloured .. 15 15

92. Mosque, Mecca, and Moot Emblem.

1973. Fifth Arab Rover Moot, Mecca. Mult.

1064. 4 p. Type **92** 8 5
1065. 6 p. Holy Ka'aba, Mecca 10 8
1066. 10 p. Rover encampment 15 15

93. Globe and Map of Palestine. **94.** Leaf and Emblem.

1973. Universal Palestine Week.

1067. **93.** 4 p. red, yellow & grey 8 5
1068. 10 p. red, yellow and blue 15 12

1973. Int. Hydrological Decade.

1069. **94.** 4 p. multicoloured .. 8 5

95. A.P.U. Emblem.

1973. Founding of Arab Postal Union at Sofar Conference. 25th Anniv.

1070. **95.** 4 p. multicoloured .. 8 5
1071. 10 p. multicoloured .. 15 12

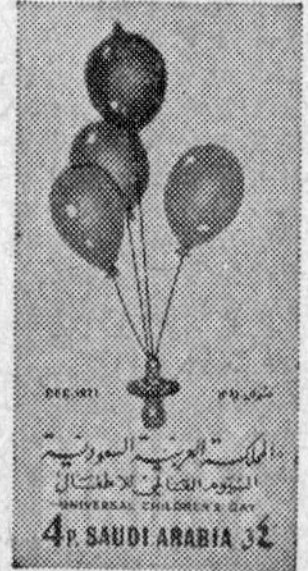

96. Balloons.

1973. Universal Children's Day (1971).

1072. **96.** 4 p. multicoloured .. 8 5

97. U.P.U. Monument and Postal Emblems.

1974. Universal Postal Union. Centenary.

1073. **97.** 3 p. multicoloured .. 5 5
1074. 4 p. multicoloured .. 8 5
1075. 10 p. multicoloured .. 15 12

98. Handclasp and U.N.E.S.C.O. Emblem.

1974. International Book Year (1972).

1076. **98.** 4 p. multicoloured .. 8 5
1077. 10 p. multicoloured .. 15 12

99. Desalination Works.

1974. Sea-water Desalination Plant, Jeddah (1971). Inaug.

1078. **99.** 4 p. blue and orange .. 8 5
1079. 6 p. lilac and green .. 10 8
1080. 10 p. black and red .. 15 12

100. Interpol Emblem. **101.** Tower, Emblem and Hand with Letter.

1974. International Criminal Police Organization (Interpol). 50th Anniv. (1973).

1081. **100.** 4 p. blue and red .. 8 5
1082. 10 p. blue and green 15 12

1974. Third Session of Arab Postal Studies Consultative Council, Riyadh.

1083. **101.** 4 p. multicoloured .. 8 5

102. New Headquarters Building.

1974. New U.P.U. Headquarters, Berne (1970). Inauguration.

1084. **102.** 3 p. multicoloured .. 5 5
1085. 4 p. multicoloured .. 8 5
1086. 10 p. multicoloured .. 15 12

103. Armed Forces and Flame.

1974. King Faisal Military Cantonment (1971).

1087. **103.** 3 p. multicoloured .. 5 5
1088. 4 p. multicoloured .. 8 5
1089. 10 p. multicoloured .. 15 12

104. Red Crescent " Flower ".

1974. Saudi Arabian Red Crescent Society. 10th Anniv. (1973).

1090. **104.** 4 p. multicoloured .. 8 5
1091. 6 p. multicoloured .. 10 8
1092. 10 p. multicoloured .. 15 12

105. Scout Emblem and Minarets.

1974. 6th Arab Rover Moot, Mecca.

1093. 105. 4 p. multicoloured .. 8 5
1094. 6 p. multicoloured .. 10 8
1095. 10 p. multicoloured .. 15 12

106. Reading Braille.

1975. Day of the Blind.

1096. 106. 4 p. multicoloured .. 8 5
1097. 10 p. multicoloured .. 20 15

107. Anemometer and U.N. Emblem as Weather Balloon.

1975. International Meteorological Co-operation. Cent. (1973).

1098. 107. 4 p. multicoloured .. 8 5

108. King Faisal. 109. Conference Emblem.

1975. King Faisal Memorial Issue.

1099. 108. 4 p. purple and green 8 5
1100. 16 p. green and violet 35 35
1101. 23 p. violet and green 50 50

1975. Sixth Islamic Conference of Foreign Ministers, Jeddah.

1103. 109. 10 p black and brown 20 15

110. Wheat and Sun.

1975. Charity Society. 29th Anniversary.

1104. 110. 4 p. multicoloured .. 10 5
1105. 10 p. multicoloured .. 25 15

111. Kaaba, Handclasp and Globe.

1975. Muslim Organisations Conf., Mecca.

1106. 111. 4 p. multicoloured .. 10 5
1107. 10 p. multicoloured .. 75 15

112. Saudia Airliner.

1975. Saudi Arabia Airline "Saudia". 30th Anniversary.

1108. 112. 4 p. multicoloured .. 10 5
1109. 10 p. multicoloured .. 25 15

113. Mecca and Riyadh.

1975. Conference Locations.

1110. 113. 10 p. multicoloured .. 25 15

114. Friday Mosque, Medina and Juwatha Mosque, al-Hasa.

1975. Islamic Holy Places.

1111. 114. 4 p. multicoloured .. 10 5
1112. 10 p. multicoloured .. 25 15

115. F.A.O. Emblem.

1975. World Food Programme. 10th Anniv. (1973).

1113. 115. 4 p. multicoloured .. 10 5
1114. 10 p. multicoloured .. 25 15

116. Conference Emblem.

1976. Islamic Solidarity Conf. of Science and Technology, Mecca.

1115. 116. 4 p. multicoloured .. 10 5

117. Map and T.V. Screen.

1976. Saudi Arabia Television Service. 10th Anniv.

1116. 117. 4 p. multicoloured .. 10 5

118. Ear of Wheat, Atomic Symbol and Graph.

1976. 2nd Five-year Plan.

1117. 118. 20 h. multicoloured .. 10 5
1118. 50 h. multicoloured .. 25 15

119. Quba Mosque, Medina.

1976.

1119. 119. 20 h. black and orange 10 5
1120. 50 h. violet and green 25 15

120. Globe and Telephones.

1976. Telephone Centenary.

1121. 120. 50 h. multicoloured .. 25 15

121. Emblem and Heads of State.

1976. Arab League Meeting.

1122. 121. 20 h. green and blue 10 5

POSTAGE DUE STAMPS

A. HEJAZ

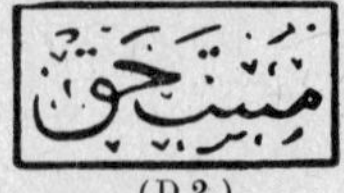

D 1. (D 2.)

1917. Arabic designs as Type D 1.

D 17. 20 pa. red 15
D 18. 1 pi. blue 15
D 19. 2 pi. claret 15

1921. Nos. D 17/9 optd. with T 2 (with or without frame-lines).

D 31. 20 pa. red .. .. 1·00
D 40. 1 pi. blue 25
D 41. 2 pi. claret 25

1923. Optd. with Type D 2.

D 47. 5. ½ pi. red 30
D 48. 1 pi blue 30
D 49. 2 pi. orange 30

1925. Nos. D 17/9 optd. with T 9.

D 88. 20 pa. red .. .. 18·00 25·00
D 91. 1 pi. blue .. .. 75 3·50
D 92. 2 pi. claret .. .. 75 3·50

1925. Nos. D 17/9 optd. with T 10.

D 93. 20 pa. red .. .. 25·00 30·00
D 94. 1 pi. blue .. .. 1·25
D 96. 2 pi. claret .. .. 1·50 5·50

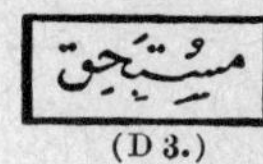

(D 3.)  (D 4.) D 5.

1925. Stamps of 1922 optd. with Type D 3.

D 149. 5. ½ pi. red .. .. 3·50
D 150. 1½ pi. violet .. .. 3·50
D 151. 2 pi. orange .. .. 12·00
D 152. 3 pi. brown .. .. 5·00
D 153. 5 pi. olive .. .. 3·50

1925. Stamps of 1922 optd. with Type D 4.

D 154. 5. ⅛ pi. brown 50
D 155. ½ pi. red 50
D 156. 1 pi. blue 65
D 157. 1½ pi. lilac 65
D 158. 2 pi. orange .. .. 1·25
D 160. 3 pi. brown 60
D 161. 5 pi. olive 60
D 162. 10 pi. brown and mauve 75

1925. Nos. D 154/62 optd. with Type D 3.

D 163. 5. ⅛ pi. brown 50
D 164. ½ pi. red 50
D 165. 1 pi. blue 50
D 166. 1½ pi. lilac 50
D 167. 2 pi. orange 50
D 169. 3 pi. brown 50
D 170. 5 pi. olive 50
D 171. 10 pi. brown and mauve 75

1925. Optd. with T 15.

D 186. D 5. ½ pi. blue 10
D 187. 1 pi. orange 10
D 188. 2 pi. brown 10
D 189. 3 pi. red 10

These stamps without overprint were not officially issued

B. HEJAZ-NEJD

D 6. D 7.

1926.

D 267. D 6. ½ pi. red 20
D 268. ½ pi. purple 75
D 269. ½ pi. orange 50
D 270. 2 pi. orange 20
D 271. 2 pi. purple 75
D 272. 6 pi. brown 20
D 273. 6 pi. purple 75
D 274. 6 pi. green 75

1926. Grand Moslem Conf. Optd. with T 20.

D 281. D 6. ½ pi. red 30
D 282. 2 pi. orange .. 30
D 283. 6 pi. brown .. 30

1927.

D 292. D 7. 1 pi. grey 20 5
D 293. 2 pi. violet 20 5

C. SAUDI ARABIA

D 8. D 9.

1937.

D 347. D 8. ½ g. brown 20 20
D 348. 1 g. blue 20 20
D 349. 2 g purple 30 30

1961.

D 449. D 9. 1 p. violet 5 5
D 450. 2 p. green 8 8
D 451. 4 p. rose 12 12

OFFICIAL STAMPS
SAUDI ARABIA

O 1. O 2.

1939.
O 347. O 1. 3 g. blue 20 20
O 348. 5 g. mauve 20 20
O 349. 20 g. brown 60 60
O 350. 50 g. blue-green 1·25 1·25
O 351. 100 g. olive .. .. 2·50 2·50
O 352. 200 g. purple .. 5·00 5·00

1961. Size 18½ × 22½ mm.
O 449. O 2. 1 p. black 5 5
O 450. 2 p. green 5 5
O 451. 3 p. bistre 8 8
O 452. 4 p. blue 10 10
O 453. 5 p. red 12 12
O 454. 10 p. maroon .. 25 25
O 455. 20 p. violet 50 50
O 456. 50 p. brown .. 1·00 1·00
O 457. 100 p. bronze .. 2·00 2·00

1964. Size 21 × 26½ mm.
O 497. O 2. 1 p. black 5 5
O 498. 2 p. green 5 5
O 499. 3 p. ochre 5 5
O 505. 4 p. blue 5 5
O 506. 5 p. vermilion .. 5 5
O 507. 6 p. purple 8 8
O 508. 7 p. emerald .. 8 8
O 509. 8 p. red 10 10
O 510. 9 p. red 10 10
O 511. 10 p. brown .. 12 12
O 512. 11 p. turquoise-green 15 15
O 513. 12 p. violet 15 15
O 514. 13 p. turquoise-blue 15 15
O 515. 14 p. violet 20 20
O 516. 15 p. orange .. 20 20
O 517. 16 p. black 20 20
O 518. 17 p. green 25 25
O 519. 18 p. yellow .. 25 25
O 520. 19 p. purple .. 25 25
O 521. 23 p. blue 30 30
O 522. 24 p. green 30 30
O 523. 26 p. bistre 30 30
O 524. 27 p. lilac 35 35
O 525. 31 p. brown .. 40 40
O 526. 33 p. apple 40 40
O 527. 50 p. olive 60 60
O 528. 100 p. olive .. 1·25 1·25

O 3.

1970.
O 1040. O 3. 1 p. brown .. 5 5
O 1041. 2 p. green 5 5
O 1042. 3 p. mauve 5 5
O 1043. 4 p. blue 8 5
O 1044. 5 p. red 8 5
O 1045. 6 p. orange .. 10 8
O 1046. 10 p. blue 15 12
O 1047. 20 p. blue 30 30
O 1048. 31 p. purple .. 45 45

SAXONY E2

A former kingdom in S. Germany. Stamps superseded in 1868 by those of the North German Federation.

10 pfennige = 1 neugroschen.
30 neugroschen = 1 thaler.

1. 2. Frederick Augustus II. 3.

1850. Imperf.
1. 1. 3 pf. red £3000 £2000

1851. Imperf.
10. 2. ½ ngr. black on grey .. 23·00 6·00
12. 1 ngr. black on rose .. 22·00 6·00
13. 2 ngr. black on blue .. £110 25·00
14. 3 ngr. black on yellow .. 85·00 10·00

1851. Imperf.
7. 3. 3 pf. green .. .. 42·00 30·00

4. Johann I. 5. 6.

1855. Imperf.
16. 4. ½ ngr. black on grey .. 4·50 1·25
18. 1 ngr. black on rose .. 4·50 1·25
21. 2 ngr. black on blue .. 6·50 13·00
23. 3 ngr. black on yellow .. 9·00 2·50
24. 5 ngr. red .. .. 38·00 20·00
28. 10 ngr. blue £120 £130

1863. Perf.
31. 5. 3 pf. green .. .. 60 6·00
36. ½ ngr. orange 25 75
39. 6. 1 ngr. rose 25 50
40. 2 ngr. blue .. .. 75 1·50
42. 3 ngr. brown .. .. 75 4·25
46. 5 ngr. purple .. .. 9·00 20·00
48. 5 ngr. grey .. .. 3·75 60·00

SCHLESWIG (SLESVIG) E3

Stamps issued during the plebiscite of 1920.

1. Arms. 2. View of Schleswig.

1920.
1. 1. 2½ pf. grey 5 5
2. 5 pf. green 5 5
3. 7½ pf. brown 5 5
4. 10 pf. red 5 8
5. 15 pf. claret 5 5
6. 20 pf. blue 5 8
7. 25 pf. orange 10 12
8. 35 pf. brown 15 15
9. 40 pf. violet 10 10
10. 75 pf. green 15 15
11. 2. 1 m. brown 15 15
12. 2 m. blue 25 25
13. 5 m. green 40 40
14. 10 m. red 70 70

1920. Values in Danish currency and optd. 1 ZONE.
29. 1. 1 ore grey 5 25
30. 5 ore green 5 12
31. 7 ore brown 5 15
32. 10 ore red 8 25
33. 15 ore claret 8 25
34. 20 ore blue 5 35
35. 25 ore orange .. .. 15 1·25
36. 35 ore brown .. .. 70 2·75
37. 40 ore violet 25 90
38. 75 ore green .. .. 35 1·75
39. 2. 1 k. brown .. .. 50 1·75
40. 2 k. blue .. .. 4·00 9·00
41. 5 k. green .. .. 2·50 9·00
42. 10 k. red .. .. 5·50 18·00

SCHLESWIG-HOLSTEIN E2

Two former grand-duchies to the S. of Denmark, annexed to Prussia in 1866. Part of Schleswig reverted to Denmark as a result of the plebiscite of 1920. The remainder is part of West Germany.

16 schillinge = 1 mark.

1. 2.

1850. Imperf.
2. 1. 1 s. blue £100 £1000
4. 2 s. rose £200 £2500

1865. Inscr. "SCHLESWIG-HOLSTEIN". Roul.
6. 2. ½ s. rose .. .. 19·00 27·00
7. 1¼ s. green .. .. 7·50 5·00
8. 1⅓ s. mauve .. .. 25·00 85·00
9. 2 s. blue .. .. 30·00 £160
10. 4 s. bistre .. .. 32·00 £550

1864. Inscr. "HERZOGTH. SCHLESWIG". Roul.
24. 2. ½ s. green .. .. 20·00 30·00
21. 1¼ s. green .. .. 25·00 7·00
25. 1¼ s. lilac .. .. 25·00 4·50
27. 1⅓ s. rose .. .. 19·00 27·00
28. 2 s. blue .. .. 12·00 16·00
22. 4 s. red .. .. 45·00 £150
29. 4 s. bistre .. .. 19·00 25·00

4. 5. 6.

1864. Imperf. or roul.
55. 4. 1¼ s. blue .. .. 28·00 23·00
59. 5. 1¼ s. blue .. .. 25·00 7·00

1865. Roul.
61. 6. ½ s. green .. .. 38·00 60·00
62. 1¼ s. mauve .. .. 25·00 8·50
63. 1⅓ s. red .. .. 38·00 23·00
64. 2 s. blue .. .. 32·00 27·00
65. 4 s. bistre .. .. 35·00 26·00

On the 1⅓ s. and 4 s. the word "SCHILLING" is inside the central oval.

1868. Inscr. "HERZOGTH. HOLSTEIN". Roul.
66. 2. 1¼ s. purple .. .. 42·00 6·50
67. 2 s. blue .. .. 80·00 £100

SELANGOR BC

A state of the Federation of Malaya, incorporated in Malaysia in 1963.

100 cents = 1 dollar (Straits or Malayan).

1881. Stamps of Straits Settlements optd. **SELANGOR.**
1. 1. 2 c. brown .. .. 5·50 6·00
35. 2 c. rose .. .. 1·25 1·25

1882. Straits Settlements stamp optd. **S.**
7. 1. 2 c. brown .. .. — £300

1891. Stamp of Straits Settlements surch. **SELANGOR Two CENTS.**
44. 1. 2 c. on 24 c. green .. 10·00 10·00

1. Tiger. 2. Tiger.

3. Elephants.

1891.
49. 1. 1 c. green 45 20
50. 2 c. red 45 25
51. 2 c. orange 35 25
52. 5 c. blue .. .. 1·00 65

1894. Surch. **3 CENTS.**
53. 1. 3 c. on 5 c. red .. 25 20

1895.
54. 2. 3 c. purple and red 75 12
55. 5 c. purple and yellow .. 20 15
56. 8 c. purple and blue .. 7·00 2·25
57. 10 c. purple and orange .. 1·10 15
58. 25 c. green and red .. 9·00 7·00
59. 50 c. green and black .. 28·00 10·00
60. 50 c. purple and black .. 5·50 4·00
61. 3. $1 green .. .. 9·00 6·50
62. $2 green and red .. 18·00 12·00
63. $3 green and yellow .. 38·00 16·00
64. $5 green and blue .. 18·00 16·00
65. $10 green and purple .. 80·00 50·00
66 $25 green and orange .. £200

1900. Surch. in words.
66a. 2. 1 c. on 5 c. purple & yell. 6·00 7·00
66b. 1 c. on 50 c. green & black 45 1·25
67. 3 c. on 50 c. green & black 1·75 1·75

4. Mosque at Palace, Klang. 5. Sultan Suleiman.

1935.
68. 4. 1 c. black 12 8
69. 2 c. green 8 8
70. 2 c. orange 8 30
71. 3 c. green 10 30
72. 4 c. orange 8 8
73. 5 c. brown 8 8
74. 4. 6 c. red 35 15
75. 8 c. grey 20 10
76. 10 c. purple 20 8
77. 12 c. blue .. .. 1·00 15
78. 15 c. blue .. .. 90 2·00
79. 25 c. purple and red 65 60
80. 30 c. purple and orange .. 90 90
81. 40 c. red and purple .. 1·00 95
82. 50 c. black on green .. 90 55
83. 5. $1 black and red on blue 2·00 55
84. $2 green and red .. 6·00 3·25
85. $5 green and red on green 13·00 8·00

6. Sultan Hisamud-din Alam Shah. 7.

1941.
86. 6. $1 black and red on blue .. 1·50 2·25
87. $2 green and red .. 4·50 6·00

1948. Silver Wedding. As T 5/6 of Aden.
88. 10 c. violet 5 5
89. $5 green .. .. 5·00 8·00

1949.
90. 7. 1 c. black 5 10
91. 2 c. orange 5 10
92. 3 c. green 5 15
93. 4 c. brown 5 5
94. 5 c. purple 5 8
95. 6 c. grey 10 8
96. 8 c. red 15 25
97. 8 c. green 12 30
98. 10 c. purple 8 5
99. 12 c. red 20 25
100. 15 c. blue 20 10
101. 20 c. black and green .. 30 25
102. 20 c. blue 35 20
103. 25 c. purple and orange 25 5
104. 30 c. red and purple .. 40 20
105. 35 c. red and purple .. 40 35
106. 40 c. red and purple .. 45 55
107. 50 c. black and blue .. 40 12
108. $1 blue and purple .. 50 15
109. $2 green and red .. 1·50 35
110. $5 green and brown .. 3·00 70

1949. U.P.U. As T 14/17 of Antigua.
111. 10 c. purple 8 8
112. 15 c. blue 8 20
113. 25 c. orange 20 30
114. 50 c. black 45 50

1953. Coronation. As T 7 of Aden.
115. 10 c. black and purple .. 5 5

1957. As Nos. 92/102 of Kedah but inset portrait of Sultan Hisamud-din Alam Shah.
116. 1 c. black 5 5
117. 2 c. red 5 5
118. 4 c. sepia 5 5
119. 5 c. lake 5 5
120. 8 c. green 5 5
121. 10 c. sepia 5 5
122. 10 c. maroon 5 5
123. 20 c. blue 12 8
124a. 50 c. black and blue .. 25 10
125. $1 blue and purple .. 40 15
126a. $2 green and red .. 70 50
127a. $5 brown and green .. 2·00 1·25

8. Sultan Salahuddin Abdul Aziz Shah.

1961. Installation of the Sultan.
128. 8. 10 c. multicoloured .. 8 5

9. Sultan Salahuddin Abdul Aziz Shah.

1961. As Nos. 116, etc., but with inset portrait of Sultan Salahuddin Abdul Aziz as in T **9.**
129. 1 c. black 5 8
130. 2 c. red 5 8
131. 4 c. sepia 5 5
132. 5 c. lake 5 5
133. 8 c. green 8 8
134. 10 c. maroon 8 5
135. 20 c. blue 8 8

10. "Vanda hookeriana".

1965. As Nos. 166/72 of Johore but with inset portrait of Sultan Salahuddin Abdul Aziz Shah as in T **10**.

136. **10.** 1 c. multicoloured .. 5 5
137. – 2 c. multicoloured .. 5 5
138. – 5 c. multicoloured .. 5 5
139. – 6 c. multicoloured .. 5 5
140. – 10 c. multicoloured .. 5 5
141. – 15 c. multicoloured .. 5 5
142. – 20 c. multicoloured .. 8 8

The higher values used in Selangor were Nos. 20/7 of Malaysia.

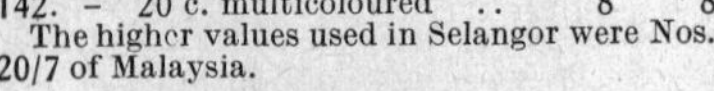

11. Clipper Butterfly.

1971. Butterflies. As Nos. 175/81 of Johore but with portrait of Sultan Salahuddin Abdul Aziz Shah as in T **11**.

146. – 1 c. multicoloured .. 5 5
147. – 2 c. multicoloured .. 5 5
148. **11.** 5 c. multicoloured .. 5 5
149. – 6 c. multicoloured .. 5 5
150. – 10 c. multicoloured .. 5 5
151. – 15 c. multicoloured .. 5 5
152. – 20 c. multicoloured .. 8 8

The higher values in use with this issue are Nos. 64/71 of Malaysia.

SENEGAL 04

A French colony incorporated in French West Africa in 1944. In 1958 Senegal became an autonomous State within the French Community and in 1959 joined the Sudan to form the Mali Federation. In 1960 the Federation broke up when Mali became an independent republic and Senegal a republic within the French Community.

1887. Stamps of French Colonies, "Commerce" type, surch. in figures.

1. **9.** 5 on 20 c. red on green .. 27·00 27·00
2. 5 on 30 c. brown .. 45·00 45·00
3. 10 on 4 c. brown on grey .. 9·50 8·50
4a. 10 on 20 c. red on green .. 80·00 80·00
5. 15 on 20 c. red on green .. 7·00 6·50

1892. Stamps of French Colonies, "Commerce" type, surch. **Senegal** and value in figures.

6. **9.** 75 on 15 c. blue .. .. 55·00 28·00
7. 1 f. on 5 c. green .. .. 55·00 28·00

1892. "Tablet" key-type inscr. "SENEGAL ET DEPENDANCES".

8. D. 1 c. black on blue .. 5 5
9. 2 c. brown on yellow .. 25 25
10. 4 c. claret on grey .. 10 10
21. 5 c. green on green .. 20 5
12. 10 c. black on lilac .. 1·10 55
22. 10 c. red .. 55 5
13. 15 c. blue .. 1·10 5
23. 15 c. grey .. 30 15
14. 20 c. red on green .. 1·00 1·00
15. 25 c. black on red .. 1·60 70
24. 25 c. blue .. 5·00 4·25
16. 30 c. brown .. 1·90 45
17. 40 c. red on yellow .. 3·25 2·40
18. 50 c. red on rose .. 4·25 3·00
25. 50 c. brown on blue .. 6·00 5·00
19. 75 c. brown on orange .. 1·90 1·75
20. 1 f. olive .. 2·10 2·00

1903. Surch. in figs. and bars.

26. D. 5 on 40 c. red on yellow .. 1·60 1·60
27. 10 on 50 c. red on rose .. 2·75 2·10
28. 10 on 75 c. brown on orge. 2·75 2·50
29. 10 on 1 f. olive .. .. 12·00 10·00

1906. "Faidherbe", "Palms" and "Balay" key-types inscr. "SENEGAL".

33. I. 1 c. grey .. 5 5
34. 2 c. brown (A) .. 5 5
34a. 2 c. brown (B) .. 25 25
35. 4 c. brown on blue .. 12 8
36. 5 c. green .. 5 5
37. 10 c. red .. 65 5
38. 15 c. violet .. 70 45
39. J. 20 c. black on blue .. 70 45
40. 25 c. blue .. 15 12
41. 30 c. brown on pink .. 75 45
42. 35 c. black on yellow .. 3·00 15
43. 40 c. red .. 1·60 1·10
44. 45 c. brown on green .. 3·00 2·25
45. 50 c. violet .. 1·40 1·10
46. 75 c. green on orange .. 60 45
47. K. 1 f. black .. .. 3·00 2·25
48. 2 f. blue on rose .. 3·50 2·50
49. 5 f. red on yellow .. 10·00 8·50

(A) has name in red: (B) in blue.

1912. Surch. in figures.

58. D. 05 on 15 c. grey 5 5
59. 05 on 20 c. red on green 8 8
60. 05 on 30 c. brown .. 5 5
61. 10 on 40 c. red on yellow 10 10
62. 10 on 50 c. red on rose .. 45 45
63. 10 on 75 c. brn. on orange 65 65

1. Market.

1914.

64. **1.** 1 c. violet and brown .. 5 5
65. 2 c. blue and black .. 5 5
66. 4 c. brown and grey .. 5 5
67. 5 c. green .. 5 5
91. 5 c. red and black .. 5 5
68. 10 c. red and orange .. 5 5
92. 10 c. green .. 5 5
113. 10 c. blue and claret .. 5 5
69. 15 c. purple and brown 5 5
70. 20 c. black and brown .. 5 5
114. 20 c. green .. 5 5
115. 20 c. blue and grey .. 5 5
71. 25 c. blue .. 5 5
93. 25 c. black and red .. 5 5
72. 30 c. red and black .. 5 5
94. 30 c. red and orange .. 5 5
116. 30 c. blue and grey .. 5 5
117. 30 c. green and olive .. 5 5
73. 35 c. violet and orange .. 5 5
74. 40 c. green and violet .. 5 5
75. 45 c. brown and blue .. 8 8
95. 45 c. blue and red .. 5 5
118. 45 c. orange and red .. 5 5
119 45 c. red and brown .. 50 50
76. 50 c. blue and purple .. 5 5
96. 50 c. blue .. 20 20
120. 50 c. green and orange 5 5
121. 60 c. violet on red .. 5 5
122. 65 c. green and red .. 25 25
77. 75 c. red and grey .. 5 5
123. 75 c. blue .. 5 5
124. 75 c. blue and red .. 15 5
125. 90 c. red and brown .. 65 65
78. 1 f. black and violet .. 5 5
126. 1 f. blue .. 5 5
127. 1 f. blue and black .. 10 5
128. 1 f. 10 black and green 50 50
129. 1 f. 25 orange and green 5 5
130. 1 f. 50 blue .. 40 35
131. 1 f. 75 green and brown 1·25 12
79. 2 f. blue and red .. 20 20
97. 2 f. brown and blue .. 25 5
132. 3 f. mauve on red .. 80 10
80. 5 f. violet and green .. 70 8

1915. Surch. **5 c.** and red cross.

89. **1.** 10 c.+5 c. red and orange 5 5
90. 15 c.+5 c. purple & brown 5 5

1922. Surch. in figures and bars.

102. **1.** 0.01 on 15 c. pur. & brn. 5 5
103. 0.02 on 15 c. pur. & brn. 5 5
104. 0.04 on 15 c. pur. & brn. 5 5
105. 0.05 on 15 c. pur. & brn. 5 5
106. 25 c. on 5 f. violet & green 5 5
98. 60 on 75 c. violet on red 5 5
99. 65 on 15 c. pur. & brown 8 8
100. 85 on 15 c. pur. & brown 8 8
101. 85 on 75 c. red and grey .. 8 8
107. 90 c. 75 c. red & brown 15 15
108. 1 f. 25 on 1 f. blue .. 5 5
109. 1 f. 50 on 1 f. blue .. 8 5
110. 3 f. on 5 f. brown & purple 25 5
111. 10 f. on 5 f. red and blue 1·00 20
112. 20 f. on 5 f. brown & mve. 1·25 75

1931. "Colonial Exn." key-types.

135. E. 40 c. green 30 30
136. F. 50 c. mauve 30 30
137. G. 90 c. red 30 20
138. H. 1 f. 50 blue 35 35

2. Faidherbe, Bridge.

4. African Landscape.

3. Senegalese Girl.

1935.

139. **2.** 1 c. blue (postage) .. 5 5
140. 2 c. brown .. 5 5
141. 3 c. violet .. 5 5
142. 4 c. blue 5 5
143. 5 c. orange .. 5 5
144. 10 c. purple .. 5 5
145. 15 c. black .. 5 5
146. 20 c. red 5 5
147. **2.** 25 c. brown 5 5
148. 30 c. green 5 5
149. **3.** 35 c. green 5 5
150. **2.** 40 c. red 5 5
151. 45 c. green 5 5
152. A. 50 c. orange 5 5
153. **3.** 55 c. brown 12 10
154. A. 60 c. violet 5 5
155. 65 c. violet 5 5
156. 70 c. brown 5 5
157. 75 c. brown 5 5
158. **3.** 80 c. violet 5 5
159. A. 90 c. red 30 30
160. **3.** 90 c. violet 5 5
161. A. 1 f. violet .. .. 1·25 15
162. **3.** 1 f. red 25 10
163. 1 f. brown 5 5
164. A. 1 f. 25 brown 15 15
165. 1 f. 25 red 5 5
166. 1 f. 40 green 5 5
167. 1 f. 50 blue 5 5
168. 1 f. 60 blue 5 5
169. 1 f. 75 green 5 5
170. **3.** 1 f. 75 blue 5 5
171. A. 2 f. blue 5 5
172. **3.** 2 f. 25 blue 5 5
173. 2 f. 50 black 12 12
174. A. 3 f. green 5 5
175. 5 f. brown 8 5
176. 10 f. red 8 5
177. 20 f. grey 10 5
178 **4.** 25 c. brown (air) .. 5 5
179. 50 c. red 5 5
180. 1 f. purple 5 5
181. 1 f. 25 green 5 5
182. 1 f. 90 blue 5 5
183. 2 f. blue 5 5
184. 2 f. 90 red 5 5
185. 3 f. green 5 5
186. B. 3 f. 50 violet 5 5
187. **4.** 4 f. 50 green 8 8
188. B. 4 f. 75 orange 5 5
189. **4.** 4 f. 90 brown 10 10
190. B. 6 f. 50 blue 10 5
191. **4.** 6 f. 90 orange 8 8
192. B. 8 f. black 15 10
193. 15 f. red 10 10

DESIGNS: A. Diourbel Mosque. B. Aeroplane over caravan.

1937. Int. Exn., Paris. As Nos. 110/15 of Cameroun.

194. 20 c. violet 10 10
195. 30 c. green 10 10
196. 40 c. red 10 10
197. 50 c. brown 15 15
198. 90 c. red 15 15
199. 1 f. 50 blue 15 15

1938. Anti-Cancer Fund. As T **10** of Cameroun.

201. 1 f. 75+50 c. blue .. 1·75 1·75

1939. Caillie Cent. As T **2** of Dahomey.

202. 90 c. orange 5 5
203. 2 f. violet 5 5
204. 2 f. 25 blue 8 8

1939. New York Fair. As T **11** of Cameroun.

205. 1 f. 25 red 5 5
206. 2 f. 25 blue 5 5

1939. French Revolution. 150th Anniv. As T **16** of Cameroun.

207. 45 c.+25 c. green (postage) 1·10 1·10
208. 70 c.+30 c. brown .. 1·10 1·10
209. 90 c.+35 c. orange .. 1·10 1·10
210. 1 f. 25+1 f. red .. 1·10 1·10
211. 2 f. 25+2 f. blue .. 1·10 1·10
212. 4 f.75+4 f. black (air) .. 1·75 1·75

1941. National Defence Fund. Surch. **SECOURS NATIONAL** and value.

213. +1 f. on 50 c. (No. 152) .. 10 10
214. +2 f. on 80 c. (No. 158) .. 65 65
215. +2 f. on 1 f. 50 (No. 167) 65 65
216. +3 f. on 2 f. (No. 171) .. 65 65

1942. Air. As T **4d** of Dahomey and similar design.

217. 50 f. olive and yellow .. 25 20
218. 100 f. blue and red .. 45 35

DESIGN—(48×26 mm.): 100 f. 'Plane landing.

1944 Stamps of 1935 and No. 202 surch.

219. **2.** 1 f. 50 on 15 c. black .. 5 5
220. – 1 f. 50 on 65 c. violet .. 5 5
221. **2.** 4 f. 50 on 15 c. black .. 10 10
222. 5 f. 50 on 2 c. brown .. 15 15
223. – 5 f. 50 on 65 c. violet .. 5 5
224. **2.** 10 f. on 15 c. black .. 20 15
226. – 20 f. on 90 c. orange .. 15 12
225. – 50 f. on 65 c. violet .. 35 20
227. – 50 f. on 90 c. orange .. 50 45

5. Savannah Buffalo.

7. Mother and Child.

6. Fish Eagle.

1960. Niokolo-Koba National Park. Animal designs inscr. as in T **5**.

228. – 5 f. mar., black & green .. 5 5
229. **5.** 10 f. mar., black & green 8 5
230. – 15 f. mar. brown & sepia 12 5
231. – 20 f. brn., grn. & chest... 15 5
232. – 25 f. chest., choc. & grn. 20 10
233. – 85 f. brn., yell., ol. & grn. 70 25

ANIMALS—VERT. 5 f. Roan antelope. 15 f. Warthog. 20 f. Derby's eland. 85 f. Waterbuck. HORIZ. 25 f. Bushbuck.

1960. Air.

234. – 50 f. multicoloured .. 45 15
235. – 100 f. multicoloured .. 90 30
236. – 200 f. multicoloured .. 1·75 1·10
237. – 250 f. multicoloured .. 2·25 1·40
238. **6.** 500 f. multicoloured .. 3·25 1·60

BIRDS—VERT. 50 f. Nubian Bee-eater. 200 f. Violet Touraco. 250 f. Franciscan. HORIZ. 100 f. Roller.

1961. Independence Commem.

239. **7.** 25 f. choc., blue & green 20 15

8. Pirogue Race.

DESIGNS: 50 c. African wrestling. 2 f. Horse race. 30 f. African dancers. 45 f. Lion game.

1961. Sports.

240. – 50 c. choc., blue & sepia 5 5
241. **8.** 1 f. mar., turq. & green 5 5
242. – 2 f. sepia, bistre and blue 5 5
243. – 30 f. maroon and red .. 20 15
244. – 45 f. blk., blue & chestnut 30 25

9. Senegal Flag, U.N. Emblem and H.Q. Building.

1962. Admission of Senegal to U.N.O. 1st Anniv.

245. **9.** 10 f. red, ochre and green 12 12
246. 30 f. green, ochre and red 25 20
247. 85 f. red, ochre, maroon and green .. 60 40

10. I.T.U. Emblems, African Map and Telephonist.

11. Boxing.

1962. 1st I.T.U. Africa Plan Sub-Committee Meeting, Dakar.

248. **10.** 25 f. multicoloured .. 20 15

1962. Air. "Air Afrique" Airline. As T **44** of Cameroun.

249. 25 f. mar., brn. & myrtle 25 15

1962. Malaria Eradication. As T **45** of Cameroun.

250. 25 f.+5 f. blue-green .. 25 25

1962. Union of African and Malagasy States. 1st Anniv. As No. 328 of Cameroun.

251. **47.** 30 f. blue-green .. 30 30

1963. Freedom from Hunger. As T **51** of Cameroun.

252. 25 f. + 5 f. olive-green, brown and violet .. 25 25

1963. Dakar Games. Inscr. as in T **11**. Centres choc.; inscr. and frame colours given.

253. **11.** 10 f. red and emerald .. 8 5
254. – 15 f. ochre and blue .. 10 8
255. – 20 f. red and blue .. 15 10
256. – 25 f. green and blue .. 20 15
257. – 30 f. red and green .. 25 15
258. – 85 f. violet-blue .. 65 45

DESIGNS—HORIZ. 15 f. Diving. 20 f. High-jumping. VERT. 25 f. Football. 30 f. Basket-ball. 85 f. Running.

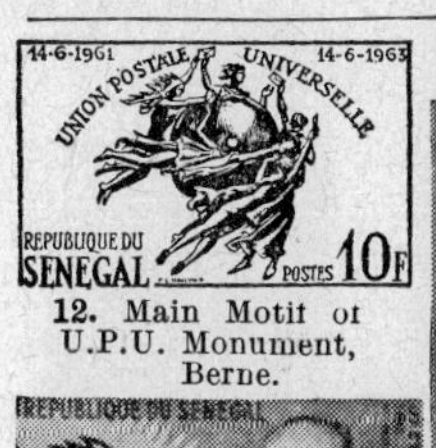

12. Main Motif of U.P.U. Monument, Berne.

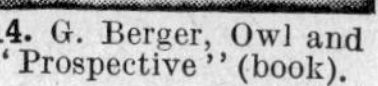
14. G. Berger, Owl and "Prospective" (book).

13. "Charaxes varanes".

1963. Admission to U.P.U. 2nd Anniv.
259. **12.** 10 f. red and green .. 10 8
260. 15 f. brown and blue .. 15 10
261. 30 f. blue and brown .. 25 15

1963. Butterflies. Butterflies in natural colours; inscr. in black; background colours given.
262. **13.** 30 f. grey-blue .. 20 10
263. – 45 f. orange .. 30 12
264. – 50 f. yellow .. 40 15
265. – 85 f. red .. 60 25
266. – 100 f. blue .. 65 35
267. – 500 f. green .. 2·75 1·25
BUTTERFLIES: 45 f. "Papillo nereus". 10 f. "Colotis danae". 85 f. "Epiphora bauhiniae". 100 f. "Junonia hierta". 500 f. "Danaus chrysippus".

1963. Air. African and Malagasian Posts and Telecommunications Union. As T **10** of Central African Republic.
268. 85 f. red, buff, brown and red-brown 55 45

1963. Prof. Gaston Berger (educationalist). 3rd Death Anniv.
269. **14.** 25 f. multicoloured .. 15 10

1963. Air. "Air Afrique" 1st Anniv. and "DC-8" Service Inaug. As T **10** of Congo Republic.
270. 50 f. black, green, drab and mauve 50 40

15. Globe, Scales of Justice and Flag.

16. Mother and Child.

1963. Declaration of Human Rights. 15th Anniv.
271. **15.** 60 f. multicoloured .. 40 30

1963. Senegalese Red Cross.
272. **16.** 25 f. multicoloured .. 20 15

17. Temple Gods, Abu Simbel.

1964. Air. Nubian Monuments Preservation Fund.
273. **17.** 25 f. + 5 f. chestnut, green and turquoise 35 25

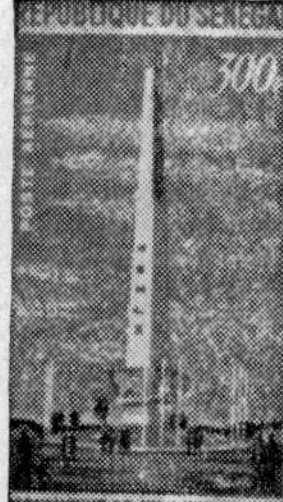

18. Independence Monument.

20. Titanium Sand Dredger.

19. Allegorical Figures of Twin Towns.

1964. Air.
274. **18.** 300 f. multicoloured 2·00 1·00

1964. Air. World Twin Towns Federation Congress, Dakar.
275. **19.** 150 f. chest., blk. & turq. 1·10 70

1964. Senegal Industries.
276. **20.** 5 f. choc., turq. & lake 5 5
277. – 10 f. indigo, brown & grn. 8 5
278. – 15 f. choc., green & blue 12 5
279. – 20 f. pur., bistre & blue 15 8
280. – 25 f. black, ochre & blue 20 5
281. – 85 f. brown, blue and red 60 30
DESIGNS: 10 f. Titanium sorting works. 15 f. Rufisque cement works. 20 f. Loading phosphate at Pallo. 25 f. Working phosphate at Taiba. 85 f. Mineral wharf, Dakar.

21. "Supporting the Globe".

1964. Air. "Europafrique".
282. **21.** 50 f. multicoloured .. 55 45

22. Basketball.

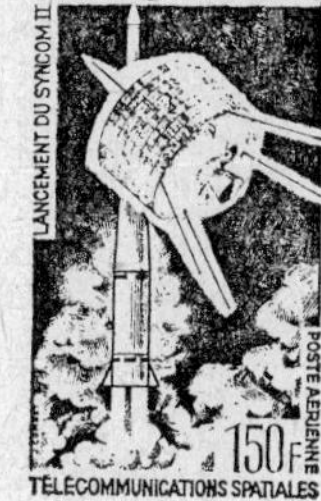

23. "Syncom II" Satellite and Rocket.

1964. Air. Olympic Games, Tokyo.
283. **22.** 85 f. brown and blue .. 65 45
284. – 100 f. maroon and green 90 55
DESIGN: 100 f. Pole-vaulting.

1964. Air. Space Telecommunications.
285. **23.** 150 f. blue, brown & grn. 1·10 65

1964. French, African and Malagasy Co-operation. As T **500** of France.
286. 100 f. choc., red and green 60 30

24. Church of Ste. Therese, Dakar.

26. Child and Microscope.

25. Pres. Kennedy.

1964. Religious Buildings.
287. **24.** 5 f. lake, green and blue 5 5
288. – 10 f. brown, black & blue 5 5
289. – 15 f. slate-blue, brown and blue 10 8
DESIGNS—HORIZ. 10 f. Touba Mosque. VERT. 15 f. Dakar Mosque.

1964. Air. Pres. Kennedy Commem.
290. **25.** 100 f. brown, yell. & grn. 75 60

1965. Anti-Leprosy Campaign.
292. **26.** 20 f. black, grn. & brn. 15 10
293. – 65 f. slate, bronze, blue and orange 50 35
DESIGN: 65 f. Peycouk Village.

27. Haute Casamance.

1965. Senegal Landscapes.
294. **27.** 25 f. green chestnut and blue (postage) .. 20 10
295. – 30 f. blue, green & brown 25 12
296. – 45 f. green & chestnut 35 25
297. – 100 f. black, green and bistre (air) 75 45
DESIGNS: 30 f. Sangalkam. 45 f. Senegal River forest region. 100 f. Banks of Gambia River, East Senegal (48 × 27 mm.).

28. A. Seck (Director of Posts, 1873-1931).

29. Berthon-Ader Telephone.

1965. Postal Services Commem.
298. **28.** 10 f. black & chocolate 8 5
299. – 15 f. brown and green.. 10 5
DESIGN—HORIZ. 15 f. P.T.T. Headquarters, Dakar.

1965. I.T.U. Cent.
300. **29.** 50 f. chest., bistre & grn. 40 20
301. – 60 f. red, green and blue 45 25
302. – 85 f. maroon, red & blue 65 40
DESIGNS: 60 f. Cable-ship "Alsace". 85 f. Picard's submarine telegraph cable relay apparatus.

30. Ploughing with Oxen.

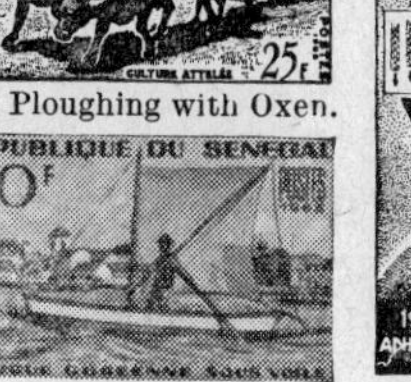

31. Goree Pirogue under Sail.

32. Woman holding Child and U.N. Emblems.

1965. Rural Development.
303. **30.** 25 f. choc., vio & bronze 20 10
304. – 60 f. indigo, chocolate, green and black .. 45 25
305. – 85 f. black, red & green 65 40
DESIGNS—VERT. 60 f. Millet cultivation. HORIZ. 85 f. Rice cultivation, Casamance.

1965. Senegal Pirogues Multicoloured.
306. 10 f. Type **31** 8 5
307. 20 f. Large pirogue at Seumbedioune 15 5
308. 30 f. One-man pirogue at Fadiouth Island .. 20 12
309. 45 f. One-man pirogue at Senegal River 35 25

1965. Air. Int. Co-operation Year.
310. **32.** 50 f. brown, grn. & blue 35 20

33. "Fruit of Cashew Tree". 34. "The Gentleman of Fashion". 35. Tom-tom Player.

1965. Fruits. Multicoloured.
311. 10 f. Type **33** 8 5
312. 15 f. Papaw 10 5
313. 20 f. Mango 12 5
314. 30 f. Groundnuts .. 20 5

1966. Goree Puppets.
315. **34.** 1 f. blue, brown & cerise 5 5
316. – 2 f. orange, brown & blue 5 5
317. – 3 f. blue, brown and red 5 5
318. – 4 f. green, brown & violet 5 5
PUPPETS: 2 f. "The Lady of Fashion". 3 f. "The Pedlar". 4 f. "The Pounder".

1966. World Festival of Negro Arts, Dakar ("Announcement").
319. **35.** 30 f. brown, red & green 20 12
See also Nos. 327/30.

36. Rocket "Diamant".

1966. Air. French Satellites.
320. **36.** 50 f. red, blue and brown 40 20
321. – 50 f. black, brown & grn. 40 20
322. – 90 f. blue, brown & slate 70 45
DESIGNS: No. 321, Satellite "A 1". 322, Rocket "Scout" and satellite "FR 1".

37. Mackerel Tuna.

39. Arms of Senegal.

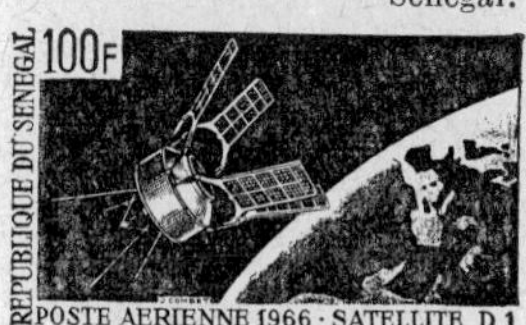

38. Satellite "D 1".

1966. Senegal Fishes. Multicoloured.
323. 20 f. Type **37** 15 8
324. 30 f. Grouper 20 12
325. 50 f. Wrasse 40 20
326. 100 f. Parrot fish 70 35

1966. World Festival of Negro Arts, Dakar. As T **35.**
327. 15 f. lake, orange and blue 10 8
328. 30 f. lake, yellow and blue 20 12
329. 75 f. black, lake and blue.. 55 30
330. 90 f. lake, black and orge. 65 40
DESIGNS: 15 f. Statuette ("Sculpture"). 30 f. Musical instrument ("Music"). 75 f. Carving ("Dance"). 90 f. Ideogram.

1966. Air. Launching of Satellite "D 1".
332. **38.** 100 f. blue, lake & violet 75 40

1966.
333. **39.** 30 f. multicoloured .. 20 8

1966. Air. "DC-8" Air Services Inaug. As T **45** of Central African Republic.
334. 30 f. yellow, black & chest. 20 10

40. "Argemone Mexicana".

42. Port of Ile de Goree.

41. Couzinet "Arc-en-Ciel" (aircraft).

1966. Flowers. Multicoloured.
335. 45 f. Type **40** 30 15
336. 55 f. "Dichrostacys glomerata" .. 40 15
337. 60 f. "Haemanthus multiflorus" .. 45 20
338. 80 f. "Adansonia digitata" 60 25

1966. Air. Disappearance of Jean Mermoz (aviator). 30th Anniv.

339. **41.** 20 f. slate, purple & blue 15 10
340. – 35 f. slate, brown & green 25 12
341. – 100 f. lake, emer. & grn. 75 30
342. – 150 f. lake, black & blue 1·00 55

DESIGNS—HORIZ. 35 f. Latecoere 300 flying-boat, "Croix du Sud". 100 f. Map of Mermoz's last flight across Atlantic Ocean. VERT. 150 f. Jean Mermoz.

1966. Tourism.

343. **42.** 20 f. lake, blue & black 15 5
344. – 25 f. sepia, green & red 20 5
345. – 30 f. blue, red and green 20 8
346. – 50 f. indigo, green & red 40 15
347. – 90 f. black, green and blue 60 25

DESIGNS: 25 f. Liner "France" at Dakar. 30 f. N'Gor Hotel and tourist cabins. 50 f. N'Gor Bay and Hotel. 90 f. Town Hall, Dakar.

43. Laying Water Mains.

1967. Int. Hydrological Decade.

348. **43.** 10 f. blue, green & chest. 10 8
349. – 20 f. chest., green & blue 20 15
350. – 30 f. blue, orge. & black 25 20
351. – 50 f. lake, flesh and blue 45 25

DESIGNS—HORIZ. 20 f. Cattle at trough. VERT. 30 f. Decade emblem. 50 f. Obtaining water from primitive well.

44. Terminal Building, Dakar-Yoff Airport.

1967. Air.

352. **44.** 200 f. indigo, blue & brn. 1·10 50

45. Lions Emblem.

1967. Lions Int. 50th Anniv.

353. **45.** 30 f. multicoloured .. 20 15

46. Blaise Diagne (statesman).

1967. Blaise Diagne. 95th Birth Anniv.

354. **46.** 30 f. mar., grn. & chest. 20 15

47. Spiny Mimosa.

1967. Air. Flowers. Multicoloured.

355. 100 f. Type **47** 75 25
356. 150 f. Barbary fig .. .. 1·10 40

48. "The Young Ladies of Avignon" (Picasso). **49.** Carved Eagle and Kudu's Head.

1967. Air.

357. **48.** 100 f. multicoloured .. 75 55

1967. "EXPO 67" World Fair, Montreal.

358. **49.** 90 f. black and red .. 60 30
359. – 150 f. multicoloured .. 1·10 55

DESIGN: 150 f. Maple Leaf and flags.

1967. Air. U.A.M.P.T. 5th Anniv. As T **55** of Central African Republic.

360. 100 f. red, green and violet 75 40

50. I.T.Y. Emblem. **51.** Currency Tokens.

1967. Int. Tourist Year.

361. **50.** 50 f. black and blue .. 40 20
362. – 100 f. black, grn. & orge. 70 35

DESIGN: 100 f. Tourist photographing hippopotamus.

1967. West African Monetary Union. 5th Anniv.

363. **51.** 30 f. violet, purple & grey 20 10

52. "Lyre" Stone, Kaffrine. **53.** Nurse feeding baby.

1967. 6th Pan-African Prehistory Congress, Dakar.

364. **52.** 30 f. red, blue and green 20 10
365. – 70 f. red, chest. & blue 50 25

DESIGN: 70 f. Ancient bowl, Bandiala.

1967. Senegalese Red Cross.

366. **53.** 50 f. lake, red and green 35 15

54. Human Rights Emblem. **55.** Chancellor Adenauer.

1968. Human Rights Year.

367. **54.** 30 f. gold and green .. 25 12

1968. Air. Adenauer Commem.

368. **55.** 100 f. sepia, red & green 70 35

56. Weather Balloon, Flourishing Plants and W.M.O. Emblem. **57.** Parliament Building, Dakar.

1968. Air. World Meteorological Day.

370. **56.** 50 f. green, blue & black 35 15

1968. Inter-Parliamentary Union Meeting, Dakar.

371. **57.** 30 f. cerise 20 10

58. Spiny Lobster. **59.** Pied Kingfisher.

1968. Marine Crustacea. Multicoloured.

372. 10 f. Type **58** 5 5
373. 20 f. Sea crawfish 10 5
374. 35 f. Prawn 20 10
375. 100 f. Gooseneck barnacle 60 30

1968. Birds. Multicoloured.

376. 5 f. Type **59** (postage) .. 5 5
377. 15 f. African jacana .. 10 5
378. 70 f. Darter 45 20
379. 250 f. Rufous-necked Whydah (air) .. .. .. 1·40 65
380. 300 f. Knob-billed duck .. 1·90 75
381. 500 f. Bateleur eagle .. 2·75 1·00

Nos. 380/81 are 45½ × 26 mm.

60. Ox and Syringe. **61.** Hurdling.

1968. Campaign for Prevention of Cattle Plague.

382. **60.** 30 f. red, green and blue 20 10

1968. Air. Olympic Games, Mexico.

383. **61.** 20 f. choc., green & blue 12 5
384. – 30 f. choc., ochre & pur. 15 12
385. – 50 f. lake, brown & blue 30 15
386. – 75 f. bistre, brn. & grn. 45 25

DESIGNS: 30 f. Throwing the javelin. 50 f. Judo. 75 f. Basketball.

1968. Air. "Philexafrique" Stamp Exn., Abidjan (1st Issue) (1969). As T **109** of Cameroun. Multicoloured.

387. 100 f. "Young Girl Reading a letter" (J. Baoux) .. 70 70

62. Senegalese Boy. **63.** Faculty Building.

1968. W.H.O. 20th Anniv.

388. **62.** 30 f. black, red & green 20 10
389. 45 f. black, green & brn. 30 15

1969. Faculty of Medicine and Pharmaceutics, and Sixth "Medical Days", Dakar.

391. **63.** 30 f. blue and green .. 20 12
392. – 50 f. green, red & brown 25 15

DESIGN—VERT. 50 f. Emblem of "Medical Days".

1969. Air. "Philexafrique" Stamp Exn., Abidjan, Ivory Coast (2nd Issue). As T **110** of Cameroun.

393. 50 f. violet, slate and green 35 35

DESIGN: 50 f. Modern Dakar and Senegal stamp of 1935.

64. Panet, Camels and Route-map.

1969. Leopold Panet, 1st Explorer of the Mauritanian Sahara. 150th Birth Anniv.

394. **64.** 75 f. brown and blue .. 45 25

65. A.I.T.Y. Emblem.

1969. Air. African Int. Tourist Year.

395. **65.** 100 f. red, green and blue 60 30

66. I.L.O. Emblem. **67.** President Lamine Gueye.

1969. Int. Labour Organization. 50th Anniv.

396. **66.** 30 f. black and turquoise 15 8
397. 45 f. black and red .. 30 12

1969. Air. President Gueye Memorial.

398. **67.** 30 f. black, buff & brown 15 8
399. – 45 f. black, blue & brown 30 12

DESIGN: 45 f. President Lamine Gueye (different).

68. Arms of Casamance.

1969. Senegal Arms. Multicoloured.

401. 15 f. Type **68** 8 5
402. 20 f. Arms of Goree .. 12 5

1969. African Development Bank. 5th Anniv. As T **118** of Cameroun.

403. 30 f. brown, emerald & slate 20 10
404. 45 f. brown and emerald .. 30 15

69. Mahatma Gandhi. **70.** "Transmission of Thought" (O. Faye).

1969. Mahatma Gandhi. Birth Cent.

405. **69.** 50 f. multicoloured .. 30 15

1969. Air. Tapestries. Multicoloured.

407. 25 f. Type **70** 15 10
408. 30 f. "The Blue Cock" (Mamadou Niang) .. 20 8
409. 45 f. "The Fairy" (Papa Sidi Diop) 30 15
410. 50 f. "Fari" (A. N'Diaye) 35 20
411. 75 f. "Lunaris" (J. Lurcat) 45 25

SIZES—VERT. 30 f., 45 f. 37 × 49 mm. HORIZ. 50 f. 49 × 37 mm.

71. Baila Bridge.

1969. Air. Europafrique.

412. **71.** 100 f. multicoloured .. 60 30

72. Rotary Emblem and "Sailing Ship".

1969. Dakar Rotary Club. 30th Anniv.

413. **72.** 30 f. yellow, blk. & blue 20 10

1969. A.S.E.C.N.A. 10th Anniv. As T **121** of Cameroun.

414. 100 f. slate 50 25

73. Cape Skiring, Casamance.

75. Dolphin.

74. Lecrivain, Aircraft and Route.

1969. Tourism.
415. 73. 20 f. green, lake & blue 15 5
416. – 30 f. lake, brown & blue 20 8
417. – 35 f. black, brown & blue 20 8
418. – 45 f. lake and blue .. 25 10
DESIGNS: 30 f. Tourist camp, Niokolo-Koba. 35 f. Herd of elephants, Niokolo-Koba Park. 45 f. Millet granaries on stilts, Fadiouth Islands.

1970. Air. Disappearance of Emile Lecrivain (aviator). 40th Anniv.
419. 74. 50 f. lake, slate & green 30 20

1970.
420. 75. 50 f. multicoloured .. 30 20

76. R. Maran (Martinique).

1970. Air. Negro Celebrities.
421. 76. 30 f. brown, green & lake 15 8
422. – 45 f. brown, blue & pink 30 12
423. – 50 f. brn., emer. & yellow 35 15
PORTRAITS: 45 f. M. Garvey (Jamaica). 50 f. Dr. P. Mars (Haiti).

77. Sailing-canoe and Obelisk.

78. Lenin.

1970. Air. Independence. 10th Anniv.
424. 77. 500 f. multicoloured .. 3·00 1·75

1970. Lenin. Birth Cent.
426. 78. 30 f. brown, stone & red 20 8

79. Bay of Naples, and Post Office, Dakar.

1970. Air. 10th "Europa" Stamp Exn., Naples.
428. 79. 100 f. multicoloured .. 55 45

1970. New U.P.U. Headquarters Building, Berne. As T 126 of Cameroun.
429. 30 f. plum, indigo and lake 15 10
430. 45 f. brn., lake and green .. 30 12

80. Nagakawa and Mt. Fuji.

1970. Air World Fair "EXPO 70", Osaka, Japan.
431. – 25 f. red, green & lake 15 8
432. 80. 75 f. red, blue & green 40 20
433. – 150 f. red, brown & blue 90 50
DESIGNS—VERT. 25 f. "Woman playing guitar" (Hokusai), and Sun tower. 150 f. "Nanboku beauty" (Shuncho).

81. Harbour Quayside, Dakar.

1970. Air. Industrial and Urban Development.
434. 81. 30 f. blue, black and red 20 8
435. – 100 f. brn., grn. & slate 60 40
DESIGN: 100 f. Aerial view of city centre, Dakar.

82. Beethoven, Napoleon and Evocation of Eroica Symphony.

1970. Air. Beethoven. Birth Bicent.
436. 82. 50 f. brn., orge. & green 35 15
437. – 100 f. red and blue .. 70 40
DESIGN: 100 f. Beethoven with quillpen and scroll.

83. Heads of Four Races.

1970. Air. United Nations. 25th Anniv.
438. 83. 100 f. multicoloured .. 70 40

84. Looms and Textile Works, Thies.

1970. "Industrialisation".
439. 84. 30 f. red, blue and green 20 5
440. – 45 f. blue, brown and red 25 10
DESIGN: 45 f. Fertiliser plant, Dakar.

85. Scouts in Camp.

86. Three Heads and Sun.

1970. 1st African Scouting Conference, Dakar. Multicoloured.
441. 30 f. Type 85 .. .. 20 8
442. 100 f. Scout badge, Lord Baden-Powell and map .. 60 30

1970. Int. Education Year.
443. 86. 25 f. brown, blue & orge. 20 8
444. – 40 f. multicoloured .. 40 10
DESIGN: 40 f. Map of Africa on Globe, and two heads.

87. Arms of Senegal.

88. De Gaulle, Map, Ears of Wheat and Cogwheel.

1970.
445. 87. 30 f. multicoloured .. 15 8
446. 35 f. multicoloured .. 20 8
446a. 50 f. multicoloured .. 35 25
446b. 65 f. multicoloured .. 30 15

1970. Air. "De Gaulle the De-coloniser". Multicoloured.
447. 50 f. Type 88 .. .. 35 25
448. 100 f. De Gaulle, and map within "sun" 65 55

89. Refugees.

90. "Mbayang" Horse.

1971. U.N. High Commissioner for Refugees. 20th Anniv. Multicoloured.
449. 40 f. Type 89 (postage) .. 25 12
450. 100 f. Building house (air) 60 40
No. 450 is 46 × 27 mm.

1971. Horse-breeding Improvement Campaign. Multicoloured.
451. 25 f. "Madjiguene" .. 12 8
452. 40 f. Type 90 .. .. 12 10
453. 100 f. "Pass" 55 25
454. 125 f. "Pepe" 65 30

91. European Girl and African Boy.

92. Phillis Wheatley.

1971. Racial Equality Year. Multicoloured.
455. 30 f. Type 91 .. .. 15 8
456. 50 f. People of four races (horiz.) (37 × 30 mm.) .. 30 12

1971. Air. Famous Negrophiles. Multicoloured.
457. 25 f. Type 92 .. .. 15 8
458. 40 f. J. E. K. Aggrey .. 20 10
459. 60 f. A. Le Roy Locke .. 35 15
460. 100 f. Booker T. Washington 55 20

93. "Telephones".

94. "Napoleon as First Consul" (Ingres).

1971. World Telecommunications Day.
461. 93. 30 f. brn., grn. & purple 15 8
462. – 40 f. brown, red & blue 25 10
DESIGN 40 f. "Telecommunications" theme.

1971. Napoleon. 150th Death Anniv. Multicoloured.
463. 15 f. Type 94 .. .. 10 8
464. 25 f. "Napoleon in 1809" (Lefevre) 20 15
465. 35 f. "Napoleon on his Death-bed" (Rouget) .. 25 20
466. 50 f. "The Awakening to Immortality" (bronze by Rude) 30 25

95. Pres. Nasser.

97. A. Nobel.

96. Hayashida (drummer).

1971. Air. Nasser Commemoration.
467. 95. 50 f. multicoloured .. 30 12

1971. 13th World Scout Jamboree, Asagiri, Japan. Multicoloured.
468. 35 f. Type 96 .. .. 20 8
469. 50 f. Japonica 30 12
470. 65 f. Judo 40 15
471. 75 f. Mt. Fuji 45 25

1971. Air. Alfred Nobel (scientist and philanthropist). 75th Birth Anniv.
472. 97. 100 f. multicoloured .. 55 30

98. Persian Flag and Senegal Arms.

1971. Air. Persian Empire. 2500th Anniv.
473. 98. 200 f. multicoloured .. 1·10 55

99. Map and Emblem.

1971. U.N.I.C.E.F. 25th Anniv. Multicoloured.
474. 35 f. Type 99 .. .. 20 12
475. 100 f. Nurse, children and U.N.I.C.E.F. emblem .. 55 25

1971. Air. U.A.M.P.T. 10th Anniv. As T 153 of Cameroun. Multicoloured.
476. 100 f. U.A.M.P.T. H.Q., Brazzaville and arms of Senegal 55 25

100. Louis Armstrong.

101. Trying for Goal.

1971. Air. Louis Armstrong Commem.
477. 100. 150 f. brown and gold 75 55

1971. 6th African Basketball Championships, Dakar. Multicoloured.

No.	Description	Unused	Used
478.	35 f. Type **101**	20	8
479.	40 f. Players reaching for ball	25	10
480.	75 f. Championships emblem	40	20

102. Ice-skating.

1971. Air. Winter Olympic Games, Sapporo, Japan. Multicoloured.

No.	Description	Unused	Used
481.	5 f. Type **102**	5	5
482.	10 f. Bob-sleighing	5	5
483.	125 f. Cross-country skiing	65	30

103. "Il Fonteghetto della Farina" (detail – Canaletto).

1972. Air. U.N.E.S.C.O. "Save Venice" Campaign. Multicoloured.

No.	Description	Unused	Used
484.	50 f. Type **103**	30	12
485.	100 f. "Giudecca e S. Giorgio Maggiore" (detail – Guardi) (vert.) ..	55	30

104. "Albouri and Queen Seb Fall" (scene from "The Exile of Albouri").

1972. Int. Theatre Day. Multicoloured.

No.	Description	Unused	Used
486.	35 f. Type **104** (postage)	20	8
487.	40 f. Scene from "The Merchant of Venice" ..	25	12
488.	150 f. Daniel Sorano as "Shylock" ("The Merchant of Venice") (vert.) (air)	85	45

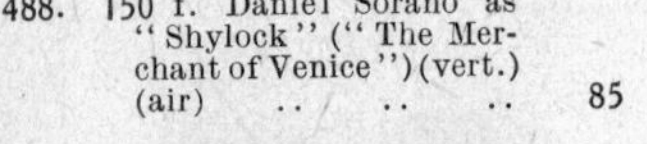

105. Human Heart.

1972. World Heart Month.

No.	Description	Unused	Used
489. **105.**	35 f. brown and blue..	20	8
490. –	40 f. mar., grn. & emer.	25	12

DESIGN: 40 f. Doctor and patient.

106. Vegetation in Desert.

1972. U.N. Environmental Conservation Conf., Stockholm. Multicoloured.

No.	Description	Unused	Used
491.	35 f. Type **106** (postage)..	20	8
492.	100 f. Oil slick on shore (air)	55	25

107. Tartarin of Tarascon shooting Lion.

1972. Alphonse Daudet (writer) 75th Death Anniv.

No.	Description	Unused	Used
493. **107.**	40 f. red, grn. & brown	25	12
494. –	100 f. brn., light bl. & bl.	50	25

DESIGN: 100 f. Daudet and scene from "Tartarin".

108. Wrestling. **109.** Emperor Haile Selassie and Flags.

1972. Olympic Games, Munich. Mult.

No.	Description	Unused	Used
496.	15 f. Type **108**	8	5
497.	20 f. Running (100 metres)	10	5
498.	100 f. Basketball ..	50	25
499.	125 f. Judo	60	30

1972. Air. Emperor Haile Selassie. 80th Birthday.

No.	Description	Unused	Used
501. **109.**	100 f. multicoloured	55	25

110. Children reading Book. **111.** "Senegalese Elegance".

1972. Int. Book Year.

No.	Description	Unused	Used
502. **110.**	50 f. multicoloured ..	30	15

1972.

No.	Description	Unused	Used
503. **111.**	25 f. black	15	5
504.	40 f. blue	25	8
504a.	60 f. green	30	15

112. Alexander Pushkin. **113.** "Amphicraspedum murrayanum".

1972. Pushkin (writer). Commem.

No.	Description	Unused	Used
505. **112.**	100 f. purple & pink ..	55	25

1972. West African Monetary Union. 10th Anniv. As Type **109** of Dahomey.

No.	Description	Unused	Used
506.	40 f. brn., grey and blue ..	20	8

1972. Protozoa and Large Fishes. Mult.

No.	Description	Unused	Used
507.	5 f. Type **113** (postage) ..	5	5
508.	10 f. "Pterocanium tricolpum"	5	5
509.	15 f. "Ceratospyris polygona"	8	5
510.	20 f. "Cortiniscus typicus"	8	5
511.	30 f. "Theopera cortina"	12	5
512.	50 f. "Xiphias gladius" (air)	25	12
513.	65 f. "Orcinus orca" ..	30	15
514.	75 f. "Rhincodon typus"	35	20
515.	125 f. "Balaenoptera physalus"	65	35

Nos. 512/15 are size 45 × 27 mm.

1972. No. 353 surch. **1872-1972** and value.

No.	Description	Unused	Used
516. **46.**	100 f. on 30 f. chocolate, green and chest. ..	45	25

114. Melchior. **115.** "Sharing the Load".

1972. Christmas. Nativity Scene and Three Kings. Multicoloured.

No.	Description	Unused	Used
517	10 f Type **114**	5	5
518.	15 f. Gaspard	8	5
519.	40 f. Balthazar	20	10
520.	60 f. Joseph	30	15
521.	100 f. Mary and Baby Jesus (African representation)	50	25

1973. Europafrique.

No.	Description	Unused	Used
522. **115.**	65 f. black and green	30	15

116. Palace of the Republic.

1973. Air.

No.	Description	Unused	Used
523. **116.**	100 f. multicoloured ..	40	20

117. Station and Aerial.

1973. Satellite Earth Station, Gandoul. Inaug.

No.	Description	Unused	Used
524. **117.**	40 f. multicoloured ..	15	10

118. Hotel Teranga.

1973. Air. Opening of Hotel Teranga, Dakar.

No.	Description	Unused	Used
525. **118.**	100 f. multicoloured..	40	20

119. "Lions" African Emblem.

1973. Air. 15th Lions Int. District 403 Congress, Dakar.

No.	Description	Unused	Used
526. **119.**	150 f. multicoloured..	55	25

120. Stages of Eclipse.

1973. Eclipse of the Sun. Multicoloured.

No.	Description	Unused	Used
527.	35 f. Type **120**	12	5
528.	65 f. Eclipse in diagramatic form	30	15
529.	150 f. Eclipse and "Skylab 1"	65	35

121. Symbolic Torch.

1973. Organization of African Unity. 10th Anniv.

No.	Description	Unused	Used
530. **121.**	75 f. multicoloured ..	30	15

1973. "Drought Relief". African Solidarity. No. 451 surch. **SECHERESSE SOLIDARITE AFRICAINE** and value.

No.	Description	Unused	Used
531.	100 f. on 25 f. multicoloured	40	20

122. "Couple with Mimosa" (Chagall).

1973. Air.

No.	Description	Unused	Used
532. **122.**	200 f. multicoloured ..	75	35

123. "Riccione 1973". **124.** W.M.O. Emblem and Child.

1973. Air. Int. Stamp Exhibition, Riccione (Italy).

No.	Description	Unused	Used
533. **123.**	100 f. violet, green & red	40	20

1973. U.A.M.P.T. As Type **182** of Cameroun.

No.	Description	Unused	Used
534.	100 f. violet, green and red	40	20

1973. World Meteorological Organization Cent.

No.	Description	Unused	Used
535. **124.**	50 f. multicoloured ..	15	8

125. Interpol H.Q., Paris. **126.** Flame Emblem and People.

1973. Int. Criminal Police Organization. (Interpol). 50th Anniv.

No.	Description	Unused	Used
536. **125.**	75 f. brn., blue & green	25	12

1973. Air. Declaration of Human Rights. 25th Anniv. Multicoloured.

No.	Description	Unused	Used
538.	35 f. Type **126** ..	10	5
539.	65 f. Emblem and drummer	20	10

127. R. Follereau (rehabilitation pioneer) and Map.

1973. Air. Discovery of Leprosy Bacillus. Cent.

No.	Description	Unused	Used
540. **127.**	40 f. brn., grn. & violet	12	8
541. –	100 f. maroon, red & grn.	30	15

DESIGN: 100 f. Dr. G. Hansen (discoverer of leprosy bacillus) and laboratory equipment.

128. "Key" Emblem. **129.** Amilcar Cabral and Weapons.

1973. Air. World Twinned Towns Congress, Dakar. Multicoloured.
542. 50 f. Type **128** 15 8
543. 125 f. Arms of Dakar and meeting of citizens (horiz.) 40 20

1974. Amilcar Cabral (Guinea Bissau guerilla leader). Commemoration.
544. **129.** 75 f. multicoloured .. 25 15

130. Grebes.

1974. Air. Birds of Djoudj Park. Mult.
545. 1 f. Type **130** 5 5
546. 2 f. White spoonbills .. 5 5
547. 3 f. Crowned cranes .. 5 5
548. 4 f. White herons 5 5
549. 250 f. Flamingoes (gold value) 90 45
550. 250 f. Flamingoes (black value) 90 45

131. "Tiger attacking Wild Horse".

1974. Air. Paintings by Delacroix. Mult.
551. 150 f. Type **131** 50 25
552. 200 f. "Tiger-hunting" .. 60 30

132. Athletes on Podium.

134. U.P.U. Emblem, Letters and Transport.

133. World Cup, Footballers and "Munich".

1974. National Youth Week. Multicoloured.
553. 35 f. Type **132** 10 5
554. 40 f. Dancer with mask .. 12 8

1974. World Cup Football Championships. Footballers and locations.
555. 25 f. Type **133** 8 5
556. 40 f. "Hamburg" 12 8
557. 65 f. "Hanover" 20 12
558. 70 f. "Stuttgart" 25 15

1974. Universal Postal Union. Centenary.
559. **134.** 100 f. green, blue and lilac 30 25

135. Archway, and Africans at Work.

136. Dakar, "Gateway to Africa".

1974. First Dakar International Fair.
560. **135.** 100 f. brown, orange & blue (postage) .. 30 25
561. **136.** 350 f. silver (air) .. 1·00
562. 1500 f. gold .. .. 4·25
Nos. 561/2 are embossed on foil.

1975. West Germany's Victory in World Cup Football Championships, Munich. No. 566 surch. **ALLEMAGNE RFA-HOLLANDE 2-1** and value.
563. 200 f. on 40 f. mult. .. 60 50

137. Pres. Senghor and King Baudouin.

1975. Visit of King Baudouin of the Belgians.
564. **137.** 65 f. blue and purple .. 25 20
565. 100 f. green and orange 40 35

138. I.L.O. Emblem.

1975. Labour Day.
566. **138.** 125 f. multicoloured .. 50 45

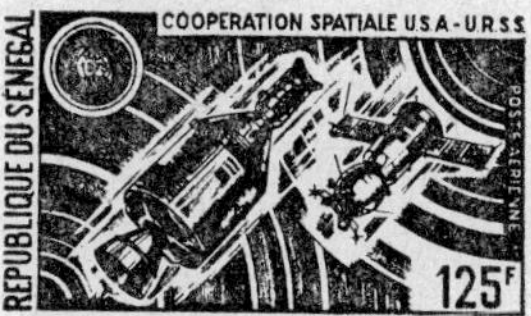
139. "Apollo" and "Soyuz".

1975. Air. "Apollo-Soyuz" Space Co-operation Project.
567. **139.** 125 f. green, blue & red 50 45

140. Spanish "Stamp" Globe and Letters.

1975. "Espana 75" (Madrid) and "Arphila 75" (Paris) International Stamp Exhibitions.
568. **140.** 55 f. red, blue & green 25 20
569. – 95 f. chocolate & brown 40 35
DESIGN: 95 f. Head of Apollo and "Arphila" emblem.

141. Classroom and Teacher.

1975. "Formation Permanente" (Technical Education).
570. **141.** 85 f. brown, blue & blk. 35 30

142. Dr. Schweitzer

1975. Dr. Albert Schweitzer. Birth Cent.
571. **142.** 85 f. lilac and green .. 35 30

143. Soldier, Flag and Map of Sinai Desert.

1975. Senegalese Battalion with U.N. (1973–74).
572. **143.** 100 f. multicoloured .. 40 35

144. Stamps and Map of Italy.

145. Woman pounding Maize.

1975. Air. Riccione Stamp Exhibition.
573. **144.** 125 f. brown, red & lilac 50 45

1975. International Women's Year. Multicoloured.
574. 55 f. Type **145** 75 20
575. 75 f. Mother and child with woman doctor (horiz.) .. 30 25

1975. Air. "Apollo-Soyuz" Space Link. Optd. **JONCTION 17 Juil. 1975.**
576. **139.** 125 f. green, blue & red 50 45

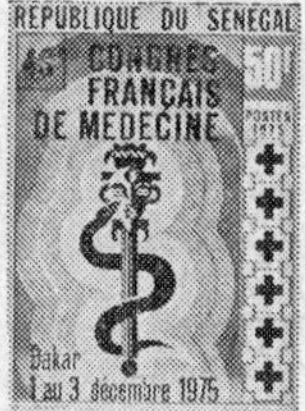
146. Stylised Caduceus.

1975. French Medical Congress, Dakar.
577. **146.** 50 f. multicoloured .. 20 15

147. Boston Massacre.

1975. Air. American Revolution. Bicent. (1st issue).
578. **147.** 250 f. brn., red & blue 1·00 95
579. – 500 f. red and blue .. 2·10 2·00
DESIGN: 500 f. Siege of Yorktown.
See also No. 593.

148. Emblem on Map.

1976. Int. Conf. on "Rights of Man" and Namibia, Dakar.
580. **148.** 125 f. multicoloured .. 60 30

149. "Concorde" and Flight Locations.

1976. Air. "Concorde's" 1st Commercial Flight, Paris–Dakar–Rio de Janeiro.
581. **149.** 300 f. multicoloured .. 1·40 70

150. Deep-sea Fishing.

1976. "Expo", Okinawa. Multicoloured.
582. 140 f. Type **150** 65 35
583. 200 f. Yacht-racing .. 95 55

151. Serval.

1976. Basse Casamance Nat. Park. Fauna. Multicoloured.
584. 2 f. Type **151** 5 5
585. 3 f. Reddish godwit (marsh bird) 5 5
586. 4 f. Wild boar 5 5
587. 5 f. Fish eagle 5 5
588. 250 f. Sitatunga (females) 1·10 55
589. 250 f. Sitatunga (males) .. 1·10 55

152. Alexander Graham Bell and Early Telephone.

1976. Telephone Centenary.
590. **152.** 175 f. multicoloured .. 80 40

153. Map of Africa.

1976. GADEF Scientific and Cultural Days.
591. **153.** 60 f. multicoloured .. 30 15

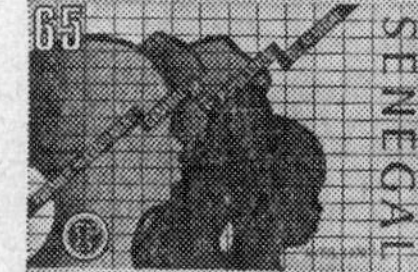
154. Family Heads on Graphs.

1976. First Population Census.
592. **154.** 65 f. multicoloured .. 30 15

155. Jefferson reading Independence Declaration.

1976. American Revolution. Bicent. (2nd issue).
593. **155.** 50 f. blk., red and blue 25 12

156. Plant Cultivation.

1976. Operation " Sahel Vert ".
594. **156.** 60 f. multicoloured .. 30 15

157. Scouts around Camp-fire.

1976. First All-African Scouts Jamboree, Jos, Nigeria. Multicoloured.
595. 80 f. Type **157** 35 20
596. 100 f. Emblem and map (vert.) 45 25

158. Tomato Harvesting.

1976. Tomatoes Production.
597. **158.** 180 f. multicoloured .. 85 45

159. Swimming.

1976. Olympic Games, Montreal. Mult.
598. 5 f. Type **159** (postage) 5 5
599. 10 f. Weightlifting .. 5 5
600. 15 f. Hurdling (horiz.) .. 5 5
601. 20 f. Horse-jumping (horiz.) 10 5
602. 25 f. Long-jumping (horiz.) 15 8
603. 50 f. Wrestling (horiz.) .. 25 12
604. 60 f. Hockey .. 30 15
605. 65 f. Gymnastics 30 15
607. 100 f. Cycling (horiz.) .. 45 25
608. 400 f. Boxing (horiz.) (air) 1·90 90
609. 500 f. Judo .. .. 2·25 1·10

160. Maps and Symbol.

1976. President Senghor's 70th Birthday. Multicoloured.
611. 40 f. Type **160** 20 10
612. 60 f. Star over world map 30 15
613. 70 f. Technicians and symbol 35 20
614. 200 f. President Senghor and extended hands .. 95 55

161. " Concorde " and Route Map.

1976. Air. Dakar International Fair.
615. **161.** 500 f. silver .. .. 2·25
616. 1,500 f. gold .. .. 6·50

162. Negro Peoples' " Charter ".

1977. Negro Peoples' Day.
617. **162.** 60 f. multicoloured .. 30 15

POSTAGE DUE STAMPS

1903. Postage Due stamps of French Colonies surch. in figures and bar.
D 30. **D 1.** 10 on 50 c. claret .. 10·00 10·00
D 31. 10 on 60 c. brown on yellow .. 10·00 10·00
D 32. 10 on 1 f. red on yell. 55·00 55·00

1906. " Natives " key-type.
D 50. **L.** 5 c. green 55 55
D 51. 10 c. claret .. .. 1·00 1·00
D 52. 15 c. blue .. .. 1·10 1·10
D 53. 20 c. black on yellow .. 1·00 1·00
D 54. 30 c. red .. .. 1·50 1·50
D 55. 50 c. violet .. .. 1·50 1·50
D 56. 60 c. black on yellow 1 50 1·50
D 57. 1 f. black .. .. 2·75 2·25

1915. " Figure " key-type.
D 81. **M.** 5 c. green 5 5
D 82. 10 c. red 5 5
D 83. 15 c. grey 5 5
D 84. 20 c. brown 5 5
D 85. 30 c. blue 20 15
D 86. 50 c. black 20 15
D 87. 60 c. orange .. 25 25
D 88. 1 f. violet 25 20

1927. Surch. in figures.
D 133. **M.** 2 f. on 1 f. purple .. 50 45
D 134. 3 f. on 1 f. brown .. 50 45

D 1. D 2.

1935.
D 194. **D 1.** 5 c. green 5 5
D 195. 10 c. orange .. 5 5
D 196. 15 c. violet 5 5
D 197. 20 c. olive 5 5
D 198. 30 c. brown 5 5
D 199. 50 c. purple .. 5 5
D 200. 60 c. yellow .. 20 20
D 201. 1 f. black 5 5
D 202. 2 f. blue 5 5
D 203. 3 f. red 15 15

1961.
D 239. **D 2.** 1 f. orange and red 5 5
D 240. 2 f. blue and red .. 5 5
D 241. 5 f. brown and red 5 5
D 242. 20 f. green and red 15 15
D 243. 25 f. purple and red 20 20

ILLUSTRATIONS
British Commonwealth and all overprints and surcharges are FULL SIZE. Foreign Countries have been reduced to ¾-LINEAR.

D 3. Lion's Head.

1966. Head in gold and black; value in black.
D 339. **D 3.** 1 f. red 5 5
D 340. 2 f. brown 5 5
D 341. 5 f. violet 5 5
D 342. 10 f. blue 5 5
D 343. 20 f. green .. 12 12
D 344. 30 f. grey 20 20

OFFICIAL STAMPS

O 1. Arms of Dakar. O 2. Baobab Tree.

1961. Figures of value in black.
O 240. **O 1.** 1 f. black and blue 5 5
O 241. 2 f. blue and yellow 5 5
O 242. 5 f. lake and emerald 5 5
O 243. 10 f. red and blue .. 8 5
O 244. 25 f. blue and red .. 15 8
O 245. 50 f. vermilion and grey 35 20
O 246. 85 f. purple and orange 55 30
O 247. 100 f. vermilion & grn. 65 40

1966.
O 339. **O 2.** 1 f. black and yellow 5 5
O 340. 5 f. black and orange 5 5
O 341. 10 f. black and red .. 5 5
O 342. 20 f. black and purple 10 5
O 342a. 25 f. black and mauve 10 5
O 343. 30 f. black and blue 12 5
O 344. 35 f. black and blue 12 8
O 344a. 40 f. black and blue 15 8
O 345. 55 f. black & emerald 25 15
O 346. 90 f. black and green 40 25
O 347. 100 f. black & brown 45 25

1969. No. O 345 surch.
O 390. **O 2.** 60 f. on 55 f. black and green 30 15

SENEGAMBIA AND NIGER O2

A French colony later re-named Upper Senegal and Niger, and later French Sudan.

1903. " Tablet " key-type inscr. " SENEGAMBIE ET NIGER ".
22. **D.** 1 c. black on blue .. 45 35
23. 2 c. brown on yellow .. 30 15
24. 4 c. claret on grey .. 40 40
25. 5 c. green 55 45
26. 10 c. red 65 55
27. 15 c. grey .. .. 2·00 1·90
28. 20 c. red on green .. 2·25 2·10
29. 25 c. blue .. .. 2·75 2·25
30. 30 c. brown .. .. 2·75 2·25
31. 40 c. red on yellow .. 2·50 2·25
32. 50 c. brown on blue .. 8·00 8·00
33. 75 c. brown on orange .. 8·00 8·00
34. 1 f. olive .. .. 10·00 10·00

For later issues see **UPPER SENEGAL AND NIGER** and **FRENCH SUDAN.**

SERBIA E3

A kingdom in the Balkans, S.E. Europe. Part of Yugoslavia since 1918, except during the Second World War when stamps were issued by a German-sponsored Government.

100 paras = 1 dinar.

1. 2. Prince Michael (Obrenovich III).

1866. Imperf.
N 3. **1.** 1 p. green on lilac-rose 8·50
N 7. 2 p. brown on lilac .. 15·00

1866. Perf.
N 17. **2.** 1 p. olive .. .. 4·50 50·00
N 18a. 2 p. brown .. .. 7·00 60·00
12. 10 p. orange .. .. 15·00 12·00
15. 20 p. red .. .. 3·00 2·00
14. 40 p. blue .. .. 3·00 1·75

1868. Imperf.
N 19. **2.** 1 p. green .. .. 6·00
N 20. 2 p. brown .. .. 8·00

3. Prince Milan 4. (Obrenovich IV). 5. King Milan I.

1869. Perf.
30. **3.** 1 p. yellow .. .. 70 3·75
45. 10 p. brown 70
48. 10 p. orange 20 30
32. 15 p. orange .. .. 3·50 1·50
49. 20 p. blue 8 15
41. 25 p. rose 20 25
35. 35 p. green 35 60
50. 40 p. mauve 20 30
37. 50 p. green 60 30

1872. Newspaper stamps. Imperf.
N 52. **3.** 1 p. yellow 60 85
N 53. **4.** 2 p. black .. .. 25 1·90

1880. Perf.
54a. **5.** 5 p. green 8 5
55. 10 p. red 8 5
56. 20 p. orange 10 5
57. 25 p. blue 8 8
58. 50 p. brown 10 10
59. 1 d. violet.. .. 75 75

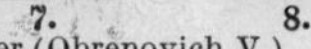

6. 7. 8. King Alexander (Obrenovich V.).

1890.
60. **6.** 5 p. green 5 5
61. 10 p. red 5 5
62. 15 p. mauve 5 5
63. 20 p. orange 5 5
64. 25 p. blue 8 8
65. 50 p. brown 40 35
66. 1 d. lilac .. .. .. 2·50 1·50

1894.
75. **7.** 1 p. red 5 5
76. 5 p. green 10 5
68. 10 p. red 50 5
78. 15 p. mauve 50 5
79. 20 p. orange 75 5
80. 25 p. blue 75 5
72. 50 p. brown .. .. 1·00 10
73. 1 d. green 12 10
74. 1 d. red on blue .. 1·75 75

1900. Surch.
82. **7.** 10 p. on 20 p. rose .. 15 5
84. 15 p. on 1 d. red on blue .. 1·25 35

1901.
85. **8.** 5 p. green 5 5
86. 10 p. red 5 5
87. 15 p. mauve 5 5
88. 20 p. orange 5 5
89. 25 p. blue 5 5
90. 50 p. yellow 5 5
91. – 1 d. brown 12 12
92. – 3 d. pink .. .. 1·60 1·25
93. – 5 d. violet .. .. 1·10 1·10
The 1 d. to 5 d. are larger.

10. King Alexander I (Obrenovich V). 11. Karageorge and Peter I.

1903. Optd. with shield.
94. **10.** 1 p. black and claret .. 8 8
95. 5 p. black and green .. 5 5
96. 10 p. black and rose .. 5 5
97. 15 p. black and grey .. 5 5
98. 20 p. black and orange 5 5
99. 25 p. black and blue .. 5 5
106. 50 p. black and grey .. 15 15
101. 1 d. black and green .. 1·40 65
102. 3 d. back and lilac .. 30 30
103. 5 d. black and brown .. 30 30

1903. Surch. **1 NAPA 1.**
104. **10.** 1 p. on 5 d. black & brown 25 25

1904. Coronation. Cent. of Karageorgevich Dynasty. Dated " 1804 1904 ".
108. **11.** 5 p. green 5 5
109. 10 p. rose 5 5
110. 15 p. purple 5 5
111. 25 p. blue 5 5
112. 50 p. brown 5 5
113. – 1 d. bistre 50 20
114. – 3 d. green 40 30
115. – 5 d. violet .. .. 1·00 60
DESIGN: 1 d., 3 d., 5 d. Karageorge and insurgents, 1804.

13. Peter I. 14. Peter I.

1905.
116. **13.** 1 p. black and grey .. 5 5
117. 5 p. black and green .. 5 5
118. 10 p. black and red .. 10 5
119. 15 p. black and mauve 20 5
120. 20 p. black and yellow 30 5
121. 25 p. black and blue .. 60 5
122. 30 p. black and green .. 35 5
123. 50 p. black and brown 35 5
124. 1 d. black and bistre .. 5 5
125. 3 d. black and green .. 5 5
126. 5 d. black and violet .. 30 20

1911.
146. **14.** 1 p. black 5 5
147. 2 p. violet 5 5
148. 5 p. green 5 5
149. 10 p. red 5 5
150. 15 p. purple 5 5
171. 15 p. black 5 5
151. 20 p. yellow 5 5
172. 20 p. brown 15 10
173. 25 p. blue 5 5
153. 30 p. green 5 5
173a. 30 p. bronze 5 5
154. 50 p. brown 5 5
174. 50 p. red 5 5
155. 1 d. orange .. .. 2·50 7·00
175. 1 d. green 25 20
156. 3 d. lake.. .. .. 7·00 12·00
176. 3 d. yellow .. .. 18·00 18·00
177. 5 d. violet .. .. 8 1·00

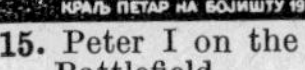

15. Peter I on the Battlefield. 16. Peter I and Prince Alexander.

1915.

178. 15. 5 p. green 5 20
179. 10 p. red 5 25

1918.

194. 16. 1 p. black 5 5
195. 2 p. olive 5 5
196. 5 p. green 5 5
197. 10 p. red 5 5
198. 15 p. sepia 5 5
199. 20 p. brown 5 5
208. 20 p. mauve 55 15
200. 25 p. blue 5 5
201. 30 p. olive 5 5
202. 50 p. mauve 5 5
203. 1 d. brown 5 5
204. 3 d. slate 25 10
205. 5 d. brown 45 15

GERMAN OCCUPATION

1941. Stamps of Yugoslavia on paper with coloured network optd. **SERBIEN** reading downwards.

1. 63. 25 p. black 5 5
2. 50 p. orange 5 5
3. 1 d. green 5 5
4. 1 d. 50 red 5 5
5. 2 d. claret 5 5
6. 3 d. brown 40 45
7. 4 d. blue 5 5
8. 5 d. blue 8 10
9. 5 d. 50 violet 8 10
10. 6 d. blue 8 10
11. 8 d. brown 35 35
12. 12 d. violet 35 35
13. 16 d. purple 55 60
14. 20 d. blue 55 60
15. 30 d. pink 2·75 3·00

1941. Air stamps of Yugoslavia on paper with coloured network, optd. **SERBIEN.**

16. 44. 50 p. brown 1·25 1·60
17. – 1 d. green (No. 361) 1·25 1·60
18. – 2 d. blue (362) 1·25 1·60
19. 46. 2 d. 50 red 1·25 1·60
20. 44. 5 d. violet 1·25 1·60
21. – 10 d. red (No. 365) 1·25 1·60
22. – 20 d. green (No. 366) 1·25 1·60
23. 46. 30 d. blue 2·75 3·25
24. – 40 d. green (No. 443) 3·25 3·50
25. – 50 d. blue (No. 444) 3·50 4·50

1941. Air. As last, but without network surch. **SERBIEN** and value.

26. – 1 d. on 10 d. red (No. 365) 90 90
27. – 3 d. on 20 d. grn. (No. 366) 90 90
28. 46. 6 d. on 30 d. blue 90 1·10
29. – 8 d. on 40 d. grn. (No. 443) 1·10 1·10
30. – 12 d. on 50 d. bl. (No. 444) 1·75 2·25

1941. As Nos. 1/15, but with **SERBIEN** reading upwards.

31. 63. 25 p. black 5 5
32. 50 p. orange 5 5
33. 1 d. green 5 5
34. 1 d. 50 red 5 5
35. 2 d. claret 5 5
36. 3 d. brown 5 8
37. 4 d. blue 5 5
38. 5 d. blue 5 8
39. 5 d. 50 violet 15 15
40. 6 d. blue 15 15
41. 8 d. brown 15 20
42. 12 d. violet 20 25
43. 16 d. purple 35 40
44. 20 d. blue 35 55
45. 30 d. pink 2·00 2·25

17. Smederevo Fortress. 18. Christ and the Virgin Mary.

1941. Smederevo Explosion Relief Fund.

46. 17. 50 p.+1 d. brown 8 10
47. – 1 d.+2 d. green 10 12
48. – 1 d. 50+3 d. purple 15 15
49. 17. 2 d.+4 d. blue 30 30

DESIGN: 1 d., 1 d. 50, Refugees.

1941. Prisoners of War Fund.

50. 18. 50 p.+1 d. 50 brown 5 5
51. 1 d.+3 d. green 5 5
52. 2 d.+6 d. red 5 5
53. 4 d.+12 d. blue 5 5

This set also exists with an optd. network, both plain and incorporating a large "E", this letter being either normal or reversed.

19. 20.

1942. Anti-Masonic Exn. Dated "22.X.1941".

54. 19. 50 p.+50 p. brown 8 5
55. – 1 d.+1 d. green 8 5
56. 20. 2 d.+2 d. red 15 20
57. – 4 d.+4 d. blue 15 20

DESIGNS—HORIZ. 1 d. Hand grasping snake. VERT. 4 d. Peasant demolishing masonic symbols.

21. Mother and Children. 22. Kalenic.

23. Ljubostinja.

1942. War Orphans Fund.

74. 21. 2 d.+6 d. violet 55 65
75. 4 d.+8 d. blue 55 65
76. 7 d.+13 d. green 55 65
77. 20 d.+40 d. red 55 65

1942. Monasteries.

58. – 50 p. violet 5 5
59. 12. 1 d. red 5 5
60. – 1 d. 50 brown 30 30
61. – 1 d. 50 green 5 5
62. – 2 d. purple 5 5
63. 23. 3 d. blue 30 30
64. 3 d. pink 5 5
65. – 4 d. blue 5 5
66. – 7 d. green 5 5
67. – 12 d. claret 10 10
68. – 16 d. black 15 15

DESIGNS—VERT. 50 p. Lazario. 1 d. 50, Ravanica. 12 d. Gornjak. 16 d. Studenica. HORIZ. 2 d. Manasija. 4 d. Sopocani. 7 d. Zica.

1942. Nos. 50/53, colours changed.

68a. 18. 0·50 d.+1·50 d. brown 25 30
68b. 1 d.+3 d. green 25 30
68c. 2 d.+6d. carmine 25 30
68d. 4 d.+12 d. blue 25 30

1942. Air. 1939 issue of Yugoslavia optd. with aeroplane and surch. new value.

69. 63. 2 on 2 d. mauve 5 5
70. 4 on 4 d. blue 5 5
71. 10 on 12 d. violet 5 5
72. 14 on 20 d. blue 5 5
73. 20 on 30 d. pink 20 20

24. Broken Sword. 25. Fallen Standard bearer.

1943. War Invalids' Relief Fund.

78. 24. 1 d. 50+1 d. 50 brown 15 20
79. 25. 2 d.+3 d. green 15 20
80. – 3 d.+5 d. magenta 20 25
81. – 4 d.+10 d. blue 35 40

DESIGNS—HORIZ. 3 d. Wounded soldier (seated). VERT. 4 d. Nurse tending soldier.

DESIGNS — HORIZ. 8 d. Horse wagon. 9 d. Railway van. 30 d. Postal motor van. 50 d. Mail 'plane.

26. Post Rider.

1943. Postal Centenary. Inscr. "15.X.1843-15.X.1943".

82. 26. 3 d. red and lilac 10 12
83. – 8 d. mauve and grey 10 12
84. – 9 d. green and brown 10 12
85. – 30 d. brown and green 10 12
86. – 50 d. blue and claret 10 12

1943. Bombing of Nish Relief Fund. Monasteries issue of 1942 on paper with network, surch. . . . **20-X-1943** and value in figures.

87. 50 p.+2 d. violet 5 5
88. 1 d.+3 d. red 5 5
89. 1 d. 50+4 d. green 5 5
90. 2 d.+5 d. purple 5 5
91. 3 d.+7 d. pink 5 8
92. 4 d.+9 d. blue 5 8
93. 7 d.+15 d. green 12 12
94. 12 d.+25 d. claret 12 12
95. 16 d.+33 d. black 20 30

OFFICIAL STAMP

GERMAN OCCUPATION

O 1.

ILLUSTRATIONS British Commonwealth and all overprints and surcharges are FULL SIZE. Foreign Countries have been reduced to ¾-LINEAR.

1943.

O 78. O 1. 3 d. claret 8 10

POSTAGE DUE STAMPS

D 1. D 2.

1895.

D 92. D 1. 5 p. mauve 5 5
D 93. 10 p. blue 15 60
D 91. 20 p. brown 5 5
D 85. 30 p. green 5 5
D 86. 50 p. red 5 5

1918.

D 227. D 2. 5 p. red 5 5
D 232. 5 p. brown 5 5
D 228. 10 p. green 5 5
D 229. 20 p. brown 5 5
D 230. 30 p. blue 5 5
D 233. 30 p. grey 5 5
D 231. 50 p. brown 5 5

GERMAN OCCUPATION

D 3. D 4. D 5.

1941. Unissued Postage Due stamps optd. **SERBIEN.**

D 16. D 3. 50 p. violet 5 5
D 17. 1 d. claret 5 5
D 18. 2 d. blue 5 5
D 19. 3 d. red 5 5
D 20. D 4. 4 d. blue 8 8
D 21. 5 d. orange 30 30
D 22. 10 d. violet 30 30
D 23. 20 d. green 40 50

1942. Types D 3 and D 4 without opt. Bottom inscription on white background.

D 69. D 3. 1 d. claret and green 5 5
D 70. 2 d. blue and red 5 5
D 71. 3 d. red and blue 5 5
D 72. D 4. 4 d. blue and red 5 5
D 73. 5 d. orange and blue 5 5
D 74. 10 d. violet and red 5 5
D 75. 20 d. green and red 15 15

1943.

D 82. D 5. 50 p. black 5 5
D 83. 3 d. violet 5 5
D 84. 4 d. blue 5 5
D 85. 5 d. green 5 5
D 86. 6 d. orange 5 5
D 87. 10 d. red 15 15
D 88. 20 d. blue 30 30

SERBIAN OCCUPATION OF HUNGARY E2

BARANYA

100 filler = 1 korona.

1919. Stamps of Hungary optd. **1919 Baranya** or surch. also.

(a) "Turul" Type.

1. 3. 6 f. drab 8 8
2. 50 f. lake on blue 5 5
3. 60 f. green on red 8 8
4. 70 f. brown on green 5 5
5. 80 f. violet 40 50

(b) War Charity stamp of 1915.

6. 3. 50+2 f. lake on blue 1·50 1·50

(c) War Charity stamps of 1916.

8. 6. 10 f. (+2 f.) red 5 5
9. – 15 f. (+2 f.) violet 5 5

(d) Harvesters and Parliament Types.

10. 11. 2 f. brown 8 8
11. 3 f. claret 8 8
12. 5 f. green 8 8
13. 6 f. blue 8 8
14. 15 f. violet 5 5
15. 20 f. brown 2·10 2·10
16. 25 f. blue 45 45
17. 35 f. brown 60 60
18. 40 f. olive 3·25 3·25
19. 45 on 2 f. brown 5 5
20. 45 on 5 f. green 5 5
21. 45 on 15 f. violet 5 5
22. 12. 50 f. purple 25 25
23. 75 f. blue 5 5
24. 80 f. green 5 5
25. 1 k. lake 5 5
26. 2 k. brown 5 5
27. 3 k. grey and violet 8 8
28. 5 k. brown 20 20
29. 60 k. lilac and brown 60 60

(e) Karl and Zita stamps.

30. 13. 10 f. red 5 5
31. 20 f. brown 5 5
32. 25 f. blue 15 15
33. 14. 40 f. olive 65 65

The following (Nos. 34/6) are also optd. **KOZTARSASAG.**

(f) Harvesters Types.

34. 11. 2 f. brown 65 65
35. 45 on 2 f. green 5 5

(g) Zita stamp.

36. 14. 40 f. olive 4·00 4·00

1919. Stamps of Hungary surch. **BARANYA** and value.

(h) Harvesters and Parliament Types.

42. 11. 20 on 2 f. green 90 90
43. 50 on 5 f. green 25 25
44. 150 on 15 f. violet 25 25
45. 12. 200 on 75 f. blue 8 8

(k) Harvester Type inscr. "MAGYAR POSTA".

46. 11. 20 on 2 f. brown 5 5
47. 30 on 6 f. blue 5 5
48. 50 on 5 f. green 5 5
49. 100 on 25 f. blue 5 5
50. 100 on 40 f. olive 5 5
51. 100 on 45 f. orange 12 12
52. 150 on 20 f. brown 15 15

(m) Karl stamp optd. **KOZTARSASAG.**

53. 13. 150 on 15 f. violet 10 10

NEWSPAPER STAMP

1919. No. N 136 surch. **BARANYA** and value.

N 54. N 3. 10 on 2 (f.) orange 8 8

EXPRESS LETTER STAMP

1919. No. E 245 optd. **1919 Baranya.**

E 37. E 1. 105 on 2 f. olive and red 12 12

1919. No. E 245 surch. **BARANYA** and value

E 55. E 1. 10 on 2 f. olive and red 8 8

SAVINGS BANK STAMP

1919. No. B 199 surch. **BARANYA** and value.

B 56. B 1. 10 on 10 f. purple 8 8

POSTAGE DUE STAMPS

1919. Nos. D 191 etc. optd. **BARANYA** or surch. also.

D 38. D 1. 2 f. red 60 60
D 39. 10 f. red and green 12 12
D 40. 20 f. red and green 12 12
D 41. 40 on 2 f. red and green 12 12

TEMESVAR

Temesvar was later occupied by Rumania which issued stamps for this area. It was then incorporated in Rumania and renamed Timosoara.

100 filler = 1 korona.

1919. Stamps of Hungary surch.

(a) War Charity stamp of 1916.

1. 6. 45 f. on 10 f. (+2 f.) red 5 5

(b) Harvesters Type.

2. 11. 10 f. on 2 f. brown 30 30
3. 30 f. on 2 f. brown 5 5
4. 1 k. 50 on 15 f. violet 10 10

(c) Karl stamp.

5. 13. 50 f. on 20 f. brown 5 5

POSTAGE DUE STAMPS

1919. No. D 191 surch.

D 6. D 1. 40 f. on 2 f. red & green 10 10
D 7. 60 f. on 2 f. red & green 10 10
D 8. 100 f. on 2 f. red & green 10 10

HAVE YOU READ THE NOTES AT THE BEGINNING OF THIS CATALOGUE?

These often provide answers to the enquiries we receive.

SEYCHELLES BC

A group of islands in the Indian Ocean, E. of Africa.

100 cents = 1 rupee.

1. 2.

1890.

No.	Description	Unused	Used
9. 1.	2 c. green and red	50	35
28.	2 c. brown and green	25	65
22.	3 c. purple and orange	20	30
10.	4 c. red and green	55	55
29.	6 c. red	65	90
11.	8 c. purple and blue	90	1·10
12.	10 c. blue and brown	1·10	1·00
23.	12 c. brown and green	50	80
13.	13 c. grey and black	1·10	1·00
24.	15 c. olive and lilac	1·10	1·10
30.	15 c. blue	2·00	1·75
6.	16 c. brown and blue	1·60	1·60
31.	18 c. blue	1·10	1·90
32.	36 c. brown and red	6·00	5·50
25.	45 c. brown and red	6·50	7·00
7.	48 c. yellow-brown & grn.	6·00	6·50
33.	75 c. yellow and violet	9·50	11·00
8.	96 c. mauve and red	9·50	11·00
34.	1 r. mauve and red	5·50	4·50
35.	1 r. 50 grey and red	14·00	16·00
36.	2 r. 25 mauve and green	14·00	16·00

1893. Surch. in figures and words in two lines.

No.	Description	Unused	Used
15. 1.	3 c. on 4 c. red and green	35	65
16.	12 c. on 16 c. brn. & blue	90	1·00
19.	15 c. on 16 c. brn. & blue	2·25	1·10
20.	45 c. on 48 c. brn. & grn.	3·00	2·25
21.	90 c. on 96 c. mauve & red	8·50	9·50

1896. Surch. in figures and words in one line.

No.	Description	Unused	Used
26. 1.	18 c. on 45 c. brown & red	2·00	2·00
27.	36 c. on 45 c. brown & red	4·00	6·00

1901. Surch. in figures and words.

No.	Description	Unused	Used
41. 1.	2 c. on 4 c. red and green	1·10	2·25
37.	3 c. on 10 c. blue & brown	55	1·10
38.	3 c. on 16 c. brown & blue	55	1·25
39.	3 c. on 36 c. brown and red	55	1·10
40.	6 c. on 8 c. purple and blue	55	1·10
42.	30 c. on 75 c. yellow & vio.	2·25	5·00
43.	30 c. on 1 r. mauve and red	2·25	5·00
44.	45 c. on 1 r. mauve and red	3·25	6·50
45.	45 c. on 2 r. mve. & green	5·00	7·00

1903.

No.	Description	Unused	Used
46. 2.	2 c. brown and green	15	30
61.	3 c. green	30	25
62.	6 c. red	25	12
49.	12 c. brown and green	75	30
64.	15 c. blue	50	1·40
65.	18 c. olive and red	1·00	1·75
66.	30 c. violet and green	2·50	2·50
67.	45 c. brown and red	2·00	3·25
54.	75 c. yellow and violet	3·25	4·50
69.	1 r. 50 black and red	6·50	7·00
56.	2 r. 25 purple and green	7·00	8·50

1903. Surch. **3 cents.**

No.	Description	Unused	Used
57. 2.	3 c. on 15 c. blue	1·10	1·60
58.	3 c. on 18 c. olive and red	3·00	3·50
59.	3 c. on 45 c. brown and red	95	2·50

3.

4.

1912. Inscr. "POSTAGE POSTAGE."

No.	Description	Unused	Used
71. 3.	2 c. brown and green	12	40
72.	3 c. green	15	10
73a.	6 c. red	90	8
74.	12 c. brown and green	55	1·60
75.	15 c. blue	75	50
76.	18 c. olive and red	45	2·00
77.	30 c. violet and green	2·25	65
78.	45 c. brown and red	1·00	2·40
79.	75 c. yellow and violet	3·25	2·00
80.	1 r. 50 black and red	1·90	1·00
81a.	2 r. 25 purple and green	9·50	4·50

1917. Inscr. "POSTAGE & REVENUE".

No.	Description	Unused	Used
98. 4.	2 c. brown and green	10	12
83.	3 c. green	8	8
100.	3 c. black	12	20
101.	4 c. green	12	20
102.	4 c. olive and red	1·00	2·75
84.	5 c. brown	8	30
85.	6 c. red	12	8
105.	6 c. mauve	8	8
106.	9 c. red	45	1·00
107.	12 c. grey	50	25
108.	12 c. red	15	10
87.	15 c. blue	12	1·00
111.	15 c. yellow	45	1·90
112. 4.	18 c. purple on yellow	1·00	2·50
113.	20 c. blue	75	1·00
114.	25 c. black & red on yellow	90	2·00
115.	30 c. purple and olive	75	2·00
116.	45 c. purple and orange	75	2·00
117.	50 c. purple and black	95	2·00
93.	75 c. black on green	1·60	2·50
119.	1 r. purple and red	4·50	5·50
121.	1 r. 50 pur. & blue on blue	4·50	6·50
122.	2 r. 25 green and violet	5·50	7·50
123.	5 r. green and blue	13·00	14·00

1935. Silver Jubilee. As T **11** of Antigua.

No.	Description	Unused	Used
128. 4.	6 c. blue and black	8	15
129.	12 c. green and blue	20	30
130.	20 c. brown and blue	25	45
131.	1 r. grey and purple	85	1·90

1937. Coronation. As T **2** of Aden.

No.	Description	Unused	Used
132.	6 c. olive	8	8
133.	12 c. orange	8	10
134.	20 c. blue	20	20

5. Coco-de-mer Palm.

DESIGNS—VERT. 3, 12, 15, 30, 75 c., 2 r. 25, Giant Tortoise. HORIZ. 6, 20, 45 c., 1 r., 5 r. Fishing Pirogue.

1938.

No.	Description	Unused	Used
135. 5.	2 c. brown	8	8
136. –	3 c. green	50	25
136a. –	3 c orange	15	12
137. –	6 c. orange	50	25
137b. –	6 c. green	8	8
138. 5.	9 c. red	75	1·00
138a.	9 c. blue	10	10
139. –	12 c. mauve	2·50	90
139b. –	15 c. red	20	15
139c. 5.	18 c. claret	10	8
140. –	20 c. blue	2·40	90
140a. –	20 c. yellow	8	10
141. 5.	25 c. brown	6·50	3·25
142. –	30 c. red	3·50	3·00
142a. –	30 c. blue	10	10
143. –	45 c. chocolate	10	12
144. 5.	50 c. slate-violet	12	12
144a.	50 c. bright violet	12	12
145. –	75 c. blue	11·00	11·00
145a. –	75 c. mauve	20	20
146. –	1 r. green	15·00	13·00
146a. –	1 r. black	25	15
147. 5.	1 r. 50 blue	50	55
148. –	2 r. 25 olive	55	60
149. –	5 r. red	2·00	2·00

1946. Victory. As T **4** of Aden.

No.	Description	Unused	Used
150.	9 c. blue	8	8
151.	30 c. blue	10	8

1948. Silver Wedding. As T **5/6** of Aden.

No.	Description	Unused	Used
152.	9 c. blue	8	30
153.	5 r. red	3·25	4·00

1949. U.P.U. As T **14/7** of Antigua.

No.	Description	Unused	Used
154.	18 c. magenta	5	8
155.	50 c. purple	20	20
156.	1 r. grey	20	30
157.	2 r. 25 olive	80	80

6. Sail-fish.

7.

1952. Full-face portrait.

No.	Description	Unused	Used
158. 6.	2 c. lilac	8	10
159. –	3 c. orange	8	10
160. –	9 c. blue	8	10
161. –	15 c. green	8	10
162. –	18 c. lake	8	10
163. –	20 c. yellow	8	10
164. –	25 c. red	10	10
165. 6.	40 c. blue	12	15
166. –	45 c. brown	12	15
167. –	50 c. violet	12	12
168. –	1 r. black	25	30
169. –	1 r. 50 blue	65	90
170. –	2 r. 25 olive	95	1·25
171. –	5 r. red	2·50	3·00
172. 6.	10 r. green	4·50	5·50

DESIGNS—VERT. 2 c., 25 c., 2 r. 25, Giant tortoise. 9 c., 50 c., 1 r. 50, Coco-de-Mer palm. HORIZ. 15 c., 20 c., 45 c. Fishing pirogue. 18 c., 1 r., 5 r. Map of Indian Ocean.

1953. Coronation. As T **7** of Aden.

No.	Description	Unused	Used
173.	9 c. black and blue	20	35

1954. Designs as 1952 but with portrait of Queen Elizabeth II.

No.	Description	Unused	Used
174.	2 c. lilac	12	12
175.	3 c. orange	15	15
175a.	5 c. violet	15	15
176.	9 c. blue	15	15
176a.	10 c. blue (as 9 c.)	15	15
177.	15 c. green	10	10
178.	18 c. lake	25	30
179.	20 c. yellow	12	15
180.	25 c. red	15	20
180a.	35 c. lake (as 18 c.)	20	25
181.	40 c. blue	30	35
182.	45 c. brown	35	35
183.	50 c. violet	35	40
183a.	70 c. brown (as 45 c.)	35	40
184.	1 r. black	45	60
185.	1 r. 50 blue	70	1·50
186.	2 r. 25 olive	1·50	2·00
187.	5 r. red	3·00	4·00
188.	10 r. green	5·50	7·00

NEW DESIGN: 5 c. "Flying Fox" (fruit bat).

1956. La Pierre de Possession. 200th Anniv.

No.	Description	Unused	Used
189. 7.	40 c. blue	25	25
190.	1 r. black	50	55

1957. No. 182 surch. **5 cents** and bars.

No.	Description	Unused	Used
191.	5 c. on 45 c. brown	30	35

8. Mauritius 6d. Stamp with Seychelles "B 64" Cancellation.

1961. First Seychelles Post Office. Cent.

No.	Description	Unused	Used
193. 8.	10 c. blue, black & purple	12	12
194.	35 c. blue, black & green	20	25
195.	2 r. 25 blue, blk. & chest.	85	95

9. Black Parrot.

10. Colony's Badge.

1962. Multicoloured.

No.	Description	Unused	Used
233.	5 c. T **9**	5	8
197.	10 c. Vanilla Vine	5	5
198.	15 c. Fisherman	5	5
199.	20 c. Denis Is. Lighthouse	5	5
200.	25 c. Clock Tower, Victoria	8	8
200a.	30 c. Anse Royal Bay	10	10
201.	35 c. Anse Royal Bay	40	40
202.	40 c. Government House	15	15
203.	45 c. Fishing Pirogue	20	20
204.	50 c. Cascade Church	20	20
236.	60 c. red, blue and brown (Flying Fox)	20	35
205.	70 c. Sail-fish	80	80
206.	75 c. Coco-de-mer Palm	25	25
237.	85 c. ultramarine and blue (Sail-fish)	30	60
207.	1 r. Cinnamon	30	30
208.	1 r. 50 Copra	60	1·00
209.	2 r. 25 Map	1·00	1·50
210.	3 r. 50 Land Settlement	1·50	2·50
211.	5 r. Regina Mundi Convent	1·75	2·50
212.	10 r. T **10**	4·50	6·00

DESIGNS: A T **9**. The 30 c., 35 c., 40 c., 85 c., 1 r., 1 r. 50, 2 r. 25, 3 r. 50 and 5 r. are horiz. No. 236 is 23 × 25 mm.

1963. Freedom from Hunger. As T **10** of Aden.

No.	Description	Unused	Used
213.	70 c. violet	40	40

1963. Red Cross Cent. As T **24** of Antigua.

No.	Description	Unused	Used
214.	10 c. red and black	10	10
215.	75 c. red and blue	45	45

1965. Surch.

No.	Description	Unused	Used
216.	45 c. on 35 c. (No. 201)	15	15
217.	75 c. on 70 c. (No. 205)	25	25

1965. I.T.U. Cent. As T **26** of Antigua.

No.	Description	Unused	Used
218.	5 c. orange and blue	8	8
219.	1 r. 50 mauve and green	60	65

1965. I.C.Y. As T **27** of Antigua.

No.	Description	Unused	Used
220.	5 c. purple and turquoise	5	5
221.	40 c. green and lavender	25	30

1966. Churchill Commem. As T **28** of Antigua.

No.	Description	Unused	Used
222.	5 c. blue	5	5
223.	15 c. green	8	8
224.	75 c. brown	35	40
225.	1 r. 50 violet	65	70

1966. World Cup Football Championships. As T **30** of Antigua.

No.	Description	Unused	Used
226.	15 c. vio., grn., lake & brn.	10	10
227.	1 r. choc., turq., lake & brn.	30	35

1966. W.H.O. Headquarters, Geneva. Inaug. As T **31** of Antigua.

No.	Description	Unused	Used
228.	20 c. black, green and blue	8	8
229.	50 c. black, purple & ochre	30	30

1966. U.N.E.S.C.O. 20th Anniv. As T **33/5** of Antigua.

No.	Description	Unused	Used
230.	15 c. violet, red, yellow and orange	8	8
231.	1 r. yellow, violet and olive	30	40
232.	5 r. black, purple and orge.	1·60	1·75

1967. Universal Adult Suffrage. Nos. 198, 203, 206 and 210 optd. **UNIVERSAL ADULT SUFFRAGE 1967.**

No.	Description	Unused	Used
238.	15 c. multicoloured	5	5
239.	45 c. multicoloured	12	15
240.	75 c. multicoloured	25	25
241.	3 r. 50 multicoloured	80	85

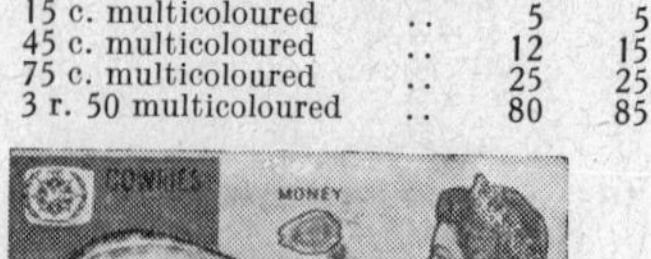

11. Cowrie Shells.

1967. Int. Tourist Year. Multicoloured.

No.	Description	Unused	Used
242.	15 c. Type **11**	5	5
243.	40 c. Cone Shells	12	15
244.	1 r. Arthritic Spider Conch	30	30
245.	2 r. 25 "Subulate auger" and Triton Shells	55	60

1968. Nos. 202/3 and 206 surch.

No.	Description	Unused	Used
246.	30 c. on 40 c. multicoloured	8	10
247.	60 c. on 45 c. multicoloured	15	20
248.	85 c. on 75 c. multicoloured	25	30

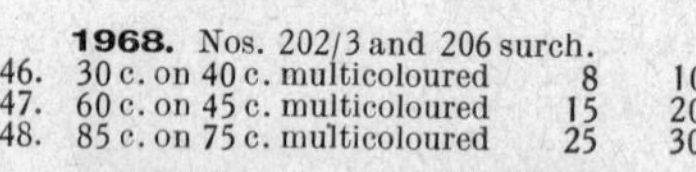

12. Farmer with Wife and Children at Sunset.

1968. Human Rights Year.

No.	Description	Unused	Used
249. 12.	20 c. multicoloured	5	8
250.	50 c. multicoloured	15	20
251.	85 c. multicoloured	25	25
252.	2 r. 25 multicoloured	50	55

13. Expedition landing at Anse Possession.

1968. First Landing on Praslin. Bicent. Multicoloured.

No.	Description	Unused	Used
253.	20 c. Type **13**	8	8
254.	50 c. Vessels at Anchor	15	20
255.	85 c. Coco-de-mer and Black Parrot	25	30
256.	2 r. 25 Vessels under Sail	65	80

14. Apollo Launching.

1969. 1st Man on the Moon. Multicoloured.
257. 5 c. Type **14** 5 5
258. 20 c. Module leaving mother-ship for the moon .. 8 8
259. 50 c. Astronauts and Space Module on the moon .. 12 15
260. 85 c. Tracking Station .. 20 25
261. 2 r. 25 Moon craters with Earth on the "Horizon" 50 55

15. Picault's Landing, 1742.

1969. Multicoloured.
262. 5 c. Type **15** 5 5
263. 10 c. U.S. Satellite-tracking Station 8 10
264. 15 c. "Konigsberg I" at Aldabra, 1914 .. .. 8 10
265. 20 c. Fleet re-fuelling off St. Anne, 1939-45 .. 8 10
266. 25 c. Exiled Ashanti king, Prempeh 8 10
267. 30 c. Laying Stone of Possession, 1756 .. .. 10 10
268. 40 c. As 30 c. 8 10
269. 50 c. Pirates and treasure 10 12
270. 60 c. Corsairs attacking merchantman 30 40
271. 65 c. As 60 c. 10 12
272. 85 c. Impressions of proposed airport 40 60
273. 95 c. As 85 c. 20 25
274. 1 r. French Governor capitulating to British naval officer, 1794 .. .. 20 25
275. 1 r. 50 "Sybille" and "Chiffone" in battle, 1801 .. .. 30 35
276. 3 r. 50 Visit of the Duke of Edinburgh, 1956 .. 50 55
277. 5 r. Chevalier Queau de Quincy 65 70
278. 10 r. Indian Ocean chart, 1574 .. .. .. 1·25 1·40
279. 15 r. Badge of Seychelles .. 1·90 2·25

NOTE: The design of No. 264 incorrectly shows the vessel "Konigsberg II" and date 1915".

16. Sea-gulls, Ship and Island.

1970. 1st Settlement, St. Anne Island. Bicent. Multicoloured.
280. 20 c. Type **16** 10 10
281. 50 c. Flying Fish, ship and island 15 20
282. 85 c. Compass and chart .. 25 30
283. 3 r. 50 Anchor on sea-bed .. 75 80

17. Girl and Optician's Chart.

1970. British Red Cross. Cent. Multicoloured.
284. 20 c. Type **17** 8 8
285. 50 c. Baby, scales and milk bottles 15 20
286. 85 c. Woman with child and umbrella (vert.) .. 25 25
287. 3 r. 50 Red Cross local headquarters building .. 70 75

18. Pitcher Plant. **19.** Piper "Navajo".

1970. Flowers. Multicoloured.
288. 20 c. Type **18** 8 8
289. 50 c. Wild Vanilla .. 15 20
290. 85 c. Tropic-Bird Orchid .. 25 25
291. 3 r. 50 Vare Hibiscus .. 1·00 1·00

1971. Airport Completion. Multicoloured.
294. 5 c. Type **19** 8 8
295. 20 c. Westland "Wessex" 8 8
296. 50 c. "Catalina" Amphibian (horiz.) 15 20
297. 60 c. Grumman "Albatross" 20 20
298. 85 c. Short "G" Class Flying-boat (horiz.) .. 25 25
299. 3 r. 50 Vickers Supermarine "Walrus" (horiz.) .. 90 90

20. Santa Claus delivering Gifts (Jean-Claude Waye Hive).

1971. Christmas. Multicoloured.
300. 10 c. Type **20** 5 5
301. 15 c. Santa Claus seated on turtle (Edison Theresine) 8 8
302. 3 r. 50 Santa Claus landing on island (Isabelle Tirant) 75 85

1971. Nos. 267, 270 and 272 surch.
303. 40 c. on 30 c. multicoloured 12 12
304. 65 c. on 60 c. multicoloured 20 20
305. 95 c. on 85 c. multicoloured 25 30

1972. Royal Visit. Nos. 265 and 277 optd. **ROYAL VISIT, 1972.**
306. 20 c. multicoloured .. 8 8
307. 5 r. multicoloured .. .. 1·00 1·10

21. Brush Warbler.

1972. Rare Seychelles Birds. Multicoloured.
308. 5 c. Type **21** 5 5
309. 20 c. Scops Owl 8 8
310. 50 c. Blue Pigeon 12 15
311. 65 c. Magpie Robin .. 20 20
312. 95 c. Paradise Flycatcher 25 30
313. 3 r. 50 Kestrel 75 90

22. Fireworks Display.

1972. "Festival '72". Multicoloured.
315. 10 c. Type **22** 5 5
316. 15 c. Pirogue race (horiz.) 5 8
317. 25 c. Floats and costumes 8 10
318. 5 r. Water skiing (horiz.) .. 1·25 1·40

1972. Royal Silver Wedding. As T **19** of Ascension, but with Giant Tortoise and Sailfish in background.
319. 95 c. blue 25 30
320. 1 r. 50 brown 35 45

1973. Royal Wedding. As T **26** of Anguilla. Multicoloured. Background colours given.
321. 95 c. brown 25 25
322. 1 r. 50 blue 30 30

23. Soldier Fish.

1974. Fishes. Multicoloured.
323. 20 c. Type **23** 8 8
324. 50 c. File Fish 15 15
325. 95 c. Butterfly Fish .. 25 30
326. 1 r. 50 Gaterin 35 40

24. Globe and Letter.

1974. U.P.U. Centenary. Multicoloured.
327. 20 c. Type **24** 5 5
328. 50 c. Globe and radio beacon 12 15
329. 95 c. Globe and postmark 20 25
330. 1 r. 50 Emblems within "UPU" 35 40

25. Sir Winston Churchill.

1974. Sir Winston Churchill. Birth Cent. Multicoloured.
331. 95 c. Type **25** 25 25
332. 1 r. 50 Profile portrait .. 35 40

1975. Visit of Liner "Queen Elizabeth II". Nos. 265, 269, 273 and 275 optd. **VISIT OF Q.E. II.**
334. 20 c. multicoloured .. 5 5
335. 50 c. multicoloured .. 15 15
336. 95 c. multicoloured .. 25 25
337. 1 r. 50 multicoloured .. 35 35

1975. Internal Self-Government. Nos. 265, 271, 274 and 276 optd. **INTERNAL SELF-GOVERNMENT OCTOBER 1975.**
338. 20 c. multicoloured .. 5 5
339. 65 c. multicoloured .. 12 15
340. 1 r. multicoloured .. 15 20
341. 3 r. 50 multicoloured .. 55 65

26. Queen Elizabeth I.

1975. International Women's Year. Mult.
342. 10 c. Type **26** 5 5
343. 15 c. Gladys Aylward .. 5 5
344. 20 c. Elizabeth Fry .. 5 5
345. 25 c. Emmeline Pankhurst 5 5
346. 65 c. Florence Nightingale 10 12
347. 1 r. Amy Johnson 15 20
348. 1 r. 50 Joan of Arc 30 35
349. 3 r. 50 Eleanor Roosevelt 55 65

27. Map of Praslin and Postmark.

1976. Seychelles Rural Posts. Multicoloured.
350. 20 c. Type **27** 5 5
351. 65 c. La Digue 12 15
352. 1 r. Mahe with Victoria postmark 15 20
353. 1 r. 50 Mahe Anse Royale postmark 25 30

Nos. 350/53 show maps and postmarks.

28. First Landing, 1609.

1976. Independence. Multicoloured.
355. 20 c. Type **28** 5 5
356. 25 c. The possession Stone 5 5
357. 40 c. First settlers, 1770 .. 8 8
358. 75 c. Chevalier Queau de Quincy 12 12
359. 1 r. Sir Bickham Sweet-Escott 15 20
360. 1 r. 25 Legislative Building 20 25
361. 1 r. 50 Seychelles badge .. 25 30
362. 3 r. 50 Seychelles flag .. 55 65

29. Flags of Seychelles and U.S.A.

1976. Seychelles Independence and American Independence. Bicent. Multicoloured.
363. 1 r. Type **29** 15 20
364. 10 r. Statehouses of Seychelles and Philadelphia 1·50 1·75

30. Swimming.

1976. Olympic Games, Montreal.
365. **30.** 20 c. blue, light blue and brown 5 5
366. – 65 c. dark green, green and grey 10 12
367. – 1 r. brown, blue & grey 15 20
368. – 3 r. 50 light red, red and grey 55 65

DESIGNS: 65 c. Hockey. 1 r. Basketball. 3 r. 50 Football.

31. Seychelles Paradise Flycatcher.

1976. 4th Pan-African Ornithological Congress, Seychelles. Multicoloured.

369. 20 c. Type **31** 5 5
370. 1 r. 25 Seychelles Sunbird (horiz.) 20 25
371. 1 r. 50 Seychelles White-eye (horiz.) 25 30
372. 5 r. Seychelles Black Parrot 75 80

POSTAGE DUE STAMPS

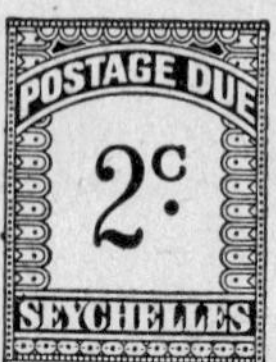

D 1.

1951. Value in red.

D 1. D 1. 2 c. red 15 20
D 2. 3 c. green 15 20
D 3. 6 c. yellow 5 5
D 4. 9 c. orange 5 5
D 5. 15 c. violet 5 5
D 6. 18 c. blue 5 5
D 7. 20 c. brown 5 8
D 8. 30 c. claret 8 10

SHANGHAI O1

A seaport on the E coast of China, which for a time had a separate postal system.

1865. 16 cash = 1 candareen.
100 candareens = 1 tael.
1890. 100 cents = 1 dollar (Chinese).

1.

1865. Value in candareens. Imperf.

28. 1. 1 cand. blue .. .. 12·00
1. 2 cand. black .. .. 20·00 50·00
31. 3 cand. brown .. .. 9·00
3. 4 cand. yellow .. .. 15·00 50·00
20. 6 cand. red .. .. 15·00
18. 6 cand. brown .. .. 12·00
4. 8 cand. green .. .. 20·00
21. 12 cand. brown .. .. 12·00
22. 16 cand. red .. .. 12·00

2. 3.

1866. Value in cents. Perf.

32. 2. 2 c. red .. .. .. 1·00 1·00
33. 4 c. lilac .. .. .. 2·25 2·50
34. 8 c. blue .. .. .. 2·75 3·00
35. 16 c. green .. .. .. 5·50 6·00

1867. Value in candareens.

37. 3. 1 cand. brown 60 70
62. 1 cand. yellow 60 85
38. 3 cand. yellow .. .. 2·25 2·50
60. 3 cand. red .. .. 3·00 3·00
39. 6 cand. grey .. .. 2·50 4·75
64. 6 cand. green .. .. 12·00
65. 9 cand. grey .. .. 12·00
40. 12 cand. brown .. .. 6·00 8·00

1873. Surch. with value in English and Chinese.

41. 2. 1 cand. on 2 c. red .. 3·25 2·25
44a. 1 cand. on 4 c. lilac .. 3·00 1·90
46. 1 cand. on 8 c. blue .. 4·00 3·25
48. 1 cand. on 16 c. green .. £200 £150
50. 3 cand. on 2 c. red .. 12·00 10·00
52. 3 cand. on 16 c. green .. £300 £300

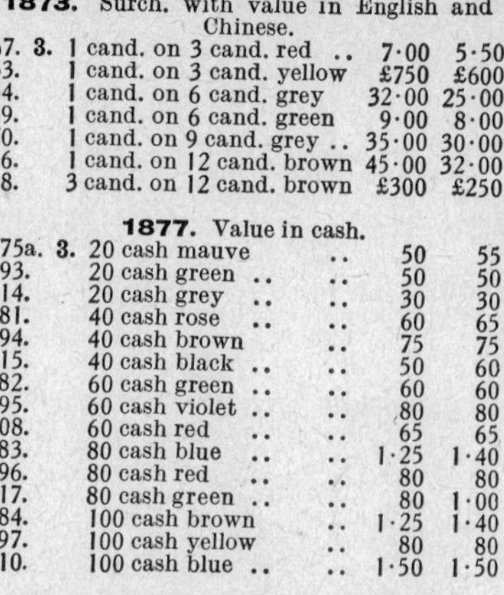

1873. Surch. with value in English and Chinese.

67. 3. 1 cand. on 3 cand. red .. 7·00 5·50
53. 1 cand. on 3 cand. yellow £750 £600
54. 1 cand. on 6 cand. grey 32·00 25·00
69. 1 cand. on 6 cand. green 9·00 8·00
70. 1 cand. on 9 cand. grey .. 35·00 30·00
56. 1 cand. on 12 cand. brown 45·00 32·00
58. 3 cand. on 12 cand. brown £300 £250

1877. Value in cash.

75a. 3. 20 cash mauve .. 50 55
93. 20 cash green 50 50
114. 20 cash grey 30 30
81. 40 cash rose 60 65
94. 40 cash brown .. 75 75
115. 40 cash black 50 60
82. 60 cash green 60 60
95. 60 cash violet 80 80
108. 60 cash red 65 65
83. 80 cash blue .. .. 1·25 1·40
96. 80 cash red 80 80
117. 80 cash green .. .. 80 1·00
84. 100 cash brown .. 1·25 1·40
97. 100 cash yellow .. 80 80
110. 100 cash blue .. 1·50 1·50

1879. Surch. in English and Chinese.

89. 3. 20 cash on 40 cash rose .. 1·25 1·40
103. 20 cash on 40 cash brown 2·00 2·00
105. 20 cash on 80 cash red .. 70 70
111. 20 cash on 80 cash green 1·00 1·00
112. 20 cash on 100 cash blue 1·00 1·00
100. 40 cash on 80 cash red .. 60 75
101. 40 cash on 100 cash yellow 80 80
90. 60 cash on 80 cash blue.. 2·00 3·00
91. 60 cash on 100 cash brown 2·50 3·00
102. 60 cash on 100 cash yellow 90 1·00

1886. Surch. **20 CASH** in English and Chinese in double-lined frame.

104. 3. 20 cash on 40 cash brown 2·00 2·00

1889. Surch. **100 CASH** over **20 CASH** in English and Chinese in double-lined frame.

113. 3. 100 cash on 20 cash on 100 cash yellow .. 5·50 5·50

4. 5. 6.

1890. Value in cents.

119. 4. 2 c. brown 20 20
142. 2 c. green 20 20
143. 5 c. red 35 35
122. 10 c. black 60 60
144. 10 c. orange 60 60
121. 15 c. blue 90 90
145. 15 c. mauve .. .. 1·00 1·00
124. 20 c. mauve 75 75
146. 20 c. brown .. .. 1·10 1·10

1892. Surch. **2 Cts.** and in Chinese.

141. 4. 2 c. on 5 c. red .. .. 6·00 5·00

1893. Surch. in words in English and Chinese.

147. 4. ½ c. on 15 c. mauve .. 90 90
148. 1 c. on 20 c. brown .. 1·00 1·00

1893. Surch. ½ **Ct.** or **1 Ct.**

152. 4. ½ c. on half of 5 c. red .. 90 60
155. 1 c. on half of 2 c. brown 15 15
156. 1 c. on half of 2 c. green 2·25 2·25

1893. Inscriptions in outer frame in black.

165. 5. ½ c. orange 8 8
166. 1 c. brown 8 8
187. 2 c. red 8 8
188. 4 c. orange on yellow .. 8 8
161. 5 c. blue 8 8
189. 6 c. red on rose 25 25
167. 10 c. green 8 8
163. 15 c. yellow 12 12
168. 20 c. mauve 12 12

1893. Jubilee of First Settlement.

176. 6. 2 c. red and black .. 15 15

1893. Optd. **1843. Jubilee 1893.** Inscriptions in outer frame in black.

177. 5. ½ c. orange 10 10
178. 1 c. brown 12 12
179. 2 c. red 15 15
180. 5 c. blue 50 60
181. 10 c. green 70 70
182. 15 c. yellow 90 90
183. 20 c. mauve .. .. 1·10 1·10

1896. Surch. in English and Chinese.

184. 5. 4 c. on 15 c. yellow .. 1·10 1·10
185. 6 c. on 20 c. mauve .. 1·10 1·10

POSTAGE DUE STAMPS

1892. Optd. **Postage Due.**

D 134. 2 c. brown 10 15
D 135. 5 c. red 40 50
D 130. 10 c. black .. .. 1·25 1·25
D 138. 10 c. orange 40 45
D 131. 15 c. blue 90 90
D 139. 15 c. mauve .. .. 1·10 1·10
D 132. 20 c. mauve 60 60
D 140. 20 c. brown .. .. 1·10 1·10

D 1.

ILLUSTRATIONS British Commonwealth and all overprints and surcharges are FULL SIZE. Foreign Countries have been reduced to ¾-LINEAR.

1893. Inscriptions in outer frame in black.

D 169. D 1. ½ c. orange .. 5 5
D 170. 1 c. brown .. 5 5
D 171. 2 c. red 5 8
D 172. 5 c. blue 8 8
D 173. 10 c. green 8 8
D 174. 15 c. yellow .. 8 10
D 175. 20 c. mauve .. 8 10

SHARJAH O4

Part of the Trucial States on the Persian Gulf. Embodies the principalities of Diba, Khor Fakkan and Kalba.

On 2nd December, 1971, Sharjah, together with six other Gulf Shaikdoms, formed the United Arab Emirates.

100 naye paise = 1 rupee.
1966. 100 dirhams = 1 riyal.

IMPERF STAMPS. Some sets exist also imperf. in limited quantities.

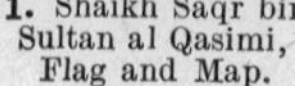

1. Shaikh Saqr bin Sultan al Qasimi, Flag and Map.
2. Mosquito and W.H.O. Emblem.

1963. Multicoloured.

1. 1. 1 n.p. (postage) 5 5
2. 2 n.p. 5 5
3. 3 n.p. 5 5
4. 4 n.p. 5 5
5. 5 n.p. 5 5
6. 6 n.p. 5 5
7. 8 n.p. 5 5
8. 10 n.p. 5 5
9. 16 n.p. 5 5
10. 20 n.p. 8 8
11. 30 n.p. 10 10
12. 40 n.p. 12 12
13. 50 n.p. 15 15
14. 75 n.p. 30 30
15. 100 n.p. 40 40
16. 1 r. (air) 30 30
17. 2 r... .. .. .. 60 60
18. 3 r... .. .. .. 85 85
19. 4 r... .. .. .. 1·10 1·10
20. 5 r... .. .. .. 1·75 1·75
21. 10 r. .. .. .. 3·25 3·25

The air stamps are as T1 but additionally inscr. "AIR MAIL" in English and Arabic, and with a hawk in flight.

1963. Malaria Eradication.

22. 2. 1 n.p. turquoise 5 5
23. 2 n.p. blue 5 5
24. 3 n.p. violet 5 5
25. 4 n.p. green 5 5
26. 90 n.p. brown .. .. 1·00 1·00

3. "Red Crescent".

1963. Red Cross Centenary.

27. 3. 1 n.p. red and purple .. 5 5
28. 2 n.p. red and turquoise.. 5 5
29. 3 n.p. red and blue .. 5 5
30. 4 n.p. red and deep green 5 5
31. 5 n.p. red and sepia .. 5 5
32. 85 n.p. red and green .. 30 30

4. Campaign Emblem between Hands.

1963. Freedom from Hunger.

33. 4. 1 n.p. green 5 5
34. 2 n.p. brown 5 5
35. 3 n.p. olive 5 5
36. 4 n.p. blue 5 5
37. 90 n.p. red 30 30

1963. Surch.

38. 4. 10 n.p. on 1 n.p. green .. 5 5
39. 20 n.p. on 2 n.p. brown .. 12 12
40. 30 n.p. on 3 n.p. olive .. 20 20
41. 40 n.p. on 4 n.p. blue .. 30 30
42. 75 n.p. on 90 n.p. red .. 60 60
43. 80 n.p. on 90 n.p. red .. 60 60
44. 2. 1 r. on 90 n.p. brown .. 85 85

1964. Air. Pres. Kennedy Memorial Issue (1st issue). Nos. 16/21 optd. **In Memoriam John F. Kennedy 1917-1963** in English and Arabic, and emblems.

45. 1. 1 r... .. .. .. 1·25 1·25
46. 2 r... .. .. .. 2·50 2·50
47. 3 r... .. .. .. 5·00 5·00
48. 4 r... .. .. .. 6·00 6·00
49. 5 r... .. .. .. 7·00 7·00
50. 10 r. .. .. .. 8·00 8·00

See also Nos. 98/100.

5. Orbiting Astronomical Observatory.

1964. Scientific Space Research.

51. 1 n.p. blue (Type **5**) .. 5 5
52. 2 n.p. olive-green & chestnut 5 5
53. 3 n.p. turquoise and black.. 5 5
54. 4 n.p. black and bistre .. 5 5
55. 5 n.p. bistre and violet .. 5 5
56. 35 n.p. violet and turquoise 40 40
57. 50 n.p. brown & olive-green 55 55

DESIGNS: 2 n.p. "Nimbus" weather satellite. 3 n.p. "Pioneer V" space probe. 4 n.p. "Explorer XIII" satellite. 5 n.p. "Explorer XII" satellite. 35 n.p. Project "Relay" satellite. 50 n.p. Orbiting solar observatory.

6. Running.

1964. Olympic Games, Tokyo (1st issue).

58. 1 n.p. blue, blue-green and yellow (Type **6**) 5 5
59. 2 n.p. red and turquoise .. 5 5
60. 3 n.p. brown & yellow-green 5 5
61. 4 n.p. blue-green & cinnamon 5 5
62. 20 n.p. blue & orange-brown 12 12
63. 30 n.p. bistre and pink .. 15 15
64. 40 n.p. violet and yellow .. 30 30
65. 1 r. chocolate & violet-blue 75 75

DESIGNS: 2 n.p. Throwing the discus. 3 n.p. Hurdling. 4 n.p. Putting the shot. 20 n.p. High-jumping. 30 n.p. Weightlifting. 40 n.p. Throwing the javelin. 1 r. High-diving.

7. Flame and World Map.

1964. Air. Human Rights Day.

66. **7.** 50 n.p. brown 20 10
67. 1 r. violet 35 35
68. 150 n.p. green 50 50

8. Girl Scouts Marching.

1964. Sharjah Girl Scouts.

69. **8.** 1 n.p. grey-green.. .. 5 5
70. 2 n.p. green 5 5
71. 3 n.p. blue 5 5
72. 4 n.p. violet 5 5
73. 5 n.p. cerise 5 5
74. 2 r. brown .. .. 1·00 1·00

9. Khor Fakkan.

1964. Air. Multicoloured.

75. 10 n.p. Type **9** 5 5
76. 20 n.p. Bedouin camp, Beni Qatab 5 5
77. 30 n.p. Dhaid oasis .. 8 8
78. 40 n.p. Kalba Castle .. 12 12
79. 75 n.p. Street and Wind tower, Sharjah .. 20 20
80. 100 n.p. Fortress .. 30 30

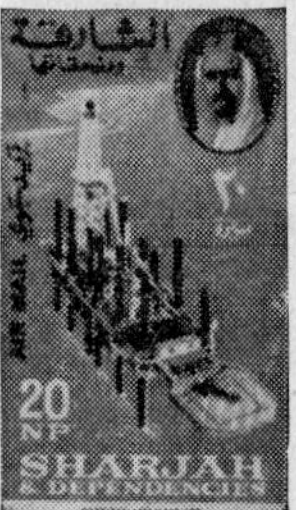

10. Oil-drilling Platform in Sea.

11. Scout at Attention.

1964. Air. New York World's Fair. Multicoloured.

81. 20 n.p. Type **10** .. 8 8
82. 40 n.p. Unisphere .. 15 15
83. 1 r. New York skyline ($85\frac{1}{2} \times 44\frac{1}{2}$ mm.) .. 40 40

1964. Sharjah Boy Scouts.

84. **11.** 1 n.p. grey-olive .. 5 5
85. – 2 n.p. green 5 5
86. – 3 n.p. blue 5 5
87. **11.** 4 n.p. violet 5 5
88. – 5 n.p. magenta 5 5
89. – 2 r. brown .. .. 1·00 1·00

DESIGNS—HORIZ. 2 n.p., 5 n.p. Scouts marching. VERT. 3 n.p., 2 r. Boy Scout.

12. Olympic Torch.

1964. Olympic Games, Tokyo (2nd issue).

90. **12.** 1 n.p. olive 5 5
91. 2 n.p. blue 5 5
92. 3 n.p. chestnut 5 5
93. 4 n.p. turquoise.. .. 5 5
94. 5 n.p. violet 5 5
95. 40 n.p. blue 20 20
96. 50 n.p. brown 30 30
97. 2 r. ochre .. .. 1·25 1·25

13. Pres. Kennedy and Statue of Liberty.

1964. Air. Pres. Kennedy Commem. (2nd issue). Inscr. in gold.

98. **13.** 40 n.p. blue, chest. & grn. 45 45
99. 60 n.p. chest., grn. & blue 65 65
100. 100 n.p. grn. bl. & chest. 1·10 1·10

14. Rock Dove.

1965. Air. Birds. Multicoloured.

101. 30 n.p. Type **14** 8 8
102. 40 n.p. Jungle fowl .. 10 10
103. 75 n.p. Hoopoe 25 25
104. 150 n.p. Type **14** .. 45 45
105. 2 r. Jungle fowl 55 55
106. 3 r. Hoopoe .. .. 1·00 1·00

15. Early Telephone.

1965. "Science, Transport and Communications".

107. **15.** 1 n.p. black and red .. 5 5
108. A. 1 n.p. black and red .. 5 5
109. B. 2 n.p. indigo and orange 5 5
110. C. 2 n.p. indigo and orange 5 5
111. D. 3 n.p. sepia and green 5 5
112. E. 3 n.p. sepia and green 5 5
113. F. 4 n.p. violet and apple 5 5
114. G. 4 n.p. violet and apple 5 5
115. H. 5 n.p. brown and green 5 5
116. I. 5 n.p. brown and green 5 5
117. J. 30 n.p. indigo and blue 10 10
118. K. 30 n.p. indigo and blue 10 10
119. L. 40 n.p. ultram. & yellow 12 12
120. M. 40 n.p. ultram. & yellow 12 12
121. N. 50 n.p. brown and blue 15 15
122. O. 50 n.p. brown and blue 15 15
123. P. 75 n.p. sepia and green 25 25
124. Q. 75 n.p. sepia and green 25 25
125. R. 1 r. ultramarine & yellow 45 45
126. S. 1 r. ultramarine & yellow 45 45

DESIGNS: A, Modern teleprinter. B, 1895 Car. C, 1964 American car. D, Early X-ray apparatus. E, T.V. X-ray machine. F, Early mailcoach. G, "Telstar" satellite. H, Early merchantman. I, Nuclear ship "Savannah". J, Early astronomers. K, Jodrel Bank radio-telescope. L, Greek messengers. M, "Relay" satellite. N, "Man's early flight" (Lilienthal's glider). O, Caravelle jetliner. P, Persian waterwheel. Q, Hydro-electric dam. R, Old steam locomotive. S, Modern diesel train.

1965. Air. Churchill Commem. (1st issue) Optd. **In Memoriam Sir Winston Churchill 1874-1965** in English and Arabic.

127. **13.** 40 n.p. bl., chest. & grn. 10 10
128. 60 n.p. chest., grn. & bl. 15 15
129. 100 n.p. grn., bl. & chest. 25 25

See also Nos. 201/4.

1965. Arab Postal Union's Permanent Office. 10th Anniv. (1964). As T **209** of Egypt.

130. 5 n.p. blue and yellow .. 5 5
131. 30 n.p. indigo and red .. 8 8
132. 65 n.p. green and orange.. 15 15

1965. Various issues of Shakh Saqr with portrait obliterated with three bars.

(a) Postage. Nos. 5, 8/13.

150. **1.** 5 n.p. multicoloured .. 5 5
151. 10 n.p. multicoloured .. 5 5
152. 16 n.p. multicoloured .. 5 5
153. 20 n.p. multicoloured .. 5 5
154. 30 n.p. multicoloured .. 8 8
155. 40 n.p. multicoloured .. 10 10
156. 50 n.p. multicoloured .. 12 12

(b) Air. (i) Nos. 16, 18/21.

157. **1.** 1 r. multicoloured .. 25 25
158. 3 r. multicoloured .. 75 75
159. 4 r. multicoloured .. 1·00 1·00
160. 5 r. multicoloured .. 1·25 1·25
161. 10 r. multicoloured .. 2·50 2·50

(ii) Nos. 75/80.

144. **9.** 10 n.p. multicoloured .. 5 5
145. – 20 n.p. multicoloured .. 5 5
146. – 30 n.p. multicoloured .. 8 8
147. – 40 n.p. multicoloured .. 10 10
148. – 75 n.p. multicoloured .. 25 25
149. – 100 n.p. multicoloured.. 30 30

16. Rameses II in his War Chariot. **17.** Cable-laying Ship "Monarch", and COMPAC Cable Route Map.

1965. Nubian Monuments Preservation.

162. **16.** 5 n.p. blue and yellow.. 5 5
163. 10 n.p. green & chestnut 5 5
164. 30 n.p. indigo & orange 8 8
165. 55 n.p. violet and blue.. 15 15

1965. I.T.U. Cent. Country name in gold.

166. **17.** 1 n.p. brown and blue.. 5 5
167. – 2 n.p. brown and blue.. 5 5
168. – 3 n.p. violet and green.. 5 5
169. – 4 n.p. brown and blue.. 5 5
170. **17.** 5 n.p. ochre and violet.. 5 5
171. – 50 n.p. purple and black 10 10
172. – 1 r. green and ochre .. 25 25
173. – 120 n.p. red and emerald 35 35

DESIGNS: 2 n.p., 120 n.p. "Relay I" satellite and tracking station, Goonhilly Down. 3 n.p., 50 n.p. "Telstar" satellite and Atlas-Agena rocket on launching pad. 4 n.p., 1 r. "Syncom" satellite, Post Office Tower (London) and horn paraboloid reflector aerial.

18. Running.

1965. Pan-Arab Games, Cairo.

174. **18.** 50 n.p. turquoise & lilac 15 15
175. – 50 n.p. green & chestnut 15 15
176. – 50 n.p. lilac and sepia 15 15
177. – 50 n.p. sepia and green 15 15
178. – 50 n.p. chestnut & turq. 15 15

SPORTS: No. 175, Pole-vaulting. 176, Boxing. 177, High-jumping. 178, Long-jumping.

19. Flags (reverse of 5 r. coin).

1966. Arabian Gulf Area Monetary Conf. Circular designs on silver foil, backed with paper inscr. "Walsall Security Paper" in English and Arabic. Imperf.

(a) Diameter $1\frac{5}{8}$ in.

179. **19.** 50 n.p. black 15 15
180. – 75 n.p. violet 25 25

(b) Diameter $2\frac{1}{16}$ in.

181. **19.** 1 r. purple 30 30
182. – 3 r. blue 90 90

(c) Diameter $2\frac{1}{2}$ in.

183. **19.** 4 r. green .. .. 1·00 1·00
184. – 5 r. orange .. .. 1·40 1·40

COINS: 75 n.p., 3 r. and 5 r. show the obverse (Pres. Kennedy).

1966. "Rendezvous in Space". Nos. 33/6 optd. **15-12-1965 Rendezvous in SPACE,** two space capsules and four bars obliterating portrait or surch. also in English and Arabic.

185. **4.** 1 n.p. green 5 5
186. 2 n.p. brown 5 5
187. 3 n.p. olive 5 5
188. 4 n.p. blue 5 5
189. 15 n.p. on 1 n.p. green .. 5 5
190. 30 n.p. on 2 n.p. brown.. 10 10
191. 50 n.p. on 3 n.p. olive .. 20 20
192. 1 r. on 4 n.p. blue .. 40 40

20. I.C.Y. Emblem and Prime Minister Harold Wilson.

1966. Int. Co-operation Year.

193. **20.** 80 n.p. sepia and violet 12 12
194. – 80 n.p. brown and green 12 12
195. – 80 n.p. olive and red .. 12 12
196. – 80 n.p. purple and blue 12 12
197. – 80 n.p. blue & vermilion 12 12
198. – 80 n.p. plum & yell.-olive 12 12
199. – 80 n.p. blue and grey .. 12 12
200. – 80 n.p. purple and ochre 12 12

DESIGNS—I.C.Y. emblem and "World Leaders": No. 194, Chancellor Erhard. 195, Pres. Nasser. 196, Pres. Johnson. 197, Pope Paul VI. 198, Pres. De Gaulle. 199, Shaikh Isa bin Sulman al-Khalifa (Bahrain). 200, King Faisal (Saudi Arabia).

21. Sir Winston Churchill, Pen and Ink, and Books.

1966. Churchill Commem. (2nd issue). Multicoloured, printed on gold foil, backed with paper.

201. 2 r. Type **21** 50 50
202. 3 r. Churchill and Houses of Parliament, pen and ink 75 75
203. 4 r. Churchill and St. Paul's Cathedral .. .. 1·00 1·00
204. 5 r. Churchill and "Big Ben" (clock tower, Houses of Parliament) and Tower Bridge .. .. .. 1·50 1·50

22. Banded Butterfly-fish.

1966. Fishes. Multicoloured.

206. 1 n.p. Type **22** 5 5
207. 2 n.p. Striped surgeon-fish 5 5
208. 3 n.p. Young imperial angel-fish 5 5
209. 4 n.p. False mouthbreeder 5 5
210. 5 n.p. Undulate trigger-fish 5 5
211. 15 n.p. Moonfish 5 5
212. 20 n.p. Clown butterfly-fish 5 5
213. 30 n.p. Moorish goddess .. 8 5
214. 40 n.p. Zebra-striped angel-fish 10 5
215. 50 n.p. False mouth breeder 12 8
216. 75 n.p. Undulate trigger-fish 15 10
217. 1 r. Zebra-striped angel-fish 25 20
218. 2 r. Moorish goddess .. 50 40
219. 3 r. Clown butterfly-fish .. 75 60
220. 4 r. Moonfish .. .. 1·00 80
221. 5 r. Young imperial angel-fish .. .. .. 1·25 1·00
222. 10 r. Type **22** .. .. 2·50 2·00

23. Arms of Munich and "Souvenir Sheet". **25.** Pres. Kennedy.

24. Greek 6th-cent. Ball-player.

1966. F.I.P. and A.I.J.P. Congresses, Munich. Multicoloured. Values expressed in naye paise and rupees.
223. 80 n.p. Type **23** 15 15
224. 120 n.p. Frauenkirche, Munich 30 30
225. 2 r. Statue and Hall of Fame, Munich (horiz. 81 × 41 mm.) 50 50

NEW CURRENCY SURCHARGES. During the latter half of 1966 various issues appeared surcharged in dirhams and riyals. The 1966 definitives with this surcharge are listed below as there is evidence of their postal use. Nos. 101, 107/126, 150/61 and 174/84 also exist with these surcharges.
Earlier in 1966 Nos. 98/100, 171/3, 193/4, 196, 198, 200/5 appeared surcharged in piastres and rials. As Sharjah did not adopt this currency their status is uncertain.

1966. Nos. 206/22 with currency names changed by overprinting in English and Arabic.
226. **22.** 1 d. multicoloured .. 5 5
227. – 2 d. multicoloured .. 5 5
228. – 3 d. multicoloured .. 5 5
229. – 4 d. multicoloured .. 5 5
230. – 5 d. multicoloured .. 5 5
231. – 15 d. multicoloured .. 5 5
232. – 20 d. multicoloured .. 5 5
233. – 30 d. multicoloured .. 8 8
234. – 40 d. multicoloured .. 10 10
235. – 50 d. multicoloured .. 12 12
236. – 75 d. multicoloured .. 15 15
237. – 1 r. multicoloured .. 25 25
238. – 2 r. multicoloured .. 50 50
239. – 3 r. multicoloured .. 75 75
240. – 4 r. multicoloured .. 1·00 1·00
241. – 5 r. multicoloured .. 1·25 1·25
242. **22.** 10 r. multicoloured .. 2·50 2·50

1966. World Cup Football Championships. Designs printed on coloured metal foil-surfaced paper. Multicoloured.
243. ½ r. Type **24** 15 12
244. ½ r. Tsu-chu "Kick-ball" game, China, circa 175 B.C. 15 12
245. ½ r. 14th-cent. ball game .. 15 12
246. ½ r. Blowing up ball-bladder (17th-cent.) 15 12
247. ½ r. Football game, Barnet, England, circa 1750 .. 15 12
248. ½ r. England v. Scotland game, Kennington Oval (London), 1879 .. .. 15 12
249. ½ r. Victorious England team, Wembley, 1966 (56 × 35½ mm.) 15 12

1966. Pres. Kennedy's 3rd Death Anniv. and Arlington Memorial Inaug. Multicoloured.
251. 50 d. Type **25** 15 12
252. 2 r. Sharjah 50 n.p. Kennedy stamp of 1964 .. .. 65 40
253. 2 r. 50 Pres. Kennedy's grave (horiz. 55 × 42 mm.) 80 55

26. Shaikh Khalid bin Mohammed al Qasimi and Arms.

1968. Multicoloured.
255. 5 d. Type **26** (postage) .. 5 5
256. 10 d. Flag 5 5
257. 15 d. Flag and arms (vert.) 5 5
258. 20 d. Decorative pattern (vert.) 5 5
259. 35 d. Type **26** (air) .. 10 10
260. 40 d. As 10 d. 10 10
261. 60 d. As 15 d. 12 12
262. 75 d. As 20 d. 15 15
363. 1 r. Type **26** 25 25
264. 2 r. As 10d. 50 50
265. 3 r As 15 d. 75 75
266. 4 r. As 20 d. .. .. 1·00 1·00
267. 5 r. Type **26** .. .. 1·25 1·25
268. 10 r. As 10 d. .. .. 2·50 2·50

OFFICIAL STAMPS

1966. Optd. **ON STATE SERVICE** in English and Arabic.
O 101. **1.** 8 n.p. 5 5
O 102. 10 n.p... .. .. 5 5
O 103. 16 n.p... .. .. 5 5
O 104. 20 n.p... .. .. 5 5
O 105. 30 n.p... .. .. 10 10
O 106 40 n.p... .. .. 12 12
O 107. 50 n.p... .. .. 15 15
O 108. 75 n.p... .. .. 25 25
O 109. 100 n.p. 30 30

For later issues see **UNITED ARAB EMIRATES.**

SIBERIA E3

Various Anti-Bolshevist governments existed in this area, culminating in Kolchaks assumption of power as "Supreme Ruler". The Kolchak Government fell in January 1920, provincial issues followed until the area was incorporated into the Soviet Union in 1922.

1919. Admiral Kolchak Govt. Arms types of Russia surch. in figures, or in figures and words (rouble values). Imperf. or perf.
5. **11.** 35 on 2 k. green 10 15
6. 50 on 3 k. red 10 20
3. 70 on 1 k. orange .. 15 15
8. **13.** 1 r. on 4 k. red 15 25
9. **11.** 3 r. on 7 k. blue 45 70
10. **4.** 5 r. on 14 k. red and blue 70 90

1920. Transbaikal Province. Ataman Semyonov regime.. Arms types of Russia surch. thus: **p. 1 p.** Perf.
11. **12.** 1 r. on 4 k red .. .. 6·00 8·00
12. **7.** 2 r. 50 on 20 k. red & blue 5·50 7·00
13. **11.** 5 r. on 5 k. claret .. 3·50 4·50
14. **4.** 10 r. on 70 k. orge. & brn. 5·00 7·00

1.

1919. Amur Province. Imperf.
15. **1.** 2 r. red .. .. .. 1·00 1·40
16. 3 r. green .. .. .. 1·00 1·40
17. 5 r. blue .. .. .. 1·00 1·40
18. 15 r. brown .. .. 1·00 1·40
19. 30 r. mauve .. .. 1·00 1·40

FAR EASTERN REPUBLIC

1920. Vladivostock issue. Optd. **D B P** in fancy letters or surch. also. Imperf. or perf. (a) On Arms types of Russia.
32. **11.** 1 k. orange .. .. 3·00 3·00
20. 2 k. green .. .. 1·25 1·25
21. 3 k. red .. .. 1·25 1·25
39. **4.** 3 k. on 35 k. grn. & purple 2·10 2·10
22. **12.** 4 k. red .. .. 1·10 1·10
40. **4.** 4 k. on 70 k. orge. & brn. 90 90
41. 7 k. on 15 k. blue & purple 90 90
23. **12.** 10 k. blue .. .. 24·00 24·00
44. **5.** 10 k. on 3 r. 50 green and brown .. .. 7·00 7·00
24. **4.** 14 k. red and blue .. 2·50 2·50
25. 15 k. blue and purple .. 1·60 1·60
26. **7.** 20 k. red and blue .. 20·00 20·00
27. **4.** 20 k. on 14 k. red & blue 1·25 1·25
28. 25 k. mauve and green .. 1·60 1·60
29. 35 k. green and purple .. 8·00 8·00
30. **7.** 50 k. green and purple .. 1·25 1·25
35. **8.** 1 r. orange and brown .. 5·00 5·00

(b) On Nos. 5 and 3 of Siberia.
37. **11.** 35 k. on 2 k. green .. 1·50 1·50
38. 70 k. on 1 k. orange .. 2·25 2·25

2.

3.

4.

1921. Chita issue. Imperf.
47. **2.** 1 k. orange 30 30
48. 3 k. red 40 40
49. **3.** 4 k. brown and red .. 12 12
50. **2.** 5 k. brown 30 30
51. 7 k. blue 15 50
52. **3.** 10 k. red and blue .. 15 15
53. **2.** 15 k. red 15 30
54. **3.** 28 k. red and blue .. 15 15
55. 30 k. red and green .. 20 30
56. 50 k. red and black .. 20 30

1922. Russian October Revolution. 5th Anniv. Optd. **1917 7-XI 1922.** Imperf.
57. **4.** 2 k. green .. .. 3·00 3·00
58. 4 k. red .. .. 3·00 3·00
59. 5 k. brown .. .. 5·00 5·00
60. 10 k. blue .. .. 5·00 5·00

PRIAMUR AND MARITIME PROVINCES
Anti-Bolshevist Government.

1921. Vladivostok issue. Imperf.
61. **4.** 2 k. green 30 25
62. 4 k. red 30 25
63. 5 k. purple 60 60
64. 10 k. blue .. .. 70 1·00

(5.)

(6. Trans. "Priamur Territory".)

Д. В.
коп. 1 коп.
ЗОЛОТОМ
(7.)

1922. Anniv. of Priamur Provisional Govt. Optd. with T **5.**
89. **4.** 2 k. green .. .. 3·50 5·00
90. 4 k. red .. .. 3·50 5·00
91. 5 k. purple .. .. 3·50 5·00
92. 10 k. blue .. .. 3·50 5·00

1922. Optd. or surch. as T **6.**
93. **4.** 1 k. on 2 k. green .. 60 80
94. 2 k. green 60 80
95. 3 k. on 4 k. red .. 60 80
96. 4 k. red 60 80
97. 5 k. purple 60 80
98. 10 k. blue 60 80

1922. Optd. as T **6.** Imperf. or perf.
(a) On Arms types of Russia.
114. **11.** 1 k. orange .. .. 1·50 1·50
115. 2 k. green .. .. 1·75 1·75
116. 3 k. red .. .. 2·25 2·25
102. **12.** 4 k. red .. .. 1·00 1·00
118. **11.** 5 k. claret .. .. 5·00 5·00
104. 7 k. blue .. .. 10·00 10·00
105. **12.** 10 k. blue .. .. 9·00 9·00
106. **4.** 14 k. red and blue .. 12·00 12·00
107. 15 k. blue and purple .. 2·10 2·10
108. **7.** 20 k. red and blue .. 3·50 3·50
109. **4.** 20 k. on 14 k. red & blue 20·00 20·00
110. 25 k. mauve and green .. 12·00 12·00
111. 35 k. green and purple .. 1·50 1·50
112. **7.** 50 k. green and purple .. 1·40 1·40
113. **4.** 70 k. orange and brown 7·00 7·00
121. **8.** 1 r. orange and brown .. 5·00 5·00

(b) On Nos. 5 and 3 of Siberia.
122. **11.** 35 k. on 2 k. green .. 16·00 16·00
123. 70 k. on 1 k. orange .. 20·00 20·00

1922. Nos. 37 and 38 optd **ПЗК** and three bars. Imperf. or perf.
125. **11.** 35 k. on 2 k. green .. 2·10 2·10
126. 70 k. on 1 k. orange .. 2·75 2·75

SOVIET UNION ISSUE FOR THE FAR EAST.

1923. Stamps of Russia surch. as T **7.** Imperf. or perf.
131. **47.** 1 k. on 100 r. red .. 25 30
128. 2 k. on 70 r. purple .. 10 20
129. **46.** 5 k. on 10 r. blue .. 10 30
130. **47.** 10 k. on 50 r. brown .. 20 20

SICILY E2

An island to the S. of Italy, which, with Naples, formed the Kingdom of the Two Sicilies, until incorporated in the Kingdom of Italy.

100 grano = 1 ducato.

1. King "Bomba".

1859. Imperf.
1d. **1.** ½ g. orange .. .. 90·00 £325
2e. 1 g. olive .. .. 32·00 50·00
3. 2 g. blue .. .. 25·00 18·00
4g. 5 g. red .. .. 60·00 £450
5. 10 g. blue .. .. £120 80·00
6. 20 g. slate £130 £150
7. 50 g. brown £100 £1800

SIERRA LEONE BC

A Br. colony on the W. coast of Africa. Achieved independence within the Br. Commonwealth in 1961. By vote of the Assembly on 19 April, 1971, Sierra Leone was proclaimed a Republic.

1964. 100 cents = 1 leone.

1.

2.

1859.
16. ½d. brown .. .. .. 90 1·75
27. ½d. green 10 8
28. 1d. red 45 12
29. 1½d. lilac .. .. .. 60 1·25
19. 2d. mauve .. .. 7·00 1·75
30. 2d. grey .. .. .. 1·75 80
31. 2½d. blue .. .. .. 1·75 15
32. 3d. yellow .. .. .. 80 1·00
21. 4d. blue .. .. .. 15·00 2·00
33. 4d. brown 80 80
37. **2.** 6d. purple .. .. 2·25 2·75
22. 1s. green .. .. .. 9·00 3·25
34. 1s. brown .. .. .. 3·25 2·00

1893. Surch. **HALF PENNY**
39. **1.** ½d. on 1½d. lilac .. .. 1·75 2·00

3.

5.

4.

1896.
41. **3.** ½d. mauve and green .. 15 15
42. 1d. mauve and red .. 20 12
43. 1½d. mauve and black .. 1·10 1·10
44. 2d. mauve and orange .. 90 85
45. 2½d. mauve and blue .. 65 40
46. 3d. mauve and grey .. 3·00 2·00
47. 4d. mauve and red .. 2·25 3·00
48. 5d. mauve andd black .. 2·25 3·00
49. 6d. mauve .. .. 3·25 3·25
50. 1s. green and black .. 3·25 3·25
51. 2s. green and blue .. 11·00 9·50
52. 5s. green and red .. 22·00 20·00
53. £1 purple on red .. .. 70·00 £100

1897. T **4** optd. **POSTAGE AND REVENUE**
54. **4.** 1 d. purple and green .. 65 75

1897. T **4** optd. **POSTAGE AND REVENUE** and surch. **2½d.** and bars.
55. **4.** 2½d. on 3d. purple & green 3·25 3·25
59. 2½d. on 6d. purple & green 3·25 3·25
63. 2½d. on 1s. purple .. .. 35·00 20·00
67. 2½d. on 2s. purple £275 £250

1903.
86. **5.** ½d. purple and green .. 1·60 40
74. 1d. purple and red .. 15 15
88. 1½d. purple and black .. 65 1·50
89. 2d. purple and orange .. 1·00 80
90. 2½d. purple and blue .. 1·10 1·25
91. 3d. purple and grey .. 2·25 1·50
92. 4d. purple and red .. 1·00 95
93. 5d. purple and black .. 2·50 1·60
94. 6d. purple .. .. 90 1·25
95. 1s. green and black .. 3·25 3·25
96. 2s. green and blue .. 6·00 5·50
97. 5s. green and red .. 20·00 18·00
98. £1 purple on red .. £100 £110

1907.
99. **5.** ½d. green 25 15
100a. 1d. red 20 12
101. 1½d. orange 50 75
102. 2d. grey 50 75
103. 2½d. blue 45 80
104. 3d. purple on yellow .. 1·10 1·10
105. 4d. black and red on yell. 80 60
106. 5d. purple and olive .. 1·10 1·75
108. 1s. black on green .. 2·50 2·25
109. 2s. purple & blue on blue 8·50 6·00
110. 5s. grn. and red on yellow 18·00 20·00
111. £1 purple & black on red 75·00 90·00

6.

7. Seal of the Colony.

1912.
131. **6.** ½d. green 20 8
113. 1d. red 35 8
132. 1d. violet 40 15
114. 1½d. orange 55 55
133. 1½d. red 30 25
115. 2d. grey 40 8
135. 2½d. blue 30 40
123. **7.** 3d. purple on yellow .. 80 1·10
136. **6.** 3d. blue 25 12
117b. 4d. blk. & red on yellow .. 45 1·10
138. 5d. purple and olive .. 45 55
139. 6d. purple 65 55
120. 7d. purple and orange .. 65 1·25
121. 9d. purple and black .. 2·25 2·00
142. 10d. purple and red .. 1·60 2·00
143. **7.** 1s. black on green .. 90 1·25
144. 2s. blue & purple on blue 3·00 2·75
145. 5s. red & green on yellow 4·50 5·50
146. 10s. red & green on green 17·00 17·00
128. £1 blk. and purple on red 35·00 38·00
129. £2 blue and purple .. £225 £250
130. £5 orange and green .. £600

8. Rice Field.

9. Palms and Kola Tree.

1932.

155.	**8.**	½d. green	15	20
156.		1d. violet	8	8
157.		1½d. red	25	45
158.		2d. brown	25	20
159.		3d. blue	30	35
160.		4d. orange	45	55
161.		5d. green	40	65
162.		6d. blue	65	80
163.		1s. claret	1·40	2·00
164.	**9.**	2s. brown	3·50	4·50
165.		5s. blue	5·00	6·00
166.		10s. green	17·00	20·00
167.		£1 purple	28·00	35·00

10. Arms of Sierra Leone.

DESIGNS VERT. 1d. "Freedom". 1½d. Map of Sierra Leone. 4d. Government Sanatorium. 5s. African Elephant. HORIZ. 2d. Old Slave Market, Freetown. 3d. Native Fruitseller. 5d. Bullam canoe. 6d. Punting near Banana Is. 1s. Govt. Buildings, Freetown. 2s. Bunce Is. 10s. King George V. £1 Freetown Harbour.

1933. Cent. of Abolition of Slavery and Death of William Wilberforce. Dated "1833 1933".

168.	**10.**	½d. green	25	40
169.	–	1d. black and brown ..	15	8
170.	–	1½d. brown	1·60	2·00
171.	–	2d. purple	90	15
172.	–	3d. blue	70	1·40
173.	–	4d. brown	2·25	3·50
174.	–	5d. green and brown ..	3·50	5·50
175.	–	6d. black and orange ..	3·50	4·00
176.	–	1s. violet	4·00	4·50
177.	–	2s. brown and blue ..	12·00	16·00
178.	–	5s. black and purple ..	50·00	80·00
179.	–	10s. black and olive ..	50·00	80·00
180.	–	£1 violet and orange ..	£225	£300

1935. Silver Jubilee. As T **11** of Antigua.

181.	1d. blue and black ..	8	8
182.	3d. brown and blue ..	40	40
183.	5d. green and blue ..	65	70
184.	1s. grey and purple ..	1·00	1·40

1937. Coronation. As T **2** of Aden.

185.	1d. orange	15	10
186.	2d. purple	15	12
187.	3d. blue	20	25

11. Freetown from the Harbour.

1938. King George VI.

188.	**11.**	½d. black and green ..	8	8
189.		1d. black and red ..	8	8
190.	–	1½d. red	2·25	15
190a.	–	1½d. mauve	8	8
191.	–	2d. mauve	4·50	1·00
191a.	–	2d. red	8	8
192.	**11.**	3d. black and blue ..	8	8
193.		4d. black and brown ..	20	25
194.	–	5d. olive	30	75
195.	–	6d. grey	10	8
196.	**11.**	1s. black and olive ..	20	15
196a.	–	1s. 3d. orange	30	15
197.	**11.**	2s. black and brown ..	45	60
198.	–	5s. brown	1·10	1·00
199.	–	10s. green	2·25	2·50
200.	**11.**	£1 blue	5·00	5·50

DESIGN: 1½d., 2d., 5d., 6d., 1s. 3d., 5s., 10s. Rice harvesting.

1946. Victory. As T **4** of Aden.

201.	1½d. lilac	8	8
202.	3d. blue	8	8

1948. Silver Wedding. As T **5/6** of Aden.

203.	1½d. mauve	8	8
204.	£1 blue	5·00	6·50

1949. U.P.U. As T **14/17** of Antigua.

205.	1½d. purple	10	12
206.	3d. blue	12	12
207.	6d. grey	30	30
208.	1s. olive	55	55

1953. Coronation. As T **7** of Aden.

209.	1½d. black and lilac ..	10	10

12. Cape Lighthouse.

1956. Centres in black.

210.	**12**	½d. lilac	5	5
211.	–	1d. olive	5	5
212.	–	1½d. blue	5	8
213.	–	2d. brown	5	5
214.	–	3d. blue	8	5
215.	–	4d. slate	8	8
216.	–	6d. violet	8	8
217.	–	1s. red	12	12
218.	–	1s. 3d. sepia	20	20
219.	–	2s. 6d. chestnut ..	40	35
220.	–	5s. green	85	85
221.	–	10s. magenta	3·00	3·25
222.	–	£1 orange	4·50	5·00

DESIGNS—HORIZ. 1d. Queen Elizabeth II Quay. 1½d. Piassava workers. 4d. Iron ore production, Marampa. 6d. Whale Bay, York Village. 1s. 3d. Aeroplane and map. 10s. Law Courts, Freetown. £1 Government House. VERT. 2d. Cotton tree, Freetown. 3d. Rice harvesting. 1s. Bullom boat. 2s. 6d. Orugu bridge. 5s. Kuranko chief.

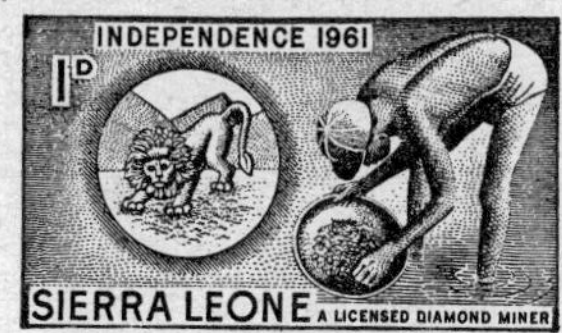

13. Licensed Diamond Miner.

1961. Independence.

223.	–	½d. choc. and blue-green	5	5
224.	**13.**	1d. brown and green ..	5	5
225.	–	1½d. black and emerald	5	8
226.	–	2d. black & ultramarine	5	5
227.	–	3d. brown and blue ..	5	5
228.	–	4d. blue and red ..	5	8
229.	–	6d. black and purple	8	8
230.	–	1s. chocolate and orange	12	12
231.	–	1s. 3d. blue and violet ..	20	20
232.	**13.**	2s. 6d. green and black	35	40
233.	–	5s. black and red ..	80	1·00
234.	–	10 s. black and green ..	1·75	2·00
235.	–	£1 red and yellow	3·50	4·00

DESIGNS—VERT. ½d., 1s. Palm fruit gathering. 1½d., 5 s. Bundu mask. 2d., 10s. Bishop Crowther and Old Fourah Bay College. £1, Forces bugler. HORIZ. 3d., 6d. Sir Milton Margai. 4d., 1s. 3d. Lumley Beach.

14. Royal Charter, 1799.

DESIGNS—As T **14**: 4d. King's Yard Gate, Freetown, 1817. As T **15**: 1s. 3d. H.M. Yacht "Britannia" at Freetown.

15. Old House of Representatives, Freetown, 1924.

1961. Royal Visit.

236.	**14.**	3d. black and red ..	8	8
237.	–	4d. black and violet ..	10	10
238.	**15.**	6d. black and orange ..	12	12
239.	–	1s. 3d. black and blue ..	25	25

16. Campaign Emblem.

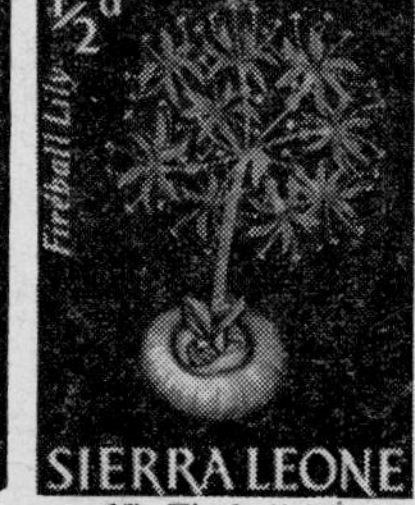

17. Fireball Lily.

1962. Malaria Eradication.

240.	**16.**	3d. red	8	8
241.		1s. 3d. green	20	20

1963. Flowers in natural colours; background colours given below.

242.	**17.**	½d. bistre	5	5
243.	–	1d. red	5	5
244.	–	1½d. emerald	5	5
245.	–	2d. olive	8	8
246.	–	3d. green	10	10
247.	–	4d. violet-blue	12	15
248.	–	6d. deep blue	12	15
249.	–	1s. yellow-green ..	20	15
250.	–	1s. 3d. bronze-green ..	20	25
251.	–	2s. 6d. dull purple ..	45	45
252.	–	5s. violet	1·00	1·25
253.	–	10s. purple	2·00	1·90
254.	–	£1 blue	4·50	5·50

FLOWERS—VERT. 1½d. Stereospermum. 3d. Beniseed. 4d. Blushing Hibiscus. 1s. Beautiful Crinum. 2s. 6d. Broken Hearts. 5s. Ra-ponthi. 10s. Blue Plumbago. HORIZ. 1d. Jina-gbo. 2d. Black-eyed Susan. 6d. Climbing Lily. 1s. 3d. Blue Bells. £1 African Tulip Tree.

18. Threshing Machine and Corn Bins.

1963. Freedom from Hunger.

255.	**18.**	3d. black and ochre ..	10	10
256.	–	1s. 3d. sepia and green ..	25	25

DESIGN: 1s. 3d. Girl with onion crop.

1963. Independence. 2nd Anniv. Stamp of 1956 surch. **2nd Year of Independence Progress Development 1963** and value in various types (except 2s. 6d.). Centres in black. (a) Postage.

257.	3d. on ½d. lilac	5	5
258.	4d. on 1½ d. blue	5	8
259.	6d. on ½d. lilac	8	8
260.	10d. on 3d. blue	15	15
261.	1s. 6d. on 3d. blue ..	25	25
262.	3s. 6d. on 3d. blue ..	50	50

(b) Air. Optd. **AIRMAIL** in addition.

263.	7d. on 1½d. blue ..	12	12
264.	1s. 3d. on 1½d. blue ..	15	20
265.	2s. 6d. chestnut	35	35
266.	3s. on 3d. blue	35	40
267.	6s. on 3d. blue	70	80
268.	11s. on 10s. magenta ..	1·75	2·00
269.	11s. on £1 orange ..	£200	£140

19. Centenary Emblem.

DESIGNS: 6d. Red Cross emblem. 1s. 3d. As T **19** but with lined background and value on left.

1963. Red Cross Cent.

270.	**19.**	3d. red and violet ..	8	8
271.	–	6d. red and black ..	12	12
272.	–	1s. 3d. red and green ..	25	30

1963. Postal Commemorations. (a) Postage. Optd. or surch. **1853-1859-1963 Oldest Postal Service Newest G.P.O. in West Africa** and value.

273.	–	3d. (No. 214)	5	5
274.	–	4d. on 1½d. (No. 212) ..	5	5
275.	–	9d. on 1½d. (No. 212) ..	12	12
276.	–	1s. on 1s. 3d. (No. 231)	15	15
277.	**12.**	1s. 6d. on ½d.	20	25
278.	–	2s. on 3d. (No. 214) ..	25	30

(b) Air. Optd. or surch. as above but **Postage Stamp** instead of **Postal Service** and **AIRMAIL** in addition.

279.	**14.**	7d. on 3d.	12	12
280.	–	1s. 3d. (No. 239) ..	15	20
281.	–	2s. 6d. on 4d. (No. 228)	40	50
282.	**14.**	3s. on 3d.	45	60
283.	**15.**	6s. on 6d.	1·00	1·25
284.	–	£1 (No. 222)	4·50	5·50

Commemoration dates:—
1853—" First Post Office ".
1859—" First Postage Stamps ".
1963—" Newest G.P.O." in West Africa.

MORE DETAILED LISTS

are given in the Stanley Gibbons Catalogues referred to in the country headings:

BC	British Commonwealth
E1, E2, E3	Europe 1, 2, 3
O1, O2, O3, O4	Overseas 1, 2, 3, 4

20. Lion Emblem and Map.

21. Globe and Map.

1964. World's Fair, New York. **Imperf.** Self-adhesive.

285.	**20.**	1d. mult. (postage) ..	5	5
286.		3d. multicoloured ..	5	5
287.		4d. multicoloured ..	5	5
288.		6d. multicoloured ..	8	5
289.		1s. multicoloured ..	12	12
290.		2s. multicoloured ..	20	25
291.		5s. multicoloured ..	50	65
292.	**21.**	7d. multicoloured (air)	8	8
293.		9d. multicoloured ..	10	10
294.		1s. 3d. multicoloured ..	15	20
295.		2s. 6d. multicoloured ..	20	30
296.		3s. 6d. multicoloured ..	40	40
297.		6s. multicoloured ..	60	70
298.		11s. multicoloured ..	1·25	2·25

Warning.—These self-adhesive stamps should be kept mint on their backing paper and used on cover or piece.

22. Inscription and Map.

23. Pres. Kennedy and Map.

1964. President Kennedy Memorial Issue. Imperf. Self-adhesive.

299.	**22.**	1d. mult. (postage) ..	5	5
300.		3d. multicoloured ..	5	5
301.		4d. multicoloured ..	5	5
302.		6d. multicoloured ..	8	8
303.		1s. multicoloured ..	12	12
304.		2s. multicoloured ..	20	25
305.		5s. multicoloured ..	50	65
306.	**23.**	7d. multicoloured (air)	8	8
307.		9d. multicoloured ..	10	10
308.		1s. 3d. multicoloured ..	15	15
309.		2s. 6d. multicoloured ..	25	30
310.	**23.**	3s. 6d. multicoloured ..	35	40
311.		6s. multicoloured ..	60	70
312.		11s. multicoloured ..	1·25	1·25

The note below No. 298 applies also to the above issue.

1964. Decimal Currency. Various stamps surch.

(i) 1st issue. Surch. in figures.

(a) Postage.

313.	–	1 c. on 6d. (No. 248) ..	5	5
314.	**14.**	2 c. on 3d.	5	5
315.	–	3 c. on 3d. (No. 246) ..	5	5
316.	–	5 c. on ½d. (No. 223) ..	8	5

317.	18.	8 c. on 3d.	10	8
318.	–	10 c. on 1s. 3d. (No. 250)	10	10
319.	–	15 c. on 1s. (No. 249) ..	15	15
320.	15.	25 c. on 6d.	30	35
321.	13.	50 c. on 2s. 6d... ..	55	60

(b) Air. Nos. 322/5 additionally optd. **AIRMAIL.**

322.	–	7 c. on 1s. 3d. (No. 256)	10	10
323.	–	20 c. on 4d. (No. 228) ..	25	25
324.	–	30 c. on 10s. (No. 234)..	35	40
325.	–	40 c. on 5s. (No. 233) ..	50	50
326.	23.	1 l. on 1s. 3d.	1·25	1·25
327.		2 l. on 11s.	2·25	2·50

(ii) 2nd issue. Surch. in figures or figures and words (Nos. 332/3).

328.	–	1 c. on 3d. (No. 227) (postage)	5	5
329.	22.	2 c. on 1d.	5	5
330.		4 c. on 3d.	8	8
331.	–	5 c. on 2d. (No. 245) ..	8	8
332.	–	1 l. on 5s. (No. 252) ..	1·25	1·25
333.	–	2 l. on £1 (No. 235) ..	2·25	2·25
334.	23.	7 c. on 7d. (air)	10	10
335.		60 c. on 9d.	75	75

(iii) Third issue. Surch. in figures.

336.	–	1 c. on 1½d. (No. 225) (postage)	5	5
337.	22.	2 c. on 3d.	8	8
338.	20.	2 c. on 4d.	8	8
339.	–	3 c. on 1d. (No. 243) ..	8	8
340.	–	3 c. on 2d. (No. 226) ..	5	5
341.		5 c. on 1s. 3d. (No. 231)	8	8
342.	22.	15 c. on 6d.	40	40
343.		15 c. on 1s.	65	65
344.	–	20 c. on 6d. (No. 229)..	25	25
345.	–	25 c. on 6d. (No. 248)	30	30
346.	–	50 c. on 3d. (No. 227)..	60	60
347.	20.	60 c. on 5s.	1·10	1·10
348.	22.	1 l. on 4d.	1·50	1·50
349.	–	2 l. on £1 (No. 235) ..	2·75	2·25
350.	21.	7 c. on 9d. (air) ..	12	12

(iv) Fourth issue. Surch in figures.

351.	20.	1 c. on 6d. (postage) ..	2·50	3·50
352.		1 c. on 2s.	2·50	3·50
353.	22.	1 c. on 2s.	2·50	3·50
354.		1 c. on 5s.	2·50	3·50
355.	21.	2 c. on 1s. 3d. (air) ..	2·50	3·50
356.	23.	2 c. on 1s. 3d.	2·50	3·50
357.		2 c. on 3s. 6d.	2·50	3·50
358.	21.	3 c. on 7d.	2·50	3·50
359.	23.	3 c. on 9d.	2·50	3·50
360.	21.	5 c. on 2s. 6d.	2·50	3·50
361.	23.	5 c. on 2s. 6d.	2·50	3·50
362.	21.	5 c. on 3s. 6d.	2·50	3·50
363.		5 c. on 6s.	2·50	3·50
364.	23.	5 c. on 6s.	2·50	3·50
		Set of 14 unused	30·00	40·00

(v) Fifth issue. No. 374 further surch. **TWO Leones.**

365.	–	2 l. on 30 c. on 6d. (air)	4·00	3·00

(**24.** Margai and Churchill).

1965. Sir Milton Margai and Sir Winston Churchill Commem. Flower stamps of 1963 surch. as T **24** on horiz. designs or with individual portraits on vert. designs as indicated. Multicoloured.

(a) Postage.

366.	–	2 c. on 1d.	5	5
367.	–	3 c. on 3d. Margai ..	5	5
368.	–	10 c. on 1s. Churchill ..	12	12
369.	–	20 c. on 1s. 3d. ..	25	25
370.	–	50 c. on 4d. Margai ..	65	65
371.	–	75 c. on 5s. Churchill ..	1·00	1·00

(b) Air. Additionally optd. **AIR MAIL.**

372.	–	7 c. on 2d.	8	8
373.	17.	15 c. on ½d. Margai ..	25	25
374.	–	30 c. on 6d.	40	40
375.	–	1 l. on £1	1·40	1·50
376.	–	2 l. on 10s. Churchill ..	3·00	3·25

25. Cola Plant and Nut.

1965. Various shapes, backed with paper bearing advertisements. Imperf. Self-adhesive.

A. Printed in green, yellow and red on silver foil. Values in colours given.

377.	25.	1 c. green (postage) ..	10	10
378.		2 c. red	10	10
379.		3 c. yellow	10	10
380.		4 c. silver on green ..	15	12
381.		5 c. silver on red ..	15	12

B. Designs 45 × 49 mm. showing Arms of Sierra Leone.

382.	–	20 c. mult. on cream (postage) ..	35	25
383.	–	50 c. mult. on cream ..	75	60
384.	–	40 c. mult. on cream (air)	75	60

C. Designs 48 × 44½ mm. showing inscription and necklace.

385.	–	7 c. multicoloured post.)	10	10
386.	–	15 c. multicoloured ..	20	20

1966. Independence 5th Anniv. Surch. **FIVE YEARS INDEPENDENCE 1961-1966** and value.

(a) Postage.

387.	–	1 c. on 6d. (No. 248) ..	5	5
388.	–	2 c. on 4d. (No. 247) ..	5	5
389.	–	3 c. on 1½d. (No. 212) ..	5	5
390.	–	8 c. on 1s. (No. 249) ..	12	12
391.	–	10 c. on 2s. 6d. (No. 251)	15	12
392.	–	20 c. on 2d. (No. 213) ..	25	25

(b) Air. Surch. **AIRMAIL** also.

393.	19.	7 c. on 3d.	10	10
394.	–	15 c. on 1s. (No. 249) ..	25	20
395.	–	25 c. on 2s. 6d. (No. 251)	35	40
396.	–	50 c. on 1½d. (No. 244)..	65	75
397.	–	1 l. on 4d. (No. 247) ..	1·40	1·50

26. Lion's Head.

1966. 1st Sierra Leone Gold Coinage Commem. Circular designs, embossed on gold foil, backed with paper bearing advertisements. Imperf. (a) Postage.

(i) ¼ golde coin. Diameter 1½ in.

398.	26.	2 c. magenta and orange	5	5
399.	–	3 c. emerald and purple	5	5

(ii) ½ golde coin. Diameter 2⅛ in.

400.	26.	5 c. vermilion & ultram.	8	8
401.	–	8 c. turquoise and black	12	12

(ii) 1 golde coin. Diameter 3¼ in.

402.	26.	25 c. violet and emerald	35	35
403.	–	1 l. orange and cerise ..	1·50	1·50

(b) Air (i) ¼ golde coin. Diameter 1½ in.

404.	26.	7 c. orange and cerise..	10	10
405.	–	10 c. cerise and blue ..	15	12

(ii) ½ golde coin. Diameter 2⅛ in.

406.	26.	15 c. orange and cerise	25	25
407.	–	30 c. purple and black..	40	45

(iii) 1 golde coin. Diameter 3¼ in.

408.	26.	50 c. green and purple..	65	65
409.	–	2 l. black and emerald	3·00	3·00

DESIGN: Nos. 399, 401, 403, 405, 407 and 409 Map of Sierra Leone.

1967. Decimal Currency Provisionals. Nos. 347/8, 369/71 and 383/4 surch.

410.	6½ c. on 75 c. on 5s. (post)	12	12
411.	7½ c. on 75 c. on 5s. ..	12	12
412.	9½ c. on 50 c. on 4d. ..	15	15
413.	12½ c. on 20 c. on 1s. 3d...	20	20
414.	17½ c. on 50 c.	1·00	1·00
415.	17½ c. on 1 l. on 4d. ..	1·00	1·00
416.	18½ c. on 1 l. on 4d. ..	1·00	1·00
417.	18½ c. on 60 c. on 5s. ..	3·50	3·50
418.	25 c. on 50 c.	35	35
419.	11½ c. on 40 c. (air) ..	15	15
420.	25 c. on 40 c.	40	40

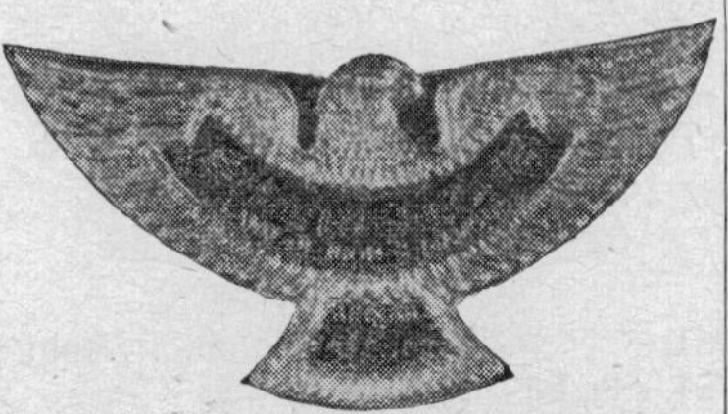

27. Eagle.
(Illustration reduced. Actual size 70 × 35 mm.)

1967. Decimal Currency. Imperf. Self-adhesive. As T **25**, but embossed on white paper, backed with paper bearing advertisements. Background colours given first, and value tablet colours in brackets.

421.	25.	½ c. red (red on white)..	8	5
422.		1 c. red (red on white)	5	5
423.		1½ c. yellow (grn. on white)	5	5
424.		2 c. red (grn. on white)	10	8
425.		2½ c. grn. (yell. on white)	8	8
426.		3 c. red (white on red)..	8	8
427.		3½ c. pur. (white on grn.)	10	10
428.		4 c. red (white on green)	10	10
429.		4½ c. grn. (grn. on white)	12	12
430.		5 c. red (yell. & white)	10	10
431.		5½ c. red (grn. on white)	12	12

1967. T **27** Embossed on black paper, backed with paper bearing advertisements; or, (No. 433), as No. 382, also with advertisements.

432.	27.	9½ c. red & gold on black	15	15
432a.		9½ c. blue & gold on blk.	20	20
433.	–	10 c. mult. (red frame)	20	20
433a.	–	10 c. mult. (black frame)	20	20
434.	27.	15 c. green & gold on blk.	30	30
434a.		15 c. red and gold on black	30	30

See also Nos. 538/44.

1968. No advertisements on back, and colours in value tablet reversed. Background colours given first, and value table colours in brackets.

435.	25.	½ c. red (white on green)	5	5
436.		1 c. red (white on red)..	5	5
437.		2 c. red (white in green)	30	30
438.		2½ c. grn. (white on yell.)	60	60
439.		3 c. red (red on white)..	5	5

On Nos. 435 and 438, the figure "½" is larger than in Nos. 421 and 425.

1968. No advertisements on back, colours changed and new value (7 c.). Background colours given.

440.	25.	2 c. pink (postage) ..	15	15
441.		2½ c. green	15	15
442.		3½ c. yellow	15	15
442a.		7 c. yellow (air) ..	15	15

On Nos. 441/2 the fraction "½" is larger than in Nos. 425 and 427.

28. Outline Map of Africa.

1968. Human Rights Year. Each value comes in six types, showing the following territories: Portuguese Guinea; South Africa: Mozambique; Rhodesia; South West Africa and Angola. Imperf. Self-adhesive.

443.	28.	½ c. multicoloured (post)	8	8
444.		2 c. multicoloured ..	8	8
445.		2½ c. multicoloured ..	8	8
446.		3½ c. multicoloured ..	8	8
447.		10 c. multicoloured ..	15	15
448.		11½ c. multicoloured ..	20	20
449.		15 c. multicoloured ..	25	25
450.		7½ c. multicoloured (air)	12	12
451.		9½ c. multicoloured ..	20	20
452.		14½ c. multicoloured ..	25	25
453.		18½ c. multicoloured ..	30	30
454.		25 c. multicoloured ..	40	40
455.		1 l. multicoloured ..	2·25	2·25
456.		2 l. multicoloured ..	6·00	6·00
		Set of 84 (6 different territories)	50·00	50·00

Nos. 443/56 were issued in sheets of 30 (6 × 5) on backing paper depicting diamonds or the coat-of-arms on the reverse. The six types occur once in each horiz. row.

1968. Mexico Olympics Participation. Nos. 383/4 surch. or optd. (Nos. 461 and 466) **OLYMPIC PARTICIPATION 1968 MEXICO** etc.

457.	6½ c. on 50 c. mult. (post.)	10	10
458.	17½ c. on 50 c. mult. ..	25	25
459.	22½ c. on 50 c. mult. ..	35	35
460.	28½ c. on 50 c. mult. ..	40	50
461.	50 c. multicoloured ..	70	85
462.	6½ c. on 40 c. mult. (air) ..	10	10
463.	17½ c. on 40 c. mult. ..	25	25
464.	22½ c. on 40 c. mult. ..	35	35
465.	28½ c. on 40 c. mult. ..	40	45
466.	40 c. multicoloured ..	60	75

29.

30.

1969. World's First Self-adhesive Postage Stamps. 5th Anniv. Self-adhesive. Imperf.

467.	29.	1 c. mult. (postage) ..	5	5
468.	–	2 c. multicoloured ..	5	5
469.	–	3½ c. multicoloured ..	5	5
470.	–	5 c. multicoloured ..	8	10
471.	–	12½ c. multicoloured ..	20	25
472.	–	1 l. multicoloured ..	1·60	1·75
473.	30.	7½ c. multicoloured (air)	12	15
474.	–	9½ c. multicoloured ..	15	20
475.	–	20 c. multicoloured ..	30	35
476.	–	30 c. multicoloured ..	45	50
477.	–	50 c. multicoloured ..	75	85
478.	–	2 l. multicoloured ..	4·25	4·50

DESIGNS—As Type **29**, Nos. 468/72. As Type **30**, Nos. 474/8.

All values are on white backing paper with advertisement printed on the reverse.

31. Ore-Ship, Globe and Flags of Sierra Leone and Japan.
(Illustration reduced. Actual size 54 × 29 mm.)

32. Ore-Ship, Map of Europe and Africa and Flags of Sierra Leone and Netherlands.
Illustration reduced. Actual size 48 × 30½ mm.)

1969. Pepel Port Improvements. Imperf. Self-adhesive, backed with paper bearing advertisements.

479.	31.	1 c. mult. (postage) ..	5	5
480.	32.	2 c. multicoloured ..	5	5
481.	–	3½ c. multicoloured ..	8	8
482.	–	10 c. multicoloured ..	12	12
483.	32.	18½ c. multicoloured ..	25	25
484.	–	50 c. multicoloured ..	65	65
485.	31.	7½ c. multicoloured (air)	10	10
486.	–	9½ c. multicoloured ..	15	15
487.	31.	15 c. multicoloured ..	25	25
488.	32.	25 c. multicoloured ..	35	35
489.	–	1 l. multicoloured ..	1·25	1·25
490.	–	2 l. multicoloured ..	2·50	2·50

The 3½, 9½ c., 2 l. and 10, 50 c., 1 l. show respectively the flags of Great Britain and West Germany instead of the Netherlands.

33. Emblem of African Development Bank.

1969. African Development Bank. 5th Anniv. Imperf. Self-adhesive, backed with paper bearing advertisements.

491. **33.** 3½ c. green, gold and black (post.) .. 15 15
492. 9½ c. violet, gold and green (air) 35 35

34. Boy Scouts Emblem in "Diamond".

1969. Boy Scouts Diamond Jubilee. Imperf. Self-adhesive.

493. **34.** 1 c. multicoloured (postage) 5 5
494. 2 c. multicoloured .. 5 5
495. 3½ c. multicoloured .. 8 8
496. 4½ c. multicoloured .. 10 10
497. 5 c. multicoloured .. 12 12
498. 75 c. multicoloured .. 3·50 3·00
499. – 7½ c. multicoloured (air) 20 20
500. – 9½ c. multicoloured .. 25 25
501. – 15 c. multicoloured .. 35 30
502. – 22 c. multicoloured .. 70 70
503. – 55 c. multicoloured .. 2·25 2·50
504. – 3 l. multicoloured .. 15·00 11·00

DESIGN—OCTAGONAL (65 × 51 mm.): Nos. 499/504, Scout saluting, Baden-Powell and badge.

1970. Air. No. 443 surch. **AIRMAIL** twice and new value.

505. **28.** 7½ c. on ½ c. mult. .. 12 12
506. 9½ c. on ½ c. mult. .. 15 15
507. 15 c. on ½ c. mult. .. 25 25
508. 28 c. on ½ c. mult. .. 35 45
509. 40 c. on ½ c. mult. .. 75 1·00
510. 2 l. on ½ c. mult. .. 3·00 3·50

Set of 36 (6 different territories) 25·00 28·00

35. Expo Symbol and Maps of Sierra Leone and Japan.

1970. World Fair, Osaka. Imperf. Self-adhesive.

511. **35.** 2 c. mult. (postage) .. 5 5
512. 3½ c. multicoloured .. 5 5
513. 10 c. multicoloured .. 12 12
514. 12½ c. multicoloured .. 15 15
515. 20 c multicoloured .. 25 25
516. 45 c. multicoloured .. 60 75
517. – 7½ c. multicoloured (air) 10 10
518. – 9½ c. multicoloured .. 12 12
519. – 15 c. multicoloured .. 20 20
520. – 25 c. multicoloured .. 40 50
521. – 50 c. multicoloured .. 75 1·00
522. – 3 l. multicoloured .. 4·50 5·00

DESIGN—CHRYSANTHEMUM (43 × 42 mm.): Nos. 517/22, Maps of Sierra Leone and Japan.

36. Diamond.

37. Palm Nut.

1970. Imperf. Self-adhesive.

523. **36.** 1 c. multicoloured .. 5 5
524. 1½ c. multicoloured .. 5 5
525. 2 c. multicoloured .. 5 5
526. 2½ c. multicoloured .. 5 5
527. 3 c. multicoloured .. 5 5
528. 3½ c. multicoloured .. 8 8
529. 4 c. multicoloured .. 8 8
530. 5 c. multicoloured .. 8 8
531. **37.** 6 c. multicoloured .. 8 8
532. 7 c. multicoloured .. 10 10
533. 8½ c. multicoloured .. 12 12
534. 9 c. multicoloured .. 12 12
535. **57.** 10 c. multicoloured .. 12 15
536. 11½ c. multicoloured .. 15 20
537. 18½ c. multicoloured .. 25 30

1970. Air. As T **27**, but on white paper.

538. **27.** 7½ c. gold and red (air) 10 10
539. 9½ c. silver and green 15 20
540. 15 c. silver and blue .. 20 25
541. 25 c. gold and purple .. 35 40
542. 50 c. green and orange 75 85
543. 1 l. blue and silver .. 1·50 1·75
544. 2 l. blue and gold .. 3·00 4·00

38. "Jewellery Box" and Sewa Diadem. (Illustration reduced. Actual size 61 × 68 mm.)

1970. Diamond Industry. Imperf. Self-adhesive.

545. **38.** 2 c. mult. (postage) .. 5 5
546. 3½ c. multicoloured .. 8 8
547. 10 c. multicoloured .. 15 15
548. 12½ c. multicoloured .. 20 20
549. 40 c. multicoloured .. 55 55
550. 1 l. multicoloured .. 1·75 1·75
551. – 7½ c. multicoloured (air) 12 12
552. – 9½ c. multicoloured .. 15 15
553. – 15 c. multicoloured .. 25 25
554. – 25 c. multicoloured .. 40 40
555. – 75 c. multicoloured .. 1·40 1·40
556. – 2 l. multicoloured .. 5·50 5·00

DESIGN—HORIZ. (63 × 61 mm.) Nos. 551/6 Diamond and Curtain.

MINIMUM PRICE

The minimum price quoted is 5p which represents a handling charge rather than a basis for valuing common stamps. For further notes about prices see introductory pages.

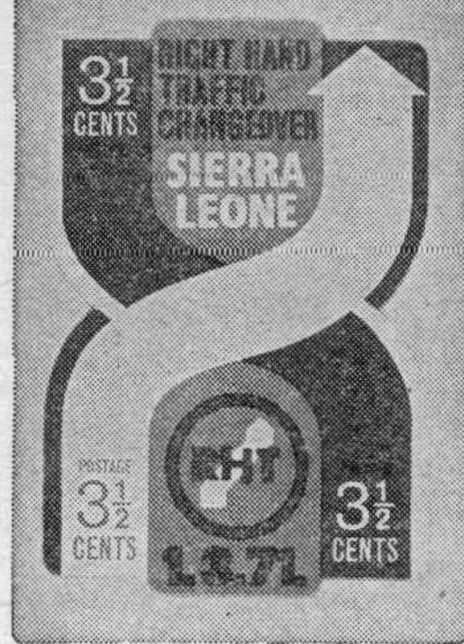

39. "Traffic Changeover".

1971. Changeover to Driving on the Right of the Road. Imperf. Self-adhesive.

557. **39.** 3½ c. orange, blue and black (postage) .. 8 8
558. **39.** 9½ c. blue, orange and black (air) 20 20

1971. Air. Various stamps surch. **AIRMAIL** and value (Nos. 559/61) or value only (Nos. 562/3).

559. 10 c. on 2d. (No. 226) .. 15 15
560. 20 c. on 1s. (No. 230) .. 30 30
561. 50 c. on 1d. (No. 243) .. 70 70
562. 70 c. on 30 c. (No. 476) .. 1·10 1·25
563. 1 l. on 30 c. (No. 476) .. 1·50 1·75

40. Flag and Lion's Head.

1971. Independence. 10th Anniv. Imperf. Self-adhesive.

564. **40.** 2 c. mult. (postage) .. 5 5
565. 3½ c. multicoloured .. 8 8
566. 10 c. multicoloured .. 15 15
567. 12½ c. multicoloured .. 20 20
568. 40 c. multicoloured .. 50 50
569. 1 l. multicoloured .. 1·10 1·25
570. – 7½ c. multicoloured (air) 12 12
571. – 9½ c. multicoloured .. 15 15
572. – 15 c. multicoloured .. 25 25
573. – 25 c. multicoloured .. 35 35
574. – 75 c. multicoloured .. 90 95
575. – 2 l. multicoloured .. 2·50 2·75

DESIGN: "Map" shaped as T **40**. Nos. 570/5, Bugles and lion's head.

41. Siaka Stevens.

1972. Multicoloured. Background colour given.

576. **41.** 1 c. lilac 5 5
577. 2 c. lavender 5 5
578. 4 c. blue 5 5
579. 5 c. brown 5 5
580. 7 c. pink 8 8
581. 10 c. brown 10 12
582. 15 c. green 15 20
583. 18 c. yellow 20 20
584. 20 c. blue 20 25
585. 25 c. orange 25 30
586. 50 c. green 55 65
587. 1 l. mauve .. .. 1·00 1·10
588. 2 l. pink .. .. 2·10 2·25
589. 5 l. cream .. .. 5·25 5·50

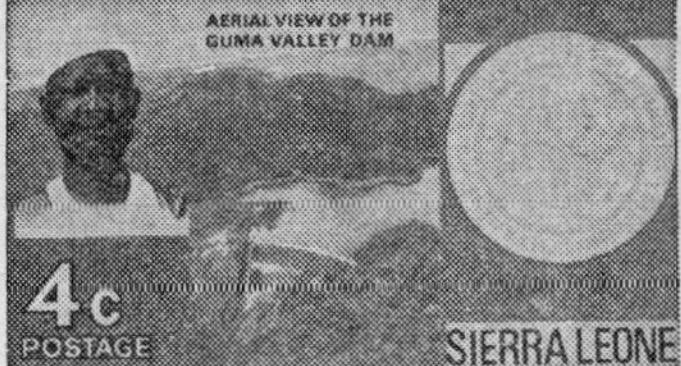

42. Guma Valley Dam and Bank Emblem.

1975. African Development Bank. 10th Anniversary.

590. **42.** 4 c. multicoloured (postage) .. .. 20·00 20·00
591. 15 c. multicoloured (air) 60 60

43. Opening Ceremony.

1975. New Congo Bridge Opening and President Stevens' 70th Birthday.

592. **43.** 5 c. multicoloured (postage) .. .. 4·50 4·50
593. 20 c. multicoloured (air) 50 50

44. Presidents Tolbert and Stevens, and Handclasp.

1975. Mano River Union.

594. **44.** 4 c. multicoloured (postage) 75 75
595. 15 c. multicoloured (air) 25 25

SINGAPORE BC

An island at the south of the Malay peninsula, formerly part of the Straits Settlements but became a Crown Colony on 1 April, 1946, when the stamps of Malaya were used until 1948. From 1 August, 1958, an internally self-governing territory designated the State of Singapore. From 16 September, 1963, part of the Malaysian Federation until 9th August, 1965, when it became an independent republic within the Commonwealth.

100 cents = 1 dollar.

1948. As T **17** of Straits Settlements, but inscr. "MALAYA SINGAPORE".

1. 1 c. black 5 5
2. 2 c. orange 5 5
3. 3 c. green 5 5
19. 4 c. brown 8 8
19a. 5 c. purple 8 8
21. 6 c. grey 8 8
6. 8 c. red 8 8
21a. 8 c. green 20 10
7. 10 c. mauve 8 8
22a. 12 c. red 8 25
8. 15 c. blue 8 8
9. 20 c. black and green .. 10 8
24a. 20 c. blue 12 8
25. 25 c. purple and orange .. 12 8
25a. 35 c. red and purple .. 40 20
11. 40 c. red and purple .. 45 60
12. 50 c. black and blue .. 40 8
13. $1 blue and purple .. 65 8
29. $2 green and red .. .. 1·10 65
30. $5 green and brown .. 3·25 90

1948. Silver Wedding. As T **5/6** of Aden.

31. 10 c. violet 8 8
32. $5 brown .. .. 4·00 4·00

1949. U.P.U. As T **14/17** of Antigua.

33. 10 c. purple 8 8
34. 15 c. blue 12 20
35. 25 c. orange 20 35
36. 50 c. black 40 55

1953. Coronation. As T **7** of Aden.

37. 10 c. black and purple .. 12 8

1. Chinese Sampan.

2. Singapore River.

1955.

38. **1.** 1 c. black 5 5
39. – 2 c. orange 5 5
40. – 4 c. brown 5 5
41. – 5 c. purple 5 5
42. – 6 c. grey 5 5
43. – 8 c. turquoise 8 10
44. – 10 c. lilac 8 5
45. – 12 c. red 15 20
46. – 20 c. blue 20 8
47. – 25 c. orange and violet .. 15 5
48. – 30 c. violet and lake .. 15 5
49. – 50 c. blue and black .. 30 8
50. – $1 blue and purple .. 75 12
51. **2.** $2 green and red .. 1·75 40
52. – $5 yell., red, brn. & black 4·00 1·00

DESIGNS—As T **1** (2 c. to 20 c. are sailing craft): 2 c. Malay kolek. 4 c. Twa-kow. 5 c. Lombok sloop. 6 c. Trengganu pinas. 8 c. Palari. 10 c. Timber tongkong. 12 c. Hainan trader. 20 c. Cocos-keeling schooner. 25 c. "Argonaut" aircraft. 30 c. Oil tanker. 50 c. M.S. "Chusan". As T **2**—VERT. $1 Raffles Statue. $5 Arms of Singapore.

3. The Singapore Lion.

1959. New Constitution. Lion in yellow and sepia.

53. **3.** 4 c. red 8 8
54. 10 c. purple 12 12
55. 20 c. blue 25 25
56. 25 c. green 40 40
57. 30 c. violet 50 50
58. 50 c. slate 85 85

4.

1960. National Day.

59. **4.** 4 c. red, yellow and blue .. 12 8
60. 10 c. red, yellow and grey 15 10

5. Clasped Hands.

1961. National Day.

61. **5.** 4 c. black, brown & yellow 12 8
62. 10 c. black, green & yellow 15 10

6. Sea-Horse.

FISH—HORIZ. 4 c. Six-banded Barb. 5 c. Clown Fish. 10 c. Harlequin. 25 c. Two-spot Gourami. VERT. 6 c. Archer Fish. 20 c. Butterfly Fish.

1962. (a) Fish as T **6**.

64. **6.** 2 c. brown and green .. 5 5
65. – 4 c. black and red .. 5 5
84. – 5 c. red and black .. 5 5
67. – 6 c. black and yellow .. 5 5
85. – 10 c. orange and black .. 8 8
71. – 20 c. orange and blue .. 10 5
86. – 25 c. black and orange .. 15 5

7. "Arachnis—Maggie Oei" (orchid).

(b) Orchids as T **7**. Multicoloured.

63. 1 c. T **7** 5 5
68. 8 c. "Vanda–Tan Chay Yan" 5 5
70. 12 c. "Grammatophyllum speciosum" 8 10
73. 30 c. "Vanda–Miss Joaquim" 20 8

The 8 c. to 30 c. are vert.

(c) Birds as T **7**. Multicoloured.

70a 15 c. Black-naped Tern .. 8 5
87. 50 c. White-rumped Shama 35 30
88. $1 White-throated Kingfisher 75 75
76. $2 Yellow-breasted Sunbird 1·50 50
77. $5 White-bellied Sea Eagle 4·00 1·25

The 15 c., $2 and $5 are vert.

8. "The Role of Labour in Nation-Building".

1962. National Day.

78. **8.** 4 c. yellow, red & black .. 12 5
79. 10 c. yellow, blue & black 15 10

9. Blocks of Flats, Singapore.

1963. National Day.

80. **9.** 4 c. red, blk., bl. & turq. 12 5
81. 10 c. red, blk., ol. & turq. 15 10

10. Dancers in National Costume.

1963. South East Asia Cultural Festival.

82. **10.** 5 c. yellow, black, green and turquoise .. 8 8

11. Workers.

1966. Republic. 1st Anniv.

89. **11.** 15 c. multicoloured .. 10 8
90. 20 c. multicoloured .. 12 15
91. 30 c. multicoloured .. 20 20

12. Flag Procession.

1967. National Day.

92. **12.** 6 c. red, brown & slate 8 8
93. 15 c. purple, brn. & slate 12 10
94. 50 c. blue, brown & slate 45 40

Nos. 92/4 are respectively inscr. "Build a Vigorous Singapore" in Chinese, Malay, and Tamil, in addition to the English inscr.

13. Skyscrapers and Afro-Asian Map.

1967. 2nd Afro-Asian Housing Congress.

95. **13.** 10 c. multicoloured .. 8 8
96. 25 c. multicoloured .. 20 15
97. 50 c. multicoloured .. 40 40

14. Symbolical Figure wielding Hammer, and Industrial outline of Singapore. 16. Sword Dance.

15. Mirudhangam.

1968. National Day. Inscription at top in Chinese (6 c.), Malay (15 c.) or Tamu (50 c.).

98. **14.** 6 c. red, black and gold 8 8
99. 15 c. green, black & gold 12 12
100. 50 c. blue, black & gold 40 40

1968.

101. **15.** 1 c. multicoloured .. 5 5
102. – 4 c. multicoloured .. 5 5
103. **16.** 5 c. multicoloured .. 5 5
104. – 6 c. blk., lemon & orge. 5 5
105. – 10 c. multicoloured .. 5 5
106. – 15 c. multicoloured .. 10 8
107. – 20 c. multicoloured .. 12 8
108. – 25 c. multicoloured .. 15 12
109. – 30 c. multicoloured .. 20 15
110. – 50 c. black, red & brown 30 30
111. – 75 c. multicoloured .. 50 50
112. – $1 multicoloured .. 50 45
113. – $2 multicoloured .. 90 90
114. – $5 multicoloured .. 2·50 2·25
115. – $10 multicoloured .. 5·00 4·50

DESIGNS—As T **15**—VERT. 4 c. Pi Pa. $2 Rebab. $10 Ta Ku. HORIZ. $5 Vina. As T **16**—VERT. 6 c. Lion Dance. 10 c. Bharatha Natyam. 15 c. Tari Payong. 20 c. Kathak Kali. 25 c. Lu Chih Shen and Lin Chung. 50 c. Tari Lilin. 75 c. Tarian Kuda Kepang. $1 Yao Chi. HORIZ. 30 c. Dragon Dance.

16. E.C.A.F.E. Emblem.

1969. Plenary Session of Economic Commission for Asia and the Far East.

116. **16.** 15 c. black, silver & blue 10 10
117. 30 c. black, silver & red 25 25
118. 75 c. black, silver & violet 60 60

17. "100000" and Slogan as Block of Flats. 18. Aircraft over Silhouette of Singapore Docks.

1969. Completion of "100,000 Homes for the People" Project.

119. **17.** 25 c. black and emerald 20 20
120. 50 c. black and blue .. 35 35

1969. Founding of Singapore. 150th Anniv.

121. **18.** 15 c. blk., verm. & yellow 8 8
122. – 30 c. black and blue .. 20 20
123. – 75 c. multicoloured 50 50
124. – $1 black and vermilion 80 80
125. – $5 vermilion and black 3·50 3·50
126. – $10 black and green .. 6·50 6·50

DESIGNS: 30 c. U.N. Emblem and outline of Singapore. 75 c. Flags and outlines of Malaysian Federation. $1 Uplifted hands holding crescent and stars. $5 Tail of Japanese aircraft and searchlight beams. $10 Bust from statue of Sir Stamford Raffles.

19. Sea Shells.

1970. World Fair, Osaka. Multicoloured.

128. 15 c. Type **19** 10 8
129. 30 c. Tropical fish .. 20 20
130. 75 c. Flamingo and Hornbill 45 45
131. $1 Orchid 75 75

20. "Kindergarten".

1970. People's Assn. 10th Anniv.

133. **20.** 15 c. agate and orange .. 10 8
134. – 50 c. blue and orange .. 35 35
135. – 75 c. purple and black .. 45 45

DESIGNS: 50 c. "Sport". 75 c. "Culture".

21. Soldier Charging.

1970. National Day. Multicoloured.

136. 15 c. Type **21** .. 8 8
137. 50 c. Soldier on assault course 35 35
138. $1 Soldier jumping .. 70 70

22. Sprinters.

1970. Festival of Sports.

139.	22.	10 c. mag., blk. & blue	5	5
140.	–	15 c. black and orange	10	10
141.	–	25 c. blk., orge and grn.	20	20
142.	–	50 c. black, grn. & mag.	40	40

DESIGNS: 15 c. Swimmers. 25 c. Tennis-players. 50 c. Racing-cars.

23. Container Berth.
(Illustration reduced. Actual size 56 × 25 mm.).

1970. Singapore Shipping.

143.	–	15 c. multicoloured ..	10	10
144.	23.	30 c. yellow and blue ..	30	30
145.	–	75 c. yellow and red ..	75	75

DESIGNS: 15 c. Ship of Neptune Orient Lines. 75 c. Shipbuilding.

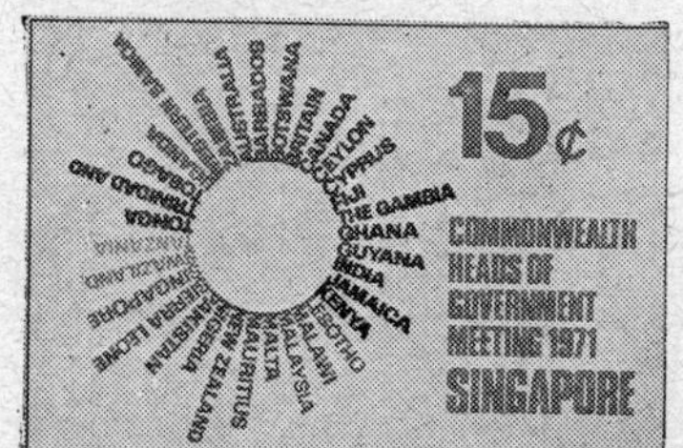

24. Country Names in Circle.

1971. Commonwealth Heads of Government Meeting, Singapore. Multicoloured.

146.	15 c. Type 24	10	10
147.	30 c. Flags in Circle ..	20	20
148.	75 c. Commonwealth Flags	45	45
149.	$1 Commonwealth Flags linked to Singapore (63 × 61 mm.)	60	60

25. Bicycle Rickshaws.

DESIGNS—SQUARE: 20 c. Houseboat "village" and boats. 30 c. Bazaar. HORIZ. (68 × 18 mm.): 50 c. Modern harbour skyline. 75 c. Religious buildings.

1971. Tourism. ASEAN Year. (ASEAN = Association of South East Asian Nations).

150.	25.	15 c. black, violet & orge.	10	10
151.	–	20 c. indigo, orge. & blue	15	15
152.	–	30 c. vermilion & maroon	20	20
153.	–	50 c. multicoloured ..	35	35
154.	–	75 c. multicoloured ..	45	45

26. Chinese New Year.

1971. Singapore Festivals. Multicoloured.

155.	15 c. Type 26	10	10
156.	30 c. Hari Raya	20	20
157.	50 c. Deepavali	35	35
158.	75 c. Christmas	50	50

27. "Dish" Aerial.

1971. Opening of Satellite Earth Station.

160.	27.	15 c. multicoloured ..	10	10
161.	–	30 c. multicoloured ..	30	30
162.	–	30 c. multicoloured ..	30	30
163.	–	30 c. multicoloured ..	30	30
164.	–	30 c. multicoloured ..	30	30

DESIGNS: Nos. 161/4 were printed in se-tenant blocks of four throughout the sheet, the four stamps forming a composite design similar to T 27. They can be identified by the colour of the face value which is: yellow (No. 161), green (No. 162), red (No. 163) or orange (No. 164).

28. "Singapore River and Fort Canning, 1843–7" (Lieut. E. A. Porcher).
(Illustration reduced. Actual size 53 × 46 mm.)

1971. Art. Multicoloured.

165.	10 c. Type 28	10	10
166.	15 c. "The Padang, 1851" (J. T. Thomson) ..	12	12
167.	20 c. "Singapore Waterfront, 1848-9" ..	15	15
168.	35 c. "View from Fort Canning, 1846" (J. T. Thomson)	30	30
169.	50 c. "View from Mt. Wallich, 1857" (P. Carpenter)	60	60
170.	$1 "Singapore Waterfront, 1861" (W. Gray) ..	1·40	1·40

The 50 c. and $1 are larger, 69 × 47 mm.

29. One-cent Coin of George V.

1972. Coins.

171.	29.	15 c. orange, blk. & grn.	10	10
172.	–	35 c. black and red ..	25	25
173.	–	$1 yellow, black & blue	60	60

DESIGNS: 35 c. One dollar of 1969. $1 One hundred and fifty dollar gold coin of 1969.

30. "Moon Festival" (Seah Kim Joo).

1972. Contemporary Art. Multicoloured.

174.	15 c. Type 30	10	10
175.	35 c. "Complementary Force" (Thomas Yeo)	30	30
176.	50 c. "Rhythm in Blue" (Yusman Aman)	40	40
177.	$1 "Gibbons" (Chen Wen Hsi)	70	70

Nos. 175/6 are 36 × 54 mm.

31. Lanterns and Fish.

1972. National Day. Designs symbolising Festivals. Multicoloured.

178.	15 c. Type 31	10	10
179.	35 c. Altar and candles ..	25	25
180.	50 c. Jug, bowl and gifts	40	40
181.	75 c. Candle	50	50

32. Student Welding.

1972. Youth.

182.	32.	15 c. multicoloured ..	10	10
183.	–	35 c. multicoloured ..	25	25
184.	–	$1 orge., violet & green	60	60

DESIGNS: 35 c. Sport. $1 Dancing.

33. "Maria Rickmers".

1972. Shipping. Multicoloured.

185.	15 c. "Neptune Ruby" (42 × 29 mm.)	10	10
186.	75 c. Type 33	50	50
187.	$1 Chinese junk	60	60

34. P.Q.R. Slogan.

1973. "Prosperity Through Quality and Reliability" Campaign. Multicoloured.

189.	15 c. Type 34	10	10
190.	35 c. Badge	25	25
191.	75 c. Text (diff.)	40	40
192.	$1 Seal	55	55

35. Jurong Bird Park.

1973. Singapore Landmarks.

193.	35.	15 c. black and orange	10	10
194.	–	35 c. black and green	25	25
195.	–	50 c. black and brown	35	35
196.	–	$1 black and purple ..	60	60

DESIGNS: 35 c. National Theatre. 50 c. City Hall. $1 Fullerton Building and Singapore River.

36. Aircraft Tail-fins.

1973. Aviation. Multicoloured.

197.	10 c. Type 36	8	8
198.	35 c. Emblems of Singapore Airlines and destinations	25	25
199.	75 c. Emblem on tail-fin ..	40	40
200.	$1 Emblems encircling the globe	55	55

37. "Culture".

1973. National Day.

201.	37.	10 c. orange and black	8	8
202.	–	35 c. orange and black	25	25
203.	–	50 c. orange and black	35	35
204.	–	75 c. orange and black	45	45

Nos. 201/204 were printed in se-tenant blocks of four within the sheet, and form a composite design representing Singapore's culture.

38. Athletics, Judo and Boxing.

1973. Seventh S.E.A.P.* Games.

205.	38.	10 c. gold, silver and blue	8	8
206.	–	15 c. gold and black ..	10	10
207.	–	25 c. gold, silver and blk.	15	15
208.	–	35 c. gold, silver and blue	25	25
209.	–	50 c. multicoloured ..	30	30
210.	–	$1 silver, blue and green	60	60

DESIGNS—As T 38. 15 c. Cycling, weightlifting, pistol-shooting and sailing. 25 c. Footballs. 35 c. Hockey stick. HORIZ. (41 × 25 mm.). 50 c. Swimmers. $1 Stadium.
*S.E.A.P. = South East Asian Peninsular.

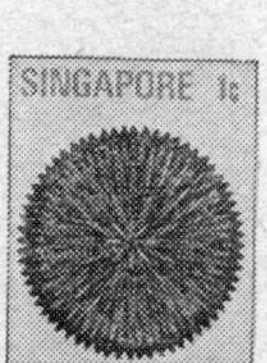

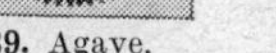

39. Agave. 40. Mangosteen.

1973. Multicoloured.

(a) Flowers and plants as T 39.

212.	1 c. Type 39	5	5
213.	5 c. "Coleus blumei" ..	5	5
214.	10 c. "Vinca rosea" ..	5	5
215.	15 c. "Helianthus angustifolius"	5	5
216.	20 c. "Licuala grandis" ..	8	8
217.	25 c. "Wedelia trilobata"	10	10
218.	35 c. "Chrysanthemum frutescens"	12	15
219.	50 c. "Costus malortieanus"	20	20
220.	75 c. "Gerbera jamesonii"	30	35

(b) Fruits as T 40.

221.	$1 Type 40	40	45
222.	$2 Jackfruit	75	90
223.	$5 Coconut	1·90	2·00
224.	$10 Pineapple	3·75	4·00

41. Tiger and Orang-utans.

1973. Singapore Zoo. Multicoloured.

225. 5 c. Type **41** .. 5 5
226. 10 c. Leopard and gazelles 8 8
227. 35 c. Panther and deer .. 25 25
228. 75 c. Horse and lion .. 45 45

42. Multicolour Guppy. **44.** U.P.U. Emblem and Multiple "Centenary".

43. Scout Badge within "9".

1974. Tropical Fish. Multicoloured.

229 5 c. Type **42** .. 5 5
230. 10 c. Half Black Guppy .. 8 8
231. 35 c. Multicolour Guppy (different) 20 20
232. $1 Black Guppy 55 55

1974. Ninth Asia-Pacific Scout Conference.

233. **43.** 10 c. multicoloured .. 8 8
234. 75 c. multicoloured .. 35 40

1974. U.P.U. Centenary.

235. **44.** 10 c. brn., pur. & gold.. 8 8
236. – 35 c. bl., dark bl. & gold 20 20
237. – 75 c. multicoloured .. 40 40

DESIGNS: 35 c. U.P.U. emblem and multiple U.N. symbols. 75 c. U.P.U. emblem and multiple peace doves.

45. Family Emblem.

1974. World Population Year. Multicoloured.

238. 10 c. Type **45** 8 8
239. 35 c. Male and female symbols 20 20
240. 75 c. World Population Map 40 40

46. "Tree and Sun" (Chia Keng San).

1974. Universal Children's Day. Mult.

241. 5 c. Type **46** 5 5
242. 10 c. "My Daddy and Mummy" (Angeline Ang) 8 8
243. 35 c. "A Dump Truck" (Si-Hoe Yeen Joong) .. 20 20
244. 50 c. "My Aunt" (Raymond Teo) 30 30

47. Street Scene.

1977. Singapore Views. Multicoloured.

246. 15 c. Type **47** 10 10
247. 20 c. Singapore River .. 12 12
248. $1 "Kelong" (fish-trap) .. 50 50

48. Emblem and Lighters' Prows.

1975. Ninth Biennial Conference of Int., Association of Ports and Harbours, Singapore. Multicoloured.

249. 5 c. Type **48** 5 5
250. 25 c. Freighter and ship's wheel 15 15
251. 50 c. Oil-tanker and flags.. 25 25
252. $1 Container-ship and ship's propellers .. 45 45

49. Satellite Earth Station, Sentosa.

1975. "Science and Industry". Multicoloured.

253. 10 c. Type **49** 8 8
254. 35 c. Oil refineries (vert.).. 20 20
255. 75 c. "Medical Sciences" 35 35

50. "Homes and Gardens".

1975. 10th National Day. Multicoloured.

256. 10 c. Type **50** 5 5
257. 35 c. "Shipping and Shipbuilding" 20 20
258. 75 c. "Communications and Technology" .. 35 35
259. $1 "Trade, Commerce and Industry" .. 45 45

51. Crowned Cranes.

1975. Birds. Multicoloured.

260. 5 c. Type **51** 5 5
261. 10 c. Great Hornbill .. 5 5
262. 35 c. Kingfishers 20 20
263. $1 Greater Sulphur-crested Cockatoo, and Blue and Yellow Macaw.. .. 45 45

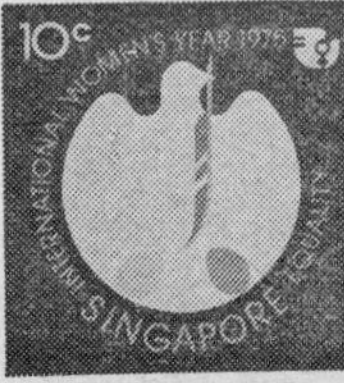

52. "Equality".

1975. International Women's Year. Multicoloured.

264. 10 c. Type **52** 5 5
265. 35 c. "Development" .. 20 20
266. 75 c. "Peace" 35 35

53. Yellow Flame. **54.** "Arachnis hookeriana x Vanda" Hilo Blue.

1976. Wayside Trees. Multicoloured.

268. 10 c. Type **53** 5 5
269. 35 c. Cabbage Tree .. 15 20
270. 50 c. Rose of India .. 25 25
271. 75 c. Variegated Coral Tree 35 35

1976. Singapore Orchids. Multicoloured.

272. 10 c. Type **54** 5 5
273. 35 c. "Arachnis Maggie Oei x Vanda insignis" .. 15 20
274. 50 c. "Arachnis Maggei Oei x Vanda" Rodman .. 20 25
275. 75 c. "Arachnis hookeriana x Vanda" Dawn Nishimura 30 35

55. Festival Symbol and Band.

1976. Singapore Youth Festival. 10th Anniv. Multicoloured.

276. 10 c. Type **55** 5 5
277. 35 c. Athletes 15 20
278. 75 c. Dancers 30 35

56. "Queen Elizabeth Walk".

1976. Paintings of Old Singapore. Mult.

279. 10 c. Type **56** 5 5
280. 50 c. "The Padang" .. 20 25
281. $1 "Raffles Place" .. 45 50

57. Chinese Costume.

1976. Bridal Costumes. Multicoloured.

283. 10 c. Type **57** 5 5
284. 35 c. Indian costume .. 15 20
285. 75 c. Malay costume .. 30 35

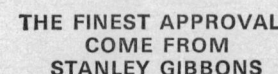

58. Radar, Missile and Soldiers.

1977. National Service. 10th Anniv. Multicoloured.

286. 10 c. Type **58** 5 5
287. 50 c. Tank and soldiers .. 20 25
288. 75 c. Soldiers, wireless operators, pilot and aircraft 30 35

POSTAGE DUE STAMPS

The postage due stamps of Malayan Postal Union were in use in Singapore from 1948 until replaced by the following issue.

D 1.

1968.

D 1. D **1.** 1 c. green 5 5
D 2. 2 c. red 5 5
D 3. 4 c. orange 5 5
D 4. 8 c. chocolate .. 5 8
D 13. 10 c. magenta .. 5 8
D 6. 12 c. violet 8 10
D 7. 20 c. blue 10 12
D 16. 50 c. drab 20 25

SIRMOOR BC

A state of the Punjab, India. Now uses Indian stamps.

1. 2.

1879.

1. **1.** 1 pice green .. .. 2·75
2. 1 pice blue .. .. 2·25 24·00

1892.

3b. **2.** 1 pice green 20 30
4. 1 pice blue 30 30

3. Raja Sir Shamsher Parkash. **4.**

1885.

6. **3.** 3 p. brown 10 5
8. 3 p. orange 10 5
12. 6 p. green 10 10
17. 1 a. blue 30 35
20. 2 a. red .. .. .. 2·25 2·25

1895.

22. **4.** 3 p. orange 65 40
23. 6 p. green 65 40
24. 1 a. blue 65 40
25. 2 a. red 80 80
26. 3 a. green .. .. .. 1·50 2·25
27. 4 a. green .. .. .. 1·50 2·25
28. 8 a. blue .. .. .. 1·75 2·75
29. 1 r. red .. .. .. 2·00 4·00

5. Raja Sir Surendar Bikram Parkash.

1899.

30. **5.** 3 a. green .. .. .. 1·00 2·75
31. 4 a. green .. .. .. 1·50 4·00
32. 8 a. blue .. .. .. 2·00 4·00
33. 1 r. red .. .. .. 4·00 5·00

OFFICIAL STAMPS

1890. Optd. **ON S.S.S.**

60. **3.** 3 p. orange 20 20
79. 6 p. green 20 20
80. 1 a. blue 20 20
81. 2 a. red .. .. .. 1·50 1·50

SLOVAKIA E3

Part of Czechoslovakia; a separate state from 1939 to 1945.

100 haleru = 1 koruna.

1939. Stamps of Czechoslovakia optd. **Slovensky stat 1939.**

2. **22.** 5 h. blue 12 15
3. 10 h. brown 5 5
4. 20 h. red 5 5
5. 25 h. green 35 55
6. 30 h. purple 5 5
7. **50.** 40 h. blue 5 5
8. **65.** 50 h. green 5 5
9. **53.** 50 h. green 5 5
10. **65.** 60 h. violet 5 5
11. 60 h. blue .. .. .. 1·10 1·40
12. **49.** 1 k. red 5 5
13. – 1 k. 20 purple (No. 354) .. 5 8
14. **51.** 1 k. 50 red 5 8
15. – 1 k. 60 olive (No. 355a) .. 35 50
16. – 2 k. green (No. 356) .. 45 60
17. – 2 k. 50 blue (No. 357) .. 10 12
18. – 3 k. chocolate (No. 358) .. 12 15
19. – 3 k. 50 violet (No. 359) .. 4·50 5·50
20. **52.** 4 k. violet .. .. 1·75 2·75
21. – 5 k. green (No. 361) .. 2·75 4·00
22. – 10 k. blue (No. 362) .. 26·00 29·00

1. Father Hlinka.

ILLUSTRATIONS
British Commonwealth and all overprints and surcharges are FULL SIZE. Foreign Countries have been reduced to ¾-LINEAR.

1939. As T 1 but inscr. "CESKO-SLOVENSKO SLOVENSKA POSTA", optd. **SLOVENSKY STAT.**

23. **1.** 50 h. green 45 10
24. 1 k. red 60 12

1939.

25. **1.** 5 h. blue 8 15
26. 10 h. olive 20 15
27a. 20 h. red 12 12
28. 30 h. violet 20 15
29. 50 h. green 25 15
33. 1 k. red 15 8
34. 2 k. 50 blue 20 8
35a. 3 k. sepia 15 5

3. Krivan. **4.** Chamois. **5.** Mgr. Tiso.

6. Weaving. **7.** Sawyer.

8. Presidential Palace, Bratislava. **9.** Rev. J. Murgas and Wireless Masts.

1939.

40. – 5 h. olive 12 5
41. **3.** 10 h. brown 5 5
125. 10 h. red 5 5
42. – 20 h. grey 5 5
126. – 20 h. blue 5 5
43. **4.** 25 h. brown 5 5
127. 25 h. maroon 5 5
44. – 30 h. brown 5 5
128. – 30 h. purple 5 5
45. **5.** 50 h. olive 5 5
129. – 50 h. green 5 5
46. **5.** 70 h. brown 5 5
47. **6.** 2 k. green .. .. .. 1·00 12
48. **7.** 4 k. brown 25 8
49. – 5 k. red 35 8
50. **8.** 10 k. blue 40 25

DESIGNS—As T 3: 5 h., 50 h. (No. 129), Zelene Pleso. 20 h. Kvety Satier (Edelweiss), 30 h. Javorina. As T 7: 5 k. Woman filling ewer at spring. Nos. 125, 126, 127, 128, and 129 are $18\frac{1}{2} \times 22\frac{1}{2}$ mm. and Nos. 40/1, 42, 43 and 44 are $17\frac{1}{2} \times 21$ mm.

1939. Rev. J. Murgas. 10th Death Anniv.

51. **9.** 60 h. violet 5 5
52. 1 k. 20 slate 15 8

1939. Child Welfare. As No. 45 but larger and inscr. "+2.50 DETOM".

54. 2 k. 50+2 k. 50 blue .. 90 90

10. Lake Csorba. **11.** Tatra Mountains. **12.** Eagle and Aeroplane.

1939. Air.

55. **10.** 30 h. violet 5 5
56. 50 h. green 5 5
57. 1 k. red 5 8
58. **11.** 2 k. green 12 12
59. 3 k. brown 15 15
60. 4 k. blue 20 20
62. **12.** 5 k. purple 15 20
63. 10 k. grey 12 15
64. 20 k. green 25 40

13. Stiavnica Castle. **14.** S. M. Daxner and Bishop Moyses.

1941.

65. **13.** 1 k. 20 claret 5 5
66. – 1 k. 50 red (Lietava) .. 5 5
67. – 1 k. 60 blue (Spissky Hrad) 5 5
68. 2 k. green (Bojnice) .. 5 5

1941. Presentation of Slovak Memorandum to Emperor Francis Joseph. 80th Anniv.

69. **14.** 50 h. olive 30 35
70. 1 k. blue .. .. .. 1·60 1·75
71. 2 k. black .. .. .. 1·40 1·40

15. Wounded Soldier and Red Cross Orderly.

1941. Red Cross Fund.

72. **15.** 50 h.+50 h. green .. 8 8
73. 1 k.+1 k. claret .. 10 12
74. 2 k.+1 k. blue .. 50 55

20. Mother and Child. **21.** Soldier with a Hlinka Youth.

1941. Child Welfare Fund.

75. **20.** 50 h.+50 h. green .. 15 20
76. 1 k.+1 k. brown .. 20 20
77. 2 k.+1 k. violet .. 25 30

1942. Hlinka Youth Fund.

78. **21.** 70 h.+1 k. brown .. 12 15
79. 1 k. 30+1 k. blue .. 12 15
80. 2 k.+1 k. red .. 40 45

1942. Father Hlinka. As T 1, but inscr. "SLOVENSKO" (without "POSTA").

81. 1 k. 30 violet 5 5

22. Boy Stamp Collector. **23.** Dove and St. Stephen's.

1942. Philatelic Exn., Bratislava. Inscr. as in T 22.

82. – 30 h. green 25 35
83. **22.** 70 h. red 25 35
84. – 80 h. violet 25 35
85. – 1 k. 30 brown 25 35

DESIGNS: 30 h., 1 k. 30, Posthorn round various arms about Bratislava. 80 h. Postmaster-General examining stamps.

1942. European Postal Congress.

86. **23.** 70 h. green 25 40
87. 1 k. 30 olive 40 55
88. 2 k. blue 50 65

24. Inaugural Ceremony. **25.** L. Stur.

1942. National Literary Society. 15th Anniv.

89. **24.** 70 h. black 5 5
90. 1 k. red 8 12
91. 1 k. 30 blue 5 8
92. 2 k. brown 8 12
93. 3 k. green 10 12
94. 4 k. violet 12 15

1943.

95. **25.** 80 h. green 5 5
96. – 1 k. red 8 8
97. – 1 k. 30 blue 5 5

PORTRAITS: 1 k. M. Razus. 1 k. 30, Father Hlinka.

26. National Costumes. **27.** Infantry.

1943. Winter Relief Fund.

98. **26.** 50 h.+50 h. green .. 5 5
99. – 70 h.+1 k. red .. 5 8
100. – 80 h.+2 k. blue .. 8 12

DESIGNS: 70 h. Mother and child. 80 h. Mother and two children.

1943. Fighting Forces.

106. **27.** 70 h.+2 k. lake .. 12 15
107. – 1 k. 30+2 k. blue .. 15 20
108. – 2 k.+2 k. olive .. 30 35

DESIGNS—HORIZ. Artillery. 1 k. 30, Air Force.

28. Railway Tunnel. **29.** Railway Viaduct.

1943. Opening of the Strazke-Presov Railway. Inscr. "5 IX 1943".

109. – 70 h. purple 8 8
110. – 80 h. blue 8 8
111. **28.** 1 k. 30 black 8 8
112. **29.** 2 k. brown 8 8

DESIGNS—HORIZ. 70 h. Presov Church. 80 h. Railway engine.

30. "The Slovak Language is our Life". **31.** National Museum.

1943. Culture Fund.

113. **30.** 30 h.+1 k. brown .. 5 5
114. **31.** 70 h.+1 k. green .. 25 30
115. – 80 h.+2 k. blue .. 5 5
116. – 1 k. 30+2 k. brown .. 5 5

DESIGNS—HORIZ. 80 h. Matica Slovenska College. VERT. 1 k. 30, Agricultural Student.

32. Prince Pribina Okolo. **33.** Footballer.

1944. Declaration of Independence. 5th Anniv.

117. **32.** 50 h. green 5 5
118. – 70 h. mauve 5 5
119. – 80 h. brown 5 5
120. – 1 k. 30 blue 5 5
121. – 2 k. blue 8 10
122. – 3 k. brown 10 15
123. – 5 k. violet 15 25
124. – 10 k. black 60 90

DESIGNS: 70 h. Prince Mojmir. 80 h. Prince Ratislav. 1 k. 30, King Svatopluk. 2 k. Prince Kocel. 3 k. Prince Mojmir II. 5 k. Prince Svatopluk II. 10 k. Prince Braslav.

1944. Sports.

130. **33.** 70 h.+70 h. olive .. 12 15
131. – 1 k.+1 k. violet .. 25 35
132. – 1 k. 30+1 k. 30 green .. 25 35
133. – 2 k.+2 k. brown .. 25 35

DESIGNS—VERT. 1 k. Ski-ing. 1 k. 30, Diving. HORIZ. 2 k. Running.

34. Symbolic of "Protection".

ILLUSTRATIONS
British Commonwealth and all overprints and surcharges are FULL SIZE. Foreign Countries have been reduced to ¾-LINEAR.

1944. Protection Series.

134. **34.** 70 h.+4 k. blue .. 25 30
135. 1 k. 30+4 k. brown .. 25 30
136. 2 k. green 5 8
137. 3 k. 80 purple 10 10

35. Children Playing. **36.** Mgr. Tiso.

1944. Child Welfare.

138. **35.** 2 k.+4 k. blue 55 70

1945.

139. **36.** 1 k. orange 25 25
140. 1 k. 50 brown 8 5
141. 2 k. green 12 5
142. 4 k. red 25 15
143. 5 k. blue 25 25
144. 10 k. purple 25 15

POSTAGE DUE STAMPS

D 1. D 2.

1939.

D 51. **D 1.** 5 h. blue 5 15
D 52. 10 h. blue 5 5
D 53. 20 h. blue 5 5
D 54. 30 h. blue 12 40
D 55. 40 h. blue 12 12
D 56. 50 h. blue 20 20
D 57. 60 h. blue 12 15
D 58. 1 k. red 40 40
D 59. 2 k. red .. .. 2·00 65
D 60. 5 k. red 65 65
D 61. 10 k. red 90 90
D 62. 20 k. red .. .. 3·25 2·25

1942.

D 89. **D 2.** 10 h. brown 5 5
D 90. 20 h. brown 5 10
D 91. 40 h. brown 5 10
D 92. 50 h. brown 40 10
D 93. 60 h. brown 8 10
D 94. 80 h. brown 8 10
D 95. 1 k. red 8 10
D 96. 1 k. 10 red 20 25
D 97. 1 k. 30 red 8 10
D 98. 1 k. 60 red 12 10
D 99. 2 k. red 8 10
D 100. 2 k. 60 red 25 15
D 101. 3 k. 50 red 30 40
D 102. 5 k. red 40 40
D 103. 10 k. red 80 55

NEWSPAPER STAMPS

1939. Nos. N 364/72 of Czechoslovakia optd. **1939. SLOVENSKY STAT.**

N 25. 2 h. brown 5 5
N 26. 5 h. blue 5 5
N 27. 7 h. orange 5 5
N 28. 9 h. green 5 5
N 29. 10 h. lake 5 5
N 30. 12 h. blue 5 5
N 31. 20 h. green 5 5
N 32. 50 h. brown 25 25
N 33. 1 k. olive .. .. 1·40 1·40

N 1. N 2. Printer's Type

1939. Imperf.

N 40. N 1. 2 h. brown 5 8
N 41. 5 h. blue 12 8
N 42. 7 h. orange 10 8
N 43. 9 h. green 8 8
N 44. 10 h. red 12 8
N 45. 12 h. blue 10 8
N 67. 15 h. purple 5 8
N 46. 20 h. green 12 8
N 69. 25 h. blue 8 8
N 70. 40 h. red 8 8
N 71. 50 h. brown 12 8
N 72. 1 k. grey 15 12
N 73. 2 k. green 15 15

1943. Imperf.

N 101. N 2. 10 h. green 8 8
N 102. 15 h. brown 8 8
N 103. 20 h. blue 8 8
N 104. 50 h. red 10 10
N 105. 1 k. green 15 15
N 106. 2 k. blue 30 30

PERSONAL DELIVERY STAMPS

P 1.

1940. Imperf.

P 65. P 1. 50 h. blue 15 25
P 66. 50 h. red 15 25

SLOVENIA E3

A province of Yugoslavia, for which stamps were issued whilst under Italian and German Occupation

ITALIAN OCCUPATION, 1941.

Co. Ci.

(1).

1941. Nos. 330/1 and 414/26 of Yugoslavia optd. with Type **1**.

1. **63.** 25 p. black 5 5
2. 50 p. orange 5 5
3. 1 d. green 5 5
4. 1 d. 50 red 5 5
5. 2 d. red 5 5
6. 3 d. brown 5 5
7. 4 d. blue 5 5
8. 5 d. blue 5 5
9. 5 d. 50 violet 5 8
10. 6 d. blue 5 8
11. 8 d. chocolate 5 8
12. **34.** 10 d. violet 5 8
13. **63.** 12 d. violet 5 8
14. **34.** 15 d. olive 27·00 28·00
15. **63.** 16 d. purple 5 5
16. 20 d. blue 20 25
17. 30 d. pink 3·75 4·50

1941. Nos. 330 and 414/26 of Yugoslavia optd. **R. Commissariato Civile Territori Sloveni occupati LUBIANA,** with four lines of dots at foot.

23. **63.** 25 p. black 5 5
24. 50 p. orange 5 5
25. 1 d. green 5 5
26. 1 d. 50 red 5 5
27. 2 d. red 5 5
28. 3 d. brown 5 5
29. 4 d. blue 5 5
30. 5 d. blue 5 5
31. 5 d. 50 violet 5 5
32. 6 d. blue 5 5
33. 8 d. chocolate 5 5
34. **34.** 10 d. violet 5 5
35. **63.** 12 d. violet 5 5
36. 16 d. purple 5 8
37. 20 d. blue 40 50
38. 30 d. pink 7·00 7·00

1941. Nos. 446/9 of Yugoslavia optd. as Nos. 23/38 but with only three lines of dots at foot.

45. 50 p.+50 p. on 5 d. violet 1·50 1·75
46. 1 d.+1 d. on 10 d. lake 1·50 1·75
47. 1 d. 50+1 d. 50 on 20 d. grn. 1·50 1·75
48. 2 d.+2 d. on 30 d. 1·50 1·75

1941. Nos. 360/7 and 443/4 of Yugoslavia optd. as Nos. 23/38, with three or four (No. 57) lines of dots at foot.

49. 50 p. brown 5 5
50. 1 d. green 5 5
51. 2 d. blue 5 5
52. 2 d. 50 red 5 8
53. 5 d. violet 12 15
54. 10 d. lake 10 12
55. 20 d. green 85 1·00
56. 30 d. blue 5·50 6·00
57. 40 d. green 42·00 48·00
58. 50 d. blue 23·00 25·00

1941. Nos. 26 and 29 surch.

59. **63.** 0 d. 50 on 1 d. 50 red 5 5
60. 0 d. 50 on 1 d. 50 red £120 £140
61. 1 d. on 4 d. blue 5 5

GERMAN OCCUPATION 1943–45.

(1.) (2.)

1944. Stamps of Italy optd. with Types **1** or **2**. (a) On Postage stamps of 1929. Nos. 239, etc.

65. **2.** 5 c. brown 5 5
66. **1.** 10 c. brown 5 5
67. **2.** 15 c. green 5 5
68. **1.** 20 c. red 5 5
69. **2.** 25 c. green 5 5
70. **1.** 30 c. brown 5 5
71. **2.** 35 c. blue 5 5
72. **1.** 50 c. violet 5 5
73. **2.** 75 c. red 5 5
74. **1.** 1 l. violet 5 5
75. **2.** 1 l. 25 blue 5 5
76. **1.** 1 l. 75 orange 30 35
77. **2.** 2 l. claret 5 5
78. **1.** 10 l. violet 35 40

Surch. with new value.

79. – 2 l. 55 on 5 c. brown 5 5
80. **2.** 5 l. on 25 c. green 5 8
81. 20 l. on 20 c. red 10 12
82. **1.** 25 l. on 2 l. claret 20 25
83. **2.** 50 l. on 1 l. 75 orange 35 45

In No. 79 the overprint inscriptions are at each side of the eagle.

(b) On Air stamps, Nos. 270, etc.

84. **2.** 25 c. green 5 5
85. **1.** 50 c. brown 65 75
86. **2.** 75 c. brown 5 5
87. **1.** 1 l. violet 65 75
88. **2.** 2 l. blue 5 5
89. **1.** 5 l. green 15 20
90. **2.** 10 l. red 25 30

(c) On Air Express stamp.

E 91. **1.** 2 l. black (No. E 370) 45 60

(d) On Express Letter stamp.

E 92. **1.** 1 l. 25 green (No. E 350) 5 5

1944. Red Cross. Express Letter stamps of Italy surch. as Types **1** or **2** with a red cross and new value alongside.

102. E **3.** 1 l. 25+50 l. green 2·00 2·50
103. 2 l. 50+50 l. orange 2·00 2·50

1944. Homeless Relief Fund. Express Letter stamps of Italy surch. as Types **1** and **2**, but in circular frame, and **DEN OBDACHLOSEN BREZDOMCEM** alongside with new value between.

104. E **3.** 1 l. 25+50 l. green 2·10 2·50
105. 2 l. 50+50 l. orange 2·10 2·50

1944. Orphans' Fund. Air stamps of Italy Nos. 270, etc., surch as Types **1** and **2**, but in circular frame between **DEN WAISEN SIROTAM** and new value.

106. – 25 c.+10 l. green 85 1·00
107. **81.** 50 c.+10 l. brown 85 1·00
108. – 75 c.+20 l. brown 85 1·00
109. – 1 l.+20 l. violet 85 1·00
110. **84.** 2 l.+20 l. blue 85 1·00
111. **81.** 5 l.+20 l. green 85 1·00

1944. Orphans' Fund. Air stamps of Italy Nos. 270, etc., surch. as Types **1** and **2**, but in circular frame between **DEN WAISEN SIROTAM** and new value.

112. – 25 c.+10 l. green 85 1·00
113. **81.** 50 c.+10 l. brown 85 1·00
114. – 75 c.+20 l. brown 85 1·00
115. – 1 l.+20 l. violet 85 1·00
116. **84.** 2 l.+20 l. blue 85 1·00
117. **81.** 5 l.+20 l. green 85 1·00

3. Railway Viaduct, Borovnice. **4.** Ribnika Church.

1945. Inscr. "PROVINZ LAIBACH".

118. – 5 c. brown 5 5
119. – 10 c. orange 5 5
120. **3.** 20 c. brown 5 5
121. – 25 c. green 5 5
122. **4.** 50 c. violet 5 5
123. – 75 c. red 5 5
124. – 1 l. green 5 5
125. – 1 l. 25 blue 5 5
126. – 1 l. 50 green 5 5
127. – 2 l. blue 5 8
128. – 2 l. 50 brown 5 5
129. – 3 l. magenta 5 8
130. – 5 l. brown 8 12
131. – 10 l. green 10 12
132. – 20 l. blue 35 55
133. – 30 l. red 14·00 14·00

DESIGNS—VERT. 5 c. Stalagmites, Krizna Jama. 1 l. 25, Kocevje. 1 l. 50, Borovnice Falls. 3 l. Castle Zuzemperk. 30 l. View and Tabor Church. HORIZ. 10 c. Zirknitz Lake. 25 c. Farm near Ljubljana. 75 c. View from Ribnica. 1 l. Old Castle, Ljubljana. 2 l. Castle, Konstajovica. 2 l. 50, Castle, Turiak. 5 l. View on River Krka. 10 l. Castle, Otocec. 20 l. Farm.

POSTAGE DUE STAMPS

1941. Postage Due stamps of Yugoslavia, Nos. D 89/93 optd. with Type **1**.

D 18. D **10.** 50 p. violet 5 5
D 19. 1 d. magenta 5 5
D 20. 2 d. blue 5 5
D 21. 5 d. orange 30 30
D 22. 10 d. chocolate 30 30

Optd. as Nos. 18/33, but with four lines of dots at top.

D 40. D **10.** 50 p. violet 5 5
D 41. 1 d. magenta 5 5
D 42. 2 d. blue 5 5
D 43. 5 d. orange 3·50 3·75
D 44. 10 d. chocolate 60 65

Optd. as Nos. D 6/10, but with narrower lettering.

D 62. D **10.** 50 p. violet 12 15
D 63. 1 d. magenta 30 35
D 64. 2 d. blue 3·75 4·25

(D 1.) (D 2.)

1944. Postage Due stamps of Italy, Nos. D 395, etc., optd. as Type D **1**.

D 93. D **6.** 5 c. brown 25 25
D 94. 10 c. blue 25 25
D 95. 20 c. red 5 5
D 96. 25 c. green 5 5
D 97. 50 c. violet 5 5
D 98. D **7.** 1 l. orange 5 5
D 99. 2 l. green 5 5

Surch. as Type D **2**.

D 100. **6.** D 30 c. on 50 c. violet 5 5
D 101. 40 c. on 5 c. brown 5 5

SOLOMON ISLANDS BC

A group of islands in the W. Pacific, E. of New Guinea, under Br. protection.

1966. 100 cents = $1 Australian.

1. Native War Canoe.

1907.

1. **1.** ½d. blue 5·50 8·50
2. 1d. red 11·00 12·00
3. 2d. blue 11·00 12·00
4. 2½d. yellow 12·00 14·00
5. 5d. green 22·00 28·00
6. 6d. chocolate 28·00 28·00
7. 1s. purple 35·00 38·00

2.

3.

1908.

8. **2.** ½d. green 40 65
9. 1d. red 85 1·10
10. 2d. grey 1·25 1·40
11. 2½d. blue 1·40 2·00
11a. 4d. red on yellow 2·50 3·50
12. 5d. olive 6·00 4·50
13. 6d. claret 5·50 4·50
14. 1s. black on green 7·00 7·00
15. 2s. purple on blue 17·00 18·00
16. 2s. 6d. red on blue 28·00 35·00
17. 5s. green on yellow 50·00 55·00

1913. Inscr. "POSTAGE POSTAGE".

18. **3.** ½d. green 90 1·40
19. 1d. red 1·00 4·00
42. 1½d. red 90 30
20. 3d. purple on yellow 1·40 3·50
21. 11d. purple and red 4·50 6·00

1914. Inscr. "POSTAGE REVENUE".

39. **3.** ½d. green 30 50
24. 1d. red 60 90
41. 1d. violet 70 1·25
43. 2d. grey 65 1·40
27. 2½d. blue 1·25 3·00
28. 3d. purple on yellow 8·00 14·00
44. 3d. blue 60 1·60
45. 4d. black & red on yellow 1·10 2·75
45a. 4½d. brown 2·75 3·50
46. 5d. purple and green 1·60 3·50
47. 6d. purple 1·60 3·50
48. 1s. black on green 2·25 4·00
49. 2s. purple and blue on blue 7·50 11·00
50. 2s. 6d. black & red on blue 9·00 13·00
51. 5s. green and red on yellow 14·00 18·00
37. 10s. green and red on green 55·00 22·00
38. £1 purple & black on red £100 £120

1935. Silver Jubilee. As T **11** of Antigua.

53. 1½d. blue and red 45 55
54. 3d. brown and blue 1·60 2·25
55. 6d. blue and olive 2·00 3·50
56. 1s. grey and purple 3·50 5·00

1937. Coronation. As T **2** of Aden.

57. 1d. violet 30 20
58. 1½d. red 30 30
59. 3d. blue 50 45

4. Spears and Shield.

1939. Portrait of King George VI.

60. **4.** ½d. blue and green 10 25
61. – 1d. brown and violet 15 25
62. – 1½d. green and red 25 25
63a.– 2d. brown and black 20 25
64. – 2½d. mauve and olive 70 60
65a.– 3d. black and blue 20 85
66. – 4½d. green and brown 3·25 4·50
67. – 6d. violet and purple 60 65
68. – 1s. green and black 85 1·00
69. – 2s. black and orange 2·75 2·75
70. – 2s. 6d. black and violet 6·00 7·50
71. – 5s. green and red 4·50 5·50
72. – 10s. green and mauve 6·50 8·50

DESIGNS—VERT. 1d. Native policeman and Chief. 4½d., 10s. Native house, Reef Islands. 6d. Coco-nut plantation. HORIZ. 1½d. Artificial Is., Malaita. 2½d. Roviana canoe. 1s. Breadfruit. 5s. Malaita canoe. LARGER—35½ × 22 mm. 2d. Canoe house. 3d. Roviana canoes. 2s. Tinakula Volcano. 2s. 6d. Megapodes.

1946. Victory. As T **4** of Aden.

73. 1½d. red 12 12
74. 3d. blue 15 15

1949. Silver Wedding. As T **5** and **6** of Aden.

75. 2d. grey 15 15
76. 10s. mauve 5·00 7·00

1949. U.P.U. As T **14** to **17** of Antigua.

77. 2d. brown 30 30
78. 3d. blue 25 40
79. 5d. green 45 55
80. 1s. black 70 80

1953. Coronation. As T **7** of Aden.

81. 2d. black and grey 35 45

5. Ysabel Canoe.

1956. Portrait of Queen Elizabeth II.

82. **5.** ½d. orange and purple 5 5
83. – 1d. grn. & brn. (As No. 65a) 5 5
84. – 1½d. slate & red (No. 62) 5 5
85. – 2d. sepia & green (No. 63) 8 10
86. – 2½d. black and blue 10 10
87. – 3d. green and red (No. 71) 12 12
88. – 5d. black and blue 35 35
89. – 6d. black and green 15 20
90. – 8d. blue and black 35 35
90a.– 9d. green and black 30 30
91. – 1s. slate and brown 35 35
91a. 1s. 3d. black and blue 35 35
92. – 2s. black and red (No. 69) 70 70
93. – 2s. 6d. grn. & pur. (No. 66) 85 1·25
94. – 5s. brown 2·50 3·50
95. – 10s. sepia (No. 61) 5·50 7·00
96. – £1 black and blue 9·50 11·00

DESIGNS—VERT. 2½d. Prow of Roviana canoe. HORIZ. 5d., 1s. 3d. Map. 6d. Trading schooner. 8d., 9d. Henderson Airfield, Guadalcanal. 1s. Chart showing voyage of H.M.S. "Swallow" in 1767. 5s. Mendana and Ship. 10s. Similar to No. 61, but policeman in different uniform, without rifle. £1 Arms.

6. Frigate Bird.

1961. New Constitution, 1960.

97. **6.** 2d. black and turquoise 8 10
98. 3d. black and red 12 15
99. 9d. black and purple 30 40

1963. Freedom from Hunger. As T **10** of Aden

100. 1s. 3d. blue 1·50 1·50

1963. Red Cross Cent. As T **24** of Antigua.

101. 2d. red and black 20 25
102. 9d. red and blue 1·25 1·40

7. Makira Food Bowl.

1965. Central design in black; background colours given.

112. 7.	½d. slate-blue and blue	5	5
113. –	1d. orange and yellow	5	5
114. –	1½d. blue and green	5	5
115. –	2d. ultramarine and blue	5	8
116. –	2½d. brown & light brown	8	8
117. –	3d. green and light green	10	10
118. –	6d. magenta and orange	12	12
119. –	9d. bluish green & yellow	20	20
120. –	1s. chocolate & magenta	25	25
121. –	1s. 3d. red	25	30
122. –	2s. purple and lilac	65	85
123. –	2s. 6d. olive-brown & brn.	80	1·25
124. –	5s. ultramarine & violet	1·50	2·00
125. –	10s. olive and yellow	2·50	3·00
126. –	£1 violet and pink	5·00	6·00

DESIGNS: 1d. "Dendrobium veratrifolium" (orchid). 1½d. Scorpion shell. 2d. Hornbill. 2½d. Ysabel shield. 3d. Rennellese club. 6d. Moorish Idol (fish). 9d. Frigate bird. 1s. "Dendrobium macrophyllum" (orchid). 1s. 3d. "Dendrobium spectabilis" (orchid). 2s. Sanford's eagle. 2s. 6d. Malaita belt. 5s. "Ornithoptera victoreae" (butterfly). 10s. White Cockatoo. £1, Western Canoe Figure-head.

1965. I.T.U. Cent. As T **26** of Antigua.

127.	2d. red and turquoise	12	15
128.	3d. turquoise and drab	25	25

1965. I.C.Y. As T **27** of Antigua.

129.	1d. purple and turquoise	5	5
130.	2s. 6d. green and lavender	50	55

1966. Churchill Commem. As T **28** of Antigua.

131.	2d. blue	8	8
132.	9d. green	20	25
133.	1s. 3d. brown	30	35
134.	2s. 6d. violet	55	60

1966. Decimal Currency. Nos. 112/26 surch.

135.	1 c. on ½d.	5	5
136.	2 c. on 1d.	5	5
137.	3 c. on 1½d.	5	8
138.	4 c. on 2d.	8	10
139.	5 c. on 6d.	12	15
140.	6 c. on 2½d.	12	15
141.	7 c. on 3d.	12	15
142.	8 c. on 9d.	12	15
143.	10 c. on 1s.	25	25
144.	12 c. on 1s. 3d.	35	35
145.	13 c. on 1s. 3d.	30	35
146.	14 c. on 3d.	25	30
147.	20 c. on 2s.	30	45
148.	25 c. on 2s. 6d.	60	70
149.	35 c. on 2d.	60	75
150.	50 c. on 5s.	1·10	1·40
151.	$1 on 10s.	1·75	2·00
152.	$2 on £1	3·25	3·50

1966. World Cup Football Championships. As T **30** of Antigua.

153.	8 c. violet, grn., lake & brn.	15	20
154.	35 c. choc., turq., lake & brn.	55	60

1966. W.H.O. Headquarters, Geneva. Inaug. As T **31** of Antigua.

155.	3 c. black, green and blue	8	8
156.	50 c. black, purple & ochre	85	90

1966. U.N.E.S.C.O. 20th Anniv. As T **33/5** of Antigua.

157.	3 c. violet, red, yell. & orge.	8	8
158.	25 c. yellow, violet & olive	40	45
159.	$1 black, purple and orange	1·40	1·60

8. Henderson Field.

1967. Guadalcanal Campaign (Pacific War). 25th Anniv. Multicoloured.

160.	8 c. Type **8**	15	20
161.	35 c. Red Beach Landings	50	50

9. Mendana off Point Cruz.

1968. Discovery of the Solomon Islands. Quater-cent.

162. 9.	3 c. multicoloured	8	8
163. –	8 c. multicoloured	10	12
164. –	35 c. multicoloured	50	55
165. –	$1 multicoloured	1·50	1·75

DESIGNS: 8 c. Arrival of Missionaries. 35 c. Pacific Campaign, World War II. $1, Proclamation of the Protectorate.

10 Vine Fishing.

1968.

166. 10.	1 c. blue, black & brown	5	5
167. –	2 c. green, black & brown	5	5
168. –	3 c. grn., myrtle & black	8	8
169. –	4 c. purple, black & brn.	8	8
170. –	6 c. multicoloured	10	10
171. –	8 c. multicoloured	15	20
172. –	12 c. ochre, red & black	25	25
173. –	14 c. red, choc. & black	30	30
174. –	15 c. multicoloured	30	30
175. –	20 c. blue, red & black	35	35
176. –	24 c. red, black & yellow	40	45
177. –	35 c. multicoloured	1·25	1·50
178. –	45 c. multicoloured	1·50	2·00
179. –	$1 blue, green and black	2·50	3·00
180. –	$2 multicoloured	5·00	6·00

DESIGNS: 2 c. Kite Fishing. 3 c. Platform Fishing. 4 c. Net Fishing. 6 c. Gold Lip Shell Diving. 8 c. Night Fishing. 12 c. Boat Building. 14 c. Cocoa. 15 c. Road Building. 20 c. Geological Survey. 24 c. Hauling Timber. 35 c. Copra. 45 c. Harvesting Rice. $1, Honiara Port. $2, Internal Air Service.

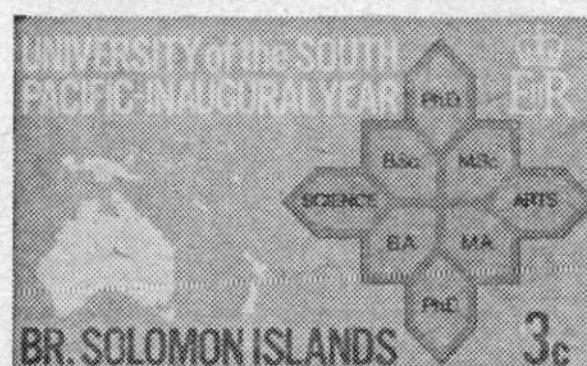

11. Map of Australasia and Diagram.

1969. South Pacific University. Inaugural Year.

181. 11.	3 c. multicoloured	8	8
182.	12 c. multicoloured	25	30
183.	35 c. multicoloured	35	60

12. Basketball Player. 13. South Sea Island with Star of Bethlehem.

1969. 3rd South Pacific Games, Port Moresby. Multicoloured.

184.	3 c. Type **12**	8	8
185.	8 c. Footballer	15	20
186.	14 c. Sprinter	25	25
187.	45 c. Rubgy player	70	75

1969. Christmas.

189. 13.	8 c. black, violet & green	20	20
190. –	35 c. multicoloured	60	60

DESIGN: 35 c. Southern Cross, "PAX" and Frigate Bird (stained glass window).

14. "Paid" Stamp, New South Wales 2d. Stamp of 1896–1906 and Tulagi Postmark. 1906–07. (Illustration reduced. Actual size 32½ × 21 mm.)

1970. New G.P.O., Honiara.

191. 14.	7 c. mag., blue and black	15	15
192. –	14 c. green, blue & black	25	25
193. –	18 c. multicoloured	35	35
194. –	23 c. multicoloured	40	40

DESIGNS: 14 c. Protectorate stamp of 1906–07 and C. M. Woodford. 18 c. Protectorate stamp of 1910–14 and Tulagi Postmark, 1913. 23 c. New G.P.O., Honiara.

15. Coat of Arms.

1970. New Constitution.

195. 15.	18 c. multicoloured	30	35
196. –	35 c. green, blue & ochre	70	70

DESIGN—HORIZ. 35 c. Map.

16. British Red Cross H.Q., Honiara.

1970. British Red Cross. Cent.

197. 16.	3 c. multicoloured	8	8
198. –	35 c. blue, vermilion & blk.	60	65

DESIGN: 35 c. Wheelchair and map.

17. Reredos (Altar Screen).

1970. Christmas.

199. –	8 c. ochre and violet	15	15
200. 17.	45 c. chestnut, orange and brown	75	80

DESIGN—HORIZ. 8 c. Carved Angel.

18. La Perouse and "La Boussole".

1971. Ships and Navigators (1st series). Multicoloured.

201.	3 c. Type **18**	8	8
202.	4 c. Astrolabe and Polynesian reed map	10	10
203.	12 c. Abel Tasman and "Heemskerk"	30	30
204.	35 c. Te puki canoe	1·00	1·10

See also Nos. 215/18, 236/9 254/7 and 272/5.

19. Bishop Patteson, J. Atkin and S. Taroaniara.

1971. Bishop Patteson. Death Cent. Multicoloured.

205.	2 c. Type **19**	5	8
206.	4 c. Last landing at Nukapu	10	10
207.	14 c. Memorial Cross and Nukapu (vert.)	30	30
208.	45 c. Knotted leaf and canoe (vert.)	75	80

20. Torch Emblem and Boxers.

1971. South Pacific Games, Tahiti. Multicoloured.

209.	3 c. Type **20**	8	8
210.	8 c. Emblem and Footballers	15	15
211.	12 c. Emblem and Runner	30	30
212.	35 c. Emblem and Skin-diver	65	70

21. Melanesian Lectern.

1971. Christmas. Multicoloured.

213.	9 c. Type **21**	20	20
214.	45 c. "United we Stand" (Margarita Bara)	75	80

1972. Ships and Navigators (2nd series). As T **18**. Multicoloured.

215.	4 c. Bougainville and "La Boudeuse"	8	8
216.	9 c. Horizontal planisphere and ivory backstaff	20	25
217.	15 c. Philip Carteret and H.M.S. "Swallow"	35	35
218.	45 c. Malaita canoe	95	1·00

22. "Cupha woodfordi" (butterfly).

1972. Multicoloured.

219.	1 c. Type **22**	5	5
220.	2 c. "Ornithoptera priamus urvillanus"	5	5
221.	3 c. "Vindula sapor"	8	8
222.	4 c. "Papilio ulyssus opsippus"	8	8
223.	5 c. Great Trevally	10	10
224.	8 c. Little Bonito	12	12
225.	9 c. Sapphire Demoiselle	15	15
226.	12 c. "Costus speciosus"	20	20
227.	15 c. Orange Anemone Fish	20	25
228.	20 c. "Spathoglottis plicata"	25	30
229.	25 c. "Ephemeratha comata"	30	35
230.	35 c. "Dendrobium cuthbertsonii"	50	55
231.	45 c. "Heliconia salomonica"	65	70
232.	$1 Blue Finned Triggerfish	1·40	1·40
233.	$2 "Ornithoptera allotti"	2·75	3·00
233a.	$5 Great Frigate Bird	6·50	7·00

The 2, 3, 4 c and $2 are butterflies; the 5, 8, 9, 15 c. and $1 are fishes, and the 12, 20, 25, 35, 45 c. are flowers.

1972. Royal Silver Wedding. As T **19** of Ascension, but with Greetings and Message Drum in background.

234.	8 c. red	15	15
235.	45 c. green	65	75

1973. Ships and Navigators (3rd series). As T **18**. Multicoloured.

236.	4 c. D. Entrecasteaux and "Recherche", 1791	8	8
237.	9 c. Ship's Hour-glass and Chronometer, 1761	20	20
238.	15 c. Lt. Shortland and "Alexander", 1788	40	40
239.	35 c. Tomoko (war canoe)	80	80

23. Pan Pipes.

1973. Musical Instruments. Multicoloured.
240. 4 c. Type **23** 8 8
241. 9 c. Castanets 20 20
242. 15 c. Bamboo flute .. 25 30
243. 35 c. Bauro gongs .. 55 60
244. 45 c. Bamboo band .. 70 75

1973. Royal Wedding. As Type **26** of Anguilla. Background colour given. Mult.
245. 4 c. blue 8 8
246. 35 c. blue 45 50

24. " Adoration of the Kings " (Jan Brueghel).

1973. Christmas. " Adoration of the Kings " by the artists listed. Multicoloured.
247. 8 c. Type **24** 20 20
248. 22 c. Peter Brueghel .. 40 45
249. 45 c. Botticelli (49 × 35 mm.) 90 90

25. Queen Elizabeth II and Map.

1974. Royal Visit.
250. **25.** 4 c. multicoloured .. 8 8
251. 9 c. multicoloured .. 20 20
252. 15 c. multicoloured .. 30 35
253. 35 c. multicoloured .. 70 75

1973. Ships and Navigators (4th series). As T **18**. Multicoloured.
254. 4 c. Commissioner landing from " S.S. Titus " .. 8 8
255. 9 c. Radar scanner .. 20 20
256. 15 c. Natives being transported to the "Blackbirder" 25 30
257. 45 c. Lieut. John F. Kennedy's " P.T. 109 " .. 75 85

26. "Postman".

1974. U.P.U. Centenary.
258. **26.** 4 c. grn., dk. grn. & blk. 8 8
259. – 9 c. lt. brn., brn. & blk. 20 20
260. – 15 c. mauve, pur. & blk. 25 30
261. – 45 c. bl., dk. bl. & blk... 60 65
DESIGNS—HORIZ. 9 c. Carrier-pigeon. 45 c. Pegasus. VERT. 15 c. St. Gabriel.

27. "New Constitution" Stamp of 1970.

1974. New Constitution.
262. **27.** 4 c. multicoloured .. 8 8
263. – 9 c. red, black & brown 20 20
264. – 15 c. red, blk. & brown 25 30
265. **27.** 35 c. multicoloured .. 55 60
DESIGN: 9 c., 15 c. "New Constitution" stamp of 1961 (inscr. "1960").

28. Golden Whistler.

1975. Birds. Multicoloured.
267. 1 c. Type **28** 5 5
268. 2 c. River Kingfisher .. 5 5
269. 3 c. Red-throated Fruit Dove 5 5
270. 4 c. Button-quail 8 8
271. $2 Duchess Lorikeet .. 2·75 3·00
See also Nos. 305/20.

1975. Ships and Navigators. (5th series). As T **18**. Multicoloured.
272. 4 c. M.V. " Walande " .. 8 8
273. 9 c. M.V. " Melanesian " .. 15 15
274. 15 c. M.V. " Marsina " .. 25 25
275. 45 c. S.S. " Himalaya " .. 65 70

29. Runner.

1975. South Pacific Games. Multicoloured.
276. 4 c. Type **29** 8 8
277. 9 c. Long jump 15 15
278. 15 c. Javelin-throwing .. 25 25
279. 45 c. Football 65 70

30. Nativity Scene and Candles.

1975. Christmas. Multicoloured.
281. 15 c. Type **30** 25 25
282. 35 c. Shepherds, angels and candles 45 45
283. 45 c. The Three Wise Men and candles 65 70

1975. Nos. 267/70, 223/32, 271 and 233a with obliterating bar over " BRITISH ". Mult.
285. 1 c. Type **28** 5 5
286. 2 c. River Kingfisher .. 5 5
287. 3 c. Red-throated Fruit Dove 5 5
288. 4 c. Button-quail 8 8
289. 5 c. Great Trevally .. 10 10
290. 8 c. Little Bonito 12 12
291. 9 c. Sapphire Demoiselle .. 15 15
292. 12 c. " Costus speciosus " 15 20
293. 15 c. Orange Anemone Fish 20 25
294. 20 c. " Spathoglottis plicata " 25 30
295. 25 c. " Ephemeratha comata " 30 35
296. 35 c. " Dendrobium cuthbertsonii " 40 45
297. 45 c. " Heliconia salomonica " 50 60
298. $1 Blue Finned Triggerfish 1·25 1·40
299. $2 Duchess Lorikeet .. 2·75 3·00
300. $5 Great Frigate Bird .. 6·50 7·00

31. Ceremonial Food-bowl.

1975. Artefacts. Multicoloured.
301. 4 c. Type **31** 8 8
302. 15 c. Chieftains' money .. 20 25
303. 35 c. Nguzu-nguzu (canoe protector spirit) (vert.) .. 45 45
304. 45 c. Nguzu-nguzu canoe prow 60 65

32. Golden Whistler.

1976. Multicoloured.
305. 1 c. Type **32** 5 5
306. 2 c. River Kingfisher .. 5 5
307. 3 c. Red-throated Fruit Dove 5 5
308. 4 c. Button Quail 5 5
309. 5 c. Willie Wagtail .. 5 5
310. 6 c. Golden Cowrie .. 5 8
311. 10 c. Glory-of-the-Sea Cone 10 12
312. 12 c. Coconut Lory .. 12 15
313. 15 c. Pearly Nautilus .. 15 20
314. 20 c. Venus Comb Murex 20 25
315. 25 c. Commercial Trochus 25 30
316. 35 c. Melon or Baler Shell 35 40
317. 45 c. Orange Spider Conch 45 50
318. $1 Pacific Triton .. .. 1·10 1·25
319. $2 Duchess Lorikeet .. 2·10 2·25
320. $5 Great Frigate Bird .. 5·50 6·00

33. Coastwatchers, 1942.

1976. American Revolution. Bicent. Mult.
321. 6 c. Type **33** 10 10
322. 20 c. " Amagiri " ramming PT 109 and Lt. J. F. Kennedy 25 30
323. 35 c. Henderson Airfield .. 45 50
324. 45 c. Map of Guadalcanal 60 70

34. Alexander Graham Bell.

1976. Telephone Centenary.
326. **34.** 6 c. multicoloured .. 10 10
327. – 20 c. multicoloured .. 25 30
328. – 35 c. brown, orge. & red 45 50
329. – 45 c. multicoloured .. 60 70
DESIGNS: 20 c. Radio telephone via satellite. 35 c. Ericson's magneto telephone. 45 c. Stick telephone and first telephone.

35. B.A.C. " 1-11 ".

1976. 1st Flight to Solomon Is. 50th Anniv. Multicoloured.
330. 6 c. Type **35** 8 8
331. 20 c. Britten-Norman " Islander " 25 30
332. 35 c. " Dakota DC3 " .. 40 45
333. 45 c. De Havilland " DH50A " 55 65

36. The Communion Plate.

1977. Silver Jubilee. Multicoloured.
334. 6 c. Queen's Visit, 1974.. 8 8
335. 35 c. Type **36** 40 45
336. 45 c. The Communion .. 55 65

POSTAGE DUE STAMPS

D 1.

1940.
D 1. **D 1.** 1d. green 30 45
D 2. 2d. red 50 75
D 3. 3d. brown 75 85
D 4. 4d. blue .. .. 90 1·10
D 5. 5d. olive .. .. 1·00 1·25
D 6. 6d. purple .. .. 1·60 2·50
D 7. 1s. violet .. .. 2·50 4·00
D 8. 1s. 6d. green .. .. 6·50 8·00

SOMALIA O4; BC

A former Italian colony in East Africa on the Gulf of Aden, including Benadir (S. Somaliland), and Jubaland. Under British Administration 1943-50. Then under United Nations control with Italian Administration. Became independent on 1st July, 1960. Following a revolution in Oct. 1969, the country was designated "Somali Democratic Republic". See also Middle East Forces.

1903. 16 annas = 1 rupee.
1905. 100 centesimi = 1 lira.
1922. 100 besa = 1 rupia.
1926. 100 centesimi = 1 lira.
1948. 100 cents = 1 shilling.
1950. 100 centesimi = 1 somalo.
1961. 100 cents = 1 Somali shilling.

1.

2.

1903.
1. **1.** 1 b. brown .. .. .. 3·00 50
2. 2 b. green 50 30
3. **2.** 1 a. red .. .. .. 1·60 80
4. 2 a. orange .. .. .. 40·00 10·00
5. $2\frac{1}{2}$ a. blue .. .. .. 1·00 1·25
6. 5 a. yellow .. .. .. 16·00 7·50
7. 10 a. lilac .. .. .. 8·50 5·00

1905. Surch. with new value without bars at top.
10. **1.** 2 c. on 1 b. brown .. 12 15
11. 5 c. on 2 b. green .. 15 12
12. 10 c. on 1 a. red .. 20 15
13. 15 c. on 2 a. orange .. 25 15
8. 15 c. on 5 a. yellow .. £700 £110
13a. 20 c. on 2 a. orange .. 1·60 15
14. 25 c. on $2\frac{1}{2}$ a. blue .. 1·00 30
9. 40 c. on 10 a. lilac .. £130 21·00
15. 50 c. on 5 a. yellow .. 2·50 80
16. 1 l. on 10 a. lilac .. 1·50 1·25
For stamps with bars at top, see Nos. 68, etc.

Nos. 19 to 160 are all, except where stated, Italian stamps, sometimes in new colours, optd. **SOMALIA ITALIANA** or **SOMALIA.**

1915. Red Cross stamps optd. or surch. **20** also.
19. **34.** 10 c. + 5 c. red 50 55
20. **35.** 15 c. + 5 c. grey .. 1·75 1·90
21. 20 c. + 5 c. orange .. 1·25 1·50
22. 20 on 15 c. + 5 c. grey .. 35 35

1916. Nos. 15 and 16 re-surcharged and with bars cancelling original surcharge.
17. **2.** 5 c. on 50 c. on 5 a. yellow 4·00 4·00
18. 20 c. on 1 l. on 10 a. lilac .. 40 45

1922. Nos. 12, etc., again surch. at top.
23. **1.** 3 b. on 5 c. on 2 b. green .. 40 75
24. **2.** 6 b. on 10 c. on 1 a. red .. 20 40
25. 9 b. on 15 c. on 2 a. orange 30 60
26. 15 b. on 25 c. on 2½ a. blue 40 60
27. 30 b. on 50 c. on 5 a. yell. 1·10 1·40
28. 60 b. on 1 l. on 10 a. lilac .. 2·50 3·75

1922. Victory stamps surch.
29. **40.** 3 b. on 5 c. green .. 20 30
30. 6 b. on 10 c. red .. 25 35
31. 9 b. on 15 c. grey .. 35 45
32. 15 b. on 25 c. blue .. 45 60

1923. Nos. 11 to 16 re-surcharged with new values and bars. (No. 33 is optd. with bars only at bottom.)
33. **1.** 2 c. on 1 b. brown 20 40
34. 2 on 2 c. on 1 b. brown .. 20 40
35. 3 on 2 c. on 1 b. brown .. 20 40
36. **2.** 5 b. on 50 c. on 5 a. yellow 20 20
37. **1.** 6 on 5 c. on 2 b. green .. 45 20
38. **2.** 18 b. on 10 c. on 1 a. red .. 45 20
39. 20 b. on 15 c. on 2 a. orge. 60 25
40. 25 b. on 15 c. on 2 a. orge. 70 35
41. 30 b. on 25 c. on 2½ a. blue 80 1·00
42. 60 b. on 1 l. on 10 a. lilac .. 1·60 3·00
43. 1 r. on 1 l. on 10 a. lilac .. 3·00 5·00

1923. Propaganda of Faith stamps surch.
44. **44.** 6 b. on 20 c. orge & grn. 1·10 2·10
45. 13 b. on 30 c. orge. & red 1·10 2·10
46. 20 b. on 50 c. orge. & vio. 95 1·60
47. 30 b. on 1 l. orge. & blue 95 1·60

1923. Fascisti stamps surch.
48. **45.** 3 b. on 10 c. green .. 40 65
49. 13 b. on 30 c. violet .. 50 75
50. 20 b. on 50 c. red .. 60 90
51. **46.** 30 b. on 1 l. blue .. .. 65 1·00
52. 1 r. on 2 l. brown .. 75 1·25
53. **47.** 3 l. on 5 f. black and blue 4·25 6·50

1924. Manzoni stamps surch.
54. **49.** 6 b. on 10 c. black & red 30 80
55. 9 b. on 15 c. black & grn. 30 80
56. 13 b. on 30 c. black .. 30 80
57. 20 b. on 50 c. blk. & brn. 30 80
58. 30 b. on 1 l. black & blue 7·50 13·00
59. 3 r. on 5 l. black & purple £110 £160

1925. Holy Year stamps surch.
60. **51.** 6 b.+3 b. on 20 c.+10 c. brown and green .. 35 60
61. 13 b.+6 b. on 30 c.+15 c. brown and chocolate .. 35 60
62. 15 b.+8 b. on 50 c.+25 c. brown & violet .. 35 60
63. 18 b.+9 b. on 60 c.+30 c. brown and red .. 35 60
64. 30 b.+15 b. on 1 l.+50 c. purple and blue .. 50 80
65. 1 r.+50 b. on 5 l.+2 l. 50 c. purple and red .. 65 1·25

1925. Royal Jubilee.
66. **53.** 60 c. red 12 25
67. 1 l. blue 30 50
67a. 1 l. 25 c. blue 15 35

1926. Nos. 10/13, and 13a/16 optd. with bars at top.
68. **1.** 2 c. on 1 b. brown .. 3·75 5·00
69. 3 c. on 2 b. green .. 2·00 2·75
70. **2.** 10 c. on 1 a. red .. 15 20
71. 15 c. on 2 a. orange .. 20 25
72. 20 c. on 2 a. orange .. 25 30
73. 25 c. on 2½ a. blue .. 40 50
74. 50 c. on 5 a. yellow .. 85 1·00
75. 1 l. on 10 a. lilac .. 1·50 1·75

1926. St. Francis of Assisi.
76. **54.** 20 c. green 25 40
77. 40 c. violet 25 40
78. 60 c. red 25 40
79. 1 l. 25 c. blue 25 40
80. 5 l.+2 l. 50 c. olive .. 1·00 1·60

1926. Colonial Propaganda stamps as T 1 of Cyrenaica, but inscr. "SOMALIA ITAL".
81. 5 c.+5 c. brown 12 25
82. 10 c.+5 c. olive 12 25
83. 20 c.+5 c. green 12 25
84. 40 c.+5 c. red 12 25
85. 60 c.+5 c. orange 12 25
86. 1 l.+5 c. blue 12 25

1926. Italian stamps optd.
87. **21.** 2 c. brown 25 50
88. **24.** 5 c. green 35 35
89. **61.** 7½ c. brown .. .. 85 1·25
90. **24.** 10 c. red 8 10
91. **26.** 20 c. purple 12 15
92. **23.** 25 c. green 8 5
92a. **26.** 30 c. black 35 45
93. **62.** 50 c. grey and brown .. 40 30
94. **61.** 50 c. mauve 50 60
95. **26.** 60 c. orange 10 15
96. **23.** 75 c. red .. .. 6·00 1·25
97. 1 l. brown and green .. 12 8
98. 1 l. 25 c. blue 30 12
99. **62.** 1 l. 75 brown .. .. 1·25 65
100. **23.** 2 l. green and orange .. 60 1·00
101. 2 l. 50 c. green & orange 70 1·10
102. 5 l. blue and red .. 5·50 3·00
103. 10 l. red and olive .. 6·50 4·50

1927. First National Defence issue.
104. **59.** 40 c.+20 c. black & brn. 35 65
105. 60 c.+30 c. brown & red 40 85
106. 1 l. 25+60 c. blk. & blue 50 1·10
107. 5 l.+2 l. 50 blk. & grn. 80 1·75

1927. Volta. Centenary.
108. **63.** 20 c. violet 65 80
109. 50 c. orange .. .. 80 1·00
110. 1 l. 25 blue .. .. 1·50 2·10

1928. 45th Anniv. Italian-African Society. As T 2 of Cyrenaica.
111. 20 c.+5 c. green .. 20 50
112. 30 c.+5 c. red .. 20 50
113. 50 c.+10 c. violet .. 20 50
114. 1 l. 25+20 c. blue .. 20 50

1929. Second National Defence issue.
115. **59.** 30 c.+10 c. black & red 35 80
116. 50 c.+20 c. black & lilac 35 80
117. 1 l. 25+50 c. blue & brn. 65 1·10
118. 5 l.+2 l. black and olive 65 1·10

1929. Montecassino Abbey.
119. 20 c. green 25 50
120. 25 c. orange 25 50
121. 50 c.+10 c. red .. 35 65
122. 75 c.+15 c. brown .. 40 85
123. 1 l. 25+25 c. purple .. 1·75 3·00
124. 5 l.+1 l. blue .. .. 1·75 3·00
125. 10 l.+2 l. brown .. 1·75 3·00

1930. Royal Wedding.
126. **80.** 20 c. green 20 40
127. 50 c.+10 c. orange .. 30 65
128. 1 l. 25+25 c. red .. 55 1·00

1930. Ferrucci.
129. **85.** 20 c. violet 20 25
130. 25 c. green (No. 283) .. 20 25
131. 50 c. black (as No. 284) 20 25
132. 1 l. 25 blue (No. 285) .. 20 25
133. 5 l.+2 l. red (as No. 286) 1·10 1·25

1930. Third National Defence issue.
134. **59.** 30 c.+10 c. grn. & olive 60 1·00
135. 50 c.+10 c. violet & olive 60 1·00
136. 1 l. 25+30 c. brown .. 80 1·75
137. 5 l.+1 l. 50 grn. & blue 6·00 11·00

3. Irrigation Canal.

1930. 25th Anniv. (1929) of Colonial Agricultural Institute.
138. **3.** 50 c.+20 c. brown .. 30 65
139. 1 l. 25+20 c. blue .. 30 65
140. 1 l. 75+20 c. green .. 30 65
141. 2 l. 55+50 c. violet .. 1·00 1·75
142. 5 l.+1 l. red .. .. 1·00 1·75

1930. Virgil. Bimillenary.
143. **89.** 15 c. violet 8 20
144. 20 c. brown 8 20
145. 25 c. green 8 20
146. 30 c. brown 8 20
147. 50 c. purple 8 20
148. 75 c. red 8 20
149. 1 l. 25 blue 8 20
150. 5 l.+1 l. 50 purple .. 95 2·00
151. 10 l.+2 l. 50 brown .. 95 2·00

1931. Portraits.
152. **70.** 25 c. green 65 35
153. **74.** 50 c. violet 65 15

1931. St. Anthony of Padua.
154. **92.** 20 c. brown 15 30
155. 25 c. green 15 30
156. 30 c. brown 15 30
157. 50 c. purple 15 30
158. 75 c. grey 15 30
159. 1 l. 25 blue 15 30
160. 5 l.+2 l. 50 brown .. 1·50 3·00

4. Tower at Mnara-Ciromo.

5. Hippopotamus.

1932.
161a. – 5 c. brown 5 5
162a. – 7½ c. violet 5 8
163a. 10 c. black 5 5
164a. – 15 c. olive 5 5
165a. **4.** 20 c. red 8 5
166a. 25 c. green 5 5
167a. 30 c. brown 5 5
168a. – 35 c. blue 12 12
169a. – 50 c. violet .. .. 1·50 5
170. – 75 c. red 25 8
171. – 1 l. 25 blue 25 5
172. – 1 l. 75 orange 25 5
173. – 2 l. red 12 8
174. – 2 l. 55 slate .. .. 2·50 3·00
175a. – 5 l. red 50 25
176. **5.** 10 l. violet .. .. 4·25 1·50
177. – 20 l. green .. .. 8·50 4·50
178. – 25 l. blue .. .. 17·00 9·50
DESIGNS—HORIZ. 5 c., 7½ c., 10 c., 15 c. Francesco Crispi Lighthouse, Cape Guardafui. 35 c., 50 c., 75 c. Governor's Residence, Mogadiscio. 25 l. Lioness. VERT. 1 l. 25, 1 l. 75, 2 l. Ant-hill. 2 l. 55, 5 l. Ostrich. 20 l. Kudu antelope.

1934. Abruzzi issue. Optd. **ONORANZE AL DUCA DEGLI ABRUZZI.**
179. 10 c. brown 40 65
180. 25 c. green 40 65
181. 50 c. mauve 40 65
182. 1 l. 25 blue 40 65
183. 5 l. black .. .. 95 1·50
184. 10 l. red .. .. .. 95 1·50
185. 20 l. blue .. .. .. 95 1·50
186. 25 l. green .. .. .. 95 1·50
DESIGNS as Nos. 163a to 178.

6. Woman and Child.

7. King Victor Emmanuel III.

8.

1934. 2nd Int. Colonial Exn., Naples.
187. **6.** 5 c. green & brown (post.) 60 1·75
188. 10 c. brown and black .. 60 1·75
189. 20 c. red and slate .. 60 1·75
190. 50 c. violet and brown .. 60 1·75
191. 60 c. brown and slate .. 60 1·75
192. 1 l. 25 blue and green .. 60 1·75
193. – 25 c. blue & orange (air) 60 1·75
194. – 50 c. green and slate .. 60 1·75
195. – 75 c. brown and orange .. 60 1·75
196. – 80 c. brown and green .. 60 1·75
197. – 1 l. red and green .. 60 1·75
198. – 2 l. blue and brown .. 60 1·75
DESIGNS: 25 c. to 75 c. Aeroplane over River Juba. 80 c. to 2 l. Cheetahs watching aeroplane.

1934. Air. Rome-Mogadiscio Flight.
199. **8.** 25 c.+10 c. green .. 70 3·00
200. 50 c.+10 c. brown .. 70 3·00
201. 75 c.+15 c. red .. 70 3·00
202. 80 c.+15 c. black .. 70 3·00
203. 1 l.+20 c. red .. .. 70 3·00
204. 2 l.+20 c. blue .. .. 70 3·00
205. 3 l.+25 c. violet .. 14·00 21·00
206. 5 l.+25 c. orange .. 14·00 21·00
207. 10 l.+30 c. purple .. 14·00 21·00
208. 25 l.+2 l. green .. 14·00 21·00

1934. King of Italy's Visit to Italian Somaliland.
209. **7.** 5 c.+5 c. black (postage) 40 80
210. 7½ c.+7½ c. purple .. 40 80
211. 15 c.+10 c. green .. 40 80
212. 20 c.+10 c. red 40 80
213. 25 c.+10 c. green .. 40 80
214. 30 c.+10 c. brown .. 40 80
215. 50 c.+10 c. violet .. 40 80
216. 75 c.+15 c. red 40 80
217. 1 l. 25+15 c. blue .. 40 80
218. 1 l. 75+25 c. orange .. 40 80
219. 2 l. 75+25 c. slate .. 6·00 10·00
220. 5 l.+1 l. claret .. .. 6·00 10·00
221. 10 l.+1 l. 80 red .. 6·00 10·00
222. – 25 l.+2 l. 75 brn. & red .. 27·00 50·00
DESIGN (36×44 mm.): 25 l. King Victor Emmanuel III on horseback.

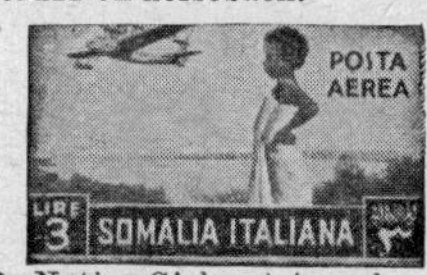

9. Native Girl and Aeroplane.

1936. Air.
223. – 25 c. green 15 8
224. – 50 c. brown 5 5
225. – 60 c. orange 25 35
226. – 75 c. brown 15 8
227. **9.** 1 l. blue 5 5
228. – 1 l. 50 violet 20 5
229. – 2 l. blue 65 15
230. **9.** 3 l. red .. .. 1·75 20
231. – 5 l. green .. .. 1·90 50
232. – 10 l. red .. .. 4·25 3·00
DESIGNS: 25 c., 1 l. 50, Banana trees. 50 c., 2 l. Native woman in cotton plantation. 60 c. 5 l. Orchard. 75 c., 10 l. Native women harvesting.

BRITISH OCCUPATION

1943. Stamps of Gt. Britain optd. **E.A.F.** (East African Forces).
S 1. **103.** 1d. pale red 5 15
S 2. 2d. pale orange .. 5 15
S 3. 2½d. light blue .. 5 15
S 4. 3d. pale violet .. 5 15
S 5. **104.** 5d. brown 5 15
S 6. 6d. purple 8 20
S 7. **105.** 9d. olive 15 60
S 8. 1s. brown 15 12
S 9. **106.** 2s. 6d. green .. .. 90 1·40
PRICES. Our prices for Nos. S 1/9 in used condition are for stamps with identifiable postmarks of the territories in which they were issued. These stamps were also used in the United Kingdom, with official sanction, from the summer of 1950, and with U.K. postmarks are worth about 25 per cent less.

BRITISH MILITARY ADMINISTRATION.

1948. Stamps of Great Britain surch. **B.M.A. SOMALIA** and new value in cents and shillings.
S 10. **103.** 5 c. on ½d. pale green 5 15
S 11. 15 c. on 1½d. pale brn. 30 75
S 12. 20 c. on 2d. pale orge. 5 35
S 13. 25 c. on 2½d. light blue 5 15
S 14. 30 c. on 3d. pale violet 35 80
S 15. **104.** 40 c. on 5d. brown .. 8 45
S 16. 50 c. on 6d. purple .. 12 55
S 17. **105.** 75 c. on 9d. olive .. 45 1·25
S 18. 1s. on 1s. brown .. 25 55
S 19. **106.** 2s. 50 c. on 2s. 6d. grn. 1·40 3·25
S 20. 5s. on 5s. red .. 2·75 5·00

BRITISH ADMINISTRATION.

1950. Stamps of Great Britain surch. **B.A. SOMALIA** and value in cents and shillings.
S 21. **103.** 5 c. on ½d. pale green 5 12
S 22. 15 c. on 1½d. pale brn. 20 60
S 23. 20 c. on 2d. pale orge. 20 50
S 24. 25 c. on 2½d. light blue 8 40
S 25. 30 c. on 3d. pale violet 30 70
S 26. **104.** 40 c. on 5d. brown .. 20 35
S 27. 50 c. on 6d. purple .. 15 35
S 28. **105.** 75 c. on 9d. olive .. 35 80
S 29. 1s. on 1s. brown .. 20 55
S 30. **106.** 2s. 50 on 2s. 6d. grn. 1·75 3·75
S 31. 5s. on 5s. red .. 3·00 4·50

ITALIAN ADMINISTRATION

10. Tower at Mnara-Ciromo.

11. Ostrich.

12. Govenor's Residence, Mogadiscio.

13. River Scene.

1950.
233. **10.** 1 c. black (postage) .. 10 8
234. **11.** 5 c. red 5 5
235. **12.** 6 c. violet 15 5
236. **10.** 8 c. green 15 8
237. **12.** 10 c. green 10 5
238. **11.** 20 c. turquoise .. 10 5
239. **10.** 35 c. red 30 12
240. **12.** 55 c. blue 30 8
241. **11.** 60 c. violet 35 8
242. **10.** 65 c. brown 45 8
243. **12.** 1 s. orange 80 10
244. **13.** 30 c. brown (air) .. 12 5
245. 45 c. red 12 10
246. 65 c. slate 15 12
247. 70 c. blue 15 12
248. 90 c. brown 20 15
249. 1 s. purple 25 8
250. 1 s. 35 violet 30 25
251. 1 s. 50 turquoise .. 40 25
252. 3 s. blue .. .. 1·00 30
253. 5 s. brown .. .. 2·10 65
254. 10 s. orange .. .. 3·50 55

14. Councillors.

15. Symbol of Fair.

1951. 1st Territorial Council.
255. **14.** 20 c. brn. & grn. (post.) 1·50 40
256. 55 c. violet and sepia .. 4·75 3·75
257. – 1 s. blue and violet (air) 1·50 80
258. – 1 s. 50 brown and green 4·75 3·25
DESIGN—Inscr. as T **14**: 1 s. and 1 s. 50, Flags and aeroplane over Mogadiscio.

1952. 1st Somali Fair, Mogadiscio.
259. **15.** 25 c. brn. & red (postage) 1·90 1·60
260. 55 c. brown and blue .. 1·90 2·10
261. – 1 s. 20 blue & bistre (air) 1·25 1·75
DESIGN: 1 s. 20, Palm tree, aeroplane and minaret.

16. Mother and Baby.

17. Native and Entrance to Fair.

1953. Anti-Tuberculosis Campaign.

No.	Type	Description		
262.	16.	5 c. brn. & vio. (postage)	5	5
263.		25 c. brown and red ..	12	10
264.		50 c. brown and blue ..	1·25	1·90
265.		1 s. 20 brn. & grn. (air)	95	95

1953. 2nd Somali Fair, Mogadiscio.

No.	Type	Description		
266.	17.	25 c. green (postage) ..	10	10
267.		60 c. blue	40	65
268.	–	1 s. 20 lake (air) ..	30	45
269.	–	1 s. 50 brown	30	45

DESIGN: 1 s. 20, 1 s. 50, Palm, aeroplane and entrance.

18. Stamps of 1903 and Map.

1953. First Stamps of Italian Somaliland. 50th Anniv. (a) Postage.

No.	Type	Description		
270.	18.	25 c. brown, red & lake	12	15
271.		35 c. brown, red & green	15	15
272.		60 c. brown, red & orge.	30	40

(b) Air. Aeroplane on Map.

No.	Type	Description		
273.	18.	60 c. brown, red & chest.	30	30
274.		1 s. brown, red & black	40	45

19. Aeroplane and Constellations.

1953. Air. U.P.U. 75th Anniv.

No.	Type	Description		
275.	19.	1 s. 20 red and buff ..	30	20
276.		1 s. 50 brown and buff ..	60	30
277.		2 s. green and blue ..	70	55

20. View of Somali Bush.

21. Alexander Is., R. Juba.

1954. Leprosy Convention.

No.	Type	Description		
278.	20.	25 c. grey-green & blue (postage)	20	25
279.		60 c. sepia and chestnut	20	35
280.	21.	1 s. 20 brn. & green (air)	30	40
281.		2 s. violet and red ..	65	1·10

22. Somali Flag.

23. "Adenium Somalense".

1954. Institution of Somali Flag.

No.	Type	Description		
282.	22.	25 c. blue, green, red yell. & black (post.)	20	20
283.		1 s. 20 blue, green, red, yellow & brown (air)	25	25

1955. Floral designs.

No.	Type	Description		
290a.	23.	1 c. red, black and blue	5	5
285.	–	5 c. mauve, grn. & blue	5	5
290c.	–	10 c. yell., grn. & lilac ..	5	5
290d.	–	15 c. yell., green & red	15	8
290e.	–	25 c. yellow, grn. & choc.	12	5
290f.	–	50 c. red, green, yellow and blue	30	15
288.	–	60 c. red, green and black	10	8
289.	–	1 s. yellow, green & mar.	15	12
290.	–	1 s. 20 yell., grn. & sepia	20	10

FLOWERS—VERT. 5 c. "Haemanthus Multiflorus Martyn." 10 c. "Grinum Scabrum". 15 c. "Adansonia Digitata". 25 c. "Poinciana Elata". 50 c. "Gloriosa Virescens". 60 c. "Calatropis Procera". 1 s. "Paneratium Trianthum Her". 1 s. 20, "Sesamothamnus Bussernus".

24. Haggard's Oribi.

24a. Lesser Kudu.

1955. Air. Antelopes. (a) As T **24**. Heads in black and orange.

No.	Type	Description		
291.	24.	35 c. green	15	12
292.	–	45 c. grey-violet ..	55	15
293.	–	50 c. violet	15	10
294.	–	75 c. red	25	15
295.	–	1 s. 20 blue-green ..	25	10
296.	–	1 s. 50 blue	35	20

ANTELOPES: 45 c. Phillips' Dik-Dik. 50 c. Speke's Gazelle. 75 c. Gerenuk (or Waller's) Gazelle. 1 s. 20, Soemmering's Gazelle. 1 s. 50, Common Waterbuck.

(b) As T **24a.**

No.	Type	Description		
296a.	24a.	3 s. slate-pur. & brn.	90	1·00
296b.	–	5 s. yellow and black	85	85

DESIGN: 5 s. Hunter's Antelope.

25. Native Weaver.

26. Voters and Map.

1955. 3rd Somali Fair.

No.	Type	Description		
297.	25.	25 c. brown (postage) ..	20	25
298.	–	30 c. green	20	25
299.	–	45 c. brown & orge. (air)	25	25
300.	–	1 s. 20 blue and pink ..	30	40

DESIGNS: 30 c. Cattle fording river. 45 c. Camels around well. 1 s. 20, Native women at well.

1956. 1st Legislative Assembly.

No.	Type	Description		
301.	26.	5 c. brn. & grey (post) ..	5	5
302.		10 c. brown and olive ..	5	5
303.		25 c. brown and red ..	8	8
304.		60 c. brown & blue (air)	15	20
305.		1 s. 20 brown & orange	15	20

27. Somali Arms.

28. Falcheiro Barrage.

1957. Inauguration of National Emblem. Arms in blue and ochre.

No.	Type	Description		
306.	27.	5 c. brown (postage) ..	5	5
307.		25 c. red	10	5
308.		60 c. violet	12	15
309.		45 c. blue (air)	15	20
310.		1 s. 20 green	15	20

1957. 4th Somali Fair.

No.	Type	Description		
311.	28.	5 c. lilac & brown (post.)	5	5
312.	–	10 c. green and bistre ..	5	8
313.	–	25 c. blue and red ..	12	15
314.	–	60 c. sepia and blue (air)	25	25
315.	–	1 s. 20 black and red ..	20	15

DESIGNS—HORIZ. 10 c. Giuba River bridge. 25 c. Silos at Margherita. 60 c. Irrigation canal. VERT. 1 s. 20, Oil well.

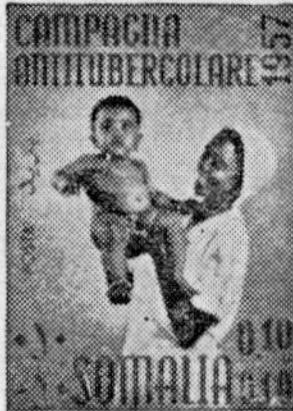

29. Somali Nurse with Baby.

30. Track running.

1957. Tuberculosis Relief Campaign.

No.	Type	Description		
316.	29.	10 c.+10 c. sepia & red (postage)	10	12
317.		25 c.+10 c. sepia & green	10	12
318.		55 c.+20 c. sepia and blue (air)	15	20
319.		1 s. 20 c.+20 c. sepia and violet	20	25

1958. Sports.

No.	Type	Description		
320.	30.	2 c. lilac (postage) ..	5	5
321.	–	4 c. green (Football) ..	5	5
322.	–	5 c. red (Discus) ..	5	5
323.	–	6 c. grey (Motor-cycling)	5	5
324.	–	8 c. blue (Fencing) ..	5	5
325.	–	10 c. orange (Archery) ..	5	5
326.	–	25 c. green (Boxing) ..	5	5
327.	–	60 c. brn. (air) (Running)	12	12
328.	–	1 s. 20 c. blue (Cycling)	15	15
329.	–	1 s. 50 c. red (Basket-ball)	20	20

The 4, 6, 10 and 25 c. are horiz. designs and the remainder vert.

31. The Constitution, and Assembly Building, Mogadiscio.

32. Stork.

1959. Opening of Constituent Assembly. Inscr. "ASSEMBLEA CONSTITUENTE".

No.	Type	Description		
330.	31.	5 c. blue & green (post.)	5	5
331.		25 c. blue & yell.-brown	8	10
332.	–	1 s. 20 c. blue & yellow-brown (air)	25	20
333.	–	1 s. 50 c. blue & ol.-grn.	25	25

DESIGN—HORIZ. 1 s. 20 c., 1 s. 50 c. Police bugler.

1959. Somali Water Birds.

No.	Type	Description		
334.	32.	5 c. black, red & yellow (postage)	5	5
335.	–	10 c. red, yell. & brown	5	5
336.	–	15 c. black and orange ..	5	5
337.	–	25 c. blk., orge. & crimson	8	8
338.	–	1 s. 20, black, red and violet (air)	25	25
339.	–	2 s. red and blue ..	30	30

BIRDS—VERT. 10 c. Senegalese stork. 15 c. Sacred ibis. 25 c. Pelicans. HORIZ. 1 s. 20, Marabou stork. 2 s. White heron.

33. Incense Tree.

34. Institute Badge.

1959. 5th Somali Fair.

No.	Type	Description		
340.	33.	20 c. blk. & orge. (post.)	8	5
341.	–	60 c. black, red & orange	20	20
342.	–	1 s. 20 black & red (air)	30	25
343.	–	2 s. blk., orge. & brown	35	30

DESIGNS—VERT. 60 c. Somali child with incense-burner. HORIZ. 1 s. 20, 15th-century censer. 2 s. Incense-burner and Mogadiscio Harbour.

1960. Opening of University Institute of Somalia, Mogadiscio. Inscr. as in T **34.**

No.	Type	Description		
344.	34.	5 c. red & brown (post.)	5	5
345.	–	50 c. brown & violet-blue	15	12
346.	–	80 c. black and red ..	30	25
347.	–	45 c. brown, black and green (air)	12	10
348.	–	1s. 20 ultram., blk. & bl.	30	30

DESIGNS—HORIZ. 45 c., 1 s. 20, Institute buildings. 50 c. Map of Africa. VERT. 80 c. Institute emblem.

35. "The Horn of Africa".

1960. World Refugee Year.

No.	Type	Description		
349.	35.	10 c. green, black and brown (postage) ..	5	5
350.	–	60 c. brn., ochre & blk.	8	10
351.	–	80 c. green, blk. & pink	12	12
352.	–	1 s. 50 red, blue and green (air)	15	25

DESIGNS—HORIZ. 60 c. Similar to T **35.** VERT. 80 c. Palm. 1 s. 50, Stork.

REPUBLIC

1960. Optd. **Somaliland Independence 26. June 1960.**

353.	10 c. yellow, green & lilac (No. 290c) (postage) ..	5·00	3·25
354.	50 c. blk., orge & violet (No. 293) (air) ..	4·50	3·50
355.	1 s. 20 blk., orge. & blue-green (No. 295)	9·50	3·50

Nos. 353/5 were only issued in the former British protectorate, which united with Somalia when the latter became independent on 1st July, 1960.

36. Gazelle and Map of Africa.

37. Olympic Flame and Somali Flag.

1960. Proclamation of Independence. Inscr. as in T **36.**

No.	Type	Description		
356.	36.	5 c. brn., bl. & lilac (post.)	10	5
357.	–	25 c. blue	15	10
358.	–	1 s. chestnut, red and green (air)	25	15
359.	–	1 s. 80 blue and orange	55	25

DESIGNS—VERT. 25 c. U.N. Flag and Headquarters Building. HORIZ. 1 s. Chamber of Deputies, Montecitorio Palace, Rome. 1 s. 80, Somalia Flag.

1960. Olympic Games. Inscr. "1960".

No.	Type	Description		
360.	37.	5 c. blue & grn. (post.) ..	5	5
361.	–	10 c. blue and yellow ..	5	5
362.	–	45 c. blue and lilac (air)	10	8
363.	–	1 s. 80 blue and red ..	25	15

DESIGNS: 10 c. Relay race. 45 c. Runner breasting tape. 1 s. 80, Runner.

38. Child drawing Giraffe.

39. Girl harvesting Paw-paw.

1960. Child Welfare. Inscr. "PRO INFANZIA".

No.	Type	Description		
364.	38.	10 c. black, brown & green (postage) ..	5	5
365.	–	15 c. blk., apple & red	5	5
366.	–	25 c. brn., blk. & yell.	8	5
367.	–	3 s. orange, black, blue and green (air) ..	50	40

ANIMALS: 15 c. Zebra. 25 c. Rhinoceros. 3 s. Leopard.

1961. Multicoloured. Designs each show a girl harvesting. 75 c. and 80 c. are horiz.

368.	5 c. T **39**	5	5
369.	10 c. Girl harvesting ..	5	5
370.	20 c. Cotton	5	5
371.	25 c. Sesame	5	5
372.	40 c. Sugar cane ..	8	5
373.	50 c. Bananas	10	5
374.	75 c. Groundnuts ..	15	8
375.	80 c. Grapefruit ..	20	10

40. "Amauris fenestrata" (butterfly).

41. Shield, Bow and Arrow, Quiver and Dagger.

42. Girl embroidering "fish" on cloth.

43. Mosquito.

1961. Butterflies. Multicoloured.

376.	60 c. Type **40**	12	8
377.	90 c. "Euryphura chalcis"	15	10
378.	1 s. "Papilio lormieri" ..	1·60	12
379.	1 s. 80 "Papilio antimachus"	40	25
380.	3 s. "Danaida morgeni" ..	55	40
381.	5 s. "Papilio ansorgei" ..	1·25	70
382.	10 s. "Charaxes cynthia"	2·50	1·25

1961. 6th Somali Trade Fair.

No.	Type	Description		
383.	41.	25 c. yellow, black and red (postage) ..	5	5
384.	–	45 c. yell., blk. & green	12	5
385.	–	1s. yell., blk. & bl. (air)	20	15
386.	–	1s. 80 brn., blk. & yellow	30	25

DESIGNS (Handicrafts)—VERT. 45 c. "Tungi" wooden vase and pottery. HORIZ. 1s. National head-dress, support and comb. 1s. 80, Statuettes of camel and man, and balancing novelty.

1962. Child Welfare. Tropical Fishes. Inscr. "PRO INFANZIA". Multicoloured.

387. 15 c. Type **42** (postage) .. 8 5
388. 25 c. Blue Angelfish .. 8 5
389. 40 c. Wrasse 25 15
390. 2 s. 70 Red Snapper (air) 85 35

1962. Malaria Eradication. Inscr. "MONDO UNITO CONTRO LA MALARIA".

391. **43.** 10 c. green & red (post) 8 5
392. – 25 c. brown and mauve 12 5
393. – 1s. brown and black (air) 30 15
394. – 1 s. 80 green and black .. 55 20

DESIGNS—VERT. 25 c. Insecticide sprayer. 1s., 1s. 80, Campaign emblem and mosquitoes.

44. Auxiliaries tending Casualty.

45. Wooden Spoon and Fork.

1963. Women's Auxiliary Forces Formation. Multicoloured.

395. 5 c. Policewoman (post.) 5 5
396. 10 c. Army auxiliary .. 5 5
397. 25 c. Policewomen with Patrol car 12 5
398. 75 c. Type **44** 20 12
399. 1 s. Policewomen marching with flag (air) 35 12
400. 1 s. 80 Army auxiliaries at attention with flag .. 55 20

The 5 c., 10 c. and 25 c. are horiz.

1963. Freedom from Hunger.

401. **45.** 75 c. chest. & grn. (post.) 20 10
402. – 1s. multicoloured (air) .. 45 20

DESIGN: 1s. Sower.

46. Pres. Osman and Arms.

47. Open-air Theatre.

1963. Independence. 3rd Anniv. Arms in blue and yellow.

403. **46.** 25 c. sepia & blue (post.) 20 10
404. 1s. sepia and red (air) .. 30 15
405. 1s. 80 sepia and green .. 50 20

1963. 7th Somali Fair.

406. **47.** 25 c. green (postage) .. 12 5
407. – 55 c. red 15 10
408. – 1s. 80 blue (air) .. 75 35

DESIGNS: 55 c. African Trade Building. 1s. 80, Government Pavilion.

48. Credit Bank, Mogadishu.

49. Running.

1964. Somali Credit Bank. 10th Anniv. Multicoloured.

409. 60 c. Type **48** (postage) .. 25 12
410. 1 s. Map of Somalia and Globe (air) 30 15
411. 1 s. 80 Bank Emblem .. 65 30

1964. Olympic Games, Tokyo. Colours sepia, chestnut and blue.

412. 10 c. Type **49** (postage) .. 5 5
413. 25 c. High-jumping .. 10 5
414. 90 c. Diving (air) .. 25 15
415. 1 s. 80 Football .. 50 25

50. Douglas "DC-3" Airliner.

1964. Somali Airlines. Inaug.

416. **50.** 2 c. blue & cerise (post) 8 5
417. – 20 c. blue and orange .. 30 5
418. – 1 s. ochre & green (air) 55 20
419. – 1 s. 80 blue and black .. 1·10 35

DESIGNS: 20 c. Passengers disembarking from "DC-3". "DC-3" in flight over: 1 s. Elephants. 1 s. 80, Mogadishu.

51. Refugees.

52. I.T.U. Emblem on Map of Africa.

1964. Somali Refugees Fund.

420. **51.** 25 c. + 10 c. red and blue (postage) 20 8
421. – 75 c. + 20 c. maroon, black and red (air) .. 40 15
422. – 1 s. 80 + 50 c. green, black and bistre .. 80 30

DESIGNS—HORIZ. 75 c. Ruined houses. VERT. 1 s. 80, Soldier with child refugees.

1965. I.T.U. Cent.

423. **52.** 25 c. blue & orge. (post) 20 5
424. 1 s. black & green (air) .. 35 12
425. 1 s. 80 brown & magenta 70 30

53. Tanning.

1965. Somali Industries.

426. **53.** 10 c. sepia and buff (post.) 5 5
427. – 25 c. sepia and pink .. 5 5
428. – 35 c. sepia and blue .. 10 5
429. – 1 s. 50 sepia & grn. (air) 40 15
430. – 2 s. sepia and mauve .. 70 20

DESIGNS: 25 c. Meat processing and canning. 35 c. Fish processing and canning. 1 s. 50, Sugar—cutting cane and refining. 2 s. Dairying—milking and bottling.

54. Hottentot Fig and Gazelle.

1965. Somali Flora and Fauna. Multicoloured.

431. 20 c. Type **54** 5 5
432. 60 c. African tulips and giraffes 12 5
433. 1 s. Ninfea and flamingoes 20 10
434. 1 s. 30 Pervincia and ostriches 25 12
435. 1 s. 80 Bignonia and zebras 40 20

55. Narina Trogon.

1966. Somali Birds. Multicoloured.

436. 25 c. Type **55** 5 5
437. 35 c. Bateleur eagle (vert.) 8 5
438. 50 c. Ruppell's griffon .. 10 5
439. 1 s. 30 "Blue jay" .. 30 12
440. 2 s. Vulturine guinea fowl (vert.) 45 20

56. Globe and U.N. Emblem.

1966. U.N. 21st Anniv. Multicoloured.

441. 35 c. Type **56** 5 5
442. 1 s. Map of Africa and U.N. emblem 15 15
443. 1 s. 50 Map of Somalia and U.N. emblem 25 20

57. Woman sitting on Crocodile.

1966. Somali Art. Showing Paintings from Caresa Museum, Mogadishu. Multicoloured.

444. 25 c. Type **57** 5 5
445. 1 s. Woman and warrior .. 12 10
446. 1 s. 50 Boy leading camel 20 15
447. 2 s. Women pounding grain 25 20

58. U.N.E.S.C.O. Emblem and Palm.

59. Abyssinian Oribi.

1966. U.N.E.S.C.O. 20th Anniv.

448. **58.** 35 c. black, red and grey 5 5
449. 1 s. black, green & yell. 12 10
450. 1 s. 80 black, blue & red 25 20

1967. Antelopes.

451. **59.** 35 c. ochre, blk. & blue 5 5
452. – 60 c. brown, black & orge. 8 5
453. – 1 s. bistre, black & red 12 10
454. – 1 s. 80 ochre, blk. & grn. 25 20

ANTELOPES: 60 c. Dik-dik. 1 s. Gerenuk, or Waller's gazelle. 1 s. 80, Soemmering's, or Ariel, gazelle.

60. Somali Dancers.

61. Badge and Scout Saluting.

1967. "Popular Dances". Designs showing dancers.

455. **60.** 25 c. multicoloured .. 5 5
456. 50 c. multicoloured .. 8 5
457. 1 s. 30 multicoloured .. 15 15
458. 2 s. multicoloured .. 20 20

1967. World Scout Jamboree. Multicoloured.

459. 35 c. Type **61** 5 5
460. 50 c. Scouts and flags .. 5 5
461. 1 s. Camp scene 15 10
462. 1 s. 80 Jamboree emblem .. 25 20

62. Pres. Schermarche and King Faisal.

1967. Visit of King Faisal of Saudi Arabia.

463. **62.** 50 c. black & blue (post.) 5 5
464. – 1 s. multicoloured .. 12 10
465. – 1 s. 80 multicoloured (air) 20 15

DESIGNS: 1 s. Somali and Saudi Arabian flags. 1 s. 80, Kaaba, Mecca and portraits as T **62**.

63. Sweetlips.

1967. Fishes. Multicoloured.

466. 35 c. Type **63** 5 5
467. 50 c. Butterfly fish .. 5 5
468. 1 s. Lunar-tailed bullseye 12 10
469. 1 s. 80 Speckled grouper .. 25 20

64. Inoculation.

65. Somali Girl with Lemons.

1968. W.H.O. 20th Anniv.

470. **64.** 35 c. blk., brn., red & bl. 5 5
471. – 1 s. black, brown & grn. 12 10
472. – 1 s. 80 blk., brn. & orge. 30 20

DESIGNS: 1 s. Chest examination. 1 s. 80 Heart examination.

1968. Agricultural Produce. Multicoloured.

473. 5 c. Type **65** 5 5
474. 10 c. Oranges 5 5
475. 25 c. Loaves of bread .. 5 5
476. 35 c. Limes 5 5
477. 40 c. Apples 5 5
478. 50 c. Grapefruit 8 5
479. 1 s. Bananas 12 10
480. 1 s. 30 Cotton bolls .. 15 12

Each design includes a Somali girl.

66. Kobus ellypsiprymnus.

67. Throwing the Javelin.

1968. Somali Antelopes. Multicoloured.

481. 1 s. 50 Type **66** 15 15
482. 1 s. 80 Gazalla spekei .. 20 15
483. 2 s. Strepsiceros imberbis 25 20
484. 5 s. Damaliscus hunteri .. 65 50
485. 10 s. Ammodorcas clarkei 1·25 1·00

1968. Olympic Games, Mexico.

486. **67.** 35 c. black, brn. & lemon 5 5
487. – 50 c. black, brn. & red 5 5
488. – 80 c. blk., brn. & purple 10 8
489. – 1 s. 50 blk., brn. & grn. 20 15

DESIGNS: 50 c. Running. 80 c. Pole-vaulting. 1 s. 50 Basketball.

68. White Stork.

69. "Pounding Meal".

1968. Air. Birds. Multicoloured.

491. 35 c. Type **68** 5 5
492. 1 s. Carmine bee-eater .. 15 10
493. 1 s. 30 Green pigeon .. 20 15
494. 1 s. 80 Paradise whydah .. 25 20

1968. Somali Art.

495. **69.** 25 c. brn., black & lilac 5 5
496. – 35 c. brown, black & red 5 5
497. – 2 s. 80 brn., blk. & grn. 35 30

DESIGNS: (wood-carvings) 35 c. "Preparing food". 2 s. 80 "Rug-making".

70. Cornflower.

1969. Flowers. Multicoloured.

498. 40 c. Type **70** 5 5
499. 80 c. Sunflower 10 8
500. 1 s. Oleander 15 10
501. 1 s. 80 Chrysanthemum .. 25 20

71. Workers at Anvil.

1969. Int. Labour Organization. 50th Anniv. Multicoloured.

502. 25 c. Type 71 .. .. 5 5
503. 1 s. Ploughing with oxen 15 10
504. 1 s. 80 Drawing water for irrigation 25 20

72. Gandhi, and Hands releasing Dove.

1969. Mahatma Gandhi. Birth Cent.

505. – 35 c. purple 5 5
506. 72. 1 s. 50 brown-orange .. 20 20
507. – 1 s. 80 olive-brown .. 25 25

DESIGNS—VERT. (Size $25\frac{1}{2} \times 36$ mm.): 35 c. Mahatma Gandhi. 1 s. 80 Gandhi seated.

SOMALI DEMOCRATIC REPUBLIC

An issue for the "Apollo 11" Moon Landing was prepared in 1970 but not issued.

73. "Nivprale vevanes".

74. Lenin with Children.

1970. Butterflies. Multicoloured.

508. 25 c. Type 73 .. .. 5 5
509. 50 c. "Leschenault" .. 8 8
510. 1 s. 50 "Papilio aeacus" .. 20 20
511. 2 s. "Urania riphaeus" .. 25 25

1970. Lenin. Birth Cent.

512. 74. 25 c. multicoloured .. 5 5
513. – 1 s. multicoloured .. 15 12
514. – 1 s. 80 black, orange and brown 20 15

DESIGNS—VERT. 1 s. Lenin making speech. HORIZ. 1 s. 80 Lenin at desk.

75. Dove feeding Young.

1970. Independence. 10th Anniv.

515. 25 c. Type 75 .. .. 5 5
516. 35 c. Dagahtur Memorial 5 5
517. 1 s. Somali arms (vert.) .. 15 15
518. 2 s. 80 Camel and star (vert.) 50 45

76. Tractor and Produce.

1970. 21st October Revolution. First Anniv.

519. 76. 35 c. multicoloured .. 5 5
520. – 40 c. black and blue .. 5 5
521. – 1 s. black and brown .. 20 12
522. – 1 s. 80 multicoloured .. 30 20

DESIGNS: 40 c. Soldier and flag. 1 s. Hand on open book. 1 s. 80 Emblems of Peace, Justice and Prosperity.

77. African within Snake's Coils.

1971. Racial Equality Year.

523. 77. 1 s. 30 multicoloured .. 20 20
524. – 1 s. 80 blk., red & brn. 30 30

DESIGN: 1 s. 80, Human figures, chain and barbed wire.

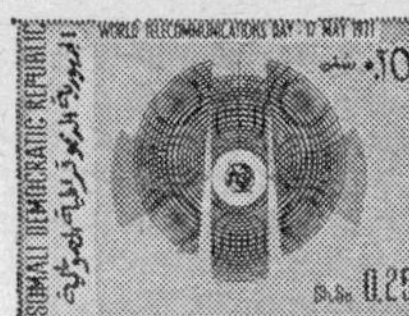

78. I.T.U. Emblem.

1971. World Telecommunications Day.

525. 78. 25 c. blk., ultram. & blue 5 5
526. – 2 s. 80 blk., bl. & green 50 45

DESIGN: 2 s. 80, Global emblem.

79. Telecommunications Map.

1971. Pan-African Telecommunications Network.

527. 79. 1 s. grn., blk. and blue 20 12
528. – 1 s. 50 blk., grn. & yellow 25 20

DESIGN: 1 s. 50 similar to T 79 but with different network pattern.

80. Rhinoceros.

1971. Wild Animals.

529. 80. 35 c. multicoloured .. 5 5
530. – 1 s. multicoloured .. 20 15
531. – 1 s. 30 black, yellow and violet 25 20
532. – 1 s. 80 multicoloured .. 30 20

DESIGNS: 1 s. Leopards. 1 s. 30 Zebras. 1 s. 80 Lion attacking camel.

81. Ancient Desert City.

1971. East and Central African Summit Conference, Mogadishu.

533. 81. 1 s. 30 brn., blk. & red 25 20
534. – 1 s. 50 multicoloured .. 25 20

DESIGN: 1 s. 50 Headquarters building, Mogadishu.

82. Memorial.

1971. Revolution. 2nd Anniv.

535. 82. 10 c. black, cobalt & bl. 5 5
536. – 1 s. multicoloured .. 15 15
537. – 1 s. 35 multicoloured .. 20 20

DESIGNS: 1 s. Agricultural workers. 1 s. 35 Building workers.

83. Inoculating Cattle.

1971. Rinderpest Control Programme. Multicoloured.

538. 40 c. Type 83 .. .. 15 5
539. 1 s. 80 Herdsmen with cattle 45 35

84. A.P.U. Emblem and Back of Airmail Envelope.

1972. African Postal Union. 10th Anniv. Multicoloured.

540. 1 s. 30 Type 84 .. .. 25 20
541. 1 s. 50 A.P.U. emblem and dove with letter 25 20

85. Mother and Child.

1972. U.N.I.C.E.F. 25th Anniv.

542. 85. 50 c. black, brown and cinnamon 8 5
543. – 2 s. 80 multicoloured .. 45 40

DESIGN—HORIZ. 2 s. 80 U.N.I.C.E.F. emblem and schoolchildren.

86. Camel.

1972. Domestic Animals.

544. 86. 5 c. multicoloured .. 5 5
545. – 10 c. multicoloured .. 5 5
546. – 20 c. multicoloured .. 5 5
547. – 40 c. black, brown & red 8 5
548. – 1 s. 70 black, green & black 30 20

DESIGNS: 10 c. Cattle on quayside. 20 c. Bull. 40 c. Black-headed sheep.

87. Child within Cupped Hands.

1972. 21st October Revolution. 3rd Anniv. Multicoloured.

549. 70 c. Type 87 .. .. 12 8
550. 1 s. Parade of standards .. 15 10
551. 1 s. 50 Youth Camps emblem 25 15

88. Folk Dancers.

1973. Folk Dances. Multicoloured.

552. 5 c. Type 88 .. .. 5 5
553. 40 c. Pair of dancers (vert.) 8 5
554. 1 s. Team of dancers (vert.) 15 12
555. 2 s. Three dancers .. 30 25

89. Old Alphabet in Flames.

1973. Introduction of New Somali Script.

556. 89. 40 c. multicoloured .. 8 5
557. – 1 s. multicoloured .. 15 10
558. – 2 s. black, stone & yellow 30 25

DESIGNS—HORIZ. 1 s. Alphabet in sun's rays. 2 s. Writing new script.

90. Soldiers and Chains within O.A.U. Emblem.

92. Somali Youth and Girl.

91. Hurdling.

1974. Organization of African Unity. 10th Anniv. (1973). Multicoloured.

559. 40 c. Type 90 .. .. 8 5
560. 2 s. Spiral on map of Africa 30 25

1974. Sports.

561. 91. 50 c. blk., red & orge-red 8 5
562. – 1 s. blk., grey-grn., & grn. 15 10
563. – 1 s. 40 blk., grey & olive-grey 20 12

DESIGNS—HORIZ. 1 s. Running. VERT. 1 s. 40 Basketball.

1974. Guulwade Youth Movement. Mult.

564. 40 c. Type 92 .. .. 8 5
565. 2 s. Guulwade members helping old woman .. 30 25

93. Map of League Members.

1974. Arab League. 30th Anniv. (1975). Multicoloured.

566. 1 s. 50 Type 93 .. .. 20 15
567. 1 s. 70 Flags of Arab League countries 25 20

94. Desert Landscape.

1974. 21 October Revolution. 5th Anniv. Multicoloured.

568. 40 c. Type 94 .. .. 8 5
569. 2 s. Somali villagers reading books 30 25

95. Doves with Letters.

96. Somali Costume.

1975. Universal Postal Union. Cent. Mult.

570. 50 c. Type 95 .. .. 10 8
571. 3 s. Mounted postman .. 60 55

1975. African Postal Union. As T 95. Multicoloured.

572. 1 s. Maps of Africa (repetitive motif) 20 15
573. 1 s. 50 Dove with letter .. 30 25

1975. Traditional Costumes.

574. 96. 10 c. multicoloured .. 5 5
575. – 40 c. multicoloured .. 8 5
576. – 50 c. multicoloured .. 10 8
577. – 1 s. multicoloured .. 20 15
578. – 5 s. multicoloured .. 85 80
579. – 10 s. multicoloured .. 1·90 1·75

DESIGNS: 40 c. to 10 s. Various costumes.

97. Indpendence Statue, Mogadishu. 98. Hassan Statue.

1976. Int. Women's Year. Multicoloured.

580.	50 c. Type **97**	12	10
581.	2 s. 30 I.W.Y. emblem (horiz.)	60	55

1976. Sayed M. A. Hassan Commemoration. Multicoloured.

582.	50 c. Type **98**	12	10
583.	60 c. Hassan directing warriors (vert.)	15	12
584.	1 s. 50 Hassan inspiring warriors (vert.) ..	40	35
585.	2 s. 30 Hassan leading attack	60	55

99. Nurse and Child. **100.** " Cypraea gracilis ".

1976. Famine Relief. Multicoloured.

586.	75 c.+25 c. Type **99** ..	25	25
587.	80 c.+20 c. Devastated land (horiz.)	25	25
588.	2 s. 40+10 c. Somali family with produce	65	65
589.	2 s. 90+10 c. Relief emblem and medical officer (horiz.)	80	80

1976. Somali Seashells. Multicoloured.

590.	50 c. Type **100**	12	10
591.	75 c. " Charonia bardayi "	20	15
592.	1 s. " Chlamys townsendi "	25	20
593.	2 s. " Cyatium ranzanii "	55	50
594.	2 s. 75 " Conus argillaceus "	75	70
595.	2 s. 90 " Strombus oldi "	75	70

AIR EXPRESS STAMP

A 1. Young Gazelles.

1958.

E 330.	A 1.	1 s. 70 c. red and black	75	85

EXPRESS LETTER STAMPS

1923. Express Letter stamps of Italy surch. **Somalia Italiana** and value.

E 44.	E 1.	30 b. on 60 c. red ..	2·10	2·10
E 45.	E 2.	60 b. on 1 l. 20 red & bl.	2·50	2·50

1924. As Express Letter stamps of Eritrea Type E 1 but inscr. "SOMALIA".

E 60.	30 b. brown and red ..	1·25	1·25
E 61.	60 b. red and blue ..	1·75	1·75

1926. Nos. E 60/1 surch.

E 104.	70 c. on 30 b. brn. & red	1·00	1·00
E 106.	1 l. 25 on 30 b. brn. & red	1·00	1·00
E 105.	2 l. 50 on 60 b. red & blue	1·25	1·25

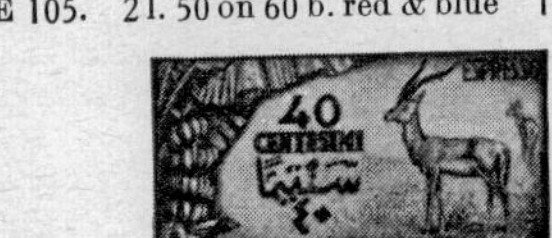

E 1. Grant's Gazelle.

1950.

E 255.	E 1.	40 c. turquoise ..	35	20
E 256.		80 c. violet	70	40

E 2. "Gardenia Lutea Fresen".

1955.

E 291.	E 2.	50 c. yell., grn. & lilac	15	20
E 292.	–	1 s. red, green & blue	25	30

FLOWER: 1 s. "Eryhrina Melanocantha Taub".

PARCEL POST STAMPS

Parcel Post stamps of Italy optd. or surch. on each half of stamp.

1920. Optd. **SOMALIA ITALIANA.**

P 23.	P 2.	5 c. brown	12	5
P 24.		10 c. blue	12	5
P 81.		20 c. black	10·00	55
P 25.		25c. red	25	5
P 85.		50 c. orange	8·50	55
P 28.		1 l. violet	1·75	20
P 29.		2 l. green	2·10	20
P 30.		3 l. yellow	3·25	35
P 31.		4 l. grey	5·00	85
P 89.		10 l. purple	2·10	65
P 90.		12 l. brown	1·75	75
P 91.		15 l. olive	1·75	75
P 92.		20 l. purple	2·10	85

1922. Optd. **SOMALIA.**

P 31.	P 2.	25 c. red	10·00	15
P 32.		50 c. orange ..	2·50	20
P 33.		1 l. violet	3·25	25
P 34.		2 l. green	4·25	55
P 35.		3 l. yellow	8·50	00
P 36.		4 l. grey	13·00	1·70

1923. Surch. **SOMALIA ITALIANA** and value.

P 44.	P 2.	3 b. on 5 c. brown ..	15	8
P 45.		5 b. on 5 c. brown ..	15	8
P 46.		10 b. on 10 c. blue	25	12
P 47.		25 b. on 25 c. red ..	35	12
P 48.		50 b. on 50 c. orange	85	15
P 49.		1 r. on 1 l. violet ..	1·75	20
P 50.		2 r. on 2 l. green ..	3·25	35
P 51.		3 r. on 3 l. yellow ..	8·50	70
P 52.		4 r. on 4 l. grey ..	10·00	1·10

1928. Optd. **SOMALIA ITALIANA.**

P 111.	P 3.	5 c. brown	40	5
P 112.		10 c. blue	40	5
P 126.		25 c. red	8·50	40
P 114.		30 c. blue	20	12
P 116.		60 c. red	25	12
P 127.		1 l. violet	1·00	2·10
P 128.		2 l. green	1·00	2·10
P 119.		3 l. yellow	25	20
P 120.		4 l. black	45	30
P 121.		10 l. mauve ..	23·00	1·40
P 122.		20 l. purple	17·00	50

P 1.

1950.

P 255.	P 1.	1 c. red	5	5
P 256.		3 c. slate	5	5
P 257.		5 c. purple	5	5
P 258.		10 c. orange ..	8	8
P 259.		20 c. brown ..	8	8
P 260.		50 c. turquoise ..	25	25
P 261.		1 s. violet	50	50
P 262.		2 s. brown	1·00	1·00
P 263.		3 s. blue	1·75	1·50

Unused prices are for complete stamps, used prices are for half stamps except in the case of Nos. P 255/63.

POSTAGE DUE STAMPS

Postage Due stamps of Italy optd. or surch.

1906. Optd. **Somalia Italiana Meridionale.**

D 17.	D 3.	5 c. purple and orange	25	35
D 18.		10 c. purple & orange	5·00	6·00
D 19.		20 c. purple & orange	1·25	1·75
D 20.		30 c. purple & orange	40	60
D 21.		40 c. purple & orange	1·40	1·90
D 22.		50 c. purple & orange	1·40	1·90
D 23.		60 c. purple & orange	3·00	4·25
D 24.	D 3.	1 l. purple and blue ..	90·00	25·00
D 25.		2 l. purple and blue ..	80·00	29·00
D 26.		5 l. purple and blue ..	70·00	29·00
D 27.		10 l. purple and blue	32·00	32·00

1909. Optd. **Somalia Italiana.**

D 28.	D 3.	5 c. purple and orange	20	40
D 29.		10 c. purple & orange	20	40
D 30.		20 c. purple & orange	20	40
D 31.		30 c. purple & orange	80	1·25
D 32.		40 c. purple & orange	80	1·25
D 33.		50 c. purple & orange	80	1·25
D 34.		60 c. purple & orange	80	1·25
D 35.		1 l. purple and blue ..	3·00	4·25
D 36.		2 l. purple and blue ..	4·25	6·50
D 37.		5 l. purple and blue ..	13·00	19·00
D 38.		10 l. purple and blue	1·75	3·25

1923. Stamps without figures of value, surch. **Somalia Italiana** and value in " besa " or " rupia " in figures and words.

D 49.	D 3.	1 b. black and orange	5	8
D 50.		2 b. black and orange	5	8
D 51.		3 b. black and orange	5	8
D 52.		5 b. black and orange	15	15
D 53.		10 b. black & orange	15	15
D 54.		20 b. black & orange	15	15
D 55.		40 b. black & orange	15	15
D 56.		1 r. black and blue ..	50	55

1926. Optd. **Somalia Italiana** and surch with figures only.

D 76.	D 3.	5 c. black and orange	2·50	2·10
D 77.		10 c. black and orange	40	30
D 78.		20 c. black and orange	35	25
D 79.		30 c. black and orange	35	25
D 80.		40 c. black and orange	40	30
D 81.		50 c. black and orange	50	40
D 82.		60 c. black and orange	65	50
D 83.		1 l. black and blue ..	3·25	1·00
D 84.		2 l. black and blue ..	4·25	1·00
D 85.		5 l. black and blue ..	4·25	1·75
D 86.		10 l. black and blue	4·25	1·90

1934. Optd. **SOMALIA ITALIANA.**

D 187.	D 6.	5 c. brown	12	15
D 188.		10 c. blue	12	15
D 189.		20 c. red	25	30
D 190.		25 c. green	20	25
D 191.		30 c. orange ..	40	50
D 192.		40 c. brown ..	50	60
D 193.		50 c. violet	55	55
D 194.		60 c. blue	1·40	1·75
D 195.	D 7.	1 l. orange	3·00	1·50
D 196.		2 l. green	3·75	3·25
D 197.		5 l. violet	7·50	8·50
D 198.		10 l. blue	8·50	9·00
D 199.		20 l. red	11·00	11·00

D 1.

1950.

D 255.	D 1.	1 c. slate	5	5
D 256.		2 c. blue	5	5
D 257.		5 c. turquoise ..	5	5
D 258.		10 c. purple ..	8	5
D 259.		40 c. violet	20	15
D 260.		1 s. brown	40	30

SOMALILAND PROTECTORATE BC

A Br. protectorate in N.E. Africa on the Gulf of Aden. Amalgamated with the Somalia Republic on 1st July, 1960, whose stamps it now uses.

16 annas = 1 rupee.
1951. 100 cents = 1 shilling.

1903. Stamps of India (Queen Victoria) optd. **BRITISH SOMALILAND.**

1.	**14.**	½ a. green	35	75
2.	–	1 a. red	50	80
3.	–	2 a. lilac	40	40
18.	–	2½ a. blue	1·25	2·50
5.	–	3 a. orange	80	1·50
6.	–	4 a. green (No. 96) ..	1·00	2·60
19.	–	6 a. brown (No. 80) ..	75	1·50
8.	–	8 a. mauve	1·50	3·00
20.	–	12 a. purple on red ..	3·00	4·00
21.	**26.**	1 r. green and red ..	4·00	5·00
11.	**27.**	2 r. red and orange ..	7·00	10·00
12.		3 r. brown and green ..	8·00	11·00
13.		5 r. blue and violet ..	9·00	13·00

1903. Stamps of India of 1902 (King Edward VII) with same opt.

25.	½ a. green (No. 122) ..	30	50
26.	1 a. red (No. 123)	30	30
27.	2 a. lilac	1·00	1·50
28.	3 a. orange	1·25	2·00
29.	4 a. olive	1·25	2·00
30.	8 a. mauve	1·50	2·50

1.

ILLUSTRATIONS
British Commonwealth and all overprints and surcharges are FULL SIZE. Foreign Countries have been reduced to ¾-LINEAR.

1904.

32.	**1.**	½ a. green	30	1·25
46.		1 a. black and red ..	30	1·50
59.		1 a. red	1·50	1·50
47.		2 a. purple	1·50	2·00
48.		2½ a. blue	1·50	2·00
36.		3 a. brown and green ..	1·25	2·50
37.		4 a. green and black ..	1·75	2·50
51.		6 a. green and violet ..	1·50	3·00
52.		8 a. black and blue ..	2·50	3·50
53.		12 a. black and orange ..		
41.		1 r. green	6·00	8·00
42.		2 r. purple	12·00	14·00
43.		3 r. green and black ..	15·00	20·00
44.		5 r. black and red ..	15·00	20·00

The rupee values are larger (26 × 31 mm.).

1912. As 1904, but portrait of King George V.

73.	½ a green	5	30
74.	1 a. red	5	30
75.	2 a. purple	40	75
76.	2½ a blue	50	1·00
64.	3 a. brown and green ..	65	1·50
65.	4 a. green and black ..	75	1·50
79.	6 a. green and violet ..	75	2·00
80.	8 a. black and blue ..	1·25	2·00
81.	12 a. black and orange ..	2·50	4·00
69.	1 r. green	1·75	3·00
83.	2 r. purple	6·00	8·00
84.	3 r. green and black ..	8·00	12·00
72.	5 r. black and red	13·00	20·00

1935. Silver Jubilee. As T **11** of Antigua.

86.	1 a. blue and red	50	60
87.	2 a. blue and grey	75	1·25
88.	3 a. brown and blue ..	1·00	2·00
89.	1 r. grey and purple ..	2·50	4·00

1937. Coronation. As T **2** of Aden.

90.	1 a. red	5	10
91.	2 a. grey	5	12
92.	3 a. blue	20	50

2. Berbera Blackhead Sheep. **4.**

3. Somaliland Protectorate.

DESIGN—As T 2; 4 a. to 12 a. Greater Kudu Antelope.

1938. Portrait faces left.

93.	**2.**	½ a. green	20	45
94.		1 a. red	20	45
95.		2 a. maroon	15	50
96.		3 a. blue	1·00	1·50
97.	–	4 a. brown	1·00	1·50
98.	–	6 a. violet	60	1·00
99.	–	8 a. grey	1·00	2·00
100.	–	12 a. orange	1·10	2·25
101.	**3.**	1 r. green	3·00	6·00
102.		2 r. purple	3·00	6·00
103.		3 r. blue	2·50	5·50
104.		5 r. black	3·50	5·50

1942. As Nos. 93/104 but with full-face portraits as in T **4**.

105.	**4.**	½ a. green	5	8
106.		1 a. red	5	8
107.		2 a. maroon	30	25
108.		3 a. blue	5	20
109.	–	4 a. brown	5	20
110.	–	6 a. violet	10	20
111.	–	8 a. grey	12	20
112.	–	12 a. orange	20	30
113.	–	1 r. green	50	60
114.	–	2 r. purple	1·00	1·50
115.	–	3 r. blue	1·00	1·75
116.	–	5 r. black	1·75	2·00

1946. Victory. As T **4** of Aden.

117.	1 a. red	5	5
118.	3 a. blue	5	5

1949. Silver Wedding. As T **5/6** of Aden

119.	1 a. red	5	5
120.	5 r. black	2·00	2·50

1949. U.P.U. As T **14/17** of Antigua surch.

121.	1 a. on 10 c. red ..	8	10
122.	3 a. on 30 c. blue ..	15	20
123.	6 a. on 50 c. purple ..	25	35
124.	12 a. on 1 s. orange ..	45	50

1951. 1942 issue surch. with figures and **Cents** or **Shillings.**

125.	5 c. on ½ a green ..	5	5
126.	10 c. on 2 a. maroon ..	5	5
127.	15 c. on 3 a. blue ..	5	8
128.	20 c. on 4 a. brown ..	5	8
129.	30 c. on 6 a. violet ..	10	15
130.	50 c. on 8 a. grey ..	12	12
131.	70 c. on 2 a. orange ..	15	20
132.	1s. on 1 r. green	20	25
133.	2s. on 2 r. purple	45	70
134.	2s. on 3 r. blue	60	70
135.	5s. on 5 r. black	1·25	1·60

1953. Coronation. As T **7** of Aden.

136.	15 c. black and green ..	20	25

5. Camel and Gurgi. **6.** Askari.

1953.

137. 5. 5 c. black 5 5
138. 6. 10 c. orange 8 8
139. 5. 15 c. green 12 15
140. 20 c. red 15 15
141. 6. 30 c. brown 25 25
142. – 35 c. blue 25 30
143. – 50 c. brown and red .. 30 30
144. – 1s. blue 35 35
145. – 1s. 30 blue and black .. 55 65
146. – 2s. brown and violet .. 95 95
147. – 5s. brown and green .. 3·00 3·00
148. – 10s. brown and violet .. 4·00 6·50

Designs—Horiz. 35 c., 2 s. Somali rock pigeon. 50 c., 5 s. Martial eagle. 1 s. Berbera Blackhead sheep. 1 s. 30, Sheikh Isaac's Tomb, Mait. 10 s. Taleh Fort.

1957. Opening of Legislative Council. Optd. **OPENING OF THE LEGISLATIVE COUNCIL 1957.**

149. 5. 20 c. red 15 20
150. 1s. blue (No. 144) .. 35 40

1960. Legislative Council's Unofficial Majority Optd. **LEGISLATIVE COUNCIL UNOFFICIAL MAJORITY. 1960.**

151. 5. 20 c. red 25 35
152. – 1 s. 30, bl. & blk. (No. 145) 35 40

OFFICIAL STAMPS

1903. Stamps of India (Queen Victoria) optd. **On H.M.S.** Further optd. **BRITISH SOMALILAND.**

O 1. 14. ½ a. blue-green .. 3·00 10·00
O 2. – 1 a. red .. .. 3·50 4·00
O 3. – 2 a. lilac .. .. 4·00 13·00
O 4. – 8 a. mauve .. .. 9·00 £120
O 5. 26. 1 r. green and red .. 9·00 90·00

1903. Stamps of India of 1902 (King Edward VII) optd. **SERVICE BRITISH SOMALILAND.**

O 6. ½ a. green (No. 122) .. 60
O 7. 1 a. red (No. 123) .. 60
O 8. 2 a. lilac 90
O 9. 8 a. mauve .. .. 9·00

1906. Stamps of 1904 optd. **O.H.M.S.**

O 10. 1. ½ a. green .. .. 2·50 15·00
O 11. 1 a. black and red .. 4·00 5·00
O 12. 2 a. purple .. .. 40·00 20·00
O 13. 8 a. black and blue .. 25·00 45·00
O 15. – 1 r. green (No. 41) .. 16·00 £150

SORUTH BC

A state of India. In 1948 the Saurashtra Union was formed which included Jasdan, Morvi, Nawanagar and Wadhwan as well as Soruth. Now uses Indian stamps.

A. JUNAGADH

1.

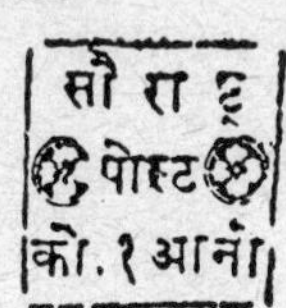

2.

1864 (?) On paper of various colours. Imperf.

1. 1. 1 a. black .. .. .. 65·00 6·00

1868. (Nos. 11 and 13 are on paper of various colours.) Imperf.

11. 2. 1 a. black .. .. .. 9·00 4·00
13. 1 a. red .. .. .. 6·50 6·50
5. 1 a. black on yellow ..
14. 4 a. black .. .. .. 35·00 40·00

3.

4.

1877. Imperf. or perf.

40. 4. 3 p. green 20 20
17. 3. 1 a. green 10 15
41. 1 a. red 20 30
26. 4. 4 a. red 30 35

1913. Surch. in words in English and in native characters.

34. 3. 3 p. on 1 a. green .. 8 8
39. 4. 1 a. on 4 a. red .. 45 45

ત્રણ પાઇ

(5.)

6. Nawab Sir Mahabat Khanji Rasulkhan.

1923. Surch. as T 5.

42. 6. 3 p. on 1 a. red .. .. 1·75 1·75

1923. Imperf. or perf.

46. 6. 3 p. mauve 10 10
47. 1 a. red .. .. .. 2·50 2·50

No. 45 is smaller.

7, Junagadh City.

8. Nawab Sir Mahabat Khanji Rasulkhan.

Designs—Horiz. ½ a., 4 a. Gir lion. 2 a., 8 a. Kathi horse.

1929. (a) Inscr. "POSTAGE".

49. 7. 3 p. black and green .. 30 10
50. – ½ a. black and blue .. 2·25 5
51. 8. 1 a. black and red .. 1·25 50
52. – 2 a. black and orange .. 3·75 70
53. 7. 3 a. black and red .. 75 15
54. – 4 a. black and purple .. 6·00 12
55. – 8 a. black and green .. 7·00 25
56. 8. 1 r. black and blue .. 3·00 1·25

1936. (b) Inscr. "POSTAGE AND REVENUE".

57. 8. 1 a. black and red .. 50 60

OFFICIAL STAMPS

1929. Nos. 49/56 optd. **SARKARI.**

O 1. 7. 3 p. black and green .. 5 5
O 2. – ½ a. black and blue .. 15 5
O 3. 8. 1 a. black and red .. 10 8
O 4. – 2 a. black and orange .. 1·25 10
O 5. 7. 3 a. black and red .. 10 10
O 6. – 4 a. black and purple .. 50 8
O 7. – 8 a. black and green .. 75 15
O 8. 8. 1 r. black and blue .. 1·00 1·00

1933. No. 57 optd. **SARKARI.**

O 13. 8. 1 a. black and red .. 75 20

B. UNION OF SAURASHTRA.

1949. Surch. **POSTAGE & REVENUE ONE ANNA.**

61. 7. 1 a. on 3 p. black & green 5·00 5·00
58. – 1 a. on ½ a. black and blue (No. 50) .. .. 2·50 60

Surch. **Postage and Revenue ONE ANNA.**

59. 1 a. on 2 a. grey and yellow (No. 52a) .. .. 2·50 50

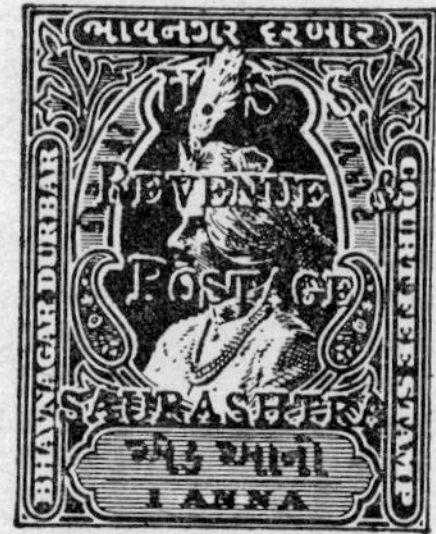

9.

1949.

60. 9. 1 s. purple .. .. .. 1·00 70

OFFICIAL STAMPS

1949. No. 59 optd. **SARKARI.**

O 22. 1 a. on 2 a. grey & yellow 12·00 7·00

1949 Official stamps of 1929 surch. **ONE ANNA.**

O 14. 1 a. on 2 a. grey & yellow 70·00 10·00
O 15. 1 a. on 3 a. black & red 70·00 10·00
O 16. 1 a. on 4 a. black & purple 70·00 10·00
O 17. 1 a. on 8 a. black & green 70·00 10·00
O 18. 1 a. on 1 r. black & blue 25·00 8·00

SOUTH AFRICA BC

The Union of S. Africa consists of the provinces of the Cape of Good Hope, Natal, the Orange Free State and the Transvaal. Became an independent republic on 31st May, 1961.

1961. 100 cents. = 1 rand.

Stamp illustrations in this country are reduced to ¾ size.

1.

2.

1910.

2. 1. 2½d. blue .. .. .. 4·00 2·00

1913.

3. 2. ½d. green 12 8
4. 1d. red 25 8
5. 1½d. brown 25 8
6. 2d. purple 75 8
7. 2½d. blue .. .. 1·25 15
8. 3d. black and red .. 1·00 15
9. 3d. blue .. .. .. 1·00 1·00
10a. 4d. orange and green .. 2·50 20
11. 6d. black and violet .. 2·50 10
12. 1s. orange .. .. 8·00 25
13. 1s. 3d. violet .. .. 12·00 7·00
14. 2s. 6d. purple and green .. 35·00 2·50
15. 5s. purple and blue .. 90·00 15·00
16. 10s. blue and olive .. £200 20·00
17. £1 green and red £500 £200

3.

ILLUSTRATIONS British Commonwealth and all overprints and surcharges are FULL SIZE. Foreign Countries have been reduced to ¾-LINEAR.

1925. Air.

26. 3. 1d. red .. .. .. 4·00 6·00
27. 3d. blue .. .. .. 6·00 7·00
28. 6d. mauve .. .. .. 12·00 15·00
29. 9d. green .. .. .. 25·00 30·00

NOTE—"Bilingual" in heading indicates that the stamps are inscribed alternately in English and Afrikaans throughout the sheet.

Our prices are for bilingual pairs, and single stamps should be considered to be worth very much less than half the price of pairs.

4. Springbok.

5. Van Riebeeck's Ship.

10. Orange Tree.

6. Union Buildings, Pretoria.

9. Groot Schuur.

8. "Hope".

1926. Bilingual. No. 33 is imperf.

			Un. pair	Us. pair
114.	4.	½d. black and green ..	12	12
115.	5.	1d. black and red ..	12	15
34.	6.	2d. grey and purple ..	15·00	15·00
44.		2d. grey and lilac ..	4·00	1·00
58.		2d. blue and violet ..	20·00	12·00
45.	9.	3d. black and red ..	15·00	12·00
45a.		3d. blue	4·00	1·75
33.	8.	4d. blue	75	75
118.	–	4d. brown ..	25	25
119.	10.	6d. green and orange ..	45	45
120.	–	1s. brown and blue ..	60	60
121.	–	2s. 6d. green and brown	8·00	6·00
49a.	–	2s. 6d. blue and brown	12·00	8·00
122.	–	5s. black and green ..	10·00	7·00
39.	–	10s. blue and brown ..	£120	£120

Designs—As T 6: 4d. (No. 118) Kaffir kraal. 1s. Gnus. 2s. 6d. Ox-wagon crossing river. 5s. Ox-wagon outspanned. 10s. Cape Town and Table Bay.

On No. 33 the English and Afrikaans inscriptions are on separate sheets, and our price is for single stamps of either language.

For ½d., 1d., 2d. 3d. and 10s. in similar designs see Nos. 105/6, 107a, 116/7 and 64ba respectively.

15. D.H. "Moth".

1929. Air.

			Us. single	Un. single
40.	15.	4d. green	2·00	2·00
41.		1s. orange	15·00	15·00

16. Church of the Vow.

20.

1933. Voortrekker Memorial Fund. Inscr as in T 16. Bilingual.

			Un. pair	Us. pair
50.	16.	½d.+½d. green	1·00	1·25
51.	–	1d.+½d. black and pink	1·50	1·50
52.	–	2d.+1d. green & purple	3·00	3·00
53.	–	3d.+1½d. green and blue	6·00	6·00

Designs: 1d. The "Great Trek". 2d Voortrekker man. 3d. Voortrekker woman.

1935. Silver Jubilee. Bilingual.

			Un. pair	Us. pair
65.	20.	½d. black and green ..	75	75
66.		1d. black and red ..	75	75
67.		3d. blue	12·00	12·00
68.		6d. green and orange ..	18·00	18·00

The positions of Afrikkaans and English inscr. are transposed on alternate stamps.

21. Gold Mine.

22. King George VI.

1936. Bilingual.

			Un. pair	Us. pair
57.	21.	1½d. green and gold ..	2·00	75

1937. Coronation. Bilingual.

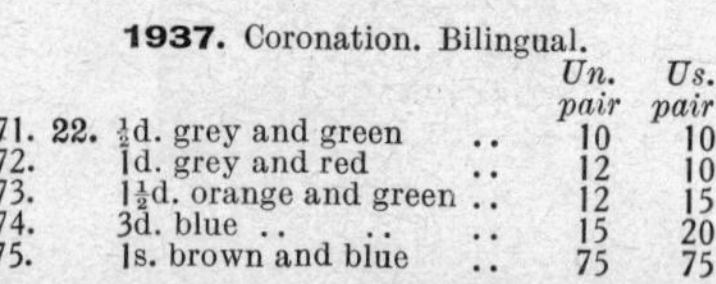

			Un. pair	Us. pair
71.	22.	½d. grey and green ..	10	10
72.		1d. grey and red ..	12	10
73.		1½d. orange and green ..	12	15
74.		3d. blue	15	20
75.		1s. brown and blue ..	75	75

23. Wagon crossing Drakensberg.

25. Signing of Dingaan-Retief Treaty.

1938. Voortrekker Centenary Fund. Dated "1838 1938". Bilingual.

No.	T	Description	Un. pair	Us. pair
76.	–	½d.+½d. blue and green	1·00	1·00
77.	23.	1d.+1d. blue and red	1·50	1·50
78.	25.	1½d.+1½d. brown & grn.	4·00	4·00
79.	–	3d.+3d. blue	5·00	5·00

DESIGNS—As T **23**: ½d. Voortrekker ploughing. As T **25**: Voortrekker Monument.

27. Voortrekker Family. **28.** "Groot Constantia".

1938. Voortrekker Commem. Bilingual.

No.	T	Description	Un. pair	Us. pair
80.	–	1d. blue and red	1·00	1·00
81.	27.	1½d. blue and brown	1·00	1·00

DESIGN: 1d. Wagon wheel.

1939. Bilingual.

No.	T	Description	Un. pair	Us. pair
64ba.	28.	10s. blue and brown	18·00	4·00

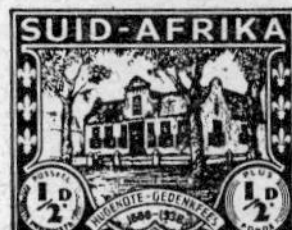

29. Old Vicarage, Paarl, now a Museum. **30.** Symbol of the Reformation.

31. Huguenot Dwelling, Drakenstein Mountain Valley.

1939. Landing of Huguenots in S. Africa. 250th Anniv. Bilingual.

No.	T	Description	Un. pair	Us. pair
82.	29.	½d.+½d. brown and green	1·25	1·25
83.	30.	1d.+1d. green and red	1·50	1·50
84.	31.	1½d.+1½d. green and pur.	3·00	4·00

32. Union Buidings, Pretoria. **33.** Groot Schuur.

1940. Bilingual.

No.	T	Description	Un. pair	Us. pair
107a.	32.	2d. slate and violet	75	1·25
116.		2d. blue and purple	15	30
117.	33.	3d. blue	30	35

34. Gold Mine. **35.** Infantry. **36.** Sailor, Destroyer and Lifebelts.

37. Women's Auxiliary Services.

1941. Bilingual.

No.	T	Description	Un. pair	Us. pair
87.	34.	1½d. green and buff	10	10

1941. War Effort. Bilingual except the 2d. and 1s. which are inscr. in both languages on each stamp.

No.	T	Description	Un. pair	Us. pair
88.	35.	½d. green	20	15
89.	–	1d. red	10	12
90.	–	1½d. green	10	10
94.	36.	2d. violet	20	5
91.	37.	3d. blue	50	75
92.	–	4d. brown	1·25	1·00
93.	–	6d. orange	1·00	1·50
95.	–	1s. brown	1·50	70

DESIGNS—As T **35**: 1d. Nurse and ambulance. 1½d. Airman. As T **36**: 4d. Artillery. 6d. Welding. As T **37**: 1s. Tank corps.

38. Infantry. **39.** Signaller.

DESIGNS—As T **38**—VERT. 1d. Nurse. 1½d. Airman. 2d. Sailor. 6d. Welder. HORIZ. 3d. Women's Auxiliary Services. 6d. Heavy gun. 1s. Tanks.

1942. War Effort. Bilingual except 4d. and 1s., which are inscr. in both languages on each stamp.

No.	T	Description	Un. unit	Us. unit
96.	38.	½d. green	20	10
97.	–	1d. red	20	10
98.	–	1½d. brown	12	12
99a.	–	2d. violet	15	20
100.	–	3d. blue	60	70
102.	–	4d. green	40	45
101.	–	6d. orange	60	60
103.	–	1s. brown	90	90
104.	39.	1s. 3d. brown	1·50	2·00

Our prices for Nos. 96, 97, 100 and 102 are for units of three. The other stamps are in units of two.

1943. As 1926, but with plain background. Bilingual.

No.	T	Description	Un. pair	Us. pair
105.	4.	½d. green	20	40
106.	5.	1d. red	30	35

49. "Victory". **50.** King George VI.

51. King George VI and Queen Elizabeth.

1945. Victory. Bilingual.

No.	T	Description	Un. pair	Us. pair
108.	49.	1d. brown and red	5	5
109.	–	2d. blue and violet	10	10
110.	–	3d. blue	10	15

DESIGNS: 2d. Man and oxen ploughing ("Peace"). 3d. Man and woman gazing at a star ("Hope").

1947. Royal Visit. Bilingual.

No.	T	Description	Un. pair	Us. pair
111.	50.	1d. black and red	5	5
112.	51.	2d. violet	5	8
113.	–	3d. blue	5	8

DESIGN—As T **51**: 3d. Queen Elizabeth II when Princess and Princess Margaret.

53. King George VI and Queen Elizabeth. **52.** Gold Mine.

54. "Wanderer" entering Durban. **55.** Hermes.

1948. Bilingual.

No.	T	Description	Un. unit	Us. unit
124.	52.	1½d. green and buff	10	20

The price for No. 124 is for a unit of four stamps.

1948. Royal Silver Wedding. Bilingual.

No.	T	Description	Un. pair	Us. pair
125.	53.	3d. blue and silver	5	8

1949. 100th Anniv. of British Settlers in Natal. Bilingual.

No.	T	Description	Un. pair	Us. pair
127.	54.	1½d. claret	10	10

1949. U.P.U. 75th Anniv. Bilingual.

No.	T	Description	Un. pair	Us. pair
128.	55.	½d. green	5	5
129.		1½d. red	10	5
130.		3d. blue	10	10

56. Wagons approaching Bingham's Berg. **57.** Union Bldgs., Pretoria.

1949. Voortrekker Monument, Pretoria. Inaug.

No.	T	Description	Un. single	Us. single
131.	56.	1d. magenta	5	5
132.	–	1½d. green	5	5
133.	–	3d. blue	5	5

DESIGNS: 1½d. Voortrekker Monument, Pretoria. 3d. Bible, candle and Voortrekkers.

1950. Bilingual.

No.	T	Description	Un. pair	Us. pair
134.	57.	2d. blue and violet	10	12

INSCRIPTIONS. In all later issues except Nos. 167 and 262/5, the stamps are inscribed in both Afrikaans and English. Our prices are for single copies, unused and used.

58. Maria de la Quellerie. **60.** Queen Elizabeth II.

1952. Landing of Van Riebeeck. Tercent. Dated "1652–1952".

No.	T	Description	Un. single	Us. single
136.	–	½d. purple and sepia	5	5
137.	58.	1d. green	5	5
138.	–	2d. violet	8	5
139.	–	4½d. blue	10	10
140.	–	1s. brown	20	20

DESIGNS—HORIZ. ½d. Seal and monogram. 2d. Arrival of Van Riebeeck's ships. 1s. Landing at the Cape. VERT. 4½d. Van Riebeeck.

1952. S. African Tercentenary Stamp Exn. No. 137 optd. **SATISE** and No. 138 optd. **SADIPU.**

No.	T	Description	Un.	Us.
141.	58.	1d. green	5	8
142.	–	2d. violet	5	12

1953. Coronation.

No.	T	Description	Un.	Us.
143a.	60.	2d. blue	8	5

61. "Cape Triangular". **62.** Merino Ram.

1953. Cape of Good Hope. Stamp Cent.

No.	T	Description	Un.	Us.
144.	61.	1d. sepia and vermilion	5	5
145.	–	4d. indigo and blue	10	10

DESIGN: 4d. as T **61** but reproducing 4d. "Triangular".

1953.

No.	T	Description	Un.	Us.
146.	62.	4½ d. purple and yellow	12	15
147.	–	1s. 3d. chocolate	60	10
148.	–	1s. 6d. vermilion & grn.	50	15

DESIGN: 1s. 3d. Springbok. 1s. 6d. Aloes.

63. Arms of Orange Free State and Scroll.

1954. Orange Free State Cent.

No.	T	Description	Un.	Us.
149.	63.	2d. sepia and vermilion	8	5
150.		4½d. purple and grey	15	15

64. Warthog. **65.** Rhinoceros.

1954. Wild Animals.

No.	T	Description	Un.	Us.
151.	64.	½d. turquoise	5	5
152.	–	1d. lake	5	5
153.	–	1½d. sepia	8	5
154.	–	2d. plum	8	5
155.	65.	3d. chocolate and blue	8	5
156.	–	4d. indigo and emerald	8	5
157.	–	4½d. indigo and blue	75	35
158.	–	6d. sepia and orange	30	5
159.	–	1s. brown and claret	40	5
160.	–	1s. 3d. brown and green	60	5
161.	–	1s. 6d. brown and pink	1·00	30
162.	–	2s. 6d. sepia and apple	1·50	30
163.	–	5s. sepia and buff	5·00	75
164.	–	10s. black and blue	10·00	2·00

DESIGNS: As T **64**—VERT. 1d. Gnu. 1½d. Leopard. 2d. Zebra. As T **65**—VERT. 4d. Elephant. 4½d. Hippopotamus. 1s. Kudu. 1s. 6d. Gemsbok. 2s. 6d. Nyala. 5s. Giraffe. 10s. Sable Antelope. HORIZ. 6d. Lion. 1s. 3d. Springbok.

66. President Kruger. **67.** A. Pretorius, Church of the Vow and Flag.

1955. Cent. of Pretoria.

No.	T	Description	Un.	Us.
165.	66.	3d. green	8	5
166.	–	6d. mar. (Pres. Pretorius)	12	10

1955. Voortrekker Covenant Celebrations Pietermaritzburg. Bilingual.

No.	T	Description	Un. pair	Us. pair
167.	67.	2d. blue and red	12	20

68. Settlers' Block-wagon and House. **69.** Arms of the Academy.

1958. Arrival of German Settlers in S. Africa. Cent.

No.	T	Description	Un. single	Us. single
168.	68.	2d. chocolate and purple	10	12

1959. S. African Academy of Science and Art, Pretoria. 50th Anniv.

No.	T	Description	Un.	Us.
169.	69.	3d. indigo & turq.-blue	8	5

70. Globe and Antarctic Scene. **71.** Union Flag.

1959. S. African National Antarctic Expedition.

No.	T	Description	Un.	Us.
178.	70.	3d. turquoise & orange	8	5

1960. Union of S. Africa. 50th Anniv.

No.	T	Description	Un.	Us.
179.	71.	4d. orange and blue	8	5
180.	–	6d. red, brown & green	8	5
181.	–	1s. blue and yellow	40	10
182.	–	1s. 6d. black and blue	1·00	75

DESIGNS—VERT. 6d. Union Arms. HORIZ. 1s. "Wheel of progress". 1s. 6d. Union Festival emblem.

See also Nos. 190 and 192/3.

72. Locomotives of 1860 and 1960.

1960. S. African Railways Cent.

183. **72.** 1s. 3d. blue .. .. 1·50 1·00

73. Prime Ministers Botha, Smuts Hertzog, Malan, Strijdom and Verwoerd.

1960. Union Day.

184. **73.** 3d. brown & light brown 8 8

1961. Types as before but new currency.

185. **64.** $\frac{1}{2}$ c. turquoise 5 5
186. – 1 c. lake (as No. 152) .. 5 5
187. – $1\frac{1}{2}$ c. sepia (as No. 153) 8 5
188. 2 c. plum (as No. 154) 8 5
189. **73.** $2\frac{1}{2}$ c. brown 8 5
190. **71.** $3\frac{1}{2}$ c. orange and blue .. 12 8
191. – 5 c. sep. & orge. (as 158) 12 8
192. – $7\frac{1}{2}$ c. red, brown and green (as No. 180) .. 30 8
193. – 10 c. bl. & yell. (as 181) 30 20
194. – $12\frac{1}{2}$ c. brn. & grn. (as 160) 50 30
195. – 20 c. brn. & pk. (as 161) 75 50
196. – 50 c. sep. & buff (as 163) 3·00 3·00
197. – 1 r. blk. & blue (as 164) 10·00 10·00

74. Natal Kingfisher.

75. Crimson-breasted Shrike.

1961. Republic issue.

237. **74.** $\frac{1}{2}$ c. blue, red and brown 5 5
238. – 1 c. red and grey .. 5 5
239. – $1\frac{1}{2}$ c. lake and purple .. 5 5
201. – 2 c. blue and yellow .. 8 5
241. – $2\frac{1}{2}$ c. violet and green .. 5 5
242. **75.** 3 c. red and indigo .. 8 5
242b. – 4 c. violet and green .. 8 5
204. – 5 c. yellow & turquoise 12 5
292. – 6 c. brown and green .. 12 12
244. – $7\frac{1}{2}$ c. brown and green .. 12 5
294. – 9 c. red, yell. & green 20 20
206. – 10 c. sepia and green .. 20 5
246. – $12\frac{1}{2}$ c. red, yell. & myrtle 20 8
247. – 15 c. black, olive & orge. 30 25
248. – 20 c. turq., red & salmon 50 40
249. – 50 c. black and blue .. 1·50 1·50
250. – 1 r. orge., green & blue 3·00 3·50

DESIGNS—As T **74**—VERT. 1 c. Kafferboom flower. HORIZ. $1\frac{1}{2}$ c. Afrikaner bull. As T **75**—HORIZ. 2 c. Pouring gold. 50 c. Capetown Harbour. 1 r. Strelitzia (flower). VERT. $2\frac{1}{2}$ c., 4 c. Groot Constantia. 5 c. Baobab tree. 6 c. $7\frac{1}{2}$ c. Maize. 9 c., $12\frac{1}{2}$ c. Protea (flower). 10 c. Capetown Castle Entrance. 15 c. Industry. 20 c. Secretary Bird.

Most values exist in two forms showing differences in the size of the inscriptions and figures of value.

See also 276/7.

76. Bleriot Monoplane and Boeing 707 Airliner over Table Mountain.

77. Folk-dancers.

1962. First South African Aerial Post. 50th Anniv.

220. **76.** 3 c. blue and red .. 8 5

1962. Volkspele (Folk-dancing) in South Africa. 50th Anniv.

221. **77.** $2\frac{1}{2}$ c. red and brown .. 8 5

HAVE YOU READ THE NOTES AT THE BEGINNING OF THIS CATALOGUE?

These often provide answers to the enquiries we receive.

78. The "Chapman".

79. Red Disa (orchid), Castle Rock and Gardens.

80. Centenary Emblem and Nurse.

1962. Unveiling of Precinct Stone, British Settlers Monument, Grahamstown.

222. **78.** $2\frac{1}{2}$ c. turquoise & purple 8 5
223. $12\frac{1}{2}$ c. blue and chocolate 25 15

1963. Kirstenbosch Botanic Gardens, Capetown. 50th Anniv.

224. **79.** $2\frac{1}{2}$ c. multicoloured .. 8 5

1963. Red Cross Cent. Inscr. "1863-1963".

225. **80.** $2\frac{1}{2}$ c. red, blk. & purple 8 5
226. – $12\frac{1}{2}$ c. red and blue .. 25 15

DESIGN—HORIZ. $12\frac{1}{2}$ c. Centenary emblem and globe.

81. Assembly Building, Umtata.

82. "Springbok" Badge of Rugby Board.

1963. 1st Meeting of Transkei Legislative Assembly.

251. **81.** $2\frac{1}{2}$ c. sepia and green .. 8 5

1964. South African Rugby Board. 75th Anniv.

252. **82.** $2\frac{1}{2}$ c. brown and green 8 5
253. – $12\frac{1}{2}$ c. black & yell.-grn. 35 25

DESIGN—HORIZ. $12\frac{1}{2}$ c. Rugby footballer making try.

83. Calvin.

84. Nurse's Lamp.

1964. Calvin (Protestant Reformer) 400th Death Anniv.

254. **83.** $2\frac{1}{2}$ c. cerise, violet & brn. 8 5

1964. South African Nursing Assn. 50th Anniv.

255. **84.** $2\frac{1}{2}$ c. blue and gold .. 8
257. – $12\frac{1}{2}$ c. blue and gold .. 30 20

DESIGN—HORIZ. $12\frac{1}{2}$ c. Nurse holding lamp.

85. I.T.U. Emblem and Satellites.

86. Pulpit in Groote Kerk, Cape Town.

1965. I.T.U. Cent.

258. **85.** $2\frac{1}{2}$ c. orange and blue 8 8
259. – $12\frac{1}{2}$ c. maroon and green 20 25

DESIGN: $12\frac{1}{2}$ c. I.T.U. Emblem and symbols.

1965. Nederduites Gereformeerde Kerk (Dutch Reformed Church) in South Africa. Tercent.

260. **86.** $2\frac{1}{2}$ c. brown and yellow 8 8
261. – $12\frac{1}{2}$ c. black, orge. & blue 25 25

DESIGN—HORIZ. $12\frac{1}{2}$ c. Church emblem.

87. Bird in Flight.

1966. Republic. 5th Anniv. Billingual.

			Un. pair	*Us. pair*
262.	–	1 c. blk., grn. & yellow	5	5
263.	**87.**	$2\frac{1}{2}$ c. blue, indigo & grn.	10	12
264.	–	3 c. red, yellow & brown	12	15
265.	–	$7\frac{1}{2}$ c. blue, ultram & yell.	30	35

DESIGNS—VERT. 1 c. Diamond. 3 c. Maize plants. HORIZ. $7\frac{1}{2}$ c. Mountain landscape.

88 Verwoerd and Union Buildings, Pretoria.

89. Martin Luther.

1966. Verwoerd Commem.

			Un. single	*Us. single*
266.	**88.**	$2\frac{1}{2}$ c. brown and turquoise	5	5
267.	–	3 c. brown and green ..	8	5
268.	–	$12\frac{1}{2}$ c. brown and blue ..	30	30

DESIGNS: 3 c. Dr. H. F. Verwoerd. $12\frac{1}{2}$ c. Verwoerd and map of South Africa.

1967. Reformation. 450th Anniv.

269. **89.** $2\frac{1}{2}$ c. black and red .. 5 5
270. – $12\frac{1}{2}$ c. black and orange 30 25

DESIGN: $12\frac{1}{2}$ c. Wittenburg Church Door.

90. Profile of Pres. Fouche.

91. Hertzog in 1902.

1968. President Fouche. Inaug.

271. **90.** $2\frac{1}{2}$ c. chocolate .. 5 5
272. – $12\frac{1}{2}$ c. blue 35 30

DESIGN: $12\frac{1}{2}$ c. Portrait of Pres. Fouche.

1968. General Hertzog Monument, Bloemfontein, Inaug.

273. **91.** $2\frac{1}{2}$ c. blk., brn. & yell. 5 5
274. – 3 c. black, brown, orge. and yellow .. 5 5
275. – $12\frac{1}{2}$ c. blk., red & orge. 35 30

DESIGNS: 3 c. Hertzog in 1924. $12\frac{1}{2}$ c. Hertzog Monument.

92. Natal Kingfisher.

93. Springbok and Olympic Torch.

1969.

276. **92.** $\frac{1}{2}$ c. blue, red and ochre 5 5
277. – 1 c. red and brown .. 8 10

DESIGN—VERT. 1 c. Kafferboom Flower.

1969. South African Games, Bloemfontein.

278. **93.** $2\frac{1}{2}$ c. black, red & green 5 5
279. $12\frac{1}{2}$ c. black, red & cinnamon 25 30

94. Professor Barnard and Groote Schuur Hospital.

1969. World's 1st Heart Transplant and 47th South African Medical Assn. Congress.

280. **94.** $2\frac{1}{2}$ c. purple and red .. 5 5
281. – $12\frac{1}{2}$ c. red and blue .. 25 25

DESIGN: $12\frac{1}{2}$ c. Hands holding heart.

95. Mail Coach.

1969. 1st Stamps of the South African Republic (Transvaal). Cent.

282. **95.** $2\frac{1}{2}$ c. yell., indigo & brn. 10 10
283. – $12\frac{1}{2}$ c. emer., gold & brn. 35 35

DESIGN—VERT. $12\frac{1}{2}$ c. Transvaal stamp of 1869.

96. "Water 70" Emblem.

97. "The Sower".

1970. Water 70 Campaign.

299. **96.** $2\frac{1}{2}$ c. grn., blue & choc. 5 5
300. – 3 c. blue and buff .. 8 8

DESIGN: 3 c. Symbolic Waves.

1970. Bible Society of South Africa. 150th Anniv. Multicoloured.

301. $2\frac{1}{2}$ c. Type **97** 5 5
302. $12\frac{1}{2}$ c. "Biblia" and Open Book (horiz.) 25 25

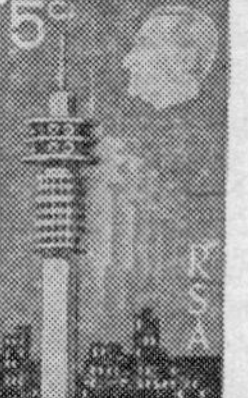

98. J. G. Strijdom and Strijdom Tower.

99. Map and Antarctic Landscape.

1971. "Interstex" Stamp Exhib.

303. **98.** 5 c. blue, black and yell. 20 15

1971. Antarctic Treaty. 10th Anniv.

304. **99.** $12\frac{1}{2}$ c. black, blue & red 20 15

100. Landing of British Settlers, 1820.

1971. Republic of South Africa. 10th Anniv.

305. **100.** 2 c. flesh and red .. 5 5
306. – 4 c. green .. 8 8

DESIGN—VERT. 4 c. Presidents Steyn and Kruger and Treaty of Vereeniging Monument.

101. View of Dam.

1972. Opening of Pres. Hendrick Verwoerd Dam. Multicoloured.

307. 4c. Type **101** 8 5
308. 5c. Aerial view of dam .. 8 5
309. 10c. View of dam and surrounding country (58×21 mm.) 20 20

102. Sheep.

103. Black and Siamese Cats.

1972. Sheep and Wool Industry.
310. 102. 4 c. multicoloured .. 8 5
311. – 15 c. stone, blue and dull blue 30 20
DESIGN: 15 c. Lamb.

1972. Societies for the Prevention of Cruelty to Animals. Cent.
312. 103. 5 c. multicoloured .. 8 8

104. Transport and Industry. 105. University Crest.

1973. ESCOM (Electricity Supply Commission). 50th Anniv. Multicoloured.
326. 4 c. Type 104 .. .. 8 5
327. 5 c. Pylon 8 8
328. 15 c. Power station .. 20 20
Nos. 327/8 are vertical designs size 21 × 28 mm.

1973. University of South Africa. Cent.
329. 105. 4 c. multicoloured .. 8 8
330. – 5 c. multicoloured .. 8 8
331. – 15 c. black and gold 20 20
DESIGNS—HORIZ. (38 × 21 mm.). 5 c. University Complex, Pretoria. VERT. As T 105. 15 c. Old University building, Cape Town.

106. Rescuing Sailors. 107. C. J. Langenhoven.

1973. Rescue by Wolraad Woltemade. Bicentenary.
332. 106. 4 c. brn., grn. & black 8 8
333. 5 c. olive, grn. & black 8 8
334. – 15 c. brn., green & blk. 20 20
DESIGNS: 5c. De Jong Thomas ' foundering 15 c. " De Jong Thomas " breaking up and sailors fleeing.

1973. C. J. Langenhoven (politician and composer of national anthem). Birth Cent.
335. 107. 4 c. multicoloured .. 8 8
336. – 5 c. multicoloured .. 8 8
337. – 15 c. multicoloured .. 20 20
Nos. 336/7 are as T 107 but with motifs re-arranged. The 5 c. is vert., 21 × 38 mm., and the 15 c. is horiz., 38 × 21 mm.

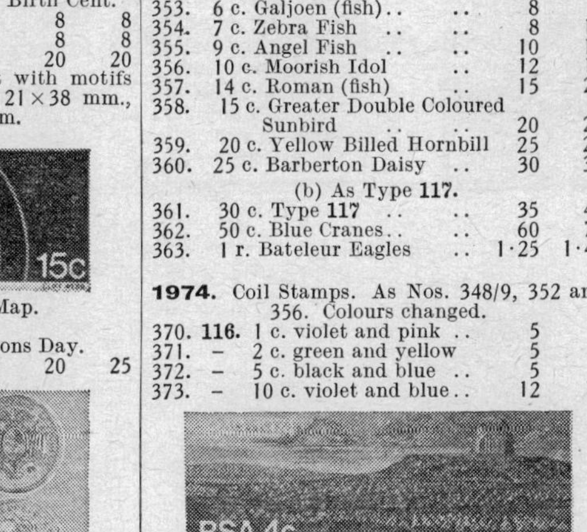

108. Communications Map.

1973. World Communications Day.
338. 108. 15 c. multicoloured .. 20 25

109. Restored Buildings. 110. Burgerspond (Obverse and Reverse).

1974. Restoration of Tulbagh. Multicoloured.
340. 4 c. Type 109 .. .. 8 5
341. 5 c. Restored Church Street (horiz. 58 × 21 mm.) .. 8 8

1974. Burgerspond (coin). Centenary.
342. 110. 9 c. brn., cream and red 15 15

111. Dr. Malan. 112. Congress Emblem.

1974. Dr. D. F. Malan (Prime Minister). Birth Cent.
343. 111. 4 c. blue and light blue 5 5

1974. 15th World Sugar Congress, Durban.
344. 112. 15 c. blue and silver .. 20 20

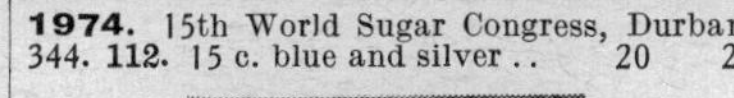

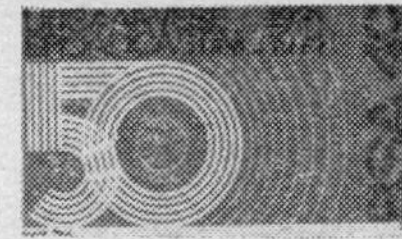

113. "50" and Radio Waves.

1974. Broadcasting in South Africa. 50th Anniv.
345. 113. 4 c. red and black .. 8 8

114. Monument Building.

1974. British Settlers' Monument, Grahamstown. Inaug.
346. 114. 5 c. red and black .. 8 8

115. Stamps of the South African Provinces.

1974. Universal Postal Union. Centenary.
347. 115. 15 c. multicoloured .. 20 25

116. Iris. 117. Bokmakieries.

1974. Multicoloured.
(a) As Type 116.
348. 1 c. Type 116 .. .. 5 5
349. 2 c. Wild Heath 5 5
350. 3 c. Geranium 5 5
351. 4 c. Arum Lily 5 5
352. 5 c. Gannet 5 5
353. 6 c. Galjoen (fish) 8 8
354. 7 c. Zebra Fish 8 10
355. 9 c. Angel Fish 10 12
356. 10 c. Moorish Idol .. 12 12
357. 14 c. Roman (fish) .. 15 20
358. 15 c. Greater Double Coloured Sunbird 20 20
359. 20 c. Yellow Billed Hornbill 25 25
360. 25 c. Barberton Daisy .. 30 35
(b) As Type 117.
361. 30 c. Type 117 .. .. 35 40
362. 50 c. Blue Cranes 60 70
363. 1 r. Bateleur Eagles .. 1·25 1·40

1974. Coil Stamps. As Nos. 348/9, 352 and 356. Colours changed.
370. 116. 1 c. violet and pink .. 5 5
371. – 2 c. green and yellow .. 5 5
372. – 5 c. black and blue .. 5 5
373. – 10 c. violet and blue .. 12 15

118. Voortrekker Monument and Encampment.

1974. Voortrekker Monument, Pretoria. 25th Anniv.
374. 118. 4 c. multicoloured .. 5 5

119. SASOL Complex.

1975. South African Coal, Oil and Gas Corporation Ltd. (SASOL). 25th Anniv.
375. 119. 15 c. multicoloured .. 20 25

120. President Diederichs. 121. Jan Smuts.

1975. State President. Inauguration.
376. 120. 4 c. brown and gold .. 8 8
377. 15 c. blue and gold .. 20 25

1975. Smuts Commemoration.
378. 121. 4 c. black and grey .. 8 8

122. " Dutch East Indiaman, Table Bay ".

1975. Thomas Baines (painter). Death Centenary. Multicoloured.
379. 5 c. Type 122 .. .. 8 8
380. 9 c. " Cradock, 1848 " .. 12 12
381. 15 c. " Thirsty Flat, 1848 " 20 20
382. 30 c. " Pretoria, 1874 " .. 35 40

123. Gideon Malherbe's House, Paarl.

1975. Genootskap van Regte Afrikaners (Afrikaner Language Movement) Cent.
384. 123. 4 c. multicoloured .. 5 5

124. " Automatic Sorting ". 125. Title Page of " Die Afrikaanse Patriot ".

1975. Postal Mechanisation.
385. 124. 4 c. multicoloured .. 5 5

1975. Language Monument, Paarl. Inaug.
386. 125. 4 c. blk., brn. and orge. 5 5
387. – 5 c. multicoloured .. 5 5
DESIGN: 5 c. " Africkaanse Taalmonument ".

126. Table Mountain.
(Illustration reduced. Actual size 57 × 20 mm.)

1975. Tourism. Multicoloured.
388. 15 c. Type 126 .. .. 20 20
389. 15 c. Johannesburg .. 20 20
390. 15 c. Cape Vineyards .. 20 20
391. 15 c. Lions in Kruger National Park 20 20

127. Globe and Satellites.

1975. Satellite Communication.
392. 127. 15 c. multicoloured .. 20 20

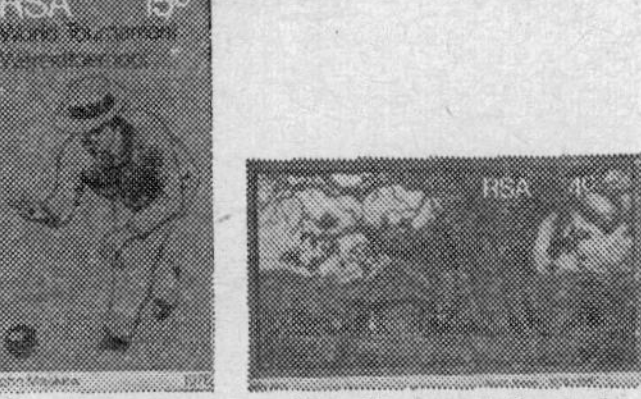

128. Bowls Player. 129. Hut and Baobab Tree.

1976. Sporting Commems.
393. 128. 15 c. black and green .. 20 20
394. – 15 c. black and green .. 20 20
395. – 15 c. black and green .. 20 20
396. – 15 c. black and green .. 20 20
DESIGNS AND EVENTS: No. 393, Type 128 (World Bowls Championships, Johannesburg). No. 394, Batsman (Organised Cricket in South Africa, Cent.), No. 395, Polo player. No. 396, Gary Player (golfer).

1976. South Africa's World Bowls Championship Victory. No. 393 optd. **WERELD-KAMPIOENE WORLD CHAMPIONS.**
398. 128. 15 c. black and green .. 20 25

1976. Ernst Mayer (painter). Birth Cent. Multicoloured.
399. 4 c. Type 129 .. .. 5 5
400. 10 c. Ox wagons 12 15
401. 15 c. Harbeespoort Dam 15 20
402. 20 c. Street scene Doornfontein 25 25

130. Cheetah.

1976. World Environment Day. Mult.
404. 3. Type 130 .. .. 5 5
405. 10 c. Black Rhino .. 12 15
406. 15 c. Bontebok .. 15 20
407. 20 c. Mountain Zebra .. 25 25

131. Emily Hobhouse. 133. Family with Globe.

132. Early Mailship.

1976. Emily Hobhouse (welfare worker). 50th Death Anniv.
408. 131. 4 c. multicoloured .. 5 5

1976. Ocean Mail Service. Centenary.
409. 132. 10 c. multicoloured .. 12 15

1976. Family Planning and Child Welfare.
410. 133. 4 c. brown & lt. brown 5 5

134. Wine glasses. 135. J. D. Du Toit.

1977. International Wine Symposium.
411. 134. 15 c. multicoloured .. 15 20

1977. Prof. Dr. J. D. Du Toit (theologian and poet). Birth Cent.
412. 135. 4 c. multicoloured .. 5 5

OFFICIAL STAMPS

1926. Optd. **OFFICIAL OFFISIEEL.**

(a) On Stamp of 1913.

			Un. single	*Us. single*
O1.	2.	2d. purple	2·00	60

(b) On various pictorial issues.

			Un. pair	*Us. pair*
O 8.	4.	½d. black and green	8	5
O 36b.	5.	1d. black and red ..	8	8
O 26a.	21.	1½d. green and gold	75	50
O 37.	33a.	1½d. green and buff	8	8
O 6.	6.	2d. grey and purple	40	70
O 27a.		2d. grey and lilac ..	25·00	15·00
O 27.		2d. blue and violet	1·00	1·00
O 27b.	32a.	2d. slate and violet	30	30
O 38.	57.	2d. blue and violet ..	8	8
O 39.	10.	6d. green and orange	15	15
O 40.	–	1s. brown & bl. (No. 120)	35	30
O 41.	–	2s. 6d. green & brown (No. 121) ..	1·50	1·00
O 20a.	–	2s. 6d. blue & brown (No. 49a) ..	6·00	6·00
O 41b.	–	5s. black and green (No. 122) ..	5·00	5·00
O 29c.	29.	10s. blue and brown	12·00	12·00

POSTAGE DUE STAMPS

D 1. D 2.

D 3.

1914. Perf. or roul.

No.	Type		*Un. single*	*Us. single*
D 11.	D 1.	½d. black and green	5	12
D 12.		1d. black and red ..	5	5
D 13.		1½d. black & chestnut	8	15
D 14.		2d. black and violet ..	8	15
D 4.		3d. black and blue ..	15	20
D 5.		5d. black and brown	65	90
D 16.		6d. black and grey ..	1·50	1·00
D 7.		1s. red and black ..	20·00	25·00

1927.

No.	Type		*Un. single*	*Us. single*
D 22.	D 2.	½d. black and green ..	5	12
D 25.		1d. black and red ..	5	5
D 19.		2d. black and mauve	8	15
D 26.		2d. black and purple	5	5
D 27.		3d. black and blue ..	1·25	40
D 28.		3d. indigo and blue ..	12	10
D 21.		6d. black and grey ..	35	60
D 29.		6d. green and brown	2·00	75
D 29a.		6d. green and orange	40	20

1943.

No.	Type		*Un. unit*	*Us. unit*
D 30.	D 3.	½d. green	20	25
D 31.		1d. red	8	25
D 32.		2d. violet	10	30
D 33.		3d. blue	20	50

The above prices are for horiz. units of three.

1948. Frame as Type **D 2**, but with bolder figures of value and capital "D".

No.		*Un. single*	*Us. single*
D 34.	½d. black and green ..	5	12
D 39.	1d. black and red ..	5	8
D 40.	2d. black and violet ..	5	5
D 41.	3d. indigo and blue ..	12	8
D 42.	4d. blue-green & emerald	15	12
D 43.	6d. green and orange ..	50	25
D 44.	1s. choc. & brown-purple	1·00	1·00

D 4.

D 5.

1961.

No.	Type		Un.	Us.
D 45.	D 4.	1 c. black and red ..	5	10
D 46.		2 c. black and violet	5	10
D 47.		4 c. blue-grn. & emer.	15	30
D 48.		5 c. indigo and blue ..	50	40
D 49.		6 c. green and orange	75	1·00
D 50.		10 c. sepia and brown	1·25	1·50

1961. Republic issue. (A) Inscr. as in Type **D 5**; (B) English at top and left, Afrikaans at bottom and right.

No.	Type		Un.	Us.
D 59.	D 5.	1 c. black and red (A)	5	5
D 60.		1 c. black and red (B)	5	5
D 61.		2 c. black & violet (A)	5	5
D 62.		2 c. black & violet (B)	5	5
D 54.		4 c. myrtle & emer. (A)	8	8
D 54a.		4 c. myrtie & emer. (B)	8	8
D 63.		4 c. black & green (A)	8	5
D 64.		4 c. black & green (B)	8	5
D 55.		5 c. indigo & blue (B)	30	35
D 65.		5 c. black and blue (A)	8	8
D 66.		5 c. black & blue (B)	8	8
D 67.		6 c. green & salmon (A)	8	8
D 68.		6 c. green & salmon (B)	8	8
D 69.		10 c. black and purple-brown (A) ..	20	20
D 70.		10 c. black & purple-brown (B)	20	20

D 6.

1972.

No.	Type		Un.	Us.
D 71.	D 6.	1 c. green	5	5
D 72.		2 c. orange	5	5
D 73.		4 c. plum	5	5
D 74.		6 c. yellow	8	8
D 75.		8 c. blue	10	12
D 76.		10 c. red	12	12

SOUTH ARABIAN FEDERATION BC

Comprising Aden and most of the territories of the former Western Aden Protectorate plus one from the Eastern Aden Protectorate. The South Arabian Federation became fully independent on 30th November, 1967.

100 cents = 1 shilling.
1965. 1000 fils = 1 dinar.

1963. Red Cross Cent. As T **24** of Antigua but without portrait. Value in English and Arabic.

No.		Un.	Us.
1.	15 c. red and black ..	12	15
2.	1s. 25 c. red and blue ..	30	45

1. Federal Crest.

2. Federal Flag.

1965.

No.	Type		Un.	Us.
3.	1.	5 f. blue	5	5
4.		10 f. lavender	5	5
5.		15 f. green	5	5
6.		20 f. emerald	5	5
7.		25 f. brown	8	5
8.		30 f. bistre	8	5
9.		35 f. chestnut	10	8
10.		50 f. red	12	12
11.		65 f. yellow-green ..	25	35
12.		75 f. red	25	45
13.	2.	100 f. multicoloured ..	25	25
14.		250 f. multicoloured ..	55	55
15.		500 f. multicoloured ..	1·50	1·40
16.		1 d. multicoloured ..	2·50	2·00

3. I.C.Y. Emblem.

1965. Int. Co-operation Year.

No.	Type		Un.	Us.
17.	3.	5 f. purple and turquoise ..	5	5
18.		65 f. green and lavender ..	25	25

4. Sir Winston Churchill and St. Paul's Cathedral in Wartime.

1966. Churchill Commem. Designs in black, cerise and gold with background in colours given.

No.	Type		Un.	Us.
19.	4.	5 f. blue	5	5
20.		10 f. green	5	5
21.		65 f. brown	20	30
22.		125 f. violet	50	60

5. Footballer's Legs, Ball and Jules Rimet Cup.

1966. World Cup Football Championships.

No.	Type		Un.	Us.
23.	5.	10 f. vio., grn., lake & brn.	5	5
24.		50 f. chocolate, turquoise, lake and brown	15	15

6. W.H.O. Building.

1966. W.H.O. Headquarters, Geneva. Inaug

No.	Type		Un.	Us.
25.	6.	10 f. black, green and blue	5	5
26.		75 f. black, purple & brown	20	25

7. "Education".

1966. U.N.E.S.C.O. 20th Anniv.

No.	Type		Un.	Us.
27.	7.	10 f. violet, red, yellow and orange	5	5
28.	–	65 f. yellow, violet & olive	20	40
29.	–	125 f. blk., purple & orge.	40	80

DESIGNS: 65 f. "Science". 125 f. "Culture".

For later issues see **SOUTHERN YEMEN**. and **YEMEN PEOPLE'S DEMOCRATIC REPUBLIC.**

SOUTH AUSTRALIA BC

A state of the Australian Commonwealth whose stamps it now uses.

1.

ILLUSTRATIONS
British Commonwealth and all overprints and surcharges are FULL SIZE.
Foreign Countries have been reduced to ¾-LINEAR.

1855. Imperf.

No.	Type		Un.	Us.
1.	1.	1d. green	£950	£130
9.		2d. red	£225	23·00
3.		6d. blue	£750	60·00
12.		1s. orange	£1100	£225

2.

3.

1858. Roul or perf.

No.	Type		Un.	Us.
20.	1.	1d. green	18·00	7·00
26.		2d. red	13·00	1·00
68.	3.	3d. on 4d. blue ..	18·00	2·50
138.		4d. violet	10·00	1·00
141.	1.	6d. blue	13·00	60
118.	2.	8d. on 9d. brown ..	14·00	1·00
123.		9d. purple	3·25	70
107.		10d. on 9d. orange ..	40·00	5·00
18.	1.	1s. orange	£215	12·00
130.		1s. brown	7·00	1·10
132.	3.	2s. red	7·00	1·25

The 3d., 8d. and 10d. are formed by surcharges: **3-PENCE, 8 PENCE** and **TEN PENCE** (curved).

4. **5.**

6.

1868. Various frames.

No.	Type		Un.	Us.
236.	4.	½d. brown	45	8
238.	5.	1d. green	25	8
294a.		1d. red	25	8
251.	6.	2d. orange	25	8
265.		2d. violet	30	8
230.	–	2½d. on 4d. green ..	55	8
255.	–	3d. green	80	8
256.	–	4d. violet		
231.	–	5d. on 6d. brown ..	1·25	55
260.	–	6d. blue	55	8

Nos. 230 and 231 are surch. in figures over straight or curved line.

1882. Surch. **HALF-PENNY** in two lines.

No.	Type		Un.	Us.
181.	5.	½d. on 1d. green	30	25

10.

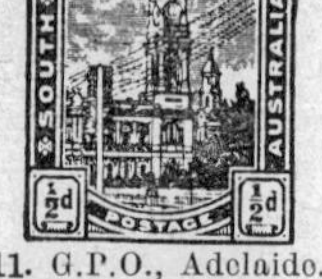

11. G.P.O., Adelaide.

12.

13.

1886.

No.	Type		Un.	Us.
195a.	10.	2s. 6d. mauve	3·50	1·75
196.		5s pink	4·50	3·50
197.		10s. green	7·00	5·00
198.		15s. brown	50·00	20·00
199.		£1 blue	35·00	10·00

1894.

No.	Type		Un.	Us.
262.	11.	½d. green	25	8
253.	12.	2½d. violet	55	8
266.		2½d. blue	95	8
258.	13.	5d. purple	45	10

1902. Inscr. "POSTAGE" at top.

No.	Type		Un.	Us.
268.	10.	3d. green	35	8
269.		4d. orange	80	25
284.		6d. green	40	25
271.		8d. blue	80	35
273.		9d. red	45	25
274.		10d. orange	80	35
303b.		1s. brown	55	8
276a.		2s. 6d. violet	2·75	1·10
290.		5s. rose	7·00	3·00
278.		10s. green	16·00	12·00
279.		£1 blue	45·00	12·00

OFFICIAL STAMPS

1874. Various postage issues optd. **O.S.**

A. Issue of 1858.

No.	Type		Un.	Us.
O 6.	1.	1d. green	—	5·50
O 7.	3.	3d. on 4d. blue ..	—	42·00
O 17.		4d. violet	95	35
O 19.	1.	6d. blue	1·75	10
O 26.	2.	8d. on 9d. brown ..	95·00	15·00
O 11.		9d. purple	32·00	6·00
O 33.	1.	1s. brown	2·75	55
O 35.	3.	2s. red	1·40	40

B. Issues of 1868-82.

No.	Type		Un.	Us.
O 66.	4.	½d. brown	40	8
O 50.	5.	½d. on 1d. green ..	70	10
O 67.		1d. green	10	8
O 81.		1d. red	10	8
O 74.		2d. orange	35	8
O 82.		2d. violet	10	8
O 58.	–	2½d. on 4d. green ..	55	10
O 84.	–	4d. violet	35	8
O 61.	–	5d. on 6d. brown ..	55	25
O 71.	–	6d. blue	45	8

C. Issue of 1886.

No.	Type		Un.	Us.
O 86.	10.	2s. 6d. mauve	£350	£350
O 87.		5s. pink	£350	£350

D. Issue of 1894.

No.	Type		Un.	Us.
O 80.	11.	½d. green	10	8
O 83.	12.	2½d. blue	65	8
O 77.	13.	5d. purple	1·00	45

INDEX

Countries can be quickly located by referring to the index at the end of this volume.

SOUTH GEORGIA BC

An island in the Antarctic, formerly one of the Falkland Islands Dependencies.

1. Reindeer.

1963.

1. 1. ½d. red 10 12
2. – 1d. blue 5 5
3. – 2d. turquoise 5 8
4. – 2½d. black.. .. .. 8 10
5. – 3d. bistre 10 12
6. – 4d. bronze 12 15
7. – 5½d. violet 20 25
8. – 6d. orange 20 25
9. – 9d. blue 30 35
10. – 1s. purple.. .. .. 30 40
11. – 2s. olive and blue .. 65 80
12. – 2s. 6d. blue .. .. 1·25 1·50
13. – 5s. brown .. .. 1·75 2·00
14. – 10s. magenta .. .. 5·50 7·00
15. – £1 blue .. .. .. 13·00 15·00
16. – £1 black .. .. .. 6·50 9·00

DESIGNS—HORIZ. 2½d. Chinstrap and King Penguin. 4d. Fin whale. 5½d. Elephant seal. 9d. Whale-catcher. 1s. Leopard seal. 2s. Shackleton's Cross. 2s. 6d. Wandering albatross. 5s. Elephant and fur seal. £1 (No. 15), Blue whale. VERT. 1d. South Sandwich Islands. 2d. Sperm whale. 3d. Fur seal. 6d. Sooty albatross. 10s. Plankton and Krill. £1 (No. 16) King Penguins.

1971. Decimal Currency. 1/14 surch.

18a. ½p. on ½d. red 12 15
19b. 1p. on 1d. blue 5 5
20a. 1½p. on 5½d. violet 5 5
21. 2p. on 2d. turquoise 5 5
22. 2½p. on 2½d. black 8 10
23. 3p. on 3d. bistre 8 10
24. 4p. on 4d. bronze 8 10
25. 5p. on 6d. orange 8 12
26. 6p. on 9d. blue 10 12
27. 7½p. on 1s. purple 12 15
28. 10p. on 2s. olive and blue.. 20 25
29. 15p. on 2s. 6d. blue .. 25 30
30. 25 p. on 5s. brown 45 50
31b. 50p. on 10s. magenta .. 85 95

2. "Endurance" beset in Weddell Sea.

1972. Sir Ernest Shackleton. 50th Death Anniv. Multicoloured.

32. 1½p. Type 2 .. .. .. 10 15
33. 5p. Launching of the long-boat "James Caird" .. 30 30
34. 10p. Route of the "James Caird" 60 60
35. 20p. Sir Ernest Shackleton and the "Quest".. .. 1·25 1·25

1972. Royal Silver Wedding. As T **19** of Ascension but with Elephant Seal and King Penguins in background.

36. 5p. green 55 90
37. 10p. violet .. .. .. 1·10 1·75

1973. Royal Wedding. As Type **26** of Anguilla. Background colours given. Multicoloured.

38. 5p. brown 15 20
39. 15 p. lilac 40 50

3. Churchill and Westminster Skyline.

1974. Sir Winston Churchill. Birth Cent. Multicoloured.

40. 15p. Type 3 .. .. 40 50
41. 25p. Churchill and warship 60 75

4. Captain Cook.

1975. Possession by Captain Cook. Bicent. Multicoloured.

43. 2p. Type 4 .. .. .. 8 8
44. 8p. H.M.S. "Resolution" 25 25
45. 16p. Possession Bay .. 40 50

5. "Discovery" and Biological Laboratory.

1976. "Discovery" Investigations. 50th Anniv. Multicoloured.

46. 2p. Type 5 .. .. .. 5 5
47. 8p. "William Scoresby" and water sampling bottle 15 15
48. 11p. "Discovery II" and plankton net 20 20
49. 25p. Biological station and krill 50 50

6. The Queen in Coronation Procession.

1977. Silver Jubilee. Multicoloured.

50. 6p. Prince Philip visiting Shackleton Memorial .. 12 12
51. 11p. The Queen with Regalia 20 20
52. 23p. Type 6 .. .. 25 25

SOUTH KASAI O4

100 centimes = 1 franc.

Region of Zaire around the town of Bakwanga. The area was declared autonomous in 1960, during the upheaval following independence, but returned to the control of the central government in Oct. 1962.

Various stamps of Belgian Congo were overprinted "ETAT AUTONOME DU SUD-KASAI" and some surcharged in addition with new values. These were put on sale at the Philatelic Bureau in Brussels and were also valid for use in South Kasai but no supplies were sent out.

1. "V" over Leopard. 2. A. D. Kalonji.

1961.

1. 1. 1 f. multicoloured 5 8
2. 1 f. 50 multicoloured .. 5 10
3. 3 f. 50 multicoloured .. 5 15
4. 8 f. multicoloured 12 30
5. 10 f. multicoloured .. 15 50

1961.

6. 2. 6 f. 50 brn., blue & black.. 10 40
7. 9 f. light brn., brn. & blk.. 12 50
8. 14 f. 50 brown, grn. & blk. 25 70
9. 20 f. light brn., bl., brn. & blk. 30 1·10

SOUTH RUSSIA E3

Stamps of various anti-Bolshevist forces and temporary governments in S. Russia after the revolution.

A. KUBAN TERRITORY: COSSACK GOVERNMENT.

1918. Arms type of Russia surch. Imperf. or perf.

1. 11. 25 k. on 1 k. orange .. 8 8
2. 50 k. on 2 k. green .. 5 8
24. 70 k. on 1 k. orange .. 25 30
10. 70 k. on 5 k. claret .. 25 30
11. 1 r. on 3 k. red .. 8 8
13. 12. 3 r. on 4 k. red .. .. 4·00 4·50
14. 10 r. on 4 k. red .. 3·50 3·75
15. 4. 10 r. on 15 k. bl. & pur. 50 60
16. 11. 25 r. on 3 k. red .. 1·75 1·50
17. 25 r. on 7 k. blue .. 12·00 14·00
18a. 4. 25 r. on 14 k. red and blue 20·00 20·00
19. 25 r. on 25 k. mve. & grn. 10·00 12·00

1919. Postal Savings Bank stamps of Russia surch.

20. 10 r. on 1 k. red on buff .. 4·50 4·50
21. 10 r. on 5 k. green on buff.. 7·00 9·00
22. 10 r. on 10 k. brown on buff 20·00 22·00

B. DON TERRITORY: COSSACK GOVERNMENT.

1919. Arms type of Russia surch. in figures only. Imperf. or perf.

25. 11. 25 k. on 1 k. orange .. 10 15
29. 25 k. on 2 k. green .. 10 15
30. 25 k. on 3 k. red .. 25 30
31. 12. 25 k. on 4 k. red .. 10 15
32. 11. 50 k. on 7 k. blue .. 80 1·00

1. T. Ermak (16th century Cossack Ataman).

1919. Currency stamp with arms and seven-line imprint on back used for postage.

33. 1. 20 k. green .. .. 4·00

C. CRIMEA: REGIONAL GOVERNMENT.

1919. Arms type of Russia surch. **35 Kon.** Imperf.

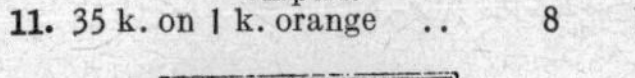

34. 11. 35 k. on 1 k. orange .. 8 15

2.

1919. Currency and postage stamp. Arms and inscription on back. Imperf.

35. 2. 50 k. brown on buff .. 4·00 4·00

D. SOUTH RUSSIA: GOVERNMENT OF GENERAL DENIKIN.

1919. Nos. 424 and 428 of Ukraine surch. in figs.

36. 3. 35 k. on 10 s. brown .. 1·25
37. 7. 70 k. on 50 s. red .. 4·00

3.

4.

1919. Imperf. or perf.

38. 3. 5 k. yellow 5 5
39. 10 k. green 5 5
40. 15 k. red 5 5
41. 35 k. blue 5 5
42. 70 k. blue 5 5
43. 4. 1 r. red and brown .. 10 20
44. 2 r. yellow and lilac .. 10 20
45. 3 r. green and brown .. 10 30
46. 5 r. violet and blue .. 15 40
47. 7 r. pink and green .. 40 70
48. 10 r. grey and red .. 25 45

Higher values similar to T **4** are bogus.

E. SOUTH RUSSIA: GOVERNMENT OF GENERAL WRANGEL.

5 ПЯТЬ рублей. (5.)

ЮГЪ РОССІИ. 100 рублей. (6.)

1920 Crimea issue. Surch. with T **5**.

(a) On Arms types of Russia. Imperf. or perf.

52. 11. 5 r. on 5 k. claret .. 75 75
54. 7. 5 r. on 20 k. red and blue 1·00 1·00

(b) On No. 41 of South Russia.

55. 3. 5 r. on 35 k. blue .. 2·00 2·50

1920. Arms type of Russia surch. with T **6**. Imperf. or perf.

56. 11. 100 r. on 1 k. orange .. 1·00

SOUTH WEST AFRICA O2; BC

(Formerly GERMAN S.W. AFRICA)

A territory in S.W. Africa, formerly a German Colony. Now administered by South Africa.

Stamp illustrations in this country are reduced to ¾ size.

GERMAN ISSUES

100 pfennig = 1 mark.

1897. Stamps of Germany optd. **Deutsch-Sudwestafrika.**

1. 6. 3 pf. brown .. .. 1·75 1·60
6. 5 pf. green 70 70
7. 7. 10 pf. red .. .. 70 1·10
4. 20 pf. blue .. .. 1·40 1·60
9. 25 pf. orange .. .. £100 90·00
10. 50 pf. brown .. .. 6·00 6·00

1900. "Yacht" key-types inscr. "DEUTSCH-SUDWESTAFRIKA".

24. N. 3 pf. brown 8 12
25. 5 pf. green 8 8
26. 10 pf. red 8 8
27. 20 pf. blue 30 60
15. 25 pf. blk. & red on yell. 55 2·25
16. 30 pf. black and orange on buff .. .. 7·00 1·25
17. 40 pf. black and red .. 55 1·40
18. 50 pf. blk. & pur. on buff 70 1·25
19. 80 pf. black & red on rose 70 2·75
29. O. 1 m. red .. .. .. 3·00 7·00
30. 2 m. blue .. .. 3·50 9·00
22. 3 m. black .. .. 10·00 9·00
32. 5 m. red and black .. 9·00 45·00

SOUTH AFRICAN ADMINISTRATION

1961. 100 cents = 1 rand.

NOTE.—Stamps overprinted for South West Africa are always South African stamps, except where otherwise indicated.

"Bilingual" in heading indicates that the stamps are inscribed alternately in English and Afrikaans throughout the sheet. "Bilingual" is not repeated in the heading where bilingual stamps of South Africa are overprinted.

Our prices are for bilingual pairs, and single stamps should be considered to be worth very much less than half the price of pairs.

1923. Optd. alternately **South West Africa** or **Zuidwest Afrika.**

		Un. pair	Us. pair
1. 2.	½d. green	30	50
2.	1d. red	20	40
31.	2d. purple	1·40	1·75
4.	3d. blue	1·75	2·75
20.	4d. orange and green ..	2·25	2·75
34.	6d. black and violet ..	3·25	3·75
35.	1s. yellow	4·75	5·50
36.	1s. 3d. violet	4·75	7·50
37.	2s. 6d. purple and green..	17·00	23·00
25.	5s. purple and blue ..	55·00	70·00
26.	10s. blue and green ..	90·00	£130
40.	£1 green and red ..	£130	£140

1926. Optd. **South West Africa** or **Suidwes Afrika** alternately.

		Un. pair	Us. pair
45. 4.	½d. black and green ..	70	90
46. 5.	1d. black and red ..	70	90
49. 6.	2d. grey and purple ..	2·25	3·75
50. –	3d. black and red ..	3·75	4·75
47. 10.	6d. green and orange ..	5·00	6·00
51. –	1s. brown and blue ..	6·50	8·00
52. –	2s. 6d. green and brown	23·00	27·00
53. –	5s. black and green ..	55·00	65·00
54. –	10s. blue and brown ..	65·00	80·00

1926. Triangular optd. **SOUTH WEST AFRICA** in two lines (E), or **SUIDWES-AFRIKA** in one line (A). Imperf. or perf.

Single stamps

		E.		A.	
44. 8.	4d. blue ..	1·00	1·00	1·00	1·00

1927. Triangular optd. **SOUTH WEST AFRIKA** in one line. Imperf.

48. 8. 4d. blue .. .. 2·75 3·75

1927. Optd. **S.W.A.**

56. 2. 1s. 3d. violet .. .. 2·75 3·75
57. £1 olive and red .. 75·00 55·00

1927. Optd. **S.W.A.** *Un. pair* *Us. pair*
58. **4.** ½d. black and green .. 70 80
59. **5.** 1d. black and red .. 70 75
60. **6.** 2d. grey and purple .. 1·75 2·25
61. – 3d. black and red .. 2·75 2·25
62. – 4d. brown .. .. 3·25 3·75
63. **10.** 6d. green and orange .. 10·00 4·50
64. – 1s. brown and blue .. 5·50 9·00
65. – 2s. 6d. green and brown 17·00 13·00
66. – 5s. black and green .. 32·00 27·00
67. – 10s. blue and brown .. 75·00 65·00

1930. Air. Optd. **S.W.A.** *Un. single* *Us. single*
72. **15.** 4d. green .. .. .. 2·25 2·75
73. 1s. orange .. .. .. 4·50 5·50

1. Gom-pauw **2.** Monoplane over Windheok.

1931. Bilingual. *Un. pair* *Us. pair*
74. **1.** ½d. black and green .. 25 25
75. – 1d. blue and red 25 25
76. – 2d. blue and brown .. 25 25
77. – 3d. blue 35 35
78. – 4d. green and purple .. 45 45
79. – 6d. blue and brown .. 55 90
80. – 1s. brown and blue .. 1·40 1·10
81. – 1s. 3d. violet and yellow 2·25 3·25
82. – 2s. 6d. red and grey .. 4·50 5·50
83. – 5s. green and brown .. 9·00 11·00
84. – 10s. brown and green .. 11·00 23·00
85. – £1 claret and green .. 35·00 45·00
DESIGNS: 1d. Cape Cross. 2d. Begenfels. 3d. Windhoek. 4d. Waterberg. 6d. Luderitz Bay. 1s. Bush scene. 1s. 3d. Elands. 2s. 6d. Zebra and gnus. 5s. Herero huts. 10s. Welwitschia plant. £1 Okuwahaken Falls.

1931. Air. Bilingual. *Un. pair* *Us. pair*
86. **2.** 3d. brown and blue .. 6·50 9·00
87. – 10d. black and brown .. 12·00 17·00
DESIGN: 10d. Biplane over Windhoek.

3.

1935. Silver Jubilee. *Un. single* *Us. single*
88. **3.** 1d. black and red .. 15 25
89. 2d. black and brown .. 25 35
90. 3d. black and blue .. 4·50 5·50
91. 6d. black and purple .. 3·75 3·75

1935. Voortrekker Memorial. Optd. **S.W.A.** *Un. pair* *Us. pair*
92. **16.** ½d.+½d. green 25 35
93. – 1d.+½d. black and pink 45 1·00
94. – 2d.+1d. green & purple 1·40 1·92
95. – 3d.+1½d. green and blue 2·75 3·25

4. Mail Transport. **5.** King George VI.

1937. Bilingual. *Un. pair* *Us. pair*
96. **4.** 1½d. brown 35 25

1937. Coronation. Bilingual. *Un. pair* *Us. pair*
97. **5.** ½d. black and green .. 10 15
98. 1d. black and red .. 10 15
99. 1½d. black and orange .. 10 15
100. 2d. black and brown .. 15 25
101. 3d. black and blue .. 20 25
102. 4d. black and purple .. 30 35
103. 6d. black and yellow .. 35 45
104. 1s. black and grey .. 75 85

1938. Voortrekker Cent. Fund. Optd. S.W.A. *Un. pair* *Us. pair*
105. – ½d.+½d. blue and green 20 30
106. **23.** 1d.+1d. blue and red 30 40
107. **25.** 1½d.+1½d. brown & grn. 75 1·00
108. – 3d.+3d. blue .. .. 1·50 2·00

1938. Voortrekker Commem. Optd. **S.W.A.** *Un. pair* *Us. pair*
109. – 1d. blue and red .. 25 30
110. **27.** 1½d. blue and brown .. 60 70

1939. Landing of Huguenots in S. Africa. 250th Anniv. Optd. **S.W.A.** *Un. pair* *Us. pair*
111. **30.** ½d.+½d. brown & green 25 50
112. **31.** 1d.+1d. green and red 50 75
113. **32.** 1½d.+1½d. grn. & purple 1·25 2·00

1941. War Effort. Optd. **S W A.**
(a) Bilingual. *Un. pair* *Us. pair*
114. **34.** ½d. green 5 10
115. – 1d. red 5 8
116. – 1½d. green 10 15
117. **36.** 3d. blue 15 25
118. – 4d. brown 30 45
119. – 6d. orange 30 90

(b) Inscr. in both English and Afrikaans. *Un. single* *Us. single*
120. **35.** 2d. violet 8 8
121. – 1s. brown 40 30

1943. War Effort. Optd. **S W A.** *Un. unit* *Us. unit*
122. **39.** ½d. green (T) 8 8
123. – 1d. red (T) 10 15
124. – 1½d. brown (P) 10 12
125a. – 2d. violet (P) 12 20
126. – 3d. blue (T) 15 25
128. – 4d. green (T) 25 30
127. – 6d. orange (P) 30 45
129b. – 1s. brown (P) 50 55
130. **47.** 1s. 3d. brown (P) .. 1·00 1·00
The units referred to above consist of pairs (P), or triplets (T).

1945. Victory. Optd. **S W A.** *Un. pair* *Us. pair*
131. **49.** 1d. brown and red .. 5 8
132. – 2d. blue and violet .. 5 10
133. – 3d. blue 8 12

1947. Royal Visit. Optd. **S W A.** *Un. pair* *Us. pair*
134. **50.** 1d. black and red .. 5 5
135. **51.** 2d. violet 5 5
136. – 3d. blue 8 8

1948. Silver Wedding. Optd. **S W A.** *Un. pair* *Us. pair*
137. **53.** 3d. blue and silver .. 5 5

1949. 75th Anniv. of U.P.U. optd. **S W A.** *Un. pair* *Us. pair*
138. **55.** ½d. green 5 8
139. 1½d. red 5 8
140. 3d. blue 10 12

1949. Inaug. of Voortrekker Monument, Pretoria. Optd. **S W A.** *Un. single* *Us. single*
141. **56.** 1d. magenta 5 8
142. – 1½d. green 5 8
143. – 3d. blue 5 8

1952. Landing of Van Riebeeck. Tercent. Optd. **S W A.**
144. – ½d. purple and sepia .. 5 5
145. **58.** 1d. green 5 8
146. – 2d. violet 5 8
147. – 4½d. blue 12 20
148. – 1s. brown 25 50

6. Queen Elizabeth II and Catophractes. **7.** "Two Bucks" (rock painting).

1953. Coronation. Native Flowers.
149. **6.** 1d. red 5 8
150. – 2d. green (Banhinia) .. 10 12
151. – 4d. magenta (Caralluma) 30 35
152. – 6d. blue (Gloriosa) .. 35 40
153. – 1s. brown (Rhigosum) .. 50 60

1954.
154. **7.** 1d. lake 5 5
155. – 2d. chocolate 5 5
156. – 3d. maroon 12 5
157. – 4d. black 12 8
158. – 4½d. blue 20 20
159. – 6d. green 15 8
160. – 1s. mauve 25 15
161. – 1s. 3d. magenta .. 25 20
162. – 1s. 6d. purple .. 50 50
163. – 2s. 6d. brown .. 1·00 1·00
164. – 5s. blue .. .. 2·00 2·00
165. – 10s. green .. .. 7·00 7·00
DESIGNS—VERT. 2d. "White Lady" (rock painting). 4½d. Karakul lamb. 6d. Ovambo woman blowing horn. 1s. Ovambo woman. 1s. 3d. Herero woman. 1s. 6d. Ovambo girl. 2s. 6d. Lioness. 5s. Gemsbok. 10s. Elephant. HORIZ. 3d. "Rhinoceros Hunt" (rock painting). 4d. "White Elephant and Giraffe" (rock painting).

8. G.P.O., Windhoek. **9.** "Agricultural Development".

1961.
202. **8.** ½ c. brown and blue .. 5 5
203. – 1 c. sepia and mauve .. 5 5
204. – 1½ c. slate-violet & salmon 5 5
205. – 2 c. green and yellow .. 5 5
206. – 2½ c. brown and blue .. 5 5
176. – 3 c. ultramarine and red 8 8
208. – 3½ c. indigo and green .. 8 5
209. – 4 c. brown and blue .. 5 5
210. – 5 c. red and grey-blue .. 5 5
211. – 6 c. sepia and yellow .. 8 5
212. – 7½ c. sepia and lemon .. 10 5
213. – 9 c. indigo and yellow .. 10 12
180. – 10 c. blue and yellow .. 20 20
181. – 12½ c. indigo and lemon 25 25
182. – 15 c. chocolate and blue 50 50
183. – 20 c. brown & red-orge. 60 60
184. – 50 c. green and orange .. 2·00 2·00
185. – 1 r. yell., maroon & blue 4·00 4·00
DESIGNS—VERT. 1 c. Finger Rock. 1½ c. Mounted Soldier Monument. 2 c. Quivertree. 3 c. Flamingoes and Swakopmund Lighthouse. 3½ c. Fishing industry. 5 c. Flamingo. 6 c., 7½ c. German Lutheran Church, Windhoek. 10 c. Diamond. 15 c. Hardap Dam. 20 c. Topaz. 50 c. Tourmaline. 1 r. Heliodor. HORIZ. 2½ c., 4 c. S.W.A. House, Windhoek. 9 c., 12½ c. Fort Namutoni.
See also Nos. 224/26.

1963. Opening of Hardap Dam.
192. **9.** 3 c. chocolate and green 8 8

10. Centenary Emblem and part of Globe. **11.** Interior of Assembly Hall.

1963. Red Cross Cent.
193. – 7½ c. red, black & blue 12 12
194. **10.** 15 c. red, blk. & salmon 25 25
DESIGN: 7½ c. Centenary emblem and Map.

1964. Opening of Legislative Assembly Hall, Windhoek.
195. **11.** 3 c. blue and salmon .. 8 5

12. Calvin (Protestant Reformer). **13.** Mail Runner of 1890.

1965. Calvin. 400th Death Anniv.
196. **12.** 2½ c. maroon and gold 5 5
197. 15 c. green and gold .. 25 35

1965. Windhoek. 75th Anniv.
198. **13.** 3 c. sepia and red .. 8 8
199. – 15 c. brown and green .. 30 30
DESIGN: 15 c. Kurt von Francois (founder).

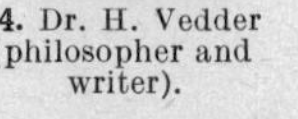

14. Dr. H. Vedder (philosopher and writer). **15.** Dr. H. F. Verwoerd.

1966. Vedder. 90th Birth Anniv.
200. **14.** 3 c. green and salmon .. 8 8
201. 15 c. sepia and blue .. 30 30

1967. Verwoerd Commem.
217. – 2½ c. black and green .. 5 5
218. – 3 c. brown and blue .. 8 5
219. **15.** 15 c. sepia and purple 25 25
DESIGNS—HORIZ. 2½ c. Camelthorn tree. VERT. 3 c. Waves breaking against rock.

16. Pres. Swart. **17.** Sand-dunes.

1968. Swart Commem. Inscr. in German, Afrikaans or English.
220. **16.** 3 c. red, blue and black 8 8
221. – 15 c. red, green and olive 25 25
DESIGN: 15 c. Pres. and Mrs. Swart.

1970. Water 70 Campaign. As Nos. 296/7 of South Africa, but inscr. "SWA".
222. 2½ c. green, blue & chocolate 8 8
223. 3 c. blue and buff 8 8

1970. As Nos. 202 etc., but with "POSGELD" "INKOMSTE" omitted and larger figure of value.
224. **8.** ½ c. brown and blue .. 5 5
225. – 1½ c. violet and salmon .. 5 5
226. – 2 c. green and yellow .. 5 5

1970. Bible Soc. of South Africa. 150th Anniv. As Nos. 298/9 of South Africa.
228. 2½ c. multicoloured .. 5 5
229. 12½ c. gold, black and blue 20 20

1971. "Interstex" Stamp Exhibition, Cape Town. As No. 300 of South Africa. Inscr. "SWA".
230. 5 c. blue, black and yellow 8 8

1971. Antarctic Treaty. 10th Anniv. As No. 301 of South Africa. Inscr. "SWA".
231. 12½ c. black, blue and red 20 20

1971. South African Republic. 10th Anniv. As Nos. 302/3 of South Africa. Inscr. "SWA".
232. 2 c. flesh and red 5 8
233. 4 c. green 8 8

1972. S.P.C.A. Cent. As No. 309 of South Africa. Inscr. "SWA".
234. 5 c. multicoloured 10 10

1973. Scenery. Paintings by Adolph Jentsch. Multicoloured.
235. 2 c. Type **17** 5 5
236. 4 c. Early morning scene 8 8
237. 5 c. Hills 8 8
238. 10 c. Schaap River (vert.) 15 15
239. 15 c. Namib Desert (vert.) 20 20

18. "Sarcocaulon rigidum". **19.** "Euphorbia virosa".

1973. Multicoloured.
(a) As T **18.**
241. 1 c. Type **18** .. 5 5
242. 2 c. "Lapidaria margaretae" 5 5
243. 3 c. "Titanopsis schwantesii" 5 5
244. 4 c. "Lithops karasmontana" 5 5
245. 5 c. "Caralluma lugardii" 5 5
246. 6 c. "Dinteranthus microspermus" .. 8 8
247. 7 c. "Conophytum gratum" 8 10
248. 9 c. "Huernia oculata" .. 10 12
249. 10 c. "Gasteria pillansii" 12 12
250. 14c. "Stapelia pedunculata" 15 20
251. 15c. "Fenestraria aurantiaca" 20 20
252. 20c. "Decabelone grandiflora" 25 25
253. 25 c. "Hoodia bainii" .. 30 35

(b) As T **19.**
254. 30 c. Type **19** 35 40
255. 50 c. "Pachypodium namaquanum" (vert.) 60 70
256. 1 r. "Walwitschia bainesii" 1·25 1·40

1973. Coil stamps. As Nos. 241/2 and 245. Colours changed.
257. **18.** 1 c. black and mauve .. 5 5
258. – 2 c. black and yellow .. 5 5
259. – 5 c. black and red .. 5 5

20. White-tailed Shrike-flycatchers.

21. Giraffe, Antelope and Spoor.

1974. Rare Bird Species of South West Africa. Multicoloured.

260.	4 c. Type **20**	5	5
261.	5 c. Rosy-faced Lovebirds	5	5
262.	10 c. Damara Rock-jumper	10	12
263.	15 c. Ruppell's Parrots ..	15	20

1974. Twyfelfontein. Rock-engravings. Mult.

264.	4 c. Type **21**	5	5
265.	5 c. Elephant, hyena, antelope and spoor	5	8
266.	15 c. Kuda cow	20	20

No. 266 is horizontal, size 38 × 21 mm.

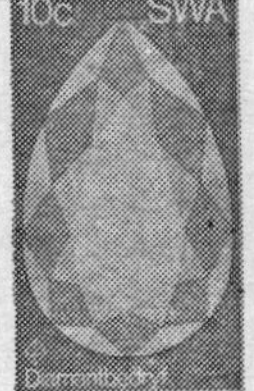

22. Cut Diamond.

23. Waggons and Map of the Trek.

1974. Diamond Mining. Multicoloured.

267.	10 c. Type **22**	12	15
268.	15 c. Diagram of shore workings	20	25

1974. Thirstland Park. Cent.

269. **23.**	4 c. multicoloured ..	5	5

24. Peregrine Falcon.

25. Kolmannskop (ghost town).

1975. Protected Birds of Prey. Multicoloured.

270.	4 c. Type **24**	8	8
271.	5 c. Black eagle	8	8
272.	10 c. Martial eagle ..	12	15
273.	15 c. Egyptian vulture ..	20	25

1975. Historic Monuments. Multicoloured.

274.	5 c. Type **25**	8	5
275.	9 c. "Martin Luther" (steam tractor) ..	10	12
276.	15 c. Kurt von Francois and Old Fort, Windhoek	20	20

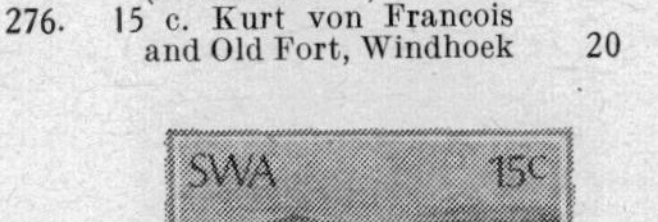

26. "View of Swakopmund".

1975. Otto Schroder (painter). Multicoloured.

277.	15 c. Type **26**	20	20
278.	15 c. "View of Luderitz"	20	20
279.	15 c. "Harbour Scene" ..	20	20
280.	15 c. "Quayside, Walvis Bay"	20	20

27. Elephants.

1976. Prehistoric Rock Paintings. Mult.

282.	4 c. Type **27**	5	5
283.	10 c. Rhinoceros	12	12
284.	15 c. Antelope	20	20
285.	20 c. Man with bow and arrow	25	25

28. Schwerinsburg.

1976. Castles. Multicoloured.

287.	10 c. Type **28**	10	12
288.	15 c. Schloss Duwisib ..	15	15
289.	20 c. Heynitzburg ..	20	25

29. Dassie.

1976. Fauna Conservation. Multicoloured.

290.	4 c. Type **29**	10	12
291.	10 c. Dik-Dik	15	15
292.	15 c. Tree Squirrel ..	20	25

30. The Augustineum, Windhoek.

1976. Modern Buildings.

293. **30.**	15 c. black and yellow..	20	25
294. –	20 c. black and yellow..	25	30

DESIGN: 20 c. Katutura Hospital, Windhoek.

31. Ovambo Water Canal System.

1976. Water and Electricity Supply. Mult.

295.	15 c. Type **31**	20	25
296.	20 c. Ruacana Falls Power Station	25	30

OFFICIAL STAMPS

1927. Pictorial and portrait (2d.) stamps alternately optd. **OFFICIAL South West Africa** or **OFFISIEEL Suidwes Afrika.**

		Un. pair	*Us. pair*
O 1. **4.**	½d. black and green ..	20·00	25·00
O 2. **5.**	1d. black and red ..	20·00	25·00
O 3. **2.**	2d. purple ..	30·00	35·00
O 4. **10.**	6d. green and orange ..	20·00	25·00

1929. Pictorial stamps alternately optd. **OFFICIAL S.W.A.** or **OFFISIEEL S.W.A.** horizontally or vertically.

		Un. pair	*Us. pair*
O 9. **4.**	½d. black and green ..	15	15
O 10.	1d. black and red ..	20	25
O 11. **6.**	2d. grey and purple ..	30	50
O 12. **10.**	6d. green and orange	35	90

1931. Optd. alternately **OFFICIAL** or **OFFISIEEL** in small capital letters.

		Un. pair	*Us. pair*
O 13. **1.**	½d. black and green..	5	10
O 14. –	1d. blue and red ..	8	10
O 15. –	2d. blue and brown ..	10	15
O 16. –	6d. blue and brown ..	25	30

1938. Optd. alternately **OFFICIAL** or **OFFISIEEL** in large capital letters.

		Un. pair	*Us. pair*
O 23. **1.**	½d. black and green ..	10	12
O 24. –	1d. blue & red (No. 75)	10	12
O 25. **16.**	1½d. brown ..	15	20
O 26. –	2d. blue & brn. (No. 76)	20	30
O 22. –	6d. blue & brn. (No. 79)	20	30

POSTAGE DUE STAMPS

1923. Postage Due stamps of Transvaal optd **South West Africa,** or **Zuidwest Afrika.**

		Un. pair	*Us. pair*
D 25. D **1.**	5d. black and violet	15	45
D 2.	6d. black and brown	1·00	2·50

1923. Postage Due stamps (Type D 1) of S. Africa optd. as last.

		Un. pair	*Us. pair*
D 8. D **1.**	½d. black and green..	10	15
D 17.	1d. black and red ..	40	80
D 7.	1½d. black & chestnut	15	30
D 30.	2d. black and violet..	15	30
D 31.	3d. black and blue..	10	20
D 20.	6d. black and grey ..	30	70

1927. Postage Due stamp of Transvaal optd. **Suidwes Afrika.***

		Un. pair	*Us. pair*
D 33. D **1.**	4d. black and violet	90	1·50

1927. Postage Due stamps of S. Africa (Type D 1 or D 2 for 1d.) optd. as last.*

		Un. pair	*Us. pair*
D 39. D **2.**	1d. black and red ..	10	20
D 34. D **1.**	1½d. black and brown	10	25
D 35.	2d. black and violet..	12	25
D 37.	3d. black and blue ..	60	1·00
D 38.	6d. black and grey ..	80	1·50

*The corresponding English overprint used here is the same, for the purposes of this catalogue, as that on No. D 25.

1928. Postage Due stamps of S. Africa (Type D 1) optd. **S.W.A.**

		Un. single	*Us. single*
D 40. D **1.**	3d. black and blue	15	25
D 41.	6d. black and grey ..	40	60

1928. Postage Due stamps of S. Africa (Type D 2) optd. **S.W.A.**

D 42. D **2**	½d. black and green ..	8	12
D 43.	1d. black and red ..	8	12
D 44.	2d. black and mauve	8	12
D 45.	3d. black and blue ..	15	25
D 46.	6d. black and grey ..	30	30

D 1.

1931. Size 19 × 23½ mm.

D 47. D **1.**	½d. black and green	8	10
D 48.	1d. black and red ..	8	10
D 49.	2d. black and violet	8	10
D 50.	3d. black and blue ..	12	12
D 51.	6d. black and slate ..	30	30

1959. As Type D 1 but smaller (17½ × 21 mm.).

D 52.	1d. black and red ..	8	10
D 53.	2d. black and violet ..	12	20
D 54.	3d. black and blue ..	15	25

1961. As Nos. D 52, etc., but value in cents.

D 57.	1 c. black and blue-green	5	8
D 58.	2 c. black and red ..	5	8
D 59.	4 c. black and violet ..	5	8
D 60.	5 c. black and blue ..	8	8
D 61.	6 c. black and green ..	8	10
D 62.	10 c. black and yellow ..	12	12

1972. As Type D 6 of South Africa. Inscr. "SWA".

D 63.	1 c. green..	5	5
D 67.	8 c. blue	10	12

SOUTHERN CAMEROONS BC

The southern area of that part of the Cameroun which was formerly under British trusteeship. Following a plebiscite it became an autonomous state on 1st October, 1960, but after another plebiscite it became part of the independent republic of Cameroun on 30th September, 1961.

1960. Stamps of Nigeria of 1953 optd. **CAMEROONS U.K.T.T.**

1. **15.**	½d. black and orange ..	5	8
2. –	1d. black and bronze ..	5	8
3. –	1½d. blue-green	5	10
4. –	2d. slate	8	10
5. –	3d. black and lilac ..	8	8
6. –	4d. black and blue ..	10	15
7. –	6d. brown and black ..	10	15
8. –	1s. black and maroon ..	20	40
9. **16.**	2s. 6d. black and green..	50	1·25
10. –	5s. black and red ..	85	2·00
11. –	10s. black and brown ..	2·00	5·00
12. **17.**	£1 black and violet ..	4·50	12·00

This issue was also on sale in Northern Cameroons.

HAVE YOU READ THE NOTES AT THE BEGINNING OF THIS CATALOGUE?

These often provide answers to the enquiries we receive.

SOUTHERN NIGERIA BC

A Br. possession on the W. coast of Africa, now incorp. in Nigeria, whose stamps it uses.

1.

1901.

1. **1.**	½d. black and green ..	25	25
2.	1d. black and red	25	30
3.	2d. black and brown ..	1·00	90
4.	4d. black and green ..	1·25	1·40
5.	6d. black and purplet ..	1·25	1·60
6.	1s. green and black ..	2·75	3·00
7.	2s. 6d. black and brown..	7·50	8·50
8.	5s. black and yellow ..	20·00	20·00
9.	10s. black & pur. on yellow	38·00	45·00

2.

3.

1903.

21. **2.**	½d. black and green ..	12	12
22.	1d. black and red ..	15	15
23.	2d. black and brown ..	40	40
24.	2½d. black and blue ..	60	65
25.	3d. brown and purple ..	2·25	1·25
14.	4d. black and green ..	1·00	1·00
27.	6d. black and purple ..	1·25	1·10
28.	1s. green and black ..	1·00	1·00
29.	2s. 6d. black and brown..	6·00	5·00
30.	5s. black and yellow ..	9·00	8·50
19.	10s. black & pur. on yellow	22·00	22·00
32.	£1 green and violet ..	55·00	70·00

1907.

33. **2.**	½d. green	35	15
34a.	1d. red	15	15
35.	2d. grey	70	50
36.	2½d. blue	70	1·25
37.	3d. purple on yellow ..	60	45
38.	4d. black & red on yellow	70	70
39.	6d. purple	1·60	1·10
40.	1s. black on green ..	1·75	85
41.	2s. 6d. black & red on blue	2·20	1·10
42.	5s. green & red on yellow	15·00	16·00
43.	10s. green & red on green	20·00	22·00
44.	£1 purple & black on red	50·00	60·00

1912.

45. **3.**	½d. green	20	20
46.	1d. red	35	12
47.	2d. grey	50	50
48.	2½d. blue	65	85
49.	3d. purple on yellow ..	40	35
50.	4d. black & red on yellow	9·00	1·00
51.	6d. purple	1·00	1·00
52.	1s. black on green.. ..	1·10	60
53.	2s. 6d. black & red on blue	4·00	4·50
54.	5s. green & red on yellow	8·00	8·50
55.	10s. green and red on green	22·00	25·00
56.	£1 purple and black on red	48·00	55·00

SOUTHERN RHODESIA BC

A Br. territory in the N. part of S. Africa, S. of the Zambesi. In 1954 became part of the Central African Federation which issued its own stamps inscribed "Rhodesia and Nyasaland" (q.v.), until 1964 when it resumed issuing its own stamps after the break-up of the Federation. In October, 1964, Southern Rhodesia was renamed Rhodesia.

1.

ILLUSTRATIONS
British Commonwealth and all overprints and surcharges are FULL SIZE. Foreign Countries have been reduced to ¾-LINEAR.

1924.

1. **1.**	½d. green	15	12
2.	1d. red	15	10
3.	1½d. brown	25	15
4.	2d. black	40	30
5.	3d. blue	1·00	80
6.	4d. black and red ..	1·00	1·25
7.	6d. black and mauve ..	1·00	75
8.	8d. purple and green ..	4·00	4·50
9.	10d. blue and red ..	4·00	4·50
10.	1s. black and blue ..	1·50	1·50
11.	1s. 6d. black and yellow..	5·00	6·00
12.	2s. black and brown ..	6·50	6·50
13.	2s. 6d. blue & grey-brown	12·00	14·00
14.	5s. blue and green ..	22·00	22·00

2.

3. Victoria Falls.

1931.

15a.	2.	½d. green	12	10
16b.		1d. red	15	10
16d.		1½d. brown	35	20
17.	3.	2d. black and brown	1·50	1·40
18.		3d. blue	3·00	3·50
19.	2.	4d. black and red	90	30
20.		6d. black and mauve	1·10	30
21.		8d. violet and green	1·50	2·00
21b.		9d. red and olive-green	3·75	3·75
22.		10d. blue and red	2·75	2·00
23.		1s. black and blue	2·50	75
24.		1s 6d. black and yellow	4·50	5·00
25.		2s. black and brown	3·50	4·00
26.		2s. 6d. blue and grey-brown	7·50	7·50
27.		5s. blue and green	12·00	12·00

4. Victoria Falls.

1932.

29.	4.	2d. green and brown	30	12
30.		3d. blue	1·50	50

5. Victoria Falls.

1935. Silver Jubilee.

31.	5.	1d. olive-green and red	15	15
32.		2d. green and brown	40	60
33.		3d. violet and blue	1·50	1·75
34.		6d. black and purple	1·60	1·75

1935. As Nos. 29/30, but inscr. "POSTAGE AND REVENUE".

35a.	4.	2d. green and brown	8	5
35b.		3d. blue	25	15

6. Victoria Falls and Railway Bridge.

1937. Coronation.

36.	6.	1d. olive and red	15	12
37.		2d. green and brown	15	15
38.		3d. violet and blue	75	1·00
39.		6d. black and purple	50	40

7. King George VI.

9. Cecil John Rhodes.

8. British South Africa Co's Arms.

1937.

40.	7.	½d. green	5	5
41.		1d. red	5	5
42.		1½d. brown	5	8
43.		4d. red	8	5
44.		6d. black	12	5
45.		8d. green	35	20
46.		9d. blue	25	15
47.		10d. purple	30	65
48.		1s. black and green	20	8
49.		1s. 6d. black and yellow	65	45
50.		2s. black and brown	70	25
51.		2s. 6d. blue and purple	1·00	40
52.		5s. blue and green	2·10	60

1940. British South Africa Co's Golden Jubilee.

53.	8.	½d. violet and green	8	5
54.	–	1d. blue and red	8	5
55.	9.	1½d. black and brown	8	8
56.	–	2d. green and violet	8	8
57.	–	3d. black and blue	10	10
58.	–	4d. green and brown	20	35
59.	–	6d. brown and green	30	50
60.	–	1s. blue and green	40	60

DESIGNS—HORIZ. 1d. Hoisting the flag; Fort Salisbury, 1890. 2d. Pioneer Fort and mail coach, Fort Victoria. 3d. Rhodes makes peace, 1896. 1s. Queen Victoria, King George VI, Lobengula's kraal and Govt. House, Salisbury. VERT. 4d. Victoria Falls Bridge. 6d. Statue of Sir Charles Coghlan.

10. Mounted Pioneer.

12. King George VI.

11. Queen Elizabeth II when Princess, and Princess Margaret.

1943. Occupation of Matabeleland. 50th Anniv.

61.	10.	2d. brown and green	5	5

1947. Royal Visit.

62.	11.	½d. black and green	5	5
63.	–	1d. black and red	5	5

DESIGN: 1d. King George VI and Queen Elizabeth.

1947. Victory. Inscr. as in T 12.

64.	–	1d. red	5	5
65.	12.	2d. slate	5	5
66.	–	3d. blue	8	8
67.	–	6d. orange	10	10

PORTRAITS: 1d. Queen Elizabeth. 3d. Queen Elizabeth II when Princess. 6d. Princess Margaret.

1949. U.P.U. As T 15/16 of Antigua.

68.		2d. green	8	8
69.		3d. blue	15	20

13. Queen Victoria, Arms and King George VI.

1950. S. Rhodesia Diamond Jubilee.

70.	13.	2d. green and brown	8	5

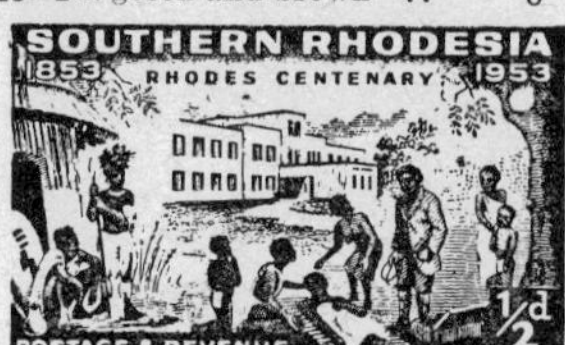

14. "Medical Services".

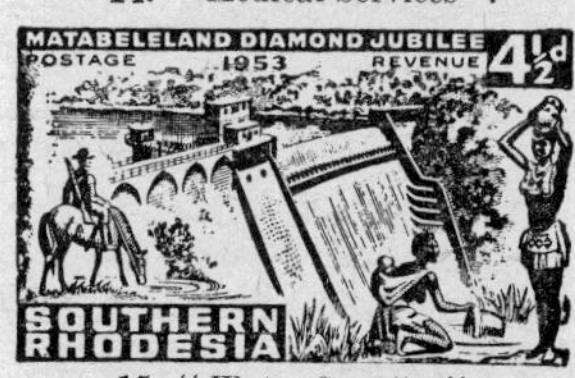

15. "Water Supplies".

1953. Cecil Rhodes. Birth Cent. Inscr. "RHODES CENTENARY".

71.	14.	½d. blue and sepia	8	20
72.	–	1d. chestnut and green	10	5
73.	–	2d. green and violet	10	10
74.	15.	4½d. green and blue	40	80
75.	–	1s. black and brown	40	50

DESIGNS: 1d. Agricultural scene and wild animals. 2d. Township and Rhodes. 1s. Ox-cart, train and aeroplane. No. 74 also commemorates the Diamond Jubilee of Matabeleland.

16. Queen Elizabeth II and Arms of S. and N. Rhodesia and Nyasaland.

1953. Rhodes Centenary Exhibition, Bulawayo.

76.	16.	6d. violet	30	40

17. Queen Elizabeth II.

1953. Coronation.

77.	17.	2s. 6d. red	75	1·50

18. Sable Antelope.

19. Rhodes's Grave.

20. Balancing Rocks.

1953.

78.	18.	½d. grey and claret	5	5
79.	–	1d. green and brown	5	5
80.	19.	2d. chestnut and violet	8	5
81.	–	3d. chocolate and red	8	10
82.	–	4d. red, green & indigo	12	8
83.	–	4½d. black and blue	20	25
84.	–	6d. olive and turquoise	15	10
85.	–	9d. blue and brown	25	30
86.	–	1s. violet and blue	30	20
87.	–	2s. purple and red	1·10	1·40
88.	–	2s. 6d. olive and chestnut	1·50	2·00
89.	–	5s. chestnut and green	3·00	4·00
90.	20.	10s. brown and olive	5·50	7·00
91.	–	£1 red and black	11·00	13·00

DESIGNS—As T 18: 1d. Tobacco planter. As T 19—HORIZ. 3d. Farm worker. 4d. Flame lily. 4½d. Victoria Falls. 9d. Lion. 1s. Zimbabwe Ruins. 2s. Birchenough Bridge. 2s. 6d. Kariba Gorge. VERT. 6d. Baobab tree. 5s. Basket maker. As T 20: £1 Coat of Arms.

21. Maize.

22. Flame Lily.

23. Cattle.

1964.

92.	21.	½d. yell., green & blue	5	5
93.	–	1d. violet and ochre	5	5
94.	–	2d. yellow and violet	5	5
95.	–	3d. chocolate and blue	5	5
96.	–	4d. orange and green	5	5
97.	22.	6d. red, yellow & green	8	8
98.	–	9d. brown, yellow & grn.	15	12
99.	–	1s. green and ochre	12	12
100.	–	1s. 3d. red, violet & grn.	30	20
101.	–	2s. blue and ochre	40	40
102.	–	2s. 6d. blue and red	45	30
103.	23.	5s. brown, yellow, blue and green	1·10	1·25
104.	–	10s. black, ochre, blue and red	2·25	2·50
105.	–	£1 brown, green, buff and red	5·00	5·50

DESIGNS—As T 21: 1d. Buffalo. 2d. Tobacco. 3d. Kudu. 4d. Citrus. As T 22: 9d. Ansellia orchid. 1s. Emeralds. 1s. 3d. Aloe. 2s. Lake Kyle. 2s. 6d. Tiger fish. As T 23: 10s. Guinea-owl. £1 Coat of Arms.

Later issues inscribed "RHODESIA" will be found listed under that name.

POSTAGE DUE STAMPS

1951. Postage due stamps of Great Britain optd. **SOUTHERN RHODESIA.**

D 1.	D 1.	½d. green	8	12
D 2.		1d. blue	10	15
D 3.		2d. black	15	20
D 4.		3d. violet	15	25
D 5.		4d. blue	20	30
D 6.		4d. grey-green	12·00	15·00
D 7.		1s. blue	35	50

For later issues see **RHODESIA.**

SOUTHERN YEMEN 04

PEOPLE'S REPUBLIC

Independent Republic comprising the areas formerly known as Aden, the Aden States and the South Arabian Federation.

From 30 November, 1970, the country was renamed The Peoples Democratic Republic of Yemen.

1968. 1000 fils = 1 dinar.

1968. Stamps of South Arabian Federation optd. **PEOPLE'S REPUBLIC OF SOUTHERN YEMEN** in English and Arabic, in four lines (Nos. 1/10) or three lines (Nos. 11/14) and bold bar.

1.	1.	5 f. blue	5	5
2.		10 f. lavender	5	5
3.		15 f. green	5	5
4.		20 f. emerald	5	5
5.		25 f. brown	8	8
6.		30 f. bistre	10	10
7.		35 f. chestnut	10	10
8.		50 f. red	15	15
9.		65 f. yellow-green	20	20
10.		75 f. red	20	20
11.	2.	100 f. multicoloured	30	30
12.		250 f. multicoloured	70	70
13.		500 f. multicoloured	1·40	1·40
14.		1 d. multicoloured	2·75	2·75

1. National Flag across Globe.

1968. Independence. Multicoloured.

15.	10 f. Type 1	5	5
16.	15 f. Revolutionary (vert.)	5	5
17.	50 f. Aden harbour	15	15
18.	100f. Cotton-picking	30	30

2. Girl Guides.

1968. Aden Girl Guides' Movement.

19.	–	10 f. blue	5	5
20.	–	25 f. indigo and chestnut	8	8
21.	2.	50 f. blue, brn. & yellow	15	15

DESIGNS—HORIZ. 10 f. Guides around camp-fire. VERT. 25 f. Brownies.

3. Revolutionary Soldier.

1968. Revolution Day.
22. **3.** 20 f. brown and blue .. 5 5
23. – 30 f. brown and green .. 10 10
24. – 100 f. vermilion & yellow 30 30
DESIGNS—HORIZ. 30 f. Radfan Mountains ("where first martyr fell"). VERT. 100 f. Open book and torch ("Freedom, Socialism and Unity").

4. Sculptured Plaque ("Assyrian influence").

1968. Antiquities.
25. – 5 f. olive 5 5
26. – 35 f. blue and claret .. 10 10
27. **4.** 50 f. buff and blue .. 15 15
28. – 65 f. green and purple .. 20 20
DESIGNS—VERT. 5 f. King Yusdqil Far'am of Ausan (statue). 35 f. Sculptured figure ("African-inspired"). HORIZ. 65 f. Bull's head ("Moon God").

5. Martyrs' Monument, Aden. **6.** Albert Thomas Memorial, Geneva.

1969. Martyr's Day.
29. **5.** 15 f. multicoloured .. 5 5
30. 35 f. multicoloured .. 10 10
31. 100 f. multicoloured .. 30 30

1969. Int. Labour Organization. 50th Anniv.
32. **6.** 10 f. sepia, black & green 5 5
33. 25 f. sepia, black & magenta 10 10

7. Teacher and Class.

1969. Int. Literacy Day.
34. **7.** 35 f. multicoloured .. 10 10
35. 100 f. multicoloured .. 30 30

8. Mahatma Gandhi. **9.** Yemeni Family.

1969. Mahatma Gandhi. Birth Cent.
36. **8.** 35 f. purple and blue .. 12 12

1969. Family Day.
37. **9.** 25 f. multicoloured .. 10 10
38. 75 f. multicoloured .. 25 25

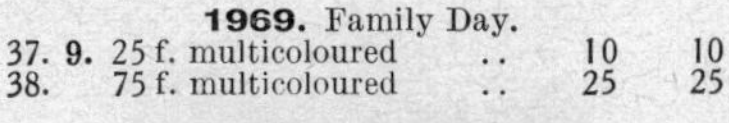

10. U.N. Headquarters, New York.

1969. United Nations Day.
39. **10.** 20 f. multicoloured .. 5 5
40. 65 f. multicoloured .. 20 20

11. Map and Flag of Southern Yemen.

1969. Independence. 2nd Anniv. Multicoloured.
41. 15 f. Type **11** 5 5
42. 35 f. Type **11** 12 12
43. 40 f. Tractors and flag .. 12 12
44. 50 f. As No. 43 .. .. 15 15

12. Map of Arab World, League Crest and Flag.

1970. Arab League. Silver Jubilee.
45. **12.** 35 f. multicoloured .. 12 12

13. Lenin. **14.** Palestinian Guerrilla.

1970. Lenin. Birth Cent.
46. **13.** 75 f. multicoloured .. 25 25

1970. Palestine Day. Multicoloured.
47. 15 f. Type **14** 5 5
48. 35 f. "Attack on airport" 12 12
49. 50 f. "Fighters reaching for flag" 15 15

15. New U.P.U. Headquarters Building.

1970. New U.P.U. Headquarters Building.
50. **15.** 15 f. emerald and orange 5 5
51. 65 f. red and buff .. 20 20

16. Girl with Pitcher.

1970. National Costumes. Multicoloured.
52. 10 f. Type **16** 5 5
53. 15 f. Woman in veil .. 5 5
54. 20 f. Girl in burnous dress 5 5
55. 50 f. Three Yemeni men 15 15

17. Camel and Calf.

1970. Fauna. Multicoloured.
56. 15 f. Type **17** 5 5
57. 25 f. Goats.. .. .. 10 10
58. 35 f. Oryx and kid .. 12 12
59. 65 f. Socotran dwarf cows.. 25 25

18. Torch and Flags.

1970. October 14th Revolution. 7th Anniv. Multicoloured.
60. 25 f. Type **18** 8 8
61. 35 f. National Front G.H.Q. (57×27 mm.) 12 12
62. 50 f. Farmer and revolutionaries (42×25 mm.) 15 15

19. U.N. H.Q. Building and Emblem.

1970. United Nations. 25th Anniv.
63. **19.** 10 f. orange and blue .. 5 5
64. 65 f. red and blue .. 20 20

For later issues see **YEMEN PEOPLE'S DEMOCRATIC REPUBLIC.**

SPAIN E3

A kingdom in S.W. Europe; twice a republic, now a National State.

1850. 8½ (later 8) cuartos = 1 real.
1866. 80 cuartos = 100 centimos de escudo = 1 escudo.
1867. 1000 milesimas = 100 centimos de escudo = 80 cuartos = 1 escudo.
1872. 100 centimos = 1 peseta.

1. **2.** **3.**
Queen Isabella II.

1850. Imperf.
2. **1.** 6 c. black .. .. .. 90·00 6·00
3. 12 c. lilac .. .. .. £650 90·00
4. **2.** 5 r. red .. .. .. £500 80·00
5. 6 r. blue £1000 £300
6. 10 r. green £1400 £600

1851. Imperf.
9. **3.** 6 c. black .. .. .. 60·00 1·40
10. 12 c. lilac .. .. .. £600 60·00
11. 2 r. red £3500 £2250
12. 5 r. red .. .. .. £700 85·00
13. 6 r. blue £1000 £350
14. 10 r. green £700 £180

4. **5.** **6.** Arms of Castile and Leon.

1852. Imperf.
16. **4.** 6 c. red .. .. .. 80·00 1·25
17. 12 c. purple .. .. £475 50·00
18. 2 r. red £3250 £1400
19. 5 r. green .. .. .. £500 45·00
20. 6 r. blue £850 £180

1853. Imperf.
22. **5.** 6 c. red .. .. . 80·00 1·00
23. 12 c. purple .. .. £450 38·00
24. 2 r. orange £2750 £900
25. 5 r. green .. .. .. £450 38·00
26. 6 r. blue £750 £160

1854. Imperf.
32. **6.** 2 c. green £550 £180
33. 4 c. red .. .. .. 75·00 1·00
34. 6 c. red .. .. .. 80·00 80
35. 1 r. blue £450 £120
36. 2 r. orange .. .. £350 38·00
37. 5 r. green .. .. .. £350 38·00
38. 6 r. blue £550 £120

7. **8.** **9.**

1855. Imperf.
58. **7.** 2 c. green .. .. .. £120 14·00
55a. 4 c. red .. .. .. 2·00 15
56. 1 r. blue .. .. .. 7·50 4·50
62. 2 r. purple .. .. 21·00 7·00

1860. Imperf.
63. **8.** 2 c. green on green .. 90·00 6·50
64. 4 c. orange on green .. 11·00 35
65. 12 c. red on buff .. .. 90·00 4·50
66. 19 c. brown on brown .. £600 £350
67. 1 r. blue on green .. 45·00 4·00
68. 2 r. lilac on lilac .. 65·00 3·50

1862. Imperf.
69. **9.** 2 c. blue on yellow .. 11·00 4·25
70. 4 c. brown on brown .. 1·00 25
71. 12 c. blue on rose .. 14·00 3·75
72. 19 c. red on lilac .. .. 55·00 55·00
73a. 1 r. brown on yellow .. 18·00 7·50
74. 2 r. green on rose .. 11·00 5·00

10. **11.** **12.**

1864. Imperf.
75. **10.** 2 c. blue on lilac .. 15·00 5·50
76. 4 c. red on red .. .. 1·00 35
77. 12 c. green on rose .. 16·00 5·00
78. 19 c. lilac on lilac .. 60·00 60·00
79. 1 r. brown on green .. 50·00 21·00
80. 2 r. blue on rose .. 10·00 3·50

1865. Imperf.
81a. **11.** 2 c. red .. .. .. 70·00 9·00
82. 12 c. red and blue .. ·£120 8·50
83. 19 c. red and brown .. £425 £200
84. 1 r. green .. .. £120 23·00
85. 2 r. mauve .. .. £110 13·00
85b. 2 r. red .. .. .. £140 25·00
85e. 2 r. yellow .. .. £130 30·00

1865. Perf.
86. **11.** 2 c. red .. .. £140 30·00
87a. 4 c. blue .. .. .. 16·00 40
88. 12 c. red and blue .. £180 22·00
89. 19 c. red and brown .. £1400 £750
90. 1 r. green £450 £120
91. 2 r. purple .. .. £300 75·00
91b. 2 r. orange £375 £110

1866. Perf.
92. **12.** 2 c. red .. .. 60·00 7·50
93. 4 c. blue .. .. .. 12·00 40
94. 12 c. orange .. .. 55·00 4·50
95. 19 c. brown £225 £100
96. 10 c. de esc. green .. 80·00 8·00
97. 20 c. de esc. lilac .. 55·00 7·00

1866. As T **10**, but dated 1866, and perf.
98. 20 c. de esc. lilac.. .. £160 20·00

13. **14.** **15.**

1867. Inscr. "CORREOS DE ESPANA". Various frames.
99. **13.** 2 c. brown .. .. 90·00 11·00
100. 4 c. blue .. .. 9·00 40
101. 12 c. orange .. .. 55·00 2·50
102. 19 c. red £325 £110
150. 19 c. brown £550 £180
103. 10 c. de esc. green .. 55·00 7·50
104. 20 c. de esc. lilac .. 30·00 3·25

1867. Various frames.
105. **14.** 5 m. green .. .. 13·00 4·50
106. 10 m. brown .. .. 13·00 3·75
107. **15.** 25 m. red and blue .. 60·00 7·25
145. 25 m. blue .. .. 65·00 5·00
108. 50 m. brown .. .. 6·50 30
146a. 50 m. purple .. .. 6·50 25
147. 100 m. brown .. .. £130 19·00
148. 200 m. green .. .. 42·00 4·00

16. **17.** **18.**

1870.
172. **16.** 1 m. lilac on rose .. 2·75 2·00
173. 2 m. black on rose .. 3·25 2·25
174. 4 m. brown .. .. 5·25 4·25
175a. 10 m. red .. .. 6·00 1·80
176a. 25 m. mauve .. 13·00 2·25
177. 50 m. blue .. .. 3·75 20
178. 100 m. red-brown .. 9·50 2·00
179. 200 m. brown .. .. 9·50 2·00
180. 400 m. green .. .. 65·00 11·00
181. 12 c. red-brown .. 55·00 2·50
182. 19 c. green .. .. £110 70·00
183. 1 esc. 600 m. lilac .. £350 £150
184. 2 esc. blue £240 £100

1872.
185. 17. ¼ c. blue 75 75
187. ¼ c. green 15 5
186a. 18. ¼ c. green 50 50

1872. As T 14, but currency in centavos de peseta.
192. 14. 2 c. lilac 9·00 4·00
193. 5 c. green 40·00 16·00

19. King Amadeo. 20. 21. "Peace".

1872.
194. 19. 5 c. red 8·50 2·50
195b. 6 c. blue 45·00 6·50
196. 10 c. lilac 75·00 32·00
197. 10 c. blue 3·00 20
199. 12 c. lilac 5·00 60
200. 20 c. lilac 35·00 13·00
201. 25 c. brown 12·00 2·75
202. 40 c. brown 11·00 2·75
203a. 50 c. green 19·00 3·50
204. 20. 1 p. lilac 32·00 11·00
205. 4 p. brown £170 £100
206. 10 p. green £425 £350

1873.
207. 21. 2 c. orange 5·25 2·25
208. 5 c. red 11·00 2·25
209. 10 c. green 3·50 20
210. 20 c. black 30·00 9·50
211. 25 c. brown 12·00 2·50
212. 40 c. purple 14·00 2·50
213. 50 c. blue 4·50 2·50
214. 1 p. lilac 16·00 7·50
215. 4 p. brown £170 £110
216. 10 p. purple £500 £400

22. "Justice". 23. 24. King Alfonso XII.

1874.
217. 22. 2 c. yellow 9·00 3·75
218a. 5 c. mauve 11·00 2·25
219. 10 c. blue 4·50 20
220. 20 c. green 45·00 13·00
221. 25 c. brown 12·50 2·75
222a. 40 c. mauve £100 3·75
223. 50 c. orange 30·00 3·75
224. 1 p. green 25·00 7·00
225. 4 p. red £180 £100
226. 10 p. black £550 £375

1874.
227. 23. 10 c. brown 6·25 40

1875.
228. 24. 2 c. brown 7·00 2·50
229. 5 c. lilac 17·00 3·75
230. 10 c. blue 3·50 20
231. 20 c. orange 85·00 32·00
232. 25 c. red 16·00 2·60
233. 40 c. brown 35·00 13·00
234. 50 c. mauve 40·00 7·50
235. 1 p. black 60·00 16·00
236. 4 p. green £130 65·00
237. 10 p. blue £400 £275

25. 26. 27.

1876.
238. 25. 5 c. brown 3·50 1·00
239. 10 c. blue 1·50 20
240. 20 c. olive 7·25 3·75
241. 25 c. brown 2·50 1·10
242. 40 c. grey 20·00 11·00
243. 50 c. green 5·50 2·00
244. 1 p. blue 6·75 2·75
245. 4 p. claret 13·00 11·00
246. 10 p. red 45·00 45·00

1878.
253. 26. 2 c. mauve 8·00 2·50
254. 5 c. yellow 13·00 2·25
255. 10 c. brown 2·25 20
256. 20 c. black 45·00 30·00
257. 25 c. olive 7·50 75
258. 40 c. brown 55·00 32·00
259. 50 c. green 24·00 3·25
260. 1 p. grey 20·00 6·50
261. 4 p. violet 60·00 37·00
262. 10 p. blue £110 £100

1879.
263. 27. 2 c. black 2·75 45
264. 5 c. green 4·25 40
265. 10 c. red 3·60 20
266. 20 c. brown 38·00 5·50
267a. 25 c. lilac 4·75 20
268. 40 c. brown 9·00 2·00
269. 50 c. orange 30·00 2·00
270. 1 p. red 32·00 75
271. 4 p. grey £130 10·00
272. 10 p. grey £375 65·00

28. 29. King Alfonso XIII. 30.

1882.
273. 28. 15 c. pink 3·00 12
273b. 15 c. yellow 12·00 30
274. 30 c. mauve 65·00 1·80
275. 75 c. violet 65·00 1·80

1889.
276. 29. 2 c. green 1·75 15
289. 2 c. black 10·00 1·50
277. 5 c. blue 3·25 5
290. 5 c. green 27·00 50
278. 10 c. brown 4·00 5
291. 10 c. red 55·00 1·50
279. 15 c. chocolate 1·40 5
280. 20 c. green 11·00 1·25
281. 25 c. blue 3·50 5
282. 30 c. grey 17·00 1·00
283. 40 c. brown 17·00 90
284. 50 c. red 18·00 40
285. 75 c. orange 35·00 1·00
286. 1 p. purple 13·00 10
287. 4 p. red £180 10·00
288. 10 p. red £250 20·00
For 15 c. yellow see No. O 13.

1900.
292. 30. 2 c. brown 1·25 10
293. 5 c. green 2·75 10
294. 10 c. red 2·75 10
295. 15 c. blue 6·00 10
296. 15 c. mauve 3·75 10
297. 15 c. violet 3·00 10
298. 20 c. grey 13·00 40
299. 25 c. blue 2·50 10
300. 30 c. green 12·00 15
301. 40 c. bistre 42·00 1·25
302. 40 c. red 85·00 60
303. 50 c. blue 15·00 15
304. 1 p. claret 13·00 15
305. 4 p. purple 90·00 6·00
306. 10 p. orange 80·00 16·00

31. Don Quixote setting out.

1905. Publication of Cervantes' "Don Quixote". Tercent.
307. 31. 5 c. green 45 25
308. – 10 c. red 1·00 50
309. – 15 c. violet 1·00 50
310. – 25 c. blue 2·50 60
311. – 30 c. green 16·00 2·50
312. – 40 c. red 32·00 7·50
313. – 50 c. grey 6·50 1·50
314. – 1 p. red £100 30·00
315. – 4 p. violet 35·00 22·00
316. – 10 p. orange 60·00 40·00
DESIGNS: 10 c. Quixote attacking windmill. 15 c. Meeting country girls. 25 c. Sancho Panza tossed in blanket. 30 c. Don Quixote knighted by innkeeper. 40 c. Tilting at sheep. 50 c On the wooden horse. 1 p. Adventure with lions. 4 p. in the bullock-cart. 10 p. The enchanted lady.

32. 33. 34. G.P.O., Madrid.

1909.
329. 32. 2 c. brown 26 5
330. 5 c. green 70 5
331. 10 c. red 85 5
332. 15 c. violet 4·00 5
333. 15 c. yellow 2·75 5
334. 20 c. green 20·00 12
335. 20 c. violet 14·00 5
336. 25 c. blue 1·75 5
337. 30 c. green 4·00 5
338. 40 c. pink 5·50 12
339. 50 c. blue 4·75 5
340. 1 p. red 13·00 5
341. 4 p. purple 35·00 1·75
342. 10 p. orange 38·00 3·75

1920. Air. Optd. **CORREO AEREO.**
353. 32. 5 c. green 50 30
354. 10 c. red 75 35
355. 25 c. blue 1·25 50
356. 50 c. blue 4·25 1·75
357. 1 p. red 15·00 7·50

1920. Imperf.
358. 33. 1 c. green 20 5

1920. U.P.U. Congress, Madrid.
361. 34. 1 c. black and blue 10 8
362. 2 c. black and brown 10 8
363. 5 c. black and green 45 40
364. 10 c. black and red 35 50
365. 15 c. black and yellow 65 50
366. 20 c. black and violet 85 50
367. 25 c. black and blue 1·00 1·00
368. 30 c. black and green 2·50 1·50
369. 40 c. black and red 5·00 2·25
370. 50 c. black and blue 12·00 7·00
371. 1 p. black and red 12·00 5·50
372. 4 p. black and brown 38·00 20·00
373. 10 p. black and orange 65·00 35·00

35. 36.

1922.
374. 35. 2 c. olive 25 5
375. 5 c. purple 1·75 5
376. 5 c. red 85 5
377. 10 c. red 70 25
378. 10 c. green 90 5
380. 15 c. slate 3·25 5
382. 20 c. violet 1·75 5
383. 25 c. red 1·75 5
387. 30 c. brown 5·50 5
388. 40 c. blue 2·00 5
389. 50 c. orange 7·00 5
391. 36. 1 p. grey 7·00 5
392. 4 p. red 30·00 1·00
393. 10 p. brown 14·00 3·00

37. Princesses Maria Christina and Beatrice. 38. King Alfonso XIII.

1926. Red Cross.
394. 37. 1 c. black 90 40
395. – 2 c. blue 75 40
396. – 5 c. purple 2·00 1·00
397. – 10 c. green 1·75 1·00
398. 37. 15 c. blue 75 40
399. – 20 c. violet 75 50
400. 38. 25 c. red 15 15
401. 37. 30 c. green 13·00 11·00
402. – 40 c. blue 9·00 5·50
403. – 50 c. orange 7·50 5·50
404. – 1 p. grey 60 35
405. – 4 p. red 20 15
406. 38. 10 p. brown 30 20
DESIGNS—VERT. 2 c., 50 c. Queen Victoria Eugenie as nurse. 5 c., 40 c., 4 p. Queen Victoria Eugenie. 10 c., 20 c., 1 p. Prince of Asturias.

39. Dornier WAL Flying-boat.

40. Route Map and Breguet 19 A2 Aircraft.

1926. Air. Red Cross and Trans-Atlantic and Madrid-Manila Flights.
407. 39. 5 c. violet and black 75 75
408. 10 c. black and blue 80 80
409. 40. 15 c. blue and orange 10 10
410. 20 c. red and green 10 10
411. 39. 25 c. black and red 10 10
412. 40. 30 c. brown and blue 10 10
413. 40 c. green and brown 10 10
414. 39. 50 c. black and red 10 10
415. 1 p. green and black 75 75
416. 40. 4 p. red and yellow 32·00 32·00

1927. Coronation. 25th Anniv. Red Cross stamps of 1926 optd. either **17-V 1902 17-V 1927 A XIII**, or same dates and **ALFONSO XIII** and laurel wreath.
417. 37. 1 c. black 2·00 2·00
418. – 2 c. blue 3·25 3·25
419. – 5 c. purple 1·00 1·00
420. – 10 c. green 18·00 18·00
421. 37. 15 c. blue 65 65
422. – 20 c. violet 1·25 1·25
423. 38. 25 c. red 20 20
424. 37. 30 c. green 40 40
425. – 40 c. blue 35 35
426. – 50 c. orange 35 35
427. – 1 p. grey 65 65
428. – 4 p. red 3·50 3·50
429. 38. 10 p. brown 12·00 12·00

1927. Red Cross stamps of 1926 optd. **17-V-1902 17-V-1927 ALFONSO XIII** and surch. also.
430. – 3 c. on 2 c. blue 4·00 4·00
431. – 4 c. on 2 c. blue 4·00 4·00
432. 38. 10 c. on 25 c. red 10 10
433. 25 c. on 25 c. red 10 10
434. – 55 c. on 2 c. blue 50 50
435. – 55 c. on 10 c. green 23·00 23·00
436. – 55 c. on 20 c. violet 23·00 23·00
437. 37. 75 c. on 15 c. blue 20 20
438. 75 c. on 30 c. green 70·00 70·00
439. – 80 c. on 5 c. purple 20·00 20·00
440. – 2 p. on 40 c. blue 40 40
441. – 2 p. on 1 p. grey 40 40
442. – 5 p. on 50 c. orange 80 80
443. – 5 p. on 4 p. red 1·10 1·10
444. 38. 10 p. on 10 p. brown 8·00 8·00

1927. Red Cross Air stamps of 1926 optd. either **17-V-1902 17-V-1927 A XIII**, or **17 MAYO 17 1902 1927 ALFONSO XIII.**
445. 39. 5 c. violet and black 60 60
446. 10 c. black and blue 75 75
447. 40. 15 c. blue and orange 10 10
448. 20 c. red and green 10 10
449. 39. 25 c. black and red 10 10
450. 40. 30 c. brown and blue 10 10
451. 40 c. green and brown 10 10
452. 39. 50 c. black and red 8 8
453. 1 p. green and black 75 75
454. 40. 4 p. red and yellow 32·00 32·00

1927. Red Cross Air stamps optd. as last and surch. **75 CTS. 75.**
455. 39. 75 c. on 5 c. vio. & blk. 1·50 1·50
456. 75 c. on 10 c. blk. & bl. 6·00 6·00
457. 75 c. on 25 c. blk. & red 10·00 10·00
458. 75 c. on 50 c. blk. & red 5·50 5·50

1927. Express Letter stamp optd. as above.
E 459. E 2. 20 c. purple 2·25 2·25

1927. Red Cross stamps of Spanish Morocco optd. as above or surch. also.
462. – 55 c. on 4 p. brown (122) 6·00 6·00
463. 38. 80 c. on 10 p. lilac (123) 6·00 6·00
460. 1 p. on 10 p. lilac (T 24) 25·00 25·00
461. – 4 p. brown (No. T 23) 10·00 10·00

1927. Red Cross stamps of Cape Juby surch. and optd. as above.
464. – 5 p. on 4 p. brown (34) 16·00 16·00
465. 38. 10 p. on 10 p. lilac (35) 11·00 11·00

1927. Red Cross stamps of Spanish Guinea surch. and optd. as above.
466. 38. 1 p. on 10 p. lilac (232) 6·00 6·00
467. – 2 p. on 4 p. brown (231) 6·00 6·00

1927. Red Cross stamps of Spanish Sahara surch. and optd. as above.
468. 38. 80 c. on 10 p. lilac (24) 8·00 8·00
469. – 2 p. on 4 p. brown (23) 6·00 6·00

41. Pope Pius XI and King Alfonso XIII.

1928. Rome Catacombs Restoration Fund.
470. 41. 2 c. black and violet 15 15
471. 2 c. black and claret 20 20
486. 2 c. red and grey 15 15
487. 2 c. red and blue 20 20
472. 3 c. violet and grey 15 15
473. 3 c. violet and blue 20 20
488. 3 c. blue and brown 15 15
489. 3 c. blue and olive 20 20
474. 5 c. violet and olive 30 30
490. 5 c. red and purple 30 30
475. 10 c. black and green 55 55
491. 10 c. blue and green 55 55
476. 15 c. violet and green 1·50 1·50
492. 15 c. red and blue 1·50 1·50
477. 25 c. violet and red 1·50 1·50
493. 25 c. blue and brown 1·50 1·50
478. 40 c. black and blue 10 10
494. 40 c. red and blue 10 10
479. 55 c. violet and brown 10 10
495. 55 c. blue and brown 10 10
480. 80 c. black and red 10 10
496. 80 c. red and black 10 10
481. 1 p. violet and grey 10 10
497. 1 p. red and yellow 10 10

No.	Type	Description	Unused	Used
482.	41.	2 p. black and brown ..	2·00	2·00
498.		2 p. blue and grey ..	2·00	2·00
483.		3 p. violet and pink ..	2·00	2·00
499.		3 p. red and violet ..	2·00	2·00
484.		4 p. black and claret ..	2·00	2·00
500.		4 p. red and claret ..	2·00	2·00
485.		5 p. violet and grey ..	2·00	2·00
501.		5 p. blue and orange ..	2·00	2·00

42. Spanish Caravel and Seville. 43. Exhibition Poster.

1929. Seville and Barcelona Exhibitions. Inscr. "EXPOSICION GENERAL (or GRAL.) ESPANOLA".

No.	Type	Description	Unused	Used
502.	42.	1 c. blue	15	15
503.	43.	2 c. green	20	20
504.	–	5 c. red	25	25
505.	–	10 c. green	30	30
506.	42.	15 c. blue	20	20
507.	43.	20 c. violet	35	35
508.	42.	25 c. red	30	30
509.	–	30 c. brown	1·75	1·75
510.	–	40 c. blue	2·00	2·00
511.	43.	50 c. orange	1·75	1·75
512.	–	1 p. grey	3·25	3·25
513.	–	4 p. red	10·00	10·00
514.	–	10 p. brown	21·00	21·00

DESIGNS—VERT. 5 c., 30 c., 1 p. View of Exhibition. HORIZ. 10 c., 40 c., 4 p., 10 p. Alfonso XIII with Barcelona in background.

46. "Spirit of St. Louis" over Coast.

1929. Air. Seville and Barcelona Exns.

No.	Type	Description	Unused	Used
515.	46.	5 c. brown	2·50	2·50
516.		10 c. red	2·75	2·75
517.		25 c. blue	3·00	3·00
518.		50 c. violet	3·75	3·75
519.		1 p. green	17·00	17·00
520.		4 p. black	13·00	13·00

1929. Meeting of Council of League of Nations at Madrid. Optd. **Sociedad de las Naciones L V reunion del Consejo Madrid.**

No.	Type	Description	Unused	Used
521.	33.	1 c. green (Imperf.) ..	30	30
522.	35.	2 c. olive	30	30
523.		5 c. red	30	30
524.		10 c. green	30	30
525.		15 c. slate	30	30
526.		20 c. violet	30	30
527.		25 c. red	20	20
528.		30 c. brown	1·25	1·25
529.		40 c. blue	1·25	1·25
530.		50 c. orange-red ..	1·25	1·25
531.	36.	1 p. grey	5·50	5·50
532.		4 p. red	5·50	5·50
533.		10 p. brown	20·00	20·00

48. 49.

1930. 11th Int. Railway Congress, Madrid

No.	Type	Description	Unused	Used
534.	48.	1 c. blue-green (postage)	25	25
535.		2 c. green	25	25
536.		5 c. claret	25	25
537.		10 c. green	25	25
538.		15 c. blue	25	25
539.		20 c. violet	25	25
540.		25 c. red	15	15
541.		30 c. brown	80	80
542.		40 c. blue	65	65
543.		50 c. orange	1·40	1·40
544.	–	1 p. grey	2·00	2·00
545.	–	4 p. red	20·00	20·00
546.	–	10 p. brown	£120	£120

The peseta values show a different view of a locomotive.

No.	Type	Description	Unused	Used
547.	49.	5 c. brown (air) ..	3·00	3·00
548.		10 c. red	3·00	3·00
549.		25 c. blue	3·00	3·00
550.		50 c. violet	6·50	6·50
551.		1 p. green	13·00	13·00
552.		4 p. black	13·00	13·00

50. Francisco Goya (after Lopez). 51.

52. "La Maja Desnuda".

1930. Goya (painter). Death Cent. (a) Postage.

No.	Type	Description	Unused	Used
553.	50.	1 c. yellow	5	5
554.		2 c. brown	5	5
555.	51.	2 c. olive	5	5
556.	50.	5 c. mauve	5	5
557.	51.	5 c. violet	5	5
558.	50.	10 c. green	15	15
559.		15 c. blue	10	10
560.		20 c. claret	10	10
561.		25 c. red	10	10
562.	51.	25 c. red	30	30
563.	50.	30 c. brown	3·25	3·25
564.		40 c. blue	3·25	3·25
565.		50 c. orange	3·25	3·25
566.		1 p. black	4·25	4·25
567.	52.	1 p. purple	60	60
568.		4 p. black	50	50
569.		10 p. brown	9·00	9·00

53. "Flight". 55. King Alfonso XIII.

(b) Air. Designs show works by Goya, all with curious flying figures.

No.	Type	Description	Unused	Used
570.	53.	5 c. yellow and red ..	5	5
571.	–	5 c. blue and olive ..	5	5
572.	–	10 c. green and blue ..	10	10
573.	53.	15 c. orange and blk. ..	10	10
574.	–	20 c. red and blue ..	10	10
575.	53.	25 c. red and claret ..	10	10
576.	–	30 c. violet and brown	30	30
577.	–	40 c. blue and violet ..	30	30
578.	–	50 c. green and red ..	30	30
579.	–	1 p. purple and plum ..	30	30
580.	–	4 p. black and claret ..	1·25	1·25
581.	–	4 p. grey and black ..	1·25	1·25
582.	–	10 p. brn. & deep brn.	5·50	5·50

The 5 c. (No. 571), 10 c., 20 c., 40 c., 1 p., 4 p. (No. 581) and 10 p. are vert. and the 30 c., 50 c. and 4 p. (No. 580) are horiz.

1930.

No.	Type	Description	Unused	Used
583.	55.	2 c. brown	5	5
584.		5 c. grey	30	5
585.		10 c. green	1·25	5
586.		15 c. blue-green ..	4·00	5
587.		20 c. violet	1·25	20
588.		25 c. red	30	5
589.		30 c. claret	4·00	35
590.		40 c. blue	7·00	25
592.		50 c. orange	7·00	30

56. "Santa Maria". 57.

58. "Nina", "Santa Maria" and "Pinta".

59. Departure from Palos.

1930. Columbus issue.

No.	Type	Description	Unused	Used
593.	56.	1 c. brown	10	10
594.		2 c. olive	10	10
595.	57.	2 c. olive	10	10
596.	56.	5 c. claret	10	10
597.	57.	5 c. claret	10	10
598.		10 c. green	45	45
599.	56.	15 c. blue	45	45
600.	57.	20 c. violet	55	55
601.	58.	25 c. red	55	55
602.	59.	30 c. brown and blue ..	2·25	2·25
603.	58.	40 c. blue	1·25	1·25
604.	59.	50 c. violet, blue & pur.	2·25	2·25
605.	58.	1 p. black	2·25	2·25
606.	–	4 p. black and blue ..	2·25	2·25
607.	–	10 p. brown and purple	12·00	12·00

DESIGN—As T 59: 4 p., 10 p. Arrival of Columbus in America.

61. Monastery of La Rabida. 62. Martin Pinzon.

64. Columbus.

1930. "Columbus" Air stamps (for Europe and Africa).

No.	Type	Description	Unused	Used
608.	61.	5 c. red	5	5
609.		5 c. brown	5	5
610.		10 c. green	10	10
611.		15 c. violet	10	10
612.		20 c. blue	10	10
613.	62.	25 c. red	10	10
614.	–	30 c. chocolate	85	85
615.	62.	40 c. blue	85	85
616.	–	50 c. orange	85	85
617.	62.	1 p. violet	85	85
618.	64.	4 p. olive	85	85
619.		10 p. brown	5·00	5·00

DESIGN—As T 62: 30 c., 50 c. Vincente Pinzon.

65. Monastery of La Rabida.

66. Columbus. 67. Columbus and the brothers Pinzon.

1930. "Columbus" Air stamps (for America and Phillippines).

No.	Type	Description	Unused	Used
620.	65.	5 c. red	5	5
621.		10 c. green	10	10
622.	66.	25 c. red	10	10
623.		50 c. grey	85	85
624.		1 p. brown	85	85
625.	67.	4 p. blue	85	85
626.		10 p. purple	4·75	4·75

68. Arms of Bolivia and Paraguay.

70. Sidar. 71. King, Queen and Columbus.

1930. Spanish-American Exn. Views of pavilions of various countries all inscr. "PRO UNION IBEROAMERICANA".

No.	Type	Description	Unused	Used
627.	68.	1 c. green (postage) ..	10	10
628.	–	2 c. brown (C. America)	10	10
629.	–	5 c. sepia (Venezuela) ..	10	10
630.	–	10 c. green (Colombia)	15	15
631.	–	15 c. blue (Dominican Republic) ..	15	15
632.	–	20 c. violet (Uruguay) ..	15	15
633.	–	25 c. red (Argentina) ..	15	15
634.	–	25 c. red (Chile) ..	15	15
635.	–	30 c. purple (Brazil) ..	60	60
636.	–	50 c. blue (Mexico) ..	35	35
637.	–	40 c. blue (Cuba) ..	35	35
638.	–	50 c. orange (Peru) ..	60	60
639.	–	1 p. blue (U.S.A.) ..	90	90
640.	–	4 p. purple (Portugal) ..	6·50	6·50
641.	–	10 p. brown	60	60

The 10 p. shows King Alfonso and Queen Victoria, map and buildings. The 2 c., 5 c., 4 p., 10 p. are vert.

No.	Type	Description	Unused	Used
643.	–	5 c. grey (air)	10	10
644.	–	10 c. olive	10	10
645.	–	25 c. blue	10	10
646.	–	50 c. blue	30	30
647.	70.	50 c. black	30	30
648.	–	1 p. red	60	60
649.	–	1 p. purple	15·00	15·00
650.	–	1 p. green	60	60
651.	71.	4 p. blue	1·00	1·00

DESIGNS: Portraits of aviators and views as T 70/71—HORIZ. 5 c. Santos Dumont. 10 c. T. Fels. 25 c. D. Godoy. 50 c. Cabral and Coutinho (No. 646). 1 p. Lindbergh (No. 650). VERT. 1 p. Jimenez and Iglesias (Nos. 648/9).

72. 73. The Fountain of the Lions.

1930.

No.	Type	Description	Unused	Used
652.	72.	5 c. black	3·00	5

1931. Optd. **REPUBLICA.**

(a) Postage.

No.	Type	Description	Unused	Used
653.	33.	1 c. green (Imperf.) ..	8	8
654.	55.	2 c. brown	10	10
655.		5 c. grey	10	10
682.	72.	5 c. black	2·00	2·00
656.	55.	10 c. green	20	20
657.		15 c. blue-green ..	70	70
658.		20 c. violet	70	70
678.		25 c. red	20	20
667.		30 c. claret	3·25	3·25
668.		40 c. blue	70	70
669.		50 c. orange	70	70
670.	36.	1 p. grey	4·50	4·50

(b) Air. On Nos. 353/6.

No.	Type	Description	Unused	Used
683.	32.	5 c. green	4·75	4·75
684.		10 c. red	4·75	4·75
685.		25 c. blue	6·00	6·00
686.		50 c. blue	8·00	8·00

1931. Optd. **Republica Espanola** in two lines continuously.

No.	Type	Description	Unused	Used
687.	55.	2 c. brown	5	5
688.		5 c. grey	20	5
689.		10 c. green	20	5
690.		15 c. blue-green ..	1·25	5
691.		20 c. violet	65	20
692.		25 c. red	20	5
693.		30 c. claret	1·75	25
694.		40 c. blue	1·75	20
695.		50 c. orange	3·00	25
696.	36.	1 p. grey	18·00	25

1931. 3rd Pan-American Postal Union Congress. Inscr. as in T **73**. (a) Postage.

No.	Type	Description	Unused	Used
697.	**73.**	5 c. maroon	8	8
698.	–	10 c. green	20	20
699.	–	15 c. violet	20	20
700.	–	25 c. red	20	20
701.	–	30 c. olive	20	20
702.	**73.**	40 c. blue	30	30
703.	–	50 c. red	30	30
704.	–	1 p. black	50	50
705.	–	4 p. purple	2·75	2·75
706.	–	10 p. brown	10·00	10·00

DESIGNS—VERT. 10 c., 25 c., 50 c. Cordoba Cathedral. HORIZ. 15 c., 1 p. Alcantara Bridge, Toledo. 30 c. Dr. F. Garcia y Santos. 4 p., 10 p. Revolutionaries hoisting republican flag (14/4/31).

75. Royal Palace and San Francisco el Grande.

(b) Air.

No.	Type	Description	Unused	Used
707.	**75.**	5 c. claret	5	5
708.		10 c. green	5	5
709.		25 c. red	5	5
710.	–	50 c. blue	20	20
711.	–	1 p. violet	25	25
712.	–	4 p. black	3·75	3·75

DESIGNS—HORIZ. 50 c., 1 p. G.P.O. and Cibeles Fountain. 4 p. The Calle de Alcala.

77. Montserrat Arms. **78.** Aeroplane above Montserrat.

1931. Montserrat Monastery. 900th Anniv. Inscr. "1031–1881–1931".

No.	Type	Description	Unused	Used
713.	**77.**	1 c. green (postage)	75	75
714.		2 c. brown	30	30
715.		5 c. brown	40	40
716.		10 c. green	40	40
717.	–	15 c. green	50	50
718.	–	20 c. purple	1·00	1·00
719.	–	25 c. claret	1·40	1·40
720.	–	30 c. red	15·00	15·00
721.	–	40 c. blue	9·00	9·00
722.	–	50 c. orange	18·00	18·00
723.	–	1 p. indigo	18·00	18·00
724.	–	4 p. magenta	£180	£180
725.	–	10 p. brown	£150	£150

DESIGNS: 15 c., 50 c. Monks planning Monastery. 20 c., 30 c. "Black Virgin" (full length), 25 c., 1 p., 10 p. "Black Virgin" (profile). 40 c., 4 p. Monastery.

No.	Type	Description	Unused	Used
726.	**78.**	5 c. brown (air)	30	30
727.		10 c. green	1·50	1·50
728.		25 c. claret	6·50	6·50
729.		50 c. orange	20·00	20·00
730.		1 p. blue	14·00	14·00

80. **80a.** **81.** Blasco Ibanez.

82. Pi y Margall. **83.** Joaquin Costa. **84.** Mariana Pineda.

85. Nicolas Salmeron. **86.** Concepcion Arenal. **87.** Ruiz Zorrilla.

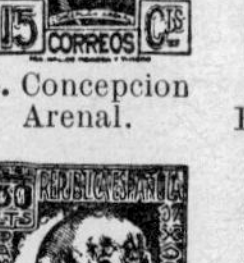

88. Pablo Iglesias. **89.** Ramon y Cajal. **90.** Azcarate.

91. Jovellanos. **92.** Pablo Iglesias. **93.** Emilio Castelar.

94. Pablo Iglesias. **95.** Velasquez. **96.** F. Salvoechia.

97. Cuenca.

1931.

No.	Type	Description	Unused	Used
770.	**80.**	1 c. green (Imperf.)	5	5
772.	**80a.**	2 c. brown	5	5
738.	**81.**	2 c. brown	5	5
771.	**80.**	2 c. brown	25	5
739.	**82.**	5 c. brown	1·50	15
740.	**81.**	5 c. chocolate	5	5
773.	**80.**	5 c. brown	5	5
741.	**83.**	10 c. green	1·75	5
742.	**84.**	10 c. green	5	5
774.	**80.**	10 c. green	5	5
744.	**85.**	15 c. blue	35	5
745.	**86.**	15 c. green	20	5
775.	**80.**	15 c. green	5	5
743.	**82.**	20 c. violet	15	5
776a.	**80.**	20 c. violet	5	5
749.	**88.**	25 c. red	14·00	5
750.	**87.**	25 c. red	30	5
777.	**80.**	25 c. mauve	5	5
751.	**88.**	30 c. red	75	5
752.	**89.**	30 c. brown	4·50	20
753.	**90.**	30 c. red	4·50	8
755.	**91.**	30 c. red	5	5
778.	**80.**	30 c. red	5	5
756.	**92.**	30 c. red	5	5
757.	**94.**	30 c. red	60	20
758.	**93.**	40 c. blue	5	5
759.		40 c. red	35	15
760.	**94.**	45 c. red	8	5
761.	**85.**	50 c. orange	13·00	10
762.		50 c. blue	75	10
763.	**95.**	50 c. blue	8	5
764.	**93.**	60 c. green	5	5
765.	**96.**	60 c. blue	35	25
766.		60 c. orange	2·75	2·00
767.	**97.**	1 p. black	12	5
768c.	–	4 p. magenta	40	25
769c.	–	10 p. brown	1·00	90

DESIGNS—As T **97**: 4 p. Castle of Segovia. 10 p. Sun Gate, Toledo.

98. Cierva Autogyro C.30 over Seville.

1935.

No.	Type	Description	Unused	Used
780.	**98.**	2 p. blue	11·00	1·50

99. De Vega's Bookplate. **100.** Scene from "Peribanez".

1935. Lope de Vega. Death Tercent.

No.	Type	Description	Unused	Used
781.	**99.**	15 c. green	4·00	15
782.	–	30 c. red	1·40	10
783.	–	50 c. blue	8·50	1·00
784.	**100.**	1 p. black	14·00	80

DESIGN—As T **99**: 30 c., 50 c. Lope de Vega.

101. Old-time Map of the Amazon.

1935. Iglesias' Amazon Expedition.

No.	Type	Description	Unused	Used
785.	**101.**	30 c. red	1·75	35

102. M. Moya. **103.** House of Nazareth and Rotary Press.

104. Pyrenean Eagle and Newspapers. **105.** Aeroplane over Press Association Building.

1936. Madrid Press Association. 40th Anniv.

No.	Type	Description	Unused	Used
786.	**102.**	1 c. red (postage)	5	5
787.	–	2 c. brown	5	5
788.	–	5 c. sepia	5	5
789.	–	10 c. green	5	5
790.	**102.**	15 c. green	10	5
791.	–	20 c. violet	10	5
792.	–	25 c. magenta	10	5
793.	–	30 c. red	5	5
794.	**102.**	40 c. orange	30	5
795.	–	50 c. blue	15	5
796.	–	60 c. olive	30	10
797.	–	1 p. black	30	10
798.	**103.**	2 p. blue	3·00	1·00
799.		4 p. claret	3·00	1·50
800.		10 p. lake	8·00	4·00

PORTRAITS: 2 c., 20 c., 50 c. T. L. de Tena. 5 c., 25 c., 60 c. F. Rodriguez. 10 c., 30 c., 1 p. A. Lerroux. SIZES: 1 c. to 10 c. 22 × 27 mm.; 15 c. to 30 c. 24 × 30 mm.; 40 c. to 1 p. 26 × 31½ mm.

No.	Type	Description	Unused	Used
801.	**104.**	1 c. red (air)	5	5
802.	**105.**	2 c. brown	5	5
803.	**104.**	5 c. sepia	5	5
804.		10 c. green	5	5
805.	–	15 c. blue	10	5
806.	**104.**	20 c. violet	10	5
807.	**105.**	25 c. magenta	10	5
808.	–	30 c. red	5	5
809.	**104.**	40 c. orange	30	15
810.	**105.**	50 c. blue	15	15
811.		60 c. olive	40	15
812.	–	1 p. black	40	15
813.	–	2 p. blue	2·25	1·00
814.	–	4 p. claret	2·50	1·50
815.	–	10 p. lake	6·00	3·00

DESIGNS: 15 c., 30 c., 50 c., 1 p. Cierva Autogyro C. 30 over House of Nazareth. 2 p., 4 p., 10 p. Don Quixote on Wooden Horse.

106. Gregorio Fernandez. **107.**

1936. Fernandez (sculptor). Death Tercent.

No.	Type	Description	Unused	Used
816.	**106.**	30 c. red	80	40

1936. First National Philatelic Exhibition. (a) Postage.

No.	Type	Description	Unused	Used
817.	**107.**	10 c. brown	25·00	25·00
818.		15 c. green	25·00	25·00

(b) Air. Optd. **CORREO AEREO.**

No.	Type	Description	Unused	Used
819.	**107.**	10 c. red	75·00	75·00
820.		15 c. blue	75·00	75·00

1936. Manila–Madrid Flight of Arnaiz and Calvo. Optd. **VUELO MANILA MADRID 1936 ARNAIZ CALVO.**

No.	Type	Description	Unused	Used
821.	**92.**	30 c. red	2·75	1·00

110. **111.** "Republic".

1937. Fiscal stamp of Asturias and Leon surch.

No.	Type	Description	Unused	Used
822.	**110.**	25 c. on 5 c. red	12·00	2·50
823.		45 c. on 5 c. red	5·50	1·75
824.		60 c. on 5 c. red	35	30
825.		1 p. on 5 c. red	25	20

1938. Surch. **45 centimos.**

No.	Type	Description	Unused	Used
826.	**80.**	45 c. on 1 c. green (imperf.)	1·75	1·75
827.		45 c. on 1 c. grn. (perf.)	20	20
830.		45 c. on 2 c. brown	4·25	4·25
831.	**80a.**	45 c. on 2 c. brown	5	5
832.	**81.**	45 c. on 2 c. brown	10·00	9·00

1938.

No.	Type	Description	Unused	Used
833.	**111.**	40 c. red	5	5
834.		45 c. red	5	5
835.		50 c. blue	5	5
836.		60 c. blue	25	25

1938. Republic. 7th Anniv. Surch. **14 ABRIL 1938 VII Aniversario de la Republica** and values. (a) Postage.

No.	Type	Description	Unused	Used
837.	**31.**	45 c. on 15 c. violet	7·25	7·25

(b) Air. Optd. **CORREO AEREO.**

No.	Type	Description	Unused	Used
838.	**31.**	2 p. 50 on 10 c. red	45·00	45·00

112. Defence of Madrid.

1938. Defence of Madrid Relief Fund. (a) Postage.

No.	Type	Description	Unused	Used
839.	**112.**	45 c. + 2 p. bl. & light bl.	35	35

(b) Air. Surch. **AEREO + 5 Pts.**

No.	Type	Description	Unused	Used
841.	**112.**	45 c. + 2 p. + 5 p. blue and light blue	95·00	95·00

1938. Labour Day. Surch. **FIESTA DEL TRABAJO 1 MAYO 1938** and values.

No.	Type	Description	Unused	Used
843.	**31.**	45 c. on 15 c. violet	1·50	1·25
844.		1 p. on 15 c. violet	2·75	2·00

113. Statue of Liberty and Flags.

1938. U.S. Constitution. 150th Anniv. (a) Postage.

No.	Type	Description	Unused	Used
845.	**113.**	1 p. black, red, yellow violet and blue	6·50	6·50

(b) Air. Surch. **AEREO + 5 Pts.**

No.	Type	Description	Unused	Used
847.	**113.**	1 p. + 5 p. black, red, yell., vio. & blue	80·00	80·00

114. **115.** Steelworks.

1938. Red Cross (a) Postage.

No.	Type	Description	Unused	Used
849.	**114.**	45 c. + 5 p. red	35	35

(b) Air. Surcharged **Aereo** and new value.

No.	Type	Description	Unused	Used
850	**114.**	45 c. + 5 p. + 3 p. red	3·00	3·00

1938. Air. No. 719 surch. with two aeroplanes and **CORREO AEREO** repeated twice and value.

No.	Type	Description	Unused	Used
851.		50 c. on 25 c. claret	12·00	12·00
852.		1 p. on 25 c. claret	60	60
853.		1 p. 25 on 25 c. claret	60	60
854.		1 p. 50 on 25 c. claret	60	60
855		2 p. on 25 c. claret	12·00	12·00

1938. In honour of Workers of Sagunto.

No.	Type	Description	Unused	Used
856.	**115.**	45 c. black	10	10
857.	–	1 p. 25 blue	10	10

DESIGN: 1 p. 25, Blast furnace and air raid victims.

115a. Submarine.

1938. Submarine Service.
857a. 115a. 1 p. blue .. .. 2·00 2·00
857b. – 2 p. brown .. .. 3·75 3·75
857c. – 4 p. orange .. 4·50 4·50
857d. – 6 p. blue .. .. 5·00 5·00
857e. – 10 p. red .. .. 15·00 15·00
857f. – 15 p. green .. £170 £170
DESIGNS: 2 p., 6 p. Submarine facing left. 4 p., 10 p. Submarine facing right.

116. Troops on the alert. 117.

1938. In honour of 43rd Division. Perf. or imperf.
858. 116. 25 c. green .. .. 4·50 4·50
859. 117. 45 c. brown .. .. 4·50 4·50

1938. Defence of Madrid. 2nd Anniv. Optd. **SECUNDO ANIVERSARIO DE LA HEROICA DEFENSA DE MADRID 7 NOV. 1938.**
860. 112. 45 c.+2 p. blue .. 1·25 1·25

1938. No. 719 surch. **2'50 PTAS** and bars and ornaments.
861. 2 p. 50 on 25 c. claret .. 10 10

117a. Man and Woman in Firing Positions.

1938. In honour of the Militia.
861b. 117a. 5 c. brown .. .. 1·50 1·50
861c. 10 c. purple .. 1·50 1·50
861d. 25 c. green .. .. 1·50 1·50
861e. – 45 c. red .. .. 1·25 1·25
861f. – 60 c. blue .. .. 2·25 2·25
861g. – 1 p. 20 black .. 50·00 50·00
861h. – 2 p. orange .. .. 16·00 16·00
861i. – 5 p. brown .. .. 75·00 75·00
861j. – 10 p. green .. .. 16·00 16·00
DESIGNS—HORIZ. 45 c., 60 c., 1 p. 20 Milicias with machine gun. VERT. 2 p., 5 p., 10 p. Grenade-thrower.

NATIONAL STATE

The Civil War began on July 17, 1936. Until it ended on April 1, 1939, the stamps listed below were current only in areas held by the forces of General Franco.

118.

119. Seville Cathedral.

120. Xavier Castle, Navarre.

121. Cordoba Cathedral.

1936.
868. 118. 1 c. green (imperf.) .. 2·00 2·00
869. 2 c. brown 20 15
862. – 5 c. brown 20 15
870. – 10 c. green 25 15
863. – 15 c. green 20 10
864. 119. 25 c. red 25 15
865. 120. 30 c. red 25 10
871. – 50 c. blue .. .. 4·75 3·25
872. 121. 60 c. green 35 25
867. – 1 p. black .. .. 1·75 80
873. – 4 p. lilac, red & yellow 16·00 9·00
874. – 10 p. brown .. .. 18·50 9·00
DESIGNS—VERT. 5 c. Burgos Cathedral. 4 p. National Flag of Malaga. HORIZ. As T 120: 15 c. Zaragoza Cathedral. 1 p. Alcantara Bridge and Alcazar, Toledo. As T 121: 10 c. Salamanca University. 50 c. Court of Lions, Granada. 10 p. Troops disembarking at Algeciras.

122.

123.

124. "El Cid".

125. Isabella the Catholic.

1937.
875. 122. 1 c. green (imperf.) .. 5 5
876. 123. 2 c. brown 5 5
877. 124. 5 c. brown 10 5
879. 10 c. green 8 5
895. 10 c. red 8 5
896. 15 c. green 8 5
880. 125. 15 c. black 10 5
881. 20 c. violet 20 8
882. 25 c. red 15 5
883. 30 c. red 20 5
885. 40 c. orange 60 8
886. 50 c. blue 60 8
887. 60 c. yellow 15 8
897. 70 c. blue 25 8
888. 1 p. blue .. .. 5·50 15
889. 4 p. mauve .. .. 6·00 1·00
891. 124. 10 p. blue .. .. 10·00 2·75

126. Santiago Cathedral.

DESIGNS—VERT. 15 c. St. James of Compostella. HORIZ. 1 p. Portico de la Gloria.

1937. Holy Year of Compostella. Inscr. "ANO JUBILAR COMPOSTELLANO".
905. – 15 c. brown 55 35
906. 126. 30 c. red .. .. 2·00 15
908. – 1 p. orange and blue 6·00 1·25

127. 128. Ferdinand the Catholic. 129.

1937. Anti-Tuberculosis Fund. Cross in red.
913. 127. 10 c. blue and black .. 1·75 40

1938.
917. 128. 15 c. green 90 5
918. 20 c. violet .. .. 6·50 40
919. 25 c. red 40 5
921. 30 c. red .. .. 2·50 5

1938. Air. Optd. **correo aereo.**
922. 123. 50 c. blue 35 15
923. 1 p. blue 75 15

1938. National Uprising. 2nd Anniv.
926. 129. 15 c. green .. .. 2·75 2·75
927. 25 c. red .. .. 2·75 2·75
928. 30 c. blue .. .. 1·25 1·25
929. 1 p. brown and yellow 35·00 35·00

130. Isabella the Catholic.

131.

1938.
930. 130. 20 c. violet 30 8
931. 25 c. red .. .. 2·50 15
932. 30 c. red 10 5
933. 40 c. mauve 10 5
934. 50 c. blue .. .. 11·00 50
935. 1 p. blue .. .. 3·25 20

1938. Anti-Tuberculosis Fund. Cross in red.
940. 131. 10 c. blue and black .. 1·25 30

132. Juan de la Cierva and Autogyro.

133. General Franco.

1939. Air.
1010. 132. 20 c. orange 10 5
1011. 25 c. red 10 5
943. 35 c. mauve 25 15
1013. 50 c. brown 20 5
945. 1 p. blue 30 10
1015. 2 p. green 60 5
1016. 4 p. blue .. .. 1·75 12
1017. 10 p. violet .. .. 1·50 20

1939.
960. 133. 5 c. brown 25 10
961. 10 c. red 70 25
962. 15 c. green 25 12
948. 20 c. violet 15 5
949. 25 c. claret 15 5
950. 30 c. red 8 5
965. 30 c. blue 10 5
1117. 35 c. blue 15 5
1118. 40 c. slate 10 5
952. 45 c. red 60 50
1119. 45 c. blue 5 5
953. 50 c. slate 10 5
1121. 60 c. orange 5 5
973. 70 c. blue 15 5
956. 1 Pts. black .. 3·00 5
974. 1 PTA. black .. 1·25 5
975. 1 PTS. grey .. 11·00 25
957. 2 Pts. brown .. 3·75 30
1124. 2 PTAS. brown .. 1·25 5
958. 4 Pts. purple .. 25·00 3·50
977a. 4 PTAS. red .. 3·75 5
959. 10 Pts. brown .. 13·00 7·50
978. 10 PTS. brown .. 25·00 1·00
1126. 10 PTAS. brown .. 75 15
For 10 c. brown imperf., see No. 981.

134. "Spain" and Wreath of Peace.

1939. Homage to the Army.
980. 134. 10 c. blue 10 5

1939. Anti-Tuberculosis Fund. Imperf.
981. 133. 10 c. brown 10 5

135. Ruins of Belchite.

1940. Zaragoza Cathedral Restoration Fund and 19th Cent. of Apparition of Virgin of El Pilar at Zaragoza. Inscr. as in T 135.

(a) Postage.
982. 135. 10 c.+5 c. brn. & blue 5 5
983. – 15 c.+10 c. olive & lilac 10 10
984. – 20 c.+10 c. bl. & violet 10 10
985. – 25 c.+10 c. brown & red 10 10
986. – 40 c.+10 c. pur. & grn. 5 5
987. – 45 c.+15 c. red & blue 15 15
988. 135. 70 c.+20 c. blk. & brn. 15 15
989. – 80 c.+20 c. violet & red 20 20
990. – 1 p.+30 c. pur. & blk. 20 20
991. – 1 p. 40+40 c. blk. & pur. 14·00 14·00
992. – 1 p. 50+50 c. pur. & bl. 30 30
993. – 2 p. 50+50 c. bl. & pur. 30 30
994. – 4 p.+1 p. slate & lilac 5·00 5·00
995. – 10 p.+4 p. brn. & blue 75·00 75·00
DESIGNS—HORIZ. 15 c., 80 c. Procession of the Rosary. 20 c., 1 p. 50, El Pilar. 25 c., 1 p. Mother Rafols praying. 40 c., 2 p. 50, Sanctuary of the Virgin. 45 c., 1 p. 40, Oath of the besieged. 4 p. Miracle of Calanda. 10 p. Virgin appearing to St. James.

(b) Air.
996. 25 c.+5 c. slate & purple 15 15
997. 50 c.+5 c. violet and red 15 15
998. 65 c.+15 c. blue & violet 15 15
999. 70 c.+15 c. violet & slate 15 15
1000. 90 c.+20 c. red & brown 15 15
1001. 1 p. 20+30 c. pur. & vio. 15 15
1002. 1 p. 40+40 c. brn. & bl. 25 25
1003. 2 p.+50 c. vio. & purple 30 30
1004. 4 p.+1 p. purple & green 3·75 3·75
1005. 10 p.+4 p. blue & brown 90·00 90·00
DESIGNS—VERT. 25 c., 70 c. Prayer during bombardment. 50 c., 1 p. 40, Caravel and Image of the Virgin. 65 c., 90 c. The Assumption. 1 p. 20, 2 p. Coronation of the Virgin. 4 p. "The Cave", after Goya. 10 p. Bombing of Zaragoza Cathedral.

136. Gen. Franco.

137. Knight and Cross of Lorrane.

1940. Anti-Tuberculosis Fund.
1006. 136. 10 c. violet & red (post.) 5 5
1007. 20 c.+5 c. grn. & red 30 25
1008. 40 c.+10 c. blue & red 40 12
1009. 136. 10 c. pink & red (air) 15 12

1941. Anti-Tuberculosis Fund.
1018. 137. 10 c. blk. & red (post.) 10 5
1019. 20 c.+5 c. violet & red 35 25
1020. 40 c.+10 c. slate & red 35 15
1021. 10 c. blue & red (air) 15 10

138. Gen. Franco.

139. St. John of the Cross.

1942.
1022. 138. 40 c. brown 15 8
1023. 75 c. blue .. .. 1·75 15
1024a. 90 c. green 15 5
1025b. 1 p. 35 violet .. 10 5

1942. St. John of the Cross. 4th Birth Cent.
1026. 139. 20 c. violet 60 5
1027. 40 c. orange .. .. 1·10 15
1028. 75 c. blue .. .. 1·10 1·00

140. Doves and Lorraine Cross.

DESIGN—HORIZ. No. 1032, Lorraine Cross and two doves in flight.

1942. Anti-T.B. Fund. Inscr. "1942-43".
1029. 140. 10 c. pink & red (post.) 12 5
1030. 20 c.+5 c. brn. & red 60 50
1031. 40 c.+10 c. grn. & red 50 10
1032. – 10 c. pink & red (air) 35 15

141.

St. James of Compostella.

142.

1943 Holy Year. Inscr. "ANO SANTO 1943".
1033. 141. 20 c. blue 15 8
1034. – 20 c. red 15 8
1035. – 20 c. lilac 15 8
1036. – 40 c. brown 40 10
1037. 142. 40 c. green 35 10
1038. – 40 c. brown 40 10
1039. – 75 c. blue .. .. 1·40 80
1040. – 75 c. blue .. .. 2·00 1·00
1041. – 75 c. blue .. .. 16·00 10·00
DESIGNS—VERT. Nos. 1034 and 1040, Details of pillars in Santiago Cathedral; 1036, St. James enthroned; 1038, Portal of Santiago Cathedral; 1039, Censer; 1041, Santiago Cathedral. HORIZ. No. 1035, Tomb of St. James.

143. 144. 10th-cent. Tower. 145. Arms of Soria.

1943. Anti-Tuberculosis Fund. Inscr. "1943-1944".
1042. 143. 10 c. vio. & red (post.) 25 15
1043. 20 c.+5 c. green & red 2·50 75
1044. 40 c.+10 c. blue & red 1·90 45
1045. – 10 c. violet and red (air) 55 40
DESIGN: No. 1045. Lorraine Cross and outline of bird.

1944. Millenary of Castile. Arms designs as T 145 inscr. "Milenario de Castilla".
1046. 144. 20 c. lilac 10 10
1047. 145. 20 c. lilac 10 10
1048. – 20 c. lilac 10 10
1049. – 40 c. brown .. .. 2·00 15
1050. – 40 c. brown .. .. 2·00 15
1051. – 40 c. brown .. .. 1·40 15
1052. – 75 c. blue .. .. 2·00 1·00
1053. – 75 c. blue .. .. 1·60 1·00
1054. – 75 c. blue .. .. 2·25 1·00

DESIGNS: No. 1048, Avila (Shield at left). 1049, Castile (Arms in centre). 1050, Segovia (Shield at left). 1051, Burgos (Shield at right). 1052, Avila (Shield at right). 1053, Fernan Gonzalez, founder of Castile (Helmet, bow and arrows at left). 1054, Santander (Shield at right).

146. "Dr. Thebussem" (Mariano de Figueros, author and postal historian).

1944. Air. Stamp Day.
1055. **146.** 5 p. blue .. .. 7·00 5·50

147.

148. Quevedo.

1944. Anti-Tuberculosis Fund. Inscr. "1944 1945". (a) Postage.
1056. **147.** 10 c. orang e& red .. 10 8
1057. 20 c.+5 c. blk. & red 20 20
1058. 40 c.+10 c. violet & red 35 10
1059. 80 c.+10 c. bl. & red 5·00 4·25

(b) Air. Inscr. "CORRESPONDENCIA AEREA".
1060. – 25 c. orange and red .. 2·50 1·75
DESIGN—HORIZ. No. 1060, Hospital.

1945. Francisco de Quevedo (author). 3rd Death Cent.
1061. **148.** 40 c. brown 40 25

149. Conde de San Luis, Mail Vehicle of 1850, and Aeroplane.

1945. Air. Stamp Day.
1062. **149.** 10 p. green .. .. 7·00 6·00

150. Carlos de Haya Gonzalez.

151. J. Garcia Morato.

1945. Air. Civil War Air Aces.
1063. **150.** 4 p. red .. .. 3·50 2·50
1064. **151.** 10 p. purple .. .. 8·00 2·75

152. St. George and Dragon.

153. Lorraine Cross and Eagle.

1945. Anti-T.B. Fund.
1065. **152.** 10 c. orge. & red (post.) 10 5
1066. 20 c.+5 c. green & red 15 10
1067. 40 c.+10 c. vio. & red 25 10
1068. 80 c.+10 c. bl. & red 5·50 4·25
1069. **153.** 25 c. red (air) .. 75 50

154. E. A. de Nebrija (compiler of first Spanish Grammar).

155. Statue of Fray Bartolome de las Casas and Indian.

1946. Stamp Day and Day of the Race.
1070. **154.** 50 c. red (postage) .. 30 10
1071. – 75 c. blue 40 20
1072. **155.** 5 p. 50 green (air) .. 1·75 1·25
DESIGN—As T **154**: 75 c. Salamanca University and signature of Fray Francisco de Vitoria (founder of International Law).

156. Self-portrait of Goya.
157. Woman and Child.
158. B. J. Feijoo y Montenegro.

1946. Goya. Birth Bicent.
1073. **156.** 25 c. red 5 5
1074. 50 c. green 10 5
1075. 75 c. blue 60 35

1946. Anti-Tuberculosis Fund. Dated. "1946 1947".
1076. **157.** 5 c. violet and red (postage) .. 5 5
1077. 10 c. grn. and red .. 5 5
1078. – 25 c. orge. & red (air) 10 8
DESIGN—HORIZ. 25 c. Eagle.

1947.
1079. **158.** 50 c. green 40 20

159. Don Quixote in Library.

160. Don Quixote.

1947. Stamp Day and 4th Birth Cent. Cervantes Inscr. "9 DE OCTUBRE DIA DEL SELLO".
1080. **159.** 50 c. brown (postage) 20 12
1081. **160.** 75 c. blue 30 25
1082. – 5 p. 50 violet (air) .. 3·25 2·00
DESIGN—HORIZ. 5 p. 50, Quixote on Wooden Horse (after Gustav Dore).

161. Manuel de Falla (composer).

162. Lorraine Cross.

163. General Franco.

1947. Air.
1083. **161.** 25 p. purple .. .. 18·00 6·00
1084. – 50 p. red .. .. 70·00 9·00
PORTRAIT: 50 p. Ignacio Zuloaga y Zabaleta (painter).

1947. Anti-Tuberculosis Fund. Dated. "1947 1948".
1085. **162.** 5 c. brn. & red (post.) 5 5
1086. – 10 c. blue and red .. 5 5
1087. – 25 c. mve. & red (air) 15 8
DESIGNS—VERT. 10 c. Deck chair in garden. HORIZ. 25 c. Sanatorium.

1948.
1088. **163.** 5 c. brown 5 5
1088a. 5 c. olive 10 5
1089. 15 c. green 5 5
1090. 50 c. brown 10 5
1091. 80 c. lake .. .. 1·10 5

164. Hernando Cortes.
165. Gen. Franco and Castillo de la Mota.
166. Ferdinand III of Castile.

1948.
1092. **164.** 35 c. black 12 5
1093. – 70 c. purple .. .. 1·40 90
PORTRAIT: 70 c. M. Aleman (writer).

1948.
1094. **165.** 25 c. orange .. 5 5
1095. 30 c. myrtle .. 5 5
1096. 35 c. green .. 5 5
1097. 40 c. brown .. 35 5
1098. 45 c. pink .. 15 5
1099. 45 c. red .. 15 5
1100. 50 c. purple .. 55 5
1101. 70 c. violet .. 75 10
1102. 75 c. blue .. 55 10
1103. 1 p. pink .. 2·50 5

1948. Institution of Castilian Navy. 7th Cent.
1104. **166.** 25 c. violet .. 25 5
1105. – 30 c. red (Admiral R. de Bonifaz) .. 12 5

167. Marquis of Salamanca.

168. Garganta de Pancorbo Viaduct.

1948. Stamp Day and Spanish Railway Cent. Inscr. "F.F.C.C. ESPAÑOLES 1848 1948".
1106. **167.** 50 c. brown (postage) 40 5
1107. **168.** 5 p. green 90 5
1108. – 2 p. red (air) .. 1·50 80
DESIGN—HORIZ. 2 p. Diesel Train.

169. Aesculapius.
170. Globe and Buildings.

1948. Anti-Tuberculosis Fund. Dated "1948 1949".
1109. **169.** 5 c. brn. & red (post.) 5 5
1110. 10 c. green and red .. 5 5
1111. 50 c.+10 c. brn. & red 60 50
1112. – 25 c. bl. & red (air) .. 20 15
DESIGN: 25 c. Aeroplane over sanatorium.

1949. Relief of War Victims. As T **124**, but larger and inscr. "AUXILIO A LAS VICTIMAS DE LA GUERRA 1946".
1113. 5 c. violet 15 5

1949. U.P.U. 75th Anniv.
1127. **170.** 50 c. brown (postage) 40 10
1128. 75 c. blue 30 20
1129. 4 p. olive (air) .. 25 15

171. Galleon.
172. San Juan de Dios and a Leper.

1949. Anti-Tuberculosis Fund. Inscr. "1949 1950".
1130. **171.** 5 c. vio. & red (post.) 5 5
1131. 10 c. green & red .. 5 5
1132. 50 c.+10 c. bis. & red 30 20
1133. – 25 c. claret & red (air) 10 8
DESIGN: 25 c. Bell.

1950. San Juan de Dios. 4th Death Cent.
1134. **172.** 1 p. violet .. .. 5·00 60

173. Ruiz de Alarcon, (author).

174. Isabella II.

1950. Portraits.
1135. 5 c. brown (postage) 5 5
1136. – 10 c. lake 5 5
1137. – 15 c. green 15 5
1138. **173.** 20 c. violet 12 5
1139. – 2 p. blue .. .. 12·00 8
1140. – 4 p. 50 maroon .. 25 20
PORTRAITS—VERT. 5 c. C. de la Barca (dramatist). 10 c. Lope de Vega (author). 15 c. T. de Molina (poet). 2 p. Dr. Ramon y Cajal (physician). 4 p. 50, Dr. Ferran y Clua (bacteriologist).

1950. Spanish Stamp Cent. Imperf.
(a) Postage Reproduction of T **1**.
1141. **174.** 50 c. violet .. 5·00 5·00
1142. 75 c. blue .. .. 5·00 5·00
1143. 10 p. black .. .. 65·00 65·00
1144. 15 p. red .. .. 65·00 65·00

(b) Air. Reproduction of T **2**.
1145. – 1 p. purple .. .. 5·00 5·00
1146. – 2 p. 50 brown .. 5·00 5·00
1147. – 20 p. blue .. .. 65·00 65·00
1148. – 25 p. green .. .. 65·00 65·00

1950. Gen. Franco's Canary Is. Visit. Nos. 1100 and 1103 surch. **VISITA DEL CAUDILLO A CANARIAS OCTUBRE 1950 SOBRETASA: DIEZ CTS** and No. A 1083 with **Correspondencia por avion** also.
1149. **165.** 10 c. on 50 c. purple (postage) .. .. 11·00 11·00
1150. 10 c. on 1 p. pink .. 11·00 11·00
1151. **161.** 10 c. on 25 p. pur. (air) £750 60·00

175. Candle and Conifer.

176. Map.

1950. Anti-T.B. Fund. Cross in red. Inscr. "1950 1951".
1152. **175.** 5 c. violet (postage) 5 5
1153. 10 c. green 5 5
1154. 50 c.+10 c. brown .. 35 20
1155. – 25 c. blue (air) .. 15 8
DESIGN: 25 c. Dove and flowers.

1951. Air. 6th Spanish-American P.U. Conf.
1156. **176.** 1 p. blue .. .. 2·00 30

177. Isabella the Catholic.

177a. St. Antonio Claret.

1951. Isabella the Catholic. 5th Birth Cent.
1157. **177.** 50 c. brown 45 12
1158. 75 c. blue 60 12
1159. 90 c. maroon 25 5
1160. 1 p. 50 orange .. .. 4·75 1·75
1161. 2 p. 80 olive .. .. 9·50 9·00

1951. Stamp Day.
1162. **177a.** 50 c. indigo .. .. 1·00 40

178. Children on Beach.

179. Isabella the Catholic.

1951. Anti-Tuberculosis Fund. Cross in red.
1163. **178.** 5 c. claret (post.) .. 5 5
1164. 10 c. green 15 5
1165. – 25 c. brown (air) .. 20 5
DESIGN: 25 c. Nurse and child.

1951. Air. Stamp Day and 500th Birth Anniv. of Isabella the Catholic.
1166. **179.** 60 c. green .. .. 2·50 10
1167. 90 c. yellow 25 10
1168. 1 p. 30 claret .. 1·90 60
1169. 1 p. 90 sepia .. 1·40 1·20
1170. 2 p. 30 blue 50 50

180. Ferdinand the Catholic.

181. St. Maria Micaela.

1952. Ferdinand the Catholic. 500th Birth. Anniv.
1171. **180.** 50 c. green .. 20 10
1172. 75 c. indigo .. 1·25 50
1173. 90 c. maroon .. 10 10
1174. 1 p. 50 orange .. 5·50 1·75
1175. 2 p. 80 brown .. 9·00 9·00

1952. 35th Int. Eucharistic Congress. Barcelona. Inscr. "XXXV CONGRESO", etc.
1176. **181.** 90 c. lake (postage) 5 5
1177. – 1 p. slate (air) .. 1·75 15
DESIGN: 1 p. "The Eucharist" (Tiepolo).

181a. St. Francis Xavier. **182.** Nurse and Baby.

1952. Air. St. Francis Xavier. 400th Death Anniv.
1178. **181a.** 2 p. blue .. .. 18·00 2·50

1952. Air. Stamp Day and 500th Anniv. of Birth of Ferdinand the Catholic. As T **179** but interior scene and portrait of Ferdinand the Catholic.
1179. 60 c. green 8 5
1180. 90 c. orange 8 5
1181. 1 p. 30 claret 8 5
1182. 1 p. 90 brown 70 40
1183. 2 p. 30 blue .. .. 3·00 2·10

1953. Anti-Tuberculosis Fund. Cross in red.
1184. **182.** 5 c. lake (postage) .. 30 5
1185. 10 c. green 30 5
1186. – 25 c. brown (air) .. 2·00 60
DESIGN: 25 c. Girl and angel.

183. J. Sorolla (painter). **184.** Bas-relief. **185.** Fray Luis de Leon.

1953. Air.
1229. – 25 p. myrtle .. .. 9·00 20
1187. **183.** 50 p. indigo .. .. £225 4·75
1230. – 50 p. indigo .. .. 4·00 45
PORTRAITS: 25 p. Fortuny (painter). No. 1230, T. Quevedo (engineer and inventor).

1953. Stamp Day and 700th Anniv. of Salamanca University. Inscr. "UNIVDAD DE SALAMANCA".
1188. **184.** 50 c. claret 25 5
1189. **185.** 90 c. green .. .. 1·50 80
1190. – 2 p. brown .. .. 9·50 70
DESIGN—As T **185**—HORIZ. 2 p. Salamanca University.

186. M. L. de Legazpi. **187.** "St. Mary Magdalene". **188.** St. James of Compostella.

1953. Air. Signing of Filipino-Spanish Postal Convention.
1191. **186.** 25 p. black .. .. 60·00 5·50

1954. Ribera (painter). Death Tercent.
1192. **187.** 1 p. 25 lake 5 5

1954. Holy Year.
1193. **188.** 50 c. brown 15 5
1194. – 3 p. blue .. .. 18·00 40
DESIGN: 3 p. Santiago Cathedral.

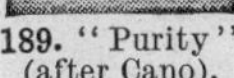

189. "Purity" (after Cano). **190.** Menendez Pelayo (Historian).

1954. Marian Year.
1195. **189.** 10 c. lake 5 5
1196. – 15 c. myrtle 5 5
1197. – 25 c. lilac 8 5
1198. – 30 c. brown 10 5
1199. – 50 c. olive 60 5
1200. – 60 c. black 10 5
1201. – 80 c. grey-green .. 1·75 5
1202. – 1 p. indigo .. .. 1·75 5
1203. – 2 p. chestnut 35 5
1204. – 3 p. blue 35 25
DESIGNS: 15 c. Virgin of Begona, Bilbao. 25 c. Virgin of the Abandoned, Valencia Cathedral. 30 c. The "Black Virgin" of Montserrat. 50 c. El Pilar Virgin, Zaragoza. 60 c. Covadonga Virgin. 80 c. Virgin of the Kings, Seville Cathedral. 1 p. Almudena Virgin, Madrid. 2 p. Virgin of Africa. 3 p. Guadelupe Virgin.

1954. Stamp Day.
1205. **190.** 80 c. green .. .. 1·75 5

191. Gen. Franco. **192.** St. Ignatius of Loyola.

1955. (a) T **191**. Imprint "F.N.M.T.".
1206. **191.** 10 c. lake 5 5
1207. 15 c. ochre 5 5
1208. 20 c. myrtle 5 5
1209. 25 c. violet 5 5
1210. 30 c. brown 5 5
1211. 40 c. purple 5 5
1212. 50 c. olive-brown .. 5 5
1213. 60 c. purple 5 5
1214. 70 c. myrtle 10 5
1215. 80 c. turquoise .. 5 5
1216. 1 p. orange 5 5
1217. 1 p. 40 magenta .. 10 8
1218. 1 p. 50 turquoise .. 5 5
1219. 1 p. 80 green 10 8
1220. 2 p. red .. .. 9·50 15
1221. 2 p. mauve 5 5
1222. 3 p. blue 5 5
1222a. 4 p. red 8 5
1223. 5 p. brown 8 5
1224. 6 p. black 15 5
1224a. 7 p. blue 15 5
1225. 8 p. violet 15 5
1226. 10 p. sage 20 5
1226a. 12 p. green 20 8
1226b. 20 p. red 40 10

(b) As T **191** but with "F.N.M.T.-B" imprint at foot.
1227. 1 p. orange 90 20
1228. 5 p. brown 90 20
Nos. 1227/8 were printed at the International Philatelic Exhibition, Barcelona, in 1960.

1955. Stamp Day and 4th Cent. of Death of St. Ignatius of Loyola.
1231. **192.** 25 c. slate 10 5
1232. – 60 c. ochre 25 5
1233. **192.** 80 c. green .. .. 1·25 5
DESIGN—HORIZ. 60 c. St. Ignatius and Loyola Castle.

193. Aeroplane and Caravel.

1955. Air.
1234. **193.** 20 c. myrtle 5 5
1235. 25 c. slate 5 5
1236. 50 c. olive-brown .. 5 5
1237. 1 p. red 5 5
1238. 1 p. 10 green 8 5
1239. 1 p. 40 magenta .. 8 5
1240. 3 p. blue 10 5
1241. 4 p. 80 yellow .. 10 5
1242. 5 p. brown 10 5
1243. 7 p. mauve 20 5
1244. 10 p. olive-green .. 30 5

194. "Telecommunications". **195.** "The Holy Family" (after El Greco). **196.**

1955. Cent. of Telegraphs in Spain.
1245. **194.** 15 c. brown 20 8
1246. 80 c. green .. .. 2·25 8
1247. 3 p. blue .. .. 5·50 30

1955. Canonization of St. Vincent Ferrer. 5th Cent. As T **187** but portrait of the Saint (after C. Vilar).
1248. 15 c. ochre 12 5

1955. Christmas.
1249. **195.** 80 c. myrtle .. .. 1·50 12

1956. Civil War. 20th Anniv.
1250. **196.** 15 c. brown and bistre 5 5
1251. 50 c. olive and green 25 15
1252. 80 c. grey-grn. & mag. 2·00 5
1253. 3 p. blue and ultram. 2·00 15

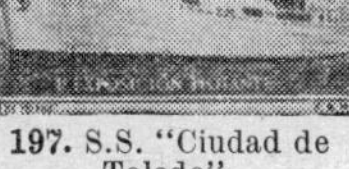

197. S.S. "Ciudad de Toledo". **198.** The "Black Virgin".

1956. First Floating Exhibition of National Products.
1254. **197.** 3 p. blue 90 25

1956. Coronation of "Black Virgin" of Montserrat. 75th Anniv.
1255. **198.** 15 c. brown 5 5
1256. – 60 c. grey-purple .. 30 15
1257. **198.** 80 c. green 30 15
DESIGN—VERT. 60 c. Montserrat Monastery.

199. Archangel Gabriel. **200.** "Statistics".

201. Hermitage and Monument. **202.** Refugee Children.

1956. Stamp Day.
1258. **199.** 80 c. green 20 10

1956. Statistics in Spain. Cent.
1259. **200.** 15 c. ochre 10 8
1260. 80 c. green .. .. 2·00 10
1261. 1 p. red .. .. 2·25 10

1956. Gen. Franco's Assumption of Office as Head of State. 20th Anniv.
1262. **201.** 80 c. grey-green .. 1·25 8

1956. Hungarian Children's Relief.
1263. **202.** 10 c. lake 5 5
1264. 15 c. brown 5 5
1265. 50 c. sepia 15 5
1266. 80 c. green 80 5
1267. 1 p. vermilion .. 80 5
1268. 3 p. blue .. .. 2·75 25

203. Apparition of the Sacred Heart. **204.** "The Great Captain".

1957. Stamp Day.
1269. **203.** 15 c. olive 5 5
1270. 60 c. slate-purple .. 20 5
1271. 80 c. green 20 5

1958. Gonzalves de Cordoba. 5th Birth Cent.
1272. **204.** 1 p. 80 green 5 5

205. Francisco Goya after Lopez. **206.** Exhibition Emblem.

1958. Stamp Day and Goya (painter) Commem. Frames in gold.
1273. – 15 c. ochre 5 5
1274. – 40 c. purple 5 5
1275. – 50 c. brown-olive .. 5 5
1276. – 60 c. slate-purple .. 5 5
1277. – 70 c. green 5 5
1278. **205.** 80 c. myrtle 10 5
1279. – 1 p. red 20 5
1280. – 1 p. 80 emerald .. 10 8
1281. – 2 p. mauve 30 15
1282. – 3 p. blue 40 35
PAINTINGS—HORIZ. 15 c. "The Sunshade". 3 p. "The Drinker". VERT. 40 c. "The Book-seller's Wife". 50 c. "The Count of Fernan-Nunez". 60 c. "The Crockery Vendor". 70 c. "Dona Isabel Cobos de Porcel". 1 p. "The Carnival Doll". 1 p. 80, "Marianito Goya". 2 p. "The Vintage".

For similar designs see Nos. 1301/10, 1333/42, 1391/1400, 1479/88, 1495/8, 1559/68, 1627/36, 1718/ 7 1770/9 1837/46 1912/21, 1968/77, 2021/30, 2077/84, 2135/42 and 2204/11.

1958. Brussels Int. Exn.
1283. **206.** 80 c. multicoloured .. 8 5
1284. 3 p. multicoloured .. 30 20

207. Emperor Charles V (after Strigell).

1958. Emperor Charles V. 4th Death Cent. Inscr. "MDLVIII + MCMLVIII".
1287. **207.** 15 c. brown and ochre 5 5
1288. – 50 c. olive and green 5 5
1289. – 70 c. green and drab 12 8
1290. – 80 c. green and brown 8 5
1291. **207.** 1 p. red and buff .. 15 5
1292. – 1 p. 80 emer. & green 8 8
1293. – 2 p. purple and grey 25 20
1294. – 3 p. blue and brown 50 35
PORTRAITS of Charles V: 50 c., 1 p. 80, At Battle of Muhlberg (after Titian). 70 c., 2 p. (after Leoni). 80 c., 3 p. (after Titian).

208. Talgo Express and Escorial Monastery.

DESIGNS — VERT. 60 c., 2 p. Diesel-electric train on viaduct, Despenaperros Gorge. HORIZ. 80 c., 3 p. Giant steam locomotive and Castillo de La Mota.

1958. 17th Int. Railway Congress, Madrid. Inscr. "XVII CONGRESO", etc.
1295. **208.** 15 c. ochre 5 5
1296. – 60 c. plum 5 5
1297. – 80 c. green 5 5
1298. **208.** 1 p. orange 15 8
1299. – 2 p. purple 12 8
1300. – 3 p. blue 35 25

1959. Stamp Day and Velasquez Commem. Designs as T **205**. Frames in gold.
1301. 15 c. sepia 5 5
1302. 40 c. purple 5 5
1303. 50 c. olive 5 5
1304. 60 c. sepia 5 5
1305. 70 c. green 5 5
1306. 80 c. myrtle 10 5
1307. 1 p. chestnut 15 5
1308. 1 p. 80 emerald .. 8 8
1309. 2 p. purple 20 15
1310. 3 p. blue 45 30
PAINTINGS—HORIZ. 15 c. "The Drunkards". VERT. 40 c. "The Seamstress". 50 c. "The Surrender of Breda". 60 c. "The Court Dwarfs". 70 c. "Balthasar Don Carlos". 80 c. Self-portrait. 1 p. "The Coronation of the Virgin". 1 p. 80, "Aesop". 2 p. "The Forge of Vulcan". 3 p. "Menippus".

209. The Holy Cross of the Valley of the Fallen.

1959. Completion of Holy Cross Monastery.
1311. **209.** 80 c. green and sepia 10 5

210. Mazarin and Luis de Haro (after tapestry by Lebrun). **211.** Guadeloupe Monastery.

1959. Treaty of the Pyrenees. Tercent.
1312. **210.** 1 p. brown and gold 10 5

1959. Entry of Franciscan Community into Guadeloupe Monastery. 50th Anniv.
1313. **211.** 15 c. brown 5
1314. – 80 c. myrtle 15 5
1315. – 1 p. red 15 5
DESIGNS: 80 c., 1 p. Different view of the monastery.

212. "The Holy Family" (after Goya). **213.** Pass with Muleta.

1959. Christmas.
1316. **212.** 1 p. chestnut .. 15 5

1960. Bullfighting.
1317. – 15 c. brown and ochre (postage) .. 5 5
1318. – 20 c. violet and blue 5 5
1319. – 25 c. black 5 5
1320. – 30 c. sepia and bistre 5 5
1321. – 50 c. violet and sepia 10 5
1322. – 70 c. blue-grn. & brn. 10 5
1323. **213.** 80 c. emerald & bl.-grn. 5 5
1324. – 1 p. chocolate & verm. 15 5
1325. – 1 p. 40 claret & brown 5 5
1326. – 1 p. 50 green and blue 5 5
1327. – 1 p. 80 blue and green 8 5
1328. – 5 p. lake and brown 25 20

1329. – 25 c. pur. & mar. (air) 5 5
1330. – 50 c. blue & turquoise 5 5
1331. – 1 p. red & vermilion 8 5
1332. – 5 p. violet and purple 25 20
DESIGNS—HORIZ. No. 1317, Fighting bull. 1318, Rounding-up bull. 1327, Placing darts from horseback. 1330, Pass with cape. 1332, Bull-ring. VERT. 1319, Corralling bulls at Pamplona. 1320, Bull entering ring. 1419, As No. 1330 (different pass). 1420, Banderillero placing darts. 1323/6, As T **213** (different passes with muleta). 1328, Old-time bull-fighter. 1329, Village bull-ring. 1331, Dedicating the bull.

1960. Stamp Day and Murillo Commem. (painter). Designs as T **205**. Frames in gold.
1333. 25 c. violet 5 5
1334. 40 c. purple 5 5
1335. 50 c. deep olive 10 5
1336. 70 c. green 10 5
1337. 80 c. blue-green 8 5
1338. 1 p. chocolate 10 5
1339. 1 p. 50 turquoise .. 8 5
1340. 2 p. 50 crimson 12 5
1341. 3 p. blue 70 30
1342. 5 p. brown 35 20
PAINTINGS—VERT. 25 c. "The Good Shepherd". 40 c. "Rebecca and Elizer". 50 c. "The Virgin of the Rosary". 70 c. "The Immaculate Conception". 80 c. "Children with Shells". 1 p. Self-portrait. 2 p. 50, "The Dice Game". 3 p. "Children Eating". 5 p. "Children with Coins". HORIZ. 1 p. 50, "The Holy Family with Bird".

214. "Christ of Lepanto". **215.** Pelota-player.

1960. Int. Philatelic Congress and Exn. Barcelona. Inscr. "CIF".
1343. **214.** 70 c. lake & grn. (post.) 65 65
1344. – 80 c. black and sage 65 65
1345. **214.** 1 p. pur. & vermilion 65 65
1346. – 2 p. 50 slate-vio. & vio. 65 65
1347. **214.** 5 p. sepia and bistre 65 65
1348. – 10 p. sepia and ochre 65 65

1349. **215.** 1 p. blk. & verm. (air) 1·40 1·40
1350. 5 p. red & choclate .. 1·40 1·40
1351. 6 p. red & black-pur. 1·40 1·40
1352. 10 p. red and green .. 1·40 1·40
DESIGN—VERT. Nos. 1344, 1346, 1348, Church of the Holy Family, Barcelona.

216. St. John of Ribera. **217.** St. Vincent de Paul. **218.** Menendez de Aviles.

1960. Canonization of St. John of Ribera.
1353. **216.** 1 p. chestnut .. 12 5
1354. 2 p. 50 magenta .. 5 5

1960. Europa. As T **279** of Belgium but size $38\frac{1}{2} \times 22$ mm.
1355. 1 p. drab and myrtle 20 8
1356. 5 p. red and brown .. 20 12

1960. St. Vincent de Paul. Death Tercent.
1357. **217.** 25 c. violet 5 5
1358. 1 p. chestnut .. 10 5

1960. Discovery and Colonization of Florida. 4th Cent. Inscr. as in T **218**.
1359. **218.** 25 c. violet and blue 5 5
1360. – 70 c. myrtle & salmon 5 5
1361. – 80 c. green and stone 5 5
1362. – 1 p. chestnut & yellow 5 5
1363. **218.** 2 p. crimson and pink 5 5
1364. – 2 p. 50 mag. & olive 10 5
1365. – 3 p. blue and green .. 35 10
1366. – 5 p. sepia and bistre 25 15
PORTRAITS: 70 c., 2 p. 50 Hernando de Soto. 80 c., 3 p. Ponce de Leon. 1 p., 5 p. Cabeza de Vaca.

219. Running.

220. Albeniz.

221. Cloisters. **222.** "The Nativity" (after Velasquez).

1960. Sports.
1367. **219.** 25 c. brown and violet-blue (postage) .. 5 5
1368. – 40 c. orange and violet 5 5
1369. – 70 c. red and emerald 10 5
1370. – 80 c. red and green 8 5
1371. – 1 p. emer. & vermilion 25 5
1372. **219.** 1 p. 50 sepia & turq. 8 5
1373. – 2 p. emerald & purple 15 5
1374. – 2 p. 50 green & mag. 8 5
1375. – 3 p. red and blue .. 10 5
1376. – 5 p. blue and chestnut 20 15
1377. – 1 p. 25 red & choc. (air) 10 5
1378. – 1 p. 50 brown & violet 10 5
1379. – 6 p. red & blkish violet 15 15
1380. – 10 p. red and olive .. 25 20
DESIGNS—HORIZ. 40 c., 2 p. Cycling. 70 c., 2 p. 50, Football. 1 p., 5 p. Hockey. 1 p. 25, 6 p. Horse-jumping. VERT. 80 c., 3 p. Gymnastics. 1 p. 50 (air), 10 p. Pelota.

1960. Isaac Albeniz (composer). Birth Cent.
1381 **220.** 25 c. slate-violet .. 5 5
1382. 1 p. chestnut .. 8 5

1960. Samos Monastery.
1383. **221.** 80 c. bl.-grn. & turq. 5 5
1384. – 1 p. lake and chestnut 30 5
1385. – 5 p. sep. & yell.-brown 20 8
DESIGNS—VERT. 1 p. Fountain. 5 p. Portico and facade.

1960. Christmas.
1386. **222.** 1 p. chestnut .. 15 5

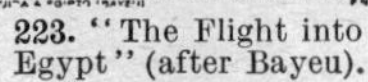

223. "The Flight into Egypt" (after Bayeu). **224.** L. F. Moratin (after Goya).

1961. World Refugee Year.
1387. **223.** 1 p. chestnut .. 12 5
1388. 5 p. chocolate .. 12 5

1961. Leandro F. Moratin (poet and dramatist). Birth Bicent.
1389. **224.** 1 p. brown-red .. 12 5
1390. 1 p. 50 turquoise .. 5 5

1961. Stamp Day and El Greco Commem. (painter). Designs as T **205**. Frames in gold.
1391. 25 c. slate-purple .. 8 5
1392. 40 c. purple 5 5
1393. 70 c. green 10 8
1394. 80 c. blue-green 10 5
1395. 1 p. maroon 80 5
1396. 1 p. 50 turquoise .. 12 5
1397. 2 p. 50 lake 15 8
1398. 3 p. blue 30 15
1399. 5 p. sepia 80 50
1400. 10 p. violet 20 15
PAINTINGS: 25 c. "St. Peter", 40 c. Part of "The Holy Family". 70 c. Part of "The Agony in the Garden". 80 c. "The Horseman". 1 p. Self-portrait. 1 p. 50, "The Baptism of Christ". 2 p. 50, "The Holy Trinity". 3 p. "Burial of the Count of Orgaz". 5 p. "The Spoliation". 10 p. "The Martyrdom of St. Maurice".

225. Velasquez. **226.** "Stamp" and "Postmark".

1961. Velasquez. Death Tercent. Inscr. "III CENTENARIO VELAZQUEZ".
1401. **225.** 80 c. blk.-grn. & ind. 12 5
1402. – 1 p. choc. & brn.-red 35 5
1403. – 2 p. 50 violet & blue .. 12 8
1404. – 10 p. green & light grn. 30 12
PAINTINGS—VERT. 1 p. "The Duke of Olivares", 2 p. 50, "Princess Margaret". HORIZ. 10 p. Part of "The Spinners".

1961. World Stamp Day.
1409. **226.** 25 c. black and red .. 5 5
1410. 1 p. red and black .. 30 5
1411. 10 p. olive-grn. & mar. 30 15

227. V. de Mella. **228.** Gen. Franco.

1961. Vazquez de Mella (politician and writer). Birth Cent.
1412. **227.** 1 p. red 20 5
1413. 2 p. 30 mauve .. 8 5

1961. National Uprising. 25th Anniv. Inscr. as in T **228**. Multicoloured.
1414. 70 c. Angel and flag .. 5 5
1415. 80 c. Straits of Gibraltar 5 5
1416. 1 p. Knight and Alcazar, Toledo 20 5
1417. 1 p. 50 Victory Arch .. 5 5
1418. 2 p. Knight crossing R. Ebro 5 5
1419. 2 p. 30 Soldier, flag and troops 8 8
1420. 2 p. 50 Shipbuilding .. 8 5
1421. 3 p. Steelworks 20 8
1422. 5 p. Map showing power stations 80 30
1423. 6 p. Irrigation (woman beside dam) 35 30
1424. 8 p. Mine 30 20
1425. 10 p. T **228** 20 20
The 5 p. is horiz. and the rest vert.

229. "Portico de la Gloria" (Cathedral of Santiago de Compostella). **230.** L. de Gongora.

1961. Council of Europe's Romanesque Art Exhibition. Inscr. as in T **229**.
1426. **229.** 25 c. violet and gold .. 5 5
1427. – 1 p. brown and gold 5 5
1428. – 2 p. purple & gold 5 5
1429. – 3 p. red, black, turq. and gold 8 8
DESIGNS: 1 p. Courtyard of Dominican Monastery, Santo Domingo de Silos. 2 p. Madonna of Irache. 3 p. "Christos Pantocrator" (from Tahull church fresco).

1961. De Gongora (poet). 400th Birth Anniv.
1430. **230.** 25 c. violet 5 5
1431. 1 p. chestnut .. 10 5

231. Doves and C.E.P.T. Emblem. **232.** Burgos Cathedral.

1961. Europa.
1432. **231.** 1 p. vermilion .. 5 5
1433. 5 p. brown 10 8

1961. 25th Anniv. of Gen. Franco as Head of State.
1434. **232.** 1 p. green and gold .. 5 5

233. S. de Belalcazar. **234.** Courtyard.

1961. Explorers and Colonizers of America (1st series).
1435. **233.** 25 c. violet and green 5 5
1436. – 70 c. green and buff .. 5 5
1437. – 80 c. green and pink .. 5 5
1438. – 1 p. blue and flesh .. 10 5
1439. **233.** 2 p. red and blue .. 30 5
1440. – 2 p. 50 purple & mve. 12 5
1441. – 3 p. blue and grey .. 20 12
1442. – 5 p. brown & yellow 30 12
PORTRAITS: 70 c., 2 p. 50, B de Lezo. 80 c., 3 p. R. de Bastidas. 1 p., 5 p. N. de Chaves.
See also Nos. 1515/22, 1587/94, 1683/90, 1738/45, 1810/17, 1877/84, 1947/51, 1997/2001 and 2054/8.

1961. Escorial.
1443. – 70 c. green and turq. 8 5
1444. **234.** 80 c. slate and green 8 5
1445. – 1 p. red and brown .. 15 5
1446. – 2 p. 50 purple & violet 12 8
1447. – 5 p. sepia and ochre .. 25 12
1448. – 6 p. purple and indigo 35 25
DESIGNS—VERT. 70 c. Patio of the Kings. 2 p. 50, Grand Staircase. 6 p. High Altar. HORIZ. 1 p. Monk's Garden. 5 p. View of Escorial.

235. King Alfonso XII Monument. **236.** Santa Maria del Naranco Church.

1961. Madrid as Capital. 400th Anniv.
1449. **235.** 25 c. pur. & grey-grn. 5 5
1450. – 1 p. brn. & yell.-brn. 12 5
1451. – 2 p. maroon and grey 10 5
1452. – 2 p. 50 violet and reddish-violet .. 8 5
1453. – 3 p. black & slate-blue 10 10
1454. – 5 p. slate-blue & brn. 25 12
DESIGNS—VERT. 1 p. King Philip II (after Pantoja. 5 p. Plaza, Madrid. HORIZ. 2 p. Town Hall, Madrid. 2 p. 50, Fountain of Cybele. 3 p. Portals of Alcala Palace.

1961. Oviedo. 1200th Anniv.
1455. **236.** 25 c. violet and green 5 5
1456. – 1 p. brown & yell.-brn. 10 5
1457. – 2 p. sepia and purple 10 5
1458. – 2 p. 50 violet & purple 10 5
1459. – 3 p. black & slate-blue 10 10
1460. – 5 p. ol.-brn. & sl.-grn. 25 12
DESIGNS: 1 p. Fruela (portrait). 2 p. Cross of the Angels. 2 p. 50, Alfonso II. 3 p. Alfonso III. 5 p. Apostles of the Holy Hall, Oviedo Cathedral.

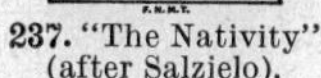

237. "The Nativity" (after Salziello). **238.** Cierva Autogyro.

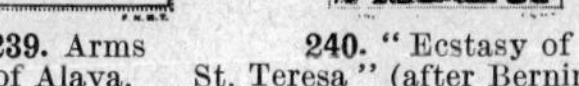

239. Arms of Alava. **240.** "Ecstasy of St. Teresa" (after Bernini).

1961. Christmas.
1461. **237.** 1 p. plum 15 5

1961. Spanish Aviation. 50th Anniv.
1462. **238.** 1 p. violet & sl.-blue.. 5 5
1463. – 2 p. green and lilac .. 10 5
1464. – 3 p. black and green.. 30 10
1465. – 5 p. purple and slate 45 30
1466. – 10 p. brown and blue 20 15
DESIGNS—HORIZ. 2 p. (Breguet 19GR) flying-boat. 3 p. Madrid–Manila flight plane "Jesus del Gran Poder". VERT. 5 p. Avro 504 k 'plane hunting wildfowl. 10 p. Madonna of Loreto (patron saint).

1962. Arms of Provincial Capitals. Mult.
1467. 5 p. T **239** 10 10
1468. 5 p. Albacete 12 10
1469. 5 p. Alicante 15 10
1470. 5 p. Almeria 15 10
1471. 5 p. Avila 15 10
1472. 5 p. Badajoz 10 10
1473. 5 p. Baleares 10 10
1474. 5 p. Barcelona 10 10
1475. 5 p. Burgos 25 10
1476. 5 p. Caceres 10 10
1477. 5 p. Cadiz 20 10
1478. 5 p. Castellon del la Plana 1·75 60
See also Nos. 1542/53, 1612/23, 1692/1703 and 1756/64.

1962. Stamp Day and Zurbaran Commem. (painter). Designs as T **205**. Frames in gold.
1479. 25 c. blackish olive .. 5 5
1480. 40 c. maroon 5 5
1481. 70 c. green 10 8
1482. 80 c. blue-green 8 5
1483. 1 p. sepia 75 5
1484. 1 p. 50 turquoise .. 10 5
1485. 2 p. 50 lake 10 5
1486. 3 p. blue 10 8
1487. 5 p. brown 25 20
1488. 10 p. olive 30 20
PAINTINGS—HORIZ. 25 c. "Martyr". VERT. 40 c. "Burial of St. Catalina". 70 c. "St. Casilda". 80 c. "Jesus crowning St. Joseph". 1 p. Self-portrait. 1 p. 50, "St. Hieronymus". 2 p. 50, "Madonna of the Grace". 3 p. Detail from "Apotheosis of St. Thomas Aquinas". 5 p. "Virgin Mary as a Child". 10 p. "The Immaculate Madonna".

1962. Teresian Reformation. 4th Cent.
1489. – 25 c. slate-violet .. 5 5
1490. **240.** 1 p. brown 5 5
1491. – 3 p. blue 30 12
DESIGNS—As T **240**: 25 c. St. Joseph's Monastery, Avila. (22×38½ mm.): 3 p. "St. Teresa of Avila" (after Velasquez).

241. Mercury. **242.** St. Benedict. **243.** El Cid (R.) Diaz de Vivar), after statue by J. Cristobal.

1962. World Stamp Day.
1492. **241.** 25 c. pink, red-purple and violet.. .. 5 5
1493. 1 p. yellow, brown and bistre-brown.. 8 5
1494. 10 p. ol., grn. & bl.-grn. 55 15

1962. Rubens Paintings. Designs as T **205** Frames in gold.
1495. 25 c. violet 10 8
1496. 1 p. brown 55 5
1497. 3 p. turquoise 55 25
1498. 10 p. green 50 20
PAINTINGS: 25 c. Ferdinand of Austria. 1 p. Self-portrait. 3 p. King Philip II. 10 p. (26×39 mm.), Duke of Lerma.

1962. Alonso Berruguete (sculptor). 4th Death Cent. Sculptures by Berruguete.
1499. **242.** 25 c. mag. & skate-blue 8 5
1500. – 80 c. green & chestnut 10 5
1501. – 1 p. brn.-red & stone 20 5
1502. – 2 p. magenta & stone 85 5
1503. – 3 p. blue and mauve 35 20
1504. – 10 p. chocolate & pink 30 15
SCULPTURES: 80 c. "The Apostle". 1 p. "St. Peter". 2 p. "St. Christopher and Child Jesus". 3 p. "Ecce Homo". 10 p. "St. Sebastian".

1962. El Cid Campeador Commem. Inscr. "EL CID".
1505. **243.** 1 p. drab & yell.-green 5 5
1506. – 2 p. black-violet & sep. 20 5
1507. – 3 p. green and blue.. 85 30
1508. – 10 p. olive-green and yellow-green .. 30 20
DESIGNS—VERT. 2 p. El Cid (equestrian statue by A. Huntingdon). HORIZ 3 p. El Cid's treasure chest. 10 p. Oath-taking ceremony at Santa Gadea.

244. Bee and Honeycomb. **245.** Throwing the Discus.

1962. Europa.
1509. **244.** 1 p. brown-red .. 5 5
1510. 5 p. green .. 15 5

1962. 2nd Spanish-American Athletic Games, Madrid.
1511. **245.** 25 c. violet-blue and pale pink 5 5
1512. – 80 c. green and yellow 10 5
1513. – 1 p. sepia and salmon 5 5
1514. – 3 p. blue & pale blue 8 10
DESIGNS: 80 c. Running. 1 p. Hurdling. 3 p. Start of sprint.

1962. Explorers and Colonizers of America (2nd series). As T **233**.
1515. 25 c. magenta & blue-grey 5 5
1516. 70 c. green & pale pink.. 15 5
1517. 80 c. green and yellow .. 12 5
1518. 1 p. chestnut & grey-green 15 5
1519. 2 p. lake and pale blue .. 40 5
1520. 2 p. 50 slate-violet and pale brown 20 5
1521. 3 p. blue and pink 50 10
1522. 5 p. brown & pale yellow 25 10
PORTRAITS: 25 c., 2 p. A. de Mendoza. 70 c., 2 p. 50, J. de Quesada. 80 c. 3 p. J. de Garay. 1 p., 5 p. P. de la Gasca.

246. U.P.A.E. Emblem. **247.** "The Annunciation (after Murillo).

1962. U.P.A.E. (Postal Union of the Americas and Spain). 50th Anniv.
1523. **246.** 1 p. sep., grn. & myrtle 8 5

1962. Mysteries of the Rosary.
1524. **247.** 25 c. choc. & vio. (post.) 5 5
1525. – 70 c. turq. & yell.-grn. 5 5
1526. – 80 c. turq. & olive .. 5 5
1527. – 1 p. sep. & yell.-green 1·50 5
1528. – 1 p. 50 grey-bl. & grn. 5 5
1529. – 2 p. sepia and violet.. 35 10
1530. – 2 p. 50 claret & mar. 10 5
1531. – 3 p. black and violet 10 5
1532. – 5 p. lake and brown.. 20 20
1533. – 8 p. black & maroon 15 15
1534. – 10 p. yell.-grn. & myrtle 20 20
1535. – 25 c. violet & slate-violet (air) .. 5 5
1536. – 1 p. olive & maroon.. 10 5
1537. – 5 p. lake & maroon.. 20 10
1538. – 10 p. yell.-grn. & grey 20 20
PAINTINGS—"Joyful Mysteries": No. 1525, "Visit of Elizabeth" (Correa). 1526, "The Birth of Christ" (Murillo). 1527, "Christ shown to the Elders" (Campana). 1528, "Jesus lost and found in the Temple" (unknown artist). "Sorrowful Mysteries": 1529, "Prayer on the Mount of Olives" (Giaquinto). 1530, "Scourging" (Cano). 1531, "The Crown of Thorns" (Tiepolo). 1532. "Carrying the cross" (El Greco). 1533, "The Crucifixion" (Murillo). "Glorious Mysteries": 1534, "The Resurrection" (Murillo). 1535, "The Ascension" (Bayeu). 1536, "The Sending-forth of the Holy Ghost" (El Greco). 1537, "The Assumption of the Virgin" (Cerezo). 1538 "The Coronation of the Virgin" (El Greco).

248. "The Nativity" (after Pedro de Mena). **249.** Campaign Emblem and Swamp.

1962. Christmas.
1539. **248.** 1 p. olive . .. 15 5

1962. Malaria Eradication.
1540. **249.** 1 p. blk., yell. & green 8 5

250. Pope John and Dome of St. Peter's. **251.** "St. Paul" (after El Greco).

1962. Ecumenical Council. Vatican City (1st issue).
1541. **250.** 1 p. slate and purple 10 5

1963. Arms of Provincial Capitals. As T **239**. Multicoloured.
1542. 5 p. Ciudad Real .. 30 10
1543. 5 p. Cordoba .. .. 1·90 60
1544. 5 p. Coruna 30 10
1545. 5 p. Cuenca 30 10
1546. 5 p. Fernando Poo .. 60 35
1547. 5 p. Gerona 10 10
1548. 5 p. Gran Canaria .. 10 10
1549. 5 p. Granada 15 10
1550. 5 p. Guadalajara .. 20 10
1551. 5 p. Guipuzcoa .. 10 10
1552. 5 p. Huelva 10 10
1553. 5 p. Huesca 10 10

1963. 1900th Anniv. of Arrival of St. Paul in Spain.
1554. **251.** 1 p. sep., ol. & brown 10 5

252. Poblet Monastery. **253.** Mail Coach.

1963. Poblet Monastery.
1555. **252.** 25 c. pur., sep. & grn. 5 5
1556. – 1 p. carmine and red 10 5
1557. – 3 p. grey-blue and violet-blue .. 25 5
1558. – 5 p. ochre and brown 45 15
DESIGNS—VERT. 1 p. Tomb. 5 p. Arch. HORIZ. 3 p. Aerial view of monastery.

1963. Stamp Day and Ribera Commem. (painter). As T **205**. Frames in gold.
1559. 25 c. violet 5 5
1560. 40 c. purple 5 5
1561. 70 c. green 10 5
1562. 80 c. bluish green .. 10 5
1563. 1 p. brown 10 5
1564. 1 p. 50 blue-green .. 10 5
1565. 2 p. 50 cerise 30 5
1566. 3 p. blue 30 5
1567. 5 p. olive-brown .. 1·00 30
1568. 10 p. brown-purple .. 40 20
PAINTINGS: 25 c. "Archimedes". 40 c. "Jacob's Flock". 70 c. "Triumph of Bacchus". 80 c. "St. Christopher". 1 p. Self-portrait. 1 p. 50, "St. Andrew". 2 p. 50, "St. John the Baptist". 3 p. "St. Onofrius". 5 p. "St. Peter". 10 p. "The Madonna".

1963. Paris Postal Conference Cent.
1569. **253.** 1 p. multicoloured .. 5 5

254. Globe.

1963. World Stamp Day.
1570. **254.** 25 c. red, blue, black and violet.. .. 5 5
1571. 1 p. vermilion, blue-grn. black and drab .. 5 5
1572. 10 p. purple, yellow, blk. & yell.-brown 20 20

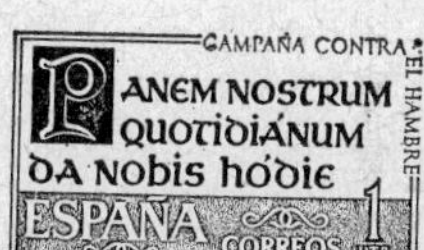

255. "Give us this day our daily bread". **256.** Pillars and Globes.

1963. Freedom from Hunger.
1573. **255.** 1 p. black, blue, red gold and green .. 5 5

1963. Spanish Cultural Institutions Congress. Multicoloured.
1574. 25 c. T **256** 5 5
1575 80 c. "Santa Maria", "Pinta" and "Nina" 5 5
1576. 1 p. Columbus 5 5

257. Civic Seals. **258.** "St. Maria of Europe".

1963. San Sebastian. 150th Anniv. Inscr. "1813–1863–1963".
1577. **257.** 25 c. blue and green.. 5 5
1578. – 80 c. red & slate-pur. 5 5
1579. – 1 p. olive-grn. & bistre 5 5
DESIGNS: 80 c. City aflame. 1 p. View of San Sebastian, 1836.

1963. Europa.
1580. **258.** 1 p. choc. & yell.-brn. 5 5
1581. 5 p. sepia and green.. 20 12

259. Arms of the Order of Mercy. **260.** Scenes from parable of the Good Samaritan.

1963. Order of Mercy. 75th Anniv. Inscr. "75 ANIV. CORONACION CANONICA".
1582. **259.** 25 c. red, gold & black 5 5
1583. – 80 c. sepia and green 5 5
1584. – 1 p. purple and indigo 8 5
1585. – 1 p. 50 olive-brown and blue 5 5
1586. – 3 p. black and violet 8 5
DESIGNS: 80 c. King Jaime I. 1 p. Our Lady of Mercy. 1 p. 50, St. Pedro Nolasco. 3 p. St. Raimundo de Penafort.

1963. Explorers and Colonizers of America (3rd series). As T **233.**

1587. 25 c. ultramarine & blue 5 5
1588. 70 c. green and salmon .. 5 5
1589. 80 c. green and cream .. 8 5
1590. 1 p. blue and salmon .. 8 5
1591. 2 p. red and blue 20 5
1592. 2 p. 50 violet and flesh .. 12 5
1593. 3 p. ultramarine and pink 25 8
1594. 5 p. brown and cream .. 30 12

PORTRAITS: 25 c., 2 p. Brother J. Serra. 70 c., 2 p. 50, Vasco Nunez de Balboa. 80 c., 3 p. J. de Galvez. 1 p., 5 p. D. Garcia de Paredes.

1963. Red Cross Cent.

1595. **260.** 1 p. violet, red & gold 5 5

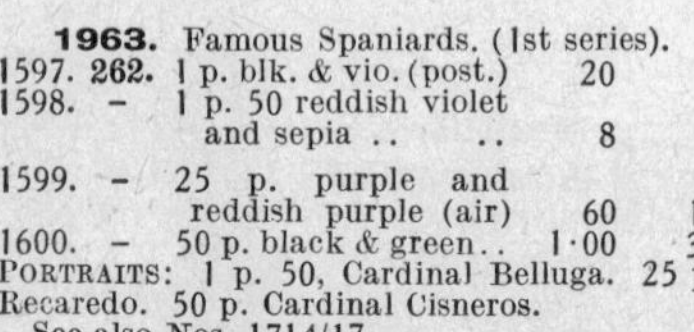

261. "The Nativity" (after sculpture by Berruguete). **262.** Fr. Raimundo Lulio.

1963. Christmas.

1596. **261.** 1 p. bronze-green .. 5 5

1963. Famous Spaniards. (1st series).

1597. **262.** 1 p. blk. & vio. (post.) 20 5
1598. – 1 p. 50 reddish violet and sepia 8 5
1599. – 25 p. purple and reddish purple (air) 60 15
1600. – 50 p. black & green .. 1·00 35

PORTRAITS: 1 p. 50, Cardinal Belluga. 25 p. Recaredo. 50 p. Cardinal Cisneros.

See also Nos. 1714/17.

263. Pope Paul and Dome of St. Peter's.

1963. Ecumenical Council, Vatican City. (2nd issue).

1601. **263.** 1 p. black & blue-grn. 5 5

264. Alcazar de Segovia. **265.** Santa Maria Monastery.

1964. Tourist Series.

1602. – 40 c. choc., blue & grn. 5 5
1603. – 50 c. sepia and indigo 5 5
1604. – 70 c. slate-blue & grn. 5 5
1605. – 70 c. chocolate & lilac 5 5
1606. – 80 c. black and blue .. 10 5
1607. **264.** 1 p. lilac and violet .. 5 5
1608. – 1 p. red and maroon 5 5
1609. – 1 p. black and green 5 5
1610. – 1 p. red and purple .. 5 5
1611. – 1 p. 50 chocolate, green and indigo .. 5 5

DESIGNS—HORIZ. No. 1602, Potes. 1604, Crypt of St. Isidore (Leon). 1608, Lion Court of the Alhambra (Granada). 1611, Gerona. VERT. 1603, Leon Cathedral. 1605, Costa Brava. 1606, "Christ of the Lanterns" (Cordoba). 1609, Drach Caves (Majorca). 1610, Mosque (Cordoba).

See also Nos. 1704/13, 1786/95, 1798/1805, 1860/6, 1867/74, 1923/7, 1938/42, 1985/9, 1993/6, 2035/9, 2040/5, 2151/55, 2187/91, 2311/6 and 2378/83.

1964. Arms of Provincial Capitals. As T **239.** Multicoloured.

1612. 5 p. Ifni 10 8
1613. 5 p. Jaen 10 8
1614. 5 p. Leon 10 8
1615. 5 p. Lerida 10 8
1616. 5 p. Logrono 10 8
1617. 5 p. Lugo 10 8
1618. 5 p. Madrid 12 8
1619. 5 p. Malaga 10 8
1620. 5 p. Murcia 12 8
1621. 5 p. Navarra 10 8
1622. 5 p. Orense 10 8
1623. 5 p. Oviedo 10 8

1964. Monastery of Santa Maria, Huerta.

1624. – 1 p. bronze and green 5 5
1625. – 2 p. sepia, black & turq. 5 5
1626. **265.** 5 p. slate & slate-vio. 20 12

DESIGNS—VERT. 1 p. Great Hall. 2 p. Cloisters.

1964. Stamp Day and Sorolla Commem. (painter). As T **205.** Frames in gold.

1627. 25 c. violet 5 5
1628. 40 c. purple 5 5
1629. 70 c. yellow-green .. 5 5
1630. 80 c. blue-green 5 5
1631. 1 p. brown 5 5
1632. 1 p. 50 greenish blue .. 5 5
1633. 2 p. 50 magenta 8 5
1634. 3 p. grey-blue 10 5
1635. 5 p. chocolate 30 25
1636. 10 p. green 20 12

PAINTINGS—VERT. 25 c. "The Earthen Jar". 70 c. "La Mancha Types". 80 c. "Valencian Fisherwoman". 1 p. Self-portrait. 5 p. "Pulling the Boat". 10 p. "Valencian Couple on Horse". HORIZ. 40 c. "Castillan Oxherd". 1 p. 50, "The Cattlepen". 2 p. 50, "And people say fish is dear" (fish market). 3 p. "Children on the Beach".

266. "25 Years of Peace".

1964. End of Spanish Civil War. 25th Anniv

1637. **266.** 25 c. gold, green and blk. 5 5
1638. – 30 c. salmon, blue and black-green 5 5
1639. – 40 c. black and gold 5 5
1640. – 50 c. blk., red, bl. & gold 5 5
1641. – 70 c. multicoloured .. 5 5
1642. – 80 c. multicoloured .. 5 5
1643. – 1 p. green, yellow, gold and black .. 10 5
1644. – 1 p. 50 olive, red & blue 5 5
1645. – 2 p. red, black, gold and blue 8 5
1646. – 2 p. 50 gold, violet-blue, blue and black 8 5
1647. – 3 p. red, bl., blk. & gold 35 20
1648. – 5 p. red, green & gold 20 5
1649. – 6 p. multicoloured .. 25 10
1650. – 10 p. multicoloured .. 25 15

DESIGNS—VERT. 30 c. Athletes ("Sport"). 50 c. Apartment-houses ("National Housing Plan"). 1 p. Graph and symbols ("Economic Development"). 1 p. 50, Rocks and tower ("Construction"). 2 p. 50, Wheatear and dam ("Irrigation"). 5 p. "Tree of Learning" ("Scientific Research"). 10 p. Gen. Franco. HORIZ. 40 c. T.V. screen and symbols ("Radio and T.V."). 70 c. Wheatears, tractor and landscape ("Agriculture"). 80 c. Tree and forests ("Reafforestation"). 2 p. Forms of transport ("Transport and Communications"). 3 p. Pylon and part of dial ("Electrification"). 6 p. Ancient buildings ("Tourism").

267. Spanish Pavilion at Fair. **268.** 6 c. Stamp of 1850 and Globe.

1964. New York World's Fair.

1651. **267.** 1 p. green & blue-grn. 25 5
1652. – 1 p. 50 chocolate & red 5 5
1653. – 2 p. 50 grey-green and grey-blue 10 5
1654. – 5 p. red 20 15
1655. – 50 p. blue & grey-blue 85 25

DESIGNS—VERT. 1 p. 50, Bullfighting. 2 p. 50, Castillo de la Mota. 5 p. Spanish dancing. 50 p. Pelota.

1964. World Stamp Day.

1656. **268.** 25 c. crimson & purple 5 5
1657. 1 p. green & grey-blue 12 5
1658. 10 p. orange and red 30 12

269. Macarena Virgin. **270.** Medieval Ship.

1964. Canonical Coronation of Macarena Virgin.

1659. **269.** 1 p. green & yell-grn. 5 5

1964. Spanish Navy Commem.

1660. **270.** 15 c. slate-vio. & pur. 5 5
1661. – 25 c. green and orange 5 5
1662. – 40 c. grey-blue & blue 5 5
1663. – 50 c. green and slate 5 5
1664. – 70 c. violet & indigo .. 5 5
1665. – 80 c. ultram. & green 5 5
1666. – 1 p. purple & chestnut 5 5
1667. – 1 p. 50 sepia and red 5 5
1668. – 2 p. black and green .. 30 5
1669. – 2 p. 50 rose and violet 5 5
1670. – 3 p. indigo and brown 5 5
1671. – 5 p. indigo and green 35 25
1672. – 6 p. violet & turquoise 25 20
1673. – 10 p. red and orange 20 12

SHIPS—VERT. 25 c. Carrack. 1 p. "Santisima Trinidad". 1 p. 50, Corvette "Atrevida" HORIZ. 40 c. "Santa Maria". 50 c. Galley. 70 c. Galleon. 80 c. Xebec. 2 p. "Isabel II". 2 p. 50, Frigate "Numancia". 3 p. Destroyer. 5 p. Isaac Peral's submarine. 6 p. Cruiser "Baleares". 10 p. Training-ship "Juan Sebastian Elcano".

271. Europa "Flower". **272.** "The Virgin of the Castle".

1964. Europa.

1674. **271.** 1 p. ochre, red & green 5 5
1675. 5 p. blue, purple & grn. 20 12

1964. Reconquest of Jerez. 700th Anniv.

1676. **272.** 25 c. brown and buff 5 5
1677. 1 p. indigo and grey .. 5 5

273. Putting the Shot. **274.** "Adoration of the Shepherds" (after Zurbaran).

1964. Olympic Games, Tokyo and Innsbruck Olympic rings in gold.

1678. **273.** 25 c. indigo & orange 5 5
1679. – 80 c. indigo and green 5 5
1680. – 1 p. blue & light blue 5 5
1681. – 3 p. indigo and buff .. 10 5
1682. – 5 p. violet-blue and reddish violet .. 15 8

DESIGNS: 80 c. Long-jumping. 1 p. Skiing (Slalom). 3 p. Judo. 5 p. Throwing the discus.

1964. Explorers and Colonizers of America (4th series). As T **233.** Inscr. "1964" at foot.

1683. 25 c. violet and pale blue 5 5
1684. 70 c. olive and pink .. 5 5
1685. 80 c. green and buff .. 10 8
1686. 1 p. violet and buff .. 8 5
1687. 2 p. olive and blue .. 8 5
1688. 2 p. 50 maroon & turq.-grn. 5 5
1689. 3 p. indigo and grey .. 20 10
1690. 5 p. brown and cream .. 20 15

PORTRAITS: 25 c., 2 p. D. de Almagro. 70 c., 2 p. 50, F. de Toledo. 80 c., 3 p. T. de Mogrovejo. 1 p., 5 p. F. Pizarro.

1964. Christmas.

1691. **274.** 1 p. brown 5 5

1965. Arms of Provincial Capitals. As T **239.** Multicoloured.

1692. 5 p. Palencia 10 8
1693. 5 p. Pontevedra 10 8
1694. 5 p. Rio Muni 10 8
1695. 5 p. Sahara 10 8
1696. 5 p. Salamanca 10 8
1697. 5 p. Santander 10 8
1698. 5 p. Segovia 10 8
1699. 5 p. Seville 10 8
1700. 5 p. Soria 10 8
1701. 5 p. Tarragona 10 8
1702. 5 p. Tenerife 10 8
1703. 5 p. Teruel 10 8

1965. Tourist Series. As T **264.**

1704. 25 c. black & ultramarine 5 5
1705. 30 c. purple-brown & turq. 5 5
1706. 50 c. purple and crimson 5 5
1707. 70 c. indigo and blue .. 5 5
1708. 80 c. purple and magenta 5 5
1709. 1 p. maroon, red and sepia 5 5
1710. 2 p. 50 purple and brown 5 5
1711. 2 p. 50 olive and blue .. 5 5
1712. 3 p. maroon and purple .. 5 5
1713. 6 p. violet and slate .. 10 5

DESIGNS—VERT. 25 c. Columbus Monument, Barcelona. 30 c. Santa Maria Church, Burgos. 50 c. Synagogue of St. Maria la Blanca, Toledo. 80 c. Seville Cathedral. 1 p. Cudillero Port. 2 p. 50 (No. 1710), Burgos Cathedral (interior). 3 p. Bridge at Cambados (Pontevedra). 6 p. Ceiling, Lonja (Valencia). HORIZ. 70 c. Zamora. 2 p. 50 (No. 1711), Mogrovejo (Santander).

1965. Famous Spaniards (2nd series). As T **262.**

1714. 25 c. sepia and bluish green 5 5
1715. 70 c. indigo and blue .. 10 5
1716. 2 p. 50 sepia and bronze .. 10 5
1717. 5 p. bronze and green .. 15 5

PORTRAITS: 25 c. Donoso Cortes. 70 c. King Alfonso X (the Saint). 2 p. 50, G. M. de Jovellanos. 5 p. St. Dominic de Guzman.

1965. Stamp Day and J. Romero de Torres Commem. Designs as T **205.** Frames in gold.

1718. 25 c. purple 5 5
1719. 40 c. reddish purple .. 5 5
1720. 70 c. green 5 5
1721. 80 c. bluish green .. 5 5
1722. 1 p. red-brown 8 5
1723. 1 p. 50 turquoise .. 5 5
1724. 2 p. 50 magenta 5 5
1725. 3 p. blue 8 5
1726. 5 p. brown 10 8
1727. 10 p. green 20 12

PAINTINGS (by J. Romero de Torres): 25 c. "Girl with Jar". 40 c. "The Song". 70 c. "The Virgin of the Lanterns". 80 c. "Girl with Guitar". 1 p. Self-portrait. 1 p. 50, "Poem of Cordoba". 2 p. 50, "Marta and Maria". 3 p. "Poem of Cordoba" (different). 5 p. "A Little Charcoal-maker". 10 p. "Long Live the Hair!".

275. Bulls and Stamps. **276.** I.T.U. Emblem and Symbols.

1965. World Stamp Day.

1728. **275.** 25 c. multicoloured .. 5 5
1729. 1 p. multicoloured .. 8 5
1730. 10 p. multicoloured .. 25 10

1965. I.T.U. Cent.

1731. **276.** 1 p. red, black & pink 5 5

277. Pilgrim. **278.** Spanish Knight and Banners.

1965. Holy Year of Santiago de Compostella. Multicoloured.

1732. 1 p. Type **277** 5 5
1733. 2 p. Pilgrim (profile) .. 5 5

1965. Florida Settlement. 400th Anniv.

1734. **278.** 3 p. black, red & yell. 12 5

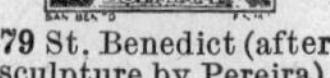

279 St. Benedict (after sculpture by Pereira). **280.** Sports Palace, Madrid.

1965. Europa.

1735. **279.** 1 p. green & emerald 5 5
1736. 5 p. violet and purple 10 8

1965. Int. Olympic Committee Meeting, Madrid.

1737. **280.** 1 p. brown, gold & grey 5 5

1965. Explorers and Colonisers of America (5th issue). As T **233**. Inscr. "1965" at foot.

1738. 25 c. violet and green .. 5 5
1739. 70 c. brown and pink .. 5 5
1740. 80 c. green and cream .. 5 5
1741. 1 p. violet and buff .. 5 5
1742. 2 p. brown and blue .. 5 5
1743. 2 p. 50 purple & turquoise 5 5
1744. 3 p. blue and grey .. 12 5
1745. 5 p. brown and yellow .. 15 5

PORTRAITS: 25 c., 2 p. Don Fadrique de Toledo. 70 c., 2 p. 50, Padre Jose de Anchieta. 80 c., 3 p. Francisco de Orellana. 1 p., 5 p. St. Luis Beltran.

281. Cloisters.

282. Spanish 1 r. Stamp of 1865.

1965. Yuste Monastery.

1746. **281.** 1 p. blue and sepia .. 5 5
1747. – 2 p. sepia and brown 8 5
1748. – 5 p. green and blue.. 12 5

DESIGNS—VERT. 2 p. Charles V room. HORIZ. 5 p. Courtyard.

1965. Spanish Perforated Stamps. Cent.

1749. **282.** 80 c. green and bronze 5 5
1750. – 1 p. brown and purple 5 5
1751. – 5 p. brown and sepia 12 12

DESIGNS: 1 p. 1865 19 c. stamp. 5 p. 1865 2 r. stamp.

283. "The Nativity" (after Mayno).

1965. Christmas.

1752. **283.** 1 p. green and blue.. 5 5

284. Madonna of Antipolo. **285.** Globe. **286.** Alvaro de Bazam.

1965. Christianity in the Philippines. 400th Anniv.

1753. **284.** 1 p.brown, blk. & buff 5 5
1754. – 3 p. blue and grey .. 8 5

DESIGN: 3 p. Father Urdaneta.

1965. 21st Ecumenical Council, Vatican City.

1755. **285.** 1 p. multicoloured .. 5 5

1966. Arms of Provincial Capitals. As T **239**. Multicoloured.

1756. 5 p. Toledo 10 5
1757. 5 p. Valencia 10 5
1758. 5 p. Valladolid 10 5
1759. 5 p. Vizcaya 10 5
1760. 5 p. Zamora 10 5
1761. 5 p. Zaragoza 10 5
1762. 5 p. Ceuta 10 5
1763. 5 p. Melilla 10 5
1764. 10 p. Spain (26 × 38½ mm.) 20 10

1966. Celebrities. (1st series).

1765. **286.** 25 c. black and blue (postage) 5 5
1766. – 2 p. violet and purple 10 5
1767. – 25 p. bronze & green (air) 55 15
1768. – 50 p. grey-blue & blue 1·25 25

PORTRAITS: 2 p. Daza de Valdes. 25 p. Seneca. 50 p. St. Damaso.

See also Nos. 1849/52.

287. Exhibition Emblem.

288. Luno Church.

1966. Graphic Arts Exn., "Graphspack", Barcelona.

1769. **287.** 1 p. green, blue & red 5 5

1966. Stamp Day and J. M. Sert Commem. Designs as T **205**. Frames in gold.

1770. 25 c. violet 5 5
1771. 40 c. purple 5 5
1772. 70 c. green 5 5
1773. 80 c. bronze 5 5
1774. 1 p. brown 5 5
1775. 1 p. 50 blue 5 5
1776. 2 p. 50 red 5 5
1777. 3 p. blue 10 8
1778. 5 p. sepia 15 8
1779. 10 p. slate-green .. 20 12

PAINTINGS (by J. M. Sert)—VERT. 25 c. "The Magic Ball". 70 c. "Christ Addressing the Disciples". 80 c. "The Balloonists". 1 p. Self-portrait. 1 p. 50, "Audacity". 2 p. 50, "Justice". 3 p. "Jacob's Struggle with the Angel". 5 p. "The Five Parts of the World". 10 p. "St. Peter and St. Paul". HORIZ. 40 c. "Memories of Toledo".

1966. Guernica. 600th Anniv. Multicoloured.

1780. 80 c. Type **288** 5 5
1781. 1 p. Arms of Guernica .. 5 5
1782. 3 p. Tree of Guernica .. 5 5

289. Postmarked 6 cuartos Stamp of 1850.

1966. World Stamp Day.

1783. **289.** 25 c. multicoloured.. 5 5
1784. – 1 p. multicoloured .. 5 5
1785. – 10 p. multicoloured.. 20 10

DESIGNS—POSTMARKED STAMPS: 1 p. 5 r. of 1850. 10 p. 10 r. of 1850.

1966. Tourist Series. As T **264**.

1786. 10 c. emerald and green 5 5
1787. 15 c. bistre and green .. 5 5
1788. 40 c. brown and chestnut 5 5
1789. 50 c. maroon and red .. 5 5
1790. 80 c. purple and mauve.. 5 5
1791. 1 p. turquoise and blue.. 5 5
1792. 1 p. 50 black and blue .. 5 5
1793. 2 p. brown and blue .. 5 5
1794. 3 p. brown and blue .. 5 5
1795. 10 p. blue and turquoise 20 10

DESIGNS—VERT. 10 c. Bohi waterfalls (Lerida). 40 c. Sigena monastery (Huesca). 50 c. Santo Domingo Church (Soria). 80 c. Golden Tower (Seville). 1 p. El Teide (Canaries). 10 p. Church of St. Gregory (Valladolid). HORIZ. 15 c. Torla (Huesca). 1 p. 50, Cathedral (Guadalupe). 2 p. University (Alcala de Henares). 3 p. La Seo Cathedral (Lerida).

290. Tree and Globe. **291.** Crown and Anchor.

1966. World Forestry Congress.

1796. **290.** 1 p. grn., choc. & brn. 5 5

1966. Naval Week, Barcelona.

1797. **291.** 1 p. blue and grey .. 5 5

292. Butron Castle (Vizcaya).

294. "Europa and the Bull".

293. Don Quixote, Dulcinea and Aldonza Lorenzo.

295. Horseman in the Sky.

1966. Spanish Castles (1st series).

1798. – 10 c. sepia and blue.. 5 5
1799. – 25 c. purple and violet 5 5
1800. – 40 c. green & turquoise 5 5
1801. – 50 c. blue and indigo 5 5
1802. – 70 c. blue & ultram... 5 5
1803. **292.** 80 c. green and violet 5 5
1804. – 1 p. olive and brown 5 5
1805. – 3 p. purple and red.. 5 5

CASTLES—HORIZ. 10 c. Guadamur (Toledo) 25 c. Alcazar (Segovia). 40 c. La Mota (Medina del Campo). 50 c. Olite (Navarra). 70 c. Monteagudo (Murcia). 1 p. Manzanares (Madrid). VERT. 3 p. Almansa (Albacete).

See also Nos. 1867/74, 1938/42, 1985/9, 2035/9 and 2151/5.

1966. 4th World Psychiatric Congress, Madrid.

1806. **293.** 1 p. 50 multicoloured 5 5

1966. Europa.

1807. **294.** 1 p. multicoloured .. 5 5
1808. 5 p. multicoloured .. 10 5

1966. 17th Int. Astronautics Federation Congress, Madrid.

1899. **295.** 1 p. 50 red, blk. & blue 5 5

1966. Explorers and Colonisers of America (6th series). As T **233**. Inscr. "1966" at foot.

1810. 30 c. bistre and brown.. 5 5
1811. 50 c. red and green .. 5 5
1812. 1 p. violet and blue .. 5 5
1813. 1 p. 20 slate and grey .. 5 5
1814. 1 p. 50 myrtle and green 5 5
1815. 3 p. blue 5 5
1816. 3 p. 50 violet and lilac .. 8 5
1817. 6 p. brown and buff .. 12 8

DESIGNS: 30 c. A. de Mendoza. 50 c. Title page of Dominican Fathers' "Christian Doctrine". 1 p. J. A. Manso de Velasco. 1 p. 20, Coins of Lima Mint (1699). 1 p. 50, M. de Castro y Padilla. 3 p. Oruro Convent. 3 p. 50, M. de Amat. 6 p. Inca postal runner.

296. R. del Valle Inclan.

297. Monastery Facade.

1966. Spanish Writers.

1818. **296.** 1 p. 50 green & black 5 5
1819. – 3 p. violet and black 5 5
1820. – 6 p. blue and black.. 12 5

WRITERS: 3 p. Carlos Arniches. 6 p. J. Benavente y Martinez.

1966. St. Mary's Carthusian Monastery, Jerez.

1821. **297.** 1 p. indigo and blue.. 5 5
1822. – 2 p. apple and green.. 5 5
1823. – 5 p. plum and purple 15 5

DESIGNS—HORIZ. 2 p. Cloisters. 5 p. Gateway.

298. "The Nativity" (after P. Duque Cornejo). **299.** Alava Costume.

1966. Christmas.

1824. **298.** 1 p. 50 multicoloured 5 5

1967. Provincial Costumes. Multicoloured.

1825. 6 p. Type **299** 12 5
1826. 6 p. Albacete 12 5
1827. 6 p. Alicante 12 5
1828. 6 p. Almeria 12 5
1829. 6 p. Avila 12 5
1830. 6 p. Badajoz 12 5
1831. 6 p. Baleares 12 5
1832. 6 p. Barcelona 12 5
1833. 6 p. Burgos 12 5
1834. 6 p. Caceres 12 5
1835. 6 p. Cadiz 12 5
1836. 6 p. Castellon de la Plana 12 5

See also Nos. 1897/1908, 1956/67, 2007/18 and 2072/6.

300. Archers.

ILLUSTRATIONS
British Commonwealth and all overprints and surcharges are FULL SIZE. Foreign Countries have been reduced to ¾-LINEAR.

1967. Stamp Day. Wall Paintings. Multicoloured.

1837. 40 c. Type **300**.. .. 5 5
1838. 50 c. Boar-hunting .. 5 5
1839. 1 p. Trees (vert.) .. 5 5
1840. 1 p. 20 Bison 5 5
1841. 1 p. 50 Hands 5 5
1842. 2 p. Hunter (vert.) .. 5 5
1843. 2 p. 50 Deer (vert.) .. 5 5
1844. 3 p. 50 Hunters .. 10 8
1845. 4 p. Chamois-hunters (vt.) 10 5
1846. 6 p. Deer-hunter (vert.).. 15 5

301. Cathedral, Palma de Mallorca, and Union Emblem.

1967. Inter-Parliamentary Union Congress, Palma de Mallorca.

1847. **301.** 1 p. 50 green .. 5 5

302. Rontgen and Ray Apparatus.

1967. Radiology Congress, Barcelona.

1848. **302.** 1 p. 50 green .. 5 5

1967. Celebrities (2nd series). As T **286**.

1849. 1 p. 20 violet and purple 5 5
1850. 3 p. 50 purple .. 5 5
1851. 4 p. sepia and brown .. 8 5
1852. 25 p. grey and blue .. 50 15

PORTRAITS: 1 p. 20, Averroes (physician and philosopher). 3 p. 50, Acosta (poet). 4 p. Maimonides (physician and philosopher). 25 p. Andres Laguna (physician).

303. Cogwheels.

305. Spanish 5 r. Stamp of 1850.

304. Fair Building.

1967. Europa.

1853. **303.** 1 p. 50 grn., brn. & red 5 5
1854. 6 p. violet, blue & mar. 12 8

1967. Valencia Int. Samples Fair. 50th Anniv.

1855. **304.** 1 p. 50 green .. 5 5

1967. World Stamp Day.

1856. **305.** 40 c. chest., bl. & blk. 5 5
1857. – 1 p. 50 lake, black and green 5 5
1858. – 6 p. blue, red & black 12 5

DESIGNS: 1 p. 50 Spanish 12 c. stamp of 1850 with crowned "M" (Madrid) postmark. 6 p. Spanish 6 r. stamp of 1850 with "I.R." postmark.

See also Nos. 1927/8, 1980/1, 2032, 2091, 2150 and 2185.

306. Sleeping Vagrant and "Guardian Angel".

307. I.T.Y. Emblem.

1967. National Day for Caritas Welfare Organisation.

1859. **306.** 1 p. 50 multicoloured 5 5

1967. Tourist Series and Int. Tourist Year.

1860. – 10 c. black and blue 5 5
1861. – 1 p. black and blue .. 5 5
1862. – 1 p. 50 black & brown 5 5
1863. – 2 p. 50 blue & turquoise 5 5
1864. **307.** 3 p. 50 ultram. & pur. 8 5
1865. – 5 p. bronze and green 10 5
1866. – 6 p. purple & mauve 15 5

DESIGNS: 10 c. Betanzos Church (Corunna). 1 p. St. Miguel's Tower (Palencia). 1 p. 50, Castellers (acrobats). 2 p. 50, Columbus Monument (Huelva). 5 p. "Enchanted City" (Cuenca). 6 p. Church of our Lady, Sanlucar (Cadiz).

1967. Spanish Castles (2nd series). As T **292.**
1867. 50 c. brown and grey .. 5 5
1868. 1 p. violet and grey .. 5 5
1869. 1 p. 50 green and blue .. 5 5
1870. 2 p. brown and vermilion 5 5
1871. 2 p. 50 brown and green 5 5
1872. 5 p. blue and purple .. 15 5
1873. 6 p. sepia and brown .. 20 5
1874. 10 p. green and blue .. 20 10
CASTLES—HORIZ. 50 c. Balsareny (Barcelona). 1 p. Jarandilla (Caceres). 1 p. 50 Almodovar (Cordoba). 2 p. 50, Peniscola (Castellon). 5 p. Coca (Segovia). 6 p. Loarre (Huesca). 10 p. Belmonte (Cuenca). VERT. 2 p. Ponferrada (Leon).

308. Globe and Snow Crystal. **309.** Map of the Americas, Spain and the Philippines.

1967. 12th Int. Refrigeration Congress, Madrid.
1875. **308.** 1 p. 50 blue 5 5

1967. 4th Spanish Portuguese, American and Philippine Municipalities Congress, Barcelona.
1876. **309.** 1 p. 50 violet.. .. 5 5

1967. Explorers and Colonisers of America (7th series). As T **233.** Inscr. "1967" at foot.
1877. 40 c. olive and orange .. 5 5
1878. 50 c. agate and grey .. 5 5
1879. 1 p. magenta and blue .. 5 5
1880. 1 p. 20 green and cream.. 5 5
1881. 1 p. 50 green and flesh .. 5 5
1882. 3 p. violet and buff .. 8 5
1883. 3 p. 50 blue and pink .. 8 5
1884. 6 p. chestnut 12 5
DESIGNS—VERT. 40 c. J. Francisco de la Bodega y Quadra. 50 c. Map of Nutka coast. 1 p. F. A. Mourelle. 1 f. 50, E. J. Martinez. 3 p. 50, Cayetano Valdes y Florez. HORIZ. 1 p. 20, View of Nutka. 3 p. Map of Californian coast. 6 p. San Elias, Alaska.

310. Ploughing with Oxen. **311.** Main Portal, Veruela Monastery.

1967. Caceres. Bimillenary. Multicoloured.
1885. 1 p. 50 Statue and archway 5 5
1886. 3 p. 50 Type **310** .. 8 5
1887. 6 p. Roman coins .. 15 5
Nos. 1885 and 1887 are vert.

1967. Centennial Annivs. Portraits as T **296.**
1888. 1 p. 20 brown and black 5 5
1889. 1 p. 50 green and black.. 5 5
1890. 3 p. 50 violet and black 8 5
1891. 6 p. blue and black .. 12 5
DESIGNS: 1 p. 20, P. de S. Jose Bethencourt. 1 p. 50, Enrique Granados. 3 p. 50, Ruben Dario. 6 p. San Ildefonso.

1967. Veruela Monastery.
1892. **311.** 1 p. 50 blue & ultram. 5 5
1893. – 3 p. 50 grey and green 8 5
1894. – 6 p. purple and brown 15 5
DESIGNS—HORIZ. 3 p. 50, Aerial view of Monastery. 6 p. Cloisters.

312. "The Canonization of San Jose de Calasanz" (from painting by Goya). **313.** "The Nativity" (Salzillo).

1967. Canonization of San Jose de Calasanz. Bicent.
1895. **312.** 1 p. 50 multicoloured 5 5

1967. Christmas.
1896. **313.** 1 p. 50 multicoloured 5 5

1968. Provincial Costumes. As T **299.** Multicoloured.
1897. 6 p. Ciudad Real .. 12 5
1898. 6 p. Cordoba 12 5
1899. 6 p. Coruna 12 5
1900. 6 p. Cuenca 12 5
1901. 6 p. Fernando Poo .. 12 5
1902. 6 p. Gerona 12 5
1903. 6 p. Las Palmas (Gran Canaria) 12 5
1904. 6 p. Granada 12 5
1905. 6 p. Guadalajara .. 12 5
1906. 6 p. Guipuzcoa 12 5
1907. 6 p. Huelva 12 5
1908. 6 p. Huesca 12 5

314. Slalom.

1968. Winter Olympic Games, Grenoble. Multicoloured.
1909. 1 p. 50 Type **314** .. 5 5
1910. 3 p. 50 Bob-sleighing (vert.) 8 5
1911. 6 p. Ice-hockey 15 5

1968. Stamp Day and Fortuny Commem. As T **205.** Frames in gold.
1912. 40 c. purple 5 5
1913. 50 c. green 5 5
1914. 1 p. brown 5 5
1915. 1 p. 20 violet 5 5
1916. 1 p. 50 green 5 5
1917. 2 p. chestnut 5 5
1918. 2 p. 50 red 5 5
1919. 3 p. 50 brown 8 8
1920. 4 p. olive 8 5
1921. 6 p. blue 12 5
Fortuny Paintings—HORIZ. 40 c. "The Vicarage". 1 p. 20, "The Print Collector". 6 p. "Queen Christina". VERT. 50 c. "Fantasia". 1 p. "Idyll". 1 p. 50, Self-portrait. 2 p. "Old Man Naked to the Sun". 2 p. 50, "Typical Calabrian". 3 p. 50, "Portrait of Lady". 4 p. "Battle of Tetuan".

315. Beatriz Galindo.

1968. Famous Spanish Women. With background scenes.
1922. **315.** 1 p. 20 brown and bistre 5 5
1923. 1 p. 50 blue & turquoise 5 5
1924. 3 p. 50 violet .. 10 5
1925. – 6 p. black and blue.. 20 5
WOMEN: 1 p. 50, Augustina de Aragon. 3 p. 50, Maria Pacheco. 6 p. Rosalia de Castro.

316. Europa "Key".

1968. Europa.
1926. **316.** 3 p. 50 gold, brn. & blue 10 5

1968. World Stamp Day. As T **305,** but stamps and postmarks changed. Inscr. "1968".
1927. 1 p. 50 black, brown & blue 5 5
1928. 3 p. 50 blue, black & grn. 8 5
DESIGNS: 1 p. 50, Spanish 6 c. stamp of 1850 with Puebla (Galicia) postmark. 3 p. 50, Spanish 6 r. stamp of 1850 with Serena postmark.

317. Emperor Galba's Coin. **318.** Human Rights Emblem.

1968. VII Roman Legion and Foundation of Leon. 1900th Anniv.
1929. – 1 p. brown and purple 5 5
1930. – 1 p. 50 brown & yellow 5 5
1931. **317.** 3 p. 50 green & ochre 10 5
DESIGNS—VERT. 1 p. Inscribed tile and town map of Leon (26×47 mm.). 1 p. 50, Legionary with standard (statue).

1968. Human Rights Year.
1932. **318.** 3 p. 50 red, grn. & blue 10 5

1968. Tourist Series. As T **264.**
1933. 50 c. brown 5 5
1934. 1 p. 20 green 5 5
1935. 1 p. 50 blue and green .. 5 5
1936. 2 p. purple 8 5
1937. 3 p. 50 purple 10 5
DESIGNS—VERT. 50 c. Count Benavente's Palace, Baeza. 1 p. 50, Sepulchre, St. Vincent's Church, Avila. 3 p. 50, Main portal, Church of Santa Maria, Sanguesa (Navarra). HORIZ. 1 p. 20, View of Salamanca. 2 p. "The King's Page" (statue), Siguenza Cathedral.

1968 Spanish Castles (3rd Series). As T **292.**
1938. 40 c. sepia and blue .. 5 5
1939. 1 p. 20 purple 5 5
1940. 1 p. 50 black and bistre 5 5
1941. 2 p. 50 bronze & green .. 5 5
1942. 6 p. turquoise and blue .. 15 5
DESIGNS—HORIZ. 40 c. Escalona. 1 p. 20, Fuensaldana. 1 p. 50, Penafiel. 2 p. 50, Villas obroso. VERT. 6 p. Frias.

319. Rifle-shooting. **320.** Monastery Building.

1968. Olympic Games, Mexico. Multicoloured.
1943. 1 p. Type **319** 5 5
1944. 1 p. 50 Horse-jumping .. 8 5
1945. 3 p. 50 Cycling .. 10 5
1946. 6 p. Sailing 20 5
The 6 p. is vert.

1968. Explorers and Colonisers of America (8th Series). As T **233** but inscr. "1968" at foot.
1947. 40 c. blue 5 5
1948. 1 p. purple and blue .. 5 5
1949. 1 p. 50 green and flesh 5 5
1950. 3 p. 50 blue and mauve 12 5
1951. 6 p. brown and yellow .. 20 5
DESIGNS—VERT. 40 c. Map of Orinoco missions. 1 p. Diego de Losada (founder of Caracas). 1 p. 50 Arms of the Losadas. 3 p. 50, Diego de Henares (builder of Caracas). HORIZ. 6 p. Old plan of Santiago de Leon de Caracas.

1968. Santa Maria del Parral Monastery.
1952. **320.** 1 p. 50 lilac and blue 5 5
1953. – 3 p. 50 brown & choc. 10 5
1954. – 6 p. brown and red .. 15 8
DESIGNS—VERT. 3 p. 50, Cloisters. 6 p. "Santa Maria del Parral".

321. "The Nativity" (Barocci).

1968. Christmas.
1955. **321.** 1 p. 50 multicoloured 5 5

1969. Provincial Costumes. As T **299.** Multicoloured.
1956. 6 p. Ifni 10 5
1957. 6 p. Jaen 10 5
1958. 6 p. Leon 10 5
1959. 6 p. Lerida 10 5
1960. 6 p. Logrono 10 5
1961. 6 p. Lugo 10 5
1962. 6 p. Madrid 10 5
1963. 6 p. Malaga 10 5
1964. 6 p. Murcia 10 5
1965. 6 p. Navarra 10 5
1966. 6 p. Orense 10 5
1967. 6 p. Oviedo 10 5

1969. Stamp Day and Alonso Cano Commem. Various paintings as T **204.** Frames gold: centre colours below.
1968. 40 c. crimson 5 5
1969. 50 c. green 5 5
1970. 1 p. sepia 8 5
1971. 1 p. 50 green 10 5
1972. 2 p. brown 12 5
1973. 2 p. 50 magenta 12 5
1974. 3 p. ultramarine 12 5
1975. 3 p. 50 purple 12 5
1976. 4 p. purple 12 5
1977. 6 p. blue 15 8
Alonso Cano paintings—VERT. 40 c. "St. Agnes". 50 c. "St. Joseph". 1 p. "Christ supported by an Angel". 1 p. 50, "Alonso Cano" (Velazquez). 2 p. "The Holy Family". 2 p. 50, "The Circumcision". 3 p. "Jesus and the Samaritan". 3 p. 50, "Madonna and Child". 6 p. "The Vision of St. John the Baptist". HORIZ. 4 p. "St. John Capistrano and St. Bernardin".

322. Molecules and Diagram.

1969. 6th European Biochemical Congress.
1978. **322.** 1 p. 50 multicoloured 5 5

323. Colonnade.

1969. Europa.
1979. **323.** 3 p. 50 multicoloured 10 5

1969. World Stamp Day. As T **305.**
1980. 1 p. 50 black, red & green 5 5
1981. 3 p. 50 green, red & blue 8 5
DESIGN: 1 p. 50, Spanish 6 c. Stamp of 1851 with "A 3 1851" Postmark. 3 p. 50, Spanish 10 r. Stamp of 1851 with "Corvera" Postmark.

324. Spectrum.

1969. 15th Int. Spectroscopical Conf., Madrid.
1982. **324.** 1 p. 50 multicoloured 5 5

325. Red Cross Symbols and Globe. **326.** Capital, Lugo Cathedral.

1969. League of Red Cross Societies. 50th Anniv.
1983. **325.** 1 p. 50 multicoloured 5 5

1969. Dedication of Galicia to Jesus Christ. 300th Anniv.
1984. **326.** 1 p. 50 brn., blk. & grn. 5 5

1969. Spanish Castles (4th Series). As T **292.**
1985. 1 p. purple and green .. 5 5
1986. 1 p. 50 blue and violet .. 5 5
1987. 2 p. 50 lilac & ultramarine 8 5
1988. 3 p. 50 brown and green 12 5
1989. 6 p. drab and green .. 20 5
CASTLES—HORIZ. 1 p. Turegano. 1 p. 50, Villalonso. 2 p. 50, Velez Blanco. 3 p. 50, Castilnovo. 6 p. Torrelobaton.

327. Franciscan Friar and Child. **328.** Rock of Gibraltar.

1969. San Diego (California). Bicent.
1990. **327.** 1 p. 50 multicoloured 5 5

1969. Aid for Spanish "ex-Gibraltar" Workers.
1991. **328.** 1 p. 50 blue 8 5
1992. – 2 p. purple 5 5
DESIGN: 2 p. Aerial view of Rock.

1969. Tourist Series. As T **264.**
1993. 1 p. 50 green and turquoise 5 5
1994. 3 p. turquoise and green 10 5
1995. 3 p. 50 blue and green .. 15 5
1996. 6 p. violet and green .. 20 5
DESIGNS—HORIZ. 1 p. 50, Alcaniz (Teruel). VERT. 3 p. Murcia Cathedral. 3 p. 50, "The Lady of Elche" (sculpture). 6 p. "Our Lady of the Redonda", Logrono.

1969. Explorers and Colonisers of America (9th series). Chile. As T **233.** Inscr. "1969" at foot.
1997. 40 c. brown on blue .. 5 5
1998. 1 p. 50 violet on flesh .. 5 5
1999. 2 p. green on mauve .. 10 5
2000. 3 p. 50 green on cream.. 12 5
2001. 6 p. brown on cream .. 20 5
DESIGNS—VERT. 40 c. Convent of Santo Domingo, Santiago de Chile. 2 p. O'Higgins. 3 p. 50. Pedro de Valdivia (founder of Santiago de Chile). HORIZ. 1 p. 50, Chilean Mint. 6 p. Caly Canto Bridge.

329. "Adoration of the Three Kings" (Maino). **330.** Las Huelgas Monastery.

1969. Christmas. Multicoloured.
2002. 1 p. 50 Type **329** .. 5 5
2003. 2 p. "The Nativity" (Gerona Cathedral) .. 8 5

1969. Las Huelgas Monastery, Burgos.
2004. **330.** 1 p. 50 slate and green 8 5
2005. – 3 p. 50 blue 12 5
2006. – 6 p. olive and green 20 5
DESIGNS—HORIZ. 3 p. 50, Tombs. VERT. 6 p. Cloisters.

1970. Provincial Costumes. As T **299**. Multicoloured.
2007. 6 p. Palencia 10 5
2008. 6 p. Pontevedra 10 5
2009. 6 p. Sahara 10 5
2010. 6 p. Salamanca 10 5
2011. 6 p. Santa Cruz de Tenerife 10 5
2012. 6 p. Santander 20 5
2013. 6 p. Segovia 12 5
2014. 6 p. Seville 12 5
2015. 6 p. Soria 12 5
2016. 6 p. Tarragona 12 5
2017. 6 p. Teruel 12 5
2018. 6 p. Toledo 12 5

331. Blessed Juan of Avila (after El Greco). (400th Death Anniv.). **332.** "St. Stephen".

1970. Spanish Celebrities.
2019. **331.** 25 p. indigo and lilac 80 15
2020. – 50 p. brown and orange 1·25 25
DESIGN: 50 p. Cardinal Rodrigo Ximenes de Rada (after J. de Borgena) (800th Birth. Anniv.).
See also Nos. 2129/31.

1970. Stamp Day and Luis de Morales Commem. Various paintings. Multicoloured.
2021. 50 c. Type **332** 5 5
2022. 1 p. "The Annunciation" 15 5
2023. 1 p. 50 "Virgin and Child with St. John" .. 12 5
2024. 2 p. "Virgin and Child" 12 5
2025. 3 p. "The Presentation of the Infant Christ" .. 10 5
2026. 3 p. 50 "St. Jerome" .. 10 5
2027. 4 p. "St. John of Ribera" 12 5
2028. 5 p. "Ecce Homo" .. 20 5
2029. 6 p. "Pieta" 20 8
2030. 10 p. "St. Francis of Assisi" 25 10
See also Nos. 2077/84, 2135/42, 2204/11, 2261/8 and 2405/12.

333. "Flaming Sun".

1970. Europa.
2031. **333.** 3 p. 50 gold & ultram. 10 5

1970. World Stamp Day. As T **305** but stamp and postmark changed.
2032. 2 p. red, black and green 8 5
DESIGN: 2 p. Spanish 12 c. stamp of 1860 with railway cachet.

334. Fair Building. **335.** Gen. Primo de Rivera.

1970. Barcelona Fair. 50th Anniv.
2033. **334.** 15 p. multicoloured .. 35 10

1970. General Primo de Rivera. Birth Cent.
2034. **335.** 2 p. grn., brn. & buff 5 5

1970. Spanish Castles (5th Series). As T **292**.
2035. 1 p. black and indigo .. 20 5
2036. 1 p. 20 blue and turq. .. 10 5
2037. 3 p. 50 brown and green 25 5
2038. 6 p. violet and brown .. 25 5
2039. 10 p. brown & chestnut 60 8
CASTLES—HORIZ. 1 p. Valencia de Don Juan. 1 p. 20 Monterrey. 3 p. 50 Mombeltran. 6 p. Sadaba. 10 p. Bellver.

1970. Tourist Series. As T **264**.
2040. 50 c. lilac and blue .. 5 5
2041. 1 p. chestnut and ochre .. 8 5
2042. 1 p. 50 green and blue .. 8 5
2043. 2 p. blue and indigo .. 20 5
2044. 3 p. 50 blue and violet .. 12 5
2045. 5 p. brown and blue .. 30 5
DESIGNS—HORIZ. 50 c. Fortress, Almeria. 1 p. Malaga Cathedral. 2 p. St. Francis' Convent, Orense. VERT. 1 p. 50 Our Lady of the Assumption, Lequeitio. 3 p. 50 The Lonja, Zaragoza. 5 p. The Portalon, Vitoria.

336. 17th-century Tailor.

1970. Int. Tailoring Congress.
2046. **336.** 2 p. violet, red & brn. 5 5

337. Diver on Map.

1970. 12th European Swimming, Diving and Water-polo Championships. Barcelona.
2047. **337.** 2 p. brn., blue and grn. 5 5

338. Concha Espina. **339.** Survey Map of Southern Spain and North Africa.

1970. Spanish Writers.
2048. **338.** 50 c. blue, brn. & buff 5 5
2049. – 1 p. violet, grn. & drab 5 5
2050. – 1 p. 50 grn., blue & drab 8 5
2051. – 2 p. olive, grn. & buff 10 5
2052. – 2 p. 50 pur., vio. & ochre 10 5
2053. – 3 p. 50 red, brn. & lilac 12 5
WRITERS: 1 p. Guillen de Castro. 1 p. 50, J. R. Jimenez. 2 p. G. A. Becquer. 2 p. 50, Miguel de Unamuno. 3 p. 50, J. M. Gabriel y Galan.

1970. Explorers and Colonisers of America (10th series). Mexico. Designs as T **233**.
2054. 40 c. grn. on pale green .. 5 5
2055. 1 p. 50 brn. on blue .. 5 5
2056. 2 p. violet on cream .. 12 5
2057. 3 p. 50 grn. on pale green 10 5
2058. 6 p. blue on pink .. 20 5
DESIGNS—VERT. 40 c. House in Queretaro. 2 p. Vasco de Quitoga. 3 p. 50, F. Juan de Zumarraga. 6 p. Morelia Cathedral. HORIZ. 1 p. 50, Cathedral, Mexico City.

1970. Spanish Geographical and Survey Institute. Cent.
2059. **339.** 2 p. multicoloured .. 5 5

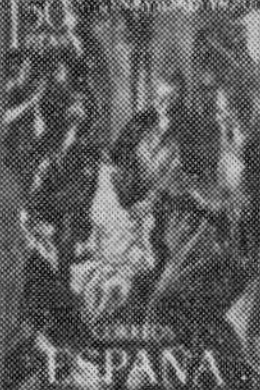

340. "The Adoration of the Shepherds". (El Greco.) **341.** U.N. Emblem and New York Headquarters.

1970. Christmas. Multicoloured.
2060. 1 p. 50 Type **340** 5 5
2061. 2 p. "The Adoration of the Shepherds" (Murillo) 5 5

1970. United Nations. 25th Anniv.
2062. **341.** 8 p. multicoloured .. 20 8

342. Ripoll Monastery. **343.** Pilgrims' Route Map.

1970. Ripoll Monastery.
2063. – 2 p. purple & violet 10 5
2064. **342.** 3 p. 50 purple & orge. 10 5
2065. – 5 p. green and slate 14 8
DESIGNS: 2 p. Entrance. 5 p. Cloisters.

1971. Holy Year of Compostela (1st issue). "St. James in Europe".
2066. **343.** 50 c. brown & blue .. 5 5
2067. – 1 p. black & brown .. 5 5
2068. – 1 p. 50 purple & green 8 5
2069. – 2 p. brown & purple .. 10 5
2070. – 3 p. indigo and blue .. 10 5
2071. – 4 p. olive 12 5
DESIGNS—VERT. 1 p. Statue of St. Brigid, Vadstena (Sweden). 1 p. 50, St. Jacques Church tower, Paris. 2 p. "St. James" (carving from altar, Pistoia, Italy). HORIZ. 3 p. St. David's Cathedral, Wales. 4 p. Carving from Ark of Charlemagne (Aachen, West Germany).
See also Nos. 2105/11 and 2121/8.

1971. Provincial Costumes. As T **299**. Multicoloured.
2072. 6 p. Valencia 12 5
2073. 8 p. Valladolid 15 8
2074. 8 p. Vizcaya 15 8
2075. 8 p. Zamora 15 8
2076. 8 p. Zaragoza 15 8

1971. Stamp Day and Ignatius Zuloaga Commem. Paintings As T **332**. Mult.
2077. 50 c. "My Uncle Daniel" 5 5
2078. 1 p. "Segovia" (horiz.) .. 5 5
2079. 1 p. 50 "The Duchess of Alba" 8 5
2080. 2 p. "Ignatius Zuloaga" (self-portrait) 10 5
2081. 3 p. "Juan Belmonte" .. 8 5
2082. 4 p. "The Countess of Noailles" 10 5
2083. 5 p. "Pablo Uranga" .. 12 5
2084. 8 p. "Boatmen's Houses, Lerma" (horiz.) .. 20 8

344. Amadeo Vives (composer).

1971. Spanish Celebrities. Multicoloured.
2085. 1 p. Type **344** 5 5
2086. 2 p. St. Teresa of Auila (mystic) 10 5
2087. 8 p. B. Perez Galdos (writer) 20 8
2088. 15 p. R. Menendez Pidal (writer) 35 10

345. Europa Chain.

1971. Europa.
2089. **345.** 2 p. brn., violet & blue 10 5
2090. 8 p. brn, emer. & grn. 20 8

1971. World Stamp Day. As T **305** but with different stamp and postmark.
2091. 2 p. black, blue & green 5 5
DESIGN: 2 p. Spanish 6 r. stamp of 1850 with letter "A" postmark.

346. Gymnast on Vaulting-horse.

1971. 9th European (Male) Gymnastics Cup Championships. Multicoloured.
2092. 1 p. Type **346** 5 5
2093. 2 p. Exercise on bar .. 8 5

347. Great Bustard.

1971. Spanish Fauna. (1st series). Mult.
2094. 1 p. Type **347** 5 5
2095. 2 p. Lynx 10 5
2096. 3 p. Brown bear 12 5
2097. 5 p. Red-legged partridge (vert.) 15 5
2098. 8 p. Spanish wild goat (vert.) 20 5
See also Nos. 2160/4, 2192/6 and 2250/4.

348. Legionaires in Battle.

1971. Spanish Foreign Legion. 50th Anniv. Multicoloured.
2101. 1 p. Type **348** 5 5
2102. 2 p. Ceremonial Parade .. 12 5
2103. 5 p. Memorial Service .. 15 5
2104. 8 p. Officer and mobile column 20 5

1971. Holy Year of Compostela (2nd issue). "En Route to Santiago". As T **343**.
2105. 50 c. purple and blue .. 5 5
2106. 6 p. blue 15 8
2107. 7 p. purple & dull purple 15 5
2108. 7 p. 50 red and purple .. 20 10
2109. 8 p. purple and green .. 20 8
2110. 9 p. violet and green .. 25 8
2111. 10 p. brown and green .. 25 8
DESGNS—HORIZ. 50 c. Pilgrims' route map of northern Spain. 7 p. 50, Cloisters, Najera Monastery. 9 p. Eunate Monastery. VERT. 6 p. "Pilgrims" (sculpture, Royal Hospital, Burgos). 7 p. Gateway, St. Domingo de la Calzada Monastery. 8 p. Statue of Christ, Puente de la Reina. 10 p. Cross of Roncesvalles.

349. "Children of the World". **350.** "Battle of Lepanto" (after L. Valdes).

1971. U.N.I.C.E.F. 25th Anniv.
2112. **349.** 8 p. multicoloured .. 20 5

1971. Battle of Lepanto. 400th Anniv.
2113. – 2 p. grn. & brn. (vert.) 5 5
2114. **350.** 5 p. chocolate & brn. 12 5
2115. – 8 p. blue & red (vert.) 25 8
DESIGNS: 2 p. "Don John of Austria" (S. Coello). 8 p. Standard of the Holy League.

351. Hockey-players. **353.** "The Nativity" (detail from altar at Avia).

352. De Havilland "DH-9" Biplane over Seville.

1971. World Hockey Cup Championships, Barcelona.
2116. **351.** 5 p. multicoloured .. 15 5

1971. Spanish Airmail Services. 50th Anniv. Multicoloured.
2117. 2 p. Type **352** 10 5
2118. 15 p. Boeing "747" "Jumbo-jet" over Madrid 35 10

1971. Christmas. Multicoloured.
2119. 2 p. Type **353** 5 5
2120. 8 p. "The Birth" (detail from altar, Sagar) .. 20 5

1971. Holy Year of Compostela (3rd issue). As Type **343.**
2121. 1 p. black and green .. 5 5
2122. 1 p. 50 violet and purple 5 5
2123. 2 p. blue and green .. 8 5
2124. 2 p. 50 violet and red .. 8 5
2125. 3 p. purple and red .. 8 5
2126. 3 p. 50 green and pink .. 8 5
2127. 4 p. brown and blue .. 12 5
2128. 5 p. black and green .. 15 5
DESIGNS—VERT. 1 p. Santiago Cathedral. 2 p. Lugo Cathedral. 3 p. Astorga Cathedral. 4 p. San Tirso, Sahagun. HORIZ. 1 p. 50, Pilgrim approaching Santiago de Compostella. 2 p. 50, Villafranca del Bierzo. 3 p. 50, San Marcos, Leon. 5 p. San Martin, Fromista.

1972. Spanish Celebrities. As Type **331.**
2129. 15 p. green and brown .. 60 10
2130. 25 p. blackish grn. & grn. 40 15
2131. 50 p. brown and red .. 80 25
CELEBRITIES: 15 p. Emilia Pardo Bazan (novelist). 25 p. Jose de Espronceda (poet). 50 p. Fernan Gonzalez (first king of Castile).

354. Ski-jumping. **355.** Title-page of "Don Quixote" (1605).

1972. Winter Olympic Games, Sapporo, Japan. Multicoloured.
2132. 2 p Type **354** 10 5
2133. 15 p. Figure-skating (vert.) 30 10

1972. Int. Book Year.
2134. **355.** 2 p. brown and lake .. 5 5

356. "Solana and Family". (self-portrait). **357.** "Abies pinsapo".

1972. Stamp Day and Solana Commem. Paintings by Solana. Multicoloured.
2135. 1 p. "Clowns" (horiz.) .. 8 5
2136. 2 p. Type **356** 10 5
2137. 3 p. "The Blind Musician" 12 5
2138. 4 p. "Return of the Fishermen" 12 5
2139. 5 p. "Decorating Masks" 12 5
2140. 7 p. "The Bibliophile" .. 15 8
2141. 10 p. "The Merchant Navy Captain" .. 25 8
2142. 15 p. "The Pombo Reunion" (horiz.) .. 30 10

1972. Spanish Flora. (1st series). Mult.
2143. 1 p. Type **357** 5 5
2144. 2 p. "Arbutus unedo" .. 8 5
2145. 3 p. "Pinus pinaster" .. 8 5
2146. 5 p. "Quercus ilex" .. 10 5
2147. 8 p. "Juniperus thurifera" 25 8
See also Nos. 2178/82 and 2278/82.

358. "Europeans".

359. Cordoba Pre-stamp Postmark.

1972. Europa. Multicoloured.
2148. 2 p. Type **358** 8 5
2149. 8 p. "Communications" .. 20 5

1972. World Stamp Day.
2150. **359.** 2 p. red, blk. & brown 5 5

1972. Spanish Castles (6th series). As T **292.**
2151. 1 p. brown and green .. 8 5
2152. 2 p. brown and green .. 8 5
2153. 3 p. brown and red .. 8 5
2154. 5 p. green and blue .. 10 5
2155. 10 p. violet and blue .. 25 10
CASTLES—VERT. 1 p. Sajazarra. HORIZ. 2 p. Santa Catalina. 3 p. Biar. 5 p. San Servando. 10 p. Pedraza.

360. Fencing.

1972. Olympic Games, Munich. Mult.
2156. 1 p. Type **360** 5 5
2157. 2 p. Weightlifting (vert.) 8 5
2158. 5 p. Rowing (vert.) .. 12 5
2159. 8 p. Pole-vaulting (vert.) 20 5

361. Genet (civet-cat).

1972. Spanish Fauna (2nd series). Mult.
2160. 1 p. Pyrenean desman (vert.) 5 5
2161. 2 p. Chamois (vert.) .. 8 5
2162. 3 p. Wolf (vert.) 10 5
2163. 5 p. Mongoose 12 5
2164. 7 p. Type **361** 20 5

362. Brigadier M. A. de Ustariz. **363.** Facade of Monastery.

1972. "Hispanidad 1972". "Spain in the New World" (1st series). Puerto Rico. 450th Anniv. Mult.
2165. 1 p. Type **362** 5 5
2166. 2 p. View of San Juan, 1870 (horiz.) 8 5
2167. 5 p. View of San Juan, 1625 (horiz.) 12 5
2168. 8 p. Map of Plaza de Bahia, 1792 (horiz.) .. 20 5

1972. Monastery of St. Thomas, Avila.
2169. **363.** 2 p. green and blue .. 8 5
2170. – 8 p. purple & brown 20 5
2171. – 15 p. blue and purple 30 10
DESIGNS—VERT. 8 p. Interior of Monastery. HORIZ. 15 p. Cloisters.

364. Grand Lyceum Theatre.

1972. Grand Lyceum Theatre, Barcelona. 125th Anniv.
2172. **364.** 8 p. brown and blue .. 20 5

365. "The Nativity".

1972. Christmas. Murals in Royal Collegiate Basilica of San Isidoro, Leon. Mult.
2173. 2 p. Type **365** 5 5
2174. 8 p. "The Annunciation" 15 5

366. J. de Herrera and Escorial.

1973. Spanish Architects.
2175. **366.** 8 p. green and sepia 20 5
2176. – 10 p. blue and brown 30 8
2177. – 15 p. blue and green 35 10
DESIGNS: 10 p. J. de Villanueva and Prado. 15 p. V. Rodriguez and Apollo Fountain, Madrid.

367. "Apollonias canariensis".

1973. Spanish Flora (2nd series). Canary Islands. Multicoloured.
2178. 1 p. Type **367** 5 5
2179. 2 p. "Myrica faya" .. 8 5
2180. 4 p. "Phoenix canariensis" 10 5
2181. 5 p. "Ilex canariensis" .. 12 5
2182. 15 p. "Dracaena drac" .. 30 10
Nos. 2179/82 are vert.

368. Roman Mosaic. **369.** Iznajar Dam.

1973. Europa.
2183. **368.** 2 p. multicoloured .. 8 5
2184. – 8 p. blue, red & black 15 5
DESIGN—HORIZ. (37 × 26 mm.) 8 p. Europa "Posthorn".

1973. World Stamp Day. As Type **305**, but with different stamp and postmark.
2185. 2 p. red, blue and black .. 5 5
DESIGN: 2 p. Spanish 6 r. stamp of 1853 with Madrid postmark.

1973. 11th Congress of Int. High Dams Commission, Madrid.
2186. **369.** 8 p. multicoloured .. 15 5

1973. Tourist Series. As Type **264.**
2187. 1 p. brown and green .. 5 5
2188. 2 p. green and dark green 5 5
2189. 3 p. brown & light brown 8 5
2190. 5 p. violet and blue .. 12 5
2191. 8 p. brown and green .. 15 5
DESIGNS—HORIZ. 1 p. Gateway, Onate University. 2 p. Town Square, Lugo. 5 p. Columbus's House, Las Palmas. 8 p. Windmills, La Mancha. VERT. 3 p. Llerena Square, Badajoz.

370. Black-bellied Sand-grouse.

1973. Spanish Fauna (3rd series). Birds. Multicoloured.
2192. 1 p. Type **370** 5 5
2193. 2 p. Black stork 5 5
2194. 5 p. Azure-winged magpie (vert.) 10 5
2195. 7 p. Imperial eagle .. 15 5
2196. 15 p. Red-crested pochard (vert.) 25 8

371. Mounted Knight, Castile, 1493.

1973. Spanish Military Uniforms (1st series) Multicoloured.
2197. 1 p. Hermandad Standard-bearer, Castile, 1488 (vert.) 5 5
2198. 2 p. Type **371** 5 5
2199. 3 p. Harquebusier, 1534 (vert.) 5 5
2200. 7 p. Mounted Harquebusier, 1560 (vert.) 15 5
2201. 8 p. Infantry sergeant, 1567 (vert.) 15 5
See also Nos. 2225/9, 2255/9, 2290/4, 2322/6, 2395/9 and 2426/30.

HAVE YOU READ THE NOTES AT THE BEGINNING OF THIS CATALOGUE?
These often provide answers to the enquiries we receive.

372. Fishes in Net.

374. "Ferdinand VII".

373. Conference Building.

1973. World Fishing Fair and Congress, Vigo.
2202. **372.** 2 p. multicoloured .. 5 5

1973. I.T.U. Conf., Torremolinos.
2203. **373.** 8 p. multicoloured .. 15 5

1973. Stamp Day and Vicente Lopez Commemoration. Paintings. Multicoloured.
2204. 1 p. Type **374** 5 5
2205. 2 p. Self-portrait 5 5
2206. 3 p. "La Senora de Carvallo" 5 5
2207. 4 p. "M. de Castelldosrrius" 8 5
2208. 5 p. "Isabella II" .. 10 5
2209. 7 p. "Goya" 15 5
2210. 10 p. "Maria Amalia of Saxony" 20 5
2211. 15 p. "The Organist, Felix Lopez" 30 8

375. Leon Cathedral, Nicaragua. **376.** Pope Gregory XI receiving St. Jerome's Petition.

1973. "Hispanidad 1973". "Spain in the New World" (2nd series). Nicaraguan Buildings. Multicoloured.
2212. 1 p. Type **375** 5 5
2213. 2 p. Subtiava Church .. 5 5
2214. 5 p. Colonial-style house (vert.) 12 5
2215. 8 p. Rio San Juan Castle 15 5

1973. Order of St. Jerome. 600th Anniv.
2216. **376.** 2 p. multicoloured .. 5 5

377. Courtyard. **378.** "The Nativity", (pillar capital, Silos).

1973. Monastery of Santo Domingo de Silos, Burgos.
2217. **377.** 2 p. red and brown .. 5 5
2218. – 8 p. purple and blue 15 5
2219. – 15 p. green 30 10
DESIGNS—HORIZ. 8 p. Cloisters. VERT. 15 p. "Three Saints" (statue).

1973. Christmas. Multicoloured.
2220. 2 p. Type **378** 5 5
2221. 8 p. "Adoration of the Kings" (bas-relief, Butrera) (horiz.) 15 5

379. Map of Spain and the Americas.

1973. Spanish Printing. 500th Anniv.

2222.	**379.**	1 p. blue and green ..	5	5
2223.	–	7 p. violet and blue..	15	5
2224.	–	15 p. green and purple	30	10

DESIGNS—VERT. 7 p. " Teacher and pupils" (ancient woodcut). 15 p. " Los Siondales" (manuscript).

1974. Spanish Military Uniforms (2nd series). As Type **371**. Multicoloured.

2225.	1 p. Mounted arquebusier, 1603	5	5
2226.	2 p. Arquebusier, 1632 ..	5	5
2227.	3 p. Mounted cuirassier, 1635	5	5
2228.	5 p. Mounted drummer, 1677	10	5
2229.	9 p. "Viejos Morados" Regiment, Musketeers, 1694	20	5

380. 14th-century Nautical Chart.

381. M. Biada (construction engineer) and Early Locomotive.

1974. Spanish Higher Geographical Council. 50th Anniv.

2230.	**380.**	2 p. multicoloured ..	5	5

1974. Barcelona-Mataro Railway. 125th Anniv.

2231.	**381.**	2 p. multicoloured ..	5	5

382. Stamp Collector, Album and Magnifier.

1974. "ESPANA 75" Int. Stamp Exhibition, Madrid.

2232.	**382.**	2 p. multicoloured ..	5	5
2233.	–	5 p. blue, blk. & brn.	15	5
2234.	–	8 p. multicoloured ..	20	5

DESIGNS—DIAMOND (43×43 mm.). 5 p. Exhibition emblem. 8 p. Globe and arrows.

383. " Woman with Offering ".

1974. Europa. Stone Sculptures. Mult.

2235.	2 p. " Woman from Baza "	5	5
2236.	8 p. Type **383**	15	5

384. 2 r. Stamp of 1854 with Seville Postmark.

1974. World Stamp Day.

2237.	**384.**	2 p. multicoloured ..	5	5

385. Jaime Balmes (philosopher) and Monastery.

386. Bramante's "Little Temple", Rome.

1974. Spanish Celebrities.

2238.	**385.**	8 p. brown and blue	15	5
2239.	–	10 p. brown and claret	20	5
2240.	–	15 p. blue and brown	25	10

DESIGNS: 10 p. Pedro Poveda (educationalist) and mountain village. 15 p. Jorge Juan (cosmographer and mariner) and shipyard.

1974. Spanish Fine Arts Academy, Rome. Cent.

2241.	**386.**	5 p. multicoloured ..	10	5

387. Roman Aqueduct, Segovia.

1974. Spain as a Province of the Roman Empire.

2242.	**387.**	1 p. black and brown	5	5
2243.	–	2 p. brown and green	5	5
2244.	–	3 p. brn. & light brn.	5	5
2245.	–	4 p. blue and green..	8	5
2246.	–	5 p. purple and blue	10	5
2247.	–	7 p. purple and green	15	5
2248.	–	8 p. green and red ..	15	5
2249.	–	9 p. brown and purple	20	5

DESIGNS—HORIZ. 2 p. Roman Bridge, Alcantara. 3 p. Marcial (poet) giving public reading. 5 p. Theatre, Merida. 7 p. Ossio, 1st Bishop of Cordoba, addressing the Synod. VERT. 4 p. Triumphal Arch, Bara. 8 p. Ruins of Curia, Talavera la Vieja. 9 p. Statue of Emperor Trajan.

388. Tortoise.

1974. Spanish Fauna (4th series). Reptiles. Multicoloured.

2250.	1 p. Type **388**	5	5
2251.	2 p. Chameleon	5	5
2252.	5 p. Gecko	10	5
2253.	7 p. Green lizard.. ..	15	5
2254.	15 p. Adder	30	8

1974. Spanish Military Uniforms (3rd series) As Type **371**. Multicoloured.

2255.	1 p. Dismounted trooper, Hussars de la Muerte, 1705	5	5
2256.	2 p. Officer, Royal Regiment of Artillery, 1710	5	5
2257.	3 p. Drummer and fifer, Granada Regiment, 1734	5	5
2258.	7 p. Guildon-bearer, Numancia Dragoons, 1737	15	5
2259.	8 p. Ensign with standard, Zamora Regiment, 1739	15	5

389. Swimmer making Rescue.

1974. 18th World Life-saving Championships, Barcelona.

2260.	**389.**	2 p. multicoloured ..	5	5

1974. Stamp Day and Eduardo Rosales. Commemoration. Various Paintings as Type **374**. Multicoloured.

2261.	1 p. "Tobias and the Angel"	5	5
2262.	2 p. Self-portrait.. ..	5	5
2263.	3 p. "Testament of Isabella the Catholic" (horiz.)..	5	5
2264.	4 p. "Nena" ..	8	5
2265.	5 p. "Presentation of Don Juan of Austria" (horiz.)	8	5
2266.	7 p. "The First Steps" (horiz.).. ..	12	5
2267.	10 p. "St. John the Evangelist"	15	5
2268.	15 p "St. Matthew the Evangelist"	25	8

390. Sobremonte's House, Cordoba (Argentina).

1974. "Hispanidad 1974". Multicoloured.

2269.	1 p. Type **390**	5	5
2270.	2 p. Town Hall, Buenos Aires (1929)	5	5
2271.	5 p. Ruins of St. Ignacio de Mini (vert.).. ..	10	5
2272.	10 p. "The Gaucho" (M. Fiervo) (vert.) ..	20	5

391. Postal Allegory.

393. " Teucriun lanigerum ".

392. Nativity, Valdavia Church.

1974. Universal Postal Union. Centenary. Multicoloured

2273.	2 p. Type **391**	5	5
2274.	8 p. U.P.U. Monument, Berne	15	5

1974. Christmas. Multicoloured.

2275.	2 p. Type **392**	5	5
2276.	3 p. Adoration of the Kings, Valcobero Church (font) (vert.)	5	5
2277.	8 p. As 3 p.	15	5

1974. Spanish Flora (3rd series). Mult.

2278.	1 p. Type **393**	5	5
2279.	2 p. "Hypericum ericoides"	5	5
2280.	4 p. "Thymus longiflorus"	8	5
2281.	5 p. "Anthyllis onobrychioides" ..	15	5
2282.	8 p. "Helianthemun paniculatum" ..	15	5

394. Leyre Monastery.

395. Spanish Stamps of 1850 and 1975.

1974. Leyre Monastery.

2283.	**394.**	2 p. grn. & bronze-grn.	5	5
2284.	–	8 p. lake & brown ..	15	5
2285.	–	15 p. myrtle & green	25	8

DESIGNS—VERT. 8 p. Pillar and bas-relief. HORIZ. 15 p. Crypt.

1975. Spanish Stamps. 125th Anniv.

2286.	**395.**	2 p. blue	5	5
2287.	–	3 p. brown & green ..	5	5
2288.	–	8 p. mauve & violet..	12	5
2289.	–	10 p. green & maroon	20	5

DESIGNS—HORIZ. 3 p. Mail-coach, 1850. 8 p. Mail-ship of Indian service. VERT. 10 p. Marcus Chapel.

1975. Spanish Military Uniforms (4th series). As Type **371**. Multicoloured.

2290.	1 p. Sergeant and grenadier, Toledo Regiment, 1750	5	5
2291.	2 p. Royal Corps of Artillery, 1762	5	5
2292.	3 p. Queen's Regt. of the Line, 1763	5	5
2293.	5 p. Fusiliers of Vitoria Regt., 1766	10	5
2294.	10 p. Dragoon of Sagunto Regt., 1775	15	5

396. Antonio Gaudi and Apartments.

1975. Spanish Architects.

2295.	**396.**	8 p. olive and green	12	5
2296.	–	10 p. brown and red	15	5
2297.	–	15 p. black and brown	25	8

ARCHITECTS: 10 p. Antonio Palacios and castle. 15 p. Secundino Zuazo and modern apartment block.

397. Almonds and Blossom.

1975. Spanish Fruits. Multicoloured.

2299.	1 p. Type **397**	5	5
2300.	2 p. Pomegranates (vert.)	5	5
2301.	3 p. Oranges (vert.) ..	5	5
2302.	4 p. Chestnuts (vert.) ..	8	5
2303.	5 p. Apples (vert.) ..	10	5

398. " Woman with Pitcher " (rock-drawing, Cave at La Aranya).

399. Early Postmark of Leon.

1975. Europa. Multicoloured.

2304.	3 p. Type **398**	5	5
2305.	12 p. " Horse " (rock-drawing, Tito Bustillo Cave) (horiz.).. ..	20	8

1975. World Stamp Day.

2306.	**399.**	3 p. multicoloured ..	5	5

400. Global Emblem.

401. Farmer, Ear of Corn and Cockerel.

1975. First General Assembly of World Tourism Organisation, Madrid.

2307.	**400.**	3 p. blue	5	5

1975. " Feria del Campo ". 25th Anniv.

2308.	**401.**	3 p. multicoloured ..	5	5

402. Women of Four Races.

1975. International Women's Year.

2309.	**402.**	3 p. multicoloured ..	5	5

403. Sanctuary, Air Force and Falangist Emblems.

1975. Defence of Virgin of Cabeza Sanctuary during Civil War.

2310.	**403.**	3 p. multicoloured ..	5	5

1975. Tourist Series. As T **264**.

2311.	1 p. black and purple ..	5	5
2312.	2 p. brown and lake ..	5	5
2313.	3 p. black and blue ..	5	5
2314.	4 p. mauve and red ..	8	5
2315.	5 p. blue and green ..	10	5
2316.	7 p. indigo and blue ..	12	5

DESIGNS—HORIZ. 1 p. Cervantes' cell, Argamasilla de Alba. 2 p. St. Martin's Bridge, Toledo. 3 p. St. Peter's Church, Tarrasa. VERT. 4 p. Alhambra archway, Granada. 5 p. Mijas village, Malaga. 7 p. St. Mary's Chapel, Tarrasa.

404. Salamander (" Salamandra salamandra ").

1975. Amphibious Fauna. Multicoloured.

2317. 1 p. Type **404** 5 5
2318. 2 p. Triton (" Triturus marmoratus ") .. 5 5
2319. 3 p. Tree-frog (" Hyla arborea ") 5 5
2320. 6 p. Toad (" Alytes obstetricans ") .. 12 5
2321. 7 p. Frog (" Rana temporaria ") 12 5

1975. Spanish Military Uniforms (5th series) As T **371**. Multicoloured.

2322. 1 p. Mounted trooper, Montesa Regt. (Linea), 1788 .. .. .. 5 5
2323. 2 p. Fusilier, Asturias Regt., 1789 .. .. 5 5
2324. 3 p. Colonel, Infantry of the Line, 1802 .. 5 5
2325. 4 p. Standard-bearer, Royal Corps of Artillery, 1803 .. .. 8 5
2326. 7 p. Sapper, Royal Engineers Regt., 1809 12 5

405. " For the Defence of Life ".

1975. Child Welfare.

2327. **405.** 3 p. multicoloured .. 5 5

406. Scroll and Emblem.

1975. Latin Notaries Congress, Barcelona.

2328. **406.** 3 p. multicoloured .. 5 5

407. " Blessing the Birds ".

1975. Gerona Cathedral. Millenium. Painted Miniatures. Multicoloured.

2329. 1 p. Type **407** 5 5
2330. 2 p. " Angel and River of Life (vert.) .. 5 5
2331. 3 p. " Angel at Gates of Paradise " (vert.) .. 5 5
2332. 4 p. " Fox seizing Cockerel " 8 5
2333. 6 p. " Daniel with Wild Bulls " 12 5
2334. 7 p. " Blessing the Multitude " (vert.) 12 5
2335. 10 p. " The Four Horsemen of the Apocalypse " (vert.) 20 8
2336. 12 p. " Peacock and Snake " (vert.) .. 20 8

408. Emblems of Industry.

1975. Spanish Industrialisation.

2337. **408.** 3 p. violet and purple 5 5

409. El Cabildo, Montevideo.

1975. " Hispanidad 1975 ". Uruguayan Independence. 150th Anniv. Multicoloured.

2338. 1 p. Type **409** 5 5
2339. 2 p. Pioneer wagon .. 5 5
2340. 3 p. St. Teresa Fortress .. 5 5
2341. 8 p. Montevideo Cathedral (vert.) 15 5

410. Monastery Building. **411.** " The Virgin and Child ", Navarre.

1975. Monastery of San Juan de la Pena.

2342. **410.** 3 p. brown and green 5 5
2343. – 8 p. violet and mauve 15 5
2344. – 10 p. red and mauve 20 8

DESIGNS—HORIZ. 8 p. Cloisters. VERT. 10 p. Columns.

1975. Christmas. Multicoloured.

2345. 3 p. Type **411** 5 5
2346. 12 p " The Flight into Egypt " (capital) (horiz.) 20 8

412. King Juan Carlos I. **413.** Virgin of Pontevedra.

1975. Proclamation of King Juan Carlos I. Multicoloured.

2347. 3 p. Type **412** 5 5
2348. 3 p. Queen Sophia .. 5 5
2349. 3 p. King Juan Carlos and Queen Sophia (30×30 mm.) 5 5
2350. 12 p. As No. 2349 .. 20 8

1975. Holy Year of Compostela.

2351. **413.** 3 p. brown and orange 5 5

414. Mountains and Emblem. **415.** Cosme Damian Churruca.

1976. Catalunya Excursion Centre. Centenary.

2352. **414.** 6 p. multicoloured .. 12 5

1976. Spanish Navigators.

2353. **415.** 7 p. green and purple 15 15
2354. – 12 p. violet and blue 25 10
2355. – 50 p. brown and green 1·10 50

NAVIGATORS—VERT. 12 p. Luis de Requesens. HORIZ. Juan Sebastian Elcano.

MINIMUM PRICE

The minimum price quoted is 5p which represents a handling charge rather than a basis for valuing common stamps. For further notes about prices see introductory pages.

416. Bell and Telephones.

1976. Telephone Centenary.

2356. **416.** 3 p. multicoloured .. 8 5

417. Care on Zebra Crossing.

1976. Road Safety. Multicoloured.

2357. 1 p. Type **417** 5 5
2358. 3 p. Dangerous overtaking (vert.) 8 5
2359. 5 p. Use of seat-belts .. 12 5

418. St. George on Horseback.

1976. St. George's Guardianship of Alcoy. 700th Anniv.

2360. **418.** 3 p. multicoloured .. 8 5

419. Talavera Pottery.

1976. Europa. Multicoloured.

2361. 3 p. Type **419** 8 5
2362. 12 p. Lace-making, Camarinas 25 10

420. Spanish 1851 6 r. Stamp and Coruna Postmark.

1976. World Stamp Day.

2363. **420.** 3 p. blue, red & black 8 5

421. Caesar Augustus Coin.

1976. Zaragoza. Bimillenary.

2364. **421.** 3 p. brown and black 8 5
2365. – 7 p. blue and black .. 15 5
2366. – 25 p. brown and black 55 20

DESIGNS—HORIZ. 7 p. Plan of Roman site and coin. VERT. 25 p. Roman mosaic.

422. Spanish Rifle of 1757.

1976. American Revolution. Bicent.

2367. **422.** 1 p. blue and brown .. 5 5
2368. – 3 p. brown and green 8 5
2369. – 5 p. green and brown 12 5
2370. – 12 p. brown and green 25 10

DESIGNS: 3 p. Bernado de Galvez and emblem. 5 p. Richmond $1 banknote of 1861. 12 p. Conquest of Pensacola.

423. Customs-house, Cadiz.

1976. Spanish Customs Buildings.

2371. **423.** 1 p. brown and black 5 5
2372. – 3 p. brown and green 8 5
2373. – 7 p. purple and brown 15 5

BUILDINGS: 3 p. Madrid. 7 p. Barcelona.

424. Savings Jar.

1976. Postal Services. Multicoloured.

2374. 1 p. Type **424** 5 5
2375. 3 p. Railway mail-sorting van 8 5
2376. 6 p. Rural mounted postman (horiz.) 12 5
2377. 10 p. Automatic letter-sorting equipment (horiz.) 20 5

1976. Tourist Series. As T **264**.

2378. 1 p. brown and grey .. 5 5
2379. 2 p. blue and green .. 5 5
2380. 3 p. brown and red .. 8 5
2381. 4 p. blue and brown .. 10 5
2382. 7 p. brown and blue .. 15 5
2383. 12 p. purple and mauve .. 25 10

DESIGNS—HORIZ. 1 p. Cloisters, San Marco, Leon. 2 p. Las Canadas, Tenerife. 4 p. Cruz de Tejeda, Las Palmas. 7 p. Gredos, Avila. 12 p. La Arruzafa, Cordoba. VERT. 3 p. Entrance, Hospice of the Catholic Kings, Santiago de Compostela.

425. King Juan Carlos I, Queen Sophia and Map of the Americas.

1976. Royal Visit to the Americas.

2384. **425.** 12 p. multicoloured .. 25 10

See also No. 2419.

426. Rowing.

1976. Olympic Games, Montreal. Multicoloured.

2385. 1 p. Type **426** 5 5
2386. 2 p. Boxing 5 5
2387. 3 p. Wrestling (vert.) .. 8 5
2388. 12 p. Basketball (vert.) .. 25 10

427. King Juan Carlos I. **428.** " Giving Blood ".

1976.
2389. **427.** 1 p. 50 cerise 5 5
2390. 2 p. blue 5 5
2391. 3 p. green 8 5
2392. 5 p. red 12 5
2393. 7 p. bistre 15 5
2394. 12 p. orange 25 10

1976. Spanish Military Uniforms (6th series). Vert. designs as T **371.** Multicoloured.
2395. 1 p. Trumpeter, Alcantara, 1815 .. .. 5 5
2396. 2 p. Infantry – sapper, Regiment of the line, 1821 .. .. 5 5
2397. 3 p. Rifleman–sapper, Gala Engineers, 1825 .. 8 5
2398. 7 p. Foot soldier, Artillery Regiment, 1828 .. 15 5
2399. 25 p. Rifleman, Light Infantry Regiment, 1830 55 20

1976. Blood Donors.
2400. **428.** 3 p. red and brown .. 5 5

429. Mosiac, Batitales.

1976. Lugo City. 2,000th Anniv.
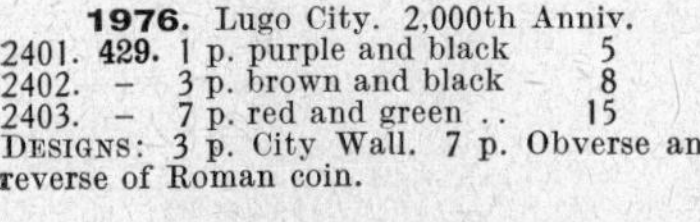
2401. **429.** 1 p. purple and black 5 5
2402. – 3 p. brown and black 8 5
2403. – 7 p. red and green .. 15 5
DESIGNS: 3 p. City Wall. 7 p. Obverse and reverse of Roman coin.

430. Parliamentary House, Madrid.

1976. 63rd Inter-Parliamentary Union Conference, Madrid.
2404. **430.** 12 p. brown and green 25 10

1976. Stamp Day and Luis Menendez Commemoration. Paintings as T **332.** Multicoloured.
2405. 1 p. "Still Life" (vert.) 5 5
2406. 2 p. "Peaches and Jar" (vert.) 5 5
2407. 3 p. "Pears and Melon" (vert.) 8 5
2408. 4 p. "Pigeons, Basket and Bowl (vert.) .. 10 5
2409. 6 p. "Fishes" 12 5
2410. 7 p. "Melon and Bread" 12 5
2411. 10 p. "Figs, Jug and Loaf" 20 5
2412. 12 p. "Fruits" 25 10

431. "The Nativity".

1976. Christmas. Multicoloured.
2413. 3 p. Type **431** 5 5
2414. 12 p. St. Christopher carrying Holy Child .. 25 10

432. Nicoya Church, Costa Rica.

1976. "Hispanidad 1976" – Links with Costa Rica. Multicoloured.
2415. 1 p. Type **432** .. 5 5
2416. 2 p. Juan Vazquez de Coronado (vert.) .. 5 5
2417. 3 p. Orosi Mission, Costa Rica 8 5
2418. 12 p. Tomas de Acosta (vert.) 25 10

1976. Royal Visit to the Americas (2nd issue). As T **425.** Multicoloured.
2419. 12 p. "Santia Maria" and South America .. 25 10

433. Monastery Building.

1976. Monastery of San Pedro de Alcantara.
2420. **433.** 3 p. brown and purple 8 5
2421. – 7 p. purple and indigo 15 5
2422. – 20 p. choc. and brown 45 20
DESIGNS—VERT. 7 p. High Altar. 20 p. San Pedro de Alcantara.

434. Hand releasing Doves.

1976. Civil War Invalids' Association.
2423. **434.** 3 p. multicoloured .. 8 5

435. Pablo Casals and Cello.

1976. Musicians' Birth Centenaries.
2424. **435.** 3 p. black and blue .. 8 5
2425. – 5 p. green and red .. 12 5
DESIGN: 5 p. Manuel de Falla and Fire Dance.

1977. Spanish Military Uniforms (7th series). Vert. designs as T **371.** Multicoloured.
2426. 1 p. Outrider, Calatrava Lancers, 1844 .. 5 5
2427. 2 p. Sapper, Engineers' Regt., 1850 .. 5 5
2428. 3 p. Corporal, Light Infantry, 1861 .. 8 5
2429. 4 p. Drum Major, Infantry of the Line, 1861 .. 10 5
2430. 20p. Captain, Horse Artillery, 1862 .. .. 45 20

EXPRESS LETTER STAMPS

E **1.** Pegasus and Arms.

1905.
E 308. E **1.** 20 c. red .. .. 20·00 15

E **2.** Spanish Royal Family.

1926. Red Cross.
E 417. E **2.** 20 c. purple .. 3·00 2·00

E **3.** Gazelle. E **4.**

1929. Seville and Barcelona Exhibitions.
E 521. E **3.** 20 c. red .. .. 6·50 6·50

1929.
E 522a. E **4.** 20 c. red .. .. 4·75 15

1929. Optd. **Sociedad de las Naciones LV reunion del Consejo Madrid.**
E 534. E **4.** 20 c. red .. .. 7·50 7·50

1930. Optd. **URGENCIA.**
E 535a. E **4.** 20 c. red .. .. 4·75 20

E **5.**

1930. Int. Railway Congress.
E 553. E **5.** 20 c. red .. .. 20·00 20·00

1930. "Goya" type optd. **URGENTE.**
E 570. **50.** 20 c. mauve .. 20 20

1930. Air. "Goya" type optd. **URGENTE.**
E 583. – 20 c. brown and grey 20 20

1930. "Columbus" type optd. **URGENTE.**
E 608. **57.** 20 c. purple .. 75 75

E **6.** Seville Exhibition.

1930. Spanish-American Exn.
E 643. E **6.** 20 c. orange .. 15 15

1931. Optd. **REPUBLICA.**
E 660. E **4.** 20 c. red (No. E 535a) 2·25 2·25
E 672. 20 c. red (No. E 522a) 2·25 2·25

1931. Optd. **Republica Espanola** in two lines continuously.
E 697. E **4.** 20 c. red (No. E 522a) 3·00 20

E **7.** E **8.**

1931. Montserrat Monastery. 9th Cent.
E 731. E **7.** 20 c. red .. .. 11·00 11·00

1934.
E 779. E **8.** 20 c. red 5 5

E **9.** Newspaper Boy. E **10.** Pegasus.

1936. Madrid Press Assoc. 40th Anniv.
E 801. E **9.** 20 c. red 20 20

1937.
E 906. E **10.** 20 c. brown .. 50 5

E **11.** Pegasus. E **12.**

1939.
E 1022. E **11.** 25 c. red 10 5

1940. Apparition of Virgin of El Pilar at Zaragoza. 19th Cent.
1006. E **12.** 25 c.+5 c. red & buff 20 20

E **13.** "Speed". E **14.** Centaur.

1956.
E 1250. E **13.** 2 p. red 8 5
E 1251. 3 p. red 10 5
E 1252. E **14.** 4 p. magenta & blk. 10 5
E 1253. E **13.** 5 p. vermilion .. 15 5
E 1254. E **14.** 6 p. 50 red and vio. 20 5

E **19.** Roman Chariot.

1971.
E 2099. E **19.** 10 p. grn., blk. & red 25 5
E 2100. – 15 p. blue, blk. & red 30 8
DESIGN—VERT. 15 p. Letter encircling Globe.

OFFICIAL STAMPS

O **1.** O **2.**

1854.
O 46. O **1.** ½ onza black on orge. 1·00 40
O 47. 1 onza black on red .. 1·50 60
O 48. 4 onza black on green 3·25 1·00
O 49. 1 libra black on blue 27·00 15·00

1855. Similar to Type O **1**, but Arms in oval frame, inscr. "CORREO OFICIAL".
O 50. ½ onza black on yellow 85 40
O 51. 1 onza black on red .. 85 40
O 52. 4 onza black on green 1·75 90
O 53. 1 libra black on lilac 6·50 3·75

1895.
O 289. **29.** 15 c. yellow .. .. 2·00 20
O 290. O **2.** (No value) Red .. 2·25 45
O 291. (No value) Blue .. 4·25 1·10

O **3.** National Library.

O **4.** Cervantes. O **5.**

1916. Cervantes. Death Tercent. (a) For use by Members of the Chamber of Deputies.
O 353. – Black and violet .. 50 50
O 354. O **3.** Black and green .. 50 50
O 355. O **4.** Black and violet .. 50 50
O 356. O **5.** Black and red .. 50 50

(b) For use by Members of the Senate.
O 357. – Black and green .. 50 50
O 358. O **3.** Black and red .. 50 50
O 359. O **4.** Black and brown .. 50 50
O 360. O **5.** Black and brown .. 50 50
DESIGN—As Type O **3**: Chamber of Deputies.

1931. 3rd Pan-American Postal Union Congress. T **73**, etc. Optd. **Oficial.**
O 707. 5 c. brown 5 5
O 708. 10 c. green 5 5
O 709. 15 c. violet 5 5
O 710. 25 c. red 5 5
O 711. 30 c. olive 5 5
O 712. 40 c. blue 10 10
O 713. 50 c. orange 10 10

O 714. 1 p. grey 10 10
O 715. 4 p. mauve 1·00 1·00
O 716. 10 p. brown 3·50 3·50

Air. T 75, etc., optd. **OFICIAL.**
O 717. 5 c. brown 5 5
O 718. 10 c. green 5 5
O 719. 25 c. red 5 5
O 720. 50 c. blue 5 5
O 721. 1 p. lilac 5 5
O 722. 4 p. grey 2·00 2·00

WAR TAX STAMPS

W 1. W 2. W 3.

1874. The 5 c. perf. or imperf.
W 217. W 1. 5 c. de p. black 2·25 25
W 218. 10 c. de p. blue 5·00 1·00

1875. As Type W 1, but large figures in bottom corners.
W 228. 5 c. de p. green 2·25 35
W 229. 10 c. de p. mauve 6·00 1·10

1876.
W 253. W 2. 5 c. de p. green 90 30
W 254. 10 c. de p. blue 90 30
W 258. W 3. 15 c. de p. claret 2·00 25
W 255. W 2. 25 c. de p. black 11·00 2·75
W 259. W 3. 50 c. de p. yellow 80·00 16·00
W 256. W 2. 1 p. lilac 50·00 11·00
W 257. 5 p. red 75·00 35·00

W 4. W 5. W 6.

1897. Inscr. "1897–98".
W 289. W 4. 5 c. green 1·25 20
W 290. 10 c. green 1·25 20
W 291. 15 c. green 85·00 32·00
W 292. 20 c. green 2·50 50

1898. Inscr. "1898–99".
W 293. W 4. 5 c. black 50 15
W 294. 10 c. black 65 15
W 295. 15 c. black 14·00 2·75
W 296. 20 c. black 1·40 60

1898.
W 297. W 5. 5 c. black 1·75 10

1938.
W 839. W 6. 10 c. red 8
W 840. 20 c. blue 8
W 841. 60 c. red 40
W 842. 1 p. blue 40
W 843. 2 p. green 40
W 844. 10 p. blue 50
Nos. W 842/3 have coloured figures of value on white backgrounds.

SPANISH GUINEA O2

A Spanish colony consisting of the islands of Fernando Poo, Annobon and the Corisco Islands off the W. coast of Africa and Rio Muni on the mainland. Fernando Poo resumed issuing stamps in 1960 (q.v.) and Rio Muni also had its own stamps in 1960.

1902. "Curly Head" key-type inscr. "GUINEA ESPANOLA 1902".
1. Z. 5 c. green 4·50 90
2. 10 c. grey 4·50 90
3. 25 c. red 25·00 6·00
4. 50 c. brown 25·00 5·00
5. 75 c. lilac 24·00 5·50
6. 1 p. red 25·00 5·50
7. 2 p. green 35·00 7·00
8. 5 p. orange 90·00 24·00

1903. "Curly Head" key-type inscr. "GUINEA CONTIAL-ESPANOLA PARA 1903".
21. Z. ¼ c. black 65 15
22. ½ c. green 65 15
23. 1 c. claret 60 12
24. 2 c. olive 60 12
25. 3 c. brown 60 12
26. 4 c. red 60 12
27. 5 c. brown 60 12
28. 10 c. brown 80 15
29. 15 c. blue 2·50 65
30. 25 c. orange 2·75 1·00
31. 50 c. claret 4·75 1·75
32. 75 c. lilac 6·50 1·90
33. 1 p. green 8·50 2·50
34. 2 p. green 10·00 2·75
35. 3 p. red 24·00 3·00
36. 4 p. blue 32·00 4·75
37. 5 p. purple 48·00 7·50
38. 10. red 75·00 10·00

1905. "Curly-Head" key-type inscr. as above but dated "1905".
39. Z. 1 c. black 15 10
40. 2 c. green 15 10
41. 3 c. claret 15 10
42. 4 c. green 15 10
43. 5 c. brown 15 10
44. 10 c. red 50 25
45. 15 c. brown 1·75 70
46. 25 c. brown 1·75 70
47. 50 c. blue 3·00 1·75
48. 75 c. orange 4·00 2·10
49. 1 p. red 4·00 2·50
50. 2 p. lilac 7·00 3·00
51. 3 p. green 17·00 7·50
52. 4 p. green 17·00 10·00
53. 5 p. red 30·00 11·00
54. 10 p. blue 48·00 30·00

1907. As T 1 of Rio de Oro, but inscr. "GUINEA CONTAL. ESPANOLA".
71. 1 c. green 40 10
72. 2 c. blue 40 10
73. 3 c. lilac 40 10
74. 4 c. green 40 10
75. 5 c. red 40 10
76. 10 c. orange 1·75 45
77. 15 c. brown 1·00 25
78. 25 c. blue 1·00 25
79. 50 c. brown 1·00 25
80. 75 c. blue 1·00 25
81. 1 p. orange 2·00 40
82. 2 p. brown 3·50 1·00
83. 3 p. black 3·50 1·00
84. 4 p. claret 4·00 1·00
85. 5 p. green 4·75 1·50
86. 10 p. purple 7·00 1·75

1908. Surch. **HABILITADO PARA** and value in figures and **CTMS.**
87. 1. 05 c. on 1 c. green 1·60 90
88. 05 c. on 2 c. blue 1·60 90
89. 05 c. on 3 c. lilac 1·60 90
90. 05 c. on 4 c. green 1·60 90
91. 05 c. on 10 c. orange 1·60 90
92. 15 c. on 10 c. orange 7·50 3·50

1909. As T 2 of Rio de Oro but in scr. "TERRITORIOS ESPANOLES DEL GOLFO DE GUINEA".
101. 1 c. brown 12 5
102. 2 c. red 12 5
103. 5 c. green 55 12
104. 10 c. red 25 10
105. 15 c. brown 25 10
106. 20 c. mauve 40 20
107. 25 c. blue 50 20
108. 30 c. brown 35 15
109. 40 c. claret 30 12
110. 50 c. lilac 25 15
111. 1 p. green 5·50 1·25
112. 4 p. orange 1·50 1·00
113. 10 p. red 1·60 1·00
This set was also issued optd. **GUINEA 1911** in an oval.

1912. As T 3 of Rio de Oro, but inscr. "TERRS. ESPANOLES DEL GOLFO DE GUINEA".
127. 1 c. black 10 5
128. 2 c. brown 10 5
129. 5 c. green 10 5
130. 10 c. red 12 8
131. 15 c. claret 20 10
132. 20 c. red 30 12
133. 25 c. blue 20 10
134. 30 c. claret 1·25 50
135. 40 c. red 80 30
136. 50 c. orange 55 15
137. 1 p. lilac 85 30
138. 4 p. mauve 1·75 70
139. 10 p. green 3·75 2·00
This set was also issued optd. **1917.**

1914. As T 4 of Rio de Oro but inscr. as 1912 issue.
140. 1 c. violet 12 10
141. 2 c. red 15 12
142. 5 c. green 15 10
143. 10 c. red 20 15
144. 15 c. purple 12 10
145. 20 c. brown 20 15
146. 25 c. blue 30 15
147. 30 c. brown 60 25
148. 40 c. green 65 25
149. 50 c. claret 30 15
150. 1 p. orange 60 50
151. 4 p. claret 1·00 45
152. 10 p. brown 1·00 55

1918. Stamps of 1912 surch. **HTADO-1917.** and value in figures and words.
166. 8. 5 c. on 40 c. red 8·50 3·50
167. 10 c. on 4 p. mauve 8·50 3·50
168. 15 c. on 20 c. red 16·00 5·50
169. 25 c. on 10 p. green 15·00 5·50

5. 6. 7.

1919.
170. 5. 1 c. violet 50 15
171. 2 c. red 50 15
172. 5 c. red 50 15
173. 10 c. purple 80 15
174. 15 c. brown 80 20
175. 5. 20 c. blue 80 25
176. 25 c. green 85 25
177. 30 c. orange 85 25
178. 40 c. orange 1·75 25
179. 50 c. red 1·75 25
180. 1 p. green 1·75 40
181. 4 p. claret 3·50 1·25
182. 10 p. brown 6·00 1·75

1920. As T 6 of Rio de Oro, but inscr. as 1909 issue.
183. 1 c. brown 10 5
184. 2 c. red 10 5
185. 5 c. green 15 5
186. 10 c. red 20 10
187. 15 c. orange 20 10
188. 20 c. yellow 20 10
189. 25 c. blue 25 10
190. 30 c. green 12·00 3·50
191. 40 c. brown 25 12
192. 50 c. purple 80 12
193. 1 p. brown 80 12
194. 4 p. red 2·00 90
195. 10 p. violet 3·50 2·00

1922.
196. 6. 1 c. brown 20 5
197. 2 c. claret 20 5
198. 5 c. green 30 8
199. 10 c. red 1·25 25
200. 15 c. orange 25 10
201. 20 c. mauve 1·00 20
202. 25 c. blue 1·50 35
203. 30 c. violet 1·50 25
204. 40 c. blue 1·00 15
205. 50 c. red 1·00 15
206. 1 p. green 1·25 15
207. 4 p. brown 4·00 1·25
208. 10 p. yellow 8·00 2·25

1925.
209. 7. 5 c. blue and brown 15 10
210. 10 c. blue and green 15 10
211. 15 c. black and red 20 10
212. 20 c. black and violet 15 10
213. 25 c. black and red 35 20
214. 30 c. black and orange 35 15
215. 40 c. black and blue 35 15
216. 50 c. black and claret 35 15
217. 60 c. black and brown 35 15
218. 1 p. black and violet 1·00 15
219. 4 p. black and blue 2·25 1·25
220. 10 p. black and green 5·00 2·25

1926. Red Cross stamps of Spain optd. **GUINEA ESPANOLA.**
221. – 5 c. grey 50 50
222. – 10 c. green 50 50
223. 37. 15 c. violet 25 25
224. – 20 c. purple 25 25
225. 38. 25 c. red 25 25
226. 37. 30 c. olive 25 25
227. – 40 c. blue 5 5
228. – 50 c. brown 5 5
229. 38. 60 c. green 5 5
230. – 1 p. red 5 5
231. – 4 p. brown 20 20
232. 38. 10 p. lilac 40 40

1929. Seville and Barcelona Exhibition. stamps of Spain (1929) optd. **GUINEA.**
233. 5 c. red 5 5
234. 10 c. green 5 5
235. 15 c. blue 5 5
236. 20 c. violet 5 5
237. 25 c. red 5 5
238. 30 c. brown 5 5
239. 40 c. blue 10 10
240. 50 c. orange 8 8
241. 1 p. grey 40 40
242. 4 p. red 1·25 1·25
243. 10 p. brown 2·00 2·00

8.

8a. Gen. Franco.

8b.

1931.
244. 8. 1 c. green 10 5
245. 2 c. brown 10 5
246. 5 c. sepia 10 5
318. 5 c. olive-grey 40 5
247. 10 c. green 12 10
248. 15 c. blue 15 8
263. 20 c. violet 12 5
250. – 25 c. red 15 5
251. – 30 c. red 25 8
252. – 40 c. blue 35 25
320. – 40 c. green 40 5
253. – 50 c. orange 75 50
292. – 50 c. blue 2·75 20
254. – 80 c. blue 1·25 65
255. – 1 p. black 2·25 10
256. – 4 p. claret 12·00 5·00
257. – 5 p. brown 6·00 4·00
DESIGNS: 25 c. to 50 c. Native drummers. 80 c. to 5 p. King Alfonso and Queen.

1931. Optd. **REPUBLICA ESPANOLA** horiz.
258. 8. 1 c. green 8 5
259. 2 c. brown 8 5
260. 5 c. grey 10 5
261. 10 c. green 12 5
262. 8. 15 c. blue 12 5
263. 20 c. violet 12 5
264. 25 c. red 12 5
265. 30 c. claret 25 15
266. 40 c. blue 60 25
267. 50 c. orange 3·25 1·75
268. 80 c. blue 1·25 60
269. 1 p. black 3·50 1·25
270. 4 p. claret 6·00 3·00
271. 5 p. brown 6·00 3·00

1933. Optd. **Republica Espanola** horiz.
272. 8. 1 c. green 10 5
273. 2 c. brown 10 5
274. 5 c. grey 15 5
275. 10 c. green 15 5
276. 15 c. blue 12 5
277. 20 c. violet 15 8
278. 25 c. red 20 10
279. 30 c. claret 20 20
280. 40 c. blue 1·10 30
281. 50 c. orange 2·50 1·40
282. 80 c. blue 1·75 1·00
283. 1 p. black 3·00 1·25
284. 4 p. claret 12·00 5·50
285. 5 p. brown 12·00 5·50

1937. Surch. **HABILITADO 30 Cts.**
293. 8. 30 c. on 40 c. (No. 252) 1·60 1·00
294. 30 c. on 40 c. (No. 266) 7·50 3·00
295. 30 c. on 40 c. (No. 280) 22·00 6·50

1939. Stamps of Spain, 1937, optd. **Territorios Espanoles del Golfo de Guinea** in script type.
296. 124. 10 c. green 1·00 15
297. 125. 15 c. black 1·00 15
298. 20 c. violet 1·75 60
299. 25 c. red 1·75 60

1939. Surch. **Habilitado 40 cts.**
300. 8. 40 c. on 80 c. (No. 268) 3·75 2·50
301. 40 c. on 80 c. (No. 282) 3·75 2·50

1940.
311. 8a. 5 c. brown 1·25 35
312. 40 c. blue 1·75 35
314. 50 c. green 8·00 3·50

1940. Fiscal stamps as T 8b inscr. "ESPECIAL MOVIL", "TIMBRE MOVIL" or "IMPUESTO SOBRE CONTRATOS" and surch. as in T 8b or optd. only.
302. 5 c. red 3·00 1·25
304. 5 c. on 35 c. green 3·50 1·50
307. 10 c. on 75 c. brown 4·25 1·60
308. 15 c. on 1 p. 50 violet 3·50 1·60
305. 25 c. on 60 c. brown 3·25 1·25
306. 50 c. on 75 c. sepia 4·25 1·75
310. 1 p. bistre 32·00 17·00
303. 1 p. on 15 c. olive 6·00 2·25
316. 1 p. on 17 p. red 25·00 9·00
315. 1 p. on 40 p. green 6·00 2·50

1941. Air. Fiscal stamp as T 8b inscr. "IMPUESTO SOBRE CONTRATOS" surch. **Habilitado para Correo Aereo Intercolonial Una Peseta** and bar.
A 317a. 1 p. on 17 p. red 12·00 2·25

1942. Surch. **Habilitado 3 Pesetas.**
321. 8. 3 p. on 20 c. vio. (No. 319) 4·25 80

1942. Stamps of Spain, 1939, optd. **Golfo de Guinea.**
322a. 133. 1 PTA. black 35 15
323. 4 PTAS. red 1·75 40

1942. Air. Air stamp of Spain optd. **Golfo de Guinea.**
324. 132. 1 p. blue 75 10

1943. Stamp of Spain, 1939, optd. **Territorios espanoles del Golfo de Guinea.**
325. 133. 2 PTAS. brown 45 15

1948. Air. Ministerial Visit. No. 323 optd. **CORREO AEREO VIAJE MINISTERIAL 10-19 ENERO 1948.**
326. 133. 4 PTAS. red 3·50 1·25

1949. Nos. 322a and 325 surch. **Habilitado para** and value in words.
327. 133. 5 c. on 1 PTA. black 15 5
328. 15 c. on 2 PTAS. brown 12 5

9. Natives Canoeing.

1949. U.P.U. 75th Anniv.
329. 9. 4 p. violet 80 25

HAVE YOU READ THE NOTES AT THE BEGINNING OF THIS CATALOGUE?
These often provide answers to the enquiries we receive.

10. Count Argalejo and San Carlos Bay.

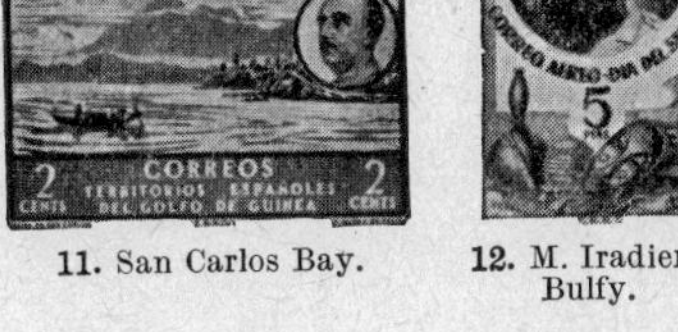

11. San Carlos Bay.

12. M. Iradier y Bulfy.

1949. Air. Colonial Stamp Day.
330. 10. 5 p. green 90 25

1949.
331. 11. 2 c. brown 5 5
332. – 5 c. violet 5 5
333. – 10 c. blue 5 5
334. – 15 c. black 10 5
335. 11. 25 c. maroon 10 5
336. – 30 c. yellow 5 5
337. – 40 c. olive 5 5
338. – 45 c. claret 5 5
339. 11. 50 c. orange 5 5
340. – 75 c. blue 8 8
341. – 90 c. green 12 10
342. – 1 p. slate 40 10
343. 11. 1 p. 35 violet .. .. 1·50 35
344. – 2 p. grey .. .. 4·00 60
345. – 5 p. mauve .. .. 5·50 1·25
346. 11. 10 p. brown .. .. 16·00 5·00
DESIGNS: 5 c., 30 c., 75 c., 2 p. Benito River rapids. 10 c., 40 c., 90 c., 5 p. Coast scene and Clarence Peak, Fernando Poo. 15 c., 45 c., 1 p. Nieparz Benito River.

1950. Air. Colonial Stamp Day.
347. 12. 5 p. brown .. .. 1·25 30

13. Hands and Natives.

14. Mt. Mioco.

1951. Native Welfare.
348. 13. 50 c.+10 c. blue .. 20 15
349. 1 p.+25 c. green .. 5·50 1·50
350. 6 p. 50+1 p. 65 orange 2·00 55

1951. Air.
351. – 25 c. yellow 5 8
352. 14. 50 c. mauve 5 5
353. – 1 p. green 5 5
354. – 2 p. blue 15 12
355. 14. 3 p. 25 violet 40 15
356. – 5 p. sepia .. .. 2·25 55
357. – 10 p. red .. .. 7·50 1·60
DESIGNS: 25 c., 2 p., 10 p. Benito Rapids. 1 p., 5 p. Santa Isabel Bay.

1951. Air. Isabella the Catholic. 500th Birth Anniv. As T 5 of Ifni.
358. 5 p. blue .. .. .. 4·00 1·00

16. Native and map.

15. Leopard.

17. Native man.

1951. Colonial Stamp Day.
359. 15. 5 c.+5 c. brown .. 5 5
360. 10 c.+5 c. orange .. 5 5
361. 60 c.+15 c. olive .. 12 12

1951. Int. W. African Conf.
362. 16. 50 c. orange 30 12
363. 5 p. blue .. .. 5·00 1·00

1952.
364. 17. 5 c. brown 5 5
365. 50 c. olive 8 5
366. 5 p. violet .. .. 1·25 15

18. "Crinum Giganteum". 19. Ferdinand the Catholic. 20. Hornbills.

1952. Native Welfare Fund.
367. 18. 5 c.+5 c. brown .. 5 5
368. 50 c.+10 c. black .. 8 8
369. 2 p.+30 c. blue.. .. 75 40

1952. Air. Ferdinand the Catholic. 500th Birth Anniv.
370. 19. 5 p. chocolate .. .. 8·00 1·90

1952. Colonial Stamp Day.
371. 20. 5 c.+5 c. brown .. 10 5
372. 10 c.+5 c. purple .. 15 8
373. 60 c.+15 c. green .. 20 15

21. Native Musician.

22. Native Woman and Dove.

23. "Tragocephala nobilis".

24. Hunting with Bow and Arrow.

1953. Native Welfare Fund. Inscr. "PRO INDIGENAS 1953".
374. 21. 5 c.+5 c. lake 5 5
375. – 10 c.+5 c. purple .. 5 5
376. 21. 15 c. olive 5 5
377. – 60 c. brown 8 8
DESIGN: 10 c., 60 c. Musician facing right.

1953.
378. 22. 5 c. orange 5 5
379. 10 c. purple 5 5
380. 60 c. brown 10 5
381. – 1 p. lilac 80 8
382. – 1 p. 90 green .. .. 1·25 20
DESIGN: 1 p., 1 p. 90, Native drummer.

1953. Colonial Stamp Day. Inscr. "DIA DEL SELLO COLONIAL 1953".
383. 23. 5 c.+5 c. blue 5 5
384. – 10 c.+5 c. purple .. 5 5
385. 23. 15 c. green 15 12
386. – 60 c. brown 15 12
DESIGN: 10, 60 c. "Papilio antimachus" (butterfly).

1954. Native Welfare Fund. Inscr. "PRO-INDIGENAS 1954".
387. 24. 5 c.+5 c. lake 5 5
388. – 10 c.+5 c. lilac.. .. 5 5
389. 24. 15 c. green 5 5
390. – 60 c. brown 15 8
DESIGN: 10, 60 c. Hunting elephant with spear.

25. Turtle.

26. M. Iradier y Bulfy.

27. Native Priest.

1954. Colonial Stamp Day. Inscr. "DIA DEL SELLO COLONIAL 1954".
391. 25. 5 c.+5 c. red 5 5
392. – 10 c.+5 c. purple .. 5 5
393. 25. 15 c. green 5 5
394. – 60 c. brown 15 10
DESIGN: 10 c., 60 c. "Leptocharias smithi" (Fish).

1955. Iradier (explorer). Birth Cent.
395. 26. 60 c. brown 25 5
396. 1 p. violet .. .. 2·25 25

1955. Apostolic Prefecture in Fernando Poo. Cent.
397. 27. 10 c.+5 c. purple .. 5 5
398. – 25 c.+10 c. violet .. 5 5
399. 27. 50 c. olive 8 5
DESIGN: 25 c. "Baptism".

28. Footballers.

29. El Pardo Palace, Madrid.

1955. Air.
400. 28. 25 c. grey 5 5
401. 50 c. olive 5 5
402. 1 p. 50 brown 40 8
403. 4 p. red.. .. .. 1·50 15
404. 10 p. green .. .. 1·10 15

1955. Treaty of Pardo, 1778.
405. 29. 5 c. brown 5 5
406. 15 c. red 5 5
407. 80 c. green 5 5

30. Titi Monkeys.

31. "Orquidea".

1955. Colonial Stamp Day. Inscr. "DIA DEL SELLO COLONIAL 1955".
408. 30. 5 c.+5 c. lake & brown 10 10
409. – 15 c.+5 c. sepia & lake 10 10
410. 30. 70 c. blue and slate .. 12 10
DESIGN—HORIZ. 15 c. Monkey and young.

1956. Native Welfare Fund. Inscr. "PRO INDIGENAS 1956".
411. 31. 5 c. + 5 c. olive .. 5 5
412. – 15 c.+5 c. ochre .. 5 5
413. 31. 20 c. turquoise.. .. 12 12
414. – 50 c. brown 20 20
DESIGN: 15 c., 50 c. "Strophantus Kombe"

32. Arms of Santa Isabel. 33. Parrot. 34. "Flight".

1956. Colonial Stamp Day. Inscr. "DIA DEL SELLO 1956".
415. 32. 5 c.+5 c. brown .. 5 5
416. – 15 c.+5 c. slate-violet 5 5
417. 32. 70 c. green 5 5
DESIGN—HORIZ. 15 c. Arms of Bata and natives.

1957. Native Welfare Fund Inscr. "PRO INDIGENAS 1957".
418. 33. 5 c.+5 c. brown-purple 5 5
419. – 15 c.+5 c. ochre .. 5 5
420. 33. 70 c. sage-green .. 10 10
DESIGN—HORIZ. 15 c. Parrot in flight.

1957. Air. Spain-Fernando Poo Flight by "Atlantida" Seaplane Squadron, 30th Anniv.
421. 34. 25 p. sepia and bistre 1·75 50

35. Elephant and Calf.

DESIGN—VERT. 15 c., 70 c. Elephant trumpeting.

1957. Colonial Stamp Day.
422. 35. 10 c.+5 c. mauve .. 5 5
423. – 15 c.+5 c. brown .. 5 5
424. 35. 20 c. blue-green .. 5 5
425. – 70 c. green 10 10

36. Doves and Arms of Valencia and Santa Isabel.

37. Boxing.

38. Missionary holding Cross.

1958. "Aid for Valencia".
426. 36. 10 c.+5 c. chestnut .. 5 5
427. 15 c.+10 c. ochre .. 5 5
428. 50 c.+10 c. olive-brn.. 10 10

1958. Sports.
429. 37. 5 c. chocolate 5 5
430. – 10 c. chestnut 5 5
431. – 15 c. yellow-brown .. 5 5
432. – 80 c. green 5 5
433. 37. 1 p. salmon 5 5
434. – 2 p. purple 10 5
435. – 2 p. 30 violet 15 5
436. – 3 p. blue 15 5
DESIGNS—VERT. 10 c., 2 p. Basket-ball. 80 c., 3 p. Running. HORIZ. 15 c., 2 p. 30, Long-jumping.

1958. Native Welfare Fund. Inscr. 1883 PRO-INDIGENAS 1958".
437. 38. 10 c.+5 c. chestnut .. 5 5
438. – 15 c.+5 c. ochre .. 5 5
439. 38. 20 c. blue-green .. 5 5
440. – 70 c. green 10 5
DESIGN: 15 c., 70 c. The Crucifixion.

39. Butterflies. 40. Digitalis. 41. Boy on "Penny-farthing" Cycle.

1958. Colonial Stamp Day. Inscr. "1958"
441. 39. 10 c.+5 c. brn.-red .. 5 5
442. – 25 c.+10 c. violet .. 5 5
443. – 50 c.+10 c. olive .. 10 8
DESIGNS: 25 c., 50 c. Different views of butterflies on plants.

1959. Child Welfare Fund. Floral designs as T 40. Inscr. "PRO-INFANCIA 1959".
444. 40. 10 c.+5 c. lake.. .. 5 5
445. – 15 c.+5 c. ochre .. 5 5
446. – 20 c. myrtle 5 5
447. 40. 70 c. green 8 8
DESIGN: 15 c., 20 c. Castor bean.

1959. Colonial Stamp Day. Inscr. "1959".
448. 41. 10 c.+5 c. lake .. 5 5
449. – 20 c.+5 c. myrtle .. 5 5
450. – 50 c.+20 c. olive .. 8 5
DESIGNS: 20 c. Racing cyclists. 50 c. Winning cyclist.

EXPRESS LETTER STAMP

E 1. Fernando Poo.

1951.
E 358. E 1. 25 c. red 12 12

SPANISH MOROCCO

O3

I. SPANISH POST OFFICES IN MOROCCO.

Nos. 2/150, except Nos. 93/8 and 124/37 are all stamps of Spain overprinted.

1903. Optd. **CORREO ESPANOL MARRUECOS.**
2. 17. $\frac{1}{4}$ c. green 5 5

1903. Optd. **CORREO ESPANOL MARRUECOS.**
3. 30. 2 c. brown 30 20
4. 5 c. green.. .. .. 35 10
5. 10 c. red.. .. .. 50 5

6. 30. 15 c. violet 65 15
7. 20 c. grey .. .. 1·00 25
8. 25 c. blue 20 8
9. 30 c. green 65 25
10. 40 c. red .. .. 1·50 45
11. 50 c. blue 75 35
12. 1 p. claret .. .. 1·60 45
13. 4 p. purple .. .. 4·50 1·00
14. 10 p. orange .. .. 4·50 1·50

1908. Stamps of Spain handstamped **TETUAN.**

15. 17. ½ c. green 1 75 60
16. 30. 2 c. brown .. .. 7·00 7·40
17. 5 c. green .. .. 8·50 4·50
18. 10 c. red .. .. 10·00 5·00
19. 15 c. violet .. .. 8·50 4·25
20. 20 c. grey .. .. 24·00 20·00
21. 25 c. blue .. .. 11·00 5·50
22. 30 c. green .. .. 24·00 10·00
23. 40 c. bistre .. .. 42·00 21·00

1908. Nos. 2/5 and 7/8 handstamped **TETUAN.**

24. 17. ½ c. green 60 60
25. 30. 2 c. brown .. .. 24·00 12·00
26. 5 c. green .. .. 21·00 9·00
27. 10 c. red .. .. 21·00 9·00
28. 20 c. grey .. .. 50·00 24·00
29. 25 c. blue .. .. 14·00 7·00

1909. Optd. as 1903.

30. 32. 2 c. brown 8
31. 5 c. green 50 35
32. 10 c. red 60 10
33. 15 c. violet .. .. 1·00 10
34. 20 c. green .. .. 2·00 20
35. 25 c. blue .. .. 38·00
36. 30 c. green 60 8
37. 40 c. pink 75 8
38. 50 c. blue .. .. 1·00 8
39. 1 p. lake .. .. 1·50 10
40. 4 p. purple .. .. 42·00
41. 10 p. orange .. .. 42·00

After the appearance of Nos. 42/54 for the Spanish Protectorate in 1914, the use of Nos. 30/41 was restricted to Tangier.

II. SPANISH PROTECTORATE (excluding Tangier).

1914. Optd. **MARRUECOS.**

42. 17. ½ c. green 5 5
43. 32. 2 c. brown 5 5
44. 5 c. green 20 10
45. 10 c. red 20 10
46. 15 c. violet 50 35
47. 20 c. green 70 50
48. 25 c. blue 50 30
49. 30 c. green 90 45
50. 40 c. pink .. .. 2·10 65
51. 50 c. blue .. .. 1·00 50
52. 1 p. red .. .. 1·00 50
53. 4 p. purple .. .. 5·50 3·00
54. 10 p. orange .. .. 7·00 3·50

1915. Optd. **PROTECTORADO ESPANOL EN MARRUECOS.**

55. 17. ½ c. green 15 5
56. 32. 2 c. brown 10 5
57. 5 c. green 15 5
58. 10 c. red 15 5
59. 15 c. violet 20 5
60. 20 c. green 35 8
61. 25 c. blue 35 10
62. 30 c. green 40 15
63. 40 c. pink 40 15
64. 50 c. blue 60 8
65. 1 p. red 60 10
66. 4 p. purple .. .. 5·50 2·40
67. 10 p. orange .. .. 8·00 3·25

1916. Optd. **ZONA DE PROTECTORADO ESPANOL EN MARRUECOS.**

68. 17. ½ c. green 5 5
69. 33. 1 c. green 45 5
70. 32. 2 c. brown 25 8
71. 5 c. green 70 8
72. 10 c. red 70 8
73. 15 c. orange 90 10
74. 20 c. violet .. .. 1·00 5
75. 25 c. blue .. .. 2·25 25
76. 30 c. green .. .. 3·25 1·00
77. 40 c. red .. .. 3·00 30
78. 50 c. blue .. .. 1·50 8
79. 1 p. red .. .. 3·00 30
80. 4 p. purple .. .. 10·00 3·25
81. 10 p. orange .. .. 21·00 7·00

1920. Optd. **PROTECTORADO ESPANOL EN MARRUECOS** perf. through centre and each half surch. in figures and words.

82. 32. 10 c.+10 c. on 20 c. green 1·50 1·50
83. 15 c.+15 c. on 30 c. green 3·50 2·00

1920. No. E 2 perf. through centre, and each half surch. **10 centimos.**

84. E 1. 10 c.+10 c. on 20 c. red 4·00 2·00

1920. Fiscal stamps showing figure of Justice, bisected and surch. **CORREOS** and value.

93. 5 c. on 5 p. blue .. 2·10 45
94. 5 c. on 10 p. green .. 15 8
95. 10 c. on 25 p. green .. 15 8
96. 10 c. on 50 p. grey .. 25 10
97. 15 c. on 100 p. red .. 25 10
98. 15 c. on 500 p. red .. 5·00 1·00

1923. Optd. as 1916.

101. 35. 2 c. olive 10 5
102. 5 c. purple 10 5
103. 10 c. green 50 5
105. 15 c. slate 50 5
106. 20 c. violet 60 5
107. 25 c. red .. .. 1·25 20
108. 40 c. blue .. .. 1·75 50
109. 50 c. orange .. .. 3·00 60
110. 36. 1 p. grey .. .. 5·50 50

1926. Red Cross stamps optd. **ZONA PROTECTORADO ESPANOL.**

111. 37. 1 c. orange 70 70
112. – 2 c. red 85 85
113. – 5 c. grey 35 35
114. – 10 c. green 35 35
115. 37. 15 c. violet 20 20
116. – 20 c. purple 20 20
117. 38. 25 c. red 20 20
118. 37. 30 c. olive 20 20
119. – 40 c. blue 5 5
120. – 50 c. brown 5 5
121. – 1 p. red 5 5
122. – 4 p. brown 20 20
123. 38. 10 p. lilac 30 30

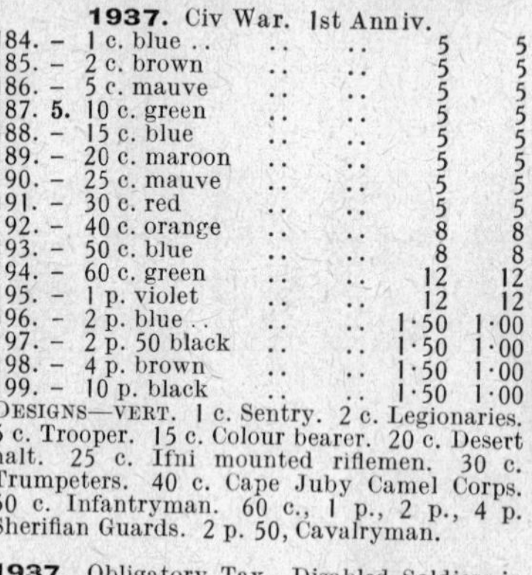

1. Mosque of Alcazarquivir. 2. Well at Alhucemas.

1928.

124. 1. 1 c. red 5 5
126. 2 c. violet 8 8
127. 5 c. blue 5 5
128. 10 c. green 5 5
129. 15 c. brown 20 5
130. – 20 c. olive 15 5
131. – 25 c. red 15 5
132. – 30 c. brown 30 8
133. – 40 c. blue 45 5
134. – 50 c. purple .. .. 1·00 5
135. 2. 1 p. green .. .. 1·75 12
136. – 2 p. 50 purple .. 5·00 80
137. – 4 p. blue .. .. 4·50 60

DESIGNS—VERT. 20 c. to 50 c. Moorish Gateway, Larache. HORIZ. 2 p. 50 Xauen. 4 p. Tetuan.

1929. Seville-Barcelona Exhibition stamps, Nos. 502/14 optd. **PROTECTORADO MARRUECOS.**

138. 1 c. blue 8 8
139. 2 c. green 5 5
140. 5 c. red 5 5
141. 10 c. green 5 5
142. 15 c. blue 5 5
143. 20 c. violet 5 5
144. 25 c. red 5 5
145. 30 c. brown 8 8
146. 40 c. blue 8 8
147. 50 c. orange 8 8
148. 1 p. grey 50 50
149. 4 p. red .. .. 1·00 1·00
150. 10 p. brown .. .. 1·50 1·50

3. Xauen.

4. Market-place, Larache.

1933.

151. 3. 1 c. red 5 5
152. – 2 c. green 5 5
153. – 5 c. magenta .. 10 5
154. – 10 c. green 15 5
155. – 15 c. yellow 40 5
156. 3. 20 c. green 25 5
157. – 25 c. red .. .. 3·75 15
165. – 25 c. violet 20 5
158. – 30 c. lake .. .. 1·00 5
166. – 30 c. red .. .. 2·25 5
159. 4. 40 c. blue .. .. 2·00 10
167. – 40 c. red .. .. 1·40 10
160. 4. 50 c. red .. .. 6·50 1·00
168. – 50 c. blue .. .. 1·50 1
169. – 60 c. green .. .. 1·40 10
161. – 1 p. grey .. .. 6·50 1·00
170. – 2 p. lake .. .. 7·00 1·00
162. – 2 p. 50 c. brown .. 4·00 1·00
163. – 4 p. green .. .. 4·00 1·00
164. – 5 p. black .. .. 5·50 1·25

DESIGNS—HORIZ. 2 c., 1 p. Xauen. 5 c., 2 p. 50 c. Arcila. 25 c. (No. 157), 5 p. Sultan and bodyguard. 30 c. (No. 166), 50 c. (No. 168), 2 p. Forest at Ketama. VERT. 10 c., 30 c. (No. 158), Tetuan. 15 c., 4 p. Alcazarquivir. 25 c. (No. 165), 40 c. (No. 167), Wayside scene at Arcila.

See also Nos. 177/83 and 213/6.

1936. Air. Surch. with new value and **18-7-36.**

171. 4. 25 c.+2 p. on 25 c. red 5·00 1·75

1936. Surch.

172. – 1 c. on 4 p. blue (137) 8 5
173. – 2 c. on 2 p. 50 pur. (136) 8 5
174. – 5 c. on 25 c. red (131) .. 5 5
175. 2. 10 c. on 1 p. green .. 2·00 1·00
176. E 1. 15 c. on 20 c. black 1·90 50

1937. Pictorials as T 3/4.

177. 1 c. green 5 5
178. 2 c. mauve 5 5
179. 5 c. orange 10 5
180. 15 c. violet 10 5
181. 30 c. red 25 5
182. 1 p. blue .. .. 1·00 10
183. 10 p. brown .. .. 14·00 3·50

DESIGNS—VERT. 1 c., 15 c. Caliph and Viziers. 30 c. Tetuan. 1 p. Arcila. 10 p. Caliph on horseback. HORIZ. 2 c. Bokoia. 5 c. Alcazarquivir.

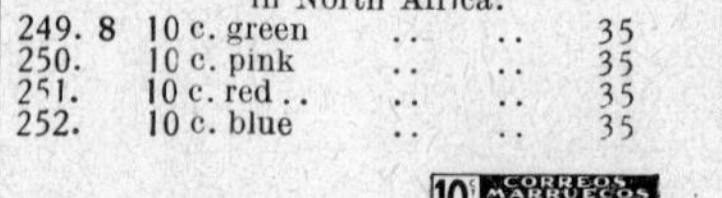

5. Volunteers. 6. General Franco.

1937. Civ War. 1st Anniv.

184. – 1 c. blue 5 5
185. – 2 c. brown 5 5
186. – 5 c. mauve 5 5
187. 5. 10 c. green 5 5
188. – 15 c. blue 5 5
189. – 20 c. maroon 5 5
190. – 25 c. mauve 5 5
191. – 30 c. red 5 5
192. – 40 c. orange 8 8
193. – 50 c. blue 8 8
194. – 60 c. green 12 12
195. – 1 p. violet 12 12
196. – 2 p. blue .. .. 1·50 1·00
197. – 2 p. 50 black .. 1·50 1·00
198. – 4 p. brown .. .. 1·50 1·00
199. – 10 p. black .. .. 1·50 1·00

DESIGNS—VERT. 1 c. Sentry. 2 c. Legionaries. 5 c. Trooper. 15 c. Colour bearer. 20 c. Desert halt. 25 c. Ifni mounted riflemen. 30 c. Trumpeters. 40 c. Cape Juby Camel Corps. 50 c. Infantryman. 60 c., 1 p., 2 p., 4 p. Sherifian Guards. 2 p. 50, Cavalryman.

1937. Obligatory Tax. Disabled Soldiers in N. Africa.

200. 6. 10 c. sepia 10 5
201. 10 c. brown 10 5
202. 10 c. blue 10 5

7. Stork over Mosque.

8. Soldier on Horseback.

1938. Air. As T 7.

203. 5 c. brown 5 5
204. 10 c. green 10 8
205. 25 c. red 8 5
206. 40 c. blue 70 15
207. 50 c. mauve 8 5
208. 75 c. blue 8 0
209. 1 p. brown 10 5
210. 1 p. 50 violet .. 50 25
211. 2 p. red 30 5
212. 3 p. black 70 15

DESIGNS—VERT. 5 c. Aeroplane over Mosque de Baja, Tetuan. 25 c. Straits of Gibraltar. 40 c. Desert natives. 1 p. Mounted postman. 1 p. 50, Stork over farmers. 2 p. Sunset. 3 p. Shadow of 'plane over city. HORIZ. 50 c. Aeroplane over Tetuan. 75 c. 'Plane over Larache.

1939. Pictorials as T 3.

213. 5 c. orange 8 5
214. 10 c. green 8 5
215. 15 c. brown 12 5
216. 20 c. blue 12 5

DESIGNS: 5 c. "Carta de Marruecos". 10 c "Carta de Espana". 15 c. Larache. 20 c. Tetuan.

1940. Pictorials as T 3, inscr. "ZONA" on back.

217. 1 c. brown 5 5
218. 2 c. olive 5 5
219. 5 c. blue 15 5
220. 10 c. lilac 15 5
221. 15 c. green 15 5
222. 20 c. violet 15 5
223. 25 c. sepia 15 5
224. 30 c. green 15 5
225. 40 c. green 50 5
226. 45 c. orange 25 5
227. 50 c. brown 25 5
228. 70 c. blue 25 5
229. 1 p. brown and blue .. 45 5
230. 2 p. 50 green and brown 2·75 75
231. 5 p. sepia and purple .. 50 15
232. 10 p. brown and olive .. 5·00 1·25

DESIGNS—VERT. 1 c. Postman. 2 c. Pillar-box. 5 c. Winter landscape. 10 c. Alcazar street. 15 c. Castle wall, Xauen. 20 c. Palace sentry, Tetuan. 25 c. Caliph on horseback. 30 c. Market-place, Larache. 40 c. Gateway, Tetuan. 45 c. Gateway, Xauen. 50 c. Street, Alcazarquivir. 70 c. Post Office. 1 p. Spanish War veterans. 2 p. 50, Flag bearers. 5 p. and 10 p. Cavalry.

1940. 4th Anniv. of Civil War. Nos. 184/99 optd. **17-VII-940 4o. ANIVERSARIO.**

233. 1 c. blue 20 20
234. 2 c. brown 20 20
235. 5 c. mauve 20 20
236. 10 c. green 20 20
237. 15 c. blue 20 20
238. 20 c. maroon 20 20
239. 25 c. mauve 20 20
240. 30 c. red 20 20
241. 40 c. orange 50 50
242. 50 c. blue 50 50
243. 60 c. green 50 50
244. 1 p. violet 50 50
245. 2 p. blue .. .. 3·50 3·50
246. 2 p. 50 black .. .. 3·50 3·50
247. 4 p. brown .. .. 3·50 5·50
248. 10 p. black .. .. 3·50 3·50

1941. Obligatory Tax for Disabled Soldiers in North Africa.

249. 8 10 c. green 35 5
250. 10 c. pink 35 5
251. 10 c. red 35 5
252. 10 c. blue 35 5

10. General Franco.

9. Larache.

11. Mules.

1941.

253. 9. 5 c. brown & dark brown 5 5
263. – 5 c. blue 5 5
254. – 10 c. vermilion and red .. 8 5
255. – 15 c. yell.-grn. & green .. 8 5
256. – 20 c. blue and ultram. .. 20 5
264. – 40 c. brown .. 4·00 5
257. – 40 c. red and purple .. 50 5

DESIGNS: 5 c. blue, 10 c. Alcazarquivir. 15 c., 40 c. brown, Larache market. 20 c. Moorish house. 40 c. purple, Gateway, Tangier.

1942. Air. New designs as T 3, optd. Z.

258. 5 c. blue 5 5
259. 10 c. brown 5 5
260. 15 c. green 5 5
261. 90 c. red 5 5
262. 5 p. black 50 50

DESIGNS—VERT. 5 c. Atlas mountains. 10 c. Mosque at Tangier. 15 c. Velez fortress. 90 c. Sanjurjo harbour. 5 p. Straits of Gibraltar.

1943. Obligatory Tax for Disabled Soldiers

265. 10. 10 c. grey 70 5
266. 10 c. slate-blue .. 70 5
267. 10 c. brown 70 5
268. 10 c. violet 70 5
283. 10 c. brown & magenta 35 5
284. 10 c. green and orange 35 5
295. 10 c. brown and blue .. 35 5
296. 10 c. lilac and grey .. 35 5

1944. Agricultural scenes.

269. – 1 c. blue and brown .. 5 5
270. – 2 c. green 5 5
271. 11. 5 c. black and brown .. 5 5
272. – 10 c. orange and blue .. 5 5
273. – 15 c. green 5 5
274. – 20 c. black and claret .. 5 5
275. – 25 c. brown and blue .. 8 5
276. – 30 c. blue and green .. 8 5
277. – 40 c. purple and brown 5 5
278. 11. 50 c. brown and blue .. 20 5
279. – 75 c. blue and green .. 25 5
280. – 1 p. brown and blue .. 25 5
281. – 2 p. 50 blue and black .. 1·10 30
282. – 10 p. black and orange 2·00 80

DESIGNS—HORIZ. 1 c., 30 c. Ploughing. 2 c., 40 c. Harvesting. 10 c., 75 c. Threshing. 15 c. 1 p. Vegetable garden. 20 c., 2 p. 50, Gathering oranges. 25 c., 10 p. Shepherd and flock.

12. Dyers.

13. Sanatorium.

14. Sanatorium.

15. Goods Train.

1946. Craftsmen.

285. – 1 c. brown and purple .. 5 5
286. 12. 2 c. violet and green .. 5 5
287. – 10 c. blue and orange .. 5 5
288. 12. 15 c. green and blue .. 5 5
289. – 25 c. blue and green .. 5 5
290. – 40 c. brown and blue .. 5 5
291. 12. 45 c. red and black .. 12 5
292. – 1 p. blue and green .. 20 5
293. – 2 p. 50 green & orange 60 25
294. – 10 p. grey and blue .. 1·00 50

DESIGNS: 1 c., 10 c., 25 c. Potters. 40 c. Blacksmiths. 1 p. Cobblers. 2 p. 50, Weavers. 10 p. Metal workers.

1946. Anti-T.B. Fund.

297. – 10 c. green and red .. 5 5
298. 13. 25 c. brown and red .. 5 5
299. – 25 c.+5 c. vio. & red .. 5 5
300. – 50 c.+10 c. blue & red 8 5
301. – 90 c.+10 c. brn. & red 15 10

DESIGNS: 10 c. Emblem and arabesque ornamentation. 25 c.+5 c. Mountain roadway. 40 c.+10 c. Fountain. 90 c.+10 c. Wayfarers.

1947. Anti-T.B. Fund.

302. – 10 c. blue and red .. 5 5
303. 14. 25 c. brn. and red .. 5 5
304. – 25 c.+5 c. lilac & red .. 5 5
305. – 50 c.+10 c. blue & red 8 5
306. – 90 c.+10 c. brn. & red 15 10

DESIGNS: 10 c. Emblem, mosque and palm tree. 25 c.+5 c. Hospital ward. 50 c.+10 c. Nurse and children. 90 c.+10 c. Arab swordsman.

1948. Transport and Commerce.

307. 15. 2 c. brown and violet .. 5 5
308. – 5 c. violet and claret .. 5 5
309. – 15 c. green and blue .. 5 5
310. – 25 c. green and black .. 5 5
311. – 35 c. black and blue .. 5 5
312. – 50 c. violet and orange 5 5
313. – 70 c. blue and green .. 5 5
314. – 90 c. green and red .. 8 5
315. – 1 p. violet and blue .. 10 5
316. 15. 2 p. 50 green and maroon 30 15
317. – 10 p. blue and black .. 60 40

DESIGNS: 5 c., 35 c. Lorry. 15 c., 70 c. Urban market. 25 c., 90 c. Country market. 50 c., 1 p. Camel caravan. 10 p. Ship at quay-side.

16. Emblem.

17. Herald.

1948. Anti-T.B. Fund.

318. 16. 10 c. green and red ..
319. – 25 c. green and red .. 60 45
320. 17. 50 c.+10 c. pur. & red 10 10
321. – 90 c.+10 c. blk. & red 25 20
322. – 2 p. 50+50 c. sep. & red 3·50 1·75
323. – 5 p.+1 p. vio. & red .. 5·00 2·50

DESIGNS: 25 c. Aeroplane over sanatorium. 90 c. Arab swordsman. 2 p. 50, Natives sitting in the sun. 5 p. Aeroplane over Ben Karrich.

18. Market Day.

19. Caliph on Horseback.

1949. Air.

324. – 5 c. grn. and purple .. 5 5
325. 18. 10 c. magenta & blk. .. 5 5
326. – 30 c. grey and blue .. 5 5
327. – 1 p. 75 blue & blk. .. 10 5
328. 18. 3 p. black and blue .. 15 5
329. – 4 p. red and black .. 30 10
330. – 6 p. 50 choc. & green .. 50 20
331. – 8 p. blue and mag. .. 90 20

DESIGNS—VERT. 5 c., 1 p. 75, Straits of Gibraltar. 30 c., 4 p. Kebira Fortress. 6 p. 50, Arrival of mail 'plane. 8 p. Galloping horseman.

1949. Caliph's Wedding Celebrations.

322. 19. 50 c.+10 c. red (postage) 10 10

333. – 1 p.+10 c. black (air) .. 35 30

DESIGN: 1 p. Wedding crowds in palace grounds.

20. Emblem. 21. Postman. 1890. 22. Morabito.

1949. Anti-T.B. Fund.

334. 20. 5 c. green and red .. 5 5
335. – 10 c. blue and red .. 5 5
336. – 25 c. black and red .. 20 8
337. – 50 c.+10 c. brn. & red 20 5
338. – 90 c.+10 c. grn. & red 30 12

DESIGNS: 10 c. Road to recovery. 25 c. Palm tree and tower. 50 c. Flag and followers. 90 c. Moorish horseman.

1950. U.P.U. 75th Anniv.

339. 21. 5 c. blue and brown .. 5 5
340. – 10 c. black and blue .. 5 5
341. – 15 c. green and black .. 5 5
342. – 35 c. black and violet .. 8 8
343. – 45 c. magenta and red .. 15 15
344. 21. 50 c. black and green .. 5 5
345. – 75 c. blue and indigo .. 10 10
346. 21. 90 c. red and black .. 5 5
347. – 1 p. green and purple .. 5 5
348. – 1 p. 50 blue and red .. 15 15
349. – 5 p. purple and black .. 20 15
350. – 10 p. blue and violet .. 2·50 1·75

DESIGNS: 10 c., 45 c., 1 p. Mounted postman, 1906. 15 c., 1 p. 50, Mail-coach, 1913. 35 c., 75 c., 5 p. Mail-van, 1914. 10 p. Mail-train, 1918.

1950. Anti-T.B. Fund.

351. – 5 c. black and red .. 5 5
352. – 10 c. green and red .. 5 5
353. – 25 c. blue and red .. 20 10
354. – 50 c.+10 c. brn. & red 10 5
355. 22. 90 c.+10 c. grn. & red 25 10

DESIGNS: 5 c. Arab horseman. 10 c. Fort. 25 c. Sanatorium. 50 c. Crowd at Fountain of Life.

23. Hunting.

25. Mounted Riflemen.

24. Emblem.

1950.

356. 23. 5 c. magenta and brown 5 5
357. – 10 c. grey and red .. 5 5
358. 23. 50 c. sepia and green .. 5 5
359. – 1 p. claret and violet .. 12 5
360. – 5 p. violet and claret .. 25 5
361. – 10 p. claret and green .. 70 20

DESIGNS: 10 c., 1 p. Hunters and hounds. 5 p. Fishermen. 10 p. Fishing boat.

1951. Anti-T.B. Fund.

362. 24. 5 c. green and red .. 5 5
363. – 10 c. blue and red .. 5 5
364. – 25 c. black and red .. 20 20
365. – 50 c.+10 c. choc. & red 5 5
366. – 90 c.+10 c. bl. & red .. 10 10
367. – 1 p.+5 p. blue & red .. 1·50 1·50
368. – 1 p. 10+25 c. sepia & red 40 40

DESIGNS: 10 c. Natives and children. 25 c. Aeroplane over Nubes. 50 c. Horseman. 90 c. Fortress. 1 p. Sailing boat. 1 p. 10, Aeroplane over caravan.

1952.

369. 25. 5 c. brown and blue .. 5 5
370. – 10 c. magenta and sepia 5 5
371. – 15 c. emerald and black 5 5
372. – 20 c. purple and green .. 5 5
373. – 25 c. blue and red .. 5 5
374. – 35 c. orange and olive .. 5 5
375. – 45 c. red .. 5 5
376. – 50 c. green and red .. 5 5
377. – 75 c. blue and purple .. 5 5
378. – 90 c. purple and blue .. 5 5
379. – 1 p. brown and blue .. 5 5
380. – 5 p. blue and red .. 50 15
381. – 10 p. black and green 1·10 25

DESIGNS—HORIZ. 10 c. Grooms leading horses. 15 c. Horse parade. 20 c. Peasants. 25 c. Monastic procession. 35 c. Native band. 45 c. Tribesmen. 50 c. Natives overlooking roof tops. 75 c. Inside a tea house. 90 c. Wedding procession. 1 p. Pilgrims on horseback. 5 p. Storyteller and audience. 10 p. Natives talking.

26. Natives at Prayer.

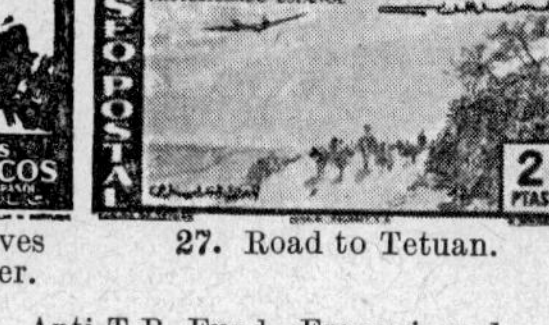
27. Road to Tetuan.

1952. Anti-T.B. Fund. Frame in red.

382. 26. 5 c. green 5 5
383. – 10 c. sepia 5 5
384. – 25 c. blue 8 8
385. – 50 c.+10 c. black .. 8 8
386. – 60 c.+25 c. green .. 20 20
387. – 90 c.+10 c. purple .. 20 20
388. – 1 p. 10+25 c. violet .. 30 30
389. – 5 p.+2 p. black .. 1·00 90

DESIGNS: 10 c. Beggars outside doorway. 25 c. Aeroplane and cactus. 50 c. Natives on horseback. 60 c. Aeroplane and palms. 90 c. Hilltop fortress. 1 p. 10, Aeroplane and agaves. 5 p. Mounted warrior.

1952. Air. Tetuan Postal Museum Fund.

390. 27. 2 p. blue and black .. 10 5
391. – 4 p. red and black .. 15 10
392. – 8 p. green and black .. 30 20
393. – 16 p. brn. and black .. 75 40

DESIGNS: 4 p. Natives watching aeroplane. 8 p. Horseman and aeroplane. 16 p. Shadow of aeroplane over Tetuan.

28. Sidi Saidi.

29.

30. Water-carrier.

1953. Air.

394. – 35 c. red and blue .. 10 5
395. 28. 60 c. green and lake .. 10 5
396. – 1 p. 10 black and blue 10 5
397. – 4 p. 50 brn. and lake .. 40 10

DESIGNS: 35 c. El Carabo (boat). 1 p. 10 Le Yunta (Ploughing). 4 p. 50, Fortress, Xauen.

1953. Air. No. 208 surch. **50.**

398. 50 c. on 75 c. blue 10 10

1953. Anti-T.B. Fund. As T 17 but inscr. "PRO TUBERCULOSOS 1953". Frame in red.

400. 5 c. green 5 5
401. 10 c. purple 5 5
402. 25 c. green 15 15
403. 50 c.+10 c. violet .. 5 5
404. 60 c.+25 c. brown .. 30 30
405. 90 c.+10 c. black .. 12 12
406. 1 p. 10+25 c. chocolate .. 50 50
407. 5 p.+2 p. blue .. .. 1·00 1·00

DESIGNS: 5 c. Herald. 10 c. Moorish horseman. 25 c. Aeroplane over Ben Karrich. 50 c. Mounted warrior. 60 c. Aeroplane over sanatorium. 90 c. Moorish horseman. 1 p. 10, Aeroplane over sea. 5 p. Arab swordsman.

1953.

408. 29. 5 c. red 5 5
409. 10 c. green 5 5

1953. 1st Pictorial Stamps of Spanish Morocco. 25th Anniv. Inscr. "1928-1953".

410. – 25 c. purple and green .. 5 5
411. 30. 50 c. green & vermilion 5 5
412. – 90 c. orange and blue .. 5 5
413. – 1 p. green and brown .. 5 5
414. – 1 p. 25 magenta & green 10 5
415. – 2 p. blue and purple .. 20 10
416. 30. 2 p. 50 orange and grey 30 10
417. – 4 p. 50 green & magenta 70 15
418. – 10 p. black and green .. 1·00 30

DESIGNS—VERT. 35 c., 1 p. 25, Mountain women. 90 c., 2 p. Mountain tribesmen. 1 p. 4 p. 50, Veiled Moorish women. 10 p. Arab dignitary.

1954. Anti-T.B. Fund. As T 17 but inscr "PRO TUBERCULOSOS 1954". Frame in red.

419. 5 c turquoise 5 5
420. 5 c.+5 c. purple 5 5
421. 10 c. sepia 5 5
422. 25 c. blue 8 8
423. 50 c.+10 c. green 15 15
424. 5 p.+2 p. black .. 1·25 1·25

DESIGNS: 5 c. Convent. 5 c.+5 c. Stork on a tower. 10 c. Moroccan family. 25 c. Aeroplane over Spanish coast. 50 c. Father and child. 5 p. Chapel.

31. Saida Gate.

32. Celebrations.

1955. Frames in black.

425. – 15 c. green 5 5
426. 31. 25 c. maroon 5 5
427. – 80 c. blue 5 5
428. 31. 1 p. magenta 5 5
429. – 15 p. turquoise 75 40

DESIGNS: 15 c., 80 c. Queen's Gate. 15 p. Ceuta Gate.

1955. Caliph's Accession. 30th Anniv.

430. 32. 15 c. olive and brown .. 5 5
431. – 25 c. lake and purple .. 5 5
432. – 30 c. green and sepia .. 5 5
433. 32. 70 c. green and myrtle .. 5 5
434. – 80 c. brown and olive .. 5 5
435. – 1 p. brown and blue .. 10 5
436. 32. 1 p. 80 violet and black 15 5
437. – 3 p. grey and blue .. 15 5
438. – 5 p. brown and myrtle .. 20 30
439. – 15 p. green and brown .. 1·10 75

DESIGNS: 25 c. 80 c., 3 p. Caliph's portrait. 30 c., 1 p., 5 p. Procession. 15 p. Coat of Arms.

EXPRESS LETTER STAMPS

Express Letter Stamps of Spain overprinted.

1914. Optd. **MARRUECOS.**

E 55. E 1. 20 c. red 75 60

1915. Optd. **PROTECTORADO ESPAÑOL EN MARRUECOS.**

E 68. E 1. 20 c. red 50 45

1923. Optd. **ZONA DE PROTECTORADO ESPANOL EN MARRUECOS.**

E 111. E 1. 20 c. red .. .. 1·40 60

1926. Red Cross. Optd. **ZONA PROTECTORADO ESPANOL.**

E 124. E 2. 20 c. black and blue 25 25

E 1. Moorish Courier.

1928.

E 138. E 1. 20 c. black .. .. 1·00 25

E 2. E 3. Moorish Courier. E 4.

1935.

E 171. E 2. 20 c. red 50 15

1937. 1st Anniv. of Civil War.

E 200. E 3. 20 c. red 8 8

1940.

E 233. E 4. 25 c. red 25 15

1940. No. E 200 optd. as Nos. 233/48 and surch. also.

E 249. E 3. 25 c. on 20 c. red .. 2·25 2·25

E 5. Air Mail 1935.

E 6. Moorish Courier.

1950. U.P.U. 75th Anniv.

E 351. E 5. 25 c. black and red .. 2·50 1·90

1952.

E 382. E 6. 25 c. red 5 5

E 7. Moorish Courier.

E 8. Tangier Gate.

1953. First Pictorial Stamps of Spanish Morocco. 25th Anniv.

E 419. E 7. 25 c. magenta & blue	12	12

1955.

E 430. E 8. 2 p. violet and black	10	10

For later issues see **MOROCCO.**

III. INTERNATIONAL ZONE OF TANGIER.

See note below No. 41 concerning the exclusive use of Nos. 30/41 in Tangier after 1914.

Postage stamps of Spain overprinted.

1921. Optd. **CORREO ESPANOL MARRUECOS.**

1. 33. 1 c. green	12	5
2. 32. 2 c. brown	16·00	
3. 15 c. yellow	80	10
4. 20 c. violet	1·00	10

1923. Optd. as 1921.

5. 35. 2 c. olive	50	5
6. 5 c. purple	50	5
7. 5 c. red	30	5
8. 10 c. green	60	5
10. 20 c. violet	45	5
11. 50 c. orange	2·00	25
12. 36. 10 p. brown	1·75	1·00

1926. Red Cross stamps optd. **CORREO ESPANOL TANGER.**

13. 37. 1 c. orange	50	50
14. – 2 c. red	55	55
15. – 5 c. grey	25	25
16. – 10 c. green	25	25
17. 37. 15 c. violet	15	15
18. – 20 c. purple	15	15
19. 38. 25 c. red	15	15
20. 37. 30 c. olive	15	15
21. – 40 c. blue	5	5
22. – 50 c. brown	5	5
23. – 1 p. red	5	5
24. – 4 p. brown	15	15
25. 38. 10 p. lilac	25	25

1929. Seville-Barcelona Exhibition stamps, Nos. 504/14 optd. **TANGER.**

27. 5 c. red	5	5
28. 10 c. green	5	5
29. 15 c. blue	5	5
30. 20 c. violet	5	5
31. 25 c. red	5	5
32. 30 c. brown	8	8
33. 40 c. blue	10	10
34. 50 c. orange	10	10
35. 1 p. grey	50	50
36. 4 p. red	1·00	1·00
37. 10 p. brown	1·50	1·50

1930. Optd. as 1921.

38. 55. 10 c. green	1·60	12
39. 15 c. blue-green	4·50	25
40. 20 c. violet	1·75	20
41. 30 c. claret	2·00	30
42. 40 c. blue	5·00	50

1933. Optd. **MARRUECOS.**

43. 80. 1 c. green (imperf.)	10	5
44. 2 c. brown	10	5
45. 82. 5 c. brown	10	5
46. 83. 10 c. green	10	5
47. 85. 15 c. blue	10	5
48. 82. 20 c. violet	10	5
49. 87. 25 c. red	10	5
50. 88. 30 c. red	5·50	70
51. 92. 40 c. blue	12	5
52. 85. 50 c. orange	20	5
53. 92. 60 c. green	20	5
54. 93. 1 p. black	20	10
55. – 4 p. magenta	1·00	40
56. – 10 p. brown	1·50	75

1937. Optd. **TANGER.**

58. 80. 1 c. green (imperf.)	15	5
59. 2 c. brown	15	5
60. 82. 5 c. brown	15	5
61. 83. 10 c. green	15	5
62. 85. 15 c. blue	15	5
63. 82. 20 c. violet	15	8
64. 87. 25 c. red	15	10
65. 91. 30 c. red	15	5
66. 93. 40 c. blue	25	12
67. 85. 50 c. orange	50	15
68. 97. 1 p. black	1·00	25
69. – 4 p. magenta (No. 768c)	55·00	
70. – 10 p. brown (No. 769c)	80·00	

1938. Optd. **Correo Espanol Tanger.**

71. 80. 5 c. brown	30	20
72. 10 c. green	35	25
73. 15 c. green	35	20
74. 20 c. violet	35	20
75. 25 c. mauve	30	15
76. 30 c. red	1·40	80
77. 111. 40 c. red	75	40
78. 45 c. red	25	12
79. 50 c. blue	25	12
80. 60 c. blue	70	35
81. 98. 2 p. blue	5·00	2·50
82. – 4 p. magenta (No. 768c)	6·00	3·00

1938. Air. Optd. **Correo Aereo TANGER.**

83. 80. 25 c. mauve	15	10
84. 111. 50 c. blue	15	10

1938. Air. Optd. **CORREO AEREO TANGER.**

86. 97. 1 p. black	15	10
85. 98. 2 p. blue	1·60	85
87. – 4 p. magenta (No. 768c)	1·50	80
88. – 10 p. brown (No. 769c)	15·00	10·00

1939. Optd. **Tanger.**

89. 80. 5 c. brown	15	8
90. 10 c. green	15	8
91. 15 c. green	15	8
92. 20 c. violet	15	8
93. 25 c. mauve	15	8
94. 30 c. red	15	8
95. 111. 40 c. red	15	8
96. 45 c. red	15	8
97. 50 c. blue	50	30
98. 60 c. blue	30	12
99. 97. 1 p. black	40	20
100. 98. 2 p. blue	7·50	4·00
101. – 4 p. magenta (No. 768c)	7·50	4·00
102. – 10 p. brown (No. 769c)	8·00	5·00

1939. Air. Optd. **Via Aerea Tanger.**

103. 80. 5 c. brown	30	25
104. 10 c. green	30	25
105. 15 c. green	25	15
106. 20 c. violet	25	15
107. 25 c. mauve	25	15
108. 30 c. red	50	30
109. 111. 40 c. red	12·00	
110. 45 c. red	12	12
111. 50 c. blue	28·00	
112. 60 c. blue	6·00	6·00
113. 97. 1 p. black	7·50	
114. – 4 p. magenta (No. 768c)	13·00	8·00
115. – 10 p. brown (No. 769c)	40·00	

1939. Air. Express Letter stamp optd. **Via Aerea Tanger.**

116. E 8. 20 c. red	75	40

1939. Various fiscal types inscr. "DERECHOS CONSULARES ESPANOLES" optd. **Correo Tanger.**

117. 50 c. pink	5·00	5·00
118. 1 p. pink	1·00	1·00
119. 2 p. pink	1·00	1·00
120. 5 p. red and green	1·40	1·40
121. 10 p. red and violet	5·00	5·00

1939. Air. Various fiscal types inscr. "DERECHOS CONSULARES ESPANOLES" optd. **Correo Aereo Tanger.**

122. 1 p. blue	14·00	14·00
123. 2 p. blue	14·00	14·00
124. 5 p. blue	1·75	1·75
125. 10 p. blue	1·75	1·75

1. Moroccan Woman.

2. Twin-engined Aeroplane.

1948.

126. – 1 c. green	5	5
127. – 2 c. orange	5	5
128. – 5 c. purple	5	5
129. – 10 c. blue	5	5
130. – 20 c. sepia	5	5
131. – 25 c. green	5	5
132. – 30 c. grey	20	5
133. – 45 c. red	20	5
134. 1. 50 c. claret	20	5
135. – 75 c. blue	25	5
136. – 90 c. green	20	5
137. – 1 p. 35 red	40	10
138. 1. 2 p. violet	1·50	25
139. – 10 p. green	4·00	70

DESIGNS: 1 c., 2 c. Woman's head facing right. 5 c., 25 c. Palm tree. 10 c., 20 c. Woman's head facing left. 30 c., 1 p. 35, Old map of Tangier. 45 c., 10 p. Street scene. 75 c., 90 c. Head of Moor.

1949. Air.

140. – 20 c. brown	12	5
141. 2. 25 c. red	12	5
142. – 35 c. green	12	5
143. – 1 p. violet	30	5
144. 2. 2 p. green	70	10
145. – 10 p. purple	1·40	40

DESIGNS: 20 c., 1 p. Aeroplane and map. 35 c., 10 p. Aeroplane in clouds.

EXPRESS LETTER STAMPS

Express Letter Stamps of Spain overprinted.

1926. Red Cross. Optd. **CORREO ESPANOL TANGER.**

E 26. E 2. 20 c. black and blue	25	25

1933. No. E 17 optd. **MARRUECOS.**

E 57. E 8. 20 c. red	70	20

E 1. Courier.

1949.

E 146. E 1. 25 c. red	15	5

SPANISH SAHARA 04

Former Spanish territory on the north-west coast of Africa, previously called Rio de Oro. Now administered jointly by Morocco and Mauritania.

1.

1924.

1. 1. 5 c. green	35	12
2. 10 c. green	35	12
3. 15 c. blue	35	12
4. 20 c. violet	50	20
5. 25 c. red	50	15
6. 30 c. brown	50	20
7. 40 c. blue	50	20
8. 50 c. orange	50	20
9. 60 c. purple	50	20
10. 1 p. claret	1·40	45
11. 4 p. brown	7·00	2·10
12. 10 p. purple	14·00	5·00

1926. Red Cross stamps of Spain optd. **SAHARA ESPANOL.**

13. – 5 c. grey	30	30
14. – 10 c. green	30	30
15. 37. 15 c. violet	15	15
16. – 20 c. purple	15	15
17. 38. 25 c. red	15	15
18. 37. 30 c. olive	15	15
19. – 40 c. blue	5	5
20. – 50 c. brown	5	5
21. 38. 60 c. green	5	5
22. – 1 p. red	5	5
23. – 4 p. brown	15	15
24. 38. 10 p. lilac	20	20

1929. Seville and Barcelona Exn. stamps of Spain. Nos. 504/14, optd. **SAHARA.**

25. 5 c. red	5	5
26. 10 c. green	5	5
27. 15 c. blue	5	5
28. 20 c. violet	5	5
29. 25 c. red	5	5
30. 30 c. brown	5	5
31. 40 c. blue	5	5
32. 50 c. orange	5	5
33. 1 p. grey	20	20
34. 4 p. red	1·10	1·10
35. 10 p. brown	1·75	1·75

1931. Optd. **Republica Espanola.**

36. 1. 5 c. green	15	10
37. 10 c. green	15	10
38. 15 c. blue	15	10
39. 20 c. violet	15	10
40. 25 c. red	20	10
41. 30 c. brown	20	10
42. 40 c. blue	55	20
43. 50 c. orange	60	35
44. 60 c. purple	55	25
45. 1 p. claret	55	25
46. 4 p. brown	5·00	1·60
47. 10 p. purple	9·00	2·75

1941. Stamps of Spain optd. **SAHARA ESPANOL.**

47a. 122. 1 c. green	45	30
47b. 123. 2 c. brown	45	30
48. 124. 5 c. brown	15	10
49. 10 c. red	45	30
50. 15 c. green	15	10
51. 133. 20 c. violet	15	10
52. 25 c. claret	20	15
53. 30 c. blue	30	20
54. 40 c. green	15	15
55. 50 c. blue	1·10	25
56. 70 c. blue	70	25
57. 1 PTA. black	2·25	45
58. 2 PTAS. brown	11·00	5·50
59. 4 PTAS. red	25·00	13·00
60. 10 PTS. brown	60·00	25·00

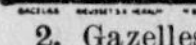

2. Gazelles.

3. Ostriches.

1943.

61. 2. 1 c. magenta & brn. (post.)	5	5
62. – 2 c. indigo and green	5	5
63. – 5 c. blue and claret	5	5
64. 2. 15 c. green and myrtle	8	8
65. – 20 c. chocolate and mauve	8	8
66. 2. 40 c. mauve and purple	12	12
67. – 45 c. red and maroon	15	15
68. – 75 c. blue and indigo	15	15
69. 2. 1 p. brown and red	35	35
70. – 3 p. green and violet	70	70
71. – 10 p. black and sepia	7·00	7·00

DESIGNS—VERT. 2 c., 20 c., 45 c., 3 p. Camel caravan. 5 c., 75 c., 10 p. Camel troops.

72. 3. 5 c. choc. and claret (air)	8	8
73. – 25 c. olive and green	8	8
74. 3. 50 c. blue-grn. & indigo	12	12
75. – 1 p. blue and mauve	12	12
76. 3. 1 p. 40 indigo and green	12	12
77. – 2 p. brown & purple	55	55
78. 3. 5 p. mauve and brown	60	60
79. – 6 p. green and blue	7·50	7·50

DESIGN: 25 c., 1 p., 2 p., 6 p. Aeroplane and camels.

4. Boy Carrying Lamb.

5. Diego Garcia de Herrera.

1950. Child Welfare.

80. 4. 50 c.+10 c. brown	20	15
81. 1 p.+25 c. claret	2·50	1·10
82. 6 p. 50+1 p. 65 green	1·40	50

1950. Air. Colonial Stamp Day.

83. 5. 5 p. violet	50	25

1951. Air. Isabella the Catholic. 500th Birth Anniv. As T 5 of Ifni.

84. 5 p. green	1·75	55

1951. Visit of Gen. Franco. As T 6 of Ifni.

85. 50 c. orange	8	5
86. 1 p. brown	20	15
87. 5 p. blue-green	3·75	1·40

6. Dromedary and Calf.

7. Native Woman.

8. Morion, Sword and Banner.

1951. Colonial Stamp Day.

88. 6. 5 c.+5 c. brown	5	5
89. 10 c.+5 c. orange	5	5
90. 60 c.+15 c. olive	8	5

1952. Child Welfare Fund.

91. 7. 5 c.+5 c. brown	8	5
92. 50 c.+10 c. black	8	8
93. 2 p.+30 c. blue	40	20

1952. Air. Ferdinand the Catholic. 5th Birth Cent.

94. 8. 5 p. brown	2·10	70

9. Head of Ostrich.

10. "Geography".

11. Native Woman Musician.

1952. Colonial Stamp Day.

95. 9. 5 c.+5 c. brown	5	5
96. 10 c.+5 c. claret	5	5
97. 60 c.+15 c. green	5	5

1953. Royal Geographical Society. 75th Anniv.

98. 10. 5 c. vermilion	5	5
99. 35 c. green	5	8
100. 60 c. brown	8	8

1953. Child Welfare Fund. Inscr. "PRO INFANCIA 1953".

101. 11. 5 c.+5 c. chestnut	5	5
102. – 10 c.+5 c. purple	5	5
103. 11. 15 c. olive	5	5
104. – 60 c. brown	5	5

DESIGN: 10 c., 60 c. Native man musician.

12.

DESIGN — HORIZ. 10 c., 60 c. Two fishes.

1953. Colonial Stamp Day. Inscr. "DIA DEL SELLO COLONIAL 1953".

105. **12.** 5 c.+5 c. violet 5 5
106. – 10 c.+5 c. green 5 5
107. **12.** 15 c. olive 5 5
108. – 60 c. orange 5 5

13. Native Hurdlers.

DESIGN — VERT. 10 c., 60 c. Runner.

1954. Child Welfare Fund. Inscr. "PRO INFANCIA 1954".

109. **13.** 5 c.+5 c. chestnut .. 5 5
110. – 10 c.+5 c. violet .. 5 5
111. **13.** 15 c. green 5 5
112. – 60 c. brown 5 5

14. Flying Fish.

DESIGNS—HORIZ 10 c., 60 c. Fish

1954. Colonial Stamp Day. Inscr. "DIA DEL SELLO COLONIAL 1954".

113. **14.** 5 c.+5 c. red 5 5
114. – 10 c.+5 c. purple .. 5 5
115. **14.** 15 c. green 5 5
116. – 60 c. brown 5 5

15. E. Bonelli.

DESIGN: 25 c. Bonelli and sailing vessel.

1955. Bonelli (explorer). Birth Cent. Inscr. "1954 CENTENARIO BONELLI".

117. **15.** 10 c.+5 c. purple .. 5 5
118. – 25 c.+10 c. violet .. 5 5
119. **15.** 50 c. olive 5 5

16. Oryx. **17.** "Antirrhinum-Romossimum".

1955. Colonial Stamp Day. Inscr. "DIA DEL SELLO COLONIAL 1955".

120. **16.** 5 c.+5 c. brown .. 5 5
121. – 15 c.+5 c. bistre .. 5 5
122. **16.** 70 c. green 8 5

DESIGN: 15 c. Oryx's head.

1956. Child Welfare Fund. Inscr. "PRO-INFANCIA 1956".

123. **17.** 5 c.+5 c. olive.. .. 5 5
124. – 15 c.+5 c. ochre .. 5 5
125. **17.** 20 c. turquoise.. .. 5 5
126. – 50 c. brown 5 5

DESIGN: 15 c., 50 c. "Sesivium Portulacastrum".

18. Arms of Aaiun and Native on Camel. **19.** Dromedaries.

1956. Colonial Stamp Day. Inscr. "DIA DEL SELLO 1956".

127. **18.** 5 c.+5 c. blk. & violet.. 5 5
128. – 15 c.+5 c. green & ochre 5 5
129. **18.** 70 c. brown and green.. 5 5

DESIGN—VERT. 15 c. Arms of Villa Cisneros and native chief.

1957. Animals.

130. **19.** 5 c. violet 5 5
131. – 15 c. ochre 5 5
132. – 50 c. olive-brown .. 5 5
133. **19.** 70 c. yellow-green .. 20 5
134. – 80 c. blue-green .. 20 5
135. – 1 p. 80 magenta .. 20 5

DESIGNS: 15 c., 80 c. Ostrich. 50 c., 1 p. 80. Gazelle.

20. Eagle. **21.** Head of Hyena.

1957. Child Welfare Fund. Inscr. "PRO-INFANCIA 1957".

136. **20.** 5 c.+5 c. red-brown .. 5 5
137. – 15 c.+5 c. yellow-brn. 5 5
138. **20.** 70 c. green 8 8

DESIGN: 15 c. Eagle in flight.

1957. Colonial Stamp Day. Inscr. "DIA DEL SELLO 1957".

139. **21.** 10 c.+5 c. purple .. 5 5
140. – 15 c.+5 c. ochre .. 5 5
141. **21.** 20 c. green 5 5
142. – 70 c. myrtle 5 5

DESIGN: 15 c., 70 c. Hyena.

22. Stork and Arms of Valencia and Aaiun. **23.** Cervantes.

1958. "Aid for Valencia".

143. **22.** 10 c.+5 c. chestnut .. 5 5
144. 15 c.+10 c. ochre .. 5 5
145. 50 c.+10 c. olive-brn. 5 5

1958. Child Welfare Fund. Inscr. "1958".

146. **23.** 10 c.+5 c. brn. & chest. 5 5
147. – 15 c.+5 c. myrtle & orge. 5 5
148. – 20 c. green & brown .. 5 5
149. **23.** 50 c. grn. & yell.-grn... 5 5

DESIGNS—VERT. 15 c. Don Quixote and Sancho Panza on horseback. HORIZ. 20 c. Don Quixote and the lion.

24. **25.** Lope de Vega (author). **26.** Heron.

1958. Colonial Stamp Day. Inscr. "1958".

150. **24.** 10 c.+5 c. red.. .. 5 5
151. – 25 c.+10 c. violet .. 5 5
152. – 50 c.+10 c. olive .. 5 5

DESIGNS—HORIZ. 25 c. and VERT. 50 c. Different views of birds on boughs.

1959. Child Welfare Fund. Inscr. "PRO INFANCIA 1959".

153. **25.** 10 c.+5 c. olive & chest. 5 5
154. – 15 c.+5 c. choc. and yellow-brown .. 5 5
155. – 20 c. sepia and green .. 5 5
156. **25.** 70 c. myrtle and green 5 5

DESIGNS—Characters from the comedy "The Star of Seville": 15 c. Spanish lady. 20 c. Caballero.

1959. Birds.

157. **26.** 25 c. violet 5 5
158. – 50 c. bronze-green .. 5 5
159 – 75 c. sepia 5 5
160 **26.** 1 p. red 5 5
161. – 1 p. 50 green 5 5
162. – 2 p. purple 25 5
163. **26.** 3 p. blue 25 5
164. – 5 p. chestnut 50 8
165. – 10 p. olive .. .. 1·75 85

DESIGNS: 50 c., 1 p. 50, 5 p. Sparrow-hawk. 75 c., 2 p., 10 p. Seagull.

27. Saharan Postman. **28.** F. de Quevedo (writer).

1959. Colonial Stamp Day. Inscr. "1959".

166. **27.** 10 c.+5 c. brn. & red.. 5 5
167. – 20 c.+5 c. brn. & grn. 5 5
168. – 50 c.+20 c. slate & olive 5 5

DESIGNS: 20 c. Postman tendering letters. 50 c. Camel postman.

1960. Child Welfare Fund. Inscr. "PRO-INFANCIA 1960".

169. **28.** 10 c.+5 c. brown-purple 5 5
170. – 15 c.+5 c. bistre-brown 5 5
171. – 35 c. grey-green .. 5 5
172. **28.** 80 c. blue-green .. 5 5

DESIGNS — VERT. (representing Quevedo's works): 15 c. Winged wheel and hour-glass. 25 c. Man in plumed hat wearing cloak and sword.

29. Leopard. **30.** Bustard. **31.** 'Plane and Camel.

1960. Stamp Day. Inscr. "1960".

173. **29.** 10 c.+5 c. magenta .. 5 5
174. – 20 c.+5 c. myrtle .. 5 5
175. – 30 c.+10 c. choc. .. 5 5
176. – 50 c.+20 c. olive-brown 5 5

DESIGNS: 20 c. Fennec. 30 c. Eagle defying leopard. 50 c. Hyena.

1961.

177. **30.** 25 c. slate-violet .. 5 5
178. – 50 c. olive-brown .. 5 5
179. **30.** 75 c. dull purple .. 5 5
180. – 1 p. vermilion .. 5 5
181. **30.** 1 p. 50 green .. 5 5
182. – 2 p. magenta .. 25 5
183. **30.** 3 p. blue 30 5
184. – 5 p. brown 35 8
185. **30.** 10 p. yellow-olive .. 70 25

DESIGN: 50 c., 1 p., 5 p. Doves.

1961. Air.

186. **31.** 25 p. sepia 90 35

32. Antelopes. **33.**

1961. Child Welfare. Inscr. "PRO-INFANCIA 1961".

187. **32.** 10 c.+5 c. red.. .. 5 5
188. – 25 c.+10 c. violet .. 5 5
189. **32.** 80 c.+20 c. green .. 5 5

DESIGN: 25 c. One antelope.

1961. 25th Anniv. of Gen. Franco as Head of State.

190. – 25 c. violet-grey .. 5 5
191. **33.** 50 c. olive 5 5
192. – 70 c. green 5 5
193. **33.** 1 p. orange 5 5

DESIGNS—VERT. 25 c. Map. 7 c. Aaiun Chapel.

34. A. Fernandez de Lugo. **35.** "Neurada procumbres Linn". **36.** Two Barred Fishes.

1961. Stamp Day. Inscr. "DIA DEL SELLO 1961".

194. **34.** 10 c.+5 c. salmon .. 5 5
195. – 25 c.+10 c. plum .. 5 5
196. **34.** 30 c.+10 c. chocolate.. 5 5
197. – 1 p.+10 c. orange .. 5 5

PORTRAIT: 25 c., 1 p. D. de Herrera.

1962. Flowers.

198. **35.** 25 c. violet 5 5
199. – 50 c. sepia 5 5
200. – 70 c. emerald 5 5
201. **35.** 1 p. orange 5 5
202. – 1 p. 50 blue-green .. 15 5
203. – 2 p. purple 55 5
204. **35.** 3 p. slate-blue 90 10
205. – 10 p. olive .. .. 1·50 35

FLOWERS: 50 c., 1 p. 50, 10 p. "Anabasis articulata moq". 70 c., 2 p. "Euphorbia resinifera".

1962. Child Welfare.

206. **36.** 25 c. violet 5 5
207. – 50 c. bronze-green .. 5 5
208. **36.** 1 p. chestnut 5 5

DESIGN—HORIZ. 50 c. Two fishes.

37. Goats. **38.** Seville Cathedral.

1962. Stamp Day.

209. **37.** 15 c. green 5 5
210. – 35 c. purple 5 5
211. **37.** 1 p. chestnut 5 5

DESIGN: 35 c. Sheep.

1963. Seville Flood Relief.

212. **38.** 50 c. olive 5 5
213. 1 p. chestnut 5 5

39. Cameleer and Camel. **40.** Dove in Hands.

1963. Child Welfare. Inscr. "PRO-INFANCIA 1963".

214. – 25 c. violet 5 5
215. **39.** 50 c. grey 5 5
216. – 1 p. orange-red .. 5 5

DESIGN: 25 c., 1 p. Three camels.

1963. "For Barcelona".

217. **40.** 50 c. blue-green .. 5 5
218. 1 p. chestnut 5 5

41. Fish ("Zeus faber").

42. Hawk Moth. **43.** Mounted Dromedary and Microphone.

1964. Stamp Day. Inscr. "DIA DEL SELLO 1963".

219. **41.** 25 c. violet 5 5
220. – 50 c. olive 5 5
221. **41.** 1 p. brown 5 5

FISH—VERT. 50 c. "Sarda unicolor".

1964. Child Welfare.

222. **42.** 25 c. violet 5 5
223. – 50 c. olive 5 5
224. **42.** 1 p. red 5 5

DESIGN—VERT. 50 c. Carpenter moths.

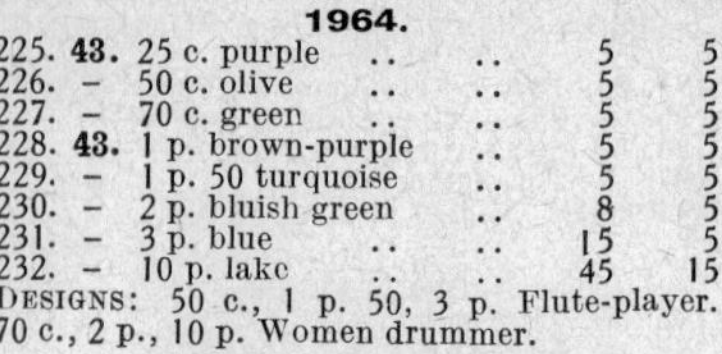

1964.

225. **43.** 25 c. purple 5 5
226. – 50 c. olive 5 5
227. – 70 c. green 5 5
228. **43.** 1 p. brown-purple .. 5 5
229. – 1 p. 50 turquoise .. 5 5
230. – 2 p. bluish green .. 8 5
231. – 3 p. blue 15 5
232. – 10 p. lake 45 15

DESIGNS: 50 c., 1 p. 50, 3 p. Flute-player. 70 c., 2 p., 10 p. Women drummer.

44. Squirrel's Head.

1964. Stamp Day.

233. – 50 c. olive 5 5
234. **44.** 1 p. lake 5 5
235. – 1 p. 50 green 5 5

DESIGN—VERT. 50 c., 1 p. 50, Squirrel eating.

45. Doctor tending Patient, and Hospital.

1965. End of Spanish Civil War. 25th Anniv. Inscr. "XXV ANOS DE PAZ".

236. – 50 c. olive 5 5
237. **45.** 1 p. red 5 5
238. – 1 p. 50 blue 5 5

DESIGNS—VERT. 50 c. Saharan Woman 1 p. 50, Desert Installation and Cameleer.

DIA DEL SELLO 1965 50 CTS CORREOS SAHARA ESPAÑA

46. "Anthia sexmaculata". **47.** Handball.

1965. Child Welfare. Insects.

239. **46.** 50 c. blue 5 5
240. – 1 p. green 5 5
241. **46.** 1 p. 50 brown .. 5 5
242. – 3 p. indigo 45 35

INSECTS—VERT. 1 p., 3 p. "Blepharopsis mendica".

1965. Stamp Day.

243. **47.** 50 c. crimson .. 5 5
244. – 1 p. purple 5 5
245. **47.** 1 p. 50 blue 5 5

DESIGN: 1 p. Arms of Spanish Sahara.

48. Bows of "Rio de Oro".

1966. Child Welfare.

246. **48.** 50 c. olive 5 5
247. 1 p. chocolate 5 5
248. – 1 p. 50 green 5 5

DESIGN: 1 p. 50 SS. "Fuerta Ventura".

49. "Parathunnus obesus" (fish). **50.** Plant.

1966. Stamp Day.

249. **49.** 10 c. blue and yellow .. 5 5
250. – 40 c. grey and salmon .. 5 5
251. **49.** 1 p. 50 choc. & green .. 5 5
252. – 4 p. purple and green .. 5 5

DESIGN—VERT. 40 c., 4 p. "Mola mola" (fish).

1967. Child Welfare. Similar floral design.

253. **50.** 10 c. yellow and indigo 5 5
254. – 40 c. purple and green 5 5
255. **50.** 1 p. 50 yellow and green 5 5
256. – 4 p. orange and blue .. 5 5

51. Quay, Aaiun.

1967. Saharan Ports. Inaug.

257. **51.** 1 p. 50 chocolate & blue 5 5
258. – 4 p. ochre and blue .. 5 5

DESIGN: 4 p. Port of Villa Cisneros.

52. Ruddy Shelduck. **53.** Dove, and Stamp within Posthorn.

1968. Stamp Day.

259. **52.** 1 p. chestnut and green 5 5
260. – 1 p. 50 magenta & black 5 5
261. – 3 p. 50 lake and brown 5 5

DESIGNS—VERT. 1 p. 50, Greater Flamingo. HORIZ. 3 p. 50, Rufous warbler.

1968. Child Welfare. Signs of the Zodiac. As T **26** of Fernando Poo.

262. 1 p. magenta on yellow .. 5 5
263. 1 p. 50 brown on pink .. 5 5
264. 2 p. 50 violet on yellow .. 5 5

DESIGNS: 1 p. Scorpio (Scorpion). 1 p. 50, Capricornus (Goat). 2 p. 50, Virgo (Virgin).

1968. Stamp Day.

265. **53.** 1 p. blue and purple .. 5 5
266. – 1 p. 50 green and apple 5 5
267. – 2 p. 50 blue and orange 5 5

DESIGNS: 1 p. 50, Postal handstamp, stamps and letter. 2 p. 50, Saharan postman.

54. Head of Gazelle.

1969. Child Welfare.

268. **54.** 1 p. brown and black .. 5 5
269. – 1 p. 50 brown and black 5 5
270. – 2 p. 50 brown and black 5 5
271. – 6 p. brown and black .. 8 8

DESIGNS: 1 p. 50, Gazelle tending young. 2 p. 50, Gazelle and camel. 6 p. Gazelle leaping.

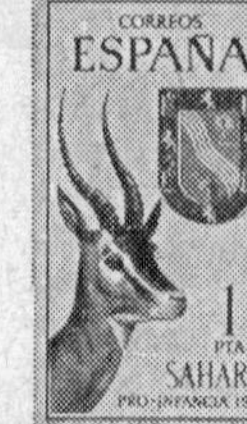

55. Woman beating Drum. **57.** Gazelle and Arms of El Aaiun.

56. "Grammodes boisdeffrei".

1969. Stamp Day.

272. **55.** 50 c. brown and bistre .. 5 5
273. – 1 p. 50 blue-green and olive-green 5 5
274. – 2 p. blue and brown .. 5 5
275. – 25 p. brown and green .. 35 10

DESIGNS—VERT. 1 p. 50, Man playing flute. HORIZ. 2 p. Drum and mounted cameleer. 25 p. Flute.

1970. Child Welfare. As T **54.**

276. 50 c. ochre and blue .. 5 5
277. 2 p. brown and blue .. 5 5
278. 2 p. 50 ochre and blue .. 5 5
279. 6 p. ochre and blue .. 8 8

DESIGNS: 50 c. Fennec. 2 p. Fennec walking. 2 p. 50, Head of Fennec. 6 p. Fennec family.

1970. Stamp Day. Butterflies. Multi-coloured.

280. 50 c. Type **56** 5 5
281. 1 p. Type **56** 5 5
282. 2 p. "Danaus chrysippus" 5 5
283. 5 p. As 2 p. 8 5
284. 8 p. "Celerio euphorbiae" 10 8

1971. Child Welfare.

285. **57.** 1 p. multicoloured .. 5 5
286. – 2 p. green and olive .. 5 5
287. – 5 p. blue, brown & grey 5 5
288. – 25 p. green, grey & blue 30 12

DESIGNS—VERT. 25 p. Smara Mosque. HORIZ. 2 p. Tourist Inn, Aaiun. 5 p. Assembly House, Aaiun.

58. Trumpeter Finch.

1971. Stamp Day. Multicoloured.

290. 1 p. 50 Type **58** 5 5
291. 2 p. Type **58** 5 5
292. 5 p. Cream-coloured courser 5 5
293. 24 p. Lanner falcon .. 30 12

59. Seated Woman. **60.** Tuareg Woman.

1972. Saharan Nomads.

294. **59.** 1 p. blk., pink & blue .. 5 5
295. – 1 p. 50 slate, lilac & brn. 5 5
296. – 2 p. blk., flesh & green .. 5 5
297. **59.** 5 p. maroon, ol. & grn. 5 5
298. – 8 p. violet, green & blk. 8 5
299. – 10 p. grn., grey & blk... 12 5
300. – 12 p. multicoloured .. 15 8
301. – 15 p. multicoloured .. 20 8
302. – 24 p. multicoloured .. 30 12

DESIGNS: 1 p. 50, 2 p. Squatting nomad. 8 p. 10 p. Head of Nomad. 12 p. Woman with bangles. 15 p. Nomad with rifle. 24 p. Woman displaying trinkets.

1972. Child Welfare. Multicoloured.

303. 8 p. Type **60** 8 5
304. 12 p. Tuareg elder .. 15 8

61. Mother and Child.

1972. Stamp Day. Multicoloured.

305. 4 p. Type **61** 5 5
306. 15 p. Nomad 20 8

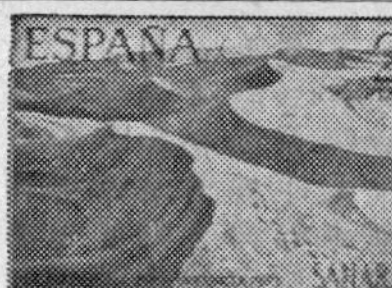

62. Sahara Desert.

1973. Child Welfare. Multicoloured.

307. 2 p. Type **62** 5 5
308. 7 p. City Gate, El Aaiun .. 8 5

63. Villa Cisneros.

1973. Stamp Day. Multicoloured.

309. 2 p. Type **63** 5 5
310. 7 p. Tuareg (vert.) .. 8 5

64. U.P.U. Monument, Berne. **65.** Archway, Smara Mosque.

1974. Universal Postal Union. Cent.

311. **64.** 15 p. multicoloured .. 20 8

1974. Child Welfare. Multicoloured.

312. 1 p. Type **65** 5 5
313. 2 p. Villa Cisneros Mosque 5 5

66. Desert Owl.

1974. Stamp Day. Multicoloured.

314. 2 p. Type **66** 5 5
315. 5 p. Vulture 5 5

67. "Espana" Emblem and Spanish Sahara Stamp.

1975. "Espana 75" International Stamp Exhibition, Madrid.

316. **67.** 8 p. yellow, blue & blk. 15 12

68. Desert Conference.

1975. Child Welfare. Multicoloured.

317. 1 p. 50 Type **68** 5 5
318. 3 p. Desert oasis 5 5

69. Tuareg Elder.

1975.
319. **69.** 3 p. pur., grn and blk... 5 5

EXPRESS LETTER STAMP

1943. Design as No. 63 inscr. " URGENTE ".
E 80. 25 c. red and myrtle .. 35 35

E 1. Despatch-rider.

1971.
E 289. **E 1.** 10 p. brown and red 12 8

SPANISH WEST AFRICA O4

Issues for use in Ifni and Spanish Sahara.

1. Native.

2. Isabella the Catholic.

1949. 75th Anniv. of U.P.U. Stamp Day.
1. **1.** 4 p. green 65 15

1949. Air. Colonial Stamp Day.
2. **2.** 5 p. brown 50 15

3. Native Tents.

1950.

3.	**3.**	2 c. brown	5	5
4.	–	5 c. violet..	5	5
5.	–	10 c. blue ..	5	5
6.	–	15 c. black	5	5
7.	**3.**	25 c. chocolate	5	5
8.	–	30 c. yellow	5	5
9.	–	40 c. olive	5	5
10.	–	45 c. claret	5	5
11.	**3.**	50 c. orange	5	5
12.	–	75 c. blue ..	5	5
13.	–	90 c. green	5	5
14.	–	1 p. grey ..	5	5
15.	**3.**	1 p. 35 violet	12	8
16.	–	2 p. sepia ..	20	20
17.	–	5 p. mauve	1·75	35
18.	**3.**	10 p. brown	4·00	1·25

DESIGNS: 5 c., 30 c., 75 c., 2 p. Palm trees, Lake Tinzgarrentz. 10 c., 40 c., 90 c., 5 p, Camel and irrigation. 15 c., 45 c., 1 p. Camel transport.

4. Camel Train.

DESIGNS: 25 c. 2 p., 10 p. Desert Camp. 1 p., 5 p. Four Camels.

1951. Air.

19.	–	25 c. yellow	8	5
20.	**4.**	50 c. magenta	5	5
21.	–	1 p. green ..	8	5
22.	–	2 p. blue ..	12	5
23.	**4.**	3 p. 25 violet	20	5
24.	–	5 p. sepia ..	1·60	15
25.	–	10 p. red ..	4·00	1·25

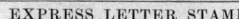

EXPRESS LETTER STAMP

E 1. Port Tilimenzo.

1951.
E 26. **E 1.** 25 c. red 8 5

SRI LANKA BC

Ceylon became a republic within the British Commonwealth in 1972 and changed its name to Sri Lanka (=" Resplendent Island ").

100 cents = 1 rupee.

123. National Flower and Mountain of the Illustrious Foot.

1972. Republic of Sri Lanka. Inaug.
591. **123.** 15 c. multicoloured .. 5 5

124. Map of World with Buddhist Flag.

1972. World Fellowship of Buddhists. 10th Conf.
592. **124.** 5 c. multicoloured .. 5 5

125. Book Year Emblem.

1972. Int. Book Year.
593. **125.** 20 c. orange & brown 5 5

126. Imperial Angelfish.

1972. Fish. Multicoloured.

594.	2 c. Type **126**	5	5
595.	3 c. Green Chromide	5	5
596.	30 c. Skipjack	5	5
597.	2 r. Black Ruby Barb	25	30

127. Memorial Hall.

1973. Bandaranaike Memorial Hall. Opening.
598. **127.** 15 c. cobalt and blue.. 5 5

128. King Vessantara Giving Away His Children.

1973. Rock and Temple Paintings. Mult.

599.	35 c. Type **128**	5	5
600.	50 c. The Prince and the Grave-digger	8	8
601.	90 c. Bearded old man	12	12
602.	1 r. 55 Two female figures	25	30

129. Bandaranaike Memorial Conference Hall.

1974. 20th Commonwealth Parliamentary Conf., Colombo.
604. **129.** 85 c. multicoloured .. 10 12

130. Prime Minister Bandaranaike.

1974.
605. **130.** 15 c. multicoloured .. 5 5

131. "UPU" and "100".

1974. U.P.U. Centenary.
606. **131.** 50 c. multicoloured .. 8 8

132. Sri Lanka Parliament Building.

1975. Inter-Parliamentary Meeting.
607. **132.** 1 r. multicoloured .. 12 15

133. Sir Ponnambalam Ramanathan.

1975. Ramanathan (politician) Commem.
608. **133.** 75 c. multicoloured .. 10 10

134. D. J. Wimalasurendra.

1975. Wimalasurendra (engineer) Commemoration.
609. **134.** 75 c. black and blue .. 10 10

135. Mrs. Bandaranaike, Map and Dove.

1975. International Women's Year.
610. **135.** 1 r. 15 multicoloured.. 15 20

136. Ma-ratmal.

1976. Indigenous Flora. Multicoloured.

611.	25 c. Type **136**	5	5
612.	50 c. Binara	5	8
613.	75 c. Daffodil orchid	8	10
614.	10 r. Diyapara	1·10	1·25

137. Mahaweli Dam.

1976. Mahaweli River Diversion.
616. **137.** 85 c. turq., blue & violet 10 12

138. Dish Aerial.

1976. Satellite Earth Station Padukka. Opening.
617. **138.** 1 r. multicoloured .. 12 15

139. Conception of the Buddha.

1976. Vesek. Multicoloured.

618. 5 c. Type **139** 5 5
619. 10 c. King Suddhodana and the astrologers .. 5 5
620. 1 r. 50 The astrologers being entertained 20 25
621. 2 r. The Queen in a palanquin 25 30
622. 2 r. 25 Royal procession.. 30 35
623. 5 r. Birth of the Buddha.. 65 75

Nos. 618/23 show paintings from the Danbava Temple.

140. Blue Sapphire.

1976. Gems of Sri Lanka. Multicoloured.

625. 60 c. Type **140** 8 8
626. 1 r. 15 Cat's Eye.. .. 15 15
627. 2 r. Star sapphire .. 25 30
628. 5 r. Ruby 55 60

141. President Mrs. S. Bandaranaike.

1976. Non-aligned Summit Conf., Colombo.

630. **141.** 1 r. 15 multicoloured.. 15 15
631. 2 r. multicoloured .. 30 35

142. Statue of Liberty.

1976. American Revolution. Bicent.

632. **142.** 2 r. 25 light blue and dark blue 30 35

143. Bell Early Telephone and Telephone lines. **144.** Maitreya (precarnate Buddha).

1976. Telephone Centenary.

633. **143.** 1 r. multicoloured .. 15 15

1976. Colombo Museum. Cent. Multicoloured.

634. 50 c. Type **144** 8 8
635. 1 r. Sundra Murti Swami (Tamil psalmist) .. 15 15
636. 5 r. Tara (goddess) .. 70 80

145. Kandyan Crown. 1798–1815.

1977. Regalia of the Kings of Kandy. Multicoloured.

637. 1 r. Type **145**. 15 15
638. 2 r. Kandyan throne, 1693–1815 .. .. .. 30 35

146. Sri Rahula.

1977. Venerable Totagamuwe Sri Rahula (poet).

639. **146.** 1 r. multicoloured .. 15 15

147. Sir Pannambalam Arunachalam.

1977. Sir Pannambalam Arunachalam (social reformer).

640. **147.** 1 r. multicoloured .. 15 15

STELLALAND BC

A temporary Boer republic annexed by the British in 1884 and later incorporated in Br. Bechuanaland.

1. Arms of the Republic.

1884.

1. **1.** 1d. red .. .. .. 50·00
2. 3d. orange .. .. .. 6·00
3. 4d. blue .. .. .. 6·00
4. 6d. mauve .. .. .. 6·00
5. 1s. green .. .. .. 10·00

1884. Surch. Twee.

6. **1.** 2d. on 4d. blue £550

STRAITS SETTLEMENTS BC

A Br. Crown colony which included portions of the mainland of the Malay Peninsula and islands off its coasts, and the island of Labuan off the N. coast of Borneo.

100 cents = 1 dollar (Straits).

1867. Stamps of India surch. with crown and value.

1. **5.** $1\frac{1}{2}$ c. on $\frac{1}{2}$ a. blue .. .. 14·00 19·00
2. 2 c. on 1 a. brown .. 16·00 16·00
3. 3 c. on 1 a. brown.. .. 18·00 18·00
4. 4 c. on 1 a. brown.. .. 27·00 21·00
5. 6 c. on 2 a. orange .. 50·00 30·00
6. 8 c. on 2 a. orange .. 27·00 13·00
7. 12 c. on 4 a. green .. 65·00 30·00
8. 24 c. on 8 a. red .. .. 42·00 17·00
9. 32 c. on 2 a. orange .. 35·00 17·00

1869 (?). No. 1 with "THREE HALF" deleted and "2" written above in manuscript.

10. **5.** 2 on $1\frac{1}{2}$ c. on $\frac{1}{2}$ a. blue .. £500 £400

1.

2.

3.

1867.

11. **1.** 2 c. brown .. .. 1·00 70
98 4 c. rose 65 25
66a. 6 c. lilac 80 70
52. 8 c. orange .. .. 1·00 25
15. 12 c. blue .. .. 7·50 2·00
68a. 24 c. green .. .. 1·10 90
69. **2.** 30 c. claret .. .. 2·00 1·50
18. **3.** 32 c. red .. .. 25·00 9·00
71. 96 c. grey .. .. 10·00 7·50

1879. Surch. in words.

20. **1.** 5 c. on 8 c. orange .. 11·00 11·00
21. **3.** 7 c. on 32 c. red .. 11·00 11·00

1880. Surch. in figures and words.

47. **1.** 5 c. on 4 c. rose .. 60·00 40·00
42. 5 c. on 8 c. orange .. 12·00 13·00
44. 10 c. on 6 c. lilac .. 6·00 4·50
45a. 10 c. on 12 c. blue .. 6·00 5·50
23. **2.** 10 c. on 30 c. claret .. 23·00 11·00

1880. Surch. in figures only.

33. **2.** "10" on 30 c. claret .. 14·00 12·00

4.

5.

1882.

63a. **1.** 2 c. rose 15 15
64. 4 c. brown .. .. 1·00 45
48. **4.** 5 c. chocolate .. .. 10·00 8·00
99. 5 c. brown 55 35
65. 5 c. blue 40 20
100. 5 c. purple 80 50
101. **1.** 8 c. blue 55 20
53. **5.** 10 c. grey 75 25
102. **1.** 12 c. purple .. .. 2·00 1·75
70. **3.** 32 c. orange .. .. 2·25 1·00

1883. Surch. in words in one line horiz. or vert. (No. 60).

58. **1.** 2 c. on 8 c. orange .. 10·00 9·00
60. **3.** 2 c. on 32 c. orange .. 40·00 22·00
109. **4.** 4 c. on 5 c. red .. 12 8

1883. Surch. with figures over words in two lines.

61. **1.** 2 c. on 4 c. rose .. 5·00 6·00
62. 2 c. on 12 c. blue .. 25·00 19·00
82. **4.** 3 c. on 5 c. blue.. .. 13·00 13·00
84. 3 c. on 5 c. purple .. 27·00 27·00
106. 4 c. on 5 c. brown .. 40 60
73. 4 c. on 5 c. blue (A)* .. 15·00 15·00
107. 4 c. on 5 c. blue (B)* .. 40 60
108b. **1.** 4 c. on 8 c. blue.. .. 55 40
74. 8 c. on 12 c. blue .. 30·00 20·00
75. 8 c. on 12 c. purple .. 30·00 20·00

* (A) "Cents" in italics (B) "cents" (with small "c") in roman type.

1884. Surch. TWO CENTS vert.

76. **4.** 2 c. on 5 c. blue.. .. 12·00 10·00

1884. Nos. 73 and 75 surch. with large figure

79. **4.** "4" on 4 c. on 5 c. blue.. — £2000
80. **1.** "8" on 8 c. on 12 c. purple 25·00 28·00

1885. Surch. with words in one line and thick bar.

93. **1.** 1 c. on 8 c. green.. .. 12 30
83a. **3.** 3 c. on 32 c. purple .. 60 60
94. 3 c. on 32 c. red .. 25 50

1887. Surch. **2 Cents** in one line.

85. **4.** 2 c. on 5 c. blue.. .. 4·00 5·00

1891. Surch. **10 CENTS** in one line and thin bar.

86. **1.** 10 c. on 24 c. green .. 55 55

1891. Surch. with words in two lines and thin bar.

88. **1.** 1 c. on 2 c. rose .. 25 35
89. 1 c. on 4 c. brown .. 70 60
90. 1 c. on 6 c. lilac .. 40 45
91. 1 c. on 8 c. orange .. 25 40
92. 1 c. on 12 c. purple .. 1·25 3·00
87. **3.** 30 c. on 32 c. orange .. 1·75 2·00

6.

7.

1892.

95. **6.** 1 c. green 15 15
96. 3 c. red 50 25
97. 3 c. brown 50 15
103a. 25 c. purple and green .. 2·00 90
104. 50 c. olive and red .. 3·50 1·10
105. $5 orange and red .. 70·00 70·00

1902.

110. **7.** 1 c. green 8 15
111. 3 c. purple and orange .. 15 20
112. 4 c. purple on red .. 75 25
113. 5 c. purple 75 20
157. 5 c. orange .. .. 1·00 20
114. 8 c. purple on blue .. 1·10 25
115. 10 c. pur. and blk. on yell. 1·40 40
159. 10 c. purple on yellow .. 25 15
116. 25 c. purple and green .. 1·75 90
161. 25 c. purple .. .. 1·50 1·00
134. 30 c. grey and red .. 2·00 1·00
162. 30 c. purple and yellow 1·00 50
135. 50 c. green and red .. 2·50 1·75
164. 50 c. black on green .. 1·10 70
136. $1 green and black .. 5·00 2·00
165. $1 black and red on blue 2·50 1·25
120. $2 purple and black .. 11·00 9·00
166. $2 green & red on yellow 5·00 4·00
138. $5 green and orange .. 20·00 12·00
167. $5 green and red on green 15·00 11·00
139. $25 green and black .. £400

8.

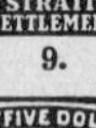

9.

10.

11.

1903.

127. **8.** 1 c. green 15 8
128. 3 c. purple 10 15
128a. 3 c. plum 65 20
153. 3 c. red 10 10
129. 4 c. purple on red .. 35 10
154. 4 c. red 10 20
155. 4 c. purple 10 10
156. 4 c. claret 35 45
131. **9.** 8 c. purple on blue .. 1·75 15
158. 8 c. blue 25 15
160. **10.** 21 c. purple .. 1·50 3·25
163. 45 c. black on green .. 1·25 2·00
168. **11.** $25 purple and blue .. £250 90·00

1907. Stamps of Labuan (Crown type) optd **STRAITS SETTLEMENTS** or surch in words also.

141. **4.** 1 c. black and purple .. 5·50 7·00
142. 2 c. black and green .. 15·00 15·00
143. 3 c. black and brown .. 3·25 4·25
144. 4 c. on 12 c. black & yell. 45 90

145. **4.** 4 c. on 16 c. green & brn. 45 1·00
146. 4 c. on 18 c. black & brn. 40 80
147. 8 c. black and orange .. 40 1·10
148. 10 c. brown and blue .. 80 1·10
149. 25 c. green and blue .. 90 2·50
150. 50 c. purple and lilac .. 2·50 4·00
151. $1 claret and orange .. 8·50 8·50

12. 13.

14. 15.

1912.

193b.**12.** 1 c. green 15 15
196a. 3 c. red 10 10
197. 4 c. purple 35 15
199. **13.** 5 c. orange 30 15
201. **14.** 8 c. blue 20 15
202. **13.** 10 c. purple on yellow 35 15
204. **15.** 21 c. purple .. .. 90 1·25
206. **13.** 25 c. purple and mauve 2·50 65
207. 30 c. purple and orange 80 65
208. **15.** 45 c. black on green .. 90 1·40
238. **13.** 50 c. black on green .. 75 20
239. $1 black and red on blue 1·75 25
211a. $2 green & red on yell. 2·25 1·50
212a. $5 green & red on green 12·00 4·00
240b. – $25 pur. & blue on blue £170 45·00

No. 240b is as T **11** but with head of King George V.

1917. Surch. **RED CROSS 2c.**

216. **12.** 2 c. on 3 c. red .. 60 1·60
217. 2 c. on 4 c. purple .. 60 1·60

1919.

218. **12.** 1 c. black 8 8
219. **14.** 2 c. green 8 8
220. 2 c. brown 60 55
221. **12.** 3 c. green 35 25
222. 4 c. red 60 15
223. 4 c. violet 10 8
224. 4 c. orange 10 8
226a.**13.** 5 c. brown 15 8
227. **14.** 6 c. claret 25 12
229. 6 c. red 55 12
230. **13.** 10 c. blue 55 12
232. **14.** 12 c. blue 40 8
236a.**15.** 35 c. purple and orange 1·25 1·25
237. 35 c. red and purple .. 2·25 1·60

1922. Optd. **MALAYA-BORNEO EXHIBITION.**

250. **12.** 1 c. black 20 35
251. **14.** 2 c. green .. .. 75 1·00
252. **12.** 4 c. red .. .. .. 85 1·40
253. **13.** 5 c. orange .. .. 1·25 1·75
244. **14.** 8 c. blue 75 90
254. **13.** 10 c. blue .. .. 1·25 2·00
245. 25 c. purple and mauve 1·75 2·00
246. **15.** 45 c. black on green .. 1·25 2·10
255. **13.** $1 black and red on blue 6·50 9·00
248. $2 green & red on yellow 7·00 8·00
249. $5 green & red on green 35·00 40·00

1935. Silver Jubilee. As T **11** of Antigua.

256. 5 c. blue and grey .. 10 10
257. 8 c. green and blue .. 35 35
258. 12 c. brown and blue .. 35 40
259. 25 c. grey and purple .. 75 70

16. 17.

1936.

260. **16.** 1 c. black 5 5
261. 2 c. green 8 8
262. 4 c. orange 10 8
263. 5 c. brown 10 5
264. 6 c. red 12 8
265. 8 c grey 20 12
266. 10 c. purple 40 12
267. 12 c. blue .. .. 1·60 45
268. 25 c. purple and red .. 60 12
269. 30 c. purple and orange 75 25
270. 40 c. red and purple .. 90 65
271. 50 c. black and green.. 1·10 55
272. $1 black & red on blue 1·75 90
273. $2 green and red .. 6·00 4·00
274. $5 green & red on green 13·00 7·50

1937. Coronation. As T **2** of Aden.

275. 4 c. orange 5 5
276. 8 c. grey 8 8
277. 12 c. blue 15 15

1937.

278. **17.** 1 c. black 8 8
279. 2 c. green 8 8
294. 2 c. orange 15 20
295. 3 c. green 20 25
280. 4 c. orange 30 10
281. 5 c. brown 20 10
282. 6 c. red 30 8
283. 8 c. grey 50 8
284. 10 c. purple 35 8
285. 12 c. blue 45 8
298. 15 c. blue .. .. 75 1·00
286. 25 c. purple and red .. 2·50 20
287. 30 c. purple and orange 1·25 40
288. 40 c. red and purple .. 1·25 65
289. 50 c. black on green 50 15
290. $1 black and red on blue 80 20
291. $2 green and red .. 3·50 1·10
292. $5 green & red on green 5·50 2·00

For subsequent issues see "Malaya".

For Japanese issues see "Japanese Occupation of Malaya".

POSTAGE DUE STAMPS

D 1.

ILLUSTRATIONS British Commonwealth and all overprints and surcharges are FULL SIZE. Foreign Countries have been reduced to ¾-LINEAR.

1924.

D 1. **D 1.** 1 c. violet 50 15
D 2. 2 c. black 40 12
D 3. 4 c. green 40 35
D 4. 8 c. red 60 20
D 5. 10 c. orange 60 25
D 6. 12 c. blue .. .. 1·10 20

For later issues see Malayan Postal Union.

SUDAN BC; O4

A territory in Africa, extending S. from Egypt towards the equator, jointly administered by Gt. Britain and Egypt until 1954 when the territory was granted a large measure of self-government. Became independent 1st Jan., 1956.

1000 milliemes = 100 piastres = £1 Sudanese.

1897. Stamps of Egypt optd. **SOUDAN** in English and Arabic.

1. **5.** 1 m. brown.. .. .. 40 50
3. 2 m. green 70 80
4. 3 m. yellow 70 70
5. 5 m. red .. .. .. 1·25 1·25
6. **4.** 1 pi. blue .. .. .. 2·50 2·50
7. – 2 pi. orange .. .. .. 11·00 8·50
8. – 5 pi. grey .. .. .. 12·00 8·50
9. **5.** 10 pi. mauve .. .. .. 11·00 10·00

1. Arab Postman. 2.

1898.

18. **1.** 1 m. brown and red .. 8 8
19. 2 m. green and brown .. 15 12
20. 3 m. mauve and green .. 35 15
21. 4 m. blue and brown .. 30 70
22. 4 m. red and brown .. 70 70
23. 5 m. red and black .. 50 8
24. 1 pi. blue and brown .. 80 15
15. 2 pi. black and blue .. 3·25 1·40
44. 2 pi. purple and orange .. 10 5
44a. 3 pi. brown and blue .. 20 10
44b. 4 pi. blue and black .. 15 5
45. 5 pi. brown and green .. 25 8
45a. 6 pi. blue and black .. 60 15
45b. 8 pi. green and black .. 65 25
46. 10 pi. black and mauve .. 50 15
46a. 20 pi. blue 90 30

1903. Surch. **5 Milliemes.**

29. **1.** 5 m. on 5 pi. brown & grn. 1·10 1·90

1921.

37. **2.** 1 m. black and orange .. 5 5
38. 2 m. yellow and brown .. 5 5
39. 3 m. mauve and green .. 5 5
40. 4 m. green and brown .. 5 5
41. 5 m. brown and black .. 5 5
42. 10 m. red and black .. 8 5
43. 15 m. blue and brown .. 8 5

For stamps as T **1** and **2** with different Arabic inscriptions see issue of 1948.

1931. Air. Optd. **AIR MAIL.**

47. **2.** 5 m. brown and black .. 70 1·00
48. 10 m. red and black .. 70 1·25
49. **1.** 2 pi. purple and yellow .. 1·00 1·60

3. Statue of General Gordon.

1931. Air.

49a. **3.** 3 m. green and brown .. 1·50 2·00
50. 5 m. black and green .. 75 75
51. 10 m. black and red .. 1·00 1·00
52a. 15 m. brown 75 40
53. 2 pi. black and orange .. 30 35
53c. 2½ pi. mauve and blue .. 70 70
54. 3 pi. black and grey .. 70 70
55. 3½ pi. black and violet .. 1·25 1·25
56. 4½ pi. brown and grey .. 5·00 6·00
57a. 5 pi. black and blue .. 1·25 1·25
57c. 7½ pi. green .. .. 2·50 2·50
57e. 10 pi. brown and blue .. 2·75 3·00

1932. Air. Surch. **AIR MAIL** and value in English and Arabic figures.

58. **1.** 2½ pi. on 2 pi. pur. & orge. 3·50 4·00

4. General Gordon. 5. Gordon Memorial College, Khartoum.

1935. Gen. Gordon 50th Death Anniv.

59. **4.** 5 m. green 35 30
60. 10 m. brown 45 45
61. 13 m. blue .. .. 1·00 2·25
62. 15 m. red 65 75
63. 2 pi. blue 70 70
64. 5 pi. orange .. .. 1·10 1·10
65. **5.** 10 pi. purple .. .. 3·25 3·00
66. – 20 pi black .. .. 14·00 16·00
67. – 50 pi. brown .. .. 30·00 30·00

DESIGN—(44 × 20 mm.): 20 pi., 50 pi. Gordon Memorial Service, Khartoum.

1935. Air. Stamps of 1931 surch. in English and Arabic.

74. **3.** 5 m. on 2½ pi. mve. & blue 20 30
68. 15 c. on 10 m. black & red 60 65
69. 2½ pi. on 3 m. green & brn. 1·25 2·00
70. 2½ pi. on 5 m. black & grn. 7·00 1·00
75. 3 pi. on 3½ pi. black & vio. 3·25 4·00
71. 3 pi. on 4½ pi. brn. & grey 2·00 3·50
76. 3 pi. on 7½ pi. green .. 70 1·10
77. 5 pi. on 10 pi. brn. & blue 90 1·25
72. 7½ pi. on 4½ pi. brn. & grey 4·50 3·50
73. 10 pi. on 4½ pi. brn. & grey 3·75 5·50

1940. Surch. **5 mills** and in Arabic.

78 **2.** 5 m. on 10 m. red & black 10 20

1940. Surch. **4½ Piastres.**

79. **2.** 4½ p. on 5 m. brown & blk. 3·50 2·50
80. **1.** 4½ p. on 8 p. green & black 3·50 2·50

7. Tuti Island, near Khartoum.

1941.

81. **7.** 1 m. black and orange .. 8 25
82. 2 m. orange and brown .. 15 25
83. 3 m. mauve and green .. 10 10
84. 4 m. green and brown .. 8 15
85. 5 m. brown and black .. 8 8
86. 10 m. red and black .. 1·50 1·25
97. 15 m. blue and brown .. 5 5
88. 2 pi purple and yellow .. 2·00 1·40
89. 3 pi. brown and blue .. 45 12
90. 4 pi. blue and black .. 40 20
91. 5 pi. brown and green .. 2·50 2·50
92. 6 pi. blue and black .. 3·50 1·25
93. 8 pi. green and black .. 3·50 1·40
94. 10 pi. black and violet .. 6·50 3·25
95. 20 pi. blue .. .. .. 11·00 9·00

The piastre values are larger (30 × 25 mm.).

8. Arab Postman. 9.

1948.

96. **8.** 1m. black and orange .. 5 8
97. 2 m. orange and brown .. 5 5
98. 3 m. mauve and green .. 5 5
99. 4 m. green and brown .. 5 5
100. 5 m. brown and black .. 5 5
101. 10 m. red and black .. 8 5
102. 15 m. blue and brown .. 8 5
103. **9.** 2 p. purple and yellow .. 20 10
104. 3 p. brown and blue .. 20 12
105. 4 p. blue and black .. 25 20
106. 5 p. orange and green .. 45 25
107. 6 p. blue and black .. 35 40
108. 8 p. green and black .. 40 60
109. 10 p. black and mauve .. 60 60
110. 20 p. blue .. .. 1·50 65
111. 50 p. red and blue .. 1·75 1·40

In this issue the Arabic inscriptions below the camel differ from those in T **1** and **2**.

10. Arab Postman. 11.

1948. Jubilee of "Camel Postman" design.

112. **10.** 2 p. black and blue .. 20 20

1948. Legislative Assembly.

113. **11.** 10 m. red and black .. 15 8
114. 5 p. orange and green .. 30 20

12. Sagia (Water Wheel).

1950. Air.

115. – 2 p. black and green .. 20 10
116. – 2½ p. blue and orange .. 20 15
117. **12.** 3 p. purple and blue .. 25 10
118. – 3½ p. sepia and brown 30 40
119. – 4 p. brown and blue .. 30 35
120. – 4½ p. black and blue .. 35 40
121. – 6 p. black and red .. 30 30
122. – 20 p. black and purple 1·00 90

DESIGNS: 2 p. Blue Nile Bridge, Khartoum. 2½ p. Kassala Jebel. 3½ p. Port Sudan. 4 p. Gordon Memorial College. 4½ p. Nile Post Boat. 6 p. Suakin. 20 p. G.P.O., Khartoum.

13. Ibex. 14. Weaving.

1951.

123. **13.** 1 m. black and orange.. 5 5
124. – 2 m. black and blue .. 5 5
125. – 3 m. black and green .. 12 15
126. – 4 m. black and emerald 5 5
127. – 5 m. black and purple.. 5 5
128. – 10 m. black and blue .. 5 5
129. – 15 m. black and chestnut 5 5
130. **14.** 2 p. blue 8 5
131. – 3 p. brown and blue .. 10 8
132. – 3½ p. green and brown.. 10 8
133. – 4 p. blue and black .. 10 8
134. – 5 p. brown and green.. 10 8
135. – 6 p. blue and black .. 12 8
136. – 8 p. blue and brown .. 25 10
137. – 10 p. black and green .. 25 15
138. – 20 p. blue-grn. & black 40 25
139. – 50 p. red and black .. 1·00 50

DESIGNS—As T **13**: 2 m. Shoebill. 3 m. Giraffe. 4 m. Baggara girl. 5 m. Shilluk warrior. 10 m. Hadendowa. 15 m. Policeman. As T **14**—HORIZ. 2 p. Cotton. 3 p. Ambatch canoe. 3½ p. Nuba wrestlers. 5 p. Saiuka farming. 6 p. Gum tapping. 8 p. Darfur Chief. 10 p. Stack Laboratory. 20 p. Nile Lechwe. VERT. 50 p. Camel postman.

15. Camel Postman. 16. "Independent Sudan".

1954. Self-Government.
140. **15.** 15 m. chestnut & green 10 10
141. 3 p. blue and indigo 20 20
142. 5 p. black and purple .. 25 20
Stamps as T **15**, but dated "1953" were released in error at the Sudan Agency in London. They had no postal validity

1956. Independence Commemoration.
143. **16.** 15 m. orange & purple 10 8
144. 3 p. orange and blue 15 12
145. 5 p. orange and green .. 25 20

17. Globe on Rhinoceros (Badge of Sudan). **18.** Sudanese Soldier and Farmer.

1958. Arab Postal Congress, Khartoum.
146. **17.** 15 m. orange and purple 12 8
147. 3 p. orange and blue .. 22 15
148. 5 p. orange and green .. 25 20

1959. Army Revolution. 1st Anniv.
149. **18.** 15 m. yellow, blue & brn. 12 8
150. 3 p. yellow, blue, brown and green .. 15 12
151. 55 m. yellow, blue, brown and maroon .. 25 20

1960. Inaug. of Arab League Centre, Cairo. As T **144** of Egypt.
152. 15 m. black and green .. 8 5

19. Refugees. **20.** Football.

1960. World Refugee Year.
153. **19.** 15 m. blue, black & brn. 8 8
154. 55 m. red, black & sepia 30 30

1960. Olympic Games, Rome.
155. **20.** 15 m. yellow, green, blue and black .. 10 8
156. 3 p. blue, green, yellow and black .. 20 15
157. 55 m. blue, yellow, grn. and black .. 30 25

21. Forest. **22.** King Ta'rhaqa

1960. 5th World Forestry Congress, Seattle.
158. **21.** 15 m. green, grey-brown and red 8 5
159. 3 p. green, grey-brown and deep green .. 15 12
160. 55 m. green, blue, brown and purple 25 20

1961 Sudanese Nubian Monuments Preservation Campaign.
161. **22.** 15 m. brown and green 10 8
162. 3 p. violet and orange .. 20 15
163. 55 m. brown and blue .. 30 25

23. Arab Girl. with Book. **24.** "The World united against Malaria".

1961. "50 Years of Girls' Education in the Sudan"
164. **23.** 15 m. mve., pur. & blue 8 5
165. 3 p. blue, orge. & black 15 12
166. 55 m. brn., green & blk. 30 25

1962. Malaria Eradication.
167. **24.** 15 m. violet, blue & blk. 8 5
168. 55 m. green, emer. & blk. 25 20

1962. Arab League Week. As T **170** of Egypt.
169. 15 m. brown-orange .. 8 5
170. 55 m. blue-green .. 25 25

25. Republican Palace. **26.** Sailing Boat.

27. Camel Postman. **28.** Campaign Emblem and "Millet" Cobs.

1962.
171. **25.** 5 m. blue 5 5
172. – 10 m. purple and blue .. 5 5
173. – 15 m. mar., orge. & bistre 5 5
174. **25.** 2 p. violet 8 5
175. – 3 p. choc. & blue-green 10 5
176. – 35 m. brown, sepia & grn. 15 5
177. – 4 p. mauve, red & blue 20 8
178. – 55 m. black and olive .. 25 8
179. – 6 p. sepia and blue 30 10
180. – 8 p. green 30 15
181. **26.** 10 p. brn., black and blue 35 20
182. – 20 p. green and bronze 65 30
183. – 50 p. olive, blue & black 1·75 60
184. **27.** £S1 chestnut and green 3·50 2·50
DESIGNS: As T **25**—HORIZ. 15 m. "Tabbaque" (food cover). 55 m., 6 p. Cattle. 8 p. Date palms. VERT. 10 m., 3 p. Cotton-picking. 35 m., 4 p. Wild game. As T **26**—HORIZ. 20 p. Bohein Temple. 50 p. Sennar Dam.

1963. Freedom from Hunger.
185. **28.** 15 m. green and brown 8 5
186. 55 m. violet, lilac & blue 20 20

29. Centenary Emblem and Medallions. **30.** "Knight".

1963. Red Cross Centenary.
187. **29** 15 m. grey-blue, red, gold and black .. 12 10
188. 55 m. grey-blue, red, gold and green .. 25 20

1964. Nubian Monuments Preservation. Frescoes from Faras Church, Nubia. Multicoloured.
189. 15 m. Type **30** 12 8
190. 30 m. "Saint" (horiz.) .. 20 15
191. 55 m. "Angel" 35 30

31. Sudan Map. **32.** Chainbreakers and Mrs. E. Roosevelt.

1964. New York World's Fair. Multicoloured.
192. 15 m. Khashm el Girba Dam 5 5
193. 3 p. Sudan Pavilion .. 10 10
194. 55 m. Type **31** 20 20
Nos. 192/3 are horiz.

1964. Mrs. Eleanor Roosevelt (Human Rights pioneer). 80th Birth Anniv.
195. **32.** 15 m. blue and black .. 5 5
196. 3 p. violet and black .. 10 10
197. 55 m. brown and black 25 20

33. Postal Union Emblem. **34.** I.T.U. Symbol and Emblems.

1964. Arab Postal Union's Permanent Bureau. 10th Anniv.
198. **33.** 15 m. black, gold & verm. 5 5
199. 3 p. black, gold & green 10 10
200. 55 m. black, gold & vio. 25 20

1965. I.T.U. Cent.
201. **34.** 15 m. brown and gold .. 5 5
202. 3 p. black and gold 10 10
203. 55 m. green and gold .. 25 20

35. Gurashi (martyr) and Demonstrators.

1965. 21st October Revolution. 1st Anniv.
204. **35.** 15 m. black and brown 5 5
205. 3 p. black and red .. 12 12
206. 55 m. black and grey .. 25 20

36. I.C.Y. Emblem. **37.** El Siddig El Mahdi.

1965. Int. Co-operation Year.
207. **36.** 15 m. lilac and black .. 5 5
208. 3 p. green and black .. 12 12
209. 55 m. red and black .. 25 20

1966. Iman El Siddig El Mahdi. 5th Death Anniv.
210. **37.** 15 m. violet-blue & blue 5 5
211. 3 p. brown and orange 12 12
212. 55 m. chestnut and grey 25 20

38. M. Zaroug (politician).

1966. Mubarak Zaroug Commem.
213. **38.** 15 m. olive and pink .. 5 5
214. 3 p. green and apple .. 12 12
215. 55 m. chocolate & chest. 25 20

39. W.H.O. Building. **40.** Crests of Upper Nile, Blue Nile and Kassala Provinces.

1966. W.H.O. Headquarters, Geneva. Inaug.
216. **39.** 15 m. blue 5 5
217. 3 p. purple 10 10
218. 55 m. brown 25 20

1967. "The Month of the South".
219. **40.** 15 m. multicoloured .. 5 5
220. – 3 p. multicoloured .. 10 8
221. – 55 m. multicoloured .. 20 15
DESIGNS (Crests of): 3 p. Equatoria, Kordofan and Khartoum Provinces. 55 m. Bahr El Gazal, Darfur and Northern Provinces.

41. Giraffe and Tourist Emblem. **42.** Handclasp Emblem.

1967. Int. Tourist Year.
222. **41.** 15 m. multicoloured .. 5 5
223. 3 p. multicoloured .. 10 8
224. 55 m. multicoloured .. 20 15

1967. Arab Summit Conf., Khartoum.
225. **42.** 15 m. multicoloured .. 5 5
226. 3 p. green and orange .. 10 8
227. 55 m. violet and yellow 20 15

43. P.L.O. Shoulder Flash.

1967. Palestine Liberation Organisation.
228. **43.** 15 m. multicoloured .. 5 5
229. 3 p. multicoloured .. 10 8
230. 55 m. multicoloured .. 20 15

44. Mohamed Nur El Din (politician).

1968. Nur El Din Commem.
231. **44.** 15 m. green and blue .. 5 5
232. 3 p. bistre and blue .. 10 8
233. 55 m. ultramarine & blue 20 15

45. Abdullahi El Fadil El Mahdi (Ansar leader).

1968. Abdullahi El Fadil El Mahdi Commem.
234. **45.** 15 m. violet & ultram. 5 5
235. 3 p. emerald & ultram. 10 8
236. 55 m. green and orange 20 15

46. Ahmed Yousif Hashim (journalist).

1968. Ahmed Yousif Hashim. 10th Death Anniv.
237. **46.** 15 m. chestnut and green 5 5
238. 3 p. brown and blue .. 8 8
239. 55 m. violet and indigo 15 12

47. Mohamed Ahmed El Mardi (politician).

1968. Mohamed Ahmed El Mardi Commem.
240. **47.** 15m. ultramarine & blue 5 5
241. 3 p. orge., ultram. & pink 10 8
242. 55 m. brown and blue .. 20 15

48. Douglas DC-3 Airliner.

1968. Sudan Airways. 20th Anniv. Multicoloured.
243. 15 m. Type **48** 5 5
244. 2 p. De Havilland "Dove" 5 5
245. 3 p. Fokker "Friendship" 10 10
246. 55 m. Comet 4-C 20 20

49. Anniversary and Bank Emblems.

1969. African Development Bank. 5th Anniv.
247. 49. 2 p. black and gold .. 5 5
248. 4 p. red and gold .. 15 10
249. 65 m. green and gold .. 20 15

50. I.L.O. Emblem.

1969. Int. Labour Organization. 50th Anniv.
250. 50. 2 p. black, red and blue 5 5
251. 4 p. black, blue & yellow 15 10
252. 65 m. black, mve. & grn. 20 15

51. "Solidarity of the People".

1970. May 25th Revolution. 1st Anniv. (1st Issue).
253. 51. 2 p. multicoloured ..
254. 4 p. multicoloured ..
255. 65 m. multicoloured Set of 3 10·00

Nos. 253/5 were withdrawn on day of issue (25 May) as being unsatisfactory. They were later replaced by Nos. 256/8 and the 1st issue may be easily distinguished by the figures of value which appear on the extreme left of the design.

52. "Solidarity of the People".

1970. May 25th Revolution. 1st Anniv. (2nd Issue).
256. 52. 2 p. brown, green & red 5 5
257. 4 p. blue, green and red 15 10
258. 65 m. green, blue & red 20 15

53. Map of Egypt, Libya and Sudan.
54. I.E.Y. Emblem.

1971. Tripoli Charter. 1st Anniv.
259. 53. 2 p. green, black & red 8 5

1971. Int. Education Year.
260. 54. 2 p. multicoloured .. 8 5
261. 4 p. multicoloured .. 15 10
262. 65 m. multicoloured .. 25 15

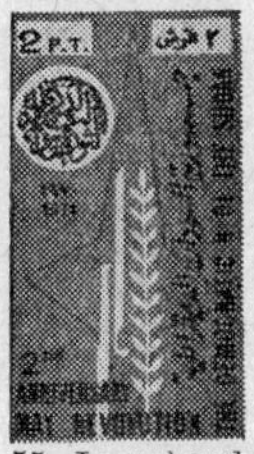

55. Laurel and Bayonets on Star.
56. Emblems of Arab League and Sudan Republic.

1971. 25th May Revolution. 2nd Anniv.
263. 55. 2 p. blk., green & yell. 8 5
264. 4 p. black, green & blue 15 10
265. 10½ p. blk., green & grey 40 25

1972. Arab League. 25th Anniv.
266. 56. 2 p. black, yell. & green 8 5
267. 4 p. multicoloured .. 15 10
268. 10½ p. multicoloured .. 40 25

57. U.N. Emblem and Text.
58. Cogwheel Emblem.

1972. United Nations. 25th Anniv.
269. 57. 2 p. green, orge. & red .. 8 5
270. 4 p. blue, orge. & red .. 15 10
271. 10½ p. blk., orge. & red 40 25

1972. World Standards Day (14.10.71).
272. 58. 2 p. multicoloured .. 8 5
273. 4 p. multicoloured .. 15 10
274. 10½ p. multicoloured .. 40 25

59. Sudanese Arms and Pres. Nemery.

1972. Presidential Elections.
275. 59. 2 p. multicoloured .. 8 5
276. 4 p. multicoloured .. 15 10
277. 10½p. multicoloured .. 40 25

60. Arms and Emblem.

1972. Socialist Union's Founding Congress (January, 1972).
278. 60. 2 p. black, yellow & blue 5 5
279. 4 p. mauve, yellow & blk. 12 10
280. 10½ p. black, yell. & grn. 35 25

61. Airmail Envelope and A.P.U. Emblem.

1972. African Postal Union. 10th Anniv. (1971).
281. 61. 2 p. multicoloured .. 5 5
282. 4 p. multicoloured .. 12 10
283. 10½ p. multicoloured .. 35 25

62. Provincial Emblems.
63. Emperor Haile Selassie.

1973. National Unity.
284. 62. 2 p. multicoloured .. 5 5
285. – 4 p. brown and black .. 12 10
286. – 10½ p. grn., orge. & silver 35 25
DESIGNS—HORIZ. 4 p. Revolutionary Council. VERT. 10½ p. Entwined trees.

1973. Emperor Haile Selassie's 80th Birthday.
287. 63. 2 p. multicoloured .. 5 5
288. 4 p. multicoloured .. 12 10
289. 10½ p. multicoloured .. 35 25

64. President Nasser.
66. Scout Emblem.

65. Ancient Gateway.

1973. Pres. Nasser. 3rd Death Anniv.
290. 64. 2 p. black 5 5
291. 4 p. black and green .. 12 10
292. 10½ p. black and violet 35 25

1973. World Food Programme. 10th Anniv.
293. 65. 2 p. multicoloured .. 5 5
294. 4 p. multicoloured .. 12 10
295. 10½ p. multicoloured .. 35 25

1973. World Scout Conference, Nairobi and Addis Ababa.
296. 66. 2 p. multicoloured .. 5 5
297. 4 p. multicoloured .. 12 10
298. 10½ p. multicoloured .. 30 25

67. Interpol Emblem.

1974. Int. Criminal Police Organization (Interpol). 50th Anniv.
299. 67. 2 p. multicoloured .. 5 5
300. 4 p. multicoloured .. 12 10
301. 10½ p. multicoloured .. 30 25

68. K.S.M. Building, Khartoum University.

1974. Faculty of Medicine, Khartoum University. 50th Anniv.
302. 68. 2 p. multicoloured .. 5 5
303. 4 p. green, brn. & red .. 12 10
304. 10½ p. red, brn. & grn. 30 25

69. African Postal Union Emblem.

1974. Universal Postal Union. Centenary. Multicoloured.
305. 2 p. Type 69 .. .. 5 5
306. 4 p. Arab Postal Union emblem 12 10
307. 10½ p. Universal Postal Union emblem 30 25

70. A. A. Latif and A. F. Elmaz (leaders).

1975. 1924 Revolution. 50th Anniv.
308. 70. 2½ p. green and blue .. 8 5
309. 4 p. red and blue .. 12 10
310. 10½ p. brown and blue .. 30 25

71. Bank and Commemorative Emblems.

1975. African Development Bank. Tenth Anniv.
311. 71. 2½ p. multicoloured .. 8 5
312. 4 p. multicoloured .. 12 10
313. 10½ p. multicoloured .. 30 25

72. Earth Station and Camel Postman.
74. Sudanese Arms and "Gold Medal".

73. Woman, Flag and Emblem.

1976. Satellite Earth Station. Inauguration.
314. 72. 2½ p. multicoloured .. 8 5
315. 4 p. multicoloured .. 12 10
316. 10½ p. multicoloured .. 30 25

1976. International Women's Year.
317. 73. 2½ p. multicoloured .. 8 5
318. 4 p. multicoloured .. 12 10
319. 10½ p. multicoloured .. 30 25

1976. Olympic Games, Montreal.
320. 74. 2½ p. multicoloured .. 8 5
321. 4 p. multicoloured .. 12 10
322. 10½ p. multicoloured .. 30 25

ARMY SERVICE STAMPS

1905. Optd. **ARMY OFFICIAL.**
A 1. 1. 1 m. brown and red .. 70 45

1906. Optd. **Army Service.**
A 6. 1. 1 m. brown and red .. 1·00 20
A 7. 2 m. green and brown .. 2·00 80
A 8. 3 m. mauve and green .. 1·75 40
A 9. 5 m. red and black .. 80 15
A 10. 1 pi. blue and brown .. 1·00 15
A 11. 2 pi. black and blue .. 4·00 3·00
A 12. 5 pi. brown and green 17·00 6·00
A 16. 10 pi. black and mauve 28·00 28·00

OFFICIAL STAMPS

1902. Optd. **O.S.G.S.**
O 5. 1. 1 m. brown and red .. 15 12
O 6. 3 m. mauve and green .. 30 15
O 7. 5 m. red and black .. 30 8
O 8. 1 pi. blue and brown .. 60 10
O 9. 2 pi. black and blue .. 1·00 20
O 10. 5 pi. brown and green 80 40
O 11. 10 pi. black and mauve 1·25 2·00

1936. Optd. **S.G.**
O 12. 2. 1 m. black and orange .. 8 8
O 13. 2 m. yellow and brown 8 8
O 14. 3 m. mauve and green .. 5 8
O 15. 4 m. green and brown 8 8
O 16. 5 m. brown and black .. 8 8
O 17. 10 m. red and black .. 15 5
O 18. 15 m. blue and brown .. 12 10
O 19. 2 pi. purple and orange 20 15
O 19a. 3 pi. brown and blue .. 30 35
O 19b. 4 pi. blue and black .. 30 20
O 20. 5 pi. brown and green 30 20
O 20a. 6 pi. blue and black .. 70 40
O 20b. 1. 8 pi. green and black .. 70 60
O 21. 10 pi. black and mauve 80 70
O 22. 20 pi. blue .. 1·75 2·00

1948. Optd. **S.G.**
O 23. 8. 1 m. black and orange .. 5 5
O 24. 2 m. orange and brown 5 5
O 25. 3 m. mauve and green .. 8 5
O 26. 4 m. green and brown .. 5 8
O 27. 5 m. brown and black .. 5 5
O 28. 10 m. red and black .. 8 5
O 29. 15 m. blue and brown .. 8 5
O 30. 9. 2 p. purple and yellow .. 8 8
O 31. 3 p. brown and blue .. 12 8
O 32. 4 p. blue and black .. 20 10
O 33. 5 p. orange and green .. 25 15
O 34. 6 p. blue and black .. 30 15
O 35. 8 p. green and black .. 35 15
O 36. 10 p. black and mauve 30 30
O 37. 20 p. blue .. .. 1·00 45
O 38. 50 p. red and blue .. 2·50 1·50

1950. Air. Nos. 115/22 optd. **S.G.**
O 39. 2 p. black and green .. 15 12
O 40. 2½ p. blue and orange .. 15 15
O 41. 3 p. purple and blue .. 15 12
O 42. 3½ p. sepia and brown .. 20 20
O 43. 4 p. brown and blue .. 25 30
O 44. 4½ p. black and blue .. 35 40
O 45. 6 p. black and red .. 30 45
O 46. 20 p. black and purple .. 1·00 1·10

1951. Nos. 123/39 optd. **S.G.**
O 47. 1 m. black and orange .. 5 5
O 48. 2 m. black and blue .. 5 5
O 49. 3 m. black and green .. 10 12
O 50. 4 m. black and emerald .. 5 5
O 51. 5 m. black and purple .. 5 5
O 52. 10 m. black and blue .. 5 5
O 53. 15 m. black and chestnut 5 5
O 54. 2 p. blue 5 5
O 55. 3 p. brown and blue .. 12 5
O 56. 3½ p. green and brown .. 15 10
O 57. 4 p. blue and black .. 15 5
O 58. 5 p. brown and green .. 15 8
O 59. 6 p. blue and black .. 20 10
O 60. 8 p. blue and brown .. 25 12
O 61. 10 p. black and green .. 40 15
O 62. 20 p. blue-green and black 70 25
O 63. 50 p. red and black .. 75 75

ح.س.
(O 1. "S.G.")

1962. Nos. 171/84 optd. with Type O 1 (larger on Nos. O 74/7).
O 185. 25. 5 m. blue 5 5
O 186. – 10 m. purple and blue 5 5
O 187. – 15 m. mar., orge. & bis. 5 5
O 188. 25. 2 p. violet .. 8 5
O 189. – 3 p. choc. & blue-green 10 5
O 190. – 35 m. brn., sepia & grn. 10 5
O 191. – 4 p. mauve, red & blue 12 10
O 192. – 55 m. black and olive 15 10
O 193. – 6 p. sepia and blue .. 20 12
O 194. – 8 p. green 25 15
O 195. 26. 10 p. brn., blk. & blue 35 20
O 196. – 20 p. green & bronze 55 45
O 197. – 50 p. olive, blue & blk. 1·75 1·10
O 198. 27. £S 1 chestnut and grn. 3·00 2·50

POSTAGE DUE STAMPS

1897. Postage Due stamps of Egypt optd. **SOUDAN** in English and Arabic.
D 1. D 2. 2 m. green 50 45
D 2. 4 m. maroon 50 55
D 3. 1 pi. blue 80 90
D 4. 2 pi. orange .. .. 1·50 1·75

D 1. Nile Steamboat. D 2.

1901.
D 9. D 1. 2 m. black and brown 8 8
D 10. 4 m. brown and green 10 10
D 11. 10 m. green and mauve 15 15
D 8. 20 m. blue and red .. 30 30

1948.
D 12. D 2. 2 m. black and brown 8 8
D 13. 4 m. brown and green 8 8
D 14. 10 m. green & mauve 8 8
D 15. 20 m. blue and red .. 10 10

The Arabic inscription in Type D 2 differs from that in Type D 1.

SUNGEI UJONG BC

A native state of the Malay Peninsula, later incorporated in Negri Sembilan.

1878. Stamp of Straits Settlements optd. with Crescent, Star and **SU** in an oval.
1. 1. 2 c. brown £450 £450

1881. Stamps of Straits Settlements optd. **SUNGEI UJONG.**
30. 1. 2 c. brown .. .. .. 6·50
45. 2 c. rose .. .. .. 1·75 2·50
8. 4 c. red £110
35. 4 c. brown .. .. 22·00 22·00
24. 8 c. orange .. .. £150 90·00
27. 5. 10 c. grey .. .. 50·00 50·00

1891. Stamp of Straits Settlements surch. **SUNGEI UJONG Two CENTS.**
49. 1. 2 c. on 24 c. green .. .. 15·00 15·00

1. Tiger. 2. Tiger.

1891.
51. 1. 2 c. red .. .. .. 1·50 1·25
52. 2 c. orange .. .. 60 1·00
56. 2. 3 c. purple and red 40 35
53. 1. 5 c. blue .. .. 65 1·10

1894. Surch. in figures and words.
54. 1. 1 c. on 5 c. green.. .. 35 30
55. 3 c. on 5 c. rose .. 35 40

SURINAM O4

A Netherlands colony on the N.E. coast of S. America also known as Dutch Guiana. In December 1954 Surinam was placed on an equal footing with Netherlands under the Crown. Independent from November 1975.

1. 2.

1873.
32. 1. 1 c. grey 80 90
33. 2 c. yellow 25 30
14. 2½ c. red 30 25
15. 3 c. green .. .. 6·00 4·00
16. 5 c. lilac .. .. 7·00 2·40
17. 10 c. bistre .. .. 1·25 90
34. 12½ c. blue .. .. 6·00 2·10
18. 15 c. grey .. .. 6·50 2·40
19. 20 c. green .. .. 12·00 11·00
20. 25 c. blue .. .. 30·00 3·00
22. 30 c. brown .. .. 12·00 12·00
23. 40 c. chocolate .. .. 11·00 11·00
12. 50 c. brown .. .. 13·00 7·00
35. 1 g. grey and brown .. 21·00 19·00
13. 2½ g. brown and green .. 35·00 30·00

1890.
44. 2. 1 c. grey 35 40
45. 2 c. brown 70 60
46. 2½ c. red 95 55
47. 3 c. green .. .. 1·75 1·50
48. 5 c. blue .. .. 11·00 80

1892. Surch. **2½ CENT.**
53. 1. 2½ c. on 50 c. brown .. £120 4·75

3. 4.

1892.
56. 3. 2½ c. black and orange .. 60 35

1892.
63. 4. 10 c. bistre .. .. 14·00 1·10
64. 12½ c. mauve .. .. 14·00 1·75
65. 15 c. grey 80 40
66. 20 c. green .. .. 1·10 70
67. 25 c. blue .. .. 4·00 1·90
68. 30 c. brown .. .. 1·10 80

1898. Surch. **10 CENT.**
69. 1. 10 c. on 12½ c. blue .. 13·00 1·50
70. 10 c. on 15 c. grey .. 30·00 26·00
71. 10 c. on 20 c. green .. 1·60 1·50
72. 10 c. on 25 c. blue .. 3·75 2·40
74. 10 c. on 30 c. brown .. 1·50 1·50

1900. Nos. 196 and 205/6 of Netherlands surch. **SURINAME** and value.
77. 11. 50 c. on 50 c. brown and olive .. .. 9·50 3·50
78. 12. 1 g. on 1 g. green .. 9·50 6·50
79. 2½ g. on 2½ g. lilac .. 7·00 5·50

1900. Surch.
83. 1. 25 c. on 40 c. chocolate .. 1·25 1·60
84. 25 c. on 50 c. brown .. 70 70
86. 50 c. on 1 g. grey & brown 12·00 12·00
82. 50 c. on 2 g. 50 brown and green .. .. 75·00 90·00

1902. As T **4** to **6** of Curacao, but inscr. "(KOLONIE) SURINAME".
87. 4. ½ c. lilac 35 30
88. 1 c. olive 80 45
89. 2 c. brown .. .. 5·50 1·50
90. 2½ c. green .. .. 1·75 20
91. 3 c. orange .. .. 2·50 1·50
92. 5 c. rose .. .. 3·25 12
93. 7½ c. grey .. .. 8·00 3·50
94. 5. 10 c. slate .. .. 6·00 45
95. 12½ c. blue 80 8
96. 15 c. brown .. .. 14·00 4·00
97. 20 c. olive .. .. 14·00 2·40
98. 22½ c. olive and brown .. 9·50 5·50
99. 25 c. violet .. .. 11·00 65
100. 30 c. brown .. .. 21·00 6·50
101. 50 c. lake .. .. 14·00 3·00
102. 6. 1 g. purple .. .. 26·00 6·00
103. 2½ g. slate .. .. 24·00 30·00

8. 9.

1909. Roul. or perf.
104. 8. 5 c. red .. .. 3·50 3·50

1911. Surch. with crown and value.
106. 2. ½ c. on 1 c. grey .. 45 45
107. ½ c. on 2 c. brown .. 3·50 4·00
108. 4. 15 c. on 25 c. blue .. 26·00 26·00
109. 20 c. on 30 c. brown .. 3·50 3·50
110. – 30 c. on 2½ g. lilac (No. 79) 60·00 60·00

1912.
113. 9. ½ c. lilac 40 40
114. 2½ c. green 40 40
115. 5 c. red .. .. 3·50 3·50
116. 12½ c. blue .. .. 4·75 4·75

1913. As T **7/9** of Curacao.
117. 7. ½ c. lilac 12 15
118. 1 c. olive 12 8
119. 1½ c. blue 12 10
120. 2 c. brown 55 65
121. 2½ c. green 25 5
124. 3 c. buff 30 25
123. 3 c. green .. .. 1·25 1·25
125. 4 c. blue .. .. 3·50 2·00
126. 5 c. rose 60 5
127. 5 c. green 60 60
128. 5 c. violet 55 8
129. 6 c. buff .. .. 1·25 1·25
130. 6 c. red 90 12
131. 7½ c. brown 40 10
132. 7½ c. red 60 20
133. 7½ c. yellow .. .. 4·00 4·25
134. 10 c. lilac .. .. 1·50 1·60
135. 10 c. red .. .. 1·25 20
136. 8. 10 c. red 65 30
137. 12½ c. blue 80 25
138. 12½ c. red .. .. 95 1·25
139. 15 c. olive 30 30
140. 15 c. blue .. .. 3·00 2·40
141. 20 c. green .. .. 1·60 1·75
142. 20 c. blue .. .. 1·25 80
143. 20 c. olive .. .. 1·60 1·25
144. 22½ c. orange .. .. 1·10 1·40
145. 25 c. mauve .. .. 1·75 20
146. 30 c. slate .. .. 2·40 55
147. 8. 32½ c. violet and orange 7·50 11·00
148. 35 c. violet and red .. 2·40 2·50
149. 9. 50 c. green .. .. 1·60 30
150. 1 g. sepia .. .. 2·10 20
151. 1½ g. purple .. .. 18·00 18·00
152a. 2½ g. red .. .. 13·00 13·00

1923. Jubilee. As T **10** of Curacao.
169a. 10. 5 c. green 35 30
170. 10 c. red 60 75
171. 20 c. blue .. .. 1·25 1·25
172a. 50 c. orange .. .. 7·00 11·00
173. 1 g. purple .. .. 11·00 6·50
174. 2 g. 50 grey .. .. 32·00 £100
175. 5 g. brown .. .. 42·00 £120

1925.
176. 7. 3 c. on 5 c. green .. 35 45
177. 8. 10 c. on 12½ c. red .. 1·25 1·25
180. 12½ c. on 22½ c. orange.. 12·00 14·00
178. 15 c. on 12½ c. blue .. 80 70
179. 15 c. on 20 c. blue .. 70 70

1926. Surch. **Frankeerzegel 12½ CENT SURINAME** in three lines with bars.
181. D 2. 12½ c. on 40 c. mauve and black. (No. D 62) .. 95 1·10

1926. No. D 162 surch. **Frankeerzegel 12½ CENT SURINAME** in four lines, but without bars.
182. D 2. 12½ c. on 40 c. lilac .. 13·00 14·00

10. 15. 18. Indigenous Disease.

1927.
183. 10. 10 c. red 40 20
184. 12½ c. orange 95 95
185. 15 c. blue .. .. 1·10 30
186. 20 c. blue .. .. 1·25 25
187. 21 c. brown .. .. 7·50 7·50
188. 22½ c. brown .. .. 4·00 4·75
189. 25 c. purple .. .. 1·75 35
190. 30 c. green .. .. 1·75 60
191. 35 c. sepia .. .. 1·90 2·00

1927. "Green Cross" Charity. Various types, with Green Cross in design.
192. 15. 2 c.+2 c. green & slate 60 75
193. – 5 c.+3 c. green & purple 60 75
194. – 10 c.+ 3 c. green & red 1·25 80

1927. Marine Insurance stamps as Type M 1 of Netherlands, but inscr. "SURINAME", surch. **FRANKEERZEGEL** and value.
195. M 1. 3 c. on 15 c. green .. 10 12
196. 10 c. on 60 c. red .. 12 15
197. 12½ c. on 75 c. brown.. 15 10
198. 15 c. on 1 g. 50 blue .. 1·25 1·25
199. 25 c. on 2 g. 25 brown 2·40 2·40
200. 30 c. on 4 g. 50 black.. 5·00 4·75
201. 50 c. on 7 g. 50 red .. 2·40 2·40

1928. "Green Cross" Charity.
202. 18. 1½ c.+1½ c. blue .. 3·00 3·00
203. 2 c.+ 2 c. green .. 3·00 3·00
204. 5 c.+3 c. violet .. 3·00 3·00
205. 7½ c.+2½ c. red .. 3·00 3·00

19. Good Samaritan. 20. Mercury and Posthorn.

1929. "Green Cross" Charity stamps.
206. 19. 1½ c.+1½ c. green .. 4·00 4·00
207. 2 c.+2 c. red .. 4·00 4·00
208. 5 c.+3 c. blue .. 4·00 4·00
209. 6 c.+4 c. black .. 4·00 4·00

1930. Surch. **6.**
210. 7. 6 c. on 7½ c. red (No. 132) 1·25 45

1930. Air.
276. 20. 10 c. red .. .. 2·10 25
212. 15 c. blue .. .. 2·00 35
213. 20 c. green 5 10
214. 40 c. orange 12 20
215. 60 c. purple 30 20
216. 1 g. black 60 75
217. 1 g. 50 brown 70 90
281. 2½ g. yellow .. .. 7·00 6·00
282. 5 g. green £130 £150
283. 10 g. bistre .. .. 19·00 28·00

1931. Air ("Do.X" flight). Optd. **Vlucht Do.X. 1931.**
218. 20. 10 c. red .. .. 12·00 8·00
219. 15 c. blue .. .. 12·00 8·00
220. 20 c. green .. .. 12·00 8·00
221. 40 c. orange .. .. 18·00 12·00
222. 60 c. purple .. .. 29·00 24·00
223. 1 g. black .. .. 35·00 27·00
224. 1 g. 50 brown .. .. 35·00 30·00

21. Mother and Child. 22. "Supplication".

1931. Child Welfare.
225. 21. 1½ c.+1½ c. black .. 3·00 3·00
226. 2 c.+2 c. red .. 3·00 3·00
227. 5 c.+3 c. blue .. 3·00 3·00
228. 6 c.+4 c. green .. 3·00 3·00

1933. William I of Orange. 4th Birth Cent. As T **50** of Netherlands.
229. 6 c. orange .. .. 3·50 80

1935. Founding of Moravian Mission in Surinam.
230. 22. 1 c.+½ c. brown .. 1·25 1·10
231. 2 c.+1 c. blue .. 1·75 1·10
232. – 3 c.+1½ c. green .. 2·10 1·60
233. – 4 c.+2 c. orange .. 2·10 1·60
234. – 5 c.+2½ c. black .. 2·10 1·75
235. 22. 10 c.+5 c. red .. 2·10 1·75

DESIGN: 3 c., 4 c., 5 c. Cross and clasped hands.

23. "Johannes van Walbeeck". 24. Queen Wilhelmina.

1936.
236. 23. ½ c. brown 12 15
237. 1 c. green 20 5
238. 1½ c. blue 30 25
239. 2 c. brown 30 12
240. 2½ c. green 5 5
241. 3 c. blue 35 20
242. 4 c. orange 40 40
243. 5 c. grey 30 12
244. 6 c. red .. .. 1·25 80
245. 7½ c. purple 5 5
246. 24. 10 c. red 40 5
247. 12½ c. green .. .. 1·60 65
248. 15 c. blue 60 30
249. 20 c. orange .. .. 1·00 30
250. 21 c. black .. .. 1·50 1·60
251. 25 c. red .. .. 1·10 55
252. 30 c. purple .. .. 1·75 40
253. 25 c. bistre .. .. 2·00 2·10
254. 50 c. green .. .. 1·75 70
255. 1 g. blue .. .. 2·75 90
256. 1 g. 50 brown .. .. 10·00 8·00
257. 2 g. 50 red .. .. 6·00 4·00

Nos. 254/7 are larger (22×33 mm.).

25. "Infant Support". 26. "Emancipation". 27. Surinam Girl.

1936. Child Welfare.
258. 25. 2 c.+1 c. green .. 1·90 1·90
259. 3 c.+1½ c. blue .. 1·90 1·90
260. 5 c.+2½ c. black .. 2·25 2·25
261. 10 c.+5 c. red .. 2·25 2·25

1938. Liberation of Slaves in Surinam and Paramaribo Girls' School Fund. 75th Anniv.
262. 26. 2½ c.+2 c. green .. 1·10 95
263. 27. 3 c.+2 c. black.. .. 1·10 95
264. 5 c.+3 c. brown .. 1·25 1·25
265. 7½ c.+5 c. blue .. 1·25 1·25

1938. Coronation. 40th Anniv. As T **71** of Netherlands.
266. 2 c. violet 30 30
267. 7½ c. red.. .. 65 65
268. 15 c. blue .. .. 1·40 1·40

MINIMUM PRICE

The minimum price quoted is 5p which represents a handling charge rather than a basis for valuing common stamps. For further notes about prices see introductory pages.

DESIGNS: 3 c. Javanese woman. 5 c. Hindu woman. 7½ c. Indian woman.

28. Creole.

1940. Charity. Inscr. "VOOR MAATSCHAPPELIJKE ZORG".
269. 28. 2½ c.+2 c. green .. 1·10 1·10
270. – 3 c.+2 c. red.. .. 1·10 1·10
271. – 5 c.+3 c. blue .. 1·10 1·10
272. – 7½ c.+5 c. red .. 1·10 1·10

1941. Prince Bernhard and "Spitfire" Funds. As T 32 of Netherlands Indies.
273. 7½ c.+7½ c. blue & orange 1·60 1·60
274. 15 c.+15 c. blue and red 1·90 1·90
275. 1 g.+1 g. blue and grey .. 9·50 9·50

1941. As T 31 of Netherlands Indies, but smaller.
342. 12½ c. blue 12 10
284. 15 c. blue .. .. 9·50 3·75

1942. Red Cross. Surch. with red cross and new values.
289. 23. 2 c.+2 c. brown (post.) 1·25 1·25
291. 2½ c.+2 c. green .. 1·25 1·25
292. 7½ c.+5 c. purple .. 1·25 1·25
293. 20. 10 c.+5 c. red (air) .. 2·00 2·25

1943. Birth of Princess Margriet. As T 20 of Curacao.
294. 20. 2½ c. orange 20 25
295. 7½ c. red 20 15
296. 15 c. red 80 90
297. 40 c. blue .. .. 1·25 1·10

1945. Surch.
298. 23. ½ c. on 1 c. green .. 5 12
299. 1½ c. on 7½ c. purple .. 5 12
300. 2½ c. on 7½ c. purple .. 1·10 1·25
301. 24. 2½ c. on 10 c. red .. 40 12
302. 5 c. on 10 c. red .. 30 25
303. 7½ c. on 10 c. red .. 35 25

1945. Air. Surch.
304. 20. 22½ c. on 60 c. purple .. 25 35
305. 1 g. on 2½ g. yellow .. 4·00 6·50
306. 5 g. on 10 g. bistre .. 9·00 12·00

1945. National Welfare Fund. Surch. **CENT/ VOOR HET/ NATIONAAL/ STEUNFONDS** and premium.
307. 29. 7½ c.+5 c. orange .. 1·25 1·25
308. 30. 15 c.+10 c. brown .. 1·10 1·25
309. 20 c.+15 c. green .. 1·10 1·25
310. 22½ c.+20 c. grey .. 1·10 1·25
311. 40 c.+35 c. red .. 1·10 1·25
312. 60 c.+50 c. violet .. 1·10 1·25

29. Sugar-cane Train.

30. Queen Wilhelmina. 31. 32. Star.

1945.
313. – 1 c. red 12 12
314. – 1½ c. red 80 90
315. – 2 c. violet 25 25
316. – 2½ c. brown 25 25
317. – 3 c. green 45 35
318. – 4 c. brown 45 40
319. – 5 c. blue 45 15
320. – 6 c. olive 90 80
321. 29. 7½ c. orange 35 12
322. 30. 10 c. blue 60 5
323. 15 c. brown 60 12
324. 20 c. green 80 8
325. 22½ c. grey .. .. 1·10 40
326. 25 c. red .. .. 3·50 1·90
327. 30 c. olive .. .. 2·40 25
328. 35 c. blue .. .. 6·00 3·50
329. 40 c. red .. .. 2·40 12
330. 50 c. red .. .. 2·40 10
331. 60 c. violet .. .. 2·40 35
332. 31. 1 g. brown .. .. 2·40 20
333. 1 g. 20 lilac .. .. 2·40 40
334. 2 g. 50 brown .. .. 4·75 45
335. 5 g. red .. .. 8·00 5·50
336. 10 g. orange .. .. 14·00 6·50

DESIGNS—HORIZ. As T 29: 1 c. Bauxite mine, Moengo. 1½ c. Natives in canoes. 2 c. Native and stream. 2½ c. Road in Coronie. 3 c. Surinam River near Berg en Dal. 4 c. Government Square, Paramaribo. 5 c. Gold mining. 6 c. Street in Paramaribo.

1946. Air. Anti-T.B. Fund. Surch. **LUCHT** premium and **POST.**
340. 30. 10 c.+40 c. blue .. 95 1·10
341. 15 c.+60 c. brown .. 95 1·10

1947. Anti-Leprosy Fund.
343. 32. 7½ c.+12½ c. orge.(post.) 1·10 1·25
344. 12½ c.+37½ c. blue .. 1·10 1·25
345. 22½ c.+27½ c. grey (air) 1·10 1·25
346. 27½ c.+47½ c. green .. 1·10 1·25

1948. Types of Nstherlands inscr. "SURINAME".
(a) Numeral type as T 99.
347. 1 c. red 5 5
348. 1½ c. purple 8 10
349. 2 c. violet 15 5
350. 2½ c. green 70 8
351. 3 c. green 8 8
352. 4 c. brown 12 10
353. 5 c. blue 60 5
354. 7½ c. orange .. .. 1·25 50

(b) Portrait of Queen Wilhelmina as T 100.
355. 5 c. blue 25 5
356. 6 c. green 35 25
357. 7½ c. red 25 5
358. 10 c. blue 35 5
359. 12½ c. blue 55 40
360. 15 c. brown 65 15
361. 17½ c. purple 75 65
362. 20 c. green 55 5
363. 22½ c. blue 55 30
364. 25 c. red 55 12
365. 27½ c. claret 55 5
366. 30 c. green 65 5
367. 37½ c. brown .. .. 1·10 95
368. 40 c. purple 75 12
369. 50 c. orange 80 12
370. 60 c. violet 95 20
371. 70 c. black .. .. 1·10 25

1948. Queen Wilhelmina's Golden Jubilee. As T 104 of Netherlands.
372. 7½ c. orange 30 30
373. 12½ c. blue 30 35

1948. As T 24 of Curacao.
374. 7½ c. orange .. .. 1·40 1·50
375. 12½ c. blue .. .. 1·40 1·50

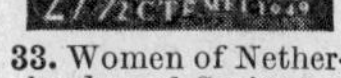

33. Women of Netherlands and Surinam. 34. Marie Curie.

1949. Air. 1st Flight on Paramaribo-Amsterdam Service.
376. 33. 27½ c. brown .. .. 2·50 1·50

1949. U.P.U. 75th Anniv. As T 3 of Netherlands Antilles.
377. 7½ c. red .. .. 2·25 1·60
378. 27½ c. blue .. .. 1·75 1·10

1950. Cancer Research Fund. Inscr. as in T 34.
379. 34. 7½ c.+7½ c. violet .. 4·50 4·50
380. – 7½ c.+22½ c. green .. 4·50 4·50
381. – 27½ c.+12½ c. blue .. 4·50 4·50
382. 34. 27½ c.+97½ c. brown .. 4·50 4·50
PORTRAIT—Nos. 380/1, Wilhelm Rontgen.

1950. Surch. **1 Cent** and bars.
383. 29. 1 c. on 7½ c. orange .. 30 30

1951. Portrait of Queen Juliana as T 108/9 of Netherlands.
395. 108. 10 c. blue 25 5
396. 15 c. brown 55 10
397. 20 c. blue-green .. 1·10 5
398. 25 c. red 75 20
399. 27½ c. lake 70 5
400. 30 c. green 70 20
401. 35 c. olive 80 60
402. 40 c. magenta 90 25
403. 50 c. orange .. .. 1·10 25
404. 109. 1 g. brown .. .. 11·00 15

1953. Netherlands Flood Relief Fund. Nos. 374/5 surch. **STORMRAMP NEDERLAND 1953** and premium.
405. 12½ c.+7½ c. on 7½ c. orange 1·40 1·60
406. 20 c.+10 c. on 12½ c. blue 1·40 1·60

35. Fisherman. 36. Surinam Stadium.

1953. Colonial Exn., Paramaribo.
407. – 2 c. sepia 5 5
408. 35. 2½ c. green 15 10
409. – 5 c. slate 15 5
410. – 6 c. blue 50 40
411. – 7½ c. violet 8 5
412. – 10 c. red.. .. .. 12 5
413. – 12½ c. indigo 60 60
414. – 15 c. red.. .. .. 35 12
415. – 17½ c. lake .. .. 1·25 95
416. – 20 c. turquoise.. .. 25 5
417. – 25 c. olive 80 40

DESIGNS—HORIZ. 2 c. Native shooting fish. 10 c. Woman gathering fruit. VERT. 5 c. Bauxite mine. 6 c. Log raft on the river. 7½ c. Ploughing with buffalo. 12½ c. "Kwie kwie", fish. 15 c. Parrot. 17½ c. Armadillo. 20 c. Native in canoe shooting rapids. 25 c. Iguana.

1953. Sports Week.
419. 36. 10 c.+5 c. claret .. 5·00 4·25
420. 15 c.+7½ c. brown .. 5·00 4·25
421. 30 c.+15 c. green .. 5·00 4·25

37. 38. Native Children.

1954. Air. Surinam Airlines. 25th Anniv.
422. 37. 15 c. blue 60 60

1954. Child Welfare Fund.
423. 38. 7½ c.+3 c. purple .. 2·75 3·00
424. 10 c.+5 c. green .. 2·75 3·00
425. 15 c.+7½ c. brown .. 2·75 3·00
426. 30 c.+15 c. blue .. 2·75 3·00

1954. Ratification of Statue for the Kingdom. As T 135 of Netherlands.
427. 7½ c. maroon 35 35

39. Doves of Peace. 40. Gathering Bananas.

1955. 10th Anniv. of Liberation of Netherlands and War Victims Relief Fund.
428. 39. 7½ c.+3½ c. red .. 1·40 1·40
429. 15 c.+8 c. blue .. 1·40 1·40

1955. 4th Caribbean Tourist Assn. Meeting.
430. 40. 2 c. green 70 70
431. – 7½ c. yellow 95 95
432. – 10 c. brown 95 95
433. – 15 c. blue 95 95

DESIGNS: 7½ c. Pounding rice. 10 c. Preparing casava. 15 c. Fishing.

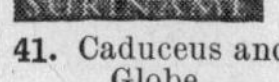

41. Caduceus and Globe. 42. Queen Juliana and Prince Bernard.

1955. Surinam Fair.
434. 41. 5 c. blue 20 20

1955. Royal Visit.
435. 42. 7½ c.+2½ c. olive .. 35 30

43. Flags and Caribbean Map. 44. Façade of 19th-century Theatre.

1956. Caribbean Commission. 10th Anniv.
447. 43. 10 c. blue and red .. 30 30

1958. "Thalia" Amateur Dramatic Society. 120th Anniv. Inscr. as in T 44.
448. 44. 7½ c.+3 c. blue & black 40 45
449. – 10 c.+5 c. purple & blk. 40 45
450. – 15 c.+7½ c. grn. & blk. 40 45
451. – 20 c.+10 c. orge. & blk. 40 45

DESIGNS: 10 c. Early 20th-century theatre. 15 c. Modern theatre. 20 c. Performance of A Midsummer Night's Dream".

1959. Surch.
452. 108. 8 c. on 27½ c. lake .. 10 10

45. Queen Juliana. 46. Symbolic Plants.

1959.
453. 45. 1 g. purple 70 8
454. 1 g. 50 brown .. .. 1·10 35
455. 2 g. 50 red .. .. 1·75 20
456. 5 g. blue .. .. 3·50 25

1959. Ratification of Statute for the Kingdom 5th Anniv.
457. 46. 20 c. red, yell., grn. & bl. 1·40 80

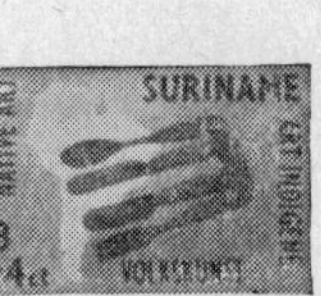

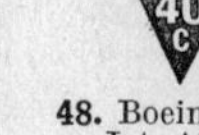

47. Wooden Utensils 48. Boeing "707" Jet Airliner.

1960. Surinam Handicrafts. Inscr. as in T 47.
458. 47. 8 c.+4 c. brown, blue, blue-grn. & yell.-grn. 65 80
459. – 10 c.+5 c. red, blue and chestnut .. 65 80
460. – 15 c.+7 c. grn., brn. & red 65 80
461. – 20 c.+10 c. blue, bistre, olive and turquoise 65 80

DESIGNS: 10 c. Indian chief's headgear. 15 c. Clay pottery. 20 c. Wooden stool.

1960. Opening of Zanderij Airport Building.
462. – 8 c. blue .. .. 1·00 1·10
463. – 10 c. green .. .. 1·10 80
464. – 15 c. red .. .. 1·10 1·10
465. – 20 c. lilac .. .. 1·40 1·10
466. 48. 40 c. brown .. .. 1·90 1·90

DESIGNS: 8 c. Charles Lindbergh's seaplane (1929). 10 c. Fokker 'plane "Snip" (1934). 15 c. Cessna 170-B 'plane (1954). 20 c. "Super-Constellation" (1957).

49. "Uprooted Tree". 50. Surinam Flag.

1960. World Refugee Year
467. 49. 8 c.+4 c. grn. & brown 25 25
468. 10 c.+5 c. green & blue 25 30

1960. Freedom Day.
469. 50. 10 c. multicoloured .. 55 55
470. – 15 c. multicoloured .. 55 60

DESIGN (30 × 25½ mm.): 15 c. Surinam Coat-of-Arms.

51. Putting the Shot. 52. Bananas.

1960. Olympic Games.
471. 51. 8 c.+4 c. brown, black and grey .. 55 55
472. – 10 c.+5 c. brown, black and orange .. 60 60
473. – 15 c.+7 c. brown, black and violet .. 65 60
474. – 20 c.+10 c. brown, black and blue .. 65 70
475. – 40 c.+20 c. brown, black and green .. 90 1·00

DESIGNS: 10 c. Basketball. 15 c. Running. 20 c. Swimming. 40 c. Football.

1961. Local Produce.
476. 52. 1 c. yellow, black and grey-green .. 5 5
477. – 2 c. grn., blk. & ol.-yell. 5 5
478. – 3 c. brown, blk. & choc. 5 5
479. – 4 c. yellow, black & blue 5 5
480. – 5 c. red, black & brown 5 5

481. – 6 c. yellow, blk. & grn. 10 10
482. – 8 c. yellow, black & blue 10 5
DESIGNS: 2 c. Citrus fruit. 3 c. Cocoa. 4 c. Sugar-cane. 5 c. Coffee. 6 c. Coconuts. 8 c. Rice.

53. Treasury.

54. Commander Shepard, Rocket and Globe.

1961. Surinam Buildings. Multicoloured.
483. 10 c. T **53** 10 5
484. 15 c. Court of Justice .. 15 8
485. 20 c. Loge Concordia (Masonic Lodge) .. 20 10
486. 25 c. Neve Shalom Synagogue 30 20
487. 30 c. Old Lock Gate, New Amsterdam .. .. 1·25 80
488. 35 c. Government Building 1·25 1·00
489. 40 c. Governor's House .. 45 30
490. 50 c. Legislative Council House 55 15
491. 60 c. Reform Church .. 70 60
492. 70 c. Zeelandia Fortress (1790) 80 60
The 10 c., 15 c., 20 c. and 30 c. are vert. and the rest horiz.

1961. Air. "Man in Space".
493. – 15 c. multicoloured .. 60 80
494. **54.** 20 c. multicoloured .. 60 80
DESIGN: 15 c. Globe and space-man in capsule.

55. Girl Scout saluting.

56. Dag Hammarskjoeld.

1961. Caribbean Girl Scout "Jamborette". Multicoloured.
495. 8 c.+2 c. Semaphoring .. 35 35
496. 10 c.+3 c. T **55** 35 35
497. 15 c.+4 c. Brownies around a "toadstool" 35 35
498. 20 c.+5 c. Camp-fire singsong 35 35
499. 25 c.+6 c. Lighting camp-fire 35 35
The 10 c. and 20 c. are vert. and the rest horiz.

1962. Hammarskjoeld Memorial Issue.
500. **56.** 10 c. black and blue .. 8 10
501. 20 c. black and violet .. 15 20

1962. Royal Silver Wedding. As T **161** of Netherlands.
502. 20 c. olive-green 30 35

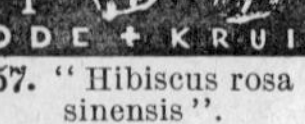

57. "Hibiscus rosa sinensis".

58. Campaign Emblem.

1962. Red Cross Fund. Flowers in natural colours. Background colours given.
503. **57.** 8 c.+4 c. olive 30 30
504. – 10 c.+5 c. blue .. 30 30
505. – 15 c.+6 c. brown .. 30 30
506. – 20 c.+10 c. violet .. 40 45
507. – 25 c.+12 c. turquoise .. 40 45
FLOWERS: 10 c. "Caesalpinia pulcherrima". 15 c. "Heliconia psittacorum". 20 c. "Lochnera rosea". 25 c. "Ixora macrothyrsa".

1962. Malaria Eradication.
508. **58.** 8 c. red 15 20
509. 10 c. blue 20 20

DESIGN: 15 c. Torarica Hotel.

59. Stoelmans Guesthouse.

1962. Opening of New Hotels.
510. **59.** 10 c. multicoloured .. 35 35
511. – 15 c. multicoloured .. 35 35

60. Sisters' Residence. 61. Wildfowl.

1962. Nunnery and Hospital of the Deaconesses. Inscr. "DIAKONESSENHAUS", etc.
512. **60.** 10 c. blk., yell., grn. & bl. 30 30
513. – 20 c. blk., yell., grn. & bl. 30 30
DESIGN: 20 c. Hospital building.

1962. Animal Protection Fund.
514. **61.** 2 c.+1 c. red and blue .. 15 15
515. – 8 c.+2 c. red and black 25 20
516. – 10 c.+3 c. black & green 25 30
517. – 15 c.+4 c. black and red 30 35
ANIMALS: 8 c. Dog. 10 c. Donkey. 15 c. Horse.

62. Emblem in Hands.

63. "Freedom".

1963. Freedom from Hunger.
518. **62.** 10 c. red 25 25
519. – 20 c. blue 25 30
DESIGN—VERT. 20 c. Tilling the land.

1963. Abolition of Slavery in Dutch West Indies. Cent.
520. **63.** 10 c. black and red .. 25 25
521. 20 c. black and green .. 25 30

64. Indian Girl.

65. U.S. "X-15" Aircraft.

67. Skipping.

66. "Camp Fire".

1963. Child Welfare Fund. Inscr. "VOOR HET KIND".
522. **64.** 8 c.+3 c. green .. 15 20
523. – 10 c.+4 c. brown .. 20 25
524. – 15 c.+10 c. blue .. 35 35
525. – 20 c.+10 c. red .. 35 40
526. – 40 c.+20 c. purple .. 60 70
PORTRAIT OF CHILDREN: 10 c. Bush negro. 15 c. Hindustan. 20 c. Indonesian. 40 c. Chinese.

1963. Kingdom of the Netherlands. 150th Anniv. As T **173** of Netherlands but smaller, size 26 × 26 mm.
528. **173.** 10 c. blk., bistre & blue 20 20

1964. Aeronautical and Astronomical Foundation, Surinam.
529. 3 c.+2 c. sepia and lake .. 12 20
530. 8 c.+4 c. sep., indigo & blue 25 25
531. 10 c.+5 c. sepia and green 25 30
532. 15 c.+7 c. sepia and brown 35 40
533. 20 c.+10 c. sepia & violet 45 50
DESIGNS: 3 c., 15 c. T **65**. 8 c. Foundation Flag. 10 c., 20 c. Agena B-Ranger rocket.

1964. Scout Jamborette, Paramaribo, and Surinam Boy Scouts Assn. 40th Anniv.
534. **66.** 3 c.+1 c. yellow & bistre 12 12
535. 8 c.+4 c. ochre, blue and deep blue 20 25
536. 10 c.+5 c. ochre, red and brown-red .. 20 25
537. 20 c.+10 c. ochre, green and indigo 40 40

1964. Child Welfare.
538. **67.** 8 c.+3 c. blue 20 20
539. – 10 c.+4 c. red 20 25
540. – 15 c.+9 c. green .. 25 30
541. – 30 c.+10 c. purple .. 30 35
DESIGNS: 10 c. Children swinging. 15 c. Child on scooter. 20 c. Child with hoop.

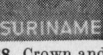

68. Crown and Wreath.

69. Expectant Mother ("Pre-natal Care").

1964. Statute of the Kingdom. 10th Anniv.
543. **68.** 25 c. red, green, yellow and grey 40 40

1965. "Het Groene Kruis" (The Green Cross). 50th Anniv.
544. **69.** 4 c.+2 c. green .. 20 20
545. – 10 c.+5 c. brown & grn. 25 25
546. – 15 c.+7 c. blue & green 25 30
547. – 25 c.+12 c. violet & grn. 30 35
DESIGNS: 10 c. Mother and baby ("Infant care"). 15 c. Young girl ("Child care"). 25 c. Old man ("Care in old age").

70. Abraham Lincoln.

71. I.C.Y. Emblem.

1965. Abraham Lincoln. Death Cent.
548. **70.** 25 c. maroon and bistre 25 30

1965. Int. Co-operation Year.
549. **71.** 10 c. orange and blue .. 10 12
550. 15 c. red and blue .. 15 20

72. Surinam Waterworks.

73. Bauxite Mine, Moengo.

1965. Air.
551. **72.** 10 c. yellow-green .. 8 5
552. – 15 c. ochre 10 5
553. – 20 c. green 15 5
554. – 25 c. indigo 20 5
555. – 30 c. turquoise-green .. 20 10
556. – 35 c. red 25 12
557. – 40 c. orange 30 10
558. – 45 c. carmine 30 40
559. – 50 c. brown-red .. 35 5
560. **72.** 55 c. emerald 40 35
561. – 65 c. yellow 45 35
562. – 75 c. blue 55 30
DESIGNS: 15 c., 65 c. Brewery. 20 c. River scene. 25 c., 75 c. Timber yard. 30 c. Bauxite mine. 35 c., 50 c. Poelepantje Bridge. 40 c. Shipping. 45 c. Jetty.

1965. Opening of Brokopondo Power Station.
563. **73.** 10 c. ochre 12 20
564. – 15 c. green 20 25
565. – 20 c. blue 25 30
566. – 25 c. red 25 30
DESIGNS: 15 c. Alum-earth works, Paranam. 20 c. Power station and dam, Afobaka. 25 c. Aluminium smeltery, Paranam.

74. Girl with Leopard.

75. Red-breasted Marsh Bird.

1965. Child Welfare.
567. **74.** 4 c.+4 c. black & green 12 12
568. – 10 c.+5 c. black & ochre 20 25
569. – 15 c.+7 c. black and red-orange 25 30
570. – 25 c.+10 c. blk. & blue 30 35
DESIGNS: 10 c. Boy with monkey. 15 c. Girl with tortoise. 25 c. Boy with rabbit.

1966. Intergovernmental Committee for European Migration (I.C.E.M.) Fund. As T **189** of Netherlands.
572. 10 c.+5 c. green & black .. 25 25
573. 25 c.+10 c. red and black 30 35

1966. Birds. Multicoloured.
575. 1 c. Type **75** 5 5
576. 2 c. Great kiskadee .. 5 5
577. 3 c. Maroon tanager .. 5 5
578. 4 c. Savannah ground dove 5 5
579. 5 c. Blue-grey tanager .. 5 5
580. 6 c. Hummingbird .. 5 5
581. 8 c. Mexican tanager .. 5 5
582. 10 c. Brown thrush .. 8 5

76. Hospital Building.

77. Father P. Donders.

1966. Opening of Central Hospital, Paramaribo. Multicoloured.
583. 10 c. Type **76** 15 15
584. 15 c. Different view .. 20 20

1966. Redemptorists Mission. Cent.
585. **77.** 4 c. black and brown .. 8 8
586. – 10 c. black, brown & red 12 12
587. – 15 c. black and ochre .. 15 20
588. – 25 c. black and lilac .. 25 30
DESIGNS: 10 c. Batavia Church, Coppename. 15 c. Mgr. J. B. Swinkels. 25 c. Paramaribo Cathedral.

78. Mary Magdalene and Disciples.

79. "Century Tree".

1966. Easter Charity.
589. **78.** 10 c.+5 c. black, red and gold 20 25
590. 15 c.+8 c. black, violet and blue 25 25
591. 20 c.+10 c. black, yellow and blue 30 30
592. 25 c.+12 c. black, green and gold 35 35
593. 30 c.+15 c. black, blue and gold 40 40
On Nos. 590/3 the emblems at bottom left differ for each value. These represent various welfare organizations.

1966. Surinam Parliament. Cent.
594. **79.** 25 c. black, green & red 25 25
595. 30 c. black, red & green 25 30

80. TV Mast, Eye and Globe.

81. Boys with Bamboo Gun.

1966. Surinam Television Service. Inaug.
596. **80.** 25 c. red and blue .. 25 25
597. 30 c. red and brown .. 25 30

1966. Child Welfare. Multicoloured.
598. 10 c.+5 c. Type **81** .. 15 15
599. 15 c.+8 c. Boy pouring liquid on another .. 30 30
600. 20 c.+10 c. Children rejoicing 25 25
601. 25 c.+12 c. Children on merry-go-round .. 40 30
602. 30 c.+15 c. Children decorating room .. 40 40
The designs symbolise New Year's Eve, the End of Lent, Liberation Day, Queen's Birthday and Christmas respectively.

82. Mining Bauxite, 1916.

83. "The Good Samaritan".

1966. Surinam Bauxite Industry. 50th Anniv.
604. **82.** 20 c. black, orge. & yell. 20 20
605. – 25 c. black, orge. & blue 25 25
DESIGN: 25 c. Modern bauxite plant.

1967. Easter Charity. Printed in black, background colours given.
606. **83.** 10 c.+5 c. yellow .. 20 20
607. – 15 c.+8 c. blue .. 25 25
608. – 20 c.+10 c. ochre .. 30 30
609. – 25 c.+12 c. pink .. 35 35
610. – 30 c.+15 c. green .. 35 35
DESIGNS—As T **83**: Various episodes illustrating the parable of "The Good Samaritan".

84. Central Bank.

1967. Surinam Central Bank. 10th Anniv.
611. **84.** 10 c. black and yellow .. 10 12
612. – 25 c. black and lilac .. 25 25
DESIGN: 25 c. Aerial view of Central Bank.

85. Amelia Earhart and Aircraft in Flight. **86.** Siva Nataraja and Ballerina's Foot.

1967. Visit of Amelia Earhart to Surinam 30th Anniv.
613. **85.** 20 c. red and yellow .. 20 20
614. 25 c. green and yellow 25 25

1967. Surinam Cultural Centre. 20th Anniv. Multicoloured.
615. 10 c. Type **86** 10 12
616. 25 c. "Bashi-Lele" mask and violin scroll .. 25 25

87. Zeelandia Fort, Paramaribo (c. 1670). **88.** Stilt-walking.

1967. Treaty of Breda. 300th Anniv. Multicoloured.
617. 10 c. Type **87** 20 20
618. 20 c. New Amsterdam (c. 1660) 20 20
619. 25 c. Breda Castle (c. 1667) 25 25

1967. Child Welfare. Multicoloured.
620. 10 c.+5 c. Type **88** .. 15 15
621. 15 c.+8 c. Playing marbles 30 30
622. 20 c.+10 c. Playing dibs 25 25
623. 25 c.+12 c. Kite-flying .. 40 40
624. 30 c.+15 c. "Cooking" game 40 40

89. "Cross of Ashes". **90.** W.H.O. Emblem.

1968. Easter Charity.
626. 10 c.+5 c. grey and violet 20 20
627. 15 c.+8 c. green and verm. 25 25
628. 20 c.+10 c. green & yellow 30 30
629. 25 c.+12 c. black and grey 35 35
630. 30 c.+15 c. brown & yellow 35 35
DESIGNS: 10 c. T **89** (Ash Wednesday); 15 c. Palm branches (Palm Sunday); 20 c. Cup and wafer (Maundy Thursday); 25 c. Cross (Good Friday); 30 c. Symbol of Christ (Easter).

1968. World Health Organization. 20th Anniv.
631. **90.** 10 c. blue and purple .. 10 12
632. 25 c. violet and blue .. 25 25

91. Chandelier, Reformed Church. **93.** Map of Joden Savanne.

92. Missionary Shop, 1768.

1968. Reformed Church, Paramaribo. 300th Anniv.
633. **91.** 10 c. blue 10 12
634. – 25 c. green 25 25
DESIGN: 25 c. No 633 reversed; chandelier on left.

1968. Evangelist Brothers' Missionary Store, G. Kersten and Co. Bicent.
635. **92.** 10 c. black and yellow .. 20 20
636. – 25 c. black and blue .. 25 25
637. – 30 c. black and mauve 30 30
DESIGNS: 25 c. Paramaribo Church and Kersten's store, 1868; 30 c. Kersten's modern store, Paramaribo.

1968. Restoration of Joden Savanne Synagogue. Multicoloured.
638. 20 c. Type **93** 25 25
639. 25 c. Synagogue, 1685 .. 25 25
640. 30 c. Gravestone at Joden Savanne, dated 1733 .. 30 30

94. Playing Hopscotch. **95.** Western Hemisphere illuminated by Full Moon.

1968. Child Welfare.
641. **94.** 10 c.+5 c. black & brn. 20 15
642. – 15 c.+8 c. black & blue 25 25
643. – 20 c.+10 c. black & pink 30 30
644. – 25 c.+12 c. black & grn. 35 35
645. – 30 c.+15 c. blk. & lilac 40 45
DESIGNS: 15 c. Forming "pyramids"; 20 c. Playing ball; 25 c. Handicrafts; 30 c. Tug-of-war.

1969. Easter Charity.
647. **95.** 10 c.+5 c. blue & pale bl. 35 35
648. 15 c.+8 c. grey & yellow 40 40
649. 20 c.+10 c. blue-green and green 45 45
650. 25 c.+12 c. brown & buff 45 45
651. 30 c.+15 c. violet & grey 50 50

96. Cayman. **97.** Mahatma Gandhi.

1969. Opening of Surinam Zoo, Paramaribo. Multicoloured.
652. 10 c. Type **96** 30 25
653. 20 c. Squirrel Monkey (vert.) 30 30
654. 25 c. Armadillo 35 35

1969. Mahatma Gandhi. Birth Cent.
655. **97.** 25 c. black and red .. 25 25

98. I.L.O. Emblem. **99.** Pillow Fight.

1969. Int. Labour Organization. 50th Anniv.
656. **98.** 10 c. green and black .. 20 20
657. 25 c. red and black .. 30 30

1969. Child Welfare.
658. 10 c.+5 c. purple and blue 20 20
659. 15 c.+8 c. brown & yellow 35 35
660. 20 c.+10 c. blue and grey 30 30
661. 25 c.+12 c. blue and pink 45 50
662. 30 c.+15 c. brown & green 45 50
DESIGNS: 10 c. Type **99**. 15 c. Eating contest. 20 c. Pole-climbing. 25 c. Sack-race. 30 c. Obstacle-race.

1969. Statute for the Kingdom. 25th Anniv. As T **213** of Netherlands but inscr. "SURINAME".
664. 25 c. multicoloured .. 35 35

100. "Flower". **101.** "1950–1970".

1970. Easter Charity. "Wonderful Nature". Multicoloured.
665. 10 c.+5 c. Type **100** .. 70 70
666. 15 c.+8 c. "Butterfly" .. 70 70
667. 20 c.+10 c. "Bird" .. 70 70
668. 25 c.+12 c. "Sun" .. 70 70
669. 30 c.+15 c. "Star" .. 70 70

1970. Secondary Education in Surinam. 20th Anniv.
670. **101.** 10 c. yellow, green & brn. 15 15
671. 25 c. yellow, blue & grn. 25 30

102. New U.P.U. Headquarters Building. **103.** U.N. "Diamond".

1970. New U.P.U. Headquarters Building.
672. **102.** 10 c. vio., blue & turq. 20 20
673. – 25 c. black and red .. 30 30
DESIGN: 25 c. Aerial view of H.Q. Building.

1970. United Nations. 25th Anniv.
674. **103.** 10 c. multicoloured .. 20 20
675. 25 c. multicoloured .. 30 30

104. Aircraft over Paramaribo Town Plan. **105.** Football Pitch (ball in centre).

1970. "40 years of Inland Airmail Flights".
676. **104.** 10 c. grey, ultram. & bl. 20 20
677. – 20 c. grey, red & yell. 25 25
678. – 25 c. grey, carmine and pink 30 30
DESIGNS: As T **104**, but showing different background maps—20 c. Totness. 25 c. Nieuw-Nickerie.

1970. Surinam Football Association. 50th Anniv.
679. **105.** 4 c. brn., yell. & black 5 5
680. – 10 c. brn., olive & black 15 15
681. – 15 c. brn., grn. & black 20 20
682. – 25 c. brn., grn. & black 30 30
DESIGNS: As T **105**, but with ball 10 c. in "corner"; 15 c. at side ("throw-in"); 25 c. at top ("goal").

106. Beethoven (1786). **107.** Heron in Flight.

1970. Child Welfare. Beethoven. Birth Bicent.
683. **106.** 10 c.+5 c. yellow, drab and green 45 45
684. – 15 c.+8 c. yellow, drab and red 70 70
685. – 20 c.+10 c. yellow, drab and blue .. 70 70
686. – 25 c.+12 c. yellow, drab and orange .. 70 70
687. – 30 c.+15 c. yellow, drab and violet .. 70 70
DESIGNS: Beethoven 15 c. 1804; 20 c. 1812; 25 c. 1814; 30 c. 1827.

1971. Netherlands – Surinam – Netherlands Antilles Air Service. 25th Anniv. Multicoloured.
689. 15 c. Type **107** 25 25
690. 20 c. Flamingo in flight .. 25 25
691. 25 c. Parrot in flight .. 35 35

108. Donkey and Palm. **109.** Morse Key.

1971. Easter. The Bible Story. Multicoloured
692. 10 c. + 5 c. Type **108** .. 45 45
693. 15 c. + 8 c. Cockerel .. 60 60
694. 20 c. + 10 c. Lamb .. 60 60
695. 25 c. + 12 c. Crown of Thorns 60 60
696. 30 c. + 15 c. Sun ("The Resurrection") 60 60

1971. World Telecommunications Day. Multicoloured.
697. 15 c. Type **109** 25 25
698. 20 c. Telephones 30 30
699. 25 c. Lunar module and telescope 30 30
EVENTS: 15 c. First National telegraph, Washington—Baltimore, 1843. 20 c. First international telephone communication, England—Sweden, 1926. 25 c. First interplanetary television communication, Earth—Moon, 1969.

1971. Prince Bernhard's 60th Birthday. Portrait as No. 1135 of the Netherlands.
700. 25 c. multicoloured .. 35 35

110. Population Map. **111.** William Mogge's Map of Surinam.

1971. First Census and Introduction of Civil Registration. 50th Anniv.
701. **110.** 15 c. blue and red .. 25 25
702. – 30 c. red and blue .. 35 35
DESIGN: 30 c. "Individual" representing civil registration.

1971. First Surinam Map. 300th Anniv.
703. **111.** 30 c. brown on yellow 40 40

112. Leap-frog. **113.** Plan of Albina.

1971. Child Welfare. Brueghel's "Children's Games". Multicoloured.
704. 10 c. + 5 c. Type **112** .. 45 45
705. 15 c. + 8 c. Strewing flowers 55 55
706. 20 c. + 10 c. Rolling hoop 55 55
707. 25 c. + 12 c. Playing ball 55 55
708. 30 c. + 15 c. Stilt-walking 55 55

1971. Albina Settlement. 125th Anniv.
710. **113.** 15 c. black on blue .. 30 30
711. – 20 c. black on green .. 35 35
712. – 25 c. black on yellow 35 35
DESIGNS—HORIZ. 20 c. Albina and Marowijne River. VERT. 25 c. August Kappler (naturalist and founder).

114. Drop of Water. **115.** Easter Candle.

1972. Surinam Waterworks. 40th Anniv.

713. **114.** 15 c. black and violet 35 35
714. – 30 c. black and blue .. 35 35

DESIGN: 30 c. Water tap.

1972. Easter Charity. Multicoloured.

715. 10 c.+5 c. Type **115** .. 45 45
716. 15 c.+8 c. "Christ teaching the Apostles" 45 45
717. 20 c.+10 c. Hands holding cup ("Christ in Gethsemane") 45 45
718. 25 c.+12 c. Fishes in net ("Miracle of the Fishes") 45 45
719. 30 c.+15 c. Pieces of silver ("Judas's Betrayal") .. 45 45

116. "Eucyane bicolor". **117.** Air-letter Motif.

1972. Air. Butterflies. Multicoloured.

720. 15 c. Type **116** 10 10
721. 20 c. "Helicopis cupido" 12 12
722. 25 c. "Papilio thoas thoas" 15 15
723. 30 c. "Urania leilus" .. 20 20
724. 35 c. "Stalachtis calliope" 25 25
725. 40 c. "Stalachtis phlegia" 25 25
726. 45 c. "Victorina steneles" 30 30
727. 50 c. "Papilio neophilus" 35 30
728. 55 c. "Anartia amathea" 40 35
729. 60 c. "Adelpha cytherea" 45 35
730. 65 c. "Heliconius doris metharmina" 45 40
731. 70 c. "Nessaea obrinus" 50 45
732. 75 c. "Ageronia feronia" 50 45

1972. 1st Airmail in Surinam. 50th Anniv.

733. **117.** 15 c. red and blue .. 25 25
734. 30 c. blue and red .. 30 30

118. Doll and Toys (kindergarten). **119.** Giant Tree.

1972. Child Welfare. Multicoloured.

735. 10 c.+5 c. Type **118** .. 35 35
736. 15 c.+8 c. Clock and abacus (primary education) .. 45 45
737. 20 c.+10 c. Blocks (primary education) 45 45
738. 25 c.+12 c. Molecule complex (secondary education) 55 55
739. 30 c.+15 c. Wrench and blue-print (technical education) 55 55

1972. Surinam Forestry Commission. 25th Anniv.

741. **119.** 15 c. brown & yellow 20 20
742. – 20 c. brn., black & blue 25 25
743. – 30 c. choc., brn. & grn. 25 25

DESIGNS: 20 c. Aerial transport of logs. 30 c. Planting tree.

120. "The Storm on the Lake". **121.** Hindu Peasant Woman.

1973. Easter Charity. Jesus's Life and Death. Multicoloured.

744. 10 c.+5 c. Type **120** .. 35 35
745. 15 c.+8 c. "Washing the Disciples' Feet" .. 40 40
746. 20 c.+10 c. "Jesus taken to Execution" 40 40
747. 25 c.+12 c. The Cross 45 45
748. 30 c.+15 c. "The Men of Emmaus" 45 45

1973. Arrival of Indian Immigrants in Surinam. Cent.

749. **121.** 15 c. violet and yellow 20 20
750. – 25 c. brown and grey 25 25
751. – 30 c. orange and blue 25 25

DESIGNS: 25 c. J. F. A. Cateau van Rosevelt, Head of Department of Immigration, holding map. 30 c. Symbols of immigration.

122. Queen Juliana.

1973. Silver Jubilee of Queen Juliana's Reign.

752. **122.** 30 c. blk., orge. & silver 30 30

123. Florence Nightingale and Red Cross. **124.** Interpol Emblem.

1973. Surinam Red Cross. 30th Anniv.

753. **123.** 30 c.+10 c. multicoloured 60 60

1973. International Criminal Police Organization (Interpol). 50th Anniv. Multicoloured.

754. 15 c. Type **124** 25 25
755. 30 c. Emblem within passport stamp 25 25

125. Flower. **126.** Carrier-pigeons.

1973. Child Welfare.

756. **125.** 10 c.+5 c. multicoloured 25 25
757. – 15 c.+8 c. green, brn. and emerald .. 30 30
758. – 20 c.+10 c. violet, blue and green 30 30
759. – 25 c.+12 c. multicoloured 40 40
760. – 30 c.+15 c. multicoloured 40 40

DESIGNS: 15 c. Tree. 20 c. Dog. 25 c. House. 30 c. Doll.

1973. Stamp Centenary.

762. **126.** 15 c. green and blue .. 20 20
763. – 25 c. multicoloured .. 25 25
764. – 30 c. multicoloured .. 30 30

DESIGNS: 25 c. Postman. 30 c. Map and postal routes.

127. "Quassia amara". **128.** Nurse and Blood Transfusion Equipment.

1974. Easter Charity Flowers. Multicoloured.

765. 10 c.+5 c. Type **127** .. 25 25
766. 15 c.+8 c. "Passiflora quadrangularis" .. 35 35
767. 20 c.+10 c. "Combretum rotundifolium" .. 35 35
768. 25 c.+12 c. "Cassia alata" 40 40
769. 30 c.+15 c. "Asclepias curassavica" 40 40

1974. Surinam Medical School. 75th Anniv. Multicoloured.

770. 15 c. Type **128** 20 20
771. 30 c. Microscope slide and oscilloscope scanner .. 25 25

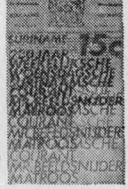

129. Aerial Crop-spraying. **130.** Commemorative Text superimposed on Early Newspaper.

1974. Mechanised Agriculture. 25th Anniv. Multicoloured.

772. 15 c. Type **129** 20 20
773. 30 c. Fertiliser plant .. 25 25

1974. Surinam's "Weekly Wednesday" Newspaper. Bicent.

774. **130.** 15 c. multicoloured .. 20 20
775. 30 c. multicoloured .. 25 25

131. Scout and Tent. **132.** G.P.O., Paramaribo.

1974. "50 Years of Scouting in Surinam". Multicoloured.

776. 10 c.+5 c. Type **131** .. 25 25
777. 15 c.+8 c. Jamboree emblem 20 30
778. 20 c.+10 c. Scouts and badge 30 30

1974. Universal Postal Union. Centenary.

779. **132.** 15 c. black and brown 15 15
780. – 30 c. black and blue .. 20 20

DESIGN: 30 c. G.P.O., Paramaribo (different view).

33. Girl with Fruit.

1974. Child Welfare.

781. **133.** 10 c.+5 c. green, emerald and pink 20 20
782. – 15 c.+8 c. brown, mve. and green 30 30
783. – 20 c.+10 c. yellow, orange and mauve .. 25 25
784. – 25 c.+12 c. brown, lilac and yellow .. 40 40
785. – 30 c.+15 c. cobalt, blue and lilac 40 40

DESIGNS: 15 c. Birds and nest. 20 c. Mother and Child with flower. 25 c. Young boy in cornfield. 30 c. Children at play.

134. Panning for Gold. **135.** "I am the Good Shepherd"

1975. Prospecting Concession Policy. Cent.

787. **134.** 15 c. brown & bistre .. 15 15
788. – 30 c. maroon & red .. 25 25

DESIGN: 30 c. Claws of modern excavator.

1975. Easter Charity.

789. **135.** 15 c.+5 c. yellow green and green 30 30
790. – 20 c.+10 c. yellow and blue 40 40
791. – 30 c.+15 c. yellow and red 40 40
792. – 35 c.+20 c. blue and violet 40 40

DESIGNS—Quotations from the New Testament. 20 c. "I do not know the man". 30 c. "He is not here; He has been raised again". 35 c. "Because you have seen me you have found faith. Happy are they who never saw Me and yet have found faith"

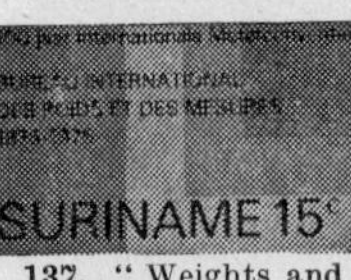

136. "Looking to Equality, Education and Peace". **137.** "Weights and Measures".

1975. International Women's Year.

793. **136.** 15 c.+5 c. blue & green 25 25
794. 30 c.+15 c. vio. & mauve 30 30

1975. Metre Convention. Cent.

795. **137.** 15 c. multicoloured .. 20 20
796. 25 c. multicoloured .. 20 20
797. 30 c. multicoloured .. 25 25

138. Caribbean Water Jug. **139.** "Labour and Technology".

1975. Child Welfare. Multicoloured.

798. 15 c.+5 c. Type **138** .. 25 25
799. 20 c.+10 c. Indian arrow-head 35 35
800. 30 c.+15 c. "Maluana" (protection against evil spirits) 40 40
801. 35 c.+20 c. Indian arrow-head (different) .. 40 40

1975. Independence. "Nation in Development". Multicoloured.

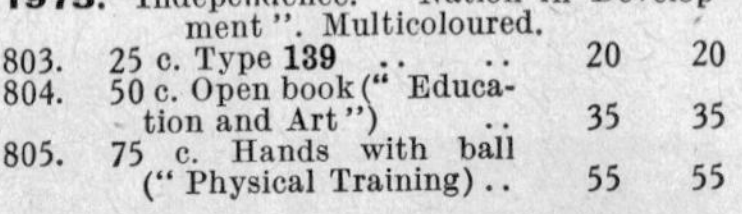

803. 25 c. Type **139** 20 20
804. 50 c. Open book ("Education and Art") .. 35 35
805. 75 c. Hands with ball ("Physical Training) .. 55 55

140. Central Bank, Paramaribo. **141.** "Oncidium lanceanum".

1975.

806. **140.** 1 g. blk., mve. and pur. 70 70
807. $1\frac{1}{2}$ g. blk., oran. & brn. 1·10 1·10
808. $2\frac{1}{2}$ g. blk., red and brn. 1·75 1·75
809. 5 g. blk., emer. & grn. 3·50 3·50
809a. 10 g. blk., bl. & dp. bl. 7·00 7·00

1976. Surinam Orchids. Multicoloured.

810. 1 c. Type **141** 5 5
811. 2 c. "Epidendrum stenopetalum" 5 5
812. 3 c. "Brassia lanceana" .. 5 5
813. 4 c. "Epidendrum ibaguense" 5 5
814. 5 c. "Epidendrum fragrans" 5 5

142. Surinam Flag. **143.** "Feeding the Hungry" (Master of Alkmaar).

1976. Multicoloured.
815. 25 c. Type **142** 20 20
816. 35 c. Surinam arms .. 25 25

1976. Easter. Paintings in Alkmaar Church. Multicoloured.
817. 20 c.+10 c. Type **143** .. 25 25
818. 25 c.+15 c. "Visting the Sick" 30 30
819. 30 c.+15 c. "Clothing the Naked" 35 35
820. 35 c.+15 c. "Burying the Dead" 40 40
821. 50 c.+25 c. "Refreshing the Thirsty" 60 60

144. "Pomacanthus semicirculatus".

1976. Fishes. Multicoloured.
823. 1 c. Type **144** (postage) .. 5 5
824. 2 c. "Adioryx diadema" 5 5
825. 3 c. "Pogonoculius zebra" 5 5
826. 4 c. "Balistes vetula" .. 5 5
827. 5 c. "Myripristis jacobus" 5 5
828. 35 c. "Chaetodon unimaculatus" (air) .. 30 30
829. 60 c. "Centropyge loriculus" 50 50
830. 95 c. "Chaetodon collare" 75 75

145. Early Telephone and Switchboard.

1976. Telephone Centenary.
831. 20 c. Type **145** 15 15
832. 35 c. Globe, satellite and modern telephone .. 30 30

146. "Anansi Tori" (A. Baag).

1976. Paintings by Surinam Artists. Mult
833. 20 c. Type **146** 15 55
834. 30 c. "Surinam Now" (R. Chang). .. 25 25
835. 35 c. "Lamentation" (N. Hatterman) (vert.) .. 30 30
836. 50 c. "Chess-players" (Q. Jan Telting) .. 40 40

147. "Divided Snake".

1976. American Revolution. Bicentenary.
837. **147.** 20 c. blk., grn. & cream 15 15
838. 60 c. black, red and cream 50 50

MORE DETAILED LISTS

are given in the Stanley Gibbons Catalogues referred to in the country headings:

BC British Commonwealth
E1, E2, E3 Europe 1, 2, 3
O1, O2, O3, O4 Overseas 1, 2, 3, 4

148. Pekinese.

1976. Child Welfare. Pet Dogs.
839. 20 c.+10 c. Type **148** .. 25 25
840. 25 c.+10 c. Alsatian .. 30 30
841. 30 c.+10 c. Dachshund .. 30 30
842. 35 c.+15 c. Surinam breed 40 40
843. 50 c.+25 c. Mongrel .. 60 60

149. "Ionopsis utricularioides".

1977. Surinam Orchids. Multicoloured.
844. 20 c. Type **149** 15 15
845. 30 c. "Rodiguezia secunda" 25 25
846. 35 c. "Oncidium pusillum" 30 30
847. 55 c. "Sobralia sessilis" .. 45 45
848. 60 c. "Octomeria surinamensis" 50 50

POSTAGE DUE STAMPS

1885. As Type D 1 of Curacao.
D 36. D **1.** 2½ c. mauve & black 1·10 1·10
D 37. 5 c. mauve and black 2·75 2·75
D 38. 10 c. mauve & black 48·00 30·00
D 39. 20 c. mauve & black 2·75 2·75
D 40. 25 c. mauve & black 4·00 4·00
D 41. 30 c. mauve & black 70 70
D 42. 40 c. mauve & black 1·90 1·90
D 43. 50 c. mauve & black 95 95

1892. As Type D 2 of Curacao.
D 57. D **2.** 2½ c. mauve & black 12 12
D 58. 5 c. mauve and black 40 35
D 59. 10 c. mauve & black 7·00 6·00
D 60. 20 c. mauve & black 75 65
D 61. 25 c. mauve & black 3·00 3·00
D 62. 40 c. mauve & black 1·25 1·60

1911. Surch. **10 cent.**
D 111. D. 1 10 c. on 30 c. mauve and black .. 35·00 35·00
D 112. 10 c. on 50 c. mauve and black .. 48·00 48·00

1913. As Type D 2 of Curacao.
D 153. D **2.** ½ c. lilac 5 5
D 154. 1 c. lilac 5 8
D 155. 2 c. lilac 8 8
D 156. 2½ c. lilac 5 5
D 157. 5 c. lilac 5 5
D 158. 10 c. lilac 8 5
D 159. 12 c. lilac 8 10
D 160. 12½ c. lilac 8 5
D 161. 15 c. lilac 12 12
D 162. 20 c. lilac 25 20
D 163. 25 c. lilac 10 5
D 164. 30 c. lilac 12 20
D 165. 40 c. lilac .. .. 4·00 5·50
D 166. 50 c. lilac 40 35
D 167. 75 c. lilac 45 45
D 168. 1 g. lilac 60 45

D 1.

D 2.

1945.
D 337. D **1.** 1 c. purple 12 12
D 338. 5 c. purple .. 1·25 60
D 339. 25 c. purple .. 3·25 12

1950. As Type D 4 of Netherlands.
D 384. 1 c. purple 80 80
D 385. 2 c. purple .. .. 1·10 70
D 386. 2½ c. purple .. 95 80
D 387. 5 c. purple .. .. 1·50 20
D 388. 10 c. purple .. 70 20
D 389. 15 c. purple .. 1·90 1·10
D 390. 20 c. purple .. 70 1·40
D 391. 25 c. purple .. 4·00 12
D 392. 50 c. purple .. 5·50 60
D 393. 75 c. purple .. 12·00 12·00
D 394. 1 g. purple .. .. 4·00 2·40

1956.
D 436. D **2.** 1 c. purple 5 5
D 437. 2 c. purple 25 10
D 438. 2½ c. purple .. 25 12
D 439. 5 c. purple 15 12
D 440. 10 c. purple .. 20 15
D 442. 15 c. purple .. 25 20
D 443. 20 c. purple .. 30 25
D 444. 25 c. purple .. 35 12
D 445. 50 c. purple .. 80 15
D 446. 75 c. purple .. 1·25 20
D 447. 1 g. purple .. .. 1·50 30

SWAZILAND BC

A kingdom in the E. part of S. Africa. Its early stamps were issued under joint control of Gt. Britain and the S. African Republic. Incorporated into the latter state in 1895 it was transferred in 1906 to the High Commissioner for S. Africa. Again issued stamps in 1933. Achieved Independence in 1968.

1961. 100 cents = 1 rand.
1974. 100 cents = 1 emalangeni.

1889. Stamps of Transvaal optd. **Swazieland.**
10. **3.** ½d. grey .. .. .. 4·00 5·00
1. 1d. red .. .. .. 6·00 7·00
2. 2d. pale brown .. .. 25·00 6·00
6. 6d. blue .. .. .. 6·00 8·00
3. 1s. green .. .. .. 4·50 5·00
7. 2s. 6d. yellow .. .. 42·00 55·00
8. 5s. blue .. .. .. 42·00 55·00
9. 10s. brown £950 £500

1.

2. Swazi Married Woman.

1933.
11. **1.** ½d. green 10 20
12. 1d. red 12 10
13. 2d. brown 20 20
14. 3d. blue 20 40
15. 4d. red 40 80
16. 6d. mauve .. .. .. 65 1·00
17. 1s. olive .. .. .. 1·10 2·25
18. 2s. 6d. violet .. .. 3·50 6·50
19. 5s. grey .. .. .. 8·00 11·00
20. 10s. brown .. .. 15·00 20·00

1935. Silver Jubilee. As T **11** of Antigua.
21. 1d. blue and red 15 20
22. 2d. blue and black .. 25 40
23. 3d. brown and blue .. 55 70
24. 6d. grey and purple .. 65 1·10

1937. Coronation. As T **2** of Aden.
25. 1d. red 10 10
26. 2d. brown 12 12
27. 3d. blue 15 15

1938. As T **1**, but with portrait of King George VI and inscr. "SWAZILAND" only below portrait.
28. ½d. green 8 10
29. 1d. red 10 12
30b. 1½d. blue 10 12
31a. 2d. brown 8 8
32b. 3d. blue 20 25
33a. 4d. orange 15 25
34b. 6d. purple 8 10
35a. 1s. olive 25 15
36a. 2s. 6d. violet 50 55
37b. 5s. grey .. .. .. 1·50 1·10
38a. 10s. brown .. .. 2·00 2·20

1945. Victory, Victory stamps of South Africa optd. **SWAZILAND.** Inscr. alternately in English or Afrikaans.
Un. pair *Us. pair*
39. **49.** 1d. brown and red .. 10 12
40. – 2d. blue & vio. (No. 109) 12 15
41. – 3d. blue (No. 110) . 15 20

1947. Royal Visit. As Nos. 32/5 of Basutoland.
Un. single *Us. single*
42. 1d. red 5 5
43. 2d. green 5 5
44. 3d. blue 12 8
45. 1s. mauve 20 20

1948. Silver Wedding. As T **5/6** of Aden.
46. 1½d. blue 8 8
47. 10s. purple .. .. 3·50 4·00

1949. U.P.U. As T **14/7** of Antigua.
48. 1½d. blue 8 8
49. 3d. blue 15 20
50. 6d. magenta 20 30
51. 1s. olive 40 45

1953. Coronation. As T **7** of Aden.
52. 2d. black and brown .. 15 20

1956.
53. – ½d. black and orange .. 5 5
54. – 1d. black and green .. 5 5
55. **2.** 2d. black and brown .. 5 5
56. – 3d. black and red .. 8 5
57. – 4½d. black and blue .. 12 20
58. – 6d. black and magenta .. 12 12
59. – 1s. black and olive .. 25 25
60. – 1s. 3d. black and sepia .. 35 35
61. – 2s. 6d. green and red .. 60 80
62. – 5s. violet and grey 1·50 1·75
63. **2.** 10s. black and violet .. 3·00 3·50
64. – £1 black and turquoise .. 6·50 9·00

DESIGNS—HORIZ. ½d., 1s. Havelock asbestos mine. 1d., 2s. 6d. Highveld view. VERT. 3d., 1s. 3d. Swazi courting couple. 4½d., 5s. Swazi warrior. 6d., £1 Kudu.

1961. Stamps of 1956 surch. in new currency.
65. ½ c. on ½d. black & orange 1·00 1·00
66. 1 c. on 1d. black & green 8 8
67. 2 c. on 2d. black & brown 10 10
68. 2½ c. on 2d. black & brown 10 10
69. 2½ c. on 3d. black and red 30 30
70. 3½ c. on 2d. black & brown 10 10
71a. 4 c. on 4½d. black and blue 15 15
72a. 5 c. on 6d. black & magenta 12 15
73. 10 c. on 1s. black & olive 3·00 4·00
74. 25 c. on 2s. 6d. green & red 60 90
75. 50 c. on 5s. violet & grey 1·00 1·25
76. 1 r. on 10s. black & violet 2·00 2·25
77. 2 r. on £1 black & turquoise 7·00 8·00

1961. As 1956 but values in new currency.
78. ½ c. black and orange (as ½d.) 5 5
79. 1 c. black and green (as 1d.) 5 5
80. 2 c. black and brown (as 2d.) 8 10
81. 2½ c. black and red (as 3d.) 15 15
82. 4 c. black and blue (as 4½d.) 20 25
83. 5 c. black & magenta (as 6d.) 20 20
84. 10 c. black and olive (as 1s.) 30 20
85. 12½ c. blk. & sep. (as 1s. 3d.) 35 40
86. 25 c. green & red (as 2s. 6d.) 80 80
87. 50 c. violet and grey (as 5s.) 1·50 1·75
88. 1 r. black & violet (as 10s.) 2·50 2·75
89. 2 r. blk. & turquoise (as £1) 6·50 7·00

3. Swazi Shields.

4. Train and Map.

1962.
90. **3.** ½ c. black, brown & buff 5 5
91. – 1 c. orange and black .. 5 5
92. – 2 c. green, black and olive 5 5
93. – 2½ c. black and red 5 5
94. – 3½ c. green and grey .. 8 5
95. – 4 c. black and turquoise 8 10
96. – 5 c. black, red & vermilion 10 10
97. – 7½ c. brown and buff .. 12 15
98. – 10 c. black and blue .. 15 20
99. – 12½ c. red and olive .. 45 50
100. – 15 c. black and mauve.. 45 50
101. – 20 c. black and green .. 45 50
102. – 25 c. black and blue .. 45 50
103. – 50 c. black and red .. 1·75 2·00
104. – 1 r. green and ochre .. 2·25 2·75
105. – 2 r. red and blue .. 4·50 5·00

DESIGNS—VERT. 1 c. Battle axe. 2 c. Forestry. 2½ c. Ceremonial head-dress. 3½ c. Musical instrument. 4 c. Irrigation. 5 c. Widow Bird. 7½ c. Rock paintings. 10 c. Secretary Bird. 12½ c. Pink Arum. 15 c. Swazi married woman. 20 c. Malaria control. 25 c. Swazi warrior. 1 r. Aloes. HORIZ. 50 c. Ground Hornbill. 2 r. Msinsi in flower.

1963. Freedom from Hunger. As T **10** of Aden.
106. 15 c. violet 40 35

1963. Red Cross Cent. As T **24** of Antigua.
107. 2½ c. red and black .. 10 12
108. 15 c. red and blue.. .. 40 40

1964. Opening of the Swaziland Railway.
109. **4.** 2½ c. green and purple .. 8 8
110. 3½ c. blue and olive 15 15
111. 15 c. orange and brown.. 30 35
112. 25 c. yellow and ultram. 40 45

1965. I.T.U. Cent. As T **26** of Antigua.
113. 2½ c. blue and bistre .. 8 8
114. 15 c. purple and rose .. 30 30

1965. I.C.Y. As T 27 of Antigua.
115. ½ c. purple and turquoise 5 5
116. 15 c. green and lavender 25 30

1966. Churchill Commem. As T 28 of Antigua.
117. ½ c. blue 5 5
118. 2½ c. green 8 8
119. 15 c. brown 30 35
120. 25 c. violet 45 50

1966. U.N.E.S.C.O. 20th Anniv. As T 33/5 of Antigua.
121. 2½ c. violet, red, yellow and orange 8 8
122. 7½ c. yellow, violet & olive 15 20
123. 15 c. black, purple & orge. 30 30

5. King Sobhuza II and Map.

1967. Protected State.
124. 5. 2½ c. multicoloured 5 5
125. – 7½ c. multicoloured 12 12
126. 5. 15 c. multicoloured 25 25
127. – 25 c. multicoloured 35 35
DESIGN—VERT. 7½ c., 25 c. King Sobhuza II.

1967. First Conferment of University Degrees. As T 3 of Botswana.
128. 2½ c. sepia, blue and orange 5 5
129. 7½ c. sepia, blue & grnsh. bl. 12 12
130. 15 c. sepia, blue and rose 25 25
131. 25 c. sepia, blue and violet 35 35

6. Incwala Ceremony.

1968. Traditional Customs.
132. 6. 3 c. silver, verm. & black 5 5
133. – 10 c. silver, brown, orange and black 20 20
134. 6. 15 c. gold, verm. & black 30 30
135. – 25 c. gold, brown, orange and black 50 50
DESIGN—VERT. 10 c., 25 c. Reed Dance.

1968. No. 96 Surch.
136. – 3 c. on 5 c. black, red and vermilion 8 10

7. Cattle Ploughing.

1968. Independence.
137. 7. 3 c. multicoloured 5 5
138. – 4½ c. multicoloured 10 12
139. – 17½ c. yell., grn. blk. & gold 35 40
140. – 25 c. slate, black & gold 50 60

1968. Nos. 90/105 optd. **INDEPENDENCE 1968** and No. 93 additionally surch. 3 c.
142. 3. ½ c. black, brown & buff 5 5
143. – 1 c. orange and black 5 5
144. – 2 c. green, black & olive 5 5
145. – 2½ c. black and red 5 5
146. – 3 c. on 2½ c. black & red 5 5
147. – 3½ c. green and grey 8 8
148. – 4 c. black and turquoise 8 10
149. – 5 c. black, red & verm. 10 10
150. – 7½ c. brown and buff 12 15
151. – 10 c. black and blue 15 15
152. – 12½ c. red and olive 25 30
153. – 15 c. black and mauve 25 30
154. – 20 c. black and green 40 50
155. – 25 c. black and blue 45 50
156. – 50 c. black and red 90 1·10
157. – 1 r. green and ochre 1·75 2·00
160. – 2 r. red and blue 3·25 4·00

8. Caracal (African Lynx).

1969. Multicoloured.
161. ½ c. Type 8 5 5
162. 1 c. Porcupine 5 5
163. 2 c. Crocodile 5 5
164. 3 c. Lion 5 5

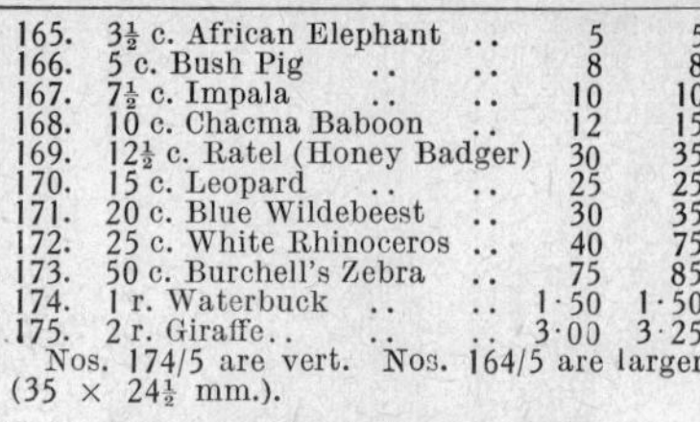
165. 3½ c. African Elephant 5 5
166. 5 c. Bush Pig 8 8
167. 7½ c. Impala 10 10
168. 10 c. Chacma Baboon 12 15
169. 12½ c. Ratel (Honey Badger) 30 35
170. 15 c. Leopard 25 25
171. 20 c. Blue Wildebeest 30 35
172. 25 c. White Rhinoceros 40 75
173. 50 c. Burchell's Zebra 75 85
174. 1 r. Waterbuck 1·50 1·50
175. 2 r. Giraffe 3·00 3·25
Nos. 174/5 are vert. Nos. 164/5 are larger (35 × 24½ mm.).

9. King Sobhuza II and Flags.

1969. Swaziland's Admission to the U.N. Multicoloured.
176. 3 c. Type 9 5 5
177. 7½ c. King Sobhuza II, U.N. building and emblem 15 15
178. 12½ c. As Type 9 25 25
179. 25 c. As 7½ c. 50 50

10. Athlete, Shield and Spears.

11. "Bauhinia galpinii".

1970. 9th Commonwealth Games. Multicoloured.
180. 3 c. Type 10 5 5
181. 7½ c. Runner 12 12
182. 12½ c. Jumper 20 20
183. 25 c. Procession of Swaziland Competitors 50 50

1971. Flowers. Multicoloured.
184. 3 c. Type 11 5 5
185. 10 c. "Crocosmia aurea" 20 20
186. 15 c. "Gloriosa superba" 30 30
187. 25 c. "Watsonia densiflora" 50 50

12. King Sobhuza II in Ceremonial Dress.

1971. King Sobhuza II's Accession. Golden Jubilee. Multicoloured.
188. 3 c. Type 12 5 5
189. 3½ c. Sobhuza II in medallion 8 8
190. 7½ c. Sobhuza II attending Incwala Ceremony 15 15
191. 25 c. Sobhuza II and aides at opening of Parliament 50 50

13. U.N.I.C.E.F. Emblem.

1972. U.N.I.C.E.F. 25th Anniv.
192. 13. 15 c. black and lilac 30 30
193. – 25 c. black and green 50 50
DESIGN: 25 c. As T 13, but inscription rearranged.

14. Local Dancers.

1972. Tourism. Multicoloured.
194. 3½ c. Type 14 8 8
195. 7½ c. Swazi beehive hut 15 15
196. 15 c. Ezulwini Valley 30 30
197 25 c. Fishing, Usutu River 50 50

15. Spraying Mosquitoes.

1973. W.H.O. 25th Anniv. Multicoloured.
198. 3½ c. Type 15 8 8
199. 7½ c. Anti-malaria vaccination 15 15

16. Mining.

1973. Natural Resources. Multicoloured.
200. 3½ c. Type 16 8 8
201. 7½ c. Cattle 12 12
202. 15 c. Water 20 25
203. 25 c. Rice 35 40

17. Coat of arms.

1973. Independence. 5th Anniv.
204. 17. 3 c. pink and black 5 8
205. – 10 c. multicoloured 15 15
206. – 15 c. multicoloured 20 25
207. – 25 c. multicoloured 35 40
DESIGNS: 10 c. King Sobhuza saluting. 15 c. Parliament buildings. 25 c. National Somhlolo stadium.

18. Flags and Mortarboard.

1973. University of Botswana, Lesotho and Swaziland. 10th Anniv. Multicoloured.
208. 7½ c. Type 18 12 12
209. 12½ c. University campus 20 20
210. 15 c. Map of Southern Africa 25 25
211. 25 c. University badge 35 35

19. King Sobhuza as College Student.

1974. King Sobhuza II. 75th Birth Anniv. Multicoloured.
212. 3 c. Type 19 5 5
213. 9 c. King Sobhuza in middle-age 12 15
214. 50 c. King Sobhuza at 75 years of age 65 70

20. New Post Office, Lobamba.

1974. U.P.U. Centenary. Multicoloured.
215. 4 c. Type 20 8 8
216. 10 c. Mbabane Temporary Post Office, 1902 15 15
217. 15 c. Carrying mail by cableway 20 20
218. 25 c. Mule-drawn mail-coach 30 35

1975. As Nos. 174/5, but in new currency.
219. 1 e. Waterbuck 1·25 1·40
220. 2 e. Giraffe 2·50 3·00

21. Umcwasho Ceremony.

1975. Swazi Youth. Multicoloured.
221. 3 c. Type 21 5 5
222. 10 c. Butimba (ritual dance) 12 15
223. 15 c. Lusekwane (preparation) (horiz.) 20 20
224. 25 c. Gcina Regiment on parade 30 35

22. Control Tower, Matsapa Airport.

1975. Internal Air Service. 10th Anniv. Multicoloured.
225. 4 c. Type 22 8 8
226. 5 c. Fire engine 8 8
227. 15 c. Douglas "Dakota" 20 20
228. 25 c. Hawker Siddeley "748" 30 30

1975. Nos. 167 and 169 surch.
230. 3 c. on 7½ c. Impala 5 5
231. 6 c. on 12½ c. Ratel 10 10

23. Elephant Symbol.

1975. International Women's Year.

232. **23.**	4 c. grey, black and blue	5	5
233. –	5 c. multicoloured ..	8	8
234. –	15 c. multicoloured ..	20	20
235. –	25 c. multicoloured ..	30	30

DESIGNS—HORIZ. 5 c. Queen Labotsibeni. VERT. 15 c. Craftswoman. 25 c. " Women in Service ".

24. Black-headed Oriole.

1976. Birds. Multicoloured.

236.	1 c. Type **24**	5	5
237.	2 c. Green Pigeon (vert.)	5	5
238.	3 c. Melba Finch	5	5
239.	4 c. Plum-coloured Starling (vert.)	5	5
240.	5 c. Black-headed Heron (vert.)	5	5
241.	6 c. Stonechat (vert.) ..	8	5
242.	7 c. Chorister Robin (vert.).	10	10
243.	10 c. Gorgeous Bush-shrike (vert.)	12	12
244.	15 c. Black-collared Barbet (vert.)	20	20
245.	20 c. Grey Heron (vert.)..	25	25
246.	25 c. Giant Kingfisher (vert.)	30	35
247.	30 c. Black Eagle (vert.)..	35	40
248.	50 c. Red Bishop (vert.)..	60	70
249.	1 e. Pin-tailed Whydah (vert.)	1·25	1·40
250.	2 e. Lilac-breasted Roller	2·50	2·75

25. Blindness from Malnutrition.

1976. Prevention of Blindness. Multicoloured.

251.	5 c. Type **25**	5	8
252.	10 c. Infected retina ..	12	15
253.	20 c. Blindness from trachoma	25	30
254.	25 c. Medicines	30	35

26. Marathon.

1976. Olympic Games, Montreal. Multicoloured.

255.	5 c. Type **26**	5	8
256.	6 c. Boxing	8	10
257.	20 c. Football	25	30
258.	25 c. Olympic torch and flame	30	35

27. Footballer Shooting.

1976. F.I.F.A. Membership. Multicoloured.

259.	4 c. Type **27**	5	8
260.	6 c. Heading	8	10
261.	20 c. Goalkeeping ..	25	30
262.	25 c. Player about to shoot	30	35

28. Bell and Telephone.

1976. Telephone Centenary.

263. **28.**	4 c. multicoloured ..	5	5
264. –	5 c. multicoloured ..	5	8
265. –	10 c. multicoloured ..	12	15
266.	15 c. multicoloured ..	20	25
267. –	20 c. multicoloured ..	25	30

Nos. 264/7 as T **28**, but showing different telephones.

29. Queen Elizabeth II and King Sobhuza II.

1977. Silver Jubilee. Multicoloured.

268.	20 c. Type **29**	25	30
269.	25 c. Coronation Coach at Admiralty Arch ..	35	40
270.	50 c. Queen in coach ..	70	80

30. Matsapa College.

1977. 50 Years of Police Training. Multicoloured.

271.	5 c. Type **30**	5	8
272.	10 c. Policemen and women on parade	12	15
273.	20 c. Royal Swaziland Police badge (vert.) ..	25	30
274.	25 c. Dog handling ..	35	40

POSTAGE DUE STAMPS

D 1.

D 2.

1933.

D 1a. D **1.**	1d. red	5	5
D 2a.	2d. violet	10	10

1961. Surch. **Postage Due 2d.**

D 3. **2.**	2d. on 2d. blk. & brown	2·50	3·50

These prices apply to stamps with large figure measuring 4½ mm. high.

1961. As Type D **1** but with value in cents.

D 4.	1 c. red	5	5
D 5.	2 c. violet	8	10
D 6.	5 c. green	10	20

1961. Surch. **Postage Due** and value in cents.

D 7. **2.**	1 c. on 2d. black & brown	45	65
D 8.	2 c. on 2d. black & brown	45	65
D 9.	5 c. on 2d. black & brown	45	65

1971.

D 13. D **2.**	1 c. red	5	5
D 14.	2 c. purple	5	5
D 15.	5 c. green	8	10

SWEDEN E3

A kingdom of N. Europe, united to Norway till 1905.

1855. 40 skilling banco = 1 riksdaler.
1858. 100 ore = 1 riksdaler.
1875. 100 ore = 1 krona.

1. **2.** **3.**

1855.

1. **1.**	3 s. b. green	£2750	£1300
2.	4 s. b. blue	£375	32·00
3a.	6 s. b. grey	£2750	£350
3b.	6 s. b. brown	£3750	£350
4.	8 s. b. orange	£1600	£180
5.	24 s. b. red	£2250	£550

1858.

6b. **1.**	5 ore green	45·00	9·50
7a.	9 ore lilac	£120	85·00
8a.	12 ore blue	45·00	1·40
9.	24 ore yellow	£110	9·50
10.	30 ore brown	95·00	11·00
11b.	50 ore red	£130	27·00

1862.

12c. **2.**	3 ore brown	23·00	7·50

1866.

13. **3.**	17 ore purple	£120	60·00
14.	17 ore grey	£225	£225
15b.	20 ore red	50·00	7·50

4.

5. King Oscar II.

6.

1872.

29. **4.**	2 ore orange	1·50	1·50
16a.	3 ore brown	7·00	1·50
31.	4 ore grey	11·00	40
32.	5 ore green	12·00	25
19b.	6 ore purple	32·00	1·60
20.	6 ore olive	£200	15·00
34. **5.**	10 ore red	30·00	8
21. **4.**	12 ore blue	7·50	15
35.	20 ore red	15·00	25
23a.	24 ore yellow	12·00	4·75
36.	30 ore brown	35·00	30
37a.	50 ore red	30·00	1·90
26. **6.**	1 r. blue and brown ..	£170	23·00
38.	1 k. blue and brown ..	27·00	60

On No. 26 the value is expressed as one riksdaler; on No. 38 the value is one krona.

1889. Surch. with new value and Arms.

39. **4.**	10 ore on 12 ore blue ..	1·50	1·90
40.	10 ore on 24 ore yellow ..	7·00	19·00

7.

8.

9.

1891.

41. **7.**	1 ore brown and blue ..	55	10
42a.	2 ore blue and yellow ..	4·75	8
43.	3 ore brown and orange..	55	40
44a.	4 ore red and blue ..	7·00	8
45c. **8.**	5 ore green	1·80	8
46.	8 ore purple	2·25	30
47.	10 ore red	3·00	8
48.	15 ore brown	14·00	8
49.	20 ore blue	11·00	8
50.	25 ore orange	12·00	8
51a.	30 ore brown	23·00	8
53.	50 ore grey	27·00	15
54. **9.**	1 k. grey and red ..	42·00	60

10. G.P.O., Stockholm.

11.

12. King Gustav V.

1903. Opening of G.P.O. at Stockholm.

57. **10.**	5 k. blue	£120	12·00

1910.

65. **11.**	1 ore black	8	8
66.	2 ore orange	8	8
67.	3 ore brown	8	8
68.	4 ore lilac	8	8
69. **12.**	5 ore green	1·50	8
70.	7 ore green	12	8
71. **12.**	8 ore mauve	12	15
72.	10 ore red	2·50	8
73.	12 ore lake	20	8
74.	15 ore brown	6·00	8
75.	20 ore blue	7·50	8
76.	25 ore orange	25	8
77.	27 ore blue	40	40
78.	30 ore brown	14·00	8
79.	35 ore violet	15·00	8
80.	40 ore olive	23·00	8
81.	50 ore grey	23·00	8
82.	55 ore blue	£450	£700
83.	65 ore olive	75	75
84.	80 ore black	£450	£700
85.	90 ore green	55	20
63.	1 k. black on yellow ..	35·00	12
64.	5 k. purple on yellow ..	2·00	90

1916. Charity. Clothing Fund for Reservists Surch. **FRIMARKE LANDSTORMEN** and value in figures and words round Arms.

86a. **4.**	5+5 on 2 ore orange ..	3·50	3·50
86b.	5+5 on 3 ore brown ..	3·50	3·50
86c.	5+5 on 4 ore grey ..	3·50	3·50
86d.	5+5 on 5 ore green ..	3·50	3·50
86e.	5+5 on 6 ore purple ..	3·50	3·50
86f.	10+10 on 12 ore blue	3·50	3·50
86g.	10+10 on 20 ore red ..	3·50	3·50
86h.	10+10 on 24 ore orange	3·50	3·50
86i.	10+10 on 30 ore brown	3·50	3·50
86j.	10+10 on 50 ore red ..	3·50	3·50

1916. Charity. Clothing Fund for Reservists. Surch. **LANDSTORMEN** and **FRIMARKE SVERIGE** in frame round Arms and value in figures and words.

86k. D **1.**	5+5 on 1 ore black ..	2·00	2·00
86l.	5+5 on 3 ore red ..	1·90	1·90
86m.	5+5 on 5 ore brown	1·90	1·90
86n.	5+10 on 6 ore yellow	2·25	2·25
86o.	5+15 on 12 ore pink	8·50	7·00
86p.	10+20 on 20 ore blue	7·50	7·50
86q.	10+40 on 24 ore lilac	25·00	42·00
86r.	10+20 on 30 ore green	2·10	2·10
86s.	10+40 on 50 ore brn.	12·00	13·00
86t.	10+90 on 1 k. bl.&brn.	55·00	85·00
86u. **10.**	10 ore+4 k. 90 ore on 5 k. blue	50·00	75·00

1917. Surch. in figures only.

87. **12.**	7 on 10 ore red	25	8
88.	12 on 25 ore orange ..	95	15
89.	12 on 65 ore olive ..	75	40
90.	27 on 55 ore blue ..	45	45
91.	27 on 65 orc olive ..	90	90
92.	27 on 80 ore black ..	55	45
93.	1.98 k. on 5 k. pur. on yell.	1·25	1·25
94.	2.12 k. on 5 k. pur. on yell.	1·25	1·25

1918. Charity. Landstorm Fund. Charity stamps of 1916 surch.

94a. **4.**	7+3 on 5 ore on 2 ore ..	3·00	3·00
94b.	7+3 on 5 ore on 3 ore ..	1·40	90
94c.	7+3 on 5 ore on 4 ore ..	1·40	90
94d.	7+3 on 5 ore on 5 ore ..	1·40	90
94e.	7+3 on 5 ore on 6 ore ..	1·40	90
94f.	12+8 on 10 ore on 12 ore	1·40	90
94g.	12+8 on 10 ore on 20 ore	1·40	90
94h.	12+8 on 10 ore on 24 ore	1·40	90
94i	12+8 on 10 ore on 30 ore	1·40	90
94j.	12+8 on 10 ore on 50 ore	1·40	90

1920. Air. Official stamps surch. **LUFTPOST** and value.

120a. O **2.**	10 on 3 ore brown ..	3·75	3·75
120b.	20 on 2 ore orange	6·00	6·00
120c.	50 on 4 ore lilac ..	27·00	7·00

PERFORATIONS. From 1920 onwards except where otherwise stated all stamps are imperf. × perf. from coils but the lower values also come perf. all round or perf. on two or three adjacent sides from booklets apart from a few values issued in the early part of the period which also come perf. all round from sheets.

13. Arms.

14. Lion.

15. King Gustav V. **16.** Crown.

1920.

95. **13.**	3 ore brown	15	15
96. **14.**	5 ore green	60	8
97a.	5 ore brown	60	15
98.	10 ore green	90	8
99.	10 ore violet	1·25	8
102. **15.**	10 ore red	6·00	12
103.	15 ore claret	40	15
104a.	20 ore blue	7·00	50
100. **14.**	25 ore orange	9·50	8
101	30 ore brown	45	8
105. **16.**	35 ore yellow	11·00	12
106.	40 ore olive	12·00	15
107.	45 ore brown	90	15
108.	60 ore purple	10·00	12

109. 16. 70 ore brown 75 75
110. 80 ore green 45 8
111. 85 ore green .. .. 2·10 12
112. 90 ore blue .. .. 15·00 8
113. 1 k. orange .. .. 5·50 8
114. 110 ore blue 60 8
115. 115 ore brown .. .. 3·00 8
116. 120 ore black .. .. 30·00 20
117. 120 ore mauve .. .. 2·25 20
118. 140 ore sepia 95 8
119. 145 ore green .. .. 2·50 25

17. Gustavus Adolfus. 18. Gustav V. 19. Gustavus Vasa.

1920. Tercent. of Swedish post between Stockholm and Hamburg.
120. 17. 20 ore blue .. .. 2·25 8

1921.
121b. 18. 15 ore violet .. .. 9·50 5
122. 15 ore red .. .. 5·50 5
123. 15 ore brown .. .. 3·75 5
124. 20 ore violet 20 5
125. 20 ore red .. .. 10·00 5
126. 20 ore orange 30 5
128. 25 ore red 45 5
129. 25 ore blue .. .. 7·00 5
131. 25 ore orange .. .. 15·00 5
134. 30 ore blue .. .. 2·25 5
133. 18. 30 ore brown .. .. 15·00 8
135. 35 ore mauve .. .. 3·75 8
136. 40 ore blue 40 15
137. 40 ore olive .. .. 7·50 15
138. 45 ore brown 90 8
139a. 50 ore black 90 8
140. 85 ore green .. .. 6·00 60
141. 115 ore brown .. .. 4·75 45
142. 145 ore green .. .. 3·50 60

1921. Liberation of Sweden. 4th Cent.
143. 19. 20 ore violet .. .. 4·75 4·75
144. 110 ore blue .. .. 23·00 2·75
145. 140 ore black .. .. 19·00 2·75

20. Old City, Stockholm. 21. Gustav V.

1924. 8th Congress of U.P.U. Perf.
146. 20. 5 ore brown .. .. 1·50 1·40
147. 10 ore green .. .. 1·50 1·40
148. 15 ore violet .. .. 1·50 1·10
149. 20 ore red .. .. 7·50 7·00
150. 25 ore orange .. .. 9·00 7·00
151. 30 ore blue .. .. 9·00 7·50
152. 35 ore black .. .. 12·00 10·00
153. 40 ore olive .. .. 15·00 14·00
154. 45 ore brown .. .. 15·00 14·00
155. 50 ore grey .. .. 15·00 14·00
156. 60 ore claret .. .. 23·00 19·00
157. 80 ore green .. .. 15·00 14·00
158. 21. 1 k. green .. .. 38·00 38·00
159. 2 k. red .. .. 75·00 75·00
160. 5 k. blue £170 £170

22. Post-rider and Aeroplane. 23. Carrier-pigeon.

1924. U.P.U. 50th Anniv. Perf.
161. 22. 5 ore brown .. .. 1·90 1·50
162. 10 ore green .. .. 1·90 1·50
163. 15 ore violet .. .. 1·50 1·10
164. 20 ore red .. .. 9·00 9·00
165. 25 ore orange .. .. 9·00 9·00
166. 30 ore blue .. .. 9·00 7·50
167. 35 ore black .. .. 15·00 14·00
168. 40 ore olive .. .. 15·00 14·00
169. 45 ore brown .. .. 15·00 14·00
170. 50 ore grey .. .. 15·00 14·00
171. 60 ore claret .. .. 23·00 19·00
172. 80 ore green .. .. 15·00 14·00
173. 23. 1 k. green .. .. 38·00 32·00
174. 2 k. red .. .. 75·00 70·00
175. 5 k. blue £170 £150

24. King Gustav V. 25. Night-flight over Stockholm.

1928. Charity. Cancer Research Fund and 70th Birthday of King Gustav V. Perf.
175a. 24. 5+5 ore green .. 3·75 3·00
175b. 10+5 ore violet .. 3·75 3·00
175c. 15+5 ore red .. 3·75 3·00
175d. 20+5 ore orange .. 5·50 1·90
175e. 25+5 ore blue .. 5·50 1·90

1930. Air. Imperf. and perf.
175f. 25. 10 ore blue 25 25
175g. 50 ore violet 60 30

26. Royal Palace, Stockholm. 27. Death of Gustavus Adolphus at Lutzen.

1931. Perf.
176. 26. 5 k. green .. .. 70·00 7·50

1932. Gustavus Adolphus. Death Tercent.
177. 27. 10 ore violet .. .. 2·25 8
178. 15 ore red .. .. 2·25 8
179. 25 ore blue .. .. 12·00 60
180. 90 ore green .. .. 27·00 95

28. Allegory of Thrift. 29. Stockholm Cathedral.

1933. Postal Savings Bank. 50th Anniv.
181. 28. 5 ore green .. .. 1·90 20

1935. First Swedish Parliament. 500th Anniv. Inscr. "RIKSDAGEN 1435–1935".
182. – 5 ore green .. .. 1·90 8
183. – 10 ore violet .. .. 2·25 8
184. 29. 15 ore red .. .. 2·50 8
185. – 25 ore blue .. .. 12·00 30
186. – 35 oreclaret .. .. 19·00 1·25
187. – 60 ore claret .. .. 19·00 90
DESIGNS: 5 ore Old Law Courts. 10 ore Exchange. 25 ore House of the Nobility. 35 ore Houses of Parliament. 60 ore Arms of Engelbrekt.

30. Axel Oxenstierna. 33. Mail-plane over Scandinavia.

1936. Postal Tercent. Inscr. "1636 20.2 1936".
188. 30. 5 ore green .. .. 1·90 12
189. – 10 ore violet .. .. 2·25 8
190. – 15 ore red .. .. 2·25 10
191. – 20 ore blue .. .. 11·00 2·75
192. – 25 ore blue .. .. 9·00 25
193. – 30 ore brown .. .. 23·00 1·90
194. – 35 ore purple .. .. 9·00 90
195. – 40 ore olive .. .. 7·00 1·25
196. – 45 ore green .. .. 10·00 1·10
197. – 50 ore grey .. .. 19·00 1·90
198. – 60 ore maroon .. .. 27·00 30
199. – 1 k. blue .. .. 11·00 3·75
DESIGNS: 10 ore Early courier. 15 ore Mounted postman. 20 ore Sailing-ship. 25 ore Paddle-steamer. 30 ore Coach. 35 ore Arms. 40 ore Train. 45 ore A. W. Roos, P.M.G., 1857–89. 50 ore Motor-bus and trailer. 60 ore Modern mail steamer. 1 k. Aeroplane.
For similar designs, but dated "1972" at foot, see Nos. 700/4.

1936. Bromma Aerodrome. Inauguration.
200. 33. 50 ore blue .. .. 3·75 3·00

34. E. Swedenborg. 35. Governor Printz and Red Indian.

1938. Swedenborg. 250th Birth Anniv.
201a. 34. 10 ore violet 30 8
202. 100 ore green .. .. 5·50 60

1938. Tercent of New Sweden, U.S.A. Inscr. as in T 35.
203. 35. 5 ore green 75 8
204. – 15 ore brown 75 8
205. – 20 ore red .. .. 3·50 40
206. – 30 ore blue .. .. 8·50 45
207. – 60 ore maroon .. .. 10·00 10
DESIGNS: 15 ore Sailing ships "Kalmar Nyckel" and "Fagel Grip". 20 ore Swedish landing in America. 30 ore First Swedish church, Wilmington. 60 ore Queen Christina.

36. King Gustav V. 37. 38. Arms of Sweden.

1938. 80th Birthday of King Gustav V.
208a. 36. 5 ore green 60 8
209a. 15 ore brown 45 8
210. 30 ore blue .. .. 12·00 40

1939.
234b. 37. 5 ore green 15 5
299. 5 ore orange 15 5
235a. 10 ore violet 15 5
300. 10 ore green 20 5
236b. 15 ore brown 25 5
237. 20 ore red 15 5
238. 25 ore orange 90 5
301. 25 ore violet 45 5
239. 30 ore blue 40 5
240. 35 ore purple 90 5
241. 40 ore olive 60 5
242. 45 ore brown 45 5
243. 50 ore grey .. .. 1·50 8
301a. 38. 50 ore grey .. .. 9·00 8
302. 55 ore brown .. .. 4·50 15
221. 60 ore red .. .. 3·75 8
302a. 65 ore green .. .. 2·50 8
302b. 70 ore blue .. .. 3·75 25
302c. 75 ore brown .. .. 3·00 25
303. 80 ore olive .. .. 1·50 8
222. 85 ore green .. .. 3·00 15
303a. 85 ore brown .. .. 3·00 25
223. 90 ore blue .. .. 2·75 8
224. 1 k. orange 45 8
303b. 1 k. 5 blue 55 15
304. 1 k. 10 ore violet .. 90 8
225. 1 k. 15 ore brown .. 55 8
226. 1 k. 20 ore purple .. 3·75 15
304a. 1 k. 20 blue 90 25
305. 1 k. 40 ore green .. 75 8
227. 1 k. 45 ore green .. 2·25 25
305a. 1 k. 50 ore purple .. 1·10 30
305b. 1 k. 50 brown 75 20
305c. 1 k. 70 ore red 75 8
306. 1 k. 75 ore blue .. 3·00 2·50
306a. 1 k. 80 blue 85 25
306b. 1 k. 85 blue 85 30
306c. 2 k. purple 75 8
306ca. 2 k. cerise 60 8
306d. 2 k. 10 ore blue .. 90 8
306e. 2 k. 15 olive .. .. 1·00 25
306f. 2 k. 30 maroon .. .. 1·10 20
306g. 2 k. 50 green .. .. 1·10 5
306h. 2 k. 55 red .. .. 1·10 25
306i. 2 k. 80 red .. .. 1·10 15
306j. 2 k. 85 orange .. .. 1·25 75
306k. 3 k. ultramarine .. 90 8

39. P. H. Ling. 40. Carl von Linnaeus. 41. Carl Michael Bellman (poet).

1939. P. H. Ling (creator of "Swedish Drill"). Death Cent.
228. 39. 5 ore green 15 10
229. 25 ore brown 60 10

1939. Swedish Academy of Sciences. Bicent.
230a. – 10 ore violet 75 10
231. 40. 15 ore brown 35 10
232. – 30 ore blue .. .. 10·00 15
233. 40. 50 ore grey .. .. 11·00 30
PORTRAIT: 10 ore, 30 ore J. J. Berzelius.

1940. C. M. Bellman. Birth Bicent.
244. 41. 5 ore green 15 8
245. 35 ore red 60 8

42. Johan Tobias Sergel. 43. Reformers presenting Bible to Gustavus Vasa.

1940. Sergel (sculptor). Birth Bicent.
246. 42. 15 ore brown .. .. 1·10 10
247. 50 ore grey .. .. 11·00 40

1941. First Authorised Version of the Bible in Swedish. 4th Cent.
248. 43. 15 ore brown 30 10
249. 90 ore blue .. .. 7·50 25

44. Hasjo Belfry. 44a. Royal Palace, Stockholm.

1941. Skansen Open Air Museum. 50th Anniv.
250. 44. 10 ore violet 30 10
251. 60 ore claret .. .. 6·00 25

1941. Perf.
252b. 44a. 5 k. blue .. .. 1·50 10

44b. Artur Hazelius. 45. St. Bridget. 45a. Flying Swans.

1941. Artur Hazelius (founder of Skansen Museum).
253. 44b. 5 ore green 15 10
254. 1 k. orange .. .. 4·75 1·50

1941. St. Bridget Commem.
255. 45. 15 ore brown 25 10
256. 120 ore purple .. .. 15·00 3·75

1942. Perf.
257. 45a. 20 k. blue .. .. 45·00 7·00

46. King Gustavus III after Alexander Roslin. 47. Count Rudenschold and Nils Mansson.

1942. National Museum, Stockholm. 150th Anniv. Inscr. "NATIONAL MUSEUM".
258. 46. 20 ore red 30 10
259. – 40 ore olive .. .. 17·00 60
PORTRAIT: 40 ore Carl Gustav Tessin (after Gustav Lundberg).

1942. Institution of National Elementary Education. Cent.
260a. 47. 10 ore red 40 25
261. 90 ore blue .. .. 2·50 1·90

48. Carl. Wilhelm Scheele. 49. King Gustav V. 50. Rifle Assn. Badge

1942. C. W. Scheele (scientist). Birth Bicent.
262. 48. 5 ore green 15 10
263. 60 ore red .. .. 5·50 12

1943. King Gustav V. 85th Birthday.
264. 49. 20 ore red 60 10
265. 30 ore blue .. .. 1·50 1·50
266. 60 ore purple .. .. 2·10 1·25

1943. National Voluntary Rifle Association. 50th Anniv.
267. 50. 10 ore purple 15 10
268. 90 ore blue .. .. 3·00 12

51. Oscar Montelius (archaeologist). 52. First Swedish Marine Chart. 53. "The Lion of Smaland".

1943. Oscar Montelius. Birth Cent.
269. 51. 5 ore green 10 10
270. 120 ore purple .. .. 4·25 90

1944. 1st Swedish Marine Chart. Tercent.
271. 52. 5 ore green 10 10
272. 60 ore red .. .. 3·75 12

1944. Swedish Fleet. Inscr. as in T 53.
273. 53. 10 ore violet 20 10
274. – 20 ore red 45 10
275. – 30 ore blue 75 55
276. – 40 ore olive .. .. 1·10 30
277. – 90 ore grey .. .. 7·00 75
DESIGNS—VERT. ($18\frac{1}{2} \times 20\frac{1}{2}$ mm.): 20 ore Portrait of Clas Fleming. HORIZ. As T 53: 30 ore Ancient sailing ship "Kung Karl". 40 ore Stern of old ship "Amphion". 90 ore Modern warship "Gustaf V".
See also Nos. 517/22.

54. Red Cross.

55. Press Symbols

1945. 80th Anniv. of Swedish Red Cross and Birthday of Prince Charles.
278. **54.** 20 ore red 70 10

1945. Swedish Press Tercent.
279. **55.** 5 ore green 10 10
280. 60 ore red .. .. 3·00 12

56. Viktor Rydberg (author).

57. Savings Banks' Symbol.

1945. Viktor Rydberg. 50th Death Anniv.
281. **56.** 20 ore red 20 10
282. 90 ore blue .. .. 3·75 12

1945. Swedish Savings Banks. 125th Anniv
283. **57.** 10 ore violet 12 10
284. 40 ore olive 60 55

58. Cathedral Model.

59. Lund Cathedral.

1946. Lund Cathedral. 800th Anniv.
285. **58.** 15 ore brown 40 15
286. **59.** 20 ore red 15 10
287. **58.** 90 ore blue .. .. 2·50 25

60. Mare and Foal.

61. Esaias Tegner (poet).

62. Alfred Nobel.

1946. Swedish Agricultural Show Cent.
288. **60.** 5 ore green 10 10
289. 60 ore red .. .. 2·50 12

1946. Esaias Tegner. Death Cent.
290. **61.** 10 ore violet 10 10
291. 40 ore olive 60 15

1946. Alfred Nobel (scientist and creator of the Nobel Foundation). 50th Death Anniv.
292. **62.** 20 ore red 45 10
293. 30 ore blue 90 25

63. E. G. Geijer.

64. King Gustav V.

65. Ploughman and Skyscraper.

1947. Erik Gustav Geijer (historian, philosopher, poet and composer). Death Cent.
294. **63.** 5 ore green 10 10
295. 90 ore blue .. .. 1·90 12

1947. Coronation of Gustav V. 40th Anniv.
296. **64.** 10 ore violet 10 10
297. 20 ore red 10 10
298. 60 ore purple .. .. 1·10 75

1948. Swedish Pioneers' Settlement in U.S.A. Cent.
307. **65.** 15 ore brown 15 10
308. 30 ore blue 50 15
309. 1 k. orange .. .. 1·25 30

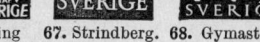

66. King Gustav V.

67. Strindberg.

68. Gymnastics.

1948. Charity. Youth Fund and King Gustav V's 90th Birthday.
309a. **66.** 10 ore + 10 ore green .. 45 45
309b. 20 ore + 10 ore red .. 55 55
309c. 30 ore + 10 ore blue .. 55 55

1949. Strindberg (dramatist). Birth Cent.
310. **67.** 20 ore red 10 10
311. 30 ore blue 45 15
312. 80 ore olive 75 12

1949. 2nd Lingiad, Stockholm
313. **68.** 5 ore blue 10 10
314. 15 ore brown 12 10

69. Globe and Hand Writing. **70.**

1949. U.P.U. 75th Anniv.
315. **69.** 10 ore green 12 10
316a. 20 ore red 15 10
317. **70.** 30 ore blue 40 20

71. King Gustav VI Adolf. **72.** Christopher Polhem. **73.**

1951. (a) Coloured lettering and figures.
318a. **71.** 10 ore green 15 5
318b. 10 ore sepia 10 5
319. 15 ore brown 25 5
388a. 15 ore red 15 5
320. 20 ore red 40 5
391a. 20 ore black 12 5
322a. 25 ore black 25 5
323a. 25 ore red 25 5
324a. 25 ore blue 12 5
392. 25 ore sepia 20 5
325. 30 ore blue 15 5
326. 30 ore sepia 15 5
326a. 30 ore red .. .. 7·00 5
327. 40 ore blue .. .. 1·10 5
328. 40 ore green 30 5

(b) White lettering and figures.
429. **71.** 15 ore red 10 5
430. **20 ore black** 10 5
431. **25 ore brown** 10 5
432. **30 ore blue** 12 5
433a. **30 ore violet** 12 5
433b. 30 ore red 25 15
434. **35 ore violet** 12 5
435. **35 ore blue** 12 5
436. **35 ore black** 20 5
437. **40 ore green** 30 5
438. **40 ore blue** 15 5
439. **45 ore orange** 15 5
439b. 45 ore blue 15 5
440. **50 ore olive** 15 5
440a. 50 ore green 15 5
440c. 55 ore red 20 5
441. **60 ore red** 75 5
441a. 65 ore blue 20 5
441c. 70 ore magenta 20 5
441d. 85 ore purple 25 5

1951. Polhem (engineer). Death Bicent.
329. **72.** 25 ore black 15 10
330. 45 ore brown 25 10

1951.
383. **73.** 5 ore rose 8 5
384. 5 ore red 8 5
386a. 10 ore blue 8 5
387a. 10 ore brown 8 5
389a. 15 ore green 8 5
390a. 15 ore brown 20 20

74. O. Petri Preaching.

75. King Gustav VI Adolf.

1952. Petri (reformer). 400th Death Anniv.
332. **74.** 25 ore black 20 10
333. 1 k. 40 ore brown .. 1·25 15

1952. 70th Birthday of King Gustav VI Adolf and Culture Fund.
333a. **75.** 10 ore + 10 ore green .. 25 25
333b. 25 ore + 10 ore red .. 25 25
333c. 40 ore + 10 ore blue .. 40 40

76. Ski-jumping.

77. Stockholm in 13th Century.

1953. Swedish Athletic Assn. 50th Anniv.
334. **76.** 10 ore green 25 10
335. – 15 ore brown 60 30
336. – 40 ore blue 70 40
337. – 1 k. 50 magenta .. 1·75 30
DESIGNS—HORIZ. 1 k. 40, Wrestling. VERT. 15 ore Ice-hockey. 40 ore Slingball.

1953. Stockholm. 700th Anniv. Inscr. "STOCKHOLM 700 AR".
338. **77.** 25 ore blue 12 10
339. – 1 k. 70 red .. .. 1·25 15
DESIGN: 1 k. 70, Seal of Stockholm (obverse and reverse).

78. "Radio".

79. Skier.

1953. Telecommunications in Sweden. Cent. Inscr. "1853–1953".
340. – 25 ore blue ("Telephones") 12 10
341. **78.** 40 ore green 65 40
342. – 60 ore red ("Telegraphs") 65 40

1954. World Ski-ing Championships. Inscr. "VM 1954".
343. **79.** 20 ore grey 25 15
344. – 1 k. blue (Women skier) 5·50 45

80. Anna Maria Lenngren.

81. Rock-carvings.

82.

1954. Anna Maria Lenngren (author). Birth Bicent.
345. **80.** 20 ore grey 15 10
346. 65 ore brown .. .. 3·00 90

1954.
347. **81.** 50 ore grey 20 5
348. 55 ore red 15 5
349. 60 ore red 25 5
350. 65 ore green 20 5
351. 70 ore yellow 20 5
352. 75 ore brown 25 5
353. 80 ore green 25 5
355. 90 ore blue 30 5
356. 95 ore violet 60 20

1955. Swedish Stamp Cent.
362. **82.** 25 ore blue 10 10
363. 40 ore green .. .. 1·10 15

83. Swedish Flag.

84. P. D. A. Atterbom (after Fogelberg).

1955. National Flag Day. Perf.
364. **83.** 10 ore yellow, bl. & grn. 20 12
365. 15 ore yellow, bl. & lake 25 12

1955. Cent. of 1st Swedish Postage Stamps and Stockholmia Philatelic Exn. As T 1 but with two rules through bottom panel. Perf.
366. **1.** 3 ore green .. .. 1·90 1·90
367. 4 ore blue .. .. 1·90 1·90
368. 6 ore grey .. .. 1·90 1·90
369. 8 ore yellow .. .. 1·90 1·90
370. 24 ore red .. .. 1·90 1·90
Nos. 366/70 were sold only at the Exhibition. in single sets, at 2 k. 45 ore (45 ore face + 2 k, entrance fee).

1955. Atterbom (poet). Death Cent.
371. **84.** 20 ore blue 20 10
372. 1 k. 40 brown .. .. 1·10 20

85. Greek Horseman.

86. Railway Construction.

1956. 16th Olympic Games Equestrian Competitions, Stockholm.
373. **85.** 20 ore red 20 10
374. 25 ore blue 20 10
375. 40 ore green .. .. 1·25 55

1956. Northern Countries' Day. As T 69 of Denmark.
376. 25 ore red 60 10
377. 40 ore blue 90 40

1956. Swedish Railways Cent. Inscr. "1856 1956".
378. **86.** 10 ore olive 25 10
379. – 25 ore blue 15 10
380. – 40 ore orange 90 70
DESIGNS: 25 ore First Swedish steam locomotive. 40 ore Arsta Bridge, Stockholm.

87. Lifeboat approaching Vessel in Distress.

1957. Swedish Life-saving Service. 50th Anniv.
381a. **87.** 30 ore blue 40 10
382. 1 k. 40 red .. .. 3·00 45

88. M.S. "Kungsholm" and Sailing Ship.

89. Postal Helicopter.

1958. Postal Services Commem.
395. **88.** 15 ore brown-red .. 20 10
396. **89.** 30 ore blue 15 10
397. **88.** 40 ore olive .. .. 3·00 75
398. **89.** 1 k. 40 brown .. .. 3·00 30

90. Footballer.

91. Bessemer tilting-furnace.

1958. World Football Championships.
399. **90.** 15 ore red 15 10
400. 20 ore green 25 10
401. 1 k. 20 blue 55 25

1958. Swedish Steel Industry Cent.
402. **91.** 30 ore blue 15 10
403. 170 ore brown .. .. 1·10 45

92. Selma Lagerlof.

93. Overhead Power Lines.

94. Henri Dunant.

1958. Selma Lagerlof (writer). Birth Cent.
404. **92.** 20 ore red 15 10
405. 30 ore blue 15 10
406. 80 ore myrtle 55 25

1959. Swedish State Power Board. 50th Anniv. Inscr. as in T 93.
407. **93.** 30 ore blue 15 10
408. – 90 ore red .. .. 1·10 15
DESIGN—HORIZ. 90 ore Dam sluice-gates.

1959. Red Cross Commem.
409. **94.** 30 ore + 10 ore red .. 90 90

95. Verner von Heidenstam.

96. Forest Trees.

97. S. Arrhenius.

1959. Von Heidenstam (poet). Birth Cent.
410. **95.** 15 ore red 30 10
411. 1 k. black .. .. 1·75 20

1959. Crown Lands and Forests Administration Cent. Inscr. as in T 96.
412. **96.** 30 ore green .. .. 1·00 10
413. – 1 k. 40 brown .. .. 1·50 15
DESIGN: 1 k. 40, Forester felling tree.

1959. Arrhenius (chemist). Birth Cent.
414. **97.** 15 ore brown 12 10
415. 1 k. 70 blue .. .. 1·40 15

98. Anders Zorn (self-portrait).

99. "Uprooted Tree".

1960. Zorn (painter and etcher). Birth Cent.
416. **98.** 30 ore grey 15 10
417. 80 ore brown .. .. 1·10 25

1960. World Refugee Year.
418. **99.** 20 ore brown 10 10
419. – 40 ore violet 40 15
DESIGN—VERT. 40 ore Refugees.

100. Target-shooting. 101. Gustav Froding.

1960. Voluntary Shooting Organization. Cent.
420. **100.** 15 ore rose 15 10
421. – 90 ore turquoise .. 75 30
DESIGN: 90 ore Members of the Organization on march.

1960. Gustav Froding (poet). Birth Cent.
422. **101.** 30 ore brown 15 10
423. 1 k. 40 bronze-green .. 75 12

1960. Europa. As T **279** of Belgium but size 27 × 21 mm.
424. 40 ore blue 15 10
425. 1 k. red .. .. .. 30 1·50

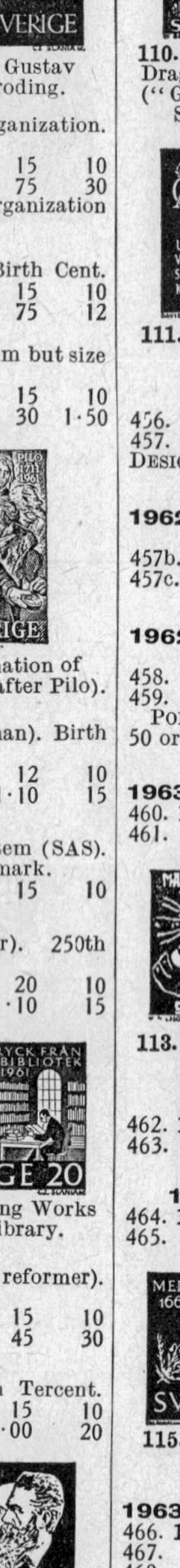

102. H. Branting. 103. "Coronation of Gustav III" (after Pilo).

1960. Hjalmar Branting (statesman). Birth Cent.
426. **102.** 15 ore rose 12 10
427. 1 k. 70 blue .. .. 1·10 15

1961. Scandinavian Airlines System (SAS). 10th Anniv. As T **81** of Denmark.
428. 40 ore blue 15 10

1961. Carl Gustav Pilo. (painter). 250th Birth Anniv.
442. **103.** 30 ore brown 20 10
443. 1 k. 40 blue .. .. 1·10 15

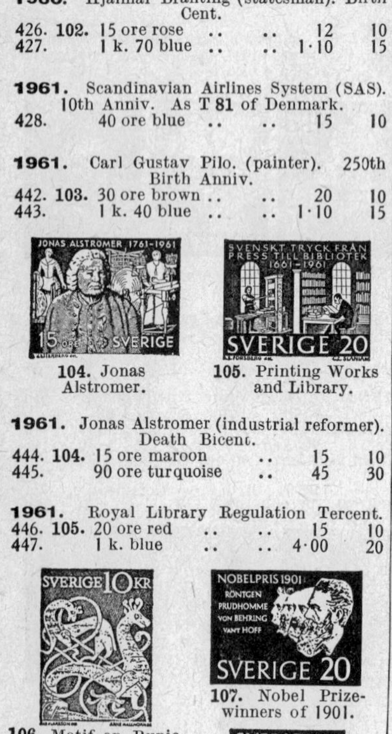

104. Jonas Alstromer. 105. Printing Works and Library.

1961. Jonas Alstromer (industrial reformer). Death Bicent.
444. **104.** 15 ore maroon .. 15 10
445. 90 ore turquoise .. 45 30

1961. Royal Library Regulation Tercent.
446. **105.** 20 ore red 15 10
447. 1 k. blue .. .. 4·00 20

106. Motif on Runic Stone on Oland. 107. Nobel Prize-winners of 1901.

108. Postman's Footprints. 109. Code, Voting Instruments and Mallet.

1961.
448. **106.** 10 k. maroon .. 3·00 60

1961. Nobel Prize-Winners.
449. **107.** 20 ore red 15 5
450. 40 ore blue 20 5
451. 50 ore green 20 5
See also Nos. 458/9, 471/2, 447/8, 488/9, 523/4, 546/7, 573/4, 602/4, 635/7, 670/2, 721/4 and 769/71.

1962. Swedish Local Mail Delivery Service. Cent.
452. **108.** 30 ore violet 15 10
453. 1 k. 70 red .. .. 1·10 15

1962. Municipal Laws Cent.
454. **109.** 30 ore blue 15 10
455. 2 k. red .. .. 1·10 15

110. St. George and Dragon, Storkyrkan ("Great Church"), Stockholm.

112. Ice-hockey Player.

111. King Gustav VI Adolf and cultural Themes.

1962. Swedish Monuments.
456. **110.** 20 ore claret .. 12 10
457. – 50 ore myrtle .. 20 10
DESIGN—HORIZ. 50 ore Skokloster Castle.

1962. King Gustav's 80th Birthday and Swedish Culture Fund.
457b. **111.** 20 ore + 10 ore brown 40 40
457c. 35 ore + 10 ore blue .. 35 35

1962. Nobel Prize-Winners. As T **107** but inscr. "NOBEL PRIS 1902".
458. 25 ore red 20 10
459. 50 ore blue 20 10
PORTRAITS: 25 ore, Mommsen, Ross. 50 ore, Fischer, Zeeman, Lorentz.

1963. World Ice-hockey Championships.
460. **112.** 25 ore blue-green .. 15 10
461. 1 k. 70 blue .. .. 1·10 20

113. Hands reaching for Wheat.

114. Symbols.

1963. Freedom from Hunger.
462. **113.** 35 ore magenta .. 15 10
463. 50 ore violet 20 10

1963. "Engineering and Industry".
464. **114.** 50 ore black 20 10
465. 1 k. 05 orange .. 60 25

115. Dr. G. F. Du Rietz.

116. Linne's Hammarby (country house).

1963. Swedish Board of Health. 300th Anniv
466. **115.** 25 ore brown 20 10
467. 35 ore blue 20 10
468. 2 k. red .. .. 1·10 15

1963. Swedish Monuments (2nd series).
469. **116.** 20 ore red 12 10
470. 50 ore bronze 20 10

1963. Nobel Prize-Winners. As T **107** but inscr. "NOBEL PRIS 1903".
471a. 25 ore bronze 25 20
472. 50 ore chocolate 20 10
PORTRAITS: 25 ore, Arrhenius, Finsen Bjornson. 50 ore, Becquerel, P. Curie, M. Curie,

117. Motif from poem "Elie Himmelsfard".

118. Seal of Archbishop Stefan.

1964. E. A. Karifeldt (poet). Birth Cent.
473a. **117.** 35 ore blue 25 10
474. 1 k. 05 red .. .. 3·00 30

1964. Archbishopric of Uppsala. 800th Anniv.
475. **118.** 40 ore bronze-green .. 20 10
476. 60 ore chestnut .. 25 15

1964. Nobel Prize-Winners. As T **107** but inscr. "NOBEL PRIS 1904".
477. 30 ore blue 20 10
478. 40 ore red 25 10
PORTRAITS: 30 ore, J. Echegaray y Eizaguirre F. Mistral, J. W. Strutt (Lord Rayleigh) 40 ore, Sir W. Ramsey, I. P. Pavlov.

119. Visby Town Wall. 120. Post-horns. 121. Telecommunications.

1965. Swedish Monuments (2rd series).
479. **119.** 30 ore cerise 15 10
480. 2 k. blue 90 12

1965.
481. **120.** 20 ore blue and yellow 10 10

1965. I.T.U. Cent.
482. **121.** 60 ore violet 20 10
483. 1 k. 40 indigo 70 15

122. Prince Eugen. (painter).

123. F. Bremer (novelist).

1965. Prince Eugen. Birth Cent.
484. **122.** 40 ore black 15 10
485. 1 k. brown 40 10

1965. Fredrika Bremer. Death Cent.
486. **123.** 25 ore violet 12 10
487. 3 k. green .. .. 1·75 15

1965. Nobel Prize-Winners. As T **107** but inscr. "NOBEL PRIS 1905".
488. 30 ore blue 20 10
489. 40 ore red 20 10
PORTRAITS: 30 ore, P. von Lenard, J. von Baeyer. 40 ore, R. Koch, H. Sienkiewicz.

124. N. Soderblom.

125. Skating.

1966. Nathan Soderblom, Archbishop of Uppsala. Birth Cent.
490. **124.** 60 ore brown 25 10
491. 80 ore green 30 10

1966. World Men's Speed Skating Championships, Gothenburg.
492. **125.** 5 ore red 10 10
493. 25 ore green 15 15
494. 40 ore blue 40 40

126. Entrance Hall, National Galley. 127. Ale's Stones, Kaseberga.

128. Louis de Geer.

1966. Opening of National Museum Building. Cent.
495. **126.** 30 ore violet 12 10
496. 2 k. 30 green .. 1·90 40

1966.
498. – 35 ore brown and blue 10 10
499. **127.** 3 k. 50 grey .. .. 1·00 12
500. – 3 k. 70 violet .. 1·25 12
501. – 4 k. 50 red .. .. 1·10 12
502. – 7 k. red & ultramarine 1·90 40
DESIGNS—HORIZ. 35 ore, Fjeld (mountains). 7 k. Gripsholm Castle. VERT. 3 k. 70, Lion fortress, Gothenburg. 4 k. 50, Uppsala Cathedral (interior).

1966. Representative Assembly Reform. Cent
510. **128.** 40 ore blue 15 10
511. 3 k. lake .. .. 2·25 25

129. Theatre Stage. 130. C. J. Almqvist (writer).

1966. Drottningholm Theatre. Bicent.
512. **129.** 5 ore red on rose .. 10 10
513. 25 ore bistre on rose .. 10 10
514. 40 ore purple on rose .. 45 45

1966. Carl Almqvist Death Cent.
515. **130.** 25 ore magenta .. 12 10
516. 1 k. green 75 10

1966. National Cancer Fund. Swedish Ships. Designs as T **53**, but with imprint "1966" at foot.
517. 10 ore red 30 30
518. 15 ore red 30 30
519. 20 ore green 30 30
520. 25 ore blue 12 12
521. 30 ore red 30 30
522. 40 ore red 30 30
SHIPS—HORIZ. 10 ore, "The Lion of Smaland" 15 ore, "Kalmar Nyckel" and "Fazel Grip". 20 ore, "Hiorten". 25 ore, "Constitution". 30 ore, "King Karl". 40 ore, Stern of "Amphion".

1966. Nobel Prize-Winners. As T **107** but inscr. "NOBEL PRIS 1906".
523. 30 ore lake 15 10
524. 40 ore green 20 10
PORTRAITS: 30 ore, J. J. Thomson, G. Carducci, 40 ore, H. Moissan, C. Golgi, R y Cajal.

131. Handball. 132. "E F T A".

1967. World Handball Championships.
525. **131.** 45 ore blue 15 10
526. 2 k. 70 mauve .. 1·10 40

1967. European Free Trade Assn. ("E.F.T.A.").
527. **132.** 70 ore orange 25 15

133. Table-Tennis Player.

134. Axeman and Beast.

1967. World Table-Tennis Championships, Stockholm.
528. **133.** 35 ore magenta .. 15 5
529. 90 ore blue 45 5

1967.
530. **134.** 10 ore blue and brown 10 5
531. – 15 ore brown and blue 15 5
532. – 30 ore magenta & brn. 15 5
533. – 35 ore brn. & magenta 20 5
DESIGNS (Ancient bronze plates found at Torslunda): 15 ore, Man between two bears. 30 ore, "Lion man" putting enemy to flight. 35 ore, Two warriors.

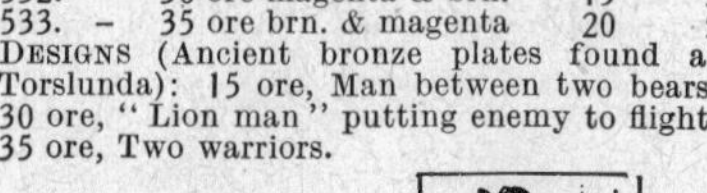

135. "Solidarity".

137. 18th-Century Postman.

136. "Keep to the Right".

1967. Finnish Settlers in Sweden.
534. **135.** 10 ore multicoloured .. 10 10
535. 35 ore multicoloured .. 15 10

1967. Adoption of Changed Rule of the Road.
536. 136. 35 ore black, orge. & bl. 12 5
537. 45 ore blk., orge. & grn. 15 5

1967.
538. 137. 5 ore black and red .. 10 5
539. – 10 ore black and blue 10 5
539b. – 20 ore black on flesh .. 10 5
540. – 30 ore red and blue .. 12 5
541. – 40 ore blue, grn. & blk. 12 5
541b. – 45 ore black and blue 15 5
542. – 90 ore brown and blue 30 5
543. – 1 k. olive 30 5
DESIGNS—As T 137: VERT. 10 ore, 17th-century ship. 20 ore, "St. Stephen" (ceiling painting, Dadesjo Church, Smaland). 30 ore, Angelica plant on coast. HORIZ. 40 ore, Haverud Aqueduct, Dalsland Canal. (27½ × 22½ mm.): 45 ore, Floating Logs. 90 ore, Elk. 1 k. Dancing cranes.

138. King Gustav VI Adolf. 139. Berwald, Violin and Music.

1967. King Gustav's 85th Birthday.
544. 138. 45 ore blue 15 5
545. 70 ore green 25 8

1967. Nobel Prize-Winners. As T 107, but inscr. "NOBEL PRIS 1907".
546. 35 ore red 15 5
547. 45 ore blue 15 5
PORTRAITS: 35 ore, E. Buchner, A. A. Michelson. 45 ore, C. L. A. Laveran, Rudyard Kipling.

1968. Franz Berwald (composer). Death Cent.
548. 139. 35 ore black and red .. 12 5
549. 2 k. black, ultramarine and yellow 75 25

140. Bank Seal. 141. Butterfly Orchids.

1968. Bank of Sweden. 300th Anniv.
550. 140. 45 ore blue 15 5
551. 70 ore black on salmon 25 8

1968. Wild Flowers.
552. 141. 45 ore green 25 5
553. – 45 ore green 25 5
554. – 45 ore red and green .. 25 5
555. – 45 ore green 25 5
556. – 45 ore green 25 5
DESIGNS: No. 553, Wood anemone. No. 554, Wild rose. No. 555, Wild cherry. No. 556, Lily of the Valley.

142. University Seal.

1968. Lund University. 300th Anniv.
557. 142. 10 ore blue 10 5
558. 35 ore red 20 20

143. Ecumenical Emblem. 144. "The Universe".

1968. World Council of Churches, Uppsala. 4th General Assembly.
559. 143. 70 ore purple 25 10
560. 90 ore blue 30 10

1968. People's College. Cent.
561. 144. 45 ore carmine .. 15 10
562. 2 k. blue 70 15

145. "Orienteer" crossing Forest. 146. "The Tug of War." (wood-carving by Axel Petersson).

1968. World "Orienteering" Championships, Linkoping.
563. 145. 40 ore lake and violet 12 10
564. 2 k. 80 violet and green 1·10 70

1968. Axel Petersson ("Doderhultarn"). Birth Cent.
565. 146. 5 ore green 10 10
566. 25 ore brown 60 60
567. 45 ore brown and sepia 20 20

147. Fox. 148. "The Worker" (A. Amelin).

1968. Bruno Liljefors' Fauna Sketches.
568. – 30 ore blue 20 5
569. – 30 ore black 20 5
570. 147. 30 ore brown 20 5
571. – 30 ore brown 20 5
572. – 30 ore blue 20 5
DESIGNS: No. 568, Hare. No. 569, Great Black-backed Gull. No. 571, Golden Eagle and Crows. No. 572, Weasel.

1968. Nobel Prize-Winners. As T 107, but inscr. "NOBEL PRIS 1908".
573. 35 ore lake 12 10
574. 45 ore green 15 10
Portraits: Nobel Prizewinners of 1908. 35 ore I. Mecnikov, P. Ehrlich, E. Rutherford. 45 ore G. Lippman, R. Eucken.

1969. Northern Countries Union. 50th Anniv. As T 125 of Denmark.
575. 45 ore brown 15 10
576. 70 ore blue 20 10

1969. Int. Labour Organization. 50th Anniv.
577. 148. 55 ore red 20 10
578. 70 ore blue 20 10

149. Colonnade. 150. A. Engstrom with Owl (self-portrait).

1969. Europa.
579. 149. 70 ore multicoloured .. 20 10
580. 1 k. multicoloured .. 30 12

1969. Albert Engstrom (painter and writer). Birth Cent.
581. 150. 35 ore black 12 10
582. 55 ore blue 20 10

151. Tjorn Bridge. 152. Helmeted Figure (Carving).

1969. Tjorn Bridges.
584. 151. 15 ore blue on blue .. 25 10
585. – 30 ore green and black on blue 25 15
586. – 55 ore black and blue on blue 40 30
DESIGNS: 30 ore Tjorn Bridge (different). LARGER (41 × 19 mm.): 55 ore Tjorn Bridges (different).

1969. Warship "Vasa" Commem.
587. 152. 55 ore red 25 8
588. – 55 ore brown 25 8
589. – 55 ore blue 25 8
590. – 55 ore brown 25 8
591. – 55 ore red 25 8
592. – 55 ore blue 25 8
DESIGNS—VERT. No. 588, Crowned Lion's Head (Carving). 590, Lion's Head (Carving). 591, Carved support. HORIZ. (46 × 28 mm.): 589, Ship's Coat-of-Arms. 592, Warship "Vasa".

153. H. Soderberg (writer).

155. "The Adventures of Nils" by S. Lagerlof (illus. by J. Bauer).

154. Lighthouses and Lightship.

1969. Hjalmar Soderberg and Bo Bergman. Birth Cents.
593. 153. 45 ore brown on cream 15 10
594. – 55 ore olive on green .. 15 10
DESIGN—HORIZ. 55 ore, Bo Bergman poet).

1969. Swedish Lighthouse Service. 300th Anniv.
595. 154. 30 ore black, red and grey 10 10
596. 55 ore blk., orge. & blue 15 10

1969. Swedish Fairy Tales.
597. – 35 ore brn., red & orge. 20 10
598. 155. 35 ore brown 20 10
599. – 35 ore brn., red & orge 20 10
600. – 35 ore brown 20 10
601. – 35 ore red and orange 20 10
DESIGNS: No. 597, "Pelle's New Suit" (written and illus. by Elsa Beskow). No. 599, "Pippi Longstocking" (by A. Lindgren, illus. by I. Vang Nyman). 600, "Vill-Vallareman, the Shepherd" from "With Pucks and Elves", illus. by J. Bauer). 601, "The Cat's Journey" (written and illus. by I. Arosenius).

156. E. Kocher and W. Ostwald. 157. Great Seal of the Middle Ages.

1969. Nobel Prize-Winners. Inscr. "NOBEL PRIS 1909".
602. 156. 45 ore green 15 5
603. – 55 ore black on flesh .. 20 5
604. – 70 ore black 20 5
DESIGNS: 55 ore Selma Lagerlof. 70 ore G. Marconi and C. F. Braun.

1970.
605. – 2 k. 55 blue 70 20
606. – 3 k. blue 95 20
607. 157. 5 k. blue-green .. 1·25 12
DESIGNS: 2 k. 55, Seal of King Magnus Ladulas. 3 k. Seal of Duke Erik Magnusson.

158. Weathervane, Soderala Church. 159. River Scene.

1970. Swedish Forgings.
608. 158. 5 ore green and brown 10 10
609. – 10 ore green and brown 10 10
610. – 30 ore black and green 20 12
611. – 55 ore brown and green 15 10
DESIGNS—HORIZ. 10 ore. As T 158, but design and country name/figures of value in reverse order. 30 ore, Memorial Cross, Eksharad Churchyard. VERT. 55 ore (larger, 17½ × 39½ mm.). 14th-century Door, Bjorksta Church.

1970. Nature Conservation Year.
612. 159. 55 ore multicoloured .. 15 10
613. 70 ore multicoloured .. 20 10

160. View of Kiruna.

1970. Sweden within the Arctic Circle.
614. 160. 45 ore brown 20 15
615. – 45 ore blue 20 15
616. – 45 ore green 20 15
617. – 45 ore brown 20 15
618. – 45 ore blue 20 15
DESIGNS: No. 615, Vita Vidder (Skiers). 616, Lappkata (lake), Stora Sjofallet National Park. 617, Reindeer herd. 618, Rocket-launching.

161. China Palace, Drottningholm.

162. Lumber Truck.

1970. Historic Buildings.
619. – 55 ore green 15 10
620. 161. 2 k. multicoloured .. 60 10
DESIGN—VERT. (21 × 27½ mm.). 55 ore, Glimmingehus (15th-century Castle).

1970. Swedish Trade and Industry.
621. 162. 70 ore brown and blue 30 15
622. – 70 ore blue, brn. & pur. 30 15
623. – 70 ore pur. and blue 30 15
624. – 70 ore blue & purple 30 15
625. – 70 ore blue & purple 30 15
626. – 70 ore brown & purple 30 15
627. – 1 k. black on cream 30 10
DESIGNS—Size as T 162: No. 623, Ship's propeller. No. 624, Dam and electric locomotive. No. 626, Technician. (44 × 20 mm.): No. 622, Loading ship at quay-side. No. 625, Mine and ore train (26 × 20 mm.): No. 627, Mining.

163. Three Hearts.

1970. United Nations. 25th Anniv.
628. 163. 55 ore red, yell. & blk. 15 10
629. – 70 ore grn., yell. & blk. 25 10
DESIGN: 70 ore, Three four-leaved clovers.

164. Blackbird. 165. Paul Heyse.

1970. Christmas. Birds. Multicoloured.
630. 30 ore Type 164 .. 20 15
631. 30 ore Great tit .. 20 15
632. 30 ore Bullfinch .. 20 15
633. 30 ore Greenfinch .. 20 15
634. 30 ore Blue tit .. 20 15

1970. Nobel Prize-Winners. Inscr. "NOBEL PRIS 1910".
635. 165. 45 ore violet 15 10
636. – 55 ore blue 15 10
637. – 70 ore black 20 10
PORTRAITS: 55 ore Otto Wallach and J. van der Waals. 70 ore A. Kossel.

165a. S.S. "Storskar" and Royal Palace, Stockholm.

1971.
638. 165a. 80 ore black & blue 25 10
639. – 4 k. black .. .. 1·10 25
639a. – 6 k. blue .. .. 1·50 45
DESIGN: 4 k. 16th-century "Blood Money" Coins. 6 k. Gustav Vasa's Dollar.

166. Kerstin Hesselgren (politician).

ILLUSTRATIONS British Commonwealth and all overprints and surcharges are FULL SIZE. Foreign Countries have been reduced to ¾-LINEAR.

1971. Swedish Women's Suffrage. 50th Anniv.
640. 166. 45 ore violet on green 15 10
641. 1 k. brown on yellow .. 30 10

167. Birds in Flight. 168. "The Prodigal Son" (painting, Sodra Rada Church).

1971. Nordic Help for Refugees Campaign.
642. 167. 40 ore red 12 10
643. 55 ore blue 15 10

1971. Art Treasures.
644. 168. 15 ore olive and green 10 8
645. – 25 ore indigo and ochre 10 8
646. – 25 ore indigo and ochre 10 8
DESIGNS—HORIZ. (Panels from Grodinge Tapestry, Swedish National History Museum): No. 645, Griffin. No. 646. Lion.

169. Container Port, Gothenburg.

1971.
647. 169. 55 ore violet and blue 15 10
648. – 60 ore brown on cream 20 10
649. – 75 ore deep green on pale green 25 10
DESIGNS: (28 x 23 mm.)—60 ore. Timber-sledge. 75 ore. Windmills, Oland.

170. Musical Score.

172. "The Three Wise Men".

171. "The Mail Coach" (after E. Schwab).

1971. Swedish Royal Academy of Music. Bicent.
650. 170. 55 ore purple .. 15 10
651. 85 ore green 25 10

1971.
652. 171. 1 k. 20 multicoloured 40 10

1971. Gotland Stone-masons Art.
653. 172. 5 ore violet & brown 10 10
654. – 10 ore violet & green 10 10
655. – 55 ore green & brown 15 10
656. – 65 ore brown & violet 20 10
DESIGNS—VERT. 10 ore "Adam and Eve". HORIZ. (40 × 21 mm.)—55 ore "Winged knight" and "Samson and the lion". 65 ore "The Flight to Egypt".

173. Child beside Lorry Wheel.

174. Gustav Vasa's State Sword, c. 1500.

1971. Road Safety.
657. 173. 35 ore black and red 12 10
658. 65 ore blue and red .. 20 10

1971. Swedish Crown Regalia. Multicoloured.
659. 65 ore Type 174 .. .. 25 10
660. 65 ore Erik XIV's sceptre, 1561 .. .. .. 25 10
661. 65 ore Erik XIV's crown, 1561 .. .. .. 25 10
662. 65 ore Erik XIV's orb, 1561 25 10
663. 65 ore Karl IX's anointing horn, 1606 .. .. 25 10

175. Santa Claus and Gifts.

176. "Nils Holgersson on Goose" (from Selma Lagerlof's "The Wonderful Adventures of Nils").

1971. Christmas. Traditional Prints.
664. 175. 35 ore red 20 10
665. – 35 ore blue 20 10
666. – 35 ore maroon .. 20 10
667. – 35 ore blue 20 10
668. – 35 ore green 20 10
DESIGNS: No. 665, Market scene. No 666, Musical evening. No. 667, Skating. No. 668, Arriving for Christmas service.

1971.
669. 176. 65 ore blue 20 5

177. M. Maeterlinck (Literature).

178. Fencing.

1971. Nobel Prize-winners Inscr. "NOBEL PRIS 1911".
670. 177. 55 ore orange .. 15 5
671. – 65 ore green .. 20 5
672. – 85 ore red 25 5
DESIGNS: 65 ore Allvar Gullstrand and Wilhelm Wien (Physics). 85 ore Marie Curie (Chemistry).
See also Nos. 721/4.

1972. Sportswomen.
673. 178. 55 ore purple .. 25 8
674. – 55 ore blue 25 8
675. – 55 ore green 25 8
676. – 55 ore purple .. 25 8
677. – 55 ore blue 25 8
DESIGNS: No. 674, Diving. No. 675, Gymnastics. No. 676, Tennis. No. 677, Figure-skating.

179. Statue of L. J. Hierta (newspaper editor).

180. Roe-deer.

1972. Anniversaries.
678. 179. 35 ore multicoloured .. 12 8
679. – 50 ore violet .. 15 8
680. – 65 ore indigo 20 8
681. – 85 ore multicoloured .. 25 10
DESIGNS AND ANNIVERSARIES—VERT. 35 ore (death cent.). 85 ore G. Stiernhielm (poet—300th death anniv.). HORIZ. 50 ore F. M. Franzen (poet and hymn-writer—birth bicent.). 65 ore Hugo Alfven (composer—birth cent.).

1972.
682. 180. 95 ore brown on cream 30 15

181. Glass-blowing.

1972. Swedish Glass Industry.
683. 181. 65 ore black 20 8
684. – 65 ore blue 20 8
685. – 65 ore red 20 8
686. – 65 ore black 20 8
687. – 65 ore blue 20 8
DESIGNS: No. 684, Glass-blowing (close-up). No. 685, Shaping glass. No. 686, Handling glass vase. No. 687, Bevelling glass vase.

182. Horses, Borgholm Castle.

1972. Tourism in South-east Sweden.
688. 182. 55 ore brown on cream 15 8
689. – 55 ore blue on cream .. 15 8
690. – 55 ore brown on cream 15 8
691. – 55 ore green on cream 15 8
692. – 55 ore blue on cream .. 15 8
DESIGNS: No. 689, Oland Bridge and sailing barque. 690, Kalmar Castle. 691, Salmon-fishing, Morrumsan. 692, Sail-training schooner "Falken", Karlskrona Naval Base.

183. Conference Emblem and Motto, "Only One Earth".

1972. U.N. Environment Conservation Conference, Stockholm.
693. 183. 65 ore blue and red on cream 20 10
694. – 85 ore mult. on cream 25 10
DESIGN—VERT. (28 × 45 mm.): 85 ore "Spring" (wooden relief).

184. Junkers "F-13".

186. Early Courier.

185. "Reindeer and Sledge" (woodcut from "Lapponia" by J. Schefferus).

1972. Swedish Mailplanes.
695. 184. 5 ore lilac 10 10
696. – 15 ore blue 10 10
697. – 25 ore blue 10 10
698. – 75 ore green 25 10
DESIGNS—HORIZ. (45 × 19 mm.). 15 ore Junkers "Ju-52". 25 ore Friedrichshafen "FF-49". 75 ore Douglas "DC-3".

1972. "Lapponia" (book by J. Schefferus). Cent.
699. 185. 1 k. 40 red on blue .. 40 10

1972. "Stockholmia 74" (1st issue) and Olle Hjortzberg (stamp designer). 100th Birth Anniv.
700. 186. 10 ore red 25 25
701. – 15 ore green 25 25
702. – 40 ore blue 25 25
703. – 50 ore brown 25 25
704. – 60 ore blue 25 25
DESIGNS: 15 ore Mounted Postman. 40 ore Train. 50 ore Motor-bus and trailer. 60 ore Mail steamer.
See also Nos. 779/82.

187. Figurehead of "Amphion" (Per Ljung).

188. Christmas Candles.

1972. Swedish 18th-cent. Art.
705. 187. 75 ore red 30 8
706. – 75 ore red 30 8
707. – 75 ore green 30 8
708. – 75 ore brown 30 8
709. – 75 ore blk., brn. & red 30 8
710. – 75 ore blk., bl. & brn. 30 8
DESIGNS: No. 706, "Quadriga" (Sergel). HORIZ. (59 × 24 mm.). No. 707, "Stockholm" (F. Martin. No. 708, "The Forge" (P. Hillestrom). VERT. (28 × 37 mm.). No. 709, "Lady with a Veil" (A. Roslin). No. 710, "Sophia Magdalena" (C. G. Pilo).

1972. Christmas. Multicoloured.
711. 45 ore Type 188 .. .. 15 8
712. 45 ore Father Christmas .. 15 8
713. 75 ore Carol-singers .. 25 8
No. 713 is size 40 × 23 mm.

189. King Gustav VI Adolf.

190. King Gustav with Book.

1972.
714. 189. 75 ore blue 25 8
715. 1 k. red 30 8

1972. King Gustav VI Adolf's 90th Birthday.
716. 190. 75 ore blue 60 60
717. – 75 ore green 60 60
718. – 75 ore brown 60 60
719. – 75 ore blue 60 60
720 – 75 ore green 60 60
DESIGNS: No. 717, Chinese objets d'art. No. 718, Opening Parliament. No. 719, Etruscan objets d'art. No. 720, King Gustav tending flowers.

1972. Nobel Prize-winners. As T 177 but inscr. "Nobelpris 1912".
721. 60 ore brown 20 5
722. 65 ore blue 20 5
723. 75 ore violet 25 5
724. 1 k. brown 25 5
DESIGNS—HORIZ. 60 ore P. Sabatier and V. Grignard. VERT. 65 ore A. Carrel. 75 ore G. Dalen. 1 k. G. Hauptmann.

191. "Tintomara" Stage Set.

192. Mail Coach, 1923.

1973. Swedish Royal Theatre. Bicent.
725. 191. 75 ore green 25 5
726. – 1 k. purple 30 5
DESIGN—HORIZ. (41 × 23 mm.). 1 k. "Orpheus" (after P. Hillestrom).

1973. Mail Coaches.
727. 192. 60 ore black on yellow 20 5
728. – 70 ore orge., bl. & grn. 20 10
DESIGN: 70 ore Mail Coach, 1973.

193. Vasa Ski Race.

194. Horse (bas relief).

1973. Tourism.
729. 193. 65 ore green 25 5
730. – 65 ore green 25 5
731. – 65 ore black 25 5
732. – 65 ore green 25 5
733. – 65 ore brown 25 5
DESIGNS: No. 730, "Going to the Church in Mora". No. 731, Church stables in Rattvik. No. 732, "The Great Pit". No. 733, "Midsummer Dance".

1973. Gottland's Picture Stores.
734. 194. 5 ore purple 5 5
735. – 10 ore blue 5 5
DESIGN: 10 ore Viking ship.

195. "Row of Willows" (P. Persson).

1973. Swedish Landscapes.
736. 195. 40 ore grey 12 5
737. – 50 ore brown & black 15 5
738. – 55 ore green 15 5
DESIGNS—VERT. (20 × 28 mm.). 50 ore, "View of Trosa" (R. Ljunggren). HORIZ. (27 × 23 mm.). 55 ore, "Trees" (O. Bergman).

196. Lumberman.

197. Observer reading Thermometer.

1973. Swedish Confederation of Trade Unions. 75th Anniv.
739. 196. 75 ore red 25 5
740. 1 k. 40 blue 40 5

1973. I.M.O./W.M.O. and Swedish Meteorological Organizations. Cent.
741. 197. 65 ore green 20 5
742. – 65 ore blue and black 20 5
DESIGN: No. 742, U.S. satellite weather picture.

198. Nordic House, Reykjavik.

1973. Nordic Countries' Postal Co-operation.
743. **198.** 75 ore multicoloured .. 25 5
744. 1 k. multicoloured .. 30 5

199. C. P. Thunberg. Japanese Flora and Scene.

1973. Swedish Explorers.
745. **199.** 1 k. brn., green and blue 30 15
746. – 1 k. brown, green & blue 30 15
747. – 1 k. brown, green & blue 30 15
748. – 1 k. multicoloured .. 30 15
749. – 1 k. brown, black & blue 30 15
DESIGNS: No. 746, A. Sparrman and island. No. 747, A. E. Nordenskjold and the "Vega". No. 748, S. A. Andree and wrecked balloon. No. 749, Sven Hedin and yaks.

200. Team of Oxen. **201.** Grey Seal.

1973. Nordic Museum. Centenary.
750. **200.** 75 ore black 30 15
751. – 75 ore brown 30 15
752. – 75 ore black 30 15
753. – 75 ore purple .. 30 15
754. – 75 ore brown 30 15
DESIGNS: No. 751, Braking flax. No. 752, Potato-planting. No. 753, Baking bread, No. 754, Spring sowing.

1973. "Save Our Animals".
755. **201.** 10 ore green 10 5
756. – 20 ore violet 10 5
757. – 25 ore green 10 5
758. – 55 ore green 15 5
759. – 65 ore violet 20 5
760. – 75 ore green 25 5
DESIGNS: 20 ore Peregrine falcon. 25 ore Lynx. 55 ore Otter. 65 ore Wolf. 75 ore Sea-eagle.

202. King Gustav VI Adolf. **204.** "Goosegirl" (Ernest Josephson.).

203. "Country Dance" (J. Nilsson).

1973. King Gustav Memorial Issue.
761. **202.** 75 ore blue 25 5
762. 1 k. purple 30 5

1973. Peasant Paintings. Multicoloured.
763. 45 ore Type **203** .. 15 5
764. 45 ore "The Three Wise Men" (A. Clemetson) .. 15 5
765. 75 ore "Gourd Plant" (B. A. Hansson) (vert.) 25 5
766. 75 ore "The Rider" (K. E. Jonsson) (vert.) .. 25 5
Nos. 765/6 are size 23 × 28 mm.

1973. Josephson Commemoration.
767. **204.** 10 k. multicoloured .. 2·50 1·00

205. Tagore.

1973. Noble Prize-winners. Inscr. "NOBELPRIS 1913".
768. – 75 ore violet 25 5
769. – 1 k. brown and sepia 30 5
770. **205.** 1 k. 40 green 45 5
DESIGNS—HORIZ. 75 ore, A. Werner and H. Kamerlingh-Onnes. VERT. 1 k. C. R. Richet.

206. Ski-jumping.

1973. "Winter Sports on Skis".
771. **206.** 65 ore green 20 5
772. – 65 ore blue 20 5
773. – 65 ore green 20 5
774. – 65 ore red 20 5
775. – 65 ore blue 20 5
DESIGNS: No. 772, Cross-country racing (men) No. 773, Relay-racing. No. 774, Downhill skiing. No. 775, Cross-country racing (women).

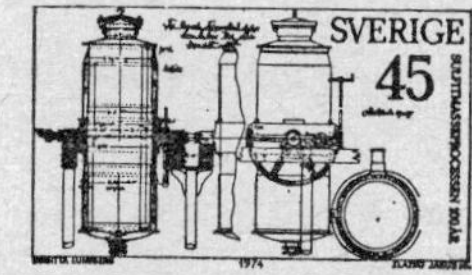

207. Ekman's Sulphite Pulping Machine.

1974. Swedish Commemorations.
776. **207.** 45 ore brown 15 5
777. – 60 ore green 20 5
778. – 75 ore red 25 5
DESIGNS AND ANNIVERSARIES: 45 ore (1st sulphite plant, Bergvik. Cent.). 60 ore, Hans Jarta and part of Government Act (birth bicent.). 75 ore, Samuel Owen and engineers (birth bicent.).

208. U.P.U. Congress Stamp of 1924.

1974. "Stockholmia '74" Stamp Exn. (2nd issue).
779. **208.** 20 ore green 20 20
780. 25 ore blue 20 20
781. 30 ore brown 20 20
782. 35 ore red 20 20

209. Great Falls. **210.** "Figure in a Storm" (B. Marklund).

1974. Tourism.
784. **209.** 35 ore black & blue .. 12 5
785. – 75 ore brown 25 5
DESIGN—HORIZ. 75 ore Ystad (town).

1974. Europa. Sculptures.
786. **210.** 75 ore maroon .. 25 5
787. – 1 k. green 30 5
DESIGN: 1 k. Picasso statue Kristinehamn.

211. King Carl XVI Gustav. **212.** Central Post Office, Stockholm.

1974.
788. **211.** 75 ore green 25 5
788b. 90 ore blue 30 5
789. 1 k. maroon 30 5
789b. 1 k. 10 red 35 5
789c. 1 k. 30 green 40 5

1974. Universal Postal Union. Cent.
790. **212.** 75 ore maroon .. 25 5
791. – 75 ore maroon .. 25 5
792. – 1 k. green 30 5
DESIGNS—As Type **212**. No. 791, Interior of Central Post Office, Stockholm. 40 × 24 mm. No. 792, Rural postman.

213. Regatta.

1974. Sweden's West Coast.
793. **213.** 65 ore red 20 5
794. – 65 ore blue 20 5
795. – 65 ore green 20 5
796. – 65 ore green 20 5
797. – 65 ore maroon 20 5
DESIGNS: No. 794, Vinga Lighthouse. No. 795, Varberg Fortress. No. 796, Seine fishing. No. 797, Mollosund.

214. "Mr. Simmons" (A. Fridell). **215.** Bobbin and Weave.

1974. Publicists' Club. Cent.
798. **214.** 45 ore black 15 5
799. 1 k. 40 red 40 20

1974. Swedish Textile and Clothing Industry.
800. **215.** 85 ore violet 25 5
801. – 85 ore black and orange 25 5
DESIGN: No. 801, Sewing-machines.

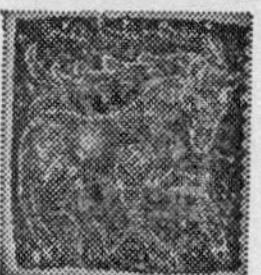

216. Reindeer.

1974. Christmas. Mosaic Embroideries.
802. **216.** 45 ore multicoloured .. 15 5
803. – 45 ore multicoloured .. 15 5
804. – 45 ore multicoloured .. 15 5
805. – 45 ore multicoloured .. 15 5
806. – 45 ore multicoloured .. 15 5
807. – 45 ore multicoloured .. 15 5
808. – 45 ore multicoloured .. 15 5
809. – 45 ore multicoloured .. 15 5
810. – 45 ore multicoloured .. 15 5
811. – 45 ore multicoloured .. 15 5
812. – 75 ore multicoloured .. 25 5
DESIGNS: Nos. 803/11, Various animals similar to Type **216**. No. 812, Animal within circular frame.

217. Swedish Tanker.

1974. Swedish Shipping. Each blue.
813. 1 k. Type **217** 30 5
814. 1 k. Liner "Snow Storm" 30 5
815. 1 k. Icebreakers "Tor" and "Atle" 30 5
816. 1 k. Train-ferry "Skanes" 30 5
817. 1 k. Tugboats in Stockholm harbour 30 5

218. Max von Laue. **219.** Sven Jerring (first announcer), Microphone and Children.

1974. Nobel Prize-winners. Inscr. "NOBELPRIS 1914".
818. **218.** 65 ore red 20 5
819. – 70 ore green 30 5
820. – 1 k. blue 30 5
PRIZE-WINNERS of 1914: 70 ore T. W. Richards. 1 k. R. Barany.

1974. Swedish Broadcasting Corporation. 50th Anniv.
821. **219.** 75 ore blue and brown 25 5
822. – 75 ore blue and brown 25 5
DESIGN: No. 822, Parliamentary debate being televised.

220. Giro Envelope.

1975. Swedish Postal Giro Office. 50th Anniv.
823. **220.** 1 k. 40 brown and black 45 5

221. Construction Workers. **222.** Helmet Decoration.

1975. International Women's Year.
824. **221.** 75 ore green 25 5
825. – 1 k. purple 30 5
DESIGN—VERT. 1 k. Jenny Lind (singer).

1975. Archaeological Discoveries. Vandal Period.
826. **222.** 10 ore red 10 5
827. – 15 ore green 10 5
828. – 20 ore violet 10 5
829. – 25 ore yellow 10 5
830. – 55 ore brown 15 5
DESIGNS: 15 ore Sword hilt and chape. 20 ore Shield buckle. 25 ore Gold effigies from excavations at Eketorp. 55 ore Iron helmet.

223. "New Year's Eve at Skansen" (E. Hallstrom).

1975. Europa. Multicoloured.
831. 90 ore Type **223** 25 5
832. 1 k. 10 "Inferno" (August Strindberg) 35 5

224. "M" Tape-Measure. **225.** Capercaillie "Cock of the Woods").

1975. Anniversaries.
833. **224.** 55 ore blue 15 5
834. – 70 ore chocolate & brn. 20 5
835. – 75 ore violet 25 5
DESIGNS AND EVENTS—HORIZ. 55 ore T **224** (cent. of Metre Convention). 70 ore Peter Hernqvist (founder) and title-page of his thesis on "Glanders" (bicent. of Swedish Veterinary Service). VERT. 75 ore "Folke Filbyter" (equestrian statue by Milles) (birth cent.).

1975.
836. **225.** 1 k. 70 blue 50 5
837. – 2 k. lake 60 10
DESIGN—VERT. 2 k. Rok Stone, Ostergotland.

226. Village Houses, Skelleftea.

1975. European Architectural Heritage Year.
838. **226.** 70 ore black 25 5
839. – 75 ore red 25 5
840. – 75 ore black 25 5
841. – 75 ore red 25 5
842. – 75 ore blue 25 5
DESIGNS: No. 839, Iron-works, Engelsberg. No. 840, Gunpowder Tower, Visby. No. 841, Pit-head gear, Falun ore mine. No. 842, Officers' Mess (1798), Old Military Barracks, Rommehed.

SVERIGE 5

227. Fire-fighting. **228.** "Fryckstad".

1975. "Watch, Guard and Help". Public Services.

843. 227. 90 ore red 30 5
844. – 90 ore blue 30 5
845. – 90 ore red 30 5
846. – 90 ore blue 30 5
847. – 90 ore green 30 5

DESIGNS: No. 844, Drug-detection. No. 845, Checking delinquents. No. 846, Hospital accident service. No. 847, Helicopter attending icebound ship.

1975. Swedish Steam Locomotives.

848. 228. 5 ore green 10 5
849. – 5 ore blue 10 5
850. – 90 ore green 30 5

DESIGNS—As T 228. No. 849, 'Gotland". (46×20 mm.). 90 ore "Prins August".

229. Water Sports. 230. Hedgehog.

1975. Scouting in Sweden. Multicoloured.

851. 90 ore Type 229 .. .. 30 5
852. 90 ore Setting-up camp .. 30 5

1975.

853. 230. 55 ore black 15 5
854. – 75 ore red 25 5
855. – 7 k. green .. .. 1·90 70

DESIGNS—HORIZ. 75 ore Player with key-fiddle. VERT. 7 k. Ballet-dancers ("The Ballet").

231. "Madonna" (Viklau Church, Gotland). 232. W. H. & W. L. Bragg (physicists).

1975. Christmas. Religious Art.

856. 231. 55 ore multicoloured .. 15 5
857. – 55 ore multicoloured .. 15 5
858. – 55 ore multicoloured .. 15 5
859. – 90 ore brown 30 5
860. – 90 ore red 30 5
861. – 90 ore blue 30 5

DESIGNS—VERT. No. 857, "Birth of Christ" (retable). No. 858, "The Sun" (retable). No. 859, "Mourning Mary". HORIZ. Nos. 860/1, "Jesse at foot of Christ's genealogical tree" (retable).

1975. Nobel Prize-winners of 1915.

862. 232. 75 ore red 25 5
863. – 90 ore blue 30 5
864. – 1 k. 10 green 35 12

DESIGNS: 90 ore Richard Willstatter (chemist) and fountain. 1 k. 10 Romain Rolland (author) and cathedral.

233. "Cave of the Winds" (sculpture by Eric Grate). 234. Guillemot and Razorbills.

1976.

865. 233. 1 k. 90 green 60 10

1976.

866. 234. 85 ore blue 25 5
867. – 1 k. purple 30 5

DESIGN—VERT. 1 k. Bobbin lace-making, Vadstena.

235. Early and Modern Hand-sets. 236. Wheat and Cornflower Seed.

1976. First Telephone Transmission. Cent.

868. 235. 1 k. 30 violet .. 40 12
869. 3 k. 40 red .. 1·00 30

1976. Swedish Seed-testing. Centenary.

870. 236. 65 ore brown 20 10
871. – 65 ore maroon & brown 20 10

DESIGN: No. 871, Seedlings.

237. Lapp Spoon. 239. Ship's Wheel.

238. View from Ringkallem.

1976. Europa. Multicoloured.

872. 1 k. Type 237 .. .. 30 10
873. 1 k. 30 Marieberg tile stove 40 12

1976. Angermanland Views.

874. 238. 85 ore green 25 5
875. – 85 ore blue 25 5
876. – 85 ore brown 25 5
877. – 85 ore blue 25 5
878. – 85 ore brown 25 5

DESIGNS: No. 875, Tug-boat hauling timber. No. 876, Hay-drying racks. No. 877, Granvagsnipen, River Angermanalven. No 878, Salmon fishing.

1976. Swedish Seamen's Church. Centenary.

879 239. 85 ore blue 25 5

240. T. Segerstedt and Newspaper.

1976. Torgny Segerstedt (Editor of Gothenburg Journal of Commerce & Shipping). Birth Cent.

880. 240. 1 k. 90 dark brn. & brn. 60 10

241. King Carl XVI and Queen Silvia. 242. "Coiled-snake" Brooch.

1976. Royal Wedding.

881. 241. 1 k. red 30 5
882. 1 k. 30 green 40 8

1976.

883. 242. 15 ore yellow 5 5
884. – 20 ore green 5 5
885. – 30 ore purple 10 5
886. – 90 ore indigo 30 5

DESIGNS: As T 242 20 ore. Pilgrim Badge. HORIZ. (30×25 mm.) 30 ore Drinking-horn. VERT. (21×28 mm.) 90 ore Chimney sweep.

243. "Girl's Head". 244. John Ericsson (inventor of ship's propeller).

245. Hands on Cogwheels.

1976. Swedish Art.

887. 243. 9 k. slate and green .. 2·75 1·50

1976. Technological Discoveries. Multicoloured.

888. 1 k. 30 Type 243 .. .. 40 8
889. 1 k. 30 H. Palmcrantz and and farm machinery (industrialist) 40 8
890. 1 k. 30 L. M. Ericsson (telephone improvements) .. 40 8
891. 1 k. 30 Wingquist inventor of spherical ball-bearings) 40 8
892. 1 k. 30 G. de Laval (inventor of milk separator and reaction turbine) .. 40 8

1976. Industrial Safety.

893. 245. 85 ore violet and orange 25 5
894. 1 k. brown and green .. 30 5

246. V. von Heidenstam (poet). 247. Archangel Michael.

1976. Nobel Prizewinner of 1916.

895. 246. 1 k. green 30 5
896. 1 k. 30 blue 40 8

1976. Christmas. Multicoloured.

897. 65 ore Type 247 .. .. 20 5
898. 65 ore St. Nicholas .. 20 5
899. 1 k. Mary visiting Elizabeth 30 5
900. 1 k. Illuminated text (Prayer to the Virgin) 30 5

Nos. 899/900 are vertical, 23×42 mm.

1977. Northern Countries' Day. As T 193 of Denmark.

901. 1 k. multicoloured .. 30 5
902. 1 k. 30 multicoloured .. 40 8

OFFICIAL STAMPS

O 1. O 2.

1874.

O 27. O 1. 2 ore orange .. 90 90
O 28. 3 ore brown .. .. 1·10 90
O 29b. 4 ore grey 90 15
O 30b. 5 ore green 90 10
O 31b. 6 ore lilac .. .. 6·00 6·00
O 32. 6 ore grey .. .. 60·00 19·00

O 33b. O1. 10 ore red .. .. 1·25 10
O 34. 12 ore blue .. .. 7·00 1·25
O 35a. 20 ore red .. .. 7·50 60
O 36. 20 ore blue 90 15
O 37. 24 ore orange .. 10·00 4·50
O 38c. 30 ore brown .. 4·75 20
O 39. 50 ore red .. .. 19·00 3·75
O 40. 50 ore grey .. .. 6·00 60
O 41c. 1 k. blue and brown 7·00 60

1889. Surch. with value in ornamental scroll between two crowns.

O 42. O 1. 10 ore on 12 ore blue 5·50 5·50
O 43b. 10 ore on 24 ore orge. 6·00 6·00

1910.

O 87. O 2. 1 ore black 12 12
O 101. 2 ore yellow 15 10
O 102. 3 ore brown 25 25
O 103. 4 ore lilac 15 15
O 104. 5 ore green 10 10
O 105. 7 ore green 30 30
O 91. 8 ore claret 45 45
O 107. 10 ore red 10 10
O 108. 12 ore red 10 10
O 109. 15 ore brown 10 10
O 110. 20 ore blue 15 10
O 111. 25 ore orange 90 20
O 112. 30 ore brown 30 10
O 113. 35 ore violet 75 20
O 114. 50 ore grey .. .. 1·50 75
O 98. 1 k. black on yellow 6·00 3·00
O 99. 5 k. red on yellow .. 4·50 2·75

POSTAGE DUE STAMPS

D 1.

1874.

D 27. D 1. 1 ore black .. .. 1·10 1·10
D 28a. 3 ore red .. .. 2·25 2·25
D 29a. 5 ore brown .. .. 1·50 1·25
D 30a. 6 ore yellow .. .. 1·50 1·25
D 31a. 12 ore red .. .. 2·75 2·75
D 32b. 20 ore blue .. .. 1·50 1·50
D 34. 24 ore grey .. .. 12·00 11·00
D 33c. 24 ore lilac .. .. 5·50 6·00
D 35. 30 ore green .. .. 1·50 1·50
D 36. 50 ore brown .. .. 2·25 2·25
D 37a. 1 k. blue and brown 14·00 10·00

SWITZERLAND E3

A federal republic of C. Europe between France and Germany.

100 Rappen = 1 Franken.
100 Centimes = 1 Franc.
100 Centesimi = 1 Franko.

These are expressions of the same currency in three languages.

For the issues under the Cantonal Administrations of Basel, Geneva and Zurich, see Stanley Gibbons' Catalogue Europe, Vol. 3.

1. 2.

1850. Inscr. "ORTS-POST". Imperf.

1. 1. 2½ r. black and red .. £700 £550

1850. As T 1, but inscr. "POSTE LOCALE". Imperf.

3. 1. 2½ r. black and red .. £600 £500

1850. As T 1, but inscr. "RAYON I, II, or III". Imperf.

6. 1. 5 r. red, black & blue (I) £500 £200
13. 5 r. red and blue (I) .. £190 60·00
10. 10 r. red, black & yell. (II) £300 55·00
23. 15 rap. red (III) .. .. £550 60·00
21. 15 cts. red (III) £3500 £400

1854. Imperf.

62. 2. 2 r. grey .. .. .. 95·00 £120
63. 5 r. brown .. .. 50·00 3·50
66. 10 r. blue .. .. .. 55·00 2·75
69. 15 r. rose .. .. 75·00 8·00
70. 20 r. orange .. .. £120 16·00
71. 40 r. green .. .. £120 19·00
44. 1 f. lilac £275 £180

3. 4. 5.

1862. Perf.

92. 3. 2 c. grey to drab .. 45 10
93. 2 c. ochre 60 15
94. 2 c. red-brown .. .. £180 75·00
77. 3 c. black .. .. 2·75 24·00
106. 5 c. brown 5 45
82. 10 c. blue .. .. 80·00 8
95. 10 c. rose 80 8
97. 15 c. yellow .. .. 1·00 6·00
84a. 20 c. orange 60 45
98. 25 c. green 55 30
86. 30 c. red .. .. £190 6·50
101. 30 c. blue .. .. 80·00 1·25
87. 40 c. green .. .. £190 13·00
102a. 40 c. grey .. .. 60 20·00
103. 50 c. purple .. .. 12·00 11·00
88. 60 c. bronze .. .. £180 55·00
90. 1 f. gold .. .. 6·00 16·00

1882.

116. 4. 2 c. olive 25 12
119. 3 c. maroon .. .. 5·00 1·90
120. 3 c. drab .. .. 65 1·00
121. 5 c. claret .. .. 3·50 12
196. 5 c. green .. .. 1·00 8
197. 10 c. red .. .. 1·00 8
198. 12 c. blue .. .. 1·10 8
131. 15 c. yellow .. .. 40·00 5·50
140. 15 c. violet .. .. 20·00 35
200. 5. 20 c. orange .. .. 1·25 35
165. 25 c. green .. .. 2·75 25
182. 25 c. blue .. .. 1·75 10
202. 30 c. brown .. .. 1·25 35
170. 40 c. grey .. .. 18·00 70
171. 50 c. blue .. .. 11·00 1·00
218. 50 c. green .. .. 2·00 1·00
175. 1 f. claret .. .. 12·00 65
219. 1 f. red .. .. 7·00 55
224. 3 f. brown .. .. 42·00 4·75

6.

ILLUSTRATIONS British Commonwealth and all overprints and surcharges are FULL SIZE. Foreign Countries have been reduced to ⅔-LINEAR.

1900. U.P.U. 25th Anniv.

191. 6. 5 c. green .. .. 1·25 20
189. 10 c. red .. .. 4·00 12
190. 25 c. blue .. .. 6·00 4·75

7. Tell's Son. 8. Helvetia. 9.

1907.

241. **7.** 2 c. bistre 12 8
242. 3 c. brown .. .. 15 2·10
243. 5 c. green .. .. 1·25 5
244. **8.** 10 c. red 90 8
245. 12 c. yellow 20 65
246. 15 c. mauve .. .. 1·10 1·10
248. **9.** 20 c. yellow and red .. 1·10 15
249. 25 c. blue .. .. 1·10 10
250. 30 c. green and brown .. 1·10 5
251. 35 c. yellow and green .. 1·10 10
252. 40 c. yellow and purple .. 6·00 12
253. 50 c. green .. .. 4·75 5
254. 70 c. yellow and brown .. 55·00 75
255. 1 f. green and claret .. 4·00 5
256. 3 f. yellow and bistre .. £250 40

For further stamps in T **9** see Nos. 314, 1910 issue.

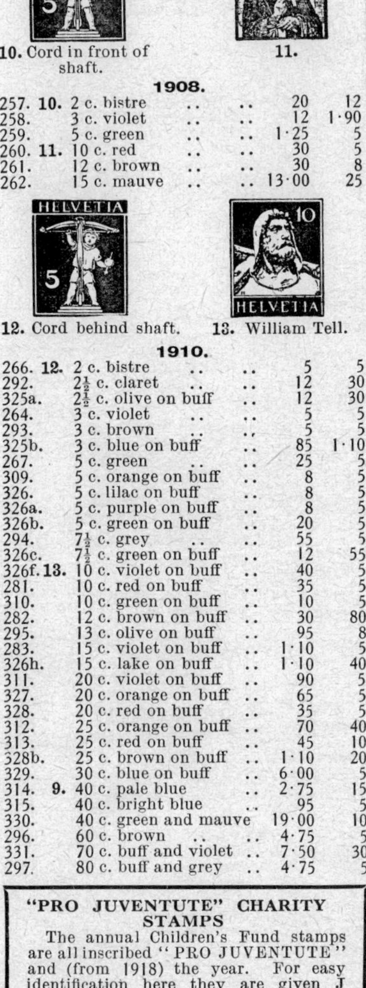

10. Cord in front of shaft. **11.**

1908.

257. **10.** 2 c. bistre 20 12
258. 3 c. violet .. .. 12 1·90
259. 5 c. green .. .. 1·25 5
260. **11.** 10 c. red 30 5
261. 12 c. brown 30 8
262. 15 c. mauve .. .. 13·00 25

12. Cord behind shaft. **13.** William Tell.

1910.

266. **12.** 2 c. bistre 5 5
292. 2½ c. claret 12 30
325a. 2½ c. olive on buff .. 12 30
264. 3 c. violet 5 5
293. 3 c. brown 5 5
325b. 3 c. blue on buff .. 85 1·10
267. 5 c. green 25 5
309. 5 c. orange on buff .. 8 5
326. 5 c. lilac on buff .. 8 5
326a. 5 c. purple on buff .. 8 5
326b. 5 c. green on buff .. 20 5
294. 7½ c. grey 55 5
326c. 7½ c. green on buff .. 12 55
326f. **13.** 10 c. violet on buff .. 40 5
281. 10 c. red on buff .. 35 5
310. 10 c. green on buff .. 10 5
282. 12 c. brown on buff .. 30 80
295. 13 c. olive on buff .. 95 8
283. 15 c. violet on buff .. 1·10 5
326h. 15 c. lake on buff .. 1·10 40
311. 20 c. violet on buff .. 90 5
327. 20 c. orange on buff .. 65 5
328. 20 c. red on buff .. 35 5
312. 25 c. orange on buff .. 70 40
313. 25 c. red on buff .. 45 10
328b. 25 c. brown on buff .. 1·10 20
329. 30 c. blue on buff .. 6·00 5
314. **9.** 40 c. pale blue .. 2·75 15
315. 40 c. bright blue .. 95 5
330. 40 c. green and mauve 19·00 10
296. 60 c. brown .. .. 4·75 5
331. 70 c. buff and violet .. 7·50 30
297. 80 c. buff and grey .. 4·75 5

"PRO JUVENTUTE" CHARITY STAMPS

The annual Children's Fund stamps are all inscribed "PRO JUVENTUTE" and (from 1918) the year. For easy identification here they are given J numbers.

14. Helvetia and Matterhorn. **15.** The Mythen.

1913. Children's Fund.

J 1. **14.** 5 c. green .. .. 3·00 2·40

1914. Mountain views.

284. **15.** 3 f. green .. .. £400 1·60
298. 3 f. red .. .. 50·00 30
285. – 5 f. blue .. .. 24·00 70
286. – 10 f. purple .. .. 90·00 80
331a. 10 f. green .. .. £160 14·00

DESIGNS: 5 f. Rutli. 10 f. Jungfrau.

1915. Surch.

287. **12.** 1 c. on 2 c. bistre .. 5 5
303. 2½ c. on 3 c. brown .. 5 5
304. 3 c. on 2½ c. olive on buff 5 30
304a. 5 c. on 2 c. bistre .. 8 40
305. 5 c. on 7½ c. grey .. 8 5
305c. 5 c. on 7½ c. grn. on buff 12 80
306. **13.** 10 c. on 13 c. olive on buff 12 35
288. **11.** 13 c. on 12 c. brown .. 12 1·50
289. **13.** 13 c. on 12 c. brn. on buff 5 5
307a. 20 c. on 15 c. vio. on buff 40 55
308. **9.** 20 c. on 25 c. blue .. 5 5
290 80 c. on 70 c. yell. & brn. 20·00 1·40

18. Appenzell. **20.** Berne. **22.** Valais.

1915. Children's Fund.

J 1a. **18.** 5 c. green on buff .. 4·75 2·40
J 2. – 10 c. red on buff .. £110 35·00

DESIGN: 10 c. Girl of Lucerne.

1916. Children's Fund.

J 3. – 3 c. violet on buff .. 6·00 12·00
J 4. **20.** 5 c. green on buff .. 12·00 3·00
J 5. – 10 c. red on buff .. 50·00 28·00

DESIGNS: 3 c., 10 c. Girls of Freiburg and Vaud.

1917. Children's Fund.

J 6. **22.** 3 c. violet on buff .. 6·00 14·00
J 7. – 5 c. green on buff .. 9·50 2·40
J 8. – 10 c. red on buff .. 24·00 8·00

DESIGNS: 5 c. Man of Unterwalden. 10 c. Girl of Ticino.

ILLUSTRATIONS
British Commonwealth and all overprints and surcharges are FULL SIZE. Foreign Countries have been reduced to ¾-LINEAR.

25. Uri.

1918. Children's Fund. Dated "1918".

J 9. **25.** 10 c. red, yellow and black on buff .. 9·00 4·75
J 10 – 15 c. violet, red, yellow and black on buff .. 9·50 3·00

ARMS: Geneva (15 c.).

1919. Air. Optd. with wings and propeller.

298a. **9.** 30 c. green and brown £130 £400
299. 50 c. green .. 38·00 32·00

27.

28.

29.

1919. Peace Celebrations.

300. **27.** 7½ c. olive and grey .. 45 45
301. **28.** 10 c. yellow and red .. 55 1·25
302. **29.** 15 c. yellow and violet .. 1·00 45

1919. Children's Fund. As T **25** but dated "1919". Cream paper.

J 11. 7½ c. red, grey and black .. 2·40 2·75
J 12. 10 c. green, red and black 2·40 2·75
J 13. 15 c. red, violet and black 2·40 1·25

ARMS: Nidwalden. (7½ c.), Vaud (10 c.) and Obwalden (15 c.).

1920. Children's Fund. As T **25** but dated "1920". Cream paper.

J 14. 7½ c. red, grey and black .. 3·00 2·50
J 15. 10 c. blue, red and black .. 4·25 2·40
J 16. 15 c. red, blue, violet & blk. 2·75 80

ARMS: Schwyz (7½ c.), Zurich (10 c.) and Ticino (15 c.).

1921. Children's Fund. As T **25** but dated "1921". Cream paper

J 17. 10 c. red, green and black 60 80
J 18. 20 c. blk., orge., red & violet 95 95
J 19. 40 c. red, blue and black 8·50 19·00

ARMS: Valais (10 c.), Berne (20 c.) and Switzerland (40 c.).

1922. Children's Fund. As T **25** but dated "1922". Cream paper.

J 20. 5 c. orange, blue and black 60 1·25
J 21. 10 c. green and black .. 45 45
J 22. 20 c. violet, blue and black 70 45
J 23. 40 c. blue, red and black .. 8·50 20·00

ARMS: Zug (5 c.), Fribourg (10 c.), Lucerne (20 c.) and Switzerland (40 c.).

43.

44.

45.

46.

1923. Air.

317. **43.** 15 c. red and green .. 1·60 1·60
317a. 20 c. green 25 12
318. 25 c. blue .. .. 4·50 4·75
319. **44.** 35 c. brown .. .. 9·50 10·00
320. 40 c. violet .. .. 12·00 14·00
321. **45.** 45 c. red and black .. 1·40 1·90
322a. 50 c. grey and red .. 80 55
323. **46.** 65 c. blue .. .. 1·25 1·60
324. 75 c. orange and purple 8·00 13·00
325. 1 f. violet .. .. 2·10 1·10

1923. Children's Fund. As T **25** but dated "1923".

J 24. 5 c. orange and black .. 30 80
J 25. 10 c. grn., red, blk. & yell. 35 45
J 26. 20 c. vio., grn., red & blk. 40 45
J 27. 40 c. blue, red and black .. 7·00 18·00

ARMS: Basel (5 c.), Glarus (10 c.), Neuchatel (20 c.) and Switzerland (40 c.).

51.

1924.

332. **51.** 90 c. red & green on green 11·00 12
333. 1 f. 20 red & lake on rose 5·50 15
334. 1 f. 50 red & blue on blue 12·00 15
335. 2 f. red & black on grey 28·00 25

52. Seat of first U.P.U. Congress. **53.**

1924. 50th Anniv. of U.P.U.

336. **52.** 20 c. red 20 25
337. **53.** 30 c. blue .. .. 35 1·10

1924. Children's Fund. As T **25** but dated "1924".

J 28. 5 c. black and lilac .. 12 30
J 29. 10 c. red, green and black on cream 12 25
J 30. 20 c. black, yellow and red on cream .. 20 25
J 31. 30 c. red, blue and black on cream .. 1·50 2·75

ARMS: Appenzell (5 c.), Solothurn (10 c.), Schaffhausen (20 c.) and Switzerland (30 c.).

1925. Children's Fund. As T **25** but dated "1925".

J 32. 5 c. green, black & violet 12 25
J 33. 10 c. black and green .. 15 25
J 34. 20 c. black, blue, yell. & red 20 25
J 35. 30 c. red, blue and black .. 1·40 2·75

ARMS: St. Gallen (5 c.), Appenzeli-Ausser-Rhoden (10 c.), Graubunden (20 c.) and Switzerland (30 c.).

1926. Children's Fund. As T **25** but dated "1926".

J 36. 5 c. pur., grn., bistre & blk. 12 30
J 37. 10 c. green, black and red 15 25
J 38. 20 c. red, black and blue .. 20 25
J 39. 30 c. blue, red and black .. 1·25 2·75

ARMS: Thurgan (5 c.), Basel (10 c.), Aargau (20 c.) and Lucerne (30 c.).

66. Forsaken Child. **67.** J. H. Pestalozzi.

69. J. H. Pestalozzi.

DESIGN—VERT As T **66**: 10 c. Orphan at Pestalozzi School.

1927. Children's Fund. Dated "1927"

J 40. **66.** 5 c. mar. & yell. on grey 12 25
J 41. – 10 c. grn. & rose on grn. 12 25
J 42. **67.** 20 c. red 20 25
J 43. **69.** 30 c. blue and black .. 1·10 2·10

70. Lausanne. **73.** J. H. Dunant.

1928. Children's Fund. Dated "1928".

J 44. **70.** 5 c. red, purple and black on buff .. 12 25
J 45. – 10 c. red, green and black on buff .. 12 25
J 46. – 20 c. black, yellow and red on buff .. 15 25
J 47. **73.** 30 c. blue and red .. 1·25 2·10

DESIGNS: As T **70**: Arms of Winterthur (10 c.) and St. Gall (20 c.).

74.

DESIGN: 2 f. Bird with letter in beak.

1929. Air.

339. **74.** 35 c. bistre and ochre 7·00 12·00
340. 40 c. green and blue 35·00 28·00
341. – 2 f. chocolate on grey 5·00 3·00

76. Mt. San Salvatore, Lake of Lugano.

DESIGNS: 10 c. Mt. Titlis, Lake of Engstlen. 20 c. Mt. Lyskamm from Riffelberg. 30 c. Nicholas de Flue.

1929. Children's Fund. Dated "1929".

J 48. **76.** 5 c. red and violet .. 12 25
J 49. – 10 c. blue and brown 15 20
J 50. – 20 c. blue and red .. 20 20
J 51. – 30 c. blue .. .. 1·50 2·75

78. Freiburg. **79.** A. Bitzius—Jeremias Gotthelf.

1930. Children's Fund. Dated "1930".

J 52. **78.** 5 c. blue, black and green on buff .. 12 25
J 53. – 10 c. yellow, red, black and violet on buff .. 15 20
J 54. – 20 c. yellow, green, black and red on buff .. 20 20
J 55. **79.** 30 c. blue .. .. 1·40 2·10

ARMS—As T **78**: Altdorf (10 c.) and Schaffhausen (20 c.).

80. The Mythen.

1931.

342. **80.** 3 f. brown .. .. 42·00 95

81. St. Moritz and Silvaplana Lakes.

DESIGNS: 10 c. The Wetterhorn. 20 c. Lac Leman. 30 c. Alexandre Vinet.

1931. Children's Fund. Dated "1931".

J 56. **81.** 5 c. green 25 25
J 57. – 10 c. violet 25 20
J 58. – 20 c. lake 35 20
J 59. – 30 c. blue .. .. 4·25 5·00

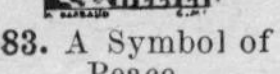

83. A Symbol of Peace. 84. "After the Darkness, Light".

85. Peace and the Air Mail.

1932. International Disarmament Conf.

343. 83. 5 c. green (postage) .. 10 10
344. 10 c. orange 15 5
345. 20 c. red 20 5
346. 30 c. blue .. .. 1·25 20
347. 60 c. sepia .. .. 12·00 35
348. 84. 1 f. grey and blue .. 15·00 2·10

349. 85. 15 c. green (air) .. 30 35
350. 20 c. red 45 45
351. 90 c. blue .. .. 9·50 12·00

86. Louis Favre. 87. Flag swinging. 89. Vaud.

1932. St. Gotthard Tunnel. 50th Anniv

352. 86. 10 c. brown 8 8
353. – 20 c. red (A. Escher) .. 15 8
354. – 30 c. blue (Emil Welti) 20 35

1932. Children's Fund. Dated "1932"

J 60. 87. 5 c. red and green .. 35 60
J 61. – 10 c. orange 60 60
J 62. – 20 c. red 60 60
J 63. – 30 c. blue .. .. 2·00 2·10

DESIGNS: 10 c. Putting the weight. 20 c. Wrestlers. 30 c. Eugen Huber.

1933. Children's Fund. Dated "1933".

J 64. 89. 5 c. green and buff .. 20 25
J 65. – 10 c. violet and buff .. 20 20
J 66. – 20 c. scarlet and buff .. 30 20
J 67. – 30 c. blue .. .. 1·75 2·40

SWISS GIRL DESIGNS: Berne (10 c.), Ticino (20 c.). 30 c. Father Gregoire Girard.

91. Staubbach Falls. 92. Appenzell. 93. A. von Haller.

1934. Landscapes.

355. 91. 3 c. olive 15 45
356. – 5 c. green 15 5
357. – 10 c. violet 25 5
358. – 15 c. orange 35 30
359. – 20 c. red 35 5
360. – 25 c. brown .. .. 8·00 1·10
361. – 30 c. blue .. .. 19·00 20

DESIGNS: 5 c. Mt. Pilatus. 10 c. Chillon Castle and Dents du Midi. 15 c. Grimsel Pass. 20 c. St. Gotthard Railway. 25 c. Viamala Gorge. 30 c. Rhine Falls near Schaffhausen.

1934. Children's Fund. Dated "1934".

J 68. 92. 5 c. green and buff .. 20 30
J 69. – 10 c. violet and buff .. 30 20
J 70. – 20 c. red and buff .. 30 20
J 71. 93. 30 c. blue .. .. 1·75 2·75

SWISS GIRL DESIGNS: 10 c. Valais. 20 c. Graubunden.

1935. Air. Surch.

362. 43. 10 on 15 c. red & green 4·25 9·00
363. 85. 10 on 15 c. green .. 30 25
364. 10 on 20 c. red 35 65
381. 46. 10 on 65 c. blue & grey 12 12
365. 85. 30 on 90 c. blue .. .. 3·25 4·00
366. 40 on 20 c. red .. .. 2·75 4·75
367. 40 on 90 c. blue .. .. 2·75 4·50

94. Stefano Franscini. 95. Freiburg Cowherd. 96. Staubbach Falls.

1935. Children's Fund. Dated "1935".

J 72. – 5 c. green and buff .. 20 25
J 73. – 10 c. violet and buff .. 25 20
J 74. – 20 c. red and buff .. 30 30
J 75. 94. 30 c. blue .. .. 1·75 2·75

DESIGNS: Costumes of Basel (5 c.), Lucerne (10 c.) and Geneva (20 c.).

1936. National Defence Fund.

368. 95. 10 c.+5 c. purple .. 30 25
369. 20 c.+10 c. red 60 60
370. 30 c.+10 c. blue .. 2·50 3·75

1936. As T 91 but redrawn with figure of value lower down. Various landscapes.

371. 96. 3 c. olive 10 5
372. – 5 c. green 10 5
489. – 5 c. brown 10 5
373b. – 10 c. purple 25 5
373c. – 10 c. brown 10 5
490. – 10 c. green 15 5
374. – 15 c. orange 30 10
375b. – 20 c. red (Railway) .. 3·00 8
375d. – 20 c. red (Lake) .. 12 5
491. – 20 c. brown 20 5
376. – 25 c. brown 40 5
492. – 25 c. red .. .. 1·25 35
377. – 30 c. ultramarine .. 65 5
493. – 30 c. greenish blue .. 6·50 60
378. – 35 c. green 65 20
379. – 40 c. grey .. .. 3·25 5
494. – 40 c. ultramarine .. 7·50 20

DESIGNS: 3 c. to 20 c. (No. 375b) as Nos. 355/9. 20 c. (Nos. 375d, 491) Lake Lugano and Mt. San Salvatore. 25 c. (No. 376), Viamala Gorge. 25 c. (No. 492), National Park. 30 c. Rhine Falls. 35 c. Mt. Neufankel stein and Klus. 40 c. Mt. Santis and Lake Seealp.

97. H. G. Nageli. 100. Mobile P.O.

1936 Children's Fund.

J 76. 97. 5 c. green 25 25
J 77. – 10 c. purple and buff 25 25
J 78. – 20 c. red and buff .. 30 25
J 79. – 30 c. blue and buff .. 3·00 4·75

DESIGNS: Costumes of Neuchatel (10 c.), Schwyz (20 c.) and Zurich (30 c.).

1937. For Mobile P.O. Mail.

380. 100. 10 c. yellow and black 25 10

101. Gen. Henri Dufour. 103. "Youth".

1937. Children's Fund.

J 80. 101. 5 c.+5 c. green .. 12 12
J 81. – 10 c.+5 c. purple .. 20 15
J 82. 103. 20 c.+5 c. red, buff and silver .. 25 15
J 83. – 30 c.+10 c. blue, buff and silver .. 1·10 2·10

DESIGNS: 10 c. Nicholas de Flue. 30 c. as T 103, but girl's head facing other way.

DESIGNS: 30 c., 60 c. Palace of League of Nations (different views). 1 f. International Labour Office.

104. International Labour Office.

1938.

382. 104. 20 c. red and buff .. 20 5
383. – 30 c. blue 35 12
384. – 60 c. brown and buff .. 1·60 25
385. – 1 f. black and buff .. 7·00 4·25

1938. Air. Surch. **1938 "PRO AERO" 75 75** and bars.

386. 45. 75 c. on 50 c. grn. & red † 3·50

108. William Tell's Chapel.

1938. National Fete. Fund for Swiss subjects abroad.

387. 108. 10 c.+10 c. violet on buff 45 25

DESIGNS: 5 f. "Assembly at Stans." 10 f. Polling booth.

109. First Act of Federal Parliament.

1938. Blue or buff paper.

388. 109. 3 f. brown .. .. 7·00 15
389. – 5 f. blue .. .. 4·75 20
390. – 10 f. green .. .. 4·75 55

110. Salomon Gessner. 111. Uri.

1938. Children's Fund. Dated "1938".

J 84. 110. 5 c.+5 c. green .. 12 12
J 85. – 10 c.+5 c. vio. and buff 15 15
J 86. 111. 20 c.+5 c. red and buff 20 15
J 87. – 30 c.+10 c. blue & buff 1·50 2·10

SWISS GIRL DESIGNS as T 111: 10 c. St. Gall. 30 c. Aargau.

112. Symbolical of Swiss Culture. 114. Crossbow and Floral Branch.

1939. National Exn. Zurich. Inscr. "EXPOSITION NATIONALE SUISSE". Inscr. in French (F.), German (G.), or Italian (I.).

	F.		G.		I.	
391. – 10 c. vio.	25	5	25	5	25	5
392. 112. 20 c. red	35	5	35	5	75	10
393. – 30 c. blue & buff	1·75	1·25	1·75	60	1·75	1·25

DESIGNS: 10 c. Group symbolic of Swiss Industry and Agriculture. 30 c. Piz Roseg and Tschirva Glacier.

1939. National Exn., Zurich. Inscr. in French (F.), German (G.) or Italian (I.).

	F.		G.		I.	
394. 114. 5 c. green	35	55	35	55	35	80
395. 10 c. pur.	55	45	55	45	60	55
396. 20 c. red	80	40	80	40	70	65
397. 30 c. blue	1·90	2·50	1·60	1·75	1·90	2·50

115. Laupen Castle.

1939. National Fete. Fund for Destitute Mothers.

398. 115. 10 c.+10 c. brown and grey 35 25

116. Geneva.

1939. Geneva (Red Cross) Convention. 75th Anniv.

399. 116. 20 c. red and buff .. 25 12
400. 30 c. blue and grey .. 45 60

117. Gen. Herzog. 118. Freiburg.

1939. Children's Fund.

J 88. 117. 5 c.+5 c. green .. 12 12
J 89. 118. 10 c.+5 c.vio. and buff 20 12
J 90. – 20 c.+5 c. red & buff 30 15
J 91. – 30 c.+10 c. blue & buff 1·50 2·40

SWISS GIRL DESIGNS: 20 c. Nidwalden. 30 c. Basel.

DESIGNS—Battle Memorials: 5 c. Sempach. 10 c. Giornico. 20 c. Calven.

119. "Les Rangiers".

1940. National Fete and Red Cross Fund. Memorial designs inscr. "FETE NATIONALE 1940" in German (5 c., 20 c.), Italian (10 c.) and French 30 c.).

401. – 5 c.+5 c. blk. & green 25 40
402. – 10 c.+5 c. black & orge. 30 20
403. – 20 c.+5 c. blk. & red .. 2·40 35
404. 119. 30 c.+10 c. blk. & blue 2·10 2·50

120. Gottfried Keller. 121. Thurgau. 122. William Tell.

1940. Children's Fund. Dated "1940".

J 92. 120. 5 c.+5 c. green .. 12 12
J 93. 121. 10 c.+5 c. brn. & buff 20 12
J 94. – 20 c.+5 c. red and buff 25 15
J 95. – 30 c.+10 c. blue & buff 1·50 2·40

SWISS GIRL DESIGNS: 20 c. Soleure. 30 c. Zug.

1941. Historical designs.

405. – 50 c. purple on green .. 5·00 8
406. 122. 60 c. brown on buff .. 6·00 5
407. – 70 c. violet on lilac .. 3·75 25
408. – 80 c. grey on grey .. 95 5
408a. – 80 c. black and violet 80 20
409. – 90 c. red on rose .. 1·10 5
409a. – 90 c. red on buff .. 80 15
410. – 1 f. green on green .. 1·25 5
411. – 1 f. 20 violet on grey 1·40 5
411a. – 1 f. 20 violet on violet 1·10 15
412. – 1 f. 50 blue on buff .. 1·75 5
413. – 2 f. lake on rose .. 2·40 5
413a. – 2 f. lake on buff .. 2·10 20

DESIGNS—(Works of Art): 50 c. "Oath of Union". 70 c. "Kneeling Warrior". 80 c. "Dying Ensign". 90 c. "Standard Bearer". Portraits: 1 f. Col. L. Pfyffer. 1 f. 20, G. Jenatsch. 1 f. 50, Lt.-Gen. F. de Reynold. 2 f. Col. J. Forrer.

123. Ploughing.

1941. Agricultural Development Plan.

414. 123. 10 c. brown and buff .. 10 8

124. The Jungfrau. 125. Chemin Creux near Kussnacht.

1941. Air. Landscapes.

415. 124. 30 c. blue on buff .. 70 5
415a. – 30 c. grey on buff .. 4·75 3·25
416. – 40 c. grey on buff .. 70 5
416a. – 40 c. blue on buff .. 15·00 1·40
417. – 50 c. olive on buff .. 70 12
418. – 60 c. brown on buff .. 95 12
419. – 70 c. violet on buff .. 1·10 25
420. – 1 f. green on buff .. 2·10 40
421. – 2 f. red on buff .. 9·50 1·40
422. – 5 f. blue on buff .. 26·00 5·00

DESIGNS: 40 c. Valais. 50 c. Lake Lenan. 60 c. Alpstein. 70 c. Ticino. 1 f. Lake Lucerne. 2 f. Engadine. 5 f. Churfirsten.

1941. Air. Special (Buochs-Payerne) Flights. No. 420, with **PRO AERO 28.V. 1941** added.

423. – 1 f. green on buff .. 6·50 11·00

1941. National Fete and Foundation of Swiss Confederation. 650th Anniv. Dated "1291 1941".

424. – 10 c.+10 c. blue, red and yellow 40 25
425. 125. 20 c.+10 c. red, brown and buff 40 25

DESIGN: 10 c. Relief Map of Lake Lucerne with Arms of Uri, Schwyz and Unterwalden.

126. Arms of Berne, Masons laying Corner-stone and Knight. 127. Johann Kaspar Lavater (philosopher).

1941. Berne. 750th Anniv.

426. 126. 10 c. blk., yell., red & ol. 10 8

1941. Children's Fund. Bicent. of Birth of Lavater and of Death of Richard (clockmaker). Dated "1941".
J 96. **127.** 5 c.+5 c. green .. 20 12
J 97. – 10 c.+5 c. brn. & buff 25 20
J 98. – 20 c.+5 c. red & buff 30 20
J 99. – 30 c.+10 c. blue .. 1·40 2·10
DESIGNS: 10 c., 20 c. Girls in costumes of Schaffhausen and Obwalden. 30 c. D. J. Richard.

128. "To survive collect salvage".

1942. Salvage Campaign. Inscr. in French (F.), German (G.) or Italian (I.).

	F.	G.	I.
427. **128.** 10 c. brn.	35 10	5 5	4·00 65

INSCRIPTIONS: (G.) Zum Durchhalten/ Alstoffe sammeln"; (I.) "PER RESISTERE/ RACCOGLIETE/LA ROBA VECCHIA".

129. Old Geneva.

130. Soldiers' Memorial at Forch, near Zurich. **131.** Nicholson Riggeubach.

1942. National Fete, National Relief Fund and Bimillenary of Geneva.
428. **129.** 10 c.+10 c. blk. & yell. 40 25
429. **130.** 20 c.+10 c. red & yell. 40 25

1942. Children's Fund. Dated "1942".
J 100. **131.** 5 c.+5 c. green .. 12 20
J 101. – 10 c.+5 c. brn. & buff 20 20
J 102. – 20 c.+5 c. red & buff 25 20
J 103. – 30 c.+10 c. blue .. 1·40 2·10
DESIGNS: 10 c. and 20 c. Girls in costumes of Appenzell-Ausser-Rhoden and Glarus. 30 c. C. E. von der Linth (statesman).

132.

1943. Swiss Cantonal Postage Stamp Cent.
430. **132.** 10 c. (4+6) black .. 8 5

132a. Intragna (Ticino).

1943. National Fete and Youths' Vocational Training Fund. Inscr. "FESTA NAZIONALE 1943".
431. **132a.** 10 c.+10 c. blk. & buff 30 25
432. – 20 c.+10 c. red & buff 40 25
DESIGN: 20 c., 1 f. Federal Palace, Berne.

1943. Air. 30th Anniv. of First Flight across Alps by Oscar Bider. As No. 432, but optd. **PRO AERO 13 VII 1943.**
433. – 1 f. red and buff .. 2·40 4·75

133. Emanuel von Fellenberg. **134.** Silver Thistle. **135.** Apollo of Olympia.

1943. Children's Fund. P. E. von Fellenberg (economist). Death Cent. As T **134**. Dated "1943".
J 104. **133.** 5 c.+5 c. green .. 12 12
J 105. **134.** 10 c.+5 c. olive, buff and grey .. 20 20
J 106. – 20 c.+5 c. red, yellow and pink 45 20
J 107. – 30 c.+10 c. blue and black .. .. 1·60 2·50
FLOWERS: 20 c. "Ladies Slipper". 30 c. Gentian.

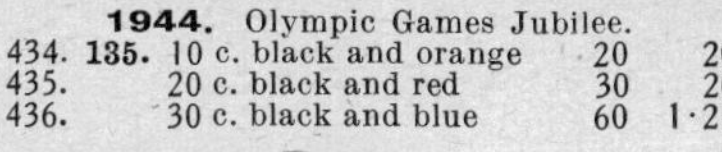
1944. Olympic Games Jubilee.
434. **135.** 10 c. black and orange 20 20
435. 20 c. black and red 30 20
436. 30 c. black and blue 60 1·25

136. Heiden.

DESIGNS: 10 c. St. Jacques on the R. Birs. 20 c. Castle Ruins, Mesocco. 30 c. Basel.

1944. National Fete and Red Cross Fund. Inscr. as in T **136**.
437. **136.** 5 c.+5 c. grn. & buff 25 55
438. – 10 c.+10 c. grey & buff 25 20
439. – 20 c.+10 c. red & buff 25 25
440. – 30 c.+10 c. blue & buff 2·50 5·00

137. D.H.3 Haefeli.

DESIGNS: 20 c. Fokker. 30 c. Lockheed - Orion. 1 f. 50 Douglas D.C.3.

1944. Air. National Air Post. 25th Anniv.
441. **137.** 10 c. brown and olive .. 10 10
442. – 20 c. red and buff .. 15 10
443. – 30 c. blue 30 30
444. – 1 f. 50 vio., pur. & red .. 7·00 9·50

138. Numa Droz. **139.** Symbolical of Faith, Hope and Charity.

1944. Children's Fund. Droz (statesman). Birth Cent. Dated "1944".
J 108. **138.** 5 c.+5 c. green .. 15 12
J 109. – 10 c.+5 c. olive, yellow and green 25 20
J 110. – 20 c.+5 c. red, yellow and grey .. 45 20
J 111. – 30 c.+10 c. blue, grey and blue .. .. 1·60 2·50
DESIGNS: 10 c. Leontopodium alpinum (Edelweiss). 20 c. Lilium Martagon. 30 c. Aquilegia alpina.

1945. War Relief Fund.
445. **139.** 10 c.+10 c. olive, black and grey .. 30 25
446. 20 c.+60 c. red, black and grey .. 1·10 1·75

140. Trans. "Peace to men of good will". **141.** Olive Branch.

1945. Peace stamps. Inscr. "PAX".
447. **140.** 5 c. green and grey .. 8 8
448. 10 c. brown and grey .. 15 8
449. 20 c. red and grey .. 25 8
450. 30 c. blue and grey .. 45 1·10
451. 40 c. orange and grey .. 60 1·75
452. **141.** 50 c. red and buff .. 2·10 6·00
453. – 60 c. grey .. .. 1·90 1·60
454. – 80 c. green and buff .. 4·75 16·00
455. – 1 f. blue and buff .. 7·00 20·00
456. – 2 f. brown and buff .. 19·00 48·00
457. – 3 f. green .. .. 24·00 14·00
458. – 5 f. brown .. .. 95·00 £110
459. – 10 f. violet .. .. 85·00 48·00
DESIGNS—As T **141**: 60 c. Keys. 80 c. Horn of plenty. 1 f. Dove. 2 f. Spade and flowers in ploughed field. 3 f. Crocuses. 5 f. Clasped hands. 10 f. Aged couple.

1945. Red Cross. As T **140**, but red cross and "5+10" in centre of stamp.
460. 5 c.+10 c. green .. 30 30

142. Silk Weaving. **143.** Ludwig Forrer.

1945. National Fete. Inscr. "1 VIII 1945".
461. **142.** 5 c.+5 c. green .. 30 55
462. – 10 c.+10 c. brn. & grey 30 25
463. – 20 c.+10 c. red & buff 35 25
464. – 30 c.+10 c. blue & grey 3·75 9·50
DESIGNS: 10 c., 20 c. Jura and Emmental farmhouses. 30 c. Timbered house.

1945. Children's Fund. Cent. of Births of Ludwig Forrer (statesman) and Susanna Orelli (social reformer). Dated "1945".
J 112. **143.** 5 c.+5 c. green .. 12 12
J 113. – 10 c.+10 c. brown 20 20
J 114. – 20 c.+10 c. red, pink and yellow .. 40 20
J 115. – 30 c.+10 c. blue, mauve and grey .. 1·60 2·75
DESIGNS: 10 c. Susanna Orelli. 20 c. Rosa alpina (Alpine Dog Rose). 30 c. Crocus albiflorus (Spring Crocus).

144. J. H. Pestalozzi. **145.** Instructional Glider.

1946. J. H. Pestalozzi (educational reformer). Birth Bicent.
465. **144.** 10 c. purple 8 5

1946. Air. Special (Lausanne, Lucerne, Locarno) Flights.
466. **145.** 1 f. 50 red and grey 11·00 14·00

146. Cheese-Making.

147. Chalet in Appenzell.

DESIGNS: 10 c. Chalet in Vaud. 30 c. Chalet in Engadine.

1946. National Fete and Fund for Swiss Citizens Abroad. Inscr. "I. VIII 1946".
467. **146.** 5 c.+5 c. green .. 30 55
468. – 10 c.+10 c. brn. & buff 30 25
469. **147.** 20 c.+10 c. red & buff 35 25
470. – 30 c.+10 c. blue & grey 3·00 3·50

148. Rudolf Toepffer. **150.** Douglas DC4 Aircraft, Statue of Liberty and St. Peter's Cathedral, Geneva.

1946. Children's Fund. Cent. of Death of Rudolf Toepffer (author and painter). T **148** and floral designs inscr. "PRO JUVENTUTE 1946".
J 116. **148.** 5 c.+5 c. green .. 15 15
J 117. – 10 c.+10 c. green, grey and orange .. 20 20
J 118. – 20 c.+10 c. red, grey and yellow .. 25 20
J 119. – 30 c.+10 c. blue, grey and mauve .. 1·50 2·40
DESIGNS: 10 c. Narcissus. 20 c. Houseleek. 30 c. Blue Thistle.

1947. Air. 1st Geneva-New York "Swissair" Flight.
472. **150.** 2 f. 50 blue and red 7·50 11·00

151. Rorschach Station.

DESIGNS: 5 c. Platelayers. 20 c. Luen-Castiel station. 30 c. Fluelen station.

1947. Charity. National Fete, and Professional Education of Invalids and Anti-Cancer Funds. Inscr. "I VIII 1947". Arms in red.
473. – 5 c.+5 c. green .. 30 55
474. **151.** 10 c.+10 c. blk. & buff 30 25
475. – 20 c.+10 c. red & buff 35 25
476. – 30 c.+10 c. blue & grey 2·75 3·25

152. "Limmat" First Swiss Steam Locomotive.

DESIGNS: 10 c. Steam freight locomotive. 20 c. Electric train crossing Melide causeway. 30 c. Railway bridge.

1947. Swiss Federal Railways Cent. Dated "1847–1947".
477. **152.** 5 c. green, yell. & black 12 20
478. – 10 c. black and brown 20 5
479. – 20 c. red, buff and lake 25 5
480. – 30 c. grey and blue .. 70 70

153. Jacob Burckhardt. **154.** Sun of St. Moritz. **155.** Ice-hockey.

1947. Children's Fund. T **153** and floral designs inscr. "PRO JUVENTUTE 1947".
J 120. **153.** 5 c.+5 c. green .. 12 12
J 121. – 10 c.+10 c. black, yellow and grey .. 20 15
J 122. – 20 c.+10 c. brown, orange and grey .. 25 20
J 123. – 30 c.+10 c. blue pink and grey .. 1·50 2·40
DESIGNS: 10 c. Alpine Primrose. 20 c. Orange Lily. 30 c. Cyclamen.

1948. Charity. Winter Olympic Games. Inscr. "ST. MORITZ OLYMPIA 1948".
481. **154.** 5 c.+5 c. brown, yellow and green .. 35 70
482. – 10 c.+10 c. blue and brown 35 60
483. **155.** 20 c.+10 c. yellow, black and claret .. 60 80
484. – 30 c.+10 c. black & bl. 1·40 1·90
DESIGNS: 10 c. Snow crystals. 30 c. Skirunner.

156. Symbol of Federal State.

DESIGNS: 5 c. J. R. Wettstein. 10 c. Neuchatel Castle. 20 c. Symbol of Helvetia.

1948. Tercent. of Treaty of Westphalia and Centenaries of the Neuchatel Revolution and Swiss Federation. 5 c. dated "1648 1948", others "1848 1948".
485. – 5 c. green 8 12
486. – 10 c. grey 10 5
487. – 20 c. red 20 5
488. **156.** 30 c. blue and brown .. 40 55

157. Frontier Guard.

158. House in Freiburg.

DESIGNS: 20 c., 30 c. Typical houses in Valais and Ticino respectively.

1948. National Fete and Anti-Tuberculosis Fund. Inscr. "I. VIII 1948". Coat of Arms in red.
495. **157.** 5 c.+5 c. green .. 25 40
496. **158.** 10 c.+10 c. grey .. 25 25
497. – 20 c.+10 c. red & buff 30 25
498. – 30 c.+10 c. bl. & grey 2·40 2·50

159. Gen. U. Wille. **160.** Glider.

1948. Children's Fund. T **159** and floral designs as T **134**. Dated "1948".

J 124. **159.** 5 c.+5 c. purple .. 12 15
J 125. – 10 c.+10 c. green yellow and grey .. 25 15
J 126. – 20 c.+10 c. brown, red and buff .. 35 20
J 127. – 40 c.+10 c. blue yellow and grey .. 1·50 2·10

FLOWERS: 10 c. Foxglove. 20 c. Rust-leaved Alpine rose. 40 c. Lily of Paradise.

1949. Air. Special (La Chaux-de-Fonds–St. Gallen–Lugano) Flights.

499. **160.** 1 f. 50 purple & yellow 13·00 15·00

161. Posthorn.

DESIGNS: 20 c. Mail coach and horses. 30 c. Postal motor coach and trailer.

1949. Federal Post Cent. Inscr. "1849 1949".

500. **161.** 5 c. yell., pink & grey 8 12
501. – 20 c. yellow and violet 25 10
502. – 30 c. yellow and brown 40 1·25

162. Main Motif of U.P.U. Monument, Berne.

DESIGNS: 25 c. Globe and ribbon. 40 c. Globe and pigeons.

1949. U.P.U. 75th Anniv. Inscr. "1874 1949".

503. **162.** 10 c. green 10 5
504. – 25 c. claret .. .. 45 2·75
505. – 40 c. blue 65 95

163. Postman.

DESIGNS: 10 c. 20 c., 40 c. Typical house in the Jura, Lucerne and Prattigau respectively.

1949. National Fete and Youth Fund. T **163** and designs as T **158**, but dated "I. VIII 1949". Arms in red

506. **163.** 5 c.+5 c. purple .. 25 45
507. – 10 c.+10 c. green .. 30 25
508. – 20 c.+10 c. brown .. 35 25
509. – 40 c.+10 c. blue .. 2·75 3·00

164. High-tension Pylons.

165. Sitter Viaducts near St. Gall.

1949. Landscapes.

510. **164.** 3 c. black .. .. 1·90 1·90
511. **165.** 5 c. orange 20 5
512. – 10 c. green 12 5
513. – 15 c. turquoise 20 5
514a. – 20 c. maroon 30 5
515. – 25 c. red 30 5
516. – 30 c. olive 35 5
517. – 35 c. brown 45 12
518. – 40 c. blue .. .. 1·50 5
519. – 50 c. grey .. .. 1·25 5
520. – 60 c. green .. .. 2·10 5
521. – 70 c. violet .. .. 1·25 12

DESIGNS: 10 c. Mountain railway, Rochers de Naye. 15 c. Rotary snow-plough. 20 c. Grimsel reservoir. 25 c. Lake Lugano and Melide Causeway. 30 c. Verbois hydro-electric power station. 35 c. Alpine road (Val d'Anniviers). 40 c. Rhine Harbour, Basel. 50 c. Suspension railway, Santis. 60 c. Railway viaduct, Landwasser. 70 c. Survey mark, Finsteraarhorn.

166. Nicholas Wengi.

167. First Federal Postage Stamps.

168. Putting the Weight.

1949. Children's Fund. T **166** and floral designs inscr. "PRO JUVENTUTE 1949".

J 128. **166.** 5 c.+5 c. lake .. 20 15
J 129. – 10 c.+10 c. grn. and yellow 30 15
J 130. – 20 c.+10 c. brown, blue and orange .. 35 20
J 131. – 40 c.+10 c. blue, mauve and yellow 1·50 2·10

DESIGNS: 10 c. Anemone sulphureous. 20 c. Alpine clematis. 40 c. Superb pink.

1950. National Fete, Red Cross Fund and Cent. of First Federal Postage Stamps. T **167** and designs, as T **168**, inscr. "I VIII 1950". Coat of arms in red.

522. **167.** 5 c.+5 c. black .. 25 30
523. **168.** 10 c.+10 c. green .. 55 30
524. – 20 c.+10 c. olive .. 60 35
525. – 30 c.+10 c. purple .. 3·50 5·00
526. – 40 c.+10 c. blue .. 3·75 4·25

DESIGNS: 20 c. Wrestling. 30 c. Sprinting. 40 c. Rifle shooting.

169. General von Bernegg.

170. Red Admiral.

1950. Children's Fund. Inscr. "PRO JUVENTUTE 1950".

J 132. **169.** 5 c.+5 c. purple .. 15 15
J 133. **170.** 10 c.+10 c. brown, red, black & blue 35 12
J 134. – 20 c.+10 c. black, violet and orange 45 12
J 135. – 30 c.+10 c. brown, grey and mauve .. 3·25 4·75
J 136. – 40 c.+10 c. yellow, brown and blue .. 2·75 3·75

DESIGNS: 20 c. Moth. 30 c. Bee. 40 c. Sulphur butterfly.

171. Arms of Zurich.

172. Valaisan Polka.

DESIGNS—As T **172**: 20 c. Flag swinging. 30 c. "Hornussen" (game). 40 c. Blowing Alphorn.

1951. National Fete, Mother's Fund and Zurich. 6th Cent. Inscr. "I. VIII 1951". Coats of arms in red.

527. **171.** 5 c.+5 c. black .. 25 25
528. **172.** 10 c.+10 c. green .. 60 30
529. 20 c.+10 c. brown .. 60 30
530. 30 c.+10 c. purple .. 3·50 4·25
531. 40 c.+10 c. blue .. 3·75 4·75

173. Johanna Spyr (authoress).

174. "Telegraph".

1951. Children's Fund. T **173** and various insects as T **170**. Inscr. "PRO JUVENTUTE 1951".

J 137. **173.** 5 c.+5 c. claret .. 15 15
J 138. – 10 c.+10 c. bl. & green 25 12
J 139. – 20 c.+10 c. crm. & mag. 35 12
J 140. – 30 c.+10 c. orange, silver and olive .. 2·40 3·25
J 141. – 40 c.+10 c. red, brown and blue 2·50 2·75

INSECTS: 10 c. Dragonfly. 20 c. Swallow-tail butterfly. 30 c. Orange-tip butterfly. 40 c. Emperor moth.

1952. Cent. of Swiss Communications. Dated "1852 1952".

532. **174.** 5 c. orange 30 25
533. – 10 c. green ("Telephone") .. 60 8
534. – 20 c. pur. ("Radio") 75 8
535. – 40 c. bl. ("Television") 2·00 2·10

175. Arms of Glarus Zandug.

176. River Doubs.

1952. Culture Funds and 600th Anniv. of Glarus and Zug joining Confederation. Inscr. "PRO PATRIA 1952".

536. **175.** 5 c.+5 c. red & black 25 30
537. **176.** 10 c.+10 c. green .. 30 20
538. – 20 c.+10 c. claret .. 35 20
539. – 30 c.+10 c. brown .. 1·90 2·50
540. – 40 c.+10 c. blue .. 2·00 2·40

DESIGNS—As T **176**. 20 c. St. Gothard Lake. 30 c. River Moesa. 40 c. Marjelen Lake.

177. "Portrait of a Boy" (Anker).

178. Zurich Airport.

1952. Children's Fund. T **177** and insects as T **170**. Inscr. "PRO JUVENTUTE 1952".

J 142. **177.** 5 c.+5 c. lake .. 15 15
J 143. – 10 c.+10 c. red, black and green .. 35 12
J 144. – 20 c.+10 c. cream, black and mauve 35 12
J 145. – 30 c.+10 c. blue, black and brown 2·40 2·75
J 146. – 40 c.+10 c. buff, brown and blue .. 2·75 2·75

INSECTS: 10 c. Ladybird. 20 c. Marbled White butterfly. 30 c. Chalkhill Blue butterfly. 40 c. Oak Eggar moth.

1953. Emigrants' Fund and 600th Anniv. of Berne joining Confederation. 5 c. as T **175** but Arms of Berne and inscr. "BERN 1353"; others as T **176** but inscr. "PRO PATRIA 1953".

541. 5 c.+5 c. red and black .. 25 30
542. 10 c.+10 c. green 30 20
543. 20 c.+10 c. claret .. 30 20
544. 30 c.+10 c. brown .. 1·90 2·50
545. 40 c.+10 c. blue .. .. 1·90 2·50

DESIGNS: 10 c. Rapids, R. Reuss. 20 c. Lac Sihl. 30 c. Aqueduct, Bisse. 40 c. Lake Leman.

1953. Inaug. of Zurich Airport.

546. **178.** 40 c. blue, grey & red 3·00 4·00

179. Alpine Postal Coach and Winter Landscape.

DESIGN: 20 c. Alpine postal coach and Summer landscape.

1953. For Mobile P.O. Mail.

547. **179.** 10 c. yell., grey & green 5 5
548. – 20 c. yellow, lake & red 12 5

1953. Children's Fund. Portraits as T **177**. and insects as T **170**. Inscr. "PRO JUVENTUTE 1953".

J 147. 5 c.+5 c. lake 15 15
J 148. 10 c.+10 c. pink, sepia and green .. 35 12
J 149. 20 c.+10 c. chocolate, buff and mauve .. 35 12
J 150. 30 c.+10 c. black, red and olive .. 2·40 2·75
J 151. 40 c.+10 c. blue .. 2·75 3·00

DESIGNS: 5 c. "Portrait of a girl" (Anker). 10 c. Nun moth. 20 c. Camberwell Beauty butterfly. 30 c. Purple Longicorn beetle. 40 c. F. Hodler (self-portrait).

180. Ear of Wheat, Leaf and Flower.

181. Rhine Map and Steering Wheel.

1954. Publicity Series. Inscr. "1954".

549. **180.** 10 c. yell., red & green 25 8
550. – 20 c. buff, black, blue and lake 95 8
551. **181.** 25 c. green, blue & red 1·50 1·75
552. – 40 c. blue, yell. & black 1·90 1·40

DESIGNS—HORIZ. 20 c. Winged spoon. 40 c. Football and world map.

These publicize the Agricultural Exn., Lucerne, Cookery Exn., Berne. 50th Anniv. of R. Rhine Navigation and World Football Championship respectively.

182. Flower, Dents du Midi and opening bars of "Swiss Hymn".

1954. Death Cent. of Father Zwyssig, composer of "Swiss Hymn" (5 c.) and Social Service Funds. T **182** and designs as T **176** inscr. "PRO PATRIA 1954".

553. 5 c.+5 c. grey 25 25
554. 10 c.+10 c. green 30 20
555. 20 c.+10 c. purple & brn. 30 20
556. 30 c.+10 c. brown .. 1·90 2·50
557. 40 c.+10 c. blue .. 1·90 2·50

DESIGNS: 10 c. Lake of Neuchatel. 20 c. Maggia River. 30 c. Taubenloch Gorge Waterfall, Schuss River. 40 c. Lake of Sils.

1954. Children's Fund. Portrait as T **173** and insects as T **170**. Inscr. "PRO JUVENTUTE 1954".

J 152. 5 c.+5 c. chocolate .. 15 12
J 153. 10 c.+10 c. sepia, blue, orange and green .. 30 12
J 154. 20 c.+10 c. black, yellow, brown and magenta .. 35 20
J 155. 30 c.+10 c. sepia, yellow, grey and violet .. 2·75 3·00
J 156. 40 c.+10 c. black, yellow, red and blue .. 2·75 3·25

DESIGNS: 5 c. "Jeremias Gotthelf" (A. Bitzius). 10 c. Garden Tiger moth. 20 c. Buff-tailed bumble-bee. 30 c. "Ascalaphus libelluloides" (fly). 40 c. Swallowtail butterfly.

183. Lausanne Cathedral.

184. Alphorn Blower.

1955. Publicity issue. Inscr. "1955".

558. **183.** 5 c. black, red, yellow and brown 20 12
559. – 10 c. yellow, red, bistre and emerald .. 20 8
560. **184.** 20 c. sepia and red .. 60 8
561. – 40 c. rose, black & blue 1·50 95

DESIGNS: 10 c. Vaud girl's hat. 40 c. Car steering-wheel. These publicize the National Philatelic Exn., Lausanne, the Wine-growers' Festival, Vevey, the Alpine Herdsmen and Costume Festival, Interlaken, and the 25th Int. Motor Show, Geneva, respectively.

185. Federal Institute of Technology, Zurich.

DESIGNS: 10 c. River Saane. 20 c. Lake Aegeri. 30 c. Lake Grappelen. 40 c. Lake of Bienne.

1955. Pro Patria. Funds for Mountain Population and Art Research. No C 562 commemorates Cent. of Federal Institute of Technology. T **185** and designs as T **176** but inscr. "PRO PATRIA 1955".

562. 5 c.+5 c. slate 25 30
563. 10 c.+10 c. green 30 20
564. 20 c.+10 c. claret .. 30 20
565. 30 c.+10 c. brown .. 2·10 2·10
566. 40 c.+10 c. blue .. .. 2·10 2·10

1955. Children's Fund. Portrait as T **173**, and insects as T **170**. Inscr. "PRO JUVENTUTE 1955".

J 157. 5 c.+5 c. lake 15 12
J 158. 10 c.+10 c. lake, sepia, yellow, blue and green 25 12
J 159. 20 c.+10 c. black, blue, yellow and red .. 40 15
J 160. 30 c.+10 c. blk., red cream and brown .. 2·25 2·50
J 161. 40 c.+10 c blk. red & bl. 2·50 2·50

DESIGNS: 5 c. C. Pictet-de-Rochemont. 10 c. Peacock butterfly. 20 c. Great Horntail. 30 c. Yellow Bear moth. 40 c. Apollo butterfly.

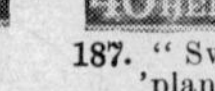

186. "Road Safety".

187. "Swissair" 'planes.

1956. Publicity Issue. Inscr. "1956".
567. – 5 c. yell., black & olive 25 15
568. – 10 c. red, green & grey 30 8
569. **186.** 20 c. yell., black & red 60 12
570. **187.** 40 c. blue and red .. 1·50 80
DESIGNS: 5 c. First postal motor coach. 10 c. Train emerging from Simplon Tunnel and Stockalper Palace. These publicize the 50th Anniv. of Postal Motor Coach Service, 50th Anniv. of Opening of Simplon Tunnel, Road Safety and the 25th Anniv. of "Swissair" Airline respectively.

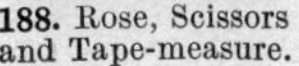
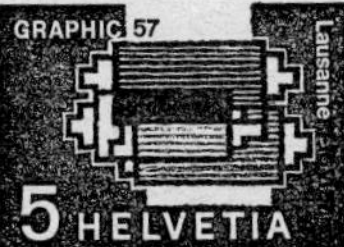

188. Rose, Scissors and Tape-measure.
189. Printing Machine's Inking Rollers.

1956. Pro Patria. Swiss Women's Fund T **188** and designs as T **176** but inscr. "PRO PATRIA 1956".
571. **188.** 5 c.+5 c. turquoise .. 25 30
572. – 10 c.+10 c. green .. 30 20
573. – 20 c.+10 c. lake .. 30 20
574. – 30 c.+10 c. brown .. 2·10 1·75
575. – 40 c.+10 c. blue .. 2·10 1·75
DESIGNS: 10 c. Rhone at St. Maurice. 20 c. Katsensee. 30 c. Rhine at Trin. 40 c. Walensee.

1956. Children's Fund. Portrait as T **173** and insects as T **170**. Inscr. "PRO JUVENTUTE 1956".
J 162. 5 c.+5 c. maroon .. 15 12
J 163. 10 c.+10 c. red, pink & green 25 12
J 164. 20 c.+10 c. violet, sepia, yellow and red .. 35 12
J 165. 30 c.+10 c. blue & yellow 1·60 2·10
J 166. 40 c.+10 c. yellow, sepia and black .. 1·90 2·10
DESIGNS: 5 c. Carlo Moderno (architect). 10 c. Burnet Moth. 20 c. Purple Emperor (butterfly). 30 c. Blue Beetle. 40 c. Large White (butterfly).

1957. Publicity Issue. Inscr. "1957".
576. **189.** 5 c. red, yellow, green, blue, black and grey 12 10
577. – 10 c. brn., grn. & turq. 1·10 5
578. – 20 c. grey and red .. 35 10
579. – 40 c. olive, purple, green and blue .. .. 1·25 70
DESIGNS: 10 c. Electric train crossing bridge. 20 c. Civil Defence shield and arms. 40 c. Munatius Plancus, Basel and Rhine. These publicize the "Graphic 57" International Exhibition, Lausanne, the 75th Anniv. of St. Gotthard Railway, Civil Defence, and the Bimillenary of Basel respectively.

190. Red Cross and Swiss Arms.
191. Symbolical of Charity.

1957. Pro Patria. Swiss Red Cross and National Cancer League Funds. Cross in red.
580. **190.** 5 c.+5 c. red & grey 25 25
581. **191.** 10 c.+10 c. lilac & grn. 30 20
582. 20 c.+10 c. grey & red 30 20
583. 30 c.+10 c. lav. & brn. 1·75 1·90
584. 40 c.+10 c. ochre & bl. 1·75 1·90

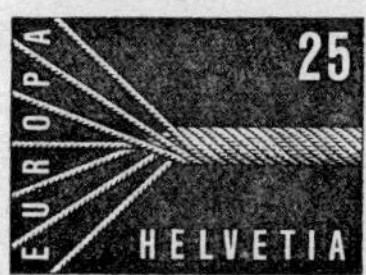

192. Symbol of Unity.
193. Nyon Castle.

1957. European Unity.
585. **192.** 25 c. red 45 15
586. 40 c. blue .. .. 1·90 10

1957. Children's Fund. Portrait as T **173** and insects as T **170**. Inscr. "PRO JUVENTUTE 1957".
J 167. 5 c.+5 c. claret.. .. 25 12
J 168. 10 c.+10 c. buff, yellow, brown and olive .. 25 12
J 169. 20 c.+10 c. yellow, brown and magenta .. 30 12
J 170. 30 c.+10 c. green & lake 1·50 1·60
J 171. 40 c.+10 c. brown, red, sepia and blue .. 1·60 1·50
DESIGNS—VERT. 5 c. L. Euler (mathematician). 10 c. Clouded Yellow butterfly. 20 c. Magpie butterfly. 30 c. Rose Chafer (beetle). 40 c. Red Underwing moth.

1958. Publicity Issue. Inscr. "1958".
587. **193.** 5 c. violet, buff & olive 12 10
588. – 10 c. myrtle, red & grn. 12 5
589. – 20 c. red, lilac & verm. 30 5
590. 40 c. indigo, red & blue 1·10 55
DESIGNS: 10 c. Woman's head with ribbons. 20 c. Crossbow. 40 c. Salvation Army bonnet. These publicize the Bimillenary of Nyon, the Saffa Exhibition, Zurich, the 25th Anniv. of crossbow as symbol of Swiss manufacture and the 75th Anniv. of Salvation Army in Switzerland respectively.

194. "Needy Mother".
195. Fluorite.

1958. Pro Patria. For Needy Mothers, T **194** and designs showing minreals, rocks and fossils as T **195**. Inscr. "PRO PATRIA 1958".
591. 5 c.+5 c. claret 20 25
592. 10 c.+10 c. yell., grn. & blk. 25 20
593. 20 c.+10 c. bistre, red & blk. 25 20
594. 30 c.+10 c. pur., ochre & blk. 1·50 1·75
595. 40 c.+10 c. turq., bl. & blk. 1·50 1·50
DESIGNS: 20 c. Ammonite. 30 c. Garnet. 40 c. Rock crystal.

196. Atomic Symbol.

1958. 2nd U.N. Atomic Conf., Geneva.
596. **196.** 40 c. red, blue & cream 35 40

197. Albrecht von Haller (naturalist).
198. Pansy.

1958. Children's Fund. T **197** and flowers as T **198**. Inscr. "PRO JUVENTUTE 1958".
J 172. **197.** 5 c.+5 c. claret .. 15 12
J 173. **198.** 10 c.+10 c. yellow, brown and green .. 25 12
J 174. – 20 c.+10 c. yellow. pink, green and lake 35 12
J 175. – 30 c.+10 c. yellow, blue, green & bistre 1·40 1·40
J 176. – 40 c.+10 c. yellow grey, green and blue 1·50 1·40
FLOWERS: 20 c. Chinese aster. 30 c. Morning glory. 40 c. Christmas rose.

199. Modern Transport.
200. "Swiss Citizens Abroad".

1959. Publicity Issue. Inscr. "1959".
597. 5 c. red, green, yell., black and slate-purple .. 12 8
598. 10 c. yellow, grey & green 20 5
599. 20 c. blue, black, brn. & red 60 8
600. 50 c. blue, violet & lt. blue 90 60
DESIGNS: 5 c. T **199** (opening of "The Swiss House of Transport and Communications"). 10 c. Lictor's fasces of the Coat-of-Arms of St. Gallen and posthorn (NABAG—National Philatelic Exn., St. Gallen). 20 c. Owl, hare and fish (Protection of Animals). 50 c. J. Calvin, Th. de Beze and University building (4th cent. of University of Geneva).

1959. Pro Patria. For Swiss Citizens Abroad. T **200** and other designs showing minerals, rocks and fossils as T **195**, and inscr. "PRO PATRIA 1959".
601. 5 c.+5 c. red and grey .. 20 25
602. 10 c.+10 c. red, orange, yellow-green and black 25 20
603. 20 c.+10 c. turq., yellow, magenta and black .. 25 20
604. 30 c.+10 c. violet, brown and black .. .. 1·25 1·25
605. 40 c.+10 c. grey-blue, blue and black .. .. 1·25 1·25
DESIGNS: 10 c. Agate. 20 c. Tourmaline 30 c. Amethyst. 40 c. Fossilized giant salamander.

201. "Europa".
202. "Campaign against Cancer".

1959. Europa.
606. **201.** 30 c. red 30 8
607. 50 c. blue 40 10

1959. European P.T.T. Conf., Montreux. Optd. **REUNION DES PTT D'EUROPE 1959.**
608. **201.** 30 c. red .. .. 1·90 1·90
609. 50 c. blue .. .. 1·90 1·90

1959. Children's Fund. Portrait as T **197** and flowers as T **198**. Inscr. "PRO JUVENTUTE 1959".
J 177. 5 c.+5 c. claret.. .. 12 12
J 178. 10 c.+10 c. yellow, brown, green and blue-green 20 12
J 179. 20 c.+10 c. red, green and purple 25 12
J 180. 30 c.+10 c. yellow, orange, green and olive .. 1·40 1·40
J 181. 50 c.+10 c. magenta, yellow green, grey and blue 1·50 1·40
DESIGNS: 5 c. Kari Hilty. 10 c. Marsh marigold. 20 c. Poppy. 30 c. Nasturtium. 50 c. Sweet pea.

1960. Publicity Issue. Inscr. "1460-1960" (20 c.) or "1960" (50 c., 75 c.).
610. 10 c. red and green .. 45 5
611. 20 c. yell., blk., brn. & red 60 8
612. 50 c. yellow, black and blue 55 70
613. 75 c. red, black and blue .. 1·40 1·40
DESIGNS: 10 c. T **202** (50th Anniv. Swiss League for Cancer Control). 20 c. Charter and sceptre (5th Cent. of Basel University). 50 c. "Uprooted tree" (World Refugee Year). 75 c. Douglas "DC-8" jet airliner ("Swissair enters the jet age").

203. 17th-century Cantonal Messenger from Fribourg.
204. Symbols of Charitable Institutions.

1960. Postal History and "Architectural Monuments". 1st Series.
614. **203.** 5 c. blue 5 5
615. – 10 c. blue-green .. 5 5
616. – 15 c. brown 8 5
617. – 20 c. magenta .. 12 5
618. – 25 c. emerald .. 20 5
619. – 30 c. red 25 5
620. – 35 c. orange-red .. 30 25
621. – 40 c. violet .. 30 5
622. – 50 c. blue 35 5
623p. – 60 c. red 40 5
624. – 70 c. orange 70 45
625. – 75 c. blue 35 12
626p. – 80 c. maroon 40 5
627p. – 90 c. olive-green .. 55 5
628p. – 1 f. buff 60 5
629. – 1 f. 20 brown-red .. 65 5
632. – 1 f. 30 chestnut on lilac 65 12
630. – 1 f. 50 emerald .. 70 20
633. – 1 f. 70 purple on lilac.. 80 12
631. – 2 f. blue .. .. 6·00 60
634. – 2 f. 20 bl.-grn. on grn. 95 30
635. – 2 f. 80 orge. on orange 1·00 25
DESIGNS—HORIZ. 10 c. 15th-century Cantonal messenger from Schwyz. 15 c. 17th-century mule-driver. 20 c. 19th-century mounted postman. 1 f. Fribourg Town Hall. 1 f. 20, Basel Gate, Solothurn. 1 f. 50, Ital Reding's house, Schwyz. 1 f. 70, 2 f., 2 f. 20 Abbey Church, Einsiedeln. VERT. 25 c. Lausanne Cathedral. 30 c. Grossmunster, Zurich. 35 c., 1 f. 30, Woodcutters Guildhall, Bienne. 40 c. St. Peter's Cathedral, Geneva. 50 c. Spalentor (gate), Basle. 60 c. Clock Tower, Berne. 70 c. Collegiate Church of St. Peter and St. Stephen, Bellinzona. 75 c. Kapellbrucke (bridge) and Water Tower, Lucerne. 80 c. St. Gall Cathedral. 90 c. Munot Fort, Schaffhausen. 2 f. 80, As 70 c. but redrawn without bell-tower.
See also Nos. 698/713.

1960. Pro Patria. For Swiss Youth. T **204** and other designs showing minerals, rocks and fossils as T **195** and inscr. "PRO PATRIA 1960".
636. 5 c.+5 c. brown, pale blue, blue and sepia 25 25
637. 10 c.+10 c. salmon, green and black.. .. 30 20
638. 20 c.+10 c. yellow, purple and black.. .. 30 20
639. 30 c.+10 c. blue, brown and black.. .. 1·60 1·40
640. 50 c.+10 c. gold and blue 1·60 1·40
DESIGNS: 5 c. Smoky quartz. 10 c. Orthoclase (feldspar). 20 c. Gryphaea (fossilized shellfish). 30 c. Azurite. 50 c. T **204** ("50 Years of National Day Collection").

1960. Europa. As T **279** of Belgium, but size 33×23 mm.
642. 30 c. red 40 10
643. 50 c. blue 40 15

1960. Children's Fund. Portrait as T**197** and flowers as T **198**. Inscr. "PRO JUVENTUTE 1960".
J 182. 5 c.+5 c. blue 15 12
J 183. 10 c.+10 c. yellow, drab and green 20 12
J 184. 20 c.+10 c. green, sepia and magenta .. 30 12
J 185. 30 c.+10 c. green, black and brown .. 1·40 1·50
J 186. 50 c.+10 c. green & blue 1·40 1·60
DESIGNS: 5 c. Alexandre Calame (painter). 10 c. Dandelion. 20 c. Phlox. 30 c. Larkspur. 50 c. Thorn apple.

205. "Aid for Development".
206. "Cultural Works of Eternity".

1961. Publicity Issue. Inscr. "1961".
644. 5 c. red, turquoise and grey 25 5
645. 10 c. yellow and turquoise 25 5
646. 20 c. multicoloured .. 40 5
647. 50 c. multicoloured .. 90 60
DESIGNS: 5 c. T **205** ("Aid to countries in process of development"). 10 c. Circular emblem ("Hyspa" Exhibition of 20th-century Hygiene, Gymnastics and Sport, Berne). 20 c. Hockey stick (World and European Ice-hockey Championships, Geneva and Lausanne). 50 c. Map of Switzerland with telephone centres as wiring diagram (Inauguration of Swiss Full-automatic Telephone Service).

1961. Pro Patria. For Swiss Cultural Works, T **206** and other designs showing minerals. rocks and fossils as T **195** and inscr. "PROPATRIA 1961".
648. 5 c.+5 c. blue 20 20
649. 10 c.+10 c. purple, green and black 30 20
650. 20 c.+10 c. red, grey-blue and black 30 20
651. 30 c.+10 c. turquoise, orange and black .. 1·10 1·10
652. 50 c.+10 c. bistre, blue and black .. .. 1·10 1·10
DESIGNS: 10 c. Fluorite. 20 c. Petrified fish. 30 c. Lazulite. 50 c. Petrified fern.

207. Doves.
208. St. Matthew.

1961. Europa.
653. **207.** 30 c. red 25 8
654. 50 c. blue 30 20

1961.
655. **208.** 3 f. magenta 95 5
656. – 5 f. blue .. .. 1·50 8
657. – 10 f. brown .. .. 3·00 40
658. – 20 f. red .. .. 5·50 1·40
WOOD-CARVINGS: 5 f. St. Mark. 10 f. St. Luke. 20 f. St. John.

1961. Children's Fund. Portrait as T **197** and figures as T **198**. Inscr. "PRO JUVENTUTE 1961".
J 187. 5 c.+5 c. blue 10 10
J 188. 10 c.+10 c. yellow, red and green 15 12
J 189. 20 c.+10 c. yellow, grey, green and red .. 20 10
J 190. 30 c.+10 c. violet, yellow, green & purple 75 95
J 191. 50 c.+10 c. yellow, green, brown and blue 75 95
DESIGNS: 5 c. J. Furrer (First President of Swiss Confederation). 10 c. Sunflower. 20 c. Lily-of-the-Valley. 30 c. Iris. 50 c. Silverweed.

209. W.H.O. Emblem and Mosquito.

1962. Publicity Issue.
659. 5 c. red, buff, black & blue 25 8
660. 10 c. bistre, purple & green 25 5
661. 20 c. slate, grey, bis. & mve. 40 5
662. 50 c. green, magenta & blue 70 60
DESIGNS: 5 c. Electric Train (Introduction of TEE Trains). 10 c. Oarsman (World Rowing Championship, Lucerne). 20 c. Jungfraujoch and Monch (50th Anniv. of Jungfraujoch Railway Station). 50 c. T **209** (Malaria Eradication).

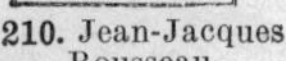

210. Jean-Jacques Rousseau.

211. Silver half taler (Obwalden).

1962. Pro Patria. For Swiss Old People's Homes and Cultural Works. Fine arts and useful arts series. Inscr. "PRO PATRIA 1962".
663. **210.** 5 c.+5 c. blue .. 12 12
664. **211.** 10 c.+10 c. grey, blue and green 25 12
665. – 20 c.+10 c. grey, yellow and red .. 25 12
666. – 30 c.+10 c. grey, myrtle and orange .. 80 80
667. – 50 c.+10 c. grey, lilac and blue .. 90 90
COINS—As T **211**: 20 c. Gold ducat (Schwyz). 30 c. Batzen (Uri). 50 c. Batzen (Nidwalden).

212. Europa "Tree".

1962. Europa.
668. **212.** 30 c. orange, yell. & brn. 35 30
669. 50 c. blue, turq. & brn. 45 40

213. "Child's World".

214. Mother and Child.

1962. Children's Fund. 50th Anniv. of Pro Juventute Foundation. T **213** and similar designs inscr. "1912-62" and T **214**.
J 192. – 5 c. + 5 c. rose, grn., yellow & slate-violet 10 12
J 193. **213.** 10 c.+10 c. red & grn. 15 12
J 194. **214.** 20 c. + 10 c. green, sepia, pink and red 30 12
J 195. – 30 c. + 10 c. red, magenta & yellow 80 80
J 196. – 50 c. + 10 c. yellow, brown and blue .. 95 95
DESIGNS—As T **213**: 5 c. Apple blossom. 30 c. "Child's World" (child in meadow). 50 c. Forsythia.

215. Campaign Emblem (Freedom from Hunger).

1963. Publicity Issue.
670. – 5 c. brn., red & grey-bl. 40 8
671. – 10 c. red, grey & green 35 5
672. – 20 c. lake, red and grey 40 5
673. **215.** 30 c. yell., ochre & grn. 80 65
674. – 50 c. red, silver & blue 70 40
675. – 50 c. grey, rose, yellow and blue 80 40
DESIGNS: 5 c. Boy scout (50th Anniv. of Swiss Boy Scout League). 10 c. Badge (Swiss Alpine Club Cent.). 20 c. Luegelkinn Viaduct (50th Anniv. of Loetschberg Railway). No. 674, Jubilee emblem (Red Cross Cent.). No. 675, Hotel des Postes, Paris, 1863 (Paris Postal Conference).

216. Dr. Anna Heer.

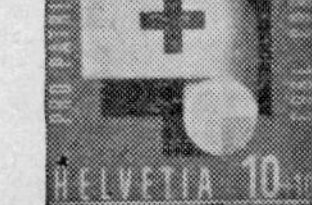

217. Roll of Bandage.

1963. Pro Patria. For Swiss Medical and Refugee Aid. T **216** and other designs as T **217** showing Red Cross activities. Inscr. "PRO PATRIA 1963".
676. 5 c.+5 c. blue 10 10
677. 10 c.+10 c. red, grey and green 12 12
678. 20 c.+10 c. red, grey, violet and pink 15 12
679. 30 c.+10 c. red, carmine, sepia and orange 65 75
680. 50 c.+10 c. red, indigo & bl. 70 70
DESIGNS: 20 c. Gift parcel. 30 c. Blood plasma. 50 c. Red Cross brassard.

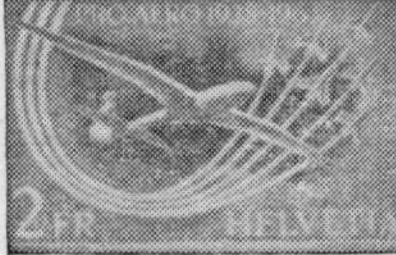

218. Glider and Jet Aircraft.

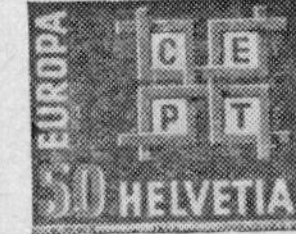

219. "Co-operation".

1963. Air. "Pro Aero" Foundation. 25th Anniv. Berne-Locarno or Langenbruck-Berne (helicopter feeder) Special Flights.
681. **218.** 2 f. yellow, red, blue and silver .. .. 2·50 2·10

1963. Europa.
682. **219.** 50 c. ochre and blue .. 60 25

220. Exhibition Emblem.

221. Great St. Bernard Tunnel.

1963. Swiss National Exn. Inscr. as in T **220**.
683. **220.** 10 c. green and sepia .. 30 5
684. 20 c. red and sepia .. 35 5
685. – 50 c. blue and red .. 35 35
686. – 75 c. violet and red .. 35 35
DESIGNS: 50 c. "Outlook" (emblem on globe and smaller globe). 75 c. "Insight" (emblem on large globe).

1963. Children's Fund. Portrait as T **197** and flowers as T **198**. Inscr. "PRO JUVENTUTE 1963".
J 197a. 5 c.+5 c. blue 10 12
J 198. 10 c.+10 c. yellow, brown, blue and green .. 15 30
J 199. 20 c.+10 c. orange, green and red 20 35
J 200. 30 c.+10 c. black, green and brown 65 60
J 201. 50 c.+10 c. purple, green and black .. 70 70
DESIGNS: 5 c. "Portrait of a Boy" (Anker). 10 c. Oxeye daisy. 20 c. Geranium. 30 c. Cornflower. 50 c. Carnation.

1964. Publicity Issue.
687. 5 c. blue, red and olive .. 12 5
688. 10 c. turquoise and blue .. 12 5
689. 20 c. multicoloured .. 25 5
690. 50 c. multicoloured .. 60 40
DESIGNS: 5 c. T **221** (Opening of Great St. Bernard Road Tunnel). 10 c. Ancient "god of the waters" (Protection of water supplies). 20 c. Swiss soldiers of 1864 and 1964 (Cent. of Swiss Association of Non-commissioned Officers). 50 c. Standards of Geneva and Swiss Confederation (Arrival of Swiss in Geneva, 150th Anniv.).

222. J. G. Bodmer (inventor).

223. Europa "Flower".

223a. Lausanne Cathedral.

1964. Pro Patria. For Swiss Mountain Aid and Cultural Funds. T **222** and vert. designs of Swiss coins as T **211**. Inscr. "PRO PATRIA 1964".
691. 5 c.+5 c. blue 8 8
692. 10 c.+10 c. drab, blk. & grn. 12 12
693. 20 c.+10 c. grey-blue black and magenta .. 15 12
694. 30 c.+10 c. grey-blue, black and orange .. 45 45
695. 50 c.+10 c. olive, brown and blue 55 55
COINS: 10 c. Copper (Zurich). 20 c. "Doppeldicken" (Basle). 30 c. Silver taler (Geneva). 50 c. half gold florin (Berne).

1964. Europa.
696. **223.** 20 c. red 12 5
697. 50 c. blue 30 12

1964. "Architectural Monuments". 2nd Series.
698. 5 c. cerise 5 5
699. 10 c. ultramarine 5 5
700. 15 c. chestnut 5 5
701. 20 c. green 8 5
702. 30 c. vermilion 10 5
703. 50 c. blue 15 5
704. 70 c. brown 25 5
705. 1 f. green 35 5
706. 1 f. 20 lake 40 5
707. 1 f. 30 ultramarine .. 80 25
708. 1 f. 50 emerald 50 10
709. 1 f. 70 red .. .. .. 1·10 20
710. 2 f. orange 65 15
711. 2 f. 20 green .. .. 1·60 30
712. 2 f. 50 green 80 20
713. 3 f. 50 purple .. .. 1·25 25
DESIGNS: As T **223a**: HORIZ. 5 c. Lenzburg Castle. 10 c. Freuler Mansion, Nafels. 15 c. Mauritius Church, Appenzell. 20 c. Planta House, Samedan. 30 c. Town Square, Gais. 50 c. Neuchatel Castle and Collegiate Church. VERT. 70 c. Lussy "Hochus", Wolfenschiessen. 1 f. Riva San Vitale Church. 1 f. 20, Payerne Abbey Church. 1 f. 30, St. Pierre-de-Clages Church. 1 f. 50, Gateway, Porrentruy. 1 f. 70, Frauenfeld Castle. 2 f. Castle Seedorf (Uri). 2 f. 20, Thomas Tower and Arch, Liestal. 2 f. 50, St. Oswald's Church, Zug. 3 f. 50, Benedictine Abbey, Engelberg.

1964. Children's Fund. Portrait as T **197** and flowers as T **198** Inscr. "PRO JUVENTUTE 1964".
J 202. 5 c.+5 c. blue 10 10
J 203. 10 c.+10 c. orange, yellow and green 12 10
J 204. 20 c.+10 c. rose, green and red 15 10
J 205. 30 c.+10 c. purple, green and brown 30 30
J 206 50 c.+10 c. multicoloured 40 40
DESIGNS: 5 c. "Portrait of a Girl" (Anker). 10 c. Daffodil. 20 c. Rose. 30 c. Red clover. 50 c. White water lily.

224. Swiss 5 r. Stamp of 1854 with "Lozenge" Cancellation.

1965. Publicity Issue.
714. – 5 c. black, red and blue 8 5
715. **224.** 10 c. brown, blue & grn. 12 5
716. – 20 c. multicoloured .. 20 5
717. – 50 c. red, black & blue 35 30
DESIGNS, etc.: 5 c. Nurse and patient ("Nursing"). 10 c. (NABRA, 1965—National Stamp Exn., Berne). 20 c. WAC officer (Women's Army Corps. 25th Anniv.). 50 c. World Telecommunications map (I.T.U. Cent.).

225. Father T. Florentini.

226. Fish-tailed Goose ("Evil").

1965. Pro Patria. For Swiss Abroad and Art Research. Inscr. "PRO PATRIA 1965".
719. **225.** 5 c.+5 c. blue .. 5 5
720. **226.** 10 c.+10 c. mult. .. 10 8
721. – 20 c.+10 c. mult. .. 15 10
722. – 30 c.+10 c. brown & bl. 30 30
723. – 50 c.+10 c. bl. & chest. 35 35
DESIGNS—As T **226**: Ceiling paintings in St. Martin's Church, Zillis (Grisons). 20 c. One of Magi journeying to Herod. 30 c. Fisherman. 50 c. The temptation of Christ.

227. Swiss Emblem and Arms of Cantons.

1965. Entry of Valais, Neuchatel and Geneva into Confederation. 150th Anniv.
724. **227.** 20 c. multicoloured .. 15 5

228. Matterhorn.

229. Europa "Sprig".

1965. Mobile P.O. Issue.
725. **228.** 10 c. black, grey, green and red 10 5
726. 30 c. black, grey, red and green 30 30
The 30 c. is inscr. "CERVIN".

1965. Europa.
727. **129.** 50 c. green and blue .. 25 20

230. I.T.U. Emblem and Satellites.

231. Figure-skating.

1965. I.T.U. Cent. Congress, Montreux. Multicoloured.
728. 10 c. Type **230** 10 5
729. 30 c. Symbols of world telecommunications .. 30 30

1965. World Figure-skating Championships, Davos.
730. **231.** 5 c. multicoloured .. 5 5

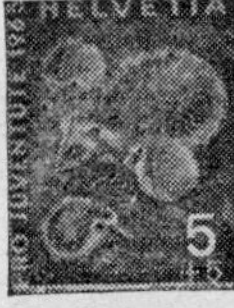

232. Hedgehogs.

233. Kingfisher.

1965. Children's Fund. Animals. Inscr. "PRO JUVENTUTE 1965".
J 207. **232.** 5 c.+5 c. ochre chocolate and red .. 8 8
J 208. – 10 c.+10 c. ochre brown, black & blue 10 10
J 209. – 20 c.+10 c. blue, brown and chestnut 15 10
J 210. – 30 c.+10 c. blue, black and yellow .. 25 25
J 211. – 50 c.+10 c. black brown and blue .. 30 30
ANIMALS: 10 c. Alpine marmots. 20 c. Red deer. 30 c. Badgers. 50 c. Alpine hares.

1966. Publicity Issue. Multicoloured.
731. 10 c. Type **233** 8 5
732. 20 c. Mercury's helmet and laurel twig 10 5
733. 50 c. Phase in nuclear fission and flags .. 25 25
PUBLICITY EVENTS: 10 c. Preservation of natural beauty. 20 c. 50th Swiss Industrial Fair, Bale (MUBA). 50 c. Int. Institute for Nuclear Research (CERN).

234. H. Federer (author).

235. Society Emblem.

1966. Pro Patria. For Aid to Mothers. Inscr. "PRO PATRIA 1966"
734. **234.** 5 c.+5 c. blue .. 8 5
735. – 10 c.+10 c. mult. .. 10 8
736. – 20 c.+10 c. mult. .. 15 10
737. – 30 c.+10 c. mult. .. 30 30
738. – 50 c.+10 c. mult. .. 35 35
DESIGNS—As T **226**: "The Flight to Egypt". Ceiling paintings in St. Martin's Church, Zillis (Grisons): 10 c. Joseph's dream. 20 c. Joseph on his way. 30 c. Virgin and Child. 50 c. Angel pointing the way.

1966. New Helvetic Society for Swiss Abroad. 50th Anniv.
739. **235.** 20 c. red and blue .. 10 5

236. Europa "Ship".

237. Finsteraarhorn.

1966. Europa.
740. **236.** 20 c. red 10 5
741. 50 c. blue 25 12

1966. "Swiss Alps".
742. **237.** 10 c. multicoloured .. 5 5

1966. Children's Fund. Animals. As T **232**, but inscr. "PRO JUVENTUTE 1966". Multicoloured.
J 212. 5 c.+5 c. Ermine .. 5 5
J 213. 10 c.+10 c. Squirrel .. 10 8
J 214. 20 c.+10 c. Fox .. 15 8
J 215. 30 c.+10 c. Field hare .. 25 25
J 216. 50 c.+10 c. Chamois .. 35 35

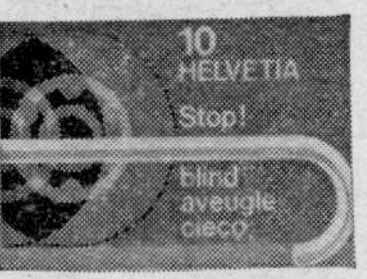

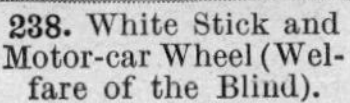

238. White Stick and Motor-car Wheel (Welfare of the Blind). **239.** C.E.P.T. Emblem and Cogwheels.

1967. Publicity Issue.

743. **238.** 10 c. multicoloured .. 5 5
744. – 20 c. multicoloured .. 10 5

DESIGN: 20 c. Flags of E.F.T.A. countries (Abolition of E.F.T.A. tariffs).

1967. Europa.

745. **239.** 30 c. blue 15 8

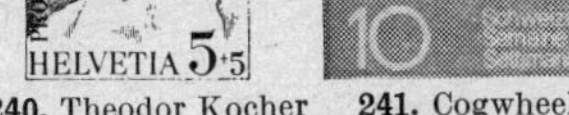

240. Theodor Kocher (surgeon). **241.** Cogwheel and Swiss Emblem.

1967. Pro Patria. For National Day Collection. Inscr. "PRO PATRIA 1967".

746. **240.** 5 c.+5 c. blue .. 8 5
747. – 10 c.+10 c. mult. .. 10 8
748. – 20 c.+10 c. mult. .. 15 10
749. – 30 c.+10 c. mult. .. 20 15
750. – 50 c.+10 c. mult. .. 35 30

DESIGNS—As T **226**: "Art and Trade". Ceiling paintings in St. Martin's Church, Zillis (Grisons). 10 c. Annunciation to the shepherds. 20 c. Christ and the woman of Samaria. 30 c. Adoration of the Magi. 50 c. Joseph seated on throne.

1967. Publicity Issue. Multicoloured.

751. 10 c. Type **241** 5 5
752. 20 c. Hour-glass and Sun .. 10 5
753. 30 c. San Bernardino highway 15 5
754. 50 c. "OCTI" emblem .. 25 20

PUBLICITY EVENTS: 10 c. 50th anniv. of Swiss Week. 20 c. 50th Anniv. of Aged People Foundation. 30 c. Opening of San Bernardino road tunnel. 50 c. 75th anniv. of Central Office for International Railway Transport (OCTI).

1967. Children's Fund. Animals. As T **232**, but inscr. "PRO JUVENTUTE 1967". Multicoloured.

J 217. 10 c.+10 c. Roe deer .. 10 8
J 218. 20 c.+10 c. Pine marten 15 10
J 219. 30 c.+10 c. Alpine ibex 20 8
J 220. 50 c.+20 c. Otter .. 35 30

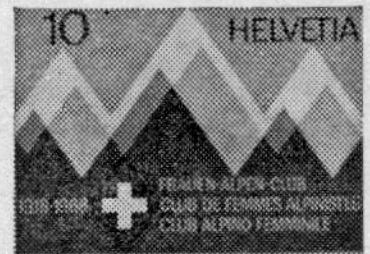

242. "Mountains" and Swiss Emblem.

1968. Publicity Issue.

755. 10 c. multicoloured .. 5 5
756. 20 c. yellow, brown & blue 12 5
757. 30 c. blue, ochre and brown 15 5
758. 50 c. red, greenish bl. & bl. 25 25

DESIGNS AND EVENTS: 10 c. T **242** (50th Anniv. of Swiss Women's Alpine Club). 20 c. Europa "Key" (Europa). 30 c. Rook and chessboard (18th Chess Olympiad, Lugano). 50 c. Dispatch "satellites" and aircraft tail-fin (Inauguration of new Geneva Air Terminal).

243. "Maius". **244.** Protective Helmet.

1968. Pro Patria. For Nat. Day Collection. Inscr. "PRO PATRIA 1968".

759. **243.** 10 c.+10 c. mult. .. 10 5
760. – 20 c.+10 c. mult. .. 15 8
761. – 30 c.+10 c. mult. .. 20 12
762. – 50 c.+20 c. mult. .. 35 30

DESIGNS: "Art and Applied Art". Stained-glass panels in the rose window, Lausanne Cathedral. 20 c. "Leo". 30 c. "Libra". 50 c. "Pisces" (symbols of the months and signs of the zodiac).

1968. Publicity Issue. Multicoloured.

763. 10 c. Type **244** 5 5
764. 20 c. Geneva and Zurich stamps of 1843 .. .. 10 5
765. 30 c. Part of Swiss map .. 15 5
766. 50 c. "Six Stars" (countries) and anchor .. 25 25

PUBLICITY EVENTS: 10 c. 50th Anniv. of Swiss Accident Insurance Company. 20 c. 125th Anniv. of Swiss stamps. 30 c. 25th Anniv. of Swiss Territorial Planning Society. 50 c. Cent. of Rhine Navigation Act.

245. Capercaillie. **246.** Guide Camp and Emblem.

1968. Children's Fund. Birds. Multicoloured.

J 221. 10 c.+10 c. Type **245** .. 10 8
J 222. 20 c.+10 c. Bullfinch .. 15 8
J 223. 30 c.+10 c. Woodchat Shrike 20 8
J 224. 50 c.+20 c. Firecrest .. 35 35

1969. Publicity Issue. Multicoloured.

767. 10 c. Type **246** 5 5
768. 20 c. Pegasus constellation 10 5
769. 30 c. Emblem of Comptoir Suisse 15 5
770. 50 c. Emblem of Gymnaestrade 30 25
771. 2 f. DH-3 "Haefeli" and DC-8 aircraft .. .. 1·25 80

247. Colonnade. **248.** "St. Francis of Assisi preaching to the Birds" (Abbey-church, Konigsfelden).

1969. Europa.

772. **247.** 30 c. multicoloured .. 15 5
773. 50 c. multicoloured .. 25 20

1969. Pro Patria. For National Day Collection. Showing Stained-glass Windows. Multicoloured.

774. 10 c.+10 c. Type **248** .. 10 8
775. 20 c.+10 c. "The People of Israel drinking . . ." (Berne Cathedral) .. 15 10
776. 30 c.+10 c. "St. Christopher" (Laufelfingen Church, Basle) 20 12
777. 50 c.+20 c. "Madonna and Child" (St. Jacob's Chapel, Grapplang, Flums) 35 30

249. Kreuzberge. **250.** H. Zwingli (Protestant reformer).

1969. Publicity and "Swiss Alps" Issues. Multicoloured.

778. 20 c. Type **249** 10 5
779. 30 c. Children crossing road 15 5
780. 50 c. Hammersmith .. 25 20

EVENTS: 30 c. Road Safety campaign for children. 50 c. Int. Labour Organization, 50th Anniv.

1969. Swiss Celebrities.

781. **250.** 10 c. violet 5 5
782. – 20 c. green 12 5
783. – 30 c. red 20 5
784. – 50 c. blue 35 35
785. – 80 c. chestnut .. 45 25

CELEBRITIES: 20 c. General H. Guisan (soldier). 30 c. B. Borromini (architect). 50 c. O. Schoeck (composer). 80 c. G. de Stael (writer).

1969. Children's Fund. Bird designs as T **245**, but inscr. "1969". Multicoloured.

J 225. 10 c.+10 c. Goldfinch .. 10 8
J 226. 20 c.+10 c. Golden oriole 15 8
J 227. 30 c.+10 c. Wall creeper 20 15
J 228. 50 c.+20 c. Jay 35 30

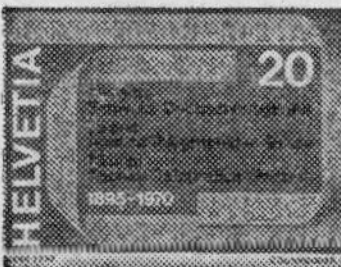

251. Telex Tape.

1970. Publicity Issue. Multicoloured.

786. 20 c. Type **251** 12 5
787. 30 c. Fireman saving child 15 5
788. 30 c. "Chained wing" emblem 15 5
789. 50 c. U.N. emblem .. 30 30
790. 80 c. New U.P.U. Headquarters 40 40

EVENTS: 20 c. Swiss Telegraphic Agency, 75th Anniv. 30 c. (No. 787), Swiss Fireman's Assn., Cent. 30 c. (No. 788), "Pro Infirmis" Foundation, 50th Anniv. 50 c. U.N. Organization, 25th Anniv. 80 c. New U.P.U. H.Q., Berne. Inaug.

252. "Flaming Sun". **253.** "Sailor" (Gian Casty).

1970. Europa.

791. **252.** 30 c. red 15 5
792. 50 c. blue 25 8

1970. Pro Patria. For National Day Collection. Glass paintings by contemporary artists. Multicoloured.

793. 10 c.+10 c. Type **253** .. 10 8
794. 20 c.+10 c. Architectonic composition (Celestino Piatti) 15 10
795. 30 c.+10 c. "Bull", symbol of Marduk, from "The Four Elements" (Hans Stocker) 20 15
796. 50 c.+20 c. "Man and Woman" (Max Hunziker and Karl Ganz) 35 25

254. Footballer (75th Anniv. of Swiss Football Association). **255.** Numeral.

1970. Publicity and "Swiss Alps" (30 c.) Issue. Multicoloured.

797. 10 c. Type **254** 5 5
798. 20 c. Census form and pencil (Federal Census) .. 12 5
799. 30 c. Piz Palu, Grisons .. 15 5
800. 50 c. Conservation Year Emblem (Nature Conservation Year) 30 25

1970. Coil Stamps.

801. **255.** 10 c. red 5 5
802. 20 c. green 8 5
803. 50 c. blue 20 20

1970. Children's Fund. "Bird" designs as Type **245**. Inscr. "1970" Multicoloured.

J 229. 10 c.+10 c. Blue tits .. 12 8
J 230. 20 c.+10 c. Hoopoe .. 20 8
J 231. 30 c.+10 c. Great spotted woodpecker 25 8
J 232. 50 c.+20 c. Great crested grebes 45 45

256. Female Gymnasts. ("Youth and Sport"). **257.** Europa Chain.

1971. Publicity Issue.

804. **256.** 10 c. multicoloured .. 12 5
805. – 10 c. multicoloured .. 12 5
806. – 20 c. multicoloured .. 10 5
807. – 30 c. multicoloured .. 15 5
808. – 50 c. brown and blue 30 20
809. – 80 c. multicoloured .. 40 35

DESIGNS AND EVENTS: 10 c. (No. 805), Male athletes ("Youth and Sport" Constitutional Amendment). 20 c. Stylized rose (Child Welfare). 30 c. "Rayon II" stamp of 1850 and bas lisk ("NABA" Philatelic Exhib., Basel). 50 c. "Co-operation" symbol (Aid for technical development). 80 c. "Intelstat 4" (I.T.U. Space Conference).

1071. Europa.

811. **257.** 30 c. yellow & magenta 15 5
812. 50 c. yellow and blue 30 15

1971. Pro Patria. For National Day Collection. Contemporary Glass Paintings. As T **253**. Multicoloured.

813. 10 c.+10 c. "Religious Abstract", (J. F. Comment) 10 8
814. 20 c.+10 c. "Cockerel", (J. Prahin) 15 10
815. 30 c.+10 c. "Fox", (K. Volk) 20 15
816. 50 c.+20 c. "Christ's Passion" (B. Schorderet) .. 35 25

258. "Telecommunications Services". **259.** Dr. A. Yersin.

1971. Publicity and "Swiss Alps".

817. – 30 c. pur., mve. & grey 15 5
818. **258.** 40 c. multicoloured .. 30 25

DESIGN: 30 c. Les Diablerets, Vaud.

No. 818 marks the 50th Anniv. of Radio-Suisse Ltd.

1971. Famous Physicians.

819. **259.** 10 c. brown 5 5
820. – 20 c. blue-green .. 10 5
821. – 30 c. red 15 5
822. – 40 c. blue 30 25
823. – 80 c. purple 40 35

PHYSICIANS: 20 c. Dr. A. Forel (psychiatrist). 30 c. Dr. J. Gonin (ophthalmologist). 40 c. Dr. Robert Koch (German bacteriologist). 80 c. Dr. F. G. Banting (Canadian physiologist).

1971. Children's Fund. Birds. As T **245**. Multicoloured.

J 233. 10 c.+10 c. Redstarts .. 12 8
J 234. 20 c.+10 c. Bluethroats 20 8
J 235. 30 c.+10 c. Peregrine falcon 25 8
J 236. 40 c.+20 c. Mallard ducks 45 45

260. Warning Triangle and Wrench. (75th Annivs. of Motoring Organisations.)

1972. Publicity Issue.

824. **260.** 10 c. multicoloured .. 5 5
825. – 20 c. multicoloured .. 10 5
826. – 30 c. orge., red & carmine 15 5
827. – 40 c. violet, grn. & blue 30 25

DESIGNS AND EVENTS: 20 c. Signal-box switch-table (125th Anniv. of Swiss Railways). 30 c. Stylized radio waves and girl's face (50th anniv. of Swiss Broadcasting). 40 c. Symbolic tree (50th "Swiss Citizens Abroad" Congress).

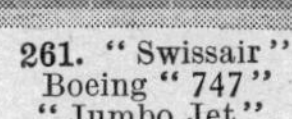

261. "Swissair" Boeing "747" "Jumbo Jet". **262.** "Communications".

1972. Air. Pro Aero Foundation and 50th Annivs. of North Atlantic and Int. Airmail Services.

828. **261.** 2 f.+1 f. multicoloured 1·40 1·40

1972. Europa.

829. **262.** 30 c. multicoloured .. 15 5
830. 40 c. multicoloured .. 25 12

263. Late Stone Age Harpoon Heads. **264.** Civil Defence Emblem.

1972. Pro Patria. For National Day Collection. Archaeological Discoveries. (1st series). Multicoloured.

831. 10 c.+10 c. Type **263** .. 12 8
832. 20 c.+10 c. Bronze water-vessel, c. 570 B.C. .. 20 8
833. 30 c.+10 c. Gold Bust of Marcus Aurelius, 2nd-cent. A.D. 25 15
834. 40 c.+20 c. Alemannic disc, 7th-cent. A.D. .. 55 55

See also Nos. 862/5, 880/3 and 894/7.

1972. Publicity and "Swiss Alps" issue. Multicoloured.
835. 10 c. Type **264** 5 5
836. 20 c. Spannorter 10 5
837. 30 c. Rescue helicopter .. 20 10
838. 40 c. The "Four Elements" (53×31 mm.) 25 20
SUBJECTS: 10 c. Swiss Civil Devence. 20 c. Tourism. 30 c. Swiss Air Rescue Service. 40 c. Protection of the environment.

265. A. Giacometti (painter).

266. "McGredy's Sunset" Rose.

1972. Swiss Celebrities.
839. **265.** 10 c. black and brown 5 5
840. – 20 c. black and bistre 10 5
841. – 30 c. black and pink .. 15 5
842. – 40 c. black and blue .. 30 25
843. – 80 c. black and purple 40 30
PORTRAITS: 20 c. C. F. Ramuz (novelist). 30 c. Le Corbusier (architect). 40 c. Albert Einstein (physicist). 80 c. A. Honegger (composer).

1972. Children's Fund. Roses. Mult.
J 237. 10 c.+10 c. Type **266** .. 15 10
J 238. 20 c.+10 c. "Miracle" rose 20 10
J 239. 30 c.+10 c. "Papa Meilland" rose .. 30 10
J 240. 40 c.+20 c. "Madame Dimitriu" rose .. 45 45

267. Dish Aerial.

1973. Publicity Issue. Multicoloured.
844. 15 c. Type **267** 12 8
845. 30 c. Quill pen 15 5
846. 40 c. Interpol emblem .. 25 20
EVENTS: 15 c. Construction of Satellite Earth Station, Leuk-Brentjong. 30 c. Swiss Association of Commercial Employees, Cent. 40 c. International Criminal Police Organisation (Interpol). 50th anniv.

268. Sottoceneri.

269. Toggenburg Inn Sign.

1973.
847. **268.** 5 c. blue and yellow .. 5 5
848. – 10 c. green and purple 5 5
849. – 15 c. blue and brown .. 5 5
850. – 25 c. violet and green .. 10 5
851. – 30 c. violet and red .. 12 5
851a. – 35 c. violet and orange 15 5
852. – 40 c. grey and blue .. 15 5
853. – 50 c. green and orange 20 5
854. – 60 c. brown and grey .. 25 8
855. – 70 c. green and purple 30 12
856. – 80 c. red and green .. 35 10
856a. – 1 f. lilac 40 20
856b. – 1 f. 10 blue 45 15
856c. – 1 f. 20 red 50 20
857. **269.** 1 f. 30 orange 55 20
857a. – 1 f. 50 green 65 25
858. – 1 f. 70 grey 70 30
859. – 1 f. 80 red 75 35
859a. – 2 f. blue 85 40
859b. – 2 f. 50 brown .. .. 1·00 60
DESIGNS—As T **268.** 10 c. Grisons. 15 c. Central Switzerland. 25 c. Jura. 30 c. Simmental. 35 c. Houses, Central Switzerland. 40 c. Vaud. 50 c. Valais. 60 c. Engadine. 70 c. Sopraceneri. 80 c. Eastern Switzerland. As T **269.** 1 f. Rose window. 1 f. 10 Portal, Basle Cathedral. 1 f. 20 Romanesque capital. 1 f. 50 Ceiling medallion. 1 f. 70 Roman Capital, Jean-Baptiste Church, Grandson. 1 f. 80 Gargoyle, Berne Cathedral. 2 f. Oriel window. 2 f. 50 Weathercock.

270. Europa "Posthorn".

1973. Europa.
860. **270.** 25 c. brown and yellow 12 10
861. 40 c. blue and yellow 20 20

1973. Pro Patria. For National Day Collection. Archaeological Discoveries. (2nd series). As T **263**, but horiz. Mult.
862. 15 c.+5 c. Rauraric jar .. 10 10
863. 30 c.+10 c. Head of a Gaul (bronze) 20 8
864. 40 c.+20 c. Alemannic "Fish" brooches .. 30 20
865. 60 c.+20 c. Gold bowl .. 40 35

271. Horological Emblem.

272. Chestnut.

1973. Publicity Issue. Multicoloured.
866. 15 c. Type **271** 8 5
867. 30 c. Skiing emblem .. 15 5
868. 40 c. Face of child .. 25 15
SUBJECTS: 15 c. Int. Horological Museum, Neuchatel. Inaug. (1974). 30 c. World Alpine Skiing Championships, St. Moritz (1974). 40 c. "Terre des Hommes" (Child-care organisation)

1973. Children's Fund. "Fruits of the Forest". Multicoloured.
J 241. 15 c.+5 c. Type **272** .. 10 8
J 242. 30 c.+10 c. Cherries .. 20 8
J 243. 40 c.+20 c. Blackberries 35 30
J 244. 60 c.+20 c. Billberries .. 40 35
See also Nos. J 245/8, J 249/53 and J 254/7.

273. "Global Hostels".

274. "Continuity" (Max Bill).

1974. Publicity Issue. Multicoloured.
869. 15 c. Type **273** 8 5
870. 30 c. Gymnast and hurdlers 15 5
871. 40 c. Pistol and target .. 25 15
SUBJECTS: 15 c. "50 Years of Swiss Youth Hostels". 30 c. Swiss Workmen's Gymnastics and Sports Assn. (S.A.T.U.S.). Cent. 40 c. World Shooting Championships, 1974.

1974. Europa. Swiss Sculptures.
873. **274.** 30 c. black and red .. 15 5
874. – 40 c. brown and blue 20 12
DESIGN: 40 c. "Amazone" (Carl Burckhardt).

275. Eugene Borel (first director of International Bureau, U.P.U.).

276. View of Berne.

1974. U.P.U. Centenary.
875. **275.** 30 c. black and pink . 15 5
876. – 40 c. black and grey .. 25 15
877. – 80 c. black and green 40 25
DESIGNS: 40 c. H. von Stephan (founder of U.P.U.). 80 c. Montgomery Blair (U.S. Postmaster-General).

1974. 17th U.P.U. Congress, Lausanne. Multicoloured.
878. 30 c. Type **276** 15 5
879. 30 c. View of Lausanne .. 15 5

1974. Pro Patria. For National Day Collection. Archaeological Discoveries (3rd series). As T **263.** Multicoloured.
880. 15 c.+5 c. Glass bowl .. 10 10
881. 30 c.+10 c. Bull's head (bronze) 20 8
882. 40 c.+20 c. Gold brooch .. 30 20
883. 60 c.+20 c. "Bird" vessel (clay) 40 35

277. "The Oath of Allegiance" (W. Witschi's iron sculpture at Fluelen).

1974. Publicity Issue. Multicoloured.
884. 15 c. Type **277** 8 5
885. 30 c. Foundation emblem 15 5
886. 30 c. Posthorn emblem and conveyor-belts 15 5
EVENTS AND COMMEMORATIONS: No. 884, Federal constitution. Cent. No. 885, Aid for Swiss Sport Foundation. No. 886, Federal posts. 125th anniv.

1974. Children's Fund. "Fruits of the Forest". Poisonous Plants. As T **272.** Inscr. "1974". Multicoloured.
J 245. 15 c.+5 c. Daphne .. 15 8
J 246. 30 c.+20 c. Belladonna 25 8
J 247. 50 c.+20 c. Laburnum 35 30
J 248. 60 c.+25 c. Mistletoe 45 35

278. "Measuring Techniques".

279. "The Monch" (F. Hodler).

1975. Publicity Issue.
887. **278.** 15 c. multicoloured .. 8 5
888. – 30 c. multicoloured .. 15 5
889. – 60 c. red, black & blue 30 12
890. – 90 c. multicoloured .. 40 20
DESIGNS AND EVENTS: 15 c. (International Metre Convention). 30 c. Women talking (International Women's Year). 60 c. Flag and barbed-wire (Diplomatic Conference on Humanitarian International Law, Geneva). 90 c. Airship "Ville de Lucerne", 1910. ("Aviation and Space Travel" Exhibition, Transport Museum, Lucerne).

1975. Europa. Paintings. Multicoloured.
891. 30 c. Type **279** 15 5
892. 50 c. "Still Life with Guitar" (R. Auberjonois) 25 15
893. 60 c. "L'effeuilleuse" (M. Barraud) 30 20

1975. Pro Patria. Archaeological Discoveries. (4th series). As T **263.** Multicoloured.
894. 15 c.+10 c. Gold brooch .. 12 10
895. 30 c.+20 c. Bronze head of Bacchus 25 20
896. 50 c.+20 c. Bronze daggers 35 35
897. 60 c.+25 c. Glass decanter 40 35

280. "Eliminate Obstacles!".

281. "Post-Brente" (postman's 'hamper").

1975. Publicity Issue. Multicoloured.
898. 15 c. Type **280** 8 5
899. 30 c. Telephone and heart emblem 15 5
900. 50 c. E.A.H.Y. emblem .. 25 15
901. 60 c. Beat Fischer von Reichenbach 30 15
SUBJECTS: 15 c. Building design for the handicapped. 30 c. Swiss Association for Pastoral Care by Telephone. 5p c. European Architectural Heritage Year. 60 c. Fisher Postal Service. 300th Anniv.

1975. Children's Fund. T **281** and "Fruits of the Forest" as T **272.** Multicoloured.
J 249. 10 c.+5 c. Type **281** .. 8 8
J 250. 15 c.+10 c. Hepatica .. 12 12
J 251. 30 c.+20 c. Rowan .. 25 20
J 252. 50 c.+20 c. Yellow dead-nettle 35 30
J 253. 60 c.+25 c. Sycamore .. 40 35

282. Woodland Scenery.

283. St. Gall Embroidery.

1976. Publicity Issue. Multicoloured.
902. 20 c. Type **282** 8 5
903. 40 c. Fruit and vegetables 15 8
904. 40 c. African child and text 15 8
905. 80 c. Early and modern telephones 30 25
EVENTS: No. 902 Federal Forest Laws. Centenary. No. 903 "Good Health" campaign against alcoholism. No. 904 Leprosy control. No. 905 Telephone centenary.

1976. Europa. Multicoloured.
906. 40 c. Type **283** 15 8
907. 80 c. Ancient pocket watch 30 25

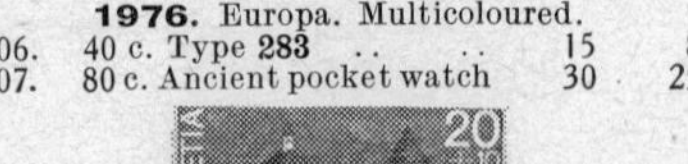

284. Kyburg Castle.

1976. Pro Patria. Swiss Castles. Mult.
908. 20 c.+10 c. Type **284** .. 10 10
909. 40 c.+20 c. Grandson .. 20 20
910. 40 c.+20 c. Morat .. 20 20
911. 80 c.+40 c. Bellinzona .. 40 40

285. Fawn, Swallow and Frog.

1976. Publicity Issues. Multicoloured.
912. 20 c. Type **285** 10 5
913. 40 c. Sun and slogans .. 20 10
914. 40 c. St. Gotthard mountains 20 10
915. 80 c. Skater at speed .. 45 40
EVENTS: 20 c. Wildlife protection campaign. 40 c. Energy-saving drive. 40 c. (914) Swiss Alps series. 80 c. World Speed Skating Championships.

1976. "Fruits of the Forest". As T **272.** Multicoloured.
J 254. 20 c.+10 c. Barberry .. 15 15
J 255. 40 c.+20 c. Black elder 30 30
J 256. 40 c.+20 c. Lime .. 30 30
J 257. 80 c.+40 c. Lungwort .. 65 65

286. Oscar Bider and Bleriot Plane.

1977. Aviation Pioneers.
916. **286.** 40 c. blk., magen. & red 20 10
917. – 80 c. blk., pur. & blue 45 40
918. – 100 c. blk., grn. & bistre 55 50
919. – 150 c. blk., brn. & turq. 80 75
DESIGNS: 80 c. Eduard Spelterini and balloon-basket. 100 c. Armand Dufaux and Dufaux biplane. 150 c. Walter Mittleholzer and Do-Merkur seaplane.

287. Blue Cross and Alcoholic receiving Treatment.

1977. Publicity Issues. Multicoloured.
920. 20 c. Type **287** 10 5
921. 40 c. Sun-shaped head of Bacchus 20 10
922. 80 c. Balloons carrying "Juphilex" letters .. 45 40
EVENTS. 20 c. Centenary of Swiss Blue Cross Society (for care of alcoholics). 40 c. Vintage Festival, Vevey. 80 c. "Juphilex '77" Youth Stamp Exhibition, Berne.

OFFICIAL STAMPS

1918. Optd. **Industrielle Kriegswirtschaft.**
O 308. **12.** 3 c. brown .. .. 1·60 2·75
O 300. 5 c. green .. .. 3·50 6·50
O 310. 7½ c. grey .. .. 2·00 2·75
O 303. **13.** 10 c. red on buff .. 5·00 6·50
O 304. 15 c. violet on buff 4·75 7·50
O 313. **9.** 20 c. yellow and red 4·00 5·50
O 314. 25 c. blue .. .. 4·00 5·50
O 315. 30 c. green and brown 6·00 11·00

1938. Optd. with Geneva Cross.
O 381. **96.** 3 c. olive 12 12
O 382. – 5 c. green (No. 372) 12 10
O 383. – 10 c. purple (No. 373b) 65 15
O 384. – 15 c. orange (No. 374) 30 65
O 385. – 20 c. red (No. 375d) .. 35 20
O 386. – 25 c. brown (No. 376) 35 45
O 387. – 30 c. ultram (No. 377) 40 40
O 388. – 35 c. green (No. 378) 45 65
O 389. 40 c. grey (No. 379) .. 45 45
O 390. **9.** 50 c. green 45 45
O 391. 60 c. brown 80 95
O 392. 70 c. buff and violet .. 80 1·90
O 393. 80 c. buff and grey .. 95 1·25
O 395. **51.** 90 c. red & grn. on grn. 1·40 1·40
O 394. **9.** 1f. green and claret 1·25 1·60
O 396. **51.** 1 f. 20 red & lake on rose 1·40 2·00
O 397. 1 f. 50 red and blue on blue .. .. 1·90 2·40
O 398. – 2 f. red & black on grey 2·40 3·00

1942. Optd. **Officiel.**
(a) Landscape designs of 1936.
O 427. 3 c. olive 25 80
O 428. 5 c. green 25 10
O 430. 10 c. brown 45 20
O 431. 15 c. orange 50 90

O 432. 20 c. red (Lake) .. 50 20
O 433. 25 c. brown .. .. 65 1·10
O 434. 30 c. ultramarine .. 70 40
O 435. 35 c. green .. .. 95 1·25
O 436. 40 c. grey .. .. 1·10 55

(b) Historical designs of 1941.

O 437. – 50 c. purple on grn. 3·50 2·00
O 438. 122. 60 c. brown on buff.. 4·25 1·90
O 439. – 70 c. violet on lilac.. 4·75 4·00
O 440. – 80 c. grey on grey .. 1·10 70
O 441. – 90 c. red on rose .. 1·25 80
O 442. – 1 f. green on green .. 1·25 95
O 443. – 1 f. 20 violet on grey 1·60 1·25
O 444. – 1 f. 50 blue on buff 1·90 1·40
O 445. – 2 f. lake on rose .. 2·50 2·00

1950. Landscape designs of 1949 optd. **Officiel.**

O 522. 165. 5 c. orange .. 20 20
O 523. – 10 c. green 30 25
O 524. – 15 c. turquoise .. 1·25 3·00
O 525. – 20 c. maroon .. 70 25
O 526. – 25 c. red .. .. 95 1·40
O 527. – 30 c. olive .. 1·25 95
O 528. – 35 c. brown .. 1·25 1·40
O 529. – 40 c. blue .. .. 1·25 95
O 530. – 50 c. grey .. .. 1·60 1·40
O 531. – 60 c. green .. .. 2·10 1·40
O 532. – 70 c. violet .. .. 4·75 4·75

For Swiss stamps overprinted for the use of officials of the League of Nations, International Labour Office and other special U.N. Agencies having their headquarters at Geneva, see under UNITED NATIONS—GENEVA HEADQUARTERS.

POSTAGE DUE STAMPS

D 1. D 2. D 3.

1878.

D 105. D 1. 1 c. blue 40 40
D 106. 2 c. blue 40 40
D 107. 3 c. blue .. .. 3·50 2·40
D 108. 5 c. blue .. .. 4·25 1·60
D 109. 10 c. blue .. .. 32·00 1·25
D 110. 20 c. blue .. .. 40·00 1·10
D 111. 50 c. blue .. .. 90·00 3·00
D 112. 100 c. blue .. .. £130 2·50
D 113. 500 c. blue .. .. £110 4·00

1883. Numerals in red.

D 188. D 1. 1 c. green 8 20
D 189. 3 c. green .. .. 1·25 1·25
D 190. 5 c. green 55 15
D 191. 10 c. green 85 20
D 192. 20 c. green .. .. 1·40 30
D 193. 50 c. green .. .. 3·50 40
D 194. 100 c. green .. 4·00 50
D 195. 500 c. green .. 32·00 3·25

The above were issued in a wide range of shades from pale blue-green to brown-olive between 1883 and 1910. A detailed list of these appears in the Stanley Gibbons Europe Catalogue Volume 3.

1910.

D 274. D 2. 1 c. green and red 5 5
D 275. 3 c. green and red 5 5
D 276. 5 c. green and red.. 5 5
D 277. 10 c. green and red 30 5
D 278. 15 c. green and red 35 25
D 279. 20 c. green and red 4·00 5
D 280. 25 c. green and red 70 20
D 281. 30 c. green and red 70 15
D 282. 50 c. green and red 95 35

1916. Surch.

D 299. D 2. 5 c. on 3 c. grn. & red 8 15
D 300. 10 c. on 1 c. grn. & red 20 1·50
D 301. 10 c. on 3 c. grn. & red 12 35
D 302. 20 c. on 50 c. green and red 45 25

1924.

D 332. D 3. 5 c. red and olive .. 30 5
D 333. 10 c. red and olive 90 5
D 334. 15 c. red and olive 70 25
D 335. 20 c. red and olive 1·75 5
D 336. 25 c. red and olive 1·10 25
D 337. 30 c. red and olive 1·10 25
D 338. 40 c. red and olive 1·50 25
D 339. 50 c. red and olive 1·50 25

1937. Surch.

D 380. D 3. 5 on 15 c. red & olive 45 80
D 381. 10 on 30 c. red & olive 45 45
D 382. 20 on 50 c. red & olive 70 1·25
D 383. 40 on 50 c. red & olive 95 1·60

D 4.

1938.

D 384. D 4. 5 c. red 20 5
D 385. 10 c. red 25 5
D 386. 15 c. red 35 45
D 387. 20 c. red 40 5
D 388. 25 c. red 60 65
D 389. 30 c. red 70 40
D 390. 40 c. red 80 12
D 391. 50 c. red 90 80

SYRIA

O4

A country at the E. end of the Mediterranean Sea, formerly Turkish territory. Occupied by the Allies in 1918 and administered under French Military Occupation. An Arab kingdom was set up in the Aleppo and Damascus area during 1919, but the Emir Faisal came into conflict with the French and was defeated in July, 1920. In April 1920, the Mandate was granted to France. Separate governments were established for the Territories of Damascus, Aleppo, the Alaouites (including Latakia), Great Lebanon and the Jebel Druze. Syria became a republic in 1934, and the Mandate ended with full Independence in 1942. In 1958 the United Arab Republic was formed which comprised Egypt and Syria. Separate stamps were issued for each territory as they employed different currencies. In 1961 Syria left the U.A.R. and the Syrian Arab Republic was established.

1919. 40 paras = 10 milliemes = 1 piastre.

1920. 100 centimes (or centiemes) = 1 piastre.

A. Egyptian currency.

1919. Stamps of France surch. **T.E.O.** and value in "Milliemes" or "Piastres".

1. 11. 1 m. on 1 c. grey .. 35·00 35·00
2. 2 m. on 2 c. claret .. 65·00 65·00
3. 3 m. on 3 c. orange .. 35·00 35·00
4. 15. 4 m. on 15 c. green .. 4·25 4·25
5. 17. 5 m. on 5 c. green .. 2·50 2·50
6. 1 p. on 10 c. red .. 5·00 5·00
7. 2 p. on 25 c. blue .. 2·25 2·25
8. 13. 5 p. on 40 c. red and blue 2·10 2·10
9. 9 p. on 50 c. brown & lav. 5·00 5·00
10. 10 p. on 1 f. red & yellow 8·50 8·50

1919. "Blanc", "Mouchon" and "Merson" key-types of French Levant surch. **T.E.O.** and value in "Milliemes" or "Piastres".

11. A. 1 m. on 1 c. grey .. 12 10
12. 2 m. on 2 c. claret .. 12 10
13. 3 m. on 3 c. orange .. 20 15
14. B. 4 m. on 15 c. red .. 10 10
15. A. 5 m. on 5 c. green .. 12 10
16. B. 1 p. on 25 c. blue .. 5 5
17. C. 2 p. on 50 c. brn. & lav.. 20 12
18. 4 p. on 1 f. red and yellow 35 25
19. 8 p. on 2 f. lilac & yellow 1·10 1·00
20. 20 p. on 5 f. blue & yellow 65·00 55·00

1920. Stamps of France surch. **O.M.F. Syrie** and value in "Milliemes" or "Piastres".

25. 11. 1 m. on 1 c. grey .. 5 5
26. 2 m. on 2 c. claret .. 15 15
27. 17. 3 m. on 5 c. green .. 10 10
28. 5 m. on 10 c. red .. 10 10
29. 13. 20 p. on 5 f. blue & yellow 15·00 15·00

1.

2.

1920. As T 1 (various sizes) and T 2.

K 88. 1. 1 m. brown 5 5
K 89. 1/10 p. green 10 10
K 90. 3/10 p. yellow 5 5
K 91. 2. 5 m. red 5 5
K 92. 1. 1 p. blue 5 5
K 93. 2 p. green 45 35
K 94. 5 p. purple 85 55
K 95. 10 p. grey 90 65

For 1 p. black as T 1, see No. KD 96.

1920. Independence Commem. Optd. with Arabic inscription.

K 98. 2. 5 m. red .. .. 20·00 20·00

B. Syrian currency.

100 piastres = 5 French francs.

1920. Stamps of France surch. **O.M.F. Syrie** and value in two lines. (a) Value in "Centimes" or "Piastres".

31. 11. 25 c. on 1 c. grey .. 12 12
32. 50 c. on 2 c. claret .. 12 12
33. 75 c. on 3 c. orange .. 12 12
35. 17. 1 p. on 5 c. green .. 5 5
36. 2 p. on 10 c. red .. 5 5
37. 2 p. on 25 c. blue .. 5 5
38. 3 p. on 25 c. blue .. 10 10
39. 15. 5 p. on 15 c. green .. 8 8
40. 13. 10 p. on 40 c. red & blue 15 20
41. 25 p. on 50 c. brn. & lav. 25 25
42. 50 p. on 1 f. red & yellow 30 30
44. 100 p. on 5 f. blue & yell. 4·50 4·50

(b) Value in "Centiemes".

45. 11. 25 c. on 1 c. grey .. 5 5
46. 50 c. on 2 c. claret .. 5 5
47. 75 c. on 3 c. orange .. 10 10

1920. Air. Nos. 35, 39/40 optd. **POSTE PAR AVION** in frame.

57. 17. 1 p. on 5 c. green .. 25·00 3·25
58. 15. 5 p. on 15 c. green .. 55·00 6·00
59. 13. 10 p. on 40 c. red & blue 55·00 10·00

C. Syrian currency revalued.

5 piastres = 1 French franc.

1921. Issued at Damascus. Nos. K 88/95 surch. **O.M.F. Syrie** and value in two lines in "Centiemes" or "Piastres".

60. 1. 25 c. on 1 m. 10 10
61. 50 c. on 1/10 p. green .. 10 12
62. 1 p. on 3/10 p. yellow .. 15 12
63. 2. 1 p. on 5 m. red .. 25 25
64. 2 p. on 5 m. red .. 25 20
65. 1. 3 p. on 1 p. blue 40 30
66. 5 p. on 2 p. green .. 70 65
67. 10 p. on 5 p. purple .. 1·00 90
68. 25 p. on 10 p. grey . 1·10 1·10

1921. Stamps of France surch. **O.M.F. Syrie** and value in two lines in "Centiemes" or "Piastres".

69. 11. 25 c. on 5 c. green .. 5 5
70. 17. 50 c. on 10 c. red .. 5 5
71. 15. 75 c. on 15 c. green .. 10 5
72. 17. 1 p. on 20 c. chocolate .. 5 5
73. 13. 2 p. on 40 c. red and blue 10 5
74. 3 p. on 60 c. violet & blue 12 8
75. 5 p. on 1 f. red & yellow 40 25
76. 10 p. on 2 f. orge. & green 55 55
77. 25 p. on 5 f. blue & yellow 27·00 27·00

1921. Air. Nos. 72, 75/6 optd. **POSTE PAR AVION** in frame.

78. 17. 1 p. on 20 c. chocolate .. 9·50 4·00
79. 13. 5 p. on 1 f. red & yellow 80·00 22·00
80. 10 p. on 2 f. orge. & grn. 80·00 22·00

1921. Stamps of France surch. **O.M.F. Syrie** and value in "Piastres" in one line.

81. 13. 2 p. on 40 c. red and blue 10 5
82. 3 p. on 60 c. violet & blue 20 10
83. 5 p. on 1 f. red and yellow 1·25 1·00
84. 10 p. on 2 f. orge & grn. 2·75 2·25
85. 25 p. on 5 f. blue & yellow 1·75 1·75

1921. Air. Nos. 72, 75/6 optd. **AVION.**

86. 17. 1 p. on 20 c. chocolate .. 8·00 1·75
87. 13. 5 p. on 1 f. red & yellow 25·00 5·00
88. 10 p. on 2 f. orge. & grn. 27·00 5·00

1922. Air. Nos. 81/5 optd. **Poste par Avion.**

89. 13. 2 p. on 40 c. red and blue 2·50 2·50
90. 3 p. on 60 c. violet & blue 2·50 2·50
91. 5 p. on 1 f. red & yellow.. 2·50 2·50
92. 10 p. on 2 f. orge. & grn. 3·50 3·50

Nos. 93/174 are all stamps of France surch.

1922. Surch. **O.M.F. Syrie** and value in two lines in "Centiemes" or "Piastres".

93. 11. 10 c. on 2 c. claret .. 5 5
94. 17. 10 c. on 5 c. orange .. 10 10
95. 25 c. on 5 c. orange .. 10 10
96. 50 c. on 10 c. green .. 8 5
96a. 1,25 p. on 25 c. blue .. 20 8
96b. 1,50 on 30 c. orange 8 5
96c. 13. 2 p. 50 on 50 c. brn. & lav. 15 15
96d. 15. 2,50 p. on 50 c. blue .. 20 12

1923. Surch. **Syrie Grand Liban** in two lines and value in "Centiemes" or "Piastres".

97. 11. 10 c. on 2 c. claret .. 5 5
98. 17. 25 c. on 5 c. orange .. 5 5
99. 50 c. on 10 c. green .. 5 5
100. 15. 75 c. on 15 c. green .. 8 8
101. 17. 1 p. on 20 c. chocolate.. 5 5
102. 1 p. 25 on 25 c. blue .. 8 8
103. 1 p. 50 on 30 c. orange 8 8
104. 1 p. 50 on 30 c. red .. 8 8
105. 15. 2 p. 50 on 50 c. blue .. 8 8

1923. Surch. **Syrie-Grand Liban** in one line and value in "Piastres".

106. 13. 2 p. on 40 c. red and blue 5 5
107. 3 p. on 60 c. violet & blue 12 12
108. 5 p. on 1 f. red & yellow 25 25
109. 10 p. on 2 f. orge. & grn. 1·10 1·10
110. 25 p. on 5 f. blue & yell. 5 00 5·00

1923. "Pasteur" issue surch. **Syrie Grand Liban** in two lines and value in "Centiemes" or "Piastres".

111. 26. 50 c. on 10 c. green .. 10 10
112. 1 p. 50 on 30 c. red .. 5 5
113. 2 p. 50 on 50 c. blue .. 8 8

1923. Air. Nos. 106/9 of Syria optd. **Poste par Avion.**

114. 13. 2 p. on 40 c. red & blue 5·00 5·00
115. 3 p. on 60 c. vio. & bl... 5·00 5·00
116. 5 p. on 1 f. red & yell... 5·00 5·00
117. 10 p. on 2 f. orange and green .. .. 5·00 5·00

THE ISSUES FOLLOWING WERE FOR USE IN SYRIA ONLY.

1924. Surch. **SYRIE** and value in two lines.

118. 11. 10 c. on 2 c. claret .. 5 5
119. 17. 25 c. on 5 c. orange .. 5 5
120. 50 c. on 10 c. green .. 5 5
121. 15. 75 c. on 15 c. green .. 8 5
122. 17. 1 p. on 20 c. chocolate 10 5
123. 1 p. 25 on 25 c. blue .. 12 12
124. 1 p. 50 on 30 c. orange 8 8
125. 1 p. 50 on 30 c. red .. 8 8
126. 15. 2 p. 50 on 50 c. blue .. 10 8

1924. Surch. **SYRIE** and value in one line.

127. 13. 2 p. on 40 c. red and blue 5 5
128. 3 p. on 60 c. violet & blue 15 15
129. 5 p. on 1 f. red & yellow 40 40
130. 10 p. on 2 f. orge. & grn. 55 50
131. 25 p. on 5 f. blue & yell. 70 70

1924. "Pasteur" issue surch. **SYRIE** and value in two lines.

132. 26. 50 c. on 10 c. green .. 5 5
133. 1 p. 50 on 30 c. red .. 5 5
134. 2 p. 50 on 50 c. blue .. 5 5

1924. Air. Nos. 127/30 of Syria optd. **Poste par Avion.**

135. 13. 2 p. on 40 c. red & blue 40 40
136. 3 p. on 60 c. vio. & blue 40 40
137. 5 p. on 1 f. red & yellow 40 40
138. 10 p. on 2 f. orge. & grn. 40 40

1924. Olympic Games issue (Nos. 401/4) surch. **SYRIE** and value in two lines.

139. 27. 50 c. on 10 c. green .. 2·25 2·25
140. – 1 p. 25 on 25 c. red .. 2·25 2·25
141. – 1 p. 50 on 30 c. red & blk. 2·25 2·25
142. – 2 p. 50 on 50 c. blue .. 2·25 2·25

1924. Surch. **Syrie** and value and **Arabic** inscription.

143. 11. 0 p. 10 on 2 c. claret .. 5 5
144. 17. 0 p. 25 on 5 c. orange .. 5 5
145. 0 p. 50 on 10 c. green .. 5 5
146. 15. 0 p. 75 on 15 c. green .. 5 5
147. 17. 1 p. on 20 c. chocolate.. 5 5
148. 1 p. 25 on 25 c. blue .. 5 5
149. 1 p. 50 on 30 c. red .. 10 10
150. 1 p. 50 on 30 c. orange 4·25 4·25
151. 2 p. on 35 c. violet .. 10 10
152. 13. 2 p. on 40 c. red and blue 5 5
153. 2 p. on 45 c. grn. & blue 40 40
154. 3 p. on 60 c. violet & blue 10 10
155. 15. 3 p. on 60 c. violet .. 5 5
156. 4 p. on 85 c. red .. 5 5
157. 13. 5 p. on 1 f. red & yellow 15 15
158. 10 p. on 2 f. orge. & grn. 20 20
159. 25 p. on 5 f. blue & yell. 25 25

1924. "Pasteur" issue surch. **Syrie** and value and Arabic inscription.

160. 26. 0 p. 50 on 10 c. green .. 10 10
161. 0 p. 75 on 15 c. green .. 15 15
162. 1 p. 50 on 30 c. red .. 10 10
163. 2 p. on 45 c. red .. 10 10
164. 2 p. 50 on 50 c. blue .. 15 15
165. 4 p. on 75 c. blue .. 15 15

1924. Olympic Games issue (Nos. 401/4) surch. **Syrie** and value and Arabic inscription.

166. 27. 0 p. 50 on 10 c. green .. 2·25 2·25
167. – 1 p. 25 on 25 c. red .. 2·25 2·25
168. – 1 p. 50 on 30 c. red & blk. 2·25 2·25
169. – 2 p. 50 on 50 c. blue .. 2·25 2·25

1924. Ronsard stamp surch. **Syrie** and value and Arabic inscription.

170. 31. 4 p. on 75 c. blue .. 10 10

1924. Air. Nos. 152, 154 and 157/8 of Syria optd. **Avion** and Arabic inscription.

171. 13. 2 p. on 40 c. red & blue 50 50
172. 3 p. on 60 c. vio. & blue 50 50
173. 5 p. on 1 f. red & yell... 50 50
174. 10 p. on 2 f. orge. & grn. 50 50

3. Hama.

4. Merkab.

5. Damascus.

1925. Views.

175. 3. 0 p. 10 violet 5 5
176. 4. 0 p. 25 black 12 12
177. – 0 p. 50 green 5 5
178. – 0 p. 75 red 5 5
179. 5. 1 p. claret 5 5
180. – 1 p. 25 green 20 20
181. – 1 p. 50 red 5 5
182. – 2 p. sepia 8 5
183. – 2 p. 50 blue 12 8
184. – 3 p. brown 5 5
185. – 5 p. violet 20 5
186. – 10 p. plum 30 5
187. – 25 p. blue 30 25

DESIGNS—As T 4: 50 c. Alexandretta. 75 c. Hama. 1 p. 25, Latakia. 1 p. 50, Damascus. 2 p., 25 p. Palmyra (different views). 2 p. 50, Kalat Yamoun. 3 p. Bridge of Daphne. 5 p., 10 p. Aleppo (different views).

1925. Air. Nos. 182 etc. optd. **AVION** and Arabic inscription.

188. 2 p. sepia 30 30
189. 3 p. brown.. .. .. 30 30
190. 5 p. violet 30 30
191. 10 p. plum.. .. .. 30 30

1926. Air. Nos. 182 etc. optd. with aeroplane.

192. 2 p. sepia 20 20
193. 3 p. brown.. .. .. 20 20
194. 5 p. violet 20 20
195. 10 p. plum.. .. .. 20 20

1926. War Refugees Fund. Nos. 176 and Nos. 192/5 etc. surch. **Secours aux Refugiés Afft,** value and Arabic inscr.

196. 4. 0 p. 25 on 0 p. 25 black (postage) 50 50
197. – 0 p. 25 on 0 p. 50 green.. 50 50
198. – 0 p. 25 on 0 p. 75 red .. 50 50
199. 5. 0 p. 50 on 1 p. claret .. 50 50
200. – 0 p. 50 on 1 p. 25 green 50 50
201. – 0 p. 50 on 1 p. 50 red .. 50 50
202. – 0 p. 75 on 2 p. sepia .. 50 50
203. – 0 p. 75 on 2 p. 50 blue.. 50 50
204. – 1 p. on 3 p. brown .. 50 50
205. – 1 p. on 5 p. violet .. 50 50

206. – 2 p. on 10 p. plum .. 50 50
207. – 5 p. on 25 p. blue .. 50 50
208. – 1 p. on 2 p. sepia (air) .. 50 50
209. – 2 p. on 3 p. brown .. 50 50
210. – 3 p. on 5 p. violet .. 50 50
211. – 5 p. on 10 p. plum .. 50 50

1926. No. 176, etc., surch. with new value in English and Arabic figures and bars
222. 1 p. on 3 p. brown .. 12 10
223. 2 p. on 1 p. 25 green .. 8 5
212. 3 p. 50 on 75 c. red .. 8 8
224. 4 p. on 25 c. black .. 10 5
215. 4 p. 50 on 75 c. red .. 5 5
216. 6 p. on 2 p. 50 blue .. 5 5
217. 7 p. 50 on 2 p. 50 blue .. 10 5
218. 12 p. on 1 p. 25 green .. 8 8
219. 15 p. on 25 p. blue .. 15 12
220. 20 p. on 1 p. 25 green .. 15 12

1928. No. 175 surch. in English and Arabic figures and single bar.
221. 05 on 0 p. 10 violet .. 5 5

1929. Air. Nos. 177, etc., optd. with aeroplane or surch. also in English and Arabic figures and bars.
225. 0 p. 50 green 8 8
226. 1 p. claret 20 20
227. 2 p. on 1 p. 25 green .. 25 25
228. 15 p. on 25 p. blue .. 55 55
229. 25 p. blue 75 75

1929. Damascus Industrial Exn. (a) Postage Nos. 117 etc. optd. **EXPOSITION INDUSTRIELLE DAMAS 1929** and Arabic inscr.
230. 0 p. 50 green 45 45
231. 1 p. claret 45 45
232. 1 p. 50 red 45 45
233. 3 p. brown 45 45
234. 5 p. violet 45 45
235. 10 p. plum 45 45
236. 25 p. blue 45 45

(b) Air. As last but optd. with aeroplane.
237. 0 p. 50 green (No. 230) .. 35 35
238. 1 p. claret (No. 231) .. 35 35
239. 2 p. sepia (No. 182) .. 35 35
240. 3 p. brown (No. 233) .. 35 35
241. 5 p. violet (No. 234) .. 35 35
242. 10 p. plum (No. 235) .. 35 35
243. 25 p. blue (No. 236) .. 35 35

6. Hama. 7. Damascus.

1930. Views.
244. 6. 0 p. 10 purple 5 5
245. – 0 p. 20 blue 5 5
245a. – 0 p. 20 red 5 5
246. – 0 p. 25 green 5 5
246a. – 0 p. 25 violet 5 5
247. – 0 p. 50 violet 5 5
247a. – 0 p. 75 red 5 5
248. – 1 p. green 5 5
248a. – 1 p. brown 5 5
249. – 1 p. 50 brown 65 60
249a. – 1 p. 50 green 10 8
250. – 2 p. violet 5 5
251. – 3 p. green 15 12
252. 7. 4 p. orange 5 5
253. – 4 p. 50 red 10 8
254. – 6 p. green 5 5
255. – 7 p. 50 blue 5 5
256. – 10 p. brown 15 5
257. – 15 p. green 20 15
258. – 25 p. claret 20 12
259. – 50 p. sepia .. .. 1·00 90
260. – 100 p. red .. .. 3·00 3·00

DESIGNS—As T **6**: 20 c. Aleppo. 25 c. Hama. As T **7**: 50 c. Alexandretta. 75 c., 4 p. 50, Homs. 1 p., 7 p. 50, Aleppo. 1 p. 50, 100 p. Damascus. 2 p., 10 p. Antioch. 3 p. Bosra. 6 p. Sednaya. 15 p. Hama. 25 p. St. Simeon. 50 p. Palmyra.

8. River Euphrates.

1931. Air. Views with aeroplane.
261. – 0 p. 50 yellow (Homs) 5 5
261a. – 0 p. 50 sepia (Homs) .. 20 15
262. – 1 p. brown (Damascus) 10 8
263. 8. 2 p. blue 45 25
264. – 3 p. green (Palmyra) .. 10 8
265. – 5 p. purple (Deir-ez-Zor) 15 8
266. – 10 p. blue (Palmyra) .. 15 10
267. – 15 p. red (Aleppo citadel) 40 40
268. – 25 p. orange (Hama) .. 40 35
269. – 50 p. black (Zebdani) .. 25 25
270. – 100 p. mauve (Telebisse) 25 25

9. Parliament House, Damascus.

10. Aboulula el Maari.

11. Aeroplane over Bloudan.

1934. Establishment of Republic.
271. 9. 0 p. 10 olive (postage) 20 20
272. 0 p. 20 black 20 20
273. 0 p. 25 red 20 20
274. 0 p. 50 blue 20 20
275. 0 p. 75 purple 20 20
276. 10. 1 p. red 50 50
277. 1 p. 50 green .. .. 1·10 1·10
278. 2 p. red .. .. .. 1·10 1·10
279. 3 p. blue .. .. 1·10 1·10
280. 4 p. violet .. .. 1·10 1·10
281. 4 p. 50 red .. .. 1·10 1·10
282. 5 p. blue .. .. 1·10 1·10
283. 6 p. brown .. .. 1·10 1·10
284. 7 p. 50 blue .. .. 1·10 1·10
285. – 10 p. brown .. .. 1·50 1·50
286. – 15 p. blue .. .. 2·00 2·00
287. – 25 p. red .. .. 3·25 3·25
288. – 50 p. brown .. .. 5·00 5·00
289. – 100 p. red .. .. 7·50 7·50

DESIGNS—As T **10**: Nos. 285/7. President Mohammed Ali Bey el Abed. Nos. 288/9, Sultan Saladin.

290. 11. 0 p. 50 brown (air) .. 45 45
291. 1 p. green 45 45
292. 2 p. blue 45 45
293. 3 p. red 45 45
294. 5 p. purple 45 45
295. 10 p. violet .. .. 5·00 5·00
296. 15 p. brown .. .. 5·00 5·00
297. 25 p. blue .. .. 5·00 5·00
298. 50 p. black .. .. 6·00 6·00
299. 100 p. red .. .. 10·00 10·00

1936. Damascus Fair. Optd. **FOIRE DE DAMAS 1936** in Arabic and French.
(a) Postage stamps of 1930.
300. – 0 p. 50 violet 60 60
301. – 1 p. brown 60 60
302. – 2 p. violet 60 60
303. – 3 p. green 60 60
304. 7. 4 p. orange 60 60
305. – 4 p. 50 red 60 60
306. – 6 p. green 60 60
307. – 7 p. 50 blue 60 60
308. – 10 p. brown 60 60

(b) Air stamps of 1931.
309. – 0 p. 50 sepia 70 70
310. – 1 p. brown 70 70
311. 8. 2 p. blue 70 70
312. – 3 p. green 70 70
313. – 5 p. purple 70 70

12. Exhibition Pavilion.

1937. Air. Paris International Exn.
314. 12. ½ p. green 30 30
315. 1 p. green 30 30
316. 2 p. brown 30 30
317. 3 p. red 30 30
318. 5 p. orange 50 50
319. 10 p. green 75 75
320. 15 p. blue 75 75
321. 25 p. violet 75 75

14. Aleppo.

DESIGN: 1, 3, 10, 25 p. Aeroplane over Damascus.

1937. Air.
322. 14. ½ p. violet 5 5
323. – 1 p. black 5 5
324. 14. 2 p. green 8 8
325. – 3 p. blue 10 10
326. 14. 5 p. mauve 15 15
327. – 10 p. brown 20 20
328. 14. 15 p. brown 75 75
329. – 25 p. blue 75 75

1938. Stamps of 1930 surch. in English and Arabic figures and bars.
330. 0 p. 25 on 0 p. 75 on 75 c. red 5 5
331. 0 p. 50 on 1 p. 50 green .. 5 5
332. 2 p. on 7 p. 50 blue .. 5 5
333. 2 p. 50 on 4 p. orange .. 5 5
334. 5 p. on 7 p. 50 blue .. 5 5
335. 10 p. on 50 p. sepia .. 10 10
336. 10 p. on 100 p. red .. 20 20

15. M. Nogues and 1st Flight Route.

16. President Atasi.

1938. Air. 1st Air Service Flight between France and Syria. 10th Anniv.
337. 15. 10 p. green 75 75

1938. Unissued stamp surch. **12.50** and in Arabic figures.
338. 16. 12 p. 50 on 10 p. blue 8 5

1938.
338a. 16. 10 p. blue 8 5
339. 20 p. sepia 12 12

17. Palmyra.

1940.
340. 17. 5 p. pink 10 5

18. Damascus Museum.

19. Deir-el-Zor Bridge.

341. 18. 0 p. 10 red (postage) .. 5 5
342. 0 p. 20 blue 5 5
343. 0 p. 25 brown 5 5
344. 0 p. 50 blue 5 5
345. – 1 p. blue 5 5
346. – 1 p. 50 brown 5 5
347. – 2 p. 50 green 5 5
348. – 5 p. violet 5 5
349. – 7 p. 50 red 15 5
350. – 50 p. purple 35 30

DESIGNS—As T **19**: 1 p., 1 p. 50, 2 p. 50, Hotel de Bloudan. 5 p., 7 p. 50, 50 p. Kasr-el-Heir Fortress.

351. 19. 0 p. 25 black (air) .. 5 5
352. 0 p. 50 blue 5 5
353. 1 p. blue 5 5
354. 2 p. brown 5 5
355. 5 p. green 12 12
356. 10 p. red 20 20
357. 50 p. violet 70 70

20. President Sheikh Taj Addin-el-Husni. 21.

1942. National Independence. Inscr. "PROCLAMATION/DE L'INDEPENDANCE/27 Septembre 1941".
358. 20. 0 p. 50 green (postage) 1·00 1·00
359. 1 p. 50 sepia .. .. 1·00 1·00
360. 6 p. red .. .. .. 1·00 1·00
361. 15 p. blue .. .. 1·00 1·00
362. – 10 p. blue (air) 65 65
363. – 50 p. purple 65 65

DESIGN: 10 p., 50 p. As T **20**, but President bareheaded and aeroplane inset.

1942. (a) Postage. Portrait in oval frame.
364. 21. 6 p. claret and pink .. 55 55
365. 15 p. blue 55 55

(b) Air. Portrait in rectangular frame.
366. 10 p. green 70 70

INDEX
Countries can be quickly located by referring to the index at the end of this volume.

22. Syria and late President's portrait.

23. Shukri Bey al-Quwatli.

1943. Union of Alaouites and Jebel Druze with Syria. (a) President bare-headed.
367. 22. 1 p. green (postage) .. 40 40
368. 4 p. brown 40 40
369. 8 p. violet 40 40
370. 10 p. orange 40 40
371. 20 p. blue 40 40

(b) President wearing turban.
372. 2 p. brown (air) 40 40
373. 10 p. purple 40 40
374. 20 p. blue 40 40
375. 50 p. pink 40 40

1943. Death of President Sheikh Taj Addin-el-Husni. Nos. 367/375 optd. with narrow black border.
376. 22. 1 p. green (postage) .. 40 40
377. 4 p. brown 40 40
378. 8 p. violet 40 40
379. 10 p. orange 40 40
380. 20 p. blue 40 40
381. 2 p. brown (air) 40 40
382. 10 p. purple 40 40
383. 20 p. blue 40 40
384. 50 p. pink 40 40

1944. Air.
385. 23. 200 p. purple .. .. 2·75 2·75
386. 500 p. blue .. .. 3·25 3·25

(24. Trans. "First Congress of Arab Lawyers, Damascus".)

(25. Trans. "Aboulula-el-Maari. Commemorative of Millenary, 363–1363".)

1944. Air. 1st Arab Lawyers' Congress. Optd. with T **24**.
387. 14. 10 p. brown 45 45
388. – 15 p. red (No. 267) .. 45 45
389. – 25 p. orge. (No. 268) .. 45 45
390. – 100 p. mauve (No. 270) 1·10 1·10
391. 23. 200 p. purple .. .. 2·00 2·00

1945. Millenary of Aboulula-el-Maari (Arab poet and philosopher). Optd. with T **25**.
392. – 2 p. 50 green (No. 347) (postage) .. 75 75
393. – 7 p. 50 red (No. 349) .. 75 75
394. – 15 p. red (No. 267) (air) 55 55
395. – 25 p. orge. (No. 268) .. 55 55
396. 23. 500 p. blue .. .. 5·00 5·00

26. Shukri Bey al-Quwatli.

27. Shukri Bey al-Quwatli.

1945. Resumption of Constitutional Govt.
397. 26. 4 p. violet (postage) .. 8 8
398. 6 p. blue 8 8
399. 10 p. red 10 10
400. 15 p. brown 15 15
401. 20 p. green 20 20
402. 40 p. orange 40 40
403. 27. 5 p. green (air) 12 12
404. 10 p. red 15 15
405. 15 p. orange 15 15
406. 25 p. blue 20 15
407. 50 p. violet 40 15
408. 100 p. brown 90 35
409. 200 p. brown .. .. 2·00 1·10

البريد السوري
POSTES SYRIE
(28.)

البريد السوري
12P.½
POSTES SYRIE
(29.)

1945. Fiscal stamps inscr. "TIMBRE FISCAL", optd. with T 28.
410. 25 p. brown .. .. 1·25 1·25
411. 50 p. on 75 p. brown .. 2·00 2·00
412. 75 p. brown .. .. 2·50 2·50
413. 100 p. green .. .. 3·00 3·00

1945. Fiscal stamps surch. as T 29 or optd. with T 28 and additional Arabic inscription.
414. 12½ p. on 15 p. green .. 35 30
415. 25 p. on 25 s. purple .. 70 85
416. 50 p. on 75 p. brown .. 30 30
417. 50 p. mauve 50 40
418. 100 p. green 80 70

POSTES SYRIE
(30.)

30a. Ear of Wheat.

31. President Shukri Bey al-Quwatli.
32. Arab Horse.

1946. Fiscal stamp optd. with T 30.
419. 200 p. blue .. .. 2·75 2·75

1946.
420. 30a. 0 p. 50 orange (postage) 5 5
421. 1 p. violet 8 5
422. 2 p. 50 grey 10 8
423. 5 p. green 15 12
424. 31. 7 p. 50 brown .. 8 5
425. 10 p. blue 10 5
426. 12 p. 50 violet .. 12 5
427. – 15 p. red 12 8
428. – 20 p. violet 20 10
429. – 25 p. blue 35 8
430. 32. 50 p. brown .. 1·10 40
431. 100 p. green .. 2·75 80
432. 200 p. purple .. 5·50 2·25
DESIGN—As T 31: 15 p., 20 p., 25 p. Pres. Shukri Bey al-Quwatli bareheaded.

433. – 3 p. brown (air) .. 25 5
434. – 5 p. green 25 5
435. – 6 p. orange 25 5
436. – 10 p. grey 10 5
437. – 15 p. red 12 8
438. – 25 p. blue 15 8
439. – 50 p. violet 25 15
440. – 100 p. green 75 25
441. – 200 p. brown .. 1·60 50
442. – 300 p. brown .. 2·25 1·10
443. – 500 p. olive .. 5·00 1·75
DESIGNS—HORIZ. 3 p., 5 p., 6 p. Flock of sheep. 10 p., 15 p., 25 p. Kattineh dam. 50 p., 100 p., 200 p. Temple ruins, Kanaouat. 300 p., 500 p. Sultan Ibrahim Mosque.

(35.)

1946. Withdrawal of Allied Forces. Optd. with T 35. (a) Postage.
444. 31. 10 p. blue 20 20
445. 12 p. 50 violet .. 30 30
446. 32. 50 p. brown 80 80

(b) Air.
447. – 25 p. blue (No. 438) .. 65 45

(36.) (37.)

1946. 8th Arab Medical Congress, Aleppo. (a) Postage. Optd. with T 36.
448. 25 p. blue (No. 429) .. 60 55

(b) Air. Optd. with T 37.
449. 25 p. blue (No. 438) .. 65 45
450. 50 p. violet (No. 439) .. 90 65
451. 100 p. green (No. 440) .. 1·75 1·10

(38.)

ILLUSTRATIONS
British Commonwealth and all overprints and surcharges are FULL SIZE. Foreign Countries have been reduced to ¾-LINEAR.

1947. 1st Anniv. of Evacuation of Allied Forces. Nos. 444/447 optd. as T 38 ("1947").
452. 31. 10 p. blue (postage) .. 20 5
453. 12 p. 50 violet 35 8
454. 32. 50 p. brown 80 30

455. – 25 p. blue (air) 65 45

39. Hercules and Lion.
40. Mosaic of the Mosque of the Omayades.

41. Courtyard of Azem Palace.
42. Congress Symbol.

1947. 1st Arab Archaeological Congress, Damascus. Inscr. "1er CONGRES ARCHEOLOGIQUE ARABE–1947".
456. 39. 12 p. 50 green (postage) 25 20
457. 40. 25 p. blue 50 40

458. – 12 p. 50 violet (air) .. 25 15
459. – 50 p. brown .. .. 1·25 65
DESIGNS—HORIZ. 12 p. 50, Window at Kasr El-Heir El-Gharbi. 50 p. King Hazekil's throne.

1947. 3rd Arab Engineers Congress Damascus. Inscr. "3e CONGRES DES INGENIEURS ARABES 1947".
460. 41. 12 p. 50 purple (post.) 25 20
461. – 25 p. blue 50 30

462. – 12 p. 50 olive (air) .. 30 20
463. 42. 50 p. violet .. .. 1·25 90
DESIGNS—HORIZ. No. 461 Telephone Exchange Building. No. 462 Fortress at Kasr El-Heir El-Charqui.

43. Parliament Building.
44. Pres. Shukri Bey al-Quwatli.

1948. Re-election of Pres. Shukri Bey al-Quwatli.
464. 43. 12 p. 50 brown & grey (postage) 25 10
465. 44. 25 p. mauve 40 25

466. 43. 12 p. 50 blue and violet (air) 20 10
467. 44. 50 p. purple and green .. 85 40

45. Syrian Arms.
46. Soldier and Flag.

1948. Compulsory Military Service.
468. 45. 12 p. 50 brown & grey (postage) 25 12
469. 46. 25 p. green, red, black and blue 40 25

470. 45. 12 p. 50 blue (air) .. 30 15
471. 46. 50 p. grn., red & black 1·00 40

1948. Surch. (a) Postage.
472. – 50 c. on 75 c. red (No. 247a) 5 5
472a. 32. 2 p. 50 on 200 p. purple 10 8
472b. 10 p. on 100 p. green .. 12 8
473. 25 p. on 200 p. purple .. 35 15

(b) Air.
474. – 2 p. 50 on 3 p. (No. 433) 5 5
475. – 2 p. 50 on 6 p. (No. 435) 5 5
475a. – 2 p. 50 on 100 p. (No. 440) 5 5
476. – 25 p. on 200 p. (No. 441) 20 10
477. – 50 p. on 300 p. (No. 442) 50 25
478. – 50 p. on 500 p. (No. 443) 50 25

47. Palmyra.
48. President Husni el Zaim and Aeroplane over Damascus.

1949. U.P.U. 75th Anniv. Inscr. "UPU. 1874 1949".
479. – 12 p. 50 violet (postage) 80 80
480. 47. 25 p. blue .. .. 1·40 1·25

481. – 12 p. 50 purple (air) .. 1·90 1·90
482. 48. 50 p. slate .. .. 6·00 4·25
DESIGNS—HORIZ. No. 479, Ain-el-Arous. No. 481, Globe and mountains.

49. President Husni el-Zaim.
50. Pres. Husni el-Zaim and Map.

52. Damascus.
51. Tel-Chehab.

1949. Revolution of 30 March, 1949.
483. 49. 25 p. blue (postage) .. 40 25

484. 50 p. brown (air) .. 1·25 1·10

1949. Presidential Election.
485. 50. 25 p. brn. & blue (post.) 80 65
486. 50 p. blue and red (air) 1·40 1·10

1949.
487. 51. 5 p. grey 5 5
488. 7 p. 50 brown 10 5
524. 7 p. 50 green 5 5
489. 52. 12 p. 50 purple .. 20 5
490. 25 p. blue 30 10

54.

53
55. Port of Latakia.

1950.
491. 53. 0 p. 50 brown 5 5
492. 2 p. 50 pink 8 5
493. – 10 p. violet 15 12
494. – 12 p. 50 green .. 25 15
495. 54. 25 p. blue 50 12
496. 50 p. black .. .. 1·50 25
DESIGN—HORIZ. 10 p., 12 p. 50, Road to Damascus.

1950. Air.
497. 55. 2 p. 50 violet 20 5
498. 10 p. turquoise-blue .. 30 5
518. 10 p. violet-blue .. 75 55
499. 15 p. brown .. .. 1·10 8
500. 25 p. blue .. .. 2·10 12

56. Parliament Building.

57. Book and Torch.

1951. New Constitution, 1950.
501. 56. 12 p. 50 black (postage) 15 10
502. 25 p. blue 25 20

503. 57. 12 p. 50 red (air) .. 15 10
504. 50 p. purple 55 45

58. Hama.

1952.
505. 58. 0 p. 50 sepia (postage) 5 5
506. 2 p. 50 slate 8 5
507. 5 p. green 12 5
508. 10 p. red 20 5
509. – 12 p. 50 black .. 25 5
510. – 15 p. claret 45 8
511. – 25 p. blue 55 12
512. – 100 p. bistre .. .. 2·25 50

513. – 2 p. 50 red (air) .. 5 5
514. – 5 p. green 10 5
515. – 15 p. violet 15 10
516. – 25 p. blue 25 10
517. – 100 p. purple .. .. 1·40 30
DESIGNS—Postage: 12 p. 50 to 100 p. Palace of Justice, Damascus. Air: 2 p. 50 to 15 p. Palmyra. 25 p., 100 p. Citadel, Aleppo.

1952. Air. United Nations Social Seminar, Damascus. Optd. **U.N.S.W.S. Damascus 8-20 Dec. 1952** and curved line of Arabic.
518. 55. 10 p. blue 75 55
519. – 15 p. vio. (No. 515) .. 75 55
520. – 25 p. blue (No. 516) .. 1·25 80
521. – 50 p. viol. (No. 439) .. 3·25 1·10

59. Qalaat el Hasn Fortress.
60. "Labour".

61. "Family".
62. "Communications".

1953. (a) Postage. View as T 59.
522. 59. 0 p. 50 red 5 5
523. 2 p. 50 brown 5 5
525. 12 p. 50 blue 8 5

527. 50 p. brown 55 15

1954.
528. 60. 1 p. olive (postage) .. 5 5
529. 2½ p. lake 5 5
530. 5 p. blue 5 5
531. 61. 7½ p. lake 8 5
532. 10 p. black 10 5
533. 12½ p. violet 15 5
534. – 20 p. claret 25 8
535. – 25 p. violet 50 12
536 – 50 p. green .. .. 1·10 30

537. 62. 5 p. violet (air) .. 8 5
538. 10 p. chocolate 10 5
539. 15 p. green 12 5
540. – 30 p. chocolate 20 8
541. – 35 p. blue 25 10
542. – 40 p. orange 30 15
543. – 50 p. purple 45 25
544. – 70 p. violet 65 25
DESIGNS—HORIZ. (As T 61): Postage. 20 p. to 50 p. "Industry". Air. 30 p. to 70 p. Syrian University.

63.
64.

1954. Air. Damascus Fair. Inscr. as in T **63**.

545. **63.** 40 p. magenta 40 20

546. – 50 p. green 55 25

DESIGN: 50 p. Mosque and Syrian flag.

1954. Cotton Festival, Aleppo. Optd. **FESTIVAL du COTON, Alep. oct. 1954** and Arab inscription.

547. **61.** 10 p. black (postage) .. 20 8

548. – 25 p. violet (No. 535) .. 25 15

549. – 50 p. brown (No. 527) (air) 45 45

550. – 100 p. pur. (No. 517) .. 90 65

1955. Arab Postal Union. As T **87** of Egypt but inscr. "SYRIE".

551. 12½ p. green (postage) .. 25 8

552. 25 p. violet 35 15

553. 5 p. brown (air) .. 10 8

1955. Air. Middle East Rotary Congress.

554. **64.** 35 p. red 35 25

555. 65 p. green 70 40

65.  **66.** "Facing the Future".

1955. Air. Rotary International. 50th Anniv.

556. **65.** 25 p. violet 25 15

557. 75 p. turquoise 80 50

1955. Air. Evacuation of Allied Forces. 9th Anniv.

558. **66.** 40 p. magenta 25 20

559. – 60 p. blue 40 25

DESIGN: 60 p. Tank and infantry attack.

See also Nos. 847/9.

67. Mother and Child.  **68.** Aeroplane, Flag and Crowd.

1955. Mothers' Day.

560. **67.** 25 p. red (postage) .. 25 12

561. 35 p. violet (air) .. 40 30

562. 40 p. black 55 35

1955. Air. Emigrants' Congress.

563. **68.** 5 p. magenta 20 10

564. – 15 p. blue 25 15

DESIGN: 15 p. Aeroplane over globe.

69. Syrian Pavilion.  **70.** Mother and Baby.

1955. Air. Int. Fair, Damascus.

565. **69.** 25 p.+5 p. black .. 25 25

566. – 35 p.+5 p. blue .. 30 30

567. – 40 p.+10 p. magenta .. 40 40

568. – 70 p.+10 p. green .. 75 75

DESIGNS: 35 p., 40 p. "Industry and Agriculture". 70 p. Exhibition pavilions and flags.

1955. Air. Int. Children's Day.

569. **70.** 25 p. blue 25 20

570. 50 p. purple 55 30

DESIGN—HORIZ. 15 p., 35 p. Globe, dove and Scales of Justice.

71. U.N. Emblem and Torch.

1955. U.N.O. 10th Anniv.

571. **71.** 7½ p. red (postage) .. 25 15

572. 12½ p. slate 35 20

573. – 15 p. blue (air) 25 12

574. – 35 p. sepia 55 25

72. Saracen Gate, Aleppo Citadel. 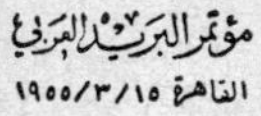 (**73.**)

1955. Installation of Aleppo Water Supply from R. Euphrates.

575. **72.** 7 p. 50 violet (postage) 10 5

576. 12 p. 50 red 15 5

577. 30 p. blue (air) 65 30

1955. 2nd Arab Postal Union Congress, Cairo. Nos. 551/553 optd. with T **73**.

578. 12½ p. green (postage) .. 10 5

579. 25 p. violet 20 15

580. 5 p. brown (air) 12 8

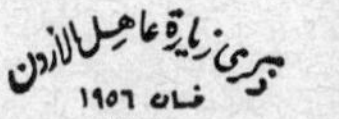

(**74.**)  **75.** Monument.

1956. Visit of King Hussein of Jordan. Nos. 551/553 optd. with T **74**.

581. 12½ p. green (postage) .. 20 20

582. 25 p. violet 35 35

583. 5 p. brown (air) 10 10

1956. Air. Evacuation of Allied Forces. 10th Anniv.

584. **75.** 35 p. sepia 25 20

585. – 65 p. red 50 45

586. – 75 p. grey 60 60

DESIGNS: 65 p. Winged female figure. 75 p. Pres. Shukri Bey al-Quwatli.

76. Pres. Shukri Bey-al-Quwatli.  **77.** Cotton.  **78.** Gate of Kasr-al-Heir, Palmyra.

1956. Air.

587. **76.** 100 p. black 55 25

588. 200 p. violet .. .. 1·10 85

589. 300 p. red .. .. 1·60 1·10

590. 500 p. green .. .. 3·25 2·50

1956. Aleppo Cotton Festival.

591. **77.** 2½ p. green 10 5

1956. Air. Nos. 565/8 with premiums obliterated by bars.

592. **69.** 25 p. black 20 12

593. – 35 p. blue 30 12

594. – 40 p. magenta 45 25

595. – 70 p. green 65 55

1956. Air. 3rd Int. Fair, Damascus.

596. **78.** 15 p. sepia 15 15

597. – 20 p. blue 20 20

598. – 30 p. green 30 30

599. – 35 p. blue 40 40

600. – 50 p. claret 45 45

DESIGNS: 20 p. Cotton mill. 30 p. Tractor. 35 p. Galley and cog-wheels. 50 p. Textiles, carpets and pottery.

DESIGNS—VERT. 30 p. Syrian legionary's helmet. HORIZ. 50 p. Lintel of Belshamine Temple, Palmyra.

79. Clay Alphabetical Tablet.

1956. Air. Int. Campaign for Museums.

601. **79.** 20 p. black 25 20

602. – 30 p. claret 40 30

603. – 50 p. sepia 65 55

1956. U.N.O. 11th Anniv. Nos. 571/574 optd. **11 eme ANNIVERSAIRE de L'ONU** in French and Arabic.

604. **71.** 7½ p. red (postage) .. 25 15

605. 12½ p. slate 30 15

606. – 15 p. blue (air) 55 25

607. – 35 p. sepia 1 10 60

80. Trees and Mosque.

81. "Resistance".  **82.** Mother and Child.

1956. Air. Afforestation Day.

608. **80.** 10 p. brown 10 8

609. 40 p. grey 30 30

1957. Syrian Defence Force.

612. **81.** 5 p. magenta 8 5

613. 20 p. slate 20 10

1957. Evacuation of Port Said. Optd. **22.12.56 EVACUATION PORT SAID** in French and Arabic.

614. **81.** 5 p. magenta 10 5

615. 20 p. slate 20 15

1957. Air. Mothers' Day.

616. – 40 p. blue 30 25

617. **82.** 60 p. red 50 40

DESIGN: 40 p. Mother fondling child.

83.  **84.** "Sword of Liberty".

1957.

610. **83.** 12½ p. purple .. 8 5

611. 15 p. black .. 12 5

1957. Air. Evacuation of Allied Forces. 11th Anniv.

618. **84.** 10 p. claret 8 8

619. – 15 p. green 12 10

620. – 25 p. violet 20 12

621. – 35 p. magenta 25 20

622. **84.** 40 p. grey 40 30

DESIGNS: 15 p., 35 p. Woman holding torch and map. 25 p. Pres. Shukri Bey al-Quwatli.

85. Ship at Quayside and Fair Emblem.  **86.** "Cotton".

1957. Air. 4th Damascus Fair.

623. **85.** 25 p. purple 15 12

624. – 30 p. brown 20 15

625. – 35 p. blue 30 20

626. – 40 p. green 30 20

627. **85.** 70 p. olive 45 40

DESIGNS—VERT. 30 p., 40 p. Girls harvesting and cotton picking. HORIZ. 35 p. Interior of processing plant.

1957. Aleppo Cotton Festival.

628. **86.** 12½ p. blk. & grn. (post.) 15 10

629. 17½ p. black & orge. (air) 20 12

630. 40 p. black and blue .. 40 20

87. Children at Work and Play.  **88.** Letter and Post-box.

1957. Int. Children's Day.

631. **87.** 12½ p. olive (postage) .. 25 12

632. 17½ p. blue (air) .. 50 20

633. 20 p. brown 50 20

1957. Int. Correspondence Week.

634. **88.** 5 p. magenta (postage) 20 10

635. – 5 p. green (air) 12 8

DESIGN: No. 635, Family writing letters.

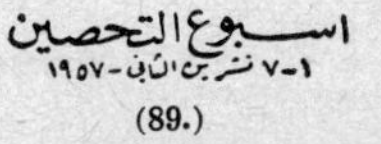

(**89.**)

91. Sailplane.  **90.** Scales of Justice, Map and Damascus Silhouette.

1957. Fortifications Week. Optd. with T **89**.

636. **81.** 5 p. magenta 5 5

637. 20 p. slate 15 10

1957. 3rd Arab Lawyers Union Congress, Damascus.

638. **90.** 12½ p. green (postage) 12 8

639. 17½ p. red (air) .. 20 10

640. 40 p. sepia 25 20

1957. Air. Gliding Festival.

641. **91.** 25 p. brown 30 12

642. 35 p. green 50 15

643. 40 p. blue 80 25

92. Torch and Map.  **93.** Khaled ibn el Walid Mosque, Homs.

1957. Afro-Asian Jurists Congress, Damascus.

644. **92.** 20 p. drab (postage) .. 20 10

645. 30 p. green (air) .. 20 15

646. 50 p. violet 30 20

1957.

647. **93.** 2½ p. brown 5 5

UNITED ARAB REPUBLIC

DESIGN—VERT. 15 p. Telephone, radio tower and telegraph pole.

94. Telecommunications Building.

1958. Five Year Plan.

648. **94.** 25 p. blue (postage) 15 12

649. 10 p. green (air) .. 10 5

650. – 15 p. brown .. 10 10

1958. Birth of United Arab Republic. As T **113** of Egypt but inscr. "SYRIA".

651. 12½ p. green & yellow (post.) 10 8

652. 17½ p. chocolate & blue (air) 20 15

DESIGN: 35 p., 45 p. Broken chain, dove and olive branch.

95. "Eternal Flame".

1958. Evacuation of Allied Forces. 12th Anniv. Inscr. as in T **95**.

653. **95.** 5 p. vio. & lemon (post.) 20 10

654. 15 p. red and green .. 30 20

655. – 35 p. black and red (air) 55 20

656. – 45 p. brown and blue .. 80 30

96. Scout fixing Tent-peg.

1958. Air. 3rd Pan-Arab Scout Jamboree

657. **96.** 35 p. sepia 80 80

658. 40 p. blue .. .. 1·40 1·40

97. Mosque, Chimneys and Cogwheel.

98. Bronze Rattle.

1958. Air. 5th Int. Fair, Damascus. Inscr. "1.9.58".
659. – 25 p. red 30 20
660. – 30 p. green 50 40
661. **97.** 45 p. violet 55 50
DESIGNS—HORIZ. 25 p. View of Fair. VERT. 30 p. Minaret, vase and emblem.

1958. Ancient Syrian Art. Inscr. as in T **98.**
662. **98.** 10 p. olive 8 5
663. – 15 p. chestnut 10 5
664. – 20 p. purple 12 5
665. – 30 p. sepia 15 8
666. – 40 p. grey 20 10
667. – 60 p. green 30 15
668. – 75 p. blue 45 20
669. – 100 p. claret 70 35
670. – 150 p. purple .. .. 1·10 45
DESIGNS: 15 p. Goddess of Spring. 20 p. "Lamgi Mari" (statue). 30 p. Mithras fighting bull. 40 p. Aspasia. 60 p. Minerva. 75 p. Ancient gourd. 100 p. Enamelled vase. 150 p. Mosaic from Omayyad Mosque, Damascus.

1958. Int. Children's Day. Optd. **R A U** and Arabic inscription.
670a. **87.** 12½ p. olive (postage) 20·00 20·00
670b. 17½ p. blue (air) .. 16·00 16·00
670c. 20 p. brown .. .. 16·00 16·00

99. Cotton and Textiles.

100. Children and Gliders.

1958. Air. Aleppo Cotton Festival.
671. **99.** 25 p. yellow and sepia 30 30
672. 35 p. red and sepia .. 50 40

1958. Republic of Iraq Commem. As T **119** of Egypt but smaller (26×42 mm.).
673. 12½ p. red 10 8

1958. Air. Gliding Festival.
674. **100.** 7½ p. green 15 10
675. 12½ p. olive 70 50

101. Damascus.

1958. 4th N.E. Regional Conf., Damascus.
676. **101.** 12½ p. green (postage) 15 8
677. 17½ p. violet (air) .. 15 10

102. U.N. Emblem and Charter.

1958. Declaration of Human Rights. 10th Anniv.
678. **102.** 25 p. purple 15 12
679. 35 p. grey 20 15
680. 40 p. brown 30 20

Stamps as Types of Egypt are easily distinguished by having values expressed in piastres.

1959. Post Day and Postal Employees' Social Fund. As T **123** of Egypt.
681. 20 p.+10 p. red, blk. & grn. 25 25

1959. United Arab Republic. As T **125** of Egypt.
682. 12½ p. red, black and green 12 8

103. Secondary School, Damascus.

1959.
683. **103.** 12½ p. green 8 5

1959. Air. Arab Telecommunications Union Commem. As T **127** of Egypt but larger (47×30 mm.).
684. 40 p. black and green .. 25 15

1959. Air. No. 684 optd. **2nd CONFERANCE DAMASCUS 1.3.1959** in English and Arabic.
685. 40 p. black and green .. 25 15

1959. Proclamation of the United Arab States (U.A.R. and Yemen). 1st Anniv. As T **128** of Egypt.
686. 12½ p. red and green .. 12 8

104. Mother with Children.

105.

1959. Arab Mothers' Day.
687. **104.** 15 p. pink 10 8
688. 25 p. grey-green .. 15 12

1959. Surch. **U.A.R. 2½ p.** and also in Arabic.
689. **60.** 2½ p. on 1 p. olive .. 5 5

1959. Air. "Evacuation 17.4.1959".
690. **105.** 15 p. green and yellow 12 8
691. – 35 p. red and grey .. 25 20
DESIGN: 35 p. Broken chain and flame.

106.

107. "Emigration".

1959. Patterns as T **106.**
692. **106.** 2½ p. violet 5 5
693. – 5 p. olive-brown .. 5 5
694. – 7½ p. blue 5 5
695. – 10 p. green 5 5
DESIGNS show different styles of ornamental scrollwork.

1959. Air. Emigrants' Congress.
696. **107.** 80 p. black, red & green 50 30

108. Oil Refinery.

1959. Air. Oil Refinery Inaug.
697. **108.** 50 p. red, black & blue 40 15

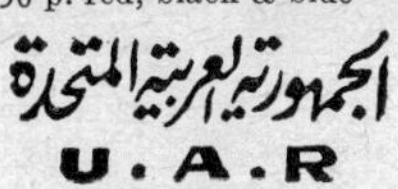
(109.)

1959. Optd. as T **109.**
698. **83** 15 p. black (postage) 15 8
699. – 50 p. green (No. 536) .. 40 30
700. – 5 p. grn. (No. 635) (air) 5
701. – 50 p. purple (No. 543).. 30 15
702. – 70 p. violet (No. 544).. 50 20

110.

111.

1959. 6th Damascus Fair.
703. **110.** 35 p. grn., vio. & grey 25 15

1959. Air. Aleppo Cotton Festival.
704. **111.** 45 p. slate-blue .. 25 15
705. 50 p. claret 30 20

112. Child and Factory.

114. Ears of Corn, Cotton and Cog-wheel.

113. Normal School for Boys, Damascus.

1959. Air. Children's Day.
706. **112.** 25 p. red, blue & lilac 15 10

1959.
707. **113.** 25 p. blue 15 10
708. – 35 p. brown 25 12
DESIGN: 35 p. Normal School for Girls, Damascus.

1959. Army Day. As T **133** of Egypt.
709. 50 p. sepia 40 20

1959. Industrial and Agricultural Production Fair, Aleppo.
710. **114.** 35 p. brn., blue & grey 25 12

115. Mosque and Trees.

116. A. R. Kawakbi.

1959. Tree Day.
711. **115.** 12½ p. brown and green 10 5

1960. A. R. Kawakbi (writer). 50th Death Anniv.
712. **116.** 15 p. grey-green .. 12 8

1960. U.A.R. 2nd Anniv. As T **142** of Egypt.
713. 12½ p. green and red .. 10 8

117. Diesel Train.

1960. Latakia-Aleppo Railway Project.
714. **117.** 12½ p. choc., blk. & bl. 15 10

1960. Arab League Centre, Cairo. Inaug. As T **144** of Egypt.
715. 12½ p. black and green .. 10 8

1960. Mothers' Day. Optd. **ARAB MOTHERS DAY 1960** in English and Arabic.
716. **104.** 15 p. pink 12 8
717. 25 p. grey-green .. 20 10

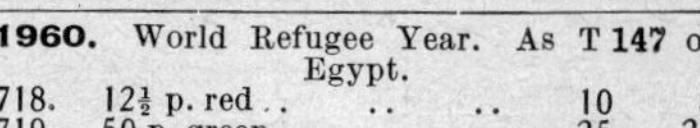
1960. World Refugee Year. As T **147** of Egypt.
718. 12½ p. red 10 8
719. 50 p. green 25 20

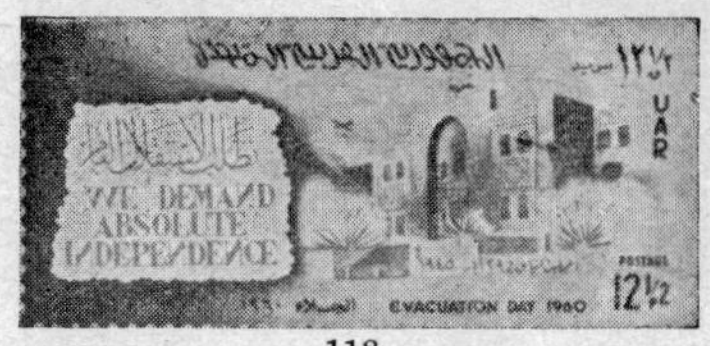
118.

1960. Evacuation of Allied Forces. 14th Anniv.
720. **118.** 12½ p. multicoloured .. 15 8

119. Hittin School.

1960.
721. **119.** 17½ p. lilac 15 5

1960. Industrial and Agricultural Production Fair, Aleppo. Optd. **1960** and in Arabic.
722. **112.** 35 p. grn., vio. & grey 20 15

120. Mobile Crane and Compasses.

(121.)

1960. Air. 7th Int. Damascus Fair.
723. **120.** 50 p. blk., bistre & red 30 20

1960. Air. Aleppo Cotton Festival. Optd. with T **121.**
724. **111.** 45 p. slate-blue .. 25 12
725. 50 p. claret 30 15

122.

123. Basketball.

1960. Children's Day.
726. **122.** 35 p. brown and green 25 15

1960. Air. Olympic Games.
727. **123.** 15 p. brn., blk. & blue 10 8
728. – 20 p. chest., blk. & blue 20 10
729. – 25 p. vio., blk. & yell. 20 10
730. – 40 p. vio., rose & blk. 35 25
DESIGNS: 20 p. Swimming. 25 p. Fencing (Arab-style). 40 p. Horse-jumping.

(124.)

125. "UN" and Globe.

1960. Tree Day. Optd. with T **124.**
731. **115.** 12½ p. brown and green 15 8

1960. Air. U.N.O. 15th Anniv.
732. **125.** 35 p. red, grn. & blue 20 12
733. 50 p. bl., ochre & red 30 20

126. Ibrahim Hanano (patriot). **127.** St. Simeon's Monastery.

1961. Air. Hanano Commem.
734. **126.** 50 p. grey-grn. & drab 30 20

1961. U.A.R. 3rd Anniv. As T **149** of Egypt.
735. 12½ p. violet 12 8

1961.
736. **127.** 12½ p. blue (postage) .. 8 5
746. – 200 p. blue (air) .. 1·10 65
DESIGN—VERT. 200 p. Entrance to St. Simeon's Monastery.

128. Raising the Flag. **129.** Eye and Hand "reading" Braille.

1961. Air. Evacuation of Allied Forces. 15th Anniv.
737. **128.** 40 p. grey-green .. 25 15

1961. Air. U.N. Campaign for Welfare of Blind.
738. **129.** 40 p. + 10 p. black and grey-green 35 35

130. Palestinian and Map. **131.** Cogwheel and Corn.

1961. Air. Palestine Day.
739. **130.** 50 p. blue and black .. 35 20

1961. Industrial and Agricultural Production Fair, Aleppo.
740. **131.** 12½ p. yellow, green, black and blue .. 10 5

132. Abou Tammam. **134.** Open Window on World.

133. Damascus University. Discus-thrower and Lyre.

1961. Air. Abou Tammam Commem.
741. **132.** 50 p. brown .. 35 15

1961. Air. 5th Universities Youth Festival.
742. **133.** 15 p. black and red .. 10 5
743. 35 p. violet and green 30 15

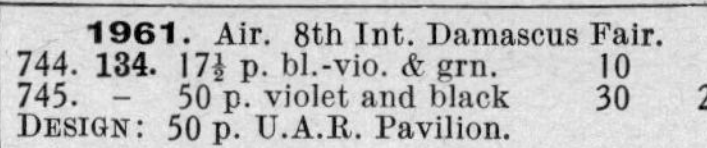

1961. Air. 8th Int. Damascus Fair.
744. **134.** 17½ p. bl.-vio. & grn. 10 8
745. – 50 p. violet and black 30 20
DESIGN: 50 p. U.A.R. Pavilion.

SYRIAN ARAB REPUBLIC

135. Assembly Chamber. **136.** The Noria, Hama.

137. Arch of Triumph, Latakia. **138.** Arab League Emblem and Headquarters, Cairo.

1961. Establishment of Syrian Arab Republic.
747. **135.** 15 p. purple .. 10 5
748. 35 p. olive 25 15

1961.
749. **136.** 2½ p. red (postage) .. 5 5
750. 5 p. blue 5 5
751. A. 7½ p. green 8 5
752. 10 p. orange 10 5
753. **137.** 12½ p. drab 25 5
754. B. 12½ p. olive 15 5
755. 15 p. blue 20 5
756. 17½ p. chocolate .. 20 5
757. 22½ p. turquoise .. 20 5
758. 25 p. red-brown .. 35 10
759. B. 45 p. olive (air) .. 25 20
760. 50 p. red 30 20
761. C. 85 p. purple 50 30
762. 100 p. purple 65 35
763. D. 200 p. green .. .. 1·10 65
764. 300 p. blue .. .. 1·40 75
764a. 500 p. purple .. .. 2·50 1·40
764b. 1000 p. black .. .. 5·00 2·50
DESIGNS: A. Khaled Ben Walid's Mosque, Homs. B, "The Beauty of Palmyra" (statue). C, Archway and columns, Palmyra. D, King Zahir Bibar's tomb.
See also Nos. 799/800.

1962. Air. Arab League Week.
765. **138.** 17½ p. blue-green and yellow-green .. 10 8
766. 22½ p. slate-vio. & blue 15 10
767. 50 p. sepia and salmon 35 20

139. Campaign Emblem. **140.** Prancing Horse.

1962. Air. Malaria Eradication.
768. **139.** 12½ p. vio., sep. & blue 10 8
769. 50 p. grn., choc. & yell. 30 25

1962. Air. Evacuation Day.
770. **140.** 45 p. orge. & violet .. 25 15
771. – 55 p. blue-violet & blue 40 20
DESIGN: 55 p. Military commander.

141. Qalb Lozah Church. **142.** Martyrs' Memorial, Swaida.

143. Jupiter Temple Gate. **144.** Globe, Monument and Handclasp.

1962.
772. **141.** 17½ p. olive 10 5
773. 35 p. blue-green .. 15 12

1962. Syrian Revolution Commem.
774. **142.** 12½ p. brown and drab 8 5
775. 35 p. blue-green & turq. 20 12

1962.
776. **143.** 2½ p. turquoise .. 5 5
777. 5 p. orange-brown .. 8 5
778. 7½ p. sepia 10 5
779. 1 p. maroon .. 5 5

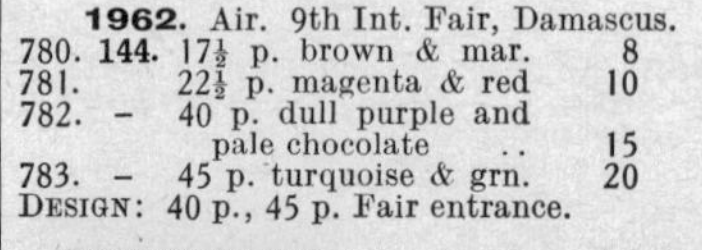

1962. Air. 9th Int. Fair, Damascus.
780. **144.** 17½ p. brown & mar. 8 5
781. 22½ p. magenta & red 10 8
782. – 40 p. dull purple and pale chocolate .. 15 12
783. – 45 p. turquoise & grn. 20 15
DESIGN: 40 p., 45 p. Fair entrance.

145. Festival Emblem. **146.** Pres. Kudsi.

1962. Air. Aleppo Cotton Festival.
784. **145.** 12½ p. yellow, maroon, black and bronze .. 10 8
785. 50 p. yellow, bronze, black and maroon .. 25 20
See also Nos. 820/1.

1962. Presidential Elections.
786. **146.** 12½ p. chocolate and blue (postage) .. 8 5
787. 50 p. indigo & buff (air) 25 15

147. Zenobia. **148.** Saadallah el-Djabiri.

1962. Air.
788. **147.** 45 p. violet 25 10
789. 50 p. red 30 15
790. 85 p. blue-green .. 40 25
791. 100 p. maroon .. 70 30
See also Nos. 801/4.

1962. Air. Saadallah el-Djabiri (revolutionary). 15th Death Anniv.
792. **148.** 50 p. grey-blue .. 25 12

149. Moharde Woman. **150.** Ears of Wheat, Hand and Globe.

1962. Air. Women in Regional Costumes. Multicoloured.
793. 40 p. Marje Sultan .. 20 12
794. 45 p. Kalamoun 20 15
795. 50 p. T **149** 25 20
796. 55 p. Jabal al-Arab .. 25 20
797. 60 p. Afrine 30 20
798. 65 p. Hauran 40 20

1963. As Nos. 750/3 (Type B) and T **147** but smaller (20 × 26 mm.).
799. B. 2½ p. slate-violet .. 5 5
800. 5 p. purple 5 5
801. **147.** 7½ p. slate 12 5
802. 10 p. drab 20 5
803. 12½ p. blue 35 5
804. 15 p. chocolate .. 50 5

1963. Freedom from Hunger.
805. **150.** 12½ p. blk. & bl. (post.) 5 5
806. – 50 p. black & red (air) 20 12
DESIGN: 50 p. Bird feeding young in nest.

151. Feris el-Khouri. **152.** S.A.R. Emblem.

1963. Air. Evacuation of Allied Forces. 17th Anniv.
807. **151.** 17½ p. sepia 12 5
808. **152.** 22½ p. turq. and black 12 8

153. Eagle. **154.** Hookah.

1963. Air. Baathist Revolution Commem.
809. **153.** 12½ p. green 5 5
810. 50 p. magenta .. 20 15

1963. Air. 10th Int. Fair, Damascus Hookah in yellow, red and black.
812. **154.** 37½ p. ultramarine .. 20 10
813. 50 p. blue 25 15

155. Ala el-Ma'ari (bust). **156.** Central Bank.

1963. Air. Honouring Ala el-Ma'ari (poet).
811. **155.** 50 p. slate-violet .. 20 15

1963. Damascus Buildings.
814. – 17½ p. violet 8 5
815. – 22½ p. blue-violet .. 10 5
816. **156.** 25 p. olive-brown .. 10 5
817. – 35 p. mauve 15 10
BUILDINGS: 17½ p. Hejaz Railway Station. 22½ p. Mouassat Hospital. 35 p. Post Office, Al-Jalaa.

157. "Red Crescent" and Centenary Emblem. **158.** Child with Ball.

1963. Air. Red Cross Centenary. Crescent in red.
818. **157.** 15 p. blk. & grey-blue 10 10
819. – 50 p. blk. & yell.-grn. 25 20
DESIGN: 50 p. "Red Crescent", globe and centenary emblem.

1963. Aleppo Cotton Festival. As T **145** but inscr. "POSTAGE" and "1963" in place of "AIRMAIL" and "1962".
820. **145.** 17½ p. multicoloured .. 8 5
821. 22½ p. multicoloured .. 12 10

1963. Children's Day.
822. **158.** 12½ p. green & emerald 5 5
823. 22½ p. green and red .. 10 5

159. Firas el-Hamadani. **160.** Flame on Head.

1963. Air. Abou Firas el-Hamadani (poet). Death Millenary.
824. **159.** 50 p. sepia and bistre 20 15

1963. Air. Declaration of Human Rights. 15th Anniv. Flame in red.
825. **160.** 17½ p. black & bl.-grey 8 8
826. 22½ p. black and green 10 8
827. 50 p. black and violet 20 12

161. Emblem and Flag.

1964. Air. 8th March Baathist Revolution. 1st Anniv. Emblem and flag in red, black and green; inscr. in black.
828. **161.** 15 p. yellow-green .. 5 5
829. 17½ p. pink 8 5
830. 22½ p. grey 15 10

162. Ugharit Princess. **163.** Chahba Thalassa Mosaic.

1964.
831. **162.** 2½ p. grey (postage) .. 5 5
832. 5 p. chocolate 5 5
833. 7½ p. purple 5 5
834. 10 p. green 5 5
835. 12½ p. violet 5 5
836. 17½ p. blue 10 5
837. 20 p. red 15 5
838. 25 p. orange 25 8

839. **163.** 27½ p. red (air) .. 10 8
840. 45 p. brown 20 10
841. 50 p. green 25 15
842. 55 p. bronze 25 20
843. 60 p. blue 30 20

164. Kaaba, Mecca and Mosque, Damascus. **165.** Abou al Zahrawi.

1964. Air. 1st Arab Moslem Wakf Ministers' Conference.
844. **164.** 12½ p. black and blue 5 5
845. 22½ p. blk. & mauve .. 10 8
846. 50 p. black and green 20 12

1964. Air. Evacuation of Allied Forces. 18th Anniv. As T **66** but larger (38½ × 26 mm.) inscr. "1964".
847. **166.** 20 p. blue 8 5
848. 25 p. magenta 10 8
849. 60 p. green 25 20

1964. Air. 4th Arab Dental and Oral Surgery Congress, Damascus.
850. **165.** 60 p. brown 20 15

166. Bronze Chimes. **167.** Cotton Plant and Symbols.

(**168.**) **169.** Aero Club Emblem.

1964. Air. 11th Int. Fair, Damascus.
851. **166.** 20 p. multicoloured .. 10 5
852. – 25 p. magenta, black, green and yellow .. 12 8
DESIGN: 25 p. Fair emblem.

1964. Air. Aleppo Cotton Festival. No. 854 is optd. with T **168.**
853. **167.** 25 p. yellow, green, black and blue .. 10 8
854. 25 p. yellow green, black and blue .. 12 8

1964. Air. Syrian Aero Club. 10th Anniv.
855. **169.** 12½ p. black and green 8 5
856. 17½ p. black and red .. 10 5
857. 20 p. black and blue .. 25 8

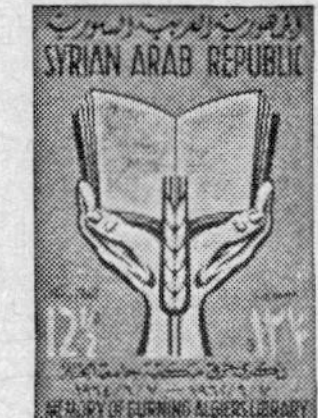

170. A.P.U. Emblem. **171.** Book within Hands.

1964. Air. Arab Postal Union. 10th Anniv.
858. **170.** 12½ p. black & orge. .. 5 5
859. 20 p. black and green 10 5
860. 25 p. black & magenta 10 8

1964. Air. Burning of Algiers Library.
861. **171.** 12½ p. black and green 5 5
862. 17½ p. black and red .. 8 5
863. 20 p. black and blue .. 10 8

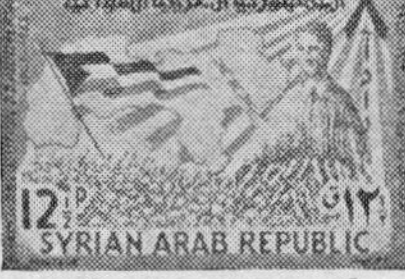

172. Tennis. **173.** Flag, Map and Revolutionaries.

1965. Air. Olympic Games, Tokyo. Multicoloured.
864. 12½ p. Type **172** 5 5
865. 17½ p. Wrestling 8 5
866. 20 p. Weightlifting .. 12 8

1965. March 8th Revolution. 2nd Anniv.
867. **173.** 12½ p. black, red, green and brown .. 5 5
868. 17½ p. black, red, green and blue .. 5 5
869. 20 p. black, red, green and grey .. 10 5

174. Rameses II in war chariot, Abu Simbel.

1965. Air. Nubian Monuments Preservation.
870. **174.** 22½ p. blk., bl. & grn. 10 8
871. – 50 p. blk., grn. & bl... 20 12
DESIGN: 50 p. Heads of Rameses II.

175. Weather Instruments and Map.

1965. World Meteorological Day.
872. **175.** 12½ p. black and purple 5 5
873. 27½ p. black and blue .. 12 8

176. Al-Radi. **177.** Evacuation Symbol.

1965. Air. Al-Sharif al-Radi. 950th Death Anniv.
874. **176.** 50 p. black 20 12

1965. Evacuation of Allied Forces. 19th Anniv.
875. **177.** 12½ p. green and blue 5 5
876. 27½ p. lilac and red .. 12 5

178. Hippocrates and Avicenna.

1965. Air. "Medical Days of the Near and Middle East",
877. **178.** 60 p. black and green 20 20

179. Dagger on Deir Yasin, Palestine. **180.** I.T.U. Emblem and Symbols.

1965. Air. Deir Yasin Massacre on 9 April, 1948.
878. **179.** 12½ p. red, black, yellow and blue .. 5 5
879. 60 p. red, black, yellow and purple .. 20 15

1965. Air. I.T.U. Cent.
880. **180.** 12½ p. red, ultramarine, black and blue .. 8 5
881. 27½ p. red, ultramarine, black and bistre .. 15 8
882. 60 p. red, ultramarine, black and green .. 30 20

181. Arab Family, Flags and Map. **182.** Hands holding Hoe and Pick.

1965. Palestine Week.
883. **181.** 12½ p.+5 p. black, red, green and brown .. 8 8
884. 25 p.+5 p. black, red, green and lilac .. 10 10

1965. Peasants' Union.
885. **182.** 2½ p. green 5 5
886. 12½ p. violet 5 5
887. 15 p. maroon 5 5
The above stamps are inscr. "RERUBLIC" for REPUBLIC".

183. Welcoming Emigrant. **184.** Fair Entrance.

1965. Air. "Welcome Arab Emigrants".
888. **183.** 25 p. blue, brown, green and violet .. 10 5
889. 100 p. blue, brown, green and olive 40 25

1965. Air. 12th Int. Fair, Damascus. Multicoloured.
890. 12½ p. Type **184** .. 5 5
891. 27½ p. Globe and compasses 10 8
892. 60 p. Syrian brassware .. 20 15

185. Cotton Boll and Shuttles. **186.** I.C.Y. Emblem and View of Damascus.

1965. Air. Aleppo Cotton Festival.
893. **185.** 25 p. multicoloured .. 10 8

1965. Air. Aleppo Industrial and Agricultural Production Fair. Optd. **INDUSTRIAL & AGRICULTURAL PRODUCTION FAIR—ALEPPO 1965** in English and Arabic.
894. **185.** 25 p. multicoloured .. 10 8

1965. Int. Co-operation Year.
895. **186.** 25 p. multicoloured .. 12 8

187. Arabs, Torch and Map. **188.** Industrial Workers.

1965. National Revolution Council.
896. **187.** 12½ p. green, red, black and blue 5 5
897. 25 p. green, red, black and bistre .. 10 5

1966. Labour Unions.
898. **188.** 12½ p. blue 5 5
899. 15 p. red 5 5
900. 20 p. lilac 8 5
901. 25 p. drab 10 10

189. Radio Aerial, Globe and Flag. **190** Dove-shaped hand holding flower.

1966. Air. Arab Information Ministers' Conf. Damascus.
902. **189.** 25 p. multicoloured .. 8 5
903. 60 p. multicoloured .. 20 15

1966. Air. March 8th Revolution. 3rd Anniv. Multicoloured.
904. 12½ p. Type **190** 5 5
905. 17½ p. Revolutionaries (horiz.) 5 5
906. 50 p. Type **190** 20 12

191. Colossi, Abu Simbel. **192.** Roman Lamp.

1966. Air. Nubian Monuments Preservation Week.
907. **191.** 25 p. blue 10 5
908. 60 p. grey 20 15

1966.
909. **192.** 2½ p. green 5 5
910. 5 p. purple 8 5
911. – 7½ p. chocolate .. 5 5
912. – 10 p. violet 5 5
DESIGN: 7½ p., 10 p. 12th-cent. Islamic vessel.

193. U.N. Emblem and Headquarters.

1966. Air. U.N. 20th Anniv.
913. **193.** 25 p. black and grey . . 8 5
914. 50 p. black and green . . 20 12

194. "Evacuation" (abstract). **195.** Workers marching across Globe.

1966. Evacuation. 20th Anniv.
916. **194.** 12½ p. multicoloured . . 5 5
917. 27½ p. multicoloured . . 10 8

1966. Air. Labour Day.
918. **195.** 60 p. multicoloured . . 20 15

196. W.H.O. Building. **197.** Traffic Signals and Map on Hand.

1966. Air. W.H.O. Headquarters, Geneva Inaug.
919. **196.** 60 p. black, blue & yell. 20 15

1966. Air. Traffic Day.
920. **197.** 25 p. multicoloured . . 8 5

198. Astarte and Tyche (wrongly inscr. "ASTRATE"). **199.** Fair Emblem.

1966. Air.
921. **198.** 50 p. brown 15 10
922. 60 p. grey 20 15

1966. Air. 13th Int. Fair, Damascus.
923. **199.** 12½ p. multicoloured . . 5 5
924. 60 p. multicoloured . . 25 15

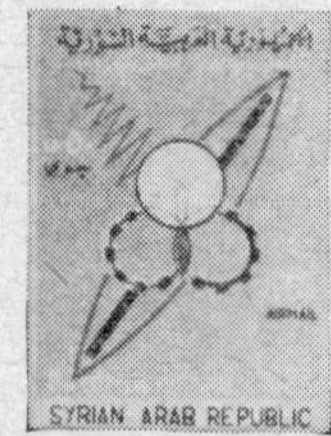

200. Shuttle (stylised). **201.** Decade Emblem.

1966. Air. Aleppo Cotton Festival.
925. **200.** 50 p. blk., red & grey . . 20 12

1966. Air. Int. Hydrological Decade.
926. **201.** 12½ p. blk., orge & grn. 5 5
927. 60 p. blk., orge. & blue 25 15

202. Emir Abd-el-kader. **203.** U.N.R.W.A. Emblem.

1966. Air. Return of Emir Abd-el-kader's Remains to Algiers.
928. **202.** 12½ p. black & green . . 5 5
929. 50 p. brown & green . . 20 15

1966. Air. U.N. Day 21st Anniv., and Refugee Week.
930. **203.** 12½ p. + 2½ p. black and blue 5 5
931. 50 p. + 5 p. black and green 20 15

204. Handclasp and Map. **205.** Doves and Oil Pipelines.

1967. Air. Solidarity Congress, Damascus
932. **204.** 20 p. multicoloured . . 8 5
933. 25 p. multicoloured . . 10 8

1967. Air. March 8th Baathist Revolution. 4th Anniv.
934. **205.** 17½ p. multicoloured . . 8 5
935. 25 p. multicoloured . . 10 8
936. 27½ p. multicoloured . . 12 8

206. Soldier and Citizens with Banner. **207.** Workers' Monument, Damascus.

1967. Air. Evacuation. 21st Anniv.
937. **206.** 17½ p. green 8 5
938. 25 p. maroon 10 8
939. 27½ p. blue 12 8

1967. Air. Labour Day.
940. **207.** 12½ p. turquoise . . 5 5
941. 50 p. magenta . . 20 15

208. Core Bust. **209.** "African woman" (vase).

210. Head of a Young Man from Amrith. **211.** Flags and Fair Entrance.

1967.
942. **208.** 2½ p. green (postage) . . 5 5
943. 5 p. red 5 5
944. 10 p. blue 5 5
945. 12½ p. brown 5 5
946. **209.** 15 p. purple 5 5
947. 20 p. blue 5 5
948. 25 p. green 8 5
949. 27½ p. ultramarine . . 12 5
950. **210.** 45 p. vermilion (air) . . 15 12
951. 50 p. magenta . . 20 12
952. 60 p. turquoise-blue . . 25 15
953. – 100 p. green 30 25
954. – 500 p. red . . . . 1·60 1·25

DESIGN—VERT. 100 p., 500 p. Bust of Princess (2nd-century bronze).

1967. Air. 14th International Damascus Fair.
955. **211.** 12½ p. multicoloured . . 5 5
956. 60 p. multicoloured . . 20 15

212. Ornina's Monument and Tourist Emblem. **213.** Cotton Boll and Cogwheel.

1967. Air. International Tourist Year.
957. **212.** 12½ p. purple, blk. & bl. 5 5
958. 25 p. red, black & blue 8 5
959. 27½ p. bl., blk. & lt. bl. 12 8

1967. Air. Aleppo Cotton Festival.
961. **213.** 12½ p. black, brown and yellow . . 5 5
962. 60 p. black, brown and greenish yellow . . 20 15

1967. Air. Industrial and Agricultural Production Fair, Aleppo. Optd. INDUSTRIAL AND AGRICULTURAL PRODUCTION FAIR—ALEPPO 1967 in English and Arabic.
963. **213.** 12½ p. blk., brn. & yell. 5 5
964. 60 p. black, brown and yellow . . 20 15

214. Ibn el-Naphis (scientist). **215.** Acclaiming Human Rights.

1967. Air. Sciences Week.
965. **214.** 12½ p. red and green . . 5 5
966. 27½ p. magenta & blue 10 8

1968. Air. Human Rights Year.
967. **215.** 12½ p. black, turquoise and blue 5 5
968. 60 p. black, red & pink 20 15

216. Learning to Read. **217.** "The Arab Revolutionary" (Damascus statue).

1968. Air. Literacy Campaign.
970. **216.** 12½ p. multicoloured . . 5 5
971. – 17½ p. multicoloured . . 5 5
972. **216.** 25 p. multicoloured . . 10 5
973. – 45 p. multicoloured . . 15 12

DESIGN: 17 p., 45 p. Flaming torch and open book.

1968. March 8th Baathist Revolution. Fifth Anniv.
974. **217.** 12½ p. brn., yell. & blk. 5 5
975. 25 p. mag., pink & black 10 5
976. 27½ p. green, light green and black . . 10 8

218. Map of Syria. **220.** Hands holding Spanner, Rifle & Torch.

219. Euphrates Dam.

1968. Al Baath Anniv.
977. **218.** 12½ p. multicoloured . . 5 5
978. 60 p. multicoloured . . 20 15

1968. Air. Euphrates Dam Project.
979. **219.** 12½ p. multicoloured . . 5 5
980. 17½ p. multicoloured . . 5 5
981. 25 p. multicoloured . . 10 5

1968. "Mobilisation Efforts".
982. **220.** 12½ p. multicoloured . . 5 5
983. 17½ p. multicoloured . . 5 5
984. 25 p. multicoloured . . 10 5

221. Railway Track and Sun. **223.** Torch, Map and Laurel.

222. Oil Pipeline Map.

1968. Evacuation of Allied Forces. 22nd Anniv.
985. **221.** 12½ p. multicoloured . . 5 5
986. 27½ p. multicoloured . . 10 5

1968. Syrian Oil Exploration.
987. **222.** 12½ p. blue, green and yellow-green . . 5 5
988. 17½ p. blue, brn. & pink 8 5

1968. Palestine Day.
989. **223.** 12½ p. multicoloured . . 5 5
990. 25 p. multicoloured . . 8 8
991. 27½ p. multicoloured . . 10 8

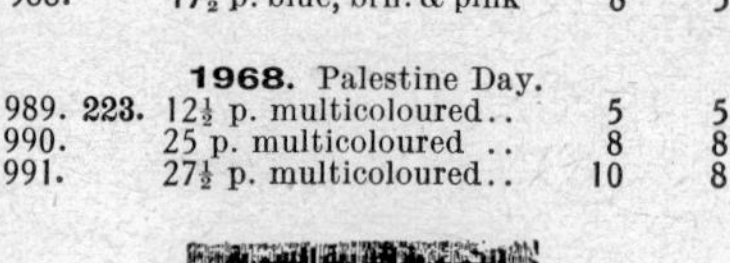

224. Refugee Family.

1968. Red Crescent. "Aid to Refugees".
992. **224.** 12½ p. + 2½ p. black, purple and blue . . 10 10
993. 27½ p. + 7½ p. black, red and violet . . 12 12

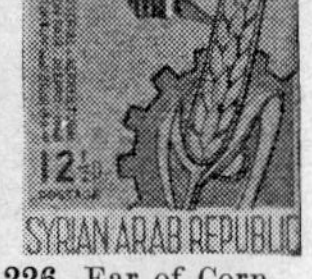

225. Avenzoar (physician) and W.H.O. Emblem. **226.** Ear of Corn, Cogwheel and Saracen Gate, Aleppo Citadel.

1968. Air. World Health Organisation. 20th Anniv.
994. **225.** 12½ p. multicoloured . . 5 5
995. – 25 p. multicoloured . . 8 5
996. – 60 p. multicoloured . . 20 15

DESIGNS—As Type **225**, but with different portraits of Arab physicians: 25 p. Razi. 60 p. Jabir.

1968. Industrial and Agricultural Production Fair, Aleppo.
997. 226. 12½ p. multicoloured.. 5 5
998. 27½ p. multicoloured.. 8 5

227. Emblems of Fair, Agriculture and Industry. **228.** Gathering Cotton.

1968. 15th Int. Damascus Fair.
999. 227. 12½ p. blk., grn. & choc. 5 5
1000. – 27½ p. black, red, green and blue .. 10 8
1001. 227. 60 p. blk., orge. & bl. 20 15
DESIGN—HORIZ. 27½ p. Flag, hand with torch and emblems.

1968. Aleppo Cotton Festival.
1002. 228. 12½ p. multicoloured 5 5
1003. 27½ p. multicoloured 10 8

229. Monastery of St. Simeon the Stylite. **230.** Oil Derrick.

1968. Air. Ancient Monuments (1st Series).
1004. 229. 15 p. brown, red, sepia and green .. 5 5
1005. – 17½ p. maroon, brown and chocolate .. 5 5
1006. – 22½ p. brown, red, sepia and stone .. 8 10
1007. – 45 p. brown, red, sepia and yellow .. 15 10
1008. – 50 p. brown, sepia and blue 15 12
DESIGNS—VERT. 17½ p. El Tekkieh Mosque, Damascus. 22½ p. Temple columns, Palmyra. HORIZ. 45 p. Chapel of St. Paul Bab Kisan. 50 p. Amphitheatre, Bosra.

See also Nos. 1026/30.

1968.
1009. 230. 2½ p. green and blue 5 5
1010. 5 p. ultram. & green 5 5
1011. 7½ p. blue and green.. 5 5
1012. 10 p. green and yellow 5 5
1013. 12½ p. red and yellow 5 5
1014. 15 p. brown and bistre 5 5
1015. 27½ p. brown & orge. 10 5

231. Al-Jahez (scientist). **232.** Throwing the Hammer.

1968. 9th Science Week.
1016. 231. 12½ p. black and olive 5 5
1017. 27½ p. black and grey 10 8

1968. Air. Olympic Games, Mexico.
1018. 232. 12½ p. black, mag. and green 5 5
1019. – 25 p. blk., red & grn. 5 5
1020. – 27½ p. black, grey and green 8 8
1021. – 60 p. multicoloured.. 20 12
DESIGNS—VERT. 25 p. Throwing the discus. 27½ p. Running. 60 p. Basketball. HORIZ. (53 × 36 mm.). 50 p. Polo.

233. Aerial View of Airport.

1969. Air. Construction of Damascus Int. Airport.
1023. 233. 12½ p. grn., bl. & yell. 5 5
1024. 17½ p. violet, verm. and green 5 5
1025. 60 p. black, magenta and yellow .. 20 12

234. Baal-Shamin Temple, Palmyra.

1969. Air. Ancient Monuments (2nd Series). Multicoloured.
1026. 25 p. Type 234 .. .. 8 5
1027. 45 p. Omayyad Mosque, Damascus 12 10
1028. 50 p. Amphitheatre, Palmyra 15 12
1029. 60 p. Khalid ibn Al-Walid Mosque, Homs 20 12
1030. 100 p. St. Simeon's Column, Djebel Samaan .. 35 25
Nos. 1027 and 1029 are vert.

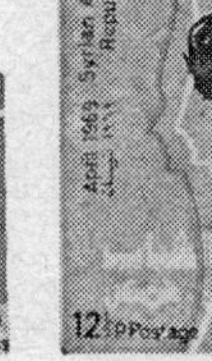

235. "Sun" and Clenched Fists in Broken Handcuffs. **236.** "Sun of Freedom".

1969. March 8th Baathist Revolution. 6th Anniv.
1031. 235. 12½ p. red, yellow, black and blue .. 5 5
1032. 25 p. red, yellow, black and grey 10 5
1033. 27½ p. red, yellow, black and green .. 10 5

1969. 5th Youth Week.
1034. 236. 12½ p. vermilion, yellow and blue 5 5
1035. 25 p. vermilion, yellow and green 8 5

237. Symbols of Progress. **238.** "Workers", Cogwheel and I.L.O. Emblem.

1969. Evacuation of Allied Forces. 23rd Anniv.
1036. 237. 12½ p. multicoloured 5 5
1037. 27½ p. multicoloured 8 5

1969. Air. Int. Labour Organisation. 50th Anniv.
1038. 238. 12½ p. multicoloured 5 5
1039. 27½ p. multicoloured 10 5

239. Russian Dancers. **240.** "Fortune" (statue).

1969. Air. 16th Int. Damascus Fair. Mult.
1041. 12½ p. Type 239.. .. 5 5
1042. 27½ p. Ballet dancers .. 10 8
1043. 45 p. Lebanese dancers.. 12 10
1044. 55 p. Egyptian dancers.. 15 12
1045. 60 p. Bulgarian dancers 20 15

1969. Air. 9th Int. Archaeological Congress, Damascus. Multicoloured.
1046. 17½ p. Type 240 .. .. 5 5
1047. 25 p. "Lady from Palmyra" (statue).. .. .. 10 8
1048. 60 p. "Motherhood" (statue) 20 15

241. Children dancing. **242.** Mahatma Gandhi.

1969. Air. Children's Day.
1049. 241. 12½ p. green, blue and turquoise 5 5
1050. 25 p. violet, bl. & red 10 5
1051. 27½ p. grey and blue 10 8

1969. Mahatma Gandhi. Birth Cent.
1052. 242. 12½ p. brown and buff 5 5
1053. 27½ p. green and yellow 10 8

243. Cotton. **244.** "Arab World" (6th Arab Science Congress).

1969. Aleppo Cotton Festival.
1054. 243. 12½ p. multicoloured 5 5
1055. 17½ p. multicoloured 5 5
1056. 25 p. multicoloured 8 8

1969. 10th Science Week.
1057. 12½ p. ultramarine and grn. 5 5
1058. 25 p. violet and pink .. 8 8
1059. 27½ p. ochre and green .. 10 8
DESIGNS: 25 p. Arab Academy (50th Anniv.). 27½ p. Damascus University (50th Anniv. of Faculty of Medicine).

245. Cockerel.

1969. Air. Damascus Agricultural Museum. Multicoloured.
1060. 12½ p. Type 245 .. .. 5 5
1061. 17½ p. Cow 5 5
1062. 20 p. Maize 8 5
1063. 50 p. Olives 15 12

246. Rising Sun, Hand and Book.

1970. March 8th Baathist Revolution. 7th Anniv.
1064. 246. 17½ p. blk., brn. & blue 5 5
1065. 25 p. blk., blue & red 8 8
1066. 27½ p. blk., brn. & grn. 10 10

247. Map of Arab World, League Emblem and Flag.

1970. Arab League. Silver Jubilee.
1067. 247. 12½ p. black, red, green and lilac 5 5
1068. 25 p. black, red, green and turquoise .. 8 8
1069. 27½ p. black, red, green and grey .. 10 10

248. Dish Aerial and Hand on Book. **249.** Lenin.

1970. Air. World Meteorological Day.
1070. 248. 25 p. blk., yell & grn. 10 8
1071. 60 p. blk., yell. & blue 25 20

1970. Air. Lenin. Birth Cent.
1072. 249. 15 p. brown and red 5 5
1073. 60 p. green and red.. 25 20

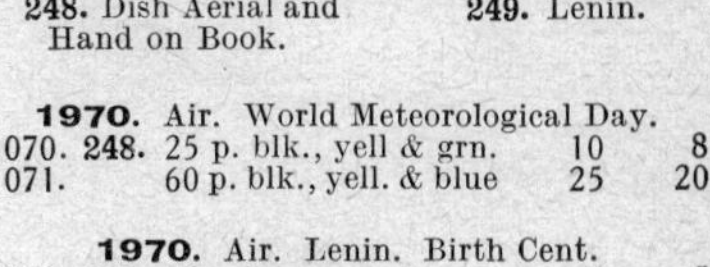

250. Battle of Hittin.

1970. Evacuation of Allied Forces. 24th Anniv.
1074. 250. 15 p. chocolate & cream 5 5
1075. 35 p. violet & cream.. 10 8

251. Emblem of Worker's Syndicate.

1970. Air. Labour Day.
1076. 251. 15 p. brown & green 5 5
1077. 60 p. brown & orange 25 15

252. Young Syrians and Map.

1970. Revolution's Youth Union. 1st Youth Week.
1078. 252. 15 p. green and ochre 5 5
1079. 25 p. brown and ochre 8 8
This issue is inscr. "YOUTH'S FIRST WEAK" in error.

253. Refugee Family.

1970. World Arab Refugee Week.
1080. 253. 15 p. multicoloured.. 5 5
1081. 25 p. multicoloured.. 8 8
1082. 35 p. multicoloured.. 12 10

254. Dish Aerial and Open Book.

1970. World Telecommunications Day.
1083. 254. 15 p. multicoloured.. 5 5
1084. 60 p. multicoloured.. 25 20

255. New U.P.U. Headquarters Building.

1970. New U.P.U. Headquarters Building.
1085. 255. 15 p. multicoloured.. 5 5
1086. 60 p. multicoloured.. 25 20

256. "Industry" and Graph.

257. Khaled Ben el Walid.

1970.

No.	Type	Description	Unused	Used
1087.	256.	2½ p. red and brown (postage)	5	5
1088.		5 p. blue and orange	5	5
1089.		7½ p. black and purple	5	5
1090.		10 p. bistre and brown	5	5
1091.		12½ p. red and blue..	5	5
1092.		15 p. purple and green	5	5
1093.		20 p. red and blue ..	8	5
1094.		22½ p. black & brown	8	8
1095.		25 p. blue and grey..	10	8
1096.		27½ p. brown & green	10	10
1097.		35 p. green and red..	12	12
1098.	257.	45 p. magenta (air)..	20	15
1099.		50 p. green	25	15
1100.		60 p. purple	30	20
1101.		100 p. blue	45	35
1102.		200 p. green	90	70
1103.		300 p. violet	1·40	1·00
1104.		500 p. black	2·00	1·75

258. Medieval Warriors.

1970. Air. Folk Tales and Legends.

No.	Type	Description	Unused	Used
1105.	258.	5 p. multicoloured ..	5	5
1106.	–	10 p. multicoloured..	5	5
1107.	–	15 p. multicoloured..	5	5
1108.	–	20 p. multicoloured..	8	8
1109.	–	60 p. multicoloured..	30	30

Nos. 1106/9 show horsemen similar to T **258**.

259. Cotton.

1970. Aleppo Agricultural and Industrial Fair. Multicoloured.

No.	Type	Description	Unused	Used
1110.		5 p. Type **259**	5	5
1111.		10 p. Tomatoes	5	5
1112.		15 p. Tobacco	5	5
1113.		20 p. Beet	8	8
1114.		35 p. Wheat	15	12

260. Mosque in Flames.

1970. Air. Burning of Al Aqsa Mosque. Jerusalem. 1st Anniv.

No.	Type	Description	Unused	Used
1115.	260.	15 p. multicoloured..	5	5
1116.		60 p. multicoloured..	25	25

261. Wood-Carving.

1970. Air. 17th Damascus Int. Fair Syrian Handicrafts. Multicoloured.

No.	Type	Description	Unused	Used
1117.		15 p. Type **261**	5	5
1118.		20 p. Jewellery	8	8
1119.		25 p. Glass-making ..	10	8
1120.		30 p. Copper-engraving ..	15	10
1121.		60 p. Shell-work	25	20

262. Scout, Encampment and Badge.

1970. 9th Pan-Arab Scout Jamboree, Damascus.

No.	Type	Description	Unused	Used
1122.	262.	15 p. grey-green ..	8	5

263. Olive Tree and Emblem.

264. I.E.Y. Emblem.

1970. World Year of Olive-oil Production.

No.	Type	Description	Unused	Used
1123.	263.	15 p. multicoloured..	5	5
1124.		25 p. multicoloured..	10	8

1970. Air. International Education Year.

No.	Type	Description	Unused	Used
1125.	264.	15 p. brn., grn. & blk.	5	5
1126.		60 p. brn., bl. & blk.	25	20

265. U.N. Emblems.

1970. Air. United Nations. 25th Anniv.

No.	Type	Description	Unused	Used
1127.	265.	15 p. multicoloured..	5	5
1128.		60 p. multicoloured..	25	20

266. Protective Shield.

267. Girl holding Garland.

1971. March 8th Baathist Revolution. 8th Anniv.

No.	Type	Description	Unused	Used
1129.	266.	15 p. multicoloured..	5	5
1130.		22½ p. multicoloured	8	8
1131.		27½ p. multicoloured	12	10

1971. Air. Evacuation. 25th Anniv.

No.	Type	Description	Unused	Used
1132.	267.	15 p. multicoloured..	5	5
1133.		60 p. multicoloured..	25	20

268. Globe and World Races.

1971. Air. Racial Equality Year.

No.	Type	Description	Unused	Used
1134.	268.	15 p. multicoloured..	5	5
1135.		60 p. multicoloured..	25	20

269. Soldier, Worker and Labour Emblems.

1971. Labour Day.

No.	Type	Description	Unused	Used
1136.	269.	15 p. multicoloured..	5	5
1137.		25 p. multicoloured..	10	8

270. Hailing Traffic.

1971. World Traffic Day.

No.	Type	Description	Unused	Used
1138.	270.	15 p. red, blue & black	5	5
1139.	–	25 p. multicoloured..	10	8
1140.	270.	45 p. red, yell. & blk.	20	15

DESIGN—VERT. 25 p. Traffic signs and signal lights.

271. Cotton, Cogwheel and Factories.

1971. Aleppo Agricultural and Industrial Fair.

No.	Type	Description	Unused	Used
1141.	271.	15 p. blk., blue & grn.	5	5
1142.		30 p. blk., red & pink	12	10

272. A.P.U. Emblem.

274. Flag and Federation Map.

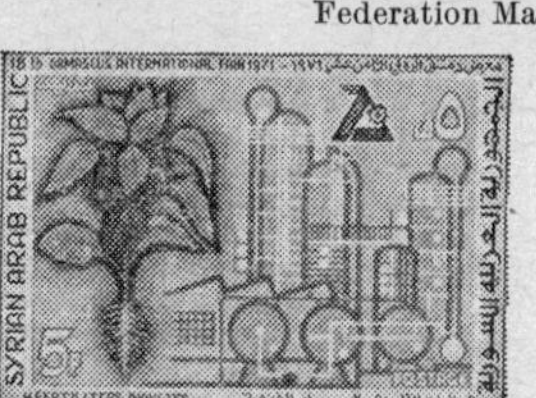

273. "Fertilizers".

1971. Sofar Conference and founding of Arab Postal Union. 25th Anniv.

No.	Type	Description	Unused	Used
1143.	272.	15 p. multicoloured..	5	5
1144.		20 p. multicoloured..	10	8

1971. 18th Damascus Int. Fair. Industries. Multicoloured.

No.	Type	Description	Unused	Used
1145.		5 p. Type **273**	5	5
1146.		15 p. TV set and telephone ("Electronics") ..	5	5
1147.		35 p. Oil lamp and dish ("Glassware") ..	15	10
1148.		50 p. Part of carpet ("Carpets")	20	15

1971. Arab Federation Referendum.

No.	Type	Description	Unused	Used
1149.	274.	15 p. black, red & grn.	5	5

275. Pres. Hafez al-Assad and People's Council Chamber.

1971. Air. People's Council and Presidential Election.

No.	Type	Description	Unused	Used
1150.	275.	15 p. multicoloured..	5	5
1151.		65 p. multicoloured..	30	20

276. Pres. Nasser.

277. "Telstar" and Dish Aerial.

1971. Air. Pres. Nasser's Death. 1st Anniv.

No.	Type	Description	Unused	Used
1152.	276.	15 p. brown & green	8	5
1153.		20 p. brown and grey	10	8

1971. U.N.E.S.C.O. 25th Anniv.

No.	Type	Description	Unused	Used
1154.	277.	15 p. multicoloured..	5	5
1155.		50 p. multicoloured..	20	15

278. Flaming Torch.

279. Quill-pen and Open Book.

1971. "Movement of 16 November 1970".

No.	Type	Description	Unused	Used
1156.	278.	15 p. multicoloured..	5	5
1157.		20 p. multicoloured..	8	8

1971. 8th Writers' Congress.

No.	Type	Description	Unused	Used
1158.	279.	15 p. brn., orge. and turquoise	5	5

280. Children with Ball.

281. Book Year Emblem.

1971. U.N.E.C.E.F. 25th Anniv.

No.	Type	Description	Unused	Used
1159.	280.	15 p. multicoloured..	5	5
1160.		25 p. multicoloured..	10	8

1972. Int. Book Year.

No.	Type	Description	Unused	Used
1161.	281.	15 p. lilac, blue & brn.	5	5
1162.		20 p. green, light green & brown	8	8

282. Emblems of Reconstruction.

283. Baath Party Emblem.

1972. 8 March Baathist Revolution. 9th Anniv.

No.	Type	Description	Unused	Used
1163.	282.	15 p. vio. & green ..	5	5
1164.		20 p. lake and brown	8	8

1972. Baath Party. 25th Anniv.

No.	Type	Description	Unused	Used
1165.	283.	15 p. multicoloured..	5	5
1166.		20 p. multicoloured..	8	8

284. Eagle, Factory Chimneys and Rifles.

285. Flowers and Broken Chain.

1972. Arab Republics Federation. 1st Anniv.

No.	Type	Description	Unused	Used
1167.	284.	15 p. gold, blk. & red	5	5

1972. Evacuation of Allied Forces. 26th Anniv.

No.	Type	Description	Unused	Used
1168.	285.	15 p. grey and red ..	5	5
1169.		50 p. grey & green ..	20	20

286. Hand with Spanner.

288. Environment Emblem.

287. Telecommunications Emblem.

1972. Labour Day.

No.	Type	Description	Unused	Used
1170.	286.	15 p. multicoloured..	5	5
1171.		50 p. multicoloured..	20	20

1972. Air. World Telecommunications Day.

No.	Type	Description	Unused	Used
1172.	287.	15 p. multicoloured..	5	5
1173.		50 p. multicoloured..	20	20

1972. U.N. Environmental Conservation Conf., Stockholm.

No.	Type	Description	Unused	Used
1174.	288.	15 p. bl., azure & pink	5	5
1175.		50 p. pur., orge. & yell.	20	20

289. Discus, Football and Swimming.

1972. Olympic Games, Munich.

1176. 289. 15 p. vio., black & brn. 5 5
1177. – 60 p. orge., blk. & bl. 20 20

DESIGN: 60 p. Running, gymnastics and fencing.

290. Dove and Factory. 291. President Hafez al-Assad.

1972. Aleppo Agricultural and Industrial Fair.

1179. 290. 15 p. multicoloured.. 5 5
1180. 20 p. multicoloured.. 8 8

1972. Air.

1181. 291. 100 p. green .. 45 25
1182. 500 p. brown .. 2·25 1·00

292. Women's Dance.

1972. 19th Damascus Int. Fair. Mult.

1183. 15 p. Type 292 .. 5 5
1184. 20 p. Tambourine dance 8 8
1185. 50 p. Men's drum dance 20 20

293. Airline Emblem. 294. Emblem of Revolution.

1972. Air. "Syrianair" Airline. 25th Anniv.

1186. 293. 15 p. blk. light bl. & blk. 5 5
1187. 50 p. blue, grey & blk. 20 20

1973. March 8th Baathist Revolution. 10th Anniv.

1188. 294. 15 p. green, red & blk. 5 5
1189. 20 p. orge., red & blk. 5 5
1190. 25 p. blue, red & blk. 8 5

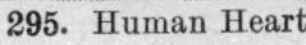

295. Human Heart. 296. Emblems of Agriculture and Industry.

1973. W.H.O. 25th Anniv.

1191. 295. 15 p. multicoloured.. 5 5
1192. 20 p. multicoloured.. 15 10

1973. Evacuation of Allied Forces. 27th Anniv.

1193. 296. 15 p. multicoloured.. 5 5
1194. 20 p. multicoloured.. 5 5

297. Globe and Workers.

1973. Labour Day.

1195. 297. 15 p. blk., pink & yell. 5 5
1196. 50 p. blk., blue & buff 15 12

298. Family and Emblems. 299. Three Heads.

1973. World Food Programme. 10th Anniv.

1197. 298. 15 p. brown and green 5 5
1198. 50 p. blue and purple 15 12

1973. Children's Day.

1199. 299. 2½ p. green 5 5
1200. – 5 p. brown 5 5
1201. – 7½ p. brown 5 5
1202. – 10 p. red 5 5
1203. 299. 15 p. blue 5 5
1204. – 25 p. blue 8 5
1205. – 35 p. blue 10 5
1206. – 55 p. green 15 10
1207. – 70 p. purple 20 12

DESIGNS—HORIZ. 7½ p., 10 p., 55 p. As Type 299, but with one head above the other two. VERT. 25 p., 35 p., 70 p. Similar to Type 299, but with heads in vertical arrangement.

300. Stock.

1973. Int. Flower Show, Damascus. Mult.

1208. 5 p. Type 300 .. .. 5 5
1209. 10 p. Gardenia 5 5
1210. 15 p. Jasmine 5 5
1211. 20 p. Rose 5 5
1212. 25 p. Narcissus 8 5

301. Cogs and Flowers.

1973. Aleppo Agricultural and Industrial Fair.

1213. 301. 15 p. multicoloured.. 5 5

302. Euphrates Dam.

1973. Euphrates Dam Project. Diversion of the River.

1214. 302. 15 p. multicoloured.. 5 5
1215. 50 p. multicoloured.. 15 10

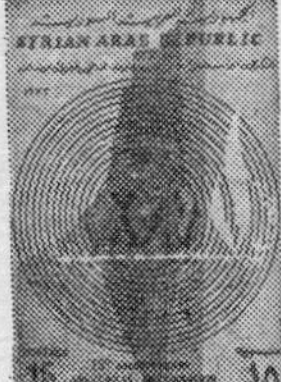

303. Deir Ezzor Costume. 304. Anniversary Emblem.

1973. 20th Damascus Int. Fair. "Costumes". Multicoloured.

1216. 5 p. Type 303 .. .. 5 5
1217. 10 p. Hassake 5 5
1218. 20 p. As Sahel 5 5
1219. 25 p. Zakie 8 5
1220. 50 p. Sarakeb 15 10

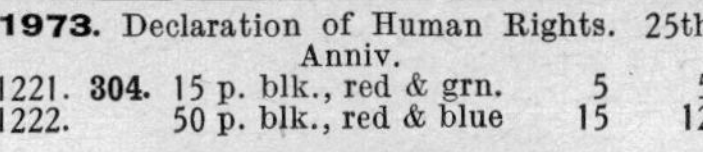

1973. Declaration of Human Rights. 25th Anniv.

1221. 304. 15 p. blk., red & grn. 5 5
1222. 50 p. blk., red & blue 15 12

305. Citadel of Ja'abar.

1973. "Save the Euphrates Monuments" Campaign. Multicoloured.

1223. 10 p. Type 305 .. 5 5
1224. 15 p. Meskeneh Minaret (vert.) .. 5 5
1225. 25 p. Psyche, Anab al-Safinah (vert.).. .. 8 5

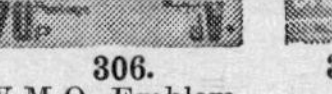

306. W.M.O. Emblem. 307. Ancient City of Maalula.

1973. World Meteorological Organization. Centenary.

1226. 306. 70 p. multicoloured.. 20 15

1973. Arab Emigrants' Congress, Buenos Aires.

1227. 307. 15 p. black and blue 5 5
1228. – 50 p. black and brown 15 12

DESIGN: 50 p. Ruins of Afamia.

308. Soldier and Workers. 309. Copernicus.

1973. November 16th Revolution. 3rd Anniv.

1229. 308. 15 p. blue & brown.. 5 5
1230. 25 p. violet and red.. 5 5

1973. 14th Science Week.

1231. 309. 15 p. black and gold.. 5 5
1232. 25 p. black and gold.. 8 8

310. National Symbols. 311. U.P.U. Monument, Berne.

1974. March 8th Baathist Revolution. 11th Anniv.

1233. 310. 20 p. blue and green 5 5
1234. 25 p. blue and green 8 5

1974. Universal Postal Union. Cent. Mult.

1235. 15 p. Type 311 .. .. 5 5
1236. 20 p. Emblem on airmail letter (horiz.) 5 5
1237. 70 p. Type 311 .. .. 20 15

312. Postal Institute.

1074. Higher Arab Postal Institute, Damascus. Inauguration.

1238. 312. 15 p. multicoloured.. 5 5

313. Sun and Monument. 314. Machine Fitter.

1974. Evacuation of Allied Forces. 28th Anniv.

1239. 313. 15 p. multicoloured.. 5 5
1240. 20 p. multicoloured.. 5 5

1974. Labour Day.

1241. 314. 15 p. multicoloured.. 5 5
1242. 50 p. multicoloured.. 15 12

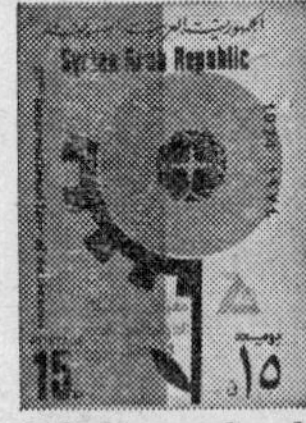

315. Abul Fida. 316. Diamond and Part of Cogwheel.

1974. Famous Arabs.

1243. 315. 100 p. green 30 25
1244. – 200 p. brown .. 60 50

DESIGN: 200 p. Al-Farabi.

1974. 21st Damascus International Fair. Multicoloured.

1245. 15 p. Type 316 .. .. 5 5
1246. 25 p. "Sun" within cogwheel 8 5

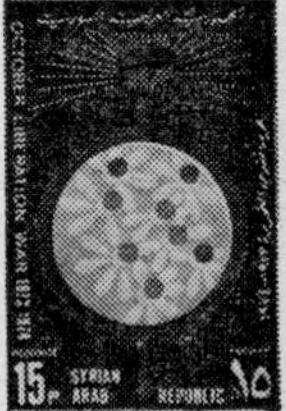

317. Figs. 318. Flowers within Drop of Blood.

1974. Aleppo Agricultural and Industrial Fair. Fruits. Multicoloured.

1247. 5 p. Type 317 .. .. 5 5
1248. 15 p. Grapes 5 5
1249. 20 p. Pomegranates .. 5 5
1250. 25 p. Cherries 8 5
1251. 35 p. Rose-hips 10 8

1974. October Liberation War. 1st Anniv. Multicoloured.

1252. 15 p. Type 318 .. .. 5 5
1253. 20 p. Flower and stars .. 5 5

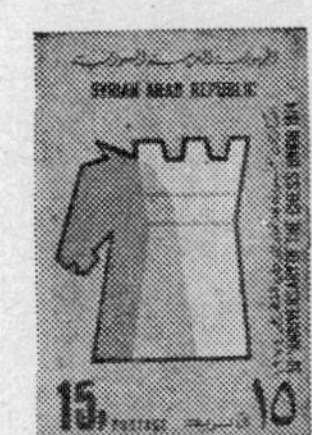

319. Knight and Rook. 320. Symbolic Figure, Globe and Emblem.

1975. Chess Union. 50th Anniv.

1254. 319. 15 p. bl., lt. bl. & blk. 5 5
1255. – 50 p. multicoloured.. 15 10

DESIGN: 50 p. Knight on chessboard.

1975. World Population Year.

1256. 320. 50 p. multicoloured.. 15 10

321. Ishtup-ilum. 322. Oil Rig and Crowd.

1975. Statuettes.
1257. **321.** 20 p. green 5 5
1258. – 55 p. brown 15 10
1259. – 70 p. blue 20 15
DESIGNS: 55 p. Woman with vase. 70 p. Ur-nina.

1975. Baathist Revolution of 8 March 1963. 12th Anniv.
1260. **322.** 15 p. multicoloured .. 5 5

323. Savings Emblem and Family (" Savings Certificates ").
324. Dove Emblem.

1975. Savings Campaign.
1261. **323.** 15 p. blk., orge. & grn. 5 5
1262. – 20 p. brn., blk. & pink 5 5
DESIGN: 20 p. Family with savings box and letter (" Postal Savings Bank ").

1975. Evacuation of Allied Forces. 29th Anniv.
1263. **324.** 15 p. multicoloured .. 5 5
1264. 25 p. multicoloured .. 10 8

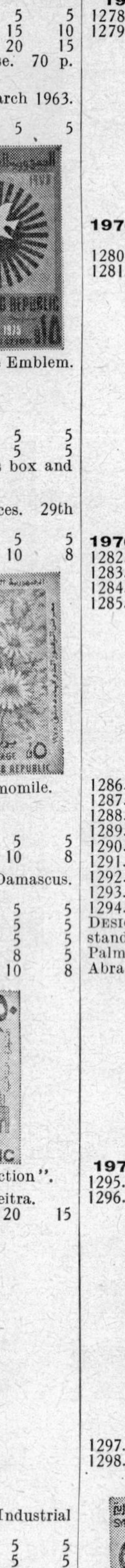

325. Worker supporting Cog.
326. Camomile.

1975. Labour Day.
1265. **325.** 15 p. multicoloured .. 5 5
1266. 25 p. multicoloured .. 10 8

1975. International Flower Show, Damascus. Multicoloured.
1267. 5 p. Type **326** 5 5
1268. 10 p. Chincherinchi .. 5 5
1269. 15 p. Carnations .. 5 5
1270. 20 p. Poppy .. 8 5
1271. 25 p. Honeysuckle .. 10 8

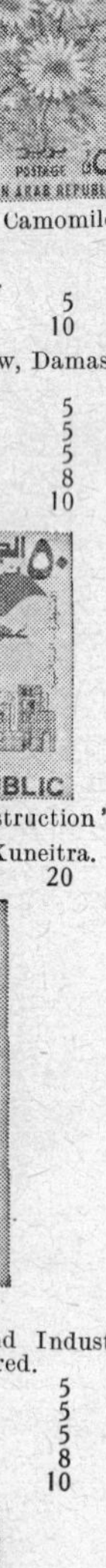

327. " Destruction and Reconstruction ".

1975. Reoccupation of Al-Kuneitra.
1272. **327.** 50 p. multicoloured .. 20 15

328. Apples.

1975. Aleppo Agricultural and Industrial Fair. Fruits. Multicoloured.
1273. 5 p. Type **328** 5 5
1274. 10 p. Qunices 5 5
1275. 15 p. Apricots 5 5
1276. 20 p. Grapes 8 3
1277. 25 p. Figs 10 8

329. Arabesque Pattern.

1975. 22nd International Damascus Fair.
1278. **329.** 15 p. multicoloured .. 5 5
1279. 35 p. multicoloured .. 15 12

330. Pres. Hafez al-Assad.

1976. " Movement of 16 November 1970 ". 5th Anniv.
1280. **330.** 15 p. multicoloured .. 5 5
1281. 50 p. multicoloured .. 25 20

331. Symbolic Woman.

1976. Int. Women's Year. Multicoloured.
1282. 10 p. Type **331** 5 5
1283. 15 p. " Motherhood " .. 5 5
1284. 25 p. " Education " .. 12 10
1285. 50 p. " Science " .. 25 20

332. Bronze " Horse " Lamp.

1976.
1286. **332.** 10 p. turquoise .. 5 5
1287. 20 p. red 10 8
1288. 25 p. blue 12 10
1289. – 30 p. brown 15 12
1290. – 35 p. olive 15 12
1291. – 50 p. turquoise .. 25 20
1292. – 75 p. orange 35 30
1293. – 500 p. grey .. .. 2·25 2·10
1294. – 1,000 p. slate .. 4·50 4·25
DESIGNS—VERT. 30 p., 35 p. Man's head inkstand. 50 p. Nike. 75 p. Hera. 500 p. Palmyrean coin of Vasalathus. 1,000 p. Abraxas coin.

333. National Theatre, Damascus.

1976. March 8th Revolution. 13th Anniv.
1295. **333.** 25 p. grn., blk. & silver 12 10
1296. 35 p. olive, blk. & silver 15 12

334. Syrian Stamp of 1920.

1976. Posts' Day.
1297. **334.** 25 p. multicoloured .. 12 10
1298. 35 p. multicoloured .. 15 12

335. Nurse and Emblem.
336. Eagle and Stars.

1976. 8th Arab Red Crescent and Red Cross Societies' Conf. Damascus.
1299. **335.** 25 p. blue, blk. & red 12 10
1300. 100 p. vio., blk. & red 45 40

1976. Allied Forces Evacuation. 30th Anniv.
1301. **336.** 25 p. multicoloured .. 12 10
1302. 35 p. multicoloured .. 15 12

337. Hand gripping Spanner.

338. Cotton Boll.

1976. Labour Day.
1303. **337.** 25 p. blue and black .. 12 10
1304. – 60 p. multicoloured .. 30 25
DESIGN: 60 p. Hand supporting globe.

1976. Aleppo Agricultural and Industrial Fair.
1305. **338.** 25 p. multicoloured .. 12 10
1306. 35 p. multicoloured .. 15 12

339. Tulips.

1976. International Flower Show, Damascus. Multicoloured.
1307. 5 p. Type **339** 5 5
1308. 15 p. Yellow daisies .. 5 5
1309. 20 p. Fuchsias 10 8
1310. 25 p. Irises 12 10
1311. 35 p. Honeysuckle .. 15 12

340. Pottery.

1976. Air. 23rd International Damascus Fair. Handicraft Industries. Multicoloured.
1312. 10 p. Type **340** 5 5
1313. 25 p. Tug-making .. 12 10
1314. 30 p. Metalware 15 12
1315. 35 p. Wickerware .. 15 12
1316. 100 p. Wood-carving .. 45 40

341. People supporting Olive Branch.

1976. Non-aligned Countries Summit Conference, Colombo. Multicoloured.
1317. 40 p. Type **341** 20 15
1318. 60 p. Symbolic arrow penetrating " Curtain " 30 25

342. Football.

1976. Fifth Pan-Arab Games. Multicoloured.
1318. 5 p. Type **342** 5 5
1320. 10 p. Swimming 5 5
1321. 25 p. Running 12 10
1322. 35 p. Basketball .. 15 12
1323. 50 p. Throwing the javelin 25 20

POSTAGE DUE STAMPS

1920. "Mouchon" and "Merson" key-types of French Levant surch. **O.M.F. Syrie Ch taxe** and value.
D 48. B. 1 p. on 10 c. red .. 22·00 22·00
D 49. 2 p. on 20 c. claret .. 22·00 22·00
D 50. 3 p. on 30 c. mauve .. 22·00 22·00
D 51. C. 4 p. on 40 c. red & blue 22·00 22·00

1920. Postage Due stamps of France surch. **O.M.F. Syrie** and value.
D 60. D **2.** 50 c. on 10 c. brown .. 10 10
D 52. 1 p. on 10 c. brown .. 25 25
D 61. 1 p. on 20 c. olive .. 10 10
D 53. 2 p. on 20 c. olive .. 25 25
D 62. 2 p. on 30 c. red .. 45 45
D 54. 3 p. on 30 c. red .. 25 25
D 63. 3 p. on 50 c. purple .. 55 55
D 55. 4 p. on 50 c. red .. 80 80
D 64. 5 p. on 1 f. claret on yellow .. .. 1·25 1·25

1920. As T **1**, but colour changed.
KD 96. **1.** 1 p. black 20 20

1921. Issued at Damascus. No. KD 5 surch. **O.M.F. Syrie Chiffre Taxe** and value.
D 69. **1.** 50 c. on 1 p. black .. 60 60
D 70. 1 p. on 1 p. black .. 30 30

1921. Issued at Damascus. Nos. 64/5 of Syria optd. **TAXE.**
D 89. **2.** 2 p. on 5 m. red .. 1·10 1·10
D 90. **1.** 3 p. on 1 p. blue .. 2·50 1·90

1923. Postage Due stamps of France surch. **Syrie Grand Liban** in two lines and value.
D 118. D **2.** 50 c. on 10 c. brown 15 15
D 119. 1 p. on 20 c. olive .. 35 35
D 120. 2 p. on 30 c. red .. 12 12
D 121. 30 p. on 50 c. purple 12 12
D 122. 5 p. on 1 f. claret on yellow 45 45

1924. Postage Due stamps of France surch. **SYRIE** and value.
D 139. D **2.** 50 c. on 10 c. brown 8 8
D 140. 1 p. on 20 c. olive .. 10 10
D 141. 2 p. on 30 c. red .. 10 10
D 142. 3 p. on 50 c. purple 12 12
D 143. 5 p. on 1 f. claret on yellow 12 12

1924. Postage Due stamps of France surch. **Syrie** and value and also in Arabic.
D 175. D **2.** 0 p. 50 on 10 c. brown 10 10
D 176. 1 p. on 20 c. olive .. 15 15
D 177. 2 p. on 30 c. red .. 15 15
D 178. 3 p. on 50 c. purple 15 15
D 179. 5 p. on 1 f. claret on yellow 20 20

D **1.** Hama.

DESIGNS—VERT. 1 p. Antioch. HORIZ. 2 p. Tarsus. 3 p. Banias. 5 p. Castle. 8 p. Ornamental design. 15 p. Lion.

1925.
D 192. D **1.** 0 p. 50 brown on yell. 5 5
D 193. – 1 p. black on red .. 5 5
D 194. – 2 p. black on blue .. 5 5
D 195. – 3 p. black on orange 8 8
D 196. – 5 p. black on green 8 8
D 197. – 8 p. black on blue .. 75 75
D 198. – 15 p. black on red .. 1·10 1·10

D **2.**

1965.
D 883. D **2.** 2½ p. blue 5 5
D 884. 5 p. sepia 5 5
D 885. 10 p. green 5 5
D 886. 17½ p. red 8 8
D 887. 25 p. blue 10 10

TAHITI O2

The largest of the Society Islands in the S. Pacific Ocean. Later renamed Oceanic Settlements.

1882. Stamps of French Colonies, " Peace and Commerce " type, surch. **25c.**
1. **8.** 25 c. on 35 c. black on orge. 55·00 50·00
3. 25 c. on 40 c. red on yellow £550 £550

1884. Stamps of French Colonies, " Commerce " type and " Peace and Commerce " type, surch. **TAHITI** and value.
4. **9.** 5 c. on 20 c. red on green .. 27·00 20·00
5. 10 c. on 20 c. red on green 50·00 42·00
2. **8.** 25 c. on 35 c. black on yell. £850 £800
6. 25 c. on 1 f. olive .. .. 90·00 80·00

1893. Stamps of French Colonies, " Commerce " type, optd. **TAHITI.**
7. **9.** 1 c. black on blue .. £140 £120
8. 2 c. brown on yellow .. £500 £350
9. 4 c. claret on grey .. £200 £140
10. 5 c. green .. .. 3·50 3·50
11. 10 c. black on lilac .. 3·50 3·50
12. 15 c. blue .. .. 3·00 3·00

13.	20 c. red on green.. ..	4·00	4·00
14.	25 c. yellow	£650	£650
15.	25 c. black on red.. ..	3·25	3·25
16.	35 c. black on orange ..	£400	£300
17.	75 c. red on rose	4·25	4·25
18.	1 f. olive	6·50	5·50

1893. Stamps of French Colonies. "Commerce" type, optd. **1893 TAHITI.**

32. 9.	1 c. black on blue.. ..	£140	£130
33.	2 c. brown on yellow ..	£500	£375
34.	4 c. claret on grey.. ..	£250	£200
35.	5 c. green	£200	£150
36.	10 c. black on lilac ..	50·00	48·00
37.	15 c. blue	3·75	3·75
38.	20 c. red on green.. ..	3·50	3·50
39.	25 c. yellow	£4000	
40.	25 c. black on red.. ..	3·50	3·50
41.	35 c. black on orange ..	£375	£300
42.	75 c. red on rose	3·25	3·25
43.	1 f. olive	4·25	4·25

1903. Stamps of Oceanic Settlements, "Tablet" key-type, surch. **TAHITI 10 centimes.**

57. D.	10 c. on 15 c. blue ..	55	55
58.	10 c. on 25 c. black on red	55	55
59.	10 c. on 40 c. red on yellow	80	80

1915. Stamps of Oceanic Settlements. "Tablet" key-type, optd. **TAHITI** and red cross.

60. D.	15 c. blue..	22·00	22·00
61.	15 c. grey	2·10	2·10

POSTAGE DUE STAMPS

1893. Postage Due stamps of French Colonies optd. **TAHITI.**

D 19. D 1.	1 c. black	60·00	60·00
D 20.	2 c. black	60·00	60·00
D 21.	3 c. black	65·00	65·00
D 22.	4 c. black	65·00	65·00
D 23.	5 c. black	65·00	65·00
D 24.	10 c. black	65·00	65·00
D 25.	15 c. black	65·00	65·00
D 26.	20 c. black	50·00	50·00
D 27.	30 c. black	65·00	65·00
D 28.	40 c. black	65·00	65·00
D 29.	60 c. black	65·00	65·00
D 30.	1 f. brown	£130	£130
D 31.	2 f. brown	£130	£130

1893. Postage Due stamps of French Colonies optd. **1893 TAHITI.**

D 44. D 1.	1 c. black	£250	£250
D 45.	2 c. black	80·00	80·00
D 46.	3 c. black	80·00	80·00
D 47.	4 c. black	80·00	80·00
D 48.	5 c. black	80·00	80·00
D 49.	10 c. black	80·00	80·00
D 50.	15 c. black	80·00	80·00
D 51.	20 c. black	80·00	80·00
D 52.	30 c. black	80·00	80·00
D 53.	40 c. black	80·00	80·00
D 54.	60 c. black	80·00	80·00
D 55.	1 f. brown	80·00	80·00
D 56.	2 f. brown	80·00	80·00

For later issues see **OCEANIC SETTLEMENTS.**

TANGANYIKA O2, BC

(Formerly GERMAN EAST AFRICA.)

A territory on the E. Coast of C. Africa, formerly a German colony. After the 1914-18 War it was under Br. Mandate until 1946 and then administered by Britain under United Nations trusteeship until 1961 when it became independent within the Br. Commonwealth. It had a common postal service with Kenya and Uganda from 1935 to 1961. For these issues see under Kenya, Uganda and Tanganyika. Renamed Tanzania in 1965.

1893.	64 pesa = 100 heller = 1 rupee.
1905.	100 heller = 1 rupee.
1915/16.	16 annas = 1 rupee.
1917.	100 cents = 1 rupee.
1922.	100 cents = 1 shilling.

GERMAN ISSUES.

1893. Stamps of Germany surch. with value in "PESA".

1. 6.	2 p. on 3 pf. brown ..	10·00	11·00
2.	3 p. on 5 pf. green.. ..	12·00	11·00
3. 7.	5 p. on 10 pf. red	7·00	4·50
5.	10 p. on 20 pf. blue ..	5·50	3·50
6.	25 p. on 50 pf. brown ..	10·00	7·00

1896. Stamps of Germany surch. **Deutsch-Ostafrika** and value in "PESA".

7. 6.	2 p. on 3 pf. brown ..	1·00	1·25
10.	3 p. on 5 pf. green ..	70	1·10
11. 7.	5 p. on 10 pf. red ..	70	1·10
12	10 p. on 20 pf. blue ..	1·75	1·40
14.	25 p. on 50 pf. brown ..	6·00	7·00

1901. "Yacht" key-type inscr. "DEUTSCH-OSTAFRIKA". Currency in pesa and rupees.

15. N.	2 p. brown . ..	35	35
16.	3 p. green	35	45
17.	5 p. red	45	50
18.	10 p. blue	90	1·10
19	15 p. black & orge. on buff	1·10	1·60
20.	20 p. black and red ..	2·00	4·50
21.	25 p. black & pur. on buff	2·00	4·50
22.	40 p. black & red on rose	2·75	6·00
23. O.	1 r. red	6·00	9·00
24.	2 r. green..	3·25	13·00
44.	3 r. black and red ..	9·0	45·000

1905. "Yacht" key-types inscr. "DEUTSCH-OSTAFRIKA". Currency in heller.

34. N.	2½ h. brown	15	20
35.	4 h. green	15	15
36.	7½ h. red	15	12
37.	15 h. blue	55	35
38.	20 h. blk. & red on yellow	45	4·50
39.	30 h. black and red ..	55	1·40
40.	45 h. black and mauve ..	1·10	6·00
33.	60 h. black & red on rose	11·00	16·00

BRITISH OCCUPATION

1915. Stamps of the Indian Expeditionary Forces optd. **G.R. POST MAFIA.**

M 33. 40.	3 p. grey	1·75	2·00
M 34. 41.	½ a. green	2·25	2·50
M 35. 42.	1 a. red	2·75	3·00
M 36. 44.	2 a. lilac	3·75	4·50
M 37. 47.	2½ a. blue	4·00	5·00
M 38. 48.	3 a. orange	4·00	4·00
M 39. 49.	4 a. olive	6·00	7·00
M 40. 52.	8 a. mauve	10·00	12·00
M 51. 53.	12 a. claret	18·00	18·00
M 52. 54.	1 r. brown and green	20·00	20·00

1916. Stamps of Nyasaland (King George V) optd. **N.F.**

33.	½d. green	45	80
34.	1d. red	35	70
35.	3d. purple on yellow ..	1·25	2·50
36.	4d. black and red on yellow	6·00	7·00
37.	1s. black on green ..	5·50	6·00

1917. Stamps of Kenya and Uganda (King George V, 1912) optd. **G.E.A.**

38.	1 c. black	10	15
40.	3 c. green	10	15
41.	6 c. red	10	15
42.	10 c. orange.. ..	10	15
43.	12 c. grey	15	40
44.	15 c. blue	15	35
45.	25 c. black and red on yellow	30	50
46.	50 c. black and lilac ..	45	90
47.	75 c. black on green ..	60	1·40
48.	1 r. black on green.. ..	90	1·75
49.	2 r. red and black on blue ..	2·00	3·50
50.	3 r. violet and green ..	3·00	4·00
51.	4 r. red and green on yellow	4·00	5·50
52.	5 r. blue and purple ..	5·50	7·50
53.	10 r. red and green on green	20·00	26·00
54.	20 r. black and purple on red	50·00	55·00
55.	50 r. red and green ..	£275	£300

BRITISH MANDATE

1. Giraffe. 2.

1922.

74. 1.	5 c. black and purple ..	25	30
89.	5 c. black and green ..	25	35
75.	10 c. black and green ..	15	20
90.	10 c. black and yellow ..	60	55
76.	15 c. black and red ..	40	8
77.	20 c. black and orange ..	30	8
78.	25 c. black	2·40	3·00
91.	25 c. black and blue ..	2·75	2·50
79.	30 c. black and blue ..	1·00	1·00
92.	30 c. black and purple ..	75	1·50
80.	40 c. black and brown ..	1·10	1·10
81.	50 c. black and grey ..	1·10	1·50
82.	75 c. black and yellow ..	2·40	2·75
83. 2.	1s. black and green ..	1·40	2·00
84.	2s. black and purple ..	2·75	3·75
85.	3s. black	3·25	4·25
86.	5s. black and red.. ..	5·00	7·00
87.	10s. black and blue ..	25·00	25·00
88.	£1 black and orange ..	48·00	48·00

3. 4.

1927.

93. 3.	5 c. black and green ..	8	5
94.	10 c. black and yellow ..	8	5
95.	15 c. black and red ..	8	5
96.	20 c. black and orange ..	15	8
97.	25 c. black and blue ..	35	30
98.	30 c. black and purple ..	45	40
98a.	30 c. black and blue ..	3·00	60
99.	40 c. black and brown ..	50	75
100.	50 c. black and grey ..	30	20
101.	75 c. black and olive ..	1·40	1·75
102. 4.	1s. black and green ..	75	50
103.	2s. black and purple ..	2·00	1·00
104.	3s. black	3·50	3·75
105.	5s. black and red ..	3·50	3·25
106.	10s. black and blue ..	11·00	12·00
107.	£1 black and orange ..	27·00	27·00

INDEPENDENT WITHIN THE COMMONWEALTH

NOTE. Stamps inscribed "UGANDA KENYA TANGANYIKA & ZANZIBAR" (or "TANZANIA UGANDA KENYA") will be found listed under East Africa.

5. Teacher and Pupils. 6. Freedom Torch over Mt. Kilimanjaro.

1961. Independence. Inscr. "UHURU 1961".

108. 5.	5 c. sepia and apple ..	5	5
109. –	10 c. blue-green	5	5
110. –	15 c. sepia and blue ..	5	5
111. –	20 c. chestnut	5	5
112. –	30 c. black, green & yell.	8	5
113. –	50 c. black and yellow ..	8	8
114. –	1s. brn., blue & ol.-yell.	15	10
115. 6.	1s. 30 red, yellow, black, brown and blue ..	35	20
116. –	2s. bl., yell., grn. & brn.	35	20
117. –	5s. blue-green and red..	85	50
118. –	10s. black, purple & blue	1·75	1·25
119. 6.	20s. red, yellow, black, brown and green..	5·00	5·00

DESIGNS—As T **5**—VERT. 10 c. District nurse and child. 15 c. Coffee-picking. 20 c. Harvesting maize. 50 c. Serengeti lions. HORIZ. 30 c. Tanganyikan Flag. As T **6**—HORIZ. 1s. "Maternity" (mother with nurse holding baby). 2s. Dar-es-Salaam Waterfront. 5s. Land tillage. 10s. Diamond mine.

7. Mr. Nyerere inaugurating Self-help Project.

DESIGNS: 50 c. Hoisting flag on Mt. Kilimanjaro. 1s. 30, Presidential emblem. 2s. 50, Independence monument.

1962. Republic. Inaug.

120. 7.	30 c. emerald	8	8
121. –	50 c. yellow, black, green, red and blue	10	10
122. –	1s. 30 multicoloured ..	20	20
123. –	2s. 30 black, red & blue	35	35

8. Map of Republic.

1964. United Republic of Tanganyika and Zanzibar Commem.

124. 8.	20 c. green and blue ..	5	5
125. –	30 c. blue and sepia ..	5	5
126. –	1s. 30 salmon and ultram.	20	25
127. 8.	2s. 50 purple and ultram.	35	35

DESIGN: 30 c., 1 s. 30, Torch and Spear Emblem.

Despite the inscription on the stamps the above issue was only on sale in Tanganyika and had no validity in Zanzibar.

OFFICIAL STAMPS

1961. Independence stamps of 1961 optd. **OFFICIAL.**

O 1.	5 c. sepia and apple ..	5	5
O 2.	10 c. blue-green	5	5
O 3.	15 c. sepia and blue ..	5	5
O 4.	20 c. chestnut	5	5
O 5.	30 c. black, green & yellow	8	10
O 6.	50 c. black and yellow ..	10	12
O 7.	1s. brn., bl. & olive-yellow	20	25
O 8.	5s. blue-green and red ..	85	1·00

For later issues see **TANZANIA.**

TANZANIA BC

A republic within the Br. Commonwealth formerly known as Tanganyika and incorporating Zanzibar.

100 cents = 1 shilling.

NOTE.—Stamps inscribed "UGANDA KENYA TANGANYIKA & ZANZIBAR" (or "TANZANIA UGANDA KENYA") will be found listed under East Africa.

A. For use in Tanzania and also valid for use in Kenya and Uganda.

9. Hale Hydro-Electric Scheme.

10. Dar-es-Salaam Harbour.

1965.

128. 9.	5 c. ultramarine & orge.	5	5
129. –	10 c. black, yellow, green and blue	5	5
130. –	15 c. multicoloured ..	5	5
131. –	20 c. sepia, green & blue	5	5
132. –	30 c. black and brown..	8	5
133. –	40 c. multicoloured ..	8	5
134. –	50 c. multicoloured ..	10	5
135.	65 c. green, brown & blue	12	15
136. 10.	1s. multicoloured ..	15	8
137. –	1s. 30 multicoloured ..	20	12
138. –	2s. 50 blue and brown..	55	45
139. –	5s. brown, green & blue	1·00	75
140. –	10s. yellow, green & blue	1·40	1·40
141. –	20s. multicoloured ..	3·25	4·50

DESIGNS—As T **9**—HORIZ. 10 c. Tanzania flag. 20 c. Road-building. 50 c. Zebras, Manyara National Park. 65 c. Mt. Kilimanjaro. VERT. 15 c. National Servicemen. 30 c. Drum, Spear, Shield and Stool. 40 c. Giraffes, Mikumi National Park. As T **10**—HORIZ. 1s. 30, Skull of Zinjanthropus and Excavations, Olduva. Gorge. 2s. 50, Fishing. 5s. Sisal Industry. 10s. State House, Dar-es-Salaam. VERT. 20s. Arms of Tanzania.

ILLUSTRATIONS British Commonwealth and all overprints and surcharges are FULL SIZE. Foreign Countries have been reduced to ¾-LINEAR.

11. Cardinal.

1967. Fishes. Multicoloured.

142. 11.	5 c. mauve, grn. & blk.	5	5
143. –	10 c. brown and bistre..	5	5
144. –	15 c. grey, blue & black	5	5
145. –	20 c. brown and green..	5	5
146. –	30 c. green and black..	5	5
147. –	40 c. yell., brn. & green	8	5
148. –	50 c. multicoloured ..	10	8
149. –	65 c. yell., grn. & black	15	15
150a. –	70 c. multicoloured ..	12	12
151a. –	1 s. brn., blue & maroon	10	10
152. –	1 s. 30 multicoloured..	25	20
153. –	1 s. 50 multicoloured..	30	25
154a. –	2 s. 50 multicoloured..	50	35
155a. –	5 s. yell., black & green	90	1·00
156. –	10 s. multicoloured ..	2·25	1·00
157. –	20 s. multicoloured ..	5·00	4·00

DESIGNS—As T **11.** 10 c. Mud Skipper. 15 c. White Spotted Puffer. 20 c. Sea Horse. 30 c. Bat Fish. 40 c. Sweetlips. 50 c. Blue Clubnosed Wrasse. 65 c. Bennett's Butterfly. 70 c. Striped Grouper. 42 × 25 mm. 1 s. Scorpion Fish. 1 s. 30 Powder Blue Surgeon. 1 s. 50 Fusilier. 2 s. 50 Red Snapper. 5 s. Moorish Idol, 10 s. Picasso Fish. 20 s. Squirrel Fish.

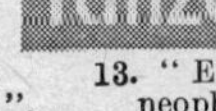

12. "Papilio hornimani". 13. "Euphaedra neophron".

1973.

(a) As T **12.**

158.	**12.**	5 c. green, blue & blk.	5	5
159.	–	10 c. multicoloured	5	5
160.	–	15 c. lavender and black	5	5
161.	–	20 c. brn., yellow & blk.	5	5
162.	–	30 c. yellow, orge. & blk.	5	5
163.	–	40 c. multicoloured	5	5
164.	–	50 c. multicoloured	5	5
165.	–	60 c. brown, yell. & lake	8	8
166.	–	70 c. green, orge. & blk.	8	8

(b) As T **13.**

167.	**13.**	1 s. multicoloured	10	12
168.	–	1 s. 50 multicoloured	15	20
169.	–	2 s. 50 multicoloured	25	30
170.	–	5 s. multicoloured	50	60
171.	–	10 s. multicoloured	1·00	1·25
172.	–	20 s. multicoloured	2·10	2·40

BUTTERFLIES: 10 c. "Colotis ione". 15 c. "Amauris makuyuensis". 20 c. "Libythea laius". 30 c. "Danaus chrysippus. 40 c. "Sallya rosa". 50 c. "Axiocerses styx". 60 c. "Eurema hecabe" 70 c. "Acraea insignis". 1 s. "Euphaedra neophron". 1 s. 50 "Precis octavia". 2 s. 50 "Charaxes eupale".5 s."Charaxes pollux". 10 s. "Salamis" parhassus". 20 s. "Papilio ophidicephalus".

1975. Nos. 165, 186/9 and 172 surch. Multicoloured.

73.	80 c. on 60 c. "Eurema hecabe"	15	15
174.	2 s. on 1 s. 50 "Precis octavia"	40	40
175.	3 s. on 2 s. 50 "Charaxes eupale"	10·00	10·00
176.	40 s. on 20 s. "Papilio ophidicephalus"	5·00	5·25

1976. Telecommunications Development. As Nos. 260/3 of Kenya.

177.	50 c. Microwave Tower	5	8
178.	1 s. Cordless switchboard	12	15
179.	2 s. Telephones	25	30
180.	3 s. Message Switching Centre	35	40

1976. Olympic Games, Montreal. As Nos. 265/8 of Kenya.

182.	50 c. Akii Bua, Ugandan hurdler	5	8
183.	1 s. Filbert Bayi, Tanzanian runner	12	15
184.	2 s. Steve Muchoki, Kenyan boxer	25	30
185.	3 s. Flags and Olympic flame	35	40

1976. Railway Transport. As Nos. 270/73 of Kenya.

187.	50 c. Tanzania-Zambia Railway	5	8
188.	1 s. Nile Bridge, Uganda	12	15
189.	2 s. Nakuru Station, Kenya	25	30
190.	3 s. Class A loco, 1896	35	40

1977. Game Fish of East Africa. As Nos. 265/8 of Kenya.

192.	50 c. Nile Perch	5	8
193.	1 s. Tilapia	12	15
194.	3 s. Sailfish	35	40
195.	5 s. Black Marlin	60	70

1977. Second World Black and African Festival of Arts and Culture. As Nos. 279/82 of Kenya.

196.	50 c. Maasai Manyatta (animal slaughter), Kenya	5	8
197.	1 s. "Heartbeat of Africa" (Ugandan dancers)	12	15
198.	2 s. Makonde sculpture, Tanzania	25	30
199.	3 s. "Early man and technology" (skinning animal)	35	40

OFFICIAL STAMPS

1965. Nos. 128, etc., optd. **OFFICIAL.**

O 9.	**9.**	5 c. ultram. & orange	5	5
O 10.	–	10 c. black, yellow, green and blue	5	5
O 11.	–	15 c. multicoloured	5	5
O 12.	–	20 c. sepia, green & blue	5	5
O 13.	–	30 c. black and brown	5	8
O 14.	–	50 c. multicoloured	10	10
O 15.	**10.**	1s. multicoloured	25	25
O 16.	–	5s. brown, green & blue	1·00	1·00

1967. Nos. 142, etc., optd. **OFFICIAL.**

O 20.	5 c. mauve, grn. & blk.	5	5
O 21.	10 c. brown & bistre	5	5
O 22.	14 c. grey, blue & black	5	5
O 23.	20 c. brown and green	5	5
O 24.	30 c. green and black	5	5
O 36.	40 c. yell., brn. & green		
O 25.	50 c. multicoloured	10	5
O 26a.	1 s. brn., blue & maroon	15	10
O 27a.	5 s. yellow, blk. & green	65	55

1973. Nos. 158 etc. optd. **OFFICIAL.**

O 40.	**12.**	5 c. green, blue & blk.	5	5
O 41.	–	10 c. multicoloured	5	5
O 42.	–	20 c. brn., yell. & blk.	5	5
O 43.	–	40 c. multicoloured	8	8
O 44.	–	50 c. multicoloured	8	8
O 45.	–	70 c. grn., orge. & blk.	10	10
O 46.	**13.**	1 s. multicoloured	12	12
O 47.	–	1 s. 50 multicoloured	20	20
O 48.	–	2 s. 50 multicoloured	30	30
O 49.	–	5 s. multicoloured	55	60

POSTAGE DUE STAMPS

The Postage Due stamps of Kenya, Uganda and Tanganyika were used in Tanganyika until January 2nd, 1967.

D 1.

1967.

D 13.	**D 1.**	5 c. red	5	5
D 14.		10 c. green	5	5
D 15.		20 c. blue	5	5
D 16.		30 c. brown	5	8
D 17.		40 c. purple	8	8
D 18.		1 s. orange	12	15

B. For use in Zanzibar only.

Z 1. Pres. Nyerere and First Vice-Pres. Karume within Bowl of Flame.

1966. United Republic. 2nd Anniv. Multicoloured.

Z 1.	30 c. Type Z 1	5	5
Z 2.	50 c. Hands supporting Bowl of Flame	8	8
Z 3.	1s. 30 As 50 c.	20	25
Z 4.	2s. 50 Type Z 1	40	45

TASMANIA BC

An island S. of Australia, one of the States of the Australian Commonwealth, whose stamps it now uses.

1. 2.

1853. Imperf.

3.	**1.**	1d. blue	£800	£180
11.	**2.**	4d. orange	£375	75·00

3. 4.

5.

ILLUSTRATIONS British Commonwealth and all overprints and surcharges are FULL SIZE. Foreign Countries have been reduced to ¾-LINEAR.

1855. Imperf.

29.	**3.**	1d. red	30·00	5·50
28.		1d. orange	30·00	5·50
34.		2d. green	45·00	17·00
37.		4d. blue	35·00	5·50
46.	**4.**	6d. lilac to grey	35·00	11·00
48.		6d. purple	70·00	12·00
41.	**5.**	1s. orange	£100	11·00

1864. Perf.

112.	**3.**	1d. red	6·00	3·00
111.		1d. orange	10·00	5·50
100.		2d. green	28·00	12·00
102.		4d. blue	28·00	3·00
93.	**4.**	6d. grey	28·00	4·00
129.		6d. purple	8·00	4·50
127.	**5.**	1s. orange	24·00	8·00

6.

7.

1870.

184.	**6.**	½d. orange	50	30
179.		1d. red	40	15
181.		2d. green	55	15
188.		3d. chocolate	65	35
135.		4d. blue	40	40
212.		4d. yellow	1·75	65
182.		8d. purple	1·00	75
227.		9d. blue	1·40	1·25
136.		10d. black	1·25	1·25
171.		5s. mauve	8·00	4·00

1889. Surch. **Halfpenny.**

201.	**6.**	½d. on 1d. red	40	30

1889. Surch. **2½d.**

207.	**6.**	2½d. on 9d. blue	60	30

1892. Various frames.

216.	**7.**	½d. orange and mauve	40	8
217.		2½d. purple	75	15
218.		5d. blue and brown	1·50	60
219.		6d. violet and black	1·75	70
220.		10d. lake and green	2·00	90
221.		1s. red and green	2·00	70
222.		2s. 6d. brown and blue	5·00	2·00
223.		5s. purple and red	7·00	4·00
224.		10s. mauve and brown	18·00	12·00
225.		£1 green and yellow	60·00	45·00

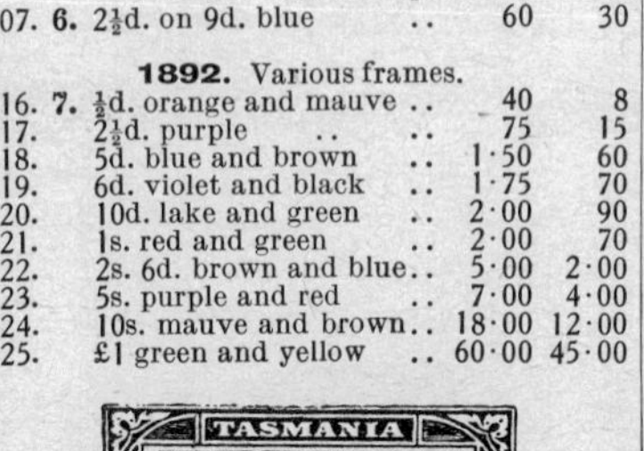

8. Lake Marion.

9. Mount Wellington.

DESIGNS—HORIZ. 2d. Hobart. 3d Spring River, Port Davey. 5d. Mt. Gould, Lake St. Clair. 6d. Dilston Falls, VERT. 2½d. Tasman's Arch. 4d. Russell Falls.

1899.

229.	**8.**	½d. green	20	8
230.	**9.**	1d. red	20	8
239.	–	2d. violet	40	8
232.	–	2½d. blue	75	40
249.	–	3d. brown	1·00	35
244a.	–	4d. orange	95	20
235.	–	5d. blue	2·00	60
250a.	–	6d. lake	2·00	75

1904. No. 218 surch. **1½d.**

257.	**7.**	1½d. on 5d. blue & brown	45	30

1912. No. 251a surch. **ONE PENNY.**

252.	1d. on 2d. violet	35	8

TCHONGKING (CHUNGKING) O1

An Indo-Chinese Post Office was opened at Chungking, in February 1902 and operated until it closed in December 1922.

1903. 100 centimes = 1 franc.
1919. 100 cents = 1 piastre.

Stamps of Indo-China surch.

1903. "Tablet" key-type surch. **TCHONGKING** and value in Chinese.

1.	**D.**	1 c. black on blue	40	40
2.		2 c. brown on buff	30	30
3.		4 c. brown on grey	30	30
4.		5 c. green	30	30
5.		10 c. red	30	30
6.		15 c. grey	40	40
7.		20 c. red on green	40	40
8.		25 c. blue	7·00	7·00
9.		25 c. black on red	30	30
10.		30 c. brown on drab	50	50
11.		40 c. red on yellow	6·00	6·00
12.		50 c. red on rose	32·00	32·00
13.		50 c. brown on blue	24·00	24·00
14.		75 c. brown on orange	5·00	5·00
15.		1 f. olive	5·00	5·00
16.		5 f. mauve on lilac	11·00	11·00

1906. Surch. **Tch'ong K'ing** and value in Chinese.

17.	**1.**	1 c. olive	20	20
18.		2 c. claret on yellow	20	20
19.		4 c. purple on blue	20	20
20.		5 c. green	20	20
21.		10 c. red	20	20
22.		15 c. brown on blue	50	40
23.		20 c. red on green	20	20
24.		25 c. blue	35	35
25.		30 c. brown on cream	35	35
26.		35 c. black on yellow	35	35
27.		40 c. black on grey	40	40
28.		50 c. brown on cream	60	60
29.	**D.**	75 c. brown on orange	2·75	2·75
30.	**1.**	1 f. green	3·00	3·00
31.		2 f. brown on yellow	3·00	3·00
32.	**D.**	5 f. mauve on lilac	18·00	18 00
33.	**1.**	10 f. red on green	24·00	24·00

1908. Native types surch. **TCHONGKING** and value in Chinese.

34.	**2.**	1 c. black and brown	5	5
35.		2 c. black and brown	5	5
36.		4 c. black and blue	8	8
37.		5 c. black and green	15	15
38.		10 c. black and red	20	20
39.		15 c. black and violet	30	30
40.	**3.**	20 c. black and violet	30	30
41.		25 c. black and blue	30	30
42.		30 c. black and brown	30	30
43.		35 c. black and green	55	55
44.		40 c. black and brown	1·75	1·75
45.		50 c. black and red	1·40	1·40
46.	**4.**	75 c. black and orange	90	90
47.		1 f. black and red	1·25	1·25
48.		2 f. black and green	11·00	11·00
49.		5 f. black and blue	3·50	3·50
50.		10 f. black and violet	45·00	45·00

1919. As last surch. in addition in figures and words.

51.	**2.**	⅖ c. on 1 c. black & brown	10	10
52.		⅘ c on 2 c. black & brown	12	12
53.		1⅗ on 4 c. black and blue	15	15
54.		2 c. on 5 c. black & green	12	12
55.		4 c. on 10 c. black and red	12	8
56.		6 c. on 15 c. black & violet	5	5
57.	**3.**	8 c. on 20 c. blk. and violet	5	5
58.		10 c. on 25 c. black & blue	15	8
59.		12 c. on 30 c. blk. & brown	15	10
60.		14 c. on 35 c. black & green	20	10
61.		16 c. on 40 c. black & brn.	25	25
62.		20 c. on 50 c. black & red	1·25	1·10
63.	**4.**	30 c. on 75 c. black & orge.	25	25
64.		40 c. on 1 f. black and red	45	45
65.		80 c. on 2 f. black & green	45	45
66.		2 p. on 5 f. black & blue	90	90
67.		4 p. on 10 f. black & violet	90	90

TETE O3

Formerly using the stamps of Mozambique, this district of Mozambique was permitted to issue its own stamps from 1913 to 1920 when Mozambique stamps were again used.

1913. Surch. **REPUBLICA TETE** and new value on "Vasco da Gama" issues of

(a) **Portuguese Colonies.**

1.	¼ c. on 2½ r. green	65	45
2.	½ c. on 5 r. red	65	45
3.	1 c. on 10 r. purple	65	45
4.	2½ c. on 25 r. green	65	45
5.	5 c. on 50 r. blue	65	45
6.	7½ c. on 75 r. brown	80	65
7.	10 c. on 100 r. brown	65	45
8.	15 c. on 150 r. yell.-brown	65	45

(b) **Macao.**

9.	¼ c. on ½ a. green	70	60
10.	½ c. on 1 a. red	70	60
11.	1 c. on 2 a. purple	70	60
12.	2½ c. on 4 a. green	70	60
13.	5 c. on 8 a. blue	70	60
14.	7½ c. on 12 a. brown	90	80
15.	10 c. on 16 a. brown	70	60
16.	15 c. on 24 a. yellow	70	60

(c) **Timor.**

17.	¼ c. on ½ c. green	70	60
18.	½ c. on 1 a. red	70	60
19.	1 c. on 2 a purple	70	60
20.	2½ c. on 4 a. green	70	60
21.	5 c. on 8 a. blue	70	60
22.	7½ c. on 12 a. brown	90	80
23.	10 c. on 16 a. brown	70	60
24.	15 c. on 24 a. yell.-brown	70	60

1914. "Ceres" key-type inscr. "TETE".

25.	**U.**	¼ c. olive	30	20
26.		½ c. black	30	20
27.		1 c. green	30	20
28.		1½ c. brown	30	20
29.		2 c. red	30	20
30.		2½ c. violet	25	15
31.		5 c. blue	30	20
32.		7½ c. brown	80	60
33.		8 c. grey	80	60
34.		10 c. brown	80	60
35.		15 c. claret	90	80
36.		20 c. green	80	60
37.		30 c. brown on green	80	70
38.		40 c. brown on rose	70	65
39.		50 c. orange on pink	80	70
40.		1 e. green on blue	1·10	80

THAILAND

O4

An independent kingdom in S.E. Asia, previously known as Siam.

1883. 32 solot = 16 atts = 8 peinung (sio) = 4 songpy (sik) = 2 fuang = 1 salung. 4 salungs = 1 tical.
1909. 100 satangs = 1 tical.
1912. 100 satangs = 1 baht.

1. King Chulalongkorn. 2.

3. King Chulalongkorn. 4.

1883.

1c. 1. 1 solot blue 60 85
2. 1 att red .. .. .. 1·25 1·40
3. 1 sio red .. .. .. 1·75 1·90
4. 2. 1 sik yellow .. .. 1·75 1·90
5a.3. 1 salung orange .. .. 2·75 2·75

1885. Surch. **1 Tical.**

7. 1. 1 t. on 1 solot blue .. 48·00 48·00

1887.

11. 4. 1 a. green 30 15
12. 2 a. green and red .. 35 25
13. 3 a. green and blue .. 70 45
14. 4 a. green and brown .. 85 70
15. 8 a. green and yellow .. 1·10 45
16. 12 a. purple and red .. 55 30
17. 24 a. purple and blue .. 70 30
18. 64 a. purple and brown .. 4·50 2·75

(5.) (6.)

1889. Surch. with T 5.

19. 1. 1 a. on 1 sio red .. 1·10 1·10

1889. Surch. as T 6.

20. 4. 1 a. on 2 a. green and red 45 45
24. 1 a. on 3 a. green and blue 85 85
29. 2 a. on 3 a. green and blue 2·75 2·75

1 Att.

(7.) (8.)

1892. Surch. with T 7.

31. 4. 4 a. on 24 a. purple & blue 4·25 4·25

1892. Surch. as T 8.

53. 4. 1 a. on 12 a. purple & red 1·75 1·40
45. 1 a. on 64 a. pur. & brown 30 30
48. 2 a. on 64 a. pur. & brown 25 25
58. 3 a. on 12 a. purple & red 85 70
59. 4 a. on 12 a. purple & red 1·25 45
33. 4 a. on 24 a. purple & blue 1·40 1·10
50. 10 a. on 24 a. purple & blue 35 25

9. 10. 11. Wat Cheng, "Temple of Light".

1899.

83. 9. 1 a. green 20 15
68. 2 a. green 25 15
84. 2 a. red and blue 45 20
69. 3 a. red and blue 50 20
85. 3 a. green .. .. .. 1·00 1·00
70. 4 a. red 45 15
86. 4 a. brown and pink .. 60 20
87. 6 a. red .. .. .. 1·00 85
71. 8 a. green and orange .. 50 15
72. 10 a. blue .. .. .. 1·10 20
73. 12 a. purple and red .. 1·40 20
88. 14 a. blue .. .. .. 2·10 2·10
74. 24 a. purple and blue .. 2·75 1·10
89. 28 a. brown and blue .. 2·50 2·10
75. 64 a. purple and brown .. 2·75 1·10

1899.

76. 10. 1 a. green .. .. 29·00 23·00
77. 2 a. green and red .. 32·00 29·00
78. 3 a. red and blue .. 70·00 55·00
79. 4 a. black and green .. 85·00 70·00
80. 10 a. red and green .. £140 £110

1905. Surch. in English and Siamese.

90. 9. 1 a. on 14 a. blue .. 45 45
91. 2 a. on 28 a. brown & blue 50 50

1905.

92. 11. 1 a. green and yellow 15 8
93. 2 a. grey and violet .. 15 8
105. 2 a. green 45 20
94. 3 a. green 20 15
106. 3 a. grey and violet .. 70 30
95. 4 a. red and sepia .. 35 8
107. 4 a. red 55 8
96. 5 a. red 35 35
97. 8 a. olive and black .. 35 12
108. 9 a. blue 85 30
98. 12 a. blue 50 15
109. 18 a. brown .. .. 2·75 1·10
99. 24 a. brown .. .. 1·00 55
100. 1 t. yellow and blue .. 2·00 25

1907. Tall Fiscal stamp with portrait and scales surch. **Siam postage** and new value.

101. 10 t. green .. .. 70·00 23·00
102. 20 t. green .. .. £140 42·00
103. 40 t. green £350 £100

1907. Surch. **1 att** and thin line.

104. 4. 1 a. on 24 s. pur. & blue 25 25

1908. Surch. in English and Siamese

110. 4. 2 a. on 24 a. pur. & blue 35 35
111. 11. 4 on 5 a. red 85 85
112. 9. 9 a. on 10 a. blue .. 1·00 85

1908. Reign of King Chulalongkorn. 40th Anniv. Optd. **Jubilee 1868-1908** in English and Siamese.

113. 11. 1 a. green and yellow .. 70 55
114. 3 a. green 85 50
115. 4 on 5 a. (No. 111) .. 1·40 70
116. 8 a. olive and black .. 5·50 4·50
117. 18 a. brown .. .. 2·75 2·75

12. 13. King Chulalongkorn.

1908.

118. 12. 1 t. violet and green .. 2·50 20
119. 2 t. orange and purple 3·50 60
120. 3 t. blue and olive .. 3·50 60
121. 5 t. green and lilac .. 5·50 1·10
122. 10 t. red and olive .. 17·00 4·00
123. 20 t. brown and grey .. 27·00 5·00
124. 40 t. black and blue .. 40·00 10·00

1909. Surch. in satangs in English and Siamese.

125. 11. 2 s. on 1 a. green & yell. 15 8
126. 2 s. on 2 a. green .. 15 10
164. 2 s. on 2 a. grey & violet 45 20
129. 3 s. on 3 a. green .. 45 30
130. 3 s. on 3 a. grey & violet 15 15
131. 6 s. on 4 a. red 15 15
133. 6 s. on 4 a. red and sepia 2·75 2·75
134. 6 s. on 5 a. red .. 30 25
138. 9. 6 s. on 6 a. red .. 85 70
135. 11. 12 s. on 8 a. olive & blk 30 15
136. 14 s. on 9 a. blue .. 30 8
137. 14 s. on 12 a. blue .. 13·00 13·00
139. 4. 14 s. on 12 a. pur. & red 11·00 11·00
140. 9. 14 s. on 14 a. blue .. 4·25 4·25

1910.

141. 13. 2 s. green and orange .. 12 5
142. 3 s. green 15 5
143. 6 s. red 25 5
144. 12 s. brown and black .. 30 5
145. 14 s. blue 35 15
146. 28 s. brown 85 45

14. King Vijiravudh. 15.

1912.

147. 14. 2 s. brown 8 5
167. 3 s. green 8 5
168. 5 s. rose 15 5
149. 6 s. red 25 8
169. 10 s. brown and black 20 5
150. 12 s. sepia and black .. 50 15
151. 14 s. blue 55 15
170. 15 s. blue 25 5
152. 28 s. brown .. .. 1·10 45
153. 15. 1 b. sepia and blue .. 2·00 20
154. 2 b. sepia and rose .. 4·00 35
155. 3 b. black and green .. 4·75 45
156. 5 b. black and violet .. 5·50 55
157. 10 b. purple and olive .. 20·00 3·50
176. 20 b. brown and green .. 38·00 7·00

1914. Surch. in English and Siamese.

165. 13. 2 s. on 14 s. blue .. 45 20
159. 14. 2 s. on 14 s. blue .. 25 8
160. 5 s. on 6 s. red 25 8
161. 10 s. on 12 s. sep. & blk. 35 8
162. 15 s. on 28 s. brown .. 45 8

1918. Optd. with small cross in circle.

177. 14. 2 s. brown 30 20
178. 3 s. green 35 25
179. 5 s. red 45 30
180. 10 s. brown and black 55 55
181. 15 s. blue 70 55
182. 15. 1 b. sepia and blue .. 3·50 2·75
183. 2 b. brown and rose .. 4·25 4·00
184. 3 b. black and green .. 7·00 6·00
185. 5 b. black and violet .. 11·00 10·00
186. 10 b. purple and olive .. 50·00 50·00
187. 20 b. brown and green .. £140 £140

1918. Optd. **VICTORY** in English and Siamese.

188. 14. 2 s. brown 15 15
189. 3 s. green 15 15
190. 5 s. red 15 15
191. 10 c. brown and black .. 55 45
192. 15 s. blue 55 45
193. 15. 1 b. sepia and blue .. 4·25 4·25
194. 2 b. brown and rose .. 6·00 6·00
195. 3 b. black and green .. 7·00 7·00
196. 5 b. black and violet .. 13·00 13·00

1919. Surch. in English and Siamese figures.

197. 14. 5 s. on 6 s. red 35 8
198. 10 s. on 12 s. sepia & blk. 35 15

Scouts Fund

(15a.) (15b.)

1920. Scouts' Fund. Various stamps handstamped.

(a) With Type **15a.**

199. 14. 2 s. (+3 s.) brown .. 8·50 7·00
200. 3 s. (+2 s.) green .. 8·50 7·00
201. 5 s. on 6 s. (+20 s.) red (No. 160) .. .. 8·50 7·00
202. 10 s. on 12 s. (+5 s.) brn and black (No. 161) .. 8·50 7·00
203. 15 s. (+5 s.) blue .. 10·00 10·00
204. 11. 1 t. (+25 s.) yell. & bl. 45·00 45·00

(b) With Type **15b.**

205. 14. 2 s. (+3 s.) brown .. 8·50 7·00
206. 3 s. (+2 s.) green .. 8·50 7·00
207. 16. 5 s. (+20 s.) red on pink 8·50 7·00
208. 14. 10 s. on 12 s. (+5 s.) brn. & blk. (No. 161) 8·50 7·00
209. 15 s. (+5 s.) blue .. 17·00 17·00
210. 11. 1 t. (+25 s.) yell. & bl. 55·00 55·00

These stamps were sold in aid of the "Wild Tiger" Scouts organisation at the premium stated.

SCOUT'S FUND

16. (16a.)

1920.

211. 16. 2 s. brown on yellow .. 12 5
212. 3 s. green on green .. 25 5
213. 3 s. brown 15 5
214. 5 s. red on pink .. 15 5
215. 5 s. green .. .. 1·00 5
216. 5 s. violet on mauve .. 25 5
217. 10 s. brown and black 50 5
218. 15 s. blue on blue .. 70 5
219. 15 s. red 85 30
220. 25 s. brown .. .. 1·40 20
221. 25 s. blue 75 25
222. 50 s. black and brown 2·75 12

1920. Scouts' Fund. Optd. with Type **16a.**

223. 16. 2 s. brown on yellow .. 7·00 7·00
224. 3 s. green on green .. 7·00 7·00
225. 5 s. red on pink .. 7·00 7·00
226. 10 s. brown and black 7·00 7·00
227. 15 s. blue on blue .. 8·50 8·50
228. 25 s. brown .. .. 20·00 20·00
229. 50 s. black and brown 42·00 42·00

17. "Garuda" Bird. 18. Coronation Stone.

1925. Air.

238. 17. 2 s. purple on yellow .. 25 8
231. 3 s. brown 55 8
239. 5 s. green 30 8
240. 10 s. orange and black 1·10 8
241. 15 s. red .. .. 1·75 12
242. 25 s. blue 55 12
243. 50 s. black and brown .. 1·10 30
237. 1 b. sepia and blue .. 2·10 1·10

1926.

244. 18. 1 t. green and lilac .. 2·40 25
245. 2 t. red .. .. 3·75 85
246. 3 t. blue and olive .. 6·50 1·10
247. 5 t. olive and violet .. 10·00 2·50
248. 10 t. brown and red .. 20·00 3·50
249. 20 t. brown and blue .. 50·00 12·00

1928. Surch. in English and Siamese.

250. 16. 5 s. on 15 s. red .. 85 30
251. 14. 10 s. on 28 s. brown .. 1·10 30

19. King Prajadhipok. 20.

1928.

252. 19. 2 s. brown 5 5
253. 3 s. green 5 5
254. 5 s. violet 8 5
255. 10 s. red 12 5
256. 15 s. blue 15 8
257. 25 s. orange and black .. 15 8
258. 50 s. black and orange .. 35 8
259. 80 s. black and blue .. 50 15
260. 20. 1 b. black and blue .. 75 20
261. 2 b. brown and red .. 1·40 45
262. 3 b. black and green .. 2·25 55
263. 5 b. brown and violet .. 5·50 85
264. 10 b. purple and olive .. 8·00 1·25
265. 20 b. brown and green .. 11·00 2·50
266. 40 b. sepia and green .. 24·00 8·50

1930. Surch. in English and Siamese.

267. 13. 10 s. on 12 s. brn. & blk. 20 15
268. 25 s. on 28 s. brown .. 45 15

21. Kings Prajadhipok and Chao Phya Chakri. 23. Chao Phya Chakri.

22. Kings Prajadhipok and Chaeo Phya Chakri.

1932. 150th Anniv. of Chakri Dynasty and of Bangkok as Capital and Opening of Memorial Bridge over Menam.

269. 21. 2 s. red 12 5
270. 3 s. green 25 8
271. 5 s. violet 30 8
272. 22. 10 s. black and red .. 45 15
273. 15 s. black and blue .. 85 15
274. 25 s. black and mauve 1·10 25
275. 50 s. black and claret .. 2·00 45
276. 23. 1 b. blue .. .. 4·25 1·10

(24.)

1939. Red Cross Fund. Membership of the International Red Cross. 75th Anniv. Surch. as T 24.

277. 15. 5+5 s. on 1 b. (193) .. 7·00 5·50
278. 10+5 s. on 2 b. (194) .. 7·00 5·50
279. 15+5 s. on 3 b. (195) .. 7·00 5·50

25. National Assembly Hall. 26. Chakri Palace and "Garuda" Bird.

1939. Constitution. Seventh Anniv. and National Day (1st issue).

280. 25. 2 s. lilac 20 15
281. 3 s. green 30 15
282. 5 s. mauve 35 8
283. 10 s. red 55 8
284. 15 s. blue .. .. 1·10 30

1940. National Day (2nd issue).

285. 26. 2 s. lilac 30 8
286. 3 s. green 35 12
287. 5 s. mauve 50 8
288. 10 s. red 70 12
289. 15 s. blue .. .. 1·00 30

27. King Ananda Mahidol. 29. Ban Pa'im Palace, Ayuthia.

28. Ploughing Rice Field. 30. Monument of Democracy.

1941.

290. 27. 2 s. brown 8 8
291. 3 s. green 8 8
292. 5 s. violet 8 8
293. 10 s. red 8 8
294. 28. 15 s. grey and blue .. 20 8
295. 25 s. orange and slate .. 35 20
296. 50 s. grey and orange .. 40 20
297. 29. 1 b. grey and blue .. 85 20
298. 2 b. grey and red .. 1·40 25
299. 3 b. grey and green .. 1·75 50
300. 5 b. red and black .. 3·50 1·00
301. 10 b. yellow and black 7·00 2·50

1942. Air.

302. 30. 2 s. brown 25 25
303. 3 s. green .. .. 2·00 1·40
304. 5 s. purple 30 15
305. 10 s. red 40 25
306. 15 s. blue 55 25

31. King Ananda Mahidol. 32. Bangkaen Monument and Ears of Rice. 33. Indo-China War Monument, Bangkok.

1943.

307. 31. 1 b. blue 85 55

1943.

311. 32. 2 s. orange 25 15
309. 33. 3 s. green 70 70
312. 32. 10 s. red 30 15

34. King Bhumibol. 35.

1947.

313. 34. 5 s. violet 8 5
314. 10 s. red 8 5
315. 20 s. brown 15 5
316. 50 s. green 30 5
317. 1 b. blue and violet .. 45 8
318. 2 b. green and blue .. 70 15
319. 3 b. black and red .. 1·10 15
320. 5 b. red and green .. 2·00 20
321. 10 b. violet and sepia .. 2·75 30
322. 20 b. lilac and black .. 7·00 55

The baht values are larger, size $21\frac{1}{2} \times 27$ mm.

1947. Coming of Age of King Bhumibol.

323. 35. 5 s. orange 55 15
324. 10 s. brown 55 15
325. 10 s. green 45 15
326. 20 s. blue 55 15
327. 50 s. green .. .. 1·00 25

36. King and Palace. 37. King Bhumibol.

1950. King's Coronation.

328. 36. 5 s. purple 5 5
329. 10 s. red 8 5
330. 15 s. violet 10 5
331. 20 s. brown 15 5
332. 80 s. green 15 15
333. 1 b. blue 25 8
334. 2 b. yellow 45 30
335. 3 b. grey 85 30

1951.

336. 37. 5 s. purple 5 5
337. 10 s. green 5 5
338. 15 s. brown 5 5
339. 20 s. chocolate .. 8 5
340. 25 s. red 8 5
341. 50 s. olive 12 5
342. 1 b. blue 25 5
343. 1 b. 15 blue 55 12
344. 1 b. 25 lake 45 12
345. 2 b. green 40 8
346. 3 b. grey 70 8
347. 5 b. red and blue .. 90 12
348. 10 b. violet and sepia 2·25 15
349. 20 b. olive and black .. 7·00 45

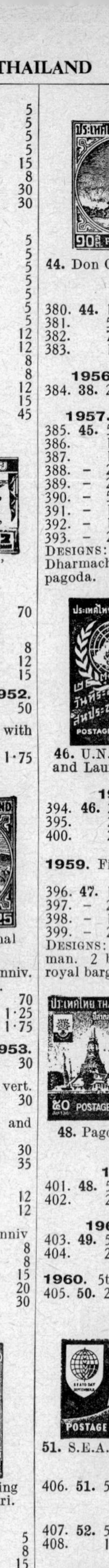

38. U.N. Emblem. 39. "Garuda" Bird.

1951. United Nations Day.

350. 38. 25 s. blue 85 70

1952. Air.

351. 39. 1 b. 50 purple .. 30 8
352. 2 b. blue 45 12
353. 3 b. grey 55 15

1952. United Nations Day. Optd. **1952.**

354. 38. 25 s. blue 70 50

1952. Constitution. 20th Anniv. Surch. with emblem and value.

355. 19. 80 s. + 20 s. black & blue 1·75 1·75

40. 41. Processional Elephant.

1953. Thai Red Cross Society. 60th Anniv. Cross in red, figure in blue and red.

356. 40. 25 s. + 25 s. cream & grn. 70 70
357. 50 s. + 50 s. cream & rose 1·25 1·25
358. 1 b. + 1 b. cream & blue 1·75 1·75

1953. United Nations Day. Optd. **1953.**

359. 38. 25 s. blue 45 30

1954. United Nations Day. Optd. **1954** vert.

360. 38. 25 s. blue 45 30

1955. Optd. **THAILAND** in English and Siamese.

361. 19. 5 s. violet 40 30
362. 10 s. red 40 35

1955. Surch.

363. 34. 5 s. on 20 s. brown .. 25 12
364. 10 s. on 20 s. brown .. 25 12

1955. King Naresuan. 400th Birth Anniv

365. 41. 25 s. red 15 8
366. 80 s. purple 35 8
367. 1 b. 25 green 45 15
368. 2 b. blue 55 20
369. 3 b. lake 85 30

42. Tao Suranari. 43. Statue of King Taksin, Thonburi.

1955. Tao Suranari Commem.

370. 42. 10 s. lilac 8 5
371. 25 s. green 25 8
372. 1 b. brown 45 15

1955. Red Cross Fair. Optd. **24 98.**

373. 40. 25 s. + 25 s. cream & grn. 1·75 1·75
374. 50 s. + 50 s. cream & rose 2·25 2·25
375. 1 b. + 1 b. cream & blue 3·50 3·50

1955. King Taksin Commem.

376. 43. 5 s. blue 5 5
377. 25 s. green 8 5
378. 1 b. 25 red 30 15

1955. U.N. Day. Optd. **1955** vert.

379. 38. 25 s. blue 25 20

44. Don Chedi Pagoda. 45. Dharmachakra and Deer.

1956.

380. 44. 10 s. green 8 5
381. 50 s. brown 20 5
382. 75 s. violet 30 12
383. 1 b. 50 chestnut .. 45 15

1956. U.N. Day. Optd. **1956** vert.

384. 38. 25 s. blue 20 15

1957. Buddhist Era. 2500th Anniv.

385. 45. 5 s. sepia 5 5
386. 10 s. claret 8 5
387. 15 s. green 12 5
388. – 20 s. orange 12 5
389. – 25 s. red-brown .. 15 5
390. – 50 s. magenta 20 5
391. – 1 b. bistre-brown .. 35 15
392. – 1 b. 25 slate-blue .. 45 20
393. – 2 b. maroon 55 25

DESIGNS: 20 s. to 50 s. Hand of Peace and Dharmachakra. 1 b. to 2 b. Nakon Phatom pagoda.

46. U.N. Emblem and Laurel Sprays. 47. Gateway to Grand Palace.

1957. United Nations Day.

394. 46. 25 s. olive 15 8
395. 25 s. brown (1958) .. 12 8
400. 25 s. indigo (1959) .. 12 8

1959. First South East Asia Peninsula Games (S.E.A.P.).

396. 47. 10 s. orange 5 5
397. – 25 s. lake 8 5
398. – 1 b. 25 green 30 15
399. – 2 b. blue 40 15

DESIGNS: 25 s. Royal parasols. 1 b. 25, Bowman. 2 b. Wat Arun (temple) and prow of royal barge.

48. Pagoda. 49. Wat Arun Temple. 50. Elephant.

1960. World Refugee Year.

401. 48. 50 s. brown 8 8
402. 2 b. green 25 25

1960. Leprosy Relief Campaign.

403. 49. 50 s. red 10 5
404. 2 b. blue 35 20

1960. 5th World Forestry Congress, Seattle.

405. 50. 25 s. green 15 8

51. S.E.A.T.O. Emblem. 52. Siamese Child.

1960. S.E.A.T.O. Day.

406. 51. 50 s. brown 15 5

1960. Children's Day.

407. 52. 50 s. mauve 12 5
408. 1 b. brown 25 15

53. Letter-writing. 54. U.N. Emblem and Globe.

1960. Int. Correspondence Week.

409. 53. 50 s. magenta 12 5
410. 2 b. blue 35 25

1960. U.N. Day.

411. 54. 50 s. violet 15 8
446. 50 s. lake (1961) .. 15 8
467. 50 s. red (1962) .. 10 8

55. King Bhumibol. 56. Children in Garden.

1961.

422. 55. 5 s. purple 5 5
423. 10 s. blue-green .. 5 5
424. 15 s. red-brown .. 5 5
425. 20 s. brown 5 5
426. 25 s. red 5 5
427. 50 s. olive 5 5
428. 80 s. orange 8 5
429. 1 b. brown and blue .. 12 5
430. 1 b. 25 yell.-olive & verm. 15 5
431. 1 b. 50 yell.-grn. & violet 20 5
432. 2 b. violet and red .. 25 8
433. 3 b. blue and brown .. 30 10
434. 4 b. black and bistre .. 45 15
435. 5 b. green and blue .. 50 20
436. 10 b. black & vermilion 1·00 35
437. 20 b. blue and emerald 2·00 70
438. 25 b. blue and green .. 2·50 1·00
439. 40 b. black and yellow 4·00 2·00

1961. Children's Day.

440. 56. 20 s. indigo 8 5
441. 2 b. violet 45 15

57. Pen, Letters and Globe. 58. Thai Scout Badge and Saluting Hand.

1961. Int. Correspondence Week.

442. – 25 s. myrtle 5 5
443. – 50 s. purple 8 8
444. 57. 1 b. red 15 8
445. 2 b. blue 35 20

DESIGN: 25 s., 50 s. Pen, and world map on envelope.

1961. Thai Scout Movement. 50th Anniv.

447. 58. 50 s. magenta 12 8
448. – 1 b. green 15 12
449. – 2 b. blue 45 20

DESIGNS—VERT. 1 b. Scout camp and scout saluting flag. 2 b. King Vajiravudh in uniform, and scout, cub and guide marching.

59. Campaign Emblem and Temple. 60. Bangkok.

1962. Malaria Eradication.

450. 59. 5 s. chestnut 5 5
451. 10 s. brown 5 5
452. 20 s. blue 5 5
453. 50 s. red 8 5
454. – 1 b. green 15 8
455. – 1 b. 50 purple .. 25 8
456. – 2 b. blue 35 12
457. – 3 b. violet 50 15

DESIGN: 1 b. to 3 b. Thailander fighting mosquitoes.

1962. "Century 21" Exhibition, Seattle.

458. 60. 50 s. purple 8 8
459. 2 b. blue 40 25

61. Thai Mother and Child. 62. Correspondence Symbols. 63. Exhibition Emblem.

1962. Children's Day.

460. 61. 25 s. turquoise 5 5
461. 50 s. buff 12 8
462. 2 b. magenta 35 15

1962. Int. Correspondence Week.
463. **62.** 25 s. violet 5 5
464. 50 s. red 8 5
465. – 1 b. olive-yellow .. 15 12
466. – 2 b. grey-green .. 30 15
DESIGN: 1 b., 2 b. Quill pen.

1962. Students' Exn., Bangkok.
468. **63.** 50 s. bistre 10 8

64. Harvesting. **65.** "Temple Guardian".

1963. Freedom from Hunger.
469. **64.** 20 s. green 8 5
470. 50 s. brown 15 8

1963. Asian-Oceanic Postal Union. 1st Anniv.
471. **65.** 50 s. green and brown .. 8 8

66. Centenary Emblem. **67.** G.P.O., Bangkok and (inset) old P.O.

1963. Red Cross Cent.
472. **66.** 50 s.+10 s. red & grey 15 12
473. – 50 s.+10 s. red & grey 15 12
DESIGNS: No. 473 As T **66** but with positions of emblem and inscr. reversed.

1963. Post and Telegraph Department. 80th Anniv.
474. **67.** 50 s. green, orange and slate-violet .. 8 5
475. 3 b. sepia, green and red 40 25

68. King Bhumibol. **69.** Children with Dolls.

1963.
476. **68.** 5 s. magenta 5 5
477. 10 s. green 5 5
478. 15 s. brown 5 5
479. 20 s. olive-brown .. 5 5
480. 25 s. red 5 5
481. 50 s. drab 5 5
482. 75 s. lilac 5 5
483. 80 s. orange 5 5
484. 1 b. brown and blue .. 8 5
485. 1 b. 25 bistre & chestnut 12 8
486. 1 b. 50 green and violet 15 5
487. 2 b. violet and red .. 15 8
488. 3 b. blue and brown .. 25 10
489. 4 b. black and bistre .. 35 15
490. 5 b. green and blue .. 45 15
491. 10 b. black & vermilion 85 20
492. 20 b. grey-blue & green 1·90 45
493. 25 b. blue and bronze .. 2·00 55
494. 40 b. black and yellow .. 4·00 1·10

1963. Children's Day.
505. **69.** 50 s. red 5 5
506. 2 b. blue 20 8

70. "Garuda" bird with Scroll in Beak.

1963. Int. Correspondence Week.
507. **70.** 50 s. purple & turquoise 8 8
508. 1 b. maroon and green .. 15 12
509. – 2 b. slate-bl. & yell.-brn. 35 25
510. – 3 b. green & orge.-brown 55 35
DESIGN: 2 b., 3 b. Thai women writing letters.

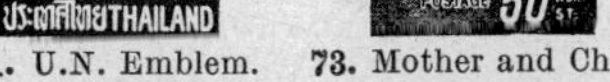

71. U.N. Emblem. **73.** Mother and Child.

72. King Bhumibol.

1963. U.N. Day.
511. **71.** 50 s. blue 8 5

1963. King Bhumibol's 36th Birthday.
512. **72.** 1 b. 50 indigo, yell. & bl. 30 12
513. 5 b. indigo, yell. & mag. 85 30

1964. U.N.I.C.E.F. 17th Anniv.
514. **73.** 50 s. blue 5 5
515. 2 b. olive 25 15

74. "Hand" of Flags, Pigeon and Globe.

1964. Int. Correspondence Week.
516. **74.** 50 s. mauve and green .. 8 5
517. – 1 b. chocolate and green 15 5
518. – 2 b. violet and yellow .. 35 12
519. – 3 b. olive and blue .. 50 15
DESIGNS: 1 b. Thai girls and map. 2 b. Map, pen and pencil. 3 b. Hand with quill pen, and globe.

75. Globe and U.N. Emblem. **76.** King Bhumibol and Queen Sirikit.

1964. United Nations Day.
520. **75.** 50 s. grey 8 5

1965. 15th Royal Wedding Anniv.
521. **76.** 2 b. multicoloured .. 35 15
522. 5 b. multicoloured .. 85 30

77. I.T.U. Emblem and Symbols.

1965. I.T.U. Cent.
523. **77.** 1 b. green 30 10

78. Goddess, Letters and Globes.

1965. Int. Correspondence Week. Multicoloured.
524. 50 s. Type **78** 8 5
525. 1 b. Type **78** 15 8
526. 2 b. Handclasp, letters and world map 35 15
527. 3 b. As 2 b. 45 20

79. Grand Palace, Bangkok. **80.** U.P.U. Monument, Berne and map of Thailand.

1965. Int. Co-operation Year.
528. **79.** 50 s. slate, yellow & blue 8 5

1965. Thailand's Admission to the U.P.U. 80th Anniv.
529. **80.** 20 s. grey-blue & mauve 5 5
530. 50 s. blk. & greenish-bl. 8 5
531. 1 b. orange & violet-blue 15 5
532. 3 b. green and ochre .. 55 20

81. Child and Lotus.

1965. Children's Day.
533. **81.** 50 s. chestnut and black 12 5
534. – 1 b. green and black .. 25 10
DESIGN: 1 b. Child mounting stairs.

82. Cycling.

1966. Publicity for 5th Asian Games, Bangkok.
535. 20 s. lake (Type **82**) .. 5 5
536. 25 s. violet (Tennis) .. 5 5
537. 50 s. red (Running) .. 8 5
538. 1 b. ultram. (Weightlifting) 15 5
539. 1 b. 25 black (Boxing) .. 15 8
540. 2 b. blue (Swimming) .. 30 12
541. 3 b. chestnut (Basketball) 40 20
542. 5 b. maroon (Football) .. 70 30
See also Nos. 553/6.

83. Emblem and Fair Buildings. **84.** "Reading and Writing".

1966. 1st Int. Trade Fair. Bangkok.
543. **83.** 50 s. purple 10 5
544. 1 b. chestnut 20 8

1966. Int. Correspondence Week.
545. – 50 s. red 8 5
546. – 1 b. chestnut 15 5
547. **84.** 2 b. violet 35 8
548. 3 b. turquoise 50 15
DESIGN: 50 s., 1 b. "Map" envelopes representing the five continents and pen.

85. U.N. Emblem. **87.** Pra Buddha Bata (monastery).

86. "Goddess of Rice".

1966. United Nations Day.
549. **85.** 50 s. ultramarine .. 10 5

1966. Int. Rice Year.
550. **86.** 50 s. blue and green .. 8 5
551. 3 b. red and maroon .. 55 30

1966. U.N.E.S.C.O. 20th Anniv.
552. **87.** 50 s. olive and black .. 8 5

88. Thai Boxing. **89.** "Channa triatus".

1966 5th Asian Games Bangkok. Each black, red and brown.
553. 50 c. Type **88** 8 5
554. 1 b. Takraw (ball game) .. 15 8
555. 2 b. "Kite fighting" .. 35 15
556. 3 b. "Cudgel play" .. 50 25

1967. Fishes. Multicoloured.
557. 1 b. Type **89** 15 5
558. 2 b. "Rastrelliger brachysomus" 35 10
559. 3 b. "Puntius gonionotus" 50 15
560. 5 b. "Betta splendens" .. 85 30
DESIGNS—HORIZ. 2 b., 3 b., 45×26 mm.

90. Djarmachakra and Globe. **91.** Great Hornbill.

1967. Establishment of Buddhist World Fellowship Headquarters in Thailand.
561. **90.** 2 b. black and yellow .. 35 12

1967. Birds. Multicoloured.
562. 20 s. Type **91** 5 5
563. 25 s. Indian mynah .. 5 5
564. 50 s. White-rumped shama 5 5
565. 1 b. Diard's fireback pheasant 12 8
566. 1 b. 50 Spotted-necked dove 25 8
567. 2 b. Sarus crane 25 12
568. 3 b. White-breasted (or stork-billed) kingfisher .. 45 25
569. 5 b. Open-billed stork .. 70 30

92. "Vandopsis parishii". **93.** Thai House.

1967. Thai Orchids. Multicoloured.
570. 20 s. Type **92** 5 5
571. 50 s. "Ascocentrum curvifolium" 5 5
572. 80 s. "Rhynchostylis retusa" 15 5
573. 1 b. "Rhynchostylis gigantea" 15 8
574. 1 b. 50 "Dendrobium falconeri" 25 8
575. 2 b. "Paphiopedilum callosum" 35 10
576. 3 b. "Dendrobium formosum" 50 15
577. 5 b. "Dendrobium primulinum" 85 25

1967. Thai Architecture.
578. **93.** 50 s. violet and blue .. 8 5
579. – 1 b. 50 chestnut & brown 20 8
580. – 2 b. blue and turquoise 35 15
581. – 3 b. sepia and yellow .. 40 15
BUILDINGS: 1 b. 50, Pagodas. 2 b. Temple bell-tower. 3 b. Temple.

94. Royal Barge and Palace. **96.** U.N. Emblem.

95. Dove, Globe, People and Letters.

1967. Int. Tourist Year.
582. **94.** 2 b. sepia and blue .. 25 15

1967. Int. Correspondence Week.
583. **95.** 50 s. multicoloured .. 8 5
584. 1 b. multicoloured .. 15 5
585. – 2 b. black and green .. 35 10
586. – 3 b. black and brown .. 50 15
DESIGN: 2 b., 3 b. Handclasp, Globe and Doves.

1967. U.N. Day.
587. **96.** 50 s. multicoloured .. 8 5

97. National Flag.

1967. Thai National Flag. 50th Anniv.
588. **97.** 50 s. red, blue & turquoise 5 5
589. 2 b. red, blue and green 25 12

98. Elephant carrying Teak Log. **99.** Satellite and Thai Tracking Station.

1968. Export Promotion.

590. **98.** 2 b. brown and red .. 20 8

See also Nos. 630, 655 and 673.

1968. "Satellite Communications".

591. **99.** 50 s. multicoloured .. 8 5
592. 3 b. multicoloured .. 45 15

100. "Goddess of the Earth".

1968. Int. Hydrological Decade.

593. **100.** 50 s. multicoloured .. 15 5

101. "Trichogaster pectoralis".

1968. Thai Fishes. Multicoloured.

594. 10 s. Type **101** 5 5
595. 20 s. "Labeo bicolor" .. 5 5
596. 25 s. "Tor tambroides" .. 5 5
597. 50 s. "Pangasius sanitwongsei" 8 5
598. 80 s. "Leiocassis siamensis" 10 5
599. 1 b. 25 "Vaimosa rambaiae" 15 8
600. 1 b. 50 "Catlocarpio siamensis" 25 8
601. 4 b. "Notopterus chitala" 55 20

102. "Papilio arcturus arcturus".

1968. Thai Butterflies. Multicoloured.

602. 50 s. Type **102** 8 5
603. 1 b. Papilio aecus 15 5
604. 3 b. Papilio memnon agenor 45 20
605. 4 b. Papilio palinurus palinurus 55 30

103. Queen Sirikit.

1968. Queen Sirikit's "Third Cycle" Anniversary. Stamps showing Queen Sirikit in different Thai costumes.

606. **103.** 50 s. multicoloured .. 8 5
607. 2 b. multicoloured .. 35 15
608. 3 b. multicoloured .. 50 30
609. 5 b. multicoloured .. 85 45

104. W.H.O. Emblem and Medical Equipment.

1968. World Health Organisation. 20th Anniv.

610. **104.** 50 s. black and olive .. 8 5

105. Globe, Letter and Pen.

1968. Int. Correspondence Week. Multicoloured.

611. 50 s. Type **105** .. 8 5
612. 1 b. Globe on pen nib .. 15 8
613. 2 b. Type **105** .. 25 12
614. 3 b. Globe on pen nib .. 40 20

106. U.N. Emblem and Flags.

108. King Rama II.

107. Human Rights Emblem and Sculpture.

1968. United Nations Day.

615. **106.** 50 s. multicoloured .. 8 5

1968. Human Rights Year. 20th Anniv.

616. **107.** 50 s. violet, red & green 8 5

1968. Birth of King Rama II. Bicent.

617. **108.** 50 s. yellow and brown 8 5

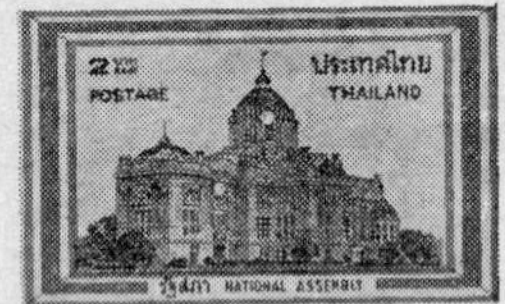

109. National Assembly Building.

1969. 1st Election Day under New Constitution.

618. **109.** 50 s. multicoloured .. 8 5
619. 2 b. multicoloured .. 30 15

110. I.L.O. Emblem within Cogwheels.

1969. Int. Labour Organisation. 50th Anniv.

620. **110.** 50 s. blue, blk. & violet 5 5

111. Ramwong Dance.

1969. Thai Classical Dances. Multicoloured.

621. 50 s. Type **111** 8 5
622. 1 b. Candle Dance .. 15 8
623. 2 b. Krathop Mai Dance .. 25 15
624. 3 b. Nohra Dance 35 20

112. "Letters by Post".

113. Globe in Hand.

1969. Int. Correspondence Week. Multicoloured.

625. 50 s. Type **112** .. 8 5
626. 1 b. Type **112** 12 8
627. 2 b. Writing and posting a letter 25 15
628. 3 b. As 2b 35 20

1969. United Nations Day.

629. **113.** 50 s. multicoloured .. 8 5

114. Tin Mine.

1969. Export Promotion and 2nd Technical Conference of the International Tin Council, Bangkok.

630. **114.** 2 b. grey-blue, purple and brown 20 15

115. Loy Krathong Festival.

1969. Thai Ceremonies and Festivals. Multicoloured.

631. 50 s. Type **115** 8 5
632. 1 b. Marriage ceremony .. 15 5
633. 2 b. Khwan ceremony .. 30 15
634. 5 b. Songkran festival .. 70 35

116. Breguet Mail-plane.

1969. Thai Airmail Services. 50th Anniv.

635. **116.** 1 b. chest., green & blue 12 8

117. "Phra Rama". **118.** "Improvement of Productivity".

1969. Nang Yai Shadow Theatre. Mult.

636. 50 s. Type **117** 8 5
637. 2 b. "Ramasura" 30 15
638. 3 b. "Mekhala" 45 15
639. 5 b. "Ongkhot" 70 30

1969. Productivity Year.

640. **118.** 50 s. multicoloured .. 8 5

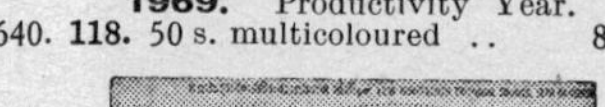

119. Thai Temples within I.C.W. Emblem.

1970. 19th Triennial Conference of Int. Council of Women, Bangkok.

641. **119.** 50 s. black and blue .. 8 5

120. Dish Aerials. **121.** Households and Data.

1970. Thai Satellite Communications. 3rd Anniv.

642. **120.** 50 s. multicoloured .. 8 5

1970. 7th Population Census.

643. **121.** 1 b. multicoloured .. 10 8

122. New Headquarters Building.

1970. New U.P.U. Headquarters Building, Berne. Inaug.

644. **122.** 50 s. blk., grn. and blue 8 5

123. Khun Ram Kamhang as Teacher.

1970. Int. Education Year.

645. **123.** 50 s. multicoloured .. 8 5

124. Swimming Stadium.

1970. Sixth Asian Games, Bangkok.

646. **124.** 50 s. lilac, red & yellow 5 5
647. – 1 b. 50 grn., red & blue 15 8
648. – 3 b. black, red & bronze 35 15
649. – 5 b. blue, red and green 55 35

STADIUMS: 1 b. 50 Velodrome. 3 b. Subhajalasaya Stadium. 5 b. Kittikachorn Indoor Stadium.

See also No. 660.

125. Boy and Girl writing Letter.

1970. Int. Correspondence Week. Multicoloured.

650. 50 s. Type **125** 5 5
651. 1 b. Woman writing letter 12 5
652. 2 b. Women reading letters 25 15
653. 3 b. Man reading letter .. 35 25

See also Nos. 683/6.

126. U.N. Emblem and Royal Palace, Bangkok. **128.** King Bhumibol lighting Flame.

127. The Heroes of Bangrachan.

1970. United Nations. 25th Anniv.

654. **126.** 50 s. multicoloured .. 8 5

1970. Export Promotion.

655. 2 b. brn., red and green .. 15 12

DESIGN: 2 b. As T **98**, but picturing rubber plantation.

1970. Heroes and Heroines of Thai History.

656. **127.** 50 s. violet and red .. 5 5
657. – 1 b. purple and violet 12 10
658. – 2 b. brown and red .. 20 15
659. – 3 b. green and blue .. 35 25

DESIGNS: 1 b. Heroines Thao Thepkrasatri and Thao Srisunthorn. 2 b. Queen Suriyothai riding an elephant. 3 b. Phraya Phichaidaphak.

1970. 6th Asian Games, Bangkok. Inaug.

660. **128.** 1 b. multicoloured .. 8 5

129. Woman playing So Sam Sai.

1970. Thai Musicians and Instruments. Multicoloured.
661. 50 s. Type **129** 5 5
662. 2 b. Khlui phiang-o (flute) 15 12
663. 3 b. Krachappi (guitar) .. 25 15
664. 5 b. Thon rammana (drums) 45 25

130. Chocolate-pointed Siamese.

1971. Siamese Cats. Multicoloured.
665. 50 s. Type **130** 5 5
666. 1 b. Blue-pointed cat .. 10 8
667. 2 b. Seal-pointed cat .. 25 15
668. 3 b. Pure White cat and kittens 35 20

131. Pagoda, Nakhon Si Thammarat.

1971. Buddhist Holy Places in Thailand. Pagodas.
669. **131.** 50 s. black, brn. & pink 5 5
670. – 1 b. brn., violet & grn. 8 8
671. – 3 b. sepia, orge. & brn. 25 15
672. – 4 b. brn., sepia & blue 35 25
DESIGNS: 1 b. Makhon Phanom. 3 b. Nakhon Pathom. 4 b. Chiang Mai.

1971. Export Promotion.
673. 2 b. multicoloured .. 15 12
DESIGN: 2 b. As Type **98**, but picturing corncob with cornfield.

132. Buddha's Birthplace, Lumbini, Nepal.

1971. World Fellowship of Buddhists. 20th Anniv.
674. **132.** 50 s. black and blue .. 5 5
675. – 1 b. black and green .. 8 8
676. – 2 b. black and yellow 15 15
677. – 3 b. black and red .. 30 20
DESIGNS: 1 b. "Place of Enlightenment", Buddha Gaya, Bihar. 2 b. "Place of First Sermon", Sarnath, Banaras. 3 b. "Place of Final Passing Away", Kusinara.

133. King Bhumibol and Thai people.
134. Floating Market, Wat Sai.

1971. Coronation. 25th Anniv.
678. **133.** 50 s. multicoloured .. 8 5

1971. Visit ASEAN Year.
679. **134.** 4 b. multicoloured .. 30 25
ASEAN = Association of South East Asian Nations.

135. King and Queen in Scout Uniform.

1971. Thai Boy Scout Movement. 60th Anniv.
680. **135.** 50 c. black, red & yell. 8 5

1971. "THAILANDAPEX 71" National Stamp Exhibition, Bangkok. Optd. **THAILANDAPEX '71** and **4-8 AUG. '71** in English and Thai, with map within "perforations", covering four stamps.
681. **55.** 80 s. orange (No. 428) 45 35
682. **68.** 80 s. orange (No. 483) 45 35
Prices are for blocks of four stamps showing the entire overprint. The overprint on No. 682 is smaller—size 23 × 26 mm.

1971. Int. Correspondence Week. As T **125**. Multicoloured.
683. 50 s. Two girls writing a letter 5 5
684. 1 b. Two girls reading letters 8 8
685. 2 b. Girl with letter on veranda 15 15
686. 3 b. Man handing letter to woman 25 15

136. Marble Temple, Bangkok.

1971. United Nations Day.
687. **136.** 50 s. multicoloured .. 8 5

137. Raising Ducks.

1971. Rural Life. Multicoloured.
688. 50 s. Type **137** 5 5
689. 1 b. Growing tobacco seedlings 8 8
690. 2 b. Cooping fish 15 15
691. 3 b. Cleaning rice-seed .. 25 20

138. Mother and Child.

1971. U.N.I.C.E.F. 25th Anniv.
692. **138.** 50 s. multicoloured .. 8 5

139. Costumes from Chaing Saen Period (17th-century).

1972. Historical Costumes. Multicoloured.
693. 50 s. Type **139** 5 5
694. 1 b. Sukhothai period (13th–14th centuries) 10 8
695. 1 b. 50 Ayudhya period (14th–17th centuries) 15 10
696. 2 b. Bangkok period (18th–19th centuries) .. 25 15

140. Globe and AOPU Emblem.
141. King Bhumibol.

1972. Asian-Oceanic Postal Union. 10th Anniv.
697. **140.** 75 s. blue 8 5

1972.
698. **141.** 10 s. green 5 5
699. 20 s. blue 5 5
700. 25 s red 5 5
701. 75 s lilac 5 5
702. 1 b. 25 pink, green and light green 8 5
703. **141.** 2 b. 75 green and red 15 12
704. 3 b. blue and sepia .. 20 12
705. 4 b. brown and blue .. 25 12
706. 5 b. brown and violet .. 30 15
707. 6 b. violet and green .. 35 15
708. 10 b. black and red .. 70 30
709. 20 b. green, orange and light orange .. 1·40 55
710. 40 b. violet and brown 2·75 1·10

142. Iko Tribe.

1972. Hill Tribes of Thailand. Multicoloured.
714. 50 s. Type **142** 5 5
715. 2 b. Musician and children, Musoe tribe 15 10
716. 4 b. Woman embroidering, Yao tribe 35 15
717. 5 b. Woman with chickens, Maeo tribe 40 20

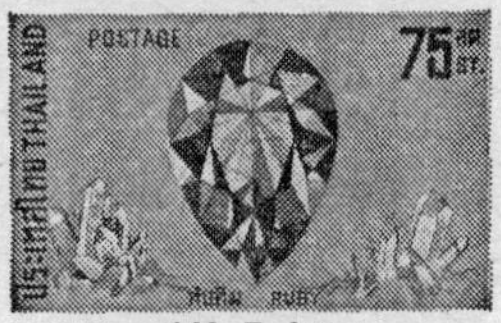

143. Ruby.

1972. Precious Stones.
718. **143.** 75 s. multicoloured .. 5 5
719. – 2 b. multicoloured .. 15 8
720. – 4 b. black and green .. 30 15
721. – 6 b. brown, black and red 50 25
DESIGNS: 2 b. Yellow sapphire. 4 b. Zircon. 6 b. Star sapphire.

144. Prince Vajiralongkorn.
145. Thai Ruan-ton Costume.

1972. Prince Vajiralongkorn's 20th Birthday.
722. **144.** 75 s. multicoloured .. 12 8

1972. Thai Women's National Costumes. Mult.
723. 75 s. Type **145** 8 5
724. 2 b. Thai Chitrlada .. 15 8
725. 4 b. Thai Chakri 30 15
726. 5 b. Thai Borompimarn .. 40 15

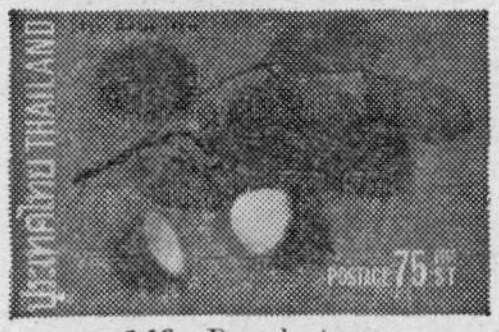

146. Rambutan.

1972. Thai Fruits. Multicoloured.
728. 75 s. Type **146** 8 5
729. 1 b. Mangosteen 10 8
730. 3 b. Durian 30 25
731. 5 b. Mango 50 25

147. Princess-Mother with Old People.

1972. Princess-Mother Sisangwan's 72nd Birthday.
732. **147.** 75 s. green and orange 8 5

148. Lod Cave, Phangnga.

1972. Int. Correspondence Week. Mult.
733. 75 s. Type **148** 8 5
734. 1 b. 25 Kang Kracharn Reservoir, Phetchaburi .. 12 5
735. 2 b. 75 Erawan Waterfall, Kanchanburi 25 15
736. 3 b. Nok-kaw Mountain, Loei 25 20

149. Globe on U.N. Emblem.
151. Crown Prince Vajiralongkorn.

150. Watphrajetubon Uimolmanklaram Rajvaramahaviharn (ancient university).

1972. E.C.A.F.E. 25th Anniv.
737. **149.** 75 s. multicoloured .. 10 5

1972. International Book Year.
738. **150.** 75 s. multicoloured .. 8 5

1972. Investiture of Crown Prince.
739. **151.** 2 b. multicoloured .. 15 12

152. Servicemen and Flag.

1973. Veterans' Day. 25th Anniv.
740. **152.** 75 s. multicoloured .. 8 5

1973. Red Cross Fair (1972). Nos. 472/3 surch.
741. **66.** 75 s. + 25 s. on 50 s. + 10 s. 25 25
742. – 75 s. + 25 s. on 50 s. + 10 s. 25 25

153. Emblem, Bank and Coin-box.

1973. Government Savings Bank. 60th Anniv.
743. **153.** 75 s. multicoloured .. 8 5

154. "Celestial Being" and Emblem.

1973. W.H.O. 25th Anniv.
744. **154.** 75 s. multicoloured .. 8 5

155. "Nymphaea pubescens".

1973. Lotus Flowers. Multicoloured.
745. 75 s. Type **155** 5 5
746. 1 b. 50 "Nymphaea pubescens" (different) .. 10 8
747. 2 b. "Nelumbo nucifera" .. 15 12
748. 4 b. "Nelumbo nucifera" (different) 30 25

156. King Bhumibol.

1973.

749. **156.** 5 s. plum 5 5
750. 20 s. blue 5 5
751. 25 s. red 5 5
752. 75 s. violet 5 5
753. 5 b. violet and brown 35 25
754. 6 b. green and lilac .. 45 25
755. 10 b. red and grey .. 75 45

157. Silverware.

1973. Thai Handicrafts. Mult.

756. 75 s. Type **157** 8 5
757. 2 b. 75 Lacquerware .. 25 20
758. 4 b. Pottery 35 15
759. 5 b. Paper umbrellas .. 45 25

158. Ramayana Mural (detail).

1973. "Ramayana" Mural, Temple of Emerald Buddha, Bangkok.

760. **158.** 25 s. multicoloured .. 5 5
761. – 75 s. multicoloured .. 8 5
762. – 1 b. 50 multicoloured 15 12
763. – 2 b. multicoloured .. 15 12
764. – 2 b. 75 multicoloured 25 15
765. – 3 b. multicoloured .. 25 15
766. – 5 b. multicoloured .. 45 30
767. – 6 b. multicoloured .. 50 35

DESIGNS: Nos. 761/7, different details from the mural.

159. "Postal Services".

1973. Thia Post and Telegraph Department. 90th Anniv. Multicoloured.

768. 75 s. Type **159** 5 5
769. 2 b. "Telecommunication Services" 15 8

160. 1 Salat Stamp of 1883.

1973. "THAIPEX 73" Nat. Stamp Exn.

770. **160.** 75 s. blue and red .. 8 5
771. – 1 b. 25 red and blue .. 12 8
772. – 1 b. 50 violet and green 15 15
773. – 2 b. green and orange 15 12

DESIGNS: 1 b. 25 6 s. stamp of 1912. 1 b. 50 5 s. stamp of 1928. 2 b. 3 s. stamp of 1941.

161. Interpol Emblem.

1973. International Criminal Police Organisation (Interpol). 50th Anniv.

775. **161.** 75 s. multicoloured .. 8 5

162. "Lilid Pralaw".

1973. Int. Correspondence Week. Characters from Thai Literature. Multicoloured.

776. 75 s. Type **162** 8 5
777. 1 b. 50 "Khun Chang, Khun Phan" 15 12
778. 2 b. "Sang Thong" .. 15 12
779. 5 b. "Pha Apai Mance" .. 45 30

163. Wat Suan Dok Temple, Chiangmai.

1973. United Nations Day.

781. **163.** 75 s. multicoloured .. 8 5

164. Schomburgk's Deer.

1973. Protected Wild Animals (1st series). Multicoloured.

782. 20 s. Type **164** 5 5
783. 25 s. Kouprey 5 5
784. 75 s. Gorals 5 5
785. 1 b. 25 Water buffaloes .. 8 8
786. 1 b. 50 Javan rhinoceros .. 10 8
787. 2 b. Eld's deer 12 8
788. 2 b. 75 Sumatran rhinoceros 15 12
789. 4 b. Serows 25 15

See also Nos. 913/16.

165. Flame Emblem.

1973. Declaration of Human Rights. 25th Anniv.

790. **165.** 75 s. multicoloured .. 5 5

166. Children within Flowers.

75+25 1973 ๒๕๑๖ (167.)

1973. Children's Day.

791. **166.** 75 s. multicoloured .. 5 5

1974. Red Cross Fair. Nos. 472/3 surch as T 167.

792. **66.** 75 s.+25 s. on 50 s.+10 s. 20 20
793. – 75 s.+25 s. on 50 s.+10 s. 20 20

168. Statue of Krom Luang Songkia Nakarin.

1974. Siriraj Hospital. 84th Anniv.

794. **168.** 75 s. multicoloured .. 5 5

169. "Pha la Phiang Lai" (vert.).

1974. Thai Classical Dance. Multicoloured.

795. 75 s. Type **169** 5 5
796. 2 b. 75 "Phra Lak Phlaeng Rit" 15 12
797. 4 b. "Chin Sao Sai" .. 25 15
798. 5 b. "Charot Phra Sumen" 30 25

170. World's Largest Teak Amphur Nam-Pad.

1974. Arbour Day.

799. **170.** 75 s. multicoloured .. 5 5

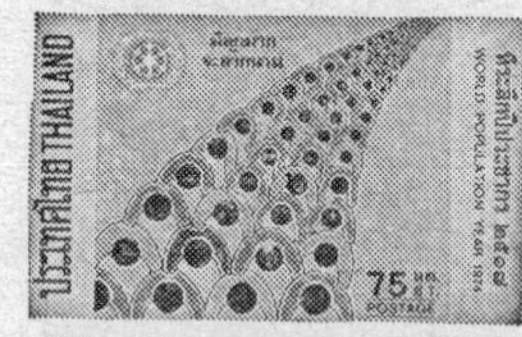

171. "Increasing Population".

1974. World Population Year.

800. **171.** 75 s. multicoloured .. 5 5

172. Royal Chariot.

1974. National Museum. Centenary. Mult.

801. 75 s. Type **172** 5 5
802. 2 b. Ban Chiang painted pottery vase 12 8
803. 2 b. 75 Avalokitesavara Bodhisattva statue .. 15 12
804. 3 b. King Mongkut Rama IV 15 12

173. "Cassia fistula".

1974. International Correspondence Week. Tropical Plants. Multicoloured.

805. 75 s. Type **173** 5 5
806. 2 b. 75 "Butea superba" .. 15 12
807. 3 b. "Jasminum sambac" 15 12
808. 4 b. "Lagerstroemia speciosa" 25 15

174. "UPU 100".

1974. Universal Postal Union. Centenary.

810. **174.** 75 s. multicoloured .. 5 5

175. Wat Suthat Thepvararam.

1974. United Nations Day.

811. **175.** 75 s. multicoloured .. 5 5

176. Elephant Round-up.

1974. Tourism.

812. **176.** 4 b. multicoloured .. 25 15

177. "Vanda coerulea".

1974. Thai Orchids (1st series). Mult.

813. 75 s. Type **177** 5 5
814. 2 b. 75 "Dendrobium aggregatum" 12 8
815. 3 b. "Dendrobium scabrilingue" 15 12
816. 4 b. "Aerides falcata" var "houlletiana" 25 15

See also Nos. 847/50.

178. Boy riding Toy Horse.

1974. Children's Day.

818. **178.** 75 c. multicoloured .. 5 5

179. Democracy Monument.

1975. Democratic Institutions Campaign. Multicoloured.

819. 75 s. Type **179** 5 5
820. 2 b. "Rights and Liberties" 12 10
821. 2 b. 75 "Freedom to choose work" 15 12
822. 5 b. Top of Monument and text 30 25

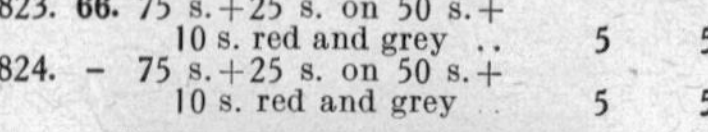

1975. Red Cross Fair 1974. Nos. 472/3 surch. **1974** and new value in English and Thai.

823. **66.** 75 s.+25 s. on 50 s.+ 10 s. red and grey .. 5 5
824. – 75 s.+25 s. on 50 s.+ 10 s. red and grey 5 5

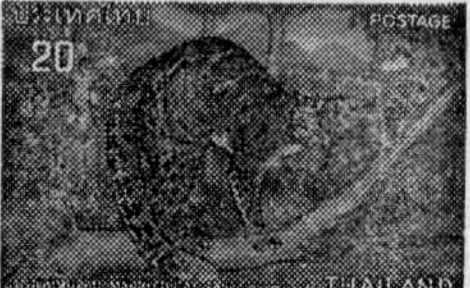

180. Marbled Tiger-cat.

1975. Protected Animals. Multicoloured.

825. 20 s. Type **180** 5 5
826. 75 s. Gaurs 5 5
827. 2 b. 75 Asiatic elephant .. 15 12
828. 3 b. Clouded leopard .. 20 15

181. "Pseudochelidon sirintirae".

1975. Thailand Birds (1st issue). Mult.

829. 75 s. Type **181** 5 5
830. 2 b. "Terpsiphone paradise" 12 10
831. 2 b. 75 "Psarisomus dalhousiae" 15 12
832. 5 b. "Melanochlora sultanae" 30 25

See also Nos. 891/4.

182. King Bhumibol and Queen Sirikit.

1975. Silver Wedding of King Bhumibol and Queen Sirikit.

833. **182.** 75 s. multicoloured .. 5 5
834. 3 b. multicoloured .. 20 15

183. " Roundhouse Kick ".

1975. Thai Boxing. Multicoloured.

835. 75 s. Type 183 .. .. 5 5
836. 2 b. 75 " Reverse Elbow " 15 12
837. 3 b. " Flying Knee " .. 20 15
838. 5 b. ' Ritual Homage " .. 30 25

184. Tosakanth.

1975. Thai Culture. Masks. Multicoloured.

839. 75 s. Type **184** 5 5
840. 2 b. Kumbhakarn .. 12 10
841. 3 b. Rama 20 15
842. 4 b. Hanuman 25 20

185. " Thaipex 75 " Emblem.

1975. Thaipex 75" National Stamp Exhibition, Bangkok. Multicoloured.

843. 75 s. Type **185** 5 5
844. 2 b. 75 Stamp designer .. 15 12
845. 4 b. Stamp printery .. 25 20
846. 5 b. " Stamp collecting " 30 25

1975. Thai Orchids (2nd series). As T **177**. Multicoloured.

847. 75 s. " Dendrobium cruentum " 5 5
848. 2 b. " Dendrobium parishii " 12 10
849. 2 b. 75 " Vanda teres " .. 15 12
850. 5 b. " Vanda denisoniana " 30 25

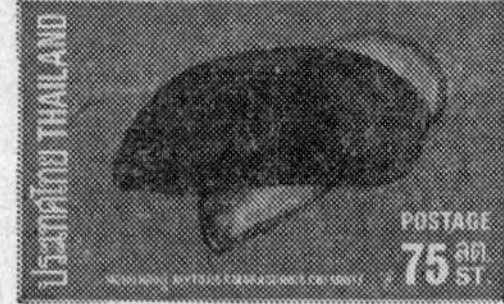

186. " Mytilus smaragdinus ".

1975. Seashells. Multicoloured.

852. 75 s. Type **186** 5 5
853. 1 b. " Turbo marmoratus " 5 5
854. 2 b. 75 " Oliva mustelina " 15 12
855. 5 b. " Cypraea moneta " .. 30 25

187. Yachting.

1975. 8th SEAP Games, Bangkok (1st issue).

856. 75 s. black and blue .. 5 5
857. 1 b. 25 black and mauve .. 8 5
858. 1 b. 50 black and red .. 10 8
859. 2 b. black and green .. 12 10

DESIGNS: 1 b. 25 Badminton. 1 b. 50 Volleyball. 2 b. Target shooting.

See also Nos. 878/81.

188. Pataya Beach.

1975. International Correspondence Week. Multicoloured.

861. 75 s. Type **188** 5 5
862. 2 b. Samila Beach .. 12 10
863. 3 b. Prachuap Bay .. 20 15
864. 5 b. Laem Singha Bay .. 30 25

189. Children within Letters " U N ".

1975. United Nations Day.

865. **189.** 75 s. multicoloured .. 5 5

190. Early Telegraph.

1975. Telegraph Service. Centenary. Multicoloured.

866. 75 s. Type **190** 5 5
867. 2 b. 75 Teleprinter and dish aerial 15 12

191. Sukhrip Khrong Muean Barge.

1975. Thai Ceremonial Barges. Mult.

868. 75 s. Type **191** 5 5
869. 1 b. Royal barge Anekchat Phuchong 5 5
870. 2 b. Royal barge Anantanakarat 12 10
871. 2 b. 75 Krabi Ran Ron Rap barge 15 12
872. 3 b. Asura Wayuphak barge 20 15
873. 4 b. Asura Paksi barge .. 25 20
874. 5 b. Royal barge Sri Suphanahong 30 25
875. 6 b. Phali Rang Thawip barge 40 35

192. Thai Flag and Arms of Chakri Royal Family.

1976. King Bhumibol's 48th Birthday. Multicoloured.

876. 75 s. Type **192** 5 5
877. 5 b. King Bhumibol in uniform 30 20

193. Putting the Shot.

1976. 8th SEAP Games, Bangkok (2nd issue).

878. **193.** 1 b. black and orange 5 5
879. – 2 b. black and green .. 12 8
880. – 3 b. black and yellow .. 20 12
881. – 4 b. black and violet .. 25 20

DESIGNS: 2 b. Table-tennis. 3 b. Cycle-racing. 4 b. Relay-running.

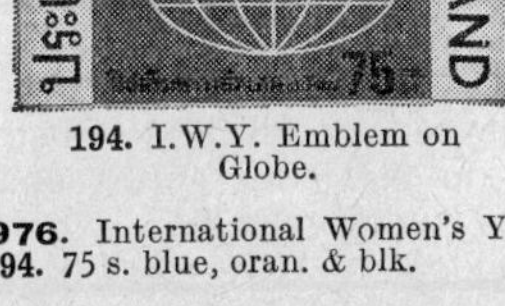

194. I.W.Y. Emblem on Globe.

1976. International Women's Year.

883. **194.** 75 s. blue, oran. & blk. 5 5

195. Children Writing.

1976. Children's Day.

884. **195.** 75 s. multicoloured .. 5 5

196. " Macrobrachium rosenbergii ".

1976. Thai Lobsters and Shrimps. Mult.

885. 75 s. Type **196** 5 5
886. 2 b. " Panaeus merguiensis " 12 8
887. 2 b. 75 " Panulirus ornatus " 15 12
888. 5 b. " Panaeus monodon " 30 20

1976. Red Cross Fair 1975. Nos. 472/3 surch. **1975** and value.

889. **66.** 75 s.+25 s. on 50 s.+10 s. red and grey .. 20 20
890. – 75 s.+25 s. on 50 s.+10 s. red and grey .. 20 20

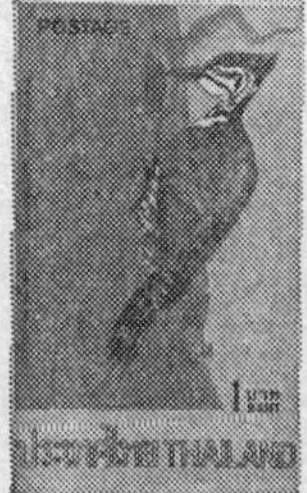

197 " Dinopium javanese ".

198 Ban Chiang Pot.

1976. Thailand Birds (2nd series). Mult.

891. 1 b. Type **197** 8 5
892. 1 b. 50 " Phaenicophaeus tristis " 12 8
893. 3 b. " Pomatorhinus hypoleucos " 25 15
894. 4 b. " Cissa chinensis " .. 30 20

1976 Ban Chiang Pottery.

895. **198.** 1 b. multicoloured .. 8 5
896. – 2 b. multicoloured .. 15 10
897. – 3 b. multicoloured .. 25 15
898. – 4 b. multicoloured .. 30 20

DESIGNS. 2 b. to 4 b. Various items of pottery.

199 Postman of 1883.

201 Drug Addiction.

200 Kinnari.

1976. Postmen's Uniforms. Multicoloured.

899. 1 b. Type **199** 8 5
900. 3 b. Postman of 1935 .. 25 15
901. 4 b. Postman of 1950 .. 30 20
902. 5 b. Postman of 1974 .. 40 30

1976. International Correspondence Week. Deities. Multicoloured.

903. 1 b. Type **200** 8 5
904. 2 b. Suphan-Mat-Cha .. 15 10
905. 4 b. Garuda 30 20
906. 5 b. Naga 40 30

1976 United Nations Day.

907. **201.** 1 b. multicoloured .. 8 5

202. Early and Modern Telphones.

1976 Telephone Centenary.

908. **202.** 1 b. multicoloured .. 8 5

203 Sivalaya.

1976. Thai Royal Halls. Multicoloured.

909. 1 b. Type **203** 8 5
910. 2 b. Cakri 15 10
911. 4 b. Mahisra 30 20
912. 5 b. Dusit 40 30

1976 Protected Wild Animals (2nd series). As T **164**. Multicoloured.

913. 1 b. Banteng 8 5
914. 2 b. Malay tapir 15 10
915. 4 b. Sambar (deer) .. 30 20
916. 5 b. Hog deer 40 30

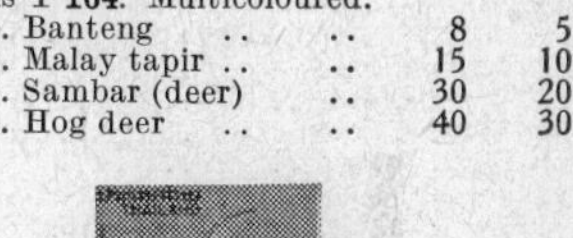

204. " From Child to Adult ".

1977. Children's Day.

917. **203.** 1 b. multicoloured .. 8 5

OFFICIAL STAMPS

O 1. (Trans. " For Government Service Statistical Research ".)

1963. No. gum.

O 495. **O 1.** 10 s. red and pink .. 8 5
O 496. 20 s. red and emerald 8 8
O 500. 20 s. green 15 20
O 497. 25 s. red and blue .. 15 20
O 501. 25 s. blue 15 35
O 502. 50 s. red 35 50
O 498. 1 b. red and silver .. 45 70
O 503. 1 b. silver 50 85
O 499. 2 b. red and bronze 70 1·00
O 504. 2 b. bistre .. .. 1·10 1·75

The above were used compulsorily by Government Departments between 1st Oct. 1963, and 31st Jan., 1964, to determine the amount of mail sent out by the different departments for the purpose of charging them in the future. They were postmarked in the usual way.

THAI OCCUPATION OF MALAYA

BC

1. War Memorial.

1943.

TM 1. **1.** 1 c. yellow .. .. 75 1·25
TM 2. 2 c. brown 55 65
TM 3. 3 c. green .. .. 1·25 2·00
TM 4. 4 c. purple .. .. 70 1·10
TM 5. 8 c. red 55 70
TM 6. 15 c. blue .. .. 75 1·25

THESSALY E3

Special stamps issued during the Turkish occupation in the Graeco-Turkish War of 1898.

40 paras = 1 piastre.

1.

1898.

M 162. **1.** 10 pa. green 75 55
M 163. 20 pa. red 75 55
M 164. 1 pi. blue 75 55
M 165. 2 pi. orange 75 55
M 166. 5 pi. violet 75 55

THRACE E3

A portion of Greece to the N. of the Aegean Sea for which stamps were issued by the Allies in 1919 and by the Greek Government in 1920. Now uses Greek stamps.

1919. 100 stotinki = 1 leva.
1920. 100 lepta = 1 drachma.

1920. Stamps of Bulgaria optd. **THRACE INTERALLIEE** in two lines.

28. **36.** 1 s. black 5 5
29. 2 s. grey 5 5
30. **37.** 5 s. green 5 5
31. 10 s. red 5 5
32. 15 s. violet 8 8
33. – 25 s. black & blue (No. 165) 8 8
34. – 1 l. brown (No. 168) .. 45 40
35. – 2 l. brown (No. 191) .. 80 65
36. – 3 l. claret (No. 192) .. 1·25 80

1920. Stamps of Bulgaria optd. **THRACE INTERALLIEE** in one line.

40. **36.** 1 s. black 20 20
41. 2 s. grey 20 20
42. **37.** 5 s. green 12 10
43. – 10 s. red 12 10
44. 15 s. violet 25 25
45. – 25 s. black & blue (No. 165) 25 25

1920. Stamps of Bulgaria optd. **THRACE Interalliee** in two lines vertically.

46. **37.** 5 s. green 5 5
47. 10 s. red 5 5
48. 15 s. violet 5 5
49. 50 s. brown 15 15

1920. Stamps of Bulgaria optd. **THRACE OCCIDENTALE.**

50. **37.** 5 s. green 5 5
51. 10 s. red 5 5
52. 15 s. violet 5 5
53. 25 s. blue 5 5
54. 30 s. brown (imperf.) .. 8 8
55. 50 s. brown 5 5

Διοίκησις
Δυτικῆς
Θράκης
(1.)

1920. 1911 stamps of Greece optd. with T **1.**

69. **24.** 1 l. green 5 5
70. **25.** 2 l. red 5 5
71. **24.** 3 l. red 5 5
72. **26.** 5 l. green 5 5
73. **24.** 10 l. red 10 8
74. **25.** 15 l. blue 8 8
75. 25 l. blue 25 15
86. **26.** 30 l. red .. .. 3·25 3·00
77. **25.** 40 l. blue 55 45
78. **26.** 50 l. purple 65 40
79. **27.** 1 d. blue .. .. 1·00 75
80. 2 d. red .. .. .. 2·50 2·50
65. 3 d. red .. .. .. 6·50 4·75
66. 5 d. blue .. .. 4·50 3·25
67. 10 d. blue .. .. 4·00 4·00
68. – 25 d. blue (No. 212) .. 13·00 10·00

The opt. on the 25 d. is in capital letters.

1920. 1916 stamps of Greece with opt. Greece T **33**, optd. with T **1.**

81. **24.** 1 l. green (No. 269) .. 10 8
82. **25.** 2 l. red 10 8
83. **24.** 10 l. red 10 8
84. **25.** 20 l. purple 35 25
85. **26.** 30 l. red 35 25
86. **27.** 2 d. red .. .. .. 4·75 3·50
87. 3 d. red .. .. .. 1·60 95
88. 5 d. blue .. .. 7·50 5·00
89. 10 d. blue .. .. 5·00 5·00

Διοίκησις
Θράκης
(2.)

Ὑπάτη Ἁρμοστεία
Θράκης
5 Λεπτὰ 5
(3.)

1920. Issue for E. Thrace. 1911 stamps of Greece optd. with T **2.**

93. **24.** 1 l. green 5 5
94. **25.** 2 l. red 5 5
95. **24.** 3 l. red 5 5
96. **26.** 5 l. green 5 5
97. **24.** 10 l. red 15 15
98. **25.** 20 l. lilac 15 15
99. 25 l. blue 40 40
100. 40 l. blue 50 50
101. **26.** 50 l. purple 75 75
102. **27.** 1 d. blue .. .. 1·90 1·90
103. 2 d. red .. .. .. 2·25 2·25
92. 25 d. blue (No. 212) .. 14·00 14·00

1920. 1916 stamps of Greece with opt. T **33** of Greece, optd. with T **2.**

104. **25.** 2 l. red (No. 270) .. 10 10
105. **26.** 5 l. green 40 40
106. **25.** 20 l. purple 20 20
107. **26.** 30 l. red 20 20
108. **27.** 3 d. red .. .. 2·25 2·25
109. 5 d. blue .. .. 4·00 4·00
110. 10 d. blue .. .. 4·00 4·00

1920. Occupation of Adrianople. Stamps of Turkey surch. as T **3.**

111. **45.** 1 l. on 5 pa. orange .. 20 20
112. – 5 l. on 3 pi. blue (No. 965) 20 20
113. – 20 l. on 1 pi. grn. (No. 964) 25 25
114. **44.** 25 l. on 5 pi. on 2 pa. blue 40 40
115. **50.** 50 l. on 5 pi. black & grn. 55 55
116. **47.** 1 d. on 20 pa. red .. 55 55
117. **12.** 2 d. on 10 pa. on 2 pa. olive 80 80
118. **53.** 3 d. on 1 pi. blue .. .. 1·60 1·60
119. **13.** 5 d. on 20 pa. red .. 1·90 1·90

POSTAGE DUE STAMPS

1919. Postage Due stamps of Bulgaria optd. **THRACE INTERALLIEE.** Perf.

D 37. **D 4.** 5 s. green 10 10
D 38. 10 s. violet 15 15
D 39. 50 s. blue 35 35

1920. Postage Due stamps of Bulgaria optd. **THRACE OCCIDENTALE.** Imperf. or perf. (10 s.).

D 56. **D 4.** 5 s. green 5 5
D 57. 10 s. violet 35 35
D 58. 20 s. orange 8 8
D 59. 50 s. blue 25 25

THURN AND TAXIS E2

The Counts of Thurn and Taxis had a postal monopoly in parts of Germany and issued special stamps.

N. District. 30 silbergroschen = 1 thaler.
S. District. 60 kreuzer = 1 gulden.

NORTHERN DISTRICT

1.

1852. Imperf.

1. **1.** $\frac{1}{4}$ s. black on brown .. 95·00 20·00
2. $\frac{1}{3}$ s. black on pink .. 42·00 £100
3. $\frac{1}{2}$ s. black on green .. £150 10·00
5. 1 s. black on blue .. £250 30·00
8. 2 s. black on rose .. £225 6·50
10. 3 s. black on yellow .. £200 5·00

1859. Imperf.

12. **1.** $\frac{1}{4}$ s. red .. .. .. 24·00 20·00
20. $\frac{1}{4}$ s. black .. .. .. 10·00 20·00
21. $\frac{1}{3}$ s. green .. .. .. 12·00 90·00
13. $\frac{1}{2}$ s. green .. .. .. £110 25·00
23. $\frac{1}{2}$ s. orange .. .. 35·00 11·00
14. 1 s. blue .. .. .. £110 9·00
25. 1 s. rose .. .. .. 23·00 7·50
15. 2 s. rose .. .. .. 55·00 21·00
27. 2 s. blue .. .. .. 20·00 25·00
17. 3 s. red .. .. .. 55·00 28·00
29. 3 s. brown .. .. .. 9·00 8·00
18. 5 s. mauve 90 £110
19. 10 s. orange 90 £250

1865. Rouletted.

31. **1.** $\frac{1}{4}$ s. black .. .. .. 5·00 £250
32. $\frac{1}{3}$ s. green .. .. .. 6·00 £140
33. $\frac{1}{2}$ s. yellow .. .. .. 6·00 19·00
42. 1 s. rose .. .. .. 75 22·00
35. 2 s. blue .. .. .. 85 20·00
36. 3 s. brown .. .. .. 1·10 10·00

SOUTHERN DISTRICT

2.

1852. Imperf.

51. **2.** 1 k. black on green .. 65·00 5·00
55. 3 k. black on blue .. £300 4·00
57. 6 k. black on rose .. £275 6·50
58. 9 k. black on yellow .. £250 3·75

1859. Imperf.

60. **2.** 1 k. green .. .. .. 9·00 2·50
62. 3 k. blue .. .. .. £225 6·50
68. 3 k. rose .. .. .. 20·00 5·00
63. 6 k. rose .. .. .. £150 21·00
70. 6 k. blue .. .. .. 5·00 7·50
65. 9 k. yellow .. .. .. £225 25·00
73. 9 k. brown .. .. .. 5·00 6·50
66. 15 k. purple .. .. .. 90 50·00
67. 30 k. orange 90 £170

1865. Roul.

79. **2.** 1 k. green .. .. .. 75 8·50
81. 3 k. rose .. .. .. 75 8·50
76. 6 k. blue .. .. .. 85 7·50
77. 9 k. brown .. .. .. 85 7·50

TIBET O1

A state lying between India and China. Now under Chinese control.

$6\frac{2}{3}$ trangka = 1 sang.

1 ($\frac{1}{6}$ t.) $\frac{1}{3}$ t. $\frac{1}{2}$ t. $\frac{2}{3}$ t. 1 t. 1 s.

1912. Imperf.

1. **1.** $\frac{1}{6}$ t. green .. .. .. 2·00 2·00
2. $\frac{1}{3}$ t. blue .. .. .. 3·00 4·50
3. $\frac{1}{2}$ t. purple .. .. .. 3·00 4·50
4. $\frac{2}{3}$ t. red .. .. .. 4·50 6·00
5. 1 t. vermilion .. .. .. 6·00 10·00
6a. 1 s. green .. .. .. 18·00 18·00

2.

1914. Imperf.

7b. **2.** 4 t. blue .. .. .. 75·00 70·00
8b. 8 t. red .. .. .. 45·00 45·00

3. (1 t.) Tibetan lion. $\frac{1}{2}$ t. $\frac{2}{3}$ t. 2 t. 4 t.

1933. Perf. or imperf.

9a. **3.** $\frac{1}{2}$ t. yellow to orange .. 2·00 2·25
10b. $\frac{2}{3}$ t. blue .. .. .. 2·00 2·25
11a. 1 t. orange to red .. 1·60 2·25
11c. 1 t. brown .. .. 15·00 10·00
12c. 2 t. orange to red .. 1·90 2·25
13d. 4 t. green .. .. .. 2·00 2·00

TIERRA DEL FUEGO O4

An island at the extreme S. of S. America. Stamp issued for use on correspondence to the mainland. Currency is expressed in centigrammes of gold dust.

1. Gold-digger's Pick and Hammer.

1891.

1. **1.** 10 c. red .. .. .. 4·00

INDEX

Countries can be quickly located by referring to the index at the end of this volume.

TIMOR O4

The eastern part of Timor in the Malay Archipelago. Administered as part of Macao until 1896, then as a separate Portuguese Overseas Province until 1975.

Following a civil war and the intervention of Indonesian forces it was proposed to incorporate Eastern Timor into Indonesia.

1885. 1000 reis = 1 milreis.
1894. 100 avos = 1 pataca
1960. 100 centavos = 1 escudo.

1885. "Crown" key-type inscr. "MACAU" and optd. **TIMOR.**

1. **P.** 5 r. black 60 50
2a. 10 r. green .. .. 1·25 1·10
13. 20 r. red .. .. .. 1·75 1·60
4. 25 r. lilac 35 25
5. 40 r. yellow .. .. 1·25 1·00
6. 50 r. blue 60 40
7. 80 r. grey .. .. 1·40 1·00
8. 100 r. purple 50 35
19. 200 r. orange .. .. 1·10 1·00
10. 300 r. brown .. .. 1·00 90

1887. "Embossed" key-type inscr. "CORREIO DE TIMOR".

21. **Q.** 5 r. black 70 50
22. 10 r. green 90 70
23. 20 r. red 90 65
24. 25 r. purple .. .. 1·40 80
25. 40 r. brown .. .. 1·60 1·00
26. 50 r. blue .. .. 1·60 1·00
27. 80 r. grey .. .. 1·60 1·10
28. 100 r. brown .. .. 2·00 1·25
29. 200 r. lilac .. .. 3·25 2·25
30. 300 r. orange .. .. 3·25 2·25

1892. "Embossed" key-type inscr. "PROVINCIA DE MACAU" surch. **TIMOR 30 30.**

32. **Q.** 30 on 300 r. orange .. 1·25 80

1894. "Figures" key-type inscr. "TIMOR".

33. **R.** 5 r. orange 40 30
34. 10 r. mauve 50 40
35. 15 r. brown 70 40
36. 20 r. lilac 70 40
37. 25 r. green 70 40
38. 50 r. blue .. .. 1·25 1·00
39. 75 r. red .. .. .. 1·50 1·25
40. 80 r. green .. .. 1·50 1·25
41. 100 r. brown on buff .. 1·50 1·25
42. 150 r. red on rose .. 2·50 2·00
43. 200 r. blue on blue .. 2·50 2·00
44. 300 r. blue on brown .. 2·75 2·50

1894. "Embossed" key-type of Timor surch. **PROVISORIO** and value in European and Chinese.

46. **Q.** 1 a. on 5 r. black .. 40 30
47. 2 a. on 10 r. green .. 60 50
48. 3 a. on 20 r red .. 80 50
49. 4 a. on 25 r. purple .. 80 40
50. 6 a. on 40 r. brown .. 1·00 60
51. 8 a. on 50 r. blue .. 1·10 60
52. 13 a. on 80 r. grey .. 1·50 1·25
53. 16 a. on 100 r. brown .. 1·50 1·25
54. 31 a. on 200 r. lilac .. 3·25 2·50
55. 47 a. on 300 r. orange .. 4·00 3·25

1895. No. 31 further surch. **5 avos PROVISORIO** and Chinese characters with bars over the original surch.

56. **Q.** 5 a. on 30 on 300 r. orge. 1·25 1·10

1898. Vasco da Gama stamps of Portugal as T 18/22, but inscr. "TIMOR" and values in local currency.

58. $\frac{1}{2}$ a. green 60 40
59. 1 a. red 60 40
60. 2 a. purple 60 40
61. 4 a. green 60 40
62. 8 a. blue 80 50
63. 12 a. brown .. .. 1·00 80
64. 16 a. brown .. .. 1·10 1·00
65. 24 a. brown .. .. 1·50 1·10

1898. "King Carlos" key-type inscr. "TIMOR".

68. **S.** $\frac{1}{2}$ a. grey 15 15
69. 1 a. orange 15 15
70. 2 a. green 15 15
71. $2\frac{1}{2}$ a. brown 50 40
72. 3 a. lilac 50 40
112. 3 a. green 60 50
73. 4 a. green 50 40
113. 5 a. red 50 40
114. 6 a. brown 60 50
74. 8 a. blue 50 40
115. 9 a. brown 60 50
75. 10 a. blue 50 40
116. 10 a. brown 60 50
76. 12 a. red .. .. 1·00 90
117. 12 a. blue .. .. 3·00 2·50
118. 13 a. purple 80 70
119. 15 a. lilac .. .. 1·40 1·00
78. 16 a. blue on blue .. 1·00 90
79. 20 a. brown on yellow .. 1·00 90
120. 22 a. brown on pink .. 1·40 1·25
80. 24 a. brown on buff .. 1·00 90
81. 31 a. purple on pink .. 1·00 90
121. 31 a. brown on yellow .. 1·40 1·10
82. 47 a. blue on pink .. 1·75 1·60
122. 47 a. purple on pink .. 3·00 2·00
83. 78 a. black on blue .. 2·50 1·60
123. 78 a. blue on yellow .. 3·00 2·00

1899. "King Carlos" key-type of Timor surch. **PROVISORIO** and value in figures and bars.

84. **S.** 10 on 16 a. blue on blue 90 80
85. 20 on 31 s. purple on pink 90 80

1902. Surch.

No.	Description	Un.	Used
88. R.	5 a. on 5 r. orange	60	50
86. Q.	5 a. on 25 r. purple	1·00	80
89. R.	5 a. on 25 r. green	50	40
91.	5 a. on 50 r. blue	80	70
87. Q.	5 a. on 200 r. lilac	1·50	1·25
95. V.	6 a. on 2½ r. brown	35	25
92. Q.	6 a. on 10 r. green	30·00	30·00
94. R.	6 a. on 20 r. lilac	70	60
93. Q.	6 a. on 300 r. orange	1·40	1·25
100. R.	9 a. on 15 r. brown	70	60
98. Q.	9 a. on 40 r. brown	1·60	1·40
101. R.	9 a. on 75 r. red	70	60
99. Q.	9 a. on 100 r. brown	1·60	1·40
124. S.	10 a. on 12 a. blue	90	80
104. R.	15 a. on 10 r. mauve	90	80
102. Q.	15 a. on 20 r. red	70	60
103.	15 a. on 50 r. blue	30·00	30·00
105. R.	15 a. on 100 r. brown on buff	90	80
106.	15 a. on 300 r. bl. on brn.	90	80
107. Q.	22 a. on 80 r. grey	2·50	2·10
108. R.	22 a. on 80 r. green	1·60	1·25
109.	22 a. on 200 r. blue on bl.	1·60	1·25

1902. Nos. 72 and 116 optd. **PROVISORIO.**

No.	Description	Un.	Used
110. S.	3 a. lilac	30	25
111.	12 a. red	1·25	1·10

1911. Nos. 68, etc., optd. **REPUBLICA.**

No.	Description	Un.	Used
125. S.	½ a. grey	15	12
126.	1 a. orange	15	12
127.	2 a. green	20	15
128.	3 a. green	20	15
129.	5 a. red	20	15
130.	6 a. brown	20	15
131.	9 a. brown	30	25
132.	10 a. brown	30	25
133.	13 a. purple	30	30
134.	15 a. lilac	60	40
135.	22 a. brown on pink	60	40
136.	31 a. brown on yellow	60	40
163.	31 a. purple on pink	80	80
137.	47 a. purple on pink	1·00	80
165.	47 a. blue on pink	1·00	90
167.	78 a. blue on yellow	1·10	1·10
168.	78 a. black on blue	1·25	1·10

1913. Provisional stamps of 1902 optd. **REPUBLICA** or **Republica.**

No.	Description	Un.	Used
194. R.	5 a. on 5 r. orange	20	20
195.	5 a. on 25 r. green	20	20
196.	5 a. on 50 r. blue	20	20
200. V.	6 a. on 2½ r. brown	20	20
201. R.	6 a. on 20 r. lilac	25	20
202.	9 a. on 15 r. brown	25	20
203.	9 a. on 75 r. red	20	20
148. S.	10 a. on 12 a. blue	40	30
204. R.	15 a. on 10 r. mauve	30	20
205.	15 a. on 100 r. brown on buff	30	20
206.	15 a. on 300 r. blue on brown	30	20
207.	22 a. on 80 r. green	70	60
151.	22 a. on 200 r. blue on bl.	1·10	80

1913. Vasco da Gama stamps of Timor optd. **REPUBLICA** or surch. also.

No.	Description	Un.	Used
169.	½ a. green	30	20
170.	1 a. red	30	20
171.	2 a. purple	30	20
172.	4 a. green	30	20
173.	8 a. blue	40	30
174.	10 a. on 12 a. brown	80	60
175.	16 a. brown	60	40
176.	24 a. yellow-brown	70	40

1914. "Ceres" key-type inscr. "TIMOR".

No.	Description	Un.	Used
211. U.	½ a. olive	8	8
212.	1 a. black	8	8
213.	1½ a. green	25	20
214.	2 a. green	8	8
180.	3 a. brown	40	35
215.	4 a. red	40	35
182.	6 a. violet	40	35
216.	7 a. green	45	35
217.	7½ a. blue	45	35
218.	9 a. blue	50	35
183.	10 a. blue	40	35
219.	11 a. grey	50	35
220.	12 a. brown	40	35
221.	15 a. mauve	1·00	90
185.	16 a. grey	60	60
222.	18 a. blue	1·10	1·00
223.	19 a. green	1·10	1·00
186.	20 a. brown	2·75	1·50
224.	36 a. blue	1·10	1·00
187.	40 a. claret	1·50	1·00
225.	54 a. brown	1·10	1·00
188.	58 a. brown on green	1·60	1·25
226.	72 a. red	2·50	2·00
189.	76 a. brown on rose	1·75	1·50
190.	1 p. orange on pink	2·50	2·25
191.	3 p. green on blue	6·00	4·25
227.	5 p. red	7·50	6·50

1915. No. 72 optd. **PROVISORIO** and **REPUBLICA.**

No.	Description	Un.	Used
192. S.	3 a. lilac	20	12

1920. No. 196 surch. **½ Avo P.P. n°. 68 19-3-1920** and bars.

No.	Description	Un.	Used
229. R.	½ a. on 5 a. on 50 r. blue	1·25	1·25

1932. "Ceres" key-type of Timor surch. with new value and bars.

No.	Description	Un.	Used
230. U.	6 a. on 72 a. red	25	20
231.	12 a. on 15 a. mauve	25	20

1935. As T 6 of Port. India ("Portugal" and San Gabriel), but inscr. "TIMOR".

No.	Description	Un.	Used
232. 6.	½ a. brown	8	5
233.	1 a. sepia	8	5
234.	2 a. green	8	5
235.	3 a. mauve	15	5
236.	4 a. black	15	12
237.	5 a. grey	15	12
238.	6 a. brown	15	12
239.	7 a. red	15	12
240.	8 a. blue	20	20
241.	10 a. red	20	20
242.	12 a. blue	25	20
243.	14 a. olive	25	20
244.	15 a. claret	25	20
245.	20 a. orange	25	20
246.	30 a. green	25	20
247.	40 a. violet	40	30
248.	50 a. brown	40	30
249.	1 p. blue	1·00	1·00
250.	2 p. brown	2·25	1·40
251.	3 p. green	3·75	2·50
252.	5 p. mauve	6·00	4·25

1938. As T 3 and 8 of Angola.

No.	Description	Un.	Used
253. 3.	1 a. olive (postage)	12	10
254. –	2 a. brown	12	10
255. –	3 a. violet	12	10
256. –	4 a. green	12	10
257. –	5 a. red	10	8
258. –	6 a. slate	12	10
259. –	8 a. purple	12	10
260. –	10 a. mauve	12	10
261. –	12 a. red	20	15
262. –	15 a. orange	20	15
263. –	20 a. blue	30	20
264. –	40 a. black	50	30
265. –	50 a. brown	60	30
266. –	1 p. red	1·10	80
267. –	2 p. olive	2·25	90
268. –	3 p. blue	2·75	1·75
269. –	5 p. brown	4·25	2·50
270. 8.	1 a. red (air)	30	20
271.	2 a. violet	30	20
272.	3 a. orange	30	20
273.	5 a. blue	30	20
274.	10 a. red	40	30
275.	20 a. green	70	60
276.	50 a. brown	1·50	1·10
277.	70 a. red	2·00	1·60
278.	1 p. mauve	2·50	2·00

DESIGNS—POSTAGE: 5 a. to 8 a. M. de Albur querque. 10 a. to 15 a. Prince Henry the Navigator. 20 a. to 50 a. "Fomento". 1 p. to 5 p. A. de Albuquerque.

1946. Stamps of Mozambique, 1938, surch. **TIMOR** and new value.

No.	Description	Un.	Used
279. 3.	1 a. on 15 c. purple (post.)	1·00	90
280. –	4 a. on 35 c. green	1·00	90
281. –	8 a. on 50 c. mauve	1·00	90
282. –	10 a. on 70 c. violet	1·00	90
283. –	12 a. on 1 e. red	1·00	90
284. –	20 a. on 1 e. 75 blue	1·00	90
285. 8.	8 a. on 50 c. orge. (air)	1·60	90
286.	12 a. on 1 e. blue	1·60	90
287.	40 a. on 3 e. green	1·60	90
288.	50 a. on 5 e. brown	1·60	90
289.	1 p. on 10 e. mauve	1·60	90

1947. Nos. 253/64 and 270/78 optd. **"LIBERTACAO".**

No.	Description	Un.	Used
290. 3.	1 a. olive (postage)	3·00	1·50
291. –	2 a. brown	4·50	2·50
292. –	3 a. violet	3·00	1·40
293. –	4 a. green	3·00	1·40
294. –	5 a. red	1·60	70
295. –	8 a. purple	40	20
296. –	10 a. mauve	1·60	70
297. –	12 a. red	1·60	70
298. –	15 a. orange	1·60	80
299. –	20 a. blue	15·00	8·00
300. –	40 a. black	3·50	1·90
301. 8.	1 a. red (air)	4·00	1·60
302.	2 a. violet	4·00	1·60
303.	3 a. orange	4·00	1·60
304.	5 a. blue	4·00	1·60
305.	10 a. red	1·40	80
306.	20 a. green	1·40	80
307.	50 a. brown	1·40	80
308.	70 a. red	3·25	1·60
309.	1p. mauve	1·60	50

1. Girl with Gong. **2.** Pottery-making.

1948. Natives.

No.	Description	Un.	Used
310. –	1 a. brown and green	30	20
311. 1.	3 a. brown and grey	60	40
312. –	4 a. green and pink	80	60
313. –	8 a. slate and red	30	20
314. –	10 a. green and orange	40	20
315. –	20 a. blue	30	20
316. –	1 p. blue and orange	3·50	1·90
317. –	3 p. brown and violet	10·00	5·00

DESIGNS: 1 a. Woman. 4 a. Girl with basket. 8 a., 10 a., 1 p., 3 p. Various chiefs. 20 a. Warrior.

1948. Honouring the Statue of Our Lady of Fatima. As T 13 of Angola.

No.	Description	Un.	Used
318.	8 a. grey	2·50	2·25

1949. U.P.U. 75th Anniv. As T 7 of Macao.

No.	Description	Un.	Used
319.	16 a. brown	4·25	3·50

1950.

No.	Description	Un.	Used
320. 2.	20 a. blue	30	20
321. –	50 a. brn. (Native woman)	70	35

1950. Holy Year. As Angola T 20/21.

No.	Description	Un.	Used
322.	40 a. green	70	40
323.	70 a. brown	1·00	70

3. "Belamcanda chinensis". **4.** Nurse weighing baby.

1950.

No.	Description	Un.	Used
324.	1 a. red, green and grey	20	12
325.	3 a. yellow, green & brown	1·10	1·00
326.	10 a. rose, green and blue	1·10	1·00
327.	16 a. red, orange, green and brown	3·00	1·60
328.	20 a. yellow, grn. & grey	1·10	1·00
329.	30 a. yellow, green & blue	1·25	1·00
330.	70 a. red, green & purple	1·60	1·25
331.	1 p. rose, yellow & green	3·25	2·50
332.	2 p. green, yellow & red	5·00	4·00
333.	5 p. pink, green and black	9·00	7·00

FLOWERS: 3 a. "Caesalpinia pulcherrima". 10 a. "Calotropis gigantea". 16 a. "Delonix regia". 20 a. "Plumeria rubra". 30 a. "Allamanda cathartica". 70 a. "Haemanthus multiflorus". 1 p. "Bauhinia". 2 p. "Eurycles amboiniensis". 5 p. "Crinum longiflorum".

1951. Holy Year. As Angola T 23.

No.	Description	Un.	Used
334.	86 a. blue	70	50

1952. 1st Tropical Medicine Congress, Lisbon.

No.	Description	Un.	Used
335. 4.	10 a. brown and green	20	15

1952. St. Francis Xavier. 400th Death Anniv. Designs as Nos. 432/4 of Macao but with background of closely spaced horiz. lines.

No.	Description	Un.	Used
336.	1 a. black and grey	8	5
337.	16 a. brown and buff	20	15
338.	1 p. claret and slate	1·00	70

5. Virgin. **6.** Map.

1953. Missionary Art Exhibition.

No.	Description	Un.	Used
339. 5.	3 a. brown and stone	5	5
340.	16 a. brown and bistre	15	12
341.	50 a. blue and stone	50	40

1954. Portuguese Postage Stamps Cent. As T 27 of Angola.

No.	Description	Un.	Used
342.	10 a. brown, lilac and grey	45	40

1954. Sao Paulo. 4th Cent. As T 28 of Angola.

No.	Description	Un.	Used
343.	16 a. black, red and blue	20	12

1956. Design multicoloured. Background colours given.

No.	Description	Un.	Used
344. 6.	1 a. salmon	5	5
345.	3 a. turquoise	5	5
346.	8 a. cream	12	10
347.	24 a. green	15	10
348.	32 a. lemon	25	10
349.	40 a. grey	40	12
350.	1 p. yellow	1·10	60
351.	3 p. slate	3·50	1·10

1958. 6th Int. Congress of Tropical Medicine. As T 35 of Angola.

No.	Description	Un.	Used
352.	32 a. orange, green, brown, red and blue	1·10	1·00

DESIGN: 32 a. "Calophyllum inophyllum" (plant).

1958. Brussels Int. Exn. As T 16 of Macao.

No.	Description	Un.	Used
353.	40 a. multicoloured	30	20

1960. New currency. Nos. 344/51 surch. thus: **$05** and bars.

No.	Description	Un.	Used
354. 6.	5 c. on 1 a. salmon	5	5
355.	10 c. on 3 a. turquoise	5	5
356.	20 c. on 8 a. cream	5	5
357.	30 c. on 24 a. green	5	5
358.	50 c. on 32 a. lemon	5	5
359.	1 e. on 40 c. grey	10	10
360.	2 e. on 40 c. grey	15	12
361.	5 e. on 1 p. yellow	20	15
362.	10 e. on 3 p. slate	1·10	70
363.	15 e. on 3 p. slate	1·40	90

7. Prince Henry's Motto.

8. Elephant Jar.

1960. Prince Henry the Navigator. 500th Death Anniv.

No.	Description	Un.	Used
364. 7.	4 e. 50 multicoloured	30	10

1961. Timor Art. Multicoloured.

No.	Description	Un.	Used
365.	5 c. T 8	5	5
366.	10 c. Model house on stilts	5	5
367.	20 c. Idol	8	5
368.	30 c. Rosary	10	5
369.	50 c. Model canoe with outrigger	5	5
370.	1 e. Casket	10	5
371.	2 e. 50 Archer (statuette)	12	5
372.	4 e. 50 Elephant (carving)	20	5
373.	5 e. Native climbing palm (carving)	40	5
374.	10 e. Timor woman (statuette)	40	12
375.	20 e. Model canoe with animals	1·25	50
376.	50 e. Model hut on stilts, bird and cat	3·50	60

The 50 c. and 20 e. are horiz.

1962. Sports. As T 41 of Angola. Multicoloured.

No.	Description	Un.	Used
377.	50 c. Game shooting	5	5
378.	1 e. Horse-riding	10	5
379.	1 e. 50 Swimming	8	5
380.	2 e. Athletes	8	5
381.	2 e. 50 Football	10	5
382.	15 e. Big-game hunting	60	30

1962. Malaria Eradication. Mosquito design as T 42 of Angola. Multicoloured.

No.	Description	Un.	Used
383.	2 e. 50 "A. sundaicus"	20	15

1964. National Overseas Bank Centenary. As Angola T 50 but portrait of M. P. Chagas.

No.	Description	Un.	Used
384.	2 e. 50 multicoloured	20	12

1965. I.T.U. Cent. As T 52 of Angola.

No.	Description	Un.	Used
385.	1 e. 50 multicoloured	50	25

1966. National Revolution. 40th Anniv. As T 56 of Angola, but showing different building. Multicoloured.

No.	Description	Un.	Used
386.	4 e. 50 Dr. V. Machado's College and Health Centre, Dili	30	20

1967. Military Naval Assn. Cent. As T 58 of Angola. Multicoloured.

No.	Description	Un.	Used
387.	10 c. G. Coutinho and warship "Patria"	5	5
388.	4 e. 50 S. Cabral and seaplane "Lusitania"	40	12

9. Sepoy Officer, 1792.

10. Pictorial Map of 1834, and Arms.

1967. Portuguese Military Uniforms. Multicoloured.

No.	Description	Un.	Used
389.	35 c. Type **9**	10	8
390.	1 e. Infantry officer, 1815	60	20
391.	1 e. 50 Infantryman 1879	12	8
392.	2 e. Infantryman, 1890	12	8
393.	2 e. 50 Infantry officer, 1903	15	8
394.	3 e. Sapper, 1918	20	8
395.	4 e. 50 Commando, 1964	20	8
396.	10 e. Parachutist, 1964	40	25

1967. Fatima Apparitions. 50th Anniv. As T 59 of Angola.

No.	Description	Un.	Used
397.	3 e. Virgin of the Pilgrims	15	10

1968. Pedro Cabral (explorer). 500th Birth Anniv. As T 63 of Angola. Multicoloured.

No.	Description	Un.	Used
398.	4 e. 50 Lopo Homem-Reineis' map, 1519 (horiz.)	40	20

1969. Admiral Gago Coutinho. Birth Cent. As T 65 of Angola. Multicoloured.

No.	Description	Un.	Used
399.	4 e. 50 Frigate "Admiral Gago Coutinho"	40	20

1969. Dili (capital). Bicent.

No.	Description	Un.	Used
400. 10.	1 e. multicoloured	5	5

1969. Vasco da Gama (explorer). 500th Anniv. Multicoloured. As T 66 of Angola.

No.	Description	Un.	Used
401.	5 e. Convent Medallion	20	10

1969. Overseas Administrative Reforms. Cent. As T **67** of Angola.
402. 5 e. multicoloured .. 20 10

1969. Manoel I. 500th Birth Anniv. As T **68** of Angola. Multicoloured.
403. 4 e. Emblem of Manoel I in Jeronimos Monastery 15 8

11. Map, Sir Ross Smith, and Arms of Britain, Timor and Australia.

1969. 1st England-Australia Flight. 50th Anniv.
404. **11.** 2 e. multicoloured .. 20 12

1970. Marshal Carmona. Birth Centenary. As T **70** of Angola.
414. 1 e. 50 Portrait in civilian dress 8 5

12. Missionaries, Natives and Ship.

1972. Camoens' "Lusiads". 400th Anniv.
415. **12.** 1 e. multicoloured .. 5 5

13. Football.

1972. Olympic Games, Munich.
416. **13.** 4 e. 50 multicoloured .. 20 8

14. Aviators G. Coutinho and S. Cabral in Seaplane.

1972. 1st Flight, Lisbon–Rio de Janeiro. 50th Anniv.
417. **14.** 1 e. multicoloured .. 5 5

1973. W.M.O. Centenary. As Type **77** of Angola.
418. 20 e. multicoloured .. 30 12

CHARITY TAX STAMPS

The notes under this heading in Portugal also apply here.

1919. No. 211 surch. **2 AVOS TAXA DA GUERRA.**
C 228. U. 2 a. on ½ a. olive .. 1·40 90

1919. No. 196 surch. **2 TAXA DE GUERRA** and bars.
C 230. R. 2 on 5 a. on 50 r. blue .. 16·00 9·00

1925. Marquis de Pombal Commem. Stamps of Portugal, but inscr. "TIMOR".
C 231. C **4.** 2 a. red 12 10
C 232. – 2 a. red 12 10
C 233. C **5.** 2 a. red 12 12

1934. Educational Tax. Fiscal stamps with values in black optd. **Instrucao D.L.n.° 7 de 3-2-1934** or surch. also.
C 234. 2 a. green .. .. 1·00 80
C 235. 5 a. green .. .. 1·10 90
C 236. 7 a. on ½ a. red .. 1·25 1·10

1936. Fiscal stamps with values in black optd. **Assistencia D.L.n°72.**
C 253. 10 a. red 80 60
C 254. 10 a. green 60 60

C **1.** C **2.** Woman and Star.

1948.
C 310. C **1.** 10 a. blue 40 40
C 311. 20 a. green 70 70
The 20 a. has a different emblem.

1960. Similar design. New currency.
C 398. 70 c. blue 10 10
C 399. 1 e. 30 green 20 20

1969.
C 405. C **2.** 30 c. blue 5 5
C 406. 50 c. purple & orge. .. 5 5
C 407. 1 c. brown & yellow .. 10 5

1970. Nos. C 398/9 surch. **D. L. No. 776** and value.
C 408. 30 c. on 70 c. blue .. 20 20
C 409. 30 c. on 1 e. 30 green .. 20 20
C 410. 50 c. on 70 c. blue .. 5 5
C 411. 50 c. on 1 e. 30 green .. 40 40
C 412. 1 e. on 70 c. blue .. 10 10
C 413. 1 e. on 1 e. 30 green .. 75 75

NEWSPAPER STAMPS

1892. "Embossed" key-type inscr. "PROVINCIA DE MACAU" surch. **JORNAES TIMOR 2½ 2½.**
N 31. Q. 2½ on 20 r. red 50 20
N 32. 2½ on 40 r. brown .. 50 20
N 33. 2½ on 80 r. grey 50 20

1893. "Newspaper" key-type inscr. "TIMOR".
N 36. V. 2½ r. brown 20 15

1895. No. N 36 surch. ½ **avo PROVISORIO.**
N 58. V. ½ a. on 2½ r. brown .. 20 15

POSTAGE DUE STAMPS

1904. "Due" key-type inscr. "TIMOR".
D 124. W. 1 a. green 15 12
D 125. 2 a. grey 15 15
D 126. 5 a. brown 40 35
D 127. 6 a. orange 50 40
D 128. 10 a. brown 50 40
D 129. 15 a. brown 80 60
D 130. 24 a. blue .. .. 1·60 1·25
D 131. 40 a. red .. .. 1·60 1·25
D 132. 50 a. orange .. .. 2·00 1·60
D 133. 1 p. lilac .. .. 3·50 2·75

1911. "Due" key-type of Timor optd. **REPUBLICA.**
D 139. W. 1 a. green 12 12
D 140. 2 a. grey 12 12
D 141. 5 a. brown 12 12
D 142. 6 a. orange 15 15
D 143. 10 a. brown 25 20
D 144. 15 a. brown 30 25
D 145. 24 a. blue 50 40
D 146. 40 a. red 70 60
D 147. 50 a. orange 70 60
D 148. 1 p. lilac .. .. 1·50 1·25

1925. Marquis de Pombal tax stamps, as Nos. C 231/3 of Timor, optd. **MULTA.**
D 231. C **4.** 4 a. red 12 10
D 232. – 4 a. red 12 10
D 233. C **5.** 4 a. red 12 10

1952. As Type D **1** of Macao, but inscr. "TIMOR PORTUGUES". Numerals in red; name in black.
D 336. 1 a. sepia and brown .. 5 5
D 337. 3 a. brown and orange .. 5 5
D 338. 5 a. green and turquoise 5 5
D 339. 10 a. green and pale grn. 5 5
D 340. 30 a. violet & pale violet 10 5
D 341. 1 p. crimson & orange .. 30 15

TOBAGO BC

An island in the Br. W. Indies, N.E. of Trinidad. Now uses stamps of Trinidad and Tobago.

1. **2.**

1879.
1. **1.** 1d. red .. .. .. 11·00 12·00
2. 3d. blue .. .. .. 13·00 12·00
3. 6d. orange .. .. .. 11·00 11·00
4. 1s. green .. .. .. £140 22·00
5. 5s. grey £300 £250
6. £1 mauve £2000

In the above issue only stamps watermarked Crown CC were issued for postal use and our prices are for stamps bearing this watermark. Stamps with watermark Crown CA are fiscals and were never admitted to postal use.

1880. No. 3 divided vertically down the centre and surch. with pen and ink.
7. **1.** 1d. on half of 6d. orange .. — £225

1880. "POSTAGE" added in design.
14. **2.** ½d. lilac .. .. 1·10 7·00
20. ½d. green 12 12
15. 1d. brown .. .. 1·25 1·25
21. 1d. red 15 12
16b. 2½d. blue 60 60
10. 4d. green .. .. 55·00 9·00
22. 4d. grey 35 40
11. 6d. pale brown 70 45
23. 6d. red-brown .. .. 90 1·75
24. 1s. olive-yellow .. 1·40 3·25

1883. Surch. in figures and words.
26. **2.** ½d. on 2½d. blue .. 1·25 2·50
30. ½d. on 4d. grey .. 5·00 8·00
27. ½d. on 6d. pale brown .. 2·00 3·25
28. ½d. on 6d. red-brown .. 14·00 15·00
29. 1d. on 2½d. blue .. 5·00 7·00
31. 2½d. on 4d. grey .. 3·50 5·00
13. 2½d. on 6d. pale brown .. 5·00 2·25

1896. Surch. ½d. **POSTAGE.**
33. **1.** ½d. on 4d. lilac and red .. 3·00 4·00

TOGO O4; BC

A territory in W. Africa, formerly a German Colony. Divided between France and Gt. Britain in 1919, the British portion being attached to the Gold Coast for administration and using the stamps of that country. In 1956 the French portion became an autonomous republic within the French Union. Full independence was achieved in April, 1960.

GERMAN ISSUES

100 pfenning = 1 mark.

1897. Stamps of Germany optd. **TOGO.**
1a. **6.** 3 pf. brown .. .. 1·60 2·10
2. 5 pf. green .. .. 1·60 90
3. **7.** 10 pf. red .. .. 1·25 1·10
4. 20 pf. blue .. .. 2·25 3·50
5. 25 pf. orange .. .. 14·00 16·00
6. 50 pf. brown .. .. 14·00 16·00

1900. "Yacht" key-types inscr. "TOGO".
7. N. 3 pf. brown 15 35
8. 5 pf. green .. .. 9·00 35
9. 10 pf. red .. .. 14·00 35
10. 20 pf. blue 35 70
11. 25 pf. blk. & red on yellow 35 4·00
12. 30 pf. blk. & oran. on red 50 3·00
13. 40 pf. black and red .. 35 3·25
14. 50 pf. black & pur. on red 50 3·25
15. 80 pf. black & red on rose 80 5·50
16. O. 1 m. red .. .. 1·25 18·00
17. 2 m. blue .. .. 2·00 27·00
18. 3 m. black .. .. 2·75 45·00
19. 5 m. red and black .. 40·00 £150

BRITISH OCCUPATION

1914. Nos. 7/19 optd. **TOGO Anglo-French Occupation.**
1. N. 3 pf. brown .. .. 65·00 45·00
2. 5 pf. green .. .. 65·00 45·00
3. 10 pf. red .. .. 80·00 55·00
4. 20 pf. blue .. .. 15·00 10·00
5. 25 pf. black & red on yell. 15·00 12·00
6. 30 pf. blk. & orge. on buff 15·00 12·00
7. 40 pf. black and red .. £140 £100
8. 50 pf. blk. & pur. on buff £3000 £2500
9. 80 pf. black & red on rose £140 £100
10. O. 1 m. red £2000 £1200
11. 2 m. blue £2700 £2200
25. 3 m. black .. ..
26. 5 m. lake and black ..

1914. Nos. 1/2 surch. in words.
27. N. ½d. on 3 pf. brown .. 12·00 9·00
28. 1d. on 5 pf. green .. 3·25 3·00

1915. Stamps of Gold Coast (King George V) optd. **TOGO ANGLO-FRENCH OCCUPATION.**
47. ½d. green 8 8
48. 1d. red 8 8
36. 2d. grey 10 12
37. 2½d. blue 15 15
38. 3d. purple on yellow .. 25 25
52. 6d. purple 25 30
53. 1s. black on green .. 60 60
54. 2s. purple & blue on blue 1·00 1·25
55. 2s. 6d. black & red on blue 1·10 1·40
56. 5s. green & red on yellow 2·00 2·25
57a. 10s. green & red on green 3·50 4·00
58. 20s. purple & black on red 10·00 12·00

FRENCH OCCUPATION

1914. Stamps of German Colonies. "Yacht" key-type, optd. **TOGO Occupation franco-anglaise** or surch. also in figures.
1. N. 05 on 3 pf. brown .. 10·00 10·00
2. 10 on 5 pf. green .. 3·25 3·25
3. 20 pf. blue .. .. 10·00 9·00
4. 25 pf. black & red on yell. 12·00 9·50
5. 30 pf. blk. & oran. on red 11·00 8·50
6. 40 pf. black and red .. £180 £110
7. 80 pf. black & red on rose £180 £110

1916. Stamps of Dahomey optd. **TOGO Occupation franco-anglaise.**
20. **1.** 1 c. black and violet .. 5 5
21. 2 c. red and brown .. 5 5
22. 4 c. brown and black .. 5 5
23. 5 c. green 5 5
24. 10 c. red and orange .. 5 5
25. 15 c. purple and brown .. 15 15
26. 20 c. brown and grey .. 8 8
27. 25 c. blue 8 8
28. 30 c. violet and purple .. 10 10
29. 35 c. black and brown .. 10 10
30. 40 c. orange and black .. 15 15
31. 45 c. blue and grey .. 8 8
32. 50 c. brown 10 10
33. 75 c. violet and blue .. 70 70
34. 1 f. black and green .. 80 80
35. 2 f. brown and yellow .. 1·50 1·50
36. 5 f. blue and violet .. 95 95

FRENCH MANDATE

1921. Stamps of Dahomey optd. **TOGO.**
37. **1.** 1 c. green and grey .. 5 5
38. 2 c. orange and blue .. 5 5
39. 4 c. orange and green .. 5 5
40. 5 c. black and red .. 5 5
41. 10 c. green 5 5
42. 15 c. red and brown .. 5 5
43. 20 c. orange and green .. 12 12
44. 25 c. orange and grey .. 5 5
45. 30 c. red and claret .. 5 5
46. 35 c. green and claret .. 15 15
47. 40 c. olive and green .. 15 15
48. 45 c. olive and claret .. 15 15
49. 50 c. blue 8 8
50. 75 c. blue and red .. 20 20
51. 1 f. blue and grey .. 20 20
52. 2 f. red and green .. 55 55
53. 5 f. black and orange .. 65 65

1922. Stamps of Dahomey optd. **TOGO** and surch. in figures.
54. **1.** 25 c. on 15 c. red & brown 5 5
55. 25 c. on 2 f. red and green 5 5
56. 25 c. on 5 f. black & orange 5 5
57. 60 on 75 c. violet .. 15 15
58. 65 on 45 c. olive and claret 15 15
59. 85 on 75 c. blue and brown 20 20

DESIGNS: 20 c. to 90 c. Cocoa trees. 1 f. to 20 f. Palm trees.

1. Coconut Palms.

1924.
60. **1.** 1 c. black and yellow .. 5 5
61. 2 c. black and red .. 5 5
62. 4 c. black and blue .. 5 5
63. 5 c. black and orange .. 5 5
64. 10 c. black and mauve .. 5 5
65. 15 c. black and green .. 5 5
66. – 20 c. black and grey .. 5 5
67. – 25 c. black & green on yell. 5 5
68. – 30 c. black and green .. 5 5
69. – 30 c. green 5 5
70 – 35 c. black and brown .. 5 5
71. – 35 c. green 5 5
72. – 40 c. black and orange .. 5 5
73. – 45 c. black and red .. 5 5
74. – 50 c. black & yell. on blue 5 5
75. – 55 c. red and blue .. 8 8
76. – 60 c. black & claret on red 5 5
77. – 60 c. red 5 5
78. – 65 c. brown and lilac .. 5 5
79. – 75 c. black and blue .. 5 5
80. – 80 c. lilac on blue .. 5 5
81. – 85 c. brown and yellow .. 5 5
82. – 90 c. rose and red .. 8 8
83. – 1 f. black & claret on blue 5 5
84. – 1 f. blue 5 5
85. – 1 f. green and lilac .. 35 30
86. – 1 f. orange and red .. 5 5
87. – 1 f. 10 brown and mauve 75 75
88. – 1 f. 25 red and claret .. 10 8
89. – 1 f. 50 blue 5 5
90. – 1 f. 75 red and bistre .. 1·10 20
91. – 1 f. 75 blue 5 5
92. – 2 f. grey on blue .. 5 5
93. – 3 f. red and green .. 8 8
94. – 5 f. blk. & oran. on blue .. 15 15
95. – 10 f. red and brown .. 20 20
96. – 20 f. black & red on yell. 25 25

1926. Surch.
98. **1.** 1 f. 25 on 1 f. blue .. 5 5

1931. "Colonial Exhibition" key-types inscr. "TOGO".
99. E. 40 c. green .. .. 1·00 1·00
100. F. 50 c. mauve .. .. 1·00 1·00
101. G. 90 c. red .. .. 1·00 1·00
102. H. 1 f. 50 blue .. .. 1·00 1·00

1937. International Exhibition, Paris. As Nos. 110/15 of Cameroun.
103. 20 c. violet 35 35
104. 30 c. green 35 35
105. 40 c. red 35 35
106. 50 c. brown 35 35
107. 90 c. red 35 35
108. 1 f. 50 blue 35 35

1938. International Anti-Cancer Fund. As T 10 of Cameroun.
109. 1 f. 75+50 c. blue .. 4·00 4·00

1939. Cent. of Death of R. Caillie. As T 2 of Dahomey.
110. 90 c. orange 15 15
111. 2 f. violet 15 15
112. 2 f. 25 blue 15 15

1939. New York World's Fair. As T 11 of Cameroun.
113. 1 f. 25 red 10 10
114. 2 f. 25 blue 10 10

1939. French Revolution. 150th Anniv. As T 16 of Cameroun.
115. 45 c.+25 c. green .. 1·00 1·00
116. 70 c.+30 c. brown .. 1·00 1·00
117. 90 c.+35 c. orange .. 1·00 1·00
118. 1 f. 25+1 f. red.. .. 1·00 1·00
119. 2 f. 25+2 f. blue .. 1·00 1·00

1940. Air. As T 3 of Dahomey.
120. 1 f. 90 blue 5 5
121. 2 f. 90 red 5 5
122. 4 f. 50 green 5 5
123. 4 f. 90 olive 5 5
124. 6 f. 90 orange 20 15

2. Pounding Meal.
3. Riverside Village.
4. Hunting.
5. Young Girl.

1940.
125. 2. 2 c. violet 5 5
126. 3 c. green 5 5
127. 4 c. black 5 5
128. 5 c. red 5 5
129. 10 c. blue 5 5
130. 15 c. brown 5 5
131. 3. 20 c. plum 5 5
132. 25 c. blue 5 5
133. 30 c. black 5 5
134. 40 c. red 5 5
135. 45 c. green 5 5
136. 50 c. brown 5 5
137. 60 c. violet 5 5
138. 4. 70 c. black 5 5
139. 90 c. violet 12 12
140. 1 f. green 5 5
141. 1 f. 25 red 15 15
142. 1 f. 40 brown 5 5
143. 1 f. 60 orange 8 8
144. 2 f. blue 5 5
145. 5. 2 f. 25 blue 8 8
146. 2 f. 50 red 10 10
147. 3 f. violet 8 8
148. 5 f. red 10 10
149. 10 f. violet 10 10
150. 20 f. black 30 30

1941. National Defence Fund. Surch. SECOURS NATIONAL and value.
151. +1 f. on 50 c. (No. 136).. 12 12
152. +2 f. on 80 c. (No. 80) .. 90 90
153. +2 f. on 1 f. 50 (No. 89) 90 90
154. +3 f. on 2 f. (No. 144) .. 90 90

1942. Air. As T 4d. of Dahomey.
154a. 50 f. violet and yellow .. 20 20

1944. Nos. 75 and 82 surch.
155. 1 f. 50 on 55 c. red & blue 12 12
156. 1 f. 50 on 90 c. rose & red 10 10

1944. No. 139 surch. in figures and ornament.
157. 4. 3 f. 50 on 90 c. violet .. 5 5
158. 4 f. on 90 c. violet .. 5 5
159. 5 f. on 90 c. violet .. 20 20
160. 5 f. 50 on 90 c. violet .. 20 20
161. 10 f. on 90 c. violet .. 20 20
162. 20 f. on 90 c. violet .. 25 25

6. Palm Oil Extraction.
7. Archer.
8. Antelopes.
9. Postal Runner and Aeroplane.

1947.
163. 6. 10 c. red (postage) .. 5 5
164. 30 c. blue 5 5
165. 50 c. green 5 5
166. 7. 60 c. pink 5 5
167. 1 f. brown 5 5
168. 1 f. 20 c. green .. 5 5
169. – 1 f. 50 c. orange.. .. 8 8
170. – 2 f. brown 10 5
171. – 2 f. 50 c. black .. 20 15
172. – 3 f. blue 5 5
173. – 3 f. 60 c. red .. 10 10
174. – 4 f. blue 5 5
175. 8. 5 f. brown 25 5
176. 6 f. blue 25 20
177. 10 f. red 25 5
178. – 15 f. green 20 5
179. – 20 f. green 30 8
180. – 25 f. pink 30 10

181. – 40 f. blue (air) .. 1·10 90
182. – 50 f. mauve and violet .. 55 40
183. – 100 f. brown and green.. 1·10 70
184. 9. 200 f. pink .. .. 2·00 1·00

DESIGNS—As T 6: 1 f. 50 to 2 f. 50, Women picking cotton. As T 8: 3 f. to 4 f. Drummer and village. 15 f. to 25 f. Trees and village. As T 9: 40 f. Elephants and aeroplane. 50 f. Two-engined aeroplane. 100 f. Four-engined aeroplane.

1949. Air. U.P.U. As T 25 of Cameroun.
185. 25 f. red, pur., grn. & blue 1·00 1·00

1950. Colonial Welfare. As Cameroun. T 26.
186. 10 f.+2 f. blue 65 65

1952. Military Medal. As T 27 of Cameroun.
187. 15 f. red, yellow and green 90 90

1954. Air. Liberation. As T 29 of Cameroun.
188. 15 f. violet and indigo .. 65 65

10. Gathering Palm Nuts.
11. Roadway through Forest.
12. Goliath Beetle.
13. Rural School.

1954.
189. 10. 8 f. maroon, lake and violet (postage) .. 20 10
190. 15 f. choc., grey & indigo 25 12

191. 11. 500 f. indigo & grn. (air) 9.00 8·00

1955. Nature Protection.
192. 12. 8 f. black and green .. 35 12

1956. Economic and Social Development Fund.
193. 13. 15 f. chocolate & chest. 80 45

AUTONOMOUS REPUBLIC

14. Togolese Woman and Flag.

1957. New National Flag.
194. 14. 15 f. brown, red & turq. 45 15

15. Native Woman and "Liberty" releasing Dove.

1957. Air. Autonomous Republic. 1st Anniv.
195. 15. 25 f. sepia, red and blue 30 30

16. Konkomba Helmet.
17. Antelope.
18. Torch and Flags.

1957.
196. 16. 30 c. vio. & claret (post.) 5 5
197. 50 c. indigo and blue.. 5 5
198. 1 f. violet and mauve.. 5 5
199. 2 f. brown and olive .. 5 5
200. 3 f. black and green .. 5 5
201. 17. 4 f. black and blue .. 30 8
202. 5 f. claret and grey .. 30 8
203. 6 f. slate and red .. 30 8
204. 8 f. violet and grey .. 30 10
205. 10 f. brown and green.. 30 12
206. – 15 f. multicoloured .. 15 12
207. – 20 f. multicoloured .. 15 12
208. – 25 f. multicoloured .. 15 15
209. – 40 f. multicoloured .. 30 15

210. 18. 50 f. multicoloured (air) 45 35
211. 100 f. multicoloured .. 85 45
212. 200 f. multicoloured .. 1·75 90
213. – 500 f. indigo, grn. & blue 5·00 3·25

DESIGNS—HORIZ. 15 f. to 40 f. Teak forest. As T 18: 500 f. Wading-bird in flight.

19. "Human Rights".
20. "Bombax".

1958. Human Rights Declaration. 10th Anniv.
214. 19. 20 f. red and green .. 35 35

1959. Tropical Flora.
215. 20. 5 f. pink, yell., grn. & bl. 5 5
216. – 20 f. yell., grn. & black 12 8

DESIGN—HORIZ. 20 f. "Tectona".

1959. As Nos. 196/213 colours changed and inscr. "REPUBLIQUE DU TOGO".
217. 16. 30 c. blue & black (post.) 5 5
218. 50 c. turquoise & orange 5 5
219. 1 f. magenta and olive 5 5
220. 2 f. olive and turquoise 5 5
221. 3 f. violet and magenta 5 5
222. 17. 4 f. purple and magenta 15 5
223. 5 f. chocolate and green 15 8
224. 6 f. grey-bl. and ultram. 15 8
225. 8 f. bistre and myrtle .. 15 8
226. 10 f. brown and violet.. 15 8
227. – 15 f. brown, orange, sepia and purple .. 10 10
228. – 20 f. green, turquoise, black and maroon .. 15 8
229. – 25 f. brown, chocolate, violet and olive .. 30 10
230. – 40 f. green, ochre, blue and chestnut .. 30 15

231. – 25 f. chocolate, emerald and blue (air) .. 15 10
232. 18. 50 f. red, blk., grn. & bl. 45 25
233. 100 f. mar., red, grn. & bl. 75 45
234. 200 f. lake, red, blue and green .. .. .. 1·60 85
235. – 500 f. sepia, grn. & pur. 4·00 1·90

DESIGN—VERT. 25 f. (No. 231) Togo flag and shadow of airliner over Africa.

21. Patient on Stretcher.
22. "The Five Continents" (after painting by Sert on ceiling of Palais des Nations Geneva).

1959. Red Cross Commem.
236. 21. 20 f.+5 f. red, orange and slate 30 0
237. – 30 f.+5 f. red, brown and blue 30 30
238. – 50 f.+10 f. red, brown and green 30 30

DESIGNS: 30 f. Mother feeding child. 50 f. Nurse superintending blood transfusion.

1959. U.N. Day. Centres in blue.
239. 22. 15 f. brown 12 12
240. 20 f. violet 15 15
241. 25 f. chestnut 15 15
242. 40 f. blue-green 25 25
243. 60 f. red 30 30

INDEPENDENT REPUBLIC

23. Ski-ing.
24. "Uprooted Tree".

1960. Olympic Games. Inscr. as in T 23 or "JEUX OLYMPIQUES ROME 1960" (10 f. to 25 f.).
244. 23. 30 c. turq., red & green 5 5
245. – 50 c. mar., red & black 5 5
246. – 1 f. green, red & black 5 5
247. – 10 f. brn., blue & indigo 8 5
248. – 15 f. maroon and green 10 8
249. – 20 f. choc., grn. & brn. 20 10
250. – 25 f. chocolate, crimson and orange .. 25 12

DESIGNS—HORIZ. 50 c. Ice-Hockey. 1 f. Tobogganing. 10 f. Cycling. 25 f. Running. VERT. 15 f. Discus-throwing. 20 f. Boxing.

1960. World Refugee Year.
251. 24. 25 f.+5 f. green, brown and blue 15 15
252. – 45 f. + 5 f. olive, black and blue 35 35

DESIGN: 45 f. As T 24 but with "TOGO" and values, etc., below tree.

25. Prime Minister, S. Olympio and Flag.
26. Benin Hotel.

1960. Independence Commem. (a) Postage. Centres mult.; backgrounds cream; inscription and frame colours given.
253. 25. 30 c. sepia 5 5
254. 50 c. brown 5 5
255. 1 f. purple 5 5
256. 10 f. blue 8 5
257. 20 f. red 12 8
258. 25 f. green 20 15

(b) Air.
259. 26. 100 f. red, yell. & green 65 45
260. 200 f. blue, yellow, green and red .. 1·25 65
261. – 500 f. brown and green 3·25 1·75

DESIGN—As T 26—VERT. 500 f. Eagle and map of Togo.

27. Union Jack and Flags of Four Powers.

1960. Four-Power "Summit" Conf., Paris. Flags and inscr. in red and blue.

262. **27.** 50 c. buff 5 5
263. – 1 f. turquoise 5 5
264. – 20 f. grey 15 10
265. – 25 f. blue 20 15

DESIGNS—As T **27** but flags of: 1 f. Soviet Union. 20 f. France. 25 f. U.S.A. The Conference did not take place.

28. Togo Flag.

29. Crowned Cranes.

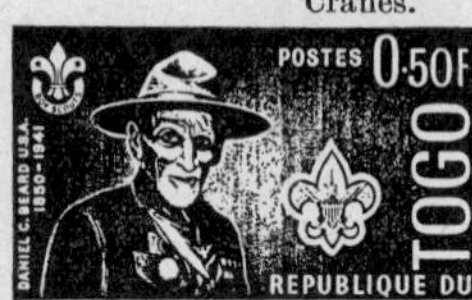

30. Papa A. de Souza. **31.** Daniel Beard (founder of American Scout Movement) and Scout Badge.

1961. Admission of Togo into U.N.O. Flag in red, yellow and green.

266. **28.** 30 c. red 5 5
267. 50 c. brown 5 5
268. 1 f. blue 5 5
269. 10 f. maroon 8 5
270. 25 f. black 20 10
271. 30 f. violet 25 15

1961.

272. **29.** 1 f. multicoloured .. 5 5
273. 10 f. multicoloured .. 10 5
274. 25 f. multicoloured .. 25 20
275. 30 f. multicoloured .. 30 25

1961. Independence. 1st Anniv.

276. **30.** 50 c. black, red & yellow 5 5
277. 1 f. black, brown & grn. 5 5
278. 10 f. black, violet & blue 8 5
279. 25 f. black, grn. & sal. 20 8
280. 30 f. black, blue & mve. 25 15

1961. Boy Scout Movement Commem.

281. **31.** 50 c. lake, green & red 5 5
282. – 1 f. violet and red .. 5 5
283. – 10 f. black and chestnut 8 5
284. – 25 f. bl., red, yell. & grn. 15 8
285. – 30 f. red, chest. & emer. 30 10
286. – 100 f. magenta and blue 80 40

DESIGNS—HORIZ. 1 f. Lord Baden Powell. 10 f. Daniel Mensah ("Rover" Scout Chief). 100 f. Scout salute. VERT. 25 f. Chief Daniel Wilson (Togolese Scout). 30 f. Campfire on triangular emblem.

32. 'Plane and Ship. **33.** U.N.I.C.E.F. Emblem.

1961. U.N. Economic Commission on Africa. Multicoloured.

287. 20 f. T **32** 12 8
288. 25 f. Electric train and gantry 20 10
289. 30 f. Excavator and pylons 25 20
290. 85 f. Microscope and atomic symbol 65 40

The designs are superimposed on a map of Africa spread over the four stamps when the 30 and 85 f. are mounted below the 20 and 25 f.

1961. U.N.I.C.E.F. 15th Anniv.

291. **33.** 1 f. blue, green & black 5 5
292. – 10 f. multicoloured .. 5 5
293. – 20 f. multicoloured .. 10 8
294. – 25 f. multicoloured .. 15 10
295. – 30 f. multicoloured .. 30 12
296. – 85 f. multicoloured .. 60 45

DESIGNS: 10 f. to 85 f. Children dancing round the globe. The six stamps, arranged in the following order, form a composite picture: Upper row, 1, 25 and 20 f. Lower row, 10, 85 and 30 f.

34. Alan Shepard.

35. Girl wearing Basket of Fruit.

1962. Space Flights Commem.

297. **34.** 50 c. green 5 5
298. – 1 f. magenta 8 8
299. **34.** 25 f. blue 15 15
300. – 30 f. violet 20 20

DESIGN: 1 f., 30 f. As T **34** but portrait of Yuri Gagarin.

1962. Col. Glenn's Space Flight. Surch. **100 F COL. JOHN H. GLENN U S A VOL ORBITAL 20 FEVRIER 1962.**

301. **34.** 100 f. on 50 c. green .. 75 75

1962. Independence. 2nd Anniv. Inscr. "27 AVRIL 1960".

303. – 50 c. ochre, black, green and mauve 5 5
304. **35.** 1 f. green and pink .. 5 5
305. – 5 f. ochre, black, green and yellow 5 5
306. **35.** 20 f. red-vio. & ol.-yell. 12 8
307. – 25 f. ochre, black, green and blue 20 8
308. **35.** 30 f. red and yellow .. 25 10

DESIGN: 50 c., 5 f., 25 f. Independence Monument.

36. Arrows piercing mosquito.

1962. Malaria Eradication

309. **36.** 10 f. multicoloured .. 8 5
310. 25 f. multicoloured .. 20 10
311. 30 f. multicoloured .. 30 15
312. 85 f. multicoloured .. 60 35

37. Presidents Kennedy and Olympio, and Capitol, Washington.

1962. Visit of President to U.S.A.

313. **37.** 50 c. slate and ochre .. 5 5
314. 1 f. slate and cobalt .. 5 5
315. 2 f. slate and red .. 5 5
316. 5 f. slate and mauve .. 5 5
317. 25 f. slate and lilac .. 20 8
318. 100 f. slate and green .. 80 55

38. Stamps of 1897 and Mail coach.

1963. Togolese Postal Services. 65th Anniv.

319. **38.** 30 c. multicoloured (post.) 5 5
320. – 50 c. multicoloured .. 5 5
321. – 1 f. multicoloured .. 5 5
322. – 10 f. multicoloured .. 8 5
323. – 25 f. multicoloured .. 20 10
324. – 30 f. multicoloured .. 25 20
325. – 100 f. multicoloured (air) 70 50

DESIGNS (Togo stamps of): 50 c. 1900 and yacht "Hohenzollern". 1 f. 1915 and mail-train. 10 f. 1924 and motor-cycle mail-carrier. 25 f. 1940 and mail-van. 30 f. 1947 and DC-3 aircraft. 100 f. 1960 and Boeing 707 aircraft.

39. Hands reaching for F.A.O. Emblem.

1963. Freedom from Hunger.

326. **39.** 50 c. multicoloured .. 5 5
327. 1 f. multicoloured .. 5 5
328. 25 f. multicoloured .. 20 12
329. 30 f. multicoloured .. 25 15

40. Lome Port and Togolese Flag. **41.** Centenary Emblem.

1963. Independence. 3rd Anniv. Flag in red, yellow and green.

330. **40.** 50 c. black and brown .. 5 5
331. 1 f. black and red .. 5 5
332. 25 f. black and blue .. 20 12
333. 50 f. black and ochre .. 45 20

1963. Red Cross Cent. Flag red, yellow and green; cross red.

334. **41.** 25 f. blue and black .. 20 15
335. 30 f. green and black .. 20 15

42. Broken Shackles and Abraham Lincoln.

43. Flame and U.N. Emblem.

44. Hibiscus. **45.** Temple and Cleopatra.

1963. American Slaves' Emancipation. Cent. Centre in grey and green.

336. **42.** 50 c. blk. & brown (post) 5 5
337. 1 f. black and blue .. 5 5
338. 25 f. black and red .. 20 12
339. **42.** 100 f. black & orge. (air) 80 55

1963. Declaration of Human Rights. 15th Anniv. Flame in red.

340. **43.** 50 c. blue & ultramarine 5 5
341. 1 f. green and black .. 5 5
342. 25 f. lilac & ultramarine 15 12
343. 85 f. gold and blue .. 65 50

1964. Multicoloured.

344. 50 c. "Odontoglossum grande" (orchid) (post.) 5 5
345. 1 f. Type **44** 5 5
346. 2 f. "Papilio dardanus" (butterfly) 5 5
347. 3 f. "Morpho aega" (butterfly) 5 5
348. 4 f. Scorpion 5 5
349. 5 f. Tortoise 8 5
350. 6 f. Strelitzia (flower) .. 5 5
351. 8 f. Python 5 5
352. 10 f. "Bunaea alcinde" (butterfly) 8 5
353. 15 f. Chameleon 12 5
354. 20 f. Octopus 15 5
355. 25 f. "Zeus faber" (fish) 20 8
356. 30 f. "Pomacanthus arcuatus" (fish) 25 8
357. 40 f. Dwarf hippopotamus 25 10
358. 45 f. African squirrel .. 30 12
359. 60 f. Antelope 40 15
360. 85 f. Monkey 60 20
361. 50 f. "Pirenestes ostrinus" (air: Birds) 45 20
362. 100 f. Blue-billed mannikin
363. 200 f. "Agapornis pullaria" 90 30
364. 250 f. African Grey Parrot 1·75 1·10
365. 500 f. Yellow-breasted barbet .. .. .. 2·25 1·25

1964. President Kennedy Memorial Issue. Optd. **En Memoire de JOHN F. KENNEDY 1917-1963.** Centre in grey and green.

366. **42.** 50 c. blk. & brn. (post.) 5 5
367. 1 f. black and blue .. 5 5
368. 25 f. black and red .. 20 15
369. 100 f. blk. & orge. (air) 90 55

1964. Nubian Monuments Preservation.

370. **45.** 20 f. red, maroon, black and green 12 8
371. – 25 f. mauve and black .. 15 10
372. – 30 f. olive, black & yell. 20 12

DESIGNS: 25 f. Queen Nefertari. 30 f. Temple of Philae.

46. Phosphate Mine, Kpeme.

1964. Independence. 4th Anniv.

373. **46.** 5 f. ochre, bistre & brn. 5 5
374. – 25 f. lake, brown & vio. 20 10
375. – 60 f. yell.-ol., ol. & grn. 45 25
376. – 85 f. blue, slate-bl. & vio. 60 35

DESIGNS: 25 f. Mine installations. 60 f. Phosphate train. 85 f. Loading phosphate from cantilever.

47. Togolese Breaking Chain. **48.** Pres. Grunitzky and Butterfly.

1964. African Heads of State Conf., Addis Ababa. 1st Anniv.

377. **47.** 5 f. sepia & orge. (post.) 5 5
378. 25 f. sepia and green .. 15 8
379. 85 f. sepia and cerise .. 60 25
380. **47.** 100 f. sepia & turq. (air) 90 55

1964. "National Union and Reconciliation".

381. **48.** 1 f. violet and magenta 5 5
382. – 5 f. sepia and ochre .. 5 5
383. – 25 f. violet and blue .. 20 10
384. **48.** 45 f. purple and red .. 35 15
385. – 85 f. bronze and green .. 60 25

DESIGNS—President and: 5 f. Dove. 25 f., 85 f. Flowers.

49. Football.

1964. Olympic Games, Tokyo.

386. **49.** 1 f. green (postage) .. 5 5
387. – 5 f. blue (Running) .. 5 5
388. – 25 f. claret (Throwing the discus) 20 10
389. **49.** 45 f. turquoise 35 15
390. – 100 f. brown (Tennis) .. (air) 90 55

1964. French, African and Malagasy Co-operation. As T **500** of France.

391. 25 f. choc., bistre & purple 20 12

50. Early Balloons and Dirigible.

1964. "Air Togo" (National Airline). Inaug.

392. **50.** 5 f. violet, brown, blue and yellow (postage) 5 5
393. 10 f. blue, lake & green 8 5
394. – 25 f. ultram., orge. & bl. 15 10
395. – 45 f. ultram., grn. & mag. 40 15
396. – 100 f. blue, red, green and yellow (air) .. 90 55

DESIGNS: 25 f., 45 f. Early flying machines and Boeing jetliner. 100 f. Boeing jetliner and Togolese flag.

51. Sun, Globe and Satellites "Ogo" and "Mariner".

1964. Int. Quiet Sun Years. Sun yellow.
397. **51.** 10 f. blue and red .. 5 5
398. – 15 f. blue, chest. & mauve 10 5
399. – 20 f. green and violet .. 12 8
400. – 25 f. pur., green and blue 15 10
401. **51.** 45 f. blue and emerald .. 30 20
402. – 50 f. green & vermilion 40 25
SATELLITES: 15 f., 25 f. "Tiros", "Telstar" and orbiting solar observatory. 20 f., 50 f. "Nimbus", "Syncom" and "Relay".

52. Pres. Grunitzky and the Mount of the Beatitudes Church.

1965. Israel-Togo Friendship. Inscr. "AMITIE ISRAEL-TOGO 1964".
403. – 5 f. maroon 5 5
404. **52.** 20 f. blue and purple .. 12 8
405. – 25 f. turq.-green & red 15 10
406. – 45 f. olive, bistre & pur. 60 30
407. – 85 f. turq.-grn. & purple 40 15
DESIGNS—VERT. 5 f. Togolese stamps being printed on Israeli press. HORIZ. 25 f., 85 f. Arms of Israel and Togo. 45 f. As T **52** but showing old synagogue, Capernaum.

53. "Syncom 3", Dish Aerial and I.T.U. Emblem.

1965. I.T.U. Cent.
408. **53.** 10 f. turq.-blue & green 8 5
409. 20 f. olive and black .. 12 8
410. 25 f. blue & ultramarine 15 10
411. 45 f. rose and red .. 35 15
412. 50 f. green and black .. 40 20

54. Abraham Lincoln.

55. Throwing the Discus.

1965. Lincoln. Death Cent.
413. **54.** 1 f. purple (postage) .. 5 5
414. 5 f. green 5 5
415. 20 f. brown 15 8
416. 25 f. indigo 20 10
417. **54.** 100 f. olive (air) .. 90 55

1965. 1st African Games, Brazzaville. Flags in red, yellow and green.
418. **55.** 5 f. purple (postage) .. 5 5
419. – 10 f. blue 8 5
420. – 15 f. brown 10 5
421. – 25 f. slate-purple .. 20 10
422. – 100 f. green (air) .. 90 55
SPORTS: 10 f. Throwing the javelin. 15 f. Handball. 25 f. Running. 100 f. Football.

56. Sir Winston Churchill.

DESIGNS—HORIZ. 10 f., 45 f. Stalin, Roosevelt and Churchill at Teheran Conference, 1943.

1965. Churchill Commem.
423. **56.** 5 f. green (postage) .. 5 5
424. – 10 f. violet and blue .. 8 5
425. **56.** 20 f. brown 15 8
426. – 45 f. blue 35 20
427. **56.** 85 f. cerise (air) .. 75 45

57. Unisphere.

1965. New York World's Fair.
428. **57.** 5 f. plum and blue .. 5 5
429. – 10 f. sepia and green .. 5 5
430. **57.** 25 f. myrtle and brown 15 8
431. – 50 f. myrtle and violet .. 35 20
432. **57.** 85 f. brown and red .. 60 35
DESIGNS: 10 f. Native dancers and drummer. 50 f. Michelangelo's "Pieta".

58. "Laying bricks of peace".

1965. Int. Co-operation Year.
433. **58.** 5 f. violet, orange, yellow and blue 5 5
434. 15 f. brown, orange, yellow and blue .. 10 5
435. – 25 f. indigo, orange, yellow and blue .. 15 8
436. – 40 f. crimson, orange, yellow and blue .. 30 15
437. – 85 f. green, orange, yellow and blue .. 60 35
DESIGNS: 25 f., 40 f. Hands supporting globe 85 f. I.C.Y. emblem.

59. Leonov with Camera.

1965. Astronauts in Space.
438. **59.** 25 f. magenta and blue 20 8
439. – 50 f. brown and green .. 40 20
DESIGN: 50 f. White with rocket-gun.

60. "ONU" and Doves.

1965. U.N. Organisation. 20th Anniv.
440. **60.** 5 f. brown, yellow and blue (postage) .. 5 5
441. – 10 f. blue, turquoise and orange 10 5
442. – 20 f. orge., grn. & apple 15 8
443. – 25 f. bl., turq. & yellow 20 10
444. – 100 f. ochre, blue and light blue (air) .. 90 45
DESIGNS: 10 f. U.N. Headquarters and emblem. 20 f. "ONU" and orchids. 25 f. U.N. Headquarters and Adlai Stevenson. 100 f. "ONU", fruit and ears of wheat.

61. Pope Paul, Aircraft and U.N. Emblem.

1966. Pope Paul's Visit to U.N. Organisation. Multicoloured.
445. 5 f. Type **61** (postage) .. 5 5
446. 15 f. Pope before microphones at U.N. (vert.) 10 5
447. 20 f. Pope and U.N. Headquarters 15 8
448. 30 f. As 15 f. 20 10
449. 45 f. Pope before microphones at U.N., and map (air) 50 25
450. 90 f. Type **61** .. .. 1·00 55

62. W.H.O. Building and Roses.

1966. W.H.O. Headquarters, Geneva. Inaug Multicoloured design showing W.H.O. Building and flower as given.
451. 5 f. Type **62** (postage) .. 5 5
452. 10 f. Alstroemerias .. 5 5
453. 15 f. Asters 10 5
454. 20 f. Freesias 12 8
455. 30 f. Geraniums 20 10
456. 50 f. Asters (air) 45 25
457. 90 f. Type **62** 65 40

63. Surgical Operation.

1966. Togolese Red Cross. 7th Anniv. Multicoloured.
459. 5 f. Type **63** (postage) .. 5 5
460. 10 f. Blood Transfusion .. 5 5
461. 15 f. Type **63** 10 5
462. 30 f. Blood transfusion .. 25 12
463. 45 f. African man & woman 40 15
464. 100 f. J. H. Dunant (air) .. 90 40

1966. Space Achievements. Nos. 438/9 optd. as below or surch. also.
465. 50 f. **(ENVOLEE SURVEYOR 1)** 40 25
466. 50 f. **(ENVOLEE GEMINI 9)** 40 25
467. 100 f. on 25 f. **(ENVOLEE LUNA 9)** 80 45
468. 100 f. on 25 f. **(ENVOLEE VENUS 3)** 80 45

64. Wood-carving.

65. Togolese Man.

1966. Togolese Arts and Crafts.
469. **64.** 5 f. brn., yell. & bl. (post.) 5 5
470. – 10 f. brn., salmon & grn. 8 5
471. – 15 f. brown, yellow & red 12 5
472. – 30 f. brown, bistre & vio. 30 12
473. – 60 f. brown, salmon and blue (air) 55 40
474. **64.** 90 f. brn., yell. & cerise 75 60
DESIGNS: 10 f., 60 f. Basket-making. 15 f. Weaving. 30 f. Pottery.

1966. Air. "DC-8" Air Services Inaug. As T **45** of Central African Republic.
475. 30 f. black, green & yellow 30 20

1966. Togolese Costumes and Dances. Multicoloured.
476. 5 f. Type **65** (postage) .. 5 5
477. 10 f. Togolese woman .. 8 5
478. 20 f. Female dancer .. 12 5
479. 25 f. Male Dancer 20 8
480. 30 f. Dancer in horned helmet 25 10
481. 45 f. Drummer 40 25
482. 50 f. Female dancer (air) .. 45 25
483. 60 f. Dancer in horned helmet 55 30

66. Footballers and Jules Rimet Cup.

1966. World Cup Football Championships, England. Showing football scenes and Jules Rimet Cup.
484. **66.** 5 f. mult. (postage) .. 5 5
485. – 10 f. multicoloured .. 8 5
486. – 20 f. multicoloured .. 15 8
487. – 25 f. multicoloured .. 20 8
488. – 30 f. multicoloured .. 30 10
489. – 45 f. multicoloured .. 40 20
490. – 50 f. mult. (air) .. 45 25
491. – 60 f. multicoloured .. 50 30

67. "Tilapia melanopleura".

1967. Fishes. Multicoloured designs showing fishes, with fishing craft in the background.
493. 5 f. Type **67** (postage) .. 5 5
494. 10 f. "Gnathodon speciosus" 8 5
495. 15 f. "Fistichodus sexfasciatus" 12 5
496. 25 f. "Hemichromis bimaculatus" 20 8
497. 30 f. Type **67** 20 12
498. 45 f. As 10 f. (air) .. 40 25
499. 90 f. As 15 f. 75 50

68. African Boy and Greyhound.

1967. U.N.I.C.E.F. 20th Anniv.
500. **68.** 5 f. multicoloured (post.) 5 5
501. – 10 f. brown, green & apple 8 5
502. **68.** 15 f. blk., brn. & magenta 10 5
503. – 20 f. blk., ultram. & blue 15 8
504. **68.** 30 f. black, blue & olive 25 10
505. – 45 f. bronze, brown and yellow (air) 40 25
506. **68.** 90 f. blk., bronze & blue 70 40
DESIGNS: 10 f. Boy and Irish setter. 20 f. Girl and dobermann. 45 f. Girl and miniature poodle.

69. Launching "Diamant" Rocket.

1967. French Space Achievements. Mult.

508. 5 f. Type **69** (postage) .. 5 5
509. 10 f. Satellite " A-1 " .. 8 5
510. 15 f. Satellite " FR-1 " .. 12 5
511. 20 f. Satellite " D-1 " .. 20 8
512. 25 f. As 10 f. 20 10
513. 40 f. As 20 f. 30 15

514. 50 f. Type **69** (air) 40 25
515. 90 f. As 15 f. 70 35

The 10 f., 20 f., 25 f. and 40 f. are horiz.

70. Bach and Organ.

1967. U.N.E.S.C.O. 20th Anniv. (1966).

517. **70.** 5 f. mult. (postage) .. 5 5
518. – 10 f. multicoloured .. 8 5
519. – 15 f. multicoloured .. 12 5
520. 20 f. multicoloured .. 20 5
521. – 30 f. multicoloured .. 25 8

522. **70.** 45 f. multicoloured (air) 40 20
523. – 90 f. multicoloured .. 70 30

DESIGNS: 10 f., 90 f., Beethoven, violin and clarinet. 15 f., 30 f. Duke Ellington, saxophone, trumpet and drums. 20 f. Debussy, grand piano and harp.

71. British Pavilion and Lilies.

1967. World Fair, Montreal. Multicoloured.

525. 5 f. Type **71** (postage) .. 5 5
526. 10 f. French Pavilion and roses 8 5
527. 30 f. " Africa Place " and strelitzia 20 8
528. 45 f. As 10 f. (air) 30 20
529. 60 f. Type **71** 60 25
530. 90 f. As 30 f. 75 40
531. 105 f. U.S. pavilion and daisies 80 45

72. " Peace ".

1967. Air. Disarmament. Designs showing sections of the " Peace " mural by J. Zanetti at the U.N. Headquarters Building Conf. Room.

533. **72.** 5 f. multicoloured .. 5 5
534. A. 15 f. multicoloured .. 12 5
535. B. 30 f. multicoloured .. 15 5
536. **72.** 45 f. multicoloured .. 25 15
537. A. 60 f. multicoloured .. 45 20
538. B. 90 f. multicoloured .. 70 30

73. Lions Emblem with Supporters.

1967. Lions Int. 50th Anniv. Multicoloured.

540. 10 f. Type **73** 8 5
541. 20 f. Flowers and Lions emblem 15 5
542. 30 f. Type **73** 20 10
543. 45 f. As 20 f. 85 15

74. Antelopes.

1967. Wildlife.

544. **74.** 5 f. brown & pur. (post.) 5 5
545. – 10 f. blue, red & yellow 8 5
546. – 15 f. black, lilac & green 12 5
547. – 20 f. blue, sepia & yellow 20 5
548. – 25 f. brn., yellow & olive 20 10
549. – 30 f. blue, violet & yell. 25 15

550. – 45 f. brown & blue (air) 35 25
551. – 60 f. black, brown & grn. 70 30

DESIGNS: 10 f., 20 f., 30 f. Montagu's harriers (birds of prey). 15 f. Zebra. 25 f. Leopard. 45 f. Lion. 60 f. Elephants.

1967. Air. U.A.M.P.T. 5th Anniv. As T **95** of Cameroun.

552. 100 f. brown, blue & green 85 40

75. Stamp Auction and Togo Stamps—1 m. (German) of 1900 and 100 f. Conference of 1964.

1967. 1st Togolese Stamps. 70th Anniv. Multicoloured.

553. 5 f. Type **75** (postage) .. 5 5
554. 10 f. Exhibition and 1d. (British) of 1915 and 50 f. I.T.U. of 1965 .. .. 8 5
555. 15 f. stamp shop and 50 c. (French) of 1924 .. 12 5
556. 20 f. Stamp-packet vending machine and 5 f. U.N. of 1965 .. .. .. 15 5
557. 30 f. As 15 f. 20 10
558. 45 f. As 10 f. 30 15

559. 90 f. Type **75** (air) .. 60 30
560. 105 f. Father and son with album and 1 f. Kennedy of 1964 .. .. .. 85 45

1967. West African Monetary Union. 5th Anniv. As T **54** of Dahomey.

562. 30 f. blue and green .. 20 12

76. Long-jumping.

1967. Olympic Games, Mexico and Grenoble (1968). Multicoloured.

563. 5 f. Type **76** (postage) .. 5 5
564. 15 f. Ski-jumping .. 8 5
565. 30 f. Relay Runners .. 20 10
566. 45 f. Bob-sleighing .. 30 12

567. 60 f. As 30 f. (air) .. 45 25
568. 90 f. Type **76** 75 40

1967. National Day (29 Sept.) Nos. 525/31 optd. **JOURNEE NATIONALE DU TOGO 29 SEPTEMBRE 1967.**

570. 5 f. multicoloured (postage) 5 5
571. 10 f. multicoloured .. 8 5
572. 30 f. multicoloured .. 25 10

573. 45 f. multicoloured (air) .. 40 15
574. 60 f. multicoloured .. 45 25
575. 90 f. multicoloured .. 65 40
576. 105 f. multicoloured .. 90 45

77. " The Gleaners " (Millet) and Benin Phosphate Mine.

1968. Paintings and Local Industries.

577. **77.** 10 f. multicoloured .. 5 5
578. A. 20 f. multicoloured .. 15 5
579. **77.** 30 f. multicoloured .. 25 8
580. A. 45 f. multicoloured .. 35 12
581. **77.** 60 f. multicoloured .. 40 15
582. A. 90 f. multicoloured .. 65 35

DESIGN: A, " The Weaver at the Loom " (Van Gogh) and textile plant, Dadia.

78. Brewing beer.

1968. Benin Brewery. Multicoloured.

583. 20 f. Type **78** 12 5
584. 30 f. " Drinking at a Bar " (detail from painting by Manet) 25 10
585. 45 f. Bottling-washing machine and bottle of Benin beer 35 20

The 30 f. is a vert. design.

79. Decade Emblem and Sunflowers. **81.** Dr. Adenauer and Europa " Key ".

80. Viking Ship and Portuguese Brigantine.

1968. Int. Hydrological Decade.

586. **79.** 30 f. mult. (postage) .. 25 10
587. 60 f. multicoloured (air) 55 25

1968. Lome Port. Inaug. Multicoloured.

588. 5 f. Type **80** (postage) .. 5 5
589. 10 f. Fulton's steamboat and modern line 8 5
590. 20 f. Quayside, Lome Port 15 8
591. 30 f. Type **80** 25 10

592. 45 f. As 10 f. (air) .. 40 25
593. 90 f. American atomic vessel " Savannah " 65 45

1968. Adenauer Commem.

595. **81.** 90 f. multicoloured .. 65 30

82. " Dr. Turp's Anatomy Lesson " (Rembrandt).

1968. World Health Organization. 20th Anniv. Paintings. Multicoloured.

596. 15 f. " Explosion from the Garden of Eden " (Michelangelo) (postage) .. 10 5
597. 20 f. Type **82** 15 8
598. 30 f. " Johann Deyman's Anatomy Lesson " (Rembrandt) 25 12
599. 45 f. " Christ healing the sick " (Raphael) .. 35 15

600. 60 f. As 30 f. (air) 50 35
601. 90 f. As 45 f. 70 25

83. Wrestling.

1968. Olympic Games, Mexico. Multicoloured.

603. 15 f. Type **83** (postage) .. 10 5
604. 20 f. Boxing 15 5
605. 30 f. Japanese wrestling .. 25 10
606. 45 f. Running 35 15

607. 60 f. Type **83** (air) .. 45 20
608. 80 f. Running 65 45

84. " Try Your Luck ". **85.** Scout and Tent.

1968. National Lottery. 2nd Anniv. Multicoloured.

610. 30 f. Type **84** 25 12
611. 45 f. Lottery ticket, horseshoe and cloverleaf .. 35 15

1968. Air. " Philexafrique " Stamp Exn., Abidjan (Ivory Coast 1969) (1st Issue). As T **109** of Cameroun. Multicoloured.

612. 100 f. " The Letter " (J. A. Franquelin) 90 75

1968. Togolese Scouts. Multicoloured.

613. 5 f. Type **85** (postage) .. 5 5
614. 10 f. Scoutmaster with cubs 8 5
615. 20 f. Giving first aid .. 15 5
616. 30 f. Scout game 25 10
617. 45 f. As 10 f. 35 15

618. 60 f. As 20 f. (air) .. 45 20
619. 90 f. As 30 f. 65 30

The 10, 20, 45 and 60 f. are horiz.

86. " The Adoration of the Shepherds " (Giorgione).

1968. Christmas Paintings. Multicoloured.

621. 15 f. Type **86** (postage) .. 10 5
622. 20 f. " The Adoration of the Kings " (Brueghel) .. 15 8
623. 30 f. " The Adoration " (Botticelli) 25 10
624. 45 f. " The Adoration " (Durer) 35 15

625. 60 f. As 20 f. (air) .. 45 20
626. 90 f. As 45 f. 65 30

87. Martin Luther King.

1969. Human Rights Year.

628. **87.** 15 f. grn. & chest. (post.) 10 5
629. – 20 f. violet & turq.-blue 15 8
630. **87.** 30 f. indigo & vermilion 20 12
631. – 45 f. cerise and olive .. 30 15

632. – 60 f. ult. & purple (air) 45 20
633. **87.** 90 f. brown and green 65 30

PORTRAITS: 20 f. Prof. Rene Cassin (Nobel Peace Prize-winner). 45 f. Pope John XXIII. 60 f. Robert F. Kennedy.

1969. Air. " Philexafrique " Stamp Exn. Abidjan, Ivory Coast (2nd Issue). As T **110** of Cameroun.

635. 50 f. red, brown and green 40 35

DESIGN: 50 f. Aledjo Rock and stamp of 1900.

88. Football.

1969. Sports Stadium, Lome. Inauguration.

636. **88.** 10 f. brn. red & grn. (post.) 5 5
637. – 15 f. brn., bl. & orge .. 10 5
638. – 20 f. brn., grn. & yell... 12 8

639. – 30 f. brn., blue & grn... 20 10
640. – 45 f. brn., vio. & orge... 30 15
641. – 60 f. brn., red & bl. (air) 45 20
642. – 90 f. brn., mauve & blue 65 30

DESIGNS: 15 f. Handball. 20 f. Volleyball. 30 f. Basketball. 45 f. Tennis. 60 f. Boxing. 90 f. Cycling.

89. Module landing on Moon.

1969. 1st Man on the Moon. Multicoloured.
644. 1 f. Type **89** (postage) .. 5 5
645. 20 f. Astronaut and module on Moon 12 5
646. 30 f. As Type **89** 20 10
647. 45 f. As No. 645 .. .. 30 15
648. 60 f. Astronaut exploring lunar surface (air) .. 50 20
649. 100 f. Astronaut gathering Moon rock 75 30

90. "The Last Supper" (Tintoretto). **91.** Bank in Hand and Emblem.

1969. Religious Paintings. Multicoloured.
651. 5 f. Type **90** 5 5
652. 10 f. "Christ's Vision at Emmaus" (Velaquez) .. 5 5
653. 20 f. "Pentecost" (El Greco) 10 5
654. 30 f. "The Assumption" (Botticelli) 15 8
655. 45 f. As 10 f. 25 15
656. 90 f. As 20 f. (air) .. 65 35

1969. Eisenhower Commem. Nos. 628/33 optd. with Eisenhower's silhouette and **EN MEMOIRE DWIGHT D. EISENHOWER 1890-1969.**
658. **87.** 15 f. grn. & chest. (post.) 8 5
659. – 20 f. violet & turq.-blue 10 8
660. **87.** 30 f. indigo & vermilion 15 10
661. – 45 f. cerise and olive .. 25 15
662. – 60 f. ultramarine and purple (air) 35 25
663. **87.** 90 f. brown and green.. 70 45

1969. African Development Bank. 5th Anniv. Multicoloured.
665. 30 f. Type 91 (post.) .. 15 8
666. 45 f. Locomotive in hand, and emblem 25 15
667. 100 f. Farmer and cattle in hand, and emblem (air) 75 30

92. Dunant and Red Cross Workers.

1969. League of Red Cross Societies. 50th Anniv. Multicoloured.
668. 15 f. Type **92** (postage) 8 5
669. 20 f. Pasteur and help for flood victims 10 8
670. 30 f. Fleming and flood control 15 10
671. 45 f. Rontgen and Red Cross post 25 15
672. 60 f. As 45 f. (air) .. 40 20
673. 90 f. Type **92** 60 35

93. Weeding Corn.

1969. Young Pioneers Agricultural Organization. Multicoloured.
675. 1 f. Type **93** (postage) .. 5 5
676. 2 f. Glidji Agricultural Centre 5 5
677. 3 f. Founding meeting .. 5 5
678. 4 f. Glidji class 5 5
679. 5 f. Student "pyramid" 5 5
680. 7 f. Students threshing .. 5 5
681. 8 f. Gardening instruction 5 5
682. 10 f. Co-op village .. 5 5
683. 15 f. Students gardening.. 5 5
684. 20 f. Cattle-breeding .. 8 5
685. 25 f. Poultry-farming .. 10 8
686. 30 f. Independence parade 12 8
687. 40 f. Boys on high-wire .. 15 10
688. 45 f. Tractor and trailer.. 20 12
689. 50 f. Co-op village .. 25 15
690. 60 f. Tractor-driving tuition 30 20
691. 90 f. Harvesting manioc (air) 55 30
692. 100 f. Gardening instruction 65 45
693. 200 f. Thinning-out corn.. 1·40 90
694. 250 f. Drummers marching 2·10 1·10
695. 500 f. Young pioneers marching .. .. 4·00 2·25

94. Books and Map. **95.** George Washington.

1969. Int. African Library Development Assn. 12th Anniv.
700. **94.** 30 f. multicoloured .. 15 12

1969. Christmas. No. 644/5 and 647/9 optd. **JOYEUX NOEL.**
701. 1 f. Type 89 (postage) .. 10 5
702. 20 f. Astronaut and module on Moon.. .. 30 15
703. 45 f. As No. 699 .. 65 30
704. 60 f. Astronaut exploring lunar surface (air) .. 90 40
705. 100 f. Astronaut gathering Moon rock .. .. 1·25 65

1969. "Leaders of World Peace". Multicoloured.
707. 15 f. Type **95** (postage) 5 5
708. 20 f. Albert Luthule .. 8 5
709. 30 f. Mahatma Gandhi .. 12 8
710. 45 f. Simon Bolivar .. 20 15
711. 60 f. Friedrich Ebert (air) 40 25
712. 90 f. As 30 f. 60 40

96. "Ploughing" (Klodt).

1970. Int. Labour Organization. 50th Anniv. Paintings. Multicoloured.
713. 5 f. Type **96** (postage) .. 5 5
714. 10 f. "Gardening" (Pissarro) 5 5
715. 20 f. "Harvesting Fruit" (Rivera) 10 5
716. 30 f. "Seeds of Spring" (Van Gogh) 15 10
717. 45 f. "Workers of the Fields" (Rivera) 25 15
718. 60 f. As 30 f (air) .. 40 20
719. 90 f. As 45 f 55 30

97. Model Coiffures.

1970. Togolese Hair styles. Multicoloured.
721. 5 f. Type **97** (postage) .. 5 5
722. 10 f. As T **97**, but different styles 5 5
723. 20 f. Fefe style 10 8
724. 30 f. Danmlongbedji style 15 10
725. 45 f. Blom style (air) .. 25 20
726. 90 f. Aklui styles .. 50 40
Nos. 723/5 are vert.

98. Togo Stamp and Independence Monument, Lome.

1970. Independence. 10th Anniv. Multicoloured.
727. 20 f. Type **98** (postage) .. 10 5
728. 30 f. Pres. Eyadema and Palace 12 8
729. 50 f. Map, dove and monument (vert.) .. 25 15
730. 60 f. Togo stamp and monument (air) 45 20

99. New U.P.U. Headquarters Building.

1970. New U.P.U. Headquarters Building.
731. **99.** 30 f. violet and orange (postage) 15 8
732. 50 f. red and blue (air) .. 35 20

100. Italy and Uruguay.

1970. World Cup Football Championships, Mexico. Multicoloured.
733. 5 f. Type **100** (postage) .. 5 5
734. 10 f. England and Brazil.. 5 5
735. 15 f. Russia and Mexico.. 8 5
736. 20 f. Germany and Morocco 10 8
737. 30 f. Rumania and Czechoslovakia 15 10
738. 50 f. Sweden and Israel (air) 30 25
739. 60 f. Bulgaria and Peru .. 35 30
740. 90 f. Belgium and Salvador 55 45

101. Lenin.

1970. Lenin. Birth Cent. Multicoloured.
742. 30 f. Type **101** (postage).. 15 12
743. 50 f. "Peasant messengers with Lenin" (Serov) (air) 35 20

102. British Pavilion.

1970. "Expo 70", Osaka, Japan. Mult.
744. 2 f. Pennants, Sanyo Pavilion (57×36 mm.).. 5 5
745. 20 f. Type **102** 10 8
746. 30 f. French Pavilion .. 15 10
747. 50 f. Soviet Pavilion .. 25 15
748. 60 f. Japanese Pavilion .. 30 20

103. Armstrong, Collins and Aldrin.

1970. "Apollo" Moon Flights. Multicoloured.
750. 1 f. Type **103** (postage) .. 5 5
751. 2 f. U.S. flag and moon-rock 5 5
752. 20 f. Astronaut and module on Moon.. .. .. 10 8
753. 30 f. Conrad, Gordon and Bean 15 10
754. 50 f. As 2 f. 30 15
755. 200 f. Lovell, Haise and Swigert ("Apollo 13") (air) .. .. .. 1·25 70

1970. Safe Return of "Apollo 13". As Nos. 750/55 but additionally inscr. FELICITATIONS BON RETOUR APOLLO XIII.
757. **103.** 1 f. multicoloured (postage) 5 5
758. – 2 f. multicoloured .. 5 5
759. – 20 f. multicoloured .. 10 8
760. – 30 f. multicoloured .. 15 8
761. – 50 f. multicoloured .. 30 15
762. – 200 f. multicoloured (air) 1·10 75

104. "Euchloron megaera".

1970. Butterflies and Moths. Multicoloured.
764. 1 f. Type **104** (postage) .. 5 5
765. 2 f. "Cymothoe sangaris" 5 5
766. 30 f. "Danaus chrysippus" 15 10
767. 50 f. "Morpho" 30 15
768. 60 f. Type **104** (air) .. 40 20
769. 90 f. "Pseudacraea boisduvali" 55 30

105. Painting by Velasquez (I.L.O.).

1970. United Nations. 25th Anniv. Multicoloured.
770. 1 f. Type **105** (postage) .. 5 5
771. 15 f. Painting by Delacroix (F.A.O.).. .. .. 5 5
772. 20 f. Painting by Holbein (U.N.E.S.C.O.) .. 10 8
773. 30 f. Painting of U.N. H.Q., New York.. .. 12 10
774. 50 f. Painting by Renoir (U.N.I.C.E.F.) 25 15
775. 60 f. Painting by Van Gogh (U.P.U.) (air) .. 40 20
776. 90 f. Painting by Carpaccio (W.H.O./O.M.S.) .. 55 30

ALBUM LISTS
Write for our latest lists of albums and accessories. These will be sent free on request.

106. " The Nativity " (Botticelli).

1970. Christmas. " Nativity " Paintings by Old Masters. Multicoloured.

778. 15 f. Type **106** (postage) .. 5 5
779. 20 f. Veronese 8 5
780. 30 f. El Greco 12 8
781. 50 f. Fra Angelico 25 10
782. 60 f. Botticelli (different) (air) 30 20
783. 90 f. Tiepolo 55 30

1971. De Gaulle Commemoration (1st issue). Nos. 708/9, 711/2 optd. **EN MEMOIRE Charles De Gaulle 1890–1970** or surch. in addition.

785. 30 f. mult. (postage) .. 15 8
786. 30 f. on 90 f. multicoloured 15 8
787. 150 f. on 20 f. multicoloured 90 40
788. 200 f. on 60 f. mult. (air) .. 1·25 80

109. De Gaulle and Churchill.

1971. De Gaulle Commemoration. (2nd issue).

789. **109.** 20 f. bl. & blk. (postage) 10 5
790. – 30 f. red and black .. 15 8
791. – 40 f. green and black 25 10
792. – 50 f. brown and black 35 15
793. – 60 f. vio. & blk. (air) 40 20
794. – 90 f. blue and black .. 55 35

DESIGNS: 30 f. De Gaulle with Eisenhower. 40 f. With Pres. Kennedy. 50 f. With Adenauer. 60 f. With Pope Paul VI. 90 f. General De Gaulle.

110. Shepard and Moon Exploration.

1971. Moon Mission of " Apollo 14 ". Mult.

796. 1 f. Type **110** (postage) .. 5 5
797. 10 f. Mitchell and rock-gathering 5 5
798. 30 f. Launch and Moon .. 12 8
799. 40 f. Launch from Moon .. 20 10
800. 50 f. " Apollo 14 " emblem (air) 30 20
801. 100 f. As 40 f. 55 35
802. 200 f. As 50 f. .. .. 1·10 60

111. "The Resurrection" (after Raphael).

1971. Easter. Paintings of "The Resurrection" by various artists. Multicoloured.

804. 1 f. Type **111** (postage) .. 5 5
805. 30 f. Master of Trebon .. 15 8
806. 40 f. Type **111** 20 10
807. 50 f. M. Grunewald (air) .. 30 15
808. 60 f. As 30 f. 45 20
809. 90 f. El Greco 55 30

112. Cocoa Tree and Pods.

1971. Int. Cocoa Day. Multicoloured.

811. 30 f. Type **112** (postage) .. 12 5
812. 40 f. Sorting beans .. 20 8
813. 50 f. Drying beans 30 15
814. 60 f. Agricultural Ministry, Lome (air) 40 20
815. 90 f. Type **112** 55 35
816. 100 f. As 40 f. 65 45

113. Airliner over Control-tower.

1971. A.S.E.C.N.A. Tenth Anniv.

817. **113.** 30 f. multicoloured (postage) 15 10
818. **113.** 100 f. multicoloured (air) 65 45

114. Napoleon.

1971. Napoleon. 150th Death Anniv. Embossed on gold foil.

819. **114.** 1,000 f. gold .. .. 5·00

115. Great Market, Lome.

1971. Tourism. Multicoloured.

821. 20 f. Type **115** (postage) .. 8 5
822. 30 f. Wooden sculpture and protea 15 8
823. 40 f. Aledjo Gorge and baboon 20 10
824. 50 f. Vale Castle and antelope (air) 20 12
825. 60 f. Lake Togo and alligator 25 15
826. 100 f. Furnace, Tokpli, and hippopotamus 45 25

116. Gbatchoume Image.

1971. Togolese Religions. Multicoloured.

827. 20 f. Type **116** (postage) .. 5 5
828. 30 f. High priest, Temple of Atta Sakuma .. 8 5
829. 40 f. "Holy Stone" ceremony 15 8
830. 50 f. Moslem worshippers, Lome Mosque (air) .. 20 12
831. 60 f. Protestants 25 15
832. 90 f. Catholic ceremony, Djogbegan Monastery 40 25

1971. Memorial Issue for "Soyuz 11" Astronauts. Nos. 799/802 optd. **EN MEMOIRE DOBROVOLSKY - VOLKOV - PATSAYEV SOYUZ 11** or surch. also.

834. 40 f. multicoloured (postage) 20 12
835. 90 f. on 50 f. multicoloured (air) 40 25
836. 100 f. multicoloured .. 45 30
837. 200 f. multicoloured .. 90 45

117. Ice-skating.

1971. Winter Games, Sapporo, Japan (1972). Multicoloured.

839. 1 f. Type **117** (postage) .. 6 5
840. 10 f. Slalom skiing 5 5
841. 20 f. Figure-skating .. 8 5
842. 30 f. Bob-sleighing .. 10 8
843. 50 f. Ice-hockey 25 12
844. 200 f. Ski-jumping (air) .. 90 45

1971. Air. African and Malagasy Posts and Telecommunications Union. 10th Anniv. As T **153** of Cameroun. Multicoloured.

845. 100 f. U.A.M.P.T. H.Q. and Adjogobo dancers .. 45 30

118. Togolese Child and Mask.

1971. Air. " Children of the World ". Embossed on gold foil.

847. **118.** 1,500 f. gold .. .. 8·00

119. Wooden Crocodile.

1971. U.N.I.C.E.F. 25th Anniv. Mult.

848. 20 f. Type **119** (postage) .. 8 5
849. 30 f. Toy " Bambi " and butterfly 12 8
850. 40 f. Toy monkey 20 10
851. 50 f. Wooden elephant on wheels 25 15
852. 60 f. Toy turtle (air) .. 25 15
853. 90 f. Toy parrot 40 20

120. " Virgin and Child " (Botticelli).

1971. Christmas. " Virgin and Child " Paintings by Old Masters. Multicoloured.

855. 10 f. Type **120** (postage) .. 5 5
856. 30 f. (Maitre de la Vie de Marie) 15 8
857. 40 f. (Durer) 20 12
858. 50 f. (Veronese) 25 15
859. 60 f. (Giorgione) (air) .. 25 20
860. 100 f. (Raphael) 45 30

INDEX

Countries can be quickly located by referring to the index at the end of this volume.

121. St. Mark's Basilica, Venice.

1972. U.N.E.S.C.O. " Save Venice " Campaign. Multicoloured.

862. 30 f. Type **121** (postage) .. 12 8
863. 40 f. Rialto Bridge .. 15 10
864. 100 f. Doge's Palace (air) .. 45 35

122. " The Crucifixion " (unknown artist).

1972. Easter. Religious Paintings. Mult.

866. 25 f. Type **122** (postage) 10 8
867. 30 f. " The Deposition " (Botticelli) 12 8
868. 40 f. Type **122** 15 10
869. 50 f. " The Resurrection " (Thomas de Coloswar) (air) 20 15
870. 100 f. " The Ascension " (Mantegna) 40 30

123. Heart Emblem and Blacksmith.

125. Washerwoman.

124. Hotel de la Paix, Lome.

1972. World Heart Month. Multicoloured.

872. 30 f. Type **123** (postage) .. 12 8
873. 40 f. Typist 15 10
874. 60 f. Javelin-thrower .. 25 15
875. 100 f. Type **123** (air) .. 45 30

1972. O.C.A.M. Summit Conf., Lome. Embossed on gold foil.

876. **124.** 1,000 f. gold, red & grn. 5·00

1972. Pres. Nixon's Visit to China. Nos. 823/4 optd. **VISITE DU PRESIDENT NIXON EN CHINE FEVRIER 1972.** and additionally surch. (No. 879).

878. 300 f. on 40 f. mult. (post.) 1·10 80
879. 50 f. multicoloured (air) .. 25 15

1972. Cassava Industries. Multicoloured.

880. 25 f. Collecting cassava (horiz.) (postage) .. 10 5
881. 40 f. Type **125** 15 10
882. 60 f. Cassava truck and factory (horiz.) (air) .. 25 15
883. 80 f. Mother with Benin tapioca cake 35 20

126. Videotelephone.

127. Basketball.

1972. World Telecommunications Day. Multicoloured.
884. 40 f. Type **126** (postage) .. 15 10
885. 100 f. "Intelsat 4" and map of Africa (air) .. 45 30

1972. Air. Pres. Nixon's Visit to Russia. No. 743, surch. **VISITE DU PRESIDENT NIXON EN RUSSIE MAI 1972,** and value.
886. 300 f. on 50 f. multicoloured 1·25 90

1972. Olympic Games, Munich. Mult.
887. 30 f. Type **127** (postage) .. 12 8
888. 40 f. Running 15 10
889. 50 f. Throwing the discus .. 20 12
890. 90 f. Gymnastics (air) .. 45 30
891. 200 f. Type **127** 90 50

128. Pin-tailed Whydah.

1972. Exotic Birds. Multicoloured.
893. 25 f. Type **128** (postage) .. 10 8
894. 30 f. Paradise whydah .. 12 10
895. 40 f. "Coliuspasser macrocercus" 15 12
896. 60 f. Sakabula (weaver bird) 25 20
897. 90 f. Ring-necked parakeet (air) 40 30

129. Paul Harris (founder). **130.** "Mona Lisa" (L. da Vinci).

1972. Rotary International. Multicoloured.
899. 40 f. Type **129** (postage) .. 15 10
900. 50 f. Rotary and Togo flags 20 12
901. 60 f. Rotary emblem, map and laurel (air) 25 15
902. 90 f. As 50 f. 40 30
903. 100 f. Type **129** 45 35

1972. Famous Paintings. Multicoloured.
905. 25 f. Type **130** (postage) .. 12 8
906. 40 f. "Virgin and Child" (Bellini) 15 10
907. 60 f. "Mystical Marriage of St. Catherine" (Master P.N.'s assistant) (air) .. 25 15
908. 80 f. "Self-portrait" (L. da Vinci) 30 20
909. 100 f. "St. Marie and Angels" (Botticelli) .. 45 30

1972. West African Monetary Union. 10th Anniv. As T **109** of Dahomey.
911. 40 f. brn., grey and red .. 15 12

131. Party H.Q. of R.P.T., Pres. Pompidou and Eyadama.

1972. Visit of President Pompidou to Togo. Multicoloured.
912. 40 f. Type **131** (postage) .. 15 12
913. 100 f. Party H.Q. rear view and portraits as T **131** (air) 45 35

MINIMUM PRICE

The minimum price quoted is 5p which represents a handling charge rather than a basis for valuing common stamps. For further notes about prices see introductory pages.

132. Goethe. **133.** "The Annunciation" (unknown artist).

1972. Air. Goethe. 140th Death Anniv.
914. **132.** 100 f. multicoloured .. 45 35

1972. Christmas. Religious Paintings. Multicoloured.
915. 25 f. Type **133** (postage) .. 10 8
916. 30 f. "The Nativity" (Master Theodor of Prague) 12 10
917. 40 f. Type **133** 15 12
918. 60 f. As 30 f. (air) 25 15
919. 80 f. "The Adoration of the Magi" (unknown artist) 35 25
920. 100 f. "The Flight into Egypt" (Giotto) 45 35

134. R. Follerau and Allegory.

1973. "World Day of the Leper".
(a) Postage. Follereau Foundation. 20th Anniv.
922. **134.** 40 f. violet and green .. 15 12
(b) Air. Hansen's bacillus Discovery. Cent.
923. – 100 f. blue and red .. 45 35
DESIGN: 100 f. Dr. Hanson, microscope and bacillus slide.

135. W.H.O. Emblem. **136.** The Crucifixion.

1973. W.H.O. 25th Anniv.
924. **135.** 30 f. multicoloured .. 12 8
925. 40 f. multicoloured .. 15 10

1973. Easter. Multicoloured.
926. 25 f. Type **136** (postage) .. 10 8
927. 30 f. The Deposition .. 12 10
928. 40 f. The Resurrection .. 15 12
929. 90 f. "Christ in Majesty" (air) 40 25

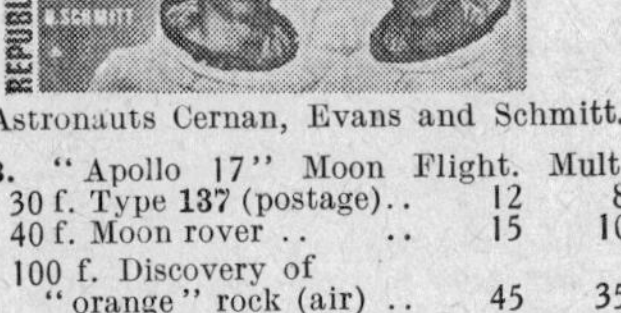

137. Astronauts Cernan, Evans and Schmitt.

1973. "Apollo 17" Moon Flight. Mult.
931. 30 f. Type **137** (postage) .. 12 8
932. 40 f. Moon rover 15 10
933. 100 f. Discovery of "orange" rock (air) .. 45 35
934. 200 f. Pres. Kennedy and lift-off 90 55

138. Erecting Tent. **139.** Heliocentric System.

1973. Int., Scout Congress. Nairobi/Addis Ababa. Multicoloured.
936. 10 f. Type **138** (postage) .. 5 5
937. 20 f. Cooking meal (horiz.) 8 5
938. 30 f. Rock-climbing .. 12 8
939. 40 f. Type **138** 15 10
940. 100 f. Canoeing (horiz.) (air) 45 35
941. 200 f. As 20 f. 90 55

1973. Copernicus. 500th Birth Anniv. Multicoloured.
943. 10 f. Type **139** (postage) .. 5 5
944. 20 f. Copernicus 8 5
945. 30 f. "Astronomy" and "Astronautics" .. 12 8
946. 40 f. Astrolabe 15 12
947. 90 f. Type **139** (air) .. 40 30
948. 100 f. As 20 f. 45 35

140. Ambulance Team.

1973. Togolese Red Cross. Multicoloured.
950. 40 f. Type **140** (postage) .. 15 10
951. 100 f. Dove of peace, sun and map (air) 45 35

1973. "Drought Relief". African Solidarity. No. 766 surch. **SECHERESSE SOLIDARITE AFRICAINE** and value.
952. 100 f. on 30 f. multicoloured 40 35

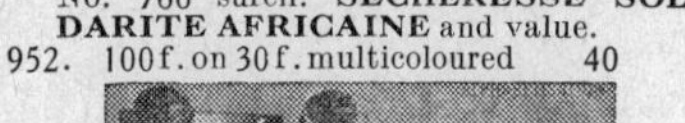

141. Classroom.

1973. Literacy Campaign. Multicoloured.
953. 30 f. Type **141** (postage) .. 15 8
954. 40 f. African reading book (vert.) 15 8
955. 90 f. Classroom (different) (air) 40 30

1973. African and Malagasy Posts and Telecommunications Union. As T **182** of Cameroun.
956. 100 f. red, yellow and pur. 45 35

142. Interpol Emblem and H.Q. Paris. **143.** W.M.O. Emblem in Weather-vane.

1973. Interpol. 50th Anniv.
957. **142.** 30 f. grn., brn. & yell. 15 8
958. 40 f. bl., mauve & grn. 15 8

1973. W.M.O. Centenary.
959. **143.** 40 f. grn., brn. & yell. (post.) 15 10
960. **143.** 200 f. brn., vio. & blue (air) 90 55

144. Togo Stamp and Locomotives.

1973. Togolese Postal Services. 75th Anniv. Multicoloured.
961. 25 f. Type **144** (postage) .. 10 8
962. 30 f. Togo stamp and mail coaches 12 8
963. 90 f. Togo stamps and mail-boats 45 35
964. 100 f. Togo stamps and mail-planes (air) .. .. 1·00 70

145. Kennedy and A. Schaerf. **146.** Flame Emblem and "People".

1973. Pres. Kennedy's 10th Death Anniv.
966. **145.** 20 f. violet and black on blue (postage) .. 10 8
967. – 30 f. brown and black on brown 12 10
968. 40 f. grn. & blk. on grn. 15 12
969. 90 f. purple and black on mauve (air) .. 40 35
970. – 100 f. blue & blk. on bl. 45 35
971. – 200 f. brn. & blk. on brn. 90 55
DESIGNS: 30 f. Kennedy and Harold Macmillan. 40 f. Kennedy and Adenauer. 90 f. Kennedy and Charles de Gaulle. 100 f. Kennedy and Konrad Nikita Kruschev. 200 f. Kennedy and "Apollo" spacecraft.

1973. Air. Declaration of Human Rights. 25th Anniv.
973. **146.** 250 f. multicoloured .. 1·10 70

147. "Virgin and Child" (anon.). **149.** "Girl Before Mirror" (Picasso).

148. Footballers.

1973. Christmas. Multicoloured.
974. 25 f. Type **147** (postage) .. 10 8
975. 30 f. "Adoration of the Magi" (Vivarini) .. 12 10
976. 90 f. "Virgin and Child" (S. di Pietro) (air) .. 40 35
977. 100 f. "Adoration of the Magi" (anon.) 45 35

1974. Lome District Rotary International Convention. Nos. 899, 901 and 903 optd. **PREMIERE CONVENTION 210eme DISTRICT FEVRIER 1974 LOME.**
979. **129.** 40 f. mult. (postage) .. 15 12
980. – 60 f. mult. (air) .. 25 20
981. **129.** 100 f. multicoloured .. 45 35

1974. World Cup Football Championships, Munich.
982. **148.** 20 f. mult. (postage) .. 10 8
983. – 30 f. multicoloured .. 12 10
984. – 40 f. multicoloured .. 15 12
985. – 90 f. mult. (air) .. 40 35
986. – 100 f. multicoloured .. 45 35
987. – 200 f. multicoloured .. 90 55
DESIGNS: Nos. 983/7, similar designs to T **148**, showing footballers in action.

1974. World Food Programme. 10th Anniv. Nos. 880/1 optd. **10e ANNIVERSAIRE DU P. A. M.** or surch. also.
989. **125.** 40 f. multicoloured .. 15 12
990. – 100 f. on 25 f. mult. .. 45 35

1974. Picasso Commemoration. Mult.
991. 20 f. Type **149** (postage) .. 10 8
992. 30 f. "The Turkish Shawl" 12 10
993. 40 f. "Mandoline and Guitar" 15 12
994. 90 f. "The Muse" (air) .. 40 35
995. 100 f. "Les Demoiselles d'Avignon" 45 35
996. 200 f. "Sitting Nude" .. 90 55

150. Kpeme Village. **151.** Togolese Postman.

1974. Coastal Scenes. Multicoloured.
998. 30 f. Type **150** (postage) 12 10
999. 40 f. Tropicana tourist village 15 12
1000. 90 f. Fisherman on Lake Togo (air) .. 40 30
1001. 100 f. Mouth of Anecho River 45 35

1974. Universal Postal Union. Centenary. Multicoloured.

1003. 30 f. Type **151** (postage) 12 10
1004. 40 f. Postman with cleft carrying-stick 15 12
1005. 50 f. Type **151** (air) .. 20 15
1006. 100 f. As 40 f. 40 30

1974. Council of Accord. 15th Anniv. As T **131** of Dahomey.

1007. 40 f. multicoloured .. 15 12

152. Hauling-in Net. **153.** Earth Station and Probe.

1974. Lagoon Fishing. Multicoloured.

1008. 30 f. Type **152** (postage) 12 10
1009. 40 f. Throwing net .. 15 12
1010. 90 f. Fishes in net (air) .. 40 30
1011. 100 f. Fishing with lines 45 35
1012. 200 f. Fishing with basket (vert.) 90 55

1974. U.S. "Jupiter" Space Mission. Mult.

1014. 30 f. Type **153** (postage) 12 10
1015. 40 f. Probe transmitting to Earth (horiz.) .. 15 12
1016. 100 f. Blast-off (air) .. 45 35
1017. 200 f. Jupiter probe (horiz.) 90 55

1974. "Internaba 1974" Stamp Exhibition Basel. Nos. 884/5 optd. **·INTERNABA 1974 · CENTENARIUM U P U** and emblem.

1019. **126.** 40 f. mult. (postage) 15 12
1020. – 100 f. mult. (air) .. 45 35

154. "Tympanotomus radula". **155.** Groom with Horses.

1974. Seashells. Multicoloured.

1021. 10 f. Type **154** (postage) 5 5
1022. 20 f. "Tonna galea" .. 8 5
1023. 30 f. "Conus mercator" .. 12 10
1024. 40 f. "Cardium costatum" 15 12
1025. 90 f. "Alcithoe ponsonbyi" (air) 40 30
1026. 100 f. "Casmaria iredalei" 45 35

1974. Horse-racing. Multicoloured.

1028. 30 f. Type **155** (postage) 12 10
1029. 40 f. Exercising horses .. 15 12
1030. 90 f. Steeple-chaser taking fence (air) 40 30
1031. 100 f. Horses racing .. 45 35

1974. Air. West Germany's Victory in World Cup Football Championships, Munich. Nos. 890/1 optd. **COUPE DU MONDE DE FOOTBALL MUNICH 1974 VAINQUEURS REPUBLIQUE FEDERALE ALLEMAGNE.**

1033. – 90 f. multicoloured .. 40 35
1034. **127.** 200 f. multicoloured 90 70

156. Leopard.

1974. Wild Animals. Multicoloured.

1036. 20 f. Type **156** (postage) 8 5
1037. 30 f. Giraffes 12 10
1038. 40 f. Two elephants .. 15 12
1039. 90 f. Lion and lioness (air) 40 30
1040. 100 f. Rhinoceros and calf 45 35

157. Herd of Cows.

1974. Pastoral Economy. Multicoloured.

1042. 30 f. Type **157** (postage) 12 10
1043. 40 f. Milking 15 12
1044. 90 f. Cattle at water-hole (air) 40 30
1045. 100 f. Village cattle-pen .. 45 35

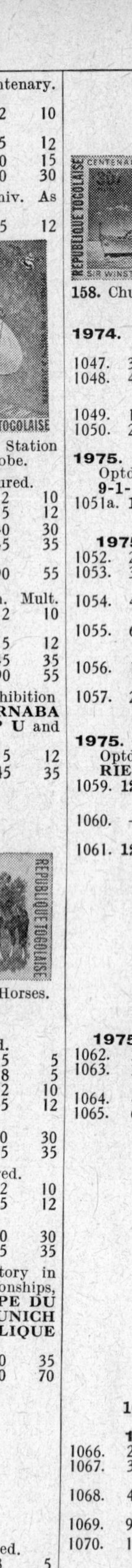

158. Churchill and Frigate. **159.** "Strelitzia reginae".

1974. Sir Winston Churchill. Birth Cent. Multicoloured.

1047. 30 f. Type **158** (postage) 12 10
1048. 40 f. Churchill and fighter aircraft 15 12
1049. 100 f. Type **158** (air) .. 45 35
1050. 200 f. As 40 f. 90 70

1975. Hotel de la Paix, Lome. Opening. Optd. **Inauguration de la l'hotel Paix 9-1-75.**

1051a. **124.** 1000 f. gold, red and green .. .. 5·00

1975. Flowers of Togo. Multicoloured.

1052. 25 f. Type **159** (postage) 10 8
1053. 30 f. "Strophanthus sarmentosus" 12 10
1054. 40 f. "Chlamydocarya macrocarpa" (horiz.) .. 15 12
1055. 60 f. "Clerodendrum scandens" (horiz.) .. 25 20
1056. 100 f. "Clerodendrum thosonae" (horiz.) (air) 45 35
1057. 200 f. "Gloriosa superba" (horiz.) 90 70

1975. Rotary International. 70th Anniv. Optd. **70e ANNIVERSAIRE 23 FEVRIER 1975.**

1059. **129.** 40 f. multicoloured (postage) 20 15
1060. – 90 f. multicoloured (No. 902) (air) .. 50 45
1061. **129.** 100 f. multicoloured 55 50

160. Radio Station, Kamina.

1975. Tourism. Views. Multicoloured.

1062. 25 f. Type **160** 15 12
1063. 30 f. Benedictine Monastery, Zogbegan .. 15 12
1064. 40 f. Causeway, Atchinedji 20 15
1065. 60 f. Ayome Waterfalls .. 35 30

161. " Jesus Mocked (El Greco).

1975. Easter. Multicoloured.

1066. 25 f. Type **161** (postage) 15 12
1067. 30 f. " The Crucifixion " (Master Janoslet) .. 15 12
1068. 40 f. " The Descent from the Cross " (Bellini) .. 20 15
1069. 90 f. " Pieta " (anon.) .. 50 45
1070. 100 f. " Christ Rising from the Grave " (Master MS) (air) 55 50
1071. 200 f. " The Holy Trinity " (detail) (Durer) .. 1·10 1·00

162. Stilt-walking.

1975. Independence. 15th Anniv. Multicoloured.

1073. 25 f. Type **162** (postage) 15 12
1074. 30 f. Dancers 15 12
1075. 50 f. Independence parade (vert.) (air) .. 30 25
1076. 60 f. Dancer (different) .. 35 30

163. Hunting Rabbits with Club.

1975. Hunting. Multicoloured.

1078. 30 f. Type **163** (postage) 15 12
1079. 40 f. Hunting beavers with bow-and-arrow .. 20 15
1080. 90 f. Running deer (air) .. 50 45
1081. 100 f. Hunting boar with shotgun 55 50

164. Pounding Palm-nuts.

1975. Palm-oil Production. Multicoloured.

1082. 30 f. Type **164** (postage) 15 12
1083. 40 f. Extracting palm-oil (vert.) 20 15
1084. 85 f. Marketing palm-oil (vert.) (air) 45 40
1085. 100 f. Oil-processing plant, Alokoegbe 55 50

165. Docking Manoeuvre.

1975. " Apollo-Soyuz " Space Link. Multicoloured.

1087. 30 f. Type **165** (postage) 15 12
1088. 50 f. " Soyuz " spacecraft (vert.) (air) .. 30 25
1089. 60 f. Astronauts Slayton, Brand and Stafford .. 35 30
1090. 90 f. Cosmonauts Leonov and Kubasov 50 45
1091. 100 f. Link-up with U.S. and Soviet flags .. 55 50
1092. 200 f. " Apollo-Soyuz " emblem and Globe .. 1·10 1·00

166. " African Woman ".

1975. International Women's Year.

1094. **166.** 30 f. multicoloured .. 15 12
1095. 40 f. multicoloured .. 20 15

167. Dr. Schweitzer, and Children drinking Milk.

1975. Dr. Albert Schweitzer. Birth Cent. Multicoloured.

1096. 40 f. Type **167** (postage) 20 15
1097. 80 f. Schweitzer playing organ (vert.) (air) .. 45 40
1098. 90 f. Schweitzer feeding pelican (vert.) .. 50 45
1099. 100 f. Schweitzer and Lambarene Hospital .. 55 50

168. " Merchant writing Letter " (V. Carpaccio). **169.** " Virgin and Child " (Mantegna).

1975. International Correspondence Week. Multicoloured.

1101. 40 f. Type **168** (postage) 20 15
1102. 80 f. " Erasmus writing Letter " (Holbein) (air) 45 40

1975. United Nations. 30th Anniv. Nos. 851/3 optd. **30eme Anniversaire des Nations-Unies.**

1103. 50 f. multicoloured (postage) 20 15
1104. 60 f. multicoloured (air) 25 20
1105. 90 f. multicoloured .. 40 35

1975. Air. World Scout Jamboree, Norway. Nos. 940/1 optd. **14eme JAMBOREE MONDIAL DES ECLAIREURS.**

1107. 100 f. multicoloured .. 45 40
1108. 200 f. multicoloured .. 90 85

1975. Christmas. " Virgin and Child " paintings by artists named. Multicoloured.

1110. 20 f. Type **169** (postage) 8 5
1111. 30 f. El Greco 12 10
1112. 40 f. Barend van Orly .. 20 15
1113. 90 f. Federigo Barocci (air) 40 35
1114. 100 f. Bellini 45 40
1115. 200 f. Correggio 90 85

170. Crashed Aircraft.

1976. Pres. Eyadema's Escape in Air-crash at Sara-kawa.

1117. **170.** 50 f. multicoloured .. 20 15
1118. 60 f. multicoloured .. 25 20

171. " Frigates forcing the Hudson Passage ".

1976. American Revolution. Bicent. Mult.

1119. 35 f. Type **171** (postage) 15 12
1120. 50 f. " George Washington " (G. Stuart) (vert.) .. 20 15
1121. 60 f. " Surrender at Burgoyne " (Trumbull) (air) 25 20
1122. 70 f. " Surrender at Trenton " (Trumbull) (vert.) 30 25
1123. 100 f. " Signing of Declaration of Independence " (Trumbull) 45 40
1124. 200 f. " Washington crossing the Delaware " (E. Leutze) 90 85

172. Cable-laying Ship.

1976. Telephone Centenary. Multicoloured.

1126. 25 f. Type **172** (postage) 10 8
1127. 30 f. Automatic telephone and tape-recording equipment 12 10
1128. 70 f. Edison and communications equipment (air) 30 25
1129. 105 f. Alexander Graham Bell, early and modern telephones 45 40

173. Blind Man and Mosquito.

174. A.C.P. and C.E.E. Emblems.

1976 World Health Day. Multicoloured.
1131. 50 f. Type **173** (postage) 20 15
1132. 60 f. Eye Examination (air) 25 20

1976. A.C.P./C.E.E. Treaty (between Togo and European Common Market). 1st Anniv. Multicoloured.
1133. 10 f. Type **174** (postage) 5 5
1134. 50 f. Map of Africa, Europe and Asia 20 15
1135. 60 f. Type **174** (air) .. 25 20
1136. 70 f. As 50 f. 30 25

175. Exhibition Hall. (10th Anniv. Marine Exhibition.)

1976 Anniversaries. Multicoloured.
1137. 5 f. Type **175** (postage).. 5 5
1138. 10 f. Electricity pylon and flags (Ghana–Togo –Dahomey Power Links. 1st Anniv. 5 5
1139. 50 f. Type **175** 20 15
1140. 60 f. As 10 f. (air) .. 25 20

1976. " Interphil '76 " International Stamp Exhibition, Philadelphia. Nos. 1121/4 optd. **INTERPHIL MAI 29 - JUIN 6 1976.**
1142. 60 f. multicoloured .. 25 20
1143. 70 f. multicoloured .. 30 25
1144. 100 f. multicoloured .. 45 40
1145. 200 f. multicoloured .. 90 85

176. Running.

1976. Olympic Games, Montreal. Mult.
1147. 25 f. Type **176** (postage) 10 8
1148. 30 f. Canoeing 12 10
1149. 50 f. High-jumping .. 20 15
1150. 70 f. Sailing (air) .. 30 25
1151. 105 f. Motorcycling .. 45 40
1152. 200 f. Fencing 90 85

177. " Titan 3 " and " Viking " Emblem.

1976. " Viking " Space Mission. Mult.
1153. 30 f. Type **177** (postage) 12 10
1154. 50 f. " Viking " en route–Earth to Mars .. 20 15
1155. 60 f. " Viking landing on Mars " (air) 25 20
1156. 70 f. Nodus Gordii .. 30 25
1157. 100 f. " Viking " over Mare Tyrrhenum 45 40
1158. 200 f. Mars landing (different) 90 85

178. " Young Routy ".

1976. Toulouse-Lautrec (painter). 75th Death Anniv. Multicoloured.
1160. 10 f. Type **178** (postage) 5 5
1161. 20 f. " Helene Vary " .. 8 5
1162. 35 f. " Louis Pascal " .. 15 12
1163. 60 f. " Carmen " (air) .. 25 20
1164. 70 f. " Maurice at the Somme " 30 25
1165. 200 f. " Messalina " .. 90 85

1976. International Children's Day. Nos. 905/1 optd. **" Journee Internationale de L'Enfance ".**
1167. **140.** 40 f. multicoloured (postage) 20 15
1168. – 100 f. multicoloured (air) 45 40

179. " Adoration of the Shepherds " (Pontormo).

1976. Christmas. Nativity scenes by artists named. Multicoloured.
1169. 25 f. Type **179** (postage) 10 8
1170. 30 f. Crivelli .. 12 10
1171. 50 f. Pontormo 20 15
1172. 70 f. Lotto (air) 30 25
1173. 105 f. Pontormo .. 45 40
1174. 200 f. Lotto 90 85

180. " Quaid-i-Azam ".

1976. Mohammad Ali Jinnah, " Quaid-i-Azam". Birth Centenary.
1176. **180.** 50 f. multicoloured .. 20 15

181. Phosphate Complex, Kpeme.

1977. Eyadema Regime. Tenth Anniv. Multicoloured.
1177. 50 f. Type **181** (postage) 20 15
1178. 60 f. Parliament Building, Lome (air) 25 20
1179. 100 f. Crowd greeting Pres. Eyadema 45 40

POSTAGE DUE STAMPS

1921. Postage Due stamps of Dahomey, " Figure " key-type, optd. **TOGO.**
D 54. M. 5 c. green 5 5
D 55. 10 c. red 8 8
D 56. 15 c. grey 12 12
D 57. 20 c. brown 45 45
D 58. 30 c. blue 45 45
D 59. 50 c. black 20 15
D 60. 60 c. orange 20 15
D 61. 1 f. violet 60 60

D **1.** Cotton Growing.

1925. Centres and inscr. in black.
D 97. D **1.** 2 c. blue 5 5
D 98. 4 c. orange 5 5
D 99. 5 c. green 5 5
D 100. 10 c. red 5 5
D 101. 15 c. yellow 5 5
D 102. 20 c. mauve 5 5
D 103. 25 c. grey 8 8
D 104. 30 c. yellow on blue 5 5
D 105. 50 c. grey 5 5
D 106. 60 c. green 10 10
D 107. 1 f. violet 10 10

1927. Surch. in figures and bars.
D 108. D **1.** " 2 f. " on 1 f. mauve and red 50 50
D 109. " 3 f. " on 1 f. blue and brown 50 50

D **2.** Native Mask. D **3.** D **4.** Kon-komba Helmet.

1940.
D 151. D **2.** 5 c. black 5 5
D 152. 10 c. green 5 5
D 153. 15 c. red 5 5
D 154. 20 c. blue 5 5
D 155. 30 c. brown 5 5
D 156. 50 c. olive 15 15
D 157. 60 c. violet 5 5
D 158. 1 f. blue 12 12
D 159. 2 f. red 8 8
D 160. 3 f. violet 8 8

1947.
D 185. D **3.** 10 c. blue 5 5
D 186. 30 c. red 5 5
D 187. 50 c. green 5 5
D 188. 1 f. brown 5 5
D 189. 2 f. red 5 5
D 190. 3 f. black 5 5
D 191. 4 f. blue 5 5
D 192. 5 f. brown 8 8
D 193. 10 f. orange .. 12 12
D 194. 20 f. blue 15 15

1957.
D 214. D **4.** 1 f. violet 5 5
D 215. 2 f. orange 5 5
D 216. 3 f. slate 5 5
D 217. 4 f. red 5 5
D 218. 5 f. blue 8 8
D 219. 10 f. green 15 15
D 220. 20 f. chocolate .. 20 20

1959. As Nos. D 214/20 but colours changed and inscr. "REPUBLIQUE DU TOGO".
D 244. D **4.** 1 f. chestnut .. 5 5
D 245. 2 f. turquoise .. 5 5
D 246. 3 f. orange 5 5
D 247. 4 f. blue 5 5
D 248. 5 f. purple 5 5
D 249. 10 f. violet 8 8
D 250. 20 f. black 12 12

D **5.** " Cardium costatum ".

D **6.** Tomatoes.

1964. Seashells. Multicoloured.
D 366. 1 f. "Conus papilionaceus" 5 5
D 367. 2 f. "Marginella faba" .. 5 5
D 368. 3 f. "Cypraea stercoraria" 5 5
D 369. 4 f. "Strombus latus" .. 5 5
D 370. 5 f. Type D **5** 5 5
D 371. 10 f. "Cancellaria cancellata" 5 5
D 372. 15 f. "Cymbium pepo" 8 8
D 373. 20 f. "Tympanotomus radula" 12 8

1969. Young Pioneers Agricultural Organization. Multicoloured.
D 696. 5 f. Type D **6** 5 5
D 697. 10 f. Corn on the cob .. 5 5
D 698. 19 f. Red pepper .. 5 5
D 699. 20 f. Peanuts 8 8

TOKELAU ISLANDS BC

Three islands situated north of Samoa. Formerly part of the Gilbert and Ellice Is. and known as the Union Is., they were declared part of New Zealand as from 1st Jan., 1949.

1. Atafu Village and Map.

1948
1. **1.** ½d. brown and purple .. 8 15
2. – 1d. red and green 12 15
3. – 2d. green and blue 15 25
DESIGNS: 1d. Nukunonu hut and map. 2d. Fakaofo village and map.

1953. Coronation. As Type **106** of New Zealand.
4. 3d. brown .. .. .. 85 1·50

1956. Surch. **ONE SHILLING.**
5. **1.** 1s. on ½d. brown and purple 60 1·40

1966. Stamps of New Zealand. Surch. **TOKELAU ISLANDS** and value.
6. **56.** 6d. blue 15 20
7. 8d. green 35 40
8. 2s. pink 60 70

1967. Decimal currency. Nos. 1/3 surch.
9. – 1 c. on 1d. (No. 2) 5 5
10. – 2 c. on 2d. (No. 3) 5 5
11. **1.** 10 c. on ½d. (No. 1) .. 20 20

2.

3. British Protectorate (1877).

1968. Arms types of New Zealand without value, surch. as in T **2.**
12. **2.** 3 c. lilac 5 8
13. 5 c. blue 10 10
14. 7 c. emerald 10 12
15. 20 c. pink 50 50

1969. History of Tokelau Islands.
16. **3.** 5 c. ultram., yellow & black 10 10
17. – 10 c. vermilion, yell. & blk. 15 15
18. – 15 c. green, yellow & black 25 25
19. – 20 c. brown, yellow & black 35 35
DESIGNS: 10 c. Annexed to Gilbert and Ellice Islands (1916). 15 c. New Zealand Administration (1925). 20 c. New Zealand Territory (1948).

1969. Christmas. As T **178** of New Zealand.
20. 2 c. multicoloured .. 10 15

1970. Christmas. As T **187** of New Zealand.
21. 2 c. multicoloured 10 15

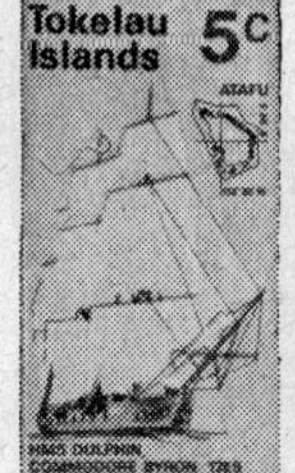

4. H.M.S. " Dolphin ", 1765.

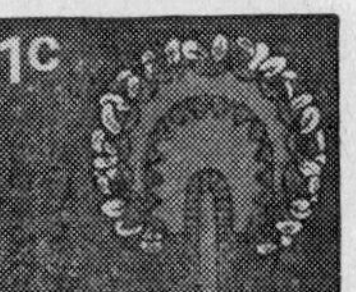

5. Fan.

1970. Discovery of Tokelau Is. Multicoloured.
22. 5 c. Type **4** 10 10
23. 10 c. H.M.S. " Pandora ", 1791 .. .. 20 20
24. 25 c. " General Jackson ", 1835 .. .. .. 45 45
The 25 c. is horiz.

1971. Handicrafts. Multicoloured.
25. 1 c. Type **5** 5 5
26. 2 c. Hand-bag 5 5
27. 3 c. Basket 5 5
28. 5 c. Hand-bag 5 5
29. 10 c. Shopping-bag .. 10 12
30. 15 c. Hand-bag 15 20
31. 20 c. Canoe 20 25
32. 25 c. Fishing hooks .. 25 30

6. Windmill Pump.

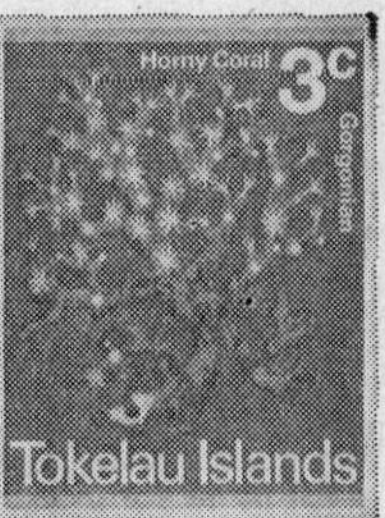

7. Horny Coral.

1972. South Pacific Commission. 25th Anniv. Multicoloured.
33. 5 c. Type **6** 10 10
34. 10 c. Community well .. 20 20
35. 15 c. Pest eradication .. 30 30
36. 20 c. Flags of member nations 25 30
In No. 35 " PACIFIC " is spelt " PACFIC ".

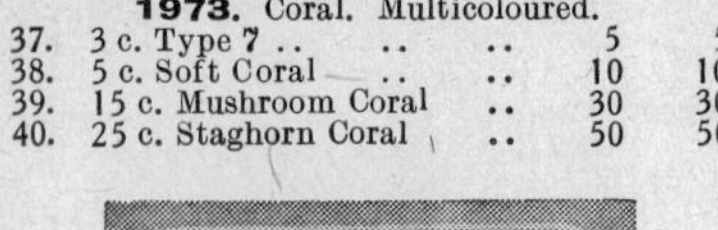

1973. Coral. Multicoloured.

37.	3 c. Type **7**	5	5
38.	5 c. Soft Coral	10	10
39.	15 c. Mushroom Coral	30	30
40.	25 c. Staghorn Coral	50	50

8. Hump-back Cowrie.

1975. "Shells of the Coral Reef" Multicoloured.

41.	3 c. Type **8**	5	5
42.	5 c. Tiger Cowrie	8	8
43.	15 c. Mole Cowrie	25	25
44.	25 c. Eyed Cowrie	35	40

9. Moorish Idol.

1975. Fishes. Multicoloured.

45.	5 c. Type **9**	5	5
46.	10 c. Long-nosed Butterfly-fish	8	10
47.	15 c. Lined Butterfly-fish	15	20
48.	25 c. Red Fire-fish	25	30

10. Canoe Making.

1976. Multicoloured.

49.	1 c. Type **10**	5	5
50.	2 c. Reef fishing	5	5
51.	3 c. Weaving preparation	5	5
52.	5 c. Uma (kitchen)	5	5
53.	9 c. Carving	8	10
54.	20 c. Husking coconuts	20	20
55.	50 c. Wash day	50	55
56.	$1 Meal time	1·00	1·10

TOLIMA O1

One of the states of the Granadine Confederation.

A department of Colombia from 1886, now uses Colombian stamps.

1.

2

3.

1870. On white or coloured paper. Imperf.

12. **1.**	5 c. black	18·00	12·00
13.	10 c. black	18·00	12·00

1871. Various frames. Imperf.

14. **2.**	5 c. brown	50	50
15. **3.**	10 c. blue	1·40	1·40
16.	50 c. green	2·25	2·25
17.	1 p. red	4·50	4·50

4.

5.

6.

7.

8.

9.

1879. Imperf.

18a.**4.**	5 c. brown	15	15
19. **5.**	10 c. blue	20	20
20a.**6.**	50 c. green	20	25
21a.**7.**	1 p. red	80	90

1883. Imperf.

22. **4.**	5 c. orange	20	20
23 **5.**	10 c. red	35	35
24. **8.**	20 c. violet	50	50

1884. Imperf.

25. **9.**	1 c. grey	8	8
26.	2 c. rose	8	8
27.	2½ c. orange	8	8
28.	5 c. brown	8	8
29a.	10 c. blue	12	15
30.	20 c. yellow	30	30
31.	25 c. black	15	15
32.	50 c. green	20	20
33.	1 p. red	25	25
34.	2 p. violet	40	30
35.	5 p. orange	25	25
36.	10 p. rose	60	60

10.

11.

1886. Condor's wings touch Arms. Perf.

37. **10.**	5 c. brown	40	40
38.	10 c. blue	1·75	1·75
39.	50 c. green	55	55
40.	1 p. red	1·25	1·25

1886. Condor's wings do not touch Arms. Perf. or imperf.

45. **11.**	1 c. grey	2·50	2·50
46.	2 c. claret	3·25	3·25
47.	2½ c. pink	9·00	11·00
48.	5 c. brown	3·50	3·50
49.	10 c. blue	6·00	6·00
50.	20 c. yellow	3·25	3·25
51.	25 c. black	3·00	3·00
52.	50 c. green	1·40	1·10
53.	1 p. red	2·25	2·25
54.	2 p. violet	4·00	4·00
55.	5 p. orange	7·50	7·50
56.	10 p. rose	3·50	3·50

12.

13.

1888. Perf.

67. **12.**	1 c. blue on rose	15	15
68.	2 c. green on green	15	15
69.	5 c. red	8	8
70.	10 c. green	20	25
71.	20 c. blue on yellow	30	30
65.	50 c. blue	45	45
72.	1 p. brown	55	55

1903. Imperf. or perf.

85. **13**	4 c. black on green	10	10
78.	10 c. blue	8	8
87.	20 c. orange	10	10
88.	50 c. black on red	12	12
81.	1 p. brown	5	5
82.	2 p. grey	5	5
91.	5 p. red	5	5
92.	10 p. black on blue	12	12
92a.	10 p. black on green	12	12

TONGA BC

(Or Friendly Is.) A group of islands in the S. Pacific Ocean. An independent Polynesian kingdom formerly under British protection, Tonga became a member of the Commonwealth in June 1970.

1967. 100 seniti = 1 pa'anga (10s.).

1. King George I.

ILLUSTRATIONS British Commonwealth and all overprints and surcharges are FULL SIZE. Foreign Countries have been reduced to ¾-LINEAR.

1886.

1b. **1.**	1d. red	30·00	8·00
2.	2d. violet	9·00	6·00
3.	6d. blue	6·00	3·00
9.	6d. orange	6·00	8·00
4ba.	1s. green	9·00	3·75

1891. Surch. with value in words.

5. **1.**	4d. on 1d. red	2·00	4·50
6.	8d. on 2d. violet	14·00	16·00

1891. Optd. with stars in upper right and lower left corners.

7. **1.**	1d. red	18·00	18·00
8.	2d. violet	17·00	17·00

2. Arms of Tonga.

3. King George I.

1892.

10a.**2.**	1d. red	6·00	9·00
11. **3.**	2d. olive	4·50	7·00
12. **2.**	4d. brown	10·00	13·00
13. **3.**	8d. mauve	20·00	22·00
14.	1s. brown	18·00	18·00

1893. Surch in figures.

15. **2.**	½d. on 1d. blue	13·00	13·00
16. **3.**	2½d. on 2d. green	7·00	6·00
18.	7½d. on 6d. red	19·00	19·00

1893. Surch. in words.

17. **2.**	5d. on 4d. orange	6·00	7·00

1894. Surch. vert. **SURCHARGE** and value in words.

21. **2.**	½d. on 4d. brown	2·00	5·00
22. **3.**	½d. on 1s. brown	2·00	6·00
25.	1d. on 2d. blue	10·00	12·00

1894 Surch. vert. **SURCHARGE** and value in figures.

26a. **3.**	1½d. on 2d. blue	11·00	12·00
27.	2½d. on 2d. blue	14·00	16·00
23.	2½d. on 8d. mauve	2·00	6·00
24b. **1.**	2½d. on 1s. green	7·00	10·00
28a. **3.**	7½d. on 2d. blue	25·00	25·00

4. King George II.

5. Arms.

6. Ovava tree, Kana-Kubolu.

11. View of Haapai.

1895.

29. **4.**	1d. green	7·00	8·00
30.	2½d. red	12·00	14·00
31.	5d. blue	6·00	7·00
32.	7½d. yellow	6·00	10·00

1895. Surch. vert. **SURCHARGE,** and value in words or figures.

33. **4.**	½d. on 2½d. red	12·00	15·00
34.	1d. on 2½d. red	8·00	12·00
35.	7½d. on 2½d. red	22·00	25·00

1896. Nos. 26a and 28a surch. with typewritten **Half-Penny** and Tongan inscription.

36. **3.**	½d. on 1½d. on 2d. blue	55·00	—
37.	½d. on 7½d. on 2d. blue	7·00	9·00

1897.

38. **5.**	½d. blue	30	30
74.	½d. green	8	12
75. **6.**	1d. black and red	15	30
42. –	2d. sepia & yellow-brown	70	1·00
43. –	2½d. black and blue	80	1·00
78. –	3d. black and green	3·00	3·50
45. –	4d. green and purple	3·00	3·50
46. –	5d. black and orange	2·75	3·50
79. –	6d. red	30	30
48. –	7½d. black and green	2·50	5·50
49. –	10d. black and red	5·00	6·00
50. –	1s. black and brown	3·50	4·50
51. **11.**	2s. black and blue	7·00	9·00
81. –	2s. 6d. purple	1·75	2·25
82. –	5s. black and red	1·25	2·00

DESIGNS—As T **14**: 2d., 2½d., 5d., 7½d., 10d., 1s. King George II. As T **6**: HORIZ. 3d. Prehistoric trilith at Haamonga. 4d. Breadfruit. VERT. 6d. Coral. As T **11**: VERT. 2s. 6d. Parrot. HORIZ. 5s. Vavau Harbour.

1899. Royal Wedding. Optd. **T-L 1 June, 1899.**

54. **6.**	1d. black and red	10·00	15·00

14.

15.

Queen Salote.

1920.

56. **14.**	1½d. black	20	60
57.	2d. slate-purple & violet	1·25	1·75
76.	2d. black and purple	10	20
58.	2½d. black and blue	1·40	3·00
77.	2½d. blue	12	25
60.	5d. black and orange	2·00	2·75
61.	7½d. black and green	80	1·40
62.	10d. black and red	2·00	2·75
80.	1s. black and brown	30	65

1923. Nos. 46 and 48/82 surch. **TWO PENCE PENI-E-UA.**

64.	2d. on 5d. black and orange	80	1·00
65.	2d. on 7½d. black and green	8·00	10·00
66.	2d. on 10d. black and red	7·00	8·50
67.	2d. on 1s. black and brown	10·00	12·00
68.	2d. on 2s. black and blue	2·00	4·00
69.	2d. on 2s. 6d. purple	2·25	3·25
70.	2d. on 5s. black and red	1·75	2·50

1938. Queen Salote's Accession. 20th Anniv. Dated "1918–1938" at foot.

71. **15.**	1d. black and red	30	70
72.	2d. black and purple	1·50	1·40
73.	2½d. black and blue	1·50	2·25

1944. Silver Jubilee of Queen Salote's Accession. Tablet at foot dated "1918–1943".

83. **15.**	1d. black and red	10	15
84.	2d. black and violet	12	20
85.	3d. black and green	15	25
86.	6d. black and orange	25	35
87.	1s. black and brown	30	45

1949. U.P.U. As T **14/7** of Antigua.

88.	2½d. blue	12	10
89.	3d. olive	20	25
90.	6d. red	25	25
91.	1s. brown	30	35

16. Queen Salote.

DESIGN — VERT. 1s. Half-length portrait of Queen.

17. Queen Salote.

1950. Queen Salote's 50th Birthday

92. **16.**	1d. red	15	25
93. **17.**	5d. green	40	45
94. –	1s. violet	50	60

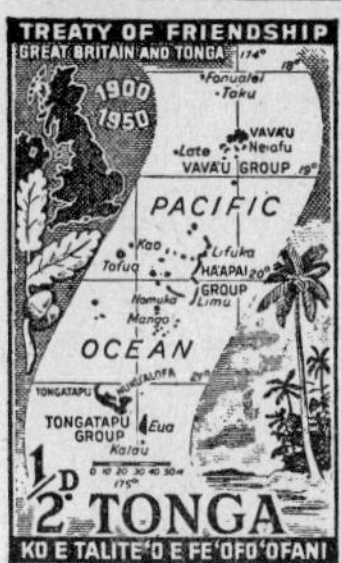

18. Map.

DESIGNS — HORIZ. 2$\frac{1}{2}$d. Beach scene. 5d. Flag and island. 1s. Arms of Tonga and G.B. VERT. 3d. H.M.N.Z.S. "Bellona".

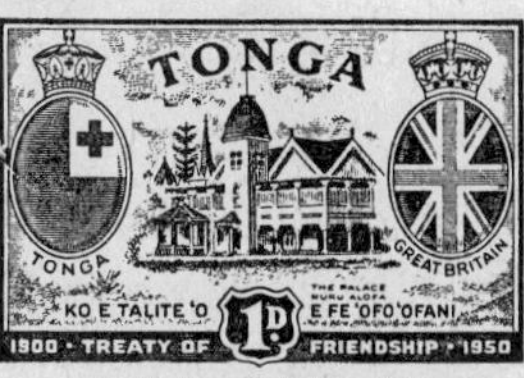

19. Palace, Nuku'alofa.

1951. Treaty of Friendship with Gt. Britain. 50th Anniv.
95. **18.** $\frac{1}{2}$d. green 20 25
96. **19.** 1d. black and red .. 30 30
97. – 2$\frac{1}{2}$d. green and brown .. 40 30
98. – 3d. yellow and blue .. 70 75
99. – 5d. red and green .. 70 90
100. – 1s. orange and violet .. 1·10 1·40

20. Royal Palace, Nuku'alofa.

1953.
101. **20.** 1d. black and brown .. 5 5
102. – 1$\frac{1}{2}$d. blue and green .. 5 5
103. – 2d. turquoise and black 5 5
104. – 3d. blue and green .. 5 5
105. – 3$\frac{1}{2}$d. yellow and red .. 5 5
106. – 4d. yellow and red .. 8 8
107. – 5d. blue and brown .. 8 8
108. – 6d. black and blue .. 8 8
109. – 8d. green and violet .. 10 10
110. – 1s. blue and black .. 12 12
111. – 2s. olive and brown .. 25 30
112. – 5s. yellow and lilac .. 70 1·25
113. – 10s. yellow and black .. 1·50 1·50
114. – £1 yellow, red and blue 2·25 2·50

DESIGNS—HORIZ. 1$\frac{1}{2}$d. Shore fishing with throw net. 2d. Ketch and canoe. 3$\frac{1}{2}$d. Map of Tongatapu. 4d. Vava'u Harbour. 5d. P.O., Nuku'alofa. 6d. Aerodrome, Fua'amotu. 8d. Nuku'alofa Wharf. 2s. Lifuka, Ha'apai. 5s. Mutiny of the "Bounty". VERT. 3d. Swallows' Cave, Vava'u. 1s. Map of Tonga Islands. 10s. Queen Salote. £1 Arms of Tonga.

21. Stamp of 1886.

1961. Tongan Postal Service. 75th Anniv.
115. **21.** 1d. red & brown-orange 10 10
116. – 2d. blue 10 12
117. – 4d. blue-green 15 15
118. – 5d. violet 15 20
119. – 1s. brown 35 40

DESIGNS: 2d. Whaler and longboat. 4d. Queen Salote and Post Office, Nuku'alofa. 5d. Mail steamer. 1s. Mailplane over Tongatapu.

1962. Emancipation Cent. Stamps of 1953 and No. 117 optd. **1862 TAU'ATAINA EMANCIPATION 1962** or surch. also.
120. 1d. black and brown .. 12 12
121. 4d. blue-green (No. 117) .. 20 20
122. 5d. blue and brown .. 20 20
123. 6d. black and blue .. 25 25
124. 8d. green and violet .. 25 25
125. 1s. blue and black .. 30 30
126. 2s. on 3d. blue and green .. 50 75
127. 5s. yellow and lilac .. 1·25 1·50

22. "Protein Foods".

1963. Freedom from Hunger.
128. **22.** 11d. blue 25 30

23. Coat of Arms.

1963. First Polynesian Gold Coinage Commemoration. Circular designs, backed with paper, inscr. overall "TONGA THE FRIENDLY ISLANDS". Imperf.

(a) Postage. $\frac{1}{4}$ koula coin. Diameter 1$\frac{5}{8}$ in.
129. **23.** 1d. red on gold .. 5 5
130. A. 2d. blue on gold .. 8 8
131. **23.** 6d. green on gold .. 12 12
132. A. 9d. purple on gold .. 15 15
133. **23.** 1s. 6d. violet on gold .. 30 35
134. A. 2s. green on gold .. 40 45

(b) Air. (i) $\frac{1}{2}$ koula coin. Diameter 2$\frac{1}{8}$ in.
135. B. 10d. red on gold .. 20 20
136. **23.** 11d. green on gold .. 25 25
137. B. 1s. 1d. blue on gold .. 25 30

(ii) 1 koula coin. Diameter 3$\frac{1}{8}$ in.
138. B. 2s. 1d. purple on gold .. 45 50
139. **23.** 2s. 4d. green on gold .. 50 55
140. B. 2s. 9d. violet on gold .. 60 70

DESIGNS: A, Queen Salote (head). B. Queen Salote (full length).

24. Red Cross Emblem.

1963. Red Cross Cent.
141. **24.** 2d. red and black .. 8 8
142. 11d. red and blue .. 25 35

25. Queen Salote.

26. Map of Tongatapu.

(Illustrations reduced to approx. $\frac{2}{3}$ size.)

1964. Pan-Pacific South-East Asia Women's Assn. Meeting, Nuku'alofa. T 25/6 backed with paper inscr. overall "TONGA THE FRIENDLY ISLANDS". Imperf.
143. **25.** 3d. pink (postage) .. 5 5
144. 9d. blue 10 12
145. 2s. yellow-green .. 25 30
146. 5s. lilac 60 70
147. **26.** 10d. blue-green (air) .. 12 12
148. 1s. 2d. black 15 20
149. 3s. 6d. cerise 40 50
150. 6s. 6d. violet 70 80

1965. "Gold Coin" stamps of 1963 surch. and with star over old value.
151. **23.** 1s. 3d. on 1s. 6d. (post.) 15 15
152. A. 1s. 9d. on 9d. 20 20
153. **23.** 2s. 6d. on 6d. 30 35
154. 5s. on 1d. .. .. 10·00 11·00
155. A. 5s. on 2d. .. .. 2·50 2·75
156. 5s. on 2s. .. .. 1·00 1·25
157. B. 2s. 3d. on 10d. (air) .. 15 20
158. **23.** 2s. 9d. on 11d. .. 20 20
159. B. 4s. 6d. on 2s. 1d. .. 10·00 10·00
160. **23.** 4s. 6d. on 2s. 4d. .. 10·00 10·00
161. B. 4s. 6d. on 2s. 9d. .. 10·00 10·00

1966. Tupou College and Secondary Education. Cent. Nos. 115/6 and 118/9 optd. or surch. **1866-1966 TUPOU COLLEGE & SECONDARY EDUCATION.**
162. **21.** 1d. red and brown-orge. (postage) .. 5 5
163. 3d. on 1d. red and brown-orange 8 8
164. – 6d. on 2d. blue .. 10 10
165. – 1s. 2d. on 2d. blue .. 15 15
166. – 2s. on 2d. blue .. 25 30
167. – 3s. on 2d. blue .. 35 40

As above optd. but with additional **AIRMAIL & CENTENARY.**
168. – 5d. violet (air) .. 5 5
169. **21.** 10d. on 1d. red and orge.-brown 12 12
170. – 1s. brown 15 15
171. – 2s. 9d. on 2d. blue .. 35 40
172. – 3s. 6d. on 5d. violet .. 40 45
173. – 4s. 6d. on 1s. brown .. 50 60

1966. Queen Salote Commem. "Women's Assn." stamps optd. (a) **IN MEMORIAM QUEEN SALOTE 1900+1965.** (b) **1900 1965**+flower emblem. or surch. also. Inscr. and new figures of value in first colour and obliterating shapes in second colour given.

(a) Postage.
174. **25.** 3d. (silver and blue) .. 5 5
175. 5d. on 9d. (silver and black) 5 5
176. 9d. (silver and black) .. 10 10
177. 1s. 7d. on 3d. (silver & blue) 20 20
178. 3s. 6d. on 9d. (silver & black) 40 45
179. 6s. 6d. on 3d. (silver & blue) 70 80

(b) Air.
180. **26.** 10d. (silver and black) .. 12 12
181. 1s. 2d. (black and gold) 15 15
182. 4s. on 10d. (silver & black) 45 50
183. 5s. 6d. on 1s. 2d. (black & gold) 60 70
184. 10s. 6d. on 1s. 2d. (gold & black) .. .. 1·25 1·40

1967. Various stamps surch. **SENITI** or **Seniti** and value.
185. 1s. on 1d. (101) 5 5
186. 2s. on 4d. (106) 5 5
187. 3s. on 5d. (107) 5 5
188. 4s. on 5d. (107) 5 5
189. 5s. on 3$\frac{1}{2}$d. (105) 5 5
190. 6s. on 8d. (109) 8 8
191. 7s. on 1$\frac{1}{2}$d. (102) 10 10
192. 8s. on 6d. (108) 10 10
193. 9s. on 3d. (104) 12 12
194. 10s. on 1s. (110) 12 12
195. 11s. on 3d. on 1d. (163) .. 15 15
196. 21s. on 3s. on 2d. (167) .. 25 30
197. 23s. on 1d. (101) 30 30
198. 30s. on 2s. (111) 50 55
199. 30s. on 2s. (111) 50 55
200. 50s. on 6d. (108) 65 70
201. 60s. on 2d. (103) 80 90

No. 198 is surch. **Seniti**, No. 199, **SENITI.**

28. Banana.

27. Coat of Arms (reverse).

1967. Coronation of King Taufa'ahau IV. Circular designs, backed with paper inscr. overall "TONGA, THE FRIENDLY ISLANDS" etc. Imperf.

Sizes:
(a) Diameter 1$\frac{1}{2}$ in. (d) Diameter 2$\frac{3}{10}$in.
(b) Diameter 1$\frac{7}{10}$ in. (e) Diameter 2$\frac{7}{10}$ in.
(c) Diameter 2 in. (f) Diameter 2$\frac{9}{10}$ in.

202. **27.** 1 s. orge. & bl. (b) (post.) 5 5
203. A. 2 s. blue & magenta (c) 5 5
204. **27.** 4 s. green and purple (d) 5 8
205. A. 15 s. turq. & violet (e) .. 20 25
206. **27.** 28 s. black & purple (a) 40 45
207. A. 50 s. red & ultram. (c) .. 65 75
208. **27.** 1 p. blue and red (f) .. 1·25 1·50
209. A. 7 s. red & black (b) (air) 10 10
210. **27.** 9 s. purple and green (c) 12 12
211. A. 11 s. blue & orange (d) 15 15
212. **27.** 21 s. black and green (e) 25 30
213. A. 23 s. purple and green (a) 35 35
214. **27.** 29 s. blue and green (c) 40 45
215. A. 2 p. purple & orge. (f) .. 2·50 2·75

DESIGN: A King Taufa'ahau IV (obverse).

The commemorative coins depicted in reverse (type 27) are inscribed in various denominations as follows: 1 s. – "20 SENITI"; 4 s. – "PA'ANGA"; 9 s. – "50 SENITI"; 21 s. – "TWO PA'ANGA"; 28 s. – "QUARTER HAU"; 29 s. "HALF HAU"; 1 p. "HAU".

1967. Arrival of U.S. Peace Corps in Tonga. As Nos. 101/13 but imperf. in different colours and surch. **The Friendly Islands welcome the United States Peace Corps** and new value (or $ only).
216. 1 s. on 1d. black & yell. (postage) 5 5
217. 2 s. on 2d. blue and red .. 5 5
218. 3 s. on 3d. brown & yellow 5 5
219. 4 s. on 4d. violet and yellow 8 8
220. 5 s. on 5d. green and yellow 10 10
221. 10 s. on 1s. red and yellow 15 15
222. 20 s. on 2s. claret and blue 25 30
223. 50 s. on 5s. sepia and yellow 65 75
224. 1 p. on 10s. orange-yellow 1·25 1·50
225. 11 s. on 3$\frac{1}{2}$d. ultram. (air) 15 15
226. 21 s. on 1$\frac{1}{2}$d. green .. 25 30
227. 23 s. on 3$\frac{1}{2}$d. ultramarine .. 30 30

1968. Various stamps surch. (a) Postage.
228. 1 s. on 1d. (No. 101) .. 5 5
229. 2 s. on 4d. (No. 106) .. 5 5
230. 3 s. on 3d. (No. 104) .. 5 5
231. 4 s. on 5d. (No. 107) .. 5 5
232. 5 s. on 2d. (No. 103) .. 5 5
233. 6 s. on 6d. (No. 108) .. 8 8
234. 7 s. on 1$\frac{1}{2}$d. (No. 102) .. 10 10
235. 8 s. on 8d. (No. 109) .. 10 12
236. 9 s. on 3$\frac{1}{2}$d. (No. 105) .. 12 12
237. 10 s. on 1s. (No. 110) .. 15 15
238. 20 s. on 5s. (No. 112) .. 25 30
239. 2 p. on 2s. (No. 111) .. 2·50 2·75

(b) Surch. with **AIRMAIL** added.
240. 11 s. on 10s. (No. 113) .. 15 15
241. 21 s. on 10s. (No. 113) .. 30 30
242. 23 s. on 10s. (No. 113) .. 35 35

1968. 50th Birthday of King Taufa'ahua IV. Nos. 202/15 optd. **H.M.'s BIRTHDAY 4 JULY 1968.**
243. **27.** 1 s. orange and blue (post.) 5 5
244. A. 2 s. blue and magenta .. 5 5
245. **27.** 4 s. green and purple .. 8 8
246. A. 15 c. turquoise & violet 20 25
247. **27.** 28 s. black and purple .. 35 40
248. A. 50 s. red and ultram. .. 65 75
249. **27.** 1 p. blue and red .. 1·25 1·40
250. A. 7 s. red and black (air) .. 10 10
251. **27.** 9 s. purple and green .. 12 12
252. A. 11 s. blue and orange .. 15 15
253. **27.** 21 s. black and green .. 25 30
254. A. 23 s. purple and green .. 30 30
255. **27.** 29 s. blue and green .. 40 45
256. A. 2 p. purple and orange .. 2·50 2·75

1968. South Pacific Games Field and Track Trials, Port Moresby, New Guinea. As Nos. 101/13 surch.
257. 5 s. on 5d. grn. & yell. (post.) 8 8
258. 10 s. on 1s. red and yellow 12 15
259. 15 s. on 2s. claret and blue 20 25
260. 25 s. on 2d. ultramarine & red 30 35
261. 50 s. on 1d. black & yellow 65 75
262. 75 s. on 10s. orge. & yellow 95 1·10
263. 6 s. on 6d. blk. & yell. (air) 8 8
264. 7 s. on 4d. violet & yellow 8 10
265. 8 s. on 8d. black & yellow 10 12
266. 9 s. on 1$\frac{1}{2}$d. emerald .. 12 12
267. 11 s. on 3d. chestnut & yell. 15 15
268. 21 s. on 3$\frac{1}{2}$d. ultramarine .. 25 30
269. 38 s. on 5s. sepia and yellow 50 60
270. 1 p. on 10s. yellow .. .. 1·25 1·40

1969. Emergency Provisionals. Various stamps (Nos. 273/6 are imperf. and in different colours), surch. (a) Postage.
271. 1 s. on 1s. 2d. ultram. (No. 165) 10 12
272. 1 s. on 2s. on 2d. ultram. (No. 166) 10 12
273. 1 s. on 6d. black and yellow (No. 108) 5 5
274. 2 s. on 3$\frac{1}{2}$d. ultram. (No. 105) 5 5
275. 3 s. on 1$\frac{1}{2}$d. green (No. 102) 5 5
276. 4 s. on 8d. black and yellow (No. 109) 8 8

(b) Air. Nos. 171/3 surch.
277. 1 s. on 2s. 9d. on 2d. ultram. 10 12
278. 1 s. on 3s. 6d. on 5d. violet 10 12
279. 1 s. on 4s. 6d. on 1s. brown 10 12

1969. Imperf. Self-adhesive.
280. **28.** 1 s. red, black and yellow 5 5
281. 2 s. green, black & yellow 5 5
282. 3 s. violet, black & yellow 8 8
283. 4 s. ultram., black & yell. 10 10
284. 5 s. grn., black & yellow 12 12

See also Nos. 325/9, O 45/9, 413/17, and O 82/6.

29. Putting the Shot.

1969. 3rd South Pacific Games, Port Moresby. Imperf., Self-adhesive.
285. **29.** 1 s. blk., red & buff (post.) 5 5
286. 3 s. green, red and buff.. 5 5
287. 6 s. green, red and buff.. 10 10
288. 10 s. ultram., red & buff 15 15
289. 20 s. blue, red and buff.. 45 45

290. – 9 s. black, violet and orange (air) 15 15
291. – 11 s. black, violet & orge. 15 15
292. – 20 s. blk., grn. & orange 30 30
293. – 60 s. black, cerise & orge. 1·00 1·00
294. – 1 p. black, green & orge. 1·60 1·60
DESIGN: Nos. 290/4, Boxing.

30. Oil Derrick and Map.

1969. Oil Search. Imperf. Self-adhesive.
295. **30.** 3 s. multicoloured (post.) 5 5
296. 7 s. multicoloured .. 12 12
297. 20 s. multicoloured .. 40 40
298. 25 s. multicoloured .. 50 50
299. 35 s. multicoloured .. 65 65

300. – 9 s. multicoloured (air) 20 20
301. – 10 s. multicoloured .. 20 20
302. – 24 s. multicoloured .. 45 45
303. – 29 s. multicoloured .. 60 60
304. – 38 s. multicoloured .. 80 80
DESIGN: Nos. 300/4, Oil Derrick and island of Tongatapu.

31. Members of the British and Tongan Royal Families.

(Reduced size illustration. Actual size 54 × 49 mm.).

1970. Royal Visit. Imperf., Self-adhesive.
305. **31.** 3 s. blue, gold and black (postage) 5 5
306. 5 s. emerald, gold & black 10 10
307. 10 s. orge., gold & black 20 20
308. 25 s. purple, gold & black 50 50
309. 50 s. red, gold and black 1·00 1·00

310. – 7 s. multicoloured (air) 15 15
311. – 9 s. multicoloured .. 20 20
312. – 24 s. multicoloured .. 50 50
313. – 29 s. multicoloured .. 60 60
314. – 38 s. multicoloured .. 80 80
DESIGN: Nos. 310/14, Queen Elizabeth II and King Taufu'ahau Tupou IV.

32. Book, Tongan Rulers and Flag.

(Reduced size illustration. Actual size 69 × 38 mm.).

1970. Entry into British Commonwealth. Imperf. Self-adhesive.
315. **32.** 3 s. multicoloured (post.) 5 5
316. 7 s. multicoloured .. 15 15
317. 15 s. multicoloured .. 30 30
318. 25 s. multicoloured .. 50 50
319. 50 s. multicoloured .. 1·00 1·00

320. – 9 s. blue, gold & red (air) 15 15
321. – 10 s. pur., gold & blue 20 20
322. – 24 s. yell., gold & green 50 50
323. – 29 s. blue, gold and red 60 60
324. – 38 s. yell., gold & green 80 80
DESIGN: ("Star" shape. Size 44 × 51 mm.). Nos. 320/24, Star and King Taufa'ahua Tupou IV.

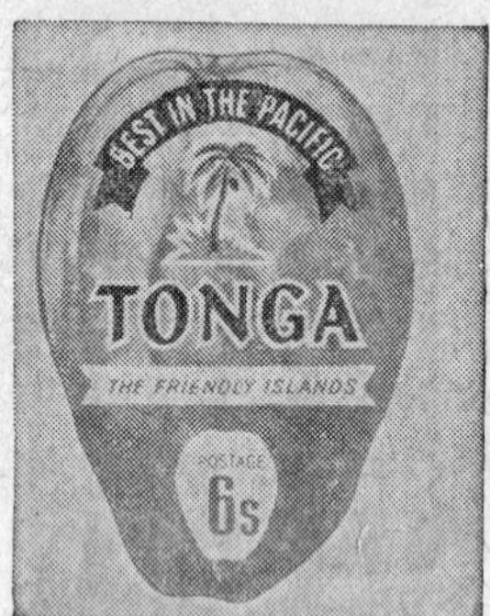

33. Coconut.

1970. Imperf. Self-adhesive.
(a) As T **28** but colours changed.
325. **28.** 1 s. yell., pur. and black 5 5
326. 2 s. yellow, blue & black 5 5
327. 3 s. yellow, brn. & blk. 5 5
328. 4 s. yell., green & black 5 5
329. 5 s. yell., red and black 8 8
(b) Multicoloured; colour of face values given.
330. **33.** 6 s. red 10 10
331. 7 s. purple 12 12
332. 8 s. violet 12 12
333. 9 s. green 15 15
334. 10 s. orange 15 15
See also Nos. 413/22.

34. "Red Cross".

1970. British Red Cross Cent. Imperf. Self-adhesive.
335. **34.** 3 s. red, black & green (postage) 5 5
336. – 7 s. red, black and blue 15 15
337. – 15 s. red, black & pur. 30 30
338. – 25 s. red, black & blue 50 50
339. 75 s. red, black & brown 1·50 1·50

340. – 9 s. red and silver (air) 20 20
341. – 10 s. red and purple .. 20 20
342. – 18 s. red and green .. 35 35
343. – 38 s. red and blue .. 80 80
344. – 1 p. red and silver .. 2·00 2·00
DESIGN: As Type **34.** Nos. 340/4 as Nos. 335/9 but with inscription rearranged and coat of arms omitted.

1971. Queen Salote. 5th Death Anniv. Nos. 174/80, 182/4 with part of old surch. obliterated and further surch. **1965† 1970** and value in seniti. On air values the surch. includes two laurel leaves.
345. **25.** 2 s. on 5d. on 9d. (post.) 5 5
346. 3 s. on 9d. 8 8
347. 5 s. on 3d. 10 10
348. 15 s. on 3s. 6d. on 9d. .. 30 30
349. 25 s. on 6s. 6d. on 3d. .. 50 50
350. 50 s on 1s. 7d. on 3d .. 1·00 1·00
351. **26.** 9 s. on 10d. (air) .. 20 20
352. 24 s. on 4s. on 10d. .. 50 50
353. 29 s. on 5s. 6d. on 1s. 2d. 60 60
354. 38 s. on 10s. 6d. on 1s. 2d. 80 80

1971. Philatokyo '71 Stamp Exhib., Japan. As Nos. 101, etc., but imperf. with colours changed and surch **PHILATOKYO '71,** emblem and value or **HONOURING JAPANESE POSTAL CENTENARY 1871-1971** (Nos. 357, 362, 364) Nos. 360/4 also surch. **AIRMAIL.**
355. 3 s. on 8d. blk. & yell. (postage) 5 5
356. 7 s. on 4d. violet and yellow 15 15
357. 15 s. on 1s. red and yellow 30 30
358. 25 s. on 1d. black & yellow 50 50
359. 75 s. on 2s. claret and blue 1·50 1·50

360. 9 s. on 1½d. green (air) .. 20 20
361. 10 s. on 4d. violet & yellow 20 20
362. 18 s. on 1s. red and yellow 35 35
363. 38 s. on 1d. black & yellow 80 80
364. 1 p. on 2s. claret and blue 2·00 2·00

35. Wristwatch.

1971. Air. Imperf. Self-adhesive.
365. **35.** 14 s. multicoloured .. 25 25
365a. 17 s. multicoloured .. 30 30
366. 21 s. multicoloured .. 35 35
366a. 38 s. multicoloured .. 55 55
See also Nos. O65/6a.

36. Pole-vaulter.

1971. 4th South Pacific Games, Tahiti. Imperf. Self-adhesive.
367. **36.** 3 s. multicoloured (postage) 5 5
368. 7 s. multicoloured .. 10 10
369. 15 s. multicoloured .. 20 25
370. 25 s. multicoloured .. 30 35
371. 50 s. multicoloured .. 65 75

372. – 9 s. multicoloured (air) 12 12
373. – 10 s. multicoloured .. 12 15
374. – 24 s. multicoloured .. 30 35
375. – 29 s. multicoloured .. 40 45
376. – 38 s. multicoloured .. 50 60
DESIGN—HORIZ. Nos. 372/6 High-jumper.

37. Medal of Merit (reverse).

1971. Investiture of Royal Tongan Medal of Merit. Multicoloured, colour of medal given. Imperf. Self-adhesive.
377. **37.** 3 s. gold (postage) .. 5 5
378. 24 s. silver 30 35
379. – 38 s. brown 50 55

380. – 10 s. gold (air) 12 15
381. – 75 s. silver .. .. 95 1·10
382. **37.** 1 p. brown .. .. 1·25 1·50
DESIGN—As Type **37.** Nos. 379/81, Obverse of the Medal of Merit.

38. Child.

1971. U.N.I.C.E.F. 25th Anniv. Imperf. Self-adhesive.
383. **38.** 2 s. multicoloured (postage) 5 5
384. 4 s. multicoloured .. 5 5
385. 8 s. multicoloured .. 10 12
386. 16 s. multicoloured .. 20 25
387. 30 s. multicoloured .. 40 45

388. – 10 s. multicoloured (air) 12 15
389. – 15 s. multicoloured .. 20 25
390. – 25 s. multicoloured .. 30 35
391. – 50 s. multicoloured .. 65 75
392. – 1 p. multicoloured .. 1·25 1·50
DESIGN—VERT. (21 × 42 mm.). Nos. 388/92. Woman.

39. Map of South Pacific, and "Olovaha". (Illustration reduced. Actual size 53 × 47 mm.).

1972. Merchant Marine Routes. Imperf. Self-adhesive.
393. **39.** 2 s. mult. (postage) .. 5 5
394. 10 s. multicoloured .. 12 15
395. 17 s. multicoloured .. 20 25
396. 21 s. multicoloured .. 25 30
397. 60 s. multicoloured .. 65 70

398. – 9 s. mult. (air) .. 12 12
399. – 12 s. multicoloured .. 15 15
400. – 14 s. multicoloured .. 20 20
401. – 75 s. multicoloured .. 80 90
402. – 90 s. multicoloured .. 1·00 1·10
DESIGN: Nos. 398/402, Map of South Pacific, and "Niuvakai".

40. ½ Hau Coronation Coin. (Illustration reduced. Actual size 60 × 40 mm).

1972. Coronation. 5th Anniv. Imperf. Self-adhesive.
403. **40.** 5 s. multicoloured (post.) 5 5
404. 7 s. multicoloured .. 8 8
405. 10 s. multicoloured .. 10 12
406. 17 s. multicoloured .. 15 20
407. 60 s. multicoloured .. 60 70

408. – 9 s. multicoloured (air) 10 10
409. – 12 s. multicoloured .. 12 12
410. – 14 s. multicoloured .. 15 20
411. – 21 s. multicoloured .. 20 25
412. – 75 s. multicoloured .. 75 85
DESIGNS: (47 × 41 mm.). Nos. 408/12. As T **40,** but with coins above inscription instead of beneath it.

41. Water Melon.

1972. Imperf. Self-adhesive.

(a) As T **28,** but inscription altered, omitting " Best in the Pacific ", and colours changed.
413. **18.** 1 s. yellow, red & black 5 5
414. 2 s. yellow, blue & black 5 5
415. 3 s. yellow, green & blk. 5 5
416. 4 s. yellow, blue & black 5 5
417. 5 s. yellow, brown & blk. 5 5

(b) As T **33** but colours changed. Multicoloured. Colour of face-value given.
418. **33.** 6 s. orange 8 8
419. 7 s. blue 8 8
420. 8 s. purple 10 10
421. 9 s. orange 12 12
422. 10 s. blue 12 12

(c) Type **41.** Multicoloured. Colour of face-value given.
423. **41.** 15 s. blue 20 20
424. 20 s. orange 25 25
425. 25 s. brown 30 30
426. 40 s. orange 50 50
427. 50 s. lemon 65 65

1972. Int. Airmail. Inaug. No. 398 surch. **NOVEMBER 1972 INAUGURAL Internal Airmail Nuku'alofa - Vava'u** and value.
428. 7 s. on 9 s. multicoloured 35 35

42. Hoisting Tongan Flag.
(Illustration reduced. Actual size 60 × 41 mm.)

1972. Proclamation of Sovereignty over Minerva Reefs. Imperf. Self-adhesive.
429. **42.** 5 s. multicoloured (post.) 8 8
430. 7 s. multicoloured .. 8 10
431. 10 s. multicoloured .. 12 15
432. 15 s. multicoloured .. 20 25
433. 40 s. multicoloured .. 50 65

434. – 9 s. multicoloured (air) 12 12
435. – 12 s. multicoloured .. 15 20
436. – 14 s. multicoloured .. 20 25
437. – 38 s. multicoloured .. 50 55
438. – 1 p. multicoloured .. 1·25 1·50
DESIGN—SPHERICAL (52 mm. diameter). Nos. 434/8, Proclamation in Govt. Gazette.

43. Coins around Bank.
(Illustration reduced. Actual size 53 × 48 mm).

1973. Bank of Tonga. Foundation. Imperf. Self-adhesive.
439. **43.** 5 s. multicoloured (post.) 8 8
440. 7 s. multicoloured .. 10 10
441. 10 s. multicoloured .. 12 12
442. 20 s. multicoloured .. 25 25
443. 30 s. multicoloured .. 35 35

444. – 9 s. multicoloured (air) 12 12
445. – 12 s. multicoloured .. 15 15
446. – 17 s. multicoloured .. 25 25
447. – 50 s. multicoloured .. 55 60
448. – 90 s. multicoloured .. 1·00 1·10
DESIGN—HORIZ. (64 × 52 mm.). Nos. 444/8, Bank and banknotes.

44. Handsnake and Scout in Canoe.
(Illustration reduced. Actual size 61 × 43 mm.).

1973. Scouting in Tonga. Silver Jubilee. Imperf. Self-adhesive.
449. **44.** 5 s. multicoloured (post.) 8 8
450. 7 s. multicoloured .. 12 12
451. 15 s. multicoloured .. 25 25
452. 21 s. multicoloured .. 35 35
453. 50 s. multicoloured .. 80 80

454. – 9 s. multicoloured (air) 15 15
455. – 12 s. multicoloured .. 20 20
456. – 14 s. multicoloured .. 25 25
457. – 17 s. multicoloured .. 30 30
458. – 1 p. multicoloured .. 2·25 2·25
DESIGN—SQUARE (53 × 53 mm.). Nos. 454/8, Scout badge.

45. Excerpt from Cook's Log-book.
(Illustration reduced. Actual size 69 × 38 mm.)

1973. Capt. Cook's Visit to Tonga. Bicentenary. Imperf. Self-adhesive.
459. **45.** 6 s. multicoloured (post.) 8 8
460. 8 s. multicoloured .. 10 10
461. 11 s. multicoloured .. 15 15
462. 35 s. multicoloured .. 40 45
463. 40 s. multicoloured .. 50 55

464. – 9 s. multicoloured (air) 12 12
465. – 14 s. multicoloured .. 20 20
466. – 29 s. multicoloured .. 35 40
467. – 38 s. multicoloured .. 50 55
468. – 75 s. multicoloured .. 90 1·00
DESIGN—VERT. Nos. 464/8, The " Resolution ".

1973. Commonwealth Games, Christchurch. Various stamps optd. **COMMONWEALTH GAMES CHRISTCHURCH 1974** and No. 474 is optd. **AIRMAIL** in addition.
469. **36.** 5 s. on 50 s. multicoloured (No. 371) (post.) .. 8 8
470. – 12 s. on 38 s. multicoloured (No. 379) .. 15 20
471. – 14 s. on 75 s. multicoloured (No. 381) .. 20 20
472. **37.** 20 s. on 1 p. multicoloured (No. 382) .. 25 30
473. 50 s. on 24 s. multicoloured (No. 378) 60 65
474. **36.** 7 s. on 25 s. multicoloured (No. 370) (air) .. 10 10
475. – 9 s. on 38 s. multicoloured (No. 376) .. 12 12
476. – 24 s. multicoloured (No. 374) 30 30
477. – 29 s. on 9s. multicoloured (No. 454) 35 40
478. – 40 s. on 14 s. multicoloured (No. 456) .. 50 55

46. Parrot.

1974. Air. Imperf. Self-adhesive.
479. **46.** 7 s. multicoloured .. 8 8
480. 9 s. multicoloured .. 12 12
481. 12 s. multicoloured .. 15 15
482. 14 s. multicoloured .. 15 15
483. 17 s. multicoloured .. 20 20
484. 29 s. multicoloured .. 35 35
485. 38 s. multicoloured .. 45 45
486. 50 s. multicoloured .. 60 60
487. 75 s. multicoloured .. 90 90

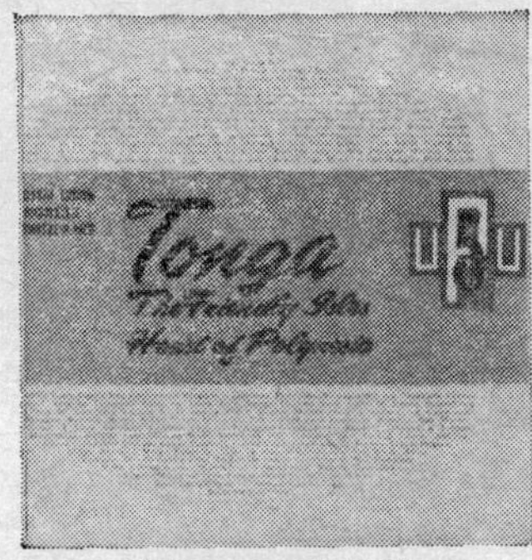

47. "Stamped Letter".

1974. U.P.U. Centenary. Imperf. Self-adhesive.
488. **47.** 5 s. mult. (postage) .. 8 8
489. 10 s. multicoloured .. 15 15
490. 15 s. multicoloured .. 20 20
491. 20 s. multicoloured .. 30 30
492. 50 s. multicoloured .. 1·00 1·00

493. – 14 s. multicoloured (air) 20 20
494. – 21 s. multicoloured .. 35 35
495. – 60 s. multicoloured .. 1·10 1·10
496. – 75 s. multicoloured .. 1·40 1·40
497. – 1 p. multicoloured .. 2·00 2·00
DESIGNS—HORIZ. Nos. 493/7, Carrier pigeon scattering letters over Tonga.

48. Girl Guides Badges.

1974. Tongan Girl Guides. Imperf. Self-adhesive.
498. **48.** 5 s. mult. (postage) .. 8 8
499. 10 s. multicoloured .. 12 12
500. 20 s. multicoloured .. 25 25
501. 40 s. multicoloured .. 45 50
502. 60 s. multicoloured .. 70 75

503. – 14 s. multicoloured (air) 20 20
504. – 16 s. multicoloured .. 20 20
505. – 29 s. multicoloured .. 35 40
506. – 31 s. multicoloured .. 40 40
507. – 75 s. multicoloured .. 85 95
DESIGNS—VERT. Nos. 503/7, Girl Guide leaders.

49. Sailing Ship.

1974. Establishment of Royal Marine Institute. Imperf. Self-adhesive.
508. **49.** 5 s. mult. (postage) .. 8 8
509. 10 s. multicoloured .. 12 12
510. 25 s. multicoloured .. 30 35
511. 50 s. multicoloured .. 55 60
512. 75 s. multicoloured .. 85 95

513. – 9 s. multicoloured (air) 12 12
514. – 14 s. multicoloured .. 20 20
515. – 17 s. multicoloured .. 20 20
516. – 60 s. multicoloured .. 70 75
517. – 90 s. multicoloured .. 1·00 1·00
DESIGNS—HORIZ. (53 × 47 mm.). Nos. 513/7, Tongan freighter "James Cook".

50. Dateline Hotel, Nuku'alofa
(Illustration reduced. Actual size 60 × 38 mm.)

1975. South Pacific Forum and Tourism. Imperf. Self-adhesive.
518. **50.** 5 s. multicoloured (postage) 8 8
519. 10 s. multicoloured .. 12 12
520. 15 s. multicoloured .. 20 20
521. 30 s. multicoloured .. 35 45
522. 1 p. multicoloured .. 1·00 1·25

523. – 9 s. multicoloured (air) 12 12
524. – 12 s. multicoloured .. 15 15
525. – 14 s. multicoloured .. 20 20
526. – 17 s. multicoloured .. 20 20
527. – 38 s. multicoloured .. 45 50
DESIGNS (46 × 60 mm.): 9, 12, 14 s. Beach. 17, 38 s. Surf and sea.

51. Boxing.
(Illustration reduced. Actual size 60 × 47 mm.)

1975. 5th South Pacific Games, Guam. Imperf. Self-adhesive.
528. **51.** 5s. multicoloured (post.) 8 8
529. 10 s. multicoloured .. 12 12
530. 20 s. multicoloured .. 25 25
531. 25 s. multicoloured .. 30 30
532. 65 s. multicoloured .. 75 75

533. – 9 s. multicoloured (air) 12 12
534. – 12 s. multicoloured .. 15 15
535. – 14 s. multicoloured .. 20 20
536. – 17 s. multicoloured .. 20 25
537. – 90 s. multicoloured .. 1·00 1·00
DESIGN: (37 × 43 mm.): Nos. 533/7, Throwing the discus.

52. Commemorative Coin.

1975. F.A.O. Commemoration. Imperf. Self-adhesive.
538. **52.** 5 s. multicoloured (postage) 5 5
539. – 20 s multicoloured .. 20 25
540. – 50 s. blue, black & silver 55 65
541. – 1 p. blue, black & silver 1·10 1·25
542. – 2 p. black and silver .. 2·25 2·50

543. – 12 s. multicoloured (air) 12 15
544. – 14 s. multicoloured .. 15 15
545. – 25 s. red, black & silver 25 30
546. – 50 s. pur., black & silver 55 65
547. – 1 p. black and silver .. 1·10 1·25
DESIGNS: Nos. 538/47 are as T **52** but showing different coins. Nos. 542 and 544 are horiz., size 75 × 42 mm.

53. Commemorative Coin.
(Illustration reduced. Actual size 58 × 58 mm.)

1975. Tongan Constitution. Centenary. Multicoloured. Imperf. Self-adhesive.

548. 5 s. Type **53** (postage) .. 5 5
549. 10 s. King George I .. 10 12
550. 20 s. King Taufa'ahau IV 20 25
551. 50 s. King George II .. 55 60
552. 75 s. Tongan arms .. 60 70
553. 9 s. King Taufa'ahau IV (air) 10 10
554. 12 s. Queen Salote .. 12 15
555. 14 s. Tongan arms .. 15 15
556. 38 s. King Taufa'ahau IV 40 45
557. 1 p. Four monarchs .. 1·10 1·25

SIZES: 60 × 40 mm., Nos. 549 and 551. 76 × 76 mm., Nos. 552 and 557. 57 × 56 mm., others.

54. Montreal Logo.

1976 First Participation in Olympic Games. Imperf. Self-adhesive.

(a). Type **54**.

558. 5 s. red, blk. & blue (postage) 5 5
559. 10 s. red, black and green 10 12
560. 25 s. red, black and brown 25 30
561. 35 s. red, black and mauve 40 45
562. 70 s. red, black and green 75 85

(b). Montreal logo optd. on Nos. 500/1, 504, 507.

563. **48.** 12 s. on 20 s. multicoloured (air) 12 15
564. – 14 s. on 16 s. multicoloured 15 20
565. – 16 s. multicoloured .. 20 20
566. **48.** 38 s. on 40 s. multicoloured 40 45
567. – 75 s. multicoloured .. 75 85

55. Signatories of Declaration of Independence.

1976. American Revolution. Bicent. Imperf. Self-adhesive.

568. **55.** 9 s. multicoloured (postage) 10 10
569. – 10 s. multicoloured .. 10 12
570. – 15 s. multicoloured .. 15 20
571. – 25 s. multicoloured .. 25 30
572. – 75 s. multicoloured .. 80 90
573. – 12 s. multicoloured (air) 12 15
574. – 14 s. multicoloured .. 15 20
575. – 17 s. multicoloured .. 20 20
576. – 38 s. multicoloured .. 40 45
577. – 1 p. multicoloured .. 1·10 1·25

DESIGNS: Nos. 569/77 show the signatories to the Declaration of Independence.

56. Nathanial Turner and John Thomas (Methodist Missionaries).

1976. Christianity in Tonga. 150th Anniv. Imperf. Self-adhesive.

578. **56.** 5 s. multicoloured (postage) 5 5
579. 10 s. multicoloured .. 10 12
580. 20 s. multicoloured .. 20 25
581. 25 s. multicoloured .. 25 30
582. 85 s. multicoloured .. 90 1·00
583. – 9 s. multicoloured (air) 10 10
584. – 12 s. multicoloured .. 12 15
585. – 14 s. multicoloured .. 15 20
586. – 17 s. multicoloured .. 20 20
587. – 38 s. multicoloured .. 40 45

DESIGNS: Nos. 583/7 show Missionary Ship "Triton".

57. Emperor Wilhelm I and King George I.

1976. Treaty of Friendship with Germany. Centenary Imperf. Self-adhesive.

588. **57.** 9 s. multicoloured (postage) 10 10
589. 15 s. multicoloured .. 15 20
590. 22 s. multicoloured .. 25 25
591. 50 s. multicoloured .. 50 55
592. 73 s. multicoloured .. 75 85
593. – 11 s. multicoloured (air) 12 15
594. – 17 s. multicoloured .. 20 20
595. – 18 s. multicoloured .. 20 25
596. – 31 s. multicoloured .. 30 35
597. – 39 s. multicoloured .. 40 45

DESIGNS—CIRCULAR: (52 mm. diameter). Nos. 593/7 show Treaty signing.

OFFICIAL STAMPS

1893. Optd. **G.F.B.**

O 1. **2.** 1d. blue .. .. .. 3·00 7·00
O 2. **3.** 2d. blue .. .. .. 6·00 11·00
O 3. **2.** 4d. blue .. .. .. 18·00 28·00
O 4. **3.** 8d. blue .. .. .. 35·00 48·00
O 5. 1s. blue .. .. .. 42·00 55·00

1893. Nos. O 1/5 variously surch.

O 6. **2.** ½d. on 1d. blue .. 3·00 7·00
O 7. **3.** 2½d. on 2d. blue .. 3·00 7·00
O 8. **2.** 5d on 4d. blue .. 2·50 7·00
O 9. **3.** 7½d. on 8d. blue .. 3·50 12·00
O 10. 10d. on 1s. blue .. 3·50 12·00

1962. Air. Stamps of 1953 and 1961 optd. as Nos. 120/7 but with **OFFICIAL AIR MAIL** in addition.

O 11. 2d. blue .. .. .. — 5·00
O 12. 5d. violet .. .. — 6·00
O 13. 1s. brown .. .. — 3·50
O 14. 5s. yellow and lilac .. — 45·00
O 15. 10s. yellow and black .. — 18·00
O 16. £1 yellow, red and blue .. — 25·00

1963. Air. First Polynesian Gold Coinage Commemoration. As No. 138 but additionally inscr. "OFFICIAL". 1 koula coin. Diameter 3½ in. Imperf.

O 17. B. 15s. black on gold .. 3·50 4·00

1965. Air. Surch. as Nos. 151/61.

O 18. B. 30s. on 15s. (No. O 17) 3·00 3·50

1966. Air. Tupou College and Secondary Education Cent. No. 117 surch. **OFFICIAL AIRMAIL** and new value, with commem. inscr. as Nos. 168/73.

O 19. 10s. on 4d. green .. 1·10 1·25
O 20. 20s. on 4d. green .. 2·25 2·40

1967. Air. No. 112 surch. **OFFICIAL AIRMAIL ONE PA'ANGA.**

O 21. 1 p. on 5s. yellow & lilac 1·25 1·25

1967. Air. No. 114 surch. **OFFICIAL AIRMAIL** and new value.

O 22. 40 s. on £1 yell., red & blue 50 60
O 23. 60 s. on £1 yell., red & blue 80 90
O 24. 1 p. on £1 yell., red & blue 1·25 1·50
O 25. 2 p. on £1 yell., red & blue 2·50 2·75

1967. Air. Arrival of U.S. Peace Corps in Tonga. As No. 114, but imperf. and background colour changed, surch. as Nos. 216/27 but with **Official Airmail** in addition.

O 26. 30 s. on £1 yellow, red, blue and green .. 40 45
O 27. 70 s. on £1 yellow, red, blue and green .. 80 90
O 28. 1 p. 50, on £1 yellow, red, blue and green .. 1·90 2·10

1968. 50th Birthday of King Taufa'ahua IV. No. 207 surch. **"HIS MAJESTY'S 50th BIRTHDAY OFFICIAL AIRMAIL"** and new value.

O 29. 40s. on 50s. red & ultram. 50 55
O 30. 60s. on 50s. red & ultram. 75 80
O 31. 1 p. on 50s. red & ultram. 1·25 1·50
O 32. 2 p. on 50s. red & ultram. 2·50 2·75

1968. Air. South Pacific Games Field and Track Trials, Port Moresby, New Guinea. As No. 114, but imperf., background colour changed, surch.

O 33. 20 s. on £1 yellow, red, ultramarine and green 30 35
O 34. 1 p. on £1 yellow, red, ultramarine and green 1·50 1·75

1969. Air. 3rd South Pacific Games, Port Moresby. As Nos. 290/4 surch. **OFFICIAL AIRMAIL.**

O 35. 70 s. red, green & turquoise 1·10 1·10
O 36. 80 s. red, orge. & turquoise 1·25 1·25

1969. Air. Oil Search. As No. 114, but imperf., background colour changed, and optd. **1969 OIL SEARCH** and new value.

O 37. 90 s. on £1 yellow, red, blue and green .. .. 2·00 2·00
O 38. 1 p. 10 on £1 yellow, red, blue and green .. 2·25 2·25

No. O 37 is additionally optd. **OFFICIAL AIRMAIL.**

1969. Air. Royal Visit. As No. 110, but imperf., colour changed, and surch. **Royal Visit MARCH 1970 OFFICIAL AIRMAIL** and new value.

O 39. 75 s. on 1s. red and yellow 1·50 1·50
O 40. 1 p. on 1s. red and yellow 2·00 2·00
O 41. 1 p. 25 on 1s. red & yellow 2·50 2·50

1970. Commonwealth Membership. As No. 112 but imperf. and surch. **Commonwealth Member, June, 1970** and **OFFICIAL AIRMAIL.**

O 42. **51.** 50 s. on 5 s. yell. & sepia 1·00 1·00
O 43. 90 s. on 5 s. yell. & sepia 1·75 1·75
O 44. $1·50 on 5 s. yellow & sepia .. .. 3·00 3·00

1970. Imperf. Self-adhesive. Colour of "TONGA" given for 6s to 10s.

O 45. **28.** 1 s. yell., pur. & blk. 5 5
O 46. 2 s. yell., blue & black 5 5
O 47. 3 s. yell., brn. & black 5 5
O 48. 4 s. yell., green & black 5 5
O 49. 5 s. yell., red and black 8 8
O 50. **33.** 6 s. blue 8 8
O 51. 7 s. mauve 10 10
O 52. 8 s. gold 10 10
O 53. 9 s. red 12 12
O 54. 10 s. silver 12 12

On the official issues Nos. O 45 to O 54, the value tablet is black (banana issue) or green (Coconut issue). On the postage issues the colour is white.

See also Nos. O 82/91.

1970. Air. British Red Cross Cent. As No. 102 and 112, but imperf. in different colours and surch **Centenary British Red Cross 1870-1970 OFFICIAL AIRMAIL** and value.

O 55. 30 s. on 5d. green .. 60 60
O 56. 80 s. on 5d. yellow & brn. 1·60 1·60
O 57. 90 s. on 5d. yellow & brn. 1·75 1·75

1971. Air. Queen Salote. 5th Death Anniv. As No. 113, but imperf and colour changed surch **OFFICIAL AIRMAIL 1965 IN MEMORIAM 1970** and value.

O 58. 20 s on 10s. orange .. 40 40
O 59. 30 s. on 10s. orange .. 60 60
O 60. 50 s. on 10s. orange .. 1·00 1·00
O 61. 2 p. on 10s. orange .. 4·00 4·00

1971. Air. Philatokyo '71 Stamp Exhib., Japan. Nos. O 55/7 optd. **PHILATOKYO '71** and Emblem.

O 62. 30 s. on 5d. green & yellow 60 60
O 63. 80 s. on 5d. green & yellow 1·60 1·60
O 64. 90 s. on 5d. green & yellow 1·75 1·75

1971 Air. As T **35** but inscr. "OFFICIAL AIRMAIL".

O 65. 14 s. multicoloured .. 20 20
O 65a. 17 s. multicoloured .. 30 30
O 66. 21 s. multicoloured .. 35 35
O 66a. 38 s. multicoloured .. 55 55

O 1. Football.

1971. Air. 4th South Pacific Games, Tahiti. Imperf. Self-adhesive.

O 67. **O 1.** 50 s. multicoloured .. 65 75
O 68. 90 s. multicoloured .. 1·10 1·25
O 69. 1 p 50 multicoloured 1·90 2·00

1971. Air. Investiture of Royal Tongan Medal of Merit. surch. **INVESTITURE 1971. OFFICIAL AIRMAIL.**

O 70. **32.** 60 s. on 3 s. mult 70 80
O 71. 80 s. on 25 s. mult. 1·00 1·10
O 72. 1 p. on 7 s. mult. 1·40 1·60

O 2. "U.N.I.C.E.F." and Emblem.

1971. Air. U.N.I.C.E.F. 25th Anniv. Imperf. Self-adhesive.

O 73. **O 2** 70 s. multicoloured .. 90 1·00
O 74. 80 s. multicoloured .. 1·00 1·10
O 75. 90 s. multicoloured .. 1·10 1·25

1972. Air. Merchant Marine Routes. As T **39**, but inscr. "OFFICIAL AIRMAIL". Imperf. Self-adhesive.

O 76. 20 s. multicoloured .. 25 30
O 77. 50 s. multicoloured .. 65 75
O 78. 1 p. 20 multicoloured .. 1·50 1·75

DESIGNS: Nos. O 76/78, Map of South Pacific, and "Aoniu".

1972. Air. Coronation. 5th Anniv. Design similar to T **41**, but inscr. "OFFICIAL AIRMAIL".

O 79. 50 s. multicoloured .. 60 65
O 80. 70 s. multicoloured .. 75 85
O 81. 1 p. 50 multicoloured .. 1·60 1·75

DESIGN: (47 × 57 mm.). Nos. O 79/81, As T **41**, but with different background.

1972. As Nos. 413/27, but inscr. "OFFICIAL POST".

(a) As. 413/17.

O 82. **28.** 1 s. yellow, red & blk. 5 5
O 83. 2 s. yellow, green & blk. 5 5
O 84. 3 s. yellow, green & blk. 5 5
O 85. 4 s. yellow and black .. 5 5
O 86. 5 s. yellow and black .. 8 8

(b) As Nos. O 50/4, but colours changed. Multicoloured. Colour of "TONGA" given.

O 87. **33.** 6 s. green 8 8
O 88. 7 s. green 8 8
O 89. 8 s. green 10 10
O 90. 9 s. green 12 12
O 91. 10 s. green 12 12

(c) As Nos. 423/7. Multicoloured. Colour of face-value given.

O 92. **41.** 15 s. blue 20 20
O 93. 20 s. orange 25 25
O 94. 25 s. brown 30 30
O 95. 40 s. orange 50 50
O 96 50 s. blue 65 65

1972. Air. Proclamation of Sovereignty over Minerva Reefs. As T **42**, but inscr. "OFFICIAL AIRMAIL".

O 97. 25 s. multicoloured .. 30 35
O 98. 75 s. multicoloured .. 85 90
O 99. 1 p. 50 multicoloured .. 1·60 1·75

1973. Air. Foundation of Bank of Tonga. No. 396 surch. **TONGA 1973 ESTABLISHMENT BANK OF TONGA OFFICIAL AIRMAIL,** star and value.

O 100. **39.** 40 s. on 21 s. mult. .. 45 50
O 101. 85 s. on 21 s. mult. .. 90 1·00
O 102. 1 p. 25 on 21 s. mult. 1·40 1·50

1973. Scouting in Tonga. Silver Jubilee. Nos. O 76, O 74 and 319 surch. or optd.

O 103. – 30 s. on 20 s. mult. 1·25 1·25
O 104. **O 2.** 80 s. multicoloured 4·00 4·00
O 105. **32.** 1 p. 40 on 50 s. mult. 6·00 6·00

OVERPRINT AND SURCHARGES: 30 s. **SILVER JUBILEE TONGAN SCOUTING 1948-1973,** scout badge and value. 80 s. **SILVER-JUBILEE 1948-1973** and scout badge. 1 p. 40 **OFFICIAL AIRMAIL 1948-1973 SILVER JUBILEE TONGAN SCOUTING** and value.

1973. Air. Capt. Cook's Visit. Bicentenary. Design similar to T **45**, but inscr. "OFFICIAL AIRMAIL".

O 106. 25 s. multicoloured .. 35 35
O 107. 80 s. multicoloured .. 95 1·10
O 108. 1 p. 30 multicoloured .. 1·60 1·75

DESIGN—HORIZ. (52×45 mm.) Nos. O 106/107, Bulk Tanker "James Cook".

1973. Air. Commonwealth Games, Christchurch. Nos. O 67/9 optd. **1974 COMMONWEALTH GAMES, CHRISTCHURCH.**

O 109. O **1** 50 s. multicoloured 60 65
O 110. 90 s. multicoloured 1·10 1·25
O 111. 1 p. 50 multicoloured 1·90 2·00

O **3** Dove of Peace.

1974. Air.

O 112. O **3.** 7 s. grn., vio. & red 8 8
O 113. 9 s. grn., vio. & brn. 12 12
O 114. 12 s. grn., vio. & brn. 15 15
O 115. 14 s. grn., vio. & yell. 15 15
O 116. 17 s. multicoloured 20 20
O 117. 29 s. multicoloured 35 35
O 118. 38 s. multicoloured 45 45
O 119. 50 s. multicoloured 60 60
O 120. 75 s. multicoloured 90 90

1974. U.P.U. Cent. As Nos. 488/97 but inscr. "OFFICIAL AIRMAIL".

O 121. 25 s. orange, grn. & blk. 50 50
O 122. 35 s. yell., red & blk. .. 65 65
O 123. 70 s. orge., bl. & blk. .. 1·40 1·40

DESIGNS—HORIZ. (43×40 mm.). Nos. 121/3, Letters "UPU".

1974. Air. Tongan Girl Guides. As Nos. 498/507 inscr. "OFFICIAL AIRMAIL".

O 124. 45 s. multicoloured .. 50 55
O 125. 55 s. multicoloured .. 60 65
O 126. 1 p. multicoloured .. 1·10 1·25

DESIGNS—OVAL (36×52 mm.). Nos. O 124/6, Lady Baden-Powell.

1974. Air. Establishment of Royal Marine Institute. Imperf. Self-adhesive.

O 127. 30 s. multicoloured .. 35 35
O 128. 35 s. multicoloured .. 40 40
O 129. 80 s. multicoloured .. 80 90

DESIGNS—HORIZ. (61×42 mm.). 30 s., 35 s. Badge and handclasp. (64×54 mm.). 80 s. Badge on Tongan banknotes.

1975. Air. South Pacific Forum and Tourism. As T **50**. Imperf. Self-adhesive.

O 130. 50 s. multicoloured .. 55 65
O 131. 75 s. multicoloured .. 85 95
O 132. 1 p. 25 multicoloured .. 1·25 1·50

DESIGNS (49×43 mm.): 50 s. Jungle arch. 75 s., 1 p. 25 Sunset scene.

1975. Air. 5th South Pacific Games. As T **51**. Imperf. Self-adhesive.

O 133. 38 s. multicoloured .. 40 50
O 134. 75 s. multicoloured .. 75 80
O 135. 1 p. 20 multicoloured .. 1·25 1·50

DESIGN—OVAL (51×27 mm.). Nos. O 133/5, Runners on track.

O **4.** Tongan Monarchs.
(Illustration reduced. Actual size 69×39 mm.)

1975. Air. Tongan Constitution. Cent. Imperf. Self-adhesive.

O 136. O **4.** 17 s. multicoloured 20 20
O 137. 60 s. multicoloured 65 75
O 138. 90 s. multicoloured 1·00 1·10

1976. Air. First Participation in Olympic Games. As Nos. 558/67 but inscr. "OFFICIAL AIRMAIL".

O 139. 45 s. multicoloured .. 50 55
O 140. 55 s. multicoloured .. 55 65
O 141. 1 p. multicoloured .. 1·10 1·25

DESIGN—OVAL (36×53 mm.). Montreal logo.

1976. Air. American Revolution. Bicent. As Nos. 568/77 but inscr. "OFFICIAL AIRMAIL".

O 142. 20 s. multicoloured .. 20 25
O 143. 50 s. multicoloured .. 55 65
O 144. 1 p. 15 multicoloured .. 1·10 1·25

1976. Air. Christianity in Tonga. 150th Anniv.

O 145. 65 s. multicoloured .. 65 75
O 146. 85 s. multicoloured .. 90 1·00
O 147. 1 p. 15 multicoloured .. 1·10 1·25

DESIGNS—HEXAGONAL (65×52 mm.). Lifuka Chapel.

1976. Air. Treaty of Friendship with Germany. Centenary.

O 148. 30 s. multicoloured .. 35 40
O 149. 60 s. multicoloured .. 60 70
O 150. 1 p. 25 multicoloured .. 1·40 1·50

DESIGN—RECTANGULAR (51×47 mm.). Text.

TRANSCAUCASIAN FEDERATION E3

A Federation of Armenia, Azerbaijan and Georgia, now part of Soviet Russia.

1. Mt. Ararat and Oilfield. 2. Mts. Ararat and Elbruz and Oil-derricks.

1923.

1. **1.** 40,000 r. purple .. .. 2·00 3·00
2. 75,000 r. green .. .. 2·00 1·50
3. 100,000 r. grey .. .. 1·00 1·00
4. 150,000 r. red 50 75
5. **2.** 200,000 r. green .. .. 1·00 1·00
6. 300,000 r. blue 25 75
7. 350,000 r. brown .. .. 25 1·50
8. 500,000 r. red .. .. 1·50 1·50

1923. Surch. **700000 RУb.**

9. **1.** 700,000 r. on 40,000 r. pur. 75 1·75
10. 700,000 r. on 75,000 r. grn. 1·00 1·75

1923. Values in gold kopecks.

11. **2.** 1 k. orange .. .. 75 1·00
12. 2 k. green .. .. 75 1·00
13. 3 k. red .. .. 1·00 75
14. 4 k. brown .. .. 50 1·00
15. **1.** 5 k. purple .. .. 50 1·00
16. 9 k. blue .. .. 25 1·00
17. 18 k. grey .. .. 50 1·00

TRANSVAAL BC

Formerly South African Republic under Boer rule, annexed by Gt. Britain in 1877, restored to the Boers in 1881 and again annexed in 1900, and since 1919 a province of the Union of S. Africa.

1.

ILLUSTRATIONS British Commonwealth and all overprints and surcharges are FULL SIZE. Foreign Countries have been reduced to ¾-LINEAR.

1869. Imperf. or roul.

64. **1.** 1d. red .. .. .. 8·50 5·50
22. 1d. black .. .. .. 5·00 6·00
53. 3d. lilac .. .. .. 18·00 15·00
54a. 6d. blue .. .. .. 15·00 8·00
31. 1s. green .. .. .. 35·00 11·00

1874. Perf.

39. **1.** 1d. red .. .. .. 27·00 15·00
171. 1d. grey-black 70 40
172. 3d. black on rose .. 3·50 1·40
173. 3d. red .. .. .. 1·75 60
173b. 3d. brown .. .. .. 8·00 1·25
40. 6d. blue .. .. .. 30·00 15·00
174. 1s. green .. .. .. 4·00 90

1877. Optd. **V. R. TRANSVAAL.** Imperf. or roul.

101. **1.** 1d. red .. .. .. 7·00 7·00
102. 3d. lilac .. .. .. 27·00 12·00
103. 6d. blue .. .. .. 32·00 12·00
113. 6d. blue on rose .. .. 22·00 14·00
104. 1s. green .. .. .. 30·00 15·00

1877. Optd. **V. R. Transvaal.** Imperf. or roul.

116. **1.** 1d. red on blue .. 18·00 9·00
117. 1d. red on orange .. 4·00 4·50
118. 3d. lilac on yellow .. 9·00 9·00
146. 3d. lilac on green .. £100 8·00
147. 3d. lilac on blue .. 15·00 10·00
124. 6d. blue on green .. 27·00 7·00
120. 6d. blue on blue .. 18·00 9·00

2.

3.

1878. Perf.

156. **2.** ½d. red .. .. .. 8·00 12·00
157a. 1d. brown .. .. .. 1·75 1·25
158. 3d. claret .. .. .. 2·20 1·25
159. 4d. olive .. .. .. 5·00 2·75
160. 6d. black .. .. .. 2·50 1·75
161. 1s. green .. .. .. 25·00 15·00
162. 2s. blue .. .. .. 30·00 24·00

1879. Surch. **1 Penny.**

168. **2.** 1d. on 6d. black .. 16·00 11·00

1882. Surch. **EEN PENNY.**

170. **2.** 1d. on 4d. olive .. .. 1·75 1·10

1885.

175. **3.** ½d. grey 5 5
176. 1d. red 5 5
177. 2d. purple 12 5
178. 2d. pale brown 12 5
179. 2½d. mauve 35 5
180. 3d. mauve 35 15
181. 4d. deep olive 60 15
182. 6d. blue 35 5
183. 1s. green 90 20
184. 2s. 6d. yellow .. .. 1·40 70
185. 5s. grey .. .. .. 2·00 90
186. 10s. brown .. .. .. 7·00 90
187. £5 green .. .. .. £1000 85·00

1885. Surch. **HALVE PENNY** vert., reading up or down.

188. **1.** ½d. on 3d. red (No. 173) 55 55
189. **3.** ½d. on 3d. mauve .. 55 55
190. **1.** ½d. on 1s. green (No. 174) 2·00 2·25

1885. Surch. with value in words and **Z.A.R.** both vert.

191. **2.** ½d. on 6d. black .. .. 3·50 4·00
192. 2d. on 6d. black 65 65

1887. Surch. **2d.** and thick bar.

194. **3.** 2d. on 3d. mauve .. 30 30

1893. Surch. **Halve Penny** and bars.

195. **3.** ½d. on 2d. pale brown .. 30 35

1893. Surch. in figures and words between bars. (A) in one line, (B) in two.

197. **3.** 1d. on 6d. blue (A) .. 5 5
198. 2½d. on 1s. green (A) .. 25 30
199. 2½d. on 1s. green (B) .. 65 60

4.

5.

1894. Waggon with shafts.

200. **4.** ½d. grey 5 5
201. 1d. red 5 5
202. 2d. pale brown 5 5
203. 6d. blue 30 35
204. 1s. green .. .. .. 1·50 1·75

1895. Waggon with pole.

205. **5.** ½d. grey 5 5
206. 1d. red 5 5
207. 2d. pale brown 5 5
208. 3d. mauve 10 5
209. 4d. black 40 35
210. 6d. blue 25 5
211. 1s. green 45 40
212. 5s. grey .. .. .. 1·75 2·00
212a. 10s. brown .. .. .. 2·00 85

1895. Surch. **Halve Penny** and bar.

213. **5.** ½d. on 1s. green 5 5

1895. Surch. **1d** and thick bar.

214. **3.** 1d. on 2½d. mauve .. 5 5

6.

ILLUSTRATIONS British Commonwealth and all overprints and surcharges are FULL SIZE. Foreign Countries have been reduced to ¾-LINEAR.

1895. Fiscal stamp optd. **POSTZEGEL.**

215. **6.** 6d. red 25 35

1896.

216. **5.** ½d. green 5 5
217. 1d. red and green .. 5 5
218. 2d. brown and green .. 5 5
219. 2½d. blue and green .. 5 5
220. 3d. purple and green .. 5 6
221. 4d. olive and green .. 5 5
222. 6d. lilac and green .. 5 5
223. 1s. pale brown and green 12 5
224. 2s. 6d. violet and green 30 30

7.

1895. Penny Postage Commem.

225. **7.** 1d. red 20 10

1900. Optd. **V.R.I.**

226. **5.** ½d. green 5 5
227. 1d. red and green .. 5 5
228. 2d. brown and green .. 5 5
229. 2½d. blue and green .. 5 5
230. 3d. purple and green .. 5 5
231. 4d. olive and green .. 25 12
232. 6d. lilac and green .. 30 12
233. 1s. pale brown and green 35 25
234. 2s. 6d. violet and green .. 75 60
235. 5s. grey .. .. .. 1·25 1·25
236. 10s. brown .. .. 2·50 2·50
237. **3.** £5 green .. .. ..

The majority of the £5 stamps, No. 237, on the market, are forgeries.

1901. Optd. **E.R.I.**

238. **5.** ½d. green 5 5
239. 1d. red and green .. 5 5
240. 3d. purple and green .. 35 35
241. 4d. olive and green .. 35 40
242. 2s. 6d. violet and green .. 1·25 1·50

1901 Surch. **E.R.I. Half Penny.**

243. **5.** ½d. on 2d. brown & green 5 5

8.

Nos. 267 and 268 onwards have the inscription "POSTAGE" on both sides. The rest are inscribed "POSTAGE" at left and "REVENUE" at right.

1902.

244. **8.** ½d. black and green .. 5 5
273. ½d. green 5 5
245. 1d. black and red .. 5 5
274. 1d. red 5 5
246. 2d. black and purple .. 20 5
275. 2d. purple 35 5
247. 2½d. black and blue .. 35 30
276. 2½d. blue .. .. .. 1·75 80
264. 3d. black and olive .. 35 5
265. 4d. black and brown .. 40 5
266a. 6d. black and orange .. 45 5
251. 1s. black and olive .. 1·40 75
267. 1s. grey and brown .. 50 5
252. 2s. black and brown .. 5·00 4·00
268. 2s. grey and yellow .. 1·75 70
253. 2s. 6d. mauve and black 2·00 3·00
270. 5s. black & pur. on yellow 4·00 80
271. 10s. black & pur. on red 9·00 1·40
272. £1 green and violet .. 20·00 2·50
259. £5 brown and violet .. £600 £225

POSTAGE DUE STAMPS

D 1.

1907.

D 1. D **1.** ½d. black and green .. 30 30
D 2. 1d. black and red .. 30 12
D 3. 2d. brown 30 20
D 4. 3d. black and blue .. 1·00 40
D 5. 5d. black and violet .. 80 85
D 6. 6d. black and brown .. 1·50 85
D 7. 1s. red and black .. 1·50 1·10

TRAVANCORE BC

A state of S.E. India.

16 cash = 1 chuckram.
28 chuckrams = 1 rupee.

1. Conch or Chank Shell. 2.

1888. Various Frames.

9. 1. 4 cash pink 10 5
24. – 5 cash olive 15 8
34. – 5 cash brown 50 20
10. 2. 6 cash brown 15 5
11. ½ ch. purple 10 5
27. – 10 cash pink 15 5
13. – ¾ ch. black 10 5
39. – ¾ ch. mauve 15 5
14. 2. 1 ch. blue 20 5
15. 1¼ ch. red 15 8
42. 1½ ch. red 20 8
16a. 2 ch. red 30 5
17. – 3 ch violet 40 5
18a 2. 4 ch. green 80 25
19. – 7 ch. claret .. .. 1·00 30
20. – 14 ch. orange .. .. 1·50 50

1906. Surch. in figures.

21. 2. ¼ on ½ ch. purple 8 5
22. ⅜ on ½ ch. purple 8 5

1921. Surch. in figures.

31. 1. 1 c. on 4 cash pink .. 10 10
57. – 1 c. on 5 cash chocolate .. 10 10
58. – 1 c. on 5 cash purple .. 10 10
50. 2. 1 c. on 1¼ ch. claret .. 8 8
59. – 2 c. on 10 cash pink .. 10 10
51. 2. 2 c. on 1¼ ch. claret .. 8 8
32. 5 c. on 1 ch. blue .. 10 10

3. Sri Padmanabha Shrine.

Design — As T 3: 10 cash, State chariot.

4. Maharaja Sir Bala Rama Varma.

1931. Coronation.

47. 3. 6 cash black and green .. 15 15
48. – 10 cash black and blue .. 15 15
49. 4. 3 ch. black and purple .. 20 20

5. Maharaja Sir Bala Rama Varma and Subramania Shrine.

1937. Temple Entry Proclamation.

60. 5. 6 cash red 10 10
61. – 12 cash blue 12 12
62. – 1½ ch. green 20 20
63. – 3 ch. violet 30 20

Designs: Portraits of the Maharaja and the temples of Sri Padmanabha (6 cash), Mahadeva (1½ ch.) and Kanyakumari (3 ch.)

6. Lake Ashtamudi.

Designs—As T 7: 1½ ch., 3 ch. Bust of Maharaja. As T 6: Sri Padmanabha Shrine (4 ch.). Bust of Maharaja and Cape Comorin (7 ch.) and Pachipari Irrigation Reservoir (14 ch.).

7. Maharaja Sir Bala Rama Varma.

1939. Maharaja's 27th Birthday.

64. 6. 1 ch. green 8 8
65. – 1½ ch. red 20 15
66. 7. 2 ch. orange 10 10
67. – 3 ch. brown 10 8
68. – 4 ch. red 25 25
69. – 7 ch. blue 45 45
70. – 14 ch. green .. .. .. 1·00 1·00

8. Maharaja and Aruvikara Falls.

1941. Maharaja's 29th Birthday.

71. 8. 6 cash violet 8 5
72. – ¾ ch. brown 8 5

Design: ¾ ch. Maharaja and Marthanda Varma Bridge, Alwaye.

1943. Stamps of 1939 and 1941 surch. in figures and capital letters.

73. – 2 cash on 1½ ch. red (65) . 8 8
74. – 4 cash on ¾ ch. brown (72) 20 8
75. 8. 8 cash on 6 cash red (as No. 71) 20 8

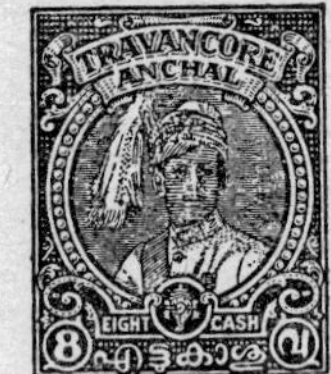

9. Maharaja Sir Bala Rama Varma.

1946. Maharaja's 34th Birthday.

76a.9. 8 cash red 50 50

1946. No. O 103 optd. **SPECIAL.**

77. 8. 6 cash violet .. .. 3·00 1·00

OFFICIAL STAMPS

1911. Optd. **On S.S.**

O 1. 1. 4 cash pink 10 8
O 14. – 5 cash olive 15 8
O 29. – 5 cash chocolate 10 10
O 15. 2. 6 cash brown 10 5
O 17. ½ ch. purple 10 5
O 18. – 10 cash pink 15 8
O 39. – ¾ ch. black 15 5
O 56. – ¾ ch. mauve 15 5
O 5. 2. 1 ch. blue 20 5
O 21. 1¼ ch. red 25 10
O 59. 1½ ch. red 25 10
O 6. 2 ch. red 20 10
O 61. – 3 ch. violet 40 10
O 10. 2. 4 ch. green 40 5
O 64. – 7 ch. claret 75 15
O 27. – 14 ch. orange .. .. 1·00 30

1932. Official stamps surch. in figures.

O 74. – 6 c. on 5 cash olive .. 75 25
O 75. – 6 c. on 5 cash chocolate 8 8
O 76. – 12 c. on 10 cash pink .. 8 8
O 77. 2. 1 ch. 8 cash on 1¼ ch. red 15 10

1939. Optd. **SERVICE.**

O 85. 2. 6 chas brown 50 8
O 86a.– ¾ ch. mauve (No. 39) 1·00 15
O 96. 6. 1 ch. green 10 5
O 97. – 1½ ch. red (No. 65) .. 15 10
O 95a.2. 1½ ch. rose 25 40
O 89. 7. 2 ch. orange 15 15
O 90. – 3 ch. brown (No. 67) .. 10 8
O 91. – 4 ch. red (No. 68) .. 25 20
O 101. – 7 ch. blue (No. 69) .. 50 25
O 102. – 14 ch. green (No. 70) .. 1·00 50

1942. Optd. **SERVICE.**

O 103. 8. 6 cash violet 15 8
O 104. – ¾ ch. brown (No. 72) .. 15 8

1942. Nos. 73/5 optd. **SERVICE.**

O 106. – 2 cash on 1½ ch. red .. 8 8
O 107. – 4 cash on ¾ ch. brown .. 20 8
O 105. 8. 8 cash on 6 cash red .. 15 8

1947. Optd. **SERVICE.**

O 108. 9. 8 cash red 75 50

TRAVANCORE—COCHIN BC

In 1949 the states of Cochin and Travancore in S.E. India were united under the name of the United States of Travancore and Cochin. Indian currency.

ONE ANNA
ഒരണ
(1.)

1949. Stamps of Travancore surch. as T 1.

1d.8. 2 p. on 6 cash violet .. 5 5
2. 9. 4 p. on 8 cash red .. 12 5
3c.6. ½ a. on 1 ch. green .. 8 5
4a.7. 1 a. on 2 ch. orange .. 10 8
5. 3. 2 a. on 4 ch. brown .. 20 15
6. – 3 a. on 7 ch. blue (No. 69) . 2·00 1·00
7. – 6 a. on 14 ch. grn. (No. 70) 1·25 50

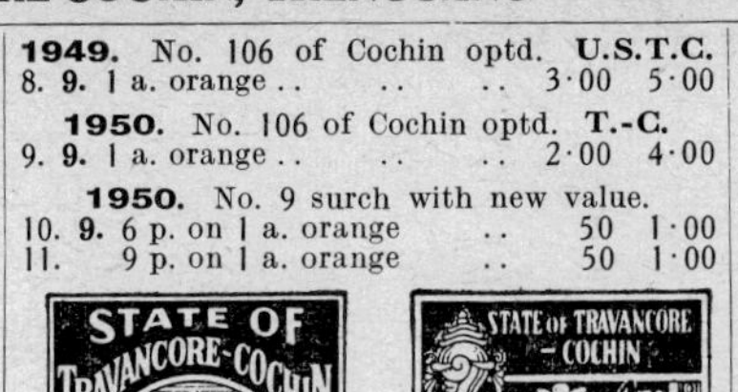

1949. No. 106 of Cochin optd. **U.S.T.C.**

8. 9. 1 a. orange .. .. 3·00 5·00

1950. No. 106 of Cochin optd. **T.-C.**

9. 9. 1 a. orange .. .. 2·00 4·00

1950. No. 9 surch with new value.

10. 9. 6 p. on 1 a. orange .. 50 1·00
11. 9 p. on 1 a. orange .. 50 1·00

2. Conch or Chank Shell. 3. Palm Trees.

1950.

12. 2. 2 p. red 75 25
13. 3. 4 p. blue .. .. .. 1·00 40

OFFICIAL STAMPS

1949. Stamps of Travancore surch. as T 1.

O 1. 8. 2 p. on 6 cash (No. 71) .. 5 5
O 10. 9. 4 p. on 8 cash (No. 76a) 5 5
O 3. 6. ½ a. on 1 ch. (No. 64) .. 5 5
O 12. 7. 1 a. on 2 ch. (No. 66) .. 12 12
O 9. – 2 a. on 4 ch. (No. 68) .. 12 10
O 6. – 3 a. on 7 ch. (No. 69) .. 40 35
O 15. – 6 a. on 14 ch. (No. 70) .. 75 40

TRENGGANU BC

A state of the Federation of Malaya, incorporated in Malaysia in 1963.

100 cents = 1 dollar (Straits or Malayan).

1. Sultan Zain ul ab din. 2.

1910.

1. 1. 1 c. green 30 35
2. 2 c. brown and purple .. 40 35
3. 3 c. red 60 40
4. 4 c. orange 80 85
5. 4 c. brown and green .. 75 1·00
5a. 4 c. red 30 40
6. 5 c. grey 55 65
7. 5 c. grey and brown .. 90 60
8. 8 c. blue .. .. 65 1·00
9a. 10 c. purple on yellow .. 70 75
10. 10 c. grn. and red on yell. 55 90
11. 20 c. mauve and purple 1·10 1·40
12. 25 c. green and purple .. 1·25 1·60
13. 30 c. purple and black .. 1·25 1·60
14. 50 c. black on green .. 1·60 2·00
15. $1 black and red on blue 3·00 3·75
16. $3 green and red on green 15·00 16·00
17. 2. $5 green and purple .. 30·00 35·00
18. $25 red and green £300

1917. Surch. **RED CROSS 2 c.**

19. 1. 2 c. on 3 c. red 25 55
20. 2 c. on 4 c. orange .. 40 60
22. 2 c. on 4 c. brown & green 70 1·40
21. 2 c. on 8 c. blue .. .. 40 1·25

3. Sultan Suleiman. 4. Sultan Ismail.

1921. (a) T 3.

48. 3. 1 c. black 15 10
26. 2 c. green 15 8
49. 3 c. green 25 30
50. 3 c. brown .. .. 75 1·10
27. 4 c. red 25 10
28. 5 c. grey and brown .. 1·10 50
51. 5 c. purple on yellow .. 45 35
52. 6 c. orange .. .. 1·50 25
53. 8 c. grey 90 40
29. 10 c. blue .. .. 1·10 10
54. 12 c. blue .. .. 1·10 1·40
30. 20 c. purple and orange .. 1·10 60
31. 25 c. green and purple .. 1·00 65
32. 30 c. purple and black .. 1·40 60
55. 35 c. red on yellow .. 1·50 2·75
33. 50 c. green and red .. 1·25 55
23 $1 purple and blue on blue 3·00 4·00
24. $3 green and red on green 11·00 14·00

(b) Larger type, as T 2, but portrait of Sultan Suleiman.

25. $5 green and red on yellow 18·00 22·00
34. $25 purple and blue .. £250 £150
35. $50 green and yellow .. £550 £550
36. $100 green and red .. £1800

1922. Optd. **MALAYA-BORNEO EXHIBITION.**

37. 3. 2 c. green .. .. .. 30 1·00
38. 4 c. red .. .. .. 90 1·25
39. 5 c. grey and brown .. 1·00 1·40
40. 1. 10 c. green & red on yellow 90 1·40
41. 20 c. mauve and purple .. 60 2·00
42. 25 c. green and purple .. 60 2·00
43. 30 c. purple and black .. 80 2·00
44. 50 c. black on green .. 90 2·25
45. $1 black and red on blue 3·00 5·00
46. $3 green and red on green 25·00 28·00
47. 2. $5 green and purple .. 45·00 50·00

1941. Surch.

59. 3. 2 c. on 5 c. purple on yellow 1·00 1·25
60. 8 c. on 10 c. blue .. .. 1·50 2·00

1948. Silver Wedding. As T 5/6 of Aden.

61. 10 c. violet 5 5
62. $5 red .. .. .. 6·00 7·00

1949. U.P.U. As T 14/17 of Antigua.

63. 10 c. purple 12 15
64. 15 c. blue 20 35
65. 25 c. orange 30 50
66. 50 c. black 45 55

1949.

67. 4. 1 c. black 5 5
68. 2 c. orange 5 5
69. 3 c. green 10 20
70. 4 c. brown 5 5
71. 5 c. purple 8 8
72. 6 c. grey 12 15
73. 8 c. red 12 20
74. 8 c. green 20 25
75. 10 c. purple 12 10
76. 12 c. red 15 20
77. 15 c. blue 15 15
78. 20 c. black and green .. 25 30
79. 20 c. blue 15 15
80. 25 c. purple and orange .. 15 20
81. 30 c. red and purple .. 30 30
82. 35 c. red and purple .. 35 40
83. 40 c. red and purple .. 60 80
84. 50 c. black and blue .. 25 35
85. $1 blue and purple .. 60 60
86. $2 green and red .. 1·75 2·50
87. $5 green and brown .. 5·50 10·00

1953. Coronation. As T 7 of Aden.

88. 10 c. black and purple .. 12 10

1957. As Nos. 92/102 of Kedah but inset portrait of Sultan Ismail.

89. 1 c. black 5 5
90. 2 c. red 5 5
91. 4 c. sepia 5 5
92. 5 c. lake 8 8
93. 8 c. green 12 15
94. 10 c. sepia 5 5
94a. 10 c. maroon 5 5
95. 20 c. blue 10 15
96ab. 50 c. black and blue .. 30 30
97. $1 blue and purple .. 50 70
98. $2 green and red .. 1·25 1·50
99a. $5 brown and green .. 2·50 2·50

5. "Vanda hookeriana".

1965. As Nos. 166/72 of Johore but inset portrait of Sultan Ismail Nasiruddin Shah as in T 5.

100. 5. 1 c. multicoloured .. 5 5
101. – 2 c. multicoloured .. 5 5
102. – 5 c. multicoloured .. 5 5
103. – 6 c. multicoloured .. 5 5
104. – 10 c. multicoloured .. 5 5
105. – 15 c. multicoloured .. 8 8
106. – 20 c. multicoloured .. 8 8

The higher values used in Trengganu were Nos. 20/7 of Malaysia.

6. Sultan of Trengganu.

1970. Installation of H.R.H. Tuanku Ismail Nasiruddin Shah as Sultan of Trengganu. 25th Anniv.
107. **6.** 10 c. multicoloured .. 5 5
108. 15 c. multicoloured .. 8 8
109. 50 c. multicoloured .. 25 25

trengganu
malaysia 6c

7. Lime Butterfly.

1971. Butterflies. As Nos. 175/81 of Johore but with portrait of Sultan Ismail Nasiruddin Shah as in T 7.
110. – 1 c. multicoloured .. 5 5
111. – 2 c. multicoloured .. 5 5
112. – 5 c. multicoloured .. 5 5
113. **7.** 6 c. multicoloured .. 5 5
114. – 10 c. multicoloured .. 5 5
115. – 15 c. multicoloured .. 8 8
116. – 20 c. multicoloured .. 8 8
The high values in use with this issue are Nos. 64/71 of Malaysia.

POSTAGE DUE STAMPS

POSTAGE DUE 1 CENT TRENGGANU

D 1.

ILLUSTRATIONS British Commonwealth and all overprints and surcharges are FULL SIZE. Foreign Countries have been reduced to ¾-LINEAR.

1937.
D 1. **D 1.** 1 c. red .. .. 40 1·00
D 2. 4 c. green .. .. 40 1·00
D 3. 8 c. yellow .. .. 2·50 5·00
D 4. 10 c. brown .. .. 3·75 9·00

TRIESTE E3

The Free Territory of Trieste situated on the Adriatic Coast between the frontiers of Italy and Yugoslavia. In 1954 when the Territory was divided between Italy and Yugoslavia, the overpinted issues were superseded by the ordinary issues of these countries in their respective zones.

For stamps of Italy surcharged **1. V.1945. TRIESTE TRST,** five-pointed star and value, see Venezia Giulia Nos. 20/32.

ZONE A

ALLIED MILITARY GOVERNMENT

Stamps of Italy variously overprinted **A.M.G. F.T.T.** or **AMG-FTT** (Allied Military Government—Free Territory of Trieste) except where otherwise stated.

1947. Opt. in two lines.
(a) Postage stamps of 1945. Nos. 647, etc.
1. 25 c. blue-green 5 5
2. 50 c. violet 5 5
3. 1 l. green 5 5
4. 2 l. brown 5 5
5. 3 l. red 5 5
6. 4 l. orange 5 5
7. 5 l. blue 5 5
8. 6 l. violet 5 5
9. 8 l. green 25 25
10. 10 l. grey 5 5
11. 10 l. red .. .. .. 2·10 5
12. 15 l. blue 12 5
13. 20 l. violet 10 5
14. 25 l. green 40 30
15. 30 l. blue .. .. .. 6·00 45
16. 50 l. purple 55 20
17. 100 l. red (No. 669) .. 1·60 65

(b) Air stamps of 1945, Nos. 670, etc.
18. 1 l. slate 5 5
19. 2 l. blue 5 5
20. 5 l. green 25 30
21. 10 l. red 25 30
22. 25 l. brown 12 15
23. 50 l. violet .. .. .. 1·60 50
24. 100 l. green .. .. .. 2·10 60
25. 300 l. mauve .. .. 2·75 2·75
26. 500 l. blue .. .. 3·25 3·25
27. 1000 l. claret .. .. 21·00 21·00

1947. Air. 50th Anniv. of Radio (Nos. 688/93).
59. 6 l. violet 5 5
60. 10 l. claret 5 5
61. 20 l. orange 40 30
62. 25 l. green 5 5
63. 35 l. blue 5 5
64. 50 l. purple 30 15

1948. Revolution Cent. (Nos. 706, etc.).
65. 3 l. brown 5 5
66. 4 l. purple 5 5
67. 5 l. blue 5 5
68. 6 l. green 12 8
69. 8 l. brown 5 5
70. 10 l. red 20 5
71. 12 l. green 20 25
72. 15 l. black .. .. .. 3·25 1·60
73. 20 l. red .. .. .. 6·00 2·50
74. 30 l. blue 12 15
75. 50 l. violet .. .. .. 80 1·00
76. 100 l. blue .. .. .. 12·00 11·00

1948. Trieste Philatelic Exn. Stamps of 1945 optd. **A.M.G. F.T.T. 1948 TRIESTE** and posthorn.
77. 8 l. green (postage) 5 5
78. 10 l. red 5 5
79. 30 l. blue 30 30
80. 10 l. red (air) 5 5
81. 25 l. brown 5 5
82. 50 l. violet 12 12

1948. Rebuilding of Bassano Bridge.
84. **171.** 15 l. green 8 8

1948. Donizetti.
85. **172.** 15 l. brown 8 8

1949. 25th Biennial Art Exhibition, Venice.
86. **174.** 5 l. lake and cream .. 10 8
87. – 15 l. green and cream 1·00 1·00
88. – 20 l. brown and cream 2·75 25
89. – 50 l. blue and cream 8·00 3·00

1949. 27th Milan Fair.
90. **173.** 20 l. sepia 40 20

1949. 75th Anniv. of U.P.U.
91. **175.** 50 l. blue .. .. 1·60 60

1949. Roman Republic Centenary.
92. **176.** 100 l. brown .. .. 21·00 21·00

1949. European Recovery Plan.
94. **177.** 5 l. green .. .. 2·50 2·75
95. 15 l. violet .. .. 2·50 2·75
96. 20 l. brown .. .. 8·00 4·25

1949. Giuseppe Mazzini.
98. **178.** 20 l. black .. .. 2·00 80

1948. Alfieri. Bicentenary.
99. **179.** 20 l. brown .. .. 1·25 60

1949. 1st Trieste Free Election.
93. **180.** 20 l. lake 45 25

1949. 2nd World Health Congress, Rome.
97. **181.** 20 l. violet .. .. 5·50 1·25

1949. Palladio's Basilica at Vicenza.
100. **182.** 20 l. violet .. .. 5·00 2·50

1949. Lorenzo de Medici.
101. **183.** 20 l. blue .. .. 1·60 60

1949. 13th Bari Fair.
102. **184.** 20 l. red .. .. 1·75 80

1949. Volta.
135. **185.** 20 l. red 80 60
136. **186.** 50 l. blue .. .. 1·75 1·75

1949. Holy Trinity Bridge, Florence.
137. **187.** 20 l. green 90 60

1949. Catullus.
138. **188.** 20 l. blue 90 60

1949. Cimarosa.
153. **189.** 20 l. slate .. .. 1·00 55

1949. Optd. in one line. (a) Postage.
103. **161.** 1 l. green 5 5
104. – 2 l. brown (No. 656) 5 5
105. – 3 l. red (No. 657) .. 5 5
106. **160.** 5 l. blue 5 5
107. **161.** 6 l. violet 5 5
108. – 8 l. green (No. 661) .. 1·25 1·25
109. **160.** 10 l. red 5 5
110. **161.** 15 l. blue 30 10
111. – 20 l. purple (No. 665) .. 12 5
112. **162.** 25 l. green .. .. 1·00 20
113. 50 l. purple .. .. 5·50 12
114. **164.** 100 l. red .. .. 6·50 45

(b) Air.
115. **163.** 10 l. red 5 5
116. – 25 l. brn. (No. 676) .. 5 5
117. **163.** 50 l. violet 12 5
118. – 100 l. grn. (No. 911) 15 5
119. – 300 l. mve. (No. 912) 1·10 1·10
120. – 500 l. blue (No. 913) .. 1·75 1·75
121. – 1,000 l. purple (No. 914) .. .. 5·00 5·00

1950. 28th Milan Fair.
154. **190.** 20 l. brown 35 25

1950. 32nd Int. Automobile Exn., Turin.
155. **191.** 20 l. violet 55 35

1950. 5th General U.N.E.S.C.O. Conf.
156. **192.** 20 l. green 60 60
157. – 55 l. blue (No. 745) .. 3·00 3·00

1950. Holy Year.
158. **193.** 20 l. violet 80 45
159. 55 l. blue .. .. 2·10 1·75

1950. Ferrari.
160. **194.** 20 l. grey 90 40

1950. Radio Conference.
161. **195.** 20 l. violet .. .. 2·75 2·50
162. 55 l. blue .. .. 5·50 5·50

1950. Muratori.
163. **196.** 20 l. brown .. .. 1·25 50

1950. D'Arezzo.
164. **197.** 20 l. green .. .. 1·25 50

1950. 14th Levant Fair, Bari.
165. **198.** 20 l. brown 90 50

1950. 2nd Trieste Fair. Optd. **A M G F T T Fiera di Trieste 1950.**
166. **161.** 15 l. blue 8 8
167. – 20 l. purple (No. 665) 10 10

1950. Wool Industry.
168. **199.** 20 l. blue 12 10

1950. Tobacco Conference. Nos. 755/7.
169. 5 l. green and claret .. 25 25
170. 20 l. green and brown .. 1·00 60
171. 55 l. brown and blue .. 7·00 6·00

1950. Fine Arts Academy.
172. **201.** 20 l. red and brown .. 30 30

1950. Augusto Righi.
173. **202.** 20 l. black and buff .. 70 35

1950. Provincial Occupations. Nos. 760/78.
176. 50 c. blue 5 5
177. 1 l. slate 5 5
178. 2 l. sepia 5 5
179. 5 l. black 5 5
180. 6 l. chocolate 8 5
181. 10 l. green 8 5
182. 12 l. green 20 8
183. 15 l. slate 20 5
184. 20 l. violet 20 5
185. 25 l. orange 35 5
186. 30 l. purple 12 12
187. 35 l. red 35 30
188. 40 l. brown 15 15
189. 50 l. violet 15 8
190. 55 l. blue 15 8
191. 60 l. red .. .. .. 1·10 40
192. 65 l. green 20 20
193. 100 l. chestnut .. .. 1·60 8
194. 200 l. olive 65 65

1951. Tuscan Stamp Cent.
195. **204.** 20 l. red and purple .. 40 40
196. 55 l. blue .. .. 3·75 3·75

1951. 33rd Int. Motor Show, Turin.
197. **205.** 20 l. green 55 35

1951. Consecration of Hall of Peace. Rome.
198. **206.** 20 l. violet 30 30

1951. 29th Milan Fair.
199. **207.** 20 l. brown 30 30
200. **208.** 55 l. blue 50 50

1951. 10th Int. Textiles Exn., Turin.
201. **209.** 20 l. violet 30 30

1951. Columbus.
202. **210.** 20 l. blue-green .. 35 25

1951. Int. Gymnastic Festival, Florence.
203. **210a.** 5 l. red and brown .. 1·75 1·90
204. 10 l. red and green .. 1·75 1·90
205. 15 l. red and blue .. 1·75 1·90

1951. Restoration of Montecassino Abbey.
206. **211.** 20 l. violet 12 12
207. – 55 l. blue (No. 791) .. 35 35

1951. 3rd Trieste Fair, Optd. **AMG-FTT FIERA di TRIESTE 1951.**
208. 6 l. choc. (No. 764) .. 5 5
209. 20 l. violet (No. 768) .. 5 5
210. 55 l. blue (No. 774) .. 15 15

1951. Perugino.
211. **212.** 20 l. brown and sepia 35 25

1951. Triennial Art Exhibition, Milan.
212. **213.** 20 l. black and green .. 20 20
213. – 55 l. pink and blue (No. 794) 50 50

1951. World Cycling Championship.
214. **214.** 25 l. grey 15 15

1951. 15th Levant Fair, Bar.
215. **215.** 25 l. blue 15 15

1951. F. P. Michetti.
216. **216.** 25 l. brown 15 15

1951. First Sardinian Postage Stamps.
217. **217.** 10 l. black and sepia .. 12 12
218. – 25 l. green & red (799) 12 12
219. – 60 l. red and blue (800) 60 60

1951. 3rd Industrial and Commercial Census.
220. **218.** 10 l. green 8 8

1951. 9th National Census.
221. **219.** 25 l. slate 12 12

1951. Forestry Festival.
222. **221.** 10 l. green and olive .. 10 10
223. – 25 l. green (No. 807) .. 12 12

1951. Verdi.
224. – 10 l. green & pur. (803) 8 8
225. **220.** 25 l. sepia and brown .. 10 10
226. – 60 l. blue & green (805) 20 20

1952. Bellini.
227. **222.** 25 l. black 12 12

1952. Caserta Palace.
228. **223.** 25 l. brown and green 30 15

1952. 1st Int. Sports Stamps Exn., Rome.
229. **224.** 25 l. brown and black 8 8

1952. 30th Milan Fair.
230. **225.** 60 l. blue 30 30

1952. Leonardo da Vinci.
231. **226.** 25 l. orange 5 5
232. – 60 l. blue (813) .. 15 15
233. **226.** 80 l. red 20 20

1952. Overseas Fair, Naples.
234. **228.** 25 l. blue 12 12

1952. Modena and Parma Stamp Cent.
235. **227.** 25 l. black and brown 30 25
236. 60 l. indigo and blue .. 55 60

1952. 26th Biennial Art Exn., Venice.
237. **229.** 25 l. black and cream .. 12 12

1952. 30th Padua Fair.
238. **230.** 25 l. red and blue .. 12 12

1952. 4th Trieste Fair.
239. **231.** 25 l. grn., red & brown 35 15

1952. 16th Levant Fair, Bari.
240. **232.** 25 l. green 12 12

1952. Savonarola.
241. **233.** 25 l. violet 12 12

1952. 1st Private Aeronautics Conf., Rome.
242. **234.** 60 l. blue & ultramarine 30 30

1952. Alpine Troops National Exn.
243. **235.** 25 l. grey 12 12

1952. Armed Forces Day.
244. **236.** 10 l. green 5 5
245. **237.** 25 l. sepia and brown .. 8 8
246. – 60 l. black & blue (827) 15 15

1952. Mission to Ethiopia.
247. **238.** 25 l. deep brown & brn. 12 12

1952. Gemito.
248. **239.** 25 l. brown 12 12

1952. Mancini.
249. **240.** 25 l. myrtle 12 12

1952. Martyrdom of Belfiore.
250. **241.** 25 l. blue and black .. 12 12

1953. Antonello Exhibition, Messina.
251. **242.** 25 l. red 12 12

1953. 20th "Mille Miglia" Car Race.
252. **243.** 25 l. violet 30 20

1953. Labour Orders of Merit.
253. **244.** 25 l. violet 25 15

1953. Corelli.
254. **245.** 25 l. brown 12 12

1953. Coin type.
255. **246.** 5 l. slate 5 5
256. 10 l. vermillion 5 5
257. 12 l. green 5 5
258. 13 l. mauve 5 5
259. 20 l. brown 5 5
260. 25 l. violet 5 5
261. 35 l. red 15 15
262. 60 l. blue 20 20
263. 80 l. chestnut 35 35

1953. St. Clare.
264. **247.** 25 l. chestnut & brown 12 12

1953. 5th Trieste Fair. Optd. **V FIERA DI TRIESTE AMG FTT 1953.**
265. 10 l. green (No. 765) .. 5 5
266. 25 l. orange (No. 769) .. 5 5
267. 60 l. red (No. 775) .. 10 10

1953. Mountains Festival.
272. **248.** 25 l. green 12 12

1953. Int. Agricultural Exn., Rome.
273. **249.** 25 l. brown 12 12
274. 60 l. blue 20 20

1953. 4th Anniv. of Atlantic Pact.
275. **250.** 25 l. slate and yellow .. 50 40
276. 60 l. blue and mauve .. 1·90 2·10

1953. Signorelli.
277. **251.** 25 l. green and brown 12 12

1953. 6th Int. Microbiological Congress, Rome.
278. **252.** 25 l. brown and slate 12 12

1953. Tourist Series, Nos. 855/60.
279. 10 l. brown and sepia .. 5 5
280. 12 l. black and blue .. 5 5
281. 20 l. brown and orange .. 8 8
282. 25 l. blue-green 8 8
283. 35 l. brown and buff .. 12 12
284. 60 l. blue and turquoise .. 15 15

1954. Lateran Treaty.
285. **254.** 25 l. brown 12 12
286. 60 l. blue 15 15

1954. Television.
287. **255.** 25 l. violet 12 12
288. 60 l. turquoise 15 15

1954. "Taxpayers' Encouragement".
289. **256.** 25 l. violet 5 5

1954. Milan-Turin Helicopter Mail Flight.
290. **257.** 25 l. grey-green .. 35 15

1954. Resistance Movement.
291. **258.** 25 l. black and brown 12 12

1954. 6th Trieste Fair. Nos. 858 and 860 of Italy optd. **AMG-FTT** and **FIERA DI TRIESTE 1954.**
292. – 25 l. blue-green .. 8 8
293. **253.** 60 l. blue and turquoise 12 12

1954. Catalani.
294. **259.** 25 l. grey-green .. 12 12

1954. Marco Polo.
295. **260.** 25 l. brown 8 8
296. 60 l. green 12 12

1954. 60th Anniv. of Italian Touring Club.
297. **261.** 25 l. green and red .. 30 15

1954. International Police Congress, Rome.

298.	**262.**	25 l. red	8	8
299.		60 l. blue	10	10

EXPRESS LETTER STAMPS

1947. Express Letter stamps optd. **A.M.G. F.T.T.** in two lines.

E 28.	–	15 l. lake (No. E 681)	12	5
E 29.	**11.**	25 l. orange	3·00	1·25
E 30.		30 l. violet	30	30
E 31.	–	60 l. red (No. E 685)	5·00	3·00

1948. Cent. of Revolution. Express Letter stamp optd. **A.M.G. F.T.T.**

E 83.	E **10.**	35 l. violet	1·25	80

1950. Express Letter stamps optd. **A.M.G.-F.T.T.** in one line.

E 174.	E **12.**	50 l. purple	20	20
E 175.	–	60 l. red (No. E 685)	20	20

PARCEL POST STAMPS

1947. Parcel Post stamps optd. **A.M.G. F.T.T.** in two lines on each half of stamp.

P 32.	P **4.**	1 l. brown	5	5
P 33.		2 l. green	5	8
P 34.		3 l. orange	10	12
P 35.		4 l. grey	10	12
P 36.		5 l. mauve	40	50
P 37.		10 l. violet	25	30
P 38.		20 l. purple	30	35
P 39.		50 l. red	35	40
P 40.		100 l. blue	55	60
P 41.		200 l. green	45·00	50·00
P 42.		300 l. purple	29·00	32·00
P 43.		500 l. brown	15·00	18·00

1949. Parcel Post stamps optd. **AMG-FTT** in one line on each half of stamp.

P 139.	P **4.**	1 l. brown	40	45
P 140.		2 l. green	5	5
P 141.		3 l. orange	5	5
P 142.		4 l. grey	5	5
P 143.		5 l. mauve	12	15
P 144.		10 l. violet	40	40
P 145.		20 l. purple	40	40
P 146.		30 l. purple	12	15
P 147.		50 l. red	20	20
P 148.		100 l. blue	30	35
P 149.		200 l. green	1·90	2·00
P 150.		300 l. purple	14·00	15·00
P 151.		500 l. brown	3·00	3·25
P 152.	P **5.**	1,000 l. blue	10·00	11·00

Unused prices are for complete stamps.

POSTAGE DUE STAMPS

1947. Postage Due stamps optd. **A.M.G. F.T.T.** in two lines.

D 44.	D **9.**	1 l. orange	5	5
D 48.	D **10.**	1 l. orange	12	8
D 49.		2 l. green	5	5
D 50.		3 l. red	35	30
D 51.		4 l. brown	30	25
D 45.	D **9.**	5 l. violet	5	5
D 52.	D **10.**	5 l. violet	10·00	1·40
D 53.		6 l. blue	3·00	2·50
D 54.		8 l. mauve	3·75	3·25
D 46.	D **9.**	10 l. blue	5	5
D 55.	D **10.**	10 l. blue	4·50	15
D 56.		12 l. brown	2·10	2·10
D 47.	D **9.**	20 l. red	1·00	8
D 57.	D **10.**	20 l. purple	50	5
D 58.		50 l. green	40	5

1949. Postage Due stamps optd. **AMG-FTT** in one line.

D 122.	D **10.**	1 l. orange	5	5
D 123.		2 l. green	5	5
D 124.		3 l. red	5	5
D 125.		5 l. violet	20	5
D 126.		6 l. blue	5	5
D 127.		8 l. mauve	5	5
D 128.		10 l. blue	5	5
D 129.		12 l. brown	80	8
D 130.		20 l. purple	35	5
D 131.		25 l. red	80	70
D 132.		50 l. green	50	5
D 133.		100 l. orange	80	5
D 134.		500 l. purple and blue	3·00	3·00

ZONE B

YUGOSLAV MILITARY GOVERNMENT

Apart from the definitive issues illustrated below the following are stamps of Yugoslavia (sometimes in new colours), variously overprinted **STT VUJA** or **VUJA-STT** or (Nos. B 65 onwards) **STT VUJNA** unless otherwise stated.

B 1. B 2.

1948. Labour Day.

B 1.	B **1.**	100 l. red on buff	80	40

Inscriptions are in either Slovene, Italian or Croat and the price for a strip of three containing one stamp in each language is £3·75 un., £1·75 us.

1948. Red Cross. No. 545 optd. and surch.

B 3a.	**85.**	2 l. on 50 p. brn. & red	1·25	1·25

1948. Air. Economic Exn., Capodistria.

B 4.	B **2.**	25 l. grey	20	12
B 5.		50 l. orange	20	12

B **3.** Hands, Hammer and Sickle. B **4.** Fishermen.

B **5.** Pack-mule. B **6.** Mew over Chimney.

1949. Labour Day.

B 6.	B **3.**	10 l. black	8	5

1949. Air.

B 7.	B **4.**	1 l. blue	12	8
B 8.	B **5.**	2 l. brown	12	10
B 9.	B **4.**	5 l. blue	10	10
B 10.	B **5.**	10 l. violet	40	30
B 11.	B **4.**	25 l. olive	50	40
B 12.	B **5.**	50 l. green	50	50
B 13.	B **6.**	100 l. purple	55	55

1949. Partisans issue.

B 14.	**77.**	50 p. olive	5	5
B 15.		1 d. green	5	5
B 16.	**78.**	2 d. red	5	5
B 17.	–	3 d. red (No. 508)	5	5
B 18.	**78.**	4 d. blue	8	5
B 19.	–	5 d. blue (No. 511)	5	5
B 20.	–	9 d. mauve (No. 514)	12	8
B 21.	–	12 d. blue (No. 515)	30	12
B 22.	**77.**	16 d. blue	25	15
B 23.	–	20 d. red (No. 517)	40	20

1949. U.P.U. 75th Anniv.

B 24.	–	5 d. blue (No. 612)	3·00	2·10
B 25.	**110.**	12 d. brown	3·00	2·10

1949. Air. Optd. **DIN** or surch. also.

B 26.	B **4.**	1 d. blue	5	5
B 27.	B **5.**	2 d. brown	5	5
B 28.	B **4.**	5 d. blue	5	8
B 29.	B **5.**	10 d. violet	12	12
B 30.	B **4.**	15 d. on 25 l. olive	1·25	1·10
B 31.	B **5.**	20 d. on 50 l. green	50	50
B 32.	B **6.**	30 d. on 100 l. purple	80	55

1950. Railway Cent.

B 33.	**112.**	2 d. green	20	12
B 34.	–	3 d. red (No. 632)	25	15
B 35.	–	5 d. blue (No. 633)	35	20
B 36.	–	10 d. orange (No. 633a)	1·60	75

B **7.** Workers. B **8.** Girl on Donkey.

1950. May Day.

B 45.	B **7.**	3 d. violet	25	15
B 46.		10 d. red	30	15

1950.

B 37.	B **8.**	50 p. slate	5	5
B 38.	–	1 d. red (Cockerel)	5	5
B 38a.	–	1 d. brown (Cockerel)	5	5
B 39a.	–	2 d. blue (Geese)	5	5
B 40.	–	3 d. brown (Bees)	12	5
B 40a.	–	3 d. red (Bees)	20	5
B 41.	–	5 d. green (Oxen)	20	5
B 42.	–	10 c. brown (Turkey)	20	5
B 43.	–	15 d. violet (Kids)	1·90	1·10
B 44.	–	20 d. olive (Silkworms)	70	30

1950. Red Cross.

B 47.	**111.**	50 p. brown and red	12	8

B **9.** Worker. B **10.** P. P. Vergerio, Jr.

1951. May Day.

B 48.	B **9.**	3 d. red	15	12
B 49.		10 d. olive	30	20

1951. Red Cross.

B 49a.	**139.**	50 p. blue and red	1·60	1·25

1951. Festival of Italian Culture.

B 50.	B **10.**	5 d. blue	30	20
B 51.		10 d. claret	30	20
B 52.		20 d. chocolate	30	20

1951. Cultural Anniversaries.

B 53	**137.**	10 d. orange	20	15
B 54.	–	12 d. blk. (As No. 699)	25	15

B **10a.** Koper Square. B **11.** Cyclists.

1952. Air. U.P.U. 75th Anniv.

B 54a.	B **10a.**	5 d. brown	3·25	3·00
B 54b.	–	15 d. blue	2·10	1·75
B 54c.	–	25 d. green	1·60	1·25

DESIGNS—VERT. 15 d. Lighthouse, Pirano. HORIZ. 25 d. Hotel, Portorose.

1952. Physical Culture Propaganda.

B 55.	B **11.**	5 d. brown	8	5
B 56.	–	10 d. green	12	5
B 57.	–	15 d. red	20	5
B 58.	–	28 d. blue	25	25
B 59.	–	50 d. lake	40	15
B 60.	–	100 d. slate	1·25	75

DESIGNS: 10 d. Footballers. 15 d. Rowing four. 28 d. Yachts. 50 d. Netballers. 100 d. Swimmer.

1952. Marshall Tito's 60th Birthday. Stamps of Yugoslavia inscr. "STT VUJA".

B 61.	**144.**	15 d. brown	12	8
B 62.	**145.**	28 d. lake	25	12
B 63.	–	50 d. green (No. 729)	40	40

1952. Children's Week.

B 64.	**146.**	15 d. red	12	8

1952. 15th Olympic Games, Helsinki. As Nos. 731/6.

B 65.	**147.**	5 d. chocolate on flesh	25	15
B 66.	–	10 d. green on green	25	15
B 67.	–	15 d. violet on mauve	25	15
B 68.	–	28 d. chocolate on buff	50	25
B 69.	–	50 d. brown on yellow	1·75	1·00
B 70.	–	100 d. blue on pink	7·00	4·25

1952. Navy Day. Nos. 737/9.

B 71.	–	15 d. purple	35	35
B 72.	**148.**	28 d. brown	50	50
B 73.	–	50 d. black	80	80

1952. Red Cross.

B 74.	**149.**	50 p. red, grey & blk.	12	8

1952. 6th Yugoslav Communist Party Congress.

B 75.	**150.**	15 d. red-brown	15	8
B 76.		15 d. turquoise	15	8
B 77.		15 d. chocolate	15	8
B 78.		15 d. blue	15	8

B **12.** Starfish.

1952. Philatelic Exn. Capodistria.

B 78a.	B **12.**	15 d. lake	30	15

1953. Tesla.

B 79.	**151.**	15 d. red	8	5
B 80.		30 d. blue	15	15

1953. Pictorials of 1950.

B 81.		1 d. grey (705)	15	15
B 86.		2 d. red (718)	5	5
B 82.		3 d. red (655)	5	5
B 87.		5 d. orange (719)	5	5
B 106.		10 d. green (721)	5	5
B 107.		15 d. red (723)	12	5
B 84.		30 d. blue (712)	12	5
B 85.		50 d. green (714)	40	12

1953. United Nations. Nos. 747/9.

B 89.	**152.**	15 d. green	12	12
B 90.	–	30 d. blue	15	12
B 91.	–	50 d. lake	40	20

1953. Adriatic Car Rally. As Nos. 750/3.

B 92.	**153.**	15 d. brown & yellow	8	5
B 93.	–	30 d. grn. & blue-grn.	12	5
B 94.	–	50 d. lake and pink	15	5
B 95.	–	70 d. indigo and blue	35	30

1953. Marshal Tito.

B 96.	**154.**	50 d. grey	30	20

1953. 38th Esperanto Congress, Zagreb.

B 97.	**155.**	15 d. green and slate (postage)	20	20
B 98.	**155.**	300 d. grn. & vio. (air)	25·00	25·00

1953. Liberation of Istria and Slovene Coast.

B 99.	**157.**	15 d. blue	12	8

1953. Radicevic.

B 100.	**158.**	15 d. black	12	8

1953. Red Cross.

B 101.	**159.**	2 d. red and brown	8	8

1953. First Republican Legislative Assembly. As Nos. 762/4.

B 102.	**160.**	15 d. slate	12	8
B 103.	–	30 d. lake	15	10
B 104.	–	50 d. green	30	20

1954. Air. As Nos. 675 etc.

B 108.		1 d. lilac	5	5
B 109.		2 d. green	5	5
B 110.		3 d. claret	5	5
B 111.		5 d. brown	5	5
B 112.		10 d. turquoise	5	5
B 113.		20 d. brown	5	5
B 114.		30 d. blue	12	10
B 115.		50 d. olive	20	12
B 116.		100 d. red	50	40
B 117.		200 d. violet	85	75
B 118.		500 d. orange	3·50	3·00

1954. Animals. As Nos. 765/76.

B 119.		2 d. slate, buff & chestnut	5	5
B 120.		5 d. brown and grey	5	5
B 121.		10 d. brown and green	5	5
B 122.		15 d. brown and turquoise	8	5
B 123.		17 d. brown and sepia	12	8
B 124.		25 d. yellow, blue & ochre	15	8
B 125.		30 d. sepia & grey-violet	20	12
B 126.		35 d. black and purple	25	12
B 127.		50 d. choc. & yell.-green	40	30
B 128.		65 d. black and brown	1·00	1·00
B 129.		70 d. brown and blue	1·10	1·10
B 130.		100 d. black and blue	6·50	4·00

1954. Serbian Insurrection. As Nos. 778/81.

B 131.	–	15 d. multicoloured	12	8
B 132.	**162.**	30 d. multicoloured	15	12
B 133.	–	50 d. multicoloured	25	20
B 134.	–	70 d. multicoloured	50	40

POSTAGE DUE STAMPS

1948. Red Cross. No. D 546 surch. **VUJA STT** and new value.

BD 4.	**85.**	2 l. on 50 p. red & grn.	19·00	15·00

1949. On 1946 issue.

BD 26.	D **14.**	50 p. orange	12	8
BD 27.		1 d. orange	12	8
BD 74.		1 d. chocoate	5	5
BD 28.		2 d. blue	12	8
BD 75.		2 d. green	5	5
BD 29.		3 d. green	12	8
BD 30.		5 d. violet	30	20
BD 76.		5 d. blue	12	5
BD 77.		10 d. red	5	5
BD 78.		20 d. violet	5	5
BD 79.		30 d. orange	8	5
BD 80.		50 d. blue	15	12
BD 81.		100 d. purple	75	55

Nos. BD 26/30 optd. **STT VUJA** and the rest **STT VUJNA.**

1950. Red Cross. No. D 617 optd. **VUJA STT.**

BD 48.	**111.**	50 p. purple and red	25	15

BD **1.** Fish.

1950.

BD 49.	–	0 d. 50 brown	12	8
BD 50.	–	1 d. green	30	20
BD 51.	BD **1.**	2 d. blue	50	35
BD 52.		3 d. blue	55	40
BD 53.		5d. purple	1·75	1·00

DESIGN: 0 d. 50, 1 d. Two fishes.

1951. Red Cross. No. D 703 optd. **STT VUJA.**

BD 50.	**139.**	50 p. green and red	19·00	18·00

The following are optd. **STT VUJNA.**

1952. Red Cross. No. D 741.

BD 82.	D **17.**	50 p. red and grey	20	15

1953. Red Cross. As No. D 760.

BD 102.	**159.**	2 d. red and purple	20	15

TRINIDAD BC

An island in the Br. W. Indies off the coast of Venezuela. Now uses stamps of Trinidad and Tobago.

1. Britannia. **2.**

1851. Imperf.

2.	**1.**	(1d.) brown	4·00	22·00
3.		(1d.) blue	3·50	16·00
5.		(1d.) grey	15·00	18·00
8.		(1d.) red	45·00	25·00
25.	**2.**	4d. lilac	28·00	£100
28.		6d. green	—	£200
29.		1s. deep blue	32·00	£110

ILLUSTRATIONS
British Commonwealth and all overprints and surcharges are FULL SIZE. Foreign Countries have been reduced to ¾-LINEAR.

3.

1852. Imperf.

18.	**3.**	(1d.) blue	—	£300
19.		(1d.) grey	—	£200
20.		(1d.) red	7·00	£175

1859. Perf.

91.	**1.**	(1d.) red	1·75	55
75.	**2.**	4d. lilac	9·00	5·00
94.		4d. grey	11·00	1·40
95.		6d. green	11·00	1·25
63.		1s. blue	£225	38·00
85.		1s. purple	22·00	4·00
97.		1s. orange	12·00	3·25

4. 5.

1869.

113.	**4.**	5s. red	4·25	6·50

1879. Surch. in words.

98.	**1.**	½d. lilac	3·50	4·00
101.		½d. red	5·00	65

1882. No. 95 surch. **1d.** with pen.

104.	**2.**	1d. on 6d. green	2·50	2·00

1883.

106.	**5.**	½d. green	25	15
107.		1d. red	40	15
108.		2½d. blue	1·00	15
110.		4d. grey	1·00	30
111.		6d. black	1·25	1·50
112.		1s. orange	2·25	1·50

6. Britannia. 7.

1896.

114.	**6.**	½d. purple and green ..	12	10
126.		½d. green	15	10
115.		1d. purple and red ..	20	10
127.		1d. black on red ..	20	8
135.		1d. red	25	10
117.		2½d. purple and blue ..	40	30
128.		2½d. purple & blue on blue	1·10	50
137.		2½d. blue	40	15
118.		4d. purple and orange ..	1·25	2·00
129.		4d. green and blue on buff	80	1·00
138.		4d. grey and red on yellow	1·10	2·00
119.		5d. purple and mauve ..	1·50	2·50
120.		6d. purple and black ..	1·50	1·50
140.		6d. purple and mauve ..	3·00	2·10
121.		1s. green and brown ..	2·25	3·25
130.		1 s. black & blue on yellow	2·25	2·10
142.		1s. purple & blue on yellow	3·50	3·50
143.		1s. black on green ..	1·00	1·25
122.	**7.**	5s. green and brown ..	13·00	16·00
131.		5s. purple and mauve ..	8·50	9·50
123.		10 s. green and blue ..	80·00	70·00
124.		£1 green and red	80·00	70·00

8. Landing of Columbus. 9.

1898. Discovery of Trinidad. 4th Cent.

125.	**8.**	2d. brown and violet ..	1·25	70

1909. Figures in corners.

146.	**9.**	½d. green	15	10
147.	–	1d. red	15	8
148.		2½d. blue	1·00	1·10

On the 1d. figures are in lower corners only.

POSTAGE DUE STAMPS

D 1.

1885.

D 1.	**D 1.**	½d. black	4·50	50
D 10.		1d. black	12	12
D 11.		2d. black	15	12
D 12.		3d. black	20	15
D 13.		4d. black	30	35
D 14.		5d. black	70	55
D 15.		6d. black	90	70
D 16.		8d. black	90	70
D 17.		1s. black	2·00	1·50

For stamps in Type D 1 but with value in cents see under Trinidad and Tobago.

OFFICIAL STAMPS

1894. Optd. **O.S.**

O 1.	**5.**	½d. green	5·50	5·50
O 2.		1d. red	6·50	6·50
O 3.		2½d. blue	7·50	7·50
O 4.		4d. grey	8·50	8·50
O 5.		6d. black	8·50	8·50
O 6.		1s. orange	13·00	13·00
O 7.	**4.**	5s. red	24·00	26·00

1909. Optd. **OFFICIAL.**

O 8.	**6.**	½d. green	20	20
O 9.		1d. red	10	10

1910. Optd. **OFFICIAL.**

O 10.	**9.**	½d. green	8	8

TRINIDAD AND TOBAGO BC

Combined issues for Trinidad and Tobago, administratively, one colony. Part of the Br. Caribbean Federation from 1958 until 31st August, 1962, on becoming independent within the Br. Commonwealth.

1935. 100 cents = 1 West Indian dollar.

1.

1913.

149.	**1.**	½d. green	12	10
150a.		1d. red	10	5
208.		1d. brown	12	10
209.		2d. grey	1·00	1·00
151a.		2½d. blue	90	50
211.		3d. blue	90	1·00
152.		4d. black & red on yellow	70	1·00
212.		6d. purple and mauve ..	90	1·00
154a.		1s. black on green ..	1·40	1·75

As T 7 of Trinidad, but inscr. "TRINIDAD & TOBAGO".

155.		5s. purple and mauve ..	6·50	8·00
156.		£1 green and red ..	45·00	50·00

1915. Optd. cross over **21.10.15.**

174.	**1.**	1d. red	20	30

1916. Optd. **19.10.16.** over cross.

175.	**1.**	1d. red	12	25

WAR TAX (2.)

WAR TAX (3.)

WAR TAX (4.)

WAR TAX (5.)

WAR TAX (6.)

War Tax (7.)

1917. T 1 optd.

177.	**3.**	½d. green	8	8
183.	**4.**	½d. green	10	12
187.	**7.**	½d. green	8	8
180.	**2.**	1d. red	8	8
178.	**3.**	1d. red	8	10
182.	**4.**	1d. red	8	8
185.	**5.**	1d. red	8	8
186.	**6.**	1d. red	8	8
188.	**7.**	1d. red	8	8

9.

1922.

218.	**9.**	½d. green	8	8
219.		1d. brown	10	5
220a.		1½d. red	15	10
222.		2d. grey	25	15
223.		3d. blue	65	25
216.		4d. black & red on yellow	40	50
225.		6d. purple and mauve	3·00	5·00
226.		6d. green & red on green	1·25	65
227.		1s. black on green ..	1·25	75
228.		5s. purple and mauve ..	8·50	9·50
229.		£1 green and red ..	45·00	48·00

10. First Boca.

1935.

230a.	**10.**	1 c. blue and green ..	5	5
231a.	–	2 c. blue and brown ..	8	8
232.	–	3 c. black and red ..	10	10
233.	–	6 c. brown and blue ..	20	20
234.	–	8 c. green and orange ..	35	30
235.	–	12 c. black and violet ..	30	40
236.	–	24 c. black & olive-green	80	80
237.	–	48 c. green	3·00	4·00
238.	–	72 c. green and red ..	6·50	7·50

DESIGNS: 2 c. Imperial College of Tropical Agriculture. 3 c. Mt. Irvine Bay, Tobago. 6 c. Discovery of Lake Asphalt. 8 c. Queen's Park, Savannah. 12 c. Town Hall, San Fernando. 24 c. Govt. House. 40 c. Memorial Park. 72 c. Blue Basin.

1935. Silver Jubilee. As T **11** of Antigua.

239.	2 c. blue and black ..	8	8
240.	3 c. blue and red	10	15
241.	6 c. brown and blue ..	35	50
242.	24 c. grey and purple ..	1·25	1·40

1937. Coronation. As T **2** of Aden.

243.	1 c. green	5	5
244	2 c. brown	12	10
245.	8 c. orange	25	25

11. First Boca.

1938. Designs as 1935 issue but with portrait of King George VI as in T **11** and without "POSTAGE & REVENUE".

246.	**11.**	1 c. blue and green ..	5	5
247.	–	2 c. blue and brown ..	5	5
248.	–	3 c. black and red ..	2·75	35
248a.	–	3 c. green and purple ..	5	5
249.	–	4 c. brown	1·25	70
249a.	–	4 c. red	15	12
249b.	–	5 c. magenta	8	5
250.	–	6 c. brown and blue ..	10	5
251.	–	8 c. olive and red ..	10	8
252a.	–	12 c. black and purple ..	40	8
253.	–	24 c. black and olive ..	35	15
254.	–	60 c. green and red ..	80	60

NEW DESIGNS: 4 c. Memorial Park. 5 c. G.P.O. and Treasury. 60 c. as No. 238.

12.

1940.

255.	**12.**	$1.20 green	1·10	50
256.		$4.80 red	6·00	3·00

1946. Victory. As T **4** of Aden.

257.	3 c. brown	5	5
258.	6 c. blue	5	5

1948. Silver Wedding. As T **5/6** of Aden.

259.	3 c. brown	5	5
260.	$4.80 red	6·50	7·50

1949. U.P.U. As T **14/17** of Antigua.

261.	5 c. purple	8	8
262.	6 c. blue	12	20
263.	12 c. violet	25	25
264.	24 c. olive	40	40

1951. B.W.I. University College. As T **18/9** of Antigua, but inscr. "TRINIDAD" only.

265.	**18.**	3 c. green and brown ..	12	8
266.	**19.**	12 c. black and violet ..	35	30

13. First Boca.

1953. Designs as 1938 and 1940 issues but with portrait of Queen Elizabeth in place of King George VI as in T **13** (1 c., 2 c., 12 c.) or facing left (others).

267.	**13.**	1 c. blue and green ..	5	5
268.	–	2 c. blue and brown ..	5	5
269.	–	3 c. green and purple ..	5	5
270.	–	4 c. red	8	8
271.	–	5 c. magenta ..	10	10
272.	–	6 c. brown and blue ..	12	10
273.	–	8 c. olive and red ..	12	10
274.	–	12 c. black and purple	15	10
275.	–	24 c. black and olive ..	30	20
276.	–	60 c. green and red ..	60	30
277a.	–	$1.20 green ..	90	45
278a.	–	$4.80 red	5·00	4·00

1953. Coronation. As T **7** of Aden.

279.	3 c. black and green ..	5	8

1956. No. 268 surch. **ONE CENT.**

280.	1 c. on 2 c. blue & brown	60	85

1958. British Caribbean Federation. As T **21** of Antigua.

281.	5 c. green	10	10
282.	6 c. blue	12	12
283.	12 c. red	25	25

14. Cipriani Memorial.

15. Humming Bird.

1960.

284.	**14.**	1 c. stone and black ..	5	5
285.	–	2 c. blue	5	5
286.	–	5 c. blue	5	5
287.	–	6 c. brown	5	5
288.	–	8 c. green	8	5
289.	–	10 c. lilac	8	5
290.	–	12 c. vermilion	8	5
291.	–	15 c. orange (A) ..	45	45
291a.	–	15 c. orange (B) ..	35	25
292.	–	25 c. red and blue ..	25	20
293.	–	35 c. emerald and black	25	15
294.	–	50 c. yell., grey & blue	35	20
295.	–	60 c. verm., grn. & ind.	45	30
296.	**15.**	$1.20 multicoloured ..	1·25	60
297.	–	$4.80 green and blue ..	4·00	3·00

DESIGNS—As T **14**—HORIZ. 2 c. Queen's Hall. 5 c. Whitehall. 6 c. Treasury Building. 8 c. Governor-General's House. 10 c. General Hospital, San Fernando. 12 c. Oil refinery. 15 c. (A) Crest, (B) Coat-of-Arms. 25 c. Scarlet ibis. 35 c. Pitch Lake. 50 c. Mohammed Jinnah Mosque. VERT. 60 c. Anthurium lilies. As T **15**: $4.80 Map of Trinidad and Tobago.

16. Scouts and Gold Wolf Badge.

1961. 2nd Caribbean Scout Jamboree. Design multicoloured. Background colours given.

298. **16.** 8 c. green 15 20
299. 25 c. blue 35 35

17. Underwater Scene after painting by Carlisle Chang.

1962. Independence.

300. **17.** 5 c. blue-green 8 8
301. – 8 c. grey 12 12
302. – 25 c. violet 25 25
303. – 35 c. brown, yellow green and black .. 25 25
304. – 60 c. red, black & blue 50 50

DESIGNS: 8 c. Piarco Air Terminal. 25 c. Hilton Hotel, Port-of-Spain. 35 c. Bird of Paradise and map. 60 c. Scarlet Ibis and map.

18. " Protein Foods ".

1963. Freedom from Hunger.

305. **18.** 5 c. red 8 5
306. 8 c. bistre 10 10
307. 25 c. blue 25 25

19. Jubilee Emblem.

1964. Golden Jubilee of Trinidad and Tobago Girl Guides' Assn.

308. **19.** 6 c. yell., ultram. & red 8 8
309. 25 c. yell., ult. & blue.. 30 30
310. 35 c. yellow, u.t. & grn. 40 45

20. I.C.Y. Emblem.

1965. Int. Co-operation Year.

311. **20.** 35 c. brown, grn. & yell. 30 30

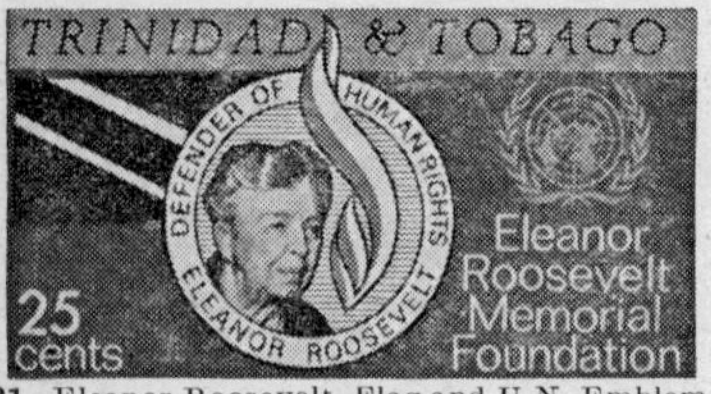

21. Eleanor Roosevelt, Flag and U.N. Emblem.

1965. Eleanor Roosevelt Memorial Foundation.

312. **21.** 25 c. black, red & blue.. 20 20

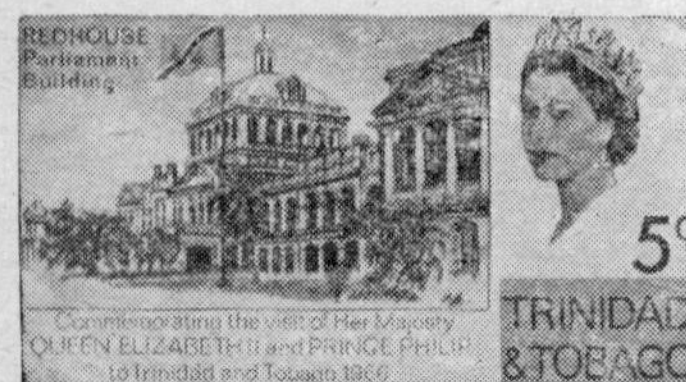

22. Parliament Building.

1966. Royal Visit. Multicoloured.

313. 5 c. Type **22** 5 5
314. 8 c. Map, H.M. Yacht "Britannia" and Arms.. 8 8
315. 25 c. Map and Flag .. 15 20
316. 35 c. Flag and Panorama.. 30 30

1967. 5th Year of Independence. Nos. 288, 289, 291a and 295 optd. **FIFTH YEAR OF INDEPENDENCE 31st AUGUST 1967.**

318. 8 c. green 8 8
319. 10 c. lilac 8 8
320. 15 c. orange 10 10
321. 60 c. verm., grn. & indigo 35 40

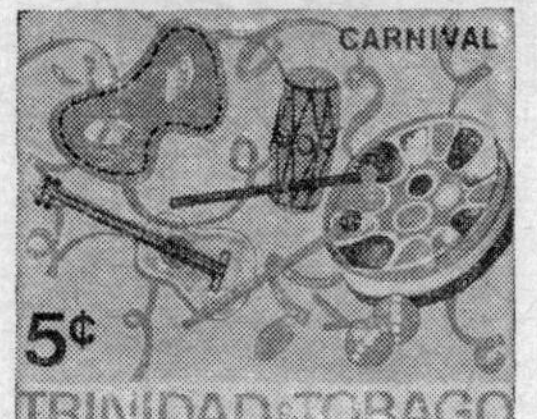

23. Musical Instruments.

1968. Trinidad Carnival. Multicoloured.

322. 5 c. Type **23** 5 5
323. 10 c. Calypso King .. 8 8
324. 15 c. Steel Band 10 8
325. 25 c. Carnival Procession 12 12
326. 35 c. Carnival King .. 2) 20
327. 60 c. Carnival Queen .. 35 35

The 10, 35 and 60 c. are vert.

24. Doctor giving Eye-Test.

1968. World Health Organisation 20th Anniv.

328. **24.** 5 c. red, brown and gold 5 5
329. 25 c. orange, brown & gold 15 15
330. 35 c. blue, black & gold 20 20

25. Peoples of the World and Emblem.

1968. Human Rights Year.

331. **25.** 5 c. cerise, blk. & yellow 5 5
332. 10 c. bl., blk. & yellow 8 8
333. 25 c. grn., blk. & yellow 20 25

26. Cycling.

1968. Olympic Games, Mexico. Multicoloured.

334. 5 c. Type **26** 5 5
335. 15 c. Weightlifting .. 10 10
336. 25 c. Relay-Racing .. 15 15
337. 35 c. Sprinting 20 20
338. $1.20 Maps of Mexico and Trinidad.. .. .. 75 90

27. Cocoa Beans.

1969. Multicoloured.

339. 1 c. Type **27** 5 5
340. 3 c. Sugar Refinery .. 5 5
341. 5 c. Cocrico 5 5
342. 6 c. Oil Refinery 5 5
343. 8 c. Fertiliser Plant .. 5 5
344. 10 c. Green Hermit .. 10 8
345. 12 c. Citrus Fruit.. .. 8 5
346. 15 c. Arms of Trinidad and Tobago 8 5
347. 20 c. Flag and outline of Trinidad and Tobago .. 10 8
348. 25 c. As 20 c. 10 10
349. 30 c. Chaconia 15 12
350. 40 c. Scarlet Ibis .. 20 15
351. 50 c. Maracas Bay .. 25 25
352. $1 Poui Tree 35 40
353. $2.50 Fishing .. .. 90 1·00
354. $5 Red House .. .. 2·00 2·25

Nos. 344/9 and 352 are vert.

28. Captain A. A. Cipriani and Entrance to Woodford Square.

1969. Int. Labour Organization. 50th Anniv.

355. **28.** 6 c. black, gold and red 5 5
356. – 15 c. black, gold & blue 12 20

DESIGN: 15 c. Arms of Industrial Court and entrance to Woodford Square.

29. Cornucopia and Fruit.

1969. C.A.R.I.F.T.A. 1st Anniv. Multicoloured.

357. 6 c. Type **29** 5 5
358. 10 c. Flags of Britain and member-nations .. 8 8
359. 30 c. Map showing C.A.R.I.F.T.A. countries 25 25
360. 40 c. Boeing "727" in flight 35 35

The 10 c. and 40 c. are horiz.

30. Space Module landing on Moon.

1969. 1st Man on the Moon. Multicoloured.

361. 6 c. Type **30** 5 5
362. 40 c. Space module and astronauts on Moon's surface 25 30
363. $1 Astronauts seen from inside space module .. 65 75

The 40 c. is vert.

31. Parliamentary Chamber, Flags and Emblems.

1969. 15th Commonwealth Parliamentary Assn. Conf., Port of Spain. Multicoloured.

364. 10 c. Type **31** 8 8
365. 15 c. J. F. Kennedy College, University of the West Indies, and emblem 10 10
366. 30 c. Parliamentary Conference emblems .. 25 25
367. 40 c. Cannon at Fort King George, Tobago & emblem 35 35

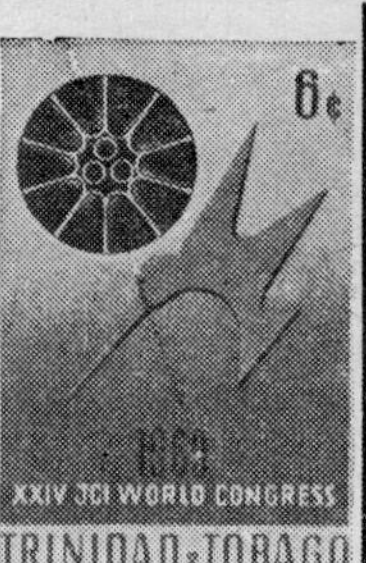

32. Congress Emblem. **33.** "Man in the Moon".

1969. Int. Congress of the Junior Chamber of Commerce.

368. **32.** 6 c. black, red and gold 5 5
369. – 30 c. gold, lake and blue 20 25
370. – 40 c. black, gold & ult. 25 30

DESIGNS: (both incorporating the Congress emblem). HORIZ. 30 c. Islands at daybreak. VERT. 40 c. Palm trees and ruin.

1970. Carnival Winners. Multicoloured.

371. 5 c. Type **33** 5 5
372. 6 c. "City beneath the sea" 5 5
373. 15 c. "Antelope" God Bamibara 10 10
374. 30 c. " Chanticleer Pheasant Queen of Malaya " .. 15 15
375. 40 c. Steel-band of the year 25 25

34. Statue of Gandhi.

1970. Gandhi Centenary Year (1969). Multicoloured.

376. 10 c. Type **34** 8 8
377. 30 c. Head of Gandhi and flag of India (horiz.) .. 20 25

35. Symbols of Culture, Science, Arts and Technology.

1970. U.N. 25th Anniv.

378. **35.** 5 c. multicoloured .. 5 5
379. – 10 c. multicoloured .. 5 5
380. – 20 c. multicoloured .. 15 15
381. – 30 c. multicoloured .. 25 25

DESIGNS AND SIZES: 10 c. Children of different races, Map and flag (34 × 25 mm.). 20 c. Noah's Ark, Rainbow and Dove (34 × 23 mm.). 30 c. New U.P.U. H.Q. Building (46 × 27½ mm.).

1970. National Commercial Bank. Inaug. No. 341 optd. **NATIONAL COMMERCIAL BANK ESTABLISHED 1.7.70.**

382. 5 c. multicoloured 8 8

36. " East Indian Immigrants ".

1970. San Fernando. 125th Anniv. Paintings by Cazabon.

383. **36.** 3 c. multicoloured .. 5 5
384. – 5 c. black, blue & ochre 5 5
385. – 40 c. black, blue & ochre 30 40

DESIGNS—HORIZ. 5 c. " San Fernando Town Hall ". 40 c. " San Fernando Harbour ".

37. "The Adoration of the Shepherds" (detail, School of Seville).

1970. Christmas. Multicoloured.

386. 3 c. Type 37 .. .. 5 5
387. 5 c. "Madonna and Child with Saints" (detail, Titian) 5 5
388. 30 c. "The Adoration of the Shepherds" (detail, Le Nain) 20 20
389. 40 c. "The Virgin and Child, St. John and an Angel" (Morando) .. 25 25
390. $1 "The Adoration of the Magi" (detail, Veronese) 60 60

38. Brocket-Deer.

1971. Trinidad Wildlife. Multicoloured.

392. 3 c. Type 38 .. .. 5 5
393. 5 c. Quenk (pig) 5 5
394. 6 c. Lappe (rodent) .. 5 5
395. 30 c. Agouti (rodent) .. 20 20
396. 40 c. Ocelot 30 30

39. A. A. Cipriani. **40.** "Virgin and Child with St. Joan" (detail Bartolommeo).

1971. Independence. 9th Anniv. Multicoloured.

397. 5 c. Type 39 .. 5 5
398. 30 c. Chaconia medal .. 20 20

1971. Christmas.

399. 40. 3 c. multicoloured .. 5 5
400. – 5 c. multicoloured .. 5 5
401. – 10 c. multicoloured .. 10 10
402. – 15 c. multicoloured .. 15 15

DESIGNS: 5 c. Local Creche. 10 c. "Virgin and Child with Saints Jerome and Dominic" (detail, Lippi). 15 c. "Virgin and Child with St. Anne" (detail Gerolamo dai Libri).

41. Satellite Earth Station, Matura.

1971. Satellite Earth Station. Multicoloured.

403. 10 c. Type 41 .. .. 8 8
404. 30 c. Dish antennae .. 20 20
405. 40 c. Satellite and the Earth 25 25

42. Morpho Hybrid.

1972. Butterflies. Multicoloured.

407. 3 c. Type 42 .. .. 5 5
408. 5 c. Purple Mort Bleu .. 5 5
409. 6 c. Jaune d'Abricot .. 5 5
410. 10 c. Purple King Shoemaker 8 8
411. 20 c. Southern White Page 15 15
412. 30 c. Little Jaune 25 25

43. S.S. "Lady McLeod" and McLeod Stamp.

1972. 1st Trinidad Postage Stamp. 125th Anniv.

413. 43. 5 c. multicoloured .. 8 8
414. – 10 c. multicoloured .. 10 10
415. – 30 c. blue, brn. & blk. 25 25

DESIGNS: 10 c. Lady McLeod stamp and Map. 30 c. Lady McLeod and inscription.

44. Trinity Cross.

1972. Independence. 10th Anniv. Mult.

417. 5 c. Type 44 .. .. 5 5
418. 10 c. Chaconia medal .. 8 8
419. 20 c. Humming-bird medal 15 15
420. 30 c. Medal of Merit .. 25 25

See also Nos. 440/3.

45. Bronze Medal, 1964 Relay.

1972. Munich Olympics. Multicoloured.

422. 10 c. Type 45 .. .. 8 8
423. 20 c. Bronze, 1964 200 metres 12 12
424. 30 c. Silver, 1952 weight-lifting 20 20
425. 40 c. Silver, 1964 400 metres 25 25
426. 50 c. Silver, 1948 weight-lifting 30 30

46. "Adoration of the Kings" (detail, Dosso).

1972. Christmas. Multicoloured.

428. 3 c. Type 46 .. .. 5 5
429. 5 c. "The Holy Family" (Titian) 8 8
430. 30 c. As 5 c. 25 25

47. E.C.L.A. Building, Chile.

1973. Anniversaries. Events described on stamps. Multicoloured.

435. 10 c. Type 47 .. .. 8 8
436. 20 c. Interpol emblem .. 12 12
437. 30 c. W.M.O. emblem .. 15 20
438. 40 c. University of the West Indies 20 20

1973. Independence. 11th Anniv. Medals as T 44. Multicoloured.

440. 10 c. Trinity Cross .. 8 8
441. 20 c. Medal of Merit .. 12 12
442. 30 c. Chaconia medal .. 15 15
443. 40 c. Humming-bird medal 20 20

48. G.P.O., Port of Spain.

1973. 2nd Commonwealth Conference of Postal Administrations, Trinidad. Mult.

445. 30 c. Type 48 .. .. 15 15
446. 40 c. Conference Hall, Chaguaramas 20 20

49. "Virgin and Child" (Murillo).

1973. Christmas.

448. 49. 5 c. multicoloured .. 5 5
449. $1 multicoloured .. 50 50

50. Berne H.Q. within U.P.U. Emblem.

1974. Universal Postal Union. Centenary. Multicoloured.

451. 40 c. Type 50 .. .. 20 20
452. 50 c. Map within emblem .. 25 25

51. "Humming Bird I" crossing Atlantic Ocean (1960).

1974. World Voyage by H. and K. La Borde. 1st Anniv. Multicoloured.

454. 40 c. Type 51 .. .. 20 20
455. 50 c. "Humming Bird II" crossing globe 25 25

52. "Sex Equality".

1975. International Women's Year.

457. 52. 15 c. multicoloured .. 5 8
458. 30 c. multicoloured .. 12 15

53. Vampire Bat, Microscope and Syringe.

1975. Isolation of Rabies Virus. Multicoloured.

459. 25 c. Type 53 .. .. 12 12
460. 30 c. Dr. Pawan, instruments and book .. 12 15

54. Route-map and Tail of Boeing "707".

1975. British West Indies Airways. 35th Anniv. Multicoloured.

461. 20 c. Type 54 .. .. 8 10
462. 30 c. "707" on ground .. 12 15
463. 40 c. "707" in flight .. 15 20

55. "From the Land of the Humming Bird".

1975. Carnival. 1974 Prizewinning Costumes. Multicoloured.

465. 30 c. Type 55 .. 15 20
466. $1 "The Little Carib" .. 45 50

56. Angostura Building, Port of Spain.

1976. Angostura Bitters. 150th Anniv. Multicoloured.

468. 5 c. Type 56 .. .. 5 5
469. 35 c. Medal, New Orleans 1885/6 .. .. .. 15 15
470. 45 c. Medal, Sydney 1879 20 20
471. 50 c. Medal Brussels 1897 20 25

1976. West Indian Victory in World Cricket Cup. As Nos. 559/60 of Barbados.

474. 35 c. Caribbean map .. 15 20
475. 45 c. Prudential Cup .. 20 25

57. "Columbus Sailing Through the Bocas" (Campins).

1976. Paintings. Multicoloured.
477. 5 c. Type 57 .. .. 5 5
478. 10 c. "Old View" (Cazabon) 5 5
479. 20 c. "Trinidad Landscape" (Cazabon) 8 10
480. 35 c. "Los Gallos Point" (Cazabon) 15 15
481. 45 c. "Corbeaux Town" (Cazabon) 20 20

58. Hasely Crawford and Olympic Gold Medal.

1977. Hasely Crawford Commemoration.
500. 58. 25 c. multicoloured .. 12 15

OFFICIAL STAMP

1913. Optd. **OFFICIAL** in various types.
O 11. 1. ½d. green 10 10

POSTAGE DUE STAMPS

1947. As Type D 1 of Trinidad, but value in cents.
D 26. 2 c. black 10 8
D 27. 4 c. black 8 8
D 28. 6 c. black 8 8
D 29a. 8 c. black 8 10
D 30a. 10 c. black 12 12
D 31aa. 12 c. black 10 10
D 32a. 16 c. black 20 40
D 33a. 24 c. black 25 25

D 1.

1969.
D 34. D 1. 2 c. green 5 5
D 35. 4 c. red 5 5
D 36. 6 c. brown 5 5
D 37. 8 c. violet 5 5
D 38. 10 c. red 5 5
D 39. 12 c. yellow 10 12
D 40. 16 c. green 5 12
D 41. 24 c. grey 12 10
D 42. 50 c. blue 20 25
D 43 60 c. green 25 30

1976. Smaller design, 17×21 mm.
D 44. D 1. 4 c. red 5 5
D 48. 12 c. orange 5 5

TRIPOLITANIA O3; BC

One of the provinces into which the Italian colony of Libya was divided. In 1943 Tripolitania was placed under British Military Administration. See also Middle East Forces. From 1952 became part of independent Libya.

Stamps optd. **Tripoli di Barberia** formerly listed here will be found under Italian P.O's in the Levant Nos. 171/81.

Nos. 1/138 except where otherwise described, are Italian stamps sometimes in new colours, overprinted **TRIPOLITANIA.**

1923. Propagation of the Faith.
1. 44. 20 c. orange and green .. 90 1·40
2. 30 c. orange and red .. 90 1·40
3. 50 c. orange and violet .. 70 1·25
4. 1 l. orange and blue .. 70 1·25

1923. Fascisti.
5. 45. 10 c. green 20 35
6. 30 c. violet 25 40
7. 50 c. red 25 50
8. 46. 1 l. brown 30 60
9. 2 l. brown 35 70
10. 47. 5 l. black and blue .. 1·40 2·00

1924. Manzoni.
11. 49. 10 c. black and red .. 20 45
12. 15 c. black and green .. 20 45
13. 30 c. black 20 45
14. 50 c. black and brown .. 20 45
15. 1 l. black and blue .. 6·50 9·00
16. 5 l. black and purple .. 90·00 £110

1925. Holy Year.
17. 51. 20 c.+10 c. brn. & green 20 35
18. 30 c.+15 c. brown & choc. 20 35
19. 50 c.+25 c. brn. & violet 20 35
20. 60 c.+30 c. brown & red 20 35
21. 1 l.+50 c. purple & olive 35 55
22. 5 l.+2 l. 50 purple & red 60 90

1925. Royal Jubilee.
23. 53. 60 c. red 8 15
24a. 1 l. blue 20 35
24c. 1 l. 25 blue 20 35

1926. St. Francis of Assisi.
25. 54. 20 c. green 15 20
26. 40 c. violet 15 20
27. 60 c. red 15 20
28. 1 l. 25 blue 15 20
29. 5 l.+2 l. 50 olive .. 70 1·00

1926. As Colonial Propaganda stamps of Cyrenaica, T 1, but inscr. "TRIPOLITANIA".
30. 5 c.+5 c. brown 8 12
31. 10 c.+5 c. olive 8 12
32. 20 c.+5 c. green 8 12
33. 40 c.+5 c. red 8 12
34. 60 c.+5 c. orange 8 12
35. 1 l.+5 c. blue 8 12

1. Port of Tripoli.

DESIGNS: 40 c. 60 c. Arch of Marcus Aurelius, 75 c., 1 l. 25. View of Tripoli.

1927. First Tripoli Exn.
36. 1. 20 c.+05 c. black & pur. 15 15
37. 25 c.+05 c. black & green 15 15
38. – 40 c.+10 c. black & choc. 15 15
39. – 60 c.+10 c. black & brown 15 15
40. – 75 c.+20 c. black and red 15 15
41. – 1 l. 25+20 c. black & blue 5·50 6·50

1927. 1st National Defence issue.
42. 59. 40+20 c. black & brown 25 50
43. 60+30 c. brown and red 25 50
44. 1 l. 25+60 c. blk. & blue 35 70
45. 5 l.+2 l. 50 blk. & green 70 1·10

1927. Volta. Death Cent.
46. 63. 20 c. violet 35 50
47. 50 c. orange 55 70
48. 1 l. 25 blue .. .. 2·00 2·50

2. Palm Tree. 3. Desert Outpost.

1928. 2nd Tripoli Exn. Inscr. "1928".
49. – 30 c.+20 c. grey & claret 30 40
50. 2. 50 c.+20 c. grey and green 30 40
51. – 1 l. 25+20 c. grey and red 30 40
52. – 1 l. 75+20 c. grey & blue 30 40
53. – 2 l. 55+50 c. grey & brown 45 65
54. 3. 5 l.+1 l. grey and violet .. 1·00 1·60
DESIGNS—As T 2: 30 c. Tripoli. 1 l. 25 c. Camel riders. As T 3: 1 l. 75, Arab citadel. 2 l. 55, Tripoli.

1928. Italian-African Society. 45th Anniv. As T 2 of Cyrenaica.
55. 20 c.+5 c. green 15 35
56. 30 c.+5 c. red 15 35
57. 50 c.+10 c. violet 15 35
58. 1 l. 25+20 c. blue 15 35

1929. 2nd National Defence issue.
59. 59. 30 c.+10 c. black and red 25 45
60. 50 c.+20 c. black & lilac 25 45
61. 1 l. 25+50 c. bl. & brown 40 70
62. 5 l.+2 l. black and olive 40 90

1929. 3rd Tripoli Trade Fair. As T 2/3 but inscr. "1929".
63. 30 c.+20 c. black & claret 35 50
64. 50 c.+20 c. black and green 35 50
65. 1 l. 25+20 c. black and red 35 50
66. 1 l. 75+20 c. black and blue 35 50
67. 2 l. 55+50 c. black & brown 35 50
68. 5 l.+1 l. black and violet 42·00 50·00
DESIGNS—As T 2: 30 c., 1 l. 25, Different trees. 50 c. Antelope. As T 3: 1 l. 75, Goats. 2 l. 55, Camel caravan. 5 l. Trees.

1929. Abbey of Montecassino.
69. 73. 20 c. green 25 35
70. 25 c. orange 25 35
71. 50 c.+10 c. red 25 45
72. 75 c.+15 c. brown .. 25 60
73. 1 l. 25+25 c. purple .. 1·10 1·40
74. 5 l.+1 l. blue .. 1·10 1·75
75. 10 l.+2 l. brown .. 1·10 2·10

1930. 4th Tripoli Trade Fair. As T 2/3 but inscr. "1930".
76. 30 c. brown 20 30
77. 50 c. violet 20 30
78. 1 l. 25 c. blue 20 30
79. 1 l. 75 c.+20 c. red .. 25 40
80. 2 l. 55 c.+45 c. green .. 2·10 2·75
81. 5 l.+1 l. orange .. 1·50 2·25
82. 10 l.+2 l. purple .. 2·75 4·25
DESIGNS—As T 2; 30 c. Gathering bananas, 50 c. Tobacco plant,. 1 l. 25, Venus of Cyrene As T 3 1 l. 75 Water-carriers. 2 l. 55. Antelopes. 5 l. Motor and camel transport. 10 l. Rome pavilion.

1930. Marriage of Prince Humbolt and Princess Marie Jose.
83. 80. 20 c. green 15 25
84. 50 c.+10 c. orange .. 25 40
85. 1 l. 25+25 c. red .. 45 70

1930. Ferrucci.
86. 85. 20 c. violet (postage) .. 15 20
87. – 25 c. green (No. 283) 15 20
88. – 50 c. black (as No. 284) 15 20
89. – 1 l. 25 blue (No. 285) .. 15 20
90. – 5 l.+2 l. red (as No. 286) 95 1·00
91. 88. 50 c. purple (air) .. 25 35
92. 1 l. blue 30 35
93. 5 l.+2 l. red .. 1·00 1·40

1930. 3rd National Defence issue.
94. 59. 30 c.+10 c. green & olive 35 55
95. 50 c.+10 c. violet & olive 35 55
96. 1 l. 25+30 c. brown .. 70 1·10
97. 5 l.+1 l. 50 grn. & blue 5·00 7·00

4.

5.

6.

1930. 25th Anniv. (1929) of Italian Colonial Agricultural Institute.
98. 4. 50 c.+20 c. brown .. 25 35
99. 1 l. 25+20 c. blue .. 25 35
100. 1 l. 75+20 c. green .. 25 35
101. 2 l. 55+50 c. violet .. 90 1·00
102. 5 l.+1 l. red .. .. 90 1·00

1930. Virgil.
103. 89. 15 c. violet (postage) .. 5 10
104. 20 c. brown 5 10
105. 25 c. green 5 10
106. 30 c. brown 5 10
107. 50 c. purple 5 10
108. 75 c. red 5 10
109. 1 l. 25 blue 5 10
110. 5 l.+1 l. 50 purple .. 65 1·00
111. 10 l.+2 l. 50 brown .. 65 1·25
112. 89. 50 c. green (air) .. 8 10
113. 1 l. red 8 10
114. 7 l. 70+1 l. 30 brown .. 40 85
115. 9 l.+2 l. grey .. .. 40 1·00

1931. Air.
116. 5. 50 c. red 8 5
117. 60 c. orange 5 5
117a. 75 c. blue 10 10
118. 80 c. purple 25 30
119. 6. 1 l. blue 8 5
120. 1 l. 20 brown 20 20
121. 1 l. 50 orange 20 20
122. 5 l. green 20 25

7. Statue of Youth.

8. Exhibition Pavilion.

1931. 5th Tripoli Trade Fair.
123. 7. 10 c. grey (postage) .. 20 35
124. – 25 c. green 20 35
125. – 50 c. violet 20 35
126. – 1 l. 25 blue 20 35
127. – 1 l. 75+25 c. red .. 55 90
128. – 2 l. 75+45 c. orange .. 70 1·00
129. – 5 l.+1 l. purple .. 1·40 2·10
130. 8. 10 l.+2 l. brown .. 9·50 16·00
131. – 50 c. blue (air) .. 20 35
DESIGNS—As T 7: 25 c. Arab musician. 50 c. View of Zeughet. 1 l. 25, Snake charmer. 1 l. 75, House and windmill. 2 l. 75, Libyan "Zaptie". 5 l. Arab horseman. As T 8: 50 c. Air, Aeroplane over desert.

1931. St. Anthony of Padua.
132. 92. 20 c. brown 12 15
133. – 25 c. green 12 15
134. – 30 c. brown 12 15
135. – 50 c. purple 12 15
136. – 75 c. grey 12 15
137. – 1 l. 25 blue 12 15
138. – 5 l.+2 l. 50 brown .. 1·00 1·75

9.

1931. Air. 25th Anniv. (1929) of Italian Colonial Agricultural Institute.
139. 9. 50 c. blue 25 30
140. 80 c. violet 25 30
141. 1 l. black 25 30
142. 2 l. green 70 95
143. 5 l.+2 l. red .. .. 4·25 5·00

10. Lioness.

1932. 6th Tripoli Trade Fair. Inscr. "1932".
144. – 10 c. brown (postage) .. 35 20
145. – 20 c. red 35 20
146. – 25 c. green 35 20
147. – 30 c. black 35 20
148. – 50 c. violet 35 20
149. – 75 c. red 35 30
150. – 1 l. 25 c. blue 35 30
151. 10. 1 l. 75 c.+25 c. brown .. 2·10 3·00
152. – 5 l.+1 l. blue .. .. 4·25 6·00
153. – 10 l.+2 l. purple .. 30·00 38·00
154. – 50 c. blue (air) 25 25
155. – 1 l. brown 25 35
156. – 2 l.+1 l. black .. .. 3·75 6·00
157. – 5 l.+2 l. red .. .. 24·00 32·00
DESIGNS. POST.—VERT. 10 c. to 50 c. Various trees. 75 c. Roman mausoleum at Ghirza. 10 l. Gazelle. HORIZ. 1 l. 25 c. Mogadiscio aerodrome. 5 l. Arab and camel. AIR—HORIZ. 50 c., 1 l. Seaplane over Bedouin camp. 2 l. 5 l. Seaplane over Tripoli.

11. Leopard.

1933. 7th Tripoli Trade Fair. Inscr. "1933".
158. – 10 c. purple (postage) .. 2·75 70
159. – 25 c. green .. .. 1·40 35
160. – 30 c. brown .. .. 1·00 35
161. – 50 c. violet .. .. 1·00 35
162. – 1 l. 25 c. blue .. .. 2·50 2·10
163. 11. 5 l.+1 l. brown .. .. 12·00 16·00
164. – 10 l.+2 l. 50 c. red .. 17·00 23·00
165. – 50 c. green (air) 35 50
166. – 75 c. red 35 50
167. – 1 l. blue 35 50
168. – 2 l.+50 c. violet .. 1·40 2·10
169. – 5 l.+1 l. brown .. .. 6·00 10·00
170. – 10 l.+2 l. 50 black .. 7·50 11·00
DESIGNS. POST.—VERT. 10 c. Ostrich. 25 c. Incense plant. 50 c. Arch of Marcus Aurelius. 1 l. 25 c. Eagle. 10 l. Tripoli and Fascist emblem. HORIZ. 30 c. Arab drummer. AIR—HORIZ. 50 c., 2 l. Seaplane over Tripoli. 75 c., 10 l. Aeroplane over Tagiura. 1 l., 5 l. Seaplane leaving Tripoli.

12. Mercury.

DESIGNS: 5 l., 15 l. Arch of Marcus Aurelius. 10 l., 20 l. "Dawn".

1933. "Graf Zeppelin" Air stamps. Inscr. "CROCIERA ZEPPELIN 1933".
171. 12. 3 l. brown .. .. 3·00 7·00
172. – 5 l. violet .. .. 3·00 7·00
173. – 10 l. green .. .. 3·00 7·00
174. – 12 l. blue .. .. 3·00 7·00
175. – 15 l. red .. .. 3·00 7·00
176. – 20 l. black .. .. 3·00 7·00

13. "Flight".

1933. Air. Balbo Transatlantic Flight.
177. 13. 19 l. 75 brown and black 13·00 35·00
178. 44 l. 75 green and blue 13·00 35·00

1934. Air. Rome-Buenos Aires Flight. Optd. with an aeroplane and **1934 XII PRIMO VOLO DIRETTO ROMA-BUENOS-AYRES**, etc., or surch. also in Italian and Arabic.
179. 6. 2 l. on 5 l. brown .. .. 1·25 3·50
180. 3 l. on 5 l. green .. .. 1·25 3·50
181. 5 l. bistre .. .. 1·25 3·50
182. 10 l. on 5 l. red .. .. 1·25 3·50

14. Water Carriers.

1934. 8th Tripoli Trade Fair.
183. 14. 10 c. brown (postage) .. 35 40
184. – 20 c. red 35 40
185. – 25 c. green 35 40
186. – 30 c. brown 35 40
187. – 50 c. violet 35 40
188. – 75 c. red 35 40
189. – 1 l. 25 blue .. 12·00 15·00
DESIGNS—VERT. 20 c. Arab. 25 c. Minaret. 50 c. Statue of Emperor Claudius. HORIZ. 30 c. 1 l. 25 Moslem Shrine. 75 c. Ruins of Ghadames.

190. 50 c. blue (air) 25 55
191. 75 c. orange 40 90
192. 5 l.+1 l. green .. 16·00 21·00
193. 10 l.+2 l. purple .. 16·00 21·00
194. 25 l.+3 l. brown .. 16·00 21·00
DESIGNS—HORIZ. 50 c., 5 l. Flying boat off Tripoli. 75 c., 10 l. Aeroplane over Mosque. VERT. 25 l. Aeroplane and Camel.

E 195. 2 l. 25 green (air express) 4·25 6·00
E 196. 4 l. 50+1 l. blue .. 4·25 6·00
DESIGN: 2 l. 25, 4 l. 50, Aeroplane over Bedouins.

1934. Oasis Flight. As Nos. 190/4 optd. **CIRCUITO DELLE OASI TRIPOLI MAGGIO 1934—XII.**
197. 50 c. red (air) .. .. 2·10 1·75
198. 75 c. yellow .. .. 1·40 1·75
199. 5 l.+1 l. brown .. .. 1·40 1·75
200. 10 l.+2 l. blue £110 £140
201. 25 l.+3 l. violet £110 £150

E 202. 2 l. 25 red (air express) .. 1·40 1·75
E 203. 4 l. 50+1 l. red .. .. 1·40 1·75

DESIGNS: 25 c. to 75 c. Shadow of aeroplane over desert. 80 c. to 2 l. Arab camel corps and aeroplane.

15. Native Village.

1934. 2nd Int. Colonial Exn., Naples. Inscr. as in T 15.
204. 15. 5 c. brn. & green (post.) 50 1·10
205. 10 c. black and brown .. 50 1·10
206. 20 c. slate and red .. 50 1·10
207. 50 c. brown and violet .. 50 1·10
208. 60 c. slate and brown .. 50 1·10
209. 1 l. 25 green and blue .. 50 1·10
210. – 25 c. orange & blue (air) 50 1·10
211. – 50 c. slate and green .. 50 1·10
212. – 75 c. red and brown .. 50 1·10
213. – 80 c. green and brown .. 50 1·10
214. – 1 l. green and red .. 50 1·10
215. – 2 l. brown and blue .. 50 1·10

16.

1934. Air. Rome-Mogadiscio Flight.
216. 16. 25 c.+10 c. green .. 50 2·50
217. 50 c.+10 c. brown .. 50 2·50
218. 75 c.+15 c. red .. 50 2·50
219. 80 c.+15 c. black .. 50 2·50
220. 1 l.+20 c. brown .. 50 2·50
221. 2 l.+20 c. blue .. 50 2·50
222. 3 l.+25 c. violet .. 10·00 14·00
223. 5 l.+25 c. orange .. 10·00 14·00
224. 10 l.+30 c. purple .. 10·00 14·00
225. 25 l.+2 l. green .. 10·00 14·00

17. Camel Transport.

1935. 9th Tripoli Exn.
226. – 10c.+10 c. brown (post) 50 1·10
227. – 20 c.+10 c. red .. .. 50 1·10
228. – 50 c.+10 c. violet .. 50 1·10
229. – 75 c.+15 c. red .. .. 50 1·10
230. – 1 l. 25+25 c. blue .. 50 1·10
231. – 2 l.+50 c. olive-green .. 50 1·10

232. – 25 c.+10 c. green (air) .. 25 40
233. 17. 50 c.+10 c. slate .. 25 40
234. – 1 l.+25 c. blue 25 40
235. – 2 l.+30 c. red 25 40
236. – 3 l.+1 l. 50 brown .. 25 40
237. – 10 l.+5 l. purple .. 7·00 12·00
DESIGNS—VERT.—POSTAGE: 10 c., 20 c. Pomegranate tree. 50 c., 2 l. Arab flautist. 75 c., 1 l. 25, Arab in burnous. AIR: 25 c., 3 l. Watch-tower. HORIZ. 1 l., 10 l. Arab girl and aeroplane.
For issue inscr. "XII FIERA CAMPIONARIA TRIPOLI" and dated "1938", see Libya Nos. 88/95.

BRITISH MILITARY ADMINISTRATION

1948. Stamps of Great Britain surch. **B.M.A. TRIPOLITANIA** and value in "M.A.L." (Military Administration lire).
T 1. 108. 1 l. on ½d. pale green 8 30
T 2. 2 l. on 1d. pale red .. 5 20
T 3. 3 l. on 1½d. pale brown 5 35
T 4. 4 l. on 2d. pale orange 5 25
T 5. 5 l. on 2½d. light blue 8 30
T 6. 6 l. on 3d. pale violet 5 30
T 7. 104. 10 l. on 5d. brown .. 5 25
T 8. 12 l. on 6d. purple .. 8 20
T 9. 105. 18 l. on 9d. olive .. 20 60
T 10. 24 l. on 1s. brown .. 30 75
T 11. 106. 60 l. on 2s. 6d. green .. 85 2·00
T 12. 120 l. on 5s. red .. 1·75 3·50
T 13. 240 l. on 10s. bright blue (No. 478a) .. 3·25 4·75

BRITISH ADMINISTRATION

1950. As Nos. T1/13 but surch. **B.A. TRIPOLITANIA** and value in M.A.L.
T 14. 103. 1 l. on ½d. pale green 10 30
T 27. 1 l. on ½d. orange .. 5 30
T 15. 2 l. on 1d. pale red .. 8 25
T 28. 2 l. on 1d. blue .. 5 30
T 16. 3 l. on 1½d. pale brn. 12 35
T 29. 3 l. on 1½d. green .. 15 30
T 17. 4 l. on 2d. pale orange 5 30
T 30. 4 l. on 2d. brown .. 10 30
T 18. 5 l. on 2½d. light blue 8 30
T 31. 5 l. on 2½d. red .. 8 30
T 19. 6 l. on 3d. pale violet 5 30
T 20. 104. 10 l. on 5d. brown .. 5 25
T 21. 12 l. on 6d. purple .. 5 25
T 22. 105. 18 l. on 9d. olive .. 12 40
T 23. 24 l. on 1s. brown .. 15 40
T 24. 106. 60 l. on 2s. 6d. green 1·25 2·50
T 25. 120 l. on 5s. red .. 2·25 4·50
T 26. – 240 l. on 10s. bright blue (No. 478a) .. 4·00 7·00

1951. Nos. 509/11 of Great Britain surch. **B.A. TRIPOLITANIA** and value in M.A.L.
T 32. 116. 60 l. on 2s. 6d. green 1·50 3·25
T 33. – 120 l. on 5s. red .. 3·50 4·25
T 34. – 240 l. on 10s. blue .. 5·00 7·50

EXPRESS LETTER STAMPS

Express stamps optd. **TRIPOLI DI BARBERIA** formerly listed here will be found under Italian P.O.s in the Levant. Nos. E 6/7.

1927. 1st Tripoli Exn. Inscr. "EXPRES".
E 1. 1 l. 25+30 c. blk. & violet 1·00 1·00
E 2. 2 l. 50+1 l. blk. & orange 1·75 2·00
DESIGN—HORIZ. as T 1: 1 l. 25, 2 l. 50, Camels and palm trees.

1931. 5th Tripoli Exn. Inscr. "EXPRESSO".
E 3. 1 l. 25+20 c. red .. 65 85
DESIGN—HORIZ. as T 8: 1 l. 25, War Memorial.

POSTAGE DUE STAMPS

1948. Postage Due stamps of Great Britain surch. **B.M.A. TRIPOLITANIA** and value in M.A.L.
TD 1. D 1. 1 l. on ½d. green .. 20 70
TD 2. 2 l. on 1d. red .. 25 70
TD 3. 4 l. on 2d. black .. 70 1·25
TD 4. 6 l. on 3d. violet .. 1·25 1·75
TD 5. 24 l. on 1s. blue .. 2·75 3·00

1950. As Nos. TD 1/5 but surch. **B.A. TRIPOLITANIA** and value in M.A.L.
TD 6. D 1. 1 l. on ½d. green .. 50 80
TD 7. 2 l. on 1d. red .. 30 75
TD 8. 4 l. on 2d. black .. 40 80
TD 9. 6 l. on 3d. violet .. 1·75 2·25
TD 10. 24 l. on 1s. blue .. 3·25 3·75

TRISTAN DA CUNHA BC

An island in the S. Atlantic Ocean west of St. Africa. Following a volcanic eruption the island was evacuated on October 10th 1961, but resettled in 1963.

1961. 100 cents=1 rand.
1963. Reverted to sterling currency.

1952. Stamps of St. Helena optd. **TRISTAN DA CUNHA.**
1. 20. ½d. violet 20 35
2. 1d. black and green .. 20 45
3. 1½d. black and red .. 20 75
4. 2d. black and red .. 20 80
5. 3d. grey 40 90
6. 4d. blue 55 10
7. 6d. blue 90 10
8. 8d. green .. .. 1·10 2·25
9. 1s. brown .. .. 1·10 3·25
10. 2s. 6d. maroon .. 6·50 7·50
11. 5s. brown .. .. 10·00 12·00
12. 10s. purple .. .. 21·00 24·00

1953. Coronation. As T 7 of Aden.
13. 3d. black and green .. 1·75 3·00

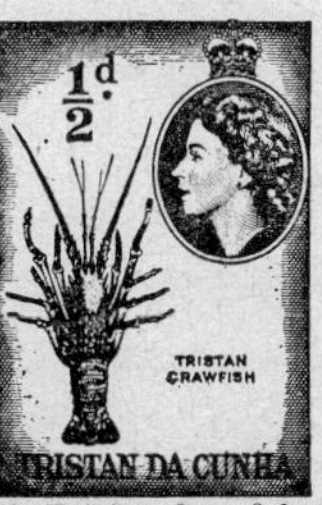

1. Tristan Crawfish.

DESIGNS—HORIZ. 1d. Carting flax. 2d. Big Beach Factory. 2½d. Mollymauk (sea-birds). 4d. Tristan from S.W. 5d. Girls on donkeys. 6d. Inaccessible Is. from Tristan. 9d. Nightingale Is. 1s. St. Mary's Church. 2s. 6d. Elephant seal at Gough Is. 5s. Flightless Rail (bird). 10s. Spinning wheel. VERT. 1½d. Rockhopper penguin. 3d. Island boat.

1954.
14. 1. ½d. vermilion and brown .. 15 20
15. – 1d. sepia and green .. 20 25
16. – 1½d. black and purple .. 30 35
17. – 2d. violet and orange .. 30 30
18. – 2½d. black and red .. 30 35
19. – 3d. blue and olive .. 30 35
20. – 4d. turquoise and blue .. 35 40
21. – 5d. emerald and black .. 40 45
22. – 6d. green and violet .. 40 45
23. – 9d. lilac and claret .. 55 70
24. – 1 s. green and sepia .. 80 90
25. – 2s. 6d. sepia and blue .. 4·00 5·00
26. – 5s. black and vermilion .. 11·00 13·00
27. – 10s. orange and purple .. 18·00 19·00

2. Starfish.

FISH: 1d. Concha Fish. 1½d. Klip Fish. 2d. Heron Fish. 2½d. Swordfish. 3d. Tristan Crawfish. 4d. Soldier Fish. 5d. "Five Finger" Fish. 6d. Mackerel. 9d. Stumpnose Fish. 1s. Blue Fish. 2s. 6d. Snoek. 5s. Shark. 10s. Atlantic Right Whale.

1960. Value, fish and inscriptions in black.
28. 2. ½d. orange 20 25
29. – 1d. purple 30 35
30. – 1½d. turquoise 30 35
31. – 2d. green 30 35
32. – 2½d. sepia 40 45
33. – 3d. red 40 45
34. – 4d. olive 45 50
35. – 5d. yellow 55 65
36. – 6d. blue 60 80
37. – 9d. rose .. .. 85 1·10
38. – 1s. brown .. .. 90 1·50
39. – 2s. 6d. blue .. .. 3·50 4·00
40. – 5s. green .. .. 8·00 9·00
41. – 10s. violet .. .. 18·00 19·00

1961. As 1960 issue but values in new currency. Value, fish and inscriptions black.
42. 2. ½ c. orange 10 12
43. – 1 c. purple (as 1d.) .. 10 15
44. – 1½ c. turquoise (as 1½d.) .. 15 25
45. – 2 c. sepia (as 2½d.) .. 20 30
46. – 2½ c. red (as 3d.) .. 25 30
47. – 3 c. olive (as 4d.) .. 30 40
48. – 4 c. yellow (as 5d.) .. 40 50
49. – 5 c. blue (as 6d.) .. 40 45
50. – 7½ c. rose (as 9d.) .. 45 70
51. – 10 c. brown (as 1s.) .. 80 1·00
52. – 25 c. blue (as 2s. 6d.) .. 3·00 4·00
53. – 50 c. green (as 5s.) .. 8·00 9·00
54. – 1 r. violet (as 10s.) .. 16·00 19·00

1963. Tristan Resettlement. Nos. 176a/88 of St. Helena optd. **TRISTA DA CUNHA RESETTLEMENT 1963.**
55. 24. 1d. blue, violet, yell. & red 5 5
56. – 1½d. yellow, green, black and drab 5 5
57. – 2d. red and grey .. 8 8
58. – 3d. blue, blk., pink & ind. 10 10
59. – 4½d. yellow-green, green brown and grey .. 10 12
60. – 6d. red, sepia and olive .. 15 20
61. – 7d. brown, black & violet 20 25
62. – 10d. maroon and blue .. 25 30
63. – 1s. lemon, green & brown 30 35
64. – 1s. 6d. grey, black and slate-blue 55 60
65. – 2s. 6d. red, yell. & turq. 1·50 1·75
66. – 5s. yellow, brown & green 3·50 2·75
67. – 10s. red, black and blue .. 4·50 5·00

1963. Freedom from Hunger. As T10 of Aden.
68. 1s. 6d. red .. .. .. 2·00 2·25

1964. Red Cross Cen. As T 24 of Antigua.
69. 3d. red and black 25 25
70. 1s. 6d. red and blue .. 2·00 2·25

3. Flagship of Tristao D'Acunha.

1965.
71. – ½d. black & ultramarine .. 5 5
72. 3. 1d. black and emerald .. 5 5
73. – 1½d. black and blue .. 5 5
74. – 2d. black and purple .. 5 5
75. – 3d. black & turquoise-blue 8 8
75a.– 4d. black and orange .. 15 20
76. – 4½d. black and brown .. 12 15
77. – 6d. black and green .. 10 12
78. – 7d. black and red .. 15 15
79. – 10d. black and chocolate 20 25
80. – 1s. black and carmine .. 20 25
81. – 1s. 6d. black and olive .. 40 45
82. – 2s. 6d. black & chestnut .. 80 90
83. – 5s. black and violet .. 1·25 1·50
84. – 10s. blue and carmine .. 3·50 3·50
84a – 10s. black & turq.-blue .. 6·50 6·50
84b.– £1 blue and brown .. 6·50 6·50

DESIGNS—HORIZ. ½d. South Atlantic Map Ships as T 3: 1½d. "Heemstede". 2d. New England Whaler. 3d. "Shenandoah". 4d. H.M.S. "Challenger". 4½d. H.M.S. "Galatea". 6d. H.M.S. "Cilicia". 7d. H.M. Yacht "Britannia". 10d. H.M.S. "Leopard". 1s. M.V. "Tjisadane". 1s. 6d. M.V. "Tristania". 2s. 6d. M.V. "Boissevain". 5s. M.S. "Bornholm". 10s. (No. 84a) Research Vessel "R.S.A.". VERT. 10s. (No. 84), £1 Queen Elizabeth II (portrait as in T 3 but larger).

1965. I.T.U. Cent. As T 26 of Antigua.
85. 3d. red and grey 30 30
86. 6d. violet and orange .. 60 60

1965. I.C.Y. As T 27 of Antigua.
87. 1d. purple and turquoise .. 15 15
88. 6d. green and lavender .. 90 90

1966. Churchill Commem. As T 28 of Antigua.
89. 1d. blue 5 5
90. 3d. green 25 10
91. 6d. brown .. .. .. 1·00 1·25
92. 1s. 6d. violet .. .. 2·25 2·00

4. Ship at Tristan and Soldier of 1816.

1966. Tristan Garrison. 150th Anniv.
93. 4 3d. multicoloured 12 12
94. 6d. multicoloured .. 30 25
95. 1s. 6d. multicoloured .. 85 60
96. 2s. 6d. multicoloured .. 1·10 85

1966. World Cup Football Championships. As T 30 of Antigua.
97. 3d. violet, grn., lake & brn. 15 15
98. 2s. 6d. chocolate, turquoise, lake and brown .. .. 1·10 1·00

1966. W.H.O. Headquarters, Geneva. Inaug. As T 31 of Antigua.
99. 6d. black, green and blue .. 25 25
100. 5s. black, purple and ochre 1·75 1·75

1966. U.N.E.S.C.O. 20th Anniv. As T33/5 of Antigua.
101. 10d. vio., red, yell. & orge. 25 25
102. 1s. 6d. yell., violet & olive 60 60
103. 2s. 6d. black, pur. & orge. 85 85

5. Calshot Harbour.

1967. Opening of Calshot Harbour.
104. 5. 6d. multicoloured .. 12 12
105. 10d. multicoloured .. 20 20
106. 1s. 6d. multicoloured .. 35 35
107. 2s. 6d. multicoloured .. 60 60

1967. No. 76 surch. **4d** and bars.
108. – 4d. on 4½d. black & brn. 10 12

6. Prince Alfred, First Duke of Edinburgh.

1967. 1st Duke of Edinburgh's Visit to Tristan. Cent.
109. 6. 3d. multicoloured .. 10 10
110. 6d. multicoloured .. 15 15
111. 1s. 6d. multicoloured .. 30 30
112. 2s. 6d. multicoloured .. 55 55

7. Wandering Albatross.

1968. Birds. Multicoloured.

113. 4d. Type 7 .. .. .. 12 12
114. 1s. Big-billed Bunting .. 30 30
115. 1s. 6d. Tristan Thrush .. 60 60
116. 2s. 6d. Great Shearwater .. 85 85

8. Union Jack and Dependency Flag.

1968. Tristan da Cunha as a Dependency of St. Helena. 30th Anniv.

117. 8. 6d. multicoloured .. 12 15
118. – 9d. sepia and blue .. 25 25
119. 8. 1s. 6d. multicoloured .. 45 45
120. – 2s. 6d. carmine and blue 75 75

DESIGN: 9d. and 2s. 6d. St. Helena and Tristan on chart.

9. Frigate.

1969. Clipper Ships.

121. 9. 4d. blue 10 10
122. – 1s. red 30 30
123. – 1s. 6d. green 45 45
124. – 2s. 6d. chocolate .. 70 70

DESIGNS: 1s. Cape Horner. 1s. 6d. Barque. 2s. 6d. Tea Clipper.

10. Sailing Ship off Tristan Da Cunha.

1969. United Society for the Propagation of the Gospel. Multicoloured.

125. 4d. Type 10 .. .. .. 10 10
126. 9d. Islanders going to First Gospel Service .. 25 25
127. 1s. 6d. Landing of the First Minister 45 45
128. 2s. 6d. Procession outside St. Mary's Church .. 75 75

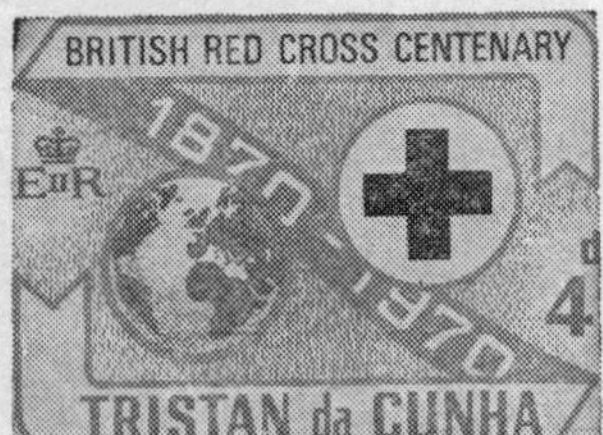

11. Globe and Red Cross Emblem.

1970. British Red Cross Cent.

129. 11. 4d. emer., red and green 10 10
130. 9d. bistre, red & green 25 25
131. – 1s. 9d. drab, red and ultramarine 45 45
132. – 2s. 6d. purple, red and ultramarine .. 70 70

DESIGNS—VERT. Nos. 131/2 "Union Jack" and Red Cross Flag.

12. Crawfish and Fishing Boat.

1970. Crawfish Industry. Multicoloured.

133. 4d. Type 12 .. .. 10 10
134. 10d. Packing and Storing Crawfish 25 25
135. 1s. 6d. Type 12 .. .. 45 45
136. 2s. 6d. As 10d. 70 70

1971. Decimal Currency. Nos. 72, etc. surch. with new values.

137. 3. ½p. on 1d. blk. & emerald 5 5
138. – 1p. on 2d. black & purple 5 5
139. – 1½p. on 4d. blk. & orange 8 8
140. – 2½p. on 6d. blk. & green 10 10
141. – 3p. on 7d. black and red 15 15
142. – 4p. on 10d. blk. & choc. 20 20
143. – 5p. on 1s. blk. & carmine 25 25
144. – 7½p. on 1s. 6d. blk. & olive 40 40
145. – 12½p. on 2s. 6d. blk. & chest. 70 70
146. – 15p. on 1½d. blk. & blue 85 85
147. – 25p. on 5s. blk. & violet 1·75 1·75
148. – 50p. on 10s. black and turq.-blue (No. 84a) 3·50 3·50

13. The "Quest".

1971. Shackleton-Rowett Expedition. 50th Anniv.

149. 13. 1½p. multicoloured .. 8 10
150. – 4p. brown, green and apple-green .. 25 25
151. – 7½p. black, pur. & grn. 50 50
152. – 12½p. multicoloured 70 75

DESIGNS—HORIZ. 4p. Presentation of Scout Troop flag. 7½p. Cachet on pair of 6d. G.B. stamps. 12½p. Shackleton, postmarks, and boat taking mail to the "Quest".

14. H.M.S. "Victory" at Trafalgar and Thomas Swain catching Nelson.

1971. Island Families. Multicoloured.

153. 1½p. Type 14 .. .. 12 12
154. 2½p. "Emily of Stonington" (P. W. Green) 30 30
155. 4p. "Italia" (Lavarello and Repetto) .. 45 45
156. 7½p. H.M.S. "Falmouth" (William Glass) 1·25 1·25
157. 12½p. American whaler (Rogers and Hagan) .. 1·75 1·75

15. Cow-Pudding.

1972. Multicoloured.

158. ½p. Type 15 .. .. 5 5
159. 1p. Peak Berry 5 5
160. 1½p. Sand Flower (horiz.) 5 5
161. 2½p. N.Z. Flax (horiz.) .. 5 5
162. 3p. Island Tree 5 5
163. 4p. Bog Fern 8 10
164. 5p. Dog Catcher 8 10
165. 7½p. Celery 12 15
166. 12½p. Pepper Tree .. 20 25
167. 25p. Foul Berry (horiz.) .. 45 50
168. 50p. Tussock 85 90
169. £1 Tussac (horiz.) .. 1·75 1·90

16. Launching.

1972. Tristan Longboats. Multicoloured.

170. 2½p. Type 16 .. .. 12 12
171. 4p. Under oars 20 20
172. 7½p. Coxswain (vert.) .. 40 40
173. 12½p. Under Sail (vert.) .. 65 70

1972. Royal Silver Wedding. As T 19 of Ascension, but with Tristan Thrushes and Wandering Albatrosses in background.

174. 2½p. brown 35 45
175. 7½p. blue .. .. 1·25 1·40

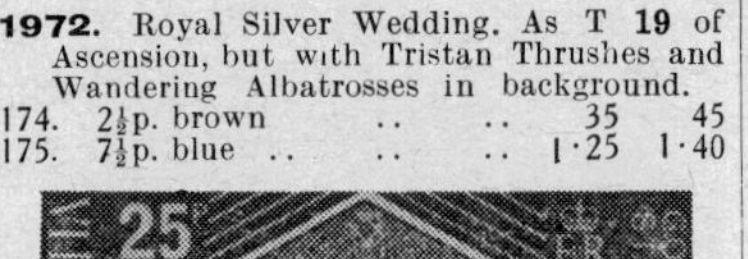

17. Church Altar.

1973. St. Mary's Church. Golden Jubilee.

176. 17. 25p. multicoloured .. 85 85

18. H.M.S. "Challenger's" Laboratory.

1973. H.M.S. "Challenger's" Visit. Cent. Multicoloured.

177. 4p. Type 18 .. .. 12 12
178. 5p. H.M.S. "Challenger" off Tristan 15 15
179. 7½p. "Challenger's" pinnace off Nightingale Is. 25 30
180. 12½p. Survey route .. 45 50

19. Approaching English Port.

1973. Return to Tristan da Cunha. 10th Anniv.

182. 19. 4p. brn., yellow & gold 12 15
183. – 5p multicoloured .. 20 20
184. – 7½p. multicoloured .. 30 30
185. – 12½p. multicoloured .. 50 55

DESIGNS: 5p. Survey party. 7½p. Embarking on "Bornholm". 12½p. Approaching Tristan.

1973. Royal Wedding. As T 26 of Anguilla. Multicoloured. Background colours given.

186. 7½p. blue 20 20
187. 12½p. green 35 35

20. Rockhopper and Egg.

1974. Penguins. Multicoloured.

188. 2½p. Type 20 .. .. 10 10
189. 5p. Rockhopper Colony Inaccessible Island .. 20 20
190. 7½p. Rockhoppers fishing .. 25 25
191. 25 p. Rockhopper and fledgling 75 75

21. Blenheim Palace.

1974. Sir Winston Churchill. Birth Centenary.

193. 21. 7½ p. yellow and black .. 25 25
194. – 25 p. black, brn. & grey 60 65

DESIGN: 25 p. Churchill with Queen Elizabeth II.

22. " Plocamium fuscorubrum.

1975. Sea Plants.

196. 22. 4p. red, lilac and black 12 12
197. – 5p. green, blue and turq. 15 15
198. – 10p. oran., brn. & pur. 30 30
199. – 20p. multicoloured 50 55

DESIGNS: 5p. " Ulva lactua ". 10p. " Epymenia flabellata ". 20p. " Macrocystis pyrifera ".

23. Killer Whale.

1975. Whales. Multicoloured.

200. 2p. Type 23 .. .. 8 8
201. 3p. Rough-toothed dolphin 8 10
202. 5p. Atlantic right whale .. 12 15
203. 20p. Finback whale .. 45 50

24. ½d. Stamp of 1952.

1976. Festival of Stamps.

204. 24. 5p. black, violet & lilac 12 15
205. – 9p. black, green & blue 20 20
206. – 25p multicoloured .. 50 60

DESIGNS—VERT. 9p. 1953 Coronation stamp. HORIZ. 25p. Mail carrier " Tristania II ".

25. Island Cottage.

1976. Paintings by Roland Svensson. Multicoloured.

207. 3p. Type 25 .. .. 5 8
208. 5p. The potato patches (horiz.) 10 12
209. 10p. Edinburgh from the sea (horiz.) 20 20
210. 20p. Huts, Nightingale Is. 40 45

26. The Royal Standard.

1977. Silver Jubilee. Multicoloured.

212. 10p. Royal Yacht " Britannia " 20 20
213. 15p. Type 26 .. .. 30 35
214. 25p. Royal Family .. 50 55

POSTAGE DUE STAMPS

1957. As Type D 1 of Barbados.

D 1. 1d. red 20 40
D 2. 2d. yellow 20 50
D 3. 3d. green 20 75
D 4. 4d. blue 25 75
D 5. 5d. lake .. .. .. 35 1·00

D 1.

1976.

D 11. D 1. 1p. purple 5 5
D 12. 2p. green 5 5
D 13. 4p. violet 8 8
D 14. 5p. blue 8 10
D 15. 10p. brown 20 20

TRUCIAL STATES BC

Seven Arab Shaikhdoms on the Persian Gulf and Gulf of Oman, in treaty relations with Great Britain. The following stamps were issued at the British Postal Agency at Dubai until it closed on 14th June, 1963.

Individual issues were later made by Abu Dhabi, Ajman, Dubai, Fujeira, Ras al Khaima, Sharjah and Umm al Qiwain.

100 naye paise = 1 rupee.

1. Palms. 2. Dhow.

1961.

1. 1. 5 n.p. green 5 5
2. 15 n.p. brown 8 8
3. 20 n.p. blue 10 12
4. 30 n.p. orange 15 20
5. 40 n.p. violet 15 20
6. 50 n.p. bistre 20 25
7. 75 n.p. grey 30 30
8. 2. 1 r. green 45 45
9. 2 r. black 85 85
10. 5 r. red .. .. .. 1·60 2·00
11. 10 r. blue .. .. .. 3·75 4·50

TUNISIA O4

Formerly a French Protectorate in N. Africa, Tunisia became an independent kingdom in 1956 and a republic in 1957.

1888. 100 centimes = 1 franc.
1959. 1000 milliemes = 1 dinar.

1.

2.

1888. Arms on plain background.

1. 1. 1 c. black on blue .. 25 25
2. 2 c. brown on yellow .. 30 30
3. 5 c. green .. .. 1·90 1·40
4. 15 c. blue .. .. 7·00 2·75
5. 25 c. black on red .. 15·00 8·00
6. 40 c. red on yellow .. 11·00 7·00
7. 75 c. red .. .. 13·00 8·00
8. 5 f. mauve on lilac .. 70·00 55·00

1888. Arms on shaded background.

9. 2. 1 c. black on blue .. 12 5
10. 2 c. brown on yellow .. 10 5
22. 5 c. green .. .. 1·00 10
12. 10 c. black on lilac .. 85 5
23. 10 c. red 80 5
14. 15 c. blue .. .. 5·00 5
24. 15 c. grey .. .. 1·60 10
15. 20 c. red on green .. 1·60 12
16. 25 c. black on red .. 2·75 20
25. 25 c. blue .. .. 2·10 20
26. 35 c. brown .. .. 3·75 15
17. 40 c. red on yellow .. 90 10
18. 75 c. red .. .. 25·00 16·00
19. 75 c. brown on orange .. 2·75 90
20. 1 f. green .. .. 3·25 90
27. 2 f. violet .. .. 25·00 18·00
21. 5 f. mauve on lilac .. 25·00 8·00

1902. Surch. **25** and bars.

28. 2. 25 on 15 c. blue 45 45

3. Mosque at Kairouan.

5. Ruins of Hadrian's Aqueduct.

4. Agriculture.

6. Carthaginian Galley.

1906.

30. 3. 1 c. black on yellow .. 5 5
31. 2 c. brown 5 5
32. 3 c. red 5 5
33. 5 c. green 5 5
72. 5 c. orange 5 5
34. 4. 10 c. red 5 5
73. 10 c. green 5 5
35. 15 c. violet 10 5
105. 15 c. brown on orange .. 5 5
36. 20 c. brown 5 5
37. 25 c. blue 20 5
74. 25 c. violet 5 5
75. 5. 30 c. violet and claret .. 10 8
76. 4. 30 c. red 12 10
38. 5. 35 c. brown and green .. 1·25 10
39. 40 c. red and brown .. 1·00 5
107. 40 c. black on red .. 10 8
108. 4. 40 c. green 5 5
77. 50 c. blue 8 5
78. 5. 60 c. violet and olive .. 5 5
109. 60 c. purple and red .. 5 5
40. 75 c. red and claret .. 8 5
110. 75 c. red 5 5
41. 6. 1 f. brown and red .. 10 5
111. 1 f. blue 5 5
42. 2 f. green and brown .. 65 30
112. 1 f. red and green on red 5 5
43. 5 f. blue and violet .. 1·40 90
113. 5 f. green and lilac .. 12 5

1908. Surch. in figures.

44. 2. 10 on 15 c. grey 15 12
45. 35 on 1 f. green 25 25
46. 40 on 2 f. violet .. .. 1·10 90
47. 75 on 5 f. mauve on lilac 65 65

1911. Surch. in figures and bar.

48. 4. 10 on 15 c. violet 35 5
60. 15 c. on 10 c. red 10 5
79. 20 c. on 15 c. violet .. 12 5

1915. Red Cross Fund. Optd. with red cross.

49. 4. 15 c. violet 10 10

1916. Red Cross Fund. Optd. with red cross and bars.

50. 3. 5 c. green 15 15

1916. Prisoners-of-War Fund. Surch. with red cross and **10 c.**

51. 4. 10 c. on 15 c. brn. on blue 5 5
52. 10 c. on 20 c. brn. on yell. 5 5
53. 10 c. on 25 c. blue on green 35 35
54. 5. 10 c. on 35 c. violet & grn. 75 75
55. 10 c. on 40 c. black & brn. 35 35
56. 10 c. on 75 c. grn. & claret 1·00 1·00
57. 6. 10 c. on 1 f. green and red 25 25
58. 10 c. on 2 f. blue & brown 11·00 11·00
59. 10 c. on 5 f. red and violet 20·00 20·00

1918. Charity. Surch. with red cross, bars and **15 c.**

61. 4. 15 c. on 20 c. blk. on grn. 5 5
62. 15 c. on 25 c. blue .. 5 5
63. 5. 15 c. on 35 c. red & olive 5 5
64. 15 c. on 40 c. blue & brown 10 10
65. 15 c. on 75 c. blk. & claret 55 55
66. 6. 15 c. on 1 f. violet & red .. 2·10 2·10
67. 15 c. on 2 f. red & brown .. 7·00 7·00
68. 15 c. on 5 f. black & violet 30·00 30·00

1919. Air. Optd. **Poste Aerienne** and wings or surch. **30 c.** and bars also.

69. 5. 30 c. on 35 c. brown & grn. 12 10
70. 30 c. blue and olive .. 8 8

7. Ruin at Dougga.

1922.

80. 7. 10 c. green 5 5
104. 10 c. red 5 5
81. 30 c. red 15 15
106. 30 c. mauve 5 5
82. 50 c. blue 8 8

1923. Charity Surch. **AFFt** and value in figures under medal.

83. 3. 0 c. on 1 c. blue .. 5 5
84. 0 c. on 2 c. brown .. 5 5
85. 1 c. on 3 c. green .. 5 5
86. 2 c. on 5 c. mauve .. 5 5
87. 7. 3 c. on 10 c. mve. on blue 5 5
88. 4. 5 c. on 15 c. green .. 5 5
89. 5 c. on 20 c. blue on red 20 20
90. 5 c. on 25 c. mauve on blue 20 20
91. 7. 5 c. on 30 c. orange .. 25 25
92. 5. 5 c. on 35 c. mve. & blue 25 25
93. 5 c. on 40 c. brn. & blue 30 30
94. 7. 10 c. on 50 c. blk. on blue 30 30
95. 5. 10 c. on 60 c. blue & brn. 35 35
96. 10 c. on 75 c. grn. & mve. 55 55
97. 6. 25 c. on 1 f. mve. & lake 55 55
98. 25 c. on 2 f. red and blue 1·60 1·60
99. 25 c on 5 f. brown & green 10·00 10·00

1923. Surch. in figures and bars.

100. 3. 10 on 5 c. green .. 5 5
101. 4. 20 on 15 c. violet .. 15 5
102. 30 on 20 c. brown .. 5 5
103. 50 on 25 c. blue .. 20 5

1925. Parcel Post stamps surch. **PROTECTION DE L'ENFANCE POSTES** and value in figures.

114. P 1. 1 c. on 5 c. red and brown on rose .. 5 5
115. 2 c. on 10 c. blue and brown on yellow .. 5 5
116. 3 c. on 20 c. red and purple on mauve .. 8 8
117. 5 c. on 25 c. red and green on green .. 10 10
118. 5 c. on 40 c. green and red on yellow .. 10 10
119. 10 c. on 50 c. green and violet on mauve .. 35 35
120. 10 c. on 75 c. brown and green on green .. 15 15
121. 25 c. on 1 f. green and blue on blue .. 20 20
122. 25 c. on 2 f. purple and red on rose .. 1·25 1·25
123. 25 c. on 5 f. brown and red on green .. 6·00 6·00

8. Arab Woman. 9. Grand Mosque, Tunis. 10. Mosque, Place Halfaouine, Tunis.

11. Amphitheatre El Djem.

1926.

124. 8. 1 c. red 5 5
125. 2 c. olive 5 5
126. 3 c. blue 5 5
127. 5 c. green 5 5
128. 10 c. claret 5 5
129. 9. 15 c. lilac 5 5
130. 20 c. red 5 5
131. 25 c. green 5 5
131a. 25 c. mauve 12 5
132. 30 c. mauve 5 5
133. 30 c. green 5 5
134. 40 c. brown 5 5
134a. 45 c. green 12 12
135. 10. 50 c. black 5 5
135a. 50 c. blue 5 5
135b. 50 c. green 5 5
135c. 60 c. red 5 5
135d. 65 c. blue 10 5
135e. 70 c. red 5 5
136. 75 c. red 5 5
136a. 75 c. purple 12 5
137. 80 c. green 10 8
137a. 80 c. brown 5 5
138. 90 c. red 5 5
138a. 90 c. blue .. .. 1·60 1·60
139. 1 f. plum 15 5
139a. 1 f. red 5 5
140. 11. 1 f. 05 claret and blue .. 5 5
141. 1 f. 25 blue 5 5
141a. 1 f. 25 red 20 20
141b. 1 f. 30 blue 5 5
141c. 1 f. 40 purple 10 10
142. 1 f. 50 blue 20 5
142a. 1 f. 50 orange and red .. 5 5
143. 2 f. brown and red .. 30 5
143a. 2 f. orange 5 5
143b. 2 f. 25 blue 10 5
143c. 2 f. 50 green 10 10
144. 3 f. orange and blue .. 30 5
144a. 3 f. violet 5 5
145. 5 f. green & red on green 45 8
145a. 5 f. brown 12 10
146. 10 f. blk. & red on blue 1·25 25
146a. 10 f. pink 10 10
146b. 20 f. red & mve. on red 35 10

For further stamps in these Types, see Nos. 220/31 and 257/286.

1927. Surch. in figures and bars.

162. 3. 3 c. on 5 c. orange .. 5 5
163. 4. 10 c. on 15 c. brown on orange 5 5
164. 7. 25 c. on 30 c. mauve .. 5 5
165. 10. 40 c. on 80 c. green .. 5 5
166. 9. 50 c. on 40 c. brown .. 75 5
167. 10. 50 c. on 75 c. red .. 5 5
147. 11. 1 f. 50 on 1 f. 25 blue .. 5 5

1927. Air. Optd. **Poste Aerienne** and aeroplane or surch. in figures and bars also.

148. 6. 1 f. blue 10 10
152. 11. 1 f. 30 mauve & orange 65 35
169. 1 f. 50 on 1 f. 30 mauve and red 50 25
170. 1 f. 50 on 1 f. 80 red and olive 60 20
171. 1 f. 50 on 2 f. 55 brown and mauve .. 1·75 40
149. 5. 1 f. 75 on 75 c. red .. 15 8
150. 6. 1 f. 75 on 5 f. green and lilac 65 50
153. 11. 1 f. 80 red and olive .. 75 15
151. 6. 2 f. red & green on red 45 40
154. 11. 2 f. 55 brown & mauve 20 15

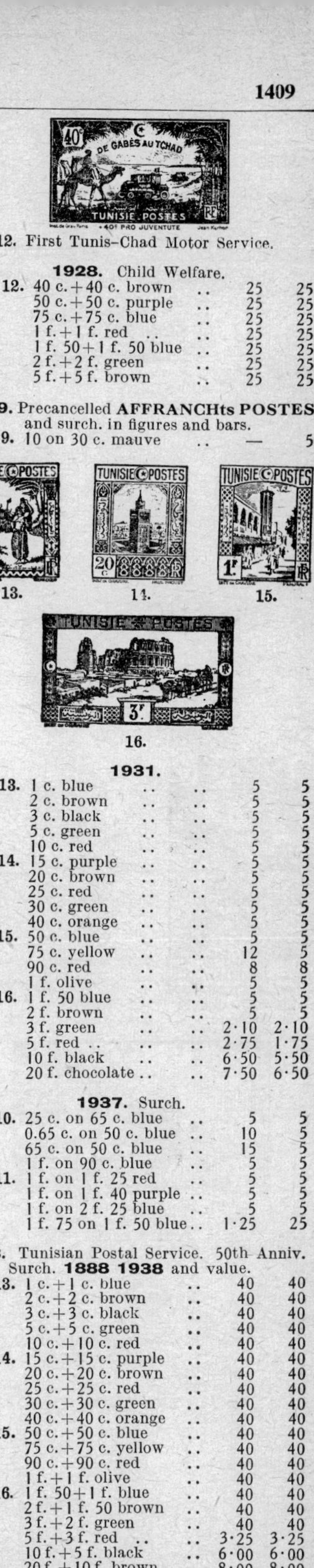
12. First Tunis–Chad Motor Service.

1928. Child Welfare.

155. 12. 40 c. + 40 c. brown .. 25 25
156. 50 c. + 50 c. purple .. 25 25
157. 75 c. + 75 c. blue .. 25 25
158. 1 f. + 1 f. red 25 25
159. 1 f. 50 + 1 f. 50 blue .. 25 25
160. 2 f. + 2 f. green .. 25 25
161. 5 f. + 5 f. brown .. 25 25

1929. Precancelled **AFFRANCHts POSTES** and surch. in figures and bars.

168. 9. 10 on 30 c. mauve .. — 5

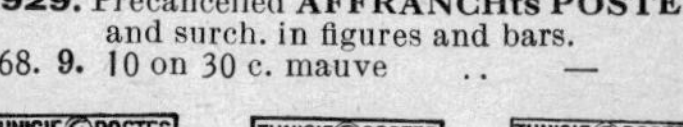

13. 14. 15.

16.

1931.

172. 13. 1 c. blue 5 5
173. 2 c. brown 5 5
174. 3 c. black 5 5
175. 5 c. green 5 5
176. 10 c. red 5 5
177. 14. 15 c. purple 5 5
178. 20 c. brown 5 5
179. 25 c. red 5 5
180. 30 c. green 5 5
181. 40 c. orange 5 5
182. 15. 50 c. blue 5 5
183. 75 c. yellow 12 5
184. 90 c. red 8 8
185. 1 f. olive 5 5
186. 16. 1 f. 50 blue 5 5
187. 2 f. brown 5 5
188. 3 f. green .. .. 2·10 2·10
189. 5 f. red .. .. 2·75 1·75
190. 10 f. black .. .. 6·50 5·50
191. 20 f. chocolate .. .. 7·50 6·50

1937. Surch.

191a. 10. 25 c. on 65 c. blue .. 5 5
192. 0.65 c. on 50 c. blue .. 10 5
193. 65 c. on 50 c. blue .. 15 5
193b. 1 f. on 90 c. blue .. 5 5
193c. 11. 1 f. on 1 f. 25 red .. 5 5
193d. 1 f. on 1 f. 40 purple .. 5 5
193e. 1 f. on 2 f. 25 blue .. 5 5
195. 1 f. 75 on 1 f. 50 blue .. 1·25 25

1938. Tunisian Postal Service. 50th Anniv. Surch. **1888 1938** and value.

196. 13. 1 c. + 1 c. blue .. 40 40
197. 2 c. + 2 c. brown .. 40 40
198. 3 c. + 3 c. black .. 40 40
199. 5 c. + 5 c. green .. 40 40
200. 10 c. + 10 c. red .. 40 40
201. 14. 15 c. + 15 c. purple .. 40 40
202. 20 c. + 20 c. brown .. 40 40
203. 25 c. + 25 c. red .. 40 40
204. 30 c. + 30 c. green .. 40 40
205. 40 c. + 40 c. orange .. 40 40
206. 15. 50 c. + 50 c. blue .. 40 40
207. 75 c. + 75 c. yellow .. 40 40
208. 90 c. + 90 c. red .. 40 40
209. 1 f. + 1 f. olive .. 40 40
210. 16. 1 f. 50 + 1 f. blue .. 40 40
211. 2 f. + 1 f. 50 brown .. 40 40
212. 3 f. + 2 f. green .. 40 40
213. 5 f. + 3 f. red .. .. 3·25 3·25
214. 10 f. + 5 f. black .. 6·00 6·00
215. 20 f. + 10 f. brown .. 8·00 8·00

1941. National Relief. Surch. **SECOURS NATIONAL 1941** and value.

216. 9. 1 f. on 45 c. green .. 8 8
217. 11. 1 f. 30 on 1 f. 25 red .. 8 8
218. 1 f. 50 on 1 f. 40 purple 8 8
219. 2 f. on 2 f. 25 blue .. 8 8

1941. As 1926 without monogram "RF".

220. 9. 30 c. red 5 5
221. 10. 1 f. 20 grey 5 5
222. 1 f. 50 brown 5 5
223. 11. 2 f. 40 pink and red .. 5 5
224. 2 f. 50 blue 5 5
225. 3 f. violet 5 5
226. 4 f. blue and black .. 5 5
227. 4 f. 50 brown and olive 5 5
228. 5 f. black 5 5
229. 10 f. violet and lilac .. 5 5
230. 15 f. lake 70 70
231. 20 f. red and violet .. 50 20

1943. As T 19 of Algeria ("UN SEUL BUT — LA VICTOIRE"), but inscr. "TUNISIE".

232. 1 f. 50 red 5 5

17. Allied Soldiers. 18. Mosque and Olive Trees.

1943. Charity. Tunisian Liberation.
233. **17.** 1 f. 50+8 f. 50 red .. 5 5

1944
234. **18.** 30 c. yellow 5 5
235. 40 c. brown 5 5
236. 60 c. orange 5 5
237. 70 c. red 5 5
238. 80 c. green 5 5
239. 90 c. violet 5 5
240. 1 f. red 5 5
241. 1 f. 50 blue 5 5
242. 2 f. 40 red 5 5
243. 2 f. 50 brown 5 5
244. 3 f. violet 5 5
245. 4 f. blue 5 5
246. 4 f. 50 green 5 5
247. 5 f. grey 5 5
248. 6 f. brown 5 5
249. 10 f. lake 5 5
250. 15 f. brown 8 5
251. 20 f. lilac .. 8 5
Nos. 234/41 are smaller ($15\frac{1}{2} \times 19$ mm.).

1944. Forces Welfare Fund. Surch. **+48 frcs pour nos Combattants.**
252. **18.** 2 f.+48 f. red 15 15

20. Sidi Mahrez Mosque.

DESIGNS—HORIZ. 4 f. Camel patrol at Fort Saint. 10 f. Mosque at Sidi-bou-Said.

21. Ramparts of Sfax.

1945. Forces Welfare Fund. Surch. **POUR NOS COMBATTANTS** and value.
253. **20.** 1 f. 50+8 f. 50 brown 12 12
254. **21.** 3 f.+12 f. green .. 12 12
255. – 4 f.+21 f. brown .. 12 12
256. – 10 f.+40 f. red .. 12 12

1945. New values and colours.
257. **10.** 10 c. brown 5 5
258. 30 c. olive 5 5
259. 40 c. red 5 5
260. 50 c. greenish blue .. 5 5
261. 60 c. blue 5 5
262. 80 c. yellow-green .. 5 5
263. 1 f. 20 brown 5 5
264. 1 f. 50 lilac 5 5
265. 2 f. green 5 5
267. **11.** 2 f. 40 red 5 5
268. **10.** 2 f. 50 brown 5 5
269. **11.** 3 f. brown 5 5
270. **10.** 3 f. red 5 5
271. **11.** 4 f. blue 5 5
272. **10.** 4 f. violet 5 5
273. **11.** 4 f. violet 5 5
273a. **10.** 4 f. orange 8 5
274. 4 f. 50 blue 5 5
275. **11.** 5 f. green 5 5
275b. **10.** 5 f. green 10 5
275a. 5 f. blue 10 5
276. **11.** 6 f. blue 5 5
277. 6 f. red 5 5
278. **10.** 6 f. red 5 5
279. **11.** 10 f. orange 5 5
280. 10 f. blue 5 5
281. 15 f. mauve 5 5
281a. **10.** 15 f. red 10 5
282. **11.** 20 f. green 8 5
283. 25 f. violet 10 5
284. 25 f. orange 15 8
285. 50 f. red 25 5
286. 100 f. red 30 5

1945. Anti-Tuberculosis Fund. Type of France optd. **TUNISIE.**
287. **202.** 2 f.+1 f. orange .. 5 5

1945. Postal Employees' War Victims' Fund. Type of France optd. **TUNISIE.**
288. **203.** 4 f.+6 f. brown .. 5 5

1945. Stamp Day. Type of France (Louis XI) optd. **TUNISIE.**
289. **208.** 2 f.+3 f. green .. 5 5

1945. War Veterans' Fund. Surch. **ANCIENS COMBATTANTS R F** and value.
290. **8.** 4 f.+6 f. on 10 c. blue 10 10
291. **10.** 10 f.+30 f. on 80 c. grn. 10 10

22. Legionary.

24. Neptune.

25. Arabesque Ornamentation from Great Mosque at Kairouan.

26. Feeding a Fledgling.

1946. Welfare Fund for French Troops in Indo- China.
292. **22.** 20 f.+30 f. black, red and green 30 30

1946. Red Cross Fund. Surch. with cross **1946** and new values.
293. **10.** 80 c.+50 c. green .. 8 8
294. 1 f. 50+1 f. 50 lilac .. 8 8
295. 2 f.+2 f. green 8 8
296. **11.** 2 f. 40+2 f. red .. 8 8
297. 4 f.+4 f. blue 8 8

1946. Stamp Day. La Varane Type of France optd. **TUNISIE.**
298. **218.** 3 f.+2 f. blue .. 10 10

1947. Stamp Day. Louvois Type of France optd. **TUNISIE.**
299. **227.** 4 f. 50+5 f. 50 brown 15 15

1947. Naval Charities. Type of France surch. **TUNISIE** and new value.
300. **213.** 10+15 on 2 f.+3 f. blue 20 20

1947. Welfare Fund. Surch. **SOLIDARITE 1947+40 F.**
301. **11.** 10 f.+40 f. black .. 25 25

1947.
302. **25.** 3 f. green .. 12 10
303. 4 f. pink and purple .. 5 5
304. **24.** 5 f. black and green .. 10 10
305. **25.** 6 f. red and brown .. 5 5
306. **24.** 10 f. black and brown .. 5 5
306a. **25.** 10 f. violet 5 5
306b. 12 f. red-brown .. 12 5
306c. 12 f. orange and brown 5 5
306d. 15 f. red and brown .. 8 5
307. **24.** 18 f. blue and green .. 12 5
307a. 25 f. green and blue .. 20 5
307b. **25.** 30 f. blue 20 10

1947. Infant Welfare Fund.
308. **26.** 4 f. 50+5 f. 50 green .. 30 30
309. 6 f.+9 f. blue 30 30
310. 8 f.+17 f. red 30 30
311. 10 f.+40 f. violet .. 30 30

1948. Stamp Day. Type of France (Arago) optd. **TUNISIE.**
312. **238.** 6 f.+4 f. red .. 20 20

1948. Anti-Tuberculosis Fund. Surch. **AIDEZ LES TUBERCULEUX + 10.**
313. **25.** 4 f.+10 f. orge. & green 20 20

27. Triumphal Arch, Sbeitla.

1948. Army Welfare Fund.
315. **27.** 10 f.+40 f. grn. & buff 25 25
316. 18 f.+42 f. blue .. 25 25

1949. Stamp Day. Type of France (Choiseul), optd. **TUNISIE.**
317. **247.** 15 f.+5 f. black .. 30 30

28. Child in Cot.

1949. Children's Welfare Fund.
318. **28.** 25 f.+50 f. green .. 45 45

29. Oued Mellegue Barrage.

1949. Tunisian Development.
319. **29.** 15 f. black 20 5

30. Bird from Antique Mosaic.

31. Globe, Mounted Postman and Aeroplane.

1949. Air.
320. **30.** 100 f. brown and green 60 10
321. 200 f. black & blue (A) 1·25 35
322. 200 f. black & blue (B) 1·10 30
In A the Arabic inscription is in two lines and in B it is in one line.

1949. U.P.U. 75th Anniv.
323. **31.** 5 f. grn. on blue (post.) 20 20
324. 15 f. brown on blue .. 20 20
325. 25 f. blue on blue (air) .. 40 40

1949. Free French Association Fund. Surch. Lorraine Cross and **FFL+15F.**
326. **24.** 10 f.+15 f. red and blue 30 30

1950. Stamp Day. Type of France (Postman) optd. **TUNISIE.**
327. **261.** 12 f.+3 f. green & blue 30 30

32. Tunisia Thanks France.

33. Old Soldier.

1950. Franco-Tunisian Relief Fund.
328. **32.** 15 f.+35 f. red .. 30 30
329. 25 f.+45 f. blue .. 30 30

1950. Old Soldiers' Relief Fund.
330. **33.** 25 f.+25 f. blue .. 50 50

34. Seal.

36. Sleeping Child.

35. Hermes of Berbera.

1950. (a) Size $21\frac{1}{2} \times 17\frac{1}{2}$ mm. (T **34**).
331. **34.** 10 c. turquoise 5 5
332. 50 c. brown 5 5
333. 1 f. violet 5 5
334. 2 f. grey 5 5
335. 3 f. brown 5 5
336. 4 f. orange 5 5
337. 5 f. green 5 5
338. 8 f. blue 5 5
339. 12 f. vermilion 20 5
340. 12 f. red 20 5
341. 15 f. red 10 5
342. 15 f. blue 10 5
346. **35.** 15 f. lake 15 10
347. 25 f. blue 20 10
348. 50 f. green 35 5

(b) Size $22\frac{1}{2} \times 18\frac{1}{4}$ mm.
343. **34.** 15 f. red 12 8
344. 15 f. blue 20 8
345. 30 f. blue 25 5

1951. Stamp Day. Type of France (Sorting Van), but colour changed optd. **TUNISIE.**
349. **268.** 12 f.+3 f. grey .. 15 15

1951. Child Welfare Fund.
350. **36.** 30 f.+15 f. blue .. 45 45

37. Gammarth National Cemetery.

38. Panel from Great Mosque at Kairouan.

1951. War Orphans' Fund.
351. **37.** 30 f.+10 f. blue .. 45 45

1952. Stamp Day. Type of France (Mail Coach), optd. **TUNISIE.**
352. **286.** 12 f.+3 f. violet .. 20 20

1952. Army Welfare Fund. Inscr. "OEUVRES SOCIALES DE L'ARMEE".
353. – 15 f.+1 f. indigo and blue (postage) .. 20 20
354. **38.** 50 f.+10 f. green and black (air) 45 45
DESIGN: 15 f. Ornamental stucco, Bardo Palace.

39. Schoolboys Clasping Hands.

40. Dr. C. Nicolle.

1952. Holiday Camp Fund.
355. **39.** 30 f.+10 f. green .. 40 40

1952. Golden Jubilee of Tunisian Medical Sciences Society.
356. **40.** 15 f. brown 20 10
357. 30 f. blue 25 15

1952. Military Medal. Type of France surch. **TUNISIE+5 F.**
358. **292.** 15 f.+5 f. green .. 25 25

1953. Stamp Day. Type of France (Count D'Argenson), optd. **TUNISIE.**
359. **297.** 12 f.+3 f. red .. 20 20

41. Tower and Flags.

42. Tozeur Mosque.

1953. 1st Int. Fair, Tunis.
360. **41.** 8 f. brown 20 20
361. 12 f. green 20 20
362. 15 f. blue 20 20
363. 18 f. violet 20 20
364. 30 f. red 20 20

1953 Air.
365. – 100 f. blue, grn. & turq. 65 20
366. – 200 f. sepia, brn. & mar. 1·25 40
367. – 500 f. brown and blue .. 5·50 2·25
368. **42.** 1000 f. green .. 8·00 5·50
DESIGNS: 100 f., 200 f. Monastir Fort. 500 f. View of Korbous.
For similar stamps but without "R F" see Nos. 423/6.

1954. Stamp Day. Type of France (Lavallette), optd. **TUNISIE.**
369. **308.** 12 f.+3 f. indigo .. 12 12

43. Courtyard, Sousse.

44. Sidi Bou Maklouf Mosque, Le Kef.

1954.
370. **43.** 50 c. green 5 5
371. 1 f. red 5 5
372. – 2 f. maroon 5 5
373. – 4 f. turquoise-blue .. 5 5
374. – 5 f. violet 5 5
375. – 8 f. black 5 5
376. – 10 f. turquoise-green .. 5 5
377. – 12 f. brown 5 5
378. – 15 f. blue (18×22 mm.) 30 5
386. – 15 f. blue (17×21½ mm.) 5 5

379. **44.** 18 f. sepia 20 15
380. – 20 f. blue 20 5
381. – 25 f. indigo 20 5
382. – 30 f. claret 20 5
383. – 40 f. turquoise 20 5
384. – 50 f. slate-violet .. 35 5
385. – 75 f. red 70 50

DESIGNS—As T **43**: 2 f., 4 f. Takrouna. 5 f., 8 f. Dwellings and Mosque, Tatahouine. 10 f., 12 f. Matmata. 15 f. Sidi Bou Said. As T **44**: 20 f., 25 f. Genoese Fort, Tabarka. 30 f., 40 f. Bab-el-Khadra Gate, Tunis. 50 f., 75 f. Four-storey dwellings, Medenine.

For similar stamps but without " R F " see Nos. 406/22.

45. Bey of Tunisia. **46.**

1954.

387. **45.** 8 f. blue 12 12
388. 12 f. grey 12 12
389. 15 f. red 12 12
390. 18 f. brown 15 15
391. 30 f. green 25 25

1955. Stamp Day. Type of France (Balloon Post) inscr. " TUNISIE " and Arabic equivalent.

392. **325.** 12 f.+3 f. brown .. 20 20

1955. " L'Essor " (Tunisian Amateur Dramatic Society). 50th Anniv.

393. **46.** 15 f. blue, lake and red 15 15

47. Tunisian Buildings and Rotary Emblem. **48.** Bey of Tunisia.

1955. Rotary Int. 50th Anniv.

394. **47.** 12 f. sepia and maroon 15 15
395. 15 f. sepia and grey .. 15 15
396. 18 f. lilac and violet .. 15 15
397. 25 f. blue 20 20
398. 30 f. indigo & turquoise 25 25

1955.

399. **48.** 15 f. blue 15 5

49. " Embroidery ". **50.** Bey of Tunisia.

1955. Int. Fair.

400. **49.** 5 f. lake 12 12
401. 12 f. blue 12 12
402. – 15 f. green 12 12
403. – 18 f. red 15 15
404. – 20 f. violet 15 15
405. – 30 f. maroon 15 15

DESIGNS: 15 f., 18 f. " Pottery ". 20 f., 30 f. " Jasmin sellers ".

INDEPENDENT KINGDOM

1956. Nos. 365/6 and 368/86 re-engraved without " RF ".

406. 50 c. green (postage) .. 5 5
407. 1 f. red 5 5
408. 2 f. maroon 5 5
409. 4 f. turquoise-blue .. 5 5
410. 5 f. violet 5 5
411. 8 f. black 5 5
412. 10 f. turquoise-green .. 5 5
413. 12 f. brown 5 5
414. 15 f. blue (A) 30 5
415. 15 f. blue (B) 5 5
416. 18 f. sepia 5 5
417. 20 f. blue 8 5
418. 25 f. indigo 10 5
419. 30 f. claret 50 5
420. 40 f. turquoise .. 40 8
421. 50 f. slate-violet .. 15 5
422. 75 f. red 25 20
423. 100 f. bl., grn. & turq. (air) 40 20
424. 200 f. sepia, brn. & maroon 70 50
425. 500 f. brown and blue .. 2·00 1·50
426. 1000 f. green .. .. 3·50 2·75

1956. Stamp Day. Type of France (Taxis) inscr. " TUNISIE " and Arabic equivalent.

427. **342.** 12 f.+3 f. green .. 20 20

1956. Autonomous Government. Inscr. as in T **50.**

428. **50.** 5 f. blue 8 5
429. – 12 f. maroon 12 5
430. **50.** 15 f. red 20 12
431. – 18 f. grey 20 12
432. **50.** 20 f. green 20 10
433. – 30 f. chestnut 30 10

DESIGN: 12 f., 18 f., 30 f. Tunisian girl releasing dove.

51. Farhat Hached. **52.** Market Scene.

1956. Labour Day.

434. **51.** 15 f. lake 20 20
435. 30 f. blue 20 20

1956. Tunisian Products.

436. – 12 f. vio., mar. & mve. 25 12
437. – 15 f. grn., brn. & indigo 25 12
438. – 18 f. ultramarine .. 25 15
439. – 20 f. chestnut 25 10
440. **52.** 25 f. chocolate 25 15
441. 30 f. blue 30 20

DESIGNS—VERT. 12 f. Bunch of grapes. 15 f. Sprig of olives. 18 f. Harvesting. 20 f. Man with basket containing wedding offering.

53. Pres. Habib Bourguiba. **54.** Pres. Bourguiba and Agricultural Workers.

1957. Independence. 1st Anniv.

442. **53.** 5 f. indigo 5 5
443. **54.** 12 f. pink 10 5
444. **53.** 20 f. blue 20 5
445. **54.** 25 f. green 25 8
446. **53.** 30 f. brown 25 15
447. **54.** 50 f. red 45 25

DESIGN—VERT. 20 f., 30 f. Handclasp and Labour Exchange.

55. Dove and Handclasp.

1957. 5th Int. Confederation of Free Trade Unions Congress.

448. **55.** 18 f. purple 15 15
449. – 20 f. red 20 20
450. **55.** 25 f. green 20 20
451. – 30 f. blue 25 25

INDEPENDENT REPUBLIC

(**56.**) **57.** Tunisian Soldiers and Flag.

1957. Tunisian Army Fortnight. No. 417 optd. with T **56.**

452. 20 f.+10 f. blue .. 20 20

1957. Proclamation of Republic.

453. **57.** 20 f. red .. .. 2·50 2·25
454. 25 f. violet .. .. 2·50 2·25
455. 30 f. brown .. .. 2·50 2·25

1957. 5th Int. Fair, Tunis. As No. 404 but additionally inscr. "5e FOIRE INTERNATIONALE" and Arabic inscriptions at sides, surch. + **10 F.**

456. 20 f.+10 f. violet .. 20 20

58. Pres. Bourguiba and Ile de la Galite. **59.** Tunisian Emblems and Map.

1958. Exile of Pres. Bourguiba. 6th Anniv.

457. **58.** 20 f. blue and chocolate 15 12
458. 25 f. blue and violet .. 15 12

1958. Independence. 2nd Anniv. Inscr. " 20 MARS 1958. 2° ANNIVERSAIRE DE L'INDEPENDANCE ".

459. **59.** 20 f. green and chocolate 15 8
460. – 25 f. brown and blue .. 15 10
461. – 30 f. brn., red-brn. & red 20 12

DESIGNS: 25 f. Mother and child. 30 f. Clenched fist holding Tunisian flag.

For 20 f. brown and blue see No. 464.

60. Andreas Vesalius (scientist) and A. ibn Khaldoun. **61.** Planting Olives.

1958. Brussels Int. Exn.

462. **60.** 30 f. green and bistre .. 20 12

1958. Labour Day.

463. **61.** 20 f. red, purple, blue, green and black .. 15 12

1958. Return of Pres. Bourguiba. 3rd Anniv. As T **59** but with inscr. altered.

464. **59.** 20 f. brown and blue .. 12 10

62. **63.** Pres Bourguiba.

1958. Proclamation of Tunisian Republic. 1st Anniv.

465. **62.** 5 f. maroon and bistre .. 20 10
466. 10 f. dp. grn. & apple-grn. 20 10
467. 15 f. brown and orange 20 10
468. 20 f. vio. olive & yellow 20 10
469. 25 f. purple 20 10

1958. Pres. Bourguiba's 55th Birthday.

470. **63.** 20 f. maroon and violet 10 8

64. Fishermen with Catch. **65.** U.N.E.S.C.O. Headquarters, Paris.

1958. 6th Int. Fair.

471. **64.** 25 f. maroon red & grn. 20 15

1958. U.N.E.S.C.O. Building. Inaug.

472. **65.** 25 f. myrtle 20 15

66. " Shedding the Veil ". **67.** Hand holding plant.

1959. Emancipation of Tunisian Women.

473. **66.** 20 m. turquoise .. 12 8

1959. Neo-Destour (Nationalist Party). 25th Anniv. and Victory Congress. Inscr. " 25 eme ANNIVERSAIRE DU NEO-DESTOUR " or " CONGRES DE LA VICTOIRE SOUSSE 1959 " (10 m.).

474. **67.** 5 m. red, brown & maroon 8 5
475. – 10 m. red, yellow, maroon and green .. 10 10
476. 20 m. blue 15 12
477. – 30 m. ind., turq. & chest. 30 25

DESIGNS—VERT. 10 m. Tunisians with flaming torch and flag on shield. 20 m. Pres. Bourguiba in exile at Borj le Boeuf, 1954. HORIZ. 30 m. Pres. Bourguiba and Borj le Boeuf, 1934.

68. " Tunisia " on Horseback.

1959. Independence. 3rd Anniv.

478. **68.** 50 m. red, black, green and bistre 30 20

69. Tunisian Horseman. **70.** " Freedom ".

1959. Designs as T **69.**

479. ½ m. choc., green & emerald 5 5
480. 1 m. yellow-brown & blue 5 5
481. 2 m. brown, yellow & blue 5 5
482. 3 m. myrtle 5 5
483. 4 m. chestnut 5 5
484. 5 m. myrtle 5 5
485. 6 m. violet 8 5
486. 8 m. maroon 5 5
487. 10 m. red, green and bistre 5 5
487a. 12 m. violet and bistre .. 8 5
488. 15 m. blue 8 5
489. 16 m. bronze-green .. 8 5
490. 20 m. turquoise 25 10
491. 20 m. mar., olive & myrtle 30 20
492. 25 m. blue, chest. & turq. 10 8
493. 30 m. choc., green & turq. 15 5
494. 40 m. green 25 10
495. 45 m. emerald 20 8
496. 50 m. blue, red, purple and turquoise 20 5
497. 60 m. chestnut and green .. 25 8
498. 70 m. grn., ol., bis. & purple 25 15
499. 75 m. olive-brown .. 30 20
500. 90 m. choc., green & blue .. 35 20
501. 95 m. red, grn., brn. & blue 35 20
502. 100 m. blue, green, brown and chestnut .. 40 25
503. 200 m. red, bistre and blue 85 35
504. ½ d. brown .. .. 2·50 1·90
505. 1 d. ochre and black-green 5·00 3·50

DESIGNS—VERT. ½ m. Ain Draham. 2 m. Camel-driver. 3 m. Saddler's shop. 5 m. T **69.** 6 m. Weavers. 8 m. Gafsa. 10 m. Woman holding pomegranates. 12 m. Turner. 20 m. (No. 491), Gabes. 40 m. Kairouan. 70 m. Carpet weaver. 75 m. Nabeul vase. 95 m. Olive-gatherer. ½ d. Sbeitla. HORIZ. 1 m. Kairouan environs. 4 m. Medenine. 15 m. Monastir. 16 m. Tunis. 20 m. (No. 490), Room in Arab house, Sidi-Bou-Said. 25 m. Sfax. 30 m. Aqueduct, Medjerda Valley. 45 m. Bizerta. 50 m. Djerba. 60 m. Le Jerid. 90 m. Le Kef. 100 m. Sidi-bou-Said highway. 200 m. Old port of Sfax. 1 d. Beja ploughman.

1959. Africa Freedom Day.

506. **70.** 40 m. chestnut and blue 25 20

71. Postman. **72.** Clenched Hands.

1959. Stamp Day.

507. **71.** 20 m.+5 m. brn. & orge. 15 15

1959. U.N. Day.

508. **72.** 80 m. chest., blue & mar. 30 30

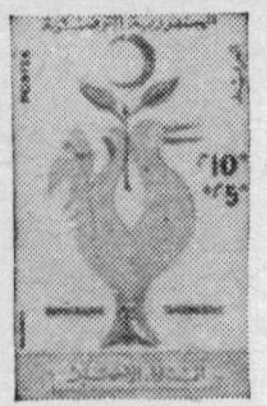

73. 74. Dancer and Coin.

1959. Red Crescent Day.

509. 73. 10 m.+5 m. blue, red, green and yellow .. 10 10

1959. Tunisian Central Bank. 1st Anniv.

510. 74. 50 m. black and blue .. 25 25

75. " Uprooted Tree ". 76. Camel Rider Telephoning.

1960. World Refugee Year. Inscr. " ANNEE MONDIALE DES REFUGIES 1959–1960 ".

511. 75. 20 m. indigo 8 5

512. – 40 m. black and purple 25 20

DESIGN—HORIZ. 40 m. Doves.

1960. Stamp Day.

513. 76. 60 m.+5 m. orange, blue and olive 30 30

77. Pres. Bourguiba signing Promulgation. 78. Fair Emblems.

1960. Promulgation of Constitution.

514. 77. 20 m. red, choc. & green 10 10

1960. 5th Sousse National Fair.

515. 78. 100 m. black and green 40 35

79. President Bourguiba. 80. Jamboree Emblems.

1960.

516. 79. 20 m. black 10 5

517. 30 m. black, red & blue 12 8

518. 40 m. black, red & green 15 10

1960. 4th Arab Scout Jamboree, Tunis.

519. 80. 10 m. turquoise .. 8 5

520. – 25 m. pur., red & green 12 10

521. – 30 m. lake, vio. & grn. 20 15

522. – 40 m. blk., blue & red.. 20 15

523. – 60 m. vio., pur. & sepia 30 25

DESIGNS: 25 m. Saluting hand with scouts as fingers. 30 m. Camp bugler. 40 m. Scout peacock badge. 60 m. Scout by camp fire.

81. Cyclist and Stadium. 82.

1960. Olympic Games.

524. 81. 5 m. chocolate and olive 5 5

525. – 10 m. pur., grn. & indigo 10 10

526. 15 m. carmine and red 12 12

527. – 25 m. slate-blue and blue 15 15

528. – 50 m. blue and green .. 35 35

DESIGNS: 10 m. Flowers composed of Olympic rings. 15 m. Girl with racquet. 25 m. Runner. 50 m. Handball player.

1960. 5th World Forestry Congress, Seattle.

529. 82. 8 m. lake, green and blue 10 8

530. – 15 m. green 12 10

531. 25 m. red, emer. & violet 20 12

532. 50 m. blue-green, brown-purple & yellow-green 30 20

DESIGNS: 15 m. Removing bark from tree. 25 m. Tree within leaf. 50 m. Diamond pattern featuring palm.

83. U.N. Emblem and People's Arms. 84. Dove of Peace.  85. Stylised Hunt over Map.

1960. U.N. Day.

533. 83. 40 m. blue, clar. & black 25 25

1961. Independence. 5th Anniv.

534. 84. 20 m. blue, bistre & mar. 12 10

535. 30 m. brown, vio. & blue 15 12

536. 40 m. ultram., bl. & grn. 25 20

537. – 75 m. blue, mve. & olive 45 35

DESIGN: 75 m. Globe and Arms of Tunisia.

1961. Africa Day and 3rd Anniv. of Accra Conference. Inscr. " JOURNEE DE L'AFRIQUE 15.4.1961 ".

538. 85. 40 m. green, chest. & brn. 20 15

539. – 60 m. black, chestnut & grey-green .. 25 20

540. – 100 m. violet, emerald and grey-green .. 35 30

541. – 200 m. chocolate & orge. 75 60

DESIGNS (all showing outline of Africa): 60 m. Profiles of negress and Arab woman. 100 m. Masks and " Africa Day " in Arabic. 200 m. Clasped hands.

86. Stamps and Magnifier. 87. " Celebration ". 88. Dag Hammarskjoeld.

1961. Stamp Day. Inscr. " JOURNEE DU TIMBRE 1961 ". Multicoloured.

542. 12 m.+4 m. Kerkennah dancer and costume of stamps 12 10

543. 15 m.+5 m. Mobile postal delivery 15 12

544. 20 m.+6 m. T 86.. .. 20 15

545. 50 m.+5 m. Postman in shirt depicting stamps 25 25

The 12 m. and 20 m. are vert. and the rest horiz.

1961. National Day.

546. 87. 25 m. brn., red & violet 10 8

547. – 50 m. brn., choc. & grn. 20 15

548. – 95 m. mve., brn. & blue 35 30

DESIGNS: 50 m. Family celebrating in street. 95 m. Girl astride crescent moon.

1961. U.N. Day.

549. 88. 40 m. blue 20 15

90. Arms of Tunisia. 91. Mosquito in Web. 92. African.

1962. Independence Campaign. 10th Anniv. Arms in red, yellow, blue and black.

550. 90. 1 m. yellow and black 5 5

551. 2 m. pink and black .. 5 5

552. 3 m. blue and black .. 5 5

553. 6 m. grey and black .. 5 5

1962. Malaria Eradication. Inscr. " LE MONDE UNI CONTRE LE PALUDISME ".

554. 91. 20 m. chocolate .. 12 10

555. – 30 m. chest., grn. & choc. 20 15

556. – 40 m. crim., grn. & choc. 30 25

DESIGNS—VERT. 30 m. " Horseman " attacking mosquito. HORIZ. 40 m. Hands destroying mosquito.

1962. Africa Day. Inscr. " JOURNEE DE L'AFRIQUE 1962 ".

557. 92. 50 m. brown and buff.. 25 20

558. – 100 m. orange, myrtle, ochre and blue .. 40 30

DESIGN: 100 m. Symbolic figure clasping ' Africa '.

93. Dancer. 94. Rejoicing Tunisians.

1962. May Day. Inscr. " FETE DU TRAVAIL 1962 ".

559. 93. 40 m. chocolate, yellow, blue and green .. 20 15

560. – 60 m. chocolate .. 25 20

DESIGN: 60 m. Worker with pneumatic drill.

1962. National Day.

561. 94. 20 m. black and salmon 8 8

95. Gabes Costume. 96. U.N. Emblem and Tunisian Flag.

1962. Republic Festival. Regional Costumes. Multicoloured.

562. 5 m. Type 95 .. .. 8 8

563. 10 m. Mahdia 10 10

564. 15 m. Kairouan 12 12

565. 20 m. Hammamet .. 15 15

566. 25 m. Djerba 20 20

567. 30 m. As 10 m. 25 25

568. 40 m. As 20 m. 30 30

569. 50 m. Type 95 .. .. 35 35

570. 55 m. Ksar Hellal.. .. 40 40

571. 60 m. Tunis 60 60

1962. U.N. Day.

572. 96. 20 m. red, black & grey 15 12

573. – 30 m. yellow, brown, blue and olive .. 20 15

574. – 40 m. blue, black & brn. 30 25

DESIGNS—HORIZ. 30 m. " Plant " with three leaves and Globe. ERT. 40 m. Globe and dove.

97. A. Q. Chabbi (poet). 98. Pres. Bourguiba.

1962. Aboul Qasim Chabbi Commem.

575. 97. 15 m. violet 8 5

1962.

576. 98. 20 m. blue 8 5

577. 30 m. claret 10 8

578. 40 m. green 15 12

99. Telephone Switch-board Operators. 100. Runners.

1962. Modernisation of Telephone System.

579. – 5 m. green, drab, violet and black 5 5

580. – 10 m. yellow, brown, blue and black 5 5

581. – 15 m. red, drab, bl. & blk. 10 8

582. 99. 50 m. flesh, chest. & blk. 25 20

583. – 100 m. blue, pur. & black 50 40

584. – 200 m. blue, stone, green and black .. .. 1·00 70

DESIGNS: 5 m. Hached Telephone Exchange. 10 m. Carthage Telephone Exchange. 15 m. Aerial equipment. 100 m. Telephone equipment as human figure. 200 m. Belvedere Telephone Exchange.

1963. 13th Int. Military Sports Council Cross-country Championships.

585. 100. 30 m. choc., grn. & blk. 10 8

101. Dove with Wheatear and Globe. 102. Centenary Emblem.

1963. Freedom from Hunger.

586. 101. 20 m. blue and brown 8 8

587. – 40 m. maroon & brown 15 12

DESIGN: 40 m. Child taking nourishment.

1963. Red Cross Cent.

588. 102. 20 m. red, grey & brown 8 8

1963. U.N. Day. Nos. 542/5 optd. **1963 O.N.U.** in English and Arabic. Multicoloured.

589. 12 m.+4 m. 8 8

590. 15 m.+5 m. 12 12

591. 20 m.+6 m. 15 15

592. 50 m.+5 m. 30 30

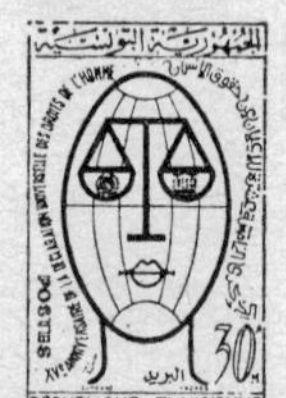

103. " Miss World ". 104. " Out of Reach ".

1963. Declaration of Human Rights. 15th Anniv.

593. 103. 30 m. chocolate & green 12 10

1964. Nubian Monuments Preservation.

594. 104. 50 m. ochre, chestnut and indigo 20 20

105. " Unsettled Forecast ". 106. Mohamed Ali (trade union leader).

1964. World Meteorological Day.

595. 105. 40 m. mauve, blue and brown 15 15

1964. Mohamed Ali. 70th Birth Anniv.

596. 106. 50 m. maroon.. .. 20 15

107. Africa within Flower. 108. Pres. Bourguiba.

1964. Addis Ababa Conference of the Organization of African Unity. 1st Anniv.
597. 107. 60 m. multicoloured .. 25 20

1964. National Day.
598. 108. 20 m. blue 5 5
599. 30 m. brown 8 5

109. "Bizerte" ("ship"). 110. Bifasciated Lark.

1964. Neo-Destour Congress, Bizerta.
600. 109. 50 m. green and black 12 10

1965. Air. Tunisian Birds. Multicoloured.
601. 25 m. Type 110 .. .. 15 10
602. 55 m. Great grey shrike 20 12
603. 55 m. Cream-coloured courser 20 12
604. 100 m. Chaffinch .. 45 20
605. 150 m. Greater flamingoes 60 35
606. 200 m. Barbary partridge 80 45
607. 300 m. Roller .. .. 1·10 80
608. 500 m. Houbara bustard .. 1·60 1·10
SIZES—As T 110: 55 m. (both). Others, 23 × 32½ mm.

111. Early Telegraphist and Aerial Mast. 112. Carthaginian Coin.

1965. I.T U Cent.
609. 111. 55 m. blue and black 15 12

1965. Festival of Popular Arts, Carthage.
610. 112. 5 m. maroon and green 5 5
611. 10 m. maroon & yellow 5 5
612. 75 m. maroon and blue 30 12

113. Girl reading Book. 114. Joined Hooks.

1965. Opening of Students' Home, Tunis.
613. 113. 25 m. blue, blk. & verm. 10 5
614. 40 m. blk., blue & verm. 15 8
615. 50 m. verm., blk. & blue 20 10

1965. Int. Co-operation Year.
617. 114. 40 m. blue, pur. & blk. 10 8

115. Woman Bathing. 117. "Independence".

116. Pres. Bourguiba and Hands.

1966. Mineral Springs. Inscr. "EAUX MINERALES".
618. 115. 10 m. red, ochre & grey 5 5
619. – 20 m. multicoloured 8 5
620. – 30 m. red, blue & yellow 10 5
621. – 100 m. olive, yell. & bl. 40 15
DESIGNS: 20 m. Man pouring water. 30 m. Woman pouring water. 100 m. Mountain and fronds of tree.

1966. Independence. 10th Anniv.
622. 116. 5 m. lilac and blue .. 5 5
623. 10 m. green and indigo 5 5
624. 117. 25 m. multicoloured .. 10 5
625. – 40 m. multicoloured .. 15 8
626. – 60 m. multicoloured .. 25 10
DESIGNS—As T 117—HORIZ. 40 m. "Development". VERT. 60 m. "Promotion of Culture" ("man" draped in books, palette, musical instruments, etc.).

118. Sectional Map of Africa. 119. U.N.E.S.C.O. Emblem of the Muses.

1966. 2nd U.N. African Regional Cartographic Conf., Tunisia.
627. 118. 15 m. multicoloured .. 5 5
628. 35 m. multicoloured .. 12 5
629. 40 m. multicoloured .. 15 8

1966. U.N.E.S.C.O. 20th Anniv.
631. 119. 100 m. brown and black 40 15

120. "Athletics".

ILLUSTRATIONS
British Commonwealth and all overprints and surcharges are FULL SIZE.
Foreign Countries have been reduced to ¾-LINEAR.

1967. Publicity for Mediterranean Games (September, 1967).
632. 120. 20 m. brown, blue & red 8 5
633. 30 m. black and blue 10 5

121. Gabes Costume and Fair Emblem. 122. Emblems of Civilisation.

1967. "Expo 67" World Fair, Montreal. T 122 and earlier designs redrawn as T 121.
634. – 50 m. mult. (As No. 586) 12 5
635. 121. 75 m. multicoloured .. 20 8
636. 122. 100 m. grn., blk. & turq. 15 10
637. 110 m. red, sep. & blue 20 10
638. – 155 m. mult. (As No. 605) 40 20

123. Tunisian Pavilion, Pres. Bourguiba and Map.

1967. "National Day at World Fair, Montreal".
639. 123. 65 m. purple and red .. 20 12
640. – 105 m. brn., red & blue 30 20
641. – 120 m. blue 40 30
642. – 200 m. blk., red & pur. 65 40
DESIGNS: 105 m. As T 123, but with profile bust of Pres. Bourguiba. Tunisian pavilion (different view) with: 120 m. Silhouette and 200 m. Bust of Pres. Bourguiba.

124. "Tunisia" holding Clover. 126. Bas-relief from Statue of Apollo.

125. Tennis Club.

1967. Republic. 10th Anniv. Multicoloured.
643. 25 m. Type 125 .. .. 8 5
644. 40 m. Woman releasing doves (vert.) .. 12 8

1967. Mediterranean Games, Tunis.
645. 125. 5 m. red and green .. 5 5
646. 10 m. multicoloured .. 5 5
647. 15 m. black 5 5
648. 35 m. turquoise, maroon and black 10 8
649. – 75 m. green, violet and claret 25 15
DESIGNS—VERT. 10 m. "Sporting Triumphs" (squared panel). HORIZ. 15 m. Olympic swimming pool. 35 m. Sports Palace. 75 m. Olympic stadium.

1967. Tunisian History (1) Punic period.
650. 126. 15 m. red, blk. & grn. 5 5
651. – 20 m. flesh, red & blue 8 5
652. – 25 m. chestnut & olive 8 5
653. – 30 m. claret and grey 10 5
654. – 40 m. lemon, yellow and maroon .. 12 8
655. – 60 m. multicoloured .. 20 10
DESIGNS: 20 m. Sea horseman (Kerkouane medallion). 25 m. Hannibal (bronze bust). 30 m. "The Sacrifice" (votive stele). 40 m. Hamilcar (coin). 60 m. Glass funeral pendant mask.

127. "Human Rights". 128. "Electronic Man".

1968. Human Rights Year.
656. 127. 25 m. vermilion .. 8 5
657. 60 m. blue 20 12

1968. Electronics in Postal Service.
658. 128. 25 m. blue, brn. & pur. 8 5
659. 40 m. black, brn. & grn. 10 5
660. 60 m. maroon, slate-blue and blue 20 12

129. "Doctor and Patient". 130. Arabian Jasmine.

1968. W.H.O. 20th Anniv.
661. 129. 25 m. emerald and bluish green 8 5
662. 60 m. carmine and lake 20 12

1968. Tunisian Flowers. Multicoloured.
663. 5 m. Flax 5 5
664. 6 m. Indian shot 5 5
665. 10 m. Pomegranate .. 5 5
666. 12 m. Type 130 .. .. 5 5
667. 15 m. Raponticum .. 5 5
668. 20 m. Geranium 8 5
669. 25 m. Madonna lily .. 8 5
670. 40 m. Almond 10 8
671. 50 m. Capers 12 8
672. 60 m. Ariana rose 15 10
673. 100 m. Jasmine 25 15

131. Globe on "Sunflower". 132. Flautist.

1968. Red Crescent Day.
674. 131. 15 m. red, green & blue 5 5
675. – 25 m. red and purple .. 8 5
DESIGN: 25 m. Red crescent on wings of dove.

1968. Stamp Day.
676. 132. 20 m. multicoloured .. 5 5
677. 50 m. multicoloured .. 12 8

133. Jackal. 134. Worker.

1968. Fauna. Multicoloured.
678. 5 m. Type 133 .. .. 5 5
679. 8 m. Porcupine 5 5
680. 10 m. Dromedary 5 5
681. 15 m. Gazelle 5 5
682. 20 m. Fennec 8 5
683. 25 m. Herisson 8 5
684. 40 m. Horse 12 8
685. 60 m. Wild boar 15 10

1969. Int. Labour Organization. 50th Anniv. Multicoloured.
686. 25 m. Type 134 .. .. 8 5
687. 60 m. Youth and girl holding "May 1" banner .. 15 8

135. Musicians and Veiled Dancers. 136. Tunisian Arms.

1969. Stamp Day.
688. 135. 100 m. multicoloured .. 30 20

1969.
689. 136. 15 m. multicoloured .. 5 5
690. 25 m. multicoloured .. 8 5
691. 40 m. multicoloured .. 12 5
692. 60 m. multicoloured .. 15 8

137. "Industrial Development". 138. Lute.

1969. African Development Bank. 5th Anniv.
693. 137. 60 m. multicoloured .. 15 5

1970. Musical Instruments. Multicoloured.
694. 25 m. Type 138 .. .. 8 5
695. 50 m. Zither 12 8
696. 70 m. Rehab 20 10
697. 90 m. Naghrat (drums) .. 25 12
Nos. 695 and 697 are horiz., size 33 × 22 mm.

139. Nurse, Caduceus and Flags. 140. New U.P.U. Headquarters Building.

1970. Sixth North-African Maghreb Medical Seminar, Tunis.
698. 139. 25 m. multicoloured .. 8 5

1970. New U.P.U. Headquarters Building, Berne.
699. 140. 25 m. brown and red 8 5

141. Mounted Postman.

1970. Stamp Day. Multicoloured.
700. 25 m. Type **141** 8 5
701. 35 m. "Postmen of yesterday and today" (23 × 38 mm.) 12 5

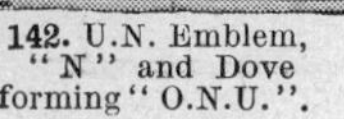

142. U.N. Emblem, "N" and Dove forming "O.N.U.". **143.** "The Flower-seller".

1970. United Nations. 25th Anniv.
702. **142.** 40 m. multicoloured .. 12 8

1970. "Tunisian Life" (1st series). Multicoloured.
703. 20 m. Type **143** 5 5
704. 25 m. "The husband's third day of marriage" 8 5
705. 35 m. "The Perfumer" .. 12 5
706. 40 m. "The Fish-seller" .. 15 5
707. 85 m. "The Coffee-house keeper" 20 10
See also Nos. 715/18, 757/62 and 819/23.

144. Lenin. **145.** Dish Aerial and Flags.

1970. Lenin. Birth Cent.
709. **144.** 60 m. lake 15 8

1971. Maghreban Posts and Telecommunications Co-ordination.
710. **145.** 25 m. multicoloured .. 8 5

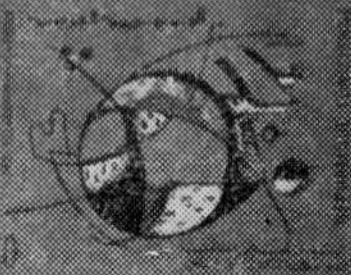

146. U.N. Building and Symbol. **147.** Globe and Satellites.

1971. Racial Equality Year.
711. **146.** 80 m. multicoloured .. 20 10

1971. World Telecommunications Day.
712. **147.** 70 m. multicoloured .. 20 8

148. Moon, Earth and Satellites.

1971. "Conquest of Space".
713. **148.** 15 m. black & blue .. 5 5
714. – 90 m. black & red .. 25 15
DESIGN: 90 m. Space allegory.

149. "The Pottery Dealer" **150.** Pres. Bourguiba.

1971. "Tunisian Life" (2nd series). Multicoloured.
715. 25 m. Type **149** 5 5
716. 30 m. "The Esparto dealer" 8 5
717. 40 m. "The Poulterer" .. 10 5
718. 50 m. "The Dyer" .. 12 8

1971. 8th P.S.D. Destourian Socialist Party Congress, Tunis. Multicoloured.
720. 25 m. Type **150** 5 5
721. 30 m. Bourguiba in bed, 1938 (horiz.) 8 5
722. 50 m. Bourguiba acclaimed 10 5
723. 80 m. Bourguiba—"Builder of the Nation" (horiz.) 20 8
SIZES: 30 m., 80 m. $13\frac{1}{2} \times 14$. 50 m. As T **150**.

151. Shah Mohammed Riza Pahlavi and Achaemenidian Effigy. **152.** Pimento.

1971. Persian Empire. 2500th Anniv. Multicoloured.
724. 25 m. Type **151** 8 5
725. 50 m. "King Bahram-Gur hunting" (14th-century) 12 5
726. 100 m. "Coronation of Louhrasap" (Persian 11th-century miniature) 25 10

1971. "Flowers, Fruits and Folklore". Multicoloured.
728. 1 m. Type **152** 5 5
729. 2 m. Mint 5 5
730. 5 m. Pear 5 5
731. 25 m. Laurel rose 5 5
732. 60 m. Quince 15 5
733. 100 m. Grapefruit 25 12
Each design includes a scene from Tunisian folklore.

153. "The Musicians of Kerkena". **154.** Telephone.

1971. Stamp Day.
735. **153.** 50 m. multicoloured .. 10 8

1971. Pan-African Telecommunications Network.
736. **154.** 95 m. multicoloured .. 20 12

155. U.N.I.C.E.F. Emblem. **157.** Olive-tree Emblem.

156. Rialto Bridge, Venice.

1971. U.N.I.C.E.F. 25th Anniv.
737. **155.** 110 m. multicoloured 25 15

1971. U.N.E.S.C.O. "Save Venice" Campaign. Multicoloured.
738. 25 m. Gondolier (vert.) .. 5 5
739. 30 m. De Medici and Palace (vert.) 8 5
740. 50 m. Prow of gondola (vert.) 15 8
741. 80 m. Type **156** .. 20 10

1972. World Olive-oil Year.
742. **157.** 60 m. multicoloured .. 15 8

158. Tunisian reading Book. **159.** Heart Emblem.

1972. Int. Book Year.
743. **158.** 90 m. multicoloured .. 20 10

1972. World Health Day. Multicoloured.
744. 25 m. Type **159** 5 5
745. 60 m. Heart within "hour-glass" 12 8

160. "Old Age". **161.** "Only One Earth".

1972. Tunisian Red Crescent.
746. **160.** 10 m. + 10 m. vio. & red 5 5
747. – 75 m. + 10 m. brn. & red 15 10
DESIGN: 75 m. Mother and Child ("Child Care").

1972. U.N. Environmental Conservation Conf., Stockholm.
748. **161.** 60 m. green and brown 12 8

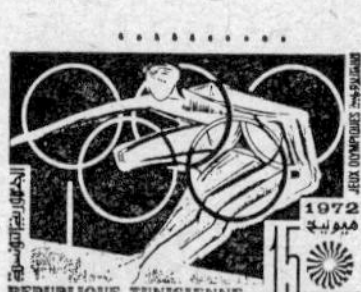

162. Hurdling. **163.** Chessboard.

1972. Olympic Games, Munich.
749. – 5 m. multicoloured .. 5 5
750. **162.** 15 m. multicoloured .. 5 5
751. – 20 m. blk., green & gold 5 5
752. – 25 m. multicoloured .. 5 5
753. – 60 m. multicoloured .. 12 8
754. – 80 m. multicoloured .. 20 10
DESIGNS—VERT. 5 m. Handball. 20 m. Athletes saluting. HORIZ. 25 m. Football. 60 m. Swimming. 80 m. Running.

1972. 20th Chess Olympiad, Skopje, Yugoslavia.
756. **163.** 60 m. multicoloured .. 12 8

164. "The Fisherman". **165.** New P.T.T. H.Q., Tunis.

1972. "Tunisian Life" (3rd series). Multicoloured.
757. 5 m. Type **164** 5 5
758. 10 m. "The Basket-maker" 5 5
759. 25 m. "The Musician" .. 8 5
760. 50 m. "The Mystic" .. 10 5
761. 60 m. "The Flower-seller" 12 8
762. 80 m. "The Berber Bride" 20 10

1972. Stamp Day.
764. **165.** 25 m. multicoloured .. 5 5

166. Dome of the Rock, Jerusalem. **167.** Globe and Beribboned Pen.

1973. Dome of the Rock Commemoration.
765. **166.** 25 m. multicoloured .. 8 5

1973. 9th Arab Writers' Congress and 11th Poetry Festival. Multicoloured.
766. 25 m. Type **167** 5 5
767. 60 m. Lyre Emblem .. 12 8

168. Heads of Family. **169.** Figures "10" and Bird feeding Young.

1973. Family Planning. Multicoloured.
768. 20 m. Type **168** 5 5
769. 25 m. Family profiles and bird 5 5

1973. World Food Programme. 10th Anniv. Multicoloured.
770. 25 m. Type **169** 5 5
771. 60 m. Symbolic "10" .. 12 8

170. Sculptured Roman Head. **171.** Red Crescent Nurse.

1973. U.N.E.S.C.O. "Save Carthage" Campaign. Multicoloured.
772. 5 m. Type **170** 5 5
773. 25 m. Carthagian mosaics 5 5
774. 30 m. "Cycle of mosaics" 5 5
775. 40 m. "Goodwill" stele (vert.) 8 5
776. 60 m. Preacher's hand (from Korba statue) .. 12 8
777. 75 m. "Malga" (17th-century potsherd) (vert.) 15 10

1973. Tunisian Red Crescent.
779. **171.** 25 m. + 10 m. mult. .. 8 5
780. – 60 m. + 10 m. red & grey 15 10
DESIGN—HORIZ. 60 m. Arms of blood donors.

172. "World Telecommunications". **173.** Smiling Youth.

1973. 5th World Telecommunications Day. Multicoloured.
781. 60 m. Type **172** 12 8
782. 75 m. "The Universe" .. 15 10

1973. 1st Pan-African Festival of Youth. Multicoloured.
783. 25 m. Festival Map .. 5 5
784. 40 m. Type **173** 10 5

174. Scout Badge. **175.** "Rover" in Car.

1973. International Scouting.
785. **174** 25 m. multicoloured 5 5

1973. 2nd Pan-Arab Rover Rally.
786. **175.** 60 m. multicoloured .. 15 10

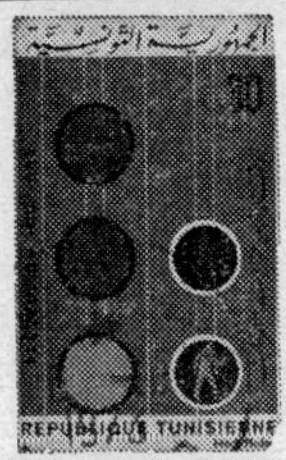
176. Traffic Lights.

177. Winged Camel.

1973. Road Safety. Multicoloured.
787. 25 m. Motorway junction (horiz.) 5 5
788. 30 m. Type **176** 8 5

1973. Stamp Day. Multicoloured.
789. 10 m. Peacock ("collectors pride") (horiz.) .. 5 5
790. 65 m. Type **177** 15 10

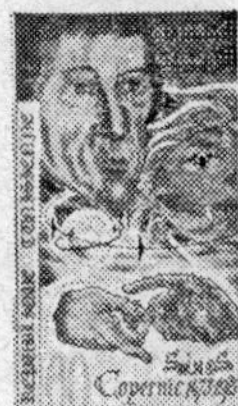
178. Copernicus.

179. O.A.U. Emblems within Arms.

1973. Copernicus. 500th Birth Anniv.
791. **178.** 60 m. multicoloured .. 15 10

1973. Organization of African Unity. 10th Anniv.
792. **179.** 25 m. multicoloured .. 5 5

180. Interpol Emblem and Handclasp.

181. Flower Offering.

1973. International Criminal Police Organization (Interpol). 50th Anniv.
793. **180.** 65 m. multicoloured .. 15 10

1973. Declaration of Human Rights. 25th Anniv.
794. **131.** 60 m. multicoloured .. 15 10

182. W.M.O. H.Q., Geneva.

1973. W.M.O. Cent. Multicoloured.
795. 25 m. Type **182** 5 5
796. 60 m. Earth and emblems 15 10

183. President Bourguiba, 1934.

184. Scientist using Microscope.

1974. Neo-Destour Party. 40th Anniv.
797. **183.** 15 m. purple, red & blk. 5 5
798. – 25 m. brn., orge. & blk. 5 5
799. – 60 m. bl., red & black .. 10 8
800. – 75 m. brn., mve. & blk. 15 10
801. – 100 m. grn., orge. & blk. 20 15
DESIGNS: Nos. 798/801, Various portraits of Pres. Bourguiba (founder), similar to Type **183**.

1974. 6th African Micro-Palaeontologica Conference, Tunis.
803. **184.** 60 m. multicoloured .. 15 10

185. "Blood Donation".

186. Telephonist holding Globe.

1974. Tunisian Red Crescent. Multicoloured.
804. 25 m. + 10 m. Type **185** .. 8 5
805. 75 m. + 10 m. "Blood Transfusion" 15 10

1974. International Automatic Telephone Service. Inauguration. Multicoloured.
806. 15 m. Type **186** 5 5
807. 60 m. Telephone dial .. 10 8

187. Population Emblems.

1974. World Population Year.
808. **187.** 110 m. multicoloured 20 15

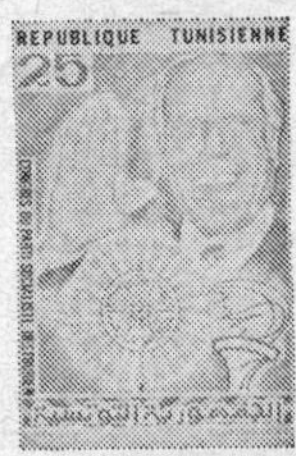
188. Pres. Bourguiba and Emblem.

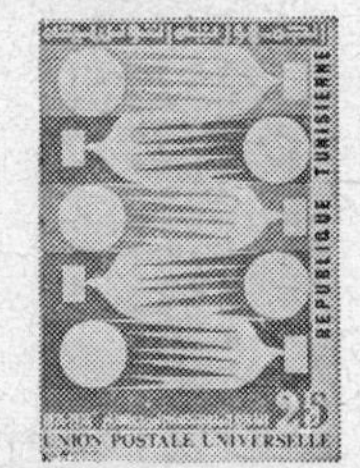
190. "Carrier-pigeons".

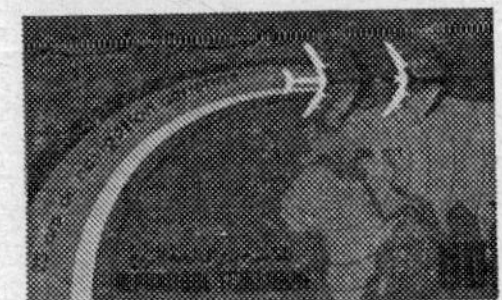
189. Aircraft crossing Globe.

1974. Destourian Socialist Party Congress.
809. **188.** 25 m. bl., turq. & blk. 5 5
810. – 60 m. red, yell. & black 10 8
811. – 200 m. pur., grn. & blk. 40 30
DESIGNS—HORIZ. 60 m. Pres. Bourguiba and sunflower. 200 m. Pres. Bourguiba and verbena.

1974. Tunisian Aviation. 25th Anniv.
813. **189.** 60 m. multicoloured .. 10 8

1974. Universal Postal Union. Centenary. Multicoloured.
814. 25 m. Type **190** 5 5
815. 60 m. Handclasp 10 8

191. Bardo Palace as "Ballot Box".

192. Postman with Parcels on Head.

1974. Legislative and Presidential Elections.
816. **191.** 25 m. bl., grn. & blk.. 5 5
817. – 100 m. blk. & orange.. 20 15
DESIGN: 100 m. Pres. Bourguiba on poll card.

1974. Stamp Day.
818. **192** 75 m. multicoloured .. 15 10

193. "The Water-carrier".

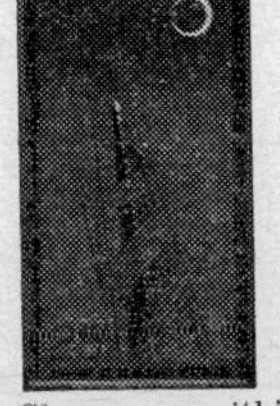
194. Skyscraper within Scaffolding.

1975. "Scenes from Tunisian Life". (4th series). Multicoloured.
819. 5 m. Type **193** 5 5
820. 15 m. "The Scent Sprinkler" 5 5
821. 25 m. "The Washerwomen" 8 5
822. 60 m. "The Potter" .. 10 8
823. 110 m. "The Fruitseller" 35 30

1975. 13th Arab Engineers' Union Conference, Tunis. Multicoloured.
825. 25 m. Type **194** 8 5
826. 65 m. Geometrical "bird" (horiz.) 20 15

195. Coffee-pot and Tray.

1975. Handicrafts. Multicoloured.
827. 10 m. Type **195** 5 5
828. 15 m. Horseman and saddlery 5 5
829. 25 m. Still life (painting) 8 5
830. 30 m. Birdcage (vert.) .. 10 8
831. 40 m. Woman's face and filigree jewellery (vert.) 12 10
832. 60 m. Textile patterns .. 20 15

196. "Good Health".

197. "Telecommunications".

1975. Tunisian Red Crescent Campaign against Malnutrition.
833. **196.** 50 m. + 10 m. multicoloured 20 20

1975. World Telecommunications Day.
834. **197.** 50 m. multicoloured .. 15 12

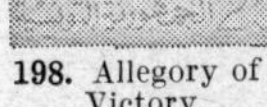
198. Allegory of Victory.

199. Tunisian Woman.

1975. "Victory". (Return of Bourguiba). 20th Anniv. Multicoloured.
835. 25 m. Type **198** 8 5
836. 65 m. President Bourguiba returning to Tunisia (horiz.) 20 15

1975. International Women's Year.
837. **199.** 110 m. multicoloured 35 30

200. Children on Road Crossing.

1975. Road Safety.
838. **200.** 25 m. multicoloured .. 8 5

201. Minaret and Yacht Marina, Jerba.

1975. "Tunisia, Yesterday and Today" (1st series). Multicoloured.
839. 10 m. Type **201** 5 5
840. 15 m. Minaret and modern hotel, Tunis 5 5
841. 20 m. Earrings, fortress and modern hotel, Monastir 5 5
842. 65 m. Old town and modern hotel, Sousse 20 15
843. 500 m. Old town and palms Tozeur .. .. .. 1·60 1·50
844. 1 d. Mosques and arches, Kairouan .. .. 3·25 3·00
See also Nos. 864/7.

202. "Athletes".

203. Bouquet.

1975. Mediterranean Games, Algiers. Multicoloured.
845. 25 m. Type **202** 8 5
846. 50 m. "Ship of sport" (horiz.) 15 12

1975. Stamp Day.
847. **203.** 100 m. multicoloured 30 25

204. College Building.

1975. Sadiki College. Centenary.
848. **204.** 25 m. multicoloured .. 8 5

205. "Duck".

206. Early and Modern Telephones.

1976. Tunisian Mosaics. Multicoloured.
849. 5 m. Type **205** 5 5
850. 10 m. "Fish" 5 5
851. 25 m. "Lioness" (40 × 27 mm.) 10 8
852. 60 m. "Gorgon" (40 × 27 mm.) 25 20
853. 75 m. "Circus Spectators" (27 × 40 mm.) 30 25
854. 100 m. "Virgil" (27 × 40 mm.) 40 35

1976. Telephone Centenary.
856. **206.** 150 m. multicoloured 60 55

207. Figures "20" and Banners.

208. Blind Man with Stick.

1976. Independence. 20th Anniv. Mult.
857. 40 m. Type **207** 15 12
858. 100 m. Figures "20" on flag 40 35
859. 150 m. Floral allegory of "Tunisia" .. 60 55

1976. World Health Day.
861. **208.** 100 m. black and red .. 40 35

209. Blood Donation. **210.** Piper and Children. " Save Medina ".

1976. Tunisian Red Crescent.
862. **209.** 40 m.+10 m. mult. 20 20

1976. " Habitat " U N. Conference on Human Settlements.
863. **242.** 40 m. multicoloured .. 15 12

211. Henna Tradition.

1976. " Tunisia Yesterday and Today " (2nd series). Multicoloured.
864. 40 m. Type **211** 15 12
865. 50 m. Diving for sponges, Jerba 20 15
866. 65 m. Weaving 25 20
867. 100 m. Pottery, Guellala .. 40 35

212. " Spirit of '76 " (Willard).

1976. American Revolution. Bicent.
868. **212.** 200 m. multicoloured 80 75

213. Running. **214.** Girl reading Book.

1976. Olympic Games, Montreal. Mult.
870. 50 m. Type **213** 20 15
871. 75 m. Olympic flags and rings 30 25
872. 120 m. Olympic " dove " 50 45

1976. Literature for Children.
873. **214.** 100 m. multicoloured 40 35

215. Heads and Bird Emblem. **216.** Mouradite (mausoleum), Tunis.

1976. 1st Non-aligned Countries Conference, Belgrade. 15th Anniv.
874. **215.** 150 m. multicoloured 60 55

1976. Cultural Heritage. Multicoloured.
875. 85 m. Type **216** 35 30
876. 100 m. Kairouan Great Mosque 40 35
877. 150 m. Ribat, Monastir .. 60 55
878. 200 m. Barber's Mosque, Kairouan 80 75

217. Emblem and Globe.

1976. U.N. Postal Administration. 25th Anniv.
879. **217.** 150 m. multicoloured 60 55

PARCEL POST STAMPS

P 1. Mail Carrier. P 2. Date Gathering.

1906.
P 44. P 1. 5 c. purple and green 5 5
P 45. 10 c. pink and red .. 20 5
P 46. 20 c. red and brown .. 25 5
P 47. 25 c. brown and blue 40 5
P 48. 40 c. red and grey .. 35 5
P 49. 50 c. violet and brown 25 5
P 50. 75 c. blue and brown 55 5
P 51. 1 f. red and brown .. 45 5
P 52. 2 f. blue and red .. 1·10 5
P 53. 5 f. brown and violet 2·50 20

1926.
P 147. P 2. 5 c. blue and brown .. 5 5
P 148. 10 c. magenta and red 5 5
P 149. 20 c. black and green 5 5
P 150. 25 c. black and brown 8 5
P 151. 40 c. green and red .. 25 10
P 152. 50 c. black and violet 20 10
P 153. 60 c. red and olive .. 40 12
P 154. 75 c. green and lilac .. 35 8
P 155. 80 c. brown and red .. 20 8
P 156. 1 f. red and green .. 20 5
P 157. 2 f. red and magenta 40 5
P 158. 4 f. black and red .. 50 5
P 159. 5 f. violet and brown 80 15
P 160. 10 f. grn. & red on grn. 1·10 12
P 161. 20 f. vio. & grn. on rose 2·50 15

POSTAGE DUE STAMPS

D 1. D 2. Carthaginian Statue. D 3. Agricultural Produce.

1901.
D 28. D 1. 1 c. black 5 5
D 29. 2 c. orange .. 5 5
D 30. 5 c. blue 5 5
D 31. 10 c. brown .. 5 5
D 32. 20 c. green 35 5
D 33. 30 c. red 10 8
D 34. 50 c. lake 15 8
D 35. 1 f. olive 8 8
D 36. 2 f. red on green .. 35 20
D 37. 5 f. black on yellow 8·00 8·00

1914. Surch. **2 FRANCS.**
D 49. D 1. 2 f. on 5 f. blk. on yell. 20 20

1923.
D 100. D 2. 1 c. black 5 5
D 101. 2 c. black on yellow 5 5
D 102. 5 c. claret 5 5
D 103. 10 c. blue 5 5
D 287. 10 c. green 5 5
D 104. 20 c. orange on yell. 5 5
D 105. 30 c. chocolate .. 8 5
D 106. 50 c. red 8 5
D 288. 50 c. violet 5 5
D 107. 60 c. mauve 5 5
D 108. 80 c. brown .. 5 5
D 109. 90 c. red 15 10
D 110. 1 f. green 5 5
D 111. D 2. 2 f. olive 5 5
D 289. 2 f. red 5 5
D 112. 3 f. violet on red .. 5 5
D 290. 4 f. blue 5 5
D 113. 5 f. violet 12 5
D 291. 10 f. lilac 8 5
D 292. 20 f. brown 15 5
D 293. 30 f. blue 25 10

1957.
D 448. D 3. 1 f. green 5 5
D 449. 2 f. brown 5 5
D 450. 3 f. slate-green .. 5 5
D 451. 4 f. indigo 8 8
D 452. 5 f. mauve 8 8
D 453. 10 f. red 10 10
D 454. 20 f. sepia 20 20
D 455. 30 f. blue 35 35

1960. Inscr. " REPUBLIQUE TUNISIENNE" and new currency.
D 534. D 3. 1 m. green 5 5
D 535. 2 m. brown 5 5
D 536. 3 m. slate-green .. 5 5
D 537. 4 m. indigo 5 5
D 538. 5 m. violet 5 5
D 539. 10 m. red 8 8
D 540. 20 m. chocolate .. 15 15
D 541. 30 m. blue 20 20

TURKEY E3

Formerly an empire, this country is now a republic, the greater part of its territory lying in the N. part of Asia Minor.

40 paras = 1 piastre = 1 grush = 1 kurus.
1942. 100 paras = 1 kurus.
1947. 100 kurus = 1 lira.

1. 2.

1863. Imperf.
1. 1. 20 pa. black on yellow .. 38·00 15·00
2. 1 pi. black on purple .. 38·00 18·00
3. 2 pi. black on blue .. 45·00 20·00
4. 5 pi. black on rose .. 50·00 25·00

1865. Perf.
11a. 2. 10 pa. green .. .. 1·50 1·50
64. 10 pa. brown 5 5
35. 10 pa. purple .. .. 5·00 65
12. 20 pa. yellow 65 50
65. 20 pa. green 5 5
94. 20 pa. grey 5 5
13. 1 pi. lilac .. .. 1·10 1·00
66. 1 pi. yellow 10 12
14. 2 pi. blue 50 65
95. 2 pi. red to orange-brown 5 5
24. 5 pi. red 50 75
39. 5 pi. blue 10 25
39c. 5 pi. grey .. .. 2·00 2·00
16. 25 pi. orange .. .. 60·00 55·00
48. 25 pi. red .. .. 11·00 12·00

1876. Surch. with value in figures and **Pre.**
77. 2. ½ pre. on 10 pa. mauve .. 65 50
78. ½ pre. on 20 pa. green .. 1·25 85
79. 1¼ pre. on 50 pa. red .. 20 45
80. 2 pre. on 2 pi. brown .. 4·25 3·25
81. 5 pre. on 5 pi. blue .. 1·50 2·75

3. 4.

1876.
89. 3. 5 pa. black and olive .. 12 15
96. 5 pa. lilac .. .. 25·00 30·00
109. 5 pa. black 12 12
113. 5 pa. green and yellow .. 12 15
82. 10 pa. black and mauve 12 30
90. 10 pa. black and green .. 12 15
123. 10 pa. green 12 8
83. 20 pa. purple and green 8·50 1·50
91. 20 pa. black and red .. 12 15
103. 20 pa. red 15 10
124. 20 pa. pink 12 8
84. 50 pa. blue and yellow .. 12 35
92. 1 pi. black and grey (A) 12 15
93. 1 pi. black and blue (B) .. 4·75 65
99. 1 pi. blue 15 8
85. 2 pi. black and orange .. 12 35
105. 2 pi. yellow 12 20
110. 2 pi. orange and blue .. 5 15
114. 2 pi. mauve and grey .. 25 15
86. 5 pi. red and blue .. 55 1·10
115. 5 pi. brown 25 35
111. 5 pi. green 12 15
87. 25 pi. purple and mauve 11·00 12·00
107. 25 pi. black .. .. 60·00 85·00
112. 25 pi. brown .. .. 10·00 12·00
116. 25 pi. red and yellow .. 10·00 12·00

(A) Inscr. " 1 PIASTRES ". (B) " 1 PIASTRE ".

1892. Various frames.
141. 4. 10 pa. green 10 5
142. 20 pa. red 8 5
143. 1 pi. blue .. .. 1·00 5
144. 2 pi. brown 8 5
145. 5 pi. purple .. .. 1·90 2·50

1897. Surch. in figures and words.
160. 4. 5 pa. on 10 pa. green .. 10 10

5. 6. 7.

1901.
167. 5. 5 pa. violet 5 5
168. 10 pa. green 5 5
169. 20 pa. red 5 5
170. 1 pi. blue 5 5
171. 2 pi. orange 8 5
172. 5 pi. mauve 12 5
173. 25 pi. brown 90 30
174. 50 pi. brown .. .. 3·75 1·25

1901.
175. 6. 5 pa. brown 25 12
176. 10 pa. green 10 10
177. 20 pa. mauve 10 10
178. 1 pi. blue 15 12
179. 2 pi. blue 15 12
180. 5 pi. brown .. .. 1·50 60
181. 25 pi. green .. .. 12·00 7·50
182. 50 pi. yellow .. .. 38·00 22·00

ب
(8.)

Some values of 1905, 1908, 1909 and 1913 issues exist optd. with the Turkish letter " B " as T 8 or smaller.

1905.
212. 7. 5 pa. orange 5 5
213. 10 pa. green 5 5
214. 20 pa. rose 5 5
215. 1 pi. blue 5 5
216. 2 pi. grey 5 5
217. 2½ pi. purple 8 5
218. 5 pi. brown 12 5
219. 10 pi. orange 20 5
220. 25 pi. olive 65 35
221. 50 pi. purple .. .. 2·00 1·00

9. 10. 11.

1908.
234. 9. 5 pa. orange 5 5
235. 10 pa. green 5 5
236. 20 pa. rose .. .. 3·00 10
237. 1 pi. blue .. .. 1·75 10
238. 2 pi. black 85 5
239. 2½ pi. chocolate .. 20 5
240. 5 pi. purple .. .. 2·50 5
241. 10 pi. red .. .. 5·00 50
242. 25 pi. green .. .. 2·25 1·25
243. 50 pi. brown .. .. 7·50 6·00

1908. Granting of Constitution.
256. 10. 5 pa. green 15 12
257. 10 pa. green 15 12
258. 20 pa. rose 35 20
259. 1 pi. blue 50 25
260. 2 pi. black .. .. 3·75 2·50

1909.
261. 11. 5 pa. orange 5 5
262. 10 pa. green 5 5
263. 20 pa. rose 5 5
264. 1 pi. blue 10 5
265. 2 pi. black 12 5
266. 2½ pi. brown .. .. 7·50 4·50
267. 5 pi. purple .. .. 1·75 12
268. 10 pi. red .. .. 3·00 25
269. 25 pi. green .. .. 55·00 35·00
270. 50 pi. brown .. .. 30·00 22·00

1910. Stamp of 1905 surch.
296. 7. 2 pa. on 5 pa. orange .. 12 10

12. G.P.O. Constantinople. 13. Mosque of Selim.

1913.
333. 12. 2 pa. green 5 5
334. 5 pa. orange 8 5
335. 10 pa. green 8 5
336. 20 pa. red 5 5
337. 1 pi. blue 5 5
338. 2 pi. grey 8 5
339. 5 pi. purple 20 15
340. 10 pi. red .. .. 1·25 55
341. 25 pi. green .. .. 3·75 1·50
342. 50 pi. brown .. .. 12·00 12·00

1913. Recapture of Adrianople.
353. 13. 10 pa. green 25 12
354. 20 pa. red 35 35
355 40 pa. blue 75 35

14. The Obelisk of the Hippodrome. 16. Leander's Tower.

1914.
499. 14. 2 pa. claret 5 5
500. – 4 pa. brown 5 5
501. 16. 5 pa. purple 5 5
502. – 6 pa. blue 10 10
516. – 10 pa. green 5 5
504. – 20 pa. red 20 5
518. – 1 pi. blue 10 5
506. – 1½ pi. grey and red .. 25 5
507. – 1¾ pi. brown and grey .. 8 8
508. – 2 pi. black and green .. 75 5
509. – 2½ pi. green and orange 35 8
510. – 5 pi. lilac .. .. 1·50 35
511. – 10 pi. brown .. .. 3·00 35
512. – 25 pi. green .. .. 10·00 2·50
513. – 50 pi. red .. .. 3·00 1·50
514. – 100 pi. blue .. .. 22·00 15·00
515. – 200 pi. black and green £200 £110

DESIGNS—VERT. 4 pa. Column of Constantine. 6 pa. Severn Towers. HORIZ. 10 pa. Lighthouse, Stamboul. 20 pa. Castle of Europe. 1 pi. Mosque of Sultan Ahmed. 1½ pi. Monument to Martyrs of Liberty. 1¾ pi. Fountains of Suleiman 2 pi. Cruiser "Hamidiye". 2½ pi. Candilli Bosphorus. 5 pi. Former Ministry of War, 10 pi. Sweet Waters of Europe. 25 pi. Suleima.. Mosques. 50 pi. Bosphorus at Rumeli-hissar. 100 pi. Sultan Ahmed's Fountain. 200 pii Sultan Mohammed V.

SIZES—As T 14: 4 pa., 6 pa.; 31½×20 mm. 10 pa. to 1 pi.; 26×21 mm. 1½ pi. to 2½ pi.; 38×24 mm. 5 pi. to 50 pi.; 40×25½ mm. 100 pi., 200 pi.

See Nos. 961/9. Some values exist optd. with small five-pointed star.

(31.)

1914. Constitution. 7th Anniv. No. 506 surch. with T 31.
521. 1 pi. on 1½ pi. grey & red .. 25 20

(32.)

1914. Abrogation of the Capitulations. Nos 501/11 optd. with T 32.
524. 5 pa. purple 35 20
526. 10 pa. green 50 20
527. 20 pa. red .. .. 1·00 25
528. 1 pi. blue .. .. 2·50 35
530. 2 pi. black and green .. 1·90 35
532. 5 pi. lilac .. .. 8·50 1·90
533. 10 pi. brown .. .. 19·00 9·50

(33.)

1915. Nos. 514/5 surch. as T 33.
534. 10 pi. on 100 pi. blue .. 7·50 3·00
535. 25 pi. on 200 pi. blk. & grn. 5·00 1·90

(34.)

1915. Various issues optd. with T 34, with or without additional opt. as T 8. There are various types of this opt. differing in the Turkish date, the shape of the star, etc.

A. On 1892 postage stamp issue.
536. 4. 5 pa. on 10 pa. green .. 5 5
537. 10 pa. green 5 5
662. 20 pa. red 5 5
663. 1 pi. blue .. .. 6·00 5·50
538. 2 pi. brown 5 5
539. 5 pi. purple 65 8

B. On 1892 postage stamp issue with additional surch. in Arabic.
630. 4. 10 pa. on 20 pa. red .. 5 5

C. On 1892 printed matter stamps optd. with Type P 3.
660. 4. 5 pa. on 10 pa. green .. 5 5
595. 10 pa. green 5 5
658. 10 pa. on 20 pa. red .. 5 5
728. 20 pa. red 8 5
596. 2 pi. brown 30 15
729. 5 pi. purple .. .. 4·75 4·50

D. On 1901 postage stamp issue.
540. 5. 5 pa. violet 5 5
541. 10 pa. green 8 5
542. 20 pa. red 5 5
543. 1 pi. blue 10 5
679. 5. 2 pi. orange 50 20
545. 5 pi. mauve 12 5
673a. 25 pi. brown 85 75
674. 50 pi. brown 75 10

E. On 1901 postage stamp issue with additional surch. in Arabic.
671a. 5. 10 pi. on 25 pi. brown .. 85 25
672. 10 pi. on 50 pi. brown .. 1·25 40

F. On 1901 printed matter stamps optd. with Type P 4.
597. 5. 5 pa. violet 5 5
731. 10 pa. green .. .. 3·00 2·50
732. 20 pa. red 5 5
733. 1 pi. blue 5 5
734. 2 pi. orange 12 5
599. 5 pi. red .. .. 1·25 55

G. On 1901 postage stamp issue.
547. 6. 5 pa. brown 5 5
676. 10 pa. green 10 5
677. 20 pa. mauve 5 5
678. 1 pi. blue 10 5
549. 2 pi. blue 10 5
550. 5 pi. brown 70 15
551. 25 pi. green .. .. 3·00 1·75

H. On 1901 postage stamp issue with additional surch. in Arabic.
680. 9. 5 pi. on 25 pi. green .. 6 00 5·50
681. 10 pi. on 25 pi. green .. 6·00 5·50

I. On 1902 printed matter stamps optd. with Type P 4.
735. 6. 5 pa. brown 5 5
600. 10 pa. green 5 5
737. 20 pa. mauve 5 5
738. 1 pi. blue 8 5
659. 5 pi. brown 35 12

J. On 1905 postage stamp issue.
552. 7. 5 pa. orange 5 5
553b. 10 pa. green 5 5
554a. 20 pa. rose 5 5
685a. 1 pi. blue 10 5
556b. 2 pi. grey 20 5
557. 2½ pi. purple 10 5
558a. 5 pi. brown 5 5
559. 10 pi. orange 70 10
690. 25 pi. olive 75 12
691. 50 pi. purple 80 12

K. On 1905 postage stamp issue with additional surch. in Arabic.
633a. 7. 10 pa. on 20 pa. rose .. 5 5
688. 10 pi. on 25 pi. olive .. 50 20
689. 10 pi. on 50 pi. purple .. 50 20

L. On 1905 printed matter stamps optd. with Type P 4.
601b. 7. 5 pa. orange 5 5
740. 10 pa. green .. .. 3·25 3·25
741. 20 pa. rose .. .. 3·25 3·25
742a. 1 pi. blue 15 5
602. 2 pi. grey .. .. 1·25 45
603. 5 pi. brown 55 10

M. On 1908 postage stamp issue.
612b. 9. 10 pa. green 5 5
640a. 20 pa. rose 5 5
569a. 2 pi. black .. .. 1·40 30
565a. 2½ pi. chocolate 10 5
613a. 5 pi. purple .. .. 2·75 90
567. 10 pi. red .. .. 1·40 30
699. 25 pi. green 90 25
700. 50 pi. brown .. .. 3·25 3·00

N. On 1908 postage stamp issue with additional surch. in Arabic.
696. 9. 10 pi. on 25 pi. green .. 1·60 1·00
697a. 10 pi. on 50 pi. brown .. 5·50 5·50
698. 25 pi. on 50 pi. brown .. 5·50 5·50

O. On 1908 printed matter stamps optd. with Type P 5.
743a. 9. 5 pa. orange .. .. 3·50 3·25
626a. 10 pa. green .. .. 14·00 5·50
604. 2 pi. black .. .. 32·00 16·00
605a. 5 pi. purple .. .. 1·25 12

P On 1908 commemorative postage stamp.
702. 10. 5 pa. orange .. .. 3·00 2·75

Q. On 1909 postage stamps.
570. 11. 5 pa. orange 5 5
616. 10 pa. green 5 5
572. 20 pa. rose 5 5
645. 1 pi. blue 8 5
574. 2 pi. black 12 5
709. 2½ pi. brown .. .. 3·25 3·00
576. 5 pi. purple 5 5
577. 10 pi. red .. .. 1·10 5
578. 25 pi. green .. .. 70·00 42·00

R. On 1909 printed matter stamps optd. with Type P 5.
606. 11. 5 pa. orange 5 5
620. 10 pa. green 8 5
608. 5 pi. purple .. .. 6·50 3·25

S. On 1913 postage stamp issue.
583. 12. 5 pa. orange 5 5
584. 10 pa. green 5 5
585. 20 pa. red 15 10
586. 1 pi. blue 15 5
587. 2 pi. grey 35 15
588. 5 pi. purple 50 20
589. 10 pi. red .. .. 2·00 50
718. 25 pi. green .. .. 1·50 30
719. 50 pi. brown .. .. 1·75 50

T. On 1913 postage stamp with additional surch. in Arabic.
717. 12. 10 pi. on 50 pi. brown .. 1·50 50

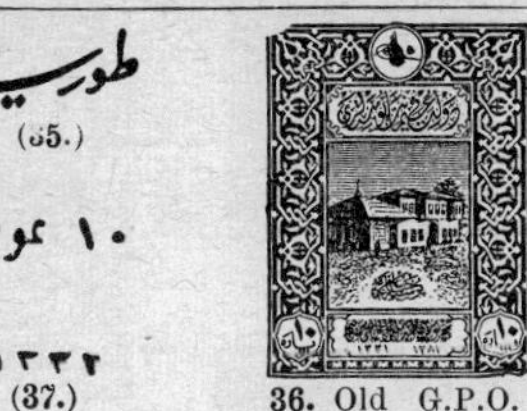

(35.) (37.) 36. Old G.P.O. Constantinople.

1916. Occupation of Sinai Peninsula. Optd. with T 35.
749. 5. 5 pa. violet 8 5
750. 10 pa. green 10 5
751. 11. 20 pa. rose 12 5
752. 1 pi. blue 15 5
753. 12. 5 pi. purple .. .. 3·25 75

1916. Jubilee of Constantinople City Post
754. 36. 5 pa. green 5 5
755. 10 pa. red 10 5
756. 20 pa. blue 12 5
757. 1 pi. black and violet 20 5
758. 5 pi. black and brown 5·00 50

1916. Jubilee stamps optd. with T 34.
654. 36. 10 pa. red 5 5
655. 20 pa. blue 5 5
656. 1 pi. black and violet 5 5
657. 5 pi. black and brown .. 75 12

1916. National Fete. Optd. with T 37.
759. 4. 10 pa. green .. .. 1·00 65
760b. 7. 20 pa. rose .. .. 1·25 50
761a. 1 pi. blue .. .. 1·25 65
762b. 2 pi. grey .. .. 1·50 25
763a. 2½ pi. purple .. .. 1·00 25

1916. Adrianople Commemorative stamps optd. with T 34.
721. 13. 10 pa. green 12 5
722. 20 pa. red 15 10
723. 40 pa. blue 30 15

1916. Constitution Commemorative of 1914 with additional surch. in Turkish.
724. 60 pa. on 1 pi. on 1½ pi. grey and red (No. 521) 25 15

1916. Postage Due stamps optd. with T 34. On Adrianople Commemorative stamps surch. in Arabic and Turkish.
745. 13. 10 on 2 pa. on 10 pa. grn. 6·00 6·00
746. 20 on 5 pa. on 20 pa. red 6·00 6·00
747. 40 on 10 pa. on 40 pa. blue .. .. 6·00 6·00
748. 40 on 20 pa. on 40 pa. blue .. .. 6·00 6·00

38. Seraglio Point. 40. Sentry.

41. Sultan Mohamed V. 39. Dolma Bagtche Palace.

1916.
721a. 38. 2 pi. blue and brown .. 10 5
764. 39. 10 pi. violet .. .. 3·00 25
765. 10 pi. green .. .. 1·25 25
766. 10 pi. brown .. .. 1·60 25
767. 40. 25 pi. red 25 12
768. 41. 50 pi. red 50 35
769. 50 pi. green .. .. 1·75 1·25
770. 50 pi. blue 20 20

42. Off to the front. (43.)

1917. Charity.
771. 42. 10 pa. purple .. 5 5

1917. Various issues optd. with T 43.

A. On postage stamp issue of 1865.
782. 2. 10 pa. purple .. .. 6·00 6·00
772a. 20 pa. yellow .. .. 6·00 6·00
783. 20 pa. green .. .. 6·00 6·00
785. 20 pa. grey .. .. 6·00 6·00
773b. 1 pi. lilac .. .. 6·00 6·00
784. 1 pi. yellow .. .. 6·00 6·00
774 2 pi. blue .. .. 6·00 6·00
780. 2 pi. red .. .. 6·00 6·00
775. 2. 5 pi. red .. .. 6·00 6·00
778. 5 pi. blue .. .. 6·00 6·00
779. 25 pi. red .. .. 6·00 6·00

B. On surch. postage stamp issue of 1876.
787. 2. ¼ pre. on 10 pa. mauve .. 6·00 6·00
788. ½ pre. on 20 pa. green .. 6·00 6·00
789. 1¼ pre. on 50 pa. red .. 6·00 6·00

C. On postage stamp issue of 1876.
790. 3. 5 pa. black and olive .. 6·00 6·00
791. 5 pa. black 8 8
792. 10 pa. black and green .. 6·00 6·00
793. 10 pa. green .. .. 6·00 6·00
794. 50 pa. blue and yellow .. 6·00 6·00
795. 2 p. black and orange .. 6·00 6·00
796. 2 pi. yellow .. .. 6·00 6·00
797. 2 pi. orange and blue .. 35 35
798. 5 pi. brown .. .. 6·00 6·00
799. 5 pi. green .. .. 6·00 6·00
801. 25 pi. purple and mauve 6·00 6·00
802. 25 pi. brown .. .. 6·00 6·00

D. On postage stamp issue of 1892.
803. 4. 20 pa. red 30 30
804. 2 pi. brown 55 55

E. On postage stamp issue of 1901.
805. 5. 5 pa. violet .. .. 6·00 6·00
806. 10 pa. green 65 50
807. 20 pa. red 12 10
808. 1 pi. blue 20 20
809. 2 pi. orange 50 40
810. 5 pi. mauve .. .. 6·00 6·00
811. 10 pi. on 50 pi. brown .. 6·00 6·00
812. 25 pi. brown 85 70

F. On postage stamp issue of 1901.
813. 6. 5 pa. brown 55 50
814. 20 pa. mauve 20 12
815. 1 pi. blue 50 35
816. 2 pi. blue 80 65
817. 5 pi. brown .. .. 6·00 6·00
818. 10 pi. on 50 pi. yellow .. 6·00 6·00
819. 25 pi. green .. .. 6·00 6·00

G. On postage stamp issue of 1905 with or without opt. as T 8.
820. 7. 5 pa. orange 5 5
830. 10 pa. green 8 8
822. 20 pa. rose 5 5
823b. 1 pi. blue 5 5
824. 2 pi. grey 40 25
825. 2½ pi. purple 65 30
826. 5 pi. brown .. .. 6·00 6·00
827. 10 pi. orange .. .. 6·00 6·00
828. 10 pi. on 50 pi. purple .. 6·00 6·00
829. 25 pi. olive .. .. 6·00 6·00

H. On postage stamp issue of 1908 with or without opt. as T 8.
834a. 9. 5 pa. orange 55 55
835. 10 pa. green 15 8
841. 1 pi. blue .. .. 6·00 6·00
842. 2 pi. black 65 50
837. 2½ pi. chocolate 55 55
838. 10 pi. on 50 pi. brown .. 6·00 6·00
839. 25 pi. green .. .. 6·00 6·00

I. On Commemorative stamp of 1908.
843. 10. 5 pa. orange 25 25

J. On postage stamp issue of 1909 with or without opt. as T 8.
844. 11. 5 pa. orange 10 10
846. 10 pa. green 12 12
847. 20 pa. rose 12 10
849. 1 pi. blue 12 10
850. 2 pi. black 55 45
851. 2½ pi. brown .. .. 6·00 6·00
852. 5 pi. purple .. .. 6·00 6·00
853. 10 pi. red .. .. 6·00 6·00

K. On postage stamp issue of 1913 with or without opt. as T 8.
858. 12. 5 pa. orange 25 25
865. 10 pa. green 35 25
860. 20 pa. red 25 25
861. 1 pi. blue 25 25
862. 2 pi. grey 55 35
863. 5 pi. purple .. .. 6·00 6·00
864. 10 pi. red .. .. 6·00 6·00

L. On Adrianople Commem. stamps of 1913.
868. 13. 10 pa. green 45 45
869. 40 pa. blue 55 55

M. On Constitution Commem. of 1914 with additional surch. in Turkish.
870. 60 pa. on 1 pi. on 1½ pi. grey and red (No. 521) 65 55

N. On postage stamp issue of 1916.
871. 40. 25 pi. red 85 20
872. 41. 50 pi. red .. .. 2·50 1·10
873. 50 pi. green .. .. 2·50 1·50
874. 50 pi. blue .. .. 5·00 2·00

O. On stamps of Eastern Roumelia of 1881 (T 3 of Turkey but inscr. "ROUMELIE ORIENTALE" at left).
876. – 5 pa. lilac .. .. 6·00 6·00
877. – 10 pa. green .. .. 6·00 6·00
875. – 20 pa. black and red .. 6·00 6·00
878. – 20 pa. red .. .. 6·00 6·00

P. On printed matter stamps of 1893 optd. with Type P 3.
879. 4. 20 pa. red (No. N 156a) .. 65 65
880. 1 pi. blue (No. N 157) .. 12 12

Q. On printed matter stamps of 1901 optd. with Type P 4.
881. 5. 5 pa. violet (No. N 183) 35 30
882. 10 pa. green (No. N 184) 3·00 2·00
883. 20 pa. red (No. N 185) .. 25 15
884. 1 pi. blue (No. N 186) .. 55 55
885. 2 pi. orange (No. N 187) 55 55
886. 5 pi. mauve (No. N 188) 6·00 6·00

R. On printed matter stamps of 1901 optd. with Type P **4**.
887. **6.** 5 pa. brown (No. N 189) 55 55
888. 10 pa. green (No. N 190) 55 55
889. 20 pa. mauve (No. N 191) 55 55
890. 2 pi. blue (No. N 193) .. 6·00 6·00

S. On printed matter stamps of 1905 optd. with Type P **4**.
891d.**7.** 5 pa. orange (No. N 222) 12 12
892. 10 pa. green (No. N 223) 25 25
893. 20 pa. rose (No. N 224).. 5 5
894. 1 pi. blue (No. N 225) .. 12 8
895. 2 pi. grey (No. N 226) .. 6·00 6·00
896. 5 pi. brown (No. N 227) 6·00 6·00

T. On printed matter stamp of 1908 optd. with Type P **5**.
897. **9.** 5 pa. orange (No. N 244) 6·00 6·00

U. On postage due stamps of 1865.
898. 20 pa. chocolate (D 18).. 5·00 5·00
899. 1 pi. chocolate (D 19) .. 5·00 5·00
900. 2 pi. chocolate (D 20) .. 5·00 5·00
901. 5 pi. chocolate (D 21) .. 5·00 5·00
902. 25 pi. chocolate (D 22) .. 5·00 5·00

V. On postage due stamps of 1869.
903. D **1.** 5 pi. brown .. .. 5·00 5·00

W. On postage due stamps of 1888.
904. **3.** 1 pi. black (D 118) .. 6·00 6·00
905. 2 pi. black (D 119) .. 6·00 6·00

X. On postage due stamps of 1892.
906. **4.** 20 pa. black (D 146) .. 25 25
907. 1 pi. black (D 148) 25 25
908. 2 pi. black (D 149) .. 25 20

Y. On Adrianople commem. issue of 1913 (postage due stamps surch. in Arabic and again in Turkish.
909. **13.** 10 on 2 pa. on 10 pa. green (D 356) .. 15 15
910. 20 on 5 pa. on 20 pa. red (D 357) 15 15
911. **13.** 40 on 10 pa. on 30 pa. blue (D 358) .. 25 15
912. 40 on 20 pa. on 40 pa. blue (D 359) .. 45 35

44. Artillery at Sedd-ul-bahr. **46.** Lighthouse.

47. Martyrs' Column. **45.** Mosque at Ortakeui.

48. Map of Gallipoli. **49.**

50. The Pyramids. **51.** In the Trenches.

1917.
916. **44.** 2 pa. violet 8 5
917. **45.** 5 pa. orange 5 5
918. **46.** 10 pa. green 8 5
919. **47.** 20 pa. red 8 5
920. **48.** 1 pi. blue 8 5
921. **49.** 50 pa. blue 8 5
922. **50.** 5 pi. brown and blue 1·90 35

1917. Surch. variously in Turkish.
913. **51.** 5 pa. on 1 pi. red .. 5 5
915. **42.** 10 pa. on 20 pa. red .. 15 5
914. **44.** 5 pi. on 2 pa. blue .. 25 8

1918. Surch. **5 Piastres 5** and in Turkish.
923. **44.** 5 pi. on 2 pa. blue .. 25 8

1918. No. 913 with additional surch.
924. **51.** 2 pa. on 5 pa. on 1 pi. red 5 8

1918. No. N 332 optd. with Sultan's toughra and surch. in Turkish.
938. **11.** 5 pa. on 2 pa. olive .. 5 5

52.

53. Sentry at Beersheba.

54. Turkish Column in Sinai.

(55.)

1918. Optd. as T **55**.
925. **52.** 20 pa. claret 5 5
926. **48.** 1 pi. blue 40 40
927. **53.** 1 pi. blue .. .. 16·00 16·00
937. D **4.** 1 pi. blue (No. D 518).. 16·00 16·00
938. **49.** 50 pa. blue 5 5
929. **38.** 2 pi. blue and brown .. 5 5
930. – 2½ pi. green & orange (No. 509) .. .. 15·00 15·00
931. **50.** 5 pi. brown and blue .. 5 5
932. **39.** 10 pi. green 35 35
933. **40.** 25 pi. red 35 35
934. **54.** 25 pi. blue .. .. 16·00 16·00
935. – 50 pi. red (No. 513) .. 16·00 16·00
936. **41.** 50 pi. green on yellow .. 40 40

56. Dome of the Rock, Jerusalem.

(57.)

1919. Optd as T **57**.
939. **52.** 20 pa. claret 25 35
940. **53.** 1 pi. blue 25 35
941. **5".** 60 pa. on 10 pa. green 25 35
942. **54.** 25 pi. blue .. .. 1·25 1·50

(58.)

(60.)

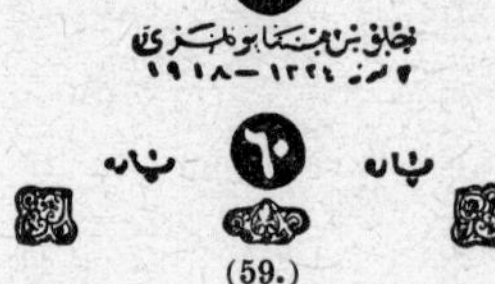

(59.)

1919. Sultan's Accession. 1st Anniv. Optd. or surch. as T **58**, **59** or **60**.
943. **44.** 2 pa. violet 5 5
944. **45.** 5 pa. orange 5 5
945. **11.** 5 pa. on 2 pa. olive .. 5 5
946. **12.** 10 pa. on 2 pa. olive .. 5 5
960a.D **2.** 10 pa. on 5 pa. purple 4·50 3·75
947. **46.** 10 pa. green 5 5
948. **47.** 20 pa. red 5 5
960b.D **3.** 20 pa. red .. 4·50 3·75
949. **48.** 1 pi. blue 5 5
960c.D **4.** 1 pi. blue .. .. 4·50 3·75
950. **49.** 60 pa. on 50 pa. blue 15 15
951. **38.** 60 pa. on 2 pi. blue and brown 5 5
952. 2 pi. blue and brown .. 8 8
960d.D **5.** 2 pi. grey .. .. 4·50 3·75
952a. – 2½ pi. green and orange (No. 509) .. .. 5·50 5·00
953. **50.** 5 pi. brown and blue.. 5 5
954. **39.** 10 pi. brown 30 20
955. **52.** 10 pi. on 20 pa. claret 5 5
956. **40.** 25 pi. red 35 25
957. **53.** 35 pi. on 1 pi. blue .. 30 12
958. **41.** 50 pi. green .. .. 1·60 1·50
958a. 50 pi. red .. .. 5·50 5·00
959. **56.** 100 pi. on 10 pa. green 1·10 1·10
960. **54.** 250 pi. on 25 pi. blue.. 2·00 1·75

1920. As 1914 pictorial issue, Nos. 501/13 but colours changed and new value.
961. 5 pa. brown 5 5
962. 10 pa. green 5 5
963. 20 pa. red 5 5
964. 1 pi. green 35 5
965. 3 pi. blue 8 5
966. 5 pi. grey .. .. 2·50 30
967. 10 pi. lilac 20 5
968. 25 pi. purple 30 20
969. 50 pi. brown .. .. 1·50 50

There are some Turkish characters at the right-hand side of the Sultan's toughra, in the frames of Nos. 501/13 which are missing from Nos. 961/4, 967 and 969.

1921. Surch. in figures and words and in Turkish characters.
970. **42.** 30 pa. on 10 pa. purple 8 8
971. – 60 pa. on 10 pa. green (No. 962) 8 8
972. **51.** 4½ pi. on 1 pi. red .. 35 25
973. – 7½ pi. on 3 pi. blue (No. 965) .. .. 1·10 40

Numerous fiscal and other stamps were surcharged or overprinted by the Turkish Nationalist Government at Angora during 1921, but as they are not often met with by general collectors we omit them.

Nos. A 79/90 and A 119/24 were the only definitive issue of the Angora Government at this period.

61. National Pact.

62. Parliament House, Sivas.

1922.
A 79. **61.** 10 pa. purple .. 12 5
A 80. – 20 pa. green .. 12 5
A 81. – 1 pi. blue .. 20 5
A 82. – 2 pi. maroon .. 35 5
A 83. – 5 pi. blue .. 40 5
A 84. – 10 pi. brown .. 3·00 12
A 85. – 25 pi. claret .. 3·00 10
A 86. **62.** 50 pi. blue (A) .. 1·50 65
A 87. 50 pi. blue (B) .. 1·90 45
A 88. – 100 pi. violet .. 19·00 75
A 89. – 200 pi. violet .. 35·00 9·50
A 90. – 500 pi. green .. 30·00 6·00

DESIGNS—HORIZ. 20 pa. Smyrna Harbour. 1 pi. Mosque, Adrianople. 10 pi. Legendary grey wolf (Boz Kurt). 25 pi. Castle, Adana. 200 pi. Map of Anatolia. VERT. 2 pi. Mosque, Konia. 5 pi. Soldier taking oath. 100 pi. Mosque, Ourfa. 500 pi. Declaration of faith from Koran.

Type (B) of the 50 pi. is as illustrated. In Type (A) the Turkish inscription is different and the figures in the value tablets are below instead of above the Turkish inscription.

72. First Parliament-house, Angora.

73.

1922.
A 119. **72.** 5 pa. mauve .. 15 10
A 120. 10 pa. green .. 20 12
A 121. 20 pa. red .. 35 15
A 122. 1 pi. orange .. 1·10 75
A 123. 2 pi. brown .. 3·75 1·10
A 124. 3 pi. red .. 1·25 30

1923.
994. **73.** 10 pa. grey .. 25 5
995. 20 pa. yellow .. 25 5
976. 1 pi. mauve .. 75 5
977. 1½ pi. green .. 35 5
1010. 2 pi. green .. 1·50 5
979. 3 pi. brown .. 1·00 5
980. 3¾ pi. cinnamon .. 1·00 12
981. 4½ pi. red .. 1·25 5
1002. 5 pi. violet .. 1·90 5
984. 7½ pi. blue .. 1·25 5
985. 10 pi. grey .. 11·00 25
1012a. 10 pi. blue .. 5·00 25
986. 11¼ pi. pink .. 1·75 30
987. 15 pi. brown .. 5·00 25
988. 18¾ pi. green .. 2·50 35
989. 22½ pi. orange .. 3·75 65
990. 25 pi. brown .. 7·50 35
991. 50 pi. grey .. 15·00 65
992. 100 pi. purple .. 25·00 75
993. 500 pi. green .. £170 38·00

74. Kemal Ataturk and View of Sakaria.

1924. Treaty of Lausanne.
1013. **74.** 1½ pi. green 35 10
1014. 3 pi. violet 50 15
1015. 4½ pi. pink .. .. 1·10 75
1016. 5 pi. brown 75 15
1017. 7½ pi. blue .. .. 1·00 50
1018. 50 pi. orange .. .. 7·50 4·00
1019. 100 pi. purple .. .. 10·00 7·50
1020. 200 pi. olive .. .. 25·00 15·00

75. Legendary Blacksmith and Grey Wolf, Boz Kurt.

76. Gorge and R. Sakaria.

77. Fortress of Ankara.

78. Kemal Ataturk.

1926.
1021. **75.** 10 pa. grey 5 5
1022. 20 pa. orange .. 10 5
1023. 1 gr. red 10 5
1024. **76.** 2 gr. green 20 5
1025. 2½ gr. black 20 5
1026. 3 gr. red 25 5
1027. **77.** 5 gr. violet .. .. 1·25 5
1028. 6 gr. red 85 5
1029. 10 gr. blue .. .. 1·25 5
1030. 15 gr. orange .. .. 1·90 5
1031. **78.** 25 gr. black and green 5·00 5
1032. 50 gr. black and red .. 6·00 15
1033. 100 gr. black and olive 8·50 50
1034. 200 gr. black and brown 22·00 1·40

(79. "1927 Smyrna Exhibition.")

(80. "Smyrna, 9 Sept., 1928.")

1927. Smyrna Exn. Optd. with T **79**.
1035. **75.** 1 gr. red 20 12
1036. **76.** 2 gr. green 25 8
1037. 2½ gr. black 40 20
1038. 3 gr. red 65 20
1039. **77.** 5 gr. violet 85 35
1040. 6 gr. red 35 15
1041. 10 gr. blue .. .. 1·90 45
1042. 15 gr. orange .. .. 1·90 65
1043. **78.** 25 gr. black and green 6·00 1·90
1044. 50 gr. black and red .. 8·50 4·00
1045. 100 gr. black and olive 21·00 12·00

1928. 2nd Smyrna Exn. Optd. with T **80** or similar type.
1053. **75.** 10 pa. grey 12 5
1054. 20 pa. orange 15 5
1055. 1 gr. red 20 8
1056. **76.** 2 gr. green 20 8
1057. 2½ gr. black 50 25
1058. 3 gr. red 50 35
1059. **77.** 5 gr. violet .. .. 1·90 1·00
1060. 6 gr. red 60 12
1061. 10 gr. blue .. .. 1·90 65
1062. 15 gr. orange .. .. 1·90 50
1063. **78.** 25 gr. black and green 6·00 85
1064. 50 gr. black and red .. 10·00 1·50
1065. 100 gr. black and olive 22·00 10·00
1066. 200 gr. black and brown 28·00 12·00

1929. Surch. with value in "Paradir" or "Kurustur".
1067. **75.** 20 par. on 1 gr. red .. 25 5
1068. **77.** 2½ kur. on 5 gr. violet 50 12
1069. 6 kur. on 10 gr. blue.. 4·00 15

81. Bridge over Kizil-Irmak.

82. Gorge and R. Sakaria.

1929. T 81/2 and 1926 stamps but inscr. reading "TURKIYE CUMHURIYETI".
1076. **75.** 10 p. green 5 5
1077. **81.** 20 p. violet 5 5
1078. 1 k. olive 25 5
1079. **75.** 1½ k. grey 15 5
1070. **81.** 2 k. black 45 8
1080. 2 k. violet .. .. 1·00 5
1071. 2½ k. green 50 8
1072. 3 k. purple 50 5
1082. 3 k. orange .. .. 2·00 5
1083. **75.** 4 k. red .. .. 2·50 5
1084. **77.** 5 k. claret .. .. 2·50 8
1073. **75.** 6 k. violet .. .. 3·75 5
1085. 6 k. blue .. .. 3·00 5
1086. **82.** 7½ k. lake 20 5
1088. **77.** 12½ k. blue 35 8
1089. 15 k. orange 35 12
1090. **82.** 17½ k. black 50 25
1091. **77.** 20 k. sepia .. .. 10·00 50
1092. **82.** 25 k. brown .. .. 1·00 12
1093. **77.** 30 k. brown .. .. 1·75 12
1094. **82.** 40 k. purple .. .. 1·10 12
1075. **78.** 50 k. black and red .. 16·00 75

83. Kemal Ataturk. **84.** **86.** Tree with Roots in Six Balkan Capitals.

1930.
1095. **83.** 50 k. black and red .. 1·90 12
1096. 100 k. black and olive 3·00 65
1097. 200 k. black and green 3·75 75
1098. 500 k. black and brown 15·00 2·75

1930. Opening of the Ankara-Sivas Railway. Surch. **Sivas D.Y. 30 ag. 930** and value.
1099. **75.** 10 p. on 10 p. green .. 5 5
1100. **81.** 10 p. on 20 p. violet .. 12 12
1101. 20 p. on 1 k. olive .. 15 12
1102. **75.** 1 k. on 1½ k. green .. 20 15
1103. **81.** 1½ k. on 2 k. violet .. 35 15
1104. 2 k. on 2½ k. green .. 35 25
1105. 2½ k. on 3 k. red .. 50 35
1106. **75.** 3 k. on 4 k. red .. 35 25
1107. **77.** 4 k. on 5 k. claret .. 75 35
1108. **75.** 5 k. on 6 k. blue .. 1·75 1·10
1109. **82.** 6 k. on 7½ k. lake .. 50 15
1110. **77.** 7½ k. on 12½ k. blue .. 85 20
1111. 12½ k. on 15 k. orange 75 20
1112. **82.** 15 k. on 17½ k. black 2·50 1·00
1113. **77.** 17½ k. on 20 k. sepia 2·50 1·00
1114. **82.** 20 k. on 25 k. brown 2·50 1·00
1115. **77.** 25 k. on 30 k. brown 2·50 1·00
1116. **82.** 30 k. on 40 k. purple 3·50 1·25
1117. **83.** 40 k. on 50 k. blk. & red 4·25 75
1118. 50 k. on 100 k. (1096) 15·00 3·75
1119. 100 k. on 200 k. (1097) 28·00 5·00
1120. 250 k. on 500 k. (1098) 18·00 3·75

1931. Surch. **1 Kurus.**
1121. **75.** 1 k. on 1½ k. green .. 1·25 12

1931.
1122. **84.** 10 p. green 5 5
1444. 10 p. maroon 5 5
1444a. 10 p. vermilion 5 5
1123. 20 p. orange 5 5
1445. 20 p. green 8 5
1445a. 20 p. yellow 5 5
1123a. 30 p. violet 8 5
1124. 1 k. green 5 5
1446. 1 k. olive 12 5
1446b. 1 k. salmon 5 5
1124a. 1½ k. lilac 5 5
1125 2 k. violet 5 5
1125a. 2 k. green 8 5
1447. 2 k. purple 20 5
1447a. 2 k. yellow 35 5
1447b. 2 k. pink 5 5
1126. 2½ k. green 5 5
1448b. 3 k. buff 30 5
1126a. 3 k. yellow 20 8
1448a. 3 k. grey 5 5
1127. 4 k. slate 10 5
1448c. 4 k. green 20 5
1128. 5 k. red 12 5
1128a. 5 k. black 15 5
1449. 5 k. blue 35 5
1449a. 5 k. purple .. .. 1·10 5
1449b. 5 k. pale blue 12 5
1129. 6 k. blue 65 5
1129a. 6 k. red 40 5
1130. 7½ k. red 20 5
1130a. 8 k. blue 50 5
1449c. 8 k. violet 10 5
1131. 10 k. black .. .. 1·50 5
1131a. 10 k. blue 75 8
1450. 10 k. brown .. .. 1·00 5
1450a. 10 k. olive 10 5
1132. 12 k. bistre 50 5
1450b. 12 k. red 15 5
1133. 12½ k. blue 30 5
1134. 15 k. yellow 35 5
1451. 15 k. violet .. .. 1·75 5
1451a. 15 k. lake .. .. 3·75 8
1451b. 15 k. chestnut 15 5
1135. 20 k. olive 35 5
1452. 20 k. blue .. .. 6·50 25
1452a. 20 k. mauve .. .. 1·00 8
1136. 25 k. blue 25 5
1137 30 k. magenta 40 5
1453. 30 k. pink .. .. 5·50 25
1453a. 30 k. green 50 5
1138. **84.** 100 k. plum .. .. 1·25 12
1139. 200 k. violet .. .. 1·60 20
1453b. 200 k. brown .. .. 4·50 50
1140. 250 k. chocolate .. 9·00 50
Some values have the inscr. above the portrait and the value beside the head.

1931. 2nd Balkan Conf.
1141. **86.** 2½ k. green 20 20
1142. 4 k. red 25 25
1143. 6 k. blue 25 12
1144. 7½ k. red 35 20
1145. 12 k. orange 25 12
1146. 12½ k. blue 50 12
1147. 30 k. violet .. .. 1·10 25
1148. 50 k. brown .. .. 1·40 30
1149. 100 k. purple .. .. 2·50 25

88. Impetus given to Industry and Agriculture by Kemal Ataturk.

1933. Turkish Republic. 10th Anniv.
1150. – 1½ k. green 25 12
1151. – 2 k. bistre 25 12
1152. **88.** 3 k. red 25 12
1153. – 6 k. blue 35 25
1154. – 12½ k. blue .. .. 1·75 75
1155. – 25 k. chocolate .. 3·75 2·50
1156. **88.** 50 k. chestnut .. .. 7·50 4·25
DESIGN—VERT. 1½, 2, 12½, 25 k. Figure "10" with rays of light and waves. (Rebirth of Turkey.)

1934. Air. Optd. **1934** and aeroplane or surch. also.
1157. **82.** 7½ k. lake 15 10
1158. **77.** 12½ k. on 15 k. orange 20 15
1159. **82.** 20 k. on 25 k. brown 25 25
1160. 25 k. brown 35 30
1161. 40 k. purple 65 50

1934. Smyrna Int. Fair. Optd. **Izmir 9 Eylul 934 Sergisi** or surch. also.
1162. **75.** 10 p. green 25 10
1163. 1 k. on 1½ k. grey .. 35 15
1164. **82.** 2 k. on 25 k. brown .. 75 25
1165. 5 k. on 7½ k. lake .. 2·25 2·25
1166. 6 k. on 17½ k. black .. 1·90 85
1167. **77.** 12½ k. blue .. .. 3·75 1·75
1168. 15 k. on 20 k. sepia .. 22·00 12·00
1169. **82.** 20 k. on 25 k. brown .. 22·00 12·00
1170. **83.** 50 k. on 100 k. black and olive .. 22·00 12·00

89. Alliance Badge. **90.** Mrs. C. Chapman Catt.

1935. 12th Congress of the Int. Women's Alliance, Istanbul.
1171. **89.** 20 p.+20 p. brown .. 20 15
1172. – 1 k.+1 k. red .. 30 20
1173. – 2 k.+2 k. slate .. 30 20
1174. – 2½ k.+2½ k. green .. 40 30
1175. – 4 k.+4 k. blue .. 65 55
1176. – 5 k.+5 k. purple .. 75 70
1177. – 7½ k.+7½ k. red .. 1·60 1·50
1178. **90.** 10 k.+10 k. orange .. 2·75 2·00
1179. – 12½ k.+12½ k. blue .. 3·50 3·00
1180. – 15 k.+15 k. violet .. 4·50 4·00
1181. – 20 k.+20 k. red .. 7·00 6·50
1182. – 25 k.+25 k. green .. 16·00 14·00
1183. – 30 k.+30 k. blue .. 75·00 55·00
1184. – 50 k.+50 k. blkish grn. 95·00 80·00
1185. – 100 k.+100 k. red .. 65·00 55·00
DESIGNS: 1 k. Woman teacher. 2 k. Woman farmer. 2½ k. Typist. 4 k. Woman pilot and policewoman. 5 k. Women voters. 7½ k. Yildiz Palace Istanbul. 12½ k. Jane Addams. 15 k. Grazia Deledda. 20 k. Selma Lagerlof. 25 k. Bertha von Suttner. 30 k. Sigrid Undset. 50 k. Mme. Curie-Sklodowska. 100 k. Kemal Ataturk.

1936. Remilitarization of Dardanelles. Surch. **BOGAZLAR MUKAVELESININ IMZASI 20/7/1936** and value in figures.
1186. **82.** 4 k. on 17½ k. black .. 85 35
1187. 5 k. on 25 k. brown .. 90 65
1188. **78.** 6 k. on 50 k. black & red 55 20
1189. **83.** 10 k. on 100 k. black and olive .. .. 2·00 40
1190. 20 k. on 200 k. black and green .. 5·00 75
1191. 50 k. on 500 k. black and brown .. 10·00 1·75

91. Stag. **92.** Arms of Turkey, Greece, Rumania and Yugoslavia.

1937. 2nd Turkish Historical Congress.
1192. **91.** 3 k. violet 70 50
1193. – 6 k. blue 85 50
1194. **91.** 7½ k. red .. .. 1·90 1·00
1195. – 12½ k. blue .. .. 2·50 2·00
DESIGN: 6 k., 12½ k. Bust of Ataturk.

1937. Balkan Entente
1196. **92.** 8 k. red .. .. 7·50 2·50
1197. 12½ k. blue .. .. 9·00 3·75

1938. Air. Surch. **1937** with aeroplane above and value.
1198. **82.** 4½ k. on 7½ k. lake .. 75 45
1199. **77.** 9 k. on 15 k. orange .. 15·00 11·00
1200. **82.** 35 k. on 40 k. purple .. 3·50 1·60

93. An Izmir Boulevard.

1938. Izmir Int. Fair. Inscr. as in T **93.**
1201. **93.** 10 p. brown 12 5
1202. – 30 p. violet 12 5
1203. – 2½ k. green 50 12
1204. – 3 k. orange 20 12
1205. – 5 k. olive 45 20
1206. – 6 k. brown 50 45
1207. – 7½ k. red 50 35
1208. – 8 k. lake 55 35
1209. – 12 k. purple .. .. 1·00 50
1210. – 12½ k. blue .. .. 1·90 1·25
DESIGNS—HORIZ. 30 p. Izmir Fair. 6 k. Woman gathering grapes. VERT. 2½ k. Fig tree. 3 k. Clock Tower, Hukunet Square. 5 k. Olive branch. 7½k. Woman gathering grapes. 8 k. Izmir Harbour. 12 k. Equestrian statue of Ataturk. 12½ k. Ataturk.

96. Railway Bridge.

1938. Proclamation of Turkish Republic. 15th Anniv. Inscr. as in T **96.**
1211. – 2½ k. green 35 20
1212. – 3 k. red 25 20
1213. – 6 k. bistre 35 35
1214. **96.** 7½ k. red 55 50
1215. – 8 k. purple .. .. 1·40 65
1216. – 12½ k. blue .. .. 1·25 95
DESIGNS—HORIZ. 2½ k. Military display. 3 k. Aerial view of Kayseri. 8 k. Scout buglers. VERT. 6 k. Ataturk driving a tractor. 12½ k. Ataturk.

97. Kemal Ataturk teaching Alphabet.

1938. Introduction of Latin Alphabet into Turkey. 10th Anniv.
1217. **97.** 2½ k. green 30 12
1218. 3 k. orange 25 12
1219. 6 k. purple 25 15
1220. 7½ k. red 45 25
1221. 8 k. red 75 30
1222. 12½ k. blue 90 95

1938. Death of Kemal Ataturk. Mourning Issue. Optd. **21-11-1938** and bar.
1223. **84.** 3 k. brown 20 10
1224. 5 k. red 20 10
1225. 6 k. blue 30 12
1226. 7½ k. red 30 25
1227. 8 k. blue 40 25
1228. 12½ k. blue 75 55

99. Presidents Ineunu and Roosevelt and Map of North America.

DESIGNS — VERT. 2½ k., 6 k. Turkish and U.S. flags. HORIZ. 7½ k., 12½ k. Ataturk and Washington.

1939. U.S. Constitution. 150th Anniv.
1229. – 2½ k. grn., red & blue 25 12
1230. **99.** 3 k. brown and blue .. 25 12
1231. – 6 k. violet, red & blue 50 15
1232. – 7½ k. red and blue .. 50 20
1233. **99.** 8 k. purple and blue .. 50 25
1234. – 12½ k. blue .. .. 1·50 1·25

1939. Cession of Hatay to Turkey. Surch. **Hatayin Anavatana Kavusmasi 23/7/1939** and new values.
1235. **82.** 3 k. on 25 k. brown 20 20
1236. **83.** 6 k. on 200 k. black and green 20 20
1237. **82.** 7½ k. on 25 k. brown .. 20 20
1238. **83.** 12 k. on 100 k. (1096) 25 20
1239. 12½ k. on 200 k. (1097) 65 40
1240. 17½ k. on 500 k. (1098) 85 65

100. Railway Bridge. **101.** Kemal Ataturk.

1939. Opening of Ankara-Erzurum Railway.
1241. **100.** 3 k. red .. .. 1·10 1·10
1242. – 6 k. brown .. .. 1·40 1·40
1243. – 7½ k. red .. .. 1·40 1·40
1244. – 12½ k. blue .. .. 2·00 2·00
DESIGNS—VERT. 6 k. Locomotive. HORIZ. 7½ k. Railway and mountain gorge. 12½ k. Tunnel entrance at Atma-Bogazi.

1939. Kemal Ataturk. 1st Death Anniv.
1245. – 2½ k. green 12 10
1246. – 3 k. blue 12 10
1247. – 5 k. brown 25 15
1248. **101.** 6 k. brown 25 35
1249. – 7½ k. red 55 25
1250. – 8 k. olive 35 25
1251. – 12½ k. blue 35 25
1252. – 17½ k. red 65 45
DESIGNS: 2½ k. Ataturk's Residence. 3 k. to 17½k. Portraits of Kemal Ataturk as T **101.**

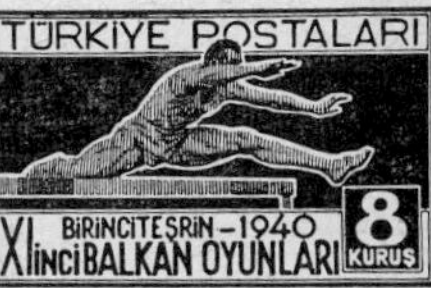

102. Namik Kemal. **103.** Hurdling.

1940. Namik Kemal (poet). Birth Cent.
1255. **102.** 6 k. brown 30 20
1256. 8 k. olive 35 25
1257. 12 k. red 45 30
1258. 12½ k. blue 85 65

1940. Balkan Entente. As T **68** of Yugoslavia. but with the torch and Arms of Turkey, Greece, Rumania and Yugoslavia rearranged.
1253. 8 k. light blue .. .. 1·90 35
1254. 10 k. deep blue .. .. 2·00 70

1940. Izmir Int. Fair. Inscr. Surch. **IZMIR ENTERNASYONAL FUARI — 1940** and value.
1259. **88.** 6 k. on 200 k. black and green 30 25
1260. 10 k. on 200 k. black and green 50 30
1261. 12 k. on 500 k. black and green 50 30

1940. 11th Balkan Games.
1266. – 3 k. olive .. .. 1·00 80
1267. – 6 k. red .. .. 3·25 3·25
1268. **103.** 8 k. brown .. .. 1·00 80
1269. – 10 k. blue .. .. 2·50 2·00
DESIGNS—VERT. 3 k. Running. 6 k. Pole-vaulting. 10 k. Discus-throwing.

104. Map and Census Figures. **105.** Postmen of 1840 and 1940.

1940. National Census.
1262. **104.** 10 p. green 15 12
1263. 3 k. orange 20 15
1264. 6 k. red 30 25
1265. 10 k. blue 65 50

1940. 1st Adhesive Postage Stamps. Cent. Inscr. "1840 1940".

1270. – 3 k. green 20 10
1271. 105. 6 k. red 30 15
1272. – 10 k. blue 50 25
1273 – 12 k. brown 85 30

DESIGNS—HORIZ. 3 k. Mail Carriers on horseback. VERT. 10 k. Modern mail boat and old-fashioned sailing vessel. 12 k. G.P.O., Istanbul.

DESIGNS — HORIZ. 30 p. Harbour. 6 k., 17½ k. Exhibition pavilions. 12 k. Girl in a field. VERT. 10 k. Equestrian statue.

106. Exhibition Building.

1941. Izmir Int. Fair.

1274. – 30 p. green 5 5
1275. 108. 3 k. grey 8 5
1276. – 6 k. red 10 8
1277. – 10 k. blue 12 10
1278. – 12 k. violet 15 10
1279. – 17½ k. brown 35 20

107. Barbarossa's Fleet at Sea. 108. Barbarossa.

1941. Barbarossa (Khair-ed-Din). 400th Death Anniv.

1280. – 20 p. violet 8 5
1281. 106. 3 k. blue 12 8
1282. 6 k. red 15 12
1283. 10 k. blue 20 15
1284. 12 k. brown 35 25
1285. 107. 17½ k. blue, grn. & brn. 90 50

DESIGN (24×37 mm.): 20 p. Barbarossa's Palace (inscr. "BARBAROSUN").

1941. Air. Surch. with aeroplane new values and squares.

1286. 82. 4½ k. on 25 k. brown .. 85 75
1287. 83. 9 k. on 200 k. blk. & grn. 5·00 4·25
1288. 35 k. on 500 k. black and brown .. .. 2·50 2·25

109. President Ineunu. 110.

1942.

1289. 109. 0.25 k. bistre .. 5 5
1290. 0.50 k. green .. 5 5
1291. 1 k. grey .. 5 5
1292. 1½ k. mauve .. 5 5
1293. 2 k. green .. 5 5
1294. 4 k. brown .. 8 5
1295. 4½ k. black .. 8 5
1296. 5 k. blue .. 50 25
1297. 6 k. red .. 20 10
1298. 6¾ k. blue .. 8 5
1299. 9 k. violet .. 25 5
1300. 10 k. blue .. 15 5
1301. 13½ k. purple .. 12 5
1302. 16 k. green .. 15 5
1303. 17½ k. red .. 20 5
1304. 20 k. purple .. 65 20
1305. 27½ k. orange .. 50 15
1306. 37 k. brown .. 30 15
1307. 50 k. violet .. 1·10 20
1308. 100 k. brown .. 2·00 1·00
1309. 110. 200 k. brown .. 3·75 1·00

111. Ankara. 112. Tile-decorating.

113. Arnavutkoy. 114. Pres. Ineunu.

1943. Inscr. "TURKIYE POSTALARI" between two crescents and stars.

1310. 111. 0.25 k. yellow .. 5 5
1311. – 0.50 k. green 12 5
1312. – 1 k. olive 5 5
1313. – 1½ k. violet 5 5
1314. – 2 k. green 5 5
1315. – 4 k. red 20 10
1316. – 4½ k. black 10 5
1317. 112. 5 k. blue 50 25
1318. – 6 k. red 20 10
1319. – 6¾ k. blue 8 5
1320. – 10 k. blue 12 5
1321. – 13½ k. mauve 12 5
1322. 113. 16 k. green 20 5
1323. – 17½ k. brown 20 5
1324. – 20 k. brown 25 5
1325. – 27½ k. orange 50 25
1326. – 37 k. brown 50 12
1327. – 50 k. purple .. .. 1·00 12
1328. – 100 k. olive .. .. 2·00 50
1329. 114. 200 k. brown .. 3·25 50

DESIGNS—VERT. 0.50 k. Mohair goats. 2 k. Oranges. 4 k. Merino sheep. 4½ k. Railway train. 6 k. Statue of Kemal Ataturk, Ankara. 6¾ k., 10 k. Full-face portrait of Pres. Ineunu. 17½ k. Republic Monument, Istanbul. 20 k. National Defence Monument, Ankara. 27½ k. P.O., Istanbul. 37 k. Monument at Afyon. 100 k. Ataturk and Ineunu. HORIZ. 7 k. Antioch. 1½ k. Ankara Reservoir. 13½ k. National Assembly Building. 50 k. People's House, Ankara.

DESIGNS — VERT. 4½ k., 13½ k. Girl eating grapes. HORIZ. 6¾ k., 27½ k. Fair Pavilion.

115. Entrance to Fair.

1943. Smyrna Int. Fair.

1330. – 4½ k. grey 25 20
1331. 115. 6 k. red 20 12
1332. – 6¾ k. blue 20 10
1333. 115. 10 k. blue 20 10
1334. – 13½ k. brown 35 25
1335. – 27½ k. grey 65 50

116. Marching Athletes. 117. Soldier guarding Flag.

1943. Republic. 20th Anniv.

1336. 116. 4½ k. olive 85 75
1337. 117. 6 k. red 30 20
1338. – 6¾ k. blue 20 15
1339. – 10 k. blue 15 10
1340. – 13½ k. olive 30 15
1341. – 27½ k. brown 45 25

DESIGNS—HORIZ. 6¾ k. Bridge. 10 k. Hospital. 13½ k. Ankara. VERT. 27½ k. Pres. Ineunu.

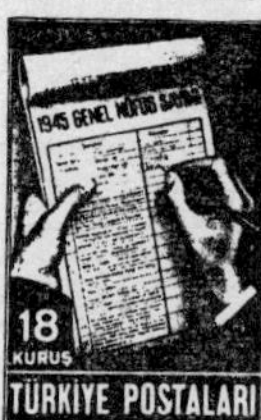

118. Filling Census Form. 119. Pres. Ineunu.

1945. National Census.

1342. 118. 4½ k. olive 30 25
1343. 9 k. violet 30 25
1344. 10 k. blue 30 25
1345. 18 k. red 60 50

1945. Surch. 4½ KURUS.

1346. 4½ k. on 6¾ k. blue (No. 1319) 12 5

1946.

1347. 119. 0.25 k. red 5 5
1348. 1 k. green 5 5
1349. 1½ k. purple 5 5
1350. 9 k. violet 15 5
1351. 10 k. blue 20 5
1352. 50 k. brown .. .. 1·10 12

120. Battleship "Missouri". 121. Sower.

1946. Visit of U.S. Battleship "Missouri" to Istanbul.

1353. 120. 9 k. violet 12 10
1354. 10 k. blue 15 12
1355. 27½ k. grey 75 35

1946. Agrarian Reform.

1356. 121. 9 k. violet 5 5
1357. 10 k. blue 8 5
1358. 18 k. olive 15 10
1359. 27½ k. orange .. 50 30

122. Dove of Peace. 123. Monument at Afyon.

1947. Izmir Int. Fair.

1360. 122. 15 k. purple and violet 8 8
1361. 20 k. blue 12 12
1362. 30 k. brown and black 20 15
1363. 1 l. olive and green 65 30

1947. Battle of Dumiupinar. 25th Anniv. Inscr. "30 AGUSTOS 1922-1947".

1364. 123. 10 k. brown 8 5
1365. – 15 k. violet and grey 10 5
1366. – 20 k. blue anb grey .. 15 5
1367. 123. 30 k. green and grey .. 20 8
1368. – 60 k. olive and brown 35 15
1369. – 1 l. green and grey .. 70 35

DESIGNS: 15 k., 60 k. Ismet Ineunu. 20 k., 1 l. Kemal Ataturk.

124. Istanbul, Grapes and Ribbon.

1947. Int. Vintners' Congress.

1370. 124. 15 k. purple 12 5
1371. 20 k. blue 20 10
1372. 60 k. brown 45 35

125. Express Train. 126. Pres. Ineunu.

127. Signing the Treaty. 128. Statue of Kemal Ataturk.

1947. Int. Railway Congress, Istanbul.

1373. 125. 15 k. purple 40 25
1374. 20 k. blue 65 40
1375. 60 k. olive .. .. 1·25 1·10

1948.

1376. 126. 0.25 k. red 5 5
1377. 1 k. black 5 5
1378. 2 k. purple 5 5
1379. 3 k. orange 5 5
1380. 4 k. green 5 5
1381. 5 k. blue 8 5
1382. 10 k. brown 10 5
1383. 12 k. red 12 5
1384. 15 k. violet 20 5
1385. 20 k. blue 20 5
1386. 30 k. brown 30 10
1387. 60 k. black 85 15
1388. 1 k. olive .. .. 2·25 30
1389. 2 l. brown .. .. 10·00 1·25
1390. 5 l. purple .. .. 6·50 4·75

The lira values are larger.

1948. Treaty of Lausanne. 25th Anniv.

1391. 127. 15 k. purple 10 8
1392. – 20 k. blue 15 12
1393. – 40 k. green 35 20
1394. 127. 1 l. brown 85 50

DESIGN: 20 k., 40 k. Lausanne Palace.

1948. Proclamation of Republic, 25th Anniv.

1395. 128. 15 k. violet 12 8
1396. 20 k. blue 20 12
1397. 40 k. green 30 20
1398. 1 l. brown 75 50

DESIGNS: 20 k. 50 k. Aeroplane over Ankara. 30 k. 1 l. Aeroplane over Istanbul.

129. Aeroplane over Izmir.

1949. Air.

1399. 129. 5 k. violet and lilac .. 5 5
1400. – 20 k. brown and lilac 30 5
1401. – 30 k. olive and grey .. 35 12
1402. 129. 40 k. blue 50 12
1403. – 50 k. brown & mauve 55 25
1404. – 1 l. green and blue .. 1·25 50

131. Galley.

130. Wrestlers. 132. Exhibition Building.

1949. 5th European Wrestling Championships. Designs depicting wrestling holds and inscr. as in T 130.

1405. 130. 15 k. mauve .. 75 50
1406. – 20 k. blue (vert.) .. 1·50 75
1407. – 30 k. brown (horiz.) 1·50 1·25
1408. – 60 k. green (horiz.) .. 2·50 2·00

1949. Navy Day.

1409. 131. 5 k. violet 20 5
1410. – 10 k. brown 30 8
1411. – 15 k. red 30 12
1412. – 20 k. blue 45 30
1413. – 30 k. slate 55 45
1414. – 40 k. olive 85 50

DESIGNS—HORIZ. 15 k. Cruiser "Hamidiye". 20 k. Submarine "Sakarya". 30 k. Battle-cruiser "Yavuz". VERT. 10 k. Frigate "Mahmudiye". 40 k. Statue of Barbarossa.

1949. Istanbul Fair.

1415. 132. 15 k. brown 12 8
1416. 20 k. blue 15 10
1417. 30 k. olive 35 25

133. U.P.U. Monument, Berne.

1949. U.P.U. 75th Anniv.

1418. – 15 k. violet 15 12
1419. – 20 k. blue 30 15
1420. 133. 30 k. red 35 35
1421. 40 k. green 75 55

DESIGN: 15 k., 20 k. as T 133 but vert.

134. Aeroplane over Bogazia.

1950. Air.

1422. 134. 2 l. 50 green and blue 7·50 6·50

135. Youth, Istanbul and Ankara. 136. Voting.

1950. 2nd World Youth Meeting.
1423. **135.** 15 k. violet 15 12
1424. 20 k. blue 30 15

1950. General Election. Inscr. as in T **136.**
1425. **136.** 15 k. chocolate .. 12 8
1426. 20 k. blue 15 10
1427. – 30 k. blue and green 25 12
DESIGN—HORIZ. 30 k. Ataturk and map.

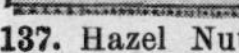

137. Hazel Nut. **138.** Map and Statistics.

1950. Izmir Fair. Inscr. "1950 IZMIR ENTERNASYONAL FUARI"
1428. **137.** 8 k. green and yellow 25 20
1429. – 12 k. red (Acorns) .. 35 30
1430. – 15 k. purple (Cotton) 55 30
1431. – 20 k. blue (Fair Symbol) 75 50
1432. – 30 k. sepia and buff (Tobacco) .. .. 1·25 75

1950. National Census.
1433. **138.** 15 k. chocolate .. 15 10
1434. 20 k. blue 25 15

139. Bird-man and Tower. **140.** Farabi (philosopher).

1950. Air. Int. Civil Aviation Congress, Istanbul. Inscr. "ICAO".
1435. **139.** 20 k. green and blue 25 15
1436. – 40 k. chocolate & blue 50 35
1437. – 60 k. violet and blue 75 50
DESIGNS—VERT. 40 k. Taurus Mts. HORIZ. 60 k. Istanbul.

1950. Farabi. 1000th Death Anniv.
1438. **140.** 15 k. multicoloured.. 50 45
1439. 20 k. multicoloured.. 75 50
1440. 60 k. multicoloured.. 2·50 2·10
1441. 1 l. multicoloured .. 3·75 3·00

141. Mithat Pasha and Deposit Bank.

1950. 3rd Co-operative Congress, Istanbul.
1442. **141.** 15 k. violet 45 45
1443. – 20 k. blue 45 45
DESIGN: 20 k. Agricultural Bank.

1951. Air. Industrial Congress, Ankara. Nos. 1399, 1401 and 1403 optd. **SANAYI KONGRESI 9-NISAN-1951.**
1454. 5 k. violet and lilac.. 75 65
1455. 30 k. olive and grey.. 75 65
1456. 50 k. brown and mauve 1·00 85

142. Mailboat.

143. Mosque of Sultan Ahmed. **144.** Count Carton de Wiart.

1951. Coastal Trading Rights. 25th Anniv.
1457. – 15 k. blue 30 15
1458. **142.** 20 k. indigo 30 15
1459. – 30 k. grey 65 35
1460. – 1 l. grey-green .. 1·25 65
DESIGNS—HORIZ. 15 k. Refloating vessel. 30 k. Diver and launch. VERT. 1 l. Lighthouse.

1951. 40th Interparliamentary Conf., Istanbul.
1461. **143.** 15 k. green 25 12
1462. – 20 k. blue 25 12
1463. **144.** 30 k. brown 35 25
1464. – 60 k. purple .. 1·00 85
DESIGNS—As T **143**: 20 k. Dolmabahce Palace. 60 k. Rumeli Tower.

145. F.A.O. Emblem and Silo. **146.** A. H. Tarhan.

1952. U.N. Economic Conf., Ankara. Inscr. "Ankara 1951".
1465. **145.** 15 k. green 65 45
1466. – 20 k. violet 65 45
1467. – 30 k. blue .. .. 1·25 85
1468. – 60 k. red .. .. 3·00 1·90
DESIGNS: 20 k. Int. Bank emblem and hydro-electric station. 30 k. U.N. emblem and New York headquarters. 60 k. Ankara University.

1952. Tarhan (writer). Birth Cent.
1469. **146.** 15 k. purple 12 5
1470. 20 k. blue 15 10
1471. 30 k. brown 25 20
1472. 60 k. green 55 40

147. Bergama. **148.** Kemal Ataturk.

1952. Views. Imperf. or perf.
1473. **147.** 1 k. orange 5 5
1474. – 2 k. olive 5 5
1475. – 3 k. brown 5 5
1476. – 4 k. green 5 5
1477. – 5 k. brown 8 5
1478. **148.** 10 k. chocolate .. 15 5
1479. 12 k. red 25 5
1480. 15 k. violet (medallion) 25 5
1481. 20 k. blue (medallion) 75 5
1482. – 30 k. myrtle 12 5
1483. – 40 k. slate 20 5
1484. – 50 k. grey 30 5
1485. – 75 k. black 45 10
1486. – 1 l. violet 65 10
1487. – 2 l. blue .. .. 1·10 25
1488. – 5 l. sepia .. .. 7·50 3·75
DESIGNS—VERT. 2 k. Ruins at Milas. 3 k. Karatay Gate, Konay. 4 k. Trees on Kozak Plateau. 5 k. Urgup. 30 k. Emirsultan Mosque, Bursa. 40 k. Yenicami Mosque, Istanbul. HORIZ. 50 k. Waterfall, Tarsus. 75 k. Rocks at Urgup. 1 l. Dolmabahce Palace, Istanbul. 2 l. Pavilion, Istanbul. 5 l. Interior of Istanbul Museum.

149. Congress Building. **150.** Turkish Sentry.

1952. Surch. **0.50 Kurus.**
1489. **147.** 0.50 k. on 1 k. orange 5 5

1952. 8th Int. Mechanics Congress, Istanbul.
1490. **149.** 15 k. violet 35 20
1491. 20 k. blue 35 25
1492. 60 k. brown 75 70

1952. Turkish Participation in Korean War.
1493. **150.** 15 k. slate 25 12
1494. – 20 k. blue 25 15
1495. – 30 k. brown 40 40
1496. – 60 k. red and green.. 65 50
DESIGNS: 20 k. Turkish soldier and flag. 30 k. Soldier and Korean child reading paper. 60 k. Soldiers planting Turkish flag.

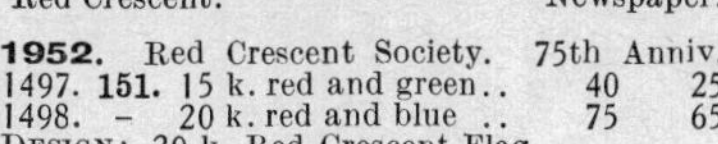

151. Doves, Hand and Red Crescent. **152.** Bas-Relief on Monument. **153.** Pigeon carrying Newspaper.

1952. Red Crescent Society. 75th Anniv.
1497. **151.** 15 k. red and green.. 40 25
1498. – 20 k. red and blue .. 75 65
DESIGN: 20 k. Red Crescent Flag.

1952. Battle of Erzurum. 75th Anniv.
1499. **152.** 15 k. violet 20 15
1500. – 20 k. blue 30 25
1501. – 40 k. grey 65 55
DESIGNS—HORIZ. 20 k. Azizye Monument, Erzurum. 40 k. View of Erzurum.

1952.
1502. **153.** 0.50 k. green .. 5 5
1503. 0.50 k. violet .. 5 5
1503a. 0.50 k. orange .. 5 5
1503b. 0.50 k. brown .. 5 5

154. Rumeli Fort.

156. Odeon Theatre, Ephesus. **155.** Sultan Mohammed II.

1953. Fall of Constantinople. 5th Cent. Inscr. "1453 1953" etc.
1504. **154.** 5 k. blue 30 10
1505. – 8 k. grey 50 10
1506. – 10 k. turquoise .. 50 10
1507. – 12 k. purple 55 10
1508. – 15 k. brown 50 8
1509. – 20 k. red 65 15
1510. – 30 k. green 65 15
1511. – 40 k. violet 75 25
1512. – 60 k. brown .. .. 1·00 35
1513. – 1 l. emerald .. .. 2·25 1·00
1514. – 2 l. green, blue & red 3·25 2·00
1515. **155.** 2½ l. yellow & brown 4·50 2·00
DESIGNS—As T **154**: HORIZ. 8 k. Turkish army at Edirne. 10 k. Horseman and sailing ships. 12 k. Army landing from galleys. 15 k. Topkapi ramparts. 40 k. Sultan Mohammed II and Patriarch Yenadios. 60 k. 15th-century map of Constantinople. 1 l. Mausoleum of Mohammed II. VERT. 20 k. Turkish entry into Constantinople. 30 k. Sultan Mohammed II Mosque. As T **155**: 2 l. Sultan Mohammed II seated on ground.

1953. Views of Ephesus. Inscr. "EFES" Multicoloured centres.
1516. **156.** 12 k. green 15 10
1517. – 15 k. violet 15 10
1518. – 20 k. slate 15 12
1519. – 40 k. turquoise .. 50 25
1520. – 60 k. blue 75 50
1521. – 1 l. red .. .. 2·75 1·75
DESIGNS: 15 k. St. John's Church and Acropolis. 20 k. Statue of Blessed Virgin. Panaya Kapulu. 40 k. Council Church ruins. 60 k. Grotto of the Seven Sleepers. 1 l. House of the Blessed Virgin, Panaya Kapulu.

DESIGN: 20 k. Pres. Bayar, Mithat Pasha and Ankara University.

157. Pres. Bayar, Mithat Pasha, Dr. Delitsch and Ankara Bank.

1953. 5th Int. Public Credit Congress.
1522. **157.** 15 k. brown 35 25
1523. – 20 k. blue-green .. 55 45

158. Berdan Barrage.

DESIGNS—HORIZ. 10 k. Combine-harvester. 20 k. Soldiers on parade. 30 k. Diesel-engined train. 35 k. Yesilkoy airport. VERT. 55 k. Kemal Ataturk.

1953. Republic. 30th Anniv.
1524. – 10 k. bistre 10 8
1525. **158.** 15 k. slate 8 5
1526. – 20 k. red 15 12
1527. – 30 k. olive 30 25
1528. – 35 k. blue 25 20
1529. – 55 k. lilac 60 40

159. Kemal Ataturk and Mausoleum.

1953. Transfer of Ashes of Kemal Ataturk to Mausoleum.
1530. **159.** 15 k. black 30 25
1531. 20 k. purple 55 35

DESIGNS: 20 k. Globe and stars. 40 k. Allegory of growth of N.A.T.O.

160. Map of World and Compass.

1954. N.A.T.O. 5th Anniv.
1532. **160.** 15 k. brown .. .. 1·90 1·25
1533. – 20 k. blue .. .. 1·90 1·25
1534. – 40 k. green .. .. 11·00 11·00

161. "Industry, Agriculture and Construction". **162.** Flying Exercise.

163. Z. Gokalp. **164.** Yesilkoy Aerodrome.

1954. Council of Europe. 5th Anniv. Inscr. "1949-1954".
1535 **161.** 10 k. brown .. .. 5·00 3·75
1536 – 15 k. green .. .. 3·75 3·00
1537. – 20 k. blue .. .. 3·75 3·00
1538. **161.** 30 k. violet .. .. 12·00 10·00
DESIGN: 15 k., 20 k. Flag and figure of "Peace and Justice".

1954. 47th Conference of Int. Aeronautical Federation. Inscr. "20.IX.1954".
1539. **162.** 20 k. black 20 12
1540. – 35 k. slate-lilac .. 30 25
1541. – 45 k. blue 50 25
DESIGNS: 35 k. Baron de la Grange and glider. 45 k. Ataturk and formation of biplanes.

1954. Gokalp (sociologist). 30th Death Anniv.
1542. **163.** 15 k. violet 12 10
1543. 20 k. green 15 12
1544. 30 k. red 30 20

1954. Air.
1545. **164.** 5 k. blue and brown.. 30 12
1546. – 20 k. blue & chestnut 12 5
1547. – 35 k. blue and green.. 15 8
1548. **164.** 40 k. blue and red .. 15 10
1549. – 45 k. blue and violet 30 20
1550. – 55 k. blue and black.. 35 25
DESIGNS: 20 k., 45 k. Frontal view of Yesilkoy Aerodrome. 35 k., 55 k. Ankara Aerodrome.

165. Kemal Ataturk. **166.** Relief Map of the Dardanelles.

1955
1551. **165.** 15 k. red 10 5
1552 20 k. blue 15 5
1553 40 k. slate 20 5
1554. 50 k. green 30 5
1555 75 k. chestnut .. 65 20

1955. Battle of Canakakle (Dardanelles). 40th Anniv. Inscr. "CANAKKALE".
1556. **166.** 15 k. green 10 5
1557. – 20 k. brown 15 12
1558. – 30 k. blue 25 20
1559. – 60 k. drab 75 40
DESIGNS—VERT. 20 k. Artilleryman loading gun. 60 k. Ataturk in uniform. HORIZ. 30 k. Minelayer.

167.
"Reconstruction".

168. Lilies.

1955. Town Planning Congress.

1560. 167. 15 k. grey 15 8
1561. 20 k. blue 15 8
1562. 50 k. brown 35 20
1563. 1 l. violet 55 30

1955. Spring Flower Festival. Inscr. "ISTANBUL 1955".

1564. – 10 k. red and green .. 30 20
1565. – 15 k. yellow and green 25 12
1566. – 20 k. red and green .. 30 15
1567. 168. 50 k. green and yellow 1·90 1·40

FLOWERS: 10 k. Carnations. 15 k. Tulips. 20 k. Roses.

DESIGN: Gulhane Military Hospital, Ankara.

169. First-aid Centre.

1955. 18th Congress of Int. Documentation Office of Military Medicine. 30 k. also inscr. "GULHANE–1898".

1568. 169. 20 k. red 20 12
1569. – 30 k. green 45 25

DESIGNS — VERT. 20 k. Footballers' badge. HORIZ. 1 l. Championship plaque.

170. Footballers.

1955. Int. Military Football Championships.

1570. 170. 15 k. blue 30 20
1571. – 20 k. red 25 15
1572. – 1 l. green .. .. 1·60 1·25

DESIGNS: 20 k Dolmabahce Palace, Istanbul. 30 k. Police College, Ankara. 45 k. Police Martyrs' Monument, Istanbul.

171. Police Monument, Ankara.

1955. Int. Police Commission Meeting, Istanbul.

1573. 171. 15 k. green 20 12
1574. – 20 k. violet 25 20
1575. – 30 k. black 30 25
1576. – 45 k. brown 75 50

172. Radio Mast.

173. Istanbul University.

1955. Telecommunications in Turkey. Cent.

1577. 15 k. olive 20 12
1578. 172. 20 k. red 20 12
1579. – 45 k. brown 35 30
1580. 172. 60 k. blue 65 40

DESIGN—HORIZ. 15 k., 45 k. Telegraph table and pole.

1955. 10th Meeting of Governors of Int. Reconstruction and Development Bank and Int. Monetary Fund.

1581. – 15 k. orange 25 12
1582. 173. 20 k. red 25 10
1583. – 60 k. purple 40 30
1584. – 1 l. blue 75 35

DESIGNS: 15 k. Faculty of Letters, Istanbul. 60 k. Hilton Hotel. 1 l. Kiz Kulesi.

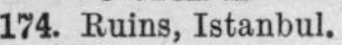

174. Ruins, Istanbul.

175.

1955. 10th Int. Congress of Byzantine Research.

1585. 174. 15 k. grey and green 20 10
1586. – 20 k. red and orange 20 12
1587. – 30 k. brown and pink 35 25
1588. – 75 k. blue 75 45

DESIGNS—VERT. 20 k. Obelisk and Sultan Ahmed Mosque. 75 k. Map of Istanbul, 1422. HORIZ. 30 k. Church of St. Sophia.

1955. 10th Int. Road Planning Congress.

1589. – 20 k. mauve 12 10
1590. 175. 30 k. green 20 15
1591. – 55 k. blue 65 45

DESIGNS: 20 k. Congress emblem. 55 k. Bridges.

176. Population Pictograph.

1955. National Census.

1592. 176. 15 k. grey and red .. 15 12
1593. 20 k. lilac and red .. 12 10
1594. 30 k. blue and red .. 20 15
1595. 60 k. green and red .. 50 30

177. Santa Clause Church, Demre.

178. Kemal Ataturk.

1955. Tourist Propaganda.

1596. – 18 k. green and blue 25 20
1597. – 20 k. brown and blue 25 20
1598. – 30 k. brown & green 30 25
1599. – 45 k. green and brown 1·50 1·10
1600. – 50 k. brown and green 25 25
1601. 177. 65 k. red and black .. 65 35

DESIGNS—VERT. 18 k. Waterfall near Antalya. 45 k. Theatre doorway ruins. 50 k. Countryside, Antalya. HORIZ. 20 k. Alanya. 30 k. Amphitheatre, Aspendos.

1955.

1602. 178. 0.50 k. pink 5 5
1603. 1 k. yellow 5 5
1604. 2 k. blue 5 5
1605. 3 k. red 5 5
1606. 5 k. brown 5 5
1606a. 6 k. green 5 5
1607. 10 k. green 5 5
1607a. 18 k. purple 12 5
1608. 20 k. blue 12 5
1609. 25 k. olive 25 5
1610. 30 k. violet 25 5
1611. 40 k. chestnut 25 5
1612. 75 k. slate .. .. 1·25 25

179.

180. Zubeyde.

181. Kemal Ataturk.

1956. Turkish Historical Association. 25th Anniv.

1613. 179. 40 k. blue 15 5

1956. Mother's Day.

1614. 180. 20 k. brown (perf.) .. 12 10
1615. 20 k. olive (imperf.) .. 65 65

1956.

1618. 181. ½ k. green 5 5
1619. 1 k. orange 5 5
1620. 3 k. olive-green .. 5 5
1621. 5 k. violet 5 5
1622. 6 k. magenta .. 8 5
1623. 10 k. purple 5 5
1624. 12 k. chestnut .. 8 5
1625. 15 k. ultramarine .. 5 5
1626. 18 k. pink 8 5
1627. 20 k. brown 5 5
1628. 25 k. emerald .. 12 5
1629. 30 k. slate 12 5
1630. 40 k. olive 15 5
1631. 50 k. orange 20 5
1632. 60 k. blue 25 8
1633. 70 k. turquoise .. 50 10
1634. 75 k. olive-brown .. 30 8

See also Nos. 1659/78.

182. Shah of Persia and Queen Soraya.

1956. Visit of Shah of Persia to Turkey.

1616. 182. 100 k. green (perf.) .. 1·25 1·00
1617. 100 k. red and green (imperf.) .. .. 7·50 5·50

183. Erenkoy Sanatorium.

1956. Turkish Post Office Health Service.

1635. 183. 50 k. blue-grn. & pink 45 20

184.

185. Serpent in Bottle.

186. Medical Clinic, Kayseri.

1956. 25th Izmir Int. Fair.

1636. 184. 45 k. green (postage) 15 15
1637. 25 k. brown (air) .. 15 12

1956. Int. Anti-Alcoholism Congress.

1638. 185. 25 k. multicoloured .. 12 8

1956. Medical Clinic Kayseri. 750th Anniv.

1639. 186. 60 k. violet & yellow 20 12

187. Sariyar Barrage.

188. Wrestling.

1956. Inaug. of Sariyar Dam.

1640. 187. 20 k. vermilion .. 8 5
1641. 20 k. blue 8 5

1956. Olympic Games. Inscr. as in T 188.

1642. 188. 40 k. sepia on green .. 35 20
1643. – 65 k. red on grey .. 45 30

DESIGN: 65 k. Another wrestling match.

189. Mehmet Akif Ersoy.

190. Vase of Troy.

1956. Ersoy (poet). 20th Death Anniv.

1644. 189. 20 k. brown & green 10 8
1645. 20 k. red and grey .. 10 8
1646. 20 k. violet and pink 10 8

Each stamp is inscribed with a different line of verse from the Turkish national anthem composed by Ersoy.

1956. Troy Commemoration. Inscr. "TRUVA (TROIA)".

1647. – 15 k. green 85 75
1648. 190. 20 k. purple 75 75
1649. – 30 k. brown 85 75

DESIGNS—HORIZ. 15 k. Troy Amphitheatre. 30 k. Trojan Horse.

191. Mobile X-ray Unit.

192. Pres. Heuss.

1957. T.B. Relief Campaign.

1650. 191. 25 k. red and drab .. 15 8

1957. Visit of President of West Germany.

1651. 192. 40 k. brown and yellow (postage) .. 25 20
1652. 40 k. pur. & sal. (air) 12 10

193. Bergama.

1957. Bergama Fair.

1653. 193. 30 k. brown 8 8
1654. – 40 k. green 10 10

DESIGN: 40 k. Folk-dancing.

194.

1957. Turkish-American Friendship.

1655. 194. 25 k. violet 12 12
1656. 40 k. blue 15 15

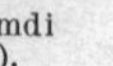
195. Osman Hamdi Bey (founder).

196. Kemal Ataturk.

1957. 75th Anniv. of Fine Arts Academy, Istanbul.

1657. 195. 20 k. drab, buff & blk. 10 10
1658. – 30 k. grey-grn. & grn. 20 12

DESIGN—HORIZ. 30 k. Hittite relic of Alacahoyuk. Inscr. "GUZEL SANATLAR AKADEMISI 75. YIL".

1957.

1659. 196. ½ k. brown 5 5
1660. 1 k. blue 5 5
1661. 2 k. slate-violet .. 5 5
1662. 3 k. orange 5 5
1663. 5 k. green 5 5
1664. 6 k. slate-green .. 5 5
1665. 10 k. violet 5 5
1666. 12 k. emerald .. 5 5
1667. 15 k. green 5 5
1668. 18 k. magenta .. 8 5
1669. 20 k. sepia 8 5
1670. 25 k. brown 10 5
1671. 30 k. blue 12 5
1672. 40 k. slate 15 5
1673. 50 k. yellow 20 5
1674. 60 k. black 25 8
1675. 70 k. purple 25 8
1676. 75 k. olive 30 8
1677. – 100 k. red 35 12
1678. – 250 k. olive .. .. 1·25 40

Nos. 1677/8 are larger (21 × 29 mm.).

197. Mohamed Zahir Shah.

198. Amasya Medical Centre.

1957. Visit of Mohamed Zahir Shah of Afghanistan.

1679. 197. 45 k. lake & pink (post.) .. 15 12
1680. 25 k. green (air) .. 12 8

1957. 11th Congress of World Medical Association. Inscr. as in T 198.

1681. 198. 25 k. red and yellow 10 5
1682. – 65 k. blue and green .. 20 15

DESIGN—HORIZ. 65 k. Sultan Mohammed School, 1557.

DESIGN—VERT. 1 l. Mimar Koca Sinan (architect).

199. Sultan Mohammed II Mosque.

1957. 400th Anniv. of the Suleiman Mosque, Istanbul. Inscr. as in T **199**.

1683. **199.** 20 k. green 8 5
1684. – 1 l. brown 35 25

1957. 2nd Philatelic Exhibition, Istanbul. Surch. **50 Kurus ISTANBUL Filatelik II. Sergisi 1957.**

1685. 50 k. on 2 l. bl. (No. 1487) 25 15

200. Forestry Map of Turkey.

1957. Cent. of Forestry Teaching.

1686. **200.** 20 k. green and brown 12 8
1687. – 25 k. green and blue 15 10

DESIGN—VERT. 25 k. Planting fir-tree.

201. Fuzuli (poet). **202.** Benjamin Franklin.

1957. Fuzuli Year.

1688. **201.** 50 k. red, yellow, violet and pink .. 35 25

1957. Franklin. 250th Birth Anniv.

1689. **202.** 65 k. purple 20 25
1690. 65 k. blue 30 25

203. Mevlana's Tomb, Konya. **204.** Adana.

1957. 750th Anniv. of Birth of Mevlana (poet).

1691. **203.** 50 k. vio., blue & grn. 20 12
1692. – 100 k. blue 30 25

DESIGN—HORIZ. 100 k. Konya Museum.

1958. Turkish Towns. As T **204**.

(a) 26 × 21 mm.

1693. 5 k. brown (Adana) .. 5 5
1694. 5 k magenta (Adapazari) .. 5 5
1695. 5 k. red (Adiyaman) .. 5 5
1696. 5 k. sepia (Afyon) .. 5 5
1697. 5 k. green (Amasya) .. 5 5
1698. 5 k. blue (Ankara) .. 5 5
1699. 5 k. turquoise (Antakya) 5 5
1700. 5 k. olive (Antalya) .. 5 5
1701. 5 k. violet (Artvin) .. 5 5
1702. 5 k. orange (Aydin) .. 5 5
1703. 5 k. violet (Balikesir) .. 5 5
1704. 5 k. olive (Bilecik) .. 5 5
1705. 5 k. sepia (Bingol) .. 5 5
1706. 5 k. blue (Bitlis) .. 5 5
1707. 5 k. purple (Bolu) .. 5 5
1708. 5 k. brown (Burdur) .. 5 5
1709. 5 k. green (Bursa) .. 5 5
1710. 5 k. ultram. (Canakkale) 5 5
1711. 5 k. plum (Cankiri) .. 5 5
1712. 5 k. blue (Corum) .. 5 5
1713. 5 k. blue (Denizli) .. 5 5
1714. 5 k. orange (Diyarbakir) 5 5
1715. 5 k. slate-violet (Edirne) 5 5
1716. 5 k. olive (Elazig) .. 5 5
1717. 5 k. blue (Erzincan) .. 5 5
1718. 5 k. orange (Erzurum) .. 5 5
1719. 5 k. green (Eskisehir) .. 5 5
1720. 5 k. olive (Gaziantep) .. 5 5
1721. 5 k. ultram. (Giresun) .. 5 5
1722. 5 k. blue (Gumosane) .. 5 5
1723. 5 k. mauve (Hakkari) .. 5 5
1724. 5 k. magenta (Isparto) .. 5 5
1725. 5 k. blue (Istanbul) .. 5 5
1726. 5 kt. ulram. (Izmir) .. 5 5
1727. 5 k. turquoise (Izmit) .. 5 5
1728. 5 k. purple (Karakose) .. 5 5
1729. 5 k. emerald (Kars) .. 5 5
1730. 5 k. cerise (Kastamonu) 5 5
1731. 5 k. myrtle (Kayseri) .. 5 5
1732. 5 k. brown (Kirklareli) .. 5 5
1733. 5 k. orange (Kirsehir) .. 5 5
1734. 5 k. ultram. (Konya) .. 5 5
1735. 5 k. violet (Kutahya) .. 5 5
1736. 5 k. brown (Malatya) .. 5 5
1737. 5 k. myrtle (Manisa) .. 5 5
1738. 5 k. purple (Maras) .. 5 5
1739. 5 k. brown (Mardin) .. 5 5
1740. 5 k. emerald (Mersin) .. 5 5
1741. 5 k. green (Mugla) .. 5 5
1742. 5 k. olive (Mus) .. 5 5
1743. 5 k. green (Nevsehir) .. 5 5
1744. 5 k. brown (Nigde) .. 5 5
1745. 5 k. ultram. (Ordu) .. 5 5
1746. 5 k. violet (Rize) .. 5 5
1747. 5 k. purple (Samsun) .. 5 5
1748. 5 k. brown (Siirt) .. 5 5
1749. 5 k. indigo (Sinop) .. 5 5
1750. 5 k. green (Sivas) .. 5 5
1751. 5 k. blue (Tekirdag) .. 5 5
1752. 5 k. red (Tokat) 5 5
1753. 5 k. violet-bl. (Trabzon) 5 5
1754. 5 k. orange (Tunceli) .. 5 5
1755. 5 k. brown (Urfa) .. 5 5
1756. 5 k. slate-green (Usak) 5 5
1757. 5 k. lake (Van) .. 5 5
1758. 5 k. red (Yozgat) .. 5 5
1759. 5 k. blue (Zonguldak) .. 5 5

(b) 32½ × 22 mm.

1760. 20 k. brown (Adana) .. 20 20
1761. 20 k. mag. (Adapazari) .. 20 20
1762. 20 k. red (Adiyaman) .. 20 20
1763. 20 k. brown (Afyon) .. 20 20
1764. 20 k. green (Amasya) .. 20 20
1765. 20 k. blue (Ankara) .. 20 20
1766. 20 k. turq. (Antakya) .. 20 20
1767. 20 k. green (Antalya) .. 20 20
1768. 20 k. indigo (Artvin) .. 20 20
1769. 20 k. orange (Aydin) .. 20 20
1770. 20 k. purple (Balikesir) 20 20
1771. 20 k. green (Bilecik) .. 20 20
1772. 20 k. slate (Bingol) .. 20 20
1773. 20 k. violet (Bitlis) .. 20 20
1774. 20 k. chocolate (Bolu) .. 20 20
1775. 20 k. olive (Burdur) .. 20 20
1776. 20 k. green (Bursa) .. 20 20
1777. 20 k. ultra. (Canakkale) 20 20
1778. 20 k. plum (Cankiri) .. 20 20
1779. 20 k. slate (Corum) .. 20 20
1780. 20 k. blue (Denizli) .. 20 20
1781. 20 k. orange (Diyarbakir) 20 20
1782. 20 k. slate (Edirne) .. 20 20
1783. 20 k. olive (Elazig) .. 20 20
1784. 20 k. blue (Erzincan) .. 20 20
1785. 20 k. orange (Erzurum) 20 20
1786. 20 k. green (Eskisehir) .. 20 20
1787. 20 k. green (Gaziantep) .. 20 20
1788. 20 k. blue (Giresun) .. 20 20
1789. 20 k. blue (Gumusane) .. 20 20
1790. 20 k. purple (Hakkari) .. 20 20
1791. 20 k. magenta (Isparta) .. 20 20
1792. 20 k. ultram. (Istanbul) 20 20
1793. 20 k. ultram. (Izmir) .. 20 20
1794. 20 k. turquoise (Izmit) .. 20 20
1795. 20 k. violet (Karakose) 20 20
1796. 20 k. emerald (Kars) .. 20 20
1797. 20 k. cerise (Kastamonu) 20 20
1798. 20 k. myrtle (Kayseri) .. 20 20
1799. 20 k. brown (Kirklareli) 20 20
1800. 20 k. chest. (Kirsehir) .. 20 20
1801. 20 k. ultram. (Konya) .. 20 20
1802. 20 k. violet (Kutahya) .. 20 20
1803. 20 k. chest. (Malatya) .. 20 20
1804. 20 k. slate (Manisa) .. 20 20
1805. 20 k. purple (Maras) .. 20 20
1806. 20 k. lake (Mardin) .. 20 20
1807. 20 k. blue-grn. (Mersin) 20 20
1808. 20 k. emerald (Mugla) .. 20 20
1809. 20 k. myrtle (Mus) .. 20 20
1810. 20 k. olive (Nevsehir) .. 20 20
1811. 20 k. lake (Nigde) .. 20 20
1812. 20 k. blue (Ordu) .. 20 20
1813. 20 k. violet (Rize) .. 20 20
1814. 20 k. purple (Samsun) .. 20 20
1815. 20 k. sepia (Siirt) .. 20 20
1816. 20 k. indigo (Sinop) .. 20 20
1817. 20 k. green (Sivas) .. 20 20
1818. 20 k. blue (Tekirdag) .. 20 20
1819. 20 k. red (Tokat) .. 20 20
1820. 20 k. vio.-blue (Trabzon) 20 20
1821. 20 k. vermilion (Tunceli) 20 20
1822. 20 k. brown (Urfa) .. 20 20
1823. 20 k. slate (Usak) .. 20 20
1824. 20 k. lake (Van) .. 20 20
1825. 20 k. red (Yozgat) .. 20 20
1826. 20 k. blue (Zonguldak) .. 20 20

205. **206.** Hierapolis at Pamukkale.

1958. 75th Anniv. of the Institute of Economics and Commerce, Ankara.

1827. **205.** 20 k. orge., bl. & bistre 8 8
1828. 25 k. bl., orge. & bistre 10 5

1958. Pamukkale Tourist Publicity. Inscr. "PAMUKKALE".

1829. **206.** 20 k. brown 10 5
1830. – 25 k. blue 12 5

DESIGN—HORIZ. 25 k. Travertins (rocks) near Denizli.

207. Katib Celebi. **208.** Letters.

1958. Katib Celebi (author). 300th Death Anniv.

1831. **207.** 50 k. + 10 k. black .. 15 15

1958. Correspondence Day.

1832. **208.** 20 k. orange and black 10 8

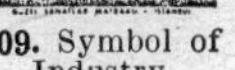

209. Symbol of Industry. **210.** Symbol of "Europa".

1958. Industrial Fair, Istanbul.

1833. **209.** 40 k. black & slate-bl. 12 8

1958. Europa.

1834. **210.** 25 k. lilac and violet 20 15
1835. 40 k. blue and ultram. 25 20

211. Bulldozer. **212.** Flame of Remembrance.

1958. Republic. 35th Anniv.

1836. **211.** 15 k. + 5 k. orange .. 5 5
1837. – 20 k. + 5 k. brown .. 8 8
1838. – 25 k. + 5 k. green .. 12 12

DESIGNS—VERT. 20 k. Portrait of Kemal Ataturk. 25 k. Army tanks and aircraft in flight.

1958. Kemal Ataturk. 20th Death Anniv. Inscr. as in T **212**.

1839. **212.** 25 k. red 5 5
1840. – 75 k. green 20 12

DESIGN: 75 k. Sword, sprig and bust of Kemal Ataturk.

213. **214.** Blackboard.

1959. Faculty of Agriculture, Ankara University. 25th Anniv.

1841. **213.** 25 k. yellow and violet 12 8

1959. Boys' High School, Istanbul. 75th Anniv.

1842. **214.** 75 k. black and yellow 15 12

BIRDS (in flight)—HORIZ. 40 k. Swallows. 65 k. Cranes. 85 k. Seagulls. VERT. 125 k. Swallows. 155 k. Stork. 195 k. Seagulls. 245 k. Buzzard.

215. Eagle.

1959. Air. Birds.

1843. – 40 k. purple & mauve 15 5
1844. – 65 k. myrtle and blue-green 30 12
1845. – 85 k. blue and black 35 12
1846. **215.** 105 k. bistre & yellow 40 20
1847. – 125 k. lilac & violet 65 25
1848. – 155 k. green & yellow-green 75 25
1849. – 195 k. ultram. & black 80 25
1850. – 245 k. brown & orge. 1·25 55

DESIGN: 25 k Portrait of Sinas and masks.

216. Theatre, Ankara.

1959. Turkish Theatre Cent.

1851. **216.** 20 k. brown and green 8 8
1852. – 25 k. green & orange 10 8

217. M.V. "Karadeniz". **218.**

1959.

1853. – 1 k. indigo 5 5
1854. **218.** 5 k. blue 5 5
1855. – 10 k. blue 5 5
1856. – 15 k. chocolate .. 5 5
1857. – 20 k. bronze-green .. 8 5
1858. – 25 k. lilac 8 5
1859. – 30 k. purple 12 5
1860. – 40 k. blue 15 5
1861. – 45 k. violet 30 5
1862. – 55 k. olive-brown .. 65 12
1863. – 60 k. green 20 5
1864. – 75 k. olive .. .. 1·10 12
1865. – 90 k. blue .. .. 1·50 25
1866. – 100 k. grey .. .. 2·00 15
1867. – 120 k. purple .. 75 10
1868. – 150 k. orange .. 2·25 25
1869. – 200 k. yellow-green .. 85 25
1870. – 250 k. brown .. 1·50 50
1871. – 500 k. blue .. .. 2·00 1·00

DESIGNS—HORIZ. 1 k. Airliner. 10 k. Grain silo. 15 k. Steel works. 20 k. Euphrates Bridge. 25 k. Zonguldak Harbour. 30 k. Oil refinery. 40 k. Rumeli Hisari Fortress. 45 k. Sugar factory. 55 k. Coal mine. 150 k. Combine-harvester. VERT. 60 k. Telegraph pole. 75 k. Railway. 90 k. Crane loading ships. 100 k. Cement factory. 120 k. Coast road. 200 k. Electric transformer. 250 k., 500 k. Portrait of Ataturk.

1959. Postage Due stamps surch. **20=20** for ordinary postage.

1872. D 8. 20 k. on 20 pa. brown 10 8
1873. 20 k. on 2 k. blue .. 10 8
1874. 20 k. on 3 k. violet 10 8
1875. 20 k. on 5 k. green .. 10 8
1876. 20 k. on 12 k. red 10 8

1959. N.A.T.O. 10th Anniv.

1877. **217.** 105 k. red 30 25
1878. 195 k. green 55 50

219. Amphitheatre, Aspendos. **220.** Basketball Players.

1959. Aspendos Festival.

1879. **219.** 20 k. violet and bistre 5 5
1880. 20 k. brown and green 8 5

1959. Council of Europe. 10th Anniv. Surch. **X. YIL** in circle of stars, **AVRUPA KONSEYI** and value.

1881. **211.** 105 k. on 15 k. + 5 k. orange 40 35

1959. 11th European and Mediterranean Basketball Championships, Istanbul

1882. **220.** 25 k. red and blue .. 20 20

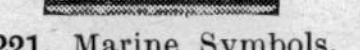

221. Marine Symbols. **222.** Goreme.

1959. Turkish Merchant Marine College. 50th Anniv. Inscr. as in T 221.
1883. 221. 30 k. gold, light blue, blue and indigo .. 12 12
1884. – 40 k. gold, light blue, blue and indigo .. 15 15
DESIGN: 40 k. As 30 k. but sea-horse in place of anchor symbol.

1959. Tourist Publicity.
1885. 222. 105 k. + 10 k. orange and violet 30 30

223. Mounted Warrior.

1959. Battle of Malazgirt (888th Anniv.).
1886. 223. 2½ l. purple and blue 65 65

224. Istanbul.

1959. 15th Int. T.B. Conf., Istanbul.
1887. 224. 105 k. + 10 k. blue and red 35 30

225. Ornamental Pattern. 226. Kemal Ataturk.

1959. 1st Int. Congress of Turkish Arts.
1888. 225. 30 k. red and black .. 10 8
1889. – 40 k. bl., blk. & ochre 12 10
1890. – 75 k. blue, yell. & red 25 20
DESIGNS—HORIZ. 40 k. Sultan Mohammed II Mosque in silhouette. VERT. 75 k. Circular ornament.

1959.
1891. 226. 500 k. blue .. .. 1·60 1·10

227. Faculty Building. 228. Crossed Sabres.

1959. Turkish Political Science Faculty Cent.
1892. 227. 40 k. brown & green 15 12
1893. 40 k. blue and brown 15 12
1894. – 1 l. ochre and violet .. 30 25
DESIGN—VERT. 1 l. "S.B.F." emblem of Faculty.

1960. Territorial War College. 125th Anniv.
1895. 228. 30 k. red and yellow 12 12
1896. – 40 k. yell., brn. & lake 15 15
DESIGN: 40 k. Bayonet in bowl of fire.

DESIGN: 105 k. "Uprooted tree" and houses representing refugee camp.

229. "Uprooted Tree" and Globe.

1960. World Refugee Year.
1897. 229. 90 k. black & turq... 30 25
1898. – 105 k. black & yellow 35 30

230. Mental Home, Manisa. 231. Carnations.

1960. Manisa Fair. Inscr. "MANISA MESIR BAYRAMI".
1899. 230. 40 k. + 5 k. vio. & mve. 12 12
1900. 40 k. + 5 k. grn. & blue 12 12
1901. – 90 k. + 5 k. pur. & mag. 25 25
1902. – 105 k. + 10 k. mult... 35 35
DESIGNS—VERT. 90 k. Sultan Mosque, Manisa. (30½ × 42½ mm.): 105 k. Merkez Mushlihid-din Effendi (portrait).

1960. Spring Flowers Festival, Istanbul. Inscr. "1960". Flowers in natural colours. Colours of inscriptions and backgrounds given.
1903. 231. 30 k. crimson & yellow 20 15
1904. – 40 k. green and grey 25 20
1905. – 75 k. red and blue .. 50 35
1906. – 105 k. green and pink 65 35
FLOWERS: 40 k. Jasmine. 75 k. Rose. 105 k. Tulips.

232. Map of Cyprus.

1960. Proclamation of Cyprus Republic. Inscr. "KIBRIS CUMHURIYETI".
1907. – 40 k. mauve and blue 15 10
1908. 232. 105 k. yell., blue & grn. 35 25
DESIGN: 40 k. Town Centre, Nicosia.

233. Globe.

1960. 16th Women's Int. Council Meeting.
1909. 233. 30 k yellow and lilac 12 10
1910. – 75 k. drab and blue .. 30 25
DESIGN: 75 k. Women, "W.I.C." emblem and nest

234. Football. 235. "Population".

1960. Olympic Games. Inscr. "1960 ROMA".
1911. 30 k. green (T 234) .. 25 20
1912. 30 k. black (Basketball) 25 20
1913. 30 k. blue (Wrestling) .. 25 20
1914. 30 k. purple (Hurdling).. 25 20
1915. 30 k. brn. (Horse-jumping) 25 20

1960. Europa. As T 279 of Belgium but size 32½ × 22½ mm.
1916. 75 k. turquoise & ol-grn. 65 65
1917. 105 k. light and deep blue 85 85

1960. National Census.
1918. – 30 k. + 5 k. red & blue 12 10
1919. 235. 50 k. + 5 k. blue & turq 15 12
DESIGN—HORIZ. 30 k. Graph showing outlines of human faces.

236. "Justice". 237. Agah Effendi and front page of newspaper "Turcamani Ahval".

1960. Trial of Ex-Government Officials.
1920. – 40 k. bistre and violet 12 5
1921. – 105 k. red & grey-grn. 35 20
1922. 236. 195 k. red and emerald 50 25
DESIGNS—HORIZ. 40 k. Badge of Turkish Army. 105 k. Trial scene.

1960. Turkish Press Cent.
1923. 237. 40 k. mar. & slate-bl. 12 10
1924. 60 k. maroon & ochre 15 15

238. U.N. Headquarters and Emblem. 239. Revolutionaries.

1960. U.N.O. 15th Anniv.
1925. – 90 k. ultram. & blue 25 20
1926. 238. 105 k. sepia and turq. 35 25
DESIGN—VERT. 90 k. U.N. emblem, "XV" and hand holding torch.

1960. Revolution of 27th May, 1960.
1927. 239. 10 k. grey and black 5 5
1928. – 30 k. violet 10 8
1929. – 40 k. red and black .. 12 12
1930. – 105 k. multicoloured 30 25
DESIGNS—HORIZ. 30 k. Kemal Ataturk and hand with torch. 105 k. Soldiers and wounded youth. VERT. 40 k. Prancing horse breaking chain.

DESIGNS — HORIZ. 40 k. Sun disc. cuneiform writing and map of Turkey. VERT. 60 k. Ataturk's statue.

240. Faculty Building.

1960. History and Geography Faculty.
1931. 240. 30 k. blk. & grey-grn. 8 8
1932. – 40 k. black and buff 15 12
1933. – 60 k. olive, buff and grey-green.. .. 20 12

241. "Communications and Transport". 242.

1961. 9th Central Treaty Organization Ministers' Meeting, Ankara.
1934. 241. 30 k. black and violet 12 12
1935. – 40 k. black and green 20 25
1936. – 75 k. black and blue 30 25
DESIGNS: 40 k. Road and rail construction, telephone and telegraph. 75 k. Parliament Building, Ankara.

1961. May 27th Revolution. 1st Anniv.
1937. 242. 30 k. multicoloured .. 12 12
1938. – 40 k. grn., cream & blk. 25 20
1939. – 60 k. red and green .. 25 20
DESIGNS—HORIZ. 40 k. Boz Kur. and warriors. VERT. 60 k. "Progress".

DESIGNS — HORIZ. 30 k. Rockets. VERT. 75 k. Ataturk, eagle and jet planes.

243. Jet 'Plane and Rocket.

1961. Turkish Air Force. 50th Anniv.
1940. – 38 k. orge., lake & blk. 20 15
1941. 243. 40 k. violet and red .. 20 20
1942. – 75 k. buff, grey & blk. 40 25

244. Old Observatory.

1961. Kandilli Observatory. 50th Anniv.
1943. 10 k. + 5 k. turq. & green 10 5
1944. 30 k. + 5 k. violet & black 12 8
1945. 40 k. + 5 k. brown & sepia 15 12
1946. 75 k. + 5 k. olive and green 25 20
DESIGNS—HORIZ. 10 k. T 245. 30 k. Observatory emblem. 75 k. Observatory building. VERT. 40 k. F. Gokmen.

245. Kemal Ataturk. 245a.

1961.
1947. 245a. 1 k. chestnut .. 5 5
1948. 5 k. blue 8 5
1949. 245. 10 k. magenta .. 10 5
1950. 245a. 10 k. sepia 10 5
1951. 30 k. grey-green .. 75 5
1952. 10 l. vio. (22 × 32 mm.) 4·50 1·40

246. Doves.

1961. Europa.
1960. 246. 30 k. blue .. .. 1·00 1·00
1961. 40 k. grey .. .. 1·00 1·00
1962. 75 k. red .. .. 1·10 1·00

247. Tulip and Cogwheel. 248. "The Constitution".

1961. Professional and Technical Schools Cent.
1963. 247. 30 k. pink, silver and slate.. .. .. 10 8
1964. – 75 k. red, blk. & blue 20 20
DESIGN—HORIZ. 75 k. Inscr. "100 Yili 1861–1961" and tulip-and-cogwheel emblem.

1961. Opening of Turkish Parliament.
1965. 248. 30 k. black, bis. & red 10 8
1966. 75 k. blk., grn. & blue 20 20

249. Insecticide-sprayers ("Malaria Eradication"). 250. N.A.T.O. and Anniversary Emblems.

1961. U.N.I.C.E.F. 15th Anniv.
1967. 249. 10 k. + 5 k. turquoise 5 5
1968. – 30 k. + 5 k. violet .. 12 12
1969. – 75 k. + 5 k. brown .. 20 20
DESIGNS—HORIZ. 30 k. Mother and child ("Child Welfare"). VERT. 75 k. Mother giving pasteurized milk to children ("Education in Nourishment").

1962. Turkish Admission to N.A.T.O. 10th Anniv.
1970. – 75 k., blk., silver & bl. 25 20
1971. 250. 105 k. blk., sil. & red 45 30
DESIGN—VERT. 75 k. Peace dove over N.A.T.O. and Anniv. emblems.

251. Mosquito on Map of Turkey. 252. "Strelitzia reginae".

1962. Malaria Eradication.
1972. 251. 30 k. + 5 k. brown .. 20 10
1973. 75 k. + 5 k. mve. & blk. 30 20

1962. Flowers. Multicoloured.
1974. 30 k. + 10 k. "Poinsettia pulcherrima" 20 15
1975. 40 k. + 10 k. T 252 .. 25 20
1976. 75 k. + 10 k. "Nymphae alba" 35 30

253. Scouts in Camp.

254. Soldier (Victory Monument, Ankara).

256. Shrine of the Virgin Mary.

255. Europa "Tree".

1962. Turkish Scout Movement. 50th Anniv. Inscr. "1912-1962".
1977. 253. 30 k. red, black & grn. 12 8
1978. – 60 k. red, blk. & lilac 20 15
1979. – 105 k. red, blk. & brn. 35 30
DESIGNS: 60 k. Two scouts with flag. 105 k. Wolf Cub and Brownie.

1962. Battle of General Command, Dumlupinar.
1980. 254. 30 k. bronze-green 10 8
1981. – 40 k. brown and black 15 10
1982. – 75 k. olive-grey 25 20
DESIGNS—HORIZ. 40 k. Ox-cart carrying ammunition (Victory Monument, Ankara). VERT. 75 k. Kemal Ataturk.

1962. Europa.
1983. 255. 75 k. sepia & emerald 25 20
1984. 105 k. sepia and red .. 35 25
1985. 195 k. sepia and blue 85 65

1962. Tourist Issue. Multicoloured.
1986. 30 k. T 256 .. .. 15 10
1989. 40 k. interior 15 12
1990. 75 k. Exterior 25 15
1991. 105 k. Statue of the Virgin 30 20
DESIGNS: The 40 and 75 k. show horiz. views of the Virgin Mary's house at Ephesus.

257. Turkish 20 pa. Stamp of 1863. 258. Julian's Column Ankara.

1963. Stamp Centenary.
1990. 257. 10 k. blk., yell. & brn. 5 5
1991. – 30 k. blk., pink & vio. 20 10
1992. – 40 k. blk., blue & turq. 20 12
1993. – 75 k. blk., pink & brn. 35 30
DESIGNS—Turkish stamps of 1863: 30 k. (1 pi.). 40 k. (2 pi.). 75 k. (5 pi.).

1963.
1994. 258. 1 k. green and olive .. 5 5
1995. 1 k. violet 5 5
1996. – 5 k. sepia & light brn. 10 5
1997. – 10 k. magenta & grn. 15 5
1998. – 30 k. black and violet 45 5
1999. – 50 k. grn., blue & yell. 85 5
2000. – 60 k. grey 75 10
2001. – 100 k. olive-brown .. 65 12
2002. – 150 k. green .. .. 2·50 25
DESIGNS—HORIZ. 5 k. Ethnographic Museum. 10 k. Citadel. 30 k. Educational Establishment, Gazi. 50 k. Ataturk's Mausoleum. 60 k. Presidential Palace, Ankara. 100 k. Ataturk's house. 150 k. National Museum, Ankara.

259. "Clinging to the World". 260. Wheat and Census Graph.

262. Ucserefili Mosque. 261. Atomic Symbol on Map.

1963. Freedom from Hunger.
2010. 259. 30 k. blue 12 8
2011. – 40 k. brown 15 10
2012. – 75 k. green 30 20
DESIGNS: 40 k. Sowers. 75 k. Emblem and Globe with hands.

1963. Agricultural Census. Unissued stamps with "KASIM 1960" obliterated with bars. Inscr. "UMUMI ZIRAAT SAYIMI".
2013. 260. 40 k.+5 k. yellow, grn., blk. & lt. grn. 12 12
2014. – 60 k.+5 k. blk. & orge. 25 15
DESIGN—HORIZ. 60 k. Wheat and chart.

1963. Opening of Turkish Nuclear Research Centre. 1st Anniv. Inscr. "1962 1963".
2015. 261. 50 k. brown 15 12
2016. – 60 k. grn., red & yell. 25 15
2017. – 100 k. blue 35 25
DESIGNS: 60 k. Various symbols. 100 k. Emblem of Turkish Atomic Energy Commission.

1963. Conquest of Edirne. 600th Anniv. Inscr. "1363 – 1963".
2018. 262. 10 k. green, ult. & bl. 8 5
2019. – 30 k. blue and red .. 15 8
2020. – 60 k. brown, red & bl. 20 15
2021. – 100 k. multicoloured 35 25
DESIGNS—HORIZ. 30 k. Meric Bridge. 60 k. Kum Kasri (building). VERT. 100 k. Sultan Amurat I.

263. Soldier and Sun.

1963. Turkish Army. 600th Anniv.
2022. 263. 50 k. black, red & slate 15 12
2023. 100 k. blk., red & bistre 35 25

264. Globe and Emblems. 265. Mithat Pasha (founder).

1963. Red Cross Cent. Multicoloured.
2024. 50 k.+10 k. Type 264 .. 15 15
2025. 60 k.+10 k. "Flowers" emblem (vert.) .. 20 15
2026. 100 k.+10 k. Three emblems on flags 35 30

1963. Turkish Agricultural Bank. Cent. Inscr. "1863-1963".
2027. – 30 k. brown, green and yellow-green .. 12 8
2028. – 50 k. blue and lilac .. 15 12
2029. 265. 60 k. green and black 20 15
DESIGNS—HORIZ. 30 k. Ploughing and irrigation. 50 k. Agricultural Bank, Ankara.

266. Exhibition Hall, Istanbul, and 5 pi. stamp of 1863.

1963. "Istanbul '63" Int. Stamp. Exn.
2030. 266. 10 k. salmon, black and yellow .. 10 5
2031. – 50 k. grn., claret & blk. 15 8
2032. – 60 k. sepia, blk. & blue 20 12
2033. – 100 k. violet & purple 35 25
2034. – 130 k. brn., orge. & yell. 40 30
DESIGNS: 50 k. Sultan Ahmed's Mosque Obelisk and 3 pi. on 2 pa. Nationalist Govt. (Angora) stamp of 1920. 60 k. Istanbul skyline and 10 pi. (Angora) stamp of 1922. 100 k. Rumeli Fort and 6 k. stamp of 1929/30. 130 k. Ankara Fort and 12½ k. air stamp of 1934.

267. "Co-operation".

268. Ataturk and Old Parliament House. 269. Kemal Ataturk.

1963. Europa.
2035. 267. 50 k. orge., blk. & red 25 20
2036. 130 k. blue, blk. & grn. 50 35

1963. Turkish Republic. 40th Anniv. Inscr. "40 YILI". Multicoloured.
2037. 30 k. Type 268 .. .. 12 8
2038. 50 k. Ataturk and flag .. 20 12
2039. 60 k. Ataturk and new Parliament House 25 15

1963. Kemal Ataturk. 25th Death Anniv.
2040. 269. 50 k. multicoloured .. 20 12
2041. 60 k. multicoloured .. 25 15

279. R. S. Dag (painter). 271. N.A.T.O. Emblem and "XV".

1964. Cultural Celebrities.
2042. – 1 k. black and red .. 5 5
2043. – 5 k. black & grey-grn. 8 5
2044. 270. 10 k. black and brown 12 5
2045. – 50 k. black and blue .. 45 10
2046. – 60 k. black and grey 30 12
2047. – 100 k. ultram. & blue 65 25
2048. – 130 k. black and green 1·25 35
PORTRAITS, etc.: 1 k. H. R. Gurpinar (romanticist, birth cent.). 5 k. J. H. Izmirli (savant, 20th birth anniv.). 10 k. (20th death anniv.). 50 k. R. Z. M. Ekrem (writer, 50th death anniv.). 60 k. A. M. Pasa (commander, 125th birth anniv.). 100 k. A. Rasim (writer, birth cent.). 130 k. S. Zeki (mathematician), birth cent.).

1964. N.A.T.O. 15th Anniv.
2049. 271. 50 k. red, vio. & turq. 25 12
2050. – 130 k. black and red 50 30
DESIGN: 130 k. N.A.T.O. emblem and laurel sprig.

272. "Europa" holding Torch.

1964. Council of Europe.
2051. 272. 50 k. ultram., brown and yellow .. 30 20
2052. – 130 k. orange ultram. and blue 65 40
DESIGN: 130 k. Torch and circlet of stars.

273. Haga Mosque, Istanbul. 274. Kars Castle.

1964. Tourist Issue.
2053. 273. 50 k. green and olive 25 15
2054. – 50 k. red and purple .. 25 15
2055. – 50 k. violet and ultram. 25 15
2056. – 60 k. grey-grn. & blk. 30 20
2057. – 60 k. chest. and sepia 30 20
DESIGNS—HORIZ. No. 2054 Zeus's Temple, Silifke. 2055, Amasra. VERT. 2056, Merzin. 2057. Augustus' Temple, Ankara.

1964. Conquest of Kars. 900th Anniv. Inscr. "1064-1964".
2058. 274. 50 k. black and lilac 20 15
2059. – 130 k. multicoloured 40 35
DESIGN: 130 k. Alpaslan warrior.

275. Europa "Flower". 276. Grazing Cattle.

1964. Europa.
2060. 275. 50 k. bl., grey & orge. 35 25
2061. 130 k. purple, ol. & bl. 75 50

1964. Animal Protection Fund. Multicoloured.
2062 10 k.+5 k. Type 276 .. 10 10
2063. 30 k.+5 k. Horned sheep 20 20
2064. 50 k.+5 k. Horses .. 30 30
2065. 60 k.+5 k. Three horned sheep 40 40
2066. 100 k.+5 k. Dairy cows .. 60 60
The 30 k. and 60 k. are vert.

277. Running. 278. Mustafa Resit.

1964. Olympic Games, Tokyo.
2067. 277. 10 k.+5 k. black red and chestnut .. 15 15
2068. – 50 k.+5 k. black, red and olive 25 20
2069. – 60 k.+5 k. black, red and blue 30 30
2070. – 100 k.+5 k. black, red and violet .. 50 45
DESIGNS—VERT. 50 k. Torch-bearer. 60 k. Wrestling. 100 k. Throwing the discus.

1964. Reformation Decrees. 125th Anniv. Multicoloured.
2071. 50 k. Mustafa Resit and the pashas (horiz. 48×32 mm.) 25 25
2072. 60 k. Type 278 .. .. 35 35
2073. 100 k. As 50 k. 45 40

279. Kemal Ataturk. 280. Glider.

1964.
2074. 279. 1 k. green 5 5
2075. 5 k. ultramarine .. 5 5
2076. 10 k. blue .. 12 5
2077. 25 k. olive-green .. 40 5
2078. 30 k. purple 25 5
2079. 50 k. brown 30 5
2080. 150 k. orange .. 1·25 20

1965. Turkish Civil Aviation League. 40th Anniv. Multicoloured.
2081. 60 k. Parachutist .. 20 15
2082. 90 k. Type 280 .. 30 25
2083. 130 k. Ataturk and squadron of aircraft .. 40 35
The 60 k. and 130 k. are vert.

281. CENTO Emblem. 282. Monument and Soldiers.

1965. Completion of CENTO Telecommunications Projects. Multicoloured.
2084. 30 k. Type 281 .. .. 12 10
2085. 50 k. Aerial mast (vert.) 15 15
2086. 75 k. Hand pressing button (inaugural ceremony) 30 25

1965. Battle of the Dardanelles. 50th Anniv. Multicoloured.
2087. 50 k.+10 k. Wreath & map 20 15
2088. 90 k.+10 k. Type 282 .. 30 25
2089. 130 k.+10 k. Dardanelles Monument and flag (vert.) 45 35

283. Beach at Ordu.

1965. Tourism. Multicoloured.
2090. 30 k Type 283 .. .. 40 35
2091. 50 k. Manavgat Falls .. 25 20
2092. 60 k. Istanbul 30 25
2093. 100 k. Urfa 45 40
2094. 130 k. Alanya 60 55

284. I.T.U. Emblem and Symbols.

1965. I.T.U. Cent
2095. 284. 50 k. multicoloured .. 20 15
2096. 130 k. multicoloured 50 35

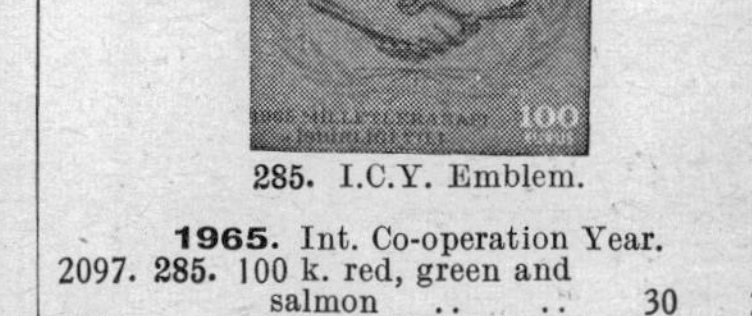

285. I.C.Y. Emblem.

1965. Int. Co-operation Year.
2097. 285. 100 k. red, green and salmon 30 25
2098. 130 k. violet, green and grey 35 35

286. "Co-operation". **287.** R. N. Guntekin.

1965. Regional Development Co-operation Pact. 1st Anniv. Multicoloured.

2099. 50 k Type **286** .. 20 15
2100. 75 k. Globe and flags of Turkey, Iran and Pakistan 30 25

1965. Cultural Celebrities.

2101. **287.** 1 k. black and red .. 5 5
2102. – 5 k. black and blue 5 5
2103. – 10 k. black & ochre.. 5 5
2104. – 25 k. black and brown 30 8
2105. – 30 k. black and grey 30 5
2106. – 50 k. black & yellow 60 5
2107. – 60 k. black and purple 45 8
2108. – 150 k. black and green 60 12
2109. – 220 k. black & brown 95 35

PORTRAITS: 5 k. Dr. B. O. Akalin. 10 k. T. Fikret. 25 k. T. Cemil. 30 k. A. V. Pasa. 50 k. O. Seyfettin. 60 k. K. Mimaroglu. 150 k. H. Z. Usakligil. 220 k. Y. K. Beyatli.

288. Kemal Ataturk and Signature. **289.** Tobacco Plant.

1965.

2110. **288.** 1 k. black and mauve 5 5
2111. 5 k. black and green.. 5 5
2112. 10 k. black and blue.. 8 5
2113. 50 k. black and gold.. 30 5
2114. 150 k. black & silver 85 10

See also Nos. 2170/4.

1965. 2nd Int. Tobacco Congress. Mult.

2115. 30 k. + 5 k. Type **289** .. 25 20
2116. 50 k. + 5 k. Leander's Tower and tobacco leaves (horiz.) 25 20
2117. 100 k. + 5 k. Tobacco leaf 50 35

290. Europa "Sprig". **291.** Civilians Supporting Map.

1965. Europa.

2118. **290.** 50 k. green, bl. & grey 25 20
2119. 130 k. grn., blk. & ochre 45 40

1965. National Census. Inscr. "GENEL NUFUS SAYIMI".

2120. **291.** 10 k. red, green, yellow and indigo.. .. 5 5
2121. – 50 k. apple, grn. & blk. 15 12
2122. – 100 k. blk., bl. & orge. 35 25

DESIGNS—HORIZ. 50 k. Year "1965". VERT. 100 k. Human eye and figure.

292. Ankara Castle and Aircraft.

1965. "Ankara '65" National Stamp Exn. Inscr. "I. MILLI PUL SERGISI".

2123. **292.** 10 k. red, yell. & violet 5 5
2124. – 30 k. red, blue, green and yellow 10 8
2125. – 50 k. blue, red & olive 20 15
2126. – 100 k. multicoloured 35 25

DESIGNS: 30 k. Archer. 50 k. Horseman. 100 k. Three thematic "stamps" and medal.

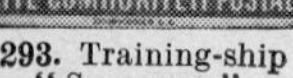

293. Training-ship "Savarona". **294.** Halide E. Adivar.

1965. Turkish Naval Society Congress

2128. **293.** 50 k. brown and blue 30 35
2129. – 60 k. indigo and blue 30 20
2130. – 100 k. brown and blue 60 30
2131. – 130 k. purple and blue 80 60
2132. – 220 k. black and blue 1·00 65

DESIGNS: 60 k. Submarine "Piri Reis". 100 k. Corvette "Alpaslan". 130 k. Destroyer "Gelibolu". 220 k. Destroyer "Gemlik".

1966. Cultural Celebrities.

2133. – 25 k. brown and grey 12 5
2134. – 30 k. brown & mauve 12 5
2135. **294.** 50 k. black and blue.. 25 8
2136. – 60 k. brown and green 65 8
2137. – 130 k. black and blue 80 15

PORTRAITS: 25 k. H. S. Arel. 30 k. K. Akdik. 60 k. Abdurrahman Seref. 130 k. Naima.

295. Roof Panel Green Mausoleum, Burs. **296.** Volleyball.

1966. Turkish Faience. Multicoloured.

2138. 50 k. Type **295** 35 20
2139. 60 k. "Spring Flowers" Sultan Mausoleum, Istanbul 75 75
2140. 130 k. 16th-cent. tile, Iznik 75 50

1966. Int. Military Volleyball Championships.

2141. **296.** 50 k. multicoloured.. 25 20

297. Bodrum. **298.** Golden Pitcher.

1966. Tourism. Multicoloured.

2142. 10 k. Type **297** 5 5
2143. 30 k. Kusadasi 55 40
2144. 50 k. Anadoluhisari .. 15 8
2145. 90 k. Marmaris 20 15
2146. 100 k. Izmir 35 20

The 50 k. and 100 k. are horiz.

1966. Ancient Works of Art. Multicoloured.

2147. 30 k. + 5 k. Ivory eagle and rabbit 30 20
2148. 50 k. + 5 k. Deity in basalt 30 25
2149. 60 k. + 5 k. Bronze bull .. 35 25
2150. 90 k. + 5 k. Type **298** .. 50 35

The 30 k. is horiz.

299. View of Dam.

1966. Keban Dam. Inaug. Multicoloured.

2151. 50 k. Type **299** 15 12
2152. 60 k. Keban valley & bridge 45 25

300. King Faisal. **301.** "Stamp" and "Postmark".

1966. Visit of King of Saudi-Arabia.

2153. **300.** 100 k. carmine & red 40 25

1966. "Balkanfila" Stamp Exn., Istanbul. Multicoloured.

2154. 50 k. Type **301** 15 10
2155. 60 k. Stamp "flower" .. 25 20
2156. 75 k. "Stamps" in form of display frames .. 35 25

302. Sultan Suleiman on Horseback. **303.** Europa "Ship".

1966. Sultan Suleiman. 400th Death Anniv. Multicoloured.

2158. 60 k. Type **302** 35 30
2159. 90 k. Mausoleum, Istanbul 70 50
2160. 130 k. Sultan Suleiman (profile) .. .. 1·10 1·10

1966. Europa.

2161. **303.** 50 k. ultam., bl. & blk. 75 65
2162. 130 k. pur., lilac & blk. 1·10 95

304. Grand Hotel, Ephesus, Izmir.

1966. 33rd Int. Fairs Union Congress, Izmir. Multicoloured.

2163. 50 k. + 5 k. Type **304** .. 15 12
2164. 60 k. + 5 k. Konak Square, Izmir (vert.) 25 20
2165. 130 k. + 5 k. Izmir Fair .. 45 30

305. "Education, Science and Culture".

1966. U.N.E.S.C.O. 20th Anniv.

2166. **305.** 130 k. chestnut, yellow and brown .. 35 30

306. University of Technology. **307.** Ataturk (equestrian statue).

1966. Middle East University of Technology 10th Anniv. Multicoloured.

2167. 50 k. Type **306** .. 15 15
2168. 100 k. Atomic symbol .. 30 20
2169. 130 k. Symbols of the sciences 55 45

1966. As Nos. 2110/4 but with imprint "KIRAL MATBAAST-IST".

2170. **288.** 25 k. black and green 12 5
2171. 30 k. black and pink 12 5
2172. 50 k. black and violet 40 5
2173. 90 k black and brown 35 5
2174. 100 k. black and drab 35 10

1966. Greetings Cards.

2175. **307.** 10 k. black and yellow 12 5

See also Nos. 2218/9, 2257/8, 2303 and 2418.

308. De Havilland "Dragon Rapide". **309.** A. Mithat (author).

1967. Air. Aircraft.

2176. **308.** 10 k. black and pink 12 5
2177. – 60 k. rose, blk. & grn. 20 8
2178. – 130 k. rose, blk. & bl. 35 15
2179. – 220 k. rose, sepia and ochre 80 45
2180. – 270 k. rose, blue and salmon .. .. 1·00 40

DESIGNS: 60 k. Fokker F-27 "Friendship". 130 k. Douglas DC 9-30. 220 k. Douglas DC-3 "Dakota". 270 k. Vickers "Viscount".

1967. Cultural Celebrities.

2181. **309.** 1 k. black and green 5 5
2182. – 5 k. black and ochre.. 10 5
2183. – 50 k. black and violet 40 5
2184. – 100 k. black & yellow 40 8
2185. – 150 k. black & yellow 60 15

PORTRAITS: 5 k. T. Reis (naval commander). 50 k. S. Mehmer (statesman). 100 k. Nedim (philosopher). 150 k. O. Hamdi (painter).

310. Karogoz and Hacivat (puppets).

1967. Int. Tourist Year. Multicoloured.

2186. 50 k. Type **310** 35 35
2187. 60 k. Sword and shield game 40 40
2188. 90 k. Military band .. 70 60
2189. 100 k. Karagoz (puppet) (vert.) .. .. .. 1·00 45

311. "Vaccination". **312.** Deer.

1967. 1st Smallpox Vaccination, Edirne. 250th Anniv.

2190. **311.** 100 k. multicoloured 25 15

1967. Game Animals. Multicoloured.

2191. 50 k. Type **312** 15 12
2192. 60 k. Ibex.. .. 30 25
2193. 100 k. Brown bear .. 30 25
2194. 130 k Wild boar.. .. 90 60

313. Emblem and Footballers. **314.** Cogwheels.

1967. 20th Int. Junior Football Tournament. Multicoloured.

2195. 50 k. Type **313** 25 20
2196. 130 k. Footballers and emblem 50 35

1967. Europa.

2197. **314.** 100 k. + 10 k. ultram., blue, black & pink 35 30
2198. 130 k. + 10 k. ultram. brown, black & grey 50 45

315. Kemal Ataturk. **316.** Road Junction on Map.

1967.

2199. **315.** 10 k. black and green 5 5
2200. 50 k. black and pink 15 5

1967. Opening of "E 5" Motorway. Mult.

2201. 60 k. + 5 k. Type **316** .. 30 30
2202. 130 k. + 5 k. Motorway map and emblem (vert.) 60 60

317. Sivas Hospital.

1967. Sivas Hospital. 750th Anniv.

2203. **317.** 50 k. multicoloured.. 20 12

318. Selim Tarcan and Olympic Rings.

1967. First Turkish Olympic Competitions, Istanbul. Multicoloured.
2204. 50 k. Type **318** 20 15
2205. 60 k. Pierre de Coubertin and Olympic rings .. 30 25

319. St. John's Church, Ephesus. **320.** Kestrel.

1967. Pope Paul VI's Visit to Virgin Mary's House, Ephesus. Multicoloured.
2206. 130 k. Interior of Virgin Mary's House, Ephesus 45 35
2207. 220 k. Type **319** 70 60

1967. Air. Birds.
2208. **320.** 10 k. brown & salmon 12 5
2209. – 60 k. brown & yellow 30 5
2210. – 130 k. maroon & blue 70 12
2211. – 220 k. sepia & green.. 1·10 30
2212. – 270 k. brown and lilac 1·40 75
DESIGNS: 60 k. Eagle. 130 k. Falcon. 220 k. Sparrow-hawk. 270 k. Buzzard.

321. Exhibition Emblem.

1967. Int. Ceramics Exn., Istanbul.
2213. **321.** 50 k. multicoloured .. 20 12

322. Emblem and Istanbul Skyline. **323.** "Stamps" and Map.

1967. Congress of Int. Large Dams Commission, Istanbul.
2214. **322.** 130 k. blue and drab 35 30

1967. "Izmir 67" Stamp Exn. Multicoloured.
2215. 50 k. Type **323** 15 12
2216. 60 k. "Stamps" and grapes 25 20

1967. Greetings Card Stamps. As T **307**.
2218. 10 k. black and green .. 10 5
2219. 10 k. black and red .. 10 5
DESIGNS: Equestrian statues of Ataturk at: No. 2218, Samsun. No. 2219, Izmir.

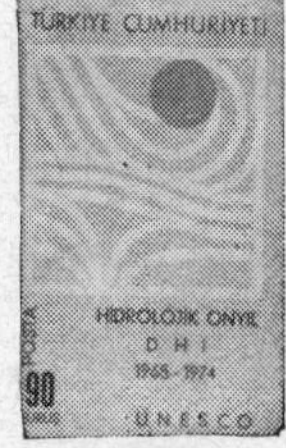

324. Decade Emblem. **325.** Girl with Angora Cat.

1967. Int. Hydrological Decade.
2220. **324.** 90 k. yell., blk. & grn. 25 20
2221. 130 k. yell., blk. & lilac 40 30

1967. Turkish Veterinary Medical Service. 125th Anniv. Multicoloured.
2222. 50 k. Type **325** 15 12
2223. 60 k. Horse 25 20

ILLUSTRATIONS
British Commonwealth and all overprints and surcharges are FULL SIZE. Foreign Countries have been reduced to ¾-LINEAR.

326. Human Rights Emblem.

1968. Human Rights Year.
2224. **326.** 50 k. orge., blk. & mve. 20 12
2225. 130 k. orge., blk. & bl. 30 30

327. Kemal Ataturk. **329.** Scales of Justice.

328. "The Investiture".

1968.
2226. **327.** 1 k. blue & pale blue 5 5
2227. 5 k. green & pale grn. 10 5
2228. 50 k. brown & yellow 70 8
2229. 200 k. brown & pink 60 15

1968. Turkish Book Miniatures. Mult.
2230. 50 k. Type **328** 25 20
2231. 60 k. "Suleman the Magnificent receiving an ambassador" 25 20
2232. 90 k. "The Sultan's Archery Practice" .. 45 30
2233. 100 k. "The Musicians" 60 35
The 60 k. is vert.

1968. Turkish Courts Cent. Multicoloured.
(a) Supreme Court.
2234. 50 k. Type **329** 20 12
2235. 60 k. Ahmet Cevdet Pasha (president) and scroll .. 25 15
(b) Court of Appeal.
2236. 50 k. Book 20 12
2237. 60 k. Mithat Pasha (first president) and scroll .. 25 15

330. W.H.O. Emblem. **331.** Europa "Key".

1968. World Health Organisation. 20th Anniv.
2238. **330.** 130 k. + 10 k. yellow, black and blue .. 40 30

1968. Europa.
2239. **331.** 100 k. yellow, red & bl. 30 25
2240. 130 k. yell., red & grn. 45 40

332. Etem Pasha and Dr. Marko.

1968. Turkish Red Crescent Fund. Mult.
2241. 50 k. + 10 k. Type **332** .. 30 20
2242. 60 k. + 10 k. Omer Pasha and Dr. Adbullah .. 45 35
2243. 100 k. + 10 k. Kemal Ataturk and Dr. Refik Saydam in front of Red Crescent Headquarters (vert.) .. 75 65

333. "Kismet". **334.** "Protection against Usury".

1968. Sadun Boro's World Voyage in Yacht. "Kismet".
2244. **333.** 50 k. multicoloured .. 25 15

1968. Pawnbroking Office, Istanbul. Cent
2245. **334.** 50 k. multicoloured .. 25 15

335. Battle of Sakarya and Obverse of Medal.

1968. Independence Medal. Multicoloured.
2246. 50 k. Type **335** 20 20
2247. 130 k. National Anthem and reverse of medal .. 35 25

336. Old and New Emblems within "100".

1968. Galatasary High School. Cent. Multicoloured.
2248. 50 k. Type **336** .. 12 10
2249. 60 k. Gulbaba offering flowers to Bayazet II .. 25 20
2250. 100 k. Kemal Ataturk and School Building .. 25 20

337. President De Gaulle. **338.** Kemal Ataturk.

1968. President De Gaulle's Visit to Turkey.
2251. **337.** 130 k. multicoloured 90 55

1968. Kemal Ataturk. 30th Death Anniv.
2252. **338.** 30 k. blk. and yellow 15 10
2253. – 50 k. black and green 15 5
2254. – 60 k. black and turq. 20 8
2255. – 100 k. black, green & bistre 45 15
2256. – 250 k. multicoloured 95 50
DESIGNS: 50 k. Ataturk's Cenotaph. 60 k. Ataturk at carriage window. (32½ × 43 mm.). 100 k. Ataturk's portrait and "address to youth". 250 k. Ataturk in military uniform.

1968. Greetings Card Stamps. As T **307** but dated "1968".
2257. 10 k. black and mauve .. 8 5
2258. 10 k. black and blue .. 8 5
DESIGNS: Equestrian statues of Ataturk at: No. 2257, Antakya. No. 2258, Zonguldak.

339. Karatay University, Konya. **340.** Dove and N.A.T.O. Emblem.

1968.
2259. – 1 k. sepia and brown 5 5
2260. – 10 k. maroon & purple 15 5
2261. **339.** 50 k. green and grey 40 5
2262. – 100 k. green.. .. 55 8
2263. – 200 k. blue .. .. 1·10 25
DESIGNS: 1 k. Ince Minara Mosque, Konya. 10 k. Doner Kumbet Tomb, Katseri. 100 k. Ortakoy Mosque, Istanbul. 200 k. Ulu Mosque, Divrigi.

1969. N.A.T.O. 20th Anniv.
2264. **340.** 50 k. + 10 k. black, blue and green .. 20 15
2265. – 130 k. + 10 k. gold and blue 45 40
DESIGN: 130 k. Stars around Globe, and N.A.T.O. Emblem.

341. "Education". **342.** I.L.O. Emblem.

1969.
2266. **341.** 1 k. black and red .. 5 5
2267. 1 k. black and green .. 5 5
2268. 1 k. black and violet 5 5
2269. 1 k. black and brown 5 5
2270. 1 k. black and grey .. 5 5
2271. – 50 k. brown and ochre 10 5
2272. – 90 k. black and olive 20 5
2273. – 100 k. red and black .. 45 5
2274. – 180 k. violet & orange 70 15
DESIGNS: 50 k. Farm workers and tractor ("Agriculture"). 90 k. Ladle, factory and cogwheel ("Industry"). 100 k. Road sign and graph ("Highways"). 180 k. Derricks ("Oil Industry").

1969. Int. Labour Organisation. 50th Anniv.
2275. **342.** 130 k. red and black 35 25

343. "Halsa Sultan" (unknown artist). **344.** Colonnade.

1969. "Halsa Sultan" (medical pioneer). Commem.
2276. **343.** 60 k. multicoloured .. 35 25

1969. Europa.
2277. **344.** 100 k. multicoloured 25 20
2278. 130 k. multicoloured 35 35

345. Kemal Ataturk in 1919. **346.** Symbolic Map of Istanbul.

1969. Kemal Ataturk's Landing at Samsun. 50th Anniv. Multicoloured.
2279. 50 k. Type **345** 12 10
2280. 60 k. S.S. Bandirma (horiz.) 20 20

1969. 22nd Int. Chambers of Commerce Congress, Istanbul.
2281. **346.** 130 k. multicoloured 35 25

347. "Suleiman the Great holding Audience" (16th-cent. Turkish miniature). **348.** Kemal Ataturk in Civilian Dress.

1969. Regional Co-operation for Development. 5th Anniv. Multicoloured.
2282. 50 k. Type **347** 25 15
2283. 80 k. "Kneeling Servant" (17th-cent. Persian) .. 30 20
2284. 130 k. "Lady on Balcony" (18th-cent. Mogul-Pakistan) 55 45

1969. Erzurum Congress. 50th Anniv.
2285. **348.** 50 k. black and violet 15 12
2286. – 60 k. black and green 20 15
DESIGN—HORIZ. 60 k. Ataturk's statue, Erzurum.

349. Red Cross Societies' Emblems.

1969. 21st Int. Red. Cross Conf., Istanbul.

2291. **349.** 100 k.+10 k. red, blue and ultramarine .. 30 20
2292. – 130 k.+10 k. mult. .. 30 30

DESIGN: No. 2292, Conference emblems and Istanbul.

350. Congress Hall.

1969. Sivas Congress. 50th Anniv.

2293. **350.** 50 k. pur., blk. & cerise 15 12
2294. – 60 k. olive, blk. & yell. 20 15

DESIGN: 60 k. Congress delegates.

351. Bar Dancers.

1969. Turkish Folk-dances. Multicoloured.

2295. 30 k. Type **351** 15 15
2296. 50 k. Caydacira "candle" dance 20 20
2297. 60 k. Halay scarf dance .. 20 20
2298. 100 k. Kilic-Kalkan sword dance 30 15
2299. 130 k. Zeybek Dance (vert.) 55 35

352. Bleriot Aeroplane, "Prince Celaleddin".

1969. 1st Turkish Airmail Service. 55th Anniv.

2300. **352.** 60 k. blue 15 12
2301. – 75 k. black and bistre 20 20

DESIGN: 75 k. 1914 First Flight covers.

353. "Kutadgu Bilig".

1969. Kutadgu Bilig" (political manual) Completion. 900th Anniv.

2302. **353.** 130 k. brown, gold and bistre 30 25

1969. Greetings Card Stamp. As T **307.**

2303. 10 k. brown and green .. 5 5

DESIGN: 10 k. Equestrian statue of Ataturk at Bursa.

355. "Ataturk's Arrival" (S. Tuna).

1969. Kemal Ataturk's Arrival in Ankara. 50th Anniv. Multicoloured.

2304. 50 k. Type **355** 30 12
2305. 60 k. Ataturk's motorcade 30 20

356. "Erosion Control".

1970. Nature Conservation Year. Multicoloured.

2306. 50 k.+10 k. Type **356** .. 25 25
2307. 60 k.+10 k. "Protection of Flora" 35 35
2308. 130 k.+10 k. "Protection of Wildlife" 65 65

357. Bosphorus Bridge (model). (Reduced size illus., actual size 79×30½ mm.).

1970. Commencement of work on Bosphorus Bridge. Multicoloured.

2309. 60 k. Type **357** 35 20
2310. 130 k. Symbolic bridge linking Europe & Asia 1·25 1·25

358. Ataturk Signature. **359.** Education Year Emblem.

1970.

2311. **358.** 1 k. brown and red .. 5 5
2312. 50 k. green and olive 15 8

1970. Int. Education Year.

2313. **359.** 130 k. blue, pur. & mve. 30 20

360. Turkish Pavilion Emblem. **361.** Kemal Ataturk.

1970. World Fair "Expo 70", Osaka, Japan. Multicoloured.

2314. 50 k. Type **360** 15 8
2315. 100 k. Turkish pavilion and Expo emblem 25 15

1970.

2316. **361.** 5 k. black on silver .. 8 5
2317. 30 k. black on bistre 15 5
2318. 50 k. black on pink .. 40 5
2319. 75 k. black on lilac .. 60 10
2320. 100 k. black on blue 85 10

362. Opening Ceremony.

1970. Turkish National Assembly. 50th Anniv. Multicoloured.

2321. 50 k. Type **362** 15 10
2322. 60 k. First Assembly in session 20 15

363. Emblem of Cartographic Directorate.

1970. "75 Years of Turkish Cartography". Multicoloured.

2323. 50 k. Type **363** 20 5
2324. 60 k. Aircraft and contour map 30 15
2325. 100 k. Survey equipment 30 15
2326. 130 k. Lt.-Gen. Mehmet Sevki Pasha and relief map of Turkey .. 75 75

Nos. 2324 and 2326 are larger, size 48×33 mm.

364. "Flaming Sun".

1970. Europa.

2327. **364.** 100 k. red, orge. & blk. 20 15
2328. 130 k. grn., orge. & blk. 40 35

365. New U.P.U. Headquarters Building. **366.** "Roe-deer" (Seker Ahmet Pasha).

1970. New U.P.U. Headquarters Building.

2329. **365.** 60 k. black and blue .. 15 12
2330. 130 k. black & green 35 25

1970. Turkish Paintings. Multicoloured.

2331. 250 k. Type **366** 65 50
2332. 250 k. "Lady with Mimosa" (Osman Hamdi) 65 50

See also Nos. 2349/50, 2364/5, 2396/7, 2416/17 and 2442/3.

367. "Turkish Folklore". **368.** Fethiye (Turkey).

1970. "Ankara 70" National Stamp Exhib. Multicoloured.

2333. 10 k. "Tree" of stamps and open album (vert.) 5 5
2334. 50 k. Type **367** .. 12 8
2335. 60 k. Ataturk statue and "stamps" 20 12

1970. Regional Co-operation for Development. 6th Anniv.

2337. 60 k. Type **368** 12 12
2338. 80 k. Seeyo-Se-Pol Bridge, Isfahan (Persia) .. 20 15
2339. 130 k. Saiful Malook Lake (Pakistan) 35 25

No. 2338 is larger (41×26 mm.).

369. Haci Bektas Veli's Tomb. **370.** Symbolic "Fencer" and Globe.

1970. Haci Bektas Veli (mystic). 700th Death Anniv. Multicoloured.

2340. 30 k. Type **369** 8 5
2341. 100 k. Sultan Balim's tomb (vert.) 20 20
2342. 180 k. Haci Bektas Veli (vert.) 50 35

No. 2342 is larger, size 32×49 mm.

1970. World Fencing Championships.

2343. **370.** 90 k.+10 k. black, blue and light blue 20 15
2344. – 130 k.+10 k. orange, green, black and blue 30 25

DESIGN: 130 k. Modern fencer, folk-dancer and globe.

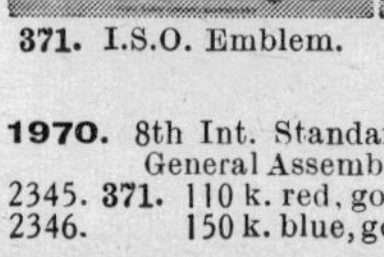

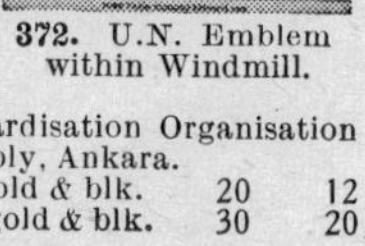

371. I.S.O. Emblem. **372.** U.N. Emblem within Windmill.

1970. 8th Int. Standardisation Organisation General Assembly, Ankara.

2345. **371.** 110 k. red, gold & blk. 20 12
2346. 150 k. blue, gold & blk. 30 20

1970. United Nations. 25th Anniv. Multicoloured.

2347. 100 k. Type **372** 20 12
2348. 220 k. World's People supporting U.N. (vert.) 40 25

1970. Turkish Paintings. As T **366.** Multicoloured.

2349. 250 k. "Fevzi Cakmak" (Avni Lifij) (vert.) .. 55 35
2350. 250 k. "Fishing-boats" (Nazmi Ziya) 55 35

No. 2350 is in a larger, horiz. size, 75×33 mm.

373. Battle Scene.

1971. Inonu. First Battle. 50th Anniv.

2351. **373.** 100 k. multicoloured 25 12

See also No. 2368.

374. Kemal Ataturk.

1971.

2352. **374.** 5 k. blue and grey .. 5 5
2353. 25 k. red and grey .. 8 5
2354. – 25 k. red and pink .. 8 5
2355. **374.** 100 k. violet and grey 20 5
2356. – 100 k. green and flesh 20 5
2357. – 250 k. blue and yellow 40 10
2358. **374.** 400 k. green & brown 60 15

DESIGNS: Nos. 2354, 2356 & 2357, portraits similar to T **374**, but larger, 21×26 mm., and with face value at bottom right.

375. "Turkish Village" (A. Sekur).

1971. Turkish Paintings. Multicoloured.

2364. 250 k. Type **375** 55 35
2365. 250 k. "Yildiz Palace Garden" (A. R. Bicakciler) 55 35

See also Nos. 2396/7, 2416/7 and 2443/4.

376. Hands enclosing "Four Races".

1971. Racial Equality Year.

2366. **376.** 100 k. multicoloured 20 12
2367. 250 k. multicoloured 40 30

1971. Inonu. Second Battle. 50th Anniv. Design similar to T **373.** Multicoloured.

2368. 100 k. Turkish machine-gunners 25 12

377. Europa Chain. **378.** Pres. C. Gursel.

1971. Europa.

2369. **377.** 100 k. vio., yell & blue 25 20
2370. 150 k. grn., red & orge. 30 25

1971. May 27th. 1960 Revolution. 11th Anniv.

2371. **378.** 100 k. multicoloured 20 12

379. Air Force Emblem and aircraft.

1971. Air. "60 Years of Turkish Aviation". Multicoloured.
2372. 110 k. "F-104G" Starfighter (vert.) .. 25 12
2373. 200 k. Victory Monument, Afyon and aircraft (vert.) 35 12
2374. 250 k. Type **379** 65 25
2375. 325 k. Starfighters and pilot .. 80 25
2376. 400 k. Bleriot "XIb" aircraft of 1911 .. 80 30
2377. 475 k. Hezarfen Celebi's "bird" flight from Galata Tower .. 1·25 40

380. "Care of Children".

1971. Children's Protection Society. 50th Anniv.
2378. **380.** 50 k.+10 k. red, pur. and black 15 10
2379. – 100 k.+15 k. mult. 20 15
2380. – 110 k.+15 k. mult. 25 20
DESIGNS—VERT. 100 k. Child standing on protective hand. HORIZ. 110 k. Mother and child.

381. Badshahi Mosque (Pakistan).

1971. Regional Co-operation for Development Pact. Mosques. 7th Anniv. Multicoloured.
2381. 100 k. Selimye Mosque, Istanbul (vert.) .. 20 12
2382. 150 k. Chaharbagh Mosque School (Persia) (vert.) 25 12
2383. 200 k. Type **381** 30 15

382. Alpaslan (Seljuk leader) and Cavalry.

1971. Battl of Malazgirt. 900th Anniv.
2384. **382.** 100 k. multicoloured 30 15
2385. – 250 k. red, yell. & blk. 60 35
DESIGN: 250 k. Seljuk mounted Archer.

383. Officer and Troop Column.

1971. Sakarya Victory. 50th Anniv.
2386. **383.** 100 k. multicoloured 20 12

384. Train Crossing Bridge (Turkey-Bulgaria Route).

1971. Int. Rail Links.
2387. **384.** 100 k. multicoloured 30 12
2388. – 110 k. violet and blue 30 20
2389. – 250 k. multicoloured 60 15
DESIGNS: 110 k. Train Ferry, Lake Van (Turkey-Iran Route). 250 k. Train and map (Turkey-Iran Route).

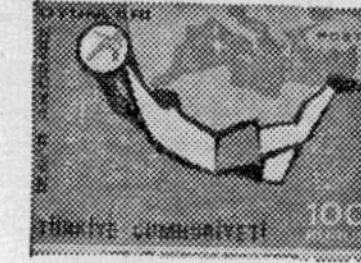

385. Football.

1971. Mediterranean Games, Izmir.
2390. **385.** 100 k. blk., vio. & bl. 25 12
2391. – 200 k. multicoloured 35 25
DESIGN—VERT. 200 k. "Athlete and stadium".

386. Tomb of Cyprus the Great.

1971. Persian Empire. 2500th Anniv.
2393. **386.** 25 k. multicoloured .. 12 5
2394. – 100 k. multicoloured 35 25
2395. – 150 k. brown & buff .. 40 35
DESIGNS—VERT. 100 k. Persian mosaic of woman. HORIZ. 150 k. Kemal Ataturk and Riza Shah Pahlavi of Persia.

387. "Sultan Mahmut I and Entourage".

1971. Turkish Paintings. Multicoloured.
2396. 250 k. Type **387** 55 35
2397. 250 k. "Cinilli Kosk Palace" 55 35

388. U.N.I.C.E.F. Emblem.

389. Yunus Emre.

1971. U.N.I.C.E.F. 25th Anniv.
2404. **388.** 100 k.+10 k. mult... 25 20
2405. 250 k.+15 k. mult... 45 30

1971. Yunus Emre (folk-poet). 650th Death Anniv.
2406. **389.** 100 k. multicoloured 20 12

390. First Turkish World Map (1072) and Book Year Emblem.

1972. Int. Book Year.
2407. **390.** 100 k. multicoloured 20 12

391. Doves and N.A.T.O. Emblem.

392. Human Heart.

1972. Turkey's Membership of N.A.T.O. 20th Anniv.
2408. **391.** 100 k. blk., grey & grn. 30 15
2409. 250 k. blk., grey & bl. 45 30

1972. World Health Day.
2410. **392.** 250 k.+25 k. red, blk. and grey 45 35

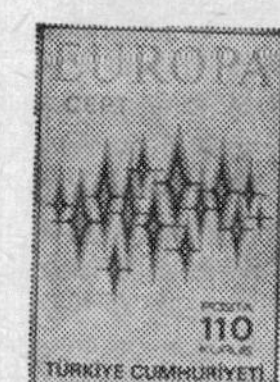

393. "Communications".

394. "Fisherman" (G. Dareli).

1972. Europa.
2414. **393.** 110 k. multicoloured 25 15
2415. 250 k. multicoloured 45 25

1972. Turkish Paintings. As T **375**. Mult.
2416. 250 k. "Gebze" (Osman Hamdi) 45 30
2417. 250 k. "Forest" (S. A. Pasa) 45 30

1972. Greetings Card stamp. As T **307**.
2418. 25 k. black and yellow .. 5 5

1972. Regional Co-operation for Development. Multicoloured.
2419. 100 k. Type **394** .. 20 12
2420. 125 k. "Will and Power" (Chunghtai) 25 12
2421. 150 k. "Iranian Woman" (Behzad) 25 20

395. Olympic Rings.

1972. Olympic Games, Munich.
2422. **395.** 100 k.+15 k. mult. .. 20 20
2423. – 110 k.+25 k. mult. .. 20 20
2424. – 250 k.+25 k. mult. .. 45 35
DESIGNS: 110 k. "Athletes". 250 k. "Stadium".

396. Observation Post.

1972. Turkish War of Independence. 50th Anniv. Multicoloured.

(a) "Grand Offensive".
2425. 100 k. Type **396** 20 10
2426. 110 k. Artillery 20 12

(b) "Commander-in-Chief's Battle".
2427. 100 k. Hand-to-hand fighting 20 10

(c) "Entry into Izmir".
2428. 100 k. Commanders in open car 20 8

397. "Diagnosis and Cure".

398. Kemal Ataturk.

1972. Fight Against Cancer.
2429. **397.** 100 k. red, blk & bl... 20 10

1972.
2430. **398.** 5 k. blue on pale blue 5 5
2431. 100 k. brown on buff 12 8
2432. 110 k. blue on pale bl. 20 8
2433. 125 k. green on grey .. 25 8
2434. 150 k. brn. on pale brn. 20 10
2435. 175 k. pur. on yellow 25 10
2436. 200 k. red on buff .. 25 10
2436a. 400 k. blue on grey .. 35 12
2437. 500 k. violet on pink 70 15
See also Nos. 7543/9.

399. U.I.C. Emblem.

400. University Emblem.

1972. International Railways Union. 50th Anniv.
2439. **399.** 100 k. red, grn & yell. 20 10

1973. Technical University, Istanbul. Bicent.
2440. **400.** 100 k.+25 k. mult. 20 10

401. Europa "Posthorn".

402. Helmet and Sword.

1973. Europa.
2441. **401.** 110 k. multicoloured 20 12
2442. 250 k. multicoloured 35 25

1973. Turkish Painters. As T **375**. Mult.
2443. 250 k. "Old Alms-house, Istanbul" (Ahmet Ziya Akbulut) (horiz.) .. 45 30
2444. 250 k. "Flowers in Vase" (Suleyman Syyit) (vert.) 45 30

1973. Land Forces Day.
2445. **402.** 90 k. grn., brn. & grey 12 10
2446. – 100 k. grn., brn. and light green .. 20 10
DESIGN: 100 k. As Type **402**, but wreath enclosing design.

403. Mausoleum of King Antiochus I (Turkey).

404. Peace Dove and "50".

1973. Regional Co-operation for Development.
2447. **403.** 100 k. multicoloured 15 10
2448. 150 k. gold, grn. & brn. 25 15
2449. – 200 k. multicoloured 35 20
DESIGNS: 150 k. Statue, Lut Desert excavations (Iran). 200 k. Main Street, Moenjodaro (Pakistan).

1973. Lausanne Peace Treaty. 50th Anniv.
2450. **404.** 100 k.+25 k. mult. 20 12

405. Destroyer "Nusret".

406. "Al-Biruni" (from 16th-century miniature).

1973. Turkish Navy. Multicoloured.
2451. 5 k. Type **405** 5 5
2452. 25 k. Destroyer "Istanbul" 5 5
2453. 100 k. M.T.B. "Simsek" 12 8
2454. 250 k. Sail-training ship "Nurud-i-Futuh" (48×32 mm.) 55 30

1973. Abu Reihan al-Biruni. Millennium.
2455. **406.** 250 k. multicoloured 30 25

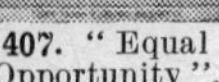

407. " Equal Opportunity ".

408. " Balkanfila " Emblem.

1973. Darussafaka High School. Cent.

2456. **407.** 100 k. multicoloured 20 10

1973. " Balkanfila IV " Stamp Exhibition, Izmir (1st issue).

2458. **408.** 100 k. multicoloured 20 10

See also Nos. 2462/3.

409. Sivas Shepherd Dog.

410. Kemal Ataturk.

1973. Multicoloured.

2459. 25 k. Type **409** .. 5 5

2460. 100 k. Angora cat .. 20 10

1973. Kemal Ataturk. 35th Death Anniv.

2461. **410.** 100 k. brown and drab 15 8

411. Bosphorus and " Stamps ".

412. " Flower " Emblem.

1973. " Balkanfila IV " Stamp Exhibition (2nd issue). Multicoloured.

2462. 110 k. Type **411** .. 15 12

2463. 250 k. " Balkanfila " in decorative script .. 30 20

1973. Republic. 50th Anniv. Mult.

2464. 100 k. Type **412** .. 12 10

2465. 250 k. " Hands " supporting " 50 " 30 20

2466. 475 k. Cogwheel and ears of corn 45 40

413. Bosphorus Bridge.

414. Bosphorus Bridge.

1973. Opening of Bosphorus Bridge, Istanbul. Multicoloured.

2468. 100 k. Type **413** 15 10

2469. 150 k. View of Bosphorus and bridge .. 20 15

1973. U.N.I.C.E.F. Ceremony. Children of Europe and Asia linked by Bosphorus Bridge.

2470. **414.** 200 k. multicoloured 30 20

415. Mevlana Celaleddin.

416. Cotton.

1973. Mevlana Celaleddin (poet and mystic). 700th Death Anniv. Multicoloured.

2471. 100 k. Tomb and " dancing dervishes " 12 10

2472. 250 k. Type **415** .. 25 25

1973. Export Products. Multicoloured.

2473. 75 k. Type **416** .. 8 10

2474. 90 k. Grapes 10 10

2475. 100 k. Figs 12 10

2476. 250 k. Citrus fruits .. 40 30

2477. 325 k. Tobacco 40 20

2478. 475 k. Hazelnuts .. 50 25

417. Fokker " Friendship " F-28.

418. President Inonu.

1973. Air. Multicoloured.

2479. 110 k. Type **417** 15 8

2480. 250 k. Douglas DC-10/10 30 15

1973. President Inonu's Death.

2481. **418.** 100 k. brown & buff .. 12 8

419. " Statue of a King " (Hittite era).

420. Doctor and Patient.

1974. Europa. Sculptures.

2482. 110 k. Type **419** 20 10

2483. 250 k. " Statuette of a Child " (c. 2000 B.C.) .. 30 25

1974. Sisli Paediatrics Hospital. 75th Anniv.

2484. **420.** 110 k. blk., grey & bl. 15 10

421. Silver and Gold Idol. 422. Population Year Emblem.

1974. Archeological Treasures. Multicoloured.

2485. 125 k. Type **421** 15 15

2486. 175 k. Painted jar (horiz.) 20 12

2487. 200 k. Bulls (statuettes) (horiz.) 25 10

2488. 250 k. Jug 40 25

1974. World Population Year.

2489. **422.** 250 k. +25 k. mult... 35 20

423. Turkish Carpet.

424. Dove and Map of Cyprus.

1974. Regional Co-operation for Development. Multicoloured.

2496. 100 k. Type **423** 12 8

2497. 150 k. Iranian carpet .. 20 12

2498. 200 k. Pakistan carpet .. 30 20

1974. Turkish Intervention in Cyprus.

2499. **424.** 250 k. multicoloured 40 20

425. " Getting to Grips. ".

426. U.P.U. " Dove ".

1974. World Free-style Wrestling Championships, Ankara. Multicoloured.

2500. 90 k. Type **425** 12 8

2501. 100 k. " Throw " (vert.) .. 15 8

2502. 250 k. " Lock " 30 20

1974. Universal Postal Union. Centenary.

2503. **426.** 110 k. gold, deep blue and blue 12 8

2504. – 200 k. green and brown 20 15

2505. – 250 k. multicoloured 25 20

DESIGNS: 200 k. Dove with fan tail. 250 k. Arrows encircling globe.

427. Law Books (" Reform of Laws ").

1974. Ataturk's Works and Reforms.

2506. **427.** 50 k. blue and black .. 5 5

2507. – 150 k. multicoloured 15 12

2508. – 400 k. multicoloured 40 30

DESIGNS—VERT. 150 k. " Tree " (" National Economy "). 400 k. Students facing Sun (" Reform of Education ").

428. Marconi.

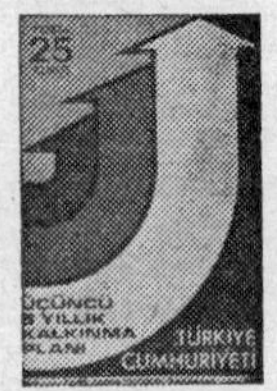

429. Rising Arrows.

1974. Guglielmo Marconi (radio pioneer). Birth Centenary.

2509. **428.** 250 k. +25 k. black, brown and red .. 30 25

1974. "Turkish Development". Multicoloured.

2510. 25 k. Type **429** 5 5

2511. 100 k. Map within cogwheel (horiz.) 15 8

430. Volleyball. 431. Dr. Schweitzer.

1974. Ball Games.

2512. **430.** 125 k. black & blue .. 15 10

2513. 175 k. blk. & orange .. 20 12

2514. – 250 k. black & green 30 15

DESIGNS: 175 k. Volleyball. 250 k. Football.

1975. Dr. Albert Schweitzer. Birth Cent.

2515. **431.** 250 k. +50 k. mult... 40 30

432. Automatic Telex Network.

1975. Posts and Telecommunications.

2516. **432.** 5 k. black and yellow 5 5

2517. — 50 k. green and orange 8 5

2518. — 100 k. black and blue 15 8

DESIGNS: 50 k. Postal cheques. 100 k. Radio link.

433. " Going to School ".

434. Karacaoglan Monument, Mut.

1975. Children's Drawings. Multicoloured.

2519. 25 k. Type **433** 5 5

2520. 50 k. " Village View " .. 8 5

2521. 100 k. " Folk-dancing " 15 8

1975. Karacaoglan Commemoration.

2522. **434.** 110 k. green, red & brn. 15 12

435. " Orange-gathering in Hatay " (C. Tollu).

1975. Europa. Paintings. Multicoloured.

2523. 110 k. Type **435** 20 12

2524. 250 k. "The Yorukas" (T. Zaim) .. 30 25

436. Turkish Porcelain Vase.

437. Namibia located on Map of Africa.

1975. Regional Co-operation for Development. Multicoloured.

2525. 110 k. Type **436** .. 12 10

2526. 200 k. Iranian tile (horiz.) 25 15

2527. 250 k. Pakistani camel-skin vase 30 20

1975. Namibia Day.

2528. **437.** 250 k. + 50 k. multicoloured .. 30 30

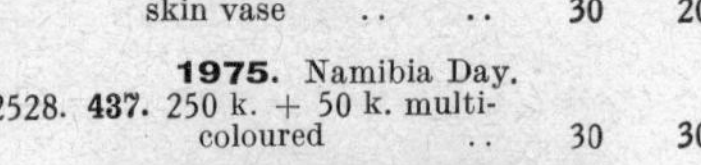

438. Horon Folk-dancers.

1975. Turkish Folk-dances. Multicoloured.

2529. 100 k Type **438** 10 8

2530. 125 k. Kasikli Oyun .. 12 10

2531. 175 k. Bengi 20 12

2532. 250 k. Kasap 20 15

2533. 325 k. Kafkas (vert.) .. 30 25

439. " St. George and the Dragon " (Oguz Khan).

440. Turbot.

1975. Tales of Dede Korkut. Multicoloured

2534. 90 k. Type **439** 8 5

2535. 175 k. Tale of Duha Koca Oglu Deli Dumrul Hikayesi (horiz.) .. 15 12

2536. 200 k. " Pillaging of Home of Salur Kazan " .. 20 15

1975. Fishes. Multicoloured.

2538. 75 k. Type **440** 8 5

2539. 90 k. Common carp .. 10 8

2540. 175 k. Trout 20 12

2541. 250 k. Red mullet .. 25 15

2542. 475 k. Red bream .. 40 35

1975.

2543. **398.** 25 k. red 5 5

2544. 100 k. grey 10 5

2545. 150 k. green 15 10

2546. 250 k. purple .. 25 15

2547. 400 k. turquoise .. 40 30

2548. 500 k. blue 45 40

2549. 10 l. mauve 90 80

The 10 l. is larger, 22 × 32 mm.

441. Two Women and Symbol.

1975. Reforms of Ataturk. Multicoloured.
2550. 100 k. Type **441** (Women's Participation in Public Life) .. 10 8
2551. 110 k. Hands holding ball (Nationalization of Insurance Companies) (vert.) .. 12 8
2552. 250 k Arrows (Orientation of the Fine Arts) 25 20

442. Z. Gokalp. **443.** Decorative Plate.

1976. Ziya Gokalp (philosopher). Birth Cent.
2553. **442.** 200 k.+25 k. multicoloured .. 20 20

1976. Europa. Multicoloured.
2554. 200 k. Type **443** .. 20 12
2555. 400 k. Dessert jug .. 35 25

444. Silhouette of Istanbul.

1976. Seventh Islamic Conf., Istanbul.
2556. **444.** 500 k. multicoloured 45 45

445. "Lunch in Field".

1976. "Samsun '76". 1st Nat. Juniors Stamp Exn. Multicoloured.
2557. 50 k. Type **445** .. 5 5
2558. 200 k. "Boats in Bosphorus" (vert.) 20 12
2559. 400 k. "Winter View" 35 25

446. Sultan Marshes.

1976. European Wetlands Conservation Year. Turkish Landscapes. Multicoloured.
2560. 150 k. Type **446** .. 15 10
2561. 200 k. Lake Manyas .. 20 12
2562. 250 k. Lake Borabay .. 25 15
2563. 400 k. Manavgat Waterfall .. 35 25

447. "Hodja with Liver". **448.** Olympic Flame.

1976. Nasreddin Hodja (humourist) Commem. "The Liver and the Kite". Multicoloured.
2564. 150 k. Type **447** .. 15 10
2565. 250 k. "Friend offers recipe" .. 25 15
2566. 600 k. "Kite takes liver, leaving recipe .. 60 55

1976. Olympic Games, Montreal. Multicoloured.
2567. 100 k. Type **448** .. 10 5
2568. 400 k. "76" and riband (horiz.) 35 25
2569. 600 k. Games emblem .. 60 55

449. Kemal Ataturk.

1976. Regional Co-operation for Development. Multicoloured.
2570. 100 k. Type **449** .. 10 5
2571. 200 k. Riza Shah Pahlavi (Iran) .. 20 12
2572. 250 k. Mohammad Ali Jinnah (Pakistan) .. 75 15

450. Peace Dove and Sword. **451.** Spoonbill.

1976. "Words and Reforms of Ataturk". Multicoloured.
2573. 100 k. Type **450** .. 10 5
2574. 200 k. "The Speeches of Ataturk" (books and listeners) .. 20 12
2575. 400 k. Peace doves and globe .. 35 25

1976. Turkish Birds. Multicoloured.
2576. 100 k.+25 k. Type **451** .. 12 12
2577. 150 k.+25 k. Roller .. 15 15
2578. 200 k.+25 k. Flamingo .. 20 20
2579. 400 k.+25 k. Bald ibis (horiz.) .. 40 40

452. "Hora".

1977. Turkish Exploration Ship.
2580. **452.** 400 k. multicoloured 35 25

OFFICIAL STAMPS

O 1. O 2. O 3. O 4.

1947.
O 1360. O 1. 10 p. brown .. 5 5
O 1361. 1 k. green .. 5 5
O 1362. 2 k. purple .. 12 5
O 1363. 3 k. orange .. 15 5
O 1364. 5 k. turquoise .. 3·75 5
O 1365. 10 k. brown .. 2·25 5
O 1366. 15 k. violet .. 55 5
O 1367. 20 k. blue .. 75 5
O 1368. 30 k. olive .. 75 5
O 1369. 50 k. blue .. 75 5
O 1370. 1 l. green .. 95 5
O 1371. 2 l. claret .. 1·25 15

1951. Postage stamps optd. **RESMI** between bars with star and crescent above.
O 1458. **126.** 25 p. red .. 5 5
O 1454. 5 k. blue .. 20 5
O 1461. 10 k. brown .. 20 5
O 1462. 15 k. violet .. 30 5
O 1456. 20 k. blue .. 30 8
O 1457. 30 k. brown .. 40 12
O 1465. 60 k. black .. 50 25

1955. Postage stamps optd. **RESMI** between wavy bars with star and crescent above or surch. also.
O 1568. **126.** 25 p. red .. 5 5
O 1587. ½ k. on 1 k. black 5 5
O 1569. 1 k. black .. 5 5
O 1570. 2 k. purple .. 5 5
O 1593. 2 k. on 4 k. green .. 5 5
O 1571. 3 k. orange .. 5 5
O 1594. 3 k. on 4 k. green .. 5 5
O 1572. 4 k. green .. 5 5
O 1573. 5 k. on 15 k. violet 5 5
O 1581. 5 k. blue .. 35 5
O 1595. 10 k. on 12 k. red .. 5 5
O 1574. 10 k. on 15 k. violet 8 5
O 1575. 15 k. violet .. 8 5
O 1576. 20 k. blue .. 15 10
O 1586. 30 k. brown .. 35 12
O 1577. 40 k. on 1 l. olive .. 20 15
O 1590. 75 k. on 1 l. olive .. 75 12
O 1578. 75 k. on 2 l. brown 50 35
O 1579. 75 k. on 5 l. purple 2·75 2·75

1957.
O 1655. O 2. 5 k blue .. 5 5
O 1843. 5 k. red .. 8 5
O 1656. 10 k. brown .. 5 5
O 1844. 10 k. olive .. 8 5
O 1657. 15 k. violet .. 5 5
O 1845. 15 k. red .. 8 5
O 1658. 20 k. red .. 5 5
O 1846. 20 k. violet .. 8 5
O 1659. 30 k. olive .. 10 5
O 1660. 40 k. purple .. 12 5
O 1847. 40 k. blue .. 12 8
O 1661. 50 k. grey .. 15 5
O 1662. 60 k. green .. 20 5
O 1848. 60 k. orange .. 30 12
O 1663. 75 k. orange .. 25 5
O 1849. 75 k. grey .. 30 12
O 1664. 100 k. green .. 30 8
O 1850. 100 k. violet .. 35 15
O 1665. 200 k. lake .. 65 15
O 1851. 200 k. brown .. 85 35

1960.
O 1916. O 3. 1 k. orange .. 5 5
O 1917. 5 k red .. 5 5
O 1918. 10 k. myrtle .. 35 5
O 1919. 30 k. brown .. 12 8
O 1920. 60 k. green .. 20 15
O 1921. 1 l. purple .. 50 25
O 1922. 1½ l. ultramarine .. 45 15
O 1923. 2½ l. violet .. 95 15
O 1924. 5 l. blue .. 1·90 45

1962.
O 1977. O 4. 1 k. olive-brown .. 5 5
O 1978. 5 k. green .. 5 5
O 1979. 10 k. brown .. 5 5
O 1980. 15 k. indigo .. 8 5
O 1981. 25 k. red .. 10 5
O 1982. 30 k. blue .. 12 5

1963. Surch.
O 2003. O 4. 50 k. on 30 k. blue 15 5
O 2004. O 3. 100 k. on 60 k. grn. 30 5

O 5. O 6. O 7.

1963.
O 2042. O 5. 1 k. bronze .. 5 5
O 2043. 5 k. chestnut .. 5 5
O 2044. 10 k. green .. 5 5
O 2045. 50 k. red .. 15 5
O 2046. 100 k. blue .. 30 5

1964.
O 2074. O 6. 1 k. grey .. 5 5
O 2075. 5 k. blue .. 5 5
O 2076. 10 k. yellow .. 5 5
O 2077. 30 k. red .. 8 5
O 2078. 50 k. green .. 12 5
O 2079. 60 k. brown .. 20 8
O 2080. 80 k. turquoise .. 25 8
O 2081. 130 k. indigo .. 45 10
O 2082. 200 k. purple .. 75 10

1965.
O 2133. O 7. 1 k. green .. 5 5
O 2134. 10 k. blue .. 5 5
O 2135. 50 k. orange .. 20 5

O 8. Usak Carpet. O 9. Doves Emblem. O 10.

1966. Turkish Carpets.
O 2175. O 8. 1 k. orange .. 5 5
O 2176. – 50 k. green .. 10 5
O 2177. – 100 k. red .. 20 8
O 2178. – 150 k. blue .. 35 12
O 2179. – 200 k. bistre .. 50 12
O 2180. – 500 k. lilac .. 1·25 40

DESIGNS (Carpets of): 50 k. Bergama. 100 k. Ladik. 150 k. Selcuk. 200 k. Nomad. 500 k. Anatolia.

1967.
O 2213. O 9. 1 k. blue & light blue 5 5
O 2214. 50 k. blue & orange 15 5
O 2215. 100 k. blue & mauve 20 8

1968.
O 2241. O 10. 50 k. brn. & grn... 12 5
O 2242. 150 k. blk. & orge. 35 5
O 2243. 500 k. brn. & blue 1·25 25

O 11. O 12. O 13.

1969.
O 2287. O 11. 1 k. red and green 5 5
O 2288. 10 k. blue and green 5 5
O 2289. 50 k. brown & green 12 5
O 2290. 100 k. magenta & grn. 20 8

1971.
O 2359. O 12. 5 k. blue & brown 5 5
O 2360. 10 k. red and blue 5 5
O 2361. 30 k. violet & orge. 12 5
O 2362. 50 k. brown & blue 20 5
O 2363. 75 k. green & buff 35 8

1971. Face-value and border colour given first.
O 2398. O 13. 5 k. blue and grey 5 5
O 2399. 25 k. green & brn. 8 5
O 2400. 100 k. brn. & grn. 20 5
O 2401. 200 k. brn. & ochre 35 8
O 2402. 250 k. pur. & vio. 40 12
O 2403. 500 k. blue & light blue .. 85 25

O 14. O 15. O 16. Trellis Motif.

1972.
O 2411. O 14. 5 k. blue & brown 5 5
O 2412. 100 k. grn. & brn. 10 5
O 2413. 200 k. red & brn. 20 5

1973.
O 2457. O 15. 100 k. blue & cream 12 5

1974.
O 2490. O 16. 10 k. brown on pink 5 5
O 2491. 25 k. pur. on blue 5 5
O 2492. 50 k. red on mauve 5 5
O 2493. 150 k. brn. on grn. 15 5
O 2494. 250 k. red on pink 25 8
O 2495. 500 k. brn. on yell. 60 25

O 17.

1975.
O 2537. O 17. 100 k red and blue 12 5

POSTAGE DUE STAMPS

1863. As T **1.** Imperf.
D 7. **1.** 20 pa. black on brown to brown-red .. 50·00 25·00
D 8. 1 pi. black on brown to brown-red .. 50·00 25·00
D 9. 2 pi. black on brown to brown-red .. £100 60·00
D 10. 5 pi. black on brown to brown-red .. 75·00 50·00

1865. As T **2.** Perf.
D 18. **2.** 20 pa. chocolate .. 12 25
D 19. 1 pi. chocolate .. 12 25
D 20. 2 pi. chocolate .. 75 1·50
D 21. 5 pi. chocolate .. 35 75
D 22. 25 pi. chocolate .. 7·50 10·00

ILLUSTRATIONS
British Commonwealth and all overprints and surcharges are FULL SIZE. Foreign Countries have been reduced to ¾-LINEAR.

D 1.

1868.
D 67. D 1. 20 pa. brown .. 1·60 35
D 73. 1 pi. brown .. 8·50 25
D 74. 2 pi. brown .. 25 50
D 70. 5 pi. brown .. 25 65
D 76. 25 pi. brown .. 5·00 6·00

1888. As T **3.**
D 117. **3.** 20 pa. black .. 8 15
D 118. 1 pi. black .. 8 15
D 119. 2 pi. black .. 8 15

1892. As T 4.

No.	Type	Description	Unused	Used
D 146.	4.	20 pa. black	50	20
D 147.		20 pa. black on red	10	10
D 148.		1 pi. black	65	30
D 149.		2 pi. black	25	12

1901. As T 5.

No.	Type	Description	Unused	Used
D 195.	5.	10 pa. black on red	40	30
D 196.		20 pa. black on red	35	25
D 197.		1 pi. black on red	12	12
D 198.		2 pi. black on red	8	5

1905. As T 7.

No.	Type	Description	Unused	Used
D 228.	7.	1 pi. black on red	50	35
D 229.		2 pi. black on red	85	75

1908. As T 9.

No.	Type	Description	Unused	Used
D 250.	9.	1 pi. black on red	1·75	65
D 251.		2 pi. black on red	35	65

1909. As T 11.

No.	Type	Description	Unused	Used
D 288.	11.	1 pi. black on red	1·90	1·90
D 287.		2 pi. black on red	15·00	15·00

1913. As T 12.

No.	Type	Description	Unused	Used
D 347.	12.	2 pa. black on red	10	10
D 348.		5 pa. black on red	10	10
D 349.		10 pa. black on red	10	10
D 350.		20 pa. black on red	10	10
D 351.		1 pi. black on red	1·25	1·00
D 352.		2 pi. black on red	2·50	1·50

1913. Adrianople issue surch.

No.	Type	Description	Unused	Used
D 356.	13.	2 pa. on 10 pa. green	25	12
D 357.		5 pa. on 20 pa. red	35	25
D 358.		10 pa. on 40 pa. blue	85	50
D 359.		20 pa. on 40 pa. blue	2·50	1·50

D 2. D 3.

D 4. D 5.

1914.

No.	Type	Description	Unused	Used
D 516.	D 2.	5 pa. purple	12	8
D 517.	D 3.	20 pa. red	20	12
D 518.	D 4.	1 pi. blue	65	35
D 519.	D 5.	2 pi. grey	65	50

D 6. D 7. Bridge over Kizil Irmak.

1921.

No.	Type	Description	Unused	Used
AD 91.	D 6.	20 pa. green	20	12
AD 92.		1 pi. green	15	15
AD 93.		2 pi. brown	65	35
AD 94.		3 pi. red	75	65
AD 95.		5 pi. indigo	85	85

1926.

No.	Type	Description	Unused	Used
D 1035.	D 7.	20 pa. orange	10	8
D 1036.		1 gr. red	12	12
D 1037.		2 gr. green	30	15
D 1038.		3 gr. purple	50	25
D 1039.		5 gr. violet	1·50	75

D 8.

1936.

No.	Type	Description	Unused	Used
D 1186.	D 8.	20 pa. brown	5	5
D 1187.		2 k. blue	5	5
D 1188.		3 k. violet	5	5
D 1189.		5 k. green	8	5
D 1190.		12 k. red	25	25

PRINTED MATTER STAMPS

(P 2.)

1891. Stamps of 1876 optd. with Type P 2.

No.	Type	Description	Unused	Used
N 132.	3.	10 pa. green	3·75	2·50
N 134.		20 pa. pink	3·00	2·00
N 136.		1 pi. blue	20·00	6·00
N 138.		2 pi. yellow	75·00	32·00
N 139.		5 pi. brown	£200	£100

1892. Stamps of 1892 optd. with Type P 2.

No.	Type	Description	Unused	Used
N 150.	4.	10 pa. green	25·00	3·75
N 151.		20 pa. red	38·00	15·00
N 152.		1 pi. blue	12·00	7·50
N 153.		2 pi. brown	15·00	7·50
N 154.		5 pi. purple	£120	75·00

(P 3.) (P 4.) (P 5.)

1894. Stamps of 1892 optd. with Type P 3.

No.	Type	Description	Unused	Used
N 161.	4.	5 pa. on 10 pa. grn. (160)	10	10
N 155.		10 pa. green	12	8
N 156a.		20 pa. red	8	8
N 157.		1 pi. blue	12	8
N 158.		2 pi. brown	3·75	1·10
N 159.		5 pi. purple	19·00	4·50

1901. Stamps of 1901 optd. with Type P 4.

No.	Type	Description	Unused	Used
N 183.	5.	5 pa. violet	25	12
N 184.		10 pa. green	1·50	20
N 185.		20 pa. red	20	12
N 186.		1 pi. blue	95	20
N 187.		2 pi. orange	6·00	1·00
N 188.		5 pi. mauve	9·00	5·50

1901. Stamps of 1901 optd. with Type P 4.

No.	Type	Description	Unused	Used
N 189.	6.	5 pa. brown	10	10
N 190.		10 pa. green	75	40
N 191.		20 pa. mauve	2·50	1·50
N 192.		1 pi. blue	4·00	2·00
N 193.		2 pi. blue	25·00	10·00
N 194.		5 pi. brown	30·00	12·00

1905. Stamps of 1905 optd. with Type P 4.

No.	Type	Description	Unused	Used
N 222.	7.	5 pa. orange	10	10
N 223.		10 pa. green	75	50
N 224.		20 pa. rose	25	10
N 225.		1 pi. blue	15	10
N 226.		2 pi. grey	7·50	2·50
N 227.		5 pi. brown	7·50	3·75

1908. Stamps of 1908 optd. with Type P 5.

No.	Type	Description	Unused	Used
N 244.	9.	5 pa. orange	2·00	15
N 245.		10 pa. green	2·00	15
N 246.		20 pa. rose	2·25	60
N 247.		1 pi. blue	3·75	90
N 248.		2 pi. black	11·00	3·75
N 249.		5 pi. purple	12·00	6·00

1909. Stamps of 1909 optd. with Type P 5.

No.	Type	Description	Unused	Used
N 276.		5 pa. orange	50	10
N 277.		10 pa. green	75	15
N 278.		20 pa. rose	4·25	1·00
N 279.		1 pi. blue	10·00	2·00
N 280.		2 pi. black	25·00	15·00
N 281.		5 pi. purple	25·00	15·00

1911. New value of 1909 issue.

No.	Type	Description	Unused	Used
N 332.	11.	2 pa. olive	10	10

1920. No. 500 surch.

No.	Type	Description	Unused	Used
N 961.	–	5 on 4 pa. brown	5	5

TURKS ISLANDS BC

A group of islands in the Br. W. Indies, S.E. of the Bahamas, now grouped with the Caicos Islands and using the stamps of Turks and Caicos Islands. A dependency of Jamaica until August, 1962, when it became a Crown Colony.

1.

1867.

No.	Type	Description	Unused	Used
4.	1.	1d. rose	15·00	15·00
55.		1d. brown	10·00	15·00
63.		1d. red	75	1·75
2.		6d. black	20	20
59.		6d. brown	3·00	3·00
3.		1s. blue	18·00	18·00
6.		1s. lilac	£1000	£500
60.		1s. brown	1·50	2·50
52.		1s. green	35·00	35·00

1881. Surch. with large figures.

No.	Type	Description	Unused	Used
17.	1.	½ on 1d. rose	12·00	12·00
7.		½ on 6d. black	22·00	25·00
9.		½ on 1s. blue	20·00	25·00
19.		½ on 1s. lilac	25·00	25·00
34.		2½ on 1d. red	75·00	
28.		2½ on 6d. black	60·00	60·00
29.		2½ on 1s. lilac	£200	£200
38.		2½ on 1s. blue	£140	
47.		4 on 1s. red	£130	£130
44.		4 on 6d. black	£140	£140
45.		4 on 1s. lilac	£150	

2.

3.

1881.

No.	Type	Description	Unused	Used
70.	2.	½d. green	25	35
56.		2½d. brown	6·00	8·00
65.		2½d. blue	1·00	95
50.		4d. blue	18·00	18·00
57.		4d. grey	2·50	3·00
71.		4d. purple and blue	1·00	3·50
72.	3.	5d. olive and red	1·00	3·50

1889. Surch. **One Penny.**

No.	Type	Description	Unused	Used
61.	2.	1d. on 2½d. brown	2·50	3·25

1893. Surch. **½d.** and bar.

No.	Type	Description	Unused	Used
67.	2.	½d. on 4d. grey	30·00	28·00

TURKS AND CAICOS ISLANDS BC

(See TURKS ISLANDS.)

1969. 100 cents—1 dollar.

1. Salt raking. 2.

1900.

No.	Type	Description	Unused	Used
110.	1.	½d. green	45	40
102.		1d. red	1·10	1·00
103.		2d. brown	1·25	1·25
104a.		2½d. blue	1·25	1·75
112.		3d. purple on yellow	1·40	3·00
105.		4d. orange	2·25	2·75
106.		6d. mauve	1·60	3·00
107.		1s. brown	1·40	3·00
108.	2.	2s. purple	25·00	30·00
109.		3s. red	25·00	28·00

3. Turk's-head Cactus. 4.

1909.

No.	Type	Description	Unused	Used
115.	3.	¼d. mauve	25	25
116.		¼d. red	12	15
162.	3.	¼d. black	10	15
117.	4.	½d. green	12	12
118.		1d. red	15	20
119.		2d. grey	1·75	2·50
120.		2½d. blue	1·10	1·75
121.		3d. purple on yellow	1·40	2·25
122.		4d. red on yellow	2·50	2·50
123.		6d. purple	4·00	3·50
124.		1s. black on green	3·00	3·50
125.		2s. red on green	14·00	17·00
126.		3s. black on red	17·00	19·00

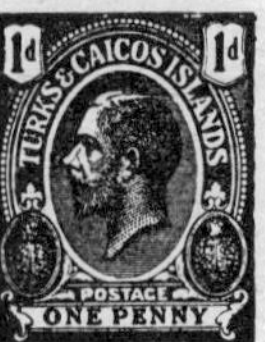

5.

1913.

No.	Type	Description	Unused	Used
129.	5.	½d. green	15	25
130b.		1d. red	70	70
131.		2d. grey	45	60
132		2½d. blue	1·75	2·00
133.		3d. purple on yellow	1·40	2·50
134a.		4d. red on yellow	1·40	2·50
159.		5d. green	2·25	3·50
136.		6d. purple	3·00	3·75
137.		1s. orange	1·40	2·50
138.		2s. red on green	5·00	6·00
139.		3s. black on red	11·00	15·00

1917. Optd. WAR TAX in one line.

No.	Type	Description	Unused	Used
143.	5.	1d. red	12	20
144.		3d. purple on yellow	25	40

WAR TAX (6.) WAR TAX (7.) WAR TAX (8.)

1918. T 5 optd.

No.	Type	Description	Unused	Used
146.	6.	1d. red	30	45
150.	7.	1d. red	12	20
152.	8.	1d. red	15	20
148.	6.	3d. purple on yellow	25	30
151.	7.	3d. purple on yellow	50	65
153.	8.	3d. purple on yellow	15	25

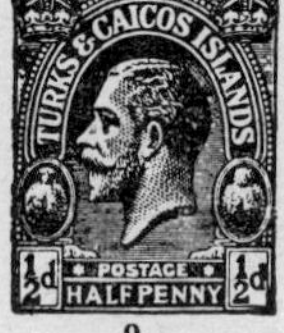

9.

10.

1922. Inscr. "POSTAGE".

No.	Type	Description	Unused	Used
163.	9.	¼d. green	15	25
164.		1d. brown	50	65
165.		1½d. red	80	85
166.		2d. grey	65	85
167.		2½d. purple on yellow	15	40
168.		3d. blue	80	90
169.		4d. red on yellow	90	1·10
170.		5d. green	80	1·50
171.		6d. purple	1·00	1·50
172.		1s. orange	1·10	2·25
173.		2s. red on green	3·50	4·50
175.		3s. black on red	4·00	5·50

1928. Inscr. "POSTAGE & REVENUE".

No.	Type	Description	Unused	Used
176.	10.	½d. green	12	12
177.		1d. brown	12	20
178.		1½d. red	20	40
179.		2d. grey	25	20
180.		2½d. purple on yellow	40	50
181.		3d. blue	40	70
182.		6d. purple	60	80
183.		1s. orange	1·00	1·50
184.		2s. red on green	4·00	5·50
185.		5s. green on yellow	16·00	20·00
186.		10s. purple on blue	22·00	25·00

1935. Silver Jubilee. As T 11 of Antigua.

No.	Type	Description	Unused	Used
187.		½d. black and green	10	15
188.		3d. brown and blue	55	70
189.		5d. blue and olive	80	90
190.		1s. grey and purple	2·25	2·75

1937. Coronation. As T 2 of Aden.

No.	Type	Description	Unused	Used
191.		½d. green	8	8
192.		2d. grey	12	15
193.		3d. blue	20	25

11. Raking Salt. 12. Salt Industry.

1938.

No.	Type	Description	Unused	Used
194.	11.	¼d. black	8	8
195a.		½d. green	8	10
196.		1d. brown	8	8
197.		1½d. red	8	10
198.		2d. grey	8	8
199a.		2½d. orange	8	8
200.		3d. blue	8	8
201.		6d. mauve	1·50	1·10
201a.		6d. brown	20	30
202.		1s. brown	1·00	2·50
202a.		1s. olive	45	50
203a.	12.	2s. red	80	1·10
204a.		5s. green	2·25	2·75
205.		10s. violet	3·00	3·75

1946. Victory. As T 4 of Aden.

No.	Type	Description	Unused	Used
206.		2d. grey	8	8
207.		3d. blue	10	8

1948. Silver Wedding. As T 5/6 of Aden.

No.	Type	Description	Unused	Used
208.		1d. brown	8	8
209.		10s. violet	3·75	6·00

13. Badge of the Dependency.

DESIGNS — HORIZ. 6d. Map of Turks and Caicos Is. 2s., 5s., 10s. Queen Victoria and King George VI.

14. Blue Ensign bearing Dependency Badge.

1948. Dependency's Separation from the Bahamas. Cent.

210. **13.** ½d. green 10 15
211. 2d. red 25 25
212. **14.** 3d. blue 30 40
213. – 6d. violet 40 50
214. – 2s. black and blue .. 75 95
215. – 5s. black and green .. 2·50 2·75
216. – 10s. black and brown .. 7·00 9·00

1949. U.P.U. As T **14/17** of Antigua.

217. 2½d. orange 10 20
218. 3d. blue 25 35
219. 6d. brown 40 50
220. 1s. olive 65 80

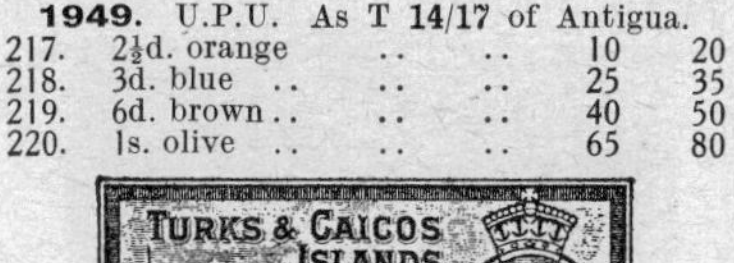

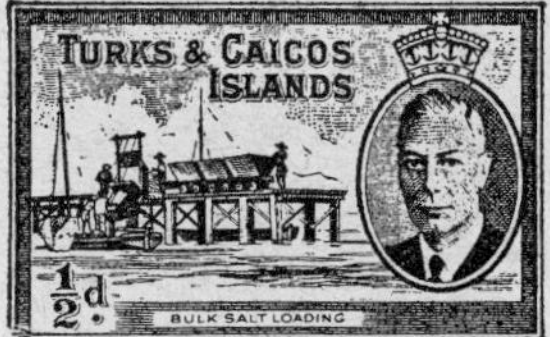

15. Bulk Salt Loading.

16. Government House.

17. Dependency's Badge.

1950.

221. **15.** ½d. green 12 12
222. – 1d. brown 12 20
223. – 1½d. red 15 25
224. – 2d. orange 12 25
225. – 2½d. olive 15 35
226. – 3d. blue 15 35
227. – 4d. black and pink .. 50 60
228. – 6d. black and blue .. 70 75
229. **16.** 1s. black and blue-green 60 75
230. – 1s. 6d. black and red .. 90 1·10
231. – 2s. green and blue .. 1·25 2·00
232. – 5s. blue and black .. 3·00 3·75
233. **17.** 10s. black and violet .. 5·00 6·00

DESIGNS—As T **15**: 1d. Salt Cay. 1½d. Caicos mail. 2d. Grand Turk. 2½d. Diving for sponges. 3d. South Creek. As T **16**: 4d. Map. 6d. Grand Turk Light. 1s. 6d. Cockburn Harbour. 2s. Govt. Offices. 5s. Loading salt.

1953. Coronation. As T **7** of Aden.

234. 2d. black and orange .. 25 40

1955. As 1950 but with portrait of Queen Elizabeth II.

235. 5d. black and green .. 30 40
236. 8d. black and brown .. 50 60

DESIGNS—HORIZ. As T **16**, 5d. M.V. "Kirksons." 8d. Flamingoes in flight.

18. Queen Elizabeth II (after Annigoni).

19. Bonefish.

20. Pelican.

1957.

237. **18.** 1d. blue and red .. 5 5
238. **19.** 1½d. grey and orange .. 5 5
239. – 2d. brown and olive .. 5 5
240. – 2½d. red and green .. 8 8
241. – 3d. turquoise & purple 8 8
242. – 4d. lake and black .. 10 10
243. – 5d. green and brown .. 12 12
244. – 6d. rose and blue .. 12 12
245. – 8d. vermilion and black 15 15
246. – 1s. blue and black .. 25 25
247. – 1s. 6d. sepia and blue 60 70
248. – 2s. blue and brown .. 80 90
249. – 5s. black and red .. 1·75 2·00
250. – 10s. black and purple 3·50 4·00
253. **20.** £1 sepia and red .. 8·00 9·00

DESIGNS—HORIZ. As T **19**: 2d. Red grouper. 2½d. Spiny lobster. 3d. Albacore. 4d. Mutton-fish snapper. 5d. Permit. 6d. Conch. 8d. Flamingoes. 1s. Spanish mackerel. 1s. 6d. Salt Cay. 2s. Caicos sloop. 5s. Cable Office. As T **20**. 10s. Dependency's Badge.

21. Map of the Turks and Caicos Is.

1959. New Constitution.

251. **21.** 6d. olive and orange .. 40 50
252. 8d. violet and orange .. 45 60

1963. Freedom from Hunger. As T **10** of Aden.

254. 8d. red 50 60

1963. Red Cross Cent. As T **24** of Antigua.

255. 2d. red and black .. 12 12
256. 8d. red and blue 70 70

1964. Shakespeare. 400th Birth Anniv. As T **25** of Antigua.

257. 8d. green 20 25

1965. I.T.U. Cent. As T **26** of Antigua.

258. 1d. red and brown .. 8 8
259. 2s. green and blue .. 60 65

1965. I.C.Y. As T **27** of Antigua.

260. 1d. purple and turquoise 5 5
261. 8d. green and lavender .. 30 35

1966. Churchill Commem. As T **28** of Antigua.

262. 1d. blue 5 5
263. 2d. green 8 8
264. 8d. brown 30 30
265. 1s. 6d. violet 60 65

1966. Royal Visit. As T **29** of Antigua.

266. 8d. black and blue .. 20 25
267. 1s. 6d. black and magenta 35 40

22. Andrew Symmers and Royal Warrant.

1966. "Ties with Britain". Bicent.

268. – 1d. blue and orange .. 5 5
269. **22.** 8d. red, blue and yellow 20 20
270. – 1s. 6d. multicoloured .. 30 35

DESIGNS: 1d. Andrew Symmers going ashore. 1s. 6d. Arms and Royal Cypher.

1966. U.N.E.S.C.O. 20th Anniv. As T **33/5** of Antigua.

271. 1d. violet, red. yell. & orge. 5 5
272. 8d. yellow violet and olive 25 30
273. 1s. 6d. black purple & orge. 40 45

23. Turk's Head Cactus.

DESIGNS—HORIZ. 1½d. Boat-building. 4d. Conch Industry. 1s. Fishing. 2s. Crawfish Industry. 3s. Maps of Turks and Caicos Islands and (inset) West Indies. 5s. Fishing Industry. 10s. Arms of Turks and Caicos Islands. VERT. 2d. Donkey Cart. 3d. Sisal Industry. 6d. Salt Industry. 8d. Skin-diving. 1s. 6d. Water-skiing. £1, Queen Elizabeth II.

1967.

274. **23.** 1d. yell., verm. & violet 5 5
275. – 1½d. brown and yellow 5 5
276. – 2d. slate & orange-yellow 5 5
277. – 3d. agate and green .. 5 5
278. – 4d. mauve, blk. & turq. 8 8
279. – 6d. sepia and blue .. 10 10
280. – 8d. yell., turq. & blue 12 12
281. – 1s. maroon and turquoise 20 20
282. – 1s. 6d. yell., brown & blue 40 40
283. – 2s. multicoloured .. 40 50
284. – 3s. maroon and blue .. 45 50
285. – 5s. ochre, blue and light blue 40 60
286. – 10s. multicoloured .. 2·00 2·50
287. – £1 blue, silver and red .. 4·00 4·50

24. Turks Islands 1d. Stamp of 1867.

1967. Stamp Cent.

288. **24.** 1d. black and magenta 5 5
289. – 6d. black and grey .. 15 20
290. – 1s. black and blue .. 30 30

DESIGNS: 6d. Queen Elizabeth "Stamp" and Turks Islands 6d. Stamp of 1867. 1s. As T **20** but shows the 1s. stamp of 1867 in place of the 1d.

25. Human Rights Emblem and Charter.

1968. Human Rights Year.

291. **25.** 1d. multicoloured .. 5 5
292. 8d. multicoloured .. 15 15
293. 1s. 6d. multicoloured .. 30 30

26. Dr. Martin Luther King and "Freedom March".

1968. Martin Luther King. Commem.

294. **26.** 2d. brown and blue .. 5 5
295. 8d. brown and lake .. 15 15
296. 1s. 6d. brn. and violet .. 30 30

1969. Decimal Currency. Nos. 274/87 surch., and new value in old design (¼ c.).

297. ¼ c. mult. (as No. 286) .. 5 5
298. 1 c. on 1d. multicoloured .. 5 5
299. 2 c. on 2d. multicoloured .. 5 5
300. 3 c. on 3d. multicoloured .. 5 5
301. 4 c. on 4d. multicoloured .. 8 8
302. 5 c. on 6d. multicoloured .. 10 10
303. 7 c. on 8d. multicoloured .. 12 12
304. 8 c. on 1½d. multicoloured 12 15
305. 10 c. on 1s. multicoloured 20 20
306. 15 c. on 1s. 6d. mult. .. 30 35
307. 20 c. on 2s. multicoloured 30 35
308. 30 c. on 3s. multicoloured 45 50
309. 50 c. on 5s. multicoloured 75 85
310. $1 on 10s. multicoloured 1·75 2·00
311a. $2 on £1 multicoloured .. 3·00 4·00

27. "The Nativity with John the Baptist".

1969. Christmas. Multicoloured.

312. 1 c. Type **27** 5 5
313. 3 c. "The Flight into Egypt" 5 5
314. 15 c. As T **27** 30 30
315. 30 c. As 3 c. 45 50

28. Coat of Arms.

1970. New Constitution.

316. **28.** 7 c. multicoloured .. 15 15
317. 35 c. multicoloured .. 55 60

29. "Christ bearing the Cross" (Durer).

1970. Easter.

318. **29.** 5 c. grey and blue .. 8 8
319. – 7 c. grey and vermilion 12 12
320. – 50 c. grey and brown .. 80 85

DESIGNS: 7 c. "Christ on the Cross" (Durer). 50 c. "The Lamentation for Christ" (Durer).

30. Dickens and Scene from "Oliver Twist".

1970. Charles Dickens. Death Cent.

321. **30.** 1 c. blk. & brn. on yell. 5 5
322. – 3 c. blk. & blue on flesh 8 8
323. – 15 c. blk. & blue on flesh 30 35
324. – 30 c. blk. & drab on blue 50 60

DESIGNS (showing Dickens and scene): 3 c. "A Christmas Carol". 15 c. "Pickwick Papers". 30 c. "The Old Curiosity Shop"

31. Ambulance – 1870.

1970. British Red Cross. Cent. Multicoloured.

325.	1 c. Type **31**	5	5
326.	5 c. Ambulance – 1970 ..	8	8
327.	15 c. Type **31**	20	30
328.	30 c. As 5 c.	40	45

32. Duke of Albemarle and Coat-of-Arms.

1970. Issue of Letters Patent. Tercent. Multicoloured.

329.	1 c. Type **32**	5	5
330.	8 c. Arms of Charles II and Elizabeth II ..	15	15
331.	10 c. Type **32**	20	25
332.	35 c As 8 c.	55	60

33. Boat-building.

1971. Decimal Currency. Designs as Nos. 274/87, but values in decimal currency as T **33**.

333.	**23.**	1 c. yellow, vermilion and violet	5	5
334.	–	2 c. slate and orange-yellow (as No. 276) ..	5	5
335.	–	3 c. agate and green (as No. 277)	5	5
336.	–	4 c. mauve, black and turquoise (as No. 278)	5	5
337.	–	5 c. sepia and blue (as No. 279)	8	8
338.	–	7 c. yellow, turquoise and blue (as No. 280)..	10	10
339.	**33.**	8 c. brown and yellow..	10	10
340.	–	10 c. maroon and turq. (as No. 281)	12	15
341.	–	15 c. yellow, brown and blue (as No. 282)	20	25
342.	–	20 c. mult. (as No. 283)	20	25
343.	–	30 c. maroon and blue (as No. 284)	40	45
344.	–	50 c. ochre, blue and light blue (as No. 285)	75	85
345.	–	$1 mult. (as No. 286) ..	1·50	1·75
346.	–	$2 blue, silver & red (as No. 287)	3·00	3·50

34. Seahorse.

1971. Tourist Development. Multicoloured.

347.	1 c. Type **34**	5	5
348.	3 c. Queen Conch shell ..	5	5
349.	15 c. Common Oyster Catcher	25	25
350.	30 c. Blue Marlin	50	50

Nos. 348/50 are horiz.

35. Pirate Sloop.

1971. Pirates. Multicoloured.

351.	2 c. Type **35**	5	5
352.	3 c. Pirate Treasure ..	8	8
353.	15 c. Marooned sailor ..	25	30
354.	30 c. Buccaneers	50	55

36. The Wilton Diptych (Left Wing).

1971. Christmas. Multicoloured.

355.	2 c. Type **36**	5	5
356.	2 c. The Wilton Diptych (Right Wing)	5	5
357.	8 c. Type **36**	12	15
358.	8 c. As No. 356	12	15
359.	15 c. Type **36**	25	25
360.	15 c. As No. 356	25	25

37. Cape Kennedy Launching Area.

1972. Colonel Glenn's Splashdown. 10th Anniv. Multicoloured.

361.	5 c. Type **37**	8	8
362.	10 c. "Friendship 7" space capsule	15	15
363.	15 c. Map of Islands and splashdown	25	25
364.	20 c. N.A.S.A. Space Medal (vert.)	35	35

38. "Christ before Pilate" (Rembrandt).

1972. Easter.

365.	**38.**	2 c. black and lilac ..	5	5
366.	–	15 c. black and pink ..	25	25
367.	–	30 c. black and yellow..	45	50

DESIGNS—HORIZ. 15 c. "The Three Crosses" (Rembrandt). VERT. 30 c. "The Descent from the Cross" (Rembrandt).

39. Christopher Columbus.

1972. Discoverers and Explorers. Mult.

368.	½ c. Type **39**	5	5
369.	8 c. Sir Richard Grenville (horiz.)	15	15
370.	10 c. Capt. John Smith ..	20	20
371.	30 c. Juan Ponce de Leon (horiz.)	60	60

1972. Royal Silver Wedding. As T **19** of Ascension but with Turk's Head Cactus and Spiny Lobster in background.

372.	10 c. blue	20	20
373.	20 c. green	40	40

40. Treasure Hunting, c. 1700.

1973. Treasure.

374.	**40.**	3 c. multicoloured ..	8	8
375.	–	5 c. pur., silver & black	10	10
376.	–	10 c. pur., silver & black	20	20
377.	–	30 c. multicoloured ..	60	60

DESIGNS: 5 c. Silver Bank medallion (obverse). 10 c. Silver Bank medallion (reverse). 30 c. Treasure hunting, 1973.

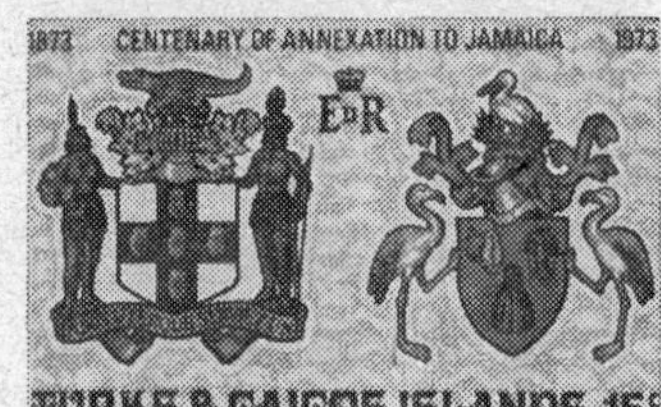

41. Arms of Turks and Caicos Islands, and Jamaica.

1973. Annexation by Jamaica. Cent.

378.	**41.**	15 c. multicoloured ..	25	25
379.		35 c. multicoloured ..	45	45

42. Sooty Tern.

1973.

381.	½ c. Type **42**	5	5
382.	1 c. Magnificent Frigate-bird	5	5
383.	2 c. Noddy Tern	5	5
384.	3 c. Blue-grey Gnatcatcher	8	8
385.	4 c. Blue Heron	5	5
386.	5 c. Catbird	5	5
387.	7 c. Black Whiskered Vireo	5	10
388.	8 c. Osprey	8	12

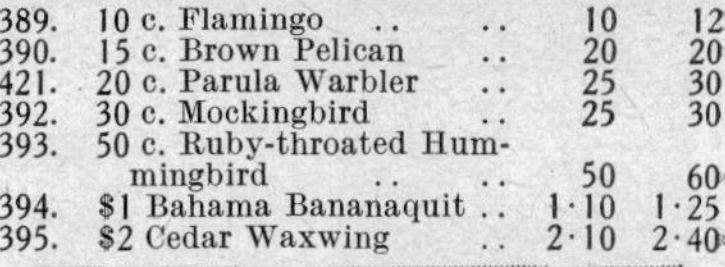

389.	10 c. Flamingo	10	12
390.	15 c. Brown Pelican ..	20	20
421.	20 c. Parula Warbler ..	25	30
392.	30 c. Mockingbird ..	25	30
393.	50 c. Ruby-throated Hummingbird	50	60
394.	$1 Bahama Bananaquit ..	1·10	1·25
395.	$2 Cedar Waxwing ..	2·10	2·40

43. Bermuda Sloop.

1973. Vessels. Multicoloured.

396.	2 c. Type **43**	5	5
397.	5 c. H.M.S. "Blanche" ..	8	8
398.	8 c. U.S. privateer "Grand Turk" and P.O. Packet "Hinchinbrooke" ..	12	12
399.	10 c. H.M.S. "Endymion"	15	15
400.	15 c. R.M.S. "Medina" ..	25	25
401.	20 c. H.M.S. "Darling" ..	30	30

1973. Royal Wedding. As T **26** of Anguilla. Multicoloured. Background colours given.

403.	12 c. blue	20	20
404.	18 c. blue	30	30

44. Duho (stool).

1974. Lucayan Remains. Multicoloured.

405.	6 c. Type **44**	8	8
406.	10 c. Broken wood bowl ..	12	12
407.	12 c. Greenstone axe ..	15	15
408.	18 c. Wood bowl	20	25
409.	35 c. Fragment of duho ..	40	45

45. G.P.O. Grand Turk.

1974. U.P.U. Centenary. Multicoloured.

426.	4 c. Type **45**	8	8
427.	12 c. Sloop and island-map	15	15
428.	18 c. "UPU" and globe..	20	25
429.	55 c. Posthorn and emblem	60	65

46. Churchill and Roosevelt.

1974. Sir Winston Churchill. Birth Centenary. Multicoloured.

430.	12 c. Type **46**	15	15
431.	18 c. Churchill and vapour-trails	25	25

47. Spanish Captain, circa 1492.

48. Ancient Windmill Salt Cay.

1975. Military Uniforms. Multicoloured.

433.		5 c. Type **47**	8	8
434.		20 c. Officer, Royal Artillery 1783	25	25
435.		25 c. Officer, 67th Foot, 1798	30	30
436.		35 c. Private, 1st West India Regiment, 1833 ..	40	45

1975. Salt-raking Industry. Multicoloured.

438.		6 c. Type **48**	10	10
439.		10 c. Salt pans drying in sun (horiz.)	12	12
440.		20 c. Salt-raking (horiz.)	25	25
441.		25 c. Unprocessed salt heaps	30	35

49. Star Coral.

1975. Island Coral. Multicoloured.

442.		6 c. Type **49**	8	8
443.		10 c. Elkhorn coral ..	12	20
444.		20 c. Brain coral ..	25	25
445.		25 c. Staghorn coral ..	30	35

50. American Schooner.

1976. American Revolution. Bicent. Mult.

446.		6 c. Type **50**	8	8
447.		20 c. British ship of the line	20	20
448.		25 c. American frigate "Grand Turk" ..	25	30
449.		55 c. British ketch ..	55	65

51. 1s. 6d. Royal Visit Stamp of 1966.

1976. Royal Visit. 10th Anniv. Multicoloured.

466.		20 c. Type **51**	20	25
467.		25 c. 8d. Royal Visit stamp	25	30

52. "Virgin and Child" (Dolci).

1976. Christmas. Multicoloured.

468.		6 c. Type **52**	5	8
469.		10 c. "Virgin and Child" (Studio of Botticelli) ..	12	15
470.		20 c. "Adoration of the Magi" (Mestre do Paraiso)	25	25
471.		25 c. "Adoration of the Magi" (French miniature)	30	35

53. Balcony Scene, Buckingham Palace.

1977. Silver Jubilee. Multicoloured.

472.		6 c. Queen presenting O.B.E. to E. T. Wood ..	5	8
473.		25 c. Queen with regalia ..	30	35
474.		55 c. Type **53**	65	75

TUSCANY E2

Formerly an independent duchy in C. Italy, now part of Italy.

1851. 60 quattrini = 20 soldi = 12 crazie = 1 Tuscan lira.
1859. 1 Tuscan lira = 1 Italian lira.

1. Arms of Tuscany.

2. Arms of Savoy.

1851. Imperf.

24.	**1.**	1 q. black	£150	£180
5.		1 s. orange	£1500	£400
6.		2 s. red	£5000	£1100
9.		1 c. red	£700	16·00
29.		2 c. blue	£250	15·00
15.		4 c. green	£700	18·00
19.		6 c. blue	£750	19·00
21.		9 c. purple	£1600	38·00
23.		60 c. red	£10000	£3750

1860. Imperf.

37.	**2.**	1 c. purple	£225	£110
39.		5 c. green	£900	38·00
43.		10 c. brown	£120	7·50
45.		20 c. blue	£550	23·00
48.		40 c. rose	£750	42·00
50.		80 c. red	£2000	£150
51.		3 l. yellow	£22000	£10000

TUVA O4

A province lying between the Sajan and Tannu Ola range. Formerly known as North Mongolia and Tannu Tuva, Tuva was incorporated into the U.S.S.R. on 11th October, 1944 and Soviet stamps are now in use.

PRICES. The prices quoted in the used column are for stamps cancelled to order where these occur. Postally used copies are worth considerably more.

1926. 100 kopecks = 1 rouble.
1935. 100 kopecks = 1 tugrik.
1936. 100 kopecks = 1 aksha.

1. Wheel of Eternity.

1926.

1.	**1.**	1 k. red	25	25
2.		2 k. blue	25	25
3.		5 k. orange	25	25
4.		8 k. green	25	25
5.		10 k. violet	25	25
6.		30 k. brown	25	25
7.		50 k. black	35	35
8.		1 r. blue-green	50	50
9.		3 r. claret	1·10	1·10
10.		5 r. blue	1·60	1·60

The rouble values are larger $22\frac{1}{2} \times 30$ mm.

1927. Surch. **TOUVA POSTAGE** and value.

11.	**1.**	8 k. on 50 k. black ..	65	65
12.		14 k. on 1 r. blue-green ..	1·00	1·00
13.		18 k. on 3 r. claret ..	1·10	1·10
14.		28 k. on 5 r. blue ..	2·00	2·00

2. Tuvan Woman.

3. Map of Tuva.

4. Mongolian Sheep and Tents.

5. Fording a River.

6. Reindeer.

1927.

15.	**2.**	1 k. brown, red and black	20	12
16.	–	2 k. brown, green & violet	30	20
17.	–	3 k. green, yellow & black	35	20
18.	–	4 k. chocolate and blue ..	20	12
19.	–	5 k. blue, black and orange	20	15
20.	**3.**	8 k. sepia, blue and claret	25	15
21.	–	10 k. red, black and green	30	20
22.	–	14 k. orange and blue ..	2·25	1·00
23.	**4.**	18 k. chocolate and blue	2·50	1·00
24.	–	28 k. sepia and green ..	1·10	40
25.	**5.**	40 k. green and red ..	70	40
26.	–	50 k. brown, black & grn.	70	40
27.	–	70 k. bistre and red ..	1·10	75
28.	**6.**	1 r. violet and brown ..	2·75	1·10

DESIGNS—As T **2**: 2 k. Stag. 3 k. Mountain goat. 4 k. Mongolian tent. 5 k. Hunters. As T **3**: 10 k. Archers. 14 k. Camel caravan. As T **4**: 28 k. Panorama. As T **5**: 50 k. Girl carpet-weaver. 70 k. Farmer.

1932. Stamps of 1927 surch. **TbBA POSTA** and value (10 k. optd. only).

29.	**5.**	1 k. on 40 k. green and red	65	65
30.	–	2 k. on 50 k. brown, black and green	65	65
31.	–	3 k. on 70 k. bistre and red	65	65
32.	**3.**	5 k. on 8 k. sep., bl. & clar.	65	65
33.	–	10 k. red, black and green	90	90
34.	–	15 k. on 14 k. orge. & blue	1·10	1·10

1932. Stamps of 1927 surch.

35.	**3.**	10 k. on 8 k. brown ..		
36.	–	15 k. on 14 k. orange & bl.		
37.	**4.**	35 k. on 18 k. choc. & blue	5·00	6·00
38.	–	35 k. on 28 k. sepia & green	5·00	6·00

1933. Fiscal stamps (20×39 mm.) surch. Posta and value.

(a) Numerals $6\frac{3}{4}$ mm. tall.

39.		15 k. on 6 k. yellow ..	5·00	5·00
40.		35 k. on 15 k. brown ..	25·00	25·00

(b) Numerals $5\frac{1}{4}$ mm. tall.

41.		15 k. on 6 k. yellow ..	8·00	8·00
42.		35 k. on 15 k. brown ..	32·00	32·00

NOTE. For many years we refrained from listing the following pictorial issues because it was known that covers and cancellations on the market originated from Moscow, using duplicate Tuva markings, and it was believed that the stamps were not in use in Tuva. However we are now satisfied, from evidence submitted by specialists, that the stamps were used in Tuva and a number of genuine covers emanating from there have been recorded.

The existence of the provisional surcharges has only been established comparatively recently and most of these are rare.

7. Mounted Hunter.

8. Interior of Tent.

9. Yak.

1934. Perf. or imperf.

43.	**7.**	1 k. orange	25	10
44.	–	2 k. green	25	10
45.	**8.**	3 k. red	25	10
46.	–	4 k. purple	90	50
47.	**9.**	5 k. blue	90	50
48.	–	10 k. chocolate	90	50
49.	–	15 k. lake	1·00	55
50.	–	20 k. black	1·25	75

DESIGNS—As T **7**. 2 k. Hunter. As T **8**. 4 k. Tractor. As T **9**. 10 k. Camel caravan. 15 k. Lassoing reindeer. 20 k. Foxhunting.

10. Yaks.

11. Turkey.

1934. Air.

51.	**10.**	1 k. red	25	15
52.	–	5 k. emerald	25	15
53.	**11.**	10 k. maroon	30	15
54.	–	15 k. red	30	15
55.	–	25 k. purple	30	15
56.	**10.**	50 k. green	30	15
57.	–	75 k. lake	60	30
58.	**10.**	1 t. blue	60	30
59.	–	2 t. ultram. (55×27 mm.)	75	45

DESIGNS (embodying monoplane). As T **10**. 5 k., 15 k. Camels. As T **11**. 25 k. Mountain sheep. 75 k. Ox-cart. 2 t. Chamois.

The 2 t. also comes larger, 60×30 mm.

1935. No. 49 surch.

60.		20 k. on 15 k. lake ..		

12. Map of Tuva.

13. Rocky Outcrop.

1935. Landscapes.

61.	12.	1 k. orange	30	20
62.	–	3 k. emerald	30	20
63.	–	5 k. red	30	25
64.	–	10 k. violet	30	25
65.	13.	15 k. green	30	25
66.	–	25 k. blue	40	30
67.	–	50 k. sepia	75	30

DESIGNS—As T **12.** 3 k., 5 k., 10 k. Views of River Yenisei. As T **13.** 25 k. Bei-kem rapids. 50 k. Mounted hunter.

14. Badger.

15. Fox.

16. Elk.

1935. Animals.

68.	14.	1 k. orange	30	20
69.	–	3 k. emerald	30	20
70.	–	5 k. red	30	20
71.	15.	10 k. crimson ..	40	20
72.	–	25 k. red	40	20
73.	–	50 k. blue	40	20
74.	16.	1 t. violet	50	20
75.	–	2 t. blue	50	20
76.	–	3 t. brown	60	25
77.	–	5 t. indigo	60	25

DESIGNS—As T **14**—VERT. 3 k. Squirrel. HORIZ. 5 k. Ermine. As T **15.** 25 k. Otter. 50 k. Lynx. LARGER (61 × 31 mm.). 2 t. Yak. 3 t. Camel. As T **16.** 5 t. Bear.

See also No. 115.

17. Arms of Republic.

18. Wrestlers.

19. Herdsman.

20. Sports Meeting.

21. Partisans.

1936. Independence. 15th Anniv. (a) Postage. Inscr. " 1921 1936 ".

78.	17.	1 k. green	30	15
79.	–	2 k. sepia	30	15
80.	–	3 k. indigo	30	15
81.	18.	4 k. red	50	20
82.	–	5 k. purple	50	20
83.	18.	6 k. green	50	20
84.	–	8 k. plum	50	20
85.	–	10 k. red	50	20
86.	–	12 k. agate	1·00	35
87.	–	15 k. green	1·00	35
88.	–	20 k. blue	1·00	35
89.	19.	25 k. red	65	25
90.	–	30 k. plum	65	25
91.	19.	35 k. red	65	25
92.	–	40 k. sepia	65	25
93.	–	50 k. indigo	65	25
94.	20.	70 k. plum	75	40
95.	–	80 k. green	75	40
96.	21.	1 a. red	75	40
97.		2 a. red	75	40
98.	–	3 a. indigo	75	40
99.	–	5 a. agate	90	50

DESIGNS—As T **17.** 2 k. Pres. Gyrmittazi. 3 k. Camel and driver. As T **18.** 5 k., 8 k. Archers. 10 k., 15 k. Fisherman. 12 k., 20 k. Bear Hunt. As T **19.** 30 k. Camel and train. 40 k., 50 k. Horse-racing. As T **20.** 80 k., 5 a, 1921 war scene. 3 a. Village.

See also Nos. 116 and 118/9.

22. Yak Transport.

23. Horseman and Airship.

MINIMUM PRICE

The minimum price quoted is 5p which represents a handling charge rather than a basis for valuing common stamps. For further notes about prices see introductory pages.

24. Seaplane over Waves.

(b) Air. Inscr. " 1921 1936 AIR MAIL ".

100.	22.	5 k. indigo and flesh ..	70	35
101.	–	10 k. pur. & cinnamon	70	35
102.	22.	15 k. agate and grey ..	70	35
103.	23.	25 k. plum and cream ..	1·10	35
104.	–	50 k. red and cream ..	1·10	35
105.	23.	75 k. emer. & yellow ..	1·10	35
106.	24.	1 a. green & blue-green	1·10	45
107.		2 a. red and cream ..	1·10	45
108.		3 a. sepia and flesh ..	1·25	65

DESIGNS—As T **22.** 10 k. Horse-drawn reaper As T **23.** 50 k. Meeting.

See also No. 117

1938. Various stamps surch. with large numerals obliterating old values.

109. 5 k. on 2 a. red (No. 97)
110. 5 k. on 2 a. red and cream (No. 107)
111. 10 k. on 1 t. blue (No. 58) .. ..
112. 20 k. on 50 k. sepia (No. 67)
113. 30 k. on 2 a. red and cream (No. 107) ..
114. 30 k. on 3 a. sepia & flesh (No. 108) .. ..

See also Nos. 120/1.

1938. Previous types with designs modified and colours changed.

115. 5 k. green (No. 70) ..
116. 10 k. indigo (No. 85) ..
117. 15 k. brown (No. 102) ..
118. 20 k. red (No. 88) ..
119. 30 k. maroon (No. 95) ..

In Nos. 116/9 the dates have been removed and in No. 117 " AIR MAIL " also.

1939. Nos. 58 and 67 surch. with small thick numerals and old values obliterated.

120. 10 k. on 1 t. blue ..
121. 20 k. on 50 k. sepia ..

See also Nos. 122/3

1940. Various stamps surch.

122. 10 k. on 1 t. blue (No. 58)
123. 20 k. on 50 k. sep. (No. 67)
124. 20 k. on 50 k. bl. (No. 73)
125. 20 k. on 50 k. indigo (No. 93) .. ..
126. 20 k. on 50 k. red on cream (No. 104) ..
127. 20 k. on 75 k. emerald and yellow (No. 105) ..
128. 20 k. on 80 k. grn. (No. 95)

1942. Nos. 98/9 surch.

129. 25 k. on 3 a. indigo ..
130. 25 k. on 5 a. agate ..

25. Tuvan Woman.

1942. Independence. 21st Anniv. Inscr. " 1921 1942 " Imperf.

131. **25.** 25 k. blue .. ..
132. – 25 k. blue .. ..
133. – 25 k. blue .. ..

DESIGNS: No. 132, Agricultural Exhibition building. 133, Government building.

26. Coat of Arms.

27. Government Building.

1943. Independence. 22nd Anniv. With or without gum.

134.	26.	25 k. blue	3·00	
135.		25 k. black	5·00	
136.		25 k. green	20·00	
137.	27.	50 k. green	15·00	

TUVALU BC

Formerly known as the Ellice Islands and sharing a joint administration with the Gilbert group. On 1st January 1976 the two island-groups separated and the Ellice Is. were renamed Tuvalu.

100 cents = $1 Australian

1. Tuvaluan and Gilbertese.

1976. Separation. Multicoloured.

1.	4 c. Type **1**	5	5
2.	10 c. Map of the Islands (vert.)	12	15
3.	35 c. Gilbert and Ellice canoes	45	50

1976. Nos. 173/87 of the Gilbert and Ellice Islands optd. **TUVALU.**

14.	1 c. Cutting toddy	5	5
20.	2 c. Lagoon fishing	5	5
21.	3 c. Cleaning pandanus leaves	5	8
22.	4 c. Casting nets	8	8
5.	5 c. Gilbertese canoe ..	10	12
15.	6 c. De-husking coconuts ..	10	12
6.	8 c. Weaving pandanus fronds	12	15
7.	10 c. Weaving a basket ..	15	20
16.	15 c. Tiger shark	25	25
23.	20 c. Beating a rolled pandanus leaf	30	35
13.	25 c. Loading copra ..	35	40
25.	35 c. Fishing at night ..	55	65
15.	50 c. Local handicrafts ..	75	85
18.	$1 Weaving coconut screen	1·50	1·75
19.	$2 Coat of Arms	3·00	3·25

2. 50 c. Coin and Octopus.

1976. New Coinage. Multicoloured.

26.	5 c. Type **2**	8	10
27.	10 c. 10 c. coin and Red-eyed Crab	15	20
28.	20 c. 20 c. coin and Flying Fish	30	35
29.	$1 $1 coin and Green Turtle	1·50	1·75

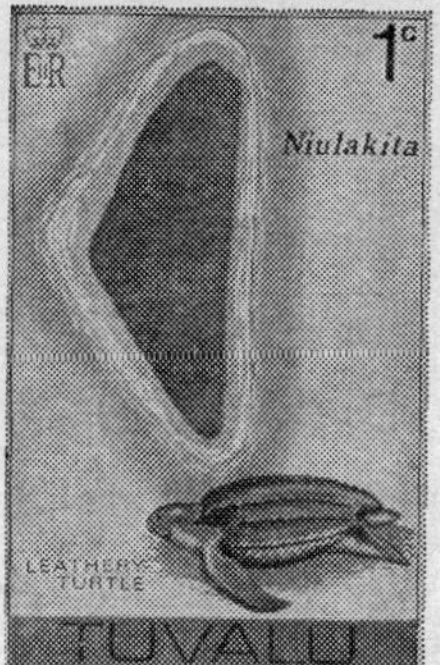

3. Niulakita and Leathery Turtle.

1976. Multicoloured.

30. 1 c. Type 3 .. 5 5
31. 2 c. Nukuulaelae and sleeping mat .. 5 5
32. 4 c. Nui and talo (vegetable) 5 8
33. 5 c. Nanumanga and grass skirt 8 8
34. 6 c. Nukufetau and Coconut Crab 8 10
35. 8 c. Funafuti and Banana tree 10 12
36. 10 c. Map of Tuvalu .. 12 15
37. 15 c. Niutao and Flying fish 20 25
38. 20 c. Vaitupu and Maneapa (house) .. 25 30
39. 25 c. Nanumea and fish-hook 35 35
40. 35 c. Te Ano (game) .. 45 50
41. 50 c. Canoe pole fishing .. 65 75
42. $1 Reef fishing by flare .. 1·25 1·40
43. $2 Living house .. 2·50 2·75
44. $5 M.V. "Nivanga" .. 6·50 7·00

4. Title Page of New Testament.

1976. Christmas. Multicoloured.

45. 5 c. Type 4 .. .. 8 10
46. 20 c. Lotolelei Church, Nanumea 30 35
47. 25 c. Kelupi Church, Nui .. 35 40
48. 30 c. Mataloa o Tuvala Church, Vaitupu 45 50
49. 35 c. Dalataise o Keliso Church, Nanumanga .. 50 55

5. The Queen and Duke of Edinburgh after Coronation.

1977. Silver Jubilee. Multicoloured.

50. 15 c. Type 5 .. .. 25 30
51. 35 c. Prince Philip carried ashore at Vaitupu 50 55
52. 50 c. The Queen leaving Buckingham Palace .. 75 80

UBANGI-SHARI O1

One of the three French colonies into which the Fr. Congo was divided in 1910. Became a part of French Equatorial Africa in 1937. In 1958 the Central African Republic was declared within the French Community.

A. UBANGI-SHARI-CHAD.

1915. Stamps of Middle Congo optd. **OUBANGUI-CHARI-TCHAD.**

1. 1. 1 c. olive and brown .. 5 5
2. 2 c. violet and brown .. 5 5
3. 4 c. blue and brown .. 5 5
4. 5 c. green and blue .. 5 5
19. 5 c. yellow and blue .. 5 5
5. 10 c. red and blue.. .. 5 5
20. 10 c. green .. 5 5
5a. 15 c. purple and red 15 15
6. 20 c. brown and blue 30 30
7. 2. 25 c. blue and green 8 8
21. 25 c. green and black .. 5 5
8. 30 c. red and green .. 5 5
22. 30 c. red 5 5
9. 35 c. brown and blue .. 55 55
10. 40 c. olive and brown .. 60 60
11. 45 c. violet and orange .. 60 60
12. 50 c. green and red .. 10 10
23. 50 c. blue and green .. 5 5
13. 75 c. chocolate and blue.. 1·50 1·50
14. 3. 1 f. green and violet .. 1·60 1·60
15. 2 f. violet and green .. 1·60 1·60
16. 5 f. blue and red .. .. 6·50 6·50

1916. Stamp of Middle Congo surch. **OUBANGUI-CHARI-TCHAD** and large cross and 5 c. in black.

17. 10 c.+5 c. red and blue.. 25 25

1916. Stamp of Middle Congo surch. **OUBANGUI-CHARI-TCHAD** and small cross and **5c.** in red.

18. 10 c.+5 c. red and blue.. 5 5

B. UBANGI-SHARI.

1922. Stamps of Middle Congo, new colours, optd. **OUBANGUI-CHARI.**

24. 1. 1 c. violet and green .. 5 5
25. 2 c. green and red.. .. 5 5
26. 4 c. brown and purple .. 8 8
27. 5 c. blue and red.. .. 10 10
28. 10 c. green 20 20
29. 15 c. red and blue .. 25 25
30. 20 c. brown and red .. 75 75
31. 2. 25 c. violet and red .. 60 60
32. 30 c. red 45 45
33. 35 c. violet and green .. 75 75
34. 40 c. blue and violet .. 75 75
35. 45 c. brown and violet .. 75 75
36. 50 c. blue 50 50
37. 60 on 75 c. violet on red.. 50 50
38. 75 c. brown and red .. 50 50
39. 3. 1 f. green and blue .. 65 65
40. 2 f. green and red .. 1·10 1·10
41. 5 f. green and brown .. 1·25 1·25

1924. Stamps of Middle Congo, new colour, optd. **OUBANGUI-CHARI** and **AFRIQUE EQUATORIALE FRANCAISE.**

42. 1. 1 c. violet and green .. 5 5
43. 2 c. green and red .. 5 5
44. 4 c. brown and purple .. 5 5
45. 1. 5 c. blue and red .. 5 5
46. 10 c. green .. 5 5
47. 10 c. red and blue .. 5 5
48. 15 c. red and blue .. 5 5
49. 20 c. brown and red .. 5 5
50. 2. 25 c. violet and red .. 5 5
51. 30 c. red 5 5
52. 30 c. brown and red .. 5 5
53. 30 c. olive and green .. 8 8
54. 35 c. violet and green .. 5 5
55. 40 c. blue and violet .. 5 5
56. 45 c. brown and violet .. 5 5
57. 50 c. blue 5 5
58. 50 c. grey and blue .. 15 15
59. 60 on 75 c. violet on red.. 5 5
60. 65 c. brown and blue .. 15 15
61. 75 c. brown and red .. 5 5
62. 75 c. blue 5 5
63. 75 c. red and brown .. 15 15
64. 90 c. red 60 60
65. 3. 1 f. green and blue .. 5 5
66. 1 f. 10 brown on blue .. 20 20
67. 1 f. 25 green and red .. 70 70
68. 1 f. 50 blue .. 70 70
69. 1 f. 75 chestnut and brown 1·00 1·00
70. 2 f. green and red.. .. 8 8
71. 3 f. mauve on red.. .. 70 70
72. 5 f. green and brown .. 30 30

1925. As last but new colours and surch.

73. 3. 65 on 1 f. violet & brown 12 12
74. 85 on 1 f. violet and brown 12 12
75. 2. 90 on 75 c. red .. 10 10
76. 3. 1 f. 25 on 1 f. blue.. .. 5 5
77. 1 f. 50 on 1 f. blue.. .. 12 12
78. 3 f. on 5 f. brown and red 25 25
79. 10 f. on 5 f. red & mauve 2·40 2·40
80. 20 f. on 5 f. mauve & grey 3·25 3·25

1931. "Colonial Exhibition" key-types inscr. "OUBANGUI-CHARI".

103. E. 40 c. green 70 70
104. F. 50 c. mauve 70 70
105. G. 90 c. red 70 70
106. H. 1 f. 50 blue 70 70

POSTAGE DUE STAMPS

1928. Postage Due type of France optd. **OUBANGUI-CHARI A.E.F.**

D 81. D 2. 5 c. blue 20 20
D 82. 10 c. brown 20 20
D 83. 20 c. olive 20 20
D 84. 25 c. red 20 20
D 85. 30 c. red 20 20
D 86. 45 c. green 20 20
D 87. 50 c. purple 20 20
D 88. 60 c. brown on cream 20 20
D 89. 1 f. claret on cream.. 45 45
D 90. 2 f. red 50 50
D 91. 3 f. violet 55 55

D 1. Mobaye.

D 2. E. Gentil.

1930.

D 92. D 1. 5 c. olive and blue .. 5 5
D 93. 10 c. brown and red.. 10 10
D 94. 20 c. brown and green 15 15
D 95. 25 c. brown and blue 15 15
D 96. 30 c. green and brown 30 30
D 97. 45 c. olive and green 45 45
D 98. 50 c. brown and mauve 75 75
D 99. 60 c. black and violet 75 75
D 100. D 2. 1 f. black and brown 30 30
D 101. 2 f. brown and mauve 50 50
D 102. 3 f. brown and red .. 70 70

UGANDA BC

A Br. Protectorate in Central Africa until it attained independence within the British Commonwealth 1962. From 1903 to 1962 used the stamps we list under "Kenya, Uganda and Tanganyika".

1895. 1,000 cowries = 2 rupees.
1896. 16 annas = 1 rupee.
1962. 100 cents = 1 shilling.

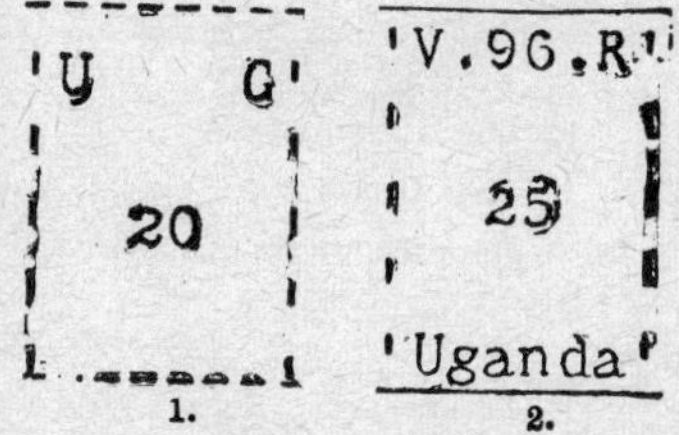

1. 2.

1895. Typewritten in black.

26. 1. 5 (c.) black .. .. 90·00
17. 5 (c.) black .. .. — £225
18. 10 (c.) black £225 £225
19. 15 (c.) black £200 £160
20. 20 (c.) black £150 £160
21. 25 (c.) black £200 £200
6. 30 (c.) black £278 £275
32. 40 (c.) black .. .. 90·00
33. 50 (c.) black .. .. 90·00
34. 60 (c.) black £100

1895. Typewritten in violet.

35. 1. 5 (c.) violet .. .. 90·00 90·00
36. 10 (c.) violet .. .. 90·00 90·00
37. 15 (c.) violet .. .. 90·00 90·00
38. 20 (c.) violet .. .. 90·00 90·00
39. 25 (c.) violet £110
40. 30 (c.) violet £110
41. 40 (c.) violet £110
42. 50 (c.) violet £110
43. 100 (c.) violet £1000

1896. Typewritten in violet.

44. 2. 5 (c.) violet .. .. 50·00 50·00
45. 10 (c.) violet .. .. 50·00 50·00
46. 15 (c.) violet .. .. 50·00 50·00
47. 20 (c.) violet .. .. 50·00 50·00
48. 25 (c.) violet .. .. 80·00
49. 30 (c.) violet .. .. 80·00
50. 40 (c.) violet .. .. 80·00
51. 50 (c.) violet .. .. 80·00
52. 60 (c.) violet £200
53. 100 (c.) violet £225 £250

U G A N D A
POSTAGE
* V R *
1 ANNA
PROTECTORATE

3.

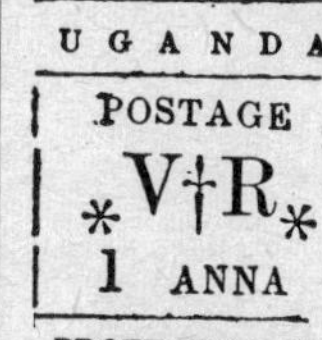

4.

1896.

55. 3. 1 a. black .. .. 2·75 3·25
56. 2 a. black .. .. 3·25 4·25
57. 3 a. black .. .. 3·25 4·25
58. 4 a. black .. .. 3·25 4·25
59. 8 a. black .. .. 4·25 5·50
60. 1 r. black .. .. 9·00 11·00
61. 5 r. black .. .. 35·00 60·00

1896. Optd. with large **L.**

70. 3. 1 a. black .. .. 8·00 15·00
71. 2 a. black .. .. 8·00 15·00
72. 3 a. black .. .. 11·00 24·00
73. 4 a. black .. .. 11·00 24·00
74. 8 a. black .. .. 24·00 26·00
75. 1 r. black .. .. 40·00 55·00
76. 5 r. black .. .. — £600

1898.

84. 4. 1 a. red 10 15
86. 2 a. brown 20 40
87a. 3 a. grey 50 70
88. 4 a. green 60 80
89. 8 a. green .. .. 1·00 2·00

Larger type with lions at either side of portrait.

90. – 1 r. blue .. .. 3·00 3·50
91. – 5 r. brown.. .. 11·00 13·00

1902. Stamps of British East Africa optd. **UGANDA**

92. 2. ½ a. green 20 25
93. 2½ a. blue 30 45

NOTE. Stamps inscribed "UGANDA KENYA TANGANYIKA & ZANZIBAR" (or "TANZANIA UGANDA KENYA") will be found listed under East Africa.

5. Ripon falls and Speke Memorial.

1962. Speke's Discovery of Source of the Nile. Cent.

95. 5. 30 c. black and red .. 8 8
96. 50 c. black and violet .. 12 12
97. 1s. 30 black and green .. 20 25
98. 2s. 50 black and blue .. 45 50

6. Murchison Falls.

DESIGNS—As T 6: 10 c. Tobacco-growing 15 c. Coffee-growing. 20 c. Ankole cattle. 30 c. Cotton. 50 c. Mountains of the moon. As T 7: 1s. 30, Cathedrals and Mosque. 2s. Makerere College. 5s. Copper mining. 10s. Cement industry. 20s. Parliamentary Buildings.

7. Mulago Hospital.

1962. Independence.

99. 6. 5 c. blue-green 5 5
100. – 10 c. brown 5 5
101. – 15 c. black, red & green.. 5 5
102. – 20 c. plum and buff .. 5 5
103. – 30 c. blue 8 5
104. – 50 c. black & turquoise.. 8 5
105. 7. 1s. sepia, red & turquoise 12 8
106. – 1s. 30 orange and violet 20 8
107. – 2s. black, red and blue 25 12
108. – 5s. verm. and deep green 75 55
109. – 10s. slate and chestnut.. 1·50 1·50
110. – 20s. brown and blue .. 5·00 5·00

8. Crowned Crane.

9. Black Bee-eater.

10. Ruwenzori Turaco.

1965. Int. Trade Fair, Kampala.

111. 8. 30 c. multicoloured .. 8 8
112. 1s. 30 multicoloured .. 25 25

1965. Birds.

113. 9. 5 c. multicoloured .. 5 5
114. – 10 c. brn., blk. and blue 5 5
115. – 15 c. yellow and brown 5 5
116. – 20 c. multicoloured .. 5 5
117. – 30 c. black and brown.. 5 5
118. – 40 c. multicoloured .. 8 5
119. – 50 c. blue and violet .. 8 5
120. – 65 c. red, black and grey 15 15

121.	10.	1s. multicoloured ..	20	10
122.	–	1s. 30 brn., blk. & yell.	20	8
123.	–	2s. 50 multicoloured ..	40	35
124.	–	5s. multicoloured	80	60
125.	–	10s. multicoloured ..	1·50	1·25
126.	–	20s. multicoloured ..	3·00	4·50

DESIGNS: As T 9—HORIZ. 10 c. African Jacana. 30 c. Sacred Ibis. 65 c. Black-winged Red Bishop. VERT. 15 c. Orange Weaver. 20 c. Narina Trogon. 40 c. Blue-breasted Kingfisher. 50 c. Whale-headed stork. As T 10—VERT. 1s. 30 African Fish Eagle. 5s. Lilac-breasted Roller. HORIZ. 2s. 50 Great Blue Turaco. 10s. Black-collared Crane. 20s. Crowned Crane.

11. Arms of Uganda.

1967. 13th Commonwealth Parliamentary Assn. Conf. Multicoloured.

127.	30 c. Carved Screen ..	5	5
128.	50 c. Type 11 ..	8	8
129.	1s. 30 Parliamentary Bldg.	25	30
130.	2s. 50 Conference Chamber	35	45

12. " Cordia abyssinica ".

13. " Acacia drepanolobium ".

1969. Flowers.

131.	12.	5 c. brown, green & yell.	5	5
132.	–	10 c. multicoloured ..	5	5
133.	–	15 c. multicoloured ..	5	5
134.	–	20 c. violet, olive & green	5	5
135.	–	30 c. multicoloured ..	5	5
136.	–	40 c. violet, grn. & grey	8	5
137.	–	50 c. multicoloured ..	8	8
138a.	–	60 c. multicoloured ..	10	10
139a.	–	70 c. multicoloured ..	12	10
140a.	13.	1s. multicoloured ..	20	15
141a.	–	1s. 50 multicoloured ..	25	20
142a.	–	2s. 50 multicoloured ..	35	35
143a.	–	5s. multicoloured ..	60	70
144a.	–	10s. multicoloured ..	1·50	1·40
145a.	–	20 s. multicoloured ..	2·75	2·75

DESIGNS—As T 12: 10 c. " Grewia similis ". 15 c. " Cassia didymobotrya ". 20 c. " Coleus barbatus ". 30 c. " Ochna ovata ". 40 c. " Ipomea spathulata ". 50 c. " Spathodea nilotica ". 60 c. " Oncoba spinosa ". 70 c. " Carissa edulis ". As T 13: 1s. 50 " Clerodendrum myricoides ". 2s. 50 " Avanthus arboreus ". 5s. " Kigelia aethiopium ". 10s. " Erythrina abyssinica ". 20s. " Monodora myristica ".

1975. Nos. 141a, 142a and 145a surch.

146.	2 s. on 1 s. multicoloured ..	45	45
147.	3 s. on 2 s. 50 multicoloured	10·00	10·00
148.	40 s. on 20 s. multicoloured	5·00	5·50

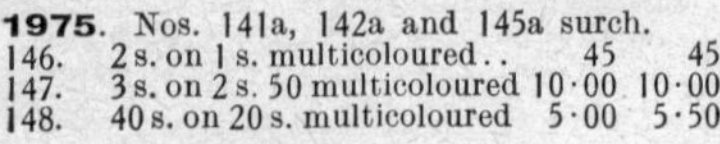

14. Millet.

15. Maize.

1976. Ugandan Crops.

149.	14.	10 c. blk., grn. and brn.	5	5
150.	–	20 c. multicoloured ..	5	5
151.	–	30 c. multicoloured ..	5	5
152.	–	40 c. multicoloured ..	5	5
153.	–	50 c. multicoloured ..	5	5
154.	–	70 c. blk., grn. and blue	8	8
155.	–	80 c. multicoloured ..	8	10
156.	15.	1s. multicoloured ..	10	12
157.	–	2s. multicoloured ..	20	25
158.	–	3s. multicoloured ..	30	35
159.	–	5s. multicoloured ..	50	60
160.	–	10s. multicoloured ..	1·00	1·25
161.	–	20s. grn., blk. and pur.	2·10	2·40
162.	–	40s. grn., bl. and oran.	4·25	4·75

DESIGNS: As T 14. 20 c. Sugar. 30 c. Tobacco. 40 c. Onions. 50 c. Tomatoes. 70 c. Tea. 80 c. Bananas. As T 15. 2s. Pineapples. 3s. Coffee. 5s. Oranges. 10s. Groundnuts. 20s. Cotton. 40s. Runner Beans.

1976. Telecommunications Development. As Nos. 260/3 of Kenya.

163.	50 c. Nicrowave tower ..	8	8
164.	1 s. Cordless switchboard	15	15
165.	2 s. Telephones ..	25	30
166.	3 s. Message Switching Centre ..	35	40

1976. Olympic Games, Montreal. As Nos. 265/8 of Kenya.

168.	50 c. Akii Bua, hurdler ..	5	8
169.	1 s. Filbert Bayi, runner ..	12	15
170.	2 s. Steve Muchoki, boxer	25	30
171.	3 s. East African flags ..	35	40

1976. Railway Transport. As Nos. 270/3 of Kenya.

173.	50 c. Tanzania-Zambia railway ..	5	8
174.	1 s. Nile Bridge, Uganda	12	15
175.	2 s. Nakuru Station, Kenya	25	30
176.	3 s. Class A loco, 1896 ..	35	40

1977. Game Fish of East Africa. As Nos. 275/8 of Kenya. Multicoloured.

178.	50 c. Nile Perch ..	5	8
179.	1 s. Tilapia ..	12	15
180.	3 s. Sailfish ..	35	40
181.	5 s. Black Marlin ..	60	65

1977. Second World Black African Festival of Arts and Culture. As Nos. 279/82 of Kenya. Multicoloured.

182.	50 c. Maasai Manyatta (animal slaughter) Kenya	5	8
183.	1 s. " Heartbeat of Africa " (Ugandan dancers) ..	12	15
184.	2 s. Makonde sculpture, Tanzania ..	25	30
185.	3 s. " Early man and technology " (skinning animal) ..	35	40

POSTAGE DUE STAMPS

The Postage Due stamps of Kenya, Uganda and Tanganyika were used in Uganda until 2nd January, 1967.

D 1.

1967.

D 12.	D 1.	5 c. red ..	5	5
D 13.		10 c. green ..	5	5
D 14.		20 c. blue ..	5	5
D 15.		30 c. brown ..	5	5
D 16.		40 c. purple ..	5	5
D 17.		1 s. orange ..	10	12

UKRAINE E3

A district of S.W. Russia, which issued stamps during its temporary independence after the Russian Revolution. Now a state forming part of Soviet Russia.

100 kopecks = 1 rouble.
100 shagiv = 1 grivna (= ½ rouble).

(1.)

(2.)

1918. Arms types of Russia optd. with Trident device in various types according to the district. Imperf. or perf.

51.	11.	1 k. orange ..	5	5
52.		2 k. green ..	5	5
53.		3 k. red ..	5	5
54.	12.	4 k. red ..	5	5
55.	11.	5 k. claret ..	5	5
138.		7 k. blue ..	5	5
57.	12.	10 k. blue ..	5	5
58.	11.	10 k. on 7 k. blue ..	8	5
159.	4.	14 k. red and blue ..	5	8
60.		15 k. blue and purple	5	5
61.	7.	20 k. red and blue	5	5
62.	4.	20 k. on 14 k. red & blue	5	5
145.		25 k. mauve and green	10	30
64.		35 k. green and purple	5	5
65.	7.	50 k. green and purple	5	5
66.	4.	70 k. orange and brown	5	5
47.	8	1 r. orange and brown	5	5
72.	5.	3 r. 50 grey and black	14·00	16·00
246.		3 r. 50 green and brown	30	60
49.	13.	5 r. blue and green	10	20
73.	5.	7 r. yellow and black	9·00	11·00
14.		7 r. pink and green	30	50
36.	13.	10 r. grey, red & yellow	3·50	5·50

3.

4.

5.

6.

7.

1918. Without inscription on back. Imperf.

G 1.	3.	10 s. brown on buff ..	5	5
G 2.	4.	20 s. brown ..	5	5
G 3.	5.	30 s. blue ..	5	5
G 4.	6.	40 s. green ..	5	5
G 5.	7.	50 s. red ..	5	5

1918. With trident and four lines of inscription on back.

G 6.	3.	10 s. brown ..	55	1·75
G 7.	4.	20 s. brown ..	55	1·75
G 8.	5.	30 s. blue ..	55	1·75
G 9.	6.	40 s. green ..	55	1·75
G 10.	7.	50 s. red ..	55	1·75

8 Trident.

10. Parliament Building.

Stamps of the above and similar designs were prepared for use but never used.

11. Spectre of famine.

12. Poet Shevchenko.

1923. Charity.

G 12.	11.	10 + 10 k. blue and black	35	90
G 13.	12.	20 + 20 k. brown & orge.	35	90
G 14.	–	90 + 30 k. black & bistre	55	1·40
G 15.	–	150 + 50 k. red and black	90	1·75

DESIGNS—VERT. 90 k. Death and peasant. 150 k. " Ukraine " (woman) distributing bread.

UMM AL QIWAIN O4

One of the Trucial States in the Persian Gulf. In July 1971 formed the United Arab Emirates with five other Gulf Shaikdoms.

100 naye paise = 1 rupee.
1967. 100 dirhams = 1 riyal.

1. Shaikh Ahmed bin Rashid al Moalla and Gazelles.

1964. Multicoloured.

(a) Size as T 1.

1.	1 n.p. Type 1 ..	5	5
2.	2 n.p. Snake ..	5	5
3.	3 n.p. Wild dog ..	5	5
4.	4 n.p. Fish ..	5	5
5.	5 n.p. Fish (different) ..	5	5
6.	10 n.p. Fish (different) ..	5	5
7.	15 n.p. Palace ..	5	5
8.	20 n.p. Town buildings ..	8	8
9.	30 n.p. Tower ..	10	10

(b) Size 42½ × 27 mm.

10.	40 n.p. Type 1 ..	12	12
11.	50 n.p. Snake ..	15	15
12.	70 n.p. Wild dog ..	20	20
13.	1 r. Fish ..	30	30
14.	1 r. 50 Fish (different) ..	40	40
15.	2 r. Fish (different) ..	55	55

(c) Size 53½ × 33½ mm.

16.	3 r. Palace ..	80	80
17.	5 r. Town buildings ..	1·60	1·60
18.	10 r. Tower ..	3·00	3·00

2 " Discus Thrower " and Stadium.

1964. Olympic Games, Tokyo. Multicoloured.

19.	50 n.p. Type 2 ..	12	12
20.	1 r. Main stadium ..	25	25
21.	1 r. 50 Swimming pool ..	40	40
22.	2 r. Main stadium ..	50	50
23.	3 r. Komazawa gymnasium	80	80
24.	4 r. Stadium entrance ..	1·25	1·25
25.	5 r. Type 2 ..	1·60	1·60

3. Cortege leaving White House.

1965. Pres. Kennedy Commem. Each black and gold on coloured paper as given below.

26.	3.	10 n.p. pale blue ..	5	5
27.	–	15 n.p. pale stone ..	5	5
28.	–	50 n.p. pale stone ..	12	12
29.	–	1 r. pale pink ..	25	25
30.	–	2 r. pale stone ..	50	50
31.	–	3 r. pale lavender ..	80	80
32.	–	5 r. pale blue ..	1·60	1·60
33.	–	7 r. 50 pale buff ..	2·00	2·00

DESIGNS (Funeral scenes): 15 n.p. Coffin-bearers. 50 n.p. Hearse. 1 r. Presidents Eisenhower and Truman. 2 r. Foreign dignitaries. (33 × 51 mm.). 3 r. Mrs. Kennedy and family at grave. 5 r. Last salute. 7 r. 50, Pres. Kennedy.

1965. Air. Designs similar to Nos. 1/9 but inscr. " AIR MAIL ". Multicoloured.

(a) Size 43 × 26½ mm.

34.	15 n.p. Type 1 ..	5	5
35.	25 n.p. Snake ..	5	5
36.	35 n.p. Wild dog ..	8	8
37.	50 n.p. Fish ..	10	10
38.	75 n.p. Fish (different) ..	15	15
39.	1 r. Fish (different)	20	20

(b) Size 53 × 34 mm.

40.	2 r. Palace ..	45	45
41.	3 r. Town buildings ..	70	70
42.	5 r. Tower ..	1·25	1·25

4. Tribute to Ruler (reverse of 10 n.p. piece).

1965. Arabian Gulf Area Monetary Conf. Circular designs on silver foil, backed with paper inscr. overall " Walsall Security Paper " in English and Arabic. Imperf.

(a) Diameter $1\frac{11}{16}$ in.

43a.	4.	10 n.p. purple and black ..	5	5
44.	–	25 n.p. blue and green ..	8	8

(b) Diameter $2\frac{3}{16}$ in.

45a.	4.	1 r. vermilion and violet ..	30	30
46.	–	2 r. green and orange ..	60	60

(c) Diameter 2½ in.
47a. 4. 3 r. blue and magenta .. 90 90
48. – 5 r. purple and ultram. .. 1·40 1·40
SILVER PIECES: Nos. 44, 46, 48 each show the obverse side (Shaikh Ahmed).

5. "Penny Black" and Egyptian 5 p. stamp of 1866.

1966. Centenary Stamp Exn., Cairo.
49. 5. 3 n.p. multicoloured .. 5 5
50. – 5 n.p. multicoloured .. 5 5
51. – 7 n.p. multicoloured .. 5 5
52. – 10 n.p. multicoloured .. 5 5
53. – 15 n.p. multicoloured .. 8 8
54. – 25 n.p. multicoloured .. 10 10
55. – 50 n.p. multicoloured .. 20 15
56. – 75 n.p. multicoloured .. 25 20
57. – 1 r. multicoloured .. 40 30
58. – 2 r. multicoloured .. 80 60
DESIGNS: As T 5, with Egyptian 5 p. stamp: 7 n.p. Brazil 30 r. "Bull's-eye" of 1843. 15 n.p. Mauritius "Post Office" One Penny of 1847. 50 n.p. Belgium 10 c. "Epaulettes" of 1849. 1 r. New South Wales One Penny and Victoria One Penny of 1850. As T 5, but with Egyptian "Pyramid and Star" watermark of 1866: 5 n.p. Basle 2½ r. "Dove" of 1845, Geneva 5 c.+5 c. "Double Eagle" and Zurich 4 r. "Numeral" of 1843. 10 n.p. U.S. St. Louis "Bears" 5 c., Baltimore 5 c. and New York 5 c. "Postmasters" stamps of 1845. 25 n.p. France 20 c. "Ceres" of 1849. 75 n.p. Bavaria 1 k. of 1850. 2 r. Spain 6 c. of 1850.

6. Sir Winston Churchill with Lord Alanbrook and Field Marshal Montgomery.

1966. Churchill Commem. Multicoloured designs, each including Churchill.
59. 3 n.p. Type 6 .. .. 5 5
60. 4 n.p. With Roosevelt and Stalin at Yalta .. 5 5
61. 5 n.p. In garden at No. 10 Downing Street, London 5 5
62. 10 n.p. With Eisenhower 5 5
63. 15 n.p. With Lady Churchill in car 5 5
64. 50 n.p. Painting in Morocco 10 5
65. 75 n.p. Walking—on holiday 20 10
66. 1 r. Funeral cortege .. 35 20
67. 3 r. Lying-in-state, Westminster Hall .. .. 1·10 60
68. 5 r. Churchill giving "Victory" sign.. .. 1·75 1·00

7. Communications Satellite.

1966. I.T.U. Cent. (in 1965). Designs showing communications satellites.
70. 7. 5 n.p. multicoloured .. 5 5
71. – 10 n.p. multicoloured .. 5 5
72. – 25 n.p. multicoloured .. 10 5
73. – 50 n.p. multicoloured .. 20 8
74. – 75 n.p. multicoloured .. 30 12
75. – 1 r. multicoloured .. 50 25
76. – 2 r. multicoloured .. 1·00 40
77. – 3 r. multicoloured .. 1·50 70
78. – 5 r. multicoloured .. 2·75 1·10

NEW CURRENCY SURCHARGES. In 1967 various issues appeared surcharged in dirhams and riyals. The 1964 definitives, 1965 air stamps and officials with this surcharge are listed as there is evidence of their postal use. Nos. 19/33 and 49/68 also exist with these surcharges.

1967. Various issues with currency names changed by overprinting.
(i) Nos. 1/18 (1964 Definitives).
80. 1 d. on 1 n.p. 5 5
81. 2 d. on 2 n.p. 5 5
82. 3 d. on 3 n.p. 5 5
83. 4 d. on 4 n.p. 5 5
84. 5 d. on 5 n.p. 5 5
85. 10 d. on 10 n.p. 5 5
86. 15 d. on 15 n.p. 5 5
87. 20 d. on 20 n.p. 8 5
88. 30 d. on 30 n.p. 10 8
89. 40 d. on 40 n.p. 12 10
90. 50 d. on 50 n.p. 20 12
91. 70 d. on 70 n.p. 25 15
92. 1 r. on 1 r. 30 20
93. 1 r. 50 on 1 r. 50 .. 50 35
94. 2 r. on 2 r. 60 45
95. 3 r. on 3 r. .. .. 1·10 70
96. 5 r. on 5 r. .. .. 1·60 1·10
97. 10 r. on 10 r. .. .. 3·00 2·25
(iv) Nos. 34/42 (Airmails).
98. 15 d. on 15 n.p. 5 5
99. 25 d. on 25 n.p. 8 5
100. 35 d. on 35 n.p. 10 8
101. 50 d. on 50 n.p. 15 8
102. 75 d. on 75 n.p. 20 12
103. 1 r. on 1 r. 25 15
104. 2 r. on 2 r. 50 25
105. 3 r. on 3 r. 70 45
106. 5 r. on 5 r. .. .. 1·40 75

8. Box Fish.

1967. Fish of the Arabian Gulf. Mult.
(a) Postage (i) Size 46×21 mm.
116. 1 d. Type 8.. .. .. 5 5
117. 2 d. Parrot fish 5 5
118. 3 d. Sweet lips 5 5
119. 4 d. Butterfly fish.. .. 5 5
120. 5 d. Soldier fish 5 5
121. 10 d. Damsel fish 5 5
122. 15 d. Picasso triggerfish .. 5 5
123. 20 d. Striped triggerfish .. 8 5
124. 30 d. Israeli puffer.. .. 10 5
(ii) Size 56×26 mm.
125. 40 d. Type 8 .. .. 12 8
126. 50 d. As 2 d. 15 8
127. 70 d. As 3 d. 20 10
128. 1 r. As 4 d.. .. .. 25 12
129. 1 r. 50 As 5 d. 35 15
130. 2 r. As 10 d. 50 25
131. 3 r. As 15 d. (No. 122) .. 75 35
132. 5 r. As 20 d. .. .. 1·25 60
133. 10 r. As 30 d. .. .. 2·50 1·25
(b) Air. Size 70×35 mm.
134. 15 d. Type 8 .. .. 5 5
135. 25 d. As 2 d. 8 5
136. 35 d. As 3 d. 10 5
137. 50 d. As 4 d. 15 8
138. 75 d. As 5 d. 20 10
139. 1 r. As 10 d. 25 12
140. 2 r. As 15 d. (No. 122) .. 50 25
141. 3 r. As 20 d. 75 35
142. 5 r. As 30 d. .. .. 1·25 60

OFFICIAL STAMPS.

1965. Designs similar to Nos. 1/9, additionally inscr. "ON STATE'S SERVICE". Multicoloured.
(a) Postage. Size 42½×26½ mm.
O 49. 25 n.p. Type 1 .. .. 8 8
O 50. 40 n.p. Snake 12 12
O 51. 50 n.p. Wild dog .. 15 15
O 52. 75 n.p. Fish 25 25
O 53. 1 r. Fish (different) .. 30 30
(b) Air. (i) Size 42½×26½ mm.
O 54. 75 n.p. Fish (different) .. 25 25
(ii) Size 53×33½ mm.
O 55. 2 r. Palace 60 60
O 56. 3 r. Town buildings .. 90 90
O 57. 5 r. Tower .. .. 1·40 1·40

1967. Nos. O 1/9 with currency names changed by overprinting.
O 107. 25 d. on 25 n.p. (postage) 8 5
O 108. 40 d. on 40 n.p. 12 8
O 109. 50 d. on 50 n.p. 15 10
O 110. 75 d. on 75 n.p. 20 15
O 111. 1 r. on 1 r. 25 20
O 112. 75 d. on 75 n.p. (air) .. 20 15
O 113. 2 r. on 2 r. 50 40
O 114. 3 r. on 3 r. 75 60
O 115. 5 r. on 5 r. .. .. 1·40 1·00

UNITED ARAB EMIRATES O4

Following the withdrawal of British forces from the Gulf and the ending of the Anglo-Trucial States treaties six of the states, Abu Dhabi, Ajman, Dubai, Fujeira, Sharjah and Umm al Qiwain, formed an independent Union on 2nd December 1971. The seventh state, Ras al Khaima, joined during February, 1972. Each emirate continued to use its own stamps, pending the introduction of a unified currency. A Union Postal administration came into being on 1st August 1972 and the first stamps appeared on 1st January 1973. (For Abu Dhabi stamps optd. U.A.E., etc., see under that heading.)

100 fils = 1 dirham.

1. U.A.E. Flag and Gulf.

1973. Multicoloured.
(a) Size 42×25 mm.
1. 5 f. Type 1 .. .. .. 5 5
2. 10 f. Type 1 .. .. 5 5
3. 15 f. Eagle emblem .. 5 5
4. 35 f. As 15 f. 8 5
(b) Size 46×30 mm.
5. 65 f. Almaqta Bridge, Abu Dhabi 15 10
6. 75 f. Khor Fakkan, Sharjah 15 10
7. 1 d. Clock Tower, Dubai .. 20 15
8. 1¼ d. Buthnah Fort, Fujeira 25 20
9. 2 d. Alfalaj Fort, Umm al Qiwain 45 35
10. 3 d. Khor Khwair, Ras al Khaima 65 35
11. 5 d. Ruler's Palace, Ajman 1·10 95
12. 10 d. President Shaikh Zaid 2·25 2·00

2. Youth and Girl within Shield.

1973. National Youth Festival. Mult.
13. 10 f. Type 2 .. .. 5 5
14. 1 d. 25 Allegory of Youth.. 30 20

3. Traffic Policeman.

1973. Traffic Week. Multicoloured.
15. 35 f. Traffic lights and road sign 8 5
16. 75 f. Pedestrian-crossing (horiz.) 20 15
17. 1 d. 25 Type 3 .. .. 30 20

4. "Three Races of the World".

1973. Declaration of Human Rights. 25th Anniv.
18. 4. 35 f. blk., yell. and blue.. 8 5
19. 65 f. black, yellow & red.. 15 12
20. 1¼ d. black, yellow & grn. 35 25

5. U.P.U. Emblem.

1974. Universal Postal Union. Centenary.
21. 5. 25 f. multicoloured .. 8 5
22. 60 f. multicoloured .. 15 12
23. 1¼ d. multicoloured .. 30 20

6. Medical Equipment. (Health Service).

1974. 3rd National Day.
24. 6. 10 f. red, brn. & lilac .. 5 5
25. – 35 f. gold, grn. & blue .. 8 5
26. – 65 f. brn., sepia and blue.. 15 12
27. – 1¼ d. multicoloured .. 25 20
DESIGNS—HORIZ. (49×30 mm.). 35 f. Children reading (Education). 65 f. Tools and buildings (Construction). 1¼ d. U.A.E. flag with emblems of U.N. and Arab League.

7. Arab Couple with Candle and Book.

1974. International Literacy Day.
28. 7. 35 f. multicoloured .. 8 5
29. – 65 f. blk., blue & brown.. 15 12
30. – 1 d. 25 black, blue & brn. 25 20
DESIGN—VERT. 65 f., 1 d. 25 Arab couple with book.

8. Oil De-gassing Installation.

1975. 9th Arab Oil Conference. Multicoloured.
31. 25 f. Type 8.. .. .. 5 5
32. 50 f. Offshore drilling platform 10 8
33. 100 f. Underwater storage tank 20 15
34. 125 f. Marine oil production platform 25 20

9. Station and Dish Aerial.

1975. Opening of Jabal Ali Satellite Earth Station. Multicoloured
36. 15 f. Type 9 .. .. 5 5
37. 35 f. Satellite beaming information to Earth .. 8 5
38. 65 f. As 35 f. 15 12
39. 2 d. Type 9 .. .. 50 45

10. Views within Eagle Emblem.

11. Symbols of Learning.

1975. 4th National Day.

40. **10.**	10 f. multicoloured ..	5	5
41. –	35 f. multicoloured ..	8	5
42. –	60 f. multicoloured ..	15	12
43. –	80 f. multicoloured ..	20	15
44. –	90 f. multicoloured ..	25	20
45. –	1 d. multicoloured ..	25	20
46. –	140 f. multicoloured ..	35	30
47. –	5 d. multicoloured ..	1·25	1·10

DESIGNS: 35 f. to 5 d. Rulers of the Emirates.

1976. Arabic Literacy Day. Multicoloured.

48.	15 f. Type **11**	5	5
49.	50 f. Arabs seeking enlightenment	12	10
50.	3 d. As 50 f.	75	70

12. Arab and Road Signals. **13.** Headphones.

1976. Traffic Week. Multicoloured.

51.	15 f. Type **12**	5	5
52.	80 f. Example of dangerous driving, and road signals (horiz.)	25	20
53.	140 f. Children on road crossing (horiz.)	45	40

1976. Int. Telecommunications Day.

54. **13.**	50 f. multicoloured ..	15	12
55.	80 f. multicoloured ..	25	20
56.	2 d. multicoloured ..	65	60

14. U.A.E. Crest. **15.** President Shaikh Zayed.

1976.

57. **14.**	5 f. brown	5	5
58.	10 f. brown	5	5
59.	15 f. pink	5	5
60.	35 f. brown	12	10
61.	50 f. violet	15	12
62.	60 f. bistre	20	15
63.	80 f. green	25	20
64.	90 f. blue	30	25
65.	1 d. grey	30	25
66.	140 f. blue	45	40
67.	150 f. violet	45	40
68.	2 d. slate	65	60
69.	5 d. turquoise	1·60	1·50
70.	10 d. magenta	3·25	3·00

1976. 5th National Day.

71. **15.**	15 f. multicoloured ..	5	5
72.	140 f. multicoloured ..	45	40

16. Falcon's Head and Arabian Gulf. **17.** Quaid-i-Azam (Mohammed-Ali-Jinnah).

1976. International Falconry Congress, Abu Dhabi.

73. **16.**	80 f. multicoloured ..	25	20
74.	2 d. multicoloured ..	65	60

1976. Quaid-i-Azam (Founder of Pakistan). Birth Centenary.

75. **17.**	50 f. multicoloured ..	15	12
76.	80 f. multicoloured ..	20	20

1977. No. 6 surch in English and Arabic.

77.	50 f. on 75 f. multicoloured	15	12

UNITED NATIONS O4; E3

A. NEW YORK HEADQUARTERS

For use on mail posted at the Post Office at U.N. Headquarters, New York.

NOTE: Similar designs, but in different colours and with values in Swiss francs (F.S.) are issues of the Geneva Office and will be found following the New York issues.

1. Peoples of the World. **2.** U.N. Emblem.

1951.

1. **1.**	1 c. magenta	5	5
2. –	1½ c. green	5	5
3. **2.**	2 c. violet	5	5
4. –	3 c. blue and purple ..	8	5
63. –	4 c. orange	5	5
5. –	5 c. blue	8	8
64. –	8 c. blue	12	10
6. **1.**	10 c. chocolate ..	35	20
7. –	15 c. blue and violet ..	30	25
8. –	20 c. brown	75	50
9. –	25 c. blue and black ..	70	70
10. –	50 c. blue	8·50	5·50
11. **2.**	$1 red	1·40	1·00

DESIGNS—VERT. 1½ c., 50 c. U.N. Headquarters, New York. 4 c., 8 c. U.N. seal. 5 c. Clasped hands. HORIZ. 3 c., 15 c., 25 c. U.N. flag. 20 c. Hemisphere and U.N. emblem.

3. Sea-gull and Aeroplane.

DESIGNS — HORIZ. 7 c. U.N. flag and airliner. 15 c., 25 c. Swallows and U.N. emblem.

1951. Air.

A 12. **3.**	6 c. red	15	15
A 53. –	7 c. blue	12	8
A 13. **3.**	10 c. green	25	15
A 14. –	15 c. blue	65	45
A 15. –	25 c. grey	2·00	1·25

4. Veteran's War Memorial Building, San Francisco.

1952. Signing of U.N. Charter. 7th Anniv.

21. **4.**	5 c. blue	55	35

5. "Flame of Freedom". **6.** Homeless Family.

1952. Human Rights Day.

13. **5.**	3 c. green	30	15
14.	5 c. blue	85	40

1953. Protection for Refugees.

15. **6.**	3 c. brown	30	15
16.	5 c. blue	2·25	85

7. "Universal Postal Union"

1953. Universal Postal Union.

17. **7.**	3 c. sepia	45	20
18.	5 c. blue	3·00	85

8. **9.** "Flame of Freedom".

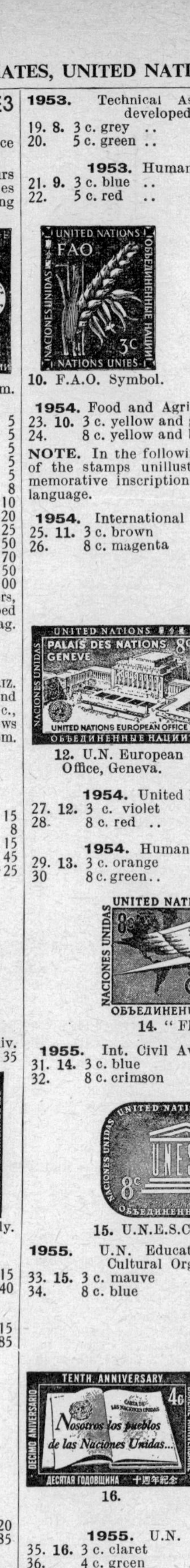

1953. Technical Assistance for Under-developed Areas.

19. **8.**	3 c. grey	30	25
20.	5 c. green	1·60	60

1953. Human Rights Day.

21. **9.**	3 c. blue	45	25
22.	5 c. red	2·75	70

10. F.A.O. Symbol. **11.** I.L.O. Symbol.

1954. Food and Agriculture Organization.

23. **10.**	3 c. yellow and green ..	45	25
24.	8 c. yellow and blue ..	1·40	65

NOTE. In the following issues the majority of the stamps unillustrated have the commemorative inscription or initials in another language.

1954. International Labour Organization.

25. **11.**	3 c. brown	35	25
26.	8 c. magenta	4·00	70

12. U.N. European Office, Geneva. **13.** Mother and Child.

1954. United Nations Day.

27. **12.**	3 c. violet	3·25	1·40
28.	8 c. red	35	30

1954. Human Rights Day.

29. **13.**	3 c. orange	19·00	2·75
30	8 c. green	55	55

14. "Flight".

1955. Int. Civil Aviation Organization.

31. **14.**	3 c. blue	4·25	55
32.	8 c. crimson	70	55

15. U.N.E.S.C.O. Symbol.

1955. U.N. Educational, Scientific and Cultural Organization.

33. **15.**	3 c. mauve	2·10	55
34.	8 c. blue	30	30

16. **17.** "Flame of Freedom".

1955. U.N. 10th Anniv.

35. **16.**	3 c. claret	4·00	70
36.	4 c. green	15	15
37.	8 c. black	30	25

1955. Human Rights Day.

39. **17.**	3 c. blue	20	15
40.	8 c. green	85	50

18. "Telecommunication".

19. Staff of Aesculapius.

1956. Int. Telecommunication Union.

41. **18.**	3 c. blue	45	30
42.	8 c. red	55	45

1956. World Health Organization.

43. **19.**	3 c. blue	12	12
44.	8 c. brown	85	50

20. General Assembly.

21. "Flame of Freedom".

22. Weather Balloon.

1956. United Nations Day.

45. **20.**	3 c. slate	8	8
46.	8 c. olive	20	15

1956. Human Rights Day.

47. **21.**	3 c. purple	5	5
48.	8 c. blue	15	10

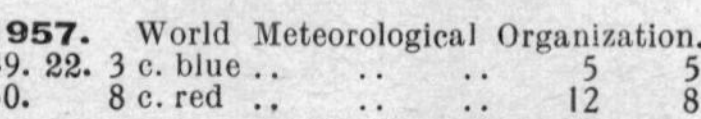

1957. World Meteorological Organization.

49. **22.**	3 c. blue	5	5
50.	8 c. red	12	8

23. U.N.E.F. Badge. **24.** "Flight".

1957. United Nations Emergency Force.

51. **23.**	3 c. blue	5	5
52.	8 c. red	12	8

1957. Air.

A 51. **24.**	4 c. brown	5	5
A 52.	5 c. red	10	5

On the 5 c. value the inscriptions are redrawn larger than those on Type **24**.

25. U.N. Emblem over Globe.

26. "Flames of Freedom".

1957. U.N. Security Council.

55. **25.**	3 c. chestnut	5	5
56.	8 c. green	12	8

1957. Human Rights Day.

57. **26.**	3 c. brown	5	5
58.	8 c. black	12	8

27. Atomic Symbol.

28. Central Hall, Westminster.

1958. Int. Atomic Energy Agency.
59. 27. 3 c. olive 5 5
60. 8 c. blue 12 8

1958. U.N. General Assembly Buildings.
61. 28. 3 c. blue 5 5
62. 8 c. purple 12 8
See also Nos. 69/70, 77/8 and 119/20.

29. Cogwheels. 30. Hands holding Globe.

1958. Economic and Social Council.
65. 29. 4 c. turquoise 5 5
66 8 c. red 15 12

1958. Human Rights Day.
67. 30. 4 c. green 5 5
68. 8 c. brown 15 12

31. New York City Building, Flushing Meadows. 32. Emblem of U.N., Industry and Agriculture.

1959. U.N. General Assembly Buildings.
69. 31. 4 c. mauve 8 5
70. 8 c. turquoise 20 15

1959. U.N. Economic Commission for Europe.
71. 32. 4 c. blue 12 12
72. 8 c. red 25 20

33. "The Age of Bronze" (after Rodin). 34. "Protection for Refugees".

1959. U.N. Trusteeship Council.
73. 33. 4 c. red 8 8
74. 8 c. bronze-green 20 15

1959. World Refugee Year.
75. 34. 4 c. red and bistre .. 8 5
76. 8 c. blue and bistre .. 15 12

35. Palais de Chaillot, Paris. 36. Steel Girder and Map.

1960. U.N. General Assembly Buildings.
77. 35. 4 c. blue and purple .. 8 5
78. 8 c. brown and green .. 15 12

1960. U.N. Economic Commission for Asia and the Far East ("ECAFE").
79. 36. 4 c. maroon, buff and turquoise 8 5
80. 8 c. green, pink and blue 15 12

37. Tree and Emblems. 38. U.N. Headquarters and Emblem.

1960. 5th World Forestry Congress, Seattle.
81. 37. 4 c. multicoloured .. 8 5
82. 8 c. multicoloured .. 15 12

1960. 15th Anniv. of U.N.
83. 38. 4 c. blue 8 5
84. 8 c. black 12 10

39. Double Block and Hook. 40. Scales of Justice.

1960. Int. Bank for Reconstruction and Development ("World Bank").
86. 39. 4 c. multicoloured .. 8 5
87. 8 c. multicoloured .. 15 12

1961. International Court of Justice.
88. 40. 4 c. black, brown & yell. 8 5
89. 8 c. black, green & yell. 15 12

41. I.M.F. Emblem.

1961. Int. Monetary Fund.
90. 41. 4 c. blue 8 5
91. 7 c. brown and yellow .. 15 12

42. "Peace". 44. Globe and Weather Vane.

43. Flags.

1961.
92. 42. 1 c. multicoloured .. 8 5
93. – 2 c. multicoloured .. 5 5
94. – 3 c. multicoloured .. 5 5
95. – 5 c. brown 20 12
96. – 7 c. brown, black & blue 8 8
97. – 10 c. black, grn. & blue .. 15 10
98. – 11 c. gold, light blue and blue 12 10
99. 43. 30 c. multicoloured .. 35 20
100. 44. 50 c. multicoloured .. 55 50

DESIGNS—HORIZ. (32×23 mm.). 2 c. Map of the World. 10 c. Three figures on globe. (30½×23½ mm.). 3 c. U.N. Flag. (36½×23½ mm.). 5 c. Hands supporting "UN" and globe. (37½×22½ mm.). 11 c. U.N. emblem across globe. VERT. (21×26 mm.). 7 c. U.N. emblem, as flowering plant.

For 1 c. in same design, but smaller, see No. 146.

45. 46. Africa Hall, Addis Ababa.

1961. Economic Commission for Latin America.
101. 45. 4 c. red, olive and blue 15 12
102. 11 c. purple, red & green 45 25

1961. Economic Commission for Africa.
103. 46. 4 c. multicoloured .. 8 8
104. 11 c. multicoloured .. 30 20

47. Bird feeding Young. 48. "Housing and Community Facilities".

1961. U.N.I.C.E.F. 15th Anniv.
105. 47. 3 c. sepia, orange, yellow and gold 5 5
106. 4 c. chocolate, blue, grn. and gold 15 8
107. 13 c. myrtle, violet, pink and gold 30 25

1962. U.N. Housing and Related Community Facilities Programme.
108. 48. 4 c. multicoloured .. 12 8
109. 7 c. multicoloured .. 25 15

49. Mosquito and W.H.O. Emblem. 50. U.N. Flag at Half-Mast.

1962. Malaria Eradication.
110. 49. 4 c. maroon, black, green, yellow and orange .. 15 8
111. 11 c. maroon, black, yell. and green 30 20

1962. Dag Hammarskjoeld Memorial Issue.
112. 50. 5 c. indigo, blue & black 15 12
113. 15 c. indigo, olive-grey and black 70 30

51. Congo on World Map. 52. "Peace in Space".

53. Conference Emblem. 54. Wheat.

1962. U.N. Congo Operation.
114. 51. 4 c. olive, orange, yellow and black 20 12
115. 11 c. turquoise, orange, yellow and black .. 65 35

1962. U.N. Committee on Peaceful Uses of Outer Space.
116. 52. 4 c. blue 8 8
117. 11 c. magenta 30 20

1963. Science and Technology Conf., Geneva.
118. 53. 5 c. multicoloured .. 12 10
119. 11 c. multicoloured .. 30 25

1963. Freedom from Hunger.
120. 54. 5 c. yellow, green & red 12 10
121. 11 c. yellow, maroon and red 30 25

55. "Flight". 56. "Bridge" over Map of West New Guinea.

1963. Air. Multicoloured.
A 122. 6 c. "Space" 8 5
A 123. 8 c. Type 55 .. .. 10 8
A 124. 13 c. "Bird" 15 12
A 125. 15 c. "Birds" in flight .. 15 15
A 126. 25 c. Aircraft and airmail envelope 35 30

SIZES—HORIZ. 6 c. As T 54. 13 c., 25 c. 30½×23 mm. VERT. 15 c. 23×30½ mm.

The 7 c. is inscr. "NATIONS UNIES"; the 8 c., 10 c., 25 c. "UNITED NATIONS" only; the others as usual.

1963. United Nations Temporary Executive Authority (UNTEA) in West New Guinea.
122. 56. 25 c. green, blue & drab 70 50

57. General Assembly Building and Flags. 58. "Flame of Freedom".

1963. U.N. General Assembly Buildings.
123. 57. 5 c. multicoloured .. 12 8
124. 11 c. multicoloured .. 30 25

1963. Declaration of Human Rights. 15th Anniv.
125. 58. 5 c. multicoloured .. 12 8
126. 11 c. multicoloured .. 30 25

59. Ships at Sea.

1964. Inter-Governmental Maritime Consultative Organization (I.M.C.O.).
127. 59. 5 c. multicoloured .. 12 8
128. 11 c. multicoloured .. 30 25

60. "Trade and Development".

1964. U.N. Trade and Development Conf., Geneva.
129. 60. 5 c. yellow, black & red 8 8
130. 11 c. yellow, black & bis. 25 25

61. Opium Poppy and Reaching Hands. 62. Atomic Explosion and Padlock.

1964. Narcotics Control.
131. 61. 5 c. red and black 8 8
132. 11 c. green and black .. 30 25

1964. Cessation of Nuclear Testing.
133. 62. 5 c. sepia and brown .. 8 8

63. "Teaching". 64. Key, Globe and "Graph".

1964. "Education for Progress".
134. 63. 4 c. multicoloured .. 8 5
135. 5 c. multicoloured .. 8 8
136. 11 c. multicoloured .. 15 15

1965. U.N. Special Fund.
137. 64. 5 c. multicoloured .. 8 8
138. 11 c. multicoloured .. 15 15

65. Cyprus "Leaves" and U.N. Emblem. 66. "From Semaphore to Satellite".

1965. Peace-keeping Force in Cyprus.
139. 65. 5 c. olive, blk. & orge. 8 8
140. 11 c. grn., blk. & lt. grn 15 15

1965. I.T.U. Cent.
141. **66.** 5 c. multicoloured .. 8 8
142. 11 c. multicoloured .. 15 15

67. I.C.Y. Emblem. **68.** "To Live Together in Peace . . .".

1965. U.N. 20th Anniv. and Int. Co-operation Year.
143. **67.** 5 c. blue 8 8
144. 15 c. magenta 25 15

1965.
146. **68.** 1 c. multicoloured .. 5 5
164. – 1½ c. multicoloured .. 5 5
165. – 5 c. multicoloured .. 8 5
166. – 6 c. multicoloured .. 12 5
167. – 13 c. blue, gold and blk. 15 8
147. – 15 c. multicoloured .. 15 15
148. – 20 c. multicoloured .. 25 20
149. – 25 c. ultram. and blue .. 30 25
150. – $1 blue and turquoise .. 1·10 1·00

DESIGNS—VERT. (23×33 mm.): 1½ c. U.N. Headquarters and World Map (23×34). 6 c. Aerial view of U.N. Headquarters. 13 c. "U.N." and emblem. (24½×30 mm.): 15 c. Scroll, "We the people . . .". (22×32 mm.): 20 c. U.N. Emblem and Headquarters. SQUARE (24×24 mm.): 25 c. U.N. emblem. HORIZ. (33×23 mm.): $1 U.N. emblem in "rippling waters". 5 c. Hands supporting letters "U.N." and Globe.

For 5 c. lake see No. 95.

69. "Expanding Population". **70.** Globe and Flags.

1965. Population Trends and Development.
151. **69.** 4 c. multicoloured .. 5 5
152. 5 c. multicoloured .. 8 5
153. 11 c. multicoloured .. 15 12

1966. World Federation of United Nations Assns. (W.F.U.N.A.)
154. **70.** 5 c. multicoloured .. 8 8
155. 15 c. multicoloured .. 25 20

71. W.H.O. Building. **72.** Coffee.

1966. W.H.O. Headquarters, Geneva. Inaug.
156. **71.** 5 c. multicoloured .. 8 8
157. 11 c. multicoloured .. 15 12

1966. Int. Coffee Agreement of 1962.
158. **72.** 5 c. multicoloured .. 8 8
159. 11 c. multicoloured .. 15 12

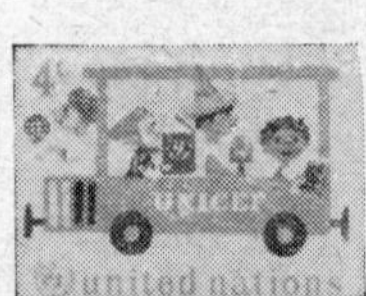

73. Military Observer. **74.** Children in Closed Rail Wagon.

1966. U.N. Military Observers.
160. **73.** 15 c. multicoloured .. 25 15

1966. U.N.I.C.E.F. 20th Anniv. Multicoloured.
161. 4 c. Type **74** 8 5
162. 5 c. Children in Locomotive and Tender .. 10 8
163. 11 c. Children in Open Rail Wagon 15 12

INDEX

Countries can be quickly located by referring to the index at the end of this volume.

75. "Progress through Development". **76.** U.N. Emblem and Fireworks.

1967. U.N. Development Programme.
168. **75.** 5 c. multicoloured .. 8 5
169. 11 c. multicoloured .. 15 12

1967. New Independent Nations Commem.
170. **76.** 5 c. multicoloured .. 8 5
171. 11 c. multicoloured .. 15 15

77. "Peace". **78.** Baggage Labels.

1967. "EXPO 67", World Fair, Montreal
(a) As T **77**.
172. **77.** 4 c. chestnut and red .. 8 8
173. – 5 c. chestnut and blue .. 10 8
174. – 8 c. multicoloured .. 20 20
175. – 10 c. chestnut & green .. 40 55
176. – 15 c. chestnut & brown 80 80

DESIGNS—VERT. 5 c. "Justice". 10 c. "Fraternity". 15 c. "Truth". HORIZ. (32×23½ mm.). 8 c. Facade of U.N. Pavilion.

The above stamps are expressed in Canadian currency and were valid for postage only from the U.N. Pavilion at the World Fair. They were also on sale at the U.N. Headquarters, New York, the Geneva Office and at U.N. sales agencies throughout the world.

1967. Int. Tourist Year.
177. **78.** 5 c. multicoloured .. 5 5
178. 15 c. multicoloured .. 15 12

79. "Towards Disarmament". **80.** "The Kiss of Peace" (part of Chagall's stained-glass window).

1967. Disarmament Campaign.
179. **79.** 6 c. multicoloured .. 8 5
180. 13 c. multicoloured .. 15 12

1967. United Nations Art (1st issue). Chagalls' Memorial Window in U.N. Secretariat Building.
181. **80.** 6 c. multicoloured .. 8 5

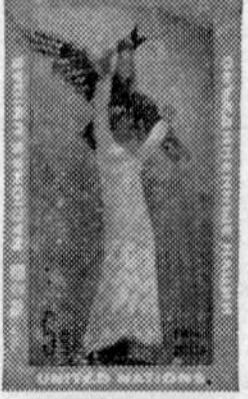

81. Globe and Diagram of U.N. Organs. **82.** Starcke's Statue.

1968. U.N. Secretariat.
183. **81.** 6 c. multicoloured .. 8 5
184. 13 c. multicoloured .. 15 8

1968. United Nations Art (2nd issue). Henrik Starcke's Statue in U.N. Trusteeship Council Chamber.
185. **82.** 6 c. multicoloured .. 8 8
186. 75 c. multicoloured .. 1·40 1·10

The 75 c. also has definitive use.

83. Industrial Skyline. **84.** "Winged" Envelopes.

85. Aircraft and U.N. Emblem.

1968. U.N. Industrial Development Organization (U.N.I.D.O.).
187. **83.** 6 c. multicoloured .. 8 5
188. 13 c. multicoloured .. 15 8

1968. Air.
A 189. **84.** 10 c. multicoloured 12 8
A 190. **85.** 20 c. multicoloured .. 25 15

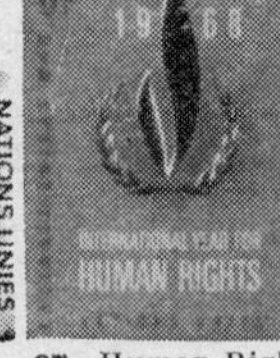

86. Radar Scanner and Globes. **87.** Human Rights Emblem.

1968. World Weather Watch.
189. **86.** 6 c. multicoloured .. 8 5
190. 20 c. multicoloured .. 25 20

1968. Human Rights Year.
191. **87.** 6 c. gold, ultram. & bl. 20 12
192. 13 c. gold, red & pink .. 20 20

88. Textbooks. **89.** U.N. Building Santiago.

1969. United Nations Institute for Training and Research (U.N.I.T.A.R.).
193. **88.** 6 c. multicoloured .. 8 8
194. 13 c. multicoloured .. 20 15

In the 13 c. the name and value panel is at foot of stamp.

1969. U.N. Building, Santiago, Chile.
195. **89.** 6 c. blue and green .. 8 8
196. 15 c. purple, red & buff 20 15

90. "Peace Through International Law".

1969. Session of U.N. Int. Law Commission. 20th Anniv.
197. **90.** 6 c. multicoloured .. 8 8
198. 13 c. multicoloured .. 20 15

91. "Labour and Development".

1969. Int. Labour Organization. 50th Anniv.
199. **91.** 6 c. gold, blue & cream 8 8
200. 20 c. gold, red & purple 30 25

92. "Ostrich". **93.** Peace Bell.

1969. United Nations Art (3rd issue). Tunisian Mosaic. Multicoloured.
201. 6 c. Type **92** 8 8
202. 13 c. "Ring-necked Pheasant" 20 15

1970. United Nations Art (4th issue). Japanese Peace Bell.
203. **93.** 6 c. multicoloured .. 8 8
204. 25 c. multicoloured .. 40 35

94. Mekong River, Power Lines and Map. **95.** "Fight Cancer".

1970. Lower Mekong Basin Development Project.
205. **94.** 6 c. multicoloured .. 8 8
206. 13 c. multicoloured .. 20 15

1970. 10th Int. Cancer Congress, Houston, Texas.
207. **95.** 6 c. black and blue .. 8 8
208. 13 c. black and olive .. 20 15

96. Laurel Branch. **97.** Scales and Olive Branch.

1970. U.N. 25th Anniv. Multicoloured.
209. 6 c. Type **96** 12 10
210. 13 c. Type **96** 20 20
211. 25 c. U.N. Emblem (vert.) 35 35

On No. 210 the inscription is in French.

1970. "Peace, Justice and Progress" (Aims of the United Nations).
213. **97.** 6 c. multicoloured .. 8 8
214. 13 c. multicoloured .. 25 20

98. U.N. Emblem on Sea-bed. **99.** "Refugees" (sculpture by Kaare Nygaard).

1971. Peaceful Uses of the Sea-bed.
215 **98.** 6 c. multicoloured .. 8 8

1971. "International Support for Refugees".
216. **99.** 6 c. black, yellow & brn. 8 8
217. 13 c. black, turq. & blue 20 15

100. Wheatsheaf on Globe. **101.** New U.P.U. H.Q. Building

1971. World Food Programme.
218. **100** 13 c. multicoloured .. 20 15

1971. New U.P.U. Headquarters Building, Berne.
219. **101.** 20 c. multicoloured .. 30 25

102. Four-leafed Clover. **103.** U.N. H.Q., New York.

1971. Racial Equality Year. Multicoloured.
220. 8 c. Type **102** 12 8
221. 13 c. Linked globes (horiz.) 20 15

1971. Multicoloured.
222. 8 c. Type **103** 10 8
223. 60 c. U.N. emblem and flags 70 50
224. 95 c. "Letter Changing Hands" .. .. .. 1·10 85

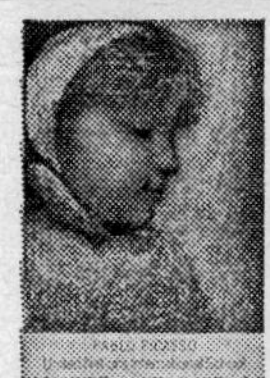

104. " Maia " (Picasso). **106.** " X " on Atomic Explosion.

1971. U.N. Int. Schools.
225. **104.** 8 c. multicoloured .. 12 8
226. 21 c. multicoloured .. 30 25

1972. Non-Proliferation of Nuclear Weapons.
227. **106.** 8 c. blue, black & pink 12 8

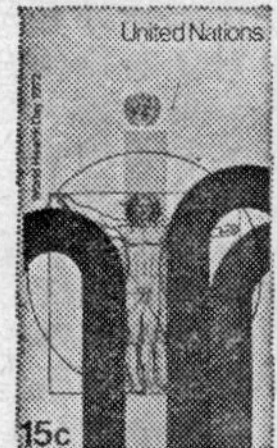

107. "Proportions of Man" (Da Vinci). **108.** Birds in Flight.

1972. World Health Day.
228. **107.** 15 c. multicoloured .. 15 15

1972. Air. Multicoloured.
A 229. 9 c. " Contemporary Flight " (vert. 23 × 31 mm)... .. 10 8
A 230. 11 c. Type **108** 12 8
A 231. 17 c. Clouds (horiz. 38 × 23 mm.).. .. 20 15
A 232. 21 c. " U.N. " jetstream (horiz. 33 × 23 mm.).. 25 20

109. Environmental Emblem. **110.** Europa " Flower ".

1972. U.N. Environmental Conservation Conf., Stockholm.
233. **109.** 8 c. multicoloured .. 10 8
234. 15 c. multicoloured .. 15 15

1972. Economic Commission for Europe (E.C.E.).
235. **110.** 21 c. multicoloured .. 25 20

111. " World United " (detail, Sert mural, Geneva). **112.** Laurel and Broken Sword.

1972. United Nations Art. (5th issue).
236. **111.** 8 c. brown, gold & lake 10 8
237. 15 c. brn., gold & grn. 15 15

1973. Disarmament Decade.
238. **112.** 8 c. multicoloured .. 12 8
239. 15 c. multicoloured .. 15 15

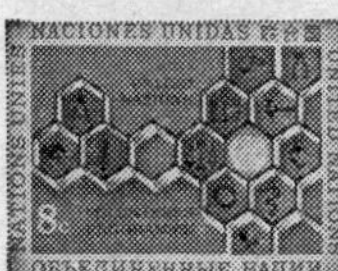

113. Skull on Poppy. **114.** Emblems within Honeycomb.

1973. " Stop Drug Abuse " Campaign.
240. **113.** 8 c. multicoloured .. 10 8
241 15 c. multicoloured .. 15 15

1973. U.N. Volunteers Progra nme.
242. **114.** 8 c. multicoloured .. 10 8
243. 21 c. multicoloured .. 25 20

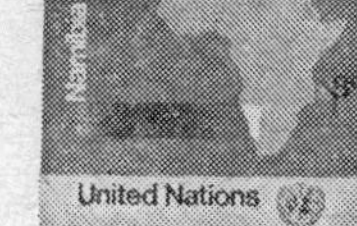

115. Namibia on Map of Africa.

1973. U.N. Resolutions on Namibia (South West Africa).
244. **115.** 8 c. multicoloured .. 10 8
245. 15 c. multicoloured .. 15 15

116. Human Rights Flame.

1973. Declaration of Human Rights. 25th Anniv.
247. **116.** 8 c. multicoloured .. 10 8
248. 21 c. multicoloured .. 25 15

117. I.L.O. H.Q., Building.

1973. New I.L.O. Headquarters Building, Geneva. Inauguration.
248. **117.** 10 c. multicoloured .. 12 8
249. 21 c. multicoloured .. 15 10

118. Globe within Posthorn.

1974. Universal Postal Union. Cent.
250. **118.** 10 c. multicoloured .. 12 8

119. "Children's Choir" (mural detail. C. Portinari).

1974. United Nations Art (6th issue). Brazilian Peace Mural, Delegates' Lobby.
251. **119.** 10 c. multicoloured .. 12 8
252. 18 c. multicoloured .. 20 15

120. Peace Dove.

1974.
253. **120.** 2 c. blue and ultram... 5 5
254. – 10 c. multicoloured .. 12 8
255. – 18 c. multicoloured .. 20 15
DESIGNS—VERT. 10 c. U.N. Headquarters. New York. 18 c. Globe over U.N. emblem and flags.

121. Globe and Jet Aircraft. **122.** Young Children with Globe.

1974. Air. Multicoloured.
A 256. 13 c. Type **121** 15 12
A 257. 18 c. " Channels of Communication " (38 × 23 mm.) 20 15
A 258. 26 c. Dove in Flight and U.N. Headquarters .. 30 20

1974. World Population Year.
259. **122.** 10 c. multicoloured .. 12 8
260. 18 c. multicoloured .. 20 15

123. Ship and Fish. **124.** Satellite, Globe and Symbols.

1974. U.N. Conference on " Law of the Sea "
261. **123.** 10 c. multicoloured .. 12 8
262. 26 c. multicoloured .. 30 20

1975. Peaceful Uses of Outer Space.
263. **124.** 10 c. multicoloured .. 12 5
264. 26 c. multicoloured 30 15

125. " Sex Equality ". **126.** " The Hope of Mankind ".

1975. International Women's Year.
265. **125.** 10 c. multicoloured .. 12 5
266. 18 c. multicoloured .. 20 10

1975. United Nations. 30th Anniv.
267. **126.** 10 c. multicoloured .. 12 5
268. 18 c. multicoloured .. 30 15

127. Cupped Hands. **128.** Wild Rose and Barbed Wire.

1975. " Namibia-U.N. Direct Responsibility"
270. **127.** 10 c. multicoloured .. 12 8
271. 18 c. multicoloured .. 20 10

1975. U.N. Peace-keeping Operations.
272. **128.** 13 c. blue 15 8
273. 26 c. mauve 30 15

129. " Bird of Peace ". **130.** Linked Ribands.

1976. Multicoloured.
274. 3 c. Type **129** 5 5
275. 4 c. " Gathering of Peoples " (39 × 23 mm.) .. 5 5
276. 30 c. U.N. flag (23 × 39 mm.) 35 15
277. 50 c. " Universal Peace " (dove and rainbow) (23 × 39 mm.).. .. 55 30

1976. World Federation of U.N. Associations.
278. **130.** 13 c. multicoloured .. 15 8
279. 26 c. multicoloured .. 30 15

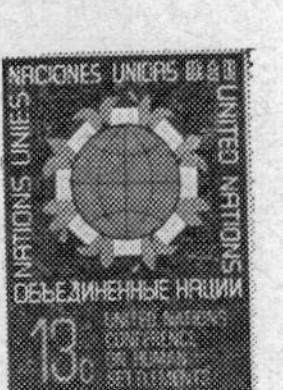

131. Globe and Crate. **132.** Houses bordering Globe.

1976. U.N. Conf. on Trade and Development.
280. **131.** 13 c. multicoloured .. 15 8
281. 31 c. multicoloured .. 35 15

1976. " HABITAT ". U.N. Conf. on Human Settlements.
282. **132.** 13 c. multicoloured .. 15 8
283. 25 c. multicoloured .. 25 15

133. Magnifying Glass and Emblem. **134.** Stylised Ear of Wheat.

1976. U.N. Postal Administration. 25th Anniv.
284. **133.** 13 c. multicoloured .. 15 8
285. 31 c. multicoloured .. 35 15

1976. World Food Council.
286. **134.** 13 c. multicoloured .. 15 8

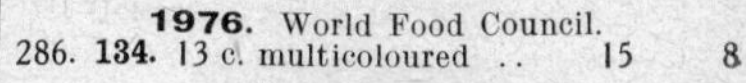

135. U.N. Emblem.

1976.
287. **135.** 9 c. multicoloured .. 10 5

B. GENEVA HEADQUARTERS

Stamps issued by the Swiss PTT for use of the Headquarters of the former League of Nations and International Labour Office, the European Office of U.N.O. and other U.N. Agencies with offices in Geneva. In Oct. 1969, the United Nations Postal Administration issued stamps for use in the Palais des Nations, Geneva, and the Swiss PTT issues for UNITED NATIONS only were withdrawn.

These stamps could not be legitimately obtained unused before February 1944.

Stamps of Switzerland overprinted for the use of international organizations. After 1955 definitive stamps were issued.

I. LEAGUE OF NATIONS

Optd. **SOCIETE DES NATIONS**

1922.
LN 1. **12.** 2½ c. olive on buff.. — 12
LN 2. 3 c. blue on buff .. — 2·75
LN 3. 5 c. orange on buff — 1·50
LN 4. 5 c. lilac on buff .. — 1·00
LN 5. 5 c. purple on buff — 75
LN 5a. 5 c. green on buff.. — 9·00
LN 6. 7½ c. green on buff — 25
LN 7. **13.** 10 c. green on buff — 25
LN 8a. 10 c. violet on buff — 65
LN 9. 15 c. lake on buff.. — 50
LN 10. 20 c. violet on buff — 1·90
LN 11. 20 c. red on buff .. — 65
LN 12. 25 c. orange on buff — 1·90
LN 13. 25 c. red on buff .. — 50
LN 14. 25 c. brown on buff — 5·50
LN 15. **9.** 30 c. green and brown — 4·50
LN 16. **13.** 30 c. blue on buff.. — 4·50
LN 17. **9.** 35 c. yellow and green — 1·50
LN 18. 40 c. bright blue .. — 65
LN 19. 40 c. green and mauve — 3·25
LN 20. 50 c. green 65 65
LN 21. 60 c. brown .. 13·00 65
LN 22. 70 c. buff and violet 75 1·00
LN 23. 80 c. buff and grey 1·10 90
LN 24. **51.** 90 c. red and green — 4·50
LN 25. **9.** 1 f. green and claret — 2·50
LN 26. **51.** 1 f. 20 red and lake 1·25 1·60
LN 27. 1 f. 50 red and blue 1·25 1·60
LN 28. 2 f. red & blk. on grey 1·60 2·10
LN 29. **15.** 3 f. red .. .. — 14·00
LN 29a. **80.** 3 f. brown.. .. — 75·00
LN 30. – 5 f. blue (No. 285) — 28·00
LN 32. – 10 f. purple (No. 286) — 55·00
LN 33. – 10 f. green (No. 331a) — 85·00

1932. Int. Disarmament Conf.
LN 34. **83.** 5 c. green .. .. — 6·50
LN 35. 10 c. orange .. — 65
LN 36. 20 c. red .. .. — 65
LN 37. 30 c. blue .. .. — 16·00
LN 38. 60 c. sepia .. — 3·25
LN 39. **84.** 1 f. grey and blue .. — 4·50

1934. Landscape designs of 1934.
LN 40. **91.** 3 c. olive .. .. — 25
LN 41. 5 c. green .. .. — 12
LN 43. 15 c. orange .. — 65
LN 45. 25 c. brown .. — 3·25
LN 46. 30 c. blue .. .. — 65

1937. Landscape designs of 1936.
LN 47. **96.** 3 c. olive 5 10
LN 48. 5 c. green 10 10
LN 49aa. 10 c. purple .. — 2·50
LN 49b. 10 c. brown .. 25 20
LN 50. 15 c. orange .. 25 15
LN 51. 20 c. red (Railway) — 65
LN 51a. 20 c. red (Lake) .. 30 25
LN 52. 25 c. brown .. 40 40
LN 53. 30 c. ultramarine .. 40 40
LN 54. 35 c. green 40 40
LN 55. 40 c. grey 40 40

1938. Nos. 382/5 optd. **SOCIETE DES NATIONS.**
LN 56. **104.** 20 c. red and buff — 50
LN 57. – 30 c. blue — 75
LN 58. – 60 c. brown and buff — 1·90
LN 59. – 1 f. black and buff — 2·50

1938. Nos. 382/5 optd. **SERVICE DE LA SOCIETE DES NATIONS** in circle.
LN 60. **104.** 20 c. red and buff.. — 65
LN 61. – 30 c. blue .. — 1·25
LN 62. – 60 c. brown and buff — 1·90
LN 63. – 1 f. black and buff.. — 2·50

1939. Nos. 388/390 optd. **SOCIETE DES NATIONS**
LN 64. **109.** 3 f. brown on buff.. 2·50 2·50
LN 65. – 5 f. blue on buff .. 3·75 5·00
LN 66. – 10 f. green on buff.. 7·50 9·50

1944. Optd. **COURRIER DE LA SOCIETE DES NATIONS.**

(a) Landscape designs of 1936.
LN 67. **96.** 3 c. olive 5 5
LN 68. 5 c. green 8 5
LN 69. 10 c. brown .. 12 12
LN 70. 15 c. orange .. 15 15
LN 71. 20 c. red (lake) .. 20 20
LN 72. 25 c. brown .. 20 20
LN 73. 30 c. ultramarine .. 35 35
LN 74. 35 c. green .. 40 40
LN 75. 40 c. grey .. 45 45

(b) Historical designs of 1941.
LN 76. – 50 c. purple on green 65 65
LN 77. **122.** 60 c. brown on buff 75 75
LN 78. – 70 c. violet on lilac 80 80
LN 79. – 80 c. grey on yellow 55 55
LN 80. 90 c. red on rose .. 55 55
LN 81. – 1 f. green on green.. 75 75
LN 82. – 1 f. 20 violet on grey 1·00 1·00
LN 83. – 1 f. 50 blue on buff 1·25 1·25
LN 84. – 2 f. lake on rose .. 1·40 1·40

(c) Parliament designs of 1938.
LN 85. **109.** 3 f. brown on buff.. 4·75 4·75
LN 86. – 5 f. blue on buff 6·50 6·50
LN 87. – 10 f green on buff 13·00 13·00

II. INTERNATIONAL LABOUR OFFICE

Optd. **S.d.N. Bureau International du Travail.**

1923.
LB 1. **12.** 2½ c. olive on buff .. — 25
LB 2. 3 c. blue on buff .. — 60
LB 3. 5 c. orange on buff.. — 25
LB 4. **12.** 5 c. purple on buff .. — 25
LB 5. 7½ c. green on buff .. — 25
LB 6. **13.** 10 c. green on buff.. — 25
LB 8. 15 c. lake on buff .. — 50
LB 9. 20 c. violet on buff .. — 2·50
LB 10. 20 c. red on buff .. — 1·60
LB 11. 25 c. red on buff .. — 65
LB 12. 25 c. brown on buff.. — 90
LB 13. **9.** 30 c. green and brown — 22·00
LB 14. **13.** 30 c. blue on buff .. — 65
LB 15. **9.** 35 c. yellow and green — 1·90
LB 16. 40 c. bright blue .. — 65
LB 17. 40 c. green and mauve — 2·50
LB 18. 50 c. green 65 75
LB 19. 60 c. brown 65 80
LB 20. 70 c. buff and violet 65 1·00
LB 21. 80 c. buff and grey .. 4·50 1·00
LB 22. **51.** 90 c. red and green.. — 1·90
LB 23 **9.** 1 f. green and claret — 1·25
LB 24. **51.** 1 f. 20 red and lake.. 3·75 2·00
LB 25. 1 f. 50 red and blue.. 1·25 1·50
LB 26. 2 f. red & blk. on grey 1·50 2·00
LB 27. **15.** 3 f. red .. .. — 14·00
LB 27a. **80.** 3 f. brown .. .. — 90·00
LB 28. – 5 f. blue (No. 285) .. — 19·00
LB 30. – 10 f. purple (No. 286) — 95·00
LB 31. – 10 f. green (No. 331a) — 75·00

1932. Int. Disarmament Conference.
LB 32. **83.** 5 c. green .. .. — 65
LB 33. 10 c. orange .. .. — 65
LB 34. 20 c. red .. .. — 75
LB 35. 30 c. blue .. .. — 3·75
LB 36. 60 c. sepia .. .. — 3·75
LB 37. **84.** 1 f. grey and blue .. — 5·00

1937. Landscape design of 1934.
LB 38. **91.** 3 c. olive .. .. — 1·90

1937. Landscape designs of 1936.
LB 39. **96.** 3 c. olive 5 10
LB 40. 5 c. green 5 10
LB 41. 10 c. purple .. .. — 65
LB 41b. 10 c. brown 15 15
LB 42. 15 c. orange .. 12 15
LB 43. 20 c. red (Mountain) — 40
LB 43a. 20 c. red (Lake) .. 40 40
LB 44. 25 c. brown .. 30 40
LB 45. 30 c. ultramarine .. 30 40
LB 46. 35 c. green 30 40
LB 47. 40 c. grey 30 45

1938. Nos. 382/5 optd. **S.d.N. Bureau International du Travail.**
LB 48. **104.** 20 c. red and buff.. — 50
LB 49. – 30 c. blue .. .. — 1·00
LB 50. – 60 c. brown and buff — 1·90
LB 51. – 1 f. black and buff.. — 2·50

1938. Nos. 382/5 optd. **SERVICE DU BUREAU INTERNATIONAL DU TRAVAIL** in circle.
LB 52. **104.** 20 c. red and buff — 75
LB 53. – 30 c. blue .. .. — 1·10
LB 54. – 60 c. brown and buff — 1·90
LB 55. – 1 f. black and buff.. — 3·00

1939. Nos. 388/390 optd. **S.d.N. Bureau International du Travail.**
LB 56. **109.** 3 f. brown on buff .. 2·50 2·50
LB 57. – 5 f. blue on buff .. 3·75 5·00
LB 58. – 10 f. green on buff 7·50 9·50

1944. Optd. **COURRIER DU BUREAU INTERNATIONAL DU TRAVAIL.**

(a) Landscape designs of 1936.
LB 59. **96.** 3 c. olive 5 5
LB 60. 5 c. green 8 8
LB 61. 10 c. brown 10 10
LB 62. 15 c. orange .. 15 15
LB 63. 20 c. red (Lake) .. 20 20
LB 64. 25 c. brown 30 30
LB 65. 30 c. ultramarine .. 35 35
LB 66. 35 c. green 45 45
LB 67. 40 c. grey 50 50

(b) Historical designs of 1941.
LB 68. **122.** 50 c. purple on green 2·50 2·50
LB 69. 60 c. brown on buff 2·50 2·50
LB 70. 70 c. violet on lilac 2·50 2·50
LB 71. 80 c. grey on grey.. 50 55
LB 72. 90 c. red on rose .. 60 60
LB 73. 1 f. green on green.. 75 80
LB 74. 1 f. 20 violet on grey 1·00 1·00
LB 75. 1 f. 50 blue on buff 1·25 1·40
LB 76. 2 f. lake on rose .. 1·75 1·50

(c) Parliament designs of 1938.
LB 77. **109.** 3 f. brown on buff.. 4·75 4·75
LB 78. 5 f. blue on buff .. 7·00 7·00
LB 79 10 f. green on buff.. 14·00 14·00

1950. Landscape designs of 1949 optd **BUREAU INTERNATIONAL DU TRAVAIL.**
LB 80. **165.** 5 c. orange.. .. 40 40
LB 81. 10 c. green .. 40 40
LB 82. 15 c. turquoise .. 50 50
LB 83. 20 c. maroon .. 75 75
LB 84. 25 c. red .. 90 90
LB 85. 30 c. bistre.. .. 1·25 1·25
LB 86. 35 c. brown .. 1·25 1·25
LB 87. 40 c. blue .. .. 1·25 1·25
LB 88. 50 c. grey .. 1·50 1·50
LB 89. 60 c. green .. 1·90 1·90
LB 90. 70 c. violet.. .. 2·50 2·50

LB 1. Miners (bas-relief).

1956. Inscr. as in Type LB 1.
LB 91. LB 1. 5 c. slate-purple.. 5 5
LB 92. 10 c. green .. 5 5
LB 93. – 20 c. scarlet .. 1·10 1·10
LB 94. – 20 c. carmine .. 8 8
LB 95. – 30 c. red .. 12 12
LB 96. LB 1. 40 c. blue .. 1·25 1·25
LB 97. 50 c. blue .. 15 15
LB 98. – 60 c. brown .. 20 20
LB 99. – 2 f. purple .. 65 65
DESIGN—HORIZ. 20 c., 30 c., 60 c. 2 f. Globe, flywheel and factory chimney.

1969. Pope Paul's Visit to Geneva. No. LB 95 optd. **Visite du Pape Paul VI Geneve 10 juin 1969.**
LB 100. LB 1. 30 c. orange .. 40 40

LB 2. New Headquarters Building.

1974. New I.L.O. Headquarters, Geneva Inaug.
LB 101. LB 2. 80 c. mult. .. 35 30

LB 3. Young Man at Lathe.

1975.
LB 102. LB 3. 30 c. brown .. 12 12
LB 103. – 60 c. blue .. 25 20
LB 104. – 1 f. green .. 50 40
DESIGNS: 60 c. Woman at drilling machine. 1 f. Surveyor with theodolite.

III. INTERNATIONAL EDUCATION OFFICE.

1944. Optd. **COURRIER DU BUREAU INTERNATIONAL D'EDUCATION.**

(a) Landscape designs of 1936.
LE 1. **96.** 3 c. olive .. 30 30
LE 2. 5 c. green .. 30 30
LE 3. 10 c. brown .. 40 40
LE 4. 15 c. orange.. 40 40
LE 5. **96.** 20 c. red (Lake) .. 40 40
LE 6. 25 c. brown .. 50 50
LE 7. 30 c. ultramarine .. 50 50
LE 8. 35 c. green .. 65 65
LE 9. 40 c. grey 95 75

(b) Historical designs of 1941.
LE 10. **122.** 50 c. purple on green 3·75 3·75
LE 11. 60 c. brown on buff 3·75 3·75
LE 12. 70 c. violet on lilac 3·75 3·75
LE 13. 80 c. grey on grey 45 45
LE 14. 90 c. red on rose .. 50 50
LE 15. 1 f. green on green 65 65
LE 16. 1 f. 20 violet on grey 80 80
LE 17. 1 f. 50 blue on buff 95 95
LE 18. 2 f. lake on rose .. 1·10 1·10

(c) Parliament designs of 1938.
LE 19. **109.** 3 f. brown on buff.. 3·75 3·75
LE 20. 5 f. blue on buff .. 6·50 6·50
LE 21. 10 f. green on buff 11·00 11·00

1946. Optd. **BIE.**
LE 22. **144.** 10 c. purple.. .. 12 15

Optd. **BUREAU INTERNATIONAL D'EDUCATION.**

1948. Landscape designs of 1936.
LE 23. **96.** 5 c. brown .. .. 1·60 1·60
LE 24. 10 c. green .. .. 1·60 1·60
LE 25. 20 c. brown .. .. 1·60 1·60
LE 26. 25 c. red .. .. 1·60 1·60
LE 27. 30 c. greenish blue .. 1·60 1·60
LE 28. 40 c. blue .. .. 1·60 1·60

1950. Landscape designs of 1949.
LE 29. **165.** 5 c. orange 20 20
LE 30. 10 c. green 25 25
LE 31. 15 c. turquoise .. 25 25
LE 32. 20 c. maroon .. 40 40
LE 33. 25 c. red 75 75
LE 34. 30 c. bistre 65 65
LE 35. 35 c. brown.. .. 75 75
LE 36. 40 c. blue 90 90
LE 37. 50 c. grey .. .. 1·00 1·00
LE 38. 60 c. green .. .. 1·50 1·50
LE 39. 70 c. violet .. .. 1·75 1·75

LE 1. Globe on Books.

1958. Inscr. as in Type E 1.
LE 40. LE 1. 5 c. slate-purple.. 5 5
LE 41. 10 c. green .. 5 5
LE 42. – 20 c. scarlet .. 1·00 1·00
LE 43. – 20 c. carmine .. 8 8
LE 44. – 30 c. red .. 12 12
LE 45. LE 1. 40 c. blue .. 1·10 1·10
LE 46. 50 c. blue .. 15 15
LE 47. – 60 c. brown .. 20 20
LE 48. – 2 f. purple .. 65 65
DESIGN—VERT. 20 c., 30 c., 60 c., 2 f. Pestalozzi Monument, Yverdon.

IV. WORLD HEALTH ORGANIZATION

Optd. **ORGANISATION MONDIALE DE LA SANTE.**

1948. (a) Landscape designs of 1936.
LH 1. 5 c. brown (No. 489) .. 1·25 1·25
LH 2. 10 c. green (No. 490) .. 1·25 1·25
LH 3. 20 c. brown (No. 491) .. 1·25 1·25
LH 4. 25 c. red (No. 492) .. 1·90 1·90
LH 5. 40 c. ultram. (No. 494).. 2·25 2·25

(b) Landscape designs of 1949.
LH 6. **165.** 5 c. orange 12 12
LH 7. – 10 c. green 25 25
LH 8. – 15 c. turquoise .. 25 25
LH 9. – 20 c. maroon .. 40 40
LH 10. – 25 c. red 75 75
LH 11. – 30 c. olive 65 65
LH 12. – 35 c. brown.. .. 75 75
LH 13. – 40 c. blue 75 75
LH 14. – 50 c. grey 75 75
LH 15. – 60 c. green .. .. 1·25 1·25
LH 16. – 70 c. violet .. .. 1·75 1·75

(c) Historical designs of 1941. Nos. 408/13
LH 17. 80 c. grey on grey .. 70 70
LH 18. 90 c. red on rose .. 2·75 2·75
LH 19. 1 f. green on green .. 80 80
LH 20. 1 f. 20 violet on grey .. 3·25 3·25
LH 21. 1 f. 50 blue on buff .. 3·75 3·75
LH 22. 2 f. lake on rose .. 1·90 1·90

(d) Parliament designs of 1938.
LH 23. **109.** 3 f. brown on buff .. 10·00 10·00
LH 24. – 5 f. blue on buff .. 4·50 4·50
LH 25. – 10 f. green on buff .. 22·00 22·00

LH 1. Staff of Aesculapius.

1957.
LH 26. LH 1. 5 c. slate-purple.. 5 5
LH 27. 10 c green .. 5 5
LH 28. 20 c. scarlet .. 1·00 1·00
LH 29. 20 c. carmine .. 8 8
LH 30. 30 c. red .. 12 12
LH 31. LH 1. 40 c. blue .. 1·00 1·00
LH 32. 50 c. blue .. 15 15
LH 33. 60 c. brown .. 20 20
LH 34. 2 f. purple .. 65 65

1962. Malaria Eradication. Optd. **ERADICATION DU PALUDISME.**
LH 35. LH 1. 50 c. blue .. 45 45

LH 2. Staff of Aesculapius.

1975.
LH 36. LH 2. 30 c. multicoloured 12 12
LH 37. 60 c. multicoloured 25 20
LH 38. 90 c. multicoloured 40 35
LH 39. 100 c. multicoloured 45 40

V. INTERNATIONAL REFUGEES ORGANIZATION.

Optd. **ORGANISATION INTERNATIONALE POUR LES REFUGIES.**

1950. (a) Landscape designs of 1949.
LR 1. **165.** 5 c. orange .. .. 4·75 4·75
LR 2. 10 c. green .. .. 4·75 4·75
LR 3. 20 c. maroon .. 4·75 4·75
LR 4. 25 c. red .. .. 4·75 4·75
LR 5. 40 c. blue .. .. 4·75 4·75

(b) Historical designs of 1941.
LR 6. **122.** 80 c. grey on grey .. 4·75 4075
LR 7. 1 f. green on green .. 4·75 4·75
LR 8. 2 f. lake on rose .. 4·75 4·75

VI. UNITED NATIONS

(a) Issues of Swiss PTT.

Optd. **NATIONS UNIES OFFICE EUROPEEN.**

1950. (a) Landscape designs of 1949.
LU 1. **165.** 5 c. orange 25 25
LU 2. 10 c. green 25 25
LU 3. 15 c. turquoise .. 40 40
LU 4. 20 c. maroon .. 40 40
LU 5. 25 c. red 50 50
LU 6. 30 c. bistre 50 50
LU 7. 35 c. brown.. .. 60 60
LU 8. 40 c. blue 70 70
LU 9. 50 c. grey .. .. 1·10 1·10
LU 10. 60 c. green .. .. 1·10 1·10
LU 11. 70 c. violet .. .. 1·40 1·40

(b) Historical designs of 1941.
LU 12. **122.** 80 c. grey on grey .. 4·50 4·50
LU 13. 90 c. red on rose .. 4·50 4·50
LU 14. 1 f. green on green .. 5·00 5·00
LU 15. 1 f. 20 violet on grey 7·50 7·50
LU 16. 1 f. 50 blue on buff.. 7·50 7·50
LU 17. 2 f. lake on rose .. 7·50 7·50

(c) Parliament designs of 1938.
LU 18. **109.** 3 f. brown .. .. 45·00 45·00
LU 19. 5 f. blue .. .. 55·00 55·00
LU 20. 10 f. green £110 £110

LU 1.

LU 2.

1955. 10th Anniv. of U.N.O.
LU 21. LU 1. 40 c. blue & yellow 2·00 2·50

1955. Nos. LU 22/3 and LU 27/8 are as Type LU 1 but without dates.
LU 22. – 5 c. purple .. 5 5
LU 23. – 10 c. green .. 5 5
LU 24. LU 2. 20 c. vermilion .. 1·90 1·90
LU 25 20 c. carmine .. 5 5
LU 26. 30 c. red .. 10 10
LU 27. – 40 c. blue .. 2·25 2·25
LU 28. – 50 c. blue .. 15 15
LU 29. LU 2. 60 c. brown .. 25 25
LU 30. 2 f. purple .. 65 65

1960. World Refugee Year. Nos. LU 25 and LU 28 optd. **ANNEE MONDIALE DU REFUGIE 1959 1960.**
LU 31. 20 c. carmine 20 20
LU 32. 50 c. blue 25 25

LU 3. Palace of Nations, Geneva.

LU 4.

1960. U.N.O. 15th Anniv.
LU 33. LU 3. 5 f. blue .. .. 1·75 1·60

1962. Opening of U.N. Philatelic Museum, Geneva.
LU 34. LU 4. 10 c. green and red 5 5
LU 35. – 30 c. orge.-red & bl. 12 12
LU 36. LU 4. 50 c. blue and red 20 20
LU 37. – 60 c. brn. & green 25 25
DESIGN—HORIZ. 30 c., 60 c. As Type LU 2 but inscr. " ONU MUSEE PHILATELIQUE ".

LU 5. U.N.C.S.A.T. Emblem.

ILLUSTRATIONS British Commonwealth and all overprints and surcharges are FULL SIZE. Foreign Countries have been reduced to ¾-LINEAR.

1963. U.N. Scientific and Technological Conference, Geneva.
LU 38. LU 5. 50 c. red and blue 50 50
LU 39. – 2 f. green & purple 90 90
DESIGN—HORIZ. 2 f. As Type LU 2, but with emblem.

(b) Issues of United Nations Postal Administration.

NOTE: References to numbers and types in this section, other than to those with " G " prefix, are to the United Nations (New York Office) listing.

G 1. Palais des Nations, Geneva.

G 2. Palais des Nations, Geneva.

1969. Existing United Nations (New York) designs adapted with new colours and values in Swiss francs (F.S.). 30 c. is new design. Multicoloured unless otherwise stated.
G 1. – 5 c. (As No. 164) .. 5 5
G 2. – 10 c. (As No. 105) .. 5 5
G 3. – 20 c. (As No. 127) .. 10 5
G 4. G 1. 30 c. multicoloured .. 15 10
G 5. G 2. 40 c. multicoloured .. 25 12
G 6. – 50 c. (As No. 147, but inscr. in French) .. 20 15
G 7. – 60 c. (As No. 107) .. 30 20
G 8. – 70 c. red, gold and black (As No. 188) 30 25
G 9. – 75 c. (As No. A 11) .. 35 25
G 10. – 80 c. (As No. 148) .. 35 30
G 11. 92. 90 c. (Inscr. in French) 40 30
G 12. – 1 f. emerald and green (As No. 149) .. 45 35
G 13. 44. 2 f. multicoloured .. 90 70
G 14. 82. 3 f. multicoloured .. 1·40 1·00
G 15. 2. 10 f. blue .. .. 4·50 3·50

1971. Peaceful Uses of the Sea-bed.
G 16. 98. 30 c. multicoloured .. 20 20

1971 United Nations Work with Refugees
G 17. 99. 50 c. blk., orge. & red 35 25

1971. World Food Programme.
G 18. 100. 50 c. multicoloured .. 35 25

1971. Opening of new U.P.U. Headquarters Building, Berne.
G 19. 101. 75 c. multicoloured .. 50 35

1971. Racial Equality Year. Designs as Nos. 220/1, with background colours changed.
G 20. 30 c. Type 102 .. 20 15
G 21. 50 c. Linked globes (horiz.) 35 25

1971. U.N. Int. Schools.
G 22. 104. 1 f. 10 multicoloured 70 50

1972. Non-Proliferation of Nuclear Weapons.
G 23. 106. 40 c. multicoloured .. 25 20

1972. World Health Day.
G 24. 107. 80 c. multicoloured .. 50 40

1972. U.N. Environmental Conservation Conf., Stockholm.
G 25. 109. 40 c. multicoloured .. 25 20
G 26. 80 c. multicoloured .. 50 40

1972. Economic Commission for Europe. (ECE).
G 27. 110. 1 f. 10 multicoloured 70 50

1972. United Nations Art. (5th issue).
G 28. 111. 40 c. multicoloured .. 25 20
G 29. 80 c. multicoloured .. 50 40

1973. Disarmament Decade.
G 30. 112. 60 c. multicoloured .. 35 30
G 31. 1 f. 10 multicoloured 65 50

1973. " No Drugs " Campaign.
G 32. 113. 60 c. multicoloured 35 30

1973. U.N. Volunteers Programme.
G 33. 114. 80 c. multicoloured .. 45 35

1973. " Namibia " (South West Africa).
G 34. 115. 60 c. multicoloured 35 30

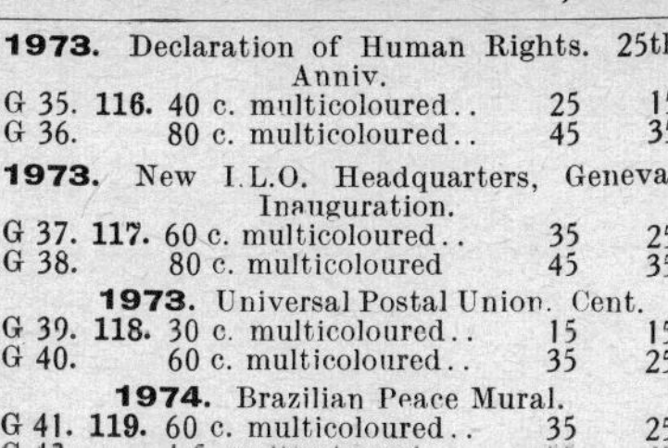

1973. Declaration of Human Rights. 25th Anniv.
G 35. 116. 40 c. multicoloured .. 25 15
G 36. 80 c. multicoloured .. 45 35

1973. New I.L.O. Headquarters, Geneva. Inauguration.
G 37. 117. 60 c. multicoloured .. 35 25
G 38. 80 c. multicoloured .. 45 35

1973. Universal Postal Union. Cent.
G 39. 118. 30 c. multicoloured .. 15 15
G 40. 60 c. multicoloured .. 35 25

1974. Brazilian Peace Mural.
G 41. 119. 60 c. multicoloured .. 35 25
G 42. 1 f. multicoloured .. 55 45

1974. World Population Year.
G 43. 122. 60 c. multicoloured .. 35 25
G 44. 80 c. multicoloured .. 45 35

1974. " Law of the Sea ".
G 45. 123. 1 f. 30 multicoloured 75 55

1975. Peaceful Uses of Outer Space.
G 46. 124. 60 c. multicoloured .. 25 25
G 47. 90 c. multicoloured .. 40 40

1975. International Women's Year.
G 48. 125. 60 c. multicoloured .. 25 25
G 49. 90 c. multicoloured .. 40 40

1975. United Nations. 30th Anniv.
G 50. 126. 60 c. multicoloured .. 25 25
G 51. 90 c. multicoloured .. 40 40

1975. " Namibi-U.N. Direct Responsibility ".
G 53. 127. 50 c. multicoloured .. 20 20
G 54. 1 f. 30 multicoloured 55 55

1975. U.N. Peace-keeping Operations.
G 55. 128. 60 c. turquoise .. 25 25
G 56. 70 c. violet 30 30

1976. World Federation of U.N. Association.
G 57. 130. 90 c. multicoloured .. 40 40

1976. U.N. Conf. on Trade and Development.
G 58. 131. 1 f. 10 multicoloured 50 35

1976. " HABITAT ". U.N. Conf. on Human Settlements.
G 59. 132. 40 c. multicoloured .. 20 15
G 60. 1 f. 50 multicoloured 70 50

G. 3. U.N. Emblem within Posthorn.

1976. U.N. Postal Administration. 25th Anniv.
G 61. G 3. 80 c. multicoloured .. 40 30
G 62. 1 f. 10 multicoloured 50 40

1976. World Food Council.
G 63. 134. 70 c. multicoloured .. 35 25

VII. WORLD METEOROLOGICAL ORGANIZATION

LM 1. " The Elements ".

LM 2. W.M.O. Emblem.

1956. Inscr. as in Type M 1.
LM 1. LM 1. 5 c. slate purple .. 5 5
LM 2. 10 c. green .. 5 5
LM 3. – 20 c. scarlet .. 1·10 1·10
LM 4. – 20 c. carmine .. 8 8
LM 5. – 30 c. red 12 12
LM 6. LM 1. 40 c. blue .. .. 1·25 1·25
LM 7. 50 c. blue 15 15
LM 8. – 60 c. brown .. 20 20
LM 9. – 2 f. purple .. 65 65
DESIGN—HORIZ. 20 c., 30 c., 60 c., 2 f. Weathervane.

1973.
LM 10. LM 2. 30 c. red .. 12 12
LM 11. 40 c. blue .. 15 15
LM 13. 1 f. brown .. 45 45

LM 3. W.M.O. Emblem.

1973. I.M.O./W.M.O. Cent.
LM 12. LM 3. 80 c. violet and red 30 30

VIII. UNIVERSAL POSTAL UNION

LP 1. U.P.U. Monument Berne.

LP 2. " Letter Post ".

1957. Inscr. as in Type P 1.
LP 1. LP 1. 5 c. slate-purple .. 5 5
LP 2. – 10 c. green .. 5 5
LP 3. – 20 c. scarlet .. 1·00 1·00
LP 4. – 20 c. carmine .. 8 8
LP 5. – 30 c. red 12 12
LP 6. LP 1. 40 c. blue .. .. 1·10 1·10
LP 7. 50 c. blue 15 15
LP 8. – 60 c. brown .. 20 20
LP 9. LP 1. 2 f. purple .. 65 65
DESIGN—HORIZ. 10 c., 20 c., 30 c., 60 c. Pegasus (sculpture).

1976. Multicoloured.
LP 10. 40 c. Type LP 2 .. 20 15
LP 11. 80 c. " Parcel Post " .. 40 30
LP 12. 90 c. " Financial Services " 40 30
LP 13. 1 f. " Technical Co-operation " 45 35

IX. INTERNATIONAL TELECOMMUNICATION UNION

LT 1. Transmitting Aerial.

LT 2. I.T.U. H.Q. Building.

1958. Inscr. as in Type 1.
LT 1. LT 1. 5 c. slate-purple .. 5 5
LT 2. 10 c. green .. 5 5
LT 3. – 20 c. scarlet .. 1·00 1·00
LT 4. – 20 c. carmine .. 8 8
LT 5. – 30 c. red 10 10
LT 6. LT 1. 40 c. blue .. .. 1·10 1·10
LT 7. 50 c. blue 12 12
LT 8. – 60 c. brown .. 15 15
LT 9. – 2 f. purple 55 55
DESIGN—VERT. 20 c., 30 c., 60 c., 2 f. Receiving aerials.

1973. I.T.U. H.Q. Building, Geneva. Inaug.
LT 10. LT 2. 80 c. blk. & blue 25 25

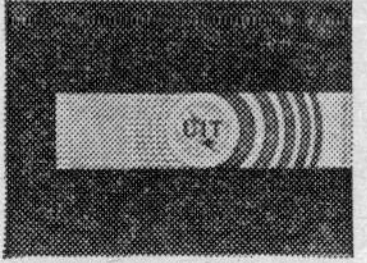
LT 3. Sound Waves.

1976. Multicoloured.
LT 11. 40 c. Type LT 3 .. 20 20
LT 12. 90 c. Airliner and ship (radio services) .. 40 40
LT 13. 1 f. " Mass media " (radio and television) .. 50 40

UNITED STATES OF AMERICA 04

A Federal Republic in N. America, consisting of 50 states and one federal district.

100 cents = 1 dollar.

PRICES. Prices throughout are for stamps in good condition, very fine copies being worth more. In issues before 1890 the gum is rarely complete and unused prices are for stamps without gum. Issues after 1890 are often badly centered and well centered stamps are worth more (and some issues very considerably more), than the prices quoted.

1. Franklin.

2. Washington.

1847. Imperf.
1. 1. 5 c. brown £400 £100
2. 2. 10 c. black £2500 £300

The 5 c. blue and 10 c. brown-orange both imperf. come from miniature sheets issued in 1947 to commemorate the Centenary Philatelic Exhibition, New York. Price per sheet of 2, 15 p. Un. or Us.

3. Franklin.

4. Washington.

5. Jefferson.

6. Washington.

7. Washington.

8. Washington.

9. Franklin.

10. Washington.

1851. Imperf.
11. 3. 1 c. blue .. .. .. 55·00 17·00
13a. 4. 3 c. red .. .. .. 26·00 1·60
14. 5. 5 c. brown £1300 £170
16. 6. 10 c. green .. .. £250 42·00
19. 7. 12 c. black .. .. £300 35·00

1857. Perf.
26. 3. 1 c. blue .. .. .. 23·00 6·00
28. 4. 3 c. red .. .. .. 9·50 1·10
33. 5. 5 c. brown .. .. 70·00 29·00
39. 6. 10 c. green .. .. 38·00 11·00
40. 7. 12 c. black .. .. 48·00 13·00
41. 8. 24 c. grey .. .. £100 45·00
42. 9. 30 c. orange .. .. £120 50·00
43. 10. 90 c. blue £250 £600

11. Franklin.

12. Andrew Jackson.

13. Washington.

14. Jefferson.

15. Washington.

16.

17. Lincoln.

18. Washington.

19. Franklin.

20. Washington.

1861. Perf.
60b. 11. 1 c. blue .. .. 19·00 4·50
69. 12. 2 c. black .. .. 20·00 4·75
61c. 13. 3 c. rose .. .. 10·00 50
63. 14. 5 c. bistre .. .. £500 50·00
72. 5 c. brown .. .. 40·00 7·00
44a. 15. 10 c. green .. .. 35·00 4·50
65. 16. 12 c. black .. .. 50·00 7·50
100. 17. 15 c. black .. .. £100 13·00
66c. 18. 24 c. blue .. .. £600 35·00
66b. 24 c. purple .. .. £100 12·00
74b. 24 c. grey .. .. 38·00 8·00
67. 19. 30 c. orange .. .. 80·00 12·00
68. 20. 90 c. blue .. .. £200 35·00

21. Franklin.

22. Post Rider.

23. Locomotive.

24. Washington.

25. Shield and Eagle.

26. S.S. " Adriatic ".

27. Landing of Columbus. 28. Declaration of Independence. 29. Lincoln.

1869.

114. **21.** 1 c. brown .. .. 48·00 14·00
115. **22.** 2 c. brown .. .. 29·00 6·00
116. **23.** 3 c. blue .. .. 20·00 1·75
117. **24.** 6 c. blue .. .. £130 16·00
118. **25.** 10 c. orange .. .. £140 16·00
119. **26.** 12 c. green .. .. £120 17·00
121. **27.** 15 c. blue and brown £130 23·00
122. **28.** 24 c. purple and green £325 £110
123. **25.** 30 c. blue and red .. £325 45·00
124. **29.** 90 c. black and red .. £1000 £225

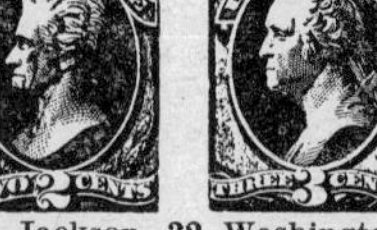
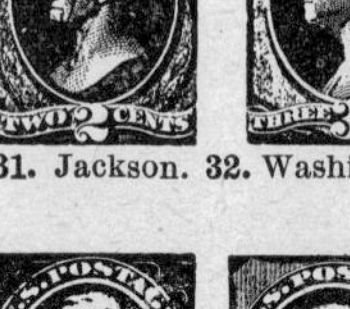

30. Franklin. 31. Jackson. 32. Washington.

33. Lincoln. 34. Stanton. 35. Jefferson.

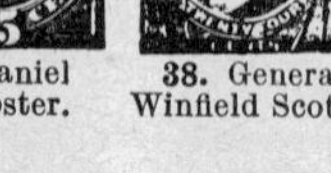

36. Henry Clay. 37. Daniel Webster. 38. General Winfield Scott.

39. Alexander Hamilton. 40. Commodore Perry. 41. General Zachary Taylor.

1870.

207. **30.** 1 c. blue .. .. 6·00 20
148. **31.** 2 c. brown .. .. 11·00 1·25
185. 2 c. red .. .. 9·50 45
160. **32.** 3 c. green .. .. 6·00 5
219. 3 c. red .. .. 8·50 5·50
161. **33.** 6 c. red .. .. 32·00 2·10
151. **34.** 7 c. red .. .. 55·00 9·00
210. **35.** 10 c. brown .. .. 9·50 85
153. **36.** 12 c. purple .. .. £100 9·00
191. **37.** 15 c. orange .. .. 20·00 3·50
155. **38.** 24 c. violet .. .. 70·00 11·00
192. **39.** 30 c. black .. .. 55·00 4·75
222. 30 c. brown .. .. 55·00 13·00
193. **40.** 90 c. red .. .. £190 35·00
223. 90 c. violet .. .. £140 35·00

1875.

181. **41.** 5 c. blue .. .. 26·00 1·60

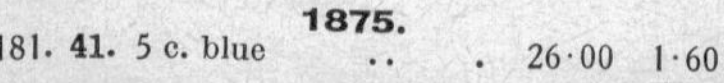

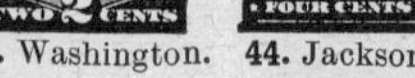

42. Franklin. 43. Washington. 44. Jackson.

45. Garfield. 46.

1882.

211. **42.** 1 c. blue .. .. 11·00 25
213. **43.** 2 c. brown .. .. 3·50 5
218. 2 c. green .. .. 2·25 5
214. **44.** 4 c. green .. .. 17·00 1·75
220. 4 c. red .. .. 13·00 2·50
211. **45.** 5 c. brown .. .. 16·00 1·25
221. 5 c. blue .. .. 14·00 1·10

1890. No triangles in upper corners.

224. **46.** 1 c. blue (Franklin) .. 3·25 5
225a. – 2 c. red (Washington).. 2·50 5
226. – 3 c. violet (Jackson) .. 10·00 1·40
227. – 4 c. sepia (Lincoln) .. 11·00 45
228. – 5 c. brown (Grant) .. 11·00 45
229. – 6 c. claret (Garfield) 10·00 3·25
230. – 8 c. purple (Sherman).. 8·00 2·25
231. – 10 c. green (Webster) 23·00 50
232. – 15 c. blue (Clay) .. 35·00 4·00
233. – 30 c. black (Jefferson) 42·00 4·75
234. – 90 c. orange (Perry) .. 80·00 23·00

47. Columbus in sight of land. 50. Jefferson.

1893 Columbus' Discovery of America. Dated "1492 1892".

235. **47.** 1 c. blue .. .. 6·50 12
236. – 2 c. purple .. .. 5·50 5
237. – 3 c green .. .. 11·00 5·00
238. – 4 c. blue .. .. 18·00 1·90
239. – 5 c. brown .. .. 18·00 2·00
240. – 6 c. violet .. .. 18·00 5·50
241. – 8 c. claret .. .. 11·00 2·50
242. – 10 c. sepia .. .. 29·00 2·10
243. – 15 c. green .. .. 42·00 14·00
244. – 30 c. orange .. .. 60·00 23·00
245. – 50 c. slate .. .. 85·00 38·00
246. – $1 red £250 £130
247. – $2 lake £275 £100
248. – $3 green £425 £200
249a. – $4 red £600 £275
250. – $5 black £650 £325

DESIGNS: 2 c. Landing of Columbus. 3 c. "Santa Maria", Flagship of Columbus. 4 c. Fleet of Columbus. 5 c. Columbus soliciting aid of Isabella. 6 c. Columbus welcomed at Barcelona, Ferdinand (left) and Balboa (right). 8 c. Columbus restored to favour. 10 c. Columbus presenting natives. 15 c. Columbus announcing his discovery. 30 c. Columbus at La Rabida. 50 c. Recall of Columbus. $1 Isabella pledging her jewels. $2 Columbus in chains. $3 Columbus describing his third voyage. $4 Isabella and Columbus. $5 Columbus, America and Liberty.

1894. Triangles in upper corners as T **50.** Same portraits as issue of 1890 except dollar values.

267. – 1 c. blue .. .. 1·60 5
283. – 1 c. green .. .. 2·00 5
284c – 2 c. red .. .. 1·25 5
271. – 3 c. violet .. .. 4·75 30
285. – 4 c. brown .. .. 3·75 25
273. – 5 c. brown .. .. 5·00 50
286. – 5 c. blue .. .. 4·00 25
287a. – 6 c. brown .. .. 5·50 65
275. – 8 c. purple .. .. 3·50 25
276. – 10 c. green .. .. 8·50 35
289. – 10 c. brown .. .. 19·00 50
277. – 15 c. blue .. .. 26·00 1·75
290. – 15 c. olive .. .. 23·00 1·60
278a. **50.** 50 c. orange .. .. 40·00 3·50
279. – $1 black (Perry) .. £110 11·00
281. – $2 blue (Madison) .. £140 55·00
282. – $5 green (Marshall) .. £300 65·00

51. Father Marquette on the Mississippi. 52. Lake Steamer.

1898. Trans-Mississippi Exposition, Omaha

291. **51.** 1 c. green .. .. 7·00 1·90
292. – 2 c. red .. .. 7·50 55
293. – 4 c. orange .. .. 29·00 6·00
294. – 5 c. blue .. .. 26·00 5·50
295. – 8 c. purple .. .. 35·00 9·50
296. – 10 c. violet .. .. 40·00 4·75
297. – 50 c. green .. .. £140 29·00
298. – $1 black £350 £120
299. – $2 brown £475 £170

DESIGNS: 2 c. Farming in West. 4 c. Indian hunting buffalo. 5 c. Fremont on Rocky Mountains. 8 c. Troops guarding emigrant train. 10 c. Hardships of emigration. 50 c. Western mining prospector. $1 Western cattle in storm. $2 Bridge at St. Louis.

1901. Pan-American Exn., Buffalo. Inscr. "COMMEMORATIVE SERIES, 1901".

300. **52.** 1 c. black and green .. 6·00 1·60
301. – 2 c. black and red .. 6·00 30
302. – 4 c. black and brown .. 23·00 4·75
303. – 5 c. black and blue .. 23·00 5·00
304. – 8 c. black and brown .. 27·00 9·50
305. – 10 c. black and brown 35·00 6·50

DESIGNS: 2 c. Empire State Express. 4 c. Automobile. 5 c. Bridge below Niagara Falls. 8 c. Locks at Sault Sainte Marie. 10 c. Liner.

53. Franklin. 54. Washington. 55. Jackson.

56. Grant. 57. Lincoln. 58. Garfield.

59. Martha Washington. 60. Webster. 61. Harrison.

62. Clay. 63. Jefferson. 64. Farragut.

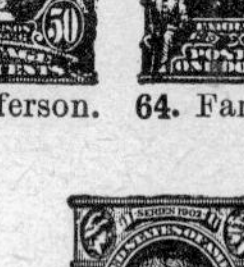

65. Madison. 66. Marshall.

1902. Inscr. "SERIES 1902".

306. **53.** 1 c. green .. .. 1·75 5
307. **54.** 2 c. red .. .. 1·90 5
308. **55.** 3 c. violet .. .. 7·00 75
309. **56.** 4 c. brown .. .. 7·00 30
310a. **57.** 5 c. blue .. .. 7·50 30
311. **58.** 6 c. lake .. .. 8·00 65
312. **59.** 8 c. violet .. .. 6·00 55
313. **60.** 10 c. brown .. .. 11·00 35
314. **61.** 13 c. purple .. .. 5·50 2·00
315. **62.** 15 c. olive .. .. 27·00 1·60
316. **6C.** 50 c. orange .. .. 70·00 6·50
317. **64.** $1 black .. .. £130 11·00
485. **65.** $2 blue .. .. 65·00 6·50
486. **66.** $5 green .. .. 48·00 7·00

67. Washington. 68. Robert R. Livingston.

1903.

326. **67.** 2 c. red .. .. .. 1·40 5

1904. Int. Exhibition, St. Louis and "Louisiana Purchase". Inscr. "COMMEMORATIVE SERIES OF 1904".

330. **68.** 1 c. green .. .. 7·50 1·90
331. – 2 c. red .. .. .. 6·50 50
332. – 3 c. violet .. .. 17·00 7·50
333. – 5 c. blue .. .. 24·00 5·00
334. – 10 c. brown .. .. 55·00 8·50

DESIGNS: 2 c. Jefferson. 3 c. Monroe. 5 c. McKinley. 10 c. Map of Louisiana Purchase.

73. Capt. John Smith, Pocahontas and Powhatan.

1907. Jamestown. 300th Anniv. Inscr. "COMMEMORATIVE SERIES 1907".

335. **73.** 1 c. green .. .. 5·50 1·90
336. – 2 c. red .. .. 7·00 1·10
337. – 5 c. blue .. .. 38·00 7·50

DESIGNS: 2 c. Founding of Jamestown, 1607. 5 c. Princess Pocahontas.

76. Franklin. 77. Washington. 78.

1908.

338. **76.** 1 c. green .. .. 1·60 5
339. **77.** 2 c. red .. .. .. 1·40 5
536. **78.** 3 c. violet 30 5
510. 4 c. brown .. .. 2·00 8
511. 5 c. blue .. .. .. 1·25 5
513. 6 c. orange .. .. 2·00 10
344. 8 c. olive .. .. 5·00 85
345. 10 c. yellow .. .. 11·00 35
346. 13 c. green .. .. 7·00 5·00
347. 15 c. blue .. .. 11·00 1·75
348. 50 c. violet .. .. 45·00 3·50
349. $1 black .. .. 80·00 16·00

79. Lincoln.

1909. Abraham Lincoln. Birth Cent.

374. **79.** 2 c. red .. .. .. 2·40 1·25

80. Wm. H. Seward. 81. The "Clermont" and "Half Moon" on Hudson River.

1909. Alaska-Yukon Pacific Exposition.

377. **80.** 2 c. red .. .. .. 3·50 85

1909. Hudson-Fulton Celebration.

379. **81.** 2 c. red .. .. .. 3·50 1·25

82. Franklin. 83.

1912.

505. **78.** 1 c. green 15 5
506. 2 c. red 15 5
514. 7 c. black .. .. 5·00 45
515. **82.** 8 c. olive .. .. 2·40 30
516. 9 c. pink .. .. 3·50 85
517. 10 c. yellow .. .. 2·40 5
518. 11 c. green .. .. 2·10 1·25
519. 12 c. claret .. .. 2·10 15
519a. 12 c. red .. .. 2·10 15
520. 13 c. green .. .. 2·75 2·25
521. 15 c. grey .. .. 7·00 35
522. 20 c. blue .. .. 6·00 8
523. 30 c. orange .. .. 6·00 35
524. 50 c. lilac .. .. 8·50 20
525. $1 black .. .. 14·00 35
527. **83.** $2 black and orange .. £130 38·00
528. $2 black and red .. 50·00 7·00
529. $5 black and green .. 50·00 6·00

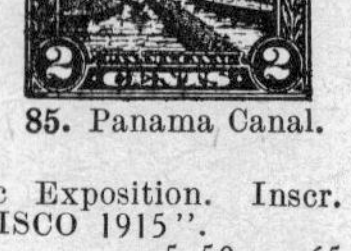

84. Balboa. 85. Panama Canal.

1913. Panama-Pacific Exposition. Inscr. "SAN FRANCISCO 1915".

423. **84.** 1 c. green .. .. 5·50 65
424. **85.** 2 c. red .. .. .. 5·50 25
425. – 5 c. blue .. .. 20·00 3·75
426. – 10 c. orange .. .. 35·00 4·00

DESIGNS: 5 c. Golden Gate, San Francisco. 10 c. Discovery of San Francisco Bay.

88. Curtiss "Jenny". 89. Liberty and Flags of the Allies.

1918. Air.
A 546. **88.** 6 c. orange .. .. 26·00 9·50
A 547. 16 c. green .. .. 42·00 13·00
A 548. 24 c. blue and red .. 38·00 12·00

1919. Victory.
546. **89.** 3 c. violet .. .. 3·50 1·90

DESIGNS: 2 c. Landing of Pilgrims. 5 c. Signing the Compact.

90. The "Mayflower"

1920. Tercent. of Landing of Pilgrim Fathers. Inscr. as in T **90.**
556. **90.** 1 c. green .. .. 2·00 1·10
557. – 2 c. red .. .. 3·50 85
558. – 5 c. blue .. .. 19·00 7·00

93. Franklin. **94** Harding. **95.** Indian Chief.

96. Statue of Liberty. **97.** Wilson.

98. Golden Gate. **99.** "America".

1922. ½ c. to 15 c. vert. 17 c. to $5 horiz
559. – ½ c. sepia (Hale) .. 5 5
602. **93.** 1 c. green 8 5
603. **103.** 1½ c. brown 25 5
685. **94.** 1½ c. brown 12 5
604. – 2 c. red (Washington) 8 5
638a. – 3 c. violet (Lincoln) .. 12 5
639. – 4 c. brown (Martha Washington) .. 45 5
686. – 4 c. brown (Taft) .. 20 5
640. – 5 c. blue (Roosevelt).. 40 5
641. – 6 c. orange (Garfield).. 50 5
642. – 7 c. black (McKinley) 50 5
643. – 8 c. olive (Grant) .. 50 5
644. – 9 c. rose (Jefferson) .. 55 5
645. – 10 c. yellow (Monroe) 75 5
571. – 11 c. blue (Hayes) .. 45 5
692. – 11 c. green (Hayes) .. 60 5
693. – 12 c. purple (Cleveland) 1·25 5
694. – 13 c. green (Harrison) 55 5
695. **95.** 14 c. blue 70 15
696. **96.** 15 c. grey .. .. 2·75 5
697. **97.** 17 c. black 90 8
698. **98.** 20 c. red .. .. 2·75 5
699. – 25 c. green (Niagara).. 1·90 5
700. – 30 c. sepia (Bison) .. 4·25 5
701. – 50 c. mve. (Arlington Amphitheatre and Unknown Warrior's Tomb) .. 11·00 5
579. – $1 brown (Lincoln Memorial) .. 9·50 15
580. – $2 blue (Capitol) .. 29·00 2·75
581. **99.** $5 blue and red .. 65·00 3·50

100. Aeroplane Radiator and Propeller. **102.** De Havilland Biplane.

1923. Air.
A 614. **100.** 8 c. green .. .. 13·00 6·00
A 615. – 16 c. blue .. .. 38·00 13·00
A 616. **102.** 24 c. red .. .. 42·00 9·00
DESIGN: 16 c. Winged Badge of Air Mail Service.

103. Harding. **104.** The "New Netherlands".

1923. President Harding Memorial.
614. **103.** 2 c. black 45 5

1924. Huguenot-Walloon Tercent.
618. **104.** 1 c. green .. .. 2·40 2·25
619. – 2 c. red .. .. 3·50 1·40
620. – 5 c. blue .. .. 17·00 8·00
DESIGNS: 2 c. Landing at Fort Orange. 5 c. Ribault Memorial, Mayport, Florida.

105. Washington at Cambridge. **107.** Sloop "Restaurationen".

1925. Battle of Lexington and Concord. 150th Anniv. Dated "1775-1925".
621. **105.** 1 c. green .. .. 2·10 1·75
622. – 2 c. red .. .. 3·75 2·40
623. – 5 c. blue .. .. 17·00 7·50
DESIGNS: 2 c. Battle of Lexington-Concord. 5 c. Statue of "Minute Man".

1925. Norse-American Centennial. Dated "1825 1925".
624. **107.** 2 c. black and red . 3·50 1·75
625. – 5 c. black and blue .. 10·00 7·00
DESIGN: 5 c. Viking galley.

109. Relief Map of U.S.A.

1926. Air.
A 628. **109.** 10 c. blue .. .. 1·75 25
A 629. 15 c. brown.. .. 1·90 1·25
A 630. 20 c. green .. .. 3·50 1·10

110. Liberty Bell.

111. Ericsson Memorial. **112.** Alexander Hamilton's Battery (after E. L. Ward).

1926. 150th Anniv. of Independence and Sesquicentennial Exhibition.
628. **110.** 2 c. red .. .. 2·40 25

1926. John Ericsson Commemoration.
629. **111.** 5 c. violet .. .. 4·75 2·40

1926. Battle of White Plains. 150th Anniv.
630. **112.** 2 c. red .. .. 1·25 1·00

112. The "Spirit of St. Louis".

1927. Lindbergh's Transatlantic Flight.
A 646. **113.** 10 c. blue .. .. 2·75 1·75

114. Green Mountain Boy. **115.** Surrender of Gen. Burgoyne.

1927. 150th Anniv. of Independence of Vermont and Battle of Bennington.
646. **114.** 2 c. red 70 65

1927. Burgoyne Campaign. 150th Anniv.
647. **115.** 2 c. red .. .. 1·75 1·25

116. Washington at Valley Forge. **117.** Air Beacon, Sherman Hill, Rocky Mountains.

1928. Valley Forge. 150th Anniv.
648. **116.** 2 c. red 55 25

1928. Air.
A 649. **117.** 5 c. blue and red .. 2·00 35

1928. Discovery of Hawaii. 150th Anniv. Optd. **HAWAII 1778-1928.**
649. 2 c. red (No. 604).. .. 2·75 2·10
650. 5 c. blue (No. 640) .. 7·50 4·25

1928. Battle of Monmouth. 150th Anniv. Optd. **MOLLY PITCHER.**
651. 2 c. red (No. 604).. .. 65 65

DESIGN: 5 c. Globe and Aeroplane.

118. Wright Aeroplane.

1928. Civil Aeronautics Conference and 25th Anniv. of Wright Bros. First Flight. Inscr. as in T **118.**
652. **118.** 2 c. red 65 50
653. – 5 c. blue .. .. 2·75 2·00

120. George Rogers Clark at Vincennes.

1929. Surrender of Fort Sackville. 150th Anniv.
654. **120.** 2 c. black and red .. 45 30

1929. Stamps of 1922 optd.

(a) **Kans.**
655. **93.** 1 c. green 55 45
656. **103.** 1½ c. brown .. .. 1·00 95
657. – 2 c. red 90 25
658. – 3 c. violet .. .. 4·75 3·75
659. – 4 c. brown .. .. 5·50 1·90
660. – 5 c. blue .. .. 3·50 2·50
661. – 6 c. orange .. .. 8·50 4·25
662. – 7 c. black .. .. 7·50 5·00
663. – 8 c. olive .. .. 24·00 20·00
664. – 9 c. rose .. .. 4·25 2·50
665. – 10 c. yellow .. .. 7·00 2·50

(b) **Nebr.**
666. **93.** 1 c. green 65 55
667. **103.** 1½ c. brown 75 60
668. – 2 c. red 50 25
669. – 3 c. violet .. .. 3·75 1·90
670. – 4 c. brown .. .. 5·50 2·75
671. – 5 c. blue .. .. 5·00 3·50
672. – 6 c. orange .. .. 8·00 5·00
673. – 7 c. black .. .. 6·00 4·00
674. – 8 c. olive .. .. 9·50 5·50
675. – 9 c. rose .. .. 9·50 5·50
676. – 10 c. yellow .. .. 24·00 5·00

121. Edison's original Lamp. **122.** Maj.-Gen. Sullivan.

1929. Edison's First Electric Lamp. 50th Anniv.
678. **121.** 2 c. red 45 12

1929. Maj.-Gen. Sullivan's Western Campaign. 150th Anniv.
680. **122.** 2 c. red 40 30

123. Gen. Wayne Memorial. **124.** Ohio River Lock.

1929. Battle of Fallen Timbers. 135th Anniv.
681. **123.** 2 c. red 55 50

1929. Ohio River Canalisation.
682. **124.** 2 c. red 35 35

125. Air Mail Pilot's Badge. **126.** Seal of the Colony.

1930. Air.
A 684. **125.** 5 c. purple .. .. 2·75 25
A 685. 6 c. orange 80 5
A 686. 8 c. olive 80 12

1930. Massachusetts Bay Colony Centenary.
683. **126.** 2 c. red 35 20

127. Settler. and Indian. **128.** "Graf Zeppelin".

1930. Settlement near Charleston. 250th Anniv.
684. **127.** 2 c. red 65 55

1930. Air. "Graf Zeppelin" Europe-Pan-American Flight. Designs as T **128.**
A 687. **128.** 65 c. green .. .. £140 90·00
A 688. – $1·30 brown .. £250 £130
A 689. – $2·60 blue £375 £200

129. George Washington. **130.** Gen. Wilhelm von Steuben. **131.** Gen. Casimir Pulaski.

1930. Battle o. Braddock's Field. 175th Anniv.
689. **129.** 2 c. red 70 50

1930. Gen. von Steuben. Birth Bicent.
690. **130.** 2 c. red 40 30

1931. Gen. Pulaski's Death. 150th Anniv.
691. **131.** 2 c. red 15 10

132. Red Cross Nurse. **133.** Rochambeau, Washington, De Grasse.

1931. American Red Cross Society. 50th Anniv.
702. **132.** 2 c. black and red .. 10 8

1931. Surrender of Cornwallis at Yorktown. 150th Anniv.
703. **133.** 2 c. black and red .. 15 12

134. **135.**

1932. George Washington. Birth Bicent. Portraits dated "1732 1932".
704. **134.** ½ c. sepia 5 5
705. **135.** 1 c. green 8 5
706. – 1½ c. brown 15 5
707. – 2 c. red 5 5
708. – 3 c. violet 20 5
709. – 4 c. brown 15 5
710. – 5 c. blue .. .. 1·00 5
711. – 6 c. orange .. .. 2·10 5
712. – 7 c. black 25 8
713. – 8 c. olive .. .. 2·10 50
714. – 9 c. red .. .. 2·10 12
715. – 10 c. yellow .. .. 7·50 5
For 3 c. as No. 707, see No. 720.

146. Skiing. **147.** Tree-planting.

1932. Winter Olympic Games.
716. **146.** 2 c. red 12 10

1932. Arbor Day. 60th Anniv.
717 **147** 2 c. red 10 8

148. Sprinter. **149.** Discus thrower. **150.** Wm. Penn.

1932. Summer Olympic Games.
718. **148.** 3 c. violet 25 5
719. **149.** 5 c. blue 45 15

1932. As No. 707, but without date.
720. 3 c. violet 8 5

1932. Penn's Arrival in America. 250th Anniv.
723. **150.** 3 c. violet 15 10

151. Webster. **152.** Gen. Oglethorpe. **153.** Washington's H.Q.

1932. Daniel Webster. 150th Birth Anniv.
724. **151.** 3 c. violet 25 15

1933. Georgia State. Bicent.
725. **152.** 3 c. violet 20 12

1933. Proclamation of Peace after War of Independence. 150th Anniv.
726. **153.** 3 c. violet 8 5

154. Fort Dearborn. **155.** Federal Building.

1933. Chicago World Exn. Perf. or imperf.
727. **154.** 1 c. green 5 5
728. **155.** 3 c. violet 10 5

156. Agriculture, Commerce and Industry.

1933. National Recovery Act.
731. **156.** 3 c. violet 8 5

157. Chicago Federal Building, "Graf Zeppelin" and Friedrichshaven Hangar.

1933. Air. "Graf Zeppelin" Chicago Flight.
A 732. **157.** 50 c. green .. .. 35·00 26·00

159. Gen. Kosciuszko.

158. Routes of Byrd Flights. **106.** "Ark" and "Dove".

1933. Byrd Antarctic Expedition. Perf. or imperf.
732. **158.** 3 c. blue 50 45

1933. Naturalization of Kosciuszko as American Citizen. 150th Anniv.
733. **159.** 5 c. blue 45 15

1934. Maryland Tercent.
735. **160.** 3 c. red 12 10

161. "Portrait of my Mother" by Whistler.

1934. Mothers' Day.
736. **161.** 3 c. violet 10 5

162. Nicolet's Landing at Green Bay.

163. "El Capitan", Yosemite. **164.** Grand Canyon.

1934. Tercentenary of Wisconsin.
738. **162.** 3 c. violet 12 5

1934. National Parks. Perf. or imperf.
739. **163.** 1 c. green 5 5
740. **164.** 2 c. red 5 5
741. – 3 c. violet 8 5
742. – 4 c. brown 25 20
743. – 5 c. blue 50 45
744. – 6 c. blue 70 50
745. – 7 c. black 50 35
762. – 8 c. green 90 85
747. – 9 c. red .. .. 1·25 30
748. – 10 c. grey .. .. 1·75 55

DESIGNS—VERT. 5 c. "Old Faithful" geyser, Yellowstone. 8 c. Great White Throne, Zion. 10 c. Mount Le Conte, Smoky Mountain. HORIZ. 3 c. Mirror Lake, Mt. Ranier. 4 c. Cliff dwellings, Mesa Verde. 6 c. Crater Lake and Wizard Is. 7 c. Acadia. 9 c. Mt. Rockwell and Two Medicine Lake Glacier.

165. The Charter Oak.

1935. Connecticut Tercent. Perf. or imperf
771. **165.** 3 c. purple 5 5

166. Exhibition Grounds, Point Loma and San Diego Bay.

1935. California Pacific Int. Exn., San Diego, Perf. or imperf.
772. **166.** 3 c. violet 5 5

168. Seal of Michigan.

167. Boulder Dam, Nevada. **169.** "China Clipper".

1935. Dedication of Boulder Dam.
773. **167.** 3 c. violet 5 5

1935. Michigan Cent. Perf. or imperf.
774. **168.** 3 c. violet 5 5

1935. Air. Trans-Pacific Air Mail.
A 775. **169.** 20 c. green .. .. 4·25 1·25
A 776. 25 c. blue .. .. 1·00 85
A 777. 50 c. red .. .. 5·00 2·75

170. S. Houston, S. F. Austin, and the Alamo.

172. First Settlement. Old State House and Capitol. **171.** Roger Williams.

1936. Declaration of Texan Independence. Cent. Perf. or Imperf.
775. **170.** 3 c. violet 5 5

1936. Rhode Island Tercent.
776. **171.** 3 c. violet 8 5

1936. Arkansas Cent.
778. **172.** 3 c. violet 5 5

173. Map of old Oregon. **174.** Susan B. Anthony.

1936. Oregon Cent.
779. **173.** 3 c. violet 5 5

1936. Woman's Suffrage. 16th Anniv.
780. **174.** 3 c. purple 5 5

175. Washington and Greene, Mt. Vernon in background.

180. Jones and Barry.

1936. Army and Navy Heroes. (a) Army.
781. **175.** 1 c. green 5 5
782. – 2 c. red 5 5
783. – 3 c. purple 8 5
784. – 4 c. grey-blue 25 12
785. – 5 c. blue 30 12

DESIGNS: 2 c. Jackson, Scott and the Hermitage. 3 c. Sherman, Grant and Sheridan. 4 c. Lee, Jackson and Stratford Hall. 5 c. West Point Military Academy.

(b) Navy.
786. **180.** 1 c. green 5 5
787. – 2 c. red 5 5
788. – 3 c. purple 8 5
789. – 4 c. grey-blue 25 12
790. – 5 c. blue 30 12

DESIGNS: 2 c. Decatur and MacDonough. 3 c. Farragut and Porter. 4 c. Sampson, Dewey and Schley. 5 c. Seal of Naval Academy and cadets.

185. Cutler, Putnam and Map of N.W. Territory. **186.** Virginia Dare.

1937. N.W. Territory Ordinance. 150th Anniv.
791. **185.** 3 c. violet 5 5

1937. Virginia Dare. 350th Birth Anniv.
792. **186.** 5 c. blue 20 15

187. Signing the Constitution.

1937. U.S. Constitution. 150th Anniv.
794. **187.** 3 c. mauve 10 5

189. Mt. McKinley, Alaska.

188. Statue to Kamehameha I, Honolulu. **190.** Fortaleza Castle, Puerto Rico.

191. Charlotte Amalie (St. Thomas), Virgin Is. **192.** Benjamin Franklin.

1937. Territorial Issue.
795. **188.** 3 c. violet 8 5
796. **189.** 3 c. violet 8 5
797. **190.** 3 c. violet 8 5
798. **191.** 3 c. mauve 8 5

1938. Presidential Series.
799. **192.** ½ c. orange 5 5
800. – 1 c. green 5 5
801. – 1½ c. brown 5 5
802. – 2 c. red 5 5
803. – 3 c. violet 5 5
804. – 4 c. purple 15 5
805. – 4½ c. grey 10 5
806. 5 c. blue 15 5
807. – 6 c. red 15 5
808. – 7 c. brown 25 5
809. – 8 c. green 25 5
810. 9 c. pink 25 5
811. – 10 c. red 25 5
812. – 11 c. blue 35 5
813. – 12 c. mauve 45 5
814. – 13 c. green 40 5
815. – 14 c. blue 45 5
816. – 15 c. slate 35 5
817. – 16 c. black 55 20
818. – 17 c. red 55 8
819. – 18 c. maroon 45 5
820. – 19 c. mauve 45 25
821. – 20 c. green 45 5
822. – 21 c. blue 65 5
823. 22 c. red 60 25
824. 24 c. black 80 12
825. – 25 c. mauve 70 5
826. – 30 c. blue .. .. 3·25 5
827. – 50 c. lilac .. .. 4·25 5
828. – $1 black and purple .. 3·50 5
830. – $2 black and green .. 13·00 2·00
831. – $5 black and red .. 50·00 1·75

DESIGNS: 1 c. Washington. 1½ c. Martha Washington. 2 c. John Adams. 3 c. Jefferson. 4 c. Madison. 4½ c. White House. 5 c. James Monroe. 6 c. John Quincey Adams. 7 c. Jackson. 8 c. Martin Van Buren. 9 c. Wm. Henry Harrison. 10 c. John Tyler. 11 c. James K. Polk. 12 c. Zachary Taylor. 13 c. Millard Fillmore. 14 c. Franklin Pierce. 15 c. James Buchanan. 16 c. Lincoln. 17 c. Johnson. 18 c. Grant. 19 c. Rutherford B. Hayes. 20 c. James A. Garfield. 21 c. Chester A. Arthur. 22 c. Grover Cleveland. 24 c. Benjamin Harrison. 25 c. Wm. McKinley. 30 c. Theodore Roosevelt. 50 c. Taft. $1 Woodrow Wilson. $2 Harding. $5 Coolidge.

224. Eagle and Shield.

1938. Air.
A 845. **224.** 6 c. red and blue .. 30 5

225. Colonial Court House. **226.** Landing of Swedes and Finns.

1938. Ratification of U.S. Constitution. 150th Anniv.
845. **225.** 3 c. violet 15 5

1938. Scandinavian Settlement in America. Tercent.
846. **226.** 3 c. magenta 12 5

227. Colonization of the West. **228.** Old Capitol Building, Iowa.

1938. Northwest Territory Sesquicent.
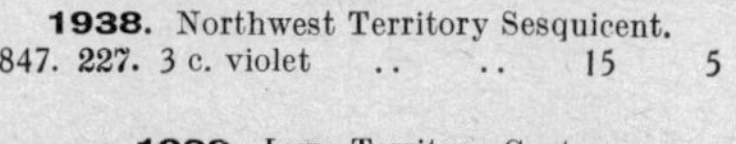
847. **227.** 3 c. violet 15 5

1938. Iowa Territory Cent.
848. **228.** 3 c. violet 15 5

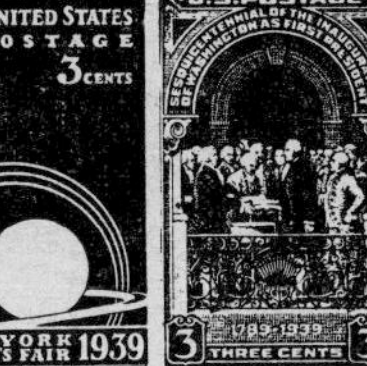

229. Tower of the Sun. 230. Trylon and Perisphere. 231. Inauguration of Washington.

1939. Golden Gate Exn., San Francisco.
849. 229. 3 c. violet 8 5

1939. New York World's Fair.
850. 230. 3 c. violet 10 5

1939. Election of Washington as First President. 150th Anniv.
851. 231. 3 c. mauve 15 5

232.

1939. Air.
A 852. 232. 30 c. blue .. .. 5·50 85

233. Baseball.

234. Theodore Roosevelt, Goethals and Gaillard Cut. 235. Stephen Daye Press.

1939. Baseball Cent.
852. 233. 3 c. violet 12 5

1939. Opening of Panama Canal. 25th Anniv.
853. 234. 3 c. violet 12 5

1939. Tercent. of Printing in Colonial America.
854. 235. 3 c. violet 8 5

236. Washington, Montana, N. and S. Dakota. 237. Washington Irving.

238. Henry W. Longfellow. 238a. Horace Mann. 238b. John James Audubon.

238c. Stephen Collins Foster. 238d. Gilbert Charles Stuart. 238e. Eli Whitney.

1939. Statehood of Washington, Montana and N. and S. Dakota. 50th Anniv.
855. 236. 3 c. mauve 8 5

1940. Famous Americans.

(a) Authors.
856. 237. 1 c. green 5 5
857. – 2 c. red 5 5
858. – 3 c. purple 8 5
859. – 5 c. blue 20 15
860. – 10 c. brown .. .. 1·50 1·50
PORTRAITS: 2 c. J. Fenimore Cooper. 3 c. Ralph Waldo Emerson. 5 c. Louisa May Alcott. 10 c. Samuel L. Clemens ("Mark Twain").

(b) Poets.
861. 238. 1 c. green 8 5
862. – 2 c. red 5 5
863. – 3 c. purple 10 5
864. – 5 c. blue 25 15
865. – 10 c. brown .. .. 1·75 1·60
PORTRAITS: 2 c. John Greenleaf Whittier. 3 c. James Russell Lowell. 5 c. Walt Whitman. 10 c. James Whitcomb Riley.

(c) Educationists.
866. 238a. 1 c. green 5 5
867. – 2 c. red 5 5
868. – 3 c. purple 15 5
869. – 5 c. blue 35 15
870. – 10 c. brown .. .. 1·25 1·25
PORTRAITS: 2 c. Mark Hopkins. 3 c. Charles W. Eliot. 5 c. Frances E. Willard. 10 c. Booker T. Washington.

(d) Scientists.
871. 238b. 1 c. green 5 5
872. – 2 c. red 5 5
873. – 3 c. purple 5 5
874. – 5 c. blue 15 15
875. – 10 c. brown .. .. 1·25 90
PORTRAITS: 2 c. Dr. Crawford W. Long. 3 c. Luther Burbank. 5 c. Dr. Walter Reed. 10 c. Jane Addams.

(e) Composers.
876. 238c. 1 c. green 5 5
877. – 2 c. red 5 5
878. – 3 c. purple 8 5
879. – 5 c. blue 30 15
880. – 10 c. brown .. .. 2·50 1·10
PORTRAITS: 2 c. John Philip Sousa. 3 c. Victor Herbert. 5 c. Edward A. MacDowell. 10 c. Ethelbert Nevin.

(f) Artists.
881. 238d. 1 c. green 5 5
882. – 2 c. red 5 5
883. – 3 c. purple 5 5
884. – 5 c. blue 25 20
885. – 10 c. brown .. .. 1·60 1·40
PORTRAITS: 2 c. James A. McNeill Whistler. 3 c. Augustus Saint-Gaudens. 5 c. Daniel Chester French. 10 c. Frederic Remington.

(g) Inventors.
886. 238e. 1 c. green 8 5
887. – 2 c. red 5 5
888. – 3 c. purple 10 5
889. – 5 c. blue 70 25
890. – 10 c. brown .. .. 5·50 1·90
PORTRAITS: 2 c. Samuel F. B. Morse. 3 c. Cyrus Hall McCormick. 5 c. Elias Howe. 10 c. Alexander Graham Bell.

239. Pony Express.

240. "The Three Graces" (Botticelli).

242. Wyoming State Seal. 241. State Capitol, Boise.

1940. Pony Express. 80th Anniv.
891. 239. 3 c. red 25 10

1940. Pan-American Union. 50th Anniv.
892. 240. 3 c. mauve 25 8

1940. Idaho. 50th Anniv.
893. 241. 3 c. violet 10 5

1940. Wyoming. 50th Anniv.
894. 242. 3 c. purple 10 5

243. "Coronado and His Captains". 244. Anti-aircraft Gun.

1940. Coronado Expedition. 400th Anniv.
895. 243. 3 c. violet 10 5

1940. National Defence.
896. – 1 c. green 5 5
897. 244. 2 c. red 5 5
898. – 3 c. violet 8 5
DESIGNS: 1 c. Statue of Liberty. 3 c. Hand holding torch.

246. State Capitol Building, Montpelier.

245. Emancipation Monument. 247.

1940. Abolition of Slavery. 75th Anniv.
899. 245. 3 c. violet 15 8

1941. Vermont. 150th Anniv.
900. 246. 3 c. violet 12 8

1941. Air.
A 901. 247. 6 c. red 12 5
A 902. 8 c. green 15 5
A 903. 10 c. violet 65 8
A 904. 15 c. red .. .. 1·40 20
A 905. 20 c. green .. .. 1·10 15
A 906. 30 c. blue .. .. 1·60 15
A 907. 50 c. orange .. .. 6·00 2·10

248. Daniel Boone views Kentucky. 249. "Victory".

1942. Kentucky. 150th Anniv.
901. 248. 3 c. violet 8 5

1942. Independence Day.
902. 249. 3 c. violet 5 5

250. Lincoln and Sun Yat-sen. 251. Allegory of Victory.

1942. Chinese War Effort.
903. 250. 5 c. blue 30 15

1943. United Nations.
904. 251. 2 c. red 5 5

252. Liberty and Torch. 253. Flag of Poland.

1943. Four Freedoms.
905. 252. 1 c. green 5 5

1943. Flags of Oppressed Nations. Frames in violet, flags in national colours.
906. 253. 5 c. Poland 15 12
907. – 5 c. Czechoslovakia .. 12 10
908. – 5 c. Norway 12 10
909. – 5 c. Luxemburg .. 12 10
910. – 5 c. Netherlands .. 12 10
911. – 5 c. Belgium 12 10
912. – 5 c. France 12 10
913. – 5 c. Greece 20 15
914. – 5 c. Yugoslavia .. 15 12
915. – 5 c. Albania 15 15
916. – 5 c. Austria 15 15
917. – 5 c. Denmark 15 15
918. – 5 c. Korea 20 15

254.

1944. 1st Transcontinental Railway. 75th Anniv.
919. 254. 3 c. violet 8 5

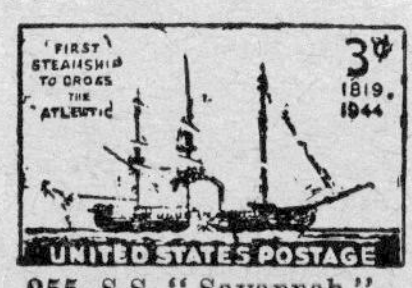

255. S.S. "Savannah".

1944. Transatlantic Crossing. 125th Anniv.
920. 255. 3 c. violet 8 5

256.

1944. Telegraph Centenary.
921. 256. 3 c. mauve 8 5

257. View of Corregidor.

1944. Final Resistance on Corregidor. Commem.
922. 257. 3 c. violet 8 5

258. Show for Troops in South Pacific.

1944. 50th Anniv. of Motion Pictures.
923. 258. 3 c. violet 8 5

259. Gates of St. Augustine, State Seal and Capital.

1945. Statehood of Florida. Cent.
924. 259. 3 c. purple 8 5

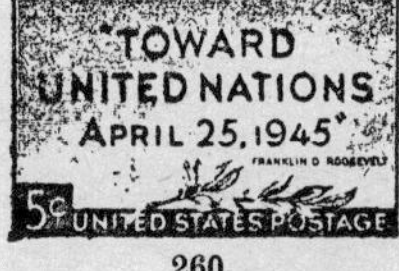

260.

1945. San Francisco Conference.
925. 260. 5 c. blue 8 5

261. Franklin D. Roosevelt and Hyde Park. 262. Raising U.S. Flag at Iwo Jima.

1945. Pres. Roosevelt Commem. Issue. Inscr. "1882 1945".
926. 261. 1 c. green 5 5
927. – 2 c. red 5 5
928. – 3 c. violet 5 5
929. – 5 c. blue 8 5
DESIGNS: 2 c. "Little White House", Warm Springs, Georgia. 3 c. "White House" Washington. 5 c. Western Hemisphere and Three Freedoms.

1945. Honouring U.S. Marines.
930. 262. 3 c. green 5 5

263. U.S. Troops Marching through Paris.

1945. Army Commemorative.
931. 263. 3 c. olive 5 5

264. U.S. Sailors.

1945. Navy Commem.
932. 264 3 c. blue 5 5

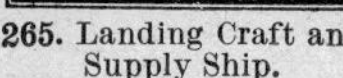

265. Landing Craft and Supply Ship. **266.** Alfred E. Smith.

1945. Coast Guard Commem.
933. **265.** 3 c. green 5 5

1945. Honouring Alfred E. Smith.
934. **266.** 3 c. violet 5 5

267. Flags of U.S.A. and Texas.

1945. Texas Statehood Cent.
935. **267.** 3 c. blue 5 5

268. Liberty Ship unloading Cargo. **269.** Honourable Discharge Emblem.

1946. U.S. Mercantile Marine.
936. **268.** 3 c. green 5 5

1946. War Veterans Commem.
937. **269.** 3 c. violet 5 5

270. Jackson and Sevier.

1946. Tennessee Statehood. 150th Anniv.
938. **270.** 3 c. violet 5 5

271. Map and Flag.

1946. Iowa Statehood Cent.
939. **271.** 3 c. blue 5 5

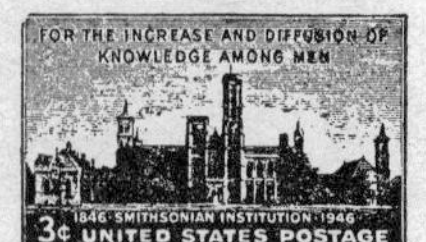

272. Smithsonian Institution.

1946. Smithsonian Institution. Cent.
940. **272.** 3 c. maroon 5 5

273. "Skymaster" Mail Plane.

1946. Air.
A 941. **273.** 5 c. red 8 5

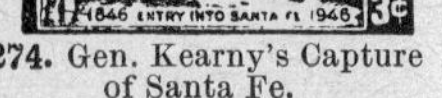

274. Gen. Kearny's Capture of Santa Fe. **275.** Thomas A. Edison.

1946. Kearny Expedition Cent.
941. **274.** 3 c. maroon 5 5

1947. Thomas Edison (inventor). Birth Cent.
942. **275.** 3 c. violet 5 5

1947. Air. As T **273**, but smaller.
A 943. 5 c. red 8 5
A 944. 6 c. red 12 5

276. Joseph Pulitzer.

1947. Joseph Pulitzer (journalist and newspaper publisher). Birth Cent.
943. **276.** 3 c. violet 5 5

77. Washington, Franklin and Evolution of Postal Transport.

1947. U.S. Stamp Centenary.
944. **277.** 3 c. blue 5 5

278. " The Doctor ".

1947. Medical Profession.
946. **278.** 3 c. maroon 5 5

279 Pioneer Caravan.

1947. Utah Cent.
947. **279.** 3 c. violet 5 5

280. Pan American Union Building, Washington.

DESIGNS: 15 c. Statue of Liberty and New York City. 25 c. San Francisco—Oakland Bay Suspension Bridge. 80 c. Diamond Head, Oahu.

1947. Air.
A 948. **280.** 10 c. black .. 25 5
A 949. – 15 c. green 35 5
A 950. – 25 c. blue 75 8
A 1005. – 80 c. purple .. 4·25 70

281. U.S. Frigate " Constitution ".

282. Heron and Map of Florida. **283.** George Washington Carver.

1947. Launching of Frigate " Constitution " (" Old Ironsides ")." 150th Anniv.
948. **281.** 3 c. green 5 5

1947. Dedication of Everglades National Park Florida.
949. **282.** 3 c. green 5 5

1948. George Washington Carver (scientist). 5th Death Anniv.
950. **283.** 3 c. violet 5 5

284. Sutter's Mill, Coloma.

1948. Discovery of Gold in California. Cent.
951. **284.** 3 c. violet 5 5

285. Gov. Winthrop Sargent, Map and Seal of Mississippi Territory.

1948. Mississippi Territory. 150th Anniv.
952. **285.** 3 c. maroon 5 5

286. Four Chaplains and S.S. " Dorchester ".

1948. Four Heroic Chaplains.
953. **286.** 3 c. black 5 5

287. Scroll and State Capitol, Madison.

1948. Wisconsin State Cent.
954. **287.** 3 c. violet 5 5

288. Pioneer and Covered Wagon.

1948. Swedish Pioneers in Middle West. Cent.
955. **288.** 5 c. blue 8 8

289. Elizabeth Stanton, Carrie C. Catt, and Lucretia Mott. **290.** Map of New York, Ring and Aeroplanes.

1948. Women's Progress. Cent.
956. **289.** 3 c. violet 5 5

1948. Air. New York City Council. Golden Anniv.
A 957. **290.** 5 c. red 12 10

291. William Allen White (editor and author). **292.** Suspension Bridge over Niagara River.

1948. Honouring W. A. White.
957. **291.** 3 c. purple 5 5

1948. U.S.A.-Canada Friendship Cent.
958. **292.** 3 c. blue 5 5

293. Francis Scott Key.

1948. Honouring F. S. Key (composer of " Star Spangled Banner ").
959. **293.** 3 c. red 5 5

294. Boy and Girl Students.

1948. Salute to Youth.
960. **294.** 3 c. blue 5 5

295. John McLoughlin, Jason Lee and Covered Wagon. **296.** Harlan Fisk Stone.

1948. Oregon Territory Cent.
961. **295.** 3 c. red 8 5

1948. Honouring H. F. Stone (Chief Justice).
962. **296.** 3 c. purple 8 5

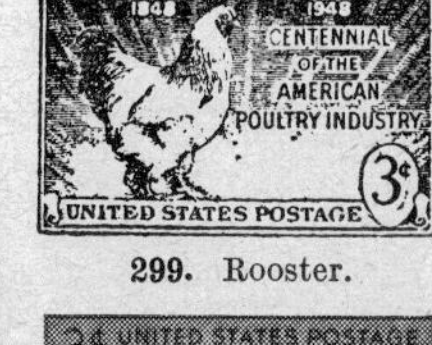

297. Mt. Palomar Observatory. **298.** Clara Barton.

1948. Dedication of Palomar Observatory.
963. **297.** 3 c. blue 15 5

1948. Honouring Clara Barton.
964. **298.** 3 c. red 5 5

299. Rooster.

300. Star and Leaf. **301.** Fort Kearney.

1948. American Poultry Industry. Cent.
965. **299.** 3 c. brown 8 5

1948. Honouring Bereaved Mothers.
966. **300.** 3 c. yellow 8 5

1948. Fort Kearney, Nebraska. Cent.
967. **301.** 3 c. violet 8 5

302. Peter Stuyvesant and Fire Engines.

1948. Volunteer Firemen. Tercent.
968. **302.** 3 c. red 8 5

303. Seals of Indian Tribes.

1948. Five Civilised Indian Tribes of Oklahoma. Cent.
969. **303.** 3 c. brown 8 5

304. Statue of Capt. William Owen O'Neill.

1948. Organization of Rough Riders. 50th Anniv.
970. **304.** 3 c. maroon 8 5

305. Juliette Gordon Low. **306.** Will Rogers.

1948. Juliette Gordon Low (founder of Girl Scouts of U.S.A.).
971. **305.** 3 c. green 8 5

1948. Honouring Will Rogers.
972. **306.** 3 c. purple 8 5

307. Rocket Testing at El Paso.
308. Moina Michael and Poppies.

1948. Fort Bliss. Cent.
973. **307.** 3 c. red 15 5

1948. Honouring Moina Michael.
974. **308.** 3 c. red 8 5

309. Abraham Lincoln and Quotation.
310. Torch and Emblem of American Turners.

1948. Lincoln's Speech at Gettysburg. 85th Anniv.
975. **309.** 3 c. blue 8 5

1948. American Turner's Society. Cent.
976. **310.** 3 c. red 8 5

311. Joel Chandler Harris.
312. Red River Ox Cart and Pioneer.

1948. J. C. Harris (author). Birth Cent.
977. **311.** 3 c. purple 8 5

1949. Territorial Status of Minnesota. Cent.
978. **312.** 3 c. green 5 5

313. Washington and Lee University.

1949. Washington and Lee University, Lexington, Virginia. Bicent.
979. **313.** 3 c. blue 5 5

314. Puerto Rican, Cog-wheel and Ballot Box.

1949. First Gubernatorial Election in Puerto Rico.
980. **314.** 3 c. green 5 5

315. Wings, Seal, Carlyle House and Gadsby's Tavern.

1949. Air. Bicent. of Alexandria, Virginia.
A 981. **315.** 6 c. red 12 8

316. Map, Ship and Shield.

1949. Annapolis, Maryland. Tercent.
981. **316.** 3 c. blue 5 5

317. Young and Old Soldiers.
318. Edgar Allan Poe (poet and author).

1949. Final National Encampment of the Grand Army of the Republic.
982. **317.** 3 c. red 5 5
For similar stamp see No. 995.

1949. Edgar Allan Poe. Death Cent.
983. **318.** 3 c. purple 5 5

DESIGNS: 15 c. Globe and birds. 25 c. Globe and aeroplane.

319. U.P.U. Monument, Berne and P.O. Department, Washington.

1949. Air. U.P.U. 75th Anniv.
A 984. **318.** 10 c. violet 30 25
A 985. – 15 c. blue 35 35
A 986. – 25 c. red 50 45

320. Wright Brothers and Aeroplane.

1949. Air. Wright Brothers' First Flight. 46th Anniv.
A 987. **320.** 6 c. purple 12 8

321. Symbolic of Investments.
322. Samuel Gompers (labour leader).

1950. American Bankers' Assn. 75th Anniv.
984. **321.** 3 c. green 5 5

1950. Samuel Gompers. Birth Cent.
985 **322.** 3 c. purple 5 5

324. The White House.

323. Statue of Freedom.
325. "Casey" Jones and Railway Trains.

1950. National Capital Sesquicentenary.
986. **323.** 3 c. blue 5 5
987. **324.** 3 c. green 5 5
988. – 3 c. violet 5 5
989. – 3 c. purple 5 5
DESIGNS—HORIZ. No. 988, U.S. Supreme Court bldg. No. 989, Capitol, Washington.

1950. Honouring Railway Engineers.
990. **325.** 3 c. maroon 5 5

326. Kansas City in 1850 and 1950.

1950. Kansas City Cent.
991. **326.** 3 c. violet 5 5

327. Scouts and Badge.

1950. Boy Scouts of America. 40th Anniv.
992. **327.** 3 c. brown 5 5

328. First Capitol and W. H. Harrison.

1950. Indiana. 150th Anniv.
993. **328.** 3 c. blue 5 5

329. Pioneers.

1950. California Centenary.
994. **329.** 3 c. yellow 5 5

1951. Final Reunion of United Confederate Veterans. As T **317**, but initials at left and in hat badge changed to "UCV".
995. **317.** 3 c. grey 5 5

330. Log Cabin.

1951. Nevada Centenary.
996. **330.** 3 c olive 5 5

331. Cadillac Disembarking.

1951. Landing of Cadillac. 250th Anniv.
997. **331.** 3 c. blue 5 5

332. Mount of Holy Cross State Seal and Capitol.

1951. Colorado. 75th Anniv.
998. **332.** 3 c. violet 5 5

333. Emblem and Chemical Plant.

1951. American Chemical Society. 75th Anniv.
999. **333.** 3 c. maroon 5 5

334. Washington at Brooklyn.

1951. Battle of Brooklyn. 175th Anniv.
1000. **334.** 3 c. violet 8 5

335. Betsy Ross and Flag.

1952. Betsy Ross. Birth Bicent.
1001. **335.** 3 c. red 8 5

336. Emblem and Club Members.

1952. 50th Anniv. of the 4-H Clubs.
1002. **336.** 3 c. green 5 5

337. Rail Transport.

1952. Baltimore and Ohio Railway. 125th Anniv.
1003. **337.** 3 c. blue 5 5

338. Cars of 1902 and 1952.
339. Torch of Freedom.

1952. American Automobile Assn. 50th Anniv.
1004. **338.** 3 c. blue 5 5

1952. N.A.T.O. 3rd Anniv.
1005. **339.** 3 c. violet 5 5

340. Grand Coulee Dam.

1952. Columbia Basin Reclamation. 50th Anniv.
1006. **340.** 3 c. green 5 5

341. Lafayette and Flags.

1952. Lafayette's Arrival in America. 175th Anniv.
1007. **341.** 3 c. blue 8 5

342. Mt. Rushmore National Memorial.
343. Bridges in 1852 and 1952.

1952. Mt. Rushmore National Memorial. 25th Anniv.
1008. **342.** 3 c. green 5 5

1952. American Society of Civil Engineers. Cent.
1009. **343.** 3 c. blue 5 5

344. Women in Uniform.

1952. Women's Services Commem.
1010. **344.** 3 c. blue 5 5

345. Guttenburg and Elector of Mainz.

1952. 500th Anniv. of Printing of First Book from Movable Type.
1011. **345.** 3 c. violet 5 5

346. Newspaperboy and Torch of Free Enterprise.

1952. Newspaperboys Commem.
1012. **346.** 3 c. violet 5 5

347. Red Cross and Globe.

1952. Int. Red Cross.
1013. **347.** 3 c. blue and red .. 5 5

348. **349.** Map and Seal of Ohio.

1953. National Guard.
1014. **348.** 3 c. blue 5 5

1953. Ohio. 150th Anniv.
1015. **349.** 3 c. sepia 5 5

350. Seal of Washington Territory and Settlers.

1953. Washington Territory. Cent.
1016. **350.** 3 c. blue-green .. 5 5

351. Monroe, Livingston and Marbois signing Transfer.

1953. Louisiana Purchase. 150th Anniv.
1017. **351.** 3 c. purple 5 5

352.

1953. Aviation. 50th Anniv.
A 1018. **352.** 6 c. red 12 8

353. Commodore Perry and Tokyo Bay.

1953. Opening of Japan to Foreign Trade Cent.
1018. **353.** 5 c. blue-green .. 8 5

354. "Wisdom", "Justine and Divine Inspiration" and "Truth".

1953. American Bar Assn. 75th Anniv.
1019. **354.** 3 c. violet 5 5

355. "Sagamore Hill".

1953. Opening of Theodore Roosevelt's Home.
1020. **355.** 3 c. green 5 5

356. Young Farmer and Landscape.

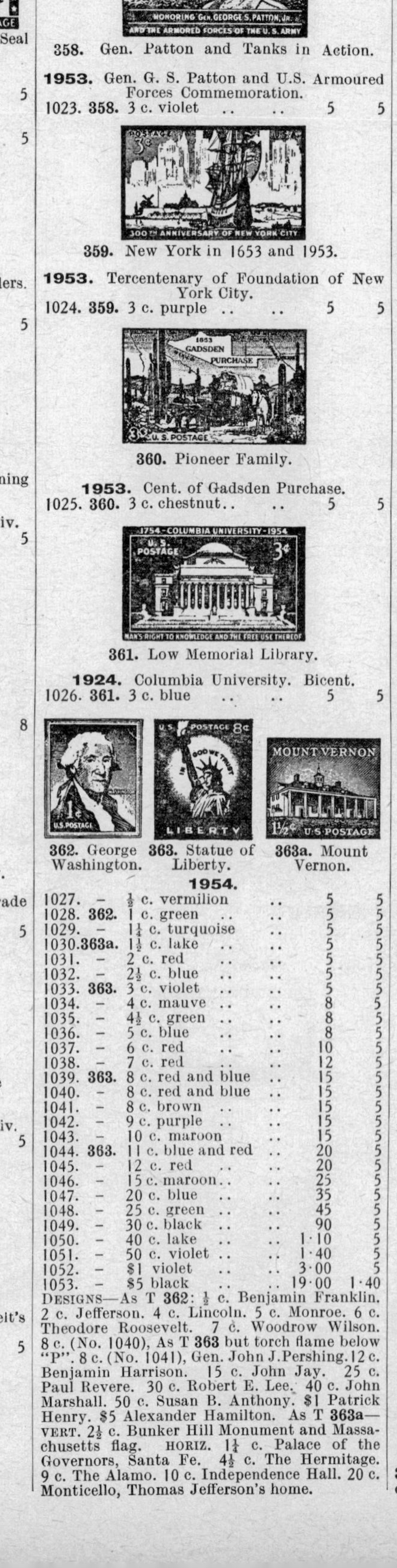

1953. "Future Farmers of America". 25th Anniv.
1021. **356.** 3 c. blue 5 5

357. Lorry and Distant City.

1953. Trucking Industry. 50th Anniv.
1022. **357.** 3 c. violet 5 5

358. Gen. Patton and Tanks in Action.

1953. Gen. G. S. Patton and U.S. Armoured Forces Commemoration.
1023. **358.** 3 c. violet 5 5

359. New York in 1653 and 1953.

1953. Tercentenary of Foundation of New York City.
1024. **359.** 3 c. purple 5 5

360. Pioneer Family.

1953. Cent. of Gadsden Purchase.
1025. **360.** 3 c. chestnut.. .. 5 5

361. Low Memorial Library.

1924. Columbia University. Bicent.
1026. **361.** 3 c. blue 5 5

362. George Washington. **363.** Statue of Liberty. **363a.** Mount Vernon.

1954.
1027. – ½ c. vermilion .. 5 5
1028. **362.** 1 c. green .. 5 5
1029. – 1¼ c. turquoise .. 5 5
1030. **363a.** 1½ c. lake .. 5 5
1031. – 2 c. red .. 5 5
1032. – 2½ c. blue .. 5 5
1033. **363.** 3 c. violet .. 5 5
1034. – 4 c. mauve .. 8 5
1035. – 4½ c. green .. 8 5
1036. – 5 c. blue .. 8 5
1037. – 6 c. red .. 10 5
1038. – 7 c. red .. 12 5
1039. **363.** 8 c. red and blue .. 15 5
1040. – 8 c. red and blue .. 15 5
1041. – 8 c. brown .. 15 5
1042. – 9 c. purple .. 15 5
1043. – 10 c. maroon .. 15 5
1044. **363.** 11 c. blue and red .. 20 5
1045. – 12 c. red .. 20 5
1046. – 15 c. maroon.. .. 25 5
1047. – 20 c. blue .. 35 5
1048. – 25 c. green .. 45 5
1049. – 30 c. black .. 90 5
1050. – 40 c. lake .. 1·10 5
1051. – 50 c. violet .. 1·40 5
1052. – $1 violet .. 3·00 5
1053. – $5 black .. 19·00 1·40

DESIGNS—As T **362**: ½ c. Benjamin Franklin. 2 c. Jefferson. 4 c. Lincoln. 5 c. Monroe. 6 c. Theodore Roosevelt. 7 c. Woodrow Wilson. 8 c. (No. 1040), As T **363** but torch flame below "P". 8 c. (No. 1041), Gen. John J. Pershing. 12 c. Benjamin Harrison. 15 c. John Jay. 25 c. Paul Revere. 30 c. Robert E. Lee. 40 c. John Marshall. 50 c. Susan B. Anthony. $1 Patrick Henry. $5 Alexander Hamilton. As T **363a**—VERT. 2½ c. Bunker Hill Monument and Massachusetts flag. HORIZ. 1¼ c. Palace of the Governors, Santa Fe. 4½ c. The Hermitage. 9 c. The Alamo. 10 c. Independence Hall. 20 c. Monticello, Thomas Jefferson's home.

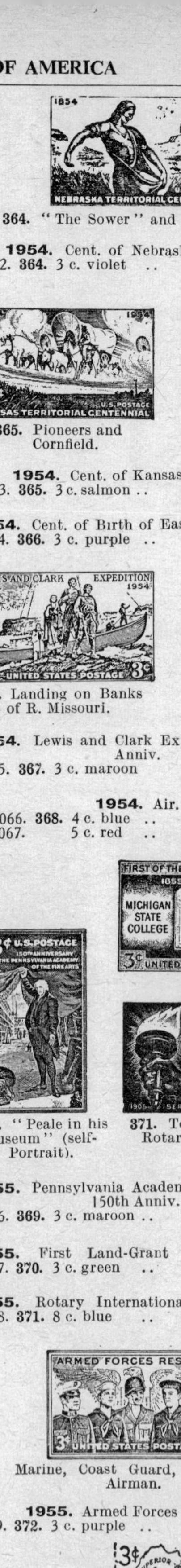

364. "The Sower" and Mitchell Pass.

1954. Cent. of Nebraska Territory.
1062. **364.** 3 c. violet 5 5

365. Pioneers and Cornfield. **366.** George Eastman.

1954. Cent. of Kansas Territory.
1063. **365.** 3 c. salmon 5 5

1954. Cent. of Birth of Eastman (inventor).
1064. **366.** 3 c. purple 5 5

367. Landing on Banks of R. Missouri. **368.** Eagle in Flight.

1954. Lewis and Clark Expedition. 150th Anniv.
1065. **367.** 3 c. maroon .. 5 5

1954. Air.
A 1066. **368.** 4 c. blue 8 8
A 1067. 5 c. red 15 5

370.

369. "Peale in his Museum" (self-Portrait). **371.** Torch, Globe and Rotary Emblem.

1955. Pennsylvania Academy of Fine Arts. 150th Anniv.
1066. **369.** 3 c. maroon 5 5

1955. First Land-Grant Colleges. Cent.
1067. **370.** 3 c. green 5 5

1955. Rotary International. 50th Anniv.
1068. **371.** 8 c. blue 15 8

372. Marine, Coast Guard, Soldier, Sailor, Airman.

1955. Armed Forces Reserve.
1069. **372.** 3 c. purple 5 5

374. Map of the Great Lakes.

373. "The Old Man of the Mountains". **375.**

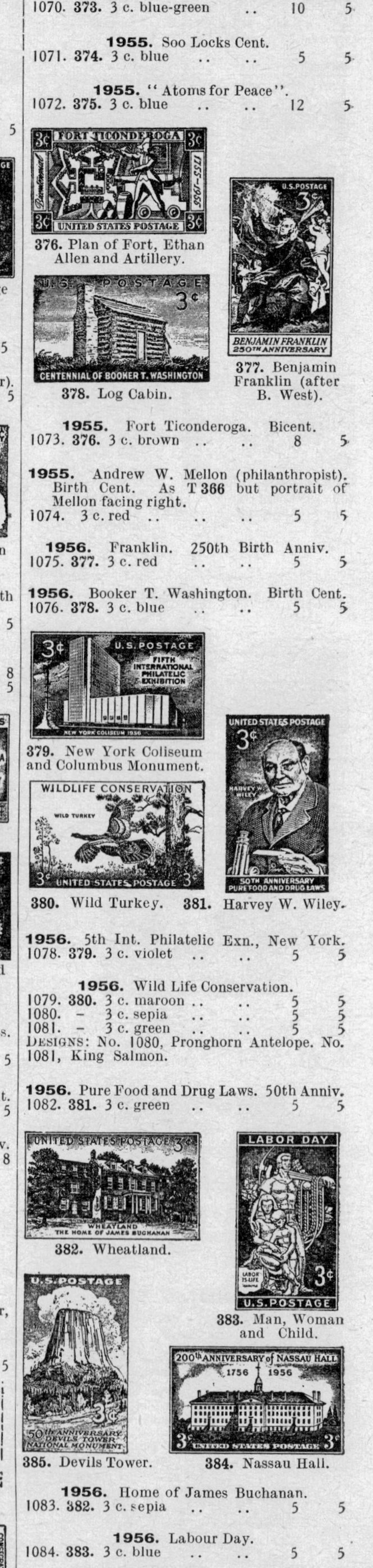

1955. 150th Anniv. of Discovery of "The Old Man of the Mountains", New Hampshire Landmark.
1070. **373.** 3 c. blue-green .. 10 5

1955. Soo Locks Cent.
1071. **374.** 3 c. blue 5 5

1955. "Atoms for Peace".
1072. **375.** 3 c. blue 12 5

376. Plan of Fort, Ethan Allen and Artillery.

378. Log Cabin. **377.** Benjamin Franklin (after B. West).

1955. Fort Ticonderoga. Bicent.
1073. **376.** 3 c. brown 8 5

1955. Andrew W. Mellon (philanthropist). Birth Cent. As T **366** but portrait of Mellon facing right.
1074. 3 c. red 5 5

1956. Franklin. 250th Birth Anniv.
1075. **377.** 3 c. red 5 5

1956. Booker T. Washington. Birth Cent.
1076. **378.** 3 c. blue 5 5

379. New York Coliseum and Columbus Monument.

380. Wild Turkey. **381.** Harvey W. Wiley.

1956. 5th Int. Philatelic Exn., New York.
1078. **379.** 3 c. violet 5 5

1956. Wild Life Conservation.
1079. **380.** 3 c. maroon 5 5
1080. – 3 c. sepia 5 5
1081. – 3 c. green 5 5

DESIGNS: No. 1080, Pronghorn Antelope. No. 1081, King Salmon.

1956. Pure Food and Drug Laws. 50th Anniv.
1082. **381.** 3 c. green 5 5

382. Wheatland.

383. Man, Woman and Child.

385. Devils Tower. **384.** Nassau Hall.

1956. Home of James Buchanan.
1083. **382.** 3 c. sepia 5 5

1956. Labour Day.
1084. **383.** 3 c. blue 5 5

1956. Nassau Hall. Bicent.
1085. **384.** 3 c. black on orange.. 5 5

1956. Devils Tower Monument. 50th Anniv.
1086. **385.** 3 c. violet 5 5

386. "The Key to World Peace."

387. Hamilton and Federal Hall, New York.

388. Woman, Children and Shield of Caduceus.

1956. Children's Friendship.
1087. **386.** 3 c. blue 5 5

1957. Alexander Hamilton. Birth Bicent.
1088. **387.** 3 c. red 5 5

1957. Infantile Paralysis Relief Campaign.
1089. **388.** 3 c. mauve .. 5 5

389. Survey Flag and Ships.

390. Ancient and Modern Capitals.

391. Eagle and Ladle.

1957. Coast and Geodetic Survey. 150th Anniv.
1090. **389.** 3 c. blue 5 5

1957. American Institute of Architects. Cent.
1091. **390.** 3 c. mauve .. 5 5

1957. American Steel Industry. Cent.
1092. **391.** 3 c. blue 5 5

392. Festival Emblem and Aircraft Carrier.

1957. Jamestown Festival and Int. Naval Review.
1093. **392.** 3 c. green 5 5

393. Arrow piercing Atomic Symbol.

1957. Oklahoma Statehood. 50th Anniv.
1094. **393.** 3 c. blue 5 5

394. Teacher with Pupils.

1957. Teachers of America Commem.
1095. **394.** 3 c. claret 5 5

395. U.S. Flag.

1957.
1096. **395.** 4 c. red and blue .. 8 5

396. B 52 Stratofortress and Three F 104 Star-fighters.

397. "Virginia of Sagadahock" and Arms of Maine.

1957. Air. U.S. Air Force. 50th Anniv.
A 1097. **396.** 6 c. blue 12 8

1957. American Shipbuilding. 350th Anniv.
1097. **397.** 3 c. violet 5 5

398. Pres. Magsaysay of the Philippines.

399. Marquis de Lafayette.

1957. Pres. Magsaysay Commemoration.
1098. **398.** 8 c. ochre, blue & red 12 8

1957. Bicent. of Birth of Marquis de Lafayette.
1099. **399.** 3 c. claret. 8 5

400. Whooping Cranes.

401. "Religious Freedom".

1957. Wildlife Conservation.
1100. **400.** 3 c. blue, orge. & grn. 5 5

1957. Flushing Remonstrance. Tercent.
1101. **401.** 3 c. black 5 5

402. "Abundance".

403. U.S. Pavilion.

1958. Gardening and Horticulture Commem.
1102. **402.** 3 c. green 5 5

1958. Brussels Int. Exn.
1103. **403.** 3 c. maroon 5 5

404. James Monroe.

405. Lake in Minnesota.

1958. Pres. James Monroe. Birth Bicent.
1104. **404.** 3 c. violet 5 5

1958. Minnesota Statehood. Cent.
1105. **405.** 3 c. green 5 5

406. Sun's Surface and Hands (after Michelangelo's "The Creation of Adam").

1958. I.G.Y.
1106. **406.** 3 c. red and black .. 12 5

407. Gunston Hall.

408. Mackinac Bridge.

1958. Gunston Hall, Virginia (home of George Mason, patriot). 200th Anniv.
1107. **407.** 3 c. green 5 5

1958. Mackinac Bridge Commem.
1108. **408.** 3 c. turquoise .. 5 5

409. Simon Bolivar.

410.

1958. Bolivar Commem.
1109. **409.** 4 c. ochre 8 5
1110. 8 c. brown, blue & red 15 10

1958. Air.
A 1111. **410.** 7 c. blue 15 5
A 1112. 7 c. red 20 5

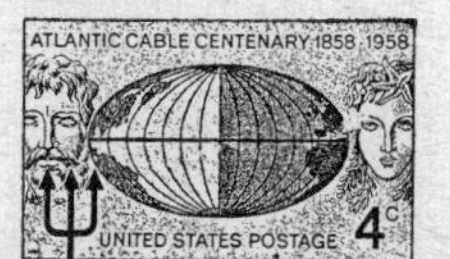

411. Globe, Neptune and Mermaid.

1958. Atlantic Cable Inaug. Cent.
1111. **411.** 4 c. purple 8 5

412. Lincoln addressing Electorate.

413. Hand with Quill Pen and Printing Press.

1958. Lincoln-Douglas Debates Cent.
1114. **412.** 4 c. brown 8 5

1958. Kossuth Commem. Medallion portrait as T **409.**
1116. 4 c. green.. .. .. 8 5
1117. 8 c. brown, blue and red.. 12 8

1958. Freedom of the Press.
1118. **413.** 4 c. black 8 5

414. Mail Coach under Attack.

415. Noah Webster (lexicographer).

1958. Overland Mail Cent.
1119. **414.** 4 c. red 8 5

1958. Noah Webster. Birth Bicent.
1120. **415.** 4 c. crimson 8 5

416. Forest Pines.

417. British Forces occupying Fort Duquesne.

1958. Forest Conservation.
1121. **416.** 4 c. yellow, grn. & brn. 8 5

1958. Fort Duquesne. Bicent.
1122. **417.** 4 c. blue 8 5

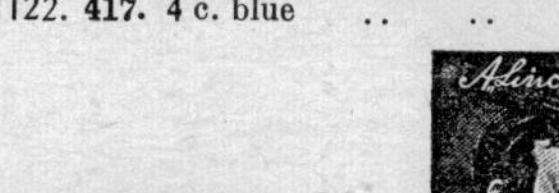

418. Stars on Alaskan Map.

419. Abraham Lincoln.

1959. Air. Alaska Statehood.
A 1123. **418.** 7 c. blue 15 5

1959. Lincoln. 150th Birth Anniv.
1112. **419.** 1 c. green .. 5 5
1113. – 3 c. claret .. 5 5
DESIGN: 3 c. Bust of Lincoln.

420. Covered Wagon and Mt. Hood.

421. N.A.T.O. Emblem.

1959. Oregon Statehood Cent.
1123. **420.** 4 c. green .. 8 5

1959. San Martin Commem. Medallion portrait as T **409.**
1124. 4 c. blue 8 5
1125. 8 c. ochre, red and blue.. 12 8

1959. N.A.T.O. 10th Anniv.
1126. **421.** 4 c. blue 8 5

422. Peary with Dog-team and Submarine "Nautilus".

1959. Arctic Explorations. Peary's Visit to N. Pole (50th Anniv.) and "Nautilus" Commem.
1127. **422.** 4 c. turquoise .. 8 5

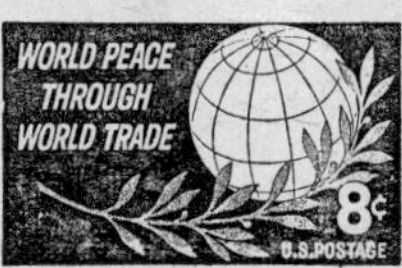

423.

1959. World Peace through World Trade.
1128. **423.** 8 c. claret 15 5

424. Lincoln Statue, Washington.

1959. Lincoln. 150th Birth Anniv. and Memorial Commem.
1115. **424.** 4 c. blue 8 5

425. Discovery of Silver at Mt. Davidson.

1959. Discovery of Silver in Nevada. Cent.
1129. **425.** 4 c. black 8 5

426. Maple Leaf linked with American Eagle.

1959. Opening of St. Lawrence Seaway.
1130. **426.** 4 c. blue and red .. 8 5

427. New U.S. Flag (with 49 stars).

1959. New United States Flag. Inaug.
1131. **427.** 4 c. red, blue & orange 8 5

428. Balloon "Jupiter".

429. Hawaiian Warrior, Map and Star.

430. "The Good Earth".

431. Oil Derrick.

1959. Air. Cent. of Balloon "Jupiter's" Mail-carrying Flight.
A 1132. **428.** 7 c. red and blue .. 15 8

1959. Air. Hawaii Statehood.
A 1133. **429.** 7 c. red 15 8

1959. Soil Conservation.
1132. **430.** 4 c. green, brown and blue 8 5

1959. Petroleum Industry Commem. and Cent. of First Oil-well at Titusville, Penn.
1133. **431.** 4 c. brown 8 5

432. Runner with Olympic Torch.

433. "Happy Children with Healthy Teeth".

1959. Air. 3rd Pan-American Games, Chicago.
A 1134. **432.** 10 c. red and blue 45 30

1959. Dental Health. Cent. of American Dental Assn.
1134. **433.** 4 c. green 8 5

1959. Ernst Reuter Commem. Medallion portrait as T **409.**
1135. 4 c grey 8 5
1136. 8 c. ochre, red and blue .. 12 8

434. "Liberty for All".

435. Dr. E. McDowell.

1959. Air.
A 1137. – 10 c. black and green 1·50 45
A 1138. – 13 c. black and red 35 8
A 1139. **434.** 15 c. blk. & orge (A) 50 5
A 1140. 15 c. blk. & orge. (B) 35 5
A 1141. – 25 c. blk. & choc... 35 5

DESIGNS: 10 c., 13 c. Freedom bell. 15 c. Statue has double frame-line (A) or single frame-line (B). 25 c. Abraham Lincoln.

1959. First Recorded Successful Abdominal Operation. 150th Anniv.
1137. **435** 4 c. purple 8 5

436.

1960. "American Credo" series.
1138. **436.** 4 c. red and blue .. 10 5
1139. – 4 c. green and bistre 10 5
1140. – 4 c. red and grey .. 10 5
1141. – 4 c. blue and red .. 10 5
1142. – 4 c. green and purple 10 5
1143. – 4 c. brown and green 10 5

INSCRIPTIONS: No. 1139, "Fear to do ill, and you need fear Nought else" (Franklin). No. 1140, "I have sworn . . . Hostility against every form of TYRANNY over the mind of man" (Jefferson). No. 1141, "And this be our Motto in GOD is our TRUST" (Francis Scott Key). No. 1142, "Those who Deny freedom in others Deserve it not for Themselves" (Lincoln). No. 1143, "Give me LIBERTY or give me DEATH" (P. Henry).

437. Scout Saluting.

438. Olympic Rings and Snow Crystal.

1960. American Boy Scout Movement. 50th Anniv.
1144. **437.** 4 c. ochre, red & blue 5 5

1960. Winter Olympic Games.
1145. **438.** 4 c. blue 5 5

1960. Thomas Masaryk Commem. Medallion portrait as T **409.**
1146. 4 c. blue 8 5
1147. 8 c. ochre, red & blue 15 8

439. "Towards the Light".

1960. World Refugee Year.
1148. **439.** 4 c. black 8 5

440. "Irrigation".

441. S.E.A.T.O. Emblem.

1960. Water Conservation Campaign.
1149. **440.** 4 c. green, chest. & bl. 8 5

1960. S.E.A.T.O. Conf.
1150. **441.** 4 c. blue 5 5

442. Mother and Child.

443. New U.S. Flag (with 50 stars).

445. Cripple operating Press.

444. Pony Express.

1960. American Womanhood Commem.
1151. **442.** 4 c. violet 8 5

1960. Inaug. of New United States Flag.
1152. **443.** 4 c. red and blue .. 8 5

1960. Pony Express Cent.
1153. **444.** 4 c. brown 8 5

1960. Cripple's Welfare Campaign.
1154. **445.** 4 c. blue 5 5

446. Congress Seal.

447. Dolores Bell (Mexico).

448. Washington Monument and Cherry Blossom.

1960. 5th World Forestry Congress, Seattle.
1155. **446.** 4 c. green 8 5

1960. Mexican Independence. 150th Anniv.
1156. **447.** 4 c. red and green .. 5 5

1960. U.S.-Japan Treaty. Cent.
1157. **448.** 4 c. red and turquoise 8 5

1960. Paderewski Commem. Medallion portrait as T **409.**
1158. 4 c. blue 8 5
1159. 8 c. ochre, red and blue .. 15 8

449. Robert A. Taft.

450. Steering Wheel, Motor Transport and Globes.

1960. Memorial Issue.
1160. **449.** 4 c. violet 5 5
1169. – 4 c. vio. (W. F. George) 5 5
1171. – 4 c. vio. (J. F. Dulles) 5 5

1960. "Wheels of Freedom" (Motor Industry).
1161. **450.** 4 c. blue 5 5

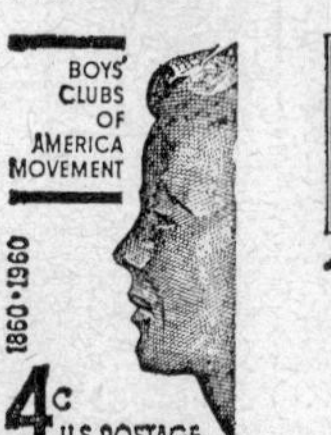

451. Boy.

452. Auto P.O., Providence, Rhode Island.

454. Andrew Carnegie.

453. Camp Fire Girls Emblem.

1960. Boys' Clubs of America Movement Cent.
1162. **451.** 4 c. red, blk. & indigo 8 5

1960. 1st U.S. Automated P.O. Inaug.
1163. **452.** 4 c. blue and red .. 5 5

1960. Marshal Mannerheim Commem. Medallion portrait as T **409.**
1164. 4 c. blue 8 5
1165. 8 c. ochre, red and blue .. 15 8

1960. Camp Fire Girls Movement. 50th Anniv.
1166. **453.** 4 c. red and blue .. 5 5

1960. Garibaldi Commem. Medallion portrait as T **409.**
1167. 4 c. green 8 5
1168. 8 c. ochre, red and blue .. 15 8

1960. Andrew Carnegie Commem.
1170. **454.** 4 c. claret 5 5

455. "Echo I" Communications Satellite.

1960. "Communications for Peace".
1172. **455.** 4 c. violet 50 5

1961. Mahatma Gandhi Commem. Medallion portrait as T **409.**
1173. 4 c. vermilion on orange 8 5
1174. 8 c. ochre, red and blue .. 15 8

456. Trail Boss and Prairie.

457. Horace Greeley (editor).

1961. Range Conservation.
1175 **456.** 4 c. blk., oran. & blue 5 5

1961. Greeley Commem.
1176. **457.** 4 c. violet 8 5

458. Sea Coast Gun.

1961. Civil War Cent. (1st issue). Fort Sumter.
1177. **458.** 4 c. green 15 5

459. Sunflower and Pioneers.

1961. Kansas Statehood Cent.
1182. **459.** 4 c. red & brn. on yell. 8 5

460. Senator G. W. Norris

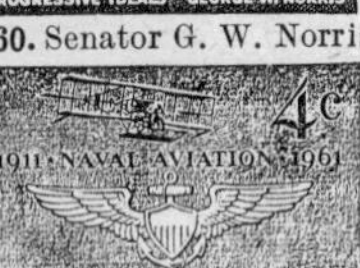

461.

462. "Balanced Judgment".

1961. Senator George W. Norris. Birth Cent.
1183. **460.** 4 c. green 5 5

1961. U.S. Naval Aviation. 50th Anniv.
1184. **461.** 4 c. blue 8 5

1961. Workmen's Compensation Law. 50th Anniv.
1185. **462.** 4 c. blue 8 5

463. "The Smoke Signal" (after Remington).

464. Dr. Sun Yat-sen.

465. Basket-ball.

1961. Frederick Remington (painter). Birth Cent.
1186. **463.** 4 c. multicoloured .. 8 5

1961. Republic of China. 50th Anniv.
1187. **464.** 4 c. blue 8 5

1961. Dr. James A. Naismith (Inventor of basketball). Birth Cent.
1188. **465.** 4 c. brown 8 5

466. Nurse lighting Candle of Dedication.

467. Ship Rock. New Mexico.

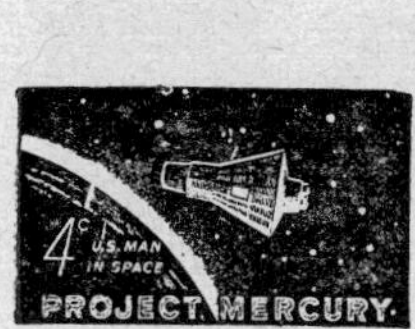

469. "U.S. Man in Space".

468. Saguaro Cactus and Flowers.

1961. Nursing Commem.
1189. **466.** 4 c. orange, black, green and blue .. 8 5

1962. Statehood of New Mexico. 50th Anniv.
1190. **467.** 4 c. lake, ochre & turq. 8 5

1962. Statehood of Arizona. 50th Anniv.
1191. **468.** 4 c. blue, green & red 10 5

1962. Project Mercury. Colonel John Glenn's Space Flight.
1192. **469.** 4 c. blue, oran. & grn. 20 5

470. U.S. and Campaign Emblems.

472. C. E. Hughes.

473. Tower and Mono-railway.

471. Soldier.

1962. Malaria Eradication.
1193. **470.** 4 c. ochre and blue .. 8 5

1962. Civil War Cent. (2nd issue). Shiloh.
1178. **471.** 4 c. black on pink .. 8 5

1962. Chief Justice Charles E. Hughes. Birth Cent.
1194. **472.** 4 c. black on buff .. 5 5

1962. "Century 21" Exn. "World's Fair"), Seattle.
1195. **473.** 4 c. blue and red .. 5 5

474. Mississippi Riverboat.

1962. Louisiana Statehood. 150th Anniv.
1196. **474.** 4 c. myrtle, red & blue 8 5

475. Settler's Homestead.

1962. Homestead Act Cent.
1197. **475.** 4 c. grey 5 5

476. Girl Scout and Flag.

1962. U.S. Girl Scouts. 50th Anniv.
1198. **476.** 4 c. red 8 5

477. Senator McMahon and Atomic Symbol.

1962. Brien McMahon Commem.
1199. **477.** 4 c. violet 8 5

478. "Transfer of Skill".

479. Sam Rayburn.

1962. National Apprenticeship Act. 25th Anniv.
1200. **478.** 4 c. black on olive .. 5 5

1962. Sam Rayburn Commem.
1201. **479.** 4 c. brown and blue .. 5 5

480. Dag Hammarskjoeld and U.N. Headquarters.

481. Christmas Laurel Wreath.

1962. Hammarskjoeld Commem.
1202. **480.** 4 c brown, yell. & black 8 5
1203. 4 c. brn., yell. & black 10 5
No. 1203 has the yellow colour inverted and comes from a special printing made after a few examples had been discovered.

1962. Christmas Issue.
1204. **481.** 4 c. green and red .. 5 5

482. "Lamp of Learning" and Map.

1962. Higher Education.
1205. **482.** 4 c. black and green .. 8 5

483. Washington (after Houdon).

484. U.S. Flag and White House.

485. Bald Eagle.

486. Capitol, Washington and Airliner.

1962.
1206. – 1 c. emerald (Andrew Jackson) (postage) 5 5
1207. **483.** 5 c. indigo 8 5
1211. **484.** 5 c. red and blue .. 8 5
A 1210. **485.** 6 c. red (air) .. 12 8
A 1211. **486.** 8 c. red 15 5

487. "Breezing Up" (after Winslow Homer).

1962.
1210. **487.** 4 c. multicoloured .. 8 5

488. Charter and Quill.

1963. Carolina Charter Tercent.
1212. **488.** 5 c. sepia and red .. 8 5

489. P.M.G. Montgomery Blair. Letters and Globe.

490. "Food for Peace".

1963. Air. Paris Postal Conferences Cent.
A 1213. **489.** 15 c. mar., blue & red 95 30

1963. Freedom from Hunger.
1213. **490.** 5 c. brown, green & red 8 5

491. Map and State Capitol, Charleston.

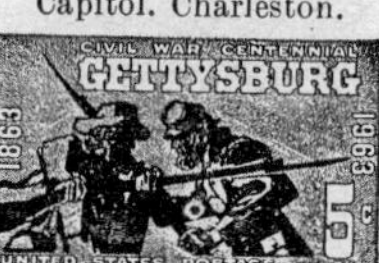

492. Armed Combat.

493. Amelia Earhart (aviator).

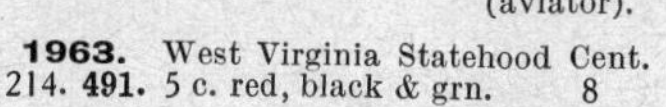

1963. West Virginia Statehood Cent.
1214. **491.** 5 c. red, black & grn. 8 5

1963. CivilWar Cent. (3rd issue). Gettysburg.
1179. **492.** 5 c. indigo and blue 8 5

1963. Air. Amelia Earhart Commem.
A 1216. **493.** 8 c. brown-pur. & red 15 8

494. Broken Link.

495. Torch of Progress.

496. Cordell Hull.

1963. Emancipation Proclamation Cent.
1215. **494.** 5 c. black, blue & red 8 5

1963. "Alliance for Progress".
1216. **495.** 5 c. green and blue .. 8 5

1963. Cordell Hull Commem.
1217. **496.** 5 c. blue-green .. 8 5

497. Eleanor Roosevelt.

498. "The Sciences".

499. City Mail Postman.

1963. Eleanor Roosevelt Commem.
1218. **497.** 5 c. violet 8 5

1963. National Academy of Science Cent.
1219. **498.** 5 c. black & turquoise 12 5

1963. City Mail Delivery Cent.
1220. **499.** 5 c. black, red & blue 8 5

500. Red Cross Flag and S.S. "Morning Light".

501. Christmas Tree.

1963. Red Cross Centenary.
1221. **500.** 5 c. black and red .. 8 5

1963. Christmas.
1222. **501.** 5 c. black, blue & red 8 5

502. Columbia Jays.

503. Sam Houston.

1963. John James Audubon Commem.
1223. **502.** 5 c. multicoloured .. 8 5
See also No. A 1304.

1964. Sam Houston Commem.
1224. **503.** 5 c. black 8 5

504. "Jerked Down".

505. Mall with Unisphere and "The Rocket Thrower" (after De Lue).

506. John Muir (naturalist), and Forest.

1964. C. M. Russell (artist). Birth Cent.
1225. **504.** 5 c. multicoloured .. 10 5

1964. New York World's Fair.
1226. **505.** 5 c. blue-green .. 10 5

1964. John Muir Commem.
1227. **506.** 5 c. brn., emer. & grn. 8 5

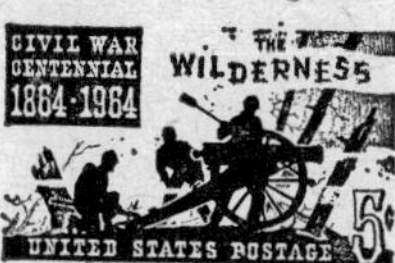

507. Artillery Team.

1964. Civil War Cent. (4th issue). The Wilderness.
1180. **507.** 5 c. black & crimson 8 5

508. Pres. Kennedy and "Eternal Flame".

509. Philip Carteret at Elizabethtown (1664).

511. U.S. Flag.

510. Virginia City in 19th Century.

1964. President Kennedy Memorial Issue.
1228. **508.** 5 c. indigo on grey .. 8 5

1964. New Jersey Tercent.
1229. **509.** 5 c. blue 8 5

1964. Nevada Statehood Cent.
1230. **510.** 5 c. multicoloured .. 8 5

1964. "Register and Vote" Campaign.
1231. **511.** 5 c. red and blue .. 8 5

512. Shakespeare.

513. Drs. William and Charles Mayo (founders of Mayo Clinic).

1964. William Shakespeare. 400th Birth Anniv.
1232. **512.** 5 c. sepia on buff .. 8 5

1964. Mayo Brothers Commem.
1233. **513.** 5 c. green 8 5

514. R. H. Goddard, "Atlas" Rocket and Launching Tower.

1964. Air. Robert H. Goddard Commem.
A 1234. **514.** 8 c. blue, red & yellow 65 8

•**515.** Lute, Horn and Music Score.

1964. American Music.
1234. **515.** 5 c. black, red and blue on pale blue .. 8 5

516. Sampler.

1964. "Homemakers" Commem.
1235. **516.** 5 c. multicoloured .. 8 5

517. Holly. **518.** Verrazano Narrows Bridge.

1964. Christmas. Each red, green and black.

1236.	5 c. Type **517**	55	5
1237.	5 c. Mistletoe	55	5
1238.	5 c. Poinsettia	55	5
1239.	5 c. Pine cone	55	5

1964. Opening of Verrazano Narrows Bridge, New York.
1240. **518.** 5 c. green 8 5

519. "Abstract Art".

1964. "To the Fine Arts".
1241. **519.** 5 c. red, black & blue 8 5

520. Radio Waves. **521.** General Jackson leading Troops into Battle.

1964. Amateur Radio.
1242. **520.** 5 c. purple 8 5

1965. Battle of New Orleans. 150th Anniv.
1243. **521.** 5 c. red, blue & black 8 5

522. Discus-thrower (Washington statue). **523.** Microscope and Stethoscope.

1965. Sokol Physical Fitness Organisation in the U.S.A. Cent.
1244. **522.** 5 c. indigo and lake.. 8 5

1965. Crusade Against Cancer.
1245. **523.** 5 c. black, violet & red 8 5

524. Soldier and Rifles. **525.** Sir Winston Churchill.

1965. Civil War Cent. (5th issue). Appomattox.
1181. **524.** 5 c. black and blue .. 12 5

1965. Churchill Commem.
1246. **525.** 5 c. black 8 5

526. Procession of Barons, and King John's Crown.

1965. Magna Carta. 750th Anniv.
1247. **526.** 5 c. black, yell. & violet 8 5

527. I.C.Y. Emblem. **528.** "One hundred years of service".

1965. Int. Co-operation Year.
1248. **527.** 5 c. black and blue .. 8 5

1965. Salvation Army Cent.
1249. **528.** 5 c. black, red & blue 8 5

529. Dante. **530.** Herbert Hoover.

1965. Dante's Birth. 700th Anniv.
1250. **529.** 5 c. red on flesh .. 8 5

1965. Hoover Commem.
1251. **530.** 5 c. red 8 5

531. Robert Fulton. **532.** Spanish Knight and Banners.

1965. Robert Fulton (inventor). Birth Cent.
1252. **531.** 5 c. black and blue.. 8 5

1965. Florida Settlement. 400th Anniv.
1253. **532.** 5 c. black, red & yellow 8 5

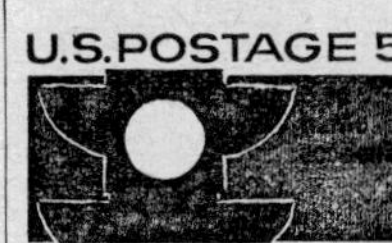

533. Traffic Signal. **534.** Elizabeth Clarke Copley (from "The Copley Family" by J. S. Copley).

1965. Traffic Safety.
1254. **533.** 5 c. red, black & green 8 5

1965. John Singleton Copley Commem.
1255. **534.** 5 c. brown, drab & blk. 8 5

535. Radio "Waves" on World Map. **536.** Adlai Stevenson.

1965. I.T.U. Cent.
1256. **535.** 11 c. red, blk. & ochre 30 5

1965. Stevenson Commem
1257. **536.** 5 c. black, blue, red and ultramarine .. 8 5

537. Archangel Gabriel (weathervane). **538.** Lincoln.

1965. Christmas.
1258. **537.** 5 c. green, ochre & red 8 5

1965. Prominent Americans (1st series).

1259.	–	1 c. green	5	5
1260.	–	1¼ c. green	10	5
1261.	–	2 c. indigo	5	5
1262.	–	3 c. violet	5	5
1263	**538.**	4 c. black	5	5
1264.	–	5 c. ultramarine ..	5	5
1266.	–	6 c. sepia	8	5
1281.	–	6 c. sepia	5	5
1267.	–	8 c. violet	10	5
1268.	–	10 c. purple	12	5
1269.	–	12 c. black	15	5
1270.	–	13 c. brown	15	5
1271.	–	15 c. maroon	15	5
1272.	–	20 c. olive	25	5
1273.	–	25 c. lake	30	5
1274.	–	30 c. purple	35	5
1275.	–	40 c. blue	45	5
1276.	–	50 c. red	55	5
1277.	–	$1 purple	1·25	5
1278.	–	$5 black	5·50	1·25

DESIGNS—VERT. 1 c. Thomas Jefferson. 1¼ c. Albert Gallatin. 2 c. Frank Lloyd Wright and Guggenheim Museum, New York. 5 c. Washington. 6 c. Franklin Roosevelt. 8 c. (1267) Prof. Albert Einstein. 10 c. Andrew Jackson. 13 c. Pres. Kennedy. 15 c. Justice Wendell Holmes. 20 c. George G. Marshall. 25 c. Frederick Douglass. 40 c. Tom Paine. 50 c. Lucy Stone. $1, Eugene O'Neill. $5, John Bassert Moore. HORIZ. 3 c. Francis Parkman. 6 c. (No. 1266), Franklin Roosevelt. 12 c. Henry Ford and Model "T" Car. 30 c. John Dewey.

See also Nos. 1383/89.

539. "Migratory Birds".

1966. Migratory Bird Treaty. 50th Anniv.
1286. **539.** 5 c. red, blue and black 8 5

INDEX

Countries can be quickly located by referring to the index at the end of this volume.

540. Dog. **541.** Seal, Emblem and Map.

542. Clown. **543.** SIPEX "Letter".

1966. Humane Treatment of Animals.
1287. **540.** 5 c. black and brown 8 5

1966. Indiana Statehood. 150th Anniv.
1288. **541.** 5 c. blue, brown & yell. 8 5

1966. The American Circus.
1289. **542.** 5 c. red, blue, pink and black 10 5

1966. 6th Int. Philatelic Exn., Washington. (SIPEX).
1290. **543.** 5 c. multicoloured .. 8 5

544. "Freedom" opposing "Tyranny". **545.** Polish Eagle.

1966. Bill of Rights. 175th Anniv.
1292. **544.** 5 c. red, indigo and blue 8 5

1966. Polish Millennium.
1293. **545.** 5 c. red 8 5

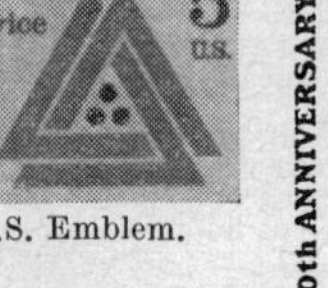

546. N.P.S. Emblem. **547.** Marines Past and Present.

549. Johnny Appleseed and Apple. **548.** Women of 1890 and 1966.

1966. National Park Service. 50th Anniv.
1294. **546.** 5 c. black, grn. & yell. 8 5

1966. Marine Corps Reserve. 50th Anniv.
1295. **547.** 5 c. multicoloured .. 8 5

1966. General Federation of Women's Clubs, 75th Anniv.
1296. **548.** 5 c. black, pink & blue 8 5

1966. Johnny Appleseed.
1297. **549.** 5 c. black, red & green 8 5

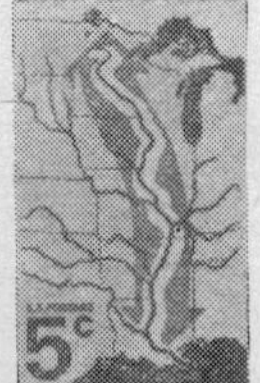

550. Jefferson Memorial, Washington. **551.** Map of Great River Road.

1966. "Beautification of America" Campaign.
1298. **550.** 5 c. black, grn. & pink 8 5

1966. Opening of Great River Road.
1299. **551.** 5 c. red, yellow & blue 10 5

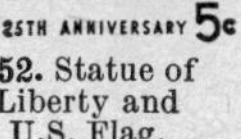

552. Statue of Liberty and U.S. Flag. **553.** "Madonna and Child" (after Memling).

1966. U.S. Savings Bank. 25th Anniv. and Tribute to U.S. Servicemen.
1300. **552.** 5 c. red, black, indigo and blue 8 5

1966. Christmas.
1301. **553.** 5 c. multicoloured .. 8 5

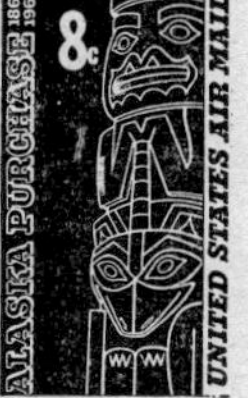

554. "The Boating Party" (after Mary Cassatt). **555.** Tlingit Totem, Southern Alaska.

1966. Mary Cassatt.
1302. **554.** 5 c. multicoloured .. 10 5

1967. Air. Alaska Purchase Cent.
A 1303. **555.** 8 c. chocolate .. 40 12

556. Recruiting Poster. **557.** "Columbia Jays" by Audubon.

1967. National Grange (farmers' organization). Cent.
1303. **556.** 5 c. multicoloured .. 8 5

1967. Air.
A 1304. **557.** 20 c. multicoloured 80 8
See also No. 1223.

558. Canadian Landscape.

1967. Canadian Centennial.
1304. **558.** 5 c. multicoloured .. 8 5

559. Canal Boat.

1967. Erie Canal. 150th Anniv.
1305. **559.** 5 c. multicoloured .. 8 5

560. Peace Dove Emblem.

1967. "Search for Peace" (Lions Int. essay theme).
1306. **560.** 5 c. black, red and blue 8 5

561. H. D. Thoreau. **563.** Radio Tower and "Waves".

562. Hereford Bull.

1967. Henry Thoreau (writer). 150th Birth Anniv.
1307. **561.** 5 c. black, red & green 8 5

1967. Nebraska Statehood Cent.
1308. **562.** 5 c. multicoloured .. 8 5

1967. "Voice of America". Radio Branch of United States Information Agency. 25th Anniv.
1309. **563.** 5 c. black, red & blue 8 5

564. Davy Crockett and Pine.

1967. Davy Crockett Commem.
1310. **564.** 5 c. black, grn. & yell. 8 5

565. Astronaut in Space. **566.** "Planned City".

1967. U.S. Space Achievements. Multicoloured.
1311. 5 c. Type **565** .. .. 1·60 12
1312. 5 c. "Gemini 4" over Earth 1·60 12
Nos. 1311/2 were issued together se-tenant, forming a composite design.

1967. Urban Planning.
1313. **566.** 5 c. ultram., blk. & bl. 10 5

567. Arms of Finland.

568. "The Biglin Brothers Racing" (after Eakins).

570. Magnolia. **569.** "Madonna and Child with Angels" (Memling).

1967. Finnish Independence. 50th Anniv.
1314. **567.** 5 c. blue 10 5

1967. Thomas Eakins.
1315. **568.** 5 c. multicoloured .. 10 5

1967. Christmas.
1316. **569.** 5 c multicoloured .. 8 5

1967. Mississippi Statehood. 150th Anniv.
1317. **570.** 5 c. brown, green and turquoise-blue .. 10 5

571. "Fifty Stars". **572.** U.S. Flag and The White House.

1968. Air.
A 1318. **571.** 10 c. red 15 5

1968. Flag Issue.
1318. **572.** 6 c. multicoloured .. 8 5
1319. – 6 c. multicoloured .. 8 5
1320. – 8 c. multicoloured .. 10 5
Nos. 1319/20 are smaller size 18 × 21 mm.

573. Homestead and Cornfield. **574.** Map of the Americas.

1968. Illinois Statehood. 150th Anniv.
1323. **573.** 6 c. multicoloured .. 15 5

1968. "HemisFair '68" Exn., San Antonio.
1324. **574.** 6 c. blue and pink .. 15 5

575. Eagle with Pennant.

1968. "Airlift".
1325. **575.** $1 brown, blue & buff 1·90 1·10
No. 1325 was issued primarily for a special reduced-rate parcels service to forces personnel overseas in Alaska, Hawaii and Puerto Rico.

576. Boys and Girls. **578.** Policeman with Small Boy.

577. Curtiss "Jenny".

1968. Youth Programme of Elks Benevolent Society.
1326. **576.** 6 c. blue and red .. 15 5

1968. Air. Scheduled Airmail Services. 50th Anniv.
A 1327. **577.** 10 c. blk., red & bl. 35 8

1968. "Law and Order".
1328. **578.** 6 c. blue, red & black 15 5

579. Eagle Weather-vane. **580.** Fort Moultrie, 1776.

1968. "Register and Vote".
1329. **579.** 6 c. gold and black .. 15 5

1968. Historic Flags.
1330. **580.** 6 c. ultramarine .. 50 15
1331. – 6 c. red & ultram. .. 50 15
1332. – 6 c. green & ultram. 50 15
1333. – 6 c. red & ultram. .. 50 15
1334. – 6 c. ultram, yell. & red 50 15
1335. – 6 c. red & u'tram. .. 50 15
1336. – 6 c. ultram., red & grn. 50 15
1337. – 6 c. red & ultram. 50 15
1338. – 6 c. ultram., red & yell. 50 15
1339. – 6 c. red, yell. & ultram. 50 15
FLAGS: No. 1331, U.S. (Fort McHenry). 1795-1818. 1332, Washington's Cruisers, 1775. 1333, Bennington, 1777. 1334, Rhode Island, 1775. 1335, First Stars and Stripes, 1777. 1336, Bunker Hill, 1775. 1337, Grand Union, 1776. 1338, Philadelphia Light Horse, 1775. 1339, First Navy Jack, 1775.

581. Walt Disney (after portrait by P. E. Wenzel). **582.** Father Jacques Marquette (explorer) with Jolliet and Indians Canoeing.

1968. Walt Disney Commem.
1340. **581.** 6 c. multicoloured .. 15 5

1968. Marquette Commem.
1341. **582.** 6 c. multicoloured .. 15 5

583. Rifle, Tomahawk, Powder-horn and Knife.

1968. Daniel Boone Commem.
1342. **583.** 6 c. red, yellow, black and cream 15 5

584. Ship's Wheel.

1968. Arkansas River Navigation Project.
1343. **584.** 6 c. black and blue 15 5

585. "Leif Erikson" (statue by Stirling Calder, Reykjavik, Iceland). **586.** Pioneers racing to Cherokee Strip.

1968. Leif Erikson Commem.
1344. **585.** 6 c. sepia and brown 15 5

1968. Opening of Cherokee Strip to Settlers. 75th Anniv.
1345. **586.** 6 c. brown 15 5

587. "Battle of Bunker's Hill" (detail) (after John Trumbull). **588.** Wood Ducks.

1968. John Trumbull.
1346. **587.** 6 c. multicoloured .. 15 5

1968. Waterfowl Conservation.
1347. **588.** 6 c. multicoloured .. 15 5

589. "The Annunciation" (Jan van Eyck). 590. "Chief Joseph" (after C. Hall).

1968. Christmas.
1348. **589.** 6 c. multicoloured .. 15 5

1968. "The American Indian".
1349. **590.** 6 c. multicoloured .. 25 5

591. "USA" and Jet Aircraft.

1968. Air.
A1350. **591.** 20 c. red, blue & black 45 5
A1351. 21 c. blue, red & black 30 8

592. Capitol and Flowers ("Cities").

1969. "Beautification of America" Campaign.
1352. **592.** 6 c. multicoloured .. 1·25 5
1353. – 6 c. multicoloured .. 1·25 5
1354. – 6 c. multicoloured .. 1·25 5
1355. – 6 c. multicoloured .. 1·25 5
DESIGNS: No. 1353, Potomac River and Flowers ("Parks"). 1354, Motorway and Flowers ("Highways"). 1355, Road and Trees ("Streets").

593. "Eagle" (U.S. Seal). 594. "July Fourth" (after Grandma Moses).

1969. American Legion. 50th Anniv.
1356. **593.** 6 c. black, blue & red 15 5

1969. Grandma Moses (Mrs. A. M. R. Moses).
1357. **594.** 6 c. multicoloured .. 15 5

595. Earth and Moon's Surface. 596. W. C. Handy (composer & musician).

1969 Moon Flight of "Apollo 8".
1358. **595.** 6 c. ochre, blue & blk. 35 5

1969. Handy Commem.
1359. **596.** 6 c. magenta, blue and violet 15 5

597. Belfry, Carmel Mission. 598. Powell exploring Colorado River.

1969. California. Bicent.
1360. **597.** 6 c. multicoloured .. 15 5

1969. John Wesley Powell (geologist). Colorado River Exploration. Cent.
1361. **598.** 6 c. multicoloured .. 15 5

599. Camellia and Yellowhammer.

1969. Alabama Statehood. 150th Anniv.
1362. **599.** 6 c. multicoloured .. 15 5

600. Ocotillo.

1969. 11th Int. Botanical Congress, Seattle. Multicoloured.
1363. 6 c. Douglas Fir .. 1·50 5
1364. 6 c. Lady's slipper .. 1·50 5
1365. 6 c. Type **600** .. .. 1·50 5
1366. 6 c. Franklinia .. .. 1·50 5

601. Astronaut setting foot on Moon.

1969. Air. 1st Man on the Moon.
A1367. **601.** 10 c. multicoloured 20 5

602. Daniel Webster and Dartmouth Hall. 603. Baseball "Batter".

1969. Dartmouth College Legal Case. 150th Anniv.
1368. **602.** 6 c. emerald .. 15 5

1969. Professional Baseball. Cent.
1369. **603.** 6 c. multicoloured .. 15 5

604. Footballer and Coach. 605. Dwight D. Eisenhower (from photograph by B. Noble).

1969. Intercollegiate Football. Cent.
1370. **604.** 6 c. green and red .. 15 5

1969. Eisenhower Commem.
1371. **605.** 6 c. black, blue & lake 15 5

606. "Winter Sunday in Norway Maine" (unknown artist).

1969. Christmas.
1372. **606.** 6 c. multicoloured .. 15 5

607. Rehabilitated Child. 608. "Old Models" (after W. Harnett).

1969. Rehabilitation of the Handicapped.
1373. **607.** 6 c. multicoloured .. 15 5
No. 1373 also commemorates the 50th anniv. of the National Society for Crippled Children and Adults.

1969. William M. Harnett.
1376. **608.** 6 c. multicoloured .. 8 5

609. Prehistoric Animals.

1970. Natural History (American Natural History Museum, Cent.). Multicoloured.
1377. 6 c. American bald eagle 15 5
1378. 6 c. African elephant herd 15 5
1379. 6 c. Haida ceremonial canoe 15 5
1380. 6 c. Type **609** .. 15 5

610. "The Lighthouse at Two Lights".

1970. Maine Statehood.
1381. **610.** 6 c. multicoloured .. 15 5

611. American Bison. 614. E. L. Masters (poet).

612. Dwight D. Eisenhower. 613. Benjamin Franklin.

1970. Wildlife Conservation.
1382. **611.** 6 c. black on brown .. 15 5

1970. Prominent Americans (2nd series).
1383. **612.** 6 c. blue 8 5
1384. **613.** 7 c. blue 8 5
1385. **612.** 8 c. brown 8 5
1390. 8 c. black, blue & red 8 5
1386. – 14 c. black 15 5
1387. – 16 c. brown 20 5
1388. – 18 c. violet 20 8
1389. – 21 c. green 25 8
DESIGNS—VERT. 14 c. F. H. La Guardia. 16 c. Ernest T. Pyle. 18 c. Dr. Elizabeth Blackwell. 21 c. Amadeo P. Giannini.

1970. Edgar Lee Masters Commem.
1401. **614.** 6 c. black and brown 15 5

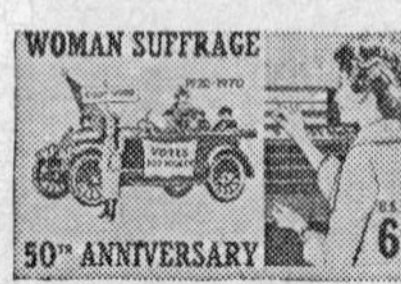

615. Suffragettes, 1920, and Woman operating Voting Machine.

1970. Women's Suffrage. 50th Anniv.
1402. **615.** 6 c. blue 15 5

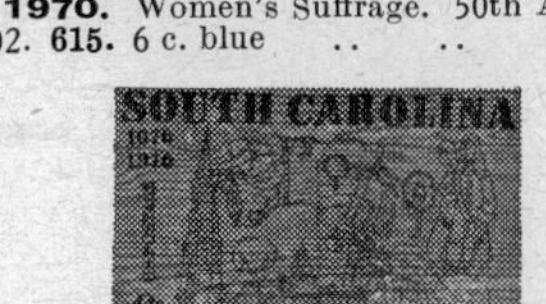

616. Symbols of South Carolina.

1970. South Carolina. 300th Anniv.
1403. **616.** 6 c. multicoloured .. 15 5

617. Stone Mountain Memorial.

1970. Dedication of Stone Mountain Confederate. Memorial.
1404. **617.** 6 c. grey 15 5

618. Fort Snelling and Barge.

1970. Fort Snelling, Minnesota. 150th Anniv.
1405. **618.** 6 c. multicoloured .. 15 5

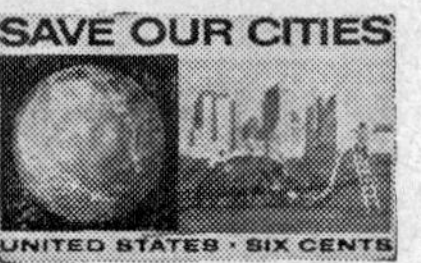

619. City Park.

1970. Prevention of Pollution.
1406. 6 c. Wheat 45 5
1407. 6 c. Type **619** 45 5
1408. 6 c. Blue-gill 45 5
1409. 6 c. Sea-gull 45 5

620. Toy Locomotive.

1970. Christmas. Multicoloured.
1410. 6 c. "The Nativity" (L. Lotto) (vert. $5\frac{1}{2} \times 9$ mm.) 15 5
1411. 6 c. Type **620** 55 5
1412. 6 c. Toy horse on wheels 55 5
1413. 6 c. Mechanised tricycle 55 5
1414. 6 c. Doll's pram 55 5

621. "U.N." and U.N. Emblem.

1970. United Nations. 25th Anniv.
1415. **621.** 6 c. red, blue and blk. 15 5

622. "Mayflower" and Pilgrims. 623. Disabled American Veterans Emblems.

1970. Landing of the Pilgrim Fathers in America. 350th Anniv.
1416. **622.** 6 c. multicoloured .. 15 5

1970. 50th Anniv. of Disabled American Veterans Organization, and Armed Forces Commemoration.
1417. **623.** 6 c. multicoloured .. 15 5
1418. – 6 c. black, blue & red 15 5
DESIGN: No. 1418, Inscriptions—"Prisoners of War", "Missing and Killed in Action".

624. Ewe and Lamb. **625.** General MacArthur.

1970. Introduction of Sheep into North America. 450th Anniv.
1419. **624.** 6 c. multicoloured .. 15 5

1971. General Douglas MacArthur. 91st Birth Anniv.
1420. **625.** 6 c. black, blue & red 15 5

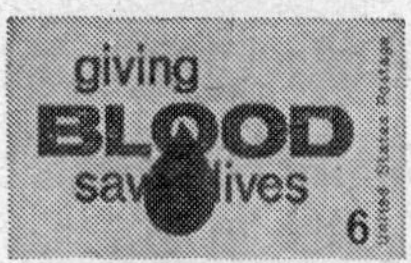

626. "Giving Blood Saves Lives".

1971. Salute to Blood Donors.
1421. **626.** 6 c. deep blue, red & bl. 15 5

627. "The Opening of the West" (detail, T. H. Benton).

1971. Missouri Statehood. 150th Anniv.
1422. **627.** 8 c. multicoloured .. 15 5

628. Jet Aircraft. **629.** Winged Letter.

1971. Air.
A 1423. – 9 c. red 15 8
A 1424. **628.** 11 c. red 15 5
A 1425. **629.** 13 c. red 25 5
DESIGN—HORIZ. 9 c. Delta-wing plane.

630. Trout.

1971. Wildlife Conservation. Multicoloured.
1428. 8 c. Type **630** 15 5
1429. 8 c. Alligator 15 5
1430. 8 c. Polar Bear and cubs 15 5
1431. 8 c. California condor .. 15 5
See also Nos. 1469/72.

631. Antarctic Map Emblem. **632.** Postal Service Emblem.

1971. Antarctic Treaty. Tenth Anniv.
1432. **631.** 8 c. red and blue .. 15 5

1971. Reorganization of U.S. Post Office as U.S. Postal Service.
1433. **632.** 8 c. multicoloured .. 15 5

633. Bicentennial Commission. **634.** Head of Statue of Liberty.

1971. American Revolution Bicent.
1434. **633.** 8 c. multicoloured .. 55 5

1971. Air.
1435. **634.** 17 c. blue, red & grn. 25 10

635. "The Wake of the Ferry". (John Sloan).

1971. John Sloan (artist). Birth Cent.
1436. **635.** 8 c. multicoloured .. 15 5

636. Landing Module on Moon. **637.** Emily Dickinson (poet).

1971. Decade of U.S. Space Achievements. Multicoloured.
1437. 8 c. Type **636** 15 5
1438. 8 c. Astronauts in lunar rover 15 5

1971. Emily Dickinson Commemoration.
1439. **637.** 8 c. multicoloured .. 15 5

638. Watch-tower, Morro Castle. **639.** Drug Victim.

1971. San Juan, Puerto Rico. 450th Anniv.
1440. **638.** 8 c. multicoloured .. 15 5

1971. Drug Abuse Prevention Week.
1441. **639.** 8 c. blk., new bl. & bl. 15 5

640. Hands reaching to "CARE". **642.** "Adoration of the Shepherds" (Giorgione).

641. Decatur House, Washington D.C.

1971. "CARE" (Co-operative for American Relief Everywhere). 25th Anniv.
1442. **640.** 8 c. multicoloured .. 15 5

1971. Historic Preservation.
1443. **641.** 8 c. blk & flesh on cream 15 5
1444. – 8 c. blk. & flesh on cream 15 5
1445. – 8 c. blk. & flesh on cream 15 5
1446. – 8 c. blk. & flesh on cream 15 5
DESIGNS: No. 1444, Whaling ship, "Charles W. Morgan", Mystic, Conn. No. 1445, San Francisco cable-car. No. 1446, San Xavier del Bac Mission, Tucson, Arizona.

1971. Christmas. Multicoloured.
1447. 8 c. Type **642** 15 5
1448. 8 c. "Partridge in a Pear Tree" (J. Wyeth) .. 15 5

643. Sidney Lanier (poet). **644.** Peace Corps Poster.

1972. Sidney Lanier. 90th Death Anniv. (1971).
1449. **643.** 8 c: blk., brn. & blue 12 5

1972. Peace Corps.
1450. **644.** 8 c. red, light bl. & bl. 12 5

645/8. Cape Hatteras National Seashore.

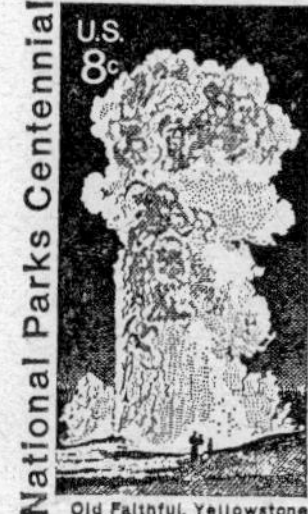

649. "Old Faithful", Yellowstone Park. **650.** Statue and Temple, City of Refuge, Hawaii.

1972. National Parks. Cent.
1451. **645.** 2 c. mult. (postage) .. 5 5
1452. **646.** 2 c. multicoloured .. 5 5
1453. **647.** 2 c. multicoloured .. 5 5
1454. **648.** 2 c. multicoloured .. 5 5
1455. – 6 c. multicoloured .. 10 5
1456. **649.** 8 c. multicoloured .. 12 5
1457. – 15 c. multicoloured .. 25 12

A 1458. **650.** 11 c. mult. (air) .. 15 5
DESIGNS—HORIZ. (As T **647**). 6 c. Theatre at Night, Wolf Trap Farm, Virginia. 15 c. Mt. McKinley, Alaska.

651. American Family. **652.** Glassblower.

1972. Family Planning.
1459. **651.** 8 c. multicoloured .. 12 5

1972. American Revolution. Bicent. American Colonial Craftsmen.
1460. **652.** 8 c. brown on yellow 12 5
1461. – 8 c. brown on yellow 12 5
1462. – 8 c. brown on yellow 12 5
1463. – 8 c. brown on yellow 12 5
DESIGNS: No. 1461, Silversmith. No. 1462, Wigmaker. No. 1463, Hatter.

653. Cycling.

1972. Olympic Games, Munich and Sapporo, Japan. Multicoloured.
1464. 6 c. Type **653** (postage) .. 12 8
1465. 8 c. Bobsleighing .. 12 5
1466. 15 c. Running 25 15
A1467. 11 c. Skiing (air) .. 15 8

654. Classroom Blackboard.

1972. Parent Teacher Assn. 75th Anniv.
1468. **654.** 8 c. black and yellow 12 5

655. Fur Seals.

1972. Wildlife Conservation. Multicoloured.
1469. 8 c. Type **655** 12 5
1470. 8 c. Cardinal (bird) .. 12 5
1471. 8 c. Brown pelicans .. 12 5
1472. 8 c. Bighorn sheep .. 12 5

656. Country Post Office and Store.

1972. Mail Order Business. Cent.
1473. **653.** 8 c. multicoloured .. 12 5

657. **658.** "Tom Sawyer" (N. Rockwell).

1972. American Osteopathics. 75th Anniv.
1474. **657.** 8 c. multicoloured .. 12 5

1972. "The Adventures of Tom Sawyer" by Mark Twain.
1475. **658.** 8 c. multicoloured .. 12 5

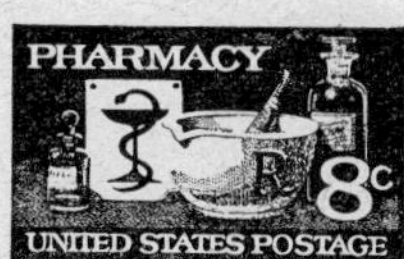

659. "Angels" from "Mary, Queen of Heaven" (Master of St. Lucy Legend). **660.** Pharmaceutical Equipment.

1972. Christmas. Multicoloured.
1476. 8 c. Type **659** 12 5
1477. 8 c. Santa Claus 12 5

1972. Amercian Pharmaceutical Association. 125th Anniv.
1478. **660.** 8 c. multicoloured .. 12 5

661. Five Cent Stamp of 1847 under Magnifier.

1972. 125th Anniv. of 1st U.S. Stamp, and Stamp Collecting Promotion.
1479. **661.** 8 c. brn., blk. and grn. 12 5

663. "LOVE".

1973. Greetings Stamp.

1480. **663.** 8 c. red, green & blue 12 5

664. Pamphleteers with Press.

1973. American Revolution. Bicent. "Spreading the Word".

1481. **664.** 8 c. grn., blue & red 12 5
1482. – 8 c. blk., red and blue 12 5
1483. – 8 c. blk., red and blue 12 5
1484. – 8 c. multicoloured .. 12 5

DESIGNS: No. 1481, Posting a Broadside. No. 1482, Post-rider. No. 1483, Drummer.

Copernicus
1473 - 1973

665. George Gershwin and scenes from "Porgy and Bess". **666.** Copernicus.

1973. American Arts Commemoration. Mult.

1485. 8 c. Type **665** 12 5
1486. 8 c. Robinson Jeffers (poet) and People of Carmel .. 12 5
1487. 8 c. Henry Tanner (painter) and Palette .. 12 5
1488. 8 c. Will Cather (novelist) and Pioneer Family .. 12 5

1973. Copernicus (astronomer). 500th Birth Anniv.

1489. **666.** 8 c. black and yellow 12 5

Harry S.Truman

U.S. Postage 8 cents
667. Counter Clerk. **668.** Harry S. Truman.

1973. Postal Service Employees. Mult.

1490. 8 c. Type **667** 12 5
1491. 8 c. Collecting mail .. 12 5
1492. 8 c. Sorting on Conveyor Belt 12 5
1493. 8 c. Sorting parcels .. 12 5
1494. 8 c. Cancelling letters .. 12 5
1495. 8 c. Sorting letters by hand 12 5
1496. 8 c. Coding desks .. 12 5
1497. 8 c. Loading Mail-van .. 12 5
1498. 8 c. City Postman .. 12 5
1499. 8 c. Rural Postman .. 12 5

1973. Pres. Harry Truman. Commemoration.

1500. **668.** 8 c. black, red & blue 12 5

669/72. Boston Tea Party. (Illustration reduced. Actual size 77 × 47 mm.).

1973. American Revolution Bicentennial. The Boston Tea Party.

1501. **669.** 8 c. multicoloured .. 12 5
1502. **670.** 8 c. multicoloured .. 12 5
1503. **671.** 8 c. multicoloured .. 12 5
1504. **672.** 8 c. multicoloured .. 12 5

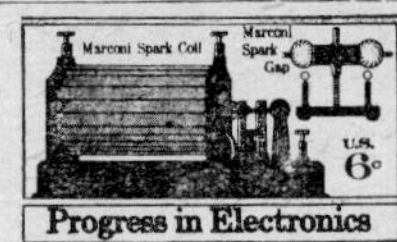

673. Marconi's Spark Coil and Gap (1901).

1973. "Progress in Electronics". Mult.

1505. 6 c. Type **673** (postage) .. 10 5
1506. 8 c. Modern Transistors circuit 12 5
1507. 15 c. Early Microphone and Radio Speaker, Radio and T.V. Camera Tubes 20 12
1508. 11 c. De Forest audions (1915) (air) 15 8

674. Lyndon B. Johnson. **675.** Angus and Longhorn Cattle.

1973. Pres. Johnson. Commem.

1509. **674.** 8 c. multicoloured .. 12 5

1973. "Rural America" Centenaries.

1510. 8 c. Type **675** .. 12 5
1511. 10 c. Institute Marquee .. 12 5
1512. 10 c. Train crossing Wheat-field 10 5

CENTENARIES: No. 1510, Introduction of Aberdeen Angus cattle into United States. No. 1511, Foundation of Chautauqua Institution (adult organization). No. 1512, Introduction of hard winter wheat into Kansas.

676. "Small Cowper Madonna" (Raphael). **677.** Christmas Tree in Needlepoint.

1973. Christmas.

1513. **676.** 8 c. multicoloured .. 12 5
1514. **677.** 8 c. multicoloured .. 12 5

678. Liberty Bell. **679.** U.S. Flags of 1777 and 1973.

680. Jefferson Memorial. **681.** Mail Transport.

1973.

1519. **678.** 6.3 c. red .. 8 5
1515. **679.** 10 c. red and blue .. 12 5
1516. **680.** 10 c. blue .. 12 5
1517. **681.** 10 c. multicoloured .. 12 5

682. Statue of Liberty.

1974. Air.

A 1521. **682.** 18 c. black, red & blue 25 8
A 1522. – 26 c. black, blue & red 35 10

DESIGN: 26 c. Mt. Rushmore National Memorial, "Shrine of Democracy".

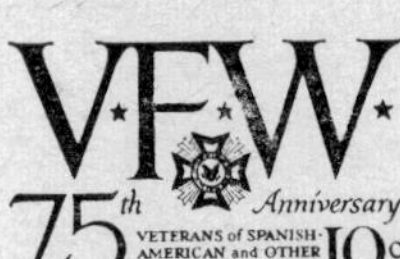

683. "VFW" and Emblem. **684.** Robert Frost.

1974. Veterans of Foreign Wars Organization. 75th Anniv.

1523. **683.** 10 c. red and blue .. 12 5

1974. Robert Frost (poet). Birth Centenary.

1524. **684.** 10 c. black 12 5

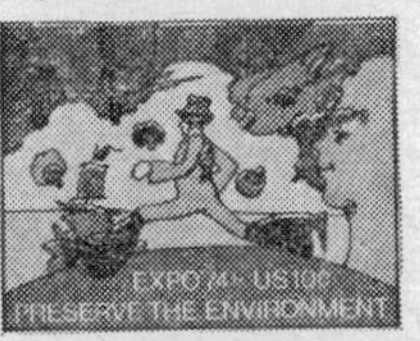

685. "Cosmic Jumper" and "Smiling Sage" ("Preserve the Environment" theme).

1974. "Expo 74" World Fair, Spokane.

1525. **685.** 10 c. multicoloured .. 12 5

686. Horse-racing.

1974. Kentucky Derby. Cent.

1526. **686.** 10 c. multicoloured .. 12 5

687. "Skylab" in Orbit.

1974. "Skylab" Space Project.

1527. **687.** 10 c. multicoloured .. 12 5

688. "Michelangelo" (detail from "School of Athens" by Raphael).

1974. Universal Postal Union. Cent. Mult.

1528. 10 c. Type **688** 12 5
1529. 10 c. "Five Feminine Virtues" (Hokusai) .. 12 5
1530. 10 c. "Old Scraps" (J. F. Peto) 12 5
1531. 10 c. "The Lovely Reader" (J. Liotard) 12 5
1532. 10 c. "Lady Writing Letter" (G. Terborch) .. 12 5
1533. 10 c. "Inkwell and Quill" (detail from "Young Boy with Top" by J. Chardin) 12 5
1534. 10 c. "Mrs. John Douglas" (T. Gainsborough) .. 12 5
1535. 10 c. "Don Antonio Noriega" (F. Goya) .. 12 5

FIRST KENTUCKY SETTLEMENT FORT HARROD 1774 1974
US 10c

689. Amethyst. **690.** Covered Wagon at Fort Harrod.

1974. Mineral Heritage. Multicoloured.

1536. 10 c. Petrified Wood .. 12 5
1537. 10 c. Tourmaline .. 12 5
1538. 10 c. Type **689** .. 12 5
1539. 10 c. Rhodochrosite .. 12 5

1974. Fort Harrod, First Settlement in Kentucky. 200th Anniv.

1540. **690.** 10 c. multicoloured .. 12 5

US 10c
WE ASK BUT FOR PEACE, LIBERTY AND SAFETY
First Continental Congress 1774
Bicentennial Era

691. "We ask for peace ..." (First Continental Congress). **692.** Slogan, Molecules and Petrol Drops.

1974. American Revolution Bicentennial. First Continental Congress.

1541. – 10 c. blue and red .. 11 5
1542. **691.** 10 c. grey, blue & red 12 5
1543. – 10 c. grey, red & blue 12 5
1544. – 10 c. red and blue 12 5

DESIGNS: No. 1541, Carpenters' Hall, Philadelphia. No. 1543, Independence Hall, Philadelphia. No. 1544, "Deriving their just powers . . ." (Declaration of Independence).

1974. Energy Conservation.

1545. **692.** 10 c. multicoloured 12 5

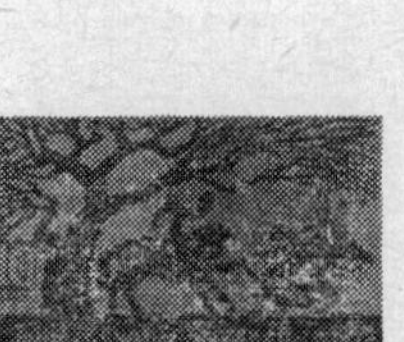

693. "The Headless Horseman". **694.** Child clasping Hand.

1974. Washington Irving's "Legend of Sleepy Hollow".

1546. **693.** 10 c. multicoloured .. 12 5

1974. Help for Retarded Children.

1547. **694.** 10 c. lake and brown 12 5

695. "The Road—Winter".

1974. Christmas. Multicoloured.

1548. 10 c. "Angel" (detail from Perussis altarpiece) .. 12 5
1549. 10 c. Type **695** .. 12 5
1550. 10 c. Dove Weathervane, Mount Vernon 12 5

No. 1550 has self-adhesive gum.

696. "Benjamin West" (self-portrait). **697.** "Pioneer" Spacecraft passing Jupiter.

1975. Benjamin West (painter). Commem.

1551. **696.** 10 c. multicoloured .. 12 5

1975. Unmanned Space Missions. Mult.

1552. **697.** 10 c. "Pioneer" Spacecraft passing Jupiter. 12 5
1553. 10 c. "Mariner 10" Venus and Mercury 12 5

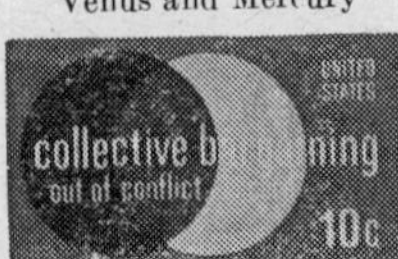

698. Overlapping Circles.

1975. Collective Bargaining in Labour Relations.

1554. **698.** 10 c. multicoloured .. 12 5

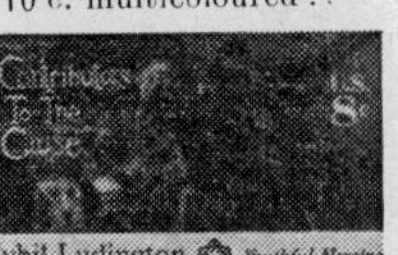

699. Sybil Ludington on Horseback.

1975. American Revolution Bicentennial Contributors to the Cause.
1555. **699.** 8 c. multicoloured .. 10 5
1556. – 10 c. multicoloured .. 10 5
1557. – 10 c. multicoloured .. 10 5
1558. – 18 c. multicoloured .. 20 10
DESIGNS: No. 1556, Salem Poor loading Musket. No. 1557, Haym Salomon writing in ledger. No. 1558, Peter Francisco carrying cannon.

700. " Lexington " (detail H. Sandham).
701. Paul Laurence Dunbar (poet).

1975. American Revolution Bicentennial. Battles of Lexington and Concord.
1559. **700.** 10 c. multicoloured .. 10 5

1975. Dunbar Commemoration.
1560. **701.** 10 c. multicoloured .. 10 5

702. D. W. Griffith (film producer).

1975. Griffith Commemoration.
1561. **702.** 10 c. multicoloured .. 10

703. " Bunker Hill " (John Trumbull).
704. Marine with Musket.

1975. American Revolution Bicent. Battle of Bunker Hill.
1562. **703.** 10 c. multicoloured .. 10 5

1975. U.S. Military Services. Bicent. Multicoloured.
1563. 10 c. Type **704** 10 5
1564. 10 c. Militiaman with musket 10 5
1565. 10 c. Soldier with flintlock 10 5
1566. 10c. Sailor with grappling-iron 10 5

705. Link-up Manoeuvre.

1975. "Apollo-Soyuz" Space Test Project. Multicoloured.
1567. 10 c. Type **705** 10 5
1568. 10 c. Link-up completed 10 5

706. " Worldwide Equality ".

1975. International Women's Year.
1569. **706.** 10 c. multicoloured .. 10 5

707. Stage-coach and Modern Truck.

1975 Postal Services. Bicent. Multicoloured.
1570. 10 c. Type **707** 10 5
1571. 10 c. Steam locomotive & modern train 10 5
1572. 10 c. Early mailplane and jet aircraft 10 5
1573. 10 c. Telecommunications satellite 10 5

708. Law Book, Gavel and Globe.

1975. " World Peace through Law ".
1574. **708.** 10 c. brown, blue & grn. 10 5

709. Coins and Engine-turned Motif.

1975. " Banking and Commerce ".
1575. **709.** 10 c. multicoloured .. 10 5
1576. – 10 c. multicoloured .. 10 5
DESIGN: No. 1576, As Type **709**, but design reversed with different coins.

710. "Madonna and Child" (Ghirlandaio).
711. "Christmas Card" (from early design by Louis Prang).

1975. Christmas.
1577. **710.** 10 c. multicoloured .. 10 5
1578. **711.** 10 c. multicoloured .. 10 5
Nos. 1577/8 were each sold at 10 c. Because of an imminent increase in the postage rates the two designs were issued without face values.

712. Early Printing Press.
713. Flag over Independence Hall.

1975.
1584. – 7.7 c. brown & yellow 8 5
1585. – 7.9 c. red on yellow.. 8 5
1586. – 9 c. green on grey .. 10 5
1588. **712.** 11 c. orange on grey.. 12 5
1590. – 13 c. brn. on pale brn. 12 5
1591. – 13 c. multicoloured .. 12 5
1593. – 24 c. red on blue .. 25 12
DESIGNS: 7.7 c. Saxhorns. 7.9 c. Drum. 9 c. Dome of Capitol. 13 c. (1590) Liberty Bell. 13 c. (1591) Eagle and Shield. 24 c. Old North Church.
Nos. 1584/5 were intended for bulk rate post.

1975.
1606. **713.** 13 c. multicoloured.. 12 5

714. Drummer Boy.
715. Aircraft & Globes.

1976. " Spirit of '76 " (painting by A. M. Willard). Multicoloured.
1607. 13 c. Type **714** 15 5
1608. 13 c. Old Drummer .. 15 5
1609. 13 c. Fifer 15 5
Nos. 1607/9 form the complete painting.

1976. Air.
A 1610. **715.** 25 c.blk., bl., & red 25 12
A 1611 – 31 c. blk., bl. & red 30 15
DESIGN: 31 c. As 25 c., but with background of U.S. flag.

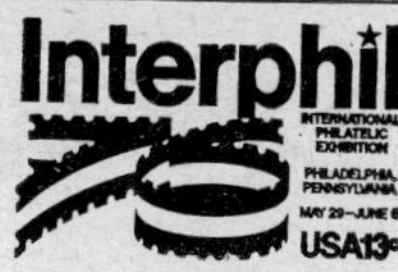

716. " Interphil 76 ".

1976. " Interphil 76 " International Stamp Exhibition, Philadelphia.
1612. **716.** 13 c. red and blue .. 15 5

717. Delaware Flag.

1976. American Revolution. Bicent. State Flags. Multicoloured.
1613. 13 c. Type **717** 15 5
1614. 13 c. Pennsylvania .. 15 5
1615. 13 c. New Jersey.. .. 15 5
1616. 13 c. Georgia 15 5
1617. 13 c. Connecticut .. 15 5
1618. 13 c. Massachusetts .. 15 5
1619. 13 c. Maryland 15 5
1620. 13 c. South Carolina .. 15 5
1621. 13 c. New Hampshire .. 15 5
1622. 13 c. Virginia 15 5
1623. 13 c. New York 15 5
1624. 13 c. North Carolina .. 15 5
1625. 13 c. Rhode Island .. 15 5
1626. 13 c. Vermont 15 5
1627. 13 c. Kentucky 15 5
1628. 13 c. Tennessee 15 5
1629. 13 c. Ohio 15 5
1630. 13 c. Louisiana 15 5
1631. 13 c. Indiana 15 5
1632. 13 c. Mississippi 15 5
1633. 13 c. Illinois 15 5
1634. 13 c. Alabama 15 5
1635. 13 c. Maine 15 5
1636. 13 c. Missouri 15 5
1637. 13 c. Arkansas 15 5
1638. 13 c. Michigan 15 5
1639. 13 c. Florida 15 5
1640. 13 c. Texas 15 5
1641. 13 c. Iowa 15 5
1642. 13 c. Wisconsin 15 5
1643. 13 c. California 15 5
1644. 13 c. Minnesota 15 5
1645. 13 c. Oregon 15 5
1646. 13 c. Kansas 15 5
1647. 13 c. West Virginia .. 15 5
1648. 13 c. Nevada 15 5
1649. 13 c. Nebraska 15 5
1650. 13 c. Colorado 15 5
1651. 13 c. North Dakota .. 15 5
1652. 13 c. South Dakota .. 15 5
1653. 13 c. Montana 15 5
1654. 13 c. Washington .. 15 5
1655. 13 c. Idaho 15 5
1656. 13 c. Wyoming 15 5
1657. 13 c. Utah 15 5
1658. 13 c. Oklahoma 15 5
1659. 13 c. New Mexico .. 15 5
1660. 13 c. Arizona 15 5
1661. 13 c. Alaska 15 5
1662. 13 c. Hawaii 15 5

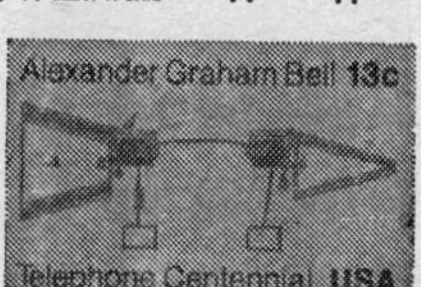

718. Bell's Telephone.

1976. First Telephone Transmission. Cent.
1663. **718.** 13 c. violet, black and red on brown .. 15 5

719. Ford-Pullman and Laird " Swallow " Aircraft.

1976. Commercial Aviation.
1664. **719.** 13 c. multicoloured .. 15 5

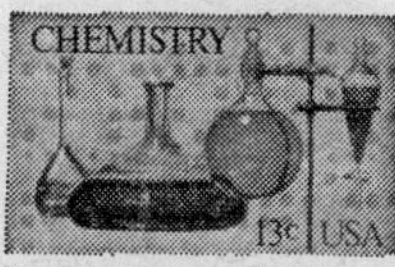

720. Laboratory Equipment.

1976. American Chemical Society. Cent.
1665. **720.** 13 c. multicoloured.. 15 5

721. Benjamin Franklin and Map of North America, 1776.

1976. American Revolution. Bicent.
1667. **721.** 13 c. multicoloured .. 15 5

722. Part of Assembly.
723. Diving.

1976. American Revolution. Bicent.
1668. **722.** 13 c. multicoloured.. 20 5
1669. – 13 c. multicoloured .. 20 5
1670. – 13 c. multicoloured .. 20 5
1671. – 13 c. multicoloured .. 20 5
DESIGNS: Nos. 1668/71 as T **722** form the complete painting " Signing of Declaration of Independence " (John Trumbull).

1976. Olympic Games, Montreal and Winter Olympic Games, Innsbruck. Multicoloured.
1672. 13 c. Type **723** 15 5
1673. 13 c. Skiing 15 5
1674. 13 c. Running 15 5
1675. 13 c. Skating 15 5

724. Clara Maas.

1976. Clara Maas (martyr to yellow fever). Birth Cent.
1676. **724.** 13 c. multicoloured .. 15 5

725. A. S. Ochs.
726. " Winter Pastime " (N. Currier).

1976. A. S. Ochs (publisher of New York Times) Commemoration.
1677. **725.** 13 c. black and grey .. 15 5

1976. Christmas.
1678. 13 c. Type **726** 15 5
1679. 13 c. " Nativity " (John S. Copley) 15 5

727. " Washington at Princeton " (Peale).

1977. American Revolution. Bicent.
1680. **727.** 13 c. multicoloured .. 15 5

NEWSPAPER STAMPS

For list of Newspaper Stamps, see the Stanley Gibbons' Overseas volume 4 Catalogue.

OFFICIAL STAMPS

For list of stamps used on correspondence of Government Departments, see the Stanley Gibbons' "Overseas" Catalogue.

C1. Letter Carrier.

1955.

C 1070. C 1. 15 c. red 35 25

Issued for recorded delivery service and still valid for ordinary postage, although the certified mail fee has been increased. No compensation is payable under this service.

PARCEL POST STAMPS

P 1. Post Office Clerk.

1912.

P 423. P 1. 1 c. red .. .. 1·10 45
P 424. – 2 c. red .. .. 1·10 25
P 425. – 3 c. red .. .. 2·75 1·75
P 426. – 4 c. red .. .. 5·50 75
P 427. – 5 c. red .. .. 4·50 50
P 428. – 10 c. red .. .. 8·00 55
P 429. – 15 c. red .. .. 8·50 2·75
P 430. – 20 c. red .. .. 18·00 3·75
P 431. – 25 c. red .. .. 8·50 1·90
P 432. – 50 c. red .. .. 35·00 10·00
P 433. – 75 c. red .. .. 9·00 6·00
P 434. – $1 red .. .. 50·00 5·50

DESIGNS: 2 c. City carrier. 3 c. Railway postal clerk. 4 c. Rural carrier. 5 c. Mail train. 10 c. Steamship and mail tender. 15 c. Automobile service. 20 c. Aeroplane carrying mail. 25 c. Manufacturing. 50 c. Dairying. 75 c. Harvesting. $1 Fruit growing.

SPECIAL HANDLING STAMPS

P 2.

1925.

SH 624. P 2. 10 c. green .. 45 35
SH 625. 15 c. green .. 50 40
SH 626. 20 c. green .. 70 70
SH 627. 25 c. green .. 3·25 1·90

PARCEL POST POSTAGE DUE STAMPS

PD 1.

1912.

PD 423. PD 1. 1 c. green .. 1·75 75
PD 424. 2 c. green .. 9·50 4·00
PD 425. 5 c. green .. 1·75 1·10
PD 426. 10 c. green .. 20·00 9·00
PD 427. 25 c. green .. 7·50 1·10

POSTAGE DUE STAMPS

D 1.

D 2.

1879.

D 221. D 1. 1 c. brown .. .. 2·40 65
D 222. 2 c. brown .. .. 1·75 60
D 209. 3 c. brown .. .. 1·40 65
D 224. 5 c. brown .. .. 14·00 1·75
D 225. 10 c. brown .. 14·00 90
D 212. 30 c. brown .. 13·00 4·25
D 213. 50 c. brown .. 26·00 9·50

1891.

D 235. D 1. 1 c. claret 65 20
D 236. 2 c. claret 75 12
D 237. 3 c. claret .. .. 1·10 90
D 238. 5 c. claret .. .. 1·60 90
D 239. 10 c. claret .. .. 4·00 1·40
D 240. 30 c. claret .. .. 29·00 14·00
D 241. 50 c. claret .. .. 32·00 17·00

1894.

D 529. D 2. ½ c. red 8 5
D 530. 1 c. red 12 5
D 531. 2 c. red 20 5
D 532. 3 c. red 50 5
D 533. 5 c. red 50 5
D 534. 10 c. red 55 8
D 535. 30 c. red .. .. 1·90 15
D 536. 50 c. red .. .. 2·40 5

D 3.

D 4.

D 5.

1931.

D 702. D 3. ½ c. red 5 5
D 703. 1 c. red 5 5
D 704. 2 c. red 5 5
D 705. 3 c. red 8 5
D 706. 5 c. red 8 5
D 707. 10 c. red 25 5
D 708. 30 c. red .. .. 1·10 5
D 709. 50 c. red .. .. 1·25 5
D 699. D 4. $1 red .. .. 2·75 8
D 700. $5 red .. .. 8·50 10

1959. Centres in black.

D 1130. D 5. ½ c. red 30 12
D 1131. 1 c. red 5 5
D 1132. 2 c. red 5 5
D 1133. 3 c. red 5 5
D 1134. 4 c. red 5 5
D 1135. 5 c. red 8 5
D 1136. 6 c. red 8 5
D 1137. 7 c. red 8 5
D 1138. 8 c. red 8 5
D 1139. 10 c. red 10 5
D 1140. 30 c. red 30 5
D 1141. 50 c. red 45 5
D 1142. $1 red 85 5
D 1143. $5 red .. .. 4·25 8

In the dollar values the numerals are double-lined and vertical.

REGISTERED LETTER STAMP

R 1. Eagle.

1911.

R 404. E 1. 10 c. blue .. .. 32·00 1·60

SPECIAL DELIVERY AIR STAMPS

SA 1. Great Seal of U.S.A.

1934.

AE 750. SA 1. 16 c. blue 55 55
AE 751. 16 c. blue and red 30 15

SPECIAL DELIVERY STAMPS

S 1.

1885. Inscr. "A SPECIAL DELIVERY OFFICE".

E 217. S 1. 10 c. blue .. .. 42·00 8·00

1888. As Type S 1, but inscr. "AT ANY POST OFFICE".

E 224. S 1. 10 c. blue .. .. 42·00 2·25
E 251. 10 c. orange .. 20·00 3·75

S 2.

1902.

E 529. S 2. 10 c. blue .. .. 3·25 12

S 3. Mercury's helmet and olive branch.

S 4. Delivery by Motor-cycle.

1908.

E 374. S 3. 10 c. green .. .. 9·50 8·50

1922.

E 648. S 4. 10 c. blue 35 5
E 648a. 10 c. violet 35 5
E 649. 13 c. blue 30 5
E 650. 15 c. orange .. 40 5
E 651. 17 c. yellow .. 2·00 70

S 5. Mail van.

1925.

E 652. S 5. 20 c. black 70 8

S 6.

1954.

E 1066. S 6. 20 c. blue 45 5
E 1067. 30 c. lake 55 5

S 7. Arrows.

1969.

E 1374. S 7. 45 c. red and blue 1·10 8
E 1375. 60 c. blue and red 70 8

CONFEDERATE STATES (N. AM.)

Stamps issued by the seceding states in the American Civil War.

1. Jefferson Davis.

2. T. Jefferson.

1861. Imperf.

1. 1. 5 c. green .. .. .. 16·00 10·00
3. 2. 10 c. blue .. .. .. 17·00 13·00

3. Jackson.

4. Jefferson Davis.

1862. Imperf.

4. 3. 2 c. green .. .. 55·00 85·00
5. 1. 5 c. blue .. .. 9·50 10·00
6. 2. 10 c. red .. .. £100 38·00

1862. Imperf.

8. 4. 5 c. blue .. .. .. 1·25 2·00

5. Jackson. 6. Jefferson Davis.

8. Washington.

1863. Imperf. or perf. (10 c.)

9. 5. 2 c. red .. .. 4·75 25·00
10. 6. 10 c. blue (TEN CENTS) .. 65·00 50·00
12. 10 c. blue (10 CENTS) .. 1·25 1·75
14. 8. 20 c. green .. .. 3·75 26·00

UNITED STATES POSTAL AGENCY IN SHANGHAI O1

These stamps were valid for use on mail despatched from the U.S. Postal Agency in Shanghai to addresses in the United States. This agency was closed down 31st December 1922.

100 cents = 1 dollar (Chinese).

1919. United States stamps of 1917/19. surch. **SHANGHAI 2 c. CHINA.**

1. 76. 2 c. on 1 c. green .. 2·40 2·75
2. 77. 4 c. on 2 c. red .. .. 2·40 2·75
3. 78. 6 c. on 3 c. violet .. 3·50 4·50
4. 8 c. on 4 c. brown .. 4·25 5·50
5. 10 c. on 5 c. blue .. 5·50 7·00
6. 12 c. on 6 c. orange .. 5·50 7·50
7. 14 c. on 7 c. black .. 5·50 7·50
8. 82. 16 c. on 8 c. olive .. 5·50 7·00
9. 18 c. on 9 c. pink .. 5·50 7·00
10. 20 c. on 10 c. yellow .. 4·25 5·00
11a. 24 c. on 12 c. red .. 5·50 7·50
12. 30 c. on 15 c. grey .. 7·00 8·50
13. 40 c. on 20 c. blue .. 7·00 8·50
14. 60 c. on 30 c. orange .. 7·50 10·00
15. $1 on 50 c. lilac .. 65·00 70·00
16. $2 on $1 black .. .. 29·00 32·00

1922. Stamps of United States of 1908/10 surch. **SHANGHAI – Cts. CHINA.**

17. 76. 2 c. on 1 c. green .. 10·00 11·00
18. 77. 4 c. on 2 c. red .. .. 11·00 12·00

UPPER SENEGAL AND NIGER O2

A French Colony in W. Africa, E. of Senegal, formerly called Senegambia and Niger, and became part of French Sudan in 1920.

1906. "Faidherbe", "Palms", and "Balay" key-types inscr. "HT.SENEGAL-NIGER".

35. I. 1 c. grey 10 10
36. 2 c. brown 10 10
37. 4 c. brown on blue .. 12 12
38. 5 c. green 45 35
39. 10 c. red 45 30
40. 15 c. violet 40 40
41. J. 20 c. black on blue .. 50 50
42. 25 c. blue .. .. 2·75 50
43. 30 c. brown on pink .. 90 90
44. 35 c. black on yellow .. 35 20
45. 40 c. red on blue .. 90 65
46. 45 c. brown on green .. 1·10 1·00
47. 50 c. violet 65 55
48. 75 c. green on orange .. 1·60 1·50
49. K. 1 f. black on blue .. 3·25 2·75
50. 2 f. blue on red .. .. 7·50 6·50
51. 5 f. red on yellow .. 16·00 15·00

1. Touareg.

ILLUSTRATIONS
British Commonwealth and all overprints and surcharges are FULL SIZE. Foreign Countries have been reduced to ¾-LINEAR.

1914.

59. 1. 1 c violet and purple .. 5 5
60. 2 c. purple and grey .. 5 5
61. 4 c. blue and black .. 5 5
62. 5 c. green 5 5
63. 10 c. red and orange .. 20 20
64. 15 c. yellow and brown .. 10 8
65. 20 c. black and purple .. 15 10
66. 25 c. blue 15 12
67. 30 c. brown 12 10
68. 35 c. violet and red .. 20 15
69. 40 c. red and grey .. 15 12
70. 45 c. brown and blue .. 12 12
71. 50 c. green and black .. 20 15
72. 75 c. brown adn yellow .. 15 12
73. 1 f. purple and brown .. 20 15
74. 2 f. blue and green .. 45 40
75. 5 f. black and violet .. 1·40 1·25

1915. Surch. **5c** and red cross.

76. 1. 10 c.+5 c. red and orange 10 10

POSTAGE DUE STAMPS

1906. "Natives" key-type inscr. "HT-SENEGAL-NIGER".

D 52. L. 5 c. green 30 30
D 53. 10 c. lake .. .. 1·40 1·10
D 54. 15 c. blue .. .. 1·60 1·40
D 55. 20 c. black on yellow 1·10 1·10
D 56. 50 c. violet .. .. 3·75 3·75
D 57. 60 c. black .. .. 2·25 2·25
D 58. 1 f. black .. .. 4·25 3·75

1915. "Figures" key-type inscr. "HT. SENEGAL-NIGER".

D 77. M. 5 c. green 12 12
D 78. 10 c. red 12 12
D 79. 15 c. grey 15 15
D 80. 20 c. brown 12 12
D 81. 30 c. blue 20 20
D 82. 50 c. black 10 10
D 83. 30 c. orange .. 40 40
D 84. 1 f. violet 45 45

For later issues see **FRENCH SUDAN.**

UPPER SILESIA O4

Stamps issued during a Plebiscite held in 1921 to decide the future of the district.

1. 2. Coal-mine in Silesia.

1920.

No.	Description	Unused	Used
1. 1.	2½ pf. grey	12	12
2.	3 pf. brown	20	20
3.	5 pf. green	5	5
4.	10 pf. brown	5	5
5.	15 pf. violet	8	8
6.	20 pf. blue	8	8
7.	50 pf. chocolate	1·75	1·75
8.	1 m. claret	1·60	1·60
9.	5 m. orange	1·60	1·60

1920. Surch.

No.	Description	Unused	Used
10. 1.	5 pf. on 15 pf. violet	3·00	3·00
12.	5 pf. on 20 pf. blue	8	8
14.	10 pf. on 20 pf. blue	8	8
16.	50 pf. on 5 m. orange	5·50	5·50

1920.

No.	Description	Unused	Used
19. 2.	2½ pf. grey	5	5
20.	3 pf. claret	5	5
21.	5 pf. green	5	5
22.	10 pf. red	5	5
23.	15 pf. violet	5	5
24.	20 pf. blue	5	5
25.	25 pf. brown	5	5
26.	30 pf. yellow	5	5
27.	40 pf. olive	5	5

Same design, but larger.

No.	Description	Unused	Used
28. 2.	50 pf. grey	5	5
29.	60 pf. blue	10	10
30.	75 pf. green	10	10
31.	80 pf. claret	10	10
32.	1 m. purple	10	10
33.	2 m. brown	10	10
34.	3 m. violet	20	12
35.	5 m. orange	40	30

1921. Optd. **Plebiscite 20 mars 1921.**

No.	Description	Unused	Used
36. 2.	10 pf. red	30	45
37.	15 pf. violet	30	45
38.	20 pf. blue	30	45
39.	25 pf. brown	55	70
40.	30 pf. yellow	55	70
41.	40 pf. olive	55	70
42.	50 pf. grey	55	70
43.	60 pf. blue	1·25	1·60
44.	75 pf. green	1·25	1·60
45.	80 pf. claret	1·40	1·60
46.	1 m. purple	1·50	1·90

1922. As last, new colours, surch.

No.	Description	Unused	Used
47. 2.	4 m. on 60 pf. green	12	12
48.	10 m. on 75 pf. red	30	30
49.	20 m. on 80 pf. orange	1·40	1·90

OFFICIAL STAMPS

1920. Official stamps of Germany (Types as O 3 and O 4 with figures "21" in corners) optd. **C.G.H.S.**

No.	Description	Unused	Used
O 25.	5 pf. green	8	12
O 26.	10 pf. red	8	12
O 27.	15 pf. brown	8	12
O 28.	20 pf. blue	8	12
O 29.	30 pf. orange on buff	8	12
O 30.	50 pf. violet on buff	20	30
O 31.	1 m. red on buff	1·75	2·50

1920. Official stamps of Germany, without figs. "21" in corners, optd. **C.G.H.S.**

No.	Description	Unused	Used
O 32.	5 pf. green	12	12
O 33.	10 pf. red	5	5
O 34.	15 pf. purple	5	5
O 35.	20 pf. blue	5	5
O 36.	30 pf. orange on buff	5	5
O 37.	40 pf. red	5	5
O 38.	50 pf. violet on buff	5	5
O 39.	60 pf. brown	5	5
O 40.	1 m. red on buff	5	5
O 41.	1 m. 25 blue on yellow	5	5
O 43.	2 m. blue	5	5
O 44.	5 m. brown on yellow	5	5

UPPER VOLTA O4

A former French colony in W. Africa, N. of Ghana, which was divided between Niger, Fr. Sudan and Ivory Coast in 1933. In 1958 it became a republic within the French Community and it attained full independence in 1960.

1920. Stamps of Upper Senegal and Niger optd. **HAUTE-VOLTA.**

No.	Description	Unused	Used
1. 1.	1 c. violet and purple	5	5
2.	2 c. purple and grey	5	5
3.	4 c. blue and black	5	5
4.	5 c. green	5	5
18.	5 c. chocolate and brown	5	5
5.	10 c. red and orange	10	10
19.	10 c. green	5	5
20.	10 c. blue and claret	5	5
6.	15 c. yellow and brown	8	5
7.	20 c. black and purple	20	15
8.	25 c. blue	20	15
21. 1.	25 c. green and black	8	8
9.	30 c. brown	20	15
22.	30 c. red and orange	5	5
23.	30 c. red and violet	5	5
23a.	30 c. green	8	8
10.	35 c. violet and red	8	8
11.	40 c. red and grey	5	5
12.	45 c. brown and blue	5	5
13.	50 c. green and black	30	20
24.	50 c. blue	5	5
25.	50 c. blue and orange	10	10
26.	60 c. red	5	5
26a.	65 c. blue and brown	8	8
14.	75 c. brown and yellow	5	5
15.	1 f. purple and brown	10	10
16.	2 f. blue and green	20	15
17.	5 f. black and violet	40	40

1922. Surch. in figures and bars.

No.	Description	Unused	Used
27. 1.	0.01 on 15 c. yellow & brn.	8	8
28.	0.02 on 15 c. yellow & brn.	8	8
29.	0.05 on 15 c. yellow & brn.	8	8
30.	25 c. on 2 f. blue & green	5	5
31.	25 c. on 5 f. black & violet	5	5
32.	60 on 75 c. violet on red	5	5
33.	65 on 45 c. brown and blue	8	8
34.	85 on 75 brown & yellow	8	8
35.	90 c. on 75 c. red	12	12
36.	1 f. 25 on 1 f. blue	5	5
37.	1 f. 50 on 1 f. blue	25	25
37a.	3 f. on 5 f. brown & red	30	30
38.	10 f. on 5 f. mauve & green	2·25	2·25
39.	20 f. on 5 f. violet & brown	2·50	2·50

1. Hausa Man. 2. Hausa Warrior.

1928.

No.	Description	Unused	Used
40. 1.	1 c. blue and green	5	5
41.	2 c. brown and mauve	5	5
42.	4 c. black and yellow	5	5
43.	5 c. blue	5	5
44.	10 c. blue and pink	12	12
45.	15 c. brown and blue	15	15
46.	20 c. brown and green	20	20
47. –	25 c. brown and yellow	25	25
48. –	30 c. green	30	30
49. –	40 c. black and pink	30	30
50. –	45 c. brown and blue	30	30
51. –	50 c. black and green	30	30
52. –	65 c. blue	30	30
53. –	75 c. black and mauve	25	25
54. –	90 c. red	30	30
55. 2.	1 f. brown and green	25	25
56.	1 f. 10 blue and mauve	30	30
57.	1 f. 50 blue	45	45
58.	2 f. black and blue	45	45
59.	3 f. brown and yellow	55	55
60.	5 f. brown and mauve	55	55
61.	10 f. black and green	3·25	3·25
62.	20 f. black and pink	4·00	4·00

DESIGN—VERT. 25 c. to 90 c. Hausa woman.

1931. "Colonial Exhibition" key-types inscr. "HAUTE-VOLTA".

No.	Description	Unused	Used
63. E.	40 c. green	50	50
64. F.	50 c. mauve	50	50
65. G.	90 c. red	50	50
66. H.	1 f. 50 blue	50	50

3. President Coulibaly. 4. Hind Mask. 5. President Yameogo.

1959. Republic. 1st Anniv.

No.	Description	Unused	Used
67. 3.	25 f. purple and black	20	5

1960. Animal Masks.

No.	Description	Unused	Used
68. 4.	30 c. violet and red	5	5
69.	40 c. purple and ochre	5	5
70.	50 c. olive and turquoise	5	5
71. –	1 f. black, brown & verm.	5	5
72. –	2 f. myrtle, yellow-green and emerald	5	5
73. –	4 f. black, violet and blue	5	5
74. –	5 f. red, brown and bistre	5	5
75. –	6 f. maroon and turquoise	8	5
76. –	8 f. brown and red	8	8
77. –	10 f. maroon and green	10	8
78. –	15 f. blue, brown and red	12	10
79. –	20 f. green and blue	15	8
80. –	25 f. maroon, green & blue	20	8
81. –	30 f. black, choc. & turq.	20	10
82. –	40 f. black, red and blue	25	10
83. –	50 f. brn., grn. & magenta	30	10
84. –	60 f. blue and brown	45	15
85. –	85 f. blue and grey-green	55	20

MASKS: 1 f. to 4 f. Wart-hog. 5 f. to 8 f. Monkey. 10 f. to 20 f. Buffalo. 25 f. Antelope. 30 f. to 50 f. Elephant. 60 f., 85 f. Secretary-bird.

1960.

No.	Description	Unused	Used
86. 5.	25 f. maroon and grey	20	15

1960. African Technical Co-operation Commission. 10th Anniv. As T **39** of Cameroun.

No.	Description	Unused	Used
87.	25 f. indigo and blue	25	25

1960. Conseil de l'Entente. 1st Anniv. As T **6** of Dahomey.

No.	Description	Unused	Used
88.	25 f multicoloured	25	25

6.

1960. Proclamation of Independence.

No.	Description	Unused	Used
89. 6.	25 f. chestnut, red & black	25	25

7. Aircraft and Map.

1961. Air.

No.	Description	Unused	Used
90. 7.	100 f. blue, green and red	75	25
91. –	200 f. brown, red & green	1·50	55
92. –	500 f. grn., red, bl. & brn.	3·75	1·60

DESIGNS: 200 f. Scene at Ouagadougou Airport. 500 f. Aerial view of Champs Elysees, Ouagadougou.

8. W.M.O. Emblem, Sun and Meteorological Instruments.

1961. 1st World Meteorological Day.

No.	Description	Unused	Used
93. 8.	25 f. red, blue and black	25	25

9. Arms of Republic.

1961. Independence Festival.

No.	Description	Unused	Used
94. 9.	25 f. multicoloured	25	25

1962. Air. "Air Afrique" Airline. As T **44** of Cameroun.

No.	Description	Unused	Used
95.	25 f. mauve, green & purple	25	20

10. W.M.O. Emblem, Weather Station and Crops.

1962. World Meteorological Day.

No.	Description	Unused	Used
96. 10.	25 f. blue, green and black	25	20

1962. Malaria Eradication. As T **45** of Cameroun.

No.	Description	Unused	Used
97.	25 f. + 5 f. red	25	25

11. Nurse and Hospital.

1962. Establishment of Red Cross in Upper Volta.

No.	Description	Unused	Used
98. 11.	25 f. brown, blue & red	25	25

12. Buffalo at Water-hole.

DESIGNS—VERT. 15 f. Defassa water buck. 85 f. Buffon's Kob. HORIZ. 10 f. Lion and lioness. 25 f. Arly Camp. 50 f. Diapaga Camp.

1962. Hunting and Tourism.

No.	Description	Unused	Used
99. 12.	5 f. green, blue & sepia	5	5
100. –	10 f. green, yell. & brn.	8	5
101. –	15 f. emer., yell. & choc.	12	5
102. –	25 f. grn., blue & maroon	20	5
103. –	50 f. grn., blue & maroon	40	12
104. –	85 f. grn., blue & brown	65	20

1962. Abidjan Games, 1961. As T **8** of Niger Republic.

No.	Description	Unused	Used
105.	20 f. choc., bl., blk. & brn.	20	20
106.	25 f. choc., bl., blk. & brn.	25	25
107.	85 f. choc., bl., blk. & brn.	60	60

DESIGNS—HORIZ. 20 f. Football. 25 f. Cycling. 85 f. Boxing.

1962. Union of African and Malagasy States. 1st Anniv. As No. 328 of Cameroun.

No.	Description	Unused	Used
108. 47.	30 f. red	55	50

13. Flag and U.N. Emblem.

1962. Air. Admission to U.N. 2nd Anniv.

No.	Description	Unused	Used
109. 13.	50 f. multicoloured	40	20
110.	100 f. multicoloured	75	45

14. G.P.O., Ouagadougou.

1962. Air. Opening of Ouagadougou P.O.

No.	Description	Unused	Used
111. 14.	100 f. brown, buff, grey, red and black	75	45

1963. Freedom from Hunger. As T **51** of Cameroun.

No.	Description	Unused	Used
112.	25 f. + 5 f. bl., brn. & myrtle	25	25

15. Rainfall Map.

17. "Hippeastrum equestre". 16. Basket-ball.

1963. 3rd World Meteorological Day.

No.	Description	Unused	Used
113. 15.	70 c. multicoloured	55	40

1963. Dakar Games. Centres in black and red.

No.	Description	Unused	Used
114. 16.	20 f. violet	15	10
115. –	25 f. ochre (Discus)	20	12
116. –	50 f. blue (Judo)	35	25

1963. Flowers. Multicoloured.

No.	Description	Unused	Used
117.	50 c. "Hibiscus rosa sinensis"	5	5
118.	1 f. "Oldemandia grandiflora"	5	5
119.	1 f. 50 "Portulaca grandiflora"	5	5
120.	2 f. "Nicotiana tabacum"	5	5
121.	4 f. "Ipomaea stolonifera"	5	5
122.	5 f. "Striga senegalensis"	5	5
123.	6 f. "Vigna"	5	5
124.	8 f. "Lepidagathis heudelotiana"	5	5
125.	10 f. "Euphorbia splendens"	8	5

126. 15 f. T 17 .. .. 10 8
127. 25 f. "Argyreia nervosa" 15 10
128. 30 f. "Quisqualis indica" 20 12
129. 40 f. "Nymphea lotus" .. 25 15
130. 50 f. "Plumeria alba" .. 35 20
131. 60 f. "Crotalaria retusa" 40 25
132. 85 f. "Hibiscus esculentus" 65 30

The 50 c. to 10 f. are vert.

18. Jetliner in Flight.

1963. Air. 1st Jet-flight, Ouagadougou-Paris.

133. 18. 200 f. multicoloured .. 1·60 80

1963. Air. African and Malagasy Post and Telecommunications Union. As T 10 of Central African Republic.

134. 85 f. red, buff, violet and deep violet 65 50

19. Centenary Emblem and Globe.

20. "Declaration universelle . . .".

1963. Red Cross Centenary.

135. 19. 25 f. black, brown, red and yellow 35 35

1963. Air. "Air Afrique". 1st Anniv. Surch. **AIR AFRIQUE 19-11-63 50F.**

136. 18. 50 f. on 200 f. mult. .. 50 50

1963. Declaration of Human Rights. 15th Anniv.

137. 20. 25 f. blue, yellow, gold and purple 20 15

21. "Europafrique".

22. "Telecommunications".

24. Barograph, Landscape and W.M.O. Emblem.

23. Rameses II, Abu Simbel.

1964. Air. "Europafrique".

138. 21. 50 f. multicoloured .. 65 55

1964. Admission of Upper Volta to I.T.U.

139. 22. 25 f. multicoloured .. 20 20

1964. Air. Nubian Monuments Preservation.

140. 23. 25 f. maroon and green 20 20
141. 100 f. brown and blue .. 85 85

1964. World Meteorological Day.

142. 24. 50 f. magenta, bl. & grn. 45 30

25. Dove and Letters.

1964. Admission to U.P.U. 1st Anniv.

143. 25. 25 f. sepia and blue .. 20 15
144. – 60 f. sepia and orange .. 45 40

DESIGN: 60 f. Aircraft and letters.

26. Head of Athlete (bronze).

27. Symbols of Solar Research.

1964. Air. Olympic Games, Tokyo.

145. 26. 15 f. green, red & sepia 12 10
146. – 25 f. green, red & sepia 20 15
147. – 85 f. green, red & brown 65 55
148. – 100 f. choc., red & brn. 75 65

DESIGNS: 25 f. Seated athlete (bronze). 85 f. "Victorious athlete" (bronze). 100 f. Venus de Milo.

1964. Int. Quiet Sun Years.

149. 27. 30 f. red, ochre & green 20 20

28. Woodpecker ("Mesopicos goertae").

29. President Kennedy.

1964. Air.

150. 28. 250 f. multicoloured .. 1·60 1·10

1964. French, African and Malagasy Co-operation. As T 500 of France.

151. 70 f. chocolate, red & blue 55 35

1964. Air. Pres. Kennedy Commem.

152. 29. 100 f. chocolate, mauve, brown and yellow .. 75 65

30. Independence Hotel.

31. Pigmy Long-tailed Sunbird.

1964. Opening of Independence Hotel, Ouagadougou.

153. 30. 25 f. multicoloured .. 65 25

1965. Birds. Multicoloured.

154. 10 f. Type 31 (postage) .. 10 10
155. 15 f. Sunbird 15 15
156. 20 f. Splendid sunbird .. 25 25
157. 500 f. Abyssinian roller (27×48 mm.) (air) .. 3·75 2·10

32. Sun and Emblems.

1965. Air. World Meteorological Day.

158. 32. 50 f. multicoloured .. 40 20

33. Grand Cascade, Banfora.

1965. Banfora Waterfalls.

159. – 5 f. brown, blue & green 5 5
160. 33. 25 f. blue, green & red 20 12

DESIGN—VERT. 5 f. Comoe Cascade.

34. Hughes Telegraph and Modern Telephone.

1965. Air. I.T.U. Cent.

161. 34. 100 f. red, green & turq. 80 50

35. I.C.Y. Emblem.

1965. Air. Int. Co-operation Year.

162. 35. 25 f. multicoloured .. 25 10
163. 100 f. multicoloured .. 70 40

36. Football, Boots and Net.

38. "Early Bird" Satellite in Orbit.

37. Sacred Alligator of Sabou.

1965. 1st African Games, Brazzaville.

164. 36. 15 f. green, red & maroon 10 10
165. – 25 f. maroon, orge. & bl. 20 12
166. – 70 f. red and green .. 50 25

DESIGNS: 25 f. Boxing-gloves and ring. 70 f. Tennis-racquets, ball and net.

1965. Air. Fauna.

167. 37. 60 f. grn., turq. & brown 40 25
168. – 85 f. brn., bistre & green 60 40

DESIGN—VERT. 85 f. Lion.

1965. Air. Space Telecommunications.

169. 38. 30 f. red, choc. and blue 25 15

39. Lincoln.

41. Dromedary.

40. President Yameogo.

1965. Abraham Lincoln. Death Cent.

170. 39. 50 f. multicoloured .. 35 25

1965. Pres. Yameogo.

171. 40. 25 f. multicoloured .. 20 12

1966. Insects and Fauna. Multicoloured.

172. 1 f. "Nemopistha imperatrix" (vert.) 5 5
173. 2 f. Python (vert.) .. 5 5
174. 3 f. "Sphodromantis lineola" 5 5
175. 4 f. "Staurocleis magnifica occidentalis" 5 5
176. 5 f. Wart-hoe (vert.) .. 5 5
177. 6 f. "Pandinus imperator" 5 5
178. 8 f. Green monkey (vert.) .. 5 5
179. 10 f. Type 41 .. .. 8 5
180. 15 f. Panther (vert.) .. 10 5
181. 20 f. Buffalo 12 8
182. 25 f. Hippopotamus (vert.) 20 10
183. 30 f. Agama (lizard) .. 25 12
184. 45 f. Viper (vert.) 30 12
185. 50 f. Chameleon (vert.) .. 35 12
186. 60 f. "Ugada limbata" (vert.) 40 20
187. 85 f. Elephant 55 20

The 1, 3, 4, 6 and 60 f. are Insects, the remainder are Fauna.

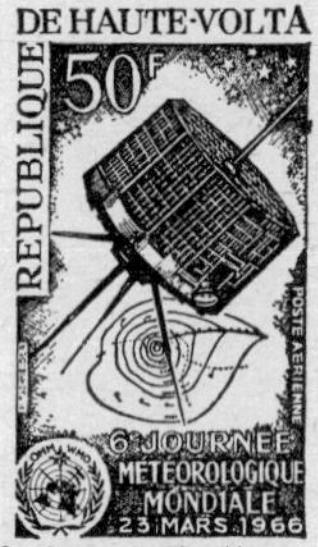

42. Communications Satellite.

43. Ritual Mask.

1966. Air. World Meteorological Day.

188. 42. 50 f. black, lake & blue 35 20

1966. World Festival of Negro Arts, Dakar. Multicoloured.

189. 20 f. Type 43 .. .. 15 10
190. 25 f. Plumed head-dress .. 20 12
191. 60 f. Dancer 45 25

44. Bobo-Dioulasso Mosque.

1966. Religious Buildings. Multicoloured.

192. 25 f. Type 44 .. .. 15 10
193. 25 f. Po Church 15 10

45. Satellite "FR 1" and Ouagadougou Tracking Station.

1966. Air. Ouagadougou Tracking Station. Inaug.

194. 45. 250 f. lake, chestnut and indigo .. .. 1·90 1·25

46. W.H.O. Building.

1966. Air. W.H.O. Headquarters, Geneva. Inaug.

195. 46. 100 f. black, blue & yell. 75 50

47. Nurse and Red Cross on Globe.

48. Scouts by Camp Fire.

1966. Red Cross.
196. **47.** 25 f. multicoloured .. 15 10

1966. Scouting.
197. **48.** 10 f. black, brown, yellow and green .. 8 5
198. – 15 f. black, brown & buff 10 5
DESIGN: 15 f. Scouts on cliff.

49. Inoculating Cattle.

1966. Prevention of Cattle Plague Campaign.
199. **49.** 25 f. black, yellow & blue 15 10

1966. Air. "DC-8" Air Services. Inaug. As T **45** of Central African Republic.
200. 25 f. olive, black and brown 20 8

50. Ploughing with Donkey.

1966. Rural Education (25 f.) and Kamboince Centre. 3rd Anniv. (30 f.). Multicoloured.
201. 25 f. Type **50** 15 8
202. 30 f. "Rotation of crops", Kamboince Centre .. 20 10

51. Sir Winston Churchill.

1966. Air. Churchill Commem.
203. **51.** 100 f. green and carmine 75 50

52. Pope Paul and Dove over U.N. General Assembly Building.

1966. Air. Pope Paul's Peace Appeal before U.N.
204. **52.** 100 f. violet and blue .. 75 50

53. U.N.E.S.C.O. Emblem. **54.** Arms of Upper Volta.

1966. U.N.E.S.C.O. and U.N.I.C.E.F. 20th Anniv.
205. **53.** 50 f. verm., blue & black 35 20
206. – 50 f. violet, purple & red 35 20
DESIGN: No. 209, U.N.I.C.E.F. emblem and child-care theme.

1967.
207. **54.** 30 f. multicoloured .. 20 8

55. Man and Woman holding emblems.

1967. Europafrique.
208. **55.** 60 f. multicoloured .. 35 20

56. Acclaiming Lions Emblem.

1967. Air. Lions Int. 50th Anniv.
209. **56.** 100 f. ultram., bl. & choc. 1·00 50

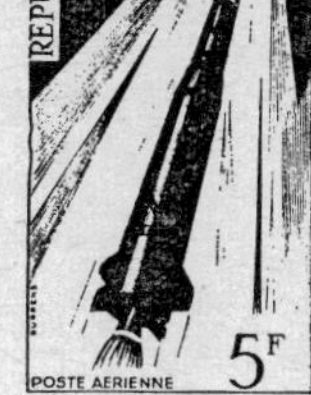

57. W.M.O. Emblem and Landscape. **58.** "Diamant" Rocket.

1967. Air. World Meteorological Day.
210. **57.** 50 f. grn., turq. & blue 35 20

1967. Air. French Space Achievements.
211. **58.** 5 f. green, orge. & blue 5 5
212. – 20 f. lilac, purple & indigo 20 10
213. – 30 f. green, blue and red 25 12
214. – 100 f. green, violet & pur. 65 30
DESIGNS—HORIZ. 20 f. "FR-1" satellite. 100 f. "D1-D" satellite. VERT. 30 f. "D1-C" satellite.

59. Dr. Schweitzer and Organ Pipes. **60.** Scout waving Hat.

1967. Air. Dr. Albert Schweitzer. 2nd Death Anniv.
215. **59.** 250 f. black and maroon 1·90 1·10

1967. World Scout Jamboree, Idaho. Multicoloured.
216. 5 f. Type **60** (postage) .. 15 8
217. 20 f. Scouts' handclasp .. 40 25
218. 100 f. Jamboree emblem and world map (48 × 27 mm.) (air) 75 40

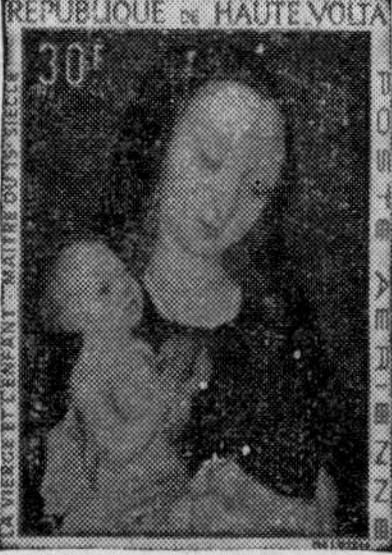

61. "Virgin and Child" by 15th century master). **63.** Postman on Cycle.

62. Bank Book and Coins.

1967. Air. Religious Paintings. Multicoloured.
219. 30 f. Type **61** 20 12
220. 50 f. "The Deposition of Christ" (Dirk Bouts) .. 35 25
221. 100 f. "Christ giving Blessing" (Bellini) 75 35
222. 250 f. "The Evangelists" (Jordaens) .. .. 1·90 1·10
See also Nos. 237/40.

1967. National Savings Bank.
223. **62.** 30 f. green, brown and orange-brown .. 20 10

1967. Air. U.A.M.P.T. 5th Anniv. As T **95** of Cameroun.
224. 100 f. green, lake and blue 65 30

1967. Stamp Day.
225. **63.** 30 f. brown, green & blue 20 10

1967. West African Monetary Union. 5th Anniv. As T **54** of Dahomey.
226. 30 f. violet and blue .. 20 10

64. "The Two Alps". **65.** Human Rights Emblem.

1967. Winter Olympic Games, Grenoble (1968).
227. – 15 f. green, blue & brown 10 5
228. **64.** 50 f. blue and green .. 35 15
229. – 100 f. green, blue & red 70 30
DESIGNS—HORIZ. 15 f. St. Nizier-du-Moucherotte. 100 f. Cable-car, Villard-de-Lans.

1968. Human Rights Year.
230. **65.** 20 f. red, gold and blue 12 10
231. 30 f. red, gold and green 20 10

66. Student and School.

1968. National School of Administration.
232. **66.** 30 f. blue, blue-grn. & brn. 20 10

67. Caravelle Airliner "Ouagadoubou".

1968. Air.
233. **67.** 500 f. blk., blue & purple 3·75 1·75

68. W.M.O. Emblem, Sun and Cloud-burst.

1968. Air. World Meteorological Day.
234. **68.** 50 f. blue, red and green 35 20

69. Human Figures and W.H.O. Emblem.

1968. W.H.O. 20th Anniv.
235. **69.** 30 f. indigo, red & blue 20 10
236. 50 f. blue, brown & grn. 30 15

1968. Air. Paintings. Old Masters in the Louvre. Multicoloured. As T **61**. Sizes given in millimetres.
237. 20 f. "Still Life" (Gauguin) (36 × 50) .. 15 10
238. 60 f. "Anne of Cleves" (Holbein the Younger) (36 × 50) 40 25
239. 90 f. "The Pawnbroker and His Wife" (Quentin Metsys) (38 × 40) .. 65 40
240. 200 f. "The Cart" (Le Nain) (50 × 37) .. 1·50 1·00

70. "Europafrique".

1968. Air. "Europafrique".
241. **70.** 50 f. red, black and ochre 25 20

71. Telephone Exchange.

1968. Automatic Telephone Exchange, Bobo-Dioulasso. Inaug.
242. **71.** 30 f. multicoloured .. 20 10

72. Colima Acrobat with Bells.

1968 Air. Olympic Games, Mexico.
243. **72.** 10 f. choc., yellow & red 10 5
244. – 30 f. blue, red and green 20 12
245. – 60 f. lake, brown & blue 40 20
246. – 100 f. lake, blue & green 65 35
DESIGNS—VERT. 30 f. Pelota-player (Veracruz). 60 f. Javelin thrower (Colima). HORIZ. 100 f. Athlete with cape (Jalisco).
The designs represent early Mexican statuary.

73. Weaving.

1968. Handicrafts.
247. – 5 f. blk., pur. & brown (postage) 5 5
248. **73.** 30 f. chocolate, orange & magenta 20 10
249. – 100 f. maroon, red and yellow (air) 55 30
250. – 150 f. blk., bl. & brown 80 55
DESIGNS—As Type **73**. 5 f. Metal-work. (48 × 27 mm.) 100 f. Pottery. 150 f. Basket-making.

1968. Air. "Philexafrique" Stamp Exn., Abidjan (Ivory Coast, 1969). (1st issue). As T **109** of Cameroun. Multicoloured.
251. 100 f. "Too Late" or "The Letter" (A. Cambon) 70 70

74. Mahatma Gandhi. **75.** "Grain for the World".

1968. Air. "Workers for Peace".
252. **74.** 100 f. blk., yell. & grn. 70 30
253. – 100 f. blk., apple & grn. 70 30
DESIGN: No. 253, Albert Luthuli.

1969. World Food Programme.
255. **75.** 30 f. maroon, slate & ultramarine 20 10

1969. Air. "Philexafrique" Stamp Exn., Abidjan (Ivory Coast) (2nd issue). As T **109** of Cameroun. Multicoloured.
256. 50 f. Dancers of Tengrela and stamp of 1928 .. 40 40

76. Loom and I.L.O. Emblem.

1969. Int. Labour Organisation. 50th Anniv.
257. 76. 30 f. indigo, lake & green 20 10

77. Cattle and Labourer.

1969. Air. World Meteorological Day.
258. 77. 100 f. choc., blue & green 65 30

79. "Lions" Emblem within Eye.

1969. Air. 12th Congress of 403 District, Lions Int., Ouagadougou.
259. 79. 250 f. multicoloured .. 1·50 85

80. Blood Donor.

1969. League of Red Cross Societies. 50th Anniv.
260. 80. 30 f. black, red and blue 20 10

81. "Mormyrops curviceps".

1969. Fishes.
261. – 20 f. buff, chocolate and blue (postage) 15 15
262. – 25 f. purple, brn. & indigo 20 20
263. 81. 30 f. black and olive .. 25 20
264. – 55 f. olive, yellow & green 40 40
265. – 85 f. blue, mag. & brown 85 65
266. – 100 f. blue, yellow and purple (air) 55 40
267. – 150 f. indigo, black & red 80 55
DESIGNS: 20 f. "Nannocharax gobioides". 25 f. "Hemigrammocharax polli". 55 f. "Alestes luteus". 85 f. "Micralestes voltae". LARGER (48 × 27 mm.): 100 f. "Phenacogrammus pabrensis". 150 f. "Synodontis arnoulti".

82. Astronaut on Moon.

1969. Air. Moon flight of "Apollo 8". Embossed on gold foil.
268. 82. 1,000 f. gold .. .. 7·00

1969. Air. 1st Man on the Moon. No. 214 optd. **L'HOMME SUR LA LUNE JUILLET 1969** and "Apollo 11".
269. 100 f. green, violet & purple 1·75 1·75

1969. Air. Napoleon Bonaparte. Birth Bicent. As T **116** of Cameroun. Multicoloured.
270. 50 f. "Bonaparte crossing the Great St. Bernard" (J. L. David) 45 35
271. 150 f. "First presentation of the Legion of Honour" (Debret) .. .. 1·10 75
272. 250 f. "Napoleon before Madrid" (C. Vernet) .. 2·10 1·25

1969. African Development Bank. 5th Anniv. As T **118** of Cameroun.
273. 30 f. brown, emerald and green 20 10

83. Millet. 84. Stylised Tree.

1969. Agricultural Produce.
274. 83. 15 f. brown, green and yellow (postage) .. 10 5
275. – 30 f. ultram. and maroon 20 10
276. – 100 f. brn. & violet (air) 55 30
277. – 200 f. yell-grn. & crimson 1·10 60
DESIGNS: 30 f. Cotton. LARGER (48 × 27 mm.): 100 f. Ground-nuts. 200 f. Rice.

1969. Air. Europafrique.
278. 84. 100 f. multicoloured .. 55 30

1969. Aerial Navigation Security Agency for Africa and Madagascar (A.S.E.C.N.A.). 10th Anniv. As T **121** of Cameroun.
279. 100 f. brown 45 30

85. "Niadale". 86. Lenin.

1970. Figurines and Masks in National Museum.
280. 85. 10 f. chocolate, orange and carmine 8 5
281. – 30 f. chocolate, blue and violet-blue .. 20 10
282. – 45 f. choc., blue & green 30 15
283. – 80 f. choc., pur. & violet 55 25
DESIGNS: 30 f. "Niaga". 45 f. "Iliu bara". 80 f. "Karan weeba".

1970. Air. Lenin. Birth Cent.
284. 86. 20 f. brown and ochre 8 5
285. – 100 f. red, blue & green 55 30
DESIGN—HORIZ.: 100 f. "Lenin addressing workers" (A. Serov.).

87. African Huts and City Buildings. 88. Cauris Dancers.

1970. Linked Cities' Day.
286. 87. 30 f. brown, blue & red 20 10

1970. Upper Volta Dances. Multicoloured.
287. 5 f. Mask of Nebwa Gnomo dance (horiz.) 5 5
288. 8 f. Type **88** 5 5
289. 20 f. Gourmantches dancers 10 5
290. 30 f. Larlle dancers (horiz.) 15 10

89. "Pupils", Sun and Emblem of Education Year.

1970. Int. Education Year. Multicoloured.
291. 40 f. Type **89** 25 15
292. 90 f. Visual Aids and emblem 50 25

90. New U.P.U. Headquarters Building, U.P.U. Monument and Abraham Lincoln.

1970. New U.P.U. Headquarters Building.
293. 90. 30 f. slate, crim. & brn. 20 10
294. 60 f. plum, grn. & brn. 35 20

91. Footballers and Cup.

1970. Air. World Cup Football Championships, Mexico.
295. 91. 40 f. pur.-brn., emer. and brown .. 20 15
296. – 100 f. brn., pur. & grn. 55 35
DESIGN: 100 f. Goalkeeper saving ball, Globe and footballers.

92. Franklin D. Roosevelt. 93. "Naval Construction".

1970. Air. Roosevelt's Death. 25th Anniv.
297. 92. 10 f. brn., blk. and grn. 5 5
298. – 200 f. red, violet & grey 1·10 65
DESIGN—HORIZ. 200 f. Roosevelt with his stamp collection.

1970. Hanover Fair.
299. 93. 15 f. multicoloured .. 8 5
300. – 45 f. green, blue & black 25 15
301. – 80 f. pur., brown & blk. 45 20
DESIGNS: 45 f. Test-tubes and retorts ("Chemistry"). 80 f. Power transmission lines and pylons ("Electro-techniques").

94. Inoculating Cattle.

1970. National Veterinary School.
302. 94. 30 f. multicoloured .. 20 12

95. "Cranes and Seashore", and Expo Monorail Coach. 96. Nurse attending Patient.

1970. Air. World Fair "EXPO 70" Osaka, Japan.
303. 50 f. Type **95** 20 15
304. 150 f. "Geisha", rocket and satellite .. 65 50

1970. Upper Volta Red Cross.
305. 96. 30 f. brown, red & grn. 20 10

INDEX

Countries can be quickly located by referring to the index at the end of this volume.

97. "Nurse and Child" (F. Hals). 98. U.N. Emblem and Dove.

1970. "Europafrique". Multicoloured.
306. 25 f. Type **97** 15 8
307. 30 f. "Courtyard in Delft" (Hoogh) 20 10
308. 150 f. "Christina of Denmark" (Holbein) .. 80 60
309. 250 f. "Hofburg Courtyard, Innsbruck" (Durer) 1·25 75

1970. Air. United Nations. 25th Anniv.
310. 98. 60 f. ultram, blue & grn. 35 20
311. – 250 f. vio., brn. & grn. 1·25 75
DESIGN—HORIZ. 250 f. U.N. emblem and two doves.

99. Front of Car.

1970. Paris Motor Show.
312. 99. 25 f. green, lake & brn. 12 8
313. – 40 f. blue, pur. & green 25 12
DESIGN: 40 f. Old and new cars.

100. "Holy Family".

1970. Air. Christmas.
314. 100. 300 f. silver .. .. 2·00
315. 1000 f. gold .. .. 6·50

101. Centre Buildings.

1970. Austro-Voltaic Centre. Inaug.
316. 101. 50 f. orange, grn. & red 25 10

102. Arms and Stork.

1970. Independence. Tenth Anniv.
317. 102. 30 f. mult. (postage) 20 10
318. – 500 f. blk., red and gold (air) .. .. .. 2·75
DESIGN—VERT. (27 × 37 mm.) Family and flag. No. 318 is embossed on gold foil.

103. U.N. "Key" and Split Globe.

1970. Air. U.N. Declaration on Colonies. 10th Anniv.
319. 103. 40 f. red, blue & brown 25 15
320. – 50 f. multicoloured .. 30 15
DESIGN: 50 f. Two maps of Africa showing African" and "European" areas.

104. Pres. Nasser.

106. Heads of Different Races.

105. Beigolo Hunting Horn.

1971. Air. Pres. Nasser Commem.

321. **104.** 100 f. multicoloured .. 45 20

1971. Musical Instruments.

322. **105.** 5 f. brn., red and blue 5 5
323. – 15 f. brn., red & green 8 5
324. – 20 f. red, slate and blue 10 5
325. – 25 f. drab, green and red 12 8

INSTRUMENTS—VERT. 15 f. Mossi "guitar". 20 f. Gurunssi "flutes". HORIZ. 25 f. Lunga "drum".

1971. Racial Equality Year.

326. **106.** 50 f. brn., red & turq. 25 15

107. "The Herons" (Egypt, 1354).

1971. Air. Muslim Miniatures. Multicoloured.

327. 100 f. Type **107** 45 30
328. 250 f. Page from the Koran (Egypt c. 1368-88) (vert.) 1·25 75

108. Telephone and Hemispheres.

110. Cutting Cane and Sugar Factory, Banfora.

109. Olympic Rings and Events.

1971. World Telecommunications Day.

329. **108.** 50 f. vio., grey & brn. 25 15

1971. Air. "Pre-Olympic Year".

330. **109.** 150 f. red, vio. and bl. 75 55

1971. Local Industries. Multicoloured.

331. 10 f. Type **110** 5 5
332. 35 f. Cotton-plant and textiles ("Voltex" project) 20 10

111. "Gonimbrasia hecate".

112. Scout and Pagodas.

1971. Butterflies. Multicoloured.

333. 1 f. Type **111** 5 5
334. 2 f. "Hamanunida daedalus" 5 5
335. 3 f. "Ophideres materna" 5 5
336. 5 f. "Danaus chrysippus" 5 5
337. 40 f. "Hypolimnas misippus" 20 10
338. 45 f. "Danaus petiverana" 20 12

1971. Air. 13th World Scout Jamboree, Asagari (Japan).

339. **112.** 45 f. multicoloured .. 25 15

113. Actor with Fan.

114. African with Seed-packet.

1971. "Philatokyo" Stamp Exhib., Tokyo. Multicoloured.

340. 25 f. Type **113**. 12 8
341. 40 f. Actor within mask .. 20 10

1971. National Seed-protection Campaign. Multicoloured.

342. 35 f. Grading seeds (horiz.) 15 10
343. 75 f. Type **114** 40 20
344. 100 f. Harvesting crops (horiz.) 50 30

1971. Volta Red Cross. 10th Anniv. Surch. **Xe ANNIVERSAIRE** and new value.

345. **96.** 100 f. on 30 f. brown, red and purple-brown .. 50 25

115. Teacher and Class

116. Soldier and Tractors.

1971. "Women's Access to Education". Multicoloured.

346. 35 f. Type **115** 15 10
347. 50 f. Family learning alphabet 25 12

1971. Dakiri Project. Military Aid for Agriculture. Multicoloured.

348. 15 f. Type **116** 8 5
349. 40 f. Soldiers harvesting (horiz.) 20 10

117. De Gaulle and Map.

1971. Air. De Gaulle Commemoration.

350. **117.** 40 f. multicoloured .. 35 35
351. – 500 f. gold and green 3·25

DESIGN—VERT. (30 × 40 mm.)—500 f. De Gaulle. No. 351 is embossed on gold foil.

1971. Air. African and Malagasy Posts and Telecommunications Union. 10th Anniv. As T **153** of Cameroun. Multicoloured.

352. 100 f. U.A.M.P.T. H.Q. and Mossi dancer 55 25

118. Tsetse-fly and Preventive Measures.

1971. Regional Anti-Onchocercose Campaign.

353. **118.** 40 f. multicoloured .. 20 10

119. Pres. Lamizana.

120. Children acclaiming Emblem.

1971.

354. **119.** 35 f. multicoloured .. 15 8

1971. U.N.I.C.E.F. 25th Anniv.

355. **120.** 45 f. multicoloured .. 25 12

121. Peulh Straw Hut.

1971. Traditional Housing (1st series). Mult.

356. 10 f. Type **121** 5 5
357. 20 f. Gourounsi house .. 10 5
358. 35 f. Mossi huts 15 10

See also Nos. 370/2.

122. Town Halls of Bobo-Dioulasso and Chalons-sur-Marne, France.

1971. "Twin Cities" Co-operation.

359. **122.** 40 f. multicoloured .. 20 10

123. Ice-hockey.

124. "La Musica" (P. Longhi).

1972. Air. Winter Olympic Games, Sapporo, Japan.

360. **123.** 150 f. pur., bl. and red 75 45

1972. Air. U.N.E.S.C.O. "Save Venice" Campaign. Multicoloured.

361. 100 f. Type **124** 50 25
362. 150 f. "Panorama da Ponte della Marina" (detail-Caffi) (horiz.) 75 35

125. Running.

127. Globe and Emblems.

126. Louis Armstrong.

1972. Air. Olympic Games, Munich.

363. **125.** 65 f. brown, blue & grn. 20 15
364. – 200 f. brown and blue 70 65

DESIGN: 200 f. Throwing the discus.

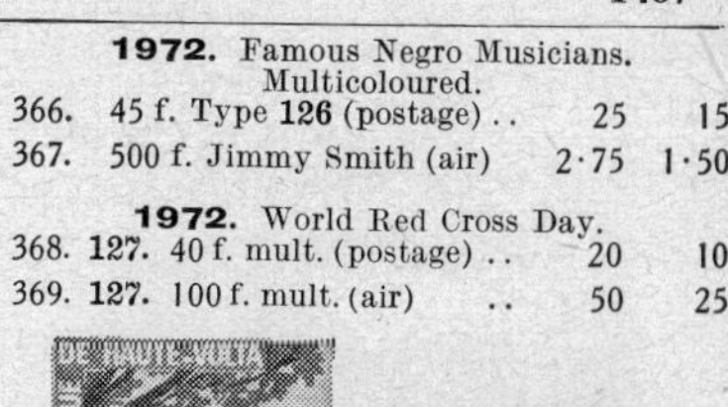

1972. Famous Negro Musicians. Multicoloured.

366. 45 f. Type **126** (postage) .. 25 15
367. 500 f. Jimmy Smith (air) 2·75 1·50

1972. World Red Cross Day.

368. **127.** 40 f. mult. (postage) .. 20 10
369. **127.** 100 f. mult. (air) .. 50 25

128. Bobo House.

129. Hair Style.

1972 Traditional Housing (2nd series). Mult.

370. 45 f. Type **128** 25 12
371. 50 f. Dagari house .. 25 12
372. 90 f. Interior of Bango house (horiz.) 45 25

1972. Upper Volta Hair Styles.

373. **129.** 25 f. multicoloured .. 12 5
374. – 35 f. multicoloured .. 15 8
375. – 75 f. multicoloured .. 35 15

DESIGNS: 35 f., 75 f. Similar hair styles.

130. "Teaching".

1972. 2nd Nat. Development Plan.

376. **130.** 10 f. maroon, green and blue-green (postage) 5 5
377. – 15 f. brown, orange-brown and green .. 8 5
378. – 20 f. brn., grn. and bl. 15 5
379. – 35 f. brn., blue & green 15 8
380. – 40 f. brn., green & pur. 12 10
381. – 85 f. blk., red & bl. (air) 40 25

DESIGNS: 15 f. Doctor and patient ("Health"). 20 f. Factory and silos ("Industry"). 35 f. Cattle ("Cattle-raising"). 40 f. Rice-planting ("Agriculture"). 85 f. Road-making machine ("Infrastructure").

1972. West African Monetary Union. 10th Anniv. As Type **109** of Dahomey.

382. 40 f. grey, blue & maroon 20 10

131. Lottery Building.

1972. Nat. Lottery. 5th Anniv.

383. **131.** 35 f. multicoloured .. 15 8

132. Pres. Pompidou and Lamizana.

1972, Air. Visit of Pres. Pompidou to Upper Volta.

384. **132.** 40 f. multicoloured .. 30 30
385. – 250 f. multicoloured .. 2·10 2·10

DESIGN: 250 f. As T **132** but frame differs and portraits are embossed on gold.

133. Mary Peters (pentathlon).

1972. Air. Gold Medal-winners, Olympic Games, Munich. Multicoloured.

386. 40 f. Type **133** 15 10
387. 65 f. Ragno-Lonzi (fencing) 25 15
388. 85 f. Touritcheva (gymnastics) 35 20
389. 200 f. Maury (sailing) .. 90 55
390. 300 f. Meyfarth (high-jumping) .. .. .. 1·25 85

134. Donkeys.

1972. Animals. Multicoloured.

392. 5 f. Type **134** 5 5
393. 10 f. Geese 5 5
394. 30 f. Goat 20 8
395. 50 f. Bull 25 12
396. 65 f. Camels 30 15

135. "The Nativity" (Della Notte).

1972. Air. Christmas. Religious Paintings. Multicoloured.

397. 100 f. Type **135** 45 20
398. 200 f. "The Adoration of the Magi" (Durer) .. 90 55

136. Mossi Hair-style and Village.

1973. Air.

399. **136.** 5 f. multicoloured .. 5 5
400. 40 f. multicoloured .. 15 10

1973. W.H.O. 25th Anniv. No. 353 surch. **O. M. S. 25· Anniversaire** and value.

401. **118.** 45 f. on 40 f. mult. .. 20 12

1973. African and Malagasy Posts and Telecommunications Union. As Type **182** of Cameroun.

402. 100 f. purple, red & yellow 45 20

1974. Council of Accord. 15th Anniv. As Type **131** of Dahomey.

403. 40 f. multicoloured .. 15 10

137. Map and Harvester.

1974. Kou Valley Project.

404. **137.** 35 f. multicoloured .. 12 10

138. Woman, Globe and Emblem.

1975. International Women's Year.

405. **138.** 65 f. multicoloured .. 30 20

139. Msgr. Jonny Thevenoud and Cathedral.

1975. Evangelisation of Upper Volta. 75th Anniv.

406. **139.** 55 f. blk., brn. and grn. 25 15
407. – 65 f. black, brn. and red 30 20

DESIGNS: 65 f. Father Guillaume Templier and Cathedral.

140. Farmer's Hat, Hoe and Emblem. **141.** Diseased Africans.

1975. Development of the Volta Valleys.

408. **140.** 15 f. multicoloured .. 8 5
409. 50 f. multicoloured .. 25 15

1976. Campaign against Onchocerciasis (round-worm).

410. **141.** 75 f. mar., oran. & grn. 35 25
411. 250 f. dark brn., oran. and brown .. .. 1·10 95

142. Globe and Emblem.

1976. Non-aligned Countries' Summit Conference, Colombo. Multicoloured.

412. 55 f. Type **142** 25 15
413. 100 f. Globe, dove and emblem 45 35

143. Washington at Trenton.

1976. "Interphil '76" International Stamp Exhibition, Philadelphia. Multicoloured.

414. 60 f. Type **143** (postage).. 30 20
415. 90 f. Seat of Government, Pennsylvania 40 30
416. 100 f. Siege of Yorktown (air) 45 35
417. 200 f. Battle of Cape St. Vincent 90 80
418. 300 f. Peter Francisco's act of bravery .. .. 1·40 1·10

144. U.P.U. and U.N. Emblems.

1976. U.N. Postal Administration. 25th Anniv.

420. **144.** 200 f. blue, bronze & red 90 80

OFFICIAL STAMPS

O **1.** Elephant.

1963.

O 112. O **1.** 1 f. sepia & chocolate 5 5
O 113. 5 f. sepia & yell.-grn. 5 5
O 114. 10 f. sepia and violet 8 8
O 115. 15 f. sepia & orange 10 10
O 116. 25 f. sepia and purple 15 15
O 117. 50 f. sepia & emerald 30 30
O 118. 60 f. sepia and red.. 35 35
O 119. 85 f. sepia and myrtle 60 60
O 120. 100 f. sepia and blue 70 70
O 121. 200 f. sepia and cerise 1·40 1·40

POSTAGE DUE STAMPS

1920. Postage Due stamps of Upper Senegal and Niger, "Figures" key-type, optd. **HAUTE-VOLTA.**

D 18. M. 5 c. green 5 5
D 19. 10 c. red 5 5
D 20. 15 c. grey 5 5
D 21. M. 20 c. brown 5 5
D 22. 30 c. blue 5 5
D 23. 50 c. black 8 8
D 24. 60 c. orange 8 8
D 25. 1 f. violet 10 10

1927. Surch.

D 40. M. "2 F." on 1 f. purple.. 45 45
D 41. "3 F." on 1 f. brown.. 45 45

1928. "Figures" key-type inscr. "HAUTE-VOLTA".

D 63. M. 5 c. green 5 5
D 64. 10 c. red 8 8
D 65. 15 c. grey 8 8
D 66. 20 c. brown 8 8
D 67. 30 c. blue 8 8
D 68. 50 c. black 40 40
D 69. 60 c. orange 60 60
D 70. 1 f. violet 70 70
D 71. 2 f. purple .. .. 1·25 1·25
D 72. 3 f. brown .. .. 1·25 1·25

D **1.** Antelope.

1962. Figures of value in black.

D 95. D **1.** 1 f. blue 5 5
D 96. 2 f. orange 5 5
D 97. 5 f. ultramarine .. 5 5
D 98. 10 f. purple.. .. 8 8
D 99. 20 f. green 12 12
D 100. 50 f. red 35 35

UPPER YAFA O4

A Sultanate of South Arabia, formerly part of the Western Aden Protectorate. Independent from September to December 1967 and then part of the People's Democratic Republic of Yemen.

1000 fils = 1 dinar.

1. Flag and Map.

1967.

UY 1. **1.** 5 f. multicoloured (post.) 5 5
UY 2. 10 f. multicoloured .. 5 5
UY 3. 20 f. multicoloured .. 5 5
UY 4. 25 f. multicoloured .. 8 8
UY 5. 40 f. multicoloured .. 10 10
UY 6. 50 f. multicoloured .. 15 15
UY 7. – 75 f. multicoloured (air) 20 20
UY 8. – 100 f. multicoloured 30 30
UY 9. – 250 f. multicoloured 70 70
UY 10. – 500 f. multicoloured 1·40 1·40

DESIGNS: UY 7/10, Arms of Sultanate.

URUGUAY O4

A republic in S. America, bordering on the Atlantic Ocean, independent since 1828.

1856. 120 centavos = 1 real.
1859. 1000 milesimos = 100 centesimos = 1 peso.
1975. 1 new peso = 100 old pesos.

1.

1856. Imperf.

1. **1.** 60 c. blue £160
2. 80 c. green .. .. .. 65·00
3. 1 r. red .. .. .. 65·00

2. **3.**

1858. Imperf.

5. **2.** 120 c. blue £100 £100
6. 180 c. green .. .. 23·00 40·00
7. 240 c. red .. .. 23·00 £110

1859. Imperf.

15. **3.** 60 c. purple .. .. 5·50 2·75
16. 80 c. yellow .. .. 9·00 8·50
17a. 100 c. red .. .. 23·00 8·50
18. 120 c. blue .. .. 9·00 4·50
12. 180 c. green .. .. 4·50 7·00
13. 240 c. red .. .. 23·00 23·00

4. **5.** **6.**

1864. Imperf.

20a. **4.** 6 c. red .. .. .. 2·75 2·75
21. 8 c. green .. .. 5·50 4·25
22. 10 c. yellow .. .. 7·00 5·50
23. 12 c. blue .. .. 3·50 2·25

1866. Surch. in figures. Imperf.

24. **4.** 5 c. on 12 c. blue .. 5·50 14·00
25. 10 c. on 8 c. green .. 5·50 14·00
26. 15 c. on 10 c. yellow .. 5·50 23·00
27a. 20 c. on 6 c. red.. .. 5·50 14·00

1866. Imperf.

28a. **5.** 1 c. black .. .. 85 1·75
29. 5 c. blue .. .. .. 1·75 85
30. 10 c. green .. .. 5·50 2·00
31. 15 c. yellow .. .. 11·00 4·25
32. 20 c. rose .. .. 11·00 4·25

1866. Perf.

37. **5.** 1 c. black .. .. 1·40 2·25
33. 5 c. blue .. .. .. 1·00 35
34. 10 c. green .. .. 1·40 35
35. 15 c. yellow .. .. 2·00 1·40
36. 20 c. rose .. .. 2·75 1·10

7. **8.**

1877. Roul. Various frames.

42. **7.** 1 c. brown 25 20
43. **8.** 5 c. green 30 15
44. **7.** 10 c. red 30 15
45. 20 c. bistre 35 25
46. 50 c. black .. .. 2·10 1·10
47. 1 p. blue .. .. .. 14·00 5·50

9. J. Suarez. **10.**

1881. Perf.

60. **9.** 7 c. blue 85 85

1882.

62. **10.** 1 c. green 45 45
63. – 2 c. red 35 35

The central device on the 2 c. is a mountain.

11. **12.** Gen. Maxime Santos.

13. General Artigas. **14.**

1883.

66. **11.** 1 c. green 35 30
67. 2 c. red 50 45
68. **12.** 5 c. blue 70 55
69. **13.** 10 c. brown 85 70

1883. Optd. **1883 Provisorio.** Roul.

75. **8.** 5 c. green 45 35

1884. Optd. **PROVISORIO 1884** or surch. **1 CENTESIMO** also.

76. 7. 1 c. on 10 c. red 15 15
77. – 2 c. red (No. 63) 45 45

1884.

79. 14. 5 c. blue 30 30

15. 16. 17. Gen. Artigas.

18. M. Santos. 19. 20.

1884. Roul.

83. 15. 1 c. grey-green 45 30
83a. 1 c. grey 35 25
100. 1 c. green 25 15
101. 16. 2 c. red 25 20
102. 15. 5 c. blue 45 15
86. 5 c. lilac 12 10
87. 17. 7 c. brown 70 55
103. 7 c. orange 50 35
88. 18. 10 c. brown 25 15
89. 19. 20 c. mauve 70 30
105. 20 c. brown 50 35
90. 20. 25 c. lilac 85 70
106. 25 c. red 85 50

21. 22.

1887. Roul.

99. 21. 10 c. mauve 85 55

1888. Roul.

104. 22. 10 c. violet 30 15

1889. Optd. **Provisorio.** Roul.

114. 15. 5 c. lilac 20 20

23. 24. 25.

26. 27. 28.

29. Figure of Justice. 30. Mercury. 31.

1889. Perf.

219. 23. 1 c. green 15 15
116. 24. 2 c. red 20 15
117. 25. 5 c. blue 25 12
118. 26. 7 c. brown 25 20
119. 27. 10 c. green 25 15
120. 28. 20 c. orange 55 30
121. 29. 25 c. red-brown 75 35
122. 30. 50 c. blue 1·60 1·25
123. 31. 1 p. violet 3·50 1·75
See also Nos 142/52, 217/24.

1891. Optd. **Provisorio 1891.** Roul.

133. 15. 5 c. lilac 15 15

1892. Optd. **Provisorio 1892** or surch. also in words.

135. 15. 1 c. green 25 25
137. 28. 1 c. on 20 c. orange 25 25
136. 26. 5 c. on 7 c. brown 20 15

32. 33. 34.

35. 36. 37.

1892. Perf.

138. 32. 1 c. green 15 12
139. 33. 2 c. red 20 15
140. 34. 5 c. blue 15 12
141. 35. 10 c. orange 70 35

1894.

142. 23. 1 c. blue 15 15
143. 24. 2 c. brown 25 20
144. 25. 5 c. rose 15 12
145. 26. 7 c. green 1·75 1·25
146. 27. 10 c. orange 1·10 25
147. 28. 20 c. brown 1·75 70
148. 29. 25 c. red 2·25 1·60
149. 30. 50 c. purple 4·25 2·00
150. 31. 1 p. blue 5·50 2·75
151. 36. 2 p. red 11·00 9·00
152. 37. 3 p. purple 11·00 9·00
See also Nos. 220, 222, 224 and 235/7.

38. Gaucho. 39. Solis Theatre. 40.

41. Typical of Cattle breeding. 42. Ceres. 43.

44. Amazon. 45. Mercury.

46. 47. Fortress of Montevideo.

48. Cathedral at Montevideo.

1895.

153. 38. 1 c. bistre 15 15
154. 39. 2 c. blue 15 15
155. 40. 5 c. red 25 15
156. 41. 7 c. green 2·00 90
157. 42. 10 c. brown 55 25
158. 43. 20 c. black and green 1·40 45
159. 44. 25 c. black and brown 1·75 55
160. 45. 50 c. black and blue 2·25 1·00
161. 46. 1 p. black and brown 2·75 2·00
162. 47. 2 p. green and violet 11·00 8·50
163. 48. 3 p. blue and red 11·00 8·50
For further stamps in these types, see Nos. 183/93 and 221.

49. J. Suarez. 50. Statue of J. Suarez. 52.

1896. Unveiling of Joaquin Suarez Monument.

177. 49. 1 c. black and claret 15 12
178. 50. 5 c. black and blue 20 15
179. – 10 c. black and lake 45 30
DESIGN: 10 c. Larger stamp showing whole Suarez Monument.

1897. Optd. **PROVISORIO 1897.**

180. 49. 1 c. black and claret 15 15
181. 50. 5 c. black and blue 20 15
182. – 10 c. black and lake 45 30

1897.

183. 38. 1 c. blue 12 12
184. 39. 2 c. purple 15 15
185. 40. 5 c. green 15 10
186. 41. 7 c. orange 1·40 55
187. 52. 10 c. red 70 30
188. 43. 20 c. black and mauve 1·10 35
189. 44. 25 c. blue and rose 70 30
190. 45. 50 c. brown and green 1·10 45
191. 46. 1 p. blue and brown 2·75 1·40
192. 47. 2 p. red and yellow 2·75 55
193. 48. 3 p. red and lilac 3·50 55
See also No. 223.

1897. End of Civil War. Optd. with palm leaf and **PAZ 1897.**

197. 38. 1 c. blue 35 35
198. 39. 2 c. purple 50 50
199. 40. 5 c. green 70 70
200. 52. 10 c. red 1·10 1·10

1898. Surch. **PROVISIONAL ½ CENTESIMO.**

209. 23. ½ c. on 1 c. blue 15 15
210. 38. ½ c. on 1 c. bistre 15 15
211. 49. ½ c. on 1 c. blk. & claret 15 15
212. 39. ½ c. on 2 c. blue 15 15
213. 50. ½ c. on 5 c. blk. & blue 20 15
214. 41. ½ c. on 7 c. green 20 15

53. Liberty. 54. Monument to Gen. Artigas.

1898.

315. 53. 5 m. rose 15 15
316. 5 m. violet 20 20

1899.

217. 54. 5 m. blue 10 8
218. 5 m. orange 8 5
220. 24. 2 c. orange 20 15
221. 40. 5 c. blue 20 8
222. 26. 7 c. red 1·00 1·00
223. 52. 10 c. purple 35 25
224. 28. 20 c. blue 40 15

1900. No. 182 surch. **1900 5 CENTESIMOS** and bar.

229. 5 c. on 10 c. black and lake 30 20

55. 56. 57.

58. 59.

1900.

230. 55. 1 c. green 25 8
231. 56. 2 c. red 15 8
232b. 57. 5 c. blue 25 5
233. 58. 7 c. brown 55 15
234. 59. 10 c. lilac 25 15
235. 29. 25 c. sepia 65 25
236. 30. 50 c. red 1·75 30
237. 31. 1 p. green 3·50 55

60. General Artigas. 61. 62.

63. 46.

65. 66.

1904.

251. 60. 5 m. yellow 12 8
252. 61. 1 c. green 30 8
253. 62. 2 c. orange 15 8
254. 63. 5 c. blue 35 5
255. 64. 10 c. lilac 30 12
256. 65. 20 c. green 70 25
257. 66. 25 c. bistre 1·00 20

1904. End of the Civil War. Optd. **Paz-1904.**

258. 61. 1 c. green 20 20
259. 62. 2 c. orange 30 25
260. 63. 5 c. blue 45 35

67. 68.

1906.

268. 67. 5 c. blue 55 8

1906.

269. 68. 5 c. blue 15 8
270. 7 c. brown 30 15
271. 50 c. rose 1·10 30

69. Cruiser "Montevideo" and Gunboat.

1908. Declaration of Independence. Roul.

279. 69. 1 c. green and red 55 55
280. 2 c. green 55 55
281. 5 c. green and orange 55 55

70. 71. Centaur.

1909. Opening of the Port of Montevideo.

282. 70. 2 c. black and brown 50 45
283. 5 c. black and red 50 45

1909. Surch. **Provisorio** and value.

284. 59. 8 c. on 10 c. violet 15 10
285. 29. 23 c. on 25 c. brown 45 25

1910. Cent. of 1810 Argentine Revolution.

286. 71. 2 c. red 25 20
287. 5 c. blue 25 20

1910. Surch. **PROVISORIO 5 MILESIMOS (or CENTESIMOS) 1910.**

294. 55. 5 m. on 1 c. green 8 8
295. 30. 5 c. on 50 c. red 15 15
296. 68. 5 c. on 50 c. rose 35 35

72. 73.

1910.

297. 72. 5 m. purple 5 5
298. 1 c. green 8 5
299. 2 c. orange-red 8 5
324. 2 c. red 8 5
319. 4 c. yellow 10 5
300. 5 c. blue 15 5
301. 8 c. black 25 8
327. 8 c. blue 15 8
302. 20 c. brown 45 10
303. 73. 23 c. blue 45 25
304. 50 c. orange 1·10 35
305. 1 p. red 2·25 45

74.

75. Liberty offering Peace to Uruguay.

1911. First Pan-American Postal Congress.

306.	74.	5 c. black and red ..	25	20

1911. Battle of Las Piedras. Cent. Surch **ARTIGAS,** value and **1811-1911.**

314.	58.	2 c. on 7 c. brown ..	25	15
315.		5 c. on 7 c. brown ..	15	15

1913. 1813 Conference. Cent. Optd. **CENTENARIO DE LAS INSTRUCCIONES DEL ANO XIII.**

332.	72.	2 c. orange-brown ..	25	15
333.		4 c. yellow	25	15
334.		5 c. blue	25	15

1918. Promulgation of New Constitution.

347.	75.	2 c. brown and green ..	30	25
348.		5 c. blue and brown ..	30	25

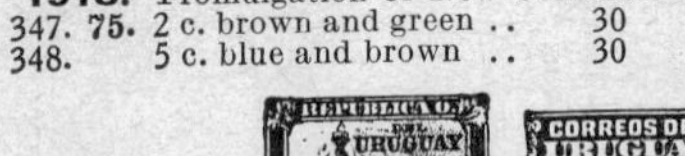

76. Montevideo Harbour.

77. Statue of Liberty, New York.

78. J. E. Rodo (writer).

1919.

349.	76.	5 m. grey and violet ..	5	5
350.		1 c. grey and green ..	5	5
351.		2 c. grey and red ..	5	5
352.		4 c. grey and orange ..	8	5
353.		5 c. grey and blue ..	12	5
354.		8 c. brown and blue ..	25	12
355.		20 c. grey and brown ..	55	20
356.		23 c. brown and green	1·00	25
357.		50 c. blue and brown ..	1·75	1·00
358.		1 p. blue and red ..	3·50	1·40

1919. Peace Commemoration.

359.	77.	2 c. brown and red ..	20	15
360.		4 c. brown and orange	20	15
361.		5 c. brown and blue ..	30	15
362.		8 c. blue and brown ..	35	20
363.		20 c. black and bistre..	50	45
364.		23 c. black and green ..	70	50

1920. Honouring J. E. Rodo.

372.	78.	2 c. black and lake ..	30	20
373.		4 c. blue and orange ..	30	20
374.		5 c. brown and blue ..	30	25

79. Mercury.

80. Damaso A. Larranaga.

1921.

378.	79.	5 m. mauve	5	5
379.		5 m. black	5	5
380.		1 c. green	8	5
381.		1 c. violet	12	5
411.		1 c. mauve	12	5
382.		2 c. orange	15	5
383.		2 c. red	15	5
384.		3 c. green	20	12
385.		4 c. yellow	15	8
386.		5 c. blue	15	5
387.		5 c. brown	15	5
414.		8 c. rose	35	30
388.		12 c. blue	70	15
389.		36 c. olive	2·25	85

1921. Air. Optd. with aeroplane and **CORREO AEREO.**

377.	29.	25 c. sepia	1·40	1·40

1921. D. A. Larranaga. 150th Birth Anniv.

390.	80.	5 c. slate	40	30

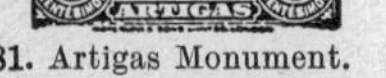

81. Artigas Monument.

82. Teru-Teru.

1923. Unveiling of Monument to Artigas.

418.	81.	2 c. brown and red ..	30	25
419.		5 c. brown and violet	30	25
420.		12 c. brown and blue ..	30	25

1923. Various sizes.

421.	82.	5 m. grey	5	5
422.		1 c. yellow	5	5
454.		1 c. pink	8	5
477.		1 c. purple	15	5
528.		1 c. violet	20	5
423.		2 c. mauve	8	5
529.		2 c. rose	8	5
530.		3 c. olive	10	5
425.		5 c. blue	8	5
532.		8 c. red	20	12
459.		10 c. green	15	12
460.		12 c. blue	20	12
461.		15 c. mauve	20	5
462.		20 c. brown	30	12
429.		36 c. green	1·40	70
463.		36 c. rose	1·10	55
430.		50 c. orange	2·75	1·10
464.		50 c. olive	1·75	85
431.		1 p. red	11·00	5·50
465.		1 p. buff	4·00	2·00
432.		2 p. green	11·00	7·00
466.		2 p. lilac	10·00	8·00

83.

84.

1923. Battle of Sarandi. Cent.

433.	83.	2 c. green	35	25
434.		5 c. red	35	25
435.		12 c. blue	35	25

1924. Air.

436.	84.	6 c. blue	55	50
437.		10 c. red	85	70
438.		20 c. green	1·75	1·40

85. "Victory" of Samothrace.

1924. Uruguayan Football Victory in Olympic Games.

450.	85.	2 c. rose	8·50	7·00
451.		5 c. purple	8·50	7·00
452.		12 c. blue	8·50	7·00

86. Landing of Lavalleja.

1925. Rising against Brazilian Rule. Cent.

467.	86.	2 c. grey and rose ..	50	45
468.		5 c. grey and mauve ..	50	45
469.		12 c. grey and blue ..	50	45

87. Parliament House.

88.

1925. Parliament House. Inaug.

470.	87.	5 c. black and violet ..	50	45
471.		12 c. black and blue ..	50	45

1925. Air. Assembly of Florida. Cent. Inscr. "MONTEVIDEO" or "FLORIDA".

472.	88.	14 c. black and blue ..	8·50	7·00

89. Gen. F. Rivera.

90. Gaucho Cavalryman at Rincon.

1925. Battle of Rincon. Cent.

474.	89.	5 c. pink (postage) ..	25	15
475.	90.	45 c. green (air) ..	—	2·25

91. Battle of Sarandi.

1925. Battle of Sarandi. Cent.

482.	91.	2 c. green	50	45
483.		5 c. mauve	50	45
484.		12 c. blue	50	45

92. Albatross.

93. The new G.P.O., Montevideo.

1926. Air. Imperf.

495.	92.	6 c. blue	55	55
496.		10 c. red	55	50
497.		20 c. green	1·40	85
498.		25 c. violet	1·40	1·00

See also Nos. 569/80.

1927. Philatelic Exn., Montevideo. Imperf.

534.	93.	2 c. green	2·00	1·60
535.		5 c. red	2·00	1·60
536.		8 c. blue	2·00	1·60

1928. Opening of San Carlos-Rocha Railway. Surch. **Inauguracion Ferrocarril SAN CARLOS a ROCHA 14/1/928** and value.

537.	82.	2 c. on 12 c. blue ..	35	30
538.		5 c. on 12 c. blue ..	35	30
539.		10 c. on 12 c. blue ..	35	30
540.		15 c. on 12 c. blue ..	35	30

ILLUSTRATIONS
British Commonwealth and all overprints and surcharges are FULL SIZE. Foreign Countries have been reduced to ¾-LINEAR.

94. Gen. F. Rivera.

1928. Cent. of Battle of Las Misiones.

541.	94.	5 c. red	12	5

95. Artigas.

96. Artigas Statue, Paysandu.

1928.

542.	95.	5 m. black	5	5
762.		5 m. brown	5	5
763.		5 m. orange	5	5
543.		1 c. violet	5	5
544.		1 c. purple	5	5
869.		1 c. blue	5	5
687.		15 m. black	8	5
545.		2 c. green	5	5
764.		2 c. brown	5	5
870.		2 c. red	5	5
546.		3 c. bistre	5	5
547.		3 c. green	5	5
548.		5 c. red	8	5
549.		5 c. olive	8	5
766.		5 c. blue	10	5
767.		5 c. blue-green ..	10	5
872.		5 c. violet	8	5
550.		7 c. red	8	5
551.		8 c. blue	12	5
552.		8 c. brown	12	5
553.		10 c. orange	15	8
554.		10 c. red	20	15
768.		12 c. blue	15	5
556.		15 c. blue	25	8
557.		17 c. violet	30	8
558.		20 c. chocolate ..	40	12
559.		20 c. lake	40	15
757.		20 c. cinnamon ..	35	12
770.		20 c. red	40	12
771.		20 c. violet	20	5
560.		24 c. red	45	15
561.		24 c. yellow	35	15
562.		36 c. olive	45	12
563.		50 c. grey	1·10	50
564.		50 c. black	95	45
565.		50 c. sepia	1·40	90
566.		1 p. green	2·25	1·00
567.	96.	2 p. brown and blue..	5·00	3·50
568.		3 p. black and red ..	7·00	5·50

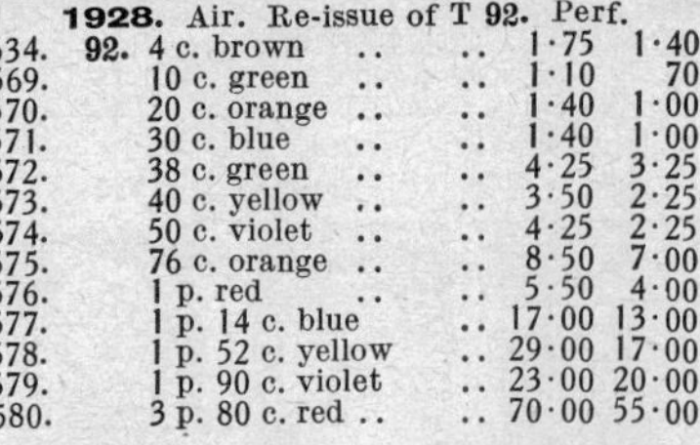

1928. Air. Re-issue of T 92. Perf.

634.	92.	4 c. brown	1·75	1·40
569.		10 c. green	1·10	70
570.		20 c. orange	1·40	1·00
571.		30 c. blue	1·40	1·00
572.		38 c. green	4·25	3·25
573.		40 c. yellow	3·50	2·25
574.		50 c. violet	4·25	2·25
575.		76 c. orange	8·50	7·00
576.		1 p. red	5·50	4·00
577.		1 p. 14 c. blue ..	17·00	13·00
578.		1 p. 52 c. yellow ..	29·00	17·00
579.		1 p. 90 c. violet ..	23·00	20·00
580.		3 p. 80 c. red	70·00	55·00

97. Garlanded Goal-posts.

98. General Garzon.

1928. Uruguayan Football Victories in 1924 and 1928 Olympic Games.

581.	97.	2 c. purple	5·50	4·50
582.		5 c. red	5·50	4·50
583.		8 c. blue	5·50	4·50

1928. Unveiling of Monument to Gen. Garzon. Imperf.

584.	98.	2 c. red	55	55
585.		5 c. green	55	55
586.		8 c. blue	55	55

99. Artigas.

100. Pegasus.

1929.

595.	99.	1 p. brown	2·00	1·10
596.		2 p. green	4·50	2·75
597.		2 p. red	7·00	4·50
760.		2 p. blue	4·50	2·25
598.		3 p. blue	8·50	5·50
761.		3 p. black	8·50	4·50
600.		4 p. violet	10·00	7·00
601.		4 p. olive	8·50	4·75
602.		5 p. brown	14·00	10·00
603.		5 p. orange	11·00	5·50
604.		10 p. blue	35·00	23·00
605.		10 p. red	35·00	29·00

1929. Air. Size $34\frac{1}{2} \times 23\frac{1}{2}$ mm.

617.	100.	1 c. mauve	15	15
659.		1 c. blue	15	15
618.		2 c. yellow	15	15
660.		2 c. olive	15	15
619.		4 c. blue	20	20
661.		4 c. lake	20	20
620.		6 c. violet	30	30
662.		6 c. brown	20	20
621.		8 c. orange	1·75	1·40
663.		8 c. grey	1·75	1·40
664.		8 c. green	20	20
622.		16 c. blue	1·10	1·10
665.		16 c. red	1·10	1·10
623.		24 c. purple	1·10	1·10
666.		24 c. violet	2·00	1·90
624.		30 c. brown	1·40	1·40
667.		30 c. green	55	35
625.		40 c. brown	2·50	2·25
668.		40 c. orange	2·25	1·90
626.		60 c. blue	2·00	2·00
669.		60 c. green	2·75	2·75
670.		60 c. red	70	70
627.		80 c. blue	4·25	3·75
671.		80 c. green	5·50	5·00
628.		90 c. blue	3·50	2·75
672.		90 c. olive	5·50	5·00
629.		1 p. red	2·75	2·50
630.		1 p. 20 olive	10·00	9·00
673.		1 p. 20 red	10·00	9·00
631.		1 p. 50 purple ..	10·00	9·00
674.		1 p. 50 sepia	4·50	4·50
632.		3 p. red	14·00	13·00
675.		3 p. blue	8·50	8·50
633.		4 p. 50 black	17·00	14·00
676.		4 p. 50 lilac	11·00	11·00
677.		10 p. blue	8·50	7·00

For stamps as T **100,** but smaller, see 1935 issue.

101. Rio Negro Bridge.

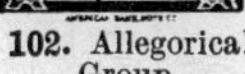

102. Allegorical Group. 103. Artigas Monument.

1930. Independence Cent.
639. 101. 5 m. black 8 8
640. – 1 c. sepia 10 8
641. 102. 2 c. lake 8 8
642. – 3 c. green 12 8
643. – 5 c. blue 15 5
644. – 8 c. red 15 12
645. – 10 c. violet 20 15
646. – 15 c. green 30 25
647. – 20 c. blue 50 30
648. – 24 c. lake 50 35
649. – 50 c. red .. .. 1·75 1·00
650. 103. 1 p. black .. .. 2·00 85
651. 2 p. blue .. .. 3·50 2·00
652. 3 p. red .. .. 5·00 3·00
653. 4 p. orange .. .. 7·00 4·25
654. 5 p. lilac .. .. 10·00 5·50
DESIGNS—HORIZ. 1 c. Allegorical group. 5 c. Head of Liberty and Uruguayan flag. 10 c. "Artigas," from picture by Blanes. 15 c. Seascape. 20 c. Montevideo Harbour, 1830. 24 c. Head of Liberty and Arms of Uruguay. 50 c. Montevideo Harbour, 1930. VERT. 3 c. Artigas Monument and buildings. 8 c. Allegorical figure with torch.

104. 105. J. Zorrilla de San Martin.

1930. Fund for Old People.
655. 104. 1 c.+1 c. violet 10 8
656. 2 c.+2 c. green .. 15 10
657. 5 c.+5 c. red 10 8
658. 8 c.+8 c. blue .. 15 10

1932.
679. 105. 1½ c. purple 8 5
680. 3 c. green 12 5
681. 7 c. blue 15 5
682. 12 c. blue 25 8
683. 1 p. brown .. .. 7·00 5·50

1932. Surch.
684. 104. 1½ c. on 2 c.+2 c. green 15 15

106. J. Zorrilla de San Martin. 107. Flag of the Race.

1933. Various portraits.
689. 95. 15 m. red (Lavalleja).. 5 5
690. 3 c. green (Rivera) .. 5 5
691. 106. 7 c. grey 8 5

1933. Columbus' Departure from Palos. 441st Anniv.
692. 107. 3 c. green 15 10
693. 5 c. red 20 12
694. 7 c. blue 15 10
695. 8 c. red 35 25
696. 12 c. blue 25 12
697. 17 c. violet 50 30
698. 20 c. lake .. .. 1·00 45
699. 24 c. orange .. .. 1·10 55
700. 36 c. red .. .. 1·40 1·00
701. 50 c. brown .. .. 1·75 1·10
702. 1 p. brown .. .. 4·25 2·75

108. Sower. 109. Map and Albatross.

1933. Opening of the 3rd National Assembly.
703. 108. 3 c. green 12 8
704. 5 c. violet 20 15
705. 7 c. blue 15 8
706. 8 c. red 35 20
707. 12 c. blue 45 25

1933. 7th Pan-American Conference, Montevideo.
708. 109. 3 c. grn., brn. & black 1·10 1·00
709. 7 c. blue, blk. & brown 1·10 1·00
710. 12 c. blue, red & grey 1·10 1·00
711. 17 c. red, blue & grey 1·75 1·40
712. 20 c. yell., grn. & blue 2·00 1·40
713. 36 c. red, yell. & black 2·50 2·00

1934. Air. Closure of the 7th Pan-American Conference. Optd. **SERVICIO POSTAL AEREO 1-1-34** in circle.
714. 109. 17 c. red, blue and grey 8·50 7·50
715. 36 c. red, yell. & black 8·50 7·50

110.

1934. Third Republic. 1st Anniv.
716. 110. 3 c. green 25 20
717. 7 c. red 25 20
718. 12 c. blue 45 30
719. 17 c. brown and pink 70 35
720. 20 c. yellow and grey 85 55
721. 36 c. violet and green 1·10 95
722. 50 c. grey and blue .. 1·75 1·10
723. 1 p. red and mauve .. 4·25 2·40

1935. Air. As T 100, but size $31\frac{1}{2} \times 21\frac{1}{2}$ mm.
725. 15 c. yellow .. .. 1·00 1·00
726. 22 c. red 55 55
727. 30 c. purple 85 85
728. 37 c. purple 45 30
729. 40 c. claret 55 50
730. 47 c. red .. .. 1·75 1·75
731. 50 c. blue 55 25
732. 52 c. blue .. .. 1·75 1·75
733. 57 c. blue 85 85
734. 62 c. olive-green .. 55 30
735. 87 c. green .. .. 2·00 2·00
736. 1 p. olive .. .. 1·10 85
737. 1 p. 12 brown .. 1·10 1·00
738. 1 p. 20 brown .. 5·00 5·00
739. 1 p. 27 brown .. 7·00 7·00
740. 1 p. 62 red .. .. 4·50 4·50
741. 2 p. lake .. .. 5·00 5·00
742. 2 p. 12 grey .. .. 7·50 7·50
743. 3 p. blue .. .. 5·00 5·00
744. 5 p. orange .. .. 14·00 14·00

111. Friendship of Uruguay and Brazil. 112. Florencio Sanchez.

1935. Visit of President Vargas of Brazil.
747. 111. 5 m. brown 45 25
748. 15 m. black 25 20
749. 3 c. green 25 20
750. 7 c. orange 25 20
751. 12 c. blue 55 35
752. 50 c. brown .. .. 2·25 1·40

1935. F. Sanchez (dramatist). 25th Death Anniv.
753. 112. 3 c. green 5 5
754. 7 c. brown 8 8
755. 12 c. blue 30 15

113. Rio Negro Dam. 114. Artigas.

1937.
780. 113. 1 c. violet (postage) .. 5 5
781. 10 c. blue 25 10
782. 15 c. red 35 15
783. 1 p. brown .. .. 2·00 1·00

793. 113. 8 c. green (air) .. 30 30
794. 20 c. green 85 45
785. 35 c. brown .. .. 4·25 2·50
786. 62 c. green 45 12
787. 68 c. orange 85 70
788. 68 c. brown 85 30
789. 75 c. violet .. .. 4·50 1·10
790. 1 p. red .. .. 1·10 85
791. 1 p. 38 c. red .. 8·50 7·00
792. 3 p. blue .. .. 5·00 85

1939. (a) Plain background.
806. 114. 5 m. orange 5 5
807. 1 c. blue 5 5
808. 2 c. violet 5 5
809. 5 c. brown 5 5
810. 8 c. red 8 5
811. 10 c. green 25 5
812. 15 c. blue 55 35
813. 1 p. brown 85 35
1008. 1 p. purple 55 25
814. 2 p. lilac .. .. 2·00 85
815. 4 p. orange .. .. 4·00 2·00
816. 5 p. red .. .. 4·50 2·50
Nos. 806/12 are size 16×19 mm. No. 1008 is 18×22 mm. and Nos. 813/6 are $24 \times 29\frac{1}{2}$ mm.

(b) Lined background. (i) Size 17×22 mm.
835. 114. 5 m. orange 5 5
848. 5 m. black 5 5
849. 5 m. blue 5 5
836. 1 c. blue 5 5
837. 1 c. purple 5 5
838. 2 c. violet 5 5
839. 2 c. orange 5 5
840. 2 c. brown 5 5
1152. 2 c. grey 5 5
841. 3 c. green 5 5
842. 5 c. brown 5 5
843. 7 c. blue 5 5
850. 8 c. red 8 5
845. 10 c. green 15 8
851. 10 c. brown 5 5
852. 12 c. blue 8 5
853. 20 c. magenta .. 20 8
846. 50 c. olive-bistre .. 2·75 1·40
847. 50 c. green .. .. 2·00 1·00
1153. 50 c. brown 8 5

(ii) Size $23\frac{1}{2} \times 29\frac{1}{2}$ mm.
1024. 114. 2 p. brown .. .. 2·75 2·00

115. Aeroplane over Covered Ox-cart.

1939. Air.
817. 115. 20 c. grey 25 20
818. 20 c. violet 35 45
819. 20 c. blue 30 20
820. 35 c. red 50 40
821. 50 c. red 45 15
822. 75 c. red 55 8
823. 1 p. blue .. .. 1·40 5
824. 1 p. 38 mauve .. 2·25 70
825. 1 p. 38 orange .. 2·75 2·25
826. 2 p. blue .. .. 3·50 40
827. 5 p. lilac .. .. 5·00 1·10
828. 5 p. green .. .. 4·50 2·00
829. 10 p. red .. .. 38·00 23·00

116. Congress of Montevideo.

1939. 1st Int. Juridical Congress, Montivideo. 50th Anniv.
830. 116. 1 c. red 8 8
831. 2 c. green 12 8
832. 5 c. red 15 12
833. 12 c. blue 30 15
834. 50 c. violet .. .. 1·25 70

117. Juan Manuel Blanes (artist). 118. Fransisco Acuna de Figueroa.

1941. Honouring Blanes.
855. 117. 5 m. brown 12 8
856. 1 c. brown 12 8
857. 2 c. green 12 8
858. 5 c. red 30 8
859. 12 c. blue 55 25
860. 50 c. violet .. .. 2·25 1·40

1942. Honouring Figueroa (author of words of National Anthem).
863. 118. 1 c. red 8 8
864. 2 c. green 8 8
865. 5 c. red 15 5
866. 12 c. blue 35 15
867. 50 c. violet .. .. 1·10 90

1943. Surch. **Valor $0,005.**
873. 114. 5 m. on 1 c. blue .. 8 8

119. 120. Clio.

1943.
874. 119. 1 c. on 2 c. brown .. 5 5
875. 2 c. on 2 c. brown .. 8 5

1943. Historical and Geographical Institute. Montevideo. Cent.
878. 120. 5 m. violet 12 5
879. 1 c. blue 12 5
880. 2 c. red 15 8
881. 5 c. brown 15 8

121. 122. Emblems of Y.M.C.A.

1944. Swiss Colony. 75th Anniv.
889. 121. 1 c. on 3 c. green .. 8 5
890. 5 c. on 7 c. brown .. 15 8
891. 10 c. on 12 c. blue .. 30 15

1944. Young Men's Christian Assn. Cent.
892. 122. 5 c. blue 8 5

1944. Air. Air stamps of 1935, Nos. 730, etc., surch.
893. 40 c. on 47 c. red.. .. 35 25
894. 40 c. on 57 c. blue .. 45 35
895. 74 c. on 1 p. 12 brown .. 45 30
896. 79 c. on 87 c. green .. 1·75 1·40
897. 79 c. on 1 p. 27 brown .. 2·75 2·25
898. 1 p. 20 on 1 p. 62 red .. 1·10 70
899. 1 p. 43 on 2 p. 12 grey .. 1·10 90

123. Legislative Palace.

1945. Air.
900. 123. 2 p. blue .. .. 1·75 85

124. Varela's Book. 125. Varela's Monument.

1945. J. P. Varela. Birth Cent.
901. 124. 5 m. green 5 5
902. – 1 c. brown (Varela) .. 5 5
903. – 2 c. red (Statue) .. 8 5
904. 125. 5 c. blue 10 5
Nos. 902/3 are vert.

126. E. Acevedo. 127. J. P. Varela.

1945.
905. – 5 m. violet 5 5
911. – 1 c. brown 5 5
912. 126. 2 c. purple 5 5
945. – 3 c. green 5 5
906. 127. 5 c. red 8 5
907. – 10 c. blue 15 5
946. – 20 c. brown and green 55 12
PORTRAITS: 5 m. S. Vazquez. 1 c. S. Blanco. 3 c. B. M. de Zabala. 10 c. J. Ellauri. 20 c Col. Luis de Larrobia.

1945. Air.. Victory. Surch. figure as "Victory of Samothrace", **1945** and new value. No. 908 optd. **VICTORIA** also.
914. 115. 14 c. on 50 c. red .. 25 20
915. 23 c. on 50 c. red .. 35 25
916. 23 c. on 1 p. 38 orange 35 25
908. 100. 44 c. on 75 c. brown .. 55 30
917. 115. 1 p. on 1 p. 38 orange.. 1·60 1·40

128. Sailing Ship "La Eolo".

1945. Air.

913.	128.	8 c. green	35	15

1946. Inaug. of Rio Negro Power Dam. Optd. **INAUGURACION DICIEMBRE, 1945** or **CORREO** and surch. also.

918.	113.	20 c. on 68 c. brown (postage)	45	30
919.		62 c. green (air) ..	40	35

1946. As T 119. (a) Postage. Optd. **CORREOS** and Caduceus.

920.	119.	5 m. orange	5	5
921.		2 c. brown	5	5
922.		3 c. green	5	5
923.		5 c. blue	5	5
924.		10 c. brown	8	5
925.		20 c. green	25	10
926.		50 c. brown	70	25
927.		3 p. red	2·75	1·75

(b) Air. Optd. **SERVICIO AEREO** and an aeroplane.

928.	119.	8 c. red	5	5
929.		50 c. brown	45	30
930.		1 p. blue	70	25
931.		2 p. olive	2·50	1·75
932.		3 p. red	2·75	2·00
933.		5 p. red	5·50	4·25

129. Four-Engined Aeroplane. 130. National Airport.

1947. Air.

947.	129.	3 c. brown	8	5
948.		8 c. red	10	8
949.		10 c. black	5	5
950.		10 c. red	8	5
951.		14 c. blue	15	12
952.		15 c. brown	8	8
953.		20 c. purple	8	8
954.		21 c. lilac	15	10
955.		23 c. green	25	15
956.		27 c. green	12	8
957.		31 c. chocolate ..	15	8
958.		36 c. blue	15	8
959.		36 c. black	15	5
960.		50 c. light blue ..	20	15
961.		50 c. deep blue ..	15	15
962.		62 c. blue	25	20
963.		65 c. red	45	25
964.		84 c. orange	20	20
941.	130.	1 p. brown and red ..	1·00	20
965.	129.	1 p. 8 c. plum ..	55	45
966.		2 p. blue	85	60
942.	130.	3 p. brown and blue ..	2·00	1·75
967.	129.	3 p. orange	1·40	1·00
943.	130.	5 p. brown & green ..	3·50	2·25
968.	129.	5 p. green	4·50	2·50
969.		5 p. slate	1·60	1·10
944.	130.	10 p. brown & purple	4·50	3·50
970.	129.	10 p. green	8·50	5·50

1947. As T 119 but surch. in figures above shield and wavy lines.

976.		2 c. on 5 c. blue ..	5	5
977.		3 c. on 5 c. blue ..	5	5

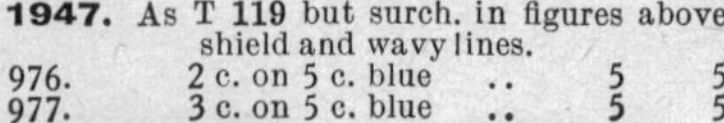

131. "Ariel". 132. Bas-reliefs.

1948. Unveiling of Monument to J. E. Rodo (writer).

978.	131.	1 c. brown and olive ..	5	5
979.	–	2 c. brown and violet	5	5
980.	132.	3 c. brown and green	8	5
981.		5 c. brown and mauve	8	5
982.		10 c. brown and red ..	12	8
983.		12 c. brown and blue	15	12
984.	131.	20 c. brown and purple	30	15
985.	–	50 c. brown and red ..	85	30

DESIGN: 2 c., 50 c. Statue of J. E. Rodo.

The 5 c. and 12 c. are as T 132 but inscr. "UN GRAN AMOR ES EL ALMA MISMA DE QUIEN AMA".

1948. Air. As T 119, optd. **AVIACION** and aeroplane.

986.	12 c. blue	12	5
987.	24 c. green	25	15
988.	36 c. grey	35	20

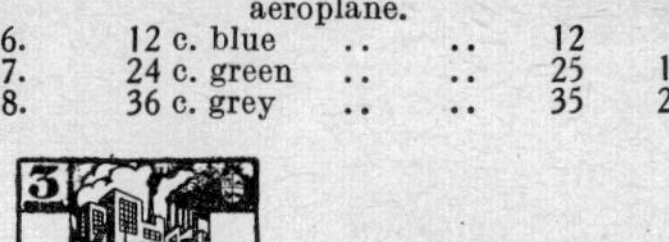

133. Factories, Steam and Sailing Vessels and Basket of Fruit. 134. River Santa Lucia Bridge.

1948. Industrial and Agricultural Exhibitions, Paysandu.

989.	133.	3 c. green	5	5
990.	–	7 c. blue	10	5

DESIGN—HORIZ. 7 c. Livestock, sower and shield.

1948. Uruguayan-Brazilian Friendship.

991.	134.	10 c. blue	12	8
992.		50 c. green	85	35

136. Medical Faculty.

DESIGNS: 15 c. Architectural faculty. 31 c. Engineering faculty. 36 c. View of University.

1949. Air. Montevideo University Centenary.

995.	–	15 c. red	8	8
996.	136.	27 c. brown	12	8
997.	–	31 c. blue	25	8
998.	–	36 c. green	25	8

135. Ploughing.

1949. 4th American Labour Conf.

993.	135.	3 c. green	10	5
994.	–	7 c. blue	15	5

DESIGN—HORIZ. 7 c. Horseman herding cattle.

137. Cannon and Buildings. 138. Kicking Football.

1950. Cordon (district of Montevideo). 200th Anniv.

1003.	137.	1 c. mauve	5	5
1004.		3 c. green	5	5
1005.		7 c. blue	8	5

1951. 4th World Football Championship.

1106.	138.	3 c. green	55	15
1007.		7 c. blue	1·10	25

139. Gen. Artigas. 140. Emigration from Eastern Provinces.

1952. Cent. of Death of Artigas. Dated "1950".

1009.	139.	5 m. indigo	5	5
1010.	–	1 c. black and blue ..	5	5
1011.	–	2 c. brown and violet	8	5
1012.	140.	3 c. sepia and green	5	5
1013.	–	5 c. black and orange	8	5
1014.	–	7 c. black and olive ..	8	5
1015.	–	8 c. black and red ..	8	5
1016.	–	10 c. red, blue & brn.	10	5
1017.	–	14 c. blue	8	5
1018.	–	20 c. red, blue & yell.	12	8
1019.	–	50 c. olive and brown	30	20
1020.	–	1 p. yell.-olive & blue	85	50

DESIGNS (all show Artigas except 10 c. and 20 c.)—As T 139: 1 c. at Las Huerfanas. 2 c. at Battle of Las Piedras. 14 c. at Cuidadela. 20 c. Arms. 50 c. in Paraguay. 1 p. Bust. As T 140: 7 c. Dictating instructions. 8 c. in Congress. 10 c. Flag.

141. Aeroplane over Mail Coach. 142. Franklin D. Roosevelt.

1952. 75th Anniv. of U.P.U.

1021.	141.	3 c. green	8	5
1022.		7 c. black	8	5
1023.		12 c. blue	12	8

1953. 5th Postal Congress of the Americas and Spain.

1025.	142.	3 c. green	5	5
1026.		7 c. blue	8	5
1027.		12 c. brown	15	8

143. Ceibo (National Flower). 144. Ombu Tree.

145. Parliament House. 146.

1954.

1028.	143.	5 m. multicoloured ..	5	5
1029.	–	1 c. black and red ..	5	5
1030.	144.	2 c. green and brown	5	5
1031.	–	3 c. multicoloured ..	5	5
1032.	145.	5 c. chocolate and lilac	5	5
1033.	–	7 c. green and brown	5	5
1034.	–	8 c. blue and red ..	45	5
1035.	144.	10 c. green and orange	12	5
1036.	–	12 c. sepia and blue	5	5
1037.	–	14 c. black and purple	12	5
1038.	143.	20 c. multicoloured ..	30	5
1039.	–	50 c. multicoloured ..	70	12
1040.	145.	1 p. brown and red ..	50	25
1041.	–	2 p. sepia and red ..	1·10	45
1042.	–	3 p. green and lilac ..	2·00	1·00
1043.	–	4 p. blue and brown ..	8·50	1·75
1044.	144.	5 p. green and blue ..	4·25	2·00

DESIGNS—As T 143: 3 c., 50 c. Passion flower. As T 144—HORIZ. 1 c., 14 c. Gaucho breaking-in horse. VERT. 7 c., 3 p. Montevideo Citadel. As T 145—VERT. 8 c., 4 p. Lighthouse and seals. HORIZ. 12 c., 2 p. Outer Gateway of Montevideo, 1836.

1956. 1st National Production Exn. Inscr. as in T 146.

1050.	146.	3 c. green (postage) ..	5	5
1051.		7 c. blue	5	5
1052.	–	20 c. blue (air) ..	15	5
1053.	–	31 c. green	30	20
1054.	–	36 c. red	55	30

DESIGN—HORIZ. Nos. 1052/41, Exn. symbol and two 'planes.

147. Uruguay's First Stamp and "Diligencia". 148. Pres. Jose Batlle y Ordonez.

1956. Air. Uruguay Stamp Centenary. Stamp in blue.

1055.	147.	20 c. green and yellow	40	20
1056.		31 c. sepia and blue	40	25
1057.		36 c. lake and pink ..	40	30

1956. Pres. Batlle y Ordonez. Birth Cent.

1058.	148.	3 c. red (postage) ..	5	5
1059.	–	7 c. sepia	5	5
1060.	–	10 c. magenta (air) ..	8	5
1061.	148.	20 c. slate	12	8
1062.	–	31 c. brown ..	20	15
1063.	–	36 c. green ..	20	15

PORTRAITS OF PRESIDENT—VERT. 7 c. Wearing overcoat. 10 c. Similar to T 148. 36 c. Profile, facing right. HORIZ. 31 c. Seated at desk.

1957. Surch. **5** or **10 Cts.**

1071.	148.	5 c. on 3 c. red ..	5	5
1072.	–	10 c. on 7 c. sepia (No. 1059)	5	5

149. High diver. 150. Dr. Eduardo Acevedo (lawyer).

1958. 14th S. American Swimming Championships, Montevideo. Inscr. as in T 149.

1073.	149.	5 c. green	8	5
1074.	–	10 c. blue	10	5

DESIGN—HORIZ. 10 c. Diving.

1958. Dr. Eduardo Acevedo. Birth Cent.

1075.	150.	5 c. black and green	5	5
1076.		10 c. black and blue	5	5

151. Flags. 152. Baygorria Dam.

1958. Air. Day of the Americas.

1077.	151.	23 c. black and blue	15	12
1078.		34 c. black and green	25	20
1079.		44 c. black and magenta	35	25

1958. Baygorria Hydro-Electric Power Station Inaug. Inscr. as in T 152.

1080.	152.	5 c. black and green	5	5
1081.		10 c. black and brown	5	5
1082.	–	1 p. black and blue ..	20	8
1083.	–	2 p. black and magenta	45	25

DESIGN: 1 p., 2 p. Aerial view of dam.

153. "Flame of Freedom". 154.

1958. Air. Declaration of Human Rights. 10th Anniv.

1084.	153.	23 c. black and blue	15	5
1085.		34 c. black and green	25	12
1086.		44 c. black and red ..	45	25

1958. Nos. 1028, 1031 and 1033 surch. with Caduceus and value.

1087.	5 c. on 3 c. yellow, rose, blue and green ..	5	5
1088.	10 c. on 7 c. grn. & brown	5	5
1089.	20 c. on 5 m. red, brown green and grey ..	5	5

1959. Air. Centres in black.

1090.	154.	3 c. brown	5	5
1091.		8 c. mauve	5	5
1092.		38 c. black	5	5
1093.		50 c. yellow	8	8
1094.		60 c. violet	12	8
1095.		90 c. olive	15	12
1096.		1 p. blue	15	15
1097.		2 p. orange	85	55
1098.		3 p. green	1·00	75
1099.		5 p. purple	1·10	1·00
1100.		10 p. red	4·25	3·25

See also T 163.

155. Santos Dumont and his Aeroplane.

1959. Air. Santos Dumont Commem.
1101. **155.** 31 c. multicoloured .. 12 8
1102. 36 c. multicoloured .. 12 8

156. "Tourism in Uruguay". **157.** Gabriela Mistral (poet).

1959. Air. Tourist Publicity and 50th Anniv. of Punta de Este. Inscr. as in T **156.**
1103. **156.** 10 c. blue and ochre .. 8 5
1104. – 38 c. buff and green .. 12 5
1105. – 60 c. buff and violet 15 12
1106. **156.** 90 c. green and red .. 15 15
1107. – 1 p. 05 buff and blue 25 15
DESIGN: 38 c., 60 c., 1 p. 05, Beach and compass.

1959. Gabriela Mistral Commem.
1108. **157.** 5 c. green 5 5
1109. 10 c. blue 5 5
1110. 20 c. red 8 5

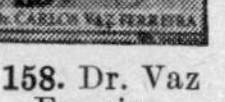

158. Dr. Vaz Ferreira. **159.** Emblem of Y.M.C.A.

1959. Honouring Dr. Carlos Vaz Ferreira (philosopher). Commem.
1111. **158.** 5 c. black and blue .. 5 5
1112. 10 c. black and ochre 5 5
1113. 20 c. black and red .. 5 5
1114. 50 c. black and violet 15 5
1115. 1 p. black and green .. 25 8

1959. Air. 50th Anniv. of Y.M.C.A. in Uruguay.
1116. **159.** 38 c. blk., grey & green 25 20
1117. 50 c. blk., grey & blue 25 25
1118. 60 c. black, grey & red 30 30

160. Boy and Dam. **161.** Artigas and Washington.

1959. National Recovery.
1119. **160.** 5 c.+10 c. green and orange (postage) .. 5 5
1120. 10 c.+10 c. blue & orge. 5 5
1121. 1 p. +10 c. vio. & orge. 20 20
1122. 38 c.+10 c. chocolate and orange (air) .. 15 8
1123. 60 c.+10 c. grn. & orge. 15 12

1960. Air. Visit of President Eisenhower.
1124. **161.** 38 c. black and red .. 15 10
1125. 50 c. black and blue .. 15 12
1126. 60 c. black and green .. 20 15

1960. Air. Surch. with Caduceus and value.
1128. **129.** 20 c. on 27 c. green .. 8 5

162. Dr. M. C. Martinez. **163.** Statue on Lanza Monument.

1960. Dr. Martin C. Martinez. Birth Cent.
1129. **162.** 3 c. black and purple 5 5
1130. 5 c. black and violet 5 5
1131. 10 c. black and blue .. 5 5
1132. 20 c. black & chocolate 5 5
1133. 1 p. black and grey .. 25 8
1134. 2 p. black and orange 40 25
1135. 3 p. black and olive 55 35
1136. 4 p. black and brown 70 35
1137. 5 p. black and red .. 85 45

1960. Air.
1138. **163.** 3 c. black and lilac .. 5 5
1139. 20 c. black and red 5 5
1140. 38 c. black & light blue 5 5
1141. 50 c. black and buff 8 8
1142. 60 c. black and green 10 8
1143. 90 c. black and claret 15 12
1144. 1 p. black and grey .. 15 10
1145. 2 p. black and green 40 30
1146. 3 p. black and purple 50 35
1147. 5 p. black and salmon 70 55
1148. 10 p. black and yellow 1·75 1·40
1149. 20 p. black and blue .. 4·00 2·75

164. Refugees. **165.** Scene of Revolution.

1960. World Refugee Year. Inscr. as in T **164.**
1150. – 10 c. black & bl. (post.) 5 5
1151. **164.** 60 c. black & mag. (air) 20 15
DESIGN: 10 c. "Uprooted tree".

1960. Argentine May Revolution. 150th Anniv.
1154. **165.** 5 c. blk., & blue (post.) 5 5
1155. 10 c. brown and blue 5 5
1156. 38 c. olive & blue (air) 12 8
1157. 50 c. red and blue .. 15 12
1158. 60 c. violet and blue 15 15

166. Pres. M. Oribe **167.** Pres. Gronchi.

1961. Honouring President Oribe.
1159. **166.** 10 c. black and blue 5 5
1160. 20 c. black and brown 5 5
1161. 40 c. black and green 8 5

1961. Air. Visit of President of Italy.
1162. **167.** 90 c. slate-purple, red, green and blue .. 25 20
1163. 1 p. 20 ochre, red, green and blue 25 25
1164. 1 p. 40 violet, red, green and blue 30 25

168. Carrasco Airport Building.

1961. Air. Carrasco National Airport.
1165. **168.** 1 p. grey and violet .. 15 8
1166. 2 p. grey and olive .. 35 20
1167. 3 p. grey and yellow .. 45 30
1168. 4 p. grey and dull purple 55 45
1169. 5 p. grey and turquoise 70 50
1170. 10 p. grey and blue .. 1·60 1·10
1171. 20 p. grey and claret 3·25 2·75

169. "Charging Horsemen" (by C. M. Herrera). **170.** Welfare, Justice and Education.

1961. February 28th Revolution. 150th Anniv.
1172. **169.** 20 c. black and blue .. 5 5
1173. 40 c. black and green 8 5

1961. Latin-American Economic Commission Conference, Punta del Este. (a) Postage. Centres in bistre.
1174. **170.** 2 c. violet 5 5
1175. 5 c. orange 5 5
1176. 10 c. red 5 5
1177. 20 c. green 5 5
1178. 50 c. lilac 8 5
1179. 1 p. blue 15 8
1180. 2 p. olive-yellow .. 30 15
1181. 3 p. purple-grey .. 45 25
1182. 4 p. blue 70 35
1183. 5 p. brown 85 55

(b) Air. Centres in black.
1184. **170.** 20 c. orange .. 5 5
1185. 45 c. green .. 8 8
1186. 50 c. purple 8 8
1187. 90 c. violet 12 10
1188. 1 p. rose 15 12
1189. 1 p. 40 lilac .. 15 15
1190. 2 p. ochre 25 25
1191. 3 p. blue 55 35
1192. 4 p. yellow 60 50
1193. 5 p. blue 70 55
1194. 10 p. apple-green .. 1·75 1·10
1195. 20 p. magenta .. 3·50 2·40

171. Gen. Rivera (First President). **172.** Symbols of Swiss Settlers.

1962. Honouring Gen. Fructuoso Rivera.
1196. **171.** 10 c. black and red .. 5 5
1197. 20 c. black and ochre 5 5
1198. 40 c. black and green 8 5

1962. First Swiss Settlers. Cent.
1199. **172.** 10 c. red, black and blue (postage) .. 5 5
1200. 20 c. red, black & green 5 5
1201. – 90 c. black, red and orange (air) .. 25 20
1202. – 1 p. 40 blk., red & blue 30 25
DESIGN—HORIZ. 90 c., 1 p. 40, Wheatsheaf, harvester and Swiss flag.

173. B. P. Berro. **174.** Red-crested Cardinal.

1962. Honouring President B. P. Berro.
1203. **173.** 10 c. black and blue 5 5
1204. 20 c. black and brown 5 5

1962. Birds.
1205. 2 c. choc., pink & blk. (post) 5 5
1206. 50 c. chestnut and black .. 8 5
1207. 1 p. brown and black .. 15 12
1208. 2 p. black, chest. & grey .. 45 30
1209. 20 c. red, blk. & grey (air) 5 5
1210. 45 c. red, blue and black .. 10 5
1211. 90 c. brown, black and red 15 8
1212. 1 p. blue, black and brown 15 8
1213. 1 p. 20 black, brown, yellow and turquoise .. 25 15
1214. 1 p. 40 brown, black & blue 25 15
1215. 2 p. yell., black & brn-red 25 15
1216. 3 p. black, yellow & brown 40 25
1217. 5 p. black, blue and green 55 50
1218. 10 p. violet-blue, yellow, black and orange .. 1·10 95
1219. 20 p. orange, black & grey 5·50 2·25
BIRDS—HORIZ. 2 c. Chocolate Ground-tyrant. 45 c. White-capped Tanager. 50 c. Rufous Ovenbird. 1 p. (1207), Mockingbird. 1 p. (1212), Shiny Cowbird. 1 p. 20, Great Kiskadee. 2 p. (1208), Rufous-collared Sparrow. 2 p. (1215), Yellow Cardinal. 3 p. Black-headed Siskin. 5 p. Blue Tanager. 10 p. Blue and Yellow Tanager. 20 p. Scarlet-headed Marsh Bird. VERT. 20 c. T **174.** 90 c. Vermilion Flycatcher. 1 p. 40 Fork-tailed Flycatcher.

Nos. 1208, 1210, 1212 and 1215 have no frame; Nos. 1206 and 1214 have a thin frame line; the others are as T **174.**

175. D. A. Larranaga.

1963. Honouring D. A. Larranaga (founder of National Library).
1220. **175.** 20 c. sepia and turquoise 5 5
1221. 40 c. sepia and drab .. 8 5

176. U.P.A.E. Emblem. **177.** Campaign Emblem.

1963. Postal Union of the Americas and Spain. 50th Anniv.
1222. **176.** 20 c. blue & black (post.) 5 5
1223. 45 c. green & blk. (air) 8 8
1224. 90 c. red and black .. 15 12

1963. Freedom from Hunger.
1225. **177.** 10 c. yell. & grn. (post.) 5 5
1226. 20 c. yellow and brown 5 5
1227. **177.** 90 c. yellow & red (air) 15 12
1228. 1 p. 40 yellow & violet 20 15

178. Anchors. **179.** Large Intestine, Congress Emblem.

1963. World Voyage of "Alferez Campora".
1229. **178.** 10 c. vio. & orge. (post.) 5 5
1230. 20 c. grey and red .. 5 5
1231. – 90 c. grn. & orge. (air) 12 10
1232. – 1 p. 40 blue and yellow 20 15
DESIGN: 90 c., 1 p. 40, "Alferez Campora" (sailing ship).

1963. 1st Uruguayan Proctological Congress, Punta del Este.
1233. **179.** 10 c. red, black & green 5 5
1234. 20 c. red, black & ochre 5 5

180. Centenary Emblem.

1964. Red Cross Centenary.
1235. **180.** 20 c. red and blue .. 5 5
1236. 40 c. red and grey .. 10 5

181. L. A. de Herrera (statesman).

1964. Luis A. de Herrera. 5th Death Anniv.
1237. **181.** 20 c. black, green & blue 5 5
1238. 40 c. black and blue .. 5 5
1239. 80 c. black, yell. & blue 10 5
1240. 1 p. black, lilac & blue 12 8
1241. 2 p. black, slate & blue 25 20

182. President de Gaulle.

1964. Air. Visit of President of France. Multicoloured.
1242. 1 p. 50 Type **182** .. 35 15
1243. 2 p. 40 Flags of France and Uruguay 70 45

183. Reliefs from Abu Simbel.

1964. Nubian Monuments Preservation. Multicoloured.
1244. 20 c. Type **183** (postage) 5 5
1245. 1 p. 30 Sphinx, Sebua (air) 12 10
1246. 2 p. Rameses II, Abu Simbel 15 20
Nos. 1245/6 are vert.

184. Arms. **185.** President Kennedy.

1965. Air.
1261. **184.** 20 p. blue, yellow, black and green .. 1·25 85
1248. – 50 p. blue, yell. & grey 2·75 2·25
DESIGN—HORIZ. (38 × 27 mm.): 50 p. National flag.

1965. Pres. Kennedy Commem. Frame and laurel in gold.
1249. **185.** 20 c. black & grn. (post.) 5 5
1250. 40 c. black and brown 5 5
1251. **185.** 1 p. 50 blk. & lilac (air) 12 10
1252. 2 p. 40 black and blue 20 20

186. "Tete-beche" Pair of Uruguayan 8 c. Stamps of 1864.

187. 6 c. "Arms-type" of 1864.

1965. 1st Rio Plate Stamp Exn., Montevideo.
(a) Postage. T **186.**
1253. 40 c. green and black .. 5 5

(b) Air. As T **187** showing Arms-type stamps of 1864 (values in brackets).
1254. 1 p. black and blue (12 c.) 8 8
1255. 1 p. black & orange (T **187**) 8 8
1256. 1 p. black & green (8 c.) .. 8 8
1257. 1 p. black & bistre (10 c.) 8 8
1258. 1 p. black and red (6 c.) .. 8 8
Nos. 1254/8 were issued together in sheets of 10 (5 × 2), each design arranged in a vertical pair with "URUGUAY" at top or bottom.

188. B. Nardone (statesman).

1965. Benito Nardone. 1st Death Anniv.
1259. **188.** 20 c. black and green .. 5 5
1260. – 40 c. black and green .. 5 5
DESIGN—VERT. 40 c. Portrait as T **188**, but Nardone with microphone.

189. Part of Artigas' speech before the 1813 Congress.

1965. Gen. Jose Artigas. Birth Bicent. (1964). Inscr. "1764–1964").
1262. **189.** 20 c. red, blue and yellow (postage) .. 5 5
1263. – 40 c. olive, black & blue 5 5
1264. – 80 c. multicoloured .. 8 5
1265. – 1 p. sepia, olive, red and blue (air) 8 5
1266. – 1 p. 50 multicoloured 12 8
1267. **189.** 2 p. 40 blue, red, sepia and brown .. 20 15
DESIGNS—HORIZ. 40 c. Bust of Artigas. 80 c. Artigas and his army flag. 1 p. 50, Bust, flag and exodus of his followers to Argentina. VERT. 1 p. Artigas' statue.

190. Football.

1965. Olympic Games, Tokyo (1964).
1269. **190.** 20 c. orange, black and green (postage) .. 5 5
1270. – 40 c. olive, black & brn. 5 5
1271. – 80 c. red, black & drab 5 5
1272. – 1 p. green, black & blue 8 5
1273. – 1 p. grey, blk. & red (air) 8 5
1274. – 1 p. 50 blue, blk. & grn. 12 5
1275. – 2 p. blue, blk. & claret 15 8
1276. – 2 p. 40 orge., blk. & bl. 15 8
1277. – 3 p. yellow, blk. & lilac 25 12
1278. – 20 p. pink, blue & indigo 1·00 60
DESIGNS: 40 c. Basketball. 80 c. Cycling. 1 p. (No. 1272) Swimming. 1 p. (No. 1273) Boxing. 1 p. 50, Running. 2 p. Fencing. 2 p. 40, Sculling. 3 p. Pistol-shooting. 20 p. Olympic "Rings".

1965. Surch. with Caduceus and value.
1280. **114.** 10 c. on 7 c. blue .. 5 5

1966. Uruguay Architects Assn. 50th Anniv. Surch. **CINCUENTENARIO Sociedad Arquitectos del Uruguay** and value.
1281. **160.** 4 c. on 5 c. + 10 c. green and orange .. 5 5

191. I.T.U. Emblem and Satellite.

1966. Air. I.T.U. Cent.
1282. **191.** 1 p. deep bl., red & blue 5 5

192. Sir Winston Churchill.

1966. Churchill Commem.
1283. **192.** 40 c. brown, red and ultramarine (post.) 5 5
1284. – 2 p. brn., red & gold (air) 8 5
DESIGN—VERT. 2 p. Churchill—full-face portrait and signed quotation.

193. Arms and View of Rio de Janeiro.

1966. Rio de Janeiro. 400th Anniv.
1285. **193.** 40 c. grn. & brn. (post.) 5 5
1286. 80 c. red & brown (air) 5 5

194. I.C.Y. Emblem.

1966. Air. I.C.Y.
1287. **194.** 1 p. black and green .. 5 5

195. Army Engineer. **196.** Pres. Shazar.

1966. Army Engineers. 50th Anniv.
1288. **195.** 20 c. red, blue, yellow and black 5 5

1966. Air. Visit of President of Israel.
1291. **196.** 7 p. black, yellow, purple and blue .. 20 15

197. Crested Screamer. **198.** Jules Rimet Cup, Ball and Globe.

1966. Air
1292. **197.** 100 p. multicoloured 2·75 2·25

1966. Air. World Cup Football Championships.
1293. **198.** 10 p. yellow and violet 25 15

199. Hereford Bull. **200.** Pres. L. B. Berres.

1966. Air. Cattle-breeding.
1294. **199.** 4 p. brn., chest. & sep. 15 5
1295. – 6 p. blk., grn. & turq. 20 8
1296. – 10 p. mar., grn. & turq. 35 15
1297. – 15 p. blk., red & orge. 55 20
1298. – 20 p. brn., yell. & grey 70 25
1299. – 30 p. brown & yellow 1·00 40
1300. – 50 p. brn., grey & grn. 1·75 70
DESIGNS (Cattle breeds): 6 p. Dutch. 10 p. Shorthorn. 15 p. Aberdeen Angus. 20 p. Norman. 30 p. Jersey. 50 p. Charolais.

1966. Former Uruguayan Presidents.
1301. **200.** 20 c. black and red .. 5 5
1302. – 20 c. black and blue 5 5
1303. – 20 c. brown and blue 5 5
PRESIDENTS: No. 1302, D. F. Crespo. 1303, W. Beltram.

201. Gutenberg Press. **202.** Capt. Boiso Lanza (pioneer military aviator).

1966. State Printing Works. 50th Anniv.
1304. **201.** 20 c. sepia, grn. & brn. 5 5

1966. Air. Honouring Boiso Lanza.
1305. **202.** 25 c. blk., bl. & ultram. 70 50

203. Fireman. **204.** General J. A. Lavalleja.

1966. Firemen's Corps. 50th Anniv.
1306. **203.** 20 c. black & vermilion 5 5

1966. 2nd Rio Plate Stamp Exn., Montevideo.
(a) Postage. No. 1253 optd. **Segunda Muestra y Jornados Rioplatenses,** etc.
1307. **187.** 40 c. green and black 5 5

(b) Air. Nos. 1254/8 optd. **CENTENARIO DEL SELLO ESCUDITO RESELLADO,** etc.
1308. 1 p. red 8 8
1309. 1 p. red 8 8
1310. 1 p. green 8 8
1311. 1 p. bistre 8 8
1312. 1 p. red 8 8
Nos. 1308/12 commemorate the cent. of Uruguay's first surcharged stamps.

1966. Heroes of War of Independence.
1313. **204.** 20 c. brn., red & blue 5 5
1314. – 20 c. blue, black & grey 5 5
1315. – 20 c. black and blue .. 5 5
DESIGNS—VERT. No. 1314, Gen. L. Gomez. HORIZ. 1315, Gen. A. Saravia on horseback.

1966. Air. Uruguayan Philatelic Club. 40th Anniv. No. 1036 surch. **40 ANIVERSARIO Club Filatelico del Uruguay $1.00 Aereo.**
1316. 1 p. on 12 c. sepia & blue 8 5

205. Dante. **206.** Sunflower.

1966. Air. Dante Commem.
1317. **205.** 50 c. brown and sepia 5 5

1967. Young Farmers' Movement. 20th Anniv.
1318. **206.** 40 c. sepia, yell. & brn. 5 5

207. Planetarium.

1967. Montevideo Planetarium. 10th Anniv.
1319. **207.** 40 c. blk. & mag. (post.) 5 5
1320. – 5 p. black & blue (air) 12 8
DESIGN: 5 p. Planetarium projector.

208. President Makarios. **209.** Dr. Schweitzer.

1967. Air. Visit of President of Cyprus.
1321. **208.** 6 p. 60 black & mauve 15 12

1967. Air. Schweitzer Commem.
1322. **209.** 6 p. multicoloured .. 10 8

210. Corriedale Ram. **212.** Church, San Carlos.

211. Uruguayan Flag and Globe.

1967. Air. Uruguayan Sheep-breeding.
1323. **210.** 3 p. blk., bistre & red 8 5
1324. – 4 p. blk., bistre & grn. 12 8
1325. – 5 p. blk., bistre & blue 15 8
1326. – 10 p. blk., bis. & yell. 35 15
DESIGNS (sheep breeds): 4 p. "Ideal". 5 p. Romney Marsh. 10 p. Australian merino.

1967. Air. Heads of State Meeting, Punta del Este.
1327. **211.** 10 p. gold, blue & blk. 20 15

1967. San Carlos. Bicent.
1328. **212.** 40 c. black, red & blue 5 5

213. E. Acevedo (lawyer and statesman). **215.** Ansina (Gen. Artigas' servant).

214. " Numeral " Stamps of 1866.

1967. Eduardo Acevedo Commem.
1329. **213.** 20 c. brown and green 5 5
1330. 40 c. green and orange 5 5

1967. Air. "Numeral Stamps of 1866. Cent.
1331. **214.** 3 p. blue, grn. & blk. 10 5
1332. – 6 p. ochre, red & blk. 12 8
DESIGN: 6 p. As T **214**, but depicting 15 c. and 20 c. stamps of 1866.

1967. Air. Honouring Ansina.
1334. **215.** 2 p. red, blue and black 5

216. Aircraft over Runway. **217.** Making Basket.

1967. Air. PLUNA Airline. 30th Anniv.
1335. **216.** 10 p. blue, red, black and yellow .. 20 15

1967. Air. World Basketball Championships, Montevideo. Multicoloured.
1336. 5 p. Type **217** 12 8
1337. 5 p. Running 12 8
1338. 5 p. Holding 12 8
1339. 5 p. Pivot 12 8
1340. 5 p. Dribbling 12 8

1967. Air. Nos. 1211 and 1223 surch. with new value in figures only.
1343. – 5 p. 90 on 45 c. red, blue and black .. 10 8
1344. **176.** 5 p. 90 on 45 c. green and black 10 8

218. Don Quixote and Sancho Panza (after Denry Torres).

1967. Air. Cervantes Commem.
1345. **218.** 8 p. brown and bistre 15 12

219. Arms of Carmelo. **220.** J. E. Rodo.

1967. Founding of Carmelo. 150th Anniv.
1346. **219.** 40 c. blue, ochre and light blue 5 5

1967. Jose E. Rodo (writer). 50th Death Anniv. Multicoloured.
1347. 1 p. Type **220** 5 5
1348. 2 p. Portrait and sculpture 5 5
The 2 p. is horiz.

221. S. Rodriguez (founder) Early Loco. and Modern Train. **222.** Child and Map of Americas.

1967. 1st National Railway Company in Uruguay. Cent.
1349. **221.** 2 p. brown and ochre 5 5

1967. Inter-American Children's Institute. 40th Anniv.
1350. **222.** 1 p. vermilion & violet 5 5

1967. No. 1033 surch. **1.00 PESO** and Caduceus.
1351. 1 p. on 7 c. green & brown 5 5

223. Primitive Club. **224.** Level Crossing and Traffic Sign.

1967. Air. Archaeological Discoveries. Each black and grey.
1352. 15 p. Type **223** 15 8
1353. 20 p. Lance-head .. 25 10
1354. 30 p. Axe-head .. 30 15
1355. 50 p. Sculptured "bird of El Polonio" 50 25
1356. 75 p. Cooking pot .. 70 35
1357. 100 p. Sculptured "bird" of Balizas .. .. 1·00 50
1358. 150 p. Spear-heads .. 1·40 80
1359. 200 p. Bolas .. .. 2·00 1·10

1967. Air. Pan American Highways Congress.
1360. **224.** 4 p. black, yellow & red 5 5

225. Lions Emblem and Map. **226.** Boy Scout.

1967. Air. Lions Int. 50th Anniv.
1361. **225.** 5 p. violet, yell. & grn. 8 5

1968. Air. Lord Baden-Powell Commem.
1362. **226.** 9 p. brown & orange 10 5

227. Great Blue Heron. **228.** Sun, Transport and U.N. Emblem.

1968. Birds.
1363. – 1 p. brown and buff.. 5 5
1364. **227.** 2 p. black and green 5 5
1365. – 3 p. pur., blk. & orge. 5 5
1366. – 4 p. black and brown 5 5
1367. – 4 p. black and orange 5 5
1368. – 5 p. black, yell. & brn. 5 5
1369. – 10 p. violet & black 8 5
BIRDS—VERT. 1 p. Great horned owl. 4 p. (No. 1367) Stilt. HORIZ. 3 p. Sea-gull. 4 p. (No. 1366), White-faced tree duck. 5 p. American jacana. 10 p. Snowy egret.

1968. Air. Int. Tourist Year (1967).
1370. **228.** 10 p. multicoloured.. 8 5

229. Presidents of Uruguay and Brazil, and Concord Bridge. **230.** Footballer.

1968. Opening of Concord Bridge between Uruguay and Brazil.
1371. **229.** 6 p. brown 5 5

1968. Penarol Clubs' Victory in Intercontinental Soccer Championships.
1372. **230.** 1 p. black and lemon 5 5

231. St. John Bosco.

1968. "Don Bosco Workshops". 75th Anniv.
1373. **231.** 2 p. black and brown 5 5

232. Octopus.

1968. Air. Uruguayan Marine Fauna.
1374. **232.** 15 p. black, blue and turq.-green .. 15 8
1375. – 20 p. brn., bl. & grn. 15 8
1376. – 25 p. orange, yellow, black and lilac .. 25 12
1377. – 30 p. black, green & bl. 30 15
1378. – 50 p. salmon, ultram. and green 50 25
DESIGNS—HORIZ. 20 p. Mackerel. 25 p. "Dorado". VERT. 30 p. "Surubi". 50 p. Squid.

233. Sailors' Monument, Montevideo.

1968. Uruguayan Navy. 150th Anniv.
1379. **233.** 2 p. black & green (postage) .. 5 5
1380. – 6 p. black and green.. 5 5
1381. – 12 p. black and blue 8 5
1382. – 4 p. blk., red & bl. (air) 5 5
1383. – 6 p. black, green, lemon and grey .. 5 5
1384. – 10 p. red, yell. & blue 8 5
1385. – 20 p. black and blue 15 10
DESIGNS—HORIZ. 4 p. Tailplane (Naval Air Force). 6 p. (No. 1383), Naval Arms. 12 p. Gunboat "Suarez". 20 p. Artigas's privateer. VERT. 6 p. (No. 1380), Buoy and lighthouse. 10 p. Mast-head and signal flags.

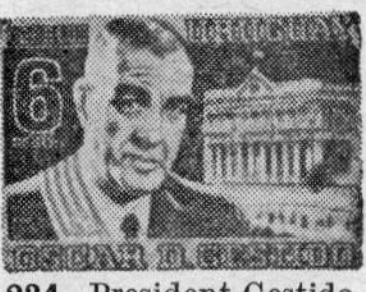

234. President Gestido.

1968. President Oscar D. Gestido. 1st Death Anniv.
1386. **234.** 6 p. brown, red & blue 5 5

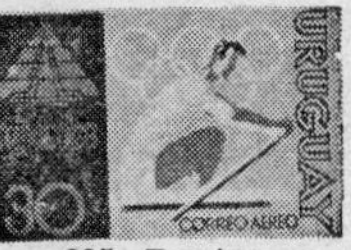

235. Rowing.

1969. Air. Olympic Games, Mexico.
1387. **235.** 30 p. black, brn. & bl. 25 15
1388. – 50 p. black, brn. & yell. 35 25
1389. – 100 p. blk., brn. & grn. 70 50
DESIGNS: 50 p. Running. 100 p. Football.

236. Cogwheel, Ear of Wheat and Two Heads.

1969. Uruguay Trades University. 25th Anniv.
1390. **236.** 2 p. black and red .. 5 5

237. Cycling.

1969. World Cycling Championships, Montevideo (1968).
1391. **237.** 6 p. blue, orange and green (postage) .. 5 5
1392. – 20 p. mult. (air) .. 15 10
DESIGN—VERT. 20 p. Cyclist and globe.

238. Efimex " Stamp " on Easel.

1969. Air. "EXFIMEX" Stamp Exn., Mexico City (1968).
1393. **238.** 20 p. verm., grn. & bl. 15 12

239. Gymnasts and Emblem. **240.** President Baltasar Brum.

1969. "L'Avenir" Gymnastics Club. 75th Anniv.
1395. **239.** 6 p. black and red .. 5 5

1969. Dr. Baltasar Brum. Commem.
1396. **240.** 6 p. black and red .. 5 5

241. Sun and Fair Emblem.

1969. 2nd World Industrial Fair, Montevideo.
1399. **241.** 2 p. yell., blk., red & bl. 5 5

242. Emblem, Quill and Book. **243.** Modern Diesel Locomotive.

1969. Air. 10th Latin-American Notaries' Congress, Montevideo.
1400. **242.** 30 p. blk., orge. & grn. 15 15

1969. Uruguayan Railways. Cent.
1401. **243.** 6 p. blk. red & blue.. 5 5
1402. – 6 p. blk., red & blue.. 5 5
DESIGN: No. 1402, Early locomotive and diesel train.

244. Automobile Club Badge. **246.** I.L.O. Emblem.

245. Jose Belloni and "Combat" (monument). (Reduced size illustration. Actual size: 72 × 23 mm.).

1969. Air. Uruguay Automobile Club. 50th Anniv.
1404. **244.** 10 p. blue and red .. 5 5

1969. Jose Belloni (sculptor). Commem.
1405. **245.** 6 p. grn., black & gold 5 5

1969. Air. Int. Labour Organization. 50th Anniv.
1406. **246.** 30 p. turquoise & black 15 15

247. Training Centre Emblem. **248.** Exhibition Emblem.

1969. Reserve Officers' Training Centre. 25th Anniv. (1967).
1407. **247.** 1 p. lemon and blue 5 5
1408. – 2 p. brown and blue 5 5
DESIGN: 2 p. Reservist in uniform and civilian dress.

1969. Air. "A.B.U.E.X.P.O. 69" Philatelic Exn., Sao Paulo, Brazil.
1409. **248.** 20 p. yell,. bl. & grn. 12 10

249. Rotary Emblem and Hemispheres. **250.** Dr. Morquio and Child.

1969. Air. South American Regional Rotary Conf., and 50th Anniv. of Rotary Club, Montevideo.
1410. **249.** 20 p. gold, ult. & blue 12 10

1969. Air. Dr. Luis Morquio (pediatrician). Birth Cent. (1967).
1411. **250.** 20 p. brown & vermilion 12 10

1969. Air. New Year. No. 1345 surch **FELIZ ANO 1970** and value.
1412. 6 p. on 8 p. brown .. 5 5

251. President Tomas Berreta. **252.** Mahatma Gandhi.

1969. Berreta Commem.
1413. **251.** 6 p. red and black .. 5 5

1970. Air. Mahatma Gandhi. Birth Cent. (1969).
1414. **252.** 100 p. brn., ochre & blue 55 50

253. Sea Lion. **254.** E. C. Ciganda.

1970. Air. Fauna.
1415. – 20 p. blk., grn. & pur. 15 10
1416. – 30 p. blk., grn. & yell. 25 15
1417. – 50 p. blk., brn. & yell. 35 25
1418. – 100 p. brown, bistre and orange .. 85 45
1419. – 150 p. brown & green 1·10 70
1420. – 200 p. blk., brn. & red 1·40 90
1421. **253.** 250 p. blk., bl. & grey 2·00 1·10
DESIGNS—VERT. 20 p. Rhea. HORIZ. 30 p. Teju Lizard. 50 p. Capybara. 100 p. Armadillo. 150 p. Puma. 200 p. Coypu.

1970. Evaristo C. Ciganda (pioneer of teachers' pensions law). Birth Cent.
1422. **254.** 6 p. brown & emerald 5 5

255. Garibaldi. **256.** Bank Emblem.

1970. Air. Garibaldi's Participation in Uruguayan Civil War. Cent.
1423. **255.** 20 p. magenta and pink 12 10

1970. 11th Inter-American Development Bank Governors' Meeting, Punta del Este.
1424. **256.** 10 p. blue and gold .. 5 5

257. Stylised Tree. **258.** Footballer and Emblem.

1970. 2nd National Forestry Exn.
1425. **257.** 2 p. black, grn. & red 5 5

1970. Air. World Cup Football Championships, Mexico.
1426. **258.** 50 p. multicoloured .. 30 25

259. Gen. Artigas' House, Sauce. **260.** "U.N.".

1970. Artigas. 120th Death Anniv.
1427. **259.** 15 p. black, blue & red 10 8

1970. Air. United Nations. 25th Anniv.
1428. **260.** 32 p. blue, gold and light blue 20 15

261. Sun, Sea and Map.

1970. Tourist Publicity.
1429. **261.** 5 p. blue 5 5

262. Eisenhower and U.S. Flag.

1970. Air. Dwight D. Eisenhower (American soldier and statesman). 1st Death Anniv.
1430. **262.** 30 p. blue, red and grey 25 15

263. First Man on the Moon.

1970. Air. Moon Landing from "Apollo 11". 1st Anniv.
1431. **263.** 200 p. multicoloured 1·40 1·00

264. Mt. Fuji.

1970. "EXPO 70" World Fair, Osaka, Japan. Each with EXPO emblem and arms of Uruguay.
1432. **264.** 25 p. blue, grn. & yell. 20 15
1433. – 25 p. blue, oran. & grn. 20 15
1434. – 25 p. blue, yell. & vio. 20 15
1435. – 25 p. blue, vio. & oran. 20 15
DESIGNS: No. 1433, Geishas. 1434, Sun tower. 1435, Youth totem.

265. Flag of 1825.

1970. Air. "Immortals" Revolt. 145th Anniv.
1436. **265.** 500 p. blk., red & blue 3·50 2·25

266. Rheumatology Congress Emblem. **267.** Street Scene.

1970. Air. 5th Pan-American Rheumatology Congress, Punta del Este.
1437. **266.** 30 p. deep blue, blue and yellow 25 15

1970. Colonia del Sacramento (first European settlement in Uruguay). 290th Anniv.
1439. **267.** 5 p. multicoloured .. 5 5

268. "Mother and Son" (statue, E. Prati). **269.** Flags of Member Countries.

1970. "Homage to Mothers".
1440. **268.** 10 p. black and green 8 5

1970. Air. Founding of Latin-American Association for Free Trade by the Montevideo Treaty. 10th Anniv.
1441. **269.** 22 p. multicoloured .. 15 12

270. "Stamp" Emblem. **272.** Dr. A. Espinola.

271. "Playing Ring-o-Roses" (Ana Gage).

1970. "URUEXPO 70" Stamp Exhib., Montevideo.
1442. **270.** 15 p. vio., blue & brn. 12 8

1970. Int. Education Year. Children's Drawings. Multicoloured.
1443. 10 p. Type **271** 10 8
1444. 10 p. "Two Girls" (Andrea Burcatovsky) (vert.) .. 10 8
1445. 10 p. "Boy at Desk" (Humberto Abel Garcia) (vert.) 10 8
1446. 10 p. "Spaceman" (Aquiles Vaxelaire) 10 8

1971 Dr. Alfonso Espinola (physician and philanthropist). Commem.
1447. **272.** 5 p. black & orange 5 5

273. "Stamps" and Poster. (Illustration reduced. Actual size 71 × 23 mm.).

1971. "EFU 71" Stamp Exhib., Montevideo.
1449. **273.** 15 p. multicoloured .. 10 8

274. 5 c. Coin of 1840 (obverse). **275.** Dr. Domingo Arena.

1971. Numismatics Day.
1450. **274.** 25 p. blk., brn. & blue 15 12
1451. – 25 p. blk., brn. & blue 15 12
DESIGN: No. 1451, Reverse of coin showing "Sun" emblem.

1971. Arena (lawyer and statesman). Birth Cent. (1970).
1452. **275.** 5 p. lake 5 5

276. Opening Bars of Anthem. **277.** Dr. J. F. Arias.

1971. National Anthem. Commem.
1453. **276.** 15 p. blk., bl. & gold 10 8

1971. Dr. Jose Arias (statesman). 1st Death Anniv.
1454. **277.** 5 p. brown 5 5

278. "Yellow Fever" (J. M. Blanes).

1971. Air. Juan Blanes (artist). 70th Death Anniv.
1455. **278.** 50 p. multicoloured .. 35 25

279. Eduardo Fabini.

1971. Eduardo Fabini (composer). Commem.
1456. **279.** 5 p. black and brown 5 5

280. " Two Races ".

1971. Air. Racial Equality Year.
1457. **280.** 27 p. blk., pink & gold 20 12

281. Congress Emblem.

1971. Air. 12th Pan-American Gastro-enterological Congress, Punta del Este.
1458. **281.** 58 p. orge., blk. & grn 40 25

282. J. E. Rodo and U.P.A.E. Emblem.

1971. Jose E. Rodo (writer and first delegate to U.P.A.E.). Birth Cent.
1459. **282.** 15 p. black and blue 10 8

283. Old Water-cart and Tap.

1971. Montevideo's Water Supply. Cent.
1460. **283.** 5 p. multicoloured .. 5 5

284. Sheep and Roll of Cloth.

1971. Wool Production.
1461. **284.** 5 p. grn., grey & lt. grn. 8 5
1462. – 15 p. grey, vio. & blue 20 12
DESIGN: 15 p. Sheep, and loading bales of cloth.

285. J. M. Elorza (sheep-breeder) and Sheep.

1971. Dr. Jose Elorza Commem.
1463. **285.** 5 p. blk., grn. and blue 8 5

286. Creole Horse.

1971. Uruguayan Horse-breeding.
1464. **286.** 5 p. blk., bl. and orge. 8 5

287. Bull, Sheep and Ears of Corn.

1971. Uruguayan Rural Association. Cent.
1465. **287.** 20 p. multicoloured .. 25 15

288. Police Emblem.

1971. Honouring Police Heroes.
1466. **288.** 10 p. bl., blk. & grey 12 10
1467. – 20 p. multicoloured .. 25 15
DESIGN: 20 p. Policeman and flag.

289. 1896 10 Peso Banknote (obverse).

1971. Uruguayan State Bank. 75th Anniv.
1468. **289.** 25 p. grn., blk. & gld. 30 20
1469. – 25 p. grn., blk. & gld. 30 20
DESIGNS: No. 1469, Reverse of banknote showing rural scene.

290. Arms and Labourer.

1971. Durazno. 150th Anniv.
1470. **290.** 20 p. multicoloured .. 25 15

291. Shield and Laurel.
(Illustration reduced. Actual size 72 × 24½ mm.).

1971. Uruguay's Victory in Liberators' Cup Football Championships.
1471. **291.** 10 p. gold, red & blue 12 8

293. Voter and Ballot-box.

1971. General Election.
1473. **293.** 10 p. black and blue 8 5
1474. – 20 p. black and blue .. 12 10
DESIGN—HORIZ. 20 p. Voters in line.

294. C.I.M.E. Emblem and Globe.

1971. Air. Inter-Governmental Committee for European Migration (C.I.M.E.). 20th Anniv.
1475. **294.** 30 p. multicoloured .. 25 15

295. Exhibition Emblem and Map of Uruguay.

296. Pres. J. L. Cuestas.

1971. "EXPO LITORAL" Industrial Exhib., Paysandu.
1476. **295.** 20 p. purple and blue 12 10

1971. Uruguayan Presidents. Each brown and blue.
1477. 10 p. Type **296** 8 5
1478. 10 p. J. Herreray Obes .. 8 5
1479. 10 p. C. Williman .. 8 5
1480. 10 p. J. Serrato .. 8 5
1481. 10 p. A. M. Trueba .. 8 5

297. Llama Emblem.

298. Olympic Symbols.

1971. Air. "EXFILIMA" Stamp Exhib., Lima, Peru.
1482. **297.** 35 p. multicoloured .. 25 15

1972. Air. Olympic Games, Munich. (1st issue).
1484. **198.** 50 p. blk., red & yell. 15 10
1485. – 100 p. multicoloured 30 20
1486. – 500 p. multicoloured 1·50 1·00
DESIGNS: 100 p. Athlete and torch. 500 p. Discus-thrower.
See also Nos. 1493/4.

299. Chemical Jar.

300. B. Hidalgo.

1972. Air. Discovery of Insulin. 50th Anniv.
1487. **299.** 27 p. multicoloured .. 8 5

1972. Bartolome Hidalgo (Gaucho poet). Commem.
1488. **300.** 5 p. multicoloured .. 5 5

301. "Flagship".

302. "Face" on Beethoven Score.

1972. Air. American Stamp Day.
1489. **301.** 37 p. multicoloured .. 12 8

1972. 12th Eastern Uruguay Choral Festival.
1491. **302.** 20 p. blk., grn. & pur. 5 5

303. Dove supporting Wounded Bird.

305. Columbus Monument, Villa Colon.

304. Footballer and 1928 Gold Medals.

1972. Dionisio Diaz (9 year-old hero). Commemoration.
1492. **303.** 10 p. multicoloured .. 5 5

1972. Air. Olympic Games, Munich. Multicoloured.
1493. 100 p. Type **304** .. 20 12
1494. 300 p. Olympic flag (vert.) 55 35

1972. Villa Colon. Cent.
1495. **305.** 20 p. black, blue & red 5 5

1972. Uruguay's Victory in Intercontinental Football Cup Championships. No. 1471, surch. **COPA INTER CONTINENTAL 1971**, and football cup.
1496. **291.** 50 p. on 10 p. gold, red and blue 12 10

306. Sapling and Spade.

308. U.N.C.T.A.D. Emblem.

307. Cross of Remembrance.

1972. Tree Planting Campaign.
1497. **306.** 20 p. blk., myrtle & grn. 5 5

1972. Air. Dan Mitrione (U.S. police instructor assassinated by terrorists in Uruguay). 2nd Death Anniv.
1498. **307.** 37 p. violet and gold 8 5

1972. Air. 3rd United Nations Conference on Trade and Development (U.N.C.T.A.D.), Santiago, Chile.
1499. **308.** 30 p. multicoloured .. 5 5

309. Brazilian "Bull's-Eye" Stamp of 1843.

1972. Air. "EXFILBRA 72" Stamp Exhib., Rio de Janeiro.
1500. **309.** 50 p. multicoloured .. 12 10

310. Compass Rose and Map of South America.

311. "Tree" and Birds' Nests.

1972. Air. Campaign for Extension of Territorial Waters to 200 Mile Limit.
1501. **310.** 37 p. multicoloured .. 10 8

1972. Nat., Building Project for Communal Dwellings.
1502. **311.** 10 p. multicoloured .. 5 5

312. Amethyst.

1972. Uruguayan Mineralogy. Rocks and Gems.
1503. **312.** 5 p. multicoloured .. 5 5
1504. – 9 p. multicoloured .. 5 5
1505. – 15 p. grn., brn. & blk. 5 5
DESIGNS: 9 p. Agate. 15 p. Chalcedony.

313. "The Three Holy Kings" (R. Barradas).

1972. Air. Christmas.

1506. 313. 20 p. multicoloured .. 5 5

314. Infantry Uniform of 1830. 315. Red Cross over Map.

1972. Military Uniforms. Multicoloured.

1509. 10 p. Type 314 .. .. 5 5
1510. 20 p. Artigas cavalry regiment uniform .. 5 5

1972. Uruguayan Red Cross. 75th Anniv.

1511. 315. 30 p. multicoloured .. 8 5

316. Open Book. 317. General Jose Artigas.

1972. Full Civil Rights for Uruguayan Women. 25th Anniv.

1513. 316. 10 p. gold, bl. & light bl. 5 5

1972.

1514.	317. 5 p. yellow ..	..	5	5
1515.	10 p. brown ..	..	5	5
1516.	15 p. green ..	..	5	5
1517.	20 p. lilac ..	..	5	5
1518.	30 p. blue ..	..	5	5
1519.	40 p. orange ..	..	8	5
1520.	50 p. red ..	..	10	5
1521.	75 p. green ..	..	12	10
1522.	100 p. green ..	..	20	12
1523.	150 p. brown ..	..	25	15
1524.	200 p. blue ..	..	30	25
1525.	250 p. violet ..	..	35	30
1526.	500 p. grey ..	..	75	55
1527.	1000 p. blue ..	..	1·50	1·10

318. Cup and Ear of Wheat on Map. 319. E. Fernandez and J. P. Varela.

1973. Int. Institute for Agricultural Sciences (I.I.C.A.). 30th Anniv.

1531. 318. 30 p. blk., yell. & red 8 5

1973. Friends of Popular Education Society (1968). Cent.

1532. 319. 10 p. blk., green & brn. 5 5

320. Columbus and Map.

1973. American Tourist Year.

1533. 320. 50 p. purple .. 12 8

321. C. M. Ramirez.

1973. Eminent Uruguayan Jurists. Each black, brown and bistre.

1534. 10 p. Type 321 .. .. 5 5
1535. 10 p. J. J. de Arechaga 5 5
1536. 10 p. J. A. Ramirez .. 5 5
1537. 10 p. J. E. de Arechaga 5 5

322. Departmental Map. 324. Priest, Indians and Soriano Church.

323. F. de los Santos (courier) and Artigas.

1973. Uruguayan Departments.

1538. 322. 20 p. multicoloured 5 5

1973. Francisco de los Santos Commem.

1540. 323. 20 p. emerald, black and green 5 5

1973. Villa Soriano (first town to be founded in Uruguay). Commemoration.

1541. 324. 20 p. blk., violet & blue 5 5

325. "SOYP" and Fish.

1973. 1st Fishery Station of Oceanographic and Fishery Service (S.O.Y.P.). Inaug.

1542. 325. 100 p. multicoloured 15 12

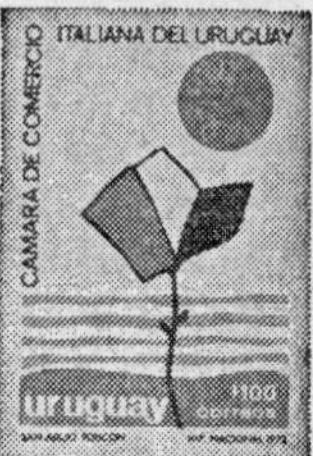

326. Flower and Sun. 327. L. A. de Herrera.

1973. Italian Chamber of Commerce in Uruguay.

1543. 326. 100 p. multicoloured 15 12

1973. Luis A. de Herrera (statesman). Birth Centenary.

1545. 327. 50 p. brn., sepia & grey 10 5

328. Festival Emblem.

1973. "Festival of Nations", Montevideo.

1546. 328. 50 p. multicoloured .. 10 5

329. Artery and Heart within "Arm". 330. "Madonna" (Rafael Barradas).

1973. 3rd Pan-American Voluntary Blood Donors' Congress.

1547. 329. 50 p. blk., red & pink 10 5

1973. Christmas.

1548. 330. 50 p. blk., yell. & grn. 10 5

331. Copernicus.

1973. Copernicus (astronomer). 500th Birth Anniv.

1549. 631. 50 p. multicoloured .. 10 5

332. Hands in Prayer, and Andes. 333. O.E.A. Emblem and Map.

1973. Rescue of Survivors from Andes Air-crash.

1550. 332. 50 p. grn., bl. & blk. 10 5
1551. – 75 p. multicoloured .. 12 8

DESIGN: 75 p. Flower with broken stem, and Christ of the Andes statue.

1974. Organisation of American States (O.E.A.). 25th Anniv.

1552. 333. 250 p. multicoloured 35 30

334. Games' Emblem.

1974. 1st International Scout Games, Montevideo.

1553. 334. 250 p. multicoloured 35 30

335. H. S. Sedes and Motor-car. 336. "The Three Gauchos".

1974. Hector Sedes (motor-racing driver). Commemoration.

1554. 335. 50 p. multicoloured .. 10 5

1974. Antonia Lussich's Poem "Los Tres Gauchos". Cent.

1560. 336. 50 p. multicoloured .. 8 5

337. Rifle, Target and Swiss Flag.

1974. Swiss Rifle Club, Nueva Helvecia. Cent.

1561. 337. 100 p. multicoloured 15 10

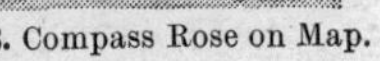

338. Compass Rose on Map. 339. Emblem and Stadium.

1974. Military Geographical Service.

1562. 338. 50 p. blk., emer. & grn. 8 5

1974. World Cup Football Championships, Munich. Multicoloured.

1563. 50 p. Type 339 .. 8 5
1564. 75 p. Emblem and foot-baller (horiz.) 12 8
1565. 1000 p. Emblem and foot-baller (diff.) (horiz.) .. 3·25 3·25

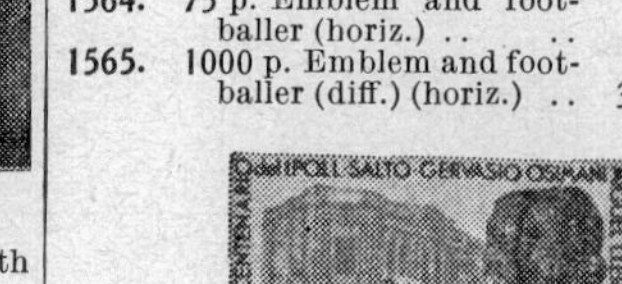

340. Old and New School Buildings, and Founders.

1974. Osimani-Llerena Technical School, Salto. Cent.

1566. 340. 75 p. black & brown 12 8

341. Carlos Gardel. 342. "Ball and Net".

1974. Carlos Gardel (singer). Commem.

1567. 341. 100 p. multicoloured 15 12

1974. 1st Women's World Cup Volleyball Championships.

1568. 342. 200 p. pur., yell. & blk. 30 25

343. "Protect Your Heart". 344. Vidal and Statue.

1974. Uruguayan "Pro Cardias" Heart Foundation.

1569. 343. 75 p. red, yell. & grn. 12 8

1974. Founding of San Jose by Eusebio Vidal. Bicent. (1973).

1570. 344. 75 p. blue & new blue 12 8

No. 1570 is incorrectly inscr. "1873–1973".

345. Artigas Monument. 346. W.P.Y. Emblem.

1974. Dedication of Artigas Monument, Buenos Aires, Argentine Republic.

1571. 345. 75 p. multicoloured .. 12 8

1974. Air. World Population Year.

1572. 346. 500 p. red, black and grey 70 55

347. Montevideo Citadel Gateway and Emblems. 348. Mast and Radio Waves.

1974. Air. Events of 1974.
1573. **347.** 200 p. multicoloured 30 25
1574. 300 p. multicoloured 40 35

1974. Broadcasting in Uruguay. 50th Anniv.
1575. **348.** 100 p. multicoloured 15 12

349. "Sheet of Stamps" and "URUEXPO 74" Emblem.

1974. "Circulo Filatelico" Journal of Montevideo Stamp Club. 10th Anniv.
1576. **349.** 100 p. bl., red & blk. 15 12

350. Envelopes and Emblem.

1974. Universal Postal Union. Cent.
1577. **350.** 100 p. multicoloured 15 12
1578. – 200 p. blk., gold & lilac 30 25
DESIGN—VERT. 200 p. U.P.U. emblem on envelope, laurel and globe.

351. Mexican Official Stamp of 1884 and Arms.

1974. Air. "EXFILMEX" Interamerican Philatelic Exn., Mexico City.
1579. **351.** 200 p. multicoloured 20 12

352. Artigas Monument and Map.

1974. Dedication of Artigas Monument, Ventura Hill, Minas.
1580. **352.** 100 p. multicoloured 15 12

353. Early Map of Montevideo.

1974. Montevideo's Fortifications. 250th Anniv.
1581. **353.** 300 p. brn., red & grn. 45 30

354. Ship in Dry-dock and Badge.

1974. Montevideo Naval Arsenal. Cent.
1582. **354.** 200 p. multicoloured 15 10

355. Balloon.

1974. History of Aviation. Multicoloured.
1583. 100 p. Type **355** 8 5
1584. 100 p. Farman biplanes .. 8 5
1585. 100 p. Castaibart monoplane 8 5
1586. 100 p. Bleriot monoplane 8 5
1587. 150 p. Military and civil pilots' "wings" .. 8 5
1588. 150 p. Nieuport biplane 8 5
1589. 150 p. Breguet-Bidon biplane 8 5
1590. 150 p. Caproni biplane .. 8 5

356. Pan de Azucar Mountain and Cross.

1974. Pan de Azucar (town). Cent.
1591. **356.** 150 p. multicoloured 8 5

357. Adoration of the Kings.

1974. Christmas. Multicoloured.
1592. 100 p. Type **357** (postage) 5 5
1593. 150 p. Kings with Gifts .. 8 5
1594. 240 p. Kings following the Star (air) 15 12

358. Rowers, Fireworks and Nike of Samothrace Statue.

1975. Montevideo Rowing Club. Cent.
1596. **358.** 150 p. multicoloured 8 5

359. "Treaty of Purification, 1817" (J. Zorrilla de San Martin).

1975. Recognition of Artigas Government by Great Britain in Treaty of Purification, 1817.
1597. **359.** 100 p. multicoloured 10 5

MINIMUM PRICE

The minimum price quoted is 5p which represents a handling charge rather than a basis for valuing common stamps. For further notes about prices see introductory pages.

360. Spanish 6 c. Stamp of 1850, and National Colours.

1975. Air. "ESPANA 75" Stamp Exhibition, Madrid.
1598. **360.** 400 p. multicoloured 30 20

361. Rose.

1975. Rosario. Bicentenary.
1600. **361.** 150 p. multicoloured 15 8

362. "The Oath of the Thirty-three" (J. M. Blanes).

1975. 1825 Liberation Movement. 150th Anniv.
1601. **362.** 150 p. multicoloured 15 8

363. Michelangelo's Motif for Floor of Capitol, Rome.

1975. Air. Michelangelo. 500th Birth Anniv.
1602. **363.** 1 np. multicoloured .. 70 50

364. Columbus and Caravel.

366. 1976 Olympics and 1978 World Cup Emblems.

365. " Sun " and Uruguay 1929 Air Stamp.

1975. Spanish-American Stamp Day.
1603. **364.** 1 n.p. multicoloured 70 50

1975. Air. Uruguayan Stamp Day.
1604. **365.** 1 n.p black yellow & grey 70 50

1975. Air. " Exfilmo-Espamer 75 " Stamp Exhibition, Montevideo. Multicoloured.
1605. 1 n.p. Type **366** 70 50
1606. 1 n.p. " Independence " (U.S. & Uruguayan flags) 70 50
1607. 1 n.p. Emblems of U.P.U. and Spanish-American Postal Union 70 50

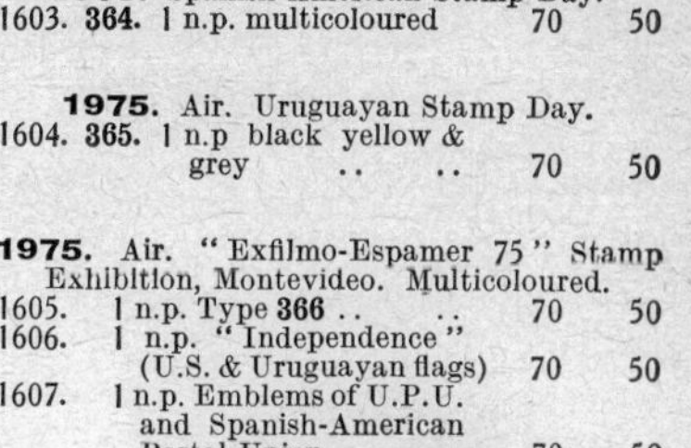

367. Jose Artigas and J. Francisco de Larrobla.

1975. Independence. 150th Anniv.
1608. **367.** 50 c. multicoloured .. 35 25

368. Col. L. Olivera and Fortress.

1975. Capture of Santa Teresa Fortress. 150th Anniv.
1609. **368.** 10 c. multicoloured .. 5 5

369. " Battle of Rincon " (D. Hequet).

1975. Battle of Rincon. 150th Anniv.
1610. **369.** 15 c. black and gold 10 8
See also Nos. 1620/1.

370. Florencio Sanchez.

1975. Florencio Sanchez (dramatist). Birth Cent. Multicoloured.
1611. 20 c. Type **370** 15 8
1612. 20 c. " En Familia " .. 15 8
1613. 20 c. " Barranca Abajo " 15 8
1614. 20 c. " M'Hijo El Dotor " 15 8
1615. 20 c. " Canillita " .. 15 8
Nos. 1612/15 show scenes from plays and are horiz., 38 × 26 mm.

1975. Surch in revalued currency.

1616. **317.**	10 c. on 20 p. lilac ..	5	5
1617.	15 c. on 40 p prange	10	5
1618.	50 c. on 50 p. red ..	30	20
1619.	1 n.p. on 1000 p. blue	60	35

1975. Artigas' Exile and Battle of Sarandi. 150th Anniv. As T **369.** Multicoloured.

1620.	15 c. Artias' house, Ibiray (Paraguay) ..	8	5
1621.	25 c. Battle scene ..	15	8

371. Maroa E. Vaz Ferreira (poetess).

1975. Birth Centenaries.

1622. **371.**	15 c. blk., yell. & pur.	10	8
1623. –	15 c. blk., oran. & pur.	10	8

DESIGN: No. 1623, Julio Herrera y Reissig (poet).

372. " Virgin and Child " (stained-glass window). **373.** Colonel L. Latorre.

1975. Christmas. Multicoloured.

1624.	20 c. Type **372**	15	8
1625.	30 c. " Virgin and Child " (different)	20	15
1626.	60 c. " Fireworks " (horiz.)	40	30

1975. Col. L. Latorre (Pres. of Uruguay, 1876–80). Commem.

1627. **373.**	15 c. multicoloured ..	10	8

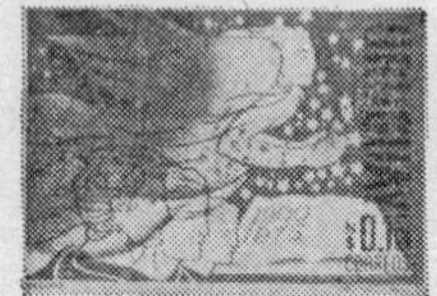

374. " Ariel ", Stars and Book.

1976. Publication of " Ariel " (by Jose Rodo). 75th Anniversary.

1628. **374.**	15 c. multicoloured ..	8	5

375. " Oncidium bifolium " (orchid).

1976. Air. Multicoloured.

1629.	50 c. Type **375**	30	20
1630.	50 c. " Felis geoffroyi paraguae " (ocelot) ..	30	20

376. Water Sports. **377.** Telephone Receiver.

1976. 23rd South American Swimming, Diving and Water-polo Championships, Maldonado

1631. **376.**	30 c. multicoloured...	20	10

1976. Telephone Centenary.

1632. **377.**	83 c. multicoloured ..	50	40

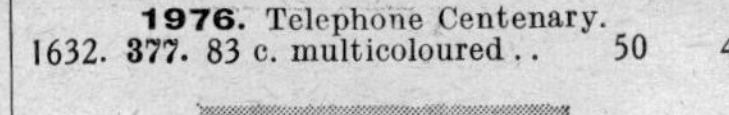

378. " Plus Ultra " Flying-boat.

1976. " Plus Ultra " Spain–South America Flight. 50th Anniversary.

1633. **378.**	83 c. multicoloured ..	50	40

379. Aircraft rising around Hour-glass. **380.** Olympic Games' Emblem.

1976. Lufthansa Airline. 50th Anniv.

1634. **379.**	83 c. multicoloured ..	50	40

1976. Commemorations. Multicoloured.

1635.	10 c. Type **380**	5	5
1636.	15 c. Telephone dial (Telephone Centenary) ..	10	8
1637.	25 c. U.N. stamp of 1951 (U.N. Postal Services, 25th Anniversary) ..	15	10
1638.	50 c. " Hands " clasping football (World Cup football championships, Argentina 1978) ..	30	20

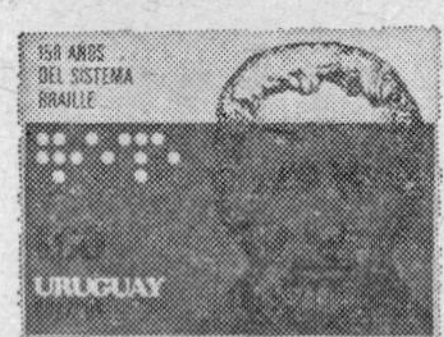

381. Louis Braille and word " Braille ".

1976. " Braille " System for the Blind. 150th Anniv.

1639. **381.**	60 c. black and brown	35	20

382. Signing of Independence Declaration.

1976. American Revolution. Bicent.

1640. **382.**	1 p. 50 multicoloured	85	50

383. " Candombe " (Pedro Figari).

1976. Abolition of Slavery. 150th Anniv.

1641. **383.**	30 c. multicoloured ..	20	12

384. Rivera Monument. **385.** Turu Bird.

1976. General Rivera Monument. Dedication.

1642. **384.**	5 p. on 10 p. mult.	3·00	2·50

1976.

1643. **385.**	1 c. violet	5	5
1644. –	5 c. green	5	5
1645. –	15 c. red	10	8
1646. –	20 c. black	15	8
1647. –	30 c. grey	20	15
1648. –	5 p. blue	3·00	2·50

DESIGNS: 5 c. Passionflower. 15 c. National flower. (sp. " Erythrina ") 20 c. Indian lance-head. 30 c. Indian statue. 5 p. Artigas.

386. Office Building and Reverse of 1840 Coin.

1976. State Accounting Office 15th Anniv.

1657. **386.**	30 c. blk., brn. & blue	20	15

387. Hand-pump within Flames.

1976. Fire Service Centenary.

1658. **387.**	20 c. black and red ..	15	8

388. Uruguay 60 c. Stamp and " Post-mark ". **389.** Championship Emblem.

1976. Uruguay Philatelic Club. 50th Anniv.

1659. **388.**	30 c. red, blue & bistre	20	15

1976. 5th World Universities' Football Championships, Montevideo.

1660. **389.**	83 c. multicoloured ..	50	40

390. Human Eye.

1976. Prevention of Blindness.

1661. **390.**	20 c. multicoloured ..	15	8

1976. Various Anniversaries. Horiz. designs as T **380.** Multicoloured.

1662.	10 c. Players and ball (Argentina '78 Football Championships) ..	5	5
1663.	30 c. Gold medals (Olympic Games, Montreal) ..	20	15
1664.	50 c. " Viking on Mars " (" Viking " Mission) ..	30	20
1665.	80 c. Nobel Prizewinners. (1st Nobel Prize Awards. 75th Anniv.) ..	50	40

391. Map of Montevideo.

1976. Montevideo. 250th Anniv. Mult.

1666.	30 c. Type **391** ..	20	15
1667.	45 c. Montevideo panorama. 1842	25	20
1668.	70 c. First settlers 1726 ..	40	30
1669.	80 c. Montevideo coin (vert.)	50	40
1670.	1 p. 15 Montevideo's first arms	70	60

LATE FEE STAMPS

L 1.

ILLUSTRATIONS
British Commonwealth and all overprints and surcharges are FULL SIZE. Foreign Countries have been reduced to ⅔-LINEAR.

1936.

L 774. **L 1.**	3 c. green	5	5
L 775.	5 c. violet	8	5
L 776.	6 c. green	8	5
L 777.	7 c. brown	10	8
L 778.	8 c. red	15	12
L 779.	12 c. blue	25	15

NEWSPAPER STAMPS

1922. Optd. **PRENSA** (=Printed Matter) or surch. also.

N 519. **82.**	3 c. olive (imperf.) ..	15	12
N 447. **78.**	3 c. on 2 c. black and lake (perf.) ..	15	12
N 403. **79.**	3 c. on 4 c. yellow (perf.)	15	8
N 448. **78.**	6 c. on 4 c. blue and orange (perf.) ..	15	12
N 449.	9 c. on 5 c. brown and blue (perf.)	15	12
N 520. **82.**	9 c. on 10 c. green (imp.)	45	30
N 521.	15 c. mauve (imperf.)	50	45

OFFICIAL STAMPS

1880. Optd. **OFICIAL.** Perf.

O 51. **5.**	15 c. yellow	1·40	1·40

1880. Optd. **OFICIAL.** Roul.

O 59. **7.**	1 c. brown	70	70
O 49. **8.**	5 c. green	30	30
O 51. **9.**	7 c. blue (perf.)	55	55
O 50. **7.**	10 c. red	55	55
O 52.	20 c. bistre	70	70
O 53.	50 c. black	5·50	5·50
O 55.	1 p. blue	5·50	5·50

1883. Optd. **OFICIAL.**

O 64. **10.**	1 c. green ..	70	55
O 65. –	2 c. red (No. 129) ..	1·00	85

1883. Optd. **OFICIAL.**

O 70. **11.**	1 c. green	9·00	9·00
O 71.	2 c. red	2·25	2·25
O 72. **12.**	5 c. blue	85	55
O 73. **13.**	10 c. brown	1·75	1·25

1884. Optd. **FRANCO** in frame.

O 74. **11.**	1 c. green	9·00	8·50

1884. Optd. **OFICIAL.**

O 80. **7.**	1 c. on 10 c. (No. 76) ..	55	55
O 81. –	2 c. red (No. 77) ..	1·25	1·00
O 82. **14.**	5 c. blue	85	75

1884. Optd. **OFICIAL.** Roul.

O 91a. **15.**	1 c. grey	2·00	2·00
O 91.	1 c. olive	55	55
O 107.	1 c. green	45	45
O 92. **16.**	2 c. red	30	30
O 93a. **15.**	5 c. blue	30	30
O 94.	5 c. lilac	1·10	1·10
O 95. **17.**	7 c. brown	55	55
O 110.	7 c. orange	55	55
O 96. **18.**	10 c. brown	30	30
O 111. **22.**	10 c. violet	2·25	2·25
O 97. **19.**	20 c. mauve	55	55
O 112.	20 c. brown	1·75	1·75
O 98. **20.**	25 c. lilac	75	75
O 113.	25 c. red	1·75	1·75

1890. Optd. **OFICIAL.** Perf.

O 124. **23.**	1 c. green	15	15
O 125. **24.**	2 c. red	15	15
O 126. **25.**	5 c. blue	55	55
O 127. **26.**	7 c. brown	35	35
O 128. **27.**	10 c. green	45	45
O 129. **28.**	20 c. orange	45	45
O 130. **29.**	25 c. red-brown ..	55	45
O 131. **30.**	50 c. blue	1·40	1·10
O 132. **31.**	1 p. violet	1·75	1·40

1891. Optd. **OFICIAL.**
O 134. **15.** 5 c. lilac (No. 113) .. 70 70

1895. Optd. **OFICIAL.**
O 164. **23.** 1 c. blue 55 55
O 165. **24.** 2 c. brown 70 70
O 166. **25.** 5 c. rose 85 85
O 167. **30.** 50 c. purple .. .. 1·40 1·10

1895. Optd. **OFICIAL.**
O 168. **38.** 1 c. bistre 8 8
O 169. **39.** 2 c. blue 8 8
O 170. **40.** 5 c. red 12 12
O 171. **41.** 7 c. green 15 15
O 172. **42.** 10 c. brown 15 15
O 173. **43.** 20 c. black and green 30 25
O 174. **44.** 25 c. black and brown 25 25
O 175. **45.** 50 c. black and blue 35 35
O 176. **46.** 1 p. black and brown 1·40 1·40

1897. Nos. 180/2 optd. **OFICIAL.**
O 194. **49.** 1 c. black and claret 55 45
O 195. **50.** 5 c. black and blue .. 55 45
O 196. – 10 c. black and lake 85 55

1897. Optd. **OFICIAL.**
O 201. **38.** 1 c. blue 20 20
O 202. **39.** 2 c. purple 30 30
O 203. **40.** 5 c. green 30 20
O 204. **52.** 10 c. red .. .. 1·00 95
O 205. **43.** 20 c. black and mauve 1·00 70
O 206. **44.** 25 c. blue and rose .. 1·00 70
O 207. **45.** 50 c. brown and green 1·00 1·00
O 208. **46.** 1 p. blue and brown 2·25 2·25

1900. Optd. **OFICIAL.**
O 226. **24.** 2 c. orange 35 30
O 227a.**40.** 5 c. blue 25 25
O 228. **52.** 10 c. purple 45 30
O 243. **28.** 20 c. blue .. .. 2·50 1·75

1901. Optd. **OFICIAL.**
O 238. **55.** 1 c. green 12 8
O 289. **56.** 2 c. red 12 8
O 240. **57.** 5 c. blue 12 8
O 241. **58.** 7 c. brown 15 15
O 242. **59.** 10 c. lilac 15 15
O 244. **29.** 25 c. sepia 30 25
O 245. **31.** 1 p. green .. .. 2·75 2·25

1905. Optd. **OFICIAL.**
O 272. **61.** 1 c. green 12 12
O 262. **62.** 2 c. orange 12 12
O 263. **63.** 5 c. blue 12 12
O 275. **64.** 10 c. lilac 8 8
O 276. **65.** 20 c. green 15 15
O 266. **66.** 25 c. bistre 35 35

1907. Optd. **OFICIAL.**
O 273. **68.** 5 c. blue 8 8
O 274. 7 c. brown 8 8
O 278. 50 c. rose 45 45

1910. Optd. **OFICIAL 1910.**
O 288. **56.** 2 c. red .. .. 2·50 2·25
O 289. **57.** 5 c. blue .. .. 2·00 85
O 290. **50.** 10 c. lilac 75 55
O 291. **28.** 20 c. green 85 55
O 292. **29.** 25 c. brown .. .. 1·40 85
O 293. **68.** 50 c. rose .. .. 1·75 1·00

O 1.

1911.
O 307. **O 1.** 2 c. brown 15 12
O 308. 5 c. blue 15 8
O 309. 8 c. slate 12 8
O 310. 20 c. brown 20 15
O 311. 23 c. claret 25 15
O 312. 50 c. orange 45 35
O 313. 1 p. red .. .. 1·40 55

1915. Optd. **Oficial.**
O 340. **72.** 2 c. red 15 12
O 341. 5 c. blue 25 15
O 342. 8 c. blue 20 8
O 343. 20 c. brown 45 15
O 344. **73.** 23 c. blue 45 20
O 345. 50 c. orange 85 50
O 346. 1 p. red .. .. 2·25 55

1919. Optd. **Oficial.**
O 365. **77.** 2 c. grey and red .. 12 8
O 366. 5 c. grey and blue .. 15 8
O 367. 8 c. brown and blue 15 8
O 368. 20 c. grey and brown 35 12
O 369. 23 c. brown & green .. 35 15
O 370. 50 c. blue and brown 60 40
O 371. 1 p. blue and red .. 1·25 40

1924. Optd. **OFICIAL** in frame. (a) Perf.
O 439. **82.** 2 c. mauve .. 15 8
O 440. 5 c. blue .. 15 12
O 593. 8 c. red .. 85 15
O 594. 10 c. green .. 1·00 15
O 441. 12 c. blue .. 15 5
O 442. 20 c. brown .. 25 12
O 443. 36 c. green .. 55 55
O 444. 50 c. orange .. 1·00 1·00
O 445. 1 p. red .. 2·75 2·00
O 446. 2 p. green .. 5·50 3·50

(b) Imperf.
O 499. **82.** 2 c. mauve .. 5 5
O 500. 5 c. blue 8 8
O 501. 8 c. red 12 12
O 502. 12 c. blue 15 15
O 503. 20 c. brown .. 45 30
O 504. 36 c. pink 55 50

PARCEL POST STAMPS

P 1. P 2.

1922. (a) Inscr. "EXTERIOR".
P 391. **P 1.** 5 c. green on buff .. 12 5
P 485. 5 c. black on yellow 12 5
P 392. 10 c. green on blue 15 5
P 486. 10 c. black on blue 30 5
P 393. 20 c. green on rose 30 12
P 488. 30 c. green on green 85 12
P 395. 50 c. green on blue 1·40 12
P 396. 1 p. green on orange 2·50 55

(b) Inscr. "INTERIOR".
P 397. **P 1.** 5 c. green on buff .. 12 5
P 398. 10 c. green on blue 15 5
P 399. 20 c. green on pink 40 8
P 400. 30 c. green on green 55 8
P 401. 50 c. green on blue 85 12
P 402. 1 p. green on orange 2·50 55

1927.
P 522. **P 2.** 1 c. blue 5 5
P 606. 1 c. violet 5 5
P 523. 2 c. green 8 5
P 524. 4 c. violet 8 5
P 609. 5 c. red 8 5
P 526. 10 c. brown 10 5
P 527. 20 c. orange 25 15

P 3. P 4. P 5. Sea and Rail Transport.

1928.
P 587. **P 3.** 5 c. black on yellow 8 5
P 588. 10 c. black on blue 12 5
P 589. 20 c. black on rose 15 5
P 590. 30 c. black on green 35 5

1929. Agricultural parcels.
P 610. **P 4.** 10 c. orange .. 30 12
P 611. 15 c. blue 30 12
P 612. 20 c. brown .. 30 15
P 613. 25 c. red 35 20
P 614. 50 c. grey .. .. 1·10 40
P 615. 75 c. violet .. .. 1·75 1·00
P 616. 1 p. olive .. .. 2·25 85

1938.
P 971. **P 5.** 5 c. orange .. 5 5
P 801. 10 c. red 12 5
P 972. 10 c. purple .. 5 5
P 1066. 10 c. green .. 8 5
P 802. 20 c. deep blue .. 15 5
P 973. 20 c. vermilion .. 12 5
P 973a. 20 c. carmine .. 12 5
P 1067. 20 c. pale blue .. 8 5
P 803. 30 c. violet .. 25 5
P 974. 30 c. blue 15 5
P 1068. 30 c. purple .. 5 5
P 804. 50 c. green .. 30 5
P 1069. 50 c. grey-green .. 5 5
P 805. 1 p. red 85 8
P 975. 1 p. deep blue .. 20 12
P 1070. 1 p. blue-green .. 8 5

P 6. P 7. University.

1943.
P 876. **P 6.** 1 c. red 5 5
P 877. 2 c. slate 5 5

1944. Optd. **ANO 1943.**
P 882. **P 4.** 10 c. orange .. 25 10
P 883. 15 c. blue 30 12
P 884. 20 c. brown .. 35 15
P 885. 25 c. red 35 15
P 886. 50 c. grey 75 25
P 887. 75 c. violet .. 1·10 75
P 888. 1 p. olive .. .. 1·40 75

1945.
P 909. **A.** 1 c. green 5 5
P 999. **P 7.** 1 c. red 5 5
P 910. 2 c. violet 5 5
P 1000. **A.** 2 c. blue 5 5
P 1047. **B.** 5 c. grey 30 5
P 1045. 5 c. brown .. 5 5
P 1001. **A.** 10 c. blue-green .. 8 5
P 1002. 10 c. olive 12 10
P 1048. **C.** 20 c. yellow .. 8 5
P 1049. 20 c. brown .. 8 5
P 1046. **D.** 1 p. blue 55 15
P 1290. 1 p. brown .. 5 5
DESIGNS—HORIZ. A, Bank. VERT. B, Custom House. C, Solis Theatre. D, Montevideo Railway Station.

P 8. Custom House. P 9. Mail Coach.

1946.
P 934. **P 8.** 5 c. blue and brown 5 5

1946.
P 935. **P 9.** 5 p. brown and red 3·75 1·10

1946. Armorial type as T **119** obliterated by arrow-head device. (a) Optd. **IMPUESTO** and **ENCOMIENDAS.**
P 936. 1 c. mauve 5 5
P 937. 2 c. brown 5 5
P 938. 5 c. blue 5 5

(b) Optd. **ENCOMIENDAS** only.
P 939. 1 p. blue 55 12
P 940. 5 p. red .. .. .. 3·50 1·40

1957. No. P 1047 surch. **$0.30.**
P 1064. 30 c. on 5 c. grey .. 15 5

P 10. National Printing Works.

1960.
P 1127. **P 10.** 30 c. green .. 5 5

1965. Surch. with Caduceus and **$5.00 ENCOMIENDAS.**
P 1268. **129.** 5 p. on 84 c. orange 25 15

1966. No. 1092 surch. with Caduceus **ENCOMIENDAS** and value.
P 1289. **154.** 1 p. on 38 c. black 5 5

P 11. Airliner and Motor-coach.

1969.
P 1397. **P 11.** 10 p. blk., red & grn. 8 5
P 1398. – 20 p. yell., blk. & bl. 15 12
DESIGN: 20 p. Side views of airliner and motor-coach.

1971. No. 1121 surch. **Encomiendas $0·60.**
P 1448. **160.** 60 c. on 1 p.+10 c. violet and orange 45 15

1971. No. 1380 surch. **IMPUESTOS A ECOMIENDAS,** diesel-engine and value.
P 1492. 60 c. on 6 p. blk. & grn. 5 5

1972. Nos. 1401/2 surch. **IMPUESTO A ENCOMIENDAS,** emblem and value.
P 1507. **243.** 1 p. on 6 p. mult. 5 5
P 1508. 1 p. on 6 p. mult. 5 5

P 12. Parcels and Arrows.

1974.
P 1555. **P 12.** 75 p. multicoloured 10 8

P 13. Mail-van.

1974. Old-time Mail Transport.
P 1556. **P 13.** 100 p. multicoloured 15 12
P 1557. – 150 p. multicoloured 25 15
P 1558. – 300 p. blk., bl. & orge. 45 30
P 1559. – 500 p. multicoloured 70 50
DESIGNS: 150 p. Steam locomotive. 300 p. Paddle-steamer. 500 p. Monoplane.

POSTAGE DUE STAMPS

D 1.

1902.
D 404a. **D 1.** 1 c. green 5 5
D 405. 2 c. red 15 10
D 796. 2 c. brown 5 5
D 491. 3 c. brown 20 15
D 797. 3 c. red 5 5
D 798. 4 c. violet 5 5
D 799. 5 c. blue 8 5
D 746. 5 c. red 15 10
D 494. 6 c. brown 20 15
D 800. 8 c. red 12 8
D 249. 10 c. blue 20 12
D 409. 10 c. green 20 12
D 250. 20 c. orange 30 30

1904. Surch. **PROVISORIO UN cent'mo.**
D 267. **D 1.** 1 c. on 10 c. blue .. 45 30

SPECIAL DELIVERY STAMPS

1921. Overprinted **MENSAJERIAS.**
E 389. **79.** 2 c. red 25

S 1. Caduceus. S 2.

1923.
E 415. **S 1.** 2 c. red 15 5
E 416. 2 c. blue 15 5

1928.
E 591. **S 2.** 2 c. black on green 8 5
E 635. 2 c. green 8 5
E 636. 2 c. blue 10 5
E 637. 2 c. pink 8 5
E 638. 2 c. brown 5 5

1957. Surch. **$0.05.**
E 1065. **S 2.** 5 c. on 2 c. brown .. 8 5

VATHY E3

A town on the island of Samos, where there was a French P.O., now closed.

1893. Stamps of France optd. **Vathy** or surch. also in figures and words.
82. **10.** 5 c. green .. .. 1·25 1·10
84. 10 c. black on lilac .. 1·75 1·75
86. 15 c. blue .. .. 1·75 1·50
87. 1 pi. on 25 c. black on red 2·40 1·25
88. 2 pi. on 50 c. red .. 4·25 3·50
89. 4 pi. on 1 f. olive .. 4·25 3·00
90. 8 pi. on 2 f. brn. on blue 11·00 9·00
91. 20 pi. on 5 f. mauve on lilac .. .. .. 15·00 15·00

VATICAN CITY E3

A small area in Rome under the independent sovereignty of the Pope since 1929.
100 centesimi = 1 lira.

1. Papal tiara, St. Peter's keys 2. Pope Pius XI. 3.

1929.
1. **1.** 5 c. brown on rose .. 20 20
2. 10 c. green on green .. 30 30
3. 20 c. violet on lilac .. 70 35
4. 25 c. blue on blue .. 90 45
5. 30 c. black on yellow .. 1·60 55
6. 50 c. black on pink .. 1·60 60
7. 75 c. red on grey .. 2·50 70

8. 2. 80 c. red .. .. .. 1·40 45
9. 1 l. 25 blue .. .. .. 3·50 1·10
10. 2 l. brown .. .. .. 9·00 2·50
11. 2 l. 50 red .. .. .. 11·00 3·75
12. 5 l. green .. .. .. 13·00 6·50
13. 10 l. black .. .. .. 16·00 10·00

1931. Surch. **C. 25** and bars.
14. 1. 25 c. on 30 c. blk. on yell. 7·50 1·00

1933. "Holy Year".
15. 3. 25 c.+10 c. green .. 8·50 4·25
16. 75 c.+15 c. red .. .. 18·00 8·50
17. 80 c.+20 c. brown .. 18·00 13·00
18. 1 l. 25+25 c. blue .. 13·00 13·00

The 80 c. and 1 l. 25 have inscriptions and frame differently arranged.

5. Papal Arms, Tiara and Keys. 6. Pope Pius XI.

1933.
19. 5. 5 c. red 5 5
20. – 10 c. black and brown .. 5 5
21. – 12½ c. black and green .. 5 5
22. – 20 c. black and orange .. 8 8
23. – 25 c. black and olive .. 8 8
24. – 30 c. brown and black .. 8 8
25. – 50 c. brown and purple .. 8 8
26. – 75 c. brown and red .. 8 8
27. – 80 c. brown and red .. 8 8
28. 6. 1 l. black and violet .. 3·25 45
29. 1 l. 25 black and blue .. 18·00 1·40
30. 2 l. black and brown .. 29·00 7·00
31. 2 l. 75 black and purple .. 35·00 27·00
32. – 5 l. green and brown .. 12 20
33. – 10 l. green and blue .. 20 25
34. – 20 l. green and black .. 25 45

DESIGNS—As T **5**: 10 c. to 25 c. Wing of Vatican Palace. 30 c. to 80 c. Vatican Gardens and Dome of St. Peter's. As T **6**: 5 l. to 20 l. St. Peter's Basilica.

1934. Surch.
35. 2. 40 c. on 80 c. red .. 2·10 1·75
36. 1 l. 30 on 1 l. 25 blue .. £180 25·00
37. 2 l. 05 on 2 l. brown .. £225 6·50
38. 2 l. 55 on 2 l. 50 red .. £140 80·00
39. 3 l. 05 on 5 l. green .. £475 £160
40. 3 l. 70 on 10 l. black .. £450 £225

7. Tribonian presenting Pandects to Justinian. 9. Doves and Bell.

1935. Int. Juridical Congress, Rome.
41. 7. 5 c. orange .. .. 2·00 55
42. 10 c. violet .. .. 2·00 35
43. 25 c. green .. .. 21·00 3·25
44. – 75 c. red .. .. £110 12·00
45. – 80 c. brown .. .. 85·00 8·00
46. – 1 l. 25 blue .. .. £140 8·00

DESIGN: 75 c., 80 c., 1 l. 25 c. Pope Gregory IX presents Decretals to jurist.

1936. Catholic Press.
47. 9. 5 c. green 50 50
48. – 10 c. black 35 35
49. – 25 c. green .. .. 40·00 1·75
50. 9. 50 c. purple 40 40
51. – 75 c. red .. .. 60·00 14·00
52. – 80 c. brown 70 90
53. – 1 l. 25 blue .. .. 1·40 1·40
54. – 5 l. brown .. .. 1·25 1·40

DESIGNS: 10 c., 75 c. Church and Bible. 25 c., 80 c. St. John Bosco. 1 l. 25, 5 l. St. Francis of Sales.

10. Statue of St. Peter. 11. Ascension of Elijah.

1938. Air.
55. 10. 25 c. brown 10 15
56. – 50 c. green 10 15
57. 11. 75 c. red 10 15
58. – 80 c. blue 10 15
59. 10. 1 l. violet 45 30
60. – 2 l. blue 55 55
61. 11. 5 l. black .. .. 1·90 1·75
62. – 10 l. purple .. .. 1·50 1·40

DESIGNS: 50 c., 2 l. Dove with olive branch and St. Peter's Square. 80 c., 10 l. Transportation of the Holy House.

12. Crypt of Basilica of St. Cecilia. 13. Coronation.

1938. Int. Christian Archaeological Congress. Inscr. "CONGRESSVS INTERNAT. ARCHAEOLOGIAE CHRIST".
63. 12. 5 c. brown 20 20
64. 10 c. orange 30 30
65. 25 c. green 30 30
66. – 75 c. red .. .. 7·50 6·00
67. – 80 c. violet .. .. 35·00 12·00
68. – 1 l. 25 blue .. .. 29·00 11·00

DESIGN: 75 c., 80 c., and 1 l. 25 Basilica of Saints Nereus and Achilles in the Catacombs of Domitilla.

1939. Death of Pope Pius XI. Optd. **SEDE VACANTE MCMXXXIX.**
69. 1. 5 c. brown on rose .. 50·00 2·75
70. 10 c. green on green .. 40 20
71. 20 c. violet on lilac .. 60 20
72. 25 c. blue on blue .. 3·50 2·75
73. 30 c. black on yellow .. 1·25 45
74. 50 c. black on pink .. 60 30
75. 75 c. red on grey .. 1·25 30

1939. Coronation of Pope Pius XII.
76. 13. 25 c. green .. .. 2·75 60
77. 75 c. red 20 60
78. 80 c. violet .. .. 4·00 1·25
79. 1 l. 25 blue 20 90

14. Arms of Pope Pius XII. 15. Pope Pius XII.

1940. Coronation of Pope Pius XII. 1st Anniv.
80. 14. 5 c. red 5 5
99. 5 c. grey 5 8
00. 30 c. brown 8 10
101. 50 c. green 8 10
81. 15. 1 l. black and violet .. 20 20
102. – 1 l. black and brown .. 8 10
82. – 1 l. 25 black and blue .. 10 10
103. – 1 l. 50 black and red .. 8 10
83. 15. 2 l. black and brown .. 1·50 1·40
104. – 2 l. 50 black and blue .. 8 10
84. 2 l. 75 black and purple 1·50 1·75
105. 15. 5 l. black and lilac .. 10 15
106. 20 l. black and green .. 15 20

DESIGN: 1 l. (No. 102) 1 l. 25, 1 l. 50, 2 l. 50 and 2 l. 75 as T **15** but with portrait of Pope facing left.

16. 17. Consecration of Archbishop Pacelli.

1942. Prisoners of War Relief Fund. 1st series. Inscr. "MCMXLII".
85. 16. 25 c. green 5 8
86. 80 c. brown 8 10
87. 1 l. 25 blue 15 20

1943. Pope's Episcopal Silver Jubilee.
88. 17. 25 c. green 8 8
89. 80 c. brown 8 8
90. 1 l. 25 blue 8 8
91. 5 l. blue and black .. 60 70

1944. Prisoners of War Relief Fund. 2nd series. Inscr. "MCMXLIII".
92. 16. 25 c. green 5 8
93. 80 c. brown 5 8
94. 1 l. 25 blue 20 25

18. Raphael. 19. St. Ignatius of Loyola.

1944. 4th Cent. of Pontifical academy of the Virtuosi of the Pantheon. Inscr. "1543–1943".
95. 18. 25 c. olive and green .. 5 5
96. – 80 c. violet and lilac .. 8 8
97. – 1 l. 25 c. blue and violet 8 8
98. – 10 l. bistre and yellow .. 80 1·10

PORTRAITS: 80 c. Sangallo (architect). 1 l. 25 c. Maratti (painter). 10 l. Canova (sculptor).

1945. Prisoners of War Relief Fund. 3rd Series. Inscr. "MCMXLIV".
107. 16. 1 l. green 5 8
108. 3 l. red 5 8
109. 5 l. blue 20 20

1946. Surch. in figures between bars.
110. 14. 20 c. on 5 c. grey .. 5 8
111. 25 c. on 30 c. brown .. 8 10
112. 1 l. on 50 c. green .. 8 10
113. – 1 l. 50 c. on 1 l. black and brown (No. 102) .. 8 10
114. – 3 l. on 1 l. 50 c. black and red (No. 103) .. 8 10
115. – 5 l. on 2 l. 50 c. black and blue (No. 104) .. 12 15
116. 15. 10 l. on 5 l. blk. & lilac 25 25
117. 30 l. on 20 l. black & grn. 60 75

1946. Inaug. of Council of Trent. 400th Anniv.
118. – 5 c. brown and bistre .. 5 8
119. – 25 c. brown and violet .. 5 8
120. – 50 c. brown and orange 5 8
121. 19. 75 c. brown and black .. 5 8
122. – 1 l. brown and purple .. 5 8
123. – 1 l. 50 c. brown and red 5 8
124. – 2 l. brown and green .. 5 8
125. – 2 l. 50 c. brown and blue 5 8
126. – 3 l. brown and red .. 5 8
127. – 4 l. brown and bistre .. 5 8
128. – 5 l. brown and blue .. 15 20
129. – 10 l. brown and red .. 15 20

DESIGNS: 5 c. Trent Cathedral. 25 c. St. Angela Merici. 50 c. St. Anthony Maria Zaccaria. 1 l. St. Cajetan of Thiene. 1 l. 50 c. St. John Fisher, Bishop of Rochester. 2 l. Cristoforo Madrussi, Bishop of Trent. 2 l. 50 c. Reginald Pole, Archbishop of Canterbury. 3 l. Marcello Cervini. 4 l. Giovanni Maria Del Monte. 5 l. Emperor Charles V. 10 l. Pope Paul III Farnese.

20. Dove with Olive Branch over St. Peter's Forecourt. 21. Swallows circling Spire of St. Peter's Basilica.

22. "Raphael accompanying Tobias" (after Botticelli).

DESIGN—VERT As T **20**: 4 l 25 l. Transportation of the Holy House.

1947. Air.
130. 20. 1 l. red 5 5
131. – 4 l. brown 8 8
132. 20. 5 l. blue 8 8
133. 21. 15 l. violet .. .. 1·25 55
134. – 25 l. green .. .. 1·40 55
135. 21. 50 l. black .. .. 3·25 1·00
136. 100 l. orange .. .. 5·00 1·25
137. 22. 250 l. black .. .. 11·00 4·25
138. 500 l. blue £325 £170

23. St. Agnes Basilica. 24. Pope Pius XII.

1949.
139. 23. 1 l. sepia 8 8
140. – 3 l. violet 8 8
141. – 5 l. orange 12 8
142. – 8 l. green 8 8
143. – 13 l. green .. .. 3·25 3·00
144. – 16 l. olive 25 25
145. – 25 l. red .. .. 4·50 60
146. – 35 l. mauve .. .. 23·00 10·00
147. – 40 l. blue 20 12
148. 24. 100 l. black .. .. 1·75 2·10

DESIGNS (Basilicas)—VERT. 3 l. St. Clement. 5 l. St. Praxedes. 8 l. St. Mary in Cosmedin. HORIZ. 13 l. Holy Cross. 16 l. St. Sebastian. 25 l. St. Laurence. 35 l. St. Paul. 40 l. St. Mary Major.

25. Angels over Globe. 26. "I Will Give You the Keys of the Kingdom".

1949. Air. U.P.U. 75th Anniv.
149. 25. 300 l. blue .. .. 29·00 8·50
150. 1,000 l. green .. .. 60·00 50·00

1949. "Holy Year".
151. 26. 5 l. chocolate & brown .. 8 8
152. – 6 l. brown and black .. 8 8
153. – 8 l. green and blue .. 50 60
154. – 10 l. blue and green .. 8 8
155. – 20 l. lake and green .. 1·25 40
156. – 25 l. blue and brown .. 90 40
157. – 30 l. purple and green .. 2·50 1·90
158. – 60 l. red and brown .. 1·60 1·50

DESIGNS: 6 l., 25 l. Four Basilicas. 8 l., 30 l. Pope Boniface VIII. 10 l., 60 l. Pope Pius XII opening the Holy Door.

27. Guards Marching. 28. Pope Proclaiming Dogma.

1950. Papal Guard. Cent.
159. 27. 25 l. sepia .. .. 16·00 12·00
160. 35 l. green .. .. 6·50 6·50
161. 55 l. brown .. .. 3·00 3·00

1951. Proclamation of Dogma of the Assumption.
162. 28. 25 l. purple 85 40
163. – 55 l. blue .. .. 7·50 7·00

DESIGN: 55 l. Angels over St. Peter's.

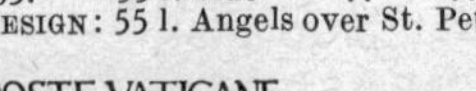

29. Pope Pius X. 30. Final Session of Council (fresco).

1951. Beatification of Pope Pius X.
164. 29. 6 l. gold and violet .. 15 20
165. 10 l. gold and green .. 25 20
166. – 60 l. gold and blue .. 8·00 6·00
167. – 115 l. gold and brown .. 9·50 8·50

DESIGN: 60 l., 115 l. Pope looking left.

1951. Council of Chalcedon. 1500th Anniv.
168. 30. 5 l. slate 20 20
169. – 25 l. brown .. .. 1·60 1·60
170. 30. 35 l. red .. .. 4·00 3·25
171. – 60 l. blue .. .. 16·00 11·00
172. 30. 100 l. brown .. .. 22·00 16·00

DESIGN: 25 l., 60 l. "Pope Leo I meeting Attila" (Raphael).

31. Gratian. 32. Mail Coach and First Stamp.

1951. Air. Decree of Gratian. 800th Anniv.
173. 31. 300 l. purple £140 £120
174. 500 l. blue .. .. 42·00 8·50

1952. No. 143 surch. **L. 12** and bars.
175. – 12 l. on 13 l. green 2·50 2·10

1952. Cent. of First Papal States' Stamp.
176. 32. 50 l. black and blue .. 5·50 5·50

33. St. Maria Goretti.

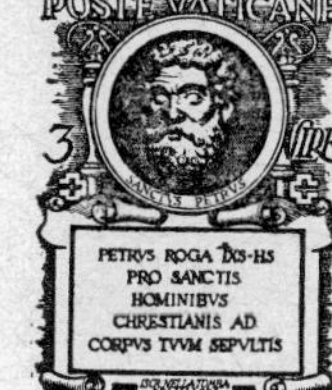

34. St. Peter and Inscription.

1953. Martyrdom of St. Maria Goretti. 50th Anniv.

177. **33.** 15 l. violet and brown .. 2·75 2·50
178. 25 l. brown and red .. 1·75 1·10

1953. Portraits of Popes and Views of St. Peter's Bascilica. Medallions in black.

179. **34.** 3 l. lake 5 5
180. – 5 l. slate 5 5
181. – 10 l. green 5 5
182. – 12 l. brown 5 5
183. – 20 l. violet 15 15
184. – 25 l. sepia 5 5
185. – 35 l. red 5 5
186. – 45 l. olive 40 45
187. – 60 l. blue 8 8
188. – 65 l. red 25 30
189. – 100 l. plum 10 8

DESIGNS—VERT. 5 l. Pius XII and sepulchre. 10 l. St. Peter and tomb. 12 l. St. Sylvester I and Constantine's Basilica. 20 l. Julius II and St. Peter's Basilica. 25 l. Paul III and apse. 35 l. Sixtus V and cupola. 45 l. Paul V and façade. 60 l. Urban VIII and baldaquin. 65 l. Alexander VII and colonnade. 100 l. Pius VI and sacristy.

35. Dome of St. Peter's.

36. St. Clare of Assisi (after Giotto).

1953. Air.

190. **35.** 500 l. chocolate .. 21·00 5·00
190a. 500 l. green .. .. 4·00 3·75
191. 1,000 l. blue .. .. 35·00 11·00
191b. 1,000 l. red .. .. 1·10 70

1953. St. Clare. 700th Death Anniv.

192. **36.** 25 l. sepia, ochre & turq. 2·10 2·10
193. 35 l. sepia, ochre and chestnut .. .. 9·00 9·00

37. "St. Bernard" (after Lippi).

38. Pier Lombardo, Bishop of Paris.

1953. St. Bernard of Clairvaux. 800th Death Anniv.

194. **37.** 20 l. maroon and olive 1·10 1·10
195. 60 l. myrtle and blue .. 4·50 4·25

1953. "Libri Sententiarum" (theological treatise). 800th Anniv.

196. **38.** 100 l. yell., blue and red 29·00 24·00

39. Pope Pius XI and Vatican City.

1954. Lateran Treaty. 25th Anniv.

197. **39.** 25 l. brown and blue .. 1·75 1·50
198. 60 l. blue and ochre .. 2·75 3·00

40. Pope Pius XII.

1954. Marian Year and Cent. of Dogma of the Immaculate Conception.

199. – 3 l. violet 5 5
200. **40.** 4 l. red 5 5
201. – 6 l. claret 5 5
202. **40.** 12 l. blue-green .. 75 70
203. – 20 l. chocolate .. 80 80
204. **40.** 35 l. blue .. .. 2·10 2·10

DESIGN: 3 l., 6 l., 20 l. Pope Pius IX facing right with different inscr. and dates "1854–1954".

41. St. Pius X.

42. Basilica of St. Francis of Assisi.

43. "St. Augustine" (after Botticelli).

44. Madonna of Ostra Vrama, Vilna, Poland.

1954. Canonization of Pope Pius X.

205. **41.** 10 l. red, yell. & brown 20 20
206. 25 l. red, yell. & violet 2·00 2·10
207. 35 l. red, yell. & green 2·75 3·00

1954. Elevation of Basilica to Papal Chapel. Bicent.

208. **42.** 20 l. black and cream .. 1·60 1·40
209. 35 l. brown and cream 1·25 1·25

1954. St. Augustine. 1600th Birth Anniv.

210. **43.** 35 l. green .. 1·10 1·10
211. 50 l. brown .. .. 1·25 1·25

1954. Termination of Marian Year.

212. **44.** 20 l. yell., bl., brn. & red 1·10 1·10
213. 35 l. yell., brn., red & bl. 5·50 5·50
214. 60 l. yell., red, bl. & brn. 8·00 8·00

45. St. Boniface and Fulda Monastery.

46. "Pope Sixtus II and St. Lawrence" (fresco).

1955. Martyrdom of St. Boniface. 1,200th Anniv.

215. **45.** 10 l. black 12 12
216. 35 l. violet .. .. 1·10 1·10
217. 60 l. turquoise .. 85 75

1955. Fra Giovanni de Fiesole ("Fra Angelico"), painter. 500th Death Anniv.

218. **46.** 50 l. red .. .. 3·00 3·00
219. 100 l. blue .. .. 1·10 1·10

47. Pope Nicholas V. (after Fra Angelico).

48. St. Bartholomew.

1955. Pope Nicholas V. 5th Death Cent.

220. **47.** 20 l. brown and blue .. 40 35
221. 35 l. brown and red .. 70 35
222. 60 l. brown and green .. 1·10 1·40

1955. St. Bartholomew the Young. 9th Death Cent.

223. **48.** 10 l. black and brown .. 8 8
224. 25 l. black and red .. 65 45
225. 100 l. black and green 1·90 2·00

49. "Annunciation" (Melozzo da Forli).

50. Corporal of the Guard.

1956. Air.

226. **49.** 5 l. black 5 5
227. A. 10 l. green 5 5
228. B. 15 l. orange 5 5
229. **49.** 25 l. red 15 5
230. A. 35 l. red 40 40
231. B. 50 l. sepia 8 8
232. **49.** 60 l. blue .. .. 1·90 1·90
233. A. 100 l. brown 12 8
234. B. 300 l. violet 30 25

PAINTINGS: A. "Annunciation" (P. Cavallini). B. "Annunciation" (Leonardo da Vinci).

1956. Swiss Guard. 450th Anniv. Inscr. as in T **50.**

235. – 4 l. red 5 5
236. **50.** 6 l. orange 5 5
237. – 10 l. blue 5 5
238. – 35 l. brown 50 50
239. **50.** 50 l. violet .. .. 1·10 1·10
240. – 60 l. green .. .. 1·25 1·25

DESIGNS: 4 l., 35 l. Captain Roust. 10 l., 60 l. Two drummers.

51. St. Rita.

52. St. Ignatius presenting Jesuit Constitution to Pope Paul III.

1956. St. Rita at Cascia. 5th Death Cent.

241. **51.** 10 l. grey 5 5
242. 25 l. brown 60 60
243. 35 l. blue 45 45

1956. St. Ignatius of Loyola. 4th Death Cent.

244. **52.** 35 l. brown 60 55
245. 60 l. slate 85 90

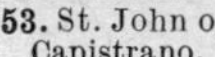

53. St. John of Capistrano.

54. Madonna and Child.

1956. St. John of Capistrano. 5th Death Cent.

246. **53.** 25 l. green and slate .. 1·75 1·60
247 35 l. brown and maroon 55 55

1956. "Black Madonna" of Czestochowa Commemoration.

248. **54.** 35 l. black and blue .. 20 20
249. 60 l. blue and green .. 55 50
250. 100 l. lake and sepia .. 60 70

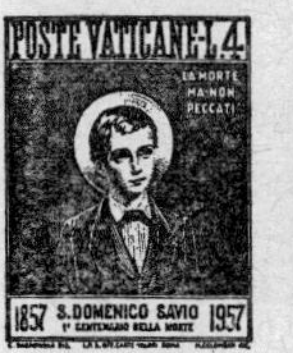

55. St. Domenico Savio.

56. Cardinal D. Capranica (founder) and Capranica College.

1957. St. Domenico Savio. Death Cent. Inscr. as in T **55.**

251. **55.** 4 l. brown 5 5
252. – 6 l. red 5 5
253. **55.** 25 l. green 35 35
254. – 60 l. blue .. .. 1·00 1·00

DESIGN: 6 l., 60 l. St. Domenico Savio and St. John Bosco.

1957. 5th Cent. of Capranica College.

255. **56.** 5 l. lake 5 5
256. – 10 l. brown 5 5
257. **56.** 35 l. slate 30 30
258. – 100 l. blue 80 80

DESIGNS—HORIZ. 10 l., 100 l. Pope Pius XII and plaque.

57. Pontifical Academy of Science.

58. Mariazell Basilica.

59. Apparition of the Virgin Mary.

1957. 20th Anniv. of the Pontifical Academy of Science.

259. **57.** 35 l. green and blue .. 55 55
260. 60 l. blue and brown 65 65

1957. Mariazell Basilica. 8th Cent.

261. **58.** 5 l. green 5 5
262. – 15 l. slate 5 5
263. **58.** 60 l. blue 30 30
264. – 100 l. violet 80 80

DESIGN: 15 l., 100 l. Statue of the Virgin of Mariazell within Sanctuary.

1958. Cent. of the Apparition of the Virgin Mary at Lourdes.

265. **59.** 5 l. blue 5 5
266. – 10 l. green 5 5
267. – 15 l. brown 5 5
268. **59.** 25 l. red 8 8
269. – 35 l. sepia 12 15
270. – 100 l. violet 12 20

DESIGNS—VERT. 10 l., 35 l. Invalid at Lourdes. 15 l., 100 l. St. Bernadette.

60. "Civitas Dei" ("City of God" at Exhibition).

61. Pope Clement XIII (from sculpture by A. Canova).

1958. Brussels International Exhibition.

271. – 35 l. claret 20 20
272. **60.** 60 l. chestnut 40 40
273. – 100 l. violet .. .. 2·00 2·25
274. – 300 l. blue .. .. 1·40 1·60

DESIGN—VERT. 35 l., 300 l. Pope Pius XII.

1958. Antonio Canova (sculptor). Birth Bicent. Inscr. "MDCCLVII MCMLVII".

275. **61.** 5 l. brown 5 5
276. – 10 r. red 5 5
277. – 35 l. grey 25 25
278. – 100 l. blue 60 60

SCULPTURES: 10 l. Pope Clement XIV. 35 l. Pope Pius VI. 100 l. Pope Pius VII.

62. St. Peter's Keys.

63. Pope John XXIII.

1958. "Vacant See."

279. **62.** 15 l. sepia on yellow .. 5·00 3·00
280. 25 l. sepia 20 20
281. 60 l. sepia on lavender .. 20 20

1959. Coronation of Pope John XXIII. Inscr. "IV-XI MCMLVIII".

282. **63.** 25 l. multicoloured .. 8 8
283. – 35 l. multicoloured .. 8 8
284. **63.** 60 l. multicoloured .. 12 12
285. – 100 l. multicoloured .. 12 12

DESIGN: 35 l., 100 l. Arms of Pope John XXIII.

64. St. Lawrence. **65.** Pope Pius XI.

1959. Martyrs' Commemoration.

286. **64.** 15 l. brown, yell. & red 5 5
287. – 25 l. brown, yell. & lilac 30 15
288. – 50 l. brn., yell., blk. & turquoise .. .. 1·25 90
289. – 60 l. brown, yell. & grn. 80 70
290. – 100 l. brn., yell. & mar. 60 40
291. – 300 l. sepia and buff .. 1·50 70

PORTRAITS: 25 l. Pope Sixtus II. 50 l. St. Agapitus. 60 l. St. Filisissimus. 100 l. St. Cyprian. 300 l. St. Fructuosus.

1959. Lateran Treaty. 30th Anniv.

292. **65.** 30 l. brown 8 10
293. 100 l. blue 35 30

66. Radio Mast. **67.** Lateran Obelisk and St. John Lateran Basilica.

1959. St. Maria di Galeria Radio Station, Vatican City. 2nd Anniv.

294. **66.** 25 l. rose, yell. & black 12 12
295. 60 l. yellow, red and blue 35 35

1959. Air. Roman Obelisks.

296. **67.** 5 l. violet 5 5
297. – 10 l. green 5 5
298. – 15 l. sepia 5 5
299. – 15 l. bronze-green .. 5 5
300. – 35 l. blue 8 8
301. **67.** 50 l. green 8 8
302. – 60 l. crimson 8 8
303. – 100 l. indigo 12 8
304. – 200 l. brown 20 20
305. – 500 l. chestnut .. 50 30

DESIGNS: 10 l., 60 l. Esquilino Obelisk and St. Mary Major Basilica. 15 l., 100 l. Vatican Obelisk and Apostolic Palace. 25 l., 200 l. Flaminio Obelisk and Churches of St. Mary in Montesanto and St. Mary of the Miracles. 35 l., 500 l. Sallustian Obelisk and Trinita del Monti Church.

68. St. Casimir Vilna Palace and Cathedral. **69.** "Christ Adored by the Magi" (after Raphael).

1959. St. Casimir (patron saint of Lithuania). 5th Birth Cent.

306. **68.** 50 l. brown 30 20
307. 100 l. green 30 20

1959. Christmas Issue.

308. **69.** 15 l. black 5 5
309. 25 l. crimson 12 12
310. 60 l. blue 50 50

70. "St. Antoninus" (after Dupre). **71.** Transept of St. John Lateran Basilica.

1960. St. Antoninus of Florence. 5th Death Cent. Inscr. "S. ANTONINUS MCDLIX MCMLIX".

311. **70.** 15 l. blue 5 5
312. – 25 l. turquoise 12 12
313. **70.** 60 l. brown 60 50
314. – 110 l. claret 90 80

DESIGN: 25 l., 110 l. "St. Antoninus preaching sermon" (after Portigiani).

1960. Roman Synod Commem.

315. **71.** 15 l. sepia 5 5
316. 60 l. black 80 55

72. "The Flight into Egypt" (after Beato Angelico). **73.** Cardinal Sarto (Pius X) leaving Venice for Conclave in Rome.

1960. World Refugee Year. Inscr. as in T **72.**

317. **72.** 5 l. green 5 5
318. – 10 l. sepia 5 5
319. – 25 l. red 8 8
320. **72.** 60 l. violet 10 10
321. – 100 l. blue .. .. 3·00 2·75
322. – 300 l. blue-green .. 1·60 1·25

DESIGNS: 10 l., 100 l. "St. Peter giving Alms". 25 l., 300 l. "Madonna of Mercy".

1960. 1st Anniv. of Transfer of Relics of Pope Pius X from Rome to Venice. Inscr. as in T **73.**

323. **73.** 15 l. brown 5 5
324. – 35 l. red 15 15
325. – 60 l. turquoise .. 30 30

DESIGNS: 35 l. Pope John XXIII kneeling before relics of Pope Pius X. 60 l. Relics in procession across St. Mark's Square, Venice.

74. "Feeding the Hungry".

1960. "Corporal Works of Mercy". Della Robbia paintings. Centres in sepia.

326. **74.** 5 l. red-brown 5 5
327. – 10 l. green 5 5
328. – 15 l. black 5 5
329. – 20 l. crimson 5 5
330. – 30 l. violet 5 5
331. – 35 l. chocolate 5 5
332. – 40 l. orange 8 8
333. – 70 l. ochre 8 8

DESIGNS: 10 l. "Giving drinks to the thirsty". 15 l. "Clothing the naked". 20 l. "Sheltering the homeless". 30 l. "Visiting the sick". 35 l. "Visiting the imprisoned". 40 l. "Burying the dead". 70 l. Pope John XXIII between 'Faith" and "Charity".

75. "The Nativity" after Gerard Honthurst (Gherardo delle Notte). **76.** St. Vincent de Paul.

1960. Christmas.

334. **75.** 10 l. black & grey-green 5 5
335. 15 l. olive-brn. & bistre 8 5
336. 70 l. blue and turquoise 50 40

1960. Death Tercent. of St. Vincent de Paul and St. Louise de Marillac.

337. **76.** 40 l. slate-violet .. 15 15
338. – 70 l. black 55 25
339. – 100 l. brown 75 65

DESIGNS: 70 l. St. Louise de Marillac. 100 l. St. Vincent giving child to care of St. Louise.

77. St. Meinrad. **78.** Pope Leo I meeting Attila (after Algardi).

1961. St. Meinrad. 11th Death Cent. Inscr. "861—JUBILAEUM S. Meinardi—1961".

340. **77.** 30 l. black 15 8
341. – 40 l. lilac 45 35
342. – 100 l. brown 95 75

DESIGNS—VERT. 40 l. The "Black Madonna". Einsiedeln Abbey. HORIZ. 100 l. Einsiedeln Abbey, Switzerland.

1961. Pope Leo I. 15th Death Cent.

343. **78.** 15 l. lake 5 5
344. 70 l. green 90 55
345. 300 l. sepia .. .. 3·00 1·50

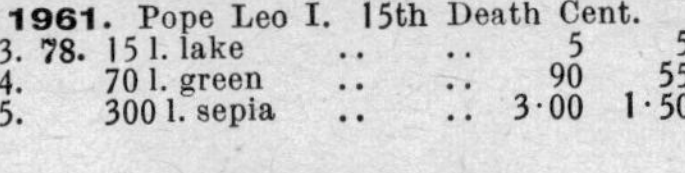

79. Route of St. Paul's Journey to Rome.

1961. St. Paul's Arrival in Rome. 19th Cent. Inscr. "LXI–MCMLXI".

346. **79.** 10 l. blue-green .. 5 5
347. – 15 l. black & pur.-brown 8 8
348. – 20 l. black and salmon 12 12
349. **79.** 30 l. blue 40 20
350. – 75 l. black and brown .. 1·25 60
351. – 200 l. black and blue .. 2·10 1·00

DESIGNS: 15 l., 75 l. St. Paul's arrival in Rome (after sculpture by Maraini). 20 l., 200 l. Basilica of St. Paul-outside-the-Walls, Rome.

80. "L'Osservatore Romano," 1861 and 1961. **81.** St. Patrick (ancient sculpture).

1961. "L'Osservatore Romano" Cent. (Vatican newspaper).

352. **80.** 40 l. black and chocolate 40 25
353. – 70 l. black and blue .. 1·25 55
354. – 250 l. black and yellow 3·25 1·25

DESIGNS: 70 l. "L'Osservatore Romano" offices. 250 l. Printing machine.

1961. St. Patrick. 15th Death Cent.

355. **81.** 10 l. green and buff .. 5 5
356. – 15 l. sepia and blue .. 10 10
357. **81.** 40 l. green and yellow .. 40 25
358. – 150 l. brown & turquoise 1·10 1·00

DESIGN: 15 l., 150 l. St. Patrick's Sanctuary. Lough Derg.

82. Arms of Roncalli Family. **83.** "The Nativity".

1961. Pope John XXIII's 80th Birthday. Inscr. as in T **82.**

359. **82.** 10 l. brown and black .. 5 5
360. – 25 l. green & bistre-brn. 8 8
362. – 30 l. violet and blue .. 15 15
362. – 40 l. blue and violet .. 25 15
363. – 70 l. brown and grey .. 75 40
364. – 115 l. black and brown 1·75 1·00

DESIGNS: 25 l. Church of St. Mary, Sotto il Monte. 30 l. Church of St. Mary, Monte Santo. 40 l. Church of Saints Ambrose and Charles, Rome. 70 l. St. Peter's Chair, Vatican Basilica. 115 l. Pope John XXIII.

1961. Christmas. Centres multicoloured.

365. **83.** 15 l. blue-green .. 5 5
366. 40 l. grey 12 8
367. 70 l. purple 35 35

84. "Annunciation" (after F. Valle). **85.** "Land Reclamation" Medal of 1588.

1962. Air.

368. **84.** 1000 l. brown .. .. 1·25 80
369. 1500 l. blue .. .. 3·75 3·00

1962. Malaria Eradication.

370. **85.** 15 l. violet 5 5
371 – 40 l. red 15 8
372. **85.** 70 l. brown 30 20
373. – 300 l. green .. .. 1·25 70

DESIGN: 40 l., 300 l. Map of Pontine Marshes reclamation project (at time of Pope Pius VI).

86. "The Good Shepherd" (statue, Lateran Museum). **87.** St. Catherine (after Il Sodoma (Bazzi)).

1962. Religious Vocations.

374. **86.** 10 l. black and violet .. 5 5
375. – 15 l. chestnut and blue 8 8
376. **86.** 70 l. black and green .. 60 35
377. – 115 l. chestnut and red 1·40 70
378. **86.** 200 l. black and brown 2·75 1·25

DESIGN: 15 l., 115 l. Wheatfield ready for harvest.

1962. St. Catherine of Siena's Canonization. 5th Cent.

379. **87.** 15 l. brown 5 5
380. 60 l. violet 55 55
381. 100 l. blue 80 80

88. Paulina M. Jaricot. **89.** St. Peter and St. Paul (from graffito on child's tomb).

1962. Paulina M. Jaricot (founder of Society for the Propagation of the Faith). Death Cent. Multicoloured centres.

382. **88.** 10 l. lilac 5 5
383 50 l. blue-green .. 35 35
384. 150 l. grey 60 60

1962. 6th Int. Christian Archaeology Congress, Ravenna.

385. **89.** 20 l. sepia and violet .. 5 5
386. – 40 l. grey-green and brn. 8 8
387. **89.** 70 l. sepia and turquoise 12 12
388. – 100 l. grey-green and red 15 15

DESIGN: 40 l., 100 l. "The Passion" (from bas relief on tomb in Domitilla cemetery, near Rome).

90. "Faith" (after Raphael). **91.** "The Nativity".

1962. Ecumenical Council.

389. **90.** 5 l. sepia and blue .. 5 5
390. – 10 l. sepia and green .. 5 5
391. – 15 l. sepia and red .. 5 5
392. – 25 l. grey and red .. 5 5
393. – 30 l. black and mauve .. 5 5
394. – 40 l. sepia and red .. 5 5
395. – 60 l. chestnut and green 8 8
396. – 115 l. red 12 12

DESIGNS—Divine Virtues: 10 l. "Hope". 15 l. "Charity" (both after Raphael). 25 l. Arms of Pope John and symbols of Evangelists. 30 l. Council Room, St. Peter's. 40 l. Pope John XXIII. 60 l. "St. Peter" (bronze in Vatican Basilica). 115 l. The Holy Ghost in form of dove.

1962. Christmas. Centres multicoloured.

397. **91.** 10 l. grey 5 5
398. 15 l. drab 5 5
399. 90 l. green 20 20

92. "Miracle of the Loaves and Fishes" (after Murillo).

93. Pope John XXIII.

1963. Freedom from Hunger.

400.	92.	15 l. sepia and brown ..	5	5
401.	–	40 l. green and red ..	5	5
402.	92.	100 l. sepia and blue ..	10	10
403.	–	200 l. green and turq...	20	20

DESIGN: 40 l., 200 l. "Miracle of the Fishes" (after Raphael).

1963. Award of Balzan Peace Prize to Pope John XXIII.

404.	93.	15 l. brown	5	5
405.		160 l. black	55	55

94. St. Peter's Keys.

95. Pope Paul VI.

1963. "Vacant See".

406.	94.	10 l. sepia	5	5
407.		40 l. sepia on yellow ..	8	10
408.		100 l. sepia on violet	12	12

1963. Coronation of Pope Paul VI. Inscr. as in T 95.

409.	95.	15 l. black	5	5
410.	–	40 l. red	15	12
411.	95.	115 l. brown	40	30
412.	–	200 l. grey	1·00	40

DESIGN: 40 l., 200 l. Arms of Pope Paul VI.

96. "The Nativity" (African terracotta statuette).

97. St. Cyril.

1963. Christmas.

413.	96.	10 l. brown and bistre ..	5	5
414.		40 l. brown and blue ..	8	8
415.		100 l. brown and olive ..	45	45

1963. Conversion of Slavs by Saints Cyril and Methodius. 1100th Anniv.

416.	97.	30 l. purple	8	8
417.	–	70 l. brown	60	45
418.	–	150 l. claret	80	55

DESIGNS: 70 l. Map of Moravia. 150 l. St. Methodius.

98. Pope Paul VI.

99. St. Peter, Pharoah's Tomb, Wadi-es-Sebua.

1964. Pope Paul's Visit to the Holy Land.

419.	98.	15 l. black	5	5
420.	–	25 l. red	5	5
421.	–	70 l. sepia	5	5
422.	–	160 l. blue	12	12

DESIGNS: 25 l. Church of the Nativity, Bethlehem. 70 l. Church of the Holy Sepulchre, Jerusalem. 160 l. Well of the Virgin Mary, Nazareth.

1964. Nubian Monuments Preservation.

423.	96.	10 l. brown and blue ..	5	5
424.	–	20 l. multicoloured ..	5	5
425.	99.	70 l. brown and olive ..	15	12
426.	–	200 l. multicoloured ..	25	20

DESIGN: 20 l., 200 l. Philae Temple.

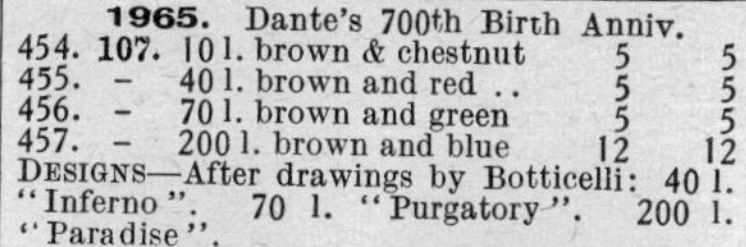

100. Pope Paul VI.

101. Michelangelo.

1964. New York World's Fair.

427.	100.	15 l. blue	5	5
428.	–	50 l. sepia	5	5
429.	100.	100 l. blue	8	8
430.	–	250 l. brown	15	15

DESIGNS: 50 l. Michelangelo's "Pieta". 250 l. Detail of Madonna's head from "Pieta".

1964. Michelangelo. 400th Death Anniv. Paintings in the Sistine Chapel.

431.	101.	10 l. black	5	5
432.	–	25 l. claret	5	5
433.	–	30 l. olive	5	5
434.	–	40 l. violet	5	5
435.	–	150 l. green	10	10

PAINTINGS: 25 l. Prophet Isaiah. 30 l. Delphic Sibyl. 40 l. Prophet Jeremiah. 150 l. Prophet Joel.

102. "The Good Samaritan" (after Emilio Greco).

103. "Christmas Scene" (after Kimiko Koseki).

105. Pope Paul at prayer.

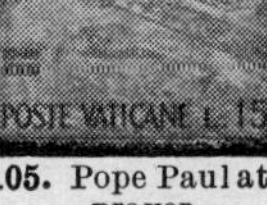

104. Cues's Birthplace.

1964. Red Cross Cent. Cross in red.

436.	102.	10 l. brown	5	5
437.		30 l. blue	5	5
438.		300 l. sepia	15	15

1964. Christmas.

439.	103.	10 l. multicoloured ..	5	5
440.		15 l. multicoloured ..	5	5
441.		135 l. multicoloured ..	15	15

1964. Nicholas Cues (Cardinal Cusanus). 500th Death Anniv.

442.	104.	40 l. green	5	5
443.	–	200 l. red	30	30

DESIGN: 200 l. Cardinal Cusanus's sepulchre, St. Peter's (relief by A. Bregno).

1964. Pope Paul's Visit to India.

444.	105.	15 l. purple	5	5
445.	–	25 l. green	5	5
446.	–	60 l. sepia	5	5
447.	–	200 l. purple	15	15

DESIGNS—HORIZ. 25 l. Public altar, "The Oval", Bombay. 60 l. "Gateway to India", Bombay. VERT. 200 l. Pope Paul walking across map of India.

106. St. Joseph Mukasa and Martyrs.

107. Dante (after Raphael).

1965. Ugandan Martyrs. T 106 and similar portrait designs.

448.	–	15 l. turquoise ..	5	5
449.	106.	20 l. brown	5	5
450.	–	30 l. blue	5	5
451.	–	75 l. black	10	10
452.	–	100 l. red	8	8
453.	–	160 l. violet	12	12

1965. Dante's 700th Birth Anniv.

454.	107.	10 l. brown & chestnut	5	5
455.	–	40 l. brown and red ..	5	5
456.	–	70 l. brown and green	5	5
457.	–	200 l. brown and blue	12	12

DESIGNS—After drawings by Botticelli: 40 l. "Inferno". 70 l. "Purgatory". 200 l. "Paradise".

108. St. Benedict (after Perugino).

109. Pope Paul.

1965. St. Benedict Commem.

458.	108.	40 l. brown	5	5
459.	–	300 l. green	15	15

DESIGN: 300 l. Monte Cassino Abbey.

1965. Pope Paul's Visit to the U.N., New York.

460.	109.	20 l. brown	5	5
461.	–	30 l. blue	5	5
462.	–	150 l. green	5	5
463.	109.	300 l. purple	10	10

DESIGN: 30 l., 150 l. U.N.O. Headquarters, New York.

110. "The Nativity" (Peruvian setting).

111. Pope Paul.

1965. Christmas.

464.	110.	20 l. lake	5	5
465.		40 l. brown	5	5
466.		200 l. green	10	10

1966.

467.	111.	5 l. sepia	5	5
468.	–	10 l. violet	5	5
469.	–	15 l. sepia	5	5
470.	–	20 l. green	5	5
471.	–	30 l. lake	5	5
472.	–	40 l. turquoise ..	5	5
473.	–	55 l. blue	8	8
474.	–	75 l. maroon	8	8
475.	–	90 l. magenta ..	10	8
476.	–	130 l. black	15	10

DESIGNS (SCULPTURES): 10 l. "Music". 15 l. "Science". 20 l. "Painting". 30 l. "Sculpture". 40 l. "Building". 55 l. "Carpentry". 75 l. "Agriculture". 90 l. "Metallurgy". 130 l. "Learning".

112. Queen Dabrowka and King Mieszko I.

113. Pope John XXIII and St. Peter's, Rome.

1966. Poland's Christian Millenium.

477.	112.	15 l. black	5	5
478.	–	25 l. violet	5	5
479.	–	40 l. red	5	5
480.	–	50 l. crimson	5	5
481.	–	150 l. slate	5	5
482.	–	220 l. brown	10	10

DESIGNS: 25 l. St. Adalbert (Wojciech), and Wroclaw and Gniezno Cathedrals. 40 l. St. Stanislas, Skalka Cathedral and Wawel Royal Palace, Cracow. 50 l. Queen Jadwiga (Hedwig), Ostra Brama Gate with Mater Misericordiae, Wilno and Jagellon University Library, Cracow. 150 l. "Black Madonna", Jasna Gora Monastery (Czestochowa) and St. John's Cathedral, Warsaw. 20 l. Pope Paul greeting Poles.

1966. Opening of Ecumenical Council 4th Anniv.

483.	113.	10 l. black and red ..	5	5
484.	–	15 l. green and brown	5	5
485.	–	55 l. magenta and sepia	5	5
486.	–	90 l. black and green	5	5
487.	–	100 l. yellow and green	8	8
488.	–	130 l. sepia and brown	8	8

DESIGNS: 15 l. Book of Prayer, St. Peter's. 55 l. Mass. 90 l. Pope Paul with Patriarch Athenagoras. 100 l. Episcopal ring. 130 l. Pope Paul at closing ceremony (12.10.65).

114. "The Nativity" (after sculpture by Scorzelli).

115. Aircraft over St. Peter's.

1966. Christmas.

489.	114.	20 l. plum	5	5
490.		55 l. green	5	5
491.		225 l. brown	10	10

1967. Air.

492.	115.	20 l. violet	5	5
493.	–	40 l. lilac and pink ..	8	8
494.	–	90 l. blue and grey ..	10	10
495.	115.	100 l. black and red ..	12	12
496.	–	200 l. lilac and grey ..	25	25
497.	–	500 l. choc. and brown	55	55

DESIGNS: 40 l., 200 l. Radio mast and St. Gabriel's statue. 90 l., 500 l. Aerial view of St. Peter's.

116. St. Peter.

117. "The Three Shepherd Children" (sculpture).

1967. Martyrdom of Saints Peter and Paul. 1900th Anniv. Multicoloured.

498.	15 l. Type 116	5	5
499.	20 l. St. Paul	5	5
500.	55 l. The two Saints ..	5	5
501.	90 l. Bernini's baldachin, St. Peter's	8	8
502.	220 l. Arnolfo di Cambio's tabernacle, St. Paul's Basilica	15	15

1967. Fatima Apparitions. 50th Anniv. Multicoloured.

503.	30 l. Type 117	5	5
504.	50 l. Basilica of Fatima ..	8	8
505.	200 l. Pope Paul VI praying before Virgin's statue at Fatima	25	25

118. Congress Emblem.

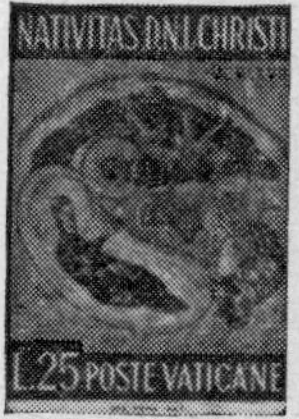

119. "The Nativity" (Byzantine carving).

1967. Third World Apostolic Laity Congress, Rome.

506.	118.	40 l. carmine	5	5
507.		130 l. blue	12	12

1967. Christmas.

508.	119.	25 l. multicoloured ..	5	5
509.		55 l. multicoloured ..	8	8
510.		180 l. multicoloured ..	20	20

120. "Angel Gabriel" (detail from "The Annunciation" by Fra Angelico).

121. Pope Paul VI.

1968. Air.

511.	120.	1000 l. carmine on cream	1·25	1·00
512.		1500 l. black on cream	2·10	1·90

1968. Pope Paul's Visit to Colombia.

513. 121. 25 l. brown and black 5 5
514. – 55 l. ochre, grey & blk. 8 8
515. – 220 l. sepia, blue & blk. 20 20

DESIGNS: 55 l. Monstrance (Raphael's "Disputa"). 220 l. Map of South America.

122. "The Holy Child of Prague".

123. "The Resurrection" (Fra Angelico).

1968. Christmas.

516. 122. 20 l. purple and red .. 5 5
517. 50 l. violet and lilac .. 8 8
518. 250 l. blue 20 20

1969. Easter.

519. 123. 20 l. carmine on buff .. 5 5
520. 90 l. green on buff .. 10 10
521. 180 l. ultramarine on buff 20 20

124. Colonnade.

125. Pope with Young Africans.

1969. Europa.

522. 124. 50 l. brown and slate .. 8 8
523. 90 l. brown and vermilion 12 12
524. 130 l. brown and green 25 25

1969. Pope Paul's visit to Uganda.

525. 125. 25 l. brown and ochre 5 5
526. – 55 l. brown and red 8 8
527. – 250 l. multicoloured .. 30 30

DESIGNS: 55 l. Pope with African bishops. 250 l. Map of Africa and olive-branch.

126. Pope Pius IX.

127. Osaka Building.

1969. St. Peter's Circle.

528. 126. 30 l. brown-red .. 5 5
529. – 50 l. slate 8 8
530. – 220 l. purple 45 45

DESIGNS: 50 l. Monogram. 220 l. Pope Paul VI.

1970. Expo 70. Multicoloured.

531. 25 l. Expo 70 Emblem .. 5 5
532. 40 l. Type 127 .. .. 8 8
533. 55 l. "Virgin and Child" (Domoto) 8 8
534. 90 l. Vatican City pavilion 10 10
535. 110 l. Mt. Fuji 60 60

128. Pope Pius IX's Arms.

129. "Christ" (R. v. d. Weyden).

1970. 1st Vatican Council. Cent.

536. – 20 l. chocolate & oran. 5 5
537. 128. 50 l. multicoloured .. 8 8
538. – 180 l. purple and red .. 25 25

DESIGNS: 20 l. Pope Pius IX's medal. 180 l. Council souvenir medal.

1970. Pope Paul's Ordination as Priest. 50th Anniv. Multicoloured.

539. 15 l. "Christ" (S. Martini) 5 5
540. 25 l. Type 129 .. .. 5 5
541. 50 l. "Christ" (Durer) .. 8 8
542. 90 l. "Christ" (El Greco) 12 12
543. 180 l. Pope Paul VI .. 35 30

130. "Adam" (Michelangelo).

131. Pope Paul VI.

1970. United Nations. 25th Anniv.

544. 20 l. Type 130 .. .. 5 5
545. 90 l. "Eve" (Michelangelo) 15 15
546. 220 l. Olive branch .. 35 35

1970. Pope Paul's Visit to Asia and Oceania. Multicoloured.

547. 25 l. Type 131 .. .. 5 5
548. 55 l. "Holy Child of Cebu" (Philippines) 8 8
549. 100 l. "Madonna and Child", Darwin Cathedral (G. Hamori) 15 15
550. 130 l. Manila Cathedral .. 20 20
551. 220 l. Sydney Cathedral .. 35 35

132. "Angel with Lectern".

133. "Madonna and Child" (F. Ghissi).

1971. Racial Equality Year. Multicoloured.

552. 20 l. Type 132 .. .. 5 5
553. 40 l. "Christ Crucified, and Doves" 8 8
554. 50 l. Type 132 .. .. 8 8
555. 130 l. As 40 l. 25 20

1971. Easter. Religious Paintings. Multicoloured.

556. 25 l. Type 133 .. .. 5 5
557. 40 l. "Madonna and Child" (Sassetta—S. di Giovanni) 8 8
558. 55 l. "Madonna and Child" (C. Crivelli) .. 10 10
559. 90 l. "Madonna and Child" (C. Maratta) .. 15 15
560. 180 l. "The Holy Family" (G. Ceracchini) 25 25

134. "St. Dominic Guzman" (Sienese School).

135. "St. Matthew".

1971. St. Dominic Guzman (founder of Preaching Friars Order). 800th Birth Anniv. Multicoloured.

561. 25 l. Type 134 .. .. 5 5
562. 55 l. Portrait by Fra Angelico 12 12
563. 90 l. Portrait by Titian .. 12 12
564. 180 l. Portrait by El Greco 30 30

1971. Air.

565. 135. 200 l. blk. and green .. 60 60
566. – 300 l. blk. and brown 80 80
567. – 500 l. black and pink 5·50 4·75
568. – 1,000 l. blk. and mve. 2·25 2·10

DESIGNS: "The Four Evangelists" (ceiling frescoes by Fra Angelico in the Niccolina Chapel, Vatican City)—300 l. "St. Mark". 500 l. "St. Luke". 1,000 l. "St. John".

136. "St. Stephen" (from chasuble in Church of Szekesfehervar, Hungary).

137. Bramante's Design of Cupola, St. Peter's.

1971. St. Stephen, King of Hungary. Millennium.

569. 136. 50 l. multicoloured .. 8 8
570. – 180 l. black and yell. 30 30

DESIGN: 180 l. "Madonna, Patroness of Hungary", (sculpture, circa 1511).

1972. Bramante Celebrations.

571. 137. 25 l. black on yellow .. 5 5
572. – 90 l. black on yellow .. 12 12
573. – 130 l. black on yellow 35 35

DESIGNS: 90 l. Donato Bramante (architect) from medal. 130 l. Spiral staircase, Innocent VIII's Belvedere, Vatican.

138. "St. Mark at Sea" (mosaic).

1972. U.N.E.S.C.O. "Save Venice" Campaign. Multicoloured.

574. 25 l. Type 138 .. .. 8 8
575. 50 l. } 15 15
576. 50 l. } Map of Venice, 15 15
577. 50 l. } 1581 (fresco) .. 15 15
578. 50 l. } 15 15
579. 80 l. St. Mark's Basilica .. 1·25 1·25

139. Gospel of St. Mark (from codex "Biblia dell" Araceoli).

1972. Int. Book Year. Illuminated Manuscripts. Multicoloured.

581. 30 l. Type 139 .. .. 5 5
582. 50 l. Gospel of St. Luke ("Biblia dell Aracoeli") 8 8
583. 90 l. 2nd Epistle of St. John (Bologna codex) 12 12
584. 100 l. Apocalypse of St. John (Bologna codex) 15 15
585. 130 l. Epistle of St. Paul to the Romans (Italian codex) .. .. 1·75 1·75

140. Luigi Orione (founder of "Caritas").

1972. Birth Centenaries. Multicoloured.

586. 50 l. Type 140 .. .. 20 12
587. 180 l. Lorenzo Perosi (composer) 40 40

141. Cardinal Bassarione (Roselli fresco, Sistine Chapel).

142. Congress Emblem.

1972. Cardinal Bassarione. 500th Death Anniv.

588. – 40 l. green 15 15
589. 141. 90 l. brown 25 25
590. – 130 l. black 40 40

DESIGNS: 40 l. "Reading of Bull of Union" (relief). 130 l. Arms of Cardinal Bassarione.

1973. Int. Eucharistic Congress, Melbourne. Multicoloured.

591. 25 l. Type 142 .. .. 5 5
592. 75 l. Michelangelo's "Pieta" 8 8
593. 300 l. Melbourne Cathedral 1·00 1·00

143. St. Theresa's Birthplace.

144. Torun (birthplace).

1973. St. Theresa of Lisieux. Birth Cent.

594. 143. 25 l. black and red .. 5 5
595. – 55 l. black and yellow 8 8
596. – 220 l. black and blue .. 50 50

DESIGNS: 55 l. St. Theresa. 220 l. Basilica of Lisieux.

1973. Copernicus. 500th Birth Anniv.

597. 144. 20 l. green 5 5
598. – 50 l. brown 8 8
599. 144. 100 l. purple 12 12
600. – 130 l. blue 50 50

DESIGN: 50 l., 130 l. Copernicus.

145. "St. Wenceslas".

1973. Prague Diocese. Millennium. Mult.

601. 20 l. Type 145 .. .. 5 5
602. 90 l. Arms of Prague Diocese 12 12
603. 150 l. Tower of Prague Cathedral 15 15
604. 220 l. "St. Adalbert" .. 45 45

146. Church of St. Hripsime.

147. "Angel" (porch of St. Mark's, Venice).

1973. St. Narsete Shnorali (Armenian patriarch). 800th Death Anniv.

605. 146. 25 l. brown on ochre .. 5 5
606. – 90 l. black on lavender 12 12
607. – 180 l. purple on green 45 45

DESIGNS: 90 l. Armenian "khatchkar" (stone stele) inscribed "Victory". 180 l. St. Narsete Shnorali.

1974. Air.

608. 147. 2500 l. multicoloured .. 3·00 3·00

148. "And There was Light".

150. "St. Thomas' School" (Fra Angelico School).

149. Noah's Ark and Doves.

1974. Int. Book Year (1973). "The Bible". Biblical Texts. Multicoloured.
609. 15 l. Type **148** 5 5
610. 25 l. "Noah entrusts himself to God" (horiz.) 5 5
611. 50 l. "The Annunciation" 8 8
612. 90 l. "The Nativity" .. 12 12
613. 180 l. "The Lord feeds His People" (horiz.) .. 45 45

1974. Universal Postal Union. Cent. Mosaics. Multicoloured.
614. 50 l. Type **149** 8 8
615. 90 l. Sheep in landscape .. 20 20

1974. St. Thomas Aquinas. 700th Death Anniv.
616. – 50 l. violet and brown 8 8
617. **150.** 90 l. violet & brown .. 15 15
618. – 220 l. violet & brown .. 35 35
DESIGNS: (21×37 mm.). 50 l. Pupils looking to right. 220 l. Pupils looking to left.

151. "Civit" (medieval quarter), Bagnoregio.

152. Christus Victor, St. Peter's.

1974. St. Bonaventura of Bagnoregio. 700th Death Anniv. Multicoloured.
619. 40 l. Type **151** 8 8
620. 90 l. "Tree of Life" (13th-century motif) 10 10
621. 220 l. "St. Bonaventura (after B. Gozzoli) .. 25 25

1974. Holy Year (1975). Multicoloured.
622. 10 l. Type **152** 5 5
623. 25 l. Christ, St. Peter's .. 5 5
624. 30 l. Christ, St. John Lateran 5 5
625. 40 l. Cross and dove, St. John Lateran .. 8 8
626. 50 l. Christ enthroned, St. Mary Major .. 8 8
627. 55 l. St. Peter, St. Mary Major 8 8
628. 90 l. St. Paul, St. Mary Major 10 10
629. 100 l. St. Peter, St. Paul Outside the Walls .. 15 15
630. 130 l. St. Paul, St. Paul outside the walls .. 20 20
631. 220 l. Arms of Pope Paul VI 25 25
632. 250 l. Pope Paul VI giving blessing (from sketch by L. Bianchi-Barriviera) .. 30 30

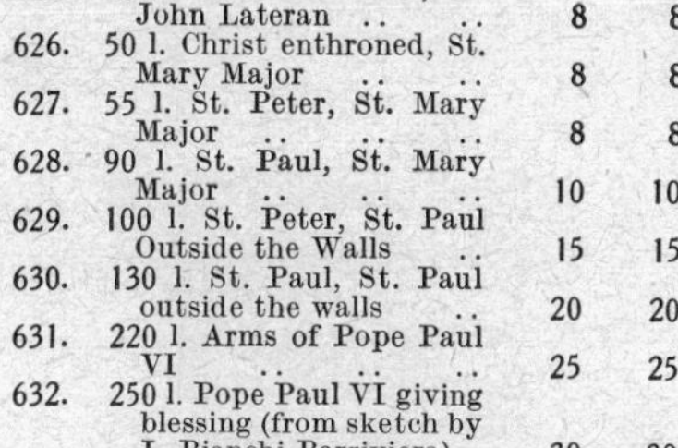

153. St. Peter's Square.

1975. European Architectural Heritage Year. Vatican Fountains.
633. **153.** 20 l. black on buff .. 5 5
634. – 40 l. black on lavender 8 8
635. – 50 l. black on red .. 10 10
636. – 90 l. black on green .. 15 15
637. – 100 l. black on green .. 20 20
638. – 200 l. black on blue .. 35 35
FOUNTAINS: 40 l. Piazza St. Martha. 50 l. Old bakery. 90 l. Belvedere courtyard. 100 l. Academy of Sciences. 200 l. "The Gallery".

154. "Pentecost" (El Greco).

155. "Miracle of Loaves and Fishes

1975. Pentecost.
639. **154.** 300 l. mauve and orange 55 55

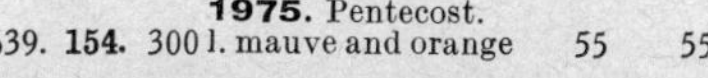

1975. Ninth International Christian Archaeological Congress. Multicoloured.
640. 30 l. Type **155** 5 5
641. 150 l. "Portrait of Christ" 25 25
642. 200 l. "Raising of Lazarus" 35 35

156. Pope Sixtus IV appointing Bartolemeo Sacchi as first Librarian.

1975. Vatican Apostolic Library. 500th Anniv.
643. **156.** 70 l. purple on blue .. 12 12
644. – 100 l. blue on green .. 20 20
645. – 250 l. brown on grey .. 45 45
DESIGNS—VERT. 100 l. "Pope Sixtus IV" (portrait from Vatican Codex). HORIZ. 250 l. Pope Sixtus IV visiting Library.

157. First Passionists' House, Mt. Argentario.

158. "Women at Prayer" (Fra Angelico).

1975. St. Paul of the Cross. Death Bicent. Multicoloured.
646. 50 l. Type **157** 10 10
647. 150 l. "St. Paul" (after Domenico della Porta) (22×28 mm.) .. 25 25
648. 300 l. Basilica of Saints John and Paul 55 55

1975. International Women's Year. Mult.
649. 100 l. Type **158** 20 20
650. 200 l. "Women in conversation" (Fra Angelico) .. 35 35

159. "The Last Judgement".

161. Eucharist and Ear of Wheat.

160. "The Madonna. (Titan).

1976. Air.
651. **159.** 500 l. brown and blue on orange 95 95
652. – 1,000 l. brown and blue on orange .. .. 1·90 1·90
653. – 2,500 l. brown and blue on orange .. .. 4·75 4·75
DESIGNS: 1,000 l. and 2,500 l. show different motifs from Michelangelo's "The Last Judgement", Sistine Chapel.

1976. Titan. 400th Death Anniv. Details from "The Madonna in Glory with the Child Jesus and Six Saints".
654. **160.** 100 l. lilac 20 20
655. – 300 l. lilac 55 55
DESIGN: 300 l. "Six Saints".

1976. 41st Int. Eucharistic Congress Philadelphia. Multicoloured.
656. 150 l. Type **161** 30 30
657. 200 l. Eucharist within protective hands 40 40
658. 400 l. "Adoration of the Eucharist" 75 75

162. "Moses".

1976. Details of Raphael's "Transfiguration". Multicoloured.
659. 30 l. Type **161** 5 5
660. 40 l. "Christ Transfigured" 8 8
661. 50 l. "Prophet Elijah" .. 10 10
662. 100 l. "Two Apostles" .. 20 20
663. 150 l. "The Relatives" .. 30 30
664. 200 l. "Landscape" .. 40 40

162. Fountain and St. John's Tower.

1976. Fountains and Buildings.
665. **162.** 50 l. black and lilac .. 10 10
666. – 100 l. sepia and pink .. 20 20
667. – 120 l. black and yellow 25 25
668. – 180 l. black and drab .. 35 35
669. – 250 l. brown and bistre 50 50
670. – 300 l. brown and mauve 55 55
DESIGNS: 100 l. Fountain of the Sacrament. 120 l. Fountain at entrance of Vatican Gardens. 180 l. Basilica, cupola of St. Peter's and Sacristy. 250 l. Borgia Tower, Sistine Chapel and Via della Fondamenta.

EXPRESS LETTER STAMPS

E 1.

1929.
E 14. **E 1.** 2 l. red .. .. 19·00 4·25
E 15. 2 l. 50 blue .. .. 14·00 2·75

E 2. Vatican City.

1933.
E 35. **E 2.** 2 l. brown and red .. 15 30
E 36. 2 l. 50 brown and blue 25 40
E 107. 3 l. 50 blue and red .. 20 25
E 108. 5 l. green and blue .. 30 35

1945. Surch. in figures over bars.
E 118. **E 2.** 6 l. on 3 l. 50 blue & red 55 70
E 119. 12 l. on 5 l. grn. & blue 65 90

E 3. Matthew Giberti, Bishop of Verona.

1946. Council of Trent. 400th Anniv.
E 130. **E 3.** 6 l. brown and green 8 10
E 131. – 12 l. brown and red 10 12
DESIGN: 12 l. Cardinal Gaspare Contarini, Bishop of Belluno.

1949. As Nos. 139/48 (Basilicas), but inscr. "ESPRESSO".
E 149. 40 l. grey .. .. 7·00 3·75
E 150. 80 l. brown .. .. 7·00 7·00
DESIGNS—HORIZ. 40 . St. Peter. 80 l. St. John.

1953. Designs as Nos. 179/89, but inscr. "ESPRESSO".
E 190. 50 l. brown and turquoise 15 15
E 191. 85 l. brown and orange 45 45
DESIGNS: 50 l. St. Peter and tomb. 85 l. Pius XII and sepulchre.

1960. Designs as Nos. 326/33 (Works of Mercy), but inscr. "ESPRESSO". Centres in sepia.
E 334. 75 l. red 8 8
E 335. 100 l. blue 12 12
DESIGN: 75 l., 100 l. Arms of Pope John XXIII between "Justice" and "Hope".

1966. Designs as Nos. 467/76, but inscr. "ESPRESSO".
E 477. – 150 l. sepia .. 15 15
E 478. **111.** 180 l. brown .. 20 20
DESIGN: 150 l. Papal Arms.

PARCEL POST STAMPS

1931. Optd. **PER PACCHI.**
P 15. **1.** 5 c. brown on rose .. 20 20
P 16. 10 c. green on green .. 20 20
P 17. 20 c. violet on lilac .. 5·50 4·25
P 18. 25 c. blue on blue .. 8·50 4·25
P 19. 30 c. black on yellow .. 8·50 3·50
P 20. 50 c. black on pink .. 8·50 3·50
P 21. 75 c. red on grey .. 2·50 2·75
P 22. **2.** 80 c. red .. .. 1·40 1·75
P 23. 1 l. 25 blue .. .. 2·10 2·50
P 24. 2 l. brown .. .. 70 1·10
P 25. 2 l. 50 red .. .. 70 1·10
P 26. 5 l. green .. .. 70 1·10
P 27. 10 l. black .. .. 70 1·10

PARCEL POST EXPRESS STAMPS

1931. Optd. **PER PACCHI.**
PE 15. **E 1.** 2 l. red .. .. 1·00 1·40
PE 16. 2 l. 50 blue .. 1·00 1·40

POSTAGE DUE STAMPS

1931. Optd. **SEGNATASSE** and cross or surch. also.
D 15. **1.** 5 c. brown on rose .. 20 20
D 16. 10 c. green on green .. 20 20
D 17. 20 c. violet on lilac .. 6·00 4·50
D 18. 40 c. on 30 c. blk. on yell. 2·50 2·50
D 19. **2.** 60 c. on 2 l. brown .. 55·00 9·00
D 20. 1 l. 10 on 2 l. 50 red .. 3·25 4·25

D 1.

D 2.

1945. Coloured network shown in brackets.
D 107. **D 1.** 5 c. black (yellow) 8 8
D 108. 20 c. black (violet) 8 8
D 109. 80 c. black (red) .. 8 8
D 110. 1 l. black (green) .. 8 8
D 111. 2 l. black (blue) .. 8 8
D 112. 5 l. black (grey) .. 8 8

1954. Coloured network shown in brackets.
D 199. **D 2.** 4 l. black (red) .. 20 20
D 200. 6 l. black (green) .. 45 35
D 201. 10 l. black (yellow) 20 20
D 202. 20 l. black (blue) .. 50 45
D 203. 50 l. black (sepia) .. 8 8
D 204. 70 l. black (chocolate) 12 12

D 3.

1968.
D 513. **D 3.** 10 l. black on grey 5 5
D 514. 20 l. black on blue 5 5
D 515. 50 l. black on pink 8 8
D 516. 60 l. black on green 10 10
D 517. 100 l. black on buff 12 12
D 518. 180 l. black on mauve 25 25

VEGLIA E1

During the period of D'Annunzio's Italian Regency of Carnaro (Fiume), separate issues were made for the island of Veglia (now Krk).

100 centesimi = 1 lira.

1920. Nos. 146, etc. of Fiume optd. **VEGLIA.**
1. 5 c. green 25 25
2. 10 c. red 80 40
3. 20 c. brown .. .. .. 1·00 60
4. 25 c. blue .. .. .. 3·25 1·90
5. 50 on 20 c. brown .. .. 1·40 80
6. 55 on 5 c. green .. .. 1·40 80

EXPRESS LETTER STAMPS

1920. Nos. E 163/4 of Fiume optd. **VEGLIA.**
E 7. 30 c. on 20 c. brown .. 20·00 7·00
E 8. 50 on 5 c. green .. .. 7·00 2·75

VENEZIA GIULIA AND ISTRIA E3

Formerly part of Italy. Stamps issued during Allied occupation, 1945-47. The Peace Treaty of 1947 established the Free Territory of Trieste (q.v.) and gave the rest of the territory to Yugoslavia.

For stamps of Austria overprinted Venezia Giulia see under Italian Austria.

A. YUGOSLAV OCCUPATION PROVISIONAL ISSUES

Issue for Trieste.

1945. Stamps of Italy, 1944, surch. **1. V. 1945 TRIESTE TRST,** five-pointed star and value.

4. – 20 c.+1 l. on 5 c. (No. 605) 5 5
5. **158.** +1 on 25 c. green .. 5 5
6. – +1 l. on 30 c. (No. 603) 5 5
7. – +1 l. on 50 c. (No. 610) 5 5
8. – +1 l. on 1 l. vio. (No. 612) 5 5
9. +2 l. on 1 l. 25 (No. 613) 5 5
2. **157.** 2+2 l. on 25 c. green .. 5 5
10. – +2 l. on 3 l. grn. (No. 614) 5 5
11. – 5+5 l. on 1 l. (No. 612) 5 5
12. – 10+10 l. on 30 c. (No. 603) 15 15
13. – 20+20 l. on 5 c. (No. 605) 65 80

Issue for Istria.

In 1945 various stamps of Italy were overprinted " ISTRA " and further surcharged for use in Istria and Pola but they were not issued. However four of these were further surcharged and issued later.

1945. Stamps of Italy surch. **ISTRA** with new value and bars obliterating old surch.

14. **70.** 4 l. on 2 l. on 1 l. (No. 249) 5 5
15. – 6 l. on 1.50 l. on 75 c. (No. 604) .. 40 40
16. – 10 l. on 0.10 l. on 5 c. (No. 605) .. .. 1·75 1·75
17. **74.** 20 l. on 1 l. on 50 c. (No. 597) 20 20

Issue for Fiume.

1945. Stamps of Italy, 1944, surch. **3-V-1945 FIUME RIJEKA,** five-pointed star over rising sun and new value.

18. **157.** 2 l. on 25 c. green .. 5 5
19. – 4 l. on 1 l. vio. (No. 612) 60 60
20. – 5 l. on 10 c. brn. (No. 606) 5 5
21. – 6 l. on 10 c. brn. (No. 606) 5 5
22. **158.** 10 l. on 25 c. green .. 5 5
23. – 16 l. on 75 c. red (No. 611) 3·75 4·25
24. **E 7.** 20 l. on 1 l. 25 c. green.. 8

B. ALLIED MILITARY GOVERNMENT

1945. Stamps of Italy optd. **A.M.G. V.G.** in two lines.

(a) Imperial Series.

26. **70.** 10 c. brown (No. 241) (post.) 5 5
27. – 10 c. brown (No. 633) .. 5 5
28. **70.** 20 c. red (No. 243) .. 5 5
30. 20 c. red (No. 640) .. 5 5
31. – 60 c. orange (No. 636) .. 5 5
32. **74.** 60 c. green (No. 641) .. 5 5
33. **70.** 1 l. violet (No. 642) .. 5 5
34. – 2 l. red (No. 644) .. 5 5
35. **69.** 5 l. red (No. 645) .. 5 5
36. – 10 l. violet (No. 646) .. 5 5
37. **70.** 20 l. green (No. 257) .. 5 5

(b) Stamps of 1945-48.

38. – 25 c. blue-green (No. 649) 5 5
39. – 2 l. brown (No. 656) .. 5 5
40. – 3 l. red (No. 657) .. 5 5
41. – 4 l. red (No. 658) .. 5 5
42. **161.** 6 l. violet (No. 660) .. 5 5
43. – 20 l. purple (No. 665) 15 15
44. **162.** 25 l. green (No. 666) .. 5 5
45. 50 l. purple (No. 668) 12 12
46. **164.** 100 l. red (No. 669) .. 40 40

1945. Air stamps of Italy, optd. as above.

47. **81.** 50 c. brn. (No. 271) (air) 5 5
48. **163.** 1 l. slate (No. 670) .. 5 5
49. – 2 l. blue (No. 671) .. 5 5
50. – 5 l. green (No. 952) .. 5 5
51. **163.** 10 l. red (No. 674) .. 5 5
52. – 25 l. blue (No. 675) .. 5 5
53. – 25 l. brown (No. 676) .. 40 45
54. **163.** 50 l. green (No. 677) .. 10 10

EXPRESS LETTER STAMPS

1946. Express Letter Stamps of Italy optd. **A.M.G. V.G.** in two lines.

E 55. – 10 l. blue (No. F 680) 5 5
E 56. **E 9.** 30 l. violet (No. E 683) 5 8

C. YUGOSLAV MILITARY GOVERNMENT

11. Grapes.

12. Pulj Harbour.

13. Tunny.

1945. Inscr. "ISTRA SLOVENSKO PRIMORJE — ISTRIA LITTORALE SLOVENO".

57. **11.** 0.25 l. green 8 5
58. – 0.50 l. brown 5 5
59. – 1 l. red 5 5
76. – 1 l. green 5 5
60. – 1.50 l. olive 10 5
61. – 2 l. green 5 5
100. – 3 l. red 5 5
62. **12.** 4 l. blue 5 5
79. 4 l. red 5 5
80. – 5 l. black 5 5
101. **11.** 6 l. blue 5 5
81. – 10 l. brown 5 5
65. **13.** 20 l. purple 50 15
82. 20 l. blue 25 12
83. – 30 l. magenta 25 15

DESIGNS—As T **11**: 0.50 l. Donkey and view. 1 l. Rebuilding damaged homes. 1.50 l. Olive-branch. 2 l. Duino Castle, near Trieste. As T **12**: 5 l. Birthplace of Vladimir Gortan at Piram. 19 l. Ploughing. As T **13**: 30 l. Viaduct over the Solkan.

1946. Stamps of 1945 surch.

96. **13.** 1 on 20 l. blue .. 25 12
97. – 2 on 30 l. mag. (No. 83) 25 12

1947. As Nos. 514 and O 540 of Yugoslavia with colours changed, surch. **VOJNA UPRAVA JUGOSLAVENSKE ARMIJE** and new value.

102. 1 l. on 9 d. pink .. 8 8
103. 1.50 l. on 50 p. blue .. 8 8
104. 2 l. on 9 d. pink .. 8 8
105. 3 l. on 50 p. blue .. 8 8
106. 5 l. on 9 d. pink .. 8 8
107. 6 l. on 50 p. blue .. 8 8
108. 10 l. on 9 d. pink .. 8 8
109. 15 l. on 50 p. blue .. 8 8
110. 35 l. on 9 d. pink .. 8 8
111. 50 l. on 50 p. blue .. 10 10

POSTAGE DUE STAMPS

1945. Stamps of 1945 surch. **PORTO** and value in " Lit ".

D 72. **13.** 0.50 l. on 20 l. purple.. 10 15
D 67. **11.** 1 l. on 0.25 l. green .. 40 20
D 73. – 2 l. on 30 l. magenta.. 10 10
D 68. – 4 l. on 0.50 l. brown .. 10 8
D 69. – 8 l. on 0.50 l. brown .. 10 8
D 70. – 10 l. on 0.50 l. brown.. 40 30
D 71. – 20 l. on 0.50 l. brown.. 40 30

1946. Stamps of 1945 surch. **PORTO** and value expressed in " Lira ".

D 90. **11.** 1 l. on 0.25 l. green .. 8 5
D 84. – 1 l. on 1 l. grn. (No. 76) 8 8
D 91. **11.** 2 l. on 0.25 l. green .. 10 10
D 85. – 2 l. on 1 l. grn. (No. 76) 8 8
D 92. **11.** 4 l. on 0.25 l. green .. 12 8
D 86. – 4 l. on 1 l. green (No. 76) 10 10
D 93. **13.** 10 l. on 20 l. blue .. 15 8
D 87. – 10 l. on 30 l. magenta (No. 83) .. 25 20
D 94. **13.** 20 l. on 20 l. blue .. 70 25
D 88. – 20 l. on 30 l. magenta (No. 83) .. 60 25
D 95. **13.** 30 l. on 20 l. blue .. 75 25
D 89. – 30 l. on 30 l. magenta (No. 83) 70 25

1947. No. D 528 of Yugoslavia with colour changed and surch. **Vojna Uprava Jugoslavenske Armije** and value.

D 112. 1 l. on 1 d. green .. 8 8
D 113. 2 l. on 1 d. green .. 8 8
D 114. 6 l. on 1 d. green .. 8 8
D 115. 10 l. on 1 d. green .. 8 8
D 116. 30 l. on 1 d. green .. 12 12

VENEZUELA O4

A republic in the N. of S. America independent since 1811.

1859. 100 centavos=8 reales=1 peso.
1879. 100 centesimos=1 venezolano.
1880. 100 centimos=1 bolivar.

1.

2.

3.

1859. Imperf.

7. **1.** ½ r. yellow .. .. 5·50 4·50
8. 1 r. blue .. .. 8·50 8·00
9. 2 r. red .. .. 11·00 10·00

1861. Imperf.

13. **2.** ½ c. green .. .. .. 7·50 30·00
14. ½ c. lilac .. .. .. 11·00 £150
15. 1 c. brown .. .. .. 13·00 £160

1863. Imperf.

16. **8.** ½ c. red .. .. .. 23·00 75·00
17. 1 c. grey .. .. .. 29·00 £100
18. ½ r. yellow .. .. 1·75 1·00
19. 1 r. blue .. .. 8·50 5·00
20. 2 r. green .. .. .. 14·00 18·00

4. **4a.** Bolivar. **5.**

1865. Imperf.

22. **4.** ½ c. green .. .. .. 85·00 £130
23. 1 c. green .. .. .. 70·00 £130
24. ½ r. rose .. .. 2·75 1·40
26. 1 r. red .. .. 11·00 3·50
27a. 2 r. yellow .. .. 45·00 28·00

1871. Optd. with inscription in very small letters. Imperf.

28. **4a.** 1 c. orange 55 25
29. 2 c. orange .. .. 1·40 25
60. 3 c. orange .. .. 2·25 1·10
61. 4 c. orange .. .. 1·60 70
62a. 5 c. orange .. .. 1·10 60
63a. 1 r. red .. .. 1·25 25
64a. 2 r. red .. .. 1·75 60
65a. 3 r. red .. .. 3·00 60
66a. 5 r. red .. .. 3·50 60
52a. 7 r. red .. .. 7·00 1·10
53a. 9 r. green .. .. 9·00 3·50
54. 15 r. green .. .. 15·00 6·00
68. 20 r. green .. .. 23·00 7·00
56. 30 r. green .. .. £150 55·00
57. 50 r. green .. .. £350 90·00

1873. Optd. with inscription in very small letters. Imperf.

74. **4.** 1 c. lilac .. .. 11·00 12·00
75a. 2 c. green .. .. 9·00 12·00
76a. ½ r. pink .. .. 2·50 1·00
77a. 1 r. red .. .. 6·00 1·50
78a. 2 r. yellow .. .. 20·00 15·00

1879. Optd. with inscription in small letters Imperf.

83. **5.** 1 c. yellow 60 12
84. 5 c. yellow .. .. 1·00 25
85. 10 c. blue .. .. 1·75 35
86. 30 c. blue .. .. 2·75 50
87. 50 c. blue .. .. 3·50 55
88. 90 c. blue .. .. 23·00 4·50
89. 1 v. red .. .. 50·00 7·50
90. 3 v. red .. .. 65·00 19·00
91. 5 v. red .. .. £100 42·00

1880. Without opt. Perf.

92. **5.** 5 c. yellow 55 12
93. 10 c. yellow 55 15
94. 25 c. yellow 55 15
95. 50 c. yellow .. .. 1·10 25
96. 1 b. blue .. .. 5·50 55
97. 2 b. blue .. .. 7·50 75
98. 5 b. blue .. .. 19·00 1·25
99. 10 b. red .. .. £100 29·00
100. 20 b. red £275 £110
101. 25 b. red £1000 £250

6.

7.

8.

Bolivar.

1880.

107. **6.** 5 c. blue .. .. 3·50 2·10
108. 10 c. red .. .. 8·50 5·00
109. 25 c. yellow .. .. 4·00 1·75
110. 50 c. brown .. .. 14·00 8·50
106. 1 b. green .. .. 23·00 14·00

1882. Various frames. Perf., roul. or imperf.

111. **7.** 5 c. green 8 5
112. 10 c. brown 8 5
113. 25 c. orange 8 5
114. 50 c. blue 10 5
115. 1 b. red 15 8
116. 3 b. violet 15 8
117. 10 b. brown 45 45
118. 20 b. purple 55 55

1882. Various frames. Perf., roul. or imperf.

119. **8.** 5 c. blue 15 8
120. 10 c. brown 15 8
121. 25 c. brown 35 12
122. 50 c. green 70 20
123. 1 b. violet .. .. 1·40 55

1892. Surch. **RESOLUCION DE 10 DE OCTUBRE DE 1892** and value in circle.

134. **7.** 25 c. on 5 c. green .. 5·00 3·25
138. **8.** 25 c. on 5 c. blue.. .. 17·00 17·00
135. **7.** 25 c. on 10 c. brown .. 5·00 3·25
139. **8.** 25 c. on 10 c. brown . 7·00 7·00
136. **7.** 1 b. on 25 c. orange .. 7·00 3·75
140. **8.** 1 b. on 25 c. brown .. 7·00 7·00
137. **7.** 1 b. on 50 c. blue .. 9·50 3·75
141. **8.** 1 b. on 50 c. green .. 7·50 7·50

1893. Optd. with coat of arms and diagonal shading.

142. **7.** 5 c. green 8 8
150. **8.** 5 c. blue 15 8
143. **7.** 10 c. brown 8 8
151. **8.** 10 c. brown 25 12
144. **7.** 25 c. orange 8 8
152. **8.** 25 c. brown 30 15
145. **7.** 50 c. blue 10 10
153. **8.** 50 c. green 40 15
146. **7.** 1 b. red 50 35
154c. **8.** 1 b. violet 85 45
147. **7.** 3 b. violet 70 35
148. 10 b. brown .. .. 2·00 1·75
149. 20 b. purple .. .. 1·75 85

9. Bolivar.

10. Bolivar.

1893. Schools Tax stamps.

155. **9** 5 c. grey 8 5
156. 10 c. green 8 5
157. 25 c. blue 8 5
158. 50 c. orange 8 5
159. 1 b. purple 25 5
160. 3 b. red 40 15
161. 10 b. violet 75 55
162. 20 b. brown .. .. 2·40 2·00

See also Nos. 227/35.

1893.

163. **10.** 5 c. brown 50 10
164. 10 c. blue .. .. 1·40 55
165. 25 c. magenta .. .. 7·00 15
166. 50 c. purple .. .. 1·40 10
167. 1 b. green .. .. 2·10 55

11. Landing of Columbus.

1893. Columbian Exposition, Chicago and Discovery of America. 400th Anniv.

168. **11.** 25 c. purple .. .. 5·50 35

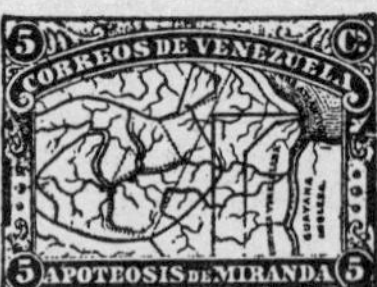

12.

13. Bolivar.

1896. Gen. Miranda Commem.

169. **12.** 5 c. green .. .. 1·25 1·25
170. 10 c. blue .. .. 1·75 1·75
171. 25 c. yellow .. .. 2·10 2·10
172. 50 c. red .. .. 13·00 6·50
173. 1 b. mauve .. .. 8·50 6·50

1899.

179. **13.** 5 c. green 35 15
180. 10 c. red 35 15
181. 25 c. blue 50 45
182. 50 c. black 35 30
183. 50 c. orange 50 25
184. 1 b. green .. .. 9·50 4·50
185. 2 b. yellow .. .. 95·00 95·00

(14.)

(15.)

1900. Stamps of 1893 optd. with T **14.**

No.	Type	Description	Unused	Used
191.	**9.**	5 c. grey	5	5
192.		10 c. green	5	5
193.		25 c. blue	5	5
194.		50 c. orange	5	5
195.		1 b. purple	15	5
196.		3 b. red	25	5
197.		10 b. violet	50	35
198.		20 b. brown	3·00	3·00

1900. Stamps of 1899 optd. with T **14.**

No.	Type	Description	Unused	Used
199.	**13.**	5 c. green	50	12
200.		10 c. red	50	12
201.		25 c. blue	2·40	30
202.		50 c. black	85	12
203.		1 b. green	70	35
204.		2 b. yellow	1·10	70

1900. Stamps of 1901 optd. **1900.**

No.	Type	Description	Unused	Used
206.	**9.**	5 c. orange	5	5
207.		10 c. blue	5	5
208.		25 c. purple	5	5
209.		50 c. green	40	5
210.		1 b. black	3·75	50
211.		3 b. brown	60	25
212.		10 b. red	3·75	1·00
213.		20 b. violet	5·00	1·40

1900. Stamps of 1899 optd. **1900.**

No.	Type	Description	Unused	Used
214.	**13.**	5 c. green	42·00	42·00
215.		10 c. red	42·00	42·00
216.		25 c. blue	£100	£100
217.		50 c. orange	9·50	50
218.		1 b. black	1·40	45

1900. Stamps of 1899 optd. with T **15.**

No.	Type	Description	Unused	Used
219.	**13.**	5 c. green	2·10	15
220.		10 c. red	1·40	15
221.		25 c. blue	1·40	15

1901. Re-issue of T **9** in new colours.

No.	Type	Description	Unused	Used
227.	**9.**	5 c. orange	5	5
228.		10 c. red	5	5
229.		10 c. blue	5	5
231.		50 c. green	5	5
232.		1 b. black	2·25	50
233.		3 b. brown	10	5
234.		10 b. red	20	10
235.		20 b. violet	50	30

1902. Stamp of 1901 optd. **1901.**

No.	Type	Description	Unused	Used
236.	**9.**	1 b. black	20	12

1904. No. 231. surch. **CORREOS Vale B 0,05 1904.**

No.	Type	Description	Unused	Used
310.	**9.**	5 c. on 50 c. green	35	15

16. General Sucre.

17. Bolivar.

1904.

No.	Type	Description	Unused	Used
311.	**16.**	5 c. green	12	5
312.		10 c. red	12	5
313.		15 c. violet	25	8
314.		25 c. blue	2·40	12
315.		50 c. claret	20	8
316.		1 b. claret	30	15

1904.

No.	Type	Description	Unused	Used
317.	**17.**	5 c. green	5	5
318.		10 c. grey	5	5
319.		25 c. red	5	5
320.		50 c. yellow	5	5
321.		1 b. claret	90	10
322.		3 bl. blue	10	8
323.		10 b. violet	20	10
324.		20 b. rose	40	20

18. President Castro.

19. Liberty.

1905. National Congress Commem.

No.	Type	Description	Unused	Used
330.	**18.**	5 c. red	1·75	1·75
331.		10 c. blue	2·75	2·25
332.		25 c. yellow	85	85

1910. Independence Cent.

No.	Type	Description	Unused	Used
333.	**19.**	25 c. blue	4·25	35

20. Miranda.

21. Blanco.

22. Bolivar.

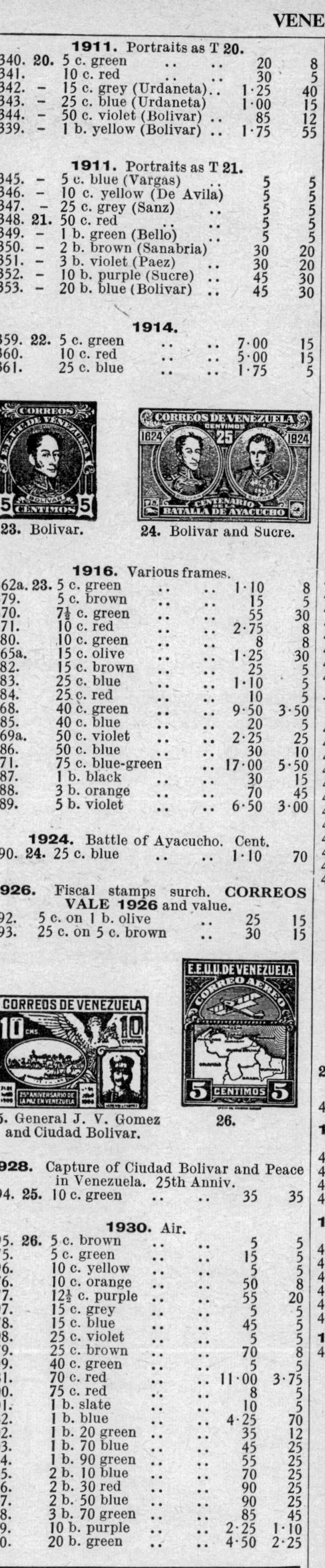

1911. Portraits as T **20.**

No.	Type	Description	Unused	Used
340.	**20.**	5 c. green	20	8
341.		10 c. red	30	5
342.	–	15 c. grey (Urdaneta)	1·25	40
343.	–	25 c. blue (Urdaneta)	1·00	15
344.	–	50 c. violet (Bolivar)	85	12
339.	–	1 b. yellow (Bolivar)	1·75	55

1911. Portraits as T **21.**

No.	Type	Description	Unused	Used
345.	–	5 c. blue (Vargas)	5	5
346.	–	10 c. yellow (De Avila)	5	5
347.	–	25 c. grey (Sanz)	5	5
348.	**21.**	50 c. red	5	5
349.	–	1 b. green (Bello)	5	5
350.	–	2 b. brown (Sanabria)	30	20
351.	–	3 b. violet (Paez)	30	20
352.	–	10 b. purple (Sucre)	45	30
353.	–	20 b. blue (Bolivar)	45	30

1914.

No.	Type	Description	Unused	Used
359.	**22.**	5 c. green	7·00	15
360.		10 c. red	5·00	15
361.		25 c. blue	1·75	5

23. Bolivar.

24. Bolivar and Sucre.

1916. Various frames.

No.	Type	Description	Unused	Used
362a.	**23.**	5 c. green	1·10	8
379.		5 c. brown	15	5
570.		7½ c. green	55	30
571.		10 c. red	2·75	8
380.		10 c. green	8	8
365a.		15 c. olive	1·25	30
382.		15 c. brown	25	5
383.		25 c. blue	1·10	5
384.		25 c. red	10	5
368.		40 c. green	9·50	3·50
385.		40 c. blue	20	5
369a.		50 c. violet	2·25	25
386.		50 c. blue	30	10
371.		75 c. blue-green	17·00	5·50
387.		1 b. black	30	15
388.		3 b. orange	70	45
389.		5 b. violet	6·50	3·00

1924. Battle of Ayacucho. Cent.

No.	Type	Description	Unused	Used
390.	**24.**	25 c. blue	1·10	70

1926. Fiscal stamps surch. **CORREOS VALE 1926** and value.

No.	Type	Description	Unused	Used
392.		5 c. on 1 b. olive	25	15
393.		25 c. on 5 c. brown	30	15

25. General J. V. Gomez and Ciudad Bolivar.

26.

1928. Capture of Ciudad Bolivar and Peace in Venezuela. 25th Anniv.

No.	Type	Description	Unused	Used
394.	**25.**	10 c. green	35	35

1930. Air.

No.	Type	Description	Unused	Used
395.	**26.**	5 c. brown	5	5
575.		5 c. green	15	5
396.		10 c. yellow	5	5
576.		10 c. orange	50	8
577.		12½ c. purple	55	20
397.		15 c. grey	5	5
578.		15 c. blue	45	5
398.		25 c. violet	5	5
579.		25 c. brown	70	8
399.		40 c. green	5	5
581.		70 c. red	11·00	3·75
400.		75 c. red	8	5
401.		1 b. slate	10	5
582.		1 b. blue	4·25	70
402.		1 b. 20 green	35	12
403.		1 b. 70 blue	45	25
404.		1 b. 90 green	55	25
405.		2 b. 10 blue	70	25
406.		2 b. 30 red	90	25
407.		2 b. 50 blue	90	25
408.		3 b. 70 green	85	45
409.		10 b. purple	2·25	1·10
410.		20 b. green	4·50	2·25

27. Simon Bolivar.

28.

1930. Bolivar. Death Cent.

No.	Type	Description	Unused	Used
411.	**27.**	5 c. yellow	35	20
412.		10 c. blue	45	8
413.		25 c. red	50	8

1932. Air. Air stamps as 1930 on paper printed with pattern as T **28.**

No.	Type	Description	Unused	Used
426.	**26.**	5 c. brown	25	8
427.		10 c. yellow	25	8
428.		15 c. grey	25	8
429.		25 c. blue	30	8
430.		40 c. green	45	8
431.		70 c. red	35	5
432.		75 c. orange	75	8
433.		1 b. slate	85	8
434.		1 b. 20 green	1·10	55
435.		1 b. 70 brown	2·25	35
436.		1 b. 80 blue	1·10	25
437.		1 b. 90 green	2·75	1·75
438.		1 b. 95 blue	3·50	1·40
439.		2 b. brown	2·25	1·10
440.		2 b. 10 blue	4·00	2·25
441.		2 b. 30 red	2·00	95
442.		2 b. 50 blue	2·75	75
443.		3 b. violet	2·75	55
444.		3 b. 70 green	3·50	3·50
445.		4 b. orange	2·75	55
446.		5 b. grey	4·50	1·10
447.		8 b. red	7·00	2·25
448.		10 b. violet	11·00	4·00
449.		20 b. green	29·00	14·00

1932. Stamps of 1916 on paper printed with pattern as T **28.**

No.	Type	Description	Unused	Used
414.	**23.**	5 c. violet	15	5
415.		7½ c. green	50	15
416.		10 c. green	25	5
417.		15 c. yellow	70	15
418.		22½ c. red	1·40	30
419.		25 c. red	50	5
420.		37½ c. blue	1·75	70
421.		40 c. blue	2·25	15
422.		50 c. olive	2·25	30
423.		1 b. blue	2·75	45
424.		3 b. brown	11·00	5·00
425.		5 b. brown	17·00	5·50

29. Arms of Bolivar.

ILLUSTRATIONS
British Commonwealth and all overprints and surcharges are FULL SIZE. Foreign Countries have been reduced to ¾-LINEAR.

1933. Bolivar. 150th Birth Anniv.

No.	Type	Description	Unused	Used
450.	**29.**	25 c. red	1·40	1·10

1933. Surch. **1933** and figures of value and old value blocked out.

No.	Type	Description	Unused	Used
451.	**23.**	7½ on 10 c. green (380)	30	8
453.		22½ on 25 c. red (384)	75	50
452.		22½ on 25 c. red (419)	95	55
454.		37½ on 40 c. blue (385)	1·10	55

1937. Air. Air stamps of 1932 surch. **1937. VALE POR** and new value.

No.	Type	Description	Unused	Used
455.	**26.**	5 c. on 1 b. 70 brown	8·50	5·50
456.		10 c. on 3 b. 70 green	8·50	5·50
457.		15 c. on 4 b. orange	4·00	2·75
458.		25 c. on 5 b. grey	4·00	2·75
459.		1 b. on 8 b. red	3·50	2·25
460.		2 b. on 2 b. 10 blue	23·00	17·00

1937. Surch. **1937 VALE POR** and value.

No.	Type	Description	Unused	Used
461.	**23.**	25 c. on 40 c. (No. 421)	75	20

30. Nurse and Child.

31. Ploughing.

32. " Flight ".

35. Caribbean Coast.

1937. (a) Postage.

No.	Type	Description	Unused	Used
463.	**30.**	5 c. violet	45	30
464.	–	10 c. green	45	15
465.	–	15 c. brown	75	35
466.	**30.**	25 c. red	55	20
467.	–	50 c. green	2·40	75
468.	**31.**	3 b. red	4·75	2·75
469.	**30.**	5 b. brown	5·50	5·00

DESIGNS—VERT. 10 c. Boats on Orinoco. 15 c. Women gathering cocoa-beans. HORIZ. 50 c. Rounding up cattle.

(b Air.

No.	Type	Description	Unused	Used
470.	**32.**	5 c. brown	25	25
471.	–	10 c. orange	12	8
472.	–	15 c. black	25	15
473.	**35.**	25 c. violet	30	12
474.	–	40 c. green	45	15
475.	**32.**	70 c. red	30	15
476.	–	75 c. bistre	1·10	55
477.	**32.**	1 b. grey	75	25
478.	–	1 b. 20 green	2·75	1·75
479.	**32.**	1 b. 80 blue	1·75	60
480.	–	1 b. 95 blue	3·50	2·25
481.	**35.**	2 b. brown	2·75	1·75
482.		2 b. 50 blue	5·50	3·50
483.	–	3 b. lilac	3·50	2·75
484.	**35.**	3 b. 70 red	5·00	5·00
485.	–	10 b. purple	5·50	4·75
486.	**32.**	20 b. black	8·50	7·00

DESIGNS—HORIZ. 10 c., 40 c., 1 b. 20, 3 b. Puerto Cabello. 15 c., 75 c., 1 b. 95, 10 b. Caracas.

36. " Venezuela welcoming La Guaira.

37. Bolivar.

38. Gathering Coffee Beans.

39. La Guaira.

1937. Acquisition of La Guaira Harbour.

No.	Type	Description	Unused	Used
487.	**36.**	25 c. blue (postage)	65	30
488.	–	70 c. green (air)	90	35
489.	–	1 b. 80 blue	1·40	75

DESIGN: 70 c., 1 b. 80, Statue of Bolivar and La Guaira Harbour.

1937. Red Cross Fund.

No.	Type	Description	Unused	Used
490.	**37.**	5 c. green	40	20

1938. (a) Postage. As T **38.**

No.	Type	Description	Unused	Used
508.	**38.**	5 c. green	15	8
509.	–	10 c. red	30	8
510.	–	15 c. violet	45	15
511.	–	25 c. light blue	30	8
512.	–	37½ c. dark blue	3·75	75
513.	–	40 c. sepia	6·50	2·75
514.	**38.**	50 c. olive	6·50	2·75
515.	–	1 b. brown	7·00	2·75
516.	**38.**	3 b. orange	42·00	20·00
517.	–	5 b. black	9·50	3·25

DESIGNS: 10 c., 25 c., 37½ c., 1 b. Bolivar. 15 c., 40 c., 5 b. G.P.O., Caracas.

(b) Air. As T **39.**

No.	Type	Description	Unused	Used
518.	**39.**	5 c. green	75	30
519.	–	10 c. red	75	30
520.	–	15 c. violet	2·10	45
521.	**39.**	25 c. blue	2·10	30
555.	–	30 c. violet	1·25	8
522.	–	40 c. violet	2·10	30
557.	**39.**	45 c. green	75	10
558.	–	50 c. blue	75	8
523.	–	70 c. crimson	45	15
524.	**39.**	75 c. brown	4·25	1·40
560.	–	90 c. orange	65	8
525.	–	1 b. olive	3·50	1·40
526.	–	1 b. 20 orange	7·00	2·75
527.	**39.**	1 b. 80 blue	1·00	30
528.	–	1 b. 90 black	2·75	1·40
529.	–	1 b. 95 blue	2·10	1·10
530.	**39.**	2 b. olive	23·00	8·50
531.	–	2 b. 50 brown	20·00	8·50
532.	–	3 b. green	11·00	4·25
533.	**39.**	3 b. 70 black	3·50	1·40
566.	–	5 b. brown	4·75	1·40
534.	–	10 b. purple	14·00	2·75
535.	–	20 b. orange	42·00	14·00

DESIGNS: 10 c., 40 c., 50 c., 1 b., 1 b. 90, 2 b. 50, 10 b. National Pantheon. 15 c., 30 c., 70 c., 90 c., 1 b. 20, 1 b. 95, 3 b., 5 b., 20 b. Oil Wells.

For other stamps in these types see Nos. 542 etc.

40. Teresa Carreno. 41. Carabobo Monuments. 42.

1938. Stamps of 1937 optd. **RESELLADO 1937-1938.**

491. 30. 5 c. violet (postage) .. 2·75 1·40
492. – 10 c. green 75 35
493. 30. 25 c. red 55 30
494. 31. 3 b. red .. .. 55·00 38·00

495. – 10 c. orange (air) .. 85 55
496. 35. 25 c. violet .. .. 1·40 1·00
497. – 40 c. green .. .. 1·40 1·10
498. 32. 70 c. red .. .. 1·10 85
499. 1 b. grey .. .. 1·75 1·10
500. – 1 b. 20 green .. .. 16·00 11·00
501. 32. 1 b. 80 blue .. .. 2·75 1·75
502. – 1 b. 95 blue .. .. 6·50 3·75
503. 35. 2 b. brown .. .. 26·00 16·00
504. 2 b. 50 blue .. .. 20·00 14·00
505. – 3 b. lilac .. .. 23·00 9·00
506. – 10 b. purple .. .. 45·00 32·00
507. 32. 20 b. blac .. .. 65·00 38·00

1938. Repatriation of (Composer) Teresa Carreno's Ashes.

567. 40. 25 c. blue .. .. 1·90 30

1938. Air. Postage stamps surch. **1938 VALE CINCO** (or other value) **CENTIMOS.**

537. 32. 5 c. on 1 b. 80 blue .. 30 20
538. 35. 10 c. on 2 b. 50 blue .. 1·40 75
539. 15 c. on 2 b. brown .. 75 35
540. – 25 c. on 40 c. green (474) 85 85
541. 35. 40 c. on 3 b. 70 red .. 1·75 1·10

1938. Re-issue of 1938 issue in new colours.

542. 38. 5 c. blue-green (post.) 15 8
544. – 15 c. olive 55 15
545. – 25 c. dark blue .. 30 15
546. – 37½ c. light blue .. 1·60 35
547. – 40 c. black .. .. 5·50 2·10
548. 38. 50 c. violet .. .. 3·75 35
549. – 1 b. sepia .. .. 4·25 55
750. – 5 b. orange .. .. 21·00 14·00
751. – 5 b. chocolate .. 7·50 3·25

550. 39. 5 c. blue-green (air) .. 8 5
551. – 10 c. red-orange .. 12 5
552. 39. 12½ c. violet 45 20
553. – 15 c. blue 85 10
554. 39. 25 c. brown 20 8
556. – 40 c. brown .. .. 1·10 10
559. 39. 75 c. olive 75 10
561. – 1 b. violet .. .. 1·00 15
562. – 1 b. 20 green 85 30
563. 39. 2 b. red .. .. 1·40 75
564. – 2 b. 50 orange .. 4·25 1·40
565. – 3 b. olive .. .. 2·75 75
566. – 5 b. red .. .. 8·50 2·75
771. – 5 b. olive .. .. 3·50 1·40
772. – 10 b. violet .. .. 13·00 4·25
773. – 10 b. yellow .. .. 5·50 2·25

DESIGNS: As for 1938 issue.

1938. Surch. **VALE BS. 0,40 1938.**

536. 30. 40 c. on 5 b. brown .. 3·25 1·10

1938. Air. Independence Issue.

583. – 20 c. brown 45 15
584. 42. 30 c. violet 75 15
585. 41. 45 c. blue 85 15
586. – 50 c. blue 75 10
587. 41. 70 c. red .. .. 10·00 7·00
588. 42. 90 c. orange .. .. 1·10 20
589. 41. 1 b. 35 black .. .. 1·00 65
590. – 1 b. 40 slate .. .. 3·75 1·40
591. 42. 2 b. 25 green .. .. 2·10 1·10

DESIGN: 20 c., 50 c., 1 b. 40, Aeroplane over Sucre Monument.

43. Allegory of Labour and Statue of Bolivar. 44. General J. I. Paz Castillo.

1938. Labour Day.

568. 43. 25 c. blue .. .. 1·90 25

1939. Venezuelan Posts. 80th Anniv.

592. 44. 10 c. red 75 25

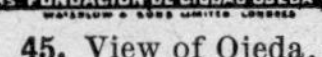

45. View of Ojeda. 46. Dr. Cristobal Mendoza.

1939. Founding of Ojeda.

593. 45. 25 c. blue .. .. 1·90 35

1939. Death of Dr. Mendoza. Cent.

594. 46. 5 c. green 35 15
595. 10 c. red 30 15
596. 15 c. violet 75 20
597. 25 c. blue 30 5
598. 37½ c. blue .. .. 7·00 2·75
599. 50 c. olive .. .. 4·25 1·75
600. 1 b. brown .. .. 3·50 2·10

47. Diego B. Urbaneja. 48. Bolivar and Carabobo Monument.

1940. Independence Issue.

601. 47. 5 c. green (postage) .. 30 8
602. 7½ c. green 45 15
603. 15 c. olive 45 8
604. 37½ c. blue 85 45
605. 40 c. blue 55 15
745. 40 c. mauve 45 12
746. 40 c. orange 30 10
606. 50 c. violet .. .. 2·50 75
607. 1 b. brown .. .. 1·40 30
748. 1 b. blue 85 15
608. 3 b. red .. .. 4·25 1·40
749. 3 b. grey .. .. 1·75 55

609. 48. 15 c. blue (air) .. 20 5
610. 20 c. olive 35 5
611. 25 c. brown .. .. 1·10 15
612. 40 c. brown 85 10
613. 1 b. lilac .. .. 2·10 30
614. 2 b. red .. .. 4·00 55

49. "Crossing the Andes". 50. Battle of Carabobo.

1940. Gen. Santander. Death Cent.

617. 49. 25 c. blue .. .. 1·40 30

1940. Gen. Paez. 150th Birth Anniv.

616. 50. 25 c. blue .. .. 1·25 30

51. "Foundation of Greater Colombia".

1940. Air. Pan-American Union. 50th Anniv.

615. 51. 15 c. brown 75 30

52. Simon Bolivar. 53. Statue of Bolivar at Caracas. 54. Symbolical of industry.

1940. 110th Anniv. of Death of Simon Bolivar. (a) Postage.

618. – 5 c. blue-green .. 20 5
738. – 5 c. yellow-green .. 10 5
739. – 5 c. blue 10 5
619. – 10 c. pink 20 5
620. – 15 c. olive 45 8
741. – 15 c. red 25 8
621. – 20 c. blue 75 5
622. 52. 25 c. blue 30 8
742. 25 c. violet 30 8
623. – 30 c. magenta .. 85 15
743. – 30 c. black 75 35
744. – 30 c. brown 25 10
624. – 37½ c. blue .. .. 1·40 30
625. – 50 c. violet .. .. 1·25 15
747. – 50 c. olive 35 15

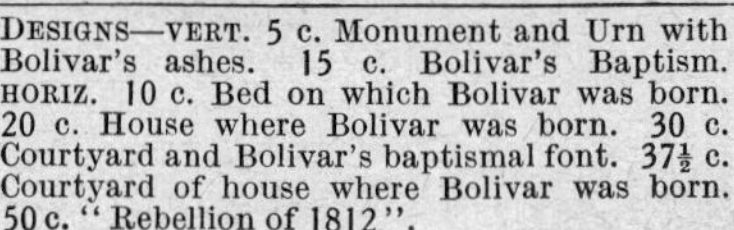
DESIGNS—VERT. 5 c. Monument and Urn with Bolivar's ashes. 15 c. Bolivar's Baptism. HORIZ. 10 c. Bed on which Bolivar was born. 20 c. House where Bolivar was born. 30 c. Courtyard and Bolivar's baptismal font. 37½ c. Courtyard of house where Bolivar was born. 50 c. "Rebellion of 1812".

(b) Air.

626. 53. 5 c. green 8 5
752. 5 c. orange 5 5
627. 10 c. red 8 5
753. 10 c. green 5 5
628. 12½ c. violet 55 30
754. 12½ c. brown 20 20
629. 15 c. blue 45 5
755. 15 c. grey 8 5
630. 20 c. brown 15 5
756. 20 c. violet 10 8
631. 25 c. brown 30 5
757. 25 c. green 10 8
632. 30 c. violet 15 5
758. 30 c. blue 30 8
633. 40 c. brown 45 5
759. 40 c. green 20 8
634. 45 c. green 20 5
760. 45 c. red 45 12
635. 50 c. blue 20 8
761. 50 c. claret 20 15
636. 70 c. rose-pink 55 15
762. 70 c. dark carmine .. 1·00 50
637. 75 c. olive .. .. 2·10 75
763. 75 c. orange .. .. 2·10 1·10
764. 75 c. violet 35 15
638. 90 c. orange 55 15
765. 90 c. black 35 15
639. 1 b. mauve 45 8
766. 1 b. blue 45 15
640. 1 b. 20 green .. .. 1·40 45
767. 1 b. 20 brown 85 40
641. 1 b. 35 black .. .. 3·50 1·75
642. 2 b. red 85 15
643. 3 b. black .. .. 2·10 75
768. 3 b. brown .. .. 2·75 1·40
769. 3 b. blue .. .. 1·40 85
644. 4 b. black .. .. 1·75 55
645. 5 b. brown .. .. 7·00 2·10

1941. Surch. **HABILITADO 1941 VALE BS.0.20.**

646. 52. 20 c. on 25 c. blue .. 45 8

1941. Optd. **HABILITADO 1940.**

647. 30. 5 c. violet .. .. 1·10 20
648. – 10 c. green (No. 464) .. 75 12

1942. National Industrial Exhibition.

652. 54. 10 c. red 55 15

55. Bolivar's Funeral. 56. Condor.

1942. Cent. of Arrival of Bolivar's Ashes at Caracas and Liberator's Monument Fund.

649. 55. 20 c. + 5 c. blue (postage) 2·10 30

650. 56. 15 c. + 10 c. brown (air) 45 20
651. 30 c. + 5 c. violet .. 45 20

57. Caracas Cathedral. 58. National and Red Cross Flags.

1943.

653. 57. 10 c. carmine 35 8
740. 10 c. orange-red .. 8 5

1943. Surch. **Habilitado Vale Bs. 0.20.**

654. 30. 20 c. on 25 c. red .. 10·00 8·50
655. 36. 20 c. on 25 c. blue .. 16·00 13·00
656. 40. 20 c. on 25 c. blue .. 5·00 2·75
657. 43. 20 c. on 25 c. blue .. 5·00 5·00

1943. Optd. **Resellado 1943.**

658. 30. 5 c. violet .. .. 8·50 4·25
659. – 10 c. green (No. 464) .. 2·75 1·40
660. – 50 c. green (No. 467) .. 4·25 2·10
661. 31. 3 b. red .. .. 17·00 8·50

1943. Air. Optd. **Resellado 1943.**

662. – 10 c. orange (No. 471) .. 55 35
663. 35. 25 c. violet 55 35
664. – 40 c. green (No. 474) .. 70 35
665. 32. 70 c. red 90 45
666. – 70 c. green (No. 488) .. 1·10 55
667. – 75 c. bistre (No. 476) .. 1·10 55
668. 32. 1 b. grey .. .. 1·40 70
669. – 1 b. 20 green (No. 478) .. 1·75 85
670. 32. 1 b. 80 blue .. .. 1·75 90
671. – 1 b. 80 blue (No. 489) .. 2·25 1·10
672. – 1 b. 95 blue (No. 480) .. 2·25 1·40
673. 35. 2 b. brown .. .. 2·75 1·75
674. 2 b. 50 blue .. .. 2·75 2·10
675. – 3 b. lilac (No. 483) .. 4·50 2·75
676. 35. 3 b. 70 red .. .. 23·00 23·00
677. – 10 b. purple (No. 485) .. 9·50 9·50
678. 32. 20 b. black .. .. 17·00 17·00

1944. Air. Red Cross Anniversaries.

680. 58. 5 c. green 5 5
681. 10 c. mauve 8 5
682. 20 c. blue 12 8
683. 30 c. blue 25 8
684. 40 c. brown 35 12
685. 45 c. green 90 50
686. 90 c. orange 80 35
687. 1 b. black .. .. 1·40 30

59. Baseball Players. 60. Charles Howarth.

1944. Air. 7th World Amateur Baseball Championship Games. Optd. **AEREO.**

688. 59. 5 c. brown 12 5
689. 10 c. green 15 8
690. 20 c. blue 25 12
691. 30 c. red 35 20
692. 45 c. purple 85 50
693. 90 c. orange .. .. 1·75 90
694. 1 b. grey .. .. 2·00 85
695. 1 b. 20 c. green .. 4·25 3·75
696. 1 b. 80 c. yellow .. 5·50 5·00

1944. Air. No. 590 surch. **Habilitado 1944//VALE/Bs.0.30.**

697. 30 c. on 1 b. 40 c. slate 55 55

1944. Air. Cent. of Rochdale Co-operative Society.

698. 60. 5 c. black 12 5
699. 10 c. violet 15 8
700. 20 c. brown 30 12
701. 30 c. green 35 15
702. 1 b. 20 yellow .. .. 1·75 1·40
703. 1 b. 80 c. blue .. .. 2·25 2·00
704. 3 b. 70 c. red .. .. 3·50 2·75

61. Antonio Jose de Sucre. 62. Antonio Jose de Sucre and Aeroplane.

1945. 150th Anniv. of Birth of Gen. Sucre.

705. 61. 5 c. yellow (postage) .. 55 15
706. 10 c. blue 70 20
707. 20 c. red 85 20

708. 62. 5 c. orange (air) .. 8 5
709. 10 c. purple 12 5
710. 20 c. black 15 5
711. 30 c. green 30 8
712. 40 c. olive 35 12
713. 45 c. brown 40 15
714. 90 c. chestnut .. .. 1·00 35
715. 1 b. mauve 70 25
716. 1 b. 20 c. black .. 1·75 1·40
717. 2 b. yellow .. .. 2·25 1·40

63. Andres Bello. 64. Gen. Rafael Urdaneta.

1946. A. Bello (educationalist). 80th Death Anniv.

718. 63. 20 c. blue (postage) .. 45 15

719. 30 c. green (air) .. 45 15

1946. Gen. R. Urdaneta. Death Cent.

720. 64. 20 c. blue (postage) .. 45 15

721. 30 c. green (air) .. 45 15

65. Allegory of Republic. 66. Western Hemisphere and Anti-Tuberculosis Inst., Maracaibo.

1946. Revolution. 1st Anniv.

722. 65. 20 c. blue (postage) .. 45 15

723. 15 c. blue (air) .. 20 8
724. 20 c. bistre 25 12
725. 30 c. violet 30 15
726. 1 b. red .. .. 1·75 1·10

Nos. 723/4 are vert.

1947. 12th Pan-American Health Conf.
727. **66.** 20 c. yell. & blue (post.) 45 20
728. 15 c. yell. & blue (air).. 35 15
729. 20 c. yellow and brown 35 15
730. 30 c. yellow and violet.. 40 20
731. 1 b. yellow and red .. 2·75 1·75
Nos 728/31 are vert.

1947. Surch. **J.R.G. CORREOS Vale Bs. 0.15 1946.**
732. **47.** 15 c. on 1 b. brown .. 30 8

1947. Air. Surch. **J.R.G. AEREO Vale Bs.**, new value, and **1946.**
733. **23.** 10 c. on 22½ c. red (No. 418) 10 8
734. **52.** 15 c. on 25 c. blue .. 20 5
735. **53.** 20 c. on 50 c. blue .. 15 8
736. **47.** 70 c. on 1 b. brown .. 50 25
737. – 20 b. on 20 b. orange (No. 535) .. .. 14·00 5·50

1947. Nos. 743 and 624 surch. **CORREOS Vale Bs.**, new value, and **1947.** (a) Postage.
776. 5 c. on 30 c. black .. 30 8
777. 5 c. on 37½ c. blue .. 20 8

(b) Air. No. 680 with **AEREO** instead of **CORREOS.**
778. 5 c. on 20 c. blue .. 12 5
779. 10 c. on 20 c. blue .. 12 5

67. M.S. "Republica de Venezuela" and Ship's Wheel. **68.**

1948. Greater Columbia Merchant Marine. 1st Anniv. Frame size 37½×22½ mm. or 22½×37½ mm. Inscr. "AMERICAN BANK NOTE COMPANY" at foot.
780. **67.** 5 c. blue (postage) .. 15 5
781. 7½ c. vermilion.. .. 25 10
782. 10 c. red 35 5
783. 15 c. grey 50 15
784. 20 c. sepia 30 8
785. 25 c. violet 45 10
786. 30 c. yellow .. .. 2·10 85
787. 37½ c. brown .. .. 1·40 1·10
788. 40 c. olive .. .. 2·10 85
789. 50 c. mauve 45 25
790. 1 b. green 85 30
791. **68.** 5 c. brown (air) .. 5 5
792. 10 c. green 5 5
793. 15 c. buff 8 5
794. 20 c. purple 15 5
795. 25 c. grey 15 5
796. 30 c. olive 20 8
797. 45 c. blue 30 12
798. 50 c. black 30 15
799. 70 c. orange 75 20
800. 75 c. blue .. .. 1·40 20
801. 90 c. red 85 30
802. 1 b. violet .. .. 1·25 45
803. 2 b. slate .. .. 1·40 55
804. 3 b. green .. .. 4·25 2·10
805. 4 b. blue .. .. 2·75 1·40
806. 5 b. vermilion .. .. 7·00 3·50
For stamps as T **67/8** in larger size and inscribed "COURVOISIER S.A." at foot, see Nos. 1012 etc.

69. Arms of Venezuela.

1948.
807. **69.** 5 c. blue.. .. .. 1·00 30
808. 10 c. red .. .. 1·10 30

70. Santos Michelena. **71.**

1949. Death Cent. of Michelena (Finance Minister) and 110th Anniv. of Int. Postal Convention, Bogota.
810. **70.** 5 c. blue (postage) .. 8 5
811. 10 c. red 30 8
812. 20 c. sepia 85 45
813. 1 b. green .. .. 3·50 1·40
814. **71.** 5 c. brown (air) .. 15 5
815. 10 c. grey 15 8
816. 15 c. orange 45 25
817. 25 c. green 75 35
818. 30 c. purple 55 25
819. 1 b. violet .. .. 4·25 75

72. Columbus, Indian, "Santa Maria" and map. **73.**

1949. Columbus' Discovery of America. 450th Anniv.
820. **72.** 5 c. blue (postage) .. 30 5
821 10 c. red .. .. 1·10 35
822. 20 c. sepia .. .. 1·10 35
823. 1 b. green .. .. 3·50 1·40
824. **73.** 5 c. brown (air) .. 20 5
825. 10 c. grey 30 8
826. 15 c. orange 45 10
827 25 c. green 55 30
828. 30 c. mauve 85 45
829. 1 b. violet .. .. 2·75 1·40

74. Hand, Bird, Aeroplane and Glove. **75.** Gen. Francisco de Miranda.

76. Declaration of Independence.

1950. Air. U.P.U. 75th Anniv.
830. **74.** 5 c. lake 5 5
831. 10 c. green 8 5
832. 15 c. brown 15 8
833. 25 c. grey 30 15
834. 30 c. olive 45 25
835. 50 c. black 30 8
836. 60 c. blue .. .. 1·10 55
837. 90 c. red .. .. 1·25 55
838. 1 b. violet .. .. 1·25 45

1950. Miranda. Birth Bicent.
839. **75.** 5 c. blue (postage) .. 20 5
840. 10 c. green 45 8
841. 20 c. brown 50 15
842. 1 b. red .. .. 2·75 1·40
843. **76.** 5 c. red (air) .. 15 5
844. 10 c. brown 20 5
845. 15 c. violet 45 10
846. 30 c. blue 55 15
847. 1 b. green .. .. 2·10 70

77. Tree. **78.** Statistical Map.

1950. Air. Protection of flora. Centres in yellow.
848. **77.** 5 c. brown 30 15
849. 10 c. green 20 8
850. 15 c. magenta 55 30
851. 25 c. green .. .. 2·10 1·10
852. 30 c. orange .. .. 4·25 2·10
853. 50 c. grey .. .. 2·75 75
854. 60 c. blue .. .. 3·50 1·10
855. 90 c. red .. .. 4·75 2·10
856. 1 b. violet .. .. 5·50 2·10

1950. Census of the Americas.
857. **78.** 5 c. blue (postage) .. 15 5
858. 10 c. grey 15 8
859. 15 c. sepia 25 8
860. 25 c. green 35 8
861. 30 c. red 45 15
862. 50 c. violet 75 20
863. 1 b. brown .. .. 1·75 55
864. **78.** 5 c. grey (air) .. 15 5
865. 10 c. green 8 5
866. 15 c. olive 30 10
867. 25 c. black 45 15
868. 30 c. orange 55 30
869. 50 c. brown 35 8
870. 60 c. blue 45 30
871. 90 c. red .. .. 1·10 45
872. 1 b. violet .. .. 1·40 65

79. Alonso de Ojeda. **80.**

1950. Discovery of Lake Maracaibo. 450th Anniv.
873. **79.** 5 c. blue (postage) .. 8 5
874. 10 c. red 15 5
875. 15 c. grey 20 10
876. 20 c. blue 75 30
877. 1 b. green .. .. 2·75 1·40
878. 5 c. brown (air) .. 15 5
879. 10 c. red 15 5
880. 15 c. sepia 20 8
881. 25 c. purple 50 25
882. 30 c. orange 75 30
883. 1 b. green .. .. 2·75 1·40

1951. Surch. **RESELLADO** and new value.
884. **67.** 5 c. on 7½ c. vermilion.. 15 8
885. 10 c. on 37½ c. brown .. 25 8

1951. Telegraph stamps surch. as in T **80.**
886. 5 c. on 5 c. brown.. .. 8 5
887. 10 c. on 10 c. emerald .. 15 5
888. 20 c. on 1 b. black .. 35 8
889. 25 c. on 25 c. red.. .. 45 8
890. 30 c. on 2 b. olive .. 55 30

81. Arms of Zulia. **82.** Statue of Bolivar.

1951. Arms issue. Federal District of Caracas. As Type **81**, showing Arms of Caracas and View.
891. 5 c. green (postage) .. 35 5
892. 10 c. red 50 5
893. 15 c. brown 75 30
894. 20 c. blue .. .. 2·75 75
895. 25 c. brown .. .. 3·75 75
896. 30 c. blue .. .. 4·25 75
897. 35 c. violet .. .. 21·00 14·00
898. 5 c. turquoise (air).. .. 55 15
899. 7½ c. green .. .. 1·75 85
900. 10 c. red 30 5
901. 15 c. brown .. .. 4·25 55
902. 20 c. blue .. .. 3·00 55
903. 30 c. blue .. .. 4·25 1·40
904. 45 c. purple .. .. 3·50 75
905. 60 c. green.. .. 10·00 1·40
906. 90 c. red .. .. 6·50 3·50
See also Nos. 922/37, 938/53, 954/69, 970/85, 991/1006, 1018/33, 1034/49, 1050/65, 1066/81, 1082/97, 1098/113, 1137/52, 1153/68, 1169/200, 1201/16, 1217/32, 1258/73, 1274/89, 1290/305, 1306/21, 1322/37 and 1338/53.

1951. Transfer of Statue of Bolivar to Central Park, New York.
907. **82.** 5 c. green (postage) .. 30 5
908. 10 c. red 45 15
909. 20 c. blue 45 15
910. 30 c. grey 55 25
911. 40 c. green 75 25
912. 50 c. brown .. .. 1·40 45
913. 1 b. black .. .. 3·50 2·10
914. 5 c. violet (air).. .. 30 8
915. 10 c. green 45 10
916. 20 c. grey 45 10
917. 25 c. olive 50 15
918. 30 c. red 55 30
919. 40 c. brown 55 30
920. 50 c. slate .. .. 1·10 35
921. 70 c. orange .. .. 1·75 85

83. Arms of Venezuela and Bolivar Statue. **84.** Isabella the Catholic.

1951. Arms issue. National Arms of Venezuela.
922. **83.** 5 c. green (postage) .. 15 8
923. 10 c. red 15 8
924. 15 c. brown .. .. 2·10 35
925. 20 c. blue .. .. 2·10 30
926. 25 c. brown .. .. 3·50 75
927. 30 c. blue .. .. 3·50 75
928. 35 c. violet .. .. 17·00 10·00
929. **83.** 5 c. turquoise (air) .. 35 8
930. 7½ c. green 85 55
931. 10 c. red 20 5
932. 15 c. brown .. .. 2·10 50
933. 20 c. blue .. .. 2·75 55
934. 30 c. blue .. .. 4·75 75
935. 45 c. purple .. .. 2·10 30
936. 60 c. green .. .. 9·50 1·75
937. 90 c. red .. .. 7·50 4·75
See also Nos. 938/53, 954/69, 970/85, 991/1006, 1018/33, 1034/49, 1050/65, 1066/81, 1082/97, 1098/113, 1137/52, 1153/68, 1169/200, 1201/16, 1217/32, 1258/73, 1274/89, 1290/305, 1306/21, 1322/37 and 1338/53.

1951. Arms issue. State of Tachira. As Types **81** and **83** showing Arms of Tachira and agricultural products.
938. 5 c. green (postage) .. 15 5
939. 10 c. red 45 8
940. 15 c. brown .. .. 1·00 35
941. 20 c. blue .. .. 1·40 30
942. 50 c. orange .. .. 85·00 14·00
943. 1 b. green .. .. 1·40 55
944. 5 b. purple.. .. 4·25 2·75
945. 5 c. turquoise (air).. .. 30 8
946. 10 c. red 15 8
947. 15 c. brown .. .. 1·10 20
948. 30 c. blue .. .. 11·00 1·75
949. 60 c. green.. .. 8·50 1·40
950. 1 b. 20 lake.. .. 7·00 5·50
951. 3 b. green .. .. 2·10 85
952. 5 b. purple.. .. 4·25 2·10
953. 10 b. violet.. .. 7·00 3·50

1951. Arms issue. State of Zulia.
954. **81.** 5 c. green (postage) .. 15 5
955. 10 c. red 20 5
956. 15 c. brown 60 30
957. 20 c. blue 85 30
958. 50 c. orange .. .. 5·50 4·25
959. 1 b. green .. .. 1·40 55
960. 5 b. purple .. .. 4·25 2·75
961. **81.** 5 c. turquoise (air) .. 35 12
962. 10 c. red 12 5
963. 15 c. brown 55 25
964. 30 c. blue .. .. 4·00 1·10
965. 60 c. green .. .. 2·25 55
966. 1 b. 20 lake .. .. 5·50 4·50
967. 3 b. green .. .. 1·40 75
968. 5 b. purple .. .. 2·75 1·75
969. 10 b. violet .. .. 5·50 2·75

1951. Arms issue. State of Carabobo. As Type **81** showing Arms of Carabobo and agricultural produce.
970. 5 c. green (postage) .. 15 5
971. 10 c. red 15 8
972. 15 c. brown 35 12
973. 20 c. blue 45 15
974. 25 c. brown 45 15
975. 30 c. blue 75 30
976. 35 c. violet.. .. 3·50 2·75
977. 5 c. turquoise (air).. .. 25 5
978. 7½ c. green.. .. 40 35
979. 10 c. red 12 5
980. 15 c. brown 35 15
981. 20 c. blue 50 25
982. 30 c. blue .. .. 1·10 30
983. 45 c. purple 55 25
984. 60 c. green .. .. 1·40 45
985. 90 c. red .. .. 2·75 1·75

1951. Air. Isabella the Catholic. 500th Birth Anniv.
986. **84.** 5 c. green 20 5
987. 10 c. red 20 5
988. 20 c. blue 35 10
989. 30 c. deep blue 35 15

1951. Arms issue. State of Anzoategui. As Type **83** showing Arms of Anzoategui and globe.
991. 5 c. green (postage) .. 15 5
992. 10 c. red 15 5
993. 15 c. brown 60 30
994. 20 c. blue.. .. 50 20
995. 40 c. orange .. .. 1·40 55
996. 45 c. purple .. .. 6·50 4·25
997. 3 b. blue .. .. 2·50 1·25
998. 5 c. turquoise (air) .. 20 5
999. 10 c. red 12 5
1000. 15 c. brown 35 12

1001.	25 c. black	55	15
1002.	30 c. blue	1·40	75
1003.	50 c. orange	1·75	60
1004.	60 c. green	1·75	30
1005.	1 b. violet	2·25	1·10
1006.	2 b. violet	3·50	1·25

86. National Stadium. 87. Juan de Villegas.

1951. Air. 3rd Bolivarian Games Caracas.

1007. 86.	5 c. green	45	10
1008.	10 c. red	45	10
1009.	20 c. brown	55	25
1010.	30 c. blue	85	30

1952. A Nos. 780/806 but frame size 38×23½ mm. or 23½×38 mm. Inscr. "COURVOISIER S.A." at foot.

1012. 67.	5 c. green (postage)	45	5
1013.	10 c. red	65	5
1014.	15 c. slate	85	5
1015. 68.	5 c. brown (air)	85	5
1016.	10 c. brown	1·25	5
1017.	15 c. olive	1·75	8

1952. Arms issue. State of Aragua. As Type **81** showing Arms of Aragua and Stylised Fauna.

1018.	5 c. green (postage)	15	5
1019.	10 c. red	20	8
1020.	15 c. brown	55	15
1021.	20 c. blue	45	15
1022.	25 c. brown	75	35
1023.	30 c. blue	85	55
1024.	35 c. violet	4·75	2·75
1025.	5 c. turquosie (air)	55	12
1026.	7½ c. green	40	30
1027.	10 c. red	12	5
1028.	15 c. brown	1·40	35
1029.	20 c. blue	55	25
1030.	30 c. blue	2·50	50
1031.	45 c. purple	1·40	25
1032.	60 c. green	2·25	55
1033.	90 c. red	14·00	9·50

1952. Arms issue. State of Bolivar. As Type **81** showing Arms of Bolivar and Iron Foundry.

1034.	5 c. green (postage)	15	5
1035.	10 c. red	20	5
1036.	15 c. brown	45	20
1037.	20 c. blue	55	15
1038.	40 c. orange	1·75	55
1039.	45 c. purple	5·50	4·25
1040.	3 b. blue	3·50	2·25
1041.	5 c. turquoise (air)	2·75	25
1042.	10 c. red	12	5
1043.	15 c. brown	45	12
1044.	25 c. black	35	5
1045.	30 c. blue	1·40	75
1046.	50 c. red	1·40	50
1047.	60 c. green	2·25	55
1048.	1 b. violet	1·75	35
1049.	2 b. violet	3·50	1·25

1952. Arms issue. State of Lara. As Type **81** showing Arms of Lara and Sisal Industry.

1050.	5 c. green (postage)	15	5
1051.	10 c. red	15	8
1052.	15 c. brown	45	20
1053.	20 c. blue	55	30
1054.	25 c. brown	75	30
1055.	30 c. blue	85	55
1056.	35 c. violet	6·50	4·25
1057.	5 c. turquoise (air)	50	15
1058.	7½ c. green	40	35
1059.	10 c. red	12	5
1060.	15 c. brown	75	12
1061.	20 c. blue	1·25	30
1062.	30 c. blue	2·25	50
1063.	45 c. purple	1·00	40
1064.	60 c. red	2·40	60
1065.	90 c. red	10·00	9·00

1952. Arms issue. State of Miranda. As Type **81** showing Arms of Miranda and Agricultural Products.

1066.	5 c. green (postage)	15	5
1067.	10 c. red	20	8
1068.	15 c. brown	45	15
1069.	20 c. blue	45	30
1070.	25 c. brown	75	35
1071.	30 c. blue	85	35
1072.	35 c. violet	4·75	2·75
1073.	5 c. turquoise (air)	25	5
1074.	7½ c. green	30	30
1075.	10 c. red	12	5
1076.	15 c. brown	55	25
1077.	20 c. blue	85	35
1078.	30 c. blue	1·75	60
1079.	45 c. purple	1·10	30
1080.	60 c. green	2·25	75
1081.	90 c. red	8·00	5·50

1952. Arms issue. State of Sucre. As Type **81** showing Arms of Sucre, Palms and Seascape.

1082.	5 c. green (postage)	10	5
1083.	10 c. red	15	5
1084.	15 c. brown	75	20
1085.	20 c. blue	55	15
1086.	40 c. orange	1·75	55
1087.	45 c. purple	7·00	4·75
1088.	3 b. blue	2·10	1·25
1089.	5 c. turquoise (air)	40	5
1090.	10 c. red	12	5
1091.	15 c. brown	35	12
1092.	25 c. black	7·00	25
1093.	30 c. blue	2·25	35
1094.	50 c. red	1·40	35
1095.	60 c. green	1·75	75
1096.	1 b. violet	2·00	60
1097.	2 b. violet	3·50	1·25

1952. Arms issue. State of Trujillo. As Type **81** showing Arms of Trujillo and Stylised Coffee Plant.

1098.	5 c. green (postage)	15	5
1099.	10 c. red	15	8
1100.	15 c. brown	85	30
1101.	20 c. blue	1·25	30
1102.	50 c. orange	4·75	3·75
1103.	1 b. green	1·40	55
1104.	5 b. purple	4·25	2·75
1105.	5 c. turquoise (air)	4·25	30
1106.	10 c. red	15	8
1107.	15 c. brown	75	15
1108.	30 c. blue	5·50	1·40
1109.	60 c. green	4·25	1·10
1110.	1 b. 20 lake	4·25	2·75
1111.	3 b. green	2·10	85
1112.	5 b. purple	4·25	2·10
1113.	10 b. violet	7·00	3·50

1952. Barquisimeto. 4th Cent.

1114. 87.	5 c. emerald (postage)	15	5
1115.	10 c. red	15	5
1116.	20 c. slate	30	8
1117.	40 c. orange	2·25	1·40
1118.	50 c. brown	1·10	45
1119.	1 b. violet	2·25	75
1120.	5 c. turquoise (air)	30	5
1121.	10 c. red	10	5
1122.	20 c. blue	20	5
1123.	25 c. black	35	10
1124.	30 c. blue	45	15
1125.	40 c. orange	1·75	1·40
1126.	50 c. olive	75	35
1127.	1 b. purple	1·40	75

88. Our Lady of Coromoto. 89. G.P.O., Caracas.

1952. Apparition of Our Lady of Coromoto. 300th Anniv.

1128. 88.	1 b. red (17×26½ mm.)	4·50	85
1129.	1 b. red (26½×41 mm.)	2·75	75
1130.	1 b. red (36×56 mm.)	2·75	75

1952. National Objective Exn. Telegraph stamps as T **80** surch. **Correos Exposicion Objetiva Nacional 1948-1952** and new value.

1131.	5 c. on 25 c. red	20	8
1132.	10 c. on 1 b. black	20	8

1952. Telegraph stamps as T **80** surch. **CORREOS HABILITADO 1952** and new value.

1133.	20 c. on 25 c. red	30	15
1134.	30 c. on 2 b. olive	1·40	1·10
1135.	40 c. on 1 b. black	75	30
1136.	50 c. on 3 b. orange	2·10	1·40

1953. Arms issue. State of Merida. As Type **81** showing Arms of Merida and church.

1137.	5 c. green (postage)	15	5
1138.	10 c. red	15	5
1139.	15 c. brown	30	15
1140.	20 c. blue	55	30
1141.	50 c. orange	2·10	1·40
1142.	1 b. green	75	35
1143.	5 b. purple	4·25	2·75
1144.	5 c. turquoise (air)	30	5
1145.	10 c. red	15	5
1146.	15 c. brown	55	15
1147.	30 c. blue	4·25	85
1148.	60 c. green	1·40	45
1149.	1 b. 20 lake	2·75	2·10
1150.	3 b. green	2·10	85
1151.	5 c. purple	4·25	2·10
1152.	10 b. violet	7·00	3·50

1953. Arms issue. State of Monagas. As Type **81** showing Arms of Monagas and horses.

1153.	5 c. green (postage)	15	5
1154.	10 c. red	15	5
1155.	15 c. brown	35	20
1156.	20 c. blue	45	20
1157.	40 c. orange	1·10	55
1158.	45 c. purple	4·25	3·50
1159.	3 b. blue	2·75	1·40
1160.	5 c. turquoise (air)	30	5
1161.	10 c. red	15	5
1162.	15 c. brown	45	15
1163.	25 c. black	50	15
1164.	30 c. blue	2·75	75
1165.	50 c. red	1·40	55
1166.	60 c. green	1·75	55
1167.	1 b. violet	2·10	75
1168.	2 c. violet	2·75	1·40

1953. Arms issue. State of Portuguesa. As Type **81** showing Arms of Portuguesa and Woodland.

1169.	5 c. green (postage)	10	5
1170.	10 c. red	15	5
1171.	15 c. brown	45	15
1172.	20 c. blue	75	20
1173.	50 c. orange	2·10	1·10
1174.	1 b. green	85	45
1175.	5 b. purple	4·25	2·75
1176.	5 c. turquoise (air)	75	15
1177.	10 c. red	15	5
1178.	15 c. brown	45	20
1179.	30 c. blue	4·25	85
1180.	60 c. green	1·75	45
1181.	1 b. 20 lake	4·75	2·75
1182.	3 b. green	2·10	85
1183.	5 b. purple	4·25	2·10
1184.	10 b. violet	7·00	3·50

1953. Arms issue. State of Delta Amacuro. As Type **83** showing Arms of Delta Amacuro and map.

1185.	5 c. green (postage)	10	5
1186.	10 c. red	15	5
1187.	15 c. brown	45	15
1188.	20 c. blue	55	30
1189.	40 c. orange	1·10	55
1190.	45 c. purple	4·25	2·75
1191.	3 b. blue	2·10	1·10
1192.	5 c. turquoise (air)	25	5
1193.	10 c. red	12	5
1194.	15 c. brown	35	12
1195.	25 c. black	50	25
1196.	30 c. blue	1·40	35
1197.	50 c. red	1·10	35
1198.	60 c. green	1·40	35
1199.	1 b. violet	1·75	85
1200.	2 b. violet	2·75	1·40

1953. Arms issue. State of Falcon. As Type **81** showing Arms of Falcon and Stylised Oil Refinery.

1201.	5 c. green (postage)	15	5
1202.	10 c. red	15	5
1203.	15 c. brown	35	15
1204.	20 c. blue	65	20
1205.	50 c. orange	2·10	1·40
1206.	1 b. green	1·25	45
1207.	5 c. purple	4·25	2·75
1208.	5 c. turquoise (air)	55	20
1209.	10 c. red	12	5
1210.	15 c. brown	35	15
1211.	30 c. blue	3·50	50
1212.	60 c. green	1·75	50
1213.	1 b. 20 lake	2·25	1·75
1214.	3 b. green	1·75	75
1215.	5 b. purple	3·50	1·75
1216.	10 b. violet	5·50	2·75

1953. Arms issue. State of Guarico. As Type **81** showing Arms of Guarico and Factory.

1217.	5 c. green (postage)	15	5
1218.	10 c. red	15	5
1219.	15 c. brown	30	20
1220.	20 c. blue	50	30
1221.	40 c. orange	1·10	55
1222.	45 c. purple	4·75	2·75
1223.	3 b. blue	2·10	1·25
1224.	5 c. turquoise (air)	30	5
1225.	10 c. red	15	5
1226.	15 c. brown	45	15
1227.	25 c. black	55	30
1228.	30 c. blue	1·75	55
1229.	50 c. red	1·10	45
1230.	60 c. green	1·75	55
1231.	1 b. violet	2·10	75
1232.	2 b. violet	2·75	1·40

1953. Insc. "EE. UU. DE VENEZUELA".

1233. 89.	5 c. green (postage)	8	5
1234.	7½ c. emerald	30	20
1235.	10 c. red	15	5
1236.	15 c. black	20	5
1237.	20 c. blue	15	5
1238.	25 c. magenta	35	5
1239.	30 c. blue	75	20
1240.	35 c. mauve	50	20
1241.	40 c. orange	55	30
1242.	45 c. violet	85	50
1243.	50 c. orange	45	15
1244. 89.	5 c. orange (air)	5	5
1245.	7½ c. green	8	8
1246.	15 c. maroon	5	5
1247.	20 c. slate	12	5
1248.	25 c. sepia	10	5
1249.	30 c. brown	1·40	75
1250.	40 c. claret	30	5
1251.	45 c. plum	30	8
1252.	50 c. vermilion	35	8
1253.	60 c. red	1·75	45
1254.	70 c. myrtle	75	20
1255.	75 c. blue	1·40	35
1256.	90 c. chestnut	60	25
1257.	1 b. violet	55	15

See also Nos. 1365/82.

1953. Arms issue. State of Cojedes. As Type **81** showing Arms of Cojedes and Cattle.

1258.	5 c. green (postage)	8	5
1259.	10 c. red	15	8
1260.	15 c. brown	20	10
1261.	20 c. blue	30	15
1262.	25 c. brown	75	30
1263.	30 c. blue	1·40	35
1264.	35 c. violet	1·75	85
1265.	5 c. turquoise (air)	1·10	45
1266.	7½ c. green	55	30
1267.	10 c. red	15	5
1268.	15 c. brown	30	15
1269.	20 c. blue	75	20
1270.	30 c. blue	1·10	30
1271.	45 c. purple	55	30
1272.	60 c. green	1·10	45
1273.	90 c. red	2·10	1·40

1954. Arms issue. State of Amazonas. As Type **83** showing Arms of Amazonas and Cattle.

1274.	5 c. green (postage)	75	8
1275.	10 c. red	75	8
1276.	15 c. brown	75	15
1277.	20 c. blue	2·10	45
1278.	40 c. orange	2·10	85
1279.	45 c. purple	4·25	2·10
1280.	3 b. blue	7·00	2·75
1281.	5 c. turquoise (air)	75	8
1282.	10 c. red	30	5
1283.	15 c. brown	1·10	20
1284.	25 c. black	1·75	30
1285.	30 c. blue	3·50	45
1286.	50 c. red	3·50	85
1287.	60 c. green	4·75	85
1288.	1 b. violet	11·00	2·75
1289.	2 b. violet	7·50	3·50

1954. Arms issue. State of Apure. As Type **83** showing Arms of Apure, Horse and Bird.

1290.	5 c. green (postage)	8	5
1291.	10 c. red	10	5
1292.	15 c. brown	30	20
1293.	20 c. blue	1·40	30
1294.	50 c. orange	1·40	85
1295.	1 b. green	75	30
1296.	5 b. purple	4·25	2·75
1297.	5 c. turquoise (air)	45	5
1298.	10 c. red	15	5
1299.	15 c. brown	75	20
1300.	30 c. blue	2·10	55
1301.	60 c. green	2·10	45
1302.	1 b. 20 lake	2·25	1·10
1303.	3 b. green	2·10	85
1304.	5 b. purple	4·25	2·10
1305.	10 b. violet	7·00	3·50

1954. Arms issue. State of Barinas. As Type **83** showing Arms of Barinas, Cow and Horse.

1306.	5 c. green (postage)	15	5
1307.	10 c. red	20	5
1308.	15 c. brown	30	20
1309.	20 c. blue	1·40	30
1310.	50 c. orange	1·50	85
1311.	1 b. green	75	30
1312.	5 b. purple	4·25	2·75
1313.	5 c. turquoise (air)	30	8
1314.	10 c. red	15	5
1315.	15 c. brown	75	20
1316.	30 c. blue	2·10	55
1317.	60 c. green	2·10	55
1318.	1 b. 20 lake	2·10	85
1319.	3 b. green	2·10	85
1320.	5 b. purple	4·25	2·10
1321.	10 b. violet	7·00	3·50

1954. Arms issue. State of Nueva Esparta. As Type **83** showing Arms of Nueva Esparta and Fish.

1322.	5 c. green (postage)	10	5
1323.	10 c. red	15	5
1324.	15 c. brown	45	20
1325.	20 c. blue	55	15
1326.	40 c orange	85	30
1327.	45 c. purple	5·50	2·75
1328.	3 b. blue	2·50	1·40
1329.	5 c. turquoise (air)	35	5
1330.	10 c. red	12	5
1331.	15 c. brown	55	15
1332.	25 c. black	1·10	30
1333.	30 c. blue	1·75	35
1334.	50 c. red	1·75	35
1335.	60 c. green	2·25	35
1336.	1 b. violet	2·75	85
1337.	2 b. violet	2·50	1·10

1954. Arms issue. State of Yaracuy. As Type **83** showing Arms of Yaracuy and Tropical foliage.

1338.	5 c. green (postage)	45	5
1339.	10 c. red	15	5
1340.	15 c. brown	20	10
1341.	20 c. blue	45	15
1342.	25 c. brown	55	30
1343.	30 c. blue	75	15
1344.	35 c. violet	1·40	75
1345.	5. c. turquoise (air)	25	5
1346.	7½ c. green	5·00	5·00
1347.	10 c. red	12	5
1348.	15 c. brown	15	8
1349.	20 c. blue	25	12
1350.	30 c. blue	35	20
1351.	45 c. purple	50	25
1352.	60 c. green	1·10	30
1353.	90 c. red	1·75	1·10

92. Simon Rodriguez.

93. Bolivar and 1824 Edict.

1954. Air. Rodriguez (Bolivar's tutor). Death Cent.
1354. **92.** 5 c. turquoise 15 5
1355. 10 c. red 20 5
1356. 20 c. blue 30 5
1357. 45 c. purple 50 12
1358. 65 c. grey-green .. 1·60 55

1954. Air. 10th Pan-American Conf., Caracas.
1359. **93.** 15 c. black and brown .. 15 8
1360. 25 c. chocolate and grey 30 12
1361. 40 c. chocolate & orange 50 10
1362. 65 c. black and blue .. 90 30
1363. 80 c. chocolate and rose 75 20
1364. 1 b. violet and mauve .. 1·40 30

1954. As T 89 but inscr. "REPUBLICA DE VENEZUELA".
1365. 5 c. green (postage) .. 8 5
1366. 10 c. red 8 5
1367. 15 c. black 8 5
1368. 20 c. blue 8 5
1369. 30 c. blue 45 12
1370. 35 c. mauve 35 8
1371. 40 c. orange 55 20
1372. 45 c. violet 45 20
1373. 5 c. yellow (air) .. 5 5
1374. 10 c. bistre 8 5
1375. 15 c. maroon 8 5
1376. 20 c. slate 15 5
1377. 30 c. brown 15 5
1378. 40 c. claret 55 12
1379. 45 c. plum 60 12
1380. 70 c. myrtle .. 1·00 50
1381. 75 c. blue 75 20
1382. 90 c. chestnut .. 45 20

94.

95.

1955. Valencia Del Rey. 400th Anniv.
1383 **94.** 5 c. green (postage) .. 35 8
1384. 20 c. blue 55 8
1385. 25 c. brown 75 10
1386. 50 c. orange 85 10
1387. 5 c. turquoise (air) .. 8 5
1388. 10 c. red 10 5
1389. 20 c. blue 15 8
1390. 25 c. black 15 8
1391. 40 c. violet 30 20
1392. 50 c. red 35 20
1393. 60 c. olive 55 20

1955. 1st Postal Convention, Caracas.
1394. **95.** 5 c. green (postage) .. 15 5
1395. 20 c. blue 20 8
1396. 25 c. lake 30 8
1397. 50 c. orange 45 15
1398. 5 c. yellow (air) .. 5 5
1399. 15 c. brown 10 5
1400. 25 c. black 15 8
1401. 40 c. red 30 12
1402. 50 c. vermilion .. 35 15
1403. 60 c. red 55 15

96. O'Leary College, Barinas.

DESIGNS—HORIZ. A. University Hospital Caracas. B. Caracas–La Guaira highway. C. Simon Bolivar Centre.

1956. Air. Public Works.
1404. **96.** 5 c. yellow 5 5
1405. 10 c. sepia 5 5
1406. 15 c. brown 8 5
1407. A. 20 c. indigo 12 5
1408. 25 c. black 15 8
1409. 30 c. chestnut .. 20 8
1410. B. 40 c. red 45 12
1411. 45 c. maroon 20 8
1412. 50 c. orange 45 10
1413. C. 60 c. olive 60 15
1414. 65 c. blue 75 30
1415. **96.** 70 c. green 85 45
1416. C. 75 c. blue .. 1·10 50
1417. A. 80 c. magenta .. 75 25
1418. B. 1 b. purple 50 15
1419. C. 2 b. claret .. 1·40 55

97.

98.

1956. First American Book Festival.
1420. **97.** 5 c. blue-green and emerald (postage) .. 8 5
1421. 10 c. purple and red .. 8 5
1422. 20 c. blue and ultram. 12 5
1423. 25 c. grey & grey-green 15 8
1424. 30 c. blue and turquoise 20 8
1425. 40 c. sepia and brown 30 15
1426. 50 c. chestnut & verm. 45 15
1427. 1 b. slate-violet & violet 75 30
1428. **98.** 5 c. brown & orge. (air) 8 5
1429. 10 c. sepia and brown 8 5
1430. 20 c. blue and turquoise 8 8
1431. 25 c. slate & slate-violet 15 8
1432. 40 c. purple and red .. 15 8
1433. 45 c. brown & chocolate 35 10
1434. 60 c. grey-grn. & ol.-grn. 55 15

99. Tamanaco Hotel. Caracas.

100. Simon Bolivar.

1957. Tamanaco Hotel, Caracas Commem.
1435. **99.** 5 c. emerald (postage) 8 5
1436. 10 c. red 8 5
1437. 15 c. black 20 5
1438. 20 c. blue 10 5
1439. 25 c. maroon 15 8
1440. 30 c. blue 20 8
1441. 35 c. lilac 20 10
1442. 40 c. orange 30 10
1443. 45 c. purple 45 20
1444. 50 c. lemon 55 15
1445. 1 b. myrtle .. 1·10 30
1446. 5 c. yellow (air) .. 8 5
1447. 10 c. brown 8 5
1448. 15 c. sepia 20 5
1449. 20 c. slate 15 5
1450. 25 c. sepia 15 8
1451. 30 c. blue 20 15
1452. 40 c. red 20 12
1453. 45 c. claret 30 12
1454. 50 c. orange-red .. 30 15
1455. 60 c. sage 60 20
1456. 65 c. orange-brown .. 75 30
1457. 70 c. grey 85 30
1458. 75 c. turquoise .. 1·10 35
1459. 1 b. maroon 85 20
1460. 2 b. black .. 1·40 30

1957. 150th Anniv. of Oath of Monte Sacro and 125th Anniv. of Death of Bolivar.
1461. **100.** 5 c. green (postage) .. 5 5
1462. 10 c. vermilion .. 8 5
1463. 20 c. blue 15 5
1464. 25 c. crimson 20 8
1465. 30 c. blue 30 8
1466. 40 c. orange 35 12
1467. 50 c. yellow 75 20
1468. 5 c. orange (air) .. 8 5
1469. 10 c. sepia 15 5
1470. 20 c. blue 35 8
1471. 25 c. slate-purple .. 75 15
1472. 40 c. red 45 12
1473. 45 c. purple 50 20
1474. 65 c. brown 75 25

101. G.P.O., Caracas.

102. Arms of Santiago de Merida.

1958.
1475. **101.** 5 c. green (postage) .. 5 5
1476. 10 c. red 5 5
1477. 15 c. grey 5 5
1478. 20 c. blue 8 5
1479. 25 c. yellow 10 5
1480. 30 c. grey-blue .. 12 5
1481. 35 c. purple 25 8
1482. 40 c. brown-red .. 30 8
1483. 45 c. violet .. 1·10 75
1484. 50 c. lemon 20 8
1485. 1 b. olive 45 25
1486. 5 c. yellow (air) .. 5 5
1487. 10 c. brown 5 5
1488. 15 c. brown 8 5
1489. 20 c. blue 8 5
1490. **101.** 25 c. grey 10 5
1491. 30 c. blue 12 5
1492. 35 c. olive 15 10
1493. 40 c. apple 15 5
1494. 50 c. red 20 8
1495. 55 c. olive-green .. 25 10
1496. 60 c. magenta .. 25 10
1497. 65 c. red 30 15
1498. 70 c. green 30 15
1499. 75 c. brown 30 15
1500. 80 c. red-brown .. 35 15
1501. 85 c. claret 35 20
1502. 90 c. violet 35 15
1503. 95 c. purple 40 25
1504. 1 b. mauve 45 15
1505. 1 b. 20 brown .. 4·75 3·50

1958. Santiago de Merida de los Caballeros. 400th Anniv.
1506. **102.** 5 c. green (postage) .. 5 5
1507. 10 c. red 8 5
1508. 15 c. grey 8 5
1509. 20 c. blue 15 5
1510. 25 c. purple 20 8
1511. 30 c. violet 20 8
1512. 35 c. reddish violet .. 25 10
1513. 40 c. orange 30 12
1514. 45 c. purple 30 15
1515. 50 c. yellow 35 15
1516. 1 b. grey-green .. 1·40 55
1517. **102.** 5 c. ochre (air) .. 8 5
1518. 10 c. drab 8 5
1519. 15 c. chocolate .. 10 5
1520. 20 c. blue 15 5
1521. 25 c. olive-brown .. 15 8
1522. 30 c. blue 20 8
1523. 40 c. lake 30 12
1524. 45 c. purple 45 12
1525. 50 c. orange 45 8
1526. 60 c. olive 35 15
1527. 65 c. chestnut .. 85 30
1528. 70 c. black 50 30
1529. 75 c. blue .. 1·10 20
1530. 80 c. violet 55 25
1531. 90 c. green 65 30
1532. 1 b. lilac 75 35

103. G.P.O. Caracas.

104. Arms of Trujillo and Bolivar Movement.

106. "Eternal Flame".

105. Caracas Stadium.

1958.
1533. **103.** 5 c. green (postage) .. 20 5
1534. 10 c. red 30 5
1535. 15 c. black 35 8
1536. 5 c. yellow (air) .. 20 8
1537. 10 c. brown 30 10
1538. 15 c. sepia 35 15

1959. 4th Cent. of Trujillo.
1539. **104.** 5 c. emerald (postage) 5 5
1540. 10 c. rose 8 5
1541. 15 c. grey 8 5
1542. 20 c. blue 12 5
1543. 25 c. mauve 15 8
1544. 30 c. blue 20 8
1545. 35 c. lilac 30 15
1546. 45 c. purple 35 15
1547. 50 c. lemon 35 10
1548. 1 b. olive 80 45
1549. 5 c. buff (air) .. 8 5
1550. 10 c. brown 8 5
1551. 15 c. chestnut .. 10 5
1552. 20 c. blue 15 5
1553. 25 c. grey 15 8
1554. 30 c. blue 20 8
1555. 40 c. apple 25 12
1556. 50 c. salmon 30 15
1557. 60 c. magenta .. 35 15
1558. 65 c. vermilion .. 90 50
1559. 1 b. violet 55 30

1959. 8th C. American and Caribbean Games.
1560. **105.** 5 c. green (postage) .. 15 8
1561. 10 c. magenta .. 15 10
1562. 20 c. turquoise .. 30 15
1563. 30 c. blue 50 20
1564. 50 c. mauve 75 30
1565. **106.** 5 c. yellow (air) .. 10 5
1566. 10 c. brown 20 10
1567. 15 c. orange 30 15
1568. 30 c. slate 55 20
1569. 50 c. green 50 25

107. Venezuelan ½ Real Stamp of 1859, Gen. J. I. Paz Castillo and Postman.

108. Alexander von Humboldt.

1959. Cent. of First Venezuelan Postage Stamps.
1570. **107.** 25 c. ochre (postage) 20 8
1571. – 50 c. blue 45 15
1572. – 1 b. red 85 30
1573. **107.** 25 c. ochre (air) .. 20 8
1574. – 50 c. blue 45 15
1575. – 1 b. red 85 30

DESIGNS: 50 c. (2), 1 real stamp of 1859, Don Jacinto Gutierrez and postman on mule. 1 b. (2), 2 reales stamp of 1859, Don Miguel Herrera, and mail train and 'plane.

1960. Von Humboldt (naturalist). Death Cent.
1576. **108.** 5 c. olive & grn. (post.) 20 5
1577. 30 c. violet & ultram. 45 12
1578. 40 c. chestnut & orange 55 20
1579. 5 c. brn. & yel.-brn. (air) 20 5
1580. 20 c. blue-green & blue 45 8
1581. 40 c. bronze and olive 75 25

108a. Bolivar Peak, Merida.

ILLUSTRATIONS
British Commonwealth and all overprints and surcharges are FULL SIZE. Foreign Countries have been reduced to ¾-LINEAR.

1960. Tourist issue.
1582. **108a.** 5 c. green (postage) 2·00 75
1583. – 15 c. grey .. 2·50 2·10
1584. – 35 c. purple .. 3·25 2·25
1585. **108a.** 30 c. indigo & bl. (air) 1·40 1·40
1586. – 50 c. brn. & orange 1·40 1·40
1587. – 65 c. red-brn. & orge. 1·40 1·40

DESIGNS: 15 c., 50 c. Caroni Falls, Bolivar. 35 c., 65 c. Cuacharo Caves, Monagas.

109. National Pantheon.

110. A. Elroy Blanco (poet).

1960. Pantheon in yellow-olive.
1588. **109.** 5 c. emerald (postage) 5 5
1589. 20 c. blue 12 5
1590. 25 c. olive 15 8
1591. 30 c. grey-blue .. 25 8
1592. 40 c. cinnamon .. 35 8
1593. 45 c. reddish violet 45 15
1594. 5 c. bistre (air) .. 5 5
1595. 10 c. brown 8 5
1596. 15 c. chestnut .. 10 5
1597. 20 c. blue 12 5
1598. 25 c. grey 15 8
1599. 30 c. violet-blue .. 20 8
1600. 40 c. apple 20 12
1601. 45 c. lilac 30 12
1602. 60 c. magenta .. 35 15
1603. 65 c. salmon 50 20
1604. 70 c. grey 55 30
1605. 75 c. grey-blue .. 85 30
1606. 80 c. blue 75 25
1607. 1 b. 20 yellow-brown 1·00 50

1960. Blanco 5th Death Anniv. Portrait in black.
1608. **110.** 5 c. emerald (postage) 10 5
1609. 30 c. grey-blue .. 20 8
1610. 50 c. yellow 45 20
1611. 20 c. blue (air) .. 20 8
1612. 75 c. turquoise .. 60 30
1613. 90 c. violet 50 25

111. 1808 Newspaper and Caracas, 1958.

112. A. Codazzi (geographer).

1960. "Gazeta de Caracas". 150th Anniv. Centres in black.
1614. **111.** 10 c. red (postage) .. 20 8
1615. 20 c. blue 30 15
1616. 35 c. violet 50 20

1617. 111. 5 c. yellow (air) .. 75 35
1618. 15 c. brown 45 20
1619. 65 c. orange 55 30

1960. Codazzi. Death Cent.

1620. 112. 5 c. grn. & emer. (post.) 5 5
1621. 15 c. black and grey .. 35 8
1622. 20 c. Prussian bl. & bl. 20 5
1623. 45 c. purple and lilac .. 35 15
1624. 5 c. brown & orge. (air) 5 5
1625. 10 c. sepia and brown 8 5
1626. 25 c. black and grey .. 20 8
1627. 30 c. indigo. & ultram. 20 8
1628. 50 c. brown and chest. 35 15
1629. 70 c. black & olive-brn. 55 30

113. Declaration of Independence.

1960. Independence. 150th Anniv. Centres multicoloured.

1630. 113. 5 c. emerald (postage) 30 8
1631. 20 c. blue 55 15
1632. 30 c. violet-blue .. 85 20
1633. 50 c. orange (air) .. 50 25
1634. 75 c. turquoise .. 55 30
1635. 90 c. violet 60 30

114. Drilling for Oil.

115. L. Caceres de Arismedni.

117. Gen. A. J. de Sucre.

116. Gen. J. A. Anzoategui.

1960. Oil Industry.

1636. 114. 5 c. myrtle and blue-green (postage) .. 75 35
1637. 10 c. brown and red .. 45 20
1638. 15 c. maroon and purple 50 20
1639. – 30 c. indigo & blue (air) 25 12
1640. – 40 c. olive & yell.-green 35 15
1641. – 50 c. chestnut & orge. 45 20

DESIGN: Nos. 1639/41, Oil refinery.

1960. Luisa Caceres de Arismendi. 94th Death Anniv. Centres multicoloured.

1642. 115. 20 c. blue (postage) .. 30 15
1643. 25 c. yellow 35 15
1644. 30 c. blue 45 20
1645. 5 c. bistre (air) .. 30 15
1646. 10 c. brown 35 15
1647. 60 c. red 45 20

1960. Gen. Anzoategui. 140th Death Anniv.

1648. 116. 5 c. olive & emer. (post.) 15 5
1649. 15 c. mar. & grey-brn. 20 5
1650. 20 c. ultramarine & blue 30 8
1651. 25 c. brn. & grey (air) 25 10
1652. 40 c. olive & yell.-olive 35 15
1653. 45 c. maroon & magenta 35 20

1960. Gen. A. J. de Sucre. 130th Death Anniv.

1654. 117. 10 c. mult. (postage) 20 15
1655. 15 c. multicoloured .. 25 10
1656. 20 c. multicoloured .. 35 15
1657. 25 c. mult. (air) .. 35 15
1658. 30 c. multicoloured .. 40 15
1659. 50 c. multicoloured .. 50 25

118. Skyscraper. **119.** " Population and Farming ".

1960. National Census. Skyscraper in orange.

1660. 118. 5 c. emerald 5 5
1661. 10 c. red 5 5
1662. 15 c. grey 8 5
1663. 20 c. blue 8 5
1664. 25 c. chestnut .. 15 8
1665. 30 c. ultramarine .. 20 8
1666. 35 c. purple 20 10
1667. 40 c. brown-red .. 35 12
1668. 45 c. violet 30 12
1669. 50 c. yellow 30 15

1960. Air. 9th Population Census and 3rd Farming Census. Animal's head and inscr. in black.

1670. 119. 5 c. yellow 5 5
1671. 10 c. brown 5 5
1672. 15 c. orange-brown .. 8 5
1673. 20 c. Prussian blue .. 8 5
1674. 25 c. grey 15 5
1675. 30 c. ultramarine .. 15 8
1676. 40 c. yellow-green .. 25 8
1677. 45 c. reddish violet .. 25 10
1678. 50 c. red-orange .. 30 10
1679. 60 c. cerise 35 15
1680. 65 c. vermilion .. 45 20
1681. 70 c. deep grey .. 55 25
1682. 75 c. turquoise .. 55 20
1683. 80 c. violet 45 25
1684. 90 c. deep violet .. 50 25

120. R. M Baralt. **121.** Arms of San Cristobal.

1961. R. M Baralt. Death Cent.

1685. 120. 5 c. turq. & grn. (post.) 8 5
1686. 15 c. chocolate & grey 15 5
1687. 35 c. violet and mauve 30 15
1688. 25 c. sepia & grey (air) 30 15
1689. 30 c. violet and blue 35 15
1690. 40 c. bronze-green and apple 40 20

1961. Air. San Cristobal. 4th Cent. Arms in red, yellow and blue.

1692. 121. 5 c. sepia and orange 5 5
1693. 55 c. black and green 40 15

122. Yellow-headed Parrot.

123. J. J. Aguerrevere (First President).

1961. Birds. Multicoloured.

1694. 30 c. T 122 (postage) .. 30 15
1695. 40 c. Snowy egret .. 45 20
1696. 50 c. Scarlet ibis .. 55 30
1697. 5 c. Troupial (air) .. 75 75
1698. 10 c. Guianan Cock-of-the-Rock 35 35
1699. 15 c. Tropical mockingbird 45 45

1961. Engineering College Cent.

1700. 123. 25 c. blue 15 8

124. Battle Scene.

1961. Battle of Carabobo. 140th Anniv. Centres multicoloured.

1702. 124. 5 c. emerald (postage) 8 5
1703. 40 c. brown .. 35 15
1704. – 50 c. ultramarine (air) 30 15
1705. – 1 b. 05 orange .. 85 45
1706. – 1 b. 50 magenta .. 60 20
1707. – 1 b. 90 violet .. 1·40 75
1708. – 2 b. sepia .. .. 1·40 75
1709. – 3 b. blue .. .. 2·10 1·10

DESIGN: 50 c. to 3 b. Cavalry charge.

125. Arms of Cardinal Quintero.

126. Archbishop Blanco.

1962. Air. Cardinal Jose Quintero Commem.

1710. 125. 5 c. magenta .. 5 5

1962. Air. Archbishop Blanco's Pastoral Letter. 4th Anniv.

1712. 126. 75 c. mauve .. 45 20

127. " Oncidium papilio Lindl ".

ILLUSTRATIONS British Commonwealth and all overprints and surcharges are FULL SIZE. Foreign Countries have been reduced to ¾-LINEAR.

1962. Orchids. Multicoloured.

1713. 5 c. Type 127 (postage) .. 5 5
1714. 10 c. " Caularthron bilamellatum (Rchb. f.). R. E. Schultes " 8 5
1715. 20 c. " Stanhopea Wardii Lodd. ex Lindl " .. 20 5
1716. 25 c. " Catasetum pileatum Rchb. f. " 35 8
1717. 30 c. " Masdevallia tovarensis Rchb. f. " 35 10
1718. 35 c. " Epidendrum Stamfordianum Batem " (horiz.) 45 15
1719. 50 c. " Epidendrum atropureum Willd " .. 50 20
1720. 3 b. " Oncidium falcipetalum Lindl. " .. .. 2·10 1·25
1721. 5 c. " Oncidium volvox Rchb. f. " (air) .. 5 5
1722. 20 c. " Cycnoches chlorochilon Kl. " 12 5
1723. 25 c. " Cattleya Gaskelliana Rchb. f. var. alba" 20 8
1724. 30 c. " Epidendrum difforme Jacq. " (horiz.) 15 8
1725. 40 c. " Catasetum callosum Lindl. " (horiz.) .. 30 15
1726. 50 c. " Oncidium bicolor Lindl. " 45 20
1727. 1 b. " Brassavola nodosa Lindl. " (horiz.) .. 45 30
1728. 1 b. 05 " Epidendrum lividum Lindl. " .. 1·40 45
1729. 1 b. 50 " Schomburgkia undulata Lindl. " .. 1·75 85
1730. 2 b. " Oncidium zebrinum Rchb. f. " .. .. 2·10 1·10

128. Signing of Independence.

1962. Declaration of Independence. 150th Anniv. Mult. centres; frame colours given.

1731. 128. 5 c. emerald (postage) 15 5
1732. 20 c. blue 35 5
1733. 25 c. orange .. 40 8
1734. 55 c. olive (air) .. 50 20
1735. 1 b. 05 magenta .. 85 45
1736. 1 b. 50 violet .. 1·00 45

1962. Air. Upata. 200th Anniv. Surch. **BICENTENARIO DE UPATA 1762 - 1962 RESELLADO AEREO VALOR Bs 2,00.**

1739. 101. 2 b. on 1 b. olive .. 85 45

129. Putting the Shot.

1962. 1st National Games, Caracas, 1961.

1740. 129. 5 c. green (postage) .. 5 5
1741. – 10 c. magenta .. 10 5
1742. – 25 c. blue 15 8
1743. – 40 c. grey (air) .. 25 10
1744. – 75 c. yellow-brown .. 45 20
1745. – 85 c. claret .. 60 35

SPORTS: 10 c. Football. 25 c. Swimming. 40 c. Cycling. 75 c. Baseball. 85 c. Gymnastics.

Each value is arranged in blocks of 4 within the sheet, with the top corners of each stamp converging to the centre of the block.

130. Vermilion Cardinal.

131. Campaign Emblem and Map.

1962. Birds. Multicoloured.

1748. 5 c. Type 130 (postage) .. 8 5
1749. 10 c. Great kiskadee .. 15 5
1750. 20 c. Glossy-back thrush 15 5
1751. 25 c. Collared trogon .. 15 8
1752. 30 c. Swallow-tanager .. 15 8
1753. 40 c. Blue-throated sylph 25 15
1754. 3 b. Common stilt .. 2·10 1·25
1755. 5 c. American kestrel (air) 5 5
1756. 20 c. Black-bellied tree duck (horiz.) .. 12 5
1757. 25 c. Amazon kingfisher .. 15 8
1758. 30 c. Rufous-vented chachalaca 20 8
1759. 50 c. Oriole blackbird .. 35 15
1760. 55 c. Pauraque 40 15
1761. 2 b. 30 Red-crowned woodpecker .. .. 2·00 90
1762. 2 b. 50 Lined quail-dove .. 1·75 85

1962. Malaria Eradication.

1763. 131. 50 c. brn. & blk. (post.) 30 15
1764. – 30 c. grn. & blk. (air) 20 8

DESIGN: As T 131 but size 26×36 mm.

132. Collared Peccary.

133. Fisherman.

1963. Venezuelan Wild Life. Multicoloured.

1766. 5 c. White-tailed deer (postage) 5 5
1767. 10 c. Type 132 .. 8 5
1768. 35 c. White-collared Titi-monkey 20 10
1769. 50 c. Giant Brazilian otter 35 15
1770. 1 b. Puma .. .. 1·10 35
1771. 3 c. Capybara .. 2·50 1·25
1772. 5 c. Spectacled bear (vert.) (air) .. 8 5
1773. 40 c. Paca 25 12
1774. 50 c. Three-toed sloth .. 30 15
1775. 55 c. Giant ant-eater .. 35 15
1776. 1 b. 50 Tapir .. 1·25 60
1777. 2 b. Jaguar .. .. 1·75 85

1963. Freedom from Hunger.

1778. 133. 25 c. bl. on pink (post.) 15 8
1779. – 40 c. red on green (air) 20 12
1780. – 75 c. sepia on yellow 35 20

DESIGNS: 40 c. Farmer with lambs. 75 c. Harvester.

134. Bocono Cathedral.

1963. Bocono. 400th Anniv.

1781. 134. 50 c. chocolate, turq. & red on buff (post.) 25 15
1782. – 1 b. mult. on buff (air) 55 30

DESIGN: 1 b. Bocono Arms.

135. St. Peter's Basilica, Vatican City. **136.** Flag.

1963. Ecumenical Council. Vatican City.

1783.	**135.** 35 c. brn. & blue (post.)	20	10
1784.	45 c. brown and green	25	12
1785.	– 80 c. multicoloured (air)	45	25
1786.	– 90 c. multicoloured ..	50	25

DESIGN: 80 c., 90 c. Arms of Vatican City and Venezuela.

1963. National Flag and Arms Cent. Mult.

1787.	30 c. Type **136** (postage) ..	15	8
1788.	70 c. Venezuela Arms (air)	45	20

137. Maracaibo Bridge. **138.** Arms, Map and Guardsman.

1963. Opening of Higher Bridge, Lake Maracaibo.

1789.	**137.** 30 c. choc. & bl. (post.)	20	8
1790.	35 c. chocolate & green	25	8
1791.	80 c. chocolate & green	55	20
1792.	– 90 c. brown & blue (air)	60	25
1793.	– 95 c. brown & lt. blue	70	30
1794.	– 1 b. brown and blue ..	50	15

DESIGN—HORIZ. 90 c. to 1 b. Aerial view of bridge and mainland.

1963. National Guard. 25th Anniv.

1795.	**138.** 50 c. green, red & blue on cream (postage)	35	15
1796.	1 b. blue and red on cream (air) ..	85	30

139. Dag Hammarskjoeld and Atlantic Map.

1963. Death of Dag Hammarskjoeld. 1st Anniv. (1962). Head in ochre.

1797.	**139.** 25 c. ind. & blue (post.)	15	8
1798.	55 c. blue-grn. & turq.	35	15
1799.	80 c. ult. & cobalt (air)	50	20
1800.	90 c. violet and blue ..	50	25

140. Dr. L. Razetti (medallion). **141.** Dr. F. A. Risquez and Centenary Emblem.

1963. Dr. Luis Razetti. Birth Cent.

1802.	**140.** 35c. brown, ochre and blue (postage)	25	10
1803.	45 c. brn., ochre & mag.	30	12
1804.	95 c. blue & mag. (air)	55	30
1805.	1 b. 05 sepia & green	60	30

DESIGN: 95 c., 1 b. 05, Portrait of Dr. Razetti.

1964. Red Cross Centenary. Multicoloured.

1806.	15 c. Type **141** (postage)	10	5
1807.	20 c. Dr. C. J. Bello ..	15	5
1808.	40 c. Sir V. K. Barrington (air)	25	12
1809.	75 c. Nurse and child ..	45	20

All designs show centenary emblem.

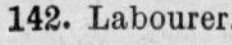

142. Labourer. **143.** Pedro Gual.

1964. Cent. of Venezuelan Ministry of Works and National Industries Exhibition, Caracas. Multicoloured.

1810.	5 c. Type **142** (postage) ..	5	5
1811.	10 c. Petrol industry ..	8	5
1812.	15 c. Building construction	8	5
1813.	30 c. Road & rail transport	15	8
1814.	40 c. Agricultural machine	25	12
1815.	5 c. Loading ship (air) ..	5	5
1816.	10 c. Tractor and maize ..	5	5
1817.	15 c. Type **142** ..	8	5
1818.	20 c. Petrol industry ..	8	5
1819.	50 c. Building construction	20	15

1964. Pedro Gual (statesman). Death Cent. (1962).

1820.	**143.** 40 c. olive (post.) ..	25	12
1821.	50 c. chestnut ..	30	15
1822.	75 c. turquoise (air) ..	35	20
1823.	1 b. magenta ..	45	30

144. C. Arvelo. **145.** Blast Furnace.

1964. Carlos Arvelo (physician). Death Cent. (1962).

1824.	**144.** 1 b. black and blue ..	55	20

1964. Orinoco Steel Works. Inaug. Multicoloured.

1825.	20 c. Type **145** (postage)	15	5
1826.	50 c. Type **145**	35	15
1827.	80 c. Cauldron & map (air)	45	15
1828.	1 b. As 80 c. ..	55	30

The 80 c. and 1 b. are vert.

146. Arms of Bolivar City. **147.** R. Gallegos (novelist).

1964. Air. Ciudad Bolivar. Bicent.

1829.	**146.** 1 b. multicoloured ..	75	45

1964. Romulo Gallegos. 80th Birth Anniv.

1830.	**147.** 5 c. green and yellow-green (postage) ..	5	5
1831.	10 c. blue & light blue	5	5
1832.	15 c. purple & mauve	12	5
1833.	– 30 c. brown & yell. (air)	20	8
1834.	– 40 c. purple and pink	25	12
1835.	– 50 c. chest. & salmon	30	15

DESIGN: Nos. 1833/5, Gallegos and book.

148. Angel Falls (Bolivar State). **149.** Eleanor Roosevelt.

1964. Tourist Publicity. Inscr. "Conozca a Venezuela Primera" ("See Venezuela First"). Multicoloured.

1836.	5 c. Type **148** ..	5	5
1837.	10 c. Tropical Landscape (Sucre) ..	5	5
1838.	15 c. Rocks, San Juan (Guarico)	8	5
1839.	30 c. Fishermen casting nets (Anzoategui) ..	20	8
1840.	40 c. Mountaineering (Merida) ..	25	12

1964. Air. Declaration of Human Rights (1963). 15th Anniv.

1841.	**149.** 1 b. orange and violet	75	45

1965. Various stamps surch. **RESELLADO VALOR** and new value. (a) Postage.

1842.	5 c. on 1 b. (No. 1485) ..	30	8
1843.	10 c. on 45 c. (1668) ..	10	8
1844.	15 c. on 55 c. (1798) ..	10	8
1845.	20 c. on 3 b. (1754) ..	15	10
1846.	25 c. on 45 c. (1623) ..	15	10
1847.	25 c. on 3 b. (1720) ..	15	10
1848.	25 c. on 1 b. (1770) ..	15	10
1849.	25 c. on 3 b. (1771) ..	15	10
1850.	30 c. on 1 b. (1516) ..	15	12
1851.	40 c. on 1 b. (1824) ..	45	15
1852.	60 c. on 80 c. (1791) ..	55	20

(b) Air.

1853.	5 c. on 55 c. (1495) ..	8	5
1854.	5 c. on 70 c. (1498) ..	8	5
1855.	5 c. on 80 c. (1500) ..	8	8
1856.	5 c. on 85 c. (1501) ..	5	5
1857.	5 c. on 90 c. (1502) ..	8	5
1858.	5 c. on 95 c. (1503) ..	8	5
1859.	5 c. on 1 b. (1796) ..	30	8
1860.	10 c. on 3 b. (804) ..	8	5
1861.	10 c. on 4 b. (805) ..	8	5
1862.	10 c. on 70 c. (1681) ..	15	5
1863.	10 c. on 90 c. (1684) ..	15	5
1864.	10 c. on 1 b. 05 (1705) ..	30	8
1865.	10 c. on 1 b. 90 (1707) ..	15	5
1866.	10 c. on 2 b. (1708) ..	15	5
1867.	10 c. on 3 b. (1709) ..	15	5
1868.	10 c. on 80 c. (1785) ..	8	5
1869.	10 c. on 90 c. (1786) ..	8	5
1870.	15 c. on 3 b. (769) ..	15	5
1871.	15 c. on 90 c. (1613) ..	15	5
1872.	15 c. on 80 c. (1799) ..	15	5
1873.	15 c. on 90 c. (1800) ..	15	5
1874.	15 c. on 1 b. (1829) ..	15	8
1875.	20 c. on 2 b. (1460) ..	30	15
1876.	20 c. on 55 c. (1693) ..	25	5
1877.	20 c. on 55 c. (1760) ..	35	15
1878.	20 c. on 2 b. 30 (1761) ..	15	8
1879.	20 c. on 2 b. 50 (1762) ..	15	8
1880.	20 c. on 70 c. (1788) ..	15	5
1881.	25 c. on 70 c. (1629) ..	15	8
1882.	25 c. on 1 b. 05 (1728) ..	15	8
1883.	25 c. on 1 b. 50 (1729) ..	15	8
1884.	25 c. on 2 b. (1730) ..	15	8
1885.	25 c. on 1 b. 50 (1776) ..	15	8
1886.	25 c. on 2 b. (1777) ..	15	8
1887.	25 c. on 95 c. (1804) ..	15	8
1888.	25 c. on 1 b. 05 (1805) ..	15	8
1889.	30 c. on 1 b. (1782) ..	15	8
1890.	40 c. on 1 b. 05 (1735) ..	15	12
1891.	50 c. on 65 c. (1603) ..	20	10
1892.	50 c. on 1 b. 20 (1607) ..	35	15
1893.	50 c. on 1 b. (1841) ..	30	15
1894.	60 c. on 90 c. (1792) ..	50	25
1895.	60 c. on 95 c. (1793) ..	45	15
1896.	75 c. on 85 c. (1745) ..	45	20

(c) Revenue stamps similar to Type **80**, additionally optd. **CORREOS.**

1897.	5 c. on 5 c. green ..	8	5
1898.	5 c. on 20 c. brown ..	8	5
1899.	10 c. on 10 c. bistre ..	8	5
1900.	15 c. on 40 c. green ..	8	5
1901.	20 c. on 3 b. blue ..	15	8
1903.	25 c. on 5 b. blue ..	20	8
1904.	60 c. on 3 b. blue ..	35	20

150. Pres. Kennedy and Alliance Emblem. **151.** Federation Emblem.

1965. "Alliance for Progress".

1905.	**150.** 20 c. black (postage)	15	8
1906.	40 c. violet	30	12
1907.	**150.** 60 c. turquoise (air)	35	15
1908.	80 c. brown	45	20

1965. Air. Venezuelan Medical Federation. 20th Anniv.

1909.	**151.** 65 c. red and black ..	35	20

152. Venezuelan Pavilion. **153.** A. Bello.

1965. Air. New York World's Fair.

1910.	**152.** 1 b. multicoloured ..	45	20

1965. Air. Andres Bello (poet). Death Cent.

1911.	**153.** 80 c. chocolate & orge.	40	20

154. Restrepo's Map 1827. **156.** Bolivar and Part of Letter.

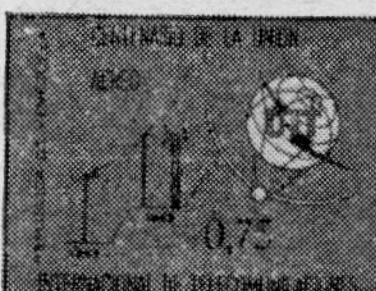

155. I.T.U. Emblem, Satellite, and Aerials of 1865 and 1965. **157.** Children on "Magic Carpet" and "Three Kings".

1965. Guayana Claim. Multicoloured.

1912.	5 c. Codazzi's map, 1840 (postage) (vert.)	5	5
1913.	15 c. Type **154** ..	8	5
1914.	40 c. L. de Surville's map, 1778	20	12
1915.	25 c. Cruz Cano's map, 1775 (air)	10	5
1916.	40 c. (50 c.) Map stamp of 1896 (vert.)	15	12
1917.	75 c. Foreign Relations Ministry map ..	30	20

1965. Air. I.T.U. Cent.

1919.	**155.** 75 c. black and green	35	20

1965. Air. Bolivar's Letter from Jamaica. 150th Anniv.

1920.	**156.** 75 c. black and blue ..	30	20

1965. Air. Children's (Christmas) Festival.

1921.	**157.** 70 c. blue and yellow	50	20

158. Father F. Toro. **159.** Sir Winston Churchill.

1965. Air. Father Fermin Toro. Death Cent.

1922.	**158.** 1 b. black and orange	45	20

1965. Air. Churchill Commem.

1923.	**159.** 1 b. black and lilac ..	55	30

160. I.C.Y. Emblem. **161.** Emblem and Map.

1965. Air. Int. Co-operation Year.

1924.	**160.** 85 c. violet and gold	50	25

1965. Air. Organisation of American States. 75th Anniv.

1925.	**161.** 50 c. gold, black & blue	35	15

162. "Papilio protesilaus leucones". **163.** Farms of 1936 and 1966.

1966. Butterflies. Multicoloured.

1926.	20 c. Type **162** (postage)	12	5
1927.	30 c. "Morpho peleides"	15	8
1928.	50 c. "Papilio zagreus"	30	15
1929.	65 c. "Siderone thebais" (air)	35	20
1930.	85 c. "Hypna rufescens"	50	25
1931.	1 b. "Caligo atreus" ..	55	30

1966. Air. Ministry of Agriculture and Husbandry. 30th Anniv.

1932.	**163.** 55 c. blk., grn. & yell.	20	12

164. Ship Crossing Atlantic.

1966. Maritime Mail. Bicent.

1933.	164.	60 c. black, blue & brn.	55	20

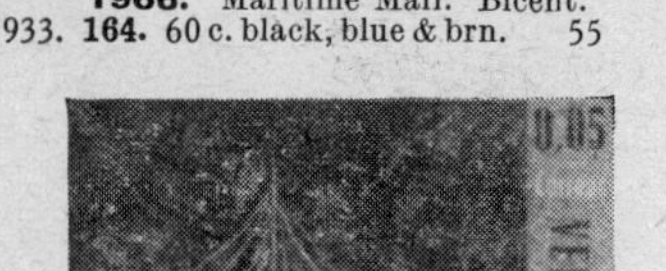

165. Sebucan Dance.

1966. "Popular Dances". Multicoloured.

1934.	5 c. Type **165** (postage) ..	5	5
1935.	10 c. Candlemas	8	5
1936.	15 c. Chichamaya ..	10	5
1937.	20 c. Carite	15	5
1938.	25 c. "Round Drum" ..	15	8
1939.	35 c. Devil Dance, Feast of Corpus Christi ..	25	10
1940.	40 c. Tamunanque (air)	25	12
1941.	50 c. Parranda de San Pedro	30	15
1942.	60 c. Las Turas	35	15
1943.	70 c. Joropo	35	20
1944.	80 c. Chimbanguele ..	45	25
1945.	90 c. "The Shepherds"	50	25

166. Title Page.

1966. Air. Jose Lamas (composer). 150th Death Anniv. (in 1964).

1946.	166.	55 c. blk., bistre & grn.	25	15
1947.		95 c. blk., bistre & mag.	35	30

167. A. Michelena (self-portrait).

168. Lincoln.

1966. Arturo Michelena (painter). Birth Cent. (in 1963), showing Michelena's paintings. Multicoloured.

1948.	95 c. sepia and cream (Type **167**) (postage) ..	55	30
1949.	1 b. "Pentesilea" (battle scene)	70	30
1950.	1 b. 05 "La Vara Rota" ("The Red Cloak") ..	75	30
1951.	95 c. "Escena de Circo" ("Circus Scene") (air)	50	25
1952.	1 b. "Miranda in La Carraca"	55	30
1953.	1 b. 05 "Carlota Corday"	55	35

Nos. 1949/53 are horiz.

1966. Air. Abraham Lincoln Death Cent. (in 1965).

1954.	168.	1 b. black and drab ..	45	30

169. Construction Worker.

170. Dr. Hernandez.

1966. 2nd O.E.A. Labour Ministers Conf.

1955.	169.	10 c. black and yellow	5	5
1956.		20 c. black & turq...	8	5
1957.	–	30 c. violet and blue ..	15	8
1958.	–	35 c. olive and yellow	25	10
1959.	–	50 c. maroon and pink	25	10
1960.	–	65 c. maroon & salmon	40	20

DESIGNS: 30 c., 65 c. Labour Monument. 35 c. Machinist. 50 c. Car assembly line.

1966. Air. Dr. Jose Hernandez (physician). Birth Cent. (in 1964).

1961.	170.	1 b. ultramarine & blue	55	30

171. Dr. M. Dagnino (founder) and Hospital.

1966. Air. Chiquinquira Hospital, Maracaibo. Cent.

1962.	171.	1 b. bronze and green	55	30

172. Marbled Cichlid.

173. R. A. Gonzalez.

1966. Fishes. Multicoloured.

1963.	15 c. Type **172** (postage)	8	5
1964.	25 c. Eye spot cichlid ..	15	8
1965.	45 c. Piranha	30	15
1966.	75 c. Head-standing fish (air) (vert.)	45	20
1967.	90 c. Swordtail characin	50	25
1968.	1 b. Butterfly dwarf cichlid	55	30

1966. Air. Rafael Arevalo Gonzalez Birth Cent.

1969.	173.	75 c. black and yellow	45	20

174. Simon Bolivar, 1816 (after anonymous artist).

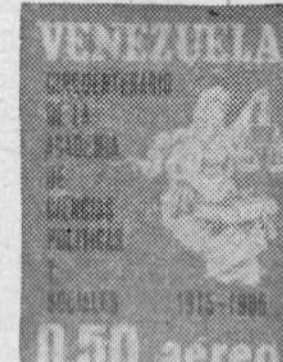

175. "Justice".

1966. Air. Bolivar Commem. Imprint "BUNDESDRUCKEREI BERLIN 1966" at foot.

1970.	174.	5 c. multicoloured ..	5	5
1971.		10 c. multicoloured ..	5	5
1972.		20 c. multicoloured ..	8	5
1973.	–	25 c. multicoloured ..	10	5
1974.	–	30 c. multicoloured ..	8	5
1975.		35 c. multicoloured ..	10	5
1976.	–	40 c. multicoloured ..	12	5
1977.	–	50 c. multicoloured ..	15	8
1978.		60 c. multicoloured ..	15	8
1979.	–	80 c. multicoloured ..	25	12
1980.	–	1 b. 20 multicoloured	50	35
1981.	–	4 b. multicoloured ..	1·75	1·10

BOLIVAR PORTRAITS: 25 c., 30 c., 35 c. After paintings by Jose Gil de Castro, 1825. 40 c., 50 c., 60 c. Anonymous artist, 1825. 80 c., 1 b. 20, 4 b. Anonymous artist, circa 1829.

For stamps in the same designs, but imprint "DRUCK BRUDER ROSENBAUM WIEN", see Nos. 2004/15.

1966. Air. Political and Social Sciences Academy. 50th Anniv.

1982.	175.	50 c. purple and lilac	35	15

176. The Nativity.

177. Globe and Communications Emblems.

1966. Christmas.

1983.	176.	65 c. black and violet	45	15

1966. Venezuelan Communications Ministry. 30th Anniv.

1984.	177.	45 c. multicoloured .	25	10

178. Angostura Bridge.

1967. Air. Opening of Angostura Bridge, Orinoco River.

1985.	178.	40 c. multicoloured ..	30	15

179. Ruben Dario (poet).

180. University Building and Arms.

1967. Ruben Dario Birth Cent.

1986.	179.	70 c. indigo and blue	40	20

1967. Zulia University. 75th Anniv.

1987.	180.	80 c. black, red & gold	45	25

181. Venezuelan Pavilion.

1967. Air. World Fair, Montreal.

1988.	181.	1 b. multicoloured ..	45	15

182. Palace of the Academies.

183. Cacique Guaicaipure (statue).

184. Francisco Esteban Gomez.

1967. Air. Caracas. 400th Anniv. Mult.

1989.	10 c. Type **182**	5	5
1990.	15 c. Type **183**	5	5
1991.	45 c. Capt. F. Fajardo ..	20	5
1992.	50 c. St. Teresa's Church	20	8
1993.	55 c. Diego de Losada (founder)	25	15
1994.	60 c. Constellations over Caracas	25	15
1995.	65 c. Arms of Caracas ..	30	20
1996.	70 c. Federal Legislative Building	35	10
1997.	75 c. University City ..	30	10
1998.	85 c. El Pulpo road junction	35	12
1999.	90 c. Map of Caracas ..	35	25
2000.	1 b. Plaza Mayor, Caracas	45	30
2001.	2 b. Avenida Libertador ..	85	30

Nos. 1991/3 and 1995 are vert. designs the rest horiz.

1967. Air. Battle of Matasiete. 150th Anniv.

2003.	184.	90 c. multicoloured	50	25

1967. Air. As Nos. 1970/81, but inscr. "DRUCK BRUDER ROSENBAUM WIEN" at foot.

2004.	5 c. multicoloured ..	5	5
2005.	10 c. multicoloured ..	5	5
2006.	20 c. multicoloured ..	12	5
2007.	25 c. multicoloured ..	15	8
2008.	30 c. multicoloured ..	15	8
2009.	35 c. multicoloured ..	15	10
2010.	40 c. multicoloured ..	35	12
2011.	50 c. multicoloured ..	45	20
2012.	60 c. multicoloured ..	85	35
2013.	80 c. multicoloured ..	75	35
2014.	1 b. 20 multicoloured ..	1·10	50
2015.	4 b. multicoloured ..	2·75	1·40

185. J. V. Gonzalez (journalist).

186. Child with Toy Windmill.

1967. Air. Juan Gonzalez. Death Cent.

2016.	185.	80 c. black and yellow	35	25

1967. Air. Children's Festival.

2017.	186.	45 c. multicoloured ..	20	12
2018.		75 c. multicoloured ..	35	20
2019.		90 c. multicoloured ..	45	25

187. "The Madonna of the Rosary" (Lochner).

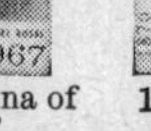

188. Dr. J. M. Nunez Ponte (educator).

1967. Air. Christmas.

2020.	187.	1 b. multicoloured ..	75	35

1968. Air. Ponte Commem.

2021.	188.	65 c. multicoloured	30	15

189. General Miranda and Printing Press.

1968. Air. General Francisco de Miranda. 150th Death Anniv. Multicoloured.

2022.	20 c. Type **189**	12	5
2023.	35 c. Portrait and Houses of Parliament, London	25	10
2024.	45 c. Portrait and Arc de Triomphe, Paris ..	30	12
2025.	70 c. Portrait (vert.) ..	45	20
2026.	80 c. Bust and Venezuelan flags (vert.)	50	25

190. Title Page and Printing Press.

1968. Newspaper "Correo del Orinoco". 150th Anniv.

2027.	190.	1 b. 50 black, ochre, maroon and green	65	45

191. "Laphygma frugiperda".

192. Keys.

1968. Insects. Multicoloured.

2028.	20 c. Type **191** (postage)	12	5
2029.	75 c. "Anthonomus grandis"	35	20
2030.	90 c. "Protoparce sexta"	45	25
2031.	5 c. "Atta sexdens" (air)	5	5
2032.	15 c. "Aeneolamia varia"	10	5
2033.	20 c. "Systena sp." ..	15	5

The 20 (air), 75 and 90 c. are horiz.

1968. Air. Office of Controller-General. 30th Anniv.

2034.	192.	95 c. multicoloured	55	30

MINIMUM PRICE

The minimum price quoted is 5p which represents a handling charge rather than a basis for valuing common stamps. For further notes about prices see introductory pages.

193. Pistol-shooting. **194.** Guayana Substation.

1968. Air. Olympic Games, Mexico. Multicoloured.

2035. 5 c. Type **193** 5 5
2036. 15 c. Running (horiz.) .. 8 5
2037. 30 c. Fencing (horiz.) .. 15 8
2038. 75 c. Boxing (horiz.) .. 35 15
2039. 5 b. Sailing .. .. 2·75 1·40

1968. Rural Electrification. Multicoloured.

2040. 15 c. Type **194** 8 5
2041. 45 c. Encantado Dam .. 30 12
2042. 50 c. Macagua Dam .. 30 15
2043. 80 c. Guri Dam .. 35 30

The 45 and 50 c. are horiz.

195. " The Holy Family " (F. J. de Lerma). **196.** House and Savings Bank.

1968. Air. Christmas.

2044. **195.** 40 c. multicoloured .. 25 12

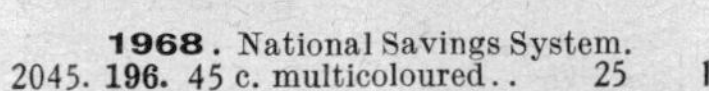

1968. National Savings System.

2045. **196.** 45 c. multicoloured .. 25 12

197. Children and Star. **198.** Planting a Tree.

1968. Air. Children's Festival.

2046. **197.** 80 c. orange and violet 35 15

1968. Conservation of Natural Resources. Multicoloured designs each incorporating central motif as in T **198**.

2047. 15 c. Type **198** (postage) 8 5
2048. 20 c. Plantation 15 5
2049. 30 c. Waterfall 20 8
2050. 45 c. Logs 25 10
2051. 55 c. Cultivated land .. 35 15
2052. 75 c. Bonito (fish) .. 35 15
2053. 15 c. Partridges (air) .. 8 5
2054. 20 c. Stork & flamingoes 10 5
2055. 30 c. Wood-carving .. 12 5
2056. 90 c. Lukuani (fish) .. 40 25
2057. 95 c. Mountain highway 55 30
2058. 1 b. Bird feeding young .. 45 30

The 15 c. (both), 20 c. (air), 30 c. (both) and 55 c. are vert. the remainder are horiz.

199. Colorada Beach, Sucre. **201.** Dr. Martin Luther King.

200. Bolivar addressing Congress.

1969. Tourism. Multicoloured.

2059. 15 c. Type **199** (postage) .. 10 5
2060. 45 c. San Francisco de Yare Church, Miranda 30 12
2061. 90 c. Houses on Stilts, Zulia 40 25
2062. 15 c. Desert lansdcape, Falcon (air) .. 12 8
2063. 30 c. Humboldt Hotel, Federal District .. 12 8
2064. 40 c. Mountain cable-car, Merida 20 12

1969. Angostura Congress. 150th Anniv.

2066. **200.** 45 c. multicoloured .. 30 15

1969. Martin Luther King (American Civil Rights Leader). 1st Death Anniv.

2067. **201.** 1 b. brown, black, red and blue 45 30

202. " Tabebuia pentaphylla ".

1969. Nature Conservation. Trees. Mult.

2068. 50 c. Type **202** (postage) .. 20 10
2069. 65 c. " Erythrina poeppigiana " .. 35 20
2070. 90 c. " Platymiscium sp. " 45 25
2071. 5 c. " Cassia grandis " (air) 5 5
2072. 20 c. " Triplaris caracasana " 10 5
2073. 25 c. " Samanea saman " 12 5

203. " The Pheasant" (after Rojas).

1969. Paintings by Cristobal Rojas. Mult.

2074. 25 c. " On the Balcony " 12 8
2075. 35 c. Type **203** 20 10
2076. 45 c. " The Christening " 30 12
2077. 50 c. " The Empty Place " 25 10
2078. 60 c. " The Tavern " .. 30 10
2079. 1 b. " The Arm " 60 30

Nos. 2074 and 2079 are vert. No. 2079 is larger, size 27 × 53 mm.

204. I.L.O. Emblem.

1969. Int. Labour Organization. 50th Anniv.

2080. **204.** 2 b. 50 black and brown 1·10 75

205. Charter and Arms of Guayana.

1969. Industrial Development. Multicoloured.

2081. 45 c. Type **205** 25 12
2082. 1 b. Sidor steel-works .. 50 30

206. Arcade, Casadel Balcon (square).

1969. Carora. 400th Anniv. Multicoloured.

2083. 20 c. Type **206** 12 5
2084. 25 c. Ruins of La Pastora Church 15 8
2085. 55 c. Chapel of the Cross .. 30 15
2086. 65 c. Museum and library building 35 20

207. " A. Von Humboldt " (J. Stieler). **208.** Arms of Maracaibo.

1969. Air. Alexander von Humboldt. Birth Bicent.

2087. **207.** 50 c. multicoloured 35 15

1969. Air. Maracaibo. 400th Anniv. Mult.

2088. 20 c. A. Alfinger, A. Pacheco and P. Maldonado (founders) 15 5
2089. 25 c. Map of Maracaibo, 1562 15 8
2090. 40 c. Type **208** 25 12
2091. 70 c. University Hospital 35 20
2092. 75 c. Cacique Mara Monument 40 25
2093. 1 b. Baralt Plaza 50 30

Nos. 2088 and 2093 are horiz.

209. Bolivar's Wedding (T. Salas).

1969. " Bolivar in Spain ".

2094. **209.** 10 c. multicoloured .. 8 5
2095. – 15 c. black and red .. 10 5
2096. – 35 c. multicoloured .. 25 8

DESIGNS—VERT. 15 c. " Bolivar as a Student " (artist unknown). 35 c. Bolivar's statue, Madrid.

210. Astronauts and Moon Landing.

1969. Air. 1st Man on the Moon.

2098. **210.** 90 c. multicoloured 55 25

211. " Virgin of the Rosary " (anon., 17th century).

1969. Air. Christmas. Multicoloured.

2100. 75 c. Type **211** 35 20
2101. 80 c. " The Holy Family " (Landeata School, Caracas, 18th century) 45 25

212. " Children and Birds ".

1969. Children's Day. Multicoloured.

2102. 5 c. Type **212** 5 8
2103. 45 c. " Children's Camp " 25 10

213. Map of Greater Colombia.

1969. Greater Colombia. 150th Anniv.

2104. **213.** 45 c. multicoloured 20 10

214. San Antonio Church, Clárines.

1970. Architecture of the Colonial Era. Mult.

2105. 10 c. Type **214** 5 5
2106. 30 c. Church of the Conception, Caroni .. 15 8
2107. 40 c. San Miguel Church, Burbusay 25 12
2108. 45 c. San Antonio Church, Maturin 25 12
2109. 75 c. San Nicolas Church, Moruy 45 20
2110. 1 b. Coro Cathedral .. 55 30

215. Seven Hills of Valera. **216.** " Simon Bolivar " (M. N. Bate).

1970. Valera. 150th Anniv.

2112. **215.** 95 c. multicoloured .. 55 25

1970. Air. Portraits of Bolivar. Stamps in purple-brown on buff; inscriptions in green; colours of country name and value given below.

2113. **216.** 15 c. brown 5 5
2114. 45 c. blue 20 10
2115. 55 c. orange 35 10
2116. – 65 c. brown 35 15
2117. – 70 c. blue 35 15
2118. – 75 c. orange .. 40 15
2119. – 85 c. brown 45 15
2120. – 90 c. blue 45 20
2121. – 95 c. orange 50 20
2122. – 1 b. brown 50 20
2123. – 1 b. 50 blue 75 30
2124. – 2 b. orange .. .. 1·40 55

PORTRAITS BY: 65, 70, 75 c. by F. Roulin. 85, 90, 95 c. J. M. Espinoza (1828). 1, 1 b. 50, 2 b. J. M. Espinoza (1830).

217. Gen. Guzman Blanco and Dr. M. J. Sanabria.

1970. Air. Free Compulsory Education in Venezuela. Cent.

2125. **217.** 75 c. black, grn. & brn. 30 10

218. Map of Venezuela.

1970. States of Venezuela. Maps and Arms of the various States. Multicoloured.

2126. 5 c. Federal District (post.) 5 5
2127. 15 c. Monagas 8 8
2128. 20 c. Nueva Esparta .. 12 5
2129. 25 c. Portuguesa (vert.) .. 10 5
2130. 45 c. Sucre 25 8
2131. 55 c. Tachira (vert.) .. 30 8
2132. 65 c. Trujillo 35 10

2133. 75 c. Yaracuy 45 10
2134. 85 c. Zulia (vert.) .. 50 12
2135. 90 c. Amazonas Federal Territory (vert.) .. 60 12
2136. 1 b. Federal Island Dependencies 70 15
2137. 5 c. Type **218** (air) .. 5 5
2138. 15 c. Apure 8 5
2139. 20 c. Aragua 12 5
2140. 20 c. Anzoategui 12 5
2141. 25 c. Barinas 15 5
2142. 25 c. Bolivar 15 8
2143. 45 c. Crabobo 25 8
2144. 55 c. Cojedes (vert.) .. 35 8
2145. 65 c. Falcon 35 10
2146. 75 c. Guarico 45 12
2147. 85 c. Lara 50 12
2148. 90 c. Merida (vert.) .. 60 12
2149. 1 b. Miranda 70 15
2150. 2 b. Amacuro Delta Federal Territory .. .. 1·40 30

219. " Monochaetum humboldtianum ". **220.** " The Battle of Boyaca " (M. Tovar y Tovar).

1970. Flowers of Venezuela. Multicoloured.
2151. 20 c. Type **219** (postage) 10 5
2152. 25 c. " Symbolanthus vasculosus " 12 5
2153. 45 c. " Cavendishia splendens " 25 10
2154. 1 b. " Befaria glauca " .. 50 15
2155. 20 c. " Epidendrum secundum " (air) .. 10 5
2156. 25 c. " Oyedaea verbesinoides " .. 12 5
2157. 45 c. " Heliconia villosa " 25 10
2158. 1 b. " Macleania nitida " 50 20

1970. Battle of Boyaca. 150th Anniv. (1969).
2159. **220.** 30 c. multicoloured .. 15 5

221. Archiepiscopal Cross. **222.** C. Parra Olmedo (T. Salas).

1970. Religious Art. Multicoloured.
2160. 35 c. Type **221** 20 8
2161. 40 c. " Out Lady of the Valley " 20 12
2162. 60 c. " Our Lady of Belen de San Mateo " .. 30 15
2163. 90 c. " The Virgin of Chiquinquira " .. 45 20
2164. 1 b. " Our Lady of Socorro de Valencia " .. 50 25

1970. Air. Caracciola Parra Olmedo (lawyer). 150th Birth Anniv.
2165. **222.** 20 c. multicoloured .. 12 5

223. Venezuelan Stamp and " EXFILCA " Emblem.

1970. " EXFILCA 70 " Philatelic Exhib., Caracas. Multicoloured.
2167. 20 c. National Flags and Exhibition emblem (vert.) 10 5
2168. 25 c. Type **223** 12 8
2169. 70 c. Air stamp and emblem (vert.) 35 20

224. " Guardian Angel " (J. P. Lopez). **225.** Aircraft of 1920, and Modern Jet.

1970. Christmas.
2171. **224.** 45 c. multicoloured .. 25 12

1970. Venezuelen Air Force. 50th Anniv.
2172. **225.** 5 c. multicoloured .. 5 5

226. People in Question Mark.

1971. National Census.
2173. **226.** 30 c. black, green and red (postage) .. 12 5
2174. – 70 c. multicoloured (air) 25 10
DESIGN: 70 c. National flag and " pin-men ".

227. Battle Scene.

228. " Cattleya gaskelliana ". **229.** Adoration of the Child.

1971. Battle of Carabobo. 150th Anniv.
2175. **227.** 2 b. multicoloured 1·10 55

1971. Air. Venezuelan Orchids. Mult.
2176. 20 c. " Cattleya percivaliana " (vert.) .. 12 5
2177. 25 c. Type **228** 15 8
2178. 75 c. " Cattleya massiae " (vert.) 45 20
2179. 90 c. " Cattleya violacea o superba " 50 25
2180. 1 b. " Cattleya lawrenceana " 55 30

1971. Christmas. Multicoloured.
2181. 25 c. Type **229** 12 5
2182. 25 c. Madonna and Child 12 5

230. Dr. L. Beauperthuy (scientist). **231.** Constitution and Government Building.

1971. Beauperthuy Commem.
2183. **230.** 1 b. multicoloured .. 50 20

1971. Air. 1961 Constitution. 10th Anniv.
2184. **231.** 90 c. multicoloured 45 20

232. Heart-shaped Globe. **233.** Arms of Venezuela and National Flags.

1972. World Heart Month.
2185. **232.** 1 b. blk., red & blue .. 45 30

1972. " Venezuela in the Americas ". Mult.
2186. 3 b. Type **233** .. .. 1·25 85
2187. 4 b. Venezuelan flag .. 1·75 1·10
2188. 5 b. National anthem .. 1·75 1·10
2189. 10 b. " Araguaney " .. (national tree) .. .. 3·50 2·75
2190. 15 b. Map of the Americas 5·50 4·25

234. Mahatma Gandhi.

1972. Mahatma Gandhi. Birth Cent. (1969).
2194. **234.** 60 c. multicoloured .. 45 12

235. Tower Blocks.

1972. Central Park. Housing Project. Mult.
2191. 30 c. Type **235** 15 8
2192. 30 c. View from ground level 15 8
2193. 30 c. Aerial view 15 8

236. Children making Music.

1972. Christmas. Multicoloured.
2195. 30 c. Type **236** .. 12 5
2196. 30 c. Children roller-skating 12 5
Nos. 2195/6 were issued together se-tenant within the sheet, forming a composite design.

237. " Drymarchon corais " (head). **238.** Planetary System.

1972. Snakes. Multicoloured.
2197. 10 c. Type **237** 5 5
2198. 15 c. " Spilotes pullatus " 8 5
2199. 25 c. " Bothrops venezuelensis " 10 8
2200. 30 c. " Micrurus dumerili carinicaudus " 12 8
2201. 60 c. " Crotalus vegrandis " 25 15
2202. 1 b. Boa constrictor .. 45 30

1973. Copernicus (astronomer). 500th Birth Anniv. Multicoloured.
2203. 5 c. Type **238** 5 5
2204. 10 c. Copernicus 5 5
2205. 15 c. Book-" De Revolutionibus Orbium Coelestium " 8 5

239. The Sun. **240.** Part of Solar System.

1973. Humboldt Planetarium. 10th Anniv. Multicoloured.

(a) As Type **239**.
2206. 5 c. Type **239** 5 5
2207. 5 c. Earth 5 5
2208. 20 c. Mars 12 5
2209. 20 c. Saturn 12 5
2210. 30 c. Asteroids 12 5
2211. 40 c. Neptune 25 5
2212. 50 c. Venus 30 8
2213. 60 c. Jupiter 35 8
2214. 75 c. Uranus 45 12
2215. 90 c. Pluto 50 12
2216. 90 c. Moon 50 12
2217. 1 b. Mercury 55 15

(b) As Type **240**.
2218. 10 c. Type **240** 5 5
2219. 15 c. Solar System (centre) 8 5
2220. 15 c. Solar System (right hand) 8 5
Nos. 2218/20 form a composite design of the Solar System.

241. O.A.S. Emblem and Map.

1973. Organisation of American States. 25th Anniv.
2221 **241.** 60 c. multicoloured .. 25 12

242. General Paez in Uniform. **244.** Bishop Ramos de Lora.

243. Admiral Padilla, Gen. Montilla and Gen. Manrique.

1973. General Jose A. Paez. Death Cent.
2222. **242.** 10 c. multicoloured .. 5 5
2223. – 30 c. gold, black & red 12 8
2224. – 50 c. blk., brn. & blue 20 10
2225. – 1 b. multicoloured .. 45 25
2226. – 2 b. multicoloured .. 85 45
DESIGNS—VERT. 30 c. Paez and horse (old engraving). 50 c. Gen. Paez in civilian dress. 1 b. Street of the Lancers, Puerto Cabello. HORIZ. 2 b. " The Charge at Centauro ".

1973. Maracaibo Naval Battle. 150th Anniv. Multicoloured.
2227. 50 c. Type **243** 20 10
2228. 1 b. " Battle of Maracaibo (M. F. Rincon) 45 20
2229. 2 b. Plan of opposing fleets 85 45

1973. Bishop Ramos de Lora. 250th Birth Anniv. (1972).
2230. **244.** 75 c. gold and brown 30 15

245. Ship, Aircraft and Map. **247.** General Paez Dam.

246. Map and Waterfall.

1973. Margarita Island, Free Zone.
2231. **245.** 5 c. multicoloured .. 5 5

1973. Completion of " Golden Highway ". Multicoloured.
2232. 5 c. Type **246** 5 5
2233. 10 c. Map and parrot .. 5 5
2234. 20 c. Map and Santa Elena Church, Vairen .. 8 5
2235. 50 c. Map and Ancient mountain sanctuary .. 25 12
2236. 60 c. As 50 c. 25 15
2237. 90 c. Map and Santa Teresita church .. 40 20
2238. 1 b. Map and flags of Venezuela and Brazil .. 45 25

1973. Completion of General Paez Dam, Merida.
2239. **247.** 30 c. multicoloured .. 12 8

248. Child on Slide.

1973. Children's Festival. Multicoloured.
2240. 10 c. Type **248** 5 5
2241. 10 c. Fairy tale animals .. 5 5
2242. 10 c. " Paginas Para Imaginar " (Childrens Books) 5 5
2243. 10 c. Holidaymakers leaving aircraft 5 5

249. King on White Horse.

251. Vase and Lace (" Handicrafts ").

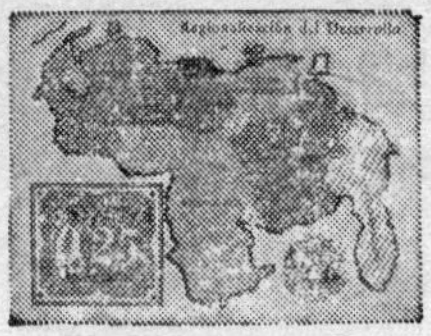

250. Regional Map.

1973. Christmas.. Multicoloured.
2244. 30 c. Type **249** 10 5
2245. 30 c. Two Kings 10 5

1973. Regional Development.
2246. **250.** 25 c. multicoloured .. 10 5

1973. Venezuelan Developments. Mult.
2247. 15 c. Type **251** 8 5
2248. 35 c. Industrial estate (" Construction ") .. 15 5
2249. 45 c. Cogwheels and chimney (" Small and medium industries ") 20 8

252. Map and Revellers.

1974. Carupano Carnival. 10th Anniv.
2250. **252.** 5 c. multicoloured .. 5 5

253. Congress Emblem.

1974. 9th Venezuelan Engineering Congress, Maracaibo.
2251. **253.** 50 c. multicoloured .. 20 8

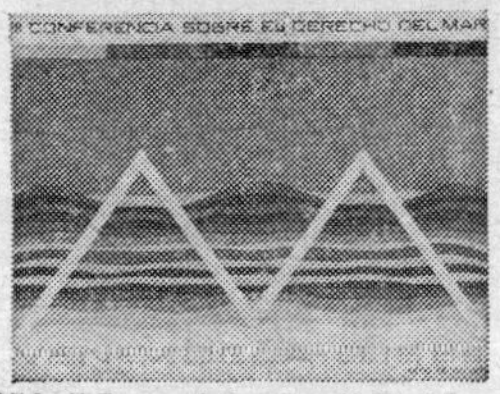

254. " Law of the Sea " Emblem.

1974. 3rd Law of the Sea Conference, Caracas, Multicoloured.
2252. 15 c. Type **254** 5 5
2253. 35 c. Fish in sea-weed .. 12 5
2254. 75 c. Sea-bird scene .. 25 10
2255. 80 c. Underwater grotto .. 30 12

255. Pupil and New School.

1974. " Pay Your Taxes " Campaign.
2256. **255.** 5 c. multicoloured .. 5 5
2257. 10 c. multicoloured .. 5 5
2258. 15 c. multicoloured .. 5 5
2259. 20 c. multicoloured .. 5 5
2260. **A.** 25 c. multicoloured .. 8 5
2261. 30 c. multicoloured .. 10 5
2262. 35 c. multicoloured .. 10 5
2263. 40 c. multicoloured .. 12 5
2264. **B.** 45 c. multicoloured .. 12 5
2265. 50 c. multicoloured .. 15 8
2266. 55 c. multicoloured .. 15 8
2267. 60 c. multicoloured .. 15 8
2268. **C.** 65 c. multicoloured .. 20 10
2269. 70 c. multicoloured .. 20 10
2270. 75 c. multicoloured .. 20 12
2271. 80 c. multicoloured .. 25 12
2272. **D.** 85 c. multicoloured .. 25 12
2273. 90 c. multicoloured .. 25 12
2274. 95 c. multicoloured .. 30 15
2275. 1 b. multicoloured .. 30 15
DESIGNS: A, Suburban housing project. B, City centre motorway. C, Sports stadium. D, Surgical team in operating theatre.

256. " Bolivar at Junin " (A. H. Tovar).

1974. Battle of Junin. 150th Anniv.
2276. **256.** 2 b. multicoloured .. 75 30

257. World Map.

1974. Universal Postal Union. Centenary. Multicoloured.
2277. 45 c. Type **257** 12 5
2278. 50 c. Mounted courier, sailing ship, modern liner and jet aircraft 15 8

258. Rufino Blanco-Fombona and Books.

1974. Rufino Blanco-Fombona (writer). Birth Centenary.
2279. **258.** 10 c. multicoloured .. 5 5
2280. – 30 c. multicoloured .. 10 5
2281. – 45 c. multicoloured .. 12 8
2282. – 90 c. multicoloured .. 25 12
DESIGNS: Nos. 2280/2, Portraits of Rufino Blanco-Fombona against a background of books similar to Type **258.**

259. Children on Paper Dart.

260. Marshal Sucre.

1974. Children's Festival.
2283. **259.** 70 c. multicoloured .. 20 12

1974. Battle of Ayacucho. 150th Anniv. Multicoloured.
2284. 30 c. Type **260** 10 5
2285. 50 c. South American flag on globe 15 8
2286. 1 b. Map showing battle sites 30 15
2287. 2 b. " Battle of Ayacucho" ($43\frac{1}{2} \times 22$ mm.) .. 55 30

261. " Shepherds ".

1974. Christmas. Details from " The Adoration of the Shepherds " (J. B. Mayno). Multicoloured.
2288. 30 c. Type **261** 10 5
2289. 30 c. " Holy Family " .. 10 5

262. Road Construction, 1905, and El Ciempies Junction, 1972.

1974. Ministry of Public Works. Centenary. Multicoloured.
2290. 5 c. Type **262** 5 5
2291. 20 c. J. Munoz Tebar (first Minister of Public Works) 5 5
2292. 25 c. Bridges on Caracas-La Guaira Road, 1912 and 1953 .. .. .. 8 5
2293. 40 c. Views of Caracas, 1874 and 1974 .. .. 12 5
2294. 70 c. Tucacas Railway Station, 1911, and projected Caracas terminal 20 10
2295. 80 c. Anatomical Institute, 1911, and Social Security Hospital, 1969 .. .. 25 12
2296. 85 c. Quininari River bridge, 1904, and Orinoco River bridge, 1967 .. .. .. 25 12
2297. 1 b. As 20 c. 30 15

263. Women in Profile.

1975. International Women's Year.
2298. **263.** 90 c. multicoloured .. 30 20

264. " Scout Camp ".

1975. 14th World Scout Jamboree.
2299. **264.** 20 c. multicoloured .. 8 5
2300. 80 c. multicoloured .. 30 20

265. " The Nativity ".

266. Red Cross Nurse.

1975. Christmas. Multicoloured.
2301. 30 c. Type **265** 12 8
2302. 30 c. " The Shepherds " 12 8

1975. Venezuelan Red Cross.
2303. **266.** 30 c. + 15 c. mult. .. 15 15
2304. 50 c. + 25 c. mult. .. 30 30

267. National Pantheon.

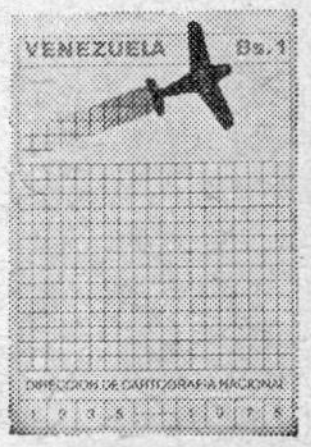

269. Aerial Cartography.

268. Flag Panels.

1976. National Pantheon. Centenary.
2305. **267.** 30 c. grey and blue .. 12 8
2306. 1 b. 05 brown and red 40 30

1976. Bolivian Independence (1975). 150th Anniv.
2307. **268.** 60 c. multicoloured .. 25 15

1976. Nat. Cartographic Institute (1975). 40th Anniv.
2308. **269.** 1 b. black and blue .. 40 30

270. Gen. Ribas' Signature.

1976. General Jose Ribas. Birth Bicent. Multicoloured.
2309. 40 c. Type **270** 15 10
2310. 55 c. General Ribas (43×31 mm.) 20 12

271. " Musicians of the Chacao School " (A. Barrios).

1976. Jose Lamas (composer). Birth Centenary.
2311. **271.** 75 c. multicoloured .. 30 20
2312. – 1 b. 25 red and grey on buff 50 40
DESIGN: 1 b. 25 Lamas's colophon.

272. Bolivar (after Jose Maria Espinoza).

274. C. A. Fernadez de Leoni (founder).

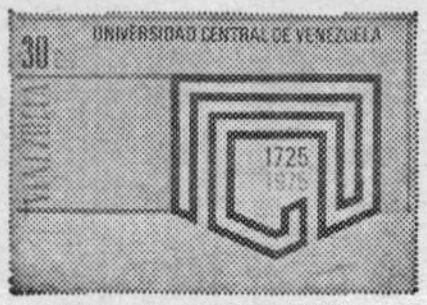

273. Symbolic Maze.

1976.

2313. 272. 5 c turquoise .. 5 5
2314. 10 c. magenta .. 5 5
2315. 15 c. brown 5 5
2316. 20 c. black 8 5
2317. 25 c. orange 10 5
2318. 30 c. violet 12 8
2319. 45 c. lilac 20 12
2320. 50 c. orange 20 12
2321. 65 c. blue 25 15
2322. 1 b. red 40 30
2323. 2 b. grey 80 70
2324. 3 b. blue .. .. 1·25 1·00
2325. 4 b. orange .. .. 1·60 1·40
2326. 5 b. red .. .. 2·00 1·75
2327. 10 b. slate .. .. 4·00 3·50
2328. 15 b. blue .. .. 6·00 5·00
2329. 20 b. red .. .. 8·00 7·00

1976. Venezuela's Central University. 250th Anniv.

2330. 273. 30 c. multicoloured .. 12 8
2331. – 50c. blk., oran. & yell. 20 12
2332. – 90 c. black and yellow 35 25

DESIGNS: 50 c. University buildings. 90 c. Faculty symbols.

1976. Children's Foundation. Multicoloured.

2333. 30 c.+15 c. Type 274 .. 20 20
2334. 50 c.+25 c. Children in "home" 30 30

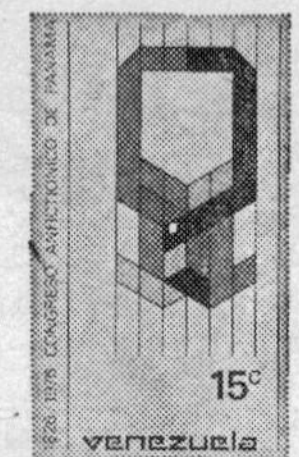

275. Unity Emblem.

1976. Panama Amphictyonic Congress. 150th Anniv.

2335. 275. 15 c. multicoloured .. 5 5
2336. – 45 c. multicoloured .. 20 12
2337. – 1 b. 25 multicoloured 50 40

DESIGN: 45 c., 1 b. 25 As Type 275, but with different "Unity" emblems.

276. George Washington.

277. Oil Valve.

1976. American Revolution. Bicent.

2338. 276. 1 b. black and brown 40 30
2339. – 1 b. black and green .. 40 30
2340. – 1 b. black and purple 40 30
2341. – 1 b. black and blue .. 40 30
2342. – 1 b. black and olive .. 40 30

DESIGNS: No. 2339, Thomas Jefferson. No. 2340, Abraham Lincoln. No. 2341, Franklin D. Roosevelt. No. 2342, John F. Kennedy.

1976. Oil Nationalisation

2343. 277. 10 c. multicoloured .. 5 5
2344. – 30 c. multicoloured .. 12 8
2345. – 35 c. multicoloured .. 15 10
2346. – 40 c. multicoloured .. 15 10
2347. – 55 c. multicoloured .. 20 12
2348. – 90 c. multicoloured .. 35 25

DESIGNS: 30 c. to 90 c. Various computer drawings of valves and pipelines.

278. "The Nativity" (B. Rivas).

279. T.B. Patient.

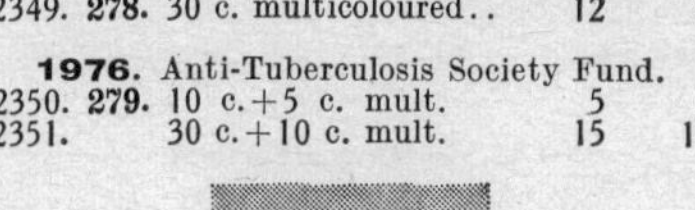

1976. Christmas.

2349. 278. 30 c. multicoloured .. 12 8

1976. Anti-Tuberculosis Society Fund.

2350. 279. 10 c.+5 c. mult. 5 5
2351. 30 c.+10 c. mult. 15 15

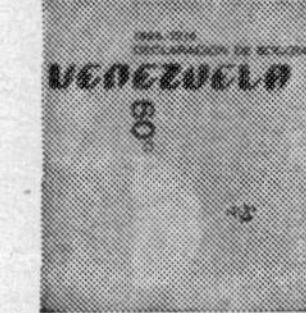

280. Emblem.

1976. Bogota Declaration. 10th Anniv.

2352. 280. 60 c. black and yellow 25 15

EXPRESS LETTER STAMPS

E 1.

E 2.

1949.

E 809. E 1. 30 c. lake 30 15

1961.

E 1691. E 2. 30 c. orange .. 15 12

OFFICIAL STAMPS

O 1.

ILLUSTRATIONS
British Commonwealth and all overprints and surcharges are FULL SIZE. Foreign Countries have been reduced to ½-LINEAR.

1898.

O 174. O 1. 5 c. black and green 45 45
O 175. 10 c. black and rose 55 55
O 176. 25 c. black and blue 85 85
O 177. 50 c. black and yellow 1·40 1·40
O 178. 1 b. black and mauve 1·40 1·40

1899. Surch. **1899** and new value.

O 187. O 1. 5 c. on 50 c. black and yellow .. 3·25 3·25
O 188. 5 c. on 1 b. black and mauve .. 11·00 11·00
O 189. 25 c. on 50 c. black and yellow .. .. 11·00 11·00
O 190. 25 c. on 1 b. black and mauve .. 5·50 5·50

1900. Optd. **1900** in upper corners.

O 222. O 1. 5 c. black and green 15 15
O 223. 10 c. black and rose 15 15
O 224. 25 c. black & blue .. 15 15
O 225. 50 c. black and yell. 30 30
O 226. 1 b. black & mauve 35 35

O 2.

O 3.

1904.

O 325. O 2. 5 c. black & green .. 15 15
O 326. 10 c. black and red .. 30 30
O 327. 25 c. black & blue .. 30 30
O 328. 50 c. black & red .. 2·10 2·10
O 329. 1 b. black & lake .. 85 85

1912.

O 354. O 3. 5 c. black & green .. 15 15
O 355. 10 c. black & red .. 15 15
O 356. 25 c. black & blue .. 15 15
O 357. 50 c. black & violet 30 20
O 358. 1 b. black & yellow 35 35

REGISTRATION STAMPS

R 1. Bolivar.

1899.

R 186. R 1. 25 c. brown .. .. 2·10 1·75

1899. Optd. with T 14.

R 205. R 1. 25 c. brown 85 85

VICTORIA BC

The S.E. state of the Australian Commonwealth, whose stamps it now uses.

1.

2. Queen on throne.

1850. Imperf.

22a. 1. 1d. red to brown .. £100 16·00
6. 2d. lilac to grey .. .. £225 40·00
17. 2d. brown .. .. £110 30·00
25b. 3d. blue .. .. .. 90·00 15·00

1857. Perf.

28. 1. 3d. blue .. .. .. — 40·00

1852. Imperf.

37. 2. 2d. brown to lilac .. 36·00 11·00

3.

4. Queen on throne.

1854. Imperf.

39. 3. 1s. blue .. .. .. 32·00 11·00

1859. Perf.

41a. 3. 1s. blue .. .. .. 17·00 5·50

1856. Imperf.

42. 4. 1d. green .. .. .. 20·00 9·00

1858. Rouletted.

43. 4. 6d. blue .. .. .. 13·00 5·50

5.

6. Emblems in corners.

1854. Imperf.

44a. 5. 6d. orange .. .. 20·00 5·50
49. 2s. green .. .. .. £250 60·00

1857. Roul.

45a. 5. 6d. orange .. .. — 15·00
50. 2 s. green .. .. .. — £160

1859. Perf.

104. 5. 6d. black .. .. .. 32·00 9·00
51. 2s. green .. .. .. 90·00 16·00
147. 2s. blue on green .. 12·00 1·50

1857. Imperf.

55. 6. 1. green .. .. .. 13·00 7·00
64a. 2d. lilac .. .. .. 55·00 5·50
57. 4d. red .. .. .. 50·00 4·00

1857. Roul.

68. 6. 1d. green .. .. .. 55·00 7·00
79. 2d. lilac .. .. .. 15·00 3·25
76b. 4d. red .. .. .. 24·00 1·10

1857. Perf.

96. 6. 1d. green .. .. .. 13·00 2·25
99a. 2d. lilac .. .. .. 24·00 1·75
99. 2d. grey .. .. .. 21·00 1·75
90. 4d. red .. .. .. 24·00 3·00

7.

8.

1860. Perf.

100. 7. 3d. blue .. .. .. 15·00 2·50
101. 3d. claret .. .. .. 15·00 7·50
102a. 4d. red .. .. .. 15·00 55
103. 6d. orange .. .. £400 90·00
105. 6d. black .. .. .. 32·00 1·75

1861.

109. 8. 1d. green .. .. .. 11·00 1·75

9.

10.

1862.

113a. 9. 6d. black .. .. 13·00 1·10

1863.

122b. 10. 1d. green .. .. 4·00 1·10
179. 2d. lilac .. .. 2·75 55
124a. 4d. red .. .. 7·50 65
125. 8d. orange .. .. 24·00 10·00
193. 8d. brown on rose .. 5·50 1·50

11.

12.

13.

14.

1865.

150. 11. 3d. lilac .. .. 11·00 5·50
187. 3d. yellow .. .. 2·75 65
192. 12. 6d. blue .. .. 2·00 20
134. 10d. grey .. .. 32·00 18·00
138. 10d. brown on rose .. 7·00 70
139. 13. 1s. blue on blue .. 8·00 1·10
162. 14. 5s. blue on yellow .. 55·00 65·00
198a. 5s. blue and red .. 11·00 3·75

1871. Surch. in figures and words.

201. 10. ½d. on 1d. grn. (No. 122b) 2·75 1·50
186. 12. 9d. on 10d. brn. on rose 20·00 3·00

15.

16.

1870.

206a. 15. 2d. lilac .. .. 2·75 15
207b. 16. 9d. brown on rose .. 8·00 1·75

1876. Surch. in figures and words.

212. 16. 8d. on 9d. brown on rose 18·00 4·00

17.

18.

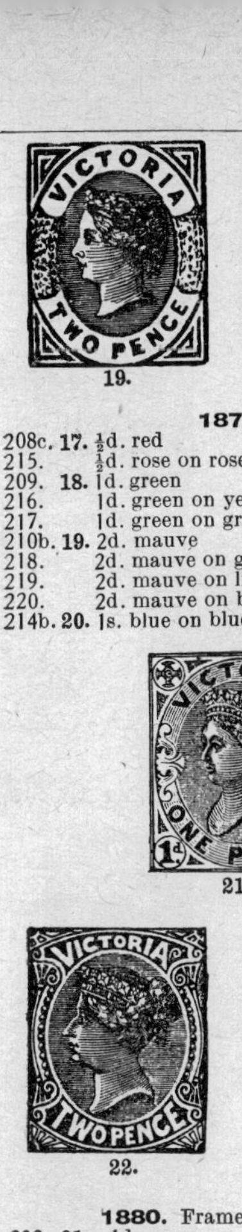

19. 20.

1873.

No.	Type	Description	Unused	Used
208c.	**17.**	½d. red ..	65	20
215.		½d. rose on rose ..	2·00	1·00
209.	**18.**	1d. green	1·50	20
216.		1d. green on yellow ..	5·00	2·00
217.		1d. green on grey ..	8·00	7·50
210b.	**19.**	2d. mauve	1·50	5
218.		2d. mauve on green ..	7·50	1·00
219.		2d. mauve on lilac ..	—	65·00
220.		2d. mauve on brown ..	7·50	1·50
214b.	**20.**	1s. blue on blue ..	3·25	60

21.

22. 23.

1880. Frame differs in 4d.

No.	Type	Description	Unused	Used
232.	**21.**	1d. green	1·50	12
228.	**22.**	2d. brown	65	5
223e.		2d. mauve	70	5
225a.		4d. red	2·25	70
226.	**23.**	2s. blue on green ..	8·00	2·50

24. 25.

26. 27.

28. 29.

1884. Inscr. "STAMP DUTY".

No.	Type	Description	Unused	Used
243.	**24.**	½d. red	65	12
244.	**25.**	1d. green	70	10
245.	**26.**	2d. mauve	1·75	5
246a.	**25.**	3d. yellow	1·00	12
247.	**27.**	4d. magenta	2·50	80
249a.	**25.**	6d. blue..	2·75	65
239.	**28.**	8d. red on rose.. ..	1·50	65
240.	**26.**	1s. blue on yellow ..	3·25	1·00
251.	**28.**	2s. green on green ..	2·00	65
253.		2s. green on white ..	1·50	1·00
254b.	**29.**	2s. 6d. orange	2·00	90

1885. Optd. **STAMP DUTY.**

No.	Type	Description	Unused	Used
237.	**11.**	3d. yellow	5·00	2·00
238.	**22.**	4d. red	5·00	2·00
234.	**20.**	1s. blue on blue ..	7·50	4·00
236.	**23.**	2s. blue on green ..	5·50	2·50

30.

31.

32.

33.

34.

35. 36.

1886. Inscr. "STAMP DUTY".

No.	Type	Description	Unused	Used
283.	**30.**	½d. lilac	75	35
304.		½d. red..	20	5
330.		½d. green	12	5
285a.	**31.**	1d. green	70	5
286d.	**32.**	2d. purple	55	5
309.	**33.**	4d. red..	70	5
288b.	**34.**	6d. blue	60	5
289.	**35.**	1s. chocolate	2·75	55
339.		1s. red	80	35
290.	**36.**	1s. 6d. blue	8·00	5·00
340.		1s. 6d. orange.. ..	1·10	1·00

37.

38.

39.

40.

1890. Inscr. "STAMP DUTY", except T **38.**

No.	Type	Description	Unused	Used
297.	**37.**	1d. orange-brn. on red	30	5
298c.		1d. brown to orange ..	12	5
331.		1d. red	12	5
306.	**38.**	1½d. green	15	20
327.		1½d. red on yellow ..	20	20
300a.	**39.**	2½d. red on yellow ..	55	5
333.		2½d. blue	20	5
336.	**40.**	5d. chocolate	40	5

41.

42.

(T **41** to **44** are reduced in size.)

1897. Charity.

No.	Type	Description	Unused	Used
325.	**41.**	1d. (1s.) blue	5·00	5·00
326.	**42.**	2½d. (2s. 6d.) brown ..	18·00	18·00

43.

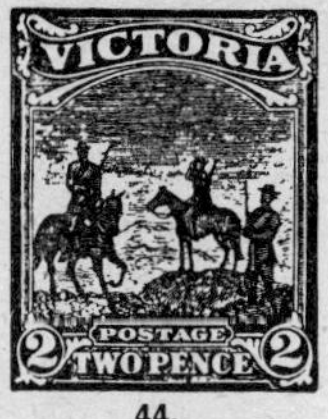

44.

1900. Charity.

No.	Type	Description	Unused	Used
346.	**43.**	1d. (1s.) brown ..	12·00	12·00
347.	**44.**	2d. (2s.) green	30·00	35·00

1901.

No.	Type	Description	Unused	Used
349.	**17.**	½d. green	12	5
361.	**37.**	1d. olive	80	65
351.	**11.**	3d. orange	40	10
362.	**25.**	3d. green	1·25	1·10
352.	**22.**	4d. yellow	55	20
353.	**12.**	6d. green	55	35
302.	**16.**	9d. green	2·75	1·00
338.		9d. red	65	20
354.	**20.**	1s. orange	70	40
348.	**23.**	2s. blue on rose ..	1·50	1·25
355.	**14.**	5s. red and blue ..	7·00	3·00

1901. As previous types, but inscr. "POSTAGE" instead of "STAMP DUTY".

No.	Type	Description	Unused	Used
363.	**17.**	½d. green	20	5
400.	**21.**	1d. red	12	5
366a.	**38.**	1½d. red on yellow ..	20	5
367a.	**22.**	2d. mauve	20	5
359a.	**39.**	2½d. blue	20	5
368a.	**11.**	3d. orange-brown ..	80	5
403.		3d. yellow	55	5
369.	**22.**	4d. yellow	55	5
360a.	**40.**	5d. chocolate	40	5
370.	**12.**	6d. green	60	5
407a.	**16.**	9d. red	80	10
408.	**20.**	1s. orange	75	8
374.	**23.**	2s. blue on rose ..	1·00	12
375a.	**14.**	5s. red and blue ..	5·00	1·50

57.

1901. Frame differs for £2.

No.	Type	Description	Unused	Used
410.	**57.**	£1 red	75·00	65·00
412.	–	£2 blue	£130	£110

1912. Surch. **ONE PENNY.**

No.	Type	Description	Unused	Used
454.	**22.**	1d. on 2d. mve. (No. 367a)	10	8

POSTAGE DUE STAMPS

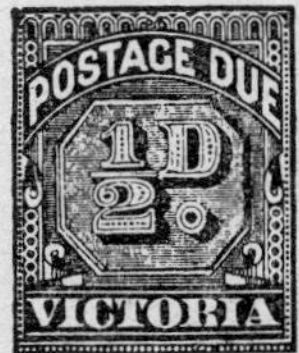

D 1.

ILLUSTRATIONS
British Commonwealth and all overprints and surcharges are FULL SIZE. Foreign Countries have been reduced to ¾-LINEAR.

1890.

No.	Type	Description	Unused	Used
D 11.	**D 1.**	½d. blue and red ..	20	20
D 12.		1d. blue and red ..	20	12
D 13.		2d. blue and red ..	55	20
D 4.		4d. blue and red ..	55	35
D 5.		5d. blue and red ..	65	35
D 6.		6d. blue and red ..	40	20
D 7.		10d. blue and red ..	3·50	2·00
D 8.		1s. blue and red ..	1·25	1·00
D 9.		2s. blue and red ..	24·00	20·00
D 10.		5s. blue and red ..	40·00	24·00

1895.

No.	Type	Description	Unused	Used
D 63.	**D 1.**	½s. red and green ..	8	8
D 30.		1d. red and green ..	5	5
D 17.		2d. red and green ..	10	5
D 32.		4d. red and green ..	12	8
D 29.		5d. red and green ..	40	20
D 34.		6d. red and green ..	35	20
D 21.		10d. red and green ..	80	75
D 22.		1s. red and green ..	80	90
D 23.		2s. red and green ..	7·00	6·50
D 24.		5s. red and green ..	12·00	14·00

REGISTRATION STAMP

R 1.

1854. Imperf. or rouletted.

No.	Type	Description	Unused	Used
52.	R 1.	1s. red and blue ..	£250	26·00

TOO LATE STAMP

1855. As Type R 1, but inscribed "TOO LATE". Imperf.

No.	Type	Description	Unused	Used
54.		6d. lilac and green ..	£110	55·00

VICTORIA LAND BC

Stamps issued in connection with Capt. Scott's Antarctic Expedition.

1911. Scott Expedition. Stamps of New Zealand optd. **VICTORIA LAND.**

No.	Type	Description	Unused	Used
A 2.	**41.**	½d. green	£250	£200
A 3.	**42.**	1d. red	20·00	20·00

VIETNAM O4

1. DEMOCRATIC REPUBLIC.

The Democratic republic was proclaimed by the Viet Minh Nationalists on 2 September 1945 and recognised by France on 6 March, 1946, as a free state within the Indo-China Federation. It consisted of Tongking, Annam and Cochin-China.

Currency: 1945. 100 cents = 1 piastre.
1945. 100 xu = 10 hao = 1 dong.

Stamps of Indo-China overprinted.

VIET-NAM
DAN-CHU CONG-HOA
DOC-LAP
TU-DO HANH-PHUC
BUU-CHINH III

(1.)

("DAN-CHU CONG-HOA" = Democratic Republic: "DOC-LAP TU-DO HANH-PHUC = Independence, Freedom, Happiness; "BUU-CHINH" = Postage.)

1945. Independence. Variously optd. as T 1 (all with **DOC-LAP TU-DO HANH-PHUC** in opt.).

No.	Type	Description	Unused	Used
1.	**26.**	1 c. brown	5	5
2.	–	2 c. mauve (No. 315) ..	5	5
3.	–	3 c. brown (Courbet) ..	5	5
4.	–	4 c. brown (No. 316) ..	5	5
5.	–	5 c. sepia (De Genouilly)	5	5
6.	–	6 c. red (No. 304) ..	5	5
7.	–	6 c. red (No. 305) ..	12	12
8.	–	10 c. green (No. 307) ..	15	15
9.	–	10 c. green (No. 322) ..	5	5
10.	–	20 c. red (No. 309) ..	15	15
11.	**31.**	40 c. blue..	5	5
12.	–	$1 green (No. 311) ..	12	12

Nos. 3 and 5 were not issued without opt. and are as Nos. 304 and 305 of Indo-China respectively.

1945, Variously optd. as follows:—

(a) **VIET-NAM DAN-CHU CONG-HOA.**

No.	Type	Description	Unused	Used
13.	**34.**	10 c. purple and yellow..	1·00	1·00
14.	–	15 c. purple (No. 292) ..	5	5
15.	–	30 c. brown (No. 294) ..	5	5
16.	**34.**	50 c. red	1·00	1·00
17.	–	$1 green (No. 295) ..	8	10

(b) **VIET-NAM DAN-CHU CONG-HOA BUU-CHINH.**

No.	Type	Description	Unused	Used
18.	**26.**	3 c. brown	5	5
19.	–	4 c. yellow (No. 317) ..	5	5
20.	**26.**	6 c. red	5	5
21.		10 c. green	15	15
22.	–	10 c. green (No. 320) ..	10	10
23.	–	20 c. red (Pavie).. ..	5	5
24.	**26.**	40 c. blue..	10	10
25.		40 c. grey	25	25

No. 23 was not issued without opt. and is as No. 320 of Indo-China.

VIET-NAM
DAN-CHU
3$00 CONG-HOA

CUU-DOI

(2.)

("CUU-DOI" = Famine Relief.)

1945. Famine Relief. Surch. as **T 2.**

No.	Type	Description	Unused	Used
26.	**35.**	"2 $00" on 15 c. + 60 c. purple	60	60
27.		"3 $00" on 40 c. + 1 $10 c. blue	75	75

1945. War wounded. Surch. as **T 2** but with **Binh-si Bi-nan** (= Fund for War Wounded).

No.	Type	Description	Unused	Used
28.	**35.**	"5 $00" on 15 c. + 60 c. purple	1·50	1·50

1945. Surch in new currency and variously optd. as before (except Nos. 43/7).

(a) **VIET-NAM DAN-CHU CONG-HOA BUU-CHINH.**

29. **31.** 30 x. on 1 c. brown .. 8 8
30. – 30 x. on 15 c. purple (Garnier) 5 5
31. **32.** 50 x. on 1 c. brown .. 10 10
32. – 60 x. on 1 c. brown (313) 15 15
33. – 1 d. on 5 c. brown (303).. 30 30
34. – 1 d. 60 x. on 10 c. green (319) 8 8
35. **31.** 3 d. on 15 c. purple .. 25 25
36. **32.** 3 d. on 15 c. purple .. 12 12
37. – 4 d. on 1 c. brown (302) 10 10
38. – 5 d. on 1 c. brown (301).. 25 25

(b) **VIET-NAM DAN-CHU CONG-HOA.**

39. – 1 d. on 5 c. purple (318) 5 5
40. **21.** 2 d. on 3 c. brown .. 1·00 1·25
41. – 2 d. on 10 c. green (321).. 10 15
42. **21.** 4 d. on 6 c. red .. .. 1·00 1·00

(c) Surch. only.

43. **28.** 50 x. on 1 c. brown .. 8 8
44. 2 d. on 6 c. red 50 65
45. **20.** 5 d. on 1 c. orange .. 45 45
46. 10 d. on 6 c. violet .. 50 50
47. 15 d. on 25 c. blue .. 1·00 1·00

No. 30 was not issued without opt. and is as No. 301 of Indo-China.

OVERPRINT. Nos. 48/55 are all optd. **VIET-NAM DAN-CHU CONG-HOA** with varying additional words as noted in headings.

1945. National Defence (**Quoc-Phong**).

48. **21.** "+5 d." on 3 c. brown .. 25 35
49. "+10 d." on 6 c. red .. 25 35

1946. People's Livelihood. (**DAN SINH**).

50. **23.** "30 xu.+3 d." on 6 c. red 25 25
51. **27.** "30 xu.+3 d." on 6 c. red 25 25

1946. Campaign against Illiteracy (**Chong nan mu chu**).

52. **22.** "+4 dong" on 6 c. red.. 20 25

1946. New Life Movement (**Doi song moi**).

53. **30.** "+4 dong" on 6 c. red.. 30 35

1946. Child Welfare (**Bao-Anh**).

54. – "+2 dong" on 6 c. red (290) 12 12

1946. War Wounded (**Binh si bi nan**).

55. – "+3 dong" on 20 c. red (293) 35 35

Definitive issues.

3. Ho Chi Minh.

ILLUSTRATIONS
British Commonwealth and all overprints and surcharges are FULL SIZE. Foreign Countries have been reduced to ¾-LINEAR.

1946.

56. **3.** 1 h. green 5 8
57. 3 h. red 5 8
58. 9 h. yellow 5 8

1946. National Defence.

59. **3.** 4+6 h. blue 12 15
60. 6+9 h. brown 12 15

The Viet-Minh Government was at war with the French from 19 December, 1946, until July, 1954, and the stamps issued by the Democratic Republic in this period are listed as North Viet-Nam Nos. N 1/13, NO 1/9 and ND 1/4.

II. INDEPENDENT STATE.

On 14 June, 1949, Vietnam, comprising Tongking, Annam and Cochin-China, became an independent state within the French Union under Emperor Bao-Dai. Until the 1951 issue Indo-Chinese stamps continued in use.

By the Geneva Declaration of 21 July, 1954, Viet-Nam was partitioned near the 17th Parallel, and all authority of Bao-Dai's Government north of that line ended. Later issues are therefore those of SOUTH VIET-NAM and NORTH VIET-NAM.

Currency: 100 cents = 1 piastre.

4. Bongour Falls, Dalat.

1951.

61. **4.** 10 c. bronze 5 5
62. – 20 c. purple 5 5
63. – 30 c. blue 5 5
64. – 50 c. red 5 5
65. **4.** 60 c. sepia 5 5
66. – 1 p. brown 5 5
67. – 1 p. 20 c. brown 45 40
68. – 2 p. violet 10 5
69. – 3 p. blue 45 5
70. **4.** 5 p. green 20 8
71. – 10 p. red 55 8
72. – 15 p. brown .. .. 3·25 1·00
73. – 30 p. green .. .. 6·00 1·10

DESIGNS—HORIZ. 20 c., 2 p., 10 p. Imperial Palace, Hue. 30 c., 15 p. Small Lake, Hanoi. 50 c., 1 p. Temple of Remembrance, Saigon. VERT. 1 p. 20, 3 p. 30 p. Emperor Bao-Dai.

5.

1952. Air.

74. **5.** 3 p. 30 c. green and lake.. 12 10
75. 4 p. yellow and brown .. 20 5
76. 5 p. 10 c. pink and blue 30 10
77. 6 p. 30 c. red and yellow (symbolic of airlines) .. 30 20

6. Empress Nam Phuong. **7.** Globe and Lightning.

1952.

78. **6.** 30 c. brown, yell. & purple 8 8
79. 50 c. brown, yell. & blue 20 8
80. 1 p. 50 brown, yell. & olive 40 8

1952. Admission of Vietnam into I.T.U. 1st Anniv.

81. **7.** 1 p. blue .. .. .. 1·25 60

8. Dragon.

1952. Air. Day of Wandering Souls.

82. **8.** 40 c. red 35 15
83. 70 c. green 35 15
84. 80 c. blue 35 15
85. 90 c. brown 35 20
86. – 3 p. 70 c. purple 25 15

DESIGN—VERT. 3 p. 70 c. Dragon.

9. U.P.U. Monument, Berne, and Coastline.

1952. Admission of Vietnam into U.P.U. 1st Anniv.

87. **9.** 5 p. brown.. .. .. 1·40 30

1952. Red Cross. T 6 surch. with red cross and +**50 c.**

88. **6.** 1 p. 50+50 c. brown, yellow and blue .. 1·00 1·00

10. Emperor Bao-Dai and Gateway.

11. Sabres and Flag.

12. Crown Prince Bao-Long.

1952. 40th Birthday of Emperor.

89. **10.** 1 p. 50 purple 65 35

1952. Wounded Soldiers' Relief Fund.

90. **11.** 3 p. 30+1 p. 70 lake .. 50 50

1954.

91. **12.** 40 c. turquoise 12 12
92. 70 c. lake 20 20
93. 80 c. sepia 25 25
94. – 90 c. green 75 55
95. – 20 p. red .. .. 3·50 2·50
96. – 50 p. violet .. .. 9·00 4·25
97. **12.** 100 p. violet-blue .. 20·00 10·00

PORTRAIT: 90 c. to 50 p. Crown Prince in uniform.

POSTAGE DUE STAMPS

D 1. Dragon.

1952.

D 78. **D 1.** 10 c. green and red .. 5 5
D 79. 20 c. yellow & green .. 5 5
D 80. 30 c. orange & violet 5 5
D 81. 40 c. pink and green .. 5 5
D 82. 50 c. grey and lake .. 5 5
D 83. 1 p. silver and blue .. 5 5

SOUTH VIETNAM

Currency: 100 cents = 1 piastre.

A. INDEPENDENT STATE. (Within the French Union).

1. Turtle.

1955. Govt. of Ngo Dinh Diem. 1st Anniv.

S 1. **1.** 30 c. maroon 8 8
S 2. 50 c. green 40 25
S 3. 1 p. 50 c. blue 30 8

2. Phoenix.

1955. Air.

S 4. **2.** 4 p. magenta and violet .. 20 5

3. Refugees.

1955. Arrival of Refugees from North Vietnam. 1st Anniv.

S 5. **3.** 70 c. red 10 5
S 6. 80 c. maroon 40 12
S 7. 10 p. indigo 60 35
S 8. 20 p. brn., orge. & violet 1·25 45
S 9. 35 p. sepia, yell. & blue 3·25 1·50
S 10. 100 p. pur., orge. & grn. 5·50 4·00

No. S 9 is inscribed "CHIEN-DICH-HUYNE-DE" in margin at foot. See also No. S 26.

B. REPUBLIC. (From 26th October, 1955.)

4. G.P.O., Saigon.

5. Pres. Ngo-Dinh Diem.

1956. Entry of Vietnam into U.P.U. 5th Anniv.

S 11. **4.** 60 c. green 25 15
S 12. 90 c. violet 45 30
S 13. 3 p. brown 70 40

1956

S 14. **5.** 20 c. chestnut 5 5
S 15. 30 c. purple 5 5
S 16. 50 c. red 5 5
S 17. 1 p. violet 5 5
S 18. 1 p. 50 c. violet .. 8 5
S 19. 3 p. sepia 10 5
S 20. 4 p. indigo 15 5
S 21. 5 p. brown 25 8
S 22. 10 p. blue 30 12
S 23. 20 p. black 65 20
S 24. 35 p. green .. .. 2·00 40
S 25. 100 p. brown .. .. 3·75 1·90

1956. No. S 9 with bottom marginal inscription obliterated by bar.

S 26. **3.** 35 p. sepia, yell. & blue 1·90 1·00

1956. Optd. **Cong-thu Buu-dien** (="Government Postal Building").

S 27. **4.** 60 c. green 35 15
S 28. 90 c. violet 65 15
S 29. 3 p. brown .. .. 1·00 25

6. Bamboo.

7. Refugee Children.

1956. 1st Anniv. of Republic.

S 30. **6.** 50 c. red 5 5
S 31. 1 p. 50 c. purple.. .. 8 5
S 32. 2 p. green 12 5
S 33. 4 p. blue 20 8

1956. United Nations "Operation Brotherhood".

S 34. **7.** 1 p. magenta 12 5
S 35. 2 p. turquoise 15 5
S 36. 6 p. violet 30 8
S 37. 35 p. blue .. .. 1·25 50

8. Hunters on Elephants.

9. Ship's Cargo being off-loaded at Saigon.

1957. Govt. of Ngo Dinh Diem. 3rd Anniv.

S 38. **8.** 20 c. purple and green .. 5 5
S 39. 30 c. claret and bistre .. 8 5
S 40. – 90 c. sepia and green .. 12 5
S 41. – 2 p. blue and green .. 20 8
S 42. – 3 p. brown and violet .. 25 15

DESIGN—VERT. 90 c. to 3 p. Mountain hut.

1957. 9th Colombo Plan Conf., Saigon.

S 43. **9.** 20 c. purple 5 5
S 44. 40 c. olive 5 5
S 45. 50 c. red 5 5
S 46. 2 p. blue 8 5
S 47. 3 p. green 12 5

10. Torch and Constitution.

11. Youth Felling Tree.

1957. National Assembly. Inaug.

S 48. **10.** 50 c. salmon, grn. & blk. 5 5
S 49. 80 c. pur., blue & black 5 5
S 50. 1 p. rose, green & black 8 5
S 51. 4 p. chest., myrtle & blk. 10 8
S 52. 5 p. olive, turq. & black 20 8
S 53. 10 p. brown-red, blue and black 35 20

1958. Better Living Standards.

S 54. **11.** 50 c. green 5 5
S 55. 1 p. violet 8 5
S 56. 2 p. blue 10 5
S 57. 10 p. red 35 15

12. Young Girl with Chinese Lantern. **13.**

1958. Children's Festival.

S 58. **12.** 30 c. lemon 5 5
S 59. 50 c. claret 5 5
S 60. 2 p. red 8 5
S 61. 3 p. green 15 8
S 62. 4 p. olive 20 8

1958. United Nations Day.

S 63. **13.** 1 p. light brown 5 5
S 64. 2 p. turquoise.. .. 8 5
S 65. 4 p. rose 25 8
S 66. 5 p. purple 30 13

14. U.N.E.S.C.O. Emblem and Building.

15. U.N. Emblem and "Torch of Freedom".

1958. U.N.E.S.C.O. Headquarters Building. Inaug.
S 67. **14.** 50 c. blue 5 5
S 68. 2 p. red 8 5
S 69. 3 p. purple 15 8
S 70. 6 p. violet 20 12

1958. Declaration of Human Rights. 10th Anniv.
S 71. **15.** 50 c. blue 5 5
S 72. 1 p. lake 5 5
S 73. 2 p. green 8 5
S 74. 6 p. purple 20 15

16. Phu-Cam Cathedral.

17. Saigon Museum.

1958.
S 75. **16.** 10 c. slate 5 5
S 76. – 30 c. green 5 5
S 77. **17.** 40 c. green 5 5
S 78. – 50 c. emerald 5 5
S 79. – 2 p. blue 10 5
S 80. – 4 p. lilac 15 10
S 81. **17.** 5 p. red 20 12
S 82. **16.** 6 p. brown 20 15
DESIGNS—HORIZ. 30 c., 4 p. Thien-Mu Pagoda. 50 c., 2 p. Palace of Independence, Saigon.

18. Trung Sisters (national heroines) on Elephants.

1959. Trung Sisters Commem.
S 83. **18.** 50 c. multicoloured .. 15 5
S 84. 2 p. multicoloured .. 25 12
S 85. 3 p. multicoloured .. 40 25
S 86. 6 p. multicoloured .. 55 30

20.

21. Diesel-electric Train.

24. Scout climbing Mountain.

23. Tilling the Land.

1959. Agricultural Reform.
S 87. **20.** 70 c. purple 5 5
S 88. 2 p. green and blue .. 8 5
S 89. 3 p. olive-green .. 10 8
S 90. 6 p. red and vermilion 20 15

1959. Re-opening of Trans-Vietnam Railway. Centres in green.
S 91. **21.** 1 p. violet 5 5
S 92. 2 p. grey 8 5
S 93. 3 p. blue 10 5
S 94. 4 p lake 20 5

1959. Republic. 4th Anniv.
S 95. **23.** 1 p. chest., grn. & blue 5 5
S 96. 2 p. vio., grn. & orange 8 5
S 97. 4 p. indigo, bl. & bistre 15 8
S 98. 5 p. choc., olive & brn. 20 12

1959. 1st National Scout Jamboree, Trang Bom.
S 99. **24.** 3 p. green 15 5
S 100. 4 p. magenta 20 8
S 101. 8 p. magenta & maroon 35 20
S 102. 20 p. blue-grn. & turq. 80 40

25. "Family Code".

1960. Family Code. 1st Anniv.
S 103. **25.** 20 c. green 5 5
S 104. 30 c. blue 5 5
S 105. 2 p. red and orange .. 8 5
S 106. 6 p. violet and red .. 20 15

26. Fleeing Refugee Family.

27. Henri Dunant.

1960. World Refugee Year.
S 107. **26.** 50 c. magenta .. 5 5
S 108. 3 p. green 10 8
S 109. 4 p. red 15 10
S 110. 5 p. violet-blue .. 20 15

1960. Red Cross Day. Cross in red.
S 111. **27.** 1 p. blue 10 5
S 112. 3 p. green 20 10
S 113. 4 p. red 20 15
S 114. 6 p. magenta .. 25 20

ILLUSTRATIONS
British Commonwealth and all overprints and surcharges are FULL SIZE. Foreign Countries have been reduced to ¾-LINEAR.

28. Co-operative Farm.

1960. Establishment of Co-operative Rice Farming.
S 115. **28.** 50 c. blue 5 5
S 116. 1 p. green 5 5
S 117. 3 p. orange 15 8
S 118. 7 p. magenta .. 30 12

29. X-ray Camera and Patient.

30. Flag and Map.

1960. National T.B. Relief Campaign Day.
S 119. **29.** 3 p.+50 c. grn. & red 12 12

1960. Republic. 5th Anniv. Flag and map in red and yellow.
S 120. **30.** 50 c. turquoise .. 5 5
S 121. 1 p. blue 5 5
S 122. 3 p. violet 10 5
S 123. 7 p. green 20 8

31. Woman with Rice.

1960. F.A.O. Regional Conf., Saigon.
S 124. **31.** 2 p. turquoise & emer. 10 5
S 125. 4 p. ultram. and blue .. 20 10

32. Crane carrying Letter.

1960. Air.
S 126. **32.** 1 p. olive-green .. 10 5
S 127. 4 p. blue & blue-green 15 10
S 128. 5 p. violet and brown .. 20 15
S 129. 10 p. mauve 50 35

33. Farm Tractor.

34. Child and Plant.

35. Pres. Ngo Dinh Diem.

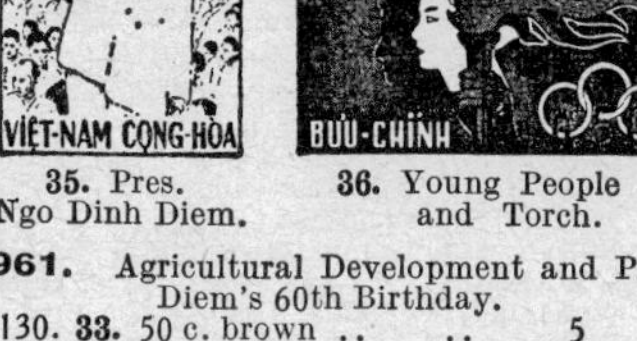

36. Young People and Torch.

1961. Agricultural Development and Pres. Diem's 60th Birthday.
S 130. **33.** 50 c. brown 5 5
S 131. 70 c. mauve .. 5 5
S 132. 80 c. rose 5 5
S 133. 10 p. magenta .. 30 15

1961. Child Welfare.
S 134. **34.** 70 c. blue 5 5
S 135. 80 c. ultramarine .. 5 5
S 136. 4 p. bistre 8 5
S 137 7 p. yell.-grn. & turq. 20 12

1961. 2nd Term of Pres. Ngo Dinh Diem
S 138. **35.** 50 c. blue 12 5
S 139. 1 p. red 20 5
S 140. 2 p. purple 25 8
S 141. 4 p. violet 45 10

1961. Sports and Youth.
S 142. **36.** 50 c. red 5 5
S 143. 70 c. magenta .. 5 5
S 144. 80 c. crimson & red .. 8 5
S 145. 8 p. purple & crimson 20 15

37. Bridge over Mekong.

1961. Saigon-Bien Hoa Motor Highway Inaug.
S 146. **37.** 50 c. green 5 5
S 147. 1 p. brown 5 5
S 148. 2 p. blue 10 5
S 149. 5 p. purple 15 8

38. Alexander of Rhodes.

39. Vietnamese with Torch.

1961. Alexander of Rhodes. Death Tercent.
S 150. **38.** 50 c. red 5 5
S 151. 1 p. maroon 5 5
S 152. 3 p. bistre 5 5
S 153. 6 p. green 15 8

1961. Youth Moral Rearmament.
S 154. **39.** 50 c. red 5 5
S 155. 1 p. green 5 5
S 156. 3 p. red 5 5
S 157. 8 p. chocolate & purple 15 8

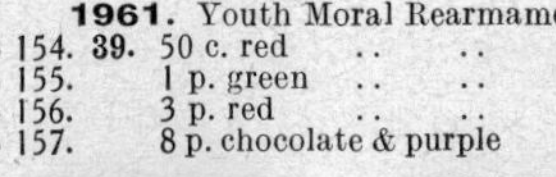

40. Gateway of Van-Mieu Temple, Hanoi.

41. Tractor and Cottages.

1961. U.N.E.S.C.O. 15th Anniv.
S 158. **40.** 1 p. green 5 5
S 159. 2 p. red 5 5
S 160. 5 p. olive 15 8

1961. Rural Reform.
S 161. **41.** 50 c. green 5 5
S 162. 1 p. lake and blue .. 5 5
S 163. 2 p. brown and green 5 5
S 164. 10 p. turquoise .. 25 15

42. Attack on Mosquito.

43. Postal Cheque Building, Saigon.

1962. Malaria Eradication.
S 165. **42.** 50 c. magenta .. 5 5
S 166. 1 p. orange 5 5
S 167. 2 p. green 10 5
S 168. 6 p. blue 20 15

1962. Postal Cheque Service. Inaug.
S 169. **43.** 70 c. green 5 5
S 170. 80 c. chocolate .. 5 5
S 171. 4 p. purple 10 5
S 172. 7 p. red 20 15

44. St. Mary of La-Vang.

45. Armed Guards and Fortified Village.

1962. St. Mary of La-Vang Commem.
S 173. **44.** 50 c. red and violet .. 5 5
S 174. 1 p. indigo and brown 5 5
S 175. 2 p. lake and chocolate 5 5
S 176. 8 p. blue & blue-green 20 10

1962. "Strategic Villages".
S 177. **45.** 50 c. red 5 5
S 178. 1 p. bronze 5 5
S 179. 1 p. 50 purple .. 5 5
S 180. 7 p. blue 15 10

46. Gougah Waterfalls, Dalat.

47. Trung Sisters Monument.

1963. Pres. Ngo Dinh Diem's 62nd Birthday and Spring Festival.
S 181. **46.** 60 c. red 5 5
S 182. 1 p. indigo 5 5

1963. Women's Day.
S 183. **47.** 50 c. green 5 5
S 184. 1 p. claret 5 5
S 185. 3 p. purple 8 5
S 186. 8 p. blue 15 10

48. Harvest Scene and Campaign Emblem.

1963. Freedom from Hunger.
S 187. **48.** 50 c. red 5 5
S 188. 1 p. claret 5 5
S 189. 3 p. purple 8 5
S 190. 5 p. violet 15 8

49. Sword and Fortress.

50. Soldier and Emblem.

1963. Communal Defence and 9th Anniv. of Inaug. of Pres. Diem.
S 191. **49.** 30 c. bistre 5 5
S 192. 50 c. magenta .. 5 5
S 193. 3 p. green 10 5
S 194. 8 p. red 20 12

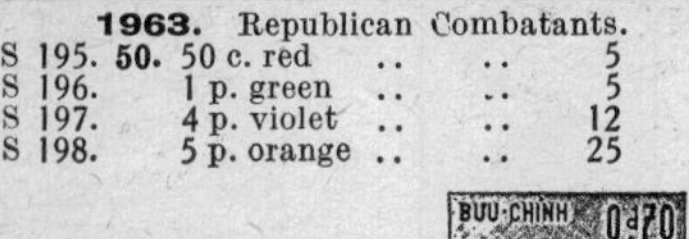

1963. Republican Combatants.

S 195. **50.** 50 c. red 5 5
S 196. 1 p. green 5 5
S 197. 4 p. violet 12 8
S 198. 5 p. orange 25 20

51. Centenary Emblem and Globe. **52.** Scales of Justice and Book.

1963. Red Cross Centenary. Cross in Red.

S 199. **51.** 50 c. blue 5 5
S 200. 1 p. red 5 5
S 201. 3 p. orange 8 5
S 202. 6 p. brown 20 15

1963. Declaration of Human Rights. 15th Anniv.

S 203. **52.** 70 c. orange 5 5
S 204. 1 p. magenta .. 5 5
S 205. 3 p. green 5 5
S 206. 8 p. ochre 15 12

53. Danhim Hydro-Electric Station.

1964. Danhim Hydro-Electric Station. Inaug.

S 207. **53.** 40 c. red 5 5
S 208. 1 p. brown 5 5
S 209. 3 p. violet 8 5
S 210. 8 p. green 15 12

54. Atomic Reactor.

1964. Peaceful Uses of Atomic Energy.

S 211. **54.** 80 c. olive 5 5
S 212. 1 p. 50 brown .. 5 5
S 213. 3 p. purple-brown .. 8 5
S 214. 7 p. blue 15 12

55. "Meteorology". **56.** "Unification".

1964. World Meteorological Day.

S 215. **55.** 50 c. ochre 5 5
S 216. 1 p. red 5 5
S 217. 1 p. 50 lake .. 8 5
S 218. 10 p. green 25 15

1964. Partition of Vietnam. 10th Anniv.

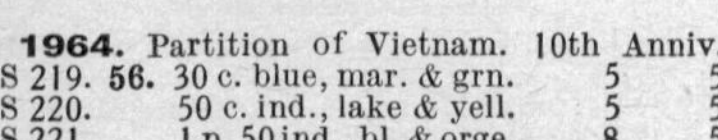

S 219. **56.** 30 c. blue, mar. & grn. 5 5
S 220. 50 c. ind., lake & yell. 5 5
S 221. 1 p. 50 ind., bl. & orge. 8 5

57. Hatien Beach.

1964.

S 222. **57.** 20 c. blue 5 5
S 223. 3 p. green 8 5

58. "Support of the People".

1964. Revolution of 1st November, 1963. 1st Anniv.

S 224. **58.** 50 c. indigo and purple 8 5
S 225. – 80 c. brown and lilac 10 5
S 226. – 3 p. chestnut and blue 20 10

DESIGNS—HORIZ. 80 c. Soldier breaking chain. VERT. 3 p. Allegory of Revolution.

59. Temple and Monument, Botanic Gardens, Saigon.

1964. Monuments and views.

S 227. **59.** 50 c. brn., grn. & blue 5 5
S 228. – 1 p. slate-blue & bistre 5 5
S 229. – 1 p. 50 green and drab 8 5
S 230. – 3 p. red, green & violet 15 8

DESIGNS: 1 p. Tomb of Minh Mang, Hue. 1 p. 50, Phan Thiet waterfront. 3 p. General Le Van Duyet Temple, Gia Dinh.

60. Face of bronze drum.

1965. Hung Vuong (legendary founder of Vietnam, 2000 B.C.).

S 231. **60.** 3 p. orange and lake .. 35 20
S 232. 100 p. violet & maroon 4·50 2·25

61. Dharmachakra and "Fire of Clemency". **62.** I.T.U. Emblem and Symbols.

1965. Buddhism.

S 233. **61.** 50 c. red 5 5
S 234. – 1 p. 50 orange, ultramarine and blue .. 5 5
S 235. – 3 p. chocolate, sepia and brown .. 8 5

DESIGNS—HORIZ. 1 p. 50, Dharmachakra, lotus and globe. VERT. 3 p. Dharmachakra and flag.

1965. I.T.U. Cent.

S 236. **62.** 1 p. red and bistre .. 5 5
S 237. 3 p. red, mar. & chest. 10 8

63. "World Solidarity". **64.** Ixora.

1965. Int. Co-operation Year.

S 238. **63.** 50 c. indigo and brown 5 5
S 239. 1 p. sepia and brown 5 5
S 240. 1 p. 50 red and grey .. 8 5

1965. Mid-Autumn Festival.

S 241. **64.** 70 c. red, grn. & emer. 5 5
S 242. – 80 c. pur., grn. & mar. 5 5
S 243. – 1 p. yell., ind. & blue 5 5
S 244. – 1 p. 50 green & olive .. 8 5
S 245. – 3 p. orange and green 15 8

FLOWERS—VERT. 80 c. Orchid. 1 p. Chrysanthemum. 3 p. "Ochna harmandii". HORIZ. 1 p. 50, Nenuphar.

65. Student and University Building.

1965. Re-opening of Vietnam University.

S 246. **65.** 50 c. brown 5 5
S 247. 1 p. green 5 5
S 248. 3 p. red 8 5
S 249. 7 p. violet 15 12

66. Young Farmers.

1965. "4-T" Rural Youth Clubs 10th Anniv.

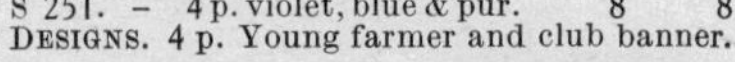

S 250. **66.** 3 p. red and green .. 8 8
S 251. – 4 p. violet, blue & pur. 8 8

DESIGNS. 4 p. Young farmer and club banner.

67. Basketball. **68.** Aerial Mast and Equipment.

1965. 3rd S.E. Asia Peninsular Games, Kuala Lumpur (Malaysia).

S 252. **67.** 50 c. cinnamon, brown and red 5 5
S 253. – 1 p. lake and brown .. 5 5
S 254. – 1 p. 50 green .. 8 5
S 255. – 10 p. lake and purple 20 15

DESIGNS: 1 p. Throwing the javelin. 1 p. 50, "Physical Culture" (gymnasts and Olympic Games' symbols). 10 p. Pole-vaulting.

1966. Saigon Microwave Station. 1st Anniv.

S 256. **68.** 3 p. sepia, blue & brn. 8 5
S 257. – 4 p. plum, red & grn. 10 5

DESIGN: 4 p. Aerial mast, Telephone dial and map.

69. Hook and Hemispheres. **70.** Help for Refugees.

1966. "Free World's Aid to Vietnam".

S 258. **69.** 3 p. lake and slate .. 5 5
S 259. 4 p. violet and brown 8 5
S 260. 6 p. blue and green .. 10 8

1966. Refugee Aid.

S 261. **70.** 3 p. olive, mar. & brn. 5 5
S 262. 7 p. violet, choc. & mar. 15 8

71. Paper "Soldiers".

1966. Wandering Soul's Festival.

S 263. **71.** 50 c. bistre, chest. & red 5 5
S 264. – 1 p. 50 red, grn. & brn. 5 5
S 265. – 3 p. verm., crim. & red 8 5
S 266. – 5 p. brn., ochre & chest. 10 8

DESIGNS: 1 p. 50, Obeisance. 3 p. Pool of candles. 5 p. Votive offering.

72. "Violinist".

1966. Ancient Musical Instruments.

S 267. **72.** 1 p. choc., mar. & brn. 5 5
S 268. – 3 p. violet and purple 5 5
S 269. – 4 p. brown and claret 8 5
S 270. – 7 p. ultram. and blue 15 8

DESIGNS: 3 p. "Harpist". 4 p. Small band. 7 p. "Flautists".

For 3 p. in smaller size, see No. S 302.

73. W.H.O. Building.

1966. W.H.O. Headquarters, Geneva. Inaug.

S 271. **73.** 50 c. plum, violet & red 5 5
S 272. – 1 p. 50 blk., blue & lake 5 5
S 273. – 8 p. blue, sepia & turq. 10 8

DESIGNS—VERT. 1 p. 50, W.H.O. Building and flag. 8 p. U.N. flag and W.H.O. Building.

74. Spade in Hand, and Soldiers. **75.** U.N.E.S.C.O. Emblem and Tree.

1966. Overthrow of Diem Government. 3rd. Anniv.

S 274. **74.** 80 c. chestnut & bistre 5 5
S 275. – 1 p. 50 mar., red & yell. 5 5
S 276. – 3 p. grn., brn. & chest. 8 5
S 277. – 4 p. lake, black & plum 12 8

DESIGNS—HORIZ. 1 p. 50, Agricultural workers, soldier and flag. VERT. 3 p. Soldier, tractor and labourers. 4 p. Soldier and horseman.

1966. U.N.E.S.C.O. 20th Anniv.

S 278. **75.** 1 p. brown and lake .. 5 5
S 279. – 3 p. chest., turq. & blue 5 5
S 280. – 7 p. indigo, turq. & red 12 10

DESIGNS—VERT. 3 p. Globe and laurel sprigs. HORIZ. 7 p. Pagoda.

76. Cashew Apples. **77.** Phan-boi-Chau.

1967. Exotic Fruits.

S 281. **76.** 50 c. red, green & blue 5 5
S 282. – 1 p. 50 orge., grn. & brn. 5 5
S 283. – 3 p. brown, grn. & choc. 5 5
S 284. – 20 p. olive, grn. & lake 25 20

FRUITS—HORIZ. 1 p. 50, Bitter "cucumbers". 3 p. Cinnamon apples. 20 p. Areca-nuts.

1967. Vietnamese Patriots.

S 285. **77.** 1 p. mar., chest. & crim. 5 5
S 286. – 20 p. blk., vio. & grn. 30 20

DESIGN: 20 p. Phan Chau Trinh (portrait and making speech).

78. Itinerant Merchant. **79.** Pottery-making.

1967. Life of the People.

S 287. **78.** 50 c. ultram., bl. & grn. 5 5
S 288. – 1 p. vio., grn. & myrtle 5 5
S 289. – 3 p. lake and red .. 5 5
S 290. – 8 p. violet and red .. 15 8

DESIGNS: 1 p. Market-place. 3 p. Horse-cab. 8 p. Pastoral activities.

1967. Arts and Crafts. Multicoloured.

S 291. 50 c. Type **79** 5 5
S 292. 1 p. 50 Wicker basket and vase 5 5
S 293. 3 p. Weavers and potters 5 5
S 294. 35 p. Baskets and pottery 45 35

The 3 p. is a horiz. design.

80. Wedding Procession.

1967. Vietnamese Wedding.

S 295. **80.** 3 p. red, violet & pur. 5 5

81. "Culture".

1967. Foundation of Vietnamese Cultural Institute.
S 296. **81.** 10 p. black, red, blue and grey-blue .. 15 8

82. "Freedom and Justice". 83. Lions Emblem and Pagoda.

1967. Democratic Elections. Multicoloured.
S 297. 4 p. Type **82** 5 5
S 298. 5 p. Vietnamese and hands casting votes .. 8 5
S 299. 30 p. Two Vietnamese with Constitution and flaming torch 40 30

1967. Lions Int. 50th Anniv.
S 300. **83.** 3 p. multicoloured .. 5 5

84. Class on Globe.

1967. World Literacy Day (Sept. 8th).
S 301. **84.** 3 p. multicoloured .. 5 5

1967. Mobile Post Office Inaug. As No. S 268 but smaller size 23 × 17 mm.
S 302. 3 p. violet and purple .. 80 80

85. Tractor.

1968. Rural Development. Multicoloured.
S 303. 1 p. Type **85** 5 5
S 304. 9 p. Bulldozer 10 8
S 305. 10 p. Workers with wheel-barrow and tractor .. 15 8
S 306. 20 p. Building construction 25 15

86. W.H.O. Emblem.

1968. W.H.O. 20th Anniv.
S 307. **86.** 10 p. yell., blk. & grn. 12 8

87. Flags of Allied Nations.

1968. Thanks for International Aid. Mult.
S 308. 1 p. Handclasp, flags and soldiers 5 5
S 309. 1 p. 50 S.E.A.T.O. emblem and flags .. 5 5
S 310. 3 p. Handclasp & flags 5 5
S 311. 50 p. Type **87**. .. 45 35

88. Farmers, Farm, Factory and Transport. **89.** Human Rights Emblem.

1968. Development of Private Ownership. Multicoloured.
S 318. 80 c. Type **88** .. 5 5
S 319. 2 p. Motor vehicles and labourers 5 5
S 320. 10 p. Tractor and tri-car 10 8
S 321. 30 p. Motor vehicles and labourers 40 15

1968. Human Rights Year. Multicoloured.
S 322. 10 p. Type **89** .. 8 5
S 323. 16 p. Men of all races acclaiming Human Rights Emblem .. 15 8

90. Children with U.N.I.C.E.F. "Kite".

1968. U.N.I.C.E.F. Day. Multicoloured.
S 324. 6 p. Type **90** 8 5
S 325. 16 p. Mother and Child 15 8

91. Train, Map and Mechanical Loader. **92.** Peasant Woman.

1968. Re-opening of Trans-Vietnam Railway. Multicoloured.
S 326. 1 p. 50 Type **91** .. 5 5
S 327. 3 p. Type **91** 5 5
S 328. 9 p. Train and permanent way workers .. 8 5
S 329. 20 p. As No. S 328 .. 20 12

1969. Vietnamese Women.
S 331. **92.** 50 c. violet, ochre & bl. 5 5
S 332. – 1 p. brown & green .. 5 5
S 333. – 3 p. blk., bl. and sepia 5 5
S 334. – 20 p. black, lake, purple and green .. 20 15
DESIGNS—VERT. 1 p. Tradeswoman. 20 p. "Ladies of fashion". HORIZ. 3 p. Nurse.

93. Family welcoming Soldier. **94.** Vietnamese and Scales of Justice.

1969. "Open-arms" National Unity Campaign. Multicoloured.
S 335. 2 p. Soldier and militiaman 5 5
S 336. 50 p. Type **93** 45 5

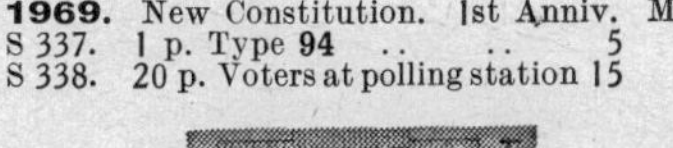

1969. New Constitution. 1st Anniv. Mult.
S 337. 1 p. Type **94** 5 5
S 338. 20 p. Voters at polling station 15 8

95. Mobile Post Office Van in Street.

1969. Vietnamese Mobile Post Offices System. Multicoloured.
S 339. 1 p. Type **95** 5 5
S 340. 3 p. Clerk serving customers 5 5
S 341. 4 p. Child with letter, and mobile post office .. 5 5
S 342. 20 p. Queue at mobile post office, and post mark 15 10

HAVE YOU READ THE NOTES AT THE BEGINNING OF THIS CATALOGUE?
These often provide answers to the enquiries we receive.

96. Djarai Woman.

1969. Ethnic Minorities' Statute. 2nd Anniv. Multicoloured.
S 343. 1 p. Type **96** 5 5
S 344. 6 p. Mnong-Gar woman 10 8
S 345. 50 p. Bahnar man .. 85 35

97. "Civilians to Soldiers". **98.** I.L.O. Emblem and Globe.

1969. General Mobilisation.
S 346. **97.** 1 p. 50 multicoloured .. 5 5
S 347. – 3 p. multicoloured .. 5 5
S 348. – 5 p. brown, red & yell. 5 5
S 349. – 10 p. multicoloured .. 10 5
DESIGNS: 3 p. Bayonet practice. 5 p. Recruits arriving at depot. 10 p. Happy conscripts.

1969. Int. Labour Organization. 50th Anniv.
S 350. **98.** 6 p. black, grey & green 5 5
S 351. 20 p. black, grey & red 20 10

99. Imperial Palace, Hue.

1970. Reconstruction of Hue.
S 552. **99.** 1 p. blue and brown .. 40 40

100. Hornbill.

1970. Birds of Vietnam. Multicoloured.
S 353. 2 p. Type **100** 5 5
S 354. 6 p. Chim Ao Da 10 8
S 355. 7 p. Hong Hoang (hornbill) 10 8
S 356. 30 p. Chim Se Se 50 25

101. Ruined House and Family.

1970. Aid for Victims of Communist Tet Offensive. Multicoloured.
S 357. 10 p. Type **101** 10 8
S 358. 20 p. Refugee family, and First Aid 20 15

102. Traditional Costume. **103.** Builders and Pagodas.

1970. Vietnamese Traditional Costumes. Multicoloured.
S 359. 1 p. Type **102** 5 5
S 360. 2 p. Seated woman (horiz.) 5 5
S 361. 3 p. Three women with carved lion (horiz.) .. 5 5
S 362. 100 p. Man and woman (horiz.) .. .. 1·00 55

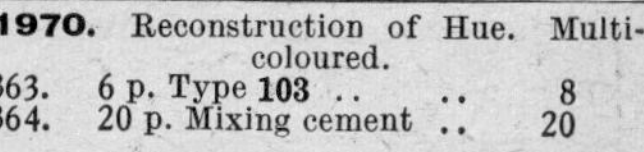

1970. Reconstruction of Hue. Multicoloured.
S 363. 6 p. Type **103** 8 5
S 364. 20 p. Mixing cement .. 20 15

104. Ploughing Paddyfield. **105.** Scaffolding and New Building.

1970. "Land to the Tiller". Agrarian Reform Law.
S 365. **104.** 6 p. blk., grn. & brn. 8 5

1970. Reconstruction after Tet Offensive. Multicoloured.
S 366. 8 p. Type **105** 8 5
S 367. 16 p. Construction workers 15 10

106. A.P.Y. Symbol.

1970. Asian Productivity Year.
S 368. **106.** 10 p. multicoloured 10 5

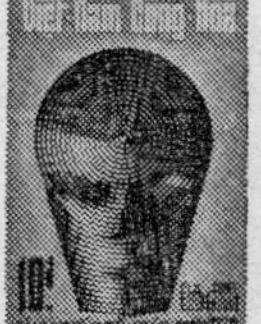

107. Nguyen Dinh Chieu and Poems. **108.** I.E.Y. Emblem.

1970. Nguyen Dinh Chieu (poet). Commem.
S 369. **107.** 6 p. brn., red & violet 8 5
S 370. 10 p. brn., red & grn. 10 5

1970. Int. Education Year.
S 371. **108.** 10 p. blk., yell. & brn. 10 5

109. Senate House. **110.** Two Dancers.

1970. Ninth Council Meeting and 6th General Assembly of Asiatic Interparliamentary Union, Saigon. Multicoloured.
S 372. 6 p. Type **109** 8 5
S 373. 10 p. House of Representatives 10 5

1971. Vietnamese Traditional Dances.
S 374. **110.** 2 p. multicoloured .. 5 5
S 375. – 6 p. brn., blue & grn. 8 5
S 376. – 7 p. red, blue & brn... 10 8
S 377. – 10 p. multicoloured .. 15 10
DESIGNS—HORIZ. 6 p. Drum dance. 7 p. Drum dancers in various positions. VERT. 10 p. Flower dance.

111. Paddyfield, Peasants and Agrarian Law.

1971. "Land to the Tiller" Agrarian Reform Law. 1st Anniv. Multicoloured.
S 378. 2 p. Type **111** 5 5
S 379. 3 p. Tractor and Law .. 5 5
S 380. 16 p. Peasants ringing Law 15 8

112. Postal Courier. **114.** Deer.

113. Armed Forces on Map of Vietnam.

1971. History of Vietnam Postal Service. Multicoloured.

S 381. 2 p. Type 112 .. .. 5 5
S 382. 6 p. Mounted courier with banner 5 5

1971. Armed Forces Day.

S 383. 113. 3 p. multicoloured .. 5 5
S 384. 40 p. multicoloured .. 45 25

1971. Vietnamese Fauna. Multicoloured.

S 385. 9 p. Type 114 .. .. 8 5
S 386. 30 p. Tiger 30 15

115. Rice Harvesters.

1971. " The Rice Harvest ".

S 387. 115. 1 p. multicoloured .. 5 5
S 388. – 30 p. lilac, blk. & red 30 15
S 389. – 40 p. brn., yell. & blue 40 20

DESIGNS: 30p Threshing and winnowing rice. 40 p. Harvesters in paddyfield.

116. New U.P.U. H.Q. Building.

1971. New U.P.U. Headquarters Building, Berne.

S 390. 116. 20 p. multicoloured .. 25 15

117. Ca Nau.

118. Cycle postman delivering letter.

1971. Vietnam Fishes. Multicoloured.

S 391. 2 p. Ca Bong (vert.) .. 5 5
S 392. 10 p. Type 117 .. .. 12 5
S 393. 100 p. Ca Ong Tien .. 1·10 65

1971. Development of Rural Post System. Multicoloured.

S 387. 5 p. " Local delivery " .. 5 5
S 388. 10 p. Symbolic crane .. 15 8
S 389. 20 p. Type 118 .. .. 20 12

119. Trawl Net.

1972. Vietnamese Fishing Industry. Mult.

S 397. 4 p. Fishermen in Boat, and Modern Trawler .. 5 5
S 398. 7 p. Fishermen hauling net 8 5
S 399. 50 p. Type 119 .. .. 55 30

120. Community Workers.

121. Emperor Quang-Trung.

1972. Community Development Projects.

S 400. 120. 3 p. multicoloured .. 5 5
S 401. 8 p. multicoloured .. 8 5

1972. Emperor Quang-Trung (victor of Dong Da). Commemoration.

S 402. 121. 6 p. multicoloured .. 5 5
S 403. 20 p. multicoloured .. 25 15

122. Harvesting Rice.

1972. Farmer's Day. Multicoloured.

S 405. 1 p. Type 122 .. .. 5 5
S 406. 10 p. Sowing rice .. 10 8

123. Jetliner over Saigon.

1972. Viet-Nam Airlines. 20th Anniv. Mult.

S 407. 10 p. Jetliner over Dalat 12 8
S 408. 10 p. Jetliner over Ha Tien 12 8
S 409. 10 p. Jetliner over Hue .. 12 8
S 410. 10 p. Type 123 .. .. 12 8
S 411. 25 p. As No. S 407 .. 30 20
S 412. 20 p. As. No S 408 .. 30 20
S 413. 25 p. As No. S 409 .. 30 20
S 414. 25 p. Type 123 .. .. 30 20

124. Vietnamese Scholar.

125. Sentry.

1972. Vietnamese Scholars. Multicoloured.

S 415. 5 p Type 124 .. .. 5 5
S 416. 20 p. Scholar with pupils 20 12
S 417. 50 p. Scholar with scroll 50 25

1972. Civilian Defence Force. Multicoloured.

S 418. 2 p. Type 125 .. .. 5 5
S 419. 6 p. Young volunteer and badge (horiz.) 5 5
S 420. 20 p. Volunteers at rifle practice 20 12

126. Hands supporting Savings Bank.

1972. Treasury Bonds Savings Scheme.

S 421. 126. 10 p. multicoloured 10 5
S 422. 25 p. multicoloured 20 15

127. Pikeman.

128. Wounded Soldier.

1972. Traditional Vietnamese Frontier Guards. Multicoloured.

S 423. 10 p. Three guards with horse (horiz.) 8 5
S 424. 30 p. Type 127 .. .. 15 10
S 425. 40 p. Guards on parade (horiz.) 90 60

1972. Vietnamese War Veterans. Mult.

S 426. 9 p. Type 128 .. .. 8 5
S 427. 16 p. Soldier on crutches 15 10
S 428. 100 p. Veteran's memorial 90 60

129. Soldiers on Tank, and Memorial.

1972. Victory at Binh Long. Multicoloured.

S 429. 5 p. Type 129 .. .. 5 5
S 430. 10 p. Soldiers on map of An Loc (vert.) .. 10 5

130. " Books for Everyone ".

1972. Int. Book Year. Multicoloured.

S 431. 2 p. Type 130 .. .. 5 5
S 432. 4 p. Book Year emblems encircling Globe .. 5 5
S 433. 5 p. Emblem, books and Globe 5 5

131.

132.

" 200,000th Returnees ". Soldiers raising Flag.

1973. 200,000th Returnees under " Open Arms " National Unity Campaign.

S 434. 131. 10 p. multicoloured .. 10 5

1973. Victory at Quang Tri. Multicoloured.

S 435. 3 p. Type 132 .. .. 5 5
S 436. 10 p. Map and defenders 10 8

133. Satellite and Globe.

1973. World Meteorological Day.

S 437. 133. 1 p. multicoloured .. 5 5

134. Programme Emblem and Farm-workers.

1973. Five-Year Agricultural Development Programme. Multicoloured.

S 438. 2 p. Type 134 .. .. 5 5
S 439. 5 p. Ploughing in paddy-field 5 5

135. Emblem and H.Q. Paris.

1973. International Criminal Police Organization. (Interpol). 50th Anniv. Mult.

S 440. 1 p. Type 135 .. .. 5 5
S 441. 2 p. " INTERPOL 1923 1973 " 5 5
S 442. 25 p. Emblem and view of Headquarters (different) 15 10

136. I.T.U. Emblem.

137. Lamp in Hand.

1973. World Telecommunications Day.

S 443. 136. 1 p. multicoloured .. 5 5
S 444. – 2 p. black and blue .. 5 5
S 445. – 3 p. multicoloured .. 5 5

DESIGNS: 2 p. Globe. 3 p. I.T.U. Emblem in frame.

1973. National Development.

S 446. 137. 8 p. multicoloured .. 5 5
S 447. – 10 p. blue, blk. & brn. 5 5
S 448. – 15 p. multicoloured .. 5 5

DESIGNS: 10 p. " Agriculture, Industry and Fisheries ". 15 p. Workers on power pylon.

INDEX

Countries can be quickly located by referring to the index at the end of this volume.

138. Water-buffaloes and Calf.

1973. " Year of the Buffalo ". Multicoloured.

S 449. 5 p. Type 138 .. .. 5 5
S 450. 10 p. Water-buffalo .. 5 5

139. Flame Emblem and " Races of the World ".

1973. Declaration of Human Rights. 25th Anniv. Multicoloured.

S 451. 15 p. Type 139 .. .. 12 5
S 452. 100 p. Flame emblem and scales of justice (vert.) 30 25

140. Emblem within " 25 ".

1973. W.H.O. 25th Anniv.

S 453. 140. 8 p. multicoloured .. 5 5
S 454. – 15 p. blue, red & brn. 5 5

DESIGN: 15 p. W.H.O. emblem and inscription.

141. Sampan crossing River.

1974. Vietnamese Sampan Women. Mult.

S 455. 5 p. Type 141 .. .. 5 5
S 456. 10 p. Sampan passengers 5 5

142. Flags and Soldiers of Allies.

1974. Allies Day. Multicoloured.

S 457. 8 p. Type 142 .. .. 5 5
S 458. 15 p. Soldiers and flags .. 5 5
S 459. 15 p. Allied Nations Monument 5 5
S 460. 60 p. Raising South Vietnamese flag, and map (vert.) 15 12

143. Trung Sisters on Elephant.

1974. Trung Sisters' Festival.

S 461. 143. 8 p. grn., yell. & blk. 5 5
S 462. 15 p. red, yell. & blk. 5 5
S 463. 80 p. bl., pink & blk. 20 15

144. Pres. Thieu holding Agrarian Reform Law.

1974. Farmers' Day. Multicoloured.

S 464. 10 p. Type **144** 5 5

S 465. 20 p. Farm-workers (32×22 mm.).. .. 5 5

S 466. 70 p. Girl harvesting rice (22×32 mm.).. .. 15 12

145. King Hung Vuong.

1974. King Hung Vuong (first Vietnamese monarch). Commemoration. Multicoloured.

S 467. 20 p. Type **145** 5 5

S 468. 100 p. Banner inscribed "Hung Vuong, National Founder" 30 25

146. National Library. **147.** Allied Nations Memorial, Saigon.

1974. New National Library Building. Mult.

S 469. 10 p. Type **146** 5 5

S 470. 15 p. Library and Phoenix bas-relief 5 5

1974. Surch.

S 489. **115.** 25 p. on 1 p. mult. ..

S 504. **133.** 25 p. on 1 p. mult...

S 490. **135.** 25 p. on 1 p. mult...

S 505. **136.** 25 p. on 1 p. mult...

S 478. – 25 p. on 7 p. red, blue and brown (No. S 376)

S 506. **142.** 25 p. on 8 p. mult..

S 507. – 25 p. on 16 p. mult. (No. S 380) ..

S 471. – 25 p. on 16 p. mult. (No. S 427) ..

1974. International Aid Day. Multicoloured.

S 472. 10 p. Type **147** 5 5

S 473. 20 p. Flags on crane (horiz.) 5 5

S 474. 60 p. Crate on hoist .. 20 15

148. "Tourist Attractions".

1974. Tourism. Multicoloured.

S 475. 5 p. Type **148** 5 5

S 476. 10 p. Xom Bong Bridge Nhatrang 5 5

S 477. 15 p. Thien Mu Pagoda, Hue (vert.) 5 5

149. "Rynchostylla is gigantea".

1974. Orchids. Multicoloured.

S 479. 10 p. Type **149** 5 5

S 480. 20 p. "Cypripedium callosum" (vert.) .. 5 5

S 481. 200 p. "Dendrobium nobile" 40 30

150. "International Exchange of Mail".

1974. Universal Postal Union. Centenary. Multicoloured.

S 486. 20 p. Type **150** 5 5

S 487. 30 p. "U.P.U. letter" and Hemispheres" .. 10 8

S 488. 300 p. U.P.U. emblem and Vietnamese girl (vert.) 60 50

151. Hien Lam Pavilion, Hue.

1975. Historical Sites. Multicoloured.

S 491. 25 p. Type **151** 5 5

S 492. 30 p. Throne Room, Imperial Palace, Hue 8 5

S 493. 60 p. Tu Duo's Pavilion, Hue 12 10

152. Conference Emblem.

1975. International Conference on Children and National Development, Saigon. Mult.

S 494. 20 p. Type **152** 5 5

S 495. 70 p. Vietnamese family (32×22 mm.).. .. 15 12

153. Unicorn Dance.

1975. Vietnamese New Year Festival. Mult.

S 496. 20 p. Type **153** 5 5

S 497. 30 p. Letting-off firecrackers (vert.) .. 10 8

S 498. 100 p. New Year greeting custom (vert.) .. 25 20

154. Military Mandarin ("San Hau" play).

1975. "Hat Bo" Vietnamese Traditional Theatre. Multicoloured.

S 499. 25 p. Type **154** 5 5

S 500. 40 p. Two characters from "Tam Ha Nam Duong" (vert.) 10 8

S 501. 100 p. Heroine, "Luu Kim Giai Gia Tho Chau" (vert.).. .. 25 20

155. Produce from Export and Map.

1975. Farmers Day. Multicoloured.

S 502. 10 p. Type **155** 5 5

S 503. 50 p. Ancient and modern irrigation 12 10

POSTAGE DUE STAMPS

D 1. Dragon. **D 2.** Butterfly. **D 3.** Butterflies.

1955.

SD 1. D 1. 2 p. yell. & magenta 10 10

SD 2. 3 p. turquoise & vio. 15 15

SD 3. 5 p. yellow & violet 20 20

SD 4. 10 p. red and green 30 25

SD 14. – 20 p. green and red 80 45

SD 15. – 30 p. yellow & grn. 1·10 80

SD 16. – 50 p. yellow & brn. 1·60 1·40

SD 17. – 100 p. yellow & vio. 3·25 3·25

The 20 p. to 100 p. are inscribed "BUU-CHINH" instead of "TIMBRE TAXE".

1968.

SD 312. D **2.** 50 c. multicoloured 8 8

SD 313. 1 p. multicoloured 8 8

SD 314. 2 p. multicoloured 12 12

SD 315. D **3.** 3 p. multicoloured 15 15

SD 316. 5 p. multicoloured 40 40

SD 317. 10 p. multicoloured 70 70

1974. Surch.

SD 482. D **3.** 5 p. on 3 p. mult...

SD 483. D **2.** 10 p. on 50 c. mult.

SD 484. 40 p. on 1 p. mult.

SD 485. 60 p. on 2 p. mult.

MILITARY FRANK STAMPS

MF 1. Soldier and Barracks.

1961. No value indicated. Roul.

SMF 142. MF 1. (–) yell., brown green & black 1·75 1·40

SMF 143. (–) yell., brown, and green .. 1·75 1·40

NATIONAL FRONT FOR THE LIBERATION OF SOUTH VIETNAM

The National Front for the Liberation of South Vietnam was formed by the Communists, known as the Vietcong, in December 1960. With the support of troops from North Vietnam the Vietcong gradually gained control of more and more territory within South Vietnam until the surrender of the last South Vietnamese Republican forces in May 1975 enabled them to take control of the entire country. The following stamps were used in those areas controlled by the National Liberation Front.

1963. 100 xu = 1 dong.

The value of the N·L.F. dong fluctuated considerably and was not on parity with the North Vietnamese currency.

1. Vietcong Flag.

1963. National Liberation Front. 3rd Anniv.

NLF 1. **1.** 20 x. multicoloured (English inscr.) .. 2·25 1·50

NLF 2. 20 x. multicoloured (French inscr.) .. 2·25 1·50

NLF 3. 20 x. multicoloured (Spanish inscr.) .. 2·25 1·50

2. Attack on Village.

1963. Revolutionary Struggle in South Vietnam. 3rd Anniv. Multicoloured.

NLF 4. 10 x. Type **2** .. .. 1·25 75

NLF 5. 10 x. Attack on U.S. helicopter .. .. 1·25 75

3. Demonstrators with Banner.

1964. National Liberation Front. 4th Anniv.

NLF 6. 10 x. Type **3** 75 75

NLF 7. 20 x. multicoloured .. 1·00 1·00

NLF 8. 30 x. green and blue .. 2·25 1·25

DESIGNS: 20 x. Harvesting rice. 30 x. Sinking of U.S.S. "Card".

4. Attack on Bien Hoa Airfield.

1965. National Liberation Front. 5th Anniv.

NLF 9. 10 x. Type **4** 50 50

NLF 10. 20 x. black, grey & red 1·00 1·00

NLF 11. 40 x. multicoloured .. 3·00 3·00

DESIGNS: 20 x. Nguyen Van Troi facing firing squad. 40 x. Vietcong flags.

5. Vietcong Soldiers on U.S. Tanks. **6.** "Guerrilla".

1967. National Liberation Front. 7th Anniv. Multicoloured.

NLF 12. 20 x. Type **5** 50 50

NLF 13. 20 x. Vietcong guerrillas (horiz.) 50 50

NLF 14. 30 x. Crowd with banners 70 70

1968. "The Struggle for Freedom". Paintings. Multicoloured.

NLF 15. 10 x. Type **6** 15 15

NLF 16. 20 x. "Jungle Patrol" (horiz.) 20 20

NLF 17. 30 x. "Woman Soldier" 25 25

NLF 18. 40 x. "Towards the Future" (horiz.) .. 30 30

7. Casting Votes.

1968. National Liberation Front. 8th Anniv. Multicoloured.

NLF 19. 20 x. Type **7** 20 20

NLF 20. 20 x. Bazooka crew and burning aircraft .. 20 20

NLF 21. 30 x. Vietcong flag and crowd (French inscr.) 25 25

NLF 22. 30 x. Vietcong flag and crowd (English inscr.) 25 25

8. Lenin and Vietcong Flag.

1970. Lenin. Birth Cent. (1970).

NLF 23. **8.** 20 x. multicoloured 12 8

NLF 24. 30 x. multicoloured 20 10

NLF 25. 50 x. multicoloured 30 20

NLF 26. 2 d. multicoloured.. 1·00 60

9. Ho Chi Minh watering Kainito Plant. **10.** Vietcong "Lightning Flash".

1970. Ho Chi Minh. 80th Birth Anniv.

NLF 27. **9.** 20 x. multicoloured 12 8

NLF 28. 30 x. multicoloured 20 10

NLF 29. 50 x. multicoloured 30 20

NLF 30. 2 d. multicoloured.. 1·00 60

1970. National Liberation Front. 10th Anniv.

NLF 31. **10.** 20 x. multicoloured 10 8

NLF 32. 30 x. multicoloured 15 12

NLF 33. 50 x. multicoloured 20 15

NLF 34. 3 d. multicoloured 1·25 75

11. Home Guards defending Village.

1971. People's Liberation Armed Forces. 10th Anniv. Multicoloured.

NLF 35.		20 x. Type **11**	10	8
NLF 36.		30 x. Surrender of U.S. tank	15	12
NLF 37.		50 x. Agricultural workers	20	15
NLF 38.		1 d. Vietcong ambush	40	30

12. Children in School. 13. Harvesting Rice.

14. Ho Chi Minh with Vietcong Soldiers.

1971. Provisional Government. 2nd Anniv. Life in Liberated Areas. Multicoloured.

NLF 39.		20 x. Type **12**	10	8
NLF 40.		30 x. Women sewing Vietcong flag ..	15	12
NLF 41.		40 x. Fortifying village	15	12
NLF 42.		50 x. Medical clinic ..	20	15
NLF 43.		1 d. Harvesting	40	30

1974. Provisional Government. 5th Anniv. Multicoloured.

NLF 44.		10 p. Type **13** ..	5	5
NLF 45.		10 p. Demonstrators with banner ..	5	5
NLF 46.		10 p. Schoolchildren ..	5	5
NLF 47.		10 p. Women home guards	5	5
NLF 48.		10 p. Vietcong conference delegate ..	5	5
NLF 49.		10 p. Soldiers and tanks	5	5
NLF 50.		10 p. Type **14** ..	5	5
NLF 51.		20 p. Type **14**	8	5

For other values as Type **14**, see Nos. NLF 57/60.

15. Ho Chi Minh watering Kainito Plant.

1975. Ho Chi Minh. 85th Birth Anniv. (1st issue).

NLF 52.	**15.**	5 d. multicoloured	5	5
NLF 53.		10 d. multicoloured	8	5

1975. Ho Chi Minh. 85th Birth Anniv. (2nd issue) As T 282 North Vietnam, but inscr. " MIEN NAM VIET NAM ".

NLF 55.		30 d. multicoloured ..	20	15
NLF 56.		60 d. multicoloured ..	40	30

1975. National Front for Liberation of South Vietnam. 15th Anniv. As T **14** but 35½ × 26 mm.

NLF 57.	**14.**	15 d. black & green	10	8
NLF 58.		30 d. black and red	20	10
NLF 59.		60 d. black and blue	40	30
NLF 60		300 d. black & yell.	2·00	1·90

16. " Cosos nucifera ".

1976. Fruits. Multicoloured.

NLF 61.		20 d. Type **16** ..	12	10
NLF 62.		30 d. " Garcina magostana "	20	15
NLF 63.		60 d. " Mangifera indica "	40	30

1976. First Elections to United National Assembly. As Nos. N 858/60 of North Vietnam, but inscr. " MIEN NAM VIET NAM ".

NLF 64.		6 x. red and blue (as N 858)	5	5
NLF 65.		6 x. yellow and red (as N 859) ..	5	5
NLF 66.		12 x. red and green (as N 860)	5	5

17. Flag of Provisional Revolutionary Government.

1976. Liberation of South Vietnam. First Anniv.

NLF 67.	**17.**	30 d. multicoloured	20	15

1976. Unified National Assembly. First Session. As Nos. N 861/2 of North Vietnam, but inscr. " MIEN NAM VIET NAM ".

NLF 68.		6 x. brn., red & yell.	5	5
NLF 69.		12 x. turq., red & yell.	5	5

The unified National Assembly proclaimed the reunification of Vietnam on 2 July 1976 and the united country was then known as the Socialist Republic of Vietnam.

NORTH VIETNAM

(Viet-Nam Democratic Republic.)

Issues before October 1954 were made in Northern Tongking (or in Central Annan where specified). From 21st July, 1954, French troops withdrew from north of the 17th Parallel, and the Ho Chi Minh Government assumed complete control.

1946. 100 cents. = 1 dong.
1959. 100 xu = 1 dong.

GUM. All stamps, except No. N 1, were issued without gum unless otherwise stated.

1946. No. 190 of Indo-China optd. **V VIET-NAM N DAN-CHU CONG-HOA BUU CHINH.**

N 1.		25 c. blue	8·00	8·00

1. Ho Chi Minh. 2. Ho Chi Minh and Vietnam Map.

1948.

N 2a.	**1.**	2 d. brown	4·50	9·00
N 3a.		5 d. red	4·50	9·00

1951. Imperf. or perf.

N 4.	**2.**	100 d. green	75	75
N 5.		100 d. brown	75	75
N 6.		200 d. red	75	75

3. Ho Chi Minh. 4. Blacksmith.

1952. Issue for Central Annam. Unissued values surch. in figures. Imperf.

N 7.	**3.**	30 d. on 5 d. green ..	75·00	60·00
N 8.		60 d. on 1 d. violet ..	90·00	75·00

1952. Issue for Central Annam. Imperf.

N 9.	**3.**	300 d. blue	65·00	65·00
N 10.		500 d. red	75·00	75·00

1953. Production Campaign.

N 11.	**4.**	100 d. violet	70	20
N 12.		500 d. brown	1·10	75

5. Malenkov, Ho Chi Minh, Mao Tse-Tung and Flags.

1954. Friendship Month.

N 14.	**5.**	100 d. red	2·75	2·75

6.

1954.

N 15.	**6.**	50 d. brown and red ..	2·00	2·00
N 16.		100 d. red and yellow ..	2·50	2·50

7. Battlefield.

1954. Dien Bien Phu Victory. Imperf. or perf.

N 16a.	**7.**	10 d. bistre and red ..	1·25	40
N 17a.		50 d. ochre and red ..	1·25	75
N 18d.		150 d. blue and brown ..	1·25	90

See also No. NO 24.

1954. (a) Handstamped thus: **10 dNH.**

N 19.	**2.**	10 d. on 100 d. green ..	70	70
N 20.		10 d. on 100 d. brown ..	2·75	2·75
N 21.		20 d. on 200 d. red ..	70	70

(b) Handstamped thus: **10 d.**

N 22.	**2.**	10 d. on 100 d. green ..	1·10	1·10
N 25.		10 d. on 100 d. brown ..	2·25	2·25
N 28.		20 d. on 200 d. red ..	2·50	2·50

See also Nos. N 46/9.

8. Pagoda of the Lost Sword, Hanoi.

1955. Proclamation of Hanoi as Capital.

N 30.	**8.**	10 d. blue	65	65
N 31.		50 d. green	65	65
N 32.		150 d. red	1·10	1·10

9. Distribution of Title Deeds.

1955. Land Reform.

N 33.	**9.**	5 d. green	40	1·40
N 34.		10 d. grey	55	55
N 35.		20 d. orange	90	90
N 36.		50 d. magenta	2·00	2·00
N 37.		100 d. brown	3·25	3·25

See also Nos. NO 39/9.

10. Crowd Welcoming Train.

1956. Hanoi-China Railway Re-opening.

N 38.	**10.**	100 d. blue	1·75	1·75
N 39.		200 d. turquoise ..	1·90	1·90
N 40.		300 d. violet	4·00	4·00
N 41.		500 d. brown	4·50	4·50

11. Parade, Ba Dinh Square, Hanoi.

1956. Return of Govt. to Hanoi.

N 42.	**11.**	1,000 d. violet ..	10·00	8·00
N 43.		1,500 d. blue ..	12·00	11·00
N 44.		2,000 d. turq.-blue ..	14·00	11·00
N 45.		3,000 d. turq.-green ..	16·00	12·00

1956. Surch. thus: **10 d** in frame.

N 46.	**2.**	10 d. on 100 d. green ..	2·75	2·75
N 48.		10 d. on 100 d. brown ..	6·50	6·50
N 49.		20 d. on 200 d. red ..	4·00	4·00

12. Tran Danh Ninh (patriot). 13. Mac Thi Buoi.

1956. 1st Anniv. of Tran Danh Ninh's Death.

N 50.	**12.**	5 d. green	50	30
N 51.		10 d. red	60	40
N 52.		20 d. brown	90	50
N 53.		100 d. blue	1·10	65

1956. Mac Thi Buoi (guerilla heroine). 5th Death Anniv.

N 54.	**13.**	1,000 d. red ..	2·75	2·00
N 55.		2,000 d. brown ..	3·75	2·75
N 56.		4,000 d. green ..	7·00	4·25
N 57.		5,000 d. blue ..	8·50	7·00

14. Bai Thuong Dam. 15. Cotton Mill.

1956. Reconstruction of Bai Thuong Dam.

N 58.	**14.**	100 d. violet and brown	1·00	65
N 59.		200 d. claret and black	1·40	90
N 60.		300 d. red and lake	2·25	1·75

1956. Surch. **50 DONG.**

N 61.	**1.**	50 d. on 5 d. red ..	5·00	8·00

1957. Opening of Nam-Dinh Mill. 1st Anniv.

N 62.	**15.**	100 d. brown and lake	80	50
N 63.		200 d. slate and blue ..	1·25	1·10
N 64.		300 d. pale grn. & grn.	1·40	1·25

16. Pres. Ho Chi Minh. 17. Arms of Republic.

1957. President's 67th Birthday.

N 65.	**16.**	20 d. green	35	25
N 66.		60 d. bistre	35	25
N 67.		100 d. blue	55	40
N 68.		300 d. brown	90	70

Nos. N 67/8 commemorate President's 67th Birthday.

1957. Democratic Republic. 12th Anniv.

N 69.	**17.**	20 d. green	55	45
N 70.		100 d. red	1·25	85

18. Congress Emblem.

1957. 4th World T.U. Congress, Leipzig.

N 71.	**18.**	300 d. purple	90	80

See also Nos. NO 69/72.

19. Presidents Voroshilov and Ho Chi Minh.

1957. Russian Revolution. 40th Anniv.
N 72. **19.** 100 d. red .. .. 1·10 70
N 73. 500 d. chocolate .. 1·75 1·00
N 74. 1,000 d. orange-red .. 3·50 2·25

20. Open-air Class. **21.** Girl Gymnast.

1958. Education Campaign.
N 75. **20.** 50 d. blue .. .. 1·40 1·10
N 76. 150 d. red .. .. 2·00 1·75
N 77. 1,000 d. brown .. 4·00 3·50

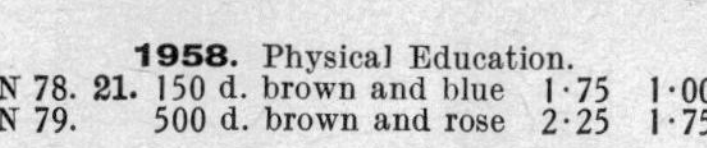

1958. Physical Education.
N 78. **21.** 150 d. brown and blue 1·75 1·00
N 79. 500 d. brown and rose 2·25 1·75

22. **23.** Congress Emblem.

1958. Labour Day.
N 80. **22.** 50 d. yellow and red.. 70 50
N 81. 150 d. red and yellow 1·50 1·25

1958. 4th Int. Congress of Democratic Women, Vienna.
N 82. **23.** 150 d. blue 60 45

24. Cup, Basket and Lace. **25.** Hanoi-Saigon Railway Reconstruction.

1958. Arts and Crafts Fair, Hanoi.
N 83. **24.** 150 d. sepia and turq. 50 40
N 84. 2,000 d. black and lilac 2·25 1·40

1958. Re-unification of Vietnam Propaganda.
N 85. **25.** 50 d. blue 30 20
N 86. 150 d. chestnut .. 40 30

26. Revolution in Hanoi.

1958. Vietnamese Revolution. 13th Anniv.
N 87. **26.** 150 d. red 40 30
N 88. 500 d. blue 75 45

27. Woman Potter.

1958. Handicrafts Exn.
N 89. **27.** 150 d. lake and rose.. 30 20
N 90. 1,000 d. choc. & ochre 1·75 75

28. Vo Thi Sau and Crowd. **29.** Tran Hung Dao.

1958. South Vietnam Resistance Movement. 13th Anniv.
N 91. **28.** 50 d. green and buff .. 45 25
N 92. 150 d. lake and orange 70 30

1958. Tran Hung Dao. 658th Death Anniv.
N 93. **29.** 150 d. grey and blue.. 30 12

30. Hanoi Factories. **31.** Harvesting Rice.

1958. Hanoi Mechanical Engineering Plant.
N 94. **30.** 150 d. sepia 30 12

1958. Mutual Aid Teams.
N 95. **31.** 150 d. lake .. .. 1·00 25
N 96. 500 d. brown .. .. 1·60 60

32. Temple of Jade. Hanoi. **33.** Furniture-makers.

1958.
N 97. **32.** 150 d. green 85 25
N 98. – 150 d. blue 35 8
N 99. – 350 d. brown .. 50 25
N 100. **32.** 2,000 d. green .. 5·50 1·40
DESIGN—HORIZ. 150 d. blue, 350 d. Bay of Halong.

1958. Furniture Co-operatives.
N 101. **33.** 150 d. blue 65 12

34. Cam Pha Coal Mines. **35.** The Trung Sisters.

1959.
N 102. **34.** 150 d. blue 35 8

1959. Trung Sisters Commem.
N 103. **35.** 5 x. red and yellow .. 10 8
N 104. 8 x. chocolate & brown 25 12

36. Mother and Child.

1959. World Peace Movement. 10th Anniv.
N 105. **36.** 12 x. violet 12 8

37. Xuan Quan Dam.

1959. Bac Hung Hai Irrigation Project.
N 106. **37.** 6 x. yell., green & vio. 40 8
N 107. 12 x. ochre, bl. & grey 1·00 15

38. Victims in Phu Loi Concentration Camp.

40. Hien-Luong Bridge. **39.** Radio Mast.

1959. The Phu Loi Massacre on 1st December 1958.
N 108. **38.** 12 x. salmon, ol. & blk. 40 8
N 109. 20 x. ochre, grey & blk. 1·00 20

1959. Me Tri Radio Station.
N 110. **39.** 3 x. green & orange.. 20 5
N 111. 12 x. sepia and blue.. 40 12

1959. Vietnam Day.
N 112. **40.** 12 x. red and black.. 25 25

41. Rifle-shooting.

DESIGNS: 6 x. Swimming. 12 x. Wrestling.

1959. Sports.
N 113. **41.** 1 x. ultram. & blue.. 15 10
N 114. – 6 x. olive and red .. 20 15
N 115. – 12 x. red and rose .. 35 25

42. Balloons. **43.** Coconuts.

1959. Chinese People's Republic. 10th Anniv.
N 116. **42.** 12 x. red, yell. & grn. 15 5

1959. Fruits. Multicoloured.
N 117. 3 x. T **43**.. .. 20 10
N 118. 12 x. Bananas 35 15
N 119. 30 x. Pineapple.. .. 60 30

44. Convair Airliner.

1959. Air.
N 120. **44.** 20 x. black and blue 1·10 65

45. Soldiers. **46.** Sailing Ship.

1959. N. Vietnam People's Army. 15th Anniv.
N 121. **45.** 12 x. yell., brn. & blue 30 15

1959. N. Vietnam Workers' Party. 30th Anniv.
N 122. **46.** 2 x. red, yellow, green and drab 20 12
N 123. 12 x. red, yellow, blue and drab 70 50

47. Girl in " E—De " Costume. **48.** Women of Vietnam.

1960. National Costumes.
N 124. **47.** 2 x. red, blue & pur. 12 8
N 125. – 10 x. blue, orge. & grn. 15 10
N 126. – 12 x. blue and brown 20 15
N 127. – 12 x. indigo and buff 20 15
COSTUMES: No. N 125, " Meo "; No. N 126, " Thai "; No. N 127, " Tay ".

1960. National Census.
N 128. **48.** 1 x. green 5 5
N 129. – 12 x. brown and red 12 5
DESIGN: 12 x. Workers and factories.

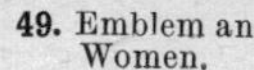

49. Emblem and Women. **50.** Hung Vuong Temple.

1960. Int. Women's Day. 50th Anniv.
N 130. **49** 12 x. multicoloured.. 12 5

1960. Hung Vuong Anniversary Day.
N 131. **50.** 12 x. green and buff 90 60
N 132. 4 d. brown and blue.. 8·00 4·50

51. Lenin. **52.** Ballot Box.

1960. Lenin. 90th Birth Anniv.
N 133. **51.** 5 x. claret and blue 12 8
N 134. 12 x. blue and buff.. 20 15

1960. 2nd Election of Parliamentary Deputies.
N 135. **52.** 12 x. chocolate, red, yellow and olive .. 15 10

53. Red Cross Nurse. **54.** Pres. Ho Chi Minh.

1960. Int. Red Cross Commem.
N 136. **53.** 8 x. blue, red & bistre 12 5
N 137. 12 x. green, red and grey-green .. 15 12

1960. President Ho Chi Minh's 70th Birthday
N 138. **54.** 4 x. lilac and green.. 5 5
N 139. 12 x. maroon and rose 15 8
N 140. – 12 x. multicoloured.. 15 8
DESIGN: ($24\frac{1}{2} \times 39$ mm.): No. N 140, Ho Chi Minh and children.

55. " New Constitution ".

1960. Opening of 2nd National Assembly.
N 141. **55.** 12 x. sepia and ochre 35 20

56. Pres. Ho Chi Minh at Microphone.

1960. Viet-Nam Democratic Republic. 15th Anniv.

N 142. **56.** 4 x. black, red, ochre and yellow .. 25 15
N 143. 12 x. black, red, green and ochre 55 30
N 144. – 12 x. deep blue & blue 55 30
N 145. – 12 x. grey-green & yell. 55 30
N 146. – 12 x. indigo and brown 55 30

DESIGNS: No. N 144, Ploughing. N 145, Electricity Works, Vietri. N 146, Classroom.

57. Workers and Flags.

1960. 3rd Vietnam Workers' Party Congress.

N 147. **57.** 1 x. brn., red, yell. & green 30 15
N 148. 12 x. chocolate, red, yellow and brown 70 35

58. Handclasp of three Races.

1960. W.F.T.U. 15th Anniv.

N 149. **58** 12 x. black and red .. 1·10 80

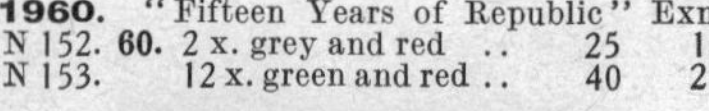

59. Dragon. **60.** Exhibition Entrance.

1960. Hanoi. 950th Anniv.

N 150. **59.** 8 x. yell., brn. & turq. 25 15
N 151. 12 x. yell., brn. & blue 40 30

1960. "Fifteen Years of Republic" Exn.

N 152. **60.** 2 x. grey and red .. 25 15
N 153. 12 x. green and red .. 40 25

61. Badge, Dove and Flag.

1960. World Federation of Democratic Youth. 15th Anniv.

N 154. **61.** 12 x. multicoloured .. 40 20

62. Emblem of Vietnamese Trade Unions. **63.** Woman, Globe and Dove.

1961. 2nd National Congress of Trade Unions.

N 155. **62.** 12 x. red, bl. & yellow 40 20

1961. 3rd National Congress of Women.

N 156. **63.** 6 x. olive-grn. & blue 35 5
N 157. 12 x. olive-grn. & sal. 40 10

IMPERF. STAMPS. Many issues from here onwards also exist imperf.

64. Deer. **65.** Ly Tu Trong (revolutionary).

1961. Vietnamese Fauna.

N 158. **64.** 12 x. buff, black and deep olive .. 25 20
N 159. – 20 x. indigo, bistre, black and chestnut 40 25
N 160. – 50 x. grey-green, black, and deep grey-green 65 40
N 161. – 1 d. blk., grey & emer. 1·10 70

DESIGNS: 20 x. Malayan bear. 50 x. Elephant. 1 d. Black Gibbon ape.

1961. 3rd Congress of Vietnam Labour Youth Union.

N 162. **65.** 2 x. olive and blue .. 20 12
N 163. 12 x. olive and salmon 50 25

66. Bugler and Drummer. **67.** Disabled Soldier learning to use Crutches.

1961. Vietnam Youth Poineers. 20th Anniv.

N 164. **66.** 1 x. red, blue, grey and yellow .. 25 12
N 165. 12 x. red, blue, black and turquoise .. 50 35

1961. Proposal for Int. Red Cross. 101st Anniv.

N 166. **67.** 6 x. brown-red, olive, yellow and red .. 35 12
N 167. 12 x. green, olive, grey and red .. 65 30

68. Nurse weighing Baby. **69.** Major Yuri Gagarin.

1961. Int. Children's Day.

N 168. **68.** 4 x. green, blk. & red 25 15
N 169. 12 x. yell., blk. & red 80 50

1961. World's First Manned Space Flight.

N 170. **69.** 6 x. red and violet .. 3·00 1·25
N 171. 12 x. red and green .. 3·00 1·25

70. South Vietnamese Woman. **71.** Vietnamese Women.

72. Mother and Child. **73.** Prospecting Team.

1961. Vietnam Reunification Campaign.

N 172. **70.** 12 x. green, orange blue and yellow .. 12 5
N 173. 2 d. green, orange, myrtle and yellow 2·25 1·00

1961. Tripling of Hanoi, Hue and Saigon.

N 174. **71.** 12 x. chocolate, myrtle, lilac & violet 50 35
N 175. 3 d. chocolate, myrtle and emerald .. 5·00 4·50

1961. National Savings, Campaign.

N 176. **72.** 3 x. red, indigo, olive and blue 15 10
N 177. 12 x. red, black, myrtle and blue .. 40 25

1961. Geological Research.

N 178. **73.** 2 x. grn., bl. & sl.-pur. 20 10
N 179. 12 x. brn., blk. & turq. 45 20

74. Thien Mu Tower, Hue. **75.** Workers and Rocket.

1961. Ancient Towers.

N 180. **74.** 6 x. choc. & chestnut 15 12
N 181. – 10 x. olive and buff.. 25 20
N 182. – 12 x. ol.-grn. & emer. 30 20
N 183. – 12 x. brown and blue 30 20

TOWERS: No. N 181, Pen-Brush, Bac Ninh. N 182, Binh Son, Vinh Phuc. N 183, Cham, Phan Rang.

1961. 22nd Communist Party Congress, Moscow.

N 184. **75.** 12. red and black .. 50 35

76. Major Titov and Rocket. **77.** Ship at Haiphong.

1961. 2nd Manned Space Flight.

N 185. **76.** 6 x. orange, ultram., slate-blue & black 40 35
N 186. 12 x. orange, blue, chocolate & violet 80 60

1961. Haiphong Port Commem.

N 187. **77.** 5 x. grey-blue, grey-green and myrtle 20 12
N 188. 12 x. brown, light brown and sepia .. 35 25

78. Cymbalist. **79.** Congress Emblem.

1961. Third Writers and Artists Congress. Multicoloured.

N 189. 12 x. T **78** 30 20
N 190. 12 x. Flautist 35 25
N 191. 30 x. Fan dancer .. 65 50
N 192. 50 x. Guitarist .. .. 1·10 80

1961. 5th W.F.T.U. Congress, Moscow.

N 193. **79.** 12 x. magenta & drab 20 15

80. Resistance Fighters. **81.** "Pigs" (after folk-engraving).

1961. National Resistance. 15th Anniv.

N 194. **80.** 4 x. black, yellow, orange and brown 5 5
N 195. 12 x. black, yellow, red and purple .. 15 10

1962. New Year.

N 196. **81.** 6 x. violet, red, yellow and green .. 20 15
N 197. – 12 x. red, green and black on yellow .. 60 45

DESIGN: 12 x. "Poultry" (after folk-engraving).

82. Watering Tree. **83.** Tea Plant.

1962. Tree-Planting Festival.

N 198. **82.** 12 x. black, buff, green and mauve.. 20 15
N 199. 40 x. black, buff, green and blue-green .. 60 45

1962. Multicoloured.

N 200. 2 x. T **83** 10 5
N 201. 6 x. Aniseed 35 20
N 202. 12 x. Coffee 60 45
N 203. 12 x. Castor-oil.. .. 60 45
N 204. 30 x. Lacquer-tree .. 1·25 1·00

84. Gong Dance. **85.** Hibiscus.

1962. Folk-Dancing. Multicoloured.

N 205. 12 x. T **84** 30 20
N 206. 12 x. Bamboo Dance .. 30 20
N 207. 30 x. Hat Dance .. 60 40
N 208. 50 x. Parasol Dance .. 90 65

1962. Flowers. Multicoloured.

N 209. 12 x. T **85** 60 45
N 210. 12 x. Frangipani .. 60 45
N 211. 20 x. Chrysanthemum.. 75 60
N 212. 30 x. Lotus 90 80
N 213. 50 x. Ipomoea .. .. 1·25 1·00

86. Kim Lien Flats, Hanoi. **87.** Workers and Rose.

1962. 1st Five-Year Plan (1st issue).

N 214. **86.** 1 x. blue, black and grey-brown .. 5 5
N 215. – 3 x. ochre, chestnut, sepia & grey-brown 10 8
N 216. – 3 x. vio., blk. & stone 25 20

DESIGNS: 3 x. State agricultural farm. 8 x. Institute of Hydraulic and Electro-Dynamic Studies.

See also Nos. N 245/8, N 251/2, N 270/1 and N 294/6.

1962. 3rd National "Heroes of Labour" Congress.

N 217. **87.** 12 x. orge., olive & red 15 5

88. Dai Lai Dam.

1962.

N 218. **88.** 12 x. turq. and brown 25 20

89. "Plough of Perfection".

1962.

N 219. **89.** 6 z. black & turquoise 15 10

DESIGNS: 20 x. Pres. Ho Chi Minh pinning medal on Titov. 30 x. Titov in space-suit.

90. Titov greeting Children.

1962. Visit of Major Titov.
N 220. **90.** 12 x. sepia and blue . . 25 15
N 221. – 20 x. sepia and salmon 30 20
N 222. – 30 x. sepia and green 55 40

91. Mosquito and Red Cross.

1962. Malaria Eradication.
N 223. **91.** 8 x. red, black & blue 30 15
N 224. 12 x. red, black and violet-blue . . 40 20
N 225. 20 x. red, blk. & pur. 60 25

92. Factory and Soldiers. **93.** Ban Gioc Falls.

1962. Geneva Vietnamese Agreements. 8th Anniv.
N 226. **92.** 12 x. black, red, olive and salmon . . 20 10

1962. Viet-Namese Scenery.
N 227. – 12 x. purple and blue 20 10
N 228. **93.** 12 x. sepia & turquoise 20 10
DESIGN—HORIZ. (32½ × 23 mm). No. N 227, Ba Be Lake.

93a. Weightlifting.

1962. Int. Military Sports Festival of Socialist States, Prague.
N 228a. **93a.** 12 x. black, red, brown and buff . . 20·00

94. Quang Trung. **95.** Groundnuts.

1962. National Heroes.
N 229. **94.** 3 x. yell., brn. & grey 5 5
N 230. – 3 x. orge., blk. & ochre 5 5
N 231. **94.** 12 x. yell., grn. & grey 20 8
N 232. – 12 x. orge., blk. & grey 20 8
PORTRAIT: Nos. N 230, N 232, Nguyen Trai.

1962. Multicoloured.
N 233. 1 x. Type **95** 8 5
N 234. 4 x. Haricot beans . . 20 10
N 235. 6 x. Sweet potatoes . . 30 15
N 236. 12 x. Maize . . 60 40
N 237. 30 x. Manioc . . . . 1·00 70

DESIGNS: No. N 239, Woman tending pigs. N 240, Herd-girl with oxen. N 241, Boy feeding buffalo.

96. Girl Feeding Poultry.

1962. Farm Stock-breeding.
N 238. **96.** 2 x. red, grey & blue 5 5
N 239. – 12 x. ochre, turquoise and blue 30 12
N 240. – 12 x. brown, pale and deep green . . 30 12
N 241. – 12 x. buff, mauve and sepia 30 12

DESIGNS—HORIZ. 20 x. Nikolaev in "Vostock 3". VERT. 30 x. "Vostocks 3 and 4".

97. Popovich in "Vostock 4".

1962. First "Team" Manned Space Flights.
N 242. **97.** 12 x. purple, violet, turquoise & black 12 5
N 243. – 20 x. ochre, bl. & blk. 20 10
N 244. – 30 x. red, blue & blk. 30 15

98. Teacher and Students.

99. Tree Felling.

1962. 1st Five Year Plan (2nd issue). Higher Education and Land Cultivation.
N 245. **98.** 12 x. black & yellow 20 5
N 246. **99.** 12 x. blk., brn. & buff 20 5

100. Guerrilla Fighter. **101.** Hoang Hoa Tham.

1963. 1st Five Year Plan (3rd issue). National Defence.
N 247. **100.** 5 x. green and grey 12 5
N 248. 12 x. brown and buff 20 5

1963. Hoang Hoa Tham (freedom fighter). 50th Death Anniv.
N 249. **101.** 6 x. myrtle and blue 12 8
N 250. 12 x. blk. & pale choc. 20 10

102. Workers in Field.

103. Lam Thao Fertiliser Factory.

104. Karl Marx.

1963. 1st Five Year Plan (4th issue). Agricultural and Chemical Manufacture.
N 251. **102.** 12 x. multicoloured 25 15
N 252. **103.** 12 x red, mauve and black . . 15 10

1963. Karl Marx. 80th Death Anniv.
N 253. **104.** 3 x. olive-black and grey-green . . 12 8
N 254. 12 x olive-black and drab on pink . . 20 10

105. Castro and Vietnamese Soldiers.

107. Nurse tending Child.

106. Doves and Labour Emblem.

1963. Vietnamese–Cuban Friendship.
N 255. **105.** 12 x. multicoloured 12 8

1963. Labour Day.
N 256. **106.** 12 x. orge., blk. & bl. 15 10

1963. Red Cross Centenary.
N 257. **107.** 12 x. red, blk. & blue 20 12
N 258. – 12 x. red, blk. & turq. 20 12
N 259. – 20 x. red, grey green and yellow . . 30 15
DESIGNS: No. N 258 Child, and syringe inscr. "BCG". 20 x. (25 × 42 mm.), Centenary emblem.

108. "Mars 1" Interplanetary Station.

1963. Launching of Soviet Rocket "Mars 1". Multicoloured.
N 260. 6 x. Type **108** 12 8
N 261. 12 x. Type **108** . . 25 15
N 262. 12 x. "Mars 1" in space (vert.) 25 15
N 263. 20 x. "Mars 1" in space (vert.) 40 25

109. Carp. **110.** Pres. Ho Chi Minh embracing Prof. Nguen Van Hien of South Vietnam.

1963. Fishing Industry. Multicoloured.
N 264. 12 x. Type **109** 55 30
N 265. 12 x. Fishes and trawler 55 30

1963. Campaign for reunification of Vietnam.
N 266. **110.** 12 x. blk., bl. & turq. 20 12

DESIGNS: 20 x. Nikolaev and "eagle" motif. 30 x. Popovich and "phoenix" motif.

111. Globe and "Vostoks 3 and 4".

1963. "Team" Manned Space Flights. 1st Anniv.
N 267. **111.** 12 x. blk., brn. & yell. 15 8
N 268. – 20 x. blk., bl. & grn. 25 15
N 269. – 30 x. blk., vio. & bl. 50 25

DESIGN: 12 x. Viet Tri chemical factory.

112. Viet Tri Insecticide Factory.

1963. 1st Five-Year Plan (5th issue).
N 270. **112.** 3 x. buff, brn. & blue 5 5
N 271. – 12 x. pink, chocolate and bistre . . 15 5

113. Black Amur.

1963. Freshwater Fish Culture. Multicoloured
N 272. 12 x. Type **113** 25 12
N 273. 12 x. Carp 25 12
N 274. 12 x. Silver Carp . . 25 12
N 275. 20 x. Snakehead . . 40 25
N 276. 30 x. Mozambique mouthbreeder . . 60 35

114. Stephenson's Francolin. **115.** Broken Chain and Map.

1963. Birds. Multicoloured.
N 277. 12 x. Type **114** . . 30 15
N 278. 12 x. Chinese crested mynah . . 30 15
N 279. 12 x. White-throated kingfisher . . 30 15
N 280. 20 x. Diard's Fireback pheasant (horiz.) . . 50 30
N 281. 30 x. Little egret . . 70 50
N 282. 40 x. Alexandrine parakeet 90 70

1963. W.F.T.U. Assembly, Hanoi.
N 283. **115.** 12 x. black, brown, yellow and red . . 15 10

116. Football. **117.** 'Ravwolfia verticillata'.

1963. "GANEFO" Athletic Games, Jakarta.
N 284. **116.** 12 x. blk., grey & ochre 15 10
N 285. – 12 x. blk., grey & orge. 15 10
N 286. – 12 x. blk., grey & blue 15 10
N 287. – 30 x. blk., grey & mag. 25 20
DESIGNS—VERT. No. N 285, Volleyball. HORIZ. 286, Swimming. 287, High-jumping.

1963. Medicinal Plants. Multicoloured.
N 288. **117.** 6 x. green, yell. & vio. 12 8
N 289. – 12 x. "Chenopodium ambrosioides" . . 25 12
N 290. – 12 x. "Sophora japonica" . . 25 12
N 291. – 12 x. "Fibraurea tinctoria" . . 25 12
N 292. – 20 x. "Momordica cochinchinensis" 40 20

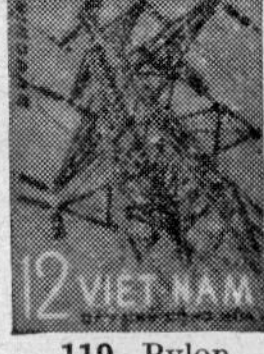

118. "Solidarity". **119.** Pylon.

1963. South Vietnam Liberation National Front. 3rd Anniv.
N 293. **118.** 12 x. blk., brn. & ochre 15 10

1964. 1st Five-Year Plan (6th issue).
N 294. – 6 x. blk., red & pur. 12 8
N 295. – 12 x. multicoloured 25 12
N 296. **119.** 12 x. blk., grey & orge. 25 12
DESIGNS—HORIZ. (40 × 22½ mm.): 6 x. Tapping cast-iron. No. N 295, Thai Ngyuen Iron and Steel Works.

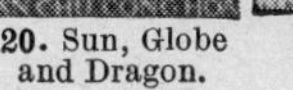

120. Sun, Globe and Dragon. **121.** Twin Space Flights.

1964. Int. Quiet Sun Years.
N 297. **120.** 12 x. orge., blk. & grn. 15 10
N 298. 50 x. drab., blk. & pur. 60 30

1964. Space Flights of Bykovsky and Tereshkova. Multicoloured.
N 299. 12 x. Type **121** .. 20 12
N 300. 12 x. Bykovsky and "Vostok 5" 20 12
N 301. 30 x. Tereshkova and "Vostok 6" 50 25

122. "Hibiscus mutabilis". **123.** Rural Costume.

1964. Flowers. Multicoloured.
N 302. 12 x. Type **122** .. 20 10
N 303. 12 x. "Persica vulgaris" 20 10
N 304. 12 x. "Saraca dives" .. 20 10
N 305. 12 x. "Passiflora hispida" 20 10
N 306. 20 x. "Michelia champaca" .. 40 20
N 307. 30 x. "Camellia amplexicaulis" .. 50 25

1964. National Costumes. Multicoloured.
N 308. 6 x. Type **123** 5 5
N 309. 12 x. "Ceremonial" 12 5
N 310. 12 x. "Everyday" .. 12 5

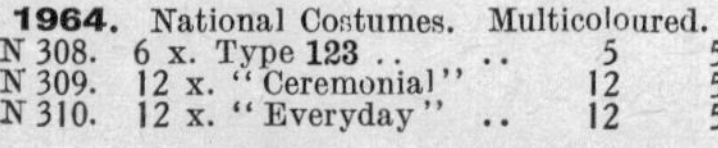

124. Artillery.

1964. Battle of Dien Bien Phu. 10th Anniv.
N 311. **124.** 3 x. black and red .. 10 5
N 312. – 6 x. black and blue .. 15 8
N 313. – 12 x. black & yellow 20 12
N 314. – 12 x. black & purple 20 12
DESIGNS: 6 x. Machine-gun post. No. N 313, Bomb-disposal. No. N 314, Dien Bien Phu and tractor.

125. Ham Rong Bridge.

1964. Inaug. of reconstructed Ham Rong Bridge.
N 315. **125.** 12 x. multicoloured 5 5

126. Spotted Deer. **127.** Women Fighters, Map, Industrial Scene and Watch-Towers.

1964. Wild Animals. Multicoloured.
N 316. 12 x. Type **126** .. 20 10
N 317. 12 x. Tapir (horiz.) .. 20 10
N 318. 12 x. Tiger 20 10
N 319. 20 x. Water-buffalo (horiz.) 40 20
N 320. 30 x. Rhinoceros (horiz.) 50 25
N 321. 40 x. Bison (horiz.) .. 60 30

1964. Geneva Agreements on Vietnam. 10th Anniv.
N 322. **127.** 12 x. black, red, brown and ochre 20 12
N 323. – 12 x. drab, blue, red and yellow .. 20 12
DESIGN—VERT. (23×45 mm.): N 323, Map of Vietnam, T.U. emblem and flag, inscr. ("NHAN DAN MIEN NAM") etc.

128. Nhu Quynh Pumping Station.

1964. Irrigation for Agriculture.
N 324. **128.** 12 x. slate-blue and black 12 8

129. Populace Greeting Soldiers.

1964. Liberation of Hanoi. 10th Anniv. Multicoloured.
N 325. 6 x. Type **129** 12 10
N 326. 12 x. Building construction 25 20

130. Rowing.

1964. "National Defence" Games.
N 327. **130.** 5 x. black, grey & bl. 12 5
N 328. – 12 x. blk., grey & yell. 20 10
N 329. – 12 x. blk., brn. & bl. 20 10
N 330. – 12 x. black, pink, grey and green .. 20 10
DESIGNS—HORIZ. No. N 328, Pistol-shooting. VERT. N 329, Gliding. N 330, Parachuting.

131. "Guarcinia mangostana".

1964. Tropical Fruits. Multicoloured.
N 331. 12 x. Type **131** .. 20 12
N 332. 12 x. "Mangifera indica" 20 12
N 333. 12 x. "Nephelium litchi" 20 12
N 334. 20 x. "Anona squamosa" 30 15
N 335. 50 x. "Citrus medica" 50 25

132. Conference Building.

1964. World Solidarity Conf., Hanoi. Multicoloured.
N 336. 12 x. Type **132** .. 20 10
N 337. 12 x. Soldier greeting workers .. 20 10
N 338. 12 x. Clenched fist, ships and aircraft 20 10

133. Soldiers with Standard. **134.** Cuban Revolutionaries.

1964. Viet-Namese People's Army. 20th Anniv. Multicoloured.
N 339. 12 x. Type **133** .. 20 10
N 340. 12 x. Coastguards .. 20 10
N 341. 12 x. Frontier guards (vert.) 20 10

1965. Cuban Republic. 6th Anniv.
N 342. **134.** 12 x. blk., red & blue 20 10
N 343. – 12 x. blue, red, yellow and black .. 20 10
DESIGN: No. N 343, Flags of Cuba and North Vietnam.

135. Le Hong Phong. **136.** Party Flag.

1965. Vietnamese Workers' Party. 35th Anniv. (a) As T **135**. Portraits and inscr. purple-brown; background colours given.
N 344. **135.** 6 x. grey 8 8
N 345. – 6 x. yellow-brown 8 8
N 346. – 6 x. drab 8 8
N 347. – 6 x. brown 8 8
N 348. – 6 x. lilac 8 8
DESIGNS: No. N 345, Tran Phu. N 346 Hoang van Thu. N 347, Ngo Gia Tu. N 348 Nguyen van Cu (Party leaders).

(b) As T **136**.
N 349. **136.** 12 x. yellow, red and magenta 15 12
N 350. 12 x. magenta, yellow and red 15 12
DESIGN: No. N 350, Foundryman and guerilla fighter.

137. Women tending Maize. **138.** Locomotive and Nguyen Van Troi (patriot).

1965. Populating Mountain Settlements.
N 351. **137.** 2 x. black, orange, drab and green 5 5
N 352. 3 x. black, orange, drab and blue .. 8 5
N 353. – 12 x. indigo, orange and blue 15 12
DESIGN: 12 x. Young girls going to school.

1965. Transport Ministers' Congress, Hanoi.
N 354. **138.** 12 x. blue and red .. 15 10
N 355. – 30 x. black and green 30 20
DESIGN: 30 x. As T **138** but position of locomotive, portrait and value transposed.

139. Cosmonauts Komarov, Feoktistov, Yegorov, and "Voskhod I".

1965. Three-manned Space Flight.
N 356. **139.** 20 x. violet, grn. & bl. 20 10
N 357. – 1 d. violet, red & mag. 1·10 60
DESIGN: 1 f. "Voskhod I" and cosmonauts.

140. Lenin with Red Guards. **141.** Pres. Ho Chi Minh.

1965. Lenin's 95th Birth Anniv.
N 358. **140.** 8 x. maroon & buff 10 8
N 359. 12 x. maroon & grey 15 12

1965. Pres. Ho Chi Minh's 75th Birthday.
N 360. **141.** 6 x. vio., yell. & grn. 10 5
N 361. 12 x. vio., yell. & buff 20 10

142. Hands clasping Serpent. **143.** Two Soldiers advancing.

1965. Afro-Asian Conf., Bandung. 10th Anniv.
N 362. **142.** 12 x. yellow, black, sepia and brown 15 10

1965. Trade Union Conf., Hanoi.
N 363. **143.** 12 x. blue & purple 12 8
N 364. – 12 x. black, red, olive and violet .. 12 8
N 365. – 12 x. red, blk. & grn. 12 8
DESIGNS—HORIZ. No. N 364, Sea battle. N 365. "Peoples of the world" on Globe, and soldiers.

144. "Martes flavigula".

1965. Fauna Protection. Multicoloured.
N 366. 12 x. Type **144** 15 10
N 367. 12 x. "Chrotogale owstoni" 15 10
N 368. 12 x. "Manis pentadactyla" 15 10
N 369. 12 x. "Presbytis delacouri" 15 10
N 370. 20 x. "Petaurista lylei" 25 15
N 371. 50 x. "Nycticebus pygmaeus" 60 40
Nos. N 369/71 are vert.

145. Marx and Lenin. **146.** Nguyen Van Troi (patriot).

1965. Postal Ministers Congress, Peking.
N 372. **145.** 12 x. multicoloured 20 12

1965. Nguyen Van Troi Commem.
N 373. **146.** 12 x. sep., brn. & grn. 15 10
N 374. 50 x. sep., brn. & ochre 40 25
N 375. 4 d. sepia and red .. 2·75 1·90

147. "Rhynchocoris humeralis". **148.** Revolutionaries.

1965. Noxious Insects. Multicoloured.
N 376. 12 x. Type **147** 15 10
N 377. 12 x. "Tessaratoma papillosa" .. 15 10
N 378. 12 x. "Poeciliocoris latus" 15 10
N 379. 12 x. "Tosena melanoptera" 15 10
N 380. 20 x. "Cicada sp." .. 20 12
N 381. 30 x. "Fulgora candelaria" 40 25
Nos. N 379/81 are vert. (20½ × 38 mm.).

1965. August Revolution. 20th Anniv.
N 382. **148.** 6 x. sep., blk. & blue 8 5
N 383. 12 x. black and red 15 10

149. Prawn. **150.** Air Battle.

1965. Marine Life. Multicoloured.
N 384. 12 x. Type **149** 15 12
N 385. 12 x. Shrimp 15 12
N 386. 12 x. Swimming Crab .. 15 12
N 387. 12 x. Serrate Swimming Crab 15 12
N 388. 20 x. Spiny Lobster .. 30 20
N 389. 50 x. Fiddler Crab .. 60 45

1965. 500th U.S. Aircraft Brought Down over North Vietnam.
N 390. **150.** 12 x. green and lilac 50 35

151. Foundryman ("Heavy Industries").

1965. Republic. 20th Anniv. and Completion of 1st Five Year Plan. Inscr. "1961–1965".

N 391. **151.** 12 x. black & orange 12 8
N 392. – 12 x. black & green 12 8
N 393 – 12 x. black & purple 12 8

DESIGNS: No. N 392, Irrigation, pylon and power station ("Hydro-electric Power"). N 393, Nurse examining child ("Social Medicine").

See also Nos. N 417/9.

152. Drummer and Peasants.

1965. Movement of Nghe An and Ha Tinh Soviet Peasants. 35th Anniv.

N 394. **152.** 10 x. multicoloured 10 5
N 395. 12 x. multicoloured 12 8

153. Girls and Flags.

1965. Friendship between China and Vietnam. 16th Anniv. Multicoloured.

N 396. 12 x. Type **153** .. 12 10
N 397. 12 x. Vietnamese and Chinese girls with flags (vert.) 12 10

154. Tsiolkovsky and "Sputnik 1".

1965. Space Flight of "Voskhod 2".

N 398. **154.** 12 x. blue & purple 12 8
N 399. – 12 x. ochre and blue 12 8
N 400. – 50 x. blue & green.. 50 35
N 401. – 50 x. blue & turquoise 50 35

DESIGNS: No. N 399, Leonov, Beliaiev and "Voskhod 2". N 400, Gagarin. N 401, Leonov in space.

155. Lacewing.

1965. Butterflies. Multicoloured.

N 402. 12 x. Type **155**.. .. 15 10
N 403. 12 x. Leopard lacewing 15 10
N 404. 12 x. Common bluebottle 15 10
N 405. 12 x. India purple emperor 15 10
N 406. 20 x. Paris peacock .. 30 20
N 407. 30 x. Common rose .. 50 35

156. N. R. Morrison and Demonstrators.

157. Birthplace of Nguyen Du (poet).

1965. Homage to Norman R. Morrison (American Quaker who immolated himself).

N 408. **156.** 12 x. black and red 15 8

1965. Nguyen Du Commem. Multicoloured.

N 409. 12 x. Type **157**.. .. 12 8
N 410. 12 x. Nguyen-Du Museum 12 8
N 411. 20 x. "Kieu" (volume of poems) 20 15
N 412. 1 d. Scene from "Kieu" 60 40

158. Pres. Ho Chi Minh.

159. Rice-field and Insecticide-sprayer ("Agriculture").

1965. Engels' 145th Birth Anniv. Mult.

N 413. 12 x. Type **158** .. 12 8
N 414. 12 x. Marx 12 8
N 415. 12 x. Lenin 12 8
N 416. 50 x. Engels 45 30

1965. Completion of First Five-Year Plan (2nd issue).

N 417. **159.** 12 x. orange & green 15 8
N 418. – 12 x. blue and red.. 15 8
N 419. – 12 x. orange & blue 15 8

DESIGNS: N 418, Factory-worker ("Light Industries"). N 419, Children at play and students ("Social Education").

160. Soldier and Demonstrators.

161. Casting Votes.

162. "Dendrobium moschatum".

1965. South Vietnam National Liberation Front. 5th Anniv.

N 420. **160.** 12 x. violet and lilac 15 8

1966. 1st Vietnamese General Elections. 20th Anniv.

N 421. **161.** 12 x. black and red 12 5

1966. Orchids. Multicoloured.

N 422. 12 x. Type **162**.. .. 15 10
N 423. 12 x. "Vanda teres".. 15 10
N 424. 12 x. "Dendrobium crystallnium" .. 15 10
N 425. 12 x. "Dendrobium nobile" .. 15 10
N 426. 20 x. "Vandopsis gigantea" 30 20
N 427. 30 x. "Dendrobium".. 50 35

163. Child on Rocking-Horse.

164. "Physignathus cocincinus".

1966. New Year.

N 428. **163.** 12 x. multicoloured 10 5

1966. Protection of Nature—Reptiles. Multicoloured.

N 429. 12 x. Type **164** .. 15 10
N 430. 12 x. "Trionyx sincensis" 15 10
N 431. 12 x. Gecko (inscr. "GEKKO GECKO") 15 10
N 432. 12 x. "Testudo elongata" 15 10
N 433. 20 x. "Varanus salvator" 30 20
N 434. 40 x. "Eretmochelys imbricata" .. 60 40

165. Wrestling.

166. Ly Tu Trong (revolutionary), Badge and Banner.

1966. National Games.

N 435. **165.** 12 x. violet, red, green and drab .. 12 5
N 436. – 12 x. black, emerald, green and yellow 12 5
N 437. – 12 x. blue, green, salmon and pink 12 5

GAMES: No. N 436, Archery (with crossbow). N 437, "Fencing".

1966. Labour Youth Union. 35th Anniv.

N 438. **166.** 12 x. multicoloured 12 5

167. Aircraft in Flames.

1966. "1,000th U.S. Aircraft Brought Down over North Vietnam.

N 439. **167.** 12 x. multicoloured 20 15

168. Worker with Rifle.

170. Children and Banners.

169. Battle Scene on Con Co Island.

1966. Labour Day.

N 440. **168.** 6 x. black, vermilion and salmon .. 5 5

1966. Defence of Con Co ("Steel Island").

N 441. **169.** 12 c. multicoloured 10 5

1966. Vietnam Youth Pioneers. 25th Anniv.

N 442. **170.** 12 x. black and red 10 5

171. View of Dien An (Yenan).

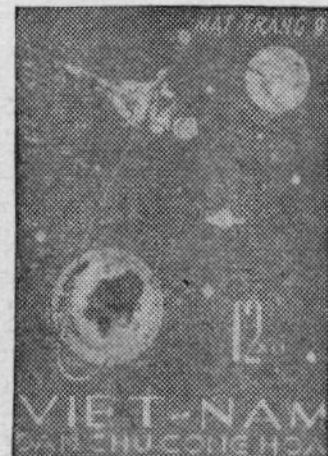

172. "Luna 9" in Space.

1966. Chinese Communist Party. 45th Anniv. Multicoloured. Inscr. "1921–1966".

N 443. 3 x. Type **171** .. 5 5
N 444. 12 x. Ho Chi Minh and Mao Tse-tung .. 12 10

1966. "Luna 9". Space Flight. Multicoloured. Inscr. "MAT TRANG 9".

N 445. 12 x. Type **172**.. .. 12 8
N 446. 50 x. "Luna 9" on Moon 45 35

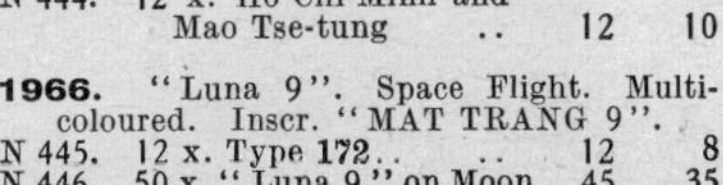

173. Aircraft in Flames.

174. Liberation Fighter.

1966. "1,500th U.S. Aircraft Brought Down over North Vietnam".

N 447. **173.** 12 x. multicoloured 45 35
N 448. 12 x. mult. (optd. **NGAY 14.10. 1966)** 60 55

1966. Victories of Liberation Army. Inscr. "1965–1966".

N 449. **174.** 1 x. maroon .. 5 5
N 450. 12 x. multicoloured 8 5
N 451. – 12 x. multicoloured 12 8

DESIGN: No. N 451, Soldier escorting prisoners-of-war.

See also No. N 646.

175. Women from different Regions, and Child.

1966. Vietnamese Women's Union. 20th Anniv.

N 452. **175.** 12 x. black & salmon 12 5

176. Blue-winged Pittas.

1966. Birds. Multicoloured.

N 453. 12 x. Type **176**.. .. 12 5
N 454. 12 x. Black-naped orioles 12 5
N 455. 12 x. Kingfisher .. 12 5
N 456. 12 x. Long-tailed broadbill 12 5
N 457. 20 x. Hoopoe 35 25
N 458. 30 x. Maroon orioles .. 50 35

Nos. N 454/5 and N 457 are vert.

177. Football.

1966. Ganefo Games. Multicoloured.

N 459. 12 x. Type **177** 12 5
N 460. 12 x. Rifle-shooting .. 12 5
N 461. 30 x. Swimming .. 25 12
N 462. 30 x. Running 25 12

178. Harvesting Rice.

1967. Agricultural Production.

N 463. **178.** 12 x. multicoloured 10 5

179. Ho Chi Minh Text and Fighters.

1967. Ho Chi Minh's Appeal.

N 464. **179.** 12 x. purple and red 12 8
N 465. – 12 x. purple and red 12 8

DESIGNS: No. N 465, Ho-Chi-Minh text and marchers with banners.

See also Nos. 519/22.

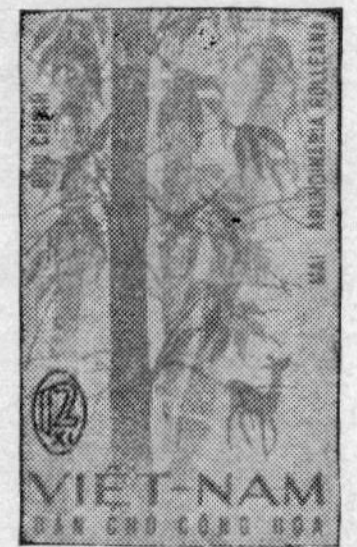

180. Bamboo ("Arundinaria rolleana").

1967. Bamboo. Multicoloured.

N 466. 12 x. Type **180** 10 5
N 467. 12 x. "Arundinaria racemosa" 10 5
N 468. 12 x. "Bambusa bingami" 10 5
N 469. 12 x. "Bambusa arundinaceu" 10 5
N 470. 30 x. "Bambusa nutans" 35 20
N 471. 50 x. "Dendrocalamus patellaris" .. 40 30

181. "Cuon rutilans".

1967. Wild Animals. Multicoloured.

N 472. 12 x. Type **181** 12 8
N 473. 12 x. "Artictis binturong" 12 8
N 474. 12 x. "Arctonix collaris" 12 8
N 475. 20 x. "Viverra zibetha" 30 20
N 476. 40 x. "Macaca speciosa" 50 40
N 477. 50 x. "Neofelis nebulosa" 60 50

182. Captured Pilot. **183.** Rocket Launching and Agricultural Scene.

1967. "2,000th U.S. Aircraft Brought Down over North Vietnam.

N 478. **182.** 6 x. blk. & red on pink 15 12
N 479. 12 x. blk. & red on grn. 15 12

1967. Launching of Chinese Rocket at Ogive. Multicoloured.

N 480. 12 x. Type **183** .. 10 5
N 481. 30 x. Rocket launching, and Gate of Heavenly Peace, Peking .. 25 12

184. Siamese Tiger Fish. **185.** Lenin and Revolutionary Soldiers.

1967. Vietnamese Fishes. Multicoloured.

N 482. 12 x. Type **184** 10 5
N 483. 12 x. Spanish Mackerel 10 5
N 484. 12 x. Lizard Fish .. 10 5
N 485. 20 x. Spangled Emperor 25 15
N 486. 30 x. German Fish .. 30 20
N 487. 50 x. Golden-Striped Snapper 50 40

1967. October Revolution. 50th Anniv. Multicoloured.

N 488. 6 x. Type **185** 5 5
N 489. 12 x. Lenin and revolutionaries 10 8
N 490. 12 x. Lenin, Marx and Vietnamese soldiers .. 10 8
N 491. 20 x. Cruiser "Aurora" 25 10

186. Air Battle.

1967. "2,500th U.S. Aircraft Brought Down over North Vietnam.

N 492. **186.** 12 x. blk., red & grn. 25 15
N 493. – 12 x. blk., red & blue 25 15

DESIGN—VERT. No. N 493, Aircraft falling in flames.

187. Atomic Symbol and Heavenly Gate, Peking.

1967. First Chinese "H"-Bomb Test. Mult.

N 494. 12 x. Type **187** 10 5
N 495. 20 x. Chinese lantern, atomic symbol & dove (30×35 mm.) .. 20 10

188. Factory Anti-Aircraft Unit.

1967. Anti-aircraft Defences. Multicoloured.

N 496. 12 x. Type **188** 10 5
N 497. 12 x. Rifle-fire from trenches 10 5
N 498. 12 x. Seaborne gun-crew 10 5
N 499. 12 x. Militiawoman with captured U.S. pilot .. 10 5
N 500. 20 x. Air battle .. 20 12
N 501. 30 x. Military anti-aircraft post 35 25

189. Chickens.

1968. Domestic Fowl. Multicoloured designs showing cocks and hens.

N 502. 12 x. Type **189** 12 8
N 503. 12 x. Inscr. "Ga ri" .. 12 8
N 504. 12 x. Inscr. "Ga trong thien ri" 12 8
N 505. 12 x. Inscr. "Ga den chanchi" 12 8
N 506. 20 x. Junglefowl .. 25 12
N 507. 30 x. Hen 30 15
N 508. 40 x. Hen and chicks .. 40 25
N 509. 50 x. Two hens .. 55 30

190. Gorky.

1968. Maxim Gorky. Birth Cent.

N 510. **190.** 12 x. black & brown 10 8

191. Burning Village.

1968. Victories of 1966-67.

N 511. **191.** 12 x. chocolate & lake 10 8
N 512. – 12 x. chocolate & lake 10 8
N 513. – 12 x. chocolate & lake 10 8
N 514. – 12 x. chocolate & lake 10 8
N 515. – 12 x. black & violet 10 8
N 516. – 12 x. black & violet 10 8
N 517. – 12 x. black & violet 10 8
N 518. – 12 x. black & violet 10 8

DESIGNS: No. N 512, Firing mortars. No. N 513, Attacking tanks with rocket-gun. No. N 514, Sniping. No. N 515, Attacking gun-site. No. N 516, Escorting prisoners. No. N 517, Interrogating refugees. No. N 518 Civilians demonstrating.

192. Ho Chi Minh Text and Fighters. **193.** Rose.

1968. Intensification of Production.

N 519. **192.** 6 x. blue on yellow .. 5 5
N 520. 12 x. blue 12 8
N 521. 12 x. maroon .. 12 8
N 522. 12 x. red 12 8

1968. Roses.

N 523. **193.** 12 x. multicoloured 12 8
N 524. – 12 x. multicoloured 12 8
N 525. – 12 x. multicoloured 12 8
N 526. – 20 x. multicoloured 20 12
N 527. – 30 x. multicoloured 30 20
N 528. – 40 x. multicoloured 40 30

DESIGNS: Nos. N 524/8, Different species of rose similar to type **193.**

194. Ho Chi Minh and Flag. **195.** Karl Marx.

1968. Ho Chi Minh's New Year Message.

N 529. **194.** 12 x. brown & violet 12 8

1968. Karl Marx. 150th Birth Anniv.

N 530. **195.** 12 x. black & green 12 8

196. Anti-aircraft Machine-gun Crew.

1968. 3,000th U.S. Aircraft Brought Down over North Vietnam. Multicoloured.

N 531. 12 x. Type **196** 25 15
N 532. 12 x. Women manning anti-aircraft gun .. 25 15
N 533. 40 x. Aerial dogfight .. 60 45
N 534. 40 x. Anti-aircraft missile 60 45

197. Rattan-cane Work.

1968. Arts and Crafts. Multicoloured.

N 535. 6 x. Type **197** 5 5
N 536. 12 x. Bamboo work .. 12 8
N 537. 12 x. Pottery .. 12 8
N 538. 20 x. Ivory carving .. 15 10
N 539. 30 x. Lacquer work .. 25 20
N 540. 40 x. Silverware .. 30 25

198. Quarter-staff Contest.

1968. Traditional Sports. Multicoloured.

N 541. 12 x. Type **198** 12 8
N 542. 12 x. Dagger fighting .. 12 8
N 543. 12 x. Duel with sabres.. 12 8
N 544. 30 x. Unarmed combat 25 20
N 545. 40 x. Scimitar fighting.. 30 25
N 546. 50 x. Sword and buckler 35 30

199. Temple, Khue.

1968. Vietnamese Architecture. Multicoloured.

N 548. 12 x. Type **199** 12 8
N 549. 12 x. Bell tower, Keo Pagoda 12 8
N 550. 20 x. Bridge, Bonze Pagoda (horiz.) .. 15 10
N 551. 30 x. Mot Cot Pagoda, Hanoi 20 12
N 552. 40 x. Gateway, Ninh Phuc Pagoda (horiz.) 25 15
N 553. 50 x. Tay Phuong Pagoda (horiz.) 30 20

200. Vietnamese Militia. **201.** "Ploughman with Rifle".

1968. Cuban-North Vietnamese Friendship. Multicoloured. With gum.

N 554. 12 x. Type **200** 10 5
N 555. 12 x. Cuban revolutionary (vert.) 10 5
N 556. 20 x. "Revolutionary Solidarity" (vert.) .. 15 10

1968. "The War Effort". Paintings. With gum.

N 557. **201.** 12 x. blk., bl. & yell. 10 5
N 558. – 12 x. multicoloured 10 5
N 559. – 30 x. brown, blue and greenish-blue 25 15
N 560. – 40 x. multicoloured 30 20

DESIGNS—HORIZ. No. N 558, "Defending the Mines". No. N 559, "Repairing the Track". No. N 560, "Crashed Aircraft".

202. Nam Ngai shooting down aircraft.

1969. Lunar New Year. Victories of the National Liberation Front. Multicoloured.

N 561. 12 x. Type **202** .. 8 5
N 562. 12 x. Tay Nguyen throwing grenade 8 5
N 563. 12 x. Insurrection of Tri Thien 8 5
N 564. 40 x. Insurgents, Tay Ninh 25 15
N 565. 50 x. Home Guards .. 30 20

203. Loading Timber Lorries.

1969. North Vietnamese Timber Industry. Multicoloured.

N 566. 6 x. Type **203** 5 5
N 567. 12 x. Log raft on River 8 5
N 568. 12 x. Tug "towing log train" 8 5
N 569. 12 x. Elephant hauling logs 8 5
N 570. 12 x. Insecticide spraying 8 5
N 571. 20 x. Buffalo hauling log 15 10
N 572. 30 x. Logs on overhead cable 65 40

204. " Young Guerrilla ". (Co Tan Long Chau).

1969. " South Vietnam—Land and People " Paintings. Multicoloured.

N 573. 12 x. Type **204** — .. 8 5
N 574. 12 x. " Scout on patrol " (Co Tan Long Chau) .. 8 5
N 575. 20 x. " Woman guerrilla " (Le Van Chuong) (vert.) 15 10
N 576. 30 x. " Soldiers in Camp " (Co Tan Long Chau) .. 25 15
N 577. 40 x. " Soldiers playing cards " (Co Tan Long Chau) 30 20
N 578. 50 x. " A liberated Hamlet " (Huynh Phuong Dong) 35 25

205. Woman Soldier, Ben Tre. 207. Grapefruit.

208. Tribunal Emblem and Falling plane. 206. Soldier defending Hanoi.

1969. Victories in Tet Offensive (1968).

N 579. **205.** 8 x. blk., grn. & pink 8 5
N 580. 12 x. blk., emer. & green 8 5
N 581. – 12 x. multicoloured 8 5
N 582. – 12 x. multicoloured 8 5
N 583. – 12 x. multicoloured 8 5

DESIGNS—VERT. No. N 581, Urban guerilla and attack on U.S. Embassy, Saigon. No. N 582, Two soldiers with flag, Hue. No. N 583, Mortar crew, Khe Sanh.

1969. Liberation of Hanoi. 15th Anniv.

N 584. **206.** 12 x. black and red 30 15
N 585. – 12 x. multicoloured 30 15

DESIGN: No. N 585, Children with construction toy.

1969. Fruits. Multicoloured.

N 586. 12 x. Type **207** 8 5
N 587. 12 x. Pawpaw 8 5
N 588. 20 x. Tangerines .. 12 8
N 589. 30 x. Oranges .. 15 10
N 590. 40 x. Lychees .. 25 15
N 591. 50 x. Persimmons .. 30 20

See also Nos. N 617/21 and N 633/6.

1969. Int. War Crimes Tribunal, Stockholm and Roskilde.

N 592. **208.** 12 x. black, red & brn. 8 5

209. Ho Chi Minh in 1924.

1970. Vietnamese Workers' Party. 40th Anniv. Multicoloured.

N 593. 12 x. Type **209** 8 5
N 594. 12 x. Ho Chi Minh in 1969 8 5
N 595. 12 x. Le Hong Phong .. 8 5
N 596. 12 x. Tran Phu 8 5
N 597. 12 x. Nguyne van Cu .. 8 5

Nos. N 595/7 are smaller than T **201**, size 40 × 24 mm.

210. Playtime in Nursery School. 211. Lenin and Red Flag.

1970. Children's Activities. Multicoloured

N 598. 12 x. Type **210** .. 8 5
N 599. 12 x. Playing with toys 8 5
N 600. 20 x. Watering plants .. 12 8
N 601. 20 x. Pasturing buffalo .. 12 8
N 602. 30 x. Feeding chickens .. 20 10
N 603. 40 x. Making music .. 25 15
N 604. 50 x. Flying model aircraft 30 20
N 605. 60 x. Going to school .. 40 25

1970. Lenin. Birth Cent.

N 606. **211.** 12 x. pur., red, yell. and blue 8 5
N 607. – 1 d. pur., red & yell. 40 25

DESIGN: 1 d. Portrait of Lenin.

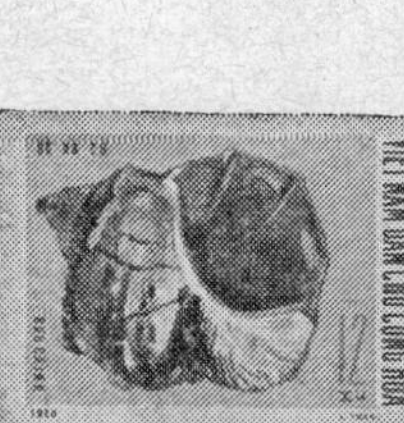

212. Oc Xa Cu Sea-shell. 213. Ho Chi Minh in 1930.

1970. Sea-shells. Multicoloured.

N 608. 12 x. Type **212** 8 5
N 609. 12 x. Oc Con Lon shell .. 8 5
N 610. 20 x. Oc Tien shell .. 12 8
N 611. 1 d. Oc Tu Va shell .. 40 25

1970. Ho Chi Minh's 80th Birth Anniv.

N 612. **213.** 12 x. blk., brn. & flesh 8 5
N 613. – 12 x. blk., bl. & grn. 8 5
N 614. – 2 d. blk., ochre & yell. 75 50

PORTRAITS: No. N 613, In 1945 with microphone No. N 614, In 1969.

214, Vietcong Flag.

1970. National Liberation Front Provisional Government in South Vietnam. 1st Anniv.

N 616. **214.** 12 x. multicoloured 8 5

215. Water-melon. 216. Power Linesman (" Electricity ").

1970. Fruits. Multicoloured.

N 617. 12 x. Type **215** .. 8 5
N 618. 12 x. Pumpkin .. 8 5
N 619. 20 x. Cucumber .. 12 8
N 620. 50 x. Courgette .. 25 15
N 621. 1 d. Charantais melon 40 25

1970. North Vietnamese Industries.

N 622. **216.** 12 x. blue andred .. 8 5
N 623. – 12 x. red, yell. & bl. 8 5
N 624. – 12 x. blk., oran. & bl. 8 5
N 625. – 12 x. yell., pur. & grn. 8 5

DESIGNS—VERT. No. N 623, Hands winding thread on bobbin (" Textiles "). No. N 624, Stoker and power station (" Electric Power "). No. N 625, Workers and lorry (" More coal for the Fatherland ").

217. Peasant Girl with Pigs. 219. Chuoi Tieu Bananas.

218. Pres. Ho Chi Minh.

1970. North Vietnamese Agriculture.

N 626. **217.** 12 x. multicoloured 8 5

1970. Democratic Republic of Vietnam. 25th Anniv.

N 627. **218.** 12 x. blk., brn. & red 8 5
N 628. – 12 x. dark brown, brown and green 8 5
N 629. – 12 x. brn., grey and red-brown .. 8 5
N 630. – 12 x. dark brown, brown and green 8 5
N 631. – 20 x. brn., red & bistre 12 8
N 632. – 1 d. brown, drab & chestnut 40 25

DESIGNS: No. 628, Vo Thi Sau facing firing-squad. No. N 629, Nguyen Van Troi and captors. No. N 630, Phan Giot attacking pill-box. No. N 631, Nguyen Viet Xuan encouraging troops. No. N 632, Nguyen Van Be attacking tank.

1970. Bananas. Multicoloured.

N 633. 12 x. Type **219** .. 8 5
N 634. 12 x. Chuoi Tay .. 8 5
N 635. 50 x. Chuoi Ngu .. 20 15
N 636. 1 d. Chuoi Mat .. 40 25

220. Flags, and Bayonets in Helmet.

1970. Indo-Chinese People's Summit Conf.

N 637. **220.** 12 x. multicoloured 8 5

221. Engels and Signature.

1970. Friedrich Engels. 150th Birth Anniv.

N 638. **221.** 12 x. blk. brn. & red 8 5
N 639. 1 d. blk., brn. & grn. 40 25

222. " Akistrodon ciatus ". 223. Mother and Child with Flag.

1970. Snakes. Multicoloured.

N 640. 12 x. Type **222** 8 5
N 641. 20 x. " Calliophis macclellandii " .. 10 8
N 642. 50 x. " Bungarus faciatus " 20 15
N 643. 1 d. " Trimeresurus gramineus " .. 40 25

1970. National Front for Liberation of South Vietnam. 10th Anniv. Multicoloured.

N 644. 6 x. Type **223** 5 5
N 645. 12 x. Vietcong flag and torch (horiz.) 8 5

1971. Victories of Liberation Army. As No. N 449, but value and colours changed.

N 646. **174.** 2 x. black & orange 5 5

224. Satellite in Earth Orbit.

1971. Launching of Chinese Satellite. 1st Anniv.

N 649. **224.** 12 x. multicoloured 8 5
N 650. 50 x. multicoloured 20 8

225. Ho Chi Minh Medal.

1971. Pres. Ho Chi Minh. 81st Birth Anniv.

N 652. **225.** 1 x. multicoloured 5 5
N 653. 3 x. multicoloured 5 5
N 654. 10 x. multicoloured 5 5
N 655. 12 x. multicoloured 8 5

226. Emperor Quang Trung liberating Hanoi.

1971. Tay Son Rising. Bicent.

N 657. **226.** 6 x. multicoloured 5 5
N 658. 12 x. multicoloured 8 5

227. Karl Marx and Music of " L'Internationale ".

1971. Paris Commune. Cent.

N 659. **227.** 12 x. blk., red & pink 8 5

228. Hai Thuong Lan Ong.

1971. Hai Thuong Lan Ong (physician). 250th Birth Anniv.

N 660. **228.** 12 x. blk., grn. & brn. 8 5
N 661. 50 x. multicoloured 20 8

229. "Kapimala". 230. Pres. Ho Chi Minh, Banner and Young Workers.

1971. Folk Sculptures in Tay Phuong Pagoda. Multicoloured.
N 662. 12 x. Type **229** .. 8 5
N 663. 12 x. "Sangkayasheta" 8 5
N 664. 12 x. "Vasumitri" .. 8 5
N 665. 12 x. "Dhikaca" .. 8 5
N 666. 30 x. "Bouddha Nandi" 15 10
N 667. 40 x. "Rahulata" .. 20 15
N 668. 50 x. "Sandha Nandi" .. 20 15
N 669. 1 d. "Cakyamuni" .. 40 30

1971. Ho Chi Minh Working Youth Union. 40th Anniv.
N 670. **230.** 12 x. multicoloured 8 5

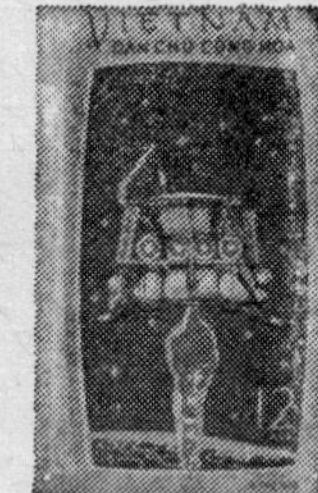

231. "Luna 16" on Moon. 232. "Luna 17" landing on Moon.

1971. Moon Flight of "Luna 16".
N 671. – 12 x. multicoloured 8 5
N 672. – 12 x. multicoloured 8 5
N 673. **231.** 1 d. brn., bl. & turq. 35 20
DESIGNS: No. N 671, Flight to Moon. No. N 672 Return to Earth.
Nos. N 671/2 were issued horizontally se-tenant forming a composite design, within the sheet.

1971. Moon Flight of "Luna 17".
N 674. – 12 x. red, bl. & grn. 8 5
N 675. – 12 x. pink, green & myrtle .. 8 5
N 676. **232.** 1 d. pink, brn. & grn. 35 20
DESIGNS—VERT. No. N 674, "Luna 17" Landing on Moon. HORIZ. No. N 675, "Luna 17" on Moon.

233. "White Tiger".

1971. "The Five Tigers" (folk-art paintings). Multicoloured.
N 679. 12 x. Type **233** .. 8 5
N 680. 12 x. "Yellow Tiger" 8 5
N 681. 12 x. "Red Tiger" .. 8 5
N 682. 40 x. "Green Tiger" .. 15 10
N 683. 50 x. "Grey Tiger" .. 20 12
N 684. 1 d. "Five Tigers" .. 35 20

234. Flags and Gate of Heavenly Peace, Peking. 235. Mongolian Emblem.

1971. Chinese Communist Party. 50th Anniv.
N 686. **234.** 12 x. multicoloured 8 5

1971. Mongolian People's Republic. 50th Anniv.
N 687. **235.** 12 x. multicoloured 8 5

236. "Drum Procession".

1972. Dong Ho Folk Engravings.
N 688. **236.** 12 x. pink, brn. & blk. 5 5
N 689. – 12 x. pink and black 5 5
N 690. – 12 x. multicoloured 5 5
N 691. – 12 x. multicoloured 5 5
N 692. – 40 x. multicoloured 10 5
N 693. – 50 x. multicoloured 12 8
DESIGNS—HORIZ. No. N 689, "Traditional wrestling". No. N 692, "Wedding of mice". No. N 693, "The Toad school". VERT. No. N 690, "Jealous Attack". No. N 691, "Gathering coconuts".

237. Workers. 238. Planting Vegetables.

1972. 3rd Vietnamese Trade Unions Congress.
N 694. **237.** 1 x. black and blue 5 5
N 695. – 12 x. black and orange 5 5
DESIGN: 12 x. As T **229**, but design reversed.

1972. Nat. Resistance. 25th Anniv.
N 696. **238.** 12 x. multicoloured 5 5
N 697. – 12 x. multicoloured 5 5
N 698. – 12 x. multicoloured 5 5
N 699. – 12 x. turq., red & pink 5 5
DESIGNS: No. N 697, Munitions worker. No. N 698, Soldier with flame-thrower. No. N 699, Text of Ho Chi Minh's Appeal.

239. Ho Chi Minh's Birthplace.

1972. Ho Chi Minh. 82nd Birth Anniv.
N 700. **329.** 12 x. black, drab & ochre 5 5
N 701. – 12 x. blk., grn. & pink 5 5
DESIGN: No. N 701, Ho Chi Minh's House, Hanoi.

240. Captured Pilot and Falling Aircraft. 241. G. Dimitrov.

1972. "3,500th U.S. Aircraft Brought Down over North Vietnam."
N 702. **240.** 12 x. green and red 10 5
N 703. 12 x. black & red .. 10 5
No. N 703 has the inscription, amended to record the actual date on which the 3,500th aircraft was brought down–20.4.1972.

1972. Georgi Dimitrov (Bulgarian statesman). 90th Birth Anniv.
N 704. **241.** 12 x. brown & green 5 5
N 705. – 12 x. black & pink .. 5 5
DESIGN: No. N 705, Dimitrov at Leipzig Court, 1933.

242. Falcated Teal. 243. Anti-Aircraft Gunner.

1972. Vietnamese Birds. Multicoloured.
N 706. 12 x, Type **242** .. 5 5
N 707. 12 x. Red-wattled lapwing 5 5
N 708. 30 x. Cattle egret .. 12 8
N 709. 40 x. Watercock .. 15 10
N 710. 50 x. Purle gallinule .. 20 12
N 711. 1 s. Adjutant-bird (stock) 35 20

1972. "4,000th U.S. Aircraft Brought Down over North Vietnam".
N 712. **243.** 12 x. blk., mve. & pink 10 5
N 713. – 12 x. grn., blk. & orge. 10 5
DESIGN: No. N 713, Gunner holding shell.

244. Umbrella Dance.

1972. Tay Nguyen Folk Dances. Mult.
N 714. 12 x. Type **244** 5 5
N 715. 12 x. Drum dance .. 5 5
N 716. 12 x. Shield dance .. 5 5
N 717. 20 x. Galloping-horse dance 8 5
N 718. 30 x. Ka-dong dance .. 10 8
N 719. 40 x. Grinding-rice dance 12 10
N 720. 50 x. Gong dance .. 15 12
N 721. 1 d. Cham rong dance 30 20

245. "Soyuz 11" Spacecraft.

1972. Space Flight of "Soyuz 11".
N 722. **245.** 12 x. blue and lilac .. 5 5
N 723. – 1 d. brown and flesh 30 20
DESIGN: 1 d. "Soyuz 11" astronauts.

246. Wild-Hill-dog.

1973. Wild Animals (1st series). Mult.
N 724. 12 x. Type **246** .. 5 5
N 725. 30 x. Leopard .. 10 8
N 726. 50 x. Leopard-cat .. 15 12
N 727. 1 d. Otter 30 20
See also Nos. N736/9.

247. Copernicus and Globe.

1973. Copernicus (astronomer). 500th Birth Anniv.
N 728. **247.** 12 x. blk., red & brn. 5 5
N 729. – 12 x. blk., red & brn. 5 5
N 730. – 30 x. black & brown 10 8
DESIGNS—HORIZ. 12 x. (No. N 729), Copernicus and sun. VERT. 30 x. Copernicus and facsimile signature.

248. "Drummers".

1973. Engravings from Ngoc Lu Bronze Drums. Each yellow and green.
N 731. 12 x. Type **248** .. 5 5
N 732. 12 x. "Pounding rice" 5 5
N 733. 12 x. "Folk-dancing" 5 5
N 734. 12 x. "War canoe" .. 5 5
N 735. 12 x. "Birds and beasts" 5 5

249. Chevrotain. 250. Grass Warblers ("Megalurus palustris").

1973. Wild Animals (2nd series). Mult.
N 736. 12 x. Type **249** .. 5 5
N 737 30 x. Serow 10 8
N 738. 50 x. Wild boar .. 15 12
N 739. 1 d. Musk deer 30 20

1973. Birds Useful to Agriculture. Mult.
N 740. 12 x. Type **250** .. 5 5
N 741. 12 x. Red-whiskered bulbuls 5 5
N 742. 20 x. Shamus 8 5
N 743. 40 x. Collared fantails .. 12 10
N 744. 50 x. Great tits .. 15 12
N 745. 1 d. Japanese white-eyes 30 20

251. "Ready to Learn".

1973. "Three Readies" Youth Movement.
N 748. **251.** 12 x. brown & green 5 5
N 749. – 12 x. violet and blue 5 5
N 750. – 12 x. green & mauve 5 5
DESIGNS: No. 749, Soldiers on the march ("Ready to Fight"). No. N 750, Road construction ("Ready to Work").

252. Flags of North Vietnam and North Korea.

1973. People's Republic of Korea. 25th Anniv.
N 751. **252.** 12 x. multicoloured 5 5

253. Bomber exploding over Haiphong.

1973. Victory over U.S. Air Force.
N 752. – 12 x. multicoloured 5 5
N 753. **253.** 12 x. multicoloured 5 5
N 754. – 12 x. multicoloured 5 5
N 755. – 1 d. black and red .. 30 20
DESIGNS: No. N 752, Dogfight over Hanoi. No. N 754, Anti-aircraft gun. No. N 755, Aircraft wreckage in China Sea.

254. Elephant hauling logs. 255. Dahlia.

1974. Vietnamese Elephants. Multicoloured.
N 758. 12 x. Type **254** 5 5
N 759. 12 x. War elephant .. 5 5
N 760. 40 x. Elephant rolling logs 12 8
N 761. 50 x. Circus elephant .. 15 10
N 762. 1 d. Elephant carrying war supplies 30 20

1974. Flowers.
N 763. **255.** 12 x. red, lake & grn. 5 5
N 764. – 12 x. red, lake & grn. 5 5
N 765. – 12 x. yell., grn. & bl. 5 5
N 766. – 12 x. multicoloured 5 5
N 767. – 12 x. multicoloured 5 5
FLOWERS: No. N 764, Rose. No. N 765, Chrysanthemum. No. N 766, Bach Mi. No. N 767, Dai Doa.

256. Soldier planting Flag. **257.** Armed Worker and Peasant.

1974. Victory at Dien Bien Phu. 20th Anniv.
N 768. 12 x. Type **256** 5 5
N 769. 12 x. Victory badge .. 5 5

1974. "Three Responsibilities" Women's Movement.
N 770. **257.** 12 x. blue and pink 5 5
N 771. – 12 x. blue and pink 5 5
DESIGN: No. N 771, Woman operating loom.

258. Cuc Nau Chrysanthemum. **259.** "Corchorus capsularis".

1974. Vietnamese Chrysanthemums. Mult.
N 772. 12 x. Type **258** 5 5
N 773. 12 x. Cuc Vang 5 5
N 774. 20 x. Cuc Ngoc Khong Tuoc 8 5
N 775. 30 x. Cuc Trang 10 5
N 776. 40 x. Kim Cuc 12 8
N 777. 50 x. Cuc Hong Mi .. 15 10
N 778. 60 x. Cuc Gam 20 12
N 779. 1 d. Cuc Tim 30 20

1974. Textile Plants.
N 780. **259.** 12 x. brown, green and olive-brown .. 5 5
N 781. – 12 x. brn., grn. & pink 5 5
N 782. – 30 x. brn., grn. & yell. 10 5
DESIGNS: No. N 781, "Cyperus tojet jormis". No. N 782, "Morus alba".

260. Nike Statue, Warsaw.

1974. People's Republic of Poland, 30th Anniv.
N 783. **260.** 1 x. purple, pink and red 5 5
N 784. 2 x. red, pink and verm. 5 5
N 785. 3 x. brown, pink and red 5 5
N 786. 12 x. lt. red, pink & red 5 5

261. Flags of China and Vietnam.

1974. People's Republic of China. 25th Anniv.
N 787. **261.** 12 x. multicoloured 5 5

262. Handclasp with Vietnamese and East German Flags.

1974. German Democratic Republic. 25th Anniv.
N 788. **262.** 12 x. multicoloured 5 5

263. Woman Bricklayer. **264.** Pres. Allende with Chilean Flag.

1974. Liberation of Hanoi. 20th Anniv. Multicoloured.
N 789. 12 x. Type **263** 5 5
N 790. 12 x. Soldier with child 5 5

1974. Salvador Allende (President of Chile) and Pablo Neruda (Chilean poet). 1st Death Annivs.
N 791. **264.** 12 x. blue and red .. 5 5
N 792. – 12 x. blue (Pablo Neruda) 5 5

265. "Rhizostoma".

1974. Marine Life. Multicoloured.
N 793. 12 x. Type **265** 5 5
N 794. 12 x. "Loligo" 5 5
N 795. 30 x. "Haleotis" .. 10 5
N 796. 40 x. "Pteria martensii" 12 8
N 797. 50 x. "Sepia officinalis" 15 10
N 798. 1 d. "Palinurus japonicus" .. 30 20

266. Flags of Algeria and Vietnam. **267.** Albanian Emblem.

1974. Algerian War of Liberation. 20th Anniv.
N 799. **266.** 12 x. multicoloured 5 5

1974. People's Republic of Albania. 30th Anniv. Multicoloured.
N 800. 12 x. Type **267** 5 5
N 801. 12 x. Girls from Albania and North Vietnam 5 5

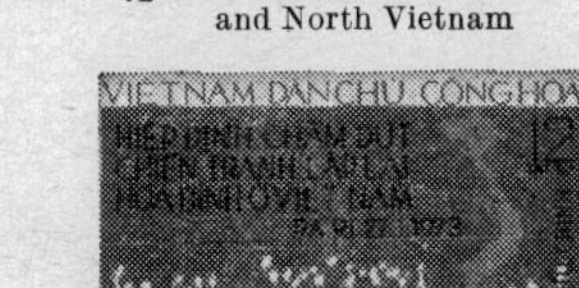

268. Signing of Paris Agreement.

1975. Paris Agreement on Vietnam. 2nd Anniv.
N 802. **268.** 12 x. blk., grn. & emerald 5 5
N 803. – 12 x. blk., blue and grey-blue 5 5
DESIGN: No. N 803, International Conference in session.

269. Tran Phu.

1975. Vietnamese Workers' Party. 45th Anniv.
N 804. **269.** 12 x. brn., red & pink 5 5
N 805. – 12 x. brn., red & pink 5 5
N 806. – 12 x. brn., red & pink 5 5
N 807. – 12 x. brn., red & pink 5 5
N 808. – 60 x. brown, chestnut and pink 25 12
PORTRAITS—HORIZ. No. N 805, Nguyen Van Cu. No. N 806, Le Hong Phong. No. N 807, Ngo Gia Tu. VERT. No. N 808, Ho Chi Minh in 1924.

280. "Costus speciosus". **281.** "Achras sapota".

1975. Medicinal Plants. Multicoloured.
N 809. 12 x. Type **280** 5 5
N 810. 12 x. "Rosa laevigata" 5 5
N 811. 12 x. "Curcuma zedoaria" 5 5
N 812. 30 x. "Erythrina indica" 10 5
N 813. 40 x. "Lilium brownii" 12 8
N 814. 50 x. "Hibiscus sagittifolius" .. 15 10
N 815. 60 x. "Papaveer somniferum" .. 20 12
N 816. 1 d. "Belamcanda chinensis" 30 20

1975. Fruits. Multicoloured.
N 817. 12 x. Type **281** 5 5
N 818. 12 x. "Persica vulgaris" 5 5
N 819. 20 x. "Eugenia jambos" 8 5
N 820. 30 x. "Chrysophyllum cainito" 12 8
N 821. 40 x. "Lucuma mamosa" 15 10
N 822. 50 x. "Prunica granitum" 20 12
N 823. 60 x. "Durio ziberthinus" 25 15
N 824. 1 d. "Prunus salicina" 35 25

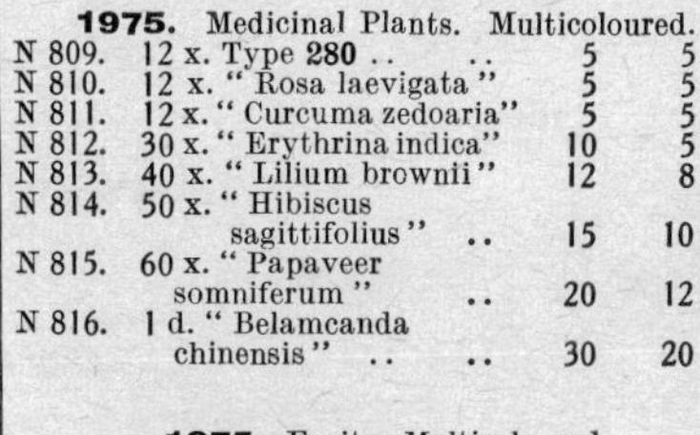

282. Ho Chi Minh. **283.** Ho Chi Minh proclaiming Independence, 1945.

1975. Ho Chi Minh. 85th Birth Anniv.
N 825. **282.** 12 x. multicoloured 5 5
N 826. 60 x. multicoloured 25 15

1975. Democratic Republic of Vietnam. 30th Anniv. Multicoloured.
N 827. 12 x. Type **283** 5 5
N 828. 12 x. Democratic Republic emblem 5 5
N 829. 12 x. Democratic Republic flag 5 5

284. "Dermochelys coriacea". **285.** Arms of Hungary.

1975. Reptiles. Multicoloured.
N 831. 12 x. Type **284** 5 5
N 832. 12 x. "Physignathus cocincinus" 5 5
N 833. 20 x. "Hydrophis brookii" 10 8
N 834. 30 x. "Platysternum megacephalum" .. 15 12
N 835. 40 x. "Leiolepis belliana" 20 15
N 836. 50 x. "Python molurus" 25 20
N 837. 60 x. "Naja hannah" 30 25
N 838. 1 d. "Draco maculatus" 45 35

1975. Liberation of Hungary. 30th Anniv.
N 839. **285.** 12 x. multicoloured 5 5

286. "Pathysa antiphates".

1976. Butterflies. Multicoloured.
N 840. 12 x. Type **286** 5 5
N 841. 12 x. "Danais plexippus" 5 5
N 842. 20 x. "Gynautocera papilionaria" .. 10 8
N 843. 30 x. "Maenas salaminia" 15 12
N 844. 40 x. "Papilio machaon" 20 15
N 845. 50 x. "Ixias pyrene" .. 25 20
N 846. 60 x. "Eusemia Vetula" 30 25
N 847. 1 d. "Eriboea hbn" .. 45 35

287. Lan Hoang Orchid. **288.** "Paguma Larvata".

1976. Lunar New Year.
N 848. **287.** 6 x. yell., grn. & blue 5 5
N 849 12 x. yell., grn. & red 5 5

1976. Wild Animals. Multicoloured.
N 850. 12 x. Type **288** 5 5
N 851. 12 x. "Callosiurus erythraeus" .. 5 5
N 852. 20 x. "Macaca mulatta" 10 8
N 853. 30 x. "Hystrix hodgsoni" 15 12
N 854. 40 x. "Nyctereutes procyonoides" .. 20 15
N 855. 50 x. "Selenarctos thibetanus" 25 20
N 856. 60 x. "Panthera pardus" 30 25
N 857. 1 d. "Cyoocephalus variegatus" 45 35

289. Voters and Map.

1976. Unified National Assembly. First Elections.
N 858. **289.** 6 x. red and sepia .. 5 5
N 859. – 6 x. yellow and red 5 5
N 860. **289.** 12 x. red and blue .. 5 5
DESIGN: 35 × 24 mm. No. 859, Map and ballot box.

See also Nos. NLF 64/6 of National Front for the Liberation of South Vietnam.

290. Map and Text.

1976. Unified National Assembly. First Session.
N 861. **290.** 6 x. pur., red & yell. 5 5
N 862. 12 x. turq., red & yell. 5 5
N 863. – 12 x. bistre, red & yell. 5 5
DESIGN—VERT. (27 × 42 mm.) No. 863, Vietnam map and design from Ngoc Lu Drum. No. 862 shows different text from Type **290**.

See also Nos. NLF 55/6 of National Front for the Liberation of South Vietnam.

291. "Dendrobium devonianum".

1976. Orchids. Multicoloured.

N 864. 12 x. Type **291** 5 5
N 865. 12 x. "Habenaria rhodocheila" .. 5 5
N 866. 20 x. "Dendrobium tortile" 10 8
N 867. 30 x. "Doritis pulcherrima" 15 12
N 868. 40 x. "Dendrobium farmeri" 20 15
N 869. 50 x. "Dendrobium aggregatum" .. 25 20
N 870. 60 x. "Eria pannea" .. 30 25
N 871. 1 d. "Paphiopedilum concolor" 45 35

FRANK STAMPS

F 1. F 2. Invalids in Rice-field.

1958. No value indicated.

NF 82. F **1.** (–) Red, yellow and green .. .. 2·00 75

Issued to war-disabled persons for private correspondence.

1959. No value indicated.

NF 105. F **2.** (–) Brown 45 30
NF 106. (–) Olive & grey-blue 90 40

Issued to invalids in agriculture for private correspondence.

F 3. Invalids' Badge.

1971. No value indicated.

NF 647. F **3.** (–) Brown and red 8 8

Issued to disabled ex-servicemen for private correspondence.

F 4. "Returning Home". F 5. Disabled soldier with drill.

1973.

NF 746. F **4.** 12 x. blk. and red 5 5
NF 747. F **5.** 12 x. black & blue 5 5

Issued to disabled veterans for private correspondence.

MILITARY FRANK STAMPS

MF 1. Soldier and Train.

1959. No value indicated.

NMF 112. MF **1.** (–) Black & grn. 45 35

MF 2. Mounted Frontier Guard. MF 3. Military Medal and Invalid's Badge.

1961. No value indicated.

NMF 154. MF **2.** (–) Multicoloured 1·25 60

1963.

NMF 277. MF **3.** 12 x. multicoloured 40 40

For use on disabled soldiers' mail.

MF 4. Soldier and Army Badge.  MF 5. Soldier in Action.

1964. No value indicated.

NMF 325. MF **4.** (–) Green, black and orange .. 30 25

1965. No value indicated.

NMF 373. MF **5.** (–) Black & red 20 5
NMF 374. (–) Black & grn. 20 5

MF 6. Soldiers and Weapons.

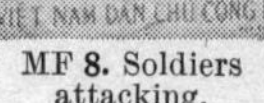

MF 8. Soldiers attacking.  MF 7. "Star" Badge of People's Army.

1966. No value indicated.

NMF 447. MF **6.** (–) Violet & blue 12 8

1967. No value indicated.

NMF 488. MF **7.** (–) Multicoloured 12 8

1968. No value indicated.

NMF 547. MF **8.** (–) Lilac .. 8 8

MF 9. Nguyen Van Be attacking Tank.

1971. No value indicated.

NMF 648. MF **9.** (–) Black, red & drab.. .. 8 8

MF 10. Disabled Soldier with Baby.

1971. No value indicated.

NMF 651. MF **10.** (–) Brown, red and yellow .. 8 8

MF 11. Nguyen Viet Yuan and Anti-aircraft Gun.

1971. No value indicated.

NMF 677. MF **11.** (–) Black, pink and buff .. 8 5
NMF 678. (–) Brown & grn. 5 5

MF 12. Sub-machine Gun and Tanks.

1974. No value indicated.

NMF 756. – (–) Black, yell. and blue .. 5 5
NMF 757. MF **12.** (–) Black, red and brown 5 5
NMF 758. – (–) Black, flesh and red .. 5 5

DESIGN: Nos. NMF 756 and 758; Soldier with bayonet advancing. No. NMF is 32×22 mm.; No. NMF 758 31×21 mm.

OFFICIAL STAMPS

The values on Nos. NO 11/16 to NO 34 are in kilogrammes of rice, the basis of the State's economy.

O 1. "Family Left Behind" O 2. Rice-harvester.

1952. Issue for Central Annam. Imperf.

NO 11. O **1.** 0.050 k. red.. .. — 60·00
NO 12. 0.300 k. red.. .. — 60·00
NO 13. 0.300 k. violet .. — 60·00
NO 14. 0.600 k. green .. — 60·00
NO 16. 1,000 k. green .. — 90·00

1953. Production and Economy Campaign.

NO 17. O **2.** 0.600 k. red.. .. 40 30
NO 18. 1.000 k. brown .. 50 30
NO 19. 2.000 k. orange .. 75 40
NO 20. 5.000 k. slate 1·50 80

1954. Issue for Central Annam. No. N 12 surch. **TEMSU VU O. k 300 THOC.**

NO 21. **3.** 0.300 k. on 30 d. on 5 d. green .. .. £140 90·00

1954. Dien-Bien-Phu Victory. As T 7 but value in "KILO". Imperf.

NO 24. 0.600 k. ochre and sepia 1·00 70

1955. Surch. **O k, 100 THOC**

NO 33. **1.** 0.100 k. on 2 d. brown 50·00 25·00
NO 34. 0.100 k. on 5 d. red .. 50·00 25·00

1955. Land Reform. As T 9 but inscr. "SU YU".

NO 38. 40 d. blue .. .. 1·00 1·00
NO 39. 80 d. rose .. .. 2·00 2·00

O 3. Cu Chinh Lan (Tank Destroyer).

1956. Cu-Chinh-Lan Commem.

NO 50. O **3.** 20 d. green & turq. 40 30
NO 51. 80 d. maroon & rose 40 30
NO 52. 100 d. sepia & drab 60 50
NO 53. 500 d. bl. & pale bl. 3·00 3·00
NO 54. 1,000 d. brn. & salm. 2·75 2·25
NO 55. 2,000 d. pur. & grn. 7·00 6·00
NO 56. 3,000 d. lake & lilac 10·00 8·00

1957. 4th World T.U. Conf., Leipzig. As T 18 but inscr. "SU VU".

NO 69. 20 d. green .. 25 25
NO 70. 40 d. blue .. 35 35
NO 71. 80 d. lake .. 50 50
NO 2. 100 d. brown .. 70 70

O 4. Moi Cot Pagoda, Hanoi. O 5. Lathe.

1957.

NO 75a. O **4.** 150 d. brown & grn. 1·10 55
NO 76. 150 d. black & yell. 1·40 70

1958. Arts and Crafts Fair, Hanoi.

NO 83. O **5.** 150 d. black & pink 35 25
NO 84. 200 d. blue & orange 50 35

O 6. Congress Symbol.

1958. 1st World Congress of Young Workers, Prague.

NO 85. O **6.** 150 d. red and green 60 30

O 7. Soldier, Factory and Crops.

1958. Military Service.

NO 91. O **7.** 50 d. sl.-bl. & mag. 35 25
NO 92. 150 d. chest. & grn. 45 30
NO 93. 200 d. red & yellow 55 35

O 8. Footballer and Hanoi Stadium.

1958. Opening of New Hanoi Stadium.

NO 102. O **8.** 10 d. lilac & grey-bl. 8 5
NO 103. 20 d. olive & salmon 10 5
NO 104. 80 d. brn. & ochre 20 5
NO 105. 150 d. brn. & turq. 35 20

O 9. Armed Forces on Boat. O 10. Woman with Rice-planter.

1962. Military Service.

NO 223. O **9.** 12 x. red, black, brown & blue .. 60 40

1962. Rural Service.

NO 229. O **10.** 3 x. red .. 8 5
NO 230. 6 x. blue-green .. 12 5
NO 231. 12 x. olive .. 20 12

O 11. Postman delivering Letter.

1966. Rural Service.

NO 445. O **11.** 3 x. purple, bistre and lilac .. 5 5
NO 446. – 6 x. purple, bistre and turquoise.. 10 10

DESIGN: 6 x. As Type O 11 but design reversed.

POSTAGE DUE STAMPS

1952. Handstamped **TT** in diamond frame.

ND 33. **2.** 100 d. green .. .. 4·50 4·50
ND 34. 100 d. brown .. 4·50 4·50
ND 35. **4.** 100 d. violet .. 9·00 9·00
ND 36. **2.** 200 d. red .. 9·00 9·00

D 1. Letter Scales. D 2.

1955.

ND 40. D **1.** 50 d. brown & lemon 1·00 75

1958.

ND 101. D **2.** 10 d. red and violet 20 20
ND 102. 20 d. green & orange 30 30
ND 103. 100 d. re dand slate 70 70
ND 104. 300 d. red and olive 1·00 1·00

SOCIALIST REPUBLIC OF VIETNAM

Following elections held in April 1976 a National Assembly representing the whole of Vietnam met in Hanoi on 24th June 1976 and on 2 July proclaimed the reunification of the country as the Socialist Republic of Vietnam, with Hanoi as capital.

100 xu = 1 dong.

13. Red Cross and Vietnam Map on Globe.

1976. Vietnamese Red Cross. 30th Anniv.
99. **13.** 12 x. red, blue and green 5 5

14. " Lutjanus sebae ".

1976. Marine Fishes. Multicoloured.
102. 12 x. Type **14** 5 5
103. 12 x. " Dampaeria melanotaeia ".. .. .. 5 5
104. 20 x. " Therapon theraps " 10 8
105. 30 x. " Amphiprion bifasciatus ".. .. .. 15 12
106. 40 x. " Abudefduf sexfasciatus ".. .. .. 20 15
107. 50 x. " Heniochus acuminatus ".. .. .. 25 20
108. 60 x. " Amphiprion macrostoma " 30 25
109. 1 d. " Symphorus spilurus " 45 35

15. Party Flag and Map. **16.** Workers and Flag.

1976. 4th Congress of Vietnam Workers' Party (1st issue). Flag in yellow and red, background colours given below.
111. **15.** 2 x. turquoise 5 5
112. 3 x. purple 5 5
113. 5 x. turquoise 5 5
114. 10 x. green 5 5
115. 12 x. myrtle 5 5
116. 20 x. green 10 8

1976. 4th Congress of Vietnam Workers' Party (2nd issue). Multicoloured.
117. 12 x. Type **16** 5 5
118. 12 x. Industry and agriculture 5 5

FRANK STAMPS

F 1. Invalid's Badge.

1976. For use by disabled veterans. Dated " 27.7.75 ". No value indicated.
F 100. **F 1.** (–) Red and blue .. 5 5
F 101. – (–) Myrtle, light green and olive.. .. 5 5

DESIGN: No. F 101, Disabled veteran in factory.

MILITARY FRANK STAMP

MF 1. Soldier and Map of Vietnam.

1976. No value indicated.
MF 110. **MF 1.** (–) Black and red 5 5

VIRGIN ISLANDS BC

A group of the Leeward Is., Br. W. Indies. Used general issues for Leeward Is. concurrently with Virgin Is. stamps until 1st July, 1956. A Crown Colony.

1951. 100 cents = 1 West Indian dollar.
1962. 100 cents = 1 U.S. dollar.

1. St. Ursula.

2.

3.

4.

1866.
8. **1.** 1d. green .. .. .. 25·00 28·00
16. **2.** 4d. red .. .. .. 17·00 24·00
7. **3.** 6d. red .. .. .. 25·00 35·00
11. **4.** 1s. black and red .. 90·00 £100

1867. With heavy coloured border
18. **4.** 1s. black and red .. 18·00 25·00

5.

6.

1880.
26. **5.** ½d. yellow.. .. .. 18·00 23·00
27. ½d. green .. .. .. 1·75 3·50
24. 1d. green .. .. .. 14·00 20·00
29. 1d. red .. .. .. 6·50 7·50
25. 2½d. brown .. .. 20·00 25·00
31. 2½d. blue .. .. .. 2·25 3·50

1887.
32. **1.** 1d. red .. .. .. 2·50 2·75
35. **2.** 4d. brown.. .. .. 9·00 11·00
39. **3.** 6d. violet .. .. 9·00 13·00
41. **4.** 1s. brown .. .. 14·00 17·00

1888. No. 18 surch. **4D.**
42. **4.** 4d. on 1s. black and red.. 35·00 50·00

1899.
43. **6.** ½d. green 40 80
44. 1d. red .. .. .. 1·75 1·75
45. 2½d. blue .. .. .. 5·50 6·00
46. 4d. brown .. .. .. 5·50 7·00
47. 6d. violet .. .. .. 4·00 5·00
48. 7d. green .. .. .. 5·50 5·50
49. 1s. yellow .. .. .. 9·00 9·00
50. 5s. blue .. .. .. 20·00 22·00

7.

8

1904.
54. **7.** ½d. purple and green .. 35 40
55. 1d. purple and red .. 60 65
56. 2d. purple and brown .. 2·75 4·50
57. 2½d. purple and blue .. 2·00 3·00
58. 3d. purple and black .. 2·50 3·50
59. 6d. purple and brown .. 3·00 4·00
60. 1s. green and red.. .. 4·50 6·00
61. 2s. 6d. green and black .. 15·00 18·00
62. 5s. green and blue .. 27·00 32·00

1913.
63. **8.** ½d. green 35 50
65. 1d. red 35 55
70. 2d. grey .. .. .. 1·40 3·00
72. 2½d. blue .. .. .. 1·40 2·50
73. 3d. purple on yellow .. 90 2·50
74. 6d. purple .. .. 1·40 2·75
75. 1s. black on green .. 2·50 3·50
76. 2s. 6d. blk. & red on blue 11·00 13·00
77. 5s. green & red on yellow 24·00 27·00

1917. Optd. **WAR STAMP.**
78a. **8.** 1d. red 15 35
79. 3d. purple on yellow .. 25 80

9.

10. King George VI and Badge of Colony.

1922.
86. **9.** ½d. green 10 15
87. 1d. red 12 35
88. 1d. violet .. .. 70 1·10
90. 1½d. red.. .. .. 1·25 1·50
91. 1½d. brown .. .. 1·50 1·50
92. 2d. grey 55 70
93. 2½d. blue .. .. 1·40 2·75
94. 2½d. orange .. .. 1·00 65
82. 3d. purple on yellow .. 25 75
97. 5d. purple and olive .. 3·75 7·00
98. 6d. purple .. .. 85 1·75
83. 1s. black on green .. 85 2·50
84. 2s. 6d. blk. & red on blue 2·75 4·00
101. 5s. green & red on yellow 11·00 13·00

1935. Silver Jubilee. As T **11** of Antigua.
103. 1d. blue and red .. 10 15
104. 1½d. blue and grey .. 12 25
105. 2½d. brown and blue .. 35 45
106. 1s. grey and purple .. 1·50 2·00

1937. Coronation. As T **2** of Aden.
107. 1d. red 8 8
108. 1½d. brown 20 15
109. 2½d. blue . .. 25 30

1938.
110. **10.** ½d. green 8 8
111. 1d. red 8 8
112. 1½d. brown 8 8
113. 2d. grey 8 8
114. 2½d. blue 12 10
115. 3d. orange 12 12
116. 6d. mauve 20 20
117. 1s. brown 35 35
118. 2s. 6d. brown .. 1·40 1·25
119. 5s. red .. .. 1·75 1·75
120. 10s. blue .. .. 3·50 4·00
121. £1 black .. .. 7·50 8·50

1946. Victory. As T **4** of Aden.
122. 1½d. brown 8 8
123. 3d. yellow 8 8

1949. Silver Wedding. As T **5/6** of Aden.
124. 2½d. blue 8 8
125. £1 grey .. .. .. 5·50 8·00

1949. U.P.U. As T **14/17** of Antigua.
126. 2½d. blue 15 12
127. 3d. orange 25 20
128. 6d. magenta 40 35
129. 1s. olive 75 80

1951. Inaug. of B.W.I. University College. As T **18/19** of Antigua.
130. 3 c. black and red .. 12 10
131. 12 c. black and violet .. 40 40

11. Map.

1951. Restoration of Legislative Council
132. **11.** 6 c. orange 15 25
133. 12 c. purple 15 40
134. 24 c. olive 40 65
135. $1.20 red .. .. 2·00 2·75

12. Jost Van Dyke Is.

1952.
136. – 1 c. black 12 15
137. **12.** 2 c. green 25 15
138. – 3 c. black and brown .. 15 20
139. – 4 c. red 25 30
140. – 5 c. claret and black .. 40 50
141. – 8 c. blue 20 25
142. – 12 c. violet 25 40
143. – 24 c. brown 30 45
144. – 60 c. green and blue .. 60 1·00
145. – $1.20 black and blue .. 2·00 2·50
146. – $2.40 green and brown 3·00 3·50
147. – $4.80 blue and red .. 5·50 7·00

DESIGNS—VERT. 1 c. Sombrero lighthouse. 24 c. Badge of Presidency. HORIZ. VIEWS: 3 c. Sheep. 5 c. Cattle. 60 c. Dead Man's Chest (Is.). $1.20 Sir Francis Drake Channel. $2.40 Road Town. HORIZ. MAPS: 4 c. Anegada Is. 8 c. Virgin Gorda Is. 12c. Tortola Is. $4.80 Virgin Is.

1953. Coronation. As T **7** of Aden.
148. 2 c. black and green .. 25 25

13. Map of Tortola Is.

14. Brown Pelican.

1956.
149. **13.** ½ c. black and purple .. 5 5
150. – 1 c. turquoise and slate 5 5
151. – 2 c. vermilion and black 5 8
152. – 3 c. blue and olive .. 8 8
153. – 4 c. chocolate & turq. .. 10 10
154. – 5 c. black 10 10
155. – 8 c. orange and blue .. 10 12
156. – 12 c. blue and red .. 12 15
157. – 24 c. green and chestnut 30 30
158. – 60 c. indigo and orange 1·10 1·10
159. – $1.20 green and red .. 2·00 2·50
160. **14.** $2.40 lemon and purple 3·75 4·50
161. – $4.80 sepia & turquoise 7·50 9·00

DESIGNS—HORIZ. As T **13**: 1 c. Virgin Islands sloop. 2 c. Nelthrop Red Poll bull. 3 c. Rood Harbour. 4 c. Mountain travel. 5 c. Badge of the Presidency. 8 c. Beach scene. 12 c. Boat launching. 24 c. White Cedar Tree. 60 c. Bonito (fish). $1.20 Treasury Square. As T **14**: $4.80 Man-o'-War Bird.

1962. New Currency. Nos. 149/53, 155/61 surch. in U.S. Currency.
162. **13.** 1 c. on ½ c. blk. & purple 5 5
163. – 2 c. on 1 c. turquoise and slate-violet 5 5
164. – 3 c. on 2 c. verm. & blk. 5 8
165. – 4 c. on 3 c. blue & olive 10 10
166. – 5 c. on 4 c. choc. & turq. 10 12
167. – 8 c. on 8 c. orange & blue 15 15
186. – 10 c. on 12 c. blue & red 20 25
169. – 12 c. on 24 c. grn. & chest. 20 25
170. – 25 c. on 60 c. ind. & orge. 40 45
171. – 70 c. on $1.20 grn. & red 2·50 3·00
172. **14.** $1.40 on $2.40 lemon and purple .. .. 2·50 3·00
173. – $2.80 on $4.80 sepia and turquoise .. .. 5·50 6·00

1963. Freedom from Hunger. As T **10** of Aden.
174. 25 c. violet 50 50

1963. Red Cross Cent. As T **24** of Antigua.
175. 2 c. red and black.. .. 10 12
176. 25 c. red and blue.. .. 55 60

1964. Shakespeare. 400th Birth Anniv. As T **25** of Antigua.
177. 10 c. blue 20 25

15. Bonito.

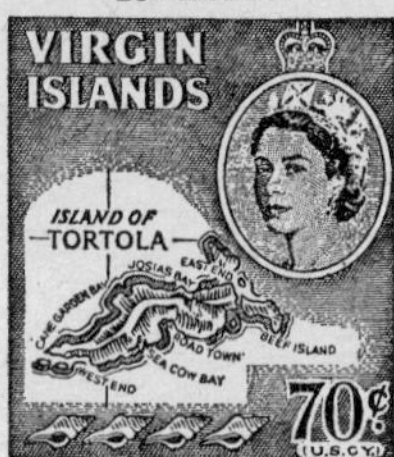

16. Map of Tortola.

1964.

178. 15. 1 c. blue and olive .. 5 5
179. – 2 c. olive and red .. 5 5
180. – 3 c. sepia & turquoise.. 5 5
181. – 4 c. black and red .. 5 8
182. – 5 c. black and green .. 8 10
183. – 6 c. black and orange .. 10 12
184. – 8 c. black and magenta 12 15
185. – 10 c. lake and lilac .. 20 25
186. – 12 c. green & violet-blue 20 25
187. – 15 c. green and black.. 25 30
188. – 25 c. green and purple.. 30 35
189. 16. 70 c. black and brown.. 1·00 1·10
190. – $1 green and chestnut.. 1·75 2·00
191. – $1.40 blue and red .. 2·50 3·00
192. – $2.80 black and purple 5·00 6·00

DESIGNS—HORIZ. As T **15**: 2 c. Soper's Hole. 3 c. Brown Pelican. 4 c. Dead Man's Chest. 5 c. Road Harbour. 6 c. Fallen Jerusalem. 8 c. The Baths, Virgin Gorda. 10 c. Map of Virgin Islands. 12 c. Tortola–St. Thomas Ferry. 15 c. The Towers, Tortola. 25 c. Beef Island Airfield. VERT. As T **16**: $1, Virgin Gorda. $1.40, Yachts at anchor. $2.80, Badge of the Colony (27½ × 37½ mm.).

1965. I.T.U. Cent. As T **26** of Antigua.

193. 4 c. yellow and turquoise.. 10 10
194. 25 c. blue and buff.. .. 40 50

1965. I.C.Y. As T **27** of Antigua.

195. 1 c. purple and turquoise.. 5 5
196. 25 c. green and lavender.. 40 45

1966. Churchill Commem. As T **28** of Antigua.

197. 1 c. blue 5 5
198. 2 c. green 8 8
199. 10 c. brown 30 30
200. 25 c. violet.. .. .. 55 60

1966. Royal Visit. As T **29** of Antigua.

201. 4 c. black and blue .. 10 10
202. 70 c. black and magenta.. 90 1·00

17. R.M.S. "Atrato", 1866.

1966. Stamp Cent. Multicoloured.

203. 5 c. Type **17** 10 10
204. 10 c. 1d. and 6d. stamps of 1866 .. .. .. 15 20
205. 25 c. Mail transport, Beef Island, and 6d. stamp of 1866 .. .. .. 35 40
206. 60 c. Landing mail at Road-town, 1866 .. .. 85 90

1966. Nos. 189 and 191/2 surch.

207. 16. 50 c. on 70 c. blk. & brn. 90 1·00
208. – $1·50 on $1·40 blue & red 2·00 2·25
209. – $3 on $2·80 blk. & pur. 4·00 4·50

1966. U.N.E.S.C.O. 20th Anniv. As T **33/5** of Antigua.

210. 2 c. violet, red, yell. & orge. 8 8
211. 12 c. yellow, violet & olive 20 25
212. 60 c. black, purple & orge. 80 85

18. Map of Virgin Islands.

1967. New Constitution.

213. 18. 2 c. multicoloured .. 5 5
214. 10 c. multicoloured .. 20 20
215. 25 c. multicoloured .. 40 40
216. $1 multicoloured .. 1·25 1·40

19. Cable Ship and Caribbean Map.

1967. Bermuda-Tortola Telephone Service. Inaug. Multicoloured.

217. 4 c. Type **19** 8 8
218. 10 c. Chalwell Telecommunications Station 15 20
219. 50 c. Cable Ship 60 65

20. Blue Marlin.

1968. Game Fishing. Multicoloured.

220. 2 c. Type **20** 5 5
221. 10 c. Cobia 15 20
222. 25 c. Wahoo 35 40
223. 40 c. Fishing launch and map 55 60

1968. Human Rights Year. Nos. 185 and 188 optd. **1968 INTERNATIONAL YEAR FOR HUMAN RIGHTS.**

224. 10 c. lake and lilac.. .. 15 20
225. 25 c. green and purple .. 35 40

21. Dr. Martin Lutner King, Bible, Sword and Armour Gauntlet.

1968. Martin Luther King. Commem.

226. 21. 4 c. multicoloured .. 8 8
227. 25 c. multicoloured .. 35 40

22. DHC-6 Twin Otter.

1968. Opening of Beef Island Airport Extension. Multicoloured.

228. 2 c. Type **22** 5 5
229. 10 c. HS 748 Airliner .. 15 20
230. 25 c. HS Heron 35 40
231. $1 Royal Engineers' Cap Badge .. .. .. 1·25 1·40

23. Long John Silver and Jim Hawkins.

1969. Robert Louis Stevenson. 75th Death Anniv.

232. 23. 4 c. blue, yellow & red.. 8 8
233. – 10 c. multicoloured .. 15 20
234. – 40 c. brown, black & blue 55 60
235. – $1 multicoloured .. 1·40 1·75

DESIGNS—HORIZ. 10 c. Jim Hawkins escaping from the Pirates. $1 Treasure Trove. VERT. 40 c. The Fight with Israel Hands.

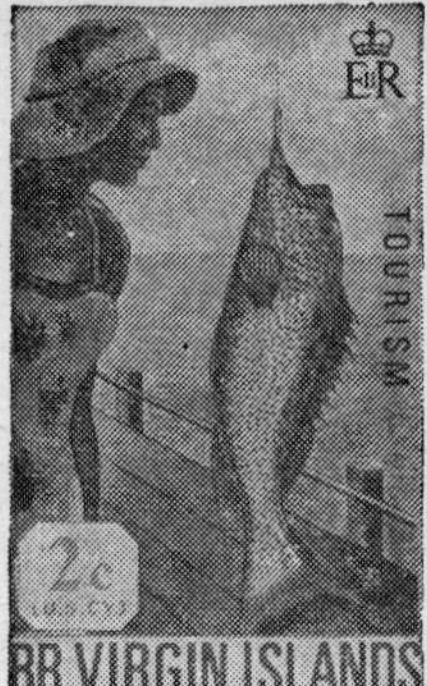

24. Tourist and Rock Grouper (fish).

1969. Tourism. Multicoloured.

236. 2 c. Type **24** 5 5
237. 10 c. Yachts in Road Harbour, Tortola 15 20
238. 20 c. Sun-bathing at Virgin Gorda National Park .. 25 30
239. $1 Tourist and Pipe Organ cactus, at Virgin Gorda 1·25 1·50

Nos. 237/8 are horiz.

25. Carib Canoe.

1970.

240. 25. ½ c. buff, brn. & sepia.. 5 5
241. – 1 c. blue and green .. 5 5
242. – 2 c. orange, brn. & slate 8 8
296. – 3 c. red, cobalt & sepia 8 8
244. – 4 c. greenish-blue, blue and brown 10 10
245. – 5 c. emerald, pink & blk. 10 10
246. – 6 c. violet, mauve & grn. 10 10
247. – 8 c. green, yellow & sepia 12 12
299. – 10 c. blue and brown .. 20 20
300. – 12 c. yellow, crim. & brn. 25 25
250. – 15 c. grn., orge. & brown 25 25
251. – 25 c. green, blue & plum 30 35
252. – 50 c. mag., green & brown 60 70
253. – $1 salmon, green & brown 1·10 1·25
254. – $2 buff, slate and grey.. 2·25 2·50
255. – $3 ochre, blue and sepia 3·25 4·00
256. – $5 violet and grey .. 5·50 6·00

DESIGNS: 1 c. "Santamariagallante" (Columbus' Flagship). 2 c. "Elizabeth Bonaventure" (Drake's Flagship). 3 c. Dutch Buccaneer, c. 1660. 4 c. "Thetis", 1827 (after etching by E. W. Cooke). 5 c. Henry Morgan's ship (17th-cent.). 6 c. H.M. Frigate "Boreas" (Capt. Nelson, 1784). 8 c. H.M. Schooner "Eclair", 1804. 10 c. H.M.S. "Formidable", 1782. 12 c. H.M. Sloop "Nymph", 1778. 15 c. "Windsor Castle", Post Office Packet, 1807. 25 c. H.M. Frigate "Astrea", 1808. 50 c. Wreck of R.M.S. "Rhone", 1860. $1 Tortola Sloop. $2 H.M. Cruiser "Frobisher". $3 Merchant Tanker "Booker Viking", 1967 $5 Hydrofoil "Sun Arrow".

26. "A Tale of Two Cities".

1970. Charles Dickens. Death Cent.

257. 26. 5 c. black, rose and grey 10 10
258. – 10 c. black, blue & green 25 30
259. – 25 c. blk., grn. & yellow 60 65

DESIGNS: 10 c. "Oliver Twist". 25 c. "Great Expectations".

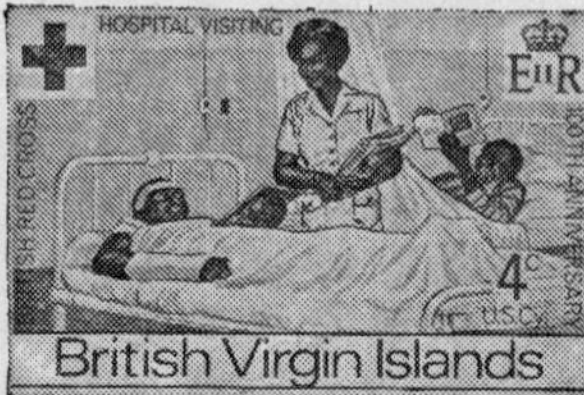

27. Hospital Visit.

1970. British Red Cross Cent. Multicoloured.

260. 4 c. Type **27** 8 8
261. 10 c. First Aid class .. 20 20
262. 25 c. Red Cross and Coat of arms 40 40

28. Mary Read.

1970. Pirates. Multicoloured.

263. ½ c. Type **28** 5 5
264. 10 c. George Lowther .. 15 25
265. 30 c. Edward Teach (Blackbeard) 40 45
266. 60 c. Henry Morgan .. 80 80

29. Children and "UNICEF".

1971. U.N.I.C.E.F. 25th Anniv.

267. 29. 15 c. multicoloured .. 25 30
268. 30 c. multicoloured .. 40 45

1972. Royal Visit of Princess Margaret. Nos. 244 and 251 optd. **VISIT OF H.R.H. THE PRINCESS MARGARET 1972 1972.**

269. 4 c. bl. chalky bl. and brn. 10 10
270. 25 c. green, blue and plum 45 45

30. Seamen of 1800.

1972. "Interpex" Stamp Exhib., New York. Naval Uniforms. Multicoloured.

271. ½ c. Type **30** 5 5
272. 10 c. Boatswain, 1787-1807 15 15
273. 30 c. Captain, 1795-1812 40 40
274. 60 c. Admiral, 1787-95 .. 75 80

1972. Royal Silver Wedding. As T **19** of Ascension, but with Sailfish and the Yacht "Sir Winston Churchill" in background.

275. 15 c. blue 20 25
276. 25 c. turquoise 35 40

31. Blue Marlin.

1972. Game Fish. Multicoloured.

277. ½ c. Type **31** 5 5
278. ½ c. Wahoo 5 5
279. 15 c. Allison Tuna .. 25 30
280. 25 c. White Marlin .. 40 50
281. 50 c. Sailfish 70 90
282. $1 Dolphin .. .. 1·40 1·60

32. J. C. Lettsom.

1973. "Interpex 1973" (Quakers). Mult.

284.	½ c. Type **32**	5	5
285.	10 c. Lettsom house (horiz.)	15	20
286.	15 c. Dr. Thornton	25	30
287.	30 c. Dr. Thornton and Capitol, Washington (horiz.)	40	45
288.	$1 William Penn (horiz.)	1·25	1·40

33. "Green-throated Carib and Antillean Crested Hummingbird" on 1 c. coin.

1973. 1st Issue of Coinage. Coins and local scenery. Multicoloured.

289.	1 c. Type **33**	5	5
290.	5 c. "Zenaida Dove" (5 c. coin)	10	10
291.	10 c. "Ringed Kingfisher" (10 c. coin)	12	15
292.	25 c. "Mangrove Cuckoo" (25 c. coin)	30	35
293.	50 c. "Brown Pelican" (50 c. coin)	60	65
294.	$1 "Magnificent Frigate-bird ($1 coin)	1·40	1·25

1973. Royal Wedding. As T **26** of Anguilla. Multicoloured. Background colours given.

301.	5 c. brown	10	10
302.	50 c. blue	60	65

34. "Virgin and Child" (Pintoricchio).

1973. Christmas. Multicoloured.

303.	½ c. Type **34**	5	5
304.	3 c. "Virgin and Child" (Lorenzo di Credi)	8	8
305.	25 c. "Virgin and Child" (Crivelli)	30	35
306.	50 c. "Virgin and Child with St. John" (Luini)	60	65

35. Crest of the "Canopus" (French).

1974. "Interpex 1974" (Naval Crests). Multicoloured.

307.	5 c. Type **35**	10	10
308.	18 c. U.S.S. "Saginaw"	25	30
309.	25 c. H.M.S. "Rothesay"	30	40
310.	50 c. H.M.C.S. "Ottawa"	60	75

36 Christopher Columbus.

1974. Historical Figures.

312. **36.**	5 c. orange and black	10	10
313. –	10 c. blue and black	15	15
314. –	25 c. violet and black	30	35
315. –	40 c. brown & dark brown	45	50

PORTRAITS: 10 c. Sir Walter Raleigh. 25 c. Sir Martin Frobisher. 40 c. Sir Francis Drake.

37. Trumpet Triton.

1974. Seashells. Multicoloured.

317.	5 c. Type **37**	10	10
318.	18 c. West Indian Murex	25	30
319.	25 c. Bleeding Tooth	30	35
320.	75 c. Virgin Islands Latirus	85	90

38. Churchill and St. Mary, Aldermanbury, London.

1974. Sir Winston Churchill. Birth Centenary. Multicoloured.

322.	10 c. Type **38**	15	15
323.	50 c. St. Mary, Fulton, Missouri	60	65

39. H.M.S. "Boreas".

1975. "Interpex 1975" Stamp Exhibition, New York. Ships' Figure-heads. Mult.

325.	5 c. Type **39**	25	25
326.	18 c. "Golden Hind"	40	40
327.	40 c. H.M.S. "Superb"	45	50
328.	85 c. H.M.S. "Formidable"	70	75

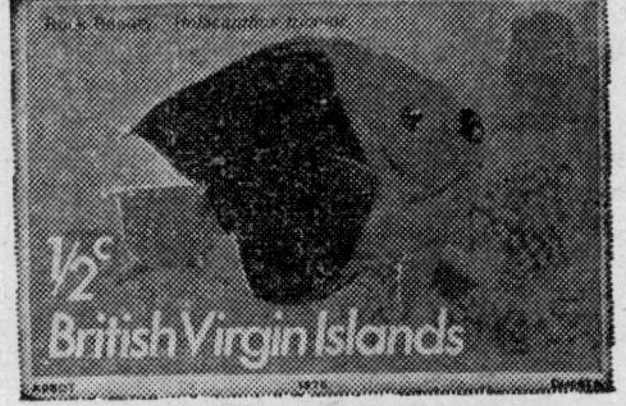

40. Rock Beauty.

1975. Fishes. Multicoloured.

330.	½ c. Type **40**	5	5
331.	1 c. Squirrelfish	5	5
332.	3 c. Queen Triggerfish	5	5
333.	5 c. Blue Angelfish	5	5
334.	8 c. Stoplight Parrotfish	8	10
335.	10 c. Queen Angelfish	10	12
336.	12 c. Nassau Grouper	12	15
337.	13 c. Blue Tang	12	15
338.	15 c. Sergeant Major	15	20
339.	18 c. Jewfish	20	20
340.	20 c. Bluehead Wrasse	20	25
341.	25 c. Grey Angelfish	25	30
342.	60 c. Glasseye Snapper	65	75
343.	$1 Blue Chromis	1·10	1·25
344.	$2·50 French Angelfish	2·50	2·75
345.	$3 Queen Parrotfish	3·25	3·50
346.	$5 Four-eye Butterfly Fish	5·50	6·00

41. St. George's Parish School (First meeting-place, 1950).

1975. Legislative Council Restoration. 25th Anniversary. Multicoloured.

347.	5 c. Type **41**	8	8
348.	25 c. Legislative Council Building	30	35
349.	40 c. Mace and gavel	25	50
350.	75 c. Commemorative scroll	75	80

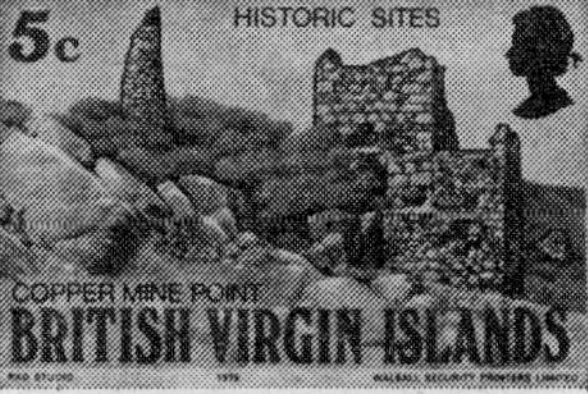

42. Copper Mine Point.

1976. Historic Sites. Multicoloured.

351.	5 c. Type **42**	8	8
352.	18 c. Pleasant Valley	20	20
353.	50 c. Callwood Distillery	50	50
354.	75 c. The Dungeon	70	75

43. Masachusetts Brig "Hazard".

1976. American Revolution. Bicent. Multicoloured.

355.	8 c. Type **43**	10	10
356.	22 c. American Privateer "Spy"	25	30
357.	40 c. Continental Navy frigate "Raleigh"	45	50
358.	75 c. Frigate "Alliance" and H.M.S. "Trepasy"	80	90

44. Government House, Tortola.

1976. Friendship Day with U.S. Virgin Is. Fifth Anniv. Multicoloured.

360.	8 c. Type **44**	10	12
361.	15 c. Government House, St. Croix (vert.)	20	20
362.	30 c. Flags (vert.)	35	40
363.	75 c. Government seals	90	1·00

45. Royal Visit, 1966.

1977. Silver Jubilee. Multicoloured.

364.	8 c. Type **45**	10	12
365.	30 c. The Holy Bible	35	40
366.	60 c. Presentation of Holy Bible	75	85

WADHWAN BC

A state of Kathyiawar India. Now uses Indian stamps.

4 pic = 1 anna.

1.

1888.

6. **1.**	½ pice black	1·00	

WALLIS AND FUTUNA ISLANDS O4

A group of French Islands in the Pacific Ocean, N.E. of Fiji Islands, a dependency of New Caledonia.

1920. Stamps of New Caledonia overprinted ILES WALLIS et FUTUNA.

1. **2.**	1 c. black on green	5	5
2.	2 c. claret	5	5
3.	4 c. blue on orange	5	5
4.	5 c. green	5	5
18.	5 c. blue	5	5
5.	10 c. red	5	5
19.	10 c. green	5	5
6.	15 c. lilac	5	5
7. **3.**	20 c. brown	5	5
8.	25 c. blue on green	5	5
21.	25 c. red on yellow	5	5
9.	30 c. brown on orange	5	5
22.	30 c. red	5	5
23.	30 c. orange	5	5
24.	30 c. green	10	10
10.	35 c. black on yellow	5	5
11.	40 c. red on green	5	5
12.	45 c. claret	5	5
13.	50 c. red on orange	5	5
25.	50 c. blue	5	5
26.	50 c. grey	8	8
27.	65 c. blue	25	25
14.	75 c. olive	8	8
15. **4.**	1 fr. blue on green	30	30
28.	1 f. 10 chestnut	25	25
16.	2 fr. red on blue	45	45
17.	5 fr. black on orange	75	75

1922. As last surch. in figs. and bars.

29. **2.**	0.01 on 15 c. lilac	5	5
30.	0.02 on 15 c. lilac	5	5
31.	0.04 on 15 c. lilac	5	5
32.	0.05 on 15 c. lilac	5	5
33. **4.**	25 c. on 2fr. red on blue	5	5
34.	25 c. on 5 fr. black on orge.	5	5
35. **3.**	65 on 40 c. red on green	5	5
36.	85 on 75 c. olive	5	5
37.	90 on 75 c. red	10	10
38. **4.**	1 f. 25 on 1 fr. blue	5	5
39.	1 f. 50 on 1 fr. blue	20	20
40.	3 fr. on 5 fr. magenta	30	30
41.	10 fr. on 5 fr. brn. on mve.	2·75	2·75
42.	20 fr. on 5 fr. red on yellow	3·25	3·25

1930. Stamps of New Caledonia overprinted ILES WALLIS et FUTUNA.

43. **5.**	1 c. blue and purple	5	5
44.	2 c. green and brown	5	5
45.	3 c. blue and red	5	5
46.	4 c. blue and orange	5	5
47.	5 c. brown and blue	5	5
48.	10 c. brown and lilac	5	5
49.	15 c. blue and brown	5	5
50.	20 c. brown and red	5	5
51.	25 c. brown and green	5	5

52. 6. 30 c. green 5 5
53. 35 c. green 5 5
54. 40 c. olive and red .. 5 5
55. 45 c. red and blue .. 5 5
56. 45 c. green 5 5
57. 50 c. brown and mauve .. 5 5
58. 55 c. red and blue .. 12 12
59. 60 c. red and blue .. 5 5
60. 65 c. blue and brown .. 10 10
61. 70 c. brown and mauve .. 5 5
62. 75 c. olive and blue .. 20 20
63. 80 c. green and maroon .. 5 5
64. 85 c. brown and green .. 30 30
65. 90 c. red 8 8
66. 90 c. red and brown .. 5 5
67. 7. 1 fr. red and brown .. 30 30
68. 1 fr. red 15 15
69. 1 fr. green and red .. 5 5
70. 1 f. 10 c. brown and green 2·50 2·50
71. 1 f. 25 c. green and brown 15 15
72. 1 f. 25 c. red .. 5 5
73. 1 f. 40 c. red and blue .. 5 5
74. 1 f. 50 blue .. 8 8
75. 1 f. 60 c. brown and green 5 5
76. 1 f. 75 c. red and blue .. 85 85
77. 1 f. 75 c. blue .. 20 20
78. 2 fr. brown and orange .. 8 8
79. 2 f. 25 c. blue .. 5 5
80. 2 f. 50 c. brown .. 5 5
81. 3 fr. brown and claret .. 10 10
82. 5 fr. brown and blue .. 8 8
83. 10 fr. brn. & mve. on pink 15 15
84. 20 fr. brn. & red on yellow 30 30

1931. "Colonial Exhibition" key-types.
85. E. 40 c. green 60 60
86. F. 50 c. mauve 60 60
87. G. 90 c. red 60 60
88. H. 1 f. 50 blue 60 60

1939. New York World's Fair. As T **11** of Cameroun.
89. 1 f. 27 red 25 25
90. 2 f. 25 blue 25 25

1939. French Revolution. 150th Anniv. As T **16** of Cameroun.
91. 45 c.+25 c. green .. 1·00 1·00
92. 70 c.+30 c. brown .. 1·00 1·00
93. 90 c.+35 c. orange .. 1·00 1·00
94. 1 f. 25 c.+1 f. red .. 1·00 1·00
95. 2 f. 25 c.+2 f. blue .. 1·00 1·00

1941. Optd. stamps of New Caledonia of 1930 overprinted **France Libre**.
96. 5. 1 c. blue and purple .. 10 5
97. 2 c. green and brown .. 10 5
98. 4 c. blue and orange .. 10 5
99. 5 c. brown and blue .. 10 8
100. 10 c. brown and lilac .. 10 5
101. 15 c. blue and brown .. 10 8
102. 20 c. brown and red .. 30 20
103. 25 c. brown and green .. 30 20
104. 6. 30 c. green 30 20
105. 35 c. green 10 8
106. 40 c. olive and red .. 30 20
107. 45 c. red and blue .. 30 20
108. 50 c. brown and mauve .. 10 8
109. 55 c. red and blue .. 10 8
110. 65 c. blue and brown .. 10 8
111. 70 c. brown and mauve .. 10 8
112. 75 c. olive and blue .. 30 20
113. 6. 80 c. green and maroon .. 10 8
114. 85 c. brown and green .. 30 20
115. 90 c. red 25 15
116. 7. 1 fr. red 20 10
117. 1 f. 25 c. green and brown 20 15
118. 1 f. 50 c. blue .. 10 8
119. 1 f. 75 c. blue .. 10 8
120. 2 fr. brown and orange .. 10 8
121. 2 f. 50 c. brown .. .. 14·00 14·00
122. 3 fr. brown and claret .. 8 8
123. 5 fr. brown and blue .. 55 45
124. 10 fr. brown and mauve on pink .. 5·50 5·50
125. 20 fr. brn. & red on yell. 5·50 5·50

1. Native Ivory Head.

1944. Free French Administration.
126. 1. 5 c. brown 5 5
127. 10 c. blue 5 5
128. 25 c. green 5 5
129. 30 c. orange 5 5
130. 40 c. green 5 5
131. 80 c. maroon 5 5
132. 1 f. purple 5 5
133. 1 f. 50 c. red 5 5
134. 2 f. black 5 5
135. 2 f. 50 blue 5 5
136. 4 f. violet 5 5
137. 5 f. yellow 5 5
138. 10 f. brown 5 5
139. 20 f. green 8 8

1944. Mutual Aid and Red Cross Funds. As T **19** of Cameroun.
140. 5 f.+20 f. orange .. 20 20

1945. Surch. with new values in figures.
141. 1. 50 c. on 5 c. brown .. 5 5
142. 60 c. on 5 c. brown .. 5 5
143. 70 c. on 5 c. brown .. 5 5
144. 1 f. 20 c. on 5 c. brown .. 5 5
145. 2 f. 40 c. on 25 c. green .. 5 5
146. 3 f. on 25 c. green .. 5 5
147. 4 f. 50 c. on 25 c. green .. 8 8
148. 15 f. on 2 f. 50 c. blue .. 12 12

1946. Air. Victory. As T **21** of Cameroun.
149. 8 f. violet 15 15

1946. Air. From Chad to the Rhine. As T **22** of Cameroun.
150. 5 f. violet 10 10
151. 10 f. green 10 10
152. 15 f. purple 12 12
153. 20 f. blue 20 20
154. 25 f. orange 20 20
155. 50 f. red 35 35

1949. Air. U.P.U. As T **25** of Cameroun.
156. 10 f. blue, green, brown and emerald .. 75 75

1949. Air. Nos. 325/6 of New Caledonia, with colours changed, optd. **WALLIS ET FUTUNA.**
157. 12. 50 f. red and yellow .. 95 95
158. – 100 f. brown and yellow 1·90 1·90

1952. Military Medal. Cent. As T **27** of Cameroun.
159. 2 f. turquoise, yell & green 30 30

1954. Air. Liberation. 10th Anniv. As T **29** of Cameroun.
160. 3 f. maroon and brown .. 70 70

2. Making Tapa (cloth).

4. "Charonia tritonis".

3. Father Chanel.

1955. (a) Postage as T **2.**
161. – 3 f. pur., mve. & magenta 5 5
162. 2. 5 f. choc., brown & green 8 8
163. – 7 f. chocolate & blue-grn. 12 12
164. – 9 f. slate-purple, blue and chocolate .. 15 15
165. – 17 f. crim., pur., grn. & bl. 25 25
166. – 19 f. turquoise and lake .. 30 30

(b) Air. as T **3.**
167. 3. 14 f. blue, green & indigo 25 25
168. – 21 f. bistre and blue .. 45 45
168a.– 27 f. green, blue & brown 60 60
169. – 33 f. choc., blue & turq. 75 75
DESIGNS—HORIZ. 3 f., 9 f. Wallisian and island view. 7 f. Preparing kava. 17 f. Dancers. 21 f. View of Mata-Utu, Queen Amelia and Mgr. Bataillou. 27 f. Wharf, Mata-Utu. 33 f. Map of Wallis and Futuna Islands and sailing ship. VERT. 19 f. Paddle dance.

1958. Tropical Flora. As T **21** of Fr. Equatorial Africa.
170. 5 f. red, grn., yell. & blue 30 25
DESIGN—HORIZ. 5 f. "Montrouziera".

1958. Declaration of Human Rights. 10th Anniv. As T **5** of Comoro Is.
171. 17 f. blue and ultramarine 70 70

1962. 5th South Pacific Conference. Pago Pago. As T **6** of French Polynesia.
172. 16 f. multicoloured .. 50 50

1962. Marine Fauna.
173. 4. 25 c. brn. & myrtle (post.) 5 5
174. – 1 f. red and green .. 5 5
175. – 2 f. chestnut and blue .. 5 5
176. – 4 f. chestnut & turquoise 10 10
177. – 10 f. orge., brn., vlo. & grn. 25 25
178. – 20 f. chestnut and ultram. 60 60
179. – 50 f. chest., turq. & bl. (air) 1·00 1·00
180. – 100 f. blue, green & purple 2·25 2·25
DESIGNS: 1 f. "Mitra episcopalis". 2 f. "Cypraecassis rufa". 4 f. "Murex tenuispina". 10 f. "Oliva erythrostoma". 20 f. "Cypraea tigris". 50 f. "Harpa ventricosa" (26½ × 48 mm.). 100 f. Fishing under water for trochus shells. (48 × 26½ mm.).

1962. Air. 1st Trans-Atlantic TV Satellite Link. As T **18** of Andorra.
181. 12 f. blue, maroon and violet 45 45

1963. Red Cross Cent. As Type F **2** of New Hebrides.
182. 12 f. red, grey and purple 35 35

1963. Declaration of Human Rights. 15th Anniv. As T **10** of Comoro Islands.
183. 29 f. ochre and red .. 90 90

1964. "PHILATEC 1964" Int. Stamp Exn., Paris. As T **481** of France.
184. 9 f. red, green & grey-green 40 40

5. Throwing the Javelin.

6. Inter-island Ship, "Reine Amelia".

1964. Air. Olympic Games, Tokyo.
185. 5. 31 f. maroon, red & grn. 1·00 1·00

1965.
186. 6. 11 f. multicoloured .. 30 30

1965. Air. I.T.U. Cent. As T **15** of Comoro Islands.
187. 50 f. chocolate, red & purple 2·10 2·10

1966. Air. Launching of 1st French Satellite. As No. 1696/7 (plus se-tenant label) of France.
188. 7 f. red, claret & vermilion 40 40
189. 10 f. red, claret & vermilion 45 45

1966. Air. Launching of Satellite "D1". As T **521** of France.
190. 10 f. red, lake and green .. 40 40

7. W.H.O. Building.

1966. Air. W.H.O. Headquarters, Geneva. Inaug.
191. 7. 30 f. lake, orange and blue 65 65

8. Art Students.

1966. Air. U.N.E.S.C.O. 20th Anniv.
192. 8. 50 f. purple, yellow & grn. 90 90

9. Athlete and Decorative Pattern.

1966. Air. South Pacific Games, Noumea.
193. 9. 32 f. blk., mar., cerise & bl. 65 65
194. – 38 f. emerald and magenta 70 70
DESIGN: 38 f. Woman with ball, and decorative pattern.

10. Samuel Wallis's ship at Uvea.

1967. Air. Discovery of Wallis Islands. Bicent.
195. 10. 12 f. multicoloured .. 25 25

1968. W.H.O. 20th Anniv. As T **21** of Comoro Islands.
196. 17 f. purple, orange & green 40 40

1968. Human Rights Year. As T **23** of Comoro Islands.
197. 19 f. brown, plum & mag. 40 40

1969. Air. 1st Flight of "Concorde". As T **27** of Comoro Islands.
198. 20 f. black and purple .. 60 60

11. Launching Outrigger canoe.

12. Weightlifting.

1969. "Scenes of Everyday Life". Mult.
199. 1 f. Type **11** (postage) .. 5 5
200. 20 f. Gathering Coconuts (air) 35 25
201. 32 f. Horse-riding 55 30
202. 38 f. Wood-carving .. 65 45
203. 50 f. Fishing 90 65
204. 100 f. Marketing Fruit .. 1·90 1·10
Nos. 200/4 are larger, 48 × 27 mm.

1969. Int. Labour Organization. 50th Anniv. As Type **28** of Comoro Islands.
205. 9 f. blue, brown and salmon 20 20

1970. New U.P.U. Headquarters Building. As T **126** of Cameroun.
206. 21 f. brn., indigo & pur. .. 45 45

1971. Surch.
207. 12 f. on 19 f. (No. 166) (postage) .. 25 25
208. 21 f. on 33 f. (No. 169) (air) 40 40

1971. 4th South Pacific Games, Papeete, Tahiti.
209. 12. 24 f. brown, indigo and green (postage) .. 45 45
210. – 36 f. bl., olive and red .. 55 55
211. – 48 f. brn., grn. & lilac (air) 70 55
212. – 54 f. red, pur. and blue 95 75
DESIGNS—VERT. (As Type 12). 36 f. Basketball. HORIZ. (48 × 27 mm.). 48 f. Pole-vaulting. 54 f. Archery.

1971. De Gaulle Commem. As Nos. 1937/40 of France.
213. 30 f. black and blue .. 55 45
214. 70 f. black and blue .. 1·10 90

1972. Air. South Pacific Commission. 25th Anniv. As T **46** of French Polynesia.
215. 44 f. multicoloured .. 60 40

13. Pacific Island Dwelling.

14. Child's Pirogue.

1972. Air. South Pacific Arts Festival, Fiji.
216. 13. 60 f. violet, grn. & red 85 65

1972. Sailing Pirogues. Multicoloured.
217. 14 f. Type **14** (postage) .. 20 15
218. 16 f. Children with model pirogues 20 15
219. 18 f. Racing pirogue .. 25 20
220. 200 f. Pirogue race (47 × 27 mm.) (air) .. 2·75 2·75

15. Samuel Wallis and "Dolphin".

1973. Air. Explorers of the Pacific.
221. – 22 f. brn., grey & red .. 25 20
222. 15. 28 f. grn., red & blue .. 35 30
223. – 40 f. brown, blue and bright blue 50 45
224. – 72 f. brn., blue & violet 95 80
DESIGNS: 22 f. La Perouse and "La Boussole". 40 f. Dumont D'Urville and "L'Astrolabe". 72 f. Bougainville and "La Boudeuse".

16. General De Gaulle.

1973. Air. De Gaulle. 3rd Death Anniv.
225. 16. 107 f. maroon and brn. 1·40 1·10

INDEX

Countries can be quickly located by referring to the index at the end of this volume.

17. " Plumeria rubra ".

1973. Air. Flora of Wallis Islands. Mult.
226. 12 f. Type **17** 15 12
227. 17 f. " Hibiscus tiliaceus " 20 15
228. 19 f. " Phaeomeria magnifica " 25 20
229. 21 f. " Hibiscus rosa sinensis " 25 20
230. 23 f. " Allamanda cathartica " 30 25
231. 27 f. " Barringtonia asiatica " 30 25
232. 39 f. Bouquet in vase .. 50 40

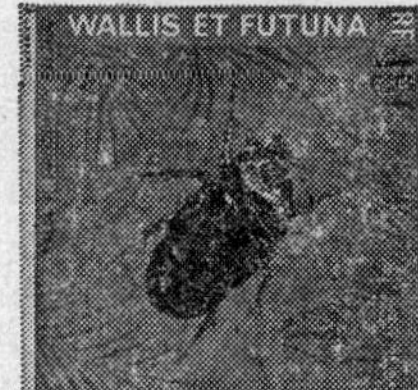

18. " Oryctes rhinoceros ".

1974. Insects. Multicoloured.
233. 15 f. Type **18** 20 12
234. 25 f. " Cosmopolites sordidus " 25 15
235. 35 f. " Ophideres fullonica " 40 30
236. 45 f. " Pantala flavescens " 50 40

19. " Flower Hand " holding Letter.

1974. Air. Universal Postal Union. Cent.
237. **19.** 51 f. purple, brn. & grn. 60 50

20. " Holy Family " (Kamalielf-Filimoehala).

1974. Air.. Christmas.
238. **20.** 150 f. multicoloured .. 1·60 1·40

21. Tapa Pattern.

1975. Air. Tapa Mats. Each brown, gold and yellow.
239. 3 f. Type **21** 5 5
240. 24 f. " Villagers " 25 15
241. 36 f. " Fishes " 40 30
242. 80 f. " Fishes and Dancers" 85 60

22. Aircraft in Flight. 23. Volley ball.

1975. Air. First regular Noumea-Wallis Noumea Air Service.
243. **22.** 100 f. bl.,blk. orge. & grn. 90 80

1975. Air. Fifth South Pacific Games, Guam. Multicoloured.
244. 26 f. Type **23** 25 15
245. 44 f. Football 40 30
246. 56 f. Throwing the javelin 50 40
247. 105 f. Aqua-diving .. 1·00 90

1976. Pres. Pompidou. Commemoration. As T **73** of French Polynesia.
248. 50 f. grey and blue .. 60 50

24. Lalolalo Lake, Wallis.

1976. Air. Landscapes. Multicoloured.
249. 10 f. Type **24** 12 8
250. 29 f. Vasavasa, Futuna .. 35 25
251. 41 f. Sigave Bay, Futuna 50 40
252. 68 f. Gahi Bay, Wallis .. 85 75

25. " Concorde " in Flight.

1976. Air. First Commercial Flight of " Concorde ", Paris–Rio de Janeiro.
253. **25.** 250 f. blue, green and red 3·00 2·50

26. Washington and Battle of Yorktown.

1976. American Revolution. Bicentenary.
254. **26.** 19 f. green, blue and red 25 15
255. – 47 f. purple, red and blue 60 50
DESIGN: 47 f. Lafayette and sea battle of the Virginian Capes.

27. Throwing the Hammer.

1976. Air. Olympic Games, Montreal.
256. **27.** 31 f. purple, blue and red 40 30
257. – 39 f. mauve, red & mar. 45 35
DESIGN: 39 f. High diving.

28. " Conus ammiralis ".

1976. Seashells. Multicoloured.
258. 20 f. Type **28** 25 15
259. 23 f. " Cyprae assellus " .. 30 20
260. 43 f. " Turbo petholatus " 50 40
261. 61 f. " Mitra papalis " .. 75 65

POSTAGE DUE STAMPS

Postage Due stamps of New Caledonia optd. **ILES WALLIS et FUTUNA.**

1920.
D 18. D 1. 5 c. blue 5 5
D 19. 10 c. brown 5 5
D 20. 15 c. green 5 5
D 21. 20 c. black on yellow 5 5
D 22. 30 c. red 5 5
D 23. 50 c. blue on cream 15 15
D 24. 60 c. green on blue 20 20
D 25. 1 f. green on cream .. 35 35

1927. Surch. in figures.
D 43. D 1. 2 f. on 1 f. mauve .. 1·00 1·00
D 44. 3 f. on 1 f. brown .. 1·00 1·00

1930.
D 85. D 2. 2 c. brown and blue .. 5 5
D 86. 4 c. green and red .. 5 5
D 87. 5 c. grey and orange .. 5 5
D 88. 10 c. blue and claret 5 5
D 89. 15 c. red and green .. 5 5
D 90. 20 c. olive and claret 5 5
D 91. 25 c. blue and brown 5 5
D 92. 30 c. brown and green 5 5
D 93. 50 c. red and brown .. 5 5
D 94. 60 c. red and mauve .. 10 10
D 95. 1 f. green and blue .. 10 10
D 96. 2 f. brown and red .. 10 10
D 97. 3 f. brown and violet 10 10

D 1. " Zanclus cornutus ".

1963. Fish designs.
D 182. D 1. 1 f. blk., yell. & blue 5 5
D 183. – 3 f. verm., grn. & blue 8 8
D 184. – 5 f. orange, blk. & bl. 12 12
FISH—HORIZ. 3 f. " Thalassoma lunare ". 5 f. " Amphiprion percula ".

WENDEN E3

Formerly part of W. Russia now in the Latvian Soviet Republic.

1863. Rectangle inscr. " Briefmarke des WENDEN-schen Kreises ". Imperf.
1. 2 k. black and red .. .. 50·00 38·00

1863. Similar rectangle, but inscr. " Packenmarke des WENDEN-schen Kreises". Imperf.
2. 4 k. black and green .. .. 19·00 17·00

1. 2. 3.

1863. Imperf.
6. **1.** 2 k. green and red .. .. 11·00 6·50

1864. As T **1**, but with horse in central oval. Imperf.
5. 2 k. green and red .. .. 25·00 22·00

1871. Imperf.
7. **2.** 2 k. green and red .. .. 5·50 5·00

1872. Perf.
8. **3.** 2 k. red and green .. .. 5·50 5·00

4. Arms of Wenden. 5. 6. Castle of Wenden.

1875.
9. **4.** 2 k. green and red 65 65

1878.
10. **5.** 2 k. green and red 65 65
11. 2 k. red, brown and green 65 65
13. 2 k. green, black and red .. 65 55

1901.
14. **6.** 2 k. brown and green .. 90 90
15. 2 k. red and green .. 80 80
16. 2 k. purple and green .. 80 80

WEST IRIAN O2

The following stamps supersede Nos. 1/19 of West New Guinea, after the former Dutch territory became part of Indonesia.

1963. Stamps of Indonesia optd. **IRIAN BARAT,** or surch. also.
1. – 1 s. on 70 s. red (No. 724) 5 5
2. – 2 s. on 90 s. grn. (No. 727) 5 5
3. – 5 s. grey-blue (No. 830) 5 5
4. – 6 s. on 20 s. yell-brown (No. 833) 5 5
5. – 7 s. on 50 s. blue (No. 835) 5 5
6. – 10 s. brown (No. 831) .. 5 5
7. – 15 s. maroon (No. 832) .. 5 5
8. **92.** 25 s. green 10 10
9. – 30 s. on 75 s. red (No. 836) 12 12
10. – 40 s. on 1 r. 15 crimson (No. 837) 15 15
11. **59.** 1 r. mauve 35 35
12. 2 r. green 75 75
13. 3 r. blue 95 95
14. 5 r. brown .. .. 1·60 1·60

1963. Acquisition of West Irian. Designs as Nos. 962/4 of Indonesia, additionally inscr. " IRIAN BARAT ".
21. **114.** 12 s. orange-red, red and black 5 5
22. 17 s. orange-red, red and black 8 8
23. – 20 s. blue, green and grey-purple 12 12
24. – 50 s. blue, green and grey-purple 20 20
25. – 60 s. brown, yell. & green 35 35
26. – 75 s. brown, yell. & green 40 40
DESIGNS: 20 s., 50 s. Parachutist. 60 s., 75 s. Bird of Paradise.

1. " Manilitoa gemmipara ". 3. Mother and Child Figurine.

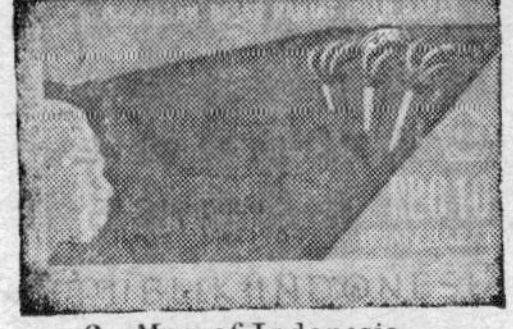
2. Map of Indonesia.

1968. Flora and Fauna.
27. **1.** 5 s. maroon and green .. 5 5
28. – 15 s. violet and green .. 5 5
29. – 30 s. green and orange .. 5 5
30. – 40 s. violet and yellow .. 5 5
31. – 50 s. black and cerise .. 5 5
32. – 75 s. black and blue .. 5 5
33. – 1 r. black and brown .. 12 12
34. – 3 r. black and green .. 50 50
35. – 5 r. multicoloured .. 60 70
36. 10 r. multicoloured .. 1·25 1·10
DESIGNS: 15 s. " Dendrobium lancifolium ". 30 s. " Gardenia gjellerupii ". 40 s. " Manitoa gemmipara " (blossom). 50 s. Phalanger. 75 s. Cassowary. 1 r. Kangaroo. 3 r. Crown pigeons. 5 r. Red lory. 10 r. Great Bird of Paradise.

1968. West Irian People's Pledge of 9 May 1964.
43. **2.** 10 s. gold and ultram. .. 15 15
44. 25 s. gold and red .. 15 15

1970. West Irian Wood-carvings. Multicoloured.
45. 5 s. Type **3** 5 5
46. 6 s. Carved shield 5 5
47. 7 s. Man and serpents .. 5 5
48. 10 s. Drum 5 5
49. 25 s. Seated warrior .. 5 5
50. 30 s. " Female " drum .. 5 5
51. 50 s. Bamboo vessel .. 5 5
52. 75 s. Seated man and tree .. 5 5
53. 1 r. Decorated shield .. 12 12
54. 2 r. Seated figure 25 25
Nos. 45/54 are inscr. " I.B." (" Irian Barat ").

POSTAGE DUE STAMPS

1963. Postage Due Stamps as Type D 2 of Indonesia, optd. **IRIAN BARAT.**
D 15. 1 s. slate-purple 5 5
D 16. 5 s. brown-olive 5 5
D 17. 10 s. turquoise 5 5
D 18. 25 s. slate 12 15
D 19. 40 s. orange 20 25
D 20. 100 s. brown 50 55

1968. As Type D 2 of Indonesia, but with coloured network background incorporating " 1968 ", optd. **IRIAN BARAT.**
D 37. 1 s. blue and green .. 5 5
D 38. 5 s. green and pink .. 5 5
D 39. 10 s. red and grey .. 5 5
D 40. 25 s. emerald and yellow 5 5
D 41. 40 s. maroon and green 5 5
D 42. 100 s. red and olive .. 10 10

WEST NEW GUINEA O2

U.N. Administration of former Netherlands New Guinea from 1st Oct. 1962 to 30th April 1963, when it became known as West Irian and became part of Indonesia.

1962. "United Nations Temporary Executive Authority". Stamps of Netherlands New Guinea optd. **UNTEA.**

1. **1.** 1 c. yellow and red .. 20 15
21. **99.** 2 c. orange 25 15
3. **1.** 5 c. yellow and sepia .. 25 20
4. – 7 c. purple, blue and chestnut (No. 60) .. 30 30
5. – 10 c. brn. & bl. (No. 27) 30 30
6. – 12 c. purple, blue and green (No. 61) .. 50 40
7. – 15 c. brn. & lemon (No. 28) 60 50
8. – 17 c. purple, blue and black (No. 62) .. 50 40
9. – 20 c. brn. & grn. (No. 29) 60 60
10. **2.** 25 c. red 35 35
11. 30 c. blue 50 50
12. 40 c. orange 70 70
32. 45 c. brown .. .. 1·25 1·25
14. 55 c. turquoise .. .. 1·00 1·00
15. 80 c. violet-grey .. 8·00 6·00
16. 85 c. maroon .. .. 3·00 3·00
17. 1 g. purple .. .. 2·00 2·00
18. **109.** 2 g. brown .. .. 10·00 8·00
19. 5 g. green .. .. 5·00 5·00

For later issues see **WEST IRIAN.**

WEST UKRAINE E3

Before the 1914/18 War this district, known as E. Galicia, was part of Austria. It achieved temporary independence after the war when stamps were issued.

(1.)

1919. Stamps of Austria 1916 optd. with T 1.

70. **26.** 3 h. violet 15
71. 5 h. green 15
72. 6 h. orange 15
73. 10 h. claret 15
74. 12 h. blue 15
75. **30.** 15 h. red 15
76. 20 h. green 15
77. 25 h. blue 15
78. 30 h. violet 15
79. **28.** 40 h. olive 20
80. 50 h. green 20
81. 60 h. blue 20
82. 80 h. red-brown .. 25
83. 90 h. purple 25
84. 1 k. red on yellow .. 30
85. **29.** 2 k. blue 35
86. 3 k. red 35
87. 4 k. green 70
88. 10 k. violet 90

For other issues, which were mainly of a local character, see Stanley Gibbons' Europe Stamp Catalogue, Volume 3.

WESTERN AUSTRALIA BC

The Western State of the Australian Commonwealth, whose stamps it now uses.

1.

2.

3.

1854. Imperf. or roul.

1. **1.** 1d. black .. .. .. £500 80·00
25. 2d. orange .. .. .. 27·00 27·00
3. **2.** 4d. blue .. .. .. 80·00 42·00
26. **1.** 4d. blue .. .. .. 70·00 £180
28. 6d. green £400 £180
5. **3.** 1s. brown .. .. .. £110 80·00

4.

5.

1857. Imperf. or roul.

15. **4.** 2d. brown on red £700 £225
17. 6d. bronze £600 £275

1861. Perf.

49. **1.** 1d. red .. .. .. 12·00 4·00
81. 1d. yellow .. .. 3·00 8
33. 2d. blue .. .. .. 30·00 11·00
82. 2d. yellow .. .. .. 3·50 8
56. 4d. red .. .. .. 8·00 1·50
34. 6d. brown .. .. 55·00 13·00
87. 6d. violet .. .. 14·00 60
61. 1s. green .. .. .. 18·00 4·00

1872.

95. **1.** 1d. pink .. .. 2·50 15
96. 2d. grey .. .. 3·00 45
141. **5.** 3d. brown 90 12
97. **1.** 4d. brown .. .. 35·00 5·00

1875. Surch. **ONE PENNY.**

7. **1.** 1d. on 2d. yellow £200 £180

1884. Surch. in figures.

89. **1.** "½" on 1d. yellow .. 2·75 1·00
92. **5.** 1d. on 3d. brown .. 4·00 2·00

6.

7.

8.

9.

1885.

98a. **6.** ½d. green 15 5
115. **7.** 1d. red 25 8
100a. **8.** 2d. grey 30 5
113. 2d. yellow 45 8
101a. **9.** 2½d. blue .. .. 2·00 5
102. 4d. brown .. .. 2·25 5
103. 5d. yellow .. .. 2·25 20
104. 6d. violet .. .. 2·25 15
106. 1s. green .. .. 2·25 20

1893. Surch. in words.

110a. **5.** ½d. on 3d. brown .. 1·25 60
107. 1d. on 3d. brown 2·50 80

10.

11.

12.

14.

15.

16.

17.

18.

19.

1901.

140. **10.** 2d. yellow 30 10
114. **11.** 2½d. blue 90 8
142. **12.** 4d. brown .. .. 1·40 20
143. **9.** 5d. olive .. .. 2·25 20
164. **11.** 6d. violet .. .. 3·50 20
144. **6.** 8d. green .. .. 2·25 1·10
145. **12.** 9d. orange .. .. 2·25 50
146. **11.** 10d. red .. .. 5·00 2·00
169. **14.** 1s. green .. .. 6·00 1·00
122a. **15.** 2s. red on yellow .. 8·00 2·25
123. **16.** 2s. 6d. blue on rose .. 9·00 2·50
124. **17.** 5s. green .. .. 11·00 7·00
125. **18.** 10s. mauve .. .. 32·00 10·00
126. **19.** £1 orange .. .. 55·00 32·00

1906. Surch. **ONE PENNY.**

170. **10.** 1d. in 2d. yellow .. 30 8

WURTTEMBERG E2

Formerly an independent kingdom of S. Germany, now part of West Germany.

1851. 60 kreuzer = 1 gulden.
1875. 100 pfennige = 1 mark.

1.

2.

1851. Imperf.

1. **1.** 1 k. black on buff .. £150 25·00
3. 3 k. black on yellow .. 55·00 1·25
5. 6 k. black on green .. £375 10·00
7. 9 k. black on rose .. £1500 10·00
9. 18 k. black on lilac .. £300 £250

1857. Imperf.

10. **2.** 1 k. brown .. .. £100 22·00
24. 3 k. orange .. .. £110 1·50
15. 6 k. green .. .. £130 15·00
17. 9 k. red .. .. £250 16·00
19. 18 k. blue £425 £300
85. 70 k. purple £450 £750

1859. Perf.

37. **2.** 1 k. brown .. .. £110 38·00
40. 3 k. yellow .. .. 21·00 12·00
41. 6 k. green .. .. .. 38·00 15·00
42. 9 k. red .. .. .. £150 55·00
43. 9 k. purple .. .. £200 80·00
44. 18 k. blue £300 £225

1863. Perf. or Roul.

60. **2.** 1 k. green .. .. 9·00 2·00
63. 3 k. red .. .. .. 7·50 90
54. 6 k. blue .. .. .. 45·00 8·50
66. 7 k. blue .. .. £180 35·00
57. 9 k. brown .. .. 45·00 12·00
59. 18 k. orange £170 £110

3.

4.

1869. Roul. or perf. (1 k.).

72. **3.** 1 k. green .. .. 5·00 65
74. 2 k. orange .. .. 20·00 17·00
77. 3 k. rose .. .. .. 5·50 30
78. 7 k. blue .. .. .. 19·00 5·50
80. 9 k. bistre .. .. .. 17·00 8·00
82. 14 k. yellow .. .. 25·00 16·00

1875. Perf.

123. **4.** 2 pf. grey 15 10
89. 3 pf. green .. .. 3·00 40
124. 3 pf. brown 10 5
91. 5 pf. mauve .. .. 2·50 20
127. 5 pf. green 12 5
93. 10 pf. red 25 5
95. 20 pf. blue 25 5
97. 25 pf. brown .. .. 14·00 3·00
130. 25 pf. orange 30 35
151. 30 pf. black and orange .. 90 1·25
152. 40 pf. black and red .. 90 1·25
99. 50 pf. grey .. .. 85·00 6·00
101. 50 pf. green .. .. 8·50 1·10
132. 50 pf. brown 40 15
102. 2 m. yellow £275 £120
103. 2 m. red on orange .. £300 60·00
121. 2 m. black on orange .. 1·90 2·50
122. 5 m. black and blue .. 25·00 60·00

For issues of 1947–49 see Germany (French Zone).

MUNICIPAL SERVICE STAMPS

M 1.

1875.

M 168. M **1.** 2 pf. grey 5 5
M 170. 3 pf. brown .. 5 5
M 104. 5 pf. mauve .. 8·50 75
M 171. 5 pf. green 5 5
M 173. 10 pf. red 5 5
M 177. 25 pf. orange .. 12 15

1906. Cent. of Wurttemberg becoming a Kingdom. Optd. **1806 - 1906** under crown.

M 153. M **1.** 2 pf. grey .. 10·00 22·00
M 154. 3 pf. brown .. .. 2·00 3·75
M 155. 5 pf. green 60 75
M 156. 10 pf. red 60 75
M 157. 25 pf. orange .. 10·00 22·00

1906.

M 169. M **1.** 2½ pf. grey 5 5
M 172. 7½ pf. orange .. 5 5
M 245. 10 pf. orange .. 5 15
M 174. 15 pf. brown .. 30 15
M 175. 15 pf. violet .. 5 5
M 176. 20 pf. blue 5 5
M 247. 20 pf. green .. 5 20
M 178. 25 pf. black & brown 12 25
M 179. 35 pf. brown .. 25 6·00
M 248. 40 pf. red 5 8
M 180. 50 pf. maroon .. 60 3·75
M 249. 50 pf. purple .. 10 25
M 250. 60 pf. olive .. 10 60
M 251. 1 m. 25 green .. 10 35
M 252. 2 m. grey 10 30
M 253. 3 m. brown 12 30

1916. Surch. **25 Pf.**

M 199. M **1.** 25 pf. on 25 pf. orange 1·00 1·25

M 2.

M 3.

1916. Jubilee of King William.

M 202. M **2.** 2½ pf. grey .. .. 50 4·25
M 203. 7½ pf. red 15 35
M 204. 10 pf. red .. .. 15 3·00
M 205. 15 pf. bistre 15 70
M 206. 20 pf. blue .. .. 15 3·00
M 207. 25 pf. grey .. .. 30 5·50
M 208. 50 pf. brown .. 55 32·00

1919. Surch. with large figure **2.**

M 219. M **1.** 2 on 2½ pf. grey .. 5 75

1919. Optd. **Volksstaat Wurttemberg.**

M 222. M **1.** 2½ pf. grey 5 75
M 223. 3 pf. brown .. 1·25 5·00
M 224. 5 pf. green 5 12
M 225. 7½ pf. orange .. 5 1·25
M 226. 10 pf. red 5 15
M 227. 15 pf. violet 5 15
M 228. 20 pf. blue 5 15
M 229. 25 pf. black & brown 5 70
M 230. 35 pf. brown .. 15 5·00
M 231. 50 pf. maroon .. 30 3·00

1920.

M 254. M **3.** 10 pf. claret .. .. 25 3·75
M 255. 15 pf. brown .. 25 2·00
M 256. 20 pf. blue 25 50
M 257. 30 pf. green .. 25 6·00
M 258. 50 pf. yellow .. 25 17·00
M 259. 75 pf. bistre .. .. 40 40·00

1922. Surch.
M 270. M 1. 5 m. on 10 pf. orange 5 20
M 271. 10 m. on 15 pf. mauve 5 12
M 272. 12 m. on 40 pf. red .. 12 50
M 273. 20 m. on 10 pf. orange 8 1·25
M 274. 25 m. on 20 pf. green 5 12
M 275. 40 m. on 20 pf. green 12 1·75
M 275. 50 m. on 60 pf. olive 5 12
M 277. 60 m. on 1 m. 25 grn. 5 35
M 278. 100 m. on 40 pf. red 5 25
M 279. 200 m. on 2 m. grey 5 35
M 280. 300 m. on 50 pf. pur. 5 35
M 281. 400 m. on 3 m. brown 10 75
M 282. 1000 m. on 60 pf. olive 12 60
M 283. 2000 m. on 1 m. 25 grn. 8 15

1923. Surch. with new value (T = Thousand; M = Million; Md. = Milliard).
M 284. M 1. 5 T. on 10 pf. orange 12 2·50
M 285. 20 T. on 40 pf. red .. 12 1·25
M 286. 50 T. on 15 pf. mauve 35 6·00
M 287. 75 T. on 2 m. grey .. 60 25
M 288. 100 T. on 20 pf. green 8 3·00
M 289. 250 T. on 3 m. brown 5 45
M 290. 1 M. on 60 pf. olive .. 20 6·00
M 291. 2 M. on 50 pf. purple 5 12
M 292. 5 M. on 1 m. 25 green 15 1·50
M 293. 4 Md. on 50 pf. purple 75 25·00
M 294. 10 Md. on 3 m. brn. 50 3·00

1923. Surch. in figures, representing gold pfennige.
M 295. M 1. 3 pf. on 25 pf. orange 25 3·00
M 296. 5 pf. on 25 pf. orange 5 25
M 297. 10 pf. on 25 pf. orange 5 25
M 298. 20 pf. on 25 pf. orange 15 1·50
M 299. 50 pf. on 25 pf. orange 50 £160

OFFICIAL STAMPS

O 1. O 2. King William.

1881.
O 181. O 1. 2 pf. grey 5 5
O 108. 3 pf. green .. .. 3·00 1·60
O 183. 3 pf. brown 5 5
O 112. 5 pf. mauve .. 1·40 25
O 184. 5 pf. green .. 5 5
O 186. 10 pf. rose 5 5
O 190. 20 pf. blue .. 20 20
O 117. 25 pf. brown .. 5·00 1·90
O 191. 25 pf. orange 5 5
O 193. 30 pf. black & orange 5 5
O 195. 40 pf. black and red 5 5
O 119. 50 pf. green .. 6·50 3·75
O 141. 50 pf. brown .. 75·00 £150
O 196. 50 pf. maroon .. 10 12
O 120. 1 m. yellow .. 45·00 75·00
O 197. 1 m. violet .. .. 60 2·00
See also Nos. O 36/52.

1906. Optd. **1806-1906** under crown.
O 158. O 1. 2 pf. grey .. .. 7·50 12·00
O 159. 3 pf. brown .. 90 1·50
O 160. 5 pf. green .. 25 35
O 161. 10 pf. rose .. 25 35
O 162. 20 pf. blue .. 75 90
O 163. 25 pf. orange .. 1·75 3·75
O 164. 30 pf. black & orange 1·75 3·75
O 165. 40 pf. black and red 10·00 15·00
O 166. 50 pf. maroon .. 10·00 15·00
O 167. 1 m. violet .. .. 15·00 25·00

1906.
O 182. O 1. 2½ pf. grey 5 5
O 185. 7½ pf. orange .. 5 5
O 187. 15 pf. brown .. 5 5
O 188. 15 pf. purple .. 5 5
O 192. 25 pf. black & brown 5 5
O 194. 35 pf. brown .. 5 5
O 198. 1 m. black and grey 35 5·00

1916. Surch.
O 200. O 1. 25 pf. on 25 pf. orge. 25 1·00
O 201. 50 pf. on 50 pf. mar. 20 3·75

1916. 25th Year of Reign.
O 209. O 2. 2½ pf. grey .. .. 25 2·50
O 210. 7½ pf. red 5 20
O 211. 10 pf. red .. .. 5 1·50
O 212. 15 pf. bistre .. 5 20
O 213. 20 pf. blue .. .. 5 1·25
O 214. 25 pf. grey .. .. 25 3·00
O 215. 30 pf. green .. 25 5·00
O 216. 40 pf. claret .. 50 5·00
O 217. 50 pf. brown .. 60 10·00
O 218. 1 m. mauve .. .. 90 12·00

1919. Surch. in large figures.
O 220. O 1. 2 on 2½ pf grey .. 5 2·50
O 221. 75 on 3 pf. brn. (O 68) 20 15·00

1919. Optd. **Volksstaat Wurttemberg.**
O 232. O 1. 2½ pf. grey 5 50
O 233. 3 pf. brown .. .. 1·25 5·00
O 234. 5 pf. green 5 5
O 235. 7½ pf. orange .. 12 1·25
O 236. 10 pf. rose 5 5
O 237. 15 pf. purple .. 5 5
O 238. 20 pf. blue 5 5
O 239. 25 pf. black & brown 5 60
O 240. 30 pf. black & orange 5 60
O 241. 35 pf. brown .. 10 3·50
O 242. 40 pf. black and red .. 10 1·75
O 243. 50 pf. maroon .. 8 1·75
O 244. 1 m. black and grey .. 12 3·00

O 3. Ulm.

VIEWS: 10 pf., 50 pf., 2 m. 50, 3 m. Stuttgart, 20 pf., 1 m. Tubingen. 30 pf., 1 m. 25, Ellwangen.

1920.
O 260. – 10 pf. claret .. 15 3·00
O 261. O 3. 15 pf. brown .. 15 4·50
O 262. – 20 pf. blue .. .. 15 1·50
O 263. – 30 pf. green .. 15 8·50
O 264. – 50 pf. yellow .. 15 15·00
O 265. O 3. 75 pf. bistre .. 30 15·00
O 266. – 1 m. red .. 30 15·00
O 267. – 1 m. 25 violet .. 30 19·00
O 268. – 2 m. 50 blue .. .. 50 20·00
O 269. – 3 m. green .. .. 50 30·00

YEMEN 04

A republic in S.W. Arabia, ruled as a kingdom and imamate until 1962. From 1962 stamps were issued concurrently by the Republican Government and the Royalists. The latter are listed after the Republican issues.

1926. 40 bogaches = 1 imadi.
1964. 40 bogaches = 1 rial.
1975. 100 fils = 1 riyal.

KINGDOM

1. 2. 3.

1926. Imperf. or perf.
1. 1. 2½ b. black on white .. 5·00 5·00
2. 2½ b. black on orange .. 5·00 5·00
3. 5 b. black on white .. 5·00 5·00

1930. The 6 b. to 1 im. values are larger
10. 2. ½ b. orange 8 8
4. 1 b. green 20 20
11. 1 b. olive 10 8
5. 2 b. olive 20 20
12. 2 b. brown 15 10
13. 3 b. lilac 20 8
6. 4 b. vermilion 45 30
14. 4 b. carmine 25 12
15. 5 b. grey 40 25
7. 6 b. blue 65 40
17. 8 b. claret 45 35
8. 10 b. brown 90 65
18. 10 b. orange 55 40
19. 20 b. olive .. .. 2·25 1·75
9. 1 im. blue and brown .. 4·00 4·00
20. 1 im. olive and claret .. 4·00 3·25

1939. Surch. with T 3.
27. 2. 4 b. on ½ b. orange .. 1·40 70
65. 4 b. on 1 b. olive .. 70 50
66. 4 b. on 2 b. brown .. 5·50 2·50
67. 4 b. on 3 b. lilac .. 1·10 65
68. 4 b. on 5 b. grey .. 1·10 65

4. Flags of Arab Allies. 5.

6.

1939. Arab Alliance. 2nd Anniv.
21. 4. 4 b. blue and red 35 35
22. 6 b. blue and slate .. 40 40
23. 10 b. blue and brown .. 60 60
24. 14 b. blue and olive .. 90 90
25. 20 b. blue and green .. 1·10 1·10
26. 1 im. blue and purple .. 2·25 2·25

1940.
28. 5. ½ b. blue and orange .. 8 8
29. 1 b. red and green .. 12 12
30. 2 b. violet and bistre .. 12 12
31. 3 b. blue and mauve .. 12 12
32. 4 b. green and red .. 15 15
33. 5 b. bistre and green .. 20 15
34. 6. 6 b. orange and blue .. 20 15
35. 8 b. blue and maroon .. 25 20
36. 10 b. olive and orange .. 30 20
37. 14 b. violet and olive .. 35 25
38. 18 b. black and green .. 50 50
39. 20 b. red and green .. 70 60
40. 1 im. red, olive & maroon 1·40 1·25

The 5 b. (for which there had originally been no postal use) was released in 1957 to serve as 4 b., without surcharge.

6a. 7.

1942.
41. 6a. 1 b. olive and orange .. 8 8
42. 2 b. olive and orange .. 10 10
43. 4 b. olive and orange .. 15 15
44. 6 b. blue and orange .. 20 20
45. 8 b. blue and orange .. 30 30
46. 10 b. blue and orange .. 40 40
47. 12 b. blue and orange .. 50 50
48. 20 b. blue and orange .. 70 70

These stamps, formerly listed under Nos. D 1/8, although inscribed "TAXE A PERCEVOIR" were only used for ordinary postage purposes as there is no postage due system in Yemen.

1945. Surch. with T 3.
49. 5. 4 b. on ½ b. blue & orange 40 40
50. 4 b. on 1 b. red and green 60 35
51. 4 b. on 2 b. violet & bistre 40 30
52. 4 b. on 3 b. blue & mauve 50 35
53. 4 b. on 5 b. bistre and green 50 35

1946. Inauguration of Yemenite Hospital.
54. 7. 4 b. black and green .. 40 30
55. 6 b. red and green .. 50 35
56. 10 b. blue and green .. 65 50
57. 14 b. olive and green .. 1·00 80

8. Coffee Plant. 10. View of Sana Parade Ground.

9. Aeroplane over Sana.

1947.
58. 8. ½ b. brown (postage) .. 40 30
59. 1 b. purple 55 40
60. 2 b. violet 70 50
61. – 4 b. red .. .. 1·25 1·00
62. – 5 b. blue 30 30
62a. 8. 6 b. green .. .. 1·25 60
63. 9. 10 b. blue (air) .. .. 2·25 2·25
64. 20 b. green .. .. 3·25 3·25

DESIGN—VERT. 4 b., 5 b. Palace, Sana.

The 5 b. was put on sale in 1957 to serve as 4 b., without surcharge.

1949. Surch. as T 3.
68a. 8. 4 b. on ½ b. brown .. 1·00 1·00
69. 4 b. on 1 b. purple .. 1·00 1·00
70. 4 b. on 2 b. violet .. 1·75 1·60

1951. (a) Postage.
71. 10. 1 b. brown 10 8
72. 2 b. chestnut 12 10
73. 3 b. magenta 15 10
74. – 5 b. red and blue .. 25 15
75. – 6 b. red and purple .. 35 20
76. – 8 b. green and blue .. 40 25
77. – 10 b. purple 50 30
78. – 14 b. turquoise 75 45
79. – 20 b. red .. .. 1·50 60
80. – 1 am. violet .. .. 2·10 1·00

DESIGNS—HORIZ. 5 b. Yemenite flag. 10 b. Mosque, Sana. 14 b. Walled City of Sana. 20 b., 1 am. Taiz and Citadel. VERT. 6 b. Eagle and Yemenite flag. 8 b. Coffee plant.

(b) Air. With aeroplane.
81. 6 b. blue 40 25
82. 8 b. sepia 50 30
83. 10 b. green 70 40
84. 12 b. blue 80 45
85. 16 b. purple .. .. 1·00 55
86. 20 b. orange .. .. 1·40 1·00
87. 1 am. red .. .. 2·50 1·75

DESIGNS—HORIZ. 6 b., 8 b. Sana. 10 b. Trees. 16 b. Taiz Palace. VERT. 12 b. Palace of the Rock, Wadi Dhahr. 20 b. Crowd of people. 1 am. Landscape.

The 5 b. postage stamp was released in 1956 to serve as 4 b. without surcharge and it was again put on sale as 8 b. in 1957. The 6 b. and 8 b. air stamps were released in 1957 to serve as ordinary postage stamps.

11. Flag and View of San's and Hodeidah.

1952. Accession of King Ahmed. 4th Anniv. Flag in red. Perf. or imperf.
88. 11. 1 im. blk. & lake (post.) 1·75 1·75
89. 1 im. blue & brown (air) 2·00 2·00

1952. 4th Anniv. of Victory. As T 11, but inscr. "COMMEMORATION OF VICTORY". Flag in red. Perf. or imperf.
90. 30 b. green & lake (post.) .. 1·50 1·50
91. 30 b. blue & green (air) .. 1·75 1·75

12. Palace of the Rock, Wadi Dhahr.

ILLUSTRATIONS
British Commonwealth and all overprints and surcharges are FULL SIZE. Foreign Countries have been reduced to ¾-LINEAR.

1952. Sky in blue. Perf. or imperf.
92. 12. 12 b. grn. & sepia (post.) 1·00 1·00
93. – 20 b. brown and red .. 1·40 1·40
94. 12. 12 b. brn. & green (air) .. 1·25 1·25
95. – 20 b. brown and blue .. 1·50 1·50

DESIGN: 20 b. (2), Walls of Ibb.

1952. Surch. as T 3.
95a. 10. 4 b. on 1 b. brown .. 50 50
96. 4 b. on 2 b. chestnut .. 50 50
97. 4 b. on 3 b. magenta .. 50 50

1953. Surch. as T 3.
98. 6a. 4 b. on 1 b. olive & orge. 1·25 70
99. 4 b. on 2 b. olive & orge. 1·25 70

13. 13a. Bab al-Yemen Gate, Sana'a.

1953.
100. 13. 4 b. orange (postage) .. 25 25
101. 6 b. blue 35 35
102. 8 b. turquoise 50 50
103. 10 b. red (air) 60 60
104. 12 b. blue 70 70
105. 20 b. bistre .. .. 1·25 1·25

1956. Unissued official stamps issued for ordinary postal use without surch.
105a. 13a. 1 b. brown 12
105b. 5 b. turquoise-blue .. 15
105c. 10 b. blue 30

The 1 and 5 b. were each sold for use as 4 b. and the 10 b. as 10 b. for inland registered post.

1957. Arab Postal Union. As T 87 of Egypt but inscr. "YEMEN" at top and inscriptions in English.
106. 4 b. brown 60 60
107. 6 b. green 75 75
108. 16 b. violet 90 90

1959. Proclamation of United Arab States (U.A.R. and Yemen). 1st Anniv. As T **128** of Egypt.
109. 1 b. black and lake (postage) 8 8
110. 2 b. black and green .. 12 12
111. 4 b. red and green .. 20 20
112. 6 b. black and orange (air) 40 40
113. 10 b. black and red .. 60 60
114. 16 b. red and violet .. 75 75

1959. Arab Telecommunications Union Commem. As T **127** of Egypt.
115. 4 b. red 25 20

1959. Inaug. of Automatic Telephone, Sana'a. Optd. **AUTOMATIC TELEPHONE INAUGURATION SANAA MARCH 1959** in English and Arabic.
116. **2.** 6 b. blue 60 60
117. 8 b. claret 70 70
118. 10 b. orange 90 90
119. 20 b. olive .. .. 1·75 1·75
120. 1 im. olive and claret .. 2·50 2·50

1960. Air. Optd. **AIR MAIL 1959** in English and Arabic and aeroplane.
121. **2.** 6 b. blue 60 60
122. 10 b. brown .. .. 1·00 1·00

1960. Inaug. of Arab League Centre, Cairo. As T **144** of Egypt but with different arms.
123. 4 b. black and green .. 25 25

IMPERF. STAMPS. From this point many issues also exist imperf. This applies also to Republican and Royalist issues.

1960. World Refugee Year. As T **145** of Egypt.
124. 4 b. brown 35 35
125. 6 b. green 50 50

14. Olympic Torch.

1960. Olympic Games, Rome.
126. **14.** 2 b. red and black .. 10 10
127. 4 b. yellow and black .. 15 15
128. 6 b. orange and black .. 20 20
129. 8 b. turquoise and black 30 30
130. 20 b. orange and violet 80 80

15. U.N. Emblem.

1961. U.N. 15th Anniv.
131. **15.** 1 b. violet 8 8
132. 2 b. green 10 10
133. 3 b. turquoise 12 12
134. 4 b. blue 15 15
135. 6 b. purple 20 20
136. 14 b. red 40 40
137. 20 b. sepia 65 65

16. Hodeida Port.

1961. Hodeida Port Inaug.
138. **16.** 4 b. red, blk., bl. & yell. 20 20
139. 6 b. red, blk., bl. & grn. 35 35
140. 16 b. red, black, blue and light blue 80 80

17. Alabaster Death-mask. **18.**

1961. Statues of Marib.
141. 1 b. black & orange (post.) 5 5
142. 2 b. black and violet .. 8 8
143. 4 b. black and brown .. 15 15
144. 8 b. black and magenta 35 35
145. 10 b. black and yellow .. 40 40
146. 12 b. black and violet-blue 60 60
147. 20 b. black and grey .. 80 80
148. 1 im. black and grey-green 1·75 1·75
149. 6 b. black & turquoise (air) 25 25
150. 16 b. black and blue .. 60 60

DESIGNS: 1 b. T **17**. 2 b. Horned head (8th-century B.C. frieze, Temple of the Moon God. 4 b. Bronze head of the Himyaritic emperor, of 1st or 2nd-century. 6 b. "Throne of Bilqis" (8th-century B.C. limestone columns, Moon God Temple). 8 b. Bronze figure of Himyaritic Emperor Dhamar Ali, 2nd or 3rd-century. 10 b. Alabaster statuette of 2nd or 3rd-century child. 12 b. Entrance to Moon God Temple. 16 b. Control tower and spillway, Marib dam. 20 b. 1st-century alabaster relief of boy with dagger riding legendary monster, Moon God Temple. 1 im. 1st-century alabaster relief of woman with grapes, Moon God Temple.

1961. Yemeni Buildings.
151. 4 b. blk., grn. & turq. (post.) 15 15
152. 8 b. black, green and cerise 35 35
153. 10 b. black, green & orange 40 40
154. 6 b. black, green & bl. (air) 25 25
155. 16 b. black, green & rose .. 60 60

DESIGNS—VERT. 4 b. T **18**. 10 b. Palace on hill-top. 16 b. Palace on rock. HORIZ. 6 b. City gateway. 8 b. Palace and trees.

19. Hodeida-Sana'a Highway.

1961. Hodeida-Sana'a Highway. Inaug.
156. **19.** 4 b. brown, yellow, blue and violet 20 20
157. 6 b. brown, yellow, blue and emerald .. 30 30
158. 10 b. brown, yellow, blue and red .. 45 45

20. Nubian Temple.

1962. U.N.E.S.C.O. Campaign for Preservation of Nubian Monuments.
159. **20.** 4 b. brown 35 35
160. 6 b. green 35 35

1962. Arab League Week. As T **170** of Egypt.
161. 4 b. green 20 20
162. 6 b. blue 25 25

21. Nurse weighing Child.

1962. Maternity and Child Centre. Mult.
164. 2 b. Putting child to bed .. 8 8
164. 4 b. T 21 .. .. .. 12 12
165. 6 b. Taking child's temperature 20 20
166. 10 b. Weighing baby .. 30 30

1962. Malaria Eradication. As T **174** of Egypt.
167. 4 b. orange and black .. 12 12
168. 6 b. green and sepia .. 20 20

1962. U.N. 17th Anniv. Nos. 131/7 optd. **1945–1962** in English and Arabic with bars over old dates.
169. **15.** 1 b. violet 70 70
170. 2 b. green 70 70
171. 3 b. turquoise 70 70
172. 4 b. blue 70 70
173. 6 b. purple 70 70
174. 14 b. red 70 70
175. 20 b. sepia 70 70

REPUBLIC

الجمهورية العربية اليمنية
١٩٦٢/٩/٢٧-١٣٨٢/٤/٢٨
Y.A.R. 27.9.1962
(**22.**)

1963. Various issues optd. as T **22**.
(a) Nos. 141/50.
176. 1 b. black & orange (post.)
177. 2 b. black and violet ..
178. 4 b. black and brown ..
179. 8 b. black and magenta ..
180. 10 b. black and yellow ..
181. 12 b. black and violet-blue
182. 20 b. black and grey ..
183. 1 im. black and grey-green
184. 6 b. black & turquoise (air)
185. 16 b. black and blue ..
Set of 10 .. .. 5·00 5·00

(b) Nos. 151/5.
186. 4 b. blk., grn. & turq. (post.)
187. 8 b. black, green & cerise
188. 10 b. black, green & orange
189. 6 b. blk., green & blue (air)
190. 16 b. black, green and rose
Set of 5 .. .. .. 2·75 2·75

(c) Nos. 163/6.
191. 2 b. multicoloured ..
192. 4 b. multicoloured ..
193. 6 b. multicoloured ..
194. 10 b. multicoloured ..
Set of 4 .. .. 2·50 2·50

23. "Torch of Freedom".

1963. "Proclamation of Republic".
195. – 4 b. brn. & mag. (post.) 12 12
196. – 6 b. red and blue .. 15 15
197. – 8 b. black & purple (air) 25 25
198. **23.** 10 b. red & deep violet 30 30
199. – 16 b. red and green .. 45 45

DESIGNS—VERT. 4 b. Soldier with flag. 6 b. Tank and flag. 8 b. Bayonet and torch. HORIZ. b 16. Flag and torch.

1963. Freedom from Hunger. As Nos. 762/3 of Egypt but inscr. "Y.A.R." instead of "UAR".
200 **190.** 4 b. chestnut and red .. 10 10
201. – 6 b. yellow and violet 20 20

1963. Various issues optd.

الجمهورية العربية اليمنية
Y.A.R.
١٩٦٢/٩/٢٧-١٣٨٢/٤/٢٨
27-9-1962
(**24.**)

الجمهورية
العربية اليمنية
١٣٨٢/٤/٢٨
١٩٦٢/٩/٢٧
Y. A. R.
27. 9. 1962
بريد اليمن
(**25.**)

(a) With T **24**. On Nos. 161/2.
202. 4 b. green 75 75
203. 6 b. blue .. .. .. 1·40 1·40

(b) With T **25**.
207. **2.** 5 b. grey 15 15
204. 6 b. blue 20 20
208. 8 b. claret 25 25
205. 10 b. brown 30 30
209. 10 b. orange 30 30
210. 20 b. olive 50 50
206. 1 im. blue and brown .. 1·10 1·10
211. 1 im. olive and claret .. 1·10 1·10

(c) As T **25** but with lowest line of inscription at top.
212. **7.** 6 b. red and green .. 30 30
213. 10 b. blue and green .. 50 50
214. 14 b. olive and green .. 85 85

(d) As T **25**, but with lowest line of inscription omitted and bar at top. On Nos. 167/8.
215. 4 b. orange and black .. 80 80
216. 6 b. green and sepia .. 1·10 1·10

الجمهورية العربية اليمنية
١٩٦٢-٩-٢٧ — ١٣٨٢-٤-٢٨
Y. A. R 27. 9. 1962
(**26.**)

(e) With T **26**. (i) On Nos. 139/40.
217. **16.** 6 b. red, blk., bl. & green 15 15
218. 16 b. red, blk., bl. & lt. bl. 40 40

(ii) On Nos. 157/8.
219. **19.** 6 b. brown, yellow, green and emerald .. 15 15
220. 10 b. brown, yellow, green and red .. 35 35

(f) As T **26**, but with only one bar over old inscription. (i) Nos. 126/8.
221. **14.** 2 b. red and black 2·00 2·00
222. 4 b. yellow and black 2·00 2·00
223. 6 b. orange and black 2·00 2·00

(ii) Nos. 159/60.
224. **20.** 4 b. brown .. .. 2·75 2·75
225. 6 b. green .. .. 3·75 3·75

AIR MAIL
Y.A.R.
(**28.**)

29. Flag, Torch and Candle.

(g) Air. With T **28**.
226. **4.** 6 b. blue and slate .. 25 25
227. 10 b. blue and brown .. 35 35
228. 14 b. blue and olive .. 60 60
229. 20 b. blue and green .. 70 70
230. 1 im. blue and purple .. 1·40 1·40

1963. Revolution. 1st Anniv.
231. **29.** 2 b. red, green & black 8 8
232. – 4 b. red, black & green 15 15
233. – 6 b. red, black & green 20 20

DESIGNS—HORIZ. 4 b. Flag, torch and broken chain. VERT. 6 b. Flag and laurel sprig.

30. Hands reaching for Centenary Emblem. **32.** Globe and Scales of Justice.

31.

1963. Red Cross Centenary. Crescent red; inscriptions black.
234. **30.** ¼ b. blue 5 5
235. ½ b. brown 8 8
236. ½ b. grey 8 8
237. – 4 b. lilac 15 15
238. – 8 b. ochre 20 20
239. – 20 b. green 65 65

DESIGN: 4 b. to 20 b. Centenary emblem.

1963. Air. "Honouring Astronauts". T **31** and similar designs showing rockets, etc.
240. **31.** ¼ b. multicoloured .. 10 10
241. – ⅓ b. multicoloured .. 10 10
242. – ½ b. multicoloured .. 10 10
243. – 4 b. multicoloured .. 20 20
244. – 20 b. multicoloured .. 1·90 1·90

1963. Declaration of Human Rights. 15th Anniv.
245. – 4 b. black, orge. & lilac 15 15
246. **32.** 6 b. black and green .. 20 20

DESIGN: 4 b. As T **32** but differently arranged

33. Darts.

1964. "Local Sports".
247. ¼ b. bronze-green, brown and orange (postage) .. 5 5
248. ⅓ b. brown, blue and violet 5 5
249. ½ b. brown, blue & magenta 5 5
250. 1 b. brown, green and blue 5 5
251. 1½ b. red, brown and grey 5 5

252. 4 b. brn-red, blk. & bl. (air) 8 8
253. 20 b. blue, indigo & brown 50 50
254. 1 r. red, brn. & blue-green 1·75 1·75
DESIGNS—HORIZ. ¼ b. T **33**. ⅓ b. Table-tennis. 4 b. Horse-racing. 20 b. Pole-vaulting. VERT. ½ b. Running. 1 b. Volley-ball. 1½ b. Football. 1 r. Basketball. All designs include the Olympic "Rings" symbol.

34. Factory and Cloth. **35.** Aircraft on Runway.

1964. Bagel Spinning and Weaving Factory. Inaug.
255. **34.** 2 b. blue & yellow (post.) 5 5
256. – 5 b. blue and lemon .. 15 15
257. – 6 b. emerald and brown 20 20

258. 16 b. salmon, indigo and grey (air) 45 45
DESIGNS—VERT. 4 b. Loom. 6 b. Factory, bobbins and cloth. HORIZ. 16 b. Factory and lengths of cloth.

1964. Hodeida Airport Inaug.
259. **35.** 4 b. yellow and blue .. 15 15
260. – 6 b. green and ultram... 20 20
261. – 10 b. blue, yell. & indigo 30 30
DESIGNS: 6 b. Control tower and aircraft on runway. 10 b. Control tower, aircraft and ship.

1964. Air. President Kennedy Memorial Issue. Nos. 240/2 optd. **JOHN F. KENNEDY 1917 1963** in English and Arabic and with portrait and laurel.
262. **31.** ¼ b. multicoloured .. 35 35
263. – ⅓ b. multicoloured .. 35 35
264. – ½ b. multicoloured .. 35 35

36. Aircraft, New York and Sana'a.

1964. New York World's Fair.
265. **36.** ¼ b. brn., bl. & grn. (post.) 5 5
266. – ⅓ b. black, red & green 5 5
267. – ½ b. blue-green, red & bl. 5 5
268. **36.** 1 b. indigo, blue & green 5 5
269. – 4 b. indigo red & green 15 15

270. – 16 b. brn., red & bl. (air) 60 60
271. **36.** 20 b. purple, blue & grn. 75 75
DESIGNS: ⅓ b., 4 b. Flag, Empire State Building, New York and Mosque, Sana'a. ½ b., 16 b. Ship, Statue of Liberty, New York. and Harbour, Hodeida.

37. Globe and Flags. **38.** Scout hoisting Flags.

1964. Olympic Games, Tokyo. Multicoloured.
272. ¼ b. Type **37** (postage) .. 5 5
273. ⅓ b. Olympic torch .. 5 5
274. ½ b. Discus-thrower .. 5 5
275. 1 b. Yemeni flag 8 8
276. 1½ b. Swimming (horiz.) .. 10 10

277. 4 b. Swimming (horiz.) (air) 20 20
278. 6 b. Olympic torch .. 30 30
279. 12 b. Type **37** 65 65
280. 20 b. Discus-thrower .. 1·10 1·10

1964. Yemeni Scouts. Multicoloured.
281. ¼ b. Type **38** (postage) .. 5 5
282. ⅓ b. Scout badge and scouts guarding camp 5 5
283. ½ b. Bugler 5 5
284. 1 b. As No. 277 .. .. 5 5
285. 1½ b. Scouts by camp-fire 8 8

286. 4 b. Type **38** (air) 15 15
287. 6 b. As No. 277 .. .. 20 20
288. 16 b. Bugler 55 55
289. 20 b. Scouts by camp-fire 70 70

39. Monkeys.

1964. Animals.
290. **39.** ¼ b. brn. & lilac (post.) 5 5
291. – ⅓ b. brown and blue .. 5 5
292. – ½ b. sepia and orange .. 5 5
293. – 1 b. brown and blue .. 8 8
294. – 1½ b. brown and blue .. 10 10

295. – 4 b. red & green (air) .. 20 20
296. – 12 b. drab and buff .. 60 60
297. – 20 b. brown and blue .. 1·10 1·10
ANIMALS: ½ b. Arab horses. ½ b., 12 b. Bullock. 1 b., 20 b. Lion and lioness. 1½ b., 4 b. Gazelles.

40. Aircraft over Mountains.

1964. Sana'a Int. Airport. Inaug.
306. **40.** 1 b. brn. & blue (post.) 5 5
307. – 2 b. chestnut & indigo .. 8 8
308. – 4 b. brown and blue .. 12 12
309. **40.** 8 b. brown and blue .. 25 25

310. – 6 b. chest. & blue (air) 20 20
DESIGNS: 2 b., 4 b. Aircraft over runway. 6 b. Aircraft in flight and on ground.

41. A.P.U. Emblem. **42.** Flags and Dove.

1964. Arab Postal Union. 10th Anniv.
311. **41.** 4 b. black, red and orange (postage) .. 12 12

312. **41.** 6 b. black, green and turquoise (air) .. 20 20

1964. 2nd Arab Summit Conf.
313. **42.** 4 b. green 12 12
314. – 6 b. brown 20 20
DESIGN: 6 b. Arms within conference emblem and map.

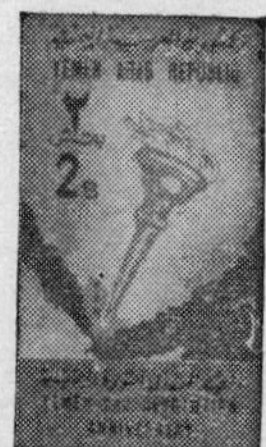

43. Flaming Torch. **44.** Gentian.

1964. Revolution. 2nd Anniv.
315. **43.** 2 b. ochre and blue .. 8 8
316. – 4 b. grey-grn. & yellow 12 12
317. – 6 b. rose, red and green 20 20
DESIGNS: 4 b. Yemeni soldier. 6 b. Candles on map.

1965. Flowers. Multicoloured.
298. ¼ b. Type **44** (postage) .. 5 5
299. ⅓ b. Lily 5 5
300. ½ b. Poinsettia 5 5
301. 1 b. Rose 8 8
302. 1½ b. Viburnum 12 12

303. 4 b. Rose (air) 20 20
304. 12 b. Poinsettia 60 60
305. 20 b. Viburnum .. .. 1·10 1·10

45. Reef Herons.

1965. Birds. Multicoloured.
318. ¼ b. Type **45** (postage) .. 5 5
319. ½ b. Arabian red-legged partridge.. .. .. 5 5
320. ¾ b. Eagle owl (vert.) .. 5 5
321. 1 b. Hammerhead .. 5 5
322. 1½ b. Yemen linnets .. 5 5
323. 4 b. Hoopoes 20 20

324. 6 b. Amethyst starlings (air) 20 20
325. 8 b. Bald ibis (vert.) .. 30 30
326. 12 b. Arabian woodpecker (vert.) 55 55
327. 20 b. Bateleur eagle (vert.) 80 80
328. 1 r. Bruce's green pigeon .. 1·75 1·75

1965. Deir Yasin Massacre. As T **230** of Egypt, but inscr. "YAR" in English and Arabic.
329. 4 b. purple & blue (postage) 15 15

330. 6 b. red and orange (air) .. 20 20

46. I.T.U. Emblem and Symbols.

1965. I.T.U. Cent.
331. – 4 b. red and blue .. 12 12
332. **46.** 6 b. emerald and red .. 20 20
DESIGN—VERT. 4 b. As T **46** but rearranged.

1965. Burning of Algiers Library. As T **232** of Egypt, but inscr. "YAR" in English and Arabic.
333. 4 b. green, red & black (post.) 12 12

334. 6 b. blue and red (air) .. 20 20

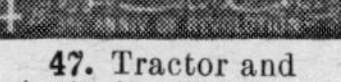

47. Tractor and Agricultural Produce. **48.** I.C.Y. and U.N. Emblems.

1965. Revolution. 3rd Anniv.
335. **47.** 4 b. blue and yellow .. 12 12
336. – 6 b. blue and yellow .. 20 20
DESIGN: 6 b. Tractor and landscape.

1965. Int. Co-operation Year.
337. **48.** 4 b. green and orange .. 12 12
338. – 6 b. brown and blue .. 20 20
DESIGN: 6 b. U.N. Headquarters and General Assembly Building, New York.

49. Pres. Kennedy, Map and Rocket-launching. **50.** Beliaiev and Rocket.

1965. Pres. Kennedy Commem. Designs each include portraits of Pres. Kennedy. Multicoloured.
339. ¼ b. Type **49** (postage) .. 5 5
340. ¼ b. Rocket gantries .. 5 5
341. ¼ b. Rocket 5 5
342. ⅓ b. Type **49** 5 5
343. ½ b. Rocket 5 5
344. 4 b. Capsule and U.S. flag 40 40

345. 8 b. Capsule in ocean (air) 80 80
346. 12 b. Rocket gantries .. 1·00 1·00

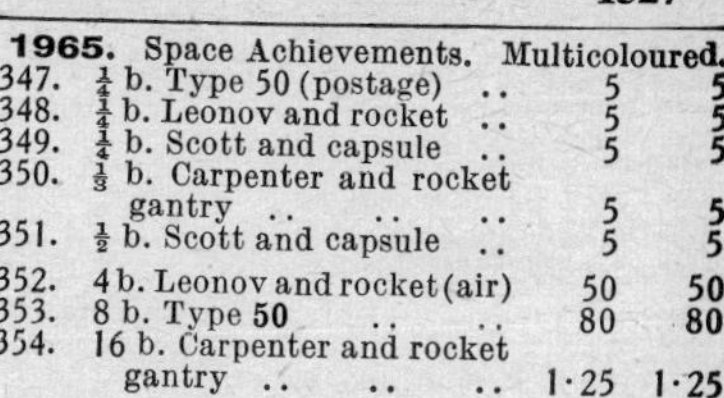

1965. Space Achievements. Multicoloured.
347. ¼ b. Type 50 (postage) .. 5 5
348. ¼ b. Leonov and rocket .. 5 5
349. ¼ b. Scott and capsule .. 5 5
350. ⅓ b. Carpenter and rocket gantry 5 5
351. ½ b. Scott and capsule .. 5 5

352. 4 b. Leonov and rocket (air) 50 50
353. 8 b. Type **50** 80 80
354. 16 b. Carpenter and rocket gantry .. .. .. 1·25 1·25

1966. Anti T.B. Campaign. Nos. 200/1 optd. **Tuberculous Campaign 1965** in English and Arabic.
356. **190.** 4 b. chestnut and red 12 12
357. – 6 b. yellow and violet 20 20

51. Torch Signalling.

1966. Telecommunications.
359. **51.** ¼ b. black & red (postage) 5 5
360. – ¼ b. black and blue .. 5 5
361. – ¼ b. black and ochre .. 5 5
362. – ⅓ b. black and red .. 5 5
363. – ½ b. black and blue .. 8 8

364. – 4 b. black & green (air) 25 25
365. – 6 b. black and brown .. 40 40
366. – 20 b. black and blue .. 1·40 1·40
DESIGNS: No. 360, Morse telegraphy. 361, Early telephone. 362, Wireless telegraphy. 363. Television. 364, Radar. 365, Telex. 366, "Early Bird" Satellite.

1966. Prevention of Cruelty to Animals. Nos. 318/20 optd. **Prevention of Cruelty to Animals** in English and Arabic.
368. **45.** ¼ b. multicoloured .. 5 5
369. – ½ b. multicoloured .. 5 5
370. – ¾ b. multicoloured .. 8 8

1966 3rd Arab Summit Conf. Nos. 305/6 optd. **3rd Arab Summit Conference 1965**, in English and Arabic.
371. **42.** 4 b. green 15 15
372. – 6 b. brown 30 30

52. Pres. Kennedy and Globe.

1966. "Builders of World Peace".
(a) Postage. Size 39 × 28½ mm.
374. **52.** ¼ b. chestnut 5 5
375. – ¼ b. green 5 5
376. – ¼ b. indigo 5 5
377. – ⅓ b. brown 5 5
378. – ½ b. purple 5 5
379. **52.** 4 b. reddish purple .. 25 25

(b) Air. Size 51 × 38 mm.
381. – 6 b. brown and green .. 40 40
382. – 10 b. brown and blue .. 75 75
383. – 12 b. brown & magenta 90 90
PORTRAITS: Nos. 375, 377, Dag Hammarskjoeld. 376, 378, Nehru. 381, Ralph Bunche. 382, U Thant. 383, Pope Paul VI.

53. Cockerel.

1966. Animals and Insects.
(a) Postage. Multicoloured.
385. ¼ b. Type **53** 5 5
386. ¼ b. Hare 5 5
387. ¼ b. Pony 5 5
388. ⅓ b. Cat 5 5
389. ½ b. Sheep and lamb .. 5 5
390. 4 b. Dromedary 25 25

(b) Air. Various butterflies.
391. 6 b. multicoloured .. 25 25
392. 8 b. multicoloured .. 35 35
393. 10 b. multicoloured .. 50 50
394. 16 b. multicoloured .. 65 65

1966. Space Flight of "Luna 9". Nos. 347/54 optd. **LUNA IX 3 February 1966** in English and Arabic, and space-craft.

396. **50.** ¼ b. multicoloured (post.) 5 5
397. – ¼ b. multicoloured .. 5 5
398. – ¼ b. multicoloured .. 5 5
399. – ⅓ b. multicoloured .. 5 5
400. – ½ b. multicoloured .. 5 5
401. – 4 b. multicoloured (air) 20 20
402. **50.** 8 b. multicoloured .. 40 40
403. – 16 b. multicoloured .. 1·00 1·00

54. Jules Rimet Cup. **55.** Traffic Signals.

1966. World Cup Football Championships.

405. **54.** ¼ b. multicoloured (post) 5 5
406. – ¼ b. multicoloured .. 5 5
407. – ¼ b. multicoloured .. 5 5
408. – ⅓ b. multicoloured .. 5 5
409. – ½ b. multicoloured .. 5 5
410. – 4 b. multicoloured (air) 30 30
411. – 5 b. multicoloured .. 40 40
412. – 20 b. multicoloured .. 1·50 1·50

DESIGNS: Nos. 406/11 Footballers in play (all different). 412, World Cup emblem.

1966. Traffic Day.

414. **55.** 4 b. red, emerald & grn. 12 12
415. 6 b. red, emerald & grn. 20 20

1966. Space Flight of "Surveyor 1". Nos. 347/51 surch. **SURVEYOR 1 2 June 1966** space-craft and new value in English and Arabic.

417. **50.** 1 b. on ¼ b. multicoloured 25 25
418. – 1 b. on ¼ b. multicoloured 25 25
419. – 1 b. on ¼ b. multicoloured 25 25
420. – 3 b. on ⅓ b. multicoloured 70 70
421. – 4 b. on ½ b. multicoloured 90 90

56. Yemeni Flag.

1966. Revolution. 4th Anniv.

422. **56.** 2 b. black, red & green 5 5
423. – 4 b. blk., bl., grn. & orge. 10 10
424. – 6 b. blk., bl., grn. & yell. 15 15

DESIGNS—VERT. (25×42 mm.): 4 b. Automatic weapon. 6 b. "Agriculture and Industry".

1966. "World Fair. Sana'a, 1965". Nos. 265/71 optd. **1965 SANA'A** in English and Arabic.

425. **36.** ¼ b. brn., bl. & grn. (post.) 5 5
426. – ⅓ b. black, red & green 5 5
427. – ½ b. green, red and blue 5 5
428. **36.** 1 b. indigo, blue & green 10 10
429. – 4 b. indigo, red & green 40 40
430. – 16 b. brn., red & bl. (air) 2·00 2·00
431. **36.** 20 b. purple, blue & grn. 2·75 2·75

57. Galen, Helianthus and W.H.O. Building.

1966. W.H.O. Headquarters, Geneva. Inaug. Multicoloured designs incoporating W.H.O. Building.

433. ¼ b. Type **57** (postage) .. 5 5
434. ¼ b. Hippocrates and Ipomoeas 5 5
435. ¼ b. Ibn Sina and Peonies 5 5
436. 4 b. Type **57** (air).. .. 15 15
437. 8 b. As No. 434 .. .. 30 30
438. 16 b. As No. 435 .. .. 70 70

58. Space-craft Launching.

1966. Space Flight of "Gemini 6 and 7". Multicoloured.

440. ¼ b. Type **58** (postage) .. 5 5
441. ¼ b. Astronauts (vert.) .. 5 5
442. ¼ b. "Gemini" space-craft (horiz.) 5 5
443. ⅓ b. "Gemini 6 and 7" (horiz.) 5 5
444. ½ b. Recovery operations at sea (vert.) 5 5
445. 2 b. As ⅓ b... .. .. 10 10
446. 8 b. As ½ b. (air) 30 20
447. 12 b. "Gemini 6 and 7" link (horiz.) 45 30

1966. Space Flight of "Gemini 9". Nos. 440/7 optd. **GEMINI IX CERNAN-STAFFORD JUNE 3–1966** in English and Arabic.

449. **58.** ¼ b. multicoloured (post.) 5 5
450. – ¼ b. multicoloured .. 5 5
451. – ¼ b. multicoloured .. 5 5
452. – ⅓ b. multicoloured .. 5 5
453. – ½ b. mulitcoloured .. 5 5
454. – 2 b. multicoloured .. 12 12
455. – 8 b. multicoloured (air) 40 40
456. – 12 b. multicoloured .. 65 65

59. Figs.

1967. Fruits. Multicoloured.

458. ¼ b. Type **59** (postage) .. 5 5
459. ¼ b. Quinces 5 5
460. ¼ b. Grapes.. .. .. 5 5
461. ⅓ b. Dates 5 5
462. ½ b. Apricots 5 5
463. 2 b. Quinces 10 10
464. 4 b. Oranges 25 25
465. 6 b. Bananas (air).. .. 50 50
466. 8 b. Type **59** 60 60
467. 10 b. Grapes .. .. 1·00 1·00

1967. Arab League Day. As Type **265** of Egypt.

471. 4 b. brown and violet .. 25 25
472. 6 b. brown and violet .. 50 50
473. 8 b. brown and violet .. 60 60
474. 20 b. brown and green .. 1·25 1·00
475. 40 b. black and green .. 2·50 2·00

60. Ploughing and Sunset.

1967.

476. **60.** 1 b. multicoloured .. 5 5
477. 2 b. multicoloured .. 8 5
478. 4 b. multicoloured .. 15 5
479. 6 b. multicoloured .. 25 8
480. 8 b. multicoloured .. 35 10
481. 10 b. multicoloured .. 50 15
482. 12 b. multicoloured .. 60 25
483. 16 b. multicoloured .. 75 30
484. 20 b. multicoloured .. 1·00 45
485. 40 b. multicoloured .. 2·00 1·00

61. Pres. Al-Salal and Soldiers.

1968. Revolution. 6th Anniv. Multicoloured.

486. 2 b. Type **61** 5 5
487. 4 b. Yemen Arab Republic flag 10 10
488. 6 b. Pres. Abdullah al-Salal (vert.) 15 15

62. Map of Yemen and Dove.

1969. Revolution. 7th Anniv. Multicoloured.

490. 2 b. Type **62** 5 5
491. 4 b. Government building (horiz.) 10 10
492. 6 b. Yemeni workers (horiz.) 15 15

63. "Lenin addressing Crowd".

1970. Air. Lenin Birth Cent. Multicoloured.

494. 6 b. Type **63** 15 15
495. 10 b. "Lenin with Arab Delegates" 40 40

64. Arab League Flag, Arms and Map.

1970. Arab League. 25th Anniv.

496. **64.** 5 b. purple, green & pink 12 12
497. 7 b. brown, green & blue 15 15
498. 16 b. blue, grn. & olive 40 40

65. Yemeni Castle.

1971. Revolution. 8th Anniv. Multicoloured.

500. 5 b. Type **65** (postage) .. 60 30
501. 7 b. Yemeni workers and soldier (air) 70 40
502. 16 b. Clasped hands, flag and torch 90 60

1971. Air. Proclamation of First Permanent Constitution. No. 502 optd. **PROCLAMATION OF THE INSTITUTION 1.11.1390H 28.12.1970.**

504. 16 b. multicoloured .. 1·00 60

66. U.N. Emblems and Globe.

1971. United Nations. 25th Anniv. (1970).

505. **66.** 5 b. purple, green and olive 12 12
506. 7 b. indigo, green & blue 15 15

67. View of Sana'a.

1972. Revolution. 9th Anniv. Multicoloured.

508. 7 b. Type **67** 25 25
509. 18 b. Military parade .. 75 75
510. 24 b. Mosque, Sana'a .. 1·00 1·00

68. A.P.U. Emblem and Flags.

1972. Founding of Arab Postal Union at Sofar Conference. 25th Anniv. (1971).

512. **68.** 3 b. multicoloured .. 10 10
513. 7 b. multicoloured .. 20 20
514. 10 b. multicoloured .. 35 35

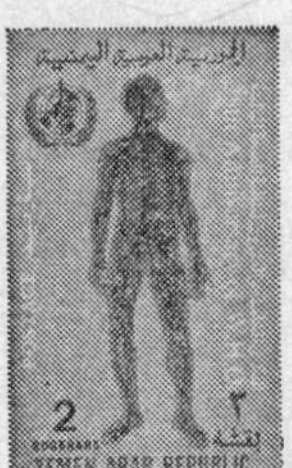

69. Arms and Flags. **70.** Skeleton and Emblem.

1972. Revolution. 10th Anniv.

516. **69.** 7 b. mult. (postage) .. 20 20
517. 10 b. multicoloured .. 35 35
518. **69.** 21 b. multicoloured (air) 90 90

1972. World Health Organisation. 25th Anniv.

519. **70.** 2 b. multicoloured .. 10 10
520. 21 b. multicoloured .. 60 60
521. 37 b. multicoloured .. 1·00 1·00

71. Al-Aqsa Mosque, Jerusalem.

1973. Burning of Al-Aqsa Mosque, Jerusalem. 2nd Anniv.

522. **71.** 7 b. multicoloured (post.) 15 15
523. 18 b. multicoloured .. 50 50
524. **71.** 24 b. multicoloured (air) 65 65

72. Arab Child with Book.

1973. U.N.I.C.E.F. 25th Anniv. (1971).

526. **72.** 7 b. multicoloured (post.) 20 20
527. 10 b. multicoloured .. 30 30
528. **72.** 18 b. multicoloured (air) 50 50

HAVE YOU READ THE NOTES AT THE BEGINNING OF THIS CATALOGUE?

These often provide answers to the enquiries we receive.

73. Modern Office Building.

1973. Air. Revolution. 11th Anniv.
530. **73.** 7 b. red and green .. 12 12
531. – 10 b. pink and green .. 20 20
532. – 18 b. violet and green .. 40 40
DESIGNS: 10 b. Factory. 18 b. Flats.

74. U.P.U. Emblem. **75.** Yemeni Town and Emblem.

1974. Universal Postal Union. Centenary.
533. **74.** 10 b. red, blk. & blue .. 5 5
534. 30 b. red, black & green 15 15
535. 40 b. red, black & yell. 20 20

1975. F.A.O. World Food Programme. 10th Anniv.
536. **75.** 10 b. multicoloured .. 5 5
537. 30 b. multicoloured .. 12 12
538. 63 b. multicoloured .. 30 30

76. Janad Mosque.

1975. Revolution. 12th Anniv. Mult.
539. 25 f. Type **76** 20 20
540. 75 f. Althawra Hospital .. 55 55

1975. Various stamps surch.
541. **69.** 75 f. on 7 b. multicoloured (postage) 55 55
542. **71.** 278 f. on 18 b. multicoloured .. .. 2·25 2·25
543. **72.** 75 f. on 18 b. multicoloured (air) .. 55 55
544. **73.** 90 f. on 7 b. red & green 70 70
545. – 120 f. on 18 b. violet and green (No. 532) .. 90 90

77. Early and Modern Telephones. **78.** Coffee Beans.

1976. Telephone Centenary.
546. **77.** 25 f. black and purple .. 20 20
547. 75 f. black and green .. 55 55
548. 160 f. black and blue .. 1·25 1·25

1976.
550. **78.** 1 f. multicoloured .. 5 5
551. 3 f. multicoloured .. 5 5
552. 5 f. multicoloured .. 5 5
553. 10 f. multicoloured .. 8 8
554. 25 f. multicoloured .. 20 20
555. 50 f. multicoloured .. 30 30
556. 75 f. multicoloured .. 55 55
557. 1 r. multicoloured .. 75 75
558. 1 r. 50 multicoloured .. 1·10 1·10
559. 2 r. multicoloured .. 1·50 1·50
560. 5 r. multicoloured .. 3·75 3·75
Nos. 557/60 are larger, 22 × 30 mm.

79. "Clasped Hands". **80.** Emblem of National Institute of Public Administration.

1976. Reformation Movement. 2nd Anniv. Multicoloured.
561. 75 f. Type **79** 55 55
562. 135 f. Hand holding pick .. 1·00 1·00

1976. Revolution. 14th Anniv. Mult.
564. 25 f Type **80** 20 20
565. 75 f. Yemeni family (Housing and population census) 55 55
566. 160 f. Shield Emblem (Sana'a university) .. 1·25 1·25

POSTAGE DUE STAMPS

1964. Designs as Nos. 303/5, but inscr. "POSTAGE DUE". Multicoloured.
D 306. 4 b. Roses 20 12
D 307. 12 b. Poinsettia 60 30
D 308. 20 b. Viburnum 85 45

1964. Designs as Nos. 291, 295/6 (Animals), but inscr. "POSTAGE DUE".
D 298. 4 b. brown and green .. 20 12
D 299. 12 b. brown & orge.-brown 70 35
D 300. 20 b. black and violet .. 1·10 70
DESIGNS: 4 b. Gazelles. 12 b. Bullock. 20 b. Arab horses.

1966. Nos. 324/8 optd. **POSTAGE DUE** in English and Arabic.
D 371. 6 b. multicoloured .. 20 20
D 372. 8 b. multicoloured .. 50 50
D 373. 12 b. multicoloured .. 70 70
D 374. 20 b. multicoloured .. 1·25 1·25
D 375. 1 r. multicoloured .. 2·50 2·50

1966. Designs as Nos. 410/12 (Football), but inscr. "POSTAGE DUE".
D 414. 4 b. multicoloured .. 20 12
D 415. 5 b. multicoloured .. 50 30
D 416. 20 b. multicoloured .. 1·00 50

1967. Designs as Nos. 465/7, but inscr. "POSTAGE DUE" instead of "AIR MAIL". Multicoloured.
D 468. – 6 b. Bananas .. 50 50
D 469. **59.** 8 b. Figs .. 60 60
D 470. – 10 b. Grapes .. 1·00 70

ROYALIST ISSUES

Fighting continued between the Royalists and Republicans until 1970. In 1970 Saudi Arabia recognised the Republican government as the rulers of Yemen, and the royalist position crumbled.

1962. Various issues optd. (i) Optd. **FREE YEMEN FIGHTS FOR GOD, IMAM, COUNTRY** in English and Arabic.
R 1. **14.** 2 b. red and black .. 55 55
R 3. 4 b. yellow and black .. 55 55

(ii) Optd. **FREE YEMEN FIGHTS FOR GOD, IMAM & COUNTRY** in English and Arabic. (a) Nos. 156/8.
R 5. **19.** 4 b. brown, yellow, blue and violet 80 80
R 6. 6 b. brown, yellow, blue and emerald 80 80
R 7. 10 b. brown, yellow, blue and red 80 80

(b) Nos. 159/60.
R 8. **20.** 4 b. brown .. .. 4·50 4·50
R 9. 6 b. green .. .. 5·50 5·50

(c) Nos. 161/2.
R 10. 4 b. green 60 60
R 11. 6 b. blue 60 60

(d) Nos. 167/8.
R 12. 4 b. orange and black .. 90 90
R 13. 6 b. green and sepia .. 90 90

(e) Nos. 126/30.
R 14. **14.** 2 b. red and black ..
R 15. 4 b. yellow and black ..
R 16. 6 b. orange and black
R 17. 8 b. turquoise and black
R 18. 20 b. orange and violet
Set of 5 .. .. 35·00 35·00

(f) Nos. 169/75.
R 19. **15.** 1 b. violet .. ..
R 20. 2 b. green .. ..
R 21. 3 b. turquoise .. ..
R 22. 4 b. blue .. ..
R 23. 6 b. purple .. ..
R 24. 14 b. red .. ..
R 25. 20 b. sepia .. ..
Set of 7 .. 5·00 5·00

R **1.** Five Ears of Wheat.

1963. Air. Freedom from Hunger.
R 26. R **1.** 4 b. red, grn. & ochre 35 35
R 27. 6 b. red, green & blue 45 45

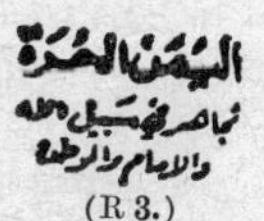

(R **2.**) (R **3.**)

1963. Nos. 195/6 variously optd.
(a) No. 195 optd. with Type R **2.**
R 28. 4 b. brown and magenta 2·00 2·00
(b) No. 196 optd. with Type R **2** with first line of Arabic inscr. repeated at foot.
R 29. 6 b. red and blue .. 3·00 3·00
(c) No. 196 optd. with Types R **2** and R **3.**
R 30. 6 b. red and blue .. ..

1963. Surch. in figures with stars over old value, for use on circulars.
R 31. R **1.** 1 b. on 4 b. red, green and ochre 20 20
R 32. 2 b. on 6 b. red, green and blue 50 50

R **4.** Red Cross Field Post.

1963. Red Cross Cent. Flags in red; inscr. in black.
R 33. R **4.** ⅛ b. violet (postage) 5 5
R 34. ¼ b. magenta .. 5 5
R 35. ½ b. brown 5 5
R 36. 4 b. turquoise .. 15 15
R 37. 6 b. blue (air) .. 25 25

R **5.**

1963. Issued at Qara. Consular Fee stamp optd. **YEMEN** in English and 'POSTAGE 1383" (Moslem Year) in Arabic with bar over old inscr., as in Type R **5.**
R 38. R **5.** 10 b. black and red .. 5·00 5·00

R **6.** Troops in Action.

1964. Air. "The Patriotic War". Flags and emblem in red.
R 39. R **6.** ½ b. emerald 5 5
R 40. 1 b. black 5 5
R 41. 2 b. slate-purple .. 8 8
R 42. 4 b. blue-green .. 12 12
R 43. 6 b. blue 20 20

1964. Air. Surch. **AIR MAIL,** red cross. **1963-64 HONOURING BRITISH RED CROSS SURGICAL TEAM** and value and Arabic equivalent.
R 44. R **6.** 10 b. on 4 b. blue-grn. 75 75
R 45. 18 b. on ½ b. emerald 1·00 1·00

1964. Air. Surch. **AIR MAIL** and value in English and Arabic with aeroplane motif.
R 46. R **4.** 10 b. on ⅛ b. violet .. 75 75
R 47. 18 b. on ¼ b. magenta 1·00 1·00
R 48. 28 b. on ½ b. brown .. 1 40 1·40

1964. Air. Surch. **4 REVALUED** in English and Arabic with dotted frameline around stamp.
R 49. R **6.** 4 b. on ½ b. emerald 80 80
R 50. 4 b. on 1 b. black .. 80 80
R 51. 4 b. on 2 b slate-purple 80 80

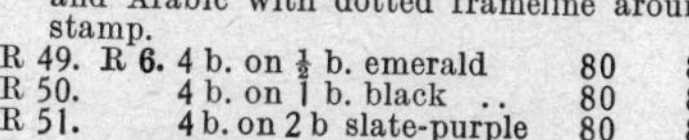

R **7.** Olympic Flame and "Rings"

1964. Olympic Games, Tokyo.
R 52. R **7.** 2 b. blue (postage) .. 30 30
R 53. 4 b. violet 50 50
R 54. R **7.** 6 b. brown (air) .. 85 85

R **8.** Rocket.

1964. Astronauts.
R 55. R **8.** 2 b. chestnut, violet and black (postage) 25 25
R 56. 4 b. chestnut, blue and black .. 40 40
R 57. R **8.** 6 b. yellow & blk. (air) 70 70

R **9.** (Actual size 80 × 26 mm.).

1964. Issued at Qara. Consular Fee stamps optd. across a pair as in Type R **9.**
R 58. R **9.** 10 b. (5 b.+5 b.) pur. 8·00 8·00
Owing to a shortage of 10 b. postage stamps, 5 b. Consular Fee stamps were optd. across pairs with **YEMEN** in English and "POSTAGE 1383" (Moslem Year) in Arabic, in frame, together with the Ministry of Communications' Royal Arms seal and a bar over old inscription at foot. Price is for horiz. or vert. pair.

1965. Air. British Yemen Relief Committee. Nos. R 46/8 additionally optd. **HONOURING BRITISH YEMEN RELIEF COMMITTEE 1963 1965,** in English and Arabic.
R 59. R **4.** 10 b. on ⅛ b. violet .. 30 30
R 60. 18 b. on ¼ b. magenta 50 50
R 61. 28 b. on ½ b. brown .. 65 65

R **10.** Seif-al-Islam Ali. R **11.** Kennedy as young man.

1965. Prince Seif al-Islam Ali Commem.
R 62. R **10.** 4 b. grey and red .. 12 12

1965. Pres. Kennedy Commem.
R 63. R **11.** ⅛ b. black, magenta and gold (postage) 5 5
R 64. – ¼ b. vio., turq. & gold 5 5
R 65. – ½ b. brn., blue & gold 5 5
R 66. – 4 b. sep., yell. & gold 55 55
R 67. – 6 b. black, apple and gold (air) .. .. 1·00 1·00
DESIGNS (Kennedy): ¼ b. As naval officer. ½ b. Sailing with Mrs. Kennedy. 4 b. In rocking-chair. 6 b. Full-face portrait.

1965. Churchill Commem. (1st issue). No. R 62, with colours changed, optd. **IN MEMORY OF SIR WINSTON CHURCHILL 1874-1965,** in English and Arabic.
R 68. R **10.** 4 b. blue and red .. 5·00 5·00

R **12.** Satellite and Emblems.

1965. I.T.U. Cent.
R 69. R **12.** 2 b. yellow, violet and black (postage) .. 30 30
R 70. 4 b. red, blue and blk. 50 50
R 71. 6 b. green, violet and black (air) 85 85

R **13.** Hammerhead.

1965. Birds. Multicoloured.

R 72. ⅛ b. Type R **13** (postage) .. 5 5
R 73. ¼ b. Goldfinch 5 5
R 74. ½ b. Hoopoe 5 5
R 75. 4 b. Kingfisher 20 20

R 76. 6 b. Rock thrush (air) .. 30 30

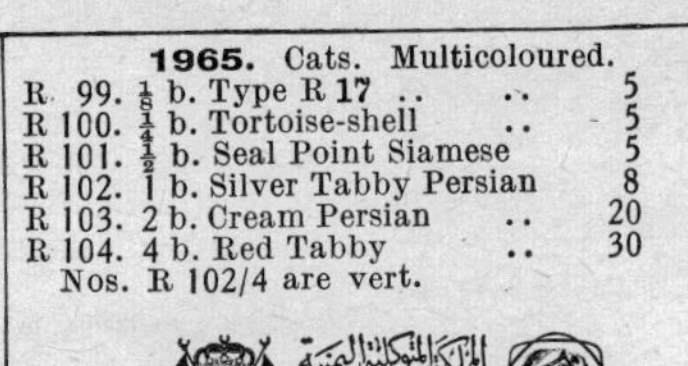

R **14.** Sir Winston Churchill and St. Paul's Cathedral.

1965. Churchill Commem. (2nd issue). Multicoloured.

R 77. ⅛ b. Type R **14** 8 8
R 78. ¼ b. Churchill and Houses of Parliament .. 10 10
R 79. ½ b. Full-face portrait .. 10 10
R 80. 1 b. Type R **14** 12 12
R 81. 2 b. Churchill and Houses of Parliament 20 20
R 82. 4 b. Full-face portrait .. 45 45

R **15.** Imam Al-Badr.

DESIGNS—VERT. 2 b., 18 b. Royal arms. HORIZ. 6 b., 24 b. Flag.

1965.

R 83. R **15.** 1 b. blk. & blue (post.) 5 5
R 83a. 1½ b. black & green 5 5
R 84. – 2 b. red and green .. 8 8
R 85. R **15.** 4 b. black and purple 15 15

R 86. – 6 b. red & violet (air) 20 20
R 87. – 18 b. red and brown 65 65
R 88. – 24 b. red and blue .. 80 80

1965. Space Flight of "Mariner 4". Nos. R 55/7 optd. **MARINER 4** in English and Arabic.

R 89. R **8.** 2 b. chestnut, violet and black (postage) 20 20
R 90. 4 b. chest., blue & blk. 45 45

R 91. 6 b. yell. & blk. (air) 70 70

R **16.** I.C.Y. Emblem, King Faisal of Saudi Arabia and Imam Al-Badr.

1965. Int. Co-operation Year.

R 92. R **16.** 2 b. indigo and brown (postage) 12 12
R 93. 4 b. lake and green 25 25
R 94. 6 b. sepia & bl. (air) 45 45

1965. Space Flight of "Gemini 5". Nos R 69/71 optd. **'GEMINI -V' GORDON COOPER & CHARLES CONRAD AUGUST 21-29, 1965** and space capsule.

R 95. R **12.** 2 b. yellow, violet and black (postage) 35 35
R 96. 4 b. red, blue and black .. 65 65

R 97. 6 b. green, violet and black (air) .. 90 90

R **17.** Black Persian.

1965. Cats. Multicoloured.

R 99. ⅛ b. Type R **17** 5 5
R 100. ¼ b. Tortoise-shell .. 5 5
R 101. ½ b. Seal Point Siamese 5 5
R 102. 1 b. Silver Tabby Persian 8 8
R 103. 2 b. Cream Persian 20 20
R 104. 4 b. Red Tabby .. 30 30

Nos. R 102/4 are vert.

R **18.**

1965. Flowers. Multicoloured.

R 106. ⅛ b. Verbena 5 5
R 107. ¼ b. Dianthus 5 5
R 108. ½ b. Dahlia 5 5
R 109. 1 b. Nasturtium 5 5
R 110. 2 b. Type R **18** 10 10
R 111. 4 b. Wild rose 20 20

Nos. R 109/11 are vert.

R **19.** Flag and Globe.

1965. Pope Paul's Visit to U.N. Organisation.

R 113. R **19.** 2 b. red, blk. & grn. 20 20
R 114. 4 b. red, blk. & vio. 35 35
R 115. 6 b. red, blk. & blue 50 50

R **20.** Moon Landing.

1965. Space Achievements. Multicoloured.

(a) Postage. (i) Size as Type R **18.**

R 117. ⅛ b. Type R **20** 8 8
R 118. ¼ b. Astronauts on Moon 10 10
R 119. ½ b. Pres. Kennedy and Cape Kennedy (vert.) 20 20

(ii) Size 48 × 28 mm.

R 120. 4 b. Beliaiev and Leonov in space 45 45

(b) Air. Size 48 × 28 mm.

R 121. 6 b. White and Mcdivitt in space 70 70

R **21.** Football and Gold Medal.

1965. "Winners of Olympic Games, Tokyo" (1964). Each design showing a sport with a gold medal. Multicoloured.

R 123. ⅛ b. Type R **21** (postage) 5 5
R 124. ¼ b. Running 5 5
R 125. ½ b. Throwing the discus 10 10
R 126. 2 b. Judo 25 25
R 127. 4 b. Wrestling 55 55

R 128. 6 b. Horse-jumping (air) 1·10 1·10

R **22.** Arms.

1966. Air. Imperf.

R 130. R **22.** 10 b. red on white
R 131. 10 b. violet on white
R 132. 10 b. red on yellow
R 133. 10 b. violet on orange
R 134. 10 b. violet on mag.

These handstamps were also applied directly to envelopes and aerogrammes.

R **23.** Nehru.

1966. "Builders of World Peace" (1st Series). Portraits in gold and black; inscr. in black.

R 136. R **23.** ⅛ b. apple 5 5
R 137. – ¼ b. brown .. 5 5
R 138. – ½ b. grey 12 12
R 139. – 1 b. blue 30 30
R 140. – 4 b. green 90 90

DESIGNS: ⅛ b. Dag Hammarskjoeld. ¼ b. Pope John XXIII. 1 b. Sir Winston Churchill. 4 b. Pres. Kennedy.

See also Nos. R 146/51.

1966. Nos. R 63/5 and R 67 surch. with new values in English and Arabic.

R 142. R **11.** 4 b. on ⅛ b. mult. (postage) .. 25 25
R 143. – 8 b. on ¼ b. mult. .. 25 25
R 144. – 10 b. on ½ b. mult. 60 60

R 145. – 1 r. on 6 b. mult. (air) 1·00 1·00

1966. "Builders of World Peace" (2nd Series). As Type R **23.** Portraits in black and gold; inscr. in black.

R 146. ⅛ b. yellow 10 10
R 147. ¼ b. flesh 10 10
R 148. ½ b. mauve 12 12
R 149. 1 b. blue 15 15
R 150. 1 b. blue-green 15 15
R 151. 4 b. green 60 60

PORTRAITS: ⅛ b Pres. Lubke. ¼ b. Pres. De Gaulle. ½ b. Pope Paul VI. 1 b. (R 149) Pres. Johnson. 1 b. (R 150) King Faisal of Saudi Arabia. 4 b. U Thant.

1966. Newspaper Stamps. Optd. **PERIODICALS** in English and Arabic in frame.

(a) Similar to Nos. R 26/7, but imperf.

R 153. R **1.** 4 b. red, grn. & ochre
R 154. 6 b. red, green & blue

(b) Unissued 1963 Red Cross Cent. issue (Nos. R 26/7 surch.)

R 155. R **1.** 1 b. on 4 b. red, green and ochre ..
R 156. 2 b. on 6 b. red, green and blue ..

1966. Air. Olympic Games Preparation, Mexico (1968). Nos. R 123/5 in new colours surch. **AIR MAIL OLYMPIC GAMES PREPARATION MEXICO 1968** and new value in English and Arabic with aircraft and flag.

R 158. R **21.** 12 b. on ⅛ b. mult. 40 40
R 159. – 28 b. on ¼ b. mult. 1·10 1·10
R 160. – 34 b. on ½ b. mult. 1·25 1·25

R **24.** Yemeni Cannon.

1966. Shaharah Fortress. Frame and stars in red.

R 162. R **24.** ⅛ b. bistre (postage) 8 5
R 163. – 1 b. grey 12 5
R 164. – 1½ b. blue .. 15 8
R 165. – 2 b. brown .. 20 8
R 166. – 4 b. green .. 30 12

R 167. – 6 b. violet (air) .. 50 15
R 168. – 10 b. black .. 60 20

DESIGNS—VERT. 1 b. Bombed Mosque. 2 b. Victory Gate. 4 b. Yemeni cannon (different). 10 b. Bombed houses. HORIZ. 1½ b. Shararah Fortress. 6 b. Yemeni cannon (different).

1966. R 33/5 surch. **4 B REVALUED** in English and Arabic within border of stars. Flags red; inscr. in black.

R 170. R **4.** 4 b. on ⅛ b. violet ..
R 171. 4 b. on ¼ b. magenta
R 172. 4 b. on ½ b. brown ..

R **25.** President Kennedy.

1967. Pres. Kennedy's Death. 3rd Anniv. and Inaug. of Arlington Grave.

R 173. R **25.** 12 b. multicoloured 25 15
R 174. 28 b. multicoloured 60 35
R 175. 34 b. multicoloured 70 40

1967. England's Victory in World Cup Football Championships (1966). Nos. R 123/8 optd. **WORLD CHAMPIONSHIP CUP ENGLAND 1966** in English and Arabic, **ENGLAND WINNER** in English only and World Cup emblem.

R 177. R **21.** ⅛ b. mult. (postage) 8 5
R 178. – ¼ b. multicoloured 8 5
R 179. – ½ b. multicoloured 8 5
R 180. – 2 b. multicoloured 50 40
R 181. – 4 b. multicoloured 1·00 75

R 182. – 6 b. mult. (air) .. 1·75 90

1967. Surch. **4 B REVALUED** in English and Arabic within border of stars.

(a) Nos. R 123/5.

R 183. R **21.** 4 b. on ⅛ b. mult...
R 184. – 4 b. on ¼ b. mult...
R 185. – 4 b. on ½ b. mult...

(b) Nos. R 177/9.

R 186. R **21.** 4 b. on ⅛ b. mult...
R 187. – 4 b. on ¼ b. mult...
R 188. – 4 b. on ½ b. mult...

R **26.** "Freedom Fighter".

1967. "Freedom Fighters". Designs showing Freedom Fighters with various weapons.

R 189. R **26.** 4 b. multicoloured 10 8
R 190. – 4 b. multicoloured 10 8
R 191. – 4 b. multicoloured 10 8
R 192. – 4 b. multicoloured 10 8
R 193. – 4 b. multicoloured 10 8
R 194. – 4 b. multicoloured 10 8
R 195. – 4 b. multicoloured 10 8
R 196. – 4 b. multicoloured 10 8

R **27.** Rembrandt—Self Portrait.

1967. "AMPHILEX" Stamp Exn., Amsterdam. Rembrandt Paintings. Multicoloured.

(a) Borders in gold.

R 198. 2 b. "An Elderly Man as St. Paul" 8 5
R 199. 4 b. Type R **27** .. 12 5
R 200. 6 b. "Portrait of Jacob Trip" .. 15 8
R 201. 10 b. "An Old Man in an Armchair" .. 25 12
R 202. 12 b. Self-portrait (different) 35 20
R 203. 20 b. "A Woman Bathing" 50 25

(b) Borders in silver.

R 205.		2 b. As No. R 198 ..	8	5
R 206.		4 b. Type R 27	12	5
R 207.		6 b. As No. R 200 ..	15	8
R 208.		10 b. As No. R 201 ..	25	12
R 209.		12 b. As No. R 202 ..	35	20
R 210.		20 b. As No. R 203 ..	50	25

1967. Pres. Kennedy's 50th Birth Anniv. Nos. R 173/5 optd. **50th ann. 29 MAY** in English only.

R 212.	R 25.	12 b. multicoloured	40	30
R 213.		28 b. multicoloured	70	50
R 214.		34 b. multicoloured	90	70

R 28. Trigger Fish.

1967. Red Sea Fish. Multicoloured.

R 216.		⅛ b. Type R 28 (postage)	5	5
R 217.		¼ b. Rudder fish ..	5	5
R 218.		½ b. Butterfly fish ..	5	5
R 219.		1 b. Grouper	5	5
R 220.		4 b. Dragon fish ..	12	5
R 221.		6 b. Dark Clown fish ..	15	5
R 222.		10 b. Violet-hued Berycid	25	5
R 223.		12 b. As No. R 222 (air)	30	5
R 224.		14 b. Cuckoo Wrasse ..	40	5
R 225.		16 b. Deepwater Squirrel fish	50	8
R 226.		18 b. As No. R 221 ..	60	10
R 227.		24 b. As No. R 220 ..	70	15
R 228.		34 b. As No. R 219 ..	90	20

Nos. R 216/22 are are Type R 29; Nos. R 223/8 are larger, size 58 × 42 mm.

R 29. The Gipsy Girl (Frans Hals).

1967. Air. Famous Paintings. Multicoloured.

R 230.		8 b. Type R 29 ..	20	12
R 231.		10 b. "The Zouave" (Van Gogh)	25	15
R 232.		12 b. Self portrait (Rubens)	30	15
R 233.		14 b. "Boys Eating Melon" (Murillo) ..	35	15
R 234.		16 b. "The Knight's Dream" (Raphael) ..	40	20
R 235.		20 b. "St. George and the Dragon" (Ucello) ..	45	25

The 20 b. is a horiz.

1967. "For Poison Gas Victims". Surch. **FOR POISON GAS VICTIMS** and surcharge in English and Arabic, with Skull and Crossbones within frame.

R 236.	R 24.	½ b. + 1 b. (No. R162) (postage) ..		
R 237.	–	1 b. + 1 b. (R 163)		
R 238.	–	1½ b. + 1 b. (R 164)		
R 239.	–	2 b. + 1 b. (R 84) ..		
R 240.	–	2 b. + 1 b. (R 126)		
R 241.	–	2 b. + 1 b. (R 165)		
R 242.	R 10.	4 b. + 2 b. (R 62)		
R 243.	–	4 b. + 2 b. (R 66)		
R 244.	R 10.	4 b. + 2 b. (R 68)		
R 245.	R 15.	4 b. + 2 b. (R 85)		
R 246.	R 21.	4 b. + 2 b. (R 93)		
R 247.	–	4 b. + 2 b. (R 127)		
R 248.	–	4 b. + 2 b. (R 166)		
R 249.	–	6 b. + 3 b. (R 86) (air)		
R 250.	–	6 b. + 3 b. (R 128)		
R 251.	–	6 b. + 3 b. (R 167)		
R 252.	R 22.	10 b. + 5 b. (R 130)		
R 253.	–	10 b. + 5 b. (R 168)		
R 254.	R 19.	12 b. + 6 b. (R 158)		
R 255.	–	18 b. + 9 b. (R 87)		
R 256.	R 6.	24 b. + 12 b. red and blue (Imperf. Size 57 × 36 mm.)		
R 257.	–	24 b. + 12 b. (R 88)		
R 258.	–	28 b. + 14 b. (R 159)		
R 259.	–	34 b. + 17 b. (R 160)		

The amount of surcharge was 50 per cent of the face value of each stamp (except Nos. R 236/8 where the surcharge was 1 b. each). Some of the higher values have two handstamps, which, when added together make up the 50 per cent.

1967. Jordan Relief Fund. Surch. **JORDAN RELIEF FUND** and surch. in English and Arabic, with Crown.

(a) No. R 66 (Kennedy).

R 261.	–	4 b. + 2 b. sepia, yellow and gold	1·40	1·00

(b) Nos. R 75/6 (Birds).

R 262.	–	4 b. + 2 b. mult. (post.)	12	10
R 263.	–	6 b. + 3 b. mult. (air)	20	15

(c) Nos. R 92/4 (I.C.Y.).

R 265.	R 21.	2 b. + 1 b. indigo & brown (postage)	10	8
R 266.		4 b. + 2 b. lake and green	12	10
R 267.		6 b. + 3 b. sepia and blue (air) ..	20	15

(d) Nos. R 102/4 (Cats).

R 269.	–	1 b. + 1 b. mult. ..	8	8
R 270.	–	2 b. + 1 b. mult. ..	10	8
R 271.	–	4 b. + 2 b. mult. ..	12	10

(e) R 109/11 (Flowers).

R 273.	–	1 b. + 1 b. mult. ..	8	8
R 274.	R 17.	2 b. + 1 b. mult. ..	10	8
R 275.	–	4 b. + 2 b. mult. ..	12	10

(f) Nos. R 136/40 ("Builders").

R 277.	R 23.	⅛ b. + 1 b. gold, black and apple ..	10	8
R 278.	–	¼ b. + 1 b. gold, black and brown ..	10	8
R 279.	–	½ b. + 1 b. gold, black and grey ..	10	8
R 280.	–	1 b. + 1 b. gold, black and blue ..	20	15
R 281.	–	4 b. + 2 b. gold, black and green ..	90	70

(g) Nos. R 146/51 ("Builders").

R 283.	–	⅛ b. + 1 b. gold, black and yellow ..	5	5
R 284.	–	¼ b. + 1 b. gold, black and flesh ..	5	5
R 285.	–	½ b. + 1 b. gold, black and mauve ..	5	5
R 286.	–	1 b. + 1 b. gold, black and blue ..	8	8
R 287.	–	1 b. + 1 b. gold, black and blue-green	8	8
R 288.	–	4 b. + 2 b. gold, black and green ..	12	10

R 30. "The Pharmacy".

1967. Air. Paintings. Multicoloured.

(a) Asiatic Paintings.

R 290.		⅛ b. "Mountains and Forests" (Wang Houei)	5	5
R 291.		¼ b. "Tiger" (Sim Sajoug)	5	5
R 292.		½ b. "Mountain Views" (Tony K'itch'ang) ..	5	5
R 293.		¾ b. "Rama Laksnama and Shiva" (Indian 16th century) ..	8	5
R 294.		1 b. "Ladies" (T. Kiyomitsu)	10	5

(b) Arab Paintings.

R 295.		1½ b. "Bayad plays the Oud and sings" ..	12	8
R 296.		2 b. Type R 30	12	8
R 297.		3 b. "Dioscorides and a Student" ..	20	8
R 298.		4 b. "The Scribe" ..	30	10
R 299.		6 b. "Abu Zayd asks to be taken over a boat"	50	12

The ⅛ b., 1½ b. and 6 b. are horiz. and the remainder vert.

R 31. Bugler.

1967. World Scout Jamboree. Idaho. Mult.

R 301.		¼ b. Type R 31 (postage)	5	5
R 302.		½ b. Camp-fire	5	5
R 303.		4 b. Type R 31	15	10
R 304.		6 b. As ½ b.	20	12
R 305.		⅛ b. Scout badge and Yemeni flag (air) ..	5	5
R 306.		10 b. as ⅛ b.	25	15
R 307.		20 b. Scout and satellite	50	30

1967. Jordan Refugees Relief Fund. Surch. **JORDAN REFUGEES RELIEF FUND** and surch. in English and Arabic, and Refugee Emblem.

(a) Nos. R 52/4 (Olympic Games).

R 309.	R 7.	2 b. + 2 b. blue (post.)	10	10
R 310.		4 b. + 4 b. violet ..	20	20
R 311.		6 b. + 6 b. brown (air)	25	25

(b) Nos. R 55/7 (Astronauts).

R 313.	R 8.	2 b. + 2 b. chestnut, violet & blk. (post.)	10	10
R 314.		4 b. + 4 b. chestnut, blue and black ..	20	20
R 315.		6 b. + 6 b. yellow and black (air) ..	25	25

(c) Nos. R 63/7 (Kennedy).

R 317.	R 11.	⅛ b. + ⅛ b. black, mag. & gold (post.)	5	5
R 318.	–	¼ b. + ¼ b. violet, turquoise & gold	5	5
R 319.	–	½ b. + ½ b. brown, blue and gold ..	5	5
R 320.	–	4 b. + 4 b. sepia, yellow and gold	20	20
R 321.	–	6 b. + 6 b. black, apple & gold (air)	25	25

(d) No. R 68 (Churchill opt.).

R 323.	R 10.	4 b. + 4 b. bl. & red		

(e) R 69/71 (I.T.U.).

R 324.	R 12.	2 b. + 2 b. yell., violet and black (post.)	10	10
R 325.		4 b. + 4 b. red, blue and black ..	20	20
R 326.		6 b. + 6 b. grn., violet and black (air) ..	25	25

(f) R 77/82 (Churchill).

R 328.	R 14.	⅛ b. + ⅛ b. mult. ..	5	5
R 329.	–	¼ b. + ¼ b. mult. ..	5	5
R 330.	–	½ b. + ½ b. mult. ..	8	8
R 331.	R 14.	1 b. + 1 b. mult. ..	10	10
R 332.	–	2 b. + 2 b. mult. ..	20	20
R 333.	–	4 b. + 4 b. mult. ..	40	40

R 32. Gaucho.

1967. Olympic Games, Mexico (1968). Multicoloured.

R 335.		⅛ b. Type R 32 (post.)	5	5
R 336.		¼ b. Fishermen on Lake Patzcuaro	5	5
R 337.		½ b. Football	5	5
R 338.		4 b. Avenida de la Reforma, Mexico City ..	8	5
R 339.		8 b. Fine Arts Theatre, Mexico City	20	5
R 340.		12 b. Mayan ruins (air) ..	25	8
R 341.		16 b. Type R 32 ..	35	8
R 342.		20 b. As ¼ b.	50	8

The ½ b. is a vert.

R 33. Moor slaying Knight.

1967. Moorish Art in Spain. Multicoloured.

R 344.		2 b. Type R 33 (postage)	5	5
R 345.		4 b. Arab Kings of Granada	8	5
R 346.		6 b. Playing chess ..	12	5
R 347.		10 b. Battle scene ..	15	5
R 348.		12 b. Moors with prisoners	25	5
R 349.		20 b. Meeting of Moor and Christian (air) ..	50	8
R 350.		22 b. Bullfight	50	8
R 351.		24 b. Lute-players ..	60	10

The 10 b. to 24 b. values are vert.

YEMEN PEOPLE'S DEMOCRATIC REPUBLIC O4

The former People's Republic of Southern Yemen was known by the above title from 30 November, 1970.

1000 fils = 1 dinar

20. Temple of Isis, Philae, Egypt.

1971. Preservation of Philae Temples Campaign.

65.	20.	5 f. multicoloured ..	5	5
66.		35 f. multicoloured ..	12	12
67.		65 f. multicoloured ..	20	20

21. Symbols of Constitution.

1971. Introduction of First Constitution.

68.	21.	10 f. multicoloured ..	5	5
69.		15 f. multicoloured ..	5	5
70.		35 f. multicoloured ..	12	12
71.		50 f. multicoloured ..	20	20

22. Heads of Three Races and Flame. **23.** Map, Flag and products.

1971. Racial Equality Year.

72.	22.	20 f. multicoloured ..	5	5
73.		35 f. multicoloured ..	12	12
74.		75 f. multicoloured ..	25	25

1971.

75.	23.	5 f. multicoloured ..	5	5
76.		10 f. multicoloured ..	5	5
77.		15 f. multicoloured ..	5	5
78.		20 f. multicoloured ..	5	5
79.		25 f. multicoloured ..	5	5
80.		35 f. multicoloured ..	10	10
81.		40 f. multicoloured ..	12	12
82.		50 f. multicoloured ..	15	15
83.		65 f. multicoloured ..	20	20
84.		80 f. multicoloured ..	20	20
85.	–	125 f. multicoloured ..	30	30
86.	–	250 f. multicoloured ..	60	60
87.	–	500 f. multicoloured ..	1·25	1·25
88.	–	1 d. multicoloured ..	2·50	2·50

DESIGNS—HORIZ. (42 × 25 mm.): Nos. 85/8, "Dam-el-Akhawain" tree, Socotra.

24. Hand holding Sub-machine Gun and Map. **25.** Hands supporting Cogwheel.

1971. Revolutionary Activity in Arabian Gulf Area. 6th Anniv. Multicoloured.

89.		15 f. Type 24 ..	5	5
90.		45 f. Girl guerilla and emblem (horiz.) ..	15	15
91.		50 f. Guerilla on the march	20	20

1971. "Corrective Move" in Revolutionary Government. 2nd Anniv. Multicoloured.

92.		15 f. Type 25 ..	5	5
93.		25 f. Torch and emblems ..	8	8
94.		65 f. Salt-works and windmill	20	20

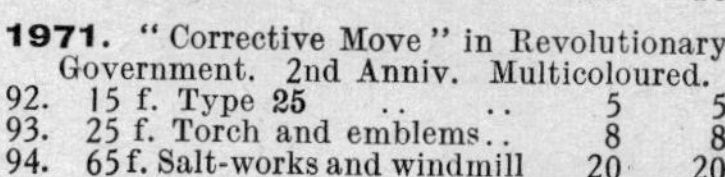

26. Eagle and Flags. **27.** Gamal Nasser.

1971. 26th September Revolution. 9th Anniv. Multicoloured.
95. 10 f. Type **26** 5 5
96. 40 f. Flag on "United Yemen" 12 12

1971. Gamal Nasser (Egyptian statesman). 1st Death Anniv.
97. **27.** 65 f. multicoloured .. 20 20

28. "Children of the World". **29.** White Pigeons.

1971. U.N.I.C.E.F. 25th Anniv.
98. **28.** 15 f. black, red & orange 5 5
99. 40 f. black, pur. & blue 10 10
100. 50 f. black, red & green 15 15

1971. Birds.
101. **29.** 5 f. black, pur. & blue .. 5 5
102. – 40 f. multicoloured .. 12 12
103. – 65 f. black, red & green 20 20
104. – 100 f. multicoloured .. 30 30
DESIGNS: 40 f. Partridge. 65 f. Guineafowl and partridge. 100 f. Glede (kite).

30. Dhow-building.

1972. Dhow-building in Aden. Multicoloured.
105. 25 f. Type **30** 8 8
106. 80 f. Dhow at sea (vert.) .. 25 25

31. Singer with "Oodh" (lute). and Band.

1972. Folk Dances. Multicoloured.
107. 10 f. Type **31** 5 5
108. 25 f. Yemeni girls dancing 5 5
109. 40 f. Dancing teams .. 12 12
110. 80 f. Festival dance .. 25 25

32. Palestinian Guerrilla and Barbed-wire.

1972. Palestine Day.
111. **32.** 5 f. multicoloured .. 5 5
112. 20 f. multicoloured .. 5 5
113. 65 f. multicoloured 20 20

33. Police Colour Party.

1972. Police Day. Multicoloured.
114. 25 f. Type **33** 5 5
115. 80 f. Girls of People's Militia on parade 25 25

34. Start of Cycle Race.

1972. Arab Youth Week. Multicoloured.
117. 10 f. Type **34** 5 5
118. 15 f. Girls on parade .. 5 5
119. 40 f. Guides and scouts .. 12 12
120. 80 f. Acrobats (vert.) .. 25 25

35. Turtle.

1972. Marine Life. Multicoloured.
121. 15 f. Type **35** 5 5
122. 40 f. Sailfish 12 12
123. 65 f. Kingfish 25 25
124. 125 f. Lobster 35 35

36. Book Year Emblem.

1972. Int. Book Year.
125. **36.** 40 f. multicoloured .. 12 12
126. 65 f. multicoloured .. 20 20

37. Farm Workers and Field.

1972. Land's Day.
127. **37.** 10 f. multicoloured .. 5 5
128. 25 f. multicoloured .. 5 5
129. 40 f. multicoloured .. 12 12

38. Soldiers advancing.

1972. Independence. Fifth Anniv. Mult.
130. 5 f. Type **38** 5 5
131. 20 f. Soldier and town .. 5 5
132. 65 f. Vignettes of Yemeni Life (vert.) 20 20

39. Population Graph. **40.** W.H.O. Emblem within "25".

1973. Population Census.
134. **39.** 25 f. emerald, red & grn. 5 5
135. 40 f. new blue, red and blue 12 12

1973. W.H.O. 25th Anniv. Multicoloured.
136. 5 f. Type **40** 5 5
137. 25 f. W.H.O. emblem on globe (horiz.) 5 5
138. 125 f. "25" and W.H.O. emblem (horiz.) .. 35 35

41. Shibam Town.

1973. Tourism. Multicoloured.
139. 20 f. Taweela Tanks, Aden (vert.) 5 5
140. 25 f. Type **41** 8 8
141. 40 f. Elephant Bay, Aden 12 12
142. 100 f. Al-Mohdar Mosque, Tarim 30 30

42. Modern Apartments and Slum Clearance.

1973. Nationalisation of Buildings (1972). Multicoloured.
143. 20 f. Type **42** 5 5
144. 80 f. Street scene (vert.) .. 25 25

43. Women's Corps on Parade.

1973. Peoples Army. Multicoloured.
145. 10 f. Type **43** 5 5
146. 20 f. Soldiers marching .. 5 5
147. 40 f. Naval contingent .. 12 12
148. 80 f. Tank column 25 25

44. Quayside Crane.

1973. World Food Programme. 10th Anniv. Multicoloured.
149. 20 f. Type **44** 5 5
150. 80 f. Granary workers .. 25 25

45. "U.P.U. Letter".

1974. Universal Postal Union. Centenary. Multicoloured.
151. 5 f. Type **45** 5 5
152. 20 f. "100" formed of people and U.P.U. emblems 5 5
153. 40 f. U.P.U. emblem and Yemeni flag (vert.) .. 10 10
154. 125 f. Map of People's Republic (vert.) 30 30

46. Irrigation Canal.

1974. Agricultural Progress. Multicoloured.
155. 10 f. Type **46** 5 5
156. 20 f. Bulldozers clearing land 5 5
157. 100 f. Tractors with harrows 25 25

47. Lathe Operator. **48.** Yemeni Woman.

1975. Industrial Progress. Multicoloured.
158. 10 f. Type **47** 5 5
159. 40 f. Workers in clothing factory 10 10
160. 80 f. Women textile workers (horiz.) 25 25

1976. Women's Costumes.
161. **48.** 5 f. brown and black .. 5 5
162. – 10 f. violet and black .. 5 5
163. – 15 f. yellow and black .. 5 5
164. – 25 f. purple and black .. 10 10
165. – 40 f. blue and black .. 15 15
166. – 50 f. brown and black .. 20 20
DESIGNS: Nos. 162/6 show different costumes.

49. Machine Worker.

1976. Int. Women's Year.
167. **49.** 40 f. brown and black .. 15 15
168. 50 f. green and black .. 20 20

50. Footballer. **51.** Lunar Launch.

1976. Yemeni Football.
169. **50.** 5 f. multicoloured .. 5 5
170. – 40 f. multicoloured .. 15 15
171. – 80 f. multicoloured .. 30 30
DESIGNS: Nos. 170/1 show footballers in different positions.

1976. Soviet Cosmonauts and Space Programmes.
172. **51.** 10 f. purple and black .. 5 5
173. – 15 f. brown and mauve 5 5
174. – 40 f. brown and green .. 15 15
175. – 65 f. brown and blue .. 25 25
DESIGNS—VERT. 15 f. Alexander Satalov. 65 f. Valentina Tereshkova and rocket. HORIZ. 40 f. Lunar vehicle.

YUGOSLAVIA E3

The kingdom of the Serbs, Croats and Slovenes, in S.E. Europe, established after the 1914–18 war and comprising Serbia, Montenegro, Bosnia, Herzegovina and parts of pre-war Hungary. A republic since 1945.

100 filler (or heller) = 1 krone.
100 paras = 1 dinar.

I. ISSUES FOR BOSNIA AND HERZEGOVINA.

(Currency. 100 heller = 1 kruna.)

1918. 1910 commem. stamps of Bosnia (with date labels) optd. **DRZAVA S.H.S. 1918 Bosna i Hercegovina** or the same in Cyrillic characters or surch. also.
1. 3 h. olive (No. 345) .. 25 25
2. 5 h. green 5 5
3. 10 h. red 5 5
4. 20 h. sepia .. 5 5
5. 25 h. blue .. 5 5
6. 30 h. green .. 5 5
7. 40 h. orange .. 5 5
8. 45 h. red .. 5 5
9. 50 h. purple .. 10 12
10. 60 h. on 50 h. purple .. 8 10
11. 80 h. on 6 h. brown .. 5 8
12. 90 h. on 35 h. green .. 5 8
13. 2 k. green .. 12 20
14. 3 k. on 3 h. olive .. 20 25
15. 4 k. on 1 k. lake .. 75 85
16. 10 k. on 2 h. violet .. 1·40 1·60

1918. Newspaper stamps of Bosnia for Express: 5 h. optd. as last and **HELERA** and 2 h. the same but in Cyrillic.
17. **N 2.** 2 h. red .. .. 1·40 1·60
18. 5 h. green 65 50
These were issued for use as ordinary postage stamps.

1918. Bosnian War Invalids Fund stamps optd. **DRAVA S.H.S. Bosna Hercegovina** or the same in Cyrillic characters.
19. **12.** 5 h. (+2 h.) green .. 75·00 75·00
20. – 10 h. (+2 h.) claret .. 25·00 25·00
21. – 10 h. (+2 h.) blue .. 25 40
22. **12.** 15 h (+2 h.) brown .. 65 65

1918. Newspaper stamps of Bosnia of 1913 surch. Imperf.
50. **N 1.** 2 on 6 h. mauve .. 75·00 75·00
51. 2 on 10 h. red .. .. 28·00 28·00
52. 2 on 20 h. green .. 1·25 1·25
23. 3 on 2 h. blue .. 5 8
24. 5 on 6 h. mauve .. 5 8
Most of these were used for ordinary postage purposes.

1919. As Type **N 1** of Bosnia without opt. but perf.
25. **N 1.** 2 h. blue 5 5
26. 6 h. mauve 40 40
27. 10 h. red 20 20
28. 20 h. green 20 20
The above were issued for use as ordinary postage stamps.
These stamps imperforate were issued as Newspaper stamps for Bosnia q.v.

КРАЉЕВСТВО

С. Х. С

(1.)

1919. Types of Bosnia optd. with T 1 or similar type with wording **KRALJEVSTVO S.H.S.**, or surch. also.

29. **10.** 3 h. lake 5 12
30. 5 h. green 5 5
31. 10 on 6 h. black 5 5
32. **11.** 20 on 35 h. green 5 12
33. **10.** 25 h. blue 5 12
34. 30 h. red 12 20
35. **11.** 45 h. brown 10 20
36. **14.** 45 on 80 h. brown 5 5
37. **11.** 50 h. blue 15·00 18·00
38. 50 on 72 h. blue 5 5
39. 60 h. purple-brown 5 10
40. **14.** 80 h. brown 5 10
41. 90 h. purple 5 10
42. – 2 k. green (No. 200) 12 25
43. **11.** 3 k. red on green 25 40
44. **15.** 4 k. red on green 1·00 90
45. **11.** 5 k. lilac on grey 1·00 90
46. **15.** 10 k. violet on grey 2·00 1·50

1919. War Victims' Fund. Stamps of Bosnia of 1906 surch. **KRALJEVSTVO Srba. Hrvata i Slovenaca** or same in Cyrillic characters and new value.

47. – 10 x. + 10 x. on 40 h. orange (No. 196) 90 90
48. – 20 x. + 10 x. on 20 h. sepia (No. 192) 40 40
49. **5.** 45 x. + 15 x. on 1 k. lake 2·50 2·50

II. ISSUES FOR CROATIA.

The provisional issues on Hungarian stamps were sold in Yugoslavian "heller" and "krone" currency, but as this is not expressed on the stamps (except for Nos. 69/73) we have retained the Hungarian descriptions to facilitate reference to the original stamps.

1918. Various issues of Hungary optd. **HRVATSKA SHS** and bar or wheel.

"Turul" issue of 1900.

53. **3.** 6 f. olive 50 50
54. 50 f. lake on blue 75 75

"Harvesters" and "Parliament" issue of 1916.

55. **11.** 2 f. brown 5 5
56. 3 f. claret 5 5
57. 5 f. green 5 5
58. 6 f. green 5 5
59. 10 f. red 1·25 1·00
60. 15 f. violet (No. 244) 12·00 12·00
61. 15 f. violet (No. 251) 5 5
62. 20 f. brown 5 5
63. 25 f. blue 5 5
64. 35 f. brown 5 5
65. 40 f. olive 8 8
66. **12.** 50 f. purple 5 5
67. 75 f. blue 5 5
68. 80 f. green 5 5
69. 1 k. lake 5 5
70. 2 k. brown 5 10
71. 3 k. grey and violet 12 15
72. 5 k. brown 75 75
73. 10 k. lilac and brown 4·50 5·00

The kroner values are overprinted **KRUNA** or **KRUNE** also.

"Charles" and "Zita" issue of 1918.

74. **13.** 10 f. red 5 5
75. 20 f. brown 5 5
76. 25 f. blue 20 20
77. **14.** 40 f. olive 5 5

1918. Stamps of Hungary optd. **HRVATSKA SHS. ZF. ZA NAROD. VIJECE.**

War Charity issue of 1916.

78. **6.** 10+2 f. red 15 15
79. – 15+2 f. violet 5 5
80. **8.** 40+2 f. lake 8 12

Coronation issue of 1916.

81. **9.** 10 f. mauve 21·00 21·00
82. – 15 f. red 21·00 21·00

2. "Freedom of Yugoslavia".

1918. Freeing of the Yugoslavs.

83. **2.** 10 h. lake 1·00 1·00
84. 20 h. violet 1·50 1·00
85. 25 h. blue 2·50 1·75
86. 45 h. black 25·00 21·00

3. "Freedom". **4.** Sailor with Standard and Falcon. **5.** Falcon ("Liberty").

1919.

87. **3.** 2 h. brown 8 8
88. 3 h. mauve 8 8
89. 5 h. green 8 8
90. **4.** 10 h. red 8 8
91. 20 h. brown 8 8
92. 25 h. blue 8 8
93. 45 h. olive 12 12
94. **5.** 1 k. red 15 15
95. – 3 k. purple 30 30
96. – 5 k. brown 55 55

DESIGN: 3 k., 5 k. as T **5** but light background behind falcon.

III. ISSUES FOR SLOVENIA.

(Currency. 100 vinar = 1 krona).

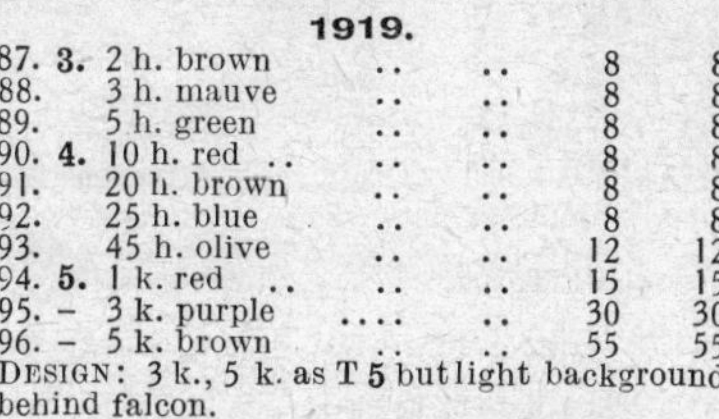

6. Chainbreakers. **7.**

8. "Freedom" **9.** **10.** King Peter I.

1919. Perf. or rouletted.

97a. **6.** 3 v. violet 5 5
127. 3 v. purple 5 5
98a. 5 v. green 5 5
99b. 10 v. red 10 5
100. 15 v. blue 5 5
101. **7.** 20 v. brown 15 5
102. 25 v. blue 8 5
103. 30 v. pink 8 5
111. 30 v. red 8 5
104a. 40 v. yellow 10 5
122. **8.** 50 v. green 5 5
113b. 60 v. violet 20 8
114b. **9.** 1 k. red 15 5
120. 2 k. blue 15 5
126. **10.** 5 k. red 20 5
139a. 10 k. blue 90 25
105. 15 k. green 2·50 2·50
106. 20 k. purple 75 75

(New currency. 100 paras = 1 dinar.)

11. Chainbreaker. **12.** "Freedom". **13.** King Peter I.

1920. Perf. (2 d. to 10 d.) or roul.

150. **11.** 5 p. olive 5 5
151. 10 p. green 5 5
152. 15 p. brown 5 5
153. 20 p. red 25 25
154. 25 p. brown 8 8
155. **12.** 40 p. violet 5 5
156. 45 p. yellow 5 5
157. 50 p. blue 5 5
158. 60 p. brown 5 5
159. **13.** 1 d. brown 5 5
160. – 2 d. black 5 5
161. **13.** 4 d. slate 20 20
162. – 6 d. olive 10 12
163. – 10 d. brown 20 20

The 2, 6 and 10 d. are as T **13** but larger.

1920. Carinthian Plebiscite Newspaper stamps of Yugoslavia of 1919 surch. **GKCA** in dotted circle and new value. Imperf.

163a. **N 2.** 5 p. on 4 h. grey 5 5
163b. 15 p. on 4 h. grey 5 5
163c. 25 p. on 4 h. grey 5 12
163d. 45 p. on 2 h. grey 12 20
163e. 50 p. on 2 h. grey 10 20
163f. 2 d. on 2 h. grey 90 1·25

These stamps were sold at three times face value in aid of the Plebiscite Propaganda Fund.

IV KINGDOM OF THE SERBS, CROATS AND SLOVENES.

14. King Alexander when Prince. **16.**

1921. Inscr. "KRALJEVSTVO" at foot.

164. **14.** 2 p. brown 5 5
165. 5 p. green 5 5
166. 10 p. red 5 5
167. 15 p. purple 5 5
168. 20 p. black 5 5
169. 25 p. blue 5 5
170. 50 p. olive 8 5
171. 60 p. red 5 5
172. 75 p. violet 5 5
173. – 1 d. orange 20 5
174. – 2 d. olive 25 5
175. – 4 d. green 65 5
176. – 5 d. red 2·50 10
177. – 10 d. brown 5·00 30

DESIGN: 1 d. to 10 d. as T **14** but portrait of King Peter I.

1921. Disabled Soldiers' Fund.

178. **16.** 10+10 p. red 5 5
179. – 15+15 p. brown 5 5
180. – 25+25 p. blue 12 12

DESIGNS: 10 p. Kosovo maiden, 1939. 15 p. Albanian retreat, 1915. 25 p. National Unity.

1922. Nos. 178/80 surch.

181. 1 d. on 10 p. red 5 5
183. 1 d. on 15 p. brown 8 8
182. 1 d. on 25 p. blue 8 5
184. 3 d. on 15 p. brown 25 8
186. 8 d. on 15 p. brown 2·00 12
187. 20 d. on 15 p. brown 8·50 40
188. 30 d. on 15 p. brown 19·00 1·25

1923. As T **14**, but inscr. "KRALJEVINA" at foot.

189. **14.** 1 d. brown 1·00 5
190. 5 d. red 2·50 20
191. 8 d. purple 9·00 25
192. 20 d. green 25·00 50
193. 30 d. orange 90·00 1·50

1924. Nos. 171 and 191 surch.

195. **14.** 20 p. on 60 p. red 25 5
196. 5 d. on 8 d. purple 7·50 45

17. King Alexander. **18.**

1924.

197. **17.** 20 p. black 5 5
198. 50 p. brown 5 5
199. 1 d. red 5 5
200. 2 d. green 25 5
201. 3 d. blue 25 5
202. 5 d. brown 1·90 5
203. – 10 d. violet 15·00 8
204. – 15 d. olive 11·00 10
205. – 20 d. orange 11·00 10
206. – 30 d. green 6·00 75

The 10 d. to 30 d. have the head in a square panel.

1925. Surch.

207. **17.** 25 p. on 3 d. blue 20 5
208. 50 p. on 3 d. blue 20 5

1926.

209. **18.** 25 p. green 5 5
210. 50 p. sepia 10 5
211. 1 d. red 25 5
212. 2 d. black 25 5
213. 3 d. blue 40 5
214. 4 d. orange 75 5
215. 5 d. violet 1·50 5
216. 8 d. brown 5·00 8
217. 10 d. olive 2·50 5
218. 15 d. chocolate 12·00 5
219. 20 d. purple 15·00 15
220. 30 d. yellow 75·00 40

1926. Danube Flood Fund. Surch.

221. **18.** 25 p.+0.25 green 5 5
222. 50 p.+0.50 sepia 5 5
223. 1 d.+0.50 red 20 5
224. 2 d.+0.50 black 40 8
225. 3 d.+0.50 blue 25 12
226. 4 d.+0.50 orange 40 10
227. 5 d.+0.50 violet 55 10
228. 8 d.+0.50 brown 1·00 40
229. 10 d.+1.00 olive 3·00 12
230. 15 d.+1.00 chocolate 7·50 50
231. 20 d.+1.00 purple 6·00 40
232. 30 d.+1.00 yellow 25·00 1·25

1928. Nos. 223/32 optd. **XXXX** over previous surch.

233. **18.** 1 d. red 25 10
234. 2 d. black 50 10
235. 3 d. blue 75 25
236. 4 d. orange 2·50 30
237. 5 d. violet 2·00 12
238. 8 d. brown 5·00 50
239. **18.** 10 d. olive 6·00 12
240. 15 d. chocolate 75·00 1·25
241. 20 d. purple 38·00 1·40
242. 30 d. yellow 85·00 2·25

V. KINGDOM OF YUGOSLAVIA.

19. Duvno Cathedral.

DESIGNS—As T **19**: 3 d. King Tomislav. HORIZ. (34×23 mm.): 1 d. Kings Tomislav and Alexander I.

1929. Millenary of Croatian Kingdom (1925).

243. **19.** 50 p.+50 p. olive 40 25
244. – 1 d.+50 p. red 65 40
245. – 3 d.+1 d. blue 1·50 65

22. Dobropolje. **23.** War Memorial.

1931. Serbian War Memorial (Paris) Fund.

246. **22.** 50 p.+50 p. green 5 5
247. **23.** 1 d.+50 p. red 8 8
248. – 3 d.+1 d. blue 12 12

DESIGN—As T **22**: 3 d. Kajmaktchalan.

25. King Alexander. **26.** Rowing "four" on Lake Bled.

1931.

249. **25.** 25 p. black 12 5
250. 50 p. green 5 5
262. 75 p. green 25 5
251. 1 d. red 8 5
263. 1 d. 50 rose 50 5
263b. 1 d. 75 red 75 25
252. 3 d. blue 2·50 5
263c. 3 d. 50 blue 1·00 12
253. 4 d. orange 3·00 5
254. 5 d. violet 3·25 5
255. 10 d. olive 10·00 5
256. 15 d. brown 9·00 8
257. 20 d. purple 18·00 12
258. 30 d. claret 10·00 55

1931. Optd. **KRALJEVINA JUGOSLAVIJA** and also in Cyrillic characters.

259. **19.** 50 p.+50 p. olive 5 5
260. – 1 d.+50 p. red 5 8
261. – 3 d.+1 d. blue 40 20

1932. European Rowing Championship. Inscr. ending "EUROPE 1932".

264. – 75 p.+50 p. green 40 35
265. **26.** 1 d.+½ d. red 40 35
266. – 1½ d.+½ d. red 50 35
267. – 3 d.+1 d. blue 1·25 90
268. – 4 d.+1 d. blue & orge. 5·00 3·75
269. – 5 d.+1 d. lilac & violet 2·50 1·75

DESIGNS—HORIZ. 75 p. Single-sculler on Danube at Smederevo. 1½ d. Rowing "eight" on Danube at Belgrade. 3 d. Rowing "pair" at Split harbour. VERT. 4 d. Rowing "pair" on river and Zagreb Cathedral. 5 d. Prince Peter.

1933. 11th Int. Pen Club Congress, Dubrovnik. As T **25** with additional value and **XI. int. kongres Pen-Klubova u Dubrovniku 1933** below in Roman or Cyrillic characters.

270. **25.** 50 p.+25 p. black 3·75 3·50
271. 75 p.+25 p. green 3·85 3·50
272. 1 d. 50+50 p. red 3·75 3·50
273. 3 d+1 d. blue 3·75 3·50
274. 4 d.+1 d. green 3·75 3·50
275. 5 d.+1 d. yellow 3·75 3·50

28. King Peter II when Prince. **29.**

1933. "Sokol" Meeting, Ljubljana.

276. **28.** 75 p.+25 p. green 30 25
277. 1½d.+½ d. red 30 25

1933. Optd. **JUGOSLAVIJA** in Roman and Cyrillic characters. (a) Postage.

No.	Type	Description	Unused	Used
278.	18.	25 p. green	10	5
279.		50 p. sepia	12	5
280.		1 d. red	40	5
281.		2 d. black	75	10
282.		3 d. blue	2·25	8
283.		4 d. orane	1·25	8
284.		5 d. violet	2·50	8
285.		8 d. brown	5·00	50
286.		10 d. olive	12·00	8
287.		15 d. chocolate	12·00	75
288.		20 d. purple	28·00	40
289.		30 d. yellow	24·00	40

(b) Charity stamps, Nos. 221/3.

No.	Type	Description	Unused	Used
290.	18.	25 p.+0.25 green ..	25	5
291.		50 p.+0.50 sepia ..	15	5
292.		1 d.+0.50 red	50	10

1933. Red Cross.

No.	Type	Description	Unused	Used
293.	29.	50 p. red and blue ..	8	5

30. Falcon over R. Bosna.  **31.** Athlete and Falcon.

1934. "Sokol" Games, Sarajevo. 20th Anniv.

No.	Type	Description	Unused	Used
294.	30.	75 p.+25 p. green ..	3·75	1·00
295.		1 d. 50+50 p. red ..	5·00	1·25
296.		1 d. 75+25 p. brown ..	10·00	2·25

1934. Croat "Sokol" Games, Zagreb. 60th Anniv.

No.	Type	Description	Unused	Used
297.	31.	75 p.+25 p. green ..	2·50	50
298.		1 d. 50+50 p. red ..	3·75	1·00
299.		1 d. 75+25 p. brown ..	10·00	2·25

32. Dubrovnik.  **33.** Mostar Bridge.

1934. Air.

No.	Type	Description	Unused	Used
300.	32.	50 p. purple	25	20
301.	–	1 d. green	20	20
302.	–	2 d. red	45	25
303.	–	3 d. blue	85	40
304.	33.	10 d. orange	2·00	1·25

DESIGNS: 1 d. Lake of Bled. 2 d. Waterfall at Jajce. 3 d. Oplenats.

1934. King Alexander Mourning issue. With black margins.

No.	Type	Description	Unused	Used
305.	25.	25 p. black (postage) ..	5	5
306.		50 p. green	5	5
307.		75 p. green	5	5
308.		1 d. red	5	5
309.		1 d. 50 p. rose ..	10	5
310.		1 d. 75 p. red ..	10	5
311.		3 d. blue	12	5
312.		3 d. 50 p. blue ..	40	5
313.		4 d. orange	40	5
314.		5 d. violet	65	5
315.		10 d. olive	2·00	5
316.		15 d. brown	3·75	15
317.		20 d. purple	6·00	15
318.		30 d. red	3·75	40
319.	–	3 d. blue (No. 303) (air)	3·00	1·25

34. King Peter II.  **35.** King Alexander.

1935.

No.	Type	Description	Unused	Used
320.	34.	25 p. black	5	5
321.		50 p. orange	5	5
322.		75 p. green	10	5
323.		1 d. brown	10	5
324.		1 d. 50 red	8	5
325.		1 d. 75 red	25	8
325a.		2 d. claret	12	5
326.		3 d. orange	15	5
327.		3 d. 50 blue	35	8
328.		4 d. green	90	8
329.		4 d. blue	20	5
330.		10 d. violet	40	5
331.		15 d. brown	65	8
332.		20 d. blue	3·50	20
333.		30 d. pink	90	20

1935. King Alexander's Assassination. 1st Anniv.

No.	Type	Description	Unused	Used
334.	35.	75 p. green	15	8
335.		1 d. 50 red	20	8
336.		1 d. 75 brown	40	25
337.		3 d. 50 blue	1·25	50
338.		7 d. 50 claret	1·00	70

36.  **37.** Queen Marie.

1935. Winter Relief Fund.

No.	Type	Description	Unused	Used
339.	36.	1 d. 50+1 d. brown ..	1·00	55
340.		3 d. 50+1 d. 50 blue ..	2·00	70

1936. Child Welfare.

No.	Type	Description	Unused	Used
341.	37.	75 p.+25 p. green ..	40	20
342.		1 d. 50+50 p. red ..	40	20
343.		1 d. 75+75 p. brown ..	90	50
344.		3 d. 50+1 d. blue ..	1·50	65

38. Nicola Tesla (physicist).  **39.** Prince Paul.  **40.** Dr. V. Georgevitch.

1936. Dr. Tesla's 80th Birthday.

No.	Type	Description	Unused	Used
345.	38.	75 p. brown and green ..	25	10
346.		1 d. 75 black and blue ..	40	15

1936. Red Cross Fund.

No.	Type	Description	Unused	Used
347.	39.	75 p.+50 p. green ..	15	12
348.		1 d.50+50 p. red ..	20	12

1936. Jubilee of Serbian Red Cross. Compulsory Tax.

No.	Type	Description	Unused	Used
349.	40.	50 p. brown	10	5

41. Princes Tomislav and Andrew.  **42.** Oplenats.

1937. Child Welfare. T **41** and similar horiz. portrait.

No.	Type	Description	Unused	Used
350.	–	25 p.+25 p. brown ..	12	8
351.	–	75 p.+75 p. orange ..	35	12
352.	41.	1 d. 50+1 d. orange ..	35	25
353.		2 d.+1 d. purple ..	45	35

1937. Little Entente.

No.	Type	Description	Unused	Used
354.	42.	3 d. green	40	10
355.		4 d. blue	40	15

44. St. Naum Convent, Lake Ochrida.  **46.** Laibach (Ljubljana).

1937. Air.

No.	Type	Description	Unused	Used
360.	44.	50 p. brown	5	5
361.	–	1 d. green	5	5
362.	–	2 d. blue	5	8
363.	46.	2 d. 50 red	10	8
364.	44.	5 d. violet	12	12
365.	–	10 d. red	25	20
366.	–	20 d. green	40	25
367.	46.	30 d. blue	75	45

DESIGNS—VERT. 1 d., 10 d. Rab (Arbe) Harbour. HORIZ. 2 d., 20 d. Sarajevo.

47. Arms of Yugoslavia, Greece, Rumania and Turkey.

1937. Balkan Entente.

No.	Type	Description	Unused	Used
368.	47.	3 d. green	50	12
369.		4 d. blue	75	25

48.  **49.**

1938. Child Welfare.

No.	Type	Description	Unused	Used
370.	48.	50 p.+50 p. brown ..	20	12
371.	49.	1 d.+1 d. green ..	20	12
372.	48.	1 d. 50+1 d. 50 red ..	50	40
373.	49.	2 d.+2 d. mauve ..	1·00	65

50. Searchlight Display and Parachute Tower.  **51.** Entrance to Demir Kapija Cliff.

1938. Int. Aeronautical Exn. and Yugoslav Air Club Fund.

No.	Type	Description	Unused	Used
374.	50.	1 d.+50 p. green ..	45	30
375.		1 d. 50 p.+1 d. red ..	55	40
376.		2 d.+1 d. magenta ..	1·25	75
377.		3 d.+1 d. 50 p. blue ..	1·50	1·10

1938. Railway Employees' Hospital Fund.

No.	Type	Description	Unused	Used
378.	51.	1 d.+1 d. green ..	40	25
379.	–	1 d. 50+1 d. 50 red ..	65	40
380.	–	2 d.+2 d. mauve ..	1·50	1·00
381.	–	3 d. + 3 d. blue ..	1·25	85

DESIGNS—HORIZ. 1 d. 50 p. Demir Kapija Hospital. VERT. 2 d. Runner carrying torch. 3 d. King Alexander.

54. Hurdling.

DESIGNS—HORIZ. 1 d. 50 p. Pole vault. VERT. 50 p. Runner. 2 d. Putting the Shot.

1938. IX Balkan Games.

No.	Type	Description	Unused	Used
382.	–	50 p.+50 p. orange ..	65	50
383.	54.	1 d.+1 d. green ..	1·25	1·00
384.	–	1 d. 50+1 d. 50 mauve	2·00	1·50
385.	–	2 d.+2 d. blue	2·50	2·25

55. Maiden oi Kosovo.

1938. Red Cross.

No.	Type	Description	Unused	Used
386.	55.	50 p. red, green, yellow and blue	20	5
386a.		50 p. red and blue ..	25	5

1938. Child Welfare. Optd. **SALVATE PARVULOS.**

No.	Type	Description	Unused	Used
387.	48.	50 p.+50 p. brown ..	20	15
388.	49.	1 d.+1 d. green ..	25	20
389.	48.	1 d. 50+1 d. 50 red ..	40	30
390.	49.	2 d.+2 d. mauve ..	1·00	55

56. Mail-carrier.

DESIGNS: 50 p. Mounted postmen. 1 d. 50, Mail train. 2 d. Mail coach. 4 d. Mail 'plane.

1939. Postal Cent.

No.	Type	Description	Unused	Used
391.	–	50 p.+50 p. orange and brown	35	30
392.	56.	1 d.+1 d. green & black	35	30
393.	–	1 d. 50 p.+1 d. 50 p. red	90	45
394.	–	2 d.+2 d. purple & violet	1·25	75
395.	–	4 d.+4 d. blue	2·25	1·75

57. Meal-time.  **59.** Milosh Obilich.

1939. Child Welfare.

No.	Type	Description	Unused	Used
396.	57.	1 d.+1 d. green ..	40	40
397.	–	1 d. 50 + 1 d. 50 red and brown	2·50	1·50
398.	–	2 d.+2 d. mauve & brn.	1·40	1·00
399.	–	4 d.+4 d. blue	2·25	1·75

DESIGNS—HORIZ. 2 d. Carpenter. VERT. 1 d. 50, Children on sands. 4 d. Children whispering.

1939. Battle of Kosova. 550th Anniv Inscr. "1389–1939".

No.	Type	Description	Unused	Used
400.	–	1 d.+1 d. green ..	1·25	50
401.	59.	1 d. 50+1 d. 50 red ..	1·25	75

DESIGN: 1 d. King Lazar.

60. Motor Cycle and Sidecar.  **61.** Sailing-ship "Jadran".

1939. 1st International Motor Races, Belgrade. Inscr. "I. MEDUNARODNE AUTO I MOTO", etc.

No.	Type	Description	Unused	Used
402.	60.	50 p. + 50 p. orange and brown	50	35
403.	–	1 d.+1 d. green & black	75	45
404.	–	1 d. 50+1 d. 50 red ..	1·25	80
405.	–	2 d.+2 d. blue	2·50	2·00

DESIGNS—HORIZ. 1 d., 2 d. Racing cars. VERT. 1 d. 50, Motor cycle.

1939. King's Birthday and Adriatic Guard Fund Inscr. "ZA JADRANSKU STRAZU".

No.	Type	Description	Unused	Used
406.	61.	50 p.+50 p. red ..	65	25
407.	–	1 d.+50 p. green ..	65	25
408.	–	1 d. 50+1 d. red ..	1·00	75
409.	–	2 d.+1 d. 50 blue ..	1·50	1·25

DESIGNS: 1 d. Tourist ship "King Alexander". 1 d. 50, Mail-boat "Triglav". 2 d. Destroyer "Dubrovnik".

62. Unknown Warrior's Tomb, Avala.  **63.** King Peter II.

1939. King Alexander. 5th Death Anniv. War Invalids' Fund.

No.	Type	Description	Unused	Used
410.	62.	1 d.+50 p. green ..	90	75
411.		1 d. 50+1 d. red ..	90	75
412.		2 d.+1 d. 50 purple ..	1·40	1·00
413.		3 d.+2 d. blue	1·90	1·25

1939.

No.	Type	Description	Unused	Used
414.	63.	25 p. black	5	5
415.		50 p. orange	5	5
416.		1 d. green	5	5
417.		1 d. 50 red	5	5
418.		2 d. mauve	10	5
419.		3 d. brown	12	5
420.		4 d. blue	15	5
420a.		5 d. blue	25	15
420b.		5 d. 50 violet ..	25	5
421.		6 d. blue	50	5
422.		8 d. brown	50	5
423.		12 d. violet	1·00	5
424.		16 d. purple	1·25	20
425.		20 d. blue	1·25	20
426.		30 d. pink	2·00	35

65. Delivering Letters.  **66.** Arrival of Thorval.

1940. Belgrade Postal Employees' Fund. Inscr. "ZA DOM P.T.T. ZVAN. I SLUZ'".

No.	Type	Description	Unused	Used
427.	65.	50 p.+50 p. orge. & brn.	55	35
428.	–	1 d.+1 d. green & black	60	50
429.	–	1 d. 50+1 d. 50 red and brown	1·00	1·00
430.	–	2 d.+2 d. mauve & pur.	1·75	1·00
431.	–	4 d.+4 d. blue and grey	3·25	1·60

DESIGNS—VERT. 1 d. Collecting letters. 4 d. Telegraph linesman. HORIZ. 1 d. 50, Mail-van. 2 d. Mail-train.

1940. Zagreb Postal Employees' Fund. Inscr. "ZA DOM P.T.T. CINOV U ZAGREBU".

No.	Type	Description	Unused	Used
432.	66.	50 p.+50 p. brown ..	25	15
433.	–	1 d.+1 d. green ..	25	15
434.	–	1 d. 50 p.+1 d. 50 p. red	65	50
435.	–	2 d.+2 d. red	90	75
436.	–	4 d.+2 d. blue	1·00	95

DESIGNS—VERT. 1 d. King Tomislav enthroned. 1 d. 50 p. Death of M. Gubac. HORIZ. 2 d. Radich Brothers. 4 d. Map of Yugoslavia.

DESIGN — VERT. 1 d., 2 d. Summer Games (Children on sands.)

67. Winter Games.

1940. Child Welfare. Inscr. "ZA NASU DECU".
437. **67.** 50 p. + 50 p. orange and brown 15 12
438. – 1 d. + 1 d. green 15 15
439. **67.** 1 d. 50 + 1 d. 50 red and brown 40 25
440. – 2 d. + 2 d. mauve 85 75

68. Arms of Yugoslavia, Greece, Rumania and Turkey. **68a.** Zagreb Cathedral.

1940. Balkan Entente. Inscr. "JUGOSLAVIJA" alternately at top in Cyrillic (I) or Roman (II) throughout the sheet.

		I.		II.	
441. **68.** 3 d. blue		40	15	40	12
442. 4 d. blue		40	15	40	12

1940. Air.
443. **68a.** 40 d. green .. .. 2·00 1·75
444. – 50 d. blue .. .. 2·50 2·25
DESIGN: 50 d. Suspension Bridge at Belgrade.

68b. Obod, scene of early Press, 1493.

1940. Invention of Printing Press by Johannes Gutenberg. 5th Centenary.
445. **68b.** 5 d. 50 green .. .. 1·90 1·10

1940. Anti-T.B. Fund. Nos. 364/7 surch.
446. **44.** 50 p. + 50 p. on 5 d. violet 25 12
447. – 1 d. + 1 d. on 10 d. red 40 20
448. – 1 d. 50 + 1 d. 50 on 20 d. green 50 30
449. **46.** 2 d. + 2 d. on 30 d. blue 75 40

68c. St. Peter's Cemetery, Ljubljana. **69.** Kamenita Gate, Zagreb.

1941. Ljubljana War Veterans' Fund.
450. **68c.** 50 p. + 50 p. green .. 25 12
451. – 1 d. + 1 d. red .. 40 20
452. – 1 d. 50 + 1 d. 50 green 50 30
453. – 2 d. + 2 d. lilac and blue 75 60
DESIGNS—HORIZ. 2 d. War Memorial, Bresje. VERT. 1 d. Croat, Serb and Slav national costumes. 1 d. 50, Memorial Chapel, Kajmakcalan.

1941. Philatelic Exhibs.
(a) 2nd Croatian Philatelic Exhib., Zagreb.
454. **69.** 1 d. 50 + 1 d. 50 brown .. 60 60
455. – 4 d. + 3 d. black 60 60

(b) 1st Philatelic Exhib., Slav Brod.
456. **69.** 1 d. 50 + 1 d. 50 black .. 8·50 8·50
457. – 4 d. + 3 d. brown .. 8·50 8·50
DESIGNS: 4 d. (2) Zagreb Cathedral.

NOTE. From 1941 until 1945 Yugoslavia ceased to exist as a stamp-issuing entity, except for the following series, Nos. 468/81 which were issued by the exiled government for the use of the Yugoslav Merchant Navy working with the Allies.

70. King Peter II. **71.** Vodnik.

1943. 2nd Anniv. of Overthrow of Regency and King Peter's Assumption of Power.
468. **70.** 2 d. blue 10 10
469. 3 d. grey 15 20
470. 5 d. red 15 30
471. 10 d. black 30 60

1943. Red Cross Fund. Surch. **CRVENI KRST + 12.50.**
472. **70.** 2 d. + 12 d. 50 blue .. 1·00 1·25
473. 3 d. + 12 d. 50 grey .. 1·00 1·25
474. 5 d. + 12 d. 50 red .. 1·00 1·25
475. 10 d. + 12 d. 50 black .. 1·00 1·50

1944. Union of Yugoslavia. 25th Anniv. 19th-century Patriots.
476. **71.** 1 d. black and red .. 12
477. 2 d. black and green .. 15
478. 3 d. black and blue .. 20
479. 4 d. brown and violet .. 50
480. 5 d. brown and purple .. 50
481. 10 d. brown .. .. 1·00
PORTRAITS: 2 d. Njegos. 3 d. Gaj. 4 d. Karadjic. 5 d. Strosmajer. 10 k. Karageorge.

VI. DEMOCRATIC FEDERAL REPUBLIC

(a) **REGIONAL ISSUES**

BOSNIA AND HERZEGOVINA

Currency: Croatian Kunas

1945. Mostar Issue. Stamps of Croatia surch. **Demokratska Federativna Jugoslavija 50 KUNA 50.**

(a) Pictorial stamps of 1941-43.
R 1. 10 k. on 25 b. red .. 30 30
R 2. 10 k. on 50 b. green .. 8 8
R 3. 10 k. on 2 k. red .. 15 15
R 4. 10 k. on 3 k. 50 brown 40 40
R 5. 40 k. on 1 k. green .. 8 8
R 6. 50 k. on 4 k. blue .. 2·50 2·50
R 7. 50 k. on 5 k. blue .. 12·00 12·00
R 8. 50 k. on 6 k. green .. 2·50 2·50
R 9. 50 k. on 7 k. red .. 80·00 80·00
R 10. 50 k. on 8 k. brown .. 75·00 75·00
R 11. 50 k. on 10 k. violet .. 50 50

(b) Famous Croats issue of 1943.
R 12. 30 k. on 1 k. blue .. 25 25
R 13. 30 k. on 3 k. 50 red .. 8 8

(c) Boskovic issue of 1943.
R 14. **21.** 30 k. on 3 k. 50 brown .. 75 75
R 15. 30 k. on 12 k. 50 purple 60 60

(d) War Victims Charity Tax stamps of 1944.
R 16. **27.** 20 k. on 1 k. green .. 8 8
R 17. **28.** 20 k. on 2 k. red .. 20 20
R 18. 20 k. on 5 k. green .. 15 15
R 19. 20 k. on 10 k. blue .. 15 15
R 20. 20 k. on 20 k. brown 40 40

CROATIA.

Currency: Kunas.

DEMOKRATSKA FEDERATIVNA

20 KUNA

(R 1.)

1945. Split issue. Stamps of Croatia 1941-43 surch as T R 1.
R 21. 10 k. on 25 b red .. 5 5
R 22. 10 k. on 50 b. green .. 5 5
R 23. 10 k. on 75 b. green .. 5 5
R 24. 10 k. on 1 k. green .. 5 5
R 25. 20 k. on 2 k. red .. 5 5
R 26. 20 k. on 3 k. brown .. 5 5
R 27. 20 k. on 3 k. 50 brown .. 5 5
R 28. 20 k. on 4 k. blue .. 5 5
R 29. 20 k. on 5 k. blue .. 15 15
R 30. 20 k. on 6 k. green .. 3·25 3·25
R 31. 30 k. on 7 k. red .. 5 5
R 32. 30 k. on 8 k. brown .. 6·00 6·00
R 33. 30 k. on 10 k. violet .. 5 5
R 34. 30 k. on 12 k. 50 black .. 5 5
R 35. 40 k. on 20 k. brown .. 10 10
R 36. 40 k. on 30 k. brown .. 20 20
R 37. 50 k. on 50 k. green .. 12 12

1945. Zagreb issue. Stamps of Croatia, 1941-43, surch. **DEMOKRATISKA FEDERATIVNA JUGOSLAVIJA KN 80 KN** and star.
R 38. 20 k. on 5 k. blue .. 12 12
R 39. 40 k. on 1 k. green .. 5 5
R 40. 60 k. on 3 k. 50 brown .. 5 5
R 41. 80 k. on 2 k. red .. 5 5
R 42. 160 k. on 50 b. green .. 15 15
R 43. 200 k. on 12 k. 50 black 20 20
R 44. 400 k. on 25 b. red .. 20 20

MONTENEGRO

Currency: Italian Lire.

Демократска Федеративна Југославија

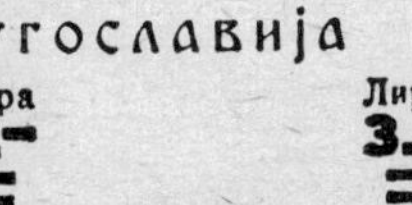

(R 2.)

1945. Cetinje issue. Stamps of Italian Occupation surch. with TR 2.

(a) National Poem Issue on 1943.
R 50. 1 l. on 10 c. green .. 65 65
R 51. 2 l. on 25 c. green .. 40 40
R 52. 3 l. on 50 c. mauve .. 40 40
R 53. 5 l. on 1 l. 25 blue .. 40 40
R 54. 10 l. on 15 c. brown .. 65 65
R 55. 15 l. on 20 c. orange .. 65 65
R 56. 20 l. on 2 l. green .. 65 65

(b) Air stamps of 1943, for use as ordinary postage stamps.
R 57. 3 l. on 50 c. brown .. 2·00 2·00
R 58. 6 l. on 1 l. blue .. .. 2·00 2·00
R 59. 10 l. on 2 l. red .. .. 2·00 2·00
R 60. 20 l. on 5 l. green .. 2·00 2·00

SERBIA

Currency: Hungarian Filler

1944. Senta issue. Various stamps of Hungary optd. with a large Star, **8.X.1944** and "Yugoslavia" in Cyrillic characters.
R 63. 1 f. grey .. .. .. 3·75 3·75
R 64. 2 f. red .. .. .. 3·75 3·75
R 65. 3 f. blue .. .. .. 3·75 3·75
R 66. 4 f. brown .. .. 3·75 3·75
R 67. 5 f. red .. .. .. 3·75 3·75
R 68. 8 f. green .. .. 3·75 3·75
R 69. 10 f. brown .. .. 50·00 50·00
R 70. 24 f. brown .. .. 38·00 38·00
R 71. 24 f. purple .. .. 6·00 6·00
R 72. 30 f. red .. .. .. 50·00 50·00

SLOVENIA

Currencies: Italian (Ljubljana)
German (Maribor)
Hungarian (Murska Sobota)

(R 3.)

1945. Ljubljana issue. Pictorial stamps of German Occupation, 1945, optd. as T R 3.
R 74. 5 c. brown 5 5
R 75. 10 c. orange 5 5
R 76. 20 c. brown 5 5
R 77. 25 c. green 5 5
R 78. 50 c. violet 5 5
R 79. 75 c. red 40 40
R 80. 1 l. green 12 12
R 81. 1 l. 25 blue 25 20
R 82. 1 l. 50 green 10 10
R 83. 2 l. blue 20 15
R 84. 2 l. 50 brown 8 8
R 85. 3 l. mauve 25 25
R 86. 5 l. brown 40 35
R 87. 10 l. green 30 30
R 88. 20 l. blue .. .. 1·90 2·00
R 89. 30 l. red .. .. 10·00 12·00

1945. Maribor issue. Hitler stamps of Germany, 1941-44, optd. **SLOVENIJA 9.5.1945 JUGOSLAVIJA** and star.
R 90. **128.** 1 pf. grey .. .. 1·75 1·75
R 91. 3 pf. brown 20 20
R 92. 4 pf. grey .. .. 1·25 1·25
R 93. 5 pf. green .. .. 1·00 1·00
R 94. 6 pf. violet 5 5
R 95. 8 pf. red 40 40
R 96. 10 pf. brown (775) 1·00 1·00
R 97. 12 pf. red (776) .. 5 5
R 98. 15 pf. brown .. 2·25 2·25
R 99. 20 pf. blue .. .. 1·75 1·75
R 100. 24 pf. brown .. 1·25 1·25
R 101. 25 pf. blue .. .. 5·00 5·00
R 102. 30 pf. green 40 40
R 103. 40 pf. mauve 40 40
R 104. **179.** 42 pf. green 30 30
R 105. **128.** 50 pf. green 90 90
R 106. 60 pf. brown 40 40
R 107. 80 pf. blue 75 50

1945. Murska Sobota issue. Various stamps of Hungary optd. As Nos. R 90/107.
R 108. 1 f. grey .. .. 2·00 2·00
R 109. 4 f. brown 12 12
R 110. 5 f. red .. .. 2·00 2·00
R 111. 10 f. brown 12 12
R 112. 18 f. black 12 12
R 113. 20 f. brown 12 12
R 114. 30 f. red 12 12
R 115. 30 f. red 12 12
R 116. 50 f. blue .. .. 2·50 2·50
R 117. 70 f. brown .. .. 2·50 2·50
R 118. 80 f. brown .. .. 25·00 25·00
R 119. 1 p. green .. .. 1·50 1·50

VI. DEMOCRATIC FEDERAL REPUBLIC.

(72.)

1944. Stamps of Serbia, 1942, surch. as T **72.**
482. **23.** 3 d. + 2 d. pink 8 5
485. – 4 d. + 21 d. bl. (No. 70) 8 5
483. – 7 d. + 3 d. grn. (No. 71) 8 5

73. Marshal Tito. **74.** Chapel at Prohor.

1945.
491. **73.** 25 p. green 30 20
492. 50 p. green 30 10
493. 1 d. red .. .. .. 3·75 15
494. 2 d. red 30 8
495. 4 d. blue 40 10
487. 5 d. green 5 5
496. 6 d. violet 50 10
497 9 d. brown .. .. 1·40 40
488. 10 d. red 8 8
498. 20 d. yellow .. .. 3·25 1·50
489. 25 d. violet 12 12
490. 30 d. blue 40 40

1945. Anti-Fascist Chamber of Deputies, Macedonia. 1st Anniv.
499. **74.** 2 d. red .. .. .. 1·50 12

75. Partisans. **76.** Flags of Russia and Yugoslavia.

1945. Red Cross Fund.
500. **75.** 1 d. + 4 d. blue .. .. 1·50 1·00
501. – 2 d. + 6 d. red .. .. 1·50 1·00
DESIGN—VERT. Child's head.

1945. Liberation of Belgrade. 1st Anniv.
518. **76.** 2 d. + 5 d. brown, red, blue and buff .. 1·25 75

77. Partisans. **78.** Marshal Tito.

1945. Partisans Commem.
502. **77.** 50 p. olive 8 8
503. 1 d. green 10 8
504. – 1 d. 50 p. brown .. 15 8
505. **78.** 2 d. red 10 8
506. – 2 d. 50 orange 50 8
507. – 3 d. brown .. .. 1·25 8
508. – 3 d. red 50 8
509. **78.** 4 d. blue 25 8
510. – 5 d. green 85 8
511. – 5 d. blue .. .. 1·50 8
512. – 6 d. black 50 8
513. – 8 d. yellow .. .. 1·25 8
514. – 9 d. mauve 45 10
515. – 12 d. blue 75 8
516. **77.** 16 d. blue 75 10
517. – 20 d. red .. .. 1·50 15
DESIGNS—As T **77**: 1 d. 50, 12 d., 20 d., Riflemen. VERT. 3 d., 5 d. Town of Jajce, inscr. "29-XI-1943". HORIZ. 2 d. 50 p., 6 d., 8 d, 9 d. Girl with flag.

79. "Industry and Agriculture". **80.**

1945. Meeting of the Constituent Assembly. Inscr. in Cyrillic at top and Roman characters at foot (I) or vice versa (II).

	I		II	
519. **79.** 2 d. red	4·00	3·00	4·00	3·00
520. 4 d. blue	4·00	3·00	4·00	3·00
521. 6 d. green	4·00	3·00	4·00	3·00
522. 9 d. orange	4·00	3·00	4·00	3·00
523. 16 d. blue	4·00	3·00	4·00	3·00
524. 20 d. brown	4·00	3·00	4·00	3·00

1946. Type of 1945 (Girl with flag), surch.
525. 2 d. 50 on 6 d. red .. 1·90 10
526. 8 d. on 9 d. orange .. 2·25 12

1946. Victory over Fascism. 1st Anniv. Star in red.

527. **80.** 1 d. 50 orange .. .. 1·00 60
528. 2 d. 50 red .. .. 1·50 75
529. 5 d. blue .. .. 3·00 2·25

81. "Communications". **82.** Railway Construction. **83.** S. Markovic.

1946. Postal Congress.

530. **81.** 1 d. 50+1 d. green .. 4·50 3·00
531. 2 d. 50+1 d. 50 red .. 4·50 3·00
532. 5 d.+2 d. blue.. .. 4·50 3·00
533. 8 d.+3 d. 50 brown .. 4·50 3·00

1946. Volunteer Workers' Railway Reconstruction Fund.

534. **82.** 50 p.+50 p. brown, red and blue .. 4·50 3·00
535. 1 d. 50+1 d. green, blue and red .. 4·50 1·60
536. 2 d. 50+2 d. lilac, red and blue .. 4·50 1·60
537. 5 d.+3 d. grey, red & bl. 4·50 3·00

1946. Svetozar Markovic. Birth Cent.

538. **83.** 1 d. 50 green .. .. 1·75 50
539. 2 d. 50 purple .. .. 2·50 75

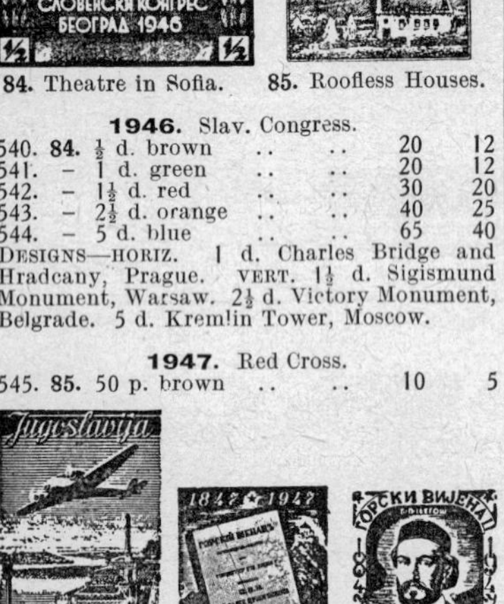

84. Theatre in Sofia. **85.** Roofless Houses.

1946. Slav. Congress.

540. **84.** ½ d. brown 20 12
541. – 1 d. green 20 12
542. – 1½ d. red 30 20
543. – 2½ d. orange 40 25
544. – 5 d. blue 65 40

DESIGNS—HORIZ. 1 d. Charles Bridge and Hradcany, Prague. VERT. 1½ d. Sigismund Monument, Warsaw. 2½ d. Victory Monument, Belgrade. 5 d. Kremlin Tower, Moscow.

1947. Red Cross.

545. **85.** 50 p. brown 10 5

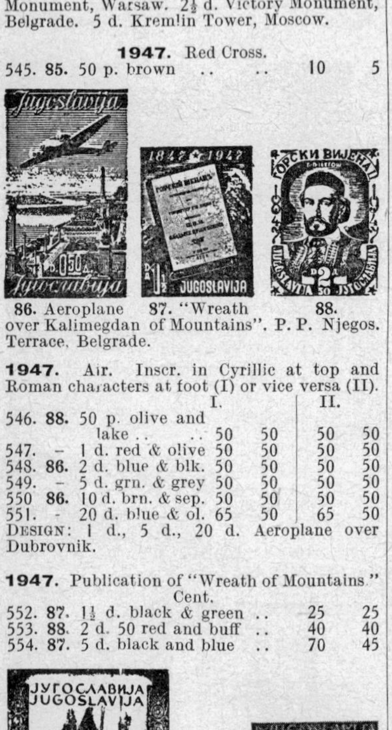

86. Aeroplane over Kalimegdan Terrace, Belgrade. **87.** "Wreath of Mountains". **88.** P. P. Njegos.

1947. Air. Inscr. in Cyrillic at top and Roman characters at foot (I) or vice versa (II).

			I.		II.	
546.	**88.**	50 p. olive and lake ..	50	50	50	50
547.	–	1 d. red & olive	50	50	50	50
548.	**86.**	2 d. blue & blk.	50	50	50	50
549.	–	5 d. grn. & grey	50	50	50	50
550.	**86.**	10 d. brn. & sep.	50	50	50	50
551.	–	20 d. blue & ol.	65	50	65	50

DESIGN: 1 d., 5 d., 20 d. Aeroplane over Dubrovnik.

1947. Publication of "Wreath of Mountains" Cent.

552. **87.** 1½ d. black & green .. 25 25
553. **88.** 2 d. 50 red and buff .. 40 40
554. **87.** 5 d. black and blue .. 70 45

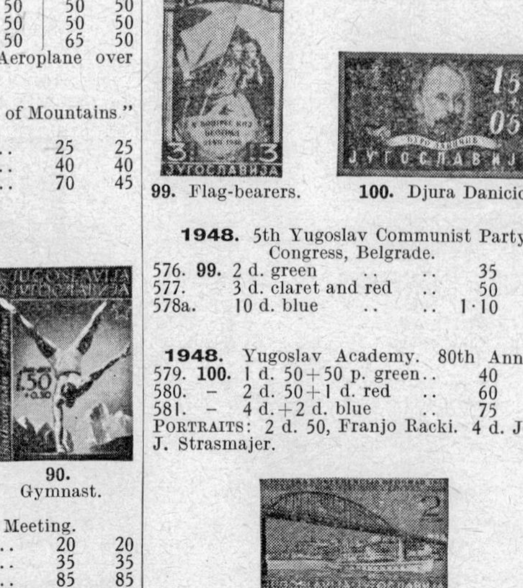

89. Girl Athlete, Star and Flags. **90.** Gymnast.

1947. Federal Sports Meeting.

555. – 1 d. 50 brown 20 20
556. **89.** 2 d. 50 red 35 35
557. – 4 d. blue 85 85

DESIGNS—VERT. 1 d. 50, Physical training groups. HORIZ. 4 d. Parade of athletes.

1947. Balkan Games.

558. **90.** 1 d. 50+50 p. green .. 50 35
559. 2 d. 50+50 p. red .. 70 50
560. 4 d.+50 p. blue .. 85 65

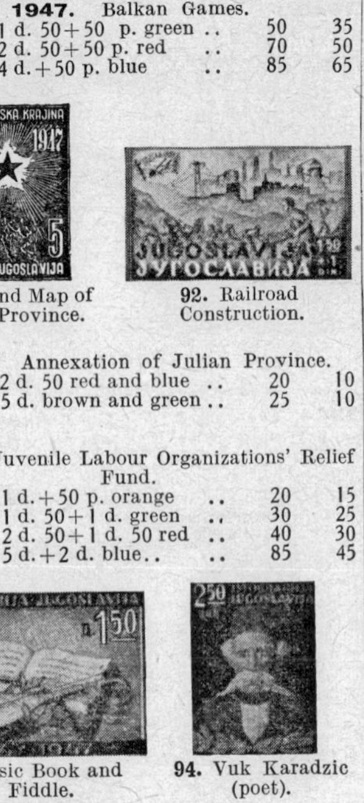

91. Star and Map of Julian Province. **92.** Railroad Construction.

1947. Annexation of Julian Province.

561. **91.** 2 d. 50 red and blue .. 20 10
562. 5 d. brown and green .. 25 10

1947. Juvenile Labour Organizations' Relief Fund.

563. **92.** 1 d.+50 p. orange .. 20 15
564. 1 d. 50+1 d. green .. 30 25
565. 2 d. 50+1 d. 50 red .. 40 30
566. 5 d.+2 d. blue.. .. 85 45

93. Music Book and Fiddle. **94.** Vuk Karadzic (poet).

1947. Serbian Literature. Cent.

567. **93.** 1 d. 50 green 40 20
568. **94.** 2 d. 50 red 60 35
569. **93.** 5 d. blue 80 60

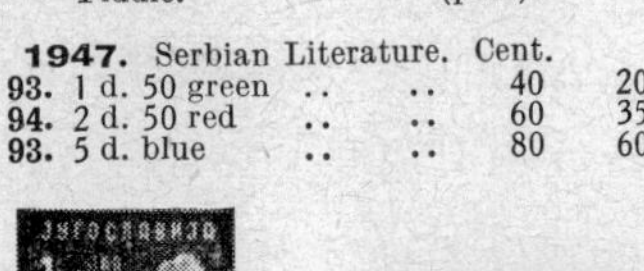

95. "B.C.G. Vaccine Defeating Tuberculosis". **96.** "Illness and Recovery".

97. "Fight against Tuberculosis". **98.** Map of Yugoslavia and Symbols of Industry and Agriculture.

1948. Anti-T.B. Fund.

570. **95.** 1 d. 50+1 d. green & red 30 15
571. **96.** 2 d. 50+2 d. green & red 40 25
572. **97.** 5 d.+3 d. blue and red 65 65

1948. Int. Fair, Zagreb.

573. **98.** 1 d. 50 grn., blue & red 12 5
574. 2 d. 50 pur., blue & red 15 8
575. 5 d. indigo, blue and red 25 15

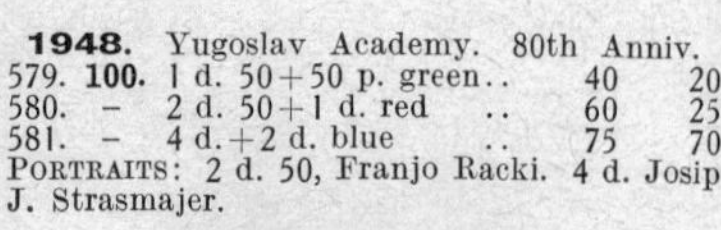

99. Flag-bearers. **100.** Djura Danicic.

1948. 5th Yugoslav Communist Party Congress, Belgrade.

576. **99.** 2 d. green 35 25
577. 3 d. claret and red .. 50 35
578a. 10 d. blue .. .. 1·10 65

1948. Yugoslav Academy. 80th Anniv.

579. **100.** 1 d. 50+50 p. green.. 40 20
580. – 2 d. 50+1 d. red .. 60 25
581. – 4 d.+2 d. blue .. 75 70

PORTRAITS: 2 d. 50, Franjo Racki. 4 d. Josip J. Strasmajer.

101. Danube Bridge.

1948. Danube Conf.

582. **101.** 2 d. green 30 20
583. 3 d. red 40 25
584. 5 d. blue 70 55
585. 10 d. brown .. .. 1·10 1·10

102. Laurence Kosir. **103.** Kosir and Mountain Homestead.

1948. 80th Death Anniv. of Laurence Kosir ("Ideological creator of first postage stamp").

586. **102.** 3 d. purple (postage).. 20 12
587. 5 d. blue 35 40
588. 10 d. orange 40 20
589. 12 d. green 95 65
590. **103.** 15 d. mauve (air) .. 60 45

104. Putting the shot. **105.** **106.** Arms of Montenegro.

1948. Projected Balkan Games.

591. **104.** 2 d.+1 d. green .. 60 60
592. – 3 d.+1 d. red.. .. 60 60
593. – 5 d.+2 d. blue .. 90 90

DESIGNS: 3 d. Girl hurdler. 5 d. Pole-vaulting.

1948. Red Cross.

594. **105.** 50 p. red and blue .. 5 5

1948. Resolution for Federation. 5th Anniv. Arms.

595. – 3 d. blue (Serbia) .. 90 90
596. – 3 d. red (Croatia) .. 90 90
397. – 3 d. orange (Slovenia) 90 90
598. – 3 d. green (Bosnia and Herzegovina) .. 90 90
599. – 3 d. mauve (Macedonia) 90 90
600. **106.** 3 d. black (Montenegro) 90 90
601. – 10 d. claret (Yugoslavia) 3·00 3·00

No. 601 is larger (24½×34½ mm.).

107. F. Presern. **108.** Ski-jump, Planica.

1949. Francis Presern. Death Cent.

602. **107.** 3 d. blue 30 15
603. 5 d. orange 50 25
604. 10 d. sepia 80 80

1949. Ski-jumping Competition Planica.

605. **108.** 10 d. magenta .. 1·40 1·25
606. 12 d. slate (Ski-jumper) 1·75 1·25

109. Soldiers. **110.** Globe, Letters and Forms of Transport.

1949. Liberation of Macedonia. 5th Anniv. Inscr. "1944-1949". (a) Postage.

607. **109.** 3 d. red 50 50
608. – 5 d. blue 75 15
608a. – 12 d. brown .. .. 3·75 3·75

DESIGNS: 5 d. Industrial and agricultural workers. 12 d. Arms and flags of Yugoslavia and Macedonia.

(b) Air. Optd. with aeroplane and **AVIONSKA POSTA.**

609. **109.** 3 d. red .. .. 2·25 2·25
610. – 5 d. blue (No. 608) .. 2·25 2·25
610a. – 12 d. brown (608a) .. 2·50 2·50

1949. U.P.U. 75th Anniv.

611. **110.** 3 d. red .. .. 3·25 2·75
612. – 5 d. blue 65 40
613. **110.** 12 d. brown 65 40

DESIGN—HORIZ. 5 d. Aeroplane, railway-train and mail-coach.

1949. Surch. with bold figures and bars.

614. O **1.** 3 d. on 8 d. brown .. 15 5
615. 3 d. on 12 d. violet .. 20 5

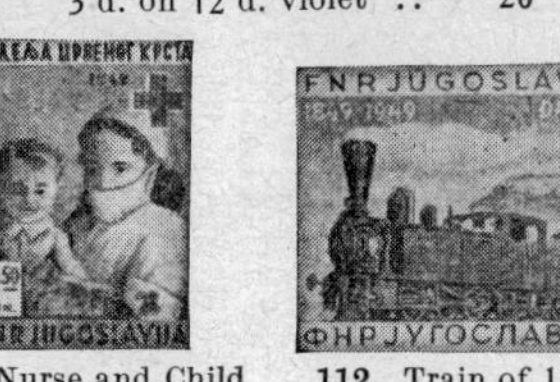

111. Nurse and Child. **112.** Train of 1849.

1949. Red Cross.

616. **111.** 50 p. brown and red .. 5 5

1949. National Railways Cent.

631. **112.** 2 d. green 75 25
632. – 3 d. red 75 25
633. – 5 d. blue .. .. 3·75 50
633a. – 10 d. orange .. .. 10·00 9·00

DESIGNS: 3 d. Modern steam locomotive. 5 d. Diesel train. 10 d. Electric loco.

ФНР ЈУГОСЛАВИЈА

≡ D3 FNR JUGOSLAVIJA (**113.**)

F N R D10 JUGOSLAVIJA (**114.**)

1949. Surch. with T **113** or **114.**

617. – 3 d. on 8 d. yellow (No. 513) .. 30 10
618. 10 d. on 20 d. red (No. 517) .. 40 10

F N R JUGOSLAVIJA (**115.**)

ФНР

FNR JUGOSLAVIJA (**116.**) F N R (**117.**)

1949. Optd. with T **116** on 2 d., **117** on 3 d. and 5 d., or **115** on others.

619. **77.** 50 p. olive 5 5
620. 1 d. green 5 5
621. 1 d. orange 5 5
622. **78.** 2 d. red 10 5
623. 2 d. green 10 5
624. – 3 d. red (No. 508) .. 10 5
625. – 3 d. pink 10 5
626. – 5 d. dark blue (No. 511) 25 20
627. – 5 d. light blue 25 20
628. – 12 d. violet (No. 515) 20 5
629. **77.** 16 d. light blue .. 95 40
630. 20 d. red 40 20

118. Surveying.

DESIGNS: 3 d. Map, road and car. 5 d. Youth and flag.

1950. Completion of Belgrade-Zagreb Road.

634. **118.** 2 d. green 65 20
635. – 3 d. pink 40 25
636. – 5 d. blue .. .. 1·75 70

119. Marshal Tito. **120.** A Child Eating.

1950. May Day.

637. **119.** 3 d. red .. .. 1·25 60
638. 5 d. blue .. .. 1·25 60
639. 10 d. brown .. .. 12·00 7·50
640. 12 d. black .. .. 2·50 2·50

1950. Child Welfare.

641. **120.** 3 d. red 65 10

121. Launching Glider. **122.** Chess-board.

1950. 3rd Aeronautical Meeting.
642. 121. 2 d. green 50 35
643. – 3 d. red 50 35
644. – 5 d. violet 80 50
645. – 10 d. brown .. .. 1·90 1·25
646. – 20 d. blue .. .. 14·00 7·50
DESIGNS—VERT. 3 d. Glider in flight. 5 d. Parachutists. 10 d. Woman pilot. 20 d. Gliding over water.

1950. World Chess Championships, Dubrovnik.
647. 122. 2 d. claret 50 35
648. – 3 d. yellow and sepia .. 50 35
649. – 5 d. yell., blue & green 90 50
650. – 10 d. yell., blue & pur. 1·90 1·25
651. – 20 d. yellow and blue .. 15·00 7·50
DESIGNS—VERT. 3 d. Castle and flags. 5 d. Chess-board and globe. 10 d. Chequered globe and players. 20 d. Knight and flags.

123. Girl Harvester. 124. Train and Map.

1950.
652. – 0 d. 50 brown .. 5 5
653. – 1 d. green 12 5
705. – 1 d. grey 8 5
654. 123. 2 d. orange 12 5
718. 2 d. red 25 5
655. – 3 d. red 20 5
656. – 5 d. blue 40 5
719. – 5 d. orange .. .. 1·10 5
657. – 7 d. grey 40 5
720. – 8 d. blue .. .. 5·50 25
658. – 10 d. chocolate .. 75 5
721. – 10 d. green .. .. 3·75 15
722. – 12 d. purple .. .. 2·00 12
723. – 15 d. red .. .. 6·00 50
660. – 16 d. blue .. .. 2·50 20
723a. – 17 d. maroon .. 7·50 12
661. – 20 d. olive .. .. 3·00 25
710. – 20 d. purple .. 2·00 5
711a. 123. 25 d. bistre .. .. 4·75 5
662. – 30 d. brown .. .. 6·00 50
712. – 30 d. blue .. .. 1·25 5
713. – 35 d. brown .. .. 1·75 10
662a. – 50 d. violet .. .. 18·00 16·00
714. – 50 d. green .. .. 1·25 5
715. – 75 d. violet .. .. 2·25 12
716. – 100 d. sepia .. .. 3·00 30
DESIGNS—VERT. 0 d. 50, 100 d. Metallurgy. 1 d. Electrician. 3 d., 35 d. Man and woman with wheelbarrow. 5 d. Fishing. 7 d., 8 d. Mining. 10 d. Apple-picking. 12 d., 75 d. Lumbering. 14 d., 16 d. Picking sunflowers. 17 d., 20 d. Woman and farm animals. 30 d. Girl printer. 50 d. Dockers unloading cargo.

1950. Zagreb Exhibition.
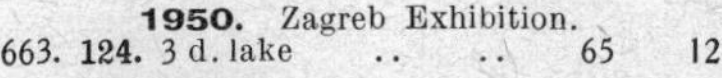
663. 124. 3 d. lake 65 12

125. National Costume. 126. Galleon.

1950. Red Cross.
664. 125. 50 p. green and red .. 5 5

1950. Navy Day.
665. 126. 2 d. purple 25 25
666. 3 d. brown 15 12
667. – 5 d. green 20 12
668. – 10 d. blue 35 35
669. – 12 d. grey .. .. 1·50 75
670. – 20 d. claret .. .. 4·75 2·75
DESIGNS: 3 d. Combat boat. 5 d. Cargo ship. 10 d. Liner. 12 d. Yachts. 20 d. Gunner.

127. Patriots of 1941. 128. Stane-Rozman.

1951. Revolt against Pact with Axis. 10th Anniv.
671. 127. 3 d. claret and red .. 8·50 4·00

1951. Partisan Rising in Slovenia. 10th Anniv. Dated "1941-1951".
672. 128. 3 d. brown 65 10
673. – 5 d. blue (Boy courier) 1·00 15

129. Children Painting.

ILLUSTRATIONS
British Commonwealth and all overprints and surcharges are FULL SIZE. Foreign Countries have been reduced to ¾-LINEAR.

1951. International Children's Day.
674. 129. 3 d. red .. .. 1·75 25

130. Iron Gates, Danube. 131. Z. Jovanovic.

1951. Air.
675. 130. 1 d. orange 8 5
676. – 2 d. green 8 5
677. – 3 d. red 15 5
677a. – 5 d. brown 12 5
678. – 6 d. blue .. .. 2·50 1·25
679. – 10 d. brown 30 5
690. – 20 d. grey 30 5
681. – 30 d. claret .. .. 1·25 5
682. – 50 d. violet .. .. 1·75 8
683. – 100 d. grey (40×27 mm.) .. .. 27·00 10·00
683a. – 100 d. green .. .. 1·25 10
683b. – 200 d. claret .. .. 1·40 35
683c. – 500 d. blue (39½×26 mm.) .. .. 3·25 75
DESIGNS—HORIZ. All show aeroplane. 2 d., 5 d. Plitvice Cascades. 3 d., 100 d. green, Gozd-Martuljak (mountain village). 6 d. 200 d. Old Bridge, Mostar. 10 d. Ochrida. 20 d. Kotor Bay. 30 d. Dubrovnik. 50 d. Bled. 100 d. grey, 500 d. Belgrade.

1951. Air. Zagreb Philatelic Exn., No. 678 in new colour optd. **ZEFIZ 1951.**
684. 6 d. green .. .. 1·50 55

1951. Serbian Insurrection. 10th Anniv. Dates "1941 7 VII 1951".
685. 131. 3 d. brown 80 25
686. – 5 d. blue .. .. 1·25 50
DESIGN—HORIZ. 5 d. Armed insurgents.

132. Mt. Kopaonik, Serbia. 133. S. Kovacevic.

1951. Air. Int. Mountaineering Assn. Meeting, Bled. Inscr. "UIAA-1951".
687. 132. 3 d. magenta .. .. 2·50 1·90
688. – 5 d. blue .. .. 2·50 1·90
689. – 20 d. green .. .. 70·00 45·00
DESIGNS: 5 d. Mt. Triglav. 20 d. Mt. Kalnik.

1951. Montenegin Insurrection. 10th Anniv. Dated "1941 13-VII 1951".
690. 133. 3 d. red 80 25
691. – 5 d. blue .. .. 1·40 50
DESIGN—HORIZ. 5 d. Partisan and mountains.

134. M. Oreskovic Statue. 135. S. Solaj.

1951. Croatian Insurrection. 10th Anniv.
692. 134. 3 d. claret 85 25
693. – 5 d. dark green .. 1·40 50
DESIGN—VERT. 5 d. Statue: "Transport of a Wounded Man".

1951. Insurrection of Bosnia and Herzegovina. 10th Anniv.
694. 135. 3 d. red 75 30
695. – 5 d. blue .. .. 1·25 40
DESIGN—VERT. 5 d. Group of insurgents.

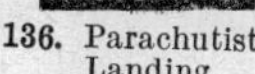

136. Parachutists Landing. 137. P. Trubar (Author).

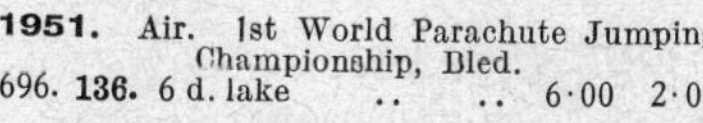
1951. Air. 1st World Parachute Jumping Championship, Bled.
696. 136. 6 d. lake .. .. 6·00 2·00

No. 682 in new colour optd. **I SVETSKO TAKMICENJE PADOBRANACA 1951.**
697. 50 d. blue .. .. 65·00 35·00

1951. Cultural Annivs.
698. 137. 10 d. slate .. .. 1·10 85
699. – 12 d. orange .. .. 1·10 85
700. – 20 d. violet .. .. 8·50 4·75
PORTRAITS: 12 d. M. Marulic poet). 20 d. Tsar Stefan Duzan.

138. National Products. 139. Hoisting the Flag.

1951. Zagreb Int. Fair.
701. 138. 3 d. yellow, red & blue 7·00 60

1951. Red Cross.
702. 139. 50 p. blue and red .. 5 5

140. M. Acev. 141. P. P. Njegos.

1951. Macedonian Insurrection. 10th Anniv. Dates "1941 II.X 1951"
703. 140. 3 d. magenta 85 65
704. – 5 d. violet .. .. 1·50 65
DESIGN—HORIZ. 5 d. War Victims' Monument, Skopje.

1951. Njegos (poet). Death Cent.
724. 141. 15 d. purple .. .. 2·75 1·00

142. Soldier. 143. Marshal Tito.

1951. Army Day.
725. 142. 15 d. red (postage) .. 65 8

726. 143. 150 d. blue (air) .. 8·00 5·00

144. Marshal Tito. 145.

1952. Marshal Tito's 60th Birthday.
727. 144. 15 d. brown .. .. 1·25 85
728. 145. 28 d. lake .. .. 3·00 1·75
729. – 50 d. green .. .. 9·50 8·00
DESIGN—As T 144: 50 d. Statue of Marshal Tito.

146. 147. Gymnastics.

1952. Children's Week.
730. 146. 15 d. red .. .. 8·00 75

1952. 15th Olympic Games, Helsinki. Inscr. "XV OLIMPIJADA 1952".
731. 147. 5 d. chocolate on buff 65 35
732. – 10 d. brown on yellow 75 35
733. – 15 d. blue on pink .. 1·10 50
734. – 28 d. chocolate on flesh 2·50 1·25
735. – 50 d. green on green .. 7·50 2·50
736. – 100 d. brown on mauve 15·00 7·00
DESIGNS: 10 d. Running. 15 d. Swimming. 28 d. Boxing. 50 d. Basket-ball. 100 d. Football.

148. "Fishing-boat" (sculpture). 148a. Belgrade in the 16th century.

1952. Navy Day. Views inscr. "1952".
737. – 15 d. purple .. .. 2·50 65
738. 148. 28 d. brown .. .. 3·75 1·00
739. – 50 d. black .. .. 13·00 9·00
DESIGNS: 15 d. Split, Dalmatia. 50 d. Sveti Stefan, Montenegro.

1952. Philatelic Exn., Belgrade.
739a. 148a. 15 d. purple .. 18·00 9·50
No. 739a was only sold at the Exhibition at 35 d. (20 d. entrance fee).

149. 150. Workers in Procession. 151. N. Tesla.

1952. Red Cross.
740. 149. 50 p. red, grey & black 8 5

1952. 6th Yugoslavia Communist Party Congress.
741. 150. 15 d. red-brown .. 3·25 1·60
742. 15 d. turquoise .. 3·25 1·60
743. 15 d. chocolate .. 3·25 1·60
744. 15 d. blue .. .. 3·25 1·60

1953. Tesla (inventor). 10th Anniv.
745. 151. 15 d. lake .. .. 1·10 20
746. 30 d. blue .. .. 3·50 40

152. Fresco, Sopocani Monastery. 153. Saloon Car.

1953. United Nations.
747. 152. 15 d. green .. .. 1·75 30
748. – 30 d. blue .. .. 2·75 45
749. – 50 d. lake .. .. 12·00 3·25
DESIGNS—VERT. 30 d. Fresco, St. Panteleimon Church, Nerezim, Skopje. 50 d. Fresco, St. Dimitri Church, Pec.

1953. Adriatic Car and Motor-cycle Rally.
750. 153. 15 d. lake and pink .. 20 5
751. – 30 d. indigo and blue .. 30 8
752. – 50 d. brown and yellow 1·00 12
753. – 70 d. green & blue-grn. 4·25 1·00
DESIGNS—HORIZ. 30 d. Motorcycle. 50 d. Sports car. 70 d. Saloon car descending.

154. Marshal Tito

155.

1953. Marshal Tito Commem.
754. **154.** 50 d. violet .. .. 8·50 95

1953. 38th Esperanto Congress, Zagreb.
755. **155.** 15 d. grn. & blk. (post.) 4·25 3·00
756. **155.** 300 d. grn. & blue (air) £200 £180

156. "Insurrection" (painting).

157.

1953. Macedonian Insurrection. 50th Anniv.
757. **156.** 15 d. maroon .. .. 2·25 90
758. – 30 d. green .. .. 6·00 2·10
DESIGN: 30 d. N. Karev (revolutionary).

1953. Liberation of Istria and Slovene Coast. 10th Anniv.
759. **157.** 15 d. green .. .. 35·00 3·50

158. B. Radicevic.

159. Blood-transfusion.

1953. Radicevic (poet). Death Cent.
760. **158.** 15 d. purple .. .. 11·00 1·25

1953. Red Cross.
761. **159.** 2 d. red and purple .. 15 5

160. Jajce. **161.** Ground Squirrel.

1953. 1st Republican Legislative Assembly. 10th Anniv.
762. **160.** 15 d. green .. .. 2·25 75
763. – 30 d. red .. .. 3·25 1·75
764. – 50 d. sepia .. .. 13·00 10·00
DESIGNS: 30 d. Assembly building. 50 d. Marshal Tito addressing assembly.

1954. Animals.
765. **161.** 2 d. slate, buff & green 8 5
766. – 5 d. brown & grey-green 20 10
767. – 10 d. brown and slate 30 15
768. – 15 d. brown & grey-blue 45 20
769. – 17 d. sepia and purple 90 25
770. – 25 d. yell., blue & violet 1·00 30
771. – 30 d. sepia and blue .. 1·25 40
772. – 35 d. black and brown 1·50 50
773. – 50 d. choc. and bronze 8·50 2·50
774. – 65 d. black and lake .. 16·00 7·50
775. – 70 d. chestnut & turq. 15·00 5·50
776. – 100 d. black and blue 21·00 16·00
DESIGNS—HORIZ. 5 d. Lynx. 10 d. Red Deer. 15 d. Bear. 17 d. Chamois. 25 d. Pelican. VERT. 30 d. Bearded Eagle. 35 d. Black Beetle. 50 d. Grasshopper. 65 d. Black Dalmatian Lizard. 70 d. Blind cave-dwelling salamander. 100 d. Trout.

161a. Ljubljana in the 17th century.

1954. Philatelic Exn., Ljubljana.
777. **161a.** 15 d. brn., grn. & blk. 19·00 18·00
No. 777 was only sold at the Exhibition at 35 d. (20 d. entrance fee).

162. Cannon, 1804.

1954. Serbian Insurrection. 150th Anniv. Inscr. "1804 1954". Multicoloured.
778. 15 d. Serbian flag .. .. 2·00 35
779. 30 d. Type **162** .. .. 4·25 75
780. 50 d. Seal of insurgents council .. .. .. 6·00 1·00
781. 70 d. Karageorge .. .. 27·00 9·00

162a. **163.**

1954. Children's Week.
781a. **162a.** 2 d. red 75 55

1954. Red Cross.
782. **163.** 2 d. red and green .. 10 5

164. V. Lisinski (composer).

165. Scene from Shakespeare's "Midsummer Night's Dream".

1954. Cultural Anniversaries.
783. **164.** 15 d. green .. .. 5·00 1·25
784. – 30 d. chocolate .. 5·00 2·50
785. – 50 d. maroon .. .. 6·00 3·75
786. – 70 d. blue .. .. 12·00 7·50
787. – 100 d. violet .. .. 27·00 22·00
PORTRAITS—VERT. 30 d. A. Kacic-Miosic (writer). 50 d. J. Vega (mathematician). 70 d. Z. J. Jovanovic (poet). 100 d. F. Visnjic (poet).
See also Nos. 975/80.

1955. Dubrovnik Festival. Inscr. as in **T 165.**
788. – 15 d. lake .. .. 2·00 70
789. **165.** 30 d. blue .. .. 6·00 2·25
DESIGN—VERT. 15 d. Scene from "Robinja" by Hanibal Lucic.

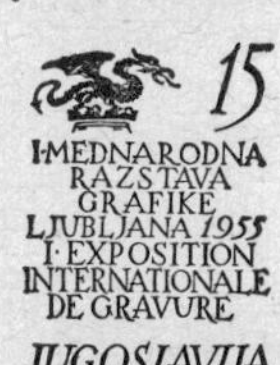

166. **167.**

1955. 1st Int. Exn. of Engraving, Ljubljana.
790. **166.** 15 d. brown and green on grey .. .. 7·00 1·40

1955. 2nd World Congress of the Deaf.
791. **167.** 15 d. lake .. .. 3·00 35

168. Hops. **169.** Laughing Girl.

1955. Vert. floral designs as **T 168.**
792. 5 d. green & brown (**T 168**) 10 5
793. 10 d. maroon, green & buff 12 5
794. 15 d. bl., grn., mar. & brn. 15 5
795. 17 d. buff, green and lake .. 25 5
796. 25 d. yell., green and blue 30 10
797. 30 d. pur., grn., blk. & violet 70 15
798. 50 d. red, green & brown .. 3·00 1·10
799. 70 d. orange, green & choc. 3·75 1·50
800. 100 d. red, yell., grn. & grey 10·00 6·00
FLOWERS—10 d. Tobacco. 15 d. Opium Poppy. 17 d. Linden. 25 d. Camomile. 30 d. Sage. 50 d. Wild rose. 70 d. Gentian. 100 d. Adonis.

1955. Children's Week.
801. **169.** 2 d. red 8 5

170. Peace Monument, New York. **171.** Red Cross Nurse.

1955. United Nations. 10th Anniv.
802. **170.** 30 d. black and blue .. 3·00 1·10

1955. Red Cross.
803. **171.** 2 d. blue, grey and red 12 5

172. Woman and Dove.

173. St. Donat's Church, Zadar.

1955. 10th Anniv. of Republic.
804. **172.** 15 d. violet 70 10

1956. Yugoslav Art.
805. **173.** 5 d. grey 25 12
806. – 10 d. myrtle 25 12
807. – 15 d. brown 25 12
808. – 20 d. lake 35 25
809. – 25 d. sepia 35 25
810. – 30 d. claret 35 25
811. – 35 d. olive 75 35
812. – 40 d. lake 85 35
813. – 50 d. brown .. .. 1·50 75
814. – 70 d. green .. .. 9·00 3·75
815. – 100 d. maroon .. 21·00 9·50
816. – 200 d. blue .. .. 40·00 24·00
DESIGNS—VERT. 10 d. Bas-relief of Croat King, Diocletian Palace, Split. 15 d. Church portal, Studenica, Serbia. 20 d. Master Radovan's portal, Trogir Cathedral. 25 d. Fresco, Sopocani, Serbia. 30 d. Monument, Radimlje, Herzegovina. 50 d. Detail from Bozidarevic Triptych, Dubrovnik. 70 d. Carved figure, Belec Church, Croatia. 100 d. Self-portrait of R. Jakopic. 200 d. Peace Monument by A. Augustincic, New York. HORIZ. 35d. Heads from Cathedral cornice, Sibenik, Dalmatia. 40 d. Frieze, Kotor Cathedral, Montenegro.

174. Zagreb through the Centuries.

175.

1956. Yugoslav Int. Philatelic Exn., Zagreb.
817. **174.** 15 d. brown, orange & black (postage) 60 20
818. 30 d. blue, red and black (air) .. 2·75 1·25

1956. Red Cross.
819. **175.** 2 d. sepia and red .. 5 5

176. "Technical Education".

177. Induction Motor.

1956. Air. 10 years of Technical Advance.
820. **176.** 30 d. red and black .. 3·00 1·50

1956. Tesla (inventor). Birth Cent. Inscr. as in **T 177.**
821. **177.** 10 d. olive 30 5
822. – 15 d. brown 30 5
823. – 30 d. blue 75 20
824. – 50 d. purple .. .. 2·75 1·25
DESIGNS: 15 d. Transformer. 30 d. "Telekomanda" (invention). 50 d. Portrait.

178. Sea-horse. **179.**

1956. Adriatic Sea Fish. Multicoloured.
825. 10 d. Type **178** 10 5
826. 15 d. Paper nautilus .. 15 5
827. 20 d. Rock lobster .. 20 5
828. 25 d. "Sea-prince" .. 30 12
829. 30 d. Perch 35 12
830. 35 d. Red mullet .. 80 25
831. 50 d. Scorpion fish .. 2·25 1·10
832. 70 d. Wrasse .. .. 3·75 2·40
833. 100 d. Dory .. .. 11·00 5·50

1956. Children's Week.
834. **179.** 2 d. olive-green .. 10 5

180. Running. **181.**

1956. Olympic Games. Horiz. designs inscr. "1956". Figures, values and country name in orchre.
835. **180.** 10 d. red 5 5
836. – 15 d. indigo (Canoeing) 8 5
837. – 20 d. blue (skiing) .. 8 5
838. – 30 d. grey-green (Swimming) .. 20 5
839. – 35 d. sepia (Football) 25 8
840. – 50 d. green (Water-polo) 60 12
841. – 70 d. maroon (Table-tennis) .. .. 3·75 1·40
842. – 100 d. red (Shooting) .. 8·00 4·00

1957. Red Cross.
843. **181.** 2 d. red, black and blue 10 5

182. Centaury.

183. Factory in Worker's Hand.

1957. Flowers. Multicoloured.
844. 10 d. Type **182** 8 5
845. 15 d. Belladonna .. 10 5
846. 20 d. Autumn crocus .. 12 8
847. 25 d. Marsh-mallow .. 20 8
848. 30 d. Valerian 35 12
849. 35 d. Woolly foxglove .. 50 12
850. 50 d. Fern .. .. 1·25 35
851. 70 d. Green-winged orchid 2·75 75
852. 100 d. Pyrethrum .. 8·50 4·75

1957. 1st Congress of Workers' Councils. Belgrade.
853. **183.** 15 d. lake 30 12
854. 30 d. blue .. .. 1·50 25

184. Gymnastics.

1957. 2nd Gymnastics Festival, Zagreb Vert. designs as **T 184** inscr. "II. GYMNAESTRADA 1957".
855. **184.** 10 d. olive and black .. 25 5
856. – 15 d. brown and black 25 5
857. – 30 d. blue and black .. 65 5
858. – 50 d. brown and black 4·50 1·60

186. Musician and Dancers of Slovenia.

187. Children.

1957. Yugoslav Costumes (1st series).
860. – 10 d. red, blue, brown and buff 15 5
861. – 15 d. red black, brown and buff 25 5
862. – 30 d. green, red, brown and buff 25 10
863. – 50 d. grn., brn. & buff 75 30
864. – 70 d. blk., brn. & buff 85 45
865. **186.** 100 d. red, green, brown and buff .. .. 5·50 3·00

DESIGNS—HORIZ. 10 d. Montenegrin musician, man and woman. 15 d. Macedonian dancers. 30 d. Croatian shepherdess and shepherd boys. VERT. 50 d. Serbian peasants. 70 d. Bosnian villagers.
See also Nos. 1020/5.

1957. Children's Week.
866. **187.** 2 d. slate and red .. 8 5

188. Revolutionaries. **189.** S. Gregorcic (poet).

1957. Russian Revolution. 40th Anniv.
867. **188.** 15 d. red and ochre .. 1·00 10

1957. Cultural Anniversaries.
868. **189.** 15 d. sepia 25 5
869. – 30 d. indigo 50 5
870. – 50 d. brown .. .. 1·25 8
871. – 70 d. violet .. .. 7·00 1·90
872. – 100 d. green .. .. 19·00 12·00

PORTRAITS—VERT. 30 d. A. Linhart (dramatist). 50 d. O. Kucera (physicist). 70 d. S. Mokranjac (compo..er). 100 d. J. Popovic (writer).

190.

191. Fresco of Sopotchyani Monastery.

1958. 7th Yugoslav Communist Party Congress.
877. **190.** 15 d. maroon .. 55 8

1958. Red Cross.
878. **191.** 2 d. multicoloured .. 12 5

192. Mallard.

193.

1958. Yugoslav Game Birds. Birds in natural colours. Background colours given below.
879. **192.** 10 d. brown 8 5
880. – 15 d. mag. (Capercailzie) 10 5
881. – 20 d. indigo (Pheasant) 15 5
882. – 25 d. green (Coot) .. 25 5
883. – 30 d. blue-green (Water rail) .. 35 12
884. – 35 d. bistre (Bustard) 50 12
885. – 50 d. purple (Mountain Partridge) .. .. 1·60 65
886. – 70 d. blue (Woodcock) 2·00 1·25
887. – 100 d. chestnut & black (Crane) .. .. 10·00 4·75

The 25, 35, 50 and 100 d. values are vert.
See also Nos. 956/64 and 1047/55.

1958. Opening of Postal Museum, Belgrade.
888. **193.** 15 d. black 75 15

194. Battle Flag.

195. Pomet, hero of Drzic's comedy "Dundo Maroje", and ancient fountain at Dubrovnik.

1958. Battle of Sutjeska River. 15th Anniv.
889. **194.** 15 d. lake 60 8

1958. Marin Drzic (writer). 450th Birth Anniv
890. **195.** 15 d. brown and black 75 15

196. **197.** Children at play.

1958.
891. – 2 d. olive 5 5
892. – 5 d. brown 5 5
983. – 5 d. orange 35 5
893. – 8 d. reddish purple .. 12 5
984. – 8 d. slate-violet .. 35 5
894. **196.** 10 d. green 35 5
895. 10 d. grey-green .. 15 5
985. 10 d. chocolate .. 35 5
896. – 15 d. red 20 5
897. – 15 d. deep green .. 25 5
986. – 15 d. emerald .. 35 5
898. – 17 d. claret 12 5
899. – 20 d. red 35 5
987. – 20 d. violet-blue .. 35 5
987a. – 20 d. emerald .. 20 5
900. – 25 d. grey 20 5
988. – 25 d. vermilion .. 35 5
901. – 30 d. indigo 20 5
989. – 30 d. brown 35 5
989a. – 30 d. vermilion .. 40 5
902. – 35 d. red 20 5
903. – 40 d. pink 35 5
904. – 40 d. blue 70 5
990. – 40 d. maroon .. 25 5
905. – 50 d. blue 35 5
991. – 50 d. blue 50 5
906. – 55 d. red .. .. 1·10 5
992. – 65 d. blue-green .. 25 5
907. – 70 d. red 65 5
908. – 80 d. red .. .. 2·00 5
909. – 100 d. green 85 8
993. – 100 d. olive .. .. 2·25 5
994. – 150 d. red 75 25
910. – 200 d. brown .. .. 1·75 20
995. – 200 d. slate-blue .. 65 5
996. – 300 d. olive-green .. 1·00 12
911. – 500 d. blue .. .. 3·75 35
997. – 500 d. violet .. 1·10 8
998. – 1000 d. sepia .. .. 2·50 35
999. – 2000 d. purple .. 4·75 1·25

DESIGNS—VERT. No. 891, 993, Oil derricks, Nafta. 892/983, Shipbuilding. 893, 984, 898, Timber industry, cable railway. 896, 899, 987, 987a, Jablanica Dam. 897, 986, 900, Ljubljana-Zagreb motor road. 988, Cable industry. 901, 989, 989a, "Litostroj" turbine factory, Ljubljana. 902, 990, Coke plant, Lukavac. 991, Iron foundry, Zenica. 992, Furnace, Sovojno. HORIZ. 903/4, 994, Hotel, Titograd. 905, 906, 995, Skopje. 907/8, 996, Sarajevo railway station and obelisk. 909, 997, Bridge, Ljubljana. 910, 998, Theatre, Zagreb. 911, 999, Parliament House, Belgrade.

1958. Children's Week.
912. **197.** 2 d. black, olive & yell. 8 5

198. Ship with Oceanographic equipment.

199. "Human Rights".

1958. I.G.Y. Inscr. as in T **198.**
913. **198.** 15 d. maroon (postage) 1·10 15
914. – 300 d. blue (air) .. 6·00 2·50

DESIGN: 300 d. Moon and earth with orbital tracks of artificial satellites.

1958. Declaration of Human Rights. 10th Anniv.
915. **199.** 30 d. green .. .. 1·10 65

200. Old City Dubrovnik.

201. Communist Party Emblem and Red Flags.

1959. Tourist Publicity Series. Views.
916. **200.** 10 d. olive-yellow & red 5 5
917. – 10 d. blue and green .. 5 5
918. – 15 d. violet and blue .. 8 5
919. – 15 d. green and blue .. 8 5
920. – 20 d. green and brown 12 5
921. – 20 d. green & turquoise 12 5
922. – 30 d. violet and buff .. 40 8
923. – 30 d. sage-grn. & blue 40 8
924. – 70 d. black & turquoise 3·75 1·10

DESIGNS: No. 917, Bled. 918, Postojna grottoes. 919, Ohrid. 920, Plitvice Lakes. 921, Opatija. 922, Split. 923, Sveti Stefan. 924, Belgrade.
See also Nos. 1033/41 and 1080/5.

1959. Yugoslav Communist Party. 40th Anniv.
925. **201.** 20 d. multicoloured .. 30 8

202. "Family Assistance".

203. Dubrovnik (XV Cent.).

1959. Red Cross.
926. **202.** 2 d. blue and red .. 10 5

1959. Philatelic Exhibition, Dubrovnik ("JUFIZ IV").
927. **203.** 20 d. myrtle, yellow-green and blue .. 1·50 75

204. Lavender.

205. Tug-of-War.

1959. Medicinal Plants.
928. **204.** 10 d. vio., grn. & blue 5 5
929. – 15 d. maroon, red, green and yellow .. 5 5
930. – 20 d. mar., grn. & bis. 8 5
931. – 25 d. lilac, grn. & olive 15 8
932. – 30 d. grn., blue & pink 20 12
933. – 35 d. blue, grn. & brn. 30 15
934. – 50 d. yell., grn. & choc. 1·25 35
935. – 70 d. red, green, yellow and ochre .. .. 1·75 60
936. – 100 d. grey, grn. & brn. 5·50 2·50

FLOWERS: 15 d. Black alder. 20 d. Scopolia. 25 d. Monk's hood. 30 d. Bilberry. 35 d. Juniper. 50 d. Cowslip. 70 d. Pomegranate. 100 d. Thorn-apple.

1959. "Partisan" Physical Culture Festival, Belgrade.
937. **205.** 10 d. black and ochre 5 5
938. – 15 d. blue and sepia .. 5 5
939. – 20 d. violet and brown 5 5
940. – 35 d. maroon and grey 12 5
941. – 40 d. violet and grey .. 15 5
942. – 55 d. green and brown 20 12
943. – 80 d. olive and slate .. 1·25 50
944. – 100 d. violet and ochre 3·75 1·50

DESIGNS—HORIZ. 15 d. High-vaulting and running. 20 d. Gymnasium exercise. 35 d. Female exercises with hoops. 40 d. Sailors' exercises. 55 d. Handball and basketball. 80 d. Swimming and diving. VERT. 100 d. "Partisan" Association insignia.

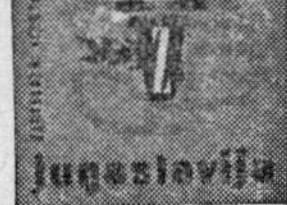
206. Fair Emblem. **207.**

1959. Zagreb Int. Fair.
945. **206.** 20 d. black and blue .. 45 10

1959. Children's Week.
946. **207.** 2 d. slate and yellow .. 8 5

208. Athletes. **209.** "Reconstruction" (sculpture).

1960. Olympic Games.
947. **208.** 15 d. yellow, buff and slate-violet 5 5
948. – 20 d. drab, lav. & blue 5 5
949. – 30 d. bl., stone & ultram. 10 5
950. – 35 d. grey, brn. & purple 20 12
951. – 40 d. drab, green and bronze 25 15
952. – 55 d. blue, drab & grn. 30 15
953. – 80 d. ochre, grey & red 85 45
954. – 100 d. ochre, drab and violet .. .. 1·00 55

DESIGNS: 20 d. Swimming. 30 d. Skiing. 35 d. Graeco-Roman wrestling. 40 d. Cycling. 55 d. Yachting. 80 d. Horse-riding. 100 d. Fencing.
Nos. 948, 950, 952 and 954 are inscr. in Cyrillic characters.

1960. Red Cross.
955. **209.** 2 d. indigo and red .. 10 5

1960. Yugoslav Forest Mammals. As T **193.** Animals in natural colours. Background colours given.
956. 15 d. indigo (Hedgehog) .. 5 5
957. 20 d. bronze-grn. (Squirrel) 8 5
958. 25 d. blue-green (Pine Marten) 10 5
959. 30 d. grey-olive (Hare) .. 15 8
960. 35 d. chocolate (Red fox) 20 10
961. 40 d. lake (Badger) .. 35 15
962. 55 d. blue (Wolf) .. 40 30
963. 80 d. violet (Roe deer) .. 50 35
964. 100 d. red (Wild boar) .. 2·00 1·40

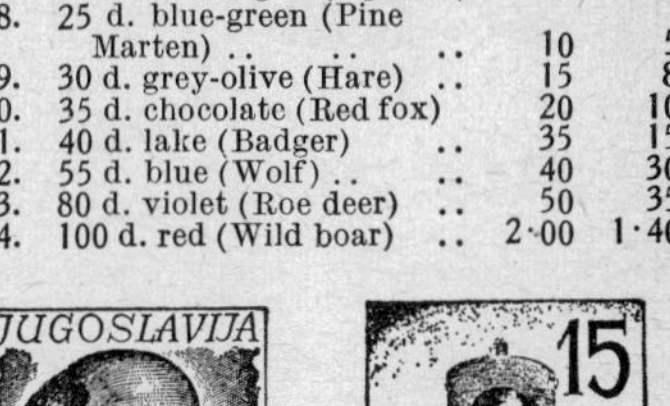

210. Lenin. **211.** Accelerator.

1960. Lenin. 90th Birth Anniv.
965. **210.** 20 d. grey-grn. & green 15 5

1960. Nuclear Energy Exn., Belgrade.
966. **211.** 15 d. green 8 5
967. – 20 d. claret 10 8
968. – 40 d. blue 50 15

DESIGNS: 20 d. Neutrons generator. 40 d. Nuclear reactor.

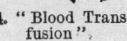

212. Young Girl.

213. Serbian National Theatre, Novi Sad (Centenary).

1960. Children's Week.
969. **212.** 2 d. red 8

1960. Jubilee Annivs.
970. **213.** 15 d. black 5 5
971. – 20 d. sepia 8 5
972. – 40 d. indigo 15 5
973. – 55 d. maroon 30 10
974. – 80 d. green 40 12

DESIGNS: 20 d. Part of "Illyrian Renaissance" (allegorical figure), after V. Bukovac (Cent of Croa National Theatre, Zagreb). 40 d. Edward Rusijan and "Bleriot" plane (50th Anniv. of 1st Flight in Yugoslavia). 55 d. Symbolic hand holding fruit (15th Anniv. of Republic). 80 d. Symbol of nuclear energy (15th Anniv. of U.N.O.).

1960. Cultural Annivs. Portraits as T **164**
975. 15 d. green 5 5
976. 20 d. chestnut 8 5
977. 40 d. bistre-brown 12 5
978. 55 d. crimson 20 5
979. 80 d. blue 35 12
980. 100 d. turquoise 60 35

PORTRAITS: 15 d. I. Cankar (writer). 20 d. S. S. Kranjcevic (poet). 40 d. P. Jovanovic (painter). 55d. D. Jaksic (writer). 80 d. M. Pupin (physician). 100 d. R. Boskovic (savant).

214. "Blood Transfusion".

215. "Atomic Energy".

1961. Red Cross. Perf. or imperf.
981. **214.** 2 d. red, yellow, orange and brown 5 5

1961. Int. Nuclear Electronic Conf., Belgrade.
982. **215.** 25 d. blue, red and grey 25 8

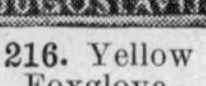

216. Yellow Foxglove. **217.** Stevan Filipovic (statue by V. Bakic).

1961. Medicinal Plants. Multicoloured.
1000. 10 d. Type **216** .. 5 5
1001. 15 d. Marjoram 5 5
1002. 29 d. Hyssop 8 5
1003. 25 d. Whitethorn .. 12 5
1004. 40 d. Rosemallow .. 20 8
1005. 50 d. Soapwort 25 12
1006. 60 d. Clary-sage 35 15
1007. 80 d. Blackthorn .. 65 25
1008. 100 d. Marigold .. 1·25 50
See also Nos. 1074/9.

1961. Yugoslav Insurrection. 20th Anniv. Inscr. "1941–1961". Inscriptions in gold.
1009. **217.** 15 d. brown and red .. 5 5
1010. – 20 d. yellow and sepia 8 5
1011. – 25 d. grey-green and blue-green .. 12 8
1012. – 60 d. violet and blue 30 20
1013. – 100 d. indigo and blue 80 30
DESIGNS: 20 d. Insurrection Monument, Bosansko Grahovo (relief by S. Stojanovic). 25 d. Executed Inhabitants Monument, Kragujevac (by A. Grzetic). 60 d. Nova Gradiska Victory Monument (by A. Augustincic). 100 d. Marshal Tito (Revolution Monument, Titovo Uzice, statue by F. Krsinic).

218.

219. St. Clement.

1961. Non-Aligned Countries Conf., Belgrade.
1014. **218.** 25 d. sepia (postage) 15 5
1015. – 50 d. green 30 5

1016. **218.** 250 d. slate-pur. (air) 1·00 75
1017. – 500 d. blue .. .. 2·40 1·75
DESIGN: 50 d., 500 d. National Assembly Building, Belgrade.

1961. 12th Int. Congress of Byzantine Studies, Ochrida.
1018. **219.** 25 d. sepia and olive 25 8

220. Bird with Flower in Beak. **221.** L. Vukalovic (revolutionary).

1961. Children's Week.
1019. **220.** 2 d. orange and violet 5 5

1961. Yugoslav Costumes (2nd series). As T **186** inscr. "1941–1961".
1020. 15 d. red, blk., sep. & brn. 5 5
1021. 25 d. black, red-brn. & brn. 5 5
1022. 30 d. sep , brn.-red & brn 8 5
1023. 50 d. red, blk., sep. & brn. 20 8
1024. 65 d. red, yell., brn. & sep. 30 15
1025. 100 d. brown-red, sepia, blue-green & brown .. 1·25 70
DESIGNS—HORIZ. Costumes of: 15 d. Serbia. 25 d. Montenegro. 30 d. Bosnia and Herzegovina. 50 d. Macedonia. 65 d. Croatia. 100 d. Slovenia.

1961. Herzegovina Insurrection Cent.
1026. **221.** 25 d. black 20 8

222. Hands holding Flower and Rifle. **223.** Miladinovci Brothers (after monument).

1961. Yugoslav Partisan Army. 20th Anniv.
1027. **222.** 25 d. violet-blue & red 15 5

1961. Macedonian National Songs by brothers Miladinovci. Cent.
1028. **223.** 25 d. purple and buff 15 8

224. "Mother's Play" (after F. Krainio). **225.** Mosquito.

1962. U.N.I.C.E.F. 15th Anniv.
1029. **224.** 50 d. black on buff .. 35 10

1962. Malaria Eradication.
1030. **225.** 50 d. black on blue 35 10

226. Cleopatra with Head-dress of Isis. **227.** Bandages and Symbols.

1962. U.N.E.S.C.O. 15th Anniv.
1031. **226.** 25 d. bronze-green on cream 25 8
1032. – 50 d. brown on buff .. 45 15
DESIGN: 50 d. Rameses II (Nubian monument) and U.N.E.S.C.O. emblem.

1962. Tourist Publicity Issue. Views as T **200**. Inscr. "1941–1961".
1033. 15 d. olive-brown and blue 8 5
1034. 15 d. olive-bistre & turq. 8 5
1035. 25 d. brown and blue .. 10 5
1036. 25 d. blue and light blue 10 5
1037. 30 d. blue & yellow-brown 15 5
1038. 30 d. blue and slate-purple 25 5
1039. 50 d. greenish bl. & olive-bis. 65 8
1040. 50 d. blue and bistre .. 65 8
1041. 100 d. bl.-grey & blk'sh grn. 4·50 70
VIEWS: No. 1033, Portoroz. 1034, Jajce. 1035, Zadar. 1036, Popova Sapka. 1037, Hvar. 1038, Kotor Bay. 1039, Derdap. 1040, Rab. 1041 Zagreb.

1962. Red Cross.
1042. **227.** 5 d. red, brn.-red & grey 8 5

228. Marshal Tito (after sculpture by A. Augustincic). **229.** Pole-vaulting.

1962. Marshal Tito's 70th Birthday.
1043. **228.** 25 d. blue-green .. 5 5
1044. – 50 d. brown 12 5
1045. **228.** 100 d. blue 70 20
1046. – 200 d. myrtle .. 1·60 1·00
DESIGN: 50 d., 200 d. As T **228** but profile view of bust.

1962. Yugoslav Amphibians and Reptiles. As T **193**. Inscr. "1962". Animals in natural colours. Background colours given.
1047. 15 d. green (Crested Newt) 5 5
1048. 20 d. violet (Spotted salamander) 5 5
1049. 25 d. chocolate (Yellow-bellied toad) 5 5
1050. 30 d. blue (Marsh frog) 8 5
1051. 50 d. brown-red (Pond Tortoise) 20 8
1052. 65 d. emerald (Wall lizard) 25 10
1053. 100 d. black (Green Lizard) 45 30
1054. 150 d. brn. (Leopard snake) 1·10 60
1055. 200 d. red (Common viper) 2·10 1·25

1962. 7th European Athletic Championships, Belgrade. Sportsmen in black.
1056. **229.** 15 d. blue 5 5
1057. – 25 d. purple .. 5 5
1058. – 30 d. green 5 5
1059. – 50 d. red 10 5
1060. – 65 d. bright blue .. 12 5
1061. – 100 d. blue-green .. 35 20
1062. – 150 d. orange .. 60 40
1063. – 200 d. brown .. 1·25 75
DESIGNS—HORIZ. 25 d. Throwing the discus. 50 d. Throwing the javelin. 100 d. Start of sprint. 200 d. High jumping. VERT. 30 d. Running. 65 d. Putting the shot. 150 d. Hurdling.

230. Physical Culture. **231.** "Bathing the Newborn Child" (Decani Monastery).

1962. Children's Week.
1064. **230.** 25 d. black and red 20 8

1962. Yugoslavia Art. Multicoloured.
1065. 25 d. Situla of Vace (detail from bronze vessel) .. 8 5
1066. 30 d. Golden Mask of Trebiniste (5th-cent. burial mask) (horiz.) .. 12 8
1067. 50 d. The God Kairos (Trogir Monastery) .. 25 12
1068. 65 d. Pigeons of Nerezi (detail from series of frescoes, "The Visitation", Nerezi Church, Skopje) 35 25
1069. 100 d. T **231** 65 60
1070. 150 d. Icon of Ohrid (detail from 14th-cent. icon, "The Annunciation") 1·90 1·10
The 25 d., 30 d. and 150 d. are horiz.
See also Nos. 1098/1103.

232. Ear of Wheat and Parched Earth. **233.** Dr. A. Mohorovicic (meteorologist).

1963. Freedom from Hunger.
1071. **232.** 50 d. blk.-pur. on stone 25 5

1963. World Meteorological Day.
1072. **233.** 50 d. ultram. on grey 25 5

234. Centenary Emblem. **235.** Partisans in file.

1963. Red Cross Cent. and Red Cross Week.
1073. **234.** 5 d. red, grey and ochre 12 5

1963. Medicinal Plants. As T **216** but dated "1963". Flowers in natural colours. Colours of backgrounds, panels and inscr. given.
1074. 15 d. dull green, grn. & blk. 5 5
1075. 25 d. cobalt, blue & violet 8 5
1076. 30 d. lavender-grey & indigo 10 5
1077. 50 d. pale choc. & chocolate 15 10
1078. 65 d. pale brown and brown 50 20
1079. 100 d. slate and deep slate 1·50 50
FLOWERS: 15 d. Lily of the Valley. 25 d. Iris. 30 d. Bistort. 50 d. Henbane. 65 d. St. John's wort. 100 d. Caraway.

1963. Tourist Publicity Issue. Views as T **200**. Inscr. "1963". Multicoloured.
1080. 15 d. Pula 5 5
1081. 25 d. Vrnjacka Banja .. 5 5
1082. 30 d. Crikvenica .. 5 5
1083. 50 d. Korcula 15 8
1084. 65 d. Durmitor 20 12
1085. 100 d. Ljubljana 75 30

1963. Battle of Sutjeska River. 20th Anniv.
1086. **235.** 15 d. green and drab 5 5
1087. – 25 d. green 5 5
1088. – 50 d. violet & pale brn. 15 10
DESIGNS—VERT. 25 d. Sutjeska Gorge. HORIZ. 50 d. Partisans in battle.
See also No. 1125.

236. Gymnast on "horse". **237.** "Mother".

1963. 5th European Cup Gymnastic Championships.
1089. **236.** 25 d. green and black 8 5
1090. – 50 d. blue and black .. 20 12
1091. – 100 d. olive-brn. & blk. 65 45
DESIGNS (Gymnast): 50 d. on parallel bars. 100 d. exercising with rings.

1963. Sculptures by Ivan Mestrovic. Inscr. as in T **237**.
1092. **237.** 25 d. bistre on pale brn. 5 5
1093. – 50 d. olive on pale olive 20 10
1094. – 65 d. green on pale blue 70 35
1095. – 100 d. blk. on pale grey 1·25 85
SCULPTURES: 50 d. "Reminiscence" (nude female figure). 65 d. "Kraljevic Marko" (head). 100 d. "Indian on horseback".

238. Children with Toys. **239.** Soldier and Emblem.

1963. Children's Week.
1096. **238.** 25 d. multicoloured .. 20 5

1963. Yugoslav Democratic Federation. 20th Anniv.
1097. **239.** 25 d. red, olive & drab 5 5

1963. Yugoslav Art. Designs as T **231** inscr. "1963". Multicoloured.
1098. 25 d. "Man", relief on Radimlje tombstone (13th–15th cents.) .. 5 5
1099. 30 d. Detail of relief on door of Split Cathedral, after A. Buvina (13th-cent.) 8 5
1100. 50 d. Detail of fresco in Beram Church (15th cent.) 10 5
1101. 65 d. Archangel Michael, from plaque in Dominican Monastery, Dubrovnik (15th-cent.) .. 30 10
1102. 100 d. Figure of man on Baroque fountain, by F. Robba, Ljubljana (18th-cent.) 45 20
1103. 150 d. Archbishop Eufraise—detail of mosaic in Porec Basilica (6th-cent.) .. .. .. 1·25 1·00
The 30 d. and 50 d. are horiz.

240. D. Obradovic (writer). **241.** Parachute.

1963. Cultural Celebrities.
1104. **240.** 25 d. blk. on pale buff 5 5
1105. – 30 d. blk. on pale blue 8 5
1106. – 50 d. blk. on pale cream 12 5
1107. – 65 d. blk. on pale lilac 50 25
1108. – 100 d. blk. on pale pink 75 55
PORTRAITS: 30 d. V. S. Karadzic (language reformer). 50 d. F. Miklosic (philologist) 65 d. L. Gaj (writer). 100 d. P. P. Njegos (poet).
See also Nos. 1174/9.

1964. Red Cross Week and 20th Anniv. of Yugoslav Red Cross.
1109. **241.** 5 d. red, mar. & blue 5 5

242. "Vanessa io". 243. Fireman saving Child.

1964. Butterflies. Multicoloured.
1110. 25 d. Type 242 .. .. 5 5
1111. 30 d. "Vanessa antiopa" 8 5
1112. 40 d. "Daphnis nerii" .. 10 5
1113. 50 d. "Parnassius apollo" 15 5
1114. 150 d. "Saturnia pyri" .. 50 35
1115. 200 d. "Papilio machaon" 75 50

1964. Voluntary Fire Brigade. Cent.
1116. **243.** 25 d. sepia and red .. 12 5

244. Running. 245. "Reconstruction"

1964. Olympic Games, Tokyo.
1117. **244.** 25 d. yellow, blk. & grey 5 5
1118. – 30 d. violet, blk. & grey 5 5
1119. – 40 d. green, blk. & grey 8 5
1120. – 50 d. red, pink, black and grey 15 5
1121. – 150 d. ochre, buff, black and grey .. 50 30
1122. – 200 d. blue, blk. & grey 75 40
DESIGNS: 30 d. Boxing. 40 d. Rowing. 50 d. Basketball. 150 d. Football. 200 d. Water-polo.

1964. Skopje Earthquake. 1st Anniv.
1123. **245.** 25 d. brown 8 5
1124. – 50 d. blue 20 8
DESIGN: 50 d. "International Aid" (U.N. flag over town).

1964. Occupation of Vis Island. 20th Anniv. As T **235** but inscr. "VIS 1944–1964" at foot.
1125. 25 d. lake and grey .. 10 5

246. Costumes of Kosovo-Metohija (Serbia). 247. F. Engels.

1964. Yugoslav Costumes (3rd series). As T **246**. Multicoloured.
1126. 25 d. Type **246** 5 5
1127. 30 d. Slovenia 5 5
1128. 40 d. Bosnia and Herzegovina 8 5
1129. 50 d. Hrvatska (Croatia) 15 5
1130. 150 d. Macedonia .. 40 20
1131. 200 d. Crna Gora (Montenegro) 80 55

1964. "1st International". Cent.
1132. **247.** 25 d. black on cream 8 5
1133. – 50 d. black on lilac .. 20 8
DESIGN: 50 d. Karl Marx.

248. Children on Scooter. 249. "Victor" (after Ivan Mestrovic).

1964. Children's Week.
1134. **248.** 25 d. grn., blk. & red 20 5

1964. Liberation of Belgrade. 20th Anniv.
1135. **249.** 25 d. black and olive on pink 12 5

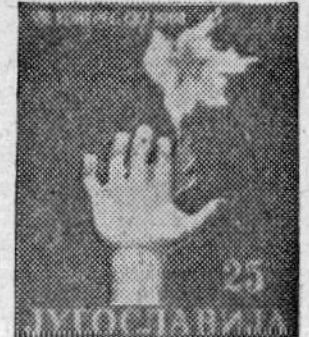

250. Initial of Hilander's Gospel (13th cent.). 251. "Hand of Equality".

1964. Yugoslav Art. Inscr. "1964". Multicoloured.
1136. 25 d. Type **250** 5 5
1137. 30 d. Initial of Miroslav's gospel (12th cent.) .. 5 5
1138. 40 d. Detail from Cetinje octateuch (15th cent.) 8 5
1139. 50 d. Miniature from Trogir's gospel (13th cent.) .. 15 8
1140. 150 d. Miniature from Hrvoe's missal (15th cent.) 40 25
1141. 200 d. Miniature from Herman Priory, Bistrica (14th cent.) (horiz.) .. 80 50

1964. 8th Yugoslav Communist League Congress. Multicoloured.
1142. 25 d. Type **251** 8 5
1143. 50 d. Dove and factory ("Peace & Socialism") 15 5
1144. 100 d. Industrial plant ("Socialism") .. 45 25

252. Table-tennis Player. 253. Children around Red Cross.

1965. World Table-tennis Championships, Ljubljana.
1145. **252.** 50 d. brown, turquoise, grey and red .. 15 8
1146. – 150 d. violet, blue grey and red .. 55 25
DESIGN: 150 d. As T **252** but design arranged in reverse.

1965. Red Cross Week.
1147. **253.** 5 d. red and brown .. 5 5

254. Titograd. 255. Young Partisan.

1965. Liberation. 20th Anniv. Yugoslav Capitals. Inscr. "15.V.1945–1965".
1148. **254.** 25 d. purple 5 5
1149. – 30 d. brown 5 5
1150. – 40 d. violet 8 5
1151. – 50 d. green 15 8
1152. – 150 d. violet 45 25
1153. – 200 d. indigo .. 70 50
CAPITALS: 30 d. Skopje. 40 d. Sarajevo. 50 d. Ljubljana. 150 d. Zagreb. 200 d. Belgrade.

1965. "Twenty Years of Freedom". Pioneer Games.
1154. **255.** 25 d. blk. & brn. on buff 12 5

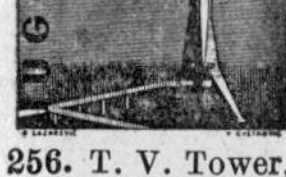

256. T. V. Tower, Avala (Belgrade). 258. Yarrow.

257. Djerdab Gorge.

1965. I.T.U. Cent.
1155. **256.** 50 d. indigo 20 5

1965. Djerdap Hydro-Electric Project. Inaug.
1156. **257.** 25 d. (30 b.) grn. & grey 5 5
1157. – 50 d. (55 b.) red & grey 12 5
DESIGN: 50 d. Djerdap Dam.
Nos. 1156/7 were issued simultaneously in Rumania.

1965. Medicinal Plants. Multicoloured.
1158. 25 d. Type **258** 5 5
1159. 30 d. Rosemary 5 5
1160. 40 d. Inula 8 5
1161. 50 d. Belladonna .. 10 5
1162. 150 d. Mint 45 15
1163. 200 d. Digitalis 90 75

259. I.C.Y. Emblem. 260. Sibenik.

1965. Int. Co-operation Year.
1164. **259.** 50 d. violet-blue, indigo and blue .. 15 5

1965. Tourist Publicity. Multicoloured.
1165. 25 d. Rogaska Slatina .. 5 5
1166. 30 d. Type **260** 5 5
1167. 40 d. Prespa Lake .. 5 5
1168. 50 d. Prizren 10 5
1169. 150 d. Skadar Lake .. 45 15
1170. 200 d. Sarajevo 80 60

261. Cat. 262. Marshal Tito.

1965. Children's Week.
1171. **261.** 30 d. lake and yellow 20 5

1965. Nos. 984 and 988 surch.
1172. – 5 d on 8 d. slate-violet 20 5
1173. – 50 d. on 25 d. verm... 35 8

1965. Cultural Celebrities. Portraits as T **240**.
1174. 30 d. red on pink 5 5
1175. 50 d. slate-blue on blue .. 10 5
1176. 60 d. sepia on brown .. 12 5
1177. 85 d. lilac on blue .. 15 5
1178. 200 d. olive on pale olive 35 15
1179. 500 d. maroon on purple 1·00 65
PORTRAITS: 30 d. B. Nusic (author and dramatist). 50 d. A. G. Matos (poet). 60 d. I. Mazuranic (author). 85 d. F. Levstik. 200 d. J. Pancic (botanist). 500 d. D. Tucovic (politician).

(Currency revalued. 100 paras = 1 dinar (= 100 old dinars).

1966.
1180. **262.** 20 p. green 25 5
1181. 30 p. red 30 5

263. Jumping (Balkan Games, Sarajevo). 264. "T", 15th-cent. Psalter.

1966. Sports Events.
1182. **263.** 30 p. red 5 5
1183. – 50 p. violet 8 5
1184. – 1 d. green 12 5
1185. – 3 d. brown 50 12
1186. – 5 d. blue .. .. 1·00 65
DESIGNS AND EVENTS: 50 p. Ice-Hockey and 3 d. Ice-hockey sticks and puck. (World Ice-hockey Championships—Jesenice, Ljubljana, Zagreb). 1 d. Rowing and 5 d. Oras (World Rowing Championships, Bled).

1966. Yugoslav Art. Manuscript Initials. Multicoloured.
1187. 30 p. Type **264** 5 5
1188. 50 p. "V", 14th-cent. Divos gospel 8 5
1189. 60 p. "R", 12th-cent. Libri moralium of Gregory 10 5
1190. 85 p. "P", 12th-cent. Miroslav gospel .. 15 8
1191. 2 d. "B", 13th-cent. Radomir gospel .. 35 15
1192. 5 d. "F", 11th-cent. passional .. .. 1·00 55

265. Red Cross Emblem. 266. Beam Aerial on Globe.

1966. Obligatory Tax. Red Cross Week.
1193. **265.** 5 p multicoloured .. 5 5

1966. As Nos. 983, etc., but values expressed "0.05" etc., colours changed and new values.
1194. 5 p. orange 5 5
1195. 10 p. brown 5 5
1196. 15 p. blue 5 5
1197. 20 p. emerald 8 5
1198. 30 p. vermilion 20 5
1199. 40 p. maroon 10 5
1200. 50 p. blue 12 5
1201. 60 p. brown 15 5
1202. 65 p. green 20 5
1203. 85 p. plum 25 5
1204. 1 d. olive 35 5
NEW VALUES: 60 p. as No. 988, 85 p. as No. 984.

1966. Int. Amateur Radio Union Regional Conf., Opatija.
1205. **266.** 85 p. blue 20 8

267. Stag Beetle. 268. Serbian 1 para Stamp of 1866.

1966. Yugoslav Insects. Multicoloured.
1206. 30 p. Type **267** 5 5
1207. 50 p. Rose Chafer .. 8 5
1208. 60 p. Violet Oil Beetle .. 10 5
1209. 85 p. Seven Spotted Ladybird 15 5
1210. 2 d. Alpine Longhorn .. 50 15
1211. 5 d. Diving Beetle .. 95 60

1966. Serbian Stamp Cent.
1212. **268.** 30 p. green, lake & brn. 5 5
1213. – 50 p. lake, bis. & ochre 8 8
1214. – 60 p. orange and green 12 12
1215. – 85 p. red and blue .. 40 20
1216. – 2 d. bl., bronze & grn. 1·10 45
DESIGNS (Serbian stamps of 1866): 50 p.—2 p. 50 p.—10 p. 85 p.—20 p. 2 d.—40 p.

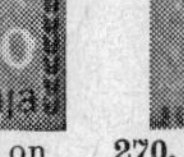

269. Rebels on Shield. 270. Strossmayer and Racki (founders).

1966. Yugoslav Insurrection. 25th Anniv.
1218. **269.** 20 p. brn., gold & grn. 5 5
1219. 30 p. mag., gold & buff 5 5
1220. 85 p. blue, gold & stone 12 8
1221. 2 d. violet, gold & blue 35 25

1966. Yugoslav Academy. Cent.
1222. **270.** 30 p. black and drab 12 5

271. Old Bridge, Mostar. 271a. Medieval View of Sibenik.

1966. Old Bridge, Mostar. 400th Anniv.
1223. **271.** 30 p. red .. .. 2·10 20

1966. Sibenik. 900th Anniv.
1224. **271a.** 30 p. maroon .. 40 5

272. "The Girl in Pigtails".

1966. Children's Week.
1225. 272. 30 p. multicoloured.. 1·10 10

273. U.N.E.S.C.O. Emblem. 274. Stylised Winter Landscape.

1966. U.N.E.S.C.O. 20th Anniv.
1226. 273. 85 p. blue 20 10

1966. Christmas.
1227. 274. 15 p. yellow and blue 5 5
1228. – 20 p. yellow and blue 8 5
1229. – 30 p. yellow and green 8 5
DESIGNS: 20 p. Father Christmas. 30 p. Stylised Christmas tree.
See also Nos. 1236/8.

275. Dinar of Durad I Balsic. 276. Flower between Red Crosses.

1966. Yugoslav Art. Designs showing different coins.
1230. 275. 30 p. multicoloured.. 5 5
1231. – 50 p. multicoloured.. 8 5
1232. – 60 p. multicoloured.. 8 5
1233. – 85 p. multicoloured.. 12 5
1234. – 2 d. multicoloured .. 35 12
1235. – 5 d. multicoloured .. 85 65
MEDIEVAL COINS (Dinars of): 50 p. King Stefan Tomasevic. 60 p. Durad Brankovic. 85 p. Ljubljana. 2 d. Split. 5 d. Emperor Stefan Dusan.

1966. New Year. As Nos. 1227/9 but colours changed.
1236. 15 p. gold, blue & indigo 35 35
1237. 20 p. gold, red and pink 35 35
1238. 30 p. gold, myrtle & green 35 35

1967. Red Cross Week.
1239. 276. 5 p. red, green & blue 5 5

277. "Arnica montana". 278. President Tito.

1967. Youth Day. Medicinal Plants. Multicoloured.
1240. 30 p. Type 277 .. .. 5 5
1241. 50 p. "Linum usititassimum" 8 5
1242. 85 p. "Nerium oleander" 12 5
1243. 1 d. 20 "Gentiana cruciata" 20 8
1244. 3 d. "Laurus nobilis" .. 45 12
1245. 5 d. "Peganum harmala" 85 70

1967. Pres. Tito's 75th Birthday.
(a) Size as Type 278.
1256. 278. 5 p. orange 5 5
1257. 10 p. brown 5 5
1258. 15 p. violet 5 5
1259a. 20 p. green 5 5
1260. 20 p. ultramarine .. 5 5
1261. 25 p. claret 5 5
1262a. 30 p. vermilion .. 5 5
1263. 30 p. myrtle 5 5
1264. 40 p. black 8 8
1265. 50 p. turquoise .. 15 12
1266. 50 p. vermilion .. 8 5
1267. 60 p. plum 12 8
1268. 75 p. sepia 20 5
1269. 75 p green 20 5
1270. 80 p. olive-brown .. 25 5
1270a. 80 p. red 8 5

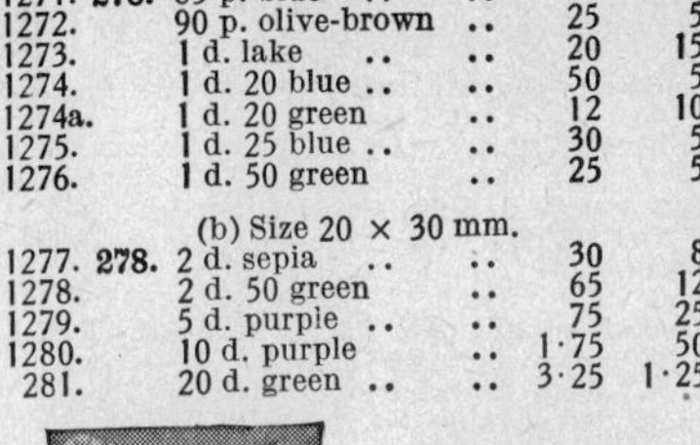
1271. 278. 85 p. blue 20 20
1272. 90 p. olive-brown .. 25 5
1273. 1 d. lake 20 15
1274. 1 d. 20 blue 50 5
1274a. 1 d. 20 green .. 12 10
1275. 1 d. 25 blue 30 5
1276. 1 d. 50 green .. 25 5

(b) Size 20 × 30 mm.
1277. 278. 2 d. sepia 30 8
1278. 2 d. 50 green .. 65 12
1279. 5 d. purple 75 25
1280. 10 d. purple .. 1·75 50
1281. 20 d. green .. .. 3·25 1·25

279. "Sputnik 1" and "Explorer 1". 280. St. Tripun's Church, Kotor.

1967. World Fair, Montreal. Space Achievements. Multicoloured.
1282. 30 p. Type 279.. .. 5 5
1283. 50 p. "Tiros", "Telstar" and "Molyna" .. 8 5
1284. 85 p. "Luna 9" and lunar orbiter 12 5
1285. 1 d. 20 "Mariner 4" and "Venus 3" 20 8
1286. 3 d. "Vostok 1" and Gemini-Agena space vehicle.. .. .. 45 30
1287. 5 d. Leonov in space .. 1·00 85

1967. Int. Tourist Year.
1288. 280. 30 p. olive and blue.. 5 5
1289. – 50 p. violet and brown 8 5
1290. – 85 p. purple and blue 12 5
1291. – 1 d. 20 brown & mar. 20 5
1292. – 3 d. olive and brown 45 20
1293. – 5 d. brn. & olive-brn. 90 75
DESIGNS: 50 p. Town Hall, Maribor. 85 p. Trogir Cathedral. 1 d. 20, Fortress gate, Nis. 3 d. Bridge, Visegrad. 5 d. Ancient bath, Skopje.

281. Partridge. 282. Congress Emblem.

1967. Int. Hunting and Fishing Exn. and Fair, Novi Sad. Multicoloured.
1294. 3 p. Type 281 .. .. 5 5
1295. 50 p. Pike.. .. .. 8 5
1296. 1 d. 20 Stag 15 10
1297. 5 d. Peregrine falcon .. 50 45

1967. Int. Astronautical Federation Congress, Belgrade.
1298. 282. 85 p. gold light blue and blue 10 5

283. Old Theatre Building. 284. "Winter Landscape" (A. Becirovic).

1967. Slovene National Theatre, Ljubljana. Cent.
1299. 283. 30 p. brown and green 10 5

1967. Children's Week.
1300. 284. 30 p. multicoloured 50 5

285. "Lenin" (from bust by Ivan Mestrovic). 286. Four-leaved Clover.

1967. October Revolution. 50th Anniv.
1301. 285. 30 p. violet 8 5
1302. 85 p. olive-brown .. 15 5

1967. New Year. Inscr. "1968".
1304. 286. 20 p. gold, blue & grn. 5 5
1305. – 30 p. gold, violet and yellow 5 5
1306. – 50 p. gold, red and lilac 15 5
DESIGNS: 30 p. Sweep with ladder. 50 p. Horseshoe and flower.
See also Nos. 1347/9.

287. "The Young Sultana" (V. Bukovac).

1967. Yugoslav Paintings (1st Series). Multicoloured.
1307. 85 p. "The Watchtower" (D. Jaksic) 12 12
1308. 1 d. Type 287 .. .. 20 15
1309. 2 d. "At Home" (J. Petkovsek) .. 25 25
1310. 3 d. "The Cock-fight" (P. Jovanovic) .. 50 35
1311. 5 d. "Summer" (I. Kobilca) .. .. 1·25 1·10
The 85 p. and 5d. are vert.
See also Nos. 1337/41, 1378/83, 1399/1404 and 1438/43.

288. Ski-jumping.

1968. Winter Olympic Games. Grenoble.
1312. 288. 50 p. purple & indigo 5 5
1313. – 1 d. olive and brown 15 10
1314. – 2 d. lake and black .. 30 15
1315. – 5 d. blue and olive .. 90 70
DESIGNS: 1 d. Figure-skating (pairs). 2 d. Downhill skiing. 5 d. Ice-hockey.

289. "The Madonna and Child" (St. George's Church, Prizren). 290. Honeycomb on Red Cross.

1968. Medieval Icons. Multicoloured.
1316. 50 p. Type 289 .. .. 8 5
1317. 1 d. "The Annunciation" (Ohrid Museum) .. 20 5
1318. 1 d. 50 "St. Sava and St. Simeon" (Belgrade Museum) 30 5
1319. 2 d. "The Descent" (Ohrid Museum) .. 40 5
1320. 3 d. "The Crucifixion" (St. Clement's Church, Ohrid) 65 8
1321. 5 d. "The Madonna and Child" (Gospe od zvonika Church, Split) .. 1·25 1·50

1968. Obligatory Tax. Red Cross Week.
1322. 290. 5 p. multicoloured .. 5 5

291. Bullfinch. 292. Running (Women's 800 metres).

1968. Song Birds. Multicoloured.
1323. 50 p. Type 291 .. .. 5 5
1324. 1 d. Goldfinch 10 5
1325. 1 d. 50 Chaffinch .. 20 5
1326. 2 d. Greenfinch 25 10
1327. 3 d. Crossbill 50 15
1328. 5 d. Hawfinch 75 80

1968. Olympic Games. Mexico.
1329. 50 p. mar. & brn. on cream 5 5
1330. 1 d. ol. & turq.-bl. on grn. 12 5
1331. 1 d. 50 sep. & bl. on flesh 20 5
1332. 2 d. green. & bis. on cream 25 5
1333. 3 d. indigo & violet on blue 45 10
1334. 5 d. pur. & grn. on mauve 95 80
DESIGNS: 50 p. Type 292. 1 d. Basketball. 1 d. 50, Gymnastics. 2 d. Sculling. 3 d. Water-polo. 5 d. Wrestling.

293. Rebel Cannon. 294. "Mother and Children" (fresco in Hrastovlje Church, Slovenia).

1968. Ilinden Uprising. 65th Anniv.
1335. 293. 50 p. chestnut and gold 10 5

1968. Partisan Occupation of Istria and Slovenian Littoral. 25th Anniv.
1336. 294. 50 p. multicoloured.. 10 5

295. "Lake of Klansko" (M. Pernhart).

1968. Yugoslav Paintings (2nd Series). 19th-cent. Landscapes. Multicoloured.
1337. 1 d. Type 295 .. .. 12 5
1338. 1 d. 50 "Bavarian Landscape" (M. Popovic) .. 20 5
1339. 2 d. "Gateway, Zadar" (F. Quiquerez) .. 30 8
1340. 3 d. "Triglav from Bohinj" (A. Karinger) .. 65 20
1341. 5 d. "Studenica Monastery" (D. Krstic) .. 1·25 1·00

296. A. Santic. 297. "Promenade" (Marina Cudov).

1968. Aleksa Santic (poet). Birth Cent.
1342. 296. 50 p. blue 10 5

1968. Children's Week.
1343. 297. 50 p. multicoloured.. 15 5

298. Karl Marx (after sculpture by N. Mitric). 299. Aztec Emblem and Olympic Rings.

1968. Karl Marx. 150th Birth Anniv.
1344. 298. 50 p. lake 10 5

1968. Obligatory Tax. Olympic Games Fund.
1345. 299. 10 p. multicoloured.. 10 5

300. Old Theatre and view of Kalimegdan. 301. Hasan Brkic.

1968. Serbian National Theatre, Belgrade. Cent.
1346. 300. 50 p. bistre and green 10 5

1968. New Year. Designs as Nos. 1304/6 but colours changed and inscr. "1969".
1347. 20 p. gold, blue and lilac 5 5
1348. 30 p. gold, violet & green 8 5
1349. 50 p. gold, cerise & lemon 10 5

1968. Yugoslav National Heroes.
1350. **301.** 50 p. violet 8 5
1351. – 75 p. black 12 5
1352. – 1 d. 25 brown .. 20 5
1353. – 2 d. indigo 35 12
1354. – 2 d. 50 green .. 50 25
1355. – 5 d. lake .. .. 1·50 1·75
PORTRAITS: 75 p. Milutinovic. 1 d. 25, R. Koncar. 2 d. K. Josifovski. 2 d. 50, T. Tomsic. 5 d. M. Pijade.

302. "Family" and Human Rights Emblem. **303.** I.L.O. Emblem.

1968. Human Rights Year.
1357. **302.** 1 d. 25 blue 20 12

1969. Int. Labour Organisation. 50th Anniv.
1358. **303.** 1 d. 25 black and red 20 10

304. Dove on Hammer and Sickle Emblem **305.** "St. Nikita" (Manasija Monastery).

1969. Yugoslav Communist Party. 50th Anniv.
1359. **304.** 50 p. red and black.. 8 5
1360. – 75 p. black and ochre 10 5
1361. – 1 d. 25 black and red 25 10
DESIGNS: 75 p. "Tito" and star (wall graffiti). 1 d. 25 Five-pointed crystal formation.

1969. Medieval Frescoes in Yugoslav Monasteries. Multicoloured.
1363. 50 p. Type **305** 8 5
1364. 75 p. "Jesus and the Apostles" (Sopocani).. 12 5
1365. 1 d. 25 "The Crucifixion" (Studenica) 20 5
1366. 2 d. "Cana Wedding Feast" (Kalenic) .. 35 8
1367. 3 d. "Angel guarding Tomb" (Milesava) .. 65 10
1368. 5 d. "Mourning over Christ" (Nerezi) .. 1·50 1·25

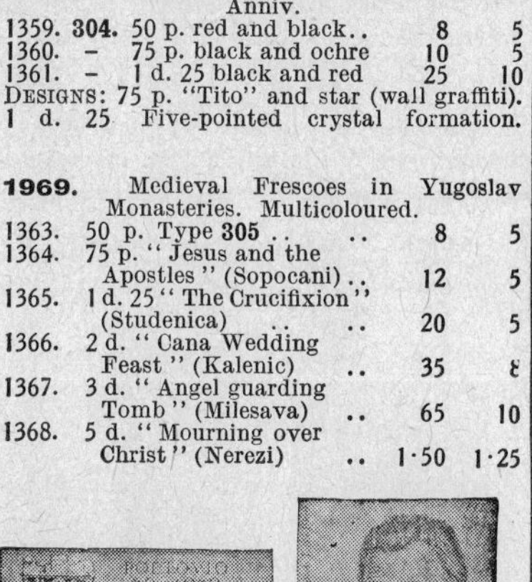

306. Roman Memorial and View of Ptuj. **307.** Vasil Glavinov.

1969. Ptuj (Poetovio) (Slovene town). 1900th Anniv.
1369. **306.** 50 p. brown 20 8

1969. Vasil Glavinov (Macedonian revolutionary). Birth Cent.
1370. **307.** 50 p. purple & brown 15 8

308. Globe between Hands. **309.** Single Peony.

1969. Obligatory Tax. Red Cross Week.
1371. **308.** 20 p. black, carmine and red 5 5

1969. Flowers. Multicoloured.
1372. 50 p. Type **309** 5 5
1373. 75 p. Coltsfoot 8 5
1374. 1 d. 25 Primrose 15 5
1375. 2 d. Christmas Rose .. 25 5
1376. 2 d. 50 Violet 35 10
1377. 5 d. Pasque flower .. 90 90

310. "Eber" (V. Ivankovic).

1969. Dubrovnik Summer Festival. Sailing Ships. Multicoloured.
1378. 50 p. Type **310** 5 5
1379. 1 d. 25 "Tare in Storm" (Franasovic) 15 5
1380. 1 d. 50 "Brig Sela" (Ivankovic) 20 5
1381. 2 d. 50 "16th-century Drubrovnik Galleon" 30 8
1382. 3 d. 25 "Frigate Madre Mimbelli" (A. Roux) 40 25
1383. 5 d. "Shipwreck" (16th-century icon) .. 1·10 1·25

311. Games' Emblem. **312.** Bosnian Mountain Horse.

1969. 9th World Deaf and Dumb Games, Belgrade.
1384. **311.** 1 d. 25 lilac and lake 30 12

1969. Veterinary Faculty, Zagreb. 50th Anniv. Multicoloured.
1385. 75 p. Type **312** 10 5
1386. 1 d. 25 Lipizzaner Horse 20 5
1387. 3 d. 25 Ljutomer trotter 50 10
1388. 5 d. Yugoslav Half-breed 75 65

313. Children and Chicks. **314.** Arms of Belgrade.

1969. Children's Week.
1389. **313.** 50 p. multicoloured.. 12 8

1969. Yugoslav Liberation. 25th Anniv. Arms of Regional Capitals. Multicoloured.
1390. 50 p. Type **314** 15 5
1391. 50 p. Skopje 15 5
1392. 50 p. Titograd (Podgorica) 15 5
1393. 50 p. Sarajevo 12 5
1394. 50 p. Zagreb 10 5
1395. 50 p. Ljubljana 10 5

315. Dr. Josip Smodlaka. **316.** Torch, Globe and Olympic Rings.

1969. Dr. Josip Smodlaka (politician). Birth Cent.
1397. **315.** 50 p. blue .. . 10 5

1969. Obligatory Tax. Olympic Games Fund.
1398. **316.** 10 p. multicoloured.. 5 5

317. "Gipsy Girl" (N. Martinoski).

1969. Yugoslav Nude Paintings. Multicoloured.
1399. 50 p. Type **317** 10 8
1400. 1 d. 25 "Girl in Red Armchair" (S. Sumanovic) 30 10
1401. 1 d. 50 "Girl Brushing Hair" (M. Tartaglia).. 40 20
1402. 2 d. 50 "Olympia" (M. Kraljevic) 55 35
1403. 3 d. 25 "The Bather" (J. Bijelic) 85 65
1404. 5 d. "Woman on a Couch" (M. Sternen) .. .. 3·00 2·75
Nos. 1402 and 1404 are horiz.
See also Nos. 1489/94.

318. University Building.

1969. Ljubljana University. 50th Anniv.
1405. **318.** 50 p. green 10 5

319. University "Seal". **320** Colonnade.

1969. Zagreb University. 300th Anniv.
1406. **319.** 50 p. gold, mar. & blue 10 5

1969. Europa.
1407. **320.** 1 d. 25 brown & green 1·10 85
1408. 3 d. 25 blue, grey & pur. 4·00 3·00

321. Jovan Cvijic (geographer). **322.** "Punishment of Dirka" (4th-cent mosaic).

1970. Famous Yugoslavs.
1409. **321.** 50 p. purple .. 5 5
1410. – 1 d. 25 black .. 15 5
1411. – 1 d. 50 purple .. 20 10
1412. – 2 d. 50 olive .. 30 15
1413. – 3 d. 25 brown .. 40 20
1414. – 5 d. ultramarine .. 65 75
CELEBRITIES: 1 d. 25, Dr. A. Stampar (hygienist). 1 d. 50, J. Krcovski (author). 2 d. 50, M. Miljanov (soldier). 3 d. 25. V. Pelagic (socialist revolutionary). 5 d., O. Zupancic (poet).

1970. Mosaics. Multicoloured.
1415. 50 p. Type **322** 5 5
1416. 1 d. 25 "Cerberus" (5th cent.) (horiz.) 15 5
1417. 1 d. 50 "Angel of Annunciation" (6th-cent.) 20 8
1418. 2 d. 50 "Hunters" (4th-cent.) 30 12
1419. 3 d. 25 "A Bull beside Cherries" (5th-cent.) (horiz.).. .. 55 25
1420. 5 d. "Virgin and Child Enthroned" (6th cent.) 1·40 1·25

323. Lenin (after sculpture by S. Stojanovic). **324.** Trying for Goal.

1970. Lenin. Birth Cent.
1421. **323.** 50 p. lake 8 5
1422. – 1 d. 25 blue 20 8
DESIGN: 1 d. 25. As T **323**, but showing left side of Lenin's bust.

1970. 6th World Basketball Championships.
1423. **324.** 1 d. 25 red 25 10

325. Red Cross Trefoil. **326.** "Flaming Sun".

1970. Obligatory Tax. Red Cross Week.
1424. **325.** 20 p. multicoloured.. 5 5

1970. Europa.
1425. **326.** 1 d. 25 blue & turq... 20 8
1426. 3 d. 25 brn., vio. & pur. 65 40

327. Istrian Short-haired Hound. **328.** Olympic Flag.

1970. Yugoslav Dogs. Multicoloured.
1427. 50 p. Type **327** 5 5
1428. 1 d. 25 Yugoslav tricolour hound 15 5
1429. 1 d. 50 Istrian hard-haired hound 20 8
1430. 2 d. 50 Balkan hound .. 30 12
1431. 3 d. 25 Dalmatian .. 40 12
1432. 5 d. Shara mountain dog 85 85

1970. Obligatory Tax. Olympic Games Fund.
1433. **328.** 10 p. multicoloured.. 5 5

329. Telegraph Key. **330.** "Bird in Meadow".

1970. Montenegro Telegraph Cent.
1434. **329.** 50 p. gold, blk. & brn. 8 5

1970. Children's Week.
1435. **330.** 50 p. multicoloured.. 10 8

331. "Gymnast" (Championships emblem). **332.** "Hand Holding Dove" (Macota).

1970. 17th World Gymnastic Championships, Ljubljana
1436. **331.** 1 d. 25 blue & purple 20 12

1970. United Nations. 25th Anniv.
1437. **332.** 1 d. 25 multicoloured 20 12

1970. Yugoslav Paintings (3rd Series). Baroque Period. Designs as T **287.** Mult.
1438. 50 p. "The Ascension" (T. D. Kracun) 5 5
1439. 75 p. "Abraham's Sacrifice" (F. Benkovic) .. 8 5
1440. 1 d. 25 "The Holy Family" (F. Jelovsek) 15 5
1441. 2 d. 50 "Jacob's Dream" (H. Zefarovic) .. 35 8
1442. 3 d. 25 "Christ's Baptism" (Serbian village artist) 45 8
1443. 5 d. 75 "Coronation of the Virgin" (T. Kokolja) .. 1·00 1·00

333. Rusty-leaved Alpenrose.

1970. Nature Conservation Year. Multicoloured.
1444. 1 d. 25 Type **333** .. .. 1·75 1·50
1445. 3 d. 25 Bearded vulture or lammergeyer .. 5·00 3·75

334. F. Supilo.

1971. Frano Supilo (politician). Birth Cent.
1446. **334.** 50 p. brown and buff 10 5

335. Different Nations' Satellites ("International Co-operation"). **336.** "Proclamation of the Commune" (A. Dodenarde, after Lamy).

1971. Space Developments. Multicoloured.
1447. 50 p. Type **335** 12 5
1448. 75 p. Telecommunications satellite 20 8
1449. 1 d. 25 Unmanned Space Flights.. .. .. 30 12
1450. 2 d. 50 Exploration of Mars and Venus (horiz.) 65 35
1451. 3 d. 25 Space-station (horiz.) .. .. .. 1·00 85
1452. 5 d. 75 "Astronauts on the Moon" (horiz.) .. 1·60 1·50

1971. Paris Commune Cent.
1453. **336.** 1 d. 25 brn. & oran. 20 12

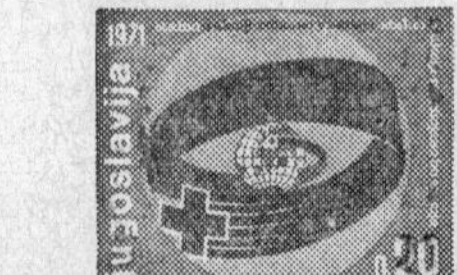

337. Red Cross Riband.

1971. Obligatory Tax. Red Cross Week.
1454. **337.** 20 p. multicoloured.. 5 5

338. Europa Chain. **339.** Congress Emblem (A Pajvancic).

1971. Europa.
1455. **338.** 1 d. 50 multicoloured 25 8
1456. 4 d. pink, pur. & mve. 65 50

1971. Yugoslav "Self-Managers" Movement. 20th Anniv.
1457. **339.** 50 p. red, blk. & gold 45 20
1458. – 1 d. 25 red. blk. & gold 1·40 85
DESIGN: 1 d. 25. "Self-Managers" emblem (designed by M. Miodragovic).

340. Common Mallow. **341.** Olympic "Spiral" and Rings.

1971. Flowers. Multicoloured.
1459. 50 p. Type **340** 8 5
1460. 1 d. 50 Buckthorn .. 20 5
1461. 2 d. Water-lily 25 5
1462. 2 d. 50 Wild poppy .. 30 15
1463. 4 d. Wild chicory .. 65 15
1464. 6 d. Bladder-herb .. 85 1·10

1971. Obligatory Tax. Olympic Games Fund.
1465. **341.** 10 p. blk., pur. & blue 5 5

342. Krk, Dalmatia. **343.** "Prince Lazar Hrebeljanovic" (from fresco, Lazarica Church).

1971. Tourism.
1466. – 5 p. orange 5 5
1467. – 10 p. brown 10 5
1468. – 20 p. violet 5 5
1469. **342.** 30 p. green 20 5
1470. – 30 p. brown .. 5 5
1471. – 35 p. brown .. 5 5
1472. – 40 p. brown 5 5
1473. – 50 p. red 30 5
1474. – 50 p. green 12 5
1475. – 60 p. purple .. 5 5
1476. – 75 p. green 12 5
1477. – 80 p. red 20 5
1478. – 1 d. purple 20 8
1479. – 1 d. 20 green .. 30 20
1480. – 1 d. 25 blue 15 12
1481. – 1 d. 50 black .. 12 8
1482. – 2 d. blue 20 12
1483. – 2d. 50 violet .. 25 25
Designs: 5 p. Krusevo, Macedonia. 10 p. Gradacac. 20 p. Bohinj Slovenia. 30 p. (No. 1470), Krk, Dalmatia. 35 p. Omis Dalmatia. 40 p. Pec. 50 p. (2). Krusevac, Serbia. 60 p. Logarska Valley. 75 p. Bohinj Slovenia. 80 p. Piran. 1 d. Bitola Macedonia. 1 d. 20 Pocitelj. 1 d. 25 Herceg-Novi. 1 d. 50 Herceg Nova, Dalmatia. 2 d. Novi Sad. 2 d. 50 Rijeka Crnojeria Montenegro.

1971. City of Krusevac. 600th Anniv.
1487. **343.** 50 p. multicoloured.. 10 5

344. Emperor Constantine's Head. **345.** Children in Balloon.

1971. Bronze Archaeological Discoveries. Multicoloured.
1488. 50 p. Type **344** 5 5
1489. 1 d. 50 "Boy with Fish" 12 5
1490. 2 d. "Hercules" .. 15 8
1491. 2 d. 50 "Satyr" .. 20 12
1492. 4 d. Goddess Aphrodite's head 30 25
1493. 6 d. "Emona Citizen" 1·40 1·10

1971. Children's Week and U.N.I.C.E.F. 25th Anniv.
1494. **345.** 50 p. multicoloured.. 12 8

1971. Yugoslav Portraits. As T **317.** Mult.
1495. 50 p. "Girl in Serbian Dress" (K. Ivanovic) .. 5 5
1496. 1 d. 50 "Ivanesevic the Merchant" (A. Bocaric) 12 12
1497. 2 d. "Anna Kresic" (V. Karas) 15 15
1498. 2 d. 50 "Pavla Jagodic" (K. Danil) 25 20
1499. 4 d. "Louise Pasjakova" (M. Stroj) 35 30
1500. 6 d. "Old Man at Ljubljana" (M. Langus) .. .. 1·50 1·50

346. "Postal Codes". **347.** Dame Gruev.

1971. Introduction of Postal Codes.
1501. **346.** 50 p. multicoloured.. 5 5

1971. Dame Gruev (Macedonian revolutionary). Birth Cent.
1502. **347.** 50 p. indigo .. 5 5

348. Speed-skating.

1972. Winter Olympic Games. Sapporo, Japan. Multicoloured.
1503. 1 d. 25 Type **348** .. 35 35
1504. 6 d. Slalom-skiing .. 1·90 1·90

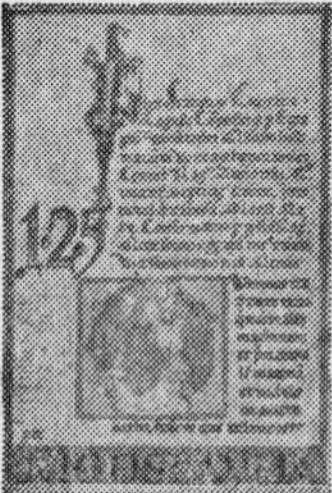

349. First Page of Statute. **350.** Ski-jump, Planica.

1972. Dubrovnik Statute. 700th Anniv.
1505. **349.** 1 d. 25 multicoloured 15 10

1972. 1st World Ski-jumping Championships, Planica.
1506. **350.** 1 d. 25 multicoloured 15 10

351. Water-polo. **352.** Red Cross and Hemispheres.

1972. Olympic Games, Munich. Multicoloured.
1507. 50 p. Type **351** 5 5
1508. 1 d. 25 Basketball .. 10 10
1509. 2 d. 50 Swimming .. 25 25
1510. 3 d. 25 Boxing .. 35 30
1511. 5 d. Running .. 50 50
1512. 6 d. 50 Sailing .. 1·25 85

1972. Obligatory Tax. Red Cross Week.
1513. **352.** 20 p. multicoloured.. 5 5

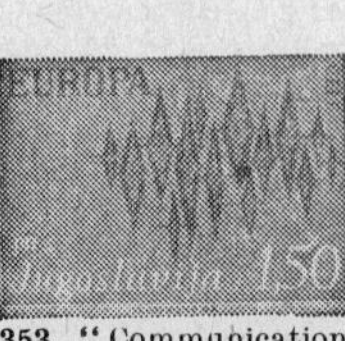

353. "Communications". **354.** Wall Creeper.

1972. Europa.
1514. **353.** 1 d. 50 multicoloured 20 15
1515. 5 d. multicoloured 75 70

1972. Birds. Multicoloured.
1516. 50 p. Type **354** .. 5 5
1517. 1 d. 25 Little bustard .. 10 10
1518. 2 d. 50 Chough .. 20 20
1519. 3 d. 25 Spoonbill .. 35 30
1520. 5 d. Eagle owl .. 65 50
1521. 6 d. 50 Ptarmigan .. 85 75

355. President Tito. **356.** Communications Tower, Olympic Rings and 1972 Games' Emblems.

1972. President Tito's 80th Birthday.
1522. **355.** 50 p. brown and buff 12 10
1523. 1 d. 25 blue and grey 30 20

1972, Obligatory Tax. Olympic Games Fund.
1525. **356.** 10 p. multicoloured.. 5 5

357. Locomotive No. 1 "King of Serbia", 1882. **359.** Pawn.

358. Glider in Flight.

1972. Int. Railway Union. 50th Anniv. Multicoloured.
1526. 1 d. 50 Type **357**.. .. 15 12
1527. 5 d. Modern "Bo-Bo" electric locomotive .. 65 45

1972. 13th World Gliding Championships, Vrasac.
1528. **358.** 2 d. black, blue & gold 25 15

1972. Chess Olympics Skopje.
1529. **359.** 1 d. 50 brown, violet and maroon .. 30 15
1530. – 6 d. black, blue and dark blue.. .. 1·00 70
DESIGN: 6 d. Chessboard, "King" and "Queen".

360. "Child on Horse" (B. Zlatec). **361.** G. Delcev.

1972. Children's Week.
1531. **360.** 80 p. multicoloured.. 10 5

1972. Goca Delcev (Macedonian revolutionary). Birth Cent.
1532. **361.** 80 p. black and green 10 5

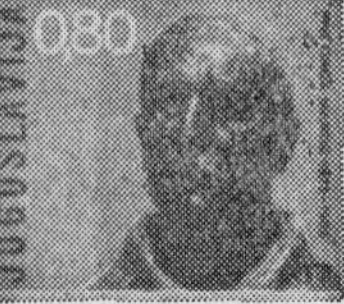

362. Father Martica.

1972. Father Grge Martica (politician). 150th Birth Anniv.
1533. **362.** 80 p. black, green. & red 12 5

363. National Library.

1972. Re-opening of Nat. Library, Belgrade. 140th Anniv.

1534. **363.** 50 p. brown 5 5

364. "Fruit Dish and Broken Majolica Vase" (M. Tenkovic).

1972. Yugoslav Art. Still Life. Multicoloured.

1535. 50 p. Type **364** 5 5
1536. 1 d. 25 "Mandoline and Book" (J. Petkovsek) (vert.) 10 10
1537. 2 d. 50 "Basket with Grapes" (K. Javanovic) 25 20
1538. 3 d. 25 "Water-melon" (K. Danil) 35 30
1539. 5 d. "In a Stable" (N. Masic) 60 45
1540. 6 d. 50 "Scrap-books" (C. Medovic) 85 60

365. Battle of Stubica.

1973. Slovenian Peasant Risings. 500th Anniv. and Croatian-Slovenian Rebellion. 400th Anniv. Multicoloured.

1541. 2 d. Type **365** 30 20
1542. 6 d. Battle of Krsko .. 85 65

366. R. Domanovic.

368. "Nov Sad". (P. Demetrovic).

367. Skofja Loka.

1973. Radoje Domanovic (Serbian satirist). Birth Cent.

1543. **366.** 80 p. brown and drab 40 8

1973. Skofja Loka. Millennium.

1544. **367.** 80 p. brown 40 8

1973. Old Engravings of Yugoslav Towns. Each black and gold.

1545. 50 p. Type **368** 5 5
1546. 1 d. 25 "Zagreb" (J. Szeman) 10 10
1547. 2 d. 50 "Koror" (P. Montier) 20 20
1548. 3 d. 25 "Belgrade" (Mancini) 30 30
1549. 5 d. "Split" (L. F. Cassas) 45 45
1550. 6 d. 50 "Kranj" M. Merian) 65 60

369. Table-tennis Bat and Ball.

1973. 32nd World Table-tennis Championships, Sarajevo.

1551. **369.** 2 d. multicoloured .. 25 15

370. Red Cross Emblem.

371. Europa "Posthorn".

1973. Obligatory Tax. Red Cross Week.

1552. **370.** 20 p. multicoloured .. 5 5

1973. Europa.

1553. **371.** 2 d. blue, purple & grn. 30 20
1554. 5 d. 50 maroon, pink and green .. 1·25 75

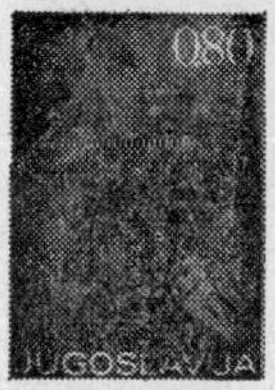

372. "Aristolochia clematatis".

373. Globe and Olympic Rings.

1973. Flora. Medicinal Plants. Mult.

1555. 80 p. Type **372** 5 5
1556. 2 d. "Echinops ritro" .. 20 20
1557. 3 d. "Olea europaea" .. 30 25
1558. 4 d. "Corydalis cava" .. 45 35
1559. 5 d. "Viscum album" .. 55 45
1560. 6 d. "Symphytum officinale" .. .. 1·00 85

1973. Obligatory Tax. Olympic Games Fund.

1561. **373.** 10 p. multicoloured .. 5 5

374. A. Jansa and Bee.

375. Aquatic Symbol.

1973. Anton Jansa (apiculturist). Death Bicent.

1562. **374.** 80 p. black 15 8

1973. 1st World Aquatic Championships, Belgrade.

1563. **375.** 2 d. multicoloured .. 20 15

376. "Child on Boat".

377. Posthorn.

1973. Children's Week.

1564. **376.** 80 p. multicoloured .. 15 8

1973.

1565. **377** 30 p. brown 5 5
1566. 50 p. blue 5 5
1567. 80 p. red 5 5
1567a. 1 d. 20 red 10 8

378. J. Dalmatinac.

379. "N. Petrovic" (self portrait).

1973. Juraj Dalmatinac (sculptor and architect). 500th Death Anniv.

1568. **378.** 80 p. olive and green 12 8

1973. Nadezda Petrovic (painter). Birth Cent.

1569. **379.** 2 d. multicoloured .. 20 15

380. "The Plaster Head" (M. Celebonovic).

1973. Yugoslav Art. Interiors. Multicoloured.

1570. 80 p. Type **380** 5 5
1571. 2 d. "St. Duja Church" (E. Vidovic) 15 15
1572. 3 d. "Slovenian House-wife" (M. Tartaglia) .. 25 25
1573. 4 d. "Dedicated at Karas"—painter at easel (M. Stancic) 30 30
1574. 5 d. "My Studio" (M. Konjovic) 40 40
1575. 6 d. "Tavern in Stara Loka" (F. Slana) .. 75 50

381. D. Dudic.

382. "M" for "Metrication".

1973. National Heroes.

(a) Each black.

1576. 80 p. Type **381** 5 5
1577. 80 p. S. Pindzur 5 5
1578. 80 p. B. Kidric 5 5
1579. 80 p. D. Dakic 5 5

(b) Each red.

1580. 2 d J. Mazar-sosa .. 15 15
1581. 2 d Z. Zrenjanin .. 15 15
1582. 2 d D. Emin 15 15
1583. 2 d I. Lola Ribar .. 15 15

1974. Introduction of Metric System in Yugoslavia. Cent.

1584. **382.** 80 p. multicoloured .. 10 8

383. Skater.

384. Sutjeska Monument.

1974. European Figure-skating Championships, Zagreb.

1585. **383.** 2 d. multicoloured .. 40 20

1974. Monuments.

1586. – 3 d. green 50 8
1587. – 4 d. 50 brown .. 85 10
1588. – 5 d. violet 65 12
1589. **384.** 10 d. green 65 25
1590. – 20 d. purple .. .. 1·40 35
1591. – 50 d. blue .. .. 3·50 1·25

DESIGNS—VERT. 3 d. Ljubljana. 4 d. 50 Kozara. 5 d. Belcista. HORIZ. 20 d. Podgaric. 50 d. Kragujevac.

385. Mailcoach.

1974. Universal Postal Union. Cent.

1592. **385.** 80 p. black & yellow 5 5
1593. – 2 d. black and red .. 20 15
1594. – 8 d. black and blue .. 1·10 80

DESIGNS: 2 d. U.P.U. H.Q., Building. 8 d. Yugoslav jetliner.

386. Montenegro 2 n. Stamp of 1874.

1974. Montenegro Stamp Centenary Mult.

1595 80 p. Type **386** 10 8
1596. 6 d. Montenegro 25 n. stamp of 1874 .. .. 75 60

387. President Tito. 388. Lenin.

1974.

1597. **387.** 50 p. green 5 5
1598. 80 p. red 5 5
1599. 1 d. 20 green 8 5
1600. 2 d. blue 15 8

1974. Lenin. 50th Death Anniv.

1601. **388.** 2 d. black and silver 20 15

389. Red Cross Emblems.

1974. Obligatory Tax. Red Cross Week.

1602. **389.** 20 p. multicoloured .. 5 5

390. "Dwarf" (Lepenski settlement, c. 4950 B.C.).

391. Great Tit.

1974. Europa. Sculptures. Multicoloured.

1603. 2 d. Type **390** 45 35
1604. 6 d. "Widow and Child" (I. Mestrovic) .. .. 1·40 1·25

1974. Youth Day. Multicoloured.

1605. 80 p. Type **391** 15 15
1606. 2 d. Roses 40 40
1607. 6 d. Cabbage White (butterfly) .. .. 1·40 1·40

392. Congress Poster.

393. Olympic Rings and Stadium.

1974. 10th Yugoslav League of Communists' Congress, Belgrade.

1608. **392.** 80 p. multicoloured .. 5 5
1609. 2 d. multicoloured .. 20 20
1610. 6 d. multicoloured .. 65 55

1974. Obligatory Tax. Olympic Games Fund.

1611. **393.** 10 p. multicoloured .. 5 5

394. Dish Aerial, Ivanjica.

395. World Cup.

1974. Satellite Communications Station, Ivanjica. Inaug.

1612. **394.** 80 p. blue 20 20
1613. – 6 d lilac .. .. 1·25 1·25

DESIGN: 6 d. "Intelstat 4" in orbit.

1974. World Cup Football Championships, West Germany.

1614. **395.** 4 d. 50 multicoloured 85 35

396. Edelweiss and Klek Mountain.

1974. Croatian Mountaineers' Society. Cent.

1615 **396.** 2 d. multicoloured .. 20 15

397. "Children's Dance" (J. Knjazovic).

1974. Yugoslav Paintings. Multicoloured.
1616. 80 p. Type 397 .. .. 5 5
1617. 2 d. "Crucified Hen" (I. Generalic) 25 15
1618. 5 d. "Laundresses" (I. Lackovic) 50 40
1619. 8 d. "Village Dance" (J. Brasic) .. .. .. 1·00 65
Nos. 1617/8 are vert.

398. "Chicken and Flower". 399. Interior of Library.

1974. Children's Week. Multicoloured.
1620. 1 d. 20 Type 398 .. .. 10 10
1621. 3 d. 20 "Boy and Girl" (vert.) 25 25
1622. 5 d. "Cat and kitten" .. 55 45

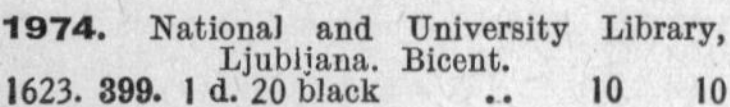

1974. National and University Library, Ljubljana. Bicent.
1623. 399. 1 d. 20 black .. 10 10

400. "White Peonies" (P. Dobrovic). 402. Dove facing Map of Europe.

401. Title-page and View of Nova Sad.

1974. Yugoslav Paintings. Flowers. Mult.
1624. 80 p. Type 400 .. .. 5 5
1625. 2 d. "Carnations" (V. Gecan) 15 15
1626. 3 d. "Flowers" (M. Konjovic) 25 25
1627. 4 d. "White Vase" (S. Sumanovic) 30 30
1628. 5 d. "Branching Larkspurs" (S. Kregar) .. 40 40
1629. 8 d. "Roses" (P. Lubarda) 75 65

1975. Matica Sipska Annals. 150th Anniv.
1630. 401. 1 d. 20 green .. 8 8

1975. 11th Interparliamentary Union Conf., Belgrade.
1631. 402. 3 d. 20 grey, red & bl. 50 50
1632. 8 d. grey, grn & orge. 1·50 1·50

403. Gold-plated Bronze Ear-ring. 404. S. Markovic.

1975. Museum Treasures. Multicoloured.
1633. 1 d. 20 Type 403 .. .. 10 10
1634. 2 d. 10 Silver bracelet .. 15 15
1635. 3 d. 20 Gold-plated silver buckle 25 25
1636. 5 d. Radulov's (gold-plated) ring 35 35
1637. 6 d. Silver-and-paste necklace 50 50
1638. 8 d. Gold-plated bronze and jewelled bracelet .. 75 75

1975. Svetozar Markovic (author and politician). Death Cent.
1639. 404. 1 d. 20 blue 10 8

405. "Fettered" (F. Krsinic). 406. Ohrid.

1975. International Women's Year.
1640. 405. 3 d. 20 brn. & gold .. 25 20

1975.
1640a. – 25 p. red 5 5
1641. 406. 1 d. violet 8 5
1641a. 1 d. violet 8 5
1641b. – 1 d. 50 red 12 10
1642. – 2 d. 10 green .. 15 12
1643. – 3 d. 20 blue 25 20
1643a. – 4 d. 90 blue 40 35
DESIGNS: 25 p. Budva. 1 d. 50 Bihac. 2 d. 10 Hvar. 3 d. 20 Skofja Loka. 4 d. 90 Nepact.

407. "Still Life with Eggs" (M. Pijade).

1975. Europa. Multicoloured.
1644. 3 d. 20 Type 407 .. .. 35 35
1645. 8 d. "The Three Graces" (I. Radovic) 85 85

408. Red Cross and Hands.

1975. Obligatory Tax. Red Cross Week.
1646. 408. 20 p. multicoloured .. 5 5

409. Liberation. Monument. 410. Garland-Flower.

1975. "Victory over Fascism" and Liberation of Yugoslavia. 30th Anniv.
1647. 409. 3 d. 20 multicoloured 25 25

1975. Youth Day. Forest Plants. Mult.
1648. 1 d. 20 Type 410 .. .. 10 10
1649. 2 d. 10 Touch-me-not .. 15 15
1650. 3 d. 20 Rose-mallow .. 25 25
1651. 5 d. Mourning Widow .. 35 35
1652. 6 d. Crocus 40 40
1653. 8 d. Rose-bay 75 75

411. Olympic Rings. 412. Canoeing.

1975. Obligatory Tax. Olympic Games Fund.
1654. 411. 10 p. multicoloured .. 5 5

1975. World Canoeing Championships, Macedonia.
1655. 412. 3 d. 20 multicoloured 25 20

413. "Ambush" (F. Quiquerez).

1975. Bosnia-Herzegovina Uprising. Cent.
1656. 413. 1 d. 20 multicoloured 12 10

414. "Earthquake in Skopje". 415. S. M. Ljubisa.

1975. Obligatory Tax. Solidarity Weeks.
1657. 414. 30 p, blk., blue & grey 5 5

1975. Yugoslav Writers.
1658. 415. 1 d. 20 black and lake 8 8
1659. – 2 d. 10 blk. and grn. 15 12
1660. – 3 d. 20 blk. & brown 25 20
1661. – 5 d. blk. & orange .. 35 30
1662. – 6 d. black and green 45 40
1663. – 8 d. black and blue .. 60 50
PORTRAITS: 2 d. 10 I. Prijatelj. 3 d. 20 J. Ignjatociv. 5 d. D. Jarnevic. 6 d. S. Corovic. 8 d. I. Brlic-Mazuranic.

416. "Young Lion".

1975. Children's Week "Joy of Europe" Meeting, Belgrade. Multicoloured.
1664. 3 d. 20 Type 416 .. .. 20 20
1665. 6 d. "Child in Pram" .. 65 50

417. Dove of Peace within "EUROPA".

1975. European Security and Co-operation Conference, Helsinki.
1666. 417. 3 d. 20 multicoloured 20 20
1667. 8 d. multicoloured .. 55 50

418. Red Cross and Map within "100".

1975. Yugoslav Red Cross. Cent. Mult.
1668. 1 d. 20 Type 418 .. .. 8 8
1669. 8 d. "Seeking Refuge" (people approaching Red Cross) 55 50

419. "Folk Kitchen" (D. Andrejevic-Kun).

1975. Yugoslav Art. Social Paintings. Mult.
1670. 1 d. 20 Type 419 .. .. 8 8
1671. 2 d. 10 "On the Doorstep" (V. Grdan) 15 15
1672. 3 d. 20 "The Drunken Coachload" (M. Detoni) (horiz.) 20 20
1673. 5 d. "Lunch" (T. Kralj) (horiz.) 35 35
1674. 6 d. "Waterwheel" (L. Licenoski) 40 40
1675. 8 d. "Justice" (lynching K. Hegedusic) 70 50

420. Diocletian's Palace, Split.

1975. European Architectural Heritage Year.
1676. 420. 1 d. 20 brown .. 10 8
1677. – 3 d. 20 black 20 20
1678. – 8 d. violet 55 55
DESIGNS—VERT. 3 d. 20 19th-century house, Ohrid. HORIZ. 8d. Gracanica Monastery, Kosovo.

421. Ski-jumping.

1976. Winter Olympic Games, Innsbruck.
1679. 421. 3 d. 20 blue 20 20
1680. – 8 d. lake 60 55
DESIGN: 8 d. Pairs figure-skating.

422. Red Flag.

1976. Red Flag Insurrection, Kragujevac. Cent.
1681. 422. 1 d. 20 red, mar. & bl. 10 8

423. S. Miletic.

1976. Svetozar Miletic (politician). 150th Birth Anniv.
1682. 423. 1 d. 20 green and grey 8 8

424. B. Stankovic.

1976. Boran Stankovic (Serbian writer). Birth Cent.
1683. 424. 1 d. 20 maroon & brn. 10 5

425. "King Matjaz". (sculpture).

1976. Europa. Multicoloured.
1684. 3 d. 20 Type 425 .. 25 20
1685. 8 d. 14th-century beaker 60 55

426. I. Canker.

1976. Ivan Canker (Slovenian writer). Birth Cent.
1686. 426. 1 d. 20 lilac and brown 10 5

427. Train crossing Viaduct.

1976. Opening of Belgrade-Bar Railway.

1687.	427.	3 d. 20 brown	25	20
1688.	–	8 d. blue	60	55

DESIGN: 8 d. Train crossing bridge (in other direction).

428. Dragonfly.

429. V. Nazor.

1976. Youth Day. Freshwater Fauna. Multicoloured.

1689.		1 d. 20 Type 428	10	5
1690.		2 d. 10 Winkle	15	12
1691.		3 d. 20 Rudd	25	20
1692.		5 d. Green frog	40	35
1693.		6 d. Ferruginous duck	45	40
1694.		8 d. Muskrat	60	55

1976. Vladimir Nazor (Croatian writer). Birth Cent.

1695.	429.	1 d. 20 blue and lilac	10	5

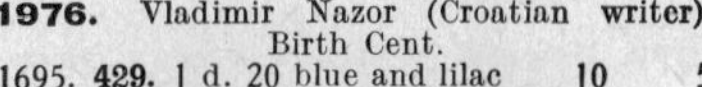

430. " Battle of Vucji Dol " (from journal " Eagle " of 1876).

1976. Montenegrin Liberation Wars. Centenary.

1696.	430.	1 d. 20 multicoloured	10	5

431. Aleksandrovac Water-jug.

1976. Yugoslav Pottery. Museum Pieces. Multicoloured.

1697.		1 d. 20 Type 431	10	5
1698.		2 d. 10 Ptuj pitcher	15	12
1699.		3 d. 20 Visnjica coffee-pot	25	20
1700.		5 d. Backi Breg pitcher	40	35
1701.		6 d. Vranestice goblet	45	40
1702.		8 d. Prizren jug	60	55

432. N. Tesla.

1976. Nikola Tesla (scientist). 120th Birth Anniv.

1703.	432.	5 d. blue and green	40	35

433. Long-jumping.

1976. Olympic Games, Montreal.

1704.	433.	1 d. 20 purple	10	5
1705.	–	3 d. 20 brown	25	20
1706.	–	5 d. brown	40	35
1707.	–	8 d. blue	60	55

DESIGNS: 3 d. 20 Handball. 5 d. Rifle-shooting. 8 d. Rowing.

434. Global Emblem.

1976. 5th Non-aligned Countries' Summit Conf., Colombo.

1708.	434.	4 d. 90 multicoloured	40	35

435. " Submarine ".

1976. Children's Week. " Joy of Europe " Meeting, Belgrade. Multicoloured.

1709.		4 d. 90 Type 435	40	35
1710.		8 d. " Children's Trains "	60	55

436. " Battle of the Montenegrins " (D. Jaksic).

437. P.M. Nenadovic.

1976. Yugoslav Art. Historical Paintings. Multicoloured.

1711.		1 d. 20 Type 436	10	5
1712.		2 d. 10 " Herzegovian Fugitives " (U. Predic)	15	12
1713.		3 d. 20 " Nikola Subic Zrinski at Siget " (O. Ivelovic) (horiz.)	25	20
1714.		5 d. " The Razlovci Uprising " (B. Lazeki) (horiz.)	40	35
1715.		6 d. " Enthronement of the Slovenian Duke at Gosposvetsko Field " (A. G. Kos) (horiz.)	45	40
1716.		8 d. " Breach of the Solun Front " (C. V. Stanojevic) (horiz.)	60	55

1976. No. 1203 surch.

1717.		1 d. on 85 p. plum	8	5

1977. P. M. Nenadovic (soldier and diplomat). Birth Bicent.

1718.	437.	4 d. 90 multicoloured	40	35

438. R. Zinifov.

1977. Rajko Zinifov (writer). Death Cent.

1719.	438.	1 d.50 brown and sepia	12	10

EXPRESS LETTER STAMP

CROATIA

1918. Express Letter stamp of Hungary optd. **HRVATSKA SHS ZURNO.**

E 84.	E 1.	2 f. olive and red	5	5

NEWSPAPER STAMPS

CROATIA

1918. Newspaper stamp of Hungary optd **HRVATSKA SHS.**

N83.	N 3.	2 f orange	5	5

N 1.

ILLUSTRATIONS British Commonwealth and all overprints and surcharges are FULL SIZE. Foreign Countries have been reduced to ¾-LINEAR.

1919. Imperf.

N 97.	N 1.	2 h. yellow	5	5

SLOVENIA

1919. Imperf.

N 150.	N 2.	2 v. grey	5	5
N 155.		2 v. blue	5	5
N 151.		4 v. grey	5	5
N 156.		4 v. blue	35	35
N 152.		6 v. grey	1·25	1·50
N 157a		6 v. blue	12·00	14·00
N 153.		10 v. grey	5	5
N 158.		10 v. blue	45	45
N 154.		30 v. grey	5	5

N 3.

N 4.

1920. Surch. as Type N 3 (2 to 6 p.) or Type N 4 (10 p. and 30 p.).

N 164.	N 2.	2 p. on 2 v. grey	25	25
N 169.		2 p. on 2 v. blue	5	5
N 165.		4 p. on 2 v. grey	25	25
N 170.		4 p. on 2 v. blue	5	5
N 166.		6 p. on 2 v. grey	40	40
N 171.		6 p. on 2 v. blue	5	5
N 167.		10 p. on 2 v. grey	65	65
N 172.		10 p. on 2 v. blue	12	12
N 168.		30 p. on 2 v. grey	65	65
N 173.		30 p. on 2 v. blue	20	20

POSTAGE DUE STAMPS.

BOSNIA AND HERZEGOVINA

ДРЖАВА С.Х.С.
БОСНА И
ХЕРЦЕГОВИНА

хелера
(D 1.)

КРАЉЕВСТВО
СРБА. ХРВАТА
И СЛОВЕНАЦА

ПОРТО

5 X
(D 2.)

1918. Postage Due stamps of Bosnia optd. as Type D 1 or **DRZAVA S.H.S. BOSNA I HERCEGOVINA HELERA.**

D 19.	D 2.	2 h. red	5	5
D 20.		4 h. red	25	50
D 21.		5 h. red	5	5
D 22.		6 h. red	35	25
D 23.		10 h. red	5	5
D 24.		15 h. red	2·75	2·25
D 25.		20 h. red	5	5
D 26.		25 h. red	25	25
D 27.		30 h. red	25	25
D 28.		40 h. red	10	10
D 29.		50 h. red	50	50
D 30.		1 k. blue	25	25
D 31.		3 k. blue	20	20

1919. "Eagle" type of Bosnia surch. as Type D 2 or **KRALJEVSTVO SRBA, HRVATA I SLOVENACA PORTO** and value.

D 50.	2.	2 h. on 35 h. blue	15	20
D 51.		5 h. on 45 h. blue	40	40
D 52.		10 h. on 10 h. red	5	5
D 53.		15 h. on 40 h. orange	12	15
D 54.		20 h. on 5 h. green	5	5
D 55.		25 h. on 20 h. pink	12	15
D 56.		30 h. on 30 h. brown	12	15
D 57.		1 k. on 50 h. purple	8	20
D 58.		3 k. on 25 h. blue	15	20

КРАЉЕВСТВО
СРБА, ХРВАТА
И СЛОВЕНАЦА
40

40 хелера 40
(D 3.)

1919. Postage Due stamps of Bosnia surch or optd. as Type D 3 or **KRALJEVSTVO SRBA HRVATA SLOVENACA** and value.

D 59.	D 1.	40 h. on 6 h. black, red and yellow	5	5
D 60.		50 h. on 8 h. black, red and yellow	5	5
D 61.		200 h. blk., red & grn.	2·50	2·25
D 62.		4 k. on 7 h. black, red and yellow	12	15

CROATIA

1919. Postage Due stamps of Hungary, with figures in red (except 50 f. in black), optd. **HRVATSKA SHS.**

D 85.	D 1.	1 f. green (No. D 190)	7·50	7·50
D 86.		2 f. green	85	85
D 87.		10 f. green	65	65
D 88.		12 f. green	38·00	38·00
D 89.		15 f. green	50	50
D 90.		20 f. green	50	50
D 91.		30 f. green	1·25	1·25
D 92.		50 f. green (No. D 177)	11·00	11·00

SLOVENIA

D 4.

1919.

D 150.	D 4.	5 v. red	5	5
D 151.		10 v. red	5	5
D 152.		20 v. red	5	5
D 153.		50 v. red	5	5
D 154.		1 k. blue	20	20
D 155.		5 k. blue	35	12
D 156.		10 k. blue	65	40

(D 5.)

(D 6.)

1920. Stamps of 1919 issue surch. as Types D 5 or D 6.

D 164.	6.	5 p. on 15 v. blue	5	5
D 165.		10 p. on 15 v. blue	50	50
D 166.		20 p. on 15 v. blue	12	8
D 167.		50 p. on 15 v. blue	5	5
D 168.	7.	1 d. on 30 v. pink (or red)	12	8
D 169.		3 d. on 30 v. pink (or red)	15	12
D 170.		8 d. on 30 v. pink (or red)	1·10	45

KINGDOM OF THE SERBS, CROATS AND SLOVENES

D 8. King Alexander I when Prince.

D 9.

1921.

D 182.	D 8.	10 on 5 p. green	20	5
D 183.		30 on 5 p. green	25	5

1921.

D 184.	D 9.	10 p. red	8	5
D 185.		30 p. green	20	5
D 197.		50 p. violet	8	5
D 187.		1 d. brown	25	5
D 188.		2 d. blue	30	5
D 189.		5 d. orange	2·25	5
D 190.		10 d. brown	9·50	15
D 191.		25 d. pink	38·00	1·00
D 192.		50 d. green	35·00	1·00

There are two issues in this type, differing in the lettering, etc.

1928. Surcharged **10**.

D 233.	D 9.	10 on 25 d. pink	5·00	25
D 234.		10 on 50 d. green	5·00	25

D 10.

(D 11.)

1931.

D 259.	D 10.	50 p. violet	5	5
D 260.		1 d. rose	5	5
D 261.		2 d. blue	5	5
D 262.		5 d orange	12	8
D 263.		10 d. brown	25	10

1933. Optd. with Type D 11

D 293.	D 9.	50 p violet	25	5
D 294a.		1 d brown	20	5
D 295b.		2 d. blue	40	5
D 296.		5 d. orange	1·10	12
D 297a.		10 d. brown	5·00	8

1933. Red Cross. As T 29, but inscr. "PORTO" in Latin and Cyrillic characters.

D 298.	29.	50 p. red and green	12	5

(a) REGIONAL ISSUES.

CROATIA.

1945. Zagreb issue. Croatian Postage Due stamps of 1943-44 surch. **DEMOKRATSKA FEDERATIVNA JUGOSLAVIJA KN 80 KN** and star.

RD 45.	D 2.	40 k. on 50 b. brn. and blue	5	5
RD 46.		60 k. on 1 k. brown and blue	5	5

RD 47. D 2. 80 k. on 2 k. brown and blue 10 10
RD 48. 100 k. on 5 k. brown and blue 12 12
RD 49. 200 k. on 6 k. brown and blue 20 20

MONTENEGRO

1945. Cetinje issue. National Poem issue of Italian Occupation surch as T R 4, with "PORTO" in addition.
RD 61. 10 l. on 5 c. violet .. £120 £120
RD 62. 20 l. on 5 l. red on brn. 38·00 38·00

SERBIA

1944. Senta issue. No. D 684 of Hungary optd. with a large Star, **8.X.1944** and "Yugoslavia" in Cyrillic characters, and surch. in addition.
RD 73. D 4. 10 (f.) on 2 f. brn. 30·00 30·00

(b) GENERAL ISSUES

D 12. D 13. D 14.

1944. Postage Due stamps of Serbia optd. in Cyrillic characters, as Type D 12.
D 487. 10 d. red 50 25
D 488. 20 d. blue 50 25

1945. (a) Value in black.
D 489. D 13. 2 d. brown .. 5 5
D 490. 3 d. violet 5 5
D 491. 5 d. green 5 5
D 492. 7 d. brown .. 5 5
D 493. 10 d. lilac .. 10 5
D 494. 20 d. blue .. 12 5
D 495. 30 d. green .. 25 10
D 496. 40 d. red .. 30 12

(b) Value in colour.
D 497. D 13. 1 d. green 8 5
D 498. 1 d. 50 blue .. 8 5
D 499. 2 d. red 15 5
D 500. 3 d. brown 30 10
D 501. 4 d. violet 40 12

1946.
D 527. D 14. 50 p. orange .. 5 5
D 528. 1 d. orange .. 5 5
D 724. 1 d. chocolate .. 10 5
D 529. 2 d. blue .. 8 5
D 725. 2 d. green .. 10 5
D 530. 3 d. green .. 15 5
D 531. 5 d. violet .. 15 5
D 726. 5 d. blue .. 20 5
D 532. 7 d. red .. 35 5
D 533. 10 d. pink .. 75 12
D 727. 10 d. red .. 50 5
D 534. 20 d. lake .. 1·00 35
D 1030. 20 d. violet .. 65 10
D 1031. 30 d. orange .. 1·40 10
D 1032. 50 d. blue .. 2·25 35
D 1033. 100 d. purple .. 4·75 65

1947. Red Cross. As No. 545, but with "PORTO" added. Colour changed.
D 546. 85. 50 p. green and red 15 5

1948. Red Cross. As No. 594, but inscr. "PORTO".
D 595. 105. 50 p. red and green 15 5

1949. Red Cross. As Type 111, but inscr. "PORTO".
D 617. 111. 50 p. purple & red 12 5

ФНРЈУГОСЛАВИЈА

FNR JUGOSLAVIJA

(D 15.) D 16. Map. D 17.

1950. Optd. with Type D 15.
D 637. D 13. 1 d. 50 p. blue .. 5 5
D 638. 3 d. brown .. 8 5
D 639. 4 d. violet .. 15 5

1950. Red Cross.
D 665. D 16. 50 p. brown & red 12 5

1951. Red Cross. Inscr. "PORTO".
D 703. 139. 50 p. green and red 12 5

1952. Red Cross.
D 741. D 17. 50 p. red and grey 15 5

1953. Red Cross. Inscr. "PORTO".
D 762. 159. 2 d. red and brown .. 25 5

1954. Red Cross. Inscr. "PORTO".
D 783. 163. 2 d. red and lilac .. 15 8

1955. Children's Week. Inscr. "PORTO".
D 802. 169. 2 d. green 15 5

1955. Red Cross. Inscr. "PORTO".
D 804. 171. 2 d. brn., claret & red 25 8

1956. Red Cross. Inscr. "PORTO".
D 820. 175. 2 d. green and red .. 15 5

1956. Children's Week. Inscr. "PORTO".
D 835. 179. 2 d. chocolate .. 15 5

1957. Red Cross. Inscr. "PORTO".
D 844. 181. 2 d. red, black, grey 15 5

1957. Children's Week. Inscr. "PORTO"
D 847. 187. 2 d. brown and blue 15 8

1958. Red Cross. Inscr. "PORTO".
D 879. 191. 2 d. multicoloured .. 25 8

D 18. Child with Toy.

1958. Children's Week.
D 913. D 18. 2 d. black and blue 15 5

1959. Red Cross. Inscr. "PORTO".
D 927. 202. 2 d. orange and red 15 5

1959. Children's Week. As T 207. Inscr. "PORTO".
D 947. 2 d. purple and yellow 15 5
DESIGN: Tree, cockerel and ears of wheat.

1960. Red Cross. Inscr. "PORTO".
D 956. 209. 2 d. purple and red 15 8

1960. Children's Week. As T 212. Inscr. "PORTO".
D 970. 2 d. slate-bl. (Young boy) 10 5

1961. Red Cross. Inscr. "PORTO". Perf. or Imperf.
D 982. 214. 2 d. multicoloured 8 5

1961. Children's Week. Inscr. "PORTO"
D 1020. 220. 2 d. green and sepia 12 5

1962. Red Cross. Inscr. "PORTO".
D 1043. 227. 5 d. red, brown-purple and blue .. 12 5

1963. Red Cross Cent. and Week. Inscr. "PORTO".
D 1074. 234. 5 d. red, purple and orange 15 5

OFFICIAL STAMPS

O 1.

1946.
O 540. O 1. 50 p. orange .. 20 5
O 541. 1 d. green .. 20 5
O 542. 1 d. 50 olive .. 35 5
O 543. 2 d. 50 red .. 35 5
O 544. 4 d. brown .. 50 5
O 545. 5 d. blue .. 75 5
O 546. 8 d. brown .. 1·25 15
O 547. 12 d. violet .. 1·50 30

YUNNANFU O1

Yunnanfu (formerly Yunnansen), the chief city of the Chinese province of Yunnan, had an Indo-Chinese Post Office from 1900 to 1922.

Stamps of Indo-China surcharged.

1903. "Tablet" key-type surch. **YUNNANSEN** and value in Chinese.
1. D. 1 c. black on blue .. 80 80
2. 2 c. brown on yellow .. 65 65
3. 4 c. claret on grey .. 65 55
4. 5 c. green 65 45
5. 10 c. red 65 45
6. 15 c. grey 75 60
7. 20 c. red on green .. 1·10 95
8. 25 c. blue .. .. 1·10 80
9. 30 c. brown on drab .. 1·10 80
10. 40 c. red on yellow .. 7·00 5·50
11. 50 c. red on rose .. 60·00 55·00
12. 50 c. brown on blue .. 25·00 24·00
13. 75 c. brown on orange .. 6·00 5·00
14. 1 f. olive .. .. 7·00 6·50
15. 5 f. mauve on lilac .. 12·00 12·00

1906. Surch. **Yunnan-Fou** and value in Chinese.
16. 1. 1 c. olive 25 25
17. 2 c. claret on yellow .. 20 20
18. 4 c. purple on blue .. 40 40
19. 5 c. green 40 40
20. 10 c. red 35 35
21. 15 c. brown on blue .. 50 50
22. 20 c. red on green .. 50 50
23. 25 c. blue 50 50
24. 30 c. brown on cream .. 60 60
25. 35 c. black on yellow .. 75 75
26. 40 c. black on grey .. 75 75
27. 50 c. brown on cream .. 75 75
28. D. 75 c. brown on orange .. 6·00 6·00
29. 1. 1 f. green .. .. 2·75 2·75
30. 2 f. brown on yellow .. 4·00 4·00
31. D. 5 f. mauve on lilac .. 9·00 9·00
32. 1. 10 f. red on green .. 10·00 10·00

1908. Native types surch. **YUNNANFOU** and value in Chinese.
33. 2. 1 c. black and brown .. 10 10
34. 2 c. black and brown .. 10 10
35. 4 c. black and blue .. 10 10
36. 5 c. black and green .. 20 20
37. 10 c. black and red .. 12 12
38. 15 c. black and violet .. 40 30
39. 3. 20 c. black and violet .. 50 40
40. 25 c. black and blue .. 60 50
41. 30 c. black and brown .. 60 50
42. 35 c. black and green .. 70 50
43. 40 c. black and brown .. 90 80
44. 50 c. black and red .. 90 80
45. 4. 75 c. black and orange .. 1·25 1·00
46. 1 f. black and red .. 2·00 1·75
47. 2 f. black and green .. 2·75 2·50
48. 5 f. black and blue .. 7·00 5·00
49. 10 f. black and violet .. 15·00 15·00

1919. As last, surch. in addition with value in figures and words.
50. 2. ⅖ c. on 1 c. blk. & brown 8 8
51. ⅘ c. on 2 c. blk. & brown 12 12
52. 1⅗ c. on 4 c. black & blue 20 20
53. 2 c. on 5 c. black & grn. 20 20
54. 4 c. on 10 c. black & red 12 12
55. 6 c. on 15 c. blk. & violet 15 15
56. 3. 8 c. on 20 c. blk. & violet 20 25
57. 10 c. on 25 c. blk. & blue 35 30
58. 12 c. on 30 c. blk. & brown 25 25
59. 14 c. on 35 c. blk. & grn. 55 55
60. 16 c. on 40 c. blk. & brn. 60 60
61. 20 c. on 50 c. blk. & red 20 20
62. 4. 30 c. on 75 c. blk. & orge. 55 55
63. 40 c. on 1 f. blk. & red .. 70 70
64. 80 c. on 2 f. blk. & grn. 1·25 1·25
65. 2 p. on 5 f. black & blue 6·00 6·00
66. 4 p. on 10 f. blk. & violet .. 1·75 1·75

ZAIRE O4

During 1971 the Congo Republic (Kinshasa) formerly Belgian Congo, became known as Zaire.

100 sengi = 1 (li) kuta. 100 (ma) kuta = 1 zaire.

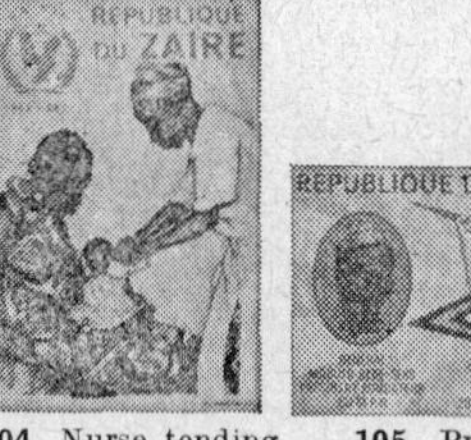

104. Nurse tending Child. 105. Pres. Mobutu, Memorial and Emblem.

1971. U.N.I.C.E.F. 25th Anniv. Multicoloured.
788. 4 k. Type 104 .. .. 10 10
789. 14 k. Zaire Republic on map of Africa 30 30
790. 17 k. Child in African village 40 40

1972. Revolution. Fifth Anniv.
791. 105. 4 k. multicoloured .. 10 10
792. 14 k. multicoloured .. 30 30
793. 22 k. multicoloured .. 55 55

106. Arms. 107. Pres. Mobutu.

1972.
794. 106. 10 s. orange and black 5 5
795. 40 s. blue and black 5 5
796. 50 s. yellow and black 5 5
797. 107. 1 k. multicoloured .. 5 5
798. 2 k. multicoloured .. 5 5
799. 3 k. multicoloured .. 5 5
800. 4 k. multicoloured .. 8 5
801. 5 k. multicoloured .. 10 8
802. 6 k. multicoloured .. 12 8
803. 8 k. multicoloured .. 15 10
804. 9 k. multicoloured .. 20 12
805. 10 k. multicoloured .. 20 12
806. 14 k. multicoloured .. 30 20
807. 17 k. multicoloured .. 40 25
808. 20 k. multicoloured .. 45 30
809. 50 k. multicoloured .. 1·10 65
810. 100 k. multicoloured .. 2·25 1·40

108. Inga Dam.

1973. Inga Dam. Completion of 1st Stage.
811. 108. 0.04 z. multicoloured 8 8
812. 0.14 z. multicoloured 30 25
813. 0.18 z. multicoloured 70 55

1973. As T 107 but face values in Zaires.
814. 0.01 z. multicoloured .. 5 5
815. 0.02 z. multicoloured .. 5 5
816. 0.03 z. multicoloured .. 8 5
817. 0.04 z. multicoloured .. 10 5
818. 0.10 z. multicoloured .. 20 15
819. 0.14 z. multicoloured .. 30 25

109. Africa on World Map.

1973. 3rd International Fair, Kinshasa.
820. 109. 0.04 z. multicoloured 10 8
821. 0.07 z. multicoloured 15 12
822. 0.18 z. multicoloured 45 35

110. Emblem on Hand.

1973. International Criminal Police Organization (Interpol). 50th Anniv.
823. 110. 0.06 z. multicoloured 15 8
824. 0.14 z. multicoloured 35 25

111. Leopard with Football on Globe.

1974. World Cup Football Championships, Munich.
825. 111. 1 k. multicoloured .. 5 5
826. 2 k. multicoloured .. 5 5
827. 3 k. multicoloured .. 5 5
828. 4 k. multicoloured .. 8 5
829. 5 k. multicoloured .. 10 8
830. 14 k. multicoloured .. 30 20

112. Muhamed Ali and George Foreman.

1974. World Heavyweight Boxing Title Fight, Kinshasa.
831. 112. 1 k. multicoloured .. 5 5
832. 4 k. multicoloured .. 8 5
833. 6 k. multicoloured .. 12 10
834. 14 k. multicoloured .. 30 20
835. 20 k. multicoloured .. 45 35

1975. World Heavyweight Boxing Title Fight, Kinshasa. Optd. with amended date **25-9-74.**
836. 112. 1 k. multicoloured .. 5 5
837. 4 k. multicoloured .. 8 5
838. 6 k. multicoloured .. 12 10
839. 14 k. multicoloured .. 30 20
840. 20 k. multicoloured .. 45 35

Nos. 836/40 differ from Type 112 by having the face values expressed as decimals of the zaire.

113. Okapis.

1975. Virunga National Park. 50th Anniv.
841. 113. 1 k. multicoloured .. 5 5
842. 2 k. multicoloured .. 5 5
843. 3 k. multicoloured .. 10 8
844. 4 k. multicoloured .. 12 10
845. 5 k. multicoloured .. 15 12

114. Female Judge with Barristers.

1975. Int. Women's Year.
863. 114. 1 k. multicoloured .. 5 5
864. 2 k. multicoloured .. 5 5
865. 4 k. multicoloured .. 12 10
866. 14 k. multicoloured .. 45 40

115. Waterfall. **116.** Sozacom Building.

1975. 12th U.C.I.N. General Assembly.
867. 115. 1 k. multicoloured .. 5 5
868. 2 k. multicoloured .. 5 5
869 3 k. multicoloured .. 10 8
870. 4 k. multicoloured .. 12 10
871. 5 k. multicoloured .. 15 12

1976. "New Regime". Multicoloured.
872. 1 k. Type 116 .. 5 5
873. 2 k. Siderma Maluku Industrial Complex (horiz.).. 5 5
874. 3 k. Flour-mill, Matadi .. 10 8
875. 4 k. Women parachutists (horiz.) .. 12 10
876. 8 k. Pres. Mobutu with Mao Tse-Tung 25 20
877. 10 k. Soldiers clearing vegetation along the Salongo (horiz.) .. 35 30
878. 14 k. Pres. Mobutu addressing U.N. General Assembly, 4 October 1973 (horiz.) 45 40
879. 15 k. Rejoicing crowd .. 50 45

117. Pende Statuette.

1977. Zaire Masks and Statuettes. Multicoloured.
880. 2 k. Type 117 .. .. 5 5
881. 4 k. Type 117 .. .. 12 10
882. 5 k. Tshokwe mask .. 15 12
883. 7 k. As 5 k. .. 25 20
884. 10 k. Suku mask .. 35 30
885. 14 k. As 10 k. .. 45 40
886. 15 k. Kongo statuette .. 50 45
887. 18 k. As 15 k. 60 55
888. 20 k. Kuba mask.. .. 65 60
889. 25 k. As 20 k. 85 80

OFFICIAL STAMPS

O 1.

1975. Nos. 794/810 opt. **SP.**
O 846. 106. 10 s. orange & black 5 5
O 847. 40 s. blue and black 5 5
O 848. 50 s. yellow & black 5 5
O 849. 107. 1 k. multicoloured.. 5 5
O 850. 2 k. multicoloured.. 5 5
O 851. 3 k. multicoloured.. 10 10
O 852. 4 k. multicoloured.. 12 12
O 853. 5 k. multicoloured.. 15 15
O 854. 6 k. multicoloured.. 20 20
O 855. 8 k. multicoloured.. 25 25
O 856. 9 k. multicoloured.. 30 30
O 857. 10 k. multicoloured 35 35
O 858. 14 k. multicoloured 45 45
O 859. 17 k. multicoloured 55 55
O 860. 20 k. multicoloured 65 65
O 861. 50 k. multicoloured 1·60 1·60
O 862. 100 k. multicoloured 3·25 3·25

ZAMBEZIA O3

Formerly administered by the Zambezia Co. This district of Portuguese E. Africa was later known as Quelimane and is now part of Mozambique.

1894. "Figures" key -type inscr. "ZAMBEZIA".
1. R. 5 r. orange 12 12
2. 10 r. mauve 15 15
3. 15 r. brown 35 30
4. 20 r. lilac 35 30
12. 25 r. green 60 50
13. 50 r. blue 60 50
14. 75 r. red .. .. 1·60 1·50
15. 80 r. green .. .. 1·10 90
8. 100 r. brown on buff .. 80 70
16. 150 r. red on rose .. 1·40 1·25
17. 200 r. blue on blue .. 1·40 1·25
18. 300 r. blue on brown .. 2·50 1·75

1898. "King Carlos" key-type inscr. "ZAMBEZIA".
20. S. 2½ r. grey 15 10
21. 5 r. orange 15 10
22. 10 r. green 15 10
23 15 r. brown 40 35
55. 15 r. green 40 30
24. 20 r. lilac 35 25
25. 25 r. green 35 25
56. 25 r. red 25 20
26. 50 r. blue 40 30
57. 50 r. brown 90 80
58. 65 r. blue .. .. 2·00 1·75
27. 75 r. red .. .. 1·75 1·60
59. 75 r. purple 90 60
28. 80 r. mauve .. .. 1·25 1·00
29. 100 r. blue on blue .. 50 50
60. 115 r. brown on pink .. 1·60 1·40
61. 130 r. brown on yellow .. 1·60 1·40
30. 150 r. brown on yellow .. 1·25 1·00
31. 200 r. purple on pink .. 1·25 1·00
32. 300 r. blue on pink .. 1·75 1·00
62. 400 r. blue on yellow .. 2·00 1·60
33. 500 r. black on blue .. 2·00 1·75
34. 700 r. mauve on yellow .. 2·50 1·90

1902. Surch.
63. S. 50 r. on 65 r. blue .. 90 80
35. R. 65 r. on 10 r. mauve .. 1·50 1·25
36. 65 r. on 15 r. brown .. 1·50 1·25
37. 65 r. on 20 r. lilac.. .. 1·50 1·25
38. 65 r. on 300 r. blue on brn. 1·50 1·25
40. 115 r. on 5 r. orange .. 1·50 1·25
41. 115. r. on 25 r. green .. 1·50 1·25
42. 115 r. on 80 r. green .. 1·50 1·25
46. V. 130 r. on 2½ r. brown .. 1·50 1·25
43. R. 130 r. on 75 r. red .. 1·75 1·25
45. 130 r. on 150 r. red on rose 1·50 1·25
47. 400 r. on 50 r. blue .. 50 40
49. 400 r. on 100 r. brn. on buff 50 40
50. 400 r. on 200 r. blue on bl. 50 40

1902. 1898 issue optd. **PROVISORIO.**
51. S. 15 r. brown 40 30
52. 25 r. blue 40 30
53. 50 r. blue 40 30
54. 75 r. red .. .. 1·00 70

1911. 1898 issue optd. **REPUBLICA.**
64. S. 2½ r. grey 15 12
65. 5 r. orange 15 12
66. 10 r. green 15 12
67. 15 r. green 15 12
68. 20 r. lilac 15 12
69. 25 r. red 45 15
108. 25 r. green .. .. 2·75 2·40
70. 50 r. brown 15 12
71. 75 r. purple 20 15
72. 100 r. blue on blue .. 20 15
73. 115 r. brown on pink .. 20 15
74. 130 r. brown on yellow .. 20 15
75. 200 r. purple on pink .. 20 15
76. 400 r. blue on cream .. 35 25
77. 500 r. black on blue .. 35 25
78. 700 r. mauve on yellow .. 35 25

1914. 1898 issue optd **PROVISORIO** and **REPUBLICA.**
94. S. 50 r. blue 12 10
81. 75 r red 25 15

1914. Provisionals of 1902 optd. **REPUBLICA.**
95. S. 50 r. on 65 r. blue .. 60 50
96. R. 115 r. on 5 r. orange .. 12 10
97. 115 r. on 25 r. green .. 12 10
98. 115 r. on 80 r. green .. 12 10
99. V. 130 r. on 2½ r. brown .. 12 10
100. R. 130 r. on 75 r. red .. 12 10
102. 130 r. on 150 r. red on rose 12 10
90. 400 r. on 50 r. blue .. 50 30
92. 400 r. on 100 r. brn. on buff 50 30
93. 400 r. on 200 r. bl. on blue 50 30

NEWSPAPER STAMP

1893. "Newspaper" key-type inscr. "ZAMBEZIA".
N 1. V. 2½ r. brown 15 12

ZAMBIA BC

Formerly Northern Rhodesia, attained independence on 24th October, 1964, and changed its name to Zambia.

1968. 100 ngwee = 1 kwacha.

1. Pres. Kaunda and Victoria Falls. **3.** Tobacco Worker.

2. Maize—Farmer and Silo.

1964. Independence.
91. 1. 3d. sepia, green and blue.. 5 5
92. – 6d. violet and yellow .. 10 10
93. – 1s. 3d. red, blk., sep. & orge. 20 20
DESIGNS—HORIZ. 6d. College of Further Education, Lusaka. VERT. 1s. 3d. Barotse Dancer.

1964.
94. 2. ½d. red, black and green 5 5
95. – 1d. brown, black & blue 5 5
96. – 2d. red, brown & orange 5 5
97. – 3d. black and red .. 5 5
98. – 4d. black, brown & orge. 5 5
99. – 6d. orange, brown and bluish green 8 5
100. – 9d. red, black and blue.. 12 10
101. – 1s. black, bistre & blue.. 20 10
102. 3. 1s. 3d. red, yell., blk. & bl. 25 15
103. – 2s. blue, blk., brn. & orge. 30 15
104. – 2s. 6d. black and yellow 40 35
105. – 5s. black, yellow & green 70 65
106. – 10s. black and orange .. 2·00 1·25
107. – £1 black, brown, yell. & red 3·50 3·50
DESIGNS—As T 2: VERT. 1d. Health—Radiographer. 2d. Chinyau Dancer. 3d. Cotton-picking. HORIZ. 4d. Angoni Bull. As T 3: HORIZ. 6d. Communications, Old and New. 9d. Zambezi Sawmills and Redwood Flower. 1s. Fishing at Mpulungu. 2s. 6d. Luangwa Game Reserve. 5s. Education — Student. 10 s. Copper Mining. VERT. 2s. Tonga Basket-making. £1, Makishi Dancer.

4. I.T.U. Emblem and Symbols.

1965. I.T.U. Cent.
108. 4. 6d. violet and gold .. 10 10
109. 2s. 6d. grey and gold .. 30 35

5. I.C.Y. Emblem.

1965. Int. Co-operation Year.
110. 5. 3d. turquoise and gold .. 8 8
111. 1s. 3d. blue and gold .. 20 25

6. State House, Lusaka.

1965. Independence. 1st Anniv. Multicoloured.
112. 3d. Type 6 .. .. 5 5
113. 6d. Fireworks, Independence Stadium 8 8
114. 1s. 3d. Clematopsis (vert.) 20 25
115. 2s. 6d. "Tithonia diversifolia" (vert.) .. 35 45

7. W.H.O. Building and U.N. Flag.

1966. W.H.O. Headquarters, Geneva. Inaug.
116. 7. 3d. brown, gold and blue 5 5
117. 1s. 3d. violet, gold & blue 25 25

8. University Building.

1966. Opening of Zambia University.
118. 8. 3d. green and bronze .. 5 5
119. 1s. 3d. violet and bronze 20 20

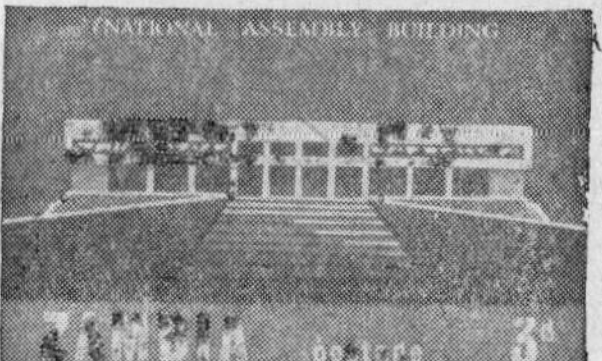

9. National Assembly Building.

1967. National Assembly Building. Inaug.
120. 9. 3d. black and gold .. 5 5
121. 6d. green and gold .. 8 8

10. Airport Scene.

1967. Lusaka Int. Airport. Opening.
122. 10. 6d. blue and bronze .. 8 8
123. 2s. 6d. brown & bronze 40 40

11. Youth Service Badge. **12.** Lusaka Cathedral.

1967. National Development.
124. 11. 4d. black, red and gold 5 5
125. – 6d. black, gold and blue 8 10
126. – 9d. black, blue & silver 12 15
127. – 1s. multicoloured .. 15 20
128. – 1s. 6d. multicoloured .. 25 30
DESIGNS—HORIZ. 6d. "Co-operative Farming". 1s. 6d. Road link with Tanzania. VERT. 9d. "Communications". 1s. Coalfields.

1968. Decimal Currency.
129. 12. 1 n. multicoloured .. 5 5
130. – 2 n. multicoloured .. 5 5
131. – 3 n. multicoloured .. 8 8
132. – 5 n. brown and bronze 10 10
133. – 8 n. multicoloured .. 15 15
134. – 10 n. multicoloured .. 20 15
135. – 15 n. multicoloured .. 25 25
136. – 20 n. multicoloured .. 35 30
137. – 25 n. multicoloured .. 40 35
138. – 50 n. brown, orange and bronze 85 75

139. – 1 k. blue and bronze .. 1·75 1·50
140. – 2 k. black and bronze.. 3·25 3·00

DESIGNS—As T 12—VERT. 2 n. Baobab Tree. 5 n. National Museum, Livingstone. 8 n. Vimbuza Dancer. 10 n. Tobacco picking. HORIZ. 3 n. Zambia Airways Jetliner. LARGER (32×26 mm.): 15 n. "Nudaurelia zambesina" (butterfly). 1 k. Kafue Railway Bridge. 2 k. Eland. (26×32 mm.): 20 n. Crowned Cranes. 25 n. Angoni warrior. 50 n. Chokwe Dancer.

13. Ndola on Outline of Zambia.

1968. Trade Fair, Ndola.
141. **13.** 15 n green and gold .. 25 30

14. Human Rights Emblem and Heads.

1968. Human Rights Year
142. **14.** 3 n. blue, violet and gold 12 2

15. W.H.O. Emblem.

1968. World Health Organization. 20th Anniv.
143. **15.** 10 n. gold and violet .. 20 20

16. Group of Children.

1968. U.N.I.C.E.F. 21st Anniv.
144. **16.** 25 n. black, gold & blue 45 55

17. Copper Miner.

1969. Int. Labour Organisation. 50th Anniv.
145. **17.** 3 n. gold and violet .. 8 8
146. – 25 n. yellow, gold & brn. 45 50

DESIGN—HORIZ. 25 n. Poling a furnace.

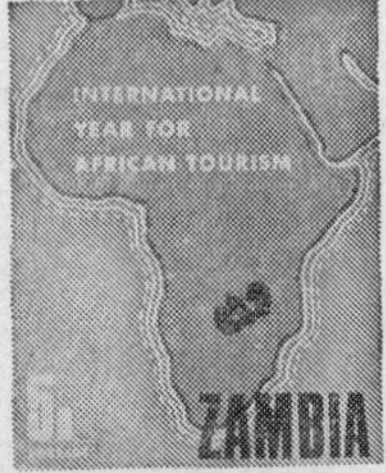

18. Zambia outlined on Map of Africa.

1969. Int. African Tourist Year. Multicoloured.
147. 5 n. Type **18** 10 10
148. 10 n. Defassa Waterbuck, Kafue National Park .. 15 15
149. 15 n. Golden Perch, Kasaba Bay 25 25
150. 25 n. Carmine Bee-Eater, Luangwa Valley .. 45 45

Nos. 148/50 are horiz.

19. Satellite "Nimbus III" orbiting the Earth.

1970. World Meteorological Day.
151. **19.** 15 n. multicoloured .. 30 25

20. Woman collecting Water from Well.

1970. Preventive Medicine.
152. **20.** 3 n. multicoloured .. 8 8
153. – 15 n. multicoloured .. 25 25
154. – 25 n. blue, rosine & sepia 45 45

DESIGNS: 15 n. Child on scales. 25 n. Child being immunised.

21. Mural (Gabriel Ellison).

1970. Conference of Non-Aligned Nations.
155. **21.** 15 n. multicoloured .. 25 30

22. Ceremonial Axe.

1970. Traditional Crafts. Multicoloured.
156. 3 n. Type **22** 8 8
157. 5 n. Clay smoking-pipe bowl 10 10
158. 15 n. Makishi mask .. 25 30
159. 25 n. Kuomboka ceremony 45 45

SIZES-HORIZ. 5 n. as T **22**. 25 n. 72×19 mm. VERT. 15 n. 30×47 mm.

23. Dag Hammarskjoeld and U.N. General Assembly.

1971. Dag Hammarskjoeld. 10th Death Anniv. Multicoloured.
161. 4 n. Type **23** 8 8
162. 10 m. Tail of aircraft 15 15
163. 15 n. Dove of Peace .. 25 25
164. 25 n. Memorial tablet .. 45 45

24. Red-breasted Bream.

1971. Fish. Multicoloured.
165. 4 n. Type **24** 8 8
166. 10 n. Green-headed Bream 15 20
167. 15 n. Tiger fish 25 30

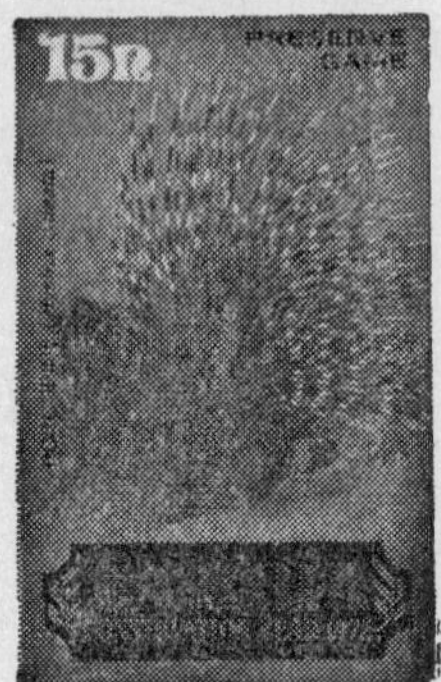

25. Porcupine.

1972. Conservation Year (1st issue). Multicoloured.
168. 4 n. Cheetah (horiz.) .. 8 8
169. 10 n. Lechwe (antelope) (horiz.) 15 20
170. 15 n. Type **25** 25 25
171. 25 n. Elephant 40 45

Nos. 168/9 are size 58×21 mm.

1972. Conservation Year (2nd issue). As T **25**. Multicoloured.
172. 4 n. Soil conservation .. 8 8
173. 10 n. Forestry 20 20
174. 15 n. Water 25 30
175. 25 n. Maize 45 45

Nos. 174/5 are size 58×21 mm.

26. Zambian Flowers.

1972. Conservation Year (3rd series). Multicoloured.
177. 4 n. Type **26** 8 8
178. 10 n. Citrus Swallowtail Butterfly 20 20
179. 15 n. Bees 25 25
180. 25 n. Red Locusts .. 45 45

27. Mary and Joseph.

1972. Christmas. Multicoloured.
181. 4 n. Type **27** 8 8
182. 9 n. Mary, Joseph and Jesus 15 15
183. 15 n. Mary, Joseph and the shepherds.. .. 25 25
184. 25 n. The Three Wise Men 45 45

28. "Oudenodon" and "Rubidgea".

1973. Zambian Prehistoric Animals. Mult.
185. 4 n. Type **28** 10 10
186. 9 n. Broken Hill Man .. 15 15
187. 10 n. "Zambiasaurus" .. 20 25
188. 15 n. "Luangwa drysdalli" 35 35
189. 25 n. "Glossopteris" .. 50 50

Nos. 186/9 are smaller (38×21 mm.) and show fossils.

29. "Dr. Livingstone I Presume".

1973. Livingstone's Death Cent. Mult.
190. 3 n. Type **29** 8 8
191. 4 n. Scripture Lesson .. 8 8
192. 9 n. Victoria Falls .. 15 15
193. 10 n. Scattering slavers .. 20 20
194. 15 n. Healing the sick .. 30 30
195. 25 n. Burial place of Livingstone's heart 45 50

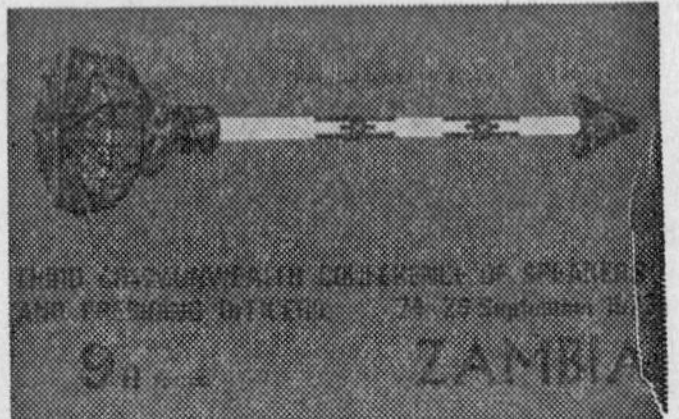

30. Parliamentary Mace.

1973. 3rd Commonwealth Conf., of Speakers and Presiding Officers, Lusaka.
196. **30.** 9 n. multicoloured .. 15 15
197. 15 n. multicoloured .. 25 30
198. 25 n. multicoloured .. 45 50

31. Inoculation.

1973. W.H.O. 25th Anniv. Multicoloured.
199. 4 n. Mother washing baby (vert.) .. .. .. 3·50 1·25
200. 9 n. Nurse weighing baby (vert.) 20 20
201. 10 n. Type **31** 25 25
202. 15 n. Child eating meal .. 30 35

32. U.N.I.P. Flag.

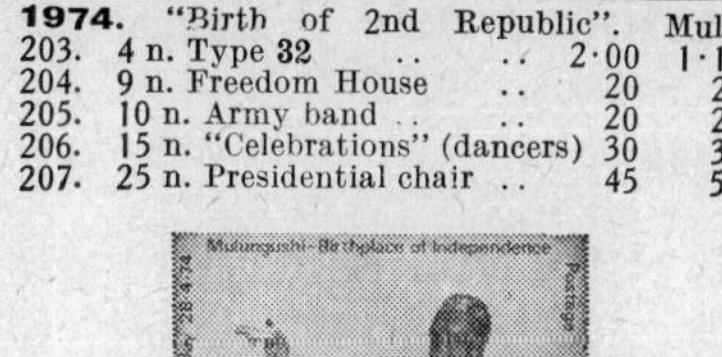

1974. "Birth of 2nd Republic". Mult.

203. 4 n. Type **32** 2·00 1·10
204. 9 n. Freedom House 20 20
205. 10 n. Army band 20 20
206. 15 n. "Celebrations" (dancers) 30 35
207. 25 n. Presidential chair 45 50

33. President Kaunda at Mulungushi.

1974. President Kaunda's 50th Birthday. Multicoloured.

208. 4 n. Type **33** 8 8
209. 9 n. President's former residence 15 15
210. 15 n. President holding Independence flame 25 30

34. Nakambala Sugar Estate.

1974. Independence. Multicoloured.

211. 3 n. Type **34** 8 8
212. 4 n. Local market 8 8
213. 9 n. Kapiri glass factory 15 15
214. 10 n. Kafue hydro-electric scheme 20 20
215. 15 n. Kafue hook bridge 25 30
216. 25 n. Non-aligned Conference, Lusaka (1970) 40 45

35. Mobile Post-van.

1974. U.P.U. Centenary. Multicoloured.

218. 4 n. Type **35** 8 8
219. 9 n. Aeroplane on tarmac 15 15
220. 10 n. Chipata Post Office 20 20
221. 15 n. Modern training centre 25 30

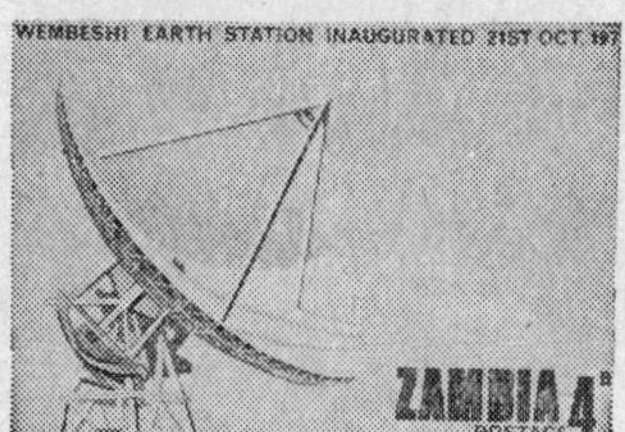

36. Dish Aerial.

1974. Opening of Mwembeshi Earth Station Multicoloured.

222. 4 n. Type **36** 8 8
223. 9 n. View at dawn 15 15
224. 15 n. View at dusk 25 30
225. 25 n. Aerial view 40 45

37. Rhinoceros and Calf.

38. Independence Monument.

1974. Multicoloured.

226. 1 n. Type **37** 5 5
227. 2 n. Guinea-fowl 5 5
228. 3 n. National Dancing Troupe 5 5
229. 4 n. Fish Eagle 5 5
230. 5 n. Knife-edge Bridge 8 8
231. 8 n. Sitatunga (antelope) 10 12
232. 9 n. Elephant, Kasaba Bay 12 12
233. 10 n. Giant Pangolin 12 15
234. 15 n. Type **38** 20 25
235. 20 n. Harvesting groundnuts 25 30
236. 25 n. Tobacco-growing 35 40
237. 50 n. Flying Doctor service 60 70
238. 1 k. Lady Ross's Turaco 1·25 1·50
239. 2 k. Village scene 2·75 3·00

Nos. 234/239 are as T **38**.

39. Map of Namibia.

1975. Namibia Day.

240. **39.** 4 n. green and yellow 8 8
241. 9 m. blue and green 15 15
242. 15 n. orange & yellow 25 25
243. 25 n. red and orange 40 45

40. Erection of Sprinkler Irrigation.

1975. Int. Commission on Irrigation and Drainage. Silver Jubilee. Multicoloured.

244. 4 n. Type **40** 8 8
245. 9 n. Sprinkler irrigation 15 15
246. 15 n. Furrow irrigation 40 45

41. Mutondo.

1976. World Forestry Day. Multicoloured.

247. 3 n. Type **41** 8 8
248. 4 n. Mukunyu 8 8
249. 9 n. Mukusi 15 15
250. 10 n. Mopane 20 20
251. 15 n. Musuku 25 25
252. 25 n. Mukwa 40 45

42. Passenger Train.

1976. Tanzania-Zambia Railway. Opening Multicoloured.

253. 4 n. Type **42** 8 8
254. 9 n. Copper exports 15 20
255. 15 n. Machinery imports 25 30
256. 25 n. Goods train 40 45

43. Kayowe Dance.

1977. Second World Black and African Festival of Arts and Culture, Nigeria. Multicoloured.

258. 4 n. Type **43** 8 8
259. 9 n. Lilombola dance 15 20
260. 15 n. Initiation ceremony 25 30
261. 25 n. Munkhwele dance 40 45

POSTAGE DUE STAMPS

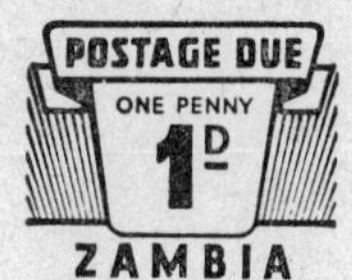

D 1.

1964.

D 11. **D 1.** 1d. orange 5 8
D 12. 2d. blue 5 8
D 13. 3d. lake 5 8
D 14. 4d. ultramarine 8 10
D 15. 6d. purple 12 15
D 16. 1s. green 25 35

ZANZIBAR BC

A Br. Protectorate consisting of several islands off the coast of Tanganyika. E. Africa. Independent in 1963 and a republic within the Br. Commonwealth in 1964. The "United Republic of Tanganyika and Zanzibar" was proclaimed in July, 1964, and the country was later renamed Tanzania. Separate issues for Zanzibar ceased on 1st Jan., 1968, and Tanzania stamps became valid for the whole country

1895. **16 annas = 1 rupee.**
1908. **100 cents = 1 rupee.**
1936. **100 cents = 1 shilling.**

1895. Stamps of India (Queen Victoria) optd. **Zanzibar.**

3. **14.** $\frac{1}{2}$ a. blue-green 90 1·25
4. 1 a. purple 1·00 1·10
5. $1\frac{1}{2}$ a. brown 90 90
6. – 2 a. blue 75 75
8. – $2\frac{1}{2}$ a. green 1·25 1·00
10. – 3 a. orange 1·40 2·50
12. – 4 a. green (No. 96) 2·25 2·75
13. – 6 a. brown (No. 80) 2·50 3·00
15. – 8 a. mauve 3·00 3·50
16. – 12 a. purple on red 3·00 2·50
17. – 1 r. grey 20·00 24·00
18. **26.** 1 r. green and red 3·50 4·00
19. **27.** 2 r. red and orange 7·00 8·00
20. 3 r. brown and green 7·00 7·50
21. 5 r. biue and violet 7·00 7·50

1895. Nos. 4/6 surch. **$2\frac{1}{2}$.**

23. $2\frac{1}{2}$ on 1 a. purple 20·00 14·00
22. $2\frac{1}{2}$ on $1\frac{1}{2}$ a. brown 5·00 5·00
26. $2\frac{1}{2}$ on 2 a. blue 6·50 6·50

1896. Stamps of British East Africa (Queen Victoria) optd. **Zanzibar.**

41. **2.** $\frac{1}{2}$ a. green 7·00 6·50
42. 1 a. red 7·00 6·50
43. $2\frac{1}{2}$ a. blue 16·00 13·00
44. $4\frac{1}{2}$ a. yellow 6·50 6·50
45. 5 a. brown 7·00 7·00
46. $7\frac{1}{2}$ a. mauve 7·50 7·50

1. Sultan Seyyid Hamed-bin-Thwain.

3. Sultan Seyyid Hamoud-bin-Mahommed bin Said.

1896. The Rupee values are larger.

178. **1.** $\frac{1}{2}$ a. green and red 15 15
179. 1 a. blue and red 25 15
180. 2 a. brown and red 30 35
181. $2\frac{1}{2}$ a. blue and red 30 25
182. 3 a. grey and red 45 45
183. 4 a. green and red 45 50
184. $4\frac{1}{2}$ a. orange and red 70 40
185. 5 a. brown and red 85 70
167. $7\frac{1}{2}$ a. mauve and red 75 75
168. 8 a. olive and red 65 65
169. – 1 r. blue and red 2·50 3·00
171. – 2 r. green and red 3·00 3·00
172. – 3 r. purple and red 6·50 5·00
173. – 4 r. red 6·50 5·50
174. – 5 r. brown and red 10·00 7·00

1896. Surch. **$2\frac{1}{2}$.**

175. **1.** $2\frac{1}{2}$ on 4 a. green and red 6·50 6·50

1899. The Rupee values are larger.

188. **3.** $\frac{1}{2}$ a. green and red 12 15
189. 1 a. blue and red 30 15
190. 1 a. red 25 12
191. 2 a. brown and red 30 20
192. $2\frac{1}{2}$ a. blue and red 30 25
193. 3 a. grey and red 50 70
194. 4 a. green and red 45 65
195. $4\frac{1}{2}$ a. orange and red 1·10 1·10
196. $4\frac{1}{2}$ a. black and red 1·25 1·40
197. 5 a. brown and red 80 90
198. $7\frac{1}{2}$ a. mauve and red 1·10 1·60
199. 8 a. olive and red 95 1·60
200. – 1 r. blue and red 6·50 6·50
201. – 2 r. green and red 6·50 6·50
202. – 3 r. purple and red 6·50 6·50
203. – 4 r. red 10·00 10·00
204. – 5 r. brown and red 12·00 12·00

1904. Surch. in words.

205. **3.** 1 on $4\frac{1}{2}$ a. orange and red 70 1·00
206. 1 on $4\frac{1}{2}$ a. black and red 2·00 2·50
207. 2 on 4 a. green and red 6·50 6·50
208. $2\frac{1}{2}$ on $7\frac{1}{2}$ a. mauve and red 6·00 6·50
209. $2\frac{1}{2}$ on 8 a. olive and red 7·00 8·00

5. Monogram of Sultan Seyyid **Ali bin** Hamoud bin Naherud.

1904. The Rupee values are larger.

210. **5.** $\frac{1}{2}$ a. green 15 10
211. 1 a. red 15 8
212. 2 a. brown 40 35
213. $2\frac{1}{2}$ a. blue 40 25
214. 3 a. grey 50 55
215. 4 a. green 70 65
216. $4\frac{1}{2}$ a. black 1·00 1·00
217. 5 a. brown 1·10 1·10
218. $7\frac{1}{2}$ a. mauve 1·75 1·75
219. 8 a. olive 1·25 1·25
220. 1 r. blue and red 4·00 3·00
221. – 2 r. green and red 5·50 6·00
222. – 3 r. violet and red 13·00 13·00
223. – 4 r. claret and red 15·00 15·00
224. – 5 r. brown and red 18·00 20·00

7.

9. Sultan Ali Hamoud.

8.

10. View of Port.

1908.

No.	Type	Description	Unused	Used
225.	7.	1 c. grey	8	8
226.		3 c. green	10	8
227.		6 c. red	15	8
228.		10 c. brown	60	85
229.		12 c. violet	50	25
230.	8.	15 c. blue	55	45
231.		25 c. brown	1·00	65
232.		50 c. green	1·60	1·40
233.		75 c. black	2·25	2·25
234.	9.	1 r. green	2·75	2·40
235.		2 r. violet	6·00	6·00
236.		3 r. brown	9·50	9·50
237.		4 r. red	13·00	13·00
238.		5 r. blue	15·00	15·00
239.	10.	10 r. green and brown	45·00	45·00
240.		20 r. black and green	£100	£100
241.		30 r. black and brown	£180	£170
242.		40 r. black and orange	£450	
243.		50 r. black and mauve	£400	
244.		100 r. black and blue	£600	
245.		200 r. black and blue	£950	

11. Sultan Kalif bin Harub. 12. Native Craft.

13. Native Craft.

1913.

No.	Type	Description	Unused	Used
246.	11.	1 c. grey	8	8
247.		3 c. green	8	8
278.		3 c. orange	8	8
279.		4 c. green	20	25
263a.		6 c. red	8	8
281.		6 c. purple on blue	15	8
264.		8 c. purple on yellow	25	30
249.		10 c. brown	25	25
265.		10 c. green on yellow	30	15
250.		12 c. violet	12	10
284.		12 c. red	30	20
251.		15 c. blue	25	25
286.		20 c. blue	50	30
252.		25 c. brown	30	25
288.		50 c. green	50	55
254.		75 c. black	55	50
290.	12.	1 r. green	70	80
291.		2 r. violet	80	1·25
292.		3 r. brown	1·50	2·00
293.		4 r. red	3·25	4·00
294.		5 r. blue	5·00	6·00
295.	13.	10 r. green and brown	9·00	9·00
296.		20 r. black and green	65·00	65·00
297.		30 r. black and brown	95·00	95·00
260c.		40 r. black and orange	£180	£170
260d.		50 r. black and purple	£190	£180
260e.		100 r. black and blue	£300	£225
260f.		200 r. brown and black	£650	£550

14. Sultan Kalif bin Harub. 15.

1926.

No.	Type	Description	Unused	Used
299.	14.	1 c. brown	8	8
300.		3 c. orange	8	8
301.		4 c. green	10	12
302.		6 c. violet	8	8
303.		8 c. grey	45	60
304.		10 c. olive	35	12
305.		12 c. red	35	10
306.		20 c. blue	15	10
307.		25 c. purple on yellow	60	30
308.		50 c. claret	45	35
309.		75 c. brown	45	1·10

1936.

No.	Type	Description	Unused	Used
310.	15.	5 c. green	5	5
311.		10 c. black	5	5
312.		15 c. red	5	12
313.		20 c. orange	5	5
314.		25 c. purple on yellow	5	10
315.		30 c. blue	5	8
316.		40 c. brown	8	15
317.		50 c. claret	8	5
318.	12.	1 s. green	15	15
319.		2 s. violet	30	30
320.		5 s. red	1·75	1·60
321.		7 s. 50 c. blue	3·00	3·25
322.	13.	10 s. green and brown	2·50	2·50

In T 15 the letters of the word "CENTS" are without serifs in T 14 they have serifs.

18. Sultan Kalif bin Harub.

1936. Silver Jubilee of Sultan.

No.	Type	Description	Unused	Used
323.	18.	10 c. black and olive	20	20
324.		20 c. black and purple	20	25
325.		30 c. black and blue	20	25
326.		50 c. black and red	15	30

19. Native Craft.

1944. Bicentenary of Al Busaid Dynasty.

No.	Type	Description	Unused	Used
327.	19.	10 c. blue	10	12
328.		20 c. red	10	12
329.		50 c. green	8	12
330.		1s. purple	10	12

1946. Victory. Optd. **VICTORY ISSUE 8th JUNE 1946.**

No.	Type	Description	Unused	Used
331.	15.	10 c. black	8	8
332.		30 c. blue	8	8

1949. Silver Wedding. As T 5/6 of Aden.

No.	Type	Description	Unused	Used
333.		20 c. orange	8	10
334.		10s. brown	2·00	2·50

1949. U.P.U. As T 14/17 of Antigua.

No.	Type	Description	Unused	Used
335.		20 c. orange	10	12
336.		30 c. blue	10	15
337.		50 c. magenta	12	20
338.		1s. green	15	30

20. Sultan Kalif bin Harub.

21. Seyyid Khalifa Schools, Beit-el-Ras.

1952.

No.	Type	Description	Unused	Used
339.	20.	5 c. black	5	5
340.		10 c. orange	5	5
341.		15 c. green	5	5
342.		20 c. red	5	5
343.		25 c. purple	5	5
344.		30 c. green	8	10
345.		35 c. blue	10	12
346.		40 c. brown	20	30
347.		50 c. violet	12	12
348.	21.	1s. green and brown	20	25
349.		2s. blue and purple	35	45
350.		5s. black and red	85	1·00
351.		7s. 50 black and emerald	1·75	3·00
352.		10s. red and black	1·90	2·40

22. Sultan Kalif bin Harub.

1954. Sultan's 75th Birthday.

No.	Type	Description	Unused	Used
353.	22.	15 c. green	10	10
354.		20 c. red	12	12
355.		30 c. blue	15	20
356.		50 c. purple	25	25
357.		1s. 25 vermilion	50	70

23. Cloves. 25. Dimbani Mosque.

24. Dhows.

1957.

No.	Type	Description	Unused	Used
358.	23.	5 c. orange and green	5	5
359.		10 c. emerald and red	5	5
360.	24.	15 c. green and sepia	5	5
361.	–	20 c. blue	5	5
362.	–	25 c. chestnut and black	5	5
363.	24.	30 c. red and black	8	5
364.	–	35 c. slate and emerald	8	8
365.	–	40 c. brown and black	12	12
366.	–	50 c. blue and myrtle	12	10
367.	25.	1s. red and black	20	15
368.	24.	1s. 25 c. slate and red	25	20
369.	25.	2s. orange and green	35	30
370.	–	5s. blue	70	75
371.	–	7s. 50 c. green	1·25	1·60
372.	–	10s. red	1·60	1·40

DESIGNS—As T 25—HORIZ. 20 c. Sultan's Barge. 25 c., 35 c., 50 c. Map of E. African coast. VERT. 40 c. Minaret Mosque. As T 24—VERT. 5s., 7s. 50 c., 10s. Kibweni Palace.

26. Sultan Seyyid Sir Abdulla bin Khalifa.

1961. As 1957 issue but with portrait of Sultan Sir Abdulla as in T 26.

No.	Type	Description	Unused	Used
373.		5 c. orange and green	5	5
374.		10 c. emerald and red	5	5
375.		15 c. green and sepia	5	5
376.		20 c. blue	5	5
377.		25 c. chestnut and black	5	5
378.		30 c. red and black	8	8
379.		35 c. slate and emerald	8	8
380.		40 c. brown and black	10	8
381.		50 c. blue and myrtle	12	10
382.		1s. red and black	20	15
383.		1s. 25 slate and red	25	20
384.		2s. orange and green	35	30
385.		5s. blue	70	55
386.		7s. 50 green	1·40	1·60
387.		10s. red	1·50	1·75
388.		20s. sepia (Kibweni Palace)	3·50	3·75

27. "Protein Foods".

1963. Freedom from Hunger.

No.	Type	Description	Unused	Used
389.	27.	1s. 30 sepia	25	30

28. Zanzibar Clove.

1963. Independence. Inscr. "UHURU 1963". Multicoloured.

No.	Type	Description	Unused	Used
390.		30 c. Type 28	5	5
391.		50 c. "To Prosperity" (Zanzibar doorway)	10	10
392.		1s. 30 "Religious Tolerance" (mosque and churches)	15	30
393.		2s. 50 "Towards the Light" (Mangapwani Cave)	35	60

No. 392 is horiz.

JAMHURI 1964 (29.) "Republic" **JAMHURI 1964** (30.)

1964 (a) Nos. 373/88 optd. with T 29.

No.	Type	Description	Unused	Used
394.		5 c. orange and green	5	5
395.		10 c. emerald and red	5	5
396.		15 c. green and sepia	5	5
397.		20 c. blue	8	8
398.		25 c. chestnut and black	8	8
399.		30 c. red and black	10	10
400.		35 c. slate and emerald	12	12
401.		40 c. brown and black	12	12
402.		50 c. blue and myrtle	15	8
403.		1s. red and black	20	15
404.		1s. 25 slate and red	30	15
405.		2s. orange and green	25	30
406.		5s. blue	60	70
407.		7s. 50 green	90	1·00
408.		10s. red	1·25	1·40
409.		20s. sepia	2·40	2·50

(b) Nos. 390/3 optd. with T 29.

No.	Type	Description	Unused	Used
410.		30 c. multicoloured	8	8
411.		50 c. multicoloured	12	12
412.		1s. 30 multicoloured	20	20
413.		2s. 50 multicoloured	30	35

(c) Nos. 373/88 optd. with T 30.

No.	Type	Description	Unused	Used
414.		5 c. orange and green	5	5
415.		10 c. emerald and red	5	5
416.		15 c. green and sepia	5	5
417.		20 c. blue	5	5
418.		25 c. chestnut and black	8	8
419.		30 c. red and black	8	8
420.		35 c. slate and emerald	10	10
421.		40 c. brown and black	12	12
422.		50 c. blue and myrtle	12	12
423.		1s. red and black	15	15
424.		1s. 25 slate and red	20	15
425.		2s. orange and green	30	30
426.		5s. blue	60	70
427.		7s. 50 green	90	1·00
428.		10s. red	1·25	1·40
429.		20s. sepia	2·40	2·50

(d) Nos. 390/3 optd. with T 30.

No.	Type	Description	Unused	Used
430.		30 c. multicoloured	8	8
431.		50 c. multicoloured	12	12
432.		1s. 30 multicoloured	20	20
433.		2s. 50 multicoloured	30	35

The opt. is in two lines on Nos. 421, 423, 425/429. 430, 431, 433.

NOTE. For the set inscribed "UNITED REPUBLIC OF TANGANYIKA & ZANZIBAR" see Nos. 124/7 of Tanganyika and for stamps inscribed "UGANDA KENYA TANGANYIKA & ZANZIBAR" (or "TANZANIA UGANDA KENYA") see under East Africa. For Zanzibar stamps inscribed "TANZANIA". see Tanzania No. Z 1 onwards.

31. Axe, Spear and Dagger.

The 1s. 30, 2s., 5s. and 20s. are horiz.

1964. Multicoloured.

No.	Type	Description	Unused	Used
434.		5 c. Type 31	5	5
435.		10 c. Bow and arrow breaking chains	5	5
436.		15 c. Type 31	5	5
437.		20 c. As 10c.	5	5
438.		25 c. Zanzibari with rifle	8	8
439.		30 c. Zanzibari breaking manacles	8	8
440.		40 c. As 25 c.	10	10
441.		50 c. As 30 c.	12	15
442.		1s. Zanzibari, flag and sun	15	15
443.		1s. 30 Hands breaking chains	20	20
444.		2s. Hand waving flag	25	30
445.		5s. Map of Zanzibar and Pemba on flag	60	70
446.		10s. Flag on map	1·25	1·40
447.		20s. National flag	2·40	2·50

32. Soldier and Maps.

1965. Revolution. 1st Anniv.

No.	Type	Description	Unused	Used
448.	32.	20 c. apple-green & grn.	5	5
449.	–	30 c. choc. & yell-orge.	5	5
450.	32.	1s. 30 blue & ultramarine	15	20
451.	–	2s. 50 violet and rose	30	35

DESIGN—VERT. 30 c., 2s. 50, Building Construction.

33. Planting Rice.

1965. Agricultural Development.

452.	**33.**	20 c. sepia and blue ..	5	5
453.	–	30 c. sepia and magenta	5	5
454.	–	1s. 30 sepia and orange	15	20
455.	**33.**	2s. 50 sepia and green ..	30	35

DESIGN: 30 c. and 1s. 30. Hands holding rice.

34. Ship, Tractor, Factory, and Open Book and Torch.

1966. Revolution. 2nd Anniv. Multicoloured.

456.	20 c. Type **34**	5	5
457.	50 c. Soldier	8	8
458.	1s. 30 Type **34**	15	20
459.	2s. 50 Soldier	30	35

35. Tree-felling.

1966.

460.	**35.**	5 c. maroon and olive ..	5	5
461.	–	10 c. maroon & emerald	5	5
462.	–	15 c. maroon and blue ..	5	5
463.	–	20 c. ultramarine & orge.	5	5
464.	–	25 c. maroon & yellow ..	5	5
465.	–	30 c. maroon & yellow	5	5
466.	–	40 c. brown and red ..	5	5
467.	–	50 c. green and yellow ..	8	8
468.	–	1s. maroon and blue ..	12	15
469.	–	1s. 30 maroon & turquoise	15	20
470.	–	2s. maroon and green ..	25	30
471.	–	5s. red and blue ..	60	70
472.	–	10s. crimson and yellow	1·25	1·40
473.	**35.**	20s. brown and magenta	2·40	2·50

DESIGNS—HORIZ. 10 c., 1s. Clove cultivation. 15 c., 40 c. Chair-making. 20 c., 5s. Lumumba College. 25 c., 1s. 30, Agriculture. 30 c., 2s. Agricultural workers. VERT. 50 c., 10s. Zanzibar Street.

36. "Education".

1966. Introduction of Free Education.

474.	**36.**	50 c. black, blue & orge.	8	8
475.		1s. 30 black, blue & grn.	15	25
476.		2s. 50 black, blue & pink	30	50

37. A.S.P. Flag.

1967. Afro-Shirazi Party. 10th Anniv.

477.	**37.**	30 c. multicoloured ..	5	5
478.	–	50 c. multicoloured ..	8	8
479.	–	1s. 30 multicoloured ..	20	30
480.	**37.**	2s. 50 multicoloured ..	35	45

DESIGN—VERT. 50 c., 1 s. 30, Vice-President M. A. Karume of Tanzania, flag and crowd.

38. Workers.

1967. Voluntary Workers Brigade.

481.	**38.**	1s. 30 multicoloured ..	15	20
482.		2 s. 50 multicoloured ..	30	35

POSTAGE DUE STAMPS

Insufficiently prepaid.
Postage due.
1 cent.

D 1.

1930. Roul. or roul. × imperf.

D 1.	D **1.**	1 c. black on orange ..	60	
D 2.		2 c. black on orange ..	60	
D 18.		2 c. black on pink ..	50	1·00
D 3.	D **1.**	3 c. black on orange ..	60	
D 19.		3 c. black on red ..	60	1·25
D 21.		6 c. black on yellow ..	70	1·50
D 5.		9 c. black on orange ..	60	
D 22.		12 c. black on blue ..	95	1·50
D 6.		12 c. black on orange		
D 7.		12 c. black on green ..	25·00	14·00
D 8.		15 c. black on orange	60	70
D 9.		18 c. black on pink ..	2·50	2·75
D 10.		18 c. black on orange	1·00	1·40
D 11.		20 c. black on orange	1·00	1·40
D 12.		21 c. black on orange	1·00	1·40
D 23.		25 c. black on rose ..	2·50	3·00
D 14.		25 c. black on orange		
D 24.		25 c. black on lilac ..	1·50	3·00
D 15.		31 c. black on orange	2·25	
D 16.		50 c. black on orange	6·00	
D 17.		75 c. black on orange	12·00	

D 2.

1936.

D 25.	D **2.**	5 c. violet	12	12
D 26.		10 c. red	12	12
D 27.		20 c. green	12	12
D 28a.		30 c. brown ..	12	12
D 29a.		40 c. blue	15	12
D 30a.		1s. grey	30	30

ZULULAND BC

A territory of S.E. Africa, annexed by Great Britain in 1887, and incorporated in Natal in 1897.

1888. Stamps of Gt. Britain (Queen Victoria) optd. **ZULULAND.**

1.	**54.**	½d. red	2·00	2·50
2.	**60.**	1d. lilac	5·00	5·00
3.	**58.**	2d. green and red ..	7·00	8·00
4.	**57.**	2½d. purple on blue ..	8·00	9·00
5.	**58.**	3d. purple on yellow ..	10·00	12·00
6.	**59.**	4d. green and brown ..	11·00	13·00
7.	**61.**	5d. purple and blue ..	25·00	25·00
8.	**62.**	6d. purple on red ..	14·00	14·00
9.	**63.**	9d. purple and blue ..	35·00	35·00
10.	**65.**	1s. green	50·00	55·00
11.	–	5s. red (No. 181) ..	£130	£140

1888. Natal stamps optd. **ZULULAND.**

12.	**5.**	½d. green	9·00	11·00
16.	–	6d. lilac (No. 103) ..	22·00	22·00

1.

ILLUSTRATIONS British Commonwealth and all overprints and surcharges are FULL SIZE. Foreign Countries have been reduced to ¾-LINEAR.

1894.

20.	**1.**	½d. mauve and green ..	1·25	1·25
21.		1d. mauve and red ..	3·50	1·00
22.		2½d. mauve and blue ..	6·00	6·00
23.		3d. mauve and brown ..	8·00	3·50
24.		6d. mauve and black ..	8·00	9·00
25.		1s. green	11·00	13·00
26.		2s. 6d. green and black ..	30·00	30·00
27.		4s. green and red	40·00	50·00
28.		£1 purple on red	£160	£180
29.		£5 purple & black on red ..	£1500	£550

APPENDIX

We record in this Appendix stamps from countries which either persist in issuing far more stamps than can be justified by postal need or have failed to maintain control over their distribution so that they have not been available to the public in reasonable quantities at face value.

A policy statement about this was published in the February 1968 issue of Gibbons "Stamp Monthly" and Stanley Gibbons Ltd. do not maintain stocks of the stamps recorded here. Hence no prices are quoted and the information is merely intended as a record. Miniature sheets and imperforate stamps are excluded.

The policy of the countries concerned is kept under continuous review and if circumstances improve or there is evidence of regular postal use of the stamps in the Appendix consideration is given to including them in the body of the catalogue.

ADEN PROTECTORATE STATES

SEIYUN

1967.

Hunting. 20 f.

Olympic Games, Grenoble. Postage 10, 25, 35, 50, 75 f.; Air 100, 250 f.

Scout Jamboree, Idaho. Air. 150 f.

Paintings—Renoir. Postage 10, 35, 50, 65, 75 f.; Air 100, 200, 250 f.

Paintings—Toulouse-Lautrec. Postage 10, 35, 50, 65, 75 f.; Air 100, 200, 250 f.

Stated to have been occupied by the N.L.F. on 1st October, 1967.

HADHRAMAUT

1967.

Stampex, London. Postage 5, 10, 15, 20, 25 f.; Air 50, 65 f.

Amphilex, Amsterdam. Air 75 f.

Olympic Games, Mexico (1968). 75 f.

Famous Paintings. Postage 5, 10, 15, 20, 25 f.; Air 50, 65 f.

Scout Jamboree, Idaho. Air. 35 f.

Space Research. Postage 10, 25, 35, 50, 75 f.; Air 100, 250 f.

Stated to have been occupied by the N.L.F. on 17th September, 1967.

MAHRA

1967.

Scout Jamboree, Idaho. 15, 75, 100, 150 f.

Kennedy. Postage 10, 15, 25, 50, 75, 100, 150 f.; Air 250, 500 f.

Olympic Games, Mexico (1968). Postage 10, 25, 50 f.; Air 250, 500 f.

Stated to have been occupied by the N.L.F. on 1st October, 1967.

Although the British Government did not officially relinquish control over Eastern Aden Protectorate (which comprises the above states) until 30th November, 1967, to the National Liberation Front (later the Southern Yemen Republic), that Government claimed that the N.L.F. were in control of them on the dates given above and repudiated the contract under which the former rulers authorised some further new issues which were placed on the market. However, despite this claim there is some uncertainty as to whether any of these later issues were delivered and actually used for postal purposes.

AFGHANISTAN

1961.

Agriculture Day. Fauna and Flora. 2, 2, 5, 10, 15, 25, 50, 100, 150, 175 p.

Child Welfare. Sports and Games. 2, 2, 5, 10, 15, 25, 50, 100, 150, 175 p.

U.N.I.C.E.F. Surch. on 1961 Child Welfare issue. 2+25, 2+25, 5+25, 10+25, 15 p.+25 p.

Women's Day. 50, 175 p.

Independence Day. Mohamed Nadir Shah. 50, 175 p.

Int. Exhib., Kabul. 50, 175 p.

Pashtunistan Day. 50, 175 p.

Nat. Assembly. 50, 175 p.

Anti-Malaria Campaign. 50, 175 p.

Shah's 47th Birthday. 50, 175 p.

Red Crescent Day. Fruits. 2, 2, 5, 10, 15, 25, 50, 100, 150, 175 p.

Afghan Red Crescent Fund. 1961 Red Crescent Day issue surch. 2+25, 2+25, 5+25, 10+25, 15 p. + 25 p.

United Nations Day. 1, 2, 3, 4, 50, 75, 175 p.

Teachers' Day. Flowers and Educational Scenes. 2, 2, 5, 10, 15, 25, 50, 100, 150, 175 p.

U.N.E.S.C.O. 1961 Teachers' Day issue surch. 2+25, 2+25, 5+25, 10+25, 15 p.+25 p.

1962.

U.N.E.S.C.O. 15th Anniv. (1961). 2, 2, 5, 10, 25, 50, 75, 100 p.

Ahmed Shah Baba. 50, 75, 100 p.

Agriculture Day. Animals and Products. 2, 2, 5, 10, 15, 25, 50, 75, 100, 125 p.

Independence Day. Marching Athletes. 25, 50, 150 p.

Women's Day. Postage 25, 50 p.; Air 100, 175p.

Pashtunistan Day. 25, 50, 150 p.

Malaria Eradication. 2, 2, 5, 10, 15, 25, 50, 75, 100, 150, 175 p.

National Assembly. 25, 50, 75, 100, 125 p.

Fourth Asian Games, Jakarta, Indonesia. Postage 1, 2, 3, 4, 5 p.; Air 25, 50, 75, 100, 150, 175 p.

Children's Day. Sports and Produce. Postage 1, 2, 3, 4, 5 p.; Air 75, 150, 200 p.

Shah's 48th Birthday. 25, 50, 75, 100 p.

Red Crescent Day. Fruits and Flowers. Postage 1, 2, 3, 4, 5 p.; Air 25, 50, 100 p.

Boy Scouts' Day. Postage 1, 2, 3, 4 p.; Air 25, 50, 75, 100 p.

Hammarskjold's Death. First Anniv. Surch on 1961 U.N.E.S.C.O. issue. 2+20, 2+20, 5+20, 10+20, 15+20, 25+20, 50+20, 75+20, 100 p.+20 p.

United Nations Day. Postage 1, 2, 3, 4, 5 p.; Air 75, 100, 125 p.

Teachers' Day. Sport and Flowers. Postage 1, 2, 3, 4, 5 p.; Air 100, 150 p.

World Meteorological Day. 50, 100 p.

1963.

Famous Afghans Pantheon, Kabul. 50, 75, 100 p.

Agriculture Day. Sheep and Silkworms. Postage 1, 2, 3, 4, 5 p.; Air 100, 150, 200 p.

Freedom from Hunger. Postage 2, 3, 300 p.; Air 500 p.

Malaria Eradication Fund. 1962 Malaria Eradication issue surch. 2+15, 2+15, 5+15, 10+15, 15+15, 25+15, 50+15, 75+15, 100+15, 150+15, 175 p.+15 p.

World Meteorological Day. Postage 1, 2, 3, 4, 5 p.; Air 200, 300, 400, 500 p.

"GANEFO" Athletic Games, Jakarta, Indonesia. Postage 2, 3, 4, 5, 10 p., 9 a.; Air 300, 500 p.

Red Cross Cent. Postage 2, 3, 4, 5, 10 p.; Air 100, 200 p., 4, 6 a.

Nubian Monuments Preservation. Postage 100, 200, 500 p.; Air 5 a., 7 a. 50.

1964.

Women's Day (1963). 2, 3, 4, 5, 10 p.

Afghan Boy Scouts and Girl Guides. Postage 2, 3, 4, 5, 10 p.; Air 2, 2, 2 a. 50, 3, 4, 5, 12 a.

Child Welfare Day (1963). Sports and Games. Postage 2, 3, 4, 5, 10 p.; Air 200, 300 p.

Afghan Red Crescent Society. Postage 100, 200 p.; Air 5 a., 7 a. 50.

Teachers' Day (1963). Flowers. Postage 2, 3, 4, 5, 10 p.; Air 3 a., 3 a. 50.

United Nations Day (1963). Postage 2, 3, 4, 5, 10 p.; Air 100 p., 2, 3 a.

Human Rights Declaration. 15th Anniv. Surch on 1964 United Nations Day issue. Postage 2+50, 3+50, 4+50, 5+50, 10 p.+50 p.; Air 100 p.+50 p., 2 a+50 p., 3 a.+50 p.

U.N.I.C.E.F. (dated 1963). Postage 100, 200 p.; Air 5 a, 7 a. 50.

Malaria Eradication (dated 1963). Postage 2, 3, 4, 5 p., 10 p. on 4 p.; Air 2, 10 a.

AJMAN

1967.

J. F. Kennedy. 50th Birth Anniv. Air 10, 20, 40, 70 d., 1, 1 r. 50, 2, 3, 5 r.

Paintings. Postage. Arab Paintings 1, 2, 3, 4, 5, 30, 70 d.; Air. Asian Paintings 1, 2, 3, 5 r.; Indian Paintings 10 r.

Tales from "The Arabian Nights". Postage 1, 2, 3, 10, 30, 50, 70 d.; Air 90 d., 1, 2, 3 r.

World Scout Jamboree, Idaho. Postage 30, 70 d., 1 r.; Air 2, 3, 4 r.

Olympic Games, Mexico (1968). Postage 35, 65, 75 d., 1 r.: Air 1 r. 25, 2, 3, 4 r.

Winter Olympic Games, Grenoble (1968). Postage 5, 35, 60, 75 d.; Air 1, 1 r. 25, 2, 3 r.

Pres. J. Kennedy Memorial. Die-stamped on gold foil. Air 10 r.

Paintings by Renoir and Terbrughen. Air 35, 65 d., 1, 2 r. × 3.

1968.

Paintings by Velasquez. Air 1 r × 2, 2 r. × 2.

Winter Olympic Games, Grenoble. Die-stamped on gold foil. Air 7 r.

Paintings from Famous Galleries. Air. 1 r × 4, 2 r. × 6.

Costumes. Air 30 d. × 2, 70 d. × 2, 1 r. × 2, 2 r. × 2.

Olympic Games, Mexico, Postage 1 r. × 4.; Air 2 r. × 4.

Satellites and Spacecraft. Air 30 d. × 2, 70 d. × 2, 1 r. × 2, 2 r. × 2, 3 r. × 2.

Paintings. Hunting Dogs. Air 2 r. × 6.

Paintings. Adam and Eve. Air 2 r. × 4.

Human Rights Year. Kennedy Brothers and Martin Luther King. Air 1 r. × 3, 2 r. × 3.

Kennedy Brothers Memorial. Postage 2 r.; Air 5 r.

Sports Champions. Inter-Milano Football Club. Postage 5, 10, 15, 20, 25 d.; Air 10 r.

Sports Champions. Famous Footballers. Postage 15, 20, 50, 75 d., 1 r.; Air 10 r.

Cats. Postage 1, 2, 3 d.; Air 2, 3 r.

Olympic Games, Mexico. Die-stamped on gold foil. 5 r.

Pres. J. Kennedy. Fifth Death Anniv. On gold foil. Air 10 r.

Paintings of the Madonna. Air 30, 70 d., 1, 2, 3 r.

Space Exploration. Postage 5, 10, 15, 20, 25 d.; Air 15 r.

Olympic Games, Mexico. Gold Medals. Postage 2 r × 4: Air 5 r. × 4.

Christmas. Air 5 r.

1969.

Sports Champions. Cyclists. Postage 1, 2, 5, 10, 15, 20 d.; Air 12 r.

Sports Champions. German Footballers. Postage 5, 10, 15, 20, 25 d.; Air 10 r.

Sports Champions. Motor-racing Drivers. Postage 1, 5, 10, 15, 25 d.; Air 10 r.

Motor-racing Cars. Postage 1, 5, 10, 15, 25 d.; Air 10 r.

Sports Champions. Boxers. Postage 5, 10, 15, 20 d.; Air 10 r.

Sports Champions. Baseball Players. Postage 1, 2, 5, 10, 15 d.; Air 10 r.

Birds. Air 1 r. × 11.

Roses. 1 r. × 6.

Wild Animals. Air 1 r. × 6.

Paintings. Italian Old Masters. 5, 10, 15, 20 d., 10 r.

Paintings. Famous Composers. Air 5, 10, 25 d., 10 r.

Paintings. French Artists. 1 r × 4.

Paintings. Nudes. Air 2 r × 4.

Three Kings Mosaic. Air 1 r. × 2, 3 r. × 2.

Kennedy Brothers. Air 2, 3, 10 r.

Olympic Games, Mexico. Gold Medal Winners. Postage 1, 2 d., 10 r.; Air 10 d., 5, 10 r.

Paintings of the Madonna. Postage 10 d.; Air 10 r.

Space Flight of "Apollo 9". Optd. on 1968 Space Exploration issue. Air 15 r.

Space Flight of "Apollo 10". Optd. on 1968 Space Exploration issue. Air 15 r.

Gagarin. First Death Anniv. Optd. on 1968 Space Exploration issue. 5 d.

Edward White. Second Death Anniv. Optd. on 1968 Space Exploration issue. 10 d.

Robert Kennedy. First Death Anniv. Optd. on 1969 Kennedy Brothers issue. Air 2 r.

European Football Championship. Optd. on 1968 Famous Footballers issue. Air 10 r.

Olympic Games, Munich (1972). Optd. on 1969 Mexico Gold Medal Winners issue. Air 10 d., 5, 10 r.

Moon Landing of "Apollo 11". Air 1, 2, 5 r.

Moon Landing of "Apollo 11". Circular designs on gold or silver foil. Air 3 r. × 3, 5 r. × 3, 10 r. × 14.

Paintings. Christmas. Postage 1, 2, 3, 4, 5, 15 d.; Air 2, 3 r.

1970.

"Apollo" Space Flights. Postage 1, 2, 4, 5, 10 d.; Air 3, 5 r.

Napoleon Bonaparte. Birth Bicent. Die-stamped on gold foil. Air 20 r.

Paintings. Easter. Postage 5, 10, 12, 30, 50, 70 d.; Air 1, 2 r.

Moon Landing. Die-stamped on gold foil. Air 20 r.

Paintings by Michelangelo. Postage 1, 2, 4, 5, 8, 10 d.; Air 3, 5 r.

World Cup Football Championships, Mexico. Air 25, 50, 75 d., 1, 2, 3 r.

"Expo 70" World Fair, Osaka, Japan. Japanese Paintings. Postage 1, 2, 3, 4, 5, 10, 15 d.; Air 1, 5 r.

Napoleon Bonaparte. Birth Bicent. Postage 1, 2, 4, 5, 10 d.; Air 3, 5 r.

Paintings. Old Masters. Postage 1, 2, 6, 5, 10 d.; Air 1, 2, 3r.

Space Flight of "Apollo 13". Air 50, 75, 80 d., 1, 2, 3 r.

World Cup Football Championships, Mexico. Die-stamped on gold foil. Air 20 r.

Olympic Games, 1960-1972. Postage 15, 30, 50, 70 d.; Air 2, 5 r.

"Expo 70" World Fair, Osaka, Japan. Pavilions. 1, 2, 3, 4, 10, 15 d.; Air 1, 3 r.

Brazil's Victory in World Cup Football Championships. Optd. on 1970 World Football Cup issue. Air 25, 50, 75 d. 1, 2, 3 r.

"Gemini" and "Apollo" Space Flights. Postage 1, 2, 3, 4, 5, 6, 8, 10, 12, 15, 20, 25, 30, 35, 40, 50 d.; Air 1, 1 r. 50, 2, 3 r.

Vintage and Veteran Cars. Postage 1, 2, 4, 5, 8, 10 d.; Air 2, 3 r.

Pres. D. Eisenhower Commem. Postage 30, 50, 70 d.; Air 1, 2, 3 r.

Paintings by Ingres. Air 25, 30, 35, 50, 70, 85 d., 1, 2 r.

Albrecht Durer. 500th Birth Anniv. (1971). Air 25, 30, 35 50, 70, 85 d., 1, 2 r.

Christmas Paintings. Air 25, 30, 35, 50, 70, 85 d., 1, 2 r.

Winter Olympic Games, Sapporo, Japan (1972). Die-stamped on gold foil. Air 20 r.

Meeting of Eisenhower and De Gaulle, 1942. Die-stamped on gold foil Air 20 r.

General De Gaulle Commem. Air 25, 50, 75 d., 1, 2, 3 r.

Winter Olympic Games, Sapporo, Japan (1972). Sports. Postage 1, 2, 5, 10 d.; Air 3, 5 r.

J. Rindt, World Formula 1 Motor-racing Champion. Die-stamped on gold foil. Air 20 r.

1971.

"Philatokyo" Stamp Exhibition Tokyo. Japanese Paintings. Air 25, 30, 35, 50, 70, 85 d. 1, 2 r.

Mars Space Project. Air 50, 75, 80 d., 1, 2, 3 r.,

Napoleonic Military Uniforms. Postage 5, 10, 15, 20, 25, 30 d.; Air 2, 3 r.

Olympic Games, Munich (1972). Sports. Postage 10, 15, 25, 30, 40 d.; Air 1, 2, 3 r.

Paintings by Modern Artists. Air 25, 30, 35, 50, 70, 85 d.; 1, 2 r.

Paintings by Famous Artists. Air 25, 30, 35, 50, 70, 85 d., 1, 2 r.

United Nations. 25th Anniv. Optd. on 1971 Modern Artists issue. Air 25, 30, 35, 50, 70, 85 d., 1, 2 r.

Olympic Games, Munich (1972). Sports. Postage 1, 2, 3, 4, 5, 6, 8, 10, 12, 15, 20, 25, 30, 35, 40, 50 d.; Air 1, 1 r. 50, 2, 3 r.

Butterflies. Air 25, 30, 35, 50, 70, 85 d., 1, 2 r.

Space Flight of "Apollo 14". Postage 15, 25, 50, 60, 70 d.; Air 5 r.

Winter Olympic Games, 1924-1968. Postage 30, 40, 50, 75 d., 1 r.; Air 2 r.

Signs of the Zodiac. 1, 2, 5, 10, 12, 15, 25, 30, 35, 45, 50, 60 h.

Famous Men. Air 65, 70, 75, 80, 85, 90 d., 1, 1 r. 25, 1 r. 50, 2, 2 r. 50, 3 r.

Beethoven. Death Bicent. 20, 30, 40, 60 d., 1 r. 50, 2 r.

Dr. Albert Schweitzer Commem. 20, 30, 40, 60 d. 1 r. 50, 2 r.

Tropical Birds. Postage 1, 2, 3, 4' 5, 10 d.; Air 2, 3 r.

Paintings by French Artists. Postage 1, 2, 3, 4, 5, 10 d.; Air 2, 3 r.

Paintings by Modern Artists. Postage 1, 2, 3, 4. 5, 10 d.; Air 2, 3 r.

Paintings by Degas. Postage 1, 2, 3, 4, 5, 10 d.; Air 2, 3 r.

Paintings by Titian. Postage 1, 2, 3, 4, 5, 10 d.; Air 2, 3 r.

Paintings by Renoir. Postage 1, 2, 3, 4, 5, 10 d.; Air 2, 3 r.

Space Flight of "Apollo 15" Postage 25, 40, 50, 60 d., 1 r.; Air 6 r.

"Philatokyo" Stamp Exhibition, Tokyo. Stamps. Postage 10, 15, 20, 30, 35, 50, 60, 80 d.; Air 1, 2 r.

Tropical Birds. Postage 1, 2, 3, 5, 7, 10, 12, 15, 20, 25, 30, 40 d.; Air 50, 80 d., 1, 3 r.

Paintings depicting Venus. Postage 1, 2, 3, 4, 5, 10 d.; Air 2, 3 r.

13th World Scout Jamboree, Asagiri, Japan. Scouts. Postage 1, 2, 3, 5, 7, 10, 12, 15, 20, 25, 30, 35, 40, 50, 65, 80 d.; Air 1, 1 r. 25, 1 r. 50, 2 r.

Lions International Clubs. Optd. on 1971 Famous Paintings issue. Air 25, 30, 35, 50, 70, 85 d., 1, 2 r.

13th World Scout Jamboree, Asagiri, Japan. Japanese Paintings. Postage 20, 30, 40, 60, 75 d.; Air 3 r.

U.N.I.C.E.F. 25th Anniv. Optd. on 1971 Scout Jamboree (paintings) issue. Postage 20, 30, 40, 60, 75 d.; Air 3 r.

Christmas 1971. (1st series. Plain frames.) Portraits of Popes. Postage 1, 2, 3, 4, 5, 10 d.; Air 2, 3 r.

Modern Cars. Postage 10, 15, 25, 40, 50 d.; Air 3 r.

Olympic Games, Munich (1972). Show-jumping. Embossed on gold foil. Air 20 r.

Exploration of Outer Space. Postage 15, 25, 50, 60 70 d.; Air 5 r.

Royal Visit of Queen Elizabeth II to Japan. Postage 1, 2, 3, 4, 5, 10 d.; Air 2, 3 r.

Meeting of Pres. Nixon and Emperor Hirohito of Japan in Alaska. Design as 3 r. value of 1970 Eisenhower issue but value changed and optd. with commemorative inscr. Air 5 r. (silver optd.), 5r. (gold opt.).

"Apollo" Astronauts. Postage 5, 20, 35, 40, 50 d.; Air 1, 2, 3 r.

Discoverers of the Universe. Astronomers and Space-scientists. Postage 5, 10, 15, 20, 25, 30 d.; Air 2, 5 r.

"ANPHILEX 71" Stamp Exhibition, New York. Air 2 r. 50.

Christmas 1971. Portraits of Popes (2nd series. Ornamental frames). Postage 1, 2, 3, 4, 5, 10 d.; Air 2, 3 r.

Royal Silver Wedding of Queen Elizabeth II and Prince Philip (1972). Air 1, 2, 3 r.

Space Flight of "Apollo 16". Postage 20, 30, 40, 50, 60 d.; Air 3, 4 r.

Fairy Tales. "Baron Munchhausen" stories. Postage 1, 2, 4, 5, 10 d.; Air 3 r.

World Fair, Philadelphia (1976). Paintings. Postage 25, 50, 75 d.; Air 5 r.

Fairy Tales. Stories of the Brothers Grimm. Postage 1, 2, 4, 5, 10 d.; Air 3 r.

European Tour of Emperor Hirohito of Japan. Postage 1, 2, 4, 5, 10 d.; Air 6 r.

13th World Scout Jamboree, Asagiri, Japan. Postage 5, 10, 15, 20, 25 d.; Air 5 r.

Winter Olympic Games, Sapporo, Japan (1972). Postage 5, 10, 15, 20, 25 d.; Air 5 r.

Olympic Games, Munich (1972). Postage 5, 10, 15, 20, 25 d.; Air 5 r.

"Japanese Life". Postage 10 d. × 4, 20 d. × 4. 30 d. × 4, 40 d. × 4, 50 d. × 4; Air 3 r. × 4.

Space Flight of "Apollo 15". Postage 5, 10, 15, 20, 25, 50 d.; Air 1, 2, 3, 5 r.

"Soyuz 11" Disaster. Air 50 d., 1 r., 1 r. 50.

"The Future in Space". Postage 5, 10, 15, 20, 25, 50 d.

Persian Empire. 2500th Anniv. Postage 10, 20, 30, 40, 50 d.; Air 3 r.

Cats. Postage 10, 15, 20, 25 d.; Air 50 d., 1 r.

Tutankhamun Tomb Discovery. 50th Anniv. Postage 1, 2, 3, 4, 5, 6, 7, 8, 9, 10, 11, 12, 13, 14, 15, 16 d.; Air 1 r × 4.

Johannes Kepler (astronomer). 400th Anniv. Postage 50 d.; Air 5 r. Famous Men. Air 1 r × 5.

1972.

150th Death Anniv. of Napoleon (1971). Postage 10. 20, 30, 40 d.; Air 1, 2, 3, 4 r.

General De Gaulle. First Death Anniv. Postage 10, 20, 30, 40 d.; Air 1, 2, 3, 4 r.

Wild Animals (1st series). Postage 5, 10, 15, 20, 25, 30, 35, 40 d.

Tropical Fish. Postage 5, 10, 15, 20, 25 d.; Air 50, 75 d., 1 r.

Famous Musicians. Postage 5 d. × 3, 10 d. × 3, 15 d. × 3, 20 d. × 3, 25 d. × 3, 30 d. × 3, 35 d. × 3, 40 d. × 3.

Easter. Postage 5, 10, 15, 20, 25 d.; Air 5 r.

Wild Animals (2nd series). Postage 5, 10, 15, 20, 25 d.; Air 5 r.

"Tour de France" Cycle Race. Postage 5, 10, 15, 20, 25, 30, 35, 40, 45, 50, 55 d.; Air 60, 65, 70, 75, 80, 85, 90, 95 d., 1 r.

Many other issues were released between 1 September 1971, and 1 August 1972, but their authenticity has been denied by the Ajman Postmaster-General. Certain issues of 1967-69, exist overprinted to commemorate other events but the Postmaster-General states that these are unofficial.

Ajman joined the United Arab Emirates on 1 August 1972 and Ministry of Communications assumed responsibility for the postal services. Further stamps inscribed "Ajman" issued after that date were released without authority and had no validity.

BHUTAN

1968.

Bhutan Pheasants. 1, 2, 4, 8, 15 ch., 2, 4, 5, 7, 9 n.

Winter Olympic Games Grenoble. Optd. on 1966 Abominable Snowmen issue. 40 ch., 1 n. 25, 3, 6 n.

Mythological Creatures. Postage 2, 3, 4, 5, 15, 20, 30, 50 ch., 1 n. 25, 2 n.; Air 1 n. 50, 2 n 50, 4, 5, 10 n.

Butterflies (plastic-surfaced). Postage 15, 50 ch., 1 n. 25, 2 n., Air 3, 4, 5, 6 n.

Paintings (relief-printed). Postage 2, 4, 5, 10 45, 80 ch., 1 n. 05, 1 n. 40, 2, 3, 4, 5 n.; Air 1 n. 50, 2 n. 50, 6, 8 n.

Olympic Games, Mexico. 5, 45, 60, 80 ch., 1 n. 05, 2, 3, 5 n.

Human Rights Year. Die-stamped surch. on unissued "Coins". 15 ch. on 50 n.p., 33 ch. on 1 r., 9 n. on 3 r. 75.

Flood Relief. Surch. on 1968 Mexico Olympics issue. 5 ch. + 5 ch., 80 ch. + 25 ch., 2 n. + 50 ch.

Rare Birds. Postage 2, 3, 4, 5, 15, 20, 30, 50 ch., 1 n. 25, 2 n.; Air 1 n. 50, 2 n. 50, 4, 5, 10 n.

1969.

Fish (plastic-surfaced). Postage 15, 20, 30 ch.; Air 5, 6, 7 n.

Insects (plastic-surfaced). Postage 10, 75 ch., 1 n. 25, 2 n.; Air 3, 4, 5, 6 n.

Admission of Bhutan to Universal Postal Union. 5, 10, 15, 45, 60 ch., 1 n. 05, 1 n. 40, 4 n.

5000 Years of Steel Industry. On steel foil. Postage 2, 5, 15, 45, 75 ch., 1 n 50, 1 n. 75, 2 n.; Air 3, 4, 5, 6 n.

Birds (plastic-surfaced). Postage 15, 50 ch., 1 n. 25, 2 n.; Air 3, 4, 5, 6 n.

Buddhist Prayer Banners. On silk rayon. 15, 75 ch., 2, 5, 6 n.

Moon Landing of "Apollo 11" (plastic-surfaced). Postage 3, 5, 15, 20, 25, 45, 50 ch., 1 n. 75; Air 3, 4, 5, 6 n.

1970.

Famous Paintings (plastic-surfaced). Postage 5, 10, 15 ch., 2 n. 75; Air 3, 4, 5, 6 n.

New U.P.U. Headquarters Building, Berne. 3, 10, 20 ch., 2 n. 50.

Flower Paintings (relief-printed). Postage 2, 3, 5, 10, 15, 75 ch., 1 n., 1 n. 40; Air 80, 90 ch., 1 n. 10, 1 n. 40, 1 n. 60, 1 n. 70, 3 n. 50.

Animals (plastic-surfaced). Postage 5, 10, 20, 25, 30, 40, 65, 75, 85 ch.; Air 2, 3, 4, 5 n.

Conquest of Space (plastic-surfaced). Postage 2, 5, 15, 25, 30, 50, 75 ch., 1 n. 50; Air 2, 3, 6, 7 n.

1971.

History of Sculpture (plastic-moulded). Postage 10, 75 ch., 1 n. 25, 2 n.; Air 3, 4, 5, 6 n.

Moon Vehicles (plastic-moulded). Postage 10 ch., 1 n. 70; Air 2 n. 50, 4 n.

History of the Motor Car (plastic-surfaced). Postage 2, 5, 10, 15, 20, 30, 60, 75, 85 ch., 1 n., 1 n. 20, 1 n. 55, 1 n. 80, 2 n., 2 n. 50; Air 4, 6, 7, 9, 10 n.

Bhutan's Admission to United Nations. Postage 5, 10, 20 ch., 3 n; Air 2 n. 50, 5, 6 n.

Boy Scout Movement. 60th Anniv. 10, 20, 50, 75 ch., 2, 6 n.

World Refugee Year. Opt. on 1971 United Nations issue. Postage 5, 10, 20 ch., 3 n.; Air 2 n. 50, 5, 6 n.

1972.

Famous Paintings (relief-printed). Postage 15, 20, 90 ch., 2 n. 50; Air 1 n. 70, 4 n. 60, 5 n. 40, 6 n.

Famous Men (plastic-moulded). Postage 10, 15, 55 ch.; Air 2, 6, 8 n.

Olympic Games, Munich. Postage 10, 15, 20, 30, 45 ch.; Air 35 ch., 1 n. 35, 7 n.

Space Flight of "Apollo 16" (plastic-surfaced). Postage 15, 20, 90 ch., 2 n. 50; Air 1 n. 70, 4 n. 60, 5 n. 40, 6 n.

Bhutan Dogs. 5, 10, 15, 25, 55 ch., 8 n.

1973.

Dogs. 2, 3, 15, 20, 30, 99 ch., 2 n. 50, 4 n.

Roses (on scent-impregnated paper). Postage 15, 25, 30 ch., 3 n.; Air 7, 9 n.

Moon Landing of "Apollo 17" (plastic-surfaced). Postage 10, 15, 25 ch., 1 n. 25, 7, 8 n.; Air 3, 9 n.

"Talking Stamps" (miniature records). Postage 10, 25 ch., 1 n. 25, 7, 8 n.; Air 6, 8 n.

Death of King Jigme Dorji Wangchuk. Embossed on gold foil. Postage 10, 25 ch. 3 n.; Air 6, 8 n.

Mushrooms. 15, 25, 30 ch., 3, 6, 7 n.

"Indipex '73" Stamp Exhibition, New Delhi. Postage 5, 10, 15, 25 ch., 1 n. 25, 3 n.; Air 5, 6 n.

1974.

1 Letter-writing". Paintings. 1, 2, 3, 5, 10, 15, 25, 50, 60, 80 ch., 1 n., 1 n. 25.

CHAD

1970.

"Apollo Programme". Postage 40 f.; Air 15, 25 f.

Napoleon. Birth Bicent. Air 10, 25, 32 f.

World Cup Football Championships, Mexico. Air 5 f.

World Cup. Previous Winners. 1, 4, f., 5 f. × 2.

"Expo '70" World Fair Osaka, Japan. Japanese Paintings. 50 c., 1, 2 f.

Christmas. Paintings. Postage 3, 25 f.; Air 32 f.

Past Olympic Venues. Postage 3, 8, 20 f.; Air 10, 35 f.

1971.

Space Exploration. 8, 10, 35 f.

Winter Olympic Games, Sapporo, Japan Japanese Paintings. 50 c., 1, 2 f.

Kings and Queens of France. Postage 25 f. × 2, 30, 32, 35 f. 40 f. × 2, 50 f. × 4, 60 f.; Air 40, 50, 60, 70, 75, 80 f. 100 f. × 5, 150 f., 200 f. × 4.

Napoleon. 150th Death Anniv. Air 10 f.

Famous Paintings. 1, 4, 5 f.

Past Olympic Venues. Postage 15, 20 f.; Air 25, 50 f.

Winter Olympic Games, Sapporo, Japan. "Expo '70" Japanese Paintings issue (1970) optd. 50 c., 1, 2 f.

Olympic Games Munich. World Cup Previous Winners issue (1970) optd. 1 f.

1972.

Moon Flight of "Apollo 15". Air 40, 80, 150, 250, 300, 500 f.

"Soyuz 11" Disaster. Air 30, 50, 100, 200, 300 400 f.

Pres. Tombalbaye. Postage 30, 40 f.; Air 70, 80 f.

Winter Olympic Games, Sapporo, Japan. Postage 25, 75, 150 f.; Air 130, 200 f.

13th World Scout Jamboree, Asagiri, Japan (1971). Postage 30, 70, 80 f.; Air 100, 200 f.

Medal Winners, Sapporo Winter Olympics. Postage 25, 75, 100, 130 f.; Air 150, 200 f.

Olympic Games, Munich. Postage 20, 40, 60 f.; Air 100, 120, 150 f.

African Animals. Air 20, 30, 100, 130, 150 f.

Medal Winners, Munich Olympics (1st series). Postage 10, 20, 40, 60 f.; Air 150, 250 f.

Medal Winners, Munich Olympics (2nd series). Gold frames, Postage 20, 30, 50 f.; Air 150, 250 f.

Other issues exist, which were prepared by various agencies, but these were never placed on sale in Chad. These include further values in the "Kings and Queens of France" series.

COMORO ISLANDS

1975.

Various stamps optd. "ETAT COMORIEN" or surch. also.

Birds issue (No. 60). 10 f. on 20 f.

Fishes issue (No. 71). Air 50 f.

Birds issue (No. 99). 40 f.

Comoro Landscapes issue (Nos. 102/4). Air 75 f. on 65 f., 100 f. on 85 f., 100 f.

Tropical Plants issue (Nos. 105/9). Postage 5 f. on 1 f., 5 f. on 3 f.; Air 75 f. on 60 f., 100 f. on 85 f.

Seashells issue (No. 114). 75 f. on 60 f.

Aquatic Sports issue (No. 122). Air 75 f. on 70 f.

Anjouan Landscapes issue (Nos. 126/8). Air 40 f., 75 f. on 60 f., 100 f.

Said Mohamed Cheikh issue (Nos. 129/30). Air 20 f., 35 f.

Great Comoro Landscapes issue (Nos. 134 and 136). Postage 35 f.; Air 200 f. on 135 f.

Moroni Buildings issue (No. 139). 20 f.

Karthala Volcano issue (No. 140). Air 200 f. on 120 f.

Hansen issue (No. 141). Air 100 f.

Copernicus issue (No. 142). Air 400 f. on 150 f.

Picasso issue (No. 143). Air 200 f.

Mosques issue (Nos. 145/6). 15 f. on 20 f., 25 f. on 35 f.

Star of Anjouan issue (No. 147). 590 f.

Said Omar Ben Soumeth issue (Nos. 148/9). Air 100 f. on 135 f., 200 f.

Shaikh Said Mohamed issue (No. 150). 25 f. on 35 f.

Handicrafts issue (Nos. 153/5). 20 f., 30 f. on 35 f., 35 f., 75 f.

Mayotte Landscapes issue (Nos. 157/60). Air 10 f. on 20 f. 30 f. on 35 f., 100 f. on 90 f., 200 f. on 120 f.

U.P.U. Centenary issue (No. 161). 500 f. on 30 f.

Air Service issue (No. 162). Air 100 f. on 135 f.

Rotary issue (No. 163). Air 400 f. on 250 f.

Handicrafts issue (Nos. 164/7). 15 f. on 20 f., 30 f. on 35 f., 100 f. on 120 f., 200 f. on 135 f.

Moheli Landscapes issue (Nos. 168/71). Postage 30 f., 50 f., 50 f. on 55 f.; Air 200 f. on 230 f.

Coelacanth issue (No. 172). 50 f.

Unissued Folk-dances issue. 100 f., 100 f. on 150 f.

1976.

"Apollo-Soyuz" Space Test Project. Postage 10, 30, 50 f.; Air 100, 200, 400 f.

ECUADOR

1966.

I.T.U. Cent. Postage 10, 10, 80 c.; Air 1 s. 50, 3, 4 s.

Space Achievements. Postage 10 c., 1 s.; Air 1 s. 30, 2 s., 2 s. 50, 3 s. 50.

Dante and Galileo. Postage 10, 80 c.; Air 2, 3 s.

Pope Paul VI. Postage 10 c.; Air 1 s. 30, 3 s. 50.

Famous Persons. Postage 10 c., 1 s.; Air 1 s. 50, 2 s. 50, 4 s.

Olympic Games. Postage 10, 10, 80 c.; Air 1 s. 30, 3 s., 3 s. 50.

Winter Olympics. Postage 10 c., 1 s.; Air 1 s. 50, 2 s., 2 s. 50, 4 s.

Franco-American Space Research. Postage 10 c.; Air 1 s. 50, 4 s.

Italian Space Research. Postage 10 c.; Air 1 s. 30, 3 s. 50.

Exploration of the Moon's Surface. Postage 10, 80 c., 1 s.; Air 2 s., 2 s. 50, 3 s. 50.

1967.

Olympic Games, Mexico. Postage 10 c., 1 s.; Air 1 s. 30, 2 s., 2 s. 50, 3 s. 50.

Olympic Games, Mexico. Postage 10, 10, 80 c.; Air 1 s. 50, 3, 4 s.

Eucharistic Conference. Postage 10, 60, 80 c., 1 s.; Air 1 s. 50, 2 s.

Paintings of the Madonna. Postage 10, 40, 50 c.; Air 1 s. 30, 2 s. 50, 3 s.

Famous Paintings. Postage 10 c., 1 s.; Air 1 s. 50, 2 s., 2 s. 50, 4 s.

J. Kennedy. 50th Birth Anniv. Postage 10, 10, 80 c.; Air 1 s. 30, 3 s., 3 s. 50.

"Year of Government". 80 c., 1 s., 1 s. 30, 2 s.

1968.

Religious Paintings and Sculptures. Postage 10, 80 c., 1 s.; Air 1 s. 30, 1 s. 50, 2 s.

COTAL Tourist Organization Congress. Postage 20, 30, 40, 50, 60, 80 c., 1 s.; Air 1 s. 30, 1 s. 50, 2 s.

1969.

Visit of Pope Paul VI to Latin America. Postage 40, 60 c.; Air 1 s. 30.

39th Int. Eucharistic Congress, Bogota. Postage 1 s.; Air 2 s.

Paintings of the Virgin Mary. Postage 40, 60 c., 1 s.; Air 1 s. 30, 2 s.

EQUATORIAL GUINEA

1972.

Space Flight of "Apollo 15". Postage 1, 3, 5, 8, 10 p.; Air 15, 25 p.

Winter Olympic Games, Sapporo, Japan. Postage 1, 2, 3, 5, 8 p.; Air 15, 50 p.

Christmas 1971. Paintings. Postage 1, 3, 5, 8, 10 p.; Air 15, 25 p.

Easter. Postage 1, 3, 5, 8, 10 p.; Air 15, 25 p.

Olympic Games, Munich 1972. Augsburg Events. Postage 1, 2, 3, 5, 8 p.; Air 15, 50 p.

Winter Olympic Games, Sapporo, Japan. Gold medal winners. Postage 1, 2, 3, 5, 8 p.; Air 15, 50 p.

Olympic Games, Munich 1972. Buildings and previous medal winners. Postage 1, 2, 3, 5, 8 p.; Air 15, 50 p.

Olympic Games 1972. Sailing and rowing, Kiel. Postage 1, 2, 3, 5, 8 p.; Air 15, 50 p.

Olympic Games Munich, 1972. Modern sports. Postage 1, 2, 3, 5, 8 p.; Air 15, 50 p.

Olympic Games Munich, 1972. Equestrian sports. Postage 1, 2, 3, 5, 8 p.; Air 15, 50 p.

Japanese Railway Centenary. Various steam locomotives. Postage 1, 3, 5, 8, 10 p.; Air 15, 50 p.

Olympic Games, Munich 1972. Gold medal winners. Postage 1, 2, 3, 5, 8 p.; Air 15, 50 p.

Christmas 1972. Paintings by Cranach. Postage 1, 3, 5, 8, 10 p.; Air 15, 25.

Cosmonauts Memorial. Designs with black borders. Postage 1, 3, 5, 8, 10 p.; Air 15, 25 p.

1973.

Transatlantic Yacht Race 1972. Postage 1, 2, 3, 5, 8 p.; Air 15, 50 p.

Renoir Paintings. Postage 1, 2, 3, 5, 8 p.; Air 15, 50 p.

Conquest of Venus. Postage 1, 3, 5, 8, 10 p.; Air 15, 25 p.

Easter. Religious Paintings by Old Masters. Postage 1, 3, 5, 8, 10 p.; Air 15, 25 p.

"Tour de France" Cycle Race. Postage 1, 2, 3, 5, 8 p.; Air 15, 50 p.

Paintings by European Old Masters. Postage 1, 2, 3, 5, 8 p.; Air 15, 50 p.

World Football Cup Competition, Munich, 1974. Previous Finals. Postage 5, 10, 15, 20, 25, 55, 60 c.; Air 5, 70 p.

Paintings by Rubens. Postage 1, 2, 3, 5, 8 p.; Air 15, 50 p.

Christmas. Religious Paintings. Postage 1, 3, 5, 8, 10 p.; Air 15, 25 p.

The Equatorial Guinea peseta was renamed the ekuele in October, 1973.

World Cup Football Championships, Munich (1974). Famous players. Postage 30, 35, 40, 45, 50, 65, 70 c.; Air 8, 60 p.

Paintings by Picasso. Postage 30, 35, 40, 45, 50 c.; Air 8, 60 e.

1974.

500th Birth Anniv. of Nicolas Copernicus. (Astronomer). Postage 5, 10, 15, 20 c.; Air 4, 10, 70 e.

World Cup Football Championships, West Germany (3rd issue). Venues of Qualifying Matches. Postage 75, 80, 85, 90, 95 c., 1 e., 1 e. 25; Air 10, 50 e.

Easter. Postage 1, 3, 5, 8, 10 p.; Air 15, 25 p.

Holy Year. Postage 5, 10, 15, 20 c., 3 e. 3, e. 50; Air 10, 70 e.

World Cup Football Championships, West Germany (4th issue). Famous Players. Postage 1 e. 50, 1 e. 75, 2 e., 2 e. 25, 2 e. 50, 3 e., 3 e. 50; Air 10, 60 e.

Centenary of Universal Postal Union (1st issue). Postage 60, 70, 80 c., 1 e., 1 e. 50; Air 30, 50 e.

First Death Anniv. of Picasso. Postage 55, 60, 65, 70, 75 c.; Air 10, 50 e.

"The Wild West". Postage 30, 35, 40, 45, 50 c.; Air 8, 60 p.

Protected Flowers. Postage 5, 10, 15, 20, 25 c., 1, 3, 5, 8, 10 p.; Air 5, 15, 25, 70 p.

Christmas. Postage 60, 70, 80 c., 1 e., 1 e. 50; Air 30, 50 e.

75th Anniv. of FC Barcelona. Postage 1, 3, 5, 8, 10 e.; Air 15, 60 e.

Centenary of Universal Postal Union (2nd issue) and "Espana '75" International Stamp Exhibition, Madrid. Postage 1 e 25, 1 e. 50, 1 e. 75, 2 e., 2 e. 25; Air 35, 60 e.

Nature Protection (1st series). Australian Animals. Postage 80, 85, 90, 95 c., 1 e.; Air 15, 40 e.

Nature Protection (2nd series). African Animals. Postage 50, 60, 65, 70, 75 c.; Air 10, 70 e.

Nature Protection (3rd series). South American and Australian Birds. Postage 1 p. 25, 1 p. 50, 1 p. 75, 2 p., 2 p. 25, 2 p. 50, 2 p. 75, 3 p., 3 p. 50, 4 p.; Air 20, 25, 30, 35 p.

Nature Protection (4th series). Endangered Species. Postage 10, 15, 20, 25, 30, 35, 40, 45, 50, 55, 60 c., 1 e.; Air 2, 10, 70 e.

1975.

Paintings by Picasso. Postage 5, 10, 15, 20, 25 c.; Air 5, 70 e. Easter. Postage 60, 70, 80 c., 1 e. 1 e. 50; Air 30, 50 e.

Winter Olympic Games, Innsbruck (1976). 5, 10, 15, 20, 25, 30, 35, 40, 45 c., 25, 70 e.

Paintings of Don Quixote. Postage 30, 35, 40, 45, 50 c.; Air 25, 60 e.

Bicentenary of American Revolution (1st issue). Postage 5, 20, 40, 75 c., 2, 5, 8 e.; Air 25, 30 e.

Bullfighting. Postage 80, 85, 90 c., 8 e.; Air 35, 40 e.

"Apollo-Soyuz" Space Test Project. Postage 1, 2, 3, 5 e., 5 e. 50, 7 e., 7 e. 50, 9, 15 e.; Air 20, 30 e.

Bicentenary of American Revolution (2nd issue). Postage 10, 30, 50 c., 1, 3, 6, 10 e.; Air 12, 40 e.

Nude Paintings. Postage 5, 10, 15, 20, 25, 30, 35, 40, 45, 50, 55, 60 c., 1, 2 e.; Air 10, 70 e.

Ships. Postage 30, 40, 45, 50, 55, 60, 65, 70, 75 c.; Air 8, 10, 50, 60 e.

Christmas. Postage 60, 70, 80 c., 1 e., 1 e. 50; Air 30, 50 e.

1976.

Olympic Games, Montreal. Postage 50, 60, 70, 80, 90 c.; Air 35, 60 e.

FUJEIRA

1967.

"One Thousand and One Nights". Postage 10, 15, 30, 75 d., 1 r., 1 r. 50; Air 25, 50, 75 d., 1 r., 1 r. 25, 2 r.

Famous Paintings. Postage 25, 50, 75 d., 1, 1 r. 50; Air 2, 3, 5 r.

Cats. Postage 10, 35, 50 d., 1, 1 r. 50; Air 1 r. 25, 2 r. 75, 3 r. 50.

1968.

Winter Olympic Games, Grenoble. 25, 50, 75 d., 1, 1 r. 50, 2, 3 r.

Famous Paintings (square designs). Postage 50, 75 d., 1, 2, 3 r.; Air 1 r. 50, 2 r. 50, 3 r. 50, 4, 5 r.

Ships. Postage 15, 25, 50, 75 d., 1 r.; Air 2, 3, 4, 5 r.

Olympic Games, Mexico. Optd. on Nos. 22/6 and four values of 1968 Winter Olympics issue. Postage 1, 1 r. 50, 2, 3, 5 r.; Air 1, 1 r. 50, 2, 3 r.

Prehistoric Animals. Postage 15, 25, 50, 75 d., 1 r. 50; Air 1, 2 r. 50, 3, 4, 5 r.

Robert Kennedy Memorial issue. Optd. on Nos. 34/7. 1, 2, 3, 5 r.

Olympic Games, Mexico. Postage 15, 25, 35, 50, 75 d., 1 r.; Air 1 r. 50, 2, 3, 5 r.

International Letter-writing Week. Paintings. Postage 25, 50, 75 d., 1 r.; Air 1 r. 50, 2, 3, 5 r.

"EFIMEX" Int. Stamp Exhibition, Mexico. Optd. on 1968 Letter-writing Week issue, Postage 25, 50, 75 d., 1 r. 50; Air 1 r. 50, 2, 3. 5 r.

Gold Medal Winners, Olympic Games, Mexico. Optd. on 1968 Olympic Games, Mexico issue. Postage 15, 25, 35, 50 75 d., 1 r.; Air 1 r. 50, 2, 3, 5 r.

1969.

Wild Animals of the World. Postage 15, 25, 50, 75 d., 1 r.; Air 1 r. 50, 2, 3, 5 r.

Scenes from Shakespeare's Plays. Postage 25, 50, 75 d., 1, 2 r.; Air 1 r. 25, 2 r. 50, 3, 5 r.

Olympic Games, Munich (1969). Optd. on 1968 Olympic Games, Mexico issue. Postage 15, 25, 35, 50, 75 d., 1 r.; Air 1 r. 50, 2 r. 50, 3, 5 r.

Famous Railway Locomotives. Postage 15, 25, 50, 75 d., 1 r.; Air 2, 3, 5 r.

Moon Flight of "Apollo 8". Optd. or surch. on Nos. 76/83. 50, 75 n.p., 1, 2, 2 r. 50 on 25 n.p., 3 r on 15 n.p., 4 r. on 10 n.p., 5 r. on 5 n.p.

Winter Olympic Games, Sapporo, Japan (1972). Optd. on 1968 Winter Olympic Games, Grenoble issue. 25, 50, 75 d., 1, 1 r. 50, 2, 3 r.

Birds. Postage 25, 50 d., 1 r., 1 r. 50, 2 r.; Air 1 r. 25, 2 r. 50, 3, 5 r.

Pres. Eisenhower Memorial issue. Postage 25, 50 d., 1 r., 1 r. 50, 2 r.; Air 1 r. 25, 2 r. 50, 3, 5 r.

Champions of Peace. 25, 50, 75 d., 1, 2, 3, 5 r.

Human Rights Year. Optd. on 1969 Champions of Peace issue. 25, 50, 75 d., 1, 2, 3, 5 r.

Flowers. Postage 25, 50 d., 1, 1 r. 50, 2 r.; Air 1 r. 25, 2 r. 50, 3, 5 r.

"Apollo" Space Flights. Postage 10, 25, 50 d., 1, 2 r.; Air 2 r. 50, 3, 4, 5 r.

Space Flight of "Apollo 10". Optd. on 1969 "Apollo" Space Flights issue. Postage 10, 25, 50 d.. 1, 2 r.; Air 2 r. 50, 3, 4, 5 r.

Moon Landing. Optd. on 1969 "Apollo" Space Flights issue. Postage 10, 25, 50 d., 1, 2 r.; Air 2 r. 50, 3, 4, 5 r.

First Man on the Moon. 1969 "Apollo" Space Flights issue optd. with various commemoration inscriptions. Postage 10, 25, 50 d., 1 2 r.; Air 2 r. 50, 3, 4, 5 r.

1970.

Birth Bicentenary of Napoleon Bonaparte. 15, 25, 50, 75 d., 1, 1 r. 50 2 r.

General De Gaulle Commemoration. Air 35, 60, 75 d., 1 r. 25, 2 r. 50, 3, 5 r.

Bible Stories. Postage 15 d., 1 r.; Air 35, 75 d., 1 r. 25, 1 r. 50, 2 r. 50, 3 r.

"Expo 70" World Fair, Osaka, Japan. Japanese Art. Postage 15, 25, 50, 75 d., 1, 2 r.; Air 75 d., 1 r. 25, 2 r. 50, 4 r.

Exploration of the Moon. 25, 50 d., 1, 2, 3, 4, 5 r.

Space Flight of "Apollo 13". Optd. on 1970 Moon Exploration issue. 25, 50 d., 1, 2, 3, 4, 5 r.

Moon Mission of "Apollo 14". Optd on 1970 Moon Exploration issue. 25, 50 d., 1, 2, 3, 4, 5 r.

"Expo 70" World Fair, Osaka, Japan Pavilions. 10, 20, 70 d., 1 r. × 2, 2 r.

World Football Cup, Mexico. 10, 20, 70 d., 1 r. × 2, 2 r.

Pres. Gamal Nasser Memorial issue. Postage 10, 20, 30, 40, 50 d.; Air 5 r.

Horses. Postage 10, 20 d.; Air 70 d., 1, 2 r.

Cats. Postage 30, 70 d.; Air 1, 2, 3 r.

Dogs. Postage 30, 70 d.; Air 1, 2, 3 r.

Paintings of the Madonna. 30, 70 d., 1, 2, 3 r.

Stations of the Cross. 1 r. × 15.

Christmas. Paintings. Postage 30, 70 d., 1 r.; Air 2, 3 r.

1971.

American and European Cars. Postage 5, 20, 30 d., 4 r.; Air 30, 50, 70 d., 1 r. 50, 2 r. 50, 4 r.

Space Exploration. Air 40, 60 d., 1, 2, 5 r.

History of Railways. 10, 20, 70 d., 2, 3 r.

General De Gaulle Memorial issue. Air 30, 70 d. 1, 2, 3 r.

Moon Mission of "Apollo 14, Air 70 d., 1, 2, 3, 4 r.

Wild Animals. Air 20, 40, 60 d., 1, 2, 3 r.

Olympic Games, Munich (1972) (square designs). Postage 50 d., 1 r.; Air 2, 3, 4 r.

Winter Olympic Games, Sapporo, Japan (1972). Postage 5, 10, 15, 20, 30, 50 d.; Air 70 d., 4 r.

500th Birth Anniv. of Durer. Paintings. Air 70 d., 1, 2, 3, 4 r.

Birth Bicentenary of Beethoven. Portraits and instruments. Postage 30, 70 d.; Air 1, 3, 4 r.

Mozart Commemoration. Postage 30, 70 d., 1 r.; Air 3, 4 r.

Frazier v Mohammed Ali World Heavyweight Boxing Championship Fight. Air 1, 2, 3 r.

World Scout Jamboree, Asagiri, Japan. Postage 20, 30, 50, 70 d., 1 r. × 2, 2 r. × 2; Air 3, 4 r.

Butterflies. Air 70 d., 1, 2, 3, 5 r.

Birds. 30, 70 d., 1, 2, 3 r.

Cats and Dogs. 10, 20, 30 d., 1, 2, 3 r.

Monkeys. 30, 70 d., 1, 2, 3 r.

Wild Animals. 30, 70 d., 1, 2, 3 r.

Horses. 70 d., 1, 2, 3, 4 r.

Olympic Games, Munich, Sports. 1, 2, 3, 4, 5, 6, 7, 8, 9, 10, 11, 12, 13, 14, 15, 16, 17, 18, 19, 20, 21, 22, 23, 24, 25, 26, 27, 28, 29, 30 d.

Olympic Games, Munich. Sports and Arenas. Postage 35, 60 d., 2, 3 r.; Air 4 r.

Christmas. Postage 40, 60 d., 2 r.; Air 3, 4 r.

International Labour Day. Paintings. Postage 40, 60 d., 2, 3 r.; Air 2, 3, 4 r.

1972.

400th Birth Anniv. of Kepler. Postage 35, 75 d., 1, 2 r.; Air 3, 5 r.

Moon Mission of "Apollo 15". Postage 30, 70 d.; Air 1, 2, 5 r.

2500th Anniv. of the Persian Empire. Postage 35, 65, 75 d.; Air 1 r. 25, 2, 3 r.

Historical Costumes. 30, 70 d., 1, 2, 3 r.

Winter Olympic Games, Sapporo, Japan. Postage 25, 30, 70 d.; Air 1 r. 25, 2, 3 r.

Children's Day. Paintings. Postage 10, 30, 60 d.; Air 4, 5 r.

Sculptures. Postage 30, 70 d.; Air 1, 2, 6 r.

Paintings of the Madonna. Postage 20, 30, 50 d.; Air 4, 5 r.

Nude Paintings. 50 d., 1, 2, 3, 4 r.

Gold Medal Winners, Winter Olympic Games, Sapporo. Optd. on 1972 Winter Olympic Games, Sapporo issue. Postage 25, 30, 70 d.; Air 1 r. 25, 2, 3 r.

Olympic Games, Munich. Discus-thrower. Air 8 r.

Space Exploration. Postage 5, 10, 15, 20, 25, 30, 35, 40, 45, 50, 55, 60 d.; Air 65, 70, 75 d., 1, 2, 3, 4, 5 r.

Walt Disney Cartoon Characters. Postage 1, 2, 3, 4, 5, 10, 15, 20, 25, 30 d.; Air 45, 55, 65, 70 d., 1, 1 r. 50, 2, 3, 4, 5 r.

History of the Olympic Games Postage 1, 2, 3, 4, 5, 10, 15, 20, 25, 30, 45, 55 d.; Air 65, 70 d., 1, 1 r. 50, 2, 3, 5 r.

Summit Meeting of Pres. Nixon and Mao Tse-tung. Air 2, 3, 5 r.

Pres. Nixon's Visit of Russia. Optd. on 1972 Nixon-Mao Tse-tung Meeting issue. Air 2, 3, 5 r.

150th Death Anniv. of Napoleon Bonaparte (1971). Air 10 r.

2nd Death Anniv. of General De Gaulle. Air 10 r.

Olympic Games, Munich, Javelin-thrower, Air 10 r.

Gold Medal Winners, Olympic Games, Munich. Optd. on 1972 Discus-thrower issue. Air 8 r.

Moon Mission of "Apollo 16". Air 10 r.

A number of issues on gold and silver foil also exist, but it is understood that these were mainly for presentation purposes, although valid for postage.

During 1970 a number of other sets came on to the market, but their official status is in doubt.

HAITI

1968.

Medal Winners, Winter Olympic Games, Grenoble. Postage 5, 10, 20, 25, 50 c., 1 g. 50; Air 2 g.

1969.

Moon Landing by "Apollo 11". Optd. on 1969 Birds issue. Nos. 1132/5. Air 50 c., 1 g., 1 g. 50, 2 g.

Space Flights of "Apollo 7" and "Apollo 8". Postage 10, 15, 20, 25 c.; Air 70 c., 1 g., 1 g 25, 1 g. 50.

1970.

Moon Mission of "Apollo 12". Postage 5, 10, 15, 20, 25, 30, 40, 50 c.; Air 25, 30, 40, 50, 75 c., 1 g., 1 g. 25, 1 g. 50.

1971.

Safe Return of "Apollo 13". Optd. on 1970 "Apollo 12" issue. Postage 5, 10, 15, 20, 25, 30, 40, 50 c.; Air 25, 30, 40, 50, 75 c., 1 g., 1 g. 25, 1 g. 50.

1972.

Gold Medal Winners Olympic Games, Munich. Air 50, 75 c., 1 g. 50, 2 g. 50, 5 g.

1973.

American and Russian Space Exploration. Postage 5, 10, 20, 25, 50 c., 2 g. 50, 5 g.; Air 50, 75 c., 1 g. 50, 2 g. 50, 5 g.

Moon Mission of "Apollo 17". 50 c., 2 g. 50, 5 g.

HONDURAS

1968.

Centenary of International Telecommunications Union (1965). Air 1, 2, 3, 5, 8, 10, 20 30 c., 1 l., 1 l. 50.

1969.

Robert Kennedy Commemoration. Optd. on 1968 I.T.U. issue. Air 1, 10, 20 c., 1 l. 50.

Gold Medal Winners, Olympic Games, Mexico. Optd. on 1968 I.T.U. issue. Air 2, 3, 5, 8, 30 c., 1 l.

First Man on the Moon. Air 5, 10, 12, 20, 24, 30 c., 1 l., 1 l. 50.

1970.

Safe Return of "Apollo 13". Optd. on 1969 Moon Landing issue. Air 5, 10, 12, 20, 24, 30 c., 1 l., 1 l. 50.

KHMER REPUBLIC (CAMBODIA)

1972.

Moon Landing of "Apollo 16". Embossed on gold foil. Air 900 r. × 2.

Olympic Games, Munich. Embossed on gold foil. Air 900 r. × 2.

1973.

Gold Medal Winners, Munich Olympics. Embossed on gold foil. Air 900 r. × 2.

World Cup Football Championships, West Germany (1974). Embossed on gold foil. Air 900 r. × 4.

1974.

Pres. Kennedy and "Apollo 11". Embossed on gold foil. Air 1100 r. × 2.

Nicholas Copernicus (astronomer). 500th Birth Anniv. Postage 1, 5, 10, 25, 50, 100, 150 r.; Air 200, 250 r., 1200 r. embossed on gold foil.

Universal Postal Union. Cent. Postage 10, 60 r.; Air 700 r.

1975.

World Cup Football Championships, West Germany (1974). Postage 1, 5, 10, 25 r.; Air 50, 100, 150, 200, 250 r., 1200 r. embossed on gold foil.

Olympic Games, Montreal (1976). Postage 5, 10, 15, 25 r.; Air 50, 100, 150, 200, 250 r., 1200 r. embossed on gold foil.

KHOR FAKKAN

1965.

Views. Nos. 75/80 of Sharjah optd. Air 10, 20, 30, 40, 75, 100 n.p.

Boy and Girl Scouts. Nos. 74 and 89 of Sharjah optd. 2, 2 r.

Birds. Nos. 101/6 of Sharjah optd. Air 30, 40, 75, 150 n.p. 2, 3 r.

Olympic Games, Tokyo 1964. Nos. 95/7 of Sharjah optd. 40, 50 n.p. 2 r.

New York World's Fair. Nos. 81/3 of Sharjah optd. Air 20, 40 n.p. 1 r.

Pres. Kennedy Commem. Nos. 98/100 of Sharjah optd. Air 40, 60, 100 n.p.

I.T.U. Cent., Sharjah. Postage 1, 2, 3, 4, 5, 50 n.p., 1 r., 120 n.p.

Pan-Arab Games, Cairo. 50 p. × 5.

1966.

International Co-operation Year. 50 n.p. × 8.

Churchill Commemoration. 2, 3, 4, 5 r.

Roses. 20, 35, 60, 80 n.p. 1 r., 125 n.p.

Fish. 1, 2, 3, 4, 5, 15, 20, 30, 40, 50, 75 n.p., 1, 2, 3, 4, 5, 10 r.

Int. Stamp Exhibition, Washington D.C., (SIPEX). 80, 120 n.p., 2 r.

New Currency Surcharges in Rials and Piastres.

(a) 1965 I.T.U. Cent., issue. 10 p. on 50 n.p., 16 p. on 120 n.p., 1 r. on 1 r.

(b) Churchill issue. 1 r. on 2 r., 2 r. on 3 r., 3 r. on 4 r., 4 r. on 5 r.

(c) Roses issue. 1 p. on 20 n.p., 2 p. on 35 n.p., 4 p. on 60 n.p., 6 p. on 80 n.p., 10 p. on 125 n.p., 12 p. on 1 r.

New Currency Surcharges in Dirhams and Riyals.

(a) 1965 Pan-Arab Games issue. 20 d. on 50 p. × 5.

(b) Fish issue. 1 d. on 1 n.p., 2 d. on 2 n.p., 3 d. on 3 n.p., 4 d. on 4 n.p., 5 d. on 5 n.p., 15 d. on 15 n.p., 20 d. on 20 n.p., 30 d. on 30 n.p., 40 d. on 40 n.p., 50 d. on 50 n.p., 75 d. on 75 n.p., 1 r. on 1 r., 2 r. on 2 r., 3 r. on 3 r., 4 r. on 4 r., 5 r. on 5 r., 10 r. on 10 r.

Pres. J. Kennedy. 3rd Death Anniv. Optd. on 1966 Int. Stamp Exhibition issue. 80 d. on 80 n.p., 120 d. on 120 n.p., 2 r. on 2 r.

World Football Cup Championships, London. ½ r. × 7.

1967.

Pres. J. Kennedy. 4th Death Anniv. Optd. on 1966 Int. Stamp Exhibition issue. 80 d. on 80 n.p., 120 d. on 120 n.p., 2 r. on 2 r.

1968.

Famous Paintings. Optd. on Sharjah. Postage 1, 2, 3, 4, 5, 30, 40, 60, 75 d.; Air 1, 2, 3, 4, 5 r.

Winter Olympic Games, Grenoble. Optd. on Sharjah. Postage 1, 2, 3, 4, 5 d.; Air 1, 2, 3 r.

Previous Olympic Games. Optd. on Sharjah. Air 25, 50, 75 d., 1 r. 50, 3, 4 r.

Olympic Games, Mexico. Optd. on Sharjah. 10, 20, 30 d., 2, 2 r. 40, 5 r.

1969.

12th World Jamboree. Optd. on 1968 issue of Sharjah. Postage 1, 2, 3, 4, 5, 10 d.; Air 30, 50, 60 d., 1 r. 50.

Martyrs of Liberty. Optd. on 1968 issue of Sharjah. Air 35 d. × 4, 60 d. × 4, 1 r. × 4.

Sportsmen and women. Optd. on 1968 issue of Sharjah. Postage 20, 30, 40, 60 d., 1 r. 50, 2 r. 50; Air 35, 50 d., 1, 2, 3 r. 25, 4, 4 r.

A number of issues on gold or silver foil also exist, but it is understood that these were mainly for presentation purposes, although valid for postage.

In common with the other states of the United Arab Emirates the Khor Fakkan stamp contract was terminated on 1st August 1972, and any further new issues released after that date were unauthorised.

MANAMA

1966.

New Currency Surcharges. Stamps of Ajman surch. **Manama** in English and Arabic and new value.

(*a*) Nos. 19/20 and 22/4 (Kennedy). 10 d. on 10 n.p., 15 d. on 15 n.p., 1 r. on 1 r., 2 r. on 2 r., 3 r. on 3 r.

(*b*) Nos. 27, 30 and 35/6 (Olympics). 5 d. on 5 n.p., 25 d. on 25 n.p., 3 r. on 3 r., 5 r. on 5 r.

(*c*) Nos. 70/2 and 75 (Churchill). 50 d. on 50 n.p., 75 d. on 75 n.p., 1 r. on 1 r., 5 r. on 5 r.

(*d*) Nos. 85/8 (Space). Air 50 d. on 50 n.p., 1 r. on 1 r., 3 r. on 3 r., 5 r. on 5 r.

1967.

World Scout Jamboree, Idaho. Postage 30, 70 d., 1 r.; Air 2, 3, 4 r.

Olympic Games, Mexico (1968). Postage 35, 65, 75 d., 1 r.; Air 1 r. 25, 2, 3, 4 r.

Winter Olympic Games, Grenoble (1968) Postage 5, 35, 60, 75 d.; Air 1, 1 r. 25, 2, 3 r.

Paintings by Renoir and Terbrughen. Air 35, 65 d., 1, 2 r. × 3.

1968.

Paintings by Velazquez. Air 1 r. × 2, 2 r. × 2.

Costumes. Air 30 d. × 2, 70 d. × 2, 1 r. × 2, 2 r. × 2.

Olympic Games, Mexico. Postage 1 r. × 4; Air 2 r. × 4.

Satellites and Spacecraft. Air 30 d. × 2, 70 d. × 2, 1 r. × 2, 2 r. × 2, 3 r. × 2.

Human Rights Year. Kennedy Brothers and Martin Luther King. Air 1 r. × 3, 2 r. × 3.

Sports Champions, Famous Footballers. Postage 15, 20, 50, 75 d., 1 r.; Air 10 r.

Heroes of Humanity. Circular designs on gold or silver foil. 60 d. × 12.

Olympic Games, Mexico. Circular designs on gold or silver foil. Air 3 r. × 8.

Mothers' Day. Paintings. Postage 1 r × 6.

Kennedy Brothers Commem. Postage 2 r.; Air 5 r.

Cats. Postage 1, 2, 3 d.; Air 2, 3 r.

Pres. Kennedy. Fifth Death Anniv. Air 10 r.

Space Exploration. Postage 5, 10, 15, 20, 25 d.; Air 15 r.

Olympic Games, Mexico. Gold Medals. Postage 2 r. × 4; Air 5 r. × 4.

Christmas. Air 5 r.

1969.

Sports Champions. Cyclists. Postage 1, 2, 5, 10, 15, 20 d.; Air 12 r.

Sports Champions. German Footballers. Postage 5, 10, 15, 20, 25 d.; Air 10 r.

Sports Champions. Motor-racing Drivers. Postage 1, 5, 10, 15, 25 d.; Air 10 r.

Motor-racing Cars. Postage 1, 5, 10, 15, 25 d.; Air 10 r.

Sports Champions. Boxers. Postage 5, 10, 15, 20 d.; Air 10 r.

Sports Champions. Baseball Players. Postage 1, 2, 5, 10, 15 d.; Air 10 r.

Birds. Air 1 r. × 11.

Roses. Postage 1 r. × 6.

Animals. Air 1 r. × 6.

Paintings by Italian Artists. Postage 5, 10, 15, 20 d., 10 r.

Great Composers. Air 5, 10, 25 d., 10 r.

Paintings by French Artists. Postage 1 r. × 4.

Nude Paintings. Air 2 r. × 4.

Kennedy Brothers. Air 2, 3, 10 r.

Olympic Games, Mexico. Gold Medal Winners. Postage 1, 2 d., 10 r.; Air 10 d., 5, 10 r.

Paintings of the Madonna. Postage 10 d.; Air 10 r.

Space Flight of "Apollo 9". Optd. on 1968 Exploration issue. Air 15 r.

Space Flight of "Apollo 10". Optd. on 1968 Space Exploration issue. Air 15 r.

Gagarin. First Death Anniv. Optd. on 1968 Space Exploration issue. Postage 5 d.

Edward White (astronaut). Second Death Anniv. Optd. on 1968 Space Exploration issue. Postage 10 d.

Robert Kennedy. First Death Anniv. Optd. on 1969 Kennedy Brothers issue. Air 2 r.

Olympic Games, Munich (1972). Optd. on 1969 Mexico Gold Medal Winners issue. Air 10 d., 5, 10 r.

Moon Mission of "Apollo 11". Air 1, 2, 3 r.

Christmas. Paintings by Brueghel. Postage 1, 2, 4, 5, 10 d.; Air 6 r.

1970.

"Soyuz" and "Apollo" Space Programmes. Postage 1, 2, 4, 5, 10 d.; Air 3, 5 r.

Kennedy and Eisenhower Commem. Embossed on gold foil. Air 20 r.

Lord Baden-Powell Commem. Embossed on gold foil. Air 20 r.

World Cup Football Championships, Mexico. Postage 1, 20, 40, 60, 80 d.; Air 3 r.

Brazil's Victory in World Cup Football Championships. Optd. on 1970 World Cup issue. Postage 1, 20, 40, 60, 80 d.; Air 3 r.

Paintings by Michelangelo. Postage 1, 2, 4, 5, 10 d.; Air 5 r.

World Fair "EXPO 70", Osaka, Japan. Air 25, 50, 75 d., 1, 2, 3, 12 r.

Paintings by Renoir. Postage 1, 2, 5, 6, 10 d.; Air 5, 12 r.

Christmas. Flower Paintings by Brueghel. Postage 5, 20, 25, 30, 50 d.; Air 60 d., 1, 2 r.

1971.

Roses. Postage 5, 10, 25, 30, 50 d.; Air 60 d., 1, 2 r.

Birds. Postage 5, 20, 25, 30, 50 d.; Air 60 d. 1, 2 r.

Paintings by Modigliani. Air 25, 50, 60, 75 d., 1 r. 50, 3 r.

Paintings by Rubens. Postage 1, 2, 3, 4, 5, 10 d.; Air 2, 3 r.

United Nations. 25th Anniv. Optd. on 1970 Christmas issue. Postage 5, 20, 25, 30, 50 d.; Air 60 d., 1, 2 r.

British Military Uniforms. Postage 5, 20, 25, 30, 50 d.; Air 60 d., 1, 2 r.

Space Flight of "Apollo 14". Postage 15, 25, 50, 60, 70 d.; Air 5 r.

Space Flight of "Apollo 15". Postage 25, 40, 50, 60 d.; Air 1, 6 r.

13th World Scout Jamboree, Asagiri, Japan. Postage 1, 2, 3, 5, 7, 10, 12, 15, 20, 25, 30, 35, 40, 50, 65, 80 d.; Air 1, 1 r. 25, 1 r. 50, 2 r.

Lions International Clubs. Optd. on 1971 Uniforms issue. Postage 5, 20, 25, 30, 50 d;. Air 60 d., 1, 2 r.

Royal Visit of Queen Elizabeth II to Japan. Postage 10, 20, 30, 40, 50 d.; Air 2, 3 r.

Fairy Tales. Stories by Hans Andersen. Postage 1, 2, 4, 5, 10 d.; Air 3 r.

World Fair, Philadelphia (1976). American Paintings. Postage 20, 25, 50, 60, 75 d.; Air 3 r.

Fairy Tales. Well-known stories. Postage 1, 2, 4, 5, 10 d.; Air 3 r.

Space Flight of "Apollo 16". Postage 20, 30, 40, 50, 60 d.; Air 3, 4 r.

European Tour of Emperor Hirohito of Japan. Postage 1, 2, 4, 5, 10 d.; Air 6 r.

Meeting of Pres. Nixon and Emperor Hirohito of Japan in Alaska. Optd. on 1971 Emperor's Tour issue. Air 6 r.

Persian Empire. 2500th Anniv. Postage 10, 20, 30, 40, 50 d.; Air 3 r.

Space Flight of "Apollo 15" and Future Developments in Space. Postage 10, 15, 20, 25, 50 d.; Air 1, 2 r.

1972.

150th Death Anniv. of Napoleon (1971). Postage 10, 20, 30, 40 d.; Air 1, 2, 3, 4 r.

Gen. de Gaulle. First Death Anniv. Postage 10, 20, 30, 40 d.; Air 1, 2, 3, 4 r.

Paintings from the "Alte Pinakothek", Munich. Postage 5, 10, 15, 20, 25 d.; Air 5 r.

"Tour de France" Cycle Race. Postage 5, 10, 15, 20, 25, 30, 35, 40, 45, 50, 55, 60 d.; Air 65, 70, 75, 80, 85, 90, 95 d., 1 r.

Many other issues inscribed "Manama" were made during this period, but we have yet to establish their authenticity.

The United Arab Emirates Ministry of Communications took over the Manama postal service on 1 August 1972. Further stamps inscribed "Manama" issued after that date were released without authority and had no validity.

PANAMA

1964.

Satellites. Postage ½, 1 c.; Air 5, 10, 21, 50 c.

1965.

Tokyo Olympic Games Medal Winners. Postage ½, 1, 2, 3, 4 c.; Air 5, 6, 7, 10, 21, 31 c.

Space Research. Postage ½, 1, 2, 3 c.; Air 5, 10, 11, 31 c.

Galileo. 400th Birth Anniv. Air 10, 21 c.

Peaceful Uses of Atomic Energy. Postage ½, 1, 4 c.; Air 6, 10, 21 c.

Nobel Prize Medals. Air 10, 21 c.

Pres. John Kennedy. Postage ½, 1 c.; Air 10+5 c., 21+10 c., 31+15 c.

1966.

Pope Paul's Visit to U.N. in New York. Postage ½, 1 c.; Air 5, 10, 21, 31 c.

Famous Men. Postage ½ c.; Air 10, 31 c.

Famous Paintings. Postage ½ c.; Air 10, 31 c.

World Cup. Postage ½, ½ c.; Air 10, 10, 21, 21 c.

Italian Space Research. Postage ½, 1 c.; Air 5, 10, 21 c.

I.T.U. Centenary. Air 31 c.

World Cup Winners. Optd. on 1966 World Cup Issue. Postage ½, ½ c.; Air 10, 10, 21, 21 c.

Religious Paintings. Postage ½, 1, 2, 3 c.; Air 21, 21 c.

Churchill and Space Research. Postage ½ c.; Air 10, 31 c.

Pres. John Kennedy. 3rd Death Anniv. Postage ½, 1 c.; Air 10, 31 c.

Jules Verne and Space Research. Postage ½, 1 c.; Air 5, 10, 21, 31 c.

1967.

Religious Paintings. Postage ½, 1 c.; Air 5, 10, 21, 31 c.

Mexico Olympics. Postage ½, 1 c.; Air 5, 10, 21, 31 c.

Famous Paintings. Postage 5 c.×3; Air 21 c.×3.

Goya's Paintings. Postage 2, 3, 4 c.; Air 5, 8, 10, 13, 21 c.

1968.

Religious Paintings. Postage 1, 1, 3 c.; Air 4, 21, 21 c.

Mexican President's Visit. Air 50 c., 1 b.

Winter Olympic Games, Grenoble. Postage ½, 1 c.; Air 5, 10, 21, 31 c.

Butterflies. Postage ½, 1, 3, 4 c.; Air 5, 13 c.

Ship Paintings. Postage ½, 1, 3, 4 c.; Air 5, 13 c.

Fishes. Postage ½, 1, 3, 4 c.; Air 5, 13 c.

Winter Olympic Medal Winners. Postage 1, 2, 3, 4, 5, 6, 8 c.; Air 13, 30 c.

Paintings of Musicians. 5, 10, 15, 20, 25, 30 c.

Satellite Transmissions from Panama T.V. (a) Olympic Games, Mexico. Optd. on 1964 Satellites Issue. Postage ½ c.; Air 50 c. (b) Pope Paul's Visit to Latin America. Postage ½ c.; Air 21 c. (c) Panama Satellite Transmissions. Inaug. (i) Optd. on Space Research Issue of 1965. Postage 5 c.; Air 31 c. (ii) Optd. on Churchill and Space Research Issue of 1966. Postage ½ c.; Air 10 c.

Hunting Paintings. Postage 1, 3, 5, 10 c.; Air 13, 30 c.

Horses and Jockeys. Postage 5, 10, 15, 20, 25, 30 c.

Mexico Olympics. Postage 1, 2, 3, 4, 5, 6, 8 c.; Air 13, 30 c.

1969.

1st Int. Philatelic and Numismatic Exhibition optd. on 1968 Issue of Mexican Presidents' Visit. Air 50 c., 1 b.

Telecommunications Satellites. Air 5, 10, 15, 20, 25, 30 c.

Provisionals. Surch. "Decreto No. 112 (de 6 de marzo de 1969)" and new values on No. 781 and 10 c.+5 c. and 21 c.+10 c. of 1965 Issue of 3rd Death Anniv. of Pres. John Kennedy. Air 5 c. on 5 c.+5 c., 5 c. on 10 c.+5 c., 10 c., on 21 c.+10 c.

Pope Paul VI visit to Latin America. Religious Paintings. Postage 1, 2, 3, 4, 5 c.; Air 6, 7, 8, 10 c.

PARAGUAY

1962.

Manned Spacecraft. Postage 15, 25, 30, 40, 50 c.; Air 12 g. 45, 18 g. 15, 36 g.

Previous Olympic Games. (First series) Postage 15, 25, 30, 40, 50 c.; Air 5, 10 g., 12 g. 45, 18 g. 15, 36 g.

Europa. Postage 4 g.; Air 36 g.

Solar System. Postage 10, 20, 25, 30, 50 c.; Air 12 g. 45, 36 g., 50 g.

1963.

Previous Olympic Games. (Second series). Postage 15, 25, 30, 40, 50 c.; Air 12 g. 45, 18 g. 15, 36 g.

Satellites and Space Flights. Postage 10, 20, 25, 30, 50 c.; Air 12 g. 45, 36 g., 50 g.

Previous Winter Olympic Games. Postage 10, 20, 25, 30, 50 c.; Air 12 g. 45, 36 g., 50 g.

Freedom from Hunger. Postage 10, 25, 50, 75 c.; Air 18 g. 15, 36 g., 50 g.

"Mercury" Space Flights. Postage 15, 25, 30, 40, 50 c.; Air 12 g. 45, 18 g. 15, 50 g.

Winter Olympic Games. Postage 15, 25, 30, 40, 50 c.; Air 12 g. 45, 18 g. 15, 50 g.

1964.

Tokyo Olympic Games. Postage 15, 25, 30, 40, 50 c.; Air 12 g. 45, 18 g. 15, 50 g.

Red Cross Cent. Postage 10, 25, 30, 50 c.; Air 18 g. 15, 36 g., 50 g.

"Gemini", "Telstar" and "Apollo" Projects. Postage 15, 25, 30, 40, 50 c.; Air 12 g. 45, 18 g. 15, 50 g.

Spacecraft Developments. Postage 15, 25, 30, 40, 50 c.; Air 12 g. 45, 18 g. 15, 50 g.

United Nations. Postage 15, 25, 30, 40, 50 c.; Air 12 g. 45, 18 g. 15, 50 g.

American Space Research. Postage 10, 15, 20, 30, 40, 50 c.; Air 12 g. 45+6 g., 18 g. 15+9 g., 20 g.+10 g.

Eucharistic Conference. Postage 20 g.+10 g., 30 g.+15 g., 50 g.+25 g., 100 g.+50 g.

Pope John Memorial Issue. Postage 20 g.+10 g., 30 g.+15 g., 50 g.+25 g., 100 g.+50 g

1965.

Scouts. Postage 10, 15, 20, 30, 50 c.; Air 12 g. 45, 18 g. 15, 36 g.

Tokyo Olympic Games Medals. Postage 15, 25, 30, 40, 50 c.; Air 12 g. 45, 18 g. 15, 50 g.

Famous Scientists. Postage 10, 15, 20, 30, 40 c.; Air 12 g. 45+6 g., 18 g. 15+9 g., 20 g.+10 g.

Orchids and Trees. Postage 20, 30, 90 c., 1 g. 50, 4 g. 50; Air 3 g., 4 g., 66 g.

Kennedy and Churchill. Postage 15, 25, 30, 40, 50 c.; Air 12 g. 45, 18 g. 15, 50 g.

I.T.U. Cent. Postage 10, 15, 20, 30, 40 c.; Air 12 g. 45+6 g., 18 g.+15+9 g., 20 g.+10 g.

Pope Paul VI visit to United Nations. Postage 10, 15, 20, 30, 50 c.; Air 12 g. 45, 18 g. 15, 36 g.

1966.

"Gemini" Space Project. Postage 15, 25, 30, 40, 50 c.; Air 12 g. 45, 18 g. 15, 50 g.

Events of 1965. Postage 10, 15, 20, 30, 50 c.; Air 12 g. 45, 18 g. 15, 36 g.

Mexico Olympic Games. Postage 10, 15, 20, 30, 50 c.; Air 12 g. 45, 18 g. 15, 36 g.

German Space Research. Postage 10, 15, 20, 30, 50 c.; Air 12 g. 45, 18 g. 15, 36 g.

Famous Writers. Postage 10, 15, 20, 30, 50 c.; Air 12 g. 45, 18 g. 15, 36 g.

Italian Space Research. Postage 10, 15, 20, 30, 50 c.; Air 12 g. 45, 18 g. 15, 36 g.

Moon Missions. Postage 10, 15, 20, 30, 50 c.; Air 12 g. 45, 18 g. 15, 50 g.

Sports Commemorative Issue. Postage 10, 15, 20, 30, 50 c.; Air 12 g. 45, 18 g. 15, 36 g.

Pres. John Kennedy. 3rd Death Anniv. Postage 10, 15, 20, 30, 50 c.; Air 12 g. 45, 18 g. 15, 36 g.

Famous Paintings. Postage 10, 15, 20, 30, 50 c.; Air 12 g. 45, 18 g. 15, 36 g.

1967.

Religious Paintings. Postage 10, 15, 20, 30, 50 c.; Air 12 g. 45, 18 g. 15, 36 g.

16th cent. Religious Paintings. Postage 10, 15, 20, 30, 50 c.; Air 12 g. 45, 18 g. 15, 36 g.

Impressionist Paintings. Postage 10, 15, 20, 30, 50 c.; Air 12 g. 45, 18 g. 15, 36 g.

European Paintings of 17th and 18th Cent. Postage 10, 15, 20, 25, 30, 50 c.; Air 12 g. 45, 18 g. 15, 36 g.

Pres. John Kennedy. Birth Anniv. Postage 10, 15, 20, 25, 30, 50 c.; Air 12 g. 45, 18 g. 15, 36 g.

Sculpture. Postage 10, 15, 20, 25, 30, 50 c.; Air 12 g. 45, 18 g. 15, 50 g.

Mexico Olympic Games. Archaeological Relics. Postage 10, 15, 20, 25, 30, 50 c.; Air 12 g. 45, 18 g. 15, 36 g.

1968.

Religious Paintings. Postage 10, 15, 20, 25, 30, 50 c.; Air 12 g. 45, 18 g. 15, 36 g.

Winter Olympic Games, Grenoble. Postage 10, 15, 20, 25, 30, 50 c.; Air 12 g. 45, 18 g. 15, 36 g.

Paraguayan Stamps from 1870–1970. Postage 10, 15, 20, 25, 30, 50 c.; Air 12 g. 45, 18 g. 15, 36 g.

Mexico Olympic Games, Paintings of Children. Postage 10, 15, 20, 25, 30, 50 c.; Air 12 g. 45, 18 g. 15, 36 g. (Sailing ship and Olympic Rings).

Visit of Pope Paul VI to Eucharistic Congress. Religious Paintings. Postage 10, 15, 20, 25, 30, 50 c.; Air 12 g. 45, 18 g. 15, 36 g.

Important Events of 1968. Postage 10, 15, 20, 25, 30, 50 c.; Air 12 g. 45, 18 g. 15, 50 g.

1969.

Gold Medal Winners of 1968 Mexico Olympic Games. Postage 10, 15, 20, 25, 30, 50 c.; Air 12 g. 45, 18 g. 15, 50 g.

Int. Projects in Outer Space. Postage 10, 15, 20, 25, 30, 50 c.; Air 12 g. 45, 18 g. 15, 50 g.

Latin American Wildlife. Postage 10, 10, 15, 15, 20, 20, 25, 25, 30, 30, 50, 50, 75, 75 c.; Air 12 g. 45×2, 18 g. 15×2.

Gold Medal Winners in Olympic Football, 1900–1968. Postage 10, 15, 20, 25, 30, 50, 75 c.; Air 12 g. 45, 18 g. 15.

Paraguayan Football Champions, 1930–1966. Postage 10, 15, 20, 25, 30, 50, 75 c.; Air 12 g. 45, 18 g. 15.

Paintings by Goya. Postage 10, 15, 20, 25, 30, 50, 75 c.; Air 12 g. 45, 18 g. 15.

Christmas. Religious Paintings. Postage 10, 15, 20, 25, 30, 50, 75 c.; Air 12 g. 45, 18 g. 15.

1970.

Moon Walk. Postage 10, 15, 20, 25, 30, 50, 75 c.; Air 12 g. 45, 18 g. 15.

Easter. Paintings Postage 10, 15, 20, 25, 30, 50, 75 c.; Air 12 g. 45, 18 g. 15.

Munich, Olympic Games. Postage 10, 15, 20, 25, 30, 50, 75 c.; Air 12 g. 45, 18 g. 15.

Paintings from the Pinakothek Museum in Munich. Postage 10, 15, 20, 25, 30, 50, 75 c.; Air 12 g. 45, 18 g. 15.

"Apollo" Space Programme. Postage 10, 15, 20, 25, 30, 50, 75 c.; Air 12 g. 45, 18 g. 15.

Space Projects in the Future. Postage 10, 15, 20, 25, 30, 50, 75 c.; Air 12 g. 45, 18 g. 15.

"EXPO '70" World Fair, Osaka, Japan. Japanese Paintings. Postage 10, 15, 20, 25, 30, 50, 75 c.; Air 12 g. 45, 18 g. 15, 50 g.

Flower Paintings. Postage 10, 15, 20, 25, 30, 50, 75 c.; Air 12 g. 45, 18 g. 15, 50 g.

Paintings from Prado Museum, Madrid. Postage 10, 15, 20, 25, 30, 50, 75 c.; Air 12 g. 45, 18 g. 15, 50 g.

Paintings by Durer. Postage 10, 15, 20, 25, 30, 50, 75 c.; Air 12 g. 45, 18 g. 15, 50 g.

1971.

Christmas 1970/71. Religious Paintings. Postage 10, 15, 20, 25, 30, 50, 75 c.; Air 12 g. 45, 18 g. 15, 50 g.

Munich Olympic Games 1972. Postage 10, 15, 20, 25, 30, 50, 75 c.; Air 12 g. 45, 18 g. 15, 50 g.

Paintings of Horses and Horsemen. Postage 10, 15, 20, 25, 30, 50, 75 c.; Air 12 g. 45, 18 g. 15, 50 g.

Famous Paintings from the Louvre, Paris. Postage 10, 15, 20, 25, 30, 50, 75 c.; Air 12 g. 45, 18 g. 15, 50 g.

Paintings in the National Museum, Asuncion. Postage 10, 15, 20, 25, 30, 50, 75 c.; Air 12 g. 45, 18 g. 15, 50 g.

Hunting Paintings. Postage 10, 15, 20, 25, 30, 50, 75 c.; Air 12 g. 45, 18 g. 15, 50 g.

Philatokyo '71, Stamp Exhibition, Tokyo. Japanese Paintings. Postage 10, 15, 20, 25, 30, 50, 75 c.; Air 12 g. 45, 18 g. 15, 50 g.

Winter Olympic Games, Sapporo 1972. Japanese Paintings. Postage 10, 15, 20, 25, 30, 50, 75 c.; Air 12 g. 45, 18 g. 15, 50 g.

Napoleon. 150th Death Anniv. Paintings. Postage 10, 15, 20, 25, 30, 50, 75 c.; Air 12 g. 45, 18 g. 15, 50 g.

Famous Paintings from the Dahlem Museum, Berlin. Postage 10, 15, 20, 25, 30, 50, 75 c.; Air 12 g. 45, 18 g. 15, 50 g.

1972.

Locomotives (First series). Postage 10, 15, 20, 25, 30, 50, 75 c.; Air 12 g. 45, 18 g. 15, 50 g.

Winter Olympic Games, Sapporo. Postage 10, 15, 20, 25, 30, 50, 75 c.; Air 12 g. 45, 18 g. 15, 50 g.

Racing Cars. Postage 10, 15, 20, 25, 30, 50, 75 c.; Air 12 g. 45, 18 g. 15, 50 g.

Famous Sailing Ships. Postage 10, 15, 20, 25, 30, 50, 75 c.; Air 12 g. 45, 18 g. 15, 50 g.

Famous Paintings from the Vienna Museum. Postage 10, 15, 20, 25, 30, 50, 75 c.; Air 12 g. 45, 18 g. 15, 50 g.

Famous Paintings from the Asuncion Museum. Postage 10, 15, 20, 25, 30, 50, 75 c.; Air 12 g. 45, 18 g. 15, 50 g.

Visit of the Argentine President to Paraguay. Postage 10, 15, 20, 25, 30, 50, 75 c.; Air 12 g. 45, 18 g. 15.

Visit of President of Paraguay to Japan. Postage 10, 15, 20, 25, 30, 50, 75 c.; Air 12 g. 45, 18 g. 15.

Paintings of Animals and Birds. Postage 10, 15, 20, 25, 30, 50, 75 c.; Air 12 g. 45, 18 g. 15.

Locomotives (Second series). Postage 10, 15, 20, 25, 30, 50, 75 c.; Air 12 g. 45, 18 g. 15.

South American Fauna. Postage 10, 15, 20, 25, 30, 50, 75 c.; Air 12 g. 45, 18 g. 15.

1973.

Famous Paintings from the Florence Museum. Postage 10, 15, 20, 25, 30, 50, 75 c.; Air 5, 10, 20 g.

South American Butterflies. Postage 10, 15, 20, 25, 30, 50, 75 c.; Air 5, 10, 20 g.

Cats. Postage 10, 15, 20, 25, 30, 50, 75 c.; Air 5, 10, 20 g.

Portraits of Women. Postage 10, 15, 20, 25, 30, 50, 75 c.; Air 5, 10, 20 g.

World Cup Football Championships, Munich (1974) (1st issue). Postage 10, 15, 20, 25, 30, 50, 75 c.; Air 5, 10, 15 g.

Paintings of Women. Postage 10, 15, 20, 25, 30, 50, 75 c.; Air 5, 10, 15 g.

Birds. Postage 10, 15, 20, 25, 30, 50, 75 c.; Air 5, 10, 15 g.

"Apollo" Moon Missions and Future Space Projects. Postage 10, 15, 20, 25, 30, 50 75 c.; Air 5, 10, 15 g.

Visit of Pres. Stroessner to Europe and Morocco. 5, 10, 25, 50, 150 g.

Folk Costume. 25, 50, 75 c., 1 g., 1 g. 50, 1 g. 75, 2 g. 25.

Flowers. 10, 20, 25, 30, 40, 50, 75 c.

1974.

World Cup Football Championships, Munich (2nd issue). Air 5, 10, 20 g.

Roses. 10, 15, 20, 25, 30, 50, 75 c.

Famous Paintings from the Gulbenkian Museum, New York. Postage 10, 15, 20, 25, 30, 50, 75 c.; Air 5, 10, 20 g.

U.P.U. Cent. Postage 10, 15, 20, 25, 30, 50, 75 c.; Air 5, 10, 20 g.

Famous Masterpieces. Postage 10, 15, 20, 25, 30, 50, 75 c.; Air 5, 10, 20 g.

Visit of Pres. Stroessner to France. Air 100 g.

World Cup Football Championships, Munich (3rd issue). Air 4, 5, 10 g.

Ships. Postage 5, 10, 15, 20, 25, 35, 40, 50 c.

Events of 1974. Air 4 g. (U.P.U.), 5 g. (President of Chile's visit), 10 g. (Pres. Stroessners' visit to South Africa).

Universal Postal Union. Centenary. Air 4, 5, 10 g.

RAS AL KHAIMA

1967.

"The Arabian Nights". Paintings. Air 30, 70 d., 1, 2, 3 r.

Cats. Postage 1, 2, 3, 4, 5d.; Air 3 r.

Arab Paintings. 1, 2, 3, 4, 10, 20, 30 d.

European Paintings. Air 60, 70 d., 1, 2, 3, 5, 10 r.

Pres. John F. Kennedy. 50th Birth Anniv. Optd. on 1965 Pres. Kennedy Commem. 2, 3, 4 r.

World Scout Jamboree, Idaho. Postage 1, 2 3, 4 d.; Air 35, 75 d., 1 r.

U.S. "Apollo" Disaster. Optd. on 1968 American Astronauts issue. 25 d. on 25 n.p., 50 d. on 50 n.p., 75 d. on 75 n.p., 1, 2, 3, 4, 5 r.

Summer Olympics Preparation, Mexico 1968. Postage 10, 20, 30, 40 d.; Air 1, 2 r.

Winter Olympics Preparation, Grenoble 1968. Postage 1, 2, 3, 4, 5, d.; Air 85 d., 2, 3 r.

1968.

Mothers' Day. Paintings. Postage 20, 30 40, 50 d.; Air 1, 2, 3, 4 r.

Int. Human Rights Year. 2 r.×3.

Int. Museum Campaign. Paintings. 15, 15, 20, 25, 35, 40, 45, 60, 70, 80, 90 d., 1, 1 r. 25, 1 r. 50, 2 r. 50, 2 r. 75.

Winter Olympic Medal Winners, Grenoble. 50 d., 1, 1 r. 50, 2, 2 r. 50, 3 r.

Olympic Games, Mexico. Air 1, 2, 2, 3, 3, 4 r.

Pres. John F. Kennedy. 5th Death Anniv. Air 2, 3 r.

Christmas. Religious Paintings. Postage 20, 30, 40, 50, 60 d., 1 r.; Air 2, 3, 4 r.

1969.

Famous Composers (1st series). Paintings. 25, 50, 75 d., 1 r. 50, 2 r. 50.

Famous Operas. 20, 40, 60, 80 d., 1, 2 r.

Famous Men. Postage 20, 30, 50 d.; Air 1 r. 50, 2, 3, 4, 5 r.

Int. Philatelic Exhib., Mexico 1968 (EFIMEX). Postage 10, 10, 25, 35, 40, 50, 60, 70 d.; Air 1, 2, 3, 5, 5 r.

Int. Co-operation in Olympics. 1, 2, 3, 4 r.

Int. Co-operation in Space. Air 1 r. 50, 2 r. 50, 3 r. 50, 4 r. 50.

Napoleon. 200th Birth Anniv. Paintings. Postage 1 r. 75, 2 r. 75, 3 r. 75; Air 75 d.

"Apollo" Moon Missions. Air 2, 2 r. 50, 3, 3 r. 50, 4, 4 r. 50, 5, 5 r. 50.

"Apollo 11" Astronauts. Air 2 r. 25, 3 r. 25, 4 r. 25, 5 r. 25.

"Apollo 12" Astronauts. Air 60 d., 2 r. 60, 3 r. 60, 4 r. 60, 5 r. 60.

1970.

Christmas 1969. Religious Paintings. Postage 50 d.; Air 3, 3 r. 50.

World Cup, Mexico. Air 1, 2, 3, 4, 5, 6 r.

Easter. Religious Paintings. Postage 50 d.; Air 3, 3 r. 50.

Paintings by Titian and Tiepolo. Postage 50, 50 d.; Air 3, 3, 3 r. 50, 3 r. 50.

Winter Olympics, Sapporo 1972. Air 1, 2, 3, 4, 5, 6 r.

Olympic Games, Munich 1972. Air 1, 2, 3, 4, 5, 6 r.

Paul Gauguin's Paintings. Postage 50 d.; Air 3, 3 r. 50.

Christmas. Religious Paintings. Postage 50 d.; Air 3, 3 r. 50.

"World Cup Champions, Brazil". Optd. on Mexico World Cup issue. Air 1, 2, 3, 4, 5, 6 r.

"EXPO" World Fair, Osaka, Japan (1st issue). Postage 40, 45, 50, 55, 60, 65, 70, 75 d.; Air 80, 85, 90, 95 d., 1 r. 60, 1 r. 65, 1 r. 85, 2 r.

"EXPO 70" World Fair, Osaka, Japan (2nd issue). Postage 55, 65, 75 d.; Air 25, 85, 95 d., 1 r. 50, 1 r. 75.

Space Programmes. Air 1 r.×6, 2 r.×6, 4 r.×6.

Famous Frenchmen. Air 1 r.×4, 2 r.×4, 2 r. 50×2, 3 r.×2, 4 r.×4, 5 r. 50×2.

Int. Philatelic Exhib. (Philympia '70). Air 1 r.×4, 1 r. 50×4, 2 r. 50×4, 3 r.×4, 4 r.×4.

Events in the Life of Christ. Religious Paintings. 5, 10, 25, 50 d., 1, 2, 5 r.

"Stages of the Cross". Religious Paintings. 10, 20, 30, 40, 50, 60, 70, 80 d., 1, 1 r. 50, 2, 2 r. 50, 3, 3 r. 50.

The Life of Mary. Religious Paintings. 10, 15, 30, 60, 75 d., 3, 4 r.

1971.

Easter. "Stages of the Cross" (1970) but with additional inscr. "Easter". 10, 20, 30, 40, 50, 60, 70, 80 d., 1, 1 r. 50, 2, 2 r. 50, 3, 3 r. 50.

Charles de Gaulle Memorial. Postage 50 d.; Air 1, 1 r. 50, 2, 3, 4 r.

Safe return of "Apollo 14". Postage 50 d.; Air 1, 1 r. 50, 2, 3, 4 r.

U.S.A.—Japan Baseball Friendship. Postage 10, 25, 30, 80 d.; Air 50, 70 d., 1, 1 r. 50.

Munich Olympics, 1972. Postage 50 d.; Air 1, 1 r. 50, 2, 3, 4 r.

Cats. 35, 60, 65, 110, 120, 160 d.

13th World Jamboree, Japan. Postage 30, 50, 60, 75 d.; Air 1, 1 r. 50, 3. 4 r.

Sapporo Olympic Gold Medal Winners. Optd. on 1970 Winter Olympics, Sapporo 1972, issue. Air 1, 2, 3, 4, 5, 6 r.

Munich Olympic Medal Winners, Optd. on 1970 Summer Olympics, Munich 1972, issue. Air 1, 2, 3, 4, 5, 6 r.

Japanese Locomotives. Postage 30, 35, 75 d.; Air 90 d., 1, 1 r. 75.

"Soyuz 11" Russian Cosmonauts Memorial. Air 1, 2, 3, 4 r.

"Apollo 15". Postage 50 d.; Air 1, 1 r. 50, 2, 3, 4 r.

Dogs. 5, 20, 75, 85, 185, 200 d.

Durers' Paintings. Postage 50 d.; Air 1, 1 r. 50 2, 3, 4 r.

Famous Composers (2nd series). Postage 50 d.; Air 1, 1 r. 50, 2, 3, 4 r.

"Soyuz 11" and "Salyut" Space Projects. Postage 50 d.; Air 1, 1 r. 50, 2, 3, 4 r.

Butterflies. Postage 15, 20, 70 d.; Air 1 r. 25, 1 r. 50, 1 r. 70.

Wild Animals. 10, 40, 80 d., 1 r. 15, 1 r. 30, 1 r. 65.

Fishes. 30, 50, 60, 90 d., 1 r. 45, 1 r. 55.

Ludwig Van Beethoven. Portraits. Postage 50 d.; Air 1, 1 r. 50. 2. 3. 4 r.

1972.

Birds. 50, 55, 80, 100, 105, 190 d.

Winter Olympics, Sapporo (1st issue). Postage 20, 30, 50 d.; Air 70, 90 d., 2 r. 50.

Winter Olympics, Sapporo (2nd issue). Postage 5, 60, 80, 90 d.; Air 1 r. 10, 1 r. 75.

Mozart. Portraits. Postage 50 d.; Air 1, 1 r. 50, 2, 3, 4 r.

Olympic Games, Munich. Postage 50 d.; Air 1, 1 r. 50, 2, 3, 4 r.

"In Memory of Charles de Gaulle" Optd. on 1971 Charles de Gaulle memorial issue. Postage 50 d.; Air 1, 1 r. 50, 2, 3, 4 r.

Winter Olympics, Sapporo (3rd issue). Postage 15, 45 d.; Air 65, 75 d., 1 r. 20, 1 r. 25.

Horses. Postage 10, 25, 30 d.; Air 1 r. 40, 1 r. 80, 1 r. 95.

Parrots. 40, 45, 70, 95 d., 1 r. 35, 1 r. 75.

"Apollo 16". Postage 50 d.; Air 1, 1 r. 50, 2, 3, 4 r.

European Footballers. Postage 50 d.; Air 1, 1 r. 50, 2, 3, 4 r.

A number of issues on gold or silver foil also exist, but it is understood that these were mainly for presentation purposes, although valid for postage.

In common with the other states of the United Arab Emirates the Ras al Khaima stamp contract was terminated on 1st August 1972, and any further new issues released after that date were unauthorised.

SHARJAH

1967.

Post Day. Japanese Paintings. 1 r.×3.

United Nations. 22nd Anniv. 10, 30, 60 d.

Olympics Preparation, Mexico 1968. Postage 1, 2, 3, 10 d.; Air 30, 60 d., 2 r.

Flowers and Butterflies. Postage 1, 2, 3, 4, 5, 10, 20 d.; Air 30, 60 d., 1, 2 r.

Famous Paintings. Postage 1, 2, 3, 4, 5, 30, 40, 60, 75 d.; Air 1, 2, 3, 4, 5 r.

1968.

Winter Olympic Games, Grenoble. Postage 1, 2, 3, 4, 5 d.; Air 1, 2, 3 r.

12th World Jamboree. Postage 1, 2, 3, 4, 5, 10 d.; Air 30, 50, 60 d., 1 r. 50.

Grenoble Olympic Medal Winners. Optd. on Winter Olympics, Grenoble issue. Postage 1, 2, 3, 4, 5 d.; Air 1, 2, 3 r.

Mothers' Day. Paintings. Postage 10, 20, 30, 40 d.; Air 1, 2, 3, 4 r.

American Paintings. Postage 20, 30, 40, 50, 60 d.; Air 1, 4, 5 r.

Egyptian Art. 15, 25, 35, 45, 55, 65, 75, 95 d.

Martyrs of Liberty. Air 35 d.×4, 60 d.×4, 1 r.×4.

Olympic Games, Mexico. 10, 20, 30 d., 2 r., 2 r. 40, 5 r.

Previous Olympic Games. Air 25, 50, 75 d., 1 r. 50, 3, 4 r.

Sportsmen and women. Postage 20, 30, 40, 60 d., 1 r. 50, 2 r. 50; Air 25, 50 d., 1, 2 r., 3 r. 25, 4, 4 r.

Robert Kennedy Memorial. Optd. on American Paintings issue. Air 4 r.

Olympic Medal Winners, Mexico. 35, 50, 60 d., 1, 2, 4 r.

1969.

Famous Men and Women. Postage 10, 20, 25, 35, 50, 60 d.; Air 1, 2, 3, 4, 5, 6 r.

"Apollo 8" Moon Mission. Postage 5 d.×6; Air 10, 15, 20 d., 2, 3, 4 r.

"Apollo 11" Moon Mission (1st series). Postage 5 d.×8; Air 75 d.×8, 1 r.×8.

Post Day. Famous Ships. Postage 5 d.×8; Air 90 d.×8.

1970.

U.N.I.C.E.F. Paintings of Children. Postage 5 d.×9; Air 20, 25, 35, 40, 50, 60, 75 d., 1, 3 r.

Animals. Postage 3 d.×14, 10, 10, 15, 15 d.; Air 20, 20, 35, 35 d., 1, 1, 2, 2 r.

"EXPO 70" World Fair, Osaka, Japan (1st series). Japanese Paintings. Postage 3 d.×4; Air 1 r.×4.

"EXPO 70" World Fair, Osaka, Japan (2nd series). Pavilions. Postage 2, 2, 3, 3 d.; Air 40 d.×4.

Paintings of Napoleon. Postage 3 d.×5; Air 20, 30, 40, 60 d., 2 r.

De Gaulle Commemoration. Postage 3 d.×5; Air 20, 30, 40, 60 d., 2 r.

Ruler's Accession. 5th Anniv. Postage 5 d.×5; Air 20 d., 35 d.×5, 40 d.×5, 60 d.×5.

"Mercury" and "Vostok" Moon Missions. Postage 1, 2, 3, 4, 5 d.; Air 25, 40, 85 d., 1, 2 r.

"Gemini" Space Programme. Postage 1, 2, 3, 4, 5 d.; Air 25, 40, 85 d., 1, 2 r.

"Apollo", "Voskhod" and "Soyuz" Projects. Postage 1, 2, 3, 4, 5 d.; Air 25, 40, 85 d., 1, 2 r.

Events of 1970. Postage 1 d.×5, 5 d.; Air 75 d., 1, 2, 3 r.

Beethoven. 200th Birth Anniv. Postage 3 d.×5; Air 35, 40, 60 d., 1, 2 r.

Mozart. Postage 3 d.×5; Air 35, 40, 60 d., 1, 2 r.

The Life of Christ (1st series). Postage 1, 2, 3, 4, 5 d.; Air 25, 40, 60 d., 1, 2 r.

1971.

"Apollo 14" Moon Mission. Optd. on 1969, "Apollo 11" issue. Postage 5 d.×4; Air 75 d.×4.

Post Day 1970. Cars. Postage 1, 2, 3, 4, 5 d.; Air 25, 50, 60 d., 2, 3 r.

Post Day (1st series). American Cars. Postage 1, 2, 3, 4, 5 d.; Air 35, 50 d., 1, 2, 3 r.

Post Day (2nd series). Trains. Postage 1, 2, 3, 4, 5 d.; Air 25, 50, 60 d., 1, 2 r.

Pres. Nasser Commemoration. Postage 5d. × 5; Air 20, 35, 40, 60 d., 2 r.

Safe return of "Apollo 13". Optd. on 1969, "Apollo 8" issue. Air 10, 15, 20 d., 2, 3, 4 r.

De Gaulle Memorial. Postage 3, 4, 5, 6, 7 d.; Air 40, 60, 75 d., 1, 2 r.

Olympics Preparation, Munich 1972. Postage 2, 3, 4, 5, 6 d.; Air 35, 40, 60 d., 1, 2 r.

Miracles of Christ. Postage 1, 2, 3, 4, 5 d.; Air 25, 40, 60 d., 1, 2 r.

1972.

Sport. Postage 2, 3, 4, 5, 6 d.; Air 35, 40, 60 d. 1, 2 r.

The Life of Christ (2nd series). Postage 1, 2, 3, 4, 5 d.; Air 25, 40, 60 d., 1, 2 r.

Winter Olympics Preparation, Sapporo Postage 2, 3, 4, 5, 6 d.; Air 35, 40, 60 d., 1, 2 r.

Safe return of "Apollo 14". Optd. on 1969, "Apollo 11" issue. Postage 5 d.×4; Air 1 r.×4.

Previous World Cup Winners. Postage 5, 10, 15, 20, 25 d.; Air 35, 75 d., 1, 2, 3 r.

Sapporo Olympic Medal Winners. Paintings. Postage 5, 10, 15, 20, 25 d.; Air 35, 75 d., 1, 2, 3 r.

Famous people, Churchill, De Gaulle and John Kennedy. Postage 5 d.×4, 10 d.×4, 35 d.×4; Air 75 d.×4, 1 r.×4, 3 r.×4.

Olympic Games, Munich. Postage 5, 10, 15, 20, 25 d.; Air 35, 75 d., 1, 2, 3 r.

Cats. Postage 20, 25 d.; Air 75 d., 1, 2 r.

Birds (1st series). Postage 20, 25, 75 d.; Air 1, 2 r.

"Apollo 11" Moon Mission (2nd series). Air 1 r.×5.

"Apollo 16" Moon Mission. Air 1 r.×5.

Dogs. Postage 20, 25 d.; Air 75 d., 1, 2 r.

"Apollo 17" Moon Mission. Postage 1, 1 r.; Air 1 r.×3.

Munich Olympic Medal Winners. Air 5 r.×20.

Horses. Postage 20, 25 d.; Air 75 d., 1, 2 r.

"Apollo 17" Astronauts. Postage 1, 1 r.; Air 1 r.×3.

Butterflies. Postage 20, 25 d.; Air 75 d., 1, 2 r.

"Luna 9" Soviet Space Programme. Postage 1, 1 r.; Air 1 r.×3.

Monkeys. Postage 20, 25 d.; Air 75 d., 1, 2 r.

Birds (2nd series). Air 25, 25, 35, 35, 50, 50, 65, 65 d., 1 r.×6, 3, 3 r.

Fish. Air 25, 35, 50, 65 d., 1 r.×5, 3 r.

Insects. Air 25, 35, 50, 65 d., 1, 3 r.

Flowers. Postage 25, 35, 50, 65 d., 1, 3 r.; Air 1 r.×4.

Fruit. Air 1 r.×4.

Children. Air 1 4 r.×4.

Eastern Antiquities. Air 25, 35, 40, 65, 75 d., 3 r., 1 r.×4.

Planetary Exploration. Postage 1 r.×3; Air 1, 1 r.

13th World Jamboree. Postage 2 d.×3, 3 d.×3, 4 d.×3, 5 d.×3, 6 d.×3; Air 35 d.×3, 75 d.×3, 1 r.×3, 2 r.×3, 3 r.×3.

A number of issues on gold or silver foil also exist, but it is understood that these were mainly for presentation purposes, although valid for postage.

In common with the other states of the United Arab Emirates the Sharjah stamp contract was terminated on 1st August 1972, and further new issues released after that date were unauthorised.

UMM AL QIWAIN

1967.

Self-Portraits of Famous Painters. Postage 10, 15, 25, 50, 75 d., 1, 1 r. 50; Air 1 r. 25, 2, 2 r. 50, 3, 5 r.

Dogs. Postage 15, 25, 50, 75 d., 1 r.; Air 1 r. 25, 2 r. 50, 4 r.

"EXPO 67" World Fair, Montreal. Famous Paintings. 25, 50, 75 d., 1, 1 r. 50, 2, 3 r.

1968.

Falcons. Postage 15, 25, 50, 75 d., 1 r.; Air 1 r. 50, 3, 5 r.

Winter Olympic Games, Grenoble. Postage 10, 25, 75 d., 1 r.; Air 1 r. 50, 2, 3, 5 r.

Famous Paintings. Postage 25, 50, 75 d., 1, 1 r. 50, 2 r. 50; Air 1, 2, 3, 4, 5 r.

Olympic Games, Mexico (1st issue). Optd. on (a) 1964 Tokyo Olympic Games issue. Postage 1 r. 50, 2, 4, 5 r. (b) 1968 Winter Olympic Games issue. Air 1 r. 50, 2, 5 r.

Robert Kennedy Memorial. Optd. on 1965 Pres. Kennedy issue. Postage 3, 5, 7 r. 50.

Olympic Games, Mexico (2nd issue). Postage 10, 25, 50 d., 1, 2 r.; Air 2 r. 50, 3, 4, 5 r.

Still Life Paintings. Postage 25, 50 d., 1, 1 r. 50, 2 r.; Air 1 r. 25, 2 r. 50, 3, 3 r. 50, 5 r.

Mexico Olympic Medal Winners. Optd. on Olympic Games, Mexico issue. Postage 10, 25, 50 d., 1, 2 r.; Air 2 r. 50, 3, 4, 5 r.

Aviation History. Aircraft. Postage 25, 50 d., 1, 1 r. 50, 2 r.; Air 1 r. 25, 2 r. 50, 3, 5 r.

1969.

"Apollo 8" Moon Orbit. Optd. on 1968 Aviation History issue. Postage 25, 50 d., 1, 1 r. 50, 2 r.; Air 1 r. 25, 2 r. 50, 3, 5 r.

Horses (1st series). Postage 25, 50, 75 d., 1, 2 r.; Air 1 r. 50, 2 r. 50, 4, 5 r.

Olympic Games, Munich, 1972 (1st issue). Optd. on 1968 Olympic Games, Mexico issue, Postage 10, 25, 50 d., 1, 2 r.; Air 2 r. 50, 3, 4, 5 r.

Winter Olympic Games, Sapporo, 1972 (1st issue). Optd. on 1968 Winter Olympics, Grenoble issue. Postage 10, 25, 75 d., 1 r.; Air 1 r. 50, 2, 3, 5 r.

Veteran and Vintage Cars. Postage 15 d.×8, 25 d.×8, 50 d.×8, 75 d.×8; Air 1 r.×8, 2 r.×8.

Famous Films. Postage 10, 15, 25, 50, 75 d., 1 r.; Air 1 r. 50, 2, 2 r. 50, 3, 4, 5 r.

"Apollo 12" Moon Landing. 10, 20, 30, 50, 75 d., 1 r.

1970.

"Apollo 13" Astronauts. 10, 30, 50 d.

"EXPO 70" World Fair, Osaka Japan. 5, 10, 20, 40 d., 1, 1 r. 25.

British Landing on Trucial Coast. 150th Anniv. Uniforms. 10, 20, 30, 50, 75 d., 1 r.

1971.

Animals. Postage 10, 15, 20, 25 d.; Air 5 r.

Winter Olympic Games, Sapporo, 1972 (2nd issue). Postage 5, 10, 15, 20, 25 d.; Air 50, 75 d., 1, 3, 5 r.

Olympic Games, Munich, 1972 (2nd issue). Postage 5, 10, 15, 20, 25 d.; Air 50, 75 d., 1, 3, 5 r.

1972.

Durer's Religious Paintings. Postage 5, 10, 15, 20, 25 d.; Air 3 r.

Horses (2nd series). Postage 10, 15, 20, 25 d.; Air 50 d., 3 r.

Locomotives (plastic surfaced). Postage 5, 10, 20, 40, 50 d.; Air 6 r.

Winter Olympic Games, Sapporo, 1972 (3rd issue) (plastic surfaced). Postage 5, 10, 20, 40, 50 d.; Air 6 r.

Easter, Religious Paintings. Postage 5, 10, 20, 50 d.; Air 1, 3 r.

Kennedy brothers memorial. Postage 5, 10, 15, 20 d.; Air 1, 3 r.

Winston Churchill memorial. Postage 5, 10, 15, 20 d.; Air 3 r.

Arab rulers. Postage 5 d.×6, 10 d.×6, 15 d.×6, 20 d.×6; Air 3 r.×6.

13th World Jamboree, 1971 (plastic surfaced). Postage 5, 10, 20, 40, 50 d.; Air 6 r.

Fish. Postage 5, 10, 20, 40, 50 d.; Air 6 r.

Internationa Airlines. Postage 5, 10, 15, 20, 25 d.; Air 50 d.

"Apollo 15" Moon Mission. Postage 5, 10, 15, 20, 25 d.; Air 50, 75 d., 1, 3, 5 r.

Olympic Games, Munich, 1972 (3rd issue) (plastic surfaced). Postage 5, 10, 20, 40, 50 d.; Air 6 r.

Founding of Persian Empire. 2500th Anniv. Postage 10, 20, 30, 40, 50, 60 d.; Air 1 r.

Portraits of Charles de Gaulle. 5, 10, 15, 20, 25 d.

Paintings of Napoleon. Postage 5, 10, 15, 20, 25 d.; Air 5 r.

Butterflies. Postage 5, 10, 15, 20, 25 d.; Air 3 r.

Penguins. Postage 5, 10, 15, 20 d.; Air 50 d., 4 r.

Cars. Postage 5, 10, 15, 20, 25 d.; Air 3 r.

Masks (1st series). Postage 5, 10, 15, 20, 25 d.; Air 50 d., 1, 3 r.

Dogs and Cats. Postage 5, 5, 10, 10, 15, 15, 20, 20, 25, 25 d.; Air 5, 5 r.

Roses. Postage 10, 15, 20, 25 d.; Air 50 d., 5 r.

Marine Fauna. Postage 5, 10, 15, 20, 25, 50 d.; Air 1, 3 r.

Masks (2nd series). Postage 5, 10, 15, 20, 25 d.; Air 50 d., 1, 3 r.

UPPER VOLTA

1973.

Gold Medal Winners, Munich Olympic Games (2nd series). Air 50, 60, 90, 150, 350 f.

Christmas 1972. Paintings of the Madonna and Child. Air 50, 75, 100, 125, 150 f.

Moon Mission of "Apollo 17". 50, 65, 100, 150, 200 f.

Gold Medal Winners, Munich Olympic Games (3rd series). Air 35, 45, 75, 250, 400 f.

Exploration of the Moon. Air 50, 65, 100, 150, 200 f.

Wild Animals. Air 100, 150, 200, 250, 500 f.

Organization of African Unity. 10th Anniv. Air 45 f.

Europafrique. European Paintings. Air 50, 65, 100, 150, 200 f.

Historic Railway Locomotives, French Railway Museum, Mulhouse. Air 10, 40, 50, 150, 250 f.

Upper Volta Boy Scouts. Postage 20 f.; Air 40, 75, 150, 200 f.

Pan-African Drought Relief. Surch. on values of 1973 Europafrique issue. Air 100 f. on 65 f., 200 f. on 150 f.

International Police Organization (Interpol). 50th Anniv. 50, 65, 70, 150 f.

Tourism. Postage 35, 40 f.; Air 100 f.

Religious Buildings. Postage 35, 40 f.; Air 200 f.

Folk-dancers. Postage 35, 40 f.; Air 100, 225 f.

Famous Men. 5, 10, 20, 25, 30, 50, 60, 75, 100, 175, 200, 250 f.

1974.

World Cup Football Championships, Munich (1st issue). Postage 5, 40 f.; Air 75, 100, 250 f.

Pres. De Gaulle Commemoration. Postage 35, 40, 60 f.; Air 300 f.

World Cup Football Championships (2nd issue). Postage 10, 20, 50 f.; Air 150, 300 f.

Universal Postal Union. Centenary. Postage 35, 40, 85 f.; Air 100, 200, 300 f.

World Cup Football Championships (3rd issue). Previous Finals. Postage 10, 25, 50 f.; Air 150, 200, 250 f.

Berne Convention. Centenary. 1974 U.P.U. issue optd. Postage 35, 40, 85 f.; Air 100, 200, 300 f.

Bouquets of Flowers. Postage 5, 10, 30, 50 f.; Air 300 f.

1975.

Sir Winston Churchill. Centenary. 50, 75, 100, 125, 300 f.

United States of America. Bicentenary. 35, 40, 75, 100, 200, 300 f.

UPPER YAFA

1967.

Olympic Games, Mexico (1968). Postage 15, 25, 50, 75 f.; Air 150 f.

Sculptures. Postage 10, 30 60, 75 f.; Air 150 f.

Paintings from the Louvre. Postage 50 f.; Air 100, 150, 200, 250 f.

World Cup Football Championships, London (1966). Postage 5, 10, 50 f.; Air 100 f.

Paintings by Old Masters. Postage 10, 15, 20, 25, 30, 40, 50, 60, 75 f.; Air 150 f.

Human Rights Year and 5th Death Anniv. of J. F. Kennedy. Postage 5, 10, 50 75 f.; Air 125 f.

Persian Miniatures. 10, 20, 30, 40, 50 f.

Ballet Paintings. 20, 30, 40, 50, 60 f.

Portraits by Old Masters. Postage 25, 50, 75 f.; Air 100, 125, 150, 175, 200, 225, 250 f.

Winter Olympic Games, Grenoble (1968). 1967 World Cup issue optd. Postage 5 f. × 2, 10 f. × 2, 50 f. × 2; Air 100 f. × 2.

20th Anniv. of U.N.I.C.E.F. Paintings. Postage 50, 75 f.; Air 100, 125, 250 f.

Flower Paintings. Postage 5, 10, 50 f.; Air 100, 150 f.

YEMEN

REPUBLIC

1967.

5th Anniv. of Revolution. Nos. 476/81 optd. in Arabic. 1, 2, 4, 6, 8, 10 b.

Paintings by Flemish Masters. Postage ¼, ⅓, ½ b.; Air 3, 6 b.

Paintings by Florentine Masters. Postage ¼, ⅓, ½ b.; Air 3, 6 b.

Paintings by Spanish Masters. Postage ¼, ⅓, ½ b.; Air 3, 6 b.

Winter Olympic Games, Grenoble (1968) (1st issue). Embossed on gold foil. Air 5, 10, 15, 50 b.

Winter Olympic Games, Grenoble (1968) (2nd issue). Sports ¼, ⅓, ½, 3, 6 b.

Chancellor Adenauer Commemoration (1st issue). Embossed on gold foil. Air 50 b.

Yemen Red Cresent. Embossed on gold foil. Air 5, 10, 15, 50 b.

1968.

Paintings by Gauguin. Postage ¼, ¼, ⅓, ⅓, ½, ½ b.; Air 3, 3, 6, 6 b.

Paintings by Van Gogh. Postage ¼, ¼, ⅓, ⅓, ½, ½ b.; Air 3, 3, 6, 6 b.

Paintings by Rubens. Postage ¼, ¼, ⅓, ⅓, ½ ½ b.; Air 3, 3, 6, 6 b.

Provisionals. Various 1930/31 values optd. "Y.A.R." and date in English and Arabic. ½, 1, 1, 2, 2, 3, 4, 4, 5, 6, 6, 10, 10, 20 b., 1, 1 i.

Gold Medal Winners, Winter Olympic Games, Grenoble (1st issue). 1967 Winter Olympic Games (1st issue) optd. with names of various winners. Air 50 b. × 4.

1st Death Anniv. of Vladimir Komarov (Russian cosmonaut). Air 5, 10, 15, 50 b.

International Human Rights Year. Air 5, 10, 15, 50 b.

Chancellor Adenauer Commemoration (2nd issue). Air 5, 10, 15 b.

Refugee Relief. Adenauer (2nd issue) optd. in Arabic only. Air 5, 10, 15, 50 b.

Olympic Games, Mexico (1st issue). Chariot-racing. Air 5, 10, 15, 50 b.

Paintings of Horses. Postage ¼, ⅓, ½ b.; Air 3, 6 b.

Paintings by Raphael. Postage ¼, ⅓, ½ b.; Air 3, 6 b.

Paintings by Rembrandt. Postage ¼, ⅓, ½ b.; Air 3, 6 b.

Dr. Martin Luther King Commemoration (1st issue). Human Rights issue optd. Air 50 b.

Gold Medal Winners, Winter Olympic Games, Grenoble (2nd issue). Postage ¼, ⅓, ½, 2 b.; Air 3, 4 b.

Olympic Games, Mexico (2nd issue). Greek and Mexican Folk-lore. Postage ¼, ⅓, ½, 2 b.; Air 3, 4 b.

Gold Medal Winners, Olympic Games, Mexico (1st issue). Mexico Olympics (1st issue) optd. with names of various winners. Air 50 b. × 4.

Gold Medal Winners, Olympic Games, Mexico (2nd series). Postage ¼, ⅓, ½, 2 b.; Air 3, 4 b.

Dr. Martin Luther King Commemoration (2nd issue). Embossed on gold foil. 16 b.

Emblems of Winter Olympic Games. Postage ¼, ⅓, ½, 2 b.; Air 3, 4 b.

Emblems of Olympic Games. Postage ¼, ⅓, ½, 2 b.; Air 3, 4 b.

Dag Hammarskjold and Kennedy Brothers Commemoration. ½, 2, 6, 14 b.

Dr. Christian Barnard's Heart Transplant Operations. ¼, ¾, 8, 10 b.

Dr. Martin Luther King Commemoration (3rd issue). 1, 4, 12, 16 b.

John and Robert Kennedy Commemoration. Embossed on gold foil. 10 b.

1969.

Paintings from the Louvre, Paris. Postage ¼, ⅓, ½, 2 b.; Air 3, 4 b.

1st Death Anniv. of Yuri Gagarin (Russian cosmonaut). Optd. on 1968 Komarov issue. Air 50 b.

Paintings from the Uffizi Gallery, Florence. Postage ¼, ⅓, ½, 2 b.; Air 3, 4 b.

Paintings from the Prado, Madrid. Postage ¼, ⅓, ½, 2 b.; Air 3, 4 b.

Birth Bicentenary of Napoleon (1st issue). Embossed on gold foil. Air 4 b.

Space Exploration (1st series). Inscr. "DISCOVERIES OF UNIVERSE". Postage ¼, ¼, ⅓, ⅓ b.; Air 3, 6, 10 b.

Space Exploration (2nd series). Inscr. "FLIGHTS TO THE PLANETS". Postage ¼, ¼, ⅓, ⅓ b.; Air 2, 4, 22 b.

First Man on the Moon (1st issue). Embossed on gold foil. Air 10 b.

50th Anniv. of International Labour Organization. Postage 1, 2, 3, 4 b.; Air 6, 8, 10 b.

Space Exploration (3rd series). Inscr. "MAN IN SPACE". Postage ¼, ¼, ⅓, ⅓ b.; Air 3, 6, 10 b.

Birth Bicentenary of Napoleon (2nd issue). Postage ¼, ⅓, ½, ¾ b.; Air 4, 8, 10 b.

Space Exploration (4th series). "Apollo" Moon Flights. Postage ¼, ¼, ⅓, ⅓ b.; Air 2, 4, 22 b.

Winter Olympic Games, Sapporo (1972) Preparation. Optd. on 1967 Grenoble Winter Olympics issue. Air 50 b.

Olympic Games, Munich (1972) Preparation. Optd. on 1968 Mexico Olympics issue. Air 50 b.

Paintings from the National Gallery, Washington. Postage ¼, ⅓, ½, 2 b.; Air 3, 4 b.

Paintings from the National Gallery, London. Postage ¼, ⅓, ½, 2 b.; Air 3, 4 b.

French Monarchs and Statesmen. Postage 1¾, 2, 2¼, 2½ b.; Air 3½, 5, 6 b.

1970.

Tutankhamun Exhibition, Paris. Postage ¼, ⅓, ½, 2 b.; Air 3, 4 b.

Indian Sculptures. Postage ¼, ⅓, ½, 2 b.; Air 3, 4 b.

"EXPO 70" World Fair, Osaka, Japan (1st issue). Japanese Paintings. Postage ¼, ⅓, ½, 2 b.; Air 3, 4 b.

"EXPO 70" World Fair, Osaka, Japan (2nd issue). Japanese Puppets. Postage ¼, ⅓, ½, 2 b.; Air 3, 4 b.

World Cup Football Championships, Mexico (1st issue). Views and Maps. Postage 1¾, 2, 2¼, 2½ b.; Air 3½, 5, 6, 7, 8 b.

World Cup Football Championships, Mexico (2nd issue). Jules Rimet. Embossed on gold foil. Air 10 b.

"United Europe". Postage 1⅓, 1¾, 2¼, 2½, 5 b.; Air 7, 8, 10 b.

25th Anniv. of Victory in Second World War. Gen. De Gaulle. Embossed on gold foil. Air 6 b.

Moon Mission of "Apollo 12". Postage 1, 1¼, 1⅓, 1½ b.; Air 4, 4½, 7 b.

World Cup Football Championships, Mexico (3rd issue). Teams. Postage ¼, ⅓, ½, ¾ b.; Air 4, 4½ b.

World Cup Football Championships, Mexico (4th issue). Beckenbauer and Pele. Embossed on gold foil. Air 10 b.

World Cup Football Championships, Mexico (5th issue). Footballers and Mexican Antiquities. Postage 1, 1¼, 1⅓, 1½ b.; Air 3, 10 b.

Interplanetary Space Travel. Postage 1¾, 2, 2¼, 2½ b.; Air 5, 8, 10, 22 b.

Inauguration of New U.P.U. Headquarters Building, Berne. Postage ⅓, 1¼, 1½, 2 b.; Air 3½, 4½, 6 b.

"Philympia 70" Stamp Exhibition, London. Postage ¼, ½, ¾, 1, 3 b.; Air 4 b.

8th Anniv. of Revolution. Flowers. ¼ b. × 5.

Olympic Games, Munich (1972) (1st issue). Buildings. Postage 1, 1¾, 2½, 3, 3½ b.; Air 8, 10 b.

Olympic Games, Munich (2nd issue). Statue. Embossed on gold foil. Air 6 b.

25th Anniv. of United Nations. Human Rights Year issue of 1968 optd. Air 50 b.

Winter Olympic Games, Sapporo (1st issue). Buildings and Emblem. Postage 1½, 2½, 4½, 5, 7 b.; Air 8, 10 b.

Winter Olympic Games, Sapporo (2nd issue). Snow Sculpture. Embossed on gold foil. Air 4 b.

General Charles de Gaulle Commemoration. 1970. 25th Anniv. of Victory issue optd. Air 6 b.

German Gold Medal Winners in Olympic Games. Postage ¼, ¾, ⅓, ⅓ b.; Air 6 b.

1971.

Pres. Gamal Nasser of Egypt Commemoration. Postage ¼ b. × 4, ½ b. × 2; Air 1, 2, 5, 7, 10, 16 b.

International Sporting Events. Postage ¼, ⅓, ½, 2 b.; Air 3, 4 b.

Olympic Games, Munich (3rd issue). Theatre Productions. Postage ½, 1¼, 1¾, 2¼, 4½ b.; Air 5, 6 b.

Moon Mission of "Apollo 14". 1969 Moon Landing issue optd. Air 10 b.

Olympic Games, Munich (4th issue). Paintings from the Pinakothek. Postage ¼, ⅓, ¾, 1½, 2 b.; Air 4, 7 b.

Chinese Paintings. Postage ¼, ⅓, ½, 2 b.; Air 3, 4 b.

Winter Olympic Games, Sapporo (3rd issue). Winter Sports and Japanese Works of Art. Postage ¼, ½, 1, 1⅓, 2 b.; Air 3, 4 b.

Winter Olympic Games, Sapporo (4th issue) Japanese Skier. Embossed on gold foil. Air 8 b.

Launching of Soviet "Salyut" Space Station. Interplanetary issue of 1970 optd. Air 22 b.

Olympic Games, Munich (5th issue). Sports and Sculptures. Postage ⅓, 1, 1⅓, 1¾, 2¼ b.; Air 4½, 7, 10 b.

Olympic Games, Munich (6th issue). Gold Medals. Embossed on gold foil. Air 8 b.

Exploration of Outer Space. Postage ¼, ⅓, ½, ¾ b.; Air 3, 3½, 6 b.

Birth Bicentenary of Beethoven. Postage ¼ b. × 4, ½ b. × 2; Air 1, 2, 5, 7, 10 b.

Indian Paintings. Postage ¼, ⅓, ½, 2 b.; Air 3, 4 b.

Olympic Games, Munich (7th issue). Sailing Events at Kiel. Postage ¼, ½, 1¼, 2, 3 b.; Air 4 b.

Winter Olympic Games, Sapporo (5th issue). Sports. Postage ⅓, ¾, 1¼, 1¾, 2¼ b.; Air 3½, 6 b.

Winter Olympic Games, Sapporo (6th issue). Slalom Skier. Embossed on gold foil. Air 10 b.

Persian Miniatures. Postage ¼, ⅓, ½, 2 b.; Air 3, 4 b.

Olympic Games, Munich (8th issue). Sports. Postage ¾, 1½, 2½, 3½, 5 b.; Air 6, 8 b.

Olympic Games, Munich (9th issue). Discus-thrower. Embossed on gold foil. Air 10 b.

Italian Gold Medal Winners in Olympic Games. Postage ¼ b. × 2, ⅓ b. × 2; Air 22 b.

1972.

French Gold Medal Winners in Olympic Games. Postage 2, 3 b.; Air 4, 10 b.

Works of Art. Postage 1, 1¼, 1⅓, 1½ b.; Air 3, 4½, 7 b.

ROYALIST ISSUES

1967.

Visit of Queen of Sheba to Solomon. ⅛, ¼, ½, 4, 6, 20, 24 b.

Arab Horses. ⅛, ¼, ½, 4, 10 b.

1968.

Winter Olympic Games, Grenoble (1st issue). Nos. R216/29 optd. Postage ⅛, ¼, ½, 1, 4, 6, 10 b.; Air 12, 14, 16, 24, 34 b.

Butterflies. Air 16, 20, 40 b.

Postage Due. Butterflies and Horse. 4, 16, 20 b.

Winter Olympic Games, Grenoble (2nd issue). Sports. Postage 1, 2, 3, 4, 6 b.; Air 10, 12, 18, 24, 28 b.

Gold Medal Winners, Grenoble Winter Olympics. Winter Olympic Games, Grenoble (2nd issue) optd. with names of various medal winners. Postage 1, 2, 3, 4, 6 b.; Air 10, 12, 18, 24, 28 b.

20th Anniv. of U.N.E.S.C.O. ½, 1, 1½, 2, 3, 4, 6, 10 b.

Mothers' Day. Paintings. Postage 2, 4, 6 b.; Air 24, 28, 34 b.

Olympic Games, Mexico (1st issue). Sports. Postage 1, 2, 3, 4, 6 b.; Air 10, 12, 18, 24, 28 b.

U.N.E.S.C.O. "Save Florence" Campaign. Paintings. Postage 2, 4, 6 b.; Air 10, 12, 18 b.

U.N.E.S.C.O. "Save Venice" Campaign. Paintings. Postage ½, 1, 1½, 24 b.; Air 28, 34 b.

Olympic Games, Mexico (2nd issue). Athletes and Flags. 4 b. × 11.

Winter Olympic Games since 1924. Competitors and Flags. Postage 1, 2, 3, 4, 6 b.; Air 10, 12, 18, 24, 28 b.

International Human Rights Year. 2 b. × 4, 4 b. × 4, 6 b. × 4.

Paintings by European and American Artists. Postage 1, 2, 3, 4, 6, 10 b.; Air 12, 18. 24, 28 b.

Coronation of Shah of Iran. Postage 1, 2, 3, 4 b.; Air 24, 28 b.

International Philately. Postage 1, 2, 3, 4, 6 b.; Air 10, 12, 18, 24, 28 b.

World Racial Peace. Postage 4, 6, 18 b.; Air 10 b.

Children's Day. Paintings. Postage 1, 2, 3, 4 b.; Air 6, 10, 12, 18, 24, 28 b.

Gold Medal Winners, Mexico Olympic Games (1st issue). Mexico Olympics (1st issue) optd. with names of various medal winners. Postage 1, 2, 3, 4, 6 b.; Air 10, 12, 18, 24, 28 b.

Gold Medal Winners, Mexico Olympics (2nd issue). Athletes and Medals. Air 12, 18, 24, 28, 34 b.

Gold Medal Winners. Mexico Olympics (3rd issue). Embossed on gold foil. 28 b.

"EFIMEX 68" Stamp Exhibition, Mexico City. Air 12, 18, 24, 28, 34 b.

1969.

Motor-racing Drivers. Postage 1, 2, 3, 4, 6 b.; Air 10, 12, 18, 24, 28 b.

Space Flight of "Apollo 7". 4, 8, 12, 24, 28 b.

Space Flight of "Apollo 8" (1st issue). 4, 6, 10, 18, 34 b.

Space Flight of "Apollo 8" (2nd issue). Embossed on gold foil. 28 b.

5th Anniv. of Imam's Meeting with Pope Paul VI at Jerusalem (1st issue). Scenes from Pope's Visit. ⅛, ¼, ¼, 1, 1½, 2, 3, 4, 5, 6 b.

5th Anniv. of Imam's Meeting with Pope Paul VI at Jerusalem (2nd issue). Paintings of the Life of Christ. Postage 1, 2, 3, 4, 5, 6, 7, 8, 9, 10 b.; Air 11, 12, 13, 14, 15, 16, 17, 18, 19, 20, 21, 22, 23, 24, 25, 26, 27, 28, 29, 30 b.

5th Anniv. of Imam's Meeting with Pope Paul VI at Jerusalem (3rd issue). Abraham's Tomb, Hebron. 4 b.

Paintings by Rembrandt (1st series). Postage 1, 2, 4 b.; Air 6, 12 b., 1 i.

Paintings by Rembrandt (2nd series). Embossed on gold foil. 20 b.

Paintings by European Artist. Postage ½, 1½, 3, 5 b.; Air 10, 18, 24, 28, 34 b.

"Apollo" Moon Programme. Postage 1, 2, 3, 4, 5 b.; Air 6, 7, 8, 9, 10, 11, 12, 13, 14, 15 b.

Moon Flight of "Apollo 10". Postage 2, 4, 6 b.; Air 8, 10, 12, 18, 24, 28, 34 b.

Olympic Games, Munich (1972). Athletes and Olympic Rings. Postage 1, 2, 4, 5, 6 b.; Air 10, 12, 18, 24, 34 b.

World Wildlife Conservation. Postage ½ b.×2, 1 b.×2, 2 b.×2, 4 b.×2, 6 b.×2; Air 8 b.×2, 10 b.×2, 18 b.×2.

First Man on the Moon (1st issue). Air 6, 10, 12, 18 b.

First Man on the Moon (2nd issue). Air 6, 10, 12, 18, 24 b.

First Man on the Moon (3rd issue). Embossed on foil. 24 b.×2.

First Man on the Moon (4th issue). Embossed on gold foil. 28 b.

First Man on the Moon (5th issue). Air 10, 12, 18, 24 b.

Palestine Holy Places. Postage 4 b.×6, 6 b.×10; Air 12 b.×8.

Famous Men. Postage 4 b.×4, 6 b.×10, Air 12 b.×2.

History of Space Exploration. Air 6 b.×27

Olympic Sports. Postage 1, 2, 4, 5, 6 b.; Air 10, 12, 18, 24, 34 b.

World Cup Football Championships, Mexico. Air 12 b.×8.

Christmas. Ikons. Postage ½, 1, 1½, 2, 4, 5, 6 b.; Air 10, 12, 18, 24, 28, 34 b.

Burning of Al-Aqsa Mosque, Jerusalem. Postage 4 b.+2 b., 6 b.+3 b.; Air 10 b.+5 b.

1970.

Brazil's Victory in World Cup Football Championships, Mexico. 1969 World Cup issue optd. Air 12 b.×3.

Dogs. Postage 2, 4, 6 b.; Air 8, 12 b.

Paintings of Horses. Postage 2, 4, 6 b.; Air 8, 12 b.

On 23 July 1970 the Saudi Arabian Government transferred their support from the Royalists to the unified government of the Yemen Republic. About this time the Saudi Arabian mail transit facilities to the Royalist areas were closed, and it therefore seems likely that after this Royalist stamps could not be used on external mail and it is even doubtful if supplies of new issues could enter these areas and be used internally during the intervening period before the unified government gained effective control. It is known that such stamps found on philatelic covers had the cancellations applied in another country and were inserted into international mails.

ADDENDA AND CORRIGENDA

AITUTAKI

14. Bell and First Telephone.

1977. First Telephone Transmission. Cent.
218. **14.** 25 c. black, gold and red 25 30
219. – 70 c. black, gold & lilac 75 85
DESIGN: 70 c. Satellite and Earth station.

15. " Calvary " (detail).

1977. Easter. Rubens. 400th Birth Anniv. Multicoloured.
221. 15 c. Type **15** 15 20
222. 20 c. " Lamentation for Christ " 20 25
223. 35 c. " Christ with Straw " 40 45

ALBANIA

323. Demonstrators attacking Police. **324.** Party Flag.

1976. Hoxha's Anti-Fascist Demonstration. 35th Anniv. Multicoloured.
1844. 25 q. Type **323** 5 5
1845. 1 l. 90 Crowd with flag .. 60 35

1976. 7th Albanian Labour Party Congress. Multicoloured.
1846. 25 q. Type **324** 5 5
1847. 1 l. 20 Hand holding Party symbols, and flag .. 35 20

325. Communist Advance.

1976. Albanian Communist Party. Mult.
1848. 15 q. Type **325** 5 5
1849. 25 q. Hands holding emblems, and revolutionary army 5 5
1850. 80 q. " Reconstruction " 30 15
1851. 1 l. 20 " Heavy Industry and Agriculture " .. 35 20
1852. 1 l. 70 " The Arts "-ballet 50 25

326. Young Communist.

1976. Albanian Young Communists' Organization. 25th Anniv. Multicoloured.
1853. 80 q. Type **326** 30 15
1854. 1 l. 25 Young Communists in action 35 20

327. Ballet Dancers.

1976. Albanian Ballet.
1855. **327.** 10 q. multicoloured .. 5 5
1856. – 15 q. multicoloured .. 5 5
1857. – 20 q. multicoloured .. 5 5
1858. – 25 q. multicoloured .. 5 5
1859. – 80 q. multicoloured .. 30 15
1860. – 1 l. 20 multicoloured 35 20
1861. – 1 l. 40 multicoloured 40 25
DESIGNS: 15 q. to 1 l. 40 Various ballet scenes.

328. Bashtoves Castle. **329.** Skanderberg's Shield and Spear.

1976. Albanian Castles.
1863. **328.** 10 q. black and blue .. 5 5
1864. – 15 q. black and green 5 5
1865. – 20 q. black and grey 5 5
1866. – 25 q. black and ochre 5 5
1867. – 80 q. black and red .. 30 15
1868. – 1 l. 20 black and blue 35 20
1869. – 1 l. 40 black and red .. 40 25
DESIGNS: 15 q. Gjirokastres. 20 q. Ali Pash Tepelenes. 25 q. Petreles. 80 q. Beratit. 1 l. 20 Durresit. 1 l. 40 Krujes.

1977. Skanderbeg's Army Commemoration. Multicoloured.
1870. 15 q. Type **329** 5 5
1871. 80 q. Helmet, sword and scabbard 30 15
1872. 1 l. Halberd, spear, bow and arrows 30 15

ALGERIA

207. Text on Open Book.

208. Soldiers planting seedlings.

1976. The Constitution.
705. **207.** 2 d. multicoloured .. 50 25

1976. " Green Barrier against the Sahara ".
706. **208.** 1 d. 40 multicoloured .. 30 15

209. Arabic Cartouche.

1976. Election of President Boumedienne.
707. **209.** 2 d. multicoloured .. 50 25

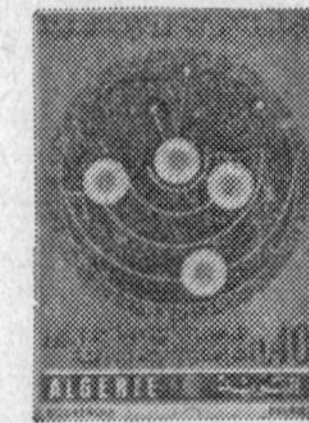

210. Telephone Centres Map. **211.** " Pyramid " of Heads.

1977. Inauguration of Automatic Telephone Dialling System.
708. **210.** 40 c. multicoloured .. 10 5

1977. 2nd General Population and Housing Census.
709. **211.** 60 c. multicoloured .. 15 5

212. Museum Building. **213.** El Kantara Gorges.

1977. Saharan Museum, Ouargla.
710. **212.** 60 c. multicoloured .. 15 5

1977. Booklet stamps.
711. **213.** 20 c. green and cream 5 5
712. 60 c. purple and cream 15 5
713. 1 d. brown and cream 25 12

214. Assembly in Session.

1977. National Popular Assembly.
714. **214.** 2 d. multicoloured .. 50 25

215. Soldiers with Flag.

1977. Solidarity with the People of Zimbabwe.
715. **215.** 2 d. multicoloured .. 50 25

ANDORRA

I. FRENCH POST OFFICES

F 59. " Euvanessa antiopa ".

1976. Nature Protection. Butterflies. Multicoloured.
F 277. 80 c. " Parnassius apollo " .. 20 20
F 278. 1 f. 40 Type **F 59** .. 30 30

II. SPANISH POST OFFICES

23. Canoeing.

1976. Olympic Games, Montreal. Mult.
99. 7 p. Slalom skiing (vert.) 20 15
100. 15 p. Type **23** 40 35

24. "The Nativity".

1976. Christmas. Multicoloured.
101. 3 p. Type **24** 5 5
102. 25 p. "The Adoration" .. 60 50

ANGOLA

83. President Neto.

1976. Independence. 1st Anniv.
735. **83.** 50 c. black and grey .. 5 5
736. 2 e. purple and grey 8 5
737. 3 e. blue and grey .. 12 5
738. 5 e. brown and buff 20 10
739. 10 e. brown and drab 40 20

ANGUILLA

37. Two French Ships approaching Anguilla.

1976. Battle of Anguilla. Bicent. Mult.
255. 1 c. Type **37** 5 5
256. 3 c. Sailing boat leaving for Antigua to fetch help 5 5
257. 15 c. H.M.S. "Lapwing" engaging French Ships 5 8
258. 25 c. "La Vaillante forced aground off St. Martin .. 12 15
259. $1 H.M.S. "Lapwing" .. 40 45
260. $1.50 French frigate "Le Desius" burning .. 60 70

38. Christmas Carnival.

1976. Christmas. Children's Paintings. Multicoloured.
262. 1 c. Type **38** 5 5
263. 3 c. Dreams of Christmas gifts 5 5
264. 15 c. Carolling 5 8
265. 25 c. Candle-light procession 12 15
266. $1 Going to church, Christmas Eve 40 45
267. $1.50 Coming home for Christmas 60 70

INDEX

Countries can be quickly located by referring to the index at the end of this volume.

39. Prince Charles and H.M.S. "Minerva".

1977. Silver Jubilee. Multicoloured.
269. 25 c. Type **39** 12 15
270. 40 c. Prince Philip landing by launch at Road Bay, 1964 .. .. .. 20 25
271. $1.20 "Long live the Queen" 45 50
272. $2.50 Map of Anguilla and coronation regalia .. 1·00 1·10

40. Yellow-crowned Night-heron.

1977. Multicoloured.
274. 1 c. Type **40** 5 5
275. 2 c. Great Barracuda .. 5 5
276. 3 c. Queen Conch .. 5 5
277. 4 c. Spanish Bayonet .. 5 5
278. 5 c. Trunkfish 5 5
279. 6 c. Cable and Wireless building 5 5
280. $10 Red-billed Tropic-bird 3·50 4·00

ANTIGUA

82. Angel appearing to Mary.

1976. Christmas. Multicoloured.
514. 8 c. Type **82** 5 5
515. 10 c. The Holy Family fleeing to Bethlehem .. 5 5
516. 15 c. The Three Wise Men 5 8
517. 50 c. The Shepherds 20 25
518. $1 The Three Wise Men presenting their gifts .. 40 45

83. U.N.P.A. 25th Anniv.

1976. Special Events. Multicoloured.
519. ½ c. Type **83** 5 5
520. 1 c. 75th Anniv. of Nobel Prize 5 5
521. 10 c. Viking space mission to Mars 5 5
522. 50 c. Achievements in cricket 20 25
523. $1 Telephone transmission centenary 40 45
524. $2 "Freelance". Operation Sail, U.S. Bicentennial 80 90

84. The Royal Family.

1977. Silver Jubilee. Multicoloured.
526. 10 c. Type **84** 5 5
527. 30 c. The Queen and Prince Philip on Royal Visit .. 12 15
528. 50 c. The Queen during Coronation 20 25
529. 90 c. The Queen after Coronation 35 40
530. $2.50 The Queen and Prince Charles .. .. 1·00 1·10

ARGENTINE REPUBLIC

Add to No. 1474.
1474a. **472.** 300 p. multicoloured 2·25 1·25
1474b. – 500 p. multicoloured 3·75 2·00
DESIGN—HORIZ. 500 p. Admiral Brown Scientific Station, Antarctica.

Add to Nos. 1494/504.
1501a. **481.** 30 p. blue & black .. 25 12

1976. As T **396**, but values in peso.
1518. **396.** 3 p. blue 5 5
1519. – 12 p. green 10 5
1520. – 12 p. red 10 5
1521. – 15 p. red 12 5
1522. **396.** 40 p. green 20 10
1523. – 70 p. blue 60 30
DESIGNS: 12 p. (both), 15 p. Jose de San Martin. 70 p. Guillermo Brown.

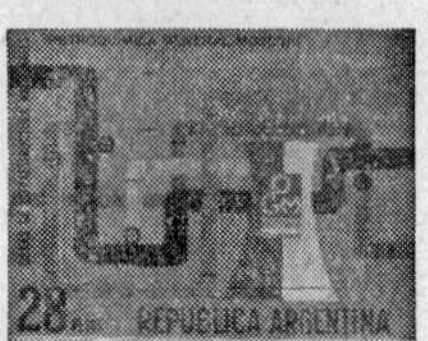

489. Cooling Tower and Pipelines.

1976. General Mosconi Petrochemical Project.
1524. **489.** 28 p. multicoloured .. 25 12

490. P.T. Fels and Bleriot Monoplane.

1976. Air Force Day.
1525. **490.** 15 p. multicoloured .. 12 5

491. "Nativity".

1976. Christmas.
1526. **491.** 20 p. multicoloured .. 15 8

MORE DETAILED LISTS

are given in the Stanley Gibbons Catalogues referred to in the country headings:

BC	British Commonwealth
E1, E2, E3	Europe 1, 2, 3
O1, O2, O3, O4	Overseas 1, 2, 3, 4

ASCENSION

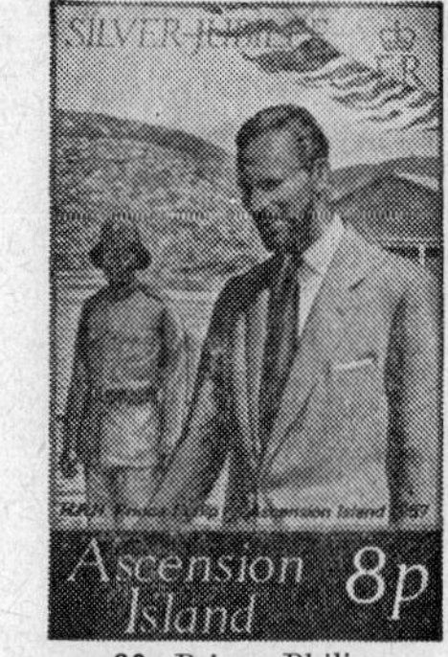

30. Prince Philip on Ascension, 1957.

1977. Silver Jubilee. Multicoloured.
222. 8 p. Type **30** 20 25
223. 12 p. The Queen leaving Buckingham Palace (horiz.) 30 35
224. 25 p. The Queen in Coronation Coach (horiz.) .. 55 60

AUSTRALIA

240. Madonna and Child.

1976. Christmas. Multicoloured.
635. 15 c. Type **240** 20 25
636. 45 c. Christmas objects .. 55 45

241. John Gould. **242.** "Music".

1976. Famous Australians. Scientists. Multicoloured.
637. 18 c. Type **241** 25 30
638. 18 c. Thomas Laby .. 25 30
639. 18 c. Sir Baldwin Spencer 25 30
640. 18 c. Griffith Taylor .. 25 30

1977. Performing Arts. Multicoloured.
641. 20 c. Type **242** 25 30
642. 30 c. Drama 40 45
643. 40 c. Dance 50 55
644. 60 c. Opera 75 80

243. Queen Elizabeth II.

244. Fielder and Wicket Keeper.

1977. Silver Jubilee. Multicoloured.
645. 18 c. Type **243** 25 30
646. 45 c. The Queen and Duke of Edinburgh 55 45

1977. Australia–England Test Cricket. Cent. Multicoloured.
647. 18 c. Type **244** 25 30
648. 18 c. Umpire and batsman 25 30
649. 18 c. Fielders 25 30
650. 18 c. Batsman and umpire 25 30
651. 18 c. Bowler and fielder .. 25 30
652. 45 c. Batsman facing bowler 55 45

AUSTRIA

Add to Nos. 1675 to 1689.
1682. – 4 s. 50 green and turq. 25 5
1688. – 11 s. red and orange.. 65 15
DESIGNS: 4 s. 50 Windmill, Retz. 11 s. Enns.

468. Bohemian Court Chancellery, Vienna.

1976. Administrative Court. Cent.
1766. **468.** 6 s. brown 35 25

469. " Cancer the Crab ". **470.** UN Emblem and Bridge.

1976. Fight against Cancer.
1768. **469.** 2 s. 50 multicoloured 15 10

1976. U.N.I.D.O. Tenth Anniv.
1769. **470.** 3 s. blue and gold .. 20 12

471. " Apa " and Tapes over Europe.

1976. Austrian Press Agency. 30th Anniv.
1770. **471.** 1 s. 50 multicoloured 8 8

472. V. Kaplan.

1976. Viktor Kaplan (inventor of turbine). Birth Cent.
1771. **472.** 2 s. 50 multicoloured 15 10

473. " The Birth of Christ " altar-painting, Konrad von Friesach).

1976. Christmas.
1772. **473.** 3 s. multicoloured .. 20 12

474. Postillion's Hat and Posthorn.

1976. Stamp Day.
1773. **474.** 6 s.+2 s. black & violet 50 50

475. R. M. Rilke. **476.** " Augustin the Piper " (Arik Brauer).

1976. Rainer M. Rilke (poet). 50th Death Anniv.
1774. **475.** 3 s. violet 20 12

1976. Modern Austrian Art.
1775. **476.** 6 s. multicoloured .. 35 25

477. City Synagogue.

1976. Vienna City Synagogue. 150th Anniv.
1776. **477.** 1 s. 50 multicoloured 8 8

BAHAMAS

54. The Queen with Cloth of Gold Canopy.

1977. Silver Jubilee. Multicoloured.
487. 8 c. Type **54** 8 10
488. 16 c. The Crowning .. 15 20
489. 21 c. Taking the oath .. 20 25
490. 40 c. The Queen with emblems of sovereignty 45 50

BAHRAIN

Add to Nos. 224/31.
228a. **29.** 60 f. black and green.. 20 20
229a. 100 f. black and red .. 30 30

33. Shaikh Isa. **34.** Housing Ministry Emblem, Houses and Mosque.

1976.
241. **33.** 300 f. green & pale green 90 90
242. 400 f. purple and pink.. 1·25 1·25
243. 500 f. blue and pale blue 1·50 1·50
244. 1 d. black and grey .. 3·00 3·00

1976. National Day.
245. **34.** 40 f. multicoloured .. 10 10
246. 80 f. multicoloured .. 25 25

BANGLADESH

Add to Nos. 49/50 (Revised inscriptions).
50a. 5 t. blue (As No. 34) .. 50 55

Add to Nos. 63, etc. Redrawn in smaller size.
68. 60 p. slate (As No. 29) .. 5 5
69. 75 p. orange (As No. 30) .. 8 10
70. 90 p. brown (As No. 31) .. 8 10
73. 5 t. turquoise (As No. 50a) 50 55
74. 10 t. pink (As No. 35, but inscr. redrawn) .. .. 1·00 1·10
Nos. 68/70 are 18×23 mm. and Nos. 73/4 32×21 mm.

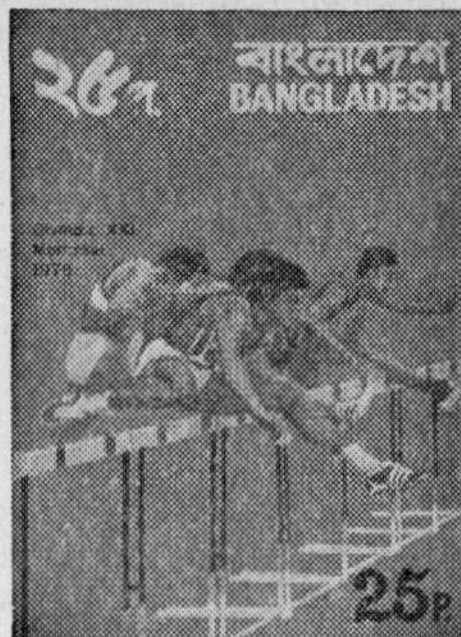

22. Hurdling.

1976. Olympic Games, Montreal. Mult.
86. 25 p. Type **22** 5 5
87. 30 p. Running (horiz.) .. 5 5
88. 1 t. Pole vaulting 12 15
89. 2 t. 25 Swimming (horiz.).. 25 30
90. 3 t. 50 Gymnastics.. .. 45 50
91. 5 t. Football 55 65

23. The Blessing.

1977. Silver Jubilee. Multicoloured.
92. 30 p. Type **23** 5 5
93. 2 t. 25 Queen Elizabeth II 25 30
94. 10 t. The Queen and Prince Philip .. .. .. 1·10 1·25

OFFICIAL STAMPS

1973. Nos. 22, etc. optd. **SERVICE.**
O 1. **6.** 2 p. black 5 5
O 2. – 3 p. green 5 5
O 3. – 5 p. brown 5 5
O 4. – 10 p. black 5 5
O 5. – 20 p. green 5 5
O 6. – 25 p. mauve 5 5
O 7. – 60 p. grey 5 5
O 8. – 75 p. orange 8 10
O 9. **7.** 1 t. violet 10 12
O 10. – 5 t. blue 50 55

1974. Nos. 49/50a. optd. **SERVICE.**
O 11. **13.** 1 t. violet 10 12
O 12. – 2 t. olive 20 25
O 13. – 5 t. blue 50 55

1976. Nos. 63/72 optd. **SERVICE.**
O 14. – 5 p. green 5 5
O 15. – 10 p. black 5 5
O 16. – 20 p. green 5 5
O 17. – 25 p. mauve 5 5
O 18. – 50 p. purple 5 5
O 19. **13.** 1 t. blue 10 12

BARBADOS

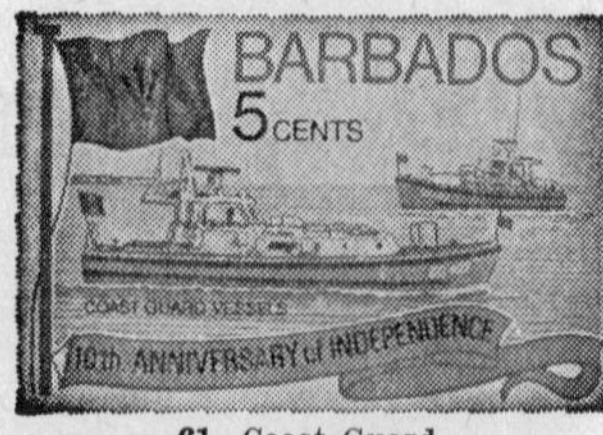

61. Coast Guard Vessels.

1976. Independence. Tenth Anniv. Mult.
569. 5 c. Type **61** 5 5
570. 15 c. Reverse of currency note 8 10
571. 25 c. Barbados national anthem 15 15
572. $1 Independence parade.. 55 65

62. Arrival at Westminster Abbey.

1977. Silver Jubilee. Multicoloured.
574. 15 c. Queen knighting Garfield Sobers 8 10
575. 50 c. Type **62** 30 35
576. $1 The Queen entering Abbey 55 65

BARBUDA

1976. Christmas. Nos. 514/8 of Antigua optd. **BARBUDA.**
281. **82.** 8 c. multicoloured .. 5 5
282. – 10 c. multicoloured .. 5 5
283. – 15 c. multicoloured .. 5 5
284. – 50 c. multicoloured .. 20 25
285. – $1 multicoloured .. 40 45

1976. Olympic Games, Montreal. Nos. 495/501 of Antigua optd. **BARBUDA.**
286. **79.** ½ c. brn., yell. and blk. 5 5
287. – 1 c. violet and black .. 5 5
288. – 2 c. green and black .. 5 5
289. – 15 c. blue and black .. 8 10
290. – 30 c. brn., yell. and blk. 15 20
291. – $1 oran., red and black 50 55
292. – $2 red and black .. 90 1·00

23. Bell, P.O. Tower and Telephones.

1977. First Telephone Transmission. Centenary. Multicoloured.
294. 75 c. Type **23** 30 35
295. $1 25 T.V. Transmission by Satellite 50 60
296. $2 Globe showing satellite transmission scheme .. 90 1·00

24. St. Margarets', Westminster.

1977. Silver Jubilee. Multicoloured.
298. 75 c. Type **24** 30 35
299. 75 c. Street decorations.. 30 35
300. 75 c. Westminster Abbey 30 35
301. $1.25 Part of Coronation procession 50 60
302. $1.25 Coronation Coach.. 50 60
303. $1.25 Postillions 50 60

BELGIUM

Add to Nos. 2207/23.
2218a. 11 f. green 30 5
2219b. 14 f. green 35 5

561. " Virgin of the Parrot ". **562.** William the Silent, Prince of Orange.

1976. Peter Paul Rubens. 400th Birth Anniv. (1st issue). Multicoloured.

2438. 4 f. 50+1 f. 50 " Descent from the Cross " .. 20 30
2439. 6 f. 50+3 f. " Adoration of the Shepherds " .. 30 30
2440. 6 f. 50+3 f. Type **561** .. 30 30
2441. 10 f.+5 f. " Adoration of the Kings " .. 45 45
2442. 10 f.+5 f. " Last Communion of St. Francis " 45 45
2443. 30 f.+15 f. " Madonna and Child " .. .. 1·50 1·50

Nos. 2438 and 2443 are larger, 35×52 mm.

1976. Pacification of Ghent. 400th Anniv.

2444. **562.** 10 f. green 30 12

563. Modern Electric Train.

1976. National Belgian Railway Company. 50th Anniv.

2445. **563.** 6 f. 50 multicoloured 20 5

564. Underground Train.

565. " The Young Musician " (W. C. Duyster).

1976. Opening of Brussels " Metro ".

2446. **564.** 6 f. 50 multicoloured 20 5

1976. " Philately for the Young " and Young Musicians' Movement.

2447. **565.** 4 f. 50 multicoloured 15 5

566. Charles Bernard (writer) (birth cent.).

567. " Child with Impediment " (Velasquez).

1976. Cultural Annivs.

2448. **566.** 5 f. purple 15 5
2449. – 5 f. lake 15 5
2450. – 6 f. 50 brown .. 20 5
2451. – 6 f. 50 green.. .. 20 5

DESIGNS—VERT. No. 2449, Fernand Toussaint van Boelaere (writer) (birth cent. 1975). No. 2450, " St. Jerome in Mountain Landscape " (J. le Patinier) (Charles Plisnier Foundation. 25th Anniv.). HORIZ. No. 2451, "Story of the Blind " (P. Brueghel) 25th Anniv. of " Vereniging voor Beschaafde Omgangstaal " (Dutch language organisation).

1976. Tourist Publicity. As T **496**.

2452. 4 f. 50 multicoloured .. 15 5
2453. 4 f. 50 multicoloured .. 15 5
2454. 5 f. brown and blue .. 15 5
2455. 5 f. brown and olive .. 15 5

DESIGNS—HORIZ. No. 2452, Hunnegem Priory, Grammont. No. 2454, River Lys, Sint-Martens-Latem. No. 2455, Chateau, Ham-sur-Heure. VERT. No. 2453, Remouchamps Caves.

1976. National Association for Aid to the Mentally Handicapped.

2456. **567.** 14 f.+6 f. mult. .. 60 60

568. " The Nativity " (Master of Flemalle).

1976. Christmas.

2457. **568.** 5 f. violet 15 5

569. Monogram.

1977. Peter Paul Rubens. 400th Birth Anniv. (2nd issue).

2458. **569.** 6 f. 50 black and lilac 20 5

RAILWAY PARCELS STAMPS

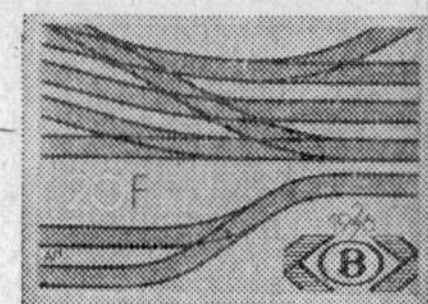

P 38. Railway Junction.

1976.

P 2431. **P 38.** 20 f. blk., bl. & lilac 60 30
P 2432. 50 f. blk., grn and turquoise .. 1·50 75
P 2433. 100 f. blk. & oran. 3·00 1·50
P 2434. 150 f. blk., mauve and magenta .. 4·50 2·50

BELIZE

CORRECTION: Add prices for Nos. 442/4.

442. 20 25
443. 30 35
444. 55 65

41. The Queen and Bishops.

1977. Silver Jubilee. Multicoloured.

448. 10 c. Royal Visit, 1975 .. 5 5
449. 35 c. Procession through the Nave 20 25
450. $2 Type **41** .. .. 1·10 1·25

1977. No. 387, surch.

451. 5 c. on 15 c. multicoloured 5 5

BENIN

1976. Various Dahomey stamps optd. **POPULAIRE DU BENIN**, surch. in addition or surch. only.

614. **85.** 50 f. on 1 f. multicoloured (postage) .. 20 12
615. – 60 f. on 2 f. multicoloured (No. 415) .. 25 15
616. – 135 f. brown, purple and blue (No. 590) (air).. 70 40
617. – 210 f. on 300 f. brown, red and blue (No. 591) 1·10 65
618. – 380 f. on 500 f. brown, red and grn. (No. 592) 1·90 90

164. Blood Bank, Cotonou.

1976. National Days of Blood Transfusion Service. Multicoloured.

624. 5 f. Type **164** 5 5
625. 50 f. Casualty and blood clinic 20 12
626. 60 f. Donor, patient and ambulance 25 15

INDEX

Countries can be quickly located by referring to the index at the end of this volume.

165. Manioc.

166. " Apollo " Emblem and Rocket.

1976. National Products Campaign Year. Multicoloured.

627. 20 f. Type **165** 10 5
628. 50 f. Maize cultivation .. 20 12
629. 60 f. Cocoa trees 25 15
630. 150 f. Cotton plantation.. 75 45

1976. Air. " Apollo 14 " Space Mission. 5th Anniv.

631. 130 f. lake, brn. and blue 65 35
632. 270 f. blue, turq. and red 1·40 70

DESIGN: 270 f. Landing on Moon.

167. Classroom

168. Antelope.

1976. " Kparo "-rural Bariba magazine. 3rd Anniv.

633. **167.** 50 f. multicoloured .. 20 12

1976. Mammals in Pendjari National Park. Multicoloured.

634 10 f Type **168** 5 5
635. 30 f. Buffalo 15 8
636. 50 f. Hippopotamus (horiz.) 20 12
637. 70 f. Lion 35 20

169. " Freedom ".

170. " The Annunciation " (Master of Jativa).

1976. Proclamation of Republic. 1st Anniv. Multicoloured.

638. 40 f. Type **169** 20 12
639. 150 f. Maize cultivation.. 75 45

1976. Air. Christmas. Multicoloured.

640. 50 f. Type **170** 20 12
641. 60 f. " The Nativity " (David) 30 15
642. 270 f. " Adoration of the Magi " (Dutch school).. 1·40 70
643. 300 f. " The Flight into Egypt " (Fabriano) (horiz.) 1·50 80

171. Table Tennis and Games Emblem.

1976. West African University Games, Cotonou. Multicoloured.

644. 10 f. Type **171** 5 5
645. 50 f. Sports Hall, Cotonou 20 12

BERMUDA

48. The Queen at Queen's View.

1977. Silver Jubilee. Multicoloured.

378. 5 c. Type **48** 5 5
379. 20 c. St. Edward's Crown 20 25
380. $1 The Queen in Chair of Estate .. .. .. 1·10 1·25

BHUTAN

35. Bhutan Orchid.

1976. Bhutan Orchids.

309. **35.** 1 ch. multicoloured .. 5 5
310. – 2 ch. multicoloured .. 5 5
311. – 3 ch. multicoloured .. 5 5
312. – 4 ch. multicoloured .. 5 5
313. – 5 ch. multicoloured .. 5 5
314. – 2 n. multicoloured .. 30 30
315. – 4 n. multicoloured .. 60 60
316. – 6 n. multicoloured .. 90 90

DESIGNS: 2 ch. to 6 n. Various Orchids.

36. Double Carp Emblem.

1976. Colombo Plan. 25th Anniv.

318. **36.** 3 ch. multicoloured .. 5 5
319. – 4 ch. multicoloured .. 5 5
320. – 5 ch. multicoloured .. 5 5
321. – 25 ch. multicoloured .. 5 5
322. – 1 n. 25 multicoloured.. 20 20
323. – 2 n. multicoloured .. 30 30
324. – 2 n. 50 multicoloured.. 35 35
325. – 3 n. multicoloured .. 45 45

DESIGNS: 4 ch. to 3 n. Similar Bhutanese emblems.

37. Bandaranaike Conference Hall.

1976. Non-aligned Countries Summit Conference, Colombo.

326. **37.** 1 n. 25 multicoloured .. 20 20
327. 2 n. 50 multicoloured .. 35 35

MORE DETAILED LISTS

are given in the Stanley Gibbons Catalogues referred to in the country headings:

BC	British Commonwealth
E1, E2, E3	Europe 1, 2, 3
O1, O2, O3, O4	Overseas 1, 2, 3, 4

38. Dragon Mask.

1976. Ceremonial Masks. Laminated prismatic – ribbed plastic surface.

328.	38.	5 ch. multicoloured (postage)	5	5
329.	–	10 ch. multicoloured ..	5	5
330.	–	15 ch. multicoloured ..	5	5
331.	–	20 ch. multicoloured ..	5	5
332.	–	25 ch. multicoloured ..	5	5
333.	–	30 ch. multicoloured ..	5	5
334.	–	35 ch. multicoloured ..	5	5
335.	–	1 n. multicoloured (air)	15	15
336.	–	2 n. multicoloured ..	30	30
337.	–	2 n. 50 multicoloured ..	35	35
338.	–	3 n. multicoloured ..	45	45

DESIGNS: 10 ch. to 3 n. Similar Bhutanese masks.

BOLIVIA

171. Bolivian Family. 172. Brother Vicente Bernedo (missionary).

1976. National Census.
994. 171. 2 p. 50 multicoloured 20 10

1976. Bernedo Commemoration.
995. 172. 1 p. 50 multicoloured 12 10

173. Rainbow and Police Handler with Dog.

1976 Police Service. 150th Anniv.
996. 173. 2 p. 50 multicoloured 20 10

174. Arms, Bolivar and Sucre.

1976. International Societies' Congress.
997. 174. 1 p. 50 multicoloured .. 12 10

175. Pedro Poveda (educator).

1976. Poveda Commemoration.
998. 175. 1 p. 50 multicoloured .. 12 10

BOTSWANA

35. Coronation Coach in Procession.

1977. Silver Jubilee. Multicoloured.

391.	4 t. The Queen and Sir Seretse Khama ..	5	5
392.	25 t. Type 35	30	35
393.	40 t. Recognition scene ..	50	55

BRAZIL

766. Christmas Scene.

1976. Christmas.

1619.	766.	80 c. multicoloured ..	10	5
1620.	–	80 c. multicoloured ..	10	5
1621.	–	80 c. multicoloured ..	10	5
1622.	–	80 c. multicoloured ..	10	5
1623.	–	80 c. multicoloured ..	10	5

DESIGNS: Nos. 1620/3, Various scenes.

768. " Our Lady of Monte Serrat " (Friar A. da Pesdade).

1976. Brazilian Sculpture. Multicoloured.

1625.	80 c. Type 768	10	5
1626.	5 cr. " St. Joseph " (unknown artist) (25 × 37 mm.)	60	35
1627.	5 cr. 60 " The Dance " (J. Bernardelli) (square)	70	40
1628.	6 cr. 50 " The Caravel " (B. Giorgi) (As 5 cr.) ..	80	50

769. Hands in Prayer. 770. Sailor of 1840.

1976 Thanksgiving Day.
1629. 769. 80 c. multicoloured .. 10 5

1976. Brazilian Navy Commemoration. Multicoloured.

1630.	80 c. Type 769 ..	10	5
1631.	2 cr. Marine of 1800 ..	25	15

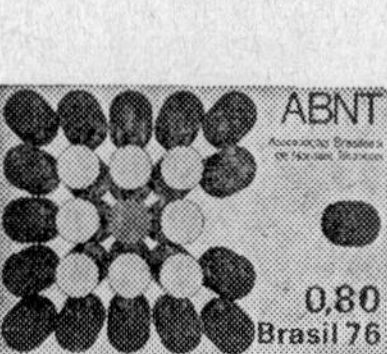

771. " Natural Resources ". 772. " Wheel of Life " (wood-carving).

1976. Brazilian Bureau of Standards.
1632. 771. 80 c. multicoloured .. 10 5

1977. 2nd World Black and African Festival of Arts and Culture, Lagos (Nigeria). Multicoloured.

1633.	5 cr. Type 772	60	35
1634.	5 cr. 60 " The Beggar " (wood-carving) ..	70	40
1635.	6 cr. 50 Benin pectoral mask	80	50

773. Airport Layout. 774. Seminar Emblem.

1977. International Airport, Rio de Janeiro. Inaug.
1636. 773. 6 c. 50 green and blue 80 50

1977. 6th Interamerican Budget Seminar.
1637. 774. 1 cr. 10 turquoise, blue and stone 12 5

BRITISH ANTARCTIC TERRITORY

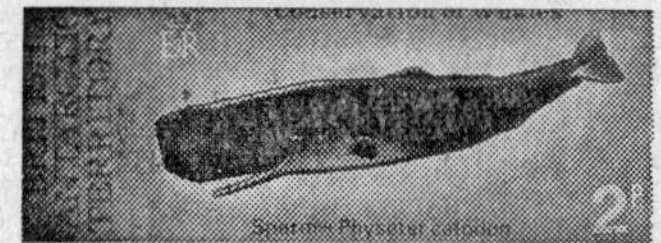

6. Sperm Whale.

1977. Conservation of Whales. Multicoloured.

65.	2 p. Type 6	5	5
66.	8 p. Fin Whale	15	20
67.	11 p. Humpback Whale ..	25	30
68.	25 p. Blue Whale	50	60

7. The Queen Before Taking the Oath.

1977. Silver Jubilee. Multicoloured.

69.	6 p. Duke of Edinburgh in Antarctic, 1956/7 ..	12	15
70.	11 p. The Coronation Oath	25	30
71.	33 p. Type 7	70	75

BULGARIA

702. Fish on line. 703. St. Theodor.

1976. World Sports Fishing Congress, Varna.
2505. 702. 5 s. multicoloured .. 5 5

1976. Semene Frescoes. Multicoloured.

2506.	2 st. Type 703 ..	5	5
2507.	3 st. St. Paul and Apostle	5	5
2508.	5 st. St. Joachim ..	5	5
2509.	13 st. Prophet Melchisedek	15	8
2510.	19 st. St. Porphyrius ..	20	10
2511.	28 st. Queen Dos ..	30	15

704. Legal Document. 705. " The Pianist ".

1976. State Archives. 25th Anniv.
2513. 704. 5 s. multicoloured .. 5 5

1976. Alex Jhendov (caricaturist). 75th Birth Anniv.

2514.	705.	2 s. deep green, cream and green	5	5
2515.	–	5 s. deep violet, violet and lilac	5	5
2516.	–	13 s. blk., pink and red	15	8

DESIGNS: 5 s. " Trick or Treat ". 13 s. " The Leader ".

706. " Aesculus hippocastanum ".

1976. Wild Flowers. Multicoloured.

2517.	1 s. Type 706 ..	5	5
2518.	2 s. " Pontentilla fruiticosa "	5	5
2519.	5 s. " Ilex aquifolium " ..	5	5
2520.	8 s. " Taxus baccata " ..	8	5
2521.	13 s. " Daphne pontica "	15	8
2522.	23 s. " Cercis siliquastrum "	25	12

BURUNDI

88. " Battle of Bunker Hill " (Trumbull). 89. " Virgin and Child " (Dirk Bouts).

1976. Air. American Revolution. Bicent. Multicoloured.

1141.	18 f. } Type 88	25	20
1142.	18 f. }	25	20
1143.	26 f. } Franklin, Jefferson	40	35
1144.	26 f. } and John Adams	40	35
1145.	36 f. } " Signing of Declar-		
1146.	36 f. } ation of Independence " (Trumbull)	45	40
		45	40

The two designs of each value form composite pictures. T 88 is the left-hand portion of the painting.

1976. Christmas. Multicoloured.

1148.	5 f. Type 89 (postage) ..	8	5
1149.	13 f. " Virgin of the Trees " (Bellini)	20	15
1150.	27 f. " Virgin and Child " (C. Crivelli)	40	35
1151.	18 f. " Virgin and Child " with St. Anne " (Leonardo) (air) ..	25	20
1152.	31 f. " Holy Family with Lamb " (Raphael) ..	45	40
1153.	40 f. " Virgin with Basket " (Correggio)	55	45

1976. Christmas (2nd issue). Nos. 1148/53 surch. + 1F.

1155.	89.	5 f. + 1 f. multicoloured (postage)	8	5
1156.	–	13 f. + 1 f. multicoloured	20	15
1157.	–	27 f. + 1 f. multicoloured	40	35
1158.	–	18 f. + 1 f. multicoloured (air)	25	20
1159.	–	31 f. + 1 f. multicoloured	45	40
1160.	–	40 f. + 1 f. multicoloured	55	45

CAMEROUN

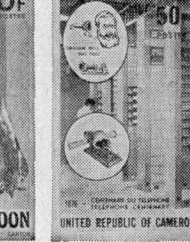

216. Masked Dancer.

217. Telephone Equipment.

1976. Cameroun Dances. Multicoloured.

770. 40 f. Type **216** (postage) .. 20 12
771. 50 f. Drummers and singers (air) 30 20
772. 100 f. Female dancer .. 55 45

1976. Air. Telephone Cent.

773. **217.** 50 f. multicoloured .. 30 20

218. Building Construction.

1976. National Youth Day. Tenth Anniv. Multicoloured.

774. 40 f. Type **218** 20 12
775. 45 f. Gathering palm leaves 25 15

219. Dr. Adenauer.

1976. Dr. Konrad Adenauer. Birth Cent.

776. **219.** 100 f. multicoloured .. 55 45

220. "Adoration of the Shepherds" (Le Brun).

1976. Air. Christmas.

777. 30 f. Type **220** 15 10
778. 60 f. "Adoration of the Magi" (Rubens) .. 30 20
779. 70 f. "Virgin and Child" (Bellini) 35 20
780. 500 f. "The New-born" (G. de la Tour) .. .. 2·75 2·25

221. Pres. Ahidjo and Douala Party H.Q.

1976. Cameroun National Union. Tenth Anniv. Multicoloured.

782. 50 f. Type **221** 30 20
783. 50 f. Pres. Ahidjo and Yaounde Party H.Q. .. 30 20

222. Bamoun Pipe. **223.** Ostrich.

1977. 2nd World Black and African Festival of Arts and Culture. Lagos (Nigeria). Multicoloured.

784. 50 f. Type **222** (postage) .. 30 20
785. 60 f. Traditional chief (air) 30 20

1977. Cameroun Birds. Multicoloured.

786. 30 f. Type **223** 15 10
787. 50 f. Crowned cranes .. 30 20

CANADA

298. "Northcote".

1976. Inland Vessels.

851. **298.** 10 c. black, red & brn. 12 12
852. – 10 c. black, light blue and blue 12 12
853. – 10 c. black, violet and blue 12 12
854. – 10 c. blk., yell. & grn. 12 12

DESIGNS: No. 852, "Chicora". No. 853, "Passport". No. 854, "Athabasca".

299. Queen Elizabeth II. **300.** Queen Elizabeth II.

1977. Silver Jubilee.

855. **299.** 25 c. multicoloured .. 35 30

1977.

862. **300.** 12 c. grey, blk. & blue 15 10

301. Eastern Cougar.

1977. Endangered Wildlife.

876. **301.** 12 c. multicoloured .. 15 10

CAPE VERDE ISLANDS

19. Cabral and Map.

1976. PAIGC (Revolutionary Party). 20th Anniv.

431. **19.** 1 e. multicoloured .. 8 5

CAYMAN ISLANDS

65. The Queen and Interior of Westminster Abbey.

1977. Silver Jubilee. Multicoloured.

427. 8 c. The Prince of Wales 10 12
428. 30 c. Type **65** 40 45
429. 50 c. Preparation for the Anointing (horiz.) 65 75

CENTRAL AFRICAN REPUBLIC

164. French Hussar.

165. "Drurya antimachus".

1976. Butterflies. Multicoloured.

422. 30 f. Type **165** (postage) .. 15 8
423. 40 f. "Argema mittrei" (vert.) 20 10
424. 50 f. "Acherontia atropos" and "Saturnia pyri" (air) 25 12
425. 100 f. "Papilio nireus" and "Heniocha marnois" 45 25

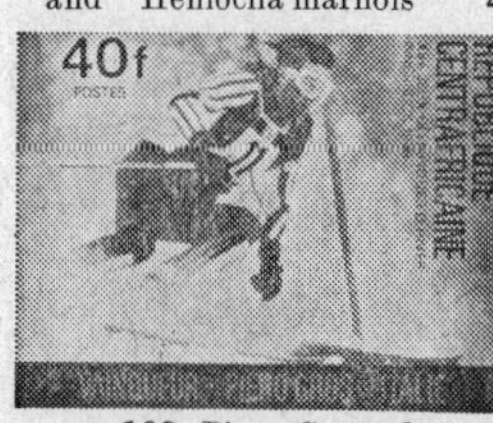

166. Piero Gros of Italy (slalom).

1976. Medal Winners, Winter Olympic Games, Innsbruck. Multicoloured.

426. 40 f. Type **166** (postage) .. 20 10
427. 60 f. Karl Schnabl and Toni Innauer of Austria (ski-jumping) 30 15
428. 100 f. Dorothy Hamill of U.S.A. (Figure-skating) (vert.) (air) 45 25
429. 200 f. Alexandre Gorshkov and Ludmilla Pakhomova (figure-skating, pairs) .. 90 50
430. 300 f. John Curry of Great Britain (figure-skating) (vert.) .. .. 1·40 75

167. "Mail Transport".

1976. World U.P.U. Day.

432. **167.** 100 f. multicoloured .. 45 25

168. Assembly of "Viking".

1976. "Viking" Space Mission to Mars. Multicoloured.

433. 40 f. Type **168** (postage) .. 20 10
434. 60 f. Launch of "Viking" 30 15
435. 100 f. Parachute descent on Mars (air) 45 25
436. 200 f. "Viking" on Mars (horiz.) 90 50
437. 300 f. "Viking" operating gravel scoop .. .. 1·40 75

CHAD

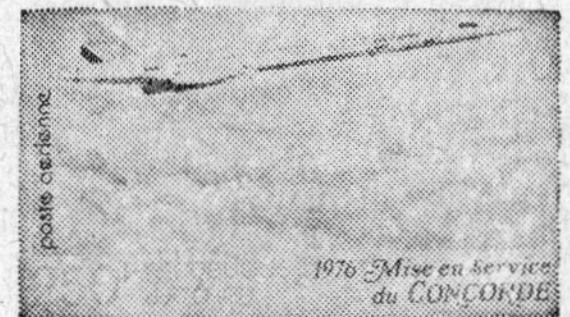

124. "Concorde" in Flight.

1976. Air. "Concorde's" First Commercial Flight.

465. **124.** 250 f. blue, red & blk. 1·75 1·50

125. Gourd and Ladle.

1976. Pyrograved Gourds.

466. **125.** 30 f. multicoloured .. 20 10
467. – 60 f. multicoloured .. 40 20
468. – 120 f. multicoloured .. 90 80

DESIGNS: 60 f., 120 f. Gourds with different decorations.

126. Robert Koch (Medicine, 1905).

1976. Nobel Prizewinners. Multicoloured.

469. 45 f. Type **126** (postage) .. 30 20
470. 90 f. Anatole France (Literature, 1921) .. 65 55
471. 100 f. Albert Einstein (Physics, 1921) (air) .. 70 60
472. 200 f. Dag Hammerskjold (Peace, 1961) .. .. 1·40 1·10
473. 300 f. Dr. S. Tomonaga (Physics, 1965) .. .. 2·10 2·00

127. "The Nativity" (Altdorfer).

1976 Air. Christmas. Multicoloured.
475. 30 f. Type **127** 20 10
476. 60 f. " The Nativity " (Holbein) 40 20
477. 120 f. " Adoration of the Shepherds " (Honthorst) (horiz.) 90 80
478. 150 f. " Adoration of the Magi " (David) (horiz.) 1·00 90

128. " Lesdiguieres Bridge " (J. B. Jongkind).

1976. Air. " Impressionism in Art ". Cent. Multicoloured.
479. 100 f. Type **128** 70 60
480. 120 f. " Warship " (J. B. Jongkind) 90 80

CHILE

Add to Nos. 765/8
765a. **208.** 20 c. lilac 5 5
765b. 30 c. orange 5 5
767a. 1 p. 50 pink 25 12

214. Indian Warrior.

1976. Military Junta. Third Anniv. Mult.
778. 1 p. Type **214** 15 8
779. 2 p. Condor with broken chain 30 15
780. 3 p. Winged woman (" Rebirth of the Country ") .. 45 25

215. Chilean Base, Antarctica.

1977. Presidential Visit to Antarctica.
781. **215.** 2 p. multicoloured .. 30 15

CHINA

PEOPLE'S REPUBLIC

420. Lu Hsun. **421.** Peasant arranging Young Farmer's Headband.

1976. Lu Hsun (revolutionary leader). 95th Birth Anniv.
2672. 8 f. Type **420** 8 5
2673. 8 f. Lu Hsun in study .. 8 5
2674. 8 f. Lu Hsun workers and soldier 8 5

1976. Chinese Country Life. Multicoloured.
2675. 4 f. Type **421** 5 5
2676. 8 f. Young peasant (horiz.) 8 5
2677. 8 f. Irrigation survey .. 8 5
2678. 8 f. Agricultural student (horiz.) 8 5
2679. 10 f. Shepherd-girl feeding lamb 10 5
2680. 20 f. Frontier guards (horiz.) 20 10

422. Mao Tse-tung's Birthplace.

1976. Shaoshan Revolutionary Sites. Mult.
2681. 4 f. Type **422** 5 5
2682. 8 f. School building .. 8 5
2683. 8 f. Peasants' association building 8 5
2684. 10 f. Railway station .. 10 5

423. Chou En-lai. **424.** Statue of Lui Hu-Lan.

1977. Chou En-lai. 1st Death Anniv. Multicoloured.
2685. 8 f. Type **423** 8 5
2686. 8 f. Chou En-lai making report 8 5
2687. 8 f. Chou meeting " Iron Man " – Wang Chin-hsi (horiz.) 8 5
2688. 8 f. Chou with provincial representatives (horiz.) 8 5

1977. Lin Hu-Lan (heroine and martyr). 30th Death Anniv. Multicoloured.
2689. 8 f. Type **424** 8 5
2690. 8 f. Text by Mao Tse-tung 8 5
2691. 8 f. Lin Hu-Lan and people 8 5

TAIWAN

Add to Nos. 1020/28:
(Present No. 1028a to become 1028e.)
1028a. $5 Steel Mill, Kaohsung 20 12
1028b. $6 Taoyuan international airport (horiz.) .. 25 15
1028c. $7 Giant shipyard, Kaohsiung (horiz.) .. 30 20
1028d. $8 Petrochemical works, Kaohsiung 30 20

274. Brazen Serpent. **275.** " Bird and Plum Blossom " (Ch'en Hung-shou).

1976. New Year's Greetings.
1129. **274.** $1 multicoloured .. 5 5
1130. $5 multicoloured .. 20 12

1977. Ancient Chinese Paintings. " Three Friends of Winter ".
1131. $2 Type **275** 8 5
1132. $8 " Wintery Days " (Yang Wei-chen) .. 30 20
1133. $10 " Rock and Bamboo " (Hsia Ch'ang) 35 25

276. Black-naped Orioles.

1977. Taiwan Birds. Multicoloured.
1134. $ 2 Type **276** 8 5
1135. $ 8 Kingfisher 30 20
1136. $ 10 Chinese Pheasant-tailed Jacana 35 25

277. Emblems of Industry and Commerce.

1977. Industry and Commerce Census.
1137. **277.** $ 2 multicoloured .. 8 5
1138. $ 10 multicoloured .. 35 25

POSTAGE DUE STAMPS

Add to Nos. D588/93.
D 594. **D 9.** $10 mauve and pale mauve 35 25

COLOMBIA

347. University Emblem and " 90 ". **348.** " Callicore sp."

1976. Air. Colombia University. 90th Anniv.
1395. **347.** 5 p. multicoloured .. 25 10

1976. Colombian Fauna and Flora. Mult.
1396. 3 p. Type **348** 15 5
1397. 5 p. " Morpho sp." (butterfly) 25 10
1398. 20 p. " Anturio negro " (plant) .. .. .. 1·00 60

349. M. Samper. **350.** Early Telephone.

1976. Air. Miguel Samper (statesman and writer). 150th Birth Anniv.
1399. **349.** 3 p. multicoloured .. 15 5

1976. Air. Telephone Cent.
1400. **350.** 3 p. multicoloured .. 15 5

351. Purace Indians, Cauca.

1976.
1401. **351.** 1 p. 50 multicoloured 8 5

352. Rotary Emblem (vert.).

1976. Colombian Rotary Club. 50th Anniv.
1402. **352.** 1 p. multicoloured .. 5 5

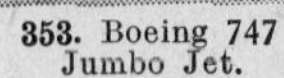

353. Boeing 747 Jumbo Jet. **354.** Arms of Tunja City.

1976. Air. Inauguration of Avianca Jumbo Jet Service.
1403. **353.** 2 p. multicoloured .. 10 5

1976. Tunja City Arms. 535th Anniv.
1404. **354.** 1 p. 20 multicoloured 8 5

355. " Signing of Declaration of Independence " (detail, Trumbull). **356.** Police Handler and Dog.

1976. American Revolution. Bicentennial. Multicoloured.
1405. **355.** 30 p. " Signing the 1·50 90
1406. – 30 p. Declaration of 1·50 90
1407. 30 p. Independence " 1·50 90
DESIGNS: Nos. 1406/7 show different portions of the painting.

1976. National Police.
1408. **356.** 1 p. 50 multicoloured 8 5

357. Convent of St. Francis.

1976. Air. Panama Congress. 150th Anniv.
1409. **357.** 6 p. multicoloured .. 30 12

COMORO ISLANDS

59. Athlete and Athens 1896 Motifs.

1976. Olympic Games – Munich (1972) and Montreal (1976). Multicoloured.
175. 20 f. Type **59** (postage) .. 8 5
176. 25 f. Running 10 5
177. 40 f. Athlete and Paris 1900 motif 15 8
178. 75 f. High-jumping .. 30 20
179. 100 f. Exercises and World's Fair, St. Louis 1904 motif (air) 40 30
180. 500 f. Gymnast on bars .. 2·00 1·50

60. Government House, Flag and Map.

1976. Independence. 1st Anniv. Mult.
182. **60.** 30 f. multicoloured .. 10 8
183. 50 f. multicoloured .. 20 15

61. Agricultural Scene and U.N. F.A.O. Stamp.

1976. U.N. Postal Services. 25th Anniv. Multicoloured.

184. 15 f. Type **61** (postage) .. 5 5
185. 30 f. Surgery scene and U.N. W.H.O. stamp .. 10 8
186. 50 f. Village scene and U.N.I.C.E.F. stamp .. 20 15
187. 75 f. Telecommunications satellite and U.N.I.T.U. stamp 30 20
188. 200 f. " Concorde ", Graf Zeppelin " and U.N. I.C.A.O. stamp (air) .. 80 60
189. 400 f. Lufthansa mailplane and U.N. U.P.U. stamp 1·60 1·25

62. Copernicus, and Rocket on Launch-pad. **63.** Comoro Flag and U.N. Headquarters.

1976. " Success of Operating Viking, and American Revolution Bicent. Multicoloured.

191. 5 f. Type **62** (postage) .. 5 8
192. 10 f. Einstein, Sagan and Young (horiz.) .. 5 5
193. 25 f, "Viking" orbiting Mars 10 5
194. 35 f. Vikings discovery of America (horiz.) 12 10
195. 500 f. First colour photograph of Martian terrain (horiz.) (air) .. .. 2·00 1·50

1976. Comoro Islands Admission to United Nations. 1st Anniv.

197. **63.** 40 f. multicoloured .. 15 8
198. 50 f. multicoloured .. 20 15

CONGO

BRAZZAVILLE

188. Congolese Woman. **189.** Pole-vaulting.

1976. Congolese Women's Hair-styles.

521. **188.** 35 f. multicoloured .. 15 10
522. – 60 f. multicoloured .. 30 20
523. – 95 f. multicoloured .. 45 35
524. – 100 f. multicoloured .. 45 35

DESIGNS: 60 f. to 100 f. Various Congolese Women's hair-styles.

1976. 1st Central African Games, Yaounde. Multicoloured.

525. 60 f. Type **189** (postage) .. 30 20
526. 95 f. Long-jumping .. 45 35
527. 150 f. Running (air) .. 70 50
528. 200 f. Throwing the discus 90 70

190. Antelope. **191.** Jabirus.

1976. Congolese Fauna. Multicoloured.

529. 5 f. Type **190** 5 5
530. 10 f. Buffaloes 5 5
531. 15 f. Hippopotami .. 8 5
532. 20 f. Warthog 10 5
533. 25 f. Elephants 12 8

1976. Birds. Multicoloured.

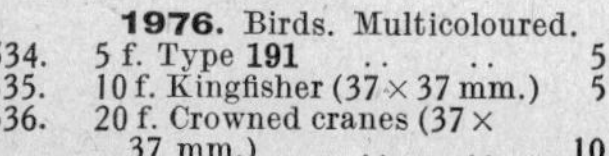

534. 5 f. Type **191** 5 5
535. 10 f. Kingfisher (37 × 37 mm.) 5 5
536. 20 f. Crowned cranes (37 × 37 mm.) 10 8

192. O.U.A. Building on Map. **193.** " Nympheas micrantha ".

1976. Air. O.U.A. 13th Anniv.

537. **192.** 60 f. multicoloured .. 30 20

1976. Tropical Flowers. Multicoloured.

538. 5 f. Type **193** 5 5
539. 10 f. " Heliotrope " .. 5 5
540. 15 f. " Strelitzia reginae " 8 5

194. Pioneers' Emblem. **196.** Cycling.

195. " Spirit of 76 " (Willard).

1976. National Pioneers Movement.

541. **194.** 35 f. multicoloured .. 15 10

1976. American Revolution. Bicent. Multicoloured.

542. 100 f. Type **195** 45 35
543. 125 f. Destruction of George III's statue .. 60 45
544. 150 f. Gunners-Battle of Princeton .. 70 50
545. 175 f. Wartime generals .. 80 60
546. 200 f. Surrender of Gen. Burgoyne, Saratoga .. 90 70

1976. Central African Games, Libreville. Multicoloured.

548. 35 f. Type **196** 15 10
549. 60 f. Handball 30 20
550. 80 f. Running 40 30
551. 95 f. Football 45 35

197. Start of Race.

1977. Pirogue Racing. Multicoloured.

552. 35 f. Type **197** 15 10
553. 60 f. Race in progress .. 30 20

COOK ISLANDS

79. Obverse and Reverse of $5 Coin.

1976. Wildlife Conservation Day.

563. **79.** $1 multicoloured .. 1·10 1·25

80. Imperial State Crown.

1977. Silver Jubilee. Multicoloured.

564. 25 c. Type **80** 25 30
565. 25 c. The Queen with regalia 25 30
566. 50 c. Westminster Abbey 50 60
567. 50 c. Coronation coach .. 50 60
568. $1 The Queen and Prince Philip .. .. .. 1·10 1·25
569. $1 Investiture of Sir Albert Henry, Cook Islands premier .. .. .. 1·10 1·25

81. " The Crucifixion."

1977. Easter. Rubens' 400th Birth Anniv. Multicoloured.

571. 7 c. Type **81** 8 8
572. 15 c. " Christ Between Two Thieves " .. 15 20
573. 35 c. " The Descent from the Cross " 40 45

COSTA RICA

180. Emblems and Costa Rica 2 c. Error of 1901

1976. Air. 7th National Philatelic Exhibition.

1040. **180.** 50 c. multicoloured .. 10 5
1041. 1 col. multicoloured .. 20 10
1042. 2 col. multicoloured .. 40 20

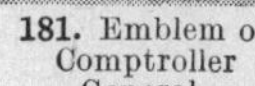

181. Emblem of Comptroller General. **182.** " Girl in Wide-brimmed Hat " (Renoir).

1976. Air. Comptroller General. 25th Anniv.

1044. **181.** 35 c. blue and black .. 8 5
1045. – 2 col. blk., brn. & blue 40 20

DESIGN—VERT. 2 col. Amadeo Quiros Blanco (1st Comptroller).

1976. Obligatory Tax. Christmas.

1046. **182.** 10 c. lake 5 5
1047. – 10 c. purple 5 5
1048. – 10 c. slate 5 5
1049. – 10 c. blue 5 5

DESIGNS: No. 1047, " Virgin and Child " (Hans Memling). No. 1048, " Meditation " (Floria Pinto de Herrero). No. 1049, " Gaston de Mezerville " (Lolita Zeller de Peralta).

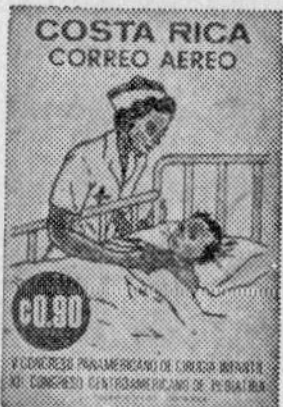

183. Nurse tending Child. **184.** " L.A.C.S.A. " encircling Globe.

1976. Air. 5th Pan-American Children's Surgery Congress. Multicoloured.

1050. 90 c. Type **183** 20 10
1051. 1 col. 10 National Children's Hospital (horiz.) .. 20 12

1976. Air. L.A.C.S.A. Airline. 30th Anniv. Multicoloured.

1052. 1 col. Type **184** 20 10
1053. 1 col. 20 Route-map of L.A.C.S.A. service .. 25 12
1054. 3 col. L.A.C.S.A. emblem and Costa Rican flag .. 60 30

184. Boston Tea Party.

1976. Air. American Revolution Bicent. Multicoloured.

1055. 2 col. 20 Type **183** .. 45 25
1056. 5 col. Declaration of Independence .. .. 1·00 90
1057. 10 col. Ringing the Independence Bell (vert.) .. 2·00 1·75

CUBA

521. School Activities.

1976. " Camilo Cienfuegos " Military School. Tenth Anniv.

2318. **521.** 3 c. multicoloured .. 5 5

522. Cuban Freighter.

1976. Development of Cuban Merchant Marine.

2319. **522.** 1 c. multicoloured .. 5 5
2320. – 2 c. multicoloured .. 5 5
2321. – 3 c. multicoloured .. 5 5
2322. – 5 c. multicoloured .. 10 5
2323. – 13 c. multicoloured .. 25 12
2324. – 30 c. multicoloured .. 60 45

DESIGNS: 2 c., to 30 c. Cuban cargo and passenger ships.

523. Emblem and Part of Cine Film.

1976. 8th International Cinematographic Festival of Socialist Countries, Havana.

2325. **523.** 3 c. multicoloured .. 5 5

524. Scene from " Apollo ".

1976. 5th International Ballet Festival, Havana.

2326. 1 c. Type **524** 5 5
2327. 2 c. " The River and the Forest " (vert.) .. 5 5
2328. 3 c. " Giselle " 5 5
2329. 5 c. " Oedipus Rex " (vert.) 10 5
2330. 13 c. " Carmen " (vert.) 25 12
2331. 30 c. " Vital Song " (vert.) 60 45

525. Soldier and Sportsmen.

1976. Third Military Games.

2332. **525.** 3 c. multicoloured .. 5 5

526. Map of Cuba.

1976. Constitution of Popular Government.

2333. **526.** 13 c. multicoloured .. 25 12

527. Landing Craft.

1976. " Granma " Landings. 20th Anniv.

2334. **527.** 1 c. multicoloured .. 5 5
2335. – 3 c. multicoloured .. 5 5
2336. – 13 c. multicoloured .. 25 12
2337. – 30 c. multicoloured .. 60 45

DESIGNS: 3 c. to 30 c. Different scenes showing guerrillas.

528. Handball.

1976. Cuban Victories in Montreal Olympic Games. Multicoloured.

2339. 1 c. Type **528** 5 5
2340. 2 c. Hurdling 5 5
2341. 3 c. Start of race .. 5 5
2342. 8 c. Boxing 15 10
2343. 13 c. Finish of race .. 25 12
2344. 30 c. Judo 60 45

529. " Golden Cross Inn " (S. Scott).

1976. National Museum Paintings. Mult.

2346. 1 c. Type **529** 5 5
2347. 3 c. " Portrait of a Man " (J. Verspronck) (vert.) 5 5
2348. 5 c. " Venetian Landscape " (F. Guardi) .. 10 5
2349. 10 c. " Valley Corner " (H. Cleenewerck) (vert.) 20 12
2350. 13 c. " F. Xaviera Paula " (anon.) (vert.) .. 25 12
2351 30 c. " F de Medici " (C. Allori) (vert.) .. 60 45

The vertical designs are slightly larger, 27 × 43 mm.

CYPRUS

110. " Cyprus 74 ", (wood engraving by A. Tassos).

1977. Refugee Fund.

481. **110.** 10 m. black 5 5

CZECHOSLOVAKIA

618. Code Emblem.

619. " Guernica 1937 " (I. Weiner-Kral).

1976. Coil Stamps. Postal Codes.

2302. **618.** 30 h. green 5 5
2303. – 60 h. red 12 5

DESIGN: 60 h. Codes map.

1976. International Brigades in Spain. 40th Anniv.

2304. **619.** 5 k. multicoloured .. 1·00 1·00

1976. Prague Castle. Art Treasures (12th series). As T **508**. Multicoloured.

2305. 3 k. " Hradcany Castle " (engraving by F. Hoogenberghe, 1572) 60 60
2306. 3 k. 60 " Satyrs " (sculptured balustrade relief) 70 70

620. Zebra.

1976. " Czechoslovak Safari ". Wild Animals. Multicoloured.

2307. 10 h. Type **620** 5 5
2308. 20 h. Elephant (vert.) .. 5 5
2309. 30 h. Leopard and head.. 5 5
2310. 40 h. Giraffe (vert.) .. 8 5
2311. 60 h. Rhinoceros .. 12 5
2312. 3 k. Bongo (antelope) (vert.) 60 25

621. " Flowers in Vase " (P. Matejka).

1976. " Praga 1978 ". International Stamp Exhibition (2nd series). Floral Art. Multicoloured.

2313. 1 k. Type **621** 20 5
2314. 1 k. 40 " Oleander Blossoms " (C. Bouda) .. 30 10
2315. 2 k. " Flowers in Vase " (J. Brueghel) .. 40 12
2316. 3 k. 60 " Tulips and Daffodils " (J. R. Bys) 70 35

622. Postal Emblem, Postillion and Satellite.

1976. Stamp Day.

2317. **622.** 1 k. blue, mauve & gold 20 5

623. " Hockey ".

624. Arms of Vranov.

1977. 6th Winter Spartakiad of Warsaw Pact Armies. Multicoloured.

2318. 60 h. Type **623** 12 5
2319. 1 k. " Biathlon " .. 20 5
2320. 1 k. 60 " Ski jumping " 30 8
2321. 2 k. " Slalom " 40 12

1977. Coats of Arms of Czechoslovak Towns. Multicoloured.

2322. 60 h. Type **624** 12 5
2323. 60 h. Kralupy and Vlatavou 12 5
2324. 60 h. Jicin 12 5
2325. 60 h. Valasske Mezirici.. 12 5

DENMARK

192. Moulding Glass.

193. Five Water Lilies.

1976. Danish Glass Production.

632. **192.** 60 ore black 15 5
633. – 80 ore brown 20 5
634. – 130 ore blue 30 15
635. – 150 ore brown .. 35 20

DESIGNS: 80 ore, Removing glass from blowpipe. 130 ore, Cutting glass at foot. 150 ore, Blowing glass in mould.

1977. Northern Countries' Day.

636. **193.** 100 ore multicoloured 25 10
637. 130 ore multicoloured 30 15

DOMINICA

63. Island Craft Co-operative.

1976. National Day. Multicoloured.

550. 10 c. Type **63** 5 5
551. 50 c. Castle Bruce Co-operative, Harvesting .. 20 25
552. $1 Bourne Farmers' Co-operative 40 45

64. Common Sundial.

1976. Shells. Multicoloured.

554. ½ c. Type **64** 5 5
555. 1 c. Flame Helmet .. 5 5
556. 2 c. Mouse Cone 5 5
557. 20 c. Caribbean Vase .. 8 10
558. 40 c. West Indian Fighting Conch 15 20
559. 50 c. Short Coral Shell .. 20 25
560. $3 Apple Murex .. .. 1·25 1·40

65. The Queen Crowned and Enthroned.

1976. Silver Jubilee. Multicoloured.

562. ½ c. Type **65** 5 5
563. 1 c. Imperial State Crown 5 5
564. 45 c. The Queen and Princess Anne 20 25
565. $2 Coronation Ring .. 80 90
566. $2.50 Ampulla and spoon 1·10 1·25

DOMINICAN REPUBLIC

328. Commemorative Text and Emblem.

1976. Dominican Radio Club. 50th Anniv.

1271. **328.** 6 c. black and red (postage) 8 5
1272. **328.** 10 c. blk. & blue (air) 12 10

329. Maps and Ships.

331. Virgin and Child.

330. Boxing.

1976. " Hispanidad 1976 ". Multicoloured.

1273. 6 c. Type **329** (postage).. 8 5
1274. 21 c. Heads of Spaniard and Dominicans (air).. 25 15

1976. Olympic Games, Montreal. Multicoloured.

1275. 2 c. Type **330** (postage).. 5 5
1276. 3 c. Weightlifting .. 5 5
1277. 10 c. Running (air) .. 12 10
1278. 25 c. Basketball.. .. 30 20

1976. Christmas. Multicoloured.

1279. 2 c. Type **331** (postage).. 5 5
1280. 6 c. The Three Kings (22 × 32 mm.).. .. 8 5
1281. 10 c. Angel with bells (22 × 32 mm.) (air) .. 12 10

ECUADOR

CORRECTION: Change Nos. 1654/5, T **276**, to 1657/8, T **277**.

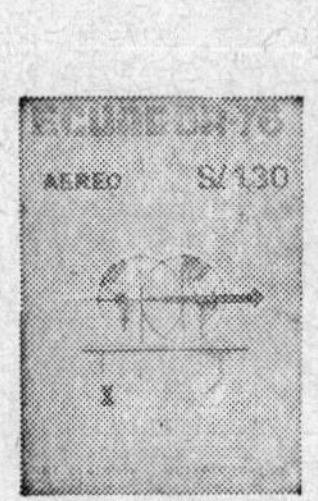

276. Congress Emblem.

278. Bolivar Memorial.

1976. Air. 10th Interamerican Construction Industry Congress, Quito.
1654. **276.** 1 s. 30 multicoloured 8 5
1655. 3 s. multicoloured .. 15 10

1976. Air. Andino Group Agricultural Ministers Meeting, Quito
1659. **278.** 3 s. multicoloured .. 15 10

279. Dr. H. Noguchi.

280. Dr. Luis Cordero.

1976. Air. Dr. Hideyo Noguchi. Birth Cent.
1661. **279.** 3 s. multicoloured .. 15 10

1976. Air. Pres. Cordero Commemoration.
1663. **280.** 2 s. multicoloured .. 10 8

281. M. F. Cordero.

1976. Air. Mariuxi Cordero—South American Swimming Champion.
1664. **281.** 3 s. multicoloured .. 15 10

EGYPT

460. Akhnaton.

461. Patrolman and Police Car.

1977. Post Day.
1304. **460.** 20 m. brown and plum 8 5
1305. – 30 m. brown and plum 12 8
1306. – 55 m. brown & purple 15 10
1307. – 110 m. brown & purple 30 20
DESIGNS: 30 m. Daughter of Akhnaton. 55 m. Nefertiti. 110 m. Akhnaton (Full-face).

1977. Police Day.
1308. **461.** 20 m. blue and red .. 8 5

462. Pharaonic Ship.

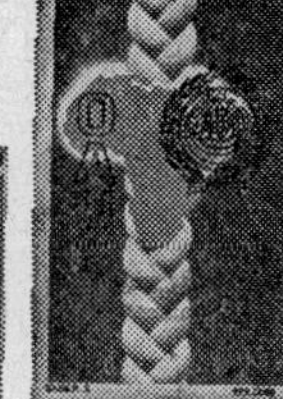
463. Arab League and O.A.U. Emblem on Map.

1977. Cairo. International Fair.
1309. **462.** 20 m. grn., blk. & red 8 5

1977. Afro-Arab Summit Conference, Cairo.
1310. **463.** 55 m. blue, blk. & oran. 15 10

464. King Faisal.

1977. King Faisal of Saudi Arabia Commemoration.
1311. **464.** 20 m. bistre and blue 8 5

EL SALVADOR

188. Fair Emblem.

189. Post-classical. Lead Vase (San Salvador).

1976. 7th International Fair.
1505. **188.** 10 c. multicoloured (postage) 5 5
1506. 30 c. multicoloured .. 15 12
1507. **188.** 25 c. multicoloured (air) 15 12
1508. 70 c. multicoloured .. 35 25

1976. Pre-Columbian Art. Multicoloured.
1509. 10 c. Type **189** (postage) 5 5
1510. 15 c. Brazier with classical effigy (Tazumal) .. 8 5
1511. 40 c. Vase with classical effigy (Tazumal) .. 20 15
1512. 25 c. Brazier with pre-classical effigy (El Trapiche) (air) 15 12
1513. 50 c. Kettle with pre-classical effigy (Atiquizaya) 30 25
1514. 70 c. Classical whistling vase (Tazumal) .. 35 25

190. Child beside Christmas Tree.

1976. Christmas.
1515. **190.** 10 c. multicoloured (postage) 5 5
1516. 15 c. multicoloured .. 8 5
1517. 30 c. multicoloured .. 15 12
1518. 40 c. multicoloured .. 20 15
1519. **190.** 25 c. multicoloured (air) 15 12
1520. 50 c. multicoloured .. 30 25
1521. 60 c. multicoloured .. 30 25
1522. 75 c. multicoloured .. 40 35

ETHIOPIA

CORRECTION: Nos. 983/7, T **161** should be renumbered 1001/5, T **162**.
Add to Nos. 974/7.
975a. **159.** 25 c. multicoloured .. 15 12

161. Crest with Sunburst.

163. Tortoise.

1976.
983. **161.** 5 c. gold, grn. & blk. 5 5
984 10 c. gold, oran. & blk. 5 5
985. 15 c. gold, blue & blk. 8 5
986. 20 c. gold, lilac & blk. 10 8
987. 25 c. gold, grn. & blk. 15 12
988. 30 c. gold, red & blk. 20 15
989. 35 c. gold, yell. & blk. 20 15
990. 40 c. gold, olive & blk. 25 20
991. 45 c. gold, grn. & blk. 25 20
992. 50 c. gold, mve. & blk. 30 25
993. 55 c. gold, blue & blk. 30 25
994. 60 c. gold, brn. & blk. 35 30
995. 70 c. gold, pink & blk. 45 40
996. 90 c. gold, blue & blk. 55 45
997. $1 gold, grn. & blk.. 60 50
998. $2 gold, grey & black 1·25 1·00
999. $3 gold, purple & blk. 1·75 1·50
1000. $5 gold, blue & black 3·00 2·50

1976. Reptiles. Multicoloured.
1006. 10 c. Type **163** 5 5
1007. 20 c. Chameleon .. 10 8
1008. 30 c. Python 20 15
1009. 40 c. Monitor (lizard) .. 25 20
1010. 80 c. Crocodile 50 40

164. Aircraft dropping Supplies.

1976. Relief and Rehabilitation. Mult.
1011. 5 c. Type **164** 5 5
1012. 10 c. Carved hand with hammer 5 5
1013. 45 c. Child supported by banknote 25 20
1014. 60 c. Map of Ogaden region and desert tracks .. 35 30
1015. 80 c. Waif within broken eggshell, camera & film 50 40

FALKLAND ISLANDS

39. The Queen Awaiting Anointment.

1977. Silver Jubilee. Multicoloured.
347. 6 p. Duke of Edinburgh riding in the Falklands 12 12
348. 11 p. Ampulla and Anointing Spoon 25 25
349. 33 p. Type **39** 65 70

FIJI

54. The Queen receiving a bouquet.

1977. Silver Jubilee. Multicoloured.
536. 10 c. Type **54** 12 12
537. 25 c. King Edward's chair 30 35
538. 30 c. The Queen wearing Cloth of Gold Supertunica 40 45

55. Map of the World.

1977. EEC/ACP Council of Ministers Conference. Multicoloured.
539. 4 c. Type **55** 5 5
540. 30 c. Map of the Fiji Islands 40 45

FINLAND

Add to Nos. 866 etc.
871. **305.** 90 p. violet 30 8

329. Hugo Alvar Aalto and Finlandia Hall, Helsinki.

1976. Hugo Alvar Aalto (architect) Commemoration.
910. **329.** 80 p. multicoloured .. 30 5

330. Weathercock (vert.).

1977.
911. **330.** 5 m. multicoloured .. 1·75 60

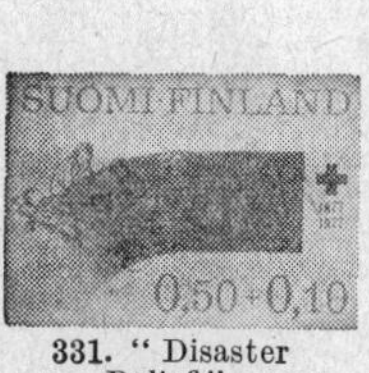

331. " Disaster Relief ".

332. Figure-Skating

1977. Finnish Red Cross. Cent. Red Cross Fund. Multicoloured.
912. 50 p.+10 p. Type **331** .. 20 20
913. 80 p.+15 p. " Community Work " 35 35
914. 90 p.+20 p. " Blood Transfusion Service " .. 45 45

1977. European Figure-Skating Championships, Helsinki.
915. **332.** 90 p. multicoloured .. 30 8

1977. Northern Countries' Day. As **193** of Denmark.
916. 90 p. multicoloured .. 30 8
917. 1 m. multicoloured .. 40 10

FRANCE

737. Fair Emblem.

738. St. Barbara.

1976. French Fairs and Exhibitions Federation. 50th Anniv.
2145. 737. 1 f. 50 blue, grn. & brn. 30 12

1976. Red Cross Fund. Statuettes in Brou Church.
2146. 738. 80 c. + 20 c. vio. & red 20 15
2147. – 1 f. + 25 c. brn. & red 25 20
DESIGN: 1 f. + 25 c. "Cumaean Sybil".

739. "Douane".

1976. Customs Service.
2148. 738. 1 f. 10 multicoloured 75 8

740. Museum and "Duchess Anne".

1976. Atlantic Museum, Port Louis.
2149. 740. 1 f. 45 brn., blue & blk. 30 12

1977. Regions of France. As T 708.
2150. 1 f. 45 mauve and green 30 12
2151. 1 f. 50 multicoloured .. 30 12
2152. 2 f. 10 yellow, blue & grn. 40 12
2153. 2 f. 40 brn., green & blue 50 15
2154. 2 f. 50 multicoloured .. 50 15
2155. 2 f. 75 green 55 20
2157. 3 f. 90 lake, brown & blue 80 25
DESIGN—HORIZ. 1 f. 45 Birds and flowers (Reunion). 2 f. 40 Coastline (Bretagne). VERT. 2 f. 75 Mountains (Rhone – Alpes). 1 f. 50 Banana tree (Martinique). 2 f. 10 Arms and transport (Franche – Comte). 2 f. 50 Fruit and yachts (Languedoc—Roussillon). 3 f. 90 Village church (Alsace).

741. Centre Building.

1977. Opening of Georges-Pompidou National Centre of Art and Culture, Paris.
2158. 741. 1 f. red, blue & green 20 8

1977. French Art. As T 445.
2159. 2 f. multicoloured .. 45 25
DESIGN—HORIZ. 2 f. "Mantes Bridge" (Corot).

742. Dunkirk Harbour.

743. Torch and Dagger Emblem.

1977. Dunkirk Port Extensions.
2161. 742. 50 c. blue, brn. & red 10 5

1977. "Le Souvenir Français" (Movement perpetuating the memory of those who died for France).
2162. 743. 80 c. brn., red & blue 15 5

744. Marckolsheim Post Relay Sign.

745. "Pisces".

1977. Stamp Day.
2163. 744. 1 f. + 20 c. grey & blue 25 20

1977. Precancelled. Signs of the Zodiac.
2164. 745. 54 c. blue 10 5
2165. – 68 c. brown 15 5
2166. – 1 f. 05 mauve .. 20 8
2167. – 1 f. 85 green 30 12
DESIGNS: 68 c. Taurus. 1 f. 05 Scorpio. 1 f. 85 Aquarius.

746. "Geometric Design" (Victor Vasarely).

1977. "Philatelic Creations". Works of Art by Modern Artists.
2168. 746. 3 f. green and mauve 60 25

COUNCIL OF EUROPE STAMPS

CORRECTION: No. C 18 to become No. C 19. Add to Nos. C 7/19.
C 18. C 1. 1 f. blue, yellow, red and brown .. 20 20

C 2. New Council of Europe Building, Strasbourg.

1977.
C 20. C 2. 80 c. red, yell. & brn. 15 15
C 21. 1 f. brn., blue & grn. 20 20
C 22. 1 f. 40 grey, grn. & brn. 25 25

UNESCO STAMPS

U 4. Sun, Moon and Flame.

1976.
U 16. U 4. 80 c. brn., blue & blk. 15 15
U 17. 1 f. oran., grn. & blue 20 20
U 18. 1 f. 40 pur., brn. & oran. 25 25

FRENCH POLYNESIA

81. Marquezes Pirogue.

1976. Ancient Pirogues. Multicoloured.
227. 25 f. Type 81 .. .. 35 20
228. 30 f. Raiatea pirogue .. 40 25
229. 75 f. Tahiti pirogue .. 1·00 60
230. 100 f. Tuamotu pirogue .. 1·40 80

82. "Murex steeriae".

1977. Air. Seashells. Multicoloured.
231. 25 f. Type 82 .. .. 35 20
232. 27 f. "Conus gauguini" .. 35 20
233. 35 f. "Conus marchionatus" 45 30

FRENCH SOUTHERN AND ANTARCTIC TERRITORIES

32. Captain Cook.

34. First Ascent of Mt. Ross.

33. Kerguelen Island.

1976. Cook Commemoration.
109. 32. 70 c. blue, brn. & yellow 12 12

1976. Air. Cook's Passage to Kerguelen. Bicent.
110. 33. 3 f. 50 slate and blue .. 70 70

1976. Ross Commemoration.
111. 34. 30 c. red, brown & blue 5 5
112. – 3 f. violet, brown & blue 60 60
DESIGN: 3 f. Sir James Clark Ross.

35. Blue Rorqual.

1976. Marine Mammals.
113 35. 1 f. 10 deep blue & blue 20 20
114. – 1 f. 50 indigo, blue & brn. 30 30
DESIGN: 1 f. 50 Commerson's dolphin.

FRENCH TERRITORY OF AFARS AND THE ISSAS

Add to Nos. 627/32b.
627a. 5 f. brown and blue .. 5 5
630a. 20 f. brown and green .. 15 10
630b. 30 f. brown, lake & green 25 15
632c. 70 f. brown, blue & black 55 40
DESIGNS: 5 f. "Murex palmarosa". 20 f. "Cypraea exhusta". 30 f. "Conus betulinus". 70 f. "Conus striatus".

1976. "Diurnal" Butterflies. As T 34. Multicoloured.
667. 50 f. "Acraea anemosa" 35 25
668. 150 f. "Vanessa cardui" 1·00 85

MINIMUM PRICE

The minimum price quoted is 5p which represents a handling charge rather than a basis for valuing common stamps. For further notes about prices see introductory pages.

40. Motor-cyclist on Course.

1977. Motor-Cross Racing.
669. 40. 200 f. multicoloured .. 1·50 1·00

GABON

177. Ricefield and Plant.

1976. Agriculture. Multicoloured.
599. 50 f. Type 177 .. .. 20 12
600. 60 f. Pepper grove and plant 25 12

178. "Presentation at the Temple".

1976. Air. Christmas. Wood-carvings. Multicoloured.
601. 50 f. Type 178 .. .. 20 12
602. 60 f. "The Nativity" .. 25 12

179. Control Panel.

1976. Air. Inauguration of Oklo Fossil Reactor.
603. 179. 60 f. multicoloured .. 25 12

180. "The Last Supper" (Juste de Gand).

1977. Air. Easter. Multicoloured.
604. 50 f. Type 180 .. .. 20 12
605. 100 f. "The Deposition" (N. Poussin) 45 30

GAMBIA

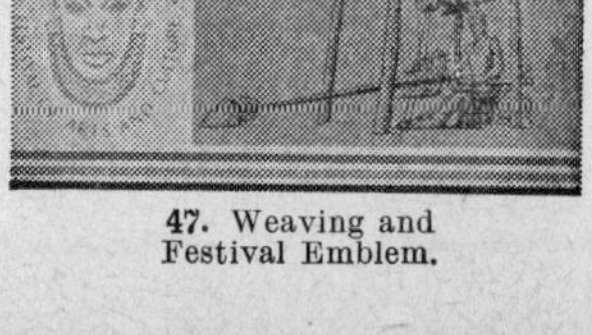

47. Weaving and Festival Emblem.

1977. 2nd World Black and African Festival of Arts and Culture, Lagos.

361.	47.	25 b. black, green, blue, red and dull blue ..	12	15
362.		50 b. black, green, blue, red and turquoise ..	25	30
363.		1 d. 25 black, green, blue, red and lilac	60	70

48. The Spurs and Jewelled Sword.

1977. Silver Jubilee. Multicoloured.

365.	25 b. The Queen's visit to Gambia, 1961	12	15
366.	50 b. Type **48**	25	30
367.	1 d. 25 Oblation of the Sword	60	70

49. Wassu Stone Circles, Kuntaur.

1977. Tourism. Multicoloured.

368.	25 b. Type **49**	12	15
369.	50 b. Ruined Fort, James Island	25	30
370.	1 d. 25 Mungo Park Monument	60	70

GERMANY

II WEST GERMANY

535. Posthouse Sign, Hochst-am-Main. **536.** Phlox.

1976. Stamp Day.

1795	535.	10 pf. multicoloured ..	5	5

1976. Humanitarian Relief Funds. Garden Flowers. Multicoloured.

1796.	30 pf. + 15 pf. Type **536** ..	25	25
1797.	40 pf. + 20 pf. Marigolds	30	30
1798.	50 pf. + 25 pf. Dahlias ..	40	40
1799.	70 pf. + 35 pf. Pansies ..	55	55

537. Caroline Neuber (" Medea ").

1976. Stage Actresses. Multicoloured.

1800.	30 pf. Type **537**	15	10
1801.	40 pf. Sophie Schroder (" Sappho ")	20	12
1802.	50 pf. Louise Dumont (" Hedda Gabler ") ..	25	15
1803.	70 pf. Hermine Korner (" Macbeth ")	35	25

III WEST BERLIN

B 122. Iris. **B 123.** Sailing Boat on the Havel.

1976. Humanitarian Relief Funds. Garden Flowers. Multicoloured.

B 508.	30 pf. + 15 pf. Type **B 122**	25	25
B 509.	40 pf. + 20 pf. Wallflower	30	30
B 510.	50 pf. + 25 pf. Dahlia ..	40	40
B 511.	70 pf. + 35 pf. Larkspur	55	55

1976. Berlin Views.

B 512.	**B 123.**	30 pf. blk. & blue	15	10
B 513.	–	40 pf. blk. & brn.	20	12
B 514.	–	50 pf. blk. & grn.	25	15

DESIGNS: 40 pf. Spandau Citadel. 50 pf. Tiergarten.

IV. EAST GERMANY

E 563. Point-tail Guppy. **E 565.** The Miller and the King.

E 564. Ceramic Pots.

1976. Aquarium Fishes – Guppies. Multicoloured.

E 1891.	10 pf. Type **E 563** ..	5	5
E 1892.	15 pf. Double-sword ..	5	5
E 1893.	20 pf. Flagtail ..	8	5
E 1894.	25 pf. Swordtail ..	12	10
E 1895.	35 pf. Triangle ..	18	12
E 1896.	70 pf. Roundtail ..	3·00	3·00

1976. Archaeological Discoveries in D.D.R. Multicoloured.

E 1897.	10 pf. Type **E 564** ..	5	5
E 1898.	20 pf. Bronze urn on wheels	8	5
E 1899.	25 pf. Roman gold coin	12	10
E 1900.	35 pf. Gold locket ..	15	12
E 1901.	70 pf. Painted glass beaker	2·50	2·50

1976. Fairy Tales (11th series). " Rumpelstiltskin ".

E 1902.	**E 565.**	5 pf. multicoloured	35	35
E 1903.	–	10 pf. multicoloured	35	35
E 1904.		15 pf. multicoloured	35	35
E 1905.	–	20 pf. multicoloured	35	35
E 1906.	–	25 pf. multicoloured	35	35
E 1907.	–	30 pf. multicoloured	35	35

DESIGNS: 10 pf. to 30 pf. Scenes from the fairy tale.

E 566. " Air " (R. Carriera).

1976. Art Treasures – Dresden Gallery. Multicoloured.

E 1908.	10 pf. Type **E 566** ..	5	5
E 1909.	15 pf. " Virgin and Child " (Murillo)	5	5
E 1910.	20 pf. " The Bass Viol Player " (B. Strozzi)	5	5
E 1911.	25 pf. " Ariadne Forsaken " (A. Kauffman)	10	5
E 1912.	35 pf. " Old Man in Black Cap " (B. Nazzari) ..	15	12
E 1913.	70 pf. " Officer reading a Letter " (G. Terborch)	3·00	3·00

E 567. Arnold Zweig (author).

1977. German Celebrities.

E 1914.	**E 567.**	10 pf. blk. & pink	5	5
E 1915.	–	20 pf. blk. & grey	5	5
E 1916.	–	35 pf. blk. & grn.	15	12
E 1917.	–	40 pf. blk. & blue	95	95

DESIGNS:—20 pf. Otto von Guericke (scientist). 35 pf. Albrecht D. Thaer (agriculturalist). 40 pf. Gustav Hertz (physicist).

GHANA

133. A. G. Bell and " Gallows Flame " Telephone.

1976. First Telephone Transmission. Cent. Multicoloured.

786.	8 p. Type **133**	5	8
787.	30 p. A. G. Bell and 1895 telephone	25	30
788.	60 p. A. G. Bell and 1929 telephone	50	55
789.	1 c. A. G. Bell and modern telephone	85	95

134. Letting off Fireworks, Christmas Eve.

1976. Christmas. Multicoloured.

791.	6 p. Type **134**	5	5
792.	8 p. Opening gifts ..	5	8
793.	30 p. Christmas feast ..	25	30
794.	1 c. As 8 p.	85	95

135. Dipo Girls Dancing Klama.

1977. Second World Black and African Festival of Arts and Culture, Lagos. Multicoloured.

796.	8 p. Type **135**	5	8
797.	30 p. African arts and crafts	25	30
798.	60 p. Traditional music and dance	50	55
799.	1 c. Traditional African architecture ..	85	95

1977. Olympic Winners. Nos. 773/6 optd. **WINNERS** and Country name.

801.	**1307.**	7 p. multicoloured ..	5	5
802.	–	30 p. multicoloured ..	25	30
803.	–	60 p. multicoloured ..	50	55
804.	–	1 c. multicoloured ..	85	95

OPTD. 7 p., 30 p. **EAST GERMANY.** 60 p. **USSR.** 1 c. **USA.**

GIBRALTAR

47. The Queen, Royal Arms and Gibraltar.

1977. Silver Jubilee. Multicoloured.

371.	47.	6p. red	12	15
372.		£1 blue	2·00	2·25

48. " Orchis tridentata ".

1977. Birds, Flowers, Fish and Butterflies. Multicoloured.

373.	½p. Type **48**	5	5
374.	1p. " Mullus surmuletus " (horiz.)	5	5
375.	2p. " Maculinea arion " (horiz.)	5	5
376.	2½p. " Sylvia melanocephala "	5	5
377.	3p. " Scilla peruviania " ..	5	5
378.	4p. " Crenilabrus cinerceus " (horiz.)	8	8
379.	5p. " Vanessa atalanta " (horiz.)	8	8
380.	6p. " Milvus migrans " ..	10	10
381.	9p. " Coronilla valentina "	15	15
382.	10p. " Zeus faber " (horiz.)	20	20
383.	12p. " Colias crocea " (horiz.)	20	25
384.	20p. " Larus audouinii "	35	40
385.	25p. " Iris sisgrinchium "	45	50
386.	50p. " Xiphias gladius " (horiz.)	85	90
387.	£1 " Papilio machaon " (horiz.)	1·75	2·00
388.	£2 " Upupa epops " ..	3·50	4·00

GILBERT ISLANDS

5. The Queen in Coronation Robes.

1977. Silver Jubilee. Multicoloured.

47.	8 c. Prince Charles ..	10	12
48.	20 c. Prince Philip ..	30	25
49.	40 c. Type **5**	60	70

GREAT BRITAIN

236.

1977.

1026. **236.** £1. olive and green .. 1·50 85
1027. £2. brown and green 3·00 1·50
1028. £5. blue and pink .. 7·50 4·00

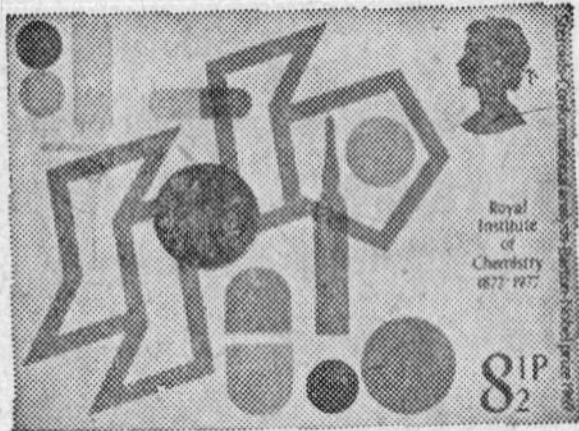

237. Chemical Structures.

1977. Royal Institute of Chemistry. Cent. Multicoloured.

1029. 8½p. Type **237** 12 15
1030. 10p. Vitamin C molecular structure 15 20
1031. 11p. Partition chromatography and graph .. 15 20
1032. 13p. Chemical model of salt crystal 20 25

238. Queen Elizabeth II and Decorated Initials.

1977. Silver Jubilee. Multicoloured.

1033. 8½p. Type **238** 12 15
1035. 10p. " Leaf " initials .. 15 20
1036. 11p. " Star " initials .. 15 20
1037. 13p. " Oak " initials .. 20 25

239. Symbolic " Gathering of the Nations " (vert.).

1977. Commonwealth Heads of Government Meeting, London.

1038. **239.** 13p. red, black, green and silver 20 25

GUERNSEY

The above illustrates T **30.**

INDEX

Countries can be quickly located by referring to the index at the end of this volume.

JERSEY

The above illustrates T **34.**

35. Thirteenth-shilling (1871) and Twelfth-shilling (1877).

1977. Currency Reform. Centenary. Multicoloured.

171. 5p. Type **35** 10 10
172. 7p. Obverse and reverse of 1949 Liberation penny 15 15
173. 11p. Obverse and reverse of 1966 crown 20 25
174. 13p. Obverse and reverse of 1972 Silver Wedding £2 25 30

ISLE OF MAN

The above illustrates T **22.**

GREECE

256. " The Magi talking to the Jews ". **257.** Open Book.

1976. Christmas. Multicoloured.

1352. 4 d. Type **256** 15 10
1353. 7 d. " The Adoration of the Magi " 20 12

1976. Printing of First Greek Book. 500th Anniv.

1354. **257.** 4 d. multicoloured .. 15 10

258. Heinrich Schliemann (archaeologist). **259.** Patients visiting Asclepius.

1976. Schliemann Commemoration. Multicoloured.

1355. 2 d. Type **258** 8 5
1356. 4 d. Gold bracelet (horiz.) 15 10
1357. 5 d. Silver brooch .. 20 12
1358. 7 d. Gold diadem (horiz.) 20 12
1359. 11 d. Gold mask .. 45 35

1977. International Rheumatism Year. Multicoloured.

1360. 50 l. Type **259** 5 5
1361. 1 d. Ancient Clinic .. 5 5
1362. 1 d. 50. Asclepius curing young man 5 5
1363. 2 d. The young Hercules accompanied by an old nurse 8 5
1364. 20 d. Cured man offering likeness of his leg .. 70 50

Nos. 1361/3 are smaller. 22×27 m.

GREENLAND

Add to Nos. 75 etc.

78a. 2 k. blue 30 30

DESIGN—HORIZ: 2 k. Helicopter.

GRENADA

91. A. G. Bell and Telephone.

1976. First Telephone Transmission. Cent. Multicoloured.

847. ½ c. Type **91** 5 5
848. 1 c. The telephone in use around the world .. 5 5
849. 2 c. Telephone, satellite and world map 5 5
850. 18 c. Telephone viewer and console 8 8
851. 40 c. Satellite transmitter-receiver 15 20
852. $1 Modern telephone and surface-satellite-water transmitting 40 45
853. $2 Modern telephone and transmitter-receiver .. 80 90

92. The Queen at Coronation.

1977. Silver Jubilee. Multicoloured. (a) Perf.

854. ½ c. Type **92** 5 5
855. 1 c. Sceptre and Orb .. 5 5
856. 35 c. The Queen taking salute at Trooping the Colour 15 20
857. $2 Spoon and Ampulla .. 80 90
858. $2.50 The Queen and Duke of Edinburgh .. .. 1·00 1·10

(b) Roul. Self-adhesive.

860. 35 c. As $2.50 .. .. 15 20
861. 50 c. As $2 .. .. 20 20
862. $3 As 35 c. .. .. 1·25 1·50

Nos. 860/2 come from booklets.

GRENADINES OF GRENADA

16. A. G. Bell and First Telephone.

1977. First Telephone Transmission. Cent. Multicoloured.

207. ½ c. Type **16** 5 5
208. 1 c. A. G. Bell and 1895 telephone 5 5
209. 2 c. A. G. Bell and 1900 telephone 5 5
210. 35 c. A. G. Bell and 1915 telephone 15 20
211. 75 c. A. G. Bell and 1920 telephone 30 35
212. $1 A. G. Bell and 1929 telephone 40 45
213. $2 A. G. Bell and 1963 telephone 80 90

17. Coronation Coach.

1977. Silver Jubilee. Multicoloured.

215. 35 c. Type **17** 15 20
216. $2 Queen entering Abbey 80 90
217. $4 The Queen crowned .. 1·60 1·75

GUATEMALA

Add to Nos. 897/9:

899b. **161.** 50 c. mauve & brown 60 50

184. Quetzal Coin.

1976. Air. Quetzal Currency. 50th Anniv.

1045. **184.** 8 c. blk., oran. & blue 10 8
1046. 20 c. blk., mve. & blue 25 15

185. " The Engineers " (sculpture).

1976. Air. Engineering School, Guatemala City. Centenary.

1047. **185.** 9 c. blue 10 8
1048. 10 c. green 12 8

GUINEA

96. " Collybia fusipes ".

1977. Mushrooms. Multicoloured.

912. 5 s. Type **96** (postage) .. 30 15
913. 7 s. " Lycoperdon perlatum " 50 30
914. 9 s. " Boletus edulis " .. 60 35
915. 9 s. 50 " Lactarius deliciosus " 60 35
916. 11 s. 50 " Agaricus campestris " 80 45
917. 10 s. " Morchella esculenta " (air) 60 35
918. 12 s. " Lepiota procera " 80 45
919. 15 s. " Cantharellus cibarius " 90 60

MINIMUM PRICE

The minimum price quoted is 5p which represents a handling charge rather than a basis for valuing common stamps. For further notes about prices see introductory pages.

GUYANA

51. Musical Instruments and Festival Emblem.

1977. Second World Black and African Festival of Arts and Culture, Lagos.

666. **51.** 10 c. red, black and gold 5 5
667. 25 c. blue, black & gold 15 20
668. 50 c. blue, black & gold 20 20
669. $1. green, black & gold 40 45

HONG KONG

44. Snake entwined in Branch.

1977. Chinese New Year ("Year of the Snake"). Multicoloured.

359. 20 c. Type **44** 5 8
360. $1.30 Snake entwined in branch 25 40

45. Presentation of the Orb.

1977. Silver Jubilee. Multicoloured.

361. 20 c. Type **45** 5 8
362. $1.30 The Queen dotting eye of ceremonial dragon 25 40
363. $2 The Orb (vert.) .. 40 45

HUNGARY

585. "Sigl" Locomotive.

1976. Gyor-Sopron Railway. Cent. Multicoloured.

3069. 40 fl. Type **585** 5 5
3070. 60 fl. Steam train .. 5 5
3071. 1 fo. Ganz rail-bus .. 15 5
3072. 2 fo. Hanomag steam locomotive 30 12
3073. 3 fo. Ganz rail-car .. 45 20
3074. 4 fo. Ganz express rail-car 60 25
3075. 5 fo. Raba rail-car .. 75 30

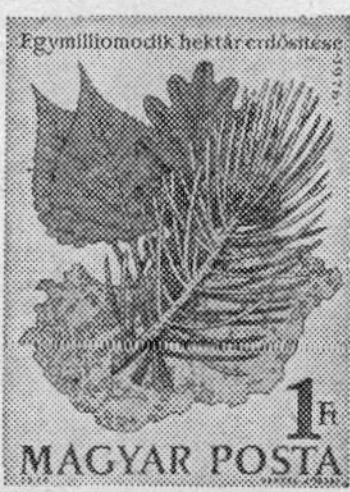

586. Foliage of Poplar, Oak and Pine.

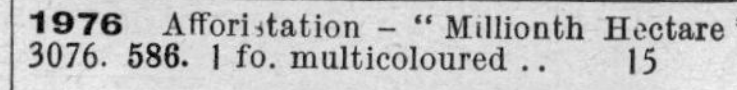

1976 Afforestation – "Millionth Hectare".

3076. **586.** 1 fo. multicoloured .. 15 5

587. Weightlifting and Wrestling (silver medals).

1976. Olympic Games, Montreal. Hungarian Medal-winners. Multicoloured.

3077. 40 fl. Type **587** 5 5
3078. 60 fl. Kayak-canoeing – men's singles, women's doubles (silver medals) 5 5
3079. 1 fo. Gymnastics (gold medal) 15 5
3080. 4 fo. Women's fencing (gold medal) 60 25
3081. 6 fo. Javelin-throwing (gold medal) 90 50

ICELAND

131. Emblem and "workers".

1976. Icelandic Labour Federation. 60th Anniv.

550. **131.** 100 k. multicoloured.. 90 90

1977. Northern Countries' Day. As T **193** of Denmark.

551. 35 k. multicoloured .. 30 30
552. 45 k. multicoloured .. 35 35

INDIA

425. Painting from "Panchatantra" (story).

1976. Children's Day.

831. **425.** 25 p. multicoloured .. 5 5

426. Hiralal Shastri.

1976. Hiralal Shastri (politician).

832. **426.** 25 p. brown 5 5

427. Dr. Hari Singh Gour.

1976. Dr. Hari Singh Gour (lawyer).

833. **427.** 25 p. purple 5 5

428. A300 B2 Airbus.

1976. Inauguration of Indian Airlines Airbus.

834. **428.** 2 r. multicoloured .. 20 25

429. Coconut Palm.

1976 Coconut Research. Diamond Jubilee.

835. **429.** 25 p. multicoloured .. 5 5

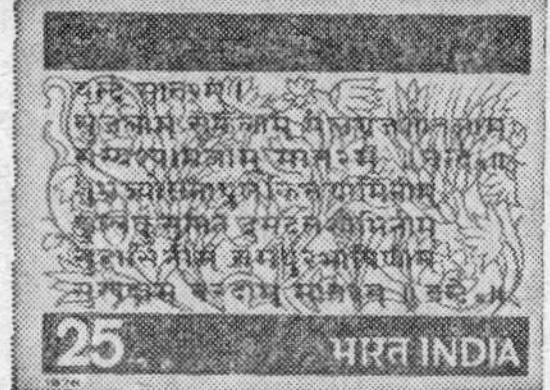

430. First Stanza of "Vande Mataram".

1976. "Vande Mataram" (patriotic song).

836. **430.** 25 p. yellow, orange, green and blue .. 5 5

431. Globe and Film Strip.

1977. Sixth International Film Festival.

827. **431.** 2 r. multicoloured. .. 20 25

432. Seismograph Recording Drum.

1977. Sixth World Conference on Earthquake Engineering.

838. **432.** 2 r. lilac 20 25

433. Tarun Ram Phookun.

1977. Tarun Ram Phookun (politican).

827 **433.** 25 p. grey 5 5

434. Paramansa Yoganda.

1977. Paramansa Yoganda (religious leader).

840. **434.** 25 p. orange 5 5

435. Asian Regional Red Cross Emblem.

1977. 1st Asian Regional Red Cross Conference, New Delhi.

841. **435.** 2 r. red, pink and blue 20 25

436. Fakhruddin Ali Ahmed.

1977. Death of President Fakhruddin Ali Ahmed.

842. **436.** 25 p. multicoloured .. 5 5

INDONESIA

228. Stylised Tree.

230. Open Book.

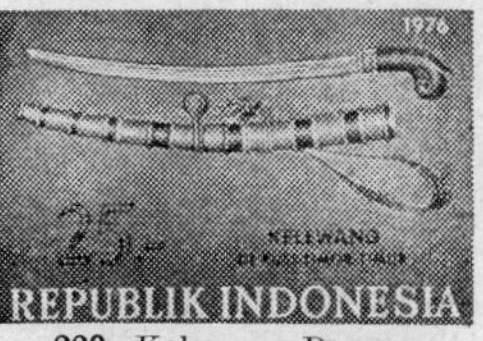

229. Kelewang Dagger and Sheath (Timor).

1976. Reafforestation Week.

1445. **228.** 20 r. multicoloured .. 5 5

1976. Historic Daggers and Sheaths. Multicoloured..

1446. 25 r. Type **229** 8 5
1447. 40 r. Mandau dagger and sheath (Borneo) .. 12 8
1448. 100 r. Rencong dagger and sheath (Aceh) .. 30 15

1976. Books for Children. multicoloured

1449. 20 r. Type **230** 5 5
1450. 40 r. Children reading book 12 8

231. UNICEF Emblem.

1976. UNICEF. 30th Anniv.
1451. **231.** 40 r. violet & turquoise 12 8

IRAN

479. U.P.U. Emblem and Iranian Stamp on Envelope.

1976. International Post Day.
1998. **479.** 10 r. multicoloured .. 15 12

480. Crown Prince presenting Cup.

1976. Society of Village Culture Houses.
1999. **480.** 6 r. multicoloured .. 10 8

481. Riza Shah Pahlavi, Shah Mohammed Riza Pahlavi and Railway Train (horiz.).

1976. Railway Day.
2000. **481.** 8 r. multicoloured .. 12 8

482. Emblem and Capital. **483.** Census Symbols.

1976. Festival of Arts and Culture, Persepolis.
2001. **482.** 14 r. multicoloured .. 20 8

1976. National Census.
2002. **483.** 2 r. multicoloured .. 5 5

484. Flowers and Birds. **485.** Quaid-i-Azam (Mohammad Ali Jinnah).

1976. Children's Week. Multicoloured.
2003. 2 r. Type **484** 5 5
2004. 2 r. Flowers and bird .. 5 5
2005. 2 r. Flowers and butterfly 5 5

1976. Mohammad Ali Jinnah. Birth Centenary.
2006. **485.** 10 r. multicoloured .. 15 12

IRAQ

CORRECTION: Nos. 1256/8 to be renumbered 1255/7.

237. Emblem within " 15 ". **238.** Children with Banner.

1976. Iraqi Students' Union. 15th Anniv.
1263. **237.** 30 f. multicoloured .. 15 10
1264. 70 f. multicoloured .. 30 15

1976. Books for Children. Multicoloured.
1265. 10 f. Type **238** 5 5
1266. 25 f. Children in garden .. 10 5
1267. 75 f. Children with Iraqi flag 30 20

239. Tanker " Rumaila " and Emblems.

1976. First Iraqi Oil Tanker (4th anniv.) and Basrah Petroleum Co. Nationalisation (1st anniv.). Multicoloured.
1268. 10 f. Type **239** 5 5
1269. 15 f. Type **239** 8 5
1270. 25 f. Oil jetty and installations 10 5
1271. 50 f. As 25 f. 20 15

ISRAEL

251. " Grandfather's Carrot ".

1977. Voluntary Service.
650. **251.** I£2.60 multicoloured .. 40 30

252. Arab and Jew shaking Hands.

1977. " My Peace ". Multicoloured.
651. 50 a. Type **252** 8 5
652. I£1.40 Arab and Jew holding hands 20 15
653. I£2.70 Peace dove, Arab and Jew 50 45

253. " By the Rivers of Babylon".

1977. Paintings by E. M. Lilien.
654. **253.** I£1.70 brn., blk. & grey 25 20
655. – I£1.80 blue, brn. & yell. 25 20
656. – I£2.10 grn., yell. & blue 35 25
PAINTINGS—VERT. I£1.80 " Abraham ". HORIZ: I£2.10 " May Our Eyes Behold ".

ITALY

553. Net of Serpents obscuring the Sun.

1977. Drug Control Campaign. Mult.
1506. 120 l. Type **553** 25 8
1507. 170 l. Puppet and poppy 35 12

554. Pietro Micca about to light Gunpowder in Turin Citadel. **555.** Globe and Cross.

1977. Pietro Micca. Birth Tercentenary.
1508. **554.** 170 l. multicoloured 35 12

1977. Salesiana Missionaries. Multicoloured
1509. 70 l. Type **555** 15 5
1510. 120 l. St. John Bosco embracing all races .. 25 8

IVORY COAST

Add to No. 435. As **T 128**, but portrait reversed.
435a. 60 f. brn., red and green 25 20
435b. 65 f. brn., green and red 30 25

155. Motorway Bridge.

1976. 3rd African Roads Conference, Abidjan.
470. **155.** 60 f. multicoloured .. 25 30

156. John Paul Jones and American Marine.

1976. American Revolution. Bicentenary. Multicoloured.
471. 100 f. Type **156** 45 35
472. 125 f. Comte de Rochambeau and grenadier 60 50
473. 150 f. Admiral D'Estaing and French marine .. 70 60
474. 175 f. Marquis de Lafayette and grenadier 80 70
475. 200 f. Thomas Jefferson and soldier 90 80

157. Independence Motif.

1976. Independence. 16th Anniv.
477. **157.** 60 f. multicoloured .. 25 20

158. Ife Bronze Mask.

1977. 2nd World Festival of Negro-African Arts, Lagos.
478. **158.** 65 f. multicoloured .. 30 25

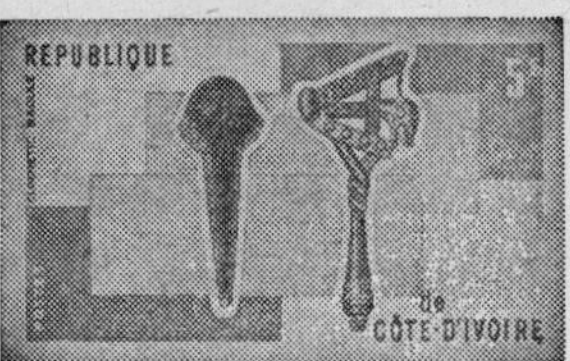

159. Baoule Handbells.

1977. Musical Instruments.
479. **159.** 5 f. brown and green .. 5 5
480. – 10 f. black and red .. 5 5
481. – 20 f. black and violet .. 8 5
DESIGNS: 10 f. Senoufo balafon (xylophone). 20 f. Dida tom-tom.

JAMAICA

1977. 17th Cent. Maps of Jamaica. As **T 105**.
425. 9 c. red, brn., buff & blue 10 10
426. 10 c. red, brown and buff .. 12 15
427. 25 c. blk., blue & pale blue 30 35
428. 40 c. black, blue & green .. 50 60
DESIGNS: 9 c. Hickeringill map, 1661. 10 c. Ogilby map, 1671. 25 c. Visscher map, 1680. 40 c. Thornton map, 1689.

1977. Butterflies (2nd series). As **T 103**. Multicoloured..
429. 10 c. " Eurema elathea " 12 15
430. 20 c. " Dynamine egaea egaea " 25 30
431. 25 c. " Atlantea pantoni " 30 35
432. 40 c. " Hypolimnas misippus " 50 60

JAPAN

708. Ship laying Cable.

1976. Opening of Sino-Japanese Cable.
1437. **708.** 50 y. multicoloured .. 20 15

709. Man-zai-raku (classical dance). **710.** Children in Kindergarten.

1976. Golden Jubilee of Emperor's Accession. Multicoloured.
1438. 50 y. Type **709** 20 15
1439. 50 y. Coronation coach .. 20 15

1976. Japanese Kindergarten. Cent.
1441. **710.** 50 y. multicoloured .. 20 15

711. " Good Health " Family. **712.** Bamboo " Snake " Toy.

1976. " 50 Years of Health Insurance ".
1442. **711.** 50 y. multicoloured .. 20 15

1976. New Year's Greetings.
1443. **712.** 20 y. multicoloured .. 10 8

713. East Pagoda of Yakushiji Temple.

1976. National Treasures. (1st series). Multicoloured.
1445. 50 y. Type **713** 20 15
1446. 100 y. Deva King holding weapon (33×48 mm.) 40 30

714. Toshodai-ji Temple.

1977. National Treasures (2nd series). Multicoloured.
1447. 50 y. Type **714** 20 15
1448. 100 y. Dedication of Sutra (33×48 mm.) 40 30

JORDAN

154. Tennis.

1976. " Sports and Youth ". Multicoloured.
1197. 5 f. Type **154** 5 5
1198. 10 f. " Strong man " within laurel 5 5
1199. 15 f. Football .. 5 5
1200. 20 f. Horse-riding .. 10 8
1201. 30 f. Weightlifting .. 15 10
1202. 100 f. Stadium, Amman 50 40

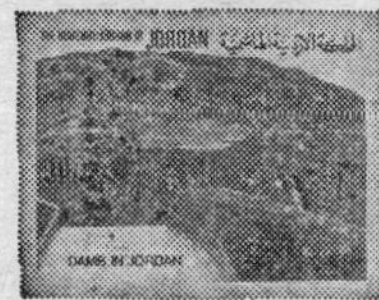

155. Jordan Dam.

1976. Jordan Dams.
1203. **155.** 30 f. multicoloured .. 15 10
1204. – 60 f. multicoloured .. 30 25
1295. – 100 f. multicoloured 50 40
DESIGNS: 60 f., 100 f. Different dams.

KENYA

35. Nile Perch.

1977. Game Fish of East Africa. Mult.
275. 50 c. Type **35** 5 8
276. 1 s. Tilapia 12 15
277. 3 s. Sailfish 35 40
278. 5 s. Black Marlin 60 70

36. Maasai Manyatta (animal slaughter), Kenya.

1977. Second World Black and African Festival of Arts and Culture, Lagos. Multicoloured.
279. 50 c. Type **36** 5 8
280. 1 s. " Heartbeat of Africa " (Ugandan dancers) .. 12 15
281. 2 s. Makonde sculpture, Tanzania 25 30
282. 3 s. Early man and technology (skinning animal) 35 40

37. Villages waving-on a Competitor.

1977. Safari Rally. 25th Anniv. Mult.
284. 50 c. Type **37** 5 8
285. 1 s. The start/finish line .. 12 15
286. 2 s. Car splashing through water 25 30
287. 5 s. Car scattering elephants 60 70

KOREA

SOUTH KOREA

465. " Training Technicians ". **466.** Satellite Antenna.

1977. 4th Five-Year Economic Development Plan. Multicoloured.
1271. 20 w. Type **465** 8 5
1272. 20 w. Oil Tanker (" Heavy Industries ") 8 5

1977. Korea's I.T.U. Membership. 25th Anniv.
1273. **466.** 20 w. multicoloured .. 8 5

467. Korean Broadcasting Centre. **468.** Grape Jar.

1977. Broadcasting in Korea. 50th Anniv.
1274. **467.** 20 w. multicoloured .. 8 5

1977. Korean Ceramics (1st series). Multicoloured.
1275. 20 w. Type **468** 8 5
1276. 20 w. Celadon flask .. 8 5

KUWAIT

165. Ethnic Heads and Map of Sri Lanka.

1976. Non-Aligned Countries' Colombo Conference.
689. **165.** 20 f. multicoloured .. 10 8
690. 30 f. multicoloured .. 20 15
691. 45 f. multicoloured .. 30 20

INDEX

Countries can be quickly located by referring to the index at the end of this volume.

166. Torch, U.N.E.S.C.O. Emblem and Kuwaiti Arms.

1976. U.N.E.S.C.O. 30th Anniv.
692 **166.** 20 f. multicoloured .. 10 8
693. 45 f. multicoloured .. 30 20

LAOS

111. Thatiang, Vien-Tran.

1976. Lao Pagodas. Multicoloured.
427. 1 k. Type **111** 5 5
428. 2 k. Phonsi, Luang Prabang 5 5
429. 30 k. Type **111** 8 5
430. 80 k. As 2 k. 15 12
431. 100 k. As 2 k. 20 15
432. 300 k. Type **111** 55 45

LESOTHO

41. Rock Rabbit.

1977. Animals. Multicoloured.
329. 4 c. Type **41** 5 5
330. 5 c. Porcupine 5 5
331. 10 c. Polecat 12 15
332. 15 c. Klipspringer .. 20 25
333. 25 c. Baboon 35 40

LIBERIA

Add to Nos. 1069/70
1070a. 10 c. Rubber tree and tyre 10 8
1070b. 25 c. Mesurado shrimps 25 20

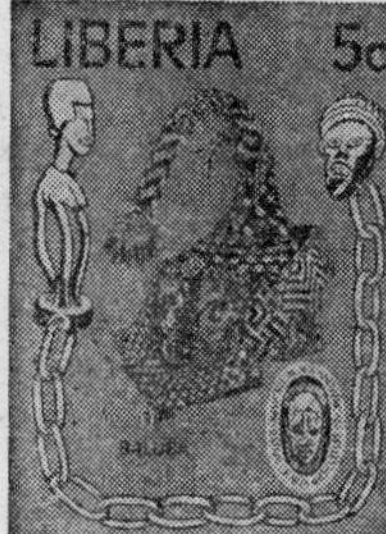

225. Baluba Masks.

1977. Second World Black and African Festival of Arts and Culture, Lagos (Nigeria). Tribal Masks. Multicoloured.
1081. 5 c. Type **225** 5 5
1082. 10 c. Bateke 10 8
1083. 15 c. Basshilele 15 12
1084. 20 c. Igungun 20 15
1085. 25 c. Maisi 25 20
1086. 50 c. Kifwebe 50 45

226. Latham's Francolin.

1977. Liberian Wild Birds. Multicoloured.
1088. 5 c. Type **226** 5 5
1089. 10 c. Narina trogon .. 10 8
1090. 15 c. Rufus-crowned roller 15 12
1091. 20 c. Brown-cheeked hornbill 20 15
1092. 25 c. Pepper bird .. 25 20
1093. 50 c. Fish eagle 50 45

LIBYA

161. Global " Tree ". **162.** " Agriculture and Industry ".

1976. Non-Aligned Countries' Colombo Conference.
705. **161.** 115 dh. multicoloured 60 55

1976. Revolution. 7th Anniv.
706. **162.** 30 dh. multicoloured .. 15 12
707. 40 dh. multicoloured .. 20 15
708. 100 dh. multicoloured 50 45

163. Sports. **164.** Chessboard and Pieces.

1976. 5th Arab Games, Damascus.
710. **163.** 15 dh. multicoloured .. 8 5
711. 30 dh. multicoloured .. 15 12
712. 100 dh. multicoloured 50 45

1976. Arab Chess Olympiad.
714. **164.** 15 dh. multicoloured .. 8 5
715. 30 dh. multicoloured .. 15 12
716. 100 dh. multicoloured 50 45

165. Ratima. **167.** Holy Ka'aba and Pilgrims.

166. Emblem and Text.

1976. Libyan Flora. Multicoloured.
717. 15 dh. Type **165** 8 5
718. 20 dh. " Sword of Crow " 10 8
719. 35 dh. Lasef 15 12
720. 40 dh. Yadid 20 15
721. 70 dh. Esparto grass .. 35 30

1976. International Archives Council.
722. **166.** 15 dh. multicoloured .. 8 5
723. 35 dh. multicoloured .. 15 12
724. 70 dh. multicoloured .. 35 30

1976. Pilgrimage to Mecca.
729. **167.** 15 dh. multicoloured .. 8 5
730. 30 dh multicoloured .. 15 12
731. 70 dh. multicoloured .. 35 30
732. 100 dh. multicoloured 50 45

168.

1977. Coil Stamps.
733. **168.** 5 dh. multicoloured .. 5 5
734. 20 dh. multicoloured .. 10 8
735. 50 dh. multicoloured .. 25 20

169. Basket (vert.).

1977. 15th International Trade Fair, Tripoli. Multicoloured.
736. 10 dh. Type **169** 5 5
737. 20 dh. Leather bag .. 10 8
738. 30 dh. Vase 15 12
739. 40 dh. Slippers 20 15
740. 50 dh. Saddle 25 20

POSTAGE DUE

D 3. Men in Boat.

1976. Ancient Mosaics. Multicoloured.
D 725. 5 dh. Type **D 3** .. 5 5
D 726. 10 dh. Head of Medusa 5 5
D 727. 20 dh. Peacock .. 10 10
D 728. 50 dh. Fish 25 25

LIECHTENSTEIN

OFFICIAL STAMPS

O 2. Government Building, Vaduz.

1976.
O 652. **O 2.** 10 r. brown & violet 5 5
O 653. 20 r. red and blue .. 8 8
O 654. 35 r. blue and red .. 15 15
O 655. 40 r. lilac and green 15 15
O 656. 50 r. grey & mauve 20 20
O 657. 70 r. brown & green 25 25
O 658. 80 r. green & purple 30 30
O 659. 90 r. violet & turq. 35 35
O 660. 1 f. olive & purple .. 40 40
O 661. 1 f. 10 brown & blue 45 45
O 662. 1 f. 50 green & red .. 60 60
O 663. 2 f. red and blue .. 75 75

LUXEMBOURG

220. Goethe.

1977. Cultural Series. Famous Visitors to Luxembourg.
981. **220.** 2 f. brown 8 5
982. – 5 f. violet 15 10
983. – 5 f. blue 20 12
984. – 12 f. violet 40 30
DESIGNS: 5 f. J. M. Turner. 6 f. Victor Hugo. 12 f. Franz Liszt.

MACAO

30. Pou Chai Pagoda. **31.** Macao Cathedral.

1976.
529. 10 p. Type **30** .. .. 2·50 2·25
530. 20 p. Tin Hau Pagoda .. 5·00 4·50

1976. Macao Diocese. 400th Anniv.
531. **31.** 1 p. multicoloured .. 25 25

MALAGASY REPUBLIC

New Currency 5 francs = 1 ariary

157. Rainandriampandry (Foreign Minister). **158.** Doves over Globe.

1976.
382. **157.** 5 a. multicoloured .. 12 10

1976. Indian Ocean – "Zone of Peace". Multicoloured.
383. 12 a. Type **158** 25 20
384. 32 a. Doves flying across Indian Ocean (horiz.) .. 70 65

1976. Olympic Games Medal – winners. Nos. 338/342 optd. with names of two winners on each stamp.
385. **149.** 40 f. multicoloured (postage) 15 12
386. – 50 f. multicoloured .. 20 15
387. – 100 f. multicoloured (air) 40 35
388. – 200 f. multicoloured .. 80 75
389. – 300 f. multicoloured .. 1·25 1·10
OPTS.: **40 f. V. DIBA, A. ROGOV.** 50 f. **H. CRAWFORD, J. SCHALLER.** 100 f. **U. BEYER, A. ROBINSON.** 200 f. **N. COMANECI, N. ANDRIANOV.** 300 f. **K. DIBIASI, E. VAYT-SEKHOVSKAYA.**

159. Malagsy Arms.

1976. Malagasy Democratic Republic. 1st Anniv.
390. **159.** 5 a. multicoloured .. 12 10

MALAWI

59. Ebony Carving of Man and Woman.

1977. Handicrafts. Multicoloured.
541. 4 t. Type **59** 5 5
542. 10 t. Ebony elephant (horiz.) 12 15
543. 20 t. Wooden antelope .. 25 30
544. 40 t. Ebony rhinoceros (horiz.) 50 55

MALI

207. Moto Guzzi 254.

1976. Motorcycling.
556. **207.** 90 f. red, grey & brown 20 15
557. – 120 f. vio., blue & blk. 30 25
558. – 130 f. red, grey & grn. 30 25
559. – 140 f. blue, grn. & grey 35 30
DESIGNS: 120 f. B.M.W. 900. 130 f. Honda "Egli". 140 f. Motobecane LT3.

208. "Nativity" (Taddeo Gaddi).

1976. Air. Christmas. Religious Paintings. Multicoloured.
560. 280 f. Type **208** 65 60
561. 300 f. "Adoration of the Magi" (Hans Memling) 70 65
562. 320 f. "Nativity" (Carlo Crivelli) 80 75

209. Muscat Fishing Boat.

1976. Ships.
563. **209.** 160 f. pur., grn. & blue 35 30
564. – 180 f. grn., red & blue 40 35
565. – 190 f. pur., blue & grn. 45 40
566. – 200 f. grn., red & blue 50 45
DESIGNS: 180 f. Cochin-chinese coaster. 190 f. Dunkirk lightship. "Ruytingen". 200 f. Nile boat.

210. Rocket in Flight.

1976. Air. Operation "Viking".
567. **210.** 500 f. blue, red & lake 1·25 1·10
568. – 1,000 f. lake, blue and deep blue .. .. 2·50 2·25
DESIGN: 1,000 f. Spacecraft on Mars.

211. Pres. Giscard d'Estaing and Sankore Mosque, Timbuktu.

1977. Air. Visit of Pres. Giscard d'Estaing of France.
570. **211.** 430 f. multicoloured .. 1·00 90

212. Queen Elizabeth II and Duke of Edinburgh.

1977. Air. "Personalities of Decolonisation". Multicoloured.
571. 180 f. Type **212** 40 35
572. 200 f. General De Gaulle (vert.) 50 45
573. 250 f. Queen Wilhelmina of the Netherlands (vert.) 65 60
574. 300 f. King Baudouin and Queen Fabiola of Belgium 70 65
575. 480 f. Crowning of Queen Elizabeth II (vert.) .. 1·10 1·00

213. Isaac Newton, Apple, and Rocket on Launch-pad.

1977. Air. Isaac Newton. 250th Death Anniv.
576. **213.** 400 f. pur., red & grn. 95 90

MALTA

107 Jean de la Valette's Armour.

1977. Suits of Armour. Multicoloured.
572. 2 c. Type **107** 5 8
573. 7 c. Aloph de Wignacourt's armour 15 20
574. 11 c. Jean Jacques de Verdelin's armour .. 25 30

1977. No. 336 surch.
575. 1 c. 7 on 4d. multicoloured 5 5

108. "Annunciation".

1977. Flemish Tapestries by Rubens. Mult.
576. 2 c. Type **108** 5 8
577. 7 c. "Four Evangelists" 15 20
578. 11 c. "Nativity" .. 25 30
579. 20 c. "Adoration of the Magi" 50 55

MAURITANIA

132. A. Graham Bell, Early Telephone and Satellite. **134.** Hare.

133. Mission Control.

1976 Telephone Cent.
528. **132.** 10 u. blue, lake and red 25 20

1977. "Viking" Space Mission. Mult.
529. 10 u. Type **133** (postage) .. 25 20
530. 12 u. Capsule assembly (vert.) 30 25
531. 20 u. "Viking" in flight (air) 50 45
532. 50 u. "Viking" over Mars 1·25 1·10
533. 60 u. Parachute descent (vert.) .. .. .. 1·50 1·40

1977. Mauritanian Animals. Multicoloured.
535. 5 u. Type **134** 12 10
536. 10 u. Jackals 25 20
537. 12 u. Warthog 30 25
538. 14 u. Lion 35 30
539. 15 u. Elephant 35 30

MEXICO

Add to Nos. 1355a etc.
1361aa. 5 p. blue and yellow .. 85 80
DESIGN: 5 p. Motor vehicles.

375. Figures "40" and Emblem.

1976. National Polytechnic Institute. 40th Anniv.
1387. **375.** 80 c. blk., red and grn. 12 10

MORE DETAILED LISTS

are given in the Stanley Gibbons Catalogues referred to in the country headings:

BC British Commonwealth
E1, E2, E3 Europe 1, 2, 3
O1, O2, O3, O4 Overseas 1, 2, 3, 4

376. Blast Furnace.

1976. Inauguration of Lazaro Cardenas Steel Mill, Las Truchas.
1388. **376.** 50 c. multicoloured .. 8 5

377. Natural Elements.

1976. Air. World Urbanisation Day.
1389. **377.** 1 p. 60 multicoloured 25 20

MONACO

Add to Nos. 1145/52.
1146a. **281.** 80 c. green 15 10
1147a. 1 f. pink 20 12
1148a. 1 f. 25 blue 25 15
1149a. 2 f. 50 grey 50 30
Add to Nos. 1153/8.
1154a. **283.** 1 f. 10 blue, brown and green .. 25 15

MONGOLIA

198. John Naber (U.S.).

1976. Olympic Games Gold-medal Winners. Multicoloured.
996. 10 m. Type **198** .. 10 8
997. 20 m. Nadia Comaneci (Rumania) 20 15
998. 30 m. Kornelia Enders (East Germany) .. 30 25
999. 40 m. Mitsuo Tsukahara (Japan) 40 35
1000. 60 m. Gregor Braun (West Germany) .. 60 55
1001. 80 m. Lasse Viren (Finland) 80 75
1002. 1 t. Nikolai Andrianov (Russia) .. .. 1·00 95

199. Tablet on Tortoise.

1976. Archaeology.
1004. **199.** 50 m. brown and blue 50 45
1005. – 60 m. black and green 60 55
DESIGN: 60 m. 6th-century stele.

200. "R – 1" Biplane.

1976. Mongolian Aircraft. Multicoloured.
1006. 10 m. Type **200** 10 8
1007. 20 m. "R – 5" biplane .. 20 15
1008. 30 m. "K – 5" monoplane 30 25
1009. 40 m. "Po – 2" biplane 40 35
1010. 60 m. "I – 16" fighter 60 35
1011. 80 m. "Jak – 6" monoplane 80 75
1012. 1 t. Junkers "Ju – 13" monoplane .. .. 1·00 95

1977. "50 Years of Communications" Nos. 616/22 optd. **1975-7-15** and Mongolian inscr.
1013. **133.** 20 m. multicoloured .. 20 15
1014. – 30 m. multicoloured .. 30 25
1015. – 40 m. multicoloured .. 40 35
1016. – 50 m. multicoloured .. 50 45
1017. – 60 m. multicoloured .. 60 55
1018. – 80 m. multicoloured .. 80 75
1019. – 1 t. multicoloured .. 1·00 95

MOROCCO

1976. Moroccan Fauna. Birds. As T **160**. Multicoloured.
466. 40 f. Chanting goshawk .. 10 5
467. 1 d. Purple gallinule .. 25 12

173. King Hassan, Emblems and Map. **175.** African Nations Cup.

174. Globe and Peace Dove.

1976. "Green March". 1st Anniv.
468. **173.** 40 f. multicoloured .. 10 5

1976. Fifth African Tuberculosis Conference. Nos. 414/15 optd. **1976** and Arabic inscr.
469. 25 f. multicoloured .. 5 5
470. 70 f. multicoloured .. 20 10

1976. Conference of Non-Aligned Countries Colombo.
471. **174.** 1 d. red, black and blue 25 12

1976. African Nations Football Championship.
472. **175.** 1 d. multicoloured .. 25 12

MOZAMBIQUE

42. Mozambique Stamp of 1876 and Emblem. **43.** Weapons and Flag.

1976. Stamp Cent.
671. **42.** 1 e. 50 multicoloured .. 8 5
672. 6 e. multicoloured .. 50 30

1976. Army Day.
673. **43.** 3 e. multicoloured .. 25 15

1976. "FACIM" Industrial Fair. optd. **FACIM 1976.**
674. **39.** 2 e. 50 multicoloured .. 15 5

MINIMUM PRICE

The minimum price quoted is 5p which represents a handling charge rather than a basis for valuing common stamps. For further notes about prices see introductory pages.

NEPAL

137. Nepalese Lily. **138.** King Birendra.

1976.
339. **137.** 30 p. multicoloured .. 5 5

1976. King Birendra's 32nd Birthday.
340. **138.** 5 p. green 5 5
341. 30 p. lake, brn. & yell. 5 5

139. Liberty Bell.

1976. American Revolution. Bicent.
342. **139.** 10 r. multicoloured .. 1·25 1·15

1977. Flowers. As T **137**. Multicoloured.
343. 30 p. "Meconopsis grandis" 5 5
344. 30 p. "Cardiocrinum giganteum" (horiz.) .. 5 5
345. 30 p. "Megacodon stylophorus" (horiz.) .. 5 5

140. Kazi Amar Singh Thapa (national hero).

1977. Thapa Commemoration.
346. **140.** 10 p. brn. & light brn. 5 5

NETHERLANDS ANTILLES

104. Price Carnival.

1977. Carnival.
628. **104.** 25 c. multicoloured .. 25 25
629. – 35 c. multicoloured .. 35 35
630. – 40 c. multicoloured .. 40 40
DESIGNS: 35 c., 40 c. Women in Carnival costumes.

NEW CALEDONIA

102. Old Town Hall, Noumea.

1976. Air. Old and New Town Halls, Noumea. Multicoloured.
574. 75 f. Type **102** .. .. 1·00 60
575. 125 f. New Town Hall .. 1·75 1·00

103. Water Carnival.

1977. Air. Summer Festival, Noumea.

576.	**103.**	11 f. multicoloured ..	15	8

104. " Pseudophyllanax imperialis ".

1977. Insects.

577.	**104.**	26 f. grn., yell. & brn.	35	20
578.	–	31 f. brn., sepia & grn.	40	20

DESIGN: 31 f. " Agrianome fairmairei ".

OFFICIAL STAMPS

Add to Nos. O525/O531:

O530a.	O **2.**	11 f. grn., blk. & vio.	15	15
O531a.		15 f. green, black and light green ..	20	20
O531b.		20 f. grn., blk. & red	25	25
O531c.		24 f. grn., blk. & blue	35	35
O531d.		26 f. grn., blk. & yell.	35	35
O531e.		36 f. grn., blk. & mve.	45	45
O531f.		42 f. grn., blk. & brn.	55	55
O531g.		50 f. grn., blk. & blue	70	70
O531h.		100 f. grn., blk. & red	1·40	1·40
O531i.		200 f. green, black & orange	2·75	2·75

NEW ZEALAND

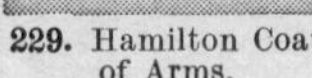

229. Hamilton Coat of Arms.

230. Physical Education, Maori Culture and Recreation Training.

1977. Anniversaries. Multicoloured.

1132.	8 c. Type **229**	8	10
1133.	8 c. Gisborne coat of arms	8	10
1134.	8 c. Masterton coat of arms	8	10
1135.	10 c. Automobile Association emblem	10	12
1136.	10 c. Royal Australasian College of Surgeons coat of arms	10	12

ANNIVERSARIES: No. 1132, Hamilton Cent. No. 1133, Gisborne Cent. No. 1134, Masterton Cent. No. 1135, A.A. in New Zealand. 75th Anniv. No. 1136, R.A.C.S. 50th Anniv.

1977. Education. Multicoloured.

1138.	8 c. Type **230**	8	10
1139.	8 c. Old Government Buildings., geography, science and manual training ..	8	10
1140.	8 c. Special schools, manual training and pre-school activity	8	10
1141.	8 c. Tertiary and language classes	8	10
1142.	8 c. Home science, correspondence school and teacher training ..	8	10

NICARAGUA

163. Mauritius Two Pence " Post Office ".

1976. Rare and Famous Stamps. Multicoloured.

2086.	1 c. Type **163** (postage) ..	5	5
2087.	2 c. Western Australia " Inverted Swan " ..	5	5
2088.	3 c. Mauritius One Penny " Post Office " ..	5	5
2089.	4 c. Jamaica 1s. Inverted Frame	5	5
2090.	5 c. U.S. 24 c. Inverted Aircraft	5	5
2091.	10 c. Swiss Basel " Dove "	5	5
2092.	25 c. Canada Seaway Inverted Centre	8	5
2093.	40 c. Hawaiian 2 c. " Missionary " " air " ..	15	12
2094.	1 cor. G.B. " Penny Black "	35	30
2095.	2 cor. British Guiana 1 c. Black on magenta ..	70	65
2096.	5 cor. Honduras Airmail 25 c. on 10 c... ..	1·75	1·50
2097.	10 cor. Newfoundland " Hawker " Airmail stamp	3·50	3·25

NIGER

CORRECTION: Nos. 646/8, should be renumbered as Nos. 651/3.

1976. International Literacy Day. Nos. 603/7 optd. **JOURNEE INTERNATIONALE DE L'ALPHABETISATION.**

646.	**206.**	25 f. multicoloured ..	12	5
647.	–	30 f. multicoloured ..	15	8
648.	–	40 f. multicoloured ..	20	10
649.	–	50 f. multicoloured ..	25	12
650.	–	60 f. multicoloured ..	30	15

219. Wall Paintings.

1976. " Archaeology ". Multicoloured.

654.	40 f. Type **219**	20	10
655.	50 f. Neolithic statuettes	25	12
656.	60 f. Skeleton of dinosaur	30	15

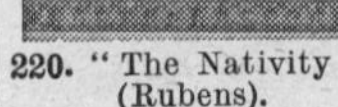

220. " The Nativity " (Rubens).

221. Ife Bronze Mask.

1976. Air. Christmas. Multicoloured.

657.	50 f. Type **220**	25	12
658.	100 f. " Holy Night " (Correggio)	50	25
659.	150 f. " Adoration of the Magi " (David) (horiz.)	75	40

1977. 2nd World Festival of Negro-African Arts, Lagos.

660.	**221.**	40 f. brown	20	10
661.	–	50 f. blue	25	12

DESIGNS—HORIZ. 50 f. Nigerian stick dance.

222. Students in Class.

223. Diagnosis and Treatment.

1977. Alphabetisation Campaign.

662.	**222.**	40 f. multicoloured ..	20	10
663.		50 f. multicoloured ..	25	12
664.		60 f. multicoloured ..	30	15

1977. Village Health. Multicoloured.

665.	40 f. Type **223**	20	10
666.	50 f. Child care	25	12

224. Marabou Stork.

1977. Fauna Protection.

667.	**224.**	80 f. sepia, bistre & red	40	20
668.	–	90 f. brown and turq.	45	25

DESIGN: 90 f. Harnessed antelopes.

225. Satellite and Weather Symbols.

1977. World Meteorological Day.

669.	**225.**	100 f. blue, blk. & turq.	50	25

226. Gymnastic Exercise.

1977. 2nd Youth Festival, Tahoua. Multicoloured.

670.	40 f. Type **226**	20	10
671.	50 f. High jumping ..	25	12
672.	80 f. Choral ensemble ..	40	20

NIGERIA

88. General Murtala Muhammed and Map of Nigeria.

1977. General Murtala Remat Muhammed, late Head of State. Multicoloured.

349.	5 k. Type **88**	8	10
350.	18 k. The General in uniform of Commander-in-Chief (vert.)	30	35
351.	30 k. The General in battle dress (vert.)	55	65

89. Scouts Saluting.

1977. First All-Africa Scout Jamboree. Multicoloured.

352.	5 k. Type **89**	8	10
353.	18 k. Scouts cleaning a dirty street (horiz.) ..	30	35
354.	25 k. Scouts working on a farm (horiz.) ..	45	50
355.	30 k. African World Scout Jamboree emblem (horiz.)	55	65

NORFOLK ISLAND

Add to Nos. 179/94

180.	2 c. " Utetheisa pulchelloides vaga "	5	5
185.	15 c. " Pyrrhorachis pyrrhogona "	15	20
187.	17 c. " Pseudocoremia christiani "	15	20
189.	19 c. " Simplicia caeneusalis buffetti "	20	20
190.	20 c. " Austrocidaria raistonae "	20	25
191.	30 c. " Hippotion scrofa "	30	35
192.	40 c. " Papilio ilioneus ilioneus "	40	45
193.	50 c. " Tiracola plagiata "	50	55

NORWAY

1977. Northern Countries' Day. As Type **193** of Denmark.

770.	1 k. 25 multicoloured ..	30	5
771.	1 k. 40 multicoloured ..	35	20

198. Akershus Castle, Oslo (horiz.).

1977.

772.	**198.**	1 k. 25 red	30	5
773.	–	1 k. 30 brown	30	8
774.	–	1 k. 80 blue	45	10

DESIGNS—HORIZ. 1 k. 30 Steinviksholm, Asen Fjord. VERT. 1 k. 80 Great and Small Torungen lighthouses, Arendal.

OFFICIAL STAMP

Add to Nos. O458/84. Colour changed.

O731g.	O **6**	5 k. blue	1·25	75

OMAN

17. Presenting Colours and Opening of Seeb-Nizwa Highway.

1976. National Day. Multicoloured.

201.	25 b. Type **17**	8	8
202.	40 b. Parachutists and harvesting	12	12
203.	75 b. Helicopter squadron and Victory Day procession	25	25
204.	150 b. Road construction and Salalah T.V. Station	50	50

18. Great Bath, Moenjodaro.

1977. " Save Moenjodaro " Campaign.

205.	**18.**	125 b. multicoloured ..	40	40

PANAMA

168. Nicanor Villalaz (designer of Panama Arms).

169. National Lottery Building, Panama City.

1976. Villalaz Commemoration.

1130.	**168.**	5 c. blue	8	5

1976. " Progressive Panama ".

1131.	**169.**	6 c. multicoloured ..	10	5

170. Cerro Colorado Copper Mine.

1976. Air.

1132. **170.** 23 c. multicoloured .. 35 25

PAPUA NEW GUINEA

78. The Queen and Papua New Guinea Flag.

1977. Silver Jubilee. Multicoloured.

320. 7 t. Type **78** 10 12
321. 15 t. The Queen and national crest 20 25
322. 35 t. The Queen and map of P.N.G. 50 50

PENRHYN ISLAND

10. The Queen in Coronation Robes.

1977. Silver Jubilee. Multicoloured.

100. 50 c. Type **10** 55 65
101. $1 The Queen and Prince Philip .. .. .. 1·10 1·25
102. $2 Queen Elizabeth II .. 2·25 2·50

PERU

1977. Air. Surch.

1300. 2 s. on 2 s. 60 green (No. 926) 5 5
1301. 3 s. on 2 s. 60 green (No. 926) 10 5
1302. 6 s. on 4s. 60 orange (No. 928) 20 12

1977. Air. Surch.

1303. 2 s. on 4 s. 60 orange (No. 928) 5 5
1304. 4 s. on 3 s. 60 purple (No. 927) 12 8
1305. 4 s. on 4 s. 60 orange (No. 928) 12 8
1306. 5 s. on 4 s. 30 orange (No. 878) 15 10
1307. 7 s. on 4 s. 30 orange (No. 878) 20 12
1308. 10 s. on 4 s. 30 orange (No. 878) 30 20
1309. 50 s. on 2 s. 60 green (No. 926) .. .. .. 1·60 1·40

259. Military Monument and Symbols.

1977. Air. Army Day.

1310. **259.** 20 s. black, buff & red 60 40

260. Map and Scroll.

1977. Air. Visit of Peruvian President to Venezuela.

1311. **260.** 12 s. multicoloured .. 35 25

PHILIPPINE ISLANDS

1977. Surch.

1423. 1 p. 20 on 1 p. 10 blue (No. 1316) 40 25
1424. 3 p. on 5 p. blue (No. 1320) 1·10 90

PORTUGAL

268. Map of Member Countries. **269.** Bottle within Human Body.

1977. Admission of Portugal to the Council of Europe.

1638. **268.** 8 e. 50 multicoloured 40 30
1639. 10 e. multicoloured .. 50 40

1977. Portuguese Anti-Alcoholic Society. Tenth Anniv. Multicoloured.

1640. 3 e. Type **269** 15 10
1641. 5 e. Broken body and bottle 25 15
1642. 15 e. Sun behind bars and bottle 75 65

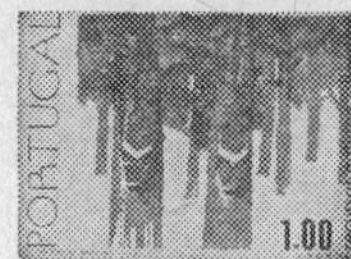

270. Forest Scene.

1977. Natural Resources. Forests. Multicoloured.

1643. 1 e. Type **270** 5 5
1644. 4 e. Cork oaks 20 12
1645. 7 e. Logs and trees .. 35 25
1646. 15 e. Trees by the sea .. 75 65

QATAR

90. Shaikh Khalifa. **91.** Shaikh Khalifa.

1977. Amir's Accession. 5th Anniv.

622. **90.** 20 d. multicoloured .. 8 8
623. 1 r. 80 multicoloured .. 70 70

1977.

624. **91.** 5 d. multicoloured .. 5 5
625. 10 d. multicoloured .. 5 5
626. 35 d. multicoloured .. 15 15
627. 80 d. multicoloured .. 30 30
628. 1 r. multicoloured .. 40 40
629. 5 r. multicoloured .. 2·00 2·00
630. 10 r. multicoloured .. 4·00 4·00

Nos. 628/30 are larger. 25×31 mm.

RUMANIA

769. Spiru Haret. **771.** Arms of Alba.

770. Red Deer.

1976. Spiru Haret (mathematician). 125th Birth Anniv.

4250. **769.** 20 b. brn., oran. & blue 5 5

1976 Endangered Animals. Multicoloured.

4251. 20 b. Type **770** 5 5
4252. 40 b. Brown Bear .. 5 5
4253. 55 b. Chamois 8 5
4254. 1 l. 75 Boar 25 12
4255. 2 l. 75 Fox 40 20
4256. 3 l. 60 Lynx 55 25

1976. Rumanian Districts' Coats of Arms. Multicoloured.

4257. 55 b. Type **771** .. 8 5
4258. 55 b. Arad 8 5
4259. 55 b. Arges 8 5
4260. 55 b. Bacau 8 5
4261. 55 b. Bihor 8 5
4262. 55 b. Bisitrita-Nassaud .. 8 5
4263. 55 b. Botonsani 8 5
4264. 55 b. Brasov 8 5
4265. 55 b. Braila 8 5
4266. 55 b. Buzau 8 5
4267. 55 b. Caras-Severin .. 8 5
4268. 55 b. Cluj 8 5
4269. 55 b. Constante 8 5
4270. 55 b. Covosna 8 5
4271. 55 b. Dimbovita .. 8 5

772. Ox Cart.

1977. Paintings by Nicola Grigorescu. Multicoloured.

4272. 55 b. Type **772** 8 5
4273. 1 l. Self portrait (vert.) .. 12 5
4274. 1 l. 50 " Shepherdess " .. 20 10
4275. 2 l. 15 " Girl with distaff " 30 15
4276. 3 l. 40 " Shepherd " (vert.) 50 25
4277. 4 l. 80 " Halt at the Well " 70 35

773. Installations and Aerial at Cheia.

1977. Cheia Telecommunications Station.

4278. **773.** 55 b. multicoloured .. 8 5

774. ICAR—1 Glider.

1977. Rumanian Gliders. Multicoloured.

4279. 20 b. Type **774** 5 5
4280. 40 b. IS–3d 5 5
4281. 55 b. RG–5 .. .. 8 5
4282. 1 l. 50 IS–11 .. .. 20 10
4283. 3 l. IS–29D 40 20
4284. 3 l. 40 IS–28B 50 25

RUSSIA

1713. A. S. Novikov-Priboy. **1714.** " Welcome " (N. M. Soloninkin).

1977. A. S. Novikov-Priboy (author). Birth Cent.

4620. **1713.** 4 k multicoloured .. 8 5

1977. " Folk Trades ". Paintings from Fedoskino Multicoloured.

4621. 4 k. Type **1714** 8 5
4622. 6 k. " Along the Street " (V. D Antonov) (horiz) 10 5
4623. 10 k. " Northern Song " (I. V. Karapaev) .. 15 8
4624. 12 k. " Fairy Tale about Tzar Saltan " (A. I. Kkozlov) 20 8
4625. 14 k. " Summer Troika " (V. A. Nalimov) (horiz.) 20 8
4626. 16 k. " Red Flower " (V. D. Lipitsky) .. 25 12

1715. Emblem, Dam, Power Line and Generator Plant.

1977. World Congress of Electronics.

4627. **1715.** 6 k. red, silver, & blue 10 5

1716. " On the Red Square " (K Filatov).

1977. Lenin. 107th Birth Anniv.

4628. **1716.** 4 k. multicoloured .. 8 5

1717. Yuri Gagarin and " Sputniks 1, 2 and 3 ".

1977. Cosmonautics Day.

4629. **1717.** 6 k. grey, mve. & red 10 5

RWANDA

1977. World Water Conference. Nos. 688/95 optd. **CONFERENCE MONDIALE DE L'EAU.**

805. **85.** 20 c. multicoloured .. 5 5
806. – 30 c. multicoloured .. 5 5
807. – 50 c. multicoloured .. 5 5
808. – 5 f. multicoloured .. 10 10
809. – 8 f. multicoloured .. 15 15
810. – 10 f. multicoloured .. 20 20
811. – 26 f. multicoloured .. 50 50
812. – 100 f. multicoloured .. 2·00 2·00

ST. KITTS-NEVIS

49. " Christ on the Cross " (Nicollo di Liberatore).

1977. Easter. Paintings from National Gallery, London. Multicoloured.

370.	25 c. Type **49**	10	12
371.	30 c. " The Resurrection " (after Mantegna) ..	12	15
372.	50 c. " The Resurrection " (Ugolino) (horiz.) ..	20	25
373.	$1 " Christ Rising from the Tomb " (Gaudenzio) ..	40	45

SAN MARINO

Add to Nos. 1040/9. New Values.

1042a.	70 l. blk. & red (as 50 l.) ..	10	10
1042b.	90 l. blk. & pink (as 220 l.)	15	15
1043a.	120 l. blk. & blue (as 100 l.)	20	20
1044a.	160 l. blk. & grn. (as 20 l.)	25	25
1044b.	170 l. blk. & oran. (as 150 l.)	30	30
1047a.	320 l. blk. & vio. (as 300 l.)	50	50

201. Panorama of Mount Titano and " San Marino '77 Emblem ".

1977. " San Marino '77 " Stamp Exhibition.

1062.	**201.**	80 l. red, olive and turquoise (postage)	12	12
1063.		170 l. yell., blue & vio.	25	25
1064.		200 l. orange, light blue and deep blue	30	30
1065.	**201.**	200 l. ochre, blue and green (air)	30	30

202. " San Marino " (Ghirlandaio).

1977. Europa. Multicoloured.

1066.	170 l. Type **202**	30	30
1067.	200 l. " San Marino " (Geurcino)	30	30

SENEGAL

163. Mohammed Ali and Joe Frazier.

1977. World Boxing Champion – Mohammed Ali.

618.	**163.**	60 f. black and blue ..	30	15
619.	–	150 f. black and green	70	40

DESIGN—HORIZ. 150 f. Mohammed Ali landing punch.

164. Dancer and Musicians.

1977. 2nd World Black and African Festival of Arts and Culture, Lagos (Nigeria). Multicoloured.

620.	50 f. Type **164**	25	12
621.	75 f. Statuette and masks	35	20
622.	100 f. Statuette and dancers	45	25

SOLOMON ISLANDS

37. Carved Wooden Figure of a Man.

1977. Artifacts. Multicoloured.

337.	6 c. Type **37**	8	8
338.	20 c. Wood-carving of Sea Adaro or spirit ..	25	30
339.	35 c. Carved figure of shark-headed man	40	45
340.	45 c. Carved wooden image	55	65

SOUTH WEST AFRICA

32. Coastline (horiz.).

1977. Namib Desert.

297.	**32.**	4 c. multicoloured ..	10	12
298.	–	10 c. multicoloured ..	15	15
299.	–	15 c. multicoloured ..	20	25
300.	–	20 c. multicoloured ..	25	30

DESIGNS: 10 c. to 20 c. Various desert scenes.

SPAIN

Add to Nos. 2389/94. New values.

2388a.	**427.**	10 c. orange ..	5	5
2388b.		50 c. mauve ..	5	5
2388c.		1 p. green	5	5
2391a.		4 p. turquoise ..	10	5

436. King James and Arms of Aragon.

1977. King James I. 700th Death Anniv.

2431.	**436.**	4 p. oran., brn. & mve.	10	5

437. Jacinto Verdaguer (Catalan poet).

438. Marquis de Penaflorida.

1977. Spanish Celebrities.

2432.	**437.**	5 p. red and violet ..	12	5
2433.	–	7 p. green and brown	15	5
2434.	–	12 p. turquoise & blue	25	10
2435.	–	50 p. brown & green	1·00	50

DESIGNS: 7 p. Miguel Servet (theologian and physician). 12 p. Pablo Sarasate (violinist). 50 p. Francisco Tarrega (guitarist).

1977. Founding of Economic Society of the Friends of the Land. 200th Anniv.

2436.	**438.**	4 p. green and brown	10	5

SRI LANKA

148. Brass Lamps.

1977. Handicrafts. Multicoloured.

641.	20 c. Type **148**	5	5
642.	25 c. Jewellery box ..	5	5
643.	50 c. Caparisoned elephant	8	8
644.	5 r. A mask	75	75

SURINAM

150. Costume with Sash.

1977. Surinam Costumes.

849.	**150.**	10 c. multicoloured ..	8	8
850.	–	15 c. multicoloured ..	12	12
851.	–	35 c. multicoloured ..	30	30
852.	–	60 c. multicoloured ..	50	50
853.	–	75 c. multicoloured ..	60	60
854.	–	1 g. multicoloured ..	75	75

DESIGNS: 15 c. to 1 g. Various women's festival costumes.

SWEDEN

Add to Nos. 788 etc. New Value.

789d.	**211.**	1 k. 40 blue	40	12

248. Tailor.

1977.

903.	**248.**	2 k. 10 brown	70	20

SYRIA

343. Muhammad Kurd-Ali.

344. Woman hoisting Flag.

1977. Muhammad Kurd-Ali (philospher). Birth Centenary.

1325.	**343.**	25 p. multicoloured ..	12	10

1977. 18th March Revolution. 14th Anniv.

1326.	**344.**	35 p. multicoloured ..	15	12

TANZANIA

1977. Safari Rally. 25th Anniv. As Nos. 284/7 of Kenya. Multicoloured.

201.	50 c. Villagers waving on a competitor	5	8
202.	1 s. The start/finish line ..	12	15
203.	2 s. Car splashing through water	25	30
204.	5 s. Car scattering elephants	60	70

TOGO

1977. Gold Medal Winners, Montreal Olympic Games. Nos. 1149/50 and 1152 optd. **CHAMPIONS OLYMPIQUES** with events and countries.

1181.	50 f. multicoloured (postage)	20	15
1182.	70 f. multicoloured (air)	30	25
1183.	200 f. multicoloured ..	90	85

OPTD. 50 f. **SAUT EN HAUTEUR POLOGNE.** 70 f. **YACHTING - FLYING DUTCHMAN REPUBLIQUE FEDERALE ALLEMAGNE.** 200 f. **ESCRIME-FLEURET PAR EQUIPES REPUBLIQUE FEDERALE ALLEMAGNE.**

TRINIDAD AND TOBAGO

59. Sikorsky S – 38.

1977. 50 Years of Airmail. Multicoloured.

502.	20 c. Type **59**	8	10
503.	35 c. Charles Lindbergh delivering mail to the island	15	15
504.	40 c. " Boeing 707 " ..	15	20
505.	50 c. " Boeing 747 " ..	25	30

POSTAGE DUES

Add to Nos. 44 etc.

D 43a.	**D 1**	2 c. turquoise ..	5	5
D 45.		6 c. brown	5	5
D 46.		8 c. violet	5	5
D 47.		10 c. red	5	5

TURKEY

453. Violin Soundhole and Keyboard.

1977. Presidential Symphony Orchestra. 150th Anniv.

2581.	**453.**	200 k. black, blue silver and brown ..	20	12

UGANDA

1977. Safari Rally. 25th Anniv. As Nos. 284/7 of Kenya. Multicoloured.

187.	50 c. Villagers waving on a competitor	5	8
188.	1 s. The start/finish line ..	12	15
189.	2 s. Car splashing through water	25	30
190.	5 s. Car scattering elephants	60	70

INDEX

Countries can be quickly located by referring to the index at the end of this volume.

MINIMUM PRICE

The minimum price quoted is 5p which represents a handling charge rather than a basis for valuing common stamps. For further notes about prices see introductory pages.

UNITED STATES OF AMERICA

728. Early Gramophone.

1977. Sound Recording Centenary.

1681.	**728.** 13 c. multicoloured ..	15	5

729. Zia Pot.

1977. Pueblo Art.

1682.	13 c. Type **729**	15	5
1683.	13 c. San Ildefonso pot ..	15	5
1684.	13 c. Hopi pot	15	5
1685.	13 c. Acoma pot ..	15	5

VATICAN CITY

163. " The Lord's Creatures ".

1977. St. Francis of Assisi. 750th Death Anniv. Multicoloured.

671.	50 l. Type **163**	10	10
672.	70 l. " Brother Sun " ..	15	15
673.	100 l. " Sister Moon and Stars "	20	20
674.	130 l. " Sister Water " ..	25	25
675.	170 l. " Praise in Infirmities and Tribulations "	35	35
676.	200 l. " Praise for Bodily Death "	40	40

YUGOSLAVIA

439. Phlox.

440. Institute Building.

1977. Flowers. Multicoloured.

1720.	1 d. 50 Type **439** ..	12	10
1721.	3 d. 40 Lily	25	20
1722.	4 d. 90 Dicentra	40	35
1723.	6 d. Zinnia	45	40
1724.	8 d. Marigold	60	55
1725.	10 d. Geranium	80	75

1977. Croatian Music Institute. 150th Anniv.

1726.	**440.** 4 d. 90 blue and sepia	40	35

441. Alojz Kraigher.

1977. Alojz Kraigher (author). Birth Centenary.

1727.	**441.** 1 d. 50 red and buff ..	12	10

NOTE. The first supplement containing new issues not in this catalogue or the Addenda appeared in the July 1977 number of *Stamp Monthly*.

INDEX